Collins

175 YEARS OF DICTIONARY PUBLISHING

Thesaurus *of the* English Language

Collins

HarperCollins Publishers
Westerhill Road
Bishopbriggs
Glasgow
G64 2QT

Third edition 2008

Reprint 10 9 8 7 6 5 4 3 2 1 0

ISBN 978-0-00-728101-5

Collins® is a registered trademark of HarperCollins Publishers Limited

www.collinslanguage.com

A catalogue record for this book is available from the British Library

Designed by Wolfgang Homola

Typeset by Davidson Pre-Press, Glasgow

Printed and bound in Italy by LEGO Spa, Lavis (Trento), Italy

Acknowledgements
We would like to thank those authors and publishers who kindly gave permission for copyright material to be used in the Collins Word Web. We would also like to thank Times Newspapers Ltd for providing valuable data.

Contents

Editorial Staff

EDITORS

Ian Brookes
Leonie Dunlop
Robert Groves
Helen Hucker
Cormac McKeown
Elspeth Summers

FOR THE PUBLISHER

Lucy Cooper
Elaine Higgleton

The editors would like to acknowledge the work of the lexicographers who compiled the previous editions of this book, notably Jeremy Butterfield and Lorna Gilmour.

Introduction

When the **Collins English Thesaurus** was first published in 1995, it revolutionized the whole concept of the thesaurus. As well as continuing the A–Z arrangement of main entry words which we had pioneered, thereby making the thesaurus as easy to look up as a dictionary, it included an entirely new dimension of fascinating and useful information connected with the entry words. The Thesaurus was completely revised in 2002 to give you even more ways of expanding your vocabulary and adding richness and variety to your language, with a clear and attractive layout which highlights the many extra features. This third edition has been further revised with special attention given to areas of interest to the modern user including technology, communications, and the environment.

The headword list was selected on the basis of frequency as verified by our unique language database of 2.5 billion words of written and spoken language, which means that the entry words given are those most likely to be looked up by the user.

The key synonym for each sense is shown first, which not only offers you the most helpful alternative but also lets you identify the sense in question at a glance. Other synonyms are arranged in order of their frequency of occurrence, with the more literary or unfamiliar ones coming towards the end. In this way the thesaurus becomes a powerful aid to help you express yourself in the most suitable style for your purpose.

The thesaurus offers extensive coverage of English as a world language, with words and phrases from all over the English-speaking world making this a truly international language resource.

A wide range of phrases and idioms is also included, both as lookup points and as alternatives, to add colour and interest to your language.

Every sense of every entry word also includes an illustrative example, which shows how the word is used in real English, taken from our unique language database.

As well as generous synonym lists, the inclusion of short antonym lists for many key words provides another way of expressing yourself. But the new **Collins Thesaurus** gives you much more than just a wide choice of synonyms and antonyms.

At many entries, we offer lists of 'related words', enabling you to find information such as adjectives, collective nouns, manias, and phobias connected with many entry words. Such words are usually hard to find unless you already have an idea of what the related word might be, but by looking up, for instance, the entry for **spider**, you will find that its related adjective is **arachnoid** and that fear of spiders is **arachnophobia**. The arrangement of such words under the main entry word enables you to go to it straight away.

Informative and comprehensive subject word lists provide a wealth of material connected with or relevant to many entry words, adding an extra dimension to your vocabulary. For example, look up the entry **game** and you will find not only a choice of synonyms for the word itself, but fascinating lists of **party games**, **word games** and **other games**. Similarly, the entry **orchestra** offers a list of **instruments in a full orchestra**. With hundreds of such lists, the thesaurus is an invaluable crossword aid, but these lists also provide information not normally available in such a helpful form in a single reference book. A full table of the lists included in the thesaurus, and where you will find them, is given on pages x–xv.

A wide range of quotations and proverbs is also included at many key words – nearly 3000 in all. These quotations have been specially selected to add sparkle, interest, and humour, and give you instant access to the wit and wisdom of centuries.

Features of the Thesaurus

Entry words

bedrock 1 = **first principle**, rule, basis, basics, principle, essentials, roots, core, fundamentals, cornerstone, nuts and bolts *(informal)*, sine qua non *(Latin)*, rudiment • *Mutual trust is the bedrock of a relationship.*

Foreign words and phrases

Key synonyms

2 = **bottom**, bed, foundation, underpinning, rock bottom, substructure, substratum • *It took five years to drill down to bedrock.*

bee

Related words expand your vocabulary

▸ **RELATED ADJECTIVE**: apian
▸ **COLLECTIVE NOUNS**: swarm, grist
▸ **NAME OF HOME**: hive, apiary
▸ **RELATED MANIA**: apimania
▹ *See panel* **Ants, bees and wasps**

beef **AS A NOUN** = **complaint**, dispute, grievance, problem, grumble, criticism, objection, dissatisfaction, annoyance, grouse, gripe *(informal)*, protestation, grouch *(informal)*, remonstrance • *I really don't have a beef with Wayne.*

Parts of speech

▸ **AS A VERB** = **complain**, carp, fuss, moan, bitch *(slang)*, groan, grieve, lament, grumble, whine, growl, deplore, grouse, gripe *(informal)*, bemoan, whinge *(informal)*, bleat, find fault, bewail, kick up a fuss *(informal)*, grouch *(informal)*, bellyache *(slang)*, kvetch *(U.S. slang)* • *She was beefing about what he had done.*

Fixed phrases

▸ **IN PHRASES: beef something up** = **strengthen**, increase, build up, enhance, reinforce, intensify, heighten, bolster, augment, give a boost to • *a campaign to beef up security*

beefy = **brawny**, strong, powerful, athletic, strapping, robust, hefty *(informal)*, muscular, sturdy, stalwart, bulky, burly, stocky, hulking, well-built, herculean, sinewy, thickset • *The place was packed with beefy ex-footballers*
OPPOSITES: weak, frail, scrawny

Synonyms offer a wide range of alternatives

beehive = **hive**, colony, comb, swarm, honeycomb, apiary • *The reproductive product of a beehive is a swarm.*

beer = **ale**, brew, swipes *(Brit. slang)*, wallop *(Brit. slang)*, hop juice, amber fluid *or* nectar *(Austral. informal)*, tinnie *or* tinny *(Austral. slang)* • *We have quite a good range of beers.*

International English from all regions of the world where English is spoken

QUOTATIONS

And malt does more than Milton can
To justify God's ways to man
[A E Housman *A Shropshire Lad*]

They who drink beer will think beer
[Washington Irving *The Sketch Book of Geoffrey Crayon*]

Then to the spicy nut-brown ale
[John Milton *L'Allegro*]

Quotations add wit, sparkle and originality

▹ *See panel* **Beers**

beer parlour = **tavern**, inn, bar, pub *(informal, chiefly Brit.)*, public house, watering hole *(facetious slang)*, boozer *(Brit., Austral. & N.Z. informal)*, beverage room *(Canad.)*, hostelry, alehouse *(archaic)*, taproom

beetle
▹ *See panel* **Beetles**

Cross references

befall = **happen to**, fall upon, occur in, take place in, ensue in, transpire in *(informal)*, materialize in, come to pass in • *the disaster that befell the island of Flores*

befit = **be appropriate for**, become, suit, be fitting for, be suitable for, be seemly for, behove *(U.S.)* • *He writes beautifully, as befits a poet.*

befitting = **appropriate to**, right for, suitable for, fitting for, fit for, becoming to, suitable to, seemly for, proper for, apposite to, meet *(archaic)* • *They offered him a post befitting his seniority and experience.*

Lists of opposites

OPPOSITES: wrong for, irrelevant to, unsuitable for

Features of the Thesaurus

BATS

barbastelle	hammerhead	noctule
false vampire	horseshoe bat	pipistrelle
flying fox	insectivorous bat	serotine
fruit bat	kalong	vampire bat

Subject word lists add an extra dimension to your vocabulary

batch = **group**, set, lot, crowd, pack, collection, quantity, bunch, accumulation, assortment, consignment, assemblage, aggregation • *the current batch of trainee priests*

Illustrative examples from real English show how the entry word is used

bath AS A NOUN 1 = **bathtub**, tub, sauna, jacuzzi, hot tub • *They would regularly sing in the bath.*
2 = **wash**, cleaning, washing, soaping, shower, soak, cleansing, scrub, scrubbing, bathe, shampoo, sponging, douse, douche, ablution • *Have a bath every morning.*
▸ AS A VERB = **clean**, wash, soap, shower, soak, cleanse, scrub, bathe, tub, sponge, rinse, douse, scrub down, lave (*archaic*) • *Don't feel you have to bath your child every day.*
▸ RELATED ADJECTIVE: balneal or balneary

bathe AS A VERB 1 = **swim**, dip, go swimming, take a dip • *small ponds for the birds to bathe in*
2 = **wash**, clean, bath, soap, shower, soak, cleanse, scrub, tub, sponge, rinse, scrub down, lave (*archaic*) • *Back home, Shirley plays with, feeds and bathes the baby.*
3 = **cleanse**, clean, wash, soak, rinse • *She paused long enough to bathe her blistered feet.*
4 = **cover**, flood, steep, engulf, immerse, overrun, permeate, suffuse, wash over • *The arena was bathed in warm sunshine.*
▸ AS A NOUN = **swim**, plunge, dip, paddle, dook (*Scot.*) • *an early-morning bathe*

Usage labels identify areas of usage

Sense numbers

Regional labels

bathing costume *or* **bathing suit** = **swimming costume**, bikini, cossie (*informal*), swimming togs (*informal*), trunks, swimsuit, swimwear, swimming trunks • *She wore a one-piece white bathing costume.*

bathos = **anticlimax**, disappointment, sentimentality, letdown, comedown (*informal*), mawkishness, false pathos • *There was an element of bathos about the much-acclaimed speech.*

bathroom = **lavatory**, toilet, loo (*Brit. informal*), washroom, can (*U.S. & Canad. slang*), john (*slang, chiefly U.S. & Canad.*), head(s) (*Nautical slang*), shower, convenience (*chiefly Brit.*), bog (*slang*), bogger (*Austral. slang*), brasco (*Austral. slang*), privy, cloakroom (*Brit.*), latrine, rest room, powder room, crapper (*taboo slang*), dunny (*Austral. & N.Z. old-fashioned*), water closet, khazi (*slang*), comfort station (*U.S.*), pissoir (*French*), Gents *or* Ladies, little boy's room *or* little girl's room (*informal*), (public) convenience, W.C. • *She had gone to use the bathroom.*

Idioms and phrases to add colour to your language

baton = **stick**, club, staff, stake, pole, rod, crook, cane, mace, wand, truncheon, sceptre, mere (*N.Z.*), patu (*N.Z.*) • *I could see a baton being used vigorously.*

battalion 1 = **company**, army, force, team, host, unit, division, troop, squad, corps, brigade, regiment, legion, contingent, squadron, military force, garrison, horde, multitude, detachment, throng • *He was ordered to return to his battalion.*
2 = **crowd**, army, host, pack, mass, mob, herd, swarm, horde, multitude, throng, troupe, rabble, bevy • *battalions of highly paid publicists*

Lists in the Thesaurus

Lists in the Thesaurus

Lists in the Thesaurus

Lists in the Thesaurus

Lists in the Thesaurus

Lists in the Thesaurus

175 YEARS OF DICTIONARY PUBLISHING

William Collins' dream of knowledge for all began with the publication of his first book in 1819. A self-educated mill worker, he not only enriched millions of lives, but also founded a flourishing publishing house. Today, staying true to this spirit, Collins books are packed with inspiration, innovation, and practical expertise. They place you at the centre of a world of possibility and give you exactly what you need to explore it.

Language is the key to this exploration, and at the heart of Collins Dictionaries is language as it is really used. New words, phrases, and meanings spring up every day, and all of them are captured and analysed by the Collins Word Web. Constantly updated, and with over 2.5 billion entries, this living language resource is unique to our dictionaries.

Words are tools for life. And a Collins Dictionary makes them work for you.

Collins. Do more.

Aa

aback IN PHRASES: **taken aback = surprised**, thrown, shocked, stunned, confused, astonished, staggered, startled, bewildered, astounded, disconcerted, bowled over *(informal)*, stupefied, floored *(informal)*, knocked for six, dumbfounded, left open-mouthed, nonplussed, flabbergasted *(informal)* • *He was taken aback when a man answered the phone.*

abandon AS A VERB **1 = leave**, strand, ditch, leave behind, walk out on, forsake, jilt, run out on, throw over, turn your back on, desert, dump, leave high and dry, leave in the lurch • *He claimed that his parents had abandoned him.*
2 = stop, drop, give up, halt, cease, cut out, pack in *(Brit. informal)*, discontinue, leave off, desist from • *The authorities have abandoned any attempt to distribute food.*
OPPOSITES: continue
3 = give up, resign from, yield, surrender, relinquish, renounce, waive, cede, forgo, abdicate • *efforts to persuade him to abandon his claim to the presidency*
OPPOSITES: take, keep, hold
▸ AS A NOUN **= recklessness**, dash, wildness, wantonness, unrestraint, careless freedom • *He has splashed money around with gay abandon.*
OPPOSITES: control, restraint, moderation
▸ IN PHRASES: **abandon ship = evacuate**, quit, withdraw from, vacate, depart from • *The crew prepared to abandon ship.*
▸ AS A VERB
OPPOSITES: maintain, defend, uphold
abandon yourself to something = indulge in, give way to, yield to, wallow in, give free rein to, lose yourself in, give yourself up to • *We are scared to abandon ourselves to our feelings.*

abandoned 1 = unoccupied, empty, deserted, vacant, derelict, uninhabited • *abandoned buildings that become a breeding ground for crime*
OPPOSITES: kept, claimed, occupied
2 = deserted, dropped, rejected, neglected, stranded, ditched, discarded, relinquished, left, forsaken, cast off, jilted, cast aside, cast out, cast away • *a newsreel of abandoned children suffering from cold and hunger*
3 = uninhibited, wild, uncontrolled, unbridled, unrestrained, unconstrained • *people who enjoy wild, abandoned lovemaking*
OPPOSITES: conscious, restrained, inhibited

abandonment 1 = desertion, leaving, forsaking, jilting • *memories of her father's complete abandonment of her*
2 = evacuation, leaving, quitting, departure, withdrawal • *the abandonment of two North Sea oilfields*
3 = stopping, cessation, discontinuation • *Rain forced the abandonment of the next day's competitions.*
4 = renunciation, giving up, surrender, waiver, abdication, cession, relinquishment • *their abandonment of the policy*

abasement = humiliation, lowering, reduction, shaming, humbling, disgrace, put-down, degradation, dishonour, mortification, debasement, belittlement • *her abasement of a man she claims to love*

QUOTATIONS
abasement: decent and customary mental attitude in the presence of wealth and power
[Ambrose Bierce *The Devil's Dictionary*]

abashed = embarrassed, confused, humbled, humiliated, dismayed, ashamed, bewildered, confounded, disconcerted, taken aback, chagrined, perturbed, mortified, discomfited, shamefaced, discomposed • *He seemed both abashed and delighted at the gift.*
OPPOSITES: confident, bold, unabashed

abate 1 = decrease, decline, relax, ease, sink, fade, weaken, diminish, dwindle, lessen, slow, wane, subside, ebb, let up, slacken, attenuate, taper off • *The storms soon abated.*
OPPOSITES: increase, strengthen, intensify
2 = reduce, slow, relax, ease, relieve, moderate, weaken, dull, diminish, decrease, lessen, alleviate, quell, mitigate, attenuate • *a government programme to abate greenhouse gas emissions*
OPPOSITES: increase, boost, add to

abatement 1 = decrease, slowing, decline, easing, sinking, fading, weakening, relaxation, dwindling, lessening, waning, subsiding, ebbing, cessation, let-up, slackening, diminution, tapering off, attenuation • *Demand for the product shows no sign of abatement.*
2 = reduction, slowing, relief, easing, weakening, dulling, decrease, lessening, cutback, quelling, moderation, remission, slackening, mitigation, diminution, curtailment, alleviation, attenuation, extenuation • *noise abatement*

abattoir = slaughterhouse, shambles, butchery • *The report said that conditions in the abattoir were appalling.*

abbey = monastery, convent, priory, cloister, nunnery, friary • *a memorial service at Westminster Abbey*

abbot
▸ RELATED ADJECTIVE: abbatial

abbreviate = shorten, reduce, contract, trim, cut, prune, summarize, compress, condense, abridge • *He abbreviated his first name to Alec.*
OPPOSITES: extend, expand, prolong

abbreviated = shortened, shorter, reduced, brief, potted, trimmed, pruned, cut, summarized, compressed, concise, condensed, abridged • *It was an abbreviated document without detailed proposals.*
OPPOSITES: increased, expanded, prolonged

abbreviation = shortening, reduction, résumé, trimming, summary, contraction, compression, synopsis, précis, abridgment • *The postal abbreviation for Kansas is KS.*
▹ *See panel* **Abbreviations**

ABC 1 = basics, principles, elements, essentials, fundamentals, rudiments • *the ABC of Marxism*
2 = alphabet, letters • *By this age children should be able to count to ten and recite their ABC.*

a

ABBREVIATIONS

Classified advertisements

Abbreviation	Meaning
AMC *or* amc	all mod cons
deps	deposit
exc *or* excl	excluding
f/f	furnished flat
GCH	gas central heating
inc *or* incl	including
pcm	per calendar month
pw	per week

Lonely hearts column abbreviations

Abbreviation	Meaning
GSOH	good sense of humour
GWM	gay white male
LTR	long term relationship
NS *or* N/S	non-smoker
SOH	sense of humour
SWF	single white female
VGSOH	very good sense of humour
WLTM	would like to meet
WSOH	wicked *or* weird sense of humour
1-2-1	one-to-one

abdicate 1 = **resign**, retire, quit, step down *(informal)* • *The last French king abdicated in 1848.*
2 = **give up**, yield, hand over, surrender, relinquish, renounce, waive, vacate, cede, abjure • *Edward chose to abdicate the throne, rather than give Mrs Simpson up.*
3 = **renounce**, give up, abandon, surrender, relinquish, waive, forgo, abnegate • *Many parents simply abdicate all responsibility for their children.*

abdication 1 = **resignation**, quitting, retirement, retiral *(chiefly Scot.)* • *the abdication of Edward VIII*
2 = **giving up**, yielding, surrender, waiving, renunciation, cession, relinquishment, abjuration • *Edward was titled Duke of Windsor after his abdication of the throne.*
3 = **renunciation**, giving up, surrender, abandonment, waiver, abnegation, relinquishment • *There had been a complete abdication of responsibility.*

abdomen = **stomach**, guts *(slang)*, belly, tummy *(informal)*, midriff, midsection, makutu *(N.Z.)*, puku *(N.Z.)* • *He underwent tests for pains in his abdomen.*
▸ **RELATED ADJECTIVES:** abdominal, coeliac

abdominal = **gastric**, intestinal, visceral • *vomiting, diarrhoea and abdominal pain*

abduct = **kidnap**, seize, carry off, run off with, run away with, make off with, snatch *(slang)* • *She was charged with abducting a six-month-old child.*

abduction = **kidnapping**, seizure, carrying off • *the abduction of four black youths from a church hostel in Soweto*

aberrant 1 = **abnormal**, odd, strange, extraordinary, curious, weird, peculiar, eccentric, queer, irregular, erratic, deviant, off-the-wall *(slang)*, oddball *(informal)*, anomalous, untypical, wacko *(slang)*, outré, daggy *(Austral. & N.Z. informal)* • *His rages and aberrant behaviour worsened.*
2 = **depraved**, corrupt, perverted, perverse, degenerate, deviant, debased, debauched • *aberrant sexual crimes*

aberration 1 = **anomaly**, exception, defect, abnormality, inconsistency, deviation, quirk, peculiarity, divergence, departure, irregularity, incongruity • *The incident was not just an aberration, not just a single incident.*
2 = **oddity**, abnormality, rarity, peculiarity, phenomenon, freak • *Single people are treated as an aberration and made to pay extra.*
3 = **lapse**, mistake, error • *an aberration of judgment*

abet 1 = **help**, aid, encourage, sustain, assist, uphold, back, second, incite, egg on, succour • *We shall strike hard at terrorists and those who abet them.*
2 = **encourage**, further, forward, promote, urge, boost, prompt, spur, foster, incite, connive at • *The media have abetted the feeling of unreality.*

abetting = **help**, backing, support, aid, assistance, encouragement, abetment, abettal • *They see blasphemy – and the abetting of it – as a most serious crime.*

abeyance **IN PHRASES:** **in abeyance** = **shelved**, pending, on ice *(informal)*, in cold storage *(informal)*, hanging fire, suspended • *The matter was left in abeyance until the next meeting.*

abhor = **hate**, loathe, despise, detest, shrink from, shudder at, recoil from, be repelled by, have an aversion to, abominate, execrate, regard with repugnance *or* horror • *He was a man who abhorred violence.*
OPPOSITES: like, love, enjoy

abhorrence = **hatred**, hate, horror, disgust, loathing, distaste, animosity, aversion, revulsion, antipathy, enmity, abomination, repugnance, odium, detestation, execration • *They are anxious to show their abhorrence of racism.*

abhorrent = **hateful**, hated, offensive, disgusting, horrible, revolting, obscene, distasteful, horrid, repellent, obnoxious, despicable, repulsive, heinous, odious, repugnant, loathsome, abominable, execrable, detestable • *Many people find the idea of abortion abhorrent.*

abide **AS A VERB** 1 = **tolerate**, suffer, accept, bear, endure, brook, hack *(slang)*, put up with, take, stand, stomach, thole *(Scot.)* • *I can't abide people who can't make up their minds.*
2 = **last**, continue, remain, survive, carry on, endure, persist, keep on • *to make moral judgements on the basis of what is eternal and abides*
▸ **IN PHRASES:** **abide by something** = **obey**, follow, agree to, carry out, observe, fulfil, stand by, act on, comply with, hold to, heed, submit to, conform to, keep to, adhere to, mind • *They have got to abide by the rules.*

abiding = **enduring**, lasting, continuing, remaining, surviving, permanent, constant, prevailing, persisting, persistent, eternal, tenacious, firm, fast, everlasting, unending, unchanging • *one of my abiding memories of him*
OPPOSITES: passing, brief, temporary

ability 1 = **capability**, power, potential, facility, capacity, qualification, competence, proficiency, competency, potentiality • *No one had faith in his ability to do the job.*
OPPOSITES: inability, incompetence
2 = **skill**, talent, know-how *(informal)*, gift, expertise, faculty, flair, competence, energy, accomplishment, knack, aptitude, proficiency, dexterity, cleverness, potentiality, adroitness, adeptness • *Her drama teacher spotted her ability.*

ab initio = **from the beginning**, from the start, from the first, from scratch *(informal)*, from the word go *(informal)*, from first principles • *They do more advanced work with their students ab initio.*

abject 1 = **wretched**, miserable, hopeless, dismal, outcast, pitiful, forlorn, deplorable, pitiable • *Both of them died in abject poverty.*
2 = **servile**, humble, craven, cringing, fawning, submissive, grovelling, subservient, slavish, mean, low, obsequious • *He sounded abject and eager to please.*
OPPOSITES: high, great, dignified
3 = **despicable**, base, degraded, worthless, vile, sordid, debased, reprehensible, contemptible, dishonourable, ignoble, detestable, scungy *(Austral. & N.Z.)* • *the kind of abject low-life that preys on children*

abjure 1 = **give up**, deny, reject, abandon, relinquish, renounce, throw off, forsake, retract, disown, renege on, disavow, recant, disclaim, forswear, wash your hands of, abnegate • *He abjured the Protestant faith in 1594.*

2 = refrain from, avoid, eschew, abstain from, abnegate • *countries whose officials abjure bribery*

ablaze **1 = on fire**, burning, flaming, blazing, fiery, alight, aflame, afire • *Shops, houses and vehicles were ablaze.* **2 = bright**, brilliant, flashing, glowing, sparkling, illuminated, gleaming, radiant, luminous, incandescent, aglow • *The chamber was ablaze with light.* **3 = passionate**, excited, stimulated, fierce, enthusiastic, aroused, animated, frenzied, fervent, impassioned, fervid • *He was ablaze with enthusiasm.*

able **1 = capable**, experienced, fit, skilled, expert, powerful, masterly, effective, qualified, talented, gifted, efficient, clever, practised, accomplished, competent, tasty *(Brit. informal)*, skilful, adept, masterful, strong, proficient, adroit, highly endowed • *They are bright, intelligent, able and confident.* OPPOSITES: weak, inadequate, incapable **2** *with* **to = in a position to**, capable of, allowed to, free to, up to • *I'd like to be able to study in peace.*

able-bodied **= strong**, firm, sound, fit, powerful, healthy, strapping, hardy, robust, vigorous, sturdy, hale, stout, staunch, hearty, lusty, right as rain *(Brit. informal)*, tough, capable, sturdy, Herculean, fighting fit, sinewy, fit as a fiddle • *The gym can be used by both able-bodied and disabled people.* OPPOSITES: weak, tender, fragile

ablutions **= washing**, bathing, wash, bath, showering, toilet, cleansing, scrubbing, purification, lavation • *He spent about 15 minutes doing his daily ablutions.*

abnegation **1 = giving up**, surrender, refusal, rejection, abandonment, renunciation, sacrifice, forbearance, disallowance, relinquishment, eschewal, abjuration • *He attacked 'society' for its abnegation of responsibility.* **2 = abstinence**, continence, temperance, renunciation, self-denial • *These monks took to abnegation and scourging as expiation for the sins of the world.*

abnormal **= unusual**, different, odd, strange, surprising, out there *(slang)*, extraordinary, remarkable, bizarre, unexpected, curious, weird, exceptional, peculiar, eccentric, unfamiliar, queer, irregular, phenomenal, uncommon, erratic, monstrous, singular, unnatural, deviant, unconventional, off-the-wall *(slang)*, oddball *(informal)*, out of the ordinary, left-field *(informal)*, anomalous, atypical, aberrant, untypical, wacko *(slang)*, outré, daggy *(Austral. & N.Z. informal)* • *a child with an abnormal fear of strangers* OPPOSITES: normal, common, average

abnormality **1 = strangeness**, deviation, eccentricity, aberration, peculiarity, idiosyncrasy, irregularity, weirdness, singularity, oddness, waywardness, unorthodoxy, unexpectedness, queerness, unnaturalness, bizarreness, unusualness, extraordinariness, aberrance, atypicalness, uncommonness, untypicalness, curiousness • *Further scans are required to confirm any abnormality.* **2 = anomaly**, flaw, rarity, deviation, oddity, aberration, exception, peculiarity, deformity, monstrosity, irregularity, malformation • *Genetic abnormalities are usually associated with paternal DNA.*

abnormally **= unusually**, oddly, strangely, extremely, exceptionally, extraordinarily, overly, excessively, peculiarly, particularly, bizarrely, disproportionately, singularly, fantastically, unnaturally, uncannily, inordinately, uncommonly, prodigiously, freakishly, atypically, subnormally, supernormally • *This stops the cells from growing abnormally.*

abode **= home**, house, quarters, lodging, pad *(slang)*, residence, habitat, dwelling, habitation, domicile, dwelling place • *I went round the streets and found his new abode.*

abolish **= do away with**, end, destroy, eliminate, shed, cancel, axe *(informal)*, get rid of, ditch *(slang)*, dissolve, junk *(informal)*, suppress, overturn, throw out, discard, wipe out, overthrow, void, terminate, drop, trash *(slang)*, repeal, eradicate, put an end to, quash, extinguish, dispense with, revoke, stamp out, obliterate, subvert, jettison, repudiate, annihilate, rescind, exterminate, invalidate, bring to an end, annul, nullify, blot out, expunge, abrogate, vitiate, extirpate, kennet *(Austral. slang)*, jeff *(Austral. slang)* • *They voted to abolish the death penalty.* OPPOSITES: found, continue, establish

abolition **= eradication**, ending, end, withdrawal, destruction, removal, overturning, wiping out, overthrow, voiding, extinction, repeal, elimination, cancellation, suppression, quashing, termination, stamping out, subversion, extermination, annihilation, blotting out, repudiation, erasure, annulment, obliteration, revocation, effacement, nullification, abrogation, rescission, extirpation, invalidation, vitiation, expunction • *the abolition of slavery*

abominable **= detestable**, shocking, terrible, offensive, foul, disgusting, horrible, revolting, obscene, vile, horrid, repellent, atrocious, obnoxious, despicable, repulsive, base, heinous, hellish, odious, hateful, repugnant, reprehensible, loathsome, abhorrent, contemptible, villainous, nauseous, wretched, accursed, execrable, godawful *(slang)* • *The President described the killings as an abominable crime.* OPPOSITES: good, pleasing, pleasant

abominably **= dreadfully**, badly, terribly, horribly, vilely, awfully, woefully, wickedly, offensively, foully, hideously, shockingly, frightfully, shamefully, disgracefully, horrendously, monstrously, wretchedly, abysmally, disgustingly, unforgivably, nauseatingly, deplorably, revoltingly, obnoxiously, repulsively, despicably, reprehensibly, horridly, odiously, contemptibly, heinously, unpalatably, abhorrently, detestably, execrably, repugnantly, disreputably • *Chloe has behaved abominably.* OPPOSITES: perfectly, wonderfully, admirably

abominate **= hate**, dislike, loathe, despise, detest, abhor, shudder at, recoil from, regard with repugnance, feel repelled by, have an aversion to, execrate, feel hostile to • *'I abominate dogma,' he said.* OPPOSITES: love, admire, treasure

abomination **1 = outrage**, bête noire, horror, evil, shame, plague, curse, disgrace, crime, atrocity, torment, anathema, barbarism, bugbear • *What is happening is an abomination.* **2 = hatred**, hate, horror, disgust, dislike, loathing, distaste, animosity, aversion, revulsion, antagonism, antipathy, enmity, ill will, animus, abhorrence, repugnance, odium, detestation, execration • *He had become an object of abomination.*

aboriginal AS A NOUN **= original inhabitant**, native, aborigine, indigene • *He remained fascinated by the Aboriginal's tales.* ▸ AS AN ADJECTIVE **= indigenous**, first, earliest, original, primary, ancient, native, primitive, pristine, primordial, primeval, autochthonous • *Most people acknowledge that the aboriginal people have had a rotten deal.*

aborigine **= original inhabitant**, native, aboriginal, indigene • *the rights of Australia's aborigines*

abort **1 = terminate** *(a pregnancy)*, miscarry • *the latest date at which a foetus can be aborted* **2 = stop**, end, finish, check, arrest, halt, cease, bring *or* come to a halt *or* standstill, axe *(informal)*, pull up, terminate, call off, break off, cut short, pack in *(Brit. informal)*, discontinue, desist • *The take-off was aborted.*

abortion **1 = termination**, feticide, aborticide, miscarriage, deliberate miscarriage • *They had been going out a year when she had an abortion.* **2 = failure**, disappointment, fiasco, misadventure, vain effort • *the abortion of the original nuclear project* **3 = monstrosity**

abortive **= failed**, failing, useless, vain, unsuccessful, idle, ineffective, futile, fruitless, unproductive, ineffectual, miscarried, unavailing, bootless • *an abortive attempt to prevent him from taking office*

abound AS A VERB = **be plentiful**, thrive, flourish, be numerous, proliferate, be abundant, be thick on the ground, superabound • *Stories abound about when he was in charge.*
▸ IN PHRASES: **abound with** *or* **in something** = **overflow with**, be packed with, teem with, be crowded with, swell with, crawl with, swarm with, be jammed with, be infested with, be thronged with, luxuriate with • *Venice abounds in famous hotels.* • *In troubled times, the roads abounded with highwaymen and brigands.*

abounding = **abundant**, full, rich, filled, flowing, rank, flourishing, flush, lavish, ample, prolific, overflowing, plentiful, exuberant, teeming, copious, replete, bountiful, luxuriant, profuse, well-provided, well-supplied, thick on the ground, bounteous, superabundant, plenteous • *a garden abounding with colour*

about AS A PREPOSITION 1 = **regarding**, on, re, concerning, touching, dealing with, respecting, referring to, relating to, concerned with, connected with, relative to, with respect to, as regards, anent *(Scot.)* • *She knew a lot about food.*
2 = **around**, over, through, round, throughout, all over • *For 18 years, he wandered about Germany, Switzerland and Italy.*
3 = **round**, around • *She threw her arms about him.*
4 = **near**, around, close to, bordering, nearby, beside, close by, adjacent to, just round the corner from, in the neighbourhood of, alongside of, contiguous to, within sniffing distance of *(informal)*, at close quarters to, a hop, skip and a jump away from *(informal)* • *The restaurant is somewhere about here.*
▸ AS AN ADVERB 1 = **approximately**, around, almost, nearing, nearly, approaching, close to, roughly, just about, more or less, in the region of, in the vicinity of, not far off • *The rate of inflation is running at about 2.7 per cent.*
2 = **everywhere**, around, all over, here and there, on all sides, in all directions, to and fro, from place to place, hither and thither • *The house isn't big enough with three children running about.*
▸ AS AN ADJECTIVE = **around**, present, active, stirring, in motion, astir • *There were a lot of people about.*
▸ IN PHRASES: **about to** = **on the point of**, ready to, intending to, on the verge *or* brink of • *I think he's about to leave.*

about-turn AS A NOUN = **change of direction**, reverse, reversal, turnaround, U-turn, right about (turn), about-face, volte-face, turnabout, paradigm shift • *The decision was seen as an about-turn for the government.*
▸ AS A VERB = **change direction**, reverse, about-face, volte-face, face the opposite direction, turn about *or* around, turn through 180 degrees, do *or* perform a U-turn *or* volte-face • *She about-turned abruptly and left.*

above AS A PREPOSITION 1 = **over**, upon, beyond, on top of, exceeding, higher than, atop • *He lifted his arms above his head.*
OPPOSITES: under, below, beneath
2 = **more than**, over, exceeding, higher than, greater than, upwards of, beyond • *The temperature crept up to just above 40 degrees.*
3 = **senior to**, over, ahead of, in charge of, higher than, surpassing, superior to, more powerful than • *the people above you in the organization*
OPPOSITES: less than, lesser than, subordinate to
4 = **better than**, superior to • *She thought she was above doing the cleaning.*
5 = **exempt from**, superior to, beyond, immune to, not subject to, out of reach of, not exposed to, not liable to, not in danger of, not vulnerable to, insusceptible to • *He was a respected academic and above suspicion.*
6 = **before**, more than, rather than, beyond, instead of, sooner than, in preference to • *I want to be honest, above everything else.*
▸ AS AN ADVERB 1 = **overhead**, upward, in the sky, on high, in heaven, atop, aloft, up above, skyward • *A long scream sounded from somewhere above.*
2 = **earlier mentioned**, previously mentioned, formerly mentioned, foregoing • *For additional information, contact any of the above.*
▸ AS AN ADJECTIVE = **preceding**, earlier, previous, prior, foregoing, aforementioned, aforesaid • *Write to the above address.*
▸ IN PHRASES: **above all** = **most of all**, chiefly, mainly, especially, essentially, basically, principally, primarily, in the first place, first of all, at the end of the day *(informal)*, predominantly, most importantly, in essence, firstly and foremost, at bottom, when all is said and done *(informal)*, before everything, beyond everything, elementally • *Above all, chairs should be comfortable.*
above yourself = **arrogant**, lordly, assuming, proud, swaggering, pompous, pretentious, contemptuous, conceited, blustering, imperious, overbearing, haughty, scornful, disdainful, presumptuous, high-handed, insolent, supercilious, high and mighty *(informal)*, overweening, uppish *(Brit. informal)*, too big for your boots *or* breeches • *I think you're getting a little bit above yourself.*
▸ RELATED PREFIXES: super-, supra-, sur-

above board AS AN ADJECTIVE = **honest**, straight, frank, square, genuine, proper, legitimate, straightforward, authentic, open, true, upright, honourable, overt, candid, truthful, forthright, upfront *(informal)*, trustworthy, on the level *(informal)*, bona fide, kosher *(informal)*, dinkum *(Austral. & N.Z. informal)*, fair and square, guileless, on the up and up, veracious, honest to goodness • *His financial dealings were always above board.*
OPPOSITES: secret, crooked, dishonest
▸ AS AN ADVERB = **honestly**, frankly, truly, legitimately, legally, uprightly, openly, cleanly, overtly, in good faith, ethically, truthfully, candidly, lawfully, honourably, straightforwardly, forthrightly, by fair means, with clean hands, without guile, veraciously • *It was clear that they had acted above board.*

ab ovo = **from the beginning**, from the start, from the first, from scratch *(informal)*, from the word go *(informal)*, ab initio *(Latin)*, from the egg, from first principles

abrade = **scrape**, grind, skin, file, scratch, erode, graze, erase, scour, wear off, rub off, wear down, scuff, wear away, scrape away, scrape out • *The rough rock had abraded her skin.*

abrasion 1 = **graze**, scratch, trauma *(Pathology)*, scrape, scuff, chafe, surface injury • *He had severe abrasions to his right cheek.*
2 = **rubbing**, wear, scratching, scraping, grating, friction, scouring, attrition, corrosion, wearing down, erosion, scuffing, chafing, grinding down, wearing away, abrading • *The sole of the shoe should be designed to take constant abrasion.*

abrasive AS AN ADJECTIVE 1 = **harsh**, cutting, biting, tough, sharp, severe, bitter, rough, hard, nasty, cruel, annoying, brutal, stern, irritating, unpleasant, grating, abusive, galling, unkind, hurtful, caustic, vitriolic, pitiless, unfeeling, comfortless • *She was unrepentant about her abrasive remarks.*
2 = **rough**, scratching, scraping, grating, scuffing, chafing, scratchy, frictional, erosive • *an all-purpose non-abrasive cleaner*
▸ AS A NOUN = **scourer**, grinder, burnisher, scarifier, abradant • *Avoid abrasives, which can damage the tiles.*

abreast AS AN ADVERB = **alongside**, level, beside, in a row, side by side, neck and neck, shoulder to shoulder • *a group of youths riding four abreast*
▸ IN PHRASES: **abreast of** *or* **with** = **informed about**, in touch with, familiar with, acquainted with, up to date with, knowledgeable about, conversant with, plugged-in to *(slang)*, up to speed with *(informal)*, in the picture about, *au courant* with, *au fait* with, keeping your finger on the pulse of • *We'll keep you abreast of developments.*

abridge = **shorten**, reduce, contract, trim, clip, diminish, decrease, abstract, digest, cut down, cut back, cut, prune, concentrate, lessen, summarize, compress, curtail, condense, abbreviate, truncate, epitomize, downsize, précis, synopsize *(U.S.)* • *We don't abridge any of the stories we publish.*
OPPOSITES: extend, expand, prolong

abridged = **shortened**, shorter, reduced, brief, potted *(informal)*, trimmed, diminished, pruned, summarized, cut, compressed, curtailed, concise, condensed, abbreviated • *an abridged version of her new novel*
OPPOSITES: increased, expanded, prolonged

abridgment = **shortening**, reduction, résumé, outline, restriction, diminishing, decrease, limitation, summary, abstract, digest, contraction, cutting, lessening, epitome, abbreviation, condensation, compendium, synopsis, diminution, curtailment, précis, conspectus • *The issue of abridgment is in the author's hands.*

abroad 1 = **overseas**, out of the country, beyond the sea, in foreign lands • *About 65 per cent of our sales come from abroad.*
2 = **about**, everywhere, circulating, at large, here and there, current, all over, in circulation • *There is still a feeling abroad that this change must be recognised.*

QUOTATIONS
Abroad is unutterably bloody and foreigners are fiends
[Nancy Mitford *The Pursuit of Love*]
PROVERBS
Go abroad and you'll hear news of home

abrogate = **revoke**, end, recall, withdraw, reverse, cancel, scrap *(informal)*, abolish, set aside, override, void, repeal, renounce, quash, take back, call back, retract, repudiate, negate, rescind, invalidate, annul, nullify, recant, obviate, disclaim, countermand, declare null and void • *The next prime minister could abrogate the treaty.*

abrogation = **revocation**, ending, withdrawal, scrapping *(informal)*, setting aside, overriding, voiding, abolition, reversal, repeal, cancellation, quashing, retraction, repudiation, annulment, countermanding, nullification, rescission, invalidation • *a dereliction of duty and an abrogation of responsibility*

abrupt 1 = **sudden**, unexpected, hurried, rapid, surprising, quick, swift, rash, precipitate, hasty, impulsive, headlong, unforeseen, unanticipated • *His abrupt departure is bound to raise questions.*
OPPOSITES: easy, slow, thoughtful
2 = **curt**, direct, brief, sharp, rough, short, clipped, blunt, rude, tart, impatient, brisk, concise, snappy, terse, gruff, succinct, pithy, brusque, offhand, impolite, monosyllabic, ungracious, discourteous, uncivil, unceremonious, snappish • *He was abrupt to the point of rudeness.*
OPPOSITES: civil, polite, gracious
3 = **steep**, sharp, sheer, sudden, precipitous • *narrow valleys and abrupt hillsides*
OPPOSITES: gradual
4 = **uneven**, broken, irregular, disconnected, jerky, discontinuous • *the rather abrupt patting she displayed*

abruptly 1 = **suddenly**, short, unexpectedly, all of a sudden, hastily, precipitately, all at once, hurriedly • *He stopped abruptly and looked my way.*
OPPOSITES: slowly, gradually, progressively
2 = **curtly**, bluntly, rudely, briskly, tersely, shortly, sharply, brusquely, gruffly, snappily • *'Good night then,' she said abruptly.*
OPPOSITES: politely, courteously

abscess = **boil**, infection, swelling, blister, ulcer, inflammation, gathering, whitlow, blain, carbuncle, pustule, bubo, furuncle *(Pathology)*, gumboil, parulis *(Pathology)* • *In the case of an abscess, seek medical treatment immediately.*

abscond = **escape**, flee, get away, bolt, fly, disappear, skip, run off, slip away, clear out, flit *(informal)*, make off, break free *or* out, decamp, hook it *(slang)*, do a runner *(slang)*, steal away, sneak away, do a bunk *(Brit. slang)*, fly the coop *(U.S. & Canad. informal)*, skedaddle *(informal)*, take a powder *(U.S. & Canad. slang)*, go on the lam *(U.S. & Canad. slang)*, make your getaway, do a Skase *(Austral. informal)*, make *or* effect your escape • *A dozen inmates have absconded from the jail in the past year.*

QUOTATIONS
abscond: to 'move in a mysterious way', commonly with the property of another
[Ambrose Bierce *The Devil's Dictionary*]

absence 1 = **time off**, leave, break, vacation, recess, truancy, absenteeism, nonappearance, nonattendance • *A bundle of letters had arrived for me in my absence.*
2 = **lack**, deficiency, deprivation, omission, scarcity, want, need, shortage, dearth, privation, unavailability, nonexistence • *In the absence of a will, the courts decide who the guardian is.*

QUOTATIONS
Absence makes the heart grow fonder,
Isle of Beauty, Fare thee well!
[Thomas Haynes Bayly *Isle of Beauty*]
Absence is to love what wind is to fire; it extinguishes the small, it inflames the great
[Comte de Bussy-Rabutin *Histoire amoureuse des Gaules*]
Among the defects of the Bill, which were numerous, one provision was conspicuous by its presence and another by its absence
[Lord John Russell *Speech to his constituents, 1859*]

absent AS AN ADJECTIVE 1 = **away**, missing, gone, lacking, elsewhere, unavailable, not present, truant, nonexistent, nonattendant • *He has been absent from his desk for two weeks.*
OPPOSITES: present, attendant, in attendance
2 = **absent-minded**, blank, unconscious, abstracted, vague, distracted, unaware, musing, vacant, preoccupied, empty, absorbed, careless, bemused, oblivious, negligent, dreamy, daydreaming, faraway, thoughtless, inadvertent, unthinking, neglectful, heedless, inattentive, unmindful, unobservant, unheeding • *'Nothing,' she said in an absent way.*
OPPOSITES: aware, conscious, alert
▸ IN PHRASES: **absent yourself** = **stay away**, withdraw, depart, keep away, truant, abscond, play truant, slope off *(informal)*, bunk off *(slang)*, remove yourself • *He pleaded guilty to absenting himself without leave.*

QUOTATIONS
Greater things are believed of those who are absent
[Tacitus *Histories*]

absentee = **nonattender**, stay-at-home, truant, no-show, stayaway • *Minnihoma is the most notable absentee from this Saturday's race.*

absently = **distractedly**, dreamily, absent-mindedly, vacantly, blankly, vaguely, unconsciously, bemusedly, abstractedly, emptily, heedlessly, obliviously, inattentively, unheedingly • *He nodded absently.*

absent-minded = **forgetful**, absorbed, abstracted, vague, absent, distracted, unaware, musing, preoccupied, careless, bemused, oblivious, dreamy, faraway, engrossed, unthinking, neglectful, heedless, inattentive, unmindful, unheeding, apt to forget, in a brown study, ditzy *or* ditsy *(slang)* • *In his later life he became even more absent-minded.*
OPPOSITES: alert, awake, wary

absent-mindedness = **forgetfulness**, musing, preoccupation, abstraction, daydreaming, carelessness, vagueness, inattention, dreaminess, obliviousness, lapse of memory, absence of mind, woolgathering, heedlessness, distractedness • *You will have to put up with her absent-mindedness.*

absolute 1 = **complete**, total, perfect, entire, pure, sheer, utter, outright, thorough, downright, consummate, unqualified, full-on *(informal)*, out-and-out, unadulterated, unmitigated, dyed-in-the-wool, thoroughgoing, unalloyed, unmixed, arrant, deep-dyed *(usually derogatory)* • *A sick person needs to have absolute trust in a doctor.*
2 = **supreme**, sovereign, unlimited, ultimate, full, utmost, unconditional, unqualified, predominant, superlative, unrestricted, pre-eminent, unrestrained, tyrannical, peerless, unsurpassed, unquestionable, matchless, peremptory, unbounded • *He ruled with absolute power.*
3 = **autocratic**, supreme, unlimited, autonomous, arbitrary, dictatorial, all-powerful, imperious, domineering, tyrannical, despotic, absolutist, tyrannous, autarchical • *the doctrine of absolute monarchy*
4 = **definite**, sure, certain, positive, guaranteed, actual, assured, genuine, exact, precise, decisive, conclusive, unequivocal, unambiguous, infallible, categorical, unquestionable, dinkum *(Austral. & N.Z. informal)*, nailed-on *(slang)* • *He brought the absolute proof that we needed.*
5 = **universal**, general, common, total, entire, worldwide, widespread, omnipresent, all-embracing, overarching • *There are no absolute truths.*

absolutely 1 = **completely**, totally, perfectly, quite, fully, entirely, purely, altogether, thoroughly, wholly, utterly, consummately, every inch, to the hilt, a hundred per cent, one hundred per cent, unmitigatedly, lock, stock and barrel • *She is absolutely right.*
OPPOSITES: probably, fairly, somewhat
2 = **definitely**, surely, certainly, clearly, obviously, plainly, truly, precisely, exactly, genuinely, positively, decidedly, decisively, without doubt, unquestionably, undeniably, categorically, without question, unequivocally, conclusively, unambiguously, beyond any doubt, infallibly • *'It's worrying, isn't it?' 'Absolutely.'*

absolution = **forgiveness**, release, freedom, liberation, discharge, amnesty, mercy, pardon, indulgence, exemption, acquittal, remission, vindication, deliverance, dispensation, exoneration, exculpation, shriving, condonation • *She felt as if his words had granted her absolution.*

absolutism = **dictatorship**, tyranny, totalitarianism, authoritarianism, despotism, autocracy, arbitrariness, absolute rule, absoluteness, autarchy • *the triumphal reassertion of royal absolutism*

absolve = **excuse**, free, clear, release, deliver, loose, forgive, discharge, liberate, pardon, exempt, acquit, vindicate, remit, let off, set free, exonerate, exculpate • *The judicial inquiry absolved the soldiers.*
OPPOSITES: charge, blame, condemn

absorb 1 = **soak up**, drink in, devour, suck up, receive, digest, imbibe, ingest, osmose • *Refined sugars are absorbed into the bloodstream very quickly.*
2 = **assimilate**, take in, incorporate, accommodate, homogenize, intermix • *an economy capable of absorbing thousands of immigrants*
3 = **cushion**, suppress, soften, pillow, bolster, stifle, dampen, muffle, buttress, deaden • *footwear to absorb the impact of a hard pavement*
4 = **consume**, use, use up, spend, waste, employ, drain, exhaust, squander, utilize, expend, eat up, fritter away • *The campaign absorbed vast amounts of capital.*
5 = **engross**, hold, involve, fill, arrest, fix, occupy, engage, fascinate, preoccupy, engulf, fill up, immerse, rivet, captivate, monopolize, enwrap • *a second career which absorbed her more completely than acting ever had*

absorbed 1 = **engrossed**, lost, involved, fixed, concentrating, occupied, engaged, gripped, fascinated, caught up, intrigued, wrapped up, preoccupied, immersed, riveted, captivated, enthralled, rapt, up to your ears • *They were completely absorbed in each other.*
2 = **digested**, soaked up, devoured, assimilated, received, exhausted, incorporated, consumed, imbibed • *Cook until all the liquid is absorbed by the rice.*

absorbency = **permeability**, receptiveness, retentiveness, ability to soak up *or* take in, sponginess, porousness, permeableness, perviousness • *You can use two nappies for extra absorbency at night.*
OPPOSITES: imperviousness, impermeability, impermeableness

absorbent = **porous**, receptive, imbibing, spongy, permeable, absorptive, blotting, penetrable, pervious, assimilative • *The towels are highly absorbent.*

absorbing = **fascinating**, interesting, engaging, gripping, arresting, compelling, intriguing, enticing, preoccupying, enchanting, seductive, riveting, captivating, alluring, bewitching, engrossing, spellbinding • *Children will find other exhibits equally absorbing.*
OPPOSITES: boring, dull, tedious

absorption 1 = **soaking up**, consumption, digestion, sucking up, osmosis • *Vitamin C increases absorption of iron.*
2 = **assimilation**, integration, inclusion, fusion, incorporation, amalgamation • *Two new camps were set up for the absorption of refugees.*
3 = **immersion**, holding, involvement, concentration, occupation, engagement, fascination, preoccupation, intentness, captivation, raptness • *He was struck by the artists' total absorption in their work.*

abstain from = **refrain from**, avoid, decline, give up, stop, refuse, cease, do without, shun, renounce, eschew, leave off, keep from, forgo, withhold from, forbear, desist from, deny yourself, kick *(informal)* • *Abstain from sex or use condoms.*
OPPOSITES: yield, give in, abandon yourself

abstemious = **temperate**, sparing, moderate, sober, austere, frugal, ascetic, self-denying, abstinent, continent • *They want to live a quiet, abstemious life.*
OPPOSITES: greedy, self-indulgent, incontinent

abstemiousness = **temperance**, restraint, austerity, moderation, plain *or* simple living, self-control, abstinence, self-discipline, sobriety, continence, self-denial, self-restraint, forbearance, asceticism, frugality • *self-discipline, abstemiousness and family values*
OPPOSITES: excess, drunkenness, self-indulgence

abstention 1 = **abstaining**, non-voting, refusal to vote • *Abstention is traditionally high in Columbia.*
2 = **abstinence**, refraining, avoidance, forbearance, eschewal, desistance, nonindulgence • *The goal is complete abstention from all mind-altering substances.*

abstinence = **abstention**, continence, temperance, self-denial, self-restraint, forbearance, refraining, avoidance, moderation, sobriety, asceticism, teetotalism, abstemiousness, soberness • *six months of abstinence*
OPPOSITES: abandon, excess, self-indulgence

QUOTATIONS

Refrain to-night, And that shall lend a kind of easiness To the next abstinence: the next more easy; For use almost can change the stamp of nature
[William Shakespeare *Hamlet*]

Abstinence is as easy to me, as temperance would be difficult
[Samuel Johnson *Correspondence with Mrs. Hannah More*]

To many, total abstinence is easier than perfect moderation
[St. Augustine of Hippo *On the Good of Marriage*]

abstract AS AN ADJECTIVE 1 = **theoretical**, general, complex, academic, intellectual, subtle, profound, philosophical, speculative, unrealistic, conceptual, indefinite, deep, separate, occult, hypothetical, generalized, impractical, arcane, notional, abstruse, recondite, theoretic, conjectural, unpractical, nonconcrete • *starting with a few abstract principles*
OPPOSITES: real, material, actual

2 = **symbolic**, figurative, emblematic, impressionistic, non-representational • *a modern abstract painting*
▸ AS A NOUN = **summary**, résumé, outline, extract, essence, summing-up, digest, epitome, rundown, condensation, compendium, synopsis, précis, recapitulation, review, abridgment • *If you want to submit a paper, you must supply an abstract.*
OPPOSITES: expansion, enlargement
▸ AS A VERB = **extract**, draw, pull, remove, separate, withdraw, isolate, pull out, take out, take away, detach, dissociate, pluck out • *The author has abstracted poems from earlier books.*
OPPOSITES: add, combine, inject

abstracted = **preoccupied**, withdrawn, remote, absorbed, intent, absent, distracted, unaware, wrapped up, bemused, immersed, oblivious, dreamy, daydreaming, faraway, engrossed, rapt, absent-minded, heedless, inattentive, distrait, woolgathering • *The same abstracted look was still on her face.*

abstraction 1 = **concept**, thought, idea, view, theory, impression, formula, notion, hypothesis, generalization, theorem, generality • *Is it worth fighting in the name of an abstraction?*
2 = **absent-mindedness**, musing, preoccupation, daydreaming, vagueness, remoteness, absence, inattention, dreaminess, obliviousness, absence of mind, pensiveness, woolgathering, distractedness, bemusedness • *He noticed her abstraction and asked, 'What's bothering you?'*

abstruse = **obscure**, complex, confusing, puzzling, subtle, mysterious, concealed, abstract, vague, deep, dark, hidden, unclear, ambiguous, enigmatic, esoteric, perplexing, opaque, incomprehensible, arcane, hazy, cryptic, unfathomable, recondite, Delphic, clear as mud *(informal)* • *Meetings keep reverting to discussions about abstruse resolutions.*
OPPOSITES: open, clear, plain

absurd = **ridiculous**, crazy *(informal)*, silly, incredible, outrageous, foolish, unbelievable, daft *(informal)*, hilarious, ludicrous, meaningless, unreasonable, irrational, senseless, preposterous, laughable, funny, stupid, farcical, illogical, incongruous, comical, zany, idiotic, nonsensical, inane, dumb-ass *(slang)*, cockamamie *(slang, chiefly U.S.)* • *They go to absurd lengths just to avoid paying a few pounds.*
OPPOSITES: smart, wise, sensible

absurdity = **ridiculousness**, nonsense, malarkey, folly, stupidity, foolishness, silliness, idiocy, irrationality, incongruity, meaninglessness, daftness *(informal)*, senselessness, illogicality, ludicrousness, unreasonableness, preposterousness, farcicality, craziness *(informal)*, bêtise *(rare)*, farcicalness, illogicalness • *I get angry at the absurdity of a situation.*

QUOTATIONS
absurdity: a statement of belief manifestly inconsistent with one's own opinion
[Ambrose Bierce *The Devil's Dictionary*]

absurdly = **ridiculously**, incredibly, unbelievably, foolishly, ludicrously, unreasonably, incongruously, laughably, irrationally, implausibly, preposterously, illogically, inanely, senselessly, idiotically, inconceivably, farcically • *Prices were still absurdly low, in his opinion.*

abundance 1 = **plenty**, heap *(informal)*, bounty, exuberance, profusion, plethora, affluence, fullness, opulence, plenitude, fruitfulness, copiousness, ampleness, cornucopia, plenteousness, plentifulness • *a staggering abundance of food*
OPPOSITES: need, lack, shortage
2 = **wealth**, money, funds, capital, cash, riches, resources, assets, fortune, possessions, prosperity, big money, wad *(U.S. & Canad. slang)*, affluence, big bucks *(informal, chiefly U.S.)*, opulence, top dollar *(informal)*, megabucks *(U.S. & Canad. slang)*, tidy sum *(informal)*, lucre, wonga *(slang)*, pretty penny *(informal)*, pelf, top whack *(informal)* • *What customers want is a display of lushness and abundance.*

abundant = **plentiful**, full, rich, liberal, generous, lavish, ample, infinite, overflowing, exuberant, teeming, copious, inexhaustible, bountiful, luxuriant, profuse, rank, well-provided, well-supplied, bounteous, plenteous • *There is an abundant supply of cheap labour.*
OPPOSITES: few, short, scarce

abundantly 1 = **exceptionally**, very, highly, greatly, quite, severely, terribly, utterly, unusually, manifestly, extraordinarily, intensely, markedly, awfully *(informal)*, acutely, exceedingly, excessively, inordinately, uncommonly • *He made it abundantly clear that he didn't like me.*
OPPOSITES: moderately, reasonably
2 = **plentifully**, greatly, freely, amply, richly, liberally, fully, thoroughly, substantially, lavishly, extensively, generously, profusely, copiously, exuberantly, in plentiful supply, luxuriantly, unstintingly, bountifully, bounteously, plenteously, in great *or* large numbers • *The pages are abundantly illustrated with colour photos.*
OPPOSITES: rarely, scarcely, sparsely

abuse AS A NOUN 1 = **maltreatment**, wrong, damage, injury, hurt, harm, spoiling, bullying, exploitation, oppression, imposition, mistreatment, manhandling, ill-treatment, rough handling • *an investigation into alleged child abuse*
2 = **insults**, blame, slights, curses, put-downs, libel, censure, reproach, scolding, defamation, indignities, offence, tirade, derision, slander, rudeness, vilification, invective, swear words, opprobrium, insolence, upbraiding, aspersions, character assassination, disparagement, vituperation, castigation, contumely, revilement, traducement, calumniation • *I was left shouting abuse as the car sped off.*
3 = **misuse**, corruption, perversion, misapplication, misemployment, misusage • *an abuse of power*
▸ AS A VERB 1 = **ill-treat**, wrong, damage, hurt, injure, harm, mar, oppress, maul, molest, impose upon, manhandle, rough up, brutalize, shit on *(taboo slang)*, maltreat, handle roughly, knock about *or* around • *She had been abused by her father.*
OPPOSITES: protect, care for
2 = **insult**, injure, offend, curse, put down, smear, libel, slate *(informal, chiefly Brit.)*, slag (off) *(slang)*, malign, scold, swear at, disparage, castigate, revile, vilify, slander, diss *(slang, chiefly U.S.)*, defame, upbraid, slight, flame *(informal)*, inveigh against, call names, traduce, calumniate, vituperate • *He alleged that he was verbally abused by other soldiers.*
OPPOSITES: respect, praise, acclaim
3 = **exploit**, take advantage of, manipulate, misuse • *He showed how the rich and powerful can abuse their position.*

abusive 1 = **violent**, wild, rough, cruel, savage, brutal, vicious, destructive, harmful, maddened, hurtful, unrestrained, impetuous, homicidal, intemperate, raging, furious, injurious, maniacal • *her cruel and abusive husband*
OPPOSITES: kind, caring, gentle
2 = **insulting**, offensive, rude, degrading, scathing, maligning, scolding, affronting, contemptuous, disparaging, castigating, reviling, vilifying, invective, scurrilous, defamatory, insolent, derisive, censorious, slighting, libellous, upbraiding, vituperative, reproachful, slanderous, traducing, opprobrious, calumniating, contumelious • *He was alleged to have used abusive language.*
OPPOSITES: approving, praising, complimentary

abut = **adjoin**, join, touch, border, neighbour, link to, attach to, combine with, connect with, couple with, communicate with, annex, meet, unite with, verge on, impinge, append, affix to • *He lived in a house abutting our hotel.*

abysmal = **dreadful**, bad, terrible, awful, appalling, dismal, dire, ghastly, hideous, atrocious, godawful *(informal)* • *The general standard was abysmal.*

abyss 1 = **chasm**, gulf, split, crack, gap, pit, opening, breach, hollow, void, gorge, crater, cavity, ravine, cleft, fissure, crevasse, bottomless depth, abysm • *She leapt to her death in a nearby abyss.*
2 = **cataclysm**, collapse, disaster, catastrophe, upheaval, debacle, calamity, convulsion • *The country was on the brink of an abyss.*
3 = **gap**, difference, gulf, split, disagreement, disparity, divergence • *How big is the abyss between them?*

academia = **academic life**, learning, scholarship, academe *(literary)*, university life, the groves of Academe *(literary)* • *strong links between industry and academia*

academic AS AN ADJECTIVE 1 = **scholastic**, school, university, college, educational, campus, collegiate • *the country's richest and most famous academic institutions*
2 = **scholarly**, learned, intellectual, literary, erudite, highbrow, studious, lettered, swotty *(Brit. informal)* • *The author has settled for a more academic approach.*
3 = **studious**, serious, intellectual, eager, hard-working, scholarly, thoughtful, earnest, reflective, diligent, meditative, bookish, assiduous, swotty *(Brit. informal)*, sedulous • *The system is failing less academic children.*
4 = **theoretical**, ideal, abstract, speculative, hypothetical, impractical, notional, conjectural • *These arguments are purely academic.*
▸ AS A NOUN = **scholar**, intellectual, don, student, master, professor, fellow, pupil, lecturer, tutor, scholastic, bookworm, man of letters, egghead *(informal)*, savant, academician, acca *(Austral. slang)*, bluestocking *(usually disparaging)*, schoolman • *He is an academic who believes in winning through argument.*

academy = **college**, school, university, institution, institute, establishment, seminary, centre of learning, whare wananga *(N.Z.)* • *her experience as a police academy instructor*

accede to AS A VERB 1 = **agree to**, accept, grant, endorse, consent to, give in to, surrender to, yield to, concede to, acquiesce in, assent to, comply with, concur to • *Why didn't he accede to our demands at the outset?*
▸ IN PHRASES: **accede to the throne** 2 = **inherit**, come to, assume, succeed, come into, attain, succeed to *(of an heir)*, enter upon, fall heir to • *when Henry VIII acceded to the throne*

accelerate 1 = **increase**, grow, advance, extend, expand, build up, strengthen, raise, swell, intensify, enlarge, escalate, multiply, inflate, magnify, proliferate, snowball • *Growth will accelerate to 2.9 per cent next year.*
OPPOSITES: fall, drop, lower
2 = **expedite**, press, forward, promote, spur, further, stimulate, hurry, step up *(informal)*, speed up, facilitate, hasten, precipitate, quicken • *The government is to accelerate its privatisation programme.*
OPPOSITES: delay, hinder, obstruct
3 = **speed up**, speed, advance, quicken, get under way, gather momentum, get moving, pick up speed, put your foot down *(informal)*, open up the throttle, put on speed • *Suddenly the car accelerated.*
OPPOSITES: brake, slow down, rein in

acceleration 1 = **hastening**, hurrying, stepping up *(informal)*, expedition, speeding up, stimulation, advancement, promotion, spurring, quickening • *He has called for an acceleration of political reforms.*
2 = **speeding up**, gathering speed, opening up, increasing speed • *Acceleration to 60 mph takes a mere 5.7 seconds.*
3 = **increase**, rise, development, gain, growth, boost, expansion, extension, enlargement, escalation, upsurge, upturn, increment, intensification, augmentation • *the recent acceleration of house prices*

accent AS A NOUN 1 = **pronunciation**, tone, articulation, inflection, brogue, intonation, diction, modulation, elocution, enunciation, accentuation • *He has developed a slight American accent.*
2 = **stress**, force, beat, emphasis, rhythm, cadence, timbre, accentuation, ictus • *Talk very fast and put an accent on every third word.*
3 = **emphasis**, stress, importance, priority, significance, insistence, prominence, underscoring • *There is often a strong accent on material success.*
▸ AS A VERB = **emphasize**, stress, highlight, underline, bring home, underscore, accentuate, foreground, give emphasis to, call *or* draw attention to • *She had a round face accented by a little white cap.*

QUOTATIONS

The accent of one's birthplace lingers in the mind and in the heart as it does in one's speech
[Duc de la Rochefoucauld *Maximes*]

I don't have an English accent because this is what English sounds like when spoken properly
[Jimmy Carr *The Tonight Show with Jay Leno (US TV chat show)*]

accentuate = **emphasize**, stress, highlight, accent, underline, bring home, underscore, foreground, give emphasis to, call *or* draw attention to • *His shaven head accentuates his large round face.*
OPPOSITES: play down, minimize, gloss over

accept 1 = **receive**, take, gain, pick up, secure, collect, have, get, obtain, acquire • *All old clothes will be gratefully accepted by the organizers.*
2 = **take on**, try, begin, attempt, bear, assume, tackle, acknowledge, undertake, embark on, set about, commence, avow, enter upon • *Everyone told me I should accept the job.*
OPPOSITES: refuse, deny, reject
3 = **say yes to**, agree to, comply with • *Eventually she was persuaded to accept an offer of marriage.*
4 = **acknowledge**, believe, allow, admit, adopt, approve, recognize, yield, concede, swallow *(informal)*, buy *(slang)*, affirm, profess, consent to, buy into *(slang)*, cooperate with, take on board, accede, acquiesce, concur with • *I do not accept that there is any kind of crisis in the industry.*
5 = **stand**, take, experience, suffer, bear, allow, weather, cope with, tolerate, sustain, put up with, wear *(Brit. slang)*, stomach, endure, undergo, brook, hack *(slang)*, abide, withstand, bow to, yield to, countenance, like it or lump it *(informal)* • *Urban dwellers have to accept noise as part of city life.*
6 = **welcome**, receive, greet, embrace, hail, usher in, receive with open arms, accept gladly, bid welcome • *He was accepted into the family like a brother.*

acceptability = **adequacy**, fitness, suitability, propriety, appropriateness, admissibility, permissibility, acceptableness, satisfactoriness • *the increasing social acceptability of divorce*
OPPOSITES: inadequacy, impropriety, unacceptability

acceptable 1 = **satisfactory**, fair, all right, suitable, sufficient, good enough, standard, adequate, so-so *(informal)*, tolerable, up to scratch *(informal)*, passable, up to the mark • *There was one restaurant that looked acceptable.*
OPPOSITES: unacceptable, unsatisfactory, unsuitable
2 = **tolerable**, bearable, allowable, admissible, supportable, endurable, sufferable • *It is becoming more and more acceptable for women to drink.*
3 = **pleasant**, pleasing, welcome, satisfying, grateful, refreshing, delightful, gratifying, agreeable, pleasurable • *a most acceptable present*

acceptance 1 = **accepting**, taking, receiving, obtaining, acquiring, reception, receipt • *The party is being downgraded by its acceptance of secret donations.*
2 = **acknowledgement**, agreement, belief, approval, recognition, admission, consent, consensus, adoption, affirmation, assent, credence, accession, approbation, concurrence, accedence, stamp *or* seal of approval • *a theory that is steadily gaining acceptance*

3 = **approval**, following, support, embracing, adoption, endorsement, espousal • *Avant-garde music has not found general public acceptance.*
4 = **recognition**, appreciation, acknowledgment • *an effort to ensure that the disabled achieve real acceptance*
5 = **taking on**, admission, assumption, acknowledgement, undertaking, avowal • *a letter of acceptance*
6 = **submission**, yielding, resignation, concession, compliance, deference, passivity, acquiescence • *He thought about it for a moment, then nodded his reluctant acceptance.*

accepted = **agreed**, received, common, standard, established, traditional, confirmed, regular, usual, approved, acknowledged, recognized, sanctioned, acceptable, universal, authorized, customary, agreed upon, time-honoured • *There is no generally accepted definition of life.*
OPPOSITES: strange, unusual, unconventional

access AS A NOUN 1 = **admission**, entry, passage, entrée, admittance, ingress • *The facilities have been adapted to give access to wheelchair users.*
2 = **entrance**, road, door, approach, entry, path, gate, opening, way in, passage, avenue, doorway, gateway, portal, passageway • *a courtyard with a side access to the rear gardens*
▸ AS A VERB = **acquire**, get, gather, obtain, net, retrieve, attain, procure • *You've illegally accessed confidential security files.*

accessibility 1 = **approachability**, availability, readiness, nearness, handiness • *the town's accessibility to the city*
2 = **availability**, possibility, attainability, obtainability • *growing fears about the cost and accessibility of health care*
3 = **friendliness**, informality, cordiality, affability, approachability, conversableness • *When he was party secretary, he was famous for his accessibility.*

accessible 1 = **handy**, near, nearby, at hand, within reach, at your fingertips, at your fingertips, reachable, achievable, get-at-able (*informal*), a hop, skip and a jump away • *The shopping centre is easily accessible.*
OPPOSITES: hidden, unavailable, inaccessible
2 = **available**, possible, ready, convenient, on hand, obtainable, attainable • *The aim is to make the system accessible to more people.*
3 = **understandable**, plain, conceivable, user-friendly, intelligible, coherent, graspable • *their reputation for providing accessible theatre for young people*

accession
▸ IN PHRASES: **accession to** 1 = **succession to**, attainment of, inheritance of, elevation to, taking up of, assumption of, taking over of, taking on of • *the 40th anniversary of the Queen's accession to the throne*
2 = **joining**, admission, signing up • *a battle over Kashmir's accession to India*

accessorize = **add to**, decorate, supplement, complement, adorn, ornament, augment, embellish • *Adding extra fabrics is an easy way to accessorize your bedroom.*

accessory AS A NOUN 1 = **extra**, addition, supplement, convenience, attachment, add-on, component, extension, adjunct, appendage, appurtenance • *an exclusive range of bathroom accessories*
2 = **adornment**, trimming, trim, decoration, ornament, accompaniment, frill, festoon, embellishment • *Her accessories include earrings, a necklace and a handbag.*
3 = **accomplice**, partner, ally, associate, assistant, helper, colleague, collaborator, confederate, henchman, abettor • *She was charged with being an accessory to the embezzlement of funds.*
▸ AS AN ADJECTIVE = **supplementary**, extra, additional, accompanying, secondary, subordinate, complementary, auxiliary, abetting, supplemental, contributory, ancillary • *Minerals are accessory food factors required in maintaining health.*

accident 1 = **crash**, smash, wreck, collision, pile-up (*informal*), smash-up (*informal*) • *She was involved in a serious car accident last week.*
2 = **misfortune**, blow, disaster, tragedy, setback, calamity, mishap, misadventure, mischance, stroke of bad luck • *5,000 people die every year because of accidents in the home.*
3 = **chance**, fortune, luck, fate, hazard, coincidence, fluke, fortuity • *She discovered the problem by accident.*

QUOTATIONS
now and then there is a person born
who is so unlucky that he runs into accidents
which started out to happen to somebody else
[Don Marquis *archys life of mehitabel*]

accidental 1 = **unintentional**, unexpected, incidental, unforeseen, unintended, unplanned, unpremeditated • *The jury returned a verdict of accidental death.*
OPPOSITES: planned, expected, deliberate
2 = **chance**, random, casual, unintentional, unintended, unplanned, fortuitous, inadvertent, serendipitous, unlooked-for, uncalculated, contingent • *His hand brushed against hers; it could have been accidental.*

accidentally = **unintentionally**, casually, unexpectedly, incidentally, by accident, by chance, inadvertently, unwittingly, randomly, unconsciously, by mistake, haphazardly, fortuitously, adventitiously • *The door cannot be opened accidentally.*
OPPOSITES: deliberately, consciously, on purpose

acclaim AS A VERB = **praise**, celebrate, honour, cheer, admire, hail, applaud, compliment, salute, approve, congratulate, clap, pay tribute to, commend, exalt, laud, extol, crack up (*informal*), big up (*slang, chiefly Caribbean*), give it up for (*slang*), eulogize • *He was acclaimed as the country's greatest modern painter.*
▸ AS A NOUN = **praise**, honour, celebration, approval, tribute, applause, cheering, clapping, ovation, accolades, plaudits, kudos, commendation, exaltation, approbation, acclamation, eulogizing, panegyric, encomium • *She won critical acclaim for her performance.*
OPPOSITES: stick (*slang*); criticism, panning (*informal*)

acclaimed = **celebrated**, famous, acknowledged, praised, outstanding, distinguished, admired, renowned, noted, highly rated, eminent, revered, famed, illustrious, well received, much vaunted, highly esteemed, much touted, well thought of, lionized, highly thought of • *She has published six highly acclaimed novels.*
OPPOSITES: criticized, badly *or* poorly received, undistinguished

acclamation = **applause**, shouting, praise, cheer, cheering, cheers, approval, enthusiasm, tribute, acclaim, ovation, accolade, adulation, kudos, commendation, salutation, approbation, plaudit • *The event went ahead to universal acclamation.*

acclimatization = **adaptation**, accommodation, adjustment, naturalization, acculturation, habituation, familiarization, acclimation, inurement • *Acclimatization to higher altitudes may take several weeks.*

acclimatize 1 = **adapt**, prepare, adjust, accommodate, accustom, familiarize, inure, shape, naturalize, habituate, acculturate, jack up (*N.Z.*) • *This year he has left early to acclimatize himself.*
2 = **adapt to**, get used to, adjust to, habituate to, naturalize to, become seasoned to • *The athletes are acclimatizing to the heat.*

accolade 1 = **honour**, award, recognition, tribute • *the ultimate accolade in the sciences*
2 = **praise**, approval, acclaim, applause, compliment, homage, laud (*literary*), eulogy, congratulation, commendation, acclamation (*formal*), recognition, tribute, ovation, plaudit • *We're always pleased to receive accolades from our guests*

accommodate 1 = **hold**, take, seat, contain, have a capacity for • *The school was not big enough to accommodate all the children.*
2 = **house**, put up, take in, lodge, board, quarter, shelter, entertain, harbour, cater for, billet • *Students are accommodated in homes nearby.*
3 = **help**, support, aid, encourage, assist, befriend, cooperate with, abet, lend a hand to, lend a helping hand to, give a leg up to *(informal)* • *He has never made an effort to accommodate photographers.*
4 = **adapt**, match, fit, fashion, settle, alter, adjust, modify, compose, comply, accustom, reconcile, harmonize • *She walked slowly to accommodate herself to his pace.*

accommodating = **obliging**, willing, kind, friendly, helpful, polite, cooperative, agreeable, amiable, courteous, considerate, hospitable, unselfish, eager to please, complaisant • *Not every wife is so accommodating.*
OPPOSITES: rude, unhelpful, inconsiderate

accommodation 1 = **housing**, homes, houses, board, quartering, quarters, digs *(Brit. informal)*, shelter, sheltering, lodging(s), dwellings • *The government is to provide accommodation for 3000 homeless people.*
2 = **space**, places, seats, room • *Some trains carry bicycles, but accommodation is restricted.*
3 = **adaptation**, change, settlement, compromise, composition, adjustment, transformation, reconciliation, compliance, modification, alteration, conformity, makeover • *Religions have to make accommodations with larger political structures.*

accompaniment 1 = **backing music**, backing, support, obbligato • *He sang to the musical director's piano accompaniment.*
2 = **supplement**, extra, addition, extension, companion, accessory, complement, decoration, frill, adjunct, appendage, adornment • *The recipe makes a good accompaniment to ice cream.*

accompany 1 = **go with**, lead, partner, protect, guide, attend, conduct, escort, shepherd, convoy, usher, chaperon • *Ken agreed to accompany me on a trip to Africa.*
2 = **occur with**, belong to, come with, supplement, coincide with, join with, coexist with, go together with, follow, go cheek by jowl with • *This volume of essays was designed to accompany an exhibition.*
3 = **back**, support, play for, play with, back up • *He accompanies her on all but one song.*

accompanying = **additional**, added, extra, related, associate, associated, joint, fellow, connected, attached, accessory, attendant, complementary, supplementary, supplemental, concurrent, concomitant, appended • *She was in an accompanying car driven by a friend.*

accomplice = **partner in crime**, ally, associate, assistant, companion, accessory, comrade, helper, colleague, collaborator, confederate, henchman, coadjutor, abettor • *His accomplice was arrested after a high-speed car chase.*

accomplish = **realize**, produce, effect, finish, complete, manage, achieve, perform, carry out, conclude, fulfil, execute, bring about, attain, consummate, bring off *(informal)*, do, effectuate • *If we all work together, I think we can accomplish our goal.*
OPPOSITES: fail, give up, fall short

accomplished = **skilled**, able, professional, expert, masterly, talented, gifted, polished, practised, cultivated, tasty *(Brit. informal)*, skilful, adept, consummate, proficient • *one of the most accomplished authors of our time*
OPPOSITES: incapable, incompetent, unskilled

accomplishment 1 = **achievement**, feat, attainment, act, stroke, triumph, coup, exploit, deed • *The accomplishments of the past year are quite extraordinary.*
2 *often plural* = **talent**, ability, skill, gift, achievement, craft, faculty, capability, forte, attainment, proficiency • *She can now add basketball to her list of accomplishments.*
3 = **accomplishing**, effecting, finishing, carrying out, achievement, conclusion, bringing about, execution, completion, realization, fulfilment, attainment, consummation • *His function is vital to the accomplishment of the mission.*

accord AS A NOUN 1 = **treaty**, contract, agreement, arrangement, settlement, pact, deal *(informal)* • *The party was made legal under the 1991 peace accords.*
2 = **sympathy**, agreement, concert, harmony, accordance, unison, rapport, conformity, assent, unanimity, concurrence • *I found myself in total accord.*
OPPOSITES: conflict, disagreement, contention
▸ AS A VERB = **grant**, give, award, render, assign, present with, endow with, bestow on, confer on, vouchsafe, impart with • *On his return home, the government accorded him the rank of Colonel.*
OPPOSITES: refuse, withhold, hold back
▸ IN PHRASES: **accord with something** = **agree with**, match, coincide with, fit with, square with, correspond with, conform with, concur with, tally with, be in tune with *(informal)*, harmonize with, assent with • *Such an approach accords with the principles of Socialist ideology.*
of your own accord = **voluntarily**, freely, willingly, by choice, without being asked, without prompting, of your own free will • *He did not quit of his own accord.*
with one accord = **unanimously**, without exception, by common consent, unitedly • *With one accord they turned and walked back over the grass.*

accordance IN PHRASES: **in accordance with** = **in agreement with**, consistent with, in harmony with, in concert with, in sympathy with, in conformity with, in assent with, in congruence with • *Entries which are not in accordance with the rules will be disqualified.*

according IN PHRASES: **according to** 1 = **as claimed by**, in the opinion of, on the authority of, as stated by, as believed by, on the report of, as maintained by • *According to local gossip they haven't been in touch for years.*
2 = **in keeping with**, in line with, consistent with, in accordance with, in the manner of, in harmony with, in agreement with, in concert with, in sympathy with, in compliance with, in conformity with, in obedience to, after the manner of, in assent with, in congruence with • *They played according to the rules.*
3 = **in relation to**, depending on, in proportion to, proportional to, commensurate with • *Prices vary according to the quantity ordered.*

accordingly 1 = **consequently**, so, thus, therefore, hence, subsequently, in consequence, ergo, as a result • *We have different backgrounds. Accordingly we will have different futures.*
2 = **appropriately**, correspondingly, properly, suitably, fitly • *It is a difficult job and they should be paid accordingly.*

accost = **confront**, challenge, address, stop, approach, oppose, halt, greet, hail, solicit *(of a prostitute)*, buttonhole • *I told them that a man had accosted me in the street.*

account AS A NOUN 1 = **description**, report, record, story, history, detail, statement, relation, version, tale, explanation, narrative, chronicle, portrayal, recital, depiction, narration • *He gave a detailed account of what had happened that night.*
2 = **importance**, standing, concern, value, note, benefit, use, profit, worth, weight, advantage, rank, import, honour, consequence, substance, merit, significance, distinction, esteem, usefulness, repute, momentousness • *These obscure little groups were of no account in national politics.*
3 = **bill**, charges, reckoning, tally, invoice, note of charge • *He can't pay the account.*
4 = **ledger**, charge, bill, statement, balance, tally, invoice,

computation • *He kept a detailed account of all expenditures.*
▸ **AS A VERB** = **consider**, rate, value, judge, estimate, think, hold, believe, count, reckon, assess, weigh, calculate, esteem, deem, compute, gauge, appraise, regard as • *The first day of the event was accounted a success.*
▸ **IN PHRASES: account for something** **1** = **constitute**, make, make up, compose, comprise • *Computers account for 5% of the country's electricity consumption.*
2 = **explain**, excuse, justify, clarify, give a reason for, give an explanation for, illuminate, clear up, answer for, rationalize, elucidate • *How do you account for the company's high staff turnover?*
3 = **put out of action**, kill, destroy, put paid to, incapacitate • *The squadron accounted for seven enemy aircraft in the first week.*
on account of = **by reason of**, because of, owing to, on the basis of, for the sake of, on the grounds of • *He declined to give the speech on account of a sore throat.*
on no account = **never**, not at all, at no time, under no circumstances, no way, not on your life *(informal)*, not on your nelly *(Brit. slang)*, not for love nor money *(informal)* • *On no account should the mixture come near boiling.*

accountability = **responsibility**, liability, culpability, answerability, chargeability • *an impetus towards democracy and greater accountability*

accountable = **answerable**, subject, responsible, obliged, liable, amenable, obligated, chargeable • *The major industries should be accountable to their customers.*

accountant = **auditor**, book-keeper, bean counter *(informal)* • *I recommend you consult an accountant before you go freelance.*

accounting = **accountancy**, auditing, book-keeping • *allegations of theft and false accounting*

accoutrements = **paraphernalia**, fittings, dress, material, clothing, stuff, equipment, tackle, gear, things, kit, outfit, trimmings, fixtures, array, decorations, baggage, apparatus, furnishings, trappings, garb, adornments, ornamentation, bells and whistles, impedimenta, appurtenances, equipage • *Understated eveningwear can be dressed up with accoutrements.*

accredit **1** = **approve**, support, back, commission, champion, favour, guarantee, promote, recommend, appoint, recognize, sanction, advocate, license, endorse, warrant, authorize, ratify, empower, certify, entrust, vouch for, depute • *The degree programme is fully accredited by the Institute of Engineers.*
2 = **attribute**, credit, assign, ascribe, trace to, put down to, lay at the door of • *The discovery of runes is, in Norse mythology, accredited to Odin.*

accredited = **authorized**, official, commissioned, guaranteed, appointed, recognized, sanctioned, licensed, endorsed, empowered, certified, vouched for, deputed, deputized • *fully accredited diplomats*

accretion = **growth**, increase, growing, development, addition, expansion, supplement, evolution, heightening, proliferation, accumulation, enlargement, increment, augmentation • *The larger the animal, the greater the accretion of poison in the fat.*

accrue = **accumulate**, issue, increase, grow, collect, gather, flow, build up, enlarge, follow, ensue, pile up, amass, spring up, stockpile • *You should never let interest payments accrue.*

accumulate = **build up**, increase, grow, be stored, collect, gather, pile up, amass, stockpile, hoard, accrue, cumulate • *Lead can accumulate in the body until toxic levels are reached.*
OPPOSITES: distribute, scatter, disperse

accumulation **1** = **collection**, increase, stock, store, mass, build-up, pile, stack, heap, rick, stockpile, hoard • *accumulations of dirt*
2 = **growth**, collection, gathering, build-up, aggregation, conglomeration, augmentation • *The rate of accumulation decreases with time.*

accuracy **1** = **exactness**, precision, fidelity, authenticity, correctness, closeness, truth, verity, nicety, veracity, faithfulness, truthfulness, niceness, exactitude, strictness, meticulousness, carefulness, scrupulousness, preciseness, faultlessness, accurateness • *The text cannot be guaranteed as to the accuracy of speakers' words.*
OPPOSITES: inaccuracy, carelessness, laxity
2 = **precision**, correctness, exactitude, exactness, meticulousness, definiteness, preciseness • *weapons that could fire with accuracy at targets 3,000 yards away*

accurate **1** = **precise**, right, close, regular, correct, careful, strict, exact, faithful, explicit, authentic, spot-on, just, clear-cut, meticulous, truthful, faultless, scrupulous, unerring, veracious • *This is the most accurate description of the killer to date.*
OPPOSITES: wrong, incorrect, inaccurate
2 = **correct**, right, true, exact, faithful, spot-on *(Brit. informal)*, faultless, on the money *(U.S.)* • *Their prediction was accurate.*
3 = **on target**, exact, precise, deadly, sure, true, effective • *The rifle was extremely accurate.*

accurately **1** = **precisely**, rightly, correctly, closely, carefully, truly, properly, strictly, literally, exactly, faithfully, meticulously, to the letter, justly, scrupulously, truthfully, authentically, unerringly, faultlessly, veraciously • *The test can accurately predict what a bigger explosion would do.*
2 = **exactly**, rightly, closely, correctly, definitely, truly, properly, precisely, nicely, strictly, faithfully, explicitly, unequivocally, scrupulously, truthfully • *His concept of 'power' could be more accurately described as 'control'.*
3 = **precisely**, absolutely, unerringly • *The more accurately you can aim, the fewer civilians you will kill.*

accursed **1** = **hateful**, offensive, disgusting, horrible, revolting, obscene, vile, foul, repellent, obnoxious, despicable, repulsive, heinous, hellish, odious, repugnant, loathsome, abhorrent, abominable, execrable, detestable • *He said that it was about time he left that accursed woman.*
OPPOSITES: good, beautiful, pleasant
2 = **damned**, condemned, ruined, unhappy, unfortunate, doomed, cursed, lost, unlucky, hopeless, undone, bewitched, jinxed, bedevilled, luckless, infernal, wretched, ill-omened, anathematized, ill-fated • *How could a life marked by such love be so accursed?*
OPPOSITES: favoured, lucky, blessed

accusation = **charge**, complaint, allegation, indictment, impeachment, recrimination, citation, denunciation, attribution, imputation, arraignment, incrimination • *people who have made public accusations of rape*

accusatory = **accusing**, critical, censorious, reproachful, condemnatory, accusative, recriminatory, denunciatory, incriminatory, imputative • *Her eyes took on an accusatory stare.*

accuse **1** = **point a** *or* **the finger at**, blame for, denounce, attribute to, hold responsible for, impute blame to • *He accused her of having an affair with another man.*
OPPOSITES: deny, exonerate
2 = **charge with**, indict for, impeach for, arraign for, cite, tax with, censure with, incriminate for, recriminate for • *Her assistant was accused of theft and fraud by the police.*
OPPOSITES: vindicate, exonerate, absolve

accused **IN PHRASES: the accused** = **the defendant**, the defence, the offender, the respondent, the appellant, the litigant, the prisoner at the bar • *The accused is alleged to be a member of a right-wing gang.*

accustom = **familiarize**, train, coach, discipline, adapt, instruct, make used, school, season, acquaint, inure, habituate, acclimatize, make conversant • *He accustoms us to a mixture of humour and tragedy in one play.*

accustomed **1** = **used**, trained, familiar, disciplined, given to, adapted, acquainted, in the habit of, familiarized,

a

seasoned, inured, habituated, exercised, acclimatized • *I was accustomed to being the only child amongst adults.*
OPPOSITES: unfamiliar, unused, unaccustomed
2 = usual, established, expected, general, common, standard, set, traditional, normal, fixed, regular, ordinary, familiar, conventional, routine, everyday, customary, habitual, wonted • *He took up his accustomed position at the fire.*
OPPOSITES: odd, strange, unusual

ace **AS A NOUN 1 = one**, single point • *the ace of hearts*
2 = expert, star, champion, authority, winner, professional, master, pro *(informal)*, specialist, genius, guru, buff *(informal)*, wizard *(informal)*, whizz *(informal)*, virtuoso, connoisseur, boffin *(Brit. informal)*, hotshot *(informal)*, past master, dab hand *(Brit. informal)*, maven *(U.S.)* • *former motor-racing ace Stirling Moss*
▸ **AS AN ADJECTIVE = great**, good, brilliant, mean *(slang)*, fine, champion, expert, masterly, wonderful, excellent, cracking *(Brit. informal)*, outstanding, superb, fantastic *(informal)*, tremendous *(informal)*, marvellous *(informal)*, terrific *(informal)*, mega *(slang)*, awesome *(slang)*, dope *(slang)*, admirable, virtuoso, first-rate, brill *(informal)*, the dog's bollocks *(taboo slang)*, bitchin' *(U.S. slang)*, chillin' *(U.S. slang)*, booshit *(Austral. slang)*, exo *(Austral. slang)*, sik *(Austral. slang)*, ka pai *(N.Z.)*, rad *(informal)*, phat *(slang)*, schmick *(Austral. informal)*, beaut *(informal)*, barrie *(Scot. slang)*, belting *(Brit. slang)*, pearler *(Austral. slang)* • *It's been a while since I've seen a really ace film.*
▸ **IN PHRASES: ace in the hole = advantage**, benefit, edge, asset, blessing, superiority, boon, upper hand, pre-eminence, ace up your sleeve • *Our superior technology is our ace in the hole.*

acerbic = sharp, cutting, biting, severe, acid, bitter, nasty, harsh, stern, rude, scathing, acrimonious, barbed, unkind, unfriendly, sarcastic, sardonic, caustic, churlish, vitriolic, trenchant, acrid, brusque, rancorous, mordant, mordacious • *comments made in a spirit of acerbic wit*

ache **AS A VERB 1 = hurt**, suffer, burn, pain, smart, sting, pound, throb, be tender, twinge, be sore • *Her head was hurting and she ached all over.*
2 = suffer, hurt, grieve, sorrow, agonize, be in pain, go through the mill *(informal)*, mourn, feel wretched • *It must have been hard to keep smiling when his heart was aching.*
▸ **AS A NOUN 1 = pain**, discomfort, suffering, hurt, smart, smarting, cramp, throb, throbbing, irritation, tenderness, pounding, spasm, pang, twinge, soreness, throe *(rare)* • *You feel nausea and aches in your muscles.*
2 = anguish, suffering, pain, torture, distress, grief, misery, mourning, torment, sorrow, woe, heartache, heartbreak • *Nothing could relieve the terrible ache of fear.*
3 = longing, need, hope, wish, desire, urge, yen *(informal)*, pining, hunger, craving, yearning, itch, thirst, hankering • *an overwhelming ache for support from others*
▸ **IN PHRASES: ache for something** *or* **someone = long for**, want, desire, hope for, dream of, pine, covet, wish for, yearn for, lust for, thirst for, hunger for, crave for, hanker for, itch for, set your heart on, eat your heart out over • *She still ached for the lost intimacy of marriage.*

achievable = attainable, obtainable, winnable, reachable, realizable, within your grasp, graspable, gettable, acquirable, possible, accessible, probable, feasible, practicable, accomplishable • *It is a good idea to start with easily achievable goals.*

achieve = accomplish, reach, fulfil, finish, complete, gain, perform, earn, do, get, win, carry out, realize, obtain, conclude, acquire, execute, bring about, attain, consummate, procure, bring off *(informal)*, effectuate, put the tin lid on • *There are many who will work hard to achieve these goals.*

achievement 1 = accomplishment, effort, feat, deed, stroke, triumph, coup, exploit, act, attainment, feather in your cap • *a conference celebrating women's achievements*
2 = fulfilment, effecting, performance, production, execution, implementation, completion, accomplishment, realization, attainment, acquirement, carrying out *or* through • *It is the achievement of these goals that will bring lasting peace.*

QUOTATIONS
If there were an instrument by which to measure desire, one could foretell achievement
[Willa Cather *The Professor's House*]

achiever = success, winner, dynamo, high-flyer, doer, go-getter *(informal)*, organizer, active person, overachiever, man *or* woman of action, wheeler-dealer *(informal)* • *In school, he was not one of the achievers.*

Achilles heel = weakness, failing, lack, fault, defect, deficiency, flaw, shortcoming, blemish, imperfection, chink in your armour • *His Achilles heel was that he could not delegate.*

aching 1 = painful, suffering, hurting, tired, smarting, pounding, raw, tender, sore, throbbing, harrowing, inflamed, excruciating, agonizing • *The aching joints and fever should last no longer than a few days.*
2 = longing, anxious, eager, pining, hungering, craving, yearning, languishing, thirsting, ardent, avid, wishful, wistful, hankering, desirous • *He has an aching need for love.*

acid **AS AN ADJECTIVE 1 = sour**, sharp, tart, pungent, biting, acidic, acerbic, acrid, acetic, vinegary, acidulous, acidulated, vinegarish, acerb • *These wines are rather hard, and somewhat acid.*
OPPOSITES: sweet, pleasant, mild
2 = sharp, cutting, biting, severe, bitter, harsh, stinging, scathing, acrimonious, barbed, pungent, hurtful, sarcastic, sardonic, caustic, vitriolic, acerbic, trenchant, mordant, mordacious • *a comedy told with compassion and acid humour*
OPPOSITES: kindly, sweet, gentle
▸ **IN PHRASES: the acid test = test**, proof, trial, check, investigation, analysis, assessment, examination • *The perception of fairness is the acid test for democracy.*
▹ See panel **Acids**

acidic = acid, biting, sharp, sour, tart, pungent, acerbic, acrid, acetic, vinegary, acidulous, acidulated, vinegarish, acerb • *If the sprouts taste acidic, do not eat them.*

acidity 1 = sourness, bitterness, sharpness, pungency, tartness, acerbity, acridness, acidulousness, acridity, vinegariness, vinegarishness • *a wine with ripe acidity*
2 = sharpness, bitterness, harshness, pungency, acerbity, trenchancy, hurtfulness, causticity, mordancy, acridness, acridity, causticness • *the acidity of her remarks*

acidly = sharply, cuttingly, bitterly, harshly, tartly, bitingly, caustically, trenchantly, pungently, mordantly, hurtfully, acerbically, acridly, stingingly • *'You never did know how to be a mother,' she said acidly.*
OPPOSITES: kindly, sweetly, pleasantly

acknowledge 1 = admit, own up, allow, accept, reveal, grant, declare, recognize, yield, concede, confess, disclose, affirm, profess, divulge, accede, acquiesce, 'fess up *(U.S. slang)* • *He acknowledged that he was a drug addict.*
OPPOSITES: deny, reject, discount
2 = recognize, know, see, accept, note, celebrate, perceive • *He is acknowledged as an excellent goalkeeper.*
3 = greet, address, notice, recognize, salute, nod to, accost, tip your hat to • *He saw her but refused to even acknowledge her.*
OPPOSITES: reject, ignore, snub
4 = reply to, answer, notice, recognize, respond to, come back to, react to, write back to, retort to • *They sent me a postcard acknowledging my request.*
OPPOSITES: deny, ignore, disregard

acknowledged = accepted, admitted, established,

ACIDS

Specific acids

abietic acid
acetic acid
alginic acid
aminobenzoic acid
aspartic acid
barbituric acid
benzoic acid
boric acid
butyric acid
carbonic acid
chloric acid
chloroacetic acid
chlorous acid
cholic acid
chromic acid
cinnamic acid
citric acid
crotonic acid
cyanic acid
decanedioic acid
decanoic acid
dichromic acid
dithionous acid
deoxyribonucleic acid
dodecanoic acid
erucic acid
formic acid
fulminic acid
fumaric acid
gallic acid
glacial acetic acid
glyceric acid
heptadecanoic acid
hexanoic acid
hydnocarpic acid
hydrochloric acid
hydrofluoric acid
hypochlorous acid
hypophosphoric acid
hypophosphorous
isocyanic acid
itaconic acid
lactic acid
linoleic acid
linolenic acid
lysergic acid
manganic acid
mucic acid
nitric acid
nitrous acid
nonanoic acid
octanedioic acid
oleic acid
orthophosphoric acid
oxalic acid
pantothenic acid
para-aminobenzoic acid
pectic acid
pentanoic acid
permanganic acid
phosphoric acid
phthalic acid
picric acid
platinocyanic acid
polyphosphoric acid
propanoic acid
prussic acid
pyroboric acid
pyrophosphoric acid
pyrosulphuric acid
racemic acid
ricinoleic acid
saccharic acid
selenic acid
selenious acid
silicic acid
sorbic acid
spiraeic acid (modern salicylic acid)
stearic acid
suberic acid
succinic acid
sulphonic acid
sulphurous acid
tantalic acid
tartaric acid
telluric acid
terebic acid
terephthalic acid
thiocyanic acid
thiosulphuric acid
trichloroacetic acid
uric acid

Types of acid

amino acid
carboxylic acid
dibasic acid
dicarboxylic acid
fatty acid
iodic acid
mineral acid
nucleic acid
periodic acid
polycarboxylic acid

Amino acids

alanine
arginine
citrulline
cystine
glutamine
glycine
histidine
isoleucine
leucine
lysine
methionine
ornithine
proline
serine
threonine
triiodothyronine

confirmed, declared, approved, recognized, well-known, sanctioned, confessed, authorized, professed, accredited, agreed upon • *He is an acknowledged authority in his field.*

acknowledgment *or* **acknowledgement** 1 = **recognition**, allowing, understanding, yielding, profession, admission, awareness, acceptance, confession, realization, accession, acquiescence • *He appreciated her acknowledgement of his maturity.*
2 = **greeting**, welcome, notice, recognition, reception, hail, hailing, salute, salutation • *He smiled in acknowledgement and gave her a bow.*
3 = **appreciation**, answer, thanks, credit, response, reply, reaction, recognition, gratitude, indebtedness, thankfulness, gratefulness • *Grateful acknowledgement is made for permission to reprint.*

acme = **height**, top, crown, summit, peak, climax, crest, optimum, high point, pinnacle, culmination, zenith, apex, apogee, vertex • *His work is the acme of cinematic art.*
OPPOSITES: bottom, minimum, depths

acne = **spots**, skin disease, skin condition • *Severe acne can cause lifetime scarring.*

acolyte 1 = **follower**, fan, supporter, pupil, convert, believer, admirer, backer, partisan, disciple, devotee, worshipper, apostle, cohort (*chiefly U.S.*), fan club (*informal*), adherent, henchman, habitué, votary • *To his acolytes, he is known simply as 'The Boss'.*
2 = **attendant**, assistant, follower, helper, altar boy • *When they reached the shrine, acolytes removed the pall.*

acquaint = **tell**, reveal, advise, inform, communicate, disclose, notify, enlighten, divulge, familiarize, apprise, let (someone) know • *I want to acquaint myself with your abilities and your weaknesses.* • *Have steps been made to acquaint them with their rights?*

acquaintance 1 = **associate**, contact, ally, colleague, comrade, confrère • *He exchanged a few words with the man, an old acquaintance of his.*
OPPOSITES: good friend, intimate, buddy
2 = **relationship**, association, exchange, connection, intimacy, fellowship, familiarity, companionship, social contact, cognizance, conversance, conversancy • *He becomes involved in a real murder mystery through his acquaintance with a police officer.*
OPPOSITES: ignorance, unfamiliarity

QUOTATIONS

Should auld acquaintance be forgot,
And never brought to mind?
[Robert Burns *Auld Lang Syne*]

I look upon every day to be lost, in which I do not make a new acquaintance
[Dr. Johnson]

acquaintance: a person whom we know well enough to borrow from, but not well enough to lend to
[Ambrose Bierce *The Devil's Dictionary*]

acquainted IN PHRASES: **acquainted with** 1 = **familiar with**, aware of, in on, experienced in, conscious of, informed of, alive to, privy to, knowledgeable about, versed in, conversant with, apprised of, cognizant of, up to speed with, *au fait* with, switched-on about (*informal*) • *He was well acquainted with European literature.*
2 = **known to**, familiar with, friendly with, on good terms with • *No-one acquainted with them was allowed to talk to the Press.*

acquiesce = **submit**, agree, accept, approve, yield, bend, surrender, consent, tolerate, comply, give in, conform, succumb, go along with, bow to, cave in (*informal*), concur, assent, capitulate, accede, play ball (*informal*), toe the line, hoist the white flag • *He seemed to acquiesce in the decision.*
OPPOSITES: fight, refuse, resist

acquiescence = **agreement**, yielding, approval, acceptance, consent, harmony, giving in, submission, compliance, obedience, conformity, assent, accession, concord, concurrence • *She smiled her acquiescence and resumed her seat.*

acquiescent = **submissive**, agreeing, accepting, approving, yielding, consenting, accommodating, conforming, agreeable, meek, assenting, obedient, compliant, amenable, acceding, concurrent, ingratiating, malleable, deferential, pliant, obsequious, tractable, unresisting, bootlicking *(informal)*, obeisant • *The other men were acquiescent but he had an independent streak.*

acquire 1 = **get**, win, buy, receive, land, score *(slang)*, gain, achieve, earn, pick up, bag, secure, collect, gather, realize, obtain, attain, amass, procure, come into possession of • *The company acquired a 50% stake in Saab for $4m.*
OPPOSITES: lose, give up, surrender
2 = **learn**, pick up, master, grasp, attain, imbibe • *I've never acquired a taste for wine.*

acquisition 1 = **acquiring**, gaining, achievement, procurement, attainment, acquirement, obtainment • *the President's recent acquisition of a helicopter*
2 = **purchase**, buy, investment, property, gain, prize, asset, possession • *her latest acquisition, a bright red dress*

acquisitive = **greedy**, grabbing, grasping, hungry, selfish, avid, predatory, rapacious, avaricious, desirous, covetous • *We live in an acquisitive society.*
OPPOSITES: liberal, generous, lavish

acquisitiveness = **greed**, selfishness, avarice, rapacity, covetousness, avidity, rapaciousness, predatoriness, avidness, graspingness • *His villa is filled with evidence of his acquisitiveness.*

acquit AS A VERB = **clear**, free, release, deliver, excuse, relieve, discharge, liberate, vindicate, exonerate, absolve, exculpate • *He was acquitted of disorderly behaviour by magistrates.*
OPPOSITES: charge, sentence, find guilty
▸ IN PHRASES: **acquit yourself** = **behave**, bear yourself, conduct yourself, comport yourself • *Most men acquitted themselves well throughout the action.*

acquittal = **clearance**, freeing, release, relief, liberation, discharge, pardon, setting free, vindication, deliverance, absolution, exoneration, exculpation • *the acquittal of six police officers charged with beating a man*

acrid 1 = **pungent**, biting, strong, burning, sharp, acid, bitter, harsh, stinging, irritating, caustic, astringent, vitriolic, highly flavoured, acerb • *The room filled with the acrid smell of tobacco.*
2 = **harsh**, cutting, biting, sharp, bitter, nasty, acrimonious, caustic, vitriolic, trenchant, mordant, mordacious • *He is soured by acrid memories he has dredged up.*

acrimonious = **bitter**, cutting, biting, sharp, severe, hostile, crabbed, sarcastic, embittered, caustic, petulant, spiteful, churlish, astringent, vitriolic, acerbic, trenchant, irascible, testy, censorious, rancorous, mordant, peevish, splenetic, mordacious • *The acrimonious debate on the agenda ended indecisively.*
OPPOSITES: forgiving, benign, good-tempered

acrimony = **bitterness**, harshness, rancour, ill will, virulence, sarcasm, pungency, asperity, tartness, astringency, irascibility, peevishness, acerbity, churlishness, trenchancy, mordancy • *The council's first meeting ended in acrimony.*
OPPOSITES: liking, friendship, goodwill

acrobat = **gymnast**, balancer, tumbler, tightrope walker, rope walker, funambulist • *A high-wire acrobat fell 50 ft to his death.*

acrobatics = **gymnastics**, balancing, tumbling, tightrope walking • *Students are trained in clowning, dance and acrobatics.*

across AS A PREPOSITION 1 = **over**, on the other *or* far side of, past, beyond • *Anyone from the houses across the road could see him.*
2 = **throughout**, over, all over, right through, all through, covering, straddling, everywhere in, through the whole of, from end to end of, over the length and breadth of • *The film opens across America in December.*
▸ AS AN ADVERB = **from side to side**, athwart, transversely, crossways *or* crosswise • *Trim toenails straight across using nail clippers.*

across-the-board = **general**, full, complete, total, sweeping, broad, widespread, comprehensive, universal, blanket, thorough, wholesale, panoramic, indiscriminate, all-inclusive, wall-to-wall, all-embracing, overarching, all-encompassing, thoroughgoing, without exception *or* omission, one-size-fits-all • *The President promised across-the-board tax cuts if re-elected.*
OPPOSITES: limited, specific, restricted

act AS A VERB 1 = **do something**, perform, move, function, go about, conduct yourself, undertake something • *I have no reason to doubt that the bank acted properly.*
2 = **behave**, react, go about, acquit yourself, bear yourself, comport yourself • *a gang of youths who were acting suspiciously*
3 = **work**, serve, operate, function, be employed, do business, have a job, earn a living • *He acted as both ship's surgeon and as chaplain to the men.*
4 = **play**, seem to be, pose as, pretend to be, posture as, imitate, sham, feign, characterize, enact, personify, impersonate, play the part of • *They were just acting tough.*
5 = **perform**, be an actor, be an actress, tread the boards *(informal)*, mimic, mime • *She told her parents of her desire to act.*
▸ AS A NOUN 1 = **deed**, action, step, performance, operation, doing, move, blow, achievement, stroke, undertaking, exploit, execution, feat, accomplishment, exertion • *My insurance covers acts of sabotage.*
2 = **pretence**, show, front, performance, display, attitude, pose, stance, fake, posture, façade, sham, veneer, counterfeit, feigning, affectation, dissimulation • *His anger was real. It wasn't just an act.*
3 = **law**, bill, measure, resolution, decree, statute, ordinance, enactment, edict • *an Act of Parliament*
4 = **performance**, show, turn, production, routine, presentation, gig *(informal)*, sketch • *Numerous bands are playing, as well as comedy acts.*
▸ IN PHRASES: **act for someone** = **stand in for**, serve, represent, replace, substitute for, cover for, take the place of, fill in for, deputize for, function in place of • *Because we travel so much, we asked a broker to act for us.*
act on *or* **upon something** 1 = **obey**, follow, carry out, observe, embrace, execute, comply with, heed, conform to, adhere to, abide by, yield to, act upon, be ruled by, act in accordance with, do what is expected • *A patient will usually listen to the doctor's advice and act on it.*
2 = **affect**, change, influence, impact, transform, alter, modify • *The drug acts very fast on the central nervous system.*
act up 1 = **misbehave**, carry on, cause trouble, mess about, be naughty, horse around *(informal)*, give trouble, piss about *(taboo slang)*, piss around *(taboo slang)*, give someone grief *(Brit. & S. African)*, give bother • *I could hear him acting up downstairs.*
2 = **malfunction**, go wrong, break down, be faulty, stop, stop working, conk out *(informal)*, go phut *(informal)*, pack up *(informal)*, play up *(Brit. informal)* • *The machine was acting up again.*

acting AS A NOUN = **performance**, playing, performing, theatre, dramatics, portraying, enacting, portrayal, impersonation, characterization, stagecraft • *She has returned home to pursue her career in acting.*

▸ **AS AN ADJECTIVE** = **temporary**, substitute, intervening, interim, provisional, surrogate, stopgap, pro tem • *The new acting President has a reputation for being independent.*

QUOTATIONS

The art of acting consists in keeping people from coughing
[Ralph Richardson]

Acting deals with very delicate emotions. It is not putting up a mask. Each time an actor acts he does not hide; he exposes himself
[Jeanne Moreau *The New York Times*]

action **AS A NOUN** 1 = **deed**, move, act, performance, blow, exercise, achievement, stroke, undertaking, exploit, feat, accomplishment, exertion • *He was the sort of man who didn't like his actions questioned.*
2 = **measure**, act, step, operation, manoeuvre • *The government is taking emergency action to deal with the crisis.*
3 = **lawsuit**, case, cause, trial, suit, argument, proceeding, dispute, contest, prosecution, litigation • *a libel action brought by one of the country's top bureaucrats*
4 = **energy**, activity, spirit, force, vitality, vigour, liveliness, vim • *Hollywood is where the action is now.*
5 = **effect**, working, work, force, power, process, effort, operation, activity, movement, influence, functioning, motion, exertion • *Her description of the action of poisons is very accurate.*
6 = **battle**, war, fight, fighting, conflict, clash, contest, encounter, combat, engagement, hostilities, warfare, fray, skirmish, sortie, affray • *Ten soldiers were wounded in action.*
▸ **AS A PLURAL NOUN** = **behaviour**, ways, bearing, conduct, manners, manner, demeanour, deportment, comportment • *He showed no remorse for his actions.*

QUOTATIONS

An ounce of action is worth a ton of theory
[Friedrich Engels]

In politics, if you want anything said, ask a man. If you want anything done, ask a woman
[Margaret Thatcher]

PROVERBS

Actions speak louder than words

activate = **start**, move, trigger (off), stimulate, turn on, set off, initiate, switch on, propel, rouse, prod, get going, mobilize, kick-start *(informal)*, set in motion, impel, galvanize, set going, actuate • *video cameras that can be activated by computer*
OPPOSITES: stop, check, arrest

activation = **start**, triggering, turning on, switching on, animation, arousal, initiation, mobilization, setting in motion, actuation • *A computer controls the activation of an airbag.*

active 1 = **busy**, involved, occupied, engaged, tiring, lively, energetic, bustling, restless, on the move, strenuous, tireless, on the go *(informal)* • *Having an active youngster about the house can be quite wearing.*
OPPOSITES: slow, lazy, sluggish
2 = **energetic**, strong, spirited, quick, vital, alert, dynamic, lively, vigorous, potent, animated, vibrant, forceful, nimble, diligent, industrious, sprightly, vivacious, on the go *(informal)*, alive and kicking, spry, full of beans *(informal)*, bright-eyed and bushy-tailed *(informal)* • *the tragedy of an active mind trapped by failing physical health*
OPPOSITES: dull, dormant, inactive
3 = **enthusiastic**, committed, engaged, enterprising, devoted, activist, aggressive, ambitious, hard-working, forward, militant, energetic, assertive, forceful, two-fisted, zealous, industrious • *We should play an active role in politics.*
4 = **in operation**, working, live, running, moving, acting, functioning, stirring, at work, in business, in action, operative, in force, effectual, astir • *Guerrilla groups are active in the province.*

activism = **action**, force, exertion • *He believed in political activism to achieve justice.*

activist = **militant**, partisan, organizer, warrior • *The attack was carried out by animal rights activists.*

activity 1 = **action**, work, life, labour, movement, energy, exercise, spirit, enterprise, motion, bustle, animation, vigour, hustle, exertion, hurly-burly, liveliness, activeness • *There is an extraordinary level of activity in the market.*
OPPOSITES: inertia, inaction, lethargy
2 = **pursuit**, act, project, scheme, task, pleasure, interest, enterprise, undertaking, occupation, hobby, deed, endeavour, pastime, avocation • *Activities range from canoeing to birdwatching.*
3 = **functioning**, power, effect, strength, efficiency, capability, vitality, vigour, potency, efficacy • *She needed special instruction due to her restricted activity.*

PROVERBS

A rolling stone gathers no moss

actor *or* **actress** = **performer**, player, artiste, leading man *or* lady, Thespian, luvvie *(informal)*, trouper, thesp *(informal)*, play-actor, dramatic artist, tragedian *or* tragedienne • *You have to be a very good actor to play that part.*
▷ *See panel* **Actors**

QUOTATIONS

An actor's a guy who, if you ain't talking about him, ain't listening
[Marlon Brando]

Actors should be treated like cattle
[Alfred Hitchcock]

I'm an actor. An actress is someone who wears boa feathers
[Sigourney Weaver]

actual 1 = **genuine**, real, true, confirmed, authentic, verified, truthful, bona fide, dinkum *(Austral. & N.Z. informal)* • *They are using local actors or the actual people involved.*
OPPOSITES: made-up, probable, unreal
2 = **real**, substantial, concrete, definite, tangible • *She had written some notes, but she hadn't started the actual work.*
OPPOSITES: supposed, theoretical, hypothetical

actuality 1 = **reality**, truth, substance, verity, materiality, realness, substantiality, factuality, corporeality • *It exists in dreams rather than actuality.*
2 = **fact**, truth, reality, verity • *You may theorise, but we are concerned with actualities.*

actually 1 = **really**, in fact, indeed, essentially, truly, literally, genuinely, in reality, in truth, in actuality, in point of fact, veritably, as a matter of fact • *He had actually felt pain several times, but he had ignored it.*
2 = **surprisingly**, believe it or not, though it may seem strange • *It may sound crazy, but it actually works.*

actuate 1 = **motivate**, move, drive, influence, excite, urge, inspire, prompt, stir, spur, induce, arouse, rouse, get going, quicken, incite, instigate, impel • *They were actuated by desire.*
2 = **activate**, trigger (off), stimulate, set off, initiate, switch on, animate, kick-start *(informal)*, set in motion, set going • *The engines overheated, actuating the fire extinguishers.*

acumen = **judgment**, intelligence, perception, wisdom, insight, wit, ingenuity, sharpness, cleverness, keenness, shrewdness, discernment, perspicacity, sagacity, smartness, smarts *(slang, chiefly U.S.)*, astuteness, acuteness, perspicuity • *His sharp business acumen meant he quickly rose to the top.*

acute 1 = **serious**, important, dangerous, critical, crucial, alarming, severe, grave, sudden, urgent, decisive • *The war aggravated an acute economic crisis.*
2 = **sharp**, shooting, powerful, violent, severe, intense, overwhelming, distressing, stabbing, cutting, fierce, piercing, racking, exquisite, poignant, harrowing, overpowering, shrill, excruciating • *His back is arched as if in acute pain.*

ACTORS

Male

Woody Allen *(U.S.)*
Fred Astaire *(U.S.)*
Richard Attenborough *(English)*
Jean-Louis Barrault *(French)*
John Barrymore *(U.S.)*
Alan Bates *(English)*
Warren Beatty *(U.S.)*
Jean-Paul Belmondo *(French)*
Alan Bennett *(English)*
Dirk Bogarde *(English)*
Humphrey Bogart *(U.S.)*
Charles Boyer *(French)*
Kenneth Branagh *(English)*
Marlon Brando *(U.S.)*
Adrien Brody *(U.S.)*
Mel Brooks *(U.S.)*
Richard Burbage *(English)*
Richard Burton *(Welsh)*
Glen Byam Shaw *(English)*
James Cagney *(U.S.)*
Michael Caine *(English)*
Simon Callow *(English)*
Robert Carlyle *(Scottish)*
Jim Carrey *(U.S.)*
Charlie Chaplin *(English)*
Maurice Chevalier *(French)*
John Cleese *(English)*
George Clooney *(U.S.)*
Sean Connery *(Scottish)*
Peter Cook *(English)*
Chris Cooper *(U.S.)*
Gary Cooper *(U.S.)*
Kevin Costner *(U.S.)*
Noel Coward *(English)*
Michael Crawford *(English)*
Tom Cruise *(U.S.)*
Daniel Day-Lewis *(English/ Irish)*
James Dean *(U.S.)*
Robert De Niro *(U.S.)*
Gerard Depardieu *(French)*
Johnny Depp *(U.S.)*
Vittorio de Sica *(Italian)*
John Dexter *(English)*
Leonardo DiCaprio *(U.S.)*
Kirk Douglas *(U.S.)*
Michael Douglas *(U.S.)*
Clint Eastwood *(U.S.)*
Douglas Fairbanks Jr. *(U.S.)*
Douglas Fairbanks Snr. *(U.S.)*
WC Fields *(U.S.)*
Albert Finney *(English)*
Errol Flynn *(Australian)*
Henry Fonda *(U.S.)*
Harrison Ford *(U.S.)*
Morgan Freeman *(U.S.)*
Jean Gabin *(France)*
Clark Gable *(U.S.)*
David Garrick *(English)*
Mel Gibson *(Australian)*
John Gielgud *(English)*
Cary Grant *(English-U.S.)*
Alec Guinness *(English)*
Gene Hackman *(U.S.)*
Tom Hanks *(U.S.)*
Oliver Hardy *(U.S.)*
Rex Harrison *(English)*
Dustin Hoffman *(U.S.)*
Bob Hope *(U.S.)*
Anthony Hopkins *(Welsh)*
Michael Hordern *(English)*
Leslie Howard *(English)*
Trevor Howard *(English)*
Rock Hudson *(U.S.)*
Barry Humphries *(Australian)*
John Hurt *(English)*
Jeremy Irons *(English)*
Henry Irving *(English)*
Derek Jacobi *(English)*
Al Jolson *(U.S.)*
Tommy Lee Jones *(U.S.)*
Boris Karloff *(English)*
Edmund Kean *(English)*
Buster Keaton *(U.S.)*
Harvey Keitel *(U.S.)*
Gene Kelly *(U.S.)*
John Kemble *(English)*
Ben Kingsley *(English)*
Burt Lancaster *(U.S.)*
Charles Laughton *(English-U.S.)*
Stan Laurel *(English-U.S.)*
Bruce Lee *(U.S.)*
Christopher Lee *(English)*
Harold Lloyd *(U.S.)*
Bela Lugosi *(Hungarian)*
Ewan McGregor *(Scottish)*
Ian McKellen *(English)*
Steve McQueen *(U.S.)*
William Macready *(English)*
James Mason *(English)*
Raymond Massey *(Canadian)*
Marcello Mastroianni *(Italian)*
Bernard Miles *(English)*
John Mills *(English)*
Robert Mitchum *(U.S.)*
Dudley Moore *(English)*
Robert Morley *(English)*
Sam Neill *(N.Z.)*
Paul Newman *(U.S.)*
Jack Nicholson *(U.S.)*
Liam Neeson *(Irish)*
David Niven *(English)*
Gary Oldman *(English)*
Laurence Olivier *(English)*
Peter O'Toole *(Irish-British)*
Al Pacino *(U.S.)*
Gregory Peck *(U.S.)*
Sean Penn *(U.S.)*
Donald Pleasence *(English)*
Anthony Quayle *(English)*
Anthony Quinn *(U.S.)*
Daniel Radcliffe *(English)*
Ronald Reagan *(U.S.)*
Robert Redford *(U.S.)*
Michael Redgrave *(English)*
Fernando Rey *(Spanish)*
Ralph Richardson *(English)*
Tim Robbins *(U.S.)*
Paul Robeson *(U.S.)*
Edward G Robinson *(U.S.)*
Tim Roth *(English)*
Arnold Schwarzenegger *(Austrian – U.S.)*
Paul Scofield *(English)*
Peter Sellers *(English)*
Sam Shepard *(U.S.)*
Kevin Spacey *(U.S.)*
Sylvester Stallone *(U.S.)*
Konstantin Stanislavsky *(Russian)*
James Stewart *(U.S.)*
Donald Sutherland *(Canadian)*
Jacques Tati *(French)*
Spencer Tracy *(U.S.)*
John Travolta *(U.S.)*
Peter Ustinov *(English)*
Rudolph Valentino *(Italian-U.S.)*
Max Von Sydow *(Swedish)*
John Wayne *(U.S.)*
Johnny Weissmuller *(U.S.)*
Orson Welles *(U.S.)*
Bruce Willis *(U.S.)*
Elijah Wood *(U.S.)*

Female

Julie Andrews *(English)*
Yvonne Arnaud *(French)*
Peggy Ashcroft *(English)*
Tallulah Bankhead *(U.S.)*
Brigitte Bardot *(French)*
Ingrid Bergman *(Swedish-U.S.)*
Sarah Bernhardt *(French)*
Juliette Binoche *(French)*
Cate Blanchett *(Australian)*
Helena Bonham Carter *(English)*
Clara Bow *(U.S.)*
Fanny Brice *(U.S.)*
Glenn Close *(U.S.)*
Claudette Colbert *(French-U.S.)*
Joan Crawford *(U.S.)*
Penelope Cruz *(Spanish)*
Bette Davis *(U.S.)*
Geena Davis *(U.S.)*
Judy Davis *(Australian)*
Judi Dench *(English)*
Catherine Deneuve *(French)*
Marlene Dietrich *(German)*
Faye Dunaway *(U.S.)*
Edith Evans *(English)*
Jane Fonda *(U.S.)*
Jodie Foster *(U.S.)*
Greta Garbo *(Swedish)*
Ava Gardner *(U.S.)*
Judy Garland *(U.S.)*
Lillian Gish *(U.S.)*
Joyce Grenfell *(English)*
Jean Harlow *(U.S.)*
Goldie Hawn *(U.S.)*
Audrey Hepburn *(Belgian-U.S.)*
Katharine Hepburn *(U.S.)*
Wendy Hiller *(English)*
Holly Hunter *(U.S.)*
Isabelle Huppert *(French)*
Glenda Jackson *(English)*
Jian Qing *(Chinese)*
Diane Keaton *(U.S.)*
Grace Kelly *(U.S.)*
Fanny Kemble *(English-U.S.)*
Nicole Kidman *(Australian)*
Keira Knightley *(English)*
Jessica Lange *(U.S.)*
Gertrude Lawrence *(English)*
Vivien Leigh *(English)*
Lotte Lenya *(Austrian)*
Margaret Lockwood *(English)*
Jennifer Lopez *(Puerto Rican)*
Sophia Loren *(Italian)*
Siobhan McKenna *(Irish)*
Shirley MacLaine *(U.S.)*
Melina Mercouri *(Greek)*
Liza Minnelli *(U.S.)*
Helen Mirren *(English)*
Marilyn Monroe *(U.S.)*
Jeanne Moreau *(French)*
Michelle Pfeiffer *(U.S.)*
Mary Pickford *(U.S.)*
Joan Plowright *(English)*
Vanessa Redgrave *(English)*
Julia Roberts *(U.S.)*
Flora Robson *(English)*
Ginger Rogers *(U.S.)*
Margaret Rutherford *(English)*
Susan Sarandon *(U.S.)*
Delphine Seyrig *(French)*
Sarah Siddons *(English)*
Simone Signoret *(French)*
Maggie Smith *(English)*
Sissy Spacek *(U.S.)*
Sharon Stone *(U.S.)*
Meryl Streep *(U.S.)*
Barbra Streisand *(U.S.)*
Janet Suzman *(South African)*
Elizabeth Taylor *(English-U.S.)*
Shirley Temple *(U.S.)*
Ellen Terry *(English)*
Charlize Theron *(South African)*
Emma Thompson *(English)*
Sybil Thorndike *(English)*
Julie Walters *(English)*
Sigourney Weaver *(U.S.)*
Raquel Welch *(U.S.)*
Mae West *(U.S.)*
Billie Whitelaw *(English)*
Kate Winslet *(English)*
Peg Woffington *(Irish)*
Renée Zellwegger *(U.S.)*
Catherine Zeta-Jones *(Welsh)*

3 = **keen**, good, penetrating, finely honed • *In the dark my sense of smell and hearing become so acute.*
4 = **perceptive**, sharp, keen, smart, sensitive, clever, subtle, piercing, penetrating, discriminating, discerning, ingenious, astute, intuitive, canny, incisive, insightful, observant, perspicacious • *His relaxed exterior hides an extremely acute mind.*
OPPOSITES: slow, stupid, dull
5 = **intense**, serious, deep, concentrated, severe, extreme, fierce, harsh, intensive, excessive, profound, agonizing • *a patient with acute rheumatoid arthritis*

acutely 1 = **painfully**, clearly, markedly, excessively, alarmingly, dreadfully, distressingly • *He was acutely aware of the smell of cooking oil.*
2 = **very**, highly, greatly, severely, extremely, terribly, utterly, unusually, exceptionally, extraordinarily, intensely, markedly, awfully *(informal)*, exceedingly, excessively, inordinately, uncommonly • *It was an acutely uncomfortable journey.*

adage = **saying**, motto, maxim, proverb, dictum, precept, by-word, saw, axiom, aphorism, apophthegm • *The old adage 'Every baby brings its own love' usually turns out true.*

adamant = **determined**, firm, fixed, stiff, rigid, set, relentless, stubborn, uncompromising, insistent, resolute, inflexible, unrelenting, inexorable, unyielding, intransigent, immovable, unbending, obdurate, unshakable • *The minister is adamant that he will not resign.*
OPPOSITES: yielding, compromising, flexible

adapt 1 = **adjust**, change, match, alter, modify, accommodate, comply, conform, reconcile, harmonize, familiarize, habituate, acclimatize • *Things will be different and we will have to adapt.*
2 = **convert**, change, prepare, fit, fashion, make, shape, suit, qualify, transform, alter, modify, tailor, remodel, tweak *(informal)*, metamorphose, customize • *Shelves were built to adapt the library for use as an office.*

adaptability = **flexibility**, versatility, resilience, variability, convertibility, plasticity, malleability, pliability, changeability, pliancy, adjustability, compliancy, modifiability, adaptableness, alterability • *The adaptability of wool is one of its great attractions.*

adaptable 1 = **flexible**, variable, versatile, resilient, easy-going, changeable, modifiable, conformable • *They are adaptable foragers that can survive on a wide range of foods.*
2 = **adjustable**, flexible, compliant, malleable, pliant, plastic, modifiable, alterable • *He hopes to make the workforce more adaptable and skilled.*

adaptation 1 = **acclimatization**, naturalization, habituation, familiarization, accustomedness • *Most creatures are capable of adaptation when necessary.*
2 = **conversion**, change, shift, variation, adjustment, transformation, modification, alteration, remodelling, reworking, refitting • *He won two awards for his screen adaptation of the play.*

add AS A VERB 1 = **count up**, total, reckon, sum up, compute, add up, tot up • *Banks add all the interest and other charges together.*
OPPOSITES: reduce, remove, take away
2 = **include**, attach, supplement, increase by, adjoin, annex, amplify, augment, affix, append, enlarge by • *He wants to add a huge sports complex to the hotel.*
3 = **continue to speak**, go on, carry on, persist, keep going • *'You could tell he was very embarrassed,' she added.*
▸ IN PHRASES: **add to something** = **increase**, boost, expand, strengthen, enhance, step up *(informal)*, intensify, raise, advance, spread, extend, heighten, enlarge, escalate, multiply, inflate, magnify, amplify, augment, proliferate • *Smiles and cheerful faces added to the general gaiety.*
add up 1 = **count up**, add, total, count, reckon, calculate, sum up, compute, tally, tot up, add together • *More than a quarter of seven-year-olds cannot add up properly.*
2 = **make sense**, hold up, be reasonable, ring true, be plausible, stand to reason, hold water, bear examination, bear investigation • *They arrested her because her statements did not add up.*
3 = **expand**, grow, thrive, flourish, prosper • *Even small savings here and there can add up.*
add up to something 1 = **mean**, reveal, indicate, imply, amount to, signify • *All this adds up to very bad news for the car industry.*
2 = **amount to**, make, come to, total, run to, grow to, number, be equal to • *For a hit show, profits can add up to millions.*

added = **extra**, more, other, further, fresh, additional, supplementary, auxiliary, add-on, supplemental, ancillary • *For added protection, choose moisturising lipsticks with sunscreen.*

addendum = **addition**, supplement, extra, extension, attachment, appendix, postscript, affix, adjunct, appendage, augmentation, codicil • *If you are self-employed, you have to get an addendum to the tax form.*

addict 1 = **junkie** *(informal)*, abuser, user *(informal)*, druggie *(informal)*, freak *(informal)*, fiend *(informal)*, mainliner *(slang)*, smackhead *(slang)*, space cadet *(slang)*, pill-popper *(informal)*, head *(slang)*, pothead *(slang)*, dope-fiend *(slang)*, cokehead *(slang)*, acidhead *(slang)*, hashhead *(slang)* • *He's only 24 years old and a drug addict.*
2 = **fan**, lover, nut *(slang)*, follower, enthusiast, freak *(informal)*, admirer, buff *(informal)*, junkie *(informal)*, devotee, fiend *(informal)*, adherent, rooter *(U.S.)*, zealot, groupie *(slang)*, aficionado • *She's a TV addict and watches as much as she can.*
▸ RELATED SUFFIX: -holic

addicted 1 = **hooked**, dependent • *After a while I was no longer addicted to nicotine.*
2 = **devoted**, in love, dedicated, fond, obsessed, enthusiastic, absorbed, wild, fanatical • *I went through about four years of being addicted to video games.*
▸ RELATED SUFFIX: -holic

addiction 1 = **dependence**, need, habit, weakness, obsession, attachment, craving, vulnerability, subordination, enslavement, subservience, overreliance • *She helped him fight his drug addiction.*
2 with **to** = **love of**, passion for, attachment to, affection for, fondness for, zeal for, fervour for, ardour for • *I've developed an addiction to rollercoasters.*

QUOTATIONS
Every form of addiction is bad, no matter whether the narcotic be alcohol or morphine or idealism
[Carl Gustav Jung *Memories, Dreams, Reflections*]

addictive = **habit-forming**, compelling, compulsive, causing addiction *or* dependency, moreish *or* morish *(informal)* • *Cigarettes are highly addictive.*

addition AS A NOUN 1 = **extra**, supplement, complement, adjunct, increase, gain, bonus, extension, accessory, additive, appendix, increment, appendage, addendum • *This book is a worthy addition to the series.*
2 = **inclusion**, adding, increasing, extension, attachment, adjoining, insertion, incorporation, annexation, accession, affixing, augmentation • *It was completely refurbished with the addition of a picnic site.*
OPPOSITES: removal, deduction, detachment
3 = **counting up**, totalling, reckoning, summing up, adding up, computation, totting up, summation • *simple addition and subtraction problems*
OPPOSITES: reduction, deduction, subtraction
▸ IN PHRASES: **in addition to** = **as well as**, along with, on top of, besides, to boot, additionally, over and above, to say nothing of, into the bargain • *There's a postage and packing fee in addition to the repair charge.*

a

additional = **extra**, more, new, other, added, increased, further, fresh, spare, supplementary, auxiliary, ancillary, appended • *The US is sending additional troops to the region.*

additionally = **also**, further, in addition, as well, moreover, furthermore, on top of that, to boot • *The maintenance programme will additionally seek to keep sites graffiti-free.*

additive = **added ingredient**, artificial *or* synthetic ingredient, E number, extra, supplement • *additive-free baby foods*

addle 1 = **confuse**, bewilder, mix up, muddle, perplex, fluster, stupefy, befuddle, fuddle • *I suppose the shock had addled his poor brain.*
2 = **go off**, turn (*Brit. informal*), spoil, rot, go bad, turn bad • *The heat had addled the milk and the stink made her retch.*

addled = **confused**, silly, foolish, at sea, bewildered, mixed-up, muddled, perplexed, flustered, befuddled • *You're talking to me like an addled romantic.*

address AS A NOUN 1 = **direction**, label, inscription, superscription • *The address on the envelope was illegible.*
2 = **location**, home, place, house, point, position, situation, site, spot, venue, lodging, pad (*slang*), residence, dwelling, whereabouts, abode, locus, locale, domicile • *The workmen had gone to the wrong address at the wrong time.*
3 = **speech**, talk, lecture, discourse, sermon, dissertation, harangue, homily, oration, spiel (*informal*), disquisition • *He had scheduled an address to the people for that evening.*
▸ AS A VERB 1 = **direct**, send, post, mail, route • *Applications should be addressed to the personnel officer.*
2 = **label**, inscribe, superscribe • *She absent-mindedly addressed the envelope with the wrong name.*
3 = **give a speech to**, talk to, speak to, lecture, discourse, harangue, give a talk to, spout to, hold forth to, expound to, orate to, sermonize to • *He will address a conference on human rights next week.*
4 = **speak to**, talk to, greet, hail, salute, invoke, communicate with, accost, approach, converse with, apostrophize, korero (*N.Z.*) • *The two ministers did not address each other directly.*
5 = **take aim at**, aim at • *First, address the ball in the centre of your stance.*
▸ IN PHRASES: **address yourself to something** = **concentrate on**, turn to, focus on, take up, look to, undertake, engage in, take care of, attend to, knuckle down to, devote yourself to, apply yourself to • *We have addressed ourselves to the problem of ethics throughout.*

adduce = **mention**, offer, name, present, advance, quote, allege, cite, designate • *The evidence she adduced was authoritative.*

adept AS AN ADJECTIVE = **skilful**, able, skilled, expert, masterly, practised, accomplished, versed, tasty (*Brit. informal*), masterful, proficient, adroit, dexterous • *He is an adept guitar player.*
OPPOSITES: awkward, clumsy, unskilled
▸ AS A NOUN = **expert**, master, genius, buff (*informal*), whizz (*informal*), hotshot (*informal*), rocket scientist (*informal, chiefly U.S.*), dab hand (*Brit. informal*), maven (*U.S.*) • *He was an adept at getting people to talk confidentially to him.*

adequacy = **sufficiency**, capability, competence, suitability, tolerability, fairness, commensurateness, requisiteness, satisfactoriness • *We are concerned about the adequacy of the children's diet.*

adequate 1 = **passable**, acceptable, middling, average, fair, ordinary, moderate, satisfactory, competent, mediocre, so-so (*informal*), tolerable, up to scratch (*informal*), presentable, unexceptional • *One in four people are without adequate homes.*
OPPOSITES: lacking, inadequate, unsatisfactory
2 = **sufficient**, enough, capable, suitable, requisite • *an amount adequate to purchase another house*
OPPOSITES: short, inadequate, insufficient

adherence = **obedience**, agreement, respect, submission, compliance, accordance, deference, assent, observance, subservience, submissiveness, dutifulness, conformability • *strict adherence to the constitution and respect for our laws*

adherent AS A NOUN = **supporter**, fan, advocate, follower, admirer, partisan, disciple, protagonist, devotee, henchman, hanger-on, upholder, sectary • *Communism was gaining adherents in Latin America.*
OPPOSITES: opposition, rival, opponent
▸ AS AN ADJECTIVE = **adhering**, holding, sticking, clinging, sticky, tacky, adhesive, tenacious, glutinous, gummy, gluey, mucilaginous • *an adherent bandage*

adhere to 1 = **follow**, keep, maintain, respect, observe, be true, fulfil, obey, heed, keep to, abide by, be loyal, mind, be constant, be faithful • *All members adhere to a strict code of practice.*
2 = **be faithful**, follow, support, respect, observe, be true, obey, be devoted, be attached, keep to, be loyal • *He urged them to adhere to the values of Islam.*
3 = **stick to**, attach to, cling to, unite to, glue to, fix to, fasten to, hold fast to, paste to, cement to, cleave to, glue on to, stick fast to, cohere to • *Small particles adhere to the seed.*

adhesion = **sticking**, grip, attachment, cohesion, coherence, adherence, adhesiveness • *Better equipment will improve track adhesion.*

adhesive AS A NOUN = **glue**, cement, gum, paste, mucilage • *Glue the mirror in with a strong adhesive.*
▸ AS AN ADJECTIVE = **sticky**, holding, sticking, attaching, clinging, adhering, tacky, cohesive, tenacious, glutinous, gummy, gluey, mucilaginous • *adhesive tape*

ad hoc AS AN ADJECTIVE = **makeshift**, emergency, improvised, impromptu, expedient, stopgap, jury-rigged (*chiefly Nautical*) • *An ad hoc committee was set up to examine the problem.*
OPPOSITES: lasting, standing (*of a committee*); permanent
▸ AS AN ADVERB = **for present purposes**, when needed, as the need arises • *Most programs have common sense built in ad hoc.*

adieu = **goodbye**, parting, farewell, leave-taking, valediction, congé, haere ra (*N.Z.*) • *We said our adieus and left.*

ad infinitum = **endlessly**, always, for ever (and ever), infinitely, eternally, perpetually, for all time, in perpetuity, interminably, to infinity, evermore, unceasingly, boundlessly, unendingly, limitlessly, in perpetuum (*Latin*), without end *or* limit • *The cycle repeats itself ad infinitum.*

adjacent = **adjoining**, neighbouring, nearby, abutting • *The fire quickly spread to adjacent shops.*
OPPOSITES: separated, remote, far away

adjoin = **connect with** *or* **to**, join, neighbour (on), link with, attach to, combine with, couple with, communicate with, touch on, border on, annex, approximate, unite with, verge on, impinge on, append, affix to, interconnect with • *Fields adjoined the garden and there were no neighbours.*

adjoining = **connecting**, nearby, joined, joining, touching, bordering, neighbouring, next door, adjacent, interconnecting, abutting, contiguous • *We waited in an adjoining office.*

adjourn = **postpone**, delay, suspend, interrupt, put off, stay, defer, recess, discontinue, put on the back burner (*informal*), prorogue, take a rain check on (*U.S. & Canad. informal*) • *The proceedings have been adjourned until next week.*
OPPOSITES: open, continue, remain

adjournment = **postponement**, delay, suspension, putting off, stay, recess, interruption, deferment, deferral, discontinuation, prorogation • *The court ordered a four-month adjournment.*

adjudge = **judge**, determine, declare, decide, assign, pronounce, decree, apportion, adjudicate • *He was adjudged to be guilty.*

adjudicate 1 = **decide**, judge, determine, settle, mediate, adjudge, arbitrate • *a commissioner to adjudicate on legal rights*
2 = **judge**, referee, umpire • *The fight will be adjudicated by a top boxing referee*

adjudication = **judgment**, finding, ruling, decision, settlement, conclusion, verdict, determination, arbitration, pronouncement, adjudgment • *unbiased adjudication of unfair dismissals*

adjudicator = **judge**, referee, umpire, umpie *(Austral. slang)*, arbiter, arbitrator, moderator • *an independent adjudicator*

adjunct = **addition**, supplement, accessory, complement, auxiliary, add-on, appendage, addendum, appurtenance • *Physical therapy is an important adjunct to drug treatments.*

adjust 1 = **adapt**, change, settle, convert, alter, accommodate, dispose, get used, accustom, conform, reconcile, harmonize, acclimatize, familiarize yourself, attune • *I felt I had adjusted to the idea of being a mother very well.*
2 = **change**, order, reform, fix, arrange, alter, adapt, revise, modify, set, regulate, amend, reconcile, remodel, redress, rectify, recast, customize, make conform • *To attract investors the country has adjusted its tax laws.*
3 = **modify**, arrange, fix, tune (up), alter, adapt, remodel, tweak *(informal)*, customize • *Liz adjusted her mirror and edged the car out.*

adjustable = **alterable**, flexible, adaptable, malleable, movable, tractable, modifiable, mouldable • *The bag has adjustable straps.*

adjustment 1 = **alteration**, setting, change, ordering, fixing, arrangement, tuning, repair, conversion, modifying, adaptation, modification, remodelling, redress, refinement, rectification • *A technician made an adjustment to a smoke machine at the back.*
2 = **acclimatization**, settling in, orientation, familiarization, change, regulation, settlement, amendment, reconciliation, adaptation, accustoming, revision, modification, naturalization, acculturation, harmonization, habituation, acclimation, inurement • *He will need a period of adjustment.*

ad-lib AS A VERB = **improvise**, speak off the cuff, vamp, busk, wing it *(informal)*, extemporize, speak extemporaneously, speak impromptu • *He is rather disjointed when he ad-libs.*
▸ AS AN ADJECTIVE = **improvised**, made up, impromptu, unprepared, off-the-cuff *(informal)*, unrehearsed, extempore, off the top of your head, extemporaneous, extemporized • *Sometimes, being in an ad-lib situation is the best way.*
▸ AS A NOUN = **improvisation**, makeshift, impromptu comment, expedient • *Every time he got me out of trouble with a brilliant ad-lib.*
▸ AS AN ADVERB = **off the cuff**, spontaneously, impromptu, extempore, off the top of your head *(informal)*, without preparation, extemporaneously, without rehearsal • *I spoke from the pulpit ad-lib.*

administer 1 = **manage**, run, control, rule, direct, handle, conduct, command, govern, oversee, supervise, preside over, be in charge of, superintend • *Next summer's exams will be straightforward to administer.*
2 = **dispense**, give, share, provide, apply, distribute, assign, allocate, allot, dole out, apportion, deal out • *Sister came to watch the nurses administer the drugs.*
3 = **execute**, do, give, provide, apply, perform, carry out, impose, realize, implement, enforce, render, discharge, enact, dispense, mete out, bring off • *He is shown administering most of the blows.*

administration 1 = **management**, government, running, control, performance, handling, direction, conduct, application, command, provision, distribution, governing, administering, execution, overseeing, supervision, manipulation, governance, dispensation, superintendence • *Standards in the administration of justice have degenerated.*
2 = **directors**, board, executive(s), bosses *(informal)*, management, employers, directorate • *They would like the college administration to exert more control.*
3 = **government**, authority, executive, leadership, ministry, regime, governing body • *He served in posts in both the Ford and Carter administrations.*
4 = **distribution**, supplying, dispensation, dealing out, appointment, endowment, allotment, disbursement, apportionment, bestowal, conferment • *a complaint about the wrongful administration of drugs*

administrative = **managerial**, executive, management, directing, regulatory, governmental, organizational, supervisory, directorial, gubernatorial *(chiefly U.S.)* • *The project will have an administrative staff of eight.*

administrator = **manager**, head, official, director, officer, executive, minister, boss *(informal)*, agent, governor, controller, supervisor, bureaucrat, superintendent, gaffer *(informal, chiefly Brit.)*, organizer, mandarin, functionary, overseer, baas *(S. African)* • *He worked for 34 years as an administrator with the company.*

admirable = **praiseworthy**, good, great, fine, capital, noted, choice, champion, prime, select, wonderful, excellent, brilliant, rare, cracking *(Brit. informal)*, outstanding, valuable, superb, distinguished, superior, sterling, worthy, first-class, notable, sovereign, dope *(slang)*, world-class, exquisite, exemplary, first-rate, superlative, commendable, top-notch *(informal)*, brill *(informal)*, laudable, meritorious, estimable, tiptop, A1 *or* A-one *(informal)*, bitchin' *(U.S. slang)*, chillin' *(U.S. slang)*, booshit *(Austral. slang)*, exo *(Austral. slang)*, sik *(Austral. slang)*, ka pai *(N.Z.)*, rad *(informal)*, phat *(slang)*, schmick *(Austral. informal)*, beaut *(informal)*, barrie *(Scot. slang)*, belting *(Brit. slang)*, pearler *(Austral. slang)* • *The film tells its story with admirable economy.*
OPPOSITES: bad, disappointing, deplorable

admiration = **regard**, surprise, wonder, respect, delight, pleasure, praise, approval, recognition, affection, esteem, appreciation, amazement, astonishment, reverence, deference, adoration, veneration, wonderment, approbation • *Her eyes widened with admiration.*

admire 1 = **respect**, value, prize, honour, praise, appreciate, esteem, approve of, revere, venerate, big up *(slang, chiefly Caribbean)*, take your hat off to, have a good *or* high opinion of, think highly of • *He admired the way she had coped with life.*
OPPOSITES: despise, scorn, spurn
2 = **adore**, like, love, desire, take to, go for, fancy *(Brit. informal)*, treasure, worship, cherish, glorify, look up to, dote on, hold dear, be captivated by, have an eye for, find attractive, idolize, take a liking to, be infatuated with, be enamoured of, lavish affection on • *I admired her when I first met her and I still think she's marvellous.*
3 = **marvel at**, look at, appreciate, delight in, gaze at, wonder at, be amazed by, take pleasure in, gape at, be awed by, goggle at, be filled with surprise by • *We took time to stop and admire the view.*

admirer 1 = **fan**, supporter, follower, enthusiast, partisan, disciple, buff *(informal)*, protagonist, devotee, worshipper, adherent, votary • *He was an admirer of her grandmother's paintings.*
2 = **suitor**, lover, boyfriend, sweetheart, beau, wooer • *He was the most persistent of her admirers.*

admissible = **permissible**, allowed, permitted, acceptable, tolerated, tolerable, passable, allowable • *Convictions will rise now that photographic evidence is admissible.*
OPPOSITES: unacceptable, intolerable, inadmissible

admission 1 = **admittance**, access, entry, introduction, entrance, acceptance, initiation, entrée, ingress • *There have been increases in hospital admissions of children.*
2 = **entry fee**, entry, entrance, entrance fee, admission fee, entry charge • *Gates open at 9 and admission is free.*

3 = **confession**, admitting, profession, declaration, revelation, concession, allowance, disclosure, acknowledgement, affirmation, unburdening, avowal, divulgence, unbosoming • *She wanted an admission of guilt from her father.*

a

admit 1 = **confess**, own up, confide, profess, own up, come clean *(informal)*, avow, come out of the closet, sing *(slang, chiefly U.S.)*, cough *(slang)*, spill your guts *(slang)*, 'fess up *(U.S. slang)* • *Two-thirds of them admit to buying drink illegally.*
2 = **allow**, agree, accept, reveal, grant, declare, acknowledge, recognize, concede, disclose, affirm, divulge • *I am willing to admit that I do make mistakes.*
OPPOSITES: deny, reject, dismiss
3 = **let in**, allow, receive, accept, introduce, include, welcome, greet, take in, incorporate, initiate, give access to, allow to enter • *Security personnel refused to admit him or his wife.*
OPPOSITES: exclude, keep out

admittance = **access**, entry, way in, passage, entrance, reception, acceptance • *He is trying to gain admittance into medical school.*

admittedly = **it must be admitted**, certainly, undeniably, it must be said, to be fair *or* honest, avowedly, it cannot be denied, it must be allowed, confessedly, it must be confessed, allowedly • *It's only a theory, admittedly, but the pieces fit together.*

admonish 1 = **reprimand**, caution, censure, rebuke, scold, berate, check, chide, tear into *(informal)*, tell off *(informal)*, reprove, upbraid, read the riot act to someone, carpet *(informal)*, chew out *(U.S. & Canad. informal)*, tear someone off a strip *(Brit. informal)*, give someone a rocket *(Brit. & N.Z. informal)*, slap someone on the wrist, rap someone over the knuckles • *They admonished me for taking risks with my health.*
OPPOSITES: praise, applaud, compliment
2 = **advise**, suggest, warn, urge, recommend, counsel, caution, prescribe, exhort, enjoin, forewarn • *Your doctor may one day admonish you to improve your posture.*

admonition = **reprimand**, warning, advice, counsel, caution, rebuke, reproach, scolding, berating, chiding, telling off *(informal)*, upbraiding, reproof, remonstrance • *She is full of admonitions about smoking now that she's given up.*

ad nauseam = **again and again**, over and over (again), on and on, time and (time) again, time after time, ad infinitum, times without number • *We discussed it ad nauseum.*

ado = **fuss**, to-do, trouble, delay, bother, stir, confusion, excitement, disturbance, bustle, flurry, agitation, commotion, pother • *And now, without further ado, let me introduce our benefactor.*

adolescence = **teens**, youth, minority, boyhood, girlhood, juvenescence • *Some young people suddenly become tongue-tied in early adolescence.*

adolescent AS AN ADJECTIVE 1 = **young**, growing, junior, teenage, juvenile, youthful, childish, immature, boyish, undeveloped, girlish, puerile, in the springtime of life • *adolescent rebellion*
2 = **teenage**, young, teen *(informal)*, juvenile, youthful, immature • *An adolescent boy should have an adult in whom he can confide.*
▸ AS A NOUN = **teenager**, girl, boy, kid *(informal)*, youth, lad, minor, young man, youngster, young woman, juvenile, young person, lass, young adult • *Adolescents are happiest with small groups of close friends.*

adopt 1 = **take on**, follow, support, choose, accept, maintain, assume, select, take over, approve, appropriate, take up, embrace, engage in, endorse, ratify, become involved in, espouse • *Pupils should be helped to adopt a positive approach.*
2 = **take in**, raise, nurse, mother, rear, foster, bring up, take care of • *There are hundreds of people desperate to adopt a child.*
OPPOSITES: give up, abandon, cast off
3 = **select**, choose, pick, nominate, opt for, decide on, single out, settle on, cherry-pick • *He had adopted a new country and a new profession.*
OPPOSITES: reject, renounce, spurn

adoption 1 = **fostering**, adopting, taking in, fosterage • *They gave their babies up for adoption.*
2 = **embracing**, choice, taking on, taking up, support, taking over, selection, approval, following, assumption, maintenance, acceptance, endorsement, appropriation, ratification, approbation, espousal • *the adoption of Japanese management practices*

adorable = **lovable**, pleasing, appealing, dear, sweet, attractive, charming, precious, darling, fetching, delightful, cute, captivating, cutesy *(informal, chiefly U.S.)* • *By the age of thirty I had three adorable children.*
OPPOSITES: despicable, displeasing, hateful

adoration = **love**, honour, worship, worshipping, esteem, admiration, reverence, estimation, exaltation, veneration, glorification, idolatry, idolization • *He had been used to female adoration all his life.*

adore 1 = **love**, honour, admire, worship, esteem, cherish, bow to, revere, dote on, idolize • *She adored her parents and would do anything to please them.*
OPPOSITES: hate, loathe, despise
2 = **like**, love, enjoy, go for, dig *(slang)*, relish, delight in, revel in, be fond of, be keen on, be partial to • *I adore good books and the theatre.*
3 = **worship**, revere, glorify, reverence, exalt, venerate • *The Holy Spirit creates in us a desire to adore God.*

adoring = **admiring**, loving, devoted, worshipping, fond, affectionate, ardent, doting, venerating, enamoured, reverential, reverent, idolizing, adulatory • *She can still pull in adoring audiences.*
OPPOSITES: hating, loathing, despising

adorn = **decorate**, enhance, deck, trim, grace, array, enrich, garnish, ornament, embellish, emblazon, festoon, bedeck, beautify, engarland • *Several oil paintings adorn the walls.*

adornment 1 = **decoration**, trimming, supplement, accessory, ornament, frill, festoon, embellishment, frippery • *A building without any adornment or decoration.*
2 = **beautification**, decorating, decoration, embellishment, ornamentation • *Cosmetics are used for adornment.*

adrift AS AN ADJECTIVE 1 = **drifting**, afloat, cast off, unmoored, aweigh, unanchored • *They were spotted adrift in a dinghy.*
2 = **aimless**, goalless, directionless, purposeless • *She had the growing sense that she was adrift and isolated.*
3 = **free**, separate, divided, loose, severed, loosened, disconnected, unconnected, disjoined • *Three panels had come adrift from the base of the vehicle.*
▸ AS AN ADVERB = **wrong**, astray, off course, amiss, off target, wide of the mark • *They are trying to place the blame for a policy that has gone adrift.*

adroit = **skilful**, able, skilled, expert, bright *(informal)*, clever, tasty *(Brit. informal)*, apt, cunning, ingenious, adept, deft, nimble, masterful, proficient, artful, quick-witted, dexterous • *She is a remarkably adroit politician.*
OPPOSITES: awkward, blundering, unskilful

adroitness = **skill**, ability, craft, expertise, cunning, mastery, knack, ingenuity, proficiency, dexterity, cleverness, deftness, nimbleness, aptness, artfulness, adeptness, quick-wittedness, ingeniousness, masterfulness, ableness, skilfulness • *He governed with an adroitness that earned him the nickname 'old fox'.*

adulation = **extravagant flattery**, worship, fawning, sycophancy, fulsome praise, blandishment, bootlicking *(informal)*, servile flattery • *The book was received with adulation by the critics.*
OPPOSITES: abuse, ridicule, condemnation

adulatory = **fawning**, worshipping, flattering, sycophantic, servile, slavish, obsequious, bootlicking *(informal)*, blandishing • *adulatory reviews*

adult AS A NOUN = **grown-up**, mature person, person of mature age, grown *or* grown-up person, man *or* woman • *Children under 14 must be accompanied by an adult.*
▸ AS AN ADJECTIVE 1 = **fully grown**, mature, grown-up, of age, ripe, fully fledged, fully developed, full grown • *a pair of adult birds*
2 = **pornographic**, blue, dirty, offensive, sexy, erotic, porn *(informal)*, obscene, taboo, filthy, indecent, sensual, hard-core, lewd, carnal, porno *(informal)*, X-rated *(informal)*, salacious, prurient, smutty • *She was the adult film industry's hottest property.*

adulterate = **debase**, thin, weaken, corrupt, deteriorate, mix with, contaminate, devalue, water down, depreciate, attenuate, vitiate, bastardize, make impure • *The food had been adulterated to increase its weight.*

adulterated = **debased**, mixed, contaminated, polluted, depreciated, reduced, lowered, impure • *The least adulterated pork sausages are your best bet.*

adulterer *or* **adulteress** = **cheat** *(informal)*, love rat *(slang)*, love cheat *(slang)*, fornicator • *He was portrayed as an adulterer and a vain fool.*

adulterous = **unfaithful**, cheating *(informal)*, extramarital, fornicating, unchaste • *She had an adulterous affair with a politician.*

adultery = **unfaithfulness**, infidelity, cheating *(informal)*, fornication, playing the field *(slang)*, extramarital sex, playing away from home *(slang)*, illicit sex, unchastity, extramarital relations, extracurricular sex *(informal)*, extramarital congress, having an affair *or* a fling • *She is going to divorce him on the grounds of adultery.*
OPPOSITES: fidelity, chastity, faithfulness

QUOTATIONS
It is not marriage but a mockery of it, a merging that mixes love and dread together like jackstraws
[Alexander Theroux *An Adultery*]
Adultery is the application of democracy to love
[H.L. Mencken]
The first breath of adultery is the freest; after it, constraints aping marriage develop
[John Updike *Couples*]

adulthood = **maturity**, manhood *or* womanhood, majority, completion, fullness, maturation, full bloom, ripeness, full growth, matureness • *Few people maintain friendships into adulthood.*

advance AS A VERB 1 = **progress**, proceed, go ahead, move up, come forward, go forward, press on, gain ground, make inroads, make headway, make your way, cover ground, make strides, move onward • *Rebel forces are advancing on the capital.*
OPPOSITES: retreat, weaken, diminish
2 = **accelerate**, speed, promote, hurry (up), step up *(informal)*, hasten, precipitate, quicken, bring forward, push forward, expedite, send forward, crack on *(informal)* • *Too much protein in the diet may advance the ageing process.*
3 = **improve**, rise, grow, develop, reform, pick up, progress, thrive, upgrade, multiply, prosper, make strides • *The country has advanced from a rural society to an industrial power.*
4 = **suggest**, offer, present, propose, allege, cite, advocate, submit, prescribe, put forward, proffer, adduce, offer as a suggestion • *Many theories have been advanced as to why this is.*
OPPOSITES: hide, suppress, withhold
5 = **lend**, loan, accommodate someone with, supply on credit • *I advanced him some money, which he promised to repay.*
OPPOSITES: defer payment, withhold payment
6 = **promote**, help, further, aid, forward, champion, push, encourage, assist, plug *(informal)*, pave the way for, hasten, patronize, succour, lend support to • *He was busy advancing other people's work.*
OPPOSITES: hold back, retard, impede
▸ AS A NOUN 1 = **credit**
2 = **down payment**, credit, fee, deposit, retainer, prepayment • *She was paid a £100,000 advance for her next two novels.*
3 = **loan**, credit
4 = **increase**
5 = **attack**, charge, strike, rush, assault, raid, invasion, offensive, onslaught, advancement, foray, incursion, forward movement, onward movement • *They simulated an advance on enemy positions.*
6 = **improvement**, development, gain, growth, breakthrough, advancement, step, headway, inroads, betterment, furtherance, forward movement, amelioration, onward movement • *Air safety has not improved since the advances of the 1970s.*
7 = **increase**, rise, development, gain, growth, boost, addition, expansion, extension, enlargement, escalation, upsurge, upturn, increment, intensification, augmentation • *They clocked up a worldwide sales advance of 27 per cent.*
▸ AS A PLURAL NOUN = **overtures**, moves, offer, approach, proposal, come-on *(informal)*, invitation, proposition • *She rejected his advances during the trip to Cannes.*
▸ AS A MODIFIER = **prior**, early, previous, beforehand • *The event received little advance publicity.*
▸ AS AN ADJECTIVE = **expeditionary**, first, leading, test, forward, trial, in front, preliminary, foremost, exploratory • *a 20-strong advance party*
▸ IN PHRASES: **in advance** = **beforehand**, earlier, ahead, previously, in the lead, in the forefront • *The subject of the talk is announced a week in advance.*

advanced 1 = **sophisticated**, foremost, modern, revolutionary, up-to-date, higher, leading, recent, prime, forward, ahead, supreme, extreme, principal, progressive, paramount, state-of-the-art, avant-garde, precocious, pre-eminent, up-to-the-minute, ahead of the times • *the most advanced optical telescope in the world*
OPPOSITES: late, behind, backward
2 = **high-level**, higher, tertiary, post-graduate • *The lab has been updated to allow for more advanced courses.*

advancement 1 = **promotion**, rise, gain, growth, advance, progress, improvement, betterment, preferment, amelioration • *He cared little for social advancement.*
2 = **progress**, advance, headway, forward movement, onward movement • *her work for the advancement of the status of women*

advantage 1 = **benefit**, use, start, help, service, aid, profit, favour, asset, assistance, blessing, utility, boon, ace in the hole, ace up your sleeve • *A good crowd will be a definite advantage to the team.*
OPPOSITES: difficulty, handicap, disadvantage
2 = **lead**, control, edge, sway, dominance, superiority, upper hand, precedence, primacy, pre-eminence • *Men have created an economic position of advantage over women.*
3 = **superiority**, good, worth, gain, comfort, welfare, enjoyment, mileage *(informal)* • *The great advantage of home-grown fruit is its magnificent flavour.*

advantageous 1 = **beneficial**, useful, valuable, helpful, profitable, of service, convenient, worthwhile, expedient • *Free exchange of goods was advantageous to all.*
OPPOSITES: unfortunate, useless, unfavourable
2 = **superior**, dominating, commanding, dominant, important, powerful, favourable, fortuitous, win-win • *She was determined to prise what she could from an advantageous situation.*

advent = **coming**, approach, appearance, arrival, entrance, onset, occurrence, visitation • *The advent of war led to austerity.*

adventure AS A NOUN 1 = **venture**, experience, chance, risk, incident, enterprise, speculation, undertaking, exploit, fling, hazard, occurrence, contingency, caper, escapade • *I set off for a new adventure in the US on the first day of the year.*
2 = **excitement**, action, passion, thrill, enthusiasm, fever, warmth, flurry, animation, ferment, commotion, elation, discomposure • *A feeling of adventure and excitement.*
▸ AS A VERB = **venture**, risk, brave, dare • *The group has adventured as far as the Alps.*

QUOTATIONS
An adventure is only an inconvenience rightly considered. An inconvenience is only an adventure wrongly considered
[G.K. Chesterton *All Things Considered*]

adventurer 1 = **mercenary**, rogue, gambler, speculator, opportunist, charlatan, fortune-hunter • *ambitious political adventurers*
2 = **venturer**, hero, traveller, heroine, wanderer, voyager, daredevil, soldier of fortune, swashbuckler, knight-errant • *A round-the-world adventurer was killed when her plane crashed.*

adventurous = **daring**, dangerous, enterprising, bold, risky, rash, have-a-go (*informal*), hazardous, reckless, audacious, intrepid, foolhardy, daredevil, headstrong, venturesome, adventuresome, temerarious (*rare*) • *He had always wanted an adventurous life in the tropics.*
OPPOSITES: safe, careful, cautious

adversary = **opponent**, rival, opposer, enemy, competitor, foe, contestant, antagonist • *His political adversaries were creating trouble for him.*
OPPOSITES: friend, partner, ally

adverse 1 = **harmful**, damaging, conflicting, dangerous, opposite, negative, destructive, detrimental, hurtful, antagonistic, injurious, inimical, inopportune, disadvantageous, unpropitious, inexpedient • *The decision would have no adverse effect on the investigation.*
OPPOSITES: promising, lucky, beneficial
2 = **unfavourable**, bad, threatening, hostile, unfortunate, unlucky, ominous, unfriendly, untimely, unsuited, ill-suited, inopportune, disadvantageous, unseasonable • *Despite the adverse conditions, the road was finished in just eight months.*
3 = **negative**, opposing, reluctant, hostile, contrary, dissenting, unwilling, unfriendly, unsympathetic, ill-disposed • *Wine lakes and butter mountains have drawn considerable adverse publicity.*

adversity = **hardship**, trouble, distress, suffering, trial, disaster, reverse, misery, hard times, catastrophe, sorrow, woe, misfortune, bad luck, deep water, calamity, mishap, affliction, wretchedness, ill-fortune, ill-luck • *He showed courage in adversity.*

advert = **advertisement**, bill, notice, display, commercial, ad (*informal*), announcement, promotion, publicity, poster, plug (*informal*), puff, circular, placard, blurb • *I saw an advert for a job in an engineering company.*

advertise = **publicize**, promote, plug (*informal*), announce, publish, push (*informal*), display, declare, broadcast, advise, inform, praise, proclaim, puff, hype, notify, tout, flaunt, crack up (*informal*), promulgate, make known, apprise, beat the drum (*informal*), blazon, bring to public notice • *Religious groups are not allowed to advertise on TV.* • *It has been much advertised in specialist magazines.*

advertisement = **advert** (*Brit. informal*), bill, notice, display, commercial, ad (*informal*), announcement, promotion, publicity, poster, plug (*informal*), puff, circular, placard, blurb • *She recently placed an advertisement in the local paper.*

advertising = **promotion**, marketing, plugging (*informal*), hype, publicizing, pushing (*informal*) • *money from advertising and sponsorship*

QUOTATIONS
You can fool all the people all the time if the advertising is right and the budget is big enough
[Joseph E. Levine]
Promise, large promise, is the soul of an advertisement
[Dr. Johnson]
Advertising is the greatest art form of the twentieth century
[Marshall McLuhan *Interview in Advertising Age*]
Advertising is a racket, like the movies and the brokerage business
[F.Scott Fitzgerald *Letter to his daughter, Frances Scott Fitzgerald*]

advice 1 = **guidance**, help, opinion, direction, suggestion, instruction, counsel, counselling, recommendation, injunction, admonition • *Don't be afraid to ask for advice when ordering a meal.*
2 = **instruction**, notification, view, information, warning, teaching, notice, word, intelligence • *Most have now left the country on the advice of their governments.*

QUOTATIONS
There is nothing we receive with so much reluctance as advice
[Joseph Addison *The Spectator*]
It was, perhaps, one of those cases in which advice is good or bad only as the event decides
[Jane Austen *Persuasion*]
The best way to give advice to your children is to find out what they want and advise them to do it
[Harry S. Truman]

advisability = **wisdom**, fitness, profitability, prudence, suitability, propriety, desirability, expediency, appropriateness, soundness, aptness, judiciousness, seemliness • *He is doubtful about the advisability of interference with the system.*

advisable = **wise**, seemly, sound, suggested, fitting, fit, politic, recommended, appropriate, suitable, sensible, proper, profitable, desirable, apt, prudent, expedient, judicious • *It is advisable to book your hotel in advance.*
OPPOSITES: stupid, silly, unwise

advise 1 = **recommend**, suggest, urge, counsel, advocate, caution, prescribe, commend, admonish, enjoin • *I would strongly advise against it.*
2 = **counsel**, train, teach, guide, influence, educate, instruct, give guidance, give tips, offer suggestions, give counselling, offer opinions • *He advises university graduates on money matters.*
3 = **notify**, tell, report, announce, warn, declare, inform, acquaint, make known, apprise, let (someone) know • *I must advise you of my decision to retire.*

QUOTATIONS
Thou dost advise me, Even so as I mine own course have set down
[William Shakespeare *The Winter's Tale*]

advisedly = **deliberately**, intentionally, with intent, on purpose, by design, prudently, judiciously, after careful consideration, calculatedly, designedly, premeditatedly • *I say 'boys' advisedly because we are talking about male behaviour.*

adviser = **counsellor**, authority, teacher, coach, guide, lawyer, consultant, solicitor, counsel, aide, tutor, guru, mentor, helper, confidant, right-hand man • *a careers adviser*

advisory = **advising**, helping, recommending, counselling, consultative • *Now my role is strictly advisory.*

advocacy = **recommendation**, support, defence, championing, backing, proposal, urging, promotion, campaigning for, upholding, encouragement, justification, argument for, advancement, pleading for, propagation, espousal, promulgation, boosterism, spokesmanship • *I support your advocacy of free trade.*

advocate AS A VERB = **recommend**, support, champion, encourage, propose, favour, defend, promote, urge, advise, justify, endorse, campaign for, prescribe, speak for, uphold, press for, argue for, commend, plead for, espouse, countenance, hold a brief for *(informal)* • *He advocates fewer government controls on business.*

OPPOSITES: oppose, resist, contradict

▸ AS A NOUN 1 = **supporter**, spokesman, champion, defender, speaker, pleader, campaigner, promoter, counsellor, backer, proponent, apostle, apologist, upholder, proposer • *He was a strong advocate of free market policies.*

2 = **lawyer**, attorney, solicitor, counsel, barrister • *When she became an advocate there were only a few women practising.*

aegis = **support**, backing, wing, favour, protection, shelter, sponsorship, patronage, advocacy, auspices, guardianship • *The space programme will continue under the aegis of the armed forces.*

aeroplane = **plane**, aircraft, jet, airplane, airliner *(U.S. & Canad.)*, kite *(Brit. slang)*, flying machine • *The aeroplane crashed in the mountains, killing 29.*

aesthetic = **ornamental**, artistic, pleasing, pretty, fancy, enhancing, decorative, tasteful, beautifying, nonfunctional • *products chosen for their aesthetic appeal as well as their durability*

afar = **a distance**, a long way away • *a stranger who has loved her from afar for 23 years*

affability = **friendliness**, warmth, good humour, civility, benevolence, sociability, good nature, graciousness, cordiality, urbanity, geniality, amiability, mildness, kindliness, congeniality, approachability, courtesy, pleasantness, benignity, amicability, obligingness • *Beneath the surface affability there was a struggle for power.*

affable = **friendly**, kindly, civil, warm, pleasant, mild, obliging, benign, gracious, benevolent, good-humoured, amiable, courteous, amicable, cordial, sociable, genial, congenial, urbane, approachable, good-natured • *He is an extremely affable and approachable man.*

OPPOSITES: cold, distant, unfriendly

affair AS A NOUN 1 = **matter**, thing, business, question, issue, happening, concern, event, subject, project, activity, incident, proceeding, circumstance, episode, topic, undertaking, transaction, occurrence • *The government has mishandled the whole affair.*

2 = **occasion**, happening, experience, event, celebration, occurrence • *Breakfast will be a cheerless affair for the minister this morning.*

3 = **relationship**, romance, intrigue, fling, liaison, flirtation, amour, dalliance • *A married male supervisor was carrying on an affair with a colleague.*

4 = **concern**, problem, business, matter, worry, responsibility, look-out, headache *(informal)* • *If you want to make a fool of yourself, that is your affair.*

▸ AS A PLURAL NOUN = **concerns**, records, papers, activities, proceedings, transactions, annals, doings • *The unexpectedness of his death meant that his affairs were not in order.*

affect[1] 1 = **influence**, involve, concern, impact, transform, alter, modify, change, manipulate, act on, sway, prevail over, bear upon, impinge upon • *Millions of people have been affected by the drought.*

2 = **emotionally move**, touch, upset, overcome, stir, disturb, perturb, impress on, tug at your heartstrings *(often facetious)* • *He loved his sister, and her loss clearly still affects him.*

affect[2] = **put on**, assume, adopt, pretend, imitate, simulate, contrive, aspire to, sham, counterfeit, feign • *He listened to them, affecting an amused interest.*

affectation = **pretence**, show, posing, posturing, act, display, appearance, pose, façade, simulation, sham, pretension, veneer, artifice, mannerism, insincerity, pretentiousness, hokum *(slang, chiefly U.S. & Canad.)*, artificiality, fakery, affectedness, assumed manners, false display, unnatural imitation • *He writes well, without fuss or affectation.*

affected[1] = **pretended**, artificial, contrived, put-on, assumed, mannered, studied, precious, stiff, simulated, mincing, sham, unnatural, pompous, pretentious, counterfeit, feigned, spurious, conceited, insincere, camp *(informal)*, la-di-da *(informal)*, arty-farty *(informal)*, phoney or phony *(informal)* • *She passed by with an affected air and a disdainful look.*

OPPOSITES: real, natural, genuine

affected[2] = **touched**, influenced, concerned, troubled, damaged, hurt, injured, upset, impressed, stirred, altered, changed, distressed, stimulated, melted, impaired, afflicted, deeply moved • *Staff at the hospital were deeply affected by the tragedy.*

OPPOSITES: cured, untouched, unaffected

affecting = **emotionally moving**, touching, sad, pathetic, poignant, saddening, pitiful, pitiable, piteous • *one of the most affecting pieces of the film*

affection = **fondness**, liking, feeling, love, care, desire, passion, warmth, attachment, goodwill, devotion, kindness, inclination, tenderness, propensity, friendliness, amity, aroha *(N.Z.)* • *She thought of him with affection.*

TERMS OF AFFECTION

angel	goose	poppet
babe *or* babes	honey	precious
baby	honey bunny	princess
bean	kitten	pumpkin
beloved	kitty *or* kitty cat	puppy
bunnykins	lamb	pussycat
chicken	little one *or*	star
chicken bunny	little 'un	sugar
darling	love	sweetheart
dear	loved one	sweetie pie
dearest	lover	sweets
dearheart	munchkin	tiger
dear one	muppet	toots
doll	pepperpot	treacle
duck	pet	treasure
flower	petal	truelove
fluffy bunny	pet lamb	weasel

affectionate = **fond**, loving, kind, caring, warm, friendly, attached, devoted, tender, doting, warm-hearted • *They seemed devoted to each other and were openly affectionate.*

OPPOSITES: cold, cool, indifferent

affidavit = **statement**, declaration, testimony, proclamation • *She was asked to sign an affidavit swearing that nothing had happened.*

affiliate = **associate**, unite, join, link, ally, combine, connect, incorporate, annex, confederate, amalgamate, band together • *Staff associations may not affiliate with outside unions.* • *All youth groups will have to affiliate to the agency.*

affiliated = **associated**, united, joined, linked, allied, connected, incorporated, confederated, amalgamated, federated, conjoined • *the UN and its affiliated organisations*

affiliation = **association**, union, joining, league, relationship, connection, alliance, combination, coalition, merging, confederation, incorporation, amalgamation, banding together • *The group has no affiliation to any political party.*

affinity 1 = **attraction**, liking, leaning, sympathy, inclination, rapport, fondness, partiality, aroha *(N.Z.)* • *There is a natural affinity between the two.*

OPPOSITES: hostility, dislike, hatred

a

2 = **similarity**, relationship, relation, connection, alliance, correspondence, analogy, resemblance, closeness, likeness, compatibility, kinship • *The two plots share certain obvious affinities.*
OPPOSITES: difference, disparity, dissimilarity

affirm 1 = **declare**, state, maintain, swear, assert, testify, pronounce, certify, attest, avow, aver, asseverate, avouch • *'The place is a dump,' she affirmed.*
OPPOSITES: deny, retract
2 = **confirm**, prove, sanction, endorse, ratify, verify, validate, bear out, substantiate, corroborate, authenticate • *Everything I had accomplished seemed to affirm that opinion.*
OPPOSITES: reject, renounce, refute

affirmation 1 = **declaration**, statement, assertion, oath, certification, pronouncement, avowal, asseveration, averment • *The ministers issued a robust affirmation of their faith in the system.*
2 = **confirmation**, testimony, ratification, attestation, avouchment • *The high turnout was an affirmation of the importance of the election.*

affirmative = **agreeing**, confirming, positive, approving, consenting, favourable, concurring, assenting, corroborative • *He was eager for an affirmative answer.*
OPPOSITES: denying, negative, disagreeing

affix = **attach**, add, join, stick on, bind, put on, tag, glue, paste, tack, fasten, annex, append, subjoin • *Complete the form and affix four tokens.*
OPPOSITES: remove, take off, detach

afflict = **torment**, trouble, pain, hurt, wound, burden, distress, rack, try, plague, grieve, harass, ail, oppress, beset, smite • *There are four main problems that afflict these people.*

affliction = **misfortune**, suffering, trouble, trial, disease, pain, distress, grief, misery, plague, curse, ordeal, sickness, torment, hardship, sorrow, woe, adversity, calamity, scourge, tribulation, wretchedness • *Hay fever is an affliction that arrives at an early age.*

affluence = **wealth**, riches, plenty, fortune, prosperity, abundance, big money, exuberance, profusion, big bucks *(informal, chiefly U.S.)*, opulence, top dollar *(informal)*, megabucks *(U.S. & Canad. slang)*, pretty penny *(informal)*, wad *(U.S. & Canad. slang)* • *The postwar era was one of new affluence for the working class.*

affluent = **wealthy**, rich, prosperous, loaded *(slang)*, well-off, opulent, well-heeled *(informal)*, well-to-do, moneyed, minted *(Brit. slang)* • *Cigarette smoking used to be commoner among affluent people.*
OPPOSITES: broke *(informal)*, poor, impoverished

afford 1 = **have the money for**, manage, bear, pay for, spare, stand, stretch to • *The arts should be available at prices people can afford.*
2 = **bear**, stand, sustain, allow yourself • *We cannot afford to wait.*
3 = **give**, offer, provide, produce, supply, grant, yield, render, furnish, bestow, impart • *The room afforded fine views of the city.*

affordable = **inexpensive**, fair, cheap, reasonable, moderate, modest, low-price, low-cost, economical • *beautiful clothes at affordable prices*
OPPOSITES: dear, expensive, costly

affray = **fight**, mêlée, contest, set-to *(informal)*, encounter, outbreak of violence, scrap, disturbance, feud, quarrel, brawl, skirmish, scuffle, free-for-all *(informal)*, fracas, dogfight, tumult, shindig *(informal)*, scrimmage, shindy *(informal)*, biffo *(Austral. slang)*, bagarre *(French)* • *He caused an affray at a pub.*

affront AS A VERB = **offend**, anger, provoke, outrage, insult, annoy, vex, displease, pique, put *or* get your back up, slight • *One example that particularly affronted him was at the world championships.*
▸ AS A NOUN = **insult**, wrong, injury, abuse, offence, slight, outrage, provocation, slur, indignity, slap in the face *(informal)*, vexation • *She has taken my enquiry as a personal affront.*

affronted = **offended**, cross, angry, upset, slighted, outraged, insulted, annoyed, stung, incensed, indignant, irate, miffed *(informal)*, displeased, peeved *(informal)*, piqued, tooshie *(Austral. slang)* • *He pretended to be affronted, but inwardly he was pleased.*

aficionado = **fan**, lover, enthusiast, admirer, supporter, nut *(slang)*, follower, addict, freak *(informal)*, disciple, buff *(informal)*, fanatic, devotee, connoisseur, adherent, votary • *You are obviously a jazz aficionado.*

afield IN PHRASES: **far afield** = **distant places**, far off, far away, remote places, beyond the horizon, far-flung places, far-off places, outlying places, far-removed places • *Many of those arrested came from far afield.*

afire AS AN ADJECTIVE = **passionate**, excited, stimulated, aroused, fervent, impassioned, aglow • *All his senses were afire.*
▸ IN PHRASES: **set afire** = **set alight**, lighted, lit, ignited, set on fire, set ablaze, set burning, set aflame, set blazing • *The houses were set afire, but there were only minor injuries.*

aflame 1 = **burning**, lighted, lit, flaming, blazing, on fire, fiery, ignited, alight, ablaze, afire • *Hundreds of tightly rolled newspapers were set aflame.*
2 = **red**, flushed, inflamed, ruddy, aglow • *The shop windows were aflame with Christmas lights.*
3 = **passionate**, excited, stimulated, aroused, fervent, impassioned, afire • *Everything about this spectacular movie is aflame.*

afloat 1 = **floating**, on the surface, buoyant, keeping your head above water, unsubmerged • *Three hours is a long time to try and stay afloat.*
OPPOSITES: submerged, immersed, sunken
2 = **solvent**, in business, above water • *Efforts were being made to keep the company afloat.*
OPPOSITES: bust *(informal)*, bankrupt, out of business

afoot = **going on**, happening, current, operating, abroad, brewing, hatching, circulating, up *(informal)*, about, in preparation, in progress, afloat, in the wind, on the go *(informal)*, astir • *We all knew that something awful was afoot.*

aforementioned = **aforesaid**, previously mentioned, earlier mentioned, prior mentioned, aforenamed • *the aforementioned conference*

aforesaid = **aforementioned**, previously mentioned, earlier mentioned, prior mentioned, aforenamed • *the aforesaid organizations and institutions*

afraid 1 = **scared**, frightened, nervous, anxious, terrified, shaken, alarmed, startled, suspicious, intimidated, fearful, cowardly, timid, apprehensive, petrified, panicky, panic-stricken, timorous, faint-hearted, scared shitless *(taboo slang)*, shit-scared *(taboo slang)* • *She did not seem at all afraid.* • *He's afraid to sleep in his own bedroom.*
OPPOSITES: bold, indifferent, unafraid
2 = **reluctant**, slow, frightened, scared, unwilling, backward, hesitant, recalcitrant, loath, disinclined, unenthusiastic, indisposed • *He seems to live in an ivory tower, afraid to enter the real world.*
3 = **anxious**, concerned, worried, troubled, bothered, nervous, disturbed, tense, fearful, apprehensive, perturbed, on edge, overwrought, fretful • *I was afraid that nobody would believe me.*
4 = **sorry**, apologetic, regretful, sad, distressed, unhappy • *I'm afraid I can't help you.*
OPPOSITES: happy, pleased

afresh = **again**, newly, once again, once more, over again, anew • *The only hope for the party is to start afresh.*

after AS A PREPOSITION 1 = **at the end of**, following, subsequent to • *After breakfast she phoned for a taxi.*
OPPOSITES: before, earlier, sooner

2 = **following**, chasing, pursuing, on the hunt for, on the tail of *(informal)*, on the track of • *People were after him for large amounts of money.*
3 = **looking for**, searching for, in search of, trying to find, hunting for, seeking out, fossicking for *(Austral. & N.Z.)* • *I did eventually find what I was after.*
4 = **because of**, in the wake of, in the aftermath of, on account of, as a result of, as a consequence of • *I always have to clean up after her.*
5 = **apart from**, barring, excepting, next to, other than, excluding, besides, in addition to • *After Germany, the US is their biggest customer.*
6 = **with the same name as**, in the name of, in honour of, the same as, as a tribute to, for *(U.S.)* • *He persuaded her to name the baby after him.*
7 = **about**, concerning, re, regarding, respecting, referring to, relating to, with respect to, as regards • *He asked after my wife and daughter.*
8 = **despite**, in spite of, regardless of, notwithstanding, in defiance of, undeterred by • *After all that, we still will not be able to compete.*
▸ AS AN ADVERB 1 = **following**, later, next, succeeding, afterwards, subsequently, thereafter • *tomorrow, or the day after*
2 = **subsequently**, next, behind, afterwards, in the wake (of) • *In the vehicle behind, the chauffeur followed after.*
▸ RELATED PREFIX: post-

aftereffect *usually plural* = **consequence**, wake, trail, aftermath, hangover *(informal)*, spin-off, repercussion, afterglow, aftershock, delayed response • *He was suffering from shock as well as from the aftereffects of drugs.*

afterlife = **life after death**, heaven, paradise, nirvana *(Buddhism, Hinduism)*, bliss, immortality, next world, Zion *(Christianity)*, hereafter, Valhalla *(Norse myth)*, Happy Valley, happy hunting ground *(Native American legend)*, life to come, everlasting life, life everlasting, abode of God, Elysium *or* Elysian fields *(Greek myth)* • *The film is about proving the existence of an afterlife.*

aftermath = **effects**, end, results, wake, consequences, outcome, sequel, end result, upshot, aftereffects • *In the aftermath of the coup, troops opened fire on demonstrators.*

afterwards *or* **afterward** = **later**, after, then, after that, subsequently, thereafter, following that, at a later date *or* time • *Shortly afterwards, police arrested four suspects.*

again AS AN ADVERB 1 = **once more**, another time, anew, afresh • *He kissed her again.*
2 = **also**, in addition, moreover, besides, furthermore • *And again, that's probably part of the progress of technology.*
▸ IN PHRASES: **again and again** = **over and over**, often, repeatedly, frequently, many times, time and (time) again, time after time • *He would go over his work again and again until it was right.*
there again *or* **then again** = **on the other hand**, in contrast, on the contrary, conversely • *They may agree, but there again, they may not.*

against 1 = **beside**, on, up against, in contact with, abutting, close up to • *She leaned against him.*
2 = **opposed to**, anti *(informal)*, opposing, counter, contra *(informal)*, hostile to, in opposition to, averse to, opposite to, not in accord with • *She was very much against commencing the treatment.*
3 = **in opposition to**, resisting, versus, counter to, in the opposite direction of • *swimming upstream against the current*
4 = **in defiance of**, resisting, in spite of, in the face of, disregarding, in opposition to, in contempt of, in disobedience to • *He left hospital early against the advice of doctors.*
5 = **in preparation for**, in case of, in anticipation of, in expectation of, in provision for • *You'll need insurance against fire, flood and breakage.*
6 = **in comparison to**, in return for, in compensation for, in exchange against • *The US dollar is down against most foreign currencies.*
7 = **unfavourable to**, damaging to, harmful to, detrimental to, prejudicial to, injurious to, hurtful to, adverse to, disadvantageous to, deleterious to, inexpedient to, inopportune to • *There are few jobs, and my age is against me.*
▸ RELATED PREFIXES: anti-, contra-, counter-

agape 1 = **wide open**, wide, yawning, gaping • *She stood looking at me, her mouth agape.*
2 = **amazed**, surprised, astonished, eager, astounded, expectant, spellbound, gobsmacked *(Brit. slang)*, dumbfounded, flabbergasted, agog, thunderstruck, awe-stricken • *Her performance left us agape.*

age AS A NOUN 1 = **years**, days, generation, lifetime, stage of life, length of life, length of existence • *He's very confident for his age.*
2 = **old age**, experience, maturity, completion, seniority, fullness, majority, maturation, senility, decline, advancing years, dotage, declining years, senescence, full growth, agedness, autumn *or* evening of your life, matureness • *Perhaps he has grown wiser with age.*
OPPOSITES: youth, childhood, adolescence
3 = **time**, day(s), period, generation, era, epoch • *the age of steam and steel*
4 = **a long time**, years, forever, a lifetime, an eternity, aeons, yonks *(informal)* • *He waited what seemed an age.*
OPPOSITES: a second, a moment, a short time
▸ AS A PLURAL NOUN = **a long time** *or* **while**, years, centuries, for ever *(informal)*, aeons, donkey's years *(informal)*, yonks *(informal)*, a month of Sundays *(informal)*, an age *or* eternity • *The bus took ages to arrive.*
▸ AS A VERB 1 = **grow old**, decline, weather, fade, deteriorate, wither • *He seemed to have aged in the last few months.*
2 = **mature**, season, condition, soften, mellow, ripen • *Whisky loses strength as it ages.*
▸ IN PHRASES: **come of age** = **reach adulthood**, mature, develop, grow up, bloom, blossom, become adult • *The money was held in trust until he came of age.*

QUOTATIONS

Youth, which is forgiven everything, forgives itself nothing; age, which forgives itself anything, is forgiven nothing
[George Bernard Shaw *Maxims for Revolutionists*]

With age, the mind grows slower and more wily
[Mason Cooley *City Aphorisms*]

Age appears to be best in four things – old wood best to burn, old wine to drink, old friends to trust, and old authors to read
[Francis Bacon *Apophthegms, no. 97*]

There is still no cure for the common birthday
[John Glenn]

aged = **old**, getting on, grey, ancient, antique, elderly, past it *(informal)*, age-old, antiquated, hoary, superannuated, senescent, cobwebby • *She has an aged parent who is capable of being very difficult.*
OPPOSITES: young, adolescent, juvenile

ageing *or* **aging** AS AN ADJECTIVE = **growing old** *or* **older**, declining, maturing, deteriorating, mellowing, in decline, senile, long in the tooth, senescent, getting on *or* past it *(informal)* • *He lives with his ageing mother.*
▸ AS A NOUN = **growing old**, decline, decay, deterioration, degeneration, maturation, senility, senescence • *degenerative diseases and premature ageing*

QUOTATIONS

Grow old along with me!
The best is yet to be
[Robert Browning *Rabbi Ben Ezra*]

ageless = **eternal**, enduring, abiding, perennial, timeless, immortal, unchanging, deathless, unfading • *the ageless oceans*
OPPOSITES: passing, temporary, momentary

agency 1 = **business**, company, office, firm, department, organization, enterprise, establishment, bureau • *a successful advertising agency*
2 = **medium**, work, means, force, power, action, operation, activity, influence, vehicle, instrument, intervention, mechanism, efficiency, mediation, auspices, intercession, instrumentality • *a negotiated settlement through the agency of the UN*

agenda AS A NOUN = **programme**, list, plan, schedule, diary, calendar, timetable • *This is sure to be an item on the agenda next week.*
▸ IN PHRASES: **hidden agenda** = **hidden motive**, secret plan, secret intention, hidden ploy, ulterior motive • *They were accused of having a hidden agenda.*

agent 1 = **representative**, deputy, substitute, advocate, rep *(informal)*, broker, delegate, factor, negotiator, envoy, trustee, proxy, surrogate, go-between, emissary • *You are buying direct, rather than through an agent.*
2 = **spy**, operative, mole, secret agent, double agent, secret service agent, undercover agent, foreign agent, fifth columnist, nark *(Brit., Austral. & N.Z. slang)* • *All these years he's been an agent for the East.*
3 = **author**, officer, worker, actor, vehicle, instrument, operator, performer, operative, catalyst, executor, doer, perpetuator • *They regard themselves as the agents of change in society.*
4 = **force**, means, power, cause, instrument • *the bleaching agent in white flour*
5 = **bureau**, business, office, department, agency, organization • *a travel agent*

age-old = **ancient**, old, aged, timeworn, antique, old-fashioned, obsolete, out-of-date, archaic, bygone, antiquated, outmoded, primordial, primeval, hoary, olden, superannuated, antediluvian, cobwebby, old as the hills • *this age-old struggle for control*

agglomeration = **mass**, collection, pile, cluster, lump, stack, heap, rick, clump, accumulation • *The album is a bizarre agglomeration of styles.*

aggrandize = **exaggerate**, advance, promote, intensify, elevate, enlarge, enrich, inflate, dignify, magnify, amplify, augment, exalt, ennoble • *He would go on and on, showing off, aggrandizing himself.*

aggravate 1 = **make worse**, exaggerate, intensify, worsen, heighten, exacerbate, magnify, inflame, increase, add insult to injury, fan the flames of • *Stress and lack of sleep can aggravate the situation.*
OPPOSITES: improve, ease, calm
2 = **annoy**, bother, provoke, needle *(informal)*, irritate, tease, hassle *(informal)*, gall, exasperate, nettle, pester, vex, irk, get under your skin *(informal)*, get on your nerves *(informal)*, nark *(Brit., Austral. & N.Z. slang)*, get up your nose *(informal)*, be on your back *(slang)*, piss you off *(taboo slang)*, rub (someone) up the wrong way *(informal)*, get in your hair *(informal)*, get on your wick *(Brit. slang)*, hack you off *(informal)* • *What aggravates you most about this country?*
OPPOSITES: please, calm, assuage

aggravating 1 = **annoying**, provoking, irritating, teasing, galling, exasperating, vexing, irksome • *You don't realise how aggravating you can be.*
2 = **worsening**, exaggerating, intensifying, heightening, exacerbating, magnifying, inflaming • *Stress is a frequent aggravating factor.*

aggravation 1 = **annoyance**, grief *(informal)*, teasing, irritation, hassle *(informal)*, provocation, gall, exasperation, vexation, irksomeness • *I just couldn't take the aggravation.*
2 = **worsening**, heightening, inflaming, exaggeration, intensification, magnification, exacerbation • *Any aggravations of the injury would keep him out of the match.*

aggregate AS A NOUN = **total**, body, whole, amount, collection, mass, sum, combination, pile, mixture, bulk, lump, heap, accumulation, assemblage, agglomeration • *society viewed as an aggregate of individuals*
▸ AS AN ADJECTIVE = **collective**, added, mixed, combined, collected, corporate, assembled, accumulated, composite, cumulative • *the rate of growth of aggregate demand*
▸ AS A VERB = **combine**, mix, collect, assemble, heap, accumulate, pile, amass • *We should never aggregate votes to predict results under another system.*

aggregation = **collection**, body, mass, combination, pile, mixture, bulk, lump, heap, accumulation, assemblage, agglomeration • *Society is more than just an aggregation of individuals.*

aggression 1 = **hostility**, malice, antagonism, antipathy, aggressiveness, ill will, belligerence, destructiveness, malevolence, pugnacity • *Aggression is by no means a male-only trait.*
2 = **attack**, campaign, injury, assault, offence, raid, invasion, offensive, onslaught, foray, encroachment • *the threat of massive military aggression*

aggressive 1 = **hostile**, offensive, destructive, belligerent, unkind, unfriendly, malevolent, contrary, antagonistic, pugnacious, bellicose, two-fisted, quarrelsome, aggers *(Austral. slang)*, biffo *(Austral. slang)*, inimical, rancorous, ill-disposed, arsey *(Brit., Austral. & N.Z. slang)* • *Some children are much more aggressive than others.*
OPPOSITES: friendly, peaceful
2 = **forceful**, powerful, convincing, effective, enterprising, dynamic, bold, militant, pushing, vigorous, energetic, persuasive, assertive, zealous, pushy *(informal)*, in-your-face *(slang)*, carnivorous *(informal)* • *He is respected as a very competitive and aggressive executive.*
OPPOSITES: retiring, quiet, submissive

aggressor = **attacker**, assaulter, invader, assailant • *They have been the aggressors in this conflict.*

aggrieved = **hurt**, wronged, injured, harmed, disturbed, distressed, unhappy, afflicted, saddened, woeful, peeved *(informal)*, ill-used • *I really feel aggrieved at this sort of thing.*

aghast = **horrified**, shocked, amazed, stunned, appalled, astonished, startled, astounded, confounded, awestruck, horror-struck, thunderstruck • *His colleagues were aghast at the sackings.*

agile 1 = **nimble**, active, quick, lively, swift, brisk, supple, sprightly, lithe, limber, spry, lissom(e) • *He is not as strong and agile as he was at 20.*
OPPOSITES: heavy, slow, stiff
2 = **acute**, sharp, quick, bright *(informal)*, prompt, alert, clever, lively, nimble, quick-witted • *She was quick-witted, and had an extraordinarily agile mind.*

agility 1 = **nimbleness**, activity, suppleness, quickness, swiftness, liveliness, briskness, litheness, sprightliness, spryness • *She blinked in surprise at his agility.*
2 = **acuteness**, sharpness, alertness, cleverness, quickness, liveliness, promptness, quick-wittedness, promptitude • *His intellect and mental agility have never been in doubt.*

agitate 1 = **protest**, campaign, push, demonstrate, drive, crusade, cry out • *The women had begun to agitate for better conditions.*
2 = **stir**, beat, mix, shake, disturb, toss, rouse, churn • *Gently agitate the water with a paintbrush.*
3 = **upset**, worry, trouble, disturb, excite, alarm, stimulate, distract, rouse, ruffle, inflame, incite, unnerve, disconcert, disquiet, fluster, perturb, faze, work someone up, give someone grief *(Brit. & S. African)* • *The thought of them inheriting all these things agitated her.*
OPPOSITES: still, quiet, calm

agitated = **upset**, worried, troubled, disturbed, shaken, excited, alarmed, nervous, anxious, distressed, rattled *(informal)*, distracted, uneasy, unsettled, worked up, ruffled, unnerved, disconcerted, disquieted, edgy, flustered, perturbed, on edge, fazed, ill at ease, hot under the collar *(informal)*, in a flap *(informal)*, hot and bothered *(informal)*, antsy *(informal)*, angsty, all of a flutter *(informal)*, discomposed • *She seemed agitated about something.*
OPPOSITES: cool, collected, calm

agitation 1 = **struggle**, fight, battle, conflict, clash, contest, encounter, combat, hostilities, strife, skirmish, tussle • *Seventy students were injured in the agitation.*
2 = **turbulence**, rocking, shaking, stirring, stir, tossing, disturbance, upheaval, churning, convulsion • *Temperature is a measure of agitation of molecules.*
3 = **turmoil**, worry, trouble, upset, alarm, confusion, excitement, disturbance, distraction, upheaval, stimulation, flurry, outcry, clamour, arousal, ferment, disquiet, commotion, fluster, lather *(informal)*, incitement, tumult, discomposure, tizzy, tizz *or* tiz-woz *(informal)* • *She was in a state of emotional agitation.*

agitator = **troublemaker**, revolutionary, inciter, firebrand, instigator, demagogue, rabble-rouser, agent provocateur, stirrer *(informal)* • *a famous actress who was accused of being a political agitator*

agnostic AS A NOUN = **sceptic**, cynic, scoffer, doubter, disbeliever, unbeliever, doubting Thomas, Pyrrhonist • *He was, if not an atheist, an agnostic.*
▸ AS AN ADJECTIVE = **sceptical**, questioning, doubting, cynical, doubtful, scoffing, unconvinced, disbelieving, incredulous, quizzical, mistrustful, unbelieving • *She grew up in an agnostic household.*

ago = **previously**, back, before, since, earlier, formerly • *He was killed a few days ago in an accident.*

agog = **eager**, excited, curious, enthusiastic, impatient, enthralled, avid, expectant, in suspense • *The city was agog with rumours last night.*
OPPOSITES: indifferent, unconcerned, uninterested

agonize = **suffer**, labour, worry, struggle, strain, strive, writhe, be distressed, be in agony, go through the mill, be in anguish • *He was agonizing over the moral issues involved.*

agonized = **tortured**, suffering, wounded, distressed, racked, tormented, anguished, broken-hearted, grief-stricken, wretched • *The agonized look on his face suggested he wouldn't be playing much longer.*

agonizing = **painful**, bitter, distressing, harrowing, heartbreaking, grievous, excruciating, hellish, heart-rending, gut-wrenching, torturous • *The wait was agonizing.*

agony = **suffering**, pain, distress, misery, torture, discomfort, torment, hardship, woe, anguish, pangs, affliction, throes • *He accepted there would be agony for the remaining children.*

agrarian = **agricultural**, country, land, farming, rural, rustic, agrestic • *a highly developed agrarian economy*
OPPOSITES: industrial, urban

agree AS A VERB 1 = **concur**, engage, be as one, sympathize, assent, see eye to eye, be of the same opinion, be of the same mind • *I'm not sure I agree with you.*
OPPOSITES: deny, dispute, disagree
2 = **correspond**, match, accord, answer, fit, suit, square, coincide, tally, conform, chime, harmonize • *His second statement agrees with the facts.*
▸ IN PHRASES: **agree on something** = **shake hands on**, reach agreement on, settle on, negotiate, work out, arrive at, yield to, thrash out, accede to, concede to • *The warring sides have agreed on a ceasefire.*
agree to something = **consent to**, grant, approve, permit, accede to, assent to, acquiesce to, comply to, concur to • *All 100 senators agreed to postponement.*
agree with someone = **suit**, get on, be good for, befit • *I don't think the food here agrees with me.*

agreeable 1 = **pleasant**, pleasing, satisfying, acceptable, delightful, enjoyable, gratifying, pleasurable, congenial, to your liking, to your taste, likable *or* likeable • *more agreeable and better paid occupations*
OPPOSITES: offensive, unpleasant, horrid
2 = **pleasant**, nice, friendly, sociable, affable, congenial, good-natured, likable *or* likeable • *I've gone out of my way to be agreeable to his friends*
3 = **consenting**, willing, agreeing, approving, sympathetic, complying, responsive, concurring, amenable, in accord, well-disposed, acquiescent • *She was agreeable to the project.*

QUOTATIONS

I do not want people to be very agreeable, as it saves me the trouble of liking them a great deal
[Jane Austen]

My idea of an agreeable person is a person who agrees with me
[Benjamin Disraeli *Lothair*]

agreed AS AN ADJECTIVE = **settled**, given, established, guaranteed, fixed, arranged, definite, stipulated, predetermined • *There is a discount if goods do not arrive by the agreed time.*
OPPOSITES: variable, indefinite, negotiable
▸ AS AN INTERJECTION = **all right**, done, settled, it's a bargain *or* deal, O.K. *or* okay *(informal)*, you're on *(informal)*, ka pai *(N.Z.)* • *That means we move out today. Agreed?*

agreement 1 = **treaty**, contract, bond, arrangement, alliance, deal *(informal)*, understanding, settlement, bargain, pact, compact, covenant, entente • *a new defence agreement*
2 = **concurrence**, harmony, compliance, union, agreeing, concession, consent, unison, assent, concord, acquiescence • *The talks ended in acrimony rather than agreement.*
OPPOSITES: disagreement, division, row
3 = **correspondence**, agreeing, accord, similarity, consistency, analogy, accordance, correlation, affinity, conformity, compatibility, congruity, suitableness • *The results are generally in agreement with these figures.*
OPPOSITES: difference, diversity, discrepancy

agricultural = **farming**, country, rural, rustic, agrarian, agronomic, agronomical, agrestic • *traditional agricultural societies*

agriculture = **farming**, culture, cultivation, husbandry, tillage, agronomy, agronomics • *The country is strong in both industry and agriculture.*
▸ RELATED ADJECTIVE: geoponic

aground = **beached**, grounded, stuck, shipwrecked, foundered, stranded, ashore, marooned, on the rocks, high and dry • *The 40ft Lady Gwendoline was aground and taking in water.*

ahead AS AN ADVERB 1 = **in front**, on, forwards, in advance, onwards, towards the front, frontwards • *He looked straight ahead.*
2 = **at an advantage**, in advance, in the lead • *Children in smaller classes were 1.5 months ahead in reading.*
3 = **in the lead**, winning, leading, at the head, to the fore, at an advantage • *Australia were ahead throughout the game.*
4 = **in the future**, hence, from now on, henceforth, hereafter, in time to come, from this day forward • *We have to expect a difficult time ahead.*
5 = **in front**, before, in advance, onwards, in the lead, in the vanguard • *You go on ahead. I'll catch you up later.*
▸ IN PHRASES: **ahead of** 1 = **before**, in front of, in advance of • *There was a man a few metres ahead of me.*
2 = **in wait for**, before, waiting for, awaiting, in store for • *I tried to think of all the problems that lay ahead of me.*
3 = **before**, prior to, earlier than, in advance of • *The dish may be prepared a day ahead of time and refrigerated*

a

4 = further on, in front of, superior to, further advanced • *He generally stayed ahead of others in subjects.*

aid AS A NOUN **1 = financial assistance**, help, relief, support, funds, benefit, gifts, charity, contributions, assistance, donations, endowment, largesse, sustenance, philanthropy, hand-outs, alms, koha *(N.Z.)* • *They have already pledged millions of dollars in aid.*
2 = help, backing, support, benefit, favour, relief, promotion, assistance, encouragement, helping hand, succour • *He was forced to turn to his former enemy for aid.*
OPPOSITES: hindrance
3 = helper, supporter, assistant, aide, adjutant, aide-de-camp, second, abettor • *A young woman employed as an aid spoke hesitantly.*
▸ AS A VERB **1 = help**, second, support, serve, sustain, assist, relieve, avail, subsidize, abet, succour, be of service to, lend a hand to, give a leg up to *(informal)* • *a software system to aid managers in decision-making*
OPPOSITES: hurt, oppose, hinder
2 = promote, help, further, forward, encourage, favour, facilitate, pave the way for, expedite, smooth the path of, assist the progress of • *Calcium may aid the prevention of colon cancer.*
▸ IN PHRASES: **in aid of = in support of**, backing, helping, in promotion of, championing, in assistance of, in encouragement of • *a charity performance in aid of the local children's hospital*

aide = assistant, supporter, deputy, attendant, helper, henchman, right-hand man, adjutant, second, helpmate, coadjutor *(rare)* • *a close aide to the prime minister*

ail 1 = trouble, worry, bother, distress, pain, upset, annoy, irritate, sicken, afflict, be the matter with • *a debate on what ails the industry*
2 = be ill, be sick, be unwell, feel unwell, be crook *(Austral. & N.Z. informal)*, be indisposed, be *or* feel off colour • *He is said to be ailing at his home in the country.*

ailing 1 = weak, failing, poor, flawed, unstable, feeble, unsatisfactory, deficient, unsound • *A rise in overseas sales is good news for the ailing economy.*
2 = ill, suffering, poorly, diseased, sick, weak, crook *(Austral. & N.Z. informal)*, feeble, invalid, debilitated, sickly, unwell, infirm, off colour, under the weather *(informal)*, indisposed • *She stopped working to care for her ailing mother.*

ailment = illness, disease, complaint, disorder, sickness, affliction, malady, infirmity, lurgy *(informal)* • *The pharmacist can assist you with the treatment of common ailments.*

aim AS A VERB **1 = try for**, want, seek, work for, plan for, strive, aspire to, wish for, have designs on, set your sights on • *He was aiming for the 100 metres world record.*
2 = mean, attempt, propose, intend, resolve • *I didn't aim to get caught.*
3 = point, level, train, direct, sight, take aim (at) • *He was aiming the rifle at me.*
▸ AS A NOUN **1 = intention**, end, point, plan, course, mark, goal, design, target, wish, scheme, purpose, direction, desire, object, objective, ambition, intent, aspiration, Holy Grail *(informal)* • *a research programme that has failed to achieve its aim*
2 = aiming, directing, sight • *He used his left hand to steady his aim.*
▸ IN PHRASES: **aim something at something** *or* **someone = intend for**, address to, mean for, direct at, target at, pitch at • *Advertising aimed at children should be curbed.*

aimless = purposeless, random, stray, pointless, erratic, wayward, frivolous, chance, goalless, haphazard, vagrant, directionless, unguided, undirected • *After several hours of aimless driving they were getting low on fuel.*
OPPOSITES: decided, firm, purposeful

air AS A NOUN **1 = wind**, blast, breath, breeze, puff, whiff, draught, gust, waft, zephyr, air-current, current of air • *Draughts help to circulate air.*
2 = atmosphere, sky, heavens, aerosphere • *They fired their guns in the air.*
3 = tune, song, theme, melody, strain, lay, aria • *an old Irish air*
4 = manner, feeling, effect, style, quality, character, bearing, appearance, look, aspect, atmosphere, tone, mood, impression, flavour, aura, ambience, demeanour, vibe *(slang)* • *The meal gave the occasion an almost festive air.*
▸ AS A VERB **1 = broadcast**, show, cable, beam, transmit, relay, televise, put on the air • *Tonight, the channel will air a documentary called 'Democracy in Action'.*
2 = be broadcast, be shown, be cabled, be beamed, be transmitted, be relayed, be televised, be put on the air • *The show will air on July 23rd.*
3 = publicize, tell, reveal, exhibit, communicate, voice, express, display, declare, expose, disclose, proclaim, utter, circulate, make public, divulge, disseminate, ventilate, make known, give vent to, take the wraps off • *The whole issue was thoroughly aired at the meeting*
4 = ventilate, expose, freshen, aerate • *Once a week she cleaned and aired each room.*
▸ IN PHRASES: **up in the air = uncertain**, vague, unclear, doubtful, dubious, unsettled, unsure, unresolved, in the balance, undecided, hazy, unconfirmed, vacillating, undetermined, unfixed • *The President's trip is still very much up in the air.*
walking on air = ecstatic, entranced, joyous, enthusiastic, frenzied, fervent, joyful, elated, over the moon *(informal)*, overjoyed, transported, blissful, delirious, euphoric, rapturous, enraptured, on cloud nine *(informal)*, cock-a-hoop, blissed out, rhapsodic, in seventh heaven, floating on air, in exaltation, in transports of delight, stoked *(Austral. & N.Z. informal)* • *As soon as I got the news I was walking on air.*
▸ RELATED ADJECTIVE: aerial
▸ RELATED PHOBIA: aerophobia

PROVERBS
Fresh air keeps the doctor poor

airborne = flying, floating, soaring, in the air, hovering, gliding, in flight, on the wing, wind-borne, volitant • *The pilot did manage to get the plane airborne.*

aircraft = plane, jet, aeroplane, airplane *(U.S. & Canad.)*, airliner, kite *(Brit. slang)*, flying machine • *The return flight of the aircraft was delayed.*
▹ *See panel* **Aviation terms**

airfield = airport, airstrip, aerodrome, landing strip, air station, airdrome *(U.S.)* • *It was built as an airfield during World War II.*

airily = light-heartedly, happily, blithely, gaily, animatedly, breezily, jauntily, buoyantly, high-spiritedly • *'I'll be all right,' he said airily.*

airiness = freshness, openness, lightness, breeziness, windiness, gustiness, draughtiness • *Skylights enhance the sense of airiness.*

airing 1 = ventilation, drying, freshening, aeration • *Open the windows and give the bedroom a good airing.*
2 = exposure, display, expression, publicity, vent, utterance, dissemination • *We feel able to talk about sex, but money rarely gets an airing.*

airless = stuffy, close, heavy, stifling, oppressive, stale, breathless, suffocating, sultry, muggy, unventilated • *a dark, airless room*
OPPOSITES: open, light, airy

airliner = plane, aircraft, aeroplane, passenger jet • *The airliner crashed just after take-off.*

airman = pilot, captain, flyer, aviator • *an English airman*

airplane = plane, aircraft, jet, aeroplane, airliner, kite *(Brit. slang)*, flying machine • *The two men were accused of the airplane bombing.*

airport = airfield, aerodrome, airdrome *(U.S.)* • *the busiest international airport in the world*

AIRCRAFT

Types of Aircraft

aerodyne, aerostat, airliner, airship, amphibian, autogiro, balloon, biplane, blimp, bomber, canard, coleopter, convertiplane, cyclogiro, delta-wing, dirigible, dive bomber, drone, fighter, fighter-bomber, flying boat, flying wing, freighter, gas-filled balloon, glider, gyrodyne, hang-glider, helicopter, helicopter gunship, hot-air balloon, interceptor, jet *or* jet plane, jetliner, jumbo jet, jump jet, lifting body, light aircraft, microlight *or* microlite, monoplane, multiplane, night fighter, ornithopter *or* orthopter, rotaplane, sailplane, seaplane, skiplane, Stealth bomber, STOL, swept-wing, swing-wing, tanker, triplane, troop carrier, turbofan, turbojet, turboprop, VTOL, warplane, wing, zeppelin

Aircraft Parts

aerofoil, aerometeorograph, aerostructure, afterburner, aileron, airframe, air-intake, airlock, air scoop, airscrew, all-flying tail, altimeter, anti-icer, arrester, artificial horizon, astrodome *or* astrohatch, athodyd, autopilot, auxiliary power unit, basket, black box, blister, body, bomb bay, bombsight, bulkhead, cabin, canopy, cantilever, capsule, chassis, clamshell, cockpit, control column *or* control stick, cowling *or* cowl, dashboard, drop tank, ejection seat, elevator, elevon, empennage, engine, engine pod, fairing, fin, flap, flight deck, flight recorder, fuel tank, fuselage, galley, gondola, heat sink, hold, horn *or* horn balance, hydroplane, inclinometer, instrument panel, jet engine, jet pipe, joystick, keel, landing gear, landing light, launching shoe, longeron, main plane, nacelle, nose, nose wheel, Pitot tube, pod, propeller, pulsejet, pusher, pylon, ramjet, rotor, rudder, slat, slinger ring, spinner, spoiler, stabilizer, tab, tail, tailplane, tailskid, tail wheel, trailing edge, trim tab, turret, undercarriage, waist, wing, winglet, wing tip

airship = **zeppelin**, blimp, dirigible • *The British airship R101 crashed in France, killing 48 passengers.*

airs = **affectation**, arrogance, pretensions, pomposity, swank *(informal)*, hauteur, haughtiness, superciliousness, affectedness • *We're poor and we never put on airs.*

airtight 1 = **closed**, shut, sealed, waterproof, watertight, stopped up • *Store the biscuits in an airtight container.*
2 = **incontestable**, sure, sound, certain, safe, positive, guaranteed, absolute, undeniable, beyond doubt, foolproof, infallible, indisputable, sure-fire *(informal)*, unbreakable, irrefutable, unquestionable, incontrovertible, indubitable • *an airtight alibi*

airy 1 = **well-ventilated**, open, light, fresh, spacious, windy, lofty, breezy, uncluttered, draughty, gusty, blowy • *The bathroom is light and airy.*
OPPOSITES: close, heavy, stuffy
2 = **light-hearted**, light, happy, gay, lively, cheerful, animated, merry, upbeat *(informal)*, buoyant, graceful, cheery, genial, high-spirited, jaunty, chirpy *(informal)*, sprightly, debonair, nonchalant, blithe, frolicsome • *He sailed past, giving them an airy wave of the hand.*
OPPOSITES: sad, miserable, gloomy
3 = **insubstantial**, imaginary, visionary, flimsy, fanciful, ethereal, immaterial, illusory, wispy, weightless, incorporeal, vaporous • *'launch aid', an airy euphemism for more state handouts*
OPPOSITES: real, material, substantial

airy-fairy = **fanciful**, lightweight, shaky, feeble, flimsy, unconvincing, unsound, insubstantial, without substance, incorporeal, chimerical • *their airy-fairy principles*
OPPOSITES: firm, sound, substantial

aisle AS A NOUN = **passageway**, path, lane, passage, corridor, alley, gangway • *the frozen food aisle*
▸ IN PHRASES: **rolling in the aisles** = **roaring with laughter**, giggling, chuckling, sniggering, cracking up *(informal)*, chortling, guffawing, tittering, convulsed *(informal)*, in stitches, busting a gut *(informal)*, creasing up *(informal)*, splitting your sides • *a host of comic talent which will have you rolling in the aisles*

ajar = **open**, gaping, agape, partly open, unclosed • *He left the door ajar in case I needed him.*

akin IN PHRASES: **akin to** = **similar to**, like, related to, corresponding to, parallel to, comparable to, allied with, analogous to, affiliated with, of a piece with, kin to, cognate with, congenial with, connected with *or* to • *It's an activity more akin to gardening than to reading.*

alacrity = **eagerness**, enthusiasm, willingness, readiness, speed, zeal, gaiety, alertness, hilarity, cheerfulness, quickness, liveliness, briskness, promptness, avidity, joyousness, sprightliness • *As you can imagine, I accepted with alacrity.*
OPPOSITES: reluctance, apathy, unwillingness

à la mode = **fashionable**, in fashion, in vogue, in *(informal)*, the new, popular, with it *(informal)*, stylish, chic, all the rage *(informal)*, modish, du jour *(French)*, all the go *(informal)*, culty, the latest rage *(informal)* • *The saxophone will always be à la mode.*

a

alarm AS A NOUN 1 = **fear**, horror, panic, anxiety, distress, terror, dread, dismay, fright, unease, apprehension, nervousness, consternation, trepidation, uneasiness • *The news was greeted with alarm by MPs.*
OPPOSITES: calm, composure, calmness
2 = **danger signal**, warning, bell, alert, siren, alarm bell, hooter, distress signal, tocsin • *As soon as the door opened he heard the alarm go off.*
▸ AS A VERB = **frighten**, shock, scare, panic, distress, terrify, startle, rattle, dismay, daunt, unnerve, terrorize, put the wind up *(informal)*, give (someone) a turn *(informal)*, scare the bejesus out of *(informal)*, make (someone's) hair stand on end • *We could not see what had alarmed him.*
OPPOSITES: comfort, calm, assure

alarmed = **frightened**, troubled, shocked, scared, nervous, disturbed, anxious, distressed, terrified, startled, dismayed, uneasy, fearful, daunted, unnerved, apprehensive, in a panic • *They should not be too alarmed by the press reports.*
OPPOSITES: calm, assured, composed

alarming = **frightening**, shocking, scaring, disturbing, distressing, terrifying, appalling, startling, dreadful, horrifying, menacing, intimidating, dismaying, scary *(informal)*, fearful, daunting, fearsome, unnerving, hair-raising, bloodcurdling • *The disease has spread at an alarming rate.*

alarmist = **fatalistic**, pessimistic, scaremongering • *some of the more alarmist reports*

alas = **sadly**, unfortunately, inopportunely • *Alas, it's not that simple.*

albatross IN PHRASES: **an albatross around your neck** = **burden**, worry, trouble, trial, weight, heavy responsibility, stress, anxiety, liability, obstruction, millstone, encumbrance • *The drive towards privatization could become a political albatross around the party's neck*

albeit = **even though**, though, although, even if, notwithstanding, tho' *(U.S. poetic)* • *His letter was published, albeit in an edited form.*

album 1 = **record**, recording, CD, single, release, disc, waxing *(informal)*, LP, vinyl, EP, forty-five, platter *(U.S. slang)*, seventy-eight, gramophone record, black disc • *He has a large collection of albums and cassettes.*
2 = **book**, collection, scrapbook • *She showed me her photo album.*

alchemy = **magic**, witchcraft, wizardry, sorcery, makutu *(N.Z.)* • *Imagine that by some political alchemy, all men had been made equal.*

alcohol 1 = **drink**, spirits, liquor, intoxicant, juice *(informal)*, booze *(informal)*, the bottle *(informal)*, grog *(informal, chiefly Austral. & N.Z.)*, the hard stuff *(informal)*, strong drink, Dutch courage *(informal)*, firewater, John Barleycorn, hooch *or* hootch *(informal, chiefly U.S. & Canad.)* • *No alcohol is allowed on the premises.*
2 = **ethanol**, ethyl alcohol • *Products for dry skin have little or no alcohol.*
▸ RELATED MANIA: dipsomania
▹ *See panels* **Alcoholic drinks; Cocktails; Liqueurs; Spirits; Whiskies; Wines**

alcoholic AS A NOUN = **drunkard**, drinker, drunk, boozer *(informal)*, toper, soak *(slang)*, lush *(slang)*, sponge *(informal)*, carouser, sot, tippler, wino *(informal)*, inebriate, dipsomaniac, hard drinker, piss artist *(slang)*, tosspot *(informal)*, pisshead *(slang)*, alky *(slang)*, alko *or* alco *(Austral. slang)* • *He admitted publicly that he was an alcoholic.*
▸ AS AN ADJECTIVE = **intoxicating**, hard, strong, stiff, brewed, fermented, distilled, vinous, inebriating, spirituous, inebriant • *tea, coffee, and alcoholic beverages*
▹ *See panel* **Alcoholic drinks**

alcove = **recess**, corner, bay, niche, bower, compartment, cubicle, nook, cubbyhole • *There were bookshelves in the alcove beside the fire.*

ALCOHOLIC DRINKS

apéritif	French vermouth	nor'wester
busera	ginger wine	palm wine
Campari *(trademark)*	glogg	posset
chaser	gluhwein	pousse-café
cider, cyder, *or (U.S. & Canad.)* hard cider	grog	pulque
caudle	hippocras	sake, saké, saki, *or* rice wine
Cinzano *(trademark)*	Irish coffee *or* Gaelic coffee	samshu
cocktail	Italian vermouth	shooter
cordial	kvass, kvas, *or* quass	skokiaan
dram	liqueur	slammer
Dubonnet *(trademark)*	malt liquor	snakebite
elderberry wine	Martini *(trademark)*	soma
frappé	mead	spruce beer
	mulled wine	toddy
	negus	vermouth
		waragi

alert AS AN ADJECTIVE 1 = **attentive**, careful, awake, wary, vigilant, perceptive, watchful, ready, on the lookout, circumspect, observant, on guard, wide-awake, on your toes, on the watch, keeping a weather eye on, heedful • *He had been spotted by an alert neighbour.*
OPPOSITES: slow, unaware, careless
2 = **quick-witted**, spirited, quick, bright, sharp, active, lively, brisk, on the ball *(informal)*, nimble, agile, sprightly, bright-eyed and bushy-tailed *(informal)* • *His grandfather is still alert at 93.*
▸ AS A NOUN = **warning**, signal, alarm, siren • *Due to a security alert, the train did not stop at our station.*
OPPOSITES: all clear
▸ AS A VERB = **warn**, signal, inform, alarm, notify, tip off, forewarn • *I was hoping he'd alert the police.*
OPPOSITES: lull

alertness = **watchfulness**, vigilance, agility, wariness, quickness, liveliness, readiness, circumspection, attentiveness, spiritedness, briskness, nimbleness, perceptiveness, carefulness, sprightliness, promptitude, activeness, heedfulness • *The drugs improve mental alertness.*

algae

ALGAE

blackfish weed *(Austral.)*	gulfweed	reindeer moss
bladderwrack	Iceland moss	rockweed
brown algae	Irish moss	sargasso *or* sargassum
carrageen, carragheen, *or* carageen	kelp	sea lettuce
diatom	laver	sea tangle
dinoflagellate	lichen	seaweed
dulse	Neptune's necklace *(Austral.)*	sea wrack
euglena	oarweed	spirogyra
fucoid *or* fucus	phytoplankton *or* plankton	stonewort
green algae	red algae	wrack

alias AS A NOUN = **pseudonym**, pen name, assumed name, stage name, nom de guerre, nom de plume • *He had rented a house using an alias.*
▸ AS AN ADVERB = **also known as**, otherwise, also called, otherwise known as, a.k.a. *(informal)* • *Richard Thorp, alias Alan Turner*

alibi = **excuse**, reason, defence, explanation, plea, justification, pretext • *He had a good alibi for his absence.*

alien AS A NOUN 1 = **foreigner**, incomer, immigrant, stranger, outsider, newcomer, asylum seeker, outlander • *The woman had hired an illegal alien for child care.*
OPPOSITES: national, resident, citizen
2 = **extraterrestrial**, visitor, ET, little green man *(informal)* • *His sister was abducted by aliens.*
▸ AS AN ADJECTIVE 1 = **foreign**, outside, strange, imported, overseas, unknown, exotic, unfamiliar, not native, not naturalized • *They were afraid of the presence of alien troops in the region.*
2 = **strange**, new, foreign, novel, remote, unknown, exotic, unfamiliar, estranged, outlandish, untried, unexplored • *His work offers an insight into an alien culture*
OPPOSITES: like, similar, related
3 = **extraterrestrial**, otherworldly • *He wants to rule out the existence of alien beings.*
▸ IN PHRASES: **alien to** = **unfamiliar to**, opposed to, contrary to, separated from, conflicting with, incompatible with, inappropriate to, repugnant to, adverse to • *Such an attitude is alien to most businessmen.*

alienate AS A VERB = **antagonize**, anger, annoy, offend, irritate, hassle *(informal)*, gall, repel, estrange, piss off *(taboo slang)*, lose the affection of, disaffect, hack off *(informal)* • *The government cannot afford to alienate either group.*
▸ IN PHRASES: **alienate someone from something** = **estrange**, separate, divide, divorce, divert, break off, set against, disunite, part, drive apart, make hostile, disaffect, set at odds, make unfriendly • *His ex-wife was determined to alienate him from his two boys.*

alienation = **estrangement**, setting against, divorce, withdrawal, separation, turning away, indifference, breaking off, diversion, rupture, disaffection, remoteness • *Her sense of alienation from the world disappeared.*

alight[1] 1 = **get off**, descend, get down, disembark, dismount • *Two men alighted from the vehicle.*
2 = **land**, light, settle, come down, descend, perch, touch down, come to rest • *A thrush alighted on a branch of the pine tree.*
OPPOSITES: rise, scale, take off

alight[2] 1 = **lit up**, bright, brilliant, shining, illuminated, fiery • *Her face was alight with happiness.*
2 = **on fire**, ignited, set ablaze, lit, burning, aflame, blazing, flaming, flaring • *The rioters set several buildings alight.*

align 1 = **ally**, side, join, associate, affiliate, cooperate, sympathize • *The prime minister is aligning himself with the liberals.*
2 = **line up**, even, order, range, sequence, regulate, straighten, coordinate, even up, make parallel, arrange in line • *A tripod would be useful to align and steady the camera.*

alignment 1 = **alliance**, union, association, agreement, sympathy, cooperation, affiliation • *His alignment with the old administration cost him the election.*
2 = **lining up**, line, order, ranging, arrangement, evening, sequence, regulating, adjustment, coordination, straightening up, evening up • *a link between the alignment of the planets and events on earth*

alike AS AN ADJECTIVE = **similar**, close, the same, equal, equivalent, uniform, parallel, resembling, identical, corresponding, akin, duplicate, analogous, homogeneous, of a piece, cut from the same cloth, like two peas in a pod • *We are very alike.*
OPPOSITES: different, separate, unlike
▸ AS AN ADVERB = **similarly**, identically, equally, uniformly, correspondingly, analogously • *They even dressed alike.*
OPPOSITES: differently, distinctly, unequally

alimony = **maintenance**, keep, support, allowance, livelihood, subsistence, upkeep, sustenance, living expenses, aliment • *A great deal of his money went in alimony to his ex-wives.*

alive AS AN ADJECTIVE 1 = **living**, breathing, animate, having life, subsisting, existing, functioning, alive and kicking, in the land of the living *(informal)* • *She does not know if he is alive or dead.*
OPPOSITES: gone, dead, departed
2 = **in existence**, existing, functioning, active, operative, in force, on-going, prevalent, existent, extant • *Factories are trying to stay alive by cutting costs.*
OPPOSITES: inactive, inoperative
3 = **lively**, spirited, active, vital, alert, eager, quick, awake, vigorous, cheerful, energetic, animated, brisk, agile, perky, chirpy *(informal)*, sprightly, vivacious, full of life, spry, full of beans *(informal)*, zestful • *I never expected to feel so alive in my life again.*
OPPOSITES: dull, lifeless, inactive
▸ IN PHRASES: **alive and kicking** = **alive**, existing, functioning, breathing, animate, living, having life, subsisting, in the land of the living *(informal)* • *The secret police may still be alive and kicking.*
alive and well = **well**, strong, sound, fit, flourishing, robust, vigorous, sturdy, in good shape *(informal)*, in good condition, fighting fit, in fine form, in fine fettle, physically fit, fit as a fiddle *(informal)*, in fine feather, right as rain *(Brit. informal)* • *A man who was lost in a blizzard yesterday has been found alive and well.*
alive to = **aware of**, sensitive to, susceptible to, alert to, eager for, awake to, cognizant of, sensible of • *You must be alive to opportunity!*
alive with = **swarming with**, packed with, bristling with, teeming with, buzzing with, abounding in, overrun by, jumping with, infested with, crawling with, thronged with, bustling with, hopping with • *The river was alive with birds.*

all AS A DETERMINER 1 = **the whole amount**, everything, the whole, the total, the sum, the total amount, the aggregate, the totality, the sum total, the entirety, the entire amount, the complete amount • *I'd spent all I had, every last penny.*
2 = **every**, each, every single, every one of, each and every • *There is built-in storage space in all bedrooms.*
3 = **the whole lot**, every one, each and every one • *All are based on herbal recipes.*
4 = **each and every one**, each one, every one, the whole lot • *He was talking to all of us.*
▸ AS AN ADJECTIVE = **complete**, greatest, full, total, perfect, entire, utter • *In all fairness, she isn't dishonest.*
▸ AS AN ADVERB = **completely**, totally, fully, entirely, absolutely, altogether, wholly, utterly • *I ran away and left her all alone.*
▸ IN PHRASES: **all along** = **the whole time**, from start to finish • *I've been fooling myself all along.*
all in 1 = **tired**, exhausted, spent, done in *(informal)*, flagging, drained, fatigued, weary, sleepy, fagged *(informal)*, whacked *(Brit. informal)*, worn out, drooping, knackered *(slang)*, drowsy, clapped out *(Brit., Austral. & N.Z. informal)*, enervated, ready to drop, dog-tired *(informal)*, zonked *(slang)*, dead beat *(informal)*, asleep *or* dead on your feet *(informal)* • *Have you eaten? You look all in.*
2 = **in total**, in all, on aggregate, in sum, in entirety • *Dinner is about £25 all in.*
all there = **rational**, normal, sane, lucid, of sound mind, compos mentis, in your right mind, mentally sound, in possession of all your faculties • *They get senile. They're not all there.*
▸ RELATED PREFIXES: pan-, panto-

allay = **reduce**, quiet, relax, ease, calm, smooth, relieve, check, moderate, dull, diminish, compose, soften, blunt, soothe, subdue, lessen, alleviate, appease, quell, mitigate,

a

assuage, pacify, mollify • *He did what he could to allay his wife's fears.*

allegation = **claim**, charge, statement, profession, declaration, plea, accusation, assertion, affirmation, deposition, avowal, asseveration, averment • *The company has denied the allegations.*

allege = **claim**, hold, charge, challenge, state, maintain, advance, declare, assert, uphold, put forward, affirm, profess, depose, avow, aver, asseverate • *The accused is alleged to have killed a man.*
OPPOSITES: deny, oppose, contradict

alleged = **claimed**, supposed, declared, assumed, so-called, apparent, rumoured, stated, described, asserted, designated, presumed, affirmed, professed, reputed, hypothetical, putative, presupposed, averred, unproved • *an alleged beating*

allegedly = **supposedly**, apparently, reportedly, by all accounts, reputedly, purportedly • *His van allegedly struck her as she was crossing the street.*

allegiance = **loyalty**, duty, obligation, devotion, fidelity, homage, obedience, adherence, constancy, faithfulness, troth *(archaic)*, fealty • *a community driven by strong allegiances*
OPPOSITES: infidelity, treason, disloyalty

PROVERBS
You cannot run with the hare and hunt with the hounds

allegorical = **symbolic**, figurative, symbolizing, emblematic, parabolic • *the allegorical novel 'The Master and Margarita'*

allegory = **symbol**, story, tale, myth, symbolism, emblem, fable, parable, apologue • *The book is a kind of allegory of the country's history.*

allergic AS AN ADJECTIVE = **sensitive**, affected, susceptible, sensitized, hypersensitive • *I'm allergic to cats.*
▸ IN PHRASES: **allergic to** = **averse to**, opposed to, hostile to, loath to, disinclined to, antipathetic to • *He was allergic to risk.*

allergy 1 = **sensitivity**, reaction, susceptibility, antipathy, hypersensitivity, sensitiveness • *Food allergies result in many and varied symptoms.*
2 = **dislike**, hatred, hostility, aversion, loathing, disgust, antipathy, animosity, displeasure, antagonism, distaste, enmity, opposition, repugnance, disinclination • *I developed an allergy to the company of couples.*

alleviate = **ease**, reduce, relieve, moderate, smooth, dull, diminish, soften, check, blunt, soothe, subdue, lessen, lighten, quell, allay, mitigate, abate, slacken, assuage, quench, mollify, slake, palliate • *A great deal can be done to alleviate back pain.*

alleviation = **easing**, relief, reduction, dulling, lessening, lightening, quelling, moderation, slackening, quenching, mitigation, diminution, slaking, palliation • *They focussed on the alleviation of the refugees' misery.*

alley = **passage**, walk, lane, pathway, alleyway, passageway, backstreet • *He dragged her into an alley and tied her up.*

alleyway = **passage**, walk, lane, alley, pathway, passageway, backstreet • *The robbers ran off down an alleyway.*

alliance 1 = **union**, league, association, agreement, marriage, connection, combination, coalition, treaty, partnership, federation, pact, compact, confederation, affinity, affiliation, confederacy, concordat • *The two parties were still too much apart to form an alliance.*
OPPOSITES: break, division, split
2 = **relationship**, association, bond, connection, affinity, rapport, kinship • *an alliance between philanthropy and medicine*

QUOTATIONS
alliance: in international politics, the union of two thieves who have their hands so deeply inserted in each other's pocket that they cannot separately plunder a third
[Ambrose Bierce *The Devil's Dictionary*]

allied 1 = **united**, joined, linked, related, married, joint, combined, bound, integrated, unified, affiliated, leagued, confederate, amalgamated, cooperating, in league, hand in glove *(informal)*, in cahoots *(U.S. informal)* • *forces from three allied nations*
2 = **connected**, joined, linked, tied, related, associated, syndicated, affiliated, kindred • *doctors and other allied medical professionals*

all-important = **essential**, central, significant, key, necessary, vital, critical, crucial, pivotal, momentous, consequential • *those all-important formative years*

allocate = **assign**, grant, distribute, designate, set aside, earmark, give out, consign, allow, budget, allot, mete, share out, apportion, appropriate • *Tickets will be allocated to those who apply first.*

allocation 1 = **allowance**, share, measure, grant, portion, quota, lot, ration, stint, stipend • *During rationing we had a sugar allocation.*
2 = **assignment**, allowance, rationing, allotment, apportionment, appropriation • *Town planning and land allocation had to be co-ordinated.*

allot = **assign**, allocate, designate, set aside, earmark, mete, share out, apportion, budget, appropriate • *We were allotted half an hour to address the committee.*

allotment 1 = **plot**, patch, tract, kitchen garden • *He was just back from a hard morning's toil on his allotment.*
2 = **assignment**, share, measure, grant, allowance, portion, quota, lot, ration, allocation, stint, appropriation, stipend, apportionment • *His meagre allotment of gas had to be saved for emergencies.*

allotted = **assigned**, given, allocated, designated, set aside, earmarked, apportioned • *Meetings tend to expand to fill their allotted time.*

all-out *or* **all out** AS AN ADJECTIVE = **total**, full, complete, determined, supreme, maximum, outright, thorough, unlimited, full-scale, optimum, exhaustive, resolute, full-on *(informal)*, unrestrained, unremitting, thoroughgoing, unstinted • *He launched an all-out attack on his critics.*
OPPOSITES: cursory, perfunctory, half-hearted
▸ AS AN ADVERB = **energetically**, hard, strongly, sharply, heavily, severely, fiercely, vigorously, intensely, violently, powerfully, forcibly, forcefully, with all your might, with might and main • *We will be going all out to make sure it doesn't happen again.*

allow AS A VERB 1 = **permit**, approve, enable, sanction, endure, license, brook, endorse, warrant, tolerate, put up with *(informal)*, authorize, stand, suffer, bear • *Smoking will not be allowed.*
OPPOSITES: refuse, ban, prohibit
2 = **let**, permit, sanction, authorize, license, tolerate, consent to, countenance, concede to, assent to, give leave to, give the green light for, give a blank cheque to • *He allows her to drive his Mercedes 300SE.*
OPPOSITES: deny, forbid
3 = **give**, provide, grant, spare, devote, assign, allocate, set aside, deduct, earmark, remit, allot • *Please allow 28 days for delivery.*
4 = **acknowledge**, accept, admit, grant, recognize, yield, concede, confess, acquiesce • *He allows that the development may result in social inequality.*
▸ IN PHRASES: **allow for something** = **take into account**, consider, plan for, accommodate, provide for, arrange for, foresee, make provision for, make allowances for, make concessions for, keep in mind, set something aside for, take into consideration • *You have to allow for a certain amount of error.*

allowable = **permissible**, all right, approved, appropriate, suitable, acceptable, tolerable, admissible, sufferable, sanctionable • *It ought not to be allowable for anyone else to take the child.*

allowance AS A NOUN 1 = **portion**, lot, share, amount, measure, grant, pension, subsidy, quota, allocation, stint, annuity, allotment, remittance, stipend, apportionment • *He lives on an allowance of £70 a week.*
2 = **pocket money**, grant, fee, payment, consideration, ration, handout, remittance • *The boy was given an allowance for his own needs.*
3 = **concession**, discount, reduction, repayment, deduction, rebate • *those earning less than the basic tax allowance*
▸ IN PHRASES: **make allowances for someone** = **forgive**, excuse, tolerate, indulge, pardon, acquit, overlook, condone, pass over, turn a blind eye to, exonerate, absolve, bear with, wink at, extenuate, exculpate • *He's tired so I'll make allowances for him.*
make allowances for something = **take into account**, anticipate, allow for, bear in mind, foresee, take into consideration • *The raw exam results make no allowance for social background.*

alloy = **mixture**, combination, compound, blend, hybrid, composite, amalgam, meld, admixture • *Bronze is an alloy of copper and tin.*
▹ *See panel* **Alloys**

all-powerful = **omnipotent**, supreme, absolute, unlimited, almighty, invincible • *the all-powerful unions*
OPPOSITES: helpless, powerless, impotent

all right AS AN ADJECTIVE 1 = **satisfactory**, O.K. *or* okay *(informal)*, average, fair, sufficient, standard, acceptable, good enough, adequate, so-so *(informal)*, up to scratch *(informal)*, passable, up to standard, up to the mark, unobjectionable, ka pai *(N.Z.)* • *'How was the school you attended?' 'It was all right.'*
OPPOSITES: bad, poor, unsatisfactory
2 = **well**, O.K. *or* okay *(informal)*, strong, whole, sound, fit, safe, healthy, hale, unharmed, out of the woods, uninjured, unimpaired, up to par • *Are you all right now?*
OPPOSITES: bad, poorly, ill
3 = **permitted**, O.K. *or* okay *(informal)*, sanctioned, acceptable, legal, proper, legitimate, authorized, lawful, permissible, allowable, kosher *(informal)*, admissible, legit *(slang)*, licit • *Would it be all right if I waited here?*
▸ AS AN ADVERB 1 = **satisfactorily**, O.K. *or* okay *(informal)*, reasonably, well enough, adequately, suitably, acceptably, passably, unobjectionably • *Things have thankfully worked out all right.*
2 = **definitely**, surely, certainly, truly, absolutely, undoubtedly, positively, decidedly, without doubt, unquestionably, undeniably, without question, unequivocally, indisputably, assuredly, irrefutably • *It's an isolated spot all right.*
▸ AS AN INTERJECTION = **O.K.** *or* **okay** *(informal)*, right, yes, agreed, fine, very good, roger, very well, ya *(S. African)*, yebo *(S. African informal)*, F.A.B. *(Brit. informal)*, ka pai *(N.Z.)* • *'I think you should go now.' 'All right.'*

all-star = **famous**, celebrated, distinguished, noted, excellent, honoured, remarkable, well-known, prominent, glorious, legendary, acclaimed, notable, renowned, eminent, illustrious, much-publicized, lionized, far-famed • *an all-star cast*

all-time = **unequalled**, record, unique, exceptional, unprecedented, consummate, unparalleled, unrivalled, incomparable, unmatched, peerless, unsurpassed, matchless • *His support is at an all-time low.*

allude to = **refer to**, suggest, mention, speak of, imply, intimate, hint at, remark on, insinuate, touch upon • *She sometimes alluded to a feeling that she was to blame.*

allure AS A NOUN = **attractiveness**, appeal, charm, attraction, lure, temptation, glamour, persuasion, enchantment, enticement, seductiveness • *It's a game that has really lost its allure.*
▸ AS A VERB = **attract**, persuade, charm, win over, tempt, lure, seduce, entice, enchant, lead on, coax, captivate, beguile, cajole, decoy, inveigle • *The dog was allured by the smell of roasting meat.*

alluring = **attractive**, fascinating, enchanting, seductive, tempting, sexy, intriguing, fetching, glamorous, captivating, beguiling, bewitching, come-hither, hot *(informal)* • *The truly alluring woman is a mix of many elements.*
OPPOSITES: unattractive, repellent, repulsive

allusion = **reference**, mention, suggestion, hint, implication, innuendo, intimation, insinuation, casual remark, indirect reference • *This remark was an allusion to their longstanding hostility.*

ally AS A NOUN = **partner**, friend, colleague, associate, mate, accessory, comrade, helper, collaborator, accomplice, confederate, co-worker, main man *(slang, chiefly U.S.)*, bedfellow, cobber *(Austral. or N.Z. old-fashioned informal)*, coadjutor, abettor, E hoa *(N.Z.)* • *He is a close ally of the Prime Minister.*
OPPOSITES: rival, enemy, opponent
▸ AS A VERB = **combine**, unite, join, link, marry, mix, bond, associate, pool, bind, connect, compound, blend, integrate, merge, put together, unify, fuse, synthesize, join together, band together, meld • *We need to ally economic freedom with personal liberty.*
OPPOSITES: separate, divide
▸ IN PHRASES: **ally yourself with something** *or* **someone** = **unite with**, join, associate with, connect with, unify, league with, affiliate with, collaborate with, join forces with, confederate, band together with • *He will have to ally himself with the new movement.*

almanac = **annual**, guide, handbook, guidebook, yearbook, workbook • *Their Media Yearbook contains an almanac for the next 12 months.*

almighty 1 = **all-powerful**, supreme, absolute, unlimited, invincible, omnipotent • *Let us now confess our sins to Almighty God.*
OPPOSITES: weak, helpless, powerless
2 = **great**, terrible, enormous, desperate, severe, intense, awful, loud, excessive • *I had the most almighty row with the waitress.*
OPPOSITES: poor, slight, tame

ALLOYS

Alnico *(trademark)*	brazing solder	ferrochromium	Manganin *(trademark)*	oroide	speculum metal
amalgam	Britannia metal	ferromanganese	misch metal	osmiridium	steel
austenitic stainless steel	bronze	ferromolybdenum	Monel	permalloy	Stellite *(trademark)*
Babbit metal	chromel	ferronickel	Nichrome *(trademark)*	pewter	sterling silver
bell bronze	constantan	ferrosilicon	nickel silver	phosphor bronze	terne
bell metal	cupronickel	Invar *(trademark)*	nimonic alloy	pinchbeck	tombac
billon	Duralumin *(trademark)*	kamacite	ormolu	platina	type metal
brass	electrum	magnolia metal		platiniridium	white gold
		magnox		soft solder	zircalloy

almond
▸ RELATED ADJECTIVES: amygdaline, amygdaloid

almost = **nearly**, about, approaching, close to, virtually, practically, roughly, all but, just about, not quite, on the brink of, not far from, approximately, well-nigh, as good as • *The couple had been dating for almost three years.*

alms = **donation**, relief, gift, charity, bounty, benefaction, koha *(N.Z.)* • *Alms were distributed to those in need.*

aloft 1 = **in the air**, up, higher, above, overhead, in the sky, on high, high up, up above • *Four of the nine balloons were still aloft the next day.*
2 = **upward**, skyward, heavenward • *He lifted the cup aloft.*

alone AS AN ADJECTIVE 1 = **solitary**, isolated, sole, separate, apart, abandoned, detached, by yourself, unattended, unaccompanied, out on a limb, unescorted, on your tod *(slang)* • *He was all alone in the middle of the hall.*
OPPOSITES: accompanied, among others, escorted
2 = **lonely**, abandoned, deserted, isolated, solitary, estranged, desolate, forsaken, forlorn, destitute, lonesome *(chiefly U.S. & Canad.)*, friendless • *Never in her life had she felt so alone.*
3 = **unique**, only, single, lone, solitary, one and only, sui generis • *Am I alone in recognising these facts?*
▸ AS AN ADVERB 1 = **solely**, only, individually, singly, exclusively, uniquely • *You alone should determine what is right for you.*
2 = **by yourself**, independently, unaided, unaccompanied, without help, on your own, unassisted, without assistance, under your own steam • *He was working alone, and did not have an accomplice.*
OPPOSITES: with help, with assistance

QUOTATIONS
I want to be alone
[Greta Garbo *Grand Hotel (film)*]

along AS A PREPOSITION 1 = **for the length of**, down, up, through • *He walked along the street by himself.*
2 = **next to**, near, close to, alongside, beside, adjacent to, nearby to • *Along each wall stretched metal filing cabinets.*
▸ AS AN ADVERB 1 = **ahead**, on, forwards, in front, onwards • *She skipped and danced along.*
2 = **for companionship**, with you, as company, as a companion • *She invited everyone she knew to come along.*
▸ IN PHRASES: **along with** = **accompanied by**, accompanying, together with, in the company of, at the same time as • *She escaped along with two other children.*

alongside 1 = **next to**, near, along, close to, beside, nearby to • *Much of the industry was located alongside rivers.*
2 = **together with**, with, along with • *He had worked alongside them for years.*

aloof = **distant**, cold, reserved, cool, formal, remote, forbidding, detached, indifferent, chilly, unfriendly, unsympathetic, uninterested, haughty, unresponsive, supercilious, unapproachable, unsociable, standoffish • *He seemed aloof and detached.*
OPPOSITES: open, warm, friendly

aloud = **out loud**, clearly, plainly, distinctly, audibly, intelligibly • *'The idiot,' she said aloud.*

alpha IN PHRASES: **the alpha and omega** = **first and last**, be-all and end-all • *He was the alpha and omega of the comedy series.*

alphabet = **letters**, script, writing system, syllabary • *By the age of two-and-a-half, he knew the alphabet.*
▹ See panel **Alphabets**

alpine = **mountainous**, high, towering, soaring, steep, rocky, highland, upland • *grassy, alpine meadows*

already = **before now**, before, previously, at present, by now, by then, even now, by this time, just now, by that time, heretofore, as of now • *They've spent nearly a billion dollars on it already.*

alright *see* **all right**

also = **and**, too, further, plus, along with, in addition, as well, moreover, besides, furthermore, what's more, on top of that, to boot, additionally, into the bargain, as well as • *She's brilliant. Also, she's beautiful!*

alter 1 = **modify**, change, reform, shift, vary, transform, adjust, adapt, revise, amend, diversify, remodel, tweak *(informal)*, recast, reshape, metamorphose, transmute • *They have never altered their programmes.*
2 = **change**, turn, vary, transform, adjust, adapt, metamorphose • *Little had altered in the village.*

alteration 1 = **change**, adjustment, shift, amendment, conversion, modification • *Making some simple alterations to your diet will make you feel fitter.*
2 = **adjustment**, change, amendment, variation, conversion, transformation, adaptation, difference, revision, modification, remodelling, reformation, diversification, makeover, metamorphosis, variance, reshaping, transmutation • *Her jacket and skirt were still awaiting alteration.*

altercation = **argument**, row, clash, disagreement, dispute, controversy, contention, quarrel, squabble, wrangle, bickering, discord, dissension • *I had an altercation with some people who objected to our filming.*

alternate AS A VERB 1 = **interchange**, change, alter, fluctuate, intersperse, take turns, oscillate, chop and change, follow one another, follow in turn • *Her gentle moods alternated with calmer states.*
2 = **intersperse**, interchange, exchange, swap, stagger, rotate • *Now you just alternate layers of that mixture and eggplant.*
▸ AS AN ADJECTIVE 1 = **every other**, every second • *The course is taught in alternate years.*
2 = **alternating**, interchanging, every other, rotating, every second, sequential • *They were streaked with alternate bands of colour.*
3 = **substitute**, alternative, other, different, replacement, complementary • *alternate forms of medical treatment*
4 = **alternative**, unusual, abnormal, irregular, unconventional, off-the-wall *(slang)*, unorthodox, heterodox, uncustomary • *an alternate lifestyle*
▸ AS A NOUN = **substitute**, reserve, deputy, relief, replacement, stand-by, makeshift • *In most jurisdictions, twelve jurors and two alternates are chosen.*

alternating = **interchanging**, changing, shifting, swinging, rotating, fluctuating, occurring by turns, oscillating, vacillating, seesawing • *alternating cycles of REM and non-REM sleep*

alternation = **rotation**, change, swing, variation, oscillation, fluctuation, vacillation, vicissitude • *The alternation of sun and snow continued throughout the holiday.*

alternative AS A NOUN = **substitute**, choice, other, option, preference, recourse • *New treatments may provide an alternative to painkillers.*
▸ AS AN ADJECTIVE 1 = **different**, other, substitute, alternate • *There were alternative methods of transport available.*
2 = **unconventional**, unusual, alternate *(U.S.)*, abnormal, irregular, off-the-wall *(slang)*, unorthodox, heterodox, uncustomary • *Grunge percolated in the alternative music scene of Seattle.*
3 = **substitute**, other, different, replacement, alternate, complementary, non-standard • *alternative healthcare*

alternatively = **or**, instead, otherwise, on the other hand, if not, then again, as an alternative, by way of alternative, as another option • *Allow about 8 hours for the drive. Alternatively, you could fly.*

although = **though**, while, even if, even though, whilst, albeit, despite the fact that, notwithstanding, even supposing, tho' *(U.S. or poetic)* • *Although the shooting has stopped, the destruction is enormous.*

ALPHABETS

RELATED VOCABULARY

Cyrillic	katakana	Linear A	Nagari
hiragana	Kufic *or* Cufic	Linear B	Roman
kana	Latin	logogram *or* logograph	
kanji	lexigraphy		

ARABIC LETTERS

ا	alif	د	dāl	ض	ḍād	ك	kāf
ب	bā	ذ	dhāl	ط	ṭā	ل	lām
ت	tā	ر	rā	ظ	ẓā	م	mīm
ث	thā	ز	zā	ع	'ain	ن	nūn
ج	jīm	س	sīn	غ	ghain	ه	hā
ح	ḥā	ش	shīn	ف	fā	و	wāw
خ	khā	ص	ṣād	ق	qāf	ي	yā

GREEK LETTERS

Α,α	alpha	Η,η	eta	Ν,ν	nu	Τ,τ	tau
Β,β	beta	Θ,θ	theta	Ξ,ξ	xi	Υ,υ	upsilon
Γ,γ	gamma	Ι,ι	iota	Ο,ο	omicron	Φ,φ	phi
Δ,δ	delta	Κ,κ	kappa	Π,π	pi	Χ,χ	chi
Ε,ε	epsilon	Λ,λ	lambda	Ρ,ρ	rho	Ψ,ψ	psi
Ζ,ζ	zeta	Μ,μ	mu	Σ,σ	sigma	Ω,ω	omega

HEBREW LETTERS

א	aleph	ז	zayin	מ	mem	ק	koph *or* qoph
ב	beth	ח	heth *or* cheth	נ	nun	ר	resh
ג	gimel	ט	teth	ס	samekh	שׁ	shin
ד	daleth *or* daled	י	yod *or* yodh	ע	ayin *or* ain	שׂ	sin
ה	he	כ	kaph *or* khaph	פ	pe	ת	tav *or* taw
ו	vav *or* waw	ל	lamed *or* lamedh	צ	sadhe, sade, *or* tsade		

COMMUNICATIONS CODE WORDS FOR THE ALPHABET

Alpha	Hotel	Oscar	Victor
Bravo	India	Papa	Whiskey
Charlie	Juliet	Quebec	X-Ray
Delta	Kilo	Romeo	Yankee
Echo	Lima	Sierra	Zulu
Foxtrot	Mike	Tango	
Golf	November	Uniform	

altitude = **height**, summit, peak, elevation, loftiness • *The next day I ran my first race at high altitude.*

altogether 1 = **absolutely**, quite, completely, totally, perfectly, fully, thoroughly, wholly, utterly, downright, one hundred per cent *(informal)*, undisputedly, lock, stock and barrel • *She wasn't altogether sorry to be leaving.*
2 = **completely**, all, fully, entirely, comprehensively, thoroughly, wholly, every inch, one hundred per cent *(informal)*, in every respect • *The choice of language is altogether different.*
OPPOSITES: relatively, somewhat, partially
3 = **on the whole**, generally, mostly, in general, collectively, all things considered, on average, for the most part, all in all, on balance, in toto *(Latin)*, as a whole • *Altogether, it was a delightful town garden.*
4 = **in total**, in all, all told, taken together, in sum, everything included, in toto *(Latin)* • *Altogether seven inmates escaped.*

altruism = **selflessness**, charity, consideration, goodwill, generosity, self-sacrifice, philanthropy, benevolence, magnanimity, humanitarianism, unselfishness, beneficence, charitableness, greatheartedness, bigheartedness • *Empathy leads to altruism, caring and compassion.*
OPPOSITES: greed, self-interest, selfishness

altruistic = **selfless**, generous, humanitarian, charitable, benevolent, considerate, self-sacrificing, philanthropic, unselfish, public-spirited • *motives that are not entirely altruistic*
OPPOSITES: mean, selfish, self-interested

alumnus *or* **alumna** *(Chiefly U.S. & Canad.)* = **graduate**, valedictorian, past student, former student, graduand • *an alumnus of Edinburgh University*

always 1 = **habitually**, regularly, every time, inevitably, consistently, invariably, aye *(Scot.)*, perpetually, without exception, customarily, unfailingly, on every occasion, day in, day out • *Always lock your garage.*
OPPOSITES: hardly, rarely, seldom
2 = **forever**, ever, for keeps, eternally, for all time, evermore, for good and all *(informal)*, till the cows come home *(informal)*, everlastingly, till the end of time, till Doomsday • *We will always remember his generosity.*
3 = **continually**, constantly, all the time, forever, repeatedly, aye *(Scot.)*, endlessly, persistently, eternally, perpetually, incessantly, interminably, unceasingly, everlastingly, in perpetuum *(Latin)* • *She was always moving things around.*
4 = **as a last resort**, in the end, whatever happens • *I could always go back into the Navy or something.*

amalgam = **combination**, mixture, compound, blend, union, composite, fusion, alloy, amalgamation, meld, admixture • *I tend to make my characters an amalgam of several people.*

amalgamate = **combine**, unite, ally, compound, blend, incorporate, integrate, merge, fuse, mingle, alloy, coalesce, meld, commingle, intermix • *The firm has amalgamated with an American company.*
OPPOSITES: part, separate, divide

amalgamation = **combination**, union, joining, mixing, alliance, coalition, merger, mixture, compound, blend, integration, composite, fusion, mingling, alloy, amalgamating, incorporation, amalgam, meld, admixture, commingling • *The organization was formed by an amalgamation of two groups.*

amass = **collect**, gather, assemble, compile, accumulate, aggregate, pile up, garner, hoard, scrape together, rake up, heap up • *We didn't enquire as to how he had amassed his fortune.*

amateur AS A NOUN = **nonprofessional**, outsider, layman, dilettante, layperson, non-specialist, dabbler • *He is an amateur who dances because he feels like it.*
▸ AS AN ADJECTIVE 1 = **nonprofessional**, lay, dilettante • *an amateur dramatics society*
2 = **incompetent**, unable, cowboy *(informal)*, useless, incapable, insufficient, floundering, bungling, unfit, unfitted, inept, ineffectual, incapacitated, inexpert, skill-less, unskilful • *They gave a performance which easily capped our amateur efforts.*

amateurish = **unprofessional**, amateur, crude, bungling, clumsy, inexpert, unaccomplished, unskilful • *All the paintings were cheap and amateurish.*
OPPOSITES: experienced, professional, skilled

amaze = **astonish**, surprise, shock, stun, alarm, stagger, startle, bewilder, astound, daze, confound, stupefy, flabbergast, bowl someone over *(informal)*, boggle someone's mind, dumbfound • *He amazed us with his knowledge of local history.*

amazed = **astonished**, surprised, stunned, staggered, bewildered, astounded, dazed, confounded, perplexed, gobsmacked *(informal)*, dumbfounded, flabbergasted *(informal)*, stupefied • *I was amazed to learn that most people travel without insurance.*

amazement = **astonishment**, surprise, wonder, shock, confusion, admiration, awe, marvel, bewilderment, wonderment, perplexity, stupefaction • *I stared at her in amazement.*

amazing = **astonishing**, striking, surprising, brilliant, stunning, impressive, overwhelming, staggering, sensational *(informal)*, bewildering, eye-popping *(informal)*, breathtaking, astounding, eye-opening, wondrous *(archaic or literary)*, mind-boggling, jaw-dropping, stupefying, gee-whizz *(slang)*, startling • *It's amazing what we can remember with a little prompting.*

ambassador = **representative**, minister, agent, deputy, diplomat, envoy, consul, attaché, emissary, legate, plenipotentiary • *the German ambassador to Poland*

QUOTATIONS
An ambassador is an honest man sent to lie abroad for the commonwealth
[Henry Wotton]

amber
▸ RELATED ADJECTIVE: succinic

ambience = **atmosphere**, feel, setting, air, quality, character, spirit, surroundings, tone, mood, impression, flavour, temper, tenor, aura, complexion, vibes *(slang)*, vibrations *(slang)*, milieu • *The overall ambience of the room is cosy.*

ambient = **atmospheric**, surrounding, background • *ambient sounds of children in the background*

ambiguity = **vagueness**, doubt, puzzle, uncertainty, obscurity, enigma, equivocation, inconclusiveness, indefiniteness, dubiety, dubiousness, tergiversation, indeterminateness, equivocality, doubtfulness, equivocacy • *the ambiguities of language*

ambiguous = **unclear**, puzzling, uncertain, obscure, vague, doubtful, dubious, enigmatic, indefinite, inconclusive, cryptic, indeterminate, equivocal, Delphic, oracular, enigmatical, clear as mud *(informal)* • *His remarks clarify an ambiguous statement given earlier this week.*
OPPOSITES: clear, simple, specific

ambit = **range**, reach, sweep, extent, scope, radius • *medicines which fall outside the ambit of the price-fixing agreement*

ambition 1 = **goal**, end, hope, design, dream, target, aim, wish, purpose, desire, intention, objective, intent, aspiration, Holy Grail *(informal)* • *His ambition is to sail round the world.*
2 = **enterprise**, longing, drive, fire, spirit, desire, passion, enthusiasm, warmth, striving, initiative, aspiration, yearning, devotion, zeal, verve, zest, fervour, eagerness, gusto, hankering, get-up-and-go *(informal)*, ardour, keenness, avidity, fervency • *a mixture of ambition and ruthlessness*

QUOTATIONS
Ambition is the growth of every clime
[William Blake *King Edward the Third*]
Well is it known that ambition can creep as well as soar
[Edmund Burke *Letters on a Regicide Peace*]
Ambition, in a private man a vice,
Is in a prince the virtue
[Philip Massinger *The Bashful Lover*]
Ambition must be made to counteract ambition
[James Madison *The Federalist Papers*]
PROVERBS
Every eel hopes to become a whale

ambitious 1 = **enterprising**, spirited, keen, active, daring, eager, intent, enthusiastic, hopeful, striving, vigorous, aspiring, energetic, adventurous, avid, zealous, intrepid, resourceful, purposeful, desirous • *He's a very ambitious lad.*
OPPOSITES: lazy, apathetic, unambitious
2 = **demanding**, trying, hard, taxing, difficult, challenging, tough, severe, impressive, exhausting, exacting, bold, elaborate, formidable, energetic, strenuous, pretentious, arduous, grandiose, industrious • *Their goal was extraordinarily ambitious.*
OPPOSITES: easy, simple, modest

ambivalence = **indecision**, doubt, opposition, conflict, uncertainty, contradiction, wavering, fluctuation, hesitancy, equivocation, vacillation, irresolution • *I've never hidden my ambivalence about getting married.*

ambivalent = **undecided**, mixed, conflicting, opposed, uncertain, doubtful, unsure, contradictory, wavering, unresolved, fluctuating, hesitant, inconclusive, debatable, equivocal, vacillating, warring, irresolute • *He maintained an ambivalent attitude to religion throughout his life.*
OPPOSITES: clear, decided, definite

amble = **stroll**, walk, wander, ramble, meander, saunter, dawdle, mosey *(informal)* • *We ambled along in front of the houses.*

ambush AS A VERB = **trap**, attack, surprise, deceive, dupe, ensnare, waylay, ambuscade, bushwhack *(U.S.)* • *Rebels ambushed and killed 10 patrolmen.*
▸ AS A NOUN = **trap**, snare, attack, lure, waylaying, ambuscade • *A policeman has been shot dead in an ambush.*

ameliorate = **improve**, better, benefit, reform, advance, promote, amend, elevate, raise, mend, mitigate, make better, assuage, meliorate • *Nothing can be done to ameliorate the situation.*

amelioration = **improvement**, advance, recovery, amendment, correction, enhancement, change for the better, upswing, betterment, melioration • *a demand for amelioration of conditions*

amenable = **receptive**, open, susceptible, responsive, agreeable, compliant, tractable, acquiescent, persuadable, able to be influenced • *I've never had a long-term relationship. I'm not amenable enough.*
OPPOSITES: stubborn, intractable, inflexible

amend = **change**, improve, reform, fix, correct, repair, edit, alter, enhance, update, revise, modify, remedy, rewrite, mend, rectify, tweak *(informal)*, ameliorate, redraw, rebrand • *The committee put forward proposals to amend the penal system.*

amendment 1 = **addition**, change, adjustment, attachment, adaptation, revision, modification, alteration, remodelling, reformation, clarification, adjunct, addendum • *an amendment to the defence bill*
2 = **change**, improvement, repair, edit, remedy, correction, revision, modification, alteration, mending, enhancement, reform, betterment, rectification, amelioration, emendation • *We are making a few amendments to the document.*

amends = **compensation**, apology, restoration, redress, reparation, indemnity, restitution, atonement, recompense, expiation, requital • *He wanted to make amends for causing their marriage to fail.*

amenity 1 = **facility**, service, advantage, comfort, convenience • *The hotel amenities include a health club and banqueting rooms.*
2 = **refinement**, politeness, affability, amiability, courtesy, mildness, pleasantness, suavity, agreeableness, complaisance • *A man of little amenity.*
OPPOSITES: rudeness, bad manners, discourtesy

America

QUOTATIONS

America is a vast conspiracy to make you happy
[John Updike *How to Love America and Leave it at the Same Time*]

America is rather like life. You can usually find in it what you look for
[E.M. Forster *Two Cheers for Democracy*]

The business of America is business
[Calvin Coolidge *Speech*, 1925]

America is God's Crucible, the great Melting-Pot where all the races of Europe are melting and reforming!
[Israel Zangwill *The Melting Pot*]

America, thou half-brother of the world;
With something good and bad of every land
[Philip James Bailey *Festus*]

Europe is the unfinished negative of which America is the proof
[Mary McCarthy *On the Contrary*]

America is the most grandiose experiment the world has seen, but, I am afraid, it is not going to be a success
[Sigmund Freud]

America is a large, friendly dog in a very small room. Every time it wags its tail, it knocks over a chair
[A.J. Toynbee]

It was wonderful to find America, but it would have been more wonderful to miss it
[Mark Twain *The Tragedy of Pudd'nhead Wilson*]

There is nothing wrong with America that cannot be cured by what is right with America
[Bill Clinton *First Inaugural Speech*]

▷ *See panel* **English and American equivalences**

American AS AN ADJECTIVE = **Yankee** *or* **Yank**, U.S. • *the American ambassador at the UN*
▸ AS A NOUN = **Yankee** *or* **Yank**, Yankee Doodle • *The 1990 Nobel Prize for medicine was won by two Americans.*

amiability = **pleasantness**, charm, kindness, sweetness, good humour, attractiveness, friendliness, sociability, cheerfulness, good nature, sweetness and light *(informal)*, affability, geniality, kindliness, sweet temper, agreeableness, benignity, winsomeness, delightfulness, lovableness, amiableness, engagingness, pleasingness • *I found his amiability charming.*

amiable = **pleasant**, kind, kindly, pleasing, friendly, attractive, engaging, charming, obliging, delightful, cheerful, benign, winning, agreeable, good-humoured, lovable, sociable, genial, affable, congenial, winsome, good-natured, sweet-tempered, likable *or* likeable • *She had been surprised at how amiable and polite he had seemed.*
OPPOSITES: hostile, sour, unfriendly

amicable = **friendly**, kindly, brotherly, civil, neighbourly, peaceful, polite, harmonious, good-humoured, amiable, courteous, cordial, sociable, fraternal, peaceable • *The meeting ended on reasonably amicable terms.*
OPPOSITES: hostile, belligerent, unfriendly

amid *or* **amidst** 1 = **during**, among, at a time of, in an atmosphere of • *He cancelled a foreign trip amid growing concerns of a domestic crisis.*
2 = **in the middle of**, among, surrounded by, amongst, in the midst of, in the thick of • *a tiny bungalow amid clusters of trees*

amiss AS AN ADJECTIVE = **wrong**, mistaken, confused, false, inappropriate, rotten, incorrect, faulty, inaccurate, unsuitable, improper, defective, out of order, awry, erroneous, untoward, fallacious • *Their instincts warned them something was amiss.*
OPPOSITES: right, true, perfect
▸ IN PHRASES: **not go amiss** = **be welcome**, be appropriate, go down well • *A bit of kindness wouldn't go amiss.*
take something amiss = **take as an insult**, take wrongly, take as offensive, take out of turn • *He took it amiss when I asked to speak to someone else.*

amity = **friendship**, understanding, accord, peace, harmony, goodwill, fellowship, fraternity, brotherhood, tranquillity, friendliness, concord, comradeship, cordiality, peacefulness, kindliness, comity, amicability • *Over the past two decades the countries have lived in amity.*

ammunition 1 = **munitions**, rounds, shot, shells, powder, explosives, cartridges, armaments, materiel, shot and shell • *He had only seven rounds of ammunition for the revolver.*
2 = **evidence**, facts, information, material, arguments, fuel • *The improved trade figures have given the government fresh ammunition.*

amnesty AS A NOUN = **general pardon**, mercy, pardoning, immunity, forgiveness, reprieve, oblivion, remission, clemency, dispensation, absolution, condonation • *Activists will not automatically be granted amnesty.*
▸ AS A VERB = **pardon**, free, release, excuse, forgive, overlook, liberate, acquit, condone, reprieve, remit, let off *(informal)*, exonerate, absolve, exculpate • *Last year Parliament amnestied the plotters.*

amok *or* **amuck** IN PHRASES: **run amok** = **go mad**, go wild, turn violent, go berserk, lose control, go insane, go into a frenzy • *He was arrested after running amok with a car in the city centre.*

among *or* **amongst** 1 = **in the midst of**, with, together with, in the middle of, amid, surrounded by, amidst, in the thick of • *They walked among the crowds in the large town square.*
2 = **in the group of**, one of, part of, included in, in the company of, in the class of, in the number of • *Among the speakers was the new American ambassador.*
3 = **between**, to • *Most of the furniture was distributed among friends.*
4 = **with one another**, mutually, by all of, by the whole of, by the joint action of • *The directors have been arguing amongst themselves.*

ENGLISH AND AMERICAN EQUIVALENCES

English	American
aeroplane	airplane
American football	football
antenatal	prenatal
aubergine	eggplant
autumn	fall
bad-tempered	mean
banknote	bill
bat	paddle
benefit	welfare
bin *or* dustbin	trashcan
biscuit	cookie
black pudding	blood sausage
blinds	shades
bonnet (car)	hood
boot (car)	trunk
braces (teeth)	retainer
braces (lingerie)	suspenders
breve	double whole note
broad bean	fava bean
building society	savings and loan
burgle	burglarize
candy floss	cotton candy
car	automobile
car park	parking lot
chemist	drug store
chips	French fries
clothes peg	clothes pin
coffin	casket
condom	rubber
cornflour	corn starch
courgette	zucchini
crisps	chips *or* potato chips
crossroads	intersection
crotchet	quarter note
current account	checking account
curtains	drapes
cutlery	flatware *or* silverware
CV	résumé
dialling code	area code
dinner jacket	tuxedo
double cream	heavy cream
drapery	dry goods
draughts	checkers
drawing pin	thumb tack
dressing gown	robe

English	American
dummy	pacifier *or* soother
engaged tone	busy signal
estate agent	realtor
estate car	station wagon
fire lighter	fire starter
first floor	second floor
flat	apartment
flick knife	switch blade
football	soccer
foyer	lobby
fringe	bangs
garden	yard
gear lever	stick shift
goose pimples	goose bumps
ground floor	first floor
hair grip	bobby pin
hairpin bend	switchback
handbag	purse
hessian	burlap
high street	main street
holiday	vacation
indicator	blinker
invigilator	proctor
ironmonger	hardware store
jam	jelly
janitor	caretaker
lawyer	attorney
lift	elevator
mangetout	snowpea
mate	friend
merry-go-round	carousel
methylated spirits	denatured alcohol
mince	ground beef
minim	half note
nappy	diaper
neat (of drinks)	straight
noughts and crosses	tick-tack-toe
nursery	kindergarten
off-licence	liquor store
paraffin	kerosene
pavement	sidewalk
pepper	bell pepper
petrol	gas *or* gasoline
pissed	drunk
plait	braid
plasterboard	dry lining
plot	lot
porridge	oatmeal

English	American
postcode	zip code
postman	mail man
pub *or* public house	bar
public school	private school
purse	pocketbook
pushchair	stroller
quaver	eighth note
quilt *or* eiderdown	comforter
railway	railroad
receptionist	desk clerk
reverse charge	collect
ring road	beltway
roll *or* bap	bun
rubber	eraser
rubbish	trash *or* garbage
semibreve	whole note
semi-detached	duplex
semiquaver	sixteenth note
shop	store
silencer	muffler
skip	dumpster
skirting board	baseboard
sleeper (railway)	tie
slowcoach	slowpoke
soft drink	soda
spanner	wrench
spring onion *or* salad onion	scallion
state school	public school
stream	creek
surgical spirit	rubbing alcohol
sweet	candy
tap	faucet
tarmac	asphalt
telegram	wire
thread	cotton
tights	pantihose
timber	lumber
torch	flashlight
town centre	downtown
trainers	sneakers
tram	streetcar
trousers	pants
turn up	cuff
VAT	sales tax
vest	undershirt
waistcoast	vest
windscreen	windshield

amoral = **unethical**, nonmoral, unvirtuous • *The film was violent and amoral.*

amorous = **loving**, in love, tender, passionate, fond, erotic, affectionate, ardent, impassioned, doting, enamoured, lustful, attached, lovesick, amatory • *She is the object of his amorous intentions.*

OPPOSITES: cold, distant, indifferent

amorphous = **shapeless**, vague, irregular, nondescript, indeterminate, unstructured, nebulous, formless, inchoate, characterless, unformed, unshaped, unshapen • *A dark, amorphous shadow filled the room.*

OPPOSITES: shaped, structured, definite

amount AS A NOUN **1** = **quantity**, lot, measure, size, supply, mass, volume, capacity, extent, bulk, number, magnitude, expanse • *I still do a certain amount of work for them.*

2 = **total**, whole, mass, addition, sum, lot, extent, aggregate, entirety, totality, sum total • *If you always pay the full amount, this won't affect you.*

▸ IN PHRASES: **amount to something 1** = **add up to**, mean, total, equal, constitute, comprise, aggregate, purport, be equivalent to • *The banks have what amounts to a monopoly.*

2 = **come to**, become, grow to, develop into, advance to, progress to, mature into • *My music teacher said I'd never amount to anything.*

PROVERBS

Many a mickle makes a muckle

amour = **love affair**, relationship, affair, romance, intrigue, liaison, affaire de coeur *(French)* • *This meaningful amour had gone horribly wrong.*

amphetamine = **speed** • *He is accused of possessing amphetamine sulphate.*

amphibian

AMPHIBIANS

axolotl	Goliath frog	pipa *or* Surinam toad
brown-striped frog *(Austral.)*	hairy frog	Queensland cane toad
bullfrog	hellbender	salamander
caecilian	hyla	siren
cane toad *(Austral.)*	midwife toad	toad *or (Caribbean)* crapaud
congo eel *or* snake	mud puppy	tree frog
eft	natterjack	
frog *or (Caribbean)* crapaud	newt *or (dialect or archaic)* eft	
	olm	

ample 1 = **plenty of**, great, rich, liberal, broad, generous, lavish, spacious, abounding, abundant, plentiful, expansive, copious, roomy, unrestricted, voluminous, capacious, profuse, commodious, plenteous • *The design gave ample space for a good-sized kitchen.*
OPPOSITES: little, small, insufficient
2 = **large**, great, big, full, wide, broad, extensive, generous, abundant, voluminous, bountiful • *a young mother with a baby resting against her ample bosom*

amplification 1 = **increase**, boosting, stretching, strengthening, expansion, extension, widening, raising, heightening, deepening, lengthening, enlargement, intensification, magnification, dilation, augmentation • *a voice that needed no amplification*
2 = **explanation**, development, expansion, supplementing, fleshing out, elaboration, rounding out, augmentation, expatiation • *They demanded amplification of the imprecise statement.*

amplifier = **amp** *(informal)*, speaker, loudspeaker • *It was just a cassette deck and an amplifier, but it worked well.*

amplify 1 = **expand**, raise, extend, boost, stretch, strengthen, increase, widen, intensify, heighten, deepen, enlarge, lengthen, magnify, augment, dilate • *The music was amplified with microphones.*
OPPOSITES: reduce, decrease, cut down
2 = **go into detail**, develop, explain, expand, supplement, elaborate, augment, flesh out, round out, enlarge on, expatiate • *Intelligent guesswork must be used to amplify the facts.*
OPPOSITES: simplify, abbreviate, abridge

amplitude 1 = **extent**, reach, range, size, mass, sweep, dimension, bulk, scope, width, magnitude, compass, greatness, breadth, expanse, vastness, spaciousness, bigness, largeness, hugeness, capaciousness • *a man of great amplitude*
2 = **fullness**, abundance, richness, plethora, profusion, completeness, plenitude, copiousness, ampleness • *The character comes to imply an amplitude of meanings.*

amply = **fully**, well, greatly, completely, richly, liberally, thoroughly, substantially, lavishly, extensively, generously, abundantly, profusely, copiously, plentifully, unstintingly, bountifully, without stinting, plenteously, capaciously • *This collection of essays amply demonstrates his genius.*
OPPOSITES: poorly, thinly, insufficiently

amputate = **cut off**, remove, separate, sever, curtail, truncate, lop off • *To save his life, doctors amputated his legs.*

amuck *see* **amok**

amulet = **charm**, fetish, talisman, juju, periapt *(rare)* • *He brought forth a small gold amulet.*

amuse 1 = **entertain**, please, delight, charm, cheer, tickle, gratify, beguile, enliven, regale, gladden • *The thought seemed to amuse him.*
OPPOSITES: bore, tire, weary
2 = **occupy**, interest, involve, engage, entertain, absorb, divert, engross • *Put a selection of toys in his cot to amuse him if he wakes early.*

QUOTATIONS
We are not amused
[Queen Victoria]

amused = **entertained**, interested, involved, occupied, engaged, absorbed, diverted, beguiled, engrossed • *She was not amused by his teasing.*

amusement 1 = **enjoyment**, delight, entertainment, cheer, laughter, mirth, hilarity, merriment, gladdening, beguilement, regalement • *He watched with amusement to see the child so absorbed.*
OPPOSITES: sadness, boredom, displeasure
2 = **diversion**, interest, sport, pleasing, fun, pleasure, recreation, entertainment, gratification • *It's unacceptable to keep animals confined for our amusement.*
3 = **pastime**, game, sport, joke, entertainment, hobby, recreation, distraction, diversion, lark, prank • *People had very few amusements to choose from in those days.*

amusing = **funny**, humorous, gratifying, laughable, farcical, comical, droll, interesting, pleasing, charming, cheering, entertaining, comic, pleasant, lively, diverting, delightful, enjoyable, cheerful, witty, merry, gladdening, facetious, jocular, rib-tickling, waggish • *He had a great sense of humour and could be very amusing.*
OPPOSITES: dead, flat, boring

anaemic 1 = **pale**, weak, dull, frail, feeble, wan, sickly, bloodless, colourless, infirm, pallid, ashen, characterless, enervated, like death warmed up *(informal)* • *Losing a lot of blood makes you tired and anaemic.*
OPPOSITES: glowing, blooming, rosy
2 = **weak**, feeble, lacklustre, bland, poor, halfhearted • *We will see some economic recovery, but it will be very anaemic.*

anaesthetic AS A NOUN = **painkiller**, narcotic, sedative, opiate, anodyne, analgesic, soporific, stupefacient, stupefactive • *The operation is carried out under general anaesthetic.*
▸ AS AN ADJECTIVE = **pain-killing**, dulling, numbing, narcotic, sedative, opiate, deadening, anodyne, analgesic, soporific, sleep-inducing, stupefacient, stupefactive • *They are rendered unconscious by anaesthetic darts.*

analgesic AS AN ADJECTIVE = **pain-killing**, dulling, numbing, narcotic, palliative, deadening, anodyne, pain-relieving • *Aloe may have an analgesic effect.*
▸ AS A NOUN = **painkiller**, narcotic, palliative, anodyne, pain reliever • *The hospital advised an analgesic for shoulder pains.*

analogous = **similar**, like, related, equivalent, parallel, resembling, alike, corresponding, comparable, akin, homologous • *This kind of construction is analogous to building a bridge under water.*
OPPOSITES: different, contrasting, unlike

analogue = **representation**, picture, model, image, illustration, simulation, likeness, simulacrum • *No model can be a perfect analogue of nature itself.*

analogy = **similarity**, relation, comparison, parallel, correspondence, resemblance, correlation, likeness, equivalence, homology, similitude • *The analogy between music and fragrance has stuck.*

analyse 1 = **examine**, test, study, research, judge, estimate, survey, investigate, interpret, evaluate, inspect, work over • *This book teaches you to analyse causes of stress in your life.*

2 = break down, consider, study, separate, divide, resolve, dissolve, dissect, think through, assay, anatomize • *We haven't had time to analyse those samples yet.*

analysis **1 = study**, reasoning, opinion, judgment, interpretation, evaluation, estimation, dissection • *We did an analysis of the way they have spent money in the past.*
2 = examination, test, division, inquiry, investigation, resolution, interpretation, breakdown, scanning, separation, evaluation, scrutiny, sifting, anatomy, dissolution, dissection, assay, perusal, anatomization • *They collect blood samples for analysis at the laboratory.*

analyst **1 = commentator**, authority, commenter, reporter, specialist, adviser, consultant, special correspondent • *a political analyst*
2 = psychiatrist, therapist, psychologist, psychotherapist, psychoanalyst, psychoanalyser, headshrinker *(slang)*, shrink *(slang)* • *My analyst has helped me not to feel guilty.*

analytic *or* **analytical** **= rational**, questioning, testing, detailed, searching, organized, exact, precise, logical, systematic, inquiring, diagnostic, investigative, dissecting, explanatory, discrete, inquisitive, interpretive, studious, interpretative, expository • *I have an analytical approach to every survey.*

anarchic **= lawless**, rioting, confused, disordered, revolutionary, chaotic, rebellious, riotous, disorganized, misruled, ungoverned, misgoverned • *anarchic attitudes and disrespect for authority*
OPPOSITES: ordered, controlled, law-abiding

anarchist **= revolutionary**, rebel, terrorist, insurgent, nihilist • *a well-known anarchist poet*

anarchy **= lawlessness**, revolution, riot, disorder, confusion, chaos, rebellion, misrule, disorganization, misgovernment • *Their liberal traditions were slipping into anarchy.*
OPPOSITES: government, order, control

anathema **= abomination**, bête noire, enemy, pariah, bane, bugbear • *Violence was anathema to them.*

anatomize **= examine**, study, separate, divide, resolve, break down, analyse, dissolve, dissect, scrutinize • *a magazine devoted to anatomizing the inadequacies of liberalism*

anatomy **1 = structure**, build, make-up, frame, framework, composition • *He had worked extensively on the anatomy of living animals.*
2 = examination, study, division, inquiry, investigation, analysis, dismemberment, dissection • *a troubling essay on the anatomy of nationhood*

ancestor **1 = forefather**, predecessor, precursor, forerunner, forebear, antecedent, progenitor, tupuna *or* tipuna *(N.Z.)* • *He could trace his ancestors back seven hundred years.*
OPPOSITES: successor, offspring, descendant
2 = forerunner, predecessor, prototype, precursor • *The immediate ancestor of rock 'n' roll is rhythm and blues.*

ancestral **= inherited**, hereditary, patriarchal, antecedent, forefatherly, genealogical, lineal, ancestorial • *the family's ancestral home*

ancestry **= origin**, house, family, line, race, stock, blood, ancestors, descent, pedigree, extraction, lineage, forebears, antecedents, parentage, forefathers, genealogy, derivation, progenitors • *They can trace their ancestry back to the seventeenth century.*

anchor AS A NOUN **1 = mooring**, hook *(Nautical)*, bower *(Nautical)*, kedge, drogue, sheet anchor • *We lost our anchor, which caused the boat to drift.*
2 = support, second, stay, supporter, prop, backer, backbone, mainstay, comforter, tower of strength • *He provided an emotional anchor for her.*
3 = presenter, newscaster, reporter, commentator, broadcaster, newsreader, anchor man, anchor woman • *He was the anchor for the channel's 15-minute news programme.*
▸ AS A VERB **1 = moor**, harbour, dock, tie up, kedge • *The ship was anchored by the pier.*
2 = dock, moor, harbour, drop anchor, kedge, cast anchor, drop the hook, let go the anchor, lay anchor, come to anchor • *We anchored off the beach.*
3 = secure, tie, fix, bind, chain, attach, bolt, fasten, affix • *The child's seatbelt was not properly anchored in the car.*

anchorage **= berth**, haven, port, harbour, dock, quay, dockage, moorage, harbourage • *The vessel yesterday reached anchorage off Dubai.*

ancient **1 = classical**, old, former, past, early, bygone, primordial, primeval, olden • *They believed ancient Greece and Rome were vital sources of learning.*
2 = very old, early, aged, antique, obsolete, archaic, age-old, bygone, antiquated, hoary, olden, superannuated, antediluvian, timeworn, old as the hills • *ancient rites*
3 = old-fashioned, past, dated, outdated, obsolete, out of date, old-time, archaic, unfashionable, antiquated, outmoded, passé, musty, old hat, behind the times, fusty, superannuated, out of style, obsolescent, square *(informal)*, cobwebby, démodé *(French)*, out of the ark *(informal)*, oldfangled, (old-)fogeyish • *He produced articles and stories on his ancient typewriter.*
OPPOSITES: new, young, up-to-date

ancillary **= supplementary**, supporting, extra, additional, secondary, subsidiary, accessory, subordinate, auxiliary, contributory • *Ancillary services like cleaning are put up for competitive tender.*
OPPOSITES: major, chief, main

and **1 = also**, including, along with, together with, in addition to, as well as • *When he returned, she and her boyfriend had already gone.*
2 = moreover, plus, furthermore, besides • *These airlines fly to isolated places. And business travellers use them.*

androgynous **= hermaphrodite**, bisexual, androgyne, hermaphroditic, epicene, ambisexual • *She's always attracted to men with an androgynous quality.*

android **= robot**, automaton, humanoid, cyborg, mechanical man, bionic man *or* woman • *Star Trek's android, Data*

anecdotal **= unreliable**, untrustworthy, based on rumour • *countless anecdotal reports*

anecdote **= story**, tale, sketch, short story, yarn, reminiscence, urban myth, urban legend • *He has a talent for recollection and anecdote.*

anew **= again**, once again, once more, over again, from the beginning, from scratch, another time, afresh • *She's ready to start anew.*

angel **1 = divine messenger**, spirit, cherub, archangel, seraph, spiritual being, guardian spirit • *a choir of angels*
2 = dear, ideal, beauty, saint, treasure, darling, dream, jewel, gem, paragon • *Thank you. You're an angel.*

QUOTATIONS

Is man an ape or an angel? Now I am on the side of the angels

[Benjamin Disraeli *Speech at Oxford Diocesan Conference*]

ANGELS

Angels

Azrael	Michael	Uriel
Gabriel	Raphael	

Angelic orders

angels	*or* dominions	seraphim
archangels	powers	thrones
cherubim	principalities	virtues
dominations	*or* princedoms	

angelic **1 = pure**, beautiful, lovely, innocent, entrancing, virtuous, saintly, adorable, beatific • *an angelic little face*

2 = **heavenly**, celestial, ethereal, cherubic, seraphic • *angelic choirs*
OPPOSITES: satanic, demonic, diabolical

anger AS A NOUN = **rage**, passion, outrage, temper, fury, resentment, irritation, wrath, indignation, annoyance, agitation, ire, antagonism, displeasure, exasperation, irritability, spleen, pique, ill temper, vehemence, vexation, high dudgeon, ill humour, choler • *He cried with anger and frustration.*
OPPOSITES: liking, peace, calmness
▸ AS A VERB = **enrage**, provoke, outrage, annoy, offend, excite, irritate, infuriate, hassle *(informal)*, aggravate *(informal)*, incense, fret, gall, madden, exasperate, nettle, vex, affront, displease, rile, pique, get on someone's nerves *(informal)*, antagonize, get someone's back up, piss someone off *(taboo slang)*, put someone's back up, nark *(Brit., Austral. & N.Z. slang)*, make someone's blood boil, get in someone's hair *(informal)*, get someone's dander up *(informal)* • *The decision to allow more construction angered the residents.*
OPPOSITES: please, calm, soothe

QUOTATIONS
Usually when people are sad, they don't do anything. They just cry over their condition. But when they get angry, they bring about a change
[Malcolm X *Malcolm X Speaks*]
Anger is a short madness
[Horace *Epistles*]
Anger and jealousy can no more bear to lose sight of their objects than love
[George Eliot *The Mill on the Floss*]
PROVERBS
Never let the sun go down on your anger

angle AS A NOUN 1 = **gradient**, bank, slope, incline, inclination • *The boat was leaning at a 30-degree angle.*
2 = **intersection**, point, edge, corner, knee, bend, elbow, crook, crotch, nook, cusp • *brackets to adjust the steering wheel's angle*
3 = **point of view**, position, approach, direction, aspect, perspective, outlook, viewpoint, slant, standpoint, take *(informal)*, side • *He was considering the idea from all angles.*
▸ AS A VERB = **slant**, aim, bend, incline, tilt, skew • *You can angle the slats for more shade.*
▸ IN PHRASES: **angle for something** = **seek**, scheme, look for, hunt, invite, be after *(informal)*, try for, aim for, contrive, fish for, solicit, set your sights on, cast about *or* around for • *It sounds as if he's just angling for sympathy.*

angler = **fisherman**, fisher, piscator *or* piscatrix • *a thinking angler with tremendous ability*

angling = **fishing** • *He claimed that angling is a cruel sport.*

QUOTATIONS
a worm at one end and a fool at the other
[Dr. Johnson]
God never did make a more calm, quiet, innocent recreation than angling
[Izaak Walton]

angry 1 = **furious**, cross, heated, mad *(informal)*, raging, provoked, outraged, annoyed, passionate, irritated, raving, hacked (off) *(U.S. slang)*, choked, pissed *(taboo slang)*, infuriated, hot, incensed, enraged, ranting, exasperated, irritable, resentful, nettled, snappy, indignant, pissed off *(taboo slang)*, irate, tumultuous, displeased, uptight *(informal)*, riled, up in arms, incandescent, ill-tempered, irascible, antagonized, waspish, piqued, hot under the collar *(informal)*, on the warpath, hopping mad *(informal)*, foaming at the mouth, choleric, splenetic, wrathful, at daggers drawn, in high dudgeon, as black as thunder, ireful, tooshie *(Austral. slang)*, off the air *(Austral. slang)* • *He's an angry man.*
OPPOSITES: loving, happy, calm
2 = **inflamed**, severe, painful, nasty, swollen, sore • *He had two angry cuts across his forehead.*
3 = **threatening**, forbidding, grim, menacing, sinister, ominous, baleful, inauspicious • *Under the angry red sky he ran, into the thickening darkness.*

QUOTATIONS
When angry, count four; when very angry, swear
[Mark Twain *Pudd'nhead Wilson*]

angst = **anxiety**, worry, distress, torment, unease, apprehension, agitation, malaise, perturbation, vexation, fretfulness, disquietude, inquietude • *Many kids suffer from acne and angst.*
OPPOSITES: ease, satisfaction, peace of mind

anguish = **suffering**, pain, torture, distress, grief, misery, agony, torment, sorrow, woe, heartache, heartbreak, pang, throe • *A cry of anguish burst from her lips.*

anguished = **suffering**, wounded, tortured, distressed, tormented, afflicted, agonized, grief-stricken, wretched, brokenhearted • *She let out an anguished cry.*

angular = **skinny**, spare, lean, gaunt, bony, lanky, scrawny, lank, rangy, rawboned, macilent *(rare)* • *He had an angular face with prominent cheekbones.*

animal AS A NOUN 1 = **creature**, beast, brute • *He was attacked by wild animals.*
2 = **brute**, devil, monster, savage, beast, bastard *(informal, offensive)*, villain, barbarian, swine *(informal)*, wild man • *He was an animal in his younger days.*
▸ AS AN ADJECTIVE = **physical**, gross, fleshly, bodily, sensual, carnal, brutish, bestial • *When he was drunk, he showed his animal side.*
▸ RELATED PREFIX: zoo-
▸ RELATED MANIAS: zoomania, zoophilia
▸ RELATED ENTHUSIAST: zoophile
▸ RELATED PHOBIA: zoophobia
▹ *See panels* **Animals; Amphibians; Anteaters and other edentates; Bats; Birds; Carnivores; Cattle and other artiodactyls; Dinosaurs; Fish; Horses, rhinos and other perissodactyls; Insects; Invertebrates; Marsupials; Monkeys, apes and other primates; Rabbits and hares; Reptiles; Rodents; Sea mammals; Shrews and other insectivores; Whales and dophins**

QUOTATIONS
Animals, whom we have made our slaves, we do not like to consider our equal
[Charles Darwin]
The best thing about animals is that they don't talk much
[Thornton Wilder *The Skin of Our Teeth*]
If I could do anything about the way people behave towards each other, I would, but since I can't I'll stick to the animals
[Brigitte Bardot]
It's almost as if we're put here on earth to show how silly [animals] aren't
[Russell Hoban *Turtle Diary*]

animate AS AN ADJECTIVE = **living**, live, moving, alive, breathing, alive and kicking • *the study of animate and inanimate aspects of the natural world*
▸ AS A VERB = **enliven**, encourage, excite, urge, inspire, stir, spark, move, fire, spur, stimulate, revive, activate, rouse, prod, quicken, incite, instigate, kick-start *(informal)*, impel, energize, kindle, embolden, liven up, breathe life into, invigorate, gladden, gee up, vitalize, vivify, inspirit • *There was little about the game to animate the crowd.*
OPPOSITES: kill, check, inhibit

animated = **lively**, spirited, quick, excited, active, vital, dynamic, enthusiastic, passionate, vivid, vigorous, energetic, vibrant, brisk, buoyant, ardent, airy, fervent, zealous, elated, ebullient, sparky, sprightly, vivacious, gay, alive and kicking, full of beans *(informal)*, zestful • *Everyone became more animated.*
OPPOSITES: boring, depressed, listless

ANIMALS

Related words

ant	formic	elephant	elephantine	mite *or* tick	acaroid
ass	asinine	falcon	falconine	monkey	simian
bear	ursine	fish	piscine *or* icthyoid	ox	bovine
bee	apian	fowl	gallinaceous	parrot	psittacine
bird	avian *or* ornithic	fox	vulpine	peacock	pavonine
bull	taurine	goat	caprine *or* hircine	pig	porcine
cat	feline	goose	anserine *or* anserous	puffin	alcidine
crab	cancroid	gull	larine	seal	phocine
crow	corvine	hare	leporine	sheep	ovine
deer	cervine	hawk	accipitrine	snake	serpentine *or* ophidian
dog	canine	horse	equine	swallow	hirundine
dove	columbine	lion	leonine	wasp	vespine
eagle	aquiline	lynx	lyncean	wolf	lupine

Collective animals

antelopes	herd	giraffes	herd	pigs	litter
apes	shrewdness	gnats	swarm *or* cloud	plovers	stand *or* wing
asses	pace *or* herd	goats	herd *or* tribe	pochards	flight, rush, bunch, *or* knob
badgers	cete	goldfinches	charm	ponies	herd
bears	sloth	grouse	brood, covey, *or* pack	porpoises	school *or* gam
bees	swarm *or* grist	gulls	colony	poultry	run
birds	flock *or* congregation	hares	down *or* husk	pups	litter
bitterns	sedge *or* siege	hawks	cast	quails	bevy
boars	sounder	hens	brood	rabbits	nest
bucks	brace *or* lease	herons	sedge *or* siege	racehorses	field *or* string
buffaloes	herd	herrings	shoal *or* glean	ravens	unkindness
capercailzies	tok	hounds	pack, mute, *or* cry	roes	bevy
cats	clowder	insects	swarm	rooks	building *or* clamour
cattle	drove *or* herd	kangaroos	troop	ruffs	hill
choughs	chattering	kittens	kindle	seals	herd *or* pod
colts	rag	lapwings	desert	sheep	flock
coots	covert	larks	exaltation	sheldrakes	dopping
cranes	herd, sedge, *or* siege	leopards	leap	snipe	walk *or* wisp
crows	murder	lions	pride *or* troop	sparrows	host
cubs	litter	mallards	sord *or* sute	starlings	murmuration
curlews	herd	mares	stud	swallows	flight
curs	cowardice	martens	richesse	swans	herd *or* bevy
deer	herd	moles	labour	swifts	flock
dolphins	school	monkeys	troop	swine	herd, sounder, *or* dryft
doves	flight *or* dule	mules	barren	teal	bunch, knob, *or* spring
ducks	paddling *or* team	nightingales	watch	whales	school, gam, *or* run
dunlins	flight	owls	parliament	whelps	litter
elk	gang	oxen	yoke, drove, team, *or* herd	whiting	pod
fish	shoal, draught, *or* haul	partridges	covey	wigeon	bunch, company, *or* knob
flies	swarm *or* grist	peacocks	muster	wildfowl	plump, sord, *or* sute
foxes	skulk	pheasants	nye *or* nide	wolves	pack, rout, *or* herd
geese	gaggle *or* skein	pigeons	flock *or* flight	woodcocks	fall

Habitations

ant	ant hill *or* formicary	eagle	aerie *or* eyrie	puffin	puffinry
badger	set *or* sett	fish	redd	rabbit	warren
beaver	lodge	fox	earth	rook	rookery
bee	hive *or* apiary	otter	holt	squirrel	drey *or* dray
bird	nest	pig	sty	wasp	vespiary *or* bike

Male

ass	jack	fowl	cock	peafowl	peacock
bird	cock	fox	dog	pig	boar
cat	tom	goat	billy *or* buck	rabbit	buck
deer	hart *or* stag	goose	gander	reindeer	buck
donkey	jack	hare	buck	ruff	ruff
duck	drake	horse	stallion	sheep	ram *or* tup
elephant	bull	kangaroo	buck *or* old man	swan	cob
falcon	tercel *or* tiercel	lobster	cock	weasel	whittret
ferret	hob	ox	bull	whale	bull

ANIMALS (CONTINUED)

Female

ass	jenny	goat	nanny	rabbit	doe
bird	hen	hare	doe	ruff	reeve
cat	tabby	horse	mare	sheep	ewe
deer	doe *or* hind	leopard	leopardess	swan	pen
dog	bitch	lion	lioness	tiger	tigress
donkey	jenny	lobster	hen	whale	cow
elephant	cow	mink	sow	wolf	bitch
ferret	gill *or* jill *(dialect)*	ox	cow	wren	jenny
fowl	hen	peafowl	peahen		
fox	vixen	pig	sow		

Young

bear	cub	ferret	kit	pig	piglet
bird	chick, fledg(e)ling, *or* nestling	fish	fry *or* fingerling	pigeon	squab
butterfly	caterpillar, chrysalis, *or* chrysalid	frog	tadpole	salmon	alevin, grilse, parr, *or* smolt
cat	kitten	fox	kit *or* cub	seal	pup
cod	codling	goat	kid *or* yeanling	sheep	lamb *or* yeanling
deer	fawn	goose	gosling	sprat	brit
dog	pup *or* puppy	hare	leveret	swan	cygnet
duck	duckling	herring	alevin, brit, *or* sparling	tiger	cub
eagle	eaglet	horse	foal, colt, *or* filly	toad	tadpole
eel	elver *or* grig	kangaroo	joey	whale	calf
elephant	calf	lion	cub	wolf	cub *or* whelp
falcon	eyas	moth	caterpillar		
		owl	owlet		
		ox	calf		

animation = **liveliness**, life, action, activity, energy, spirit, passion, enthusiasm, excitement, pep, sparkle, vitality, vigour, zeal, verve, zest, fervour, high spirits, dynamism, buoyancy, elation, exhilaration, welly *(slang)*, gaiety, ardour, vibrancy, brio, zing *(informal)*, vivacity, ebullience, briskness, airiness, sprightliness, pizzazz *or* pizazz *(informal)* • *They both spoke with animation.*

animosity = **hostility**, hate, hatred, resentment, bitterness, malice, antagonism, antipathy, enmity, acrimony, rancour, bad blood, ill will, animus, malevolence, virulence, malignity • *There's a long history of animosity between the two nations.*
OPPOSITES: love, friendship, friendliness

animus = **ill will**, hate, hostility, hatred, resentment, bitterness, malice, animosity, antagonism, antipathy, enmity, acrimony, rancour, bad blood, malevolence, virulence, malignity • *He displayed a thorough animus to the Western tradition.*

ankle
▸ TECHNICAL NAME: talus

annals = **records**, history, accounts, registers, journals, memorials, archives, chronicles • *He has become a legend in the annals of military history.*

annex 1 = **seize**, take over, appropriate, acquire, occupy, conquer, expropriate, arrogate • *Rome annexed the Nabatean kingdom in 106 AD.*
2 = **join**, unite, add, connect, attach, tack, adjoin, fasten, affix, append, subjoin • *A gate goes through to the annexed garden.*
OPPOSITES: remove, separate, detach

annexation = **seizure**, takeover, occupation, conquest, appropriation, annexing, expropriation, arrogation • *the country's annexation of its neighbour*

annexe 1 = **extension**, wing, ell, supplementary building • *They are planning to set up a museum in an annexe to the theatre.*
2 = **appendix**, addition, supplement, attachment, adjunct, addendum, affixment • *The annexe lists and discusses eight titles.*

annihilate = **destroy**, abolish, wipe out, erase, eradicate, extinguish, obliterate, liquidate, root out, exterminate, nullify, extirpate, wipe from the face of the earth, kennet *(Austral. slang)*, jeff *(Austral. slang)* • *The army was annihilated.*

annihilation = **destruction**, wiping out, abolition, extinction, extinguishing, liquidation, rooting out, extermination, eradication, erasure, obliteration, nullification, extirpation • *Political leaders fear the annihilation of their people.*

anniversary = **jubilee**, remembrance, commemoration • *the 100th anniversary of the birth of Ho Chi Minh*
▹ *See panel* **Anniversaries**

annotate = **make notes on**, explain, note, illustrate, comment on, interpret, gloss, footnote, commentate, elucidate, make observations on • *Historians annotate diary selections.*

annotation = **note**, comment, explanation, observation, interpretation, illustration, commentary, gloss, footnote, exegesis, explication, elucidation • *He supplied annotations to 15,000 musical works.*

announce 1 = **make known**, tell, report, reveal, publish, declare, advertise, broadcast, disclose, intimate, proclaim, trumpet, make public, publicize, divulge, promulgate, propound, shout from the rooftops *(informal)* • *She was planning to announce her engagement to Peter.*
OPPOSITES: hide, bury, keep secret
2 = **introduce**, name, present • *A brisk voice announced the inspector.*
3 = **be a sign of**, signal, herald, warn of, signify, augur, harbinger, presage, foretell, portend, betoken • *The doorbell of the shop announced the arrival of a customer.*

announcement 1 = **statement**, communication, broadcast, explanation, publication, declaration, advertisement, testimony, disclosure, bulletin, communiqué, proclamation, utterance, intimation, promulgation, divulgence • *There has been no formal announcement by either government.*

ANNIVERSARIES

Year	Traditional	Modern
1st	Paper	Clocks
2nd	Cotton	China
3rd	Leather	Crystal, glass
4th	Linen (silk)	Electrical appliances
5th	Wood	Silverware
6th	Iron	Wood
7th	Wool (copper)	Desk sets
8th	Bronze	Linen, lace
9th	Pottery (china)	Leather
10th	Tin (aluminium)	Diamond jewellery
11th	Steel	Fashion jewellery, accessories
12th	Silk	Pearls *or* coloured gems
13th	Lace	Textile, furs
14th	Ivory	Gold jewellery
15th	Crystal	Watches
20th	China	Platinum
25th	Silver	Sterling silver
30th	Pearl	Diamond
35th	Coral (jade)	Jade
40th	Ruby	Ruby
45th	Sapphire	Sapphire
50th	Gold	Gold
55th	Emerald	Emerald
60th	Diamond	Diamond

2 = **declaration**, report, reporting, publication, revelation, disclosure, proclamation, intimation, promulgation, divulgence • *the announcement of their engagement*

announcer = **presenter**, newscaster, reporter, commentator, broadcaster, newsreader, master of ceremonies, anchor man, anchor • *The radio announcer said it was nine o'clock.*

annoy = **irritate**, trouble, bore, anger, harry, bother, disturb, provoke, get *(informal)*, bug *(informal)*, needle *(informal)*, plague, tease, harass, hassle *(informal)*, aggravate *(informal)*, badger, gall, madden, ruffle, exasperate, nettle, molest, pester, vex, displease, irk, bedevil, rile, peeve, get under your skin *(informal)*, get on your nerves *(informal)*, nark *(Brit., Austral. & N.Z. slang)*, get up your nose *(informal)*, give someone grief *(Brit. & S. African)*, make your blood boil, piss you off *(taboo slang)*, rub someone up the wrong way *(informal)*, get your goat *(slang)*, get in your hair *(informal)*, get on your wick *(Brit. slang)*, get your dander up *(informal)*, get your back up, incommode, put your back up, hack you off *(informal)* • *Try making a note of the things that annoy you.*
OPPOSITES: comfort, calm, soothe

annoyance 1 = **irritation**, trouble, anger, bother, grief *(informal)*, harassment, disturbance, hassle *(informal)*, nuisance, provocation, displeasure, exasperation, aggravation, vexation, bedevilment • *To her annoyance the stranger did not go away.*
2 = **nuisance**, bother, pain *(informal)*, bind *(informal)*, bore, drag *(informal)*, plague, tease, pest, gall, pain in the neck *(informal)*, pain in the arse *(taboo slang)* • *Snoring can be more than an annoyance.*

annoyed = **irritated**, bothered, pissed *(taboo slang)*, harassed, hassled *(informal)*, aggravated *(informal)*, maddened, ruffled, exasperated, nettled, vexed, pissed off *(taboo slang)*, miffed *(informal)*, displeased, irked, riled, harried, peeved *(informal)*, piqued, browned off *(informal)* • *She tapped her forehead and looked annoyed with herself.*

annoying = **irritating**, boring, disturbing, provoking, teasing, harassing, aggravating, troublesome, galling, maddening, exasperating, displeasing, bedevilling, peeving *(informal)*, irksome, bothersome, vexatious • *You must have found my attitude annoying.*
OPPOSITES: charming, entertaining, delightful

annual AS AN ADJECTIVE 1 = **once a year**, yearly • *the annual conference of the trade union movement*
2 = **yearlong**, yearly • *annual costs, £1,600*
▸ AS A NOUN = **almanac**, yearbook, guide, handbook, guidebook, workbook • *I looked for Wyman's picture in my high-school annual.*

annually 1 = **once a year**, yearly, each year, every year, per year, by the year, every twelve months, per annum, year after year • *Companies report to their shareholders annually.*
2 = **per year**, yearly, each year, every year, by the year, per annum • *They hire 300 staff annually.*

annul = **invalidate**, reverse, cancel, abolish, void, repeal, recall, revoke, retract, negate, rescind, nullify, obviate, abrogate, countermand, declare *or* render null and void • *The marriage was annulled last month.*
OPPOSITES: restore, bring back, reinstate

annulment = **invalidation**, voiding, abolition, reversal, repeal, cancellation, retraction, negation, recall, revocation, countermanding, nullification, abrogation, rescission, rescindment • *the annulment of the elections*

anodyne AS AN ADJECTIVE = **bland**, dull, boring, insipid, unexciting, uninspiring, uninteresting, mind-numbing *(informal)* • *Their quarterly meetings were anodyne affairs.*
▸ AS A NOUN = **painkiller**, narcotic, palliative, analgesic, pain reliever • *Leisure is a kind of anodyne.*

anoint 1 = **smear**, oil, rub, grease, spread over, daub, embrocate • *He anointed my forehead with oil.*
2 = **consecrate**, bless, sanctify, hallow, anele *(archaic)* • *The Pope has anointed him as Archbishop.*

anomalous = **unusual**, odd, rare, bizarre, exceptional, peculiar, eccentric, abnormal, irregular, inconsistent, off-the-wall *(slang)*, incongruous, deviating, oddball *(informal)*, out there *(slang)*, atypical, aberrant, outré • *For years his anomalous behaviour has baffled scientists.*
OPPOSITES: common, natural, normal

anomaly = **irregularity**, departure, exception, abnormality, rarity, inconsistency, deviation, eccentricity, oddity, aberration, peculiarity, incongruity • *Their wariness of opera is an anomaly in Europe.*

anon = **soon**, presently, shortly, promptly, before long, forthwith, betimes *(archaic)*, erelong *(archaic or poetic)*, in a couple of shakes *(informal)* • *You shall see him anon.*

anonymity 1 = **namelessness**, innominateness • *Both mother and daughter have requested anonymity.*
2 = **unremarkability** *or* **unremarkableness**, characterlessness, unsingularity • *the anonymity of the rented room*

anonymous 1 = **unnamed**, unknown, unidentified, nameless, unacknowledged, incognito, unauthenticated, innominate • *You can remain anonymous if you wish.*
OPPOSITES: known, named, identified
2 = **unsigned**, uncredited, unattributed, unattested • *I heard that an anonymous note was actually being circulated.*
OPPOSITES: signed, credited, attested
3 = **nondescript**, impersonal, faceless, colourless, undistinguished, unexceptional, characterless • *It's nice to stay in a home rather than an anonymous holiday flat.*

another 1 = **a further**, an extra, one more, an additional • *We're going to have another baby.*
2 = **a different**, an alternative, a variant • *They referred her to another therapist*

answer AS A VERB 1 = **reply**, explain, respond, resolve, acknowledge, react, return, retort, rejoin, refute • *He paused before answering.*
OPPOSITES: ask, question, query
2 = **acknowledge**, respond to, react to, reply to, write back to • *Did he answer your letter?*

3 = **pick up**, get, respond to • *She answered her phone on the first ring.*
4 = **satisfy**, meet, serve, fit, fill, suit, solve, fulfil, suffice, measure up to • *We must ensure we answer real needs.*
5 = **fit**, meet, match, agree to, conform to, correspond to, correlate to • *two men answering the description of the suspects*
6 = **defend yourself against**, refute, rebut • *He will appear in court to answer charges of trying to hide money.*
▸ AS A NOUN 1 = **reply**, response, reaction, resolution, explanation, plea, comeback, retort, report, return, defence, acknowledgement, riposte, counterattack, refutation, rejoinder • *Without waiting for an answer, he turned and went in.*
OPPOSITES: question, inquiry, query
2 = **solution**, resolution, explanation • *Simply marking an answer wrong will not help the student.*
3 = **remedy**, solution, vindication • *Prison is not the answer for most young offenders.*
4 = **defence**, response, reply, rebuttal, counter-statement • *In answer to the speculation, she boldly declared her intention.*
▸ IN PHRASES: **answer for something** 1 = **be responsible for**, be to blame for, be liable for, be accountable for, take the rap for *(slang)*, be answerable for, be chargeable for • *That child's mother has a lot to answer for.*
2 = **pay for**, suffer for, atone for, make amends for • *He must be made to answer for his terrible crimes.*
answer to someone = **be responsible to**, obey, work under, be ruled by, be managed by, be subordinate to, be accountable to, be answerable to • *He answers to a boss he has met once in 18 months.*

answerable = **responsible for** *or* **to**, to blame for, liable for *or* to, accountable for *or* to, chargeable for, subject to • *Councils should be answerable to the people who elect them.*

answer back = **be impertinent**, argue, dispute, disagree, retort, contradict, rebut, talk back, be cheeky • *I always answered my parents back when I thought they were wrong.*

ant
▸ RELATED ADJECTIVE: formic
▸ NAME OF HOME: ant hill, formicary
▹ *See panel* **Ants, bees, and wasps**

antagonism = **hostility**, competition, opposition, conflict, rivalry, contention, friction, discord, antipathy, dissension • *There is much antagonism between the unions and the companies.*
OPPOSITES: love, accord, friendship

antagonist = **opponent**, rival, opposer, enemy, competitor, contender, foe, adversary • *He had never previously lost to his antagonist.*

antagonistic = **hostile**, opposed, resistant, at odds, incompatible, set against, averse, unfriendly, at variance, inimical, antipathetic, ill-disposed • *Nearly all the women were antagonistic to the idea.*

antagonize = **annoy**, anger, insult, offend, irritate, alienate, hassle *(informal)*, aggravate *(informal)*, gall, repel, estrange, get under your skin *(informal)*, get on your nerves *(informal)*, nark *(Brit., Austral. & N.Z. slang)*, get up your nose *(informal)*, be on your back *(slang)*, piss you off *(taboo slang)*, rub (someone) up the wrong way *(informal)*, disaffect, get in your hair *(informal)*, get on your wick *(Brit. slang)*, hack you off *(informal)* • *He didn't want to antagonize her.*
OPPOSITES: calm, win over, pacify

Antarctic = **Antarctic zone**, the Ice *(N.Z.)*, Antarctica, South Pole • *A hole has opened up over the Antarctic over the past decade.*

ante IN PHRASES: **up the ante** = **raise the stakes** • *He knew he had to up the ante again in this poker game.*

anteater

ANTEATERS AND OTHER EDENTATES

aardvark
anteater
armadillo
echidna *or* spiny anteater
numbat *or* banded anteater
pangolin *or* scaly anteater
sloth *or* ai
tamandu, tamandua, *or* lesser anteater

antecedent AS AN ADJECTIVE = **preceding**, earlier, former, previous, prior, preliminary, foregoing, anterior, precursory • *They were allowed to take account of antecedent legislation.*
OPPOSITES: later, following, subsequent
▸ AS A PLURAL NOUN 1 = **ancestors**, family, line, stock, blood, descent, extraction, ancestry, forebears, forefathers, genealogy, progenitors, tupuna *or* tipuna *(N.Z.)* • *a Frenchman with Irish antecedents*
2 = **past**, history, background • *a series of conditions or antecedents which may have contributed to the situation*

antediluvian = **old-fashioned**, ancient, antique, obsolete, out-of-date, archaic, antiquated, passé, out of the ark *(informal)*, old as the hills • *those antediluvian days before television*

antelope
▸ COLLECTIVE NOUN: herd

antenna = **aerial**, sensor • *The air force are developing an antenna to protect all its aircraft.*

anterior 1 = **front**, forward, fore, frontward • *the left anterior descending artery*
2 = **earlier**, former, previous, prior, preceding, introductory, foregoing, antecedent • *memories of our anterior existences*

anteroom *or* **ante-room** = **outer room**, lobby, foyer, waiting room, reception room, vestibule, antechamber • *I was waiting in the anteroom of a radio studio.*

anthem = **song of praise**, carol, chant, hymn, psalm, paean, chorale, canticle • *the Olympic anthem*

anthology = **collection**, choice, selection, treasury, digest, compilation, garland, compendium, miscellany, analects • *an anthology of poetry*

anticipate 1 = **expect**, predict, forecast, prepare for, look for, hope for, envisage, foresee, bank on, apprehend, foretell,

ANTS, BEES, AND WASPS

Amazon ant
ant *or (archaic or dialect)* emmet
army ant *or* legionary ant
bee
blue ant *(Austral.)*
bulldog ant, bull ant, *or (Austral.)* bull Joe
bumblebee *or* humblebee
carpenter bee
cicada hunter *(Austral.)*
cuckoo bee
digger wasp
driver ant
flower wasp *(Austral.)*
gall wasp
honeypot ant *or* honey ant *(Austral.)*
honeybee *or* hive bee
horntail *or* wood wasp
ichneumon fly *or* ichneumon wasp
killer bee
kootchar *(Austral.)*
leafcutter ant
leafcutter bee
mason bee
mason wasp
minga *(Austral.)*
mining bee
mud dauber
native bee *or* sugarbag fly *(Austral.)*
Pharaoh ant
policeman fly *(Austral.)*
ruby-tail wasp
sand wasp
Sirex wasp *(Austral.)*
slave ant
spider-hunting wasp
termite *or* white ant
velvet ant
wasp
wood ant
yellow jacket *(U.S. & Canad.)*

think likely, count upon • *We could not have anticipated the result of our campaigning.*
2 = **await**, look forward to, count the hours until • *We are all eagerly anticipating the next match.*
3 = **pre-empt**, intercept, forestall, second-guess, beat (someone) to it • *You've anticipated my next question.*

a

anticipation 1 = **expectancy**, hope, expectation, apprehension, foresight, premonition, preconception, foretaste, prescience, forethought, presentiment • *There's been an atmosphere of anticipation round here for some days.*
2 = **readiness for**, expectation, preparation for • *Troops have been put on alert in anticipation of more trouble.*

anticipatory = **expectant**, foreseeing, apprehensive, provident, foretelling, forethoughtful • *anticipatory excitement at the thought of eating such delights*

anticlimax = **disappointment**, letdown, comedown *(informal)*, bathos • *His international career ended in anticlimax.*
OPPOSITES: summit, height, climax

QUOTATIONS
This is the way the world ends
Not with a bang but a whimper
[T.S. Eliot *The Hollow Men*]

antics = **clowning**, tricks, stunts, mischief, larks, capers, pranks, frolics, escapades, foolishness, silliness, playfulness, skylarking, horseplay, buffoonery, tomfoolery, monkey tricks • *She tolerated his antics.*

antidote 1 = **remedy**, cure, preventive, corrective, neutralizer, nostrum, countermeasure, antitoxin, antivenin, counteragent • *He noticed their sickness and prepared an antidote.*
2 = **cure**, remedy, corrective, nostrum, countermeasure • *Massage is a wonderful antidote to stress.*

antipathy = **hostility**, opposition, disgust, dislike, hatred, loathing, distaste, animosity, aversion, antagonism, enmity, rancour, bad blood, incompatibility, ill will, animus, repulsion, abhorrence, repugnance, odium, contrariety • *She'd often spoken of her antipathy towards London.*
OPPOSITES: bond, attraction, affinity

antiquated = **obsolete**, old, aged, ancient, antique, old-fashioned, elderly, dated, past it *(informal)*, out-of-date, archaic, outmoded, passé, old hat, hoary, superannuated, antediluvian, outworn, cobwebby, old as the hills • *The factory is so antiquated, it isn't worth saving.*
OPPOSITES: new, young, up-to-date

antique AS A NOUN = **period piece**, relic, bygone, heirloom, collector's item, museum piece, object of virtu • *a genuine antique*
▸ AS AN ADJECTIVE 1 = **vintage**, classic, antiquarian, olden • *antique silver jewellery*
2 = **old-fashioned**, old, aged, ancient, remote, elderly, primitive, outdated, obsolete, archaic, bygone, primordial, primeval, immemorial, superannuated • *Their aim is to break taboos and change antique laws.*

antiquity 1 = **distant past**, ancient times, time immemorial, olden days • *famous monuments of classical antiquity*
2 = **old age**, age, oldness, ancientness, elderliness • *a town of great antiquity*
3 = **antique**, ruin, relic • *collectors of Roman antiquities*

antiseptic AS AN ADJECTIVE = **hygienic**, clean, pure, sterile, sanitary, uncontaminated, unpolluted, germ-free, aseptic • *These herbs have strong antiseptic qualities.*
OPPOSITES: dirty, infected, unhygienic
▸ AS A NOUN = **disinfectant**, purifier, bactericide, germicide • *She bathed the cut with antiseptic.*

antisocial 1 = **unsociable**, reserved, retiring, withdrawn, alienated, unfriendly, uncommunicative, misanthropic, asocial • *a generation of teenagers who will become aggressive and anti-social*
OPPOSITES: social, friendly, sociable
2 = **disruptive**, disorderly, hostile, menacing, rebellious, belligerent, antagonistic, uncooperative • *Playing these games can lead to anti-social behaviour.*

antithesis 1 = **opposite**, contrast, reverse, contrary, converse, inverse, antipode • *They are the antithesis of the typical married couple.*
2 = **contrast**, opposition, contradiction, reversal, inversion, contrariety, contraposition • *the antithesis between instinct and reason*

antithetical or **antithetic** = **opposite**, opposed, contrasted, contrasting, counter, reverse, contrary, contradictory, converse, inverse, poles apart, antipodal • *The oppressive use of power is antithetical to our ideals.*

anus ▸ RELATED ADJECTIVE: anal

anxiety = **uneasiness**, concern, care, worry, doubt, tension, alarm, distress, suspicion, angst, unease, apprehension, misgiving, suspense, nervousness, disquiet, trepidation, foreboding, restlessness, solicitude, perturbation, watchfulness, fretfulness, disquietude, apprehensiveness, dubiety • *His voice was full of anxiety.*
OPPOSITES: security, confidence, relief

anxious 1 = **eager**, keen, intent, yearning, impatient, itching, ardent, avid, expectant, desirous • *He is anxious that there should be no delay.*
OPPOSITES: reluctant, hesitant, loath
2 = **uneasy**, concerned, worried, troubled, upset, careful, wired *(slang)*, nervous, disturbed, distressed, uncomfortable, tense, fearful, unsettled, restless, neurotic, agitated, taut, disquieted, apprehensive, edgy, watchful, jittery *(informal)*, perturbed, on edge, ill at ease, twitchy *(informal)*, solicitous, overwrought, fretful, on tenterhooks, in suspense, hot and bothered, unquiet *(chiefly literary)*, like a fish out of water, antsy *(informal)*, angsty, on pins and needles, discomposed • *He admitted he was still anxious about the situation.*
OPPOSITES: certain, cool, confident

any AS A DETERMINER 1 = **a scrap of**, a bit of, a grain of, a fragment of, a small piece of, a speck of, the slightest bit of, a crumb of, an atom of, an iota of, a jot of • *We're doing all this without any support.*
2 = **whichever**, every • *Any actor will tell you that it's easier to act than to be themselves.*
3 = **a single one**, any one, a single member • *There was nothing any of us could do.*
▸ AS AN ADVERB = **at all**, somewhat, in the least, to an extent • *Things aren't getting any easier for graduates.*

anybody *see* **anyone**

anyhow 1 = **anyway**, still, nevertheless, nonetheless, in any case, for all that, in spite of everything • *Anyhow, it's no secret that he owes money.*
2 = **carelessly**, haphazardly, heedlessly • *her long legs which she displayed all anyhow getting into the car*

any more = **any longer** • *I couldn't trust him any more.*

anyone or **anybody** = **a soul**, any person • *I won't tell anyone I saw you here.*

anything = **a thing** • *We can't do anything.*

anyway = **anyhow**, regardless, in any case, for all that, at any rate, in any event • *She won't let him stay with her, and anyway he wouldn't.*

anywhere = **anyplace** • *Did you try and get help from anywhere?*

apace = **quickly**, rapidly, swiftly, speedily, without delay, at full speed, expeditiously, posthaste, with dispatch • *Summer gallops on apace.*

apart AS AN ADVERB 1 = **to pieces**, to bits, asunder, into parts • *He took the clock apart to see what was wrong with it.*
2 = **away from each other**, distant from each other • *They live 25 miles apart.*

3 = aside, away, alone, independently, separately, singly, excluded, isolated, cut off, to one side, to yourself, by itself, aloof, to itself, by yourself, out on a limb • *He saw her standing some distance apart.*
4 = separately, independently, separated, divorced • *Mum and Dad live apart.*
▸ **IN PHRASES: apart from = except for**, excepting, other than, excluding, besides, not including, aside from, but, save, bar, not counting • *The room was empty apart from one man seated beside the fire.*

apartment 1 = flat, room, suite, compartment, penthouse, duplex *(U.S. & Canad.)*, crib, bachelor apartment *(Canad.)* • *She has her own apartment and her own car.*
2 = rooms, quarters, chambers, accommodation, living quarters • *the private apartments of the Prince of Wales at St James's Palace*

apathetic = uninterested, passive, indifferent, sluggish, unmoved, stoic, stoical, unconcerned, listless, cold, cool, impassive, unresponsive, phlegmatic, unfeeling, unemotional, torpid, emotionless, insensible • *Many people feel apathetic about the candidates in both parties.*
OPPOSITES: moved, interested, concerned

apathy = lack of interest, indifference, inertia, coolness, passivity, coldness, stoicism, nonchalance, torpor, phlegm, sluggishness, listlessness, unconcern, insensibility, unresponsiveness, impassivity, passiveness, impassibility, unfeelingness, emotionlessness, uninterestedness • *the political apathy of young people these days*
OPPOSITES: feeling, interest, concern

ape AS A VERB = imitate, copy, mirror, echo, mock, parrot, mimic, parody, caricature, affect, counterfeit • *These films merely ape Hollywood.*
▸ **IN PHRASES: go ape = be furious**, storm, rage, rave, blow up *(informal)*, fume, be angry, lose it *(informal)*, fret, seethe, crack up *(informal)*, see red *(informal)*, chafe, lose the plot *(informal)*, go ballistic *(slang, chiefly U.S.)*, rant and rave, foam at the mouth, lose your temper, blow a fuse *(slang, chiefly U.S.)*, fly off the handle *(informal)*, be incandescent, go off the deep end *(informal)*, throw a fit *(informal)*, go up the wall *(slang)*, blow your top, lose your rag *(slang)*, be beside yourself, flip your lid *(slang)* • *When he found out, he went ape.*
▸ **COLLECTIVE NOUN:** shrewdness

aperture = opening, space, hole, crack, gap, rent, passage, breach, slot, vent, rift, slit, cleft, eye, chink, fissure, orifice, perforation, eyelet, interstice • *Through the aperture he could see daylight.*

apex 1 = culmination, top, crown, height, climax, highest point, zenith, apogee, acme • *At the apex of the party was the central committee.*
OPPOSITES: bottom, depths, nadir
2 = highest point, point, top, tip, summit, peak, crest, pinnacle, vertex • *She led me up a gloomy corridor to the apex of the pyramid.*
OPPOSITES: base, bottom, lowest point

aphorism = saying, maxim, gnome, adage, proverb, dictum, precept, axiom, apothegm, saw • *one of his favoured aphorisms*

aphrodisiac AS A NOUN = love potion, philtre • *Asparagus is reputed to be an aphrodisiac.*
▸ **AS AN ADJECTIVE = erotic** *or* **erotical**, exciting, stimulating, arousing, venereal • *plants with aphrodisiac qualities*

apiece = each, individually, separately, for each, to each, respectively, from each, severally • *He and I had two fish apiece.*
OPPOSITES: together, overall, all together

aplenty AS AN ADJECTIVE = in plenty, to spare, galore, in abundance, in quantity, in profusion, à gogo *(informal)* • *There were problems aplenty, and it was an uncomfortable evening.*
▸ **AS AN ADVERB = plentifully**, in abundance, abundantly, in quantity, in plenty, copiously, plenteously • *Wickets continued to fall aplenty.*

aplomb = self-possession, confidence, stability, self-confidence, composure, poise, coolness, calmness, equanimity, balance, self-assurance, sang-froid, level-headedness • *The cast executed the production with professional aplomb.*
OPPOSITES: confusion, embarrassment, self-consciousness

apocalypse = destruction, holocaust, havoc, devastation, carnage, conflagration, cataclysm • *We live in the shadow of the apocalypse.*

FOUR HORSEMEN OF THE APOCALYPSE

white – Christ	black – Famine
red – War	pale – Death

apocalyptic = disastrous, terrible, devastating, tragic, fatal, dreadful, destructive, harmful, dire, catastrophic, detrimental, calamitous, cataclysmic, unpropitious, cataclysmal • *He saw the news in apocalyptic terms.*

apocryphal = dubious, legendary, doubtful, questionable, mythical, spurious, fictitious, unsubstantiated, equivocal, unverified, unauthenticated, uncanonical • *This may well be an apocryphal story.*
OPPOSITES: true, authentic, factual

apogee = highest point, top, tip, crown, summit, height, peak, climax, crest, pinnacle, culmination, zenith, apex, acme, vertex • *The campaign reached its apogee in the 1970s*

apologetic = regretful, sorry, rueful, contrite, remorseful, penitent • *The hospital staff were very apologetic about the mistake.*

apologia = defence, case, argument, explanation, plea, apology, justification • *The left have seen the work as an apologia for privilege.*

apologist = defender, spokesman, champion, arguer, maintainer, supporter, advocate, pleader, vindicator, justifier • *the great Christian apologist Origen*

apologize = say sorry, express regret, ask forgiveness, make an apology, beg pardon, say you are sorry • *He apologized to those who had been affected.*

apology AS A NOUN = regret, explanation, excuse, confession, extenuation • *We received a letter of apology.*
▸ **IN PHRASES: apology for something** *or* **someone = mockery of**, excuse for, imitation of, caricature of, travesty of, poor substitute for • *What an apology for a leader!*

apoplectic = furious, mad, raging, boiling, fuming, frantic, frenzied, infuriated, incensed, enraged, livid *(informal)*, incandescent, beside yourself, tooshie *(Austral. slang)*, off the air *(Austral. slang)* • *My father was apoplectic when he discovered the truth.*

apoplexy 1 = fit, attack, heart attack, seizure, convulsion, paroxysm • *In 1685, Charles II died of apoplexy.*
2 = anger, rage, outrage, fury, indignation, ire, antagonism, exasperation, vexation • *He has caused apoplexy with his books on class and war.*

apostasy = desertion, defection, treachery, heresy, disloyalty, backsliding, perfidy, unfaithfulness, falseness, faithlessness, recreance *or* recreancy *(archaic)* • *a charge of apostasy*

apostate AS A NOUN = deserter, traitor, renegade, defector, heretic, turncoat, backslider, recreant *(archaic)* • *He was an early apostate, leaving the party last year.*
▸ **AS AN ADJECTIVE = disloyal**, false, untrue, treacherous, unfaithful, heretical, faithless, backsliding, perfidious, traitorous, recreant • *the writings of apostate reformers like Luther*

a

apostle 1 = **evangelist**, herald, missionary, preacher, messenger, proselytizer • *the twelve apostles*
2 = **supporter**, champion, advocate, pioneer, proponent, propagandist, propagator • *They present themselves as apostles of free trade.*
▹ *See panel* **Disciples of Jesus**

apotheosis = **deification**, elevation, exaltation, glorification, idealization, idolization • *This was the time of the star's apotheosis.*

appal = **horrify**, shock, alarm, frighten, scare, terrify, outrage, disgust, dishearten, revolt, intimidate, dismay, daunt, sicken, astound, harrow, unnerve, petrify, scandalize, make your hair stand on end *(informal)* • *She's starting to look like her mother, which appals me.*

appalled = **horrified**, shocked, stunned, alarmed, frightened, scared, terrified, outraged, dismayed, daunted, astounded, unnerved, disquieted, petrified, disheartened • *We are all appalled that these items are still on sale.*

appalling 1 = **horrifying**, shocking, terrible, alarming, frightening, scaring, awful, terrifying, horrible, grim, dreadful, intimidating, dismaying, horrific, fearful, daunting, dire, astounding, ghastly, hideous, shameful, harrowing, vile, unnerving, petrifying, horrid, unspeakable, frightful, nightmarish, abominable, disheartening, godawful *(slang)*, hellacious *(U.S. slang)* • *They have been living under the most appalling conditions.*
OPPOSITES: encouraging, comforting, reassuring
2 = **awful**, terrible, tremendous, distressing, horrible, dreadful, horrendous, ghastly, godawful *(slang)* • *I've got the most appalling headache.*

apparatus 1 = **organization**, system, network, structure, bureaucracy, hierarchy, setup *(informal)*, chain of command • *a massive bureaucratic apparatus*
2 = **equipment**, machine, tackle, gear, means, materials, device, tools, implements, mechanism, outfit, machinery, appliance, utensils, contraption *(informal)* • *He was rescued by firemen wearing breathing apparatus.*

apparel = **clothing**, dress, clothes, equipment, gear *(informal)*, habit, outfit, costume, threads *(slang)*, array *(poetic)*, garments, robes, trappings, attire, garb, accoutrements, vestments, raiment *(archaic or poetic)*, schmutter *(slang)*, habiliments • *Women's apparel is offered in petite, regular and tall sizes.*

apparent 1 = **seeming**, supposed, alleged, outward, exterior, superficial, ostensible, specious • *I was a bit depressed by our apparent lack of progress.*
OPPOSITES: real, true, actual
2 = **obvious**, marked, clear, plain, visible, bold, patent, evident, distinct, open, understandable, manifest, noticeable, blatant, conspicuous, overt, unmistakable, palpable, undeniable, discernible, salient, self-evident, indisputable, much in evidence, undisguised, unconcealed, indubitable, staring you in the face *(informal)*, plain as the nose on your face • *The presence of a star is already apparent in the early film.*
OPPOSITES: uncertain, obscure, unclear

apparently 1 = **seemingly**, outwardly, ostensibly, speciously • *The deterioration has been caused by an apparently endless recession.*
2 = **it appears that**, allegedly, it seems that, on the face of it, by all accounts, so the story goes, so I'm told • *Apparently the girls are not amused by the situation.*

apparition = **ghost**, spirit, shade *(literary)*, phantom, spectre, spook *(informal)*, wraith, chimera, revenant, visitant, eidolon, atua *(N.Z.)*, kehua *(N.Z.)* • *She recognized one of the women as the apparition she had seen.*

appeal AS A VERB = **plead**, call, ask, apply, refer, request, sue, lobby, pray, beg, petition, solicit, implore, beseech, entreat, importune, adjure, supplicate • *The UN has appealed for help from the international community.*
OPPOSITES: refuse, deny, reject
▸ AS A NOUN 1 = **plea**, call, application, request, prayer, petition, overture, invocation, solicitation, entreaty, supplication, suit, cry from the heart, adjuration • *The government issued a last-minute appeal to him to return.*
OPPOSITES: refusal, rejection, denial
2 = **attraction**, charm, fascination, charisma, beauty, attractiveness, allure, magnetism, enchantment, seductiveness, interestingness, engagingness, pleasingness • *It was meant to give the party greater public appeal.*
OPPOSITES: repulsiveness
3 = **retrial**, reconsideration • *She lost the case on appeal.*
▸ IN PHRASES: **appeal to someone** = **attract**, interest, draw, please, invite, engage, charm, fascinate, tempt, lure, entice, enchant, captivate, allure, bewitch • *The idea appealed to him.*

QUOTATIONS
appeal: in law, to put the dice into the box for another throw
[Ambrose Bierce *The Devil's Dictionary*]

appealing = **attractive**, inviting, engaging, charming, winning, desirable, endearing, alluring, winsome, prepossessing • *That's a very appealing idea.*
OPPOSITES: offensive, disgusting, repellent

appear 1 = **seem**, be clear, be obvious, be evident, look (like *or* as if), be apparent, be plain, be manifest, be patent • *It appears that some missiles have been moved.*
2 = **look (like** *or* **as if)**, seem, occur, look to be, come across as, strike you as • *She did her best to appear more confident than she felt.*
3 = **come into view**, emerge, occur, attend, surface, come out, turn out, arise, turn up, be present, loom, show *(informal)*, issue, develop, arrive, show up *(informal)*, come to light, crop up *(informal)*, materialize, come forth, come into sight, show your face • *A woman appeared at the far end of the street.*
OPPOSITES: disappear, vanish
4 = **come into being**, come out, be published, be developed, be created, be invented, become available, come into existence • *a poem which appeared in his last collection of verse*
5 = **perform**, play, act, enter, come on, take part, play a part, be exhibited, come onstage • *She appeared in several of his plays.*

appearance 1 = **look**, face, form, air, figure, image, looks, bearing, aspect, manner, expression, demeanour, mien *(literary)* • *He had the appearance of a college student.*
2 = **arrival**, appearing, presence, turning up, introduction, showing up *(informal)*, emergence, advent • *The sudden appearance of a few bags of rice could start a riot.*
3 = **occurrence**, development, emergence, manifestation • *the appearance of a number of cases of cholera*
4 = **impression**, air, front, image, illusion, guise, façade, pretence, veneer, semblance, outward show • *They gave the appearance of being on both sides.*

QUOTATIONS
Appearances are often deceiving
[Aesop *The Wolf in Sheep's Clothing*]
It is only shallow people who do not judge by appearances
[Oscar Wilde *The Picture of Dorian Gray*]

PROVERBS
You can't tell a book by its cover

appease 1 = **pacify**, satisfy, calm, soothe, quiet, placate, mollify, conciliate • *The offer has not appeased separatists.*
OPPOSITES: upset, anger, disturb
2 = **ease**, satisfy, calm, relieve, diminish, compose, quiet, blunt, soothe, subdue, lessen, alleviate, lull, quell, allay, mitigate, assuage, quench, tranquillize • *Cash is on hand to appease mounting frustration.*

appeasement 1 = **pacification**, compromise, accommodation, concession, conciliation, acceding,

propitiation, mollification, placation • *He denies there is a policy of appeasement*
2 = easing, relieving, satisfaction, softening, blunting, soothing, quieting, lessening, lulling, quelling, solace, quenching, mitigation, abatement, alleviation, assuagement, tranquillization • *the appeasement of terror*

appellation = name, term, style, title, address, description, designation, epithet, sobriquet • *They called him the King of Pork. He never minded the appellation.*

append = add, attach, join, hang, adjoin, fasten, annex, tag on, affix, tack on, subjoin • *His real name hadn't been appended to the manuscript.*
OPPOSITES: remove, separate, detach

appendage = attachment, addition, supplement, accessory, appendix, auxiliary, affix, ancillary, adjunct, annexe, addendum, appurtenance • *Upon marriage she became an appendage of her husband.*

appendix[1] = supplement, add-on, postscript, adjunct, appendage, addendum, addition, codicil • *Details of the investigation are set out in the appendix.*

appendix[2]
▸ RELATED ADJECTIVE: appendicular

appertain AS A VERB
▸ IN PHRASES: **appertain to something = relate to**, refer to, be part of, belong to, apply to, have to do with, be connected to, pertain to, be relevant to, be characteristic of, touch upon, bear upon, be pertinent to, inhere in, be proper to • *The book covers everything appertaining to the cinema.*

appetite 1 = hunger, taste, palate, voracity, the munchies *(slang)*, hungriness, ravenousness • *a slight fever, headache and loss of appetite*
2 = desire, liking, longing, demand, taste, passion, stomach, hunger, willingness, relish, craving, yearning, inclination, zeal, zest, propensity, hankering, proclivity, appetence, appetency • *our growing appetite for scandal*
OPPOSITES: disgust, dislike, distaste

QUOTATIONS
The appetite grows by eating
[François Rabelais *Gargantua*]

appetizer = hors d'oeuvre, titbit, antipasto, canapé • *Seafood soup is a good appetizer.*

appetizing = delicious, appealing, inviting, tempting, tasty, savoury, succulent, palatable, mouthwatering, scrumptious *(informal)*, yummo *(Austral. slang)* • *the appetizing smell of freshly baked bread*
OPPOSITES: distasteful, unsavoury, unpalatable

applaud 1 = clap, encourage, praise, cheer, hail, acclaim, laud, give it up for *(slang)*, give (someone) a big hand • *The audience laughed and applauded.*
OPPOSITES: pan *(informal)*, boo, hiss
2 = praise, celebrate, approve, acclaim, compliment, salute, commend, extol, crack up *(informal)*, big up *(slang, chiefly Caribbean)*, eulogize • *He should be applauded for his courage.*
OPPOSITES: blast, condemn, criticize

applause = ovation, praise, cheering, cheers, approval, acclaim, clapping, accolade, big hand, commendation, hand-clapping, approbation, acclamation, eulogizing, plaudit • *They greeted him with thunderous applause.*

apple IN PHRASES: **the apple of your eye = favourite**, pick, choice, dear, pet, darling, beloved, idol, fave *(informal)*, blue-eyed boy *(informal)* • *Her only son was the apple of her eye.*
▹ *See panel* **Apples**

appliance 1 = device, machine, tool, instrument, implement, mechanism, apparatus, gadget, waldo • *He could learn to use the washing machine and other household appliances.*
2 = application, use, practice, exercise, employment, discharge, implementation, accomplishment, fulfilment, exertion, utilization • *They were the result of the intellectual appliance of science.*

APPLES

biffin *(Brit.)*	Fuji	Prince Albert
Blenheim Orange	Golden Delicious	Red Delicious
Braeburn	Granny Smith	Red Ellison
bramley	Greensleeves	Rosemary
Charles Ross	Grenadier	Russet
codlin	Idared	Royal Gala
costard	James Grieve	russet
Cox's orange pippin	Jonathon	Spartan
crab apple	Jonagold	sturmer
Discovery	Laxton Superb	sunset
Egremont Russet	Lobo	sweeting
Elstar	Lord Lambourne	Worcester Pearmain
Empire	Pink Lady	
	pippin	

applicable = appropriate, fitting, fit, suited, useful, suitable, relevant, to the point, apt, pertinent, befitting, apposite, apropos, germane, to the purpose • *What is reasonable for one family is not applicable for another.*
OPPOSITES: wrong, irrelevant, inappropriate

applicant = candidate, entrant, claimant, suitor, petitioner, aspirant, inquirer, job-seeker, suppliant, postulant • *The successful applicant will have excellent interpersonal skills.*

application 1 = request, claim, demand, appeal, suit, inquiry, plea, petition, requisition, solicitation • *His application for membership was rejected.*
2 = relevance, use, value, practice, bearing, exercise, purpose, function, appropriateness, aptness, pertinence, appositeness, germaneness • *Students learned the practical application of the theory.*
3 = effort, work, study, industry, labour, trouble, attention, struggle, pains, commitment, hard work, endeavour, dedication, toil, diligence, perseverance, travail *(literary)*, attentiveness, assiduity, blood, sweat, and tears *(informal)* • *his immense talent and unremitting application*
4 = utilization, use, practice, exercise, employment, discharge, implementation, appliance, accomplishment, fulfilment, exertion • *With repeated application of the product, the weeds were overcome.*
5 = program, package, software • *applications that can convert a TV screen into an internet terminal*

apply AS A VERB **1 = request**, seek, appeal, put in, petition, inquire, solicit, claim, sue, requisition, make application • *I am continuing to apply for jobs.*
2 = be relevant, concern, relate, refer, be fitting, be appropriate, be significant, fit, suit, pertain, be applicable, bear upon, appertain • *The rule applies where a person owns stock in a company.*
3 = use, exercise, carry out, employ, engage, implement, practise, execute, assign, administer, exert, enact, utilize, bring to bear, put to use, bring into play • *The government appears to be applying the same principle.*
4 = put on, work in, cover with, lay on, paint on, anoint, spread on, rub in, smear on, shampoo in, bring into contact with • *Applying the dye can be messy, particularly on long hair.*
5 = exert, place, put on • *Apply direct pressure to the wound.*
▸ IN PHRASES: **apply yourself = work hard**, concentrate, study, pay attention, try, commit yourself, buckle down *(informal)*, be assiduous, devote yourself, be diligent, dedicate yourself, make an effort, address yourself, be industrious, persevere • *If you apply yourself, there's no reason why you shouldn't pass.*

appoint 1 = assign, name, choose, commission, select, elect, install, delegate, nominate • *It made sense to appoint a banker to this job.*

OPPOSITES: fire, dismiss, sack *(informal)*
2 = **decide**, set, choose, establish, determine, settle, fix, arrange, specify, assign, designate, allot • *We met at the time appointed.*
OPPOSITES: cancel

a

appointed 1 = **decided**, set, chosen, established, determined, settled, fixed, arranged, assigned, designated, allotted • *The appointed hour for the ceremony was drawing near.*
2 = **assigned**, named, chosen, commissioned, selected, elected, installed, delegated, nominated • *The recently appointed captain led by example in the first game.*
3 = **equipped**, provided, supplied, furnished, fitted out • *beautiful, well-appointed houses*

appointment 1 = **selection**, naming, election, choosing, choice, commissioning, delegation, nomination, installation, assignment, allotment, designation • *his appointment as foreign minister in 1985*
2 = **job**, office, position, post, situation, place, station, employment, assignment, berth *(informal)* • *He is to take up an appointment as a researcher with the Society.*
3 = **meeting**, interview, date, session, arrangement, consultation, engagement, fixture, rendezvous, tryst *(archaic)*, assignation • *She has an appointment with her accountant.*
4 = **appointee**, candidate, representative, delegate, nominee, office-holder • *He is the new appointment at RSA.*

apportion = **divide**, share, deal, distribute, assign, allocate, dispense, give out, allot, mete out, dole out, measure out, parcel out, ration out • *They are even-handed in apportioning the blame.*

apportionment = **division**, sharing, distribution, assignment, allocation, dispensing, allotment, meting out, doling out, dealing out, measuring out, parcelling out, rationing out • *the apportionment of resources*

apposite = **appropriate**, fitting, suited, suitable, relevant, proper, to the point, apt, applicable, pertinent, befitting, apropos, germane, to the purpose, appertaining • *Recent events have made his central theme even more apposite.*
OPPOSITES: irrelevant, inappropriate, unsuitable

appraisal 1 = **assessment**, opinion, estimate, judgment, evaluation, estimation, sizing up *(informal)*, recce *(slang)* • *Self-appraisal is never easy.*
2 = **valuation**, pricing, rating, survey, reckoning, assay • *He has resisted being drawn into the business of cost appraisal.*

appraise = **assess**, judge, review, estimate, survey, price, rate, value, evaluate, inspect, gauge, size up *(informal)*, eye up, assay, recce *(slang)* • *Many companies were prompted to appraise their recruitment policies.*

appreciable = **significant**, marked, obvious, considerable, substantial, visible, evident, pronounced, definite, noticeable, clear-cut, discernible, measurable, material, recognizable, detectable, perceptible, distinguishable, ascertainable, perceivable • *This has not had an appreciable effect on production.*
OPPOSITES: small, minute, insignificant

appreciably = **significantly**, obviously, definitely, considerably, substantially, evidently, visibly, markedly, noticeably, palpably, perceptively, measurably, recognizably, discernibly, detectably, distinguishably, perceivably, ascertainably • *Travel had not mellowed him appreciably.*

appreciate 1 = **enjoy**, like, value, regard, respect, prize, admire, treasure, esteem, relish, cherish, savour, rate highly • *Anyone can appreciate our music.*
OPPOSITES: scorn, disdain, denigrate
2 = **be aware of**, know, understand, estimate, realize, acknowledge, recognize, perceive, comprehend, take account of, be sensitive to, be conscious of, sympathize with, be alive to, be cognizant of • *She never really appreciated the depth of the conflict.*
OPPOSITES: misunderstand, be unaware of, underrate
3 = **be grateful for**, be obliged for, be thankful for, give thanks for, be indebted for, be in debt for, be appreciative of • *I'd appreciate it if you didn't mention that.*
OPPOSITES: be ungrateful for
4 = **increase**, rise, grow, gain, improve, mount, enhance, soar, inflate • *There is little confidence that houses will appreciate in value.*
OPPOSITES: fall, deflate, depreciate

appreciation 1 = **admiration**, liking, respect, assessment, esteem, relish, valuation, enjoyment, appraisal, estimation, responsiveness • *He whistled in appreciation.*
2 = **gratitude**, thanks, recognition, obligation, acknowledgment, indebtedness, thankfulness, gratefulness • *the gifts presented to them in appreciation of their work*
OPPOSITES: ingratitude
3 = **awareness**, understanding, regard, knowledge, recognition, perception, sympathy, consciousness, sensitivity, realization, comprehension, familiarity, mindfulness, cognizance • *They have a strong appreciation of the importance of economic incentives.*
OPPOSITES: ignorance, incomprehension
4 = **increase**, rise, gain, growth, inflation, improvement, escalation, enhancement • *You have to take capital appreciation of the property into account.*
OPPOSITES: fall, decline, devaluation
5 = **review**, report, notice, analysis, criticism, praise, assessment, recognition, tribute, evaluation, critique, acclamation • *I had written an appreciation of his work for a magazine.*

appreciative 1 = **enthusiastic**, understanding, pleased, aware, sensitive, conscious, admiring, sympathetic, supportive, responsive, knowledgeable, respectful, mindful, perceptive, in the know *(informal)*, cognizant, regardful • *There is a murmur of appreciative laughter.*
2 = **grateful**, obliged, thankful, indebted, beholden • *We are very appreciative of their support.*

apprehend 1 = **arrest**, catch, lift *(slang)*, nick *(slang, chiefly Brit.)*, capture, seize, run in *(slang)*, take, nail *(informal)*, bust *(informal)*, collar *(informal)*, pinch *(informal)*, nab *(informal)*, take prisoner, feel your collar *(slang)* • *Police have not apprehended her killer.*
OPPOSITES: free, release, discharge
2 = **understand**, know, think, believe, imagine, realize, recognize, appreciate, perceive, grasp, conceive, comprehend, get the message, get the picture • *Only now can I begin to apprehend the power of these forces.*
OPPOSITES: miss, misunderstand, be unaware of

apprehension 1 = **anxiety**, concern, fear, worry, doubt, alarm, suspicion, dread, unease, mistrust, misgiving, disquiet, premonition, trepidation, foreboding, uneasiness, pins and needles, apprehensiveness • *It reflects real anger and apprehension about the future.*
OPPOSITES: confidence, assurance, composure
2 = **arrest**, catching, capture, taking, seizure • *information leading to the apprehension of the alleged killer*
OPPOSITES: release, liberation, discharge
3 = **awareness**, understanding, knowledge, intelligence, ken, perception, grasp, comprehension • *the sudden apprehension of something*
OPPOSITES: incomprehension

apprehensive = **anxious**, concerned, worried, afraid, alarmed, nervous, suspicious, doubtful, uneasy, fearful, neurotic, disquieted, foreboding, twitchy *(informal)*, mistrustful, antsy *(informal)* • *People are still terribly apprehensive about the future.*
OPPOSITES: confident, assured, composed

apprentice = **trainee**, student, pupil, novice, beginner, learner, neophyte, tyro, probationer • *I started off as an apprentice and worked my way up.*
OPPOSITES: expert, master, pro

apprenticeship = **traineeship**, probation, studentship, novitiate *or* noviciate • *He served an apprenticeship as a toolmaker.*

apprise = **make aware**, tell, warn, advise, inform, communicate, notify, enlighten, acquaint, give notice, make cognizant • *Have the customers been fully apprised of the advantages?*

approach AS A VERB 1 = **move towards**, come to, reach, near, advance, catch up, meet, come close, gain on, converge on, come near, push forward, draw near, creep up on • *When I approached they fell silent.*
2 = **make a proposal to**, speak to, apply to, appeal to, proposition, solicit, sound out, make overtures to, make advances to, broach the matter with • *When he approached me about the job, my first reaction was disbelief.*
3 = **set about**, tackle, undertake, embark on, get down to, launch into, begin work on, commence on, make a start on, enter upon • *The bank has approached the issue in a practical way.*
4 = **approximate**, touch, be like, compare with, resemble, come close to, border on, verge on, be comparable to, come near to • *They race at speeds approaching 200mph.*
▸ AS A NOUN 1 = **advance**, coming, nearing, appearance, arrival, advent, drawing near • *At their approach the little boy ran away and hid.*
2 = **access**, way, drive, road, passage, entrance, avenue, passageway • *The path serves as an approach to the boat house.*
3 *often plural* = **proposal**, offer, appeal, advance, application, invitation, proposition, overture • *There had already been approaches from interested buyers.*
4 = **way**, means, course, style, attitude, method, technique, manner, procedure, mode, modus operandi • *We will be exploring different approaches to information-gathering.*
5 = **approximation**, likeness, semblance • *the nearest approach to an apology we have so far heard*

approachable 1 = **friendly**, open, cordial, sociable, affable, congenial • *We found him very approachable and easy to talk to.*
OPPOSITES: reserved, cool, unfriendly
2 = **accessible**, attainable, reachable, get-at-able *(informal)*, come-at-able *(informal)* • *It is approachable on foot for only a few hours a day.*
OPPOSITES: remote, out-of-the-way, inaccessible

approbation = **approval**, support, favour, praise, sanction, recognition, acceptance, acclaim, encouragement, applause, endorsement, ratification, assent, congratulation, commendation • *The result has not met with universal approbation.*
OPPOSITES: blame, dislike, condemnation

appropriate AS AN ADJECTIVE = **suitable**, right, fitting, fit, suited, correct, belonging, relevant, proper, to the point, in keeping, apt, applicable, pertinent, befitting, well-suited, well-timed, apposite, apropos, opportune, becoming, seemly, felicitous, germane, to the purpose, appurtenant, congruous • *It is appropriate that Irish names dominate the list.*
OPPOSITES: irrelevant, inappropriate, unsuitable
▸ AS A VERB 1 = **seize**, take, claim, assume, take over, acquire, confiscate, annex, usurp, impound, pre-empt, commandeer, take possession of, expropriate, arrogate • *Several other newspapers have appropriated the idea.*
OPPOSITES: give, relinquish, cede
2 = **allocate**, allow, budget, devote, assign, designate, set aside, earmark, allot, share out, apportion • *He is sceptical that Congress will appropriate more money for this.*
OPPOSITES: withhold
3 = **steal**, take, nick *(slang, chiefly Brit.)*, pocket, trouser *(slang)*, pinch *(informal)*, pirate, poach, swipe *(slang)*, lift *(informal)*, knock off *(slang)*, heist *(U.S. slang)*, embezzle, blag *(slang)*, pilfer, misappropriate, snitch *(slang)*, purloin, filch, plagiarize, thieve, peculate • *What do they think about your appropriating their music and culture?*

appropriateness = **suitability**, fitness, relevance, correctness, felicity, rightness, applicability, timeliness, aptness, pertinence, fittingness, seemliness, appositeness, properness, germaneness, opportuneness, becomingness, congruousness, felicitousness, well-suitedness • *He wonders about the appropriateness of every move he makes.*

appropriation 1 = **setting aside**, assignment, allocation, earmarking, allotment, apportionment • *The government raised defence appropriations by 12 per cent.*
2 = **seizure**, taking, takeover, assumption, annexation, confiscation, commandeering, expropriation, pre-emption, usurpation, impoundment, arrogation • *fraud and illegal appropriation of land*

approval 1 = **consent**, agreement, sanction, licence, blessing, permission, recommendation, concession, confirmation, mandate, endorsement, leave, compliance, the go-ahead *(informal)*, countenance, ratification, the green light, assent, authorization, validation, acquiescence, imprimatur, concurrence, O.K. *or* okay *(informal)* • *The proposed modifications met with widespread approval.*
2 = **favour**, liking, regard, respect, praise, esteem, acclaim, appreciation, encouragement, admiration, applause, commendation, approbation, good opinion • *an obsessive drive to win his father's approval*
OPPOSITES: dislike, dissatisfaction, disapproval

approve AS A VERB = **agree to**, second, allow, pass, accept, confirm, recommend, permit, sanction, advocate, bless, endorse, uphold, mandate, authorize, ratify, go along with, subscribe to, consent to, buy into *(informal)*, validate, countenance, rubber stamp, accede to, give the go-ahead to *(informal)*, give the green light to, assent to, concur in, greenlight, O.K. *or* okay *(informal)* • *MPs approved the bill by a majority of 97.*
OPPOSITES: veto, disallow, discountenance
▸ IN PHRASES: **approve of something** *or* **someone** = **favour**, like, support, respect, praise, appreciate, agree with, admire, endorse, esteem, acclaim, applaud, commend, be pleased with, big up *(slang, chiefly Caribbean)*, have a good opinion of, regard highly, think highly of • *Not everyone approves of the festival.*

approved = **accepted**, received, agreed, common, standard, established, traditional, confirmed, normal, regular, usual, acknowledged, recognized, sanctioned, conventional, universal, authorized, customary, agreed upon, time-honoured • *The approved method of cleaning is industrial sand-blasting.*

approving = **favourable**, admiring, applauding, respectful, appreciative, commendatory, acclamatory • *an approving nod*

approximate AS AN ADJECTIVE = **rough**, close, general, near, estimated, loose, vague, hazy, sketchy, amorphous, imprecise, inexact, almost exact, almost accurate • *The times are approximate only.*
OPPOSITES: specific, correct, exact
▸ IN PHRASES: **approximate to** = **resemble**, reach, approach, touch, come close to, border on, come near, verge on • *Something approximating a just outcome will be ensured.*

approximately = **almost**, about, around, generally, nearly, close to, relatively, roughly, loosely, just about, more or less, in the region of, in the vicinity of, not far off, in the neighbourhood of • *Approximately $150,000 will be spent on improvements.*

approximation 1 = **likeness**, approach, correspondence, resemblance, semblance • *That's a fair approximation of the way the next boss will be chosen.*
2 = **guess**, estimate, conjecture, estimation, guesswork, rough idea, rough calculation, ballpark figure *(informal)*, ballpark estimate *(informal)* • *That's an approximation, but my guess is there'll be a reasonable balance.*

a priori AS AN ADJECTIVE = **deduced**, deductive, inferential • *There is no a priori hypothesis to work with.*
▸ AS AN ADVERB = **theoretically**, in theory • *One assumes, a priori, that a parent would be better at dealing with problems.*

apron = **pinny**, overall, pinafore *(informal)* • *She put on an apron and rolled up her sleeves.*

apropos AS AN ADJECTIVE = **appropriate**, right, seemly, fitting, fit, related, correct, belonging, suitable, relevant, proper, to the point, apt, applicable, pertinent, befitting, apposite, opportune, germane, to the purpose • *It was a verse from the book of Job. Very apropos.*
▸ IN PHRASES: **apropos of** = **concerning**, about, re, regarding, respecting, on the subject of, in respect of, as to, with reference to, in re, in the matter of, as regards, in *or* with regard to • *Apropos of the party, have you had any further thoughts on a venue?*
apropos of nothing = **arbitrarily**, randomly, for no reason, irrelevantly • *Suddenly, apropos of nothing, he said, 'You're such an optimist.'*

apt 1 = **appropriate**, timely, right, seemly, fitting, fit, related, correct, belonging, suitable, relevant, proper, to the point, applicable, pertinent, befitting, apposite, apropos, opportune, germane, to the purpose • *The words of this report are as apt today as they were in 1929.*
OPPOSITES: irrelevant, inappropriate, unsuitable
2 = **inclined**, likely, ready, disposed, prone, liable, given, predisposed, of a mind • *She was apt to raise her voice and wave her hands about.*
3 = **gifted**, skilled, expert, quick, bright, talented, sharp, capable, smart, prompt, clever, intelligent, accomplished, tasty *(Brit. informal)*, ingenious, skilful, astute, adroit, teachable • *She was never a very apt student.*
OPPOSITES: slow, stupid, dull

aptitude = **gift**, ability, talent, capacity, intelligence, leaning, bent, tendency, faculty, capability, flair, inclination, disposition, knack, propensity, proficiency, predilection, cleverness, proclivity, quickness, giftedness, proneness, aptness • *He discovered an aptitude for working in accounts.*

aquatic = **sea**, water, ocean, marine, maritime, oceanic, saltwater, ocean-going, seagoing, pelagic, briny • *aquatic plants and fish*

aqueduct = **conduit**, channel, passage, canal, waterway, duct, sluice • *an old Roman aqueduct*

arable = **productive**, fertile, fruitful, fecund, cultivable, farmable, ploughable, tillable • *arable farmland*

arachnid
▹ *See panel* **Spiders and other arachnids**

arbiter 1 = **judge**, referee, umpire, umpie *(Austral. slang)*, arbitrator, adjudicator • *the court's role as arbiter in the law-making process*
2 = **authority**, expert, master, governor, ruler, dictator, controller, lord, pundit • *Sequins have often aroused the scorn of arbiters of taste.*

arbitrary 1 = **random**, chance, optional, subjective, unreasonable, inconsistent, erratic, discretionary, personal, fanciful, wilful, whimsical, capricious • *Arbitrary arrests were common.*
OPPOSITES: reasoned, sound, logical
2 = **dictatorial**, absolute, unlimited, uncontrolled, autocratic, dogmatic, imperious, domineering, unrestrained, overbearing, tyrannical, summary, magisterial, despotic, high-handed, peremptory, tyrannous • *the virtually unlimited arbitrary power of slave owners*

arbitrate = **decide**, judge, determine, settle, referee, umpire, mediate, adjudicate, adjudge, pass judgment, sit in judgment • *He arbitrates between investors and members of the association.*

arbitration = **decision**, settlement, judgment, determination, adjudication, arbitrament • *The matter is likely to go to arbitration.*

arbitrator = **judge**, referee, umpire, umpie *(Austral. slang)*, arbiter, adjudicator • *He served as an arbitrator in a series of commercial disputes in India.*

arbour = **alcove**, corner, bay, shelter, retreat, niche, bower, compartment, recess, cubicle, nook, grotto, gazebo, cubbyhole • *The plan is to make an arbour of kiwi fruit vines.*

arc = **curve**, bend, bow, arch, crescent, half-moon • *The 71 offices are spread out in an arc around London.*

arcade 1 = **gallery**, mall, cloister, portico, colonnade, covered walk, peristyle • *mansions with vaulted roofs and arcades*
2 = **complex**, centre, precinct • *a shopping arcade*

arcane = **mysterious**, secret, hidden, esoteric, occult, recondite, cabbalistic • *the arcane world of contemporary music*

arch[1] AS A NOUN 1 = **archway**, curve, dome, span, vault • *The theatre is located under old railway arches in the East End.*
2 = **curve**, bend, bow, crook, arc, hunch, sweep, hump, curvature, semicircle • *Train the cane supports to form an arch.*
▸ AS A VERB = **curve**, bridge, bend, bow, span, arc • *the domed ceiling arching overhead*

TYPES OF ARCH

acute, gothic, lancet, pointed arch, *or* ogive	keel arch	proscenium arch
horseshoe arch	Norman *or* Roman arch	Roman arch
	gee arch	skew arch
		triumphal arch

arch[2] = **playful**, joking, teasing, humorous, sly, mischievous, saucy, tongue-in-cheek, jesting, jokey, pert, good-natured, roguish, frolicsome, waggish • *a slightly amused, arch expression*

arch- = **chief**, first, highest, greatest, lead, leading, head, top, major, main, prime, central, key, grand, expert, master, premier, primary, supreme, principal, superior, accomplished, paramount, big-time *(informal)*, foremost, consummate, predominant, pre-eminent • *his arch enemy*

archaeology = **prehistory**, protohistory • *She is keen on anything to do with history and archaeology.*
▹ *See panel* **Archaeology**

archaic 1 = **old**, ancient, antique, primitive, bygone, olden *(archaic)* • *archaic sculpture and porcelain*
OPPOSITES: new, present, modern
2 = **old-fashioned**, obsolete, out of date, antiquated, outmoded, passé, old hat, behind the times, superannuated • *These archaic practices are advocated by people of limited outlook.*
OPPOSITES: new, latest, up-to-date

arched = **curved**, domed, vaulted • *an arched roof*

archer = **bowman** *(archaic)*, toxophilite *(formal)* • *infantry, archers and cavalrymen*

archetypal *or* **archetypical** = **typical**, standard, model, original, normal, classic, ideal, exemplary, paradigmatic, prototypal, prototypic *or* prototypical • *Cricket is the archetypal English game.*

archetype = **prime example**, standard, model, original, pattern, classic, ideal, norm, form, prototype, paradigm, exemplar • *He is the archetype of the successful businessman.*

architect 1 = **designer**, planner, draughtsman, master builder • *Employ an architect to make sure the plans comply with regulations.*
2 = **creator**, father, shaper, engineer, author, maker, designer, founder, deviser, planner, inventor, contriver, originator, prime mover, instigator, initiator • *the country's chief architect of economic reform*

ARCHAEOLOGY

ARCHAEOLOGICAL PERIODS

Acheulean *or* Acheulian
Asturian
Aurignacian
Azilian
Bronze Age
chalcolithic
Châtelperronian
Eneolithic
Gravettian
Helladic
Ice age
Iron Age
La Tène
Levalloisian *or* Levallois
Magdalenian
Mesolithic
Minoan
Mousterian
Mycenaean
Neo-Babylonian
Neolithic *or* New Stone Age
Old Babylonian
Palaeolithic *or* Old Stone Age
Solutrean

ARCHAEOLOGICAL TERMS

acropolis
alignment
arcade
archaeomagnetism *or* archeomagnetism
barrow
baulk
bifacial
blade
bogman
bracteate
burin
cairn
callais
cartouch *or* cartouche
caveman
celt
cirque
cist *or* kist
clovis point
core
cromlech
cross-dating
dolmen
earthwork
eolith
flake
flint
graffito
henge
hillfort
hogback
hut circle
larnax
ley line
microlith
megalith
mound
neolith
obelisk
palmette
palstave
patella
pylon
radiocarbon dating
retouch
robber trench
sondage
souterrain
stela *or* stele
stone circle
stratigraphy
tribrach
tumulus
vallum

QUOTATIONS

architect: one who drafts a plan of your house, and plans a draft of your money
[Ambrose Bierce *The Devil's Dictionary*]

architecture 1 = **design**, planning, building, construction, architectonics • *He studied architecture and design at college.*
2 = **construction**, design, style • *a fine example of Moroccan architecture*
3 = **structure**, design, shape, make-up, construction, framework, layout, anatomy • *the architecture of muscle fibres*
▷ *See panels* **Architecture; Types of arch**

QUOTATIONS

Architecture in general is frozen music
[Friedrich von Schelling *Philosophie der Kunst*]
Architecture is the art of how to waste space
[Philip Johnson *New York Times*]
Architecture, of all the arts, is the one which acts the most slowly, but the most surely, on the soul
[Ernest Dimnet *What We Live By*]

archive AS A NOUN = **record office**, museum, registry, repository • *I decided I would go to the archive and look up the issue.*
▸ AS A PLURAL NOUN = **records**, papers, accounts, rolls, documents, files, registers, deeds, chronicles, annals • *the archives of the Imperial War Museum*

arctic = **freezing**, cold, frozen, icy, chilly, frosty, glacial, frigid, gelid, frost-bound, cold as ice • *The bathroom is positively arctic.*

Arctic = **polar**, far-northern, hyperborean • *Arctic ice*

ardent 1 = **enthusiastic**, keen, eager, avid, zealous, keen as mustard • *an ardent opponent of the war*
OPPOSITES: indifferent, lukewarm, apathetic
2 = **passionate**, warm, spirited, intense, flaming, fierce, fiery, hot, fervent, impassioned, ablaze, lusty, vehement, amorous, hot-blooded, warm-blooded, fervid • *an ardent lover*
OPPOSITES: cold, cool, frigid

ardour 1 = **passion**, feeling, fire, heat, spirit, intensity, warmth, devotion, fervour, vehemence, fierceness • *The sexual ardour had cooled.*
2 = **enthusiasm**, zeal, eagerness, earnestness, keenness, avidity • *my ardour for football*

arduous = **difficult**, trying, hard, tough, tiring, severe, painful, exhausting, punishing, harsh, taxing, heavy, steep, formidable, fatiguing, rigorous, troublesome, gruelling, strenuous, onerous, laborious, burdensome, backbreaking, toilsome • *The task was more arduous than he had calculated.*
OPPOSITES: light, easy, simple

area 1 = **region**, land, quarter, division, sector, district, stretch, territory, zone, plot, province, patch, neighbourhood, sphere, turf *(U.S. slang)*, realm, domain, tract, locality, neck of the woods *(informal)* • *the large number of community groups in the area*
2 = **part**, section, sector, portion • *You will notice that your baby has two soft areas on its head.*
3 = **range**, reach, size, sweep, extent, scope, sphere, domain, width, compass, breadth, parameters *(informal)*, latitude, expanse, radius, ambit • *Although large in area, the flat did not have many rooms.*
4 = **realm**, part, department, field, province, arena, sphere, domain • *She wanted to be involved in every area of my life.*

arena 1 = **ring**, ground, stage, field, theatre, bowl, pitch, stadium, enclosure, park *(U.S. & Canad.)*, coliseum, amphitheatre • *the largest indoor sports arena in the world*
2 = **scene**, world, area, stage, field, theatre, sector, territory, province, forum, scope, sphere, realm, domain • *He has no intention of withdrawing from the political arena.*

argot = **jargon**, slang, dialect, idiom, vernacular, patter, parlance, cant, lingo *(informal)*, patois • *the argot of the university campus*

arguable 1 = **tenable**, reasonable, rational, viable, plausible, believable, justifiable, defensible, defendable, maintainable • *It was arguable that this was not as grave as it might seem.*
2 = **questionable**, controversial, uncertain, suspicious, doubtful, suspect, dubious, dodgy *(Brit., Austral. & N.Z. informal)*, unreliable, debatable, paradoxical, unproven, fishy *(informal)*, moot, iffy *(informal)*, equivocal, problematical, disputable, controvertible, dubitable • *It is arguable whether he ever had much control.*

arguably = **possibly**, potentially, conceivably, plausibly, feasibly, questionably, debatably, deniably, disputably, contestably, controvertibly, dubitably, refutably • *They are arguably the most successful band of the decade.*

argue AS A VERB 1 = **quarrel**, fight, row, clash, dispute, disagree, feud, squabble, spar, wrangle, bicker, have an argument, cross swords, be at sixes and sevens, fight like cat and dog, go at it hammer and tongs, bandy words, altercate • *They were still arguing. I could hear them down the road.*
2 = **discuss**, debate, dispute, thrash out, exchange views on, controvert • *The two of them were arguing this point.*

ARCHITECTURE

Architectural styles

Art Deco
Art Nouveau
Baroque
Bauhaus
brutalist
Byzantine
churrigueresque *or* churrigueresco
classical
colonial
Composite
Corinthian
Decorated
Doric
Early Christian
Early English
Edwardian
Elizabethan
Empire
Federation (*Austral.*)
functionalism
Georgian
Gothic
Gothic Revival
Greek Revival
International Style *or* Modernist
Ionic
Jacobean
Louis Quatorze
Louis Quinze
Louis Seize
Louis Treize
Mannerist
moderne
Moorish *or* Morisco
Mudéjar
neoclassicist
new brutalist
Norman
Palladian
perpendicular
postmodernist
Queen-Anne
Regency
Renaissance
Rococo
Roman
Romanesque
Saracen
Saxon
transition *or* transitional
Tudor
Tuscan
Victorian

Architectural terms

abutment *or* abuttal
architectonic
architectonics
architectural
astylar
bolster
bracket
castellated *or* castled
cinquecento
cloistered
colossal *or* giant
composite
cradling
crenellate *or* (*U.S.*) crenelate
denticulate
diastyle
diminish
dipteral
discharge
drum
elevation
engaged
eurhythmy
fenestrated
filler
flamboyant
floor plan
floriated *or* floreated
florid
fluted
foliated
foliation
galilee
galleria
ground plan
hexastyle
high-pitched
hip
hipped
hypostyle
imbricate *or* imbricated
intercolumniation
invert
joggle post *or* king post
lanceted
lierne
lintel *or* summer
listed
loggia
member
module
Moresque
naos
order
orientation
polychromy
postiche
profile
prostyle
pulvinate *or* pulvinated
queen post
rampant
rendering
respond
return
rhythm
ribbon development
rise
rusticate
sexpartite
shaft
shafting
shell
soffit
springing, spring, springing line, *or* springing point
stilted
storey
stria
stringer, string, *or* string course
stylobate
subbase
summer *or* summer tree
supercolumnar
surbase
tailpiece *or* tail beam
trabeate *or* trabeated
tympanic
underpitch vault

Architectural features

abacus
acanthus
accolade
acroter
aisle
ambulatory
amphiprostyle
amphistylar
ancon *or* ancone
annulet
anta
antefix
anthemion
apophyge *or* hypophyge
apse *or* apsis
apteral
arcade
arcature
arch
architrave
archivolt
arcuation
arris
articulation
astragal
atlas (*plural* atlantes) *or* telamon
atrium
attic
baguette *or* baguet
balcony
baldachin
balk
ballflower
baluster
band
banderole, banderol, *or* bannerol
barge couple
barge course
barrel vault, tunnel vault, *or* wagon vault
base
basement
bay window
bead
beak
bed moulding
belfry
bezant, bezzant, *or* byzant
billet
binder
bolection *or* bilection
bottom house
bow
bow window
bracket
brattishing
breast
broach
buttress
caisson, coffer, *or* lacuna
calotte
canopy
cantilever
capital, chapiter, *or* cap
cartouche
caryatid
case *or* casing
casement
Catherine wheel
cavetto
ceiling
cella *or* naos
cellar
channel
chaplet
cheek
chevron *or* dancette
choir
choir loft
cinquefoil
clerestory
cloister
colonnade
columbarium
column
columniation
compass window
concha *or* conch
congé
corbeil *or* corbeille
corbel *or* truss
corbie gable
corbie-step, corbel step, *or* crow step
cordon, string course, belt course, *or* table
cornice
corona
cove *or* coving
crenel *or* crenelle
cresting
crocket *or* crochet
crossing
crown
cullis
cupola
curb roof
curtail step
curtain wall
cushion
cusp
cuspidation
cyma
cymatium
dado
decastyle
dentil
die
dogtooth
drip
dripstone, label, *or* hood mould
echinus
ectype
egg and dart, egg and tongue, *or* egg and anchor
ell
embrasure
entablature
entasis
exedra
extrados
facade
facet
fan
fanlight
fantail
fan tracery

a

Architectural features (continued)

fan *or* palm vaulting
fascia *or* facia
fascial *or* facial
fenestella
fenestra
festoon
fillet *or* listel
finial
flèche
fluting
flying buttress *or* arc-boutant
foil
footing
footstall
French windows *or* doors
frieze
frontispiece
frustum
gable
gable end
gable window
gadroon *or* godroon
gallery
gambrel
gargoyle
garret
garth
gatehouse
gazebo
glyph
gradin
griffe
groin
grotto
gutta
half landing
haunch *or* hance
headstone
headwork
helicline
hipped *or* hip roof
imperial
impost
intrados
jube
keystone, quoin, *or* headstone
lancet arch, Gothic arch, *or* ogive
lancet window
landing
lantern
leaded
loggia
long-and-short work
louvre
lucarne
machicolation
mansard
meander
medallion
metope
minaret
modillion
moulding
mullion
mutule
narthex
neck
necking *or* gorgerin
newel
niche
Norman arch *or* Roman arch
obelisk
oeil-de-boeuf
offset
ogee, ogee arch, *or* talon
ogive
onion dome
oriel *or* oriel window
ovolo, quarter round, *or* thumb
pace
parapet
patio
pedestal
pediment
pendant
penthouse
peristyle
perpend
perron
piazza
pier
pillar
pinnacle
platform
plinth
podium
predella
pylon
quad
poppyhead
porch *or* portico
portal
porte-cochere
postern
propylaeum
quadrangle
quatrefoil
quirk
quoin, coign, *or* coigne
reed
reeding
reglet
relief
respond
return
reveal
rib
ridge
rose window, rosace, *or* rosette
rotunda
roundel
saddle roof *or* saddleback
sash window
scotia
screen
scrollwork
semidome
shaft
shafting
sill
skew arch
skylight
soffit
spandrel *or* spandril
spire
splay
springer
squinch
squint *or* hagioscope
steeple
stele *or* stela
stoa
straining piece
strap work
stria
strigil
stylobate *or* stereobate
summer
taenia *or* (*U.S.*) tenia
tambour
tellamon
term, terminal, *or* terminus
torus *or* tore
tracery
transept
traverse
trefoil
tribune
triforium
triglyph
trophy
trumeau
turret
tympanum *or* tympan
underpitch vault
vault
veranda *or* verandah
verge
vignette
volute *or* helix
water table
web
whispering gallery
xyst

Architects

Alvar Aalto (*Finnish*)
(Leslie) Patrick Abercrombie (*English*)
James Adam (*Scottish*)
Robert Adam (*Scottish*)
William Adam (*Scottish*)
Leon Battista Alberti (*Italian*)
Anthemias of Tralles (*Greek*)
Arnolfo di Cambio (*Italian*)
Erik Gunnar Asplund (*Swedish*)
Herbert Baker (*English*)
Charles Barry (*English*)
Frédéric August Bartholdi (*French*)
Peter Behrens (*German*)
Hendrick Petrus Berlage (*Dutch*)
Gian Lorenzo Bernini (*Italian*)
Francesco Borromini (*Italian*)
Etienne-Louis Boulle (*French*)
Donato Bramante (*Italian*)
Marcel Lajos Breuer (*Hungarian-U.S.*)
Salomon de Brosse (*French*)
Filippo Brunelleschi (*Italian*)
David Bryce (*Scottish*)
David Hudson Burnham (*U.S.*)
Decimus Burton (*English*)
William Butterfield (*English*)
Callicrates (*Greek*)
Jacob van Campen (*Dutch*)
Felix Candela (*Mexican*)
Hugh (Maxwell) Casson (*English*)
William Chambers (*Scottish*)
Serge Chermayeff (*U.S.*)
Don Jose Churriguera (*Spanish*)
Wells Wintemute Coates (*English*)
Charles Robert Cockerell (*English*)
Pietro Berrettini da Cortona (*Italian*)
Francois de Cuvillies (*Bavarian*)
Daedalus (*Greek*)
George Dance (the Elder) (*English*)
George Dance (the Younger) (*English*)
Philibert Delorme *or* de l'Orme (*French*)
Theo van Doesburg (*Dutch*)
Balkrishna Vithaldas Doshi (*Indian*)
Willem Marinus Dudok (*Dutch*)
Johann Carl Ludwig Engel (*Finnish*)
Arthur Charles Erickson (*Canadian*)
Johann Bernhard Fischer von Erlach (*Austrian*)
Norman Foster (*English*)
(Richard) Buckminster Fuller (*U.S.*)
Ange-Jacques Gabriel (*French*)
Tony (Antoine) Garnier (*French*)
Antonio Gaudí (*Spanish*)
Patrick Geddes (*Scottish*)
Frederick Gibberd (*English*)
James Gibbs (*English*)
Cass Gilbert (*U.S.*)
Friedrich Gilly (*German*)
Francesco di Giorgio (*Italian*)
Giotto (di Bondone) (*Italian*)
Giulio Romano (*Italian*)
Walter Gropius (*German*)
Guarino Guarini (*Italian*)
Thomas Hamilton (*Scottish*)
Georges Eugene Haussmann (*French*)
Nicholas Hawksmoor (*English*)
Johann Lukas von Hildebrandt (*Austrian*)
Josef Hoffmann (*Austrian*)
Henry Holland (*English*)
Victor Horta (*Belgian*)
Ebenezer Howard (*English*)
Ictinus (*Greek*)
Imhotep (*Egyptian*)
Arne Jacobsen (*Danish*)
Philip Cortelyou Johnson (*U.S.*)
Inigo Jones (*English*)
Louis I(sadore) Kahn (*U.S.*)
William Kent (*English*)
(Pierre Francois) Henri Labrouste (*French*)
Denys Lasdun (*English*)

Architects (continued)

Le Corbusier *(French)*
Claude Nicolas Ledoux *(French)*
Leonardo da Vinci *(Italian)*
Pierre Lescot *(French)*
William Richard Lethaby *(English)*
Louis Levau *(French)*
Adolf Loos *(Austrian)*
Robert Stodart Lorimer *(Scottish)*
Edwin Lutyens *(English)*
Charles Rennie Mackintosh *(Scottish)*
Arthur Heygate Mackmurdo *(English)*
Carlo Maderna or Maderno *(Italian)*
François Mansart *(French)*
Jules Hardouin Mansart *(French)*
Eric Mendelsohn *(German)*
Michelangelo *(Italian)*
Michelozzo *(Italian)*
Ludwig Mies van der Rohe *(German-U.S.)*
Charles Willard Moore *(U.S.)*
John Nash *(English)*
Pier Luigi Nervi *(Italian)*
Johann Balthasar Neumann *(German)*
Oscar Niemeyer *(Brazilian)*
Andrea Orcagna *(Italian)*
Jacobus Johann Pieter Oud *(Dutch)*
Andrea Palladio *(Italian)*
Joseph Paxton *(English)*
I(eoh) M(ing) Pei *(Chinese-U.S.)*
Auguste Perret *(French)*
Baldassare Tommaso Peruzzi *(Italian)*
Pietro da Cortona *(Italian)*
Giambattista Piranesi *(Italian)*
Andrea Pisano *(Italian)*
Nicola Pisano *(Italian)*
William Henry Playfair *(Scottish)*
Hans Poelzig *(German)*
Augustus (Welby Northmore) Pugin *(English)*
Raphael *(Italian)*
James Renwick *(U.S.)*
Gerrit Thomas Rietveld *(Dutch)*
Richard Rogers *(English)*
Eero Saarinen *(Finnish-U.S.)*
Michele Sanmicheli *(Italian)*
Jacopo Sansovino *(Italian)*
Karl Friederich Schinkel *(German)*
Scopas *(Greek)*
George Gilbert Scott *(English)*
Giles Gilbert Scott *(English)*
Sebastiano Serlio *(Italian)*
Richard Norman Shaw *(English)*
Robert Smirke *(English)*
Robert Smythson *(English)*
John Soane *(English)*
Ettore Sottsass Jr. *(Italian)*
Jacques Germain Soufflot *(French)*
Basil (Unwin) Spence *(Scottish)*
James Stirling *(Scottish)*
George Edmund Street *(English)*
James Stuart *(English)*
Louis (Henri) Sullivan *(U.S.)*
Kenzo Tange *(Japanese)*
(John) Quinlan Terry *(English)*
Alexander (Greek) Thomson *(Scottish)*
Jorn Utzon *(Danish)*
John Vanbrugh *(English)*
Henry van de Velde *(Belgian)*
Giorgio Vasari *(Italian)*
Robert Venturi *(U.S.)*
Giacomo Barozzi da Vignola *(Italian)*
Eugène Emmanuel Viollet-le-Duc *(French)*
Marcus Vitruvius Pollio *(Roman)*
Charles (Francis Annesley) Voysey *(English)*
Otto Wagner *(Austrian)*
Alfred Waterhouse *(English)*
Aston Webb *(English)*
Philip Webb *(English)*
John Wood (the Elder) *(English)*
John Wood (the Younger) *(English)*
Christopher Wren *(English)*
Frank Lloyd Wright *(U.S.)*
James Wyatt *(English)*
Minoru Yamasaki *(U.S.)*

3 = **claim**, question, reason, challenge, insist, maintain, hold, allege, plead, assert, contend, uphold, profess, remonstrate, expostulate • *His lawyers are arguing that he is unfit to stand trial.*
4 = **demonstrate**, show, suggest, display, indicate, imply, exhibit, denote, evince • *Eventually they argued me into going.*
▸ **in phrases: argue someone into something = persuade someone to**, convince someone to, talk someone into, prevail upon someone to, talk someone round to

argument **as a noun** 1 = **reason**, case, reasoning, ground(s), defence, excuse, logic, justification, rationale, polemic, dialectic, line of reasoning, argumentation • *There's a strong argument for lowering the price.*
2 = **debate**, questioning, claim, row, discussion, dispute, controversy, pleading, plea, contention, assertion, polemic, altercation, remonstrance, expostulation, remonstration • *The issue has caused heated political argument.*
3 = **quarrel**, fight, row, clash, dispute, controversy, disagreement, misunderstanding, feud, barney *(informal)*, squabble, wrangle, bickering, difference of opinion, tiff, altercation • *She got into a heated argument with a stranger.*
opposites: accord, agreement, concurrence
▸ **in phrases: without argument = without question**, without debate, without confusion, without dispute, without query, without contention • *He complied without argument.*

quotations
Argument seldom convinces anyone contrary to his inclinations
[Thomas Fuller *Gnomologia*]
The aim of argument, or of discussion, should not be victory, but progress
[Joseph Joubert *Pensées*]

argumentative = **quarrelsome**, contrary, contentious, belligerent, combative, opinionated, litigious, disputatious • *You're in an argumentative mood today!*
opposites: obliging, accommodating, easy-going

aria = **song**, air, tune, melody • *an Italian operatic aria*

arid 1 = **dry**, desert, dried up, barren, sterile, torrid, parched, waterless, moistureless • *the arid zones of the country*
opposites: rich, fertile, lush
2 = **boring**, dull, tedious, dreary, dry, tiresome, lifeless, colourless, uninteresting, flat, uninspired, vapid, spiritless, jejune, as dry as dust • *She had given him the only joy his arid life had ever known.*
opposites: interesting, spirited, exciting

arise 1 = **happen**, start, begin, follow, issue, result, appear, develop, emerge, occur, spring, set in, stem, originate, ensue, come about, commence, come to light, emanate, crop up *(informal)*, come into being, materialize • *if a problem arises later in pregnancy*
2 = **get to your feet**, get up, rise, stand up, spring up, leap up • *I arose from the chair and left.*
3 = **get up**, wake up, awaken, get out of bed • *He arose at 6:30 a.m. as usual.*
4 = **ascend**, rise, lift, mount, climb, tower, soar, move upward • *the flat terrace, from which arises the volume of the house*

aristocracy = **upper class**, elite, nobility, gentry, peerage, ruling class, patricians, upper crust *(informal)*, noblesse *(literary)*, haut monde *(French)*, patriciate, body of nobles • *a member of the aristocracy*
opposites: masses, working classes, commoners

quotations
An aristocracy in a republic is like a chicken whose head has been cut off; it may run about in a lively way, but in fact it is dead
[Nancy Mitford *Noblesse Oblige*]
There is a natural aristocracy among men. The grounds of this are virtue and talent
[Thomas Jefferson *Letter to John Adams*]

aristocrat = **noble**, lord, lady, peer, patrician, grandee, nobleman, aristo *(informal)*, childe *(archaic)*, noblewoman, peeress • *He is the archetypal English aristocrat.*

aristocratic 1 = **upper-class**, lordly, titled, gentle *(archaic)*, elite, gentlemanly, noble, patrician, blue-blooded, well-born, highborn • *a wealthy, aristocratic family*
OPPOSITES: common, working-class, lower-class
2 = **refined**, fine, polished, elegant, stylish, dignified, haughty, courtly, snobbish, well-bred • *He laughed it off with aristocratic indifference.*
OPPOSITES: common, crude, vulgar

arm[1] AS A NOUN 1 = **upper limb**, limb, appendage • *She stretched her arms out.*
2 = **sleeve** • *I pulled the arm of her coat.*
3 = **branch**, part, office, department, division, section, wing, sector, extension, detachment, offshoot, subdivision, subsection • *the research arm of Congress*
4 = **authority**, might, force, power, strength, command, sway, potency • *Local people say the long arm of the law was too heavy-handed.*
5 = **inlet**, bay, passage, entrance, creek, cove, fjord, bight, ingress, sea loch *(Scot.)*, firth or frith *(Scot.)* • *At the end of the other arm of Cardigan Bay is Bardsey Island.*
▸ IN PHRASES: **an arm and a leg = a lot of money**, a bomb *(Brit. slang)*, a fortune, a pile *(informal)*, big money, a packet *(slang)*, a bundle *(slang)*, big bucks *(informal, chiefly U.S.)*, a tidy sum *(informal)*, a king's ransom, a pretty penny *(informal)* • *A week at a health farm can cost an arm and a leg.*
would give your right arm for something = would do anything for, would kill for, would sell your own grandmother for *(informal)*, would give your eye teeth for • *I would give my right arm for a car like that.*
▸ TECHNICAL NAME: brachium
▸ RELATED ADJECTIVE: brachial

arm[2] AS A VERB 1 = **equip**, provide, supply, outfit, rig, array, furnish, issue with, deck out, accoutre • *She had armed herself with a loaded rifle.*
2 = **provide**, prime, prepare, protect, guard, strengthen, outfit, equip, brace, fortify, forearm, make ready, gird your loins, jack up *(N.Z.)* • *She armed herself with all the knowledge she could gather.*
▸ AS A PLURAL NOUN = **weapons**, guns, firearms, weaponry, armaments, ordnance, munitions, instruments of war • *The organization has an extensive supply of arms.*

armada = **fleet**, navy, squadron, flotilla • *An armada of allied ships participated in the invasion.*

armaments = **weapons**, arms, guns, ammunition, weaponry, ordnance, munitions, materiel • *global efforts to reduce nuclear armaments*

armed AS AN ADJECTIVE = **carrying weapons**, provided, prepared, supplied, ready, protected, guarded, strengthened, equipped, primed, arrayed, furnished, fortified, in arms, forearmed, fitted out, under arms, girded, rigged out, tooled up *(slang)*, accoutred • *The rebels are organized and armed.*
▸ IN PHRASES: **armed to the teeth = well-equipped**, loaded up, well-furnished, tooled up *(informal)* • *They are armed to the teeth with high-tech equipment.*

armistice = **truce**, peace, ceasefire, suspension of hostilities • *Finally, they signed an armistice with their longstanding enemy.*

armour = **protection**, covering, shield, sheathing, armour plate, chain mail, protective covering • *a medieval suit of armour*

armoured = **protected**, mailed, reinforced, toughened, bulletproof, armour-plated, steel-plated, ironclad, bombproof • *armoured vehicles carrying troops*

armoury or *(U.S.)* **armory** = **arsenal**, magazine, ammunition dump, arms depot, ordnance depot • *'Her bedroom was an armoury,' the court heard.*

ARMOUR

armet	cuisse *or* cuish	mail
basinet *or* bascinet	culet	nosepiece
breastplate	gauntlet	pavloron
camail	gorget	poleyn
chamfrain, chamfron, *or* chanfron	greave	roundel
coat-of-mail	gusset	sabaton
corselet *or* corslet	helmet	sword belt
couter	jack	tasset, tasse, *or* tace
crinet	jambeau, jambart, *or* jamber	umbo
cuirass	jupon	vambrace
	lance rest	ventail
		visor *or* vizor

armpit = **underarm**, oxter *(Scot., Irish & Northern English dialect)*, pit • *I saw the dark wisps of his armpit hair.*
▸ TECHNICAL NAME: axilla
▸ RELATED ADJECTIVE: axillary

army 1 = **soldiers**, military, troops, armed force, legions, infantry, military force, land forces, land force, soldiery • *After returning from abroad, he joined the army.*
2 = **vast number**, host, gang, mob, flock, array, legion, swarm, sea, pack, horde, multitude, throng • *data collected by an army of volunteers*
PROVERBS
An army marches on its stomach

aroma = **scent**, smell, perfume, fragrance, bouquet, savour, odour, redolence • *the wonderful aroma of freshly baked bread*

aromatic = **fragrant**, perfumed, spicy, savoury, pungent, balmy, redolent, sweet-smelling, sweet-scented, odoriferous • *a shrub with aromatic leaves*
OPPOSITES: rank, offensive, smelly

around AS A PREPOSITION 1 = **approximately**, about, nearly, close to, roughly, just about, in the region of, circa *(of a date)*, in the vicinity of, not far off, in the neighbourhood of • *My salary was around £19,000.*
2 = **surrounding**, about, enclosing, encompassing, framing, encircling, on all sides of, on every side of, environing • *a prosperous suburb built around a new mosque*
3 = **about**, all over, everywhere in • *I've been walking around Moscow and the town is terribly quiet.*
▸ AS AN ADVERB 1 = **in the opposite direction**, the other way • *I turned around and wrote the title on the board.*
2 = **everywhere**, about, throughout, all over, here and there, on all sides, in all directions, to and fro • *What are you doing following me around?*
3 = **near**, close, nearby, handy, at hand, close by, close at hand • *It's important to have lots of people around.*
▸ RELATED PREFIX: circum-

arousal = **stimulation**, movement, response, reaction, excitement, animation, stirring up, provocation, inflammation, agitation, exhilaration, incitement, enlivenment • *Thinking angry thoughts can provoke strong physiological arousal.*

arouse 1 = **stimulate**, encourage, inspire, prompt, spark, spur, foster, provoke, rouse, stir up, inflame, incite, instigate, whip up, summon up, whet, kindle, foment, call forth • *His work has aroused intense interest.*
OPPOSITES: still, end, quell
2 = **inflame**, move, warm, excite, spur, provoke, animate, prod, stir up, agitate, quicken, enliven, goad, foment • *He apologized, saying this subject always aroused him.*
3 = **excite sexually**, thrill, stimulate, provoke, turn on *(slang)*, tease, please, get going, tickle, inflame, tantalize, make wild • *Some men are aroused by their partner saying erotic words to them.*

4 = **awaken**, wake up, rouse, waken • *We were aroused from our sleep by a knocking at the door.*

arraign = **accuse**, charge, prosecute, denounce, indict, impeach, incriminate, call to account, take to task • *He was arraigned for criminally abetting a traitor.*

arraignment = **accusation**, charge, complaint, prosecution, indictment, impeachment, denunciation, incrimination • *The men are scheduled for arraignment on October 5th.*

arrange 1 = **plan**, agree, prepare, determine, schedule, organize, construct, devise, contrive, fix up, jack up (*N.Z. informal*) • *She arranged an appointment for Friday afternoon.*
2 = **put in order**, group, form, order, sort, class, position, range, file, rank, line up, organize, set out, sequence, exhibit, sort out (*informal*), array, classify, tidy, marshal, align, categorize, systematize, jack up (*N.Z. informal*) • *He started to arrange the books in piles.*
OPPOSITES: disturb, scatter, disorganize
3 = **adapt**, score, orchestrate, harmonize, instrument • *The songs were arranged by a well-known pianist.*

arrangement 1 *often plural* = **plan**, planning, provision, preparation • *I am in charge of all the travel arrangements.*
2 = **agreement**, contract, settlement, appointment, compromise, deal (*informal*), pact, compact, covenant • *The caves can be visited only by prior arrangement.*
3 = **display**, grouping, system, order, ordering, design, ranging, structure, rank, organization, exhibition, line-up, presentation, array, marshalling, classification, disposition, alignment, setup (*informal*) • *an imaginative flower arrangement*
4 = **adaptation**, score, version, interpretation, instrumentation, orchestration, harmonization • *an arrangement of a well-known piece by Mozart*

arrant = **total**, complete, extreme, absolute, gross, notorious, utter, outright, thorough, infamous, rank, blatant, monstrous, vile, downright, atrocious, out-and-out, flagrant, egregious, unmitigated, undisguised, thoroughgoing, deep-dyed (*usually derogatory*) • *That's the most arrant nonsense I've ever heard.*

array AS A NOUN 1 = **arrangement**, show, order, supply, display, collection, exhibition, line-up, mixture, parade, formation, presentation, spectacle, marshalling, muster, disposition • *the markets with their wonderful arrays of fruit and vegetables*
2 = **clothing**, dress, clothes, threads (*slang*), garments, apparel, attire, garb, finery, regalia, raiment (*archaic or poetic*), schmutter (*slang*) • *Bathed, dressed in his finest array, he was ready.*
▸ AS A VERB 1 = **arrange**, show, group, order, present, range, display, line up, sequence, parade, exhibit, unveil, dispose, draw up, marshal, lay out, muster, align, form up, place in order, set in line (*Military*) • *Here are arrayed such 20th century relics as Madonna's bustier.*
2 = **dress**, supply, clothe, wrap, deck, outfit, decorate, equip, robe, get ready, adorn, apparel (*archaic*), festoon, attire, fit out, garb, bedeck, caparison, accoutre • *a priest arrayed in white vestments*

arrears AS A PLURAL NOUN = **debt**, claim, bill, due, duty, obligation, liability, debit • *They have promised to pay the arrears over the next five years.*
▸ IN PHRASES: **in arrears** = **behind**, overdue, in debt, behindhand • *They are more than six months in arrears with their mortgage.*

arrest AS A VERB 1 = **capture**, catch, lift (*slang*), nick (*slang, chiefly Brit.*), seize, run in (*slang*), nail (*informal*), bust (*informal*), collar (*informal*), take, detain, pinch (*informal*), nab (*informal*), apprehend, take prisoner, take into custody, lay hold of • *Seven people were arrested for minor offences.*
OPPOSITES: free, release, let go
2 = **stop**, end, hold, limit, check, block, slow, delay, halt, stall, stay, interrupt, suppress, restrain, hamper, inhibit, hinder, obstruct, retard, impede • *The new rules could arrest the development of good research.*
OPPOSITES: encourage, promote, speed up
3 = **fascinate**, hold, involve, catch, occupy, engage, grip, absorb, entrance, intrigue, rivet, enthral, mesmerize, engross, spellbind • *As he reached the hall, he saw what had arrested her.*
▸ AS A NOUN 1 = **capture**, bust (*informal*), detention, seizure, apprehension • *information leading to the arrest of the bombers*
OPPOSITES: freeing, release
2 = **stoppage**, halt, suppression, obstruction, inhibition, blockage, hindrance • *a cardiac arrest*
OPPOSITES: promotion, encouragement, acceleration

arresting = **striking**, surprising, engaging, dramatic, stunning, impressive, extraordinary, outstanding, remarkable, noticeable, conspicuous, salient, jaw-dropping, gee-whizz (*slang*)
OPPOSITES: unremarkable, unimpressive, inconspicuous

arrival 1 = **appearance**, coming, arriving, entrance, advent, materialization • *the day after his arrival*
2 = **coming**, happening, taking place, dawn, emergence, occurrence, materialization • *They celebrated the arrival of the New Year.*
3 = **newcomer**, arriver, incomer, visitor, caller, entrant, comer, newbie (*slang*), visitant • *A high proportion of the new arrivals are skilled professionals.*
4 = **birth**, delivery, childbirth, nativity, parturition • *a couple anticipating the arrival of a new child*

arrive AS A VERB 1 = **come**, appear, enter, turn up, show up (*informal*), materialize, draw near • *Fresh groups of guests arrived.*
OPPOSITES: go, leave, depart
2 = **occur**, happen, take place, ensue, transpire, fall, befall • *They needed to be much further forward before winter arrived.*
3 = **succeed**, make it (*informal*), triumph, do well, thrive, flourish, be successful, make good, prosper, cut it (*informal*), reach the top, become famous, make the grade (*informal*), get to the top, crack it (*informal*), hit the jackpot (*informal*), turn out well, make your mark (*informal*), achieve recognition, do all right for yourself (*informal*) • *These are cars which show you've arrived.*
▸ IN PHRASES: **arrive at something** 1 = **reach**, make, get to, enter, land at, get as far as • *She arrived at the airport early this morning.*
2 = **achieve**, get, come to, reach, effect, complete, obtain, accomplish, execute, bring about, attain, consummate • *The jury could not arrive at a unanimous decision.*

arriviste = **upstart**, would-be, climber, social climber, status seeker, adventurer *or* adventuress, parvenu *or* parvenue • *a woman regarded by some as a pushy arriviste*

arrogance = **conceit**, pride, swagger, pretension, presumption, bluster, hubris, pomposity, insolence, hauteur, pretentiousness, high-handedness, haughtiness, loftiness, imperiousness, pompousness, superciliousness, lordliness, conceitedness, contemptuousness, scornfulness, uppishness (*Brit. informal*), disdainfulness, overweeningness • *At times, the arrogance of those in power is quite blatant.*
OPPOSITES: modesty, humility, shyness

arrogant = **conceited**, lordly, assuming, proud, swaggering, pompous, pretentious, stuck up (*informal*), cocky, contemptuous, blustering, imperious, overbearing, haughty, scornful, puffed up, egotistical, disdainful, self-important, presumptuous, high-handed, insolent, supercilious, high and mighty (*informal*), overweening, immodest, swollen-headed, bigheaded (*informal*), uppish (*Brit. informal*) • *an air of arrogant indifference*
OPPOSITES: modest, shy, humble

arrogate = **seize**, demand, assume, appropriate, presume, usurp, commandeer, expropriate, claim unduly • *He arrogated the privilege to himself alone.*

arrow 1 = **dart**, flight, reed *(archaic)*, bolt, shaft *(archaic)*, quarrel • *warriors armed with bows and arrows*
2 = **pointer**, indicator, marker • *A series of arrows point the way to his grave.*
▸ RELATED ADJECTIVE: sagittal

arse = **bottom**, bum *(Brit. slang)*, behind *(informal)*, seat, rear, tail *(informal)*, butt *(U.S. & Canad. informal)*, ass *(U.S. & Canad. taboo slang)*, buns *(U.S. slang)*, buttocks, backside, rump, rear end, posterior, derrière *(euphemistic)*, tush *(U.S. slang)*, fundament, jacksy *(Brit. slang)* • *You can't do business sitting on your arse all day.*

arsenal 1 = **store**, stock, supply, magazine, stockpile • *an impressive arsenal of guns*
2 = **armoury**, storehouse, ammunition dump, arms depot, ordnance depot • *Terrorists had broken into the arsenal and stolen a range of weapons.*

arson = **pyromania**, incendiarism • *a terrible wave of rioting, theft and arson*

arsonist = **pyromaniac**, incendiary, firestarter • *A convicted arsonist set fire to a top security hospital last night.*

art 1 = **artwork**, style of art, fine art, creativity • *the first exhibition of such art in the West*
2 = **skill**, knowledge, method, facility, craft, profession, expertise, competence, accomplishment, mastery, knack, ingenuity, finesse, aptitude, artistry, artifice *(archaic)*, virtuosity, dexterity, cleverness, adroitness • *the art of seduction and romance*

QUOTATIONS

Art is a jealous mistress
[Ralph Waldo Emerson *Conduct of Life*]

All art constantly aspires towards the condition of music
[Walter Pater *Studies in the History of the Renaissance*]

Art is a lie that makes us realise the truth
[Pablo Picasso]

Life is short, the art long
[Hippocrates *Aphorisms*]

Art does not reproduce the visible; rather, it makes visible
[Paul Klee *Inward Vision*]

Art is a revolt against fate
[André Malraux *Les Voix du silence*]

Art is...pattern informed by sensibility
[Herbert Read *The Meaning of Art*]

We must have ... art for art's sake ... the beautiful cannot be the way to what is useful, or to what is good, or to what is holy; it leads only to itself
[Victor Cousin *Sorbonne lecture, 1818*]

Art is meant to disturb. Science reassures
[Georges Braque *Pensées sur l'art*]

True art selects and paraphrases, but seldom gives a verbatim translation
[Thomas Bailey Aldrich *Ponkapog Papers*]

Art enlarges experience by admitting us to the inner life of others
[Walter Lippmann *The Golden Rule and After*]

▹ *See panel* **Art**

artefact = **item**, thing, article, object, entity, ornament • *He realised that the 'ancient artefacts' were fakes.*

artery 1 = **vein**, blood vessel • *patients suffering from blocked arteries*
2 = **route**, way, course, round, road, passage, avenue • *one of the north-bound arteries of the central business district*
▸ RELATED ADJECTIVE: arterial

artful 1 = **cunning**, designing, scheming, sharp, smart, clever, subtle, intriguing, tricky, shrewd, sly, wily, politic, crafty, foxy, deceitful • *the smiles and artifices of a subtly artful woman*
OPPOSITES: open, simple, straightforward
2 = **skilful**, masterly, smart, clever, subtle, ingenious, adept, resourceful, proficient, adroit, dexterous • *There is also an artful contrast of shapes.*
OPPOSITES: clumsy, unskilled, artless

Arthurian
▹ *See panel* **Arthurian legend**

article AS A NOUN 1 = **feature**, story, paper, piece, item, creation, essay, composition, discourse, treatise • *a newspaper article*
2 = **thing**, piece, unit, item, object, device, tool, implement, commodity, gadget, utensil • *household articles*
3 = **clause**, point, part, heading, head, matter, detail, piece, particular, division, section, item, passage, portion, paragraph, proviso • *article 50 of the UN charter*
▸ IN PHRASES: **the genuine article** = **authentic**, real, genuine, legitimate, the real thing, on the level *(informal)*, bona fide, dinkum *(Austral. & N.Z. informal)*, the real McCoy *(informal)* • *The vodka was the genuine article.*

ART

ART STYLES AND MOVEMENTS

abstract expressionism	conceptual art	Impressionism	neoplasticism	romanticism
abstractionism	constructivism	Jugendstil	op art	Suprematism
Art Deco	cubism	mannerism	pointillism	surrealism
Arte Povera	Dada *or* Dadaism	minimal art	pop art	symbolism
Art Nouveau	De Stijl	modernism	postimpressionism	synthetism
Barbizon School	divisionism	Nabis	postmodernism	ukiyo-e
baroque	expressionism	naturalism	Pre-Raphaelite	vorticism
Der Blaue Reiter	Fauvism	Nazarene	realism	
Brücke	futurism	neoclassicism	rococo	
classicism	Gothic	neoimpressionism	Romanesque	

ART EQUIPMENT

acrylic	crayon	ink	paintbrush	spatula
airbrush	drawing paper	lay figure	palette	spray gun
brush	easel	linseed oil	palette knife	varnish
canvas	fixative	oil paint	pastel	watercolour
chalk	glaze	paint	pencil	
charcoal	ground	paintbox	sketchbook	

ARTHURIAN LEGEND

Characters in Arthurian legend

Arthur
Bedivere
Bors
Caradoc
Elaine
Galahad
Gareth (of Orkney)
Gawain *or* Gawayne
Guinevere
Igraine
Lancelot *or* Launcelot du Lac
Launfal
Merlin
Modred
Morgan Le Fay
Nimue
Parsifal *or* Perceval
Tristan *or* Tristram
Uther Pendragon
Viviane *or* the Lady of the Lake

Places in Arthurian legend

Astolat
Avalon
Camelot
Glastonbury
Lyonnesse
Tintagel

articulate AS AN ADJECTIVE = **expressive**, clear, effective, vocal, meaningful, understandable, coherent, persuasive, fluent, eloquent, lucid, comprehensible, communicative, intelligible • *She is an articulate young woman.*
OPPOSITES: halting, silent, incoherent
▸ AS A VERB 1 = **express**, say, tell, state, word, speak, declare, phrase, communicate, assert, pronounce, utter, couch, put across, enunciate, put into words, verbalize, asseverate • *He failed to articulate an overall vision.*
2 = **pronounce**, say, talk, speak, voice, utter, enunciate, vocalize, enounce • *He articulated each syllable.*

articulated = **attached**, joined, coupled, jointed, hinged • *an articulated lorry*

articulation 1 = **expression**, delivery, pronunciation, speech, saying, talking, voicing, speaking, utterance, diction, enunciation, vocalization, verbalization • *an actor able to sustain clear articulation over long periods*
2 = **voicing**, statement, expression, verbalization • *a way of restricting their articulation of grievances*
3 = **joint**, coupling, jointing, connection, hinge, juncture • *The articulation of different modes of production*

artifice 1 = **cunning**, scheming, trick, device, craft, tactic, manoeuvre, deception, hoax, expedient, ruse, guile, trickery, duplicity, subterfuge, stratagem, contrivance, chicanery, wile, craftiness, artfulness, slyness, machination • *His photographs are full of artifice.*
2 = **cleverness**, skill, facility, invention, ingenuity, finesse, inventiveness, deftness, adroitness • *a combination of theatrical artifice and dazzling cinematic movement*

artificial 1 = **synthetic**, manufactured, plastic, man-made, non-natural • *free from artificial additives and flavours*
2 = **insincere**, forced, affected, assumed, phoney *or* phony (*informal*), put on, false, pretended, hollow, contrived, unnatural, feigned, spurious, meretricious • *The voice was affected, the accent artificial.*
OPPOSITES: true, natural, genuine
3 = **fake**, mock, imitation, bogus, simulated, phoney *or* phony (*informal*), sham, pseudo (*informal*), fabricated, counterfeit, spurious, ersatz, specious • *The sauce was glutinous and tasted artificial.*
OPPOSITES: authentic

artillery = **big guns**, battery, cannon, ordnance, gunnery, cannonry • *the sound of artillery fire*

artisan = **craftsman**, technician, mechanic, journeyman, artificer, handicraftsman, skilled workman • *They have been restored by a stonemason and artisan.*

artist 1 = **creator**, master, maker, craftsman, artisan (*obsolete*), fine artist • *the studio of a great artist*
2 = **master**, expert, pro (*informal*), ace (*informal*), genius, wizard, adept, maestro, virtuoso, grandmaster, doyen, past master, dab hand (*Brit. informal*), wonk (*informal*), maven (*U.S.*), fundi (*S. African*) • *He's an outstanding barber, an artist with shears*

QUOTATIONS

The artist must be in his work as God is in creation, invisible and all-powerful; one must sense him everywhere but never see him
[Gustave Flaubert]

The true artist will let his wife starve, his children go barefoot, his mother drudge for his living at seventy, sooner than work at anything but his art
[George Bernard Shaw *Man and Superman*]

▷ *See panel* **Artists**

artiste = **performer**, player, entertainer, Thespian, trouper, play-actor • *a Parisian cabaret artiste*

artistic 1 = **creative**, cultured, original, sensitive, sophisticated, refined, imaginative, aesthetic, discerning, eloquent, arty (*informal*) • *They encourage boys to be sensitive and artistic.*
OPPOSITES: untalented
2 = **beautiful**, fine, pleasing, lovely, creative, elegant, stylish, cultivated, imaginative, decorative, aesthetic, exquisite, graceful, expressive, ornamental, tasteful • *an artistic arrangement*
OPPOSITES: unattractive, tasteless, inelegant

artistry = **skill**, art, style, taste, talent, craft, genius, creativity, touch, flair, brilliance, sensibility, accomplishment, mastery, finesse, craftsmanship, proficiency, virtuosity, workmanship, artistic ability • *his artistry as a cellist*

artless 1 = **natural**, simple, fair, frank, plain, pure, open, round, true, direct, genuine, humble, straightforward, sincere, honest, candid, unaffected, upfront (*informal*), unpretentious, unadorned, dinkum (*Austral. & N.Z. informal*), guileless, uncontrived, undesigning • *his artless air and charming smile*
OPPOSITES: affected, artificial, unnatural
2 = **unskilled**, awkward, crude, primitive, rude, bungling, incompetent, clumsy, inept, untalented, maladroit • *a spiritless and artless display of incompetence*
OPPOSITES: sophisticated, artistic, artful

artwork = **art**, design, cover art • *The artwork for the LP was done by an old friend of ours.*

arty = **artistic**, arty-farty (*informal*), arty-crafty (*informal*) • *an arty French film*

as AS A CONJUNCTION 1 = **when**, while, just as, at the time that, during the time that • *All eyes were on him as he continued.*
2 = **in the way that**, like, in the manner that • *Behave towards them as you would like to be treated.*
3 = **since**, because, seeing that, considering that, on account of the fact that • *This is important as it sets the mood for the day.*
4 = **although**, while, though • *Try as he might, he couldn't escape.*

a

ARTISTS

Agostino di Duccio *(Italian)*
Josef Albers *(German-U.S.)*
Leon Battista Alberti *(Italian)*
Washington Allston *(U.S.)*
Lawrence Alma-Tadema *(Dutch-English)*
Albrecht Altdorfer *(German)*
Fra Angelico *(Italian)*
Pietro Annigoni *(Italian)*
Antonello da Messina *(Italian)*
Apelles *(Greek)*
Karel Appel *(Dutch)*
Aleksandr Porfiryevich Archipenko *(Russian)*
Giuseppe Arcimboldo *(Italian)*
Jean *or* Hans Arp *(French)*
John James Audubon *(U.S.)*
Frank Auerbach *(English-German)*
Francis Bacon *(Irish)*
Leon Nikolayevich Bakst *(Russian)*
Balthus *(Polish-French)*
Frédéric August Bartholdi *(French)*
Fra Bartolommeo *(Italian)*
Max Beckmann *(German)*
Vanessa Bell *(English)*
Giovanni Bellini *(Italian)*
Thomas Hart Benton *(U.S.)*
Gian Lorenzo Bernini *(Italian)*
Joseph Beuys *(German)*
Peter Blake *(English)*
William Blake *(English)*
Umberto Boccioni *(Italian)*
David Bomberg *(English)*
Rosa Bonheur *(French)*
Pierre Bonnard *(French)*
Richard Parkes Bonnington *(English)*
Gutzon Borglum *(U.S.)*
Hieronymus Bosch *(Dutch)*
Sandro Botticelli *(Italian)*
Francois Boucher *(French)*
Eugène Boudin *(French)*
Arthur Boyd *(Australian)*
Donato Bramante *(Italian)*
Constantin Brancusi *(Romanian)*
Georges Braque *(French)*
Brassaï *(French)*
Agnolo Bronzino *(Italian)*
Ford Madox Brown *(English)*
Jan Brueghel *(Flemish)*
Pieter Brueghel the Elder *(Flemish)*
Pieter Brueghel the Younger *(Flemish)*
Bernard Buffet *(French)*
Edward Burne-Jones *(English)*
Edward Burra *(English)*
Reg Butler *(English)*
Alexander Calder *(U.S.)*
Callimachus *(Greek)*
Robert Campin *(Flemish)*
Antonio Canova *(Italian)*
Michelangelo Merisi da Caravaggio *(Italian)*
Anthony Caro *(English)*
Vittore Carpaccio *(Italian)*
Agostino Carracci *(Italian)*
Annibale Carracci *(Italian)*
Ludovico Carracci *(Italian)*
Mary Cassatt *(U.S.)*
Pietro Cavallini *(Italian)*
Benvenuto Cellini *(Italian)*
Lynn Chadwick *(English)*
Marc Chagall *(Russian-French)*
Philippe de Champaigne *(French)*
Jean-Baptiste Siméon Chardin *(French)*
Giorgio de Chirico *(Italian)*
Giovanni Cimabue *(Italian)*
Claude Lorrain *(French)*
François Clouet *(French)*
Jean Clouet *(French)*
John Constable *(English)*
John Copley *(U.S.)*
Jean Baptiste Camille Corot *(French)*
Antonio Allegri da Corregio *(Italian)*
Gustave Courbet *(French)*
David Cox *(English)*
Antoine Coypel *(French)*
Lucas Cranach *(German)*
Walter Crane *(English)*
John Crome *(English)*
Aelbert Cuyp *or* Kuyp *(Dutch)*
Paul Cézanne *(French)*
Richard Dadd *(English)*
Salvador Dalí *(Spanish)*
Francis Danby *(Irish)*
Charles François Daubigny *(French)*
Honoré Daumier *(French)*
Jacques Louis David *(French)*
Peter de Wint *(English)*
Hilaire Germain Edgar Degas *(French)*
Eugène Delacroix *(French)*
Paul Delaroche *(French)*
Robert Delaunay *(French)*
Paul Delvaux *(Belgian)*
Maurice Denis *(French)*
André Derain *(French)*
William Dobell *(Australian)*
Domenichino *(Italian)*
Domenico del Barbiere *(Italian)*
Donatello *(Italian)*
Gerrit Dou *(Dutch)*
George Russell Drysdale *(Australian)*
Jean Dubuffet *(French)*
Duccio di Buoninsegna *(Italian)*
Marcel Duchamp *(French-U.S.)*
Raoul Dufy *(French)*
Albrecht Dürer *(German)*
Thomas Eakins *(U.S.)*
El Greco *(Greek-Spanish)*
James Ensor *(Belgian)*
Jacob Epstein *(British)*
Max Ernst *(German)*
Henri Fantin-Latour *(French)*
Lyonel Feininger *(U.S.)*
John Flaxman *(English)*
Jean Fouquet *(French)*
Jean Honoré Fragonard *(French)*
Lucian Freud *(English)*
Caspar David Friedrich *(German)*
Roger Fry *(English)*
Henry Fuseli *(Swiss)*
Naum Gabo *(Russian-U.S.)*
Thomas Gainsborough *(English)*
Henri Gaudier-Brzeska *(French)*
Paul Gauguin *(French)*
Gentile da Fabriano *(Italian)*
Lorenzo Ghiberti *(Italian)*
Domenico Ghirlandaio *(Italian)*
Alberto Giacometti *(Swiss)*
Giambologna *(Italian)*
Grinling Gibbons *(Dutch)*
Gilbert (Proesch) and George (Passmore) *(English)*
Eric Gill *(English)*
Giorgione da Castelfranco *(Italian)*
Giotto di Bondone *(Italian)*
Giulio Romano *(Italian)*
Hugo van der Goes *(Flemish)*
Julio González *(Spanish)*
Arshile Gorky *(U.S.)*
Francisco de Goya *(Spanish)*
Jan van Goyen *(Dutch)*
Duncan Grant *(Scottish)*
Jean Baptiste Greuze *(French)*
Juan Gris *(Spanish)*
Antoine Jean Gros *(French)*
George Grosz *(German-U.S.)*
Grünewald *(German)*
Francesco Guardi *(Italian)*
François Gérard *(French)*
Théodore Géricault *(French)*
Frans Hals *(Dutch)*
Richard Hamilton *(English)*
Ando Hiroshige *(Japanese)*
Damien Hirst *(English)*
Meindert Hobbema *(Dutch)*
David Hockney *(English)*
Hans Hofmann *(German-U.S.)*
William Hogarth *(English)*
Katsushika Hokusai *(Japanese)*
Hans Holbein *(German)*
Winslow Homer *(U.S.)*
Pieter de Hooch *or* Hoogh *(Dutch)*
Edward Hopper *(U.S.)*
Jean Antoine Houdon *(French)*
William Holman Hunt *(English)*
Jean Auguste Dominique Ingres *(French)*
Augustus John *(Welsh)*
Gwen John *(Welsh)*
Jasper Johns *(U.S.)*
Johan Barthold Jongkind *(Dutch)*
Jacob Jordaens *(Flemish)*
Wassily Kandinsky *(Russian)*
Angelica Kauffmann *(Swiss)*
Ernst Ludwig Kirchner *(German)*
Ron B. Kitaj *(U.S.)*
Paul Klee *(Swiss)*
Gustav Klimt *(Austrian)*
Franz Kline *(U.S.)*
Godfrey Kneller *(German-English)*
Laura Knight *(English)*
Oscar Kokoschka *(Austrian)*
Willem de Kooning *(Dutch-U.S.)*
Leon Kossoff *(English)*
Georges de La Tour *(French)*
Edwin Landseer *(English)*
Thomas Lawrence *(English)*
Charles Lebrun *(French)*
Fernand Léger *(French)*
Wilhelm Lehmbruck *(German)*
Frederic Leighton *(English)*

a

ARTISTS (CONTINUED)

Peter Lely *(Dutch-English)*
Leonardo da Vinci *(Italian)*
Wyndham Lewis *(British)*
Roy Lichtenstein *(U.S.)*
Norman Alfred William Lindsay *(Australian)*
Jacques Lipchitz *(Lithuanian-U.S.)*
Filippino Lippi *(Italian)*
L(awrence) S(tephen) Lowry *(English)*
Lysippus *(Greek)*
Jan Mabuse *(Flemish)*
Charles Rennie Mackintosh *(Scottish)*
René Magritte *(Belgian)*
Aristide Maillol *(French)*
Kasimir Severinovich Malevich *(Russian)*
Edouard Manet *(French)*
Andrea Mantegna *(Italian)*
Franz Marc *(German)*
John Martin *(English)*
Simone Martini *(Italian)*
Masaccio *(Italian)*
Quentin Massys *(Flemish)*
Henri Matisse *(French)*
Hans Memling *or* Memlinc *(Flemish)*
Franz Xavier Messerschmidt *(Austrian)*
Ivan Mestrovic *(Yugoslav-U.S.)*
Michelangelo Buonarroti *(Italian)*
Michelozzi Michelozzo *(Italian)*
John Everett Millais *(English)*
Jean François Millet *(French)*
Joan Miró *(Spanish)*
Amedeo Modigliani *(Italian)*
László Moholy-Nagy *(Hungarian)*
Piet Mondrian *(Dutch)*
Claude Oscar Monet *(French)*
Henry Moore *(British)*
Gustave Moreau *(French)*
Berthe Morisot *(French)*
William Morris *(English)*
Samuel Finley Breese Morse *(U.S.)*
Grandma Moses *(U.S.)*
Edvard Munch *(Norwegian)*
Alfred Munnings *(English)*
Bartolomé Esteban Murillo *(Spanish)*
Myron *(Greek)*
Paul Nash *(English)*
Ernst Wilhelm Nay *(German)*
Barnett Newman *(U.S.)*
Ben Nicholson *(English)*
Sidney Nolan *(Australian)*
Emil Nolde *(German)*
Joseph Nollekens *(Dutch-English)*
Georgia O'Keefe *(U.S.)*
Claes Oldenburg *(Swedish-U.S.)*
Orcagna *(Italian)*
José Clemente Orozco *(Mexican)*
Jean Baptiste Oudry *(French)*
Palma Vecchio *(Italian)*
Samuel Palmer *(English)*
Eduardo Paolozzi *(Scottish)*
Parmigianino *(Italian)*
Victor Pasmore *(English)*
Joachim Patinir *or* Patenier *(Flemish)*
Perugino *(Italian)*
Baldassare Peruzzi *(Italian)*
Antoine Pevsner *(Russian-French)*
Phidias *(Greek)*
Francis Picabia *(French)*
Pablo Picasso *(Spanish)*
Piero della Francesca *(Italian)*
Piero di Cosimo *(Italian)*
Pietro da Cortona *(Italian)*
Jean Baptiste Pigalle *(French)*
Germain Pilon *(French)*
Pinturicchio *(Italian)*
John Piper *(English)*
Pisanello *(Italian)*
Andrea Pisano *(Italian)*
Giovanni Pisano *(Italian)*
Nicola Pisano *(Italian)*
Camille Pissarro *(French)*
Antonio del Pollaiuolo *(Italian)*
Piero del Pollaiuolo *(Italian)*
Jackson Pollock *(U.S.)*
Polyclitus *(Greek)*
Polygnotus *(Greek)*
Pontormo *(Italian)*
Paulus Potter *(Dutch)*
Nicolas Poussin *(French)*
Praxiteles *(Greek)*
Pierre Paul Prud'hon *(French)*
Pierre Puget *(French)*
Pierre Puvis de Chavannes *(French)*
Jacopa della Quercia *(Italian)*
Arthur Rackham *(English)*
Henry Raeburn *(Scottish)*
Allan Ramsay *(Scottish)*
Raphael *(Italian)*
Robert Rauschenberg *(U.S.)*
Man Ray *(U.S.)*
Odilon Redon *(French)*
Rembrandt Harmensz van Rijn *(Dutch)*
Guido Reni *(Italian)*
Pierre Auguste Renoir *(French)*
Joshua Reynolds *(English)*
José de Ribera *(Spanish)*
Bridget Riley *(English)*
Diego Rivera *(Mexican)*
Andrea della Robbia *(Italian)*
Luca della Robbia *(Italian)*
Alexander Mikhailovich Rodchenko *(Russian)*
Auguste Rodin *(French)*
George Romney *(English)*
Salvator Rosa *(Italian)*
Dante Gabriel Rossetti *(English)*
Mark Rothko *(U.S.)*
Georges Rouault *(French)*
Louis-François Roubiliac *or* Roubillac *(French)*
Henri Julien Rousseau *(French)*
Théodore Rousseau *(French)*
Peter Paul Rubens *(Flemish)*
Rublyov *or* Rublev Andrei *(Russian)*
Jacob van Ruisdael *(Dutch)*
Philipp Otto Runge *(German)*
Salomen van Ruysdael *(Dutch)*
John Singer Sargent *(U.S.)*
Egon Schiele *(Austrian)*
Martin Schongauer *(German)*
Kurt Schwitters *(German)*
Scopas *(Greek)*
Maurice Sendak *(U.S.)*
Sesshu *(Japanese)*
Georges Seurat *(French)*
Ben Shahn *(U.S.)*
Walter Richard Sickert *(British)*
Paul Signac *(French)*
Luca Signorelli *(Italian)*
David Alfaro Siqueiros *(Mexican)*
Alfred Sisley *(French)*
John Sloan *(U.S.)*
Claus Sluter *(Dutch)*
David Smith *(U.S.)*
Chaim Soutine *(Lithuanian-French)*
Stanley Spencer *(English)*
Jan Steen *(Dutch)*
Veit Stoss *(German)*
George Stubbs *(English)*
Graham Sutherland *(English)*
Yves Tanguy *(French)*
Vladimir Tatlin *(Russian)*
David Teniers the Elder *(Flemish)*
David Teniers the Younger *(Flemish)*
Gerard Ter Borch *or* Terborch *(Dutch)*
Hendrik Terbrugghen *(Dutch)*
James Thornhill *(English)*
Bertel Thorvaldsen *(Danish)*
Giambattista Tiepolo *(Italian)*
Jacopo Tintoretto *(Italian)*
James Jacques Joseph Tissot *(French)*
Titian *(Italian)*
Henri Marie Raymond de Toulouse-Lautrec *(French)*
J(oseph) M(allord) W(illiam) Turner *(English)*
Paolo Uccello *(Italian)*
Utagawa Kuniyoshi *(Japanese)*
Maurice Utrillo *(French)*
Adriaen van de Velde *(Dutch)*
Willem van de Velde the Elder *(Dutch)*
Willem van de Velde the Younger *(Dutch)*
Rogier van der Weyden *(Flemish)*
Anthony Van Dyck *(Flemish)*
Jan van Eyck *(Flemish)*
Vincent van Gogh *(Dutch)*
Victor Vasarely *(Hungarian-French)*
Giorgio Vasari *(Italian)*
Diego Rodríguez de Silva y Velázquez *(Spanish)*
Jan Vermeer *(Dutch)*
Paolo Veronese *(Italian)*
Andrea del Verrocchio *(Italian)*
Élisabeth Vigée-Lebrun *(French)*
Jacques Villon *(French)*
Maurice de Vlaminck *(French)*
Andy Warhol *(U.S.)*
Jean Antoine Watteau *(French)*
George Frederick Watts *(English)*
Benjamin West *(U.S.)*
James Abbott McNeill Whistler *(U.S.)*
Richard Wilson *(Welsh)*
Joseph Wright *(English)*
Xia Gui *or* Hsia Kuei *(Chinese)*
Zeuxis *(Greek)*
Johann Zoffany *(German)*
Anders Zorn *(Swedish)*
Gaetano Giulio Zumbo *(Italian)*
Francisco Zurbarán *(Spanish)*

▸ **AS A PREPOSITION** = **in the role of**, being, under the name of, in the character of • *I had natural ability as a footballer.*
▸ **IN PHRASES:** **as for** *or* **to** = **with regard to**, about, re, concerning, regarding, respecting, relating to, with respect to, on the subject of, with reference to, in reference to, in the matter of, apropos of, as regards, anent *(Scot.)* • *As for giving them guns, I don't think that's a very good idea.*
as it were = **in a way**, to some extent, so to speak, in a manner of speaking, so to say • *I understood the words, but I didn't, as it were, understand the question.*

ascend 1 = **climb**, scale, mount, go up • *I held her hand as we ascended the steps.*
OPPOSITES: go down, descend
2 = **slope upwards**, come up, rise up • *A number of steps ascend from the cobbled street.*
OPPOSITES: go down, slope downwards, descend
3 = **move up**, rise, go up • *Keep the drill centred as it ascends and descends in the hole.*
OPPOSITES: fall, drop, move down
4 = **float up**, rise, climb, tower, go up, take off, soar, lift off, fly up • *They ascended 55,900 feet in their balloon.*
OPPOSITES: fall, drop, descend

ascendancy *or* **ascendence** = **influence**, power, control, rule, authority, command, reign, sovereignty, sway, dominance, domination, superiority, supremacy, mastery, dominion, upper hand, hegemony, prevalence, pre-eminence, predominance, rangatiratanga *(N.Z.)* • *The extremists are gaining ascendancy.*
OPPOSITES: weakness, inferiority, subordination

ascendant *or* **ascendent** **AS AN ADJECTIVE** = **influential**, controlling, ruling, powerful, commanding, supreme, superior, dominant, prevailing, authoritative, predominant, uppermost, pre-eminent • *Radical reformers are once more ascendant.*
▸ **IN PHRASES:** **in the ascendant** = **rising**, increasing, growing, powerful, mounting, climbing, dominating, commanding, supreme, dominant, influential, prevailing, flourishing, ascending, up-and-coming, on the rise, uppermost, on the way up • *Geography, drama, art and English are in the ascendant.*

ascension 1 = **rise**, rising, mounting, climb, ascending, ascent, moving upwards • *the resurrection and ascension of Jesus Christ*
2 = **succession**, taking over, assumption, inheritance, elevation, entering upon • *fifteen years after his ascension to the throne*

ascent 1 = **climbing**, scaling, mounting, climb, clambering, ascending, ascension • *He led the first ascent of K2.*
2 = **upward slope**, rise, incline, ramp, gradient, rising ground, acclivity • *It was a tough course over a gradual ascent.*
3 = **rise**, rising, climb, ascension, upward movement • *He pressed the button and the elevator began its slow ascent.*

ascertain = **find out**, learn, discover, determine, confirm, settle, identify, establish, fix, verify, make certain, suss (out) *(slang)*, ferret out • *Try to ascertain what services the bank is offering.*

ascetic **AS A NOUN** = **recluse**, monk, nun, abstainer, hermit, anchorite, self-denier • *He left the luxuries of court for a life as an ascetic.*
OPPOSITES: hedonist, sensualist, voluptuary
▸ **AS AN ADJECTIVE** = **self-denying**, severe, plain, harsh, stern, rigorous, austere, Spartan, self-disciplined, celibate, puritanical, frugal, abstemious, abstinent • *priests practising an ascetic life*
OPPOSITES: abandoned, comfortable, self-indulgent

asceticism = **self-denial**, austerity, rigour, celibacy, abstinence, self-discipline, harshness, puritanism, frugality, plainness, self-abnegation, abstemiousness, self-mortification, mortification of the flesh, rigorousness • *a life of uncompromising asceticism and absolute poverty*

ascribe = **attribute**, credit, refer, charge, assign, put down, set down, impute • *Doctors ascribed the child's death to a hole in the heart.*

asexual = **sexless**, neutral, neuter • *asexual parasites*

ash = **ashes**, embers, cinders • *a cloud of volcanic ash*
▸ **RELATED ADJECTIVE:** cinereous

ashamed 1 = **embarrassed**, sorry, guilty, upset, distressed, shy, humbled, humiliated, blushing, self-conscious, red-faced, chagrined, flustered, mortified, sheepish, bashful, prudish, crestfallen, discomfited, remorseful, abashed, shamefaced, conscience-stricken, discountenanced • *She was ashamed that she looked so shabby.*
OPPOSITES: pleased, honoured, proud
2 = **reluctant**, afraid, embarrassed, scared, unwilling, loath, disinclined • *Women are often ashamed to admit they are being abused.*

ashen = **pale**, white, grey, wan, livid, pasty, leaden, colourless, pallid, anaemic, ashy, like death warmed up *(informal)* • *He fell back, shocked, his face ashen.*
OPPOSITES: red, glowing, rosy

ashore = **on land**, on the beach, on the shore, aground, to the shore, on dry land, shorewards, landwards • *Once ashore, the vessel was thoroughly inspected.*

aside **AS AN ADVERB** 1 = **to one side**, away, alone, separately, apart, alongside, beside, out of the way, on one side, to the side, in isolation, in reserve, out of mind • *She closed the book and laid it aside.*
2 = **apart**, notwithstanding • *Emotional arguments aside, here are the facts.*
▸ **AS A NOUN** = **interpolation**, remark, parenthesis, digression, interposition, confidential remark • *She mutters an aside to the camera.*
▸ **IN PHRASES:** **aside from** = **apart from**, but, save, other than, excluding, besides, except for, not counting • *Aside from these few niggles, all is clear.*

asinine = **stupid**, silly, foolish, daft *(informal)*, senseless, goofy *(informal)*, idiotic, inane, fatuous, moronic, imbecile, gormless *(Brit. informal)*, brainless, imbecilic, braindead *(informal)*, dumb-ass *(slang)*, dead from the neck up *(informal)*, thickheaded, dunderheaded, halfwitted, thick-witted • *I have never heard such an asinine discussion.*
OPPOSITES: bright, sharp, intelligent

ask 1 = **inquire**, question, quiz, query, interrogate • *'How is Frank?' he asked.*
OPPOSITES: answer, reply, respond
2 = **put**, propose, pose • *I wasn't the only one asking questions.*
3 = **request**, apply to, appeal to, plead with, demand, urge, sue, pray, beg, petition, crave, solicit, implore, enjoin, beseech, entreat, supplicate • *We had to ask him to leave.*
4 = **invite**, bid, summon • *She asked me back to her house.*

askance 1 = **suspiciously**, doubtfully, dubiously, sceptically, disapprovingly, distrustfully, mistrustfully • *They have always looked askance at the western notion of democracy.*
2 = **out of the corner of your eye**, sideways, indirectly, awry, obliquely, with a side glance • *'Do you play chess?' he asked, looking askance at me.*

askew **AS AN ADJECTIVE** = **crooked**, awry, oblique, lopsided, off-centre, cockeyed *(informal)*, skewwhiff *(Brit. informal)* • *She stood there, hat askew.*
OPPOSITES: even, right, straight
▸ **AS AN ADVERB** = **crookedly**, to one side, awry, obliquely, off-centre, aslant • *Some of the doors hung askew.*
OPPOSITES: evenly, right, straight

asleep = **sleeping**, napping, dormant, crashed out *(slang)*, dozing, slumbering, snoozing *(informal)*, fast asleep, sound asleep, out for the count, dead to the world *(informal)*, in a deep sleep • *My daughter was asleep on the sofa.*

aspect 1 = **feature**, point, side, factor, angle, characteristic, facet • *Climate affects every aspect of our lives.*

a

2 = position, view, situation, scene, bearing, direction, prospect, exposure, point of view, outlook • *The house has a south-west aspect.*
3 = appearance, look, air, condition, quality, bearing, attitude, cast, manner, expression, countenance, demeanour, mien *(literary)* • *The snowy tree assumed a dumb, lifeless aspect.*

asperity = sharpness, bitterness, severity, irritability, acrimony, harshness, roughness, sourness, ruggedness, sullenness, irascibility, peevishness, acerbity, churlishness, moroseness, crossness, crabbedness • *'I told you he had no idea,' she remarked with some asperity.*

aspersion = slander, abuse, smear, censure, slur, reproach, defamation, vilification, denigration, calumny, character assassination, disparagement, vituperation, obloquy, detraction, traducement • *He has flatly denied casting aspersions on the star's character.*

asphyxiate = suffocate, choke, strangle, stifle, smother, throttle, strangulate • *Three people were asphyxiated in the crush.*

asphyxiation = suffocation, strangulation, throttling • *A post mortem found that she died from asphyxiation.*

aspirant AS A NOUN **= candidate**, applicant, hopeful, aspirer, seeker, suitor, postulant • *He is among the few aspirants with administrative experience.*
▸ AS AN ADJECTIVE **= hopeful**, longing, ambitious, eager, striving, aspiring, endeavouring, wishful • *aspirant politicians*

aspiration = aim, longing, end, plan, hope, goal, design, dream, wish, desire, object, intention, objective, ambition, craving, endeavour, yearning, eagerness, Holy Grail *(informal)*, hankering • *the needs and aspirations of our pupils*

QUOTATIONS
An aspiration is a joy for ever, a possession as solid as a landed estate, a fortune which we can never exhaust and which gives us year by year a revenue of pleasurable activity
[Robert Louis Stevenson *El Dorado*]

aspire to = aim for, desire, pursue, hope for, long for, crave, seek out, wish for, dream about, yearn for, hunger for, hanker after, be eager for, set your heart on, set your sights on, be ambitious for • *people who aspire to public office*

aspiring = hopeful, longing, would-be, ambitious, eager, striving, endeavouring, wannabe *(informal)*, wishful, aspirant • *an aspiring young artist*

ass 1 = donkey, moke *(slang)*, jennet • *She was led up to the sanctuary on an ass.*
2 = fool, dope *(informal)*, jerk *(slang, chiefly U.S. & Canad.)*, idiot, plank *(Brit. slang)*, berk *(Brit. slang)*, prick *(derogatory slang)*, wally *(slang)*, prat *(slang)*, charlie *(Brit. informal)*, plonker *(slang)*, coot, geek *(slang)*, twit *(informal, chiefly Brit.)*, bonehead *(slang)*, dunce, oaf, simpleton, airhead *(slang)*, jackass, dipstick *(Brit. slang)*, dickhead *(slang)*, gonzo *(slang)*, schmuck *(U.S. slang)*, dork *(slang)*, nitwit *(informal)*, dolt, blockhead, ninny, divvy *(Brit. slang)*, pillock *(Brit. slang)*, halfwit, nincompoop, dweeb *(U.S. slang)*, putz *(U.S. slang)*, fathead *(informal)*, weenie *(U.S. informal)*, eejit *(Scot. & Irish)*, thicko *(Brit. slang)*, dumb-ass *(slang)*, gobshite *(Irish taboo slang)*, numpty *(Scot. informal)*, doofus *(slang, chiefly U.S.)*, daftie *(informal)*, fuckwit *(taboo slang)*, dickwit *(slang)*, nerd *or* nurd *(slang)*, numbskull *or* numskull, twerp *or* twirp *(informal)*, dorba *or* dorb *(Austral. slang)*, bogan *(Austral. slang)* • *He was regarded as a pompous ass.*
▸ RELATED ADJECTIVE: asinine
▸ NAME OF MALE: jack
▸ NAME OF FEMALE: jenny
▸ COLLECTIVE NOUNS: pace, herd

assail 1 = criticize, abuse, blast, flame *(informal)*, put down, malign, berate, revile, vilify, tear into *(informal)*, diss *(slang, chiefly U.S.)*, impugn, go for the jugular, lambast(e) • *These newspapers assail the government each day.*
2 = attack, charge, assault, invade, set about, beset, fall upon, set upon, lay into *(informal)*, maltreat, belabour • *He was assailed by a young man with a knife.*
3 = plague, trouble, pain, harry, bother, disturb, torture, haunt, annoy, tease, torment, harass, hassle *(informal)*, afflict, badger, persecute, molest, pester, vex, bedevil, give someone grief *(Brit. & S. African)* • *She is assailed by self-doubt and emotional insecurity.*

assailant = attacker, assaulter, invader, aggressor, assailer • *Other party-goers rescued the man from his assailant.*

assassin = murderer, killer, slayer, liquidator, executioner, hit man *(slang)*, eliminator *(slang)*, hatchet man *(slang)* • *He memorized the number of the assassin's car.*

assassinate = murder, kill, eliminate *(slang)*, take out *(slang)*, terminate, hit *(slang)*, slay, blow away *(slang, chiefly U.S.)*, liquidate • *a plot to assassinate the President*

assassination = murder, killing, slaughter, purge, hit *(slang)*, removal, elimination *(slang)*, slaying, homicide, liquidation • *She would like to investigate the assassination of her husband.*

QUOTATIONS
Assassination is the quickest way
[Molière *Le Sicilien*]
Assassination is the extreme form of censorship
[George Bernard Shaw *The Rejected Statement*]

assault AS A NOUN **1 = attack**, campaign, strike, rush, storm, storming, raid, invasion, charge, offensive, onset, onslaught, foray, incursion, act of aggression, inroad • *The rebels are poised for a new assault.*
OPPOSITES: defence, protection, resistance
2 = battery, attack, beating, mugging, physical violence, GBH *(Brit.)*, ABH *(Brit.)* • *At the police station, I was charged with assault.*
3 = abuse, attack, blame, criticism, censure, vilification, denigration, calumny, character assassination, stick *(slang)*, sideswipe, impugnment • *He levelled a verbal assault against his opponents.*
▸ AS A VERB **1 = strike**, attack, beat, knock, punch, belt *(informal)*, bang, batter, clip *(informal)*, slap, bash *(informal)*, deck *(slang)*, sock *(slang)*, chin *(slang)*, smack, thump, set about, lay one on *(slang)*, clout *(informal)*, cuff, flog, whack, lob, beset, clobber *(slang)*, smite *(archaic)*, wallop *(informal)*, swat, fall upon, set upon, lay into *(informal)*, tonk *(slang)*, lambast(e), belabour, beat *or* knock seven bells out of *(informal)* • *The gang assaulted him with iron bars.*
2 = attack, charge, storm, invade, fall on, strike at, swoop on, assail • *They would be compelled to assault the capital from the south.*
OPPOSITES: protect, defend, resist

assay = analyse, examine, investigate, assess, weigh, evaluate, inspect, try, appraise • *She sat down and assayed me with her large brown eyes.*

assemblage = group, company, meeting, body, crowd, collection, mass, gathering, rally, assembly, flock, congregation, accumulation, multitude, throng, hui *(N.Z.)*, conclave, aggregation, convocation, runanga *(N.Z.)* • *an assemblage of German officers*

assemble 1 = gather, meet, collect, rally, flock, accumulate, come together, muster, convene, congregate, foregather • *There was nowhere for students to assemble before classes.*
OPPOSITES: dismiss, break up *(informal)*, scatter
2 = bring together, collect, gather, rally, summon, accumulate, round up, marshal, come together, muster, convene, amass, congregate, call together, foregather, convoke • *The assembled multitude cheered as the leaders arrived.*
3 = put together, make, join, set up, manufacture, build up, connect, construct, erect, piece together, fabricate, fit together • *She was trying to assemble the bomb when it went off.*
OPPOSITES: divide, take apart, disassemble

assembly 1 = **gathering**, group, meeting, body, council, conference, crowd, congress, audience, collection, mass, diet, rally, convention, flock, company, house, congregation, accumulation, multitude, throng, synod, hui *(N.Z.)*, assemblage, conclave, aggregation, convocation, runanga *(N.Z.)* • *He waited until quiet settled on the assembly.*
2 = **putting together**, joining, setting up, manufacture, construction, building up, connecting, erection, piecing together, fabrication, fitting together • *workers in car assembly plants*

assent AS A NOUN = **agreement**, accord, sanction, approval, permission, acceptance, consent, compliance, accession, acquiescence, concurrence • *He gave his assent to the proposed legislation.*
OPPOSITES: refusal, objection, denial
▸ IN PHRASES: **assent to something** = **agree to**, allow, accept, grant, approve, permit, sanction, O.K., comply with, go along with, subscribe to, consent to, say yes to, accede to, fall in with, acquiesce in, concur with, give the green light to • *I assented to the publisher's request to write this book.*

assert AS A VERB 1 = **state**, argue, maintain, declare, allege, swear, pronounce, contend, affirm, profess, attest, predicate, postulate, avow, aver, asseverate, avouch *(archaic)* • *He asserted that the bill violated the First Amendment.*
OPPOSITES: deny, refute, rebut
2 = **insist upon**, stress, defend, uphold, put forward, vindicate, press, stand up for • *The republics began asserting their right to govern themselves.*
OPPOSITES: retract, disavow, disclaim
▸ IN PHRASES: **assert yourself** = **be forceful**, put your foot down *(informal)*, put yourself forward, make your presence felt, exert your influence • *He's speaking up and asserting himself much more now.*

assertion 1 = **statement**, claim, allegation, profession, declaration, contention, affirmation, pronouncement, avowal, attestation, predication, asseveration • *assertions that the recession is truly over*
2 = **insistence**, defence, stressing, maintenance, vindication • *They have made the assertion of ethnic identity possible.*

assertive = **confident**, firm, demanding, decided, forward, can-do *(informal)*, positive, aggressive, decisive, forceful, emphatic, insistent, feisty *(informal, chiefly U.S. & Canad.)*, pushy *(informal)*, in-your-face *(Brit. slang)*, dogmatic, strong-willed, domineering, overbearing, self-assured, carnivorous *(informal)* • *an assertive style of management*
OPPOSITES: reserved, retiring, meek

assertiveness = **confidence**, insistence, aggressiveness, firmness, decisiveness, dogmatism, forcefulness, positiveness, pushiness *(informal)*, forwardness, self-assuredness, decidedness, domineeringness • *Her assertiveness stirred up his sense of inadequacy.*
OPPOSITES: insecurity, modesty, meekness

assess 1 = **judge**, determine, estimate, fix, analyse, evaluate, rate, value, check out, compute, gauge, weigh up, appraise, size up *(informal)*, eye up • *The test was to assess aptitude rather than academic achievement.*
2 = **evaluate**, rate, tax, value, demand, estimate, fix, impose, levy • *What is the assessed value of the property?*

assessment 1 = **judgment**, analysis, determination, evaluation, valuation, appraisal, estimation, rating, opinion, estimate, computation • *He was remanded to a mental hospital for assessment.*
2 = **evaluation**, rating, rate, charge, tax, demand, fee, duty, toll, levy, tariff, taxation, valuation, impost • *inflated assessments of mortgaged property*

assessor = **examiner**, tester, inspector, investigator, analyser, surveyor, appraiser, checker • *external assessors of exam results*

asset = **benefit**, help, service, aid, advantage, strength, resource, attraction, blessing, boon, good point, strong point, ace in the hole, feather in your cap, ace up your sleeve • *Her leadership qualities were the greatest asset to the party.*
OPPOSITES: burden, handicap, disadvantage

assets = **property**, goods, means, holdings, money, funds, effects, capital, riches, finance, reserves, resources, estate, wealth, valuables, possessions • *By 1989 the group had assets of 3.5 billion francs.*

assiduity = **diligence**, industry, application, persistence, perseverance, constancy, steadiness, attentiveness, industriousness, indefatigability, studiousness, assiduousness, laboriousness, tirelessness, sedulity, sedulousness • *those with the ability and the assiduity to make it big*

assiduous = **diligent**, constant, steady, hard-working, persistent, attentive, persevering, laborious, industrious, indefatigable, studious, unflagging, untiring, swotty *(Brit. informal)*, sedulous, unwearied • *an assiduous student*
OPPOSITES: lazy, slack, idle

assign 1 = **give**, set, grant, allocate, give out, consign, allot, apportion • *Later in the year, she'll assign them research papers.*
2 = **allocate**, give, determine, fix, appoint, distribute, earmark, mete • *He assigned her all his land.*
3 = **select for**, post, commission, elect, appoint, delegate, nominate, name, designate, choose for, stipulate for • *Did you choose this country or were you simply assigned here?*
4 = **attribute**, credit, put down, set down, ascribe, accredit • *Assign the letters of the alphabet their numerical values.*

assignation = **secret meeting**, rendezvous, tryst *(archaic)*, clandestine meeting, illicit meeting • *She had an assignation with her boyfriend.*

assignment 1 = **task**, work, job, charge, position, post, commission, exercise, responsibility, duty, mission, appointment, undertaking, occupation, chore • *The course involves written assignments and practical tests.*
2 = **selection**, choice, option, appointment, delegation, nomination, designation • *I only ever take photos on assignment.*
3 = **giving**, issuing, grant, distribution, allocation, earmarking, allotment, designation, consignment, dealing out, assignation *(Scots law)*, apportionment • *The state prohibited the assignment of licences to competitors.*

assimilate 1 = **adjust**, fit, adapt, accommodate, accustom, conform, mingle, blend in, become like, homogenize, acclimatize, intermix, become similar, acculturate • *They had been assimilated into the nation's culture.*
2 = **learn**, absorb, take in, incorporate, digest, imbibe *(literary)*, ingest • *My mind could only assimilate one possibility at a time.*

assist 1 = **help**, back, support, further, benefit, aid, encourage, work with, work for, relieve, collaborate with, cooperate with, abet, expedite, succour, lend a hand to, lend a helping hand to, give a leg up to *(informal)* • *They decided to assist me with my chores.*
2 = **facilitate**, help, further, serve, aid, forward, promote, promote, boost, ease, sustain, reinforce, speed up, pave the way for, make easy, expedite, oil the wheels, smooth the path of, assist the progress of • *a chemical that assists in the manufacture of proteins*
OPPOSITES: resist, frustrate, hinder

assistance = **help**, backing, service, support, benefit, aid, relief, boost, promotion, cooperation, encouragement, collaboration, reinforcement, helping hand, sustenance, succour, furtherance, abetment • *He's been operating the shop with the assistance of volunteers.*
OPPOSITES: opposition, resistance, hindrance

assistant 1 = **helper**, partner, ally, colleague, associate, supporter, deputy, subsidiary, aide, aider, second, accessory, attendant, backer, protagonist, collaborator, accomplice, confederate, auxiliary, henchman, right-hand man, adjutant, helpmate, coadjutor *(rare)*, abettor, cooperator • *He had been accompanied to the meeting by an assistant.*

2 = **salesperson**, shop assistant, checkout person, retail assistant • *The assistant checked the price on the back cover of the book.*

associate AS A VERB 1 = **connect**, couple, league, link, mix, relate, pair, ally, identify, unite, join, combine, attach, affiliate, fasten, correlate, confederate, yoke, affix, lump together, cohere, mention in the same breath, conjoin, think of together • *We've got the idea of associating progress with the future.*
OPPOSITES: separate, distance, divorce
2 = **affiliate**, unite, join, link, ally, combine, connect, incorporate, confederate, band together • *I haven't been associated with the project over the last year.*
3 = **socialize**, mix, hang (*informal, chiefly U.S.*), accompany, hang out (*informal*), run around (*informal*), mingle, be friends, befriend, consort, hang about, hobnob, fraternize • *They found out they'd been associating with a murderer.*
OPPOSITES: avoid, break off, part company
▸ AS A NOUN = **partner**, friend, ally, colleague, mate (*informal*), companion, comrade, affiliate, collaborator, confederate, co-worker, workmate, main man (*slang, chiefly U.S.*), cobber (*Austral. & N.Z. old-fashioned or informal*), confrère, compeer, E hoa (*N.Z.*) • *the restaurant owner's business associates*

associated = **connected**, united, joined, leagued, linked, tied, related, allied, combined, involved, bound, syndicated, affiliated, correlated, confederated, yoked • *the Associated Press*

association 1 = **group**, company, club, order, union, class, society, league, band, set, troop, pack, camp, collection, gathering, organization, circle, corporation, alliance, coalition, partnership, federation, bunch, formation, faction, cluster, syndicate, congregation, batch, confederation, cooperative, fraternity, affiliation, posse (*slang*), clique, confederacy, assemblage • *the British Olympic Association*
2 = **friendship**, relationship, link, tie, relations, bond, connection, partnership, attachment, intimacy, liaison, fellowship, affinity, familiarity, affiliation, companionship, comradeship, fraternization • *The association between the two companies stretches back 30 years.*
3 = **connection**, union, joining, linking, tie, mixing, relation, bond, pairing, combination, mixture, blend, identification, correlation, linkage, yoking, juxtaposition, lumping together, concomitance • *the association of the colour black with death*

assorted = **various**, different, mixed, varied, diverse, diversified, miscellaneous, sundry, motley, variegated, manifold, heterogeneous • *swimsuits, sizes 12-18, in assorted colours*
OPPOSITES: like, same, similar

assortment = **variety**, choice, collection, selection, mixture, diversity, array, jumble, medley, mixed bag (*informal*), potpourri, mélange (*French*), miscellany, mishmash, farrago, hotchpotch, salmagundi, pick 'n' mix • *an assortment of cheeses*

assuage 1 = **relieve**, ease, calm, moderate, temper, soothe, lessen, alleviate, lighten, allay, mitigate, quench, palliate • *She was trying to assuage her guilt.*
OPPOSITES: increase, intensify, worsen
2 = **calm**, still, quiet, relax, satisfy, soften, soothe, appease, lull, pacify, mollify, tranquillize • *The meat they'd managed to procure assuaged their hunger.*
OPPOSITES: provoke, infuriate, aggravate

assume 1 = **presume**, think, believe, expect, accept, suppose, imagine, suspect, guess (*informal, chiefly U.S. & Canad.*), take it, fancy, take for granted, infer, conjecture, postulate, surmise, presuppose • *It is a mistake to assume that the two are similar.*
OPPOSITES: know, prove
2 = **take on**, begin, accept, manage, bear, handle, shoulder, take over, don, acquire, put on, take up, embrace, undertake, set about, attend to, take responsibility for, embark upon, enter upon • *He will assume the role of Chief Executive.*
3 = **simulate**, affect, adopt, put on, imitate, mimic, sham, counterfeit, feign, impersonate • *He assumed an air of superiority.*
4 = **take over**, take, appropriate, acquire, seize, hijack, confiscate, wrest, usurp, lay claim to, pre-empt, commandeer, requisition, expropriate, arrogate • *If there is no president, power will be assumed by extremist forces.*
OPPOSITES: leave, give up, hand over

assumed = **false**, affected, made-up, pretended, fake, imitation, bogus, simulated, sham, counterfeit, feigned, spurious, fictitious, make-believe, pseudonymous, phoney or phony (*informal*) • *The articles were published under an assumed name.*
OPPOSITES: real, natural, actual

assuming = **if**, provided, providing, allowing, whether, admitting, supposing, granting, whenever, in case, wherever, on the assumption that, on condition that • *Assuming you're right, there's not much I can do about it.*

assumption 1 = **presumption**, theory, opinion, belief, guess, expectation, fancy, suspicion, premise, acceptance, hypothesis, anticipation, inference, conjecture, surmise, supposition, presupposition, premiss, postulation • *They are wrong in their assumption that we are all alike.*
2 = **taking on**, managing, handling, shouldering, putting on, taking up, takeover, acquisition, undertaking, embracing, acceptance, adoption, entering upon • *He is calling for 'a common assumption of responsibility'.*
3 = **seizure**, taking, takeover, acquisition, appropriation, wresting, confiscation, commandeering, expropriation, pre-empting, usurpation, arrogation • *the government's assumption of power*

assurance 1 = **promise**, statement, guarantee, commitment, pledge, profession, vow, declaration, assertion, oath, affirmation, protestation, word, word of honour • *an assurance that other forces will not move into the territory*
OPPOSITES: lie, falsehood
2 = **confidence**, conviction, courage, certainty, self-confidence, poise, assertiveness, security, faith, coolness, nerve, aplomb, boldness, self-reliance, firmness, self-assurance, certitude, sureness, self-possession, positiveness, assuredness • *He led the orchestra with assurance.*
OPPOSITES: doubt, uncertainty, self-doubt
3 = **insurance**, cover, security, guarantee, protection, provision, coverage, safeguard, warranty, indemnity, indemnification • *endowment assurance*

assure 1 = **convince**, encourage, persuade, satisfy, comfort, prove to, reassure, soothe, hearten, embolden, win someone over, bring someone round • *'Everything's going to be okay,' he assured me.*
2 = **make certain**, ensure, confirm, guarantee, secure, make sure, complete, seal, clinch • *Last night's victory has assured their promotion.*
3 = **promise to**, pledge to, vow to, guarantee to, swear to, attest to, confirm to, certify to, affirm to, give your word to, declare confidently to • *We can assure you of our best service at all times.*

assured 1 = **confident**, certain, positive, bold, poised, assertive, complacent, fearless, audacious, pushy (*informal*), brazen, self-confident, self-assured, self-possessed, overconfident, dauntless, sure of yourself • *He was much more assured than in recent appearances.*
OPPOSITES: retiring, timid, self-conscious
2 = **certain**, sure, ensured, confirmed, settled, guaranteed,

fixed, secure, sealed, clinched, made certain, sound, in the bag *(slang)*, dependable, beyond doubt, irrefutable, unquestionable, indubitable, nailed-on *(slang)* • *Our victory is assured; nothing can stop us.*
OPPOSITES: uncertain, doubtful, unsettled

asteroid = **planetoid**, minor planet • *It's only a matter of time before a giant asteroid destroys the Earth.*

ASTEROIDS

Ceres	Hesperia	Phaethon
Eros	Juno	
Hermes	Pallas	

astonish = **amaze**, surprise, stun, stagger, bewilder, astound, daze, confound, stupefy, boggle the mind, dumbfound, flabbergast *(informal)* • *Her dedication astonishes me.*

astonished = **amazed**, surprised, staggered, bewildered, astounded, dazed, stunned, confounded, perplexed, gobsmacked *(informal)*, dumbfounded, flabbergasted *(informal)*, stupefied • *I was astonished by his stupidity.*

astonishing = **amazing**, striking, surprising, brilliant, stunning, impressive, overwhelming, staggering, startling, sensational *(informal)*, bewildering, breathtaking, astounding, eye-opening, wondrous *(archaic or literary)*, jaw-dropping, stupefying, gee-whizz *(slang)* • *an astonishing display of physical strength*

astonishment = **amazement**, surprise, wonder, confusion, awe, consternation, bewilderment, wonderment, stupefaction • *'What?' she asked in astonishment.*

astound = **amaze**, surprise, overwhelm, astonish, stagger, bewilder, daze, confound, stupefy, stun, take your breath away, boggle the mind, dumbfound, flabbergast *(informal)* • *He used to astound us with feats of physical endurance.*

astounded = **astonished**, surprised, shocked, stunned, alarmed, staggered, startled, bewildered, dazed, confounded, electrified, bowled over *(informal)*, dumbfounded, flabbergasted, stupefied • *I was astounded by its beauty.*

astounding = **amazing**, striking, surprising, brilliant, impressive, astonishing, staggering, sensational *(informal)*, bewildering, stunning, breathtaking, wondrous *(archaic or literary)*, jaw-dropping, eye-popping *(informal)*, stupefying, gee-whizz *(slang)* • *The results are quite astounding.*

astray AS AN ADJECTIVE
▸ **AS AN ADVERB** = **off the right track**, adrift, off course, off the mark, amiss • *Many items of mail being sent to her have gone astray.*
▸ **IN PHRASES: lead someone astray** = **lead into sin**, lead into error, lead into bad ways, lead into wrong, lead off the straight and narrow • *The judge thought he'd been led astray by others.*

astringent 1 = **contractive**, contractile, styptic • *an astringent lotion*
2 = **severe**, strict, exacting, harsh, grim, stern, hard, rigid, rigorous, stringent, austere, caustic, acerbic • *an astringent satire on Hollywood*

astrologer = **stargazer** • *In a way, being an astrologer means being a counsellor.*

astrology = **stargazing**, astromancy, horoscopy • *He has always taken a keen interest in astrology.*
▹ *See panels* **Astrology terms; Zodiac**

astronaut = **space traveller**, cosmonaut, spaceman, spacewoman, space pilot • *The shuttle explosion killed seven astronauts.*

ASTROLOGY TERMS

air	earth	ruling planet
Ascendant *or* Ascendent	element	satellitium
aspect	fire	square
birthchart	fixed	stars
cardinal	horoscope	star sign
conjunction	house	sun sign
cusp	Midheaven *or* MC	trine
Descendant *or* Descendent	mutable	water
	opposition	zodiac
	quintile	

astronomical *or* **astronomic** = **huge**, great, giant, massive, vast, enormous, immense, titanic, infinite, gigantic, monumental, colossal, boundless, galactic, Gargantuan, immeasurable • *Houses here are going for astronomical prices.*

astronomy
▹ *See panels* **Astronomy terms; Planets; Stars and constellations**

astute = **intelligent**, politic, bright, sharp, keen, calculating, clever, subtle, penetrating, knowing, shrewd, cunning, discerning, sly, on the ball *(informal)*, canny, perceptive, wily, crafty, artful, insightful, foxy, adroit, sagacious • *He made a series of astute business decisions.*
OPPOSITES: slow, stupid, dull

astuteness = **intelligence**, knowledge, insight, cunning, penetration, subtlety, brightness, sharpness, acumen, cleverness, keenness, shrewdness, discernment, sagacity, perceptiveness, canniness, adroitness, craftiness, artfulness, slyness, wiliness, foxiness • *With characteristic astuteness, he spoke separately to all involved.*

asunder AS AN ADVERB
▸ **AS AN ADJECTIVE** *(Literary)* = **to pieces**, apart, torn, rent, to bits, to shreds, in pieces, into pieces • *a dress rent asunder from shoulder to hem*

asylum 1 = **mental hospital**, hospital, institution, psychiatric hospital, madhouse *(informal)*, funny farm *(facetious)*, loony bin *(slang)*, nuthouse *(slang)*, rubber room *(U.S. slang)*, laughing academy *(U.S. slang)* • *He spent the rest of his life in a mental asylum.*
2 = **refuge**, security, haven, safety, protection, preserve, shelter, retreat, harbour, sanctuary • *He applied for asylum after fleeing his home country.*

asylum seeker = **refugee**, exile, runaway, fugitive, escapee, émigré, displaced person • *an asylum seeker swam ashore in a bid to enter the country*

asymmetrical = **uneven**, odd, unbalanced, lopsided, out of true, not parallel • *asymmetrical shapes*

atheism = **nonbelief**, disbelief, scepticism, infidelity, paganism, unbelief, freethinking, godlessness, irreligion, heathenism • *He pondered atheism before becoming a minister.*

atheist = **nonbeliever**, pagan, sceptic, disbeliever, heathen, infidel, unbeliever, freethinker, irreligionist • *She is an ex-nun who is now an atheist.*

QUOTATIONS

An atheist is a man who has no invisible means of support
[John Buchan *On Being a Real Person*]

By night an atheist half believes a God
[Edward Young *The Complaint: Night Thoughts*]

No one has ever died an atheist
[Plato *Laws*]

There are no atheists in the foxholes
[William Thomas Cummings *I Saw the Fall of the Philippines*]

ASTRONOMY TERMS

achondrite
aerolite
aerospace
aerosphere
albedo
almucantar *or* almacantar
altitude
analemma
annular eclipse
anthelion
aphelion
apocynthion
apolune
appulse
apapsis
apsis *or* apse
asteroid
asteroid belt
astrobleme
atmosphere
aureola *or* aureole
aurora
aurora australis
aurora borealis
azimuth
barycentre
basin
binary star
black drop
black hole
blue straggler
bolide
brown dwarf
burst
cataclysmic variable
Cepheid variable
Chandrasekhar limit
chemosphere
chondrite
chromosphere
circumlunar
circumpolar
circumsolar
circumstellar
cislunar
cluster
collapsar
colour index
colure
coma
comet
companion
conjunction
constellation
cooordinate system
Copernican system
corona
cosmic
cosmogony
cosmology
crater
crescent
crust
culmination
cusp
dwarf
dynamics
eccentric
ecosphere
effective temperature
ejecta
ellipse
elongation
emersion
ephemeris
epoch
equator
escape velocity
equinox
evection
evolved star
exosphere
extinction
facula
farside
filament
fireball
flare
flocculus
galactic centre
galactic equator
galactic rotation
galaxy
giant
gravitation
heliocentric system
heliosphere
immersion *or* ingress
inclination
inequality
inertia
inferior planet
inner planet
insolation
interplanetary
interstellar
ionosphere
jet
light year
limb
lodestar *or* loadstar
luminosity
lunar
lunar eclipse
magnetosphere
magnitude
major planet
maria
mass
mass loss
mass transfer
merger
meridian
meridian passage
mesosphere
metallicity
metal ratio
meteor
meteorite
meteoroid
meteoroid stream
meteor shower
meteor storm
missing mass
molecular cloud
moonquake
moving cluster
multiple star
nadir
naked singularity
nearside
nebula
neutron star
new moon
node
north celestial pole
northern hemisphere
northern lights
northing
north polar distance
nova
nucleosynthesis
nucleus
nutation
oblateness
obliquity
observatory
occultation
octant
open cluster
opposition
orbit
orbital elements
orbital velocity
oscillating universe
outer planet
parallax
partial eclipse
penumbral eclipse
periapsis
periastron
percentre
perigee
perihelion
photosphere
physical libration
plages
planetary
planetary alignment
planetary system
planetesimal
planetoid
plasmasphere
plerion
polar axis
pole
precession
precession of the equinoxes
primary
prominence
proper motion
protogalaxy
protoplanet
protostar
Ptolemaic system
pulsating universe
pulsating variable
quadrature
quarter
quasar
quasi-stellar object
quiet
radiant
radio source
ray
reciprocal mass
red giant
red supergiant
regolith
retardation
revolution
ring
ring plain
rising
rotation
rupes
saros
satellite
Schwarzschild radius
scintillation
secondary
sextile
Seyfert galaxy
shell star
shepherd satellite
sidereal time
singularity
solar
solar constant
solar eclipse
solar spectrum
solar system
solstice
south celestial pole
southern hemisphere
southern lights
southing
south polar distance
space
spacetime
spectral type *or* spectral class
spherule
spicule
spinar
spray
star
star cloud
stellar
stellar evolution
stellar structure
stellar wind
Strömgren sphere
sublunar point
subsolar point
substellar point
sunspot
sunspot cycle
supercluster
supergiant
superior planet
supernova
symbiotic star
synodic period
syzygy
telluric line
terminator
terrestrial planet
tidal capture
tidal force
tidal friction
tide
total eclipse
total magnitude
thermosphere
train
transient lunar phenomena
triple star
tropical year
troposphere
universal time
universe
variable star
variation
velocity dispersion
vertical circle
visual magnitude
white dwarf
white hole
zenith
zenith distance

atheistic = **nonbelieving**, sceptic, disbelieving, faithless, heathen, infidel, godless, irreligious, unbelieving, freethinking, paganistic, nullifidian • *atheistic philosophers*

athlete = **sportsperson**, player, runner, competitor, contender, sportsman, contestant, gymnast, games player, sportswoman • *He was a great athlete.*

athletic 1 = **fit**, strong, powerful, healthy, active, trim, strapping, robust, vigorous, energetic, muscular, two-fisted, sturdy, husky *(informal)*, lusty, herculean, sinewy, brawny, able-bodied, well-proportioned • *He was tall, with an athletic build.*

OPPOSITES: delicate, frail, feeble
2 = sporting, games, sports, competitive • *They have been given scholarships purely on athletic ability.*

ATHLETIC EVENTS

60 metres	5000 metres	long jump
100 metres	10 000 metres	marathon
110 metres hurdles	cross-country running	orienteering
200 metres	decathlon	pentathlon
400 metres	discus	pole vault
400 metres hurdles	half marathon	relay
800 metres	hammer	shot put
1500 metres	heptathlon	steeplechase
3000 metres	high jump	triathlon
	javelin	triple jump
		walking

athletics = **sports**, games, races, exercises, contests, sporting events, gymnastics, track and field events, games of strength • *intercollegiate athletics*
atmosphere 1 = **air**, sky, heavens, aerosphere • *These gases pollute the atmosphere of towns and cities.*
2 = feeling, feel, air, quality, character, environment, spirit, surroundings, tone, mood, climate, flavour, aura, ambience, vibes *(slang)* • *The muted decor adds to the relaxed atmosphere.*

REGIONS OF THE ATMOSPHERE

ionosphere	stratosphere
mesosphere	thermosphere
ozone layer *or* ozonosphere	troposphere

atmospheric = **ambient**, surrounding, background • *beautiful, atmospheric music*
atom = **particle**, bit, spot, trace, scrap, molecule, grain, dot, fragment, fraction, shred, crumb, mite, jot, speck, morsel, mote, whit, tittle, iota, scintilla *(rare)* • *one carbon atom attached to four hydrogens*
atone = **make amends**, pay, do penance, make reparation, make redress • *He felt he had atoned for what he had done.*
atonement = **amends**, payment, compensation, satisfaction, redress, reparation, restitution, penance, recompense, expiation, propitiation • *True guilt is marked by a willingness to make atonement.*
atop = **on top of**, over, upon, higher than • *Atop a sheet of paper lay an envelope.*
atrocious 1 = **shocking**, terrible, appalling, horrible, horrifying, grievous, execrable, detestable • *The food here is atrocious.*
OPPOSITES: fine, admirable, tasteful
2 = cruel, savage, brutal, vicious, ruthless, infamous, monstrous, wicked, barbaric, inhuman, diabolical, heinous, flagrant, infernal, fiendish, villainous, nefarious, godawful *(slang)*, hellacious *(U.S. slang)* • *The treatment of the prisoners was atrocious.*
OPPOSITES: good, kind, gentle
atrocity 1 = **act of cruelty**, wrong, crime, horror, offence, evil, outrage, outrage, cruelty, brutality, obscenity, wrongdoing, enormity, monstrosity, transgression, abomination, barbarity, villainy • *Those who committed this atrocity should be punished.*
2 = cruelty, wrong, horror, brutality, wrongdoing, enormity, savagery, ruthlessness, wickedness, inhumanity, infamy, transgression, barbarity, viciousness, villainy, baseness, monstrousness, heinousness, nefariousness, shockingness, atrociousness, fiendishness, barbarousness, grievousness, villainousness • *stomach-churning tales of atrocity and massacre*
atrophy AS A VERB 1 = **waste away**, waste, shrink, diminish, deteriorate, decay, dwindle, wither, wilt, degenerate, shrivel • *His muscle atrophied, and he was left lame.*
2 = decline, waste, fade, shrink, diminish, deteriorate, dwindle, wither, wilt, degenerate, shrivel, waste away • *If you let your mind stagnate, this talent will atrophy.*
▸ AS A NOUN 1 = **wasting away**, decline, wasting, decay, decaying, withering, deterioration, meltdown *(informal)*, shrivelling, degeneration, diminution • *exercises to avoid atrophy of cartilage*
2 = wasting, decline, decay, decaying, withering, deterioration, meltdown *(informal)*, shrivelling, degeneration, diminution, wasting away • *levels of consciousness which are in danger of atrophy*
attach AS A VERB 1 = **affix**, stick, secure, bind, unite, add, join, couple, link, tie, fix, connect, lash, glue, adhere, fasten, annex, truss, yoke, append, make fast, cohere, subjoin • *Attach labels to things before you file them away.*
OPPOSITES: remove, separate, detach
2 = ascribe, connect, attribute, assign, place, associate, lay on, accredit, invest with, impute • *They have attached much significance to your visit.*
▸ IN PHRASES: **attach yourself to** *or* **be attached to something** = **join**, accompany, associate with, combine with, join forces with, latch on to, unite with, sign up with, become associated with, sign on with, affiliate yourself with • *He attached himself to a group of poets known as the Martians.*
attached AS AN ADJECTIVE = **spoken for**, married, partnered, engaged, accompanied • *I wondered if he was attached.*
▸ IN PHRASES: **attached to** = **fond of**, devoted to, affectionate towards, full of regard for • *She is very attached to her family and friends.*
attachment 1 = **fondness**, liking, feeling, love, relationship, regard, bond, friendship, attraction, loyalty, affection, devotion, fidelity, affinity, tenderness, reverence, predilection, possessiveness, partiality, aroha *(N.Z.)* • *As a teenager she formed a strong attachment to one of her teachers.*
OPPOSITES: hostility, hatred, aversion
2 = accessory, fitting, extra, addition, component, extension, supplement, fixture, auxiliary, adaptor *or* adapter, supplementary part, add-on, adjunct, appendage, accoutrement, appurtenance • *Some models come with attachments for dusting.*
3 = assignment, charge, commission, transfer, appointment, secondment, detail • *During her course she worked on attachment at the botanical gardens.*
4 = fastening, coupling, link, linking, tie, bond, fixing, joint, binding, union, connection, junction, fusion, concatenation, ligature, affixation • *Measure from the point of attachment of the rope.*
5 = seizure, taking, grabbing, appropriation, annexation, confiscation, commandeering • *Attachment of earnings is a common method of debt collection.*
attack AS A VERB 1 = **assault**, strike (at), mug, set about, ambush, assail, tear into, fall upon, set upon, lay into *(informal)* • *He bundled her into a hallway and brutally attacked her.*
OPPOSITES: support, protect, defend
2 = invade, occupy, raid, infringe, charge, rush, storm, encroach • *The infantry's aim was to slow attacking forces.*
3 = criticize, blame, abuse, blast, pan *(informal)*, condemn, knock *(informal)*, slam *(slang)*, flame *(informal)*, put down, slate *(informal)*, have a go (at) *(informal)*, censure, malign, berate, disparage, revile, vilify, tear into *(informal)*, slag off *(Brit. slang)*, diss *(slang, chiefly U.S.)*, find fault with, impugn, go for the jugular, lambast(e), pick holes in, excoriate, bite

someone's head off, snap someone's head off, pick to pieces • *He publicly attacked the people who've been calling for a secret ballot.*
4 = **infect**, affect, poison, contaminate, pollute, touch, blight, taint, spread to *or* among • *The virus seems to have attacked his throat.*
5 = **deal with**, concentrate on, look after, take care of, see to, attend to, get to work on, devote yourself to, apply yourself to, occupy yourself with • *Any attempt to attack the problem will have to deal with these issues.*
▸ **AS A NOUN** 1 = **assault**, charge, campaign, strike, rush, raid, invasion, offensive, aggression, blitz, onset, onslaught, foray, incursion, inroad • *a campaign of air attacks on strategic targets*
OPPOSITES: support, defence, withdrawal
2 = **criticism**, panning *(informal)*, slating *(informal)*, censure, disapproval, slagging *(slang)*, abuse, knocking *(informal)*, bad press, vilification, denigration, calumny, character assassination, sideswipe, disparagement, impugnment • *He launched an attack on businesses for failing to invest.*
3 = **infection**, poison, pollution, contamination, contagion, septicity • *The body is open to attack from other infections.*
4 = **bout**, fit, access, spell, stroke, seizure, spasm, convulsion, paroxysm • *It brought on an attack of asthma.*

PROVERBS
Attack is the best form of defence

attacker = **assailant**, assaulter, raider, intruder, invader, aggressor, mugger • *There were signs that she had struggled with her attacker.*

attain 1 = **obtain**, get, win, reach, effect, land, score *(slang)*, complete, gain, achieve, earn, secure, realize, acquire, fulfil, accomplish, grasp, reap, procure • *He's halfway to attaining his pilot's licence.*
2 = **reach**, achieve, realize, acquire, arrive at, accomplish • *attaining a state of calmness and confidence*

attainable = **achievable**, possible, likely, potential, accessible, probable, at hand, feasible, within reach, practicable, obtainable, reachable, realizable, graspable, gettable, procurable, accomplishable • *It is unrealistic to believe perfection is a attainable goal.*
OPPOSITES: impossible, unlikely, unattainable

attainment 1 = **achievement**, getting, winning, reaching, gaining, obtaining, acquisition, feat, completion, reaping, accomplishment, realization, fulfilment, arrival at, procurement, acquirement • *the attainment of independence*
2 = **skill**, art, ability, talent, gift, achievement, capability, competence, accomplishment, mastery, proficiency • *their educational attainments*

attempt **AS A VERB** = **try**, seek, aim, struggle, tackle, take on, experiment, venture, undertake, essay, strive, endeavour, have a go at *(informal)*, make an effort, make an attempt, have a crack at, have a shot at *(informal)*, try your hand at, do your best to, jump through hoops *(informal)*, have a stab at *(informal)*, take the bit between your teeth • *We attempted to do something like that here.*
▸ **AS A NOUN** 1 = **try**, go *(informal)*, shot *(informal)*, effort, trial, bid, experiment, crack *(informal)*, venture, undertaking, essay, stab *(informal)*, endeavour • *a deliberate attempt to destabilize defence*
2 = **attack**, assault, strike, offensive • *an attempt on the life of the Prime Minister*

attempted = **tried**, ventured, undertaken, endeavoured, assayed • *a case of attempted murder*

attend **AS A VERB** 1 = **be present**, go to, visit, be at, be there, be here, frequent, haunt, appear at, turn up at, patronize, show up at *(informal)*, show yourself, put in an appearance at, present yourself at • *Thousands of people attended the funeral.*
OPPOSITES: miss, be absent, play truant
2 = **pay attention**, listen, follow, hear, mark, mind, watch, note, regard, notice, observe, look on, heed, take to heart, pay heed, hearken *(archaic)* • *I'm not sure what he said – I wasn't attending.*
OPPOSITES: ignore, discount, neglect
3 = **escort**, conduct, guard, shadow, accompany, companion, shepherd, convoy, usher, squire, chaperon • *horse-drawn coaches attended by liveried footmen*
▸ **IN PHRASES: attend to someone** = **look after**, help, mind, aid, tend, nurse, care for, take care of, minister to, administer to • *The main thing is to attend to the injured.*
attend to something 1 = **apply yourself to**, concentrate on, look after, take care of, see to, get to work on, devote yourself to, occupy yourself with • *You had better attend to the matter in hand.*
2 = **deal with**, manage, address, tackle, cope with, take care of, see to • *There are more pressing needs to be attended to today.*

attendance **AS A NOUN** 1 = **presence**, being there, attending, appearance • *Her attendance at school was sporadic.*
2 = **turnout**, audience, gate, congregation, house, crowd, throng, number present • *Some estimates put attendance at 60,000.*
▸ **IN PHRASES: in attendance** = **here**, there, present, near, available, ready, nearby, accounted for, to hand, at hand, in attendance • *Several fire engines were in attendance.*

attendant **AS A NOUN** = **assistant**, guide, guard, servant, companion, aide, escort, follower, steward, waiter, usher, warden, helper, auxiliary, custodian, page, menial, concierge, underling, lackey, chaperon, flunky • *He was working as a car-park attendant.*
▸ **AS AN ADJECTIVE** = **accompanying**, related, associated, accessory, consequent, resultant, concomitant • *His victory, and all the attendant publicity, were deserved.*

attention **AS A NOUN** 1 = **thinking**, thought, mind, notice, consideration, concentration, observation, scrutiny, heed, deliberation, contemplation, thoughtfulness, attentiveness, intentness, heedfulness • *He turned his attention to the desperate state of housing in the province.*
2 = **care**, support, concern, treatment, looking after, succour, ministration • *a demanding baby who wants attention 24 hours a day*
3 = **awareness**, regard, notice, recognition, consideration, observation, consciousness • *Let me draw your attention to some important issues.*
OPPOSITES: distraction, disregard, inattention
▸ **AS A PLURAL NOUN** = **courtesy**, compliments, regard, respect, care, consideration, deference, politeness, civility, gallantry, mindfulness, assiduities • *He was flattered by the attentions of a younger woman.*
OPPOSITES: discourtesy, impoliteness

attentive 1 = **intent**, listening, concentrating, careful, alert, awake, mindful, watchful, observant, studious, on your toes, heedful, regardful • *I wish you would be more attentive to detail.*
OPPOSITES: distracted, preoccupied, heedless
2 = **considerate**, kind, civil, devoted, helpful, obliging, accommodating, polite, thoughtful, gracious, conscientious, respectful, courteous, gallant • *At parties he is always attentive to his wife.*
OPPOSITES: negligent, thoughtless, neglectful

attenuate = **weaken**, reduce, contract, lower, diminish, decrease, dilute, lessen, sap, water down, adulterate, enfeeble, enervate, devaluate • *Preparation and training can attenuate risk.*

attenuated 1 = **slender**, extended, thinned, slimmed, refined, stretched out, lengthened, drawn out, spun out, elongated, rarefied • *rounded arches and attenuated columns*
2 = **weakened**, reduced, contracted, lowered, diminished, decreased, dilute, diluted, lessened, devalued, sapped, watered down, adulterated, enfeebled, enervated • *The vaccination contains attenuated strains of the target virus.*

attest = **testify**, show, prove, confirm, display, declare, witness, demonstrate, seal, swear, exhibit, warrant, assert, manifest, give evidence, invoke, ratify, affirm, certify, verify, bear out, substantiate, corroborate, bear witness, authenticate, vouch for, evince, aver, adjure • *Records attest to his long history of violence.*
OPPOSITES: deny, contradict, disprove

attic = **loft**, garret, roof space • *Gallons of water cascaded from the attic.*

attire = **clothes**, wear, dress, clothing, gear *(informal)*, habit, uniform, outfit, costume, threads *(slang)*, array *(poetic)*, garments, robes, apparel, garb, accoutrements, raiment *(archaic or poetic)*, vestment, schmutter *(slang)*, habiliments • *women dressed in their finest attire*

attired = **dressed**, clothed, turned out, equipped, costumed, arrayed, robed, got ready, fitted out, decked out, garbed, rigged out, apparelled *(archaic)*, accoutred • *He was faultlessly attired in black coat and striped trousers.*

attitude 1 = **opinion**, thinking, feeling, thought, view, position, approach, belief, mood, perspective, point of view, stance, outlook, viewpoint, slant, frame of mind • *the general change in attitude towards them*
2 = **manner**, air, condition, bearing, aspect, carriage, disposition, demeanour, mien *(literary)* • *He has a gentle attitude.*
3 = **position**, bearing, pose, stance, carriage, posture • *scenes of the king in various attitudes of worshipping*

attorney = **lawyer**, solicitor, counsel, advocate, barrister, counsellor, legal adviser • *a prosecuting attorney*

attract 1 = **allure**, interest, draw, invite, persuade, engage, charm, appeal to, fascinate, win over, tempt, lure *(informal)*, induce, incline, seduce, entice, enchant, endear, lead on, coax, captivate, beguile, cajole, bewitch, decoy, inveigle, pull, catch (someone's) eye • *Summer attracts visitors to the countryside.*
OPPOSITES: disgust, revolt, repel
2 = **pull**, draw, magnetize • *Anything with strong gravity attracts other things to it.*

attraction 1 = **appeal**, interest, draw, pull *(informal)*, come-on *(informal)*, charm, incentive, invitation, lure, bait, temptation, fascination, attractiveness, allure, inducement, magnetism, enchantment, endearment, enticement, captivation, temptingness, pleasingness • *It was never a physical attraction, just a meeting of minds.*
2 = **pull**, draw, magnetism • *the gravitational attraction of the Sun*
3 = **entertainment**, feature, delight, distraction, amusement, diversion, honeypot • *The walled city is an important tourist attraction*

attractive 1 = **seductive**, charming, tempting, interesting, pleasing, pretty, fair, beautiful, inviting, engaging, likable *or* likeable, lovely, winning, sexy *(informal)*, pleasant, handsome, fetching, good-looking, glamorous, gorgeous, magnetic, cute, irresistible, enticing, provocative, captivating, beguiling, alluring, bonny, winsome, comely, prepossessing, hot *(informal)*, fit *(Brit. informal)* • *He was always very attractive to women.*
OPPOSITES: unattractive, ugly, unsightly
2 = **appealing**, pleasing, inviting, fascinating, tempting, enticing, agreeable, irresistible • *Co-operation was more than just an attractive option.*
OPPOSITES: offensive, unpleasant, unappealing

attractiveness 1 = **seductiveness**, appeal, beauty, charm, good looks, fairness, allure, magnetism, desirability, loveliness, prettiness, gorgeousness, handsomeness, pulchritude *(formal or literary)*, winsomeness, comeliness, engagingness, glamorousness *or* glamourousness, likableness *or* likeableness, prepossessingness, takingness, winningness • *Physical attractiveness can play a major part in how we react to people.*
OPPOSITES: ugliness, unsightliness, unbecomingness
2 = **appeal**, magnetism, pleasantness, agreeableness, agreeability, enticingness, pleasingness • *The forest enhances the attractiveness of the region.*
OPPOSITES: unpleasantness, offensiveness, repulsiveness

attributable = **ascribable**, accountable, applicable, traceable, explicable, assignable, imputable, blamable *or* blameable, placeable, referable *or* referrable • *deaths attributable to smoking*

attribute AS A VERB = **ascribe**, apply, credit, blame, refer, trace, assign, charge, allocate, put down, set down, allot, impute • *They attribute their success to external causes such as luck.*
▸ AS A NOUN = **quality**, point, mark, sign, note, feature, property, character, element, aspect, symbol, characteristic, indication, distinction, virtue, trait, hallmark, facet, quirk, peculiarity, idiosyncrasy • *He has every attribute a footballer could want.*

attribution = **ascription**, charge, credit, blame, assignment, attachment, placement, referral, assignation, imputation • *There was attribution of evil intent to those with different views.*

attrition = **wearing down**, harrying, weakening, harassment, thinning out, attenuation, debilitation • *a war of attrition against the government*

attune = **accustom**, set, accord, tune, adjust, adapt, regulate, coordinate, modulate, harmonize, familiarize, acclimatize • *Meditation helps me to attune myself to the patient.*

attuned = **accustomed**, adjusted, coordinated, in tune, in harmony, in accord, harmonized, familiarized, acclimatized • *I have become attuned to the industrial aspect of the city.*

atypical = **unusual**, exceptional, uncommon, singular, deviant, unconventional, unique, unorthodox, uncharacteristic, out of the ordinary, unrepresentative, out of keeping, uncustomary, nonconforming, unconforming • *The economy of the province was atypical because it was so small.*
OPPOSITES: standard, model, normal

auburn = **reddish-brown**, tawny, russet, henna, rust-coloured, copper-coloured, chestnut-coloured, Titian red, nutbrown • *a tall woman with long auburn hair*
▹ See panel **Shades of red**

au courant IN PHRASES: *au courant* **with** = **up-to-date with**, acquainted with, abreast of, knowledgeable about, well-informed about, conversant with, well up on, up to speed with, in the know about, enlightened of, *au fait* with, in the swim about • *He was so wonderfully au courant with the European scene.*

auction AS A NOUN = **sale**, deal, selling, transaction, disposal, marketing, vending • *He bought the picture at an auction.*
▸ AS A VERB = **sell**, trade, exchange • *We'll auction them for charity.*

audacious 1 = **daring**, enterprising, brave, bold, risky, rash, adventurous, reckless, courageous, fearless, intrepid, valiant, daredevil, death-defying, dauntless, venturesome • *an audacious plan to win the presidency*
OPPOSITES: guarded, frightened, timid
2 = **cheeky**, presumptuous, impertinent, insolent, impudent, forward, fresh *(informal)*, assuming, rude, defiant, brazen, in-your-face *(Brit. slang)*, shameless, sassy *(U.S. informal)*, pert, disrespectful • *Audacious thieves stole her car from under her nose.*
OPPOSITES: gracious, unassuming, tactful

audacity 1 = **daring**, nerve, courage, guts *(informal)*, bravery, boldness, recklessness, face *(informal)*, front, enterprise, valour, fearlessness, rashness, adventurousness, intrepidity, audaciousness, dauntlessness, venturesomeness • *I was shocked at the audacity of the gangsters.*

a

2 = **cheek**, nerve, defiance, gall *(informal)*, presumption, rudeness, chutzpah *(U.S. & Canad. informal)*, insolence, impertinence, neck *(informal)*, impudence, effrontery, brass neck *(Brit. informal)*, shamelessness, sassiness *(U.S. informal)*, forwardness, pertness, audaciousness, disrespectfulness • *He had the audacity to look at his watch while I was talking.*

QUOTATIONS
Being tactful in audacity is knowing how far one can go too far
[Jean Cocteau *Le Rappel à l'ordre*]

audible = **clear**, distinct, discernible, detectable, perceptible, hearable • *There was an audible sigh of relief.*
OPPOSITES: inaudible, faint, imperceptible

audience 1 = **spectators**, company, house, crowd, gathering, gallery, assembly, viewers, listeners, patrons, congregation, turnout, onlookers, throng, assemblage • *The entire audience broke into loud applause.*
2 = **public**, market, following, fans, devotees, fanbase, aficionados • *She began to find a receptive audience for her work.*
3 = **interview**, meeting, hearing, exchange, reception, consultation • *The Prime Minister will seek an audience with the Queen today.*

audit AS A VERB = **inspect**, check, review, balance, survey, examine, investigate, go through, assess, go over, evaluate, vet, verify, appraise, scrutinize, inquire into • *Each year they audit our accounts and certify them as true and fair.*
▸ AS A NOUN = **inspection**, check, checking, review, balancing, search, survey, investigation, examination, scan, scrutiny, supervision, surveillance, look-over, verification, once-over *(informal)*, checkup, superintendence • *The bank is carrying out an internal audit.*

audition = **test**, screen test • *They gave him the role after hearing him perform just once in audition.*

auditor = **inspector**, critic, investigator, supervisor, superintendent, censor, examiner, scrutinizer, checker, overseer, scrutineer • *They were singled out for criticism in the auditor's report.*

auditorium = **hall**, theatre, chamber, concert hall, meeting place, assembly room • *The hall is a huge auditorium.*

au fait IN PHRASES: *au fait with* = **fully informed about**, in touch with, familiar with, abreast of, knowledgeable about, well-acquainted with, well up on, up to speed with, in the know about, on the ball about *(informal)*, conversant about, *au courant* with, clued-up about *(informal)*, switched-on about *(informal)* • *I am au fait with fashion.*

augment = **increase**, grow, raise, extend, boost, expand, add to, build up, strengthen, enhance, reinforce, swell, intensify, heighten, enlarge, multiply, inflate, magnify, amplify, dilate • *She was searching for a way to augment her income.*
OPPOSITES: reduce, contract, diminish

augmentation = **increase**, rise, growth, inflation, boost, addition, build-up, strengthening, expansion, extension, swelling, heightening, reinforcement, enlargement, enhancement, accession, intensification, magnification, multiplication, amplification, dilation • *the augmentation of the army*

augur = **bode**, promise, predict, herald, signify, foreshadow, prophesy, harbinger, presage, prefigure, portend, betoken, be an omen of • *Already there were problems. It didn't augur well.*

august = **noble**, great, kingly, grand, excellent, imposing, impressive, superb, distinguished, magnificent, glorious, splendid, elevated, eminent, majestic, dignified, regal, stately, high-ranking, monumental, solemn, lofty, exalted • *the august surroundings of the Liberal Club*

aura = **air**, feeling, feel, quality, atmosphere, tone, suggestion, mood, scent, aroma, odour, ambience, vibes *(slang)*, vibrations *(slang)*, emanation • *She had an aura of authority.*

auspices = **support**, backing, control, charge, care, authority, championship, influence, protection, guidance, sponsorship, supervision, patronage, advocacy, countenance, aegis • *a peace conference under the auspices of the UN*

auspicious = **favourable**, timely, happy, promising, encouraging, bright, lucky, hopeful, fortunate, prosperous, rosy, opportune, propitious, felicitous • *His career had an auspicious start.*
OPPOSITES: bad, black, unpromising

austere 1 = **stern**, hard, serious, cold, severe, formal, grave, strict, exacting, harsh, stiff, forbidding, grim, rigorous, solemn, stringent, inflexible, unrelenting, unfeeling • *an austere, distant, cold person*
OPPOSITES: kindly, sweet, flexible
2 = **plain**, simple, severe, spare, harsh, stark, bleak, subdued, economical, Spartan, unadorned, unornamented, bare-bones • *The church was austere and simple.*
OPPOSITES: comfortable, luxurious, indulgent
3 = **ascetic**, strict, continent, exacting, rigid, sober, economical, solemn, Spartan, unrelenting, self-disciplined, puritanical, chaste, strait-laced, abstemious, self-denying, abstinent • *The life of the troops was comparatively austere.*
OPPOSITES: abandoned, loose, immoral

austerity 1 = **plainness**, economy, simplicity, severity, starkness, spareness, Spartanism • *abandoned buildings with a classical austerity*
2 = **asceticism**, economy, rigidity, abstinence, self-discipline, chastity, sobriety, continence, puritanism, solemnity, self-denial, strictness, abstemiousness, chasteness, exactingness, Spartanism • *the years of austerity which followed the war*

authentic 1 = **real**, true, original, actual, pure, genuine, valid, faithful, undisputed, veritable, lawful, on the level *(informal)*, bona fide, dinkum *(Austral. & N.Z. informal)*, pukka, the real McCoy, true-to-life • *patterns for making authentic border-style clothing*
OPPOSITES: supposed, false, fake
2 = **accurate**, true, certain, reliable, legitimate, authoritative, factual, truthful, dependable, trustworthy, veracious • *authentic details about the birth of the organization*
OPPOSITES: misleading, fraudulent, fictitious

authenticate 1 = **verify**, guarantee, warrant, authorize, certify, avouch • *All the antiques have been authenticated.*
OPPOSITES: invalidate, annul, render null and void
2 = **vouch for**, confirm, endorse, validate, attest • *He authenticated the accuracy of various details.*

authenticity 1 = **genuineness**, purity, realness, veritableness • *Some factors have cast doubt on the statue's authenticity.*
2 = **accuracy**, truth, certainty, validity, reliability, legitimacy, verity, actuality, faithfulness, truthfulness, dependability, trustworthiness, authoritativeness, factualness • *The film's authenticity of detail has impressed critics.*

author 1 = **writer**, composer, novelist, hack, creator, columnist, scribbler, scribe, essayist, wordsmith, penpusher, littérateur, man *or* woman of letters • *She's the author of the book 'Give your Child Music'.*
2 = **creator**, father, parent, mother, maker, producer, framer, designer, founder, architect, planner, inventor, mover, originator, prime mover, doer, initiator, begetter, fabricator • *the authors of the plan*
▸ RELATED ADJECTIVE: auctorial

QUOTATIONS
There is probably no hell for authors in the next world – they suffer so much from critics and publishers in this
[C.N. Bovee]

authoritarian AS AN ADJECTIVE = **strict**, severe, absolute, harsh, rigid, autocratic, dictatorial, dogmatic, imperious, domineering, unyielding, tyrannical, disciplinarian, despotic,

doctrinaire • *There was a coup to restore authoritarian rule.*
OPPOSITES: democratic, liberal, lenient
▸ **AS A NOUN** = **disciplinarian**, dictator, tyrant, Big Brother, control freak, despot, autocrat, absolutist • *He became an overly strict authoritarian.*

authoritative 1 = **commanding**, lordly, masterly, imposing, dominating, confident, decisive, imperative, assertive, autocratic, dictatorial, dogmatic, imperious, self-assured, peremptory • *He has a deep, authoritative voice.*
OPPOSITES: weak, humble, timid
2 = **official**, approved, sanctioned, legitimate, sovereign, authorized, commanding • *The first authoritative study was published in 1840.*
OPPOSITES: unofficial, unauthorized, unsanctioned
3 = **reliable**, learned, sound, true, accurate, valid, scholarly, faithful, authentic, definitive, factual, truthful, veritable, dependable, trustworthy • *The evidence she uses is highly authoritative.*
OPPOSITES: unreliable, deceptive, undependable

authority 1 *usually plural* = **powers that be**, government, police, officials, the state, management, administration, the system, the Establishment, Big Brother *(informal)*, officialdom • *This was a pretext for the authorities to cancel the elections.*
2 = **prerogative**, right, influence, might, force, power, control, charge, rule, government, weight, strength, direction, command, licence, privilege, warrant, say-so, sway, domination, jurisdiction, supremacy, dominion, ascendancy, mana *(N.Z.)* • *The judge has no authority to order a second trial.*
3 = **expert**, specialist, professional, master, ace *(informal)*, scholar, guru, buff *(informal)*, wizard, whizz *(informal)*, virtuoso, connoisseur, boffin *(Brit. informal)*, arbiter, hotshot *(informal)*, fundi *(S. African)* • *He's an authority on Russian affairs.*
4 = **command**, power, control, rule, management, direction, grasp, sway, domination, mastery, dominion • *He has no natural authority.*
5 = **permission**, leave, permit, sanction, licence, approval, go-ahead *(informal)*, liberty, consent, warrant, say-so, tolerance, justification, green light, assent, authorization, dispensation, carte blanche, a blank cheque, sufferance • *He must first be given authority from his own superiors.*

QUOTATIONS
Authority is never without hate
[Euripides *Ion*]
I am a man under authority, having soldiers under me;
and I say to this man, Go, and he goeth; and to another,
Come, and he cometh; and to my servant,
Do this, and he doeth it
[*Bible: St. Matthew*]

authorization = **permission**, right, leave, power, authority, ability, strength, permit, sanction, licence, approval, warrant, say-so, credentials, a blank cheque • *a request for authorization to use military force*

authorize 1 = **empower**, commission, enable, entitle, mandate, accredit, give authority to • *They authorized him to use force if necessary.*
2 = **permit**, allow, suffer, grant, confirm, agree to, approve, sanction, endure, license, endorse, warrant, tolerate, ratify, consent to, countenance, accredit, vouch for, give leave, give the green light for, give a blank cheque to, give authority for • *We are willing to authorize a police raid.*
OPPOSITES: ban, exclude, forbid

authorized = **official**, commissioned, approved, licensed, ratified, signed and sealed • *The application will be processed by one of our authorized agents.*

auto = **car**, machine, motor, vehicle, wheels *(informal)*, automobile, jalopy *(informal)*, motorcar • *the auto industry*

autobiography = **life story**, record, history, résumé, memoirs • *He published his autobiography last autumn.*

QUOTATIONS
An autobiography is an obituary in serial form with the last instalment missing
[Quentin Crisp *The Naked Civil Servant*]

autocracy = **dictatorship**, tyranny, despotism, absolutism • *Many poor countries are abandoning autocracy.*

autocrat = **dictator**, tyrant, Big Brother, control freak, despot, absolutist • *Her management style was that of an unapologetic autocrat.*

autocratic = **dictatorial**, absolute, unlimited, all-powerful, imperious, domineering, tyrannical, despotic, tyrannous • *They have grown intolerant of his autocratic ways.*

autograph = **signature**, moniker *(informal)* • *He went backstage and asked for her autograph.*

automated = **automatic**, mechanical, robot, mechanized, push-button, self-regulating, self-propelling, self-activating, self-moving, self-acting • *highly automated production lines*

automatic 1 = **mechanical**, robot, automated, mechanized, push-button, self-regulating, self-propelling, self-activating, self-moving, self-acting • *Modern trains have automatic doors.*
OPPOSITES: human, physical, done by hand
2 = **involuntary**, natural, unconscious, mechanical, spontaneous, reflex, instinctive, instinctual, unwilled • *the automatic body functions, such as breathing*
OPPOSITES: conscious, voluntary, deliberate
3 = **inevitable**, certain, necessary, assured, routine, unavoidable, inescapable • *They should face an automatic charge of manslaughter*

automobile = **car**, machine, motor, vehicle, wheels *(informal)*, auto *(U.S.)*, jalopy *(informal)*, motorcar • *He seems to have bought up half America's automobile production.*

autonomous = **self-ruling**, free, independent, sovereign, self-sufficient, self-governing, self-determining • *They declared themselves part of a new autonomous province.*

autonomy = **independence**, freedom, sovereignty, self-determination, self-government, self-rule, self-sufficiency, home rule, rangatiratanga *(N.Z.)* • *They stepped up their demands for local autonomy.*
OPPOSITES: dependency, subjection, foreign rule

autopsy = **postmortem**, dissection, postmortem examination, necropsy • *The autopsy report gave the cause of death as poisoning.*

autumn
▸ **RELATED ADJECTIVE:** autumnal

auxiliary **AS AN ADJECTIVE** 1 = **supplementary**, reserve, emergency, substitute, secondary, back-up, subsidiary, fall-back • *auxiliary fuel tanks*
2 = **supporting**, helping, aiding, assisting, accessory, ancillary • *the army and auxiliary forces*
OPPOSITES: first, leading, primary
▸ **AS A NOUN** = **helper**, partner, ally, associate, supporter, assistant, companion, accessory, subordinate, protagonist, accomplice, confederate, henchman • *a nursing auxiliary*

avail **AS A NOUN** = **benefit**, use, help, good, service, aid, profit, advantage, purpose, assistance, utility, effectiveness, mileage *(informal)*, usefulness, efficacy • *His efforts were to no avail.*
▸ **IN PHRASES: avail yourself of something** = **make use of**, use, employ, exploit, take advantage of, profit from, make the most of, utilize, have recourse to, turn to account • *Guests should feel at liberty to avail themselves of your facilities.*

availability = **accessibility**, readiness, handiness, attainability, obtainability • *the easy availability of guns*

available 1 = **accessible**, ready, to hand, convenient, handy, vacant, on hand, at hand, free, applicable, to be had, achievable, obtainable, on tap *(informal)*, attainable, at your

fingertips, at your disposal, ready for use • *There are three small boats available for hire.*
OPPOSITES: taken, occupied, in use
2 = **free**, around, unoccupied, contactable • *He is on holiday and is not available for comment.*
OPPOSITES: busy, engaged, unavailable

a

avalanche 1 = **snow-slide**, landslide, landslip, snow-slip • *Four people died when an avalanche buried them alive last week.*
2 = **large amount**, barrage, torrent, deluge, inundation • *He was greeted with an avalanche of publicity.*

avant-garde = **progressive**, pioneering, way-out *(informal)*, experimental, innovative, unconventional, far-out *(slang)*, ground-breaking, innovatory • *avant-garde concert music*
OPPOSITES: conservative, traditional, conventional

avarice = **greed**, meanness, penny-pinching, parsimony, acquisitiveness, rapacity, cupidity, stinginess, covetousness, miserliness, greediness, niggardliness, graspingness, close-fistedness, penuriousness • *a month's rent – just enough to satisfy the landlord's avarice*
OPPOSITES: generosity, extravagance, liberality

QUOTATIONS
The love of money is the root of all evil
[Bible: I Timothy]
avarice, the spur of industry
[David Hume *Essays: Moral and Political*]

avaricious = **grasping**, greedy, acquisitive, stingy, mean, miserable, rapacious, penny-pinching, parsimonious, miserly, niggardly, covetous, penurious, close-fisted, tight-arsed *(taboo slang)*, tight-assed *(U.S. taboo slang)*, snoep *(S. African informal)*, tight as a duck's arse *(taboo slang)* • *He sacrificed his career so that his avaricious brother could succeed.*

avenge = **get revenge for**, revenge, repay, retaliate for, take revenge for, hit back for, requite, pay (someone) back for, get even for *(informal)*, even the score for, get your own back for, take vengeance for, take satisfaction for, pay (someone) back in his *or* her own coin for • *He spent five years avenging his daughter's death.*

avenue 1 = **street**, way, course, drive, road, pass, approach, channel, access, entry, route, path, passage, entrance, alley, pathway, boulevard, driveway, thoroughfare • *It is set in landscaped grounds at the end of a tree-lined avenue.*
2 = **method**, line, approach, direction, path • *He was presented with 80 potential avenues of investigation.*

aver = **state**, say, maintain, declare, protest, allege, swear, assert, proclaim, pronounce, affirm, profess, avow, asseverate, avouch • *Her friends aver that men find her fascinating.*

average AS A NOUN = **standard**, normal, usual, par, mode, mean, rule, medium, norm, run of the mill, midpoint • *The pay is about the average for a service industry.*
▸ AS AN ADJECTIVE 1 = **usual**, common, standard, general, normal, regular, ordinary, typical, commonplace, unexceptional • *The average man burns 2000 calories a day.*
OPPOSITES: great, bad, unusual
2 = **mean**, middle, medium, intermediate, median • *Of the US's million millionaires, the average age was 63.*
OPPOSITES: minimum, maximum
3 = **mediocre**, fair, ordinary, moderate, pedestrian, indifferent, not bad, middling, insignificant, so-so *(informal)*, banal, second-rate, middle-of-the-road, tolerable, run-of-the-mill, passable, undistinguished, uninspired, unexceptional, bog-standard *(Brit. & Irish slang)*, no great shakes *(informal)*, fair to middling *(informal)* • *I was only average academically.*
▸ AS A VERB = **make on average**, be on average, even out to, do on average, balance out to • *pay increases averaging 9.75%*
▸ IN PHRASES: **on average** = **usually**, generally, normally, typically, for the most part, as a rule • *On average we would be spending $200 a day.*

averse = **opposed**, reluctant, hostile, unwilling, backward, unfavourable, loath, disinclined, inimical, indisposed, antipathetic, ill-disposed • *He's not averse to publicity.*
OPPOSITES: willing, keen, favourable

aversion = **hatred**, hate, horror, disgust, hostility, opposition, dislike, reluctance, loathing, distaste, animosity, revulsion, antipathy, repulsion, abhorrence, disinclination, repugnance, odium, detestation, indisposition • *Many people have an aversion to insects.*
OPPOSITES: liking, love, desire

avert 1 = **ward off**, avoid, prevent, frustrate, fend off, preclude, stave off, forestall • *A fresh tragedy was narrowly averted yesterday.*
2 = **turn away**, turn, turn aside • *He kept his eyes averted.*

aviary = **bird enclosure** • *There is also an aviary with parrots, macaws and peacocks.*

aviation = **flying**, flight, aeronautics, powered flight • *the aviation industry*
▹ *See panels* **Aircraft; Aviation terms**

aviator = **pilot**, flyer, airman, airwoman, aeronaut • *He was a pioneer aviator – the first to fly across the Channel.*

avid 1 = **enthusiastic**, keen, devoted, intense, eager, passionate, ardent, fanatical, fervent, zealous, keen as mustard • *an avid collector of art*
OPPOSITES: indifferent, lukewarm, apathetic
2 = **insatiable**, hungry, greedy, thirsty, grasping, voracious, acquisitive, ravenous, rapacious, avaricious, covetous, athirst • *He was avid for wealth.*

avoid 1 = **prevent**, stop, frustrate, hamper, foil, inhibit, head off, avert, thwart, intercept, hinder, obstruct, impede, ward off, stave off, forestall, defend against • *He had to take emergency action to avoid a disaster.*
2 = **refrain from**, bypass, dodge, eschew, escape, duck (out of) *(informal)*, fight shy of, shirk from • *He managed to avoid giving them an idea of what he was up to.*
3 = **elude**, escape, ignore, hide from, keep away from, keep aloof from • *She had to lock herself in to avoid him.*
OPPOSITES: find, face, confront
4 = **keep away from**, dodge, shun, evade, steer clear of, sidestep, circumvent, bypass, slip through the net, body-swerve *(Scot.)*, give a wide berth to • *He had ample time to swerve and avoid the woman.*

avoidable 1 = **preventable**, stoppable, avertible *or* avertable • *The tragedy was entirely avoidable.*
OPPOSITES: unstoppable, unpreventable
2 = **escapable**, evadable • *Smoking is an avoidable cause of disease and death.*
OPPOSITES: necessary, inevitable, unavoidable

avoidance 1 = **refraining**, dodging, shirking, eschewal • *tax avoidance*
2 = **prevention**, safeguard, precaution, anticipation, thwarting, elimination, deterrence, forestalling, prophylaxis, preclusion, obviation • *Improve your health by stress avoidance*

avow = **state**, maintain, declare, allege, recognize, swear, assert, proclaim, affirm, profess, aver, asseverate • *a public statement avowing neutrality*

avowal 1 = **statement**, allegation, recognition, profession, declaration, maintenance, assertion, oath, affirmation, proclamation, asseveration, averment • *He made an avowal to set himself right once again.*
2 = **confession**, owning, admission, acknowledgment • *an avowal of error*

avowed = **declared**, open, admitted, acknowledged, confessed, sworn, professed, self-proclaimed • *She is an avowed vegetarian.*

await 1 = **wait for**, expect, look for, look forward to, anticipate, stay for • *Little was said as we awaited the arrival of the chairman.*
2 = **be in store for**, wait for, be ready for, lie in wait for, be in readiness for • *A nasty surprise awaited them.*

AVIATION TERMS

aerobatics
air corridor
air miss
airside
airspeed
air traffic control
anhedral
approach *or* approach path
attitude
automatic pilot *or* autopilot
autorotation
bank
barrel roll
batsman
belly landing
bird strike
boarding pass
bunt
ceiling
chandelle
charter flight
clearway
contact flight
copilot
crab
crash-dive
crash-land
cruise
dihedral
ditch
dive
drogue
feather
flameout
flight
flight management systems
flight path
fly-by-wire
gate
glide
groundspeed
head-up display
holding pattern
hunt
Immelmann turn *or* Immelmann
in-flight
landing
landside
loading
loop
Mach
navigator
nose dive
overfly
overshoot
pancake landing
pilot
pitch
pitch axis
power dive
rake
redeye *or* redeye flight
reheat
roll
roll axis
runway
SBA *or* standard beam approach
scheduled flight
shockstall
sideslip
snap roll
sonic boom
sound barrier
spin
stack
stall
subsonic
supersonic
tailspin
takeoff
taxi
taxiway
trim
undershoot
vapour trail
victory roll
wide-body
wingover
yaw
yaw axis

awake AS A VERB **1 = wake up**, come to, wake, stir, awaken, rouse • *I awoke to the sound of the wind in the trees.*
2 = alert, excite, stimulate, provoke, revive, arouse, activate, awaken, fan, animate, stir up, incite, kick-start *(informal)*, enliven, kindle, breathe life into, call forth, vivify • *He had awoken interest in the sport again.*
3 = stimulate, excite, provoke, activate, alert, animate, fan, stir up, incite, kick-start *(informal)*, enliven, kindle, breathe life into, call forth, vivify • *The aim was to awaken an interest in foreign cultures.*
▸ AS AN ADJECTIVE **1 = not sleeping**, sleepless, wide-awake, aware, waking, conscious, aroused, awakened, restless, restive, wakeful, bright-eyed and bushy-tailed • *I don't stay awake at night worrying about that.*
OPPOSITES: sleeping, asleep, unconscious
2 = alert, aware, on the lookout, alive, attentive, on the alert, observant, watchful, on guard, on your toes, heedful, vigilant • *They are awake to the challenge of stemming the exodus.*

awaken = awake, wake, wake up, revive, arouse, rouse • *He was snoring when I awakened him.*

awakening = stirring up, birth, waking, waking up, revival, awaking, animating, rousing, stimulation, provocation, arousal, enlivening, activation, kindling, incitement, vivification • *the awakening of national consciousness in people*

award AS A VERB **1 = present with**, give, grant, gift, distribute, render, assign, decree, hand out, confer, endow, bestow, allot, apportion, adjudge • *She was awarded the prize for both films.*
2 = grant, give, render, assign, decree, accord, confer, adjudge • *The contract has been awarded to a British shipyard.*
▸ AS A NOUN **1 = grant**, subsidy, scholarship, hand-out, endowment, stipend • *this year's annual pay award*
2 = prize, gift, trophy, decoration, grant, bonsela *(S. African)*, koha *(N.Z.)* • *She presented a bravery award to the schoolgirl.*
3 = settlement, payment, compensation • *workmen's compensation awards*
4 = giving, presentation, allotment, bestowal, conferment, conferral • *the award of the man of the match trophy*

aware AS AN ADJECTIVE **= informed**, enlightened, knowledgeable, learned, expert, versed, up to date, in the picture, plugged-in *(slang)*, in the know *(informal)*, erudite, well-read, au fait *(French)*, in the loop, well-briefed, au courant *(French)*, clued-up *(informal)* • *They are politically very aware.*
OPPOSITES: unaware, ignorant, oblivious
▸ IN PHRASES: **aware of = knowing about**, familiar with, conscious of, wise to *(slang)*, alert to, mindful of, acquainted with, alive to, awake to, privy to, hip to *(slang)*, appreciative of, attentive to, conversant with, apprised of, cognizant of, sensible of • *They are well aware of the dangers.*

awareness IN PHRASES: **awareness of = knowledge of**, understanding of, appreciation of, recognition of, attention to, perception of, consciousness of, acquaintance with, enlightenment with, sensibility to, realization of, familiarity with, mindfulness of, cognizance of, sentience of • *The 1980s brought an awareness of green issues.*

awash 1 = flooded, drowned, engulfed, submerged, immersed, afloat, inundated, deluged, submersed • *The bathroom floor was awash.*
2 = overburdened, overwhelmed, swamped • *a company which is awash with cash*

away AS AN ADJECTIVE **= absent**, out, gone, elsewhere, abroad, not there, not here, not present, on vacation, not at home • *She was away on a business trip.*
▸ AS AN ADVERB **1 = off**, elsewhere, abroad, hence, from here • *She drove away before he could speak again.*
2 = aside, out of the way, to one side • *I put my journal away and prepared for bed.*
3 = at a distance, far, apart, remote, isolated • *They live thirty miles away from town.*
4 = continuously, repeatedly, relentlessly, incessantly, interminably, unremittingly, uninterruptedly • *He would work away on his computer well into the night.*

awe AS A NOUN **= wonder**, fear, respect, reverence, horror, terror, dread, admiration, amazement, astonishment, veneration • *She gazed in awe at the great stones.*
OPPOSITES: contempt, arrogance, scorn
▸ AS A VERB **= impress**, amaze, stun, frighten, terrify, cow, astonish, horrify, intimidate, daunt • *I am still awed by his courage.*

awed = impressed, shocked, amazed, afraid, stunned, frightened, terrified, cowed, astonished, horrified, intimidated, fearful, daunted, dumbfounded, wonder-struck • *The crowd listened in awed silence.*

awe-inspiring = impressive, striking, wonderful, amazing, stunning *(informal)*, magnificent, astonishing, intimidating, awesome, daunting, breathtaking, eye-popping *(informal)*, fearsome, wondrous *(archaic or literary)*, jaw-dropping, gee-whizz *(slang)* • *a museum with an awe-inspiring display of jewellery*
OPPOSITES: flat, boring, unimpressive

awesome = awe-inspiring, striking, shocking, imposing, terrible, amazing, stunning, wonderful, alarming, impressive, frightening, awful, overwhelming, terrifying, magnificent, astonishing, horrible, dreadful, formidable, horrifying, intimidating, fearful, daunting, breathtaking, majestic, solemn, fearsome, wondrous *(archaic or literary)*, redoubtable, jaw-dropping, stupefying, gee-whizz *(slang)* • *the awesome responsibility of sending men into combat*

a

awestruck *or* **awe-stricken** = **impressed**, shocked, amazed, stunned, afraid, frightened, terrified, cowed, astonished, horrified, intimidated, fearful, awed, daunted, awe-inspired, dumbfounded, struck dumb, wonder-struck • *I was awestruck that anyone could be so beautiful.*

awful AS AN ADJECTIVE 1 = **disgusting**, terrible, tremendous, offensive, gross, nasty, foul, horrible, dreadful, unpleasant, revolting, stinking, sickening, hideous, vulgar, vile, distasteful, horrid, frightful, nauseating, odious, repugnant, loathsome, abominable, nauseous, detestable, godawful *(slang)*, hellacious *(U.S. slang)*, festy *(Austral. slang)*, yucko *(Austral. slang)* • *an awful smell of paint*
2 = **bad**, poor, terrible, appalling, foul, rubbish *(slang)*, shit *(taboo slang)*, dreadful, unpleasant, dire, crap *(taboo slang)*, horrendous, ghastly, from hell *(informal)*, atrocious, deplorable, abysmal, frightful, shite *(taboo slang)*, hellacious *(U.S. slang)* • *Even if the weather's awful there's still lots to do.*
OPPOSITES: great *(informal)*, wonderful, excellent, ka pai *(N.Z.)*
3 = **shocking**, serious, alarming, distressing, dreadful, horrifying, horrific, hideous, harrowing, gruesome • *Her injuries were massive; it was awful.*
4 = **unwell**, poorly *(informal)*, ill, terrible, sick, ugly, crook *(Austral. & N.Z. informal)*, unhealthy, unsightly, queasy, out of sorts *(informal)*, off-colour, under the weather *(informal)*, green about the gills • *I looked awful and felt quite sleepy.*
▸ AS AN ADVERB = **very**, highly, really, deeply, particularly, seriously *(informal)*, truly, extremely, absolutely, terribly, remarkably, unusually, jolly *(Brit.)*, wonderfully, profoundly, decidedly, awfully *(informal)*, acutely, exceedingly, excessively, eminently, superlatively, uncommonly • *Gosh, you're awful pretty.*

awfully 1 = **very**, extremely, terribly, exceptionally, quite, very much, seriously *(informal)*, greatly, immensely, exceedingly, excessively, dreadfully • *That caramel looks awfully good.*
2 = **badly**, woefully, dreadfully, inadequately, disgracefully, wretchedly, unforgivably, shoddily, reprehensibly, disreputably • *I played awfully, and there are no excuses.*

awhile = **for a while**, briefly, for a moment, for a short time, for a little while • *He worked awhile as a pharmacist.*

awkward 1 = **embarrassing**, difficult, compromising, sensitive, embarrassed, painful, distressing, delicate, uncomfortable, tricky, trying, humiliating, unpleasant, sticky *(informal)*, troublesome, perplexing, disconcerting, inconvenient, thorny, untimely, ill at ease, discomfiting, ticklish, inopportune, toe-curling *(slang)*, barro *(Austral. slang)*, cringeworthy *(Brit. informal)* • *There was an awkward moment when people had to decide where to stand.*
OPPOSITES: comfortable, pleasant
2 = **inconvenient**, difficult, troublesome, cumbersome, unwieldy, unmanageable, clunky *(informal)*, unhandy • *It was heavy enough to make it awkward to carry.*
OPPOSITES: easy, convenient, handy
3 = **clumsy**, stiff, rude, blundering, coarse, bungling, lumbering, inept, unskilled, bumbling, unwieldy, ponderous, ungainly, gauche, gawky, uncouth, unrefined, artless, inelegant, uncoordinated, graceless, cack-handed *(informal)*, unpolished, clownish, oafish, inexpert, maladroit, ill-bred, all thumbs, ungraceful, skill-less, unskilful, butterfingered *(informal)*, unhandy, ham-fisted *or* ham-handed *(informal)*, unco *(Austral. slang)* • *She made an awkward gesture with her hands.*
OPPOSITES: graceful, skilful, adept
4 = **uncooperative**, trying, difficult, annoying, unpredictable, unreasonable, stubborn, troublesome, perverse, prickly, exasperating, irritable, intractable, vexing, unhelpful, touchy, obstinate, obstructive, bloody-minded *(Brit. informal)*, chippy *(informal)*, vexatious, hard to handle, disobliging • *She's got to an age where she's being awkward.*
5 = **embarrassed**, nervous, uncomfortable, uneasy, self-conscious • *He was rather awkward with his godson.*

awkwardness 1 = **clumsiness**, stiffness, rudeness, coarseness, ineptness, ill-breeding, artlessness, gaucheness, inelegance, gaucherie, gracelessness, oafishness, gawkiness, uncouthness, maladroitness, ungainliness, clownishness, inexpertness, uncoordination, unskilfulness, unskilledness • *He displayed all the awkwardness of adolescence.*
2 = **embarrassment**, difficulty, discomfort, delicacy, unpleasantness, inconvenience, stickiness *(informal)*, painfulness, ticklishness, uphill *(S. African)*, thorniness, inopportuneness, perplexingness, untimeliness • *It was a moment of some awkwardness in our relationship.*

awning = **canopy**, tester, covering, shade, sunshade, baldachin • *They leapt from a first-floor window on to a shop awning.*

awry AS AN ADVERB = **askew**, to one side, off course, out of line, obliquely, unevenly, off-centre, cockeyed *(informal)*, out of true, crookedly, skew-whiff *(informal)* • *He was concerned that his hair might go awry.*
▸ AS AN ADJECTIVE = **askew**, twisted, crooked, to one side, uneven, off course, out of line, asymmetrical, off-centre, cockeyed *(informal)*, misaligned, out of true, skew-whiff *(informal)* • *His dark hair was all awry.*
▸ AS AN ADVERB
▸ AS AN ADJECTIVE = **wrong**, amiss • *a plan that had gone awry*

axe AS A NOUN = **hatchet**, chopper, tomahawk, cleaver, adze • *She took an axe and wrecked the car.*
▸ AS A VERB 1 = **abandon**, end, pull, eliminate, cancel, scrap, wind up, turn off *(informal)*, relegate, cut back, terminate, dispense with, discontinue, pull the plug on • *Community projects are being axed by the government.*
2 = **dismiss**, fire *(informal)*, sack *(informal)*, remove, get rid of, discharge, throw out, oust, give (someone) their marching orders, give the boot to *(slang)*, give the bullet to *(Brit. slang)*, give the push to, give someone his *or* her P45 *(informal)*, kennet *(Austral. slang)*, jeff *(Austral. slang)* • *She was axed by the Edinburgh club in October after her comments about a referee.*
▸ IN PHRASES: **an axe to grind** = **pet subject**, grievance, ulterior motive, private purpose, personal consideration, private ends • *I've got no axe to grind with him.*
the axe = **the sack** *(informal)*, dismissal, discharge, wind-up, the boot *(slang)*, cancellation, cutback, termination, the chop *(slang)*, the (old) heave-ho *(informal)*, the order of the boot *(slang)* • *one of the four doctors facing the axe*

axiom = **principle**, fundamental, maxim, gnome, adage, postulate, dictum, precept, aphorism, truism, apophthegm • *the long-held axiom that education leads to higher income*

axiomatic = **self-evident**, given, understood, accepted, certain, granted, assumed, fundamental, absolute, manifest, presupposed, unquestioned, indubitable, apodictic *or* apodeictic • *It is axiomatic that as people grow older they become less agile.*

axis = **pivot**, shaft, axle, spindle, centre line • *the axis of the Earth*

axle = **shaft**, pin, rod, axis, pivot, spindle, arbor, mandrel • *The engine, gearbox and black axle needed to be replaced.*

azure = **sky blue**, blue, clear blue, ultramarine, cerulean, sky-coloured • *warm azure seas and palm-fringed beaches*
▹ *See panel* **Shades of blue**

Bb

baas = **master**, bo *(informal)*, chief, ruler, commander, head, overlord, overseer • *The word 'baas' is now regarded as an expression of servility.*

babble AS A VERB **1** = **gabble**, chatter, gush, spout, waffle *(informal, chiefly Brit.)*, splutter, gaggle, burble, prattle, gibber, rabbit on *(Brit. informal)*, jabber, prate, earbash *(Austral. & N.Z. slang)* • *They all babbled simultaneously.*
2 = **gurgle**, lap, bubble, splash, murmur, ripple, burble, plash • *a brook babbling only yards from the door*
▸ AS A NOUN **1** = **gabble**, chatter, burble, prattle, blabber • *He couldn't make himself heard above the babble.*
2 = **gibberish**, waffle *(informal, chiefly Brit.)*, drivel, twaddle • *lots of babble about strategies and tactics*

babe **1** = **darling**, love, baby, dear, dearest, honey, sweetheart, sweetie *(informal)* • *I'm sorry, babe. I didn't mean it.*
2 = **attractive young woman**, siren, charmer, vamp *(informal)*, femme fatale *(French)*, temptress, Lorelei, seductress, Circe • *This is not a case of idle babe worship among howling teens.*
3 = **baby**, child, innocent, infant, bairn *(Scot. & Northern English)*, tacker *(Austral. slang)*, suckling, newborn child, babe in arms, nursling • *innocent as newborn babes*

baby AS A NOUN **1** = **child**, infant, babe, wean *(Scot.)*, little one, bairn *(Scot. & Northern English)*, suckling, newborn child, babe in arms, sprog *(slang)*, neonate, rug rat *(U.S. & Canad. informal)*, ankle biter *(Austral. slang)*, tacker *(Austral. slang)* • *My wife has just had a baby.*
2 = **darling**, love, dear, dearest, honey, babe, sweetheart, sweetie *(informal)* • *You have to wake up now, baby.*
3 = **youngest**, smallest, junior member, littlest • *It's very evident he is the baby of the family.*
▸ AS AN ADJECTIVE = **small**, little, minute, tiny, mini, wee, miniature, dwarf, diminutive, petite, midget, teeny *(informal)*, pocket-sized, undersized, teeny-weeny *(informal)*, Lilliputian, teensy-weensy *(informal)*, pygmy *or* pigmy • *Serve with baby new potatoes.*
▸ AS A VERB = **spoil**, pamper, cosset, coddle, pet, humour, indulge, spoon-feed, mollycoddle, overindulge, wrap up in cotton wool *(informal)* • *He'd always babied her.*

QUOTATIONS

A baby is God's opinion that life should go on
[Carl Sandburg *Remembrance Rock*]

Every baby born into the world is a finer one than the last
[Charles Dickens *Nicholas Nickleby*]

The invisible bond that gives the baby rein to discover his place in the world also brings the creeping baby back to home base
[Louise J. Kaplan *Oneness and Separateness: From Infant to Individual*]

People who say they sleep like a baby usually don't have one
[Leo Burke]

babyish = **childish**, young, simple, soft *(informal)*, silly, spoiled, juvenile, foolish, immature, boyish *or* girlish, infantile, sissy, puerile, namby-pamby, baby • *I'm ashamed of the babyish nonsense I write.*
OPPOSITES: adult, mature, grown-up

baby-sit = **child mind** • *I promised to baby-sit for Mrs Plunkett.*

bachelor

QUOTATIONS

A bachelor never quite gets over the idea that he is a thing of beauty and a boy forever
[Helen Rowland *A Guide to Men*]

The confirmed bachelor is ... quite as often the victim of a too profound appreciation of the infinite charmingness of woman, as made solitary for life by the legitimate empire of a cold and tasteless temperament
[Herman Melville *Pierre*]

back AS AN ADVERB **1** = **backwards**, in reverse, towards the rear, towards the back, rearwards • *She stepped back from the door expectantly.*
2 = **again**, as before • *Denise hopes to be back at work by the time her daughter is one.*
3 = **at a distance**, far, away, apart, out of the way • *Keep back from the edge of the platform.*
4 = **ago**, before, earlier, in the past, previously • *He was wounded in that terrorist attack a few years back.*
▸ AS A NOUN **1** = **spine**, backbone, vertebrae, spinal column, vertebral column • *Three of the victims were shot in the back.*
2 = **rear**, other side, back end, rear side • *a room at the back of the shop*
OPPOSITES: head, face, front
3 = **end**, tail end • *the customers at the back of the queue*
4 = **reverse**, rear, other side, wrong side, underside, flip side, verso • *Send your answers on the back of a postcard.*
▸ AS AN ADJECTIVE **1** = **rear** • *a path leading to the back garden*
OPPOSITES: front, advance, fore
2 = **rearmost**, hind, hindmost • *She could remember sitting in the back seat of their car.*
3 = **previous**, earlier, former, past, out of date, elapsed • *A handful of back copies will give an indication of property prices.*
OPPOSITES: later, future
4 = **tail**, end, rear, posterior, dorsal • *They had transmitters taped to their back feathers.*
▸ AS A VERB **1** = **support**, help, second, aid, champion, encourage, favour, defend, promote, sanction, sustain, assist, advocate, endorse, side with, stand up for, espouse, stand behind, countenance, abet, stick up for *(informal)*, take up the cudgels for • *He is backed by the civic movement.*
OPPOSITES: attack, combat, oppose
2 = **subsidize**, help, support, finance, sponsor, assist, underwrite • *Murjani backed him to start the new company.*
3 = **gamble on**, bet (money) on, speculate on, punt on *(chiefly Brit.)*, put money on, take a risk on, put your shirt on,

stake money on, chance money on, wager money on, pledge money on, venture money on • *It is upsetting to discover that you have backed a loser.*

▸ IN PHRASES: **back away** = **move back**, go back, retire, withdraw, shrink, recede, pull back, back off, recoil, draw back, give ground, turn tail • *The girls hastily backed away.*

back away from something = **retreat**, withdraw, shrink, depart, pull back, back off, draw back • *He's backing away from the policies and styles of his predecessor.*

back down = **give in**, collapse, withdraw, yield, concede, submit, surrender, comply, cave in *(informal)*, capitulate, accede, admit defeat, back-pedal • *It's too late now to back down.*

back off = **recoil**, go back, retire, withdraw, shrink back, move back, recede, pull back, back away, draw back, turn tail • *They backed off in horror.*

back off from something = **retreat from**, withdraw from, depart from, shrink from, pull back from, draw back from • *The union has publicly backed off from that demand.*

back out = **withdraw**, retire, give up, pull out, retreat, drop out, renege, cop out *(slang)*, chicken out *(informal)*, detach yourself • *I've already promised I'll go – I can't back out now.*

back out of something 1 = **withdraw from**, abandon, cancel, pull out of, retire from, resign from, drop out of, give up on, retreat from, go back on, renege on, flip-flop on *(informal, chiefly U.S.)*, backtrack on, chicken out of *(informal)*, cop out of *(slang)*, detach yourself from, recant on, disengage yourself from • *They backed out of the deal.*

2 = **withdraw from**, retire from, reverse from, retreat from, pull back from, back off from, back away from, recoil from, draw back from, turn tail from • *The two men backed out of the shop.*

back someone up = **support**, second, aid, assist, stand by, bolster, side with, vouch for • *The girl denied being there, and the men backed her up.*

back something up = **substantiate**, support, prove, confirm, reinforce, validate, bear out, corroborate, attest to, authenticate • *Her views are backed up by a report on crime.*

behind someone's back = **secretly**, covertly, surreptitiously, furtively, conspiratorially, sneakily, deceitfully • *You enjoy her hospitality, and then criticize her behind her back.*

▸ RELATED ADJECTIVE: dorsal

backbiting = **slander**, abuse, spite, gossip, smearing, malice, maligning, defamation, vilification, denigration, bitchiness *(slang)*, calumny, disparagement, muckraking, vituperation, spitefulness, cattiness *(informal)*, scandalmongering, detraction, calumniation • *Corporate backbiting is nothing new.*

backbone 1 = **spinal column**, back, spine, vertebrae, vertebral column • *She doubled over, snapping her backbone and breaking her arm.*

2 = **foundation**, support, base, basis, mainstay, bedrock • *the economic backbone of the nation*

3 = **strength of character**, will, balls *(taboo slang)*, character, bottle *(Brit. slang)*, resolution, resolve, nerve, daring, courage, determination, guts, pluck, stamina, grit, bravery, fortitude, toughness, tenacity, willpower, mettle, boldness, firmness, spunk *(informal)*, fearlessness, steadfastness, moral fibre, hardihood, ballsiness *(taboo slang)*, dauntlessness • *You might be taking drastic measures and you've got to have the backbone to do that.*

back-breaking = **exhausting**, hard, difficult, wearing, tiring, draining, punishing, crippling, fatiguing, wearying, gruelling, debilitating, strenuous, arduous, laborious, toilsome • *Many months of back-breaking work still face them.*

backdrop = **environment**, situation, circumstances, background, atmosphere • *The election will take place against a backdrop of increasing instability.*

backer 1 = **supporter**, second, ally, angel *(informal)*, patron, promoter, subscriber, underwriter, helper, benefactor • *I was looking for a backer to assist me in the attempted buy-out.*

2 = **advocate**, supporter, patron, sponsor, promoter, protagonist • *He became a backer of reform at the height of the crisis.*

backfire 1 = **fail**, founder, flop *(informal)*, rebound, fall through, fall flat, boomerang, miscarry, misfire, go belly-up *(slang)*, turn out badly, meet with disaster • *The President's tactics could backfire.*

2 = **misfire** • *The car backfired.*

background AS A NOUN 1 = **upbringing**, history, culture, environment, tradition, circumstances, breeding, milieu • *Moulded by his background, he could not escape traditional values.*

2 = **experience**, grounding, education, preparation, qualifications, credentials • *His background was in engineering.*

3 = **circumstances**, history, conditions, situation, atmosphere, environment, framework, equation, ambience, milieu, frame of reference • *The meeting takes place against a background of political violence.*

4 = **backdrop**, surrounding, backcloth • *roses patterned on the blue background*

▸ IN PHRASES: **in the background** 1 = **in the distance** • *I kept hearing applause in the background.*

2 = **behind the scenes**, unnoticed, out of the limelight, out of the spotlight • *Rosemary likes to stay in the background.*

backhanded 1 = **ambiguous**, ironic, indirect, sarcastic, oblique, sardonic, double-edged, equivocal, with tongue in cheek • *a backhanded compliment*

2 = **indirect**, rambling, roundabout, meandering, devious, oblique, circuitous, circumlocutory, periphrastic • *In a backhanded way, he raises yet another objection.*

backing 1 = **support**, seconding, championing, promotion, sanction, approval, blessing, encouragement, endorsement, patronage, accompaniment, advocacy, moral support, espousal • *He said the president had the full backing of his government.*

2 = **assistance**, support, help, funds, aid, grant, subsidy, sponsorship, patronage • *She brought her action with the financial backing of the BBC.*

3 = **lining**, reinforcement, underlay • *Remove the backing.*

4 = **accompaniment**, harmony, orchestration • *Tapes provided the backing.*

backlash = **reaction**, response, resistance, resentment, retaliation, repercussion, counterblast, counteraction, retroaction • *a right-wing backlash*

backlog = **build-up**, stock, excess, accumulation, accretion • *There is a backlog of repairs and maintenance in schools.*

back-pedal 1 = **backtrack**, go back, reverse, reconsider, climb down, have second thoughts, change your mind, flip-flop *(informal, chiefly U.S.)*, do a U-turn • *He appeared to back-pedal on that statement.*

2 = **break your word**, go back on your word, default, back out, repudiate, welsh *(slang)*, flip-flop *(informal, chiefly U.S.)*, break a promise • *He's back-pedalled twice already.*

backside = **buttocks**, behind *(informal)*, seat, bottom, rear, tail *(informal)*, cheeks *(informal)*, butt *(U.S. & Canad. informal)*, bum *(Brit. slang)*, ass *(U.S. & Canad. taboo slang)*, buns *(U.S. slang)*, arse *(taboo slang)*, rump, fanny *(slang, chiefly U.S. & Canad.)*, rear end, posterior, haunches, hindquarters, derrière *(euphemistic)*, tush, fundament, gluteus maximus *(Anatomy)*, coit *(Austral. slang)*, nates *(technical)*, jacksy *(Brit. slang)*, keister or keester *(slang, chiefly U.S.)* • *I've got a sportscar under my backside and the world's my oyster.*

backslide = **relapse**, slip, weaken, go wrong, stray, lapse, revert to old habits, fall back, degenerate, slip back to old ways, regress, go astray, retrogress • *Keep these things in mind to help prevent you from backsliding.*

backslider = **relapser**, renegade, reneger, deserter, fallen angel, turncoat, apostate • *I've never heard of him punishing a backslider.*

backtrack 1 *often with* **on** = **retract**, withdraw, retreat, draw back, recant, back-pedal • *The finance minister backtracked on his decision.*
2 = **retrace your steps**, go back, reverse, retreat, move back, back-pedal • *We had to backtrack to the corner and cross the street.*

backup 1 = **support**, backing, help, aid, reserves, relief, assistance, reinforcement, auxiliaries • *There's no emergency backup immediately available if something goes wrong.*
2 = **substitute**, reserve, relief, stand-in, replacement, stand-by, understudy, second string, locum • *He was added to the squad as a backup.*

backward 1 = **reverse**, inverted, inverse, back to front, rearward • *He did a backward flip.*
OPPOSITES: forward, frontward
2 = **regressive**, negative, downward, for the worse, degenerative, retrograde, retrogressive • *a backward step into unskilled work*
3 = **underdeveloped**, primitive, undeveloped, unsophisticated • *We need to accelerate the pace of change in our backward country.*
4 = **slow**, behind, stupid, retarded, deficient, underdeveloped, subnormal, half-witted, behindhand, slow-witted, intellectually handicapped *(Austral.)* • *I was slow to walk and my parents thought I was backward.*

backwardness 1 = **lack of development**, underdevelopment, lack of sophistication, primitiveness • *I was astonished at the backwardness of our country at the time.*
2 = **slowness**, learning difficulties, underdevelopment, retardation, arrested development • *Her parents were concerned about her backwardness in practical and physical activities.*
OPPOSITES: brightness, quickness, smartness

backwards *or* **backward** 1 = **towards the rear**, behind you, in reverse, rearwards • *Bess glanced backwards.*
2 = **in reverse order**, back to front, in the opposite way from usual • *He works backwards, building a house from the top downwards.*
3 = **to the past**, back • *unshakable traditions that look backward rather than ahead*

backwater = **isolated place**, backwoods, remote place, sleepy town, secluded spot • *a quiet rural backwater*

backwoods = **sticks** *(informal)*, outback, back country *(U.S.)*, back of beyond, backlands *(U.S.)* • *the backwoods of Louisiana*

bacteria = **microorganisms**, viruses, bugs *(slang)*, germs, microbes, pathogens, bacilli • *Chlorine is added to kill bacteria.*

bad AS AN ADJECTIVE 1 = **harmful**, damaging, dangerous, disastrous, destructive, unhealthy, detrimental, hurtful, ruinous, deleterious, injurious, disadvantageous • *Divorce is bad for children.*
OPPOSITES: good, sound, beneficial
2 = **severe**, serious, terrible, acute, extreme, intense, painful, distressing, fierce, harsh • *The pain is often so bad she wants to scream.*
3 = **poor**, unwise, unsound • *Of course politicians will sometimes make bad decisions.*
4 = **unfavourable**, troubling, distressing, unfortunate, grim, discouraging, unpleasant, gloomy, adverse • *The closure of the project is bad news for her staff.*
5 = **inferior**, poor, inadequate, pathetic, faulty, duff *(Brit. informal)*, unsatisfactory, mediocre, defective, second-class, deficient, imperfect, second-rate, shoddy, low-grade, erroneous, substandard, low-rent *(informal, chiefly U.S.)*, two-bit *(U.S. & Canad. slang)*, crappy *(slang)*, end-of-the-pier *(Brit. informal)*, poxy *(slang)*, dime-a-dozen *(informal)*, piss-poor *(slang)*, bush-league *(Austral. & N.Z. informal)*, tinhorn *(U.S. slang)*, half-pie *(N.Z. informal)*, bodger *or* bodgie *(Austral. slang)*, strictly for the birds *(informal)* • *Many old people in Britain are living in bad housing.*
OPPOSITES: fair, adequate, satisfactory
6 = **incompetent**, poor, useless, crap *(slang)*, incapable, unfit, inexpert • *He was a bad driver.*
7 = **grim**, severe, hard, tough, harsh, unpleasant • *Being unable to hear doesn't seem as bad as being unable to see.*
8 = **wicked**, criminal, evil, corrupt, worthless, base, vile, immoral, delinquent, sinful, depraved, debased, amoral, egregious, villainous, unprincipled, iniquitous, nefarious, dissolute, maleficent • *I was selling drugs, but I didn't think I was a bad person.*
OPPOSITES: good, moral, virtuous
9 = **naughty**, defiant, perverse, wayward, mischievous, wicked, unruly, impish, undisciplined, roguish, disobedient • *You are a bad boy for repeating what I told you.*
OPPOSITES: good, obedient, well-behaved
10 = **foul**, irritable, grotty • *She is in a bit of a bad mood because she's just given up smoking.*
11 = **guilty**, sorry, ashamed, apologetic, rueful, sheepish, contrite, remorseful, regretful, shamefaced, conscience-stricken • *You don't have to feel bad about relaxing.*
12 = **injured**, damaged, diseased, hurt, sick, weak, disabled, ailing, lame, unhealthy, dicky *(Brit. informal)* • *He has a bad back so we have a hard bed.*
13 = **rotten**, off, rank, sour, rancid, mouldy, fetid, putrid, festy *(Austral. slang)* • *They bought so much beef that some went bad.*
14 = **offensive**, nasty, insulting, disgusting, crude, rude, abusive, coarse, indecent, unsavoury, objectionable, uncouth, impolite, discourteous, indelicate, uncivil, indecorous • *I don't like to hear bad language in the street.*
15 = **null and void**, false, fake, bogus, worthless, dud, counterfeit, null, not binding, fallacious • *She wrote another bad cheque.*
▸ IN PHRASES: **not bad** = **O.K.** *or* **okay**, fine, middling, average, fair, all right, acceptable, moderate, adequate, respectable, satisfactory, so-so, tolerable, passable, fair to middling *(informal)* • *These are not bad for cheap shoes.*
too bad 1 = **a shame**, a crime *(informal)*, a pity, a sin, a crying shame, a bummer *(slang)*, a sad thing • *It is too bad that she had to leave so soon.*
2 = **hard luck**, tough luck, hard cheese • *'But I haven't finished yet.' 'Too bad.'*

QUOTATIONS
When I'm good, I'm very, very good, but when I'm bad I'm better
[Mae West *I'm No Angel*]

baddie *or* **baddy** *(Informal)* = **villain**, criminal, rogue, bad guy, scoundrel, miscreant, antihero, evildoer, wrong 'un *(Austral. slang)* • *All the characters, even the baddies, are a little too nice.*
OPPOSITES: hero, heroine, goodie *or* goody

badge 1 = **image**, brand, stamp, identification, crest, emblem, insignia • *a badge depicting a party leader*
2 = **mark**, sign, indication, token, indicator, trademark, hallmark • *sporting a sword as their badge of citizenship*
3 = **brooch**, pin, button *(U.S.)*, breast pin • *He handed me a computer-printed name badge.*

badger = **pester**, worry, harry, bother, bug *(informal)*, bully, plague, hound, get at, harass, nag, hassle *(informal)*, chivvy, importune, bend someone's ear *(informal)*, be on someone's back *(slang)* • *She badgered her doctor time and again, pleading with him.*
▸ COLLECTIVE NOUN: cete
▸ NAME OF HOME: set or sett

badinage = **banter**, joking, teasing, mockery, chaff, pleasantry, repartee, wordplay, drollery, raillery, persiflage • *She tried to respond to his light-hearted badinage.*

badly 1 = **poorly**, incorrectly, carelessly, inadequately, erroneously, imperfectly, ineptly, shoddily, defectively, faultily • *I was angry because I played so badly.*
OPPOSITES: well, properly, satisfactorily
2 = **severely**, greatly, deeply, seriously, gravely, desperately, sorely, dangerously, intensely, painfully, acutely, exceedingly • *It was a gamble that went badly wrong.*
3 = **much**, seriously, desperately • *Why do you want to go so badly?*
4 = **cruelly**, savagely, brutally, unkindly, viciously, mercilessly, ferociously, cold-bloodedly, callously, unmercifully, sadistically, pitilessly, spitefully, heartlessly, barbarously, brutishly • *Why were they treated so badly?*
5 = **unfavourably**, unsuccessfully • *The male sex comes out of the film very badly.*
6 = **poorly**, meanly, inadequately, insufficiently, unsatisfactorily • *You may have to work part-time, in a badly paid job with unsociable hours.*
7 = **mischievously**, perversely, wickedly, playfully, annoyingly, impishly, exasperatingly, naughtily, waywardly, disobediently • *Children who behave badly need help, not criticism.*

bad manners = **rudeness**, disrespect, insolence, impertinence, bluntness, impudence, coarseness, discourtesy, abruptness, boorishness, incivility, brusqueness, churlishness, curtness, indelicacy, impoliteness • *You mistook his bad manners for masculinity.*
OPPOSITES: courtesy, politeness, good manners

badness = **wickedness**, wrong, evil, corruption, sin, impropriety, immorality, villainy, naughtiness, sinfulness, foulness, baseness, rottenness, vileness, shamefulness • *They only recognize badness when they perceive it in others.*
OPPOSITES: good, virtue, excellence

bad-tempered = **irritable**, cross, angry, tense, crabbed, fiery, grumbling, snarling, prickly, exasperated, edgy, snappy, sullen, touchy, surly, petulant, sulky, ill-tempered, irascible, cantankerous, tetchy, ratty (*Brit. & N.Z. informal*), tooshie (*Austral. slang*), testy, chippy (*informal*), fretful, grouchy (*informal*), querulous, peevish, crabby, huffy, dyspeptic, choleric, splenetic, crotchety (*informal*), oversensitive, snappish, ill-humoured, liverish, narky (*Brit. slang*), out of humour • *a crusty, bad-tempered, ill-humoured old gentleman*
OPPOSITES: happy, pleasant, good-tempered

baffle = **puzzle**, beat (*slang*), amaze, confuse, stump, bewilder, astound, elude, confound, perplex, disconcert, mystify, flummox, boggle the mind of, dumbfound • *An apple tree producing square fruit is baffling experts.*
OPPOSITES: explain, interpret, clarify

baffling = **puzzling**, strange, confusing, weird, mysterious, unclear, bewildering, elusive, enigmatic, perplexing, incomprehensible, mystifying, inexplicable, unaccountable, unfathomable • *I was constantly ill, with a baffling array of symptoms.*
OPPOSITES: clear, easy, understandable

bag AS A NOUN 1 = **sack**, container, poke (*Scot.*), sac, receptacle • *She left the hotel carrying a shopping bag.*
2 = **handbag**, purse, shoulder bag, clutch bag, evening bag • *Meg drew a long, knitted scarf out of her leather bag.*
3 = **luggage**, chest, container, trunk, suitcase, baggage, crate, rucksack, backpack, holdall, knapsack, coffret, overnighter • *The airline lost my bag so I didn't have any training gear.*
▸ AS A VERB 1 = **get**, take, land, score (*slang*), gain, pick up, secure, obtain, capture, acquire, get hold of, come by, procure, make sure of, win possession of • *The smart ones will have already bagged their seats.*
2 = **catch**, get, kill, shoot, capture, acquire, trap, snare, pick off, ensnare • *Bag a rabbit for supper.*

TYPES OF BAG

backpack	holdall *or* (*U.S. & Canad.*) carryall	sea bag
bergen	kitbag	shoulder bag
briefcase	knapsack	suitcase
bum bag	nunny bag (*Canad.*)	tucker bag
carpetbag	pikau (*N.Z.*)	valise
carrier bag	reticule	vanity bag,
clutch bag	rucksack	vanity case, *or* vanity box
ditty bag	sabretache	water bag
duffel bag	saddlebag	workbag
Gladstone bag	satchel	
handbag		
haversack		

baggage = **luggage**, things, cases, bags, equipment, gear, trunks, suitcases, belongings, paraphernalia, accoutrements, impedimenta • *excess baggage*

baggy = **loose**, hanging, slack, loosened, bulging, not fitting, sagging, sloppy, floppy, billowing, roomy, slackened, ill-fitting, droopy, oversize, not tight • *a baggy jumper*
OPPOSITES: close, tight, narrow

bail[1] AS A NOUN = **security**, bond, guarantee, pledge, warranty, indemnity, surety, guaranty • *He was freed on bail pending an appeal.*
▸ IN PHRASES: **bail out** = **escape**, withdraw, get away, retreat, make your getaway, break free *or* out, make *or* effect your escape • *The pilot bailed out safely.*
bail something *or* **someone out** = **save**, help, free, release, aid, deliver, recover, rescue, get out, relieve, liberate, salvage, set free, save the life of, extricate, save (someone's) bacon (*Brit. informal*) • *They will discuss how to bail the economy out of its slump.*

bail[2] *or* **bale** = **scoop**, empty, dip, ladle, drain off • *We kept her afloat for a couple of hours by bailing frantically.*

bait AS A NOUN = **lure**, attraction, incentive, carrot (*informal*), temptation, bribe, magnet, snare, inducement, decoy, carrot and stick, honeypot, enticement, allurement • *bait to attract audiences for advertisements*
▸ AS A VERB = **tease**, provoke, annoy, irritate, guy (*informal*), bother, needle (*informal*), plague (*informal*), mock, rag, rib (*informal*), wind up (*Brit. slang*), hound, torment, harass, ridicule, taunt, hassle (*informal*), aggravate (*informal*), badger, gall, persecute, pester, goad, irk, bedevil, take the mickey out of (*informal*), take the piss out of (*taboo slang*), chaff, gibe, get on the nerves of (*informal*), nark (*Brit., Austral. & N.Z. slang*), be on the back of (*slang*), piss you off (*taboo slang*), get in the hair of (*informal*), get *or* take a rise out of, hack you off (*informal*) • *He delighted in baiting his mother.*

bake 1 = **cook** • *How did you learn to bake cakes?*
2 = **get too hot**, roast, warm up, overheat, grow hot • *If you closed the windows you baked.*

baked = **dry**, desert, seared, dried up, scorched, barren, sterile, arid, torrid, desiccated, sun-baked, waterless, moistureless • *her feet dancing over the baked earth*

baking = **scorching**, burning, heated, boiling, roasting, searing, blistering, torrid, sultry, sweltering • *the baking Jordanian desert*

bakkie = **truck**, pick-up, van, lorry, pick-up truck • *They stole the farmer's chickens and carried them off in a bakkie.*

balance AS A VERB 1 = **stabilize**, support, level, steady • *He balanced a football on his head.*
OPPOSITES: upset, outweigh, overbalance
2 = **offset**, match, square, make up for, compensate for, counteract, neutralize, counterbalance, even up, equalize, counterpoise • *Balance spicy dishes with mild ones.*
3 = **weigh**, consider, compare, estimate, contrast, assess,

evaluate, set against, juxtapose • *She carefully tried to balance religious sensitivities against democratic freedom.*
4 = calculate, rate, judge, total, determine, estimate, settle, count, square, reckon, work out, compute, gauge, tally • *He balanced his budget by rigid control over public expenditure.*
▸ AS A NOUN **1 = equilibrium**, stability, steadiness, evenness, equipoise, counterpoise • *The medicines you are currently taking could be affecting your balance.*
OPPOSITES: instability, unbalance, disproportion
2 = stability, equanimity, constancy, steadiness • *the ecological balance of the forest*
3 = parity, equity, fairness, impartiality, equality, correspondence, equivalence • *her ability to maintain the political balance*
4 = remainder, rest, difference, surplus, residue, outstanding amount • *They were due to pay the balance on delivery.*
5 = composure, stability, restraint, self-control, poise, self-discipline, coolness, calmness, equanimity, self-restraint, steadiness, self-possession, self-mastery, strength of mind or will • *a balance of mind*

balanced 1 = unbiased, just, fair, equal, objective, neutral, detached, open-minded, equitable, impartial, disinterested, even-handed, nonpartisan, unprejudiced, without fear or favour, nondiscriminating • *a fair, balanced, comprehensive report*
OPPOSITES: weighted, unfair, biased
2 = varied, mixed, healthy, sensible • *a balanced diet*
3 = calm, together *(slang)*, cool, collected, reasonable, steady, sensible, composed, sane, dependable, unflappable *(informal)*, self-possessed, even-tempered, grounded • *I have to prove myself as a respectable, balanced person.*

balance sheet = statement, report, account, budget, ledger, financial statement, credits and debits sheet • *They needed a strong balance sheet.*

balcony 1 = terrace, veranda, loggia • *He appeared on a second floor balcony to appeal to the crowd to be calm.*
2 = upper circle, gods, gallery • *We took our seats in the balcony.*

bald 1 = hairless, smooth, bare, shorn, clean-shaven, tonsured, depilated, glabrous *(Biology)*, baldheaded, baldpated • *The man's bald head was beaded with sweat.*
2 = plain, direct, simple, straight, frank, severe, bare, straightforward, blunt, rude, outright, downright, forthright, unadorned, unvarnished, straight from the shoulder • *The bald truth is that he's just not happy.*

balderdash = nonsense, balls *(taboo slang)*, bull *(slang)*, rubbish, shit *(taboo slang)*, rot, crap *(slang)*, garbage *(informal)*, trash, bunk *(informal)*, bullshit *(taboo slang)*, hot air *(informal)*, tosh *(slang, chiefly Brit.)*, waffle, pap, cobblers *(Brit. taboo slang)*, bilge *(informal)*, malarkey, drivel, twaddle, tripe *(informal)*, gibberish, guff *(slang)*, moonshine, claptrap *(informal)*, hogwash, bizzo *(Austral. slang)*, bull's wool *(Austral. & N.Z. slang)*, hokum *(slang, chiefly U.S. & Canad.)*, piffle *(informal)*, poppycock *(informal)*, bosh *(informal)*, eyewash *(informal)*, kak *(S. African taboo slang)*, tommyrot, horsefeathers *(U.S. slang)*, bunkum or buncombe *(chiefly U.S.)* • *What a load of balderdash!*

balding = losing your hair, receding, thin on top, becoming bald • *a balding man with a dense mat of body hair*

baldness = hairlessness, alopecia *(Pathology)*, baldheadedness, baldpatedness, glabrousness *(Biology)* • *He wears a cap to cover a spot of baldness.*

bale *see* **bail²**

baleful = menacing, threatening, dangerous, frightening, evil, deadly, forbidding, intimidating, harmful, sinister, ominous, malignant, hurtful, vindictive, pernicious, mournful, malevolent, noxious, venomous, ruinous, intimidatory, minatory, maleficent, bodeful, louring or lowering, minacious • *He had a baleful look.*
OPPOSITES: friendly, healthy, beneficial

balk or **baulk** *usually with* **at = recoil**, resist, hesitate, dodge, falter, evade, shy away, flinch, quail, shirk, shrink, draw back, jib • *Even biology graduates may balk at animal experiments.*
OPPOSITES: accept, yield, submit

ball¹ 1 = sphere, drop, globe, pellet, orb, globule, spheroid • *a golf ball* • *He screwed the letter up into a ball.*
2 = projectile, shot, missile, bullet, ammunition, slug, pellet, grapeshot • *A cannon ball struck the ship*

ball² = dance, social, hop *(informal)*, disco, knees-up *(Brit. informal)*, discotheque, dancing party, B and S *(Austral. informal)* • *You're going to a ball dressed like that?*

ballad = song, saga, ditty, folk song, canzone • *one of the most beautiful ballads he ever wrote*

ballast = counterbalance, balance, weight, stability, equilibrium, sandbag, counterweight, stabilizer • *She may have to discharge some ballast to make her lighter.*

ballet
▸ RELATED MANIA: balletomania
▸ RELATED ENTHUSIAST: balletomane
▹ *See panel* **Ballet steps and terms**

BALLET STEPS AND TERMS

abstract *or* absolute ballet
adagio *or* adage
allegro
allongé
aplomb
arabesque
assemblé
attitude
balancé
ballerina
ballet blanc
ballet d'action
ballet de cour
ballon
ballonné
ballotté *or* pas ballotté
battement
batterie
battu
Benesh notation
brisé *or* pas de brisé
cabriole
Cecchetti method
changement *or* changement de pieds
chassé *or* pas de chassé
ciseaux *or* pas ciseaux
classical ballet
contretemps
cou-de-pied
coupé *or* pas coupé
croisé
croisé derrière
croisé devant
déboulé
decor
défilé de corps de ballet
dégagé
demi-plié
demi-pointe
détournée
développé *or* temps développé
ecarté
échappé *or* pas échappé
emboîté
elevation
enchaînement
en couronne
en dedans
en dehors
en l'air
en pointe
en tire-bouchon
entrechat
entrée de ballet
failli
figurant
foudroyant
fouetté en tournant
gargouillade
glissade
grand écart
grande plié
jeté
ouvert
pas
pas de bourée
pas de bourée couru
pas de chat
pas de deux
pas de sissonne
passé
pirouette
plié
pointe
ports de bras
premier danseur *or* *(fem.)* première danseuse
prima ballerina
prima ballerina assoluta
raccourci
relevé
romantic ballet
rond de jambe
sickling
soubresaut
soutenu
Stepanov notation
sur place
temps de cuisse
temps de flèche
temps de poisson
temps levé
temps lié
terre à terre
toe-dance
tombé
tour en l'air
turn-out
variation
Von Laban notation

ball game
▹ See panel **Ball games**

ballistic IN PHRASES: **go ballistic** 1 = **go mad**, go wild, go ape *(slang)*, go berserk, go apeshit *(slang)* • *The singer went ballistic.*
2 = **go through the roof**, go mental *(slang)*, go mad, go bananas *(slang)*, go out of control • *August registrations have gone ballistic.*

balloon AS A NOUN = **airship**, hot-air balloon, Montgolfier, weather balloon • *the first to attempt to circle the Earth non-stop by balloon*
▸ AS A VERB = **expand**, rise, increase, extend, swell, mushroom, blow up, enlarge, inflate, bulge, billow, dilate, be inflated, puff out, become larger, distend, bloat, grow rapidly • *The budget deficit has ballooned to $25 million.* • *Her weight ballooned from 8 stone to 11 stone.*

ballot AS A NOUN = **vote**, election, voting, poll, polling, referendum, show of hands • *The result of the ballot will not be known for two weeks.*
▸ AS A VERB = **poll**, canvass • *The union said they will ballot members on whether to strike.*

balls AS A PLURAL NOUN 1 = **bravery**, face *(informal)*, spirit, bottle *(slang)*, resolution, nerve, daring, courage, guts *(informal)*, pluck, grit, backbone, fortitude, toughness, mettle, boldness, firmness, valour, spunk *(informal)*, fearlessness, intrepidity, cojones *(Spanish)*, hardihood, ballsiness *(taboo slang)*, dauntlessness, lion-heartedness • *I never had the balls to do anything like this.*
2 = **nonsense**, stuff, bull, malarkey, rubbish, shit *(taboo slang)*, pants *(slang)*, rot, crap *(slang)*, garbage *(informal)*, folly, trash, bunk *(informal)*, bullshit *(taboo slang)*, hot air *(informal)*, tosh *(slang, chiefly Brit.)*, absurdity, waffle *(informal, chiefly Brit.)*, bollocks *(Brit. taboo slang)*, pap, cobblers *(Brit. taboo slang)*, bilge *(informal)*, drivel, twaddle, tripe *(informal)*, gibberish, guff *(slang)*, bombast, moonshine, claptrap *(informal)*, hogwash, bizzo *(Austral. slang)*, bull's wool *(Austral. & N.Z. slang)*, hokum *(slang, chiefly U.S. & Canad.)*, codswallop *(Brit. slang)*, piffle *(informal)*, poppycock *(informal)*, balderdash *(slang)*, bosh *(informal)*, senselessness, eyewash *(informal)*, kak *(S. African taboo slang)*, ludicrousness, fatuity, tommyrot, horsefeathers *(U.S. slang)*, bunkum *or* buncombe *(chiefly U.S.)* • *What complete and utter balls!*
3 = **testicles**, bollocks *or* ballocks *(taboo slang)*, testes, rocks *(U.S. taboo slang)*, nuts *(taboo slang)*, cobblers *(Brit. taboo slang)*, gonads, goolies *(taboo slang)*, family jewels *(slang)*, cojones *(Spanish)*, nads *(U.S. taboo slang)* • *I kneed him in the balls.*
▸ IN PHRASES: **balls something up** = **mess up**, bungle, botch, cock up *(Brit. slang)*, fuck up *(offensive taboo slang)*, make a hash of *(informal)*, muck up *(Brit. slang)*, make a pig's ear of *(informal)* • *I have no intention of letting you balls it up.*

ballyhoo 1 = **fuss**, to-do, performance *(informal)*, noise, stir, excitement, flap *(informal)*, racket, bustle, furore, babble, commotion, rumpus, tumult, hubbub, brouhaha, hullabaloo, hue and cry, hoo-ha • *The announcement was made amongst much ballyhoo.*
2 = **hype**, promotion, build-up, plugging *(informal)*, propaganda campaign, PR campaign, razzmatazz *(slang)*, brouhaha • *a big ballyhoo in the press*

balm 1 = **ointment**, cream, lotion, salve, emollient, balsam, liniment, embrocation, unguent, cerate • *The balm is very soothing.*
2 = **comfort**, support, relief, cheer, consolation, solace, palliative, anodyne, succour, restorative, curative • *This place is a balm to the soul.*

balmy = **mild**, warm, calm, moderate, pleasant, clement, tranquil, temperate, summery • *a balmy summer's evening*
OPPOSITES: rough, harsh, stormy

bamboozle 1 = **cheat**, do *(informal)*, kid *(informal)*, skin *(slang)*, trick, fool, take in *(informal)*, con *(informal)*, stiff, sting *(informal)*, mislead, rip off *(slang)*, thwart, deceive, fleece, hoax, defraud, dupe, beguile, gull *(archaic)*, delude, swindle, stitch up *(slang)*, victimize, hoodwink, double-cross *(informal)*, diddle *(informal)*, take for a ride *(informal)*, do the dirty on *(Brit. informal)*, bilk, pull a fast one on *(informal)*, cozen • *He was bamboozled by con men.*
2 = **puzzle**, confuse, stump, baffle, bewilder, confound, perplex, mystify, befuddle, flummox, nonplus • *He bamboozled Mercer into defeat.*

ban AS A VERB 1 = **prohibit**, black, bar, block, restrict, veto, forbid, boycott, suppress, outlaw, banish, disallow, proscribe, debar, blackball, interdict, criminalize • *Last year arms sales were banned.*
OPPOSITES: let, allow, permit
2 = **bar**, prohibit, prevent, exclude, forbid, disqualify, preclude, debar, declare ineligible • *He was banned from driving for three years.*
▸ AS A NOUN = **prohibition**, block, restriction, veto, boycott, embargo, injunction, censorship, taboo, suppression, stoppage, disqualification, interdiction, interdict, proscription, disallowance, rahui *(N.Z.)*, restraining order *(U.S. Law)* • *The General also lifted a ban on political parties.*
OPPOSITES: sanction, approval, permission

banal = **unoriginal**, stock, ordinary, boring, tired, routine, dull, everyday, stereotypical, pedestrian, commonplace, mundane, tedious, vanilla *(slang)*, dreary, stale, tiresome, monotonous, humdrum, threadbare, trite, unimaginative, uneventful, uninteresting, clichéd, old hat, mind-numbing, hackneyed, ho-hum *(informal)*, vapid, repetitious, wearisome, platitudinous, cliché-ridden, unvaried • *The text is banal.*
OPPOSITES: new, interesting, original

banality 1 = **unoriginality**, predictability, dullness, ordinariness, triviality, staleness, vapidity, triteness • *the banality of life*
2 = **cliché**, commonplace, platitude, truism, bromide *(informal)*, old chestnut, stock phrase, trite phrase • *His ability to utter banalities never ceased to amaze me.*

banana IN PHRASES: **go bananas** = **go crazy**, go nuts *(slang)*, go insane, go bonkers *(slang, chiefly Brit.)*, go mental *(slang)*, go barmy *(slang)*, go loopy *(informal)*, go round the bend *(Brit. slang)*, go frantic, go batty *(slang)*, go doolally *(slang)*, go round the twist *(Brit. slang)*, go nutty *(slang)* • *People went bananas with boredom.*

BALL GAMES

American football, Australian Rules, badminton, bagatelle, bar billiards, baseball, billiards, boules, bowling, bumble-puppy, Canadian football, crazy golf, croquet, fives, football *or (U.S.)* soccer, goalball, golf, handball, hockey, hurling, korfball, lacrosse, netball, paintball, piggy in the middle, pinball, pocket billiards, punchball, pushball, pyramid, rounders, snooker, squash, Subbuteo *(trademark)*, tennis, volleyball

band[1] AS A NOUN **1 = ensemble**, group, orchestra, combo • *Local bands provide music for dancing.*
2 = gang, company, group, set, party, team, lot, club, body, association, crowd, troop, pack, camp, squad, crew *(informal)*, assembly, mob, horde, troupe, posse *(informal)*, clique, coterie, bevy • *bands of government soldiers*
▸ IN PHRASES: **band together = unite**, group, join, league, ally, associate, gather, pool, merge, consolidate, affiliate, collaborate, join forces, cooperate, confederate, pull together, join together, federate, close ranks, club together • *People living in a foreign city band together for company.*

band[2] **1 = headband**, tie, strip, ribbon, fillet • *She was wearing a trouser suit and a band around her forehead.*
2 = bandage, tie, binding, strip, belt, strap, cord, swathe, fetter • *He placed a metal band around the injured kneecap.*
3 = strip, belt • *bands of natural vegetation between strips of crops*

bandage AS A NOUN **= dressing**, plaster, sling, compress, gauze, lint, tourniquet • *His chest was swathed in bandages.*
▸ AS A VERB **= dress**, cover, bind, wrap, swathe, strap up, put a bandage on • *Apply a dressing to the wound and bandage it.*

bandit = robber, gunman, crook, outlaw, pirate, raider, gangster, plunderer, mugger *(informal)*, hijacker, looter, highwayman, racketeer, desperado, marauder, brigand, freebooter, footpad • *Reports say he was killed in an attack by armed bandits.*

bandy = exchange, trade, pass, throw, truck, swap, toss, shuffle, commute, interchange, barter, reciprocate • *The prosecution and defense were bandying accusations back and forth.*

bane = plague, bête noire, trial, disaster, evil, ruin, burden, destruction, despair, misery, curse, pest, torment, woe, nuisance, downfall, calamity, scourge, affliction • *Spots can be the bane of a teenager.*
OPPOSITES: support, relief, blessing

bang AS A NOUN **1 = explosion**, report, shot, pop, clash, crack, blast, burst, boom, slam, discharge, thump, clap, thud, clang, peal, detonation • *I heard four or five loud bangs.*
2 = blow, hit, box, knock, stroke, punch, belt *(informal)*, rap, bump, bash *(informal)*, sock *(slang)*, smack, thump, buffet, clout *(informal)*, cuff, clump *(slang)*, whack, wallop *(informal)*, slosh *(Brit. slang)*, tonk *(informal)*, clomp *(slang)* • *a nasty bang on the head*
▸ AS A VERB **1 = resound**, beat, crash, burst, boom, echo, drum, explode, thunder, thump, throb, thud, clang • *The engine spat and banged.*
2 = slam, crash, thump • *the sound of doors banging*
3 = bump, knock, elbow, jostle • *I didn't mean to bang into you.*
4 *often with* **on = hit**, pound, beat, strike, crash, knock, belt *(informal)*, hammer, slam, rap, bump, bash *(informal)*, thump, clatter, pummel, tonk *(informal)*, beat *or* knock seven bells out of *(informal)* • *We could bang on the desks and shout until they let us out.*
▸ AS AN ADVERB **1 = exactly**, just, straight, square, squarely, precisely, slap, smack, plumb *(informal)* • *bang in the middle of the track*
2 = completely, quite, totally, fully, entirely, absolutely, altogether, thoroughly, wholly, utterly, every inch, a hundred per cent, one hundred per cent, down to the ground • *It's as bang up-to-date as you can get.*
3 = suddenly, promptly, instantly, abruptly, all of a sudden, all at once, without warning, in a flash, in an instant, on the spur of the moment • *Email: I click on 'send', and bang, it's there!*

banish 1 = exclude, bar, ban, dismiss, expel, throw out, oust, drive away, eject, evict, shut out, ostracize • *I was banished from the small bedroom upstairs.*
2 = expel, transport, exile, outlaw, deport, drive away, expatriate, excommunicate • *He was banished from England.*
OPPOSITES: receive, accept, admit
3 = get rid of, remove, eliminate, eradicate, shake off, dislodge, see the back of • *a public investment programme intended to banish the recession*
4 = dismiss, drop, ban, reject, shelve, discard, set aside, disregard, dispel, cast out, lay aside, put out of your mind • *He has now banished all thoughts of retirement.*

banishment = expulsion, exile, dismissal, removal, discharge, transportation, exclusion, deportation, eviction, ejection, extrusion, proscription, expatriation, debarment • *banishment from political and industrial life*

banisters = railing, rail, balustrade, handrail, balusters • *I still remember sliding down the banisters.*

bank[1] AS A NOUN **1 = financial institution**, building society, merchant bank, repository, high-street bank, depository • *I had money in the bank.*
2 = store, fund, stock, source, supply, reserve, pool, reservoir, accumulation, stockpile, hoard, storehouse • *one of the largest data banks in the world*
▸ AS A VERB **= deposit**, keep, clear, save, pay in • *The agency has banked your cheque.*
▸ IN PHRASES: **bank on something = rely on**, trust (in), depend on, look to, believe in, count on, be sure of, lean on, be confident of, have confidence in, swear by, reckon on, repose trust in • *She is clearly banking on her past to be the meal ticket for her future.*
bank with someone = deal with, do business with, have an account with, be a customer of • *My husband has banked with them since before the war.*

bank[2] AS A NOUN **1 = side**, edge, margin, shore, brink, lakeside, waterside • *an old warehouse on the banks of the canal*
2 = mound, banking, rise, hill, mass, pile, heap, ridge, dune, embankment, knoll, hillock, kopje *or* koppie *(S. African)* • *resting indolently upon a grassy bank*
3 = mass, accumulation • *a bank of fog off the north-east coast*
▸ AS A VERB **= tilt**, tip, pitch, heel, slope, incline, slant, cant, camber • *A single-engine plane took off and banked above the highway.*

bank[3] **= row**, group, line, train, range, series, file, rank, arrangement, sequence, succession, array, tier • *The typical labourer now sits in front of a bank of dials.*

banknote = paper money, greenback *(U.S.)* • *He thrust the banknote back into his pocket.*

bankrupt AS AN ADJECTIVE **1 = insolvent**, broke *(informal)*, spent, ruined, wiped out *(informal)*, impoverished, beggared, in the red, on the rocks, destitute, gone bust *(informal)*, in receivership, gone to the wall, in the hands of the receivers, on your uppers, in queer street • *He was finally declared bankrupt.*
OPPOSITES: sound, wealthy, solvent
2 = lacking, wanting, deprived, in need, bereft, destitute • *He really thinks that European civilisation is morally bankrupt.*
▸ AS A VERB **= ruin**, break, impoverish, make bankrupt, make insolvent • *The move to the market nearly bankrupted the firm and its director.*
▸ AS A NOUN **= bankrupt person**, debtor, insolvent • *Three years later he was declared a bankrupt.*

bankruptcy 1 = insolvency, failure, crash, disaster, ruin, liquidation, indebtedness • *Many established firms were facing bankruptcy.*
2 = emptiness, want, vacuum, deficiency, void, shortcoming, deprivation, dearth, destitution, vacuity • *The massacre laid bare the moral bankruptcy of the regime.*

banner 1 = flag, standard, colours, jack, pennant, ensign, streamer, burgee, pennon, banderole, fanion, gonfalon • *A big banner was draped across one of the streets.*
2 = placard • *banners proclaiming "Welcome to Milan"*

banquet = feast, spread *(informal)*, dinner, meal, entertainment, revel, blowout *(slang)*, repast, slap-up meal *(Brit. informal)*, hakari *(N.Z.)* • *Last night he attended a state banquet.*

b

banter AS A NOUN **=joking**, kidding *(informal)*, ribbing *(informal)*, teasing, jeering, quipping, mockery, derision, jesting, chaff, pleasantry, repartee, wordplay, joshing, badinage, chaffing, raillery, persiflage • *She heard them exchanging good-natured banter.*
▸ AS A VERB **=joke**, kid *(informal)*, rib *(informal)*, tease, taunt, jeer, quip, josh *(slang, chiefly U.S. & Canad.)*, jest, take the mickey *(informal)*, chaff • *They shared a cocktail and bantered easily.*

b

baptism 1 **=christening**, naming, sprinkling, purification, immersion • *We are at a site of baptism, a place of worship.*
2 **=initiation**, beginning, debut, introduction, admission, dedication, inauguration, induction, inception, rite of passage, commencement, investiture, baptism of fire, instatement • *The new boys face a tough baptism against Leeds.*

baptize 1 **=christen**, cleanse, immerse, purify, besprinkle • *I think your mother was baptized a Catholic.*
2 **=initiate**, admit, introduce, invest, recruit, enrol, induct, indoctrinate, instate • *baptized into the Church of England*

bar AS A NOUN 1 **=public house**, pub *(informal, chiefly Brit.)*, counter, inn, local *(Brit. informal)*, lounge, saloon, tavern, canteen, watering hole *(facetious slang)*, boozer *(Brit., Austral. & N.Z. informal)*, beer parlour *(Canad.)*, roadhouse, hostelry *(archaic or facetious)*, alehouse *(archaic)*, taproom • *the city's most popular country and western bar*
2 **=counter**, stand, table • *He leaned forward across the bar.*
3 **=rod**, staff, stick, stake, rail, pole, paling, shaft, baton, mace, batten, palisade, crosspiece • *a crowd throwing stones and iron bars*
4 **=piece**, bit, block, slice, cake, quantity, portion, tablet, chunk, slab • *a bar of soap*
5 **=obstacle**, block, barrier, hurdle, hitch, barricade, snag, deterrent, obstruction, stumbling block, impediment, hindrance, interdict • *one of the fundamental bars to communication*
OPPOSITES: help, benefit, aid
6 **=measure** *(U.S.)*, snatch of music • *Another bar of music trills forth.*
▸ AS A VERB 1 **=lock**, block, secure, chain, attach, anchor, bolt, blockade, barricade, fortify, fasten, latch, obstruct, make firm, make fast • *For added safety, bar the door to the kitchen.*
2 **=block**, restrict, hold up, restrain, hamper, thwart, hinder, obstruct, impede, shut off • *He stepped in front of her, barring her way.*
3 **=exclude**, ban, forbid, prohibit, keep out of, disallow, shut out of, ostracize, debar, blackball, interdict, black • *They have been barred from the country since 1982.*
OPPOSITES: let, allow, admit
▸ AS A PREPOSITION **=except**, but, saving, save *(archaic)*, barring, excepting, apart from, other than, excluding, besides, omitting, with the exception of, exclusive of • *They provide everything the independent investor wants, bar advice.*

Bar IN PHRASES: **the Bar =barristers**, court, lawyers, solicitors, counsel, judgment, advocates, tribunal, legal advisers, body of lawyers • *Gareth Williams QC, chairman of the Bar*

barb 1 **=point**, spur, needle, spike, spine, thorn, bristle, quill, prickle, tine, prong • *Apply gentle pressure on the barb with the point of the pliers.*
2 **=dig**, abuse, slight, insult, put-down, snub, sneer, scoff, rebuff, affront, slap in the face *(informal)*, gibe, aspersion • *The barb stung her exactly the way he hoped it would.*

barbarian AS A NOUN 1 **=savage**, monster, beast, brute, yahoo, swine, ogre, sadist • *Our maths teacher was a bully and a complete barbarian.*
2 **=lout**, hooligan, illiterate, vandal, yahoo, bigot, philistine, ned *(Scot. slang)*, hoon *(Austral. & N.Z.)*, cougan *(Austral. slang)*, scozza *(Austral. slang)*, bogan *(Austral. slang)*, ruffian, ignoramus, boor, boot boy, lowbrow, vulgarian • *The visitors looked upon us all as barbarians.*
▸ AS AN ADJECTIVE **=uncivilized**, wild, rough, savage, crude, primitive, vulgar, illiterate, barbaric, philistine, uneducated, unsophisticated, barbarous, boorish, uncouth, uncultivated, lowbrow, uncultured, unmannered • *rude and barbarian people*
OPPOSITES: cultured, civil, civilized

barbaric 1 **=brutal**, fierce, cruel, savage, crude, vicious, ruthless, coarse, vulgar, heartless, inhuman, merciless, bloodthirsty, remorseless, barbarous, pitiless, uncouth • *a particularly barbaric act of violence*
2 **=uncivilized**, wild, savage, primitive, rude, barbarian, barbarous • *a prehistoric and barbaric world*
OPPOSITES: cultured, sophisticated, civilized

barbarism **=cruelty**, outrage, atrocity, brutality, savagery, ruthlessness, wickedness, inhumanity, barbarity, viciousness, coarseness, crudity, monstrousness, heinousness, fiendishness, barbarousness • *Not the death penalty: barbarism must not be met with barbarism.*

barbarity 1 **=viciousness**, horror, cruelty, brutality, ferocity, savagery, ruthlessness, inhumanity • *the barbarity of war*
2 **=atrocity**, cruelty, horror, inhumanity • *the barbarities committed by the invading army*

barbarous 1 **=uncivilized**, wild, rough, gross, savage, primitive, rude, coarse, vulgar, barbarian, philistine, uneducated, brutish, unsophisticated, uncouth, uncultivated, unpolished, uncultured, unmannered • *He thought the poetry of Whitman barbarous.*
2 **=brutal**, cruel, savage, vicious, ruthless, ferocious, monstrous, barbaric, heartless, inhuman, merciless, remorseless, pitiless • *It was a barbarous attack on a purely civilian train.*

barbecue AS A NOUN 1 **=brazier**, rotisserie • *The heat of the barbecue travelled to where he was sitting.*
2 **=meal cooked outdoors**, barbie *(informal)*, BBQ • *On these fine evenings we usually have a barbecue.*
▸ AS A VERB **=chargrill**, broil *(U.S.)*, cook outdoors, charbroil *(U.S.)* • *Tuna can be grilled, fried or barbecued.*

barbed 1 **=cutting**, pointed, biting, critical, acid, hostile, nasty, harsh, savage, brutal, searing, withering, scathing, unkind, hurtful, belittling, sarcastic, caustic, scornful, vitriolic, trenchant, acrid, catty *(informal)*, mordant, mordacious • *barbed comments*
2 **=spiked**, pointed, toothed, hooked, notched, prickly, jagged, thorny, pronged, spiny, snaggy • *The factory was surrounded by barbed wire.*

bard **=poet**, singer, rhymer, minstrel, lyricist, troubadour, versifier • *the epic and myth which formed the bard's repertoire*

bare 1 **=naked**, nude, stripped, exposed, uncovered, shorn, undressed, divested, denuded, in the raw *(informal)*, disrobed, unclothed, buck naked *(slang)*, unclad, scuddy *(slang)*, without a stitch on *(informal)*, in the bare scud *(slang)*, naked as the day you were born *(informal)* • *She seemed unaware that she was bare.*
OPPOSITES: covered, dressed, clothed
2 **=simple**, basic, stripped, severe, plain, spare, stark, austere, spartan, unadorned, unfussy, unvarnished, unembellished, unornamented, unpatterned, bare-bones • *bare wooden floors*
OPPOSITES: adorned
3 **=empty**, wanting, mean, lacking, deserted, vacant, void, scarce, barren, uninhabited, unoccupied, scanty, unfurnished • *a bare, draughty interviewing room*
OPPOSITES: full, abundant, plentiful
4 **=desolate**, dry, waste, empty, desert, unproductive, unfruitful • *a bare landscape*
5 **=plain**, hard, simple, cold, basic, essential, obvious, sheer, patent, evident, stark, manifest, bald, literal, overt, unembellished • *reporters were given nothing but the bare facts*
6 **=absolute**, very, simple, sheer • *a bare minimum of forces*

bare-faced = **flagrant**, open, obvious, naked, bold, patent, outrageous, glaring, manifest, bald, transparent, blatant, palpable, brazen, shameless, out-and-out, undisguised, unconcealed • *crooked politicians who tell bare-faced lies*
OPPOSITES: covered, secret

barely = **only just**, just, hardly, scarcely, at a push, almost not • *His voice was barely audible.*
OPPOSITES: completely, amply, fully

bargain AS A NOUN 1 = **good buy**, discount purchase, good deal, good value, steal *(informal)*, snip *(informal)*, giveaway, cheap purchase • *At this price the wine is a bargain.*
2 = **agreement**, deal *(informal)*, understanding, promise, contract, negotiation, arrangement, settlement, treaty, pledge, convention, transaction, engagement, pact, compact, covenant, stipulation • *The treaty was based on a bargain between the governments.*
▸ AS A VERB 1 = **haggle**, deal, sell, trade, traffic, barter, drive a hard bargain • *Shop in small local markets and don't be afraid to bargain.*
2 = **negotiate**, deal, contract, mediate, covenant, stipulate, arbitrate, transact, cut a deal • *They prefer to bargain with individual clients, for cash.*
▸ IN PHRASES: **bargain for** *or* **on something** = **anticipate**, expect, look for, imagine, predict, plan for, forecast, hope for, contemplate, be prepared for, foresee, foretell, count upon • *The effects of this policy were more than they had bargained for.* • *He didn't bargain on an undercover investigation.*
into the bargain = **too**, also, further, in addition, as well, moreover, besides, furthermore, what's more • *She is rich. Now you say she is a beauty into the bargain.*

barge AS A NOUN = **canal boat**, lighter, narrow boat, scow, flatboat • *He lives on a barge and only works when he has to.*
▸ AS A VERB = **force**, break, push, blast, thrust • *Students tried to barge their way into the secretariat building.*
▸ IN PHRASES: **barge in (on something** *or* **someone)** = **interrupt**, break in (on), muscle in (on) *(informal)*, intrude (on), infringe (on), burst in (on), butt in (on), impose yourself (on), force your way in (on), elbow your way in (on) • *Sorry to barge in like this, but I need your advice.* • *He just barged in on us while we were having a private conversation.*
barge into someone = **bump into**, drive into, press, push against, shoulder, thrust, elbow into, shove into, collide with, jostle with, cannon into • *He would barge into them and kick them in the shins.*

bark[1] AS A VERB 1 = **yap**, bay, howl, snarl, growl, yelp, woof • *Don't let the dogs bark.*
2 = **shout**, snap, yell, snarl, growl, berate, bawl, bluster, raise your voice • *I didn't mean to bark at you.*
▸ AS A NOUN = **yap**, bay, howl, snarl, growl, yelp, woof • *The Doberman let out a string of roaring barks.*

bark[2] AS A NOUN = **covering**, casing, cover, skin, protection, layer, crust, housing, cortex *(Anatomy, Botany)*, rind, husk • *The spice comes from the inner bark of the tree.*
▸ AS A VERB = **scrape**, skin, strip, rub, scratch, shave, graze, scuff, flay, abrade • *She barked her shin off the edge of the drawer.*

barmy *or* **balmy** *(Slang)* 1 = **stupid**, bizarre, foolish, silly, daft *(informal)*, irresponsible, irrational, senseless, preposterous, impractical, idiotic, inane, fatuous, dumb-ass *(slang)* • *This policy is absolutely barmy.*
2 = **insane**, odd, crazy, stupid, silly, nuts *(slang)*, loony *(slang)*, nutty *(slang)*, goofy *(informal)*, idiotic, loopy *(informal)*, crackpot *(informal)*, out to lunch *(informal)*, dippy, out of your mind, gonzo *(slang)*, doolally *(slang)*, off your trolley *(slang)*, round the twist *(Brit. slang)*, up the pole *(informal)*, off your rocker *(slang)*, off the air *(Austral. slang)*, wacko *or* whacko *(informal)*, a sausage short of a fry-up *(slang)*, porangi *(N.Z.)* • *He used to say I was barmy, and that really got to me.*
OPPOSITES: reasonable, sensible, sane

barn = **grainstore**, store, shed, grange, outbuilding • *She's down at the barn.*

baron 1 = **nobleman**, lord, peer, noble, aristocrat, patrician, grandee • *Yes, our friend the baron has his problems.*
2 = **tycoon**, leader, chief, fat cat *(slang, chiefly U.S.)*, mogul, bigwig *(informal)*, big shot *(informal)*, big cheese *(slang, old-fashioned)*, plutocrat, nabob *(informal)*, Mister Big *(slang, chiefly U.S.)* • *the battle against the drug barons*

baroque = **ornate**, fancy, bizarre, elegant, decorated, elaborate, extravagant, flamboyant, grotesque, convoluted, flowery, rococo, florid, bedecked, overelaborate, overdecorated • *He was a baroque figure dressed in theatrical, but elegant, clothes.*

barrack = **heckle**, abuse, mock, bait, criticize, boo, taunt, jeer, shout down, diss *(slang, chiefly U.S.)*, flame *(informal)* • *Fans gained more enjoyment barracking him than cheering on the team.*

barracks = **camp**, quarters, garrison, encampment, billet, cantonment, casern • *an army barracks in the north of the city*

barrage AS A NOUN 1 = **bombardment**, attack, bombing, assault, shelling, battery, volley, blitz, salvo, strafe, fusillade, cannonade, curtain of fire • *a barrage of anti-aircraft fire*
2 = **torrent**, attack, mass, storm, assault, burst, stream, hail, outburst, rain, spate, onslaught, deluge, plethora, profusion • *a barrage of angry questions from the floor*
3 = **barrier**, wall, dam, obstruction, embankment • *a hydro-electric tidal barrage*
▸ AS A VERB = **harass**, harry, bug *(informal)*, annoy, hound, badger, pester • *Doctors are complaining about being barraged by drug-company salesmen.*

barrel = **cask**, drum, butt, vat, cylinder, tub, keg, firkin • *barrels of pickled fish*

barren 1 = **desolate**, empty, desert, bare, waste • *the Tibetan landscape of the high barren mountains*
2 = **unproductive**, dry, useless, sterile, fruitless, arid, unprofitable, unfruitful, unprolific • *He also wants to use water to irrigate barren desert land.*
OPPOSITES: rich, useful, fertile
3 = **dull**, boring, commonplace, tedious, dreary, stale, lacklustre, monotonous, uninspiring, humdrum, uninteresting, vapid, unrewarding, as dry as dust • *My life has become barren.*
OPPOSITES: interesting, instructive
4 = **empty**, clear, vacant, void, unfilled • *one loaf of bread on the otherwise barren shelves*
5 = **infertile**, sterile, childless, unproductive, nonproductive, infecund, unprolific • *a three-year-old barren mare*

barricade AS A NOUN = **barrier**, wall, railing, fence, blockade, obstruction, rampart, fortification, bulwark, palisade, stockade • *Large areas of the city have been closed off by barricades.*
▸ AS A VERB 1 = **bar**, block, defend, secure, lock, bolt, blockade, fortify, fasten, latch, obstruct • *The doors had been barricaded.*
2 = **shut**, lock, confine, enclose, imprison, pound, wall off *or* up, impound • *The students have barricaded themselves into the building.*

barrier 1 = **obstacle**, bar, block, handicap, hurdle, limitation, hitch, drawback, snag, obstruction, stumbling block, impediment, hindrance • *Duties and taxes are the most obvious barriers to free trade.*
2 = **barricade**, wall, bar, block, railing, fence, pale, boundary, obstacle, ditch, blockade, obstruction, rampart, bulwark, palisade, stockade • *The demonstrators broke through the heavy police barriers.*

barring = **except for**, saving, bar, excepting, apart from, but for, other than, excluding, besides, omitting, save for *(archaic)*, exclusive of, if there is *or* are no • *Barring accidents, I believe they will succeed.*

barrister = **advocate**, lawyer, attorney, solicitor, counsel, Queen's Counsel, Q.C. • *The report has been written by a senior barrister.*

barrow = **cart**, trolley, wheelbarrow, handcart, pushcart • *He tried to push four crates up a steep hill on a barrow.*

barter = **trade**, sell, exchange, switch, traffic, bargain, swap, haggle, drive a hard bargain • *They have been bartering wheat for cotton and timber.*

b

base[1] AS A NOUN 1 = **bottom**, floor, lowest part, deepest part • *Line the base and sides of a 20cm deep round cake tin with paper.*
OPPOSITES: top, crown, summit
2 = **underside**, sole, underneath, lower side • *Plunge the base of the pan into a bowl of very cold water.*
3 = **support**, stand, foot, rest, bed, bottom, foundation, pedestal, groundwork • *The mattress is best on a solid bed base.*
4 = **foundation**, institution, organization, establishment, bedrock, starting point • *The family base was crucial to my development.*
5 = **centre**, post, station, camp, settlement, headquarters, barracks, encampment • *Gunfire was heard at an army base close to the airport.*
6 = **home**, house, territory, pad *(slang)*, residence, home ground, abode, stamping ground, dwelling place • *For most of the spring and early summer her base was in Scotland.*
7 = **essence**, source, basis, concentrate, root, core, extract • *Oils may be mixed with a base and massaged into the skin.*
▸ AS A VERB 1 = **ground**, found, build, rest, establish, depend, root, construct, derive, hinge • *He based his conclusions on the evidence given by the prisoners.*
2 = **place**, set, post, station, establish, fix, locate, install, garrison • *We will base ourselves in the town.*

base[2] = **dishonourable**, evil, corrupt, infamous, disgraceful, vulgar, shameful, vile, immoral, scandalous, wicked, sordid, abject, despicable, depraved, ignominious, disreputable, contemptible, villainous, ignoble, discreditable, scungy *(Austral. & N.Z.)* • *Love has the power to overcome the baser emotions.*
OPPOSITES: good, just, honourable

baseless = **unfounded**, false, fabricated, unconfirmed, spurious, unjustified, unproven, unsubstantiated, groundless, unsupported, trumped up, without foundation, unjustifiable, uncorroborated, ungrounded, without basis • *The government has described the reports as completely baseless.*
OPPOSITES: supported, proven, well-founded

basement = **cellar**, crypt, lower ground floor *(Brit.)*, vault, underground room • *They live in a basement in North London.*

bash AS A NOUN 1 = **party**, do *(informal)*, social, at-home, gathering, function, celebration, reception, rave *(Brit. slang)*, get-together *(informal)*, festivity, knees-up *(Brit. informal)*, beano *(Brit. slang)*, social gathering, shindig *(informal)*, soirée, rave-up *(Brit. slang)*, hooley *or* hoolie *(chiefly Irish & N. Z.)* • *one of the biggest showbiz bashes of the year*
2 = **knock**, stroke, punch, belt *(informal)*, bang, rap, sock *(slang)*, smack, thump, buffet, clout *(informal)*, clump *(slang)*, whack *(informal)*, wallop *(informal)*, slosh *(Brit. slang)*, tonk *(informal)*, clomp *(slang)* • *She gave him a bash on the head.*
3 = **attempt**, go *(informal)*, try, shot *(informal)*, bid, crack *(informal)*, stab *(informal)* • *He's prepared to have a bash at discussing it intelligently.*
▸ AS A VERB 1 = **hit**, break, beat, strike, knock, smash, punch, belt *(informal)*, crush, deck *(slang)*, batter, slap, sock *(slang)*, chin *(slang)*, smack, thump, clout *(informal)*, whack *(informal)*, biff *(slang)*, clobber *(slang)*, wallop *(informal)*, slosh *(Brit. slang)*, tonk *(informal)*, lay one on *(slang)*, beat *or* knock seven bells out of *(informal)* • *If he tries to bash you he'll have to bash me as well.*
2 = **criticize**, pan *(informal)*, condemn, slam *(slang)*, knock *(informal)*, flame *(informal)*, carp, put down, slate *(informal)*, have a go at *(informal)*, censure, disparage, tear into *(informal)*, diss *(slang, chiefly U.S.)*, find fault with, lambast(e), give (someone *or* something) a bad press • *He continued to bash them as being soft on crime.*

bashful = **shy**, reserved, retiring, nervous, modest, shrinking, blushing, constrained, timid, self-conscious, coy, reticent, self-effacing, aw-shucks, diffident, sheepish, mousy, timorous, abashed, shamefaced, easily embarrassed, overmodest • *a bashful young lady*
OPPOSITES: forward, confident, aggressive

bashfulness = **shyness**, reserve, embarrassment, constraint, hesitation, modesty, nervousness, lack of confidence, reticence, self-consciousness, timidity, diffidence, coyness, timorousness, mousiness, sheepishness, timidness • *Suddenly overcome with bashfulness, he lowered his voice.*

basic AS AN ADJECTIVE 1 = **fundamental**, main, key, essential, primary, vital, principal, constitutional, cardinal, inherent, elementary, indispensable, innate, intrinsic, elemental, immanent • *Access to justice is a basic right.*
2 = **vital**, needed, important, key, necessary, essential, primary, crucial, fundamental, elementary, indispensable, requisite • *shortages of even the most basic foodstuffs*
3 = **essential**, central, key, vital, fundamental, underlying, indispensable • *There are certain ethical principles that are basic to all the great religions.*
OPPOSITES: supporting, minor, secondary
4 = **main**, key, essential, primary • *There are three basic types of tea.*
5 = **plain**, simple, classic, ordinary, severe, crude, straightforward, Spartan, unpretentious, uncluttered, unadorned, unfussy, bog-standard *(informal)*, unembellished, without frills, bare-bones • *the extremely basic hotel room*
6 = **lowest**, starting, lowest level • *the basic pay of a typical coalface worker*
▸ AS A PLURAL NOUN = **essentials**, facts, principles, fundamentals, practicalities, requisites, nuts and bolts *(informal)*, hard facts, nitty-gritty *(informal)*, rudiments, brass tacks *(informal)*, necessaries • *Let's get down to basics and stop horsing around.*

basically = **essentially**, firstly, mainly, mostly, principally, fundamentally, primarily, at heart, inherently, intrinsically, at bottom, in substance, au fond *(French)* • *It's basically a vegan diet.*

basin 1 = **bowl**, dish, vessel, container, receptacle • *a pudding basin*
2 = **washbasin**, sink • *a cast-iron bath with a matching basin and WC*
3 = **valley**, hollow, gorge, ravine • *the Amazon basin*
4 = **bed**, depression, trough, concavity • *countries around the Pacific Basin*

basis AS A NOUN 1 = **arrangement**, way, system, footing, agreement • *We're going to be meeting there on a regular basis.*
2 = **foundation**, support, base, ground, footing, theory, bottom, principle, premise, starting point, groundwork, point of departure, principal element, chief ingredient • *The UN plan is a possible basis for negotiation.*
▸ IN PHRASES: **on the basis of** = **based on**, because of, due to, thanks to, going by, owing to, on account of, by reason of • *Our conclusions were drawn on the basis of these medical reports.*

bask AS A VERB = **lie**, relax, lounge, sprawl, loaf, lie about, swim in, sunbathe, recline, loll, laze, outspan *(S. African)*, warm yourself, toast yourself • *Crocodiles bask on the small sandy beaches.*
▸ IN PHRASES: **bask in** = **enjoy**, relish, delight in, savour, revel in, wallow in, rejoice in, luxuriate in, indulge yourself in, take joy in, take pleasure in *or* from • *He smiled and basked in her approval.*

basket = **wickerwork box**, box, pannier, punnet, creel, trug, flax kit *(N.Z.)*, kete *(N.Z.)* • *a laundry basket*

bass = **deep**, low, resonant, sonorous, low-pitched, deep-toned • *a bass guitar*

bastard AS A NOUN **1** = **rogue**, criminal, sharper, fraud, cheat, devil, crook *(informal)*, villain, charlatan, rascal, profligate, scoundrel, con man *(informal)*, scally *(Northwest English dialect)*, fraudster, wretch *(slang)*, swindler, libertine, knave *(archaic)*, ne'er-do-well, reprobate, scumbag, miscreant, scamp, malefactor, blackguard, evildoer, grifter *(slang, chiefly U.S. & Canad.)*, rapscallion, caitiff *(archaic)*, skelm *(S. African)*, rorter *(Austral. slang)*, wrong 'un *(Austral. slang)* • *I don't trust the bastard.*
2 = **illegitimate child**, love child, by-blow *(archaic)*, natural child, child born out of wedlock, whoreson *(archaic)* • *He was a bastard, disowned by his father.*
3 = **nuisance**, pain, bore, drag *(informal)*, bother, headache *(informal)*, pest, irritation, gall, annoyance, aggravation, pain in the neck *(informal)*, pain in the arse *(taboo slang)*, vexation • *Life can be a real bastard at times.*
▸ AS AN ADJECTIVE = **illegitimate**, fatherless, born out of wedlock, misbegotten *(literary)*, born on the wrong side of the blanket, baseborn • *his bastard son*

bastardize = **corrupt**, shame, disgrace, distort, pervert, degrade, devalue, demean, drag down, debase, dishonour, defile, cheapen, adulterate, abase • *We are not about to bastardize the game.*

bastion = **stronghold**, support, defence, rock, prop, refuge, fortress, mainstay, citadel, bulwark, tower of strength, fastness • *The army is still one of the last male bastions.*

bat[1] = **club**, stick, racket • *a baseball bat*

bat[2]
▸ RELATED ADJECTIVE: chiropteran

BATS

barbastelle	hammerhead	noctule
false vampire	horseshoe bat	pipistrelle
flying fox	insectivorous bat	serotine
fruit bat	kalong	vampire bat

batch = **group**, set, lot, crowd, pack, collection, quantity, bunch, accumulation, assortment, consignment, assemblage, aggregation • *the current batch of trainee priests*

bath AS A NOUN **1** = **bathtub**, tub, sauna, jacuzzi, hot tub • *They would regularly sing in the bath.*
2 = **wash**, cleaning, washing, soaping, shower, soak, cleansing, scrub, scrubbing, bathe, shampoo, sponging, douse, douche, ablution • *Have a bath every morning.*
▸ AS A VERB = **clean**, wash, soap, shower, soak, cleanse, scrub, bathe, tub, sponge, rinse, douse, scrub down, lave *(archaic)* • *Don't feel you have to bath your child every day.*
▸ RELATED ADJECTIVE: balneal or balneary

bathe AS A VERB **1** = **swim**, dip, go swimming, take a dip • *small ponds for the birds to bathe in*
2 = **wash**, clean, bath, soap, shower, soak, cleanse, scrub, tub, sponge, rinse, scrub down, lave *(archaic)* • *Back home, Shirley plays with, feeds and bathes the baby.*
3 = **cleanse**, clean, wash, soak, rinse • *She paused long enough to bathe her blistered feet.*
4 = **cover**, flood, steep, engulf, immerse, overrun, permeate, suffuse, wash over • *The arena was bathed in warm sunshine.*
▸ AS A NOUN = **swim**, plunge, dip, paddle, dook *(Scot.)* • *an early-morning bathe*

bathing costume *or* **bathing suit** = **swimming costume**, bikini, cossie *(informal)*, swimming togs *(informal)*, trunks, swimsuit, swimwear, swimming trunks • *She wore a one-piece white bathing costume.*

bathos = **anticlimax**, disappointment, sentimentality, letdown, comedown *(informal)*, mawkishness, false pathos • *There was an element of bathos about the much-acclaimed speech.*

bathroom = **lavatory**, toilet, loo *(Brit. informal)*, washroom, can *(U.S. & Canad. slang)*, john *(slang, chiefly U.S. & Canad.)*, head(s) *(Nautical slang)*, shower, convenience *(chiefly Brit.)*, bog *(slang)*, bogger *(Austral. slang)*, brasco *(Austral. slang)*, privy, cloakroom *(Brit.)*, latrine, rest room, powder room, crapper *(taboo slang)*, dunny *(Austral. & N.Z. old-fashioned)*, water closet, khazi *(slang)*, comfort station *(U.S.)*, pissoir *(French)*, Gents *or* Ladies, little boy's room *or* little girl's room *(informal)*, (public) convenience, W.C. • *She had gone to use the bathroom.*

baton = **stick**, club, staff, stake, pole, rod, crook, cane, mace, wand, truncheon, sceptre, mere *(N.Z.)*, patu *(N.Z.)* • *I could see a baton being used vigorously.*

battalion **1** = **company**, army, force, team, host, unit, division, troop, squad, corps, brigade, regiment, legion, contingent, squadron, military force, garrison, horde, multitude, detachment, throng • *He was ordered to return to his battalion.*
2 = **crowd**, army, host, pack, mass, mob, herd, swarm, horde, multitude, throng, troupe, rabble, bevy • *battalions of highly paid publicists*

batten[1] AS A NOUN = **rod**, bar, stick, stake, rail, pole, paling, shaft, palisade, crosspiece • *Timber battens can be fixed to the wall.*
▸ AS A VERB *usually with* **down** = **fasten**, unite, fix, secure, lock, bind, chain, connect, attach, seal, tighten, anchor, bolt, clamp down, affix, nail down, make firm, make fast, fasten down • *The roof was never securely battened down.*

batten[2] AS A VERB
▸ IN PHRASES: **batten on something** *or* **someone** = **thrive**, grow, develop, gain, advance, succeed, get on, boom, do well, flourish, bloom, wax, prosper, burgeon, fatten, grow rich • *battening on fears about mass immigration and unemployment*

batter **1** = **beat**, hit, strike, knock, assault, smash, punch, belt *(informal)*, deck *(slang)*, bang, bash *(informal)*, lash, thrash, pound, lick *(informal)*, buffet, flog, maul, pelt, clobber *(slang)*, smite, wallop *(informal)*, pummel, tonk *(informal)*, cudgel, thwack, lambast(e), belabour, dash against, beat the living daylights out of, lay one on *(slang)*, drub, beat *or* knock seven bells out of *(informal)* • *He battered her around the head.*
2 = **damage**, destroy, hurt, injure, harm, ruin, crush, mar, wreck, total *(slang)*, shatter, weaken, bruise, demolish, shiver, trash *(slang)*, maul, mutilate, mangle, mangulate *(Austral. slang)*, disfigure, deface, play (merry) hell with *(informal)* • *a storm that's been battering the Northeast coastline*

battered **1** = **beaten**, injured, harmed, crushed, bruised, squashed, beat-up *(informal)*, oppressed, manhandled, black-and-blue, ill-treated, maltreated • *research into the experiences of battered women*
2 = **damaged**, broken-down, wrecked, beat-up *(informal)*, ramshackle, dilapidated • *a battered leather suitcase*

battery **1** = **power unit** • *The shavers come complete with batteries.*
2 = **artillery**, ordnance, gunnery, gun emplacement, cannonry • *They stopped beside a battery of abandoned guns.*
3 = **range**, lot, collection, variety, selection, array, assortment, gamut • *Crack is part of a battery of drugs used by addicts.*
4 = **series**, set, course, chain, string, sequence, suite, succession • *We give a battery of tests to each patient.*
5 = **beating**, attack, assault, aggression, thumping, onslaught, physical violence • *He has served three years for assault and battery.*

battle AS A NOUN **1 = fight**, war, attack, action, struggle, conflict, clash, set-to *(informal)*, encounter, combat, scrap *(informal)*, biffo *(Austral. slang)*, engagement, warfare, fray, duel, skirmish, head-to-head, tussle, scuffle, fracas, scrimmage, sparring match, bagarre *(French)*, melee *or* mêlée, boilover *(Austral.)* • *a gun battle between police and drug traffickers*
OPPOSITES: accord, peace, agreement
2 = conflict, campaign, struggle, debate, clash, dispute, contest, controversy, disagreement, crusade, strife, head-to-head, agitation • *a renewed political battle over their attitude to Europe*
3 = campaign, war, drive, movement, push, struggle • *the battle against crime*
▸ AS A VERB **1 = wrestle**, war, fight, argue, struggle, dispute, contest, combat, contend, feud, grapple, agitate, clamour, scuffle, lock horns • *Many people battled with police.*
2 = struggle, work, fight, labour, strain, strive, go for it *(informal)*, toil, make every effort, go all out *(informal)*, bend over backwards *(informal)*, go for broke *(slang)*, bust a gut *(informal)*, give it your best shot *(informal)*, break your neck *(informal)*, exert yourself, make an all-out effort *(informal)*, work like a Trojan, knock yourself out *(informal)*, do your damnedest *(informal)*, give it your all *(informal)*, rupture yourself *(informal)* • *Doctors battled throughout the night to save her life.*
▹ *See panel* **Famous battles**

battle-axe = harridan, witch, fury, nag, scold, virago, shrew, tartar, disciplinarian, vixen, termagant, ballbreaker *(slang)* • *an old battle-axe who hasn't smiled in decades*

battle cry 1 = slogan, motto, watchword, catch phrase, tag-line, catchword, catchcry *(Austral.)* • *the ideological battle cry of Hong Kong*
2 = war cry, rallying cry, war whoop • *He screamed out a battle cry and charged.*

battlefield = battleground, front, field, war zone, combat zone, field of battle • *the battlefields of the Somme*

battlement = rampart, wall, defence, fence, fort, barricade, stronghold, barbican, bastion, embankment, parapet, fortification, bulwark, earthwork, breastwork, bartizan, crenellation, fortified pa *(N.Z.)* • *Guns could also be seen behind the battlements of the fort itself.*

battleship = warship, gunboat, man-of-war, ship of the line, capital ship • *the rumble of a great battleship going down the slipway*

batty = crazy, odd, mad, eccentric, bats *(slang)*, out there *(slang)*, nuts *(slang)*, barking *(slang)*, peculiar, daft *(informal)*, crackers *(Brit. slang)*, queer *(informal)*, insane, lunatic, loony *(slang)*, barmy *(slang)*, off-the-wall *(slang)*, touched, nutty *(slang)*, potty *(Brit. informal)*, oddball *(informal)*, off the rails, cracked *(slang)*, bonkers *(slang, chiefly Brit.)*, cranky *(U.S., Canad. & Irish informal)*, dotty *(slang, chiefly Brit.)*, loopy *(informal)*, crackpot *(informal)*, out to lunch *(informal)*, barking mad *(slang)*, out of your mind, outré, gonzo *(slang)*, screwy *(informal)*, doolally *(slang)*, off your trolley *(slang)*, off the air *(Austral. slang)*, round the twist *(Brit. slang)*, up the pole *(informal)*, off your rocker *(slang)*, not the full shilling *(informal)*, as daft as a brush *(informal, chiefly Brit.)*, wacko *or* whacko *(slang)*, porangi *(N.Z.)*, daggy *(Austral. & N.Z. informal)* • *some batty uncle of theirs*

bauble = trinket, ornament, trifle, toy, plaything, bagatelle, gimcrack, gewgaw, knick-knack, bibelot, kickshaw • *The trees are decorated with fairy lights and coloured baubles.*

baulk *see* **balk**

bawdy = rude, blue, dirty, gross, crude, erotic, obscene, coarse, filthy, indecent, vulgar, improper, steamy *(informal)*, pornographic, raunchy *(U.S. slang)*, suggestive, racy, lewd, risqué, X-rated *(informal)*, salacious, prurient, lascivious, smutty, lustful, lecherous, ribald, libidinous, licentious,

FAMOUS BATTLES

Battle	Date	Battle	Date	Battle	Date
Aboukir Bay *or* Abukir Bay	1798	Hastings	1066	Plataea	479 B.C.
Actium	31 B.C.	Hohenlinden	1800	Poltava	1709
Agincourt	1415	Imphal	1944	Prestonpans	1745
Alamo	1836	Inkerman	1854	Pydna	168 B.C.
Arnhem	1944	Issus	333 B.C.	Quatre Bras	1815
Atlantic	1939-45	Jemappes	1792	Ramillies	1706
Austerlitz	1805	Jena	1806	Roncesvalles	778
Balaklava *or* Balaclava	1854	Killiecrankie	1689	Sadowa *or* Sadová	1866
Bannockburn	1314	Kursk	1943	Saint-Mihiel	1918
Barnet	1471	Ladysmith	1899-1900	Salamis	480 B.C.
Bautzen	1813	Le Cateau	1914	Sedgemoor	1685
Belleau Wood	1918	Leipzig	1813	Sempach	1386
Blenheim	1704	Lepanto	1571	Shiloh	1862
Borodino	1812	Leyte Gulf	1944	Shipka Pass	1877-78
Bosworth Field	1485	Little Bighorn	1876	Somme	1916; 1918
Boyne	1690	Lützen	1632	Stalingrad	1941-42
Britain	1940	Manassas	1861; 1862	Stamford Bridge	1066
Bulge	1944-45	Mantinea *or* Mantineia	418 B.C.; 362 B.C.	Stirling Bridge	1297
Bull Run	1861;1862			Tannenberg	1410; 1914
Bunker Hill	1775	Marathon	490 B.C.	Tewkesbury	1471
Cannae	216 B.C.	Marengo	1800	Thermopylae	480 B.C.
Crécy	1346	Marston Moor	1644	Tobruk	1941; 1942
Culloden	1746	Missionary Ridge	1863	Trafalgar	1805
Dien Bien Phu	1954	Naseby	1645	Trenton	1776
Edgehill	1642	Navarino	425 B.C.	Verdun	1916
El Alamein	1942	Omdurman	1898	Vitoria	1813
Falkirk	1298; 1746	Passchendaele	1917	Wagram	1809
Flodden	1513	Philippi	42 B.C.	Waterloo	1815
Gettysburg	1863	Plains of Abraham	1759	Ypres	1914; 1915; 1917; 1918
Guadalcanal	1942-3	Plassey	1757	Zama	202 B.C.

indelicate, near the knuckle *(informal)*, indecorous • *We got arrested once, for singing bawdy songs in a cemetery.*
OPPOSITES: good, seemly, clean

bawl 1 = shout, call, scream, roar, yell, howl, bellow, bay, clamour, holler *(informal)*, raise your voice, halloo, hollo, vociferate • *They were shouting and bawling at each other.*
2 = cry, weep, sob, wail, whine, whimper, whinge *(informal)*, keen, greet *(Scot. or archaic)*, squall, blubber, snivel, shed tears, yowl, mewl, howl your eyes out • *One of the toddlers was bawling, and another had a runny nose.*

bay[1] = inlet, sound, gulf, entrance, creek, cove, fjord, arm (of the sea), bight, ingress, natural harbour, sea loch *(Scot.)*, firth or frith *(Scot.)* • *a short ferry ride across the bay*
▹ *See panel* **Bays**

bay[2] = recess, opening, corner, niche, compartment, nook, alcove, embrasure • *Someone had placed the device in a loading bay behind the shop.*

bay[3] AS A VERB = howl, cry, roar *(of a hound)*, bark, lament, cry out, wail, growl, bellow, quest, bell, clamour, yelp • *A dog suddenly howled, baying at the moon.*
▸ **AS A NOUN = cry**, bell, roar *(of a hound)*, quest, bark, lament, howl, wail, growl, bellow, clamour, yelp • *She trembled at the bay of the dogs.*
▸ **IN PHRASES: at bay = away**, off, at arm's length • *Eating oranges keeps colds at bay.*

bayonet AS A NOUN = sword, knife, blade, lance, brand • *The sentry held his bayonet in front of his chest.*
▸ **AS A VERB = stab**, cut, wound, knife, slash, pierce, run through, spear, transfix, impale, lacerate, stick • *soldiers bayoneting unarmed prisoners to death*

bazaar 1 = market, exchange, fair, marketplace, mart • *He was a vendor in Egypt's open-air bazaar.*
2 = fair, fête, gala, festival, garden party, bring-and-buy • *a church bazaar*

be 1 = exist, be present, be extant • *There are two kinds of company pension.*
2 = be alive, live, exist, survive, breathe, last, be present, continue, endure, be living, be extant, happen • *It hurt so badly he wished to cease to be.*
3 = take place, happen, occur, arise, come about, transpire *(informal)*, befall, come to pass • *The film's premiere is next week.*
4 = remain, last, stand, continue, stay, endure, prevail, persist, abide, bide • *How long have you been here?*
5 = be situated, be set, be placed, be located, be installed, be positioned • *The church is on the other side of the town.*
6 = attend, go to, be at, be there, be present, frequent, haunt • *He's at university now.*
7 = cost, come to, sell at, set (someone) back *(informal)*, command a price of • *How much is this?*
8 = amount to, become, come to, total, equal, add up to • *Eight plus eight is sixteen.*

beach AS A NOUN = shore, coast, sands, margin, strand, seaside, shingle, lakeside, water's edge, lido, foreshore, seashore, plage, littoral, sea *(chiefly U.S.)* • *a beautiful sandy beach*
▸ **AS A VERB = land**, founder, be stuck, be stranded, come to rest, run aground, be on the rocks, be beached, run ashore, be high and dry • *The boat beached on a mud flat.*
▸ **RELATED ADJECTIVE:** littoral

beachcomber = scavenger, wanderer, tramp, forager, loafer, vagrant, scrounger, vagabond • *Beachcombers will note creeping vines beside the beach.*

beached = stranded, grounded, abandoned, deserted, wrecked, ashore, marooned, aground, high and dry • *A beached whale is a creature to be loved, rescued and cared for.*

beacon 1 = signal, sign, rocket, beam, flare, bonfire, smoke signal, signal fire • *The full moon beams like a beacon in the clear sky.*
2 = lighthouse, pharos, watchtower • *a lonely beacon on the rocks*

bead AS A NOUN 1 = ball, pearl, globe, sphere, pellet, orb, pill, spherule • *The beads scattered all over the floor.*
2 = drop, tear, bubble, pearl, dot, drip, blob, droplet, globule, driblet • *beads of blood*
▸ **AS A PLURAL NOUN = necklace**, pearls, pendant, choker, necklet, chaplet • *baubles, bangles and beads*

beady = bright, powerful, concentrated, sharp, intense, shining, glittering, gleaming, glinting • *She felt the old woman's beady eyes on her.*

beak[1] 1 = bill, nib, neb *(archaic or dialect)*, mandible • *a black bird with a yellow beak*
2 = nose, snout, hooter *(slang)*, snitch *(slang)*, conk *(slang)*, neb *(archaic or dialect)*, proboscis, schnozzle *(slang, chiefly U.S.)* • *his sharp, aristocratic beak*

beak[2] = magistrate, justice, sheriff • *The beak told him he'd go down if he did anything like it again.*

beaker = cup, glass, mug, tumbler • *a beaker of hot milk, well-laced with brandy*

beam AS A VERB 1 = smile, grin, be all smiles • *She beamed at her friend with undisguised admiration.*
2 = transmit, show, air, broadcast, cable, send out, relay,

BAYS

Aboukir or Abukir Bay
Bay of Acre
Algoa Bay
Ariake Bay
Baffin Bay
Bay of Bengal
Bay of Biscay
Biscayne Bay
Bombetoka Bay
Botany Bay
Buzzards Bay
Bay of Cádiz
Caernarvon Bay
Callao Bay
Bay of Campeche
Cape Cod Bay
Cardigan Bay
Carmarthen Bay
Casco Bay
Chesapeake Bay
Cienfuegos Bay
Colwyn Bay
Corpus Christi Bay
Delagoa Bay
Delaware Bay
Discovery Bay
Dublin Bay
Dundalk Bay
Dvina Bay
Encounter Bay
Bay of Espírito Santo
False Bay
Famagusta Bay
Florida Bay
Bay of Fundy
Galway Bay
Bay of Gdansk
Georgian Bay
Bay of Gibraltar
Guanabara Bay
Guantánamo Bay
Hangzhou Bay
Hawke Bay
Hudson Bay
Inhambane Bay
Ise Bay
James Bay
Jervis Bay
Jiazhou Bay
Bay of Kaválla
Korea Bay
Kuskokwim Bay
Lobito Bay
Lützow-Holm Bay
Magdalena Bay
Manila Bay
Massachusetts Bay
Milne Bay
Mobile Bay
Montego Bay
Morecambe Bay
Moreton Bay
Narragansett Bay
Newark Bay
Bay of Naples
New York Bay
Omura Bay
Osaka Bay
Passamaquoddy Bay
Bay of Pigs
Bay of Plenty
Port Phillip Bay
Poverty Bay
Quiberon Bay
San Francisco Bay
San Pedro Bay
Santiago Bay
Setúbal Bay
Sligo Bay
St Austell Bay
Bay of St Michel
Swansea Bay
Table Bay
Tampa Bay
Tasman Bay
Thunder Bay
Tokyo Bay
Toyama Bay
Tralee Bay
Bay of Trincomalee
Ungava Bay
Urado Bay
Vigo Bay
Bay of Vlorë
Vyborg Bay
Walvis or Walfish Bay
Whitley Bay
Wick Bay

televise, radio, emit, put on the air • *The interview was beamed live across America.*
3 = radiate, flash, shine, glow, glitter, glare, gleam, emit light, give off light • *A sharp white spotlight beamed down on a small stage.*
▸ AS A NOUN **1 = ray**, bar, flash, stream, glow, radiation, streak, emission, shaft, gleam, glint, glimmer • *a beam of light*
2 = rafter, support, timber, spar, plank, girder, joist • *The ceilings are supported by oak beams.*
3 = smile, grin • *She knew he had news, because of the beam on his face.*

beaming 1 = smiling, happy, grinning, pleasant, sunny, cheerful, cheery, joyful, chirpy *(informal)*, light-hearted • *his mother's beaming eyes*
2 = radiating, bright, brilliant, flashing, shining, glowing, sparkling, glittering, gleaming, glimmering, radiant, glistening, scintillating, burnished, lustrous • *An engraved and beaming sun rose out of the sea.*

bean
▹ *See panel* **Beans and other pulses**

bear[1] AS A VERB **1 = carry**, take, move, bring, lift, transfer, conduct, transport, haul, transmit, convey, relay, tote *(informal)*, hump *(Brit. slang)*, lug • *a surveyor and his assistant bearing a torch*
OPPOSITES: drop, shed, put down
2 = hold, carry, pack • *the constitutional right to bear arms*
3 = support, carry, shoulder, sustain, endure, hold up, keep up, uphold, withstand, bear up under • *The ice was not thick enough to bear the weight of marching men.*
OPPOSITES: drop, give up, abandon
4 = display, have, show, hold, carry, possess, exhibit • *notepaper bearing the President's seal*
5 = suffer, feel, experience, go through, sustain, stomach, endure, undergo, admit, brook, hack *(slang)*, abide, put up with *(informal)* • *He bore his sufferings manfully.*
6 = bring yourself to, allow, accept, permit, endure, tolerate, hack *(informal)*, abide, be doing with *(informal)*, countenance • *He can't bear to talk about it, even to me.*
7 = take on, support, carry, accept, shoulder, sustain, absorb • *She should bear that responsibility alone.*
8 = produce, give, provide, develop, generate, yield, bring forth, give forth • *The plants grow and start to bear fruit.*
9 = earn, make, get, receive, gain, net, collect, realize, obtain, yield, bring in, gross, reap, procure • *The eight-year bond will bear annual interest of 10.5%.*
10 = give birth to, produce, deliver, breed, bring forth, beget, be delivered of • *She bore a son called Karl.*
11 = exhibit, hold, maintain, entertain, harbour, cherish • *She bore no ill will. If they didn't like her, too bad.*
12 = conduct, carry, move, deport • *There was elegance and simple dignity in the way he bore himself.*
13 = turn, tack, veer, swerve, change direction, change course, shift, sheer • *Go left on the A107 and bear left into Seven Sisters Road.*
▸ IN PHRASES: **bear down on someone = advance on**, attack, approach, move towards, close in on, converge on, move in on, come near to, draw near to • *A group of half a dozen men entered the pub and bore down on her.*
bear down on something *or* **someone = press down**, push, strain, crush, compress, weigh down, encumber • *She felt as if a great weight was bearing down on her shoulders.*
bear on something = be relevant to, involve, concern, affect, regard, refer to, be part of, relate to, belong to, apply to, be appropriate, befit, pertain to, touch upon, appertain to • *The remaining 32 examples do not bear on our problem.*
bear something out = support, prove, confirm, justify, endorse, uphold, vindicate, validate, substantiate, corroborate, legitimize • *His photographs do not quite bear this out.*
bear up = cope, suffer, manage, survive, carry on, persevere, bear the brunt, grin and bear it *(informal)*, take it on the chin *(informal)*, hold your own, keep your chin up, go through the mill • *She felt that she would be unable to bear up under the pain.*
bear with someone = be patient with, suffer, wait for, hold on *(informal)*, stand by, tolerate, put up with *(informal)*, make allowances for, hang fire • *If you'll bear with me, Frank, I can explain everything.*

bear[2]
▸ RELATED ADJECTIVE: ursine
▸ NAME OF YOUNG: cub
▸ COLLECTIVE NOUN: sloth

bearable = tolerable, acceptable, sustainable, manageable, passable, admissible, supportable, endurable, sufferable • *A cool breeze made the heat pleasantly bearable.*
OPPOSITES: too much *(informal)*, unacceptable, intolerable

beard = whiskers, bristles, stubble, goatee, facial hair, five-o'clock shadow • *Charlie's bushy black beard*

bearded = unshaven, hairy, whiskered, stubbly, bushy, shaggy, hirsute, bristly, bewhiskered • *a bearded 40-year-old sociology professor*

bearer 1 = agent, carrier, courier, herald, envoy, messenger, conveyor, emissary, harbinger • *I hate to be the bearer of bad news.*
2 = carrier, runner, servant, porter, transporter • *a flag bearer*
3 = holder, owner, possessor • *The identity documents state the bearer's profession.*
4 = payee, beneficiary, consignee • *the chief cashier's promise to pay the bearer*

bearing AS A NOUN **1** *usually with* **on** *or* **upon = relevance**, relation, application, connection, import, reference, significance, pertinence, appurtenance • *My father's achievements don't have any bearing on what I do.*
OPPOSITES: irrelevance, irrelevancy, non sequitur
2 = manner, attitude, conduct, appearance, aspect, presence, behaviour, tone, carriage, posture, demeanour, deportment, mien *(literary)*, air, comportment • *She later wrote warmly of his bearing and behaviour.*
3 = position, heading, course, direction, path, orientation, point of compass • *I'm flying on a bearing of ninety-three degrees.*
▸ AS A PLURAL NOUN **= way**, course, position, situation, track, aim, direction, location, orientation, whereabouts, sense of direction • *I lost my bearings and was just aware of cars roaring past.*

BEANS AND OTHER PULSES

adzuki bean *or* adsuki bean
black bean
black-eyed bean *or* *(U.S.)* black-eyed pea
bobby bean
borlotti bean
broad bean
butter bean
cannelini bean
chick pea *or* garbanzo
continental lentil
dhal
field bean
flageolet bean
French bean
gram
green bean
green lentil
haricot bean *or* *(U.S.)* navy bean
kidney bean
lentil
lima bean
mangetout *or* snow pea
marrowfat pea
mung bean
petit pois
pigeon pea
pinto bean
puy lentil
red kidney bean *or* *(U.S.)* red bean
red lentil
runner bean
soya bean
split pea
string bean
sugar snap pea

bearish = **falling**, declining, slumping, weakening, dwindling • *the market's recent bearish trend*

beast 1 = **animal**, creature, brute • *the threats our ancestors faced from wild beasts*
2 = **brute**, monster, savage, barbarian, fiend, swine, ogre, ghoul, sadist • *a sex beast who subjected two sisters to a terrifying ordeal*

QUOTATIONS
And what rough beast, its hour come round at last,
Slouches towards Bethlehem to be born?
[W.B. Yeats *The Second Coming*]

beastly 1 = **unpleasant**, mean, terrible, awful, nasty, foul, rotten, horrid, disagreeable, irksome, shitty *(taboo slang)* • *The weather was beastly.*
OPPOSITES: good, fine, pleasant
2 = **cruel**, mean, nasty, harsh, savage, brutal, coarse, monstrous, malicious, insensitive, sadistic, unfriendly, unsympathetic, uncaring, spiteful, thoughtless, brutish, barbarous, unfeeling, inconsiderate, bestial, uncharitable, unchristian, hardhearted • *He must be wondering why everyone is being so beastly to him.*
OPPOSITES: sensitive, humane

beat AS A VERB 1 = **batter**, break, hit, strike, knock, punch, belt *(informal)*, whip, deck *(slang)*, bruise, bash *(informal)*, sock *(slang)*, lash, chin *(slang)*, pound, smack, thrash, cane, thump, lick *(informal)*, buffet, clout *(informal)*, flog, whack *(informal)*, maul, clobber *(slang)*, wallop *(informal)*, tonk *(informal)*, cudgel, thwack *(informal)*, lambast(e), lay one on *(slang)*, drub, tan *(informal)*, lam *(informal)*, beat *or* knock seven bells out of *(informal)* • *They were beaten to death with baseball bats.*
2 = **pound**, strike, hammer, batter, thrash, pelt • *The rain was beating on the window pains.*
3 = **throb**, pulse, tick, thump, tremble, pound, quake, quiver, vibrate, pulsate, palpitate • *I felt my heart beat faster.*
4 = **hit**, play, strike, bang, rap, hammer • *When you beat the drum, you feel good.*
5 = **whisk**, mix, stir, fold, whip, blend, fluff up • *Beat the eggs and sugar until they start to thicken.*
6 = **flap**, thrash, flutter, agitate, wag, swish • *Its wings beat slowly.*
7 = **defeat**, outdo, trounce, overcome, stuff *(slang)*, master, tank *(slang)*, crush, overwhelm, conquer, lick *(informal)*, undo, subdue, excel, surpass, overpower, outstrip, clobber *(slang)*, vanquish, outrun, subjugate, run rings around *(informal)*, wipe the floor with *(informal)*, knock spots off *(informal)*, make mincemeat of *(informal)*, pip at the post, outplay, blow out of the water *(slang)*, put in the shade *(informal)*, bring to their knees • *She was easily beaten into third place.*
8 = **exceed**, best, top, cap, eclipse, surpass, transcend, outdo, go one better than *(informal)*, put in the shade • *He was as eager as his captain to beat the record.*
▸ AS A NOUN 1 = **pounding**, striking, hammering, battering, thrashing, thumping • *the rhythmic beat of the surf*
2 = **throb**, pounding, pumping, pulse, thumping, vibration, pulsating, palpitation, pulsation • *He could hear the beat of his heart.*
3 = **rhythm**, time, measure *(Prosody)*, movement, pattern, swing, metre, accent, pulse, tempo, cadence, lilt • *the dance beats of the last two decades*
4 = **route**, way, course, rounds, path, circuit • *I was a relatively new PC on the beat, stationed in Hendon.*
▸ IN PHRASES: **beat it** = **go away**, leave, depart, get lost *(informal)*, piss off *(taboo slang)*, shoo, exit, go to hell *(informal)*, fuck off *(offensive taboo slang)*, hook it *(slang)*, bugger off *(taboo slang)*, scarper *(Brit. slang)*, pack your bags *(informal)*, make tracks, hop it *(slang)*, scram *(informal)*, get on your bike *(Brit. slang)*, bog off *(Brit. slang)*, skedaddle *(informal)*, sling your hook *(Brit. slang)*, vamoose *(slang, chiefly U.S.)*, voetsek *(S. African offensive)*, rack off *(Austral. & N.Z. slang)* • *Beat it before it's too late.*
beat someone up = **assault**, attack, batter, thrash, set about, do over *(Brit., Austral. & N.Z. slang)*, work over *(slang)*, clobber *(slang)*, assail, set upon, lay into *(informal)*, put the boot in *(slang)*, lambast(e), duff up *(Brit. slang)*, beat the living daylights out of *(informal)*, knock about *or* around, fill in *(Brit. slang)*, beat *or* knock seven bells out of *(informal)* • *Then they actually beat her up as well.*
beat something out = **put out**, stifle, smother, extinguish, snuff out • *His brother beat out the flames with a blanket.*
beat yourself up = **torture yourself**, suffer, worry, struggle, be distressed, go through the mill, be in anguish • *Don't beat yourself up about it.*

beaten 1 = **well-trodden**, worn, trodden, trampled, well-used, much travelled • *Before you is a well-worn path of beaten earth.*
2 = **stirred**, mixed, whipped, blended, whisked, frothy, foamy • *Cool a little and slowly add the beaten eggs.*
3 = **shaped**, worked, formed, stamped, hammered, forged • *brightly painted beaten metal*
4 = **defeated**, overcome, frustrated, overwhelmed, cowed, thwarted, trounced, vanquished, disheartened • *They had looked a beaten side with just seven minutes left.*

beatific = **blissful**, happy, heavenly, glorious, enchanted, ecstatic, sublime, serene, joyous, exalted, joyful, elated, euphoric, rapturous, rapt, enraptured, blissed out, stoked *(Austral. & N.Z. informal)* • *He smiled an almost beatific smile.*

beating 1 = **thrashing**, hiding *(informal)*, belting *(informal)*, whipping *(slang)*, slapping, tanning, lashing, smacking, caning, pasting *(slang)*, flogging, drubbing, corporal punishment, chastisement • *the savage beating of a suspect by police officers*
2 = **defeat**, ruin, overthrow, pasting *(slang)*, conquest, rout, downfall • *A beating at Wembley would be too much of a trauma for them.*
3 = **throb**, pounding, pumping, pulse, thumping, vibration, pulsating, palpitation, pulsation • *High in the stands there came the beating of a drum.*

beau = **boyfriend**, man, guy *(informal)*, date, lover, young man, steady, escort, admirer, fiancé, sweetheart, suitor, swain, toy boy, leman *(archaic)*, fancy man *(slang)* • *She appeared with her new beau.*

beautiful 1 = **attractive**, pretty, lovely, stunning *(informal)*, charming, tempting, pleasant, handsome, fetching, good-looking, gorgeous, fine, pleasing, fair, magnetic, delightful, cute, exquisite, enticing, seductive, graceful, captivating, appealing, radiant, alluring, drop-dead *(slang)*, ravishing, bonny, winsome, comely, prepossessing, hot *(informal)*, fit *(Brit. informal)* • *a beautiful red-haired woman kneeling at her mother's feet*
OPPOSITES: ugly, unpleasant, hideous
2 = **bright**, clear, fine, summery, unclouded, sunshiny, without a cloud in the sky • *It was a beautiful morning*
3 = **wonderful**, great, excellent, superb, marvellous, sensational *(informal)*, mega *(slang)*, cracking *(Brit. informal)*, awesome *(slang)*, topping *(Brit. slang)*, world-class, first-rate, brill *(informal)*, mean *(slang)*, booshit *(Austral. slang)*, exo *(Austral. slang)*, sik *(Austral. slang)*, rad *(informal)*, phat *(slang)*, schmick *(Austral. informal)*, beaut *(informal)*, barrie *(Scot. slang)*, belting *(Brit. slang)*, pearler *(Austral. slang)* • *That's a beautiful shot!*
OPPOSITES: bad, terrible, awful

QUOTATIONS
Remember that the most beautiful things in the world are the most useless; peacocks and lilies for instance
[John Ruskin *Stones of Venice*]

I never saw an ugly thing in my life: for let the form of an object be what it may, – light, shade, and perspective will always make it beautiful
[John Constable]
Things are beautiful if you love them
[Jean Anouilh *Mademoiselle Colombe*]

beautify = **make beautiful**, enhance, decorate, enrich, adorn, garnish, ornament, gild, embellish, grace, festoon, bedeck, glamorize • *Claire worked to beautify the garden.*

beauty 1 = **attractiveness**, appeal, charm, grace, bloom, glamour, fairness, elegance, symmetry *(formal or literary)*, allure, loveliness, prettiness, seductiveness, gorgeousness, pleasantness, handsomeness, pulchritude, winsomeness, comeliness, exquisiteness, seemliness, pleasingness, prepossessingness • *an area of outstanding natural beauty*
OPPOSITES: ugliness, unpleasantness, repulsiveness
2 = **good-looker**, looker *(informal, chiefly U.S.)*, lovely *(slang)*, sensation, dazzler, belle, goddess, Venus, peach *(informal)*, cracker *(slang)*, wow *(slang, chiefly U.S.)*, dolly *(slang)*, knockout *(informal)*, heart-throb, stunner *(informal)*, charmer, smasher *(informal)*, humdinger *(slang)*, glamour puss, beaut *(Austral. & N.Z. slang)* • *She is known as a great beauty.*
3 = **advantage**, good, use, benefit, profit, gain, asset, attraction, blessing, good thing, utility, excellence, boon • *the beauty of such water-based minerals*
OPPOSITES: disadvantage, flaw, detraction

QUOTATIONS
A thing of beauty is a joy forever;
Its loveliness increases; it will never
Pass into nothingness
[John Keats *Endymion*]
If you get simple beauty and nought else,
You get about the best thing God invents
[Robert Browning *Fra Lippo Lippi*]
'Beauty is truth, truth beauty,' – that is all
Ye know on earth, and all ye need to know
[John Keats *Ode on a Grecian Urn*]
The truth isn't always beauty, but the hunger for it is
[Nadine Gordimer *A Bolter and the Invincible Summer*]
It is amazing how complete is the delusion that beauty is goodness
[Leo Tolstoy *The Kreutzer Sonata*]
Beauty vanishes; beauty passes
[Walter de la Mare *Epitaph*]
Beauty is a precious trace that eternity causes to appear to us and that it takes away from us
[Eugène Ionesco *Present Past – Past Present*]
Beauty is the moment of transition, as if the form were just ready to flow into other forms
[Ralph Waldo Emerson *The Conduct of Life*]
Beauty is mysterious as well as terrible. God and devil are fighting there, and the battlefield is the heart of man
[Fedor Dostoevsky *The Brothers Karamazov*]
All changed, changed utterly;
A terrible beauty is born
[W.B. Yeats *Easter 1916*]
Beauty is feared, more than death
[William Carlos Williams *Paterson*]
Beauty halts and freezes the melting flux of nature
[Camille Paglia *Sexual Personae*]
Beauty is no quality in things themselves. It exists merely in the mind which contemplates them
[David Hume *Essays, Moral, Political, and Literary*]
Ask a toad what is beauty ...; he will answer that it is a female with two great round eyes coming out of her little head, a large flat mouth, a yellow belly and a brown back
[Voltaire *Philosophical Dictionary*]
I always say beauty is only sin deep
[Saki (H.H. Munro) *Reginald*]
Beauty is nothing other than the promise of happiness
[Stendhal *On Love*]
beauty: the power by which a woman charms a lover and terrifies a husband
[Ambrose Bierce *The Devil's Dictionary*]
Beauty is all very well at first sight; but who ever looks at it when it has been in the house three days?
[George Bernard Shaw *Man and Superman*]
Beauty is an ecstasy; it is as simple as hunger. There is really nothing to be said about it
[W.Somerset Maugham *Cakes and Ale*]

PROVERBS
Beauty is in the eye of the beholder
Beauty is only skin deep

beaver AS A VERB
▸ IN PHRASES: **beaver away** = **work**, sweat, slave, persist, graft *(informal)*, toil, slog (away), persevere, plug away *(informal)*, drudge, hammer away, peg away, exert yourself, break your back, keep your nose to the grindstone • *They are beavering away to get everything ready for us.*
▸ NAME OF HOME: lodge

becalmed = **still**, stuck, settled, stranded, motionless • *We found ourselves becalmed off Dungeness for several hours.*

because AS A CONJUNCTION = **since**, as, in that, seeing as • *They could not obey the command because they had no ammunition.*
▸ IN PHRASES: **because of** = **as a result of**, on account of, by reason of, thanks to, owing to • *He failed because of a lack of money.*

beckon 1 = **gesture**, sign, wave, indicate, signal, nod, motion, summon, gesticulate • *He beckoned to the waiter.*
2 = **lure**, call, draw, pull, attract, invite, tempt, entice, coax, allure • *All the attractions of the peninsula beckon.*
3 = **draw near**, near, move towards someone, come close, gain on someone, come near • *Old age beckons.*

become AS A VERB 1 = **come to be**, develop into, be transformed into, grow into, change into, evolve into, alter to, mature into, metamorphose into, ripen into • *After leaving school, he became a professional footballer.*
2 = **suit**, look good on, fit, enhance, flatter, ornament, embellish, grace, harmonize with, look right on, set off • *Does khaki become you?*
▸ IN PHRASES: **become of something** *or* **someone** = **happen to**, befall, be the fate of, betide • *What will become of him?*

becoming 1 = **flattering**, pretty, attractive, enhancing, elegant, neat, stylish, graceful, tasteful, well-chosen, comely • *Softer fabrics are much more becoming than stiffer ones.*
OPPOSITES: ugly, unattractive, unflattering
2 = **appropriate**, right, seemly, fitting, fit, correct, suitable, decent, proper, worthy, in keeping, compatible, befitting, decorous, comme il faut *(French)*, congruous, meet *(archaic)* • *This behaviour is not becoming among our politicians.*
OPPOSITES: inappropriate, unfit, unsuitable

bed AS A NOUN 1 = **bedstead**, couch, berth, cot, the sack *(informal)*, bunk, the hay *(informal)*, pallet, divan • *She went in to her bedroom and lay down on the bed.*
2 = **plot**, area, row, strip, patch, ground, land, garden, border • *beds of strawberries and rhubarb*
3 = **bottom**, ground, floor • *the bare bed of a dry stream*
4 = **base**, footing, basis, bottom, foundation, underpinning, groundwork, bedrock, substructure, substratum • *a sandstone bed*
5 = **layer**, mass, pile, heap, mound • *Heat the curry thoroughly and serve it on a bed of rice.*
▸ AS A VERB = **fix**, set, found, base, plant, establish, settle, root, sink, insert, implant, embed • *The slabs can then be bedded on mortar to give rigid paving.*

▸ **IN PHRASES: bed down = sleep**, lie down, retire, turn in *(informal)*, settle down, kip *(Brit. slang)*, hit the hay *(slang)* • *They bedded down in the fields.*
go to bed = retire, turn in *(informal)*, go to sleep, hit the sack *(slang)*, go to your room, kip down *(Brit. slang)*, hit the hay *(slang)* • *I go to bed quite early.*
go to bed with someone = have sex with, fuck *(taboo slang)*, screw *(taboo slang)*, shag *(taboo slang, chiefly Brit.)*, hump *(taboo slang)*, bonk *(informal)*, have intercourse with, copulate with, ball *(taboo slang, chiefly U.S.)* • *Do you really want to go to bed with a girl you don't fancy?*

QUOTATIONS
And so to bed
[Samuel Pepys *Diary*]
'Tis very warm weather when one's in bed
[Jonathan Swift *Journal to Stella*]
PROVERBS
As you make your bed, so you must lie in it

▹ *See panel* **Types of bed**

bedclothes = bedding, covers, sheets, blankets, linen, pillow, quilt, duvet, pillowcase, bed linen, coverlet, eiderdown • *He moved his body gently under the bedclothes.*

bedding = bedclothes, covers, sheets, blankets, linen, pillow, quilt, duvet, pillowcase, bed linen, coverlet, eiderdown • *They carried food, bedding and clothing with them.*

bedeck = decorate, grace, trim, array, enrich, adorn, garnish, ornament, embellish, festoon, beautify, bedight *(archaic)*, bedizen *(archaic)*, engarland • *Flags bedeck the balcony*

bedevil = plague, worry, trouble, frustrate, torture, irritate, torment, harass, hassle *(informal)*, aggravate *(informal)*, afflict, pester, vex, irk, give someone grief *(Brit. & S. African)* • *His career was bedevilled by injury.*

bedlam = pandemonium, noise, confusion, chaos, turmoil, clamour, furore, uproar, commotion, rumpus, babel, tumult, hubbub, ruction *(informal)*, hullabaloo, hue and cry, ruckus *(informal)* • *He is causing bedlam at the hotel.*

bedraggled = messy, soiled, dirty, disordered, stained, dripping, muddied, muddy, drenched, ruffled, untidy, sodden, sullied, dishevelled, rumpled, unkempt, tousled, disarranged, disarrayed, daggy *(Austral. & N.Z. informal)* • *a bedraggled group of journalists*

bedridden = confined to bed, confined, incapacitated, laid up *(informal)*, flat on your back • *bedridden patients*

bedrock 1 = first principle, rule, basis, basics, principle, essentials, roots, core, fundamentals, cornerstone, nuts and bolts *(informal)*, sine qua non *(Latin)*, rudiment • *Mutual trust is the bedrock of a relationship.*
2 = bottom, bed, foundation, underpinning, rock bottom, substructure, substratum • *It took five years to drill down to bedrock.*

bee
▸ **RELATED ADJECTIVE:** apian
▸ **COLLECTIVE NOUNS:** swarm, grist
▸ **NAME OF HOME:** hive, apiary
▸ **RELATED MANIA:** apimania
▹ *See panel* **Ants, bees and wasps**

beef AS A NOUN = complaint, dispute, grievance, problem, grumble, criticism, objection, dissatisfaction, annoyance, grouse, gripe *(informal)*, protestation, grouch *(informal)*, remonstrance • *I really don't have a beef with Wayne.*
▸ **AS A VERB = complain**, carp, fuss, moan, bitch *(slang)*, groan, grieve, lament, grumble, whine, growl, deplore, grouse, gripe *(informal)*, bemoan, whinge *(informal)*, bleat, find fault, bewail, kick up a fuss *(informal)*, grouch *(informal)*, bellyache *(slang)*, kvetch *(U.S. slang)* • *She was beefing about what he had done.*
▸ **IN PHRASES: beef something up = strengthen**, increase, build up, enhance, reinforce, intensify, heighten, bolster, augment, give a boost to • *a campaign to beef up security*

beefy = brawny, strong, powerful, athletic, strapping, robust, hefty *(informal)*, muscular, sturdy, stalwart, bulky, burly, stocky, hulking, well-built, herculean, sinewy, thickset • *The place was packed with beefy ex-footballers*
OPPOSITES: weak, frail, scrawny

beehive = hive, colony, comb, swarm, honeycomb, apiary • *The reproductive product of a beehive is a swarm.*

beer = ale, brew, swipes *(Brit. slang)*, wallop *(Brit. slang)*, hop juice, amber fluid *or* nectar *(Austral. informal)*, tinnie *or* tinny *(Austral. slang)* • *We have quite a good range of beers.*

QUOTATIONS
And malt does more than Milton can
To justify God's ways to man
[A E Housman *A Shropshire Lad*]
They who drink beer will think beer
[Washington Irving *The Sketch Book of Geoffrey Crayon*]
Then to the spicy nut-brown ale
[John Milton *L'Allegro*]

▹ *See panel* **Beers**

beer parlour = tavern, inn, bar, pub *(informal, chiefly Brit.)*, public house, watering hole *(facetious slang)*, boozer *(Brit., Austral. & N.Z. informal)*, beverage room *(Canad.)*, hostelry, alehouse *(archaic)*, taproom

beetle
▹ *See panel* **Beetles**

befall = happen to, fall upon, occur in, take place in, ensue in, transpire in *(informal)*, materialize in, come to pass in • *the disaster that befell the island of Flores*

befit = be appropriate for, become, suit, be fitting for, be suitable for, be seemly for, behove *(U.S.)* • *He writes beautifully, as befits a poet.*

befitting = appropriate to, right for, suitable for, fitting for, fit for, becoming to, suitable to, seemly for, proper for, apposite to, meet *(archaic)* • *They offered him a post befitting his seniority and experience.*
OPPOSITES: wrong for, irrelevant to, unsuitable for

before AS A PREPOSITION 1 = earlier than, ahead of, prior to, in advance of • *Annie was born a few weeks before Christmas.*
OPPOSITES: after, following, succeeding
2 = in front of, ahead of, in advance of, to the fore of • *They stopped before a large white villa.*
3 = in the presence of, in front of, before the eyes of • *The Government will appear before the committee.*

TYPES OF BED

air bed, bassinet, berth, box bed, bunk, bunk bed, camp bed, captain's bed, cot, couchette, cradle, crib, day bed, divan bed, double bed, feather bed, field bed, foldaway bed, folding bed, four-poster bed, futon, hammock, hospital bed, king-size *or* king-sized bed, litter, loft bed, Murphy bed *(U.S. & Canada)*, pallet, platform bed, put-u-up, queen-size *or* queen-sized bed, shake down, single bed, sleigh bed, sofa bed, trestle bed, truckle *or* trundle bed, twin bed, water bed

b

BEERS

ale
barley wine
Bière de Garde
black and tan
bock beer *or* bock
boilermaker
bottle-conditioned beer *or* ale
brown ale
cask-conditioned beer *or* ale
Christmas beer *or* ale
draught beer
eighty shilling *or* eighty
export
fruit beer
guest beer
gueuze
half-and-half
heavy *(Scot.)*
home-brew
ice beer
India Pale Ale *or* IPA
Kaffir beer
keg beer
Kölsch
lager
lambic
light *(Scot.)*
light ale
mild
milk stout
nog *or* nogg *(dialect)*
pale ale
Pils
Pilsner *or* Pilsener
plain *(Irish)*
porter
Rauchbier
real ale
seventy shilling *or* seventy
shandy
shebeen *or* shebean *(Irish & U.S.)*
sixty shilling *or* sixty
special
stingo
stout
sweet stout
Trappist beer
Weissbier
Weizenbier
wheat beer

4 = ahead of, in front of, in advance of • *I saw before me an idyllic life.*
5 = in preference to, over, rather than, above, instead of, sooner than, over and above • *Her husband, her children, and the Church come before her needs.*
▸ AS AN ADVERB **1 = previously**, earlier, sooner, in advance, formerly • *The war had ended only a month or so before.*
OPPOSITES: after, later, afterwards
2 = in the past, earlier, once, previously, formerly, at one time, hitherto, beforehand, a while ago, heretofore, in days *or* years gone by • *I've been here before.*
▸ RELATED PREFIXES: ante-, fore-, pre-

beforehand = in advance, before, earlier, already, sooner, ahead, previously, in anticipation, before now, ahead of time • *How could she tell beforehand that I was going to go out?*

befriend = make friends with, back, help, support, benefit, aid, encourage, welcome, favour, advise, sustain, assist, stand by, uphold, side with, patronize, succour • *It's about an elderly woman and a young nurse who befriends her.*

befuddle = confuse, puzzle, baffle, bewilder, muddle, daze, perplex, mystify, disorient, faze, stupefy, flummox, bemuse, intoxicate • *He liked to befuddle his readers.*
OPPOSITES: resolve, interpret, make clear

befuddled = confused, upset, puzzled, baffled, at sea, bewildered, muddled, dazed, perplexed, taken aback, intoxicated, disorientated, disorganized, muzzy *(U.S. informal)*, groggy *(informal)*, flummoxed, woozy *(informal)*, at sixes and sevens, fuddled, inebriated, thrown off balance, discombobulated *(informal, chiefly U.S. & Canad.)*, not with it *(informal)*, not knowing if you are coming or going • *I was befuddled with drink.*

beg 1 = implore, plead with, beseech, desire, request, pray, petition, conjure, crave, solicit, entreat, importune, supplicate, go on bended knee to • *I begged him to come back to England with me.*
2 = scrounge, bum *(informal)*, blag *(slang)*, touch (someone) for *(slang)*, mooch *(slang)*, cadge, forage for, hunt around (for), sponge on (someone) for, freeload *(slang)*, seek charity, call for alms, solicit charity • *I was surrounded by people begging for food.*
OPPOSITES: give, present, award
3 = dodge, avoid, get out of, duck *(informal)*, hedge, parry, shun, evade, elude, fudge, fend off, eschew, flannel *(Brit. informal)*, sidestep, shirk, equivocate, body-swerve *(Scot.)* • *The research begs a number of questions.*

beget 1 = cause, bring, produce, create, effect, lead to, occasion, result in, generate, provoke, induce, bring about, give rise to, precipitate, incite, engender • *Poverty begets debt.*
2 = father, breed, generate, sire, get, propagate, procreate • *He wanted to beget an heir.*

beggar AS A NOUN **= tramp**, bankrupt, bum *(informal)*, derelict, drifter, down-and-out, pauper, vagrant, hobo *(chiefly U.S.)*, vagabond, bag lady *(chiefly U.S.)*, dosser *(Brit. slang)*, derro *(Austral. slang)*, starveling • *Now I am a beggar, having lost everything except life.*
▸ AS A VERB **= defy**, challenge, defeat, frustrate, foil, baffle, thwart, withstand, surpass, elude, repel • *The statistics beggar belief.*

begin AS A VERB **1 = start**, commence, proceed • *He stood up and began to walk around the room.*
OPPOSITES: end, stop, finish
2 = commence, start, initiate, embark on, set about, instigate, inaugurate, institute, make a beginning, set on foot • *The US wants to begin talks immediately.*
3 = start talking, start, open, initiate, commence, lead off, begin business, get *or* start the ball rolling • *He didn't know how to begin.*

BEETLES

ambrosia beetle
Asiatic beetle
bacon beetle
bark beetle
bee beetle
black beetle *or (N.Z.)* kekerengu *or* Māori bug
blister beetle
bloody-nosed beetle
boll weevil
bombardier beetle
burying beetle *or* sexton
cabinet beetle
cardinal beetle
carpet beetle *or (U.S.)* carpet bug
carrion beetle
chafer
Christmas beetle *or* king beetle
churchyard beetle
click beetle, snapping beetle, *or* skipjack
cockchafer, May beetle, *or* May bug
Colorado beetle *or* potato beetle
curculio
deathwatch beetle
devil's coach-horse
diving beetle
dor
dung beetle *or* chafer
elater
firefly
flea beetle
furniture beetle
glow-worm
gold beetle *or* goldbug
goldsmith beetle
goliath beetle
ground beetle
Hercules beetle
huhu
Japanese beetle
June bug, June beetle, May bug, *or* May beetle
ladybird *or (U.S. & Canad.)* ladybug
larder beetle
leaf beetle
leather beetle
longicorn (beetle) *or* long-horned beetle
May beetle, cockchafer, *or* June bug
museum beetle
oil beetle
pill beetle
rhinoceros beetle
rose chafer *or* rose beetle
rove beetle
scarab
scavenger beetle
snapping beetle
snout beetle
soldier beetle
Spanish fly
stag beetle
tiger beetle
timberman beetle
tortoise beetle
vedalia
water beetle
weevil *or* snout beetle
weevil, pea weevil, *or* bean weevil
whirligig beetle

4 = come into existence, start, appear, emerge, spring, be born, arise, dawn, be developed, be created, originate, commence, be invented, become available, crop up *(informal)*, come into being • *It began as a local festival.*
5 = emerge, start, spring, stem, derive, issue, originate • *The fate line begins close to the wrist.*
OPPOSITES: cease, end, finish
▸ IN PHRASES: **to begin with 1 = at first**, to start with, in the first place • *It was great to begin with but now it's difficult.*
2 = firstly • *To begin with, they doubt it's going to work.*

beginner = **novice**, student, pupil, convert, recruit, amateur, initiate, newcomer, starter, trainee, apprentice, cub, fledgling, learner, freshman, neophyte, tyro, probationer, greenhorn *(informal)*, novitiate, newbie *(slang)*, tenderfoot, proselyte • *I am a complete beginner to bird-keeping.*
OPPOSITES: authority, professional, expert

beginning 1 = start, opening, break *(informal)*, chance, source, opportunity, birth, origin, introduction, outset, starting point, onset, overture, initiation, inauguration, inception, commencement, opening move • *Think of this as a new beginning.*
OPPOSITES: ending, end, closing
2 = outset, start, opening, birth, onset, prelude, preface, commencement, kickoff *(informal)* • *The question was raised at the beginning of this chapter.*
3 = origins, family, beginnings, stock, birth, roots, heritage, descent, pedigree, extraction, ancestry, lineage, parentage, stirps • *His views come from his own humble beginnings.*

begrudge 1 = resent, envy, grudge, be jealous of, be envious of, be resentful of • *I certainly don't begrudge him the Nobel Prize.*
2 = be bitter about, object to, be angry about, be pissed (off) about *(taboo slang)*, give reluctantly, bear a grudge about, be in a huff about, give stingily, have hard feelings about • *She spends £2,000 a year on it and she doesn't begrudge a penny.*

beguile 1 = charm, please, attract, delight, occupy, cheer, fascinate, entertain, absorb, entrance, win over, amuse, divert, distract, enchant, captivate, solace, allure, bewitch, mesmerize, engross, enrapture, tickle the fancy of • *His paintings beguiled the Prince of Wales.*
2 = fool, trick, take in, cheat, con *(informal)*, mislead, impose on, deceive, dupe, gull *(archaic)*, delude, bamboozle, hoodwink, take for a ride *(informal)*, befool • *He used his newspapers to beguile his readers.*
OPPOSITES: alarm, alert, enlighten

beguiling = **charming**, interesting, pleasing, attractive, engaging, lovely, entertaining, pleasant, intriguing, diverting, delightful, irresistible, enchanting, seductive, captivating, enthralling, winning, eye-catching, alluring, bewitching, delectable, winsome, likable *or* likeable • *Mombasa is a town with a beguiling Arabic flavour.*

behalf IN PHRASES: **on behalf of something** *or* **someone** *or* **on something** *or* **someone's behalf 1 = as a representative of**, representing, in the name of, as a spokesperson for • *She made an emotional public appeal on her son's behalf.* • *On behalf of my wife and myself, I'd like to thank you all.*
2 = for the benefit of, for the sake of, in support of, on the side of, in the interests of, on account of, for the good of, in defence of, to the advantage of, for the profit of • *The honour recognizes work done on behalf of classical theatre.* • *The pupils were enthusiastic in their fund-raising efforts on the charity's behalf.*

behave 1 = act, react, conduct yourself, acquit yourself, comport yourself • *He'd behaved badly.*
2 *often reflexive* = **be well-behaved**, be good, be polite, mind your manners, keep your nose clean, act correctly, act politely, conduct yourself properly • *You have to behave.* • *Sit down and behave yourself.*
OPPOSITES: carry on *(informal)*, be bad, misbehave

behaviour 1 = conduct, ways, actions, bearing, attitude, manner, manners, carriage, demeanour, deportment, mien *(literary)*, comportment • *He was asked to explain his extraordinary behaviour.*
2 = action, working, running, performance, operation, practice, conduct, functioning • *This process modifies the cell's behaviour.*

QUOTATIONS
Perfect behaviour is born of complete indifference
[Cesare Pavese *This Business of Living*]

behead = **decapitate**, execute, guillotine, truncate, decollate *(archaic)* • *Charles I was beheaded by the Cromwellians.*

behemoth = **giant**, monster, mammoth, titan, Hercules, colossus, leviathan, Brobdingnagian • *The city is a sprawling behemoth with no heart.*

behest IN PHRASES: **at someone's behest = at someone's command**, by someone's order, at someone's demand, at someone's wish, by someone's decree, at someone's bidding, at someone's instruction, by someone's mandate, at someone's dictate, at someone's commandment • *He did it at his wife's behest.*

behind AS A PREPOSITION **1 = at the rear of**, at the back of, on the other side of, on the far side of, at the heels of • *They were parked behind the truck.*
2 = after, following, in the wake of, on the heels of, to the rear of • *Keith wandered along behind him.*
3 = supporting, for, backing, on the side of, in agreement with • *He had the state's judicial power behind him.*
4 = causing, responsible for, the cause of, initiating, at the bottom of, to blame for, instigating • *I'd like to know who was behind this plot.*
5 = less advanced than, slower than, inferior to, weaker than • *Food production is behind population growth.*
6 = later than, after • *The work is 22 weeks behind schedule*
▸ AS AN ADVERB **1 = the back**, the rear • *She was attacked from behind.*
2 = after, next, following, afterwards, subsequently, in the wake (of) • *The troopers followed behind.*
OPPOSITES: in front of, prior to, in advance of
3 = behind schedule, delayed, running late, behind time • *The accounts are more than three months behind.*
OPPOSITES: earlier, sooner, ahead
4 = overdue, in debt, in arrears, behindhand • *They were falling behind with their mortgage payments.*
▸ AS A NOUN = **bottom**, seat, bum *(Brit. slang)*, ass *(U.S. & Canad. taboo slang)*, butt *(U.S. & Canad. informal)*, buns *(U.S. slang)*, arse *(taboo slang)*, buttocks, rump, posterior, tail *(informal)*, derrière *(euphemistic)*, tush *(U.S. slang)*, jacksy *(Brit. slang)* • *jeans that actually flatter your behind*
▸ IN PHRASES: **put something behind you = put something in the past**, put something down to experience, pay no heed to something, regard something as water under the bridge • *Maureen put the nightmare behind her.*

behindhand = **behind schedule**, late, slow, delayed, running late, tardy, dilatory, remiss, behind time • *He got terribly behindhand with his appointments.*

behold = **look at**, see, view, eye, consider, study, watch, check, regard, survey, witness, clock *(Brit. slang)*, examine, observe, perceive, gaze, scan, contemplate, check out *(informal)*, inspect, discern, eyeball *(slang)*, scrutinize, recce *(slang)*, get a load of *(informal)*, take a gander at *(informal)*, take a dekko at *(Brit. slang)*, feast your eyes upon • *He was a joy to behold.*

beholden = **indebted**, bound, owing, grateful, obliged, in debt, obligated, under obligation • *He was made beholden to the Mafia.*

behove = **be fitting**, benefit, be necessary, be wise, befit, be advisable, be obligatory, be incumbent upon, beseem • *I think it behoves us, sir, to get out of here with all speed.*

beige AS A NOUN
▸ AS AN ADJECTIVE = **fawn**, coffee, cream, sand, neutral, mushroom, tan, biscuit, camel, buff, cinnamon, khaki, oatmeal, ecru, café au lait *(French)* • *a pair of beige shorts*
▹ *See panels* **Shades of brown; Shades of yellow**

being 1 = **individual**, thing, body, animal, creature, human being, beast, mortal, living thing • *beings from outer space*
2 = **life**, living, reality, animation, actuality • *the complex process by which the novel is brought into being*
OPPOSITES: oblivion, nothingness, nonexistence
3 = **soul**, spirit, presence, substance, creature, essence, organism, entity • *The music seemed to touch his very being.*

belabour 1 = **beat**, hit, strike, knock, punch, belt *(informal)*, whip, deck *(slang)*, batter, thrash, pound, flog, clobber *(slang)*, tonk *(informal)*, cudgel, thwack, lambast(e), lay one on *(slang)*, drub, beat *or* knock seven bells out of *(informal)* • *Men began to belabour his shoulders with sticks.*
2 = **attack**, blast, put down, criticize, have a go (at) *(informal)*, censure, malign, berate, castigate, revile, vilify, flame *(informal)*, tear into *(informal)*, lay into *(informal)*, flay, diss *(slang, chiefly U.S.)*, go for the jugular, lambast(e), excoriate • *They have been belaboured on all sides for withdrawing from the cup.*
3 = **dwell on**, go on about, linger over, harp on about, over-elaborate, over-emphasize, tarry over • *I will not belabour the point.*

belated = **late**, delayed, overdue, late in the day, tardy, behind time, unpunctual, behindhand • *a belated birthday present*

belch AS A VERB 1 = **burp**, eructate, eruct • *He covered his mouth with his hand and belched discreetly.*
2 = **emit**, discharge, erupt, send out, throw out, vent, vomit, issue, give out, gush, eject, diffuse, emanate, exude, give off, exhale, cast out, disgorge, give vent to, send forth, spew forth, breathe forth • *Tired old trucks belched black smoke.*
▸ AS A NOUN = **burp**, hiccup, eructation • *He drank and stifled a belch.*

beleaguered 1 = **harassed**, troubled, plagued, tormented, hassled *(informal)*, aggravated *(informal)*, badgered, persecuted, pestered, vexed, put upon • *There have been seven attempts against the beleaguered government.*
2 = **besieged**, surrounded, blockaded, encompassed, beset, encircled, assailed, hemmed in, hedged in, environed • *The rebels continue to push their way towards the beleagured capital.*

belie 1 = **misrepresent**, disguise, conceal, distort, misinterpret, falsify, gloss over, airbrush • *Her looks belie her 50 years.*
2 = **disprove**, deny, expose, discredit, contradict, refute, repudiate, negate, invalidate, rebut, give the lie to, make a nonsense of, gainsay *(archaic or literary)*, prove false, blow out of the water *(slang)*, controvert, confute • *The facts of the situation belie his testimony.*

belief 1 = **trust**, confidence, faith, conviction, reliance, hopefulness • *a belief in personal liberty*
OPPOSITES: doubt, disbelief, scepticism
2 = **faith**, principles, doctrine, ideology, creed, dogma, tenet, credence, credo • *He refuses to compete on Sundays because of his religious beliefs.*
3 = **opinion**, feeling, idea, view, theory, impression, assessment, notion, judgment, point of view, sentiment, persuasion, presumption • *It is my belief that a common ground can be found.*

believable = **credible**, possible, likely, acceptable, reliable, authentic, probable, plausible, imaginable, trustworthy, creditable • *believable evidence*
OPPOSITES: incredible, fabulous, unbelievable

believe AS A VERB 1 = **think**, consider, judge, suppose, maintain, estimate, imagine, assume, gather, guess *(informal, chiefly U.S. & Canad.)*, reckon, conclude, deem, speculate, presume, conjecture, postulate, surmise • *I believe you have something of mine.*
2 = **accept**, hold, buy *(slang)*, trust, credit, depend on, rely on, swallow *(informal)*, count on, buy into *(slang)*, have faith in, swear by, be certain of, be convinced of, place confidence in, presume true, take as gospel, take on *(U.S.)* • *Don't believe what you read in the papers.*
OPPOSITES: question, doubt, disbelieve
▸ IN PHRASES: **believe in someone** = **trust in**, have faith in, place reliance on, place your trust in, pin your faith on, place confidence in • *If you believe in yourself you can succeed.*
believe in something = **advocate**, champion, approve of, swear by • *He believed in marital fidelity.*

QUOTATIONS

To believe with certainty we must begin with doubting
[Stanislaus I of Poland *Maxims*]

Man can believe the impossible, but man can never believe the improbable
[Oscar Wilde *The Decay of Lying*]

We can believe what we choose. We are answerable for what we choose to believe
[Cardinal Newman *Letter to Mrs William Froude*]

It is necessary to the happiness of man that he be mentally faithful to himself. Infidelity does not consist in believing, or in disbelieving, it consists in professing to believe what one does not believe
[Thomas Paine *The Age of Reason*]

Except ye see signs and wonders, ye will not believe
[*Bible: St. John*]

Though ye believe not me, believe the works
[*Bible: St. John*]

believer = **follower**, supporter, convert, disciple, protagonist, devotee, worshipper, apostle, adherent, zealot, upholder, proselyte • *I made no secret of the fact that I was not a believer.*
OPPOSITES: sceptic, atheist, disbeliever

belittle = **run down**, dismiss, diminish, put down, underestimate, discredit, ridicule, scorn, rubbish *(informal)*, degrade, minimize, downgrade, undervalue, knock *(informal)*, deride, malign, detract from, denigrate, scoff at, disparage, decry, sneer at, underrate, deprecate, depreciate, defame, derogate • *We mustn't belittle her outstanding achievement.*
OPPOSITES: praise, elevate, magnify

belle = **beauty**, looker *(informal)*, lovely, good-looker, goddess, Venus, peach *(informal)*, cracker *(informal)*, stunner *(informal)*, charmer • *She was the belle of her Sunday school class.*

bellicose = **aggressive**, offensive, hostile, destructive, defiant, provocative, belligerent, combative, antagonistic, pugnacious, hawkish, warlike, quarrelsome, militaristic, sabre-rattling, jingoistic, warmongering, aggers *(Austral. slang)* • *bellicose statements threatening tough action*

belligerence = **aggressiveness**, hostility, animosity, antagonism, destructiveness, pugnacity, combativeness, offensiveness, unfriendliness • *He could be accused of passion, but never belligerence.*

belligerent AS AN ADJECTIVE = **aggressive**, hostile, contentious, combative, unfriendly, antagonistic, pugnacious, argumentative, bellicose, quarrelsome, aggers *(Austral. slang)*, biffo *(Austral. slang)*, litigious • *He was almost back to his belligerent mood of twelve months ago.*
OPPOSITES: friendly, benign, harmonious
▸ AS A NOUN = **fighter**, battler, militant, contender, contestant, combatant, antagonist, warring nation, disputant • *The belligerents were due to settle their differences.*

bellow AS A VERB = **shout**, call, cry (out), scream, roar, yell, howl, shriek, clamour, bawl, holler *(informal)* • *He bellowed the information into the telephone.*
▸ AS A NOUN = **shout**, call, cry, scream, roar, yell, howl, shriek, bell, clamour, bawl • *a bellow of tearful rage*

bell-ringing
▸ RELATED ENTHUSIAST: campanologist

belly AS A NOUN = **stomach**, insides *(informal)*, gut, abdomen, tummy, paunch, vitals, breadbasket *(slang)*, potbelly, corporation *(informal)*, puku *(N.Z.)* • *a horse with its belly ripped open*
▸ IN PHRASES: **go belly up** = **go bankrupt**, break, fail, be ruined, go bust, become insolvent • *I really can't afford to see this company go belly up.*
▸ TECHNICAL NAME: venter
▸ RELATED ADJECTIVE: ventral

belong AS A VERB **1** = **go**, fit in, have a home, have a rightful place • *This piece really belongs in a museum.*
2 = **go with**, fit into, be part of, relate to, attach to, be connected with, pertain to, have as a proper place • *The judges could not decide which category it belonged in.*
▸ IN PHRASES: **belong to someone** = **be the property of**, be owned by, be held by, be in the possession of, be at the disposal of, be in the ownership of • *The house has belonged to her family for four generations.*
belong to something = **be a member of**, be associated with, be included in, be allied to, be affiliated to, be an adherent of • *I used to belong to a youth club.*

belonging = **fellowship**, relationship, association, partnership, loyalty, acceptance, attachment, inclusion, affinity, closeness, rapport, affiliation, kinship • *a man utterly without a sense of belonging*

belongings = **possessions**, goods, things, effects, property, stuff, gear, paraphernalia, personal property, accoutrements, chattels, goods and chattels • *I collected my belongings and left.*

beloved AS AN ADJECTIVE = **dear**, loved, valued, prized, dearest, sweet, admired, treasured, precious, darling, worshipped, adored, cherished, revered • *He lost his beloved wife last year.*
▸ AS A NOUN = **darling**, love, sweet, lover, angel, loved one, sweetheart, truelove, dear one, inamorata *or* inamorato • *He takes his beloved in his arms.*

below AS A PREPOSITION **1** = **under**, beneath, underneath, lower than • *The boat dipped below the surface of the water.*
2 = **less than**, under, lower than, smaller than, not as much as • *Night temperatures can drop below 15 degrees Celsius.*
3 = **subordinate to**, under, subject to, inferior to, subservient to, lesser than • *white-collar staff below chief officer level*
▸ AS AN ADVERB **1** = **lower**, down, under, beneath, underneath, downstairs, further down, at a lower level • *Spread out below was a huge crowd.*
2 = **beneath**, following, at the end, underneath, at the bottom, further on • *Please write to me at the address below.*

belt AS A NOUN **1** = **waistband**, band, strap, sash, girdle, girth, cummerbund, ceinture, cincture • *He wore a belt with a large brass buckle.*
2 = **conveyor belt**, band, loop, fan belt, drive belt • *The turning disc is connected by a drive belt to an electric motor.*
3 = **zone**, area, region, section, sector, district, stretch, strip, layer, patch, portion, tract • *a belt of trees*
4 = **blow**, knock, punch, rap, smack, thump, clout *(informal)*, whack, swipe, wallop *(informal)* • *He gave me a belt over the head with a scrubbing brush.*
▸ AS A VERB **1** = **strike**, beat, punch, deck *(slang)*, bang, bash *(informal)*, sock *(slang)*, smack, thump, clout *(informal)*, whack, thud, clobber *(slang)*, wallop *(informal)*, thwack, lay one on *(slang)*, beat *or* knock seven bells out of *(informal)* • *Is it true that she belted old George in the stomach?*
2 = **rush**, run, race, fly, speed, spring, tear, bound, dash, hurry, barrel (along) *(informal, chiefly U.S. & Canad.)*, sprint, bolt, dart, hasten • *We belted down the street to where the motor was.*
▸ IN PHRASES: **below the belt** = **unfair**, foul, crooked *(informal)*, cowardly, sly, fraudulent, unjust, dishonest, deceptive, unscrupulous, devious, unethical, sneaky, furtive, deceitful, surreptitious, dishonourable, unsporting, unsportsmanlike, underhanded, not playing the game *(informal)* • *Do you think it's a bit below the belt, what they're doing?*
belt something out = **blast out**, scream, boom out, sing out loud • *belting out Sinatra and Beatles hits*
belt up = **be quiet**, shut up *(informal)*, hush, button it *(slang)*, pipe down *(slang)*, hold your tongue, put a sock in it *(Brit. slang)*, keep your trap shut *(slang)*, cut the cackle *(informal)*, button your lip *(slang)* • *'Belt up!' he snapped.*

bemoan = **lament**, regret, complain about, rue, deplore, grieve for, weep for, bewail, cry over spilt milk, express sorrow about, moan over • *He continually bemoans his lot in life.*

bemuse = **puzzle**, stun, confuse, overwhelm, stump, baffle, bewilder, muddle, daze, confound, perplex, mystify, flummox, nonplus, amaze • *It doesn't bemuse readers with pompous language.*

bemused = **puzzled**, stunned, confused, stumped, baffled, at sea, bewildered, muddled, preoccupied, dazed, perplexed, mystified, engrossed, clueless, stupefied, nonplussed, absent-minded, flummoxed, half-drunk, fuddled • *He was looking at the boys with a bemused expression.*

bemusement = **puzzlement**, surprise, confusion, uncertainty, amazement, questioning, bewilderment, perplexity, bafflement, mystification, stupefaction, befuddlement • *A look of bemusement mixed with alarm spread across their faces.*

bench AS A NOUN **1** = **seat**, stall, pew • *He sat down on a park bench.*
2 = **worktable**, stand, table, counter, slab, trestle table, workbench • *the laboratory bench*
▸ IN PHRASES: **the bench** = **court**, judge, judges, magistrate, magistrates, tribunal, judiciary, courtroom • *It shows how seriously the bench viewed these offences.*

benchmark = **reference point**, gauge, yardstick, measure, level, example, standard, model, reference, par, criterion, norm, touchstone • *The truck industry is a benchmark for the economy.*

bend AS A VERB **1** = **twist**, turn, wind, lean, hook, bow, curve, arch, incline, arc, deflect, warp, buckle, coil, flex, stoop, veer, swerve, diverge, contort, inflect, incurvate • *Bend the bar into a horseshoe.*
2 = **wind**, turn, twist, arch, arc, swerve • *The road bent slightly to the right.*
3 = **submit**, yield, bow, surrender, give in, give way, cede, capitulate, resign yourself • *Congress has to bend to his will.*
4 = **force**, direct, influence, shape, persuade, compel, mould, sway • *He's very decisive. You cannot bend him.*
▸ AS A NOUN = **curve**, turn, corner, hook, twist, angle, bow, loop, arc, zigzag, camber • *The crash occurred on a sharp bend.*
▸ IN PHRASES: **bend over backwards** = **try**, endeavour, try hard, toil, make every effort, go all out *(informal)*, do your best, bust a gut *(informal)*, do all you can, give it your best shot *(informal)*, jump through hoops *(informal)*, break your neck *(informal)*, exert yourself, do your utmost, do your damnedest *(informal)*, give it your all *(informal)*, rupture yourself *(informal)*, drive someone round the bend • *People are bending over backwards to please customers.*

beneath AS A PREPOSITION **1** = **under**, below, underneath, lower than • *She found pleasure in sitting beneath the trees.*
OPPOSITES: over, above, upon
2 = **inferior to**, below, secondary to, not good enough for, lower in status than, not as important as • *She decided he was beneath her.*
3 = **unworthy of**, unfitting for, unsuitable for, inappropriate for, unbefitting • *Many find themselves having to take jobs far beneath them.*

▸ **AS AN ADVERB** = **underneath**, below, further down, in a lower place • *On a shelf beneath he spotted a photo album.*
▸ **RELATED PREFIX:** sub-

benediction 1 = **blessing**, favour, grace, prayer, devotion, gratitude, thanksgiving, communion, litany, invocation, consecration, supplication, thankfulness, benedictus *(Latin)*, benison, orison • *The minister pronounced the benediction.*
2 = **beatitude**, favour, grace, felicity, exaltation, beatification, saintliness, holy joy • *She could only raise her hand in a gesture of benediction.*

benefactor = **supporter**, friend, champion, defender, sponsor, angel *(informal)*, patron, promoter, contributor, backer, helper, subsidizer, philanthropist, upholder, well-wisher • *In his old age he became a benefactor of the arts.*

beneficent = **charitable**, benign, benevolent, philanthropic, bountiful, bounteous, munificent • *In 1909 nuns were running more than 1,000 beneficent institutions.*

beneficial = **favourable**, useful, valuable, helpful, profitable, benign, wholesome, advantageous, expedient, salutary, win-win, healthful, serviceable, salubrious, gainful • *vitamins which are beneficial to health*
OPPOSITES: useless, harmful, detrimental

beneficiary 1 = **recipient**, receiver, payee, assignee, legatee • *The main beneficiaries of pension equality so far have been men.*
2 = **heir**, inheritor • *a sole beneficiary of a will*

benefit **AS A NOUN** 1 = **good**, use, help, profit, gain, advantage, favour, reward, utility, merit, boon, mileage *(informal)*, avail • *I'm a great believer in the benefits of this form of therapy.*
OPPOSITES: loss, damage, harm
2 = **advantage**, interest, aid, gain, favour, assistance, betterment • *This could now work to his benefit.*
3 = **social security payments**, welfare, the dole *(informal)*, unemployment benefit, state benefit, Jobseeker's Allowance, JSA, pogey *(Canad.)* • *the removal of benefit from school-leavers*
▸ **AS A VERB** 1 = **profit from**, make the most of, gain from, do well out of, reap benefits from, turn to your advantage • *Both sides have benefited from the talks.*
2 = **help**, serve, aid, profit, improve, advance, advantage, enhance, assist, avail, be of service to, be of assistance to, be to the advantage of • *a variety of government schemes benefiting children*
OPPOSITES: damage, injure, harm

benevolence = **kindness**, understanding, charity, grace, sympathy, humanity, tolerance, goodness, goodwill, compassion, generosity, indulgence, decency, altruism, clemency, gentleness, philanthropy, magnanimity, fellow feeling, beneficence, kindliness, kind-heartedness, aroha *(N.Z.)* • *A bit of benevolence from people in power is not what we need.*
OPPOSITES: selfishness, ill will, malevolence

benevolent = **kind**, good, kindly, understanding, caring, liberal, generous, obliging, sympathetic, humanitarian, charitable, benign, humane, compassionate, gracious, indulgent, amiable, amicable, lenient, cordial, considerate, affable, congenial, altruistic, philanthropic, bountiful, beneficent, well-disposed, kind-hearted, warm-hearted, bounteous, tender-hearted • *a most benevolent employer*

benighted = **uncivilized**, crude, primitive, backward, uncultivated, unenlightened • *the terrible circumstances of that benighted country*

benign 1 = **benevolent**, kind, kindly, warm, liberal, friendly, generous, obliging, sympathetic, favourable, compassionate, gracious, amiable, genial, affable, complaisant • *Critics of the scheme take a less benign view.*
OPPOSITES: bad, severe, unkind
2 = **harmless**, innocent, superficial, innocuous, curable, inoffensive, not dangerous, remediable • *It wasn't cancer, only a benign tumour.*
OPPOSITES: malignant
3 = **favourable**, good, encouraging, warm, moderate, beneficial, clement, advantageous, salutary, auspicious, propitious • *relatively benign economic conditions*
OPPOSITES: bad, unlucky, unfavourable

bent **AS AN ADJECTIVE** 1 = **misshapen**, twisted, angled, bowed, curved, arched, crooked, crippled, distorted, warped, deformed, tortuous, disfigured, out of shape • *The trees were all bent and twisted from the wind.*
OPPOSITES: even, level, straight
2 = **stooped**, bowed, arched, hunched, stooping • *a bent, frail, old man*
3 = **corrupt**, crooked *(informal)*, rotten, shady *(informal)*, fraudulent, dishonest, unscrupulous, unethical, venal, unprincipled, bribable • *a bent accountant*
4 = **gay**, homosexual, queer *(informal, derogatory)* • *an actor who was as bent as a nine-bob note*
▸ **AS A NOUN** = **inclination**, ability, taste, facility, talent, leaning, tendency, preference, faculty, forte, flair, knack, penchant, bag *(slang)*, propensity, aptitude, predisposition, predilection, proclivity, turn of mind • *his bent for natural history*
▸ **IN PHRASES:** **bent on** = **intent on**, committed to, set on, fixed on, hell bent on *(informal)*, predisposed to, obsessive about, fixated on, resolved on, insistent on • *He's bent on suicide.*

bequeath 1 = **leave**, will, give, grant, commit, transmit, hand down, endow, bestow, entrust, leave to by will • *He bequeathed all his silver to his children.*
2 = **give**, offer, accord, grant, afford, contribute, yield, lend, pass on, transmit, confer, bestow, impart • *It is true that colonialism did not bequeath much to Africa.*

bequest = **legacy**, gift, settlement, heritage, trust, endowment, estate, inheritance, dower, bestowal, koha *(N.Z.)* • *Only one in eight leaves a bequest to charity.*

berate = **scold**, rebuke, reprimand, reproach, blast, carpet *(informal)*, put down, criticize, slate *(informal, chiefly Brit.)*, censure, castigate, revile, chide, harangue, tear into *(informal)*, tell off *(informal)*, rail at, flame *(informal)*, diss *(slang, chiefly U.S.)*, read the riot act to, reprove, upbraid, slap on the wrist, lambast(e), bawl out *(informal)*, excoriate, rap over the knuckles, chew out *(U.S. & Canad. informal)*, tear (someone) off a strip *(Brit. informal)*, give a rocket *(Brit. & N.Z. informal)*, vituperate • *Marion berated Joe for the noise he made.*
OPPOSITES: approve, praise, cheer

bereaved = **mourning**, suffering, grieving, lamenting, sorrowful • *He visited the bereaved family to offer comfort.*

bereavement = **loss**, death, misfortune, deprivation, affliction, tribulation • *those who have suffered a bereavement*

bereft **IN PHRASES:** **bereft of** = **deprived of**, without, minus, lacking in, devoid of, cut off from, parted from, sans *(archaic)*, robbed of, empty of, denuded of • *The place seemed to be utterly bereft of human life.*

berg = **mountain**, peak, mount, height, ben *(Scot.)*, horn, ridge, fell *(Brit.)*, alp, pinnacle, elevation, eminence • *a wind coming down off the berg*

berserk = **crazy**, wild, mad, frantic, ape *(slang)*, insane, apeshit *(slang)*, barro *(Austral. slang)*, off the air *(Austral. slang)*, porangi *(N.Z.)* • *When I saw him I went berserk.*

berth **AS A NOUN** 1 = **bunk**, bed, cot *(Nautical)*, hammock, billet • *Golding booked a berth on the first boat he could.*
2 = **anchorage**, haven, slip, port, harbour, dock, pier, wharf, quay • *A ship has applied to leave its berth.*
3 = **job**, position, post, situation, employment, appointment, living • *some of the players who tried for a berth on the team*
▸ **AS A VERB** = **anchor**, land, dock, moor, tie up, drop anchor • *The ship berthed in New York.*
▸ **IN PHRASES:** **give something a wide berth** = **avoid**, shun, steer clear of, sidestep, keep away from, keep aloof from • *She gives showbiz parties a wide berth.*

beseech = **beg**, ask, petition, call upon, plead with, solicit, implore, entreat, importune, adjure, supplicate • *She beseeched him to cut his drinking and smoking.*

beset = **plague**, trouble, embarrass, torture, haunt, torment, harass, afflict, badger, perplex, pester, vex, entangle, bedevil • *The country is beset by severe economic problems.*

besetting = **chronic**, persistent, long-standing, prevalent, habitual, ingrained, deep-seated, incurable, deep-rooted, inveterate, incorrigible, ineradicable • *my besetting sins*

beside AS A PREPOSITION = **next to**, near, close to, neighbouring, alongside, overlooking, next door to, adjacent to, at the side of, abreast of, cheek by jowl with • *On the table beside an empty plate was a pile of books.*
▸ IN PHRASES: **beside yourself** = **distraught**, desperate, mad, distressed, frantic, frenzied, hysterical, insane, crazed, demented, unbalanced, uncontrolled, deranged, berserk, delirious, unhinged, very anxious, overwrought, apoplectic, out of your mind, at the end of your tether • *He was beside himself with anxiety.*

besides AS A PREPOSITION = **apart from**, barring, excepting, other than, excluding, as well (as), in addition to, over and above • *I think she has many good qualities besides being beautiful.*
▸ AS AN ADVERB = **also**, too, further, otherwise, in addition, as well, moreover, furthermore, what's more, into the bargain • *Besides, today's young people have grown up knowing only a Conservative government.*

besiege 1 = **harass**, worry, trouble, harry, bother, disturb, plague, hound, hassle *(informal)*, badger, pester, importune, bend someone's ear *(informal)*, give someone grief *(Brit. & S. African)*, beleaguer • *She was besieged by the press and the public.*
2 = **surround**, confine, enclose, blockade, encompass, beset, encircle, close in on, hem in, shut in, lay siege to, hedge in, environ, beleaguer, invest *(rare)* • *The main part of the army moved to besiege the town.*

besmirch = **tarnish**, damage, soil, stain, smear, taint, blacken, daub, slander, sully, dishonour, defame, drag through the mud, smirch • *Lawyers can besmirch reputations.*

besotted = **infatuated**, charmed, captivated, beguiled, doting, smitten, bewitched, bowled over *(informal)*, spellbound, enamoured, hypnotized, swept off your feet • *He was completely besotted.*

bespeak 1 = **indicate**, show, suggest, evidence, reveal, display, predict, imply, exhibit, proclaim, signify, denote, testify to, foretell, evince, betoken • *His large ears bespeak his ability to hear all.*
2 = **engage**, solicit, prearrange, order beforehand • *I'm already bespoken to take you tomorrow morning.*

best AS AN ADJECTIVE 1 = **finest**, leading, top, chief, supreme, principal, first, foremost, superlative, pre-eminent, unsurpassed, most accomplished, most skilful, most excellent • *He was the best player in the world for most of the 1950s.*
2 = **most fitting**, right, most desirable, most apt, most advantageous, most correct • *the best way to end the long-running war*
▸ AS A NOUN 1 = **utmost**, most, greatest, hardest, highest endeavour • *You must do your best to protect yourselves.*
2 = **most sensible thing**, wisest thing, most desirable thing, most advisable thing, most prudent thing • *The best we can do is try to stay cool and muddle through.*
▸ AS AN ADVERB 1 = **most highly**, most, most fully, to the highest degree, most deeply • *The thing I liked best about the show was the music.*
2 = **most advantageously**, most fittingly, most usefully, most profitably, most beneficially • *Studying is best done alone.*
▸ IN PHRASES: **the best** = **the finest**, the pick, the choice, the flower, the cream, the elite, the crème de la crème *(French)* • *We only offer the best to our clients.*

bestial = **brutal**, low, animal, gross, savage, beastly, primitive, degraded, sensual, vile, sordid, barbaric, inhuman, depraved, carnal, brutish, barbarous, scungy *(Austral. & N.Z.)*, beastlike • *the bestial conditions into which the city has sunk*

bestiality 1 = **brutality**, atrocity, cruelty, ferocity, savagery, ruthlessness, barbarism, depravity, inhumanity, barbarity, viciousness, carnality, brutishness, beastliness, bloodthirstiness, savageness • *He now became accustomed to the bestiality of his troops.*
2 = **zoophilia**, zooerastia • *a video featuring bestiality*

bestow = **present**, give, accord, award, grant, commit, hand out, lavish, confer, endow, entrust, impart, allot, honour with, apportion • *The Queen has bestowed a knighthood on him.*
OPPOSITES: make, get, obtain

bestseller = **success**, hit *(informal)*, winner, smash *(informal)*, belter *(slang)*, sensation, blockbuster *(informal)*, wow *(slang)*, market leader, smash hit *(informal)*, chart-topper *(informal)*, runaway success, number one • *an international bestseller*
OPPOSITES: failure, turkey *(slang, chiefly U.S. & Canad.)*, flop *(informal)*

bestselling = **successful**, top, hit *(informal)*, smash *(informal)*, flourishing, lucrative, smash-hit *(informal)*, chart-topping *(informal)*, moneymaking, number one, highly successful • *a best-selling romantic novelist*

bet AS A VERB 1 = **gamble**, chance, stake, venture, hazard, speculate, punt *(chiefly Brit.)*, wager, put money, risk money, pledge money, put your shirt • *I bet on a horse called Premonition.*
2 = **imagine**, expect, suspect, assume, guess *(informal, chiefly U.S. & Canad.)*, fancy, deem, infer, deduce, conjecture • *I bet you were good at games when you were at school.*
▸ AS A NOUN 1 = **gamble**, risk, stake, venture, pledge, speculation, hazard, flutter *(informal)*, ante, punt, wager, long shot • *He made a 30 mile trip to the casino to place a bet.*
2 = **option**, plan, choice, alternative, course of action • *Your best bet is to choose a guest house.*
3 = **guess**, feeling, view, opinion, prediction • *My bet is that next year will be different.*

bête noire = **pet hate**, horror, nightmare, devil, curse, dread, bogey, scourge, aversion, nemesis, anathema, bane, abomination, bogeyman, bugbear, bugaboo, thorn in the flesh *or* side • *Our real bête noire is the car-boot sale.*

betide = **happen**, chance, occur, take place, overtake, ensue, crop up *(informal)*, transpire *(informal)*, befall, come to pass, supervene, bechance • *Woe betide anyone who got in his way.*

betoken = **indicate**, mark, suggest, evidence, promise, represent, declare, manifest, signify, denote, typify, bode, bespeak, augur, presage, portend, prognosticate • *His demeanour betokened embarrassment at his prosperity.*

betray 1 = **be disloyal to**, break with, grass on *(Brit. slang)*, dob in *(Austral. slang)*, double-cross *(informal)*, stab in the back, be unfaithful to, sell down the river *(informal)*, grass up *(slang)*, shop *(slang, chiefly Brit.)*, put the finger on *(informal)*, inform on *or* against • *He might be seen as having betrayed his mother.*
2 = **give away**, tell, show, reveal, expose, disclose, uncover, manifest, divulge, blurt out, unmask, lay bare, tell on, let slip, evince • *She studied his face, but it betrayed nothing.*

QUOTATIONS
To betray, you must first belong
[Kim Philby]

betrayal 1 = **disloyalty**, sell-out *(informal)*, deception, treason, treachery, trickery, duplicity, double-cross *(informal)*, double-dealing, breach of trust, perfidy, unfaithfulness, falseness, inconstancy • *She felt that what she had done was a betrayal of Patrick.*
OPPOSITES: loyalty, devotion, allegiance

2 = **giving away**, telling, revelation, disclosure, blurting out, divulgence • *She saw his newspaper piece as a betrayal of her confidence.*
OPPOSITES: keeping, guarding, keeping secret

QUOTATIONS
If I had to choose between betraying my country and betraying my friend, I hope I should have the guts to betray my country
[E.M. Forster *Two Cheers for Democracy*]

betrayer = **traitor**, deceiver, informer, renegade, defector, conspirator, Judas, deserter, double-crosser *(informal)*, turncoat, quisling, apostate, miscreant, snake in the grass, back-stabber, fizgig *(Austral. slang)* • *a traitor and betrayer*

betrothal = **engagement**, promise, vow, plight, espousal *(archaic)*, troth, affiancing, betrothing, marriage contract • *The betrothal was secret.*

betrothed AS AN ADJECTIVE *(Old-fashioned)* = **engaged**, promised, pledged, plighted, affianced • *She was betrothed to his brother.*
▸ AS A NOUN = **fiancé** *or* **fiancée**, intended, prospective spouse, wife- *or* husband-to-be, future wife *or* husband • *She is here without her betrothed.*

better AS AN ADVERB 1 = **to a greater degree**, more completely, more thoroughly • *I like your interpretation better than the one I was taught.*
2 = **in a more excellent manner**, more effectively, more attractively, more advantageously, more competently, in a superior way • *If we had played better we might have won.*
OPPOSITES: worse
▸ AS AN ADJECTIVE 1 = **well**, stronger, improving, progressing, recovering, healthier, cured, mending, fitter, fully recovered, on the mend *(informal)*, more healthy, less ill • *He is better now.*
OPPOSITES: worse
2 = **superior**, finer, nicer, worthier, higher-quality, surpassing, preferable, more appropriate, more useful, more valuable, more suitable, more desirable, streets ahead, more fitting, more expert • *I've been able to have a better car than I otherwise could have.*
OPPOSITES: worse, lesser, inferior
▸ AS A VERB = **beat**, top, exceed, excel, surpass, outstrip, outdo, trump, improve on *or* upon, cap *(informal)*, forward, reform, advance, promote, correct, amend, mend, rectify, augment, ameliorate, meliorate • *Our parents came here with the hope of bettering themselves.*
OPPOSITES: worsen, lower, depress
▸ IN PHRASES: **get the better of someone** = **defeat**, beat, surpass, triumph over, outdo, trounce, outwit, best, subjugate, prevail over, outsmart *(informal)*, get the upper hand, score off, run rings around *(informal)*, wipe the floor with *(informal)*, make mincemeat of *(informal)*, blow out of the water *(slang)* • *He usually gets the better of them.*

betterment = **improvement**, gain, advancement, enhancement, edification, amelioration, melioration • *His research is for the betterment of mankind.*

between 1 = **amidst**, among, mid, in the middle of, betwixt • *She left the table to stand between the two men.*
2 = **connecting**, uniting, joining, linking • *the relationship between doctors and patients*
▸ RELATED PREFIX: inter-

bevel = **slant**, angle, slope, diagonal, oblique, cant, mitre, bezel, chamfer • *The stone must be along the bevel so as to keep clear of the blade.*

beverage = **drink**, liquid, liquor, refreshment, draught, bevvy *(dialect)*, libation *(facetious)*, thirst quencher, potable, potation • *food and beverages*

beverage room = **tavern**, inn, bar, pub *(informal, chiefly Brit.)*, public house, watering hole *(facetious slang)*, boozer *(Brit., Austral. & N.Z. informal)*, beer parlour *(Canad.)*, hostelry, alehouse *(archaic)*, taproom

bevy = **group**, company, set, party, band, crowd, troop, pack, collection, gathering, gang, bunch *(informal)*, cluster, congregation, clump, troupe, posse *(slang)*, clique, coterie, assemblage • *a bevy of little girls*

bewail = **lament**, regret, complain about, moan about, mourn, rue, wail about, deplore, bemoan, repent, grieve for, cry over, weep over, express sorrow for • *All your songs seem to bewail a dissatisfaction in love.*

beware 1 = **be careful**, look out, watch out, be wary, be cautious, take heed, guard against something • *Beware, this recipe is not for slimmers.*
2 = **avoid**, mind, shun, refrain from, steer clear of, guard against • *Beware using plastic cards in foreign cash machines.*

bewilder = **confound**, surprise, stun, confuse, puzzle, baffle, mix up, daze, perplex, mystify, stupefy, befuddle, flummox, bemuse, dumbfound, nonplus, flabbergast *(informal)* • *The silence from Alex had hurt and bewildered her.*

bewildered = **confused**, surprised, stunned, puzzled, uncertain, startled, baffled, at sea, awed, muddled, dizzy, dazed, perplexed, disconcerted, at a loss, mystified, taken aback, speechless, giddy, disorientated, bamboozled *(informal)*, nonplussed, flummoxed, at sixes and sevens, thrown off balance, discombobulated *(informal, chiefly U.S. & Canad.)* • *Some shoppers look bewildered by the variety of goods on offer.*

bewildering = **confusing**, surprising, amazing, stunning, puzzling, astonishing, staggering, eye-popping *(informal)*, baffling, astounding, perplexing, mystifying, stupefying • *The choice of excursions was bewildering.*

bewilderment = **confusion**, puzzlement, disorientation, perplexity, bemusement, mystification, befuddlement • *He shook his head in bewilderment.*

bewitch = **enchant**, attract, charm, fascinate, absorb, entrance, captivate, beguile, allure, ravish, mesmerize, hypnotize, cast a spell on, enrapture, spellbind • *She was not moving, as if someone had bewitched her.*
OPPOSITES: disgust, offend, repulse

bewitched = **enchanted**, charmed, transformed, fascinated, entranced, possessed, captivated, enthralled, beguiled, ravished, spellbound, mesmerized, enamoured, hypnotized, enraptured, under a spell • *The doctor is bewitched by Maya's beauty.*

beyond AS A PREPOSITION 1 = **on the other side of**, behind, on the far side of, outwith *(Scot.)* • *They heard footsteps in the main room, beyond a door.*
2 = **after**, over, past, above, later than, upwards of • *Few jockeys continue riding beyond the age of forty.*
3 = **past**, outside, outwith *(Scot.)*, outside the range of • *His interests extended beyond the fine arts.*
4 = **except for**, but, save, apart from, other than, excluding, besides, aside from • *I knew nothing beyond a few random facts.*
5 = **exceeding**, surpassing, superior to, out of reach of • *What he had done was beyond my comprehension.*
6 = **outside**, over, above, outwith *(Scot.)*, outside the range of • *The situation was beyond her control.*
▸ AS AN ADVERB = **further away**, far away, far off, at a distance • *People come from Renfrewshire and beyond to see his grave.*

bias AS A NOUN 1 = **prejudice**, leaning, bent, tendency, inclination, penchant, intolerance, bigotry, propensity, favouritism, predisposition, nepotism, unfairness, predilection, proclivity, partiality, narrow-mindedness, proneness, one-sidedness • *There were fierce attacks on the BBC for alleged political bias.*
OPPOSITES: equity, equality, impartiality
2 = **slant**, cross, angle, diagonal line • *The fabric, cut on the bias, hangs as light as a cobweb.*
▸ AS A VERB = **influence**, colour, weight, prejudice, distort, sway, warp, slant, predispose • *We mustn't allow it to bias our teaching.*

biased = **prejudiced**, weighted, one-sided, partial, distorted, swayed, warped, slanted, embittered, predisposed, jaundiced • *The judge was biased.*

Bible

QUOTATIONS

Thy word is a lamp unto my feet, and a light unto my path
[*Bible: Psalms 119*]

the English Bible, a book which, if everything else in our language should perish, would alone suffice to show the whole extent of its beauty and power
[Lord Macaulay *Miscellaneous Writings*]

I've often thought the Bible ought to have a disclaimer in the front saying this is fiction
[*Sir Ian McKellen*]

No man ever believes that the Bible means what it says: he is always convinced that it says what he means
[*George Bernard Shaw*]

▹ *See panel* **Bible**

bibliography = **book list**, record, catalogue, list of books, list of suggested reading • *a select bibliography of useful books*

biceps

▸ RELATED ADJECTIVE: bicipital

bicker = **quarrel**, fight, argue, row (*informal*), clash, dispute, scrap (*informal*), disagree, fall out (*informal*), squabble, spar, wrangle, cross swords, fight like cat and dog, go at it hammer and tongs, altercate • *The two women bickered constantly.*
OPPOSITES: agree, accord, get on

bicycle = **bike**, cycle, racer, mountain bike, two-wheeler, push bike, pedal cycle, bone-shaker • *He was cycling round on his old bicycle.*

BICYCLES

Bicycle parts

bell	kickstand	rat-trap
bicycle chain	mileometer	saddle
bicycle pump	mudguard	saddlebag
crossbar	pannier	stabilizer
handlebars	pedal	wheel

Types of bicycle

autocycle	chopper	penny-farthing
bicycle	exercise bike	roadster
BMX	fairy cycle	tandem
boneshaker	mountain bike	velocipede

bid AS A NOUN **1** = **attempt**, try, effort, venture, undertaking, go (*informal*), shot (*informal*), stab (*informal*), crack (*informal*), endeavour • *a bid to silence its critics*
2 = **offer**, price, attempt, amount, advance, proposal, sum, tender, proposition, submission • *He made an agreed takeover bid of £351 million.*
▸ AS A VERB **1** = **make a bid for**, attempt, seek, strive • *I don't think she is bidding to be Prime Minister again.*
2 = **make an offer**, offer, propose, put up, submit, tender, proffer • *She wanted to bid for it.*
3 = **wish**, say, call, tell, greet • *I bade her goodnight.*
4 = **tell**, call, ask, order, charge, require, direct, desire, invite, command, summon, instruct, solicit, enjoin • *I dare say he did as he was bidden.*

bidding 1 = **order**, call, charge, demand, request, command, instruction, invitation, canon, beck, injunction, summons, behest, beck and call • *the bidding of his backbenchers*
2 = **offer**, proposal, auction, tender • *The bidding starts at £2 million.*

big 1 = **large**, great, huge, giant, massive, vast, enormous, considerable, substantial, extensive, immense, spacious, gigantic, monumental, mammoth, bulky, burly, colossal, stellar (*informal*), prodigious, hulking, ponderous, voluminous, fuck-off (*offensive taboo slang*), elephantine, ginormous (*informal*), humongous *or* humungous (*U.S. slang*), sizable *or* sizeable, supersize • *Australia's a big country.*
OPPOSITES: little, small, tiny
2 = **important**, serious, significant, grave, urgent, paramount, big-time (*informal*), far-reaching, momentous, major league (*informal*), weighty • *Her problem was just too big for her to tackle on her own.*
OPPOSITES: ordinary, minor, unimportant
3 = **powerful**, important, prime, principal, prominent, dominant, influential, paramount, eminent, puissant, skookum (*Canad.*) • *Their father was very big in the army.*
4 = **difficult**, long, learned, formal, complicated, scholarly, erudite • *They use a lot of big words.*
5 = **grown-up**, adult, grown, mature, elder, full-grown • *He's a big boy now.*
OPPOSITES: young, immature
6 = **generous**, good, princely, noble, heroic, gracious, benevolent, disinterested, altruistic, unselfish, magnanimous, big-hearted • *They describe him as an idealist with a big heart.*

QUOTATIONS

The bigger they come, the harder they fall
[Robert Fitzsimmons]

big fish = **powerful person**, authority, leader, important person, supreme person, influential person • *a big fish in the murky pool of high finance*

bighead = **boaster**, know-all (*informal*), swaggerer, self-seeker, egomaniac, egotist, braggart, braggadocio, narcissist, swell-head (*informal*), blowhard (*informal*), self-admirer, figjam (*Austral. slang*) • *You really are a bighead.*

bigheaded = **boastful**, arrogant, swaggering, bragging, cocky, vaunting, conceited, puffed-up, bumptious, immodest, crowing, overconfident, vainglorious, swollen-headed, egotistic, full of yourself, too big for your boots *or* breeches • *What an arrogant, bigheaded man, she thought.*

big-hearted = **kind**, caring, warm, generous, noble, charitable, compassionate, gracious, benevolent, considerate, affable, altruistic, philanthropic, open-hearted, bountiful, unselfish, magnanimous, beneficent, well-disposed, kind-hearted, great-hearted, warm-hearted, bounteous, tender-hearted • *a bluff, big-hearted Irishman*
OPPOSITES: mean, selfish, uncharitable

big name = **celebrity**, star, personality, superstar, name, dignitary, luminary, bigwig (*informal*), celeb (*informal*), face (*informal*), big shot (*informal*), personage, megastar (*informal*), lion, V.I.P. • *all the big names in rock and pop*

bigot = **fanatic**, racist, extremist, sectarian, maniac, fiend (*informal*), zealot, persecutor, dogmatist • *a narrow-minded bigot with pretensions to power*

QUOTATIONS

There is nothing more dangerous than the conscience of a bigot
[George Bernard Shaw]

bigoted = **intolerant**, twisted, racist, prejudiced, biased, warped, sectarian, dogmatic, opinionated, narrow-minded, obstinate, xenophobic, chauvinistic, small-minded, illiberal, uncharitable, racialist • *He was bigoted and racist.*
OPPOSITES: tolerant, open-minded, equitable

bigotry = **intolerance**, discrimination, racism, prejudice, bias, ignorance, injustice, sexism, unfairness, xenophobia, chauvinism, fanaticism, sectarianism, jingoism, racialism, dogmatism, provincialism, narrow-mindedness, mindlessness, pig-ignorance (*slang*), illiberality • *He deplored religious bigotry.*
OPPOSITES: tolerance, forbearance, permissiveness

BIBLE

Books of the Bible (Old Testament)

Genesis
Exodus
Leviticus
Numbers
Deuteronomy
Joshua
Judges
Ruth
1 Samuel
2 Samuel
1 Kings
2 Kings
1 Chronicles
2 Chronicles
Ezra
Nehemiah
Esther
Job
Psalms
Proverbs
Ecclesiastes
Song of Solomon
Isaiah
Jeremiah
Lamentations
Ezekiel
Daniel
Hosea
Joel
Amos
Obadiah
Jonah
Micah
Nahum
Habakkuk
Zephaniah
Haggai
Zechariah
Malachi

Books of the Bible (New Testament)

Matthew
Mark
Luke
John
Acts
Romans
1 Corinthians
2 Corinthians
Galatians
Ephesians
Philippians
Colossians
1 Thessalonians
2 Thessalonians
1 Timothy
2 Timothy
Titus
Philemon
Hebrews
James
1 Peter
2 Peter
1 John
2 John
3 John
Jude
Revelation

Books of the Bible (Apocrypha)

Tobit
Judith
1 Maccabees
2 Maccabees
Wisdom
Ecclesiasticus
Baruch
Daniel and Susanna
Daniel, Bel and the Snake
Song of the Three
Esdras
Manasseh

Characters in the Bible

Aaron
Abednego
Abel
Abigail
Abraham
Absalom
Achitophel *or* Ahithophel
Adam
Ahab
Ahasuerus
Ammon
Amos
Ananias
Andrew
Asher
Balaam
Balthazar
Barabbas
Bartholomew
Baruch
Bathsheba
Beelzebub
Belial
Belshazzar
Benjamin
Boanerges
Boaz
Caiaphas
Cain
Caspar
Cush *or* Kush
Dan
Daniel
David
Deborah
Delilah
Dinah
Dives
Dorcas
Elias
Elijah
Elisha
Enoch
Enos
Ephraim
Esau
Esther
Eve
Ezekiel
Ezra
Gabriel
Gad
Gideon
Gilead
Gog and Magog
Goliath
Good Samaritan
Habakkuk
Hagar
Haggai
Ham
Hannah
Herod
Hezekiah
Hiram
Holofernes
Hosea
Isaac
Isaiah
Ishmael
Issachar
Jacob
Jael
James
Japheth
Jehoshaphat
Jehu
Jephthah *or* Jephte
Jeremiah
Jeroboam
Jesse
Jesus Christ
Jethro
Jezebel
Joab
Job
Joel
John
John the Baptist
Jonah *or* Jonas
Jonathan
Joseph
Joshua
Josiah
Jubal
Judah
Judas Iscariot
Jude
Judith
Laban
Lazarus
Leah
Levi
Lot
Lot's wife
Luke
Magus
Malachi
Manasseh
Mark
Martha
Mary
Mary Magdalene
Matthew
Matthias
Melchior
Melchizedek *or* Melchisedech
Meshach
Methuselah
Micah
Midian
Miriam
Mordecai
Moses
Nabonidus
Naboth
Nahum
Naomi
Naphtali
Nathan
Nathanael
Nebuchadnezzar *or* Nebuchadrezzar
Nehemiah
Nicodemus
Nimrod
Noah
Obadiah
Paul
Peter
Philip
Potiphar
Prodigal Son
Queen of Sheba
Rachel
Rebecca
Reuben
Ruth
Salome
Samson
Samuel
Sarah
Saul
Seth
Shadrach
Shem
Simeon
Simon
Solomon
Susanna
Tetragrammaton
Thaddeus *or* Thadeus
Thomas
Tobit
Tubal-cain
Uriah
Virgin Mary
Zacharias, Zachariah, *or* Zachary
Zebedee
Zebulun
Zechariah
Zedekiah
Zephaniah
Zilpah

Place names in the Bible

Aceldama
Antioch
Aram
Ararat
Arimathaea *or* Arimathea
Babel
Bashan
Bethesda
Bethlehem
Calvary
Cana
Canaan
Capernaum
Eden
Galilee
Garden of Eden
Gath
Gaza
Gehenna
Gethsemane
Golgotha
Gomorrah *or* Gomorrha
Goshen
Horeb
Jericho
Jerusalem
Judaea *or* Judea
Judah
land of milk and honey
land of Nod
Moab
Nazareth
On
Ophir
Rabbath Ammon
Samaria
Shiloh
Shinar
Shittim
Sodom
Tadmor
Tophet *or* Topheth
wilderness

QUOTATIONS
Bigotry may roughly be defined as the anger of men who have no opinions
[G.K. Chesterton *Heretics*]
Bigotry tries to keep truth safe in its hand
With a grip that kills it
[Rabindranath Tagore *Fireflies*]

big time = **fame**, glory, celebrity, prominence, stardom, renown, public esteem • *the first player from Japan to hit the big time*

bigwig = **important person**, somebody, celebrity, heavyweight *(informal)*, notable, big name, mogul, big gun *(informal)*, dignitary, celeb *(informal)*, big shot *(informal)*, personage, nob *(slang)*, big cheese *(old-fashioned slang)*, big noise *(informal)*, big hitter *(informal)*, heavy hitter *(informal)*, panjandrum, notability, V.I.P. • *a former communist bigwig who heads the local parliament*
OPPOSITES: nothing, nobody, nonentity

bijou = **desirable**, pleasing, elegant, fashionable, profitable, stylish, chic, sought-after, to die for *(informal)*, covetable • *bijou shops and boutiques*

bike *see* bicycle

bile = **bitterness**, anger, hostility, resentment, animosity, venom, irritability, spleen, acrimony, pique, nastiness, rancour, virulence, asperity, ill humour, irascibility, peevishness, churlishness • *He aims his bile at religion, drugs and politics.*

bilge = **trash**, rubbish, rot, garbage *(informal)*, tosh *(slang, chiefly Brit.)*, trivia, drivel, twaddle, tripe *(informal)*, dross, moonshine, hogwash, bunkum *or* buncombe *(chiefly U.S.)* • *I supported the family by writing bilge for women's magazines.*

bilious 1 = **gaudy**, flash *(informal)*, loud, garish, glaring, vulgar, brash, tacky *(informal)*, flashy, lurid, tasteless, naff *(Brit. slang)*, brassy • *the bilious green overstuffed sofas*
2 = **sick**, nauseated, queasy, out of sorts, nauseous, liverish • *She appears to be suffering a bilious attack.*
3 = **bad-tempered**, cross, angry, nasty, irritable, edgy, grumpy, touchy, petulant, ill-tempered, irascible, cantankerous, tetchy, ratty *(Brit. & N.Z. informal)*, tooshie *(Austral. slang)*, testy, chippy *(informal)*, short-tempered, grouchy *(informal)*, peevish, crabby, choleric, splenetic, crotchety, ill-humoured, chippy *(informal)* • *a bilious, rancorous attack*

bilk = **cheat**, do *(slang)*, skin *(slang)*, fool, con *(informal)*, stiff *(slang)*, sting, mislead, rip off *(slang)*, deceive, fleece, defraud, dupe, stitch up *(slang)*, rook *(slang)*, bamboozle *(informal)*, hoodwink, double-cross *(informal)*, diddle *(informal)*, do the dirty on *(Brit. informal)*, sell a pup to, pull a fast one on *(informal)*, cozen *(informal)*, trick, take in *(informal)*, swindle, take for a ride *(informal)* • *trusts that secretly conspired to bilk the public*

bill[1] AS A NOUN 1 = **charges**, rate, costs, score, account, damage *(informal)*, statement, reckoning, expense, tally, invoice, note of charge • *They couldn't afford to pay the bills.*
2 = **banknote**, green-back *(U.S.)*, note • *The case contained a large quantity of US dollar bills.*
3 = **act of parliament**, measure, proposal, piece of legislation, draft law, projected law • *The bill was opposed by a large majority.*
4 = **list**, listing, programme, card, schedule, agenda, catalogue, inventory, roster, syllabus • *He is topping the bill at a dusk-to-dawn party.*
5 = **advertisement**, notice, poster, leaflet, bulletin, circular, handout, placard, handbill, playbill • *A sign forbids the posting of bills.*
▸ AS A VERB 1 = **charge**, debit, invoice, send a statement to, send an invoice to • *Are you going to bill me for this?*
2 = **advertise**, post, announce, push *(informal)*, declare, promote, plug *(informal)*, proclaim, tout, flaunt, publicize, crack up *(informal)*, give advance notice of • *They bill it as Britain's most exciting museum.*
▸ IN PHRASES: **fit the bill** = **be suitable**, fit, be right, be suited, be cut out for • *If you think you fit the bill, send a CV.*
foot the bill = **pay**, cough up *(informal)*, meet the cost • *Who is footing the bill for her extravagant holiday?*

bill[2] = **beak**, nib, neb *(archaic or dialect)*, mandible • *Its legs and feet are grey, its bill brownish-yellow.*

billet AS A VERB = **quarter**, post, station, locate, install, accommodate, berth, garrison • *The soldiers were billeted in private homes.*
▸ AS A NOUN = **quarters**, accommodation, lodging, barracks • *We hid the radio in Hut 10, which was our billet.*

billow AS A VERB 1 = **surge**, roll, expand, swell, balloon, belly, bulge, dilate, puff up, bloat • *the billowing sails*
2 = **flow**, course, rush, stream, emit, run, gush, spout, spew • *thick plumes of smoke billowing from factory chimneys*
▸ AS A NOUN 1 = **surge**, wave, flow, rush, flood, cloud, gush, deluge, upsurge, outpouring, uprush • *billows of almost solid black smoke*
2 = **wave**, surge, tide, swell, roller, crest, breaker • *a wild sea, with immense billows breaking upon our ship*

billowing = **roll**, rise, rush, swell, swirl, gush, heave • *the billowing dust*

bimbo = **Barbie (doll)**, dumb blonde, airhead, birdbrain, featherbrain • *I'm not some blonde bimbo.*

bin = **dustbin**, bucket *(Scot.)*, garbage can, wastepaper basket, circular file • *He screwed the paper up and chucked it in the bin.*

bind AS A VERB 1 = **unite**, join, link, consolidate, unify • *It is the threat of persecution that binds them together.*
2 = **oblige**, make, force, require, engage, compel, prescribe, constrain, necessitate, impel, obligate • *The treaty binds them to respect their neighbour's independence.*
3 = **tie**, unite, join, stick, secure, attach, wrap, rope, knot, strap, lash, glue, tie up, hitch, paste, fasten, truss, make fast • *Bind the ends of the card together with thread.*
OPPOSITES: free, release, untie
4 = **restrict**, limit, handicap, confine, detain, restrain, hamper, inhibit, hinder, impede, hem in, keep within bounds or limits • *All are bound by the same strict etiquette.*
5 = **trim**, finish, edge, border • *Each volume is bound in bright-coloured stock.*
6 = **fuse**, join, stick, bond, cement, adhere • *These compounds bind with genetic material in the liver.*
7 = **bandage**, cover, dress, wrap, swathe, encase • *Her mother bound the wound with a rag soaked in iodine.*
8 = **edge**, finish, border, trim, hem • *Bind the edges of the blind with braid or fringing.*
▸ AS A NOUN = **nuisance**, inconvenience, hassle *(informal)*, drag *(informal)*, spot *(informal)*, difficulty, bore, dilemma, pest, hot water *(informal)*, uphill *(S. African)*, predicament, annoyance, quandary, pain in the neck *(informal)*, pain in the arse *(taboo slang)*, pain in the backside *(informal)*, pain in the butt *(informal)* • *It is expensive to buy and a bind to carry home.*

binding = **compulsory**, necessary, mandatory, imperative, obligatory, conclusive, irrevocable, unalterable, indissoluble • *a legally binding commitment*
OPPOSITES: free, voluntary, optional

binge AS A NOUN *(Informal)* = **bout**, session, spell, fling, feast, stint, spree, orgy, bender *(informal)*, jag *(slang)*, beano *(Brit. slang)*, sesh *(slang)*, blind *(slang)* • *She went on occasional drinking binges.*
▸ AS A VERB = **overeat**, pig out *(slang)* • *I binged on pizzas and milkshakes.*

biography = **life story**, life, record, account, profile, memoir, CV, life history, curriculum vitae • *an unauthorised biography*

QUOTATIONS
Biography is all about cutting people down to size.
Getting an unruly quart into a pint pot
[Alan Bennett]

Biography is: a system in which the contradictions of a human life are unified
[José Ortega y Gasset *The Dehumanization of Art and Other Essays*]

Read no history: nothing but biography, for that is life without theory
[Benjamin Disraeli *Contarini Fleming*]

Discretion is not the better part of biography
[Lytton Strachey]

biology

▹ *See panel* **Biology**

bird = feathered friend, birdie, fledgling, fowl, warbler, songbird • *a rare bird*

▸ **RELATED ADJECTIVES:** avian, ornithic
▸ **NAME OF MALE:** cock
▸ **NAME OF FEMALE:** hen
▸ **NAME OF YOUNG:** chick, fledgeling or fledgling nestling
▸ **COLLECTIVE NOUNS:** flock, congregation, flight, volery
▸ **NAME OF HOME:** nest
▸ **RELATED MANIA:** ornithomania
▸ **RELATED PHOBIA:** ornithophobia

▹ *See panels* **Birds; Sea birds; Types of fowl**

QUOTATIONS

No ladder needs the bird but skies
To situate its wings,
Nor any leader's grim baton
Arraigns it as it sings
[Emily Dickinson]

Who wills devoutly to absorb, contain,
birds give him pain
[Richard Wilbur *The Beautiful Changes*]

I know what the caged bird feels, alas!
[Paul Lawrence Dunbar *Sympathy*]

PROVERBS

A bird in the hand is worth two in the bush
Birds of a feather flock together

bird of prey

▸ **RELATED ADJECTIVE:** raptorial

birth AS A NOUN **1 = childbirth**, birthing, delivery, confinement, nativity, parturition, accouchement • *She weighed 5lb 7oz at birth.*

OPPOSITES: end, death, passing

BIOLOGY

Branches of biology

actinobiology, aerobiology, agrobiology, astrobiology, bacteriology, biochemistry, biodynamics, biogeography, biometry, biophysics, biostatics, botany, chronobiology, cryobiology, cytogenetics, cytology, ecology, entomology, genetics, histology, microbiology, morphology, oceanography, organography, organology, palaeontology, parasitology, photobiology, photodynamics, radiobiology, sociobiology, somatology, stoichiology, taxonomy, teratology, zoology

Biology terms

aerobic, agglutination, albino, allele *or* allelomorph, anaerobic, anterior, asexual reproduction, assimilation, bacteria, binary fission, biomass, blood, blood vessel, bone, cell, chromosome, circulation, circulatory system, class, clone, codominance, cold-blooded, conception, copulation, cytoplasm, diffusion, digestion, diploid, division, DNA *or* deoxyribonucleic acid, dominant, dorsal, ecosystem, egg, embryo, environment, enzyme, epidermis, evolution, excretion, family, fermentation, fertilization, flower, foetus, food chain, fossil, fruit, fungus, gamete, gene, genus, germination, gestation, gland, gonad, growth, haploid, heredity, hermaphrodite, hormone, hybrid, inheritance, invertebrate, kingdom, Krebs cycle, life cycle, meiosis, menstruation, metabolism, metamorphosis, mitosis, muscle, mutation, natural selection, nitrogen cycle, nucleus, order, organ, osmosis, ovulation, ovum, parasite, pathogen, pectoral, photosynthesis, phylum, poikilothermic, pollen, pollination, pollution, posterior, predator, pregnancy, progeny, propagation, protein, protoplasm, puberty, recessive, reproduction, respiration, RNA *or* ribose nucleic acid, ribosome, root, seed, sexual reproduction, skeleton, skin, soil, species, spermatozoon *or* sperm, spore, symbiosis, translocation, transpiration, ventral, vertebrate, virus, vitamin, viviparous, warm-blooded, X-chromosome, Y-chromosome, zygote

Biologists

David Baltimore *(U.S.)*
George Well Beadle *(U.S.)*
Paul Berg *(U.S.)*
John Boyd Orr *(Scottish)*
Alexis Carrel *(French)*
Rachel Carson *(U.S.)*
Albert Claude *(U.S.)*
Francis Harry Compton Crick *(English)*
Charles (Robert) Darwin *(English)*
Max Delbrück *(U.S.)*
Theodosius Dobzhansky *(U.S.)*
Renato Dulbecco *(U.S.)*
Alexander Fleming *(Scottish)*
Ernst Heinrich Haeckel *(German)*
Albrecht von Haller *(Swiss)*
William Harvey *(English)*
Andrew Fielding Huxley *(English)*
Julian Huxley *(English)*
Thomas Henry Huxley *(English)*
Robert Koch *(German)*
Hans Adolf Krebs *(British)*
Anton van Leeuwenhoek *(Dutch)*
Linnaeus (Carl von Linné) *(Swedish)*
Trofim Denisovich *(Russian)*
Robert McCredie May *(Australian)*
Gregor Mendel *(Austrian)*
Thomas Hunt Morgan *(U.S.)*
Louis Pasteur *(French)*
James Dewey Watson *(U.S.)*

b

BIRDS

accentor
amazon
amokura *(N.Z.)*
ani
apostle bird *or* happy family bird *(Austral.)*
avadavat *or* amadavat
avocet
axebird *(Austral.)*
babbler
Baltimore oriole
banded dotterel *(N.Z.)*
banded rail *(N.Z.)*
barbet
beccafico
bee-eater
bellbird *or (N.Z.)* koromako *or* makomako
bird of paradise
bishopbird
bittern
blackbird
blackcap
blackcock
black-fronted tern *or* tara *(N.Z.)*
black grouse
blackpoll
black robin *(N.Z.)*
bluebird
blue duck, mountain duck, whio *or* whistling duck *(N.Z.)*
blue grouse
blue jay
bluethroat
bluetit
boatbill *or* boat-billed heron
bobolink
bobwhite
bokmakierie
boobook *(Austral.)*
bowerbird
brain-fever bird *or (Austral.)* pallid cuckoo
brambling
broadbill
brolga, Australian crane, *or (Austral.)* native companion
brown creeper *or* pipipi *(N.Z.)*
brown duck *(N.Z.)*
brown kiwi *(N.Z.)*
budgerigar *or (Austral.)* zebra parrot
bulbul
bullfinch
bunting
bush shrike
bushtit
bush wren *(N.Z.)*
bustard *or (Austral.)* plain turkey, plains turkey, *or* wild turkey
button quail *or (Austral.)* bustard quail
cacique
Californian quail *(N.Z.)*
canary
Cape Barren goose
Cape pigeon
capercaillie *or* capercailzie
Cape sparrow
capuchin
cardinal *or* cardinal grosbeak
carrion crow
cassowary
catbird
chaffinch
chat
chickadee
chicken *or (Austral. informal)* chook
chiffchaff
chimney swallow *or* chimney swift
chipping sparrow
chough
chuck-will's-widow
chukar
cliff swallow
coal tit *or* coletit
cockatiel, cockateel, *or* cockatoo-parrot
cockatoo
cock-of-the-rock
collared dove
coly *or* mousebird
conure
coppersmith
coquette
corella
corn bunting
corncrake
cotinga *or* chatterer
coucal, pheasant coucal, *or* swamp pheasant
cowbird
crake
crane
crested tit
crocodile bird
crombec
crossbill
crow *or (Scot.)* corbie
cuckoo
cuckoo-shrike
cumulet
curassow
curlew
currawong *or* bell magpie
dabchick
darter, anhinga, *or* snakebird
demoiselle (crane) *or* Numidian crane
diamond bird *or* pardalote
dipper *or* water ouzel
diver
dollarbird
dotterel *or* dottrel
dove *or (archaic or poetic)* culver
dowitcher
drongo
dunlin *or* red-backed sandpiper
egret
emperor penguin
emu
emu-wren
fantail *or (N.Z.)* piwakawaka
fernbird *(N.Z.)*
fieldfare
fig-bird
finch
finfoot
firebird
firecrest
flamingo
flower-pecker
flycatcher
francolin
friarbird
frogmouth
galah *or (Austral.)* galar *or* gillar
gang-gang
gnatcatcher
go-away bird
godwit
goldcrest
golden oriole
goldfinch
Gouldian finch, painted finch, *or* purple-breasted finch
grackle *or* crow blackbird
grassfinch
grassquit
great crested grebe *or* loon
great northern diver
great tit
grebe
greenfinch
green leek
greenlet
greenshank
green woodpecker
grey-crowned babbler, happy family bird, Happy Jack, *or* parson bird *(Austral.)*
grey warbler *or* riroriro *(N.Z.)*
grosbeak
grouse
guan
guinea fowl
hadedah
hawfinch
hazelhen
hedge sparrow *or* dunnock
helldiver, pie-billed grebe, *or* dabchick
hen harrier *or (U.S. & Canad.)* marsh harrier
heron
hill myna
hoatzin *or* hoactzin
homing pigeon
honey creeper
honeyeater
honey guide
honeysucker
hooded crow
hoopoe
hornbill
house martin
house sparrow
hummingbird *or* trochilus
ibis
jabiru *or (Austral.)* policeman bird
jacamar
jaçana *or* lily-trotter
jackdaw
jacksnipe
Jacobin
jaeger *(U.S. & Canad.)*
Java sparrow
jay
junco
jungle fowl
kagu
kaka *(N.Z.)*
kakapo *(N.Z.)*
kakariki *(N.Z.)*
karoro *or* blackbacked gull *(N.Z.)*
kea *(N.Z.)*
killdeer
kingbird
kingfisher *or (N.Z.)* kotare
king penguin
kiwi *or* apteryx
knot
koel *or (Austral.)* black cuckoo *or* cooee bird
kokako *or* blue-wattled crow *(N.Z.)*
kookaburra, laughing jackass, *or (Austral.)* bushman's clock, settler's clock, goburra, *or* great brown kingfisher
kotuku *or* white heron *(N.Z.)*
Lahore
lapwing *or* green plover
lark
limpkin *or* courlan
linnet
locust bird
loggerhead shrike
longspur
long-tailed tit
lorikeet
lory
lourie
lovebird
lyrebird *or (Austral.)* buln-buln
macaw
magpie *or (Austral.)* piping shrike *or* piping crow-shrike
magpie lark *or (Austral.)* mudlark, Murray magpie, mulga, *or* peewit

b

BIRDS (CONTINUED)

Major Mitchell *or* Leadbeater's cockatoo
makomako *(Austral.)*
marabou
marsh tit
martin
meadowlark
meadow pipit
metallic starling *or* shining starling *(Austral.)*
minivet
miromiro *(N.Z.)*
mistle thrush *or* missel thrush
mistletoe bird *(Austral.)*
mockingbird
mohua *or* bush canary *(N.Z.)*
monal *or* monaul
motmot *or* sawbill
mourning dove
myna, mynah, *or* mina
New Zealand pigeon *or* kereru *(N.Z.)*
nighthawk, bullbat, *or* mosquito hawk
night heron
nightingale
nightjar, *(U.S. & Canad.)* goatsucker, *or (Austral.)* nighthawk
noddy
noisy friarbird *or* leatherhead
noisy miner *or (Austral.)* micky *or* soldier bird
notornis
nun
nutcracker
nuthatch
oil bird *or* guacharo
oriole
ortolan *or* ortolan bunting
ostrich
ouzel *or* ousel
ovenbird
oxpecker *or* tick-bird
paradise duck *or* putangitangi *(N.Z.)*
parakeet *or* parrakeet
pardalote *(Austral.)*
parrot
partridge
peacock
peafowl
peewit
pelican
penguin
phalarope
pheasant
pied goose *or* magpie goose
pied wagtail
pigeon
pipit *or (N.Z.)* pihoihoi
pipiwharauroa *or* bronze-winged cuckoo *(N.Z.)*
pitta *(Austral.)*
plover
pratincole
ptarmigan
puffbird
puffin
pukeko
purple gallinule
pyrrhuloxia
quail
quarrian *or* quarrion
quetzal
racket-tail
rail
rainbow bird
rainbow lorikeet
raven
red-backed shrike
redbreast
red grouse
red-legged partridge
redpoll
redshank
redstart
redwing
reedbird
reed bunting
reedling *or* bearded tit
reed warbler
regent-bird *or* regent bowerbird
regent honeyeater
rhea *or* American ostrich
ricebird
riflebird
rifleman *or (N.Z.)* titipounamu
ringed plover
ring-necked pheasant
ringneck parrot, Port Lincoln parrot, *or* buln-buln *(Austral.)*
ring ouzel
roadrunner *or* chaparral cock
robin *or* robin redbreast
rock dove *or* rock pigeon
rockhopper
roller
rook
rosella
rosy finch
ruff
ruffed grouse
runt
saddleback
saddlebill *or* jabiru
sage grouse
sanderling
sandgrouse
sand martin
sandpiper
sapsucker
satin bowerbird
Scandaroon
scarlet tanager
scrub bird
sedge warbler
seriema
serin
sheathbill
shoebill
shore bird *or (Brit.)* wader
shrike *or* butcherbird
sicklebill
silver-eye *(Austral.)*
siskin *or (formerly)* aberdevine
sitella *or* tree-runner
skimmer
skylark
snipe
snow bunting
snowy egret
solitaire
song sparrow
song thrush *or* mavis
sora
sparrow
spoonbill
spotted crake *or (Austral.)* water crake
spotted flycatcher
spotted sandpiper *or (U.S.)* peetweet
squacco
starling
stilt
stint
stock dove
stonechat
stone curlew *or* thick-knee
stork
sugar bird
sulphur-crested cockatoo *or* white cockatoo
sunbird
sun bittern
superb blue wren *(Austral.)*
superb lyrebird *(Austral.)*
surfbird
swallow
swift
swiftlet
swordbill
tailorbird
takahe
tanager
tattler
tawny pippit
tern
thornbill
thrasher
thrush *or (poetic)* throstle
tit
titmouse
tody
topknot pigeon *(Austral.)*
toucan
touraco, turaco, *or* plantain-eater
towhee
tragopan
tree creeper
tree sparrow
trochilus
trogon
tropicbird
troupial
trumpeter
tui *or* parson bird *(N.Z.)*
turtledove
twite
umbrella bird
veery
verdin
wader *or* wading bird
wagtail
wall creeper
warbler
water rail
water thrush
wattlebird
waxbill
waxwing
weaverbird *or* weaver
weka, weka rail, Māori hen, *or* wood hen *(N.Z.)*
wheatear
whimbrel
whinchat
whip bird
whippoorwill
white-eye *or (N.Z.)* blighty, silvereye, tauhou *or* waxeye
white-fronted tern *or* kahawai bird *(N.Z.)*
whitethroat
whooping crane
willet
willow grouse
willow tit
willow warbler
wonga-wonga *or* wonga pigeon
woodchat *or* woodchat shrike
woodcock
wood ibis
woodlark
woodpecker
wood pigeon, ringdove, cushat, *(Scot.)* cushie-doo, *or (English dialect)* quist
woodswallow
wood warbler
wren
wrybill
wryneck
yellowhammer
yellowtail *or* yellowtail kingfisher *(Austral.)*
zebra finch

BIRDS (CONTINUED)

Extinct birds

archaeopteryx
archaeornis
dodo
great auk
huia *(N.Z.)*
ichthyornis
moa
notornis
passenger pigeon
piopio *(N.Z.)*
solitaire

b

2 = beginning, start, rise, source, origin, emergence, outset, genesis, initiation, inauguration, inception, commencement, fountainhead • *the birth of popular democracy*
3 = ancestry, line, race, stock, blood, background, breeding, strain, descent, pedigree, extraction, lineage, forebears, parentage, genealogy, derivation • *men of low birth*
▸ **in phrases: give birth = deliver**, have, mother, produce, bear, bring into the world, be delivered of • *She's just given birth to a baby girl.*
▸ **related adjective:** natal

quotations

Our birth is but a sleep and a forgetting:
The Soul that rises with us, our life's Star,
Hath had elsewhere its setting,
And cometh from afar:
[William Wordsworth *Ode: Intimations of Immortality*]

Birth, and copulation, and death.
That's all the facts when you come to brass tacks:
Birth, and copulation and death.
I've been born, and once is enough.
[T.S. Eliot *Sweeney Agonistes*]

It is as natural to die as to be born; and to a little infant, perhaps, the one is as painful as the other
[Francis Bacon *On Death*]

birthmark = naevus, mole, blemish, port wine stain, strawberry mark • *a routine operation to remove a birthmark*
birthplace = native land, homeland, cradle, fatherland, whenua *(N.Z.)*, Godzone *(Austral. informal)* • *Athens, the birthplace of the ancient Olympics.*
birthright = right, due, heritage, privilege, patrimony • *Freedom is the natural birthright of every human.*
biscuit
▹ *See panel* **Biscuits**
bisect = cut in two, cross, separate, split, halve, cleave, cut across, intersect, cut in half, split down the middle, divide in two, bifurcate • *The main street bisects the town.*
bisexual, ambisexual **= bi** *(slang)*, ambidextrous *(slang)*, swinging both ways *(slang)*, AC/DC *(slang)* • *a road movie about two bisexual women*

quotations

[Bisexuality] immediately doubles your chances for a date on Saturday night
[Woody Allen]

bishop = prelate, metropolitan, diocesan, suffragen • *I'm just a retired bishop.*
▸ **related adjective:** episcopal
bishopric = diocese, see, primacy, episcopate, episcopacy • *Do you think I should resign from the bishopric?*
bit[1] as a noun 1 = slice, segment, fragment, crumb, mouthful, small piece, morsel • *a bit of cake*
2 = piece, scrap, small piece • *crumpled bits of paper*
3 = jot, whit, tittle, iota • *All it required was a bit of work.*
4 = part, moment, period • *The best bit was the car chase.*
5 = little while, time, second, minute, moment, spell, instant, tick *(Brit. informal)*, jiffy *(informal)* • *Let's wait a bit.*
▸ **in phrases: a bit = somewhat**, rather, quite, kind of *(informal)*, pretty, fairly, slightly, moderately, to some extent • *This girl was a bit strange.*
bit by bit = little by little, slowly, progressively, steadily, step by step, by degrees • *Bit by bit I began to understand what they were trying to do.*
do your bit = aid, help, assist, cooperate, lend a hand, lend a helping hand • *She always tried to do her bit.*
bit[2] as a noun = curb, check, brake, restraint, snaffle • *The horse can be controlled by a snaffle bit and reins.*
▸ **in phrases: take the bit in** *or* **between your teeth = get to grips with something**, get stuck in *(informal)*, tackle something, get down to something, set about something, make a start on something • *I got the bit between my teeth and did my best*
bitch as a noun 1 *(Informal)* **= cow**, devil, vixen • *I was a rich little spoiled bitch.*
2 = nightmare, pig, bastard *(offensive, informal)*, swine, bummer • *It was a bitch of a winter that year.*
▸ **in phrases: bitch about something** *or* **someone = criticize**, condemn, slam *(slang)*, put down, knock *(informal)*, disparage, slag off *(slang)*, flame *(informal)*, diss *(slang, chiefly U.S.)*, pick holes in, pick to pieces, be cruel about, be spiteful about • *They're forever bitching about everyone else.*
bitchy = spiteful, mean, nasty, cruel, vicious, malicious, barbed, vindictive, malevolent, venomous, snide, rancorous, catty *(informal)*, backbiting, shrewish, ill-natured, vixenish, snarky *(informal)* • *Women are not the only ones who say bitchy things about each other.*
opposites: kindly, nice, generous
bite as a verb 1 = nip, cut, tear, wound, grip, snap, crush, rend, pierce, champ, pinch, chew, crunch, clamp, nibble, gnaw, masticate • *Llamas won't bite or kick.*
2 = sting, wound, prick • *We were all badly bitten by mosquitoes.*

BISCUITS

abernethy
amaretti
bannock *(Scot.)*
Bath Oliver
bourbon
brandy snap
captain's biscuit
caramel wafer
chocolate digestive
cookie *(chiefly U.S. & Canad.)*
cracker
cracknel
cream cracker
crispbread
digestive
Empire biscuit
fairing
farl
flapjack
Florentine
garibaldi
gingerbread man
ginger nut *or* ginger snap
graham cracker *(U.S.)*
hardtack, ship's biscuit, pilot biscuit, *or* sea biscuit
Jaffa cake *(trademark)*
langue de chat
lebkuchen
love letter
macaroon
matzo
oatcake
petit four
pretzel
ratafia
rich tea
rusk
shortbread
shortcake
soda biscuit
sweetmeal biscuit *or* digestive
Tararua biscuit *(N.Z.)*
tea biscuit
wafer
water biscuit

3 = take effect, work, be effective, take hold, come into force, produce results, have the desired effect, become operative • *As the sanctions begin to bite there will be more difficulties.*
4 = eat, burn, smart, sting, erode, tingle, eat away, corrode, wear away • *nylon biting into the flesh*
5 = take the bait, be lured, be enticed, rise to the bait • *The fish stopped biting.*
▸ **AS A NOUN 1 = nibble**, taste, peck, munch, gnaw • *He took another bite of the apple.*
2 = snack, food, piece, taste, refreshment, mouthful, morsel, titbit, light meal • *a bite to eat*
3 = wound, sting, pinch, nip, prick • *The boy had suffered a snake bite but he made a quick recovery.*
4 = chill, nip, sharpness, coolness, coldness, rawness, crispness • *There was a bite in the air, a smell perhaps of snow.*
5 = edge, interest, force, punch *(informal)*, sting, zest, sharpness, keenness, pungency, incisiveness, acuteness • *The novel seems to lack bite and tension.*
6 = kick *(informal)*, edge, punch *(informal)*, spice, relish, zest, tang, sharpness, piquancy, pungency, spiciness • *I'd have preferred a bit more bite and not so much sugar.*

biting 1 = piercing, cutting, cold, sharp, freezing, frozen, bitter, raw, chill, harsh, penetrating, arctic, nipping, icy, blighting, chilly, wintry, gelid, cold as ice • *a raw, biting northerly wind*
2 = sarcastic, cutting, sharp, severe, stinging, withering, scathing, acrimonious, incisive, virulent, caustic, vitriolic, trenchant, mordant, mordacious • *This was the most biting criticism made against her.*

bitter 1 = grievous, hard, severe, distressing, fierce, harsh, cruel, savage, ruthless, dire, relentless, poignant, ferocious, galling, unrelenting, merciless, remorseless, gut-wrenching, vexatious, hard-hearted • *the scene of bitter fighting*
OPPOSITES: pleasant, fortunate
2 = resentful, hurt, wounded, angry, offended, sour, put out, sore, choked, crabbed, acrimonious, aggrieved, sullen, miffed *(informal)*, embittered, begrudging, peeved *(informal)*, piqued, rancorous • *She is said to be very bitter about the way she was sacked.*
OPPOSITES: happy, friendly, sweet
3 = great, awful, unpleasant, sore • *The statement was greeted with bitter disappointment.*
4 = freezing, biting, severe, intense, raw, fierce, chill, stinging, penetrating, arctic, icy, polar, Siberian, glacial, wintry • *a night in the bitter cold*
OPPOSITES: gentle, pleasant, mild
5 = sour, biting, sharp, acid, harsh, unpleasant, tart, astringent, acrid, unsweetened, vinegary, acidulated, acerb • *The leaves taste rather bitter.*
OPPOSITES: sweet, pleasant, mild

bitterly 1 = grievously, harshly, cruelly, savagely, terribly, ruthlessly, mercilessly, distressingly • *a bitterly fought football war*
2 = resentfully, sourly, sorely, tartly, grudgingly, sullenly, testily, acrimoniously, caustically, mordantly, irascibly • *They bitterly resented their loss of power.*
3 = greatly, terribly, sorely, awfully • *I was bitterly disappointed.*
4 = intensely, freezing, severely, fiercely, icy, bitingly • *It's been bitterly cold here in Moscow.*

bittern
▸ **COLLECTIVE NOUN:** sedge or siege

bitterness 1 = trauma, tragedy, grief, misery, sadness, sorrow, anguish, unhappiness, unpleasantness, awfulness • *the growing bitterness of the dispute*
2 = resentment, hurt, anger, hostility, indignation, animosity, venom, acrimony, pique, rancour, ill feeling, bad blood, ill will, umbrage, vexation, asperity • *I still feel bitterness and anger.*
3 = sourness, acidity, sharpness, tartness, acerbity, vinegariness • *the strength and bitterness of the drink*
4 = intense cold, bite, chill, sting, sharpness, bitter cold, frostiness, iciness • *the bitterness of the British climate*

bitty = disjointed, confused, fragmented, rambling, incomplete, jumbled, patchy, disconnected, sketchy, unconnected, incoherent, scrappy, fragmentary, fitful • *It was bitty and absolutely meaningless.*
OPPOSITES: complete, comprehensive, coherent

bizarre = strange, odd, unusual, out there *(slang)*, extraordinary, fantastic, curious, weird, way-out *(informal)*, peculiar, eccentric, abnormal, ludicrous, queer *(informal)*, irregular, rum *(Brit. slang)*, uncommon, singular, grotesque, perplexing, uncanny, mystifying, off-the-wall *(slang)*, outlandish, comical, oddball *(informal)*, off the rails, zany, unaccountable, off-beat, left-field *(informal)*, freakish, wacko *(slang)*, outré, cockamamie *(slang, chiefly U.S.)*, daggy *(Austral. & N.Z. informal)* • *That book you lent me is really bizarre.*
OPPOSITES: common, standard, normal

blab 1 = tell, reveal, disclose, divulge, blurt out, give away, let slip, blow wide open *(slang)* • *She'll blab it all over the school.*
2 = tell all, tell, gossip, spill the beans *(informal)*, sing *(slang, chiefly U.S.)*, tattle, open your mouth, let the cat out of the bag, blow the gaff *(Brit. slang)*, spill your guts *(slang)* • *Don't blab about your plans until you are ready to make an announcement.*

black **AS AN ADJECTIVE 1 = dark**, raven, ebony, sable, jet, dusky, pitch-black, inky, swarthy, stygian, coal-black, pitchy, murky • *He had thick black hair.*
OPPOSITES: light, bright
2 = gloomy, sad, depressing, distressing, horrible, grim, bleak, hopeless, dismal, ominous, sombre, morbid, mournful, morose, lugubrious, joyless, funereal, doleful, cheerless • *After the tragic death of her son, she fell into a black depression.*
OPPOSITES: happy, warm, cheerful
3 = terrible, bad, devastating, tragic, fatal, unfortunate, dreadful, destructive, unlucky, harmful, adverse, dire, catastrophic, hapless, detrimental, untoward, ruinous, calamitous, cataclysmic, ill-starred, unpropitious, ill-fated, cataclysmal • *He had just undergone one of the blackest days of his political career.*
4 = wicked, bad, evil, corrupt, vicious, immoral, depraved, debased, amoral, villainous, unprincipled, nefarious, dissolute, iniquitous, irreligious, impious, unrighteous • *the blackest laws in the country's history*
OPPOSITES: good, moral, pure
5 = cynical, weird, ironic, pessimistic, morbid, misanthropic, mordacious • *a black comedy*
6 = angry, cross, furious, hostile, sour, menacing, moody, resentful, glowering, sulky, baleful, louring *or* lowering • *a black look on your face*
OPPOSITES: happy, pleased, warm
7 = dirty, soiled, stained, filthy, muddy, blackened, grubby, dingy, grimy, sooty, mucky, scuzzy *(slang, chiefly U.S.)*, begrimed, skanky *(slang)*, festy *(Austral. slang)*, mud-encrusted, miry • *The whole front of him was black with dirt.*
OPPOSITES: white, clean, pure
▸ **AS A VERB = bruise**, mark, hit, injure, mar, blacken, blemish, deface, discolour, contuse • *Her husband blacked her eye.*
▸ **IN PHRASES: black out = pass out**, drop, collapse, faint, swoon, lose consciousness, keel over *(informal)*, flake out *(informal)*, become unconscious • *He felt so ill that he blacked out.*
black something out 1 = darken, cover, shade, conceal, obscure, eclipse, dim, blacken, obfuscate, make dark, make darker, make dim • *The whole city is blacked out at night.*
2 = suppress, conceal, obscure, cover up, censor, whitewash, hush up, blue-pencil, cut, expurgate,

bowdlerize • *Some activists started blacking out English-language road signs.*
in the black = in credit, solid, solvent, in funds, debt-free, financially sound, without debt, unindebted • *Until he's in the black we certainly can't afford to get married.*

SHADES FROM BLACK TO WHITE

ash	ivory	raven
black	jet	sable
charcoal	off-white	silver
cream	oyster white	slate
ebony	pearl	steel grey
eggshell	pewter	stone
grey	pitch-black	white
gunmetal	platinum	
iron	putty	

black and white AS AN ADJECTIVE **= monochrome**, grey-scale • *old black and white film footage*
▸ IN PHRASES: **in black and white 1 = in absolute terms**, unconditionally, naively, unambiguously, uncompromisingly, simplistically, in oversimplified terms • *She saw things in black and white.*
2 = in print, documented, on paper, written down, on record • *He'd seen the proof in black and white.*
blackball = remove, bar, ban, exclude, get rid of, veto, embargo, expel, throw out, oust, snub, vote against, force out, evict, disallow, shut out, repudiate, blacklist, ostracize, debar, drum out • *Members can blackball candidates in secret ballots.*
blacken 1 = darken, dim, deepen, grow black, grow dim • *He watched the blackening clouds move in.*
2 = make dark, shadow, shade, obscure, overshadow, make darker, make dim • *The smoke blackened the sky like the apocalypse.*
3 = discredit, stain, disgrace, smear, knock *(informal)*, degrade, rubbish *(informal)*, taint, tarnish, censure, slur, slag (off) *(slang)*, malign, reproach, denigrate, disparage, decry, vilify, slander, sully, dishonour, defile, defame, bad-mouth *(slang, chiefly U.S. & Canad.)*, traduce, bring into disrepute, smirch, calumniate • *They're trying to blacken our name.*
blacklist = exclude, bar, ban, reject, rule out, veto, boycott, embargo, expel, vote against, preclude, disallow, repudiate, proscribe, ostracize, debar, blackball • *the full list of blacklisted airports* • *A government official disclosed that they had secretly been blacklisted.*
black magic = witchcraft, magic, witching, voodoo, the occult, wizardry, enchantment, sorcery, occultism, incantation, black art, witchery, necromancy, diabolism, sortilege, makutu *(N.Z.)* • *I believed in black magic and white magic.*
blackmail AS A NOUN **= threat**, intimidation, ransom, compulsion, protection *(informal)*, coercion, extortion, pay-off *(informal)*, shakedown, hush money *(slang)*, exaction • *It looks like the pictures were being used for blackmail.*
▸ AS A VERB **= threaten**, force, squeeze, compel, exact, intimidate, wring, coerce, milk, wrest, dragoon, extort, bleed *(informal)*, press-gang, hold to ransom • *I thought he was trying to blackmail me into saying whatever he wanted.*
blackness = darkness, dark, shade, gloom, dusk, obscurity, nightfall, murk, dimness, murkiness, duskiness, shadiness, melanism, swarthiness, inkiness, nigrescence, nigritude *(rare)* • *The twilight had turned to a deep blackness.*
OPPOSITES: light, brilliance, brightness
blackout 1 = noncommunication, secrecy, censorship, suppression, radio silence • *a media blackout*
2 = power cut, power failure, blown fuse, electricity failure • *an electricity blackout*
3 = unconsciousness, collapse, faint, oblivion, swoon *(literary)*, loss of consciousness, syncope *(Pathology)* • *I suffered a blackout which lasted for several minutes.*
black sheep = disgrace, rebel, maverick, outcast, renegade, dropout, prodigal, individualist, nonconformist, ne'er-do-well, reprobate, wastrel, bad egg *(old-fashioned informal)*, wrong 'un *(informal)* • *the black sheep of the family*
bladder
▸ RELATED ADJECTIVE: cystic, vesical
blame AS A VERB **1 = hold responsible**, accuse, denounce, indict, impeach, incriminate, impute, recriminate, point a *or* the finger at • *They blamed the army for most of the atrocities.*
OPPOSITES: clear, excuse, absolve
2 = attribute to, credit to, assign to, put down to, ascribe to, impute to • *The police blamed the explosion on terrorists.*
3 *used in negative constructions* **= criticize**, charge, tax, blast, condemn, flame *(informal)*, put down, disapprove of, censure, reproach, chide, admonish, tear into *(informal)*, diss *(slang, chiefly U.S.)*, find fault with, reprove, upbraid, lambast(e), reprehend, express disapprobation of • *I do not blame them for trying to make some money.*
OPPOSITES: praise, acclaim, compliment
▸ AS A NOUN **= responsibility**, liability, rap *(slang)*, accountability, onus, culpability, answerability • *Bad women never take the blame for anything.*
OPPOSITES: credit, honour, praise
▸ IN PHRASES: **to blame = at fault**, responsible, guilty, culpable, blameworthy • *Who is to blame here?*
blameless = innocent, clear, clean, upright, stainless, honest, immaculate, impeccable, virtuous, faultless, squeaky-clean, unblemished, unsullied, uninvolved, unimpeachable, untarnished, above suspicion, irreproachable, guiltless, unspotted, unoffending • *a blameless life*
OPPOSITES: responsible, guilty, to blame
blanch 1 = turn pale, fade, pale, drain, bleach, wan, whiten, go white, become pallid, become *or* grow white • *She felt herself blanch at the unpleasant memories.*
2 = recoil, start, withdraw, flee, retreat, duck, shrink, back off, wince, swerve, cringe, shy away, quail, cower, shirk, draw back, baulk, blench • *Staff don't blanch at the sight of a wheelchair.*
3 = boil, scald, dunk • *Skin the peaches by blanching them.*
bland 1 = dull, boring, weak, plain, flat, commonplace, tedious, vanilla *(informal)*, dreary, tiresome, monotonous, run-of-the-mill, uninspiring, humdrum, unimaginative, uninteresting, insipid, unexciting, ho-hum *(informal)*, vapid, unstimulating, undistinctive • *It's easy on the ear but bland and forgettable.*
OPPOSITES: interesting, exciting, inspiring
2 = tasteless, weak, watered-down, insipid, flavourless, thin, unstimulating, undistinctive • *It tasted bland and insipid, like warmed card.*
blandishments = flattery, compliments, coaxing, fawning, adulation, blarney, wheedling, sweet talk *(informal)*, soft-soap *(informal)*, sycophancy, flannel *(Brit. informal)*, obsequiousness, cajolery, soft words, ingratiation, toadyism, false praise, inveiglement, honeyed words • *At first Lewis resisted their blandishments.*
blandly = impassively, coolly, indifferently, unemotionally, apathetically, unfeelingly, undemonstratively, passionlessly • *The nurse smiled blandly.*
blank AS AN ADJECTIVE **1 = unmarked**, white, clear, clean, empty, plain, bare, void, spotless, unfilled, uncompleted • *He tore a blank page from his notebook.*
OPPOSITES: full, marked, completed
2 = expressionless, empty, dull, vague, hollow, vacant, lifeless, deadpan, straight-faced, vacuous, impassive,

inscrutable, inane, wooden, poker-faced *(informal)* • *He gave him a blank look.*
OPPOSITES: interested, alert, expressive
3 = **puzzled**, lost, confused, stumped, doubtful, baffled, stuck, at sea, bewildered, muddled, mixed up, confounded, perplexed, disconcerted, at a loss, mystified, clueless, dumbfounded, nonplussed, uncomprehending, flummoxed • *Abbot looked blank. 'I don't follow, sir.'*
4 = **absolute**, complete, total, utter, outright, thorough, downright, consummate, unqualified, out and out, unmitigated, unmixed • *a blank refusal to attend*
▸ AS A NOUN 1 = **empty space**, space, gap • *Put a word in each blank to complete the sentence.*
2 = **void**, vacuum, vacancy, emptiness, nothingness, vacuity, tabula rasa • *Everything was a complete blank.*
▸ IN PHRASES: **blank something out** = **forget**, overlook, think no more of, consign to oblivion, not give another thought to • *I learned to blank those feelings out.*

blanket AS A NOUN 1 = **cover**, rug, coverlet, afghan • *There was an old blanket in the trunk of my car.*
2 = **covering**, cover, bed, sheet, coating, coat, layer, film, carpet, cloak, mantle, thickness • *The mud disappeared under a blanket of snow.*
▸ AS A VERB = **coat**, cover, hide, surround, cloud, mask, conceal, obscure, eclipse, cloak • *More than a foot of snow blanketed parts of Michigan.*
▸ AS AN ADJECTIVE = **comprehensive**, full, complete, wide, sweeping, broad, extensive, wide-ranging, thorough, inclusive, exhaustive, all-inclusive, all-embracing • *the blanket coverage of the Olympics*

blankness = **vacancy**, indifference, abstraction, lack of interest, incomprehension, vacuity, inanity, absent-mindedness, obliviousness, fatuity, inattentiveness, vacuousness, incuriousness • *His eyes have the blankness of someone half-asleep.*

blare AS A VERB = **blast**, scream, boom, roar, thunder, trumpet, resound, hoot, toot, reverberate, sound out, honk, clang, peal • *Music blared from the flat behind me.*
▸ AS A NOUN = **sound**, blast, burst, bang, roar, rumble, wail • *the blare of a radio through a thin wall*

blarney = **flattery**, coaxing, exaggeration, fawning, adulation, wheedling, spiel, sweet talk *(informal)*, flannel *(Brit. informal)*, soft soap *(informal)*, sycophancy, servility, obsequiousness, cajolery, blandishment, fulsomeness, toadyism, overpraise, false praise, honeyed words • *You're as full of blarney as my father.*

blasé = **nonchalant**, cool, bored, distant, regardless, detached, weary, indifferent, careless, lukewarm, glutted, jaded, unmoved, unconcerned, impervious, uncaring, uninterested, apathetic, offhand, world-weary, heedless, satiated, unexcited, surfeited, cloyed • *his seemingly blasé attitude*
OPPOSITES: interested, caring, affected

blaspheme = **curse**, swear, abuse, revile, profane, damn, desecrate, cuss *(informal)*, use bad language, be foul-mouthed, take the Lord's name in vain, execrate, anathematize • *He cursed and blasphemed to his last gasp.*

blasphemous = **irreverent**, cheeky *(informal)*, contemptuous, profane, disrespectful, godless, ungodly, sacrilegious, irreligious, impious • *works which they describe as blasphemous and obscene*
OPPOSITES: godly, religious, reverent

blasphemy = **irreverence**, swearing, cursing, indignity *(to God)*, disrespect, desecration, sacrilege, profanity, impiety, profanation, execration, profaneness, impiousness • *She described the killings as a blasphemy before God.*

blast AS A NOUN 1 = **explosion**, crash, burst, discharge, blow-up, eruption, detonation • *250 people were killed in the blast.*
2 = **bang**, crack, burst, discharge, volley, outburst, clap, report, salvo • *a shotgun blast*
3 = **gust**, rush, storm, breeze, puff, gale, flurry, tempest, squall, strong breeze • *Blasts of cold air swept down from the mountains.*
4 = **blare**, blow, scream, trumpet, wail, resound, clamour, hoot, toot, honk, clang, peal • *The buzzer suddenly responded in a long blast of sound.*
5 = **reprimand**, talking-to *(informal)*, lecture, wigging *(Brit. slang)*, censure, rebuke, reproach, ticking-off *(informal)*, dressing-down *(informal)*, telling-off *(informal)*, admonition, tongue-lashing, reproof, castigation, flea in the ear *(informal)*, reprehension • *Cricket: Blast for Ormerod.*
▸ AS A VERB 1 = **blow up**, bomb, destroy, burst, ruin, break up, explode, shatter, demolish, rupture, dynamite, put paid to, raze to the ground, blow sky-high • *The explosion blasted out the external supporting wall.*
2 = **hit**, kill, shoot, plug *(slang)*, blow away *(slang, chiefly U.S.)*, gun down, open fire on, zap *(slang)*, pick off, mow down, put a bullet in, pump full of lead *(slang)* • *A son blasted his father to death.*
3 = **boot**, fire, project, launch, discharge, hurl, fling, propel, punt, let fly • *He blasted the ball into the back of the net.*
4 = **criticize**, attack, put down, censure, berate, castigate, tear into *(informal)*, flay, rail at, flame *(informal)*, diss *(slang, chiefly U.S.)*, lambast(e), chew out *(U.S. & Canad. informal)* • *They have blasted the report.*
▸ IN PHRASES: **blast away** 1 = **open fire**, shoot, shell, pull the trigger • *The men pulled out pistols and began blasting away.*
2 = **roar**, scream, boom, resound, clamour • *Clock-radios blast away until you get up.*
blast off = **launch**, take off, lift off, take to the air, become airborne • *It is set to blast off on Wednesday.*
blast out = **blast**, scream, boom, roar, trumpet, sound out • *loudspeakers blasting out essential tourist facts*

blasted 1 = **damned**, bloody, freaking *(slang, chiefly U.S.)*, confounded, hateful, infernal, detestable • *I couldn't get that blasted door open.*
2 = **ruined**, destroyed, wasted, devastated, shattered, spoiled, withered, ravaged, blighted, desolated • *the blasted landscape where the battle was fought*

blastoff = **launch**, launching, take off, discharge, projection, lift-off, propelling, sendoff • *The planned launch was called off four minutes before blastoff.*

blatant = **obvious**, open, clear, plain, naked, sheer, patent, evident, pronounced, straightforward, outright, glaring, manifest, bald, transparent, noticeable, conspicuous, overt, unmistakable, flaunting, palpable, undeniable, brazen, flagrant, indisputable, ostentatious, unmitigated, cut-and-dried *(informal)*, undisguised, obtrusive, unsubtle, unconcealed • *blatant elitism*
OPPOSITES: cultured, hidden, subtle

blather AS A VERB = **chatter**, ramble, mumble, babble, waffle *(informal, chiefly Brit.)*, rabbit on *(Brit. informal)*, drivel, yap *(informal)*, tattle, jabber, gabble, blether, run off at the mouth *(slang)*, prate • *He kept on blathering about police incompetence.*
▸ AS A NOUN = **nonsense**, gossip, chatter, hot air, malarkey *(informal)*, waffle *(informal, chiefly Brit.)*, pap, bilge *(informal)*, drivel, twaddle, gibberish, guff *(slang)*, tattle, moonshine, jabbering, jabber, verbiage, gabble, claptrap *(informal)*, gobbledegook, hogwash, bizzo *(Austral. slang)*, bull's wool *(Austral. & N.Z. slang)*, hokum *(slang, chiefly U.S. & Canad.)*, piffle *(informal)*, poppycock *(informal)*, inanity, blether *(Scot.)*, bunkum or buncombe *(chiefly U.S.)* • *Anyone knows that this is all blather.*

blaze AS A VERB 1 = **burn**, glow, flare, flicker, be on fire, go up in flames, be ablaze, fire, flash, flame • *The log fire was blazing merrily.*

2 = **shine**, flash, beam, glow, flare, glare, gleam, shimmer, radiate • *The gardens blazed with colour.*
3 = **flare up**, rage, boil, explode, fume, seethe, be livid, be incandescent • *His dark eyes were blazing with anger.*
▸ AS A NOUN 1 = **inferno**, fire, flames, bonfire, combustion, conflagration • *Two firemen were hurt in a blaze which swept through a tower block.*
2 = **flash**, glow, glitter, flare, glare, gleam, brilliance, radiance • *I wanted the front garden to be a blaze of colour.*
▸ IN PHRASES: **blaze away** = **blast**, shoot, fire • *She took the gun and blazed away with deadly accuracy.*

blazing 1 = **burning**, flashing, flaming, glowing, gleaming, on fire, fiery, alight, scorching, smouldering, ablaze, aflame, afire • *a blazing fire*
2 = **shining**, brilliant, flashing, glowing, sparkling, illuminated, gleaming, radiant, luminous, incandescent, aglow, coruscating • *the blazing, brilliant rays of a new dawn*
3 = **furious**, excited, angry, raging, passionate, fuming, frenzied, incensed, enraged, seething, fervent, impassioned, wrathful • *My husband has just had a blazing row with his boss.*

bleach 1 = **lighten**, wash out, blanch, peroxide, whiten, blench, etiolate • *These products don't bleach the hair.*
2 = **whiten**, fade, pale, lighten, go white, turn pale, grow pale • *The sun will cause the hairs on your face to bleach.*

bleached = **whitened**, faded, lightened, washed-out, etiolated, stone-washed, peroxided, achromatic • *Her hair was bleached blonde.*

bleak 1 = **dismal**, black, dark, depressing, grim, discouraging, gloomy, hopeless, dreary, sombre, unpromising, disheartening, joyless, cheerless, comfortless • *The immediate outlook remains bleak.*
OPPOSITES: promising, encouraging, cheerful
2 = **exposed**, open, empty, raw, bare, stark, barren, desolate, gaunt, windswept, weather-beaten, unsheltered • *The island's pretty bleak.*
OPPOSITES: protected, sheltered, shielded
3 = **stormy**, cold, severe, bitter, rough, harsh, chilly, windy, wintry, tempestuous, intemperate • *The weather can be quite bleak on the coast.*

bleary = **dim**, blurred, fogged, murky, fuzzy, watery, misty, hazy, foggy, blurry, ill-defined, indistinct, rheumy • *Mona smiled at her through bleary eyes.*

bleat 1 = **baa**, call, cry, maa • *a small flock of bleating ewes and lambs*
2 = **complain**, carp, fuss, moan, bitch *(slang)*, groan, grieve, lament, grumble, whine, growl, grouse, gripe *(informal)*, beef *(slang)*, bemoan, whinge *(informal)*, find fault, put the boot in *(slang)*, bewail, kick up a fuss *(informal)*, grouch *(informal)*, bellyache *(slang)*, kvetch *(U.S. slang)* • *They are always bleating about 'unfair' foreign competition.*

bleed 1 = **lose blood**, flow, weep, trickle, gush, exude, spurt, shed blood • *The wound was bleeding profusely.*
2 = **blend**, run, meet, unite, mix, combine, flow, fuse, mingle, converge, ooze, seep, amalgamate, meld, intermix • *The two colours will bleed into each other.*
3 = **extort**, milk, squeeze, drain, exhaust, fleece • *They mean to bleed the British to the utmost.*

blemish AS A NOUN 1 = **mark**, line, spot, scratch, bruise, scar, blur, defect, flaw, blot, smudge, imperfection, speck, blotch, disfigurement, pock, smirch • *the blemish on his face*
OPPOSITES: improvement, perfection, purity
2 = **defect**, fault, weakness, stain, disgrace, deficiency, shortcoming, taint, inadequacy, dishonour, demerit • *the one blemish on an otherwise resounding success*
▸ AS A VERB = **dishonour**, mark, damage, spot, injure, ruin, mar, spoil, stain, blur, disgrace, impair, taint, tarnish, blot, smudge, disfigure, sully, deface, blotch, besmirch, smirch • *He wasn't about to blemish that pristine record.* • *Nobody wanted to blemish his reputation at that time.*
OPPOSITES: improve, perfect, enhance

blend AS A VERB 1 = **mix**, join, combine, compound, incorporate, merge, put together, fuse, unite, mingle, alloy, synthesize, amalgamate, interweave, coalesce, intermingle, meld, intermix, commingle, commix • *Blend the ingredients until you have a smooth cream.*
2 = **go well**, match, fit, suit, go with, correspond, complement, coordinate, tone in, harmonize, cohere • *Make sure all the patches blend together*
3 = **combine**, mix, link, integrate, merge, put together, fuse, unite, synthesize, marry, amalgamate • *a band that blended jazz, folk and classical music*
▸ AS A NOUN = **mixture**, cross, mix, combination, compound, brew, composite, union, fusion, synthesis, alloy, medley, concoction, amalgam, amalgamation, meld, mélange *(French)*, conglomeration, admixture • *He makes up his own blends of flour.*

bless 1 = **sanctify**, dedicate, ordain, exalt, anoint, consecrate, hallow, invoke happiness on • *Bless this couple and their loving commitment to one another.*
OPPOSITES: damn, curse, excommunicate
2 = **endow**, give to, provide for, grant for, favour, grace, bestow to • *If God has seen fit to bless you with this gift, you should use it.*
OPPOSITES: trouble, destroy, afflict
3 = **praise**, thank, worship, glorify, magnify, exalt, extol, pay homage to, give thanks to • *Let us bless God for so uniting our hearts.*

blessed 1 = **endowed**, supplied, granted, favoured, lucky, fortunate, furnished, bestowed, jammy *(Brit. slang)* • *He's the son of a doctor, and well blessed with money.*
2 = **happy**, contented, glad, merry, heartening, joyous, joyful, blissful • *The birth of a healthy baby is a truly blessed event.*
3 = **holy**, sacred, divine, adored, revered, hallowed, sanctified, beatified • *After the ceremony, they were declared 'blessed'.*
4 = **damned**, bloody, freaking *(slang, chiefly U.S.)*, confounded, goddamn • *No-one knows a blessed thing.*
5 = **welcome**, wanted, pleasing, appreciated, pleasant, refreshing, delightful, gratifying, pleasurable, gladly received • *The lifts will be a blessed relief.*

QUOTATIONS
Blessed are the poor in spirit: for theirs is the kingdom of heaven.
Blessed are they that mourn: for they shall be comforted.
Blessed are the meek: for they shall inherit the earth.
Blessed are they which do hunger and thirst after righteousness: for they shall be filled.
Blessed are the merciful: for they shall obtain mercy.
Blessed are the pure in heart: for they shall see God.
Blessed are the peacemakers: for they shall be called the children of God
[*Bible: St. Matthew*]

blessing 1 = **benefit**, help, service, profit, gain, advantage, favour, gift, windfall, kindness, boon, good fortune, bounty, godsend, manna from heaven • *the blessings of prosperity*
OPPOSITES: damage, harm, disadvantage
2 = **approval**, backing, support, agreement, regard, favour, sanction, go-ahead *(informal)*, permission, leave, consent, mandate, endorsement, green light, ratification, assent, authorization, good wishes, acquiescence, approbation, concurrence, O.K. *or* okay *(informal)* • *They gave their formal blessing to the idea.*
OPPOSITES: objection, disapproval, reproof
3 = **benediction**, grace, dedication, thanksgiving, invocation, commendation, consecration, benison • *He said the blessing after taking the bread.*
OPPOSITES: curse, condemnation, malediction

blight AS A NOUN 1 = **curse**, suffering, evil, depression, corruption, distress, pollution, misery, plague, hardship, woe, misfortune, contamination, adversity, scourge, affliction, bane, wretchedness • *urban blight and unacceptable poverty*
OPPOSITES: help, service, blessing
2 = **disease**, plague, pest, fungus, contamination, mildew, contagion, infestation, pestilence, canker, cancer • *the worst year of the potato blight*
▸ AS A VERB = **frustrate**, destroy, ruin, crush, mar, dash, wreck, spoil, crool *or* cruel *(Austral. slang)*, scar, undo, mess up, annihilate, nullify, put a damper on • *families whose lives were blighted by unemployment*

blind AS AN ADJECTIVE 1 = **sightless**, unsighted, unseeing, eyeless, visionless, stone-blind • *How would you describe colour to a blind person?*
OPPOSITES: seeing, sighted
2 *usually followed by* **to = unaware of**, unconscious of, deaf to, ignorant of, indifferent to, insensitive to, oblivious of, unconcerned about, inconsiderate of, neglectful of, heedless of, insensible of, unmindful of, disregardful of • *All the time I was blind to your suffering.*
OPPOSITES: concerned, aware, conscious
3 = **unquestioning**, prejudiced, wholesale, implicit, indiscriminate, uncritical, unreasoning, undiscriminating • *her blind faith in the wisdom of the church*
4 = **hidden**, concealed, obscured, dim, unseen, tucked away • *a blind corner*
OPPOSITES: open, obvious
5 = **dead-end**, closed, dark, obstructed, leading nowhere, without exit • *a dusty hotel room overlooking a blind alley*
6 = **unthinking**, wild, violent, rash, reckless, irrational, hasty, senseless, mindless, uncontrollable, uncontrolled, unchecked, impetuous, intemperate, unconstrained • *The poor man went into a blind panic.*
▸ AS A VERB 1 = **stop someone seeing**, block someone's vision, obscure someone's vision • *The sun hit the windscreen, momentarily blinding him.*
2 = **make blind**, deprive of sight, deprive of vision, render sightless • *The blast of pellets blinded him in one eye.*
3 = **intimidate**, confuse, overwhelm, baffle, bewilder, perplex, mystify, faze, flummox, nonplus • *He would try to blind us with science.*
▸ AS A NOUN = **shutter**, cover, screen, shade, canopy, louvre, awning, Venetian blind, roller blind • *Hang the blind straight.*

QUOTATIONS
If the blind lead the blind, both shall fall into the ditch
[*Bible: St. Matthew*]

PROVERBS
There's none so blind as those who will not see
A nod's as good as a wink to a blind horse

blinding 1 = **bright**, brilliant, intense, shining, glowing, blazing, dazzling, vivid, glaring, gleaming, beaming,
2 = **amazing**, striking, surprising, stunning, impressive, astonishing, eye-popping *(informal)*, staggering, sensational *(informal)*, breathtaking, wondrous *(archaic or literary)*, jaw-dropping, gee-whizz *(slang)* • *waiting for a blinding revelation that never came*
3 = **painful**, agonizing, excruciating, hellish, gut-wrenching, grievous, torturous • *a quick, blinding agony that jumped along her spine*

blindly 1 = **thoughtlessly**, carelessly, recklessly, indiscriminately, unreasonably, impulsively, unthinkingly, senselessly, heedlessly, regardlessly • *Don't just blindly follow what the banker says.*
2 = **wildly**, aimlessly, madly, frantically, confusedly • *Panicking blindly they stumbled towards the exit.*

blink AS A VERB 1 = **flutter**, wink, bat • *She was blinking her eyes rapidly.*
2 = **flash**, flicker, sparkle, wink, shimmer, twinkle, glimmer, scintillate • *Green and yellow lights blinked on the surface of the harbour.*
▸ IN PHRASES: **on the blink = not working (properly)**, faulty, defective, playing up, out of action, malfunctioning, out of order, on the fritz *(U.S. slang)* • *an old TV that's on the blink*
the blink of an eye = an instant, a second, a minute, no time, a flash, a moment, a split second, a tick *(Brit. informal)*, a twinkling, a trice, a jiffy *(informal)*, two shakes *(informal)*, a shake *(informal)*, two shakes of a lamb's tail *(informal)*, the bat of an eye *(informal)* • *It was all over in the blink of an eye.*

blinkered = **narrow-minded**, narrow, one-sided, prejudiced, biased, partial, discriminatory, parochial, constricted, insular, hidebound, one-eyed, lopsided • *They've got a very blinkered view of life.*
OPPOSITES: open-minded, impartial, broad-minded

bliss 1 = **joy**, ecstasy, euphoria, rapture, nirvana, felicity, gladness, blissfulness, delight, pleasure, heaven, satisfaction, happiness, paradise • *It was a scene of such domestic bliss.*
OPPOSITES: distress, grief, misery
2 = **beatitude**, ecstasy, exaltation, blessedness, felicity, holy joy • *the bliss beyond the now*

blissful 1 = **delightful**, pleasing, satisfying, heavenly *(informal)*, enjoyable, gratifying, pleasurable • *There's nothing more blissful than lying by that pool.*
2 = **happy**, joyful, satisfied, ecstatic, joyous, euphoric, rapturous • *a blissful smile*

blister AS A NOUN = **sore**, boil, swelling, cyst, pimple, wen, blain, carbuncle, pustule, bleb, furuncle *(Pathology)* • *The first sign of a blister is itching in the infected area.*
▸ AS A VERB = **swell** • *The affected skin turns red and may blister.*

blistering 1 = **hot**, boiling, baking, flaming, tropical, roasting, searing, scorching, sizzling, very hot, sweltering, scalding, like a furnace *or* an oven • *a blistering summer day*
OPPOSITES: freezing, arctic, icy
2 = **scathing**, cutting, biting, violent, fierce, harsh, savage, searing, withering, ferocious, caustic, vehement, scornful, vitriolic, trenchant, belittling, mordant, mordacious • *a blistering attack on his critics*
OPPOSITES: gentle, mild, bland
3 = **very fast**, flying, rapid, swift, speedy, precipitate, breakneck • *She set a blistering pace to take the lead.*

blithe 1 = **heedless**, casual, rash, reckless, indifferent, careless, oblivious, negligent, unconcerned, untroubled, thoughtless, nonchalant, unthinking, imprudent, neglectful, incautious, unmindful • *It does so with blithe disregard for best scientific practice.*
OPPOSITES: concerned, thoughtful
2 = **happy**, sunny, cheerful, merry, upbeat *(informal)*, buoyant, airy, cheery, carefree, breezy, genial, jaunty, chirpy *(informal)*, untroubled, happy-go-lucky, gay, debonair, insouciant, mirthful, light-hearted, gladsome *(archaic)* • *His spirit was anything but blithe below the surface.*
OPPOSITES: sad, depressed, gloomy

blitz 1 = **attack**, strike, assault, raid, offensive, onslaught, bombardment, bombing campaign, blitzkrieg • *Security forces are active since the bombing blitz last month.*
2 = **crackdown**, drive, campaign, push *(informal)*, crusade, onslaught, clampdown • *a blitz on incorrect grammar*

blizzard = **snowstorm**, storm, tempest • *The blizzard has not just affected the Midlands.*

bloated 1 = **puffed up**, swollen, blown-up, enlarged, inflated, puffy, dilated, distended, turgid, tumescent, tumid • *His face was bloated.*
OPPOSITES: contracted, wrinkled, shrivelled

2 = too full, stuffed *(informal)*, blown up, swollen up, uncomfortably full • *Diners do not want to leave the table feeling bloated.*

blob 1 = drop, ball, mass, pearl, lump, bead, dab, droplet, globule, glob, dewdrop • *a blob of chocolate mousse*
2 = form, blurred outline, spot, shape, shadow, silhouette • *a blob in the distance*

bloc = group, union, league, ring, alliance, coalition, axis, combine • *the former Soviet bloc*

block AS A NOUN **1 = building**, group, complex, tower, edifice • *blocks of council flats*
2 = piece, bar, square, mass, cake, brick, lump, chunk, cube, hunk, nugget, ingot • *a block of ice*
3 = batch, group, lot, collection, quantity, bunch • *Those booking a block of seats get them at reduced rates.*
4 = obstruction, bar, barrier, obstacle, impediment, hindrance • *a block to peace*
▸ AS A VERB **1 = obstruct**, close, stop, cut off, plug, choke, clog, shut off, stop up, bung up *(informal)* • *When the shrimp farm is built it will block the stream.*
OPPOSITES: open, clear, unblock
2 = obscure, bar, cut off, interrupt, obstruct, get in the way of, shut off • *a row of spruce trees that blocked his view*
3 = shut off, stop, bar, cut off, head off, hamper, obstruct, get in the way of • *The police officer blocked his path.*
4 = prevent, stop, check, bar, frustrate, foil, thwart, obstruct, forestall, nip in the bud • *All attempts to complain to his superiors were blocked.*
OPPOSITES: support, further, aid
5 = deflect, parry, repel, intercept, rebuff, repulse, obstruct • *The goalie blocked two shots.*
▸ IN PHRASES: **block something in = hem in**, surround, confine, enclose, shut in, hedge in • *Our cars get blocked in.*
block something out 1 = remove, eradicate, excise, obliterate, efface, blot out, expunge • *I had to block the thought out of my mind.*
2 = cover, block, cloud, shade, mask, conceal, eclipse, overshadow, cloak, shroud, adumbrate, befog, bedim • *Thick fog blocked out the daylight.*
block something up = clog (up), jam (up), stop up, bung up, congest • *Powdering a sweaty nose will only block up the pores.*

blockade AS A NOUN **= stoppage**, block, barrier, restriction, obstacle, barricade, obstruction, impediment, hindrance, encirclement • *They agreed to lift their blockades of main roads*
▸ AS A VERB **= bar**, block, cut off, obstruct, shut off, barricade • *Truck drivers have blockaded roads to show their anger over driving regulations.*

blockage = obstruction, block, blocking, stoppage, impediment, occlusion • *The logical treatment is to remove the blockage.*

bloke = man, person, individual, customer *(informal)*, character *(informal)*, guy *(informal)*, fellow, punter *(informal)*, chap, boy, bod *(informal)* • *He is a really nice bloke.*

blonde *or* **blond 1 = fair**, light, light-coloured, flaxen • *The baby had blonde curls.*
2 = fair-haired, golden-haired, tow-headed • *She was tall, blonde and attractive.*

blood AS A NOUN **1 = lifeblood**, gore, vital fluid • *an inherited defect in the blood*
2 = family, relations, birth, descent, extraction, ancestry, lineage, kinship, kindred • *He was of noble blood, and an officer.*
▸ IN PHRASES: **bad blood = hostility**, anger, offence, resentment, bitterness, animosity, antagonism, enmity, bad feeling, rancour, ill feeling, hard feelings, ill will, animus, dudgeon *(archaic)*, disgruntlement, chip on your shoulder • *There is, it seems, some bad blood between them.*
in cold blood = without emotion, cruelly, ruthlessly, mercilessly, callously, indifferently, unmercifully • *The crime has been committed in cold blood.*
▸ RELATED ADJECTIVES: haemal, haematic, haemic, sanguineous
▸ RELATED PHOBIA: haematophobia

PROVERBS
You cannot get blood from a stone
Blood is thicker than water

BLOOD CELLS

phagocytic white blood cell	leucocyte	poikilocyte
erythrocyte	lymphocyte	polymorph
haemocyte	macrocyte	reticulocyte
	microcyte	

blood-curdling = terrifying, shocking, frightening, scary, appalling, chilling, horrible, dreadful, horrifying, fearful, horrendous, monstrous, gruesome, horrid, frightful, hair-raising, spine-chilling • *Scottish history has its share of blood-curdling tales.*

bloodless 1 = non-violent, friendly, peaceful, harmonious, amicable, without hostility, free from strife • *The campaign would be short and bloodless.*
2 = pale, white, wan, sickly, pasty, colourless, pallid, anaemic, ashen, chalky, sallow, ashy, like death warmed up *(informal)* • *Her face was grey and bloodless.*

bloodshed = killing, murder, massacre, slaughter, slaying, carnage, butchery, blood-letting, blood bath • *an end to bloodshed and to the economic chaos*

bloodstream = circulation • *The disease releases toxins into the bloodstream.*

bloodthirsty = cruel, savage, brutal, vicious, ruthless, ferocious, murderous, heartless, inhuman, merciless, cut-throat, remorseless, warlike, barbarous, pitiless • *this bloodthirsty killer*

blood vessel = vein, artery • *He's ruptured a blood vessel.*

bloody 1 = damned, flaming, fucking *(taboo slang)*, bleeding, blooming, freaking *(slang, chiefly U.S.)*, rotten, blinking, confounded, ruddy, infernal, deuced, wretched, frigging *(taboo slang)* • *I just assumed they were bloody idiot tourists.*
2 = cruel, fierce, savage, brutal, vicious, ferocious, cut-throat, warlike, barbarous, sanguinary • *Forty-three demonstrators were killed in bloody chaos.*
3 = bloodstained, raw, bleeding, blood-soaked, blood-spattered • *His fingers were bloody and cracked.*

bloody-minded = difficult, contrary, annoying, awkward, unreasonable, stubborn, perverse, exasperating, intractable, unhelpful, obstructive, cussed *(informal)*, uncooperative, disobliging • *He was just being bloody-minded.*
OPPOSITES: reasonable, helpful, accommodating

bloom AS A NOUN **1 = flower**, bud, blossom • *Harry carefully plucked the bloom.*
2 = prime, flower, beauty, height, peak, flourishing, maturity, perfection, best days, heyday, zenith, full flowering • *in the full bloom of youth*
3 = glow, flush, blush, freshness, lustre, radiance, rosiness • *The skin loses its youthful bloom.*
OPPOSITES: whiteness, pallor, paleness
▸ AS A VERB **1 = flower**, blossom, open, bud • *This plant blooms between May and June.*
OPPOSITES: die, waste, wither
2 = grow, develop, wax, blossom • *She bloomed into an utterly beautiful creature.*
3 = succeed, flourish, thrive, prosper, fare well • *Not many economies bloomed in 1990.*
OPPOSITES: fail, decline, decay

blooming 1 = damned, bloody *(slang, chiefly Brit.)*, flaming *(informal)*, fucking *(offensive taboo slang)*, bleeding *(Brit. slang)*,

freaking *(slang, chiefly U.S.)*, rotten, blinking *(informal)*, confounded, ruddy *(informal, chiefly Brit.)*, infernal, deuced *(Brit. informal)*, wretched, frigging *(taboo slang)* • *It's a blooming nuisance because it frightens my dog to death.*
2 = **glowing**, great, fine, fantastic, radiant • *She's in blooming health.*

blossom AS A NOUN = **flower**, bloom, bud, efflorescence, floret • *the blossoms of plants, shrubs and trees*
▸ AS A VERB 1 = **bloom**, grow, develop, mature • *Why do some people take longer than others to blossom?*
2 = **succeed**, progress, thrive, flourish, prosper • *His musical career blossomed.*
3 = **flower**, bloom, bud • *Rain begins to fall and peach trees blossom.*

b

blot AS A NOUN 1 = **disgrace**, spot, fault, stain, scar, defect, flaw, taint, blemish, demerit, smirch, blot on your escutcheon • *a blot on the reputation of the architectural profession*
2 = **spot**, mark, patch, smear, smudge, speck, blotch, splodge, stain • *an ink blot*
▸ AS A VERB 1 = **soak up**, take up, absorb, draw up, dry up, mop up, suck up, sop up • *Blot any excess oils with a tissue.*
2 = **stain**, mark, spot, spoil, disgrace, tarnish, disfigure, sully, smirch • *Only one memorable slip-up has blotted his career.*
▸ IN PHRASES: **blot something out** 1 = **obliterate**, hide, shadow, disguise, obscure, blur, eclipse, block out, efface, obfuscate • *The victim's face was blotted out by a camera blur.*
2 = **erase**, cancel, eradicate, excise, obliterate, efface, expunge • *He is blotting certain memories out.*

blotch = **mark**, spot, patch, splash, stain, blot, smudge, blemish, splodge, smirch, smutch • *His face was covered in red blotches.*

blotchy = **spotty**, uneven, patchy, blemished, macular • *blotchy marks on the leaves*

blow[1] AS A VERB 1 = **gust**, blast, puff • *A chill wind blew at the top of the hill.*
2 = **move**, carry, drive, bear, sweep, toss, fling, whisk, buffet, whirl, waft • *The wind blew her hair back from her forehead.*
3 = **be carried**, move, travel, flow, float, hover, flutter, whirl, waft, flit, flitter • *Leaves were blowing around in the wind.*
4 = **exhale**, breathe, pant, puff, breathe out, expel air • *Take a deep breath and blow.*
5 = **puff out**, expel, send out, emit, give out, breathe out • *He blew a ring of blue smoke.*
6 = **play**, sound, pipe, trumpet, blare, toot • *A saboteur blew a horn to distract the hounds.*
7 = **unblock**, clear, unclog • *He took out a handkerchief and blew his nose.*
8 = **blast** • *Rival gunmen blew the city to bits.*
9 = **spend**, waste, squander, consume, run through, use up, dissipate, fritter away • *My brother lent me some money and I went and blew the lot.*
10 = **ruin**, spoil, screw up *(informal)*, botch, mess up, cock up *(Brit. slang)*, fuck up *(offensive taboo slang)*, make a mess of, muff, foul up, make a nonsense of *(informal)*, bodge *(informal)*, make a pig's ear of *(informal)*, flub *(U.S. slang)*, crool or cruel *(Austral. slang)*, louse up *(slang)* • *Oh you fool! Now you've really blown your chances!*
11 = **short-circuit**, go, break, fuse, burn out • *The fuse blew as he pressed the button.*
12 = **burst**, puncture, split, explode, blow out, rupture • *The car tyre blew.*
13 = **puff**, breathe, pant, gasp, gulp, wheeze, exhale • *He ran from door to door, puffing and blowing.*
▸ IN PHRASES: **blow over** = **die down**, end, pass, finish, cease, be forgotten, subside • *Wait, and it'll blow over.*
blow someone away 1 = **bowl over**, amaze, stun, stagger, astound, electrify *(informal)*, stupefy, flabbergast • *She just totally blew me away with her singing.*
2 = **open fire on**, kill, blast *(slang)*, bring down, zap *(slang)*, pick off, pump full of lead *(slang)* • *He'd like to get hold of a gun and blow them all away.*
blow something out = **put out**, extinguish, snuff out • *I blew out the candle.*
blow something up 1 = **explode**, bomb, blast, dynamite, detonate, blow sky-high • *He was jailed for forty-five years for trying to blow up a plane.*
2 = **inflate**, pump up, fill, expand, swell, enlarge, puff up, distend • *Other than blowing up a tyre I haven't done any car maintenance.*
3 = **exaggerate**, heighten, enlarge on, inflate, embroider, magnify, amplify, overstate, embellish, blow out of (all) proportion, make a mountain out of a molehill, make a production out of, make a federal case of *(U.S. informal)*, hyperbolize • *Newspapers blew up the story.*
4 = **magnify**, increase, extend, stretch, expand, widen, broaden, lengthen, amplify, elongate, dilate, make larger • *The image is blown up on a large screen.*
blow up 1 = **explode**, burst, go off, shatter, erupt, detonate • *The bomb blew up as they slept.*
2 = **lose your temper**, rage, erupt, lose it *(informal)*, crack up *(informal)*, see red *(informal)*, lose the plot *(informal)*, become angry, go ballistic *(slang, chiefly U.S.)*, hit the roof *(informal)*, blow a fuse *(slang, chiefly U.S.)*, fly off the handle *(informal)*, become enraged, go off the deep end *(informal)*, wig out *(slang)*, go up the wall *(slang)*, go crook *(Austral. & N.Z. slang)*, flip your lid *(slang)*, blow your top • *I'm sorry I blew up at you.*
3 = **flare up**, widen, heighten, enlarge, broaden, magnify, boil over • *The scandal blew up into a major political furore.*
blow your top = **lose your temper**, explode, blow up *(informal)*, lose it *(informal)*, see red *(informal)*, lose the plot *(informal)*, have a fit *(informal)*, throw a tantrum, fly off the handle *(informal)*, go spare *(Brit. slang)*, fly into a temper, flip your lid *(slang)*, do your nut *(Brit. slang)* • *I just asked him why he was late and he blew his top.*

blow[2] 1 = **knock**, stroke, punch, belt *(informal)*, bang, rap, bash *(informal)*, sock *(slang)*, smack, thump, buffet, clout *(informal)*, whack *(informal)*, wallop *(informal)*, slosh *(Brit. slang)*, tonk *(informal)*, clump *(slang)*, clomp *(slang)* • *He went off to hospital after a blow to the face.*
2 = **setback**, shock, upset, disaster, reverse, disappointment, catastrophe, misfortune, jolt, bombshell, calamity, affliction, whammy *(informal, chiefly U.S.)*, choker *(informal)*, sucker punch, bummer *(slang)*, bolt from the blue, comedown *(informal)* • *The ruling comes as a blow to environmentalists.*

blowout 1 = **binge** *(informal)*, party, feast, rave *(Brit. slang)*, spree, beano *(Brit. slang)*, rave-up *(Brit. slang)*, carousal, carouse, hooley or hoolie *(chiefly Irish & N.Z.)* • *Once in a while we had a major blow-out.*
2 = **puncture**, burst, flat, flat tyre, flattie *(N.Z.)* • *A lorry travelling south had a blow-out and crashed.*

blubber AS A NOUN = **fat**, fatty tissue, adipose tissue • *a thick layer of blubber*
▸ AS A VERB = **weep**, sob, wail, whimper, bawl, snivel, yowl, greet *(Scot. or archaic)*, mewl, howl your eyes out • *To their surprise, their mother started to blubber like a child.*

bludge = **slack**, skive *(Brit. informal)*, idle, shirk, gold-brick *(U.S. slang)*, bob off *(Brit. slang)*, scrimshank *(Brit. Military slang)* • *He was sacked for bludging on the job.*

bludgeon AS A VERB 1 = **club**, batter, beat, strike, belt *(informal)*, clobber *(slang)*, pound, cosh *(Brit.)*, cudgel, beat or knock seven bells out of *(informal)* • *A wealthy businessman has been found bludgeoned to death.*
2 = **bully**, force, cow, intimidate, railroad *(informal)*, hector, coerce, bulldoze *(informal)*, dragoon, steamroller, browbeat, tyrannize • *His relentless aggression bludgeons you into seeing his point.*

▸ **AS A NOUN** = **club**, stick, baton, truncheon, cosh *(Brit.)*, cudgel, shillelagh, bastinado, mere *(N.Z.)*, patu *(N.Z.)* • *I rather feel that the bludgeon has replaced the rapier.*

blue **AS AN ADJECTIVE** 1 = **depressed**, low, sad, unhappy, fed up, gloomy, dismal, melancholy, glum, dejected, despondent, downcast, down in the dumps *(informal)*, down in the mouth, low-spirited, down-hearted • *There's no earthly reason for me to feel so blue.*
OPPOSITES: happy, optimistic, sunny
2 = **smutty**, dirty, naughty, obscene, indecent, vulgar, lewd, risqué, X-rated *(informal)*, bawdy, near the knuckle *(informal)* • *a secret stash of porn mags and blue movies*
OPPOSITES: decent, respectable
▸ **AS A PLURAL NOUN** = **depression**, gloom, melancholy, unhappiness, despondency, the hump *(Brit. informal)*, dejection, moodiness, low spirits, the dumps *(informal)*, doldrums, gloominess, glumness • *Interfering in-laws are the prime sources of the blues.*
▸ **RELATED ADJECTIVE:** cyanic
▹ *See panel* **Shades of blue**

blue-collar = **manual**, industrial, physical, manufacturing, labouring • *The plant employed more than a thousand blue-collar workers.*

blueprint 1 = **scheme**, plan, design, system, idea, programme, proposal, strategy, pattern, suggestion, procedure, plot, draft, outline, sketch, proposition, prototype, layout, pilot scheme • *the blueprint of a new plan of economic reform*
2 = **plan**, scheme, project, pattern, draft, outline, sketch, layout • *The documents contain a blueprint for a nuclear device.*

bluff[1] **AS A NOUN** = **deception**, show, lie, fraud, fake, sham, pretence, deceit, bravado, bluster, humbug, subterfuge, feint, mere show • *The letter was a bluff.*
▸ **AS A VERB** = **deceive**, lie, trick, fool, pretend, cheat, con, fake, mislead, sham, dupe, feign, delude, humbug, bamboozle *(informal)*, hoodwink, double-cross *(informal)*, pull the wool over someone's eyes • *He tried to bluff his way through another test and failed it.*

bluff[2] **AS A NOUN** = **precipice**, bank, peak, cliff, ridge, crag, escarpment, promontory, scarp • *a high bluff over the Congaree River*
▸ **AS AN ADJECTIVE** = **hearty**, open, frank, blunt, sincere, outspoken, honest, downright, cordial, genial, affable, ebullient, jovial, plain-spoken, good-natured, unreserved, back-slapping • *a man with a bluff exterior*
OPPOSITES: sensitive, diplomatic, tactful

blunder **AS A NOUN** = **mistake**, slip, fault, error, boob *(Brit. slang)*, oversight, gaffe, slip-up *(informal)*, indiscretion, impropriety, howler *(informal)*, bloomer *(Brit. informal)*, clanger *(informal)*, faux pas, boo-boo *(informal)*, gaucherie, barry *or* Barry Crocker *(Austral. slang)* • *I think he made a tactical blunder.*
OPPOSITES: accuracy, correctness
▸ **AS A VERB** 1 = **make a mistake**, blow it *(slang)*, err, slip up *(informal)*, cock up *(Brit. slang)*, fuck up *(offensive taboo slang)*, miscalculate, foul up, drop a clanger *(informal)*, put your foot in it *(informal)*, drop a brick *(Brit. informal)*, screw up *(informal)* • *No doubt I had blundered again.*
OPPOSITES: be correct, get it right, be exact
2 = **stumble**, fall, reel, stagger, flounder, lurch, lose your balance • *He had blundered into the table, upsetting the flowers.*

blunt **AS AN ADJECTIVE** 1 = **frank**, forthright, straightforward, explicit, rude, outspoken, bluff, downright, upfront *(informal)*, trenchant, brusque, plain-spoken, tactless, impolite, discourteous, unpolished, uncivil, straight from the shoulder • *She is blunt about her personal life.*
OPPOSITES: sensitive, diplomatic, tactful
2 = **dull**, rounded, dulled, edgeless, unsharpened • *a blunt object*
OPPOSITES: pointed, sharp, keen
▸ **AS A VERB** = **dull**, weaken, soften, numb, dampen, water down, deaden, take the edge off • *Our appetite was blunted by the beer.*
OPPOSITES: stimulate, animate, sharpen

bluntness = **frankness**, forthrightness, openness, candour, truthfulness, plain speaking, outspokenness • *His bluntness got him into trouble.*

blur **AS A NOUN** = **haze**, confusion, fog, obscurity, dimness, cloudiness, blear, blurredness, indistinctness • *Her face is a blur.*
▸ **AS A VERB** 1 = **become indistinct**, soften, become vague, become hazy, become fuzzy • *If you move your eyes and your head, the picture will blur.*
2 = **obscure**, make indistinct, mask, soften, muddy, obfuscate, make vague, befog, make hazy • *Scientists are trying to blur the distinction between these questions.*

blurred 1 = **indistinct**, faint, vague, unclear, dim, fuzzy, misty, hazy, foggy, blurry, out of focus, ill-defined, lacking definition • *blurred black and white photographs*
2 = **indistinct**, vague, unclear, fuzzy, hazy, indistinguishable, nebulous, ill-defined, indiscernible • *The line between fact and fiction is becoming blurred.*

blurt **AS A VERB**
▸ **IN PHRASES:** **blurt something out** = **tell**, reveal, give away, cry, exclaim, leak, spill, disclose, come out with, let out, spout *(informal)*, babble, divulge, let slip, blab, utter suddenly • *Over the food, Richard blurted out what was on his mind.*

blush **AS A VERB** = **turn red**, colour, burn, flame, glow, flush, crimson, redden, go red (as a beetroot), turn scarlet • *I blushed scarlet at my stupidity.*
OPPOSITES: pale, drain, turn pale
▸ **AS A NOUN** = **reddening**, colour, glow, flush, pink tinge, rosiness, ruddiness, rosy tint • *A blush spread over Brenda's cheeks.*

QUOTATIONS
Man is the Only Animal that Blushes. Or needs to.
[Mark Twain *Following the Equator*]

blushing
▸ **RELATED PHOBIA:** ereuthophobia

bluster **AS A VERB** = **boast**, swagger, talk big *(slang)* • *He was still blustering, but there was panic in his eyes.*
▸ **AS A NOUN** = **hot air**, boasting, bluff, swagger, swaggering *(informal)*, bravado, bombast • *the bluster of their campaign*

blustery = **gusty**, wild, violent, stormy, windy, tempestuous, inclement, squally, blusterous • *a cool, blustery day*

SHADES OF BLUE

aqua	cobalt blue	heliotrope	Oxford blue	royal blue	turquoise
aquamarine	Copenhagen blue	indigo	peacock blue	sapphire	ultramarine
azure	cyan	lapis lazuli	periwinkle	saxe blue	Wedgwood blue
Cambridge blue	duck-egg blue	midnight blue	perse	sky blue	
cerulean	electric blue	navy blue	petrol blue	steel blue	
clear blue	gentian blue	Nile blue	pewter	teal	

boar
▸ **COLLECTIVE NOUN:** sounder

board AS A NOUN **1 = blackboard**, noticeboard, chalkboard, flip chart, whiteboard • *He wrote a few more notes on the board.*
2 = plank, panel, timber, piece of wood, slat, piece of timber, lath • *The floor was draughty bare boards.*
3 = management, heads, leaders, directors, managers, executives, committee, bosses *(informal)*, governors, panel, administrators, controllers, directorate • *the agenda for the October 12 meeting of the board*
4 = council, directors, committee, congress, ministry, advisers, panel, assembly, chamber, trustees, governing body, synod, directorate, quango, advisory group, conclave • *the US National Transportation Safety Board*
5 = meals, food, eats *(informal)*, provisions, refreshments, grub *(informal)*, kai *(N.Z. informal)*, sustenance, nosh *(informal)*, victuals, edibles, daily meals • *Free room and board are provided for all hotel staff.*
▸ AS A VERB **1 = get on**, enter, mount, embark, get on board, go aboard, entrain, embus, enplane • *I boarded the plane bound for England.*
OPPOSITES: land, arrive, get off
2 = stay, lodge, live, room, stop, be housed, have rooms, sojourn • *She boarded at the Lord Mayor Treloar College.*
▸ **IN PHRASES: board something up = cover up**, seal, close up, shut up • *Shopkeepers have boarded up their windows.*

board game

BOARD GAMES

acey-deucy
backgammon
bagatelle
chequers
chess
Chinese chequers
Cluedo *(trademark)*
draughts
fox and geese
go *or* I-go
halma
kriegspiel
lightning chess
ludo
Monopoly *(trademark)*
nine men's morris
Parcheesi *(trademark)*
reversi
shove-halfpenny
snakes and ladders
solitaire
speed chess

boast AS A VERB **1 = brag**, crow, vaunt, bluster, talk big *(slang)*, blow your own trumpet, show off, be proud of, flaunt, showboat, congratulate yourself on, flatter yourself, pride yourself on, skite *(Austral. & N.Z. informal)* • *She boasted about her achievements.*
OPPOSITES: cover up, deprecate, disclaim
2 = possess, offer, present, exhibit • *The houses boast the latest energy-saving technology.*
▸ AS A NOUN **= bragging**, vaunting, rodomontade *(literary)*, gasconade *(rare)* • *He was asked about earlier boasts of a quick victory.*
OPPOSITES: disclaimer

PROVERBS
A mule always boasts that its ancestors were horses

boastful = bragging, vain, crowing, swaggering, vaunting, conceited, swanky *(informal)*, puffed-up, egotistical, vainglorious, swollen-headed, full of yourself • *I am not afraid of seeming boastful.*
OPPOSITES: modest, humble, unassuming

boat AS A NOUN **= vessel**, ship, craft, barge *(informal)*, watercraft, barque *(poetic)* • *One of the best ways to see the area is in a small boat.*
▸ **IN PHRASES: in the same boat = in the same situation**, alike, even, together, equal, on a par, on equal *or* even terms, on the same *or* equal footing • *The police and I were in the same boat.*
miss the boat = miss your chance *or* **opportunity**, miss out, be too late, lose out, blow your chance *(informal)* • *Big name companies have missed the boat.*
push the boat out = celebrate, party, large it *(Brit. slang)*, have a fling, go the whole hog *(informal)*, go on a bender *(informal)*, put the flags out, kill the fatted calf, go on a beano *(Brit. slang)* • *I earn enough to push the boat out now and again.*
rock the boat = cause trouble, protest, object, dissent, make waves *(informal)*, throw a spanner in the works, upset the apple cart • *I said I didn't want to rock the boat in any way.*
▹ *See panel* **Boats and ships**

bob AS A VERB **1 = bounce**, duck, leap, hop, weave, skip, jerk, wobble, quiver, oscillate, waggle • *Balloons bobbed about in the sky*
2 = duck, drop, lower yourself, bend, bow, dodge, crouch, stoop • *She handed over a form, then bobbed down again behind a typewriter.*
3 = nod, lower, bend, bow, dip • *She bobbed her head at each passenger.*
▸ AS A NOUN **= nod**, sign, signal, greeting, gesture, indication, salute • *The young man smiled with a bob of his head.*
▸ **IN PHRASES: bob up = spring up**, rise, appear, emerge, surface, pop up, jump up, bounce up • *They will bob up like corks as they cook.*

bode = augur, portend, threaten, predict, signify, foreshadow, presage, betoken, be an omen, forebode • *Grace had dried her eyes. That boded well.*

bodily AS AN ADJECTIVE **= physical**, material, actual, substantial, fleshly, tangible, corporal, carnal, corporeal • *There's more to eating than just bodily needs.*
▸ AS AN ADVERB **= physically**, completely, entirely, wholly • *I was hurled bodily to the deck.*

body AS A NOUN **1 = physique**, build, form, figure, shape, make-up, frame, constitution, flesh and bones • *The largest organ in the body is the liver.*
2 = torso, middle, chest, stomach, trunk • *Cross your upper leg over your body.*
3 = corpse, dead body, remains, stiff *(slang)*, relics, carcass, cadaver • *His body lay in state.*
4 = organization, company, group, society, league, association, band, congress, institution, corporation, federation, outfit *(informal)*, syndicate, bloc, confederation • *the police representative body*
5 = main part, matter, heart, material, mass, substance, bulk, essence, hub • *the preface, followed by the main body of the article*
6 = expanse, area, mass, stretch, sweep, extent, tract, breadth • *It is probably the most polluted body of water in the world.*
7 = amount, measure, collection, mass, volume, quantity, bulk, corpus • *a body of evidence*
8 = mass, company, press, army, host, crowd, majority, assembly, mob, herd, swarm, horde, multitude, throng, bevy • *The great body of people moved slowly forward.*
9 = consistency, substance, texture, density, richness, firmness, solidity, viscosity • *a dry wine, with good body*
▸ **IN PHRASES: body and soul = completely**, wholeheartedly, totally, perfectly, entirely, absolutely, altogether, thoroughly, wholly, positively, utterly, every inch, heart and soul, one hundred per cent, in all respects, from first to last, lock, stock and barrel • *She was now committed to the band, body and soul.*
▸ **RELATED ADJECTIVES:** corporal, physical

QUOTATIONS
The human body is the best picture of the human soul
[Ludwig Wittgenstein *Philosophical Investigations*]
What we think and feel and are is to a great extent determined by the state of our ductless glands and our viscera
[Aldous Huxley *Music at Night*]

BOATS AND SHIPS

airboat
aircraft carrier
auxiliary
banker
barge
barque
barquentine *or* barquantine
bateau
bathyscaph, bathyscaphe, *or* bathyscape
battlecruiser
battleship
Bermuda rig
boatel
brigantine
bulk carrier
bumboat
cabin cruiser
canal boat
canoe
caravel *or* carvel
carrack
catamaran
catboat
caïque
clipper
coble
cockboat *or* cockleboat
cockleshell
coracle
corvette
crabber
cruiser
cutter
destroyer
destroyer escort
dhow
dinghy
dogger
dory
dreadnought *or* dreadnaught
dredger
drifter
dromond *or* dromon
E-boat
factory ship
faltboat
felucca
ferry
fireboat
fishing boat
flatboat
flotel *or* floatel
flyboat
fore-and-after
foyboat
freighter
frigate
galleas
galleon
galley
gig
gondola
gunboat
hooker
houseboat
hoy
hydrofoil
hydroplane
icebreaker
ice yacht *or* scooter
Indiaman
ironclad
jet-boat
jolly boat
junk
kayak
keelboat
ketch
laker
landing craft
lapstrake *or* lapstreak
launch
lifeboat
lightship
liner
longboat
longship
lugger
man-of-war *or* man o' war
maxi
merchantman
minehunter
minelayer
minesweeper
monitor
monohull
motorboat
MTB (motor torpedo boat)
multihull
MY *or* motor yacht
narrow boat
nuggar
outboard
outrigger
oysterman
packet boat
paddle steamer
pink
pocket battleship
polacre *or* polacca
powerboat
proa *or* prau
PT boat
púcán
punt
quinquereme
raft
randan
revenue cutter
rowboat
rowing boat
sailing boat *or* (*U.S. & Canad.*) sailboat
scow
schooner
scull
sealer
shallop
shell
ship of the line
sidewheeler
skiff
skipjack
sloop
speedboat
square-rigger
steamboat
steamer
steamship
stern-wheeler
submarine
supertanker
surfboat
swamp boat
tall ship
tanker
tartan
tender
threedecker
torpedo boat
torpedo-boat destroyer
towboat
trawler
trimaran
trireme
troopship
tub
tug *or* tugboat
U-boat
umiak *or* oomiak
vaporetto
vedette
VJ (vaucluse junior)
warship
weathership
whaler
wherry
windjammer
xebec, zebec, *or* zebeck
yacht
yawl

Body and spirit are twins: God only knows which is which:
The soul squats down in the flesh, like a tinker drunk in a ditch
[Algernon Charles Swinburne *The Heptalogia*]

▷ *See panels* **Blood cells; Bodily humours; Bones; Glands; Muscles; Parts of the body; Parts of the brain; Parts of the ear; Parts of the eye; Parts of the heart; Teeth**

bodyguard = **guard**, minder, defender, guardian, escort, bouncer, protector, chaperon • *Three of his bodyguards were injured in the attack.*

boffin = **expert**, authority, brain(s) (*informal*), intellectual, genius, guru, inventor, thinker, wizard, mastermind, intellect, rocket scientist (*informal, chiefly U.S.*), egghead, wonk (*informal*), brainbox, bluestocking (*usually disparaging*), maven (*U.S.*), fundi (*S. African*) • *a bumbling computer boffin*

bog AS A NOUN **1** = **marsh**, moss (*Scot. & Northern English dialect*), swamp, slough, wetlands, fen, mire, quagmire, morass, marshland, peat bog, pakihi (*N.Z.*), muskeg (*Canad.*) • *We walked steadily across moor and bog.*
2 = **lavatory**, toilet, loo (*Brit. informal*), can (*U.S. & Canad. slang*), john (*slang, chiefly U.S. & Canad.*), bogger (*Austral. slang*), brasco (*Austral. slang*), throne (*informal*), privy, latrine, crapper (*taboo slang*), khazi (*slang*), W.C. • *I'm reading it on the bog.*
3 = **bathroom**, lavatory, toilet, loo (*Brit. informal*), bogger (*Austral. slang*), brasco (*Austral. slang*), convenience, privy, outhouse, washroom, powder room, water closet, gents *or* ladies (*Brit. informal*), ladies' room, little boy's *or* little girl's room (*informal*), W.C. • *'I'm in the bog!' she heard him call.*
▸ IN PHRASES: **bog something** *or* **someone down** = **hold up**, stick, delay, halt, stall, slow down, impede, slow up • *The talks have become bogged down with the issue of military reform.*

bogey 1 = **bugbear**, bête noire, horror, nightmare, bugaboo • *Age is another bogey for actresses.*
2 = **spirit**, ghost, phantom, spectre, spook (*informal*), apparition, imp, sprite, goblin, bogeyman, hobgoblin, eidolon, atua (*N.Z.*), kehua (*N.Z.*) • *It was no bogey, no demon.*

bogged down = **entangled**, involved, overwhelmed, mixed up, embroiled, enmeshed, ensnared, encumbered • *But why get bogged down in legal details?*

boggle 1 = **wonder**, gaze, be amazed, marvel, be taken aback, be awed, be filled with surprise • *The mind boggles at the possibilities.*
2 = **confuse**, surprise, shock, amaze, stun, astonish, stagger, bewilder, astound, daze, confound, bowl over, stupefy, dumbfound, flabbergast • *The management group's decision still boggles his mind.*
3 = **hesitate**, falter, waver, dither (*chiefly Brit.*), shrink, jib, demur, vacillate, hang back • *Many people boggled at engaging in a full-scale war against all the colonies.*

boggy = **marshy**, muddy, waterlogged, spongy, swampy, soft, yielding, fenny, oozy, miry, quaggy • *a green patch at the far end of a boggy field*

bogus = **fake**, false, artificial, forged, dummy, imitation, sham, fraudulent, pseudo (*informal*), counterfeit, spurious, ersatz, phoney *or* phony (*informal*), assumed • *bogus insurance claims*
OPPOSITES: real, true, genuine

Bohemian AS AN ADJECTIVE *often not cap.*
= **unconventional**, alternative, artistic, exotic, way-out (*informal*), eccentric, avant-garde, off-the-wall (*slang*), unorthodox, arty (*informal*), oddball (*informal*), offbeat, left bank, nonconformist, outré, out there (*slang*), boho • *bohemian pre-war poets*
OPPOSITES: conservative, square (*informal*), conventional

PARTS OF THE BODY

Part of the body	Technical name	Related adjective
abdomen	–	abdominal
adenoids	pharyngeal tonsil	adenoid *or* adenoidal
alimentary canal	–	–
ankle	talus	–
anus	–	anal
appendix	vermiform appendix	appendicular
arm	brachium	brachial
armpit	axilla	axillary
artery	–	arterial
back	–	dorsal
belly	venter	ventral
bladder	urinary bladder	vesical
blood	–	haemal, haemic, *or* haematic
bone	os	osseous, osteal, *or* osteoid
brain	encephalon	cerebral
breast	–	–
buttocks	nates	natal *or* gluteal
caecum	–	caecal
calf	–	–
capillary	–	capillary
cervix	–	cervical
cheek	gena	genal
chest	–	pectoral
chin	–	genial *or* mental
clitoris	–	clitoral
colon	–	colonic
duodenum	–	duodenal
ear	–	aural
elbow	–	–
epiglottis	–	epiglottal
external ear	auricle *or* pinna	–
eye	–	ocular *or* ophthalmic
eyebrow	–	superciliary
eyelash	cilium	ciliary
eyelid	–	palpebral
Fallopian tube	oviduct	oviducal *or* oviductal
finger	–	digital
fingernail	–	ungual *or* ungular
fist	–	–
follicle	–	follicular
fontanelle *or* (*chiefly U.S.*) fontanel	–	–
foot	pes	pedal
forearm	–	cubital
forehead	–	frontal
foreskin	prepuce	preputial
gall bladder	–	–
gland	–	adenoid
glottis	–	glottic
groin	–	inguinal
gullet	oesophagus	oesophageal
gum	gingiva	gingival
hamstring	–	popliteal
hard palate	–	–
hair	–	–
half-moon	lunula *or* lunule	–
hand	manus	manual
head	caput	capital
heart	–	cardiac
heel	–	–
hip	–	–
ileum	–	ileac *or* ileal
inner ear *or* internal ear	labyrinth	–
instep	–	–
intestine	–	alvine
jaw	–	gnathic *or* gnathal
jejunum	–	jejunal
jugular vein	–	–
kidney	–	renal *or* nephritic
knee	genu	genicular
knuckle	–	–
labia majora	–	labial
labia minora	–	labial
large intestine	–	–
leg	crus	crural
lip	–	labial
liver	–	hepatic
loin	lumbus	lumbar
lung	–	pulmonary
lymph cell	lymphocyte	–
lymph node	–	–
midriff	diaphragm	–
mons pubis	–	–
mons veneris	–	–
mouth	–	stomatic
nape	nucha	nuchal
navel *or* omphalos	umbilicus	umbilical
neck	cervix	cervical
nerve	–	neural
nerve cell	neuron *or* neurone	neuronic
nipple *or* teat	mamilla *or* papilla	mamillary
nose	–	nasal
nostril	naris	narial *or* narine
occiput	–	occipital
ovary	–	ovarian
pancreas	–	pancreatic
penis	–	penile
pharynx	–	pharyngeal
pubes	–	pubic
rectum	–	rectal
red blood cell	erythrocyte	erythrocytic
ribcage	–	–
scalp	–	–
scrotum	–	scrotal
shin	–	–
shoulder	–	–
side	–	–
skin	cutis	cutaneous
small intestine	–	–
soft palate	–	–
sole	–	plantar
spleen	–	lienal *or* splenetic
stomach	–	gastric
tear duct	lacrimal duct	–
temple	–	temporal
tendon	–	–
testicle	–	testicular
thigh	–	femoral *or* crural
thorax	–	thoracic

PARTS OF THE BODY (CONTINUED)

Part of the body	Technical name	Related adjective
throat	–	guttural, gular, or jugular
thumb	pollex	pollical
toe	–	–
toenail	–	ungual *or* ungular
tongue	lingua	lingual *or* glottic
tonsil	–	tonsillar *or* tonsillary
torso	–	–
transverse colon	–	–
trunk	–	–
umbilical cord	umbilicus	–
ureter	–	ureteral *or* ureteric
urethra	–	urethral
vagina	–	vaginal
vein	vena	venous
vocal cords	glottis	glottal
voice box	larynx	laryngeal
vulva	–	vulval, vulvar, *or* vulvate
waist	–	–
white blood cell	leucocyte	leucocytic
windpipe	trachea	tracheal *or* tracheate
womb	uterus	uterine
wrist	carpus	–

▸ AS A NOUN *often not cap.* = **nonconformist**, rebel, radical, eccentric, maverick, hippy, dropout, individualist, beatnik, iconoclast, boho • *I am a bohemian. I have no roots.*

boil[1] AS A VERB 1 = **simmer**, bubble, foam, churn, seethe, fizz, froth, effervesce • *I stood in the kitchen, waiting for the water to boil.*
2 = **bring to the boil**, cook, simmer • *Peel the potatoes and boil them.*
3 = **be furious**, storm, rage, rave, fume, be angry, crack up *(informal)*, see red *(informal)*, go ballistic *(slang, chiefly U.S.)*, be indignant, fulminate, foam at the mouth *(informal)*, blow a fuse *(slang, chiefly U.S.)*, fly off the handle *(informal)*, go off the deep end *(informal)*, wig out *(slang)*, go up the wall *(slang)* • *She was boiling with anger.*
▸ IN PHRASES: **boil down to something** = **amount to**, mean, come to, equal, add up to, come down to • *What they want boils down to just one thing.*
boil something down = **reduce**, concentrate, precipitate *(Chemistry)*, thicken, condense, decoct • *He boils down red wine and uses what's left.*
boil something up = **make hot**, make, warm up, heat up • *Boil up some coffee.*

boil[2] = **pustule**, gathering, swelling, blister, blain, carbuncle, furuncle *(Pathology)* • *a boil on her nose*

boiling 1 = **very hot**, hot, burning, baking, tropical, roasting, blistering, scorching, torrid, sultry, sweltering • *It's boiling in here.*
2 = **furious**, angry, fuming, choked, infuriated, incensed, enraged, indignant, incandescent, on the warpath, foaming at the mouth, fit to be tied *(slang)*, tooshie *(Austral. slang)*, off the air *(Austral. slang)* • *She was boiling with rage.*

boisterous 1 = **unruly**, wild, disorderly, loud, noisy, wayward, rowdy, wilful, riotous, unrestrained, rollicking, impetuous, rumbustious, uproarious, obstreperous, clamorous • *a boisterous but good-natured crowd*
OPPOSITES: controlled, quiet, self-controlled
2 = **stormy**, rough, raging, turbulent, tumultuous, tempestuous, blustery, gusty, squally • *The boisterous wind had been making the sea increasingly choppy.*
OPPOSITES: quiet, calm, peaceful

bold 1 = **fearless**, enterprising, brave, daring, heroic, adventurous, courageous, gritty, gallant, gutsy *(slang)*, audacious, intrepid, valiant, plucky, undaunted, unafraid, unflinching, dauntless, ballsy *(taboo slang)*, lion-hearted, valorous • *She becomes a bold, daring rebel.*
OPPOSITES: fearful, cowardly, timid
2 = **impudent**, forward, fresh *(informal)*, confident, rude, cheeky, brash, feisty *(informal, chiefly U.S. & Canad.)*, saucy, pushy *(informal)*, brazen, in-your-face *(Brit. slang)*, shameless, sassy *(U.S. informal)*, unabashed, pert, insolent, barefaced, spirited, forceful • *Men do not like girls who are too bold.*
OPPOSITES: conservative, retiring, shy
3 = **bright**, conspicuous, strong, striking, loud, prominent, lively, pronounced, colourful, vivid, flashy, eye-catching, salient, showy • *bold, dramatic colours*
OPPOSITES: soft, pale, dull
4 = **heavy**, clear, thick, distinct, pronounced • *It's a big book with bold print.*

QUOTATIONS
Bold knaves thrive without one grain of sense,
But good men starve for want of impudence
[John Dryden *Constantine the Great*]

PROVERBS
The bold are always lucky

bolster AS A VERB = **support**, help, aid, maintain, boost, strengthen, assist, prop, reinforce, hold up, cushion, brace, shore up, augment, buttress, buoy up, give a leg up to *(informal)* • *a number of measures intended to bolster morale*
▸ AS A NOUN = **pillow**, support, pad, cushion • *Make a bolster to fit across the width of a bed.*

bolt AS A NOUN 1 = **pin**, rod, peg, screw, rivet, fastener • *details right down to the dimensions of nuts and bolts*
2 = **bar**, catch, lock, latch, fastener, sliding bar • *I heard him slide the bolt across the door.*
3 = **arrow**, missile, shaft, dart, projectile • *He pulled the crossbow bolt from his head.*
4 = **flash**, thunderbolt, burst, streak, shaft • *Suddenly a bolt of lightning crackled through the sky.*
5 = **bale**, amount, roll, quantity, reel, packet, bundle • *bolts of black silk*
6 = **dash**, race, flight, spring, rush, rush, bound, sprint, dart, spurt • *a bolt for freedom*
▸ AS A VERB 1 = **lock**, close, bar, secure, fasten, latch • *He reminded her to lock and bolt the kitchen door behind her.*
2 = **dash**, run, fly, spring, jump, rush, bound, leap, sprint, hurtle • *I made some excuse and bolted towards the exit.*
3 = **run away**, escape, flee, abscond, decamp, make a break (for it), do a runner *(slang)*, run for it, fly the coop *(U.S. & Canad. informal)*, take a powder *(U.S. & Canad. slang)*, take it on the lam *(U.S. & Canad. slang)* • *They caught the horse 200 yards from where it had bolted.*
4 = **gobble**, stuff, wolf, cram, gorge, devour, gulp, guzzle, swallow whole • *Don't bolt your food.*
▸ IN PHRASES: **a bolt from the blue** = **complete surprise**, shock, revelation, jolt, bombshell • *The decision came as a bolt from the blue.*

bomb AS A NOUN = **explosive**, charge, mine, shell, missile, device, rocket, grenade, torpedo, bombshell, projectile • *There were two bomb explosions in the city overnight.*

▸ **AS A VERB = blow up**, attack, destroy, assault, shell, blast, blitz, bombard, torpedo, open fire on, strafe, fire upon, blow sky-high • *Airforce jets bombed the city at night.*
▸ **IN PHRASES: bomb something out = blow to bits**, destroy, devastate, flatten, ravage, raze to the ground • *London has been bombed out.*
the bomb = nuclear bombs, A-bombs, atom bombs • *They are generally thought to have the bomb.*

BOMBS

atom bomb *or* A-bomb	grenade	Molotov cocktail
bangalore torpedo	hand grenade	nail bomb
blockbuster	hydrogen bomb	neutron bomb
bouncing bomb	improvised explosive device *or* IED	nuclear bomb
cluster bomb	incendiary *or* incendiary bomb	petrol bomb
depth charge	Mills bomb	pipe bomb
fusion bomb		plastic bomb
		stun grenade
		time bomb

bombard 1 = attack, assault, batter, barrage, besiege, beset, assail • *The media bombards all of us with images of violence and drugs and sex.*
2 = bomb, shell, blast, blitz, open fire, strafe, fire upon • *Rebel artillery units have regularly bombarded the airport.*
bombardment = bombing, attack, fire, assault, shelling, blitz, barrage, flak, strafe, fusillade, cannonade • *The city has been flattened by regular artillery bombardments.*
bombast = pomposity, ranting, bragging, hot air *(informal)*, bluster, grandiosity, braggadocio, grandiloquence, rodomontade *(literary)*, gasconade *(rare)*, extravagant boasting, magniloquence • *There were men aboard who could not tolerate his bombast.*
bombastic = grandiloquent, inflated, ranting, windy, high-flown, pompous, grandiose, histrionic, wordy, verbose, declamatory, fustian, magniloquent • *the bombastic style of his oratory*
bombshell = complete surprise, shock, revelation, jolt, bolt from the blue • *His resignation after thirteen years is a political bombshell.*
bona fide = genuine, real, true, legal, actual, legitimate, authentic, honest, veritable, lawful, on the level *(informal)*, kosher *(informal)*, dinkum *(Austral. & N.Z. informal)*, the real McCoy • *We are happy to donate to bona fide charitable causes.*
OPPOSITES: false, fake, bogus
bonanza = boom, jackpot, windfall, boon, good fortune, winning streak, stroke of luck • *The expected sales bonanza hadn't materialised.*
bond AS A NOUN 1 = tie, union, coupling, link, association, relation, connection, alliance, attachment, affinity, affiliation • *the bond that linked them*
2 = fastening, band, tie, binding, chain, cord, shackle, fetter, manacle • *He managed to break free of his bonds.*
3 = agreement, word, promise, contract, guarantee, pledge, obligation, compact, covenant • *I'm not about to betray my bond with my brother.*
▸ **AS A VERB 1 = form friendships**, connect, form close ties, get to know one another well, get *or* become close • *They all bonded while working together.*
2 = fix, hold, bind, connect, glue, gum, fuse, stick, paste, fasten • *Strips of wood are bonded together and moulded by machine.*
bondage = slavery, imprisonment, captivity, confinement, yoke, duress, servitude, enslavement, subjugation, serfdom, subjection, vassalage, thraldom, enthralment • *A terrible life of bondage was compounded by a guilty secret.*
bone
▸ **TECHNICAL NAME:** os
▸ **RELATED ADJECTIVES:** osseous, osteal, osteoid
▹ *See panel* **Bones**
bonhomie = geniality, happiness, warmth, good humour, exuberance, friendliness, high spirits, buoyancy, gaiety, cheerfulness, good cheer, conviviality, cordiality, affability, heartiness, congeniality, light-heartedness, jauntiness, joyousness • *his soft-spoken bonhomie*
bon mot = joke, sally, gag *(informal)*, quip, jibe, barb, jest, witticism, smart remark, witty remark, funny *(informal)*, pithy remark, sardonic remark • *He was a genius for dissolving a tense situation with a bon mot.*
bonny = beautiful, pretty, fair, sweet, appealing, attractive, lovely, charming, handsome, good-looking, gorgeous, radiant, alluring, comely, fit *(Brit. informal)* • *She was a bonny highland lassie.*
bonus 1 = extra, benefit, commission, prize, gift, reward, premium, dividend, hand-out, perk *(Brit. informal)*, bounty, gratuity, honorarium, boot money *(informal)* • *a special end-of-year bonus*

BONES

Bone	Nontechnical names	Bone	Nontechnical names	Bone	Nontechnical names
astragalus	anklebone	incus	anvil	sacrum	–
calcaneus	heel bone	innominate bone	hipbone	scapula	shoulder blade
carpal	wrist	ischium	–	skull	–
carpus	wrist	malleus	hammer	sphenoid	–
clavicle	collarbone	mandible	lower jawbone	spinal column *or* spine	backbone
coccyx	–	maxilla	upper jawbone	stapes	stirrup
costa	rib	metacarpal	–	sternum	breastbone
cranium	brainpan	metatarsal	–	talus	anklebone
cuboid	–	metatarsus	–	tarsal	–
ethmoid	–	occipital bone	–	tarsus	–
femur	thighbone	parietal bone	–	temporal bone	–
fibula	–	patella	kneecap	tibia	shinbone
frontal bone	–	pelvis	–	ulna	–
hallux	–	phalanx	–	vertebra	–
humerus	–	pubis	–	vertebral column	backbone
hyoid	–	radius	–	zygomatic bone	cheekbone
ilium	–	rib	–		

2 = advantage, benefit, gain, extra, plus, asset, perk *(Brit. informal)*, icing on the cake • *Anything else would be a bonus.*

bon vivant = gourmet, bon viveur, connoisseur, foodie *(informal)*, epicurean, hedonist, pleasure-seeker, epicure, gastronome, voluptuary, luxurist • *a garrulous book collector and bon vivant*
OPPOSITES: abstainer, celibate, ascetic

bony = thin, lean, skinny, angular, gaunt, skeletal, haggard, emaciated, scrawny, undernourished, cadaverous, rawboned, macilent *(rare)* • *an old man with a bony face and white hair*

booby = fool, jerk *(slang, chiefly U.S. & Canad.)*, idiot, berk *(Brit. slang)*, prick *(slang)*, wally *(slang)*, prat *(slang)*, plonker *(slang)*, geek *(slang)*, goof *(informal)*, twit *(informal, chiefly Brit.)*, dunce, duffer *(informal)*, oaf, simpleton, dimwit *(informal)*, dipstick *(Brit. slang)*, dickhead *(slang)*, gonzo *(slang)*, schmuck *(U.S. slang)*, dork *(slang)*, dorba *or* dorb *(Austral. slang)*, bogan *(Austral. slang)*, nitwit, blockhead, plank *(Brit. slang)*, divvy *(Brit. slang)*, pillock *(Brit. slang)*, dweeb *(U.S. slang)*, putz *(U.S. slang)*, fathead *(informal)*, weenie *(U.S. informal)*, charlie *(Brit. informal)*, coot, muggins *(Brit. slang)*, eejit *(Scot. & Irish)*, thicko *(Brit. slang)*, dumb-ass *(slang)*, gobshite *(Irish taboo slang)*, numpty *(Scot. informal)*, doofus *(slang, chiefly U.S.)*, lamebrain *(informal)*, fuckwit *(taboo slang)*, dickwit *(slang)*, nerd *or* nurd *(slang)*, numbskull *or* numskull • *Her husband is a booby.*

book AS A NOUN **1 = work**, title, guide, volume, publication, companion, manual, paperback, textbook, tract, hardback, tome, treatise • *a book about witches*
2 = notebook, album, journal, diary, pad, record book, Filofax *(trademark)*, notepad, exercise book, jotter, memorandum book • *I had several names in my little black book that I called regularly.*
▸ AS A PLURAL NOUN **= accounts**, records, balance sheet, ledger, financial statement • *He usually left the books to his managers and accountants.*
▸ AS A VERB **1 = reserve**, schedule, engage, line up, organize, charter, arrange for, procure, make reservations • *She booked herself a flight home last night.*
2 = charge • *They took him to the police station and booked him for assault.*
▸ IN PHRASES: **book in = register**, enter, enrol • *He was happy to book in at the Royal Pavilion Hotel.*
in my book = in my opinion, to me, as far as I am concerned • *He is no hero in my book*
▸ RELATED MANIA: bibliomania
▸ RELATED ENTHUSIAST: bibliophile
▸ RELATED PHOBIA: bibliophobia

QUOTATIONS

A good book is the precious life-blood of a master spirit, embalmed and treasured up on purpose to a life beyond life
[John Milton *Areopagitica*]

All books are divisible into two classes, the books of the hour, and the books of all time
[John Ruskin *Sesame and Lilies*]

There is no such thing as a moral or an immoral book. Books are well written, or badly written
[Oscar Wilde *The Picture of Dorian Gray*]

Style and Structure are the essence of a book; great ideas are hogwash
[Vladimir Nabokov]

All books are either dreams or swords,
You can cut, or you can drug, with words
[Amy Lowell *Sword Blades and Poppy Seeds*]

Some books are to be tasted, others to be swallowed, and some few to be chewed and digested
[Francis Bacon *Essays*]

The reading of all good books is like conversation with the finest men of past centuries
[René Descartes *Discourse on Method*]

All good books are alike in that they are truer than if they had really happened
[Ernest Hemingway]

Books succeed,
And lives fail
[Elizabeth Barrett Browning *Aurora Leigh*]

Books are where things are explained to you; life is where things aren't
[Julian Barnes *Flaubert's Parrot*]

Even bad books are books and therefore sacred
[Günter Grass *The Tin Drum*]

▹ *See panel* **Books**

booking = reservation, date, appointment, engagement, prior arrangement • *I suggest you tell him there was a mistake over his late booking.*

bookish = studious, learned, academic, intellectual, literary, scholarly, erudite, pedantic, well-read, donnish, swotty *(Brit. informal)* • *a bookish socialist*

booklet = brochure, leaflet, hand-out, pamphlet, folder, mailshot, handbill • *a booklet on natural pesticides*

boom AS A NOUN **1 = expansion**, increase, development, growth, advance, jump, boost, improvement, spurt, upsurge, upturn, upswing • *an economic boom*
OPPOSITES: decline, failure, crash
2 = bang, report, shot, crash, clash, blast, burst, explosion, roar, thunder, rumble, clap, peal, detonation • *The stillness of the night was broken by the boom of a cannon.*
▸ AS A VERB **1 = increase**, flourish, grow, develop, succeed, expand, strengthen, do well, swell, thrive, intensify, prosper, burgeon, spurt • *Lipstick sales have boomed even more.*
OPPOSITES: fall, fail, crash
2 = bang, roll, crash, blast, echo, drum, explode, roar, thunder, rumble, resound, reverberate, peal • *Thunder boomed like battlefield cannons over Crooked Mountain.*

boomerang = rebound, backfire, come home to roost • *The trick boomeranged, though.*

booming 1 = loud, echoing, thundering, bellowing, resounding, deafening, strident, resonant, sonorous, stentorian • *The ginger man had a large booming voice.*
2 = flourishing, successful, expanding, doing well, thriving, blooming, mushrooming, prospering, rampant, burgeoning, on the up and up *(Brit.)* • *It has a booming tourist industry.*

boon 1 = benefit, advantage, blessing, godsend, gift • *This battery booster is a boon for photographers.*
2 = gift, present, grant, favour, donation, hand-out, gratuity, benefaction • *She begged him to grant her one boon.*

boor = lout, peasant, hick *(informal, chiefly U.S. & Canad.)*, barbarian, brute, philistine, redneck *(U.S. slang)*, oaf, bumpkin, vulgarian, hayseed *(U.S. & Canad. informal)*, cougan *(Austral. slang)*, scozza *(Austral. slang)*, bogan *(Austral. slang)*, clodhopper *(informal)*, churl, clodpole • *He was a braggart, a cynic and a boor.*

boorish = loutish, gross, crude, rude, hick *(informal, chiefly U.S. & Canad.)*, coarse, vulgar, rustic, barbaric, churlish, uneducated, bearish, uncouth, unrefined, uncivilized, clownish, oafish, ill-bred, lubberly • *Crude was the word for him. Boorish.*
OPPOSITES: cultured, sophisticated, refined

boost AS A VERB **1 = increase**, develop, raise, expand, add to, build up, heighten, enlarge, inflate, magnify, amplify, augment, jack up • *They need to take action to boost sales.*
OPPOSITES: cut, drop, decrease
2 = bolster, further, raise, support, inspire, sustain, assist, improve, encourage, foster, swell, uplift, shore up, buoy up • *We need a big win to boost our confidence.*
3 = promote, improve, encourage, advance, advertise, praise, plug *(informal)*, hype, crack up *(informal)*, big up *(slang, chiefly Caribbean)* • *companies seeking to boost their product ranges*

b

BOOKS

Types of book

album, almanac, anatomy, annual, anthology, armorial, A to Z, atlas, autobiography, Baedeker, bestiary, bibelot, Bible, biography, breviary, brochure, casebook, catalogue, catechism, coffee-table book, comic book, commonplace book, companion, compendium, concordance, confessional, cookery book, copybook, diary, dictionary, directory, dispensatory, encyclopedia *or* encyclopaedia, exercise book, formulary, gazetteer, gradus, grammar, graphic novel, grimoire, guidebook, handbook, hymn book, jotter, journal, lectionary, ledger, lexicon, log *or* logbook, manual, miscellany, missal, monograph, notebook, novel, novelette, novella, ordinal, peerage, pharmacopoeia, phrase book, prayer book, primer, prospectus, psalter, reader, reference book, register, road book, score, scrapbook, service book, sketchbook, song book, speller, statute book, storybook, telephone directory, textbook, thesaurus, vade mecum, who's who, wordbook, workbook, yearbook

Parts of a book

acknowledgments, addendum, afterword, appendix, back, back matter, bibliography, binding, blurb, chapter, contents, corrigenda, cover, dedication, dust jacket *or* cover, endpaper, epigraph, epilogue, errata, flyleaf, folio, fore-edge, foreword, frontispiece, front matter, glossary, gutter, half-title, illustration, index, interleaf, introduction, leaf, margin, page, plate, postscript, preface, prelims, proem, prolegomenon, prologue, recto, rubric, running head, slipcase, spine, tail, title page, verso, wrapper

▸ **as a noun 1 = rise**, increase, advance, jump, addition, improvement, expansion, upsurge, upturn, increment, upswing, upward turn • *The paper is enjoying a boost in circulation.*
opposites: fall, decline, reduction
2 = encouragement, help, lift, spur, inspiration, bolster • *It did give me a boost to win such an event.*

boot **as a noun = wellington**, welly, gumboot, wader, jackboot, overshoe, thigh boot, galosh • *He was wearing riding pants, high boots, and spurs.*
▸ **as a verb = kick**, punt, put the boot in(to) *(slang)*, drop-kick • *One guy booted the door down.*
▸ **in phrases: boot someone out = dismiss**, sack *(informal)*, expel, throw out, oust, relegate, kick out, eject, kiss off *(slang, chiefly U.S. & Canad.)*, show someone the door, give someone the boot *(slang)*, give (someone) their marching orders, give someone the bullet *(Brit. slang)*, give someone the bum's rush *(slang)*, throw out on your ear *(informal)*, give someone the heave *or* push *(informal)*, give someone his *or* her P45 *(informal)* • *Schools are booting out record numbers of unruly pupils*
boot something up = start up, prepare, fire up, make ready, reboot • *I can boot the machine up from a floppy disk, but that's all.*
too big for your boots = overconfident, arrogant, brash, cocky, presumptuous, bumptious, cocksure, hubristic, full of yourself • *The players have become too big for their boots.*

booth = cubicle, cell, bay, chamber, niche, alcove, pigeonhole, cubbyhole, carrel • *In Darlington, queues form at some polling booths.*

bootleg = illicit, illegal, outlawed, pirate, unofficial, black-market, unlicensed, under-the-table, unauthorized, contraband, hooky *(slang)*, under-the-counter • *bootleg liquor*
opposites: official, legal, licensed

booty = plunder, winnings, gains, haul, spoils, prey, loot, takings, pillage, swag *(slang)*, boodle *(slang, chiefly U.S.)* • *Troops confiscated many works of art as war booty.*

booze **as a noun = alcohol**, drink, spirits, juice *(informal)*, the bottle *(informal)*, liquor, grog *(informal, chiefly Austral. & N.Z.)*, the hard stuff *(informal)*, strong drink, intoxicant, firewater, John Barleycorn, hooch *or* hootch *(informal, chiefly U.S. & Canad.)* • *empty bottles of booze*
▸ **as a verb = drink**, indulge, get drunk, tipple, imbibe, tope, carouse, bevvy *(dialect)*, get plastered, drink like a fish, go on the piss *(taboo slang)*, get soused, get tanked up *(informal)*, go on a binge *or* bender *(informal)*, hit the booze *or* bottle *(informal)* • *a load of drunken businessmen who had been boozing all afternoon*

boozer **1 = pub**, local *(Brit. informal)*, bar *(informal, chiefly Brit.)*, inn, tavern, beer parlour *(Canad.)*, beverage room *(Canad.)*, public house, watering hole *(facetious slang)*, roadhouse, hostelry, alehouse *(archaic)*, taproom • *She once caught him in a boozer with another woman.*
2 = drinker, toper, drunk, soak *(slang)*, alcoholic, lush *(slang)*, drunkard, sot, tippler, wino *(informal)*, alko *or* alco *(Austral. slang)*, inebriate • *We always thought he was a bit of a boozer.*

boozy = hard-drinking, tippling, red-nosed, intemperate, beery, gin-sodden • *a cheerful, boozy chain-smoker*

bop **as a noun = dance**, hop *(informal)*, knees-up *(Brit. informal)* • *People just want a good tune and a good bop.*
▸ **as a verb = dance**, rock, trip, hop, skip, caper, jig, frolic, gambol, cut a rug *(informal)* • *He was bopping around, snapping his fingers.*

bordello = brothel, whorehouse, red-light district, cathouse *(U.S. slang)*, house of ill repute, knocking shop *(slang)*, bawdy house *(archaic)*, house of prostitution, bagnio, house of ill fame, stews *(archaic)* • *the last bordello on the street*

border **as a noun 1 = frontier**, line, marches, limit, bounds, boundary, perimeter, borderline, borderland • *Clifford is enjoying life north of the border.*
2 = edge, lip, margin, skirt, verge, rim, hem, brim, flange • *pillowcases trimmed with a hand-crocheted border*
3 = flower bed, area, garden, bed, row, strip, plot, patch • *a lawn flanked by wide herbaceous borders*

▸ **AS A VERB** 1 = **adjoin**, be situated alongside, join, touch, be attached to, be connected to, abut • *the European and Arab countries bordering the Mediterranean*
2 = **edge**, bound, decorate, trim, fringe, rim, hem • *white sand bordered by palm trees and tropical flowers*
▸ **IN PHRASES: border on something = come close to**, approach, be like, resemble, be similar to, approximate, come near • *The atmosphere borders on the surreal.*

borderline **AS A NOUN** = **dividing line**, divide, boundary, cut-off point, line of demarcation • *the borderline between painting and photography*
▸ **AS AN ADJECTIVE** = **marginal**, bordering, doubtful, peripheral, indefinite, indeterminate, equivocal, inexact, unclassifiable • *someone who is a borderline case*

bore[1] **AS A VERB** = **drill**, mine, sink, tunnel, pierce, penetrate, burrow, puncture, perforate, gouge out • *Get the special drill bit to bore the correct-size hole.*
▸ **AS A NOUN** = **hole**, tunnel, shaft, borehole, drill hole • *Water is pumped out to reduce pressure around the well bore.*

bore[2] **AS A VERB** = **tire**, exhaust, annoy, fatigue, weary, wear out, jade, wear down, be tedious, pall on, send to sleep • *Dickie bored him all through the meal with stories of the Navy.*
OPPOSITES: interest, excite, fascinate
▸ **AS A NOUN** = **nuisance**, pain *(informal)*, drag *(informal)*, headache *(informal)*, yawn *(informal)*, anorak *(informal)*, pain in the neck *(informal)*, dullard, pain in the arse *(taboo slang)*, dull person, tiresome person, wearisome talker • *He's a bore and a fool.*

QUOTATIONS

Bore: a person who talks when you wish him to listen
[Ambrose Bierce *The Devil's Dictionary*]

The way to be a bore is to say everything
[Voltaire *Sept Discours en vers sur l'Homme*]

A bore is a man who, when you ask him how he is, tells you
[Bert Leston Taylor *The So-Called Human Race*]

A healthy male adult bore consumes each year one and a half times his own weight in other people's patience
[John Updike *Confessions of a Wild Bore*]

Some people can stay longer in an hour than others can in a week
[W.D. Howells]

bored = **fed up**, tired, hacked (off) *(U.S. slang)*, wearied, weary, pissed off *(taboo slang)*, uninterested, sick and tired *(informal)*, listless, browned-off *(informal)*, brassed off *(Brit. slang)*, ennuied, hoha *(N.Z.)* • *I am getting very bored with this entire business.*

boredom = **tedium**, apathy, doldrums, weariness, monotony, dullness, sameness, ennui, flatness, world-weariness, tediousness, irksomeness • *He had given up attending lectures out of sheer boredom.*
OPPOSITES: interest, entertainment, excitement

QUOTATIONS

Boredom: the desire for desires
[Leo Tolstoy *Anna Karenina*]

Boredom is a sign of satisfied ignorance, blunted apprehension, crass sympathies, dull understanding, feeble powers of attention and irreclaimable weakness of character
[James Bridie *Mr. Bolfry*]

One can be bored until boredom becomes the most sublime of all emotions
[Logan Pearsall Smith *Afterthoughts*]

Boredom is...a vital problem for the moralist, since half the sins of mankind are caused by the fear of it
[Bertrand Russell *The Conquest of Happiness*]

boring = **uninteresting**, dull, tedious, dreary, stale, tiresome, monotonous, old, dead, flat, dry, routine, uninspiring, humdrum, insipid, mind-numbing, unexciting, ho-hum *(informal)*, repetitious, wearisome, unvaried, as dry as dust • *boring television programmes*

born = **brought into this world**, delivered • *She was born in London on April 29, 1923.*

borough = **district**, area, community, quarter, region, sector, ward, parish, neighbourhood, locality, locale • *the New York City borough of Brooklyn*

borrow 1 = **take on loan**, touch (someone) for *(slang)*, scrounge *(informal)*, blag *(slang)*, mooch *(slang)*, cadge, use temporarily, take and return • *Can I borrow a pen please?*
OPPOSITES: give, return, lend
2 = **steal**, take, use, copy, adopt, appropriate, acquire, pinch *(informal)*, pirate, poach, pilfer, filch, plagiarize • *I borrowed his words for my book's title.*

QUOTATIONS

Neither a borrower nor a lender be
[William Shakespeare *Hamlet*]

bosom **AS A NOUN** 1 = **breast**, chest, front, bust, boobs *(slang)*, tits *(slang)*, teats, thorax, boobies *(slang)*, titties *(slang)* • *On my bosom laid her weeping head.*
2 = **midst**, centre, heart, safety, protection, circle, shelter, refuge • *He went back to the snug bosom of his family.*
3 = **heart**, feelings, spirit, soul, emotions, sympathies, sentiments, affections • *Something gentle seemed to move in her bosom.*
▸ **AS AN ADJECTIVE** = **intimate**, close, warm, dear, friendly, confidential, cherished, boon, very dear • *They were bosom friends.*

boss **AS A NOUN** = **manager**, head, leader, director, chief, executive, owner, master, governor *(informal)*, employer, administrator, supervisor, superintendent, gaffer *(informal, chiefly Brit.)*, foreman, overseer, kingpin, big cheese *(old-fashioned slang)*, baas *(S. African)*, numero uno *(informal)*, Mister Big *(slang, chiefly U.S.)*, sherang *(Austral. & N.Z.)* • *He cannot stand his boss.*
▸ **IN PHRASES: boss someone around = order around**, dominate, bully, intimidate, oppress, dictate to, terrorize, put upon, push around *(slang)*, browbeat, ride roughshod over, lord it over, tyrannize, rule with an iron hand • *He started bossing people around and I didn't like it.*

bossy = **domineering**, lordly, arrogant, authoritarian, oppressive, hectoring, autocratic, dictatorial, coercive, imperious, overbearing, tyrannical, despotic, high-handed • *She remembers being a rather bossy little girl.*

botany
▹ *See panel* **Botany**

botch **AS A VERB** = **spoil**, mar, bungle, fumble, screw up *(informal)*, mess up, cock up *(Brit. slang)*, balls up *(taboo slang)*, fuck up *(offensive taboo slang)*, mismanage, muff, make a nonsense of *(informal)*, bodge *(informal)*, make a pig's ear of *(informal)*, flub *(U.S. slang)*, crool *or* cruel *(Austral. slang)* • *It's a silly idea, and he has botched it.*
▸ **AS A NOUN** = **mess**, failure, blunder, miscarriage, bungle, bungling, fumble, hash, cock-up *(Brit. slang)*, balls-up *(taboo slang)*, fuck-up *(offensive taboo slang)*, pig's ear *(informal)*, pig's breakfast *(informal)* • *I rather made a botch of that whole thing.*

bother **AS A VERB** 1 = **concern yourself**, take the time, make the effort, go to the trouble, trouble yourself, burden yourself, inconvenience yourself • *Most of the papers didn't even bother reporting it.*
2 = **trouble**, concern, worry, upset, alarm, disturb, distress, annoy, dismay, gall, disconcert, vex, perturb, faze, put *or* get someone's back up • *That kind of jealousy doesn't bother me.*
3 = **pester**, plague, irritate, put out, harass, nag, hassle *(informal)*, inconvenience, molest, breathe down someone's neck, get on your nerves *(informal)*, nark *(Brit., Austral. & N.Z. slang)*, bend someone's ear *(informal)*, give someone grief *(Brit. & S. African)*, get on your wick *(Brit. slang)* • *I don't know why he bothers me with this kind of rubbish.*

b

b

BOTANY

Branches of botany

agrostology, algology, archaeobotany *or* archeobotany, astrobotany, bryology, carpology, dendrology, ethnobotany, floristics, mycology, palaeobotany, palaeoethnobotany, phytogenesis, phytogeography, phytography, phytopathology, pteridology

Botany terms

abscission, androecium, androgynous, anther, archegonium, auxin, axil, axis, berry, bulb, calyx, cambium, carpel, chlorophyll, chloroplast, corm, corolla, corona, cortex, cotyledon, cross-pollination, cuticle, dicotyledon, epidermis, filament, flower, foliation, fruit, geotropism, germination, guard cell, gynaecium, hilum, hydrotropism, inflorescence, insect pollination, integument, key, lamina, leaf, legume, lenticel, meristem, mesophyll, micropyle, monocotyledon, nastic movement, nut, operculum, ovary, ovule, palisade mesophyll, phloem, photosynthesis, phototropism, pistil, pith, plumule, pollen, pollination, raceme, radicle, receptacle, rhizome, root, root cap, root hair, root nodule, rosette, runner, sap, seed, seed capsule *or* seedcase, seed pod, seed vessel, self-pollination, sepal, shoot, spadix, spongy mesophyll, sporangium, spore, stamen, stem, stigma, stolon, stoma, style, testa, translocation, transpiration, tropism, tuber, vascular bundle, vegetative reproduction, wind pollination, xylem

Botanists

Joseph Banks *(English)*
David (James) Bellamy *(English)*
Robert Brown *(Scottish)*
Auguste Pyrame de Candolle *(Swiss)*
George Washington Carver *(U.S.)*
Charles Robert Darwin *(English)*
Hugo De Vries *(Dutch)*
August Wilhelm Eichler *(German)*
Joseph Dalton Hooker *(English)*
William Jackson Hooker *(English)*
Linnaeus (Carl von Linné) *(Swedish)*
Gregor Johann Mendel *(Austrian)*
John Ray *(English)*
John Tradescant *(English)*

OPPOSITES: help, support, further
▸ AS A NOUN **= trouble**, problem, worry, difficulty, strain, grief *(Brit. & S. African)*, fuss, pest, irritation, hassle *(informal)*, nuisance, flurry, uphill *(S. African)*, inconvenience, annoyance, aggravation, vexation • *Most men hate the bother of shaving.*
OPPOSITES: use, help, service

bothersome = troublesome, trying, demanding, difficult, distressing, annoying, irritating, aggravating, galling, exasperating, tiresome, inconvenient, vexing, irksome, vexatious • *It's all been very noisy and bothersome in Parliament this week.*
OPPOSITES: useful, helpful, convenient

bottle AS A NOUN **1 = flask**, pitcher, decanter, carafe, glass container, flagon, demijohn • *He was pulling the cork from a bottle of wine.*
2 = nerve, will, daring, courage, determination, guts *(informal)*, face *(informal)*, balls *(taboo slang)*, spirit, resolution, pluck, grit, bravery, fortitude, coolness, mettle, firmness, spunk *(informal)*, fearlessness, steadfastness, intrepidity, hardihood, gameness, ballsiness *(taboo slang)* • *Will anyone have the bottle to go through with it?*
▸ IN PHRASES: **bottle out = get cold feet**, give up, withdraw, back out, cop out *(slang)*, chicken out *(informal)* • *I haven't come all this way to bottle out.*
bottle something up = suppress, check, contain, conceal, curb, restrain, cover up, withhold, stifle, repress, smother, keep secret, shut in, keep back, sweep under the carpet *(informal)*, hold in check, hold in *or* back • *Tension in the home increases if you bottle things up.*
hit the bottle = start drinking, take to drink, go on a bender *(informal)*, drown your sorrows, fall off the bandwagon • *After my mother died my father hit the bottle.*

BOTTLES

ampulla, carboy, caster, decanter, demijohn, feeding bottle, flacon, flagon, flask, gourd, half-jack, hot-water bottle, lagena, miniature, Nansen bottle, phial, pycnometer, screw top, soda siphon, stubby, vinaigrette, water bottle, Woulfe bottle

bottleneck = block, hold-up, obstacle, congestion, obstruction, impediment, blockage, snarl-up *(informal, chiefly Brit.)*, (traffic) jam • *a town-centre bottleneck*

bottle shop = off-licence *(Brit.)*, liquor store *(U.S. & Canad.)*, bottle store *(S. African)*, package store *(U.S. & Canad.)*, offie *or* offy *(Brit. informal)* • *This place has a better-than-average range of wines for a suburban bottle shop.*

bottle store = off-licence *(Brit.)*, liquor store *(U.S. & Canad.)*, bottle shop *(Austral. & N.Z.)*, package store *(U.S. & Canad.)*, offie *or* offy *(Brit. informal)* • *He went into a bottle store to buy some whisky.*

bottom AS A NOUN **1 = lowest part**, base, foot, bed, floor, basis, foundation, depths, support, pedestal, deepest part

• *He sat at the bottom of the stairs.*
OPPOSITES: top, cover, surface
2 = **underside**, sole, underneath, lower side • *the bottom of their shoes*
3 = **end**, far end, furthest point, furthest part • *The cathedral is at the bottom of the street.*
4 = **lowest level**, lowest position, least successful part • *a contract researcher at the bottom of the pay scale*
5 = **buttocks**, behind *(informal)*, rear, butt *(U.S. & Canad. informal)*, bum *(Brit. slang)*, ass *(U.S. & Canad. taboo slang)*, buns *(U.S. slang)*, arse *(taboo slang)*, backside, rump, seat, tail *(informal)*, rear end, posterior, derrière *(euphemistic)*, tush *(U.S. slang)*, fundament, jacksy *(Brit. slang)* • *She moved her large bottom on the window-seat.*
6 = **basis**, base, cause, ground, heart, source, principle, root, origin, core, substance, essence, provenance, derivation, mainspring • *I have to get to the bottom of this mess.*
▸ AS AN ADJECTIVE = **lowest**, last, base, ground, basement, undermost • *the bottom drawer of the cupboard*
OPPOSITES: higher, highest, top

bottomless 1 = **unlimited**, endless, infinite, limitless, boundless, inexhaustible, immeasurable, unbounded, illimitable • *She does not have a bottomless purse.*
2 = **deep**, profound, yawning, boundless, unfathomable, immeasurable, fathomless, abyssal • *His eyes were like bottomless brown pools.*

boulder = **rock**, stone • *I felt myself smash against a boulder.*

boulevard = **avenue**, street, route, way, lane, highway, motorway, roadway, thoroughfare • *The boulevard is lined by parking spaces.*

bounce AS A VERB 1 = **rebound**, return, thump, recoil, ricochet, spring back, resile • *The ball bounced past the right-hand post.*
2 = **bound**, spring, jump, leap, skip, caper, prance, gambol, jounce • *Moira bounced into the office.*
3 = **force**, drive, railroad *(informal)*, coerce, strong-arm *(informal)*, dragoon, press-gang • *The aim of the exercise is to bounce him into a coalition government.*
4 = **throw out**, fire *(informal)*, turn out, expel, oust, relegate, kick out *(informal)*, drive out, eject, evict, boot out *(informal)*, show someone the door, give someone the bum's rush *(slang)*, throw out on your ear *(informal)* • *He was bounced from two programmes for unbecoming conduct.*
▸ AS A NOUN 1 = **springiness**, give, spring, bound, rebound, resilience, elasticity, recoil • *the pace and steep bounce of the pitch*
2 = **life**, go *(informal)*, energy, pep, sparkle, zip *(informal)*, vitality, animation, vigour, exuberance, dynamism, brio, vivacity, liveliness, vim *(slang)*, lustiness, vivaciousness • *the natural bounce of youth*
▸ IN PHRASES: **bounce back** = **recover**, pick up, rally, take heart, be heartened, pull through, take a turn for the better, get back on your feet • *He is young enough to bounce back.*

bouncing = **lively**, healthy, thriving, blooming, robust, vigorous, energetic, perky, sprightly, alive and kicking, fighting fit, full of beans *(informal)*, fit as a fiddle *(informal)*, bright-eyed and bushy-tailed • *They are bouncing with good health in the summer.*

bouncy 1 = **lively**, active, enthusiastic, energetic, bubbly, exuberant, irrepressible, ebullient, perky, chirpy *(informal)*, sprightly, vivacious, effervescent, chipper *(informal)*, full of beans *(informal)*, zestful, full of pep *(informal)*, bright-eyed and bushy-tailed • *She was bouncy and full of energy.*
OPPOSITES: dull, listless, unenthusiastic
2 = **springy**, flexible, elastic, resilient, rubbery, spongy • *a bouncy chair*
OPPOSITES: flat, inelastic

bound[1] AS AN ADJECTIVE 1 = **compelled**, obliged, forced, committed, pledged, constrained, obligated, beholden, duty-bound • *All members are bound by an oath of secrecy.*
2 = **tied**, fixed, secured, attached, lashed, tied up, fastened, trussed, pinioned, made fast • *Her arms were bound to her sides.*
3 = **certain**, sure, fated, doomed, destined, very likely • *There are bound to be price increases next year.*
▸ IN PHRASES: **bound up with** = **connected with**, linked to, attached to, dependent on, united with, tied up with, reliant on • *My fate was bound up with hers.*

bound[2] AS A VERB = **leap**, bob, spring, jump, bounce, skip, vault, pounce • *He bounded up the steps and pushed the bell of the door.*
▸ AS A NOUN = **leap**, bob, spring, jump, bounce, hurdle, skip, vault, pounce, caper, prance, lope, frisk, gambol • *With one bound Jack was free.*

bound[3] 1 = **surround**, confine, enclose, terminate, encircle, circumscribe, hem in, demarcate, delimit • *the trees that bounded the car park*
2 = **limit**, fix, define, restrict, confine, restrain, circumscribe, demarcate, delimit • *Our lives are bounded by work, family and television.*

bound[4] *with* **for** = **going to**, travelling to, flying to, on its way to, sailing to • *The ship was bound for Italy.*

boundary 1 = **frontier**, edge, border, march, barrier, margin, brink • *Drug traffickers operate across national boundaries.*
2 = **edges**, limits, bounds, margins, pale, confines, fringes, verges, precinct, perimeter, extremities, outer limits • *the western boundary of the wood*
3 = **limits**, bounds, confines, threshold, parameters, outer limits • *extending the boundaries of press freedom*
4 = **dividing line**, threshold, borderline, cut-off point, line of demarcation • *the boundary between childhood and adulthood.*

boundless = **unlimited**, vast, endless, immense, infinite, untold, limitless, unending, inexhaustible, incalculable, immeasurable, unbounded, unconfined, measureless, illimitable • *His zeal for reform was boundless.*
OPPOSITES: limited, bounded, restricted

bounds AS A PLURAL NOUN 1 = **limits**, restrictions, confines, limitations • *the bounds of good taste*
2 = **boundary**, line, limit, edge, border, march, margin, pale, confine, frontier, fringe, verge, rim, perimeter, periphery • *The bounds of the empire continued to expand.*
▸ IN PHRASES: **out of bounds** = **forbidden**, barred, banned, not allowed, vetoed, prohibited, taboo, closed off, off-limits *(chiefly U.S. Military)*, proscribed, verboten *(German)* • *Tibet was now virtually out of bounds to foreign journalists.*

bountiful 1 = **plentiful**, generous, lavish, ample, prolific, abundant, exuberant, copious, luxuriant, bounteous, plenteous • *The land is bountiful and no one starves.*
2 = **generous**, kind, princely, liberal, charitable, hospitable, prodigal, open-handed, unstinting, beneficent, bounteous, munificent, ungrudging • *Their bountiful host was bringing brandy, whisky and liqueurs.*

bounty 1 = **generosity**, charity, assistance, kindness, philanthropy, benevolence, beneficence, liberality, almsgiving, open-handedness, largesse *or* largess • *The aid organization would not allow such bounty.*
2 = **abundance**, plenty, exuberance, profusion, affluence, plenitude, copiousness, plenteousness • *autumn's bounty of fruits, seeds and berries*
3 = **reward**, present, grant, prize, payment, gift, compensation, bonus, premium, donation, recompense, gratuity, meed *(archaic)*, largesse *or* largess, koha *(N.Z.)* • *They paid bounties for people to give up their weapons.*

bouquet 1 = **bunch of flowers**, spray, garland, wreath, posy, buttonhole, corsage, nosegay, boutonniere • *a bouquet of dried violets*
2 = **aroma**, smell, scent, perfume, fragrance, savour, odour, redolence • *a Sicilian wine with a light red colour and a bouquet of cloves*

bourgeois = **middle-class**, conservative, traditional, conventional, provincial, suburban, small-town, materialistic, conformist, property-owning, hidebound, Pooterish • *the bourgeois ideology of individualism*

QUOTATIONS

The bourgeois treasures nothing more highly than the self

[Hermann Hesse *Steppenwolf*]

Destroy him as you will, the bourgeois always bounces up – execute him, expropriate him, starve him out en masse, and he reappears in your children

[Cyril Connolly]

How beastly the bourgeois is
Especially the male of the species

[D.H. Lawrence *How Beastly the Bourgeois Is*]

bout 1 = **period**, time, term, fit, session, stretch, spell, turn, patch, interval, stint • *I was suffering with a bout of nerves.*
2 = **round**, run, course, series, session, cycle, sequence, stint, spree • *The latest bout of violence has claimed ten lives.*
3 = **fight**, match, battle, competition, struggle, contest, set-to, encounter, engagement, head-to-head, boxing match • *This will be his eighth title bout in 19 months.*

bovine 1 = **cow-like**, taurine, calf-like, cattle-like • *an expression half bovine and half sheep-like*
2 = **dull**, heavy, slow, thick, stupid, dull, dense, sluggish, lifeless, inactive, inert, lethargic, dozy (*Brit. informal*), listless, unresponsive, stolid, torpid, slothful • *I'm depressed by the bovine enthusiasm of the crowd's response.*

bow[1] AS A VERB = **bend**, bob, nod, incline, stoop, droop, genuflect, make obeisance • *He bowed slightly before taking her bag.*
▸ AS A NOUN = **bending**, bob, nod, inclination, salaam, obeisance, kowtow, genuflection • *I gave a theatrical bow and waved.*
▸ IN PHRASES: **bow down to someone** = **grovel to**, suck up to (*slang*), fawn on, cringe to, court, toady to • *We should not have to bow down to anyone.*
bow out = **give up**, retire, withdraw, get out, resign, quit, pull out, step down (*informal*), back out, throw in the towel, cop out (*slang*), throw in the sponge, call it a day *or* night • *He bowed out gracefully when his successor was appointed.*
bow to something *or* **someone** = **give in to**, accept, comply with, succumb to, submit to, surrender to, yield to, defer to, concede to, acquiesce to, kowtow to • *She is having to bow to their terms.*

bow[2] 1 = **knot**, tie, lace, loop, ribbon, braid, rosette, ligature • *Add a length of ribbon tied in a bow.*
2 = **longbow**, crossbow • *Some of the raiders were armed with bows and arrows.*

bow[3] = **prow**, head, stem, fore, beak • *spray from the ship's bow*

bowdlerize = **censor**, cut, clean up, blue-pencil, expurgate, sanitize • *She had ceased to bowdlerize her storytelling.*

bowed = **bent**, lowered, angled, curved, arched, inclined, crooked, hunched, stooped, procumbent • *He walked aimlessly, head down and shoulders bowed.*
OPPOSITES: erect, upright, straight-backed

bowels 1 = **guts**, insides (*informal*), intestines, innards (*informal*), entrails, viscera, vitals • *Snatched sandwiches and junk food had cemented his bowels.*
2 = **depths**, hold, middle, inside, deep, interior, core, belly, midst, remotest part, deepest part, furthest part, innermost part • *deep in the bowels of the earth*

bower = **arbour**, grotto, alcove, summerhouse, shady recess, leafy shelter • *a private bower of ivy and honeysuckle*

bowl[1] 1 = **basin**, plate, dish, vessel, container, mixing bowl, receptacle • *Put all the ingredients into a large bowl.*
2 = **stadium**, park (*U.S. & Canad.*), ground, stage, field, ring, enclosure, coliseum, amphitheatre • *the Crystal Palace Bowl*

bowl[2] AS A VERB 1 = **throw**, hurl, launch, cast, pitch, toss, fling, chuck (*informal*), lob (*informal*) • *He bowled each ball so well that we won two matches.*
2 *often with* **along** = **drive**, travel, shoot, speed, tear, motor, proceed, barrel (along) (*informal, chiefly U.S. & Canad.*), trundle • *It felt just like old times, to bowl down to Knightsbridge.*
▸ IN PHRASES: **bowl someone over** 1 = **knock down**, fell, floor, deck (*slang*), overturn, overthrow, bring down • *People clung to trees as the flash flood bowled them over.*
2 = **surprise**, amaze, stun, overwhelm, astonish, stagger, startle, astound, take (someone) aback, stupefy, strike (someone) dumb, throw off balance, sweep off your feet, dumbfound • *I was bowled over by India.*

box[1] AS A NOUN = **container**, case, chest, trunk, pack, package, carton, casket, receptacle, ark (*dialect*), portmanteau, coffret, kist (*Scot. & Northern English dialect*) • *They sat on wooden boxes.*
▸ AS A VERB = **pack**, package, wrap, encase, bundle up • *He boxed the test pieces and shipped them back to Berlin.*
▸ IN PHRASES: **box something** *or* **someone in** = **confine**, contain, surround, trap, restrict, isolate, cage, enclose, restrain, imprison, shut up, incarcerate, hem in, shut in, coop up • *He was boxed in with 300 metres to go.*
the box = **television**, TV, telly (*Brit. informal*), the tube (*slang*), TV set, small screen (*informal*), gogglebox (*Brit. slang*), idiot box (*slang*) • *Did you actually go to the match or did you watch it on the box?*
▹ *See panel* **Boxes**

box[2] AS A VERB 1 = **fight**, spar, exchange blows, prizefight • *At school I boxed and played rugby.*
2 = **punch**, hit, strike, belt (*informal*), deck (*slang*), slap, sock (*slang*), buffet, clout (*informal*), cuff, whack (*informal*), wallop (*informal*), chin (*slang*), tonk (*informal*), thwack (*informal*), lay one on (*slang*) • *They slapped my face and boxed my ears.*
▸ AS A NOUN = **punch**, blow, stroke, belt (*informal*), slap, thumping, buffet, clout (*informal*), cuff, wallop (*informal*) • *His mother dealt him a violent box on the ears.*

boxer = **fighter**, pugilist, prizefighter, sparrer • *At school he had wanted to be a boxer.*

boxing = **prizefighting**, the ring, sparring, fisticuffs, the fight game (*informal*), pugilism • *I don't think boxing's better than it was in my day.*
▹ *See panel* **Boxing weights**

BOXES

ballot box	chest	ditty box	matchbox	poor box	trunk
bandbox	coffer	glory box	music box	saggar	vanity box
bulla	coffin	glove box	nest box	saltbox	window box
caisson	coin box	grass box	pouncet box	sandbox	wine box
carton	cracket	hatbox	packing case	soapbox	
cartouche	deed box	haybox	paintbox	solander	
case	desiccator	honesty box	papeterie	strongbox	
casket	dispatch box	keister	pillbox	tinderbox	

b

BOXING WEIGHTS

Weight	Amateur	Professional
Light flyweight	48 kg	49 kg
Flyweight	51 kg	51 kg
Bantamweight	54 kg	53.5 kg
Featherweight	57 kg	57 kg
Junior lightweight	–	59 kg
Lightweight	60 kg	61 kg
Light welterweight	63.5 kg	63.5 kg
Welterweight	67 kg	66.6 kg
Light middleweight	71 kg	70 kg
Middleweight	75 kg	72.5 kg
Light heavyweight	81 kg	79 kg
Cruiserweight	–	88.5 kg
Heavyweight	91 kg	+88.5 kg
Superheavyweight	+91 kg	–

boy = **lad**, kid *(informal)*, youth, fellow, youngster, chap *(informal)*, schoolboy, junior, laddie *(Scot.)*, stripling • *I knew him when he was just a little boy.*

PROVERBS

Never send a boy to do a man's job

Boys will be boys

boycott AS A VERB = **embargo**, reject, snub, refrain from, stay away from, spurn, steer clear of, blacklist, black, cold-shoulder, ostracize, refuse to take part in, turn your back on, blackball • *The main opposition parties are boycotting the elections.*
OPPOSITES: back, support, accept
▸ AS A NOUN = **embargo** • *the lifting of the economic boycott*

boyfriend = **sweetheart**, man, lover, young man, steady, beloved, valentine, admirer, suitor, beau, date, swain, toy boy, truelove, leman *(archaic)*, inamorato • *I don't know if she's got a boyfriend or not.*

boyish = **youthful**, young, innocent, adolescent, juvenile, childish, immature, green, childlike • *He has a boyish enthusiasm for life.*

brace AS A VERB 1 = **steady**, support, balance, secure, stabilize • *He braced his back against the wall.*
2 = **support**, strengthen, steady, prop, reinforce, hold up, tighten, shove, bolster, fortify, buttress, shove up • *The lights showed the old timbers, used to brace the roof.*
▸ AS A NOUN 1 = **pair**, couple, twosome • *a brace of grouse*
2 = **support**, stay, prop, bracer, bolster, bracket, reinforcement, strut, truss, buttress, stanchion • *She wears a neck brace.*
▸ IN PHRASES: **brace yourself** = **prepare (yourself)**, get ready, make (yourself) ready, steel yourself, fortify yourself, gear yourself up, gird your loins • *He braced himself for the icy plunge into the black water.*

bracelet = **bangle**, band, armlet, wristlet • *I put on the gold bracelet they had given me.*
▸ RELATED ADJECTIVE: armillary

bracing = **refreshing**, fresh, cool, stimulating, reviving, lively, crisp, vigorous, rousing, brisk, uplifting, exhilarating, fortifying, chilly, rejuvenating, invigorating, energizing, healthful, restorative, tonic, rejuvenative • *a bracing walk*
OPPOSITES: taxing, tiring, draining

bracket AS A NOUN 1 = **grouping**, limits, group, list, range, category, scope, span, sphere, classification, parameters • *Do you fall outside the age bracket?*
2 = **support**, stay, post, prop, brace, underpinning, stanchion, abutment • *adjustable wall brackets*
▸ AS A VERB = **group**, rank, arrange, grade, catalogue, classify, categorize, pigeonhole, systematize • *Austrian wines are often bracketed with those of northern Germany.*

brackish = **salty**, salt, bitter, saline, briny, undrinkable, brak *(S. African)* • *shallow pools of brackish water*
OPPOSITES: clear, clean, fresh

brag = **boast**, crow, swagger, vaunt, bluster, talk big *(slang)*, blow your own trumpet, blow your own horn *(U.S. & Canad.)* • *He'll probably go around bragging to his friends.*

braggart = **boaster**, show-off *(informal)*, bluffer, swaggerer, brag, blusterer, swashbuckler, braggadocio, hot dog *(chiefly U.S.)*, bigmouth *(slang)*, bragger, skite *or* skiter *(Austral. & N.Z. informal)*, figjam *(Austral. slang)* • *a swaggering jovial prankster and braggart*

braid AS A NOUN = **binding**, cording, cord, ribbon, yarn, twine, rickrack • *a plum-coloured uniform with lots of gold braid*
▸ AS A VERB = **interweave**, weave, lace, intertwine, plait, entwine, twine, ravel, interlace • *She had almost finished braiding Louisa's hair.*

brain AS A NOUN 1 = **cerebrum**, mind, grey matter *(informal)* • *The eye grows independently of the brain.*
2 = **intellectual**, genius, scholar, sage, pundit, thinker, mastermind, intellect, prodigy, highbrow, rocket scientist *(informal, chiefly U.S.)*, egghead *(informal)*, brainbox, clever clogs, bluestocking *(usually disparaging)* • *I've never been much of a brain myself.*
▸ AS A PLURAL NOUN = **intelligence**, mind, reason, understanding, sense, capacity, smarts *(slang, chiefly U.S.)*, wit, common sense, intellect, savvy *(slang)*, nous *(Brit. slang)*, suss *(slang)*, shrewdness, sagacity • *They were not the only ones to have brains and ambition.*
▸ AS A VERB = **hit**, strike, smash, belt *(informal)*, sock *(slang)*, clout *(informal)*, slug, swipe *(informal)*, wallop *(informal)* • *He had threatened to brain him then and there.*
▸ TECHNICAL NAME: encephalon
▸ RELATED ADJECTIVES: encephalic, cerebral

QUOTATIONS

I was taught that the human brain was the crowning glory of evolution so far, but I think it's a very poor scheme for survival

[Kurt Vonnegut]

▹ *See panel* **Parts of the brain**

brainless = **stupid**, simple, slow, thick, dull, foolish, dim, dense, dumb *(informal)*, sluggish, senseless, mindless, idiotic, simple-minded, dozy *(Brit. informal)*, inane, witless, dopey *(informal)*, moronic, cretinous, unintelligent, half-witted, braindead *(informal)*, dumb-ass *(slang)*, doltish, dead from the neck up *(informal)*, thickheaded, slow-witted • *I got treated as if I was a bit brainless.*

PARTS OF THE BRAIN

amygdala
brainstem
Broca's area
central sulcus
cerebellum
cerebral aqueduct
cerebral cortex
or (nontechnical) grey matter
cerebrospinal fluid
cerebrum
choroid plexus
corpus callosum
diencephalon
fourth ventricle
frontal lobe
hippocampus
hypothalamus
infundibulum
limbic system
mamillary body
medulla oblongata
meninges
midbrain
myelencephalon *or (nontechnical)* afterbrain
occipital lobe
optic chiasma
parietal lobe
pineal body
pituitary gland
pons Varolli
substantia alba *or (nontechnical)* white matter
temporal lobe
thalamus
third ventricle
vermis
Wernicke's area

brainpower = **intelligence**, understanding, brains (*informal*), perception, IQ, brilliance, intellect, aptitude, cleverness, mental acuity, braininess • *Ginseng boosts your brainpower and makes you feel good.*

brainwash = **indoctrinate**, condition, drill, pressurize, re-educate • *We were brainwashed to believe we were all equal.*

brainwashing = **indoctrination**, conditioning, persuasion, re-education • *Hypnotherapy can involve brainwashing or manipulation.*

b

brainwave = **idea**, thought, wheeze, bright idea, stroke of genius • *In 1980 she had a brainwave that changed her life.*

brainy = **intelligent**, quick, bright, sharp, brilliant, acute, smart, alert, clever, rational, knowing, quick-witted • *I don't class myself as being very intelligent or brainy.*

brake AS A NOUN = **control**, check, curb, restraint, constraint, rein, damper • *Illness had put a brake on his progress.*
▸ AS A VERB = **slow**, decelerate, reduce speed • *She braked to a halt and switched off.*

bran
▸ RELATED ADJECTIVE: furfuraceous

branch AS A NOUN 1 = **bough**, shoot, arm, spray, limb, sprig, offshoot, prong, ramification • *the low, overhanging branches of a giant pine tree*
2 = **office**, department, unit, wing, chapter, bureau, local office • *The local branch is handling the accounts.*
3 = **division**, part, section, subdivision, subsection • *He had a fascination for submarines and joined this branch of the service.*
4 = **discipline**, field, section, sphere, subdivision • *an experimental branch of naturopathic medicine*
▸ IN PHRASES: **branch off** = **turn off**, deviate, change direction, leave the road, take a side road, take another road, quit the road, depart from the road • *She branched off down the earth track.*
branch out = **expand**, diversify • *I continued studying moths, and branched out to other insects.*

brand AS A NOUN 1 = **trademark**, logo, brand name, marque, tradename, proprietary name • *a supermarket's own brand*
2 = **type**, make, sort, kind, class, quality, variety, species, strain, grade, cast • *the British brand of socialism*
3 = **label**, mark, sign, stamp, symbol, logo, trademark, marker, hallmark, emblem, identification marker • *The brand on the barrel stood for Elbert Anderson and Uncle Sam.*
4 = **stigma**, mark, stain, disgrace, taint, slur, blot, infamy, smirch • *the brand of shame*
▸ AS A VERB 1 = **stigmatize**, mark, label, expose, denounce, disgrace, discredit, censure, pillory, defame • *I was instantly branded as a rebel.*
2 = **mark**, burn, label, stamp, scar • *The owner couldn't be bothered to brand the cattle.*
3 = **imprint**, fix permanently, print, stamp, engrave • *That smile of his is branded on my heart.*

brandish = **wave**, raise, display, shake, swing, exhibit, flourish, wield, flaunt • *He appeared in the lounge brandishing a knife.*

brash = **bold**, forward, rude, arrogant, cocky, pushy (*informal*), brazen, presumptuous, impertinent, insolent, impudent, bumptious, cocksure, overconfident, hubristic, full of yourself • *On stage she seems hard, brash and uncompromising.*
OPPOSITES: reserved, careful, timid

brass (*Informal*) = **nerve**, face (*informal*), front, neck (*informal*), cheek, gall, presumption, audacity, rudeness, chutzpah (*U.S. & Canad. informal*), insolence, impertinence, impudence, effrontery, brass neck (*Brit. informal*), sassiness (*U.S. informal*) • *You have got some brass, mate!*

brassy 1 = **strident**, loud, harsh, piercing, jarring, noisy, grating, raucous, blaring, shrill, jangling, dissonant, cacophonous • *Musicians blast their brassy jazz from street corners.*
2 = **brazen**, forward, bold, brash, saucy, pushy (*informal*), pert, insolent, impudent, loud-mouthed, barefaced • *Alec and his brassy blonde wife*
3 = **flashy**, loud, blatant, vulgar, gaudy, garish, jazzy (*informal*), showy, obtrusive • *a woman with big brassy ear-rings*
OPPOSITES: quiet, modest, discreet

brat = **youngster**, kid (*informal*), urchin, imp, rascal, spoilt child, devil, puppy (*informal*), cub, scallywag (*informal*), whippersnapper, guttersnipe • *He's a spoilt brat.*

bravado = **swagger**, boast, boasting, swaggering, vaunting, bluster, swashbuckling, bombast, braggadocio, boastfulness, fanfaronade (*rare*) • *The threats may be an act of bravado.*

brave AS AN ADJECTIVE = **courageous**, daring, bold, heroic, adventurous, gritty, fearless, resolute, gallant, gutsy (*slang*), audacious, intrepid, valiant, plucky, undaunted, unafraid, unflinching, dauntless, ballsy (*taboo slang*), lion-hearted, valorous • *brave people who dare to challenge the tyrannical regimes*
OPPOSITES: afraid, frightened, timid
▸ AS A VERB = **confront**, face, suffer, challenge, bear, tackle, dare, endure, defy, withstand, stand up to • *She had to brave his anger and confess.*
OPPOSITES: give in to, surrender to, retreat from

QUOTATIONS

None but the brave deserves the fair
[John Dryden *Alexander's Feast*]

Fortune assists the bold
[Virgil *Aeneid*]

bravery = **courage**, nerve, daring, pluck, balls (*taboo slang*), spirit, bottle (*Brit. slang*), guts (*informal*), grit, fortitude, heroism, mettle, boldness, bravura, gallantry, valour, spunk (*informal*), hardiness, fearlessness, intrepidity, indomitability, hardihood, ballsiness (*taboo slang*), dauntlessness, doughtiness, pluckiness, lion-heartedness • *He deserves the highest praise for his bravery.*
OPPOSITES: fright, cowardice, timidity

QUOTATIONS

They are surely to be esteemed the bravest spirits who, having the clearest sense of both the pains and pleasures of life, do not on that account shrink from danger
[Thucydides *The Peloponnesian War*]

bravo = **congratulations**, well done, good for you, encore, nice one (*informal*) • *'Bravo! You're right,' the students said.*

bravura AS A NOUN = **brilliance**, energy, spirit, display, punch (*informal*), dash, animation, vigour, verve, panache, boldness, virtuosity, élan, exhibitionism, brio, ostentation • *He launched into the live transmission with operatic bravura.*
▸ AS AN ADJECTIVE = **brilliant**, outstanding, superb, magnificent, glorious, exceptional, splendid, notable • *a bravura performance*

brawl AS A NOUN = **fight**, battle, row (*informal*), clash, disorder, scrap (*informal*), fray, squabble, wrangle, skirmish, scuffle, punch-up (*Brit. informal*), free-for-all (*informal*), fracas, altercation, rumpus, broil, tumult, affray (*Law*), shindig (*informal*), donnybrook, ruckus (*informal*), scrimmage, shindy (*informal*), biffo (*Austral. slang*), bagarre (*French*), melee or mêlée • *He had been in a drunken street brawl.*
▸ AS A VERB = **fight**, battle, scrap (*informal*), wrestle, wrangle, tussle, scuffle, go at it hammer and tongs, fight like Kilkenny cats, altercate • *Gangs of youths brawled in the street*

brawn = **muscle**, might, power, strength, muscles, beef (*informal*), flesh, vigour, robustness, muscularity, beefiness (*informal*), brawniness • *He's got plenty of brains as well as brawn.*

brawny = **muscular**, strong, powerful, athletic, strapping, hardy, robust, vigorous, hefty (*informal*), sturdy, stalwart, bulky, burly, husky (*informal*), fleshy, beefy (*informal*), lusty,

well-built, sinewy, thickset, well-knit, thewy • *Oscar turned out to be a brawny young man.*
OPPOSITES: thin, weak, skinny

bray **AS A VERB** 1 = **neigh**, bellow, screech, whinny, heehaw • *The donkey brayed and tried to bolt.*
2 = **roar**, trumpet, bellow, hoot • *Neil brayed with angry laughter.*
▸ **AS A NOUN** 1 = **neigh**, bellow, screech, whinny, heehaw • *It was a strange laugh, like the bray of a donkey.*
2 = **roar**, cry, shout, bellow, screech, hoot, bawl, harsh sound • *She cut him off with a bray of laughter.*

brazen **AS AN ADJECTIVE** = **bold**, forward, defiant, brash, saucy, audacious, pushy *(informal)*, shameless, unabashed, pert, unashamed, insolent, impudent, immodest, barefaced, brassy *(informal)* • *She's just a brazen hussy.*
OPPOSITES: modest, reserved, shy
▸ **IN PHRASES: brazen it out** = **be unashamed**, persevere, be defiant, put a brave face on it, stand your ground, confront something, be impenitent, outface, outstare • *As for the scandal, he is as determined as ever to brazen it out.*

breach **AS A VERB** 1 = **break**, violate, go against, flout, infringe, contravene, disobey, fly in the face of, transgress, fail to comply with • *The film breached the criminal libel laws.*
2 = **break through**, split, rupture, burst through • *Fire may have breached the cargo tanks and set the oil ablaze.*
▸ **AS A NOUN** 1 = **nonobservance**, abuse, violation, infringement, trespass, disobedience, transgression, contravention, infraction, noncompliance • *The congressman was accused of a breach of secrecy laws.*
OPPOSITES: performance, honouring, compliance
2 = **disagreement**, difference, division, separation, falling-out *(informal)*, quarrel, alienation, variance, severance, disaffection, schism, parting of the ways, estrangement, dissension • *the breach between Tito and Stalin*
3 = **opening**, crack, break, hole, split, gap, rent, rift, rupture, aperture, chasm, cleft, fissure • *A large battering ram hammered a breach in the wall.*

QUOTATIONS
Once more unto the breach, dear friends, once more
[William Shakespeare *Henry V*]

bread 1 = **food**, provisions, fare, necessities, subsistence, kai *(N.Z. informal)*, nourishment, sustenance, victuals, nutriment, viands, aliment • *I go to work, I put bread on the table, I pay the mortgage.*
2 = **money**, funds, cash, finance, necessary *(informal)*, silver, tin *(slang)*, brass *(Northern English dialect)*, dough *(slang)*, dosh *(Brit. & Austral. slang)*, needful *(informal)*, shekels *(informal)*, wonga *(slang)*, dibs *(slang)*, ackers *(slang)*, spondulicks *(slang)*, rhino *(Brit. slang)* • *a period in which you could earn your bread by the sweat of your brow*
▹ *See panel* **Breads**

breadth 1 = **width**, spread, beam, span, latitude, broadness, wideness • *The breadth of the whole camp was 400 metres.*
2 = **extent**, area, reach, range, measure, size, scale, spread, sweep, scope, magnitude, compass, expanse, vastness, amplitude, comprehensiveness, extensiveness • *The breadth of his knowledge filled me with admiration.*

break **AS A VERB** 1 = **shatter**, separate, destroy, split, divide, crack, snap, smash, crush, fragment, demolish, sever, trash *(slang)*, disintegrate, splinter, smash to smithereens, shiver • *He fell through the window, breaking the glass.*
OPPOSITES: unite, join, repair
2 = **fracture**, crack, smash • *She broke her leg in a skiing accident.*
3 = **burst**, tear, split, puncture, perforate • *The bandage must be put on when the blister breaks.*
4 = **stop working**, break down, go wrong, give out, pack up *(Brit. informal)*, have had it, seize up, cease to function, conk out *(informal)*, die, go on the blink, go kaput, go phut • *When the clutch broke, the car was locked into second gear.*
5 = **disobey**, breach, defy, violate, disregard, flout, infringe, contravene, transgress, go counter to, infract *(Law)* • *We didn't know we were breaking the law.*
OPPOSITES: follow, observe, obey
6 = **stop**, cut, check, suspend, interrupt, cut short, discontinue • *He aims to break the vicious cycle.*
7 = **disturb**, cut, interrupt, interfere with • *The noise broke my concentration.*
8 = **end**, stop, cut, drop, give up, abandon, suspend, interrupt, terminate, put an end to, discontinue, bring to an end, pull the plug on, call a halt to • *They have yet to break the link with the trade unions.*
9 = **give up**, stop, kick, abandon, quit, cut out, pack in, leave off, say goodbye to • *If you continue to smoke, keep trying to break the habit.*
10 = **weaken**, undermine, cow, tame, subdue, demoralize, dispirit • *He never let his jailers break him.*
11 = **ruin**, destroy, crush, humiliate, bring down, bankrupt, degrade, impoverish, demote, make bankrupt, bring to ruin • *The newspapers can make or break you.*
12 = **pause**, stop briefly, stop, rest, halt, cease, take a break, have a breather *(informal)* • *They broke for lunch.*
13 = **interrupt**, stop, suspend • *We broke our journey at a small country hotel.*
14 = **cushion**, reduce, ease, moderate, diminish, temper, soften, lessen, alleviate, lighten • *She was saved by bushes which broke her fall.*
15 = **be revealed**, come out, be reported, be published, be announced, be made public, be proclaimed, be let out, be imparted, be divulged, come out in the wash • *He resigned his post as Bishop when the scandal broke.*
16 = **reveal**, tell, announce, declare, disclose, proclaim, divulge, make known • *I worried for ages and decided I had better break the news.*

BREADS

bagel *or* beigel
baguette
bap
barm cake *(dialect)*
barmbrack *(Irish)*
barm cake *(Lancashire)*
batch loaf
billy-bread *(N.Z.)*
black bread
bloomer
bridge roll
brioche
brown bread, loaf, *or* roll
bun
buttery *(Scot.)*
challah *or* hallah
chapati *or* chapatti
ciabatta
cob
coburg
corn bread, corn pone, *or* Indian bread *(U.S.)*
cottage loaf
croissant
damper *(Austral.)*
farmhouse
focaccia
French bread
French stick
fruit loaf
Granary *(trademark)*
gluten bread
griddlebread
half-quartern
johnny cake
long tin
matzo, matzoh, matza, *or* matzah
muffin
naan *or* nan
pan bread *or* loaf *(Scot.)*
paratha
pitta
plain bread *or* loaf *(Scot.)*
plait
poppadom *or* poppadum
pumpernickel
puri
quartern
roll
roti
rye bread *or* rye
schnecken
soda bread
sourdough
split tin
square tin
stollen
tortilla
unleavened bread
wheaten bread
white bread, loaf, *or* roll
wholemeal *or (esp U.S. & Canad.)* whole-wheat

17 = **beat**, top, better, exceed, go beyond, excel, surpass, outstrip, outdo, cap *(informal)* • *The film has broken all box office records.*
18 = **happen**, appear, emerge, occur, erupt, burst out, come into being, come forth suddenly • *They continued their search as dawn broke.*
19 = **pound**, crash, batter, lash, buffet • *He listened to the waves breaking against the shore.*
20 = **decode**, crack, work out, solve, interpret, decipher, unscramble, decrypt, descramble • *It was feared they could break the allies' code.*
21 = **hesitate**, shake, tremble, falter, waver, stammer, stutter, speak haltingly • *Godfrey's voice broke, and halted.*
22 = **change**, shift, alter • *I've been waiting for the weather to break.*
▸ AS A NOUN 1 = **fracture**, opening, tear, hole, split, crack, gap, rent, breach, rift, rupture, gash, cleft, fissure • *a break in the earth's surface*
2 = **let-up**, halt, pause, suspension, lessening, recess, interruption, respite, lull, cessation, remission, breathing space, slackening, hiatus • *Nothing has been discussed that might lead to a break in the deadlock.*
3 = **gap**, opening, space, hole, divide, crack, breach, rift, cleft, chink, crevice, cranny, discontinuity, interstice • *a sudden break in the clouds*
4 = **interval**, pause, recess, interlude, intermission, entr'acte • *They always play that music during the break.*
5 = **holiday**, leave, vacation, time off, recess, awayday, schoolie *(Austral.)*, accumulated day off *or* ADO *(Austral.)* • *They are currently taking a short break in Spain.*
6 = **stroke of luck**, chance, opportunity, advantage, fortune, opening • *The rain was a lucky break for the American.*
7 = **breach**, split, dispute, separation, rift, rupture, alienation, severance, disaffection, schism, estrangement, disunion • *There is some threat of a break in relations between them.*
▸ IN PHRASES: **break away** = **get away**, escape, flee, run away, break free, break loose, make your escape • *I broke away from him and rushed out into the hall.*
break down 1 = **stop working**, stop, give out, pack up *(Brit. informal)*, have had it, seize up, cease to function, conk out *(informal)*, go on the blink, go kaput *(informal)*, go phut, die, cark it *(Austral. & N.Z. slang)* • *Their car broke down.*
2 = **fail**, collapse, fall through, be unsuccessful, come unstuck, run aground, come to grief, come a cropper *(informal)*, turn out badly • *Paola's marriage broke down.*
3 = **be overcome**, lose control, crack up *(informal)*, lose it *(informal)*, go to pieces • *The young woman broke down and cried.*
break free of something *or* **someone** = **escape (from)**, leave, withdraw from, extricate yourself from, free yourself of, disentangle yourself from • *his inability to break free of his marriage*
break in 1 = **break and enter**, burst in, enter, gain access • *The thief had broken in through a first-floor window.*
2 = **interrupt**, intervene, interfere, intrude, burst in, interject, butt in, barge in, interpose, put your oar in, put your two cents in *(U.S. slang)* • *Suddenly, O'Leary broke in with a suggestion.*
break into something 1 = **burgle** • *In this country a house is broken into every 24 seconds.*
2 = **begin**, start, burst into, give way to, commence, launch into, embark upon • *The moment she was out of sight she broke into a run.*
break off = **stop talking**, pause, stumble, falter, fumble, hem and haw *or* hum and haw • *He broke off in mid-sentence.*
break out 1 = **begin**, start, happen, occur, arise, set in, commence, spring up • *He was 29 when war broke out.*
2 = **escape**, flee, bolt, burst out, break free, get free, break loose, abscond, do a bunk *(Brit. slang)*, do a Skase *(Austral. informal)* • *The two men broke out and cut through a perimeter fence.*
3 = **erupt**, gush, flare up, burst out, burst forth, pour forth • *A line of sweat broke out on her forehead.*
break someone in = **initiate**, train, accustom, habituate, show someone the ropes • *The band are breaking in a new backing vocalist.*
break something down 1 = **divide up**, split, cut up, subdivide, separate out • *These rules tell us how a sentence is broken down into phrases.*
2 = **demolish**, knock down, destroy, pull down, tear down, smash in, kick down, smash down • *His father failed to break the door down.*
3 = **remove**, destroy, get rid of, knock down, eradicate, do away with, obliterate, put paid to • *He was able to break down barriers between the two groups.*
break something in = **prepare**, condition, prime, tame • *I'm breaking in these new boots.*
break something off 1 = **detach**, separate, divide, cut off, pull off, sever, part, remove, splinter, tear off, snap off • *He broke off a large piece of the clay.*
2 = **bring to an end**, end, terminate, put an end to, discontinue, pull the plug on, call a halt to • *He doesn't seem to have the courage to break his engagement off.*
3 = **stop**, finish, suspend, halt, pause, cease, terminate, discontinue, pull the plug on, desist, belay *(Nautical)* • *They have broken off negotiations.*
break something up = **stop**, end, suspend, disrupt, dismantle, disperse, terminate, disband, diffuse • *Police used tear gas to break up a demonstration.*
break through = **succeed**, make it *(informal)*, achieve, do well, flourish, cut it *(informal)*, get to the top, crack it *(informal)*, make your mark *(informal)*, shine forth • *There is still scope for new writers to break through.*
break through something 1 = **penetrate**, go through, get past, burst through • *Protesters tried to break through a police cordon.*
2 = **pierce**, penetrate, burst through, emerge from behind • *Sunlight had broken through the clouds.*
break up 1 = **finish**, stop, be suspended, terminate, come to an end, adjourn, recess • *The meeting broke up half an hour later.*
2 = **split up**, separate, part, divorce, part company, get divorced, end a relationship • *My girlfriend and I have broken up.*
3 = **scatter**, separate, divide, dissolve • *The crowd broke up reluctantly.*
break with something *or* **someone** = **separate from**, drop *(informal)*, reject, ditch *(slang)*, renounce, depart from, break away from, part company with, repudiate, jilt • *It was a tough decision for him to break with Leeds.*

breakable = **fragile**, delicate, frail, brittle, flimsy, crumbly, friable, frangible • *My parents had a remarkable array of breakable objects.*
OPPOSITES: lasting, strong, unbreakable

breakage = **break**, cut, tear, crack, rent, breach, fracture, rift, rupture, cleft, fissure • *Use a wooden-toothed comb to avoid breakages.*

breakaway = **rebel**, revolutionary, rebellious, dissenting, insurgent, seceding, secessionist, heretical, mutinous, insubordinate, insurrectionary, schismatic • *a breakaway group*

breakdown 1 = **failure**, collapse, foundering, downfall, disintegration, lack of success • *the irretrievable breakdown of his marriage*
2 = **collapse**, nervous breakdown, crackup *(informal)* • *They often seem depressed and close to breakdown.*
3 = **hitch**, disturbance, disruption, interruption, stoppage, mishap, impediment, hindrance • *The trip was plagued by breakdowns.*
4 = **analysis**, classification, dissection, categorization, detailed list, itemization • *The organisers were given a breakdown of the costs.*

breaker = **wave**, roller, comber, billow, white horse, whitecap • *breakers on the sea wall*

break-in = **burglary**, robbery, breaking and entering, home invasion (*Austral. & N.Z.*) • *The break-in had occurred just before midnight.*

breakneck = **dangerous**, rapid, excessive, rash, reckless, precipitate, headlong, express • *Jack drove to Mayfair at breakneck speed.*

breakthrough = **development**, advance, progress, improvement, discovery, find, finding, invention, step forward, leap forwards, turn of events, quantum leap • *The breakthrough came hours before a UN deadline.*

break-up 1 = **separation**, split, divorce, breakdown, ending, parting, breaking, splitting, wind-up, rift, disintegration, dissolution, termination • *a marital break-up*
2 = **dissolution**, division, splitting, disintegration • *the break-up of British Rail*

breakwater = **sea wall**, spur, mole, jetty, groyne • *Suddenly a breakwater loomed up in front.*

breast 1 = **heart**, feelings, thoughts, soul, being, emotions, core, sentiments, seat of the affections • *Happiness flowered in her breast.*
2 = **bosom**, boob (*slang*), tit (*slang*), jug (*slang*), booby (*slang*), mammary gland, bristol (*slang*), titty (*slang*) • *a skimpy top which barely covered her breasts*
▸ RELATED ADJECTIVE: mammary

breastbone
▸ TECHNICAL NAME: sternum

breath AS A NOUN 1 = **air**, wind, oxygen, puff (*informal*) • *I had nearly run out of breath when the boat was lifted.*
2 = **inhalation**, breathing, pant, gasp, gulp, wheeze, exhalation, respiration • *He took a deep breath and began to climb the stairs.*
3 = **gust**, sigh, puff, flutter, flurry, whiff, draught, waft, zephyr, slight movement, faint breeze • *Not even a breath of wind stirred the pine branches.*
4 = **trace**, suggestion, hint, whisper, suspicion, murmur, undertone, intimation • *It was left to her to add a breath of common sense.*
5 = **odour**, smell, aroma, whiff, vapour, niff (*Brit. slang*) • *A breath of cooking smell crept to her from the kitchen.*
6 = **rest**, breather • *He had to stop for breath.*
7 = **life**, energy, existence, vitality, animation, life force, lifeblood, mauri (*N.Z.*) • *Here is no light, no breath, no warm flesh.*
▸ IN PHRASES: **take your breath away** = **amaze**, surprise, stun, astonish, stagger, startle, astound, bowl over, sweep you off your feet, dumbfound • *I heard this song on the radio and it just took my breath away.*

breathe AS A VERB 1 = **inhale and exhale**, pant, gasp, puff, gulp, wheeze, respire, draw in breath • *Always breathe through your nose.*
2 = **whisper**, say, voice, express, sigh, utter, articulate, murmur • *He never breathed a word about our conversation.*
3 = **instil**, inspire, pass on, inject, impart, infuse, imbue • *It is the readers who breathe life into a newspaper.*
▸ IN PHRASES: **breathe in** = **inhale**, gasp, respire, draw in breath • *She breathed in deeply.*

breather = **rest**, break, halt, pause, recess, breathing space, breath of air • *Relax and take a breather whenever you feel that you need one.*

breathing space = **respite**, break, rest, time to think • *We hope that it will give us some breathing space.*

breathless 1 = **out of breath**, winded, exhausted, panting, gasping, puffed, choking, gulping, wheezing, out of puff (*informal*), out of whack (*informal*), puffing and blowing, short-winded • *I was a little breathless and my heartbeat was fast.*
2 = **excited**, anxious, curious, eager, enthusiastic, impatient, agog, on tenterhooks, in suspense • *We were breathless with anticipation.*

breathtaking = **amazing**, striking, exciting, brilliant, dramatic, stunning (*informal*), impressive, thrilling, overwhelming, magnificent, astonishing, sensational, eye-popping (*informal*), awesome, wondrous (*archaic or literary*), awe-inspiring, jaw-dropping, heart-stirring • *The house has breathtaking views from every room.*

breed AS A NOUN 1 = **variety**, family, line, sort, kind, race, class, stock, type, species, strain, pedigree • *rare breeds of cattle*
2 = **kind**, sort, type, variety, order, brand, stamp, genre, calibre • *the new breed of walking holidays*
▸ AS A VERB 1 = **rear**, tend, keep, raise, maintain, farm, look after, care for, bring up, nurture, nourish • *He lived alone, breeding horses and dogs.*
2 = **reproduce**, multiply, propagate, procreate, produce offspring, bear young, bring forth young, generate offspring, beget offspring, develop • *Frogs will usually breed in any convenient pond.*
3 = **produce**, cause, create, occasion, generate, bring about, arouse, originate, give rise to, stir up • *If they are unemployed it's bound to breed resentment.*

breeding 1 = **refinement**, style, culture, taste, manners, polish, grace, courtesy, elegance, sophistication, delicacy, cultivation, politeness, civility, gentility, graciousness, urbanity, politesse • *men of low birth and no breeding*
2 = **rearing**, raising, nurturing • *There is potential for selective breeding for better yields.*
3 = **reproduction**, mating, reproducing, multiplying, propagation, procreation • *During the breeding season the birds come ashore.*

PROVERBS
You cannot make a silk purse out of a sow's ear

breeze AS A NOUN 1 = **light wind**, air, whiff, draught, gust, waft, zephyr, breath of wind, current of air, puff of air, capful of wind • *a cool summer breeze*
2 = **child's play**, piece of cake, pushover, doddle, walkover, cinch, no-brainer (*informal*) • *Making the pastry is a breeze if you have a food processor.*
▸ AS A VERB = **sweep**, move briskly, pass, trip, sail, cruise, hurry, ghost, sally, stroll, glide, flit • *Lopez breezed into the room.*

breezy 1 = **carefree**, casual, lively, sparkling, sunny, informal, cheerful, animated, upbeat (*informal*), buoyant, airy, easy-going, genial, jaunty, chirpy (*informal*), sparky, sprightly, vivacious, debonair, blithe, free and easy, full of beans (*informal*), light, light-hearted • *a bright and breezy website with serious intentions*
OPPOSITES: serious, heavy, sad
2 = **windy**, fresh, airy, blustery, blowing, gusty, squally, blowy, blusterous • *The day was breezy and warm.*
OPPOSITES: heavy, calm, oppressive

brevity 1 = **shortness**, transience, impermanence, ephemerality, briefness, transitoriness • *The bonus of this homely soup is the brevity of its cooking time.*
2 = **conciseness**, economy, crispness, concision, terseness, succinctness, curtness, pithiness • *The brevity of the letter concerned me.*
OPPOSITES: rambling, verbiage, wordiness

QUOTATIONS
Brevity is the soul of wit
[William Shakespeare *Hamlet*]
I strive to be brief, and I become obscure
[Horace *Ars Poetica*]

brew AS A VERB 1 = **boil**, make, soak, steep, stew, infuse (*tea*) • *He brewed a pot of coffee.*
2 = **make**, ferment, prepare by fermentation • *I brew my own beer.*
3 = **start**, develop, gather, loom, be on the way, be imminent, foment, be just around the corner, gather force, be impending • *At home a crisis was brewing.*

4 = develop, form, gather, loom, be imminent, foment, be impending • *We'd seen the storm brewing when we were out on the boat.*

▸ **AS A NOUN 1 = drink**, preparation, mixture, blend, liquor, beverage, infusion, concoction, fermentation, distillation • *a mild herbal brew*

2 = blend, compound, fusion, concoction, potpourri, admixture • *Most cities generate a potent brew of pollutants.*

bribe AS A NOUN **= inducement**, incentive, pay-off *(informal)*, graft *(informal)*, sweetener *(slang)*, kickback *(U.S.)*, sop, backhander *(slang)*, enticement, hush money *(slang)*, payola *(informal)*, allurement, corrupting gift, reward for treachery • *He was being investigated for receiving bribes.*

▸ **AS A VERB = buy off**, reward, pay off *(informal)*, lure, corrupt, get at, square, suborn, grease the palm *or* hand of *(slang)*, influence by gifts, oil the palm of *(informal)* • *The company bribed the workers to be quiet.*

bribery = corruption, graft *(informal)*, inducement, buying off, payola *(informal)*, crookedness *(informal)*, palm-greasing *(slang)*, subornation • *He was jailed on charges of bribery.*

bric-a-brac = knick-knacks, ornaments, trinkets, baubles, odds and ends, curios, stuff, miscellany, objets d'art *(French)*, gewgaws, bibelots, kickshaws, objects of virtu • *The rooms are choked with bric-a-brac.*

brick AS A NOUN **= kind person**, good sort, salt of the earth, star • *You were a brick, a real friend when I was in need.*

▸ **IN PHRASES: brick something up = wall up**, cover, close up, shut up • *We bricked up all our windows.*

bridal = matrimonial, marriage, wedding, marital, bride's, nuptial, conjugal, spousal, connubial, hymeneal • *the bridal party*

bride = wife, newly-wed, marriage partner, wifey *(informal)* • *We toasted the bride and groom.*

bridegroom = husband, groom, newly-wed, marriage partner • *The bride and bridegroom left in a carriage.*

bridge AS A NOUN **1 = arch**, span, viaduct, aqueduct, flyover, overpass • *He walked over the railway bridge.*

2 = link, tie, bond, connection • *They saw themselves as a bridge to peace.*

▸ **AS A VERB 1 = span**, cross, go over, cross over, traverse, reach across, extend across, arch over • *a tree used to bridge the river*

2 = reconcile, unite, resolve, overcome • *She bridged the gap between pop music and opera.*

OPPOSITES: separate, split, divide

▸ RELATED ADJECTIVE: pontine

▹ *See panel* **Bridges**

bridle AS A NOUN **= rein**, curb, control, check, restraint, trammels • *She dismounted and took her horse's bridle.*

▸ **AS A VERB 1 = get angry**, draw (yourself) up, bristle, seethe, see red, be infuriated, rear up, be indignant, be maddened, go crook *(Austral. & N.Z. slang)*, raise your hackles, get your dander up *(slang)*, get your back up • *He bridled at the shortness of her tone.*

2 = curb, control, master, govern, moderate, restrain, rein, subdue, repress, constrain, keep in check, check, keep a tight rein on, keep on a string • *I must learn to bridle my tongue.*

brief AS AN ADJECTIVE **1 = short**, fast, quick, temporary, fleeting, swift, short-lived, little, hasty, momentary, ephemeral, quickie *(informal)*, transitory • *This time their visit is brief.*

OPPOSITES: long, extensive, lengthy

2 = concise, short, limited, to the point, crisp, compressed, terse, curt, laconic, succinct, clipped, pithy, thumbnail, monosyllabic • *Write a very brief description of a typical problem.*

OPPOSITES: long, detailed, lengthy

3 = curt, short, sharp, blunt, abrupt, brusque • *He was brief, rapid, decisive.*

▸ **AS A VERB = inform**, prime, prepare, advise, fill in *(informal)*, instruct, clue in *(informal)*, gen up *(Brit. informal)*, put in the picture *(informal)*, give a rundown, keep (someone) posted, give the gen *(Brit. informal)* • *A spokesman briefed reporters.*

▸ **AS A NOUN 1 = instructions**, remit, briefing, guidelines, mandate, directive • *Hughes will be given the brief of man-marking Francesco Totti.*

2 = summary, résumé, outline, sketch, abstract, summing-up, digest, epitome, rundown, synopsis, précis, recapitulation, abridgment • *He gives me my first brief of the situation.*

3 = case, defence, argument, data, contention • *a lawyer's brief*

▸ **IN PHRASES: in brief 1 = briefly**, in summary, in synopsis, in digest form • *And now sport in brief.*

2 = in short, briefly, in essence, in a word, in a nutshell, to sum up, to come to the point, to put it briefly • *In brief, take no risks.*

briefing 1 = conference, meeting, priming, question and answer session • *They're holding a press briefing tomorrow.*

2 = instructions, information, priming, directions, instruction, preparation, guidance, preamble, rundown • *The Chancellor gives a twenty-minute briefing to his backbenchers.*

briefly 1 = quickly, shortly, precisely, casually, temporarily, abruptly, hastily, briskly, momentarily, hurriedly, curtly, summarily, fleetingly, cursorily • *He smiled briefly.*

2 = in outline, in brief, in passing, in a nutshell, concisely, in a few words • *There are four alternatives; they are described briefly below.*

briefs = knickers, pants, underpants, undies, panties, broekies *(S. African informal)*, underdaks *(Austral. slang)*, smalls • *A bra and a pair of briefs lay on the floor.*

brigade 1 = corps, company, force, unit, division, troop, squad, crew, team, outfit, regiment, contingent, squadron, detachment • *the men of the Seventh Armoured Brigade*

BRIDGES

Bridges

Brooklyn Bridge
Clifton Suspension Bridge
Forth Railway Bridge
Forth Road Bridge
Gateshead Millennium Bridge
Golden Gate Bridge
Halfpenny Bridge
Humber Bridge
London Bridge
Millennium Bridge
Oakland Bay Bridge
Rainbow Bridge
Rialto Bridge
Severn Bridge
Bridge of Sighs
Skye Bridge
Sydney Harbour Bridge
Tower Bridge
Tyne Bridge
Waterloo Bridge
Westminster Bridge

Types of bridge

aqueduct
Bailey bridge
balance, bascule, *or* counterpoise bridge
box-girder bridge
cable-stayed bridge
cantilever bridge
clapper bridge
deck bridge
drawbridge
flyover
footbridge
pivot, swing, *or* turn bridge
pontoon bridge
snow bridge
suspension bridge
truss bridge
turn bridge
viaduct

2 = **group**, party, body, band, camp, squad, organization, crew, bunch *(informal)* • *the healthy-eating brigade*

brigand = **bandit**, outlaw, robber, gangster, plunderer, highwayman, desperado, marauder, ruffian, freebooter, footpad *(archaic)* • *He looked like a scruffy brigand.*

bright 1 = **vivid**, rich, brilliant, intense, glowing, colourful, highly-coloured • *a bright red dress*
2 = **shining**, flashing, beaming, glowing, blazing, sparkling, glittering, dazzling, illuminated, gleaming, shimmering, twinkling, radiant, luminous, glistening, resplendent, scintillating, lustrous, lambent, effulgent • *Newborns hate bright lights and loud noises.*
3 = **intelligent**, smart, clever, knowing, thinking, quick, aware, sharp, keen, acute, alert, rational, penetrating, enlightened, apt, astute, brainy, wide-awake, clear-headed, perspicacious, quick-witted • *I was convinced that he was brighter than average.*
OPPOSITES: simple, slow, stupid
4 = **clever**, brilliant, smart, sensible, cunning, ingenious, inventive, canny • *There are lots of books crammed with bright ideas.*
5 = **cheerful**, happy, glad, lively, jolly, merry, upbeat *(informal)*, joyous, joyful, genial, chirpy *(informal)*, sparky, vivacious, full of beans *(informal)*, gay, light-hearted • *The boy was so bright and animated.*
6 = **promising**, good, encouraging, excellent, golden, optimistic, hopeful, favourable, prosperous, rosy, auspicious, propitious, palmy • *Both had successful careers and the future looked bright.*
7 = **sunny**, clear, fair, pleasant, clement, lucid, cloudless, unclouded, sunlit • *the bright winter sky*
OPPOSITES: dark, grey, cloudy

brighten 1 = **cheer up**, rally, take heart, perk up, buck up *(informal)*, become cheerful • *Seeing him, she seemed to brighten a little.*
OPPOSITES: sadden, blacken, become gloomy
2 = **light up**, shine, glow, gleam, clear up, lighten, enliven • *Her tearful eyes brightened with interest.*
OPPOSITES: shadow, shade, dim
3 = **enliven**, animate, make brighter, vitalize • *Planted tubs brightened the area outside the door.*
4 = **improve**, pick up, rally, look up *(informal)*, perk up, gain strength, take a turn for the better *(informal)* • *It is undeniable that the economic picture is brightening.*
5 = **become brighter**, light up, glow, gleam, clear up • *The sky above the ridge of the mountains brightened.*

brightness 1 = **vividness**, richness, intensity, brilliance, splendour, resplendence • *You'll be impressed with the brightness of the colors.*
2 = **light**, shine, sparkle, glare, brilliance, radiance, luminosity, incandescence, effulgence, refulgence • *An astronomer can determine the brightness of each star.*
OPPOSITES: dullness, dimness
3 = **intelligence**, intellect, brains *(informal)*, awareness, sharpness, alertness, cleverness, quickness, acuity, brain power, smarts *(slang, chiefly U.S.)*, smartness • *Her brightness seemed quite intimidating to me.*

brilliance *or* **brilliancy** 1 = **cleverness**, talent, wisdom, distinction, genius, excellence, greatness, aptitude, inventiveness, acuity, giftedness, braininess • *His brilliance and genius will always remain.*
OPPOSITES: folly, incompetence, stupidity
2 = **brightness**, blaze, intensity, sparkle, glitter, dazzle, gleam, sheen, lustre, radiance, luminosity, vividness, resplendence, effulgence, refulgence • *the brilliance of the sun on the water*
OPPOSITES: darkness, obscurity, dullness
3 = **splendour**, glamour, grandeur, magnificence, éclat, gorgeousness, illustriousness, pizzazz *or* pizazz *(informal)*, gilt • *The opera house was perfection, all brilliance and glamour.*

brilliant 1 = **intelligent**, sharp, intellectual, alert, clever, quick, acute, profound, rational, penetrating, discerning, inventive, astute, brainy, perspicacious, quick-witted • *She had a brilliant mind.*
OPPOSITES: simple, slow, stupid
2 = **expert**, masterly, talented, gifted, accomplished • *a brilliant pianist*
OPPOSITES: ordinary, dull, untalented
3 = **excellent**, great, good, fine, wonderful, cracking *(Brit. informal)*, superb, fantastic *(informal)*, tremendous *(informal)*, marvellous *(informal)*, terrific *(informal)*, mean *(slang)*, mega *(slang)*, awesome *(slang)*, booshit *(Austral. slang)*, exo *(Austral. slang)*, sik *(Austral. slang)*, first-rate, brill *(informal)*, topping *(Brit. slang)*, hunky-dory *(informal)*, beaut *(informal)*, barrie *(Scot. slang)*, belting *(Brit. slang)*, pearler *(Austral. slang)* • *My sister's given me a brilliant book.*
4 = **splendid**, grand, famous, celebrated, rare, supreme, outstanding, remarkable, superb, magnificent, sterling, glorious, exceptional, notable, renowned, heroic, admirable, eminent, sublime, illustrious • *a brilliant success*
5 = **bright**, shining, intense, sparkling, glittering, dazzling, vivid, radiant, luminous, ablaze, resplendent, scintillating, lustrous, coruscating, refulgent, lambent • *The event was held in brilliant sunshine.*
OPPOSITES: dark, dull, obscure

brim AS A NOUN 1 = **peak**, shade, shield, visor • *Rain dripped from the brim of his baseball cap.*
2 = **rim**, edge, border, lip, margin, verge, brink, flange • *The toilet was full to the brim with insects.*
▸ AS A VERB 1 = **be full**, spill, well over, run over, overflow, spill over, brim over • *They are brimming with confidence.*
2 = **fill**, well over, fill up, overflow • *Michael looked at him imploringly, his eyes brimming with tears.*

brimful = **full**, filled, packed, running over, brimming, overflowing, flush, overfull • *The country is brimful with highly paid doctors.*

brindled = **streaked**, spotted, patched, speckled, mottled, tabby • *a brindled cat seated on a mat*

brine = **salt water**, saline solution, pickling solution • *Soak the walnuts in brine for four or five days.*

bring AS A VERB 1 = **fetch**, take, carry, bear, transfer, deliver, transport, import, convey • *My father brought home a book for me.*
2 = **take**, lead, guide, conduct, accompany, escort, usher • *I brought him inside and dried him off.*
3 = **cause**, produce, create, effect, occasion, result in, contribute to, inflict, wreak, engender • *The revolution brought more trouble than it was worth.*
4 = **make**, force, influence, convince, persuade, prompt, compel, induce, move, dispose, sway, prevail on *or* upon • *I could not even bring myself to enter the house.*
5 = **earn**, return, produce, net, command, yield, gross, fetch • *This brings her the benefit of a higher rate of interest.*
▸ IN PHRASES: **bring someone down** 1 = **knock over**, floor, trip up • *I hooked his leg and brought him down.*
2 = **discourage**, upset, depress, crush, dash, damp, deter, dismay, daunt, dampen, lay low, cast down, put a damper on, dispirit, deject • *You'll do anything to bring me down, won't you?*
bring someone in = **introduce**, include, take in, incorporate • *The firm decided to bring in a new management team.*
bring someone round 1 = **wake up**, rouse, bring to, arouse • *I'd passed out and he'd brought me around.*
2 = **persuade**, influence, convince, convert, win over, sway, talk round • *They thought they had brought you round to their way of seeing things.*
bring someone up = **rear**, raise, support, train, develop, teach, nurse, breed, foster, educate, care for, nurture • *She brought up four children.*

b

bring something about = **cause**, produce, create, effect, manage, achieve, occasion, realize, generate, accomplish, give rise to, make happen, effectuate, bring to pass • *The two sides are attempting to bring about fundamental changes.*
bring something back 1 = **bring to mind**, evoke, summon up, remind you of, make you think of • *Talking about it brought it all back.*
2 = **revive**, restore, rekindle, revitalize, breathe new life into, bring back to life, re-awaken, reanimate • *Nothing can bring back the old order.*
bring something down 1 = **overturn**, reduce, undermine, overthrow, abase • *They were threatening to bring down the government.*
2 = **reduce**, cut, drop, lower, slash, decrease • *The air fares war will bring down prices.*
3 = **cut down**, level, fell, hew, lop, raze • *The lumberjacks brought the tree down.*
4 = **demolish**, level, destroy, dismantle, flatten, knock down, pull down, tear down, bulldoze, raze, kennet (*Austral. slang*), jeff (*Austral. slang*) • *Such forces would normally bring the building down.*
bring something forward = **put forward**, present, suggest, advance, come up with, submit, tender, proffer, propound • *The government will bring forward several proposals.*
bring something in 1 = **introduce**, start, found, launch, establish, set up, institute, organize, pioneer, initiate, usher in, inaugurate • *They brought in a controversial law.*
2 = **produce**, return, net, realize, generate, be worth, yield, gross, fetch, accrue • *The business brings in about £24,000 a year*
bring something off = **accomplish**, achieve, perform, carry out, succeed, execute, discharge, pull off, carry off, bring to pass • *They were about to bring off an even bigger coup.*
bring something on = **cause**, produce, create, effect, lead to, occasion, result in, generate, provoke, compel, motivate, induce, bring about, give rise to, precipitate, incite, engender • *Severe shock can bring on an attack of acne.*
bring something out 1 = **publish**, issue, produce, print, put out • *A journalist all his life, he's now brought out a book.*
2 = **launch**, found, establish, set up, institute, start up, inaugurate • *They've brought out a new product.*
3 = **emphasize**, highlight, accent, accentuate, foreground, give prominence to • *That shade brings out the colour of your eyes.*
bring something up = **mention**, raise, introduce, point out, refer to, allude to, broach, call attention to, speak about or of • *Why are you bringing that up now?*

brink = **edge**, point, limit, border, lip, margin, boundary, skirt, frontier, fringe, verge, threshold, rim, brim • *Their economy is teetering on the brink of collapse.*

brio = **energy**, spirit, enthusiasm, dash, pep, zip (*informal*), animation, vigour, verve, zest, panache, gusto, get-up-and-go (*informal*), élan, vivacity, liveliness, welly (*slang*) • *The performance was full of brio.*

brisk 1 = **quick**, lively, energetic, active, vigorous, animated, bustling, speedy, nimble, agile, sprightly, vivacious, spry • *The horse broke into a brisk trot.*
OPPOSITES: heavy, slow, lazy
2 = **short**, sharp, brief, blunt, rude, tart, abrupt, no-nonsense, terse, curt, gruff, pithy, brusque, offhand, monosyllabic, ungracious, uncivil, snappish • *She attempted to reason with him in a rather brisk fashion.*
3 = **busy**, good, rewarding, lucrative, paying, money-making, hectic, fruitful, gainful, remunerative • *Business had been brisk since July.*
4 = **invigorating**, fresh, biting, sharp, keen, stimulating, crisp, bracing, refreshing, exhilarating, nippy • *The breeze was cool, brisk and invigorating.*
OPPOSITES: tiring, wearisome, enervating

briskly 1 = **quickly**, smartly, promptly, rapidly, readily, actively, efficiently, vigorously, energetically, pronto (*informal*), nimbly, posthaste • *Eve walked briskly down the corridor.*
2 = **rapidly**, quickly, apace, pdq (*slang*) • *A trader said gold was selling briskly on the local market.*
3 = **brusquely**, firmly, decisively, incisively • *'Anyhow,' she added briskly, 'it's none of my business.'*

bristle AS A NOUN 1 = **hair**, spine, thorn, whisker, barb, stubble, prickle • *two days' growth of bristles*
2 = **point**, spur, needle, spike, spine, thorn, barb, prickle • *It has a short stumpy tail covered with bristles.*
▸ AS A VERB 1 = **stand up**, rise, prickle, stand on end, horripilate • *It makes the hair on the nape of my neck bristle.*
2 = **be angry**, rage, seethe, flare up, bridle, see red, be infuriated, spit (*informal*), go ballistic (*slang, chiefly U.S.*), be maddened, wig out (*slang*), get your dander up (*slang*) • *He bristled with indignation.*
3 = **abound**, crawl, be alive, hum, swarm, teem, be thick • *The country bristles with armed groups.*

bristly 1 = **prickly**, barbed, thorny, spiny, brambly, briery • *a plant with bristly pale stems and hairy toothed leaves*
2 = **hairy**, rough, bearded, whiskered, stubbly, unshaven, bewhiskered • *He lifted a beer to his bristly mouth.*

Britain = **the UK**, Great Britain, the United Kingdom, the British Isles, Blighty (*Brit. informal*) • *the volume of visitors to Britain*

Briton = **Brit.** (*informal*), limey (*U.S. & Canad. slang*), Britisher, pommy or pom (*Austral. & N.Z. slang*), Anglo-Saxon • *The three men, one Briton, are said to be close to death.*

brittle 1 = **fragile**, delicate, crisp, crumbling, frail, crumbly, breakable, shivery, friable, frangible, shatterable • *Pine is brittle and breaks easily.*
OPPOSITES: strong, flexible, tough
2 = **tense**, nervous, edgy, stiff, wired (*slang*), irritable, curt • *a brittle man*
3 = **harsh**, rough, jarring, grating, raucous, strident, rasping, discordant, croaking, guttural, dissonant, unmelodious • *Myrtle gave a brittle laugh.*

broach 1 = **bring up**, approach, introduce, mention, speak of, talk of, open up, hint at, touch on, raise the subject of • *Eventually I broached the subject of her early life.*
2 = **open**, crack, pierce, puncture, uncork • *He would ask the landlord to broach a new barrel of wine.*

broad 1 = **wide**, large, ample, generous, expansive • *His shoulders were broad and his waist narrow.*
2 = **large**, huge, comfortable, vast, extensive, ample, spacious, expansive, roomy, voluminous, capacious, uncrowded, commodious, beamy (*of a ship*), sizable or sizeable • *a broad expanse of lawn*
OPPOSITES: close, limited, narrow
3 = **full**, general, comprehensive, complete, wide, global, catholic, sweeping, extensive, wide-ranging, umbrella, thorough, unlimited, inclusive, far-reaching, exhaustive, all-inclusive, all-embracing, overarching, encyclopedic • *A broad range of issues was discussed.*
4 = **universal**, general, common, wide, sweeping, worldwide, widespread, wide-ranging, far-reaching • *a film with broad appeal*
5 = **general**, loose, vague, approximate, indefinite, ill-defined, inexact, nonspecific, unspecific, undetailed • *a broad outline of the Society's development*
6 = **strong**, heavy, thick, pronounced, noticeable • *a broad Yorkshire accent*
7 = **clear**, open, full, plain • *Militants shot a man dead in broad daylight today.*
8 = **unsubtle**, clear, straightforward, bold, obvious, blatant, overt, undisguised, unconcealed • *They've been giving broad hints about what to expect.*

9 = **vulgar**, blue, dirty, gross, crude, rude, naughty, coarse, indecent, improper, suggestive, risqué, boorish, uncouth, unrefined, ribald, indelicate, near the knuckle *(informal)*, indecorous, unmannerly • *Use wit rather than broad humour.*

broadcast AS A NOUN = **transmission**, show, programme, telecast, webcast, podcast • *a broadcast on the national radio*
▸ AS A VERB 1 = **transmit**, show, send, air, radio, cable, beam, send out, relay, televise, disseminate, put on the air, podcast • *CNN also broadcasts programmes in Europe.*
2 = **make public**, report, announce, publish, spread, advertise, proclaim, circulate, disseminate, promulgate, shout from the rooftops *(informal)* • *Don't broadcast your business outside the family.*

broaden 1 = **widen**, spread, extend, stretch, expand, enlarge, dilate, open out *or* up, become wider *or* broader • *The smile broadened to a grin.*
2 = **expand**, increase, develop, spread, extend, stretch, open up, swell, supplement, widen, enlarge, augment • *We must broaden our appeal.*
OPPOSITES: reduce, narrow, restrict

broadly 1 = **in general**, largely, generally, mainly, widely, mostly, on the whole, predominantly, in the main, for the most part • *He broadly got what he wanted out of his meeting.*
2 = **widely**, greatly, hugely, vastly, extensively, expansively • *Charles grinned broadly.*
3 = **generally**, commonly, widely, universally, popularly • *This gives children a more broadly based education.*
OPPOSITES: narrowly, exclusively
4 = **blatantly**, unsubtly, clearly, overtly • *He hinted broadly that he would like to come.*

broad-minded = **tolerant**, open-minded, flexible, liberal, catholic, cosmopolitan, responsive, indulgent, permissive, unbiased, dispassionate, free-thinking, unprejudiced, undogmatic, unbigoted • *You'll find me more broad-minded than you think.*
OPPOSITES: prejudiced, biased, narrow-minded

broadside = **attack**, criticism, censure, swipe, denunciation, diatribe, sideswipe, philippic • *She defiantly replied with a broadside.*

brochure = **booklet**, advertisement, leaflet, hand-out, circular, pamphlet, folder, mailshot, handbill • *travel brochures*

broekies = **underpants**, pants, briefs, drawers, knickers, panties, boxer shorts, Y-fronts *(trademark)*, underdaks *(Austral. slang)* • *He was wearing nothing but a pair of broekies.*

broke = **penniless**, short, ruined, bust *(informal)*, bankrupt, impoverished, in the red, cleaned out *(slang)*, insolvent, down and out, skint *(Brit. slang)*, strapped for cash *(informal)*, dirt-poor *(informal)*, flat broke *(informal)*, penurious, on your uppers, stony-broke *(Brit. slang)*, in queer street, without two pennies to rub together *(informal)*, without a penny to your name • *I'm as broke as you are.*
OPPOSITES: rich, comfortable, wealthy

broken 1 = **interrupted**, disturbed, incomplete, erratic, disconnected, intermittent, fragmentary, spasmodic, discontinuous • *nights of broken sleep*
2 = **failed**, ruined, wrecked, unsuccessful, abortive, ending in divorce • *the traumas of a broken marriage*
3 = **imperfect**, halting, hesitating, stammering, disjointed • *Eric could only respond in broken English.*
4 = **smashed**, destroyed, burst, shattered, fragmented, fractured, demolished, severed, ruptured, rent, separated, shivered • *Damp air came through the broken window.*
5 = **defective**, not working, ruined, imperfect, out of order, not functioning, on the blink *(slang)*, on its last legs, kaput *(informal)* • *a broken guitar and a rusty snare drum*
6 = **violated**, forgotten, ignored, disregarded, not kept, infringed, retracted, disobeyed, dishonoured, transgressed, traduced • *History is made up of broken promises.*
7 = **defeated**, beaten, crushed, humbled, crippled, tamed, subdued, oppressed, overpowered, vanquished, demoralized, browbeaten • *He looked a broken man.*
8 = **fractured**, cracked, splintered • *He escaped with a broken leg.*
9 = **cut**, wounded, pierced, punctured, perforated, ruptured • *The broken skin became infected.*
10 = **uneven**, rough, bumpy, rutted, not flat, not level, not smooth, pitty • *the rough broken ground in front of the flats*

broken-down = **not in working order**, old, worn out, out of order, dilapidated, not functioning, out of commission, on the blink *(slang)*, inoperative, kaput *(informal)*, in disrepair, on the fritz *(U.S. slang)* • *a broken-down car*

brokenhearted = **heartbroken**, devastated, disappointed, despairing, miserable, choked, desolate, mournful, prostrated, grief-stricken, sorrowful, wretched, disconsolate, inconsolable, crestfallen, down in the dumps *(informal)*, heart-sick • *I was brokenhearted when she left.*

broker AS A NOUN = **dealer**, marketer, agent, trader, supplier, merchant, entrepreneur, negotiator, chandler, mediator, intermediary, wholesaler, middleman, factor, purveyor, go-between, tradesman, merchandiser • *They met through a commercial marriage broker.*
▸ AS A VERB = **organize**, run, plan, set up, arrange, construct, put together, get together, marshal, get going, coordinate • *He tried to broker a peace conference.*

bromide = **platitude**, cliché, banality, truism, commonplace, chestnut *(informal)*, old saw, trite remark, hackneyed saying *or* phrase • *The same old bromides were used to justify failure.*

bronze = **reddish-brown**, copper, tan, rust, chestnut, brownish, copper-coloured, yellowish-brown, reddish-tan, metallic brown • *Her hair shone bronze and gold.*
▹ *See panel* **Shades of brown**

bronzed = **tanned**, brown, suntanned, sunburnt • *He's bronzed from a short holiday in California.*

brooch = **badge**, pin, clip, fastening, clasp • *a sapphire brooch*

brood AS A NOUN 1 = **offspring**, young, issue, breed, infants, clutch, hatch, litter, chicks, progeny • *The last brood of the pair was hatched.*
2 = **children**, family, offspring, progeny, nearest and dearest, flesh and blood, ainga *(N.Z.)* • *She flew to the defence of her brood.*
▸ AS A VERB = **think**, obsess, muse, ponder, fret, meditate, agonize, mull over, mope, ruminate, eat your heart out, dwell upon, repine • *She constantly broods about her family.*

brooding = **gloomy**, troubled, depressed, moody, glum, dejected, despondent, downcast, morose • *A heavy, brooding silence descended on them.*

brook[1] = **stream**, burn *(Scot. & Northern English)*, rivulet, gill *(dialect)*, beck, watercourse, rill, streamlet, runnel *(literary)* • *He threw the hatchet in the brook.*

brook[2] = **tolerate**, stand, allow, suffer, accept, bear, stomach, endure, swallow, hack *(slang)*, abide, put up with *(informal)*, withstand, countenance, support, thole *(dialect)* • *The army will brook no weakening of its power.*

brothel = **whorehouse**, red-light district, bordello, cathouse *(U.S. slang)*, house of ill repute, knocking shop *(slang)*, bawdy house *(archaic)*, house of prostitution, bagnio, house of ill fame, stews *(archaic)* • *a thriving brothel*

QUOTATIONS
Prisons are built with stones of Law, brothels with bricks of Religion
[William Blake *The Marriage of Heaven and Hell*]

brother 1 = **male sibling** • *Have you got any brothers and sisters?*
2 = **comrade**, partner, colleague, associate, mate, pal *(informal)*, companion, cock *(Brit. informal)*, chum *(informal)*, fellow member, confrère, compeer • *their freedom-loving brothers*

b

3 = **monk**, cleric, friar, monastic, religious, regular • *priests and religious brothers*
▸ RELATED ADJECTIVE: fraternal

brotherhood 1 = **fellowship**, kinship, companionship, comradeship, friendliness, camaraderie, brotherliness • *He believed in socialism and the brotherhood of man.*
2 = **association**, order, union, community, society, league, alliance, clan, guild, fraternity, clique, coterie • *a secret international brotherhood*

brotherly = **fraternal**, friendly, neighbourly, sympathetic, affectionate, benevolent, kind, amicable, altruistic, philanthropic • *family loyalty and brotherly love*

brow 1 = **forehead**, temple • *She wrinkled her brow inquisitively.*
2 = **top**, summit, peak, edge, tip, crown, verge, brink, rim, crest, brim • *He climbed to the brow of the hill.*

browbeat = **bully**, threaten, cow, intimidate, badger, oppress, hector, coerce, bulldoze *(informal)*, overawe, dragoon, ride roughshod over, tyrannize, overbear, domineer • *attempts to deceive, con, or browbeat the voters*
OPPOSITES: tempt, lure, coax

brown AS AN ADJECTIVE 1 = **brunette**, dark, bay, coffee, chocolate, brick, toasted, ginger, rust, chestnut, hazel, dun, auburn, tawny, umber, donkey brown, fuscous • *her deep brown eyes*
2 = **tanned**, browned, bronze, bronzed, tan, dusky, sunburnt • *rows of bodies slowly going brown in the sun*
3 = **wholemeal**, wholegrain, untreated, unrefined, coarse-grained, unpurified • *brown bread*
▸ AS A VERB = **fry**, cook, grill, sear, sauté • *He browned the chicken in a frying pan.*
▹ *See panel* **Shades of brown**

browse 1 = **skim**, scan, glance at, survey, look through, look round, dip into, leaf through, peruse, flip through, examine cursorily • *There are plenty of biographies for him to browse.*
2 = **graze**, eat, feed, crop, pasture, nibble • *three red deer stags browsing 50 yards from my lodge*

bruise AS A NOUN = **discoloration**, mark, injury, trauma *(Pathology)*, blemish, black mark, contusion, black-and-blue mark • *How did you get that bruise on your cheek?*
▸ AS A VERB 1 = **hurt**, injure, mark, blacken, discolour, contuse, make black and blue • *I had only bruised my knee.*
2 = **damage**, mark, mar, blemish, discolour • *Be sure to store them carefully or they'll get bruised.*
3 = **injure**, hurt, pain, wound, slight, insult, sting, offend, grieve, displease, rile, pique • *Men's egos are so easily bruised.*

bruiser = **tough**, heavy *(slang)*, rough *(informal)*, bully, thug, gorilla *(informal)*, hard man, rowdy, tough guy, hoodlum, bully boy, ruffian, roughneck *(slang)* • *Dad was a docker and a bit of a bruiser in his day.*

bruising AS A NOUN = **discoloration**, marking, swelling, contusion, ecchymosis • *She had quite a severe bruising and a cut lip.*
▸ AS AN ADJECTIVE = **hard**, tough, violent, rough, fierce, ferocious, rumbustious • *a bruising battle over civil rights*

brunt = **full force**, force, pressure, violence, shock, stress, impact, strain, burden, thrust • *A child's head tends to take the brunt of any fall.*

brush[1] AS A NOUN 1 = **broom**, sweeper, scrubbing brush, besom, sweeping brush • *Scrub lightly with a brush, then rinse.*
2 = **clean**, sweep, dust • *I gave it a quick brush.*
3 = **conflict**, fight, clash, set-to *(informal)*, scrap *(informal)*, confrontation, skirmish, tussle, fracas, spot of bother *(informal)*, slight engagement • *It is his third brush with the law in less than a year.*
4 = **encounter**, meeting, confrontation, rendezvous • *the trauma of a brush with death*
▸ AS A VERB 1 = **clean**, wash, polish, scrub, buff • *Have you brushed your teeth?*
2 = **coat**, cover, paint • *Brush with melted butter.*
3 = **touch**, come into contact with, sweep, kiss, stroke, glance, flick, scrape, graze, caress • *I felt her hair brushing the back of my shoulder.*
▸ IN PHRASES: **brush someone off** = **ignore**, cut, reject, dismiss, slight, blank *(slang)*, put down, snub, disregard, scorn, disdain, spurn, rebuff, repudiate, disown, cold-shoulder, kiss off *(slang, chiefly U.S. & Canad.)*, send to Coventry • *She just brushed me off.*
brush something aside = **dismiss**, ignore, discount, override, disregard, sweep aside, have no time for, kiss off *(slang, chiefly U.S. & Canad.)* • *He brushed aside my views on politics.*
brush something up *or* **brush up on something** = **revise**, study, go over, cram, polish up, read up on, relearn, bone up on *(informal)*, refresh your memory • *I had hoped to brush up my Spanish.*

brush[2] = **shrubs**, bushes, scrub, underwood, undergrowth, thicket, copse, brushwood • *a meadow of low brush and grass*

brushoff = **snub**, rebuff, rejection, dismissal, cut, slight, refusal, go-by *(slang)*, knock-back *(slang)*, repulse, cold shoulder, repudiation, kick in the teeth *(slang)*, kiss-off *(slang, chiefly U.S. & Canad.)*, bum's rush *(slang)*, the (old) heave-ho *(informal)* • *He told me he'd been given the brush-off.*

brusque = **curt**, short, sharp, blunt, tart, abrupt, hasty, terse, surly, gruff, impolite, monosyllabic, discourteous, unmannerly • *The doctors are brusque and busy.*
OPPOSITES: patient, civil, polite

brutal 1 = **cruel**, harsh, savage, grim, vicious, ruthless, ferocious, callous, sadistic, heartless, atrocious, inhuman, merciless, cold-blooded, inhumane, brutish, bloodthirsty, remorseless, barbarous, pitiless, uncivilized, hard-hearted • *He was the victim of a very brutal murder.*
OPPOSITES: kind, gentle, humane
2 = **harsh**, tough, severe, rough, rude, indifferent, insensitive, callous, merciless, unconcerned, uncaring, gruff, bearish, tactless, unfeeling, impolite, uncivil, unmannerly • *She spoke with a brutal honesty.*
OPPOSITES: sensitive, refined, polite
3 = **bestial**, animal, beastly, crude, coarse, sensual, brute, carnal, brutish • *a kind of frank and brutal passion*

SHADES OF BROWN

almond	burnt sienna	coffee	khaki	oxblood	taupe
amber	burnt umber	copper	liver	russet	tawny
auburn	butternut	cream	mahogany	rust	teak
bay	café au lait	drab	mocha	sable	terracotta
beige	camel	dun	mousy	sand	tortoiseshell
biscuit	chestnut	ecru	mushroom	seal brown	umber
bisque	chocolate	fawn	neutral	sepia	walnut
bistre	cinnabar	ginger	nutbrown	sienna	
bronze	cinnamon	hazel	nutmeg	sorrel	
buff	cocoa	henna	oatmeal	tan	

brutality = **cruelty**, atrocity, ferocity, savagery, ruthlessness, barbarism, inhumanity, barbarity, viciousness, brutishness, bloodthirstiness, savageness • *Her experience of men was of domination and brutality.*

brutalize 1 = **dehumanize**, corrupt, harden, degrade, toughen, desensitize, bestialize • *He was selfish, guarded, brutalized by his Civil War experiences.*
2 = **terrorize**, browbeat, vandalize, barbarize, threaten, bully, menace, intimidate, oppress • *The policemen brutalized him and concocted his confessions.*

brutally 1 = **cruelly**, fiercely, savagely, ruthlessly, viciously, mercilessly, ferociously, remorselessly, in cold blood, callously, murderously, pitilessly, heartlessly, inhumanly, barbarously, brutishly, barbarically, hardheartedly • *Her real parents had been brutally murdered.*
2 = **mercilessly**, fiercely, cruelly, relentlessly, ferociously, remorselessly, pitilessly • *The talks had been brutally frank.*
3 = **savagely**, cruelly, dangerously, ferociously, fiendishly, fiercely • *The early morning New York air can be brutally cold.*

brute AS A NOUN 1 = **savage**, devil, monster, beast, barbarian, fiend, swine, ogre, ghoul, sadist • *a drunken brute*
2 = **beast**, animal, creature, wild animal • *a big brute of a dog*
▸ AS AN ADJECTIVE = **physical**, bodily, mindless, instinctive, senseless, unthinking • *He used brute force to take control.*

brutish = **coarse**, stupid, gross, cruel, savage, crude, vulgar, barbarian, crass, boorish, uncouth, loutish, subhuman, swinish • *The man was brutish and coarse.*

bubble AS A NOUN = **air ball**, drop, bead, blister, blob, droplet, globule, vesicle, air pocket, air cavity • *a bubble of gas trapped under the surface*
▸ AS A PLURAL NOUN = **foam**, fizz, froth, lather, suds, spume, effervescence, head • *With bubbles and boats, children love bathtime.*
▸ AS A VERB 1 = **boil**, simmer, seethe • *Heat the seasoned stock until it is bubbling.*
2 = **foam**, fizz, froth, churn, agitate, percolate, effervesce • *The fermenting wine bubbled over the top.*
3 = **gurgle**, splash, murmur, trickle, ripple, babble, trill, burble, lap, purl, plash • *He looked at the stream bubbling through the trees nearby.*
▸ IN PHRASES: **bubble over** = **brim over**, burst, be filled, well over, overflow, gush, spill over • *He was quite tireless, bubbling over with vitality.*

bubbly AS AN ADJECTIVE 1 = **lively**, happy, excited, animated, merry, bouncy, elated, sparky, alive and kicking, full of beans *(informal)* • *a bubbly girl who likes to laugh*
2 = **frothy**, sparkling, fizzy, effervescent, carbonated, foamy, sudsy, lathery • *a nice hot bubbly bath*
▸ AS A NOUN = **champagne**, sparkling wine, champers *(informal)*, cava, spumante • *bottles of bubbly*

buccaneer = **pirate**, privateer, corsair, freebooter, sea-rover • *the villainous buccaneer with the peg-leg and the parrot*

buck[1] AS A NOUN 1 = **profit**, earnings, return, proceeds, takings, winnings • *This means big bucks for someone.*
2 = **gallant**, blood, spark, blade, beau, dandy, fop, popinjay, coxcomb • *He'd been a real hellraiser as a young buck.*
▸ AS A VERB = **resist**, oppose, defy, thwart, stand up to, struggle against, hold out against, put up a fight (against) • *He wants to be the tough rebel who bucks the system.*
▸ IN PHRASES: **buck something** *or* **someone up** = **cheer up**, encourage, brighten, hearten, enliven, perk up, gladden, raise someone's spirits, gee up, make happier, inspirit, jolly along *(informal)* • *The aim was to buck up their spirits.*
buck up 1 = **rally**, brighten, cheer up, take heart, perk up • *After half-time we started to buck up.*
2 = **hurry up**, speed up, hasten, get under way, gather momentum, get moving, get a move on, put your foot down *(informal)*, increase the tempo, shake a leg, open up the throttle, put on speed, rattle your dags *(N.Z. informal)* • *Buck up or we'll be late!*

buck[2]
▸ COLLECTIVE NOUNS: brace, lease

bucket AS A NOUN = **pail**, container, pitcher, scuttle • *We drew water in a bucket from a well outside the door.*
▸ AS A PLURAL NOUN = **loads**, floods, oceans • *He was weeping buckets.*
▸ AS A VERB *often with* **down** = **pour down**, rain heavily, lash down, pelt down, come down in torrents, teem down, torrent • *As soon as we were inside, the rain began to bucket down.*
▸ IN PHRASES: **kick the bucket** = **die**, expire, perish, pass away, buy it *(U.S. slang)*, check out *(U.S. slang)*, kick it *(slang)*, croak *(slang)*, give up the ghost, go belly-up *(slang)*, snuff it *(slang)*, peg out *(informal)*, buy the farm *(U.S. slang)*, peg it *(informal)*, decease, cark it *(Austral. & N.Z. slang)*, pop your clogs *(informal)*, breathe your last, hop the twig *(slang)* • *I don't plan on kicking the bucket for another thirty years.*

buckle AS A NOUN = **fastener**, catch, clip, clasp, hasp • *He wore a belt with a large brass buckle.*
▸ AS A VERB 1 = **fasten**, close, secure, hook, clasp • *A man came out buckling his belt.*
2 = **distort**, bend, warp, crumple, contort • *A freak wave had buckled the deck.*
3 = **collapse**, bend, twist, fold, give way, subside, cave in, crumple • *His right leg buckled under him.*
▸ IN PHRASES: **buckle down** = **apply yourself**, set to, fall to, pitch in, get busy, get cracking *(informal)*, exert yourself, put your shoulder to the wheel • *I just buckled down and got on with playing.*
buckle under = **give in**, yield, concede, submit, surrender, succumb, cave in *(informal)*, capitulate • *They accused him of buckling under to right-wing religious groups.*

bucolic = **rustic**, country, rural, agricultural, pastoral, agrarian, agrestic • *the bucolic surroundings of Chantilly*

bud AS A NOUN = **shoot**, branch, sprout, twig, sprig, offshoot, scion • *The first buds appeared on the trees.*
▸ AS A VERB = **develop**, grow, shoot, sprout, burgeon, mature, germinate, burst forth, pullulate • *The leaves were budding on the trees now.*

Buddhism

SCHOOLS OF BUDDHISM

Foism	Nichiren	Soto
Geluk	Nyingma	Tendai
Hinayana	Pure Land Buddhism	Theravada
Jodo	Rinjai	Vajrayana
Kagyü	Sakya	Zen
Lamaism	Soka Gakkai	
Mahayana		

budding = **developing**, beginning, growing, promising, potential, flowering, burgeoning, fledgling, embryonic, nascent, incipient, germinal • *The forum is now open to all budding entrepreneurs.*

buddy = **friend**, mate *(informal)*, pal, companion, comrade, chum *(informal)*, crony, main man *(slang, chiefly U.S.)*, homeboy *(slang, chiefly U.S.)*, cobber *(Austral. & N.Z. old-fashioned informal)*, E hoa *(N.Z.)* • *We became great buddies.*

budge 1 = **yield**, change, compromise, bend, concede, surrender, comply, give way, capitulate, acquiesce, change your mind • *Both sides say they will not budge.*
2 = **persuade**, influence, convince, sway • *The Prime Minister was not to be budged by the verbal assault.*

3 = **move**, roll, slide, stir, give way, change position • *The snake still refused to budge.*
4 = **dislodge**, move, push, roll, remove, transfer, shift, slide, stir, propel • *I pulled and pulled but I couldn't budge it.*

budget AS A NOUN = **allowance**, means, funds, income, finances, resources, allocation • *A designer would be beyond their budget.*
▸ AS A VERB = **plan**, estimate, allocate, cost, ration, apportion, cost out • *I'm learning how to budget my finances.*
▸ AS AN ADJECTIVE = **inexpensive**, economy, bargain, sale, reduced, keen, reasonable, low-priced, low-cost, cut-price, economical, cheapo *(informal)* • *Cheap flights are available from budget travel agents.* • *a budget price*

QUOTATIONS
Annual income twenty pounds, annual expenditure nineteen pounds nineteen six, result happiness. Annual income twenty pounds, annual expenditure twenty pound ought and six, result misery
[Charles Dickens *David Copperfield*]

budgetary = **financial**, money, economic, monetary, fiscal, pecuniary • *huge budgetary pressures*

buff[1] AS AN ADJECTIVE = **fawn**, cream, tan, beige, yellowish, ecru, straw-coloured, sand-coloured, yellowish-brown, biscuit-coloured, camel-coloured, oatmeal-coloured • *a buff envelope*
▸ AS A VERB = **polish**, clean, smooth, brush, shine, rub, wax, brighten, burnish • *He was already buffing the car's hubs.*
▸ IN PHRASES: **in the buff** = **naked**, bare, nude, in the raw *(informal)*, unclothed, in the altogether *(informal)*, buck naked *(slang)*, unclad, in your birthday suit *(informal)*, scuddy *(slang)*, without a stitch on *(informal)*, with bare skin, in the bare scud *(slang)* • *My character had to appear in the buff for some scenes.*
▹ *See panels* **Shades of brown; Shades of yellow**

buff[2] = **expert**, fan, addict, enthusiast, freak *(informal)*, admirer, whizz *(informal)*, devotee, connoisseur, boffin *(Brit. informal)*, fiend *(informal)*, grandmaster, hotshot *(informal)*, aficionado, wonk *(informal)*, maven *(U.S.)*, fundi *(S. African)* • *She is a real film buff.*

buffalo
▸ COLLECTIVE NOUN: herd

buffer AS A NOUN 1 = **safeguard**, screen, shield, cushion, intermediary, bulwark • *a multinational buffer between the two sides*
2 = **geriatric**, dinosaur, fossil *(informal)*, relic, fogey, codger, fuddy-duddy *(informal)*, antique *(informal)* • *a collection of old buffers*
▸ AS A VERB = **protect**, cover, screen, guard, defend, shelter, cushion, safeguard • *The company is buffered by long-term contracts with growers.*

buffet[1] 1 = **smorgasbord**, counter, cold table • *A cold buffet had been laid out in the dining room.*
2 = **snack bar**, café, cafeteria, brasserie, salad bar, refreshment counter • *We sat in the station buffet sipping tea.*

buffet[2] 1 = **knock**, push, bang, rap, slap, bump, smack, shove, thump, cuff, jolt, wallop *(informal)*, box • *Their plane had been severely buffeted by storms.*
2 = **beset**, trouble, plague, harass, badger, perplex, pester, entangle, bedevilbox • *buffeted by social and political upheavals*

buffoon = **clown**, fool, comic, comedian, wag, joker, jester, dag *(N.Z. informal)*, harlequin, droll, silly billy *(informal)*, joculator *or (fem.)* joculatrix, merry-andrew • *a drunken buffoon*

buffoonery = **clowning**, nonsense, jesting, silliness, tomfoolery, malarkey, drollery, waggishness • *music hall buffoonery*

bug AS A NOUN 1 = **insect**, beastie *(informal)*, creepy-crawly *(informal)*, gogga *(S. African informal)* • *a bloodsucking bug which infests poor housing*
2 = **illness**, disease, complaint, virus, infection, disorder, disability, sickness, ailment, malaise, affliction, malady, lurgy *(informal)* • *I think I've got a bit of a stomach bug.*
3 = **fault**, failing, virus, error, defect, flaw, blemish, imperfection, glitch, gremlin • *There is a bug in the software.*
4 = **bugging device**, wire, listening device, phone tap, hidden microphone • *There was a bug on the phone.*
5 = **mania**, passion, rage, obsession, craze, fad, thing *(informal)* • *I've definitely been bitten by the gardening bug.*
▸ AS A VERB 1 = **tap**, eavesdrop, listen in on, wiretap • *He heard they were planning to bug his office.*
2 = **annoy**, bother, disturb, needle *(informal)*, plague, irritate, harass, hassle *(informal)*, aggravate *(informal)*, badger, gall, nettle, pester, vex, irk, get under your skin *(informal)*, get on your nerves *(informal)*, nark *(Brit., Austral. & N.Z. slang)*, get up your nose *(informal)*, be on your back *(slang)*, piss you off *(taboo slang)*, get in your hair *(informal)*, get on your wick *(Brit. slang)*, hack you off *(informal)* • *I only did it to bug my parents.*

BUGS

bedbug *or (Southern U.S.)* chinch	*or* spittle bug	water strider, *or* water skater
cicada *or* cicala	harlequin bug	shield bug *or* stink bug
damsel bug	kissing bug	water boatman
debris bug	lace bug	water bug
froghopper, spittle insect,	leaf-hopper	water scorpion
	Māori bug	
	mealy bug	
	pond-skater,	

bugbear = **pet hate**, bête noire, horror, nightmare, devil, dread, fiend, anathema, bane, bogeyman, bugaboo, bogey • *Money is my biggest bugbear.*

build AS A VERB 1 = **construct**, make, raise, put up, assemble, erect, fabricate, form • *Developers are now proposing to build a hotel on the site.*
OPPOSITES: dismantle, demolish, tear down
2 = **establish**, start, begin, found, base, set up, institute, constitute, initiate, originate, formulate, inaugurate • *I wanted to build a relationship with my team.*
OPPOSITES: end, finish, suspend
3 = **develop**, increase, improve, extend, strengthen, intensify, enlarge, amplify, augment • *Diplomats hope the meetings will build mutual trust.*
OPPOSITES: reduce, contract, decrease
▸ AS A NOUN = **physique**, form, body, figure, shape, structure, frame • *the smallness of his build*
▸ IN PHRASES: **build on something** = **expand on**, develop, enhance, elaborate, refine, improve on, flesh out, enlarge on • *We must patiently build on our small successes piece by piece.*
build someone up = **cheer up**, encourage, boost, revive, liven up, pep up, buck up *(informal)*, gee up *(informal)* • *Build her up with kindness and a sympathetic ear.*
build something into something = **include**, incorporate, integrate, assimilate, subsume • *How much delay should we build into the plan?*
build something up = **increase**, develop, improve, extend, expand, add to, strengthen, enhance, reinforce, intensify, heighten, fortify, amplify, augment • *We can build up speed gradually and safely.*
build something *or* **someone up** = **hype**, promote, advertise, boost, plug *(informal)*, spotlight, publicize • *The media will report on it and the tabloids will build it up.*

builder = **construction worker**, engineer, producer, developer, creator, labourer, constructor • *The builders have finished the roof.*

building = **structure**, house, construction, dwelling, erection, edifice, domicile, pile • *They were on the upper floor of the building.*
▹ *See panel* **Buildings and monuments**

build-up 1 = **increase**, development, growth, expansion, accumulation, enlargement, escalation, upsurge, intensification, augmentation • *a build-up of troops*
2 = **accumulation**, amassing, accretion • *a build-up of gases in the city's sewers*
3 = **hype**, promotion, publicity, plug (*informal*), puff, razzmatazz (*slang*), brouhaha, ballyhoo (*informal*) • *the build-up for the film*

built-in 1 = **integral**, fitted, incorporated, integrated • *modern cameras with built-in flash units*
2 = **essential**, integral, included, incorporated, inherent, implicit, in-built, intrinsic, inseparable, immanent • *These corporations enjoy substantial built-in advantages.*

bulb = **tuber**, rhizome, corm • *a tulip bulb*

bulbous = **bulging**, rounded, swelling, swollen, bloated, convex • *his bulbous purple nose*

bulge AS A VERB 1 = **swell out**, project, expand, swell, stand out, stick out, protrude, puff out, distend, bag • *He bulges out of his black T-shirt.*
2 = **stick out**, project, stand out, protrude • *His eyes seemed to bulge like those of a toad.*
3 = **overflow**, be full, be packed, be stuffed, be crammed, burst at the seams, brim over, be full to bursting, be fit to burst • *They returned home with the car bulging with boxes.*
▸ AS A NOUN 1 = **lump**, swelling, bump, projection, hump, protuberance, protrusion • *Why won't those bulges on your hips and thighs go?*
OPPOSITES: hole, bowl, hollow
2 = **increase**, rise, boost, surge, intensification • *a bulge in aircraft sales*

bulk AS A NOUN 1 = **size**, volume, dimensions, magnitude, substance, vastness, amplitude, immensity, bigness, largeness, massiveness • *the shadowy bulk of an ancient barn*
2 = **weight**, size, mass, heaviness, poundage, portliness • *Despite his bulk he moved lightly on his feet.*
3 = **majority**, mass, most, body, quantity, best part, major part, lion's share, better part, generality, preponderance, main part, plurality, nearly all, greater number • *The vast bulk of imports and exports is carried by sea.*
▸ IN PHRASES: **bulk large** = **be important**, dominate, loom, stand out, loom large, carry weight, preponderate, threaten • *Propaganda bulks large in their plans.*

bulky = **large**, big, huge, heavy, massive, enormous, substantial, immense, mega (*slang*), very large, mammoth, colossal, cumbersome, weighty, hulking, unwieldy, ponderous, voluminous, unmanageable, elephantine, massy, ginormous (*informal*), humongous *or* humungous (*U.S. slang*) • *a bulky man with balding hair*
OPPOSITES: small, slim, neat

bull
▸ RELATED ADJECTIVE: taurine

bulldoze 1 = **demolish**, level, destroy, flatten, knock down, tear down, raze, kennet (*Austral. slang*), jeff (*Austral. slang*) • *She defeated developers who wanted to bulldoze her home.*
2 = **push**, force, drive, thrust, shove, propel • *He bulldozed through the Tigers' defence.*
3 = **force**, bully, intimidate, railroad (*informal*), cow, hector, coerce, dragoon, browbeat, put the screws on • *My parents tried to bulldoze me into going to college.*

bullet = **projectile**, ball, shot, missile, slug, pellet • *There are three bullet holes in the windscreen.*
▸ RELATED MANIA: ballistomania

bulletin 1 = **report**, account, statement, message, communication, announcement, dispatch, communiqué, notification, news flash • *the early morning news bulletin*
2 = **journal**, paper, review, newsletter, gazette, periodical • *a hospital bulletin*

bullish = **optimistic**, confident, positive, encouraged, can-do (*informal*), bright, hopeful, cheerful, buoyant, sanguine, expectant, looking on the bright side, buoyed up • *The market opened in bullish mood.*

bully AS A NOUN = **persecutor**, tough, oppressor, tormentor, bully boy, browbeater, coercer, ruffian, intimidator • *I fell victim to the office bully.*
▸ AS A VERB 1 = **persecute**, intimidate, torment, hound, oppress, pick on, victimize, terrorize, push around (*slang*), ill-treat, ride roughshod over, maltreat, tyrannize, overbear • *I wasn't going to let him bully me.*
2 = **force**, coerce, railroad (*informal*), bulldoze (*informal*), dragoon, pressurize, browbeat, cow, hector, press-gang, domineer, bullyrag • *She used to bully me into doing my schoolwork.*

bulwark 1 = **fortification**, defence, bastion, buttress, rampart, redoubt, outwork • *a bulwark against the English*
2 = **defence**, support, safeguard, security, guard, buffer, mainstay • *a bulwark of democracy*

bum[1] = **bottom**, backside, buttocks, behind (*informal*), rear, arse (*taboo slang*), ass (*U.S. & Canad. taboo slang*), seat, tail (*informal*), butt (*U.S. & Canad. informal*), buns (*U.S. slang*), rump, rear end, posterior, derrière (*euphemistic*), tush (*U.S. slang*), fundament, jacksy (*Brit. slang*) • *Does my bum look big in this dress?*

bum[2] AS A NOUN 1 = **vagrant**, tramp, derelict, drifter, down-and-out, hobo (*chiefly U.S.*), vagabond, bag lady (*chiefly U.S.*), dosser (*Brit. slang*), derro (*Austral. slang*) • *A bum, a derelict, is what he looked like.*
2 = **loafer**, lounger, piker (*Austral. & N.Z. slang*), dodger, drone, slouch (*informal*), shirker, slacker, couch potato (*slang*), sloth, laggard, time-waster, layabout, deadbeat (*informal, chiefly U.S. & Canad.*), skiver (*Brit. slang*), idler, malingerer, sluggard, bludger (*Austral. & N.Z. informal*), clock-watcher, slugabed, Weary Willie (*informal*), lazybones • *You're all a bunch of bums.*
▸ AS AN ADJECTIVE = **bad**, poor, inadequate, pathetic, inferior, duff (*Brit. informal*), unsatisfactory, defective,

BUILDINGS AND MONUMENTS

Admiralty House
Althorp House
Alhambra
Angel of the North
Arc de Triomphe
Barbican
Beehive
Big Ben
Blenheim Palace
Buckingham Palace
Cenotaph
Charminar
Cleopatra's Needle
Crystal Palace
Edinburgh Castle
Eiffel Tower
Elysées Palace
Empire State Building
Forbidden City
Hampton Court Palace
Hermitage
Holyroodhouse
Houses of Parliament
Kaaba
Kensington Palace
Knossos
Kremlin
Lambeth Palace
Lateran
Leaning Tower of Pisa
Longleat House
Louvre
Masada
Mansion House
Monument
Nelson's Column
Pentagon
Saint James's Palace
Scone Palace
Taj Mahal
Tower of London
Vatican
Palace of Versailles
Westminster Abbey
White House

deficient, imperfect, low-rent *(informal, chiefly U.S.)*, poxy *(slang)*, chickenshit *(U.S. slang)*, pants *(informal)*, bodger or bodgie *(Austral. slang)* • *He knows you're getting a bum deal.*
▸ AS A VERB = **scrounge**, cadge, beg, touch (someone) for *(slang)*, blag *(slang)*, sorn *(Scot.)*, freeload *(slang)* • *Mind if I bum a cigarette?*
▸ IN PHRASES: **bum around** = **hang around**, idle, take it easy, lie around, loiter, laze around, loaf around • *She went off to bum around in Europe with a boyfriend.*

bumble 1 = **stagger**, reel, weave, sway, lurch, wobble, teeter, totter • *I finally bumbled out of the little bar.*
2 = **blather**, rabbit (on) *(Brit. informal)*, ramble, waffle *(informal, chiefly Brit.)*, burble, prattle, jabber, gabble, prate • *He bumbled his way through endless takes.*

bumbling = **clumsy**, awkward, blundering, bungling, incompetent, inefficient, lumbering, inept, maladroit, unco *(Austral. slang)* • *a clumsy, bumbling, inarticulate figure*
OPPOSITES: able, fit, efficient

bump AS A VERB 1 = **knock**, hit, strike, crash, smash, slam, bang • *He bumped his head on the low beam.*
2 = **jerk**, shake, bounce, rattle, jar, jog, lurch, jolt, jostle, jounce • *We left the road again and bumped over the mountainside.*
▸ AS A NOUN 1 = **knock**, hit, blow, shock, impact, rap, collision, thump • *Small children often cry after a minor bump.*
2 = **thud**, crash, knock, smash, bang, smack, thump, clump, wallop *(informal)*, clunk, clonk • *I felt a little bump and knew instinctively what had happened.*
3 = **lump**, swelling, bulge, hump, node, nodule, protuberance, contusion • *She got a large bump on her forehead.*
4 = **hump**, lump • *The truck hit a bump and bounced.*
▸ IN PHRASES: **bump into someone** = **meet**, encounter, come across, run into, run across, meet up with, chance upon, happen upon, light upon • *I happened to bump into Mervyn Johns in the hallway.*
bump into something = **crash into**, knock, hit, strike, collide with, smash into, slam into, bang into • *They stopped moving and he almost bumped into them.*
bump someone off = **murder**, kill, assassinate, remove, do in *(slang)*, eliminate, take out *(slang)*, wipe out *(informal)*, dispatch, finish off, do away with, blow away *(slang, chiefly U.S.)*, knock off *(slang)*, liquidate, rub out *(U.S. slang)* • *They will probably bump you off anyway.*
bump something up = **increase**, raise, boost, expand, add to, heighten, enlarge, magnify, amplify, jack up, hoick • *The extra cost will bump up the price.*

bumper = **exceptional**, excellent, exo *(Austral. slang)*, massive, unusual, mega *(slang)*, jumbo *(informal)*, abundant, whacking *(informal, chiefly Brit.)*, spanking *(informal)*, whopping *(informal)*, bountiful • *a bumper crop of rice*

bumpkin = **yokel**, peasant, hick *(informal, chiefly U.S. & Canad.)*, rustic, lout, hillbilly, oaf, country bumpkin, clown, boor, hayseed *(U.S. & Canad. informal)*, clodhopper, lubber • *unsophisticated country bumpkins*

bumptious = **cocky**, forward, arrogant, brash, swaggering, vaunting, pushy *(informal)*, conceited, showy, overbearing, presumptuous, boastful, impudent, overconfident, vainglorious, self-assertive, egotistic, full of yourself • *a bumptious young man*

bumpy 1 = **uneven**, rough, pitted, irregular, rutted, lumpy, potholed, knobby • *bumpy cobbled streets*
2 = **jolting**, jarring, bouncy, choppy, jerky, bone-breaking, jolty • *a hot and bumpy journey across the desert*

bunch AS A NOUN 1 = **group**, band, crowd, party, team, troop, gathering, crew *(informal)*, gang, knot, mob, flock, swarm, multitude, posse *(informal)*, bevy • *The players were a great bunch.*
2 = **bouquet**, spray, garland, wreath, sheaf, flower arrangement • *He had left a huge bunch of flowers in her hotel room.*
3 = **cluster**, clump • *She had fallen asleep clutching a fat bunch of grapes.*
4 = **number**, lot, mass, pile, quantity, stack, heap, batch, assortment • *We did a bunch of songs together.*
▸ AS A VERB = **gather**, wrinkle, pleat, ruffle, rumple, pucker, tousle • *She clutches the sides of her skirt until it bunches around her waist.*
▸ IN PHRASES: **bunch together** or **up** = **group**, crowd, mass, collect, assemble, cluster, flock, herd, huddle, congregate • *People bunched up at all the exits.*

bundle AS A NOUN = **bunch**, group, collection, mass, pile, quantity, stack, bolt, roll, heap, rick, batch, accumulation, assortment, armful • *He gathered the bundles of clothing into his arms.*
▸ AS A VERB = **push**, thrust, shove, throw, rush, hurry, hasten, jostle, hustle • *They bundled him into a taxi.*
▸ IN PHRASES: **bundle someone up** = **wrap up**, shroud, swathe, envelop, muffle up, clothe warmly • *Harry greeted them bundled up in a long coat and a fur hat.*
bundle something up = **package**, tie, pack, bind, wrap, tie up, bale, fasten, truss, tie together, palletize • *possessions bundled up and carried in weary arms*
▸ RELATED ADJECTIVE: fascicular

bung 1 = **stopper**, top, cap, seal, cork, plug, spigot, stopple • *Pump the air out, then remove the bung.*
2 = **place**, put, stick *(informal)*, position, lay, shove, lob *(informal)* • *Wrap it in a plastic bag and bung it in the freezer.*

bunged up = **clogged**, stuffed-up, blocked up, jammed • *My nose is all bunged up.*

bungle = **mess up**, blow *(slang)*, ruin, spoil, blunder, fudge, screw up *(informal)*, botch, cock up *(Brit. slang)*, fuck up *(offensive taboo slang)*, miscalculate, make a mess of, mismanage, muff, foul up, make a nonsense of *(informal)*, bodge *(informal)*, make a pig's ear of *(informal)*, flub *(U.S. slang)*, crool or cruel *(Austral. slang)*, louse up *(slang)* • *Two prisoners bungled an escape bid last night*
OPPOSITES: achieve, succeed in, accomplish

bungler = **incompetent**, blunderer, muddler, fumbler, botcher, duffer *(informal)*, butterfingers *(informal)*, lubber • *Why is this lying bungler still in the fire service?*

bungling = **incompetent**, blundering, awkward, clumsy, inept, botching, cack-handed *(informal)*, maladroit, ham-handed *(informal)*, unskilful, ham-fisted *(informal)*, unco *(Austral. slang)* • *a bungling burglar*

bunk[1] = **berth**, bed, cot *(Nautical)*, hammock, billet • *He left his bunk and went up on deck again.*

bunk[2] IN PHRASES: **do a bunk** = **run away**, flee, bolt, clear out *(informal)*, beat it *(slang)*, abscond, decamp, do a runner *(slang)*, run for it *(informal)*, cut and run *(informal)*, scram *(informal)*, fly the coop *(U.S. & Canad. informal)*, skedaddle *(informal)*, take a powder *(U.S. & Canad. slang)*, take it on the lam *(U.S. & Canad. slang)*, do a Skase *(Austral. informal)* • *His live-in lover has done a bunk because he won't marry her.*

bunk[3] or **bunkum** = **nonsense**, rubbish, shit *(taboo slang)*, rot, crap *(slang)*, garbage *(informal)*, trash, bullshit *(taboo slang)*, balls *(taboo slang)*, hot air *(informal)*, tosh *(slang, chiefly Brit.)*, cobblers *(Brit. taboo slang)*, bilge *(informal)*, twaddle, tripe *(informal)*, guff *(slang)*, havers *(Scot.)*, moonshine, malarkey, baloney *(informal)*, hogwash, bizzo *(Austral. slang)*, bull's wool *(Austral. & N.Z. slang)*, hokum *(slang, chiefly U.S. & Canad.)*, piffle *(informal)*, tomfoolery, poppycock *(informal)*, balderdash, bosh *(informal)*, eyewash *(informal)*, kak *(S. African taboo slang)*, stuff and nonsense, hooey *(slang)*, tommyrot, horsefeathers *(U.S. slang)*, tarradiddle • *Henry Ford's opinion that 'history is bunk'*

buoy AS A NOUN = **float**, guide, signal, marker, beacon • *We released the buoy and drifted back on the tide.*
▸ IN PHRASES: **buoy someone up** = **encourage**, support, boost, cheer, sustain, hearten, cheer up, keep afloat, gee up • *They are buoyed up by a sense of hope.*

buoyancy 1 = **floatability**, lightness, weightlessness • *Air can be pumped into the diving suit to increase buoyancy.*
2 = **cheerfulness**, bounce (*informal*), pep, animation, good humour, high spirits, zing (*informal*), liveliness, spiritedness, cheeriness, sunniness • *a mood of buoyancy and optimism*
3 = **expansion**, development, strength, mushrooming, economic growth • *The slump will be followed by a period of buoyancy.*

buoyant 1 = **cheerful**, happy, bright, lively, sunny, animated, upbeat (*informal*), joyful, carefree, bouncy, breezy, genial, jaunty, chirpy (*informal*), sparky, vivacious, debonair, blithe, full of beans (*informal*), peppy (*informal*), light-hearted • *She was in a buoyant mood.*
OPPOSITES: sad, depressed, gloomy
2 = **expanding**, developing, booming, strong, thriving, mushrooming, vigorous • *a buoyant economy*
3 = **floating**, light, floatable • *a small and buoyant boat*

burden AS A NOUN 1 = **trouble**, care, worry, trial, weight, responsibility, stress, strain, anxiety, sorrow, grievance, affliction, onus, albatross, millstone, encumbrance • *Her illness will be an impossible burden on him.*
2 = **load**, weight, pack, bundle, cargo, freight, bale, consignment, encumbrance, charge • *She heaved her burden into the back.*
▸ AS A VERB = **weigh down**, worry, load, tax, strain, bother, overwhelm, handicap, oppress, inconvenience, overload, saddle with, encumber, trammel, incommode • *We decided not to burden him with the news.*
▸ RELATED ADJECTIVE: onerous

burdened = **laden**, weighed down, loaded, freighted, charged • *They arrived burdened by bags and food baskets.*

burdensome = **troublesome**, trying, taxing, difficult, heavy, crushing, exacting, oppressive, weighty, onerous, irksome • *The outlay so far has not been too burdensome.*

bureau 1 = **agency**, company, business, service, concern, firm, operation, organization • *the foreign employment bureau*
2 = **office**, department, section, branch, station, unit, division, subdivision • *the paper's Washington bureau*
3 = **desk**, writing desk, writing table, secretaire, davenport • *A simple writing bureau sat in front of the window.*

bureaucracy 1 = **government**, officials, authorities, administration, ministry, the system, civil service, directorate, officialdom, corridors of power • *State bureaucracies tend to stifle enterprise and initiative.*
2 = **red tape**, regulations, paperwork, officialdom, officialese, bumbledom • *People complain about having to deal with too much bureaucracy.*

bureaucrat = **official**, minister, officer, administrator, civil servant, public servant, functionary, apparatchik, office-holder, mandarin • *The economy is still controlled by bureaucrats.*

bureaucratic 1 = **administrative**, political, official, ministerial, governmental, red-tape • *The school is free from bureaucratic control.*
2 = **rigid**, complex, strict, stringent, uncompromising, unadaptable • *The GPs complain that the system has become too bureaucratic.*

burgeon = **develop**, increase, grow, flower, progress, mature, thrive, flourish, bloom, bud, blossom, prosper • *Japan's burgeoning satellite-TV industry*

burglar = **housebreaker**, thief, robber, pilferer, filcher, cat burglar, sneak thief, picklock • *Burglars broke into their home.*

burglary = **breaking and entering**, housebreaking, break-in, home invasion (*Austral. & N.Z.*) • *He's been arrested for burglary.*

burgle = **rob**, raid, loot, steal from, plunder, ransack • *I thought we had been burgled.*

burial = **funeral**, interment, burying, obsequies, entombment, inhumation, exequies, sepulture • *He can have a decent burial.*
▸ RELATED PHOBIA: taphephobia

burial ground = **graveyard**, cemetery, churchyard, necropolis, golgotha (*rare*), God's acre • *an ancient burial ground*

buried 1 = **absorbed**, engrossed, preoccupied, lost, committed, concentrating, occupied, devoted, caught up, intent, immersed, rapt • *She was buried in a book.*
2 = **hidden**, concealed, covered • *buried treasure*

burlesque AS A NOUN = **parody**, mockery, satire, caricature, send-up (*Brit. informal*), spoof (*informal*), travesty, takeoff (*informal*) • *The book read like a black comic burlesque.*
▸ AS AN ADJECTIVE = **satirical**, comic, mocking, mock, farcical, travestying, ironical, parodic, mock-heroic, caricatural, hudibrastic • *a trio of burlesque stereotypes*

burly = **brawny**, strong, powerful, big, strapping, hefty, muscular, sturdy, stout, bulky, stocky, hulking, beefy (*informal*), well-built, thickset • *He was a big, burly man.*
OPPOSITES: thin, weak, scrawny

burn 1 = **be on fire**, blaze, be ablaze, smoke, flame, glow, flare, flicker, go up in flames • *I suddenly realized the blanket was burning.*
2 = **set on fire**, light, ignite, kindle, incinerate, reduce to ashes • *He found out he'd won the Lottery, but he'd burnt the ticket.*
3 = **scorch**, toast, sear, char, singe, brand • *I burnt the toast.*
4 = **sting**, hurt, smart, tingle, bite, pain • *When you go to the toilet, it burns and stings.*
5 = **shine**, glow, beam, glare, gleam, shimmer, radiate, glimmer, emit light, give off light • *a single light burning in a third-story window*
6 = **blush**, be red, flush, colour, be hot, be on fire, redden, turn red, feel hot, go red (as a beetroot), turn scarlet • *Liz's face was burning.*
7 = **be passionate**, blaze, be excited, be aroused, be inflamed • *The young boy was burning with a fierce ambition.*
8 = **seethe**, boil, fume, be angry, simmer, smoulder, be wild, be livid, be beside yourself • *He was burning with rage.*
9 = **yearn**, long, desire, hunger, ache, crave, itch, hanker, have a yen for (*informal*), set your heart upon, would give your eyeteeth for • *He's burning to prove he's still the best.*

burning 1 = **very hot**, boiling, baking, flaming, tropical, roasting, searing, blistering, fiery, scorching, sizzling, red-hot, torrid, sweltering, broiling, unbearably hot • *the burning desert of central Asia*
2 = **intense**, passionate, earnest, eager, frantic, frenzied, ardent, fervent, impassioned, zealous, vehement, all-consuming, fervid • *I had a burning ambition to become a journalist.*
OPPOSITES: cool, calm, mild
3 = **blazing**, flaming, fiery, ignited, smouldering, glowing, ablaze, in flames, afire • *He was last seen alive as he ran into his burning house.*
4 = **flashing**, blazing, flaming, gleaming, fiery • *She glared at both of them with burning, reproachful eyes.*
5 = **crucial**, important, pressing, significant, essential, vital, critical, acute, compelling, urgent • *a burning question*

burnish 1 = **improve**, enhance, brighten, refine, cultivate, brush up, touch up, emend • *The company badly needs a president who can burnish its image.*
2 = **polish**, shine, buff, brighten, rub up, furbish • *His shoes were burnished, his shirt perfectly pressed.*
OPPOSITES: scratch, graze, scuff

burnt-out = **incinerated**, burnt, gutted, torched, carbonized • *a burnt-out car*

burp = **belch**, bring up wind, eructate, hiccup *or* hiccough • *Charlie burped loudly.*

burrow AS A NOUN = **hole**, shelter, tunnel, den, lair, retreat • *a rabbit's burrow*
▸ AS A VERB 1 = **dig**, tunnel, excavate • *The larvae burrow into cracks in the floor.*

2 = delve, search, dig, probe, ferret, rummage, forage, fossick *(Austral. & N.Z.)* • *He burrowed into the pile of charts.*

burst AS A VERB **1 = explode**, blow up, break, split, crack, shatter, fragment, shiver, disintegrate, puncture, rupture, rend asunder • *The driver lost control when a tyre burst.* • *She burst the balloon with a pin.*

2 = rush, run, break, pour, jet, surge, spill, break out, erupt, cascade, spout, gush forth • *Water burst through the dam and flooded their villages.*

3 = barge, charge, rush, tear, plunge, dash, shove, hurtle • *Gunmen burst into his home and opened fire.*

4 = explode, go off, blow up, detonate, go bang *(informal)* • *Every now and then you hear some bombs bursting.*

▸ AS A NOUN **1 = rush**, surge, fit, outbreak, outburst, spate, gush, torrent, eruption, spurt, outpouring • *short bursts of activity*

2 = explosion, crack, blast, blasting, bang, discharge • *a burst of machine-gun fire*

▸ AS AN ADJECTIVE **= ruptured**, flat, punctured, split, rent • *a burst tyre*

▸ IN PHRASES: **burst into tears = break down in tears**, suddenly start crying • *She burst into tears and ran from the kitchen.*

burst out 1 = exclaim, cry, call, declare, shout, proclaim, yell, utter, call out, cry out, ejaculate, vociferate • *'I want to be just like you,' she burst out.*

2 = begin, start, happen, appear, emerge, occur, arise, set in, commence, spring up • *Then war burst out.*

bursting 1 = overflowing, full, filled, packed, running over, level with, brimming, overflowing, flush, overfull • *The place appears to be bursting with women directors.*

2 = passionate, blazing, excited, aroused, aching, itching, inflamed • *I was bursting with curiosity.*

bury 1 = inter, lay to rest, entomb, sepulchre, consign to the grave, inearth, inhume, inurn • *soldiers who helped to bury the dead*

OPPOSITES: unearth, dig up, exhume

2 = hide, cover, conceal, stash *(informal)*, secrete, cache, stow away • *She buried it under some leaves.*

OPPOSITES: find, reveal, uncover

3 = sink, embed, immerse, enfold • *She buried her face in the pillows.*

4 = embed, sink, implant, drive in, submerge • *The missile buried itself deep in the grassy hillside.*

5 = forget, break with, draw a veil over, think no more of, consign to oblivion, put in the past, not give another thought to • *It is time to bury our past misunderstandings.*

6 = engross, involve, occupy, interest, busy, engage, absorb, preoccupy, immerse • *His reaction was to withdraw, to bury himself in work.*

bush AS A NOUN **= shrub**, plant, hedge, undergrowth, thicket, shrubbery • *Trees and bushes grow down to the water's edge.*

▸ IN PHRASES: **the bush = the wilds**, brush, wilderness, scrub, woodland, remote areas, the outback, backwoods, back country *(U.S.)*, scrubland, backlands *(U.S.)* • *He was shot dead while travelling in the bush.*

bushy = thick, bristling, spreading, rough, stiff, fuzzy, fluffy, unruly, shaggy, wiry, luxuriant, bristly • *a bushy tail*

busily = actively, briskly, intently, earnestly, strenuously, speedily, purposefully, diligently, energetically, assiduously, industriously • *The two saleswomen were busily trying to keep up with the demand.*

business AS A NOUN **1 = trade**, selling, trading, industry, manufacturing, commerce, dealings, merchandising • *young people seeking a career in business*

2 = establishment, company, firm, concern, organization, corporation, venture, enterprise • *The company was a family business.*

3 = profession, work, calling, job, line, trade, career, function, employment, craft, occupation, pursuit, vocation, métier • *May I ask what business you are in?*

4 = matter, issue, subject, point, problem, question, responsibility, task, duty, function, topic, assignment • *Parenting can be a stressful business.*

5 = concern, affair, problem, worry, lookout • *My sex life is my own business.*

▸ IN PHRASES: **mean business = be serious**, be determined, be resolute, be set on something • *Now people are starting to realise that he means business.*

QUOTATIONS

Boldness in business is the first, second, and third thing
[Thomas Fuller *Gnomologia*]

The business of America is business
[Calvin Coolidge *Address to the Society of Newspaper Editors*]

Dispatch is the soul of business, and nothing contributes more to Dispatch than Method
[Lord Chesterfield *Letters to His Son*]

Here's the rule for bargains: 'Do other men, for they would do you.' That's the true business precept
[Charles Dickens *Martin Chuzzlewit*]

I'll keep it short and sweet. Family. Religion. Friendship. These are the three demons you must slay if you wish to succeed in business
[C. Montgomery Burns *The Simpsons*]

PROVERBS

business before pleasure

businesslike = efficient, professional, practical, regular, correct, organized, routine, thorough, systematic, orderly, matter-of-fact, methodical, well-ordered, workaday • *Mr Penn sounds quite businesslike.*

OPPOSITES: disorderly, irregular, inefficient

businessman *or* **businesswoman = executive**, director, manager, merchant, capitalist, administrator, entrepreneur, tycoon, industrialist, financier, tradesman, homme d'affaires *(French)* • *a wealthy businesswoman*

bust[1] 1 = bosom, breasts, chest, front • *Good posture also helps your bust look bigger.*

2 = sculpture, carving, head • *a bronze bust of the Queen*

bust[2] AS A VERB **1 = break**, smash, split, crack, burst, snap, shatter, fracture, splinter, rupture, break into fragments • *They will have to bust the door to get him out.*

2 = arrest, catch, lift *(slang)*, raid, cop *(slang)*, nail *(informal)*, collar *(informal)*, nab *(informal)*, feel your collar *(slang)* • *They were busted for possession of cannabis.*

▸ AS A NOUN **= arrest**, capture, raid, cop *(slang)* • *He was imprisoned after a drug bust.*

▸ IN PHRASES: **go bust = go bankrupt**, fail, go under, break, be ruined, be wound up, go to the wall, be liquidated, go into receivership, go into liquidation, become insolvent, cease trading • *Hundreds of restaurants went bust last year.*

bustle AS A VERB **= hurry**, tear, rush, dash, scramble, fuss, flutter, beetle, hasten, scuttle, scurry, scamper • *My mother bustled around the kitchen.*

OPPOSITES: rest, relax, idle

▸ AS A NOUN **= activity**, to-do, stir, excitement, hurry, fuss, flurry, haste, agitation, commotion, ado, tumult, hurly-burly, pother • *the hustle and bustle of modern life*

OPPOSITES: inactivity, quiet, tranquillity

bustling = busy, full, crowded, rushing, active, stirring, lively, buzzing, energetic, humming, swarming, thronged, hustling, teeming, astir • *The sidewalks are bustling with people.*

busy AS AN ADJECTIVE **1 = active**, efficient, brisk, hard-pressed, tireless, diligent, industrious, hardworking, assiduous, rushed off your feet • *He's a very busy man.*

OPPOSITES: relaxed, lazy, idle

2 = occupied with, working, engaged in, on duty, employed in, preoccupied with, absorbed in, immersed in, hard at work, engrossed in, in harness, on active service, hard at work on • *Life is what happens to you while you're busy making other plans.*
OPPOSITES: off duty, unoccupied
3 = hectic, full, active, tiring, exacting, energetic, strenuous, on the go *(informal)* • *I'd had a busy day and was rather tired.*
4 = crowded, full, packed, crushed, mobbed, cramped, bustling, swarming, overflowing, thronged, teeming, congested, populous, jam-packed • *The ward was busy and Amy hardly had time to talk.*
▸ **IN PHRASES: busy yourself = occupy yourself**, be engrossed, immerse yourself, involve yourself, amuse yourself, absorb yourself, employ yourself, engage yourself, keep busy *or* occupied • *He busied himself with the camera.*

busybody = nosy parker *(informal)*, gossip, troublemaker, snoop, intriguer, intruder, pry, eavesdropper, snooper, stirrer *(informal)*, meddler, scandalmonger, tattletale *(chiefly U.S. & Canad.)* • *Some busybody tipped off the police.*

but AS A CONJUNCTION 1 = yet, however, though, although, nevertheless, even so, all the same, for all that, in spite of that, despite that, be that as it may • *You are awful. But I like you.*
2 = however, still, yet, nevertheless • *'But,' he added, 'the vast majority must accept a common future.'*
▸ **AS A PREPOSITION = except (for)**, save, bar, barring, excepting, other than, excluding, omitting, with the exception of • *He was forced to wind up everything but the hotel business.*
▸ **AS AN ADVERB = only**, just, simply, merely • *St Anton is but a snowball's throw away from Lech.*

butch = manly, masculine, virile, he-man, chauvinist • *Paul was a butch outdoor type.*

butcher AS A NOUN 1 = meat trader, slaughterer, meat merchant, meat seller • *I went to the butcher for steak for my lunch.*
2 = murderer, killer, slaughterer, slayer, destroyer, liquidator, executioner, cut-throat, exterminator • *Klaus Barbie was known in France as the Butcher of Lyon.*
▸ **AS A VERB 1 = slaughter**, prepare, carve, cut up, dress, cut, clean, joint • *Pigs were butchered, hams were hung to dry from the ceiling.*
2 = kill, slaughter, massacre, destroy, cut down, assassinate, slay, liquidate, exterminate, put to the sword • *Our people are being butchered in their own homes.*
3 = mess up, destroy, ruin, wreck, spoil, mutilate, botch, bodge *(informal)* • *I am not in Cannes because they butchered my film.*

butchery 1 = slaughter, killing, murder, massacre, bloodshed, carnage, mass murder, blood-letting, blood bath • *War is simply a legalised form of butchery.*
2 = carving, cutting up, dressing, cleaning, jointing • *a carcass hung up for butchery*

butt[1] 1 = bottom, behind *(informal)*, bum *(Brit. slang)*, arse *(taboo slang)*, ass *(U.S. & Canad. taboo slang)*, seat, rear, tail *(informal)*, buns *(U.S. slang)*, buttocks, backside, rump, rear end, posterior, derrière *(euphemistic)*, tush *(U.S. slang)*, fundament, jacksy *(Brit. slang)* • *She grinned, pinching him on the butt.*
2 = end, handle, shaft, stock, shank, hilt, haft • *Troops used tear gas and rifle butts to break up the protests.*
3 = stub, end, base, foot, tip, tail, leftover, fag end *(informal)* • *He paused to stub out the butt of his cigar.*

butt[2] = target, victim, object, point, mark, subject, dupe, laughing stock, Aunt Sally • *He is still the butt of cruel jokes about his humble origins.*

butt[3] AS A VERB = knock, push, bump, punch, buck, thrust, ram, shove, poke, buffet, prod, jab, bunt • *The male butted me.*
▸ **IN PHRASES: butt in 1 = interfere**, meddle, intrude, heckle, barge in *(informal)*, stick your nose in, put your oar in • *Nobody asked you to butt in.*
2 = interrupt, cut in, break in, chip in *(informal)*, put your two cents in *(U.S. slang)* • *Could I just butt in here and say something?*

butt[4] = cask, drum, barrel, cylinder • *The hose is great for watering your garden from your water butt.*

butter IN PHRASES: butter someone up = flatter, coax, cajole, pander to, blarney, wheedle, suck up to *(informal)*, soft-soap, brown-nose *(taboo slang)*, kiss (someone's) ass *(U.S. slang)*, fawn on *or* upon, honey up, oil your tongue • *I tried buttering her up.*
▸ **RELATED ADJECTIVE:** butyraceous

butterfly
▸ **RELATED ADJECTIVE:** lepidopterous
▸ **NAME OF YOUNG:** caterpillar, chrysalis *or* chrysalid
▸ **RELATED ENTHUSIAST:** lepidopterist
▹ *See panel* **Butterflies and moths**

buttocks = bottom, behind *(informal)*, bum *(Brit. slang)*, arse *(taboo slang)*, ass *(U.S. & Canad. taboo slang)*, backside *(informal)*, seat, rear, tail *(informal)*, butt *(U.S. & Canad. informal)*, buns *(U.S. slang)*, rump, posterior, haunches, hindquarters, derrière *(euphemistic)*, tush *(U.S. slang)*, fundament, gluteus maximus *(Anatomy)*, jacksy *(Brit. slang)* • *Squeeze buttocks lightly and draw your tailbone down.*
▸ **TECHNICAL NAME:** nates
▸ **RELATED ADJECTIVES:** natal, gluteal

BUTTERFLIES AND MOTHS

apollo
argus
bag moth *(N.Z.)*
bagworm moth
bell moth
bogong *or* bugong (moth)
brimstone
brown-tail moth
buff-tip moth
cabbage white
cactoblastis
Camberwell beauty *or (U.S.)* mourning cloak
cardinal
carpenter moth
carpet moth
cleopatra
comma butterfly
copper
cecropia moth
cinnabar
clearwing *or* clearwing moth
Clifden nonpareil
codlin(g) moth
death's-head moth
drinker moth *or* drinker
egger *or* eggar
ermine moth *or* ermine
festoon
ghost moth
gipsy moth
goldtail moth *or* yellowtail (moth)
grass moth
grayling
hairstreak
herald moth
hawk moth, sphinx moth, *or* hummingbird moth
house moth
Io moth
Kentish glory
kitten moth
lackey moth
lappet moth
large white *or* cabbage white
leopard moth
lobster moth
luna moth
magpie moth
marbled white
monarch
mother-of-pearl moth
Mother Shipton
old lady
orange-tip
painted lady
peacock butterfly
peppered moth
privet hawk
processionary moth
purple emperor
puss moth
red admiral
red underwing
ringlet
silver-Y
skipper
small white
snout
speckled wood
swallowtail
swift
tapestry moth
thorn (moth)
tiger (moth)
tussock moth
two-tailed pasha
umber (moth)
vapourer moth
wave (moth)
wax moth, honeycomb moth, *or* bee moth
wall brown
white
white admiral
winter moth
yellow
yellow underwing

button 1 = **fastening**, catch, hook, clip, clasp, fastener, hasp, press stud • *a coat with brass buttons*
2 = **switch**, control, key, handle, lever, knob • *He pressed the 'play' button.*

buttonhole = **detain**, catch, grab, intercept, accost, waylay, take aside • *It is not easy to buttonhole her for an interview.*

b

buttress AS A NOUN = **support**, shore, prop, brace, pier, reinforcement, strut, mainstay, stanchion, stay, abutment • *a buttress of rock*
▸ AS A VERB = **support**, sustain, strengthen, shore, prop, reinforce, back up, brace, uphold, bolster, prop up, shore up, augment • *His tough line is buttressed by a democratic mandate.*

buxom = **plump**, ample, voluptuous, busty, well-rounded, curvaceous, comely, bosomy, full-bosomed • *Melissa was a tall, buxom blonde.*
OPPOSITES: thin, slight, slender

buy AS A VERB 1 = **purchase**, get, score (*slang*), secure, pay for, obtain, acquire, invest in, shop for, procure • *He could not afford to buy a house.*
OPPOSITES: sell, retail, auction
2 = **accept**, believe, trust, credit, rely on, swallow (*informal*), have faith in, be persuaded of, place confidence in, presume true, take as gospel, take on • *I'm not buying any of that nonsense.*
▸ AS A NOUN = **purchase**, deal, bargain, acquisition, steal (*informal*), snip (*informal*), giveaway • *a good buy*
▸ IN PHRASES: **buy someone off** = **bribe**, square, fix (*informal*), pay off (*informal*), lure, corrupt, get at, suborn, grease someone's palm (*slang*), influence by gifts, oil the palm of (*informal*) • *policies designed to buy off the working-class*

buyer = **consumer**, client, user, patron, shopper, purchaser • *The buyer has to put down a 10% deposit.*

buzz AS A VERB 1 = **hum**, whizz, drone, whir • *Attack helicopters buzzed across the city.*
2 = **bustle**, tear, rush, stir, dash, hurry, scramble, fuss, flutter, beetle, hasten, scuttle, scurry, scamper • *A few tourists were buzzing around.*
3 = **be busy**, hum, bustle, throb, be lively • *The rehearsal studio is buzzing with activity.*
4 = **phone**, call, telephone, ring (up) (*informal, chiefly Brit.*), give someone a call, give someone a ring (*informal, chiefly Brit.*), give someone a buzz (*informal*), give someone a bell (*Brit. slang*), give someone a tinkle (*Brit. informal*), get on the blower to (*informal*) • *She said she would buzz me later.*
5 = **purr**, ring, sound, reverberate, beep, whirr • *Just then the intercom buzzed.*
▸ AS A NOUN 1 = **hum**, buzzing, murmur, drone, whir, bombilation *or* bombination (*literary*) • *the irritating buzz of an insect*
2 = **murmur**, whisper, hum • *the excited buzz of conversation*
3 = **thrill**, charge (*slang*), kick (*informal*), pleasure, glow, sensation, stimulation, tingle, titillation, flush of excitement • *Performing still gives him a buzz.*
4 = **ring**, call, phone, bell (*informal*), tinkle (*informal*) • *We'll give him a buzz when we get there.*
5 = **gossip**, news, report, latest (*informal*), word, scandal, rumour, whisper, dirt (*U.S. slang*), gen (*Brit. informal*), hearsay, scuttlebutt (*U.S. slang*), goss (*informal*) • *The buzz is that she knows something.*
▸ IN PHRASES: **buzz off** = **go away**, get lost (*informal*), piss off (*taboo slang*), fuck off (*taboo slang*), bugger off (*taboo slang*), bog off (*Brit. slang*), voetsek (*S. African offensive*), rack off (*Austral. & N.Z. slang*) • *Now be quiet and buzz off.*

by AS A PREPOSITION 1 = **through**, via, with the help of, by virtue of, with the aid of, under the aegis of, through the agency of • *The feast was served by his mother and sisters.*
2 = **via**, over, by way of • *The train passes by Oxford.*
3 = **near**, past, along, close to, closest to, neighbouring, next to, beside, nearest to, adjoining, adjacent to • *She was sitting in a rocking chair by the window.*
4 = **before**, prior to, earlier than, in advance of, no later than • *We all knew by then that the affair was practically over.*
▸ AS AN ADVERB 1 = **nearby**, close, handy, at hand, within reach • *Large numbers of security police stood by.*
2 = **away**, aside, to one side • *They did not put the money by for a rainy day.*
▸ IN PHRASES: **by and by** = **presently**, shortly, soon, eventually, one day, before long, in a while, anon, in the course of time, erelong (*archaic or poetic*) • *By and by the light gradually grew fainter.*
by yourself 1 = **alone**, separately, singly, on your own, on your tod, on your lonesome (*informal*), in a solitary state • *a dark-haired man sitting by himself in a corner*
2 = **without help**, independently, single-handedly, unassisted, without assistance, by your own effort • *She decided to learn to fly to prove she could do something all by herself.*

bygone = **past**, former, previous, lost, forgotten, ancient, of old, one-time, departed, extinct, gone by, erstwhile, antiquated, of yore, olden, past recall, sunk in oblivion • *bygone generations*
OPPOSITES: to be, coming, future

bypass AS A VERB 1 = **get round**, avoid, evade, circumvent, outmanoeuvre, body-swerve (*Scot.*) • *Regulators worry that controls could easily be bypassed.*
2 = **go round**, skirt, circumvent, depart from, deviate from, pass round, detour round • *Money for new roads to bypass cities.*
OPPOSITES: meet, unite, cross
▸ AS A NOUN = **ringroad**, detour, alternative route, relief road • *A new bypass around the city is being built.*

bystander = **onlooker**, passer-by, spectator, witness, observer, viewer, looker-on, watcher, eyewitness • *It looks like an innocent bystander was killed instead of you.*
OPPOSITES: party, participant, contributor

byword AS A NOUN = **saying**, slogan, motto, maxim, gnome, adage, proverb, epithet, dictum, precept, aphorism, saw, apophthegm • *Loyalty, support, and secrecy became the bywords of the day.*
▸ IN PHRASES: **a byword for** = **the epitome of**, synonymous with, a perfect example of, a classic case of, the personification of • *a region that had become a byword for violence and degeneracy*

Cc

cab = **taxi**, minicab, taxicab, hackney, hackney carriage • *We'd better take a cab to the station.*

cabal 1 = **clique**, set, party, league, camp, coalition, faction, caucus, junta, coterie, schism, confederacy, conclave • *He had been chosen by a cabal of fellow senators.*
2 = **plot**, scheme, intrigue, conspiracy, machination • *The left saw it as a bourgeois cabal.*

cabin 1 = **room**, berth, quarters, compartment, deckhouse • *The steward showed her to a small cabin.*
2 = **compartment**, section, carriage • *the first-class cabin of a jumbo jet*
3 = **hut**, shed, cottage, lodge, cot *(archaic)*, shack, chalet, shanty, hovel, bothy, whare *(N.Z.)* • *a log cabin in the woods*

cabinet = **cupboard**, case, locker, dresser, closet, press, chiffonier • *a display cabinet with gleaming trophies*
▷ *See panel* **Cupboards and cabinets**

Cabinet = **council**, committee, administration, ministry, assembly, board • *The radically-changed Cabinet of the Prime Minister includes eight new ministers*

cache = **store**, fund, supply, reserve, treasury, accumulation, stockpile, hoard, stash *(informal)* • *A cache of weapons and explosives was found by the police.*

cachet = **prestige**, credit, status, importance, distinction, esteem, standing, stature, eminence, kudos • *Having a PhD still gives one a certain cachet.*

cackle AS A VERB = **laugh**, giggle, chuckle • *The old lady cackled with glee.*
▸ AS A NOUN = **laugh**, giggle, chuckle • *He let out a brief cackle of triumph.*

cacophonous = **discordant**, harsh, jarring, grating, raucous, strident, dissonant, inharmonious • *screaming guitars and cacophonous vocals*

cacophony = **discord**, racket, din, dissonance, disharmony, stridency • *The whole place erupted in a cacophony of sound.*

cad = **scoundrel** *(slang)*, rat *(informal)*, bounder *(Brit. old-fashioned slang)*, cur, knave, rotter *(slang, chiefly Brit.)*, heel, scumbag *(slang)*, churl, dastard *(archaic)*, wrong 'un *(Austral. slang)* • *You're nothing but a scoundrel and a cad, sir!*

cadaverous = **deathly**, pale, ghastly, wan, blanched, gaunt, haggard, emaciated, bloodless, pallid, ashen, hollow-eyed, corpse-like, like death warmed up *(informal)*, deathlike • *a tall, thin man with a cadaverous face*

cadence 1 = **intonation**, accent, inflection, modulation • *He recognised the Polish cadences in her voice.*
2 = **rhythm**, beat, measure *(Prosody)*, metre, pulse, throb, tempo, swing, lilt • *There was a sudden shift in the cadence of the music.*

cadge = **scrounge**, beg, bum *(informal)*, blag *(slang)*, mooch *(slang)*, freeload *(slang)*, sponge *(informal)* • *He asked if he could cadge a ride from somebody.*

cadre = **group**, band, core, framework, corps, nucleus, hard core, key group • *An elite cadre of trained soldiers was standing by.*

café = **snack bar**, restaurant, cafeteria, coffee shop, brasserie, coffee bar, tearoom, lunchroom, eatery *or* eaterie • *The café also serves delicious lunches.*

cage AS A NOUN = **enclosure**, pen, coop, hutch, pound, corral *(U.S.)* • *I hate to see animals being kept in cages.*
▸ AS A VERB = **shut up**, confine, restrain, imprison, lock up, mew, incarcerate, fence in, impound, coop up, immure, pound • *Don't you think it's cruel to cage wild creatures?*
▸ IN PHRASES: **rattle someone's cage** = **annoy**, anger, bother, provoke, bug *(informal)*, needle *(informal)*, irritate, tease, harass, hassle *(informal)*, aggravate *(informal)*, gall, madden, ruffle, exasperate, nettle, vex, irk, rile, harry, get under your skin *(informal)*, get on your nerves *(informal)*, get up your nose *(informal)*, piss you off *(taboo slang)*, get your goat *(slang)*, get on your wick *(Brit. slang)*, put your back up, hack you off *(informal)* • *Ignore him – he's just trying to rattle your cage.*

cagey *or* **cagy** = **guarded**, reserved, careful, cautious, restrained, wary, discreet, shrewd, wily, reticent, noncommittal, chary • *He is cagey about what he was paid for his business.*
OPPOSITES: reckless, careless, unwary

cajole = **persuade**, tempt, lure, flatter, manoeuvre, seduce, entice, coax, beguile, wheedle, sweet-talk *(informal)*, inveigle • *It was he who cajoled Garland into making the film.*

cake AS A NOUN 1 = **gateau** • *Would you like some chocolate cake?*
2 = **block**, bar, slab, lump, cube, loaf, mass • *He bought a cake of soap.*
▸ AS A VERB 1 = **solidify**, dry, consolidate, harden, thicken, congeal, coagulate, ossify, encrust • *The blood had begun to cake and turn brown.*
2 = **cover**, coat, plaster, smear, spread • *Her hair was caked with mud.*
▷ *See panel* **Cakes and pastries**

calamitous = **disastrous**, terrible, devastating, tragic, fatal, deadly, dreadful, dire, catastrophic, woeful, ruinous, cataclysmic • *a calamitous air crash*
OPPOSITES: good, helpful, fortunate

calamity = **disaster**, tragedy, ruin, distress, reversal of fortune, hardship, catastrophe, woe, misfortune, downfall, adversity, scourge, mishap, affliction, trial, tribulation, misadventure, cataclysm, wretchedness, mischance • *This course of action could only end in calamity.*
OPPOSITES: help, benefit, advantage

QUOTATIONS

Calamities are of two kinds: misfortune to ourselves, and good fortune to others

[Ambrose Bierce *The Devil's Dictionary*]

calculable = **computable**, measurable, quantifiable, assessable, determinable, appraisable, gaugeable *or* gageable, judgeable, ratable *or* rateable, estimable *(rare)* • *The risks involved are, within reason, calculable.*

C

CAKES AND PASTRIES

almond cake	cream cake	frangipane	ladyfinger *or* sponge finger	panettone	stollen
angel cake	cream puff	French pastry	lamington (*Austral. & N.Z.*)	parkin	swiss roll
Bakewell tart	cruller (*U.S. & Canad.*)	fruitcake	lardy cake	petit four	tart
baklava	crumpet	fudge cake	layer cake	pound cake	teabread
Banbury cake	cupcake	gateau	Linzer torte	profiterole	teacake
Battenburg cake	Danish pastry	Genoa cake	Madeira cake	queencake	tipsy cake
black bun	devil's food cake	Genoese sponge	madeleine	rock cake	torte
Black forest gateau	doughnut	gingerbread	marble cake	rum baba	turnover
brownie	drop scone	hot cross bun	meringue	Sally Lunn	upside-down cake
carrot cake	dumpling	johnny cake (*Austral.*)	millefeuille	sandwich cake	Victoria sponge
cherry cake	Dundee cake	jumble	mince pie	scone	wedding cake
chocolate cake	Eccles cake	koeksister (*S. African*)	muffin	seedcake	yumyum (*Scot.*)
Christmas cake	eclair	kuchen	pancake	Selkirk bannock	
coconut cake	fairy cake	kuglehopf	pandowdy	simnel cake	
coffee kiss	flapjack			singing hinny	
				sponge cake	

calculate 1 = **work out**, value, judge, determine, estimate, count, reckon, weigh, consider, compute, rate, gauge, enumerate, figure • *From this we can calculate the total mass in the galaxy.*
2 = **plan**, design, aim, intend, frame, arrange, formulate, contrive • *Its twin engines were calculated to give additional safety.*

calculated = **deliberate**, planned, considered, studied, intended, intentional, designed, aimed, purposeful, premeditated • *a calculated strategy for winning power*
OPPOSITES: hurried, rash, unplanned

calculating = **scheming**, designing, sharp, shrewd, cunning, contriving, sly, canny, devious, manipulative, crafty, Machiavellian • *He is a cool, calculating and clever criminal.*
OPPOSITES: open, direct, frank

calculation 1 = **computation**, working out, reckoning, figuring, estimate, forecast, judgment, estimation, result, answer • *He made a quick calculation on a scrap of paper.*
2 = **planning**, intention, deliberation, foresight, contrivance, forethought, circumspection, premeditation • *an act of cold, unspeakably cruel calculation*

calf
▸ RELATED ADJECTIVE: vituline

calibrate = **measure**, gauge • *We need to calibrate the sextants on the tankers for navigation.*

calibre *or* (*U.S.*) **caliber** 1 = **worth**, quality, ability, talent, gifts, capacity, merit, distinction, faculty, endowment, stature • *I was impressed by the high calibre of the candidates.*
2 = **standard**, level, quality, grade • *The calibre of the teaching here is very high.*
3 = **diameter**, bore, gauge, measure • *Next morning she was arrested and a .44 calibre revolver was found in her possession.*

call AS A VERB 1 = **name**, entitle, dub, designate, term, style, label, describe as, christen, denominate • *They called their daughter Mischa.*
2 = **consider**, think, judge, estimate, describe as, refer to as, regard as • *His own party called him a traitor.*
3 = **cry**, announce, shout, scream, proclaim, yell, cry out, whoop • *'Boys!' she called, 'Dinner's ready!'*
OPPOSITES: whisper, mutter, murmur
4 = **phone**, contact, telephone, ring (up) (*informal, chiefly Brit.*), give (someone) a bell (*Brit. slang*) • *Will you call me as soon as you hear anything?*
5 = **send for**, contact, summon, fetch • *We'd better call the doctor.*
6 = **hail**, address, summon, contact, halloo • *He called me over the tannoy.*
7 = **summon**, gather, invite, rally, assemble, muster, convene, convoke, collect • *The group promised to call a meeting of shareholders.*
OPPOSITES: dismiss, excuse, cancel
8 = **visit**, come, go to, drop in (*informal*), stop by, pop in (*informal*) • *He called at the house every day to ask how I was.*
9 = **waken**, arouse, awaken, rouse • *I'm late for work! Why didn't you call me earlier?*
▸ AS A NOUN 1 = **telephone call**, bell (*informal*), phone call, buzz (*informal*), tinkle (*informal*), ring (*informal*) • *I got a call from him late last night.*
2 = **visit** • *He decided to pay a call on Mr Cummings.*
3 = **request**, order, demand, appeal, notice, command, announcement, invitation, plea, summons, supplication • *There was a call by the trade unions for members to stay home for the duration of the strike.*
4 *used in negative constructions* = **demand**, need, market, requirement, necessity • *I'm afraid there's not much call for that product round here.*
5 *used in negative constructions* = **need**, cause, reason, grounds, occasion, excuse, justification, claim • *There was no call for him to talk to you like he did.*
6 = **attraction**, draw, pull (*informal*), appeal, lure, attractiveness, allure, magnetism • *a sailor who could not resist the call of the sea*
7 = **cry**, shout, scream, yell, whoop • *He heard calls coming from the cellar.*
OPPOSITES: whisper, mutter, murmur
▸ IN PHRASES: **call for someone** = **fetch**, pick up, collect, uplift (*Scot.*) • *I shall call for you at 7 o'clock.*
call for something 1 = **demand**, order, request, insist on, cry out for • *They angrily called for his resignation.*
2 = **require**, need, involve, demand, occasion, entail, necessitate • *It's a situation that calls for a blend of delicacy and force.*
call on someone 1 = **request**, ask, bid, invite, appeal to, summon, invoke, call upon, entreat, supplicate • *He was frequently called on to resolve conflicts.*
2 = **visit**, look up, drop in on, look in on, see • *I'm leaving early tomorrow to call on a friend.*
call someone up 1 = **telephone**, phone, ring (*chiefly Brit.*), buzz (*informal*), dial, call up, give (someone) a ring (*informal, chiefly Brit.*), put a call through to, give (someone) a call, give (someone) a buzz (*informal*), give (someone) a bell (*Brit. slang*), give someone a tinkle (*Brit. informal*), get on the blower to (*informal*) • *He called me up to ask how I was.*
2 = **enlist**, draft, recruit, muster • *The United States has called up some 150,000 military reservists.*

call something off = **cancel**, drop, abandon, scrap, scratch, put off, forget about, abort, put on ice, countermand • *He has called off the trip.*

call the shots = **be in charge**, be in control, give the orders • *He's the one who calls the shots around here.*

calling = **profession**, work, business, line, trade, career, mission, employment, province, occupation, pursuit, vocation, walk of life, life's work, métier • *He was a serious man, dedicated to his calling as a physician.*

callous = **heartless**, cold, harsh, hardened, indifferent, insensitive, hard-boiled *(informal)*, unsympathetic, uncaring, soulless, hard-bitten, unfeeling, obdurate, case-hardened, hardhearted • *a callous and brutal attack on an old man*
OPPOSITES: understanding, caring, compassionate

callously = **heartlessly**, coldly, harshly, brutally, insensitively, obdurately, unfeelingly, soullessly, hardheartedly • *He is accused of callously ill-treating his wife.*

callousness = **heartlessness**, insensitivity, hardness, coldness, harshness, obduracy, soullessness, hardheartedness, obdurateness • *I find your statement breathtaking in its callousness and cynicism.*

callow = **inexperienced**, juvenile, naïve, immature, raw, untried, green, unsophisticated, puerile, guileless, jejune, unfledged • *Although he's 25, he still behaves like a callow youth in some ways.*

calm AS AN ADJECTIVE **1** = **cool**, relaxed, composed, sedate, undisturbed, collected, unmoved, dispassionate, unfazed *(informal)*, impassive, unflappable *(informal)*, unruffled, unemotional, self-possessed, imperturbable, equable, keeping your cool, unexcited, unexcitable, as cool as a cucumber, chilled *(informal)* • *Try to keep calm and just tell me what happened.*
OPPOSITES: worried, troubled, excited
2 = **peaceful**, quiet, tranquil, undisturbed, untroubled, free from strife • *The city appears relatively calm today.*
3 = **still**, quiet, smooth, peaceful, mild, serene, tranquil, placid, halcyon, balmy, restful, windless, pacific • *The normally calm waters of Mururoa lagoon heaved and frothed.*
OPPOSITES: wild, rough, stormy
▸ AS A NOUN **1** = **peacefulness**, peace, serenity, calmness • *He felt a sudden sense of calm and contentment.*
2 = **stillness**, peace, quiet, hush, serenity, tranquillity, repose, calmness, peacefulness • *the rural calm of Grand Rapids, Michigan*
3 = **peace**, calmness • *Church leaders have appealed for calm.*
OPPOSITES: disturbance, agitation, wildness
▸ AS A VERB **1** = **soothe**, settle, quiet, relax, appease, still, allay, assuage, quieten • *She had a drink to calm her nerves.*
OPPOSITES: excite, disturb, irritate
2 = **placate**, hush, pacify, mollify • *Officials hoped this action would calm the situation.*
OPPOSITES: stir, arouse, aggravate

calmly = **coolly**, casually, sedately, serenely, nonchalantly, impassively, dispassionately, placidly, unflinchingly, equably, imperturbably, tranquilly, composedly, collectedly, self-possessedly • *She walked up to her lover's wife and calmly shot her in the head.*

calumny = **slander**, abuse, insult, smear, libel, stigma, defamation, misrepresentation, lying, vilification, denigration, backbiting, derogation, vituperation, obloquy, aspersion, detraction, calumniation • *He alleges that he was the victim of calumny and dirty tricks.*

camaraderie = **comradeship**, fellowship, brotherhood, companionship, togetherness, esprit de corps, good-fellowship, companionability • *He missed the camaraderie of army life.*

camera
▹ *See panel* **Camera parts**

camouflage AS A NOUN **1** = **protective colouring**, mimicry, false appearance, deceptive markings • *Many animals employ camouflage to hide from predators.*

CAMERA PARTS

accessory shoe	flash gun	sprocket
amplifier	hot shoe	synchroflash
automatic exposure	intervalometer	telephoto lens
automatic focus	iris diaphragm	tripod
autowinder	lens hood	viewfinder
extension ring	macro lens	wide-angle lens
	shutter	zoom lens

2 = **disguise**, front, cover, screen, blind, mask, cloak, guise, masquerade, subterfuge, concealment • *Her merrymaking was only a camouflage to disguise her grief.*
▸ AS A VERB = **disguise**, cover, screen, hide, mask, conceal, obscure, veil, cloak, obfuscate • *This is another clever attempt to camouflage reality.*
OPPOSITES: show, reveal, display

camp[1] AS A NOUN **1** = **camp site**, tents, encampment, camping ground • *The camp was in a densely-forested area.*
2 = **bivouac**, cantonment *(Military)* • *He was held in a military camp for three days.*
3 = **faction**, group, set, party, division, section, sector, minority, gang, lobby, bloc, contingent, pressure group, junta, clique, coterie, schism, splinter group, public-interest group *(U.S. & Canad.)* • *The Republican camp is solidly in favour of capital punishment.*
▸ AS A VERB = **pitch tents**, set up camp, encamp, pitch camp • *We camped at the foot of Ben Nevis.*

camp[2] **1** = **effeminate**, campy *(informal)*, camped up *(informal)*, poncy *(slang)* • *an outrageously camp comedian*
2 = **affected**, mannered, artificial, posturing, ostentatious, campy *(informal)*, camped up *(informal)* • *All the characters are either too camp or too dull.*

campaign AS A NOUN **1** = **drive**, appeal, movement, push *(informal)*, offensive, crusade • *A new campaign has begun to encourage more people to become blood donors.*
2 = **operation**, drive, attack, movement, push, offensive, expedition, crusade, jihad • *The General's campaign against the militia has so far failed.*
▸ AS A VERB **1** = **crusade**, press, push, encourage, urge, boost, petition, back • *We are campaigning for law reform.*
2 = **canvass**, solicit votes, electioneer • *The parties can campaign for votes as long as they do so peacefully.*

campaigner = **demonstrator**, champion, advocate, activist, reformer, crusader • *She is a formidable campaigner for animal rights.*

canal = **waterway**, channel, passage, conduit, duct, watercourse • *A blockage of the canal could severely affect international shipping.*

CANALS

Berezina Canal	Grand Union Canal	Barge Canal
Bridgewater Canal	Houston Ship Canal	Canal do Norte
Caledonian Canal	Kiel Canal	Panama Canal
Champlain Canal	Manchester Ship Canal	Rhine-Herne Canal
Corinth Canal	Canal du Midi	Canal de São Gonçalo
Dortmund-Ems Canal	Mittelland Canal	Suez Canal
Erie Canal	Moscow Canal	Twente Canal
Göta Canal	New York State	Welland Canal
Grand Canal		

cancel AS A VERB **1** = **call off**, drop, abandon, scrap, scratch,

put off, forget about, abort, put on ice, countermand • *The foreign minister has cancelled his visit to Washington.*
2 = annul, abolish, repeal, abort, quash, do away with, revoke, repudiate, rescind, obviate, abrogate, countermand, eliminate • *Her insurance had been cancelled by the company.*
▸ **IN PHRASES: cancel something out = counterbalance**, offset, make up for, compensate for, redeem, neutralize, nullify, obviate, balance out • *These two opposing factors tend to cancel each other out.*

C

cancellation **1 = abandonment**, abandoning • *No reason has been given for the cancellation of the event.*
2 = annulment, abolition, repeal, elimination, quashing, revocation • *a march by groups calling for the cancellation of Third World debt*

cancer **1 = growth**, tumour, carcinoma (*Pathology*), malignancy • *Ninety percent of lung cancers are caused by smoking.*
2 = evil, corruption, rot, sickness, blight, pestilence, canker • *There's a cancer in the system.*
▸ **RELATED PREFIX:** carcino-
▸ **RELATED PHOBIA:** carcinophobia

candid **1 = honest**, just, open, truthful, fair, plain, straightforward, blunt, sincere, outspoken, downright, impartial, forthright, upfront (*informal*), unequivocal, unbiased, guileless, unprejudiced, free, round, frank • *a candid account of her life as a drug addict*
OPPOSITES: diplomatic, subtle, biased
2 = informal, impromptu, uncontrived, unposed • *There are also some candid pictures taken when he was young.*

candidate **= contender**, competitor, applicant, nominee, entrant, claimant, contestant, suitor, aspirant, possibility, runner • *We spoke to them all and John emerged as the best candidate.*

candour **= honesty**, simplicity, fairness, sincerity, impartiality, frankness, directness, truthfulness, outspokenness, forthrightness, straightforwardness, ingenuousness, artlessness, guilelessness, openness, unequivocalness, naïveté • *He spoke with disarming candour about his childhood.*
OPPOSITES: prejudice, bias, dishonesty

canker **1 = corruption**, disease, cancer, infection, rot, blight, scourge, corrosion, bane • *The canker of anti-semitism is growing again in this country.*
2 = fungal disease • *In gardens, cankers are the most prominent on apple and pear trees.*
3 = sore, blister, ulcer, lesion • *Dab a small amount of bicarbonate of soda on mouth ulcers or cankers.*

cannabis **= marijuana**, pot (*slang*), dope (*slang*), hash (*slang*), black (*slang*), blow (*slang*), smoke (*informal*), stuff (*slang*), leaf (*slang*), tea (*U.S. slang*), grass (*slang*), chronic (*U.S. slang*), weed (*slang*), hemp, gage (*U.S. dated slang*), hashish, mary jane (*U.S. slang*), ganja, bhang, kif, wacky baccy (*slang*), sinsemilla, dagga (*S. African*), charas • *Long-term heavy smoking of cannabis may lead to lung disorders.*

cannon **= gun**, big gun, artillery piece, field gun, mortar • *The rebels are using anti-aircraft guns, light cannon and heavy machine guns.*

canny **= shrewd**, knowing, sharp, acute, careful, wise, clever, subtle, cautious, prudent, astute, on the ball (*informal*), artful, judicious, circumspect, perspicacious, sagacious, worldly-wise • *He was far too canny to risk giving himself away.*
OPPOSITES: inept, unskilled, bumbling

canon **1 = rule**, standard, principle, regulation, formula, criterion, dictate, statute, yardstick, precept • *These measures offended all the accepted canons of political economy.*
2 = list, index, catalogue, syllabus, roll • *the body of work which constitutes the canon of English literature as taught in schools*

canonical **= authorized**, accepted, approved, recognized, sanctioned, orthodox, authoritative • *Caravaggio has finally attained canonical status as an artist.*

canopy **1 = awning**, covering, shade, shelter, sunshade • *The dais is covered with a silk brocade canopy.*
2 = covering, layer, blanket, mantle, overlay • *The land is thickly covered by a dense canopy of jungle.*

cant[1] **1 = hypocrisy**, pretence, lip service, humbug, insincerity, pretentiousness, sanctimoniousness, pious platitudes, affected piety, sham holiness • *Politicians are holding forth with their usual hypocritical cant.*
2 = jargon, slang, vernacular, patter, lingo, argot • *He resorted to a lot of pseudo-psychological cant to confuse me.*

cant[2] **= tilt**, angle, slope, incline, slant, bevel, rise • *The helicopter canted inward towards the landing area.*

cantankerous **= bad-tempered**, contrary, perverse, irritable, crusty, grumpy, disagreeable, cranky (*U.S., Canad. & Irish informal*), irascible, tetchy, ratty (*Brit. & N.Z. informal*), testy, quarrelsome, waspish, grouchy (*informal*), arsey (*Brit., Austral. & N.Z. slang*), peevish, crabby, choleric, crotchety (*informal*), ill-humoured, captious, difficult • *You're just a cantankerous old man.*
OPPOSITES: kindly, happy, cheerful

canter **AS A VERB = jog**, lope • *The competitors cantered into the arena.*
▸ **AS A NOUN = jog**, lope, easy gait, dogtrot • *He set off at a canter.*

canvass **1 = campaign**, solicit votes, electioneer • *I'm canvassing for the Labour Party.*
2 = poll, study, examine, investigate, analyse, scan, inspect, sift, scrutinize • *The survey canvassed the views of almost 80 economists.*

canyon **= gorge**, pass, gulf, valley, clough (*dialect*), gully, ravine, defile, gulch (*U.S. & Canad.*), coulee (*U.S.*) • *This trail leads down into the canyon.*

cap **AS A NOUN = lid**, cork, stopper, cover • *She unscrewed the cap of her water bottle.*
▸ **AS A VERB 1 = limit**, fix, restrict, curb, delimit • *the government's decision to cap levels of tax*
2 = beat, top, better, exceed, eclipse, lick (*informal*), surpass, transcend, outstrip, outdo, run rings around (*informal*), put in the shade, overtop • *He always has to cap everyone else's achievements.*
3 = top, cover, crown • *home-made scones capped with cream*
4 = complete, finish, crown • *Our team's victory capped a perfect day.*

capability **= ability**, means, power, potential, facility, capacity, qualification(s), faculty, competence, proficiency, wherewithal, potentiality • *These tasks are far beyond her capabilities.*
OPPOSITES: inability, incompetence, inefficiency

capable **1 = able**, fitted, suited, adapted, adequate • *Such a weapon would be capable of firing conventional or nuclear shells.*
OPPOSITES: incapable
2 = accomplished, experienced, masterly, qualified, talented, gifted, efficient, clever, intelligent, competent, apt, skilful, adept, proficient • *She's a very capable administrator.*
OPPOSITES: incompetent, ineffective, inept

capacious **= spacious**, wide, broad, vast, substantial, comprehensive, extensive, generous, ample, expansive, roomy, voluminous, commodious, sizable *or* sizeable • *She crammed the lot into her capacious handbag.*
OPPOSITES: small, limited, tiny

capacity **1 = ability**, power, strength, facility, gift, intelligence, efficiency, genius, faculty, capability, forte, readiness, aptitude, aptness, competence *or* competency • *Our capacity for giving care, love and attention is limited.*
2 = size, room, range, space, volume, extent, dimensions,

scope, magnitude, compass, amplitude • *an aircraft with a bomb-carrying capacity of 454 kg*
3 = function, position, role, post, appointment, province, sphere, service, office • *She was visiting in her official capacity as co-chairperson.*

cape = headland, point, head, peninsula, ness *(archaic)*, promontory • *voyages of exploration round the Cape*

caper AS A VERB **= dance**, trip, spring, jump, bound, leap, bounce, hop, skip, romp, frolic, cavort, frisk, gambol • *The children were capering about, shouting and laughing.*
▸ AS A NOUN **= escapade**, sport, stunt, mischief, lark *(informal)*, prank, jest, practical joke, high jinks, antic, jape, shenanigan *(informal)* • *Jack would have nothing to do with such childish capers.*

capercailzie
▸ COLLECTIVE NOUN: tok

capital AS A NOUN **= money**, funds, stock, investment(s), property, cash, finance, finances, financing, resources, assets, wealth, principal, means, wherewithal, wonga *(slang)* • *The company is having difficulties in raising capital.*
▸ AS AN ADJECTIVE **1 = upper case**, block • *The name and address are written in capital letters.*
2 = first-rate, fine, excellent, superb, sterling, splendid, world-class • *They had a capital time in London.*
▹ *See panel* **Capital cities**

capitalism = private enterprise, free enterprise, private ownership, laissez faire *or* laisser faire • *the two fundamentally opposed social systems, capitalism and socialism*

QUOTATIONS
I think that Capitalism, wisely managed, can probably be made more efficient for attaining economic ends than any alternative system yet in sight, but that in itself it is in many ways extremely objectionable
[John Maynard Keynes *The End of Laissez-Faire*]
You show me a capitalist, and I'll show you a bloodsucker
[Malcolm X]

capitalize AS A VERB **= sell**, put up for sale, trade, dispose of • *The company will be capitalized at £2 million.*
▸ IN PHRASES: **capitalize on something = take advantage of**, exploit, benefit from, profit from, make the most of, gain from, cash in on *(informal)* • *The rebels seemed to be trying to capitalize on the public's discontent.*

capitulate = give in, yield, concede, submit, surrender, comply, give up, come to terms, succumb, cave in *(informal)*, relent • *The club eventually capitulated and granted equal rights to women.*
OPPOSITES: resist, hold out

capitulation = surrender, yielding, submission, cave-in *(informal)* • *They criticised the government decision as a capitulation to terrorist organisations.*

caprice = whim, notion, impulse, freak, fad, quirk, vagary, whimsy, humour, fancy, fickleness, inconstancy, fitfulness, changeableness • *Her life was spent in terror of her husband's sudden caprices and mood swings.*

capricious = unpredictable, variable, unstable, inconsistent, erratic, quirky, fickle, impulsive, mercurial, freakish, fitful, inconstant • *His wife's capricious mood swings were beginning to get him down.*
OPPOSITES: firm, determined, consistent

capriciousness = unpredictability, quirkiness, fickleness, impulsiveness, inconstancy, freakishness, fitfulness, unpredictableness, changefulness, variability • *the capriciousness of Fate*
OPPOSITES: predictability, constancy, single-mindedness

capsize = overturn, turn over, invert, tip over, keel over, turn turtle, upset • *The sea got very rough and the boat capsized.*

capsule 1 = pill, tablet, lozenge, bolus • *You can also take red ginseng in convenient capsule form.*
2 = pod, case, shell, vessel, sheath, receptacle, seed case, pericarp *(Botany)* • *Each flower is globular, with an egg-shaped capsule.*

captain 1 = leader, boss, master, skipper, chieftain, head, number one *(informal)*, chief • *He is a former English cricket captain.*
2 = commander, officer, skipper, (senior) pilot • *a beefy German sea captain*

captivate = charm, attract, fascinate, absorb, entrance, dazzle, seduce, enchant, enthral, beguile, allure, bewitch, ravish, enslave, mesmerize, ensnare, hypnotize, enrapture, sweep off your feet, enamour, infatuate • *I was captivated by her sparkling personality.*
OPPOSITES: disgust, alienate, repel

captive AS AN ADJECTIVE **= confined**, caged, imprisoned, locked up, enslaved, incarcerated, ensnared, subjugated, penned, restricted • *Her heart had begun to pound inside her chest like a captive animal.*
▸ AS A NOUN **= prisoner**, hostage, convict, prisoner of war, detainee, internee • *He described the difficulties of surviving for four months as a captive.*

captivity = confinement, custody, detention, imprisonment, incarceration, internment, durance *(archaic)*, restraint • *An American missionary was released today after more than two months of captivity.*

QUOTATIONS
A robin red breast in a cage
Puts all Heaven in a rage
[William Blake *Auguries of Innocence*]

captor = jailer *or* **gaoler**, guard, keeper, custodian • *They did not know what their captors had planned for them.*

capture AS A VERB **1 = catch**, arrest, take, bag, secure, seize, nail *(informal)*, collar *(informal)*, nab *(informal)*, apprehend, lift *(slang)*, take prisoner, take into custody, feel your collar *(slang)* • *The police gave chase and captured him as he was trying to escape.*
OPPOSITES: free, release, liberate
2 = invade, take over, occupy, seize, overrun, take possession of • *The army has captured a strategic city in the north.*
3 = encapsulate, sum up, summarize, put in a nutshell, express • *Today's newspapers capture the mood of the nation.*
4 = engage, fascinate, absorb, preoccupy, rivet, engross • *the story that has captured the imagination of the whole country*
▸ AS A NOUN **= arrest**, catching, trapping, imprisonment, seizure, apprehension, taking, taking captive • *The shooting happened while the man was trying to evade capture.*

car 1 = vehicle, motor, wheels *(informal)*, auto *(U.S.)*, automobile, jalopy *(informal)*, motorcar, machine • *They arrived by car.*
2 = (railway) carriage, coach, cable car, dining car, sleeping car, buffet car, van • *Tour buses have replaced railway cars.*
▸ RELATED ENTHUSIAST: automobilist
▹ *See panel* **Cars**

carafe = jug, pitcher, flask, decanter, flagon • *He ordered a carafe of wine.*

carcass 1 = body, remains, corpse, skeleton, dead body, cadaver *(Medical)* • *A cluster of vultures crouched on the carcass of a dead buffalo.*
2 = remains, shell, framework, debris, remnants, hulk • *At one end of the camp lies the carcass of an aircraft which crashed in the mountains.*
3 = body, butt *(U.S. slang)*, ass *(U.S. slang)*, arse *(taboo slang)* • *Get your carcass back to the boathouse right now!*

card
▹ *See panel* **Cards**

cardinal = principal, first, highest, greatest, leading, important, chief, main, prime, central, key, essential, primary, fundamental, paramount, foremost, pre-eminent

C

CAPITAL CITIES

City	Country	City	Country	City	Country
Abu Dhabi	United Arab Emirates	Djibouti	Djibouti	Moscow	Russia
Abuja	Nigeria	Dodoma	Tanzania	Muscat	Oman
Accra	Ghana	Doha	Qatar	Nairobi	Kenya
Addis Ababa	Ethiopia	Douglas	Isle of Man	Nassau	Bahamas
Algiers	Algeria	Dublin	Republic of Ireland	Ndjamena	Chad
Amman	Jordan	Dushanbe	Tajikistan	Niamey	Niger
Amsterdam	Netherlands	Edinburgh	Scotland	Nicosia	Cyprus
Andorra la Vella	Andorra	Fort-de-France	Martinique	Nouakchott	Mauritania
Ankara	Turkey	Freetown	Sierra Leone	Nuku'alofa	Tonga
Antananarivo	Madagascar	Funafuti	Tuvalu	Nuuk	Greenland
Apia	Samoa	Gaborone	Botswana	Oslo	Norway
Ashkhabad	Turkmenistan	Georgetown	Guyana	Ottawa	Canada
Asmara	Eritrea	Guatemala City	Guatemala	Ouagadougou	Burkina-Faso
Astana	Kazakhstan	Hanoi	Vietnam	Palikir	Micronesia
Asunción	Paraguay	Harare	Zimbabwe	Panama City	Panama
Athens	Greece	Havana	Cuba	Paramaribo	Suriname
Baghdad	Iraq	Helsinki	Finland	Paris	France
Baku	Azerbaijan	Honiara	Solomon Islands	Phnom Penh	Cambodia
Bamako	Mali	Islamabad	Pakistan	Pishpek	Kirghizia
Bandar Seri Begawan	Brunei	Jakarta	Indonesia	Port-au-Prince	Haiti
Bangkok	Thailand	Jerusalem	Israel	Port Louis	Mauritius
Bangui	Central African Republic	Kabul	Afghanistan	Port Moresby	Papua New Guinea
Banjul	Gambia	Kampala	Uganda	Port of Spain	Trinidad and Tobago
Basseterre	St. Kitts and Nevis	Katmandu	Nepal	Porto Novo	Benin
Beijing	People's Republic of China	Khartoum	Sudan	Port Vila	Vanuatu
Beirut	Lebanon	Kiev	Ukraine	Prague	Czech Republic
Belfast	Northern Ireland	Kigali	Rwanda	Praia	Cape Verde
Belgrade	Yugoslavia (Serbia and Montenegro)	Kingston	Jamaica	Pretoria	administrative capital of South Africa
Belmopan	Belize	Kingstown	St. Vincent and the Grenadines	Pristina	Kosovo (Federal Republic of Yugoslavia)
Berlin	Germany	Kinshasa	Congo (Democratic Republic of)	Pyongyang	North Korea
Berne	Switzerland	Kishinev	Moldova	Quito	Ecuador
Bishkek	Kyrgyzstan	Koror	Palau	Rabat	Morocco
Bissau	Guinea-Bissau	Kuala Lumpur	Malaysia	Reykjavik	Iceland
Bloemfontein	judicial capital of South Africa	Kuwait	Kuwait	Riga	Latvia
Bogotá	Colombia	La Paz	administrative capital of Bolivia	Riyadh	Saudi Arabia
Brasília	Brazil	Libreville	Gabon	Rome	Italy
Bratislava	Slovakia	Lilongwe	Malawi	Roseau	Dominica
Brazzaville	Congo (Republic of)	Lima	Peru	San'a	Yemen
Bridgetown	Barbados	Lisbon	Portugal	San José	Costa Rica
Brussels	Belgium	Ljubljana	Slovenia	San Juan	Puerto Rico
Bucharest	Romania	Lomé	Togo	San Marino	San Marino
Budapest	Hungary	London	United Kingdom	San Salvador	El Slavador
Buenos Aires	Argentina	Luanda	Angola	Santiago	Chile
Bujumbura	Burundi	Lusaka	Zambia	Santo Domingo	Dominican Republic
Cairo	Egypt	Luxembourg	Luxembourg	São Tomé	São Tomé and Principe
Canberra	Australia	Madrid	Spain	Sarajevo	Bosnia and Herzegovina
Cape Town	legislative capital of South Africa	Majuro	Marshall Islands	Seoul	South Korea
Caracas	Venezuela	Malabo	Equatorial Guinea	Singapore	Singapore
Cardiff	Wales	Malé	Maldives	Skopje	Macedonia
Castries	St. Lucia	Managua	Nicaragua	Sofia	Bulgaria
Cayenne	French Guiana	Manama	Bahrain	St. George's	Grenada
Colombo	Sri Lanka	Manila	Philippines	St. John's	Antigua and Barbuda
Conakry	Guinea	Maputo	Mozambique	Stockholm	Sweden
Copenhagen	Denmark	Maseru	Lesotho	Sucre	legislative and judicial capital of Bolivia
Dakar	Senegal	Mbabane	Swaziland		
Damascus	Syria	Mexico City	Mexico		
Delhi	India	Minsk	Belarus		
Dhaka	Bangladesh	Mogadishu	Somalia		
Dili	East Timor	Monaco-Ville	Monaco		
		Monrovia	Liberia		
		Montevideo	Uruguay		
		Moroni	Comoros		

CAPITAL CITIES (CONTINUED)

City	Country	City	Country	City	Country
Suva	Fiji	Tokyo	Japan	Warsaw	Poland
Taipei	Taiwan	Tripoli	Libya	Washington DC	United States of America
Tallinn	Estonia	Tunis	Tunisia		
Tarawa	Kiribati	Ulan Bator	Mongolia	Wellington	New Zealand
Tashkent	Uzbekistan	Vaduz	Liechtenstein	Windhoek	Namibia
Tbilisi	Georgia	Valletta	Malta	Yamoussoukro	Côte d'Ivoire
Tegucigalpa	Honduras	Vatican City	Vatican City	Yangon	Myanmar
Tehran	Iran	Victoria	Seychelles	Yaoundé	Cameroon
Tel Aviv	Israel	Vienna	Austria	Yaren	Nauru
Thimphu	Bhutan	Vientiane	Laos	Yerevan	Armenia
Tirana	Albania	Vilnius	Lithuania	Zagreb	Croatia

• *As a salesman, your cardinal rule is to do everything you can to satisfy the customer.*
OPPOSITES: lowest, secondary, subordinate

care AS A VERB = **be concerned**, mind, bother, be interested, be bothered, give a damn, concern yourself • *a company that cares about the environment*
▸ AS A NOUN **1 = custody**, keeping, control, charge, management, protection, supervision, guardianship, safekeeping, ministration • *the orphans who were in her care*
2 = caution, attention, regard, pains, consideration, heed, prudence, vigilance, forethought, circumspection, watchfulness, meticulousness, carefulness • *I chose my words with care.*
OPPOSITES: abandon, neglect, carelessness
3 = worry, concern, pressure, trouble, responsibility, stress, burden, anxiety, hardship, woe, disquiet, affliction, tribulation, perplexity, vexation • *He never seemed to have a care in the world.*
OPPOSITES: pleasure, relaxation
▸ IN PHRASES: **care for someone 1 = look after**, mind, tend, attend, nurse, minister to, watch over • *They hired a nurse to care for her.*
2 = love, desire, be fond of, want, prize, find congenial • *He wanted me to know that he still cared for me.*
care for something *or* **someone = like**, enjoy, take to, relish, be fond of, be keen on, be partial to • *I don't care for seafood very much.*
take care of 1 = look after, mind, watch, protect, tend, nurse, care for, provide for, supervise, attend to, keep an eye on, take charge of • *There was no-one else to take care of their children.*
2 = deal with, manage, cope with, see to, handle • *Leave me to take care of this problem.*

QUOTATIONS
What is this life if, full of care,
We have no time to stand and stare?
[W.H. Davies *Leisure*]

career AS A NOUN **1 = occupation**, calling, employment, pursuit, vocation, livelihood, life's work • *She is now concentrating on a career as a fashion designer.*
2 = progress, course, path, procedure, passage • *The club has had an interesting, if chequered, career.*
▸ AS A VERB = **rush**, race, speed, tear, dash, barrel (along) (*informal, chiefly U.S. & Canad.*), bolt, hurtle, burn rubber (*informal*) • *The car went careering off down the track.*

carefree = untroubled, happy, cheerful, careless, buoyant, airy, radiant, easy-going, cheery, breezy, halcyon, sunny, jaunty, chirpy (*informal*), happy-go-lucky, blithe, insouciant, light-hearted • *She remembered her years of carefree youth.*
OPPOSITES: down, low, unhappy

careful 1 = cautious, painstaking, scrupulous, fastidious, circumspect, punctilious, chary, heedful, thoughtful, discreet • *One has to be extremely careful when dealing with these people.*
OPPOSITES: reckless, careless, negligent
2 = thorough, full, particular, accurate, precise, intensive, in-depth, meticulous, conscientious, attentive, exhaustive, painstaking, scrupulous, assiduous • *He decided to prosecute her after careful consideration of all the facts.*
OPPOSITES: casual, careless, inaccurate
3 = prudent, sparing, economical, canny, provident, frugal, thrifty • *Train your children to be careful with their pocket-money.*

PROVERBS
Softly, softly, catchee monkey

careless 1 = slapdash, irresponsible, sloppy (*informal*), cavalier, offhand, neglectful, slipshod, lackadaisical, inattentive • *He pleaded guilty to careless driving.*
OPPOSITES: alert, attentive, careful
2 = negligent, hasty, unconcerned, cursory, perfunctory, thoughtless, indiscreet, unthinking, forgetful, absent-minded, inconsiderate, heedless, remiss, incautious, unmindful • *She's careless about her personal hygiene.*
OPPOSITES: concerned, careful, anxious
3 = nonchalant, casual, offhand, artless, unstudied • *With a careless flip of his wrists, he sent the ball on its way.*
OPPOSITES: careful, painstaking

carelessness = negligence, neglect, omission, indiscretion, inaccuracy, irresponsibility, slackness, inattention, sloppiness (*informal*), laxity, thoughtlessness, laxness, remissness • *The accident was caused by sheer carelessness.*

PROVERBS
Don't throw out the baby with the bathwater

caress AS A NOUN = **stroke**, pat, kiss, embrace, hug, cuddle, fondling • *Margaret held my arm in a gentle caress.*
▸ AS A VERB = **stroke**, cuddle, fondle, pet, embrace, hug, nuzzle, neck (*informal*), kiss • *They kissed and caressed one another.*

caretaker AS A NOUN = **warden**, keeper, porter, superintendent, curator, custodian, watchman, janitor, concierge • *The caretaker sleeps in the building all night.*
▸ AS AN ADJECTIVE = **temporary**, holding, short-term, interim • *The administration intends to hand over power to a caretaker government.*

careworn = stressed, drawn, strained, anxious, distraught, haggard, overburdened, heavy-laden • *Their faces look old and careworn.*

cargo = load, goods, contents, shipment, freight, merchandise, baggage, ware, consignment, tonnage, lading • *The boat calls at the main port to load its cargo of bananas.*

caricature AS A NOUN = **parody**, cartoon, distortion, satire, send-up (*Brit. informal*), travesty, takeoff (*informal*), lampoon, burlesque, mimicry, farce • *The poster showed a caricature of Hitler with a devil's horns and tail.*
▸ AS A VERB = **parody**, take off (*informal*), mock, distort, ridicule, mimic, send up (*Brit. informal*), lampoon, burlesque, satirize • *Her political career has been caricatured in the newspapers.*

C

CARS

Car parts

accelerator
air bag
alternator
ammeter
anti-roll bar
ashtray
automatic choke
axle
battery
bearing
big end
body
bonnet
boot
brake
brake light
brake pad
bucket seat
bulb
bumper
camshaft
carburettor
catalytic converter
chassis
childproof lock
choke
clutch
coil
connecting rod
convertible top
cowl
crank
crankcase
crankshaft
cylinder
cylinder head
dashboard
demister
dipstick
disc brakes
distributor
distributor cap
door
door handle
driveshaft
engine
exhaust
fan
fan belt
fascia
fender (*U.S. & Canad.*)
flywheel
fog lamp
fuel gauge
fuse
fuse box
gasket
gear
gearbox
gear lever
generator
glove compartment
grille *or* radiator grille
handbrake
hard top
hazard light
headlight
headrest
heater
hood
horn
hubcap
ignition
indicator
jack
light
little end
lock
luggage rack
manifold
mileometer
mud flap
numberplate
oil filter
oil-pressure gauge
oil pump
parcel shelf
parking light
pedal
petrol cap
petrol gauge
petrol tank
piston
plug
points
radiator
radius arm
rear light
rear-view mirror
reversing light
roof
seat
seat belt
shock absorber
silencer
soft top
spare wheel
speedometer
springs
sprocket
starter
steering column
steering wheel
sump
sunroof
suspension
tailgate
tailpipe
tank
top
torsion bar
towbar
transmission
trim
tyre
universal joint
valve
wheel
wheel brace
wheel nut
wheel trim
window
windscreen
windscreen wiper
wing
wing mirror
wing nut

International car registration letters

	Country
A	Austria
ADN	Yemen
AFG	Afghanistan
AL	Albania
AND	Andorra
AUS	Australia
B	Belgium
BD	Bangladesh
BDS	Barbados
BG	Bulgaria
BH	Belize
BR	Brazil
BRN	Bahrain
BRU	Brunei
BS	Bahamas
BUR	Myanmar
C	Cuba
CDN	Canada
CH	Switzerland
CI	Côte d'Ivoire
CL	Sri Lanka
CO	Colombia
CR	Costa Rica
CY	Cyprus
CZ	Czech Republic
D	Germany
DK	Denmark
DOM	Dominican Republic
DY	Benin
DZ	Algeria
E	Spain
EAK	Kenya
EAT	Tanzania
EAU	Uganda
EC	Ecuador
ES	El Salvador
ET	Egypt
ETH	Ethiopia
EW	Estonia
F	France
FIN	Finland
FJI	Fiji
FL	Liechtenstein
FR	Faeroe Islands
GB	United Kingdom
GBA	Alderney
GBG	Guernsey
GBJ	Jersey
GBM	Isle of Man
GBZ	Gibraltar
GCA	Guatemala
GH	Ghana
GR	Greece
GUY	Guyana
H	Hungary
HK	Hong Kong
HKJ	Jordan
HR	Croatia
I	Italy
IL	Israel
IND	India
IR	Iran
IRL	Republic of Ireland
IRQ	Iraq
IS	Iceland
J	Japan
JA	Jamaica
K	Cambodia
KWT	Kuwait
L	Luxembourg
LAO	Laos
LAR	Libya
LB	Liberia
LS	Lesotho
LT	Lithuania
LV	Latvia
M	Malta
MA	Morocco
MAL	Malaysia
MC	Monaco
MEX	Mexico
MS	Mauritius
MW	Malawi
N	Norway
NA	Netherlands Antilles
NIC	Nicaragua
NL	Netherlands
NZ	New Zealand
OMAN	Oman
P	Portugal
PA	Panama
PE	Peru
PK	Pakistan
PL	Poland
PNG	Papua New Guinea
PY	Paraguay
RA	Argentina
RB	Botswana
RC	Taiwan
RCA	Central African Republic
RCB	Congo Republic
RCH	Chile
RH	Haiti
RI	Indonesia
RIM	Mauritania
RL	Lebanon
RM	Madagascar
RMM	Mali
RO	Romania
ROK	South Korea
ROU	Uruguay
RP	Philippines
RSM	San Marino
RU	Burundi
RUS	Russian Federation
RWA	Rwanda
S	Sweden
SD	Swaziland
SGP	Singapore
SK	Slovakia
SME	Suriname
SN	Senegal
SWA	Namibia
SY	Seychelles
SYR	Syria
T	Thailand
TG	Togo
TN	Tunisia
TR	Turkey
TT	Trinidad and Tobago
USA	United States of America
V	Vatican City
VN	Vietnam
WAG	Gambia
WAL	Sierra Leone
WAN	Nigeria
WD	Dominica
WG	Grenada
WL	St. Lucia
WS	Western Samoa
WV	St. Vincent and the Grenadines
YU	Yugoslavia
YV	Venezuela
Z	Zambia
ZA	South Africa
ZRE	Zaire
ZW	Zimbabwe

CARDS

Card games

auction bridge	écarté	rouge et noir
baccarat	euchre	rubber bridge
beggar-my neighbour	faro	rummy
bezique	five hundred	seven up
blackjack	gin rummy	skat
boston	happy families	slapjack
bridge	hearts	snap
canasta	loo	solo
canfield	monte	solo whist
casino	nap *or* napoleon	spoilfive
chemin-de-fer *or* chemmy	old maid	stops
cinch	ombre	strip poker
contract bridge	patience	stud poker
cooncan	pinochle	switch
cribbage	piquet	trente et quarante
duplicate bridge	poker	whist
	pontoon	
	quinze	

Bridge terms

contract	small slam	slam
double	north	south
dummy	no-trump	trick
east	redouble	trump
finesse	rubber	vulnerable
grand slam	ruff	west
little slam *or*	singleton	yarborough

Poker terms

ante	royal flush	straddle
flush	see	straight
full house	showdown	straight flush
pair	shy	
raise	stand pat	

Other card terms

ace	diamonds	queen
clubs	hand	revoke
court card	hearts	spades
cut	jack	suit
deal	joker	trey
deck	king	wild
deuce	knave	

caring = **compassionate**, loving, kindly, warm, soft, sensitive, tender, sympathetic, responsive, receptive, considerate, warmhearted, tenderhearted, softhearted, touchy-feely *(informal)* • *He is a wonderful person, very gentle and caring.*

carnage = **slaughter**, murder, massacre, holocaust, havoc, bloodshed, shambles, mass murder, butchery, blood bath • *Their peaceful protest ended in carnage.*

carnal = **sexual**, animal, sexy *(informal)*, fleshly, erotic, sensual, randy *(informal, chiefly Brit.)*, steamy *(informal)*, raunchy *(slang)*, sensuous, voluptuous, lewd, wanton, amorous, salacious, prurient, impure, lascivious, lustful, lecherous, libidinous, licentious, unchaste • *Their passion became inflamed and their carnal desires ran wild.*

carnival 1 = **festival**, fair, fête, celebration, gala, jubilee, jamboree, Mardi Gras, revelry, merrymaking, fiesta, holiday • *The town is best known for its carnivals with masked balls and firework processions.*
2 = **funfair**, circus • *a carnival with rides and games*

carnivore
▷ *See panel* **Carnivores**

carol = **song**, noel, hymn, Christmas song, canticle • *The singing of Christmas carols is ultimately of pagan origin.*

carouse = **drink**, booze *(informal)*, revel, imbibe, quaff, pub-crawl *(informal, chiefly Brit.)*, bevvy *(dialect)*, make merry, bend the elbow *(informal)*, roister, go on the piss *(taboo slang)* • *He should stay home with his wife more, instead of going out and carousing with friends.*

carp[1] = **find fault**, complain, beef *(slang)*, criticize, nag, censure, reproach, quibble, cavil, pick holes, kvetch *(U.S. slang)*, nit-pick *(informal)* • *His wife is constantly carping at him about his drinking.*
OPPOSITES: approve, praise, admire

carp[2]
▸ **RELATED ADJECTIVES:** cyprinoid, cyprinid

carpenter = **joiner**, cabinet-maker, woodworker • *a carpenter who specializes in restoring antique furniture*

carpet

CARPETS AND RUGS

Aubusson	durrie	numdah
Axminster	flat-woven	Persian carpet *or* Persian rug
broadloom	ingrain	
Brussels carpet	Kidderminster	Turkey carpet
Bukhara rug	kilim	Wilton
chenille	Kirman	

carping = **fault-finding**, critical, nagging, picky *(informal)*, nit-picking *(informal)*, hard to please, cavilling, hypercritical, captious, nit-picky *(informal)* • *They deserve recognition, not carping criticism.*

carriage 1 = **vehicle**, coach, trap, gig, cab, wagon, hackney, conveyance • *He followed in an open carriage drawn by six grey horses.*
2 = **coach**, car • *Our railway carriage was full of drunken football fans.*
3 = **transportation**, transport, delivery, conveying, freight, conveyance, carrying • *It costs £10.86 for one litre, including carriage.*
4 = **bearing**, posture, gait, deportment, air • *Her legs were long and fine, her hips slender, her carriage graceful.*
▸ **RELATED PHOBIA:** amakaphobia
▷ *See panel* **Carriages and carts**

carry AS A VERB 1 = **convey**, take, move, bring, bear, lift, transfer, conduct, transport, haul, transmit, fetch, relay, cart, tote *(informal)*, hump *(Brit. slang)*, lug • *He carried the plate through to the dining room.*
2 = **transport**, take, transfer, transmit • *The ship can carry seventy passengers.*
3 = **support**, stand, bear, maintain, shoulder, sustain, hold up, suffer, uphold, bolster, underpin • *This horse can't carry your weight.*
4 = **transmit**, transfer, spread, pass on • *Frogs eat pests which carry diseases.*
5 = **publish**, include, release, display, print, broadcast, communicate, disseminate, give • *Several magazines carried the story.*
6 = **entail**, involve, lead to, occasion, result in • *The crime of espionage carries the death penalty.*
7 = **be audible**, travel, be heard • *Even in this stillness he doubted if the sound would carry.*
8 = **be expecting**, be pregnant with • *She claims to be carrying his child.*
9 = **win**, gain, secure, capture, accomplish • *It was this point of view that carried the day.*
▸ **IN PHRASES: carry on** 1 = **continue**, last, endure, persist, keep going, persevere, crack on *(informal)* • *Her bravery has given him the will to carry on.*

CARNIVORES

aardwolf, arctic fox, badger, bear, binturong, black bear, bobcat, brown bear, cacomistle, caracal *or* desert lynx, cat ▹ *See panel* **Breeds of cat**, catamount, cheetah, cinnamon bear, civet, corsac, coyote *or* prairie wolf, dhole, dingo *or* (*Austral.*) native dog *or* warrigal, dog ▹ *See panel* **Breeds of dog**, ermine, fennec, ferret, fox, genet *or* genette, giant panda, grey fox, grey wolf *or* timber wolf, grison, grizzly bear, hog badger, hognosed skunk, hyena *or* hyaena, ichneumon, jackal, jaguar, jaguarondi *or* (*Austral.*) eyra, kinkajou, honey bear, *or* potto, Kodiak bear, kolinsky, laughing hyena *or* spotted hyena, leopard, linsang, lion, lynx, margay, marten, meerkat, mink, mongoose, mountain lion, ocelot, otter, otter shrew, palm civet, panda, panther, pine marten *or* sweet marten, polar bear *or* (*N. Canad.*) nanook, polecat, prairie dog, puma *or* cougar, raccoon, raccoon dog, rasse, ratel, red fox, rooikat, sable, sea otter, serval, silver fox, skunk, sloth bear, snow leopard, snow leopard *or* ounce, stoat, stone marten, strandwolf, sun bear, swift fox *or* kit fox, tayra, teledu, tiger, tiger cat, timber wolf, weasel, wolf, wolverine, glutton, *or* carcajou, zibeline, zibet, zorilla

2 = make a fuss, act up (*informal*), misbehave, create (*slang*), raise Cain • *She was yelling and screaming and carrying on like an idiot.*
3 = have an affair, play around, mess around, play away, commit adultery, philander • *My husband's carrying on with a girl barely older than our daughter.*
carry something on = engage in, conduct, carry out, undertake, embark on, enter into • *The consulate will carry on a political dialogue.*
carry something out = perform, effect, achieve, realize, implement, fulfil, accomplish, execute, discharge, consummate, carry through • *Commitments have been made with very little intention of carrying them out.*
carry something through = achieve, effect, finish, complete, perform, carry out, conclude, accomplish, execute, discharge, bring to completion • *The state announced a clear-cut policy and set out to carry it through.*
carry yourself = behave, act, conduct yourself, deport yourself, acquit yourself, comport yourself • *They carried themselves with great pride and dignity.*

carry-on = fuss, disturbance, racket, fracas, commotion, rumpus, tumult, hubbub, shindy (*informal*) • *What's all the carry-on down here?*

cart AS A NOUN **1 = wagon**, wain (*chiefly poetic*) • *a country where horse-drawn carts are still used*
2 = trolley, barrow, handcart • *She was pushing a shopping cart full of groceries.*
▸ AS A VERB **= carry**, take, bring, bear, haul, convey, tote (*informal*), hump (*Brit. slang*), lug • *I've been trying to reduce the amount of stuff I cart round with me.*
▹ *See panel* **Carriages and carts**

carton = box, case, pack, package, container • *A large and heavy cardboard carton had been delivered to the house.*

cartoon 1 = drawing, parody, satire, caricature, comic strip, takeoff (*informal*), lampoon, sketch • *The newspaper printed a cartoon depicting the president as a used car salesman.*
2 = animation, animated film, animated cartoon • *the X-rated TV cartoon, South Park*

cartridge 1 = shell, round, charge • *Gun and cartridge manufacturers will lose money if the game laws are amended.*
2 = container, case, magazine, cassette, cylinder, capsule • *Change the filter cartridge as often as instructed by the manufacturer.*

carve 1 = sculpt, form, cut, chip, sculpture, whittle, chisel, hew, fashion • *One of the prisoners has carved a beautiful chess set.*
2 = etch, engrave, inscribe, fashion, slash • *He carved his name on his desk.*
3 = slice, hack • *Carve the beef into slices.*

carving = sculpture, model, statue, statuette • *It was a wood carving of a human hand.*
▸ RELATED ADJECTIVE: glyptic

cascade AS A NOUN **= waterfall**, falls, torrent, flood, shower, fountain, avalanche, deluge, downpour, outpouring, cataract • *She stood still for a moment under the cascade of water.*
▸ AS A VERB **= flow**, fall, flood, pour, plunge, surge, spill, tumble, descend, overflow, gush, teem, pitch • *A waterfall cascades down the cliff from the hills.*

case[1] **1 = situation**, event, circumstance(s), state, position, condition, context, dilemma, plight, contingency,

CARRIAGES AND CARTS

barouche, brake, britzka, brougham, buckboard (*U.S. & Canad.*), buggy, cab, cabriolet, calash, Cape cart (*S. African*), cariole, carriage, carryall, cart, chaise, chariot, clarence, coach, Conestoga wagon, coupe, covered wagon (*U.S. & Canad.*), curricle, dogcart, drag, droshky, equipage, fiacre, fly, four-in-hand, gharry, gig, Gladstone, hansom, herdic (*U.S.*), jaunting car, landau, phaeton, post chaise, prairie schooner (*chiefly U.S.*), pung (*Eastern U.S. & Canad.*), quadriga, randem, ratha, rig, rockaway (*U.S.*), sledge, spider phaeton, stagecoach, sulky, surrey, tandem, tarantass, tilbury, troika, victoria, vis-à-vis, wagon, wagonette, wain (*chiefly poetic*)

predicament • *In extreme cases, insurance companies can prosecute for fraud.*
2 = **patient**, client, sufferer • *Expensive hospital cases are monitored by a case manager.*
3 = **instance**, example, occasion, specimen, occurrence • *Some cases of arthritis respond to a gluten-free diet.*
4 = **investigation**, search, inquiry, inspection • *The police have several suspects in this murder case.*
5 = **argument**, reasoning, ground(s), defence, logic, justification, line of reasoning • *Both these facts strengthen the case against hanging.*
6 = **lawsuit**, process, trial, suit, proceedings, dispute, cause, action • *He lost his case at the European Court of Human Rights.*

case[2] 1 = **cabinet**, box, chest, holder • *There was a ten-foot long stuffed alligator in a glass case.*
2 = **container**, compact, capsule, carton, cartridge, canister, casket, receptacle, coffret • *She held up a blue spectacle case.*
3 = **suitcase**, bag, grip, trunk, holdall, portmanteau, valise • *The porter brought my cases down and called for a taxi.*
4 = **crate**, box • *The winner will receive a case of champagne.*
5 = **covering**, casing, cover, shell, wrapping, jacket, envelope, capsule, folder, sheath, wrapper, integument • *Vanilla is the seed case of a South American orchid.*

cash AS A NOUN = **money**, change, funds, notes, ready *(informal)*, the necessary *(informal)*, resources, currency, silver, bread *(slang)*, coin, tin *(slang)*, brass *(Northern English dialect)*, dough *(slang)*, rhino *(Brit. slang)*, banknotes, bullion, dosh *(Brit. & Austral. slang)*, wherewithal, coinage, needful *(informal)*, specie, shekels *(informal)*, wonga *(slang)*, dibs *(slang)*, ready money, ackers *(slang)*, spondulicks *(slang)* • *He stole to get cash for his drug habit.*
▸ IN PHRASES: **cash in on something** = **exploit**, use, take advantage of, capitalize on, put to use, make capital out of, use to advantage, turn to account • *The record company is simply cashing in on the loyalty of the band's fans.*

cashier[1] = **teller**, accountant, clerk, treasurer, bank clerk, purser, bursar, banker • *The cashier said that he would fetch the manager.*

cashier[2] = **dismiss**, discharge, expel, cast off, drum out, give the boot to *(slang)* • *Many officers were cashiered on political grounds.*

casing = **covering**, case, cover, shell, container, integument • *Bullet casings lay scattered on the ground.*

cask = **barrel**, drum, cylinder, keg, firkin, hogshead • *The casks of sherry are stored one on top of the other.*

casket 1 = **box**, case, chest, coffer, ark *(dialect)*, jewel box, coffret, kist *(Scot. & Northern English dialect)* • *a jewellery casket made from French walnut*
2 = **coffin**, sarcophagus • *The casket was slowly lowered into the open grave.*

cast AS A NOUN 1 = **actors**, company, players, characters, troupe, dramatis personae • *The show is very amusing and the cast are excellent.*
2 = **type**, turn, sort, kind, style, stamp • *Hers was an essentially optimistic cast of mind.*
▸ AS A VERB 1 = **choose**, name, pick, select, appoint, assign, allot • *He has been cast in the lead role of the new Pinter play.*
2 = **bestow**, give, level, accord, direct, confer • *He cast a stern glance at the two men.*
3 = **give out**, spread, deposit, shed, distribute, scatter, emit, radiate, bestow, diffuse • *The moon cast a bright light over the yard.*
4 = **throw**, project, launch, pitch, shed, shy, toss, thrust, hurl, fling, chuck *(informal)*, sling, lob, impel, drive, drop • *She took a pebble and cast it into the water.*
5 = **mould**, set, found, form, model, shape • *This statue of Neptune is cast in bronze.*
▸ IN PHRASES: **cast around for something** = **look for**, seek, hunt, search for, fossick for *(Austral. & N.Z.)* • *She had been casting around for a good excuse to go to New York*
cast someone down = **discourage**, depress, desolate, dishearten, dispirit, deject • *I am not too easily cast down by changes of fortune.*
cast something *or* **someone aside** = **discard**, drop, abandon, dump *(informal)*, get rid of, ditch *(slang)*, chuck *(informal)*, dispose of, dispense with, jettison, throw away *or* out • *Now that she is old, she has been cast aside like an old glove.*

caste = **class**, order, race, station, rank, status, stratum, social order, lineage • *Most of these people are from the socially-disadvantaged lower castes.*

castigate = **reprimand**, blast, carpet *(informal)*, flame *(informal)*, put down, criticize, lash, slate *(informal, chiefly Brit.)*, censure, rebuke, scold, berate, dress down *(informal)*, chastise, chasten, tear into *(informal)*, diss *(slang, chiefly U.S.)*, read the riot act, slap on the wrist, lambast(e), bawl out *(informal)*, excoriate, rap over the knuckles, haul over the coals *(informal)*, chew out *(U.S. & Canad. informal)*, tear (someone) off a strip *(Brit. informal)*, give a rocket *(Brit. & N.Z. informal)* • *She castigated him for having no intellectual interests.*

castigation = **reprimand**, criticism, blast, put-down, condemnation, censure, dressing down *(informal)*, chastisement, bawling-out *(informal)*, excoriation • *Helen's merciless castigation of her staff in public*

cast-iron = **certain**, established, settled, guaranteed, fixed, definite, copper-bottomed, idiot-proof, nailed-on *(slang)* • *I can't give you any cast-iron guarantees that your job will be safe.*

castle = **fortress**, keep, palace, tower, peel, chateau, stronghold, citadel, fastness • *They were given a guided tour of the medieval castle.*
▹ *See panel* **Castles**

castrate = **neuter**, unman, emasculate, geld • *She threatened to castrate her husband with a carving knife.*

casual 1 = **careless**, relaxed, informal, indifferent, unconcerned, apathetic, blasé, offhand, nonchalant, insouciant, lackadaisical • *an easy-going young man with a casual approach to life*
OPPOSITES: concerned, serious, committed
2 = **chance**, unexpected, random, accidental, incidental, unforeseen, unintentional, fortuitous *(informal)*, serendipitous, unpremeditated • *It was just a casual meeting.*
OPPOSITES: planned, expected, fixed
3 = **informal**, leisure, sporty, non-dressy • *I bought casual clothes for the weekend.*
OPPOSITES: formal, ceremonial, dressy
4 = **temporary**, short-term, occasional, part-time, uncertain, irregular • *I've been doing casual work in a hostel for five months.*
5 = **promiscuous** • *I don't believe in having casual sex.*
6 = **perfunctory**, careless, cursory, offhand, nonchalant • *I stood up and gave a casual glance behind me.*

casualty 1 = **fatality**, death, loss, wounded • *Troops fired on the demonstrators, causing many casualties.*
2 = **victim**, sufferer • *The company has been one of the greatest casualties of the recession.*

casuistry = **sophistry**, chicanery, equivocation, speciousness, sophism • *Every system of moral rules, laws, and principles gives rise to casuistry.*

cat = **feline**, pussy *(informal)*, moggy *(slang)*, puss *(informal)*, ballarat *(Austral. informal)*, tabby • *Cats are renowned for their curiosity.*
▸ RELATED ADJECTIVE: feline
▸ NAME OF MALE: tom
▸ NAME OF FEMALE: queen
▸ NAME OF YOUNG: kitten
▸ COLLECTIVE NOUN: clowder
▸ RELATED MANIA: ailurophilia
▸ RELATED ENTHUSIAST: ailurophile
▸ RELATED PHOBIA: ailurophobia
▹ *See panel* **Breeds of cat**

C

CASTLES

Aberystwyth, Amboise, Arundel, Ashby de la Zouch, Ashford, Aydon, Ballindalloch, Balmoral, Balvenie, Barnard, Beaumaris, Beeston, Belvoir, Berkeley, Berkhamstead, Berwick-upon-Tweed, Blarney, Blois, Braemar, Brodie, Bunraity, Cabra, Caerlaverock, Caernarfon, Caerphilly, Cahir, Canossa, Carisbrooke, Carmarthen, Carrickfergus, Château-Raoul, Cheb, Chillon, Colditz, Conwy, Crathes, Culzean, Darnaway, Dinan, Drum, Dublin, Dunnottar, Dunsinane, Dunstaffnage, Durham, Edinburgh, Eilean Donan, Esterháza, Farney, Forfar, Fotheringhay, Glamis, Harlech, Heidelberg, Herstmonceux, Inverness, Kenilworth, Kilkea, Kilkenny, Killaghy, Kilravock, Lancaster, Launceston, Leamaneh, Leeds, Leicester, Lincoln, Ludlow, Malahide, Monmouth, Otranto, Pembroke, Pendennis, Pontefract, Portlick, Rait, Restormel, Richmond, Rithes, Rock of Cashel, St Mawes, Scarborough, Sherborne, Skipton, Stirling, Stuart, Taymouth, Tintagel, Torún, Trausnitz, Trim, Urquhart, Vaduz, Vincennes, Wartburg, Warwick

QUOTATIONS

Cats seem to go on the principle that it never does any harm to ask for what you want
[Joseph Wood Krutch *The Twelve Seasons*]

When I play with my cat, who knows whether she isn't amusing herself with me more than I am with her?
[Montaigne *Essais*]

PROVERBS

When the cat's away, the mice will play
The cat would eat fish, but would not wet her feet
All cats are grey in the dark

BREEDS OF CAT

Abyssinian, Angora, Bengal leopard, Burmese, colourpoint *or* (*U.S.*) Himalayan, Havana, Maine coon, Manx, Persian, ragdoll, Rex, Russian blue, Siamese, tabby, tortoiseshell, Turkish

cataclysm = **disaster**, collapse, catastrophe, upheaval, debacle, devastation, calamity • *the cataclysm that was overwhelming Europe before the Second World War*

cataclysmic = **disastrous**, devastating, catastrophic, calamitous • *Few had expected the change to be as cataclysmic as it was.*

catacombs = **vault**, tomb, crypt, ossuary • *It took six strong men to carry his coffin down into the catacombs.*

catalogue *or* (*U.S.*) **catalog** AS A NOUN = **list**, record, schedule, index, register, directory, inventory, gazetteer • *One of the authors of the catalogue is the Professor of Art History.*
▸ AS A VERB = **list**, file, index, register, classify, inventory, tabulate, alphabetize • *The Royal Greenwich Observatory was founded to observe and catalogue the stars.*

catapult AS A NOUN = **sling**, slingshot (*U.S.*), trebuchet, ballista • *They were hit twice by missiles fired from a catapult.*
▸ AS A VERB = **shoot**, pitch, plunge, toss, hurl, propel, hurtle, heave • *He was catapulted into the side of the van.*

cataract 1 = **opacity** (*of the eye*) • *a battle with blindness caused by cataracts*
2 = **waterfall**, falls, rapids, cascade, torrent, deluge, downpour, Niagara • *There was an impressive cataract at the end of the glen.*

catastrophe = **disaster**, tragedy, calamity, meltdown (*informal*), cataclysm, trouble, trial, blow, failure, reverse, misfortune, devastation, adversity, mishap, affliction, whammy (*informal, chiefly U.S.*), bummer (*slang*), mischance, fiasco • *The world is heading towards an environmental catastrophe.*

catastrophic = **disastrous**, devastating, tragic, calamitous, cataclysmic • *A tidal wave caused catastrophic damage.*

catch AS A VERB 1 = **capture**, arrest, trap, seize, nail (*informal*), nab (*informal*), snare, lift (*slang*), apprehend, ensnare, entrap, feel your collar (*slang*) • *Police say they are confident of catching the killer.*
OPPOSITES: free, release, loose
2 = **trap**, capture, snare, entangle, ensnare, entrap • *The locals were encouraged to catch and kill the birds.*
3 = **seize**, get, grab, snatch • *I jumped up to catch the ball and fell over.*
4 = **grab**, take, grip, seize, grasp, clutch, lay hold of • *He knelt beside her and caught her hand in both of his.*
OPPOSITES: release, drop, give up
5 = **hit**, strike, bang, clip (*informal*), slap, smack, whack • *He caught her on the side of her head with his fist.*
6 = **become trapped**, snag, become entangled • *Her ankle caught on a root and she almost lost her balance.*
7 = **board**, make, get on • *We made it in time to catch the ferry.*
8 = **discover**, surprise, find out, expose, detect, catch in the act, take unawares • *He caught a youth breaking into his car.*
9 = **notice**, see, note, spot, observe, recognize, perceive, detect, discern, mark • *She caught the puzzled look on her mother's face.*
10 = **make out**, get, follow, hear, take in, perceive, grasp, discern, apprehend • *Sorry, I didn't quite catch what you said.*
11 = **engage**, attract, delight, capture, charm, grip, fascinate, absorb, enchant, captivate, bewitch, engross, enrapture • *This award has caught the imagination of the public.*
OPPOSITES: bore, disgust, repel
12 = **evoke**, express, capture, conjure up, encapsulate • *His words caught the mood of the vast crowd.*
13 = **contract**, get, develop, suffer from, incur, succumb to, go down with • *The more stress you are under, the more likely you are to catch a cold.*
OPPOSITES: avoid, escape, avert
▸ AS A NOUN 1 = **fastener**, hook, clip, bolt, latch, clasp, hasp, hook and eye, snib (*Scot.*), sneck (*dialect, chiefly Scot. & Northern English*) • *Always fit windows with safety locks or catches.*
2 = **drawback**, trick, trap, disadvantage, hitch, snag, stumbling block, fly in the ointment • *It sounds too good to be true – what's the catch?*

OPPOSITES: benefit, advantage, reward
3 = haul, net, bag • *The catch included one fish over 18 pounds.*
4 = marriage prospect, match • *All my friends said what a good catch he was.*
▸ **IN PHRASES: catch on 1 = understand**, see, find out, grasp, see through, comprehend, twig (*Brit. informal*), get the picture, see the light of day • *He tried to explain it to me, but it took me a while to catch on.*
2 = become popular, take off, become trendy, come into fashion • *The idea has been around for ages without catching on.*

catchcry = catch phrase, slogan, saying, quotation, motto • *his catchcry, "If it ain't broke, don't fix it"*

catching = infectious, contagious, transferable, communicable, infective, transmittable • *There are those who think eczema is catching.*
OPPOSITES: incommunicable, non-infectious, non-contagious

catch phrase = slogan, saying, quotation, motto, catchword, catchcry (*Austral.*) • *a comedy character with the catch phrase, 'You don't want to do that'*

catchy = memorable, haunting, unforgettable, captivating • *a catchy theme song*

categorical = absolute, direct, express, positive, explicit, unconditional, emphatic, downright, unequivocal, unqualified, unambiguous, unreserved • *He issued a categorical denial that he had had an affair.*
OPPOSITES: qualified, uncertain, vague

category = class, grouping, heading, head, order, sort, list, department, type, division, section, rank, grade, classification • *The entries were organised into six different categories.*

cater IN PHRASES: cater for something *or* **someone**
1 = provide for, supply, provision, purvey, victual • *Thirty restaurants and hotels catered for the event.*
2 = take into account, consider, bear in mind, make allowance for, have regard for • *We have to cater for the demands of the marketplace.*
cater to something *or* **someone = indulge**, spoil, minister to, pamper, gratify, pander to, coddle, mollycoddle • *His parents spoil him and cater to his every whim.*

catharsis = release, cleansing, purging, purification, purgation, abreaction • *Writing acted as a catharsis for all his painful feelings.*

catholic = wide, general, liberal, global, varied, comprehensive, universal, world-wide, tolerant, eclectic, all-inclusive, ecumenical, all-embracing, broad-minded, unbigoted, unsectarian • *He was a man of catholic tastes, enjoying music and fine arts of all kinds.*
OPPOSITES: limited, exclusive, sectarian

cattle = cows, stock, beasts, livestock, bovines • *a ban on all imports of live cattle and beef from the European Community*
▸ **RELATED ADJECTIVE:** bovine
▸ **COLLECTIVE NOUNS:** drove, herd

QUOTATIONS
The cow is of the bovine ilk;
One end is moo, the other, milk
[Ogden Nash *The Cow*]

▹ *See panel* **Cattle**

catty = spiteful, mean, malicious, malevolent, venomous, bitchy (*informal*), snide, rancorous, backbiting, shrewish, ill-natured, snarky (*informal*) • *She had to put up with catty remarks about her appearance.*
OPPOSITES: kind, generous, pleasant

caucus = group, division, section, camp, sector, lobby, bloc, contingent, pressure group, junta, public-interest group (*U.S. & Canad.*) • *the Black Caucus of minority congressmen*

cause AS A NOUN 1 = origin, source, agency, spring, agent,

CATTLE

BREEDS OF CATTLE

Aberdeen Angus, Africander, Alderney, Ayrshire, Belted Galloway, Blonde d'Aquitaine, Brown Swiss, cattalo, Charolais, Devon, dexter, Durham, Friesian, Galloway, Gelbvieh, Guernsey, Hereford, Highland, Holstein, Illawarra (shorthorn), Jersey, Kerry, kyloe, Limousin, longhorn, Meuse-Rhine-Ijssel, Normandy, Norwegian Red, Red Poll, Santa Gertrudis, shorthorn, Simmental, Sussex, Texas longhorn, Wagyu

CATTLE AND OTHER ARTIODACTYLS

addax, alpaca, antelope, aoudad, argali, ariel, axis *or* chital, babirusa, Bactrian camel, bharal, bison, blacktail, blaubok, blesbok, boar, boer goat, bongo, bontebok, brocket, bubal, buffalo, bull, ▹ *See panel* **Breeds of cattle**, bushbuck, bushpig, camel *or* (*Anglo-Indian*) oont, Cape buffalo, caribou, chamois *or* izard, chevrotain *or* mouse deer, Chinese water deer, cow, deer, dik-dik, dromedary, duiker, eland, elk, gaur, gayal, gazelle, gemsbok, gerenuk, giraffe *or* (*obsolete*) camelopard, gnu, goa, goat, goral, grysbok, guanaco, harnessed antelope, hartebeest, hippopotamus, ibex, impala, Jacob, karakul, Kashmir goat, klipspringer, kob, kongoni, kouprey, kudu, llama, markhor, marshbuck, moose, mouflon, mountain goat, mule deer, muntjac *or* barking deer, musk deer, nilgai, nyala, okapi, oribi, oryx, ox, peccary, Père David's deer, pig, ▹ *See panel* **Breeds of pig**, pronghorn, pudu, razorback, red deer, reedbuck *or* nagor, reindeer, rhebok, Rocky Mountain goat, roe deer, sable antelope, saiga, sambar, sassaby, serow, sheep *or* (*Austral. slang*) jumbuck, ▹ *See panel* **Breeds of sheep**, sika, springbok, stag, steenbok, tahr, takin, vicuña, wapiti, wart hog, waterbuck, water buffalo, water ox, *or* carabao, white-tailed deer, wild boar, wildebeest, yak, zebu, zo

maker, producer, root, beginning, creator, genesis, originator, prime mover, mainspring • *Smoking is the biggest preventable cause of death and disease.*
OPPOSITES: end, result, effect
2 = **reason**, call, need, grounds, basis, incentive, motive, motivation, justification, inducement • *There is obvious cause for concern.*
3 = **aim**, movement, purpose, principle, object, ideal, enterprise, end • *His comments have done nothing to help the cause of peace.*
▸ **AS A VERB** = **produce**, begin, create, effect, lead to, occasion, result in, generate, provoke, compel, motivate, induce, bring about, give rise to, precipitate, incite, engender • *I don't want to cause any trouble.*
OPPOSITES: stop, prevent, deter

caustic 1 = **burning**, corrosive, corroding, astringent, vitriolic, acrid, mordant • *This substance is caustic; use gloves when handling it.*
2 = **sarcastic**, biting, keen, cutting, severe, stinging, scathing, acrimonious, pungent, vitriolic, trenchant, mordant • *He was well known for his abrasive wit and caustic comments.*
OPPOSITES: loving, kind, pleasing

caution **AS A NOUN** 1 = **care**, discretion, heed, prudence, vigilance, alertness, forethought, circumspection, watchfulness, belt and braces, carefulness, heedfulness • *Drivers are urged to exercise extreme caution in icy weather.*
OPPOSITES: daring, carelessness, recklessness
2 = **reprimand**, warning, injunction, admonition • *The others got off with a caution but I was fined.*
▸ **AS A VERB** 1 = **warn**, urge, advise, alert, tip off, forewarn, put you on your guard • *Banks caution young couples against opening joint bank accounts.*
2 = **reprimand**, warn, admonish, give an injunction to • *The two men were cautioned but the police say they will not be charged.*

PROVERBS
You should know a man seven years before you stir his fire
Once bitten, twice shy

cautious = **careful**, guarded, alert, wary, discreet, tentative, prudent, vigilant, watchful, judicious, circumspect, cagey *(informal)*, on your toes, chary, belt-and-braces, keeping a weather eye on • *Mr King clearly has a cautious approach to change.*
OPPOSITES: daring, bold, careless

cautiously = **carefully**, alertly, discreetly, tentatively, warily, prudently, judiciously, guardedly, circumspectly, watchfully, vigilantly, cagily *(informal)*, mindfully • *The government has reacted cautiously to the report.*

cavalcade = **parade**, train, procession, march-past • *a cavalcade of limousines and police motorcycles*

cavalier = **offhand**, lordly, arrogant, lofty, curt, condescending, haughty, scornful, disdainful, insolent, supercilious • *He has always had a cavalier attitude towards other people's feelings.*

cavalry = **horsemen**, horse, mounted troops • *They were the best-mounted cavalry in all the world.*
OPPOSITES: foot soldiers, infantrymen

cave = **hollow**, cavern, grotto, den, cavity • *creatures such as bats and moths which shelter in caves*

QUOTATIONS
Caves: Usually inhabited by thieves. Always full of snakes
[Gustave Flaubert *The Dictionary of Received Ideas*]

caveat = **warning**, caution, admonition, qualification, proviso, reservation, condition • *He added the caveat that all the figures in the survey were suspect.*

cavern = **cave**, hollow, grotto, underground chamber • *an enormous cavern, with caves running in all directions from it*

cavernous = **vast**, wide, huge, enormous, extensive, immense, spacious, expansive, capacious, commodious • *the cavernous interior of the gallery*

cavil = **find fault**, object, complain, beef *(slang)*, carp, quibble, kvetch *(U.S. slang)*, nit-pick *(informal)* • *This is not the time to cavil about petty details.*

cavity = **hollow**, hole, gap, pit, dent, crater • *The sinuses are four sets of air-filled cavities leading directly from the nose.*

cavort = **frolic**, sport, romp, caper, prance, frisk, gambol • *children cavorting on the sand*

cease 1 = **stop**, end, finish, be over, come to an end, peter out, die away • *Almost miraculously, the noise ceased.*
OPPOSITES: start, begin, continue
2 = **discontinue**, end, stop, fail, finish, give up, conclude, suspend, halt, terminate, break off, refrain, leave off, give over *(informal)*, bring to an end, desist, belay *(Nautical)* • *A small number of firms have ceased trading.*
OPPOSITES: start, begin, continue

ceaseless = **continual**, constant, endless, continuous, eternal, perennial, perpetual, never-ending, interminable, incessant, everlasting, unending, unremitting, nonstop, untiring • *Their life is a ceaseless struggle for survival.*
OPPOSITES: broken, occasional, irregular

cede = **surrender**, grant, transfer, abandon, yield, concede, hand over, relinquish, renounce, make over, abdicate • *The General had promised to cede power by January.*

celebrate 1 = **rejoice**, party, enjoy yourself, carouse, live it up *(informal)*, whoop it up *(informal)*, make merry, paint the town red *(informal)*, go on a spree, large it *(Brit. slang)*, put the flags out, roister, kill the fatted calf • *I was in a mood to celebrate.*
2 = **commemorate**, honour, observe, toast, drink to, keep • *Tom celebrated his birthday two days ago.*
3 = **perform**, observe, preside over, officiate at, solemnize, reverence • *Pope John Paul celebrated mass today in a city in central Poland.*
4 = **praise**, honour, commend *(informal)*, glorify, publicize, exalt, laud, extol, big up *(slang, chiefly Caribbean)*, eulogize • *a festival to celebrate the life and work of this great composer*

celebrated = **renowned**, popular, famous, outstanding, distinguished, well-known, prominent, glorious, acclaimed, notable, eminent, revered, famed, illustrious, pre-eminent, lionized • *He was soon one of the most celebrated young painters in England.*
OPPOSITES: forgotten, unknown, obscure

celebration 1 = **party**, festival, gala, jubilee, festivity, rave *(Brit. slang)*, junketing, beano *(Brit. slang)*, revelry, red-letter day, rave-up *(Brit. slang)*, merrymaking, jollification, carousal, -fest *(in combination)*, hooley or hoolie *(chiefly Irish & N.Z.)* • *There was a celebration in our house that night.*
2 = **commemoration**, honouring, remembrance • *This was not a memorial service but a celebration of his life.*
3 = **performance**, observance, solemnization • *the celebration of Mass in Latin*

celebrity 1 = **personality**, name, star, lion, superstar, big name, dignitary, luminary, bigwig *(informal)*, celeb *(informal)*, face *(informal)*, big shot *(informal)*, personage, megastar *(informal)*, V.I.P. • *At the age of twelve, he was already a celebrity.*
OPPOSITES: has-been, nobody, unknown
2 = **fame**, reputation, honour, glory, popularity, distinction, prestige, prominence, stardom, renown, pre-eminence, repute, éclat, notability • *She has finally achieved celebrity after 25 years as an actress.*
OPPOSITE: obscurity

QUOTATIONS
A celebrity is a person who works hard all his life to become known, then wears dark glasses to avoid being recognized
[Fred Allen *Treadmill to Oblivion*]
The celebrity is a person who is known for his well-knownness
[Daniel Boorstin *The Image*]

Celebrity: the advantage of being known by those who don't know you
[Chamfort *Maximes et pensées*]

celestial 1 = **astronomical**, planetary, stellar, astral, extraterrestrial • *the clusters of celestial bodies in the ever-expanding universe*
2 = **heavenly**, spiritual, divine, eternal, sublime, immortal, supernatural, astral, ethereal, angelic, godlike, seraphic • *gods and other celestial beings*

celibacy = **chastity**, purity, virginity, continence, singleness • *priests who take a vow of celibacy for life*
QUOTATIONS
Marriage has many pains, but celibacy has no pleasures
[Dr. Johnson *Rasselas*]

celibate = **chaste**, single, pure, virgin, continent • *He found it hard to adapt to the celibate life of a monk.*

cell 1 = **room**, chamber, lock-up, compartment, cavity, cubicle, dungeon, stall • *They took her back to the cell, and just left her there to die.*
2 = **unit**, group, section, core, nucleus, caucus, coterie • *the abolition of Communist Party cells in all work places*

cement AS A NOUN 1 = **mortar**, plaster, paste • *The stone work has all been pointed with cement.*
2 = **sealant**, glue, gum, adhesive, binder • *Stick the pieces on with tile cement.*
▸ AS A VERB = **stick**, join, bond, attach, seal, glue, plaster, gum, weld, solder • *Most artificial joints are cemented into place.*

cemetery = **graveyard**, churchyard, burial ground, necropolis, God's acre • *There was a small cemetery just outside the town.*

censor = **expurgate**, cut, blue-pencil, bowdlerize • *Most TV companies tend to censor bad language in feature films.*

censorious = **critical**, severe, carping, disapproving, scathing, disparaging, judgmental, cavilling, condemnatory, fault-finding, captious • *He is too judgmental and censorious for my liking.*

censorship = **expurgation**, blue pencil, purgation, bowdlerization *or* bowdlerisation, sanitization *or* sanitisation • *The government today announced that press censorship was being lifted.*
QUOTATIONS
Censorship is never over for those who have experienced it
[Nadine Gordimer *Censorship and Its Aftermath*]
God forbid that any book should be banned. The practice is as indefensible as infanticide
[Rebecca West *The Strange Necessity*]
Wherever books are burned, in the end people too will be burned
[Heinrich Heine *Almansor*]
Where there is official censorship it is a sign that speech is serious
[Paul Goodman *Growing Up Absurd*]

censure AS A VERB = **criticize**, blame, abuse, condemn, carpet *(informal)*, flame *(informal)*, denounce, put down, slate *(informal, chiefly U.S.)*, rebuke, reprimand, reproach, scold, berate, castigate, chide, tear into *(informal)*, diss *(slang, chiefly U.S.)*, blast, read the riot act, reprove, upbraid, slap on the wrist, lambast(e), bawl out *(informal)*, excoriate, rap over the knuckles, chew out *(U.S. & Canad. informal)*, tear (someone) off a strip *(Brit. informal)*, give (someone) a rocket *(Brit. & N.Z. informal)*, reprehend • *I would not presume to censure him for his views.*
OPPOSITES: applaud, compliment, commend
▸ AS A NOUN = **disapproval**, criticism, blame, condemnation, rebuke, reprimand, reproach, dressing down *(informal)*, stick *(slang)*, stricture, reproof, sideswipe, castigation, obloquy, remonstrance • *It is a controversial policy which has attracted international censure.*
OPPOSITES: approval, encouragement, compliment

central 1 = **inner**, middle, mid, interior • *She had a house in central London.*
OPPOSITES: outer, exterior, outermost
2 = **main**, chief, key, essential, primary, principal, fundamental, focal • *The Poll Tax was a central part of Mrs Thatcher's reform of local government.*
OPPOSITES: minor, secondary, subsidiary

centralize = **unify**, concentrate, incorporate, compact, streamline, converge, condense, amalgamate, rationalize • *In the mass production era, multinational firms tended to centralize their operations.*

centre AS A NOUN = **middle**, heart, focus, core, nucleus, hub, pivot, kernel, crux, bull's-eye, midpoint • *A large wooden table dominates the centre of the room.*
OPPOSITES: limit, edge, border
▸ IN PHRASES: **centre on something** *or* **someone** = **focus**, concentrate, cluster, revolve, converge • *Our efforts centre on helping patients to overcome illness.* • *All his thoughts are centred on himself.*

centrepiece = **focus**, highlight, hub, cynosure, star • *This year the centrepiece of the Festival will be its presentation of two rarely performed operas.*

cereal
▹ *See panel* **Rice and other cereals**

ceremonial AS AN ADJECTIVE = **formal**, public, official, ritual, stately, solemn, liturgical, courtly, ritualistic • *He represented the nation on ceremonial occasions.*
OPPOSITES: simple, relaxed, informal
▸ AS A NOUN = **ritual**, ceremony, rite, formality, solemnity • *It is difficult to imagine a more impressive ceremonial.*

ceremony 1 = **ritual**, service, rite, observance, commemoration, solemnities • *The flag was blessed in a ceremony in the local cathedral.*
2 = **formality**, ceremonial, propriety, decorum, formal courtesy • *He was crowned with great ceremony.*

certain 1 = **sure**, convinced, positive, confident, satisfied, assured, free from doubt • *She's absolutely certain she's going to make it as a singer.*
OPPOSITES: uncertain, doubtful, unsure
2 = **bound**, sure, fated, destined • *They say he's certain to get a nomination for best supporting actor.*
OPPOSITES: unlikely
3 = **inevitable**, unavoidable, inescapable, inexorable, ineluctable • *They intervened to save him from certain death.*
4 = **known**, true, positive, plain, ascertained, unmistakable, conclusive, undoubted, unequivocal, undeniable, irrefutable, unquestionable, incontrovertible, indubitable, nailed-on *(slang)* • *One thing is certain – they have the utmost respect for each other.*
OPPOSITES: uncertain, doubtful, dubious
5 = **fixed**, decided, established, settled, definite • *He has to pay a certain sum in child support every month.*
OPPOSITES: unsettled, indefinite
6 = **particular**, special, individual, specific • *A certain person has been looking for you.*

certainly = **definitely**, surely, truly, absolutely, undoubtedly, positively, decidedly, without doubt, unquestionably, undeniably, without question, unequivocally, indisputably, assuredly, indubitably, doubtlessly, come hell or high water, irrefutably • *I'll certainly do all I can to help.*

certainty 1 = **confidence**, trust, faith, conviction, assurance, certitude, sureness, positiveness, authoritativeness • *I have said with absolute certainty that there will be no change of policy.*
OPPOSITES: doubt, uncertainty, disbelief
2 = **inevitability** • *There is too little certainty about the outcome yet.*
OPPOSITES: uncertainty

3 = **fact**, truth, reality, sure thing *(informal)*, surety, banker • *A general election became a certainty three weeks ago.*

QUOTATIONS

In this world nothing is certain but death and taxes
[Benjamin Franklin]

If a man will begin with certainties, he shall end in doubts; but if he will be content to begin with doubts, he shall end in certainties
[Francis Bacon *The Advancement of Learning*]

certificate = **document**, licence, warrant, voucher, diploma, testimonial, authorization, credential(s) • *a certificate of adoption*

certify = **confirm**, show, declare, guarantee, witness, assure, endorse, testify, notify, verify, ascertain, validate, attest, corroborate, avow, authenticate, vouch for, aver • *They have certified the document as genuine.*

certitude = **certainty**, confidence, conviction, assurance, sureness, positiveness • *I cannot say with any degree of certitude what will happen next.*

cessation = **ceasing**, ending, break, halt, halting, pause, suspension, interruption, respite, standstill, stoppage, termination, let-up *(informal)*, remission, abeyance, discontinuance, stay • *They would not agree to a cessation of hostilities.*

chafe 1 = **rub**, scratch, scrape, rasp, abrade • *The shorts were chafing my thighs.*
2 = **be annoyed**, rage, fume, be angry, fret, be offended, be irritated, be incensed, be impatient, be exasperated, be inflamed, be ruffled, be vexed, be narked *(Brit., Austral. & N.Z. slang)* • *He chafed at having to take orders from someone else.*

chaff = **husks**, remains, refuse, waste, hulls, rubbish, trash, dregs • *The harvester separates the straw and chaff from the grain.*

chagrin AS A NOUN = **annoyance**, embarrassment, humiliation, dissatisfaction, disquiet, displeasure, mortification, discomfiture, vexation, discomposure • *Much to his chagrin, she didn't remember him at all.*
▸ AS A VERB = **annoy**, embarrass, humiliate, disquiet, vex, displease, mortify, discomfit, dissatisfy, discompose • *He was chagrined at missing such an easy goal.*

chain AS A NOUN 1 = **tether**, coupling, link, bond, shackle, fetter, manacle • *The dogs were growling and pulling at their chains.*
2 = **group**, multiple • *A new chain of shops is to be opened next year.*
3 = **series**, set, train, string, sequence, succession, progression, concatenation • *a horrific chain of events*
▸ AS A VERB = **bind**, confine, restrain, handcuff, shackle, tether, fetter, manacle • *We were kept in a cell, chained to the wall.*

chair
▹ *See panel* **Types of chair**

chairman *or* **chairwoman** 1 = **director**, president, chief, executive, chairperson • *I had done business with the company's chairman.*
2 = **master of ceremonies**, spokesman, chair, speaker, MC, chairperson • *The chairman declared the meeting open.*

chalk up 1 = **score**, win, gain, achieve, accumulate, attain • *The team chalked up one win after another.*
2 = **record**, mark, enter, credit, register, log, tally • *I just chalked his odd behaviour up to midlife crisis.*

challenge AS A NOUN 1 = **dare**, provocation, summons to contest, wero *(N.Z.)* • *I like a challenge, and they don't come much bigger than this.*
2 = **test**, trial, opposition, confrontation, defiance, ultimatum, face-off *(slang)* • *In December, she saw off the first challenge to her leadership.*
▸ AS A VERB 1 = **dispute**, question, tackle, confront, defy, object to, disagree with, take issue with, impugn • *The move was immediately challenged by the opposition.*
2 = **dare**, invite, provoke, defy, summon, call out, throw down the gauntlet • *He left a note at the crime scene, challenging detectives to catch him.*
3 = **test**, try, tax • *a task that would challenge his courage*
4 = **question**, interrogate, accost • *The men opened fire after they were challenged by the guard.*

chamber 1 = **hall**, room • *We are going to be in the council chamber when he speaks.*
2 = **council**, assembly, legislature, legislative body • *the main political chamber of the Slovenian parliament*
3 = **room**, bedroom, apartment, enclosure, cubicle • *We shall dine together in my chamber.*
4 = **compartment**, hollow, cavity • *The incinerator works by focusing the sun's rays onto a cylindrical glass chamber.*

champagne
▹ *See panel* **Champagne bottles**

champion AS A NOUN 1 = **winner**, hero, victor, conqueror, title holder, warrior, nonpareil • *Kasparov became a world chess champion.*
2 = **defender**, guardian, patron, backer, protector, upholder, vindicator • *He received acclaim as a champion of the oppressed.*
▸ AS A VERB = **support**, back, defend, promote, advocate, fight for, uphold, espouse, stick up for *(informal)*, endorse • *He passionately championed the poor.*

chance AS A NOUN 1 = **probability**, odds, possibility, prospect, liability, likelihood • *This partnership has a good chance of success.*
OPPOSITES: certainty, impossibility, surety
2 = **opportunity**, opening, occasion, time, scope, window • *All eligible people will get a chance to vote.*
3 = **accident**, fortune, luck, fate, destiny, coincidence, misfortune, providence • *I met him quite by chance.*
OPPOSITES: design, intention

TYPES OF CHAIR

armchair	bucket seat	dos-à-dos	kneeling chair	piano stool	swing
banquette	campaign chair	easy chair	ladder-back chair	platform rocker	swivel chair
barrel chair	camp chair	fauteuil	lounger	pouf	throne
bar stool	cane chair	fiddle-back	milking stool	reclining chair	tub chair
basket chair	carver	folding chair	Morris chair	rocking chair	wheelchair
Bath chair	cathedra	form	music stool	sedan chair	window seat
beanbag	corner chair	garden chair	office chair	settle	Windsor chair
bench	curule chair	gestatorial chair	opsitbank *(S. African)*	shooting stick	Windsor rocker
bentwood chair	deck chair	hassock	ottoman	stool	wing chair
berbice chair	dining chair	highchair	pew	straight chair	
bergère	director's chair	jampan		súgán chair	

CHAMPAGNE BOTTLES

Bottle	Capacity
magnum	2 bottles
jeroboam	2 magnums
rehoboam	3 magnums
methuselah	4 magnums
salmanazar	6 magnums
balthazar	8 magnums
nebuchadnezzar	10 magnums

4 = risk, speculation, gamble, hazard • *I certainly think it's worth taking a chance.*
▸ **AS AN ADJECTIVE = accidental**, random, casual, incidental, unforeseen, unintentional, fortuitous, inadvertent, serendipitous, unforeseeable, unlooked-for • *He describes their chance meeting as intense.*
OPPOSITES: planned, expected, designed
▸ **AS A VERB 1 = happen** • *A man I chanced to meet proved to be a most unusual character.*
2 = risk, try, stake, venture, gamble, hazard, wager • *No sniper would chance a shot from amongst that crowd.*
▸ **RELATED ADJECTIVE:** fortuitous

chancy = risky, dangerous, uncertain, dodgy (*Brit., Austral. & N.Z. slang*), hazardous, speculative, perilous, problematical, dicey (*informal, chiefly Brit.*), shonky (*Austral. & N.Z. informal*) • *Investment is becoming a chancy business.*
OPPOSITES: sure, sound, safe

change **AS A NOUN 1 = alteration**, innovation, transformation, modification, mutation, metamorphosis, permutation, transmutation, difference, revolution, transition • *They are going to have to make some drastic changes.*
2 = variety, break (*informal*), departure, variation, novelty, diversion, whole new ball game (*informal*) • *It makes a nice change to see you in a good mood for once.*
OPPOSITES: stability, uniformity, monotony
3 = exchange, trade, conversion, swap, substitution, interchange • *He stuffed a bag with a few changes of clothing.*
4 = coins, money, small change, loose change, wonga (*slang*), kembla (*Austral. slang*) • *Do you have any change for the phone?*
▸ **AS A VERB 1 = alter**, reform, transform, adjust, moderate, revise, modify, remodel, reorganize, restyle, convert • *They should change the law to make it illegal to own replica weapons.*
OPPOSITES: keep, hold
2 = shift, vary, transform, alter, modify, diversify, fluctuate, mutate, metamorphose, transmute • *We are trying to detect and understand how the climate changes.*
OPPOSITES: remain, stay
3 = exchange, trade, replace, substitute, swap, interchange • *Can we change it for another if it doesn't work properly?*

QUOTATIONS

A state without the means of some change is without the means of its conservation
[Edmund Burke *Reflections on the Revolution in France*]

Can the Ethiopian change his skin, or the leopard his spots?
[*Bible: Jeremiah*]

The more things change, the more they are the same
[Alphonse Karr *Les Guêpes*]

Change is not made without inconvenience, even from worse to better
[Dr. Johnson *Dictionary of the English Language*]

The old order changeth, yielding place to new
[Alfred, Lord Tennyson *The Passing of Arthur*]

Philosophers have only interpreted the world in various ways; the point, however, is to change it
[Karl Marx *Theses on Feuerbach*]

When it is not necessary to change, it is necessary not to change
[Lucius Cary *Discourses of Infallibility*]

PROVERBS

Don't change horses in midstream
A change is as good as a rest
A new broom sweeps clean

changeable = variable, shifting, mobile, uncertain, volatile, unsettled, unpredictable, versatile, unstable, irregular, erratic, wavering, uneven, unreliable, fickle, temperamental, whimsical, mercurial, capricious, unsteady, protean, vacillating, fitful, mutable, labile, inconstant • *He was a man of changeable moods.* • *The forecast is for changeable weather.*
OPPOSITES: regular, stable, constant

channel **AS A NOUN 1 = means**, way, course, approach, medium, route, path, avenue • *We'll be lodging a complaint through the official channels.*
2 = strait, sound, route, passage, canal, waterway, main • *Oil spilled into the channel following a collision between a tanker and a trawler.*
3 = duct, chamber, artery, groove, gutter, furrow, conduit • *Keep the drainage channel clear.*
▸ **AS A VERB = direct**, guide, conduct, transmit, convey • *Stephen is channelling all his energies into his novel.*

chant **AS A NOUN 1 = cry**, call, song, shout, slogan • *They taunted their rivals with the chant, 'You're not singing any more.'*
2 = song, carol, chorus, melody, psalm • *We were listening to a CD of Gregorian chant.*
▸ **AS A VERB 1 = shout**, call, sing • *The demonstrators chanted slogans at the police.*
2 = sing, chorus, recite, intone, carol • *Muslims chanted and prayed in the temple.*

chaos = disorder, confusion, mayhem, anarchy, lawlessness, pandemonium, entropy, bedlam, tumult, disorganization • *The country appears to be sliding towards chaos.*
OPPOSITES: organization, neatness, orderliness

QUOTATIONS

Chaos is a name for any order that produces confusion in our minds
[George Santayana *Dominations and Powers*]

Chaos often breeds life, when order breeds habit
[Henry Brooks Adams *The Education of Henry Adams*]

chaotic = disordered, confused, uncontrolled, anarchic, tumultuous, lawless, riotous, topsy-turvy, disorganized, purposeless • *My house is always a chaotic mess.*

chap = fellow, man, person, individual, type, sort, customer (*informal*), character, guy (*informal*), bloke (*Brit. informal*), cove (*slang*), dude (*U.S. & Canad. informal*) • *Her husband's a very decent chap.*

chaperone **AS A NOUN = escort**, companion, governess, duenna • *She is 15 and still in need of a chaperone.*
▸ **AS A VERB = escort**, protect, attend, accompany, shepherd, safeguard, watch over • *We were chaperoned by a tall red-haired woman.*

chapter 1 = section, part, stage, division, episode, topic, segment, instalment • *I took the title of this chapter from one of my favorite songs.*
2 = period, time, stage, phase • *It was one of the most dramatic chapters of recent British politics.*
3 = convocation, council, congress, assembly, convention, synod, conclave • *The Archbishop thanked the Dean and Chapter of Westminster for inviting him to the Abbey.*
4 = branch, part, department, section, wing, subdivision, subsection • *the Brisbane-based chapter of Hell's Angels*
▸ **RELATED ADJECTIVE:** capitular

char = scorch, sear, singe • *Halve the peppers and char the skins under a hot grill.*

character 1 = **personality**, nature, make-up, cast, constitution, bent, attributes, temper, temperament, complexion, disposition, individuality, marked traits • *There is a side to his character which you haven't seen yet.*
2 = **nature**, kind, quality, constitution, calibre • *Moscow's reforms were socialist in character.*
3 = **person**, sort, individual, type, guy *(informal)*, fellow • *What an unpleasant character he is!*
4 = **reputation**, honour, integrity, good name, rectitude, uprightness • *He's begun a series of attacks on my character.*
5 = **courage**, resolution, determination, guts *(informal)*, pluck, grit, bravery, backbone, fortitude, staying power, strength of mind, dauntlessness • *She showed real character in her refusal to give up.*
6 = **role**, part, persona • *He plays the film's central character.*
7 = **eccentric**, card *(informal)*, original, nut *(slang)*, flake *(slang, chiefly U.S.)*, oddity, oddball *(informal)*, odd bod *(informal)*, queer fish *(Brit. informal)*, wacko *or* whacko *(informal)* • *He'll be sadly missed. He was a real character.*
8 = **symbol**, mark, sign, letter, figure, type, device, logo, emblem, rune, cipher, hieroglyph • *Chinese characters inscribed on a plaque*

QUOTATIONS
Genius is formed in quiet, character in the stream of human life
[Goethe *Torquato Tasso*]
Character is much easier kept than recovered
[Thomas Paine *The American Crisis*]
A man's character is his fate
[Heraclitus *On the Universe*]
Character is like a tree and reputation like its shadow. The shadow is what we think of it; the tree is the real thing
[Abraham Lincoln]
Fate and character are the same concept
[Novalis *Heinrich von Ofterdingen*]

characteristic AS A NOUN = **feature**, mark, quality, property, attribute, faculty, trait, quirk, peculiarity, idiosyncrasy • *Genes determine the characteristics of every living thing.*
▸ AS AN ADJECTIVE = **typical**, special, individual, specific, representative, distinguishing, distinctive, signature, peculiar, singular, idiosyncratic, symptomatic • *Windmills are a characteristic feature of the landscape.*
OPPOSITES: rare, unusual, uncharacteristic

characterize 1 = **distinguish**, mark, identify, brand, inform, stamp, typify • *This election campaign has been characterized by violence.*
2 = **portray**, show, present, represent, depict • *In horror films women are usually characterized as victims.*

charade = **pretence**, farce, parody, pantomime, fake • *They went through an elaborate charade of pretending they had never met before.*

charge AS A VERB 1 = **ask for**, set, impose, levy • *The majority of traders charged a fair price.*
2 = **bill**, invoice • *Charge it to my credit card, please.*
3 = **accuse**, indict, impeach, incriminate, arraign • *They have all the evidence required to charge him.*
OPPOSITES: clear, pardon, acquit
4 = **attack**, assault, assail • *Our general ordered us to charge the enemy.*
OPPOSITES: withdraw, retreat, back off
5 = **rush**, storm, stampede • *He charged into the room.*
6 = **fill**, load, instil, suffuse, lade • *a performance that was charged with energy*
7 = **command**, order, demand, require, bid, instruct, entrust, exhort, enjoin • *Jesus charged his disciples to preach the gospel.*
▸ AS A NOUN 1 = **price**, rate, cost, amount, payment, expense, toll, expenditure, outlay, damage *(informal)* • *We can arrange this for a small charge.*
2 = **accusation**, allegation, indictment, imputation • *They appeared at court to deny charges of murder.*
OPPOSITES: clearance, pardon, acquittal
3 = **care**, trust, responsibility, custody, safekeeping • *I have been given charge of this class.*
4 = **duty**, office, concern, responsibility, remit • *I did not consider it any part of my charge to come up with marketing ideas.*
5 = **ward**, pupil, protégé, dependant • *The coach tried to get his charges motivated.*
6 = **attack**, rush, assault, onset, onslaught, stampede, sortie • *He led the bayonet charge from the front.*
OPPOSITES: withdrawal, retreat

charisma = **charm**, appeal, personality, attraction, lure, allure, magnetism, force of personality • *He does not have the charisma to inspire people.*

charismatic = **charming**, appealing, attractive, influential, magnetic, enticing, alluring • *With her striking looks and charismatic personality, she was noticed far and wide.*

charitable 1 = **benevolent**, liberal, generous, lavish, philanthropic, bountiful, beneficent • *He made large donations to numerous charitable organizations.*
OPPOSITES: mean, stingy, ungenerous
2 = **kind**, understanding, forgiving, sympathetic, favourable, tolerant, indulgent, lenient, considerate, magnanimous, broad-minded • *Some people take a less charitable view of his behaviour.*
OPPOSITES: mean, strict, unkind

charity 1 = **charitable organization**, fund, movement, trust, endowment • *The National Trust is a registered charity.*
2 = **donations**, help, relief, gift, contributions, assistance, hand-out, philanthropy, alms-giving, benefaction, largesse *or* largess, koha *(N.Z.)* • *My mum was very proud. She wouldn't accept charity.*
OPPOSITES: selfishness, meanness, stinginess
3 = **kindness**, love, pity, humanity, affection, goodness, goodwill, compassion, generosity, indulgence, bounty, altruism, benevolence, fellow feeling, benignity, bountifulness, tenderheartedness, aroha *(N.Z.)* • *He had no sense of right and wrong, no charity, no humanity.*
OPPOSITES: hatred, intolerance, ill will

QUOTATIONS
And now abideth faith, hope, charity, these three: but the greatest of these is charity
[*Bible: 1 Corinthians*]
Charity. To love human beings in so far as they are nothing. That is to love them as God does
[Simone Weil *The New York Notebook*]
Though I speak with the tongues of men and of angels, and have not charity, I am become as sounding brass, or a tinkling cymbal. And though I have the gift of prophecy, and understand all mysteries, and all knowledge; and though I have all faith; so that I could remove mountains; and have not charity, I am nothing
[*Bible: 1 Corinthians*]
Charity begins at home, but should not end there
[Thomas Fuller *Gnomologia*]
Charity suffereth long, and is kind; charity envieth not; charity vaunteth not itself, is not puffed up... Beareth all things, believeth all things, hopeth all things, endureth all things. Charity never faileth
[*Bible: 1 Corinthians*]
Charity shall cover the multitude of sins
[*Bible: 1 Peter*]
He gives the poor man twice as much good who gives quickly
[Publilius Syrus]

PROVERBS
Charity begins at home

charlatan = **fraud**, cheat, fake, sham, pretender, quack, con man *(informal)*, impostor, fraudster, swindler, mountebank, grifter *(slang, chiefly U.S. & Canad.)*, phoney *or* phony *(informal)*, rorter *(Austral. slang)*, rogue trader • *This so-called psychic was exposed as a charlatan.*

charm AS A NOUN **1** = **attraction**, appeal, fascination, allure, magnetism, desirability, allurement • *He was a man of great distinction and charm.*
OPPOSITES: unattractiveness, repulsiveness
2 = **trinket** • *She wore a silver bracelet hung with charms.*
3 = **talisman**, amulet, lucky piece, good-luck piece, fetish • *He carried a rabbit's foot as a good luck charm.*
4 = **spell**, magic, enchantment, sorcery, makutu *(N.Z.)* • *They cross their fingers and spit over their shoulders as a charm against the evil eye.*
▸ AS A VERB **1** = **attract**, win, please, delight, fascinate, absorb, entrance, win over, enchant, captivate, beguile, allure, bewitch, ravish, mesmerize, enrapture, enamour • *My brother charms everyone he meets.*
OPPOSITES: alienate, repel, repulse
2 = **persuade**, seduce, coax, beguile, cajole, sweet-talk *(informal)* • *I'm sure you'll be able to charm him into taking you.*

QUOTATIONS
You know what charm is: a way of getting the answer yes without having asked any clear question
[Albert Camus *The Fall*]
Charm ... it's a sort of bloom on a woman. If you have it, you don't need to have anything else; and if you don't have it, it doesn't much matter what else you have
[J.M. Barrie *What Every Woman Knows*]

charming = **attractive**, pleasing, appealing, engaging, lovely, winning, pleasant, fetching, delightful, cute, irresistible, seductive, captivating, eye-catching, bewitching, delectable, winsome, likable *or* likeable • *I found her a delightful and charming young woman.*
OPPOSITES: unpleasant, disgusting, unattractive

chart AS A NOUN = **table**, diagram, blueprint, graph, tabulation, plan, map • *The chart below shows the results of our survey.*
▸ AS A VERB **1** = **plot**, map out, delineate, sketch, draft, graph, tabulate • *These seas have been well charted.*
2 = **monitor**, follow, record, note, document, register, trace, outline, log, graph, tabulate • *Bulletin boards charted each executive's progress.*

charter AS A NOUN **1** = **document**, right, contract, bond, permit, licence, concession, privilege, franchise, deed, prerogative, indenture • *In Britain, city status is granted by royal charter.*
2 = **constitution**, laws, rules, code • *The Prime Minister also attacked the social charter.*
▸ AS A VERB **1** = **hire**, commission, employ, rent, lease • *He chartered a jet to fly her home.*
2 = **authorize**, permit, sanction, entitle, license, empower, give authority • *The council is chartered to promote the understanding of British culture throughout the world.*

chary = **wary**, guarded, careful, reluctant, cautious, suspicious, uneasy, scrupulous, circumspect, leery *(slang)*, heedful • *Some people are rather chary of being associated with him.*

chase AS A VERB **1** = **pursue**, follow, track, hunt, run after, course • *She chased the thief for 100 yards.*
2 = **woo**, pursue, flirt with, run after, pay court to, set your cap at • *If he's not chasing women, he's out boozing with the lads.*
3 = **drive away**, drive, expel, hound, send away, send packing, put to flight • *Some farmers chase you off their land quite aggressively.*
4 = **rush**, run, race, shoot, fly, speed, dash, sprint, bolt, dart, hotfoot • *They chased down the stairs into the alley.*
▸ AS A NOUN = **pursuit**, race, hunt, hunting • *He was arrested after a car chase.*

chasm **1** = **gulf**, opening, crack, gap, rent, hollow, void, gorge, crater, cavity, abyss, ravine, cleft, fissure, crevasse • *The chasm was deep and its sides almost vertical.*
2 = **gap**, division, gulf, split, breach, rift, alienation, hiatus • *the chasm that separates the rich from the poor*

chassis = **frame**, framework, fuselage, bodywork, substructure • *These cars have all-new tubular chassis and suspension.*

chaste **1** = **pure**, moral, decent, innocent, immaculate, wholesome, virtuous, virginal, unsullied, uncontaminated, undefiled, incorrupt • *Her character was pure, her thoughts chaste.*
OPPOSITES: dirty, corrupt, promiscuous
2 = **simple**, quiet, elegant, modest, refined, restrained, austere, unaffected, decorous • *Beyond them she could see the dim, chaste interior of the room.*

chasten = **subdue**, discipline, cow, curb, humble, soften, humiliate, tame, afflict, repress, put in your place • *He has clearly not been chastened by his punishment.*

chastise = **scold**, blame, correct, discipline, lecture, carpet *(informal)*, nag, censure, rebuke, reprimand, reproach, berate, tick off *(informal)*, castigate, chide, tell off *(informal)*, find fault with, remonstrate with, bring (someone) to book, take (someone) to task, reprove, upbraid, bawl out *(informal)*, give (someone) a talking-to *(informal)*, haul (someone) over the coals *(informal)*, chew out *(U.S. & Canad. informal)*, give (someone) a dressing-down, give a rocket *(Brit. & N.Z. informal)*, give (someone) a row *(Scot. informal)* • *I did not chastise the child for what she had done.*
OPPOSITES: reward, praise, compliment

chastity = **purity**, virtue, innocence, modesty, virginity, celibacy, continence, maidenhood • *I took a vow of chastity and celibacy when I became a priest.*
OPPOSITES: promiscuity, immorality, profligacy

QUOTATIONS
Give me chastity and continence, but not just now
[St. Augustine of Hippo *Confessions*]
chastity – the most unnatural of all the sexual perversions
[Aldous Huxley *Eyeless in Gaza*]
The essence of chastity is not the suppression of lust, but the total orientation of one's life towards a goal
[Dietrich Bonhoeffer *Letters and Papers from Prison*]
'Tis chastity, my brother, chastity;
She that has that, is clad in complete steel
[John Milton *Comus*]

chat AS A VERB = **talk**, gossip, jaw *(slang)*, natter, blather, schmooze *(slang)*, blether *(Scot.)*, shoot the breeze *(U.S. slang)*, chew the rag *or* fat *(slang)* • *I was just chatting to him the other day.*
▸ AS A NOUN = **talk**, tête-à-tête, conversation, gossip, heart-to-heart, natter, blather, schmooze *(slang)*, blether *(Scot.)*, chinwag *(Brit. informal)*, confab *(informal)*, craic *(Irish informal)*, korero *(N.Z.)* • *She asked me into her office for a chat.*

chatter AS A VERB = **prattle**, chat, rabbit on *(Brit. informal)*, babble, gab *(informal)*, natter, tattle, jabber, blather, schmooze *(slang)*, blether *(Scot.)*, run off at the mouth *(U.S. slang)*, prate, gossip • *Everyone was chattering away in different languages.*
▸ AS A NOUN = **prattle**, chat, rabbit *(Brit. informal)*, gossip, babble, twaddle, gab *(informal)*, natter, tattle, jabber, blather, blether *(Scot.)* • *She kept up a steady stream of chatter the whole time.*

chatterbox = **chatterer**, gossip, babbler, prattler, natterer, blather, blether *(Scot.)* • *My five-year-old daughter's a real little chatterbox.*

chatty = **talkative**, informal, effusive, garrulous, gabby *(informal)*, gossipy, newsy *(informal)* • *She's quite a chatty person.*
OPPOSITES: quiet, silent, taciturn

cheap 1 = **inexpensive**, sale, economy, reduced, keen, reasonable, bargain, low-priced, low-cost, cut-price, economical, cheapo *(informal)* • *Smoke detectors are cheap and easy to put up.* • *People want good service at a cheap price.*
OPPOSITES: dear, expensive, steep
2 = **inferior**, poor, worthless, second-rate, shoddy, tawdry, tatty, trashy, substandard, low-rent *(informal, chiefly U.S.)*, two-bit *(U.S. & Canad. slang)*, crappy *(slang)*, two a penny, rubbishy, dime-a-dozen *(informal)*, piss-poor *(slang)*, tinhorn *(U.S. slang)*, bodger or bodgie *(Austral. slang)* • *Don't resort to cheap copies; save up for the real thing.*
OPPOSITES: good, valuable, decent
3 = **despicable**, mean, low, base, vulgar, sordid, contemptible, scurvy, scungy *(Austral. & N.Z.)* • *That was a cheap trick to play on anyone.*
OPPOSITES: good, decent, generous

cheapen = **degrade**, lower, discredit, devalue, demean, belittle, depreciate, debase, derogate • *Love is a word cheapened by overuse.*

cheapness 1 = **inexpensiveness**, affordability, reasonableness • *the comparative cheapness of hosting your wedding reception in your own home*
2 = **inferiority**, worthlessness, shoddiness, tawdriness, commonness, poorness, tattiness, paltriness, crappiness *(slang)* • *What I object to most in this novel is the cheapness of its writing.*

cheat AS A VERB 1 = **deceive**, skin *(slang)*, trick, fool, take in *(informal)*, con *(informal)*, stiff *(slang)*, sting *(informal)*, mislead, rip off *(slang)*, fleece, hoax, defraud, dupe, beguile, gull *(archaic)*, do *(informal)*, swindle, stitch up *(slang)*, victimize, bamboozle *(informal)*, hoodwink, double-cross *(informal)*, diddle *(informal)*, take for a ride *(informal)*, bilk, pull a fast one on *(informal)*, screw *(informal)*, finagle *(informal)*, scam *(slang)* • *He cheated an old woman out of her life savings.*
2 = **foil**, check, defeat, prevent, frustrate, deprive, baffle, thwart • *He cheated death when he was rescued from the blazing cottage.*
▸ AS A NOUN = **deceiver**, sharper, cheater, shark, charlatan, trickster, con man *(informal)*, impostor, fraudster, double-crosser *(informal)*, swindler, grifter *(slang, chiefly U.S. & Canad.)*, rorter *(Austral. slang)*, chiseller *(informal)*, rogue trader • *He's nothing but a rotten cheat.*

PROVERB
Cheats never prosper

check AS A VERB 1 *often with* **out** = **examine**, test, study, look at, research, note, confirm, investigate, monitor, probe, tick, vet, inspect, look over, verify, work over, scrutinize, make sure of, inquire into, take a dekko at *(Brit. slang)* • *Check the accuracy of every detail in your CV.* • *Get a mechanic to check the car out for you before you buy it.*
OPPOSITES: ignore, overlook, neglect
2 = **stop**, control, limit, arrest, delay, halt, curb, bar, restrain, inhibit, rein, thwart, hinder, repress, obstruct, retard, impede, bridle, stem the flow of, nip in the bud, put a spoke in someone's wheel • *Sex education is expected to help check the spread of Aids.*
OPPOSITES: start, help, further
▸ AS A NOUN 1 = **examination**, test, research, investigation, inspection, scrutiny, once-over *(informal)* • *He is being constantly monitored with regular checks on his blood pressure.*
2 = **control**, limitation, restraint, constraint, rein, obstacle, curb, obstruction, stoppage, inhibition, impediment, hindrance, damper • *There is no check on the flood of new immigrants arriving in the country.*

cheek = **impudence**, face *(informal)*, front, nerve, sauce *(informal)*, gall *(informal)*, disrespect, audacity, neck *(informal)*, lip *(slang)*, temerity, chutzpah *(U.S. & Canad. informal)*, insolence, impertinence, effrontery, brass neck *(Brit. informal)*, brazenness, sassiness *(U.S. informal)* • *I'm amazed they have the cheek to ask in the first place.*
▸ TECHNICAL NAME: gena
▸ RELATED ADJECTIVES: genal, buccal, malar

cheekbone
▸ TECHNICAL NAME: zygomatic bone
▸ RELATED ADJECTIVE: malar

cheeky = **impudent**, rude, forward, fresh *(informal)*, insulting, saucy, audacious, sassy *(U.S. informal)*, pert, disrespectful, impertinent, insolent, lippy *(U.S. & Canad. slang)* • *They sat making cheeky comments about passers-by.*
OPPOSITES: civil, mannerly, respectful

cheer AS A VERB 1 = **applaud**, hail, acclaim, clap, hurrah • *Cheering crowds lined the route.*
OPPOSITES: boo, ridicule, hiss
2 = **hearten**, encourage, warm, comfort, elevate, animate, console, uplift, brighten, exhilarate, solace, enliven, cheer up, buoy up, gladden, elate, inspirit • *The people around him were cheered by his presence.*
OPPOSITES: depress, discourage, dishearten
▸ AS A NOUN 1 = **applause**, ovation • *The colonel was rewarded by a resounding cheer from his men.*
2 = **cheerfulness**, comfort, joy, optimism, animation, glee, solace, buoyancy, mirth, gaiety, merriment, liveliness, gladness, hopefulness, merry-making • *This news did not bring them much cheer.*
▸ IN PHRASES: **cheer someone up** = **comfort**, encourage, brighten, hearten, enliven, gladden, gee up, jolly along *(informal)* • *She chatted away brightly, trying to cheer him up.*
cheer up = **take heart**, rally, perk up, buck up *(informal)* • *Cheer up, things could be a lot worse.*

cheerful 1 = **happy**, bright, contented, glad, optimistic, bucked *(informal)*, enthusiastic, sparkling, gay, sunny, jolly, animated, merry, upbeat *(informal)*, buoyant, hearty, cheery, joyful, jovial, genial, jaunty, chirpy *(informal)*, sprightly, blithe, light-hearted • *They are both very cheerful in spite of their circumstances.*
OPPOSITES: down, low, sad
2 = **pleasant**, bright, sunny, gay, enlivening • *The room is bright and cheerful.*
OPPOSITES: depressing, dull, gloomy

cheerfulness = **happiness**, good humour, exuberance, high spirits, buoyancy, gaiety, good cheer, gladness, geniality, light-heartedness, jauntiness, joyousness • *He was particularly remembered for his unfailing cheerfulness.*

cheering = **encouraging**, promising, comforting, reassuring, heartening, auspicious, propitious • *It is cheering to hear some good news for once.*

cheerless 1 = **gloomy**, dark, depressing, dull, grim, bleak, dismal, dreary, sombre, austere, drab, desolate, forlorn, joyless, funereal, comfortless • *The kitchen was a dank and cheerless room.*
OPPOSITES: gay, bright, cheerful
2 = **miserable**, sad, depressed, unhappy, gloomy, dismal, melancholy, forlorn, sullen, woeful, mournful, dejected, despondent, sorrowful, disconsolate, joyless, woebegone, dolorous • *They were like a restless, cheerless throng of lost souls.*
OPPOSITES: happy, cheerful, jolly

cheery = **cheerful**, happy, pleasant, lively, sunny, upbeat *(informal)*, good-humoured, carefree, breezy, genial, chirpy *(informal)*, jovial, full of beans *(informal)* • *He is loved by everyone for his cheery disposition and sense of humour.*

cheese
▹ *See panel* **Cheeses**

chef-d'oeuvre = **masterpiece**, tour de force *(French)*, magnum opus, masterwork, crowning achievement, brainchild • *This set of lithographs is the chef-d'oeuvre of the Polish artist Rojankowski.*

chemical = **compound**, drug, substance, synthetic substance, potion • *The whole food-chain is affected by the over-use of chemicals in agriculture.*
▹ *See panel* **Chemical elements**

CHEESES

Bavarian blue	Cambazolla	Dolcelatte	Gouda	Neufchâtel	Roquefort
Bel Paese	Camembert	Double Gloucester	Gruyère	Oka	Sage Derby
Bleu d'Auvergne	canestrato	Dunlop	Havarti	Parmesan	Saint Agur
Bleu de Bresse	Cantal	Dunsyre Blue	Jarlsberg	pecorino	Samsö
blue cheese *or* blue vein	Chaumes	Edam	Lanark Blue	Port-Salut	sapsago
Blue Shropshire	Cheddar	Emmenthal	Lancashire	pot cheese	Stilton
Blue Stilton	Cheshire	Ermite	Leicester	provolone	Taleggio
Blue Vinney	chèvre	Esrom	Limburger	quark	Tornegus
Bonchester	cottage cheese	feta	mascarpone	Reblochon	Vacherin
Brie	cream cheese	fontina	Monterey jack	Red Leicester	vignotte
Caboc	crowdie	fromage frais	mousetrap	Red Windsor	wensleydale
caciocavallo	curd cheese	Gjetost	mozzarella	Ribblesdale	yarg
Caerphilly	Danish blue	goats' cheese	muenster	ricotta	
	Derby	Gorgonzola	mycella	Romano	

chemist = **pharmacist**, apothecary *(obsolete)*, pharmacologist, dispenser • *She went into a chemist's and bought some aspirin.*
▹ *See panel* **Chemistry**

chemistry
▹ *See panel* **Chemistry**

cherish 1 = **cling to**, prize, treasure, hold dear, cleave to • *I will cherish the memory of that visit for many years to come.*
OPPOSITES: hate, dislike, despise
2 = **care for**, love, support, comfort, look after, shelter, treasure, nurture, cosset, hold dear • *He genuinely loved and cherished his children.*
OPPOSITES: hate, abandon, neglect
3 = **harbour**, nurse, sustain, foster, entertain • *He cherished an ambition to be an actor.*

cherubic = **angelic**, appealing, sweet, heavenly, innocent, lovable, adorable, seraphic • *the toddler's beaming, cherubic face*

chess
▹ *See panel* **Chess pieces**

chest 1 = **breast**, front • *He crossed his arms over his chest.*
2 = **box**, case, trunk, crate, coffer, ark *(dialect)*, casket, strongbox • *At the very bottom of the chest were his carving tools.*
▸ RELATED ADJECTIVE: pectoral

chew AS A VERB = **munch**, bite, grind, champ, crunch, gnaw, chomp, masticate • *Be careful to eat slowly and chew your food well.*
▸ IN PHRASES: **chew something over** = **consider**, weigh up, ponder, mull (over), meditate on, reflect upon, muse on, ruminate, deliberate upon • *You might want to sit back and chew things over for a while.*

chewy = **tough**, fibrous, leathery, as tough as old boots • *The meat was too chewy and the vegetables overcooked.*

chic = **stylish**, smart, elegant, fashionable, trendy *(Brit. informal)*, up-to-date, new, modish, du jour *(French)*, à la mode, voguish *(informal)*, culty, hip *(slang)*, schmick *(Austral. informal)* • *Her gown was French and very chic.* • *the chic place to be seen around town*
OPPOSITES: old-fashioned, shabby, unfashionable

chicanery = **trickery**, cheating, intrigue, deception, artifice, wiles, duplicity, subterfuge, stratagems, double-dealing, skulduggery *(informal)*, sharp practice, sophistry, deviousness, wire-pulling *(chiefly U.S.)*, underhandedness • *The trial revealed a world of crime, corruption and political chicanery.*

chide = **scold**, blame, lecture, carpet *(informal)*, flame *(informal)*, put down, criticize, slate *(informal, chiefly Brit.)*, censure, rebuke, reprimand, reproach, berate, tick off *(informal)*, admonish, tear into *(informal)*, blast, tell off *(informal)*, find fault, diss *(slang, chiefly U.S.)*, read the riot act, reprove, upbraid, slap on the wrist, lambast(e), bawl out *(informal)*, rap over the knuckles, chew out *(U.S. & Canad. informal)*, tear (someone) off a strip *(Brit. informal)*, give (someone) a rocket *(Brit. & N.Z. informal)*, reprehend, give (someone) a row *(Scot. informal)* • *He is quick to chide his staff for any mistakes or oversights.*

chief AS A NOUN = **head**, leader, director, manager, lord, boss *(informal)*, captain, master, governor, commander, principal, superior, ruler, superintendent, chieftain, ringleader, baas *(S. African)*, ariki *(N.Z.)*, sherang *(Austral. & N.Z.)* • *The new leader is the deputy chief of the territory's defence force.*
OPPOSITES: subject, follower, subordinate
▸ AS AN ADJECTIVE = **primary**, highest, leading, main, prime, capital, central, key, essential, premier, supreme, most important, outstanding, principal, prevailing, cardinal, paramount, big-time *(informal)*, foremost, major league *(informal)*, predominant, uppermost, pre-eminent, especial • *Financial stress is acknowledged as a chief reason for divorce.* • *The job went to one of his chief rivals.*
OPPOSITES: least, minor, subsidiary

chiefly 1 = **especially**, essentially, principally, primarily, above all • *We are chiefly concerned with the welfare of the children.*
2 = **mainly**, largely, usually, mostly, in general, on the whole, predominantly, in the main • *a committee composed chiefly of grey-haired old gentlemen*

child 1 = **youngster**, baby, kid *(informal)*, minor, infant, babe, juvenile, toddler, tot, wean *(Scot.)*, little one, brat, bairn *(Scot.)*, suckling, nipper *(informal)*, chit, babe in arms, sprog *(slang)*, munchkin *(informal, chiefly U.S.)*, rug rat *(slang)*, nursling, littlie *(Austral. informal)*, ankle-biter *(Austral. & U.S. slang)*, tacker *(Austral. slang)* • *This film is not suitable for children.*
2 = **offspring**, issue, descendant, progeny • *How many children do you have?*
▸ RELATED ADJECTIVE: filial
▸ RELATED PREFIX: paedo-

QUOTATIONS

Children are the anchors that hold a mother to life
[Sophocles *Phaedra*]

The child is father of the man
[William Wordsworth *My Heart Leaps Up*]

Your children are not your children.
They are the sons and daughters of life's longing for itself.
They came through you but not from you
And though they are with you yet they belong not to you
[Kahlil Gibran *The Prophet*]

Children are completely egoistic; they feel their needs intensely and strive ruthlessly to satisfy them
[Sigmund Freud *The Interpretation of Dreams*]

Making terms with reality, with things as they are, is a full-time business for the child
[Milton R. Sapirstein *Paradoxes of Everyday Life*]

PROVERBS

Children should be seen and not heard
Little children, little sorrows; big children, great sorrows

CHEMICAL ELEMENTS

	Symbols	Atomic numbers		Symbols	Atomic numbers		Symbols	Atomic numbers
hydrogen	H	1	strontium	Sr	38	rhenium	Re	75
helium	He	2	yttrium	Y	39	osmium	Os	76
lithium	Li	3	zirconium	Zr	40	iridium	Ir	77
beryllium	Be	4	niobium	Nb	41	platinum	Pt	78
boron	B	5	molybdenum	Mo	42	gold	Au	79
carbon	C	6	technetium	Tc	43	mercury	Hg	80
nitrogen	N	7	ruthenium	Ru	44	thallium	Tl	81
oxygen	O	8	rhodium	Rh	45	lead	Pb	82
fluorine	F	9	palladium	Pd	46	bismuth	Bi	83
neon	Ne	10	silver	Ag	47	polonium	Po	84
sodium	Na	11	cadmium	Cd	48	astatine	At	85
magnesium	Mg	12	indium	In	49	radon	Rn	86
aluminium	Al	13	tin	Sn	50	francium	Fr	87
silicon	Si	14	antimony	Sb	51	radium	Ra	88
phosphorus	P	15	tellurium	Te	52	actinium	Ac	89
sulphur	S	16	iodine	I	53	thorium	Th	90
chlorine	Cl	17	xenon	Xe	54	protactinium	Pa	91
argon	Ar	18	caesium	Cs	55	uranium	U	92
potassium	K	19	barium	Ba	56	neptunium	Np	93
calcium	Ca	20	lanthanum	La	57	plutonium	Pu	94
scandium	Sc	21	cerium	Ce	58	americium	Am	95
titanium	Ti	22	praseodymium	Pr	59	curium	Cm	96
vanadium	V	23	neodymium	Nd	60	berkelium	Bk	97
chromium	Cr	24	promethium	Pm	61	californium	Cf	98
manganese	Mn	25	samarium	Sm	62	einsteinium	Es	99
iron	Fe	26	europium	Eu	63	fermium	Fm	100
cobalt	Co	27	gadolinium	Gd	64	mendelevium	Md	101
nickel	Ni	28	terbium	Tb	65	nobelium	No	102
copper	Cu	29	dysprosium	Dy	66	lawrencium	Lr	103
zinc	Zn	30	holmium	Ho	67	rutherfordium	Rf	104
gallium	Ga	31	erbium	Er	68	dubnium	Db	105
germanium	Ge	32	thulium	Tm	69	seaborgium	Sg	106
arsenic	As	33	ytterbium	Yb	70	bohrium	Bh	107
selenium	Se	34	lutetium	Lu	71	hassium	Hs	108
bromine	Br	35	hafnium	Hf	72	meitnerium	Mt	109
krypton	Kr	36	tantalum	Ta	73	darmstadtium	Ds	110
rubidium	Rb	37	tungsten *or* wolfram	W	74	roentgenium	Rg	111

CHEMISTRY

Branches of chemistry

analytical chemistry
astrochemistry
biochemistry
chemurgy
cytochemistry
electrochemistry
geochemistry
histochemistry
immunochemistry
inorganic chemistry
kinetics
magnetochemistry
neurochemistry
nuclear chemistry
organic chemistry
petrochemistry
phonochemistry
photochemistry
physical chemistry
phytochemistry
radiochemistry
stereochemistry
stoichiometry
thermochemistry
zoochemistry
zymurgy

Chemistry terms

acid
alcohol
alkali
alkali metal
alkaline earth metal
alkane
allotrope
alloy
amino acid
analysis
anion
anode
atom
atomic mass
atomic number
base
boiling point
bond
Brownian motion
carbohydrate
catalyst
cathode
cation
chain
chain reaction
chromatography
combustion
compound
concentrated
condensation
corrosion
covalent bond
crystal
crystallization
diffusion
dilute
distillation
electrode
electrolysis
electron
electrovalency
element
emulsion
equation
ester
ether
evaporation
fat
fatty acid
fermentation
fission
foam
formula
fuel
fusion
gas
halogen
hydrocarbon
hydrolysis
inert
inorganic
insoluble
ion
ionic bond
ionization

CHEMISTRY TERMS (CONTINUED)

isomer
isotope
lanthanide *or* rare-earth element
liquid
litmus test
melting point
metal
metalloid
mineral
mixture
molarity
mole
molecule
monomer
neutral
neutron
noble gas *or* inert gas
nonmetal
nucleus
oil
ore
organic
oxidation
periodic table
pH
plastic
polymer
precipitate
proton
radioactivity
reaction
reagent
redox reaction
reduction
salt
saponification
saturated
soap
solid
soluble
solution
solvent
sublimation
substitution reaction
sugar
suspension
synthesis
transition metal
unsaturated
valency
van der Waals forces

CHEMISTS

Philip Abelson *(U.S.)*
William Abney *(English)*
Roger Adams *(U.S.)*
Thomas Andrews *(Irish)*
Svante August Arrhenius *(Swedish)*
Francis William Aston *(English)*
Karl Auer *(Austrian)*
Lambert von Babo *(German)*
Johann Friedrich Wilhelm Adolf von Baeyer *(German)*
Derek Barton *(English)*
Antoine Baumé *(French)*
Ernst Otto Beckmann *(German)*
Friedrich (Karl Rudolph) Bergius *(German)*
James (Whyte) Black *(English)*
Joseph Black *(Scottish)*
Carl Bosch *(German)*
Robert Boyle *(Irish)*
Georg Brandt *(Swedish)*
Herbert Charles Brown *(U.S.)*
Eduard Buchner *(German)*
Robert Wilhelm Bunsen *(German)*
Adolf Frederick Johann Butenandt *(German)*
Melvin Calvin *(U.S.)*
Heinrich Caro *(German)*
Geroge Washington Carver *(U.S.)*
Hamilton Young Castner *(U.S.)*
Henry Cavendish *(English)*
(Louis Marie) Hilaire Bernigaud Chardonnet *(French)*
John Warcup Cornforth *(Australian)*
William Crookes *(English)*
Marie Curie *(French)*
Pierre Curie *(French)*
Henry Dakin *(English)*
John Dalton *(English)*
Humphrey Davy *(English)*
Peter Joseph Wilhelm Debye *(Dutch)*
James Dewar *(Scottish)*
John William Draper *(U.S.)*
Jean-Baptiste André Dumas *(French)*
Manfred Eigen *(German)*
Emil Erlenmeyer *(German)*
Richard Robert Ernst *(Swiss)*
Michael Faraday *(English)*
Emil Hermann Fischer *(German)*
Ernst Otto Fischer *(German)*
Hans Fischer *(German)*
Johan Gadolin *(Finnish)*
Joseph Louis Gay-Lussac *(French)*
Moses Gomberg *(U.S.)*
Victor Grignard *(French)*
Samuel Guthrie *(U.S.)*
Fritz Haber *(German)*
Charles Martin Hall *(U.S.)*
Jean Baptiste van Helmont *(Flemish)*
William Henry *(English)*
George von Hevesy *(Hungarian)*
Archibald Vivian Hill *(English)*
Dorothy Crowfoot Hodgkin *(English)*
Robert Hooke *(English)*
(Friedrich) August Kekulé von Stradonitz *(German)*
Petrus Jacobus Kipp *(Dutch)*
Irving Langmuir *(U.S.)*
Antoine Laurent Lavoisier *(French)*
Nicolas Leblanc *(French)*
Willard Frank Libby *(U.S.)*
Justus Liebig *(German)*
John Macadam *(Australian)*
Dmitri Ivanovich Mendeleyev *(Russian)*
Ludwig Mond *(German)*
Edward Williams Morley *(U.S.)*
Paul Hermann Müller *(Swiss)*
Robert Sanderson Mulliken *(U.S.)*
Kary Banks Mullis *(U.S.)*
Walther Hermann Nernst *(German)*
John Alexander Newlands *(English)*
Alfred Bernhard Nobel *(Swedish)*
Wilhelm Ostwald *(German)*
Louis Pasteur *(French)*
Linus Carl Pauling *(U.S.)*
Max Ferdinand Perutz *(Austrian-British)*
George Porter *(English)*
Joseph Priestley *(English)*
Joseph Louis Proust *(French)*
William Prout *(English)*
Pierre Joseph Pelletier *(French)*
Jean Félix Piccard *(U.S.)*
Ilya Prigogine *(Belgian)*
William Ramsay *(Scottish)*
Paul Sabatier *(French)*
Karl Wilhelm Scheele *(Swedish)*
Hugo Schiff *(German)*
Glenn Theodore Seaborg *(U.S.)*
Benjamin Silliman *(U.S.)*
James Smithson *(English)*
Frederick Soddy *(English)*
Ernest Solvay *(Belgian)*
Soren Peter Lauritz Sorensen *(Danish)*
Joseph Wilson Swan *(English)*
Albert von Nagyrapolt Szent-Gyorgyi *(Hungarian-American)*
Henry Tizard *(English)*
Alexander Robert Todd *(Scottish)*
Harold Clayton Urey *(U.S.)*
Jacobus Hendricus van't Hoff *(Dutch)*
Otto Heinrich Warburg *(German)*
Alfred Werner *(Swiss)*
Friedrich Wöhler *(German)*
R(obert) B(urns) Woodward *(U.S.)*
Peter Woulfe *(English)*
Carl Ziegler *(German)*
Richard Adolf Zsigmondy *(German)*

childbirth = **child-bearing**, labour, delivery, lying-in, confinement, parturition • *My grandmother died in childbirth.*

▸ **RELATED ADJECTIVES:** natal, parturient, obstetric

QUOTATIONS

In sorrow thou shalt bring forth children
[*Bible: Genesis*]

Death and taxes and childbirth! There's never any convenient time for any of them
[Margaret Mitchell *Gone with the Wind*]

childhood = **youth**, minority, infancy, schooldays, immaturity, boyhood *or* girlhood • *She had a very happy childhood.*

QUOTATIONS

Childhood is the kingdom where nobody dies.
Nobody that matters, that is
[Edna St. Vincent Millay *Childhood is the Kingdom where Nobody Dies*]

One of the great pleasures of childhood is found in the mysteries which it hides from the skepticism of the elders, and works up into small mythologies of its own
[Oliver Wendell Holmes Sr. *The Poet at the Breakfast-Table*]

childish 1 = **youthful**, young, boyish *or* girlish • *One of his most appealing qualities is his childish enthusiasm.*
2 = **immature**, silly, juvenile, foolish, trifling, frivolous, infantile, puerile • *I've never seen such selfish and childish behaviour.*
OPPOSITES: adult, mature, sophisticated

C

CHESS PIECES

Piece	Abbreviation
Bishop	B
King	K
King's bishop	KB
King's knight	KN
King's rook	KR
Knight	N
Pawn	P
Queen	Q
Queen's bishop	QB
Queen's knight	QN
Queen's rook	QR

childlike = **innocent**, trusting, simple, naive, credulous, artless, ingenuous, guileless, unfeigned, trustful • *She had never lost her childlike sense of wonder.*

chill AS A VERB **1 = cool**, refrigerate, freeze • *Chill the fruit salad until serving time.*
2 = dishearten, depress, discourage, dismay, dampen, deject • *There was a coldness in her voice which chilled him.*
▸ AS A NOUN **1 = coldness**, bite, nip, sharpness, coolness, rawness, crispness, frigidity • *September is here, bringing with it a chill in the mornings.*
2 = shiver, frisson, goose pimples, goose flesh • *He smiled an odd smile that sent a chill through me.*
3 = cold • *He caught a nasty chill.*
▸ AS AN ADJECTIVE = **chilly**, biting, sharp, freezing, raw, bleak, chilly, wintry, frigid, parky (*Brit. informal*) • *A chill wind was blowing.*
▸ IN PHRASES: **chill out = relax**, take it easy, loosen up, lighten up (*slang*), hang loose (*slang*), let yourself go (*informal*), let your hair down (*informal*), mellow out (*informal*), outspan (*S. African*) • *Take it easy, man – you need to chill out.*

chilly 1 = cool, fresh, sharp, crisp, penetrating, brisk, breezy, draughty, nippy, parky (*Brit. informal*), blowy • *It was a chilly afternoon.*
OPPOSITES: hot, warm, mild
2 = unfriendly, hostile, unsympathetic, frigid, unresponsive, unwelcoming, cold as ice • *I was slightly afraid of his chilly, distant politeness.*
OPPOSITES: welcoming, warm, friendly

chime AS A VERB = **ring** • *The Guildhall clock chimed three o'clock.*
▸ AS A NOUN = **sound**, boom, toll, jingle, dong, tinkle, clang, peal • *the chime of the Guildhall clock*

chimera = **illusion**, dream, fantasy, delusion, spectre, snare, hallucination, figment, ignis fatuus, will-o'-the-wisp • *He spent his life pursuing the chimera of perfect love.*

chin
▸ RELATED ADJECTIVES: genial, mental

china[1] = **pottery**, ceramics, ware, porcelain, crockery, tableware, service • *She collects blue and white china.*

china[2] = **friend**, pal, mate (*informal*), buddy (*informal*), companion, best friend, intimate, cock (*Brit. informal*), close friend, comrade, chum (*informal*), crony, main man (*slang, chiefly U.S.*), soul mate, homeboy (*slang, chiefly U.S.*), cobber (*Austral. & N.Z. old-fashioned informal*), bosom friend, boon companion, E hoa (*N.Z.*) • *How are you, my old china?*

Chinese
▸ RELATED PREFIX: Sino-

chink = **opening**, crack, gap, rift, aperture, cleft, crevice, fissure, cranny • *He peered through a chink in the curtains.*

chip AS A NOUN **1 = fragment**, scrap, shaving, flake, paring, wafer, sliver, shard • *His eyes gleamed like chips of blue glass.*
2 = scratch, nick, flaw, notch, dent • *The washbasin had a small chip in it.*
3 = counter, disc, token • *He gambled all his chips on one number.*
▸ AS A VERB **1 = nick**, damage, gash • *The blow chipped the woman's tooth.* • *Steel baths are light, but they chip easily.*
2 = chisel, whittle • *a sculptor chipping at a block of marble*
▸ IN PHRASES: **chip in 1 = contribute**, pay, donate, subscribe, go Dutch (*informal*) • *We'll all chip in for the petrol and food.*
2 = interpose, put in, interrupt, interject, butt in, put your oar in • *He chipped in, 'That's right,' before she could answer.*

chirp = **chirrup**, pipe, peep, warble, twitter, cheep, tweet • *The birds chirped loudly in the hedges.*

chirpy = **cheerful**, happy, bright, enthusiastic, lively, sparkling, sunny, jolly, animated, buoyant, radiant, jaunty, sprightly, in high spirits, blithe, full of beans (*informal*), light-hearted • *You're very chirpy today – have you won the lottery or something?*

chivalrous = **courteous**, knightly, gentlemanly, honourable, gallant, courtly, high-minded, magnanimous • *He was a handsome, upright and chivalrous man.*
OPPOSITES: rude, boorish, ungallant

chivalry 1 = courtesy, politeness, gallantry, courtliness, gentlemanliness • *He always treated women with old-fashioned chivalry.*
2 = knight-errantry, knighthood, gallantry, courtliness • *Our story is set in England, in the age of chivalry.*

chivvy = **nag**, annoy, plague, hound, torment, harass, hassle (*informal*), prod, badger, pester, breathe down someone's neck (*informal*), pressure (*informal*), bug (*informal*), bend someone's ear (*informal*) • *She was very assertive, endlessly chivvying her staff to work harder.*

choice AS A NOUN **1 = range**, variety, selection, assortment • *It's available in a choice of colours.*
2 = selection, preference, election, pick • *His choice of words made Rodney angry.*
3 = option, say, alternative • *If I had any choice in the matter, I wouldn't have gone.*
▸ AS AN ADJECTIVE = **best**, bad (*slang*), special, prime, nice, prize, select, excellent, elect, crucial (*slang*), exclusive, elite, superior, exquisite, def (*slang*), booshit (*Austral. slang*), exo (*Austral. slang*), sik (*Austral. slang*), hand-picked, dainty, rad (*informal*), phat (*slang*), schmick (*Austral. informal*) • *The finest array of choicest foods is to be found within their Food Hall.*

QUOTATIONS

We human beings do have some genuine freedom of choice and therefore some effective control over our own destinies
[A.J.Toynbee *Some Great 'Ifs' of History*]

We often experience more regret over the part we have left, than pleasure over the part we have preferred
[Joseph Roux *Meditations of a Parish Priest*]

As a man thinketh, so is he, and as a man chooseth so is he
[Ralph Waldo Emerson *Spiritual Laws*]

choke 1 = suffocate, stifle, smother, overpower, asphyxiate • *Dense smoke swirled and billowed, its fumes choking her.*
2 = strangle, throttle, asphyxiate • *They choked him with his tie.*
3 = block, dam, clog, obstruct, bung, constrict, occlude, congest, close, stop, bar • *The village roads are choked with traffic.*

choleric = **bad-tempered**, cross, angry, irritable, touchy, petulant, ill-tempered, irascible, tetchy, ratty (*Brit. & N.Z. informal*), tooshie (*Austral. slang*), testy, chippy (*informal*), hot-tempered, quick-tempered, chippy (*informal*) • *He plays a choleric old schoolmaster.*

choose 1 = pick, take, prefer, select, elect, adopt, opt for, designate, single out, espouse, settle on, fix on, cherry-pick, settle upon, predestine • *I chose him to accompany me on my trip.*
OPPOSITES: leave, refuse, reject

2 = **wish**, want, desire, see fit • *You can just take out the interest every year, if you choose.*

PROVERBS
If you run after two hares you will catch neither

choosy = **fussy**, particular, exacting, discriminating, selective, fastidious, picky (*informal*), finicky, faddy, nit-picky (*informal*) • *You can't afford to be too choosy about jobs these days.*
OPPOSITES: easy (*informal*), undemanding, indiscriminating

chop AS A VERB = **cut**, fell, axe, slash, hack, sever, shear, cleave, hew, lop, truncate • *We were set to work chopping wood.*
▸ IN PHRASES: **chop something up** = **cut up**, divide, fragment, cube, dice, mince • *Chop up three firm tomatoes.*
the chop = **the sack**, sacking (*informal*), dismissal, the boot (*slang*), your cards (*informal*), the axe (*informal*), termination, the (old) heave-ho (*informal*), the order of the boot (*slang*) • *I was amazed when I got the chop from the team.*

choppy = **rough**, broken, ruffled, tempestuous, blustery, squally • *A gale was blowing and the sea was choppy.*
OPPOSITES: calm, smooth, windless

chore = **task**, job, duty, burden, hassle (*informal*), fag (*informal*), errand, no picnic • *I find gardening a real chore.*

chortle AS A VERB = **chuckle**, laugh, cackle, guffaw • *He began chortling like an idiot.*
▸ AS A NOUN = **chuckle**, laugh, cackle, guffaw • *The old man broke into a wheezy chortle of amusement.*

chorus AS A NOUN 1 = **refrain**, response, strain, burden • *Everyone joined in the chorus.*
2 = **choir**, singers, ensemble, vocalists, choristers • *The chorus was singing 'The Ode to Joy'.*
▸ IN PHRASES: **in chorus** = **in unison**, as one, all together, in concert, in harmony, in accord, with one voice • *'Let us in,' they all wailed in chorus.*

chough
▸ COLLECTIVE NOUN: chattering

Christ = **Jesus Christ**, Our Lord, the Galilean, the Good Shepherd, the Nazarene • *This is the day which marks Christ's Last Supper with His disciples.*

christen 1 = **baptize**, name • *She was born in March and christened in June.*
2 = **name**, call, term, style, title, dub, designate • *a boat which he christened 'the Stray Cat'*

Christianity
▹ *See panel* **Christian denominations and sects**

Christmas = **the festive season**, Noël, Xmas (*informal*), Yule (*archaic*), Yuletide (*archaic*) • *Easter and Christmas are two very important religious festivals.*

chronic 1 = **persistent**, constant, continual, deep-seated, incurable, deep-rooted, ineradicable • *His drinking has led to chronic cirrhosis of the liver.*
2 = **habitual**, confirmed, ingrained, incessant, inveterate, incorrigible • *He has always been a chronic smoker.*
OPPOSITES: temporary, occasional, infrequent
3 = **serious**, dangerous, acute, alarming, severe, extreme • *There is a chronic shortage of police cars in this district.*
4 = **dreadful**, awful, appalling, atrocious, abysmal • *The programme was chronic, all banal dialogue and canned laughter.*

chronicle AS A VERB = **record**, tell, report, enter, relate, register, recount, set down, narrate, put on record • *The rise of collectivism in Britain has been chronicled by several historians.*
▸ AS A NOUN = **record**, story, history, account, register, journal, diary, narrative, annals, blog (*informal*) • *this vast chronicle of Napoleonic times*

chronicler = **recorder**, reporter, historian, narrator, scribe, diarist, annalist • *the chronicler of the English civil war*

chronological = **sequential**, ordered, historical, progressive, consecutive, in sequence • *These stories are arranged in chronological order.*
OPPOSITES: random, irregular, intermittent

chubby = **plump**, stout, fleshy, tubby, flabby, portly, buxom, roly-poly, rotund, round, podgy • *He used to tease me about being too chubby.*
OPPOSITES: thin, lean, skinny

chuck 1 = **throw**, cast, pitch, shy, toss, hurl, fling, sling, heave • *Someone chucked a bottle and it caught me on the side of the head.*
2 *often with* **away** *or* **out** (*informal*) = **throw out**, dump (*informal*), scrap, get rid of, bin (*informal*), ditch (*slang*), junk (*informal*), discard, dispose of, dispense with, jettison • *I chucked a whole lot of old magazines and papers.* • *Don't just chuck your bottles away – recycle them.*
3 = **give up** *or* **over**, leave, stop, abandon, cease, resign from, pack in, jack in • *Last summer, he chucked his job and went on the road.*
4 = **vomit**, throw up (*informal*), spew, heave (*slang*), puke (*slang*), barf (*U.S. slang*), chunder (*slang, chiefly Austral.*), upchuck (*U.S. slang*), do a technicolour yawn, toss your cookies (*U.S. slang*) • *It smelt so bad I thought I was going to chuck.*

chuckle AS A VERB = **laugh**, giggle, snigger, chortle, titter • *He chuckled appreciatively at her riposte.*
▸ AS A NOUN = **laugh**, giggle, snigger, chortle, titter • *She gave a soft chuckle and said, "No chance."*

chum = **friend**, mate (*informal*), pal (*informal*), companion, cock (*Brit. informal*), comrade, crony, main man (*slang, chiefly U.S.*), cobber (*Austral. & N.Z. old-fashioned informal*), E hoa (*N.Z.*) • *My dear old chum, what you tell me won't go any further.*

chummy = **friendly**, close, thick (*informal*), pally (*informal*), intimate, affectionate, buddy-buddy (*slang, chiefly U.S. & Canad.*), palsy-walsy (*informal*), matey *or* maty (*Brit. informal*) • *You two seem to be very chummy all of a sudden.*

chunk = **piece**, block, mass, portion, lump, slab, hunk, nugget, wad, dollop (*informal*), wodge (*Brit. informal*) • *Cut the melon into chunks.*

chunky 1 = **thickset**, stocky, beefy (*informal*), stubby, dumpy • *The sergeant was a chunky man in his late twenties.*
2 = **thick**, heavy • *You can't beat these big chunky sweaters for warmth.*

church 1 = **chapel**, temple, cathedral, kirk (*Scot.*), minster, basilica, tabernacle, place of worship, house of God • *one of the country's most historic churches*

CHRISTIAN DENOMINATIONS AND SECTS

Adventism
Amish
Anabaptism
Anglicanism
Baptist Church
Byzantine Church
Calvinism
Catholicism
Christadelphianism
Christian Science
Congregationalism
Coptic Church
Dutch Reformed Church
Eastern Orthodox Church
Episcopal Church
Evangelicalism
Greek Orthodox Church
Jehovah's Witnesses
Lutheranism
Maronite Church
Methodism
Moravian Church
Mormons *or* Latter-day Saints
New Jerusalem Church
Orthodox Church
Pentecostalism
Plymouth Brethren
Presbyterianism
Protestantism
Quakerism
Roman Catholicism
Russian Orthodox Church
Salvation Army
Seventh-Day Adventism
Shakerism
Society of Friends
Unification Church
Unitarianism

2 = **denomination**, belief, sect, persuasion, creed, communion, religious group, school, hauhau *(N.Z.)* • *the growing influence of the Roman Catholic Church*
▸ RELATED ADJECTIVE: ecclesiastical

churlish = **rude**, harsh, vulgar, sullen, surly, morose, brusque, ill-tempered, boorish, uncouth, impolite, loutish, oafish, uncivil, unmannerly • *It seemed churlish to refuse an offer meant so kindly.*
OPPOSITES: civil, mannerly, polite

churn 1 = **stir up**, beat, disturb, swirl, agitate • *The powerful thrust of the boat's engine churned the water.*
2 = **swirl**, boil, toss, foam, seethe, froth • *Churning seas smash against the steep cliffs.*

chute = **slope**, channel, slide, incline, runway, gutter, trough, ramp • *Passengers escaped from the plane by sliding down emergency chutes.*

cigarette = **fag** *(Brit. slang)*, smoke, gasper *(slang)*, ciggy *(informal)*, coffin nail *(slang)*, cancer stick *(slang)* • *He went out to buy a packet of cigarettes.*
▹ *See panel* **Tobacco**

cigarette cards
▸ RELATED ENTHUSIAST: cartophilist

cinema 1 = **pictures**, movies, picture-house, flicks *(slang)* • *They decided to spend an evening at the cinema.*
2 = **films**, pictures, movies, the big screen *(informal)*, motion pictures, the silver screen • *Contemporary African cinema has much to offer in its vitality and freshness.*

QUOTATIONS

Photography is truth. The cinema is truth 24 times per second
[Jean-Luc Godard *Le Petit Soldat*]

A film must have a beginning, a middle and an end. But not necessarily in that order
[Jean-Luc Godard]

To wish the movies to be articulate is about as sensible as wishing the drama to be silent
[George Jean Nathan]

Pictures are for entertainment, messages should be delivered by Western Union
[Sam Goldwyn]

Cinema is a matter of what's in the frame and what's out
[Martin Scorsese]

cipher 1 = **code**, coded message, cryptogram • *The codebreakers cracked the cipher.*
2 = **nobody**, nonentity, non-person • *They were little more than ciphers who faithfully carried out the Fuehrer's commands.*

circa = **approximately**, about, around, roughly, in the region of, round about • *The story tells of a runaway slave girl in Louisiana, circa 1850.*

circle AS A NOUN 1 = **ring**, round, band, disc, loop, hoop, cordon, perimeter, halo • *The flag was red with a large white circle.* • *The monument consists of a circle of gigantic stones.*
2 = **group**, company, set, school, club, order, class, society, crowd, assembly, fellowship, fraternity, clique, coterie • *a small circle of friends*
3 = **sphere**, world, area, range, field, scene, orbit, realm, milieu • *She moved only in the most exalted circles.*
▸ AS A VERB 1 = **go round**, ring, surround, belt, curve, enclose, encompass, compass, envelop, encircle, circumscribe, hem in, gird, circumnavigate, enwreath • *This is the ring road that circles the city.*
2 = **wheel**, spiral, revolve, rotate, whirl, pivot • *There were two helicopters circling around.*

circuit 1 = **course**, round, tour, track, route, journey • *I get asked this question a lot when I'm on the lecture circuit.*
2 = **racetrack**, course, track, racecourse • *the historic racing circuit at Brooklands*
3 = **lap**, round, tour, revolution, orbit, perambulation • *She made a slow circuit of the room.*

circuitous 1 = **indirect**, winding, rambling, roundabout, meandering, tortuous, labyrinthine • *They were taken on a circuitous route home.*
OPPOSITES: direct, straight, unswerving
2 = **oblique**, indirect • *He has a pedantic and circuitous writing style.*

circular AS AN ADJECTIVE 1 = **round**, ring-shaped, annular, discoid • *The car turned into a spacious, circular courtyard.*
2 = **circuitous**, cyclical, orbital • *Both sides of the river can be explored on this circular walk.*
▸ AS A NOUN = **advertisement**, notice, ad *(informal)*, announcement, advert *(Brit. informal)*, press release • *A circular has been sent to 1,800 newspapers.*

circulate 1 = **spread**, issue, publish, broadcast, distribute, diffuse, publicize, propagate, disseminate, promulgate, make known • *Public employees are circulating a petition calling for his reinstatement.*
2 = **get around**, spread, go around • *Rumours were already beginning to circulate about redundancies in the company.*
3 = **flow**, revolve, rotate, radiate • *Cooking odours can circulate throughout the entire house.*
4 = **mingle**, socialize • *Let me get you something to drink, then I must circulate.*

circulation 1 = **distribution**, currency, readership • *The paper once had the highest circulation of any daily in the country.*
2 = **bloodstream**, blood flow • *Anyone with circulation problems should seek medical advice before flying.*
3 = **flow**, circling, motion, rotation • *Fit a ventilated lid to allow circulation of air.*
4 = **spread**, distribution, transmission, dissemination • *measures inhibiting the circulation of useful information*

circumference = **edge**, limits, border, bounds, outline, boundary, fringe, verge, rim, perimeter, periphery, extremity • *a gold watch-face with diamond chips around its circumference*

circumlocution = **indirectness**, redundancy, euphemism, beating about the bush *(informal)*, wordiness, diffuseness, prolixity, discursiveness • *He is long-winded and prone to circumlocution in his public speeches.*

circumscribe = **restrict**, limit, define, confine, restrain, delineate, hem in, demarcate, delimit, straiten • *The monarch's powers are circumscribed by Parliament.*

circumspect = **cautious**, politic, guarded, careful, wary, discriminating, discreet, sage, prudent, canny, attentive, vigilant, watchful, judicious, observant, sagacious, heedful • *You should have been more circumspect in your dealings with him.*
OPPOSITES: daring, bold, rash

circumspection = **caution**, care, discretion, prudence, wariness, keeping your head down, canniness, chariness • *Handling difficult customers requires tact and circumspection.*

PROVERBS

Don't put all your eggs in one basket

circumstance 1 *usually plural* = **situation**, condition, scenario, contingency, state of affairs, lie of the land • *They say they will never, under any circumstances, be the first to use force.*
2 *usually plural* = **detail**, fact, event, particular, respect, factor • *I'm making inquiries about the circumstances of her murder.*
3 *usually plural* = **situation**, state, means, position, station, resources, status, lifestyle • *help and support for the single mother, whatever her circumstances*
4 = **chance**, the times, accident, fortune, luck, fate, destiny, misfortune, providence • *These people are innocent victims of circumstance.*

circumstantial 1 = **indirect**, contingent, incidental, inferential, presumptive, conjectural, founded on circumstances • *He was convicted on purely circumstantial evidence.*
2 = **detailed**, particular, specific • *The reasons for the project collapsing were circumstantial.*

circumvent 1 = **evade**, bypass, elude, steer clear of, sidestep • *Military rulers tried to circumvent the treaty.*
2 = **outwit**, trick, mislead, thwart, deceive, dupe, beguile, outflank, hoodwink • *It is a veiled attempt to change gun laws by circumventing legislators.*

cistern = **tank**, vat, basin, reservoir, sink • *He pointed to the antiquated cistern above the lavatory.*

citadel = **fortress**, keep, tower, stronghold, bastion, fortification, fastness • *The citadel at Besançon towered above the river.*

citation 1 = **commendation**, award, mention • *His citation says he showed outstanding and exemplary courage.*
2 = **quotation**, quote, reference, passage, illustration, excerpt • *The text is full of Biblical citations.*

cite 1 = **quote**, name, evidence, advance, mention, extract, specify, allude to, enumerate, adduce • *She cites a favourite poem by George Herbert.*
2 = **summon**, call, subpoena • *The judge ruled a mistrial and cited the prosecutors for gross misconduct.*

citizen = **inhabitant**, resident, dweller, ratepayer, denizen, subject, freeman, burgher, townsman • *football hooligans who terrorized citizens after the match*
▸ **RELATED ADJECTIVE:** civil

city = **town**, metropolis, municipality, conurbation, megalopolis • *Around the city small groups of police patrolled the streets.*
▸ **RELATED ADJECTIVE:** civic
▹ *See panel* **Capital cities**

QUOTATIONS
The city is not a concrete jungle, it is a human zoo
[Desmond Morris *The Human Zoo*]

civic = **public**, community, borough, municipal, communal, local • *the businessmen and civic leaders of Manchester*

civil 1 = **civic**, home, political, domestic, interior, municipal • *This civil unrest threatens the economy.*
OPPOSITES: state, military, religious
2 = **polite**, obliging, accommodating, civilized, courteous, considerate, affable, courtly, well-bred, complaisant, well-mannered • *He couldn't even bring himself to be civil to Pauline.*
OPPOSITES: unpleasant, rude, unfriendly

civility = **politeness**, consideration, courtesy, tact, good manners, graciousness, cordiality, affability, amiability, politesse, complaisance, courteousness • *Most people treat each other with at least some civility.*

QUOTATIONS
Civility costs nothing and buys everything
[Mary Wortley Montagu *Letter to her daughter*]

PROVERBS
A civil question deserves a civil answer

civilization 1 = **society**, people, community, nation, polity • *He believed Western civilization was in grave economic and cultural danger.*
2 = **culture**, development, education, progress, enlightenment, sophistication, advancement, cultivation, refinement • *a race with an advanced state of civilization*

QUOTATIONS
Civilization is a limitless multiplication of unnecessary necessities
[Mark Twain]

civilize = **cultivate**, improve, polish, educate, refine, tame, enlighten, humanize, sophisticate • *The missionaries exacted a heavy price in labour from the natives they presumed to enlighten and civilize.*

civilized 1 = **cultured**, educated, sophisticated, enlightened, humane • *All truly civilized countries must deplore torture.*
OPPOSITES: simple, wild, primitive
2 = **polite**, mannerly, tolerant, gracious, courteous, affable, well-behaved, well-mannered • *Our divorce was conducted in a very civilized manner.*

clad = **dressed**, clothed, arrayed, draped, fitted out, decked out, attired, rigged out *(informal)*, apparelled, accoutred, covered • *He was clad casually in slacks and a light blue golf shirt.*

claim AS A VERB 1 = **assert**, insist, maintain, allege, uphold, profess, hold • *He claimed that it was a conspiracy against him.*
2 = **take**, receive, pick up, collect, lay claim to • *Now they are returning to claim what is theirs.*
3 = **demand**, call for, ask for, insist on • *They intend to claim for damages against the three doctors.*
▸ AS A NOUN 1 = **assertion**, statement, allegation, declaration, contention, pretension, affirmation, protestation • *He rejected claims that he had had an affair.*
2 = **demand**, application, request, petition, call • *The office has been dealing with their claim for benefits.*
3 = **right**, title, entitlement • *The Tudors had a tenuous claim to the monarchy.*

claimant = **applicant**, pretender, petitioner, supplicant, suppliant • *the rival claimant to the French throne*

clairvoyant AS AN ADJECTIVE = **psychic**, visionary, prophetic, prescient, telepathic, fey, second-sighted, extrasensory, oracular, sibylline • *a fortune-teller who claims to have clairvoyant powers*
▸ AS A NOUN = **psychic**, diviner, prophet, visionary, oracle, seer, augur, fortune-teller, soothsayer, sibyl, prophetess, telepath • *You don't need to be a clairvoyant to see how this is going to turn out.*

QUOTATIONS
clairvoyant: a person, commonly a woman, who has the power of seeing that which is invisible to her patron – namely, that he is a blockhead
[Ambrose Bierce *The Devil's Dictionary*]

clamber = **climb**, scale, scramble, claw, shin, scrabble • *They clambered up the steep hill.*

clammy 1 = **moist**, sweating, damp, sticky, sweaty, slimy • *My shirt was clammy with sweat.*
2 = **damp**, humid, dank, muggy, close • *As you peer down into this pit, the clammy atmosphere rises to meet your skin.*

clamorous = **noisy**, loud, insistent, deafening, blaring, strident, tumultuous, vociferous, vehement, riotous, uproarious • *The clamorous din of voices filled the air.*

clamour AS A VERB = **yell**, shout, scream, howl, bawl • *My two grandsons were clamouring to go swimming.*
▸ AS A NOUN = **noise**, shouting, racket, outcry, din, uproar, agitation, blare, commotion, babel, hubbub, brouhaha, hullabaloo, shout • *Kathryn's quiet voice stilled the clamour.*

clamp AS A NOUN = **vice**, press, grip, bracket, fastener • *This clamp is ideal for holding frames and other items.*
▸ AS A VERB = **fasten**, fix, secure, clinch, brace, make fast • *U-bolts are used to clamp the microphones to the pole.*

clan 1 = **family**, house, group, order, race, society, band, tribe, sept, fraternity, brotherhood, sodality, ainga *(N.Z.)*, ngai *or* ngati *(N.Z.)* • *A clash had taken place between rival clans.*
2 = **group**, set, crowd, circle, crew *(informal)*, gang, faction, coterie, schism, cabal • *a powerful clan of industrialists from Monterrey*

clandestine = **secret**, private, hidden, underground, concealed, closet, covert, sly, furtive, underhand, surreptitious, stealthy, cloak-and-dagger, under-the-counter • *They are said to have been holding clandestine meetings for years.*

clang AS A VERB = **ring**, toll, resound, chime, reverberate, jangle, clank, bong, clash • *A little later the church bell clanged.*
▸ AS A NOUN = **ringing**, clash, jangle, knell, clank, reverberation, ding-dong, clangour • *He pulled the gates shut with a clang.*

clannish = **cliquish**, select, narrow, exclusive, sectarian, unfriendly, insular • *Teenagers can be clannish and cruel in their exclusion of others who are 'different'.*

clap 1 = **applaud**, cheer, acclaim, give it up for *(slang)*, give (someone) a big hand • *The men danced and the women clapped.* • *People lined the streets to clap the marchers.*
OPPOSITES: boo, hiss, jeer
2 = **strike**, pat, punch, bang, thrust, slap, whack, wallop *(informal)*, thwack • *He clapped me on the back and boomed, 'Well done.'*

claptrap = **nonsense**, rubbish, rot, crap *(slang)*, garbage *(informal)*, trash, bunk *(informal)*, bullshit *(taboo slang)*, balls *(taboo slang)*, bull *(slang)*, shit *(taboo slang)*, hot air *(informal)*, tosh *(slang, chiefly Brit.)*, flannel *(Brit. informal)*, pap, cobblers *(Brit. taboo slang)*, bilge *(informal)*, humbug, drivel, malarkey, twaddle, tripe *(informal)*, affectation, guff *(slang)*, blarney, bombast, moonshine, insincerity, hogwash, hokum *(slang, chiefly U.S. & Canad.)*, bizzo *(Austral. slang)*, bull's wool *(Austral. & N.Z. slang)*, piffle *(informal)*, poppycock *(informal)*, bosh *(informal)*, eyewash *(informal)*, tommyrot, horsefeathers *(U.S. slang)*, bunkum or buncombe *(chiefly U.S.)* • *He talks a lot of pretentious claptrap.*

clarification = **explanation**, interpretation, exposition, illumination, simplification, elucidation • *I have written to the union asking for clarification of my position.*

clarify 1 = **explain**, resolve, interpret, illuminate, clear up, simplify, make plain, elucidate, explicate, clear the air about, throw or shed light on • *A bank spokesman was unable to clarify the situation.*
2 = **refine**, cleanse, purify • *Clarify the butter by bringing it to a simmer in a small pan.*

clarity 1 = **clearness**, precision, simplicity, transparency, lucidity, explicitness, intelligibility, obviousness, straightforwardness, comprehensibility • *the clarity with which the author explains this technical subject*
OPPOSITES: complexity, complication, obscurity
2 = **transparency**, translucency, translucence, clearness, limpidity • *The first thing to strike me was the incredible clarity of the water.*
OPPOSITES: dullness, murkiness, cloudiness

QUOTATIONS
Everything that can be said can be said clearly
[Ludwig Wittgenstein *Tractatus Logico-Philosophicus*]

clash AS A VERB 1 = **conflict**, grapple, wrangle, lock horns, cross swords, war, feud, quarrel • *A group of 400 demonstrators clashed with police.*
2 = **disagree**, conflict, vary, counter, differ, depart, contradict, diverge, deviate, run counter to, be dissimilar, be discordant • *Don't make policy decisions which clash with company thinking.*
3 = **not go**, jar, not match, be discordant • *The red door clashed with the pink walls.*
4 = **crash**, bang, rattle, jar, clatter, jangle, clang, clank • *The golden bangles on her arms clashed and jangled.*
▸ AS A NOUN 1 = **conflict**, fight, brush, confrontation, collision, showdown *(informal)*, boilover *(Austral.)* • *There are reports of clashes between militants and the security forces in the city.*
2 = **disagreement**, difference, division, argument, dispute, dissent, difference of opinion • *Inside government, there was a clash of views.*

clasp AS A VERB = **grasp**, hold, press, grip, seize, squeeze, embrace, clutch, hug, enfold • *Mary clasped the children to her desperately.*
▸ AS A NOUN 1 = **grasp**, hold, grip, embrace, hug • *He gripped my hand in a strong clasp.*
2 = **fastening**, catch, grip, hook, snap, pin, clip, buckle, brooch, fastener, hasp, press stud • *She undid the clasp of the hooded cloak she was wearing.*

class AS A NOUN 1 = **form**, grade, study group, band, stream • *Reducing the size of classes should be a priority.*
2 = **lesson**, period, seminar, tutorial • *They put me into a remedial maths class.*
3 = **group**, grouping, set, order, league, division, rank, caste, status, sphere • *the relationship between different social classes*
4 = **type**, set, sort, kind, collection, species, grade, category, stamp, genre, classification, denomination, genus • *The navy is developing a new class of nuclear-powered submarine.*
5 = **style**, polish, dash, chic, elegance, sophistication, refinement, panache, élan, savoir-faire, stylishness, bon ton *(French)* • *This woman exudes class, style and sophistication.*
▸ AS A VERB = **classify**, group, rate, rank, brand, label, grade, designate, categorize, codify • *I would class my garden as being medium in size.*
▸ AS AN ADJECTIVE = **excellent**, expert, good, great, able, skilled, masterly, outstanding, superb, superior, accomplished, first-class, competent, world-class, tasty *(Brit. informal)*, booshit *(Austral. slang)*, exo *(Austral. slang)*, sik *(Austral. slang)*, skilful, adept, first-rate, superlative, proficient, top-notch *(informal)*, adroit, dexterous, A1 or A-one *(informal)*, rad *(informal)*, phat *(slang)*, schmick *(Austral. informal)* • *We do not have a single class player in our team.*
▹ *See panel* **Family**

QUOTATIONS
The history of all hitherto existing society is the history of class struggles
[Karl Marx and Friedrich Engels *The Communist Manifesto*]
There are but two families in the world as my grandmother used to say, the Haves and the Have-nots
[Miguel de Cervantes *Don Quixote*]
The rich man in his castle,
The poor man at his gate,
God made them, high or lowly,
And ordered their estate
[Cecil Frances Alexander *All Things Bright and Beautiful*]

classic AS AN ADJECTIVE 1 = **typical**, standard, model, regular, usual, ideal, characteristic, signature, definitive, archetypal, exemplary, quintessential, time-honoured, paradigmatic, dinki-di *(Austral. informal)* • *This is a classic example of media hype.*
2 = **masterly**, best, finest, master, world-class, consummate, first-rate • *Aldous Huxley's classic work, The Perennial Philosophy*
OPPOSITES: poor, modern, second-rate
3 = **lasting**, enduring, abiding, immortal, undying, ageless, deathless • *These are classic designs which will fit in well anywhere.*
▸ AS A NOUN = **standard**, masterpiece, prototype, paradigm, exemplar, masterwork, model • *The album is one of the classics of modern popular music.*

QUOTATIONS
A classic is something that everybody wants to have read and nobody wants to read
[Mark Twain]
Every man with a bellyful of the classics is an enemy to the human race
[Henry Miller *Tropic of Cancer*]

classical 1 = **traditional**, established, conventional, long-established, time-honoured • *They performed dance dramas in the classical style.*
2 = **Greek**, Roman, Latin, Attic, Grecian, Hellenic, Augustan • *the healers of ancient Egypt and the classical world*
▹ *See panel* **Mythology**

QUOTATIONS
The great tragedy of the classical languages is to have been born twins
[Geoffrey Madan]
That's the classical mind at work, runs fine inside but looks dingy on the surface
[Robert M. Pirsig *Zen and the Art of Motorcycle Maintenance*]

classification 1 = **categorization**, grading, cataloguing, taxonomy, codification, sorting, analysis, arrangement • *the accepted classification of the animal and plant kingdoms*

C

2 = class, grouping, heading, head, order, sort, list, department, type, division, section, rank, grade • *several different classifications of vehicles*

classify = categorize, sort, file, rank, arrange, grade, catalogue, codify, pigeonhole, tabulate, systematize • *Rocks can be classified according to their mode of origin.*

classy = high-class, select, exclusive, superior, elegant, stylish, posh *(informal, chiefly Brit.)*, swish *(informal, chiefly Brit.)*, up-market, urbane, swanky *(informal)*, top-drawer, ritzy *(slang)*, high-toned, schmick *(Austral. informal)* • *Her parents lived in Rome's classy Monte Mario quarter.*

clause = section, condition, article, item, chapter, rider, provision, passage, point, part, heading, paragraph, specification, proviso, stipulation • *There is a clause in his contract which entitles him to a percentage of the profits.*

claw AS A NOUN **1 = nail**, talon, unguis *(technical)* • *The cat's claws got caught in my clothes.*
2 = pincer, nipper • *The lobster has two large claws.*
▸ AS A VERB **= scratch**, tear, dig, rip, scrape, graze, maul, scrabble, mangle, mangulate *(Austral. slang)*, lacerate • *She struck back at him and clawed his arm with her hand.*

clay
▸ RELATED ADJECTIVE: figuline

clean AS AN ADJECTIVE **1 = hygienic**, natural, fresh, sterile, pure, purified, antiseptic, sterilized, unadulterated, uncontaminated, unpolluted, decontaminated • *Disease is not a problem because clean water is available.*
OPPOSITES: infected, contaminated, polluted
2 = spotless, fresh, washed, immaculate, laundered, impeccable, flawless, sanitary, faultless, squeaky-clean, hygienic, unblemished, unsullied, unstained, unsoiled, unspotted • *He wore his cleanest slacks and a navy blazer.*
OPPOSITES: soiled, dirty, filthy
3 = moral, good, pure, decent, innocent, respectable, upright, honourable, impeccable, exemplary, virtuous, chaste, undefiled • *I want to live a clean life, a life without sin.*
OPPOSITES: indecent, immoral, impure
4 = complete, final, whole, total, perfect, entire, decisive, thorough, conclusive, unimpaired • *It is time for a clean break with the past.*
5 = neat, simple, elegant, trim, delicate, tidy, graceful, uncluttered • *I admire the clean lines of Shaker furniture.*
OPPOSITES: disorderly, chaotic, untidy
▸ AS A VERB **= cleanse**, wash, bath, sweep, dust, wipe, vacuum, scrub, sponge, rinse, mop, launder, scour, purify, do up, swab, disinfect, deodorize, sanitize • *Her father cleaned his glasses with a paper napkin.* • *It took half an hour to clean the orange powder off the bath.*
OPPOSITES: soil, dirty, infect

clean-cut = neat, trim, tidy, chiselled • *He was handsome in a clean-cut, English way.*

cleanliness = cleanness, purity, freshness, whiteness, sterility, spotlessness • *Many of Britain's beaches fail to meet minimum standards of cleanliness.*

PROVERBS
Cleanliness is next to godliness

cleanse 1 = purify, clear, purge • *Your body is beginning to cleanse itself of tobacco toxins.*
2 = absolve, clear, purge, purify • *Confession cleanses the soul.*
3 = clean, wash, scrub, rinse, scour • *She demonstrated the proper way to cleanse the face.*

cleanser = detergent, soap, solvent, disinfectant, soap powder, purifier, scourer, wash • *Their product range includes washing powder, washing-up liquid, and cream cleanser*

clear AS AN ADJECTIVE **1 = comprehensible**, explicit, articulate, understandable, coherent, lucid, user-friendly, intelligible • *The book is clear, readable and amply illustrated.*
OPPOSITES: confused, incoherent, inarticulate
2 = distinct, audible, perceptible • *He repeated his answer in a clear, firm voice.*
OPPOSITES: inaudible, indistinct, unrecognizable
3 = obvious, plain, apparent, bold, patent, evident, distinct, pronounced, definite, manifest, blatant, conspicuous, unmistakable, express, palpable, unequivocal, recognizable, unambiguous, unquestionable, cut-and-dried *(informal)*, incontrovertible • *It was a clear case of homicide.*
OPPOSITES: hidden, obscured, ambiguous
4 = certain, sure, convinced, positive, satisfied, resolved, explicit, definite, decided • *It is important to be clear on what the author is saying here.*
OPPOSITES: confused, doubtful
5 = transparent, see-through, translucent, crystalline, glassy, limpid, pellucid • *The water is clear and plenty of fish are visible.*
OPPOSITES: muddy, opaque, cloudy
6 = unobstructed, open, free, empty, unhindered, unimpeded, unhampered • *All exits must be kept clear in case of fire or a bomb scare.*
OPPOSITES: closed, blocked, hampered
7 = bright, fine, fair, shining, sunny, luminous, halcyon, cloudless, undimmed, light, unclouded • *Most places will be dry with clear skies.*
OPPOSITES: dark, dull, cloudy
8 = untroubled, clean, pure, innocent, stainless, immaculate, unblemished, untarnished, guiltless, sinless, undefiled • *I can look back on things with a clear conscience.*
▸ AS A VERB **1 = unblock**, unclog, free, loosen, extricate, disengage, open, disentangle • *We called in a plumber to clear our blocked sink.*
2 = remove, clean, wipe, cleanse, tidy (up), sweep away • *Firemen were still clearing rubble from the scene of the explosion.*
3 = brighten, break up, lighten • *As the weather cleared, helicopters began to ferry the injured to hospital.*
4 = pass over, jump, leap, vault, miss • *The horse cleared the fence by several inches.*
5 = absolve, acquit, vindicate, exonerate • *In a final effort to clear her name, she is writing a book.*
OPPOSITES: charge, accuse, blame
6 = gain, make, earn, secure, acquire, reap • *The company cleared over £57 million profit last year.*
▸ IN PHRASES: **clear out = go away**, leave, retire, withdraw, depart, beat it *(slang)*, decamp, hook it *(slang)*, slope off, pack your bags *(informal)*, make tracks, bog off *(Brit. slang)*, take yourself off, make yourself scarce, rack off *(Austral. & N.Z. slang)* • *'Clear out!' he bawled, 'This is private property.'*
clear something out 1 = empty, sort, tidy up • *I took the precaution of clearing out my desk before I left.*
2 = get rid of, remove, dump, dispose of, throw away or out • *It'll take you a month just to clear out all this rubbish.*
clear something up 1 = tidy (up), order, straighten, rearrange, put in order • *I told you to clear up your room.*
2 = solve, explain, resolve, clarify, unravel, straighten out, elucidate • *During dinner the confusion was cleared up.*

clearance 1 = evacuation, emptying, withdrawal, removal, eviction, depopulation • *By the late fifties, slum clearance was the watchword in town planning.*
2 = permission, consent, endorsement, green light, authorization, blank cheque, go-ahead *(informal)*, leave, sanction, O.K. or okay *(informal)* • *He has a security clearance that allows him access to classified information.*
3 = space, gap, margin, allowance, headroom • *The lowest fixed bridge has 12.8m clearance.*

clear-cut = straightforward, specific, plain, precise, black-and-white, explicit, definite, unequivocal, unambiguous, cut-and-dried *(informal)* • *He won a clear-cut victory in yesterday's election.*

clearing = **glade**, space, dell • *A helicopter landed in a clearing in the jungle.*

clearly 1 = **obviously**, undoubtedly, evidently, distinctly, markedly, overtly, undeniably, beyond doubt, incontrovertibly, incontestably, openly • *He clearly believes that he is in the right.*
2 = **legibly**, distinctly • *Write your address clearly on the back of the envelope.*
3 = **audibly**, distinctly, intelligibly, comprehensibly • *Please speak clearly after the tone.*

C

cleave[1] = **split**, open, divide, crack, slice, rend, sever, part, hew, tear asunder, sunder • *The axe had cleaved open the back of his skull.*

cleave[2] AS A VERB
▸ IN PHRASES: **cleave to** = **stick to**, stand by, cling to, hold to, be devoted to, adhere to, be attached to, abide by, be true to • *She teaches the principles she has cleaved to for more than 40 years.*

cleft AS A NOUN = **opening**, break, crack, gap, rent, breach, fracture, rift, chink, crevice, fissure, cranny • *a narrow cleft in the rocks too small for a human to squeeze through*
▸ AS AN ADJECTIVE = **split**, separated, torn, rent, ruptured, cloven, riven, sundered, parted • *The cleft rock face seemed to move in the static noonday light.*

clemency = **mercy**, pity, humanity, compassion, kindness, forgiveness, indulgence, leniency, forbearance, quarter • *The prisoners' pleas for clemency were turned down.*

clement = **mild**, fine, fair, calm, temperate, balmy • *The area is usually known for its clement weather.*

clergy = **priesthood**, ministry, clerics, clergymen, churchmen, the cloth, holy orders, ecclesiastics • *The Bolsheviks closed churches and imprisoned the clergy.*
▸ RELATED ADJECTIVES: clerical, pastoral

QUOTATIONS
Clergy are men as well as other folks
[Henry Fielding *Joseph Andrews*]

clergyman = **minister**, priest, vicar, parson, reverend (*informal*), rabbi, pastor, chaplain, cleric, rector, curate, father, churchman, padre, man of God, man of the cloth, divine • *The crowds were protesting against a local clergyman being banned from preaching.*

QUOTATIONS
The clergyman is expected to be a kind of human Sunday
[Samuel Butler *The Way of All Flesh*]

clerical 1 = **administrative**, office, bureaucratic, secretarial, book-keeping, stenographic • *The hospital blamed the mix-up on a clerical error.*
2 = **ecclesiastical**, priestly, pastoral, sacerdotal • *a clergyman who had failed to carry out his clerical duties*

clever 1 = **intelligent**, quick, bright, talented, gifted, keen, capable, smart, sensible, rational, witty, apt, discerning, knowledgeable, astute, brainy (*informal*), quick-witted, sagacious, knowing, deep, expert • *My sister has always been the clever one in our family.*
OPPOSITES: slow, thick, stupid
2 = **shrewd**, bright, cunning, ingenious, inventive, astute, resourceful, canny • *It's a very clever idea.*
OPPOSITES: boring, dull, unimaginative
3 = **skilful**, able, talented, gifted, capable, inventive, adroit, dexterous • *My father was very clever with his hands.*
OPPOSITES: awkward, clumsy, inept

cleverness 1 = **intelligence**, sense, brains, wit, brightness, nous (*Brit. slang*), suss (*slang*), quickness, gumption (*Brit. informal*), sagacity, smartness, astuteness, quick wits, smarts (*slang, chiefly U.S.*) • *He congratulated himself on his cleverness.*
2 = **shrewdness**, sharpness, resourcefulness, canniness • *a policy almost Machiavellian in its cleverness*
3 = **dexterity**, ability, talent, gift, flair, ingenuity, adroitness • *The artist demonstrates a cleverness with colours and textures.*

cliché = **platitude**, stereotype, commonplace, banality, truism, bromide, old saw, hackneyed phrase, chestnut (*informal*) • *I've learned that the cliché about life not being fair is true.*

click AS A NOUN = **snap**, beat, tick, clack • *I heard a click and then the telephone message started to play.*
▸ AS A VERB 1 = **snap**, beat, tick, clack • *Camera shutters clicked all around me.*
2 = **become clear**, come home (to), make sense, fall into place • *When I saw the TV report, it all suddenly clicked.*
3 = **get on**, be compatible, hit it off (*informal*), be on the same wavelength, get on like a house on fire (*informal*), take to each other, feel a rapport • *They clicked immediately; they liked all the same things.*

client = **customer**, consumer, buyer, patron, shopper, habitué, patient • *The company requires clients to pay substantial fees in advance.*

clientele = **customers**, market, business, following, trade, regulars, clients, patronage • *This pub has a mixed clientele.*

cliff = **rock face**, overhang, crag, precipice, escarpment, scarp, face, scar, bluff • *The car rolled over the edge of a cliff.*
▸ RELATED MANIA: cremnomania

climactic = **crucial**, central, critical, peak, decisive, paramount, pivotal • *the film's climactic scene*

climate 1 = **weather**, country, region, temperature, clime • *the hot and humid climate of Cyprus*
2 = **atmosphere**, environment, spirit, surroundings, tone, mood, trend, flavour, feeling, tendency, temper, ambience, vibes (*slang*) • *A major change of political climate is unlikely.*

QUOTATIONS
You don't need a weatherman to know which way the wind blows
[Bob Dylan *Subterranean Homesick Blues*]

climax AS A NOUN = **culmination**, head, top, summit, height, highlight, peak, pay-off (*informal*), crest, high point, zenith, apogee, high spot (*informal*), acme, ne plus ultra (*Latin*) • *Reaching the Olympics was the climax of her career.*
▸ AS A VERB = **culminate**, end, finish, conclude, peak, come to a head • *They did a series of charity events climaxing in a millennium concert.*

climb AS A VERB 1 = **ascend**, scale, mount, go up, clamber, shin up • *Climbing the first hill took half an hour.*
2 = **clamber**, descend, scramble, dismount • *He climbed down from the cab.*
3 = **rise**, go up, soar, ascend, fly up • *The plane took off, lost an engine as it climbed, and crashed just off the runway.*
4 = **increase**, rise, mount, go up, rocket, soar, escalate, inflate, shoot up, snowball • *Prices have climbed by 21% since the beginning of the year.*
5 = **slope**, rise, go up, incline • *The road climbs steeply.*
▸ IN PHRASES: **climb down** = **back down**, withdraw, yield, concede, retreat, surrender, give in, cave in (*informal*), retract, admit defeat, back-pedal, eat your words, eat crow (*U.S. informal*) • *He has climbed down on pledges to reduce capital gains tax.*
▸ RELATED ADJECTIVE: scansorial

clinch AS A VERB 1 = **secure**, close, confirm, conclude, seal, verify, sew up (*informal*), set the seal on • *He is about to clinch a deal with an American engine manufacturer.*
2 = **settle**, decide, determine, tip the balance • *Evidently this information clinched the matter.*
3 = **win**, get, land, gain, achieve, bag (*informal*), acquire, accomplish, attain • *Leeds need to finish in the first three to clinch the title.*
▸ AS A NOUN = **embrace**, hug, cuddle • *They were caught in a clinch when their parents returned home unexpectedly.*

cling AS A VERB 1 = **clutch**, grip, embrace, grasp, hug, hold on to, clasp • *She had to cling onto the door handle until the pain passed.*

2 = **stick to**, attach to, adhere to, fasten to, twine round • *His sodden trousers were clinging to his shins.*
▸ **IN PHRASES: cling to something = adhere to**, maintain, stand by, cherish, abide by, be true to, be loyal to, be faithful to, cleave to • *They still cling to their beliefs.*

clinical = unemotional, cold, scientific, objective, detached, analytic, impersonal, antiseptic, disinterested, dispassionate, emotionless • *This approach is far too clinical for my liking.*

clip[1] AS A VERB 1 = trim, cut, crop, dock, prune, shorten, shear, cut short, snip, pare • *I saw an old man out clipping his hedge.*
2 = **cut out**, remove, extract • *I clipped his picture from the newspaper and carried it round with me.*
3 = **smack**, strike, box, knock, punch, belt *(informal)*, thump, clout *(informal)*, cuff, whack, wallop *(informal)*, skelp *(dialect)* • *I'd have clipped his ear for him if he'd been my kid.*
▸ **AS A NOUN 1 = extract**, scene, selection, excerpt, snippet • *an historical film clip of Lenin speaking*
2 = **smack**, strike, box, knock, punch, belt *(informal)*, thump, clout *(informal)*, cuff, whack, wallop *(informal)*, skelp *(dialect)* • *The boy was later given a clip round the ear by his father.*
3 = **speed**, rate, pace, gallop, lick *(informal)*, velocity • *They trotted along at a brisk clip.*

clip[2] = attach, fix, secure, connect, pin, staple, fasten, affix, hold • *He clipped his flashlight to his belt.*

clipping = cutting, passage, extract, excerpt, piece, article • *I found her death notice among some old newspaper clippings.*

clique = group, set, crowd, pack, circle, crew *(informal)*, gang, faction, mob, clan, posse *(informal)*, coterie, schism, cabal • *The country is run by a small clique of wealthy families.*

cloak AS A NOUN 1 = cape, coat, wrap, mantle • *She set out, wrapping her cloak about her.*
2 = **covering**, layer, blanket, shroud • *Today most of England will be under a cloak of thick mist.*
3 = **disguise**, front, cover, screen, blind, mask, shield, cover-up, façade, pretext, smoke screen, smoke and mirrors • *Individualism is sometimes used as a cloak for self-interest.*
▸ **AS A VERB 1 = cover**, coat, wrap, blanket, shroud, envelop • *The coastline was cloaked in fog.*
2 = **hide**, cover, screen, mask, disguise, conceal, obscure, veil, camouflage • *He uses jargon to cloak his inefficiency.*

clobber[1] = batter, beat, assault, smash, bash *(informal)*, lash, thrash, pound, beat up *(informal)*, wallop *(informal)*, pummel, rough up *(informal)*, lambast(e), belabour, duff up *(informal)*, beat or knock seven bells out of *(informal)* • *She clobbered him with a vase.*

clobber[2] = belongings, things, effects, property, stuff, gear, possessions, paraphernalia, accoutrements, chattels • *His house is filled with a load of old clobber.*

clock IN PHRASES: round the clock = morning, noon and night, all day, continuously, non-stop, day and night, night and day, without a break, twenty-four seven *(informal)* • *We have been working round the clock.*

clod = lump, piece, block, mass, chunk, clump, hunk • *a clod of earth from which a mass of thick plant roots protruded*

clog = obstruct, block, jam, hamper, hinder, impede, bung, stop up, dam up, occlude, congest • *The traffic clogged the Thames bridges.*

cloistered = sheltered, protected, restricted, shielded, confined, insulated, secluded, reclusive, shut off, sequestered, withdrawn, cloistral • *She was stifled by the cloistered life imposed on women at that time.*
OPPOSITES: public, social, outgoing

close[1] AS A VERB 1 = shut, lock, push to, fasten, secure • *If you are cold, close the window.*
OPPOSITES: open, widen
2 = **shut down**, finish, cease, discontinue • *Many enterprises will be forced to close because of the recession.*
3 = **wind up**, finish, axe *(informal)*, shut down, terminate, discontinue, mothball • *There are rumours of plans to close the local college.*
4 = **block up**, bar, seal, shut up • *The government has closed the border crossing.*
OPPOSITES: open, clear
5 = **end**, finish, complete, conclude, wind up, culminate, terminate • *He closed the meeting with his customary address.*
OPPOSITES: start, open, begin
6 = **clinch**, confirm, secure, conclude, seal, verify, sew up *(informal)*, set the seal on • *He needs another $30,000 to close the deal.*
7 = **come together**, join, connect • *His fingers closed around her wrist.*
OPPOSITES: part, separate, disconnect
▸ **AS A NOUN = end**, ending, finish, conclusion, completion, finale, culmination, denouement • *His retirement brings to a close a glorious chapter in British football history.*

close[2] 1 = near, neighbouring, nearby, handy, adjacent, adjoining, hard by, just round the corner, within striking distance *(informal)*, cheek by jowl, proximate, within spitting distance *(informal)*, within sniffing distance, a hop, skip and a jump away • *The plant is close to Sydney airport.*
OPPOSITES: far, future, remote
2 = **intimate**, loving, friendly, familiar, thick *(informal)*, attached, devoted, confidential, inseparable, dear • *She and Linda became very close.*
OPPOSITES: cold, cool, distant
3 = **noticeable**, marked, strong, distinct, pronounced • *There is a close resemblance between them.*
4 = **careful**, detailed, searching, concentrated, keen, intense, minute, alert, intent, thorough, rigorous, attentive, painstaking, assiduous • *His recent actions have been the subject of close scrutiny.*
5 = **even**, level, neck and neck, fifty-fifty *(informal)*, evenly matched, equally balanced • *It is still a close contest between the two leading parties.*
6 = **imminent**, near, approaching, impending, at hand, upcoming, nigh, just round the corner • *A White House official said an agreement is close.*
OPPOSITES: far, future, far away
7 = **stifling**, confined, oppressive, stale, suffocating, stuffy, humid, sweltering, airless, muggy, unventilated, fuggy, frowsty, heavy, thick • *They sat in that hot, close room for two hours.*
OPPOSITES: fresh, refreshing, airy
8 = **accurate**, strict, exact, precise, faithful, literal, conscientious • *The poem is a close translation from the original Latin.*
9 = **secretive**, private, reticent, taciturn, uncommunicative, unforthcoming • *The Colonel was very close about certain episodes in his past.*
10 = **mean**, stingy, parsimonious, illiberal, miserly, niggardly, ungenerous, penurious, tight-fisted, mingy *(Brit. informal)*, tight as a duck's arse *(taboo slang)* • *She is very close with money.*
OPPOSITES: liberal, generous, lavish

closed 1 = shut, locked, sealed, fastened • *Her bedroom door was closed.*
OPPOSITES: open, unlocked, ajar
2 = **shut down**, out of business, out of service • *The airport shop was closed.*
3 = **exclusive**, select, restricted • *No-one was admitted to this closed circle of elite students.*
4 = **finished**, over, ended, decided, settled, concluded, resolved, terminated • *I now consider the matter closed.*

closeness 1 = nearness, proximity, handiness, adjacency • *the closeness of the Chinese mainland to Hong Kong*
2 = **imminence**, nearness, impendency • *this ever-present feeling of the closeness of death*

3 = intimacy, love, devotion, confidentiality, familiarity, dearness, inseparability, aroha *(N.Z.)* • *He experienced a lack of closeness to his parents during childhood.*

closet AS A NOUN = **cupboard**, cabinet, recess, cubicle, cubbyhole • *Perhaps there's room in the broom closet.*
▸ AS AN ADJECTIVE = **secret**, private, hidden, unknown, concealed, covert, unrevealed • *He is a closet Fascist.*

closure = **closing**, end, finish, conclusion, stoppage, termination, cessation • *the closure of the Ravenscraig steelworks*

clot AS A NOUN 1 = **lump**, mass, clotting, curdling, gob, embolism, coagulation, thrombus *(technical)*, occlusion, embolus *(technical)* • *He needed emergency surgery to remove a blood clot from his brain.*
2 = idiot, fool, dope *(informal)*, jerk *(slang, chiefly U.S. & Canad.)*, ass, plank *(Brit. slang)*, berk *(Brit. slang)*, prick *(derogatory slang)*, wally *(slang)*, prat *(slang)*, plonker *(slang)*, charlie *(Brit. informal)*, coot, nit *(informal)*, geek *(slang)*, twit *(informal, chiefly Brit.)*, buffoon, dipstick *(Brit. slang)*, dickhead *(slang)*, gonzo *(slang)*, schmuck *(U.S. slang)*, dork *(slang)*, dorba *or* dorb *(Austral. slang)*, bogan *(Austral. slang)*, nitwit *(informal)*, dolt, divvy *(Brit. slang)*, pillock *(Brit. slang)*, nincompoop, dweeb *(U.S. slang)*, putz *(U.S. slang)*, fathead *(informal)*, eejit *(Scot. & Irish)*, thicko *(Brit. slang)*, dumb-ass *(slang)*, gobshite *(Irish taboo slang)*, dunderhead, numpty *(Scot. informal)*, doofus *(slang, chiefly U.S.)*, fuckwit *(taboo slang)*, dickwit *(slang)*, nerd *or* nurd *(slang)*, numbskull *or* numskull, twerp *or* twirp *(informal)* • *He has always been a bit of a clot.*
▸ AS A VERB = **congeal**, thicken, curdle, coalesce, jell, coagulate • *The patient's blood refused to clot.*

cloth = **fabric**, material, textiles, dry goods, stuff • *She covered the tray with a piece of cloth.*

clothe = **dress**, outfit, rig, array, robe, drape, get ready, swathe, apparel, attire, fit out, garb, doll up *(slang)*, accoutre, cover, deck • *He was clothed in a dashing scarlet and black uniform.*
OPPOSITES: strip, expose, undress

clothes = **clothing**, wear, dress, gear *(informal)*, habits, get-up *(informal)*, outfit, costume, threads *(slang)*, wardrobe, ensemble, garments, duds *(informal)*, apparel, clobber *(Brit. slang)*, attire, garb, togs *(informal)*, vestments, glad rags *(informal)*, raiment *(archaic or poetic)*, rigout *(informal)* • *He was dressed in casual clothes.*
▸ RELATED ADJECTIVE: vestiary

clothing = **clothes**, wear, dress, gear *(informal)*, habits, get-up *(informal)*, outfit, costume, threads *(slang)*, wardrobe, ensemble, garments, duds *(informal)*, apparel, clobber *(Brit. slang)*, attire, garb, togs *(informal)*, vestments, glad rags *(informal)*, raiment *(archaic or poetic)*, rigout *(informal)* • *The refugees were given food, clothing and shelter.*
▹ *See panels* **Clothing; Coats and cloaks; Dresses; Hats; Jackets; Religion; Shoes and boots; Skirts; Socks and tights; Suits; Sweaters; Ties and cravats; Trousers and shorts; Underwear**

QUOTATIONS
The origins of clothing are not practical. They are mystical and erotic. The primitive man in the wolf-pelt was not keeping dry; he was saying: 'Look what I killed. Aren't I the best?'
[Katherine Hamnett]
The apparel oft proclaims the man
[William Shakespeare *Hamlet*]
Clothes make the man. Naked people have little or no influence in society
[Mark Twain]
Beware of all enterprises that require new clothes, and not rather a new wearer of clothes
[Henry David Thoreau *Walden*]

cloud AS A NOUN 1 = **mist**, fog, haze, obscurity, vapour, nebula, murk, darkness, gloom • *The sun was almost entirely obscured by cloud.*
2 = billow, mass, shower, puff • *The hens darted away on all sides, raising a cloud of dust.*
3 = swarm, host, crowd, flock, horde, multitude, throng, dense mass • *He was surrounded by a cloud of buzzing flies.*
▸ AS A VERB 1 = **confuse**, obscure, distort, impair, muddle, disorient • *Perhaps anger has clouded his vision.*
2 = darken, dim, be overshadowed, be overcast • *The sky clouded and a light rain began to fall.*
▸ RELATED PHOBIA: nephophobia

QUOTATIONS
I wander'd lonely as a cloud
That floats on high o'er vales and hills
[William Wordsworth *I Wandered Lonely as a Cloud*]

TYPES OF CLOUD

altocumulus	cumulonimbus	nimbostratus
altostratus	cumulus	nimbus
cirrocumulus	false cirrus	stratocumulus
cirrostratus	fractocumulus	stratus
cirrus	fractostratus	

cloudy 1 = **dull**, dark, dim, gloomy, dismal, sombre, overcast, leaden, sunless, louring *or* lowering • *It was a cloudy, windy day.*
OPPOSITES: clear, fair, bright
2 = opaque, muddy, murky, emulsified • *She could just barely see him through the cloudy water.*
3 = vague, confused, obscure, blurred, unclear, hazy, indistinct • *The legal position on this issue is very cloudy.*
OPPOSITES: clear, obvious, plain

clout AS A VERB = **hit**, strike, punch, deck *(slang)*, slap, sock *(slang)*, chin *(slang)*, smack, thump, cuff, clobber *(slang)*, wallop *(informal)*, box, wham, lay one on *(slang)*, skelp *(dialect)* • *The officer clouted him on the head.*
▸ AS A NOUN 1 = **thump**, blow, crack, punch, slap, sock *(slang)*, cuff, wallop *(informal)*, skelp *(dialect)* • *I was half tempted to give them a clout myself.*
2 = influence, power, standing, authority, pull, weight, bottom, prestige, mana *(N.Z.)* • *The two firms wield enormous clout in financial markets.*

cloven = **split**, divided, cleft, bisected • *The tracks were made by an animal with a cloven hoof.*

clown AS A NOUN 1 = **comedian**, fool, harlequin, jester, buffoon, pierrot, dolt • *a classic circus clown with a big red nose and baggy suit*
2 = joker, comic, prankster • *He gained a reputation as the class clown.*
3 = fool, dope *(informal)*, jerk *(slang, chiefly U.S. & Canad.)*, idiot, ass, berk *(Brit. slang)*, prat *(slang)*, moron, twit *(informal, chiefly Brit.)*, imbecile *(informal)*, ignoramus, jackass, dolt, blockhead, ninny, putz *(U.S. slang)*, eejit *(Scot. & Irish)*, thicko *(Brit. slang)*, doofus *(slang, chiefly U.S.)*, dorba *or* dorb *(Austral. slang)*, bogan *(Austral. slang)*, lamebrain *(informal)*, numbskull *or* numskull • *I could do a better job than those clowns in Washington.*
▸ AS A VERB *usually with* **around** = **play the fool**, mess about, jest, act the fool, act the goat, play the goat, piss about *or* around *(taboo slang)* • *He clowned a lot and antagonized his workmates.* • *Stop clowning around and get some work done.*

cloying 1 = **sickly**, nauseating, icky *(informal)*, treacly, oversweet, excessive • *Her cheap, cloying scent enveloped him.*
2 = over-sentimental, sickly, nauseating, mushy, twee, slushy, mawkish, icky *(informal)*, treacly, oversweet • *The film is sentimental but rarely cloying.*

CLOTHING

ARTICLES OF CLOTHING

apron, baldric, basque, bathing suit, bathrobe, bib and brace, bikini, blouse, body, body stocking, bodysuit, boubou, braces *or (U.S.)* suspenders, bustier, cardigan, chapeau, chaps, chausses, chuddah, cilice, coat, coatee, codpiece, cummerbund, dolman, dress, dressing gown, dungarees, frock, galluses *(dialect)*, gambeson, garter, gilet, glove, gown, haik, halter, hauberk, hose, housecoat, jacket, jerkin, jersey, jubbah, jumper, jump suit, jupon, kaftan, kameez, kanzu, kaross, kimono, kilt, kittel, leotard, loincloth *or* breechcloth, maillot, manteau, mantle *(archaic)*, mitten, muff, negligee, nightdress, nightshirt, overall, overcoat, overskirt, oversleeve, paletot, pallium, partlet, pashmina, peignoir, plaid, pullover, pyjamas, robe, rompers, sash, sanbenito, sari, sarong, serape, shalwar, shawl, shift, shirt, shoe, shorts, skivvy *(slang, chiefly U.S.)*, slop, smock, sock, sporran, surcoat, sweater, swimming costume, swimming trunks, swimsuit, tallit, tanga, tank top, thong, tie, tights, toga, T-shirt, tunic, undergarment, waistcoat, wrap, wrapper, yashmak

PARTS OF CLOTHING

arm, armhole, armlet, bodice, buttonhole, collar, cuff, dicky, epaulette, flounce, gusset, hem, hemline, hood, jabot, lapel, leg, lining, neckline, patch pocket, pocket, seam, shawl collar, shoulder, sleeve, tail, train, waist, waistline, yoke

TYPES OF CLOTHING

academic dress, armour, baby clothes, beachwear, black tie, canonicals, civvies, clericals, coordinates, coveralls, evening dress, fancy dress, fatigues, froufrou, Highland dress, hose, hosiery, knitwear, lingerie, livery, long-coats, millinery, morning dress, mufti, neckwear, nightclothes, nightwear, overgarments, sackcloth, samfoo, separates, skivvies *(slang, chiefly U.S.)*, slops, sportswear, swaddling clothes, swimwear, undergarments, underthings, underwear, uniform, weepers, white tie, widow's weeds

club **AS A NOUN 1 = association**, company, group, union, society, circle, lodge, guild, fraternity, set, order, sodality • *He was a member of the local youth club.*
2 = team, squad • *He is a great supporter of Fulham football club.*
3 = nightclub, disco, nightspot • *It's a big dance hit in the clubs*
4 = stick, bat, bludgeon, truncheon, cosh *(Brit.)*, cudgel • *Men armed with knives and clubs attacked his home.*
▸ **AS A VERB = beat**, strike, hammer, batter, bash, clout *(informal)*, bludgeon, clobber *(slang)*, pummel, cosh *(Brit.)*, beat *or* knock seven bells out of *(informal)* • *Two thugs clubbed him with baseball bats.*

QUOTATIONS

I don't want to belong to any club that will accept me as a member

[Groucho Marx]

TYPES OF CLUB

blackjack, bludgeon, cudgel, knobkerrie, lathi, life preserver, mere *(N.Z.)*, nightstick, nulla-nulla, patu *(N.Z.)*, quarterstaff, shillelagh, truncheon, waddy

clue = indication, lead, sign, evidence, tip, suggestion, trace, hint, suspicion, pointer, tip-off, inkling, intimation • *Scientists have discovered a clue to the puzzle of why our cells get old and die.* • *a vital clue to the killer's identity*

clueless = stupid, thick, dull, naive, dim, dense, dumb *(informal)*, simple-minded, dozy *(Brit. informal)*, simple, slow, witless, dopey *(informal)*, moronic, unintelligent, half-witted, slow on the uptake *(informal)* • *He's totally clueless when it comes to women.*

clump **AS A NOUN = cluster**, group, bunch, bundle, shock • *There was a clump of trees bordering the side of the road.*
▸ **AS A VERB = stomp**, stamp, stump, thump, lumber, tramp, plod, thud, clomp • *They went clumping up the stairs to bed.*

clumsiness 1 = awkwardness, ineptitude, heaviness, ineptness, inelegance, ponderousness, gracelessness, gawkiness, ungainliness • *I was embarrassed by my clumsiness on the dance-floor.*
OPPOSITES: skill, grace, expertise
2 = insensitivity, heavy-handedness, tactlessness, gaucheness, lack of tact, uncouthness • *He cursed himself for his clumsiness and insensitivity.*

clumsy 1 = awkward, blundering, bungling, lumbering, inept, bumbling, ponderous, ungainly, gauche, accident-prone, gawky, heavy, uncoordinated, cack-handed *(informal)*, inexpert, maladroit, ham-handed *(informal)*, like a bull in a china shop, klutzy *(U.S. & Canad. slang)*, unskilful,

butterfingered *(informal)*, ham-fisted *(informal)*, unco *(Austral. slang)* • *I'd never seen a clumsier, less coordinated boxer.*
OPPOSITES: expert, competent, skilful
2 = **unwieldy**, ill-shaped, unhandy, clunky *(informal)* • *The keyboard is a large and clumsy instrument.*
3 = **insensitive**, gauche, tactless, uncouth, graceless • *a clumsy attempt at humour*

cluster AS A NOUN = **gathering**, group, collection, bunch, knot, clump, assemblage • *A cluster of men blocked the doorway.*
▸ AS A VERB = **gather**, group, collect, bunch, assemble, flock, huddle • *The passengers clustered together in small groups.*

clutch AS A VERB 1 = **hold**, grip, embrace, grasp, cling to, clasp • *She was clutching a photograph in her hand.*
2 = **seize**, catch, grab, grasp, snatch • *I staggered and had to clutch at a chair for support.*
▸ AS A NOUN = **group**, crowd, bunch, cluster, pack, load, bevy • *He was surrounded by a clutch of pretty girls.*
▸ AS A PLURAL NOUN = **power**, hands, control, grip, possession, grasp, custody, sway, keeping, claws • *He escaped his captors' clutches by jumping from a moving vehicle.*

clutter AS A NOUN = **untidiness**, mess, disorder, confusion, litter, muddle, disarray, jumble, hotchpotch • *She preferred her work area to be free of clutter.*
OPPOSITES: order, organization, neatness
▸ AS A VERB = **litter**, scatter, strew, mess up • *I don't want to clutter the room up with too much junk.*
OPPOSITES: arrange, organize, tidy

cluttered = **untidy**, confused, disordered, littered, messy, muddled, jumbled, disarrayed • *She dreaded going into that cluttered room.*

coach AS A NOUN 1 = **instructor**, teacher, trainer, tutor, handler • *He has joined the team as a coach.*
2 = **bus**, charabanc • *I hate travelling by coach.*
▸ AS A VERB = **instruct**, train, prepare, exercise, drill, tutor, cram • *He coached me for my French A levels.*

coagulate = **congeal**, clot, thicken, curdle, jell • *The blood coagulates to stop wounds bleeding.*

coalesce = **blend**, unite, mix, combine, incorporate, integrate, merge, consolidate, come together, fuse, amalgamate, meld, cohere, commingle • *Cities, if unrestricted, tend to coalesce into bigger and bigger conurbations.*

coalition = **alliance**, union, league, association, combination, merger, integration, compact, conjunction, bloc, confederation, fusion, affiliation, amalgam, amalgamation, confederacy • *He had been opposed by a coalition of about 50 civil rights organizations.*

coarse 1 = **rough**, crude, unfinished, homespun, impure, unrefined, rough-hewn, unprocessed, unpolished, coarse-grained, unpurified • *He wore a shepherd's tunic of coarse cloth.* • *a tablespoon of coarse sea salt*
OPPOSITES: soft, polished, smooth
2 = **vulgar**, offensive, rude, indecent, improper, raunchy *(slang)*, earthy, foul-mouthed, bawdy, impure, smutty, impolite, ribald, immodest, indelicate • *He has a very coarse sense of humour.*
3 = **loutish**, rough, brutish, boorish, uncivil • *They don't know how to behave, and are coarse and insulting.*
OPPOSITES: fine, cultured, well-mannered

coarseness 1 = **roughness**, unevenness • *This gadget chops vegetables to the exact degree of coarseness or fineness required.*
2 = **vulgarity**, smut, roughness, poor taste, earthiness, crudity, offensiveness, boorishness, ribaldry, bawdiness, uncouthness, indelicacy, smuttiness • *She showed a certain coarseness in sexual matters.*

coast AS A NOUN = **shore**, border, beach, strand, seaside, coastline, seaboard, littoral • *Camp sites are usually situated along the coast.*
▸ AS A VERB = **cruise**, sail, drift, taxi, glide, freewheel • *I slipped into neutral gear and coasted down the slope.*
▸ RELATED ADJECTIVE: littoral

coat AS A NOUN 1 = **jacket**, overcoat • *He put on his coat and walked out.*
2 = **fur**, hair, skin, hide, wool, fleece, pelt • *Vitamin B6 is great for improving the condition of dogs' and horses' coats.*
3 = **layer**, covering, coating, overlay • *The front door needs a new coat of paint.*
▸ AS A VERB = **cover**, spread, plaster, smear • *Coat the fish with seasoned flour.*
▹ *See panel* **Coats and cloaks**

coating = **layer**, covering, finish, skin, sheet, coat, dusting, blanket, membrane, glaze, film, varnish, veneer, patina, lamination • *We put on the second coating of lacquer.*

coat of arms = **heraldry**, crest, insignia, escutcheon, blazonry • *the family coat of arms*

coax = **persuade**, cajole, talk into, wheedle, sweet-talk *(informal)*, prevail upon, inveigle, soft-soap *(informal)*, twist (someone's) arm, flatter, entice, beguile, allure • *After lunch she coaxed him into talking about himself.*
OPPOSITES: force, threaten, bully

cobber = **friend**, pal, mate *(informal)*, buddy *(informal)*, china *(Brit. & S. African informal)*, best friend, intimate, cock *(Brit. informal)*, close friend, comrade, chum *(informal)*, crony, alter ego, main man *(slang, chiefly U.S.)*, soul mate, homeboy *(slang, chiefly U.S.)*, bosom friend, boon companion, E hoa *(N.Z.)* • *He was just acting big in front of his cobbers.*

cobble IN PHRASES: **cobble something together** = **improvise**, devise, put together, contrive, concoct, throw together • *Politicians are trying to cobble together a peace treaty.*

cock AS A NOUN 1 = **cockerel**, rooster, chanticleer • *We heard the sound of a cock crowing in the yard.*

COATS AND CLOAKS

afghan, balmacaan, bathrobe, box coat, Burberry *(trademark)*, burnous, cape, capote, capuchin, cardinal, chesterfield, coat dress, coatee, cope, covert coat, Crombie *(trademark)*, cutaway, dolman, domino, dreadnought, dress coat, dressing gown, duffel coat, duster coat, fearnought, frock coat, fun fur coat, fur coat, gabardine, greatcoat, hacking coat, himation, housecoat, Inverness, jellaba, Jodhpuri coat, joseph, loden coat, mac, Mackinaw coat, mackintosh, manta, mantelet, mantilla, mantle, morning coat, newmarket, opera cloak, overcoat, paletot, pea jacket, parka, peignoir, pelisse, peplum, poncho, Prince Albert, raglan, raincoat, redingote, roquelaure, sheepskin coat, sherwani, slicker *(U.S. & Canad.)*, snorkel, sou'wester, spencer, surcoat, surtout, swallow-tailed coat *or* tails, tippet, topcoat, trench coat, ulster, undercoat, waterproof

2 = **phallus**, member, tool *(taboo slang)*, dick *(taboo slang)*, organ, prick *(taboo slang)*, knob *(Brit. taboo slang)*, chopper *(Brit. slang)*, plonker *(slang)*, dong *(slang)*, pecker *(U.S. & Canad. taboo slang)*, John Thomas *(taboo slang)*, weenie *(U.S. slang)*, tadger *(Brit. slang)*, schlong *(U.S. slang)*, willie *or* willy *(Brit. informal)* • *She glanced at his cock, then pointed and laughed.*

▸ **AS A VERB** = **raise**, prick up, perk up • *He suddenly cocked an ear and listened.*

cockeyed 1 = **absurd**, crazy, ludicrous, preposterous, nonsensical • *She has some cockeyed delusions about becoming a big movie star.*

2 = **crooked**, squint *(informal)*, awry, lopsided, askew, asymmetrical, skewwhiff *(Brit. informal)* • *Dusty photographs were hanging at cockeyed angles on the walls.*

cockiness = **overconfidence**, vanity, arrogance, conceit, self-assurance, egotism, brashness, presumptuousness, confidence, bumptiousness, bigheadedness • *There is a fine line between confidence and an obnoxious cockiness.*

cocksure = **overconfident**, arrogant, brash, cocky, presumptuous, bumptious, hubristic, full of yourself • *a cocksure, self-confident performer*

cocktail = **mixture**, combination, compound, blend, concoction, mix, amalgamation, admixture • *The court was told she had taken a cocktail of drugs and alcohol.*

▹ *See panel* **Cocktails**

cocky[1] = **overconfident**, arrogant, brash, swaggering, conceited, egotistical, cocksure, swollen-headed, vain, full of yourself • *He was a little cocky because he was winning all the time.*

OPPOSITES: modest, hesitant, self-effacing

cocky[2] *or* **cockie** = **farmer**, smallholder, crofter *(Scot.)*, grazier, agriculturalist, rancher, husbandman • *He got some casual work with the cane cockies on Maroochy River.*

cocoon 1 = **wrap**, swathe, envelop, swaddle, pad • *She lay on the sofa, cocooned in blankets.*

2 = **protect**, shelter, cushion, insulate, screen • *I was cocooned in my own safe little world.*

cod

▸ **NAME OF YOUNG:** codling

coddle = **pamper**, spoil, indulge, cosset, baby, nurse, pet, wet-nurse *(informal)*, mollycoddle • *She coddled her youngest son dreadfully.*

code 1 = **principles**, rules, manners, custom, convention, ethics, maxim, etiquette, system, kawa *(N.Z.)*, tikanga *(N.Z.)* • *Writers are expected to observe journalistic ethics and code of conduct.*

2 = **law**, rules, regulations, constitution, charter, canon, jurisprudence • *This crime is included in the penal code on treason.*

3 = **cipher**, cryptograph • *They used elaborate secret codes.*

codify = **systematize**, catalogue, classify, summarize, tabulate, collect, organize • *The latest draft of the agreement codifies the panel's decision.*

coerce = **force**, compel, bully, intimidate, railroad *(informal)*, constrain, bulldoze *(informal)*, dragoon, pressurize, browbeat, press-gang, twist (someone's) arm *(informal)*, drive • *He argued that the government had coerced him into resigning.*

coercion = **force**, pressure, threats, bullying, constraint, intimidation, compulsion, duress, browbeating, strong-arm tactics *(informal)* • *It was vital that the elections should be free of coercion or intimidation.*

coffee

QUOTATIONS

The morning cup of coffee has an exhilaration about it which the cheering influence of the afternoon or evening cup of tea cannot be expected to reproduce
[Oliver Wendell Holmes Sr. *Over the Teacups*]

▹ *See panel* **Coffees**

coffer AS A NOUN = **chest**, case, repository, casket, treasure chest, strongbox, kist *(Scot. & Northern English dialect)*, treasury, ark *(dialect)* • *Crossing to her clothes coffer, she jerked the lid up.*

▸ **AS A PLURAL NOUN** = **funds**, finances, reserves, assets, treasury, vaults, means, capital • *The problem is the lack of hard currency in the state's coffers.*

cogent = **convincing**, strong, powerful, effective, compelling, urgent, influential, potent, irresistible, compulsive, forceful, conclusive, weighty, forcible • *He makes a cogent argument for a more egalitarian education system.*

cogitate = **think**, consider, reflect, contemplate, deliberate, muse, ponder, meditate, mull over, ruminate • *He was silent as he cogitated on what she had just said.*

cognate = **related**, similar, allied, associated, connected, alike, affiliated, akin, analogous, kindred • *Apocalypticism and millennialism are cognate theological terms.*

cognition = **perception**, reasoning, understanding, intelligence, awareness, insight, comprehension, apprehension, discernment • *processes of perception and cognition*

cognizant *or* **cognisant** = **knowledgeable**, aware, familiar, informed, conscious, versed, switched-on *(informal)*, acquainted, sussed *(Brit. slang)*, conversant, clued-up *(informal)* • *Every man must be assumed to be cognizant of the law; ignorance is no excuse.*

cohere = **be consistent**, be logical, hang together, hold good, hold water, agree, square, correspond, consolidate, be connected, harmonize • *This article fails to cohere as a single work.*

coherence = **consistency**, rationality, concordance, consonance, congruity, union, agreement, connection, unity, correspondence • *the political structure which can lend coherence to a global enterprise*

coherent 1 = **consistent**, reasoned, organized, rational, logical, meaningful, systematic, orderly • *He has failed to work out a coherent strategy for modernising the service.*

OPPOSITES: confusing, vague, inconsistent

COCKTAILS

Americano	cold duck	glogg	mojito	rickey	snowball
Bellini	collins	Harvey Wallbanger	Moscow Mule	Rusty Nail	spritzer
Black Russian	cooler	highball	negroni	sangaree	stinger
black velvet	Cuba libre	julep	nog	sangria	swizzle
Bloody Mary	cup	kir	oenomel	sazerac	syllabub
Brandy Alexander	daiquiri	Long Island Tea	old-fashioned	screwdriver	Tom Collins
buck's fizz	dry martini	manhattan	orgasm	sidecar	whiskey sour
bullshot	eggnog	margarita	piña colada	Singapore sling	whisky mac
caudle	Gibson	martini	pink gin	sling	white lady
claret cup	gimlet	milk punch	planter's punch	Slow Screw Against the Wall	zombie
cobbler	gin sling	mint julep	punch		

COFFEES

americano	brown coffee	Continental	frappuccino	Java	mochaccino
arabica	café au lait	Costa Rican	French roast	Kenyan	robusta
black coffee	café noir	decaffeinated	instant coffee	latte	skinny latte
Blue mountain	cappuccino	*or* decaf	Irish *or* Gaelic	macchiato	Turkish coffee
Brazilian	Colombian	espresso	coffee	mocha	white coffee

2 = **articulate**, lucid, comprehensible, intelligible • *He's so calm when he speaks in public. I wish I could be that coherent.*
OPPOSITES: incomprehensible, unintelligible

cohort 1 = **supporter**, partner, associate, mate, assistant, follower, comrade, protagonist, accomplice, sidekick *(slang)*, henchman • *Drake and his cohorts were not pleased at my promotion.*
2 = **group**, set, band, contingent, batch • *We now have results for the first cohort of pupils to be assessed.*

coil AS A NOUN = **loop**, twist, curl, spiral, twirl • *Tod slung the coil of rope over his shoulder.*
▸ AS A VERB 1 = **wind**, twist, curl, loop, spiral, twine • *He turned off the water and began to coil the hose.*
2 = **curl**, wind, twist, snake, loop, entwine, twine, wreathe, convolute • *A python had coiled itself around the branch of the tree.*

coin AS A NOUN = **money**, change, cash, silver, copper, dosh *(Brit. & Austral. slang)*, specie, wonga *(slang)*, kembla *(Austral. slang)* • *His pocket was full of coins.*
▸ AS A VERB = **invent**, create, make up, frame, forge, conceive, originate, formulate, fabricate, think up • *The phrase 'cosmic ray' was coined by R. A. Millikan in 1925.*
▸ RELATED ADJECTIVE: nummary
▸ RELATED ENTHUSIAST: numismatist

coincide 1 = **occur simultaneously**, coexist, synchronize, be concurrent • *The exhibition coincides with the 50th anniversary of his death.*
2 = **agree**, match, accord, square, correspond, tally, concur, harmonize • *a case in which public and private interests coincide*
OPPOSITES: part, separate, disagree

coincidence = **chance**, accident, luck, fluke, eventuality, stroke of luck, happy accident, fortuity • *By an amazing coincidence, their sons were all born on the same day.*

coincident AS AN ADJECTIVE = **coinciding**, correspondent, coordinate, concomitant, contemporaneous, synchronous • *The Moon's path through the sky is more or less coincident with the Sun's.*
▸ IN PHRASES: **coincident with something** = **in agreement with**, compatible with, harmonious with, concurring with, consonant with, in accord with • *His wishes were coincident with hers.*

coincidental = **accidental**, unintentional, unintended, unplanned, fortuitous, fluky *(informal)*, chance, casual • *Any resemblance to actual persons, places or events is purely coincidental.*
OPPOSITES: planned, calculated, deliberate

coitus = **sexual intercourse**, sex, coupling, congress, mating, nookie *(slang)*, copulation, rumpy-pumpy *(slang)*, coition, the other *(informal)*, union, poontang *(taboo slang)*, rumpo *(slang)* • *During coitus, the male ejaculates millions of sperm cells.*

cold AS AN ADJECTIVE 1 = **chilly**, biting, freezing, bitter, raw, chill, harsh, bleak, arctic, icy, frosty, wintry, frigid, inclement, parky *(Brit. informal)*, cool • *It was bitterly cold outside.*
OPPOSITES: hot, heated, warm
2 = **freezing**, frozen, chilled, numb, chilly, shivery, benumbed, frozen to the marrow • *I'm hungry, I'm cold and I have nowhere to sleep.*
3 = **distant**, reserved, indifferent, aloof, glacial, cold-blooded, apathetic, frigid, unresponsive, unfeeling, passionless, undemonstrative, standoffish • *His wife is a cold, unfeeling woman.*
OPPOSITES: open, loving, emotional
4 = **unfriendly**, indifferent, stony, lukewarm, glacial, unmoved, unsympathetic, apathetic, frigid, inhospitable, unresponsive • *The president is likely to receive a cold reception when he speaks today.*
OPPOSITES: warm, friendly, sympathetic
▸ AS A NOUN = **coldness**, chill, frigidity, chilliness, frostiness, iciness, inclemency • *He must have come inside to get out of the cold.*
▸ RELATED PHOBIA: cheimaphobia

cold-blooded = **callous**, cruel, savage, brutal, ruthless, steely, heartless, inhuman, merciless, unmoved, dispassionate, barbarous, pitiless, unfeeling, unemotional, stony-hearted • *These callous, cold-blooded killers butchered six people.*
OPPOSITES: feeling, open, caring

cold-hearted = **heartless**, harsh, detached, indifferent, insensitive, callous, unkind, inhuman, unsympathetic, uncaring, frigid, unfeeling, hardhearted, stony-hearted • *That Harriet is a cold-hearted bitch.*

collaborate 1 = **work together**, team up, join forces, cooperate, play ball *(informal)*, participate • *The two men collaborated on an album in 1986.*
2 = **conspire**, cooperate, collude, fraternize • *He was accused of having collaborated with the secret police.*

collaboration 1 = **teamwork**, partnership, cooperation, association, alliance, concert • *There is substantial collaboration with neighbouring departments.*
2 = **conspiring**, cooperation, collusion, fraternization • *rumours of his collaboration with the occupying forces during the war*

collaborator 1 = **co-worker**, partner, colleague, associate, team-mate, confederate • *My wife was an important collaborator on the novel.*
2 = **traitor**, turncoat, quisling, collaborationist, fraternizer • *Two alleged collaborators were shot dead by masked activists.*

collapse AS A VERB 1 = **fall down**, fall, give way, subside, cave in, crumple, fall apart at the seams • *A section of the Bay Bridge had collapsed.*
2 = **fail**, fold, founder, break down, fall through, come to nothing, go belly-up *(informal)* • *His business empire collapsed under a massive burden of debt.*
3 = **faint**, break down, pass out, black out, swoon *(literary)*, crack up *(informal)*, keel over *(informal)*, flake out *(informal)* • *It's common to see people in the streets collapsing from hunger.*
▸ AS A NOUN 1 = **falling down**, ruin, falling apart, cave-in, disintegration, subsidence • *Floods and a collapse of the tunnel roof were a constant risk.*
2 = **failure**, slump, breakdown, flop, downfall • *Their economy is teetering on the edge of collapse.*
3 = **faint**, breakdown, blackout, prostration • *A few days after his collapse he was sitting up in bed.*

collar = **seize**, catch, arrest, appropriate, grab, capture, nail *(informal)*, nab *(informal)*, apprehend, lay hands on • *As Kerr fled towards the exit, Boycott collared him.*

collarbone
▸ TECHNICAL NAME: clavicle

collate = **collect**, gather, organize, assemble, compose, adduce, systematize • *Roberts collated the data on which the study was based.*

collateral = **security**, guarantee, deposit, assurance, surety, pledge • *Many people here cannot borrow from banks because they lack collateral.*

colleague = **fellow worker**, partner, ally, associate, assistant, team-mate, companion, comrade, helper, collaborator, confederate, auxiliary, workmate, coadjutor *(rare)*, confrère • *Three of my colleagues have been made redundant.*

collect AS A VERB 1 = **gather**, save, assemble, heap, accumulate, aggregate, amass, stockpile, hoard • *Two young girls were collecting firewood.*
OPPOSITES: spread, distribute, scatter
2 = **fetch**, get, meet, pick up • *I collected her at the station.*
3 = **raise**, secure, gather, obtain, acquire, muster, solicit • *They collected donations for a fund to help the earthquake victims.*
4 = **assemble**, meet, rally, cluster, come together, convene, converge, congregate, flock together, foregather • *A crowd collected outside.*
OPPOSITES: scatter, disperse
▸ IN PHRASES: **collect yourself** = **recover**, pull yourself together, get *or* take a hold of yourself, regain your composure • *She paused for a moment to collect herself*

collected = **calm**, together *(slang)*, cool, confident, composed, poised, serene, sedate, self-controlled, unfazed *(informal)*, unperturbed, unruffled, self-possessed, keeping your cool, unperturbable, as cool as a cucumber, chilled *(informal)* • *Police say she was cool and collected during her interrogation.*
OPPOSITES: troubled, emotional, nervous

collection 1 = **accumulation**, set, store, mass, pile, heap, stockpile, hoard, congeries • *He has gathered a large collection of prints and paintings over the years.*
2 = **compilation**, accumulation, anthology • *Two years ago he published a collection of short stories.*
3 = **group**, company, crowd, gathering, assembly, cluster, congregation, assortment, assemblage • *A collection of people of all ages assembled to pay their respects.*
4 = **gathering**, acquisition, accumulation • *computer systems designed to speed up the collection of information*
5 = **contribution**, donation, alms • *I asked my headmaster if we could arrange a collection for the refugees.*
6 = **offering**, offertory • *I put a five-pound note in the church collection.*

collective 1 = **joint**, united, shared, common, combined, corporate, concerted, unified, cooperative • *It was a collective decision taken by the full board.*
OPPOSITES: individual, split, divided
2 = **combined**, aggregate, composite, cumulative • *Their collective volume wasn't very large.*
OPPOSITES: individual, separate, uncombined

collector
▹ *See panel* **Collectors and enthusiasts**

college
▹ *See panel* **Schools, colleges and universities**

collide 1 = **crash**, clash, meet head-on, come into collision • *Two trains collided head-on early this morning.*
2 = **conflict**, clash, be incompatible, be at variance • *It is likely that their interests will collide.*

collision 1 = **crash**, impact, accident, smash, bump, pile-up *(informal)*, prang *(informal)* • *Their van was involved in a collision with a car.*
2 = **conflict**, opposition, clash, clashing, encounter, disagreement, incompatibility • *a collision between two strong personalities*

colloquial = **informal**, familiar, everyday, vernacular, conversational, demotic, idiomatic • *He converses in colloquial Japanese as easily as in English.*

COLLECTORS AND ENTHUSIASTS

ailurophile	cats
arctophile	teddy bears
audiophile	high-fidelity sound reproduction
automobilist	cars
bibliophile	books
brolliologist	umbrellas
campanologist	bell-ringing
cartophilist	cigarette cards
cruciverbalist	crosswords
deltiologist	picture postcards
discophile	gramophone records
fusilatelist	phonecards
herbalist	herbs
lepidopterist	moths and butterflies
medallist	medals
numismatist	coins
oenophile	wine
paranumismatist	coin-like objects
philatelist	stamps
phillumenist	matchbox labels
phraseologist	phrases
scripophile	share certificates
vexillologist	flags
zoophile	animals

collude = **conspire**, scheme, plot, intrigue, collaborate, contrive, abet, connive, be in cahoots *(informal)*, machinate • *Several local officials are in jail on charges of colluding with the Mafia.*

collusion = **conspiracy**, intrigue, deceit, complicity, connivance, secret understanding • *He found no evidence of collusion between record companies and retailers.*

colonist = **settler**, immigrant, pioneer, colonial, homesteader *(U.S.)*, colonizer, frontiersman • *The apple was brought over here by the colonists when they came.*

colonize = **settle**, populate, put down roots in, people, pioneer, open up • *The first British attempt to colonize Ireland was in the twelfth century.*

colonnade = **cloisters**, arcade, portico, covered walk • *We walked down the stone pathway past the colonnade.*

colony = **settlement**, territory, province, possession, dependency, outpost, dominion, satellite state, community • *Cyprus, a former British colony, gained independence in 1960.*

colossal = **huge**, massive, vast, enormous, immense, titanic, gigantic, monumental, monstrous, mammoth, mountainous, stellar *(informal)*, prodigious, gargantuan, fuck-off *(offensive taboo slang)*, herculean, elephantine, ginormous *(informal)*, humongous *or* humungous *(U.S. slang)*, supersize • *A colossal statue stands in the square.* • *The task they face is colossal.*
OPPOSITES: little, small, tiny

colour *or (U.S.)* **color** AS A NOUN 1 = **hue**, tone, shade, tint, tinge, tincture, colourway • *The badges come in twenty different colours and shapes.*
2 = **paint**, stain, dye, tint, pigment, tincture, coloration, colourwash, colorant • *the latest range of lip and eye colours*
3 = **skin colour**, race, complexion, ethnicity, pigmentation • *His colour and ethnic origins are not the issue here.*
4 = **rosiness**, glow, bloom, flush, blush, brilliance, redness, vividness, ruddiness • *There was a touch of colour in her cheeks.*

5 = **liveliness**, life, interest, excitement, animation, zest • *The ceremony brought a touch of colour to the normally drab proceedings.*

▸ AS A PLURAL NOUN 1 = **flag**, standard, banner, emblem, ensign • *Troops raised the country's colours in a special ceremony.*
2 = **kit**, strip, uniform, regalia • *I was wearing the team's colours.*
3 = **nature**, quality, character, aspect, personality, stamp, traits, temperament • *After we were married, he showed his true colours.*

▸ AS A VERB 1 = **tint**, stain, dye • *Saffron can be used to colour the rice yellow.*
2 = **blush**, flush, crimson, redden, go crimson, burn, go as red as a beetroot • *He couldn't help noticing that she coloured slightly.*
3 = **influence**, affect, prejudice, distort, pervert, taint, slant • *The attitude of parents colours the way their children behave.*
4 = **exaggerate**, disguise, embroider, misrepresent, falsify, gloss over, airbrush • *He wrote a highly coloured account of his childhood.*

▸ RELATED PHOBIA: chromophobia

▹ *See panels* **Shades from black to white; Shades of blue; Shades of brown; Shades of green; Shades of orange; Shades of purple; Shades of red; Shades of yellow**

colourful 1 = **bright**, rich, brilliant, intense, vivid, vibrant, psychedelic, motley, variegated, jazzy *(informal)*, multicoloured, Day-glo *(trademark)*, kaleidoscopic • *Everyone was dressed in colourful clothes.*
OPPOSITES: dark, faded, drab
2 = **interesting**, rich, unusual, stimulating, graphic, lively, distinctive, vivid, picturesque, characterful • *an irreverent and colourful tale of Restoration England*
OPPOSITES: flat, boring, dull

colourless 1 = **uncoloured**, faded, neutral, bleached, washed out, achromatic • *a colourless, almost odourless liquid*
2 = **ashen**, washed out, wan, sickly, anaemic • *Her face was colourless, and she was shaking.*
OPPOSITES: healthy, glowing, radiant
3 = **uninteresting**, dull, tame, dreary, drab, lacklustre, vacuous, insipid, vapid, characterless, unmemorable • *His wife is a drab, colourless little woman.*
OPPOSITES: interesting, bright, exciting

colt
▸ COLLECTIVE NOUN: rag

column 1 = **pillar**, support, post, shaft, upright, obelisk, pilaster • *Great stone steps led past Greek columns to the main building.*
2 = **line**, train, row, file, rank, string, queue, procession, cavalcade • *There were reports of columns of military vehicles appearing on the streets.*
3 = **article**, story, feature, piece, item • *His name features frequently in the social columns of the tabloid newspapers.*

columnist = **journalist**, correspondent, editor, reporter, critic, reviewer, gossip columnist, journo *(slang)*, hackette *(derogatory)* • *He is a columnist for the Chicago Tribune.*

coma = **unconsciousness**, trance, oblivion, lethargy, stupor, torpor, somnolence, insensibility • *She had slipped into a coma by the time she reached the hospital.*

comatose 1 = **unconscious**, in a coma, out cold, insensible, insensate • *The right side of my brain had been so severely bruised that I was comatose for a month.*
2 = **inert**, stupefied, out cold, somnolent, torpid, insensible, dead to the world *(informal)*, drugged • *Granpa lies comatose on the sofa.*

comb 1 = **untangle**, arrange, groom, dress • *Her reddish hair was cut short and neatly combed.*
2 = **search**, hunt through, sweep, rake, sift, scour, rummage, ransack, forage, fossick *(Austral. & N.Z.)*, go through with a fine-tooth comb • *Officers combed the woods for the murder weapon.*

combat AS A NOUN = **fight**, war, action, battle, conflict, engagement, warfare, skirmish • *Over 16 million men died in combat during the war.*
OPPOSITES: peace, agreement, surrender

▸ AS A VERB = **fight**, battle against, oppose, contest, engage, cope with, resist, defy, withstand, struggle against, contend with, do battle with, strive against • *new government measures to combat crime*
OPPOSITES: support, accept, give up on

combatant AS A NOUN = **fighter**, soldier, warrior, contender, gladiator, belligerent, antagonist, fighting man, serviceman *or* servicewoman • *His grandfather was a Boer war combatant.*

▸ AS AN ADJECTIVE = **fighting**, warring, battling, conflicting, opposing, contending, belligerent, combative • *the monitoring of ceasefires between combatant states*

combative = **aggressive**, militant, contentious, belligerent, antagonistic, pugnacious, warlike, carnivorous *(informal)*, bellicose, truculent, quarrelsome, aggers *(Austral. slang)* • *Mrs Thatcher's combative oratorical style*
OPPOSITES: pacific, peaceful, nonaggressive

combination 1 = **mixture**, mix, compound, blend, composite, amalgam, amalgamation, meld, coalescence • *A combination of factors are to blame.*
2 = **association**, union, alliance, coalition, merger, federation, consortium, unification, syndicate, confederation, cartel, confederacy, cabal • *The company's chairman has proposed a merger or other business combination.*

combine 1 = **amalgamate**, marry, mix, bond, bind, compound, blend, incorporate, integrate, merge, put together, fuse, synthesize • *Combine the flour with water to make a paste.* • *Her tale combines a strong storyline with sly humour.*
OPPOSITES: separate, divide, dissolve
2 = **join together**, link, connect, integrate, merge, fuse, amalgamate, meld • *Disease and starvation are combining to kill thousands.*
3 = **unite**, associate, team up, unify, get together, collaborate, join forces, cooperate, join together, pool resources • *Different states or groups can combine to enlarge their markets.*
OPPOSITES: part, separate, split up

combustible = **flammable**, explosive, incendiary, inflammable • *Methane is a highly combustible gas.*

come AS A VERB 1 = **approach**, near, advance, move towards, draw near • *We heard the train coming.* • *Tom, come here and look at this.*
2 = **arrive**, move, appear, enter, turn up *(informal)*, show up *(informal)*, materialize • *Two police officers came into the hall.* • *My brother's coming from Canada tomorrow.*
3 = **reach**, extend • *The water came to his chest.*
4 = **happen**, fall, occur, take place, come about, come to pass • *Saturday's fire-bombing came without warning.*
5 = **be available**, be made, be offered, be produced, be on offer • *The wallpaper comes in black and white only.*
6 = **climax**, orgasm, ejaculate, have an orgasm, achieve orgasm • *My boyfriend always comes too soon when we have sex.*

▸ IN PHRASES: **come about** = **happen**, result, occur, take place, arise, transpire *(informal)*, befall, come to pass • *Any possible solution to the Irish question can only come about through dialogue.*

come across as something *or* **someone** = **seem**, look, seem to be, look like, appear to be, give the impression of being, have the *or* every appearance of being, strike you as (being) • *He came across as an extremely pleasant and charming young man.*

come across someone = **meet**, encounter, run into, bump into *(informal)* • *I recently came across a college friend in New York.*

come across something = **find**, discover, notice, unearth, stumble upon, hit upon, chance upon, happen upon, light upon • *He came across the jawbone of a 4.5 million-year-old marsupial.*
come along 1 = **hurry**, let's go, hurry up, get moving, get a move on, rattle your dags *(N.Z. informal)* • *Come along! There's no sense in hanging around.*
2 = **progress**, develop, get on, come on, go forward, roll up, make headway • *A spokesman says the talks are coming along well.*
3 = **recover**, improve, pick up, progress, get on, rally, mend, perk up, recuperate • *How's he coming along after his operation?*
come apart = **fall to pieces**, break, separate, tear, split, crumble, give way, fall apart, disintegrate • *The whole thing just came apart in my hands.*
come at someone = **attack**, charge, rush, go for, assault, fly at, assail, fall upon, rush at • *A madman came at him with an axe.*
come back = **return**, reappear, re-enter • *She came back half an hour later.*
come between people = **separate**, part, divide, alienate, estrange, set at odds • *It's difficult to imagine anything coming between them.*
come by something = **get**, win, land, score *(slang)*, secure, obtain, acquire, get hold of, procure, take possession of • *How did you come by that cheque?*
come clean about something = **confess to**, admit, reveal, declare, acknowledge, disclose, cough *(slang)*, divulge, own up to, come out of the closet about, spill your guts about *(slang)*, 'fess up to *(U.S.)* • *I thought it best to come clean about our affair.*
come down 1 = **decrease**, fall, drop, reduce, go down, diminish, lessen, become lower • *Interest rates are coming down.*
2 = **fall**, descend • *The rain began to come down.*
come down on someone = **reprimand**, blast, carpet *(informal)*, flame *(informal)*, put down, criticize, jump on *(informal)*, rebuke, dress down *(informal)*, tear into *(informal)*, diss *(slang, chiefly U.S.)*, read the riot act, lambast(e), bawl out *(informal)*, rap over the knuckles, chew out *(U.S. & Canad. informal)*, tear (someone) off a strip *(Brit. informal)*, give (someone) a rocket *(Brit. & N.Z. informal)* • *If she came down too hard on him, he would rebel.*
come down on something = **decide on**, choose, favour • *He clearly came down on the side of the President.*
come down to something = **amount to**, boil down to • *In the end it all comes down to a matter of personal preference.*
come down with something = **catch**, get, take, contract, fall victim to, fall ill, be stricken with, take sick, sicken with • *He came down with chickenpox.*
come forward = **volunteer**, step forward, present yourself, offer your services • *A witness came forward to say that she had seen him that night.*
come from something 1 = **be from**, originate, hail from, be a native of • *Nearly half the students come from France.*
2 = **be obtained**, be from, issue, emerge, flow, arise, originate, emanate • *Chocolate comes from the cacao tree.*
come in 1 = **arrive**, enter, appear, show up *(informal)*, cross the threshold • *They were scared when they first came in.*
2 = **finish** • *My horse came in third in the second race.*
come in for something = **receive**, get, suffer, endure, be subjected to, bear the brunt of, be the object of • *The plans have already come in for fierce criticism.*
come into something = **inherit**, be left, acquire, succeed to, be bequeathed, fall heir to • *My father has just come into a fortune.*
come off = **succeed**, work out, be successful, pan out *(informal)*, turn out well • *It was a good try but it didn't quite come off.*
come on 1 = **progress**, develop, improve, advance, proceed, make headway • *He is coming on very well at the violin.*
2 = **begin**, appear, take place • *Winter is coming on.*
come out 1 = **be published**, appear, be released, be issued, be launched • *The book comes out this week.*
2 = **be revealed**, emerge, be reported, be announced, become apparent, come to light, be divulged • *The truth is beginning to come out now.*
3 = **turn out**, result, end up, work out, pan out *(informal)* • *I'm sure it will come out all right in the end.*
come out with something = **say**, speak, utter, let out • *Everyone burst out laughing when he came out with this remark.*
come round *or* **around** 1 = **call**, visit, drop in, stop by, pop in • *Beryl came round last night to apologize.*
2 = **change your opinion**, yield, concede, mellow, relent, accede, acquiesce • *Don't worry, she'll come round eventually.* • *It looks like they're coming around to our way of thinking.*
3 = **regain consciousness**, come to, recover, rally, revive • *When I came round I was on the kitchen floor.*
come through = **succeed**, triumph, prevail, make the grade *(informal)* • *He's putting his job at risk if he doesn't come through.*
come through something = **survive**, overcome, endure, withstand, weather, pull through • *We've come through some rough times.*
come to = **revive**, recover, rally, come round, regain consciousness • *When he came to and raised his head he saw Barney.*
come to something = **amount to**, total, add up to • *The bill came to over a hundred pounds.*
come up = **happen**, occur, arise, turn up, spring up, crop up • *Sorry I'm late – something came up at home.*
come up to something = **measure up to**, meet, match, approach, rival, equal, compare with, resemble, admit of comparison with, stand *or* bear comparison with • *Her work did not come up to his exacting standards.*
come up with something = **produce**, offer, provide, present, suggest, advance, propose, submit, furnish • *Several members have come up with suggestions of their own.*

comeback 1 = **return**, revival, rebound, resurgence, rally, recovery, triumph • *Sixties singing star Petula Clark is making a comeback.*
2 = **response**, reply, retort, retaliation, riposte, rejoinder • *I tried to think of a witty comeback.*

comedian = **comic**, laugh *(informal)*, wit, clown, funny man, humorist, wag, joker, jester, dag *(N.Z. informal)*, card *(informal)* • *After a career as a comedian, he turned to serious drama.*

comedown 1 = **decline**, reverse, demotion • *His new job is a comedown after the high office he held previously.*
2 = **disappointment**, blow, humiliation, whammy *(informal, chiefly U.S.)*, letdown, anticlimax • *After all the build-up, the wedding itself was a bit of a comedown.*

comedy 1 = **light entertainment**, sitcom *(informal)*, soap opera *(slang)*, soapie *or* soapy *(Austral.)* • *Channel Four's comedy, 'Father Ted'*
OPPOSITES: opera, tragedy, melodrama
2 = **humour**, fun, joking, farce, jesting, slapstick, wisecracking, hilarity, witticisms, facetiousness, chaffing • *He and I provided the comedy with songs and monologues.*
OPPOSITES: sadness, seriousness, melancholy

QUOTATIONS

Comedy is an imitation of the common errors of our life
[Sir Philip Sidney *The Defence of Poetry*]

The world is a comedy to those that think, a tragedy to those that feel
[Horace Walpole *Letters*]

All tragedies are finish'd by a death,
All comedies are ended by a marriage
[Lord Byron *Don Juan*]

You can't be beautiful and sexy forever. You can be funny
[Diane Keaton]

comely = **good-looking**, pretty, fair, beautiful, attractive, lovely, handsome, blooming, cute, graceful, becoming, pleasing, wholesome, bonny, winsome, buxom, fit *(Brit. informal)* • *She was a large, comely girl with a mass of dark brown hair.*
OPPOSITES: homely, plain, ugly

comet
▸ RELATED PHOBIA: cometophobia

comeuppance = **punishment**, dues, deserts, retribution, chastening, recompense, due reward, requital, merit • *The central character is an evil man who gets his comeuppance in the end.*

comfort AS A NOUN 1 = **ease**, luxury, wellbeing, opulence • *She had enough money to live in comfort for the rest of her life.*
2 = **consolation**, cheer, encouragement, succour, help, support, aid, relief, ease, compensation, alleviation • *I tried to find some words of comfort to offer her.*
OPPOSITES: discomfort, irritation, annoyance
▸ AS A VERB = **console**, encourage, ease, cheer, strengthen, relieve, reassure, soothe, hearten, solace, assuage, gladden, commiserate with • *He put his arm round her, trying to comfort her.*
OPPOSITES: trouble, excite, distress

comfortable 1 = **loose-fitting**, loose, adequate, ample, snug, roomy, commodious • *Dress in loose comfortable clothes that do not make you feel restricted.*
OPPOSITES: tight, tight-fitting, skin-tight
2 = **pleasant**, homely, easy, relaxing, delightful, enjoyable, cosy, agreeable, restful • *A home should be comfortable and friendly.*
OPPOSITES: uncomfortable, inadequate, unpleasant
3 = **at ease**, happy, at home, contented, relaxed, serene • *Lie down on your bed and make yourself comfortable.*
OPPOSITES: troubled, nervous, uncomfortable
4 = **well-off**, prosperous, affluent, well-to-do, comfortably-off, in clover *(informal)* • *She came from a stable, comfortable, middle-class family.*

comforting = **consoling**, encouraging, cheering, reassuring, soothing, heart-warming, consolatory, inspiriting • *My mother had just died and I found this book very comforting.*
OPPOSITES: worrying, upsetting, alarming

comic AS AN ADJECTIVE = **funny**, amusing, witty, humorous, farcical, comical, light, joking, droll, facetious, jocular, waggish • *The novel is both comic and tragic.*
OPPOSITES: serious, touching, sad
▸ AS A NOUN = **comedian**, funny man, humorist, wit, clown, wag, jester, dag *(N.Z. informal)*, buffoon • *At that time he was still a penniless, unknown comic.*

comical = **funny**, entertaining, comic, silly, amusing, ridiculous, diverting, absurd, hilarious, ludicrous, humorous, priceless, laughable, farcical, whimsical, zany, droll, risible, side-splitting • *The whole situation suddenly struck her as being comical.*

coming AS AN ADJECTIVE 1 = **approaching**, next, future, near, due, forthcoming, imminent, in store, impending, at hand, upcoming, on the cards, in the wind, nigh, just round the corner • *This obviously depends on the weather in the coming months.*
2 = **up-and-coming**, future, promising, aspiring • *He is widely regarded as the coming man of Scottish rugby.*
▸ AS A NOUN = **arrival**, approach, advent, accession • *Most of us welcome the coming of summer.*

command AS A VERB 1 = **order**, tell, charge, demand, require, direct, bid, compel, enjoin • *He commanded his troops to attack.*
OPPOSITES: ask, appeal (to), beg
2 = **receive**, get, be given, gain • *He was an excellent physician who commanded the respect of his colleagues.*
3 = **have authority over**, lead, head, control, rule, manage, handle, dominate, govern, administer, supervise, be in charge of, reign over • *the French general who commands the UN troops in the region*
OPPOSITES: follow, be subordinate to, be inferior to
▸ AS A NOUN 1 = **order**, demand, direction, instruction, requirement, decree, bidding, mandate, canon, directive, injunction, fiat, ultimatum, commandment, edict, behest, precept • *The tanker failed to respond to a command to stop.*
2 = **domination**, control, rule, grasp, sway, mastery, dominion, upper hand, power, government • *the struggle for command of the air*
3 = **management**, power, control, charge, authority, direction, supervision • *In 1942 he took command of 108 Squadron.*
4 = **knowledge**, ability, grasp, mastery, comprehension, fluency • *His command of English was excellent.*

commandeer = **seize**, appropriate, hijack, confiscate, requisition, sequester, expropriate, sequestrate • *The soldiers commandeered vehicles in the capital.*

commander = **leader**, director, chief, officer, boss, head, captain, bass *(S. African)*, ruler, commander-in-chief, commanding officer, C in C, C.O., sherang *(Austral. & N.Z.)* • *The commander and some of his men had been released.*

commanding 1 = **dominant**, controlling, dominating, superior, decisive, advantageous, win-win • *Right now you're in a very commanding position.*
2 = **authoritative**, imposing, impressive, compelling, assertive, forceful, autocratic, peremptory • *The voice at the other end of the line was serious and commanding.*
OPPOSITES: retiring, weak, unassertive

commemorate = **celebrate**, remember, honour, recognize, salute, pay tribute to, immortalize, memorialize • *a gallery of paintings commemorating great moments in baseball history*
OPPOSITES: forget, ignore, overlook

commemoration 1 = **ceremony**, tribute, memorial service, testimonial • *A special commemoration for her will be held next week.*
2 = **remembrance**, honour, tribute • *a march in commemoration of Malcolm X*

commemorative = **memorial**, celebratory • *The Queen unveiled a commemorative plaque.*

commence 1 = **embark on**, start, open, begin, initiate, originate, instigate, inaugurate, enter upon • *They commenced a systematic search of the area.*
OPPOSITES: end, stop, finish
2 = **start**, open, begin, go ahead • *The academic year commences at the beginning of October.*
OPPOSITES: end, stop, finish

commencement = **beginning**, start, opening, launch, birth, origin, dawn, outset, onset, initiation, inauguration, inception, embarkation • *All applicants should be at least 16 years of age at the commencement of this course.*

commend 1 = **praise**, acclaim, applaud, compliment, extol, approve, big up *(slang, chiefly Caribbean)*, eulogize, speak highly of • *She was highly commended for her bravery.*
OPPOSITES: attack, knock *(informal)*, criticize
2 = **recommend**, suggest, approve, advocate, endorse, vouch for, put in a good word for • *I can commend it to you as a sensible course of action.*
3 = **entrust**, deliver, commit, yield, hand over, confide, consign • *Lord, unto Thy hands I commend my spirit.*
OPPOSITES: keep, withdraw, retain

commendable = **praiseworthy**, deserving, worthy, admirable, exemplary, creditable, laudable, meritorious, estimable • *He has acted with commendable speed.*

commendation = **praise**, credit, approval, acclaim, encouragement, Brownie points, approbation, acclamation, good opinion, panegyric, encomium • *Both teams deserve commendation for their performance.*

commensurate 1 = **equivalent**, consistent, corresponding, comparable, compatible, in accord, proportionate, coextensive • *Employees are paid salaries commensurate with those of teachers.*
2 = **appropriate**, fitting, fit, due, sufficient, adequate • *The resources available are in no way commensurate to the need.*

comment AS A VERB 1 = **remark**, say, note, mention, point out, observe, utter, opine, interpose • *Stuart commented that this was very true.*
2 *usually with* **on** = **remark on**, explain, talk about, discuss, speak about, say something about, allude to, elucidate, make a comment on • *So far Mr Cook has not commented on these reports.*
▸ AS A NOUN 1 = **remark**, statement, observation • *He made these comments at a news conference.*
2 = **note**, criticism, explanation, illustration, commentary, exposition, annotation, elucidation • *He had added a few comments in the margin.*
3 = **discussion**, talk, debate, discourse, deliberation • *There's been a lot of comment lately on miscarriages of justice.*

commentary 1 = **narration**, report, review, explanation, description, voice-over • *He gave the listening crowd a running commentary on the game.*
2 = **analysis**, notes, review, critique, treatise • *He will be writing a twice-weekly commentary on American society and culture.*
3 = **explanation**, illustration, exposition, annotation, exegesis, elucidation • *The review includes a textual commentary.*

commentator 1 = **reporter**, special correspondent, sportscaster, commenter • *a sports commentator*
2 = **critic**, interpreter, expositor, annotator • *He is a commentator on African affairs.*

commerce 1 = **trade**, business, dealing, exchange, traffic, merchandising • *They have made their fortunes from industry and commerce.*
2 (*Literary*) = **relations**, communication, dealings, intercourse, socializing • *The hours tick by in pleasant social commerce.*

commercial AS AN ADJECTIVE 1 = **mercantile**, business, trade, trading, sales • *In its heyday it was a major centre of commercial activity.*
2 = **profitable**, popular, in demand, marketable, saleable • *Whether the project will be a commercial success is still uncertain.*
3 = **materialistic**, mercenary, profit-making, venal, monetary, exploited, pecuniary • *There's a feeling among a lot of people that music has become too commercial.*
▸ AS A NOUN = **advertisement**, ad, advert • *The government has launched a campaign of television commercials and leaflets*

commiserate *often with* **with** = **sympathize**, pity, feel for, console, condole • *When I lost, he commiserated with me.*

commiseration = **sympathy**, pity, compassion, consolation, condolence, fellow feeling • *I was moved to tears of pity and deep commiseration.*

commission AS A VERB = **appoint**, order, contract, select, engage, delegate, nominate, authorize, empower, depute • *You can commission them to paint something especially for you.*
▸ AS A NOUN 1 = **duty**, authority, trust, charge, task, function, mission, employment, appointment, warrant, mandate, errand • *She approached him with a commission to write the screen play for the film.*
2 = **fee**, cut, compensation, percentage, allowance, royalties, brokerage, rake-off (*slang*) • *He got a commission for bringing in new clients.*
3 = **committee**, board, representatives, commissioners, delegation, deputation, body of commissioners • *The authorities have been asked to set up a commission to investigate the murders.*

commit AS A VERB 1 = **do**, perform, carry out, execute, enact, perpetrate • *I have never committed any crime.*
2 = **give**, deliver, engage, deposit, hand over, commend, entrust, consign • *The government have committed billions of pounds for a programme to reduce acid rain.*
OPPOSITES: receive, withhold
3 = **put in custody**, confine, imprison, consign • *His drinking caused him to be committed to a psychiatric hospital.*
OPPOSITES: free, release, let out
▸ IN PHRASES: **commit yourself to something** = **pledge to**, promise to, bind yourself to, make yourself liable for, obligate yourself to • *She didn't want to commit herself to working at weekends.*

commitment 1 = **dedication**, loyalty, devotion, adherence • *a commitment to the ideals of Bolshevism*
OPPOSITES: wavering, indecisiveness, vacillation
2 = **responsibility**, tie, duty, obligation, liability, engagement • *I've got too many commitments to take on anything more right now.*
3 = **pledge**, promise, guarantee, undertaking, vow, assurance, word • *We made a commitment to keep working together.*
OPPOSITES: negation, disavowal

PROVERBS
In for a penny, in for a pound
One might as well be hanged for a sheep as a lamb

committed 1 = **dedicated**, devoted, loyal, intent, faithful, devout, resolute, adherent, dutiful • *He said the government remained committed to attaining peace.*
2 = **pledged**, involved, promised, tied, engaged, obliged, duty-bound • *It would have meant cancelling several meetings which I was already committed to.*

committee = **group**, commission, panel, delegation, subcommittee, deputation • *My report was circulated to all committee members.*
▹ *See panel* **Family**

QUOTATIONS
a group of men who individually can do nothing but as a group decide that nothing can be done
[attributed to Fred Allen]
a group of the unwilling, chosen from the unfit, to do the unnecessary
[Richard Harkness]
Committees are to get everybody together and homogenize their thinking
[Art Linkletter *A Child's Garden of Misinformation*]

PROVERBS
A committee is a group of men who keep minutes and waste hours

commodious = **roomy**, large, comfortable, extensive, ample, spacious, expansive, capacious • *Big terraces of commodious houses went up.*

commodity *usually plural* = **goods**, produce, stock, products, merchandise, wares • *The government increased prices on several basic commodities.*

common 1 = **usual**, standard, daily, regular, ordinary, familiar, plain, conventional, routine, frequent, everyday, customary, commonplace, vanilla (*slang*), habitual, run-of-the-mill, humdrum, stock, workaday, bog-standard (*Brit. & Irish slang*), a dime a dozen • *Earthquakes are fairly common in this part of the world.*
OPPOSITES: strange, rare, unusual
2 = **popular**, general, accepted, standard, routine, widespread, universal, prevailing, prevalent • *It is common practice these days to administer vitamin K during childbirth.*
3 = **shared**, collective • *They share a common language.*
4 = **ordinary**, average, simple, typical, undistinguished, dinky-di (*Austral. informal*) • *He proclaims himself to be the voice of the common man.*
OPPOSITES: important, famous, superior

5 = vulgar, low, inferior, coarse, plebeian • *She might be a little common at times, but she was certainly not boring.*
OPPOSITES: cultured, sensitive, refined
6 = collective, public, community, social, communal • *social policies which promote the common good*
OPPOSITES: private, personal

commonplace AS AN ADJECTIVE **= everyday**, common, ordinary, widespread, pedestrian, customary, mundane, vanilla *(slang)*, banal, run-of-the-mill, humdrum, dime-a-dozen *(informal)* • *Foreign vacations have become commonplace nowadays.*
OPPOSITES: new, interesting, rare
▸ AS A NOUN **= cliché**, platitude, banality, truism • *It is a commonplace to say that the poetry of the first world war was greater than that of the second.*

common sense = good sense, sound judgment, level-headedness, practicality, prudence, nous *(Brit. slang)*, soundness, reasonableness, gumption *(Brit. informal)*, horse sense, native intelligence, mother wit, smarts *(slang, chiefly U.S.)*, wit • *Her mother acted with remarkable common sense.*

common-sense = sensible, sound, practical, reasonable, realistic, shrewd, down-to-earth, matter-of-fact, sane, astute, judicious, level-headed, hard-headed, grounded • *The secret lies in taking a common-sense approach.*
OPPOSITES: foolish, daft *(informal)*, unrealistic

commotion = disturbance, to-do, riot, disorder, excitement, fuss, turmoil, racket, upheaval, bustle, furore, uproar, ferment, agitation, ado, rumpus, tumult, hubbub, hurly-burly, brouhaha, hullabaloo, ballyhoo *(informal)*, hue and cry, perturbation • *He heard a terrible commotion outside.*

communal 1 = community, neighbourhood • *Communal violence broke out in different parts of the country*
2 = public, shared, general, joint, collective, communistic • *The inmates ate in a communal dining room.*
OPPOSITES: single, private, individual

commune = community, collective, cooperative, kibbutz • *They briefly joined a hippie commune in Denmark.*

commune with 1 = contemplate, ponder, reflect on, muse on, meditate on • *He set off from the lodge to commune with nature.*
2 = talk to, communicate with, discuss with, confer with, converse with, discourse with, parley with, korero *(N.Z.)* • *You can now commune with people from the safety of your PC.*

communicable = infectious, catching, contagious, transferable, transmittable • *communicable diseases such as Ebola*

communicate 1 = contact, talk, speak, phone, correspond, make contact, be in touch, ring up *(informal, chiefly Brit.)*, be in contact, get in contact, e-mail, text • *My natural mother has never communicated with me.* • *They communicated in sign language.*
2 = make known, report, announce, reveal, publish, declare, spread, disclose, pass on, proclaim, transmit, convey, impart, divulge, disseminate • *The result will be communicated to parents.*
OPPOSITES: sit on *(informal)*, suppress, keep secret
3 = pass on, transfer, spread, transmit • *typhus, a disease communicated by body lice*

communication AS A NOUN **1 = contact**, conversation, correspondence, intercourse, link, relations, connection • *The problem is a lack of real communication between you.*
2 = passing on, spread, circulation, transmission, disclosure, imparting, dissemination, conveyance • *Treatment involves the communication of information.*
3 = message, news, report, word, information, statement, intelligence, announcement, disclosure, dispatch, e-mail, text • *The ambassador has brought with him a communication from the President.*
▸ AS A PLURAL NOUN **= connections**, travel, links, transport, routes • *Violent rain has caused flooding and cut communications between neighbouring towns.*

communicative = talkative, open, frank, forthcoming, outgoing, informative, candid, expansive, chatty, voluble, loquacious, unreserved • *She has become a lot more tolerant and communicative.*
OPPOSITES: reserved, quiet, secretive

communion = affinity, accord, agreement, unity, sympathy, harmony, intercourse, fellowship, communing, closeness, rapport, converse, togetherness, concord • *The ancient Druids were widely known as visionaries and prophets, in communion with the gods.*

Communion = Eucharist, Mass, Sacrament, Lord's Supper • *Most villagers only took Communion at Easter.*

communiqué = announcement, report, bulletin, dispatch, news flash, official communication • *The call came in a communiqué sent to the Irish Prime Minister.*

communism *usually cap.* **= socialism**, Marxism, Stalinism, collectivism, Bolshevism, Marxism-Leninism, state socialism, Maoism, Trotskyism, Eurocommunism, Titoism • *the collapse of Communism in Eastern Europe*

QUOTATIONS

We Communists are like seeds and the people are like the soil. Wherever we go, we must unite with the people, take root and blossom among them
[Mao Tse-tung]

A spectre is haunting Europe – the spectre of Communism
[Karl Marx *The Communist Manifesto*]

Communism is Soviet power plus the electrification of the whole country
[Lenin]

One strength of the communist system of the East is that it has some of the character of a religion and inspires the emotions of a religion
[Albert Einstein *Out of My Later Life*]

Far from being a classless society, Communism is governed by an elite as steadfast in its determination to maintain its prerogatives as any oligarchy known to history
[Robert F. Kennedy *The Pursuit of Justice*]

Under capitalism, man exploits man. Under communism, it's just the opposite
[John Kenneth Galbraith]

communist *often cap.* **= socialist**, Red *(informal)*, Marxist, Bolshevik, collectivist • *Its leader is a former Communist who joined the dissident movement in 1989.*

QUOTATIONS

What is a communist? One who hath yearnings
For equal division of unequal earnings
[Ebenezer Elliot *Epigram*]

community 1 = society, people, public, association, population, residents, commonwealth, general public, populace, body politic, state, company • *He's well liked by the local community.*
2 = district, area, quarter, region, sector, parish, neighbourhood, vicinity, locality, locality, locale, neck of the woods *(informal)* • *a black township on the outskirts of the mining community*
3 = group, set, camp, circle, crowd, category • *Other organisations come to the festival to show their solidarity for the lesbian and gay community.*

commute 1 = travel • *He commutes to London every day.*
2 = reduce, cut, modify, shorten, alleviate, curtail, remit, mitigate • *His death sentence was commuted to life imprisonment.*

commuter = daily traveller, passenger, suburbanite • *The number of commuters to London has dropped.*

compact[1] AS AN ADJECTIVE **1 = closely packed**, firm, solid, thick, dense, compressed, condensed, impenetrable,

impermeable, pressed together • *a thick, bare trunk crowned by a compact mass of dark-green leaves*
OPPOSITES: loose, scattered, sprawling
2 = **small**, little, tiny, mini, wee, diminutive, petite, dinky (*informal*), pocket-sized • *a compact computer that could be tucked under the arm and carried like a notebook*
3 = **concise**, brief, to the point, succinct, terse, laconic, pithy, epigrammatic, pointed • *The strength of the series is in its concise, compact short-story quality.*
OPPOSITES: lengthy, rambling, long-winded
▸ **AS A VERB** = **pack closely**, stuff, cram, compress, condense, tamp • *The soil settles and is compacted by the winter rain.*
OPPOSITES: separate, disperse, loosen

compact[2] = **agreement**, deal, understanding, contract, bond, arrangement, alliance, treaty, bargain, pact, covenant, entente, concordat • *The Pilgrims signed a democratic compact aboard the Mayflower.*

companion 1 = **friend**, partner, ally, colleague, associate, mate (*informal*), gossip (*archaic*), buddy (*informal*), comrade, accomplice, crony, confederate, consort, main man (*slang, chiefly U.S.*), homeboy (*slang, chiefly U.S.*), cobber (*Austral. & N.Z. old-fashioned informal*) • *He has been her constant companion for the last six years.*
2 = **assistant**, aide, escort, attendant • *She was employed as companion to a wealthy old lady.*
3 = **complement**, match, fellow, mate, twin, counterpart • *The book was written as the companion to a trilogy of television documentaries.*

companionable = **friendly**, neighbourly, familiar, outgoing, cordial, sociable, genial, affable, congenial, gregarious, convivial • *They stood around the room chatting in small companionable groups.*

companionship = **fellowship**, company, friendship, fraternity, rapport, camaraderie, togetherness, comradeship, amity, esprit de corps, conviviality • *He missed the companionship of friends of his own age.*

company 1 = **business**, firm, association, corporation, partnership, establishment, syndicate, house, concern • *She worked as a secretary in an insurance company.*
2 = **group**, troupe, set, community, league, band, crowd, camp, collection, gathering, circle, crew, assembly, convention, ensemble, throng, coterie, bevy, assemblage, party, body • *He was a notable young actor in a company of rising stars.*
3 = **troop**, unit, squad, team • *The division consists of two tank companies and one infantry company.*
4 = **companionship**, society, presence, fellowship • *I would be grateful for your company on the drive back.*
5 = **guests**, party, visitors, callers • *Oh, I'm sorry, I didn't realise you had company.*

QUOTATIONS
Every man is like the company he is wont to keep
[Euripides *Phoenix*]
A wise man may look ridiculous in the company of fools
[Thomas Fuller *Gnomologia*]
Tell me thy company, and I'll tell thee what thou art
[Miguel de Cervantes *Don Quixote*]

PROVERBS
A man is known by the company he keeps
Two is company, three's a crowd

comparable 1 = **equal**, equivalent, on a par, tantamount, a match, proportionate, commensurate, as good • *They should be paid the same wages for work of comparable value.* • *Farmers were meant to get an income comparable with that of townspeople.*
OPPOSITES: different, unequal, dissimilar
2 = **similar**, related, alike, corresponding, akin, analogous, of a piece, cognate, cut from the same cloth • *The scoring systems used in the two studies are not directly comparable.*

comparative = **relative**, qualified, by comparison, approximate • *The task was accomplished with comparative ease.*

compare **AS A VERB** = **contrast**, balance, weigh, set against, collate, juxtapose • *Compare the two illustrations in Fig 60.*
▸ **IN PHRASES:** **compare to something** = **liken to**, parallel, identify with, equate to, correlate to, mention in the same breath as • *Commentators compared his work to that of James Joyce.*
compare with something = **be as good as**, match, approach, equal, compete with, come up to, vie, be on a par with, be the equal of, approximate to, hold a candle to, bear comparison, be in the same class as • *The flowers here do not compare with those at home.*

comparison 1 = **contrast**, distinction, differentiation, juxtaposition, collation • *There are no previous statistics for comparison.*
2 = **similarity**, analogy, resemblance, correlation, likeness, comparability • *There is no comparison between the picture quality of a video and that of a DVD.*

QUOTATIONS
Comparisons are odious
[John Fortescue *De Laudibus Legum Angliae*]
Comparisons are odorous
[William Shakespeare *Much Ado About Nothing*]

compartment 1 = **section**, carriage, berth • *We shared our compartment with a group of businessmen.*
2 = **bay**, chamber, booth, locker, niche, cubicle, alcove, pigeonhole, cubbyhole, cell, carrel • *I put the vodka in the freezer compartment of the fridge.*
3 = **category**, area, department, division, section, subdivision • *We usually put the mind, the body and the spirit into three separate compartments.*

compartmentalize *or* **compartmentalise** = **categorize** *or* **categorise**, classify, pigeonhole, sectionalize *or* sectionalise • *It is impossible for people to fully compartmentalize their lives.*

compass[1] = **range**, field, area, reach, scope, sphere, limit, stretch, bound, extent, zone, boundary, realm • *Within the compass of a book of this size, such a comprehensive survey is not practicable.*

compass[2]
▹ *See panel* **Compass points**

compassion = **sympathy**, understanding, charity, pity, humanity, mercy, heart, quarter, sorrow, kindness, tenderness, condolence, clemency, commiseration, fellow feeling, soft-heartedness, tender-heartedness, aroha (*N.Z.*) • *The Dalai Lama practises what he preaches: universal kindness and compassion.*
OPPOSITES: indifference, apathy, unconcern

compassionate = **sympathetic**, kindly, understanding, tender, pitying, humanitarian, charitable, humane, indulgent, benevolent, lenient, merciful, kind-hearted, tender-hearted • *My father was a deeply compassionate man.*
OPPOSITES: harsh, callous, uncaring

compatibility 1 = **agreement**, consistency, accordance, affinity, conformity, concord, congruity, accord • *National courts can freeze any law while its compatibility with European Community legislation is tested.*
2 = **like-mindedness**, harmony, empathy, rapport, single-mindedness, amity, sympathy, congeniality • *Dating allows people to check out their compatibility before making a commitment to one another.*

compatible 1 = **consistent**, in keeping, consonant, congenial, congruent, reconcilable, congruous, accordant, agreeable • *Free enterprise, he argued, was compatible with Russian values and traditions.*
OPPOSITES: inappropriate, contradictory, unfitting

C

COMPASS POINTS

Compass Point	Abbreviation	Compass Point	Abbreviation	Compass Point	Abbreviation
North	N	South East by South	SE by S	West North West	WNW
North by East	N by E	South South East	SSE	North West by West	NW by W
North North East	NNE	South by East	S by E	North West	NW
North East by North	NE by N	South	S	North West by North	NW by N
North East	NE	South by West	S by W	North North West	NNW
North East by East	NE by E	South South West	SSW	North by West	N by W
East North East	ENE	South West by South	SW by S	**Cardinal point**	**Related adjective**
East by North	E by N	South West	SW	north	arctic *or* boreal
East	E	South West by West	SW by W	east	oriental
East by South	E by S	West South West	WSW	south	meridional *or* austral
East South East	ESE	West by South	W by S	west	occidental *or* hesperidan
South East by East	SE by E	West	W		
South East	SE	West by North	W by N		

2 = **like-minded**, harmonious, in harmony, in accord, of one mind, of the same mind, en rapport *(French)* • *She and I are very compatible – we're interested in all the same things.*
OPPOSITES: unsuitable, incompatible, unharmonious

compatriot = **fellow countryman**, countryman, fellow citizen • *He beat his compatriots in the final.*

compel = **force**, make, urge, enforce, railroad *(informal)*, drive, oblige, constrain, hustle *(slang)*, necessitate, coerce, bulldoze *(informal)*, impel, dragoon • *the introduction of legislation to compel cyclists to wear a helmet*

compelling 1 = **convincing**, telling, powerful, forceful, conclusive, weighty, cogent, irrefutable • *He puts forward a compelling argument against the culling of badgers.*
2 = **pressing**, binding, urgent, overriding, imperative, unavoidable, coercive, peremptory • *Another, probably more compelling, factor is that of safety.*
3 = **fascinating**, gripping, irresistible, enchanting, enthralling, hypnotic, spellbinding, mesmeric • *Her eyes were her best feature, wide-set and compelling.* • *a violent yet compelling film*
OPPOSITES: ordinary, boring, dull

compendium = **collection**, summary, abstract, digest, compilation, epitome, synopsis, précis • *His book is a delightful compendium of miscellaneous knowledge.*

compensate 1 = **recompense**, repay, refund, reimburse, indemnify, make restitution, requite, remunerate, satisfy, make good • *To ease financial difficulties, farmers could be compensated for their loss of subsidies.*
2 = **make amends for**, make up for, atone for, pay for, do penance for, cancel out, make reparation for, make redress for • *She compensated for her burst of anger by doing even more for the children.*
3 = **balance**, cancel (out), offset, make up for, redress, counteract, neutralize, counterbalance • *The rewards more than compensated for the inconveniences involved in making the trip.*

PROVERBS
What you lose on the swings you gain on the roundabouts

compensation 1 = **reparation**, damages, payment, recompense, indemnification, offset, remuneration, indemnity, restitution, reimbursement, requital • *He received one year's salary as compensation for loss of office.*
2 = **recompense**, amends, reparation, restitution, atonement • *The present she left him was no compensation for her absence.*

compete 1 = **contend**, fight, rival, vie, challenge, struggle, contest, strive, pit yourself against • *The stores will inevitably end up competing with each other for increased market shares.*
2 = **take part**, participate, be in the running, be a competitor, be a contestant, play • *He has competed twice in the London marathon.*

competence 1 = **ability**, skill, talent, capacity, expertise, proficiency, competency, capability • *I regard him as a man of integrity and high professional competence.*
OPPOSITES: inability, incompetence
2 = **fitness**, suitability, adequacy, appropriateness • *They questioned her competence as a mother.*
OPPOSITES: inadequacy

QUOTATIONS
He has, indeed, done it very well; but it is a foolish thing well done
[Dr. Johnson]

competent 1 = **able**, skilled, capable, clever, endowed, proficient • *He was a loyal and very competent civil servant.*
OPPOSITES: cowboy *(informal)*, incapable, incompetent
2 = **fit**, qualified, equal, appropriate, suitable, sufficient, adequate • *I don't feel competent to deal with a medical emergency.*
OPPOSITES: inadequate, unqualified

competition 1 = **rivalry**, opposition, struggle, contest, contention, strife, one-upmanship *(informal)* • *There's been some fierce competition for the title.*
2 = **opposition**, field, rivals, challengers • *In this business you have to stay one step ahead of the competition.*
3 = **contest**, event, championship, tournament, quiz, head-to-head • *He will be banned from international competitions for four years.*

QUOTATIONS
A horse never runs so fast as when he has other horses to catch up and outpace
[Ovid *The Art of Love*]

competitive 1 = **cut-throat**, aggressive, fierce, ruthless, relentless, antagonistic, carnivorous *(informal)*, dog-eat-dog • *Modelling is a tough, competitive world.*
2 = **ambitious**, pushing, opposing, aggressive, two-fisted, vying, contentious, combative, carnivorous *(informal)* • *He has always been a fiercely competitive player.*

competitor 1 = **rival**, competition, opposition, adversary, antagonist • *The bank isn't performing as well as some of its competitors.*
2 = **contestant**, participant, contender, challenger, entrant, player, opponent • *One of the oldest competitors in the race won the silver medal.*

compilation = **collection**, treasury, accumulation, anthology, assortment, assemblage • *His latest album is a compilation of his jazz works over the past decade.*

compile = **put together**, collect, gather, organize, accumulate, marshal, garner, amass, cull, anthologize • *The anthology took ten years to compile.*

complacency = **smugness**, satisfaction, gratification, contentment, self-congratulation, self-satisfaction • *She warned that there was no room for complacency on inflation.*

complacent = **smug**, self-satisfied, pleased with yourself, resting on your laurels, pleased, contented, satisfied, gratified, serene, unconcerned, self-righteous, self-assured, self-contented • *We cannot afford to be complacent about our health.*
OPPOSITES: troubled, uneasy, insecure

complain = **find fault**, moan, grumble, whinge *(informal)*, beef *(slang)*, carp, fuss, bitch *(slang)*, groan, grieve, lament, whine, growl, deplore, grouse, gripe *(informal)*, bemoan, bleat, put the boot in *(slang)*, bewail, kick up a fuss *(informal)*, grouch *(informal)*, bellyache *(slang)*, kvetch *(U.S. slang)*, nit-pick *(informal)* • *She's always complaining about her husband's laziness.*

complaint 1 = **protest**, accusation, objection, grievance, remonstrance, charge • *There have been a number of complaints about the standard of service.*
2 = **grumble**, criticism, beef *(slang)*, moan, bitch *(slang)*, lament, grievance, wail, dissatisfaction, annoyance, grouse, gripe *(informal)*, grouch *(informal)*, plaint, fault-finding • *I don't have any complaints about the way I've been treated.*
3 = **disorder**, problem, trouble, disease, upset, illness, sickness, ailment, affliction, malady, indisposition • *Eczema is a common skin complaint.*

complement AS A VERB = **enhance**, complete, improve, boost, crown, add to, set off, heighten, augment, round off • *Nutmeg complements the flavour of these beans perfectly.*
▸ AS A NOUN 1 = **accompaniment**, companion, accessory, completion, finishing touch, rounding-off, adjunct, supplement • *The green wallpaper is the perfect complement to the old pine of the dresser.*
2 = **total**, capacity, quota, aggregate, contingent, entirety • *Each ship had a complement of around a dozen officers and 250 men.*

complementary = **matching**, companion, corresponding, compatible, reciprocal, interrelating, interdependent, harmonizing • *Many plain tiles and complementary borders are available.*
OPPOSITES: different, contradictory, incompatible

complete AS AN ADJECTIVE 1 = **total**, perfect, absolute, utter, outright, thorough, consummate, out-and-out, unmitigated, dyed-in-the-wool, thoroughgoing, deep-dyed *(usually derogatory)* • *He made me look like a complete idiot.*
2 = **whole**, full, entire • *A complete tenement block was burnt to the ground.*
OPPOSITES: partial
3 = **entire**, full, whole, intact, unbroken, faultless, undivided, unimpaired • *Scientists have found the oldest complete skeleton of an ape-like man.*
OPPOSITES: spoilt, incomplete, deficient
4 = **unabridged**, full, whole, entire, full-length, uncut, unexpurgated, uncondensed • *the complete works of Shakespeare*
5 = **finished**, done, ended, completed, achieved, concluded, fulfilled, accomplished • *The work of restoring the farmhouse is complete.*
OPPOSITES: unsettled, unfinished, inconclusive
▸ AS A VERB 1 = **perfect**, accomplish, finish off, round off, crown, cap • *the stickers needed to complete the collection*
OPPOSITES: mar, spoil
2 = **finish**, conclude, fulfil, accomplish, do, end, close, achieve, perform, settle, realize, execute, discharge, wrap up *(informal)*, terminate, finalize • *He had just completed his first novel.*
OPPOSITES: start, begin, initiate
3 = **fill in**, fill out • *Simply complete the coupon below.*

completely = **totally**, entirely, wholly, utterly, quite, perfectly, fully, solidly, absolutely, altogether, thoroughly, in full, every inch, en masse, heart and soul, a hundred per cent, one hundred per cent, from beginning to end, down to the ground, root and branch, in toto *(Latin)*, from A to Z, hook, line and sinker, lock, stock and barrel • *Dozens of flats have been completely destroyed.* • *I have fallen completely in love with him.*

completion = **finishing**, end, close, conclusion, accomplishment, realization, fulfilment, culmination, attainment, fruition, consummation, finalization • *The project is near completion.*

complex AS AN ADJECTIVE 1 = **compound**, compounded, multiple, composite, manifold, heterogeneous, multifarious • *His complex compositions are built up of many overlapping layers.*
2 = **complicated**, difficult, involved, mixed, elaborate, tangled, mingled, intricate, tortuous, convoluted, knotty, labyrinthine, circuitous • *in-depth coverage of today's complex issues*
OPPOSITES: clear, easy, simple
▸ AS A NOUN 1 = **structure**, system, scheme, network, organization, aggregate, composite, synthesis • *Our philosophy is a complex of many tightly interrelated ideas.*
2 = **obsession**, preoccupation, phobia, fixation, fixed idea, idée fixe *(French)* • *I have never had a complex about my weight.*

complexion 1 = **skin**, colour, colouring, hue, skin tone, pigmentation • *She had short brown hair and a pale complexion.*
2 = **nature**, character, make-up, cast, stamp, disposition • *The political complexion of the government has changed.*
3 = **perspective**, look, light, appearance, aspect, angle, slant • *This latest development puts a different complexion on things.*

complexity = **complication**, involvement, intricacy, entanglement, convolution • *a diplomatic problem of great complexity*

compliance 1 = **conformity**, agreement, obedience, assent, observance, concurrence • *The company says it is in full compliance with US labor laws.*
OPPOSITES: defiance, disobedience, non-compliance
2 = **submissiveness**, yielding, submission, obedience, deference, passivity, acquiescence, complaisance, consent • *Suddenly, he hated her for her compliance and passivity.*
OPPOSITES: opposition, resistance, defiance

compliant = **obedient**, willing, accepting, yielding, obliging, accommodating, passive, cooperative, agreeable, submissive, conformist, deferential, acquiescent, complaisant, conformable • *a docile and compliant workforce*

complicate = **make difficult**, confuse, muddle, embroil, entangle, make intricate, involve • *Don't complicate matters by getting the union involved.*
OPPOSITES: explain, clarify, simplify

complicated 1 = **involved**, difficult, puzzling, troublesome, problematic, perplexing • *The situation in Lebanon is very complicated.*
OPPOSITES: simple, straightforward, uncomplicated
2 = **complex**, involved, elaborate, intricate, Byzantine • *a complicated voting system*
OPPOSITES: clear, easy, understandable
3 = **convoluted**, labyrinthine • *the workings of his his complicated mind*
▹ *See panel* **Complex**

complication 1 = **problem**, difficulty, obstacle, drawback, snag, uphill *(S. African)*, stumbling block, aggravation • *The age difference was a complication to the relationship.*
2 = **complexity**, combination, mixture, web, confusion, intricacy, entanglement • *His poetry was characterised by a complication of imagery and ideas.*

complicity = **collusion**, conspiracy, collaboration, connivance, abetment • *evidence of their complicity with international terrorists*

compliment AS A NOUN = **praise**, honour, tribute, courtesy, admiration, bouquet, flattery, eulogy • *She blushed, but accepted the compliment with good grace.*
OPPOSITES: criticism, complaint, condemnation

C

▸ **AS A PLURAL NOUN** 1 = **greetings**, regards, respects, remembrances, good wishes, salutation • *Give my compliments to your lovely wife when you write home.*
OPPOSITES: insult
2 = **congratulations**, praise, commendation • *That was an excellent meal – my compliments to the chef.*
▸ **AS A VERB** = **praise**, flatter, salute, congratulate, pay tribute to, commend, laud, extol, crack up *(informal)*, pat on the back, sing the praises of, wax lyrical about, big up *(slang, chiefly Caribbean)*, speak highly of • *They complimented me on my performance.*
OPPOSITES: blast, condemn, criticize

complimentary 1 = **flattering**, approving, appreciative, congratulatory, laudatory, eulogistic, commendatory • *We often get complimentary remarks regarding the quality of our service.*
OPPOSITES: critical, insulting, abusive
2 = **free**, donated, courtesy, honorary, free of charge, on the house, gratuitous, gratis • *He had complimentary tickets for the show.*

comply = **obey**, follow, respect, agree to, satisfy, observe, fulfil, submit to, conform to, adhere to, abide by, consent to, yield to, defer to, accede to, act in accordance with, perform, acquiesce with • *The commander said that the army would comply with the ceasefire.*
OPPOSITES: break, fight, defy

component **AS A NOUN** = **part**, piece, unit, item, element, ingredient, constituent • *Enriched uranium is a key component of nuclear weapons.*
▸ **AS AN ADJECTIVE** = **constituent**, composing, inherent, intrinsic • *Polish workers will now be making component parts for Boeing 757s.*

comport **IN PHRASES:** **comport with something** = **suit**, fit, agree with, coincide with, accord with, square with, be appropriate to, correspond with, tally with, harmonize with • *This conclusion does not comport with my opinion.*
comport yourself = **behave yourself**, act, carry yourself, bear yourself, conduct yourself, acquit yourself • *He comports himself with great dignity.*

compose **AS A VERB** 1 = **put together**, make up, constitute, comprise, make, build, form, fashion, construct, compound • *They agreed to form a council composed of leaders of the rival factions.*
OPPOSITES: destroy, dismantle, demolish
2 = **create**, write, produce, imagine, frame, invent, devise, contrive • *He started at once to compose a reply to her letter.*
3 = **arrange**, make up, construct, put together, order, organize • *The drawing is beautifully composed.*
▸ **IN PHRASES:** **compose yourself** = **calm yourself**, be still, control yourself, settle yourself, collect yourself, pull yourself together • *She quickly composed herself before she entered the room.*

composed = **calm**, together *(slang)*, cool, collected, relaxed, confident, poised, at ease, laid-back *(informal)*, serene, tranquil, sedate, self-controlled, level-headed, unfazed *(informal)*, unflappable, unruffled, self-possessed, imperturbable, unworried, keeping your cool, as cool as a cucumber, chilled *(informal)*, grounded • *She was standing beside him, very calm and composed.*
OPPOSITES: excited, upset, agitated

composer
▹ *See panel* **Composers**

composite **AS AN ADJECTIVE** = **compound**, mixed, combined, complex, blended, conglomerate, synthesized • *The chassis is made of a complex composite structure incorporating carbon fibre.*
▸ **AS A NOUN** = **compound**, blend, conglomerate, fusion, synthesis, amalgam, meld • *Spain is a composite of diverse traditions and people.*

composition 1 = **design**, form, structure, make-up, organization, arrangement, constitution, formation, layout, configuration • *Materials of different composition absorb and reflect light differently.*
2 = **creation**, work, piece, production, opus, masterpiece, chef-d'oeuvre *(French)* • *Bach's compositions are undoubtedly among the greatest ever written.*
3 = **essay**, writing, study, exercise, treatise, literary work • *Write a composition on the subject 'What I Did on My Holidays'.*
4 = **arrangement**, balance, proportion, harmony, symmetry, concord, consonance, placing • *Let us study the composition of this painting.*
5 = **production**, creation, making, fashioning, formation, putting together, invention, compilation, formulation • *These plays are arranged in order of their composition.*

QUOTATIONS
At school, composition tests your stamina, whereas translation requires intelligence. But in later life you can scoff at those who did well in composition
[Gustave Flaubert *The Dictionary of Received Ideas*]

compost = **fertilizer**, mulch, humus • *A wormery produces excellent compost.*

composure = **calmness**, calm, poise, self-possession, cool *(slang)*, ease, dignity, serenity, tranquillity, coolness, aplomb, equanimity, self-assurance, sang-froid, placidity, imperturbability, sedateness • *Stopping briefly to regain her composure, she described her ordeal.*
OPPOSITES: impatience, nervousness, agitation

compound **AS A NOUN** = **combination**, mixture, blend, composite, conglomerate, fusion, synthesis, alloy, medley, amalgam, meld, composition • *Organic compounds contain carbon in their molecules.*
OPPOSITES: element
▸ **AS AN ADJECTIVE** = **complex**, multiple, composite, conglomerate, intricate, not simple • *a tall shrub with shiny compound leaves*
OPPOSITES: single, simple, pure
▸ **AS A VERB** 1 = **intensify**, add to, complicate, worsen, heighten, exacerbate, aggravate, magnify, augment, add insult to injury • *Additional bloodshed will only compound the misery.*
OPPOSITES: moderate, modify, lessen
2 = **combine**, unite, mix, blend, fuse, mingle, synthesize, concoct, amalgamate, coalesce, intermingle, meld • *An emotion oddly compounded of pleasure and bitterness flooded over me.*
OPPOSITES: part, divide, segregate

comprehend = **understand**, see, take in, perceive, grasp, conceive, make out, discern, assimilate, see the light, fathom, apprehend, get the hang of *(informal)*, get the picture, know • *I just cannot comprehend your attitude.*
OPPOSITES: mistake, misunderstand, misinterpret

comprehensible = **understandable**, clear, plain, explicit, coherent, user-friendly, intelligible, graspable • *He spoke abruptly, in barely comprehensible Arabic.*

comprehension = **understanding**, grasp, conception, realization, sense, knowledge, intelligence, judgment, perception, discernment • *The situation was utterly beyond her comprehension.*
OPPOSITES: misunderstanding, incomprehension, misapprehension

comprehensive = **broad**, full, complete, wide, catholic, sweeping, extensive, blanket, umbrella, thorough, inclusive, exhaustive, all-inclusive, all-embracing, overarching, encyclopedic • *The Rough Guide to Nepal is a comprehensive guide to the region.*
OPPOSITES: limited, specific, narrow

compress 1 = **squeeze**, crush, squash, constrict, press, crowd, wedge, cram • *Poor posture can compress the body's organs.*
2 = **condense**, contract, concentrate, compact, shorten, summarize, abbreviate • *Textbooks compressed six millennia of Egyptian history into a few pages.*

COMPOSERS

Classical composers

Adolphe Adam *(French)*
John Adams *(U.S.)*
Isaac Albéniz *(Spanish)*
Tomaso Albinoni *(Italian)*
Gregorio Allegri *(Italian)*
William Alwyn *(British)*
George Antheil *(U.S.)*
Thomas Arne *(English)*
Malcolm Arnold *(British)*
Daniel François Esprit Auber *(French)*
Georges Auric *(French)*
Carl Philipp Emanuel Bach *(German)*
Johann Christian Bach *(German)*
Johann Christoph Friedrich Bach *(German)*
Johann Sebastian Bach *(German)*
Wilhelm Friedemann Bach *(German)*
Mily Alexeyevich Balakirev *(Russian)*
Granville Bantock *(British)*
Samuel Barber *(U.S.)*
Béla Bartók *(Hungarian)*
Arnold Bax *(British)*
Ludwig van Beethoven *(German)*
Vincenzo Bellini *(Italian)*
Arthur Benjamin *(Australian)*
Richard Rodney Bennett *(British)*
Alban Berg *(Austrian)*
Luciano Berio *(Italian)*
Lennox Berkeley *(British)*
Hector Berlioz *(French)*
Leonard Bernstein *(U.S.)*
Heinrich Biber *(German)*
Harrison Birtwhistle *(British)*
Georges Bizet *(French)*
Arthur Bliss *(British)*
Ernest Bloch *(U.S.)*
Luigi Bocherini *(Italian)*
Arrigo Boito *(Italian)*
Francesco Antonio Bonporti *(Italian)*
Aleksandr Porfirevich Borodin *(Russian)*
Pierre Boulez *(French)*
William Boyce *(English)*
Johannes Brahms *(German)*
Havergal Brian *(British)*
Frank Bridge *(British)*
Benjamin Britten *(British)*
Max Bruch *(German)*
Anton Bruckner *(Austrian)*
John Bull *(English)*
George Butterworth *(British)*
Dietrich Buxtehude *(Danish)*
William Byrd *(English)*
John Cage *(U.S.)*
Joseph Canteloube *(French)*
John Alden Carpenter *(U.S.)*
Eliot Carter *(U.S.)*
Robert Carver *(Scottish)*
Pablo Casals *(Spanish)*
Emmanuel Chabrier *(French)*
Gustave Charpentier *(French)*
Marc-Antoine Charpentier *(French)*
Ernest Chausson *(French)*
Luigi Cherubini *(Italian)*
Frédéric Chopin *(Polish-French)*
Domenico Cimarosa *(Italian)*
Jeremiah Clarke *(English)*
Samuel Coleridge-Taylor *(British)*
Aaron Copland *(U.S.)*
Arcangelo Corelli *(Italian)*
François Couperin *(French)*
Karl Czerny *(Austrian)*
Luigi Dallapiccola *(Italian)*
Peter Maxwell Davies *(British)*
Claude Debussy *(French)*
Léo Delibes *(French)*
Frederick Delius *(British)*
Josquin des Prés *(Flemish)*
Vincent d'Indy *(French)*
Ernst von Dohnányi *(Hungarian)*
Gaetano Donizetti *(Italian)*
Antal Doráti *(U.S.)*
John Dowland *(English)*
Paul Dukas *(French)*
John Dunstable *(English)*
Henri Duparc *(French)*
Marcel Dupré *(French)*
Maurice Duruflé *(French)*
Henri Dutilleux *(French)*
Antonín Dvořák *(Czech)*
Edward Elgar *(British)*
Georges Enesco *(Romanian)*
Manuel de Falla *(Spanish)*
John Farmer *(English)*
Gabriel Fauré *(French)*
John Field *(Irish)*
Gerald Finzi *(British)*
Friedrich von Flotow *(German)*
César Franck *(Belgian-French)*
Girolamo Frescobaldi *(Italian)*
Wilhelm Furtwängler *(German)*
Andrea Gabrieli *(Italian)*
Giovanni Gabrieli *(Italian)*
George Gershwin *(U.S.)*
Carlo Gesualdo *(Italian)*
Orlando Gibbons *(English)*
Alberto Ginastera *(Argentinian)*
Philip Glass *(U.S.)*
Aleksandr Konstantinovich Glazunov *(Russian)*
Mikhail Ivanovich Glinka *(Russian)*
Christoph Willibald Gluck *(German)*
Eugene Goossens *(Belgian-British)*
Henryk Górecki *(Polish)*
Charles François Gounod *(French)*
Percy Grainger *(Australian)*
Enrique Granados *(Spanish)*
Edvard Grieg *(Norwegian)*
Ivor Gurney *(British)*
Fromental Halévy *(French)*
George Frederick Handel *(German)*
Roy Harris *(U.S.)*
Franz Joseph Haydn *(Austrian)*
Michael Haydn *(Austrian)*
Hans Werner Henze *(German)*
Hildegard of Bingen *(German)*
Paul Hindemith *(German)*
Heinz Holliger *(Swiss)*
Gustav Holst *(British)*
Arthur Honegger *(French)*
Johann Nepomuk Hummel *(German)*
Engelbert Humperdinck *(German)*
Jacques Ibert *(French)*
John Ireland *(British)*
Charles Ives *(U.S.)*
Leoš Janáček *(Czech)*
Émile Jaques-Dalcroze *(Swiss)*
Joseph Joachim *(Hungarian)*
Daniel Jones *(British)*
Aram Ilich Khachaturian *(Armenian)*
Otto Klemperer *(German)*
Oliver Knussen *(British)*
Zoltán Kodály *(Hungarian)*
Erich Korngold *(Austrian)*
Franz Krommer *(Moravian)*
Raphael Kubelik *(Czech)*
Édouard Lalo *(French)*
Constant Lambert *(British)*
Roland de Lassus *(Flemish)*
Henry Lawes *(English)*
William Lawes *(English)*
Franz Lehár *(Hungarian)*
Ruggiero Leoncavallo *(Italian)*
György Ligeti *(Hungarian)*
Franz Liszt *(Hungarian)*
George Lloyd *(British)*
Matthew Locke *(English)*
Karl Loewe *(German)*
Jean Baptiste Lully *(Italian-French)*
Witold Lutosławski *(Polish)*
Elisabeth Lutyens *(British)*
Guillaume de Machaut *(French)*
James MacMillan *(British)*
Elizabeth Maconchy *(British)*
Gustav Mahler *(Austrian)*
Luca Marenzio *(Italian)*
Frank Martin *(Swiss)*
Bohuslav Martinů *(Czech)*
Steve Martland *(British)*
Pietro Mascagni *(Italian)*
Jules Émile Frédéric Massenet *(French)*
Fanny Mendelssohn *(German)*
Felix Mendelssohn *(German)*
Gian Carlo Menotti *(Italian)*
André Messager *(French)*
Olivier Messiaen *(French)*
Giacomo Meyerbeer *(German)*
Darius Milhaud *(French)*
Claudio Monteverdi *(Italian)*
Thomas Morley *(English)*
Leopold Mozart *(Austrian)*
Wolfgang Amadeus Mozart *(Austrian)*
Thea Musgrave *(British)*
Modest Petrovich Mussorgsky *(Russian)*
Carl Otto Ehrenfried Nicolai *(German)*
Carl Nielsen *(Danish)*
Luigi Nono *(Italian)*
Michael Nyman *(British)*
Johannes Ockeghem *(Flemish)*
Jacques Offenbach *(German-French)*
John Ogdon *(British)*
Carl Orff *(German)*
Johann Pachelbel *(German)*
Ignace Jan Paderewski *(Polish)*

C

Classical composers (continued)

Niccolò Paganini *(Italian)*
Giovanni Pierluigi da Palestrina *(Italian)*
Andrzej Panufnik *(Polish-British)*
Hubert Parry *(British)*
Arvo Pärt *(Estonian)*
Krzystof Penderecki *(Polish)*
Giovanni Battista Pergolesi *(Italian)*
Francis Poulenc *(French)*
Michael Praetorius *(German)*
Sergei Sergeyevich Prokofiev *(Russian)*
Giacomo Puccini *(Italian)*
Henry Purcell *(English)*
Sergei Vassilievich Rachmaninov *(Russian)*
Jean Philippe Rameau *(French)*
Maurice Ravel *(French)*
Alan Rawsthorne *(British)*
Max Reger *(German)*
Steve Reich *(U.S.)*
Ottorino Respighi *(Italian)*
Vittorio Rieti *(Italian)*
Nikolai Andreyevich Rimsky-Korsakov *(Russian)*
Joaquín Rodrigo *(Spanish)*
Sigmund Romberg *(U.S.)*
Gioacchino Antonio Rossini *(Italian)*
Mstislav Leopoldovich Rostropovich *(Russian)*
Claude Joseph Rouget de Lisle *(French)*
Albert Roussel *(French)*
Edmund Rubbra *(British)*
Anton Grigorevich Rubinstein *(Russian)*
Camille Saint-Saëns *(French)*
Antonio Salieri *(Italian)*
Erik Satie *(French)*
Alessandro Scarlatti *(Italian)*
Domenico Scarlatti *(Italian)*
Artur Schnabel *(Austrian-U.S.)*
Alfred Schnittke *(Russian)*
Arnold Schoenberg *(Austrian)*
Franz Schubert *(Austrian)*
William Schuman *(U.S.)*
Clara Schumann *(German)*
Robert Schumann *(German)*
Heinrich Schütz *(German)*
Aleksandr Nikolayevich Scriabin *(Russian)*
Peter Sculthorpe *(Australian)*
Roger Sessions *(U.S.)*
Dmitri Dmitriyevich Shostakovich *(Russian)*
Jean Sibelius *(Finnish)*
Robert Simpson *(English)*
Bedřich Smetana *(Czech)*
Ethel Smyth *(British)*
John Philip Sousa *(U.S.)*
John Stainer *(British)*
Charles Stanford *(Irish)*
Karlheinz Stockhausen *(German)*
Oscar Straus *(French)*
Johann Strauss, the elder *(Austrian)*
Johann Strauss, the younger *(Austrian)*
Richard Strauss *(German)*
Igor Fyodorovich Stravinsky *(Russian-U.S.)*
Jan Pieterszoon Sweelinck *(Dutch)*
Karol Szymanowski *(Polish)*
Toru Takemitsu *(Japanese)*
Thomas Tallis *(English)*
John Tavener *(British)*
John Taverner *(English)*
Pyotr Ilyich Tchaikovsky *(Russian)*
Georg Philipp Telemann *(German)*
Mikis Theodorakis *(Greek)*
Ambroise Thomas *(French)*
Virgil Thomson *(U.S.)*
Michael Tippett *(British)*
Paul Tortelier *(French)*
Edgar Varèse *(French-U.S.)*
Ralph Vaughan Williams *(British)*
Giuseppi Verdi *(Italian)*
Tomás Luis de Victoria *(Spanish)*
Heitor Villa-Lobos *(Brazilian)*
Antonio Vivaldi *(Italian)*
Richard Wagner *(German)*
William Walton *(British)*
David Ward *(British)*
Peter Warlock *(British)*
Carl Maria von Weber *(German)*
Anton Webern *(Austrian)*
Thomas Weelkes *(English)*
Judith Weir *(British)*
Egon Wellesz *(Austrian-British)*
Gillian Whitehead *(New Zealand)*
Malcolm Williamson *(Australian)*
Hugo Wolf *(Austrian)*
Ermanno Wolf-Ferrari *(Italian)*
Yannis Xenakis *(Romanian-Greek)*
Alexander Zemlinsky *(Austrian)*

Popular composers, songwriters, and lyricists

Harold Arlen *(U.S.)*
Burt Bacharach *(U.S.)*
Joan Baez *(U.S.)*
John Barry *(British)*
Lionel Bart *(British)*
Irving Berlin *(Russian-U.S.)*
Leonard Bernstein *(U.S.)*
David Bowie *(English)*
Jacques Brel *(Belgian)*
Nacio Herb Brown *(U.S.)*
Sammy Cahn *(U.S.)*
Hoagy Carmichael *(U.S.)*
George Cohan *(U.S.)*
Leonard Cohen *(Canadian)*
Noel Coward *(English)*
Willie Dixon *(U.S.)*
Lamont Dozier *(U.S.)*
Vernon Duke *(Russian-U.S.)*
Bob Dylan *(U.S.)*
Duke Ellington *(U.S.)*
Stephen Foster *(U.S.)*
George Gershwin *(U.S.)*
W(illiam) S(chwenck) Gilbert *(British)*
Gerry Goffin *(U.S.)*
Elliot Goldenthal *(U.S.)*
Jerry Goldsmith *(U.S.)*
Woody Guthrie *(U.S.)*
W(illiam) C(hristopher) Handy *(U.S.)*
Marvin Hamlisch *(U.S.)*
Oscar Hammerstein *(U.S.)*
Lorenz Hart *(U.S.)*
Jerry Herman *(U.S.)*
Brian Holland *(U.S.)*
Eddie Holland *(U.S.)*
Mick Jagger *(British)*
Maurice Jarre *(French)*
Antonio Carlos Jobim *(Brazilian)*
Elton John *(British)*
Robert Johnson *(U.S.)*
Jerome (David) Kern *(U.S.)*
Carole King *(U.S.)*
Kris Kristofferson *(U.S.)*
Huddie 'Leadbelly' Ledbetter *(U.S.)*
Tom Lehrer *(U.S.)*
John Lennon *(British)*
Alan Jay Lerner *(U.S.)*
Jerry Lieber *(U.S.)*
Jay Livingston *(U.S.)*
Andrew Lloyd-Webber *(British)*
Frank Loesser *(U.S.)*
Frederick Loewe *(Austrian-U.S.)*
Paul McCartney *(British)*
Ewan McColl *(British)*
Kirsty McColl *(British)*
Jimmy McHugh *(U.S.)*
Henry Mancini *(U.S.)*
Barry Manilow *(U.S.)*
Barry Mann *(U.S.)*
Joni Mitchell *(Canadian)*
Thelonious (Sphere) Monk *(U.S.)*
Van Morrison *(Irish)*
Willie Nelson *(U.S.)*
Ivor Novello *(British)*
Doc Pomus *(U.S.)*
Cole Porter *(U.S.)*
Keith Richards *(British)*
William 'Smokey' Robinson *(U.S.)*
Tim Rice *(British)*
Richard Rodgers *(U.S.)*
Sigmund Romberg *(Hungarian-U.S.)*
Howard Shore *(Canadian)*
Paul Simon *(U.S.)*
Stephen Sondheim *(U.S.)*
Mike Stoller *(U.S.)*
Billy Strayhorn *(U.S.)*
Barrett Strong *(U.S.)*
Jule Styne *(U.S.)*
Arthur Sullivan *(British)*
Allen Toussaint *(U.S.)*
Johnny Van Heusen *(U.S.)*
Tom Waits *(U.S.)*
Harry Warren *(U.S.)*
Jimmy Webb *(U.S.)*
Cynthia Weil *(U.S.)*
Kurt Weill *(German-U.S.)*
Norman Whitfield *(U.S.)*
Hank Williams *(U.S.)*
John Williams *(U.S.)*
Brian Wilson *(U.S.)*
Vincent Youmans *(U.S.)*

compressed 1 = **squeezed**, concentrated, compact, compacted, consolidated, squashed, flattened, constricted • *a biodegradable product made from compressed peat and cellulose*
2 = **reduced**, compacted, shortened, abridged • *All those three books are compressed into one volume.*

compression = **squeezing**, pressing, crushing, consolidation, condensation, constriction • *The compression of the wood is easily achieved.*

comprise 1 = **be composed of**, include, contain, consist of, take in, embrace, encompass, comprehend • *The exhibition comprises 50 oils and watercolours.*
2 = **make up**, form, constitute, compose • *Women comprise 44% of hospital medical staff.*

compromise AS A NOUN = **give-and-take**, agreement, settlement, accommodation, concession, adjustment, trade-off, middle ground, half measures • *Be willing to make compromises between what your partner wants and what you want.*
OPPOSITES: difference, dispute, disagreement
▸ AS A VERB 1 = **meet halfway**, concede, make concessions, give and take, strike a balance, strike a happy medium, go fifty-fifty (*informal*) • *I don't think we can compromise on fundamental principles.*
OPPOSITES: argue, contest, disagree
2 = **undermine**, expose, embarrass, weaken, prejudice, endanger, discredit, implicate, jeopardize, dishonour, imperil • *He had compromised himself by accepting the money.*
OPPOSITES: support, boost, assure

PROVERBS
If the mountain will not come to Mahomet, Mahomet must go to the mountain

compulsion 1 = **urge**, need, obsession, necessity, preoccupation, drive • *He felt a compulsion to talk about his ex-wife all the time.*
2 = **force**, pressure, obligation, constraint, urgency, coercion, duress, demand • *Students learn more when they are in classes out of choice rather than compulsion.*

compulsive 1 = **obsessive**, confirmed, chronic, persistent, addictive, uncontrollable, incurable, inveterate, incorrigible • *He is a compulsive liar.*
2 = **fascinating**, gripping, absorbing, compelling, captivating, enthralling, hypnotic, engrossing, spellbinding • *This really is compulsive reading.*
3 = **irresistible**, overwhelming, compelling, urgent, neurotic, besetting, uncontrollable, driving • *He seems to have an almost compulsive desire to play tricks.*

compulsory = **obligatory**, forced, required, binding, mandatory, imperative, requisite, de rigueur (*French*) • *Many young men are trying to get away from compulsory military conscription.*
OPPOSITES: voluntary, unnecessary, optional

compunction = **guilt**, misgiving, qualm, scruples, regret, reluctance, sorrow, remorse, repentance, contrition, penitence, stab *or* sting of conscience, work out • *He had no compunction about stealing from his parents.*

compute = **calculate**, rate, figure, total, measure, estimate, count, reckon, sum, figure out, add up, tally, enumerate • *I tried to compute the cash value of the ponies and horse boxes.*

computer
▸ RELATED PREFIX: cyber-
▸ RELATED PHOBIA: cyberphobia

QUOTATIONS
The Answer to the Great Question ... Of Life, the Universe and Everything ... Is ... Forty-two
[Douglas Adams *The Hitchhiker's Guide to the Galaxy*]
A distributed system is one in which the failure of a computer you didn't even know existed can render your own computer unusable
[Leslie Lamport]
That's what's cool about working with computers. They don't argue, they remember everything, and they don't drink all your beer
[Paul Leary]

▹ *See panel* **Computers**

comrade = **companion**, friend, partner, ally, colleague, associate, fellow, mate (*informal*), pal (*informal*), buddy (*informal*), compatriot, crony, confederate, co-worker, main man (*slang, chiefly U.S.*), homeboy (*slang, chiefly U.S.*), cobber (*Austral. & N.Z. old-fashioned informal*), compeer • *Unlike so many of his comrades, he survived the war.*

comradely = **friendly**, neighbourly, pally (*informal*), amiable, cordial, genial, affable, fraternal, chummy (*informal*), companionable, palsy-walsy (*informal*), matey or maty (*Brit. informal*) • *He gave her a comradely grin.*

comradeship = **fellowship**, solidarity, fraternity, brotherhood, companionship, camaraderie, kotahitanga (*N.Z.*) • *He missed the comradeship of army life.*

con AS A VERB = **swindle**, trick, cheat, rip off (*slang*), sting (*informal*), kid (*informal*), skin (*slang*), stiff (*slang*), mislead, deceive, hoax, defraud, dupe, gull (*archaic*), rook (*slang*), humbug, bamboozle (*informal*), hoodwink, double-cross (*informal*), diddle (*informal*), take for a ride (*informal*), inveigle, do the dirty on (*Brit. informal*), bilk, sell a pup, pull a fast one on (*informal*), scam (*slang*) • *He claimed that the businessman had conned him out of his life savings.* • *The British motorist has been conned by the government.*
▸ AS A NOUN = **swindle**, trick, fraud, deception, scam (*slang*), sting (*informal*), bluff, fastie (*Austral. slang*) • *I am afraid you have been the victim of a con.*

concave = **hollow**, cupped, depressed, scooped, hollowed, excavated, sunken, indented • *Remove the flesh from the concave part of the shell.*
OPPOSITES: rounded, curving, convex

conceal 1 = **hide**, bury, stash (*informal*), secrete, cover, screen, disguise, obscure, camouflage • *The device, concealed in a dustbin, was defused by police.*
OPPOSITES: show, reveal, display
2 = **keep secret**, hide, disguise, mask, suppress, veil, dissemble, draw a veil over, keep dark, keep under your hat • *Robert could not conceal his relief.*
OPPOSITES: show, reveal, display

concealed = **hidden**, covered, secret, screened, masked, obscured, covert, unseen, tucked away, secreted, under wraps, inconspicuous • *He was filmed with a concealed camera.*

concealment 1 = **cover**, hiding, camouflage, hiding place • *The criminals vainly sought concealment from the searchlight.*
2 = **cover-up**, disguise, keeping secret • *His concealment of his true motives was masterly.*
OPPOSITES: showing, display, disclosure

concede AS A VERB 1 = **admit**, allow, accept, acknowledge, own, grant, confess • *She finally conceded that he was right.*
OPPOSITES: deny, protest, reject
2 = **give up**, yield, hand over, surrender, relinquish, cede • *The central government has never conceded that territory to the Kurds.*
OPPOSITES: beat, defeat, conquer
▸ IN PHRASES: **concede defeat** = **capitulate**, give up, yield, submit, surrender, give in, come to terms, succumb, cave in (*informal*), relent, throw in the towel • *I eventually had to concede defeat.*

conceit 1 = **self-importance**, vanity, arrogance, complacency, pride, swagger, narcissism, egotism, self-love, amour-propre, vainglory • *He knew, without conceit, that he was considered a genius.*
2 = **image**, idea, concept, metaphor, imagery, figure of speech, trope • *Critics may complain that the novel's central conceit is rather simplistic.*

C

COMPUTERS

Computer parts

analogue-digital converter
arithmetic logic unit
cartridge case
CD-rewriter
CD-Rom drive
central processing unit
chip
coaxial cable
console
control key
counter
daisywheel
DDR-RAM
digital audio player
digital camera
digitizer
DIMM
disk
disk drive
disk unit
DRAM
DVD reader
DVD writer
emulator
encoder
flatbed scanner
floppy disk
graphics card
hard drive
integrated circuit
interface
joystick
keyboard
laser printer
LCD panel
line printer
magnetic tape unit
memory
microprocessor
modem
monitor
motherboard
mouse
MP3 player
multiplexor
optical character reader
optical disk
optical scanner
port
printed circuit board
printer
processor
scanner
screen
SDRAM
SIMM
sound card
speaker
trackball
transistor
USB port
visual display unit
webcam

Computer types

desktop
laptop
notebook
Macintosh *(trademark)*
palmtop
PC
tablet

Computer terms

absolute address
access
access time
address
address bus
ADSL
adware
algorithm
alpha-test
analogue computer
AND gate
antivirus
applet
application program
architecture
archival storage
area
array
artificial intelligence
ASCII
assemble
assembler
assembly language
audio response
automatic repeat
backbone
backing store
backup
bandwidth
base address
batch processing
beta-test
binary notation
bit
black box
Bluetooth
boilerplate
bomb
boot
bottom-up processing
bpi (bits per inch)
branch instruction
broadband
buffer
bug
buggy
bulletin board
bundle
bus
bus master
byte
cache memory
capture
CD-Rom
character
chipset
clip art
clock
code
COM
command
command language
communications
compatible
compiler
complex instruction set computer
computer-aided design
computer-aided design and manufacture
computer-aided engineering
computer-aided instruction
computer-aided (*or* -assisted) learning
computer-aided management
computer-aided manufacture
computer-aided teaching
computer aided trading
computerate
computer-based training
computer conferencing
computer graphics
computer input on microfilm
computer integrated manufacture
computerize
computer science
computer typesetting
concordance
concurrent processing
condition codes
configuration
connectivity
constant
control commands
cookie
core memory
co-routine
corrupt
crash
cross assembler
cursor
cut and paste
cybercafé
cyberpunk
cyberspace
cycle
DAC
data
data bank
database
database management
databus
data capture
dataflow architecture
data processing
data protection
data structure
Datel *(trademark)*
debugging
decision support system
decision table
default
desktop
desktop publishing
development system
device
digit
digital computer
digital fount
digital imaging
digital mapping
digital watermark
digitize
digitized
direct-access *or* random-access storage
direct memory access
directory
disassembler
distributed array processor
distributed logic
dithering
document
document reader
DOS *(trademark)*
dot matrix
download
downsize
down time
dumb terminal
dump
dpi
driver
dump
duplex
EBCDIC
echo
ecommerce
edit
editor
EEPROM
electronic flight information systems
electronic mail *or* E-mail
electronic office
electronic publishing
emulator
encryption
error message
escape routine
exclusive OR circuit
exit
expansion slot
expert system
extranet
fail-safe
field
fifth-generation
file
file manager
filename
file sharing
firewall
FireWire
firmware
flag
flops
flowchart
freeware
front-end processor
FTP
function
function key
fuzzy
gate
gateway
gif
giga-
gigabyte
global search
graphical user interface
graphics
greyed out
hacker
hand-held computer
handshake
hard card
hard copy
hardware
hard-wired
help screens
hexadecimal notation
high-level language
host
hot key
hotspot
housekeeping
HTML
hybrid computer
hypermedia
hypertext
icon
idle time
IM *or* instant messaging
image enhancement
incremental plotter
incremental recorder
infect
information technology

COMPUTER TERMS (CONTINUED)

initialize, input, input device, input/output, install, instruction, intelligent knowledge-based system, intelligent terminal, interactive, interactive video, Internet, interpreter, interrupt, intranet, ISDN, job, jpeg, key in, keyword, kilo-, kilobyte, LAN, language, lapheld, laptop, legacy, linked list, liveware, load, local area network, location, logic bomb, logic circuit, logic programming, login, log in, log out, loop, low-level language, machine code, machine learning, machine readable, machine translation, macro, magnetic bubble, mail bombing, mailbox, mainframe, main memory, malware, manager, mega-, megabyte, memory mapping, menu, menu-driven, microcomputer, microprocessor, midi, minicomputer, mobile device, module, morphing, mpeg, MP3, multiaccess, multi programming, multi-threaded, multi-user, NAND circuit, neurocomputer, node, NOR gate, notebook computer, NOT gate, object program, OEM, offline, online, open, open-source, operating system, optimize, OR gate, output, overflow, package, packet, packet-switching, palette, palmtop computer, parallel processing, parameter, parity check, parser, password, patch, patch board, PC, PDA, PDF, personal computer, piggyback, pixel, platform, plug compatible, podcast, pointer, polymorphic function, pop-up, portable, power down, power up, printout, procedure, process, program, program generator, programmable read only memory, programmer, programming language, program statement, prompt, protocol, query language, queue, queuing theory, random access memory *or* RAM, Random Instruction Set Computer, raster, read in, read out, read only memory *or* ROM, real-time processing, reboot, record, remote access, rerun, reserved word, reset, restricted users group, retrieval, RISC *or* reduced instruction set computer, robustness, routine, run, run time, screensaver, scroll, SCSI, search engine, sense, sequential access, serial access memory, serial processing, server, SGML, shareware, shell program, skinning, slide-show, smart card, software, software engineering, sort, source document, source program, spam, speech recognition, spreadsheet, sprite, spyware, stack, statement, storage capacity, storage device, store, store and forward, string, subroutine, supercomputer, SWITCH, syntax, system, systems analysis, systems disk, taskbar, teleprocessing, telesoftware, terabyte, terminal, tetrabyte, text processing, 3D graphics, throughput, time out, time sharing, toggle, toolbar, top-down processing, topology, transcribe, translator, transputer, tristate, turnkey system, underflow, UNIX *(trademark)*, uptime, USB, user-defined key, user group, utility, vaccine, variable, virtual address, virtual memory, virtual reality, virtual storage, virus, visual programming, voice input, voice recognition, voice response, volatile memory, WAN, WAP, warez, webcasting, web development, Wi-Fi, wild card, window, windows icons menus pointers *or* WIMP, wireless, wizard, word, word processor, work station, World Wide Web, worm, WYSIWIG, XML

COMPUTER SCIENTISTS

Ada, Countess of Lovelace *(British)*, Howard Aiken *(U.S.)*, Charles Babbage *(British)*, Tim Berners-Lee *(English)*, Seymour Cray *(U.S.)*, John Presper Eckert *(U.S.)*, Bill Gates *(U.S.)*, Herman Hollerith *(U.S.)*, John W. Mauchly *(U.S.)*, Clive Sinclair *(British)*, Alan Mathison Turing *(British)*, John von Neumann *(U.S.)*

3 = **fancy**, thought, idea, opinion, belief, notion, fantasy, judgment, vagary, whimsy • *the conceit that God has placed the creature of His image in the center of the cosmos*

QUOTATIONS

As for conceit, what man will do any good who is not conceited? Nobody holds a good opinion of a man who has a low opinion of himself

[Anthony Trollope *Orley Farm*]

conceited = **self-important**, vain, arrogant, stuck up *(informal)*, cocky, narcissistic, puffed up, egotistical, overweening, immodest, vainglorious, swollen-headed, bigheaded *(informal)*, full of yourself, too big for your boots *or* breeches • *I thought him conceited and arrogant.*
OPPOSITES: modest, humble, unassuming

conceivable = **imaginable**, possible, credible, believable, thinkable • *It is just conceivable that a single survivor may be found.*
OPPOSITES: incredible, unbelievable, inconceivable

conceive 1 = **imagine**, envisage, comprehend, visualize, think, believe, suppose, fancy, appreciate, grasp, apprehend • *We now cannot conceive of a world without electricity.*
2 = **think up**, form, produce, create, develop, design, project, purpose, devise, formulate, contrive • *I began to conceive a plan of attack.*
3 = **become pregnant**, get pregnant, become impregnated • *Women should give up alcohol before they plan to conceive.*

concentrate 1 = **focus your attention**, focus, pay attention, be engrossed, apply yourself • *Try to concentrate on what you're doing.*

OPPOSITES: disregard, pay no attention, lose concentration
2 = **focus**, centre, converge, bring to bear • *We should concentrate our efforts on tackling crime in the inner cities.*
3 = **gather**, collect, cluster, accumulate, congregate • *Most poor people are concentrated in this area.*
OPPOSITES: scatter, disperse, spread out

concentrated 1 = **condensed**, rich, undiluted, reduced, evaporated, thickened, boiled down • *Sweeten dishes with honey or concentrated apple juice.*
2 = **intense**, hard, deep, intensive, all-out *(informal)* • *She makes a concentrated effort to keep her feet on the ground.*

C

concentration 1 = **attention**, application, absorption, single-mindedness, intentness • *His talking kept breaking my concentration.*
OPPOSITES: distraction, disregard, inattention
2 = **focusing**, centring, consolidation, convergence, bringing to bear, intensification, centralization • *This concentration of effort and resources should not be to the exclusion of everything else.*
3 = **convergence**, collection, mass, cluster, accumulation, aggregation • *The area has one of the world's greatest concentrations of wildlife.*
OPPOSITES: scattering, spreading-out, diffusion

concept = **idea**, view, image, theory, impression, notion, conception, hypothesis, abstraction, conceptualization • *She added that the concept of arranged marriages is misunderstood in the west.*

conception 1 = **understanding**, idea, picture, impression, perception, clue, appreciation, comprehension, inkling • *He doesn't have the slightest conception of teamwork.*
2 = **idea**, plan, design, image, concept, notion • *The symphony is admirable in its conception.*
3 = **impregnation**, insemination, fertilization, germination • *Six weeks after conception your baby is the size of your little fingernail.*
4 = **origin**, beginning, launching, birth, formation, invention, outset, initiation, inception • *It is six years since the project's conception.*

concern AS A NOUN 1 = **anxiety**, fear, worry, distress, unease, apprehension, misgiving, disquiet, disquietude • *The move follows growing public concern over the spread of the disease.*
2 = **worry**, care, anxiety • *His concern was that people would know that he was responsible.*
3 = **affair**, issue, matter, consideration • *Feminism must address issues beyond the concerns of middle-class whites.*
4 = **care**, interest, regard, consideration, solicitude, attentiveness • *He had only gone along out of concern for his two grandsons.*
5 = **business**, job, charge, matter, department, field, affair, responsibility, task, mission, pigeon *(informal)* • *The technical aspects are not my concern.*
6 = **company**, house, business, firm, organization, corporation, enterprise, establishment • *If not a large concern, his business was at least a successful one.*
7 = **importance**, interest, bearing, relevance • *The survey's findings are a matter of great concern.*
▸ AS A VERB 1 = **worry**, trouble, bother, disturb, distress, disquiet, perturb, make uneasy, make anxious • *It concerned her that Bess was developing a crush on Max.*
2 = **be about**, cover, deal with, go into, relate to, have to do with • *The bulk of the book concerns the author's childhood.*
3 = **be relevant to**, involve, affect, regard, apply to, bear on, have something to do with, pertain to, interest, touch • *This matter doesn't concern you, so stay out of it.*

concerned 1 = **involved**, interested, active, mixed up, implicated, privy to • *I believe he was concerned in all those matters you mention.* • *It's been a difficult time for all concerned.*
2 = **worried**, troubled, upset, bothered, disturbed, anxious, distressed, uneasy • *I've been very concerned about the situation.*
OPPOSITES: detached, indifferent, aloof
3 = **caring**, attentive, solicitous • *A concerned friend put a comforting arm around her shoulder.*

concerning = **regarding**, about, re, touching, respecting, relating to, on the subject of, as to, with reference to, in the matter of, apropos of, as regards • *issues concerning the national interest of the United States*

concert AS A NOUN = **show** • *I've been to plenty of live rock concerts*
▸ IN PHRASES: **in concert** = **together**, jointly, unanimously, in unison, in league, in collaboration, shoulder to shoulder, concertedly • *He wants to act in concert with other nations.*

concerted 1 = **coordinated**, united, joint, combined, collaborative • *He says it is time for concerted action by world leaders.*
OPPOSITES: separate, uncooperative, disunited
2 = **strenuous**, strong, determined, earnest, active, intensive, energetic, resolute • *You must make a concerted effort to curb your over-indulgence.*

concession 1 = **compromise**, agreement, settlement, accommodation, adjustment, trade-off, give-and-take, half measures • *Britain has made sweeping concessions to China in order to reach a settlement.*
2 = **privilege**, right, permit, licence, franchise, entitlement, indulgence, prerogative • *The government has granted concessions to three private telephone companies.*
3 = **reduction**, saving, grant, discount, allowance • *tax concessions for mothers who choose to stay at home with their children*
4 = **surrender**, yielding, conceding, renunciation, relinquishment • *He said there'd be no concession of territory.*

conciliate 1 = **pacify**, win over, soothe, reconcile, disarm, appease, placate, mollify, propitiate • *His duty was to conciliate the people, not to provoke them.*
2 = **mediate**, intervene, arbitrate, interpose, make the peace, restore harmony, pour oil on troubled waters, clear the air, act as middleman • *He has conciliated in more than 600 unfair dismissal cases.*

conciliation = **pacification**, reconciliation, disarming, appeasement, propitiation, mollification, soothing, placation • *He is openly sceptical about peace talks and efforts at conciliation.*

conciliatory = **pacifying**, pacific, disarming, appeasing, mollifying, peaceable, placatory, propitiatory, soothing • *The next time he spoke he used a more conciliatory tone.*

concise = **brief**, short, to the point, compact, summary, compressed, condensed, terse, laconic, succinct, pithy, synoptic, epigrammatic, compendious • *The text is concise and informative.*
OPPOSITES: lengthy, rambling, long

conclave = **(secret** *or* **private) meeting**, council, conference, congress, session, cabinet, assembly, parley, runanga *(N.Z.)* • *In the US, Nato defence ministers have just ended a lengthy conclave.*

conclude 1 = **decide**, judge, establish, suppose, determine, assume, gather, reckon *(informal)*, work out, infer, deduce, surmise • *We concluded that he was telling the truth.*
2 = **come to an end**, end, close, finish, wind up, draw to a close • *The evening concluded with dinner and speeches.*
OPPOSITES: start, open, begin
3 = **bring to an end**, end, close, finish, complete, wind up, terminate, round off • *They concluded their annual summit meeting today.*
OPPOSITES: start, open, begin
4 = **accomplish**, effect, settle, bring about, fix, carry out, resolve, clinch, pull off, bring off *(informal)* • *If the clubs cannot conclude a deal, an independent tribunal will decide.*

conclusion AS A NOUN **1 = decision**, agreement, opinion, settlement, resolution, conviction, verdict, judgment, deduction, inference • *We came to the conclusion that it was too difficult to combine the two techniques.*
2 = end, ending, close, finish, completion, finale, termination, bitter end, result • *At the conclusion of the programme, viewers were invited to phone in.*
3 = outcome, result, upshot, consequence, sequel, culmination, end result, issue • *Executives said it was the logical conclusion of a process started in 1987.*
▸ IN PHRASES: **in conclusion = finally**, lastly, in closing, to sum up • *In conclusion, walking is a cheap, safe form of exercise.*

conclusive = decisive, final, convincing, clinching, definite, definitive, irrefutable, unanswerable, unarguable, ultimate • *There is no conclusive evidence that a murder took place.*
OPPOSITES: vague, doubtful, inconclusive

concoct = make up, design, prepare, manufacture, plot, invent, devise, brew, hatch, formulate, contrive, fabricate, think up, cook up *(informal)*, trump up, project • *He said the prisoner had concocted the story to get a lighter sentence.*

concoction = mixture, preparation, compound, brew, combination, creation, blend • *This concoction helps to control skin blemishes.*

concomitant = accompanying, related, associated, connected, attendant, complementary, collateral, consequent, resultant, concurrent, associative • *New methods had to be learnt, with concomitant delays in production.*

concord 1 = harmony, accord, peace, agreement, concert, friendship, consensus, goodwill, unison, good understanding, rapport, unanimity, amity, consonance • *A climate of concord and tolerance prevails among the Muslim and Christian Egyptian citizens.*
2 = treaty, agreement, convention, compact, protocol, entente, concordat • *The Concord of Wittenberg was agreed in 1536.*

concourse 1 = gathering *or* **meeting place**, hall, lounge, foyer, rallying point • *He crossed the station's concourse towards the escalator.*
2 = crowd, collection, gathering, assembly, crush, multitude, throng, convergence, hui *(N.Z.)*, assemblage, confluence, meeting, runanga *(N.Z.)* • *The streets were filled with a fair concourse of people that night.*

concrete AS A NOUN **= cement** *(not in technical usage)* • *The posts have to be set in concrete.*
▸ AS AN ADJECTIVE **1 = specific**, precise, explicit, definite, clear-cut, unequivocal, unambiguous • *He had no concrete evidence.*
OPPOSITES: vague, indefinite, unspecified
2 = real, material, actual, substantial, sensible, tangible, factual • *using concrete objects to teach addition and subtraction*
OPPOSITES: abstract, theoretical, intangible

concubine = mistress, courtesan, kept woman, paramour, odalisque • *the custom of husbands taking a concubine or an additional wife*

concur = agree, accord, approve, assent, accede, acquiesce • *Four other judges concurred with his verdict.*

concurrent = simultaneous, coexisting, concomitant, contemporaneous, coincident, synchronous, concerted • *He will actually be serving three concurrent sentences.*

concussion 1 = shock, brain injury • *She fell off a horse and suffered a concussion.*
2 = impact, crash, shaking, clash, jarring, collision, jolt, jolting • *I was blown off the deck by the concussion of the torpedoes.*

condemn 1 = denounce, damn, criticize, disapprove, censure, diss *(slang, chiefly U.S.)*, reprove, upbraid, excoriate, reprehend, blame, flame *(informal)* • *Political leaders united yesterday to condemn the latest wave of violence.*
OPPOSITES: approve, praise, acclaim
2 = sentence, convict, damn, doom, pass sentence on • *He was condemned to life imprisonment.*
OPPOSITES: free, liberate, acquit

QUOTATIONS
Society needs to condemn a little more and understand a little less
[John Major]

condemnation = denunciation, blame, censure, disapproval, reproach, stricture, reproof, reprobation, denouncement • *There was widespread condemnation of Saturday's killings.*

condemnatory = critical, accusing, disapproving, scathing, censorious, accusatory, proscriptive • *He was justified in some of his condemnatory outbursts.*

condensation 1 = moisture, liquid, damp, dampness, wetness • *He used his sleeve to wipe the condensation off the glass.*
2 = distillation, precipitation, liquefaction • *The surface refrigeration allows the condensation of water.*
3 = abridgment, summary, abstract, digest, contraction, synopsis, curtailment, précis, encapsulation • *a condensation of a book that offers ten ways to be a better manager*
4 = concentration, reduction, consolidation, compression, crystallization • *Matter is a temporary condensation of energy.*

condense 1 = abridge, contract, concentrate, compact, shorten, summarize, compress, curtail, encapsulate, abbreviate, epitomize, précis • *The English translation has been condensed into a single more readable book.*
OPPOSITES: increase, expand, elaborate
2 = concentrate, reduce, precipitate *(Chemistry)*, thicken, boil down, solidify, coagulate • *The compressed gas is cooled and condenses into a liquid.*
OPPOSITES: thin (out), weaken, dilute

condensed 1 = abridged, concentrated, compressed, curtailed, potted, shortened, summarized, slimmed-down, encapsulated • *I also produced a condensed version of the paper.*
2 = concentrated, reduced, thickened, boiled down, precipitated *(Chemistry)* • *condensed milk*

condescend 1 = patronize, talk down to, treat like a child, treat as inferior, treat condescendingly • *a writer who does not condescend to his readers*
2 = deign, see fit, lower yourself, be courteous enough, bend, submit, stoop, unbend *(informal)*, vouchsafe, come down off your high horse *(informal)*, humble *or* demean yourself • *He never condescended to notice me.*

condescending = patronizing, lordly, superior, lofty, snooty *(informal)*, snobbish, disdainful, supercilious, toffee-nosed *(slang, chiefly Brit.)*, on your high horse *(informal)* • *I'm fed up with your condescending attitude.*

condescension = patronizing attitude, superiority, disdain, haughtiness, loftiness, superciliousness, lordliness, airs • *There was a tinge of condescension in the way the girl received me.*

condition AS A NOUN **1 = state**, order, shape, nick *(Brit. informal)*, trim • *The two-bedroom chalet is in good condition.*
2 = situation, state, position, status, circumstances, plight, status quo *(Latin)*, case, predicament • *The government has to encourage people to better their condition.*
3 = requirement, terms, rider, provision, restriction, qualification, limitation, modification, requisite, prerequisite, proviso, stipulation, rule, demand • *They had agreed to a summit subject to certain conditions.*
4 = health, shape, fitness, trim, form, kilter, state of health, fettle, order • *She was in fine condition for a woman of her age.*
5 = ailment, problem, complaint, weakness, malady, infirmity • *Doctors suspect he may have a heart condition.*
▸ AS A PLURAL NOUN **= circumstances**, situation, environment, surroundings, way of life, milieu • *The conditions in the camp are just awful.*

▸ **AS A VERB** 1 = **train**, teach, educate, adapt, accustom, inure, habituate • *We have been conditioned to believe that it is weak to be scared.*
2 = **nourish**, improve, feed • *Lecithin is a protein which is excellent for conditioning dry and damaged hair.*
▸ **IN PHRASES: on condition that** = **provided that**, if, on the understanding that, as long as • *He only spoke to reporters on condition that he was not identified.*

conditional = **dependent**, limited, qualified, contingent, provisional, with reservations • *Their support is conditional on their approval of his proposals.* • *They have made us a conditional offer.*
OPPOSITES: absolute, unconditional, unrestricted

C

conditioning = **training**, education, teaching, accustoming, habituation • *Because of social conditioning, men don't expect to be managed by women.*

condolence = **sympathy**, pity, compassion, consolation, commiseration, fellow feeling • *She sent him a letter of condolence.*

condom = **sheath**, safe *(U.S. & Canad. slang)*, rubber *(U.S. slang)*, blob *(Brit. slang)*, scumbag *(U.S. slang)*, Frenchie *(slang)*, flunky *(slang)*, French letter *(slang)*, rubber johnny *(Brit. slang)*, French tickler *(slang)* • *It's much better to use a condom every time you have sex.*

condone = **overlook**, excuse, forgive, pardon, disregard, turn a blind eye to, wink at, look the other way, make allowance for, let pass • *I couldn't condone what she was doing.*
OPPOSITES: condemn, punish, denounce

conducive = **favourable**, helpful, productive, contributory, calculated to produce, leading, tending • *Make your bedroom as conducive to sleep as possible.*

conduct **AS A VERB** 1 = **carry out**, run, control, manage, direct, handle, organize, govern, regulate, administer, supervise, preside over • *I decided to conduct an experiment.*
2 = **transmit**, carry, spread, pass on, convey, diffuse, impart • *Water conducts heat faster than air.*
3 = **accompany**, lead, escort, guide, attend, steer, convey, usher, pilot • *He asked if he might conduct us to the ball.*
▸ **AS A NOUN** 1 = **management**, running, control, handling, administration, direction, leadership, organization, guidance, supervision • *Also up for discussion will be the conduct of free and fair elections.*
2 = **behaviour**, ways, bearing, attitude, manners, carriage, demeanour, deportment, mien *(literary)*, comportment • *Other people judge you by your conduct.*
▸ **IN PHRASES: conduct yourself** = **behave yourself**, act, carry yourself, acquit yourself, deport yourself, comport yourself • *The way he conducts himself reflects on the party.*

conduit = **passage**, channel, tube, pipe, canal, duct, main • *He saw that the conduit was choked with rubbish.*

confederacy = **union**, league, alliance, coalition, federation, compact, confederation, covenant, bund • *Vienna was established as the political and cultural capital of a new confederacy of Germanic states.*

confederate **AS A NOUN** = **associate**, partner, ally, colleague, accessory, accomplice, abettor • *The conspirators were joined by their confederates.*
▸ **AS AN ADJECTIVE** = **allied**, federal, associated, combined, federated, in alliance • *We want a confederate Europe.*

confer 1 = **discuss**, talk, consult, deliberate, discourse, converse, parley • *He conferred with Hill and the others in his office.*
2 = **grant**, give, present, accord, award, hand out, bestow, vouchsafe • *An honorary degree was conferred on him by Newcastle University in 1976.*

conference = **meeting**, congress, discussion, convention, forum, consultation, seminar, symposium, hui *(N.Z.)*, convocation, colloquium • *The president summoned the state governors to a conference on education.*

confess 1 = **admit**, acknowledge, disclose, confide, own up, come clean *(informal)*, divulge, blurt out, come out of the closet, make a clean breast of, get (something) off your chest *(informal)*, spill your guts *(slang)*, 'fess up *(U.S.)*, sing *(slang, chiefly U.S.)*, cough *(slang)* • *He has confessed to seventeen murders.* • *She confesses that she only wrote those books for the money.*
OPPOSITES: cover up, deny, hide
2 = **declare**, own up, allow, prove, reveal, grant, confirm, concede, assert, manifest, affirm, profess, attest, evince, aver • *I must confess I'm not a great sports enthusiast.*

confession = **admission**, revelation, disclosure, acknowledgment, avowal, divulgence, exposure, unbosoming • *His confession was extracted under duress*

PROVERBS
Confession is good for the soul

confidant *or* **confidante** = **close friend**, familiar, intimate, crony, alter ego, main man *(slang, chiefly U.S.)*, bosom friend • *You are her closest friend and confidante.*

confide = **tell**, admit, reveal, confess, whisper, disclose, impart, divulge, breathe • *He confided his worries to me.*

confidence **AS A NOUN** 1 = **trust**, belief, faith, dependence, reliance, credence • *I have every confidence in you.*
OPPOSITES: doubt, disbelief, distrust
2 = **self-assurance**, courage, assurance, aplomb, boldness, self-reliance, self-possession, nerve • *She always thinks the worst of herself and has no confidence whatsoever.*
OPPOSITES: fear, uncertainty, shyness
3 = **secret** • *I'm not in the habit of exchanging confidences with her.*
▸ **IN PHRASES: in confidence** = **in secrecy**, privately, confidentially, between you and me (and the gatepost), (just) between ourselves • *I'm telling you all these things in confidence.*

confident 1 = **certain**, sure, convinced, positive, secure, satisfied, counting on • *I am confident that everything will come out right in time.*
OPPOSITES: not sure, uncertain, unsure
2 = **self-assured**, positive, assured, bold, self-confident, self-reliant, self-possessed, sure of yourself, can-do *(informal)* • *In time he became more confident and relaxed.*
OPPOSITES: shy, afraid, insecure

confidential 1 = **secret**, private, intimate, classified, privy, off the record, hush-hush *(informal)* • *She accused them of leaking confidential information.*
2 = **secretive**, low, soft, hushed • *He adopted a confidential tone of voice.*

confidentially = **in secret**, privately, personally, behind closed doors, in confidence, in camera, between ourselves, sub rosa • *Confidentially, I am not sure they knew what was happening.*

configuration = **arrangement**, form, shape, cast, outline, contour, conformation, figure • *The flow of water follows the configuration of the rock strata.*

confine **AS A VERB** 1 = **imprison**, enclose, shut up, intern, incarcerate, circumscribe, hem in, immure, keep, cage • *He has been confined to his barracks.*
2 = **restrict**, limit • *She had largely confined her activities to the world of big business.*
▸ **AS A PLURAL NOUN** = **limits**, bounds, boundaries, compass, precincts, circumference, edge, pale • *The movie is set entirely within the confines of the abandoned factory.*

confined = **restricted**, small, limited, narrow, enclosed, cramped • *His long legs were cramped in the confined space.*

confinement 1 = **imprisonment**, custody, detention, incarceration, internment, porridge *(slang)* • *She had been held in solitary confinement for four months.*
2 = **childbirth**, labour, travail, parturition, childbed, accouchement *(French)*, time • *His pregnant wife is near her confinement.*

confirm 1 = **prove**, support, establish, back up, verify, validate, bear out, substantiate, corroborate, authenticate • *This confirms what I suspected all along.*
2 = **affirm**, state, declare, assert, testify, pronounce, certify, attest, aver, avouch • *He confirmed that the area was now in rebel hands.*
3 = **ratify**, establish, approve, sanction, endorse, authorize, certify, validate, authenticate • *He is due to be confirmed as President on Friday.*
4 = **strengthen**, establish, settle, fix, secure, assure, reinforce, clinch, verify, fortify • *He has confirmed his position as the world's number one snooker player.*

confirmation 1 = **proof**, evidence, testimony, verification, ratification, validation, corroboration, authentication, substantiation • *He took her resignation as confirmation of their suspicions.*
OPPOSITES: denial, contradiction, repudiation
2 = **affirmation**, approval, acceptance, endorsement, ratification, assent, agreement • *She glanced over at James for confirmation of what she'd said.*
OPPOSITES: refusal, rejection, disapproval

confirmed = **long-established**, seasoned, rooted, chronic, hardened, habitual, ingrained, inveterate, inured, dyed-in-the-wool • *I'm a confirmed bachelor.*

confiscate = **seize**, appropriate, impound, commandeer, sequester, expropriate, sequestrate • *They confiscated weapons, ammunition and propaganda material.*
OPPOSITES: give, return, give back

confiscation = **seizure**, appropriation, impounding, forfeiture, expropriation, sequestration, takeover • *Anyone convicted of drug trafficking would be liable to confiscation of assets and imprisonment.*

conflagration = **fire**, blaze, holocaust, inferno, wildfire • *All the stock was destroyed in a warehouse conflagration.*

conflict AS A NOUN 1 = **dispute**, difference, opposition, hostility, disagreement, friction, strife, fighting, antagonism, variance, discord, bad blood, dissension, divided loyalties • *Try to keep any conflict between you and your ex-partner to a minimum.*
OPPOSITES: accord, agreement, harmony
2 = **struggle**, battle, clash, strife • *the anguish of his own inner conflict*
3 = **battle**, war, fight, clash, contest, set-to *(informal)*, encounter, combat, engagement, warfare, collision, contention, strife, head-to-head, fracas, boilover *(Austral.)* • *The National Security Council has met to discuss ways of preventing a military conflict.*
OPPOSITES: peace, treaty, truce
▸ AS A VERB = **be incompatible**, clash, differ, disagree, contend, strive, collide, be at variance • *He held firm opinions which sometimes conflicted with my own.*
OPPOSITES: agree, coincide, reconcile

conflicting = **incompatible**, opposed, opposing, clashing, contrary, contradictory, inconsistent, paradoxical, discordant • *There are conflicting reports on the severity of his injuries.*
OPPOSITES: agreeing, similar, consistent

confluence = **convergence**, junction, concurrence, conflux • *The 160-metre falls mark the confluence of the rivers.*

conform 1 = **fit in**, follow, yield, adjust, adapt, comply, obey, fall in, toe the line, follow the crowd, run with the pack, follow convention • *Children who can't or won't conform are often bullied.*
2 with **with** = **fulfil**, meet, match, suit, satisfy, agree with, obey, abide by, accord with, square with, correspond with, tally with, harmonize with • *These activities do not conform with diplomatic rules and regulations.*

conformation = **shape**, build, form, structure, arrangement, outline, framework, anatomy, configuration • *Poor conformation means a horse is more susceptible to injury.*

conformist = **traditionalist**, conservative, reactionary, Babbitt *(U.S.)*, stickler, yes man, stick-in-the-mud *(informal)*, conventionalist • *He's described as a conformist, an orthodox member of his party.*

conformity 1 = **compliance**, agreement, accordance, observance, conformance, obedience • *The prime minister is, in conformity with the constitution, chosen by the president.*
2 = **conventionality**, compliance, allegiance, orthodoxy, observance, traditionalism, Babbittry *(U.S.)* • *Excessive conformity is usually caused by fear of disapproval.*

confound 1 = **bewilder**, baffle, amaze, confuse, astonish, startle, mix up, astound, perplex, surprise, mystify, flummox, boggle the mind, be all Greek to *(informal)*, dumbfound, nonplus, flabbergast *(informal)* • *For many years medical scientists were confounded by these seemingly contradictory facts.*
2 = **disprove**, contradict, refute, negate, destroy, ruin, overwhelm, explode, overthrow, demolish, annihilate, give the lie to, make a nonsense of, prove false, blow out of the water *(slang)*, controvert, confute • *The findings confound all the government's predictions.*

confront 1 = **tackle**, deal with, cope with, brave, beard, face up to, meet head-on • *We are learning how to confront death.*
2 = **trouble**, face, afflict, perplex, perturb, bedevil • *the environmental crisis which confronts us all*
3 = **challenge**, face, oppose, tackle, encounter, defy, call out, stand up to, come face to face with, accost, face off *(slang)* • *She pushed her way through the mob and confronted him face to face.*
OPPOSITES: challenge, flee, evade

confrontation = **conflict**, fight, crisis, contest, set-to *(informal)*, encounter, showdown *(informal)*, head-to-head, face-off *(slang)*, boilover *(Austral.)* • *This issue could lead to a military confrontation.*

confuse 1 = **mix up with**, take for, mistake for, muddle with • *I can't see how anyone could confuse you two with each other.*
2 = **bewilder**, puzzle, baffle, perplex, mystify, fluster, faze, flummox, bemuse, be all Greek to *(informal)*, nonplus • *Politics just confuses me.*
3 = **obscure**, cloud, complicate, muddle, darken, make more difficult, muddy the waters • *His critics accused him of trying to confuse the issue.*

confused 1 = **bewildered**, puzzled, baffled, at sea, muddled, dazed, perplexed, at a loss, taken aback, disorientated, muzzy *(U.S. informal)*, nonplussed, flummoxed, at sixes and sevens, thrown off balance, discombobulated *(informal, chiefly U.S. & Canad.)*, not with it *(informal)*, not knowing if you are coming or going • *People are confused about what they should eat to stay healthy.*
OPPOSITES: aware, with it *(informal)*, enlightened
2 = **disorderly**, disordered, chaotic, mixed up, jumbled, untidy, out of order, in disarray, topsy-turvy, disorganized, higgledy-piggledy *(informal)*, at sixes and sevens, disarranged, disarrayed • *The situation remains confused as both sides claim victory.* • *Everything lay in a confused heap on the floor.*
OPPOSITES: ordered, in order, tidy

QUOTATIONS

If you are sure you understand everything that is going on, you are hopelessly confused
[Walter Mondale]

Anyone who isn't confused doesn't really understand the situation
[Ed Murrow (on the Vietnam War)]

confusing = **bewildering**, complicated, puzzling, misleading, unclear, baffling, muddling, contradictory, ambiguous, inconsistent, perplexing, clear as mud *(informal)* • *The statement they issued was highly confusing.*
OPPOSITES: clear, simple, plain

confusion 1 = **bewilderment**, doubt, uncertainty, puzzlement, perplexity, mystification, bafflement, perturbation • *Omissions in my recent article may have caused some confusion.*
OPPOSITES: solution, explanation, enlightenment
2 = **disorder**, chaos, turmoil, upheaval, muddle, bustle, shambles, disarray, commotion, disorganization, disarrangement • *The rebel leader seems to have escaped in the confusion.*
OPPOSITES: order, organization, arrangement
3 = **puzzlement**, bewilderment, perplexity, bafflement, mystification, perturbation • *I left his office in a state of confusion.*

QUOTATIONS
Confusion is a word we have invented for an order which is not understood
[Henry Miller *Tropic of Capricorn*]
with ruin upon ruin, rout on rout,
Confusion worse confounded
[John Milton *Paradise Lost*]

congeal = **thicken**, set, freeze, harden, clot, stiffen, condense, solidify, curdle, jell, coagulate • *The blood had started to congeal.*

congenial = **pleasant**, kindly, pleasing, friendly, agreeable, cordial, sociable, genial, affable, convivial, companionable, favourable, complaisant • *The food at the party was excellent, and the company congenial.*

congenital 1 = **inborn**, innate, inherent, hereditary, natural, constitutional, inherited, inbred, hard-wired • *When he was 17, he died of congenital heart disease.*
2 = **complete**, confirmed, chronic, utter, hardened, thorough, habitual, incurable, inveterate, incorrigible, deep-dyed *(usually derogatory)* • *He is a congenital liar.*

congested 1 = **packed (out)**, crowded, choked, swarming, overcrowded, teeming, jam-packed, bursting at the seams, crammed full, overpopulated, like the Black Hole of Calcutta, hoatching *(Scot.)* • *Some areas are congested with both cars and people.*
OPPOSITES: empty, half-full, uncrowded
2 = **clogged**, jammed, blocked-up, overfilled, stuffed, packed, crammed, overflowing, stuffed-up • *The arteries in his neck had become fatally congested.*
OPPOSITES: free, clear, unhindered

congestion = **overcrowding**, crowding, mass, jam, clogging, bottleneck, snarl-up *(informal, chiefly Brit.)* • *Energy consumption, road congestion and pollution have increased.*

conglomerate = **corporation**, multinational, corporate body, business, association, consortium, aggregate, agglomerate • *Fiat is Italy's largest industrial conglomerate.*

conglomeration = **mass**, combination, composite, accumulation, assortment, medley, potpourri, aggregation, miscellany, mishmash, hotchpotch • *a conglomeration of buildings, all tightly packed together*

congratulate = **compliment**, pat on the back, wish joy to • *She congratulated him on the birth of his son.*

congratulations AS A PLURAL NOUN = **good wishes**, greetings, compliments, best wishes, pat on the back, felicitations • *I offer you my congratulations on your appointment as chairman.*
▸ AS AN INTERJECTION = **good wishes**, greetings, compliments, best wishes, felicitations • *Congratulations! You have a healthy baby boy.*

congregate = **come together**, meet, mass, collect, gather, concentrate, rally, assemble, flock, muster, convene, converge, throng, rendezvous, foregather, convoke • *People were already beginning to congregate outside the cinema.*
OPPOSITES: part, separate, disperse

congregation = **parishioners**, host, brethren, crowd, assembly, parish, flock, fellowship, multitude, throng, laity, flock • *Most members of the congregation arrive a few minutes before the service.*

congress 1 = **meeting**, council, conference, diet, assembly, convention, conclave, legislative assembly, convocation, hui *(N.Z.)*, runanga *(N.Z.)* • *A lot has changed since the party congress.*
2 = **legislature**, house, council, parliament, representatives, delegates, quango, legislative assembly, chamber of deputies, House of Representatives *(N.Z.)* • *It's far from certain that the congress will approve them.*

congruence = **compatibility**, accord, agreement, harmony, coincidence, correspondence, consistency, conformity, concurrence, congruity • *the absence of the necessary congruence between political, cultural and economic forces*

congruent = **compatible**, agreeing, according, consistent, identical, coinciding, corresponding, conforming, concurrent, congruous • *The interests of landowners were by no means congruent with those of industrial capitalists.*

conical *or* **conic** = **cone-shaped**, pointed, tapered, tapering, pyramidal, funnel-shaped • *We were soon aware of a great conical shape to the north-east.*

conjectural = **speculative**, theoretical, tentative, hypothetical, supposed, academic, surmised, suppositional • *There is something undeniably conjectural about such claims.*

conjecture AS A NOUN = **guess**, theory, fancy, notion, speculation, assumption, hypothesis, inference, presumption, surmise, theorizing, guesswork, supposition, shot in the dark, guesstimate *(informal)* • *Your assertion is merely a conjecture, not a fact.*
▸ AS A VERB = **guess**, speculate, surmise, theorize, suppose, imagine, assume, fancy, infer, hypothesize • *This may or may not be true; we are all conjecturing here.*

conjugal = **marital**, nuptial, matrimonial, married, wedded, bridal, spousal, connubial • *A woman's refusal to allow her husband his conjugal rights was once grounds for divorce.*

conjunction = **combination**, union, joining, association, coincidence, juxtaposition, concurrence • *This is due to a conjunction of religious and social factors.*

conjure AS A VERB 1 = **produce**, generate, bring about, give rise to, make, create, effect, produce as if by magic • *They managed to conjure an impressive victory.*
2 *often with* **up** = **summon up**, raise, invoke, rouse, call upon • *The ouija board is used to conjure up spirits and communicate with them.*
▸ IN PHRASES: **conjure something up** = **bring to mind**, recall, evoke, recreate, recollect, produce as if by magic • *When he closed his eyes, he could conjure up almost every event of his life.*

conjuring = **magic**, juggling, trickery, sleight of hand, legerdemain, prestidigitation • *The show includes performances of conjuring, dancing, and exhibitions of strength.*

conjuror *or* **conjurer** = **magician**, illusionist • *A conjuror was hired for her sixth birthday party.*

connect 1 = **link**, join, couple, attach, fasten, affix, unite • *You can connect the machine to your hi-fi.*
OPPOSITES: part, separate, divide
2 = **associate**, unite, join, couple, league, link, mix, relate, pair, ally, identify, combine, affiliate, correlate, confederate, lump together, mention in the same breath, think of together • *There is no evidence to connect him to the robberies.* • *I wouldn't have connected the two events if you hadn't said that.*

connected = **linked**, united, joined, coupled, related, allied, associated, combined, bracketed, affiliated, akin, banded together • *skin problems connected with exposure to the sun*

connection 1 = **association**, relationship, link, relation, bond, correspondence, relevance, tie-in, correlation, interrelation • *There is no evidence of any connection between BSE and the brain diseases recently confirmed in cats.*
2 = **communication**, alliance, commerce, attachment, intercourse, liaison, affinity, affiliation, union • *I no longer

have any connection with my ex-husband's family.
3 = **link**, coupling, junction, fastening, tie • *Check radiators for small leaks, especially round pipework connections.*
4 = **contact**, friend, relation, ally, associate, relative, acquaintance, kin, kindred, kinsman, kith • *She used her connections to full advantage.*
5 = **context**, relation, reference, frame of reference • *13 men have been questioned in connection with the murder.*

connivance = **collusion**, intrigue, conspiring, complicity, abetting, tacit consent, abetment • *The crime had been carried out with police connivance.*

connive AS A VERB = **conspire**, scheme, plot, intrigue, collude • *Senior politicians connived to ensure that he was not released.*
▸ IN PHRASES: **connive at something** = **turn a blind eye to**, overlook, pass by, disregard, abet, wink at, look the other way, blink at, be a party to, be an accessory to, be in collusion with, let pass, shut your eyes to, lend yourself to, aid • *Mr Mandela suggested the government had connived at the violence.*

conniving = **scheming**, designing, plotting, calculating, conspiring, contriving • *She was seen as a conniving, greedy woman.*

connoisseur = **expert**, authority, judge, specialist, buff (*informal*), devotee, boffin (*Brit. informal*), whiz (*informal*), arbiter, aficionado, savant, maven (*U.S.*), appreciator, cognoscente, fundi (*S. African*), fancier • *I hear you're something of an art connoisseur.*
QUOTATIONS
connoisseur: a specialist who knows everything about something and nothing about anything else
[Ambrose Bierce *The Devil's Dictionary*]

connotation = **implication**, colouring, association, suggestion, significance, nuance, undertone • *It's just one of those words that's got so many negative connotations.*

connote = **imply**, suggest, indicate, intimate, signify, hint at, betoken, involve • *The term 'ladies' connotes females who are simultaneously put on a pedestal and patronised.*

conquer 1 = **seize**, obtain, acquire, occupy, overrun, annex, win • *Early in the eleventh century the whole of England was again conquered by the Vikings.*
2 = **defeat**, overcome, overthrow, beat, stuff (*slang*), master, tank (*slang*), triumph, crush, humble, lick (*informal*), undo, subdue, rout, overpower, quell, get the better of, clobber (*slang*), vanquish, subjugate, prevail over, checkmate, run rings around (*informal*), wipe the floor with (*informal*), make mincemeat of (*informal*), put in their place, blow out of the water (*slang*), bring to their knees • *a Navajo myth about a great warrior who conquers the spiritual enemies of his people*
OPPOSITES: lose to, give up to, submit to
3 = **overcome**, beat, defeat, master, rise above, overpower, get the better of, surmount, best • *I had learned to conquer my fear of spiders.*
QUOTATIONS
I came, I saw, I conquered (veni, vidi, vici)
[Julius Caesar]
To conquer with arms is to make only a temporary conquest; to conquer the world by earning its esteem is to make a permanent conquest
[Woodrow Wilson *Address to Congress*]

conqueror = **winner**, champion, master, victor, conquistador, lord • *Spain had a tradition of learning long before the arrival of their Muslim conquerors.*

conquest 1 = **takeover**, coup, acquisition, invasion, occupation, appropriation, annexation, subjugation, subjection • *He had led the conquest of southern Poland in 1939.*
2 = **defeat**, victory, triumph, overthrow, pasting (*slang*), rout, mastery, vanquishment • *This hidden treasure charts the brutal Spanish conquest of the Aztecs.*
3 = **seduction** • *people who boast about their sexual conquests*
4 = **catch**, prize, supporter, acquisition, follower, admirer, worshipper, adherent, fan, feather in your cap • *He was a womaniser whose conquests included everyone from prostitutes to princesses.*

conscience AS A NOUN 1 = **principles**, scruples, moral sense, sense of right and wrong, still small voice • *I have battled with my conscience over whether I should send this letter or not.*
2 = **guilt**, shame, regret, remorse, contrition, self-reproach, self-condemnation • *She was suffering terrible pangs of conscience about what she had done.*
▸ IN PHRASES: **in all conscience** = **in fairness**, rightly, certainly, fairly, truly, honestly, in truth, assuredly • *She could not, in all conscience, back out on her deal with him.*
QUOTATIONS
Conscience: the inner voice which warns us that someone may be looking
[H.L. Mencken *A Little Book in C Major*]
Thus conscience does make cowards of us all
[William Shakespeare *Hamlet*]
Conscience is thoroughly well-bred and soon leaves off talking to those who do not wish to hear it
[Samuel Butler]
PROVERBS
A guilty conscience needs no accuser

conscientious 1 = **thorough**, particular, careful, exact, faithful, meticulous, painstaking, diligent, punctilious • *She is generally very conscientious about her work.*
OPPOSITES: slack, irresponsible, careless
2 = **honourable**, just, responsible, moral, strict, straightforward, upright, honest, scrupulous, high-minded, incorruptible, high-principled • *I admired this noble, conscientious man.*
OPPOSITES: unscrupulous, unprincipled

conscious 1 *often with* **of** = **aware of**, wise to (*slang*), alert to, responsive to, cognizant of, sensible of, clued-up on (*informal*), percipient of • *She was very conscious of Max studying her.*
OPPOSITES: unconscious, unaware, ignorant
2 = **deliberate**, knowing, reasoning, studied, responsible, calculated, rational, reflective, self-conscious, intentional, wilful, premeditated • *Make a conscious effort to relax your muscles.*
OPPOSITES: unconscious, accidental, unintentional
3 = **awake**, wide-awake, sentient, alive • *She was fully conscious throughout the operation.*
OPPOSITES: asleep, unconscious, oblivious

consciousness 1 = **awareness**, understanding, knowledge, recognition, enlightenment, sensibility, realization, apprehension • *His political consciousness sprang from his upbringing.*
2 = **sentience**, awareness, sensibility • *She banged her head and lost consciousness.*
QUOTATIONS
Consciousness ... is the phenomenon whereby the universe's very existence is made known
[Roger Penrose *The Emperor's New Mind*]

consecrate = **sanctify**, dedicate, ordain, exalt, venerate, set apart, hallow, devote • *The church was consecrated in 1234.*

consecutive = **successive**, running, following, succeeding, in turn, uninterrupted, chronological, sequential, in sequence, seriatim • *This was their fourth consecutive meeting in the past four days.*

consensus = **agreement**, general agreement, unanimity, common consent, unity, harmony, assent, concord, concurrence, kotahitanga (*N.Z.*) • *The declaration reflects a growing consensus on the types of reform necessary in developing countries.*

consent AS A NOUN = **agreement**, sanction, approval,

go-ahead *(informal)*, permission, compliance, green light, assent, acquiescence, concurrence, O.K. *or* okay *(informal)* • *Can my child be medically examined without my consent?*
OPPOSITES: refusal, disagreement, dissent
▸ **AS A VERB** = **agree**, approve, yield, permit, comply, concur, assent, accede, acquiesce, play ball *(informal)* • *I was a little surprised when she consented to my proposal.*
OPPOSITES: refuse, decline, resist

consequence **AS A NOUN** 1 = **result**, effect, outcome, repercussion, end, issue, event, sequel, end result, upshot • *Her lawyers said she understood the consequences of her actions.*
2 = **importance**, interest, concern, moment, value, account, note, weight, import, significance, portent • *This question is of little consequence.*
3 = **status**, standing, bottom, rank, distinction, eminence, repute, notability • *He was a sad little man of no consequence.*
▸ **IN PHRASES:** **in consequence** = **consequently**, as a result, so, then, thus, therefore, hence, accordingly, for that reason, thence, ergo • *His death was totally unexpected and, in consequence, no plans had been made for his replacement.*

PROVERBS
As you sow, so shall you reap

consequent = **following**, resulting, subsequent, successive, ensuing, resultant, sequential • *The warming of the Earth and the consequent climatic changes affect us all.*

consequential 1 = **resulting**, subsequent, successive, ensuing, indirect, consequent, resultant, sequential, following • *The company disclaims any liability for incidental or consequential damages.*
2 = **important**, serious, significant, grave, far-reaching, momentous, weighty, eventful • *From a medical standpoint, a week is usually not a consequential delay.*

consequently = **as a result**, thus, therefore, necessarily, hence, subsequently, accordingly, for that reason, thence, ergo • *My grandfather sustained a broken back and, consequently, spent the rest of his life in a wheelchair.*

conservation 1 = **preservation**, saving, protection, maintenance, custody, safeguarding, upkeep, guardianship, safekeeping • *Attention must be paid to the conservation of the environment.*
2 = **economy**, saving, thrift, husbandry, careful management, thriftiness • *projects aimed at energy conservation*

conservative **AS AN ADJECTIVE** = **traditional**, guarded, quiet, conventional, moderate, cautious, sober, reactionary, die-hard, middle-of-the-road, hidebound • *People tend to be more adventurous when they're young and more conservative as they get older.*
OPPOSITES: liberal, radical, progressive
▸ **AS A NOUN** = **traditionalist**, moderate, reactionary, die-hard, middle-of-the-roader, stick-in-the-mud *(informal)* • *The new judge is regarded as a conservative.*
OPPOSITES: changer, radical, progressive

QUOTATIONS
I do not know which makes a man more conservative – to know nothing but the present, or nothing but the past
[John Maynard Keynes *The End of Laissez-Faire*]
A man who is determined never to move out of the beaten road cannot lose his way
[William Hazlitt *The Round Table*]
A conservative is a man with two perfectly good legs who, however, has never learned to walk forward
[Franklin D. Roosevelt]
The most radical revolutionary will become a conservative the day after the revolution
[Hannah Arendt]
Conservative: a statesman who is enamoured of existing evils, as distinguished from the Liberal, who wishes to replace them with others
[Ambrose Bierce *The Cynic's Word Book*]

Conservative **AS AN ADJECTIVE** = **Tory**, Republican *(U.S.)*, right-wing • *Even among Conservative voters, more than a third disapprove of the tax.*
▸ **AS A NOUN** = **Tory**, Republican *(U.S.)*, right-winger • *Up to eighty Conservatives are expected to vote against the bill.*

QUOTATIONS
I've got money so I'm a Conservative
[Lord Thomson of Fleet]
I am driven into grudging toleration of the Conservative Party because it is the party of non-politics, of resistance to politics
[Kingsley Amis]

conservatory = **greenhouse**, hothouse, glasshouse • *The plant is susceptible to frost but can be placed in a conservatory or greenhouse.*

conserve 1 = **save**, husband, take care of, hoard, store up, go easy on, use sparingly • *The factory has closed over the weekend to conserve energy.*
OPPOSITES: spend, blow *(slang)*, waste
2 = **protect**, keep, save, preserve • *an increase in US aid to help developing countries conserve their forests*

consider 1 = **think**, see, believe, rate, judge, suppose, deem, view as, look upon, regard as, hold to be, adjudge • *I had always considered myself a strong, competent woman.*
2 = **think about**, study, reflect on, examine, weigh, contemplate, deliberate, muse, ponder, revolve, meditate, work over, mull over, eye up, ruminate, chew over, cogitate, turn over in your mind • *Consider how much you can afford to pay.*
3 = **bear in mind**, remember, regard, respect, think about, care for, take into account, reckon with, take into consideration, make allowance for, keep in view • *You have to consider the feelings of those around you.*

considerable = **large**, goodly, much, great, marked, comfortable, substantial, reasonable, tidy, lavish, ample, noticeable, abundant, plentiful, tolerable, appreciable, sizable *or* sizeable • *We have already spent a considerable amount of money on repairs.*
OPPOSITES: small, insignificant, meagre

considerably = **greatly**, very much, seriously *(informal)*, significantly, remarkably, substantially, markedly, noticeably, appreciably • *Their dinner parties had become considerably less formal.*

considerate = **thoughtful**, kind, kindly, concerned, obliging, attentive, mindful, unselfish, solicitous • *I think he's the most charming, considerate man I've ever met.*
OPPOSITES: selfish, thoughtless, inconsiderate

consideration **AS A NOUN** 1 = **thought**, study, review, attention, regard, analysis, examination, reflection, scrutiny, deliberation, contemplation, perusal, cogitation • *He said there should be careful consideration of the company's future role.*
2 = **thoughtfulness**, concern, respect, kindness, friendliness, tact, solicitude, kindliness, considerateness • *Show consideration for other rail travellers.*
3 = **factor**, point, issue, concern, element, aspect, determinant • *Price was a major consideration in our choice of house.*
4 = **payment**, fee, reward, remuneration, recompense, perquisite, tip • *He does odd jobs for a consideration.*
▸ **IN PHRASES:** **take something into consideration** = **bear in mind**, consider, remember, think about, weigh, take into account, make allowance for, keep in view • *Other factors must also be taken into consideration.*

considering **AS A PREPOSITION** = **taking into account**, in the light of, bearing in mind, in view of, keeping in mind, taking into consideration • *The former hostage is in remarkably good shape considering his ordeal.*
▸ **AS AN ADVERB** = **all things considered**, all in all, taking everything into consideration, taking everything into account • *I think you've got off very lightly, considering.*

consign 1 = **put away**, commit, deposit, relegate • *For decades, many of his works were consigned to the basements of museums.*
2 = **deliver**, ship, transfer, transmit, convey • *He had managed to obtain arms in France and have them safely consigned to America.*

consignment = **shipment**, delivery, batch, goods • *The first consignment of food has already left Bologna.*

consist IN PHRASES: **consist in something** = **lie in**, involve, reside in, be expressed by, subsist in, be found *or* contained in • *His work as a consultant consists in advising foreign companies.*
consist of something = **be made up of**, include, contain, incorporate, amount to, comprise, be composed of • *My diet consisted almost exclusively of fruit.*

consistency 1 = **agreement**, harmony, correspondence, accordance, regularity, coherence, compatibility, uniformity, constancy, steadiness, steadfastness, evenness, congruity • *There's always a lack of consistency in matters of foreign policy.*
2 = **texture**, density, thickness, firmness, viscosity, compactness • *I added a little milk to mix the dough to the right consistency.*

QUOTATIONS
Consistency is the last refuge of the unimaginative
[Oscar Wilde]
A foolish consistency is the hobgoblin of little minds
[Ralph Waldo Emerson *Essays: Self-Reliance*]

consistent 1 = **steady**, even, regular, stable, constant, persistent, dependable, unchanging, true to type, undeviating • *He has never been the most consistent of players.*
OPPOSITES: changing, irregular, erratic
2 = **compatible**, agreeing, in keeping, harmonious, in harmony, consonant, in accord, congruent, congruous, accordant • *These new goals are not consistent with the existing policies.*
OPPOSITES: contrary, contradictory, incompatible
3 = **coherent**, logical, compatible, harmonious, consonant, all of a piece • *A theory should be internally consistent.*
OPPOSITES: contradictory, inconsistent, incompatible

QUOTATIONS
We cannot remain consistent with the world save by growing inconsistent with our past selves
[Havelock Ellis *The Dance of Life*]

consolation = **comfort**, help, support, relief, ease, cheer, encouragement, solace, succour, alleviation, assuagement • *After her husband's death, she found great consolation in her children.*

console = **comfort**, cheer, relieve, soothe, support, encourage, calm, solace, assuage, succour, express sympathy for • *I can console myself with the thought that I'm not alone.*
OPPOSITES: trouble, hurt, distress

QUOTATIONS
Isn't everyone consoled when faced with a trouble or fact he doesn't understand, by a word, some simple word, which tells us nothing and yet calms us?
[Luigi Pirandello *Six Characters in Search of an Author*]
Anything that consoles is fake
[Iris Murdoch *Prayer and the Pursuit of Happiness*]

consolidate 1 = **strengthen**, secure, reinforce, cement, fortify, stabilize • *The Prime Minister hopes to consolidate existing trade ties between the two countries.*
2 = **combine**, unite, join, marry, merge, unify, amalgamate, federate, conjoin • *The state's four higher education boards are to be consolidated.*

consolidation 1 = **strengthening**, reinforcement, fortification, stabilization • *Change brought about the growth and consolidation of the working class.*
2 = **combination**, union, association, alliance, merger, federation, amalgamation • *Further consolidations in the industry may follow.*

consonant = **in agreement with**, correspondent with, consistent with, compatible with, in accordance with, harmonious with, concordant with, congruous with, according with • *Their work is very much consonant with this way of thinking.*

consort AS A VERB = **associate with**, mix with, mingle with, hang with (*informal, chiefly U.S.*), go around with, keep company with, fraternize with, hang about, around *or* out with • *He regularly consorted with drug-dealers.*
▸ AS A NOUN = **spouse**, wife, husband, partner, associate, fellow, squeeze (*informal*), companion, significant other (*U.S. informal*), bidie-in (*Scot.*), wahine (*N.Z.*), wifey (*informal*) • *Queen Victoria's consort, Prince Albert*

conspicuous = **obvious**, clear, apparent, visible, patent, evident, manifest, noticeable, blatant, discernible, salient, perceptible, easily seen • *Her conspicuous lack of warmth confirmed that they were no longer friends.*
OPPOSITES: hidden, concealed, inconspicuous

conspiracy = **plot**, scheme, intrigue, collusion, confederacy, cabal, frame-up (*slang*), machination, league • *Many people believe there was a conspiracy to kill President Kennedy in 1963.*

conspirator = **plotter**, intriguer, conspirer, traitor, schemer • *the conspirators who had planned to kill the King*

conspire 1 = **plot**, scheme, intrigue, devise, manoeuvre, contrive, machinate, plan, hatch treason • *I had a persecution complex and thought people were conspiring against me.*
2 = **work together**, combine, contribute, cooperate, concur, tend, conduce • *History and geography have conspired to bring Greece to a moment of decision.*

constancy 1 = **steadiness**, stability, regularity, uniformity, perseverance, firmness, permanence, fixedness • *Climate reflects a basic struggle between constancy and change.*
2 = **faithfulness**, loyalty, devotion, fidelity, dependability, trustworthiness, steadfastness • *Even before they were married, she had worried about his constancy.*

QUOTATIONS
But I am constant as the northern star
Of whose true-fixed and resting quality
There is no fellow in the firmament
[William Shakespeare *Julius Caesar*]

constant 1 = **continuous**, sustained, endless, persistent, eternal, relentless, perpetual, continual, never-ending, habitual, uninterrupted, interminable, unrelenting, incessant, everlasting, ceaseless, unremitting, nonstop • *Women are under constant pressure to be thin.*
OPPOSITES: occasional, random, irregular
2 = **unchanging**, even, fixed, regular, permanent, stable, steady, uniform, continual, unbroken, immutable, immovable, invariable, unalterable, unvarying, firm • *The temperature should be kept more or less constant.*
OPPOSITES: changing, variable, unstable
3 = **faithful**, true, devoted, loyal, stalwart, staunch, dependable, trustworthy, trusty, steadfast, unfailing, tried-and-true • *She couldn't bear the thought of losing her constant companion.*
OPPOSITES: fickle, disloyal, undependable

constantly = **continuously**, always, all the time, invariably, continually, aye (*Scot.*), endlessly, relentlessly, persistently, perpetually, night and day, incessantly, nonstop, interminably, everlastingly, twenty-four-seven (*informal*), morning, noon and night • *The direction of the wind is constantly changing.*
OPPOSITES: sometimes, occasionally, from time to time

consternation = **dismay**, shock, alarm, horror, panic, anxiety, distress, confusion, terror, dread, fright, amazement, fear, bewilderment, trepidation • *His decision caused consternation among his colleagues.*

constituent AS A NOUN 1 = **voter**, elector, member of the electorate • *They plan to consult their constituents before taking action.*

2 = **component**, element, ingredient, part, unit, factor, principle • *Caffeine is the active constituent of drinks such as tea and coffee.*

▸ AS AN ADJECTIVE = **component**, basic, essential, integral, elemental • *The fuel is dissolved in nitric acid and separated into its constituent parts.*

constitute 1 = **represent**, be, consist of, embody, exemplify, be equivalent to • *The result of the vote hardly constitutes a victory.*

2 = **make up**, make, form, compose, comprise • *The country's ethnic minorities constitute 7 per cent of its total population.*

3 = **set up**, found, name, create, commission, establish, appoint, delegate, nominate, enact, authorize, empower, ordain, depute • *On 6 July a People's Revolutionary Government was constituted.*

constitution 1 = **laws**, code, charter, canon, body of law • *The king was forced to adopt a new constitution which reduced his powers.*

2 = **state of health**, build, body, make-up, frame, physique, physical condition • *He must have an extremely strong constitution.*

3 = **structure**, form, nature, make-up, organization, establishment, formation, composition, character, temper, temperament, disposition • *He ran a small research team looking into the chemical constitution of coal.*

constitutional AS AN ADJECTIVE = **legitimate**, official, legal, chartered, statutory, vested • *We have a constitutional right to demonstrate.*

▸ AS A NOUN = **walk**, stroll, turn, airing • *I met him as he was taking his daily constitutional.*

constrain 1 = **restrict**, confine, curb, restrain, rein, constrict, hem in, straiten, check, chain • *Women are too often constrained by family commitments.*

2 = **force**, pressure, urge, bind, compel, oblige, necessitate, coerce, impel, pressurize, drive • *Individuals will be constrained to make many sacrifices for the greater good.*

constrained = **forced**, reserved, guarded, inhibited, subdued, unnatural, reticent • *I realised, from his constrained smile, that he resented what I was saying.*

constraint 1 = **restriction**, limitation, curb, rein, deterrent, hindrance, damper, check • *Their decision to abandon the trip was made because of financial constraints.*

2 = **force**, pressure, necessity, restraint, compulsion, coercion • *People are not morally responsible for that which they do under constraint or compulsion.*

3 = **repression**, reservation, embarrassment, restraint, inhibition, timidity, diffidence, bashfulness • *She feels no constraint in discussing sexual matters.*

constrict 1 = **squeeze**, contract, narrow, restrict, shrink, tighten, pinch, choke, cramp, strangle, compress, strangulate • *Severe migraine can be treated with a drug which constricts the blood vessels.*

2 = **limit**, restrict, confine, curb, inhibit, delimit, straiten • *Senators crafting the bill were frequently constricted by budget limits.*

constriction = **tightness**, pressure, narrowing, reduction, squeezing, restriction, constraint, cramp, compression, blockage, stenosis *(Pathology)*, limitation, impediment, stricture • *Smoking tobacco products causes constriction of the arteries.*

construct 1 = **build**, make, form, create, design, raise, establish, set up, fashion, shape, engineer, frame, manufacture, put up, assemble, put together, erect, fabricate • *The boxes should be constructed from rough-sawn timber.*

OPPOSITES: level, destroy, demolish

2 = **create**, make, form, set up, organize, compose, put together, formulate • *You will find it difficult to construct a spending plan without first recording your outgoings.*

construction 1 = **building**, assembly, creation, formation, composition, erection, fabrication • *With the exception of teak, this is the finest wood for boat construction.*

2 = **structure**, building, edifice, form, figure, shape • *The British pavilion is an impressive steel and glass construction.*

3 = **interpretation**, meaning, reading, sense, explanation, rendering, take *(informal, chiefly U.S.)*, inference • *He put the wrong construction on what he saw.*

4 = **composition**, structure, arrangement • *Avoid complex verbal constructions.*

constructive = **helpful**, positive, useful, practical, valuable, productive • *Both men described the talks as frank, friendly and constructive.*

OPPOSITES: negative, useless, unproductive

construe = **interpret**, take, read, explain • *He may construe your approach as a hostile act.*

consult 1 = **ask**, refer to, turn to, interrogate, take counsel, ask advice of, pick (someone's) brains, question • *Consult your doctor before undertaking a strenuous exercise programme.*

2 = **confer**, talk, debate, deliberate, commune, compare notes, consider • *The umpires consulted quickly.*

3 = **refer to**, check in, look in • *He had to consult a pocket dictionary.*

4 = **consider**, regard, respect, take account of, take into consideration, have regard for • *They must not feel the decision has been made without consulting their feelings.*

QUOTATIONS

consult: to seek another's approval of a course already decided on

[Ambrose Bierce *The Devil's Dictionary*]

consultant = **specialist**, adviser, counsellor, authority • *He was a consultant for the Swedish government.*

consultation 1 = **discussion**, talk, council, conference, dialogue • *Next week he'll be in Florida for consultations with President Mitterrand.*

2 = **meeting**, interview, session, appointment, examination, deliberation, hearing • *A personal diet plan is devised after a consultation with a nutritionist.*

consume 1 = **eat**, swallow, devour, put away, gobble (up), eat up, guzzle, polish off *(informal)*, hoover *(informal)* • *Andrew would consume nearly two pounds of cheese per day.*

2 = **use up**, use, spend, waste, employ, absorb, drain, exhaust, deplete, squander, utilize, dissipate, expend, eat up, fritter away • *Some of the most efficient refrigerators consume 70 percent less electricity than traditional models.*

3 = **destroy**, devastate, demolish, ravage, annihilate, lay waste • *Fire consumed the building.*

4 *often passive* = **obsess**, dominate, absorb, preoccupy, devour, eat up, monopolize, engross • *I was consumed by fear.*

consumer = **buyer**, customer, user, shopper, purchaser • *If consumers demand more of a product then more of it will be supplied.*

QUOTATIONS

The consumer, so it is said, is the king ... each is a voter who uses his money as votes to get the things done that he wants done

[Paul A. Samuelson *Economics*]

Every man is a consumer, and ought to be a producer ... He is by constitution expensive, and needs to be rich

[Ralph Waldo Emerson *Wealth*]

consuming = **overwhelming**, gripping, absorbing, compelling, devouring, engrossing, immoderate • *He has developed a consuming passion for chess.*

consummate AS AN ADJECTIVE 1 = **skilled**, perfect, supreme, polished, superb, practised, accomplished, tasty *(Brit. informal)*, matchless • *He acted the part with consummate skill.*

2 = **complete**, total, supreme, extreme, ultimate, absolute, utter, conspicuous, unqualified, deep-dyed *(usually derogatory)* • *He was a consummate liar and exaggerator.*

▸**AS A VERB** = **complete**, finish, achieve, conclude, perform, perfect, carry out, crown, fulfil, end, accomplish, effectuate, put the tin lid on • *No one has yet been able to consummate a deal.*
OPPOSITES: start, begin, initiate

consummation = **completion**, end, achievement, perfection, realization, fulfilment, culmination • *We look forward to the consummation of this transaction.*

consumption 1 = **using up**, use, loss, waste, drain, consuming, expenditure, exhaustion, depletion, utilization, dissipation • *The laws have led to a reduction in fuel consumption.*
2 = **eating**, drinking, ingestion • *food and drink which is not fit for human consumption*
3 = **tuberculosis**, atrophy, T.B., emaciation • *an opera about a prostitute dying of consumption in a garret*

contact **AS A NOUN** 1 = **communication**, link, association, connection, correspondence, intercourse • *Opposition leaders are denying any contact with the government in Kabul.*
2 = **touch**, contiguity • *Hepatitis B virus is spread by contact with infected blood.*
3 = **connection**, colleague, associate, liaison, acquaintance, confederate • *Her business contacts described her as 'a very determined lady'.*
▸**AS A VERB** = **get** *or* **be in touch with**, call, reach, approach, phone, ring (up) *(informal, chiefly Brit.)*, write to, speak to, communicate with, get hold of, touch base with *(U.S. & Canad. informal)*, e-mail, text • *When she first contacted me, she was upset.*

contagion 1 = **contamination**, infection, corruption, pollution, taint • *They have been reluctant to admit AIDS patients because of unfounded fears of contagion.*
2 = **spread**, spreading, communication, passage, proliferation, diffusion, transference, dissemination, dispersal, transmittal • *He continues to isolate his country from the contagion of foreign ideas.*
▸**RELATED PHOBIA:** misophobia

contagious = **infectious**, catching, spreading, epidemic, communicable, transmissible, pestilential • *I felt like I had some contagious disease.*

contain 1 = **hold**, incorporate, accommodate, enclose, have capacity for • *Factory shops contain a wide range of cheap furnishings.*
2 = **include**, consist of, embrace, comprise, embody, comprehend • *The committee contains 11 Democrats and nine Republicans.*
3 = **restrain**, control, hold in, curb, suppress, hold back, stifle, repress, keep a tight rein on • *The city authorities said the curfew had contained the violence.*

container = **holder**, vessel, repository, receptacle • *The paint is supplied in a clear, plastic container.*

CONTAINERS FOR LIQUID

amphora	flask	rehoboam
ampulla	gourd	Salmanazar
Balthazar	half-bottle	screw-top *(informal)*
barrel	hogshead	stubby *(Austral. informal)*
bottle	jar	tantalus
can	jeroboam	tin
carafe	jug	tinny *(Austral. slang)*
carton	keg	tube *(Austral. slang)*
cask	magnum	
coldie *(Austral. slang)*	Methuselah	
decanter	miniature	
firkin	Nebuchadnezzar	
flagon	pitcher	
	polypin	

contaminate = **pollute**, infect, stain, corrupt, taint, sully, defile, adulterate, befoul, soil • *The fishing waters have been contaminated with toxic wastes.*
OPPOSITES: clean, cleanse, purify

contaminated = **polluted**, dirtied, poisoned, infected, stained, corrupted, tainted, sullied, defiled, soiled, adulterated • *More than 100,000 people could fall ill after drinking contaminated water.*

contamination = **pollution**, dirtying, infection, corruption, poisoning, decay, taint, filth, impurity, contagion, adulteration, foulness, defilement • *Acid rain is responsible for the destruction of forests and the contamination of rivers and streams.*

contemplate 1 = **consider**, plan, think of, propose, intend, envisage, foresee, have in view *or* in mind • *He contemplated a career as an army medical doctor.*
2 = **think about**, consider, ponder, mull over, reflect upon, ruminate (upon), meditate on, brood over, muse over, deliberate over, revolve *or* turn over in your mind • *He lay in his hospital bed and cried as he contemplated his future.*
3 = **look at**, examine, observe, check out *(informal)*, inspect, gaze at, behold, eye up, view, study, regard, survey, stare at, scrutinize, eye • *He contemplated his hands thoughtfully.*

contemplation 1 = **thought**, consideration, reflection, musing, meditation, pondering, deliberation, reverie, rumination, cogitation • *The garden is a place of quiet contemplation.*
2 = **observation**, viewing, looking at, survey, examination, inspection, scrutiny, gazing at • *He was lost in contemplation of the landscape.*

contemplative = **thoughtful**, reflective, introspective, rapt, meditative, pensive, ruminative, in a brown study, intent, musing, deep *or* lost in thought • *He is a quiet, contemplative sort of chap.*

contemporary **AS AN ADJECTIVE** 1 = **modern**, latest, recent, current, with it *(informal)*, trendy *(Brit. informal)*, up-to-date, present-day, in fashion, up-to-the-minute, à la mode, newfangled, happening *(informal)*, present, ultramodern • *The gallery holds regular exhibitions of contemporary art, sculpture and photography.*
OPPOSITES: old, early, old-fashioned
2 = **coexisting**, concurrent, contemporaneous, synchronous, coexistent • *The book draws upon official records and the reports of contemporary witnesses.*
▸**AS A NOUN** = **peer**, fellow, equal, compeer • *a glossary of terms used by Shakespeare and his contemporaries*

contempt = **scorn**, disdain, mockery, derision, disrespect, disregard, contumely • *I will treat that remark with the contempt it deserves.*
OPPOSITES: liking, regard, respect

contemptible = **despicable**, mean, low, base, cheap, worthless, shameful, shabby, vile, degenerate, low-down *(informal)*, paltry, pitiful, abject, ignominious, measly, scurvy, detestable, odious • *Her husband is a contemptible little man.* • *It was an utterly contemptible thing to do.*
OPPOSITES: attractive, pleasant, admirable

contemptuous = **scornful**, insulting, arrogant, withering, sneering, cavalier, condescending, haughty, disdainful, insolent, derisive, supercilious, high and mighty, on your high horse *(informal)* • *She gave a contemptuous little laugh and walked away.*
OPPOSITES: civil, mannerly, respectful

contend **AS A VERB** 1 = **argue**, hold, maintain, allege, assert, affirm, avow, aver • *The government contends that he is a fundamentalist.*
2 = **compete**, fight, struggle, clash, contest, strive, vie, grapple, jostle, skirmish • *The two main groups contended for power.*
▸**IN PHRASES:** **contend with something** = **face**, meet, deal with, oppose, tackle, cope with, confront, grapple with • *It is time, once again, to contend with racism.*

C

contender = **competitor**, rival, candidate, applicant, hopeful, contestant, aspirant • *Her trainer said yesterday that she would be a strong contender for a place in the British team.*

content[1] AS A NOUN 1 = **subject matter**, ideas, matter, material, theme, text, substance, essence, gist • *She is reluctant to discuss the content of the play.*
2 = **amount**, measure, size, load, volume, capacity • *Sunflower margarine has the same fat content as butter.*
▸ AS A PLURAL NOUN 1 = **constituents**, elements, load, ingredients • *Empty the contents of the pan into the sieve.*
2 = **subjects**, chapters, themes, topics, subject matter, divisions • *There is no initial list of contents at the start of the book.*

content[2] AS AN ADJECTIVE = **satisfied**, happy, pleased, contented, comfortable, fulfilled, at ease, gratified, agreeable, willing to accept • *I'm perfectly content with the way the campaign has gone.*
▸ AS A NOUN = **satisfaction**, peace, ease, pleasure, comfort, peace of mind, gratification, contentment • *Once he'd retired, he could potter about the garden to his heart's content.*
▸ IN PHRASES: **content yourself with something** = **satisfy yourself with**, be happy with, be satisfied with, be content with • *He had to content himself with the knowledge that he had been right.*

contented = **satisfied**, happy, pleased, content, comfortable, glad, cheerful, at ease, thankful, gratified, serene, at peace • *Whenever he returns to this place he is happy and contented.*
OPPOSITES: troubled, uncomfortable, discontented

contention AS A NOUN 1 = **assertion**, claim, stand, idea, view, position, opinion, argument, belief, allegation, profession, declaration, thesis, affirmation • *Sufficient research evidence exists to support this contention.*
2 = **dispute**, hostility, disagreement, feuding, strife, wrangling, discord, enmity, dissension • *They generally tried to avoid subjects of contention between them.*
▸ IN PHRASES: **in contention** = **in competition**, competing, contesting, in the running, in the hunt *(informal)* • *He was in contention for a place in the squad.*

contentious = **argumentative**, wrangling, perverse, bickering, combative, pugnacious, quarrelsome, litigious, querulous, cavilling, disputatious, factious, captious • *He was a sociable if rather contentious man.*

contentment = **satisfaction**, peace, content, ease, pleasure, comfort, happiness, fulfilment, gratification, serenity, equanimity, gladness, repletion, contentedness • *I cannot describe the feeling of contentment that was with me at that time.*
OPPOSITES: discomfort, discontent, dissatisfaction

QUOTATIONS
Poor and content is rich and rich enough
[William Shakespeare *Othello*]

contest AS A NOUN 1 = **competition**, game, match, trial, tournament, head-to-head • *Few contests in the recent history of British boxing have been as thrilling.*
2 = **struggle**, fight, battle, debate, conflict, dispute, encounter, controversy, combat, discord, turf war *(informal)* • *a bitter contest over who should control the state's future*
▸ AS A VERB 1 = **compete in**, take part in, fight in, go in for, contend for, vie in • *He quickly won his party's nomination to contest the elections.*
2 = **oppose**, question, challenge, argue, debate, dispute, object to, litigate, call in *or* into question • *Your former employer has to reply within 14 days in order to contest the case.*

contestant = **competitor**, candidate, participant, contender, entrant, player, aspirant • *She was a former contestant in the Miss World beauty pageant.*

context 1 = **circumstances**, times, conditions, situation, ambience • *the historical context in which Chaucer wrote*
2 = **frame of reference**, background, framework, relation, connection • *Without a context, I would have assume it was written by a man.*

contiguous = **near**, touching, bordering, neighbouring, beside, adjacent, in contact, adjoining, next door to, juxtaposed, abutting, next, juxtapositional • *The vineyards are virtually contiguous with those of Ausone.*

continence = **self-restraint**, moderation, self-control, celibacy, abstinence, chastity, temperance, asceticism • *The most widely used methods of contraception in those days were continence and coitus interruptus.*

QUOTATIONS
You command continence; give what you command, and command what you will
[St. Augustine of Hippo *Confessions*]

continent

CONTINENTS

Africa	Europe
Antarctica	North America
Asia	South America
Australia	

contingency = **possibility**, happening, chance, event, incident, accident, emergency, uncertainty, eventuality, juncture • *I need to provide for all possible contingencies.*

contingent AS A NOUN = **group**, detachment, deputation, set, body, section, bunch *(informal)*, quota, batch • *There were contingents from the navies of virtually all EC countries.*
▸ AS AN ADJECTIVE = **chance**, random, casual, uncertain, accidental, haphazard, fortuitous • *these apparently random, contingent and unexplained phenomena*
▸ IN PHRASES: **contingent on** = **dependent on**, subject to, controlled by, conditional on • *Growth is contingent on improved incomes.*

continual 1 = **constant**, endless, continuous, eternal, perpetual, uninterrupted, interminable, incessant, everlasting, unremitting, unceasing • *Despite continual pain, he refused all drugs.*
OPPOSITES: broken, erratic
2 = **frequent**, regular, repeated, repetitive, recurrent, oft-repeated • *She suffered continual police harassment.*
OPPOSITES: occasional, irregular, periodic

continually 1 = **constantly**, always, all the time, forever, aye *(Scot.)*, endlessly, eternally, incessantly, nonstop, interminably, everlastingly, twenty-four-seven *(informal)* • *The large rotating fans whirred continually.*
2 = **repeatedly**, often, frequently, many times, over and over, again and again, time and (time) again, persistently, time after time, many a time and oft *(archaic or poetic)* • *He continually changed his mind.*

continuance = **perpetuation**, lasting, carrying on, keeping up, endurance, continuation, prolongation • *The agreement guarantees the continuance of the UN mission.*

continuation 1 = **continuing**, lasting, carrying on, maintenance, keeping up, endurance, perpetuation, prolongation • *What we'll see in the future is a continuation of this trend.*
2 = **addition**, extension, supplement, sequel, resumption, postscript • *This chapter is a continuation of Chapter 8.*

continue 1 = **keep on**, go on, maintain, pursue, sustain, carry on, stick to, keep up, prolong, persist in, keep at, persevere, stick at, press on with • *Outside the hall, people continued their vigil.*
OPPOSITES: stop, give up, quit
2 = **go on**, advance, progress, proceed, carry on, keep going,

crack on *(informal)* • *As the investigation continued, the plot began to thicken.*
3 = **resume**, return to, take up again, proceed, carry on, recommence, pick up where you left off • *She looked up for a moment, then continued drawing.*
OPPOSITES: stop, give up, quit
4 = **remain**, last, stay, rest, survive, carry on, live on, endure, stay on, persist, abide • *For ten days I continued in this state.* • *He had hoped to continue as a full-time career officer.*
OPPOSITES: leave, retire, quit

continuing = **lasting**, sustained, enduring, ongoing, in progress • *We advocate a continuing process of constitutional discussion.*

continuity = **cohesion**, flow, connection, sequence, succession, progression, wholeness, interrelationship • *They want to ensure that standardization of methods and continuity of ideas will be achieved.*

continuous = **constant**, continued, extended, prolonged, unbroken, uninterrupted, unceasing • *Residents reported that they heard continuous gunfire.*
OPPOSITES: broken, occasional

contort = **twist**, knot, distort, warp, deform, misshape • *His face contorts as he screams out the lyrics.*

contortion = **twist**, distortion, deformity, convolution, bend, knot, warp • *The symptoms of the poison included facial contortions.*

contour = **outline**, profile, lines, form, figure, shape, relief, curve, silhouette • *The light of dawn began to outline the contours of the hills.*

contraband = **smuggled**, illegal, illicit, black-market, hot *(informal)*, banned, forbidden, prohibited, unlawful, bootleg, bootlegged, interdicted • *Most of the city markets were flooded with contraband goods.*

contract AS A NOUN = **agreement**, deal *(informal)*, commission, commitment, arrangement, understanding, settlement, treaty, bargain, convention, engagement, pact, compact, covenant, bond, stipulation, concordat • *The company won a prestigious contract for work on the building.*
▸ AS A VERB 1 = **agree**, arrange, negotiate, engage, pledge, bargain, undertake, come to terms, shake hands, covenant, make a deal, commit yourself, enter into an agreement • *He has contracted to lease part of the collection to a museum in Japan.*
OPPOSITES: refuse, decline, disagree
2 = **constrict**, confine, tighten, shorten, wither, compress, condense, shrivel • *New research shows that an excess of meat and salt can contract muscles.*
3 = **tighten**, narrow, knit, purse, shorten, pucker • *As we move our bodies, our muscles contract and relax.*
OPPOSITES: develop, stretch, expand
4 = **lessen**, reduce, shrink, diminish, decrease, dwindle • *Output fell last year and is expected to contract further this year.*
OPPOSITES: increase, grow, develop
5 = **catch**, get, develop, acquire, incur, be infected with, go down with, be afflicted with • *He contracted AIDS from a blood transfusion.*
OPPOSITES: avoid, escape, avert

QUOTATIONS
A verbal contract isn't worth the paper it is written on
[Sam Goldwyn]

contraction 1 = **tightening**, narrowing, tensing, shortening, drawing in, constricting, shrinkage • *Cramp is caused by contraction of the muscles.*
2 = **abbreviation**, reduction, shortening, compression, diminution, constriction, elision • *'It's' is a contraction of 'it is'.*

contradict 1 = **dispute**, deny, challenge, belie, fly in the face of, make a nonsense of, gainsay *(archaic or literary)*, be at variance with • *We knew she was wrong, but nobody liked to contradict her.* • *His comments contradict remarks he made earlier that day.*
2 = **negate**, deny, oppose, counter, contravene, rebut, impugn, controvert • *The result appears to contradict a major study carried out last December.*
OPPOSITES: support, agree, confirm

contradiction 1 = **conflict**, inconsistency, contravention, incongruity, confutation • *They see no contradiction in using violence to bring about a religious state.*
2 = **negation**, opposite, denial, antithesis • *What he does is a contradiction of what he says.*

contradictory = **inconsistent**, conflicting, opposed, opposite, contrary, incompatible, paradoxical, irreconcilable, antithetical, discrepant • *He seems to be capable of holding a number of apparently contradictory attitudes.*

contraption = **device**, instrument, mechanism, apparatus, gadget, contrivance, waldo, rig • *an interesting musical contraption called a Theremin*

contrary AS AN ADJECTIVE 1 = **opposite**, different, opposed, clashing, counter, reverse, differing, adverse, contradictory, inconsistent, diametrically opposed, antithetical • *His sister was of the contrary opinion to his.*
OPPOSITES: consistent, parallel, in agreement
2 = **perverse**, difficult, awkward, wayward, intractable, wilful, obstinate, cussed *(informal)*, stroppy *(Brit. slang)*, cantankerous, disobliging, unaccommodating, thrawn *(Scot. & Northern English dialect)*, arsey *(Brit., Austral. & N.Z. slang)* • *Why must she always be so contrary?*
OPPOSITES: willing, helpful, cooperative
▸ AS A NOUN = **opposite**, reverse, converse, antithesis • *Let me assure you that the contrary is, in fact, the case.*
▸ IN PHRASES: **contrary to** = **at odds with**, counter to, in opposition to • *Contrary to popular belief, moderate exercise actually decreases your appetite.*
on the contrary = **quite the opposite** *or* **reverse**, on the other hand, in contrast, conversely • *The government must, on the contrary, re-establish its authority.*

contrast AS A NOUN = **difference**, opposition, comparison, distinction, foil, disparity, differentiation, divergence, dissimilarity, contrariety • *The two women provided a startling contrast in appearance.*
▸ AS A VERB 1 = **differentiate**, compare, oppose, distinguish, set in opposition • *She contrasted the situation then with the present crisis.*
2 = **differ**, be contrary, be distinct, be at variance, be dissimilar • *Johnstone's easy charm contrasted with the prickliness of his boss.*

contravene 1 = **break**, violate, go against, infringe, disobey, transgress • *He said the article did not contravene the industry's code of conduct.*
2 = **conflict with**, cross, oppose, interfere with, thwart, contradict, hinder, go against, refute, counteract • *This deportation order contravenes basic human rights.*

contravention 1 = **breach**, violation, infringement, trespass, disobedience, transgression, infraction • *They are in direct contravention of the law.*
2 = **conflict**, interference, contradiction, hindrance, rebuttal, refutation, disputation, counteraction • *He denied that the new laws were a contravention of fundamental rights.*

contretemps 1 = **argument**, disagreement, quarrel, row, clash, dispute, controversy, falling out *(informal)*, barney *(informal)*, squabble, wrangle, bickering, difference of opinion, fight, altercation • *There had been a slight contretemps over who was to drive the car.*
2 = **mishap**, mistake, difficulty, accident, misfortune, uphill *(S. African)*, predicament, calamity • *His cross-country tour had its full share of comic contretemps.*

contribute AS A VERB = **give**, provide, supply, donate, furnish, subscribe, chip in *(informal)*, bestow • *They say they would like to contribute more to charity.*
▸ IN PHRASES: **contribute to something** = **be partly**

C

responsible for, lead to, be instrumental in, be conducive to, conduce to, help • *Design faults in the boat contributed to the tragedy.*

contribution = **gift**, offering, grant, donation, input, subscription, bestowal, koha *(N.Z.)* • *companies that make charitable contributions of a half million dollars or more*

contributor 1 = **donor**, supporter, patron, subscriber, backer, bestower, giver • *Redford is the institute's leading financial contributor and is active in fund-raising.*
2 = **writer**, correspondent, reporter, journalist, freelance, freelancer, journo *(slang)*, hackette *(derogatory)* • *All of the pieces by the magazine's contributors appear anonymously.*

contrite = **sorry**, humble, chastened, sorrowful, repentant, remorseful, regretful, penitent, conscience-stricken, in sackcloth and ashes • *He was so contrite that he wrote me a letter of apology.*

contrition = **regret**, sorrow, remorse, repentance, compunction, penitence, self-reproach • *The next day he'd be full of contrition for hurting her.*

contrivance 1 = **device**, machine, equipment, gear, instrument, implement, mechanism, invention, appliance, apparatus, gadget, contraption • *They wear simple clothes and shun modern contrivances.*
2 = **stratagem**, plan, design, measure, scheme, trick, plot, dodge, expedient, ruse, artifice, machination • *It is nothing more than a contrivance to raise prices.*

contrive 1 = **devise**, plan, fabricate, create, design, scheme, engineer, frame, manufacture, plot, construct, invent, improvise, concoct, wangle *(informal)* • *The oil companies were accused of contriving a shortage of gasoline to justify price increases.*
2 = **manage**, succeed, arrange, manoeuvre • *Somehow he contrived to pass her a note without her chaperone seeing it.*

contrived = **forced**, planned, laboured, strained, artificial, elaborate, unnatural, overdone, recherché • *It mustn't sound like a contrived compliment.*
OPPOSITES: natural, relaxed, genuine

control AS A NOUN 1 = **power**, government, rule, authority, management, direction, command, discipline, guidance, supervision, jurisdiction, supremacy, mastery, superintendence, charge • *The first aim of his government would be to establish control over the republic's territory.*
2 = **restraint**, check, regulation, brake, limitation, curb • *There are to be tighter controls on land speculation.*
3 = **self-discipline**, cool, calmness, self-restraint, restraint, coolness, self-mastery, self-command • *He had a terrible temper, and sometimes lost control completely.*
4 = **switch**, instrument, button, dial, lever, knob • *He adjusted the temperature control.*
▸ AS A PLURAL NOUN = **instruments**, dash, dials, console, dashboard, control panel • *He died of a heart attack while at the controls of the plane.*
▸ AS A VERB 1 = **have power over**, lead, rule, manage, boss *(informal)*, direct, handle, conduct, dominate, command, pilot, govern, steer, administer, oversee, supervise, manipulate, call the shots, call the tune, reign over, keep a tight rein on, have charge of, superintend, have (someone) in your pocket, keep on a string • *He now controls the largest retail development empire in southern California.* • *My husband tried to control me in every way.*
2 = **limit**, restrict, curb, delimit • *The government tried to control rising health-care costs.*
3 = **restrain**, limit, check, contain, master, curb, hold back, subdue, repress, constrain, bridle, rein in • *Try to control that temper of yours.*

QUOTATIONS
Who controls the past controls the future: who controls the present controls the past
[George Orwell *Nineteen Eighty-Four*]
Who can control his fate?
[William Shakespeare *Othello*]

controversial = **disputed**, contended, contentious, at issue, debatable, polemic, under discussion, open to question, hot-button *(informal)*, disputable • *Immigration is a controversial issue in many countries.*

controversy = **argument**, debate, row, discussion, dispute, contention, quarrel, squabble, strife, wrangle, wrangling, polemic, altercation, dissension • *The proposed cuts have caused considerable controversy.*

contusion = **bruise**, injury, swelling, trauma *(Pathology)*, discoloration, knock • *He had lacerations and contusions all over his arm and shoulder.*

conundrum = **puzzle**, problem, riddle, enigma, teaser, poser, brain-teaser *(informal)* • *It was a conundrum with no solution.*

convalesce = **recover**, rest, rally, rehabilitate, recuperate, improve • *After two weeks I was allowed home, where I convalesced for three months.*

convalescence = **recovery**, rehabilitation, recuperation, return to health, improvement • *He was home for three weeks' convalescence after a bout of jaundice.*

convalescent = **recovering**, getting better, recuperating, on the mend, improving, mending • *You may need vitamin supplements if you have been ill or are convalescent.*

convene 1 = **call**, gather, assemble, summon, bring together, muster, convoke • *He convened a meeting of all the managers.*
2 = **meet**, gather, rally, assemble, come together, muster, congregate • *Senior officials convened in London for an emergency meeting.*

convenience AS A NOUN 1 = **benefit**, good, interest, advantage • *He was happy to make a detour for her convenience.*
2 = **suitability**, fitness, appropriateness, opportuneness • *She was delighted with the convenience of this arrangement.*
3 = **usefulness**, utility, serviceability, handiness • *The convenience of digital cameras means that more and more people are buying them nowadays.*
OPPOSITES: inconvenience, uselessness
4 = **accessibility**, availability, nearness, handiness • *They miss the convenience of London's tubes and buses.*
5 = **appliance**, facility, comfort, amenity, labour-saving device, help • *The chalets have all the modern conveniences.*
▸ IN PHRASES: **at your convenience** = **at a suitable time**, at your leisure, in your own time, whenever you like, in your spare time, in a spare moment • *Please call me to set up an appointment at your convenience.*

convenient 1 = **suitable**, fitting, fit, handy, satisfactory, befitting • *The family found it more convenient to eat in the kitchen.*
2 = **useful**, practical, handy, serviceable, labour-saving • *Pre-prepared foods are a tempting and convenient option.*
OPPOSITES: awkward, useless, unsuitable
3 = **nearby**, available, accessible, handy, at hand, within reach, close at hand, just round the corner • *The town is convenient for Heathrow Airport.*
OPPOSITES: distant, out-of-the-way, inaccessible
4 = **appropriate**, timely, suited, suitable, beneficial, well-timed, opportune, seasonable, helpful • *She will try to arrange a mutually convenient time for an interview.*

convent = **nunnery**, religious community, religious house • *She entered a Carmelite convent at the age of 21.*

QUOTATIONS
The convent, which belongs to the West as it does to the East, to antiquity as it does to the present time, to Buddhism and Muhammadanism as it does to Christianity, is one of the optical devices whereby man gains a glimpse of infinity
[Victor Hugo *Les Misérables*]
I like convents, but I wish they would not admit anyone under the age of fifty
[Napoleon Bonaparte]

convention 1 = **custom**, practice, tradition, code, usage, protocol, formality, etiquette, propriety, kawa *(N.Z.)*, tikanga *(N.Z.)*, rule • *It's just a social convention that men don't wear skirts.*
2 = **agreement**, contract, treaty, bargain, pact, compact, protocol, stipulation, concordat • *the importance of observing the Geneva convention on human rights*
3 = **assembly**, meeting, council, conference, congress, convocation, hui *(N.Z.)*, runanga *(N.Z.)* • *I flew to Boston to attend the annual convention of the Parapsychological Association.*

conventional 1 = **proper**, conservative, correct, formal, respectable, bourgeois, genteel, staid, conformist, decorous, Pooterish • *a respectable married woman with conventional opinions*
2 = **ordinary**, standard, normal, regular, usual, vanilla *(slang)*, habitual, bog-standard *(Brit. & Irish slang)*, common • *the cost of fuel and electricity used by a conventional system*
3 = **traditional**, accepted, prevailing, orthodox, customary, prevalent, hidebound, wonted • *The conventional wisdom on these matters is being challenged.*
4 = **unoriginal**, routine, stereotyped, pedestrian, commonplace, banal, prosaic, run-of-the-mill, hackneyed, vanilla *(slang)* • *This is a rather conventional work by a mediocre author.*
OPPOSITES: abnormal, uncommon, unconventional

converge AS A VERB = **come together**, meet, join, combine, gather, merge, coincide, mingle, intersect • *As they flow south, the five rivers converge.*
▸ IN PHRASES: **converge on something** = **close in on**, arrive at, move towards, home in on, come together at • *Hundreds of coaches will converge on the capital.*

convergence = **meeting**, junction, intersection, confluence, concentration, blending, merging, coincidence, conjunction, mingling, concurrence, conflux • *Hindon lies at the convergence of eight roads.*

conversant IN PHRASES: **conversant with** = **experienced in**, familiar with, skilled in, acquainted with, practised in, knowledgeable about, versed in, well up in *(informal)*, well-informed about, proficient in, *au fait* with • *These businessmen are not conversant with basic scientific principles.*

conversation = **talk**, exchange, discussion, dialogue, tête-à-tête, conference, communication, chat, gossip, intercourse, discourse, communion, converse, powwow, colloquy, chinwag *(Brit. informal)*, confabulation, confab *(informal)*, craic *(Irish informal)*, korero *(N.Z.)* • *Our telephone conversation lasted an hour and a half.*
▸ RELATED ADJECTIVE: colloquial

QUOTATIONS

The art of conversation is the art of hearing as well as being heard
[William Hazlitt *The Plain Speaker*]

That is the happiest conversation where there is no competition, no vanity, but a calm quiet interchange of sentiments
[Samuel Johnson]

In conversation discretion is more important than eloquence
[Baltasar Gracián *The Art of Worldly Wisdom*]

conversational = **chatty**, informal, communicative, colloquial • *What is refreshing is the author's easy, conversational style.*

converse[1] = **talk**, speak, chat, communicate, discourse, confer, commune, exchange views, shoot the breeze *(slang, chiefly U.S. & Canad.)*, korero *(N.Z.)* • *They were conversing in German, their only common language.*

converse[2] AS A NOUN = **opposite**, reverse, contrary, other side of the coin, obverse, antithesis • *If that is true, the converse is equally so.*
▸ AS AN ADJECTIVE = **opposite**, counter, reverse, contrary • *Stress reduction techniques have the converse effect on the immune system.*

conversion 1 = **change**, transformation, metamorphosis, transfiguration, transmutation, transmogrification *(jocular)* • *the conversion of disused rail lines into cycle routes*
2 = **adaptation**, reconstruction, modification, alteration, remodelling, reorganization • *A loft conversion can add considerably to the value of a house.*
3 = **reformation**, rebirth, change of heart, proselytization • *his conversion to Christianity*

convert AS A VERB 1 = **change**, turn, transform, alter, metamorphose, transpose, transmute, transmogrify *(jocular)* • *a handy table which converts into an ironing board*
2 = **adapt**, modify, remodel, reorganize, customize, restyle • *By converting the loft, they were able to have two extra bedrooms.*
3 = **reform**, save, convince, proselytize, bring to God • *I resent religious people who insist on trying to convert others.*
▸ AS A NOUN = **neophyte**, disciple, proselyte, catechumen • *She was a recent convert to Roman Catholicism.*

convertible = **changeable**, interchangeable, exchangeable, adjustable, adaptable • *the need for the introduction of a convertible currency*

convex = **rounded**, bulging, protuberant, gibbous, outcurved • *The lens is flat on one side and convex on the other.*
OPPOSITES: cupped, depressed, concave

convey 1 = **communicate**, impart, reveal, relate, disclose, make known, tell • *I tried to convey the wonder of the experience to my husband.*
2 = **carry**, transport, move, bring, support, bear, conduct, transmit, fetch • *They borrowed our boats to convey themselves across the river.*
3 = **transfer**, grant, deliver, lease, devolve, bequeath, will • *Conveying a property from one owner to another calls for meticulous attention to detail.*

conveyance 1 = **vehicle**, transport • *He had never travelled in such a strange conveyance before.*
2 = **transportation**, movement, transfer, transport, transmission, carriage, transference • *the conveyance of bicycles on Regional Railway trains*

convict AS A VERB = **find guilty**, sentence, condemn, imprison, pronounce guilty • *There was sufficient evidence to convict him.*
▸ AS A NOUN = **prisoner**, criminal, con *(slang)*, lag *(slang)*, villain, felon, jailbird, malefactor • *The prison houses only lifers and convicts on death row.*

conviction 1 = **belief**, view, opinion, principle, faith, persuasion, creed, tenet, kaupapa *(N.Z.)* • *Their religious convictions prevented them from taking up arms.*
2 = **certainty**, confidence, assurance, fervour, firmness, earnestness, certitude • *He preaches with conviction.*
3 = **sentence**, ruling, decision, verdict, judgment, punishment, decree, condemnation, pronouncement • *He will appeal against the conviction.*

convince 1 = **assure**, persuade, satisfy, prove to, reassure • *I soon convinced him of my innocence.*
2 = **persuade**, induce, coax, talk into, prevail upon, inveigle, twist (someone's) arm, bring round to the idea of • *He convinced her to go ahead and marry Bud.*

convincing = **persuasive**, credible, conclusive, incontrovertible, telling, likely, powerful, impressive, probable, plausible, cogent • *Scientists say there is no convincing evidence for this theory.*
OPPOSITES: unlikely, incredible, unconvincing

convivial = **sociable**, friendly, lively, cheerful, jolly, merry, festive, hearty, genial, fun-loving, jovial, back-slapping, gay, partyish *(informal)* • *Enjoy simple but satisfying food in the bistro's convivial atmosphere.*

C

conviviality = **sociability**, cheer, festivity, gaiety, bonhomie, jollity, liveliness, cordiality, geniality, joviality, good fellowship, merrymaking, jollification • *I love the conviviality of these little canal-side pubs.*

convocation = **meeting**, congress, convention, synod, diet, assembly, concourse, council, assemblage, conclave, hui (N.Z.), runanga (N.Z.) • *He attended a convocation of the American Youth Congress.*

convolution = **twist**, complexity, intricacy, contortion, winding, curl, loop, spiral, coil, coiling, helix, undulation, curlicue • *the size, shape and convolutions of the human brain*

convoy AS A NOUN = **escort**, entourage, guard, protection, fleet, attendant, armed guard, retinue, cortege • *They travel in a convoy with armed guards.*
▸ AS A VERB = **escort**, conduct, accompany, shepherd, protect, attend, guard, pilot, usher • *He ordered the combined fleet to convoy troops to Naples.*

convulse 1 = **shake**, twist, agitate, contort • *He let out a cry that convulsed his whole body.*
2 = **twist**, contort, work • *Olivia's face convulsed in a series of spasms.*

convulsion 1 = **spasm**, fit, shaking, seizure, contraction, tremor, cramp, contortion, paroxysm • *He fell to the floor in the grip of an epileptic convulsion.*
2 = **upheaval**, disturbance, furore, turbulence, agitation, commotion, tumult • *It was a decade that saw many great social, economic and political convulsions.*

convulsive = **jerky**, violent, sporadic, fitful, spasmodic, paroxysmal • *Convulsive sobs racked her body.*

cook IN PHRASES: **cook something up** = **invent**, plot, devise, contrive, prepare, scheme, manufacture, improvise, dream up, fabricate, concoct, trump up • *He must have cooked up this scheme on the spur of the moment.*

PROVERBS
Too many cooks spoil the broth
God sends meat and the Devil sends cooks

cookery
▸ RELATED ADJECTIVE: culinary

QUOTATIONS
Cookery has become an art, a noble science; cooks are gentlemen
[Robert Burton *Anatomy of Melancholy*]
If cooking becomes an art form rather than a means of providing a reasonable diet, then something is clearly wrong
[Tom Jaine, Editor of *The Good Food Guide*]
Cooking is like love. It should be entered into with abandon or not at all
[Harriet Van Horne]
Life is too short to stuff a mushroom
[Shirley Conran *Superwoman*]

▹ *See panel* **Cookery**

cool AS AN ADJECTIVE 1 = **cold**, chilled, chilling, refreshing, chilly, nippy • *I felt a current of cool air.*
OPPOSITES: warm, sunny, lukewarm
2 = **calm**, together (slang), collected, relaxed, composed, laid-back (informal), serene, sedate, self-controlled, placid, level-headed, dispassionate, unfazed (informal), unruffled, unemotional, self-possessed, imperturbable, unexcited, chilled (informal) • *He was marvellously cool, smiling as if nothing had happened.*
OPPOSITES: troubled, excited, agitated
3 = **unfriendly**, reserved, distant, indifferent, aloof, lukewarm, unconcerned, uninterested, frigid, unresponsive, offhand, unenthusiastic, uncommunicative, unwelcoming, standoffish • *People found him too cool, aloof and arrogant.*
OPPOSITES: warm, friendly, outgoing
4 = **unenthusiastic**, indifferent, lukewarm, uninterested, apathetic, unresponsive, unwelcoming • *The idea met with a cool response.*
5 = **fashionable**, with it (informal), hip (slang), stylish, trendy (Brit. informal), chic, up-to-date, urbane, up-to-the-minute, voguish (informal), trendsetting, schmick (Austral. informal) • *He was trying to be really cool and trendy.*
6 = **impudent**, bold, cheeky, audacious, brazen, shameless, presumptuous, impertinent • *He displayed a cool disregard for the rules.*
7 = **excellent**, good, mean (slang), great, choice, brilliant, cracking (Brit. informal), crucial (slang), outstanding, superb, superior, first-class, mega (slang), dope (slang), world-class, admirable, first-rate, def (slang), superlative, top-notch (informal), brill (informal), bodacious (slang, chiefly U.S.), boffo (slang), bitchin' (U.S. slang), chillin' (U.S. slang), booshit (Austral. slang), exo (Austral. slang), sik (Austral. slang), ka pai (N.Z.), rad (informal), phat (slang), schmick (Austral. informal), beaut (informal), barrie (Scot. slang), belting (Brit. slang), pearler (Austral. slang), funky • *this summer's coolest film*
▸ AS A VERB 1 = **lose heat**, cool off • *Drain the meat and allow it to cool.*
OPPOSITES: heat (up), warm (up), thaw
2 = **make cool**, freeze, chill, refrigerate, cool off • *Huge fans are used to cool the factory.*
OPPOSITES: heat (up), warm (up), thaw
3 = **calm (down)**, lessen, abate • *Within a few minutes their tempers had cooled.*
4 = **lessen**, calm (down), quiet, moderate, temper, dampen, allay, abate, assuage • *His strange behaviour had cooled her passion.*
▸ AS A NOUN 1 = **coldness**, chill, coolness • *She walked into the cool of the hallway.*
2 = **calmness**, control, temper, composure, self-control, poise, self-discipline, self-possession • *She kept her cool and managed to get herself out of the situation.*

coolness 1 = **coldness**, freshness, chilliness, nippiness • *He felt the coolness of the tiled floor.*
OPPOSITES: sunniness, tepidity, warmness
2 = **calmness**, control, composure, self-control, self-discipline, self-possession, placidity, level-headedness, imperturbability, sedateness, placidness • *They praised him for his coolness under pressure.*
OPPOSITES: disconcertion, excitement, agitation
3 = **unfriendliness**, reserve, distance, indifference, apathy, remoteness, aloofness, frigidity, unconcern, unresponsiveness, frostiness, offhandedness • *She seemed quite unaware of the sudden coolness of her friend's manner.*
OPPOSITES: warmth, friendliness, responsiveness
4 = **impudence**, audacity, boldness, insolence, impertinence, shamelessness, cheekiness, brazenness, presumptuousness, audaciousness • *The coolness of his suggestion took her breath away.*

coop AS A NOUN = **pen**, pound, box, cage, enclosure, hutch, corral (chiefly U.S. & Canad.) • *Behind the house, the pair set up a chicken coop.*
▸ IN PHRASES: **coop someone up** = **confine**, imprison, shut up, impound, pound, pen, cage, immure • *He was cooped up in a cell with ten other inmates.*

cooperate 1 = **work together**, collaborate, coordinate, join forces, conspire, concur, pull together, pool resources, combine your efforts • *The two parties are cooperating more than they have done in years.*
OPPOSITES: fight, struggle, conflict
2 = **help**, contribute to, assist, go along with, aid, pitch in, abet, play ball (informal), lend a helping hand • *He agreed to cooperate with the police investigation.*
OPPOSITES: fight, prevent, oppose

cooperation 1 = **teamwork**, concert, unity, collaboration, give-and-take, combined effort, esprit de corps, concurrence, kotahitanga (N.Z.) • *A deal with Japan could open the door to economic cooperation with East Asia.*

COOKERY

General cookery terms

à la king	chafing dish	entrée	jardinière	offal	smoked
à la mode	chargrill	entremets	jerk	oven-ready	soup
antipasto	chasseur	fajita	julienne	panada	steam
au gratin	chef	farci	knead	parboil	stew
au jus	cobbler	fillet	ladle	Parmentier	stock
au lait	coddle	flambé	lard	paste	stroganoff
au naturel	colander	flour	lardon	poach	supreme
bake	commis	fondue	leaven	potage	sweat
barbecue *or*	confectioner	fricassee	liaison	Provençale	sweet-and-sour
(Austral. slang)	consommé	fry	luau	purée	tandoori
barbie	cook	fumet	lyonnaise	ragout	tenderize
bard	cookbook	garnish	macedoine	rijsttafel	teriyaki
baste	cook-chill	gelatine	marengo	rise	tikka
batter	corned	ghee	marinade	rissole	timbale
blackened	creole	giblets	marinate	roast	topping
blanch	cuisine	glacé	marmite	roulade	undressed
boil	cuisine minceur	glaze	mask	roux	unleavened
boil-in-the-bag	cured	goujon	mash	royal icing	unsmoked
braise	curried	goulash	médaillons	salpicon	whip
broth	custard	grate	meunière	sauce	wholemeal
browning	dice	gravy	meze	sauté	wholemeal flour
caramelize	dough	grill	mirepoix	scramble	yeast
carbonado	dressing	hors d'oeuvre	mornay	season	
casserole	en brochette	ice	Newburg	silver service	
caterer	en croute	icing	nouvelle cuisine	sippet	

Cuisines and cooking styles

balti	cuisine minceur	haute cuisine	Italian	nouvelle cuisine	Thai
Cantonese	fast food	home cooking	Japanese	Provençal	Turkish
Caribbean	French	Indian	kosher	seafood	vegan
Californian	Greek	Indonesian	Malaysian	Sichuan	vegetarian
Chinese	gutbürgerlich	international	Mediterranean	tapas	
cordon bleu	halal	ital	Mexican	Tex-Mex	

OPPOSITES: opposition, rivalry, discord
2 = help, assistance, participation, responsiveness, helpfulness • *The police asked for the public's cooperation in their hunt for the killer.*
OPPOSITES: opposition, hindrance

PROVERBS
Two heads are better than one

cooperative 1 = shared, united, joint, combined, concerted, collective, unified, coordinated, collaborative • *The visit was intended to develop cooperative relations between the countries.*
2 = helpful, obliging, accommodating, supportive, responsive, onside *(informal)* • *I made every effort to be co-operative.*

coopt *or* **co-opt = appoint**, choose, pick, select, elect • *She co-opted Natasha as her assistant.*

coordinate AS A VERB **1 = organize**, synchronize, integrate, bring together, mesh, correlate, systematize • *Officials visited the earthquake zone to coordinate the relief effort.*
2 = match, blend, harmonize • *She'll show you how to coordinate pattern and colours.*
▸ **IN PHRASES: coordinate with = go with**, match, blend with, harmonize with • *Choose a fabric that coordinates with your colour scheme.*

coot
▸ **COLLECTIVE NOUN:** covert

cope AS A VERB **= manage**, get by *(informal)*, struggle through, rise to the occasion, survive, carry on, make out *(informal)*, make the grade, hold your own • *It was amazing how my mother coped after my father died.*
▸ **IN PHRASES: cope with something = deal with**, handle, struggle with, grapple with, wrestle with, contend with, tangle with, tussle with, weather • *She has had to cope with losing all her previous status and money.*

copious = abundant, liberal, generous, lavish, full, rich, extensive, ample, overflowing, plentiful, exuberant, bountiful, luxuriant, profuse, bounteous, superabundant, plenteous • *He drank copious quantities of tea and coffee.*

cop out = avoid, dodge, abandon, withdraw from, desert, quit, skip, renounce, revoke, renege, skive *(Brit. slang)*, bludge *(Austral. & N.Z. informal)* • *He copped out of going at the last minute.*

cop-out = pretence, dodge, pretext, fraud, alibi • *She said she was too upset to talk, but that was just a cop-out.*

copper
▸ **RELATED ADJECTIVES:** cupric, cuprous
▸ **RELATED PREFIX:** cupro-

copulate = have intercourse, have sex, screw *(taboo slang)*, shag *(taboo slang, chiefly Brit.)*, ball *(taboo slang, chiefly U.S.)*, fuck *(taboo slang)*, hump *(taboo slang)*, bonk *(informal)* • *The males will copulate with every female on heat.*

copulation = sexual intercourse, love, sex, lovemaking, the other *(informal)*, coupling, congress, mating, intimacy, sex act, nookie *(slang)*, coitus, carnal knowledge, rumpy-pumpy *(slang)*, legover *(slang)*, venery *(archaic)*, coition, poontang *(taboo slang)*, rumpo *(slang)* • *Couples engaged in acts of copulation in full view of the public.*

copy AS A NOUN **= reproduction**, duplicate, photocopy, carbon copy, image, print, fax, representation, fake, replica, imitation, forgery, counterfeit, Xerox *(trademark)*,

transcription, likeness, replication, facsimile, Photostat *(trademark)* • *Always keep a copy of everything in your own files.*
OPPOSITES: model, original, pattern
▸ **AS A VERB 1 = reproduce**, replicate, duplicate, photocopy, transcribe, counterfeit, Xerox *(trademark)*, Photostat *(trademark)* • *She never participated in copying classified documents for anyone.*
OPPOSITES: create, originate
2 = imitate, act like, emulate, behave like, follow, repeat, mirror, echo, parrot, ape, mimic, simulate, follow suit, follow the example of • *We all tend to copy people we admire.* • *coquettish gestures which she had copied from actresses in soap operas*

C

coquettish = flirtatious, inviting, arch, teasing, coy, amorous, flirty, flighty, come-hither *(informal)* • *She gave him a coquettish glance.*

cord = rope, line, string, twine • *The door had been tied shut with a length of nylon cord.*

cordial 1 = warm, welcoming, friendly, cheerful, affectionate, hearty, agreeable, sociable, genial, affable, congenial, warm-hearted • *I had never known him to be so chatty and cordial.*
OPPOSITES: cold, reserved, unfriendly
2 = wholehearted, earnest, sincere, heartfelt • *She didn't bother to hide her cordial dislike of him.*

cordiality = warmth, friendliness, affability, geniality, amiability, heartiness • *They want to solve the problem in an atmosphere of cordiality.*

cordon AS A NOUN = chain, line, ring, barrier, picket line • *Police formed a cordon between the two crowds.*
▸ **IN PHRASES: cordon something off = surround**, isolate, close off, fence off, separate, enclose, picket, encircle • *The police cordoned the area off.*

core 1 = centre • *Lava is molten rock from the earth's core*
2 = heart, essence, nucleus, kernel, crux, gist, nub, pith • *He has the ability to get straight to the core of a problem.*

cork
▸ **RELATED ADJECTIVE:** suberose

corner AS A NOUN 1 = angle, joint, crook • *the corner of a door*
2 = bend, curve • *He waited until the man had turned the corner.*
3 = space, hole, niche, recess, cavity, hideaway, nook, cranny, hide-out, hidey-hole *(informal)* • *She hid it away in a corner of her room.*
4 = region, part, area, sector, district, territory, zone, neighbourhood, sphere, realm, domain, locality, neck of the woods *(informal)* • *Buyers came from all corners of the world.*
5 = tight spot, predicament, tricky situation, spot *(informal)*, hole *(informal)*, hot water *(informal)*, pickle *(informal)* • *He appears to have got himself into a tight corner.*
▸ **AS A VERB 1 = trap**, catch, run to earth, bring to bay • *The police moved in with tear gas and cornered him.*
2 = monopolize, take over, dominate, control, hog *(slang)*, engross, exercise *or* have a monopoly of • *This restaurant has cornered the market for specialist paellas.*

cornerstone = basis, key, premise, starting point, bedrock • *Effective opposition is a cornerstone of any democracy.*

corny 1 = unoriginal, banal, trite, hackneyed, dull, old-fashioned, stereotyped, commonplace, feeble, stale, cheesy *(informal)*, old hat • *I know it sounds corny, but I'm not motivated by money.*
2 = sentimental, cheesy *(informal)*, mushy *(informal)*, maudlin, slushy *(informal)*, mawkish, schmaltzy *(slang)* • *a corny old love song*

corollary = consequence, result, effect, outcome, sequel, end result, upshot • *The number of prisoners increased as a corollary of the government's crackdown on violent crime.*

corporal = bodily, physical, fleshly, anatomical, carnal, somatic, corporeal *(archaic)*, material • *We do not believe that corporal punishment should be used in schools.*

corporate = collective, collaborative, united, shared, allied, joint, combined, pooled, merged, communal • *Most boards wish to have an effective system of corporate governance.*

corporation 1 = business, company, concern, firm, society, association, organization, enterprise, establishment, corporate body • *chairman of a huge multi-national corporation*
2 = town council, council, municipal authorities, civic authorities • *The local corporation has given permission for the work to proceed.*

QUOTATIONS
corporation: an ingenious device for obtaining individual profit without individual responsibility
[Ambrose Bierce *The Devil's Dictionary*]

corporeal = physical, human, material, substantial, bodily, mortal, fleshy • *Descartes held that there are two kinds of substances in the world, mental and corporeal.*

corps = team, unit, regiment, detachment, company, body, band, division, troop, squad, crew, contingent, squadron • *an officer in the Army Medical Corps*

corpse = body, remains, carcass, cadaver, stiff *(slang)* • *The victim's corpse was pulled out of the river.*
▸ **RELATED PHOBIA:** necrophobia

corpulent = fat, large, overweight, plump, stout, bulky, burly, obese, fleshy, beefy *(informal)*, tubby, portly, roly-poly, rotund, well-padded, podgy, gross • *His rather corpulent figure betrayed his self-indulgent lifestyle.*
OPPOSITES: thin, slim, skinny

corpus = collection, body, whole, compilation, entirety, oeuvre *(French)*, complete works • *a corpus of over 450 million words of spoken and written English*

corral AS A NOUN = enclosure, yard, pen, confine, coop, fold • *As we neared the corral, the horses pranced and whinnied.*
▸ **AS A VERB = enclose**, confine, cage, fence in, impound, pen in, coop up • *The men were corralled into a hastily constructed concentration camp.*

correct AS AN ADJECTIVE 1 = accurate, right, true, exact, precise, flawless, faultless, on the right lines, O.K. *or* okay *(informal)* • *The information was correct at the time of going to press.*
OPPOSITES: wrong, false, inaccurate
2 = right, standard, regular, appropriate, acceptable, strict, proper, precise • *The use of the correct procedure is vital.*
3 = proper, seemly, standard, fitting, diplomatic, kosher *(informal)* • *They refuse to adopt the rules of correct behaviour.*
OPPOSITES: unacceptable, inappropriate, unfitting
▸ **AS A VERB 1 = rectify**, remedy, redress, right, improve, reform, cure, adjust, regulate, amend, set the record straight, emend • *He may need surgery to correct the problem.*
OPPOSITES: damage, harm, spoil
2 = rebuke, discipline, reprimand, chide, admonish, chastise, chasten, reprove, punish • *He gently corrected me for taking the Lord's name in vain.*
OPPOSITES: praise, excuse, compliment

QUOTATIONS
For whom the Lord loveth he correcteth
[*Bible: Proverbs*]

correction 1 = rectification, improvement, amendment, adjustment, modification, alteration, emendation • *He has made several corrections and additions to the document.*
2 = punishment, discipline, reformation, admonition, chastisement, reproof, castigation • *jails and other places of correction*

corrective 1 = remedial, therapeutic, palliative, restorative, rehabilitative • *He has received extensive corrective surgery to his skull.*
2 = disciplinary, punitive, penal, reformatory • *He was placed in a corrective institution for children.*

correctly = rightly, right, perfectly, properly, precisely, accurately, aright • *Did I pronounce your name correctly?*

correctness 1 = **truth**, accuracy, precision, exactitude, exactness, faultlessness • *Please check the correctness of the details on this form.*
2 = **decorum**, propriety, good manners, civility, good breeding, bon ton *(French)* • *He conducted himself with formal correctness at all times.*

correlate 1 = **correspond**, parallel, be connected, equate, tie in, match • *Obesity correlates with increased risk of heart disease and stroke.*
2 = **connect**, compare, associate, tie in, coordinate, match • *attempts to correlate specific language functions with particular parts of the brain*

correlation = **correspondence**, link, relation, connection, equivalence • *There is a correlation between smoking and lung cancer.*

correspond 1 = **be consistent**, match, agree, accord, fit, square, coincide, complement, be related, tally, conform, correlate, dovetail, harmonize • *The two maps of London correspond closely.*
OPPOSITES: vary, differ, disagree
2 = **communicate**, write, keep in touch, exchange letters, e-mail, text • *We corresponded regularly for years.*

correspondence 1 = **communication**, writing, contact • *The judges' decision is final and no correspondence will be entered into.*
2 = **letters**, post, mail • *He always replied to his correspondence promptly.*
3 = **relation**, match, agreement, fitness, comparison, harmony, coincidence, similarity, analogy, correlation, conformity, comparability, concurrence, congruity • *correspondences between Eastern religions and Christianity*

correspondent 1 = **reporter**, journalist, contributor, special correspondent, journo *(slang)*, hack, hackette *(derogatory)* • *Here is a special report from our Europe correspondent.*
2 = **letter writer**, pen friend *or* pen pal • *He wasn't a good correspondent and only wrote to me once a year.*

corresponding = **equivalent**, matching, similar, related, correspondent, identical, complementary, synonymous, reciprocal, analogous, interrelated, correlative • *March and April sales this year were up 8 per cent on the corresponding period last year.*

corridor = **passage**, alley, aisle, hallway, passageway • *He raced down the corridor towards the exit.*

corroborate = **support**, establish, confirm, document, sustain, back up, endorse, ratify, validate, bear out, substantiate, authenticate • *I had access to a wide range of documents which corroborated the story.*
OPPOSITES: contradict, refute, disprove

corroboration = **support**, establishment, confirmation, endorsement, documentation, ratification, certification, validation, authentication, substantiation • *There were no witnesses to establish corroboration of his version of the accident.*

corrode = **eat away**, waste, consume, corrupt, deteriorate, erode, rust, gnaw, oxidize • *Engineers found that the structure had been corroded by moisture.*

corrosive 1 = **corroding**, wasting, caustic, vitriolic, acrid, erosive • *Sodium and sulphur are highly corrosive elements.*
2 = **cutting**, biting, incisive, virulent, sarcastic, caustic, venomous, vitriolic, trenchant, mordant • *She had a corrosive sense of humour.*

corrugated = **furrowed**, channelled, ridged, grooved, wrinkled, creased, fluted, rumpled, puckered, crinkled • *sheets of corrugated iron*

corrupt AS AN ADJECTIVE 1 = **dishonest**, bent *(slang)*, crooked *(informal)*, rotten, shady *(informal)*, fraudulent, unscrupulous, unethical, venal, unprincipled • *corrupt police officers who took bribes*
OPPOSITES: straight, principled, honest
2 = **depraved**, abandoned, vicious, degenerate, debased, demoralized, profligate, dishonoured, defiled, dissolute • *the flamboyant and morally corrupt court of Charles the Second*
3 = **distorted**, doctored, altered, falsified • *a corrupt text of a poem by Milton*
▸ AS A VERB 1 = **bribe**, square, fix *(informal)*, buy off, suborn, grease (someone's) palm *(slang)* • *The ability to corrupt politicians, policemen, and judges was fundamental to Mafia operations.*
2 = **deprave**, pervert, subvert, debase, demoralize, debauch • *Cruelty depraves and corrupts.*
OPPOSITES: reform, correct
3 = **distort**, doctor, tamper with • *Computer hackers often break into important sites to corrupt files.*

corrupted 1 = **depraved**, abandoned, perverted, warped, degenerate, debased, demoralized, profligate, dishonoured, defiled, debauched, reprobate • *the corrupted, brutal Duvalier regime*
2 = **contaminated**, soiled, dirtied, infected, spoiled, stained, decayed, rotten, polluted, tainted, tarnished, sullied, defiled, adulterated, vitiated, putrefied • *The body's T cells kill cells corrupted by viruses.*
3 = **distorted**, altered • *The computer files had been corrupted during the upgrade.*

corruption 1 = **dishonesty**, fraud, fiddling *(informal)*, graft *(informal)*, bribery, extortion, profiteering, breach of trust, venality, shady dealings *(informal)*, crookedness *(informal)*, shadiness • *He faces 54 charges of corruption and tax evasion.*
2 = **depravity**, vice, evil, degradation, perversion, decadence, impurity, wickedness, degeneration, immorality, iniquity, profligacy, viciousness, sinfulness, turpitude, baseness • *It was a society sinking into corruption and vice.*
3 = **distortion**, doctoring, falsification • *The name 'Santa Claus' is a corruption of 'Saint Nicholas'.*

QUOTATIONS
Something is rotten in the state of Denmark
[William Shakespeare *Hamlet*]
All rising to great place is by a winding stair
[Francis Bacon *Essays*]
PROVERBS
One rotten apple spoils the barrel

corsair = **pirate**, rover, buccaneer, freebooter, sea rover • *Treasure galleons were often attacked by corsairs and pirates.*

corset = **girdle**, bodice, foundation garment, panty girdle, stays *(rare)* • *a cocktail dress with in-built corset*

cortege = **procession**, train, entourage, cavalcade, retinue, suite • *The funeral cortege wound its way through the city.*

cosmetic = **superficial**, surface, touching-up, nonessential • *It is a cosmetic measure which will not help the situation in the long run.*

cosmic 1 = **extraterrestrial**, stellar • *Inside the heliosphere we are screened from cosmic rays.*
2 = **universal**, general, omnipresent, all-embracing, overarching • *There are cosmic laws governing our world.*
3 = **vast**, huge, immense, infinite, grandiose, limitless, measureless • *It was an understatement of cosmic proportions.*

cosmonaut = **astronaut**, spaceman, space pilot, space cadet • *two cosmonauts are marooned on the Soviet space station, Mir*

cosmopolitan 1 = **international**, global, worldwide, universal • *London has always had a cosmopolitan character.*
2 = **sophisticated**, worldly, cultured, refined, cultivated, urbane, well-travelled, worldly-wise • *The family are rich, and extremely sophisticated and cosmopolitan.*
OPPOSITES: limited, restricted, unsophisticated

cosmos = **universe**, world, creation, macrocosm • *a religion which offers a sense of the place of humanity in the cosmos*

cosset = **pamper**, baby, pet, coddle, mollycoddle, wrap up in cotton wool *(informal)* • *Important clients were cosseted and pampered like royalty.*

cost AS A NOUN 1 = **price**, worth, expense, rate, charge, figure, damage *(informal)*, amount, payment, expenditure, outlay • *The cost of a loaf of bread has increased five-fold.*
2 = **loss**, suffering, damage, injury, penalty, hurt, expense, harm, sacrifice, deprivation, detriment • *a man who always looks after 'number one', whatever the cost to others*
▸ AS A PLURAL NOUN = **expenses**, spending, expenditure, overheads, outgoings, outlay, budget • *The company admits its costs are still too high.*
▸ AS A VERB 1 = **sell at**, come to, set (someone) back *(informal)*, be priced at, command a price of • *The course is limited to 12 people and costs £50.*
2 = **lose**, deprive of, cheat of • *The operation saved his life, but cost him his sight.*
▸ IN PHRASES: **at all costs** = **no matter what**, regardless, whatever happens, at any price, come what may, without fail • *We must avoid any further delay at all costs.*

costly 1 = **expensive**, dear, stiff, excessive, steep *(informal)*, highly-priced, exorbitant, extortionate • *Having curtains professionally made can be costly.*
OPPOSITES: reduced, fair, inexpensive
2 = **splendid**, rich, valuable, precious, gorgeous, lavish, luxurious, sumptuous, priceless, opulent • *the exceptionally beautiful and costly cloths made in northern Italy*
3 = **damaging**, disastrous, harmful, catastrophic, loss-making, ruinous, deleterious • *If you follow the procedures correctly you will avoid costly mistakes.*

costume = **outfit**, dress, clothing, get-up *(informal)*, uniform, ensemble, robes, livery, apparel, attire, garb, national dress • *Even from a distance, the effect of his costume was stunning.*

cosy 1 = **comfortable**, homely, warm, intimate, snug, comfy *(informal)*, sheltered • *Guests can relax in the cosy bar before dinner.*
2 = **snug**, warm, secure, comfortable, sheltered, comfy *(informal)*, tucked up, cuddled up, snuggled down • *I was lying cosy in bed with the Sunday papers.*
3 = **intimate**, friendly, informal • *a cosy chat between friends*

coterie = **clique**, group, set, camp, circle, gang, outfit *(informal)*, posse *(informal)*, cabal • *The songs he recorded were written by a small coterie of dedicated writers.*

cottage = **cabin**, lodge, hut, shack, chalet, but-and-ben *(Scot.)*, cot, whare *(N.Z.)* • *We used to have a cottage in Scotland.*

couch AS A NOUN = **sofa**, bed, chesterfield, ottoman, settee, divan, chaise longue, day bed • *He lay down on the couch.*
▸ AS A VERB = **express**, word, frame, phrase, utter, set forth • *This time his proposal was couched as an ultimatum.*

cough AS A VERB = **clear your throat**, bark, hawk, hack, hem • *He began to cough violently.*
▸ AS A NOUN = **frog** *or* **tickle in your throat**, bark, hack • *He put a hand over his mouth to cover a cough.*
▸ IN PHRASES: **cough up** = **fork out**, deliver, hand over, surrender, come across *(informal)*, shell out *(informal)*, ante up *(informal, chiefly U.S.)* • *I'll have to cough up $10,000 a year for private tuition.*

council 1 = **committee**, governing body, board, panel, quango • *The city council has voted almost unanimously in favour of the proposal.*
2 = **governing body**, house, parliament, congress, cabinet, ministry, diet, panel, assembly, chamber, convention, synod, conclave, convocation, conference, runanga *(N.Z.)* • *The powers of the King had been handed over temporarily to a council of ministers.*

counsel AS A NOUN 1 = **advice**, information, warning, direction, suggestion, recommendation, caution, guidance, admonition • *He had always been able to count on her wise counsel.*
2 = **legal adviser**, lawyer, attorney, solicitor, advocate, barrister • *The defence counsel warned that the judge should stop the trial.*
▸ AS A VERB = **advise**, recommend, advocate, prescribe, warn, urge, caution, instruct, exhort, admonish • *My advisors counselled me to do nothing.*

count AS A VERB 1 *often with* **up** = **add (up)**, total, reckon (up), tot up, score, check, estimate, calculate, compute, tally, number, enumerate, cast up • *I counted the money. It came to more than five hundred pounds.*
2 = **matter**, be important, cut any ice *(informal)*, carry weight, tell, rate, weigh, signify, enter into consideration • *It's as if your opinions just don't count.*
3 = **consider**, judge, regard, deem, think of, rate, esteem, look upon, impute • *I count him as one of my best friends.*
4 = **include**, number among, take into account *or* consideration • *The years before their arrival in prison are not counted as part of their sentence.*
▸ AS A NOUN = **calculation**, poll, reckoning, sum, tally, numbering, computation, enumeration • *At the last count the police had 247 people in custody.*
▸ IN PHRASES: **count on** *or* **upon something** *or* **someone** = **depend on**, trust, rely on, bank on, take for granted, lean on, reckon on, take on trust, believe in, pin your faith on • *I'm counting on your support.* • *We're all counting on you to do the right thing.*
count someone out = **leave out**, except, exclude, disregard, pass over, leave out of account • *If it means working extra hours, you can count me out.*

countenance AS A NOUN 1 = **face**, features, expression, look, appearance, aspect, visage, mien, physiognomy • *He met each inquiry with an impassive countenance.*
2 = **support**, assistance, backing, aid, favour, sanction, approval, endorsement • *Those who remained could hope for no countenance or advancement.*
3 = **composure**, cool *(slang)*, dignity, poise, coolness, aplomb, calmness, equanimity, self-assurance, sang-froid, self-possession, imperturbability • *I kept my countenance and remained self-possessed.*
▸ AS A VERB = **tolerate**, sanction, endorse, condone, support, encourage, approve, endure, brook, stand for *(informal)*, hack *(slang)*, put up with *(informal)* • *He would not countenance his daughter marrying while she was still a student.*

counter[1] 1 = **surface**, top, bar, worktop • *He put the money on the counter and left.*
2 = **token**, piece, chip, disc, marker, man • *Players throw dice to move their counters round the board.*

counter[2] AS A VERB 1 = **oppose**, meet, block, resist, offset, parry, deflect, repel, rebuff, fend off, counteract, ward off, stave off, repulse, obviate, hold at bay • *They discussed a plan to counter the effects of such a blockade.*
2 = **retaliate**, return, answer, reply, respond, come back, retort, hit back, rejoin, strike back • *The union countered with letters rebutting the company's claim.*
OPPOSITES: accept, yield, surrender
▸ AS AN ADVERB = **opposite to**, against, versus, conversely, in defiance of, at variance with, contrarily, contrariwise • *Their findings ran counter to all expectations.*
OPPOSITES: parallel to, in accordance with, in agreement with
▸ AS AN ADJECTIVE = **opposing**, conflicting, opposed, contrasting, opposite, contrary, adverse, contradictory, obverse, against • *These charges and counter charges are being exchanged at an important time.*
OPPOSITES: similar, parallel

counteract 1 = **act against**, check, defeat, prevent, oppose, resist, frustrate, foil, thwart, hinder, cross • *Many countries within the region are planning measures to counteract a missile attack.*

2 = offset, negate, neutralize, invalidate, counterbalance, annul, obviate, countervail • *pills to counteract high blood pressure*

counterbalance = offset, balance out, compensate for, make up for, counterpoise, countervail • *Add honey to counterbalance the acidity of the sauce.*

counterfeit AS AN ADJECTIVE **= fake**, copied, false, forged, imitation, bogus, simulated, sham, fraudulent, feigned, spurious, ersatz, phoney *or* phony *(informal)*, pseud *or* pseudo *(informal)* • *He admitted possessing and delivering counterfeit currency.*
OPPOSITES: real, original, genuine
▸ AS A NOUN **= fake**, copy, reproduction, imitation, sham, forgery, phoney *or* phony *(informal)*, fraud • *Levi Strauss says counterfeits of the company's jeans are flooding Europe.*
OPPOSITES: the real thing, the real McCoy
▸ AS A VERB **= fake**, copy, forge, imitate, simulate, sham, fabricate, feign • *He is alleged to have counterfeited video cassettes.*

countermand = cancel, reverse, override, repeal, revoke, retract, rescind, annul • *I can't countermand her orders.*

counterpart = opposite number, equal, twin, equivalent, peer, match, fellow, mate • *It is unlikely that his counterpart in India will disagree with him at this point.*

counterpoint
▸ RELATED ADJECTIVE: contrapuntal

counting
▸ RELATED MANIA: arithmomania

countless = innumerable, legion, infinite, myriad, untold, limitless, incalculable, immeasurable, numberless, uncounted, multitudinous, endless, measureless • *She brought joy to countless people through her music.*
OPPOSITES: limited, restricted, finite

countrified = rural, pastoral, picturesque, rustic, idyllic, bucolic, Arcadian • *The house was very handsome, with a lovely countrified garden.*

country AS A NOUN **1 = nation**, state, land, commonwealth, kingdom, realm, sovereign state, people • *the disputed boundary between the two countries*
2 = people, community, nation, society, citizens, voters, inhabitants, grass roots, electors, populace, citizenry, public • *Seventy per cent of this country is opposed to blood sports.*
3 = countryside, rural areas, provinces, outdoors, sticks *(informal)*, farmland, outback *(Austral. & N.Z.)*, the middle of nowhere, green belt, wide open spaces *(informal)*, backwoods, back country *(U.S.)*, the back of beyond, bush *(N.Z. & S. African)*, backlands *(U.S.)*, boondocks *(U.S. slang)* • *They live somewhere way out in the country.*
OPPOSITES: city, town, metropolis
4 = territory, part, land, region, terrain • *This is some of the best walking country in the district.*
5 = native land, nationality, homeland, motherland, fatherland, patria *(Latin)*, Hawaiki *(N.Z.)*, Godzone *(Austral. informal)* • *I am willing to serve my country.*
▸ AS AN ADJECTIVE **= rural**, pastoral, rustic, agrarian, bucolic, Arcadian • *I want to live a simple country life.*
OPPOSITES: city, urban, sophisticated
▸ RELATED ADJECTIVES: campestral, pastoral, rural
▹ *See panel* **Countries**

countryman 1 = compatriot, fellow citizen • *He beat his fellow countryman in the final.*
2 = yokel, farmer, peasant, provincial, hick *(informal, chiefly U.S. & Canad.)*, rustic, swain, hillbilly, bucolic, country dweller, hayseed *(U.S. & Canad. informal)*, clodhopper *(informal)*, husbandman, cockie *(N.Z.)*, (country) bumpkin • *He had the red face of a countryman.*

countryside = country, rural areas, outdoors, farmland, outback *(Austral. & N.Z.)*, green belt, wide open spaces *(informal)*, sticks *(informal)* • *I've always loved the English countryside.*

county AS A NOUN **= province**, district, shire • *He is living now in his mother's home county of Oxfordshire.*
▸ AS AN ADJECTIVE **= upper-class**, upper-crust *(informal)*, tweedy, plummy *(informal)*, green-wellie, huntin', shootin', and fishin' *(informal)* • *They were all upper-crust ladies, pillars of the county set.*
▹ *See panel* **Counties**

coup = masterstroke, feat, stunt, action, stroke, exploit, manoeuvre, deed, accomplishment, tour de force *(French)*, stratagem, stroke of genius • *They have scored something of a coup by persuading her to join.*

coup de grâce = final blow, clincher *(informal slang)*, kill, knockout blow, mortal blow, quietus, deathblow, mercy stroke • *His affair administered the coup de grâce to their marriage.*

coup d'état = overthrow, takeover, coup, rebellion, putsch, seizure of power, palace revolution • *The government put down an attempted coup d'état last week.*

couple AS A NOUN **1 = pair**, two, brace, span *(of horses or oxen)*, duo, twain *(archaic)*, twosome • *There are a couple of police officers standing guard.*
2 = husband and wife, pair, item • *The couple have no children.*
▸ IN PHRASES: **couple something to something = link to**, connect to, pair with, unite with, join to, hitch to, buckle to, clasp to, yoke to, conjoin to • *The engine is coupled to a semiautomatic gearbox.*
couple something with something = combine with, accompany by, mix with, join with, unite with, compound with, amalgamate with, incorporate with, link with • *Overuse of these drugs, coupled with poor diet, leads to physical degeneration.*

coupon = slip, ticket, certificate, token, voucher, card, detachable portion • *Send the coupon with a cheque for £18.50.*

courage = bravery, nerve, fortitude, boldness, balls *(taboo slang)*, bottle *(Brit. slang)*, resolution, daring, guts *(informal)*, pluck, grit, heroism, mettle, firmness, gallantry, valour, spunk *(informal)*, fearlessness, intrepidity, hardihood • *They do not have the courage to apologise for their actions.*
OPPOSITES: fear, cowardice, timidity

QUOTATIONS

No one can answer for his courage when he has never been in danger
[Duc de la Rochefoucauld *Maxims*]

Sometimes even to live is an act of courage
[Seneca *Letters to Lucilius*]

Courage is not simply one of the virtues but the form of every virtue at the testing point
[C.S. Lewis]

Screw your courage to the sticking place
[William Shakespeare *Macbeth*]

As to moral courage, I have very rarely met with two o'clock in the morning courage: I mean instantaneous courage
[Napoleon Bonaparte]

courageous = brave, daring, bold, plucky, hardy, heroic, gritty, stalwart, fearless, resolute, gallant, audacious, intrepid, valiant, indomitable, dauntless, ballsy *(taboo slang)*, lion-hearted, valorous, stouthearted • *She is clearly a very tough and courageous woman.*
OPPOSITES: yellow *(informal)*, scared, cowardly

courier 1 = messenger, runner, carrier, bearer, herald, envoy, emissary, pursuivant *(archaic)* • *The cheques were delivered to the bank by a private courier.*
2 = guide, representative, escort, conductor, chaperon, cicerone, dragoman • *He was a travel courier.*

course AS A NOUN **1 = route**, way, line, road, track, channel, direction, path, passage, trail, orbit, tack, trajectory • *For nearly four hours we maintained our course northwards.*

COUNTRIES

Afghanistan
Albania
Algeria
American Samoa
Andorra
Angola
Antigua and Barbuda
Argentina
Armenia
Australia
Austria
Azerbaijan
Bahamas
Bahrain
Bangladesh
Barbados
Belarus
Belau
Belgium
Belize
Benin
Bhutan
Bolivia
Bosnia and Herzegovina
Botswana
Brazil
Brunei
Bulgaria
Burkina-Faso
Burundi
Cambodia
Cameroon
Canada
Cape Verde
Central African Republic
Chad
Chile
Colombia
Comoros
Congo (Democratic Republic of)
Congo (Republic of)
Costa Rica
Côte d'Ivoire
Croatia
Cuba
Cyprus
Czech Republic
Denmark
Djibouti
Dominica
Dominican Republic
East Timor
Ecuador
Egypt
El Salvador
England
Equatorial Guinea
Eritrea
Estonia
Ethiopia
Fiji
Finland
France
Gabon
Gambia
Georgia
Germany
Ghana
Greece
Greenland
Grenada
Guatemala
Guinea
Guinea-Bissau
Guyana
Haiti
Honduras
Hungary
Iceland
India
Indonesia
Iran
Iraq
Israel
Italy
Jamaica
Japan
Jordan
Kazakhstan
Kenya
Kirghizia
Kiribati
Kuwait
Laos
Latvia
Lebanon
Lesotho
Liberia
Libya
Liechtenstein
Lithuania
Luxembourg
Macedonia
Madagascar
Malawi
Malaysia
Mali
Malta
Marshall Islands
Mauritania
Mauritius
Mexico
Micronesia
Moldova
Monaco
Mongolia
Morocco
Mozambique
Myanmar
Namibia
Nauru
Nepal
Netherlands
New Zealand
Nicaragua
Niger
Nigeria
Northern Ireland
North Korea
Norway
Oman
Pakistan
Panama
Papua New Guinea
Paraguay
People's Republic of China
Peru
Philippines
Poland
Portugal
Puerto Rico
Qatar
Republic of Ireland
Republic of Maldives
Romania
Russia
Rwanda
St Kitts and Nevis
St Lucia
St Vincent and the Grenadines
Samoa
San Marino
São Tomé and Principe
Saudi Arabia
Scotland
Senegal
Seychelles
Sierra Leone
Singapore
Slovakia
Slovenia
Solomon Islands
Somalia
South Africa
South Korea
Spain
Sri Lanka
Sudan
Suriname
Swaziland
Sweden
Switzerland
Syria
Taiwan
Tajikistan
Tanzania
Thailand
Togo
Tonga
Trinidad and Tobago
Tunisia
Turkey
Turkmenistan
Tuvalu
Uganda
Ukraine
United Arab Emirates
United Kingdom
United States of America
Uruguay
Uzbekistan
Vanuatu
Vatican City
Venezuela
Vietnam
Wales
Yemen
Yugoslavia (Serbia and Montenegro)
Zambia
Zimbabwe

2 = **procedure**, plan, policy, programme, method, conduct, behaviour, manner, mode, regimen • *Resignation is the only course left open to him.*
3 = **progression**, order, unfolding, development, movement, advance, progress, flow, sequence, succession, continuity, advancement, furtherance, march • *a series of naval battles which altered the course of history*
4 = **classes**, course of study, programme, schedule, lectures, curriculum, studies • *I'll shortly be beginning a course on the modern novel.*
5 = **racecourse**, race, circuit, cinder track, lap • *On the Tour de France, 200 cyclists cover a course of 2,000 miles.*
6 = **period**, time, duration, term, passing, sweep, passage, lapse • *In the course of the 1930s steel production in Britain approximately doubled.*
▸ **AS A VERB** 1 = **run**, flow, stream, gush, race, speed, surge, dash, tumble, scud, move apace • *The tears coursed down his cheeks.*
2 = **hunt**, follow, chase, pursue • *New muzzling regulations for dogs coursing hares have been introduced.*
▸ **IN PHRASES: in due course = in time**, finally, eventually, in the end, sooner or later, in the course of time • *I hope that it will be possible in due course.*
of course = naturally, certainly, obviously, definitely, undoubtedly, needless to say, without a doubt, indubitably • *There'll be the usual inquiry, of course.*

court AS A NOUN 1 = **law court**, bar, bench, tribunal, court of justice, seat of judgment • *At this rate, you could find yourself in court for assault.*
2 = **playing area**, park (*U.S. & Canad.*), ground, field, ring, arena, circus, enclosure, rink • *The hotel has several tennis and squash courts.*
3 = **palace**, hall, castle, manor • *She came to visit England, where she was presented at the court of James I.*
4 = **royal household**, train, suite, attendants, entourage, retinue, cortege • *tales of King Arthur and his court*
▸ **AS A VERB** 1 = **cultivate**, seek, flatter, solicit, pander to, curry favour with, fawn upon • *Britain's political parties are courting the vote of the lesbian and gay community.*
2 = **invite**, seek, attract, prompt, provoke, bring about, incite • *If he thinks he can remain in power by force he is courting disaster.*
3 = **woo**, go (out) with, go steady with (*informal*), date, chase, pursue, take out, make love to, run after, walk out with, keep company with, pay court to, set your cap at, pay your addresses to, step out with (*informal*) • *I was courting him at 19 and married him when I was 21.*

courteous = polite, civil, respectful, mannerly, polished, refined, gracious, gallant, affable, urbane, courtly, well-bred, well-mannered • *He gave me a courteous but firm refusal.*
OPPOSITES: rude, unkind, discourteous

courtesan = mistress, prostitute, whore, call girl, working girl (*facetious slang*), kept woman, harlot, paramour, scarlet woman, hetaera, demimondaine, fille de joie (*French*) • *a courtesan who was kept by some of 16th-century Venice's most powerful men*

COUNTIES

English counties

- Bedfordshire
- Berkshire
- Bristol
- Buckinghamshire
- Cambridgeshire
- Cheshire
- Cornwall
- Cumbria
- Derbyshire
- Devon
- Dorset
- Durham
- East Riding of Yorkshire
- East Sussex
- Essex
- Gloucestershire
- Greater London
- Greater Manchester
- Hampshire
- Herefordshire
- Hertfordshire
- Isle of Wight
- Kent
- Lancashire
- Leicestershire
- Lincolnshire
- Merseyside
- Norfolk
- Northamptonshire
- Northumberland
- North Yorkshire
- Nottinghamshire
- Oxfordshire
- Rutland
- Shropshire
- Somerset
- South Yorkshire
- Staffordshire
- Suffolk
- Surrey
- Tyne and Wear
- Warwickshire
- West Midlands
- West Sussex
- West Yorkshire
- Wiltshire
- Worcestershire

Former English counties

- Bedfordshire
- Berkshire
- Buckinghamshire
- Cambridgeshire and Isle of Ely
- Cheshire
- Cornwall
- Cumberland
- Derbyshire
- Devon
- Dorset
- Durham
- East Suffolk
- East Sussex
- East Yorkshire
- Essex
- Gloucestershire
- Greater London
- Hampshire
- Herefordshire
- Hertfordshire
- Huntingdon and Peterborough
- Kent
- Lancashire
- Leicestershire
- Lincolnshire
- Norfolk
- Northamptonshire
- Northumberland
- North Yorkshire
- Nottinghamshire
- Oxfordshire
- Rutland
- Shropshire
- Somerset
- Staffordshire
- Surrey
- Warwickshire
- Westmorland
- West Suffolk
- West Sussex
- West Yorkshire
- Wiltshire
- Worcestershire

Scottish counties

- Aberdeen City
- Aberdeenshire
- Angus
- Argyll and Bute
- City of Edinburgh
- Clackmannanshire
- Dumfries and Galloway
- Dundee City
- East Ayrshire
- East Dunbartonshire
- East Lothian
- East Renfrewshire
- Falkirk
- Fife
- Glasgow City
- Highland
- Inverclyde
- Midlothian
- Moray
- North Ayrshire
- North Lanarkshire
- Orkney
- Perth and Kinross
- Renfrewshire
- Scottish Borders
- Shetland
- South Ayrshire
- South Lanarkshire
- Stirling
- West Dunbartonshire
- Western Isles (Eilean Siar)
- West Lothian

Former Scottish counties

- Aberdeen
- Aberdeenshire
- Angus
- Argyll
- Ayrshire
- Banff *or* Banffshire
- Berwickshire
- Bute
- Caithness
- Clackmannanshire
- Dumfriesshire
- Dunbartonshire
- Dundee
- East Lothian
- Edinburgh
- Fife
- Glasgow
- Inverness-shire
- Kincardine *or* Kincardineshire
- Kinross *or* Kinross-shire
- Kirkcudbrightshire
- Lanarkshire
- Midlothian
- Moray
- Nairn *or* Nairnshire
- Orkney
- Peeblesshire
- Perthshire
- Renfrewshire
- Ross and Cromarty
- Roxburgh *or* Roxburghshire
- Selkirkshire
- Shetland
- Stirlingshire
- Sutherland
- West Lothian
- Wigtownshire

Welsh counties post-1998

- Anglesey
- Blaenau Gwent
- Bridgend
- Caerphilly
- Cardiff
- Carmarthenshire
- Ceredigion
- Conwy
- Denbighshire
- Flintshire
- Gwynedd
- Merthyr Tydfil
- Monmouthshire
- Neath Port Talbot
- Newport
- Pembrokeshire
- Powys
- Rhondda, Cynon, Taff
- Swansea
- Torfaen
- Vale of Glamorgan
- Wrexham

Former Welsh counties

- Clwyd
- Dyfed
- Gwent
- Gwynedd
- Mid Glamorgan
- Powys
- South Glamorgan
- West Glamorgan

Northern Irish counties

- Antrim
- Armagh
- Down
- Fermanagh
- Londonderry
- Tyrone

Republic of Ireland counties

- Carlow
- Cavan
- Clare
- Cork
- Donegal
- Dublin
- Galway
- Kerry
- Kildare
- Kilkenny
- Laois
- Leitrim
- Limerick
- Longford
- Louth
- Mayo
- Meath
- Monaghan
- Offaly
- Roscommon
- Sligo
- Tipperary
- Waterford
- Westmeath
- Wexford
- Wicklow

courtesy 1 = **politeness**, grace, good manners, civility, gallantry, good breeding, graciousness, affability, urbanity, courtliness • *He is a gentleman who behaves with the utmost courtesy towards ladies.*
2 = **favour**, consideration, generosity, kindness, indulgence, benevolence • *If you're not coming, at least do me the courtesy of letting me know.*

courtier = **attendant**, follower, squire, pursuivant (*archaic*), train-bearer, liegeman (*archaic*) • *a courtier who worked in the royal household*

C

QUOTATIONS
The two maxims of any great man at court are, always to keep his countenance, and never to keep his word
[Jonathan Swift *Thoughts on Various Subjects*]

courtly = **ceremonious**, civil, formal, obliging, refined, polite, dignified, stately, aristocratic, gallant, affable, urbane, decorous, chivalrous, highbred • *a large man with a gentle, courtly manner*

courtship = **wooing**, courting, suit, romance, pursuit, engagement, keeping company • *After a short courtship, she accepted his marriage proposal.*

courtyard = **yard**, square, piazza, quadrangle, area, plaza, enclosure, cloister, quad (*informal*), peristyle • *They walked through the arch and into the cobbled courtyard.*

cove[1] = **bay**, sound, creek, inlet, bayou, firth *or* frith (*Scot.*), anchorage • *the sandy cove at the north end of the beach*

cove[2] = **fellow**, type, customer, character, bloke (*Brit. informal*), chap • *I've always thought of him as a decent old cove.*

covenant AS A NOUN 1 = **promise**, contract, agreement, commitment, arrangement, treaty, pledge, bargain, convention, pact, compact, concordat, trust • *the United Nations covenant on civil and political rights*
2 = **deed**, contract, bond • *If you make regular gifts through a covenant we can reclaim the income tax.*
▸ AS A VERB = **promise**, agree, contract, pledge, bargain, undertake, engage • *In the deed of separation, he covenanted that he would not revoke his will.*

cover AS A VERB 1 = **conceal**, cover up, screen, hide, shade, curtain, mask, disguise, obscure, hood, veil, cloak, shroud, camouflage, enshroud • *the black patch which covered his left eye*
OPPOSITES: show, reveal, expose
2 = **clothe**, invest, dress, wrap, envelop • *He covered his head with a turban.*
OPPOSITES: uncover, unwrap, unclothe
3 = **overlay**, blanket, eclipse, mantle, canopy, overspread, layer • *The clouds had spread and nearly covered the entire sky.*
4 = **coat**, cake, plaster, smear, envelop, spread, encase, daub, overspread • *She was soaking wet and covered with mud.*
5 = **submerge**, flood, engulf, overrun, wash over • *Nearly a foot of water covered the streets.*
6 = **travel over**, cross, traverse, pass through *or* over, range • *It would not be easy to cover ten miles on that amount of petrol.*
7 = **protect**, guard, defend, shelter, shield, watch over • *You make a run for it and I'll cover you.*
8 = **insure**, compensate, provide for, offset, balance, make good, make up for, take account of, counterbalance • *These items are not covered by your medical insurance.*
9 = **deal with**, refer to, provide for, take account of, include, involve, contain, embrace, incorporate, comprise, embody, encompass, comprehend • *The law covers four categories of experiments.*
OPPOSITES: exclude, omit
10 = **consider**, deal with, examine, investigate, detail, describe, survey, refer to, tell of, recount • *In this lecture, I aim to cover several topics.*
11 = **report on**, write about, commentate on, give an account of, relate, tell of, narrate, write up • *He was sent to Italy to cover the World Cup.*
12 = **pay for**, fund, provide for, offset, be enough for • *Please send £1.50 to cover postage.*
▸ AS A NOUN 1 = **protection**, shelter, shield, refuge, defence, woods, guard, sanctuary, camouflage, hiding place, undergrowth, concealment • *There were barren wastes of field with no trees and no cover.*
2 = **insurance**, payment, protection, compensation, indemnity, reimbursement • *Make sure that the firm's accident cover is adequate.*
3 = **covering**, case, top, cap, coating, envelope, lid, canopy, sheath, wrapper, awning • *Put a polythene cover over it to protect it from dust.*
4 = **bedclothes**, bedding, sheet, blanket, quilt, duvet, eiderdown • *He groaned and slid farther under the covers.*
5 = **jacket**, case, binding, wrapper • *a small book with a green cover*
6 = **disguise**, front, screen, mask, cover-up, veil, cloak, façade, pretence, pretext, window-dressing, smoke screen, smoke and mirrors • *The grocery store was just a cover for their betting shop.*
▸ IN PHRASES: **cover for someone** = **stand in for**, take over, substitute, relieve, double for, fill in for, hold the fort for (*informal*) • *She did not have enough nurses to cover for those who were off sick.*
cover something up = **conceal**, hide, suppress, repress, keep secret, whitewash (*informal*), hush up, sweep under the carpet, draw a veil over, keep silent about, cover your tracks, keep dark, feign ignorance about, keep under your hat (*informal*) • *They knew they had done something wrong and lied to cover it up.*

coverage = **reporting**, treatment, analysis, description, reportage • *Now a special TV network gives live coverage of most races.*

covering AS A NOUN = **cover**, protection, coating, overlay, housing, casing, top, clothing, wrapping, wrap, shelter, layer, blanket, wrapper • *Sawdust was used as a hygienic floor covering.*
▸ AS AN ADJECTIVE = **explanatory**, accompanying, introductory, descriptive • *Include a covering letter with your CV.*

covert = **secret**, private, hidden, disguised, concealed, veiled, sly, clandestine, underhand, unsuspected, surreptitious, stealthy • *They have been supplying covert military aid to the rebels.*

cover-up = **concealment**, conspiracy, whitewash (*informal*), complicity, front, smoke screen, smoke and mirrors • *He denied there'd been any cover-up of the fraud.*

covet = **long for**, desire, fancy (*informal*), envy, crave, aspire to, yearn for, thirst for, begrudge, hanker after, lust after, set your heart on, have your eye on, would give your eyeteeth for • *She coveted his job so openly that conversations between them were tense.*

covetous = **envious**, jealous, yearning, greedy, acquisitive, rapacious, avaricious • *His sports car was attracting covetous stares.*

cow = **intimidate**, daunt, frighten, scare, bully, dismay, awe, subdue, unnerve, overawe, terrorize, browbeat, psych out (*informal*), dishearten • *She was so cowed by her husband that she meekly obeyed him in everything.*

coward = **wimp**, chicken (*slang*), scaredy-cat (*informal*), sneak, funk (*informal*), craven (*informal*), pussy (*slang, chiefly U.S.*), yellow-belly (*slang*), poltroon • *The man's just a lily-livered coward.*

QUOTATIONS
Cowards die many times before their deaths
[William Shakespeare *Julius Caesar*]
coward: one who in a perilous emergency thinks with his legs
[Ambrose Bierce *The Devil's Dictionary*]

May coward shame distain his name,
The wretch that dares not die!
[Robert Burns *McPherson's Farewell*]
All men would be cowards if they durst
[John Wilmot *A Satire against Mankind*]

cowardice = **faint-heartedness**, weakness, softness, fearfulness, pusillanimity, spinelessness, timorousness • *He openly accused his opponents of cowardice.*

QUOTATIONS
To know what is right and not to do it is the worst cowardice
[Confucius *Analects*]
I cannot do this. This is too much for me. I shall ruin myself if I take this risk. I cannot take the leap, it's impossible. All of me will be gone if I do this, and I cling to myself
[J.N.Figgis]

cowardly = **faint-hearted**, scared, spineless, gutless (*informal*), base, soft, yellow (*informal*), weak, chicken (*slang*), shrinking, fearful, craven, abject, dastardly, timorous, weak-kneed (*informal*), pusillanimous, chickenshit (*U.S. slang*), chicken-hearted, lily-livered, white-livered, sookie (*N.Z.*) • *I was too cowardly to complain.*
OPPOSITES: brave, daring, bold

cowboy 1 = **cowhand**, drover, herder, rancher, stockman, cattleman, herdsman, gaucho, buckaroo (*U.S.*), ranchero (*U.S.*), cowpuncher (*U.S. informal*), broncobuster (*U.S.*), wrangler (*U.S.*) • *Ranchers have recently been finding it impossible to recruit people to work as cowboys.*
2 = **amateur**, fraud, rogue, incompetent, bungler, nonprofessional • *Those builders we hired were nothing but a bunch of cowboys.*

cower = **cringe**, shrink, tremble, crouch, flinch, quail, draw back, grovel • *The hostages cowered in their seats.*

coy 1 = **modest**, retiring, shy, shrinking, arch, timid, self-effacing, demure, flirtatious, bashful, prudish, aw-shucks, skittish, coquettish, kittenish, overmodest • *She was demure without being coy.*
OPPOSITES: forward, bold, brash
2 = **uncommunicative**, mum, secretive, reserved, quiet, silent, evasive, taciturn, unforthcoming, tight-lipped, close-lipped • *The hotel are understandably coy about the incident.*

coyness = **shyness**, reserve, modesty, timidity, affectation, diffidence, prudery, evasiveness, prudishness, bashfulness, skittishness, primness, archness, prissiness (*informal*), coquettishness, demureness • *She discusses sexual matters without a trace of coyness.*

QUOTATIONS
Had we but world enough, and time
This coyness, lady, were no crime
[Andrew Marvell *To his Coy Mistress*]

crab
▸ RELATED ADJECTIVE: cancroid

crabby = **bad-tempered**, acid, irritable, cross, awkward, sour, prickly, snappy, surly, tetchy, ratty (*Brit. & N.Z. informal*), testy, grouchy (*informal*), unsociable, misanthropic, crotchety (*informal*), snappish, ill-humoured, nasty-tempered • *Our grandmother was a crabby, bossy old woman.*

crack AS A VERB 1 = **break**, split, burst, snap, fracture, splinter, craze, rive • *A gas main had cracked under my neighbour's garage.* • *Crack the salt crust and you will find the skin just peels off the fish.*
2 = **snap**, ring, crash, burst, explode, crackle, pop, detonate • *Thunder cracked in the sky.*
3 = **hit**, clip (*informal*), slap, smack, thump, buffet, clout (*informal*), cuff, whack, wallop (*informal*), chop • *She drew back her fist and cracked him on the jaw.* • *He cracked his head on the pavement and was knocked out.*
4 = **break**, cleave • *Crack the eggs into a bowl.*
5 = **solve**, work out, resolve, interpret, clarify, clear up, fathom, decipher, suss (out) (*slang*), get to the bottom of, disentangle, elucidate, get the answer to • *He has finally cracked the code after years of painstaking research.*
6 = **break down**, collapse, yield, give in, give way, succumb, lose control, be overcome, go to pieces • *She's calm and strong, and will not crack under pressure.*
▸ AS A NOUN 1 = **break**, chink, gap, breach, fracture, rift, cleft, crevice, fissure, cranny, interstice • *She watched him though a crack in the curtains.*
2 = **split**, break, chip, breach, fracture, rupture, cleft • *The plate had a crack in it.*
3 = **snap**, pop, crash, burst, explosion, clap, report • *Suddenly there was a loud crack and glass flew into the air.*
4 = **blow**, slap, smack, thump, buffet, clout (*informal*), cuff, whack, wallop (*informal*), clip (*informal*) • *He took a crack on the head during the game.*
5 = **attempt**, go (*informal*), try, shot, opportunity, stab (*informal*) • *I'd love to have a crack at the title next year.*
6 = **joke**, dig, insult, gag (*informal*), quip, jibe, wisecrack, witticism, funny remark, smart-alecky remark • *He made a nasty crack about her weight.*
▸ AS AN ADJECTIVE = **first-class**, choice, excellent, ace, elite, superior, world-class, first-rate, hand-picked • *He is said to be a crack shot.*
▸ IN PHRASES: **crack down on something** *or* **someone** = **suppress**, crush, curb, repress, clamp down on, put a stop to, get tough on, come down hard on, be strict on • *new laws to crack down on vice*
crack up 1 = **have a breakdown**, collapse, break down, go crazy (*informal*), go berserk, freak out (*informal*), go to pieces, go ape (*slang*), fly off the handle (*informal*), come apart at the seams (*informal*), throw a wobbly (*slang*), go off the deep end (*informal*), go apeshit (*slang*), go out of your mind, flip your lid (*slang*), go off your rocker (*slang*), go off your head (*slang*) • *He's going to crack up if he doesn't take a break soon.*
2 = **burst out laughing**, laugh, fall about (laughing), guffaw, roar with laughter, be in stitches, split your sides • *We all just cracked up when he told us.*

crackdown = **clampdown**, crushing, repression, suppression • *The government have announced a crackdown on welfare fraud.*

cracked AS AN ADJECTIVE 1 = **broken**, damaged, split, chipped, flawed, faulty, crazed, defective, imperfect, fissured • *a cracked mirror*
2 = **crazy**, nuts (*slang*), eccentric, nutty (*slang*), touched, bats (*slang*), out there (*slang*), daft (*informal*), batty (*slang*), insane, loony (*slang*), off-the-wall (*slang*), oddball (*informal*), loopy (*informal*), crackpot (*informal*), out to lunch (*informal*), round the bend (*slang*), out of your mind, gonzo (*slang*), doolally (*slang*), off your trolley (*slang*), off the air (*Austral. slang*), round the twist (*Brit. slang*), up the pole (*informal*), off your rocker (*slang*), crackbrained, off your head *or* nut (*slang*), wacko *or* whacko (*informal*), porangi (*N.Z.*), daggy (*Austral. & N.Z. informal*) • *Everyone in our family's a bit cracked.*
▸ IN PHRASES: **cracked up** = **overrated**, exaggerated, blown up, hyped (up), puffed up, overpraised • *Package holidays are not always all they're cracked up to be.*

cradle AS A NOUN 1 = **crib**, cot, Moses basket, bassinet • *The baby sleeps in the cradle upstairs.*
2 = **birthplace**, beginning, source, spring, origin, fount, fountainhead, wellspring • *New York is the cradle of capitalism.*
▸ AS A VERB = **hold**, support, rock, nurse, nestle • *I cradled her in my arms.*

craft 1 = **vessel**, boat, ship, plane, aircraft, spacecraft, barque • *Cannabis smuggling by small craft to remote sites is rising.*
2 = **occupation**, work, calling, business, line, trade, employment, pursuit, vocation, handiwork, handicraft • *All kinds of traditional crafts are preserved here.*

3 = **skill**, art, ability, technique, know-how *(informal)*, expertise, knack, aptitude, artistry, dexterity, workmanship, expertness • *Lilyanne learned her craft of cooking from her grandmother.*
4 = **cunning**, ingenuity, guile, cleverness, scheme, subtlety, deceit, ruse, artifice, trickery, wiles, duplicity, subterfuge, contrivance, shrewdness, artfulness • *They defeated their enemies through craft and cunning.*

CRAFTS

basketry *or* basket-making	dressmaking	quilling
batik	embroidery	quilting
calligraphy	flower arranging	raffia work
ceramics	knitting	sewing
cloisonnage	knotwork	spinning
crewelwork	macramé	sugarcraft
crochet	needlepoint	tapestry
decoupage	patchwork	weaving
	pottery	wickerwork

craftsman = **skilled worker**, artisan, master, maker, wright, technician, artificer, smith • *The table in the kitchen was made by a local craftsman.*
craftsmanship = **workmanship**, technique, expertise, mastery, artistry • *His carvings are known for their style, detail and craftsmanship.*
crafty = **cunning**, scheming, sly, devious, knowing, designing, sharp, calculating, subtle, tricky, shrewd, astute, fraudulent, canny, wily, insidious, artful, foxy, deceitful, duplicitous, tricksy, guileful • *That crafty old devil had taken us all for a ride.*
OPPOSITES: open, simple, frank
crag = **rock**, peak, bluff, pinnacle, tor, aiguille • *The castle sits on a rocky crag above the town.*
craggy 1 = **rocky**, broken, rough, rugged, uneven, jagged, stony, precipitous, jaggy *(Scot.)* • *The scenery is a mix of wild, craggy mountains and broad valleys.*
2 = **rugged**, lined, weathered, furrowed, leathery, rough-hewn, weather-beaten, strong-featured • *He's a very small man with a lined, craggy face.*
cram 1 = **stuff**, force, jam, ram, shove, compress, compact • *She pulled off her school hat and crammed it into a wastebasket.*
2 = **pack**, fill, stuff • *She crammed her mouth with nuts.*
3 = **squeeze**, press, crowd, pack, crush, pack in, fill to overflowing, overfill, overcrowd • *We crammed into my car and set off.*
4 = **study**, revise, swot, bone up *(informal)*, grind, con, swot up, mug up *(slang)* • *She was cramming hard for her exam.*
cramp[1] = **spasm**, pain, ache, contraction, pang, stiffness, stitch, convulsion, twinge, crick, shooting pain • *She started getting stomach cramps this morning.*
cramp[2] = **restrict**, hamper, inhibit, hinder, check, handicap, confine, hamstring, constrain, obstruct, impede, shackle, circumscribe, encumber • *Like more and more women, she believes wedlock would cramp her style.*
cramped = **restricted**, confined, overcrowded, crowded, packed, narrow, squeezed, uncomfortable, awkward, closed in, congested, circumscribed, jammed in, hemmed in • *There are hundreds of families living in cramped conditions.*
OPPOSITES: open, large, spacious
crane
▸ COLLECTIVE NOUNS: herd, sedge, siege
crank = **eccentric**, freak *(informal)*, oddball *(informal)*, weirdo or weirdie *(informal)*, case *(informal)*, character *(informal)*, nut *(slang)*, flake *(slang, chiefly U.S.)*, screwball *(slang, chiefly U.S. & Canad.)*, odd fish *(informal)*, kook *(U.S. & Canad. informal)*, queer fish *(Brit. informal)*, rum customer *(Brit. slang)*, wacko or whacko *(informal)* • *People think I'm a crank because of my beliefs.*
cranky = **eccentric**, wacky *(slang)*, oddball *(informal)*, freakish, odd, strange, funny *(informal)*, out there *(slang)*, bizarre, peculiar, queer *(informal)*, rum *(Brit. slang)*, quirky, idiosyncratic, off-the-wall *(slang)*, freaky *(slang)*, outré, wacko or whacko *(informal)*, daggy *(Austral. & N.Z. informal)* • *Vegetarianism has shed its cranky image.*
cranny = **crevice**, opening, hole, crack, gap, breach, rift, nook, cleft, chink, fissure, interstice • *The lizards fled into crannies in the rocks.*
crash AS A NOUN 1 = **collision**, accident, smash, wreck, prang *(informal)*, bump, pile-up *(informal)*, smash-up • *His elder son was killed in a car crash a few years ago.*
2 = **smash**, clash, boom, smashing, bang, thunder, thump, racket, din, clatter, clattering, thud, clang • *Two people in the flat recalled hearing a loud crash about 1.30am.*
3 = **collapse**, failure, depression, ruin, bankruptcy, downfall • *He predicted correctly that there was going to be a stock market crash.*
▸ AS A VERB 1 = **fall**, pitch, plunge, sprawl, topple, lurch, hurtle, come a cropper *(informal)*, overbalance, fall headlong • *He lost his balance and crashed to the floor.*
2 = **plunge**, hurtle, precipitate yourself • *We heard the sound of an animal crashing through the undergrowth.*
3 = **smash**, break, break up, shatter, fragment, fracture, shiver, disintegrate, splinter, dash to pieces • *Her glass fell on the floor and crashed into a thousand pieces*
4 = **collapse**, fail, go under, be ruined, go bust *(informal)*, fold up, go broke *(informal)*, go to the wall, go belly up *(informal)*, smash, fold • *When the market crashed they assumed the deal would be cancelled.*
▸ AS AN ADJECTIVE = **intensive**, concentrated, immediate, urgent, round-the-clock, emergency • *I might take a crash course in typing.*
▸ IN PHRASES: **crash into** = **collide with**, hit, bump into, bang into, run into, drive into, plough into, hurtle into • *His car crashed into the rear of a van.*
crass = **insensitive**, stupid, gross, blundering, dense, coarse, witless, boorish, obtuse, unrefined, asinine, indelicate, oafish, lumpish, doltish • *They have behaved with crass insensitivity.*
OPPOSITES: bright, sharp, sensitive
crassness = **insensitivity**, stupidity, vulgarity, coarseness, boorishness, tactlessness, grossness, oafishness, denseness, indelicacy, asininity • *We were stunned by the crassness of his conversation.*
crate AS A NOUN = **container**, case, box, packing case, tea chest • *A crane was already unloading crates and pallets.*
▸ AS A VERB = **box**, pack, enclose, pack up, encase, case • *The plane had been dismantled, crated, and shipped to London.*
crater = **hollow**, hole, depression, dip, cavity, shell hole • *A huge crater marks the spot where the explosion happened.*
crave 1 = **long for**, yearn for, hanker after, be dying for, want, need, require, desire, fancy *(informal)*, hope for, cry out for *(informal)*, thirst for, pine for, lust after, pant for, sigh for, set your heart on, hunger after, eat your heart out over, would give your eyeteeth for • *There may be certain times of day when smokers crave a cigarette.*
2 = **beg**, ask for, seek, petition, pray for, plead for, solicit, implore, beseech, entreat, supplicate • *If I may crave your lordship's indulgence, I would like to consult my client.*
craven = **cowardly**, weak, scared, fearful, abject, dastardly, mean-spirited, timorous, pusillanimous, chickenshit *(U.S. slang)*, chicken-hearted, yellow *(informal)*, lily-livered • *The craven attackers pounced on the boy and stabbed him before fleeing.*

craving = **longing**, hope, desire, urge, yen *(informal)*, hunger, appetite, ache, lust, yearning, thirst, hankering, the munchies *(slang)* • *He had a sudden craving for a glass of brandy.*

craw IN PHRASES: **stick in your craw** = **annoy**, anger, outrage, offend, irritate, infuriate, incense, enrage, madden, nettle, vex, rile, pique, nark *(Brit., Austral. & N.Z. slang)*, make your blood boil, piss you off *(taboo slang)*, get your dander up *(informal)*, get your back up, put your back up, hack you off *(informal)* • *What stuck in his craw was the implication that he was a liar.*

crawl AS A VERB **1** = **creep**, slither, go on all fours, move on hands and knees, inch, drag, wriggle, writhe, move at a snail's pace, worm your way, advance slowly, pull *or* drag yourself along • *I began to crawl on my hands and knees towards the door.*
OPPOSITES: run, race, walk
2 = **grovel**, creep, cringe, humble yourself, abase yourself, brown-nose *(taboo slang)*, kiss ass *(U.S. & Canad. taboo slang)* • *I'll apologize to him, but I won't crawl.*
▸ IN PHRASES: **be crawling with something** = **be full of**, teem with, be alive with, swarm with, be overrun with *(slang)*, be lousy with • *This place is crawling with police.*
crawl to someone = **fawn on**, pander to, suck up to *(slang)*, toady to, truckle to, lick someone's boots *(slang)*, lick someone's arse *(taboo slang)* • *I'd have to crawl to her to keep my job.*

craze = **fad**, thing, fashion, trend, passion, rage, enthusiasm, mode, vogue, novelty, preoccupation, mania, infatuation, the latest thing *(informal)* • *Aerobics is the latest fitness craze.*

crazed = **mad**, crazy, raving, insane, lunatic, demented, unbalanced, deranged, berserk, unhinged, berko *(Austral. slang)*, off the air *(Austral. slang)*, porangi *(N.Z.)* • *A crazed gunman slaughtered five people last night.*

crazy **1** = **strange**, odd, bizarre, fantastic, silly, weird, ridiculous, outrageous, peculiar, eccentric, rum *(Brit. slang)*, oddball *(informal)*, cockamamie *(slang, chiefly U.S.)*, wacko *or* whacko *(informal)*, out there *(slang)*, off the air *(Austral. slang)*, porangi *(N.Z.)*, daggy *(Austral. & N.Z. informal)* • *I ignored the crazy guy seated beside me on the bus.*
OPPOSITES: common, normal, regular
2 = **ridiculous**, wild, absurd, inappropriate, foolish, ludicrous, irresponsible, unrealistic, unwise, senseless, preposterous, potty *(Brit. informal)*, short-sighted, unworkable, foolhardy, idiotic, nonsensical, half-baked *(informal)*, inane, fatuous, ill-conceived, quixotic, imprudent, impracticable, cockeyed *(informal)*, bird-brained *(informal)*, cockamamie *(slang, chiefly U.S.)*, porangi *(N.Z.)* • *I know it sounds a crazy idea, but hear me out.*
OPPOSITES: responsible, brilliant, sensible
3 = **insane**, mad, unbalanced, deranged, touched, cracked *(slang)*, mental *(slang)*, nuts *(slang)*, barking *(slang)*, daft *(informal)*, batty *(slang)*, crazed, lunatic, demented, cuckoo *(informal)*, barmy *(slang)*, off-the-wall *(slang)*, off the air *(Austral. slang)*, nutty *(slang)*, potty *(Brit. informal)*, berserk, delirious, bonkers *(slang, chiefly Brit.)*, idiotic, unhinged, loopy *(informal)*, crackpot *(informal)*, out to lunch *(informal)*, round the bend *(slang)*, barking mad *(slang)*, out of your mind, maniacal, not all there *(informal)*, doolally *(slang)*, off your head *(slang)*, off your trolley *(slang)*, round the twist *(Brit. slang)*, up the pole *(informal)*, of unsound mind, not right in the head, off your rocker *(slang)*, not the full shilling *(informal)*, a bit lacking upstairs *(informal)*, as daft as a brush *(informal, chiefly Brit.)*, mad as a hatter, mad as a March hare, nutty as a fruitcake *(slang)*, porangi *(N.Z.)* • *If I think about it too much, I'll go crazy.* • *some crazy man who had killed his wife and family before committing suicide*
OPPOSITES: smart, wise, sane
4 = **fanatical**, wild *(informal)*, mad, devoted, enthusiastic, passionate, hysterical, ardent, very keen, zealous, smitten, infatuated, enamoured • *He's crazy about football.*
OPPOSITES: cool, indifferent, uninterested
▹ *See panel* **Mad**

creak = **squeak**, grind, scrape, groan, grate, screech, squeal, scratch, rasp • *The bed-springs creaked.*

creaky **1** = **squeaky**, creaking, squeaking, unoiled, grating, rusty, rasping, raspy • *She pushed open the creaky door.*
2 = **old-fashioned**, dated, outdated, obsolete, out of date, archaic, antiquated, outmoded, behind the times, obsolescent • *During his time in office he reformed the creaky tax system.*

cream AS A NOUN **1** = **lotion**, ointment, oil, essence, cosmetic, paste, emulsion, salve, liniment, unguent • *Gently apply the cream to the affected areas.*
2 = **best**, elite, prime, pick, flower, crème de la crème *(French)* • *The event was attended by the cream of Hollywood society.*
▸ AS AN ADJECTIVE = **off-white**, ivory, yellowish-white • *cream silk stockings*
▹ *See panel* **Shades from black to white**

creamy **1** = **milky**, buttery • *creamy mashed potato*
2 = **smooth**, soft, creamed, lush, oily, velvety, rich • *Whisk the mixture until it is smooth and creamy.*

crease AS A NOUN **1** = **fold**, ruck, line, tuck, ridge, groove, pucker, corrugation • *She frowned at the creases in her silk dress.*
2 = **wrinkle**, line, crow's-foot • *There were tiny creases at the corner of his eyes.*
▸ AS A VERB **1** = **crumple**, rumple, pucker, crinkle, fold, ridge, double up, crimp, ruck up, corrugate • *Most outfits crease a bit when you're travelling.* • *Liz sat down carefully, so as not to crease her skirt.*
2 = **wrinkle**, crumple, screw up • *His face creased with mirth.*

create **1** = **cause**, lead to, occasion, bring about • *Criticism will only create feelings of failure.*
2 = **make**, form, produce, develop, design, generate, invent, coin, compose, devise, initiate, hatch, originate, formulate, give birth to, spawn, dream up *(informal)*, concoct, beget, give life to, bring into being *or* existence • *He's creating a whole new language of painting*
OPPOSITES: destroy, demolish, annihilate
3 = **appoint**, make, found, establish, set up, invest, install, constitute • *They are about to create a scholarship fund for black students.*

creation **1** = **universe**, world, life, nature, cosmos, natural world, living world, all living things • *the origin of all creation*
2 = **invention**, production, concept, achievement, brainchild *(informal)*, concoction, handiwork, pièce de résistance *(French)*, magnum opus, chef-d'oeuvre *(French)* • *The bathroom is entirely my own creation.*
3 = **making**, generation, formation, conception, genesis • *the time and effort involved in the creation of a work of art*
4 = **setting up**, development, production, institution, foundation, constitution, establishment, formation, laying down, inception, origination • *He said all sides were committed to the creation of a democratic state.*

creative = **imaginative**, gifted, artistic, inventive, original, inspired, clever, productive, fertile, ingenious, visionary • *Like many creative people, he was never satisfied.*

creativity = **imagination**, talent, inspiration, productivity, fertility, ingenuity, originality, inventiveness, cleverness, fecundity • *American art reached a peak of creativity in the 50's and 60's.*

creator **1** = **maker**, father, author, framer, designer, architect, inventor, originator, initiator, begetter • *George Lucas, the creator of the Star Wars films*
2 *usually with cap.* = **God**, Maker • *This was the first object placed in the heavens by the Creator.*

creature **1** = **living thing**, being, animal, beast, brute, critter *(U.S. dialect)*, quadruped, dumb animal, lower animal • *Many cultures believe that every living creature possesses a spirit.*

2 = **person**, man, woman, individual, character, fellow, soul, human being, mortal, body, wight *(archaic)* • *He is one of the most amiable creatures in existence.*
3 = **minion**, tool, instrument *(informal)*, puppet, cohort *(chiefly U.S.)*, dependant, retainer, hanger-on, lackey, hireling • *We are not merely creatures of our employers.*

credence 1 = **credibility**, credit, plausibility, believability • *Further studies are needed to lend credence to this notion.*
2 = **belief**, trust, confidence, faith, acceptance, assurance, certainty, dependence, reliance • *Seismologists give this idea little credence.*

C

credentials 1 = **qualifications**, ability, skill, capacity, fitness, attribute, capability, endowment(s), accomplishment, eligibility, aptitude, suitability • *He has the right credentials for the job.*
2 = **certification**, document, reference(s), papers, title, card, licence, recommendation, passport, warrant, voucher, deed, testament, diploma, testimonial, authorization, missive, letters of credence, attestation, letter of recommendation *or* introduction • *He called at Government House to present his credentials.*

credibility = **believability**, reliability, cred *(slang)*, plausibility, trustworthiness, tenability • *The president will have to work hard to restore his credibility with voters.*

credible 1 = **believable**, possible, likely, reasonable, probable, plausible, conceivable, imaginable, tenable, thinkable, verisimilar • *This claim seems perfectly credible to me.*
OPPOSITES: unlikely, incredible, unbelievable
2 = **reliable**, honest, dependable, trustworthy, sincere, trusty • *the evidence of credible witnesses*
OPPOSITES: unreliable, dishonest, untrustworthy

credit AS A NOUN 1 = **praise**, honour, recognition, glory, thanks, approval, fame, tribute, merit, acclaim, acknowledgment, kudos, commendation, Brownie points • *It would be wrong of us to take all the credit for this result.*
2 = **source of satisfaction** *or* **pride**, asset, honour, feather in your cap • *He is a credit to his family.*
3 = **prestige**, reputation, standing, position, character, influence, regard, status, esteem, clout *(informal)*, good name, estimation, repute • *His remarks lost him credit with many people.*
4 = **belief**, trust, confidence, faith, reliance, credence • *At first this theory met with little credit.*
▸ AS A VERB = **believe**, rely on, have faith in, trust, buy *(slang)*, accept, depend on, swallow *(informal)*, fall for, bank on • *You can't credit anything he says.*
▸ IN PHRASES: **credit someone with something** = **attribute to**, assign to, ascribe to, accredit to, impute to, chalk up to *(informal)* • *You don't credit me with any intelligence at all, do you?*
credit something to someone = **attribute to**, ascribe to, accredit to, impute to, chalk up to *(informal)* • *Although the song is usually credited to Lennon and McCartney, it was written by McCartney alone.*
on credit = **on account**, by instalments, on tick *(informal)*, on hire-purchase, on the slate *(informal)*, by deferred payment, on (the) H.P. • *They bought most of their furniture on credit.*

PROVERBS
credit where credit is due

creditable = **praiseworthy**, worthy, respectable, admirable, honourable, exemplary, reputable, commendable, laudable, meritorious, estimable • *The band turned out quite a creditable performance.*

credulity = **gullibility**, naïveté *or* naivety, blind faith, credulousness • *The plot stretches credulity to the limits.*

credulous = **gullible**, trusting, unsuspecting, naive *or* naïve, uncritical, green, born yesterday *(informal)*, wet behind the ears *(informal)*, unsuspicious, as green as grass, overtrusting • *Why are westerners such credulous suckers for alternative therapies?*
OPPOSITES: suspecting, wary, sceptical

creed = **belief**, principles, profession *(of faith)*, doctrine, canon, persuasion, dogma, tenet, credo, catechism, articles of faith • *The centre is open to all, no matter what race or creed.*

creek 1 = **inlet**, bay, cove, bight, firth *or* frith *(Scot.)* • *The offshore fishermen took shelter from the storm in a creek.*
2 = **stream**, brook, tributary, bayou, rivulet, watercourse, streamlet, runnel • *Follow Austin Creek for a few miles.*

creep AS A VERB 1 = **crawl**, worm, wriggle, squirm, slither, writhe, drag yourself, edge, inch, crawl on all fours • *The rabbit crept off and hid in a hole.*
2 = **sneak**, steal, tiptoe, slink, skulk, approach unnoticed • *I went back to the hotel and crept up to my room.*
▸ AS A NOUN = **bootlicker** *(informal)*, sneak, sycophant, crawler *(slang)*, toady, brown-noser *(taboo slang)*, ass-kisser *(U.S. & Canad. taboo slang)* • *He's a smug, sanctimonious little creep.*
▸ IN PHRASES: **creep to someone** = **grovel to**, pander to, suck up to *(informal)*, kiss someone's ass *(U.S. & Canad. taboo slang)*, brown-nose *(taboo slang)*, scrape to, kowtow to, fawn on, toady to, truckle to, insinuate yourself with • *I can't stand the way he creeps to the bosses.*
give someone the creeps = **disgust**, frighten, scare, terrify, horrify, repel, repulse, make you wince, make your hair stand on end, make you squirm, make you flinch, scare the bejesus out of *(informal)*, make you quail, make you shrink • *I've always hated that painting. It gives me the creeps.*

creeper = **climbing plant**, runner, vine *(chiefly U.S.)*, climber, rambler, trailing plant • *flaming curtains of Virginia creeper*

creepy = **disturbing**, threatening, frightening, terrifying, weird, forbidding, horrible, menacing, unpleasant, scary *(informal)*, sinister, ominous, eerie, macabre, nightmarish, hair-raising, awful • *This place is really creepy at night.*

crescent AS A NOUN = **meniscus**, sickle, new moon, half-moon, old moon, sickle-shape • *a flag with a white crescent on a red ground*
▸ AS AN ADJECTIVE = **sickle-shaped**, curved, arched, semicircular, bow-shaped • *a crescent moon*

crest 1 = **top**, summit, peak, ridge, highest point, pinnacle, apex, head, crown, height • *He reached the crest of the hill.*
2 = **tuft**, crown, comb, plume, mane, tassel, topknot, cockscomb • *Both birds had a dark blue crest.*
3 = **emblem**, badge, symbol, insignia, charge, bearings, device • *On the wall is the family crest.*

crestfallen = **disappointed**, depressed, discouraged, dejected, despondent, downcast, disheartened, disconsolate, downhearted, sick as a parrot *(informal)*, choked • *He looked crestfallen when she turned him down.*
OPPOSITES: happy, encouraged, elated

crevasse = **crack**, abyss, chasm, cleft, fissure • *The climber had fallen down a crevasse on to a ledge.*

crevice = **gap**, opening, hole, split, crack, rent, fracture, rift, slit, cleft, chink, fissure, cranny, interstice • *a huge boulder with rare ferns growing in every crevice*

crew 1 = **(ship's) company**, hands, (ship's) complement • *These vessels carry small crews of around twenty men.*
2 = **team**, company, party, squad, gang, corps, working party, posse • *a two-man film crew making a documentary*
3 = **crowd**, set, lot, bunch *(informal)*, band, troop, pack, camp, gang, mob, herd, swarm, company, horde, posse *(informal)*, assemblage • *a motley crew of college friends*

crib AS A NOUN 1 = **cradle**, bed, cot, bassinet, Moses basket • *She placed the baby back in its crib.*
2 = **translation**, notes, key, trot *(U.S. slang)* • *Only desperate students take cribs into the exam with them.*
3 = **manger**, box, stall, rack, bunker • *He claimed the cribs in which the calves were kept had been approved by the RSPCA.*

▸ **AS A VERB = copy**, cheat, pirate, pilfer, purloin, plagiarize, pass off as your own work • *He had been caught cribbing in an exam.*

crick AS A NOUN = spasm, cramp, convulsion, twinge • *I've got a crick in my neck from looking up at the screen.*

▸ **AS A VERB = rick**, jar, wrench • *I cricked my back from sitting in the same position for too long.*

cricket

▹ *See panel* **Cricket terms**

crime 1 = offence, job *(informal)*, wrong, fault, outrage, atrocity, violation, trespass, felony, misdemeanour, misdeed, transgression, unlawful act, malfeasance • *He has committed no crime and poses no danger to the public.*

2 = lawbreaking, corruption, delinquency, illegality, wrong, vice, sin, guilt, misconduct, wrongdoing, wickedness, iniquity, villainy, unrighteousness, malefaction • *Much of the city's crime revolves around protection rackets.*

criminal AS A NOUN = lawbreaker, convict, con *(slang)*, offender, crook *(informal)*, lag *(slang)*, villain, culprit, sinner, delinquent, felon, con man *(informal)*, rorter *(Austral. slang)*, jailbird, malefactor, evildoer, transgressor, skelm *(S. African)*, rogue trader, perp *(U.S. & Canad. informal)* • *He was put in a cell with several hardened criminals.*

▸ **AS AN ADJECTIVE 1 = unlawful**, illicit, lawless, wrong, illegal, corrupt, crooked *(informal)*, vicious, immoral, wicked, culpable, under-the-table, villainous, nefarious, iniquitous, indictable, felonious, bent *(slang)* • *The entire party cannot be blamed for the criminal actions of a few members.*

OPPOSITES: right, legal, lawful

2 = disgraceful, ridiculous, foolish, senseless, scandalous, preposterous, deplorable • *This project is a criminal waste of time and resources.*

criminality = illegality, crime, corruption, delinquency, wrongdoing, lawlessness, wickedness, depravity, culpability, villainy, sinfulness, turpitude • *The evils of unemployment have increased criminality in the inner cities.*

cringe 1 = shrink, flinch, quail, recoil, start, shy, tremble, quiver, cower, draw back, blench • *I cringed in horror.*

2 = wince, squirm, writhe • *The idea makes me cringe.*

crinkle AS A VERB = crease, wrinkle, crumple, pucker, fold, curl, crimp • *When she laughs, her eyes crinkle.*

▸ **AS A NOUN = crease**, wrinkle, crumple, ruffle, twist, fold, curl, rumple, pucker, crimp • *The fabric was smooth, without a crinkle.*

crinkly = wrinkled, gathered, creased, fluted, ruffled, kinky, furrowed, puckered, wrinkly • *a dress made of crinkly material*

cripple 1 = disable, paralyse, lame, debilitate, mutilate, maim, incapacitate, enfeeble, weaken, hamstring • *He had been warned that another bad fall could cripple him for life.*

2 = damage, destroy, ruin, bring to a standstill, halt, spoil, cramp, impair, put paid to, vitiate, put out of action • *A total cut-off of supplies would cripple the country's economy.*

OPPOSITES: help, further, aid

crippled = disabled, handicapped, challenged, paralysed, lame, deformed, incapacitated, bedridden, housebound, enfeebled • *He looked after his senile, crippled mother.*

crisis 1 = emergency, plight, catastrophe, predicament, pass, trouble, disaster, mess, dilemma, strait, deep water, meltdown *(informal)*, extremity, quandary, dire straits, exigency, critical situation • *Strikes worsened the country's economic crisis.*

2 = critical point, climax, point of no return, height, confrontation, crunch *(informal)*, turning point, culmination, crux, moment of truth, climacteric, tipping point • *The anxiety that had been building within him reached a crisis.*

crisp 1 = firm, crunchy, crispy, crumbly, fresh, brittle, unwilted • *Bake the potatoes till they're nice and crisp.*

OPPOSITES: soft, limp, withered

2 = bracing, fresh, refreshing, brisk, invigorating • *a crisp autumn day*

OPPOSITES: warm, pleasant, mild

3 = clean, smart, trim, neat, tidy, orderly, spruce, snappy, clean-cut, well-groomed, well-pressed • *He wore a panama hat and a crisp white suit.*

4 = brief, clear, short, tart, incisive, terse, succinct, pithy, brusque • *In a clear, crisp voice, he began his speech.*

criterion = standard, test, rule, measure, principle, proof, par, norm, canon, gauge, yardstick, touchstone, bench mark • *Exam results shouldn't be the only criterion for your choice of school.*

critic 1 = judge, authority, expert, analyst, commentator, pundit, reviewer, connoisseur, arbiter, expositor • *The New York critics had praised her performance.*

2 = fault-finder, attacker, censor, censurer, detractor, knocker *(informal)* • *He became a fierce critic of the tobacco industry.*

QUOTATIONS

It's not the critic who counts. Not the man who points out where the strong man stumbled or where the doer of great deeds could have done them better
[Theodore Roosevelt]

The proper function of the critic is to save the tale from the artist who created it
[D.H. Lawrence]

A critic is a man who knows the way but can't drive the car
[Kenneth Tynan]

CRICKET TERMS

appeal	cover point	full toss	mid off	pitch	swing
Ashes	covers	glance *or* glide	mid on	pull	test match
bail	crease	googly	mid wicket	run	third man
ball	cut	gully	nightwatchman	run out	twelfth man
bat	declare	hit wicket	no ball	seam	Twenty20
batsman	doosra	hook	off break	short leg	umpire *or* *(Austral. slang)* umpie
bouncer *or* bumper	drive	in	off side	silly mid on	wicket
boundary	duck	innings	off spin	silly mid off	wicketkeeper
bowl	edge	leg before wicket	off-spinner	single	wide
bowled	extra	leg break	on side *or* leg side	six	yorker
bowler	extra cover	leg bye	opener *or* opening batsman	slip	
bye	fast bowler	leg slip	out	spin	
catch	fielder *or* fieldsman	long leg	over	square leg	
caught	fine leg	long off	pad	stump	
century	follow on	long on		stumped	
chinaman	four	maiden (over)		sweep	

critic: a person who boasts himself hard to please because nobody tries to please him
[Ambrose Bierce *The Devil's Dictionary*]
A critic is a bundle of biases held loosely together by a sense of taste
[Whitney Balliet *Dinosaurs in the Morning*]

critical 1 = **crucial**, decisive, momentous, deciding, pressing, serious, vital, psychological, urgent, all-important, pivotal, high-priority, now or never • *The incident happened at a critical point in the campaign.*
OPPOSITES: unimportant
2 = **grave**, serious, dangerous, acute, risky, hairy *(slang)*, precarious, perilous • *Ten of the injured are said to be in a critical condition.*
OPPOSITES: safe, settled, secure
3 = **disparaging**, disapproving, scathing, derogatory, nit-picking *(informal)*, censorious, cavilling, fault-finding, captious, carping, niggling, nit-picky *(informal)* • *He has apologized for critical remarks he made about the referee.*
OPPOSITES: approving, complimentary, appreciative
4 = **analytical**, penetrating, discriminating, discerning, diagnostic, perceptive, judicious, accurate, precise • *What is needed is a critical analysis of the evidence.*
OPPOSITES: undiscriminating

criticism 1 = **fault-finding**, censure, disapproval, disparagement, stick *(slang)*, knocking *(informal)*, panning *(informal)*, slamming *(slang)*, slating *(informal)*, flak *(informal)*, slagging *(slang)*, strictures, bad press, denigration, brickbats *(informal)*, character assassination, sideswipe, critical remarks, animadversion • *The policy had repeatedly come under strong criticism.*
2 = **analysis**, review, notice, assessment, judgment, commentary, evaluation, appreciation, appraisal, critique, elucidation • *Her work includes novels, poetry and literary criticism.*

criticize = **find fault with**, censure, disapprove of, knock *(informal)*, blast, pan *(informal)*, condemn, slam *(slang)*, flame *(informal)*, carp, put down, slate *(informal)*, have a go (at) *(informal)*, disparage, tear into *(informal)*, diss *(slang, chiefly U.S.)*, nag at, lambast(e), roast *(informal)*, pick holes in, excoriate, pick to pieces, give (someone *or* something) a bad press, pass strictures upon, nit-pick *(informal)* • *His mother had rarely criticized him or any of her children.*
OPPOSITES: praise, compliment, commend

QUOTATIONS
To criticize is to appreciate, to appropriate, to take intellectual possession, to establish in fine a relation with the criticized thing and to make it one's own
[Henry James *What Maisie Knew*]
PROVERBS
People in glass houses shouldn't throw stones

critique = **essay**, review, analysis, assessment, examination, commentary, appraisal, treatise • *The book is a feminist critique of Victorian lady novelists.*

croak 1 = **grunt**, squawk, caw • *Frogs croaked in the reeds.*
2 = **rasp**, gasp, grunt, wheeze, utter *or* speak harshly, utter *or* speak huskily, utter *or* speak throatily • *Daniel managed to croak, 'Help me.'*
3 = **die**, expire, pass away, perish, buy it *(U.S. slang)*, check out *(U.S. slang)*, kick it *(slang)*, go belly-up *(slang)*, peg out *(informal)*, kick the bucket *(informal)*, buy the farm *(U.S. slang)*, peg it *(informal)*, cark it *(Austral. & N.Z. slang)*, pop your clogs *(informal)*, hop the twig *(informal)* • *The old man finally croaked at the age of 92.*

crone = **old woman**, witch, hag, old bag *(derogatory slang)*, old bat *(slang)*, kuia *(N.Z.)* • *a toothless old crone sitting in the corner*

crony = **friend**, china *(Brit. slang)*, colleague, associate, mate *(informal)*, pal *(informal)*, companion, cock *(Brit. informal)*, buddy *(informal)*, comrade, chum *(informal)*, accomplice, ally, sidekick *(slang)*, main man *(slang, chiefly U.S.)*, homeboy *(slang, chiefly U.S.)*, cobber *(Austral. & N.Z. old-fashioned informal)* • *his weekend drinking sessions with his cronies*

crook AS A NOUN 1 = **criminal**, rogue, cheat, thief, shark, lag *(slang)*, villain, robber, racketeer, fraudster, swindler, knave *(archaic)*, grifter *(slang, chiefly U.S. & Canad.)*, chiseller *(informal)*, skelm *(S. African)* • *The man is a crook and a liar.*
2 = **angle**, bend, bow, curve, fork, intersection, crotch • *She hid her face in the crook of her arm.*
▸ AS A VERB = **bend**, hook, angle, bow, curve, curl, cock, flex • *He crooked his finger at her and said, 'Come here.'*
▸ AS AN ADJECTIVE = **ill**, sick, poorly *(informal)*, funny *(informal)*, weak, ailing, queer, frail, feeble, unhealthy, seedy *(informal)*, sickly, unwell, laid up *(informal)*, queasy, infirm, out of sorts *(informal)*, dicky *(Brit. informal)*, nauseous, off-colour, under the weather *(informal)*, at death's door, indisposed, peaky, on the sick list *(informal)*, green about the gills • *He admitted to feeling a bit crook.*
▸ IN PHRASES: **go (off) crook** = **lose your temper**, be furious, rage, go mad, lose it *(informal)*, seethe, crack up *(informal)*, see red *(informal)*, lose the plot *(informal)*, go ballistic *(slang, chiefly U.S.)*, blow a fuse *(slang, chiefly U.S.)*, fly off the handle *(informal)*, be incandescent, go off the deep end *(informal)*, throw a fit *(informal)*, wig out *(slang)*, go up the wall *(slang)*, blow your top, lose your rag *(slang)*, be beside yourself, flip your lid *(slang)* • *She went crook when I confessed.*

crooked 1 = **bent**, twisted, bowed, curved, irregular, warped, deviating, out of shape, misshapen • *the crooked line of his broken nose*
OPPOSITES: straight, flat
2 = **deformed**, crippled, distorted, disfigured • *Whole families went about with crooked legs or twisted shoulders.*
3 = **zigzag**, winding, twisting, meandering, tortuous • *men gathered in the bars of the crooked streets*
4 = **at an angle**, angled, tilted, to one side, uneven, slanted, slanting, squint, awry, lopsided, askew, asymmetric, off-centre, skewwhiff *(Brit. informal)*, unsymmetrical • *He gave her a crooked grin.*
5 = **dishonest**, criminal, illegal, corrupt, dubious, questionable, unlawful, shady *(informal)*, fraudulent, unscrupulous, under-the-table, bent *(slang)*, shifty, deceitful, underhand, unprincipled, dishonourable, nefarious, knavish • *She might expose his crooked business deals to the authorities.*
OPPOSITES: legal, straight, honest

croon 1 = **sing**, warble • *a nightclub singer who crooned romantic songs*
2 = **say softly**, breathe, hum, purr • *The man was crooning soft words of encouragement to his wife.*

crop AS A NOUN 1 = **yield**, produce, gathering, fruits, harvest, vintage, reaping, season's growth • *a fine crop of apples*
2 = **batch**, set, lot, pack, collection, bunch, group • *the present crop of books and documentaries on Marilyn Monroe*
3 = **whip**, stick, switch, cane • *She grabbed her riding hat and crop and led the way out.*
▸ AS A VERB 1 = **harvest**, pick, collect, gather, bring in, reap, bring home, garner, mow • *I started cropping my beans in July.*
2 = **graze**, eat, browse, feed on, nibble • *I let the horse drop his head to crop the grass.*
3 = **cut**, reduce, trim, clip, dock, prune, shorten, shear, snip, pare, lop • *She cropped her hair and dyed it blonde.*
▸ IN PHRASES: **crop up** = **happen**, appear, emerge, occur, arise, turn up, spring up • *As we get older health problems often crop up.*

cross AS A VERB 1 = **go across**, pass over, traverse, cut across, move across, travel across • *She was partly to blame for failing to look as she crossed the road.*

2 = **span**, bridge, ford, go across, extend over • *A bridge crosses the river about half a mile outside the village.*
3 = **intersect**, meet, intertwine, crisscross • *The two roads cross at this junction.*
4 = **oppose**, interfere with, hinder, obstruct, deny, block, resist, frustrate, foil, thwart, impede • *He was not a man to cross.*
5 = **interbreed**, mix, blend, cross-pollinate, crossbreed, hybridize, cross-fertilize, intercross • *These small flowers were later crossed with a white flowering species.*
▸ AS A NOUN 1 = **crucifix** • *She wore a cross on a silver chain.*
2 = **trouble**, worry, trial, load, burden, grief, misery, woe, misfortune, affliction, tribulation • *My wife is much cleverer than I am; it is a cross I have to bear.*
3 = **mixture**, combination, blend, amalgam, amalgamation • *The noise that came out was a cross between a laugh and a bark.*
4 = **crossbreed**, hybrid • *a cross between a collie and a poodle*
5 = **crossroads**, crossing, junction, intersection • *Turn left at the cross and go straight on for two miles.*
▸ AS AN ADJECTIVE = **angry**, impatient, irritable, annoyed, put out, hacked (off) *(informal)*, pissed *(taboo slang)*, crusty, snappy, grumpy, vexed, pissed off *(taboo slang)*, sullen, surly, fractious, petulant, disagreeable, short, churlish, peeved *(informal)*, ill-tempered, irascible, cantankerous, tetchy, ratty *(Brit. & N.Z. informal)*, tooshie *(Austral. slang)*, testy, fretful, waspish, in a bad mood, grouchy *(informal)*, querulous, shirty *(slang, chiefly Brit.)*, peevish, splenetic, crotchety *(informal)*, snappish, ill-humoured, liverish, captious, pettish, out of humour, hoha *(N.Z.)* • *Everyone was getting bored and cross.*
OPPOSITES: nice, civil, good-humoured
▸ IN PHRASES: **cross something out** *or* **off** = **strike off** *or* **out**, eliminate, cancel, delete, blue-pencil, score off *or* out • *He crossed her name off the list.*
▹ *See panel* **Types of cross**

cross-examine = **question**, grill *(informal)*, quiz, interrogate, catechize, pump • *The accused's lawyers will get a chance to cross-examine him.*

crosswise *or* **crossways** = **across**, sideways, diagonally, from side to side, at right angles, at an angle, crisscross, athwart, on the bias, transversely, over, aslant • *Slice the courgettes crosswise.*

crossword
▸ RELATED ENTHUSIAST: cruciverbalist

crotch = **groin**, lap, crutch • *She kicked him hard in the crotch.*

crotchety = **bad-tempered**, difficult, cross, contrary, awkward, irritable, crusty, grumpy, surly, fractious, disagreeable, cantankerous, tetchy, ratty *(Brit. & N.Z. informal)*, testy, peevish, curmudgeonly, obstreperous, crabby, liverish • *a crotchety old man*

crouch = **bend down**, kneel, squat, stoop, bow, duck, hunch • *A man was crouching behind the bushes.*

crow[1] 1 = **squawk**, cry, screech • *The cock crows and the dawn chorus begins.*
2 = **gloat**, triumph, boast, swagger, brag, vaunt, bluster, exult, blow your own trumpet • *Edwards is already crowing over his victory.*

crow[2]
▸ RELATED ADJECTIVE: corvine
▸ COLLECTIVE NOUN: murder

crowd AS A NOUN 1 = **multitude**, mass, assembly, throng, company, press, army, host, pack, mob, flock, herd, swarm, horde, rabble, concourse, bevy • *It took some two hours before the crowd was fully dispersed.*
2 = **group**, set, lot, circle, gang, bunch *(informal)*, clique • *All the old crowd from my university days were there.*
3 = **audience**, spectators, house, gate, attendance • *When the song finished, the crowd went wild.*
▸ AS A VERB 1 = **flock**, press, push, mass, collect, gather, stream, surge, cluster, muster, huddle, swarm, throng, congregate, foregather • *The hungry refugees crowded around the lorries.*
2 = **squeeze**, pack, pile, bundle, cram • *A group of journalists were crowded into a minibus.* • *Hundreds of people crowded into the building.*
3 = **congest**, pack, cram • *Demonstrators crowded the streets shouting slogans.*
4 = **jostle**, batter, butt, push, elbow, shove • *It had been a tense, restless day with people crowding her all the time.*
▸ IN PHRASES: **the crowd** = **the masses**, the people, the public, the mob, the rank and file, the populace, the rabble, the proletariat, the hoi polloi, the riffraff, the vulgar herd • *You can learn to stand out from the crowd.*
▸ RELATED MANIA: ochlomania
▸ RELATED PHOBIA: ochlophobia, demophobia

crowded = **packed**, full, busy, mobbed, cramped, swarming, overflowing, thronged, teeming, congested, populous, jam-packed, crushed • *The street was crowded and noisy.*

crown AS A NOUN 1 = **coronet**, tiara, diadem, circlet, coronal *(poetic)*, chaplet • *a beautiful woman wearing a golden crown*
2 = **laurel wreath**, trophy, distinction, prize, bays, honour, garland, laurels, wreath, kudos • *He won the middleweight crown in 1947.*
3 = **high point**, head, top, tip, summit, crest, pinnacle, apex • *We stood on the crown of the hill.*

TYPES OF CROSS

Barbée	Iona	Potent
Canterbury	Jerusalem	Raguly *or* Rarulée
Celtic	Latin	Russian Orthodox
Cercelée	Maltese	St Andrew's (Saltire)
Cross crosslet	Millvine	St Peter's
Crux ansata	Papal	Tau (St Anthony's)
Globical	Pattée	Trefly
Graded (Calvary)	Pattée formée	
Greek	Patriarchal *or* Lorraine	

▸ **AS A VERB** 1 = **install**, invest, honour, dignify, ordain, inaugurate • *He had himself crowned as Emperor.*
2 = **top**, cap, be on top of, surmount • *A rugged castle crowns the cliffs.*
3 = **cap**, finish, complete, perfect, fulfil, consummate, round off, put the finishing touch to, put the tin lid on, be the climax *or* culmination of • *The summit was crowned by the signing of the historical treaty.*
4 = **strike**, belt *(informal)*, bash, hit over the head, box, punch, cuff, biff *(slang)*, wallop • *I felt like crowning him with the frying pan.*
▸ **IN PHRASES:** **the Crown** 1 = **monarch**, ruler, sovereign, rex *(Latin)*, emperor *or* empress, king *or* queen • *loyal subjects of the Crown*
2 = **monarchy**, sovereignty, royalty • *All treasure trove is the property of the Crown.*

crowning = **supreme**, final, ultimate, sovereign, paramount, culminating, consummate, mother of all *(informal)*, climactic • *the crowning moment of an illustrious career*

crucial 1 = **vital**, important, pressing, essential, urgent, momentous, high-priority • *the most crucial election campaign in years*
2 = **critical**, central, key, psychological, decisive, pivotal, now or never • *At the crucial moment, his nerve failed.*

crucify 1 = **execute**, put to death, nail to a cross • *the day that Christ was crucified*
2 = **pan** *(informal)*, rubbish *(informal)*, ridicule, slag (off) *(slang)*, lampoon, wipe the floor with *(informal)*, tear to pieces • *She was crucified by the critics for her performance.*
3 = **torture**, rack, torment, harrow • *He had been crucified by guilt ever since his child's death.*

crude 1 = **rough**, undeveloped, basic, outline, unfinished, makeshift, sketchy, unformed • *a crude way of assessing the risk of heart disease*
2 = **simple**, rudimentary, basic, primitive, coarse, clumsy, rough-and-ready, rough-hewn • *crude wooden carvings*
3 = **vulgar**, dirty, rude, obscene, coarse, indecent, crass, tasteless, lewd, X-rated *(informal)*, boorish, smutty, uncouth, gross • *a crude sense of humour*
OPPOSITES: polished, subtle, tasteful
4 = **unrefined**, natural, raw, unprocessed, unpolished, unmilled, unprepared • *8.5 million tonnes of crude steel*
OPPOSITES: processed, fine, prepared

crudely 1 = **roughly**, basically, sketchily • *The donors can be split – a little crudely – into two groups.*
2 = **simply**, roughly, basically, coarsely, clumsily • *a crudely carved wooden form*
3 = **vulgarly**, rudely, coarsely, crassly, indecently, obscenely, lewdly, impolitely, tastelessly • *and yet she spoke so crudely*

crudity 1 = **roughness**, crudeness, primitiveness, clumsiness • *the crudity of the country's political system*
2 = **vulgarity**, obscenity, indecency, impropriety, rudeness, coarseness, crudeness, lewdness, lowness, indelicacy, smuttiness • *He had not expected such crudity from so sophisticated a woman.*

cruel 1 = **brutal**, ruthless, callous, sadistic, inhumane, hard, fell *(archaic)*, severe, harsh, savage, grim, vicious, relentless, murderous, monstrous, unnatural, unkind, heartless, atrocious, inhuman, merciless, cold-blooded, malevolent, hellish, depraved, spiteful, brutish, bloodthirsty, remorseless, barbarous, pitiless, unfeeling, sanguinary, hard-hearted, stony-hearted • *the cruel practice of bullfighting* • *the persecution of prisoners by cruel officers*
OPPOSITES: kind, caring, gentle
2 = **bitter**, severe, painful, ruthless, traumatic, grievous, unrelenting, merciless, pitiless • *Fate dealt him a cruel blow.*

QUOTATIONS
I must be cruel, only to be kind
[William Shakespeare *Hamlet*]

cruelly 1 = **brutally**, severely, savagely, viciously, mercilessly, in cold blood, callously, monstrously, unmercifully, sadistically, pitilessly, spitefully, heartlessly, barbarously • *Douglas was often treated cruelly by his fellow-pupils.*
2 = **bitterly**, deeply, severely, mortally, painfully, ruthlessly, mercilessly, grievously, pitilessly, traumatically • *His life has been cruelly shattered by an event not of his own making.*

cruelty = **brutality**, spite, severity, savagery, ruthlessness, sadism, depravity, harshness, inhumanity, barbarity, callousness, viciousness, bestiality, heartlessness, brutishness, spitefulness, bloodthirstiness, mercilessness, fiendishness, hardheartedness • *Britain had laws against cruelty to animals but not children.*

cruise **AS A NOUN** = **sail**, voyage, boat trip, sea trip • *He and his wife were planning to go on a world cruise.*
▸ **AS A VERB** 1 = **sail**, coast, voyage • *She wants to cruise the canals of France in a barge.*
2 = **travel along**, coast, drift, keep a steady pace • *A black and white police car cruised past.*

crumb 1 = **bit**, grain, particle, fragment, shred, speck, sliver, morsel • *I stood up, brushing crumbs from my trousers.*
2 = **morsel**, scrap, atom, shred, mite, snippet, sliver, soupçon *(French)* • *There is one crumb of comfort – at least we've still got each other.*

crumble 1 = **disintegrate**, collapse, break up, deteriorate, decay, fall apart, perish, degenerate, decompose, tumble down, moulder, go to pieces • *Under the pressure, the flint crumbled into fragments.* • *The chalk cliffs are crumbling.*
2 = **crush**, fragment, crumb, pulverize, pound, grind, powder, granulate • *Roughly crumble the cheese into a bowl.*
3 = **collapse**, break down, deteriorate, decay, fall apart, degenerate, go to pieces, go to rack and ruin • *Their economy crumbled under the weight of United Nations sanctions.*

crumbling = **disintegrating**, collapsing, deteriorating, decaying, eroding, decomposing, mouldering • *the building's leaking roofs, broken windows, and crumbling stonework*

crumbly = **brittle**, short *(of pastry)*, powdery, friable • *The soil is dry and crumbly.*

crummy = **second-rate**, cheap, inferior, substandard, poor, pants *(informal)*, miserable, rotten *(informal)*, duff *(Brit. informal)*, lousy *(slang)*, shoddy, trashy, low-rent *(informal, chiefly U.S.)*, for the birds *(informal)*, third-rate, contemptible, shitty *(taboo slang)*, two-bit *(U.S. & Canad. slang)*, crappy *(slang)*, rubbishy, poxy *(slang)*, dime-a-dozen *(informal)*, piss-poor *(slang)*, chickenshit *(U.S. slang)*, bodger *or* bodgie *(Austral. slang)*, bush-league *(Austral. & N.Z. informal)*, tinhorn *(U.S. slang)*, of a sort *or* of sorts, strictly for the birds *(informal)* • *This is a lot better than some of the crummy places I've stayed in.*

crumple 1 = **crush**, squash, screw up, scrumple • *She crumpled the paper in her hand.*
2 = **crease**, wrinkle, rumple, ruffle, pucker • *She sat down carefully, so as not to crumple her skirt.*
3 = **collapse**, sink, go down, fall • *He crumpled to the floor in agony.*
4 = **break down**, fall, collapse, give way, cave in, go to pieces • *Sometimes we just crumpled under our grief.*
5 = **screw up**, pucker • *She faltered, and then her face crumpled once more.*

crumpled = **crushed**, wrinkled, creased, ruffled, rumpled, puckered • *He was wearing a donkey jacket and crumpled trousers.*

crunch **AS A VERB** = **chomp**, champ, munch, masticate, chew noisily, grind • *She sucked an ice cube and crunched it loudly.*
▸ **IN PHRASES:** **the crunch** = **critical point**, test, crisis, emergency, crux, moment of truth, hour of decision • *He can rely on my support when the crunch comes.*

crusade **AS A NOUN** 1 = **campaign**, drive, movement, cause, push • *a crusade against racism on the football terraces*

2 = **holy war**, jihad • *He was leading a religious crusade that did not respect national boundaries.*
▸ **AS A VERB** = **campaign**, fight, push, struggle, lobby, agitate, work • *a newspaper that has crusaded against drug traffickers*

crusader = **campaigner**, champion, advocate, activist, reformer • *He has set himself up as a crusader for higher press and broadcasting standards.*

crush **AS A VERB** 1 = **squash**, pound, break, smash, squeeze, crumble, crunch, mash, compress, press, crumple, pulverize • *Their vehicle was crushed by an army tank.*
2 = **crease**, wrinkle, crumple, rumple, scrumple, ruffle • *I don't want to crush my skirt.*
3 = **overcome**, overwhelm, put down, subdue, overpower, quash, quell, extinguish, stamp out, vanquish, conquer • *The military operation was the first step in a plan to crush the uprising.*
4 = **demoralize**, depress, devastate, discourage, humble, put down *(slang)*, humiliate, squash, flatten, deflate, mortify, psych out *(informal)*, dishearten, dispirit, deject • *Listen to criticism but don't be crushed by it.*
5 = **squeeze**, press, embrace, hug, enfold • *He crushed her in his arms.*
▸ **AS A NOUN** 1 = **crowd**, mob, horde, throng, press, pack, mass, jam, herd, huddle, swarm, multitude, rabble • *They got separated from each other in the crush.*
2 = **infatuation**, passion, obsession, fixation • *I developed a teenage crush on one of my teachers.*

crust 1 = **heel**, end • *pieces of broken biscuit and hard crusts of bread*
2 = **layer**, covering, coating, incrustation, film, outside, skin, surface, shell, coat, caking, scab, concretion • *As the water evaporates, a crust of salt is left on the surface of the soil.*
3 = **living**, income, livelihood, subsistence, bread and butter *(informal)*, daily bread, (means of) support, (source of) income • *In the old days, he would do almost anything to earn a crust.*

crustacean
▹ See panel **Crustaceans**

crusty 1 = **crispy**, well-baked, crisp, well-done, brittle, friable, hard, short • *crusty french loaves*
2 = **irritable**, short, cross, prickly, touchy, curt, surly, gruff, brusque, cantankerous, tetchy, ratty *(Brit. & N.Z. informal)*, testy, chippy *(informal)*, short-tempered, peevish, crabby, choleric, splenetic, ill-humoured, captious, snappish *or* snappy • *a crusty old colonel with a gruff manner*

crux = **crucial point**, heart, core, essence, nub, decisive point • *He said the crux of the matter was economic policy.*

cry **AS A VERB** 1 = **weep**, sob, bawl, shed tears, keen, greet *(Scot. or archaic)*, wail, whine, whimper, whinge *(informal)*, blubber, snivel, yowl, boohoo, howl your eyes out • *I hung up the phone and started to cry.*
OPPOSITES: laugh, giggle, chuckle
2 = **shout**, call, scream, roar, hail, yell, howl, call out, exclaim, shriek, bellow, whoop, screech, bawl, holler *(informal)*, ejaculate, sing out, halloo, vociferate • *'You're under arrest!' he cried.*
OPPOSITES: whisper, mutter, murmur
3 = **beg**, plead, pray, clamour, implore, beseech, entreat • *She screamed and cried for help.*
4 = **announce**, hawk, advertise, proclaim, bark *(informal)*, trumpet, shout from the rooftops *(informal)*, bruit • *In the street below, a peddler was crying his wares.*
▸ **AS A NOUN** 1 = **weep**, greet *(Scot. or archaic)*, sob, howl, bawl, blubber, snivel • *Have a good cry if you want to.*
2 = **shout**, call, scream, roar, yell, howl, shriek, bellow, whoop, screech, hoot, ejaculation, bawl, holler *(informal)*, exclamation, squawk, yelp, yoo-hoo • *Her brother gave a cry of recognition.*
3 = **appeal**, prayer, plea, petition, entreaty, supplication • *Many other countries have turned a deaf ear to their cries for help.*
4 = **announcement**, proclamation • *the sound of car horns and street cries*
5 = **weeping**, sobbing, bawling, crying, greeting *(Scot. or archaic)*, howling, wailing, blubbering, snivelling • *The baby's cries woke him again.*
▸ **IN PHRASES: cry off** = **back out**, withdraw, quit, cop out *(slang)*, beg off, excuse yourself • *She caught flu and had to cry off at the last minute.*
PROVERBS
It is no use crying over spilt milk

crypt = **vault**, tomb, catacomb, ossuary, undercroft • *people buried in the crypt of an old London church*

cryptic = **mysterious**, dark, coded, puzzling, obscure, vague, veiled, ambiguous, enigmatic, perplexing, arcane, equivocal, abstruse, Delphic, oracular • *I wondered just what he meant by that cryptic remark.*

crystal
▸ **RELATED PHOBIA:** crystallophobia

crystallize 1 = **take shape**, form, become clear, come together, materialize • *Now my thoughts really began to crystallize.*
2 = **harden**, solidify, coalesce, form crystals • *Keep stirring the mixture or the sugar will crystallize.*

cub = **young**, baby, offspring, whelp • *three day-old lion cubs*
▸ **COLLECTIVE NOUN:** litter

cubbyhole 1 = **cubicle**, booth, den, hole, snug • *Back in her cubbyhole of an office, Nina sat down at her desk.*
2 = **compartment**, slot, niche, recess, pigeonhole • *He fetched an official form from his cubbyhole.*

cuddle **AS A VERB** 1 = **hug**, embrace, clasp, fondle, cosset • *He cuddled their newborn baby.*
2 = **pet**, hug, canoodle *(slang)*, bill and coo • *They used to kiss and cuddle in front of everyone.*
▸ **IN PHRASES: cuddle up** = **snuggle**, nestle • *My cat cuddled up to me.*

cuddly = **soft**, plump, buxom, curvaceous, huggable, cuddlesome, warm • *a small, plump, cuddly woman*

cudgel **AS A NOUN** = **club**, stick, baton, bludgeon, truncheon, cosh *(Brit.)*, shillelagh, mere *(N.Z.)*, patu *(N.Z.)* • *He has slept with a cudgel by his bed since being burgled.*
▸ **AS A VERB** = **beat**, batter, thrash, thump, bang, cane, pound, bludgeon, pummel, cosh *(Brit.)*, thwack, drub, beat *or* knock seven bells out of *(informal)* • *He used to cudgel his stepson like a dog.*

CRUSTACEANS

barnacle
crab
crayfish, crawfish, *(U.S.)* or *(Austral. & N.Z. informal)* craw
Dublin Bay prawn
freshwater shrimp
goose barnacle
gribble
hermit crab
horseshoe crab *or* king crab
king prawn
koura *(N.Z.)*
krill
land crab
langoustine
lobster
Norway lobster
opossum shrimp
oyster crab
prawn
robber crab
sand hopper, beach flea, *or* sand flea
sand shrimp
scorpion
sea spider
shrimp
soft-shell crab
spider crab
spiny lobster, rock lobster, crawfish, *or* langouste
water flea

cue = **signal**, sign, nod, hint, prompt, reminder, suggestion • *He took this as his cue to leave.*

cuff[1] IN PHRASES: **off the cuff** 1 = **impromptu**, spontaneous, improvised, offhand, unrehearsed, extempore • *I didn't mean any offence. It was just an off-the-cuff remark.*
2 = **without preparation**, spontaneously, impromptu, offhand, on the spur of the moment, ad lib, extempore, off the top of your head • *He was speaking off the cuff when he made this suggestion.*

C

cuff[2] AS A VERB = **smack**, hit, thump, punch, box, knock, bat *(informal)*, belt *(informal)*, slap, clap, clout *(informal)*, whack, biff *(slang)*, clobber *(slang)* • *He cuffed the child across the head.*
▸ AS A NOUN = **smack**, blow, knock, punch, thump, box, belt *(informal)*, rap, slap, clout *(informal)*, whack, biff *(slang)* • *He gave the dog a cuff.*

cul-de-sac = **dead end**, blind alley • *The factory was set at the end of a cul-de-sac.*

cull 1 = **select**, collect, gather, amass, choose, pick, pick up, pluck, glean, cherry-pick • *All this information had been culled from radio reports.*
2 = **slaughter**, kill, destroy, butcher, slay, exterminate, thin out • *The wildlife park is planning to cull 2,000 elephants.*

culminate = **end up**, end, close, finish, conclude, wind up, climax, terminate, come to a head, come to a climax, rise to a crescendo • *The parade will culminate in a firework display.*

culmination = **climax**, conclusion, completion, finale, consummation • *This week's events are the culmination of a long-running row between the two countries.*

culpability = **fault**, blame, responsibility, liability, accountability • *He added there was clear culpability on the part of the government.*

culpable = **blameworthy**, wrong, guilty, to blame, liable, in the wrong, at fault, sinful, answerable, found wanting, reprehensible • *Their decision to do nothing makes them culpable.*
OPPOSITES: innocent, not guilty, blameless

culprit = **offender**, criminal, villain, sinner, delinquent, felon, person responsible, guilty party, wrongdoer, miscreant, malefactor, evildoer, transgressor, perp *(U.S. & Canad. informal)* • *The real culprits in the fight have not yet been identified.*

cult 1 = **sect**, following, body, faction, party, school, church, faith, religion, denomination, clique, hauhau *(N.Z.)* • *The teenager may have been abducted by a religious cult.*
2 = **craze**, fashion, trend, fad • *The programme has become something of a cult among thirty-somethings.*
3 = **obsession**, worship, admiration, devotion, reverence, veneration, idolization • *The cult of personality surrounding pop stars leaves me cold.*

cultivate 1 = **farm**, work, plant, tend, till, harvest, plough, bring under cultivation • *She cultivated a small garden of her own.*
2 = **develop**, establish, acquire, foster, devote yourself to, pursue • *Try to cultivate a positive mental attitude.*
3 = **court**, associate with, seek out, run after, consort with, butter up, dance attendance upon, seek someone's company *or* friendship, take trouble *or* pains with • *He only cultivates people who may be of use to him.*
4 = **foster**, further, forward, encourage • *She went out of her way to cultivate his friendship.*
5 = **improve**, better, train, discipline, polish, refine, elevate, enrich, civilize • *My father encouraged me to cultivate my mind.*

cultivated = **refined**, cultured, advanced, polished, educated, sophisticated, accomplished, discriminating, enlightened, discerning, civilized, genteel, well-educated, urbane, erudite, well-bred • *His mother was an elegant, cultivated woman.*

cultivation 1 = **farming**, working, gardening, tilling, ploughing, husbandry, tillage, agronomy • *environments where aridity makes cultivation of the land difficult*
2 = **growing**, planting, production, farming • *groups that want a ban on the cultivation of GM crops*
3 = **development**, fostering, pursuit, devotion to • *the cultivation of a positive approach to life and health*
4 = **promotion**, support, encouragement, nurture, patronage, advancement, advocacy, enhancement, furtherance • *those who devote themselves to the cultivation of the arts*
5 = **refinement**, letters, learning, education, culture, taste, breeding, manners, polish, discrimination, civilization, enlightenment, sophistication, good taste, civility, gentility, discernment • *He was a man of cultivation and scholarship.*

cultural 1 = **ethnic**, national, native, folk, racial • *a deep sense of honour which was part of his cultural heritage*
2 = **artistic**, educational, elevating, aesthetic, enriching, broadening, enlightening, developmental, civilizing, edifying, educative • *This holiday was a rich cultural experience.*

culture 1 = **the arts** • *France's Minister of Culture and Education*
2 = **civilization**, society, customs, way of life • *people of different cultures*
3 = **lifestyle**, habit, way of life, mores • *Social workers say this has created a culture of dependency.*
4 = **refinement**, education, breeding, polish, enlightenment, accomplishment, sophistication, good taste, erudition, gentility, urbanity • *He was a well-travelled man of culture and breeding.*

cultured = **refined**, advanced, polished, intellectual, educated, sophisticated, accomplished, scholarly, enlightened, knowledgeable, well-informed, genteel, urbane, erudite, highbrow, well-bred, well-read • *He is a cultured man with a wide circle of friends.*
OPPOSITES: common, coarse, uneducated

culvert = **drain**, channel, gutter, conduit, watercourse • *The bomb was hidden in a culvert under a road.*

cumbersome 1 = **awkward**, heavy, hefty *(informal)*, clumsy, bulky, weighty, impractical, inconvenient, burdensome, unmanageable, clunky *(informal)*, cumbrous • *Although the machine looks cumbersome, it is easy to use.*
OPPOSITES: practical, compact, easy to use
2 = **inefficient**, unwieldy, badly organized • *an old and cumbersome computer system*
OPPOSITES: efficient, serviceable

cumulative = **collective**, increasing, aggregate, amassed, accruing, snowballing, accumulative • *Skin cancer can be caused by the cumulative effect of years of exposure to the sun.*

cunning AS AN ADJECTIVE 1 = **crafty**, sly, devious, artful, sharp, subtle, tricky, shrewd, astute, canny, wily, Machiavellian, shifty, foxy, guileful • *He's a cunning, devious, good-for-nothing so-and-so.*
OPPOSITES: frank, ethical, honest
2 = **ingenious**, subtle, imaginative, shrewd, sly, astute, devious, artful, Machiavellian • *I came up with a cunning plan.*
3 = **skilful**, clever, deft, adroit, dexterous • *The artist's cunning use of light and shadow creates perspective.*
OPPOSITES: clumsy, maladroit
▸ AS A NOUN 1 = **craftiness**, guile, trickery, shrewdness, deviousness, artfulness, slyness, wiliness, foxiness • *an example of the cunning of modern art thieves*
OPPOSITES: sincerity, candour, ingenuousness
2 = **skill**, art, ability, craft, subtlety, ingenuity, finesse, artifice, dexterity, cleverness, deftness, astuteness, adroitness • *He tackled the problem with skill and cunning.*
OPPOSITES: clumsiness

QUOTATIONS
Cunning is the dark sanctuary of incapacity
[Lord Chesterfield *Letters...to his Godson and Successor*]

cup 1 = **mug**, goblet, chalice, teacup, beaker, demitasse, bowl • *a set of matching cups and saucers*
2 = **trophy** • *First prize is a silver cup and a scroll.*

CUPS AND OTHER DRINKING VESSELS

canteen
champagne flute
chalice
copita
cup
demitasse
glass
goblet
mug
porrón
quaich
schooner
tankard
tassie
tumbler
water bottle

cupboard = **cabinet**, closet, locker, press • *The kitchen cupboard was stocked with tins of food.*
▷ *See panel* **Cupboards and cabinets**

Cupid = **god of love**, love, Eros • *Cupid's arrow may strike you at any time.*

cupidity = **avarice**, greed, acquisitiveness, rapacity, covetousness, avidity, greediness, rapaciousness • *the well-known cupidity and greed of politicians*

cupola = **dome**, onion dome • *The church tower's cupola can be seen above the trees.*

cur 1 = **mongrel**, hound, stray, canine, mutt *(slang)* • *He called my dog a mangy cur.*
2 = **scoundrel**, villain, good-for-nothing, blackguard, heel *(slang)*, rat *(informal)*, shit *(taboo slang)*, bastard *(informal, offensive)*, bugger *(taboo slang)*, son-of-a-bitch *(slang, chiefly U.S. & Canad.)*, wretch, rotter *(slang, chiefly Brit.)*, scumbag *(slang)*, bad egg *(old-fashioned informal)*, cocksucker *(taboo slang)*, wrong 'un *(informal)* • *Elliot was vilified as a cur and a scoundrel.*
▸ **COLLECTIVE NOUN:** cowardice

curative = **restorative**, healing, therapeutic, tonic, corrective, medicinal, remedial, salutary, healthful, health-giving • *The curative powers of fresh air and sunlight are well known.*

curb AS A VERB = **restrain**, control, check, contain, restrict, moderate, suppress, inhibit, subdue, hinder, repress, constrain, retard, impede, muzzle, bridle, stem the flow of, keep a tight rein on • *He must learn to curb that temper of his.*
▸ **AS A NOUN** = **restraint**, control, check, brake, limitation, rein, deterrent, bridle • *He called for much stricter curbs on immigration.*

curdle = **congeal**, clot, thicken, condense, turn sour, solidify, coagulate • *The sauce must not boil or the egg yolk will curdle.*
OPPOSITES: melt, dissolve, soften

cure AS A VERB 1 = **make better**, correct, heal, relieve, remedy, mend, rehabilitate, help, ease • *An operation finally cured his shin injury.*
2 = **restore to health**, restore, heal • *I was cured almost overnight.*
3 = **rectify**, improve, fix, remedy, right, correct, repair, amend, make good, mend, redress, put right, emend • *We need to cure our environmental problems.*
4 = **preserve**, smoke, dry, salt, pickle, kipper • *Legs of pork were cured and smoked over the fire.*
▸ **AS A NOUN** = **remedy**, treatment, medicine, healing, antidote, corrective, panacea, restorative, nostrum • *There is still no cure for the common cold.*

QUOTATIONS
It is part of the cure to wish to be cured
[Seneca *Phaedra*]
The cure is worse than the disease
[Philip Massinger *The Bondman*]

cure-all = **panacea**, elixir, nostrum, elixir vitae *(Latin)* • *He was the first physician to use leeches as a cure-all.*

curio = **collector's item**, antique, trinket, knick-knack, bibelot • *a shop which sold antiques and curios*

curiosity 1 = **inquisitiveness**, interest, prying, snooping *(informal)*, nosiness *(informal)* • *Mr Lim was a constant source of curiosity to his neighbours.*
2 = **oddity**, wonder, sight, phenomenon, spectacle, freak, marvel, novelty, rarity • *The company is a curiosity in the world of publishing.*
3 = **collector's item**, trinket, curio, knick-knack, objet d'art *(French)*, bibelot • *The mantelpieces and windowsills are adorned with curiosities.*

PROVERBS
Curiosity killed the cat

curious 1 = **inquisitive**, interested, questioning, searching, inquiring, peering, puzzled, peeping, meddling, prying, snoopy *(informal)*, nosy *(informal)* • *He was intensely curious about the world around him.*
OPPOSITES: indifferent, uninterested, incurious
2 = **strange**, unusual, bizarre, odd, novel, wonderful, rare, unique, extraordinary, puzzling, unexpected, exotic, mysterious, marvellous, peculiar, queer *(informal)*, rum *(Brit. slang)*, singular, unconventional, quaint, unorthodox • *A lot of curious things have happened here in the past few weeks.*
OPPOSITES: common, ordinary, familiar

curl AS A NOUN 1 = **ringlet**, lock • *a little girl with blonde curls*
2 = **twist**, spiral, coil, kink, whorl, curlicue • *A thick curl of smoke rose from the rusty stove.*
▸ **AS A VERB** 1 = **crimp**, wave, perm, frizz • *She had curled her hair for the event.*
2 = **twirl**, turn, bend, twist, curve, loop, spiral, coil, meander, writhe, corkscrew, wreathe • *Smoke was curling up the chimney.*
3 = **wind**, entwine, twine • *She curled her fingers round his wrist.*

curlew
▸ **COLLECTIVE NOUN:** herd

curly = **wavy**, waved, curled, curling, fuzzy, kinky, permed, corkscrew, crimped, frizzy • *She had curly dark hair and black eyes.*

curmudgeon = **grump** *(informal)*, bear, grumbler, grouser, malcontent, grouch *(informal)*, sourpuss *(informal)*, churl, crosspatch *(informal)* • *a terrible old curmudgeon*

currency 1 = **money**, coinage, legal tender, medium of exchange, bills, notes, coins • *More people favour a single European currency than oppose it.*
2 = **acceptance**, exposure, popularity, circulation, vogue, prevalence • *His theory has gained wide currency in America.*
▷ *See panel* **Currencies**

CUPBOARDS AND CABINETS

ambry
armoire
bookcase
buffet
bureau
cabinet
canterbury
cellaret
chest
chest of drawers
chest-on-chest
chiffonier *or* chiffonnier
closet
clothes-press
commode
console
Coolgardie safe
court cupboard
credence table *or* credenza
dooket *(Scot.)*
drawer
dresser
filing cabinet
étagère
garderobe *(archaic)*
highboy *(U.S.)*
larder
locker
lowboy *(U.S.)*
medicine chest
pantry
press
safe
shelf
sideboard
stand
tallboy
vitrine
wardrobe
Welsh dresser
whatnot

CURRENCIES

Country	Currency
Afghanistan	afghani
Albania	lek
Algeria	Algerian dinar
Andorra	euro
Angola	kwanza
Antigua and Barbuda	East Caribbean dollar
Argentina	peso
Armenia	dram
Australia	Australian dollar
Austria	euro
Azerbaijan	manat
Bahamas	Bahamian dollar
Bahrain	dinar
Bangladesh	taka
Barbados	Barbados dollar
Belarus	rouble
Belgium	euro
Belize	Belize dollar
Benin	CFA franc
Bhutan	ngultrum
Bolivia	boliviano
Bosnia-Herzegovina	convertible marka
Botswana	pula
Brazil	real
Brunei	Brunei dollar
Bulgaria	lev
Burkina-Faso	CFA franc
Burundi	Burundi franc
Cambodia	riel
Cameroon	CFA franc
Canada	Canadian dollar
Cape Verde	escudo
Central African Republic	CFA franc
Chad	CFA franc
Chile	peso
China	yuan
Colombia	peso
Comoros	Comorian franc
Congo (Democratic Republic of)	Congolese franc
Congo (Republic of)	CFA franc
Costa Rica	cólon
Côte d'Ivoire	CFA franc
Croatia	kuna
Cuba	peso
Cyprus	pound
Czech Republic	koruna
Denmark	krone
Djibouti	Djibouti franc
Dominica	East Caribbean dollar
Dominican Republic	peso
East Timor	U.S. dollar
Ecuador	U.S. dollar
Egypt	pound
El Salvador	cólon
Equatorial Guinea	CFA franc
Eritrea	nakfa
Estonia	kroon
Ethiopia	birr
Fiji	Fiji dollar
Finland	euro
France	euro
French Guiana	French franc
Gabon	CFA franc
Gambia	dalasi
Germany	euro
Ghana	cedi
Greece	euro
Greenland	Danish krone
Grenada	East Caribbean dollar
Guatemala	quetzal
Guinea	Guinea franc
Guinea-Bissau	CFA franc
Guyana	Guyana dollar
Haiti	gourde
Honduras	lempira
Hungary	forint
Iceland	krona
India	rupee
Indonesia	rupiah
Iran	rial
Iraq	dinar
Ireland (Republic of)	euro
Israel	shekel
Italy	euro
Jamaica	Jamaican dollar
Japan	yen
Jordan	dinar
Kazakhstan	tenge
Kenya	shilling
Kirghizia	som
Kiribati	Australian dollar
Kosovo	dinar; euro
Kuwait	dinar
Kyrgyzstan	som
Laos	kip
Latvia	lat
Lebanon	pound
Lesotho	loti
Liberia	Liberian dollar
Libya	dinar
Liechtenstein	Swiss franc
Lithuania	litas
Luxembourg	euro
Macedonia	denar
Madagascar	Malagasy franc
Malawi	kwacha
Malaysia	ringgit
Maldives (Republic of)	rufiyaa
Mali	CFA franc
Malta	lira
Marshall Islands	U.S.dollar
Mauritania	ouguiya
Mauritius	rupee
Mexico	peso
Micronesia	U.S.dollar
Moldova	leu
Monaco	French franc
Mongolia	tugrik
Montenegro	euro
Montserrat	East Caribbean dollar
Morocco	dirham
Mozambique	metical
Myanmar	kyat
Namibia	Namibian dollar
Nauru	Australian dollar
Nepal	rupee
Netherlands	euro
New Zealand	New Zealand dollar
Nicaragua	córdoba
Niger	CFA franc
Nigeria	naira
North Korea	won
Norway	krone
Oman	rial
Pakistan	rupee
Palau	U.S.dollar
Panama	balboa
Papua New Guinea	kina
Paraguay	guarani
Peru	new sol
Philippines	Philippine peso
Poland	zloty
Portugal	euro
Qatar	riyal
Romania	leu
Russia	rouble
Rwanda	Rwanda franc
St. Kitts and Nevis	East Caribbean dollar
St. Lucia	East Caribbean dollar
St. Vincent and the Grenadines	East Caribbean dollar
Samoa	tala
San Marino	euro
São Tomé and Principe	dobra
Saudi Arabia	riyal
Senegal	CFA franc
Seychelles	rupee
Sierra Leone	leone
Singapore	Singapore dollar
Slovakia	koruna
Slovenia	tolar
Solomon Islands	Solomon Islands dollar
Somalia	shilling
South Africa	rand
South Korea	won
Spain	euro
Sri Lanka	rupee
Sudan	dinar
Surinam	guilder
Swaziland	lilangeni
Sweden	krona
Switzerland	Swiss franc
Syria	pound

CURRENCIES (CONTINUED)

Country	Currency	Country	Currency	Country	Currency
Taiwan	Taiwan dollar	Turkmenistan	manat	Uzbekistan	sum
Tajikistan	somoni	Tuvalu	Australian dollar	Vanuatu	vatu
Tanzania	shilling	Uganda	shilling	Vatican City	euro
Thailand	baht	Ukraine	hryvna	Venezuela	bolívar
Togo	CFA franc	United Arab Emirates	dirham	Vietnam	dong
Tonga	pa'anga	United Kingdom	pound sterling	Yemen	riyal
Trinidad and Tobago	Trinidad and Tobago dollar	United States of America	U.S. dollar	Yugoslavia (Serbia)	dinar
Tunisia	dinar			Zambia	kwacha
Turkey	Turkish lira	Uruguay	peso	Zimbabwe	Zimbabwe dollar

current AS A NOUN 1 = **flow**, course, undertow, jet, stream, tide, progression, river, tideway • *The swimmers were swept away by the strong current.*
2 = **draught**, flow, breeze, puff • *I felt a current of cool air blowing in my face.*
3 = **mood**, feeling, spirit, atmosphere, trend, tendency, drift, inclination, vibe *(slang)*, undercurrent • *A strong current of nationalism is running through the country.*
▸ AS AN ADJECTIVE 1 = **present**, fashionable, ongoing, up-to-date, in, now *(informal)*, happening *(informal)*, contemporary, in the news, sexy *(informal)*, trendy *(Brit. informal)*, topical, present-day, in fashion, in vogue, up-to-the-minute, du jour *(French)*, culty • *current trends in the music scene*
OPPOSITES: past, old-fashioned, out-of-date
2 = **prevalent**, general, common, accepted, popular, widespread, in the air, prevailing, circulating, going around, customary, rife, in circulation • *the prevailing tide of current opinion*

curry

TYPES OF CURRY

achari	green thai	nentara
balti	jalfrezi	pasanda
biryani	jaipuri	pathia
bhoona *or* bhuna	karahi	phal
	kofta	red thai
chasni	korma	rogan josh
dhal	madras	tandoori
dhansak	masala	tikka
dopiaza	mussalman	vindaloo

curse AS A VERB 1 = **swear**, cuss *(informal)*, blaspheme, use bad language, turn the air blue *(informal)*, be foul-mouthed, take the Lord's name in vain • *He was obviously very drunk and cursed continuously at passers-by.*
2 = **abuse**, damn, scold, swear at, revile, vilify, fulminate, execrate, vituperate, imprecate • *He cursed her for having been so careless.*
3 = **put a curse on**, damn, doom, jinx, excommunicate, execrate, put a jinx on, accurse, imprecate, anathematize • *I began to think that I was cursed.*
4 = **afflict**, trouble, burden • *He's always been cursed with a bad memory.*
▸ AS A NOUN 1 = **oath**, obscenity, blasphemy, expletive, profanity, imprecation, swearword • *He shot her an angry look and a curse.*
2 = **malediction**, jinx, anathema, hoodoo *(informal)*, evil eye, excommunication, imprecation, execration • *He believes someone has put a curse on him.*
3 = **affliction**, evil, plague, scourge, cross, trouble, disaster, burden, ordeal, torment, hardship, misfortune, calamity, tribulation, bane, vexation • *The curse of alcoholism is a huge problem in Britain.*

QUOTATIONS
A plague o' both your houses
[William Shakespeare *Romeo and Juliet*]
How comes it that you curse, Frère Jean? It's only, said the monk, in order to embellish my language
[François Rabelais *Gargantua*]
PROVERBS
Curses, like chickens, come home to roost

cursed 1 = **under a curse**, damned, doomed, jinxed, bedevilled, fey *(Scot.)*, star-crossed, accursed, ill-fated • *The whole family seemed cursed.*
2 = **hateful**, damned, vile, odious, loathsome, abominable, infernal, detestable, damnable, pestilential • *I'd like to burn this whole cursed place to the ground.*

cursory = **brief**, passing, rapid, casual, summary, slight, hurried, careless, superficial, hasty, perfunctory, desultory, offhand, slapdash • *I gave the letter a fairly cursory reading.*

curt = **terse**, short, brief, sharp, summary, blunt, rude, tart, abrupt, gruff, brusque, offhand, ungracious, uncivil, unceremonious, snappish • *'The matter is closed,' was his curt reply.*

curtail = **reduce**, cut, diminish, decrease, dock, cut back, shorten, lessen, cut short, pare down, retrench • *NATO plans to curtail the number of troops being sent to the region.* • *The celebrations had to be curtailed because of bad weather.*

curtailment = **cutting**, reduction, docking, lessening, cutback, cutting short, retrenchment • *He supports the curtailment of military spending.*

curtain AS A NOUN 1 = **hanging**, drape *(chiefly U.S.)*, portière • *Her bedroom curtains were drawn.*
2 = **screen**, veil, shroud, pall • *a curtain of cigarette smoke*
▸ IN PHRASES: **curtain something off** = **conceal**, screen, hide, veil, drape, shroud, shut off • *The bed was a massive four-poster, curtained off by ragged draperies.*

curvaceous = **shapely**, voluptuous, curvy, busty, well-rounded, buxom, full-figures, bosomy, well-stacked *(Brit. slang)*, Rubenesque • *a curvaceous blonde*

curvature = **curving**, bend, curve, arching, arc • *He suffered from a curvature of the spine.*

curve AS A NOUN = **bend**, turn, loop, arc, curvature, camber • *a curve in the road*
▸ AS A VERB = **bend**, turn, wind, twist, bow, arch, snake, arc, coil, swerve • *The track curved away below him.*
▸ RELATED ADJECTIVE: sinuous

curved = **bent**, rounded, sweeping, twisted, bowed, arched, arced, humped, serpentine, sinuous, twisty • *the curved lines of the chairs*

cushion AS A NOUN 1 = **pillow**, pad, bolster, headrest, beanbag, scatter cushion, hassock, squab • *Her leg was propped up on two cushions.*

2 = **protection**, cover, security, defence, guard, barrier, shield, safeguard, buffer, bulwark • *Housing benefit provides a cushion against hardship.*
▸ **AS A VERB** 1 = **protect**, support, bolster, cradle, buttress • *The suspension is designed to cushion passengers from the effects of riding over rough roads.*
2 = **soften**, dampen, muffle, mitigate, deaden, suppress, stifle • *He spoke gently, trying to cushion the blow of rejection.*

cushy = **easy**, soft, comfortable, undemanding, jammy *(Brit. slang)* • *He's had a very cushy life so far.*

custodian = **keeper**, guardian, superintendent, warden, caretaker, curator, protector, warder, watchman, overseer • *the custodian of the holy shrine in Mecca*

custody 1 = **care**, charge, protection, supervision, preservation, auspices, aegis, tutelage, guardianship, safekeeping, keeping, trusteeship, custodianship • *I'm taking him to court to get custody of the children.*
2 = **imprisonment**, detention, confinement, incarceration • *Three people appeared in court and two of them were remanded in custody.*

custom 1 = **tradition**, practice, convention, ritual, form, policy, rule, style, fashion, usage, formality, etiquette, observance, praxis, unwritten law, kaupapa *(N.Z.)* • *The custom of lighting the Olympic flame goes back centuries.*
2 = **habit**, way, practice, manner, procedure, routine, mode, wont • *It was his custom to approach every problem cautiously.*
3 = **customers**, business, trade, patronage • *Providing discounts is not the only way to win custom.*

QUOTATIONS

Custom reconciles us to everything
[Edmund Burke *The Origin of our Ideas of the Sublime and Beautiful*]

a custom
More honoured in the breach than the observance
[William Shakespeare *Hamlet*]

customarily = **usually**, generally, commonly, regularly, normally, traditionally, ordinarily, habitually, in the ordinary way, as a rule • *Marriages in medieval Europe were customarily arranged by the families.*

customary 1 = **usual**, general, common, accepted, established, traditional, normal, ordinary, familiar, acknowledged, conventional, routine, everyday • *It is customary to offer a drink or a snack to guests.*
OPPOSITES: rare, unusual, exceptional
2 = **accustomed**, regular, usual, habitual, wonted • *She took her customary seat behind her desk.*

customer = **client**, consumer, regular *(informal)*, buyer, patron, shopper, purchaser, habitué • *Most of our customers have very tight budgets.*

customs = **import charges**, tax, duty, toll, tariff • *Some merchants imported goods without paying the full customs.*

cut **AS A VERB** 1 = **slit**, saw, score, nick, slice, slash, pierce, hack, penetrate, notch • *Thieves cut a hole in the fence.* • *You can hear the saw as it cuts through the bone.*
2 = **chop**, split, divide, slice, segment, dissect, cleave, part • *Cut the tomatoes into small pieces.*
3 = **carve**, slice • *Mr Long was cutting himself a piece of the cake.*
4 = **sever**, cut in two, sunder • *I cut the rope with scissors.*
5 = **shape**, carve, engrave, chisel, form, score, fashion, chip, sculpture, whittle, sculpt, inscribe, hew • *Geometric motifs are cut into the stone walls.*
6 = **slash**, nick, wound, lance, gash, lacerate, incise • *I cut myself shaving.*
7 = **clip**, mow, trim, dock, prune, snip, pare, lop • *The previous tenants hadn't even cut the grass.*
8 = **trim**, shave, hack, snip • *She cut his ragged hair and shaved off his beard.*
9 = **reduce**, lower, slim (down), diminish, slash, decrease, cut back, rationalize, ease up on, downsize, kennet *(Austral. slang)*, jeff *(Austral. slang)* • *The first priority is to cut costs.*
OPPOSITES: increase, expand, enlarge
10 = **abridge**, edit, shorten, curtail, condense, abbreviate, précis • *He has cut the play judiciously.*
OPPOSITES: extend, add to, fill out
11 = **delete**, take out, excise, edit out, expurgate • *The audience wants more music and less drama, so we've cut some scenes.*
12 = **stop**, suspend, interrupt, discontinue • *They used pressure tactics such as cutting food and water supplies.*
13 = **hurt**, wound, upset, sting, grieve, pain, hurt someone's feelings • *The personal criticism has cut him deeply.*
14 = **ignore**, avoid, slight, blank *(slang)*, snub, spurn, freeze (someone) out *(informal)*, cold-shoulder, turn your back on, send to Coventry, look straight through (someone) • *She just cut me in the street.*
OPPOSITES: receive, greet, embrace
15 = **cross**, interrupt, intersect, bisect • *a straight line that cuts the vertical axis*
▸ **AS A NOUN** 1 = **incision**, nick, rent, stroke, rip, slash, groove, slit, snip • *The operation involves making several cuts in the cornea.*
2 = **gash**, nick, wound, slash, graze, laceration • *He had sustained a cut on his left eyebrow.*
3 = **reduction**, fall, lowering, slash, decrease, cutback, diminution • *The economy needs an immediate 2 per cent cut in interest rates.*
4 = **share**, piece, slice, percentage, portion, kickback *(chiefly U.S.)*, rake-off *(slang)* • *The lawyers, of course, will take their cut of the profits.*
5 = **style**, look, form, fashion, shape, mode, configuration • *The cut of her clothes made her look slimmer and taller.*
▸ **IN PHRASES: a cut above something** *or* **someone** = **superior to**, better than, more efficient than, more reliable than, streets ahead of, more useful than, more capable than, more competent than • *He's a cut above the usual boys she goes out with.*
be cut out for something = **be suited for**, be designed for, be fitted for, be suitable for, be adapted for, be equipped for, be adequate for, be eligible for, be competent for, be qualified for • *She wasn't cut out for motherhood.*
cut and dried = **clear-cut**, settled, fixed, organized, automatic, sorted out *(informal)*, predetermined, prearranged • *We are aiming for guidelines, not cut and dried answers.*
cut in = **interrupt**, break in, butt in, interpose • *'That's not true,' the duchess cut in suddenly.*
cut someone down = **kill**, take out *(slang)*, massacre, slaughter, dispatch, slay *(archaic)*, blow away *(slang, chiefly U.S.)*, mow down • *He was cut down in a hail of bullets.*
cut someone down to size = **make (someone) look small**, humble, humiliate, bring (someone) low, take (someone) down a peg *(informal)*, abash, crush, put (someone) in their place, take the wind out of (someone's) sails • *It's high time someone cut that arrogant little creep down to size.*
cut someone off 1 = **separate**, isolate, sever, keep apart • *The exiles had been cut off from all contact with their homeland.*
2 = **interrupt**, stop, break in, butt in, interpose • *'But sir, I'm under orders to—' Clark cut him off. 'Don't argue with me.'*
3 = **disinherit**, renounce, disown • *His father cut him off without a penny.*
cut someone out = **exclude**, eliminate, oust, displace, supersede, supplant • *He felt that he was being cut out of the decision-making process completely.*
cut someone short = **interrupt**, stop, break in, butt in, interpose • *Veronica cut him short by saying, 'I don't want to hear about it.'*
cut someone up = **slash**, injure, wound, knife, lacerate • *They cut him up with a razor.*
cut something back 1 = **reduce**, check, lower, slash, decrease, curb, lessen, economize, downsize, retrench,

draw or pull in your horns *(informal)*, kennet *(Austral. slang)*, jeff *(Austral. slang)* • *The government has cut back on defence spending.*
2 = trim, prune, shorten • *Cut back the root of the bulb to within half an inch of the base.*
cut something down 1 = reduce, moderate, decrease, lessen, lower • *Car owners were asked to cut down their travel.*
2 = fell, level, hew, lop • *A vandal with a chainsaw cut down several trees in the park.*
cut something off = discontinue, disconnect, suspend, halt, obstruct, bring to an end • *The rebels have cut off the electricity supply from the capital.*
cut something out 1 = remove, extract, censor, delete, edit out • *All the violent scenes had been cut out of the film.*
2 = stop, cease, refrain from, pack in, kick *(informal)*, give up, sever • *You can cut that behaviour out right now.*
cut something short = bring to an end, stop, check, halt, dock, postpone, terminate, break off, abort, pull the plug on, truncate, leave unfinished • *His career was cut tragically short by a car crash.*
be cut up = be upset, be disturbed, be distressed, be stricken, be agitated, be heartbroken, be desolated, be dejected, be wretched • *Terry was very cut up by Jim's death.*
cut something up = chop, divide, slice, carve, dice, mince • *Cut the sausages up and cook them over a medium heat.*

cutback = reduction, cut, retrenchment, economy, decrease, lessening • *A 200-person cutback in staff was announced.*

cute = appealing, sweet, attractive, engaging, charming, delightful, lovable, winsome, winning, cutesy *(informal, chiefly U.S.)* • *a cute little baby*

cut-price = cheap, sale, reduced, bargain, cut-rate *(chiefly U.S.)*, cheapo *(informal)* • *a shop selling cut-price videos and CDs*

cut-throat AS AN ADJECTIVE **1 = competitive**, fierce, ruthless, relentless, unprincipled, dog-eat-dog • *the cut-throat world of international finance*
2 = murderous, violent, bloody, cruel, savage, ferocious, bloodthirsty, barbarous, homicidal, thuggish, death-dealing • *Captain Hook and his band of cut-throat pirates*
▸ AS A NOUN **= murderer**, killer, butcher, thug, assassin, slayer *(archaic)*, homicide, bravo, liquidator, executioner, hit man *(slang)*, heavy *(slang)* • *a band of cut-throats prepared to undertake the vilest crimes for money*

cutting AS A NOUN **= clipping**, extract, excerpt, piece • *Here are the press cuttings and reviews.*
▸ AS AN ADJECTIVE **1 = hurtful**, wounding, severe, acid, bitter, malicious, scathing, acrimonious, barbed, sarcastic, sardonic, caustic, vitriolic, trenchant, pointed • *People make cutting remarks to help themselves feel superior to others.*
OPPOSITES: kind, mild, flattering
2 = piercing, biting, sharp, keen, bitter, raw, chilling, stinging, penetrating, numbing • *a cutting wind*
OPPOSITES: pleasant, soothing, balmy

cycle = series of events, round *(of years)*, circle, revolution, rotation • *the necessary cycle of birth, growth, decay and death*

cyclone = typhoon, hurricane, tornado, whirlwind, tempest, twister *(U.S. informal)*, storm • *The death toll from the cyclone has now risen to one-hundred-and-forty.*

cynic = sceptic, doubter, pessimist, misanthrope, misanthropist, scoffer • *A cynic might see this as simply a ploy to make us part with more money.*

QUOTATIONS

A cynic is a man who knows the price of everything and the value of nothing
[Oscar Wilde *Lady Windermere's Fan*]

The cynic is one who never sees a good quality in a man, and never fails to see a bad one
[H.W. Beecher *Proverbs from Plymouth Pulpit*]

cynic: a blackguard whose faulty vision sees things as they are, not as they ought to be
[Ambrose Bierce *The Devil's Dictionary*]

cynical 1 = sceptical, mocking, ironic, sneering, pessimistic, scoffing, contemptuous, sarcastic, sardonic, scornful, distrustful, derisive, misanthropic • *He has a very cynical view of the world.*
OPPOSITES: trusting, green, optimistic
2 = unbelieving, sceptical, disillusioned, pessimistic, disbelieving, mistrustful • *My experiences have made me cynical about relationships.*
OPPOSITES: optimistic, hopeful

cynicism 1 = scepticism, pessimism, sarcasm, misanthropy, sardonicism • *I found Ben's cynicism wearing at times.*
2 = disbelief, doubt, scepticism, mistrust • *This talk betrays a certain cynicism about free trade.*

QUOTATIONS

Cynicism is intellectual dandyism without the coxcomb's feathers
[George Meredith *The Egoist*]

cyst = sac, growth, blister, wen, vesicle, bleb • *He had a minor operation to remove a cyst.*

Dd

dab AS A VERB **1 = pat**, press, touch, stroke, tap, wipe, mop, blot, swab • *dabbing her eyes with a tissue*
2 = apply, spread, smudge, daub, spot, stipple, bedaub • *She dabbed iodine on the cuts.*
▸ AS A NOUN **1 = spot**, little, bit, drop, touch, taste, suggestion, pat, trace, hint, dash, particle, splash, sprinkle, smear, lick, trickle, dribble, fleck, smudge, tad *(informal)*, speck, dollop *(informal)*, modicum, soupçon, smidgen *or* smidgin *(informal, chiefly U.S. & Canad.)* • *a dab of glue*
2 = touch, stroke, flick, smear, blot, smudge • *just one dab of the right fragrance*

dabble *usually with* **in** *or* **with = play (at** *or* **with)**, toy (with), potter, tinker (with), trifle (with), flirt (with), dip into, fiddle (with), dally (with), scratch the surface of, have a smattering of, potter about *or* around *or* round with • *She dabbled with drugs at University.*

dab hand = expert, master, ace *(informal)*, buff *(informal)*, wizard, adept, whizz *(informal)*, boffin *(Brit. informal)*, hotshot *(informal)*, past master, maven *(U.S.)*, fundi *(S. African)*, dabster *(dialect)* • *She was a dab hand at solving difficult puzzles.*

dad *or* **daddy** *(Informal)* **= father**, pop, old man, pa, old boy, papa, patriarch, pater *(Brit.)*, biological father, stepfather, poppa, adoptive father, foster father, begetter, male parent, paterfamilias, birth father • *He's living with his mum and dad.*
OPPOSITES: child, mother

daft AS AN ADJECTIVE **1 = stupid**, simple, crazy, silly, absurd, foolish, irrational, unwise, senseless, giddy, infantile, goofy, foolhardy, idiotic, inane, fatuous, loopy *(informal)*, witless, crackpot *(informal)*, out to lunch *(informal)*, dopey *(informal)*, puerile, imprudent, scatty *(Brit. informal)*, asinine, gonzo *(slang)*, imbecilic, doolally *(slang)*, off your head *(informal)*, off your trolley *(slang)*, up the pole *(informal)*, dumb-ass *(slang)*, wacko *or* whacko *(slang)*, off the air *(Austral. slang)* • *I wasn't so daft as to believe him.*
2 = ridiculous, foolish, impractical, ludicrous, pointless, unrealistic, unreasonable, unwise, preposterous, laughable, farcical, illogical, unworkable, foolhardy, nonsensical, half-baked, fatuous, risible, ill-conceived, impracticable, hare-brained, dumb-ass *(slang)*, cockamamie *(slang, chiefly U.S.)* • *Now there's a daft suggestion!*
3 = crazy, mad, mental *(slang)*, touched, nuts *(slang)*, barking *(slang)*, crackers *(Brit. slang)*, insane, lunatic, demented, nutty *(slang)*, deranged, unhinged, round the bend *(Brit. slang)*, barking mad *(slang)*, not right in the head, not the full shilling *(informal)*, off the air *(Austral. slang)*, porangi *(N.Z.)* • *It either sends you daft or kills you.*
▸ IN PHRASES: **daft about = enthusiastic about**, mad about, crazy about *(informal)*, doting on, besotted with, sweet on, nuts about *(slang)*, potty about *(Brit. informal)*, infatuated by, dotty about *(slang, chiefly Brit.)*, nutty about *(informal)* • *He's just daft about her.*

dag AS A NOUN **= joker**, comic, wag, wit, comedian, clown, kidder *(informal)*, jester, humorist, prankster • *He does all these great impersonations – he's such a dag.*
▸ IN PHRASES: **rattle your dags = hurry up**, get a move on, step on it *(informal)*, get your skates on *(informal)*, make haste • *You'd better rattle your dags and get on with this before the boss gets back.*

dagga = cannabis, marijuana, pot *(slang)*, dope *(slang)*, hash *(slang)*, black *(slang)*, blow *(slang)*, smoke *(informal)*, stuff *(slang)*, leaf *(slang)*, tea *(U.S. slang)*, grass *(slang)*, chronic *(U.S. slang)*, weed *(slang)*, hemp, gage *(U.S., dated, slang)*, hashish, mary jane *(U.S. slang)*, ganja, bhang, kif, wacky baccy *(slang)*, sinsemilla, charas • *people who drive while high on dagga and alcohol*

dagger AS A NOUN **= knife**, blade, bayonet, dirk, stiletto, poniard, skean • *The man raised his arm and plunged a dagger into her back.*
▸ IN PHRASES: **at daggers drawn = on bad terms**, at odds, at war, at loggerheads, up in arms, at enmity • *She and her mother were at daggers drawn.*
look daggers at someone = glare, frown, scowl, glower, look black, lour *or* lower • *The girls looked daggers at me.*

QUOTATIONS

Is this a dagger which I see before me
The handle toward my hand?
[William Shakespeare *Macbeth*]

daggy 1 = untidy, unkempt, dishevelled, tousled, disordered, messy, ruffled, scruffy, rumpled, bedraggled, ratty *(informal)*, straggly, windblown, disarranged, mussed up *(informal)* • *He turned up wearing a daggy tracksuit.*
2 = eccentric, odd, strange, bizarre, weird, peculiar, abnormal, queer *(informal)*, irregular, uncommon, quirky, out there *(slang)*, singular, unconventional, idiosyncratic, off-the-wall *(slang)*, outlandish, whimsical, rum *(Brit. slang)*, capricious, anomalous, freakish, aberrant, wacko *(slang)*, outré • *his slightly daggy hobby of collecting novelty tea towels*

daily AS AN ADJECTIVE **1 = everyday**, regular, circadian *(Biology)*, diurnal, quotidian • *the company's daily turnover*
2 = day-to-day, common, ordinary, routine, everyday, commonplace, quotidian • *factors which deeply influence daily life*
▸ AS AN ADVERB **= every day**, day by day, day after day, once a day, per diem • *The shop is open daily.*

dainty 1 = delicate, pretty, charming, fine, slight, slim, elegant, trim, neat, refined, exquisite, graceful, petite, dinky *(Brit. informal)* • *The girls were dainty and feminine.*
OPPOSITES: awkward, coarse, clumsy
2 = delectable, choice, delicious, tender, tasty, savoury, palatable, toothsome • *a dainty morsel*
3 = particular, nice, refined, fussy, scrupulous, fastidious, choosy, picky *(informal)*, finicky, anal retentive, finical • *They cater for a range of tastes, from the dainty to the extravagant.*

dais = **platform**, stage, podium, rostrum, estrade (*rare*) • *She sat on the dais along with the other guests of honour.*

dale = **valley**, glen, vale, dell, dingle, strath (*Scot.*), coomb • *farmhouses all across the dale*

dalliance 1 = **flirtation**, coquetry, amorous play • *a politician engaging in sexual dalliance with his colleague*
2 = **dabbling**, playing, toying, trifling • *a fashionable dalliance with ideas of liberty and reason*

dally AS A VERB = **waste time**, delay, fool (about *or* around), linger, hang about, loiter, while away, dawdle, fritter away, procrastinate, tarry, dilly-dally (*informal*), drag your feet *or* heels • *He did not dally long over his meal.*
OPPOSITES: run, hurry (up), hasten
▸ IN PHRASES: **dally with someone** = **flirt with**, tease, lead on, toy with, play around with, fool (about *or* around) with, trifle with, play fast and loose with (*informal*), frivol with (*informal*) • *He was dallying with some floosie.*

dam AS A NOUN = **barrier**, wall, barrage, obstruction, embankment, hindrance • *They went ahead with plans to build a dam across the river.*
▸ AS A VERB = **block up**, block, hold in, restrict, check, confine, choke, hold back, barricade, obstruct • *The reservoir was formed by damming the River Blith.*

damage AS A NOUN 1 = **destruction**, harm, loss, injury, suffering, hurt, ruin, crushing, wrecking, shattering, devastation, detriment, mutilation, impairment, annihilation, ruination • *There have been many reports of minor damage to buildings.*
OPPOSITES: gain, improvement, reparation
2 = **harm**, loss, injury, abuse, ill, impairment • *The administration wants to limit the damage done to international relations.*
3 = **cost**, price, charge, rate, bill, figure, amount, total, payment, expense, outlay • *What's the damage for these tickets?*
▸ AS A VERB 1 = **spoil**, hurt, injure, smash, harm, ruin, crush, devastate, mar, wreck, shatter, weaken, gut, demolish, undo, trash (*slang*), total (*slang*), impair, ravage, mutilate, annihilate, incapacitate, raze, deface, play (merry) hell with (*informal*) • *He damaged the car with a baseball bat.*
OPPOSITES: improve, fix, repair
2 = **harm**, ruin, mar, stain, taint, tarnish, blot, blemish, sully, smirch • *He doesn't want to damage his reputation as a political personality.*
▸ AS A PLURAL NOUN = **compensation**, fine, payment, satisfaction, amends, reparation, indemnity, restitution, reimbursement, atonement, recompense, indemnification, meed (*archaic*), requital • *He was vindicated in court and damages were awarded.*

damaging = **harmful**, detrimental, hurtful, ruinous, prejudicial, deleterious, injurious, disadvantageous • *Is the recycling process damaging to the environment?*
OPPOSITES: useful, valuable, helpful

dame 1 *with cap.* = **lady**, baroness, dowager, grande dame (*French*), noblewoman, peeress • *a Dame of the British Empire*
2 = **woman**, girl, lady, female, bird (*slang*), maiden (*archaic*), miss, chick (*slang*), maid (*archaic*), gal (*slang*), lass, lassie (*informal*), wench (*facetious*), charlie (*Austral. slang*), chook (*Austral. slang*), wahine (*N.Z.*) • *This is one classy dame you've got yourself here.*

damn AS AN ADVERB = **very**, really, particularly, highly, greatly, seriously (*informal*), truly, extremely, terribly, remarkably, unusually, jolly (*Brit.*), wonderfully, decidedly, awfully (*informal*), exceedingly, superlatively, uncommonly • *Let's have a damn good party.*
▸ AS A VERB = **criticize**, condemn, blast, pan (*informal*), slam (*slang*), flame (*informal*), denounce, put down, slate (*informal*), censure, castigate, tear into (*informal*), diss (*slang, chiefly U.S.*), inveigh against, lambast(e), excoriate, denunciate • *You can't damn him for his beliefs.*
OPPOSITES: approve, honour, praise
▸ IN PHRASES: **damn near** = **almost**, virtually, practically, all but, just about, as good as, well-nigh • *I damn near went crazy.*
not give a damn = **not care**, not mind, be indifferent, not give a hoot, not care a jot, not give two hoots, not care a whit, not care a brass farthing, not give a tinker's curse *or* damn (*slang*) • *Frankly, my dear, I don't give a damn.*

damnable = **wicked**, offensive, horrible, cursed, atrocious, despicable, culpable, hateful, abominable, accursed, execrable, detestable • *That's a damnable lie!*
OPPOSITES: fine, excellent, admirable

damnation = **condemnation**, damning, sending to hell, consigning to perdition • *She had a healthy fear of hellfire and eternal damnation.*

damned = **infernal**, accursed, detestable, revolting, infamous, confounded, despicable, abhorred, hateful, loathsome, abominable, freaking (*slang, chiefly U.S.*) • *They're a damned nuisance.*

damnedest AS A NOUN = **best**, hardest, utmost, most, highest, greatest • *I must try my damnedest.*
▸ AS AN ADJECTIVE = **oddest**, strangest, funniest, weirdest, queerest, most remarkable, most extraordinary, most curious, most peculiar • *Today I heard the damnedest thing.*

damning = **incriminating**, implicating, condemnatory, dooming, accusatorial, damnatory, implicative • *a damning report into the affair*

damp AS AN ADJECTIVE = **moist**, wet, dripping, soggy, humid, sodden, dank, sopping, clammy, dewy, muggy, drizzly, vaporous • *She wiped the table with a damp cloth.* • *damp weather*
OPPOSITES: dry, arid, watertight
▸ AS A NOUN = **moisture**, liquid, humidity, drizzle, dew, dampness, wetness, dankness, clamminess, mugginess • *There was damp everywhere in the house.*
OPPOSITES: dryness, aridity
▸ AS A VERB = **moisten**, wet, soak, dampen, lick, moisturize, humidify • *She damped a hand towel and laid it across her head.*
▸ IN PHRASES: **damp something down** = **curb**, reduce, check, cool, moderate, dash, chill, dull, diminish, discourage, restrain, inhibit, stifle, allay, deaden, pour cold water on • *He tried to damp down his panic.*

dampen 1 = **reduce**, check, moderate, dash, dull, restrain, deter, stifle, lessen, smother, muffle, deaden • *Nothing seemed to dampen his enthusiasm.*
2 = **moisten**, wet, spray, make damp, bedew, besprinkle • *She took the time to dampen a cloth and wash her face.*

damper = **discouragement**, cloud, chill, curb, restraint, gloom, cold water (*informal*), pall • *He put a damper on our hopes.*

dampness = **moistness**, damp, moisture, humidity, wetness, sogginess, dankness, clamminess, mugginess • *A chill dampness was rising from the rough grass.*
OPPOSITES: dryness, aridity, aridness

damsel = **maiden**, girl, virgin, maid, miss, nymph (*poetic*), lass, lassie (*informal*), wench • *He came to the aid of a damsel in distress.*

dance AS A VERB 1 = **prance**, rock, trip, swing, spin, hop, skip, sway, whirl, caper, jig, frolic, cavort, gambol, bob up and down, cut a rug (*informal*) • *They like to dance to the music on the radio.*
2 = **caper**, trip, spring, jump, bound, leap, bounce, hop, skip, romp, frolic, cavort, gambol • *He danced off down the road.*
3 = **sparkle**, move, flash, glitter, wink, shimmer, twinkle, glint, glisten, glister (*archaic*), scintillate • *patterns of light dancing on the river*
▸ AS A NOUN = **ball**, social, hop (*informal*), disco, knees-up (*Brit. informal*), discotheque, dancing party, B and S (*Austral.*

DANCE

Dances

allemande, apache dance, ballroom dance, barn dance, beguine, belly dance, black bottom, body popping, bogle, bolero, boogaloo, boogie, bossa nova, boston, bourrée, branle, brawl, break dance, breakdown, buck and wing, bump, bunny hug, butterfly, cachucha, cakewalk, calypso, cancan, carioca, carmagnole, carol, cha-cha-cha *or* cha-cha, chaconne, charleston, clog dance, conga, contredanse, Cossack dance, cotillion, country dance, courante, czardas, Dashing White Sergeant, ecossaise, eightsome reel, excuse-me, fan dance, fandango, farandole, flamenco, folk dance, formation dance, foxtrot, galliard, galop, gavotte, Gay Gordons, german, ghost dance, gigue, gopak, habanera, haka *(N.Z.)*, hay, Highland fling, hoedown, hokey cokey, hora, hornpipe, hula *or* hula-hula, hustle, jig, jitterbug, jive, jota, juba, kazachok, kolo, lambada, Lambeth walk, lancers, ländler, limbo, line dance, macarena, malagueña, mambo, maxixe, mazurka, merengue, minuet, Morisco, morris dance, mosh, musette, nautch, old-time dance, one-step, palais glide, paso doble, passacaglia, Paul Jones, pavane, pogo, poi dance, polka, pole dance, polonaise, pyrrhic, quadrille, quickstep, redowa, reel, rigadoon, ring-shout, robot dancing *or* robotics, ronggeng, round, round dance, roundelay *or* roundel, rumba, salsa, saltarello, samba, saraband, saunter, schottische, seguidilla, shake, shimmy, shuffle, siciliano, Sir Roger de Coverley, skank, snake dance, snowball, square dance, step dance, stomp, strathspey, strip the willow, sword dance, tambourin, tango, tap dance, tarantella, toe dance, twist, two-step, Tyrolienne, Virginia reel, vogueing, volta, waltz, war dance, Zapata

General dance steps and terms

chassé, choreography, dosido, glide, grand chain, keep step, in step, out of step, pas, pas de basque, pas seul, phrase, pigeonwing, progressive, promenade, rhythm, routine, score, sequence, set, shuffle, slip step, steps, time

informal) • *She often went to dances and parties in the village.*

▸ **IN PHRASES: lead someone a merry dance = run rings around**, mess someone about, lead someone up the garden path • *The criminals led the police a merry dance.*

▸ **RELATED ADJECTIVE:** Terpsichorean

▸ **RELATED MANIA:** choreomania

QUOTATIONS

Dancing is the loftiest, the most moving, the most beautiful of the arts, because it is no mere translation or abstraction from life; it is life itself
[Havelock Ellis *The Dance of Life*]

On with the dance! Let joy be unconfined;
No sleep till morn, when Youth and Pleasure meet
To chase the glowing hours with flying feet
[Lord Byron *Childe Harold's Pilgrimage*]

No sober man dances, unless he happens to be mad
[Cicero *Pro Murena*]

▹ *See panel* **Dance**

dancer = ballerina, hoofer *(slang)*, Terpsichorean • *His girlfriend was a ballet dancer.*

dandy AS A NOUN = fop, beau, swell *(informal)*, blood *(rare)*, buck *(archaic)*, blade *(archaic)*, peacock, dude *(U.S. & Canad. informal)*, toff *(Brit. slang)*, macaroni *(obsolete)*, man about town, popinjay, coxcomb • *a handsome young dandy*

▸ **AS AN ADJECTIVE = excellent**, great, fine, capital, splendid, first-rate • *Everything's fine and dandy.*

danger 1 = jeopardy, risk, peril, vulnerability, insecurity, precariousness, endangerment • *Your life is in danger.*
2 = hazard, risk, threat, menace, peril, pitfall • *These roads are a danger to cyclists.*
3 = possibility, chance, risk, prospect, liability, likelihood, probability • *There is a real danger that people will not be able to afford insurance.*

QUOTATIONS

danger, the spur of all great minds
[George Chapman *The Revenge of Bussy D'Ambois*]

dangerous = perilous, threatening, risky, hazardous, exposed, alarming, vulnerable, nasty, ugly, menacing, insecure, hairy *(slang)*, unsafe, precarious, treacherous, breakneck, parlous *(archaic)*, fraught with danger, chancy *(informal)*, unchancy *(Scot.)* • *a dangerous undertaking*
OPPOSITES: protected, safe, secure

QUOTATIONS

mad, bad, and dangerous to know
[Caroline Lamb (of Byron)]

dangerously 1 = seriously, badly, severely, gravely, critically, acutely, grievously • *He is dangerously ill.*
2 = perilously, alarmingly, carelessly, precariously, recklessly, daringly, riskily, harmfully, hazardously, unsafely, unsecurely • *He rushed downstairs dangerously fast.*

dangle 1 = hang, swing, trail, sway, flap, hang down, depend • *A gold bracelet dangled from his left wrist.*
2 = wave, swing, flap, wiggle, jiggle, joggle • *He dangled the keys in front of her face.*
3 = offer, flourish, brandish, flaunt, tempt someone with, lure someone with, entice someone with, tantalize someone with • *They dangled rich rewards before me.*

dangling = hanging, swinging, loose, trailing, swaying, disconnected, drooping, unconnected • *the telegraph pole with its dangling wires*

dank = **damp**, dripping, moist, soggy, clammy, dewy • *The kitchen was dank and cheerless.*

dapper = **neat**, nice, smart, trim, stylish, spruce, dainty, natty *(informal)*, well-groomed, well turned out, trig *(archaic or dialect)*, soigné • *a small, dapper man in his early fifties*
OPPOSITES: sloppy *(informal)*, untidy, dishevelled

dappled = **mottled**, spotted, speckled, pied, flecked, variegated, checkered, freckled, stippled, piebald, brindled • *He stood in the dappled sunlight of the forest.*

dare AS A VERB **1** = **risk doing**, venture, have the courage, have the nerve, be brave enough, presume, have the audacity, make bold *(archaic)*, hazard doing, brave doing, be so bold as, take the liberty of doing • *I didn't dare to tell my uncle what had happened.*
2 = **challenge**, provoke, defy, taunt, goad, throw down the gauntlet • *She dared me to ask him out.*
▸ IN PHRASES: **I dare say** *or* **I daresay** = **probably**, perhaps, maybe, likely, possibly, most likely, doubtless, in all probability, in all likelihood, perchance *(archaic)*, as likely as not • *People think I'm a fool, and I dare say they're right.*

QUOTATIONS
Who dares wins
[Motto of the British SAS regiment]

daredevil AS A NOUN = **adventurer**, show-off *(informal)*, madcap, desperado, exhibitionist, stunt man, hot dog *(chiefly U.S.)*, adrenalin junky *(slang)* • *a tragic ending for a daredevil whose luck ran out*
▸ AS AN ADJECTIVE = **daring**, bold, adventurous, reckless, audacious, madcap, death-defying • *He gets his kicks from daredevil car-racing.*

daring AS AN ADJECTIVE = **brave**, bold, adventurous, rash, have-a-go *(informal)*, reckless, fearless, audacious, intrepid, impulsive, valiant, plucky, game *(informal)*, daredevil, ballsy *(taboo slang)*, venturesome, (as) game as Ned Kelly *(Austral. slang)* • *a daring rescue attempt*
OPPOSITES: careful, cautious, timid
▸ AS A NOUN = **bravery**, nerve *(informal)*, courage, face *(informal)*, balls *(taboo slang)*, spirit, bottle *(Brit. slang)*, guts *(informal)*, pluck, grit, audacity, boldness, temerity, derring-do *(archaic)*, spunk *(informal)*, fearlessness, rashness, intrepidity, ballsiness *(taboo slang)* • *His daring may have cost him his life.*
OPPOSITES: fear, caution, timidity

dark AS AN ADJECTIVE **1** = **dim**, murky, shady, shadowy, grey, cloudy, dingy, overcast, dusky, unlit, pitch-black, indistinct, poorly lit, sunless, tenebrous, darksome *(literary)*, pitchy, unilluminated • *It was a dark and stormy night.*
2 = **black**, brunette, ebony, dark-skinned, sable, dusky, swarthy • *a tall, dark and handsome stranger*
OPPOSITES: light, fair, blonde
3 = **evil**, foul, horrible, sinister, infamous, vile, satanic, wicked, atrocious, sinful, hellish, infernal, nefarious, damnable • *magicians who harnessed dark powers*
4 = **secret**, deep, hidden, mysterious, concealed, obscure, mystic, enigmatic, puzzling, occult, arcane, cryptic, abstruse, recondite, Delphic • *the dark recesses of the mind*
5 = **gloomy**, sad, grim, miserable, low, bleak, moody, dismal, pessimistic, melancholy, sombre, morbid, glum, mournful, morose, joyless, doleful, cheerless • *His endless chatter kept me from thinking dark thoughts.*
OPPOSITES: clear, bright, cheerful
6 = **angry**, threatening, forbidding, frowning, ominous, dour, scowling, sullen, glum, glowering, sulky • *He shot her a dark glance.*
▸ AS A NOUN **1** = **darkness**, shadows, gloom, dusk, obscurity, murk, dimness, semi-darkness, murkiness • *I've always been afraid of the dark.*
2 = **night**, twilight, evening, evo *(Austral. slang)*, dusk, night-time, nightfall • *after dark*
▸ IN PHRASES: **in the dark** = **ignorant**, unaware, oblivious, uninformed, out of the loop, unenlightened, blind to something • *I managed to keep my parents in the dark.*

PROVERBS
The darkest hour is just before the dawn

darken 1 = **cloud**, shadow, shade, obscure, eclipse, dim, deepen, overshadow, blacken, becloud • *A storm darkened the sky.*
OPPOSITES: shine, glow, brighten
2 = **make dark**, shade, blacken, make darker, deepen • *She darkened her eyebrows with mascara.*
3 = **become gloomy**, blacken, become angry, look black, go crook *(Austral. & N.Z. slang)*, grow troubled • *His face suddenly darkened.*
OPPOSITES: encourage, cheer, become cheerful
4 = **sadden**, upset, cloud, blacken, cast a pall over, cast a gloom upon • *Nothing was going to darken his mood today.*

darkened = **unlit**, dark, shadowy, poorly lit, tenebrous, unilluminated • *He drove past darkened houses.*

darkness 1 = **dark**, shadows, shade, gloom, obscurity, blackness, murk, dimness, murkiness, duskiness, shadiness • *The room was plunged into darkness.*
2 = **night**, dark, dusk, nightfall, night-time, hours of darkness • *They worked all evening until darkness fell.*
▸ RELATED PHOBIA: achluophobia

darling AS A NOUN **1** = **beloved**, love, dear, dearest, angel, treasure, precious, loved one, sweetheart, sweetie, truelove, dear one • *Hello, darling!*
2 = **favourite**, pet, spoilt child, apple of your eye, blue-eyed boy, fair-haired boy *(U.S.)* • *He was the darling of the family.*
▸ AS AN ADJECTIVE **1** = **beloved**, dear, dearest, sweet, treasured, precious, adored, cherished, revered • *my darling baby boy*
2 = **adorable**, sweet, attractive, lovely, charming, cute, enchanting, captivating, cutesy *(informal, chiefly U.S.)* • *a perfectly darling little house*

darn AS A VERB = **mend**, repair, patch, stitch, sew up, cobble up • *His aunt darned his old socks.*
▸ AS A NOUN = **mend**, patch, reinforcement, invisible repair • *blue woollen stockings with untidy darns*

dart AS A NOUN **1** = **arrow**, missile, shaft, projectile • *He died after being struck by a poison dart.*
2 = **dash**, run, rush, sprint, race, bolt, spurt, sortie • *He made a dart for the finishing line.*
▸ AS A VERB **1** = **dash**, run, race, shoot, fly, speed, spring, tear, rush, bound, flash, hurry, sprint, bolt, hasten, whizz, haste, flit, scoot • *She darted away through the trees.*
2 = **shoot**, send, cast • *She darted a sly glance at him.*

dash AS A VERB **1** = **rush**, run, race, shoot, fly, career, speed, spring, tear, bound, hurry, barrel (along) *(informal, chiefly U.S. & Canad.)*, sprint, bolt, dart, hasten, scurry, haste, stampede, burn rubber *(informal)*, make haste, hotfoot • *Suddenly she dashed out into the garden.*
OPPOSITES: walk, crawl, dawdle
2 = **throw**, cast, pitch, slam, toss, hurl, fling, chuck *(informal)*, propel, project, sling, lob *(informal)* • *She dashed the doll against the stone wall.*
3 = **crash**, break, smash, shatter, shiver, splinter • *The waves dashed against the side of the ship.*
4 = **disappoint**, ruin, frustrate, crush, shatter, spoil, overturn, wipe out, foil, undo, thwart, scotch, blight, dampen, confound, put the kibosh on *(informal)*, crool *or* cruel *(Austral. slang)* • *They had their hopes raised and then dashed.*
▸ AS A NOUN **1** = **rush**, run, race, sprint, bolt, dart, spurt, sortie • *a 160-mile dash to hospital*
2 = **drop**, little, bit, shot *(informal)*, touch, spot, suggestion, trace, hint, pinch, sprinkling, tot, trickle, nip, tinge, soupçon *(French)* • *Add a dash of balsamic vinegar.*
OPPOSITES: much, lot

3 = **style**, spirit, flair, flourish, vigour, verve, panache, élan, brio, vivacity • *He played with great fire and dash.*

dashing 1 = **stylish**, smart, elegant, dazzling, flamboyant, sporty, swish *(informal, chiefly Brit.)*, urbane, jaunty, dapper, showy • *He looked very dashing in a designer jacket of soft black leather.*
2 = **bold**, spirited, daring, exuberant, gallant, plucky, swashbuckling, debonair • *the founding father of the dashing air squadron*
OPPOSITES: boring, dull, dreary

d

dastardly = **despicable**, mean, low, base, sneaking, cowardly, craven, vile, abject, sneaky, contemptible, underhand, weak-kneed *(informal)*, faint-hearted, spiritless, recreant *(archaic)*, caitiff *(archaic)*, niddering *(archaic)* • *He described the killing as a dastardly act.*

data 1 = **details**, facts, figures, materials, documents, intelligence, statistics, gen *(Brit. informal)*, dope *(informal)*, info *(informal)* • *The survey was based on data from 2,100 patients.*
2 = **information**, input

date AS A NOUN 1 = **day**, time, occasion, year, anniversary, day of the month • *There are two important dates for you to remember.*
2 = **time**, stage, period • *An inquest will be held at a later date.*
3 = **appointment**, meeting, arrangement, commitment, engagement, rendezvous, tryst, assignation • *He had made a date with the girl.*
4 = **partner**, escort, friend, young man, girlfriend, boyfriend, steady *(informal)*, squeeze *(informal)*, young lady • *She is his date for the dance.*
▸ AS A VERB 1 = **put a date on**, determine the date of, assign a date to, fix the period of, ascertain the age of • *It is difficult to date the relic.*
2 = **become dated**, become obsolete, show its age, become old-fashioned, obsolesce • *It always looks smart and will never date.*
3 = **go out with**, take out, go around with, be romantically involved with, go steady with, step out with *(informal)* • *He's been dating her for three months.*
▸ IN PHRASES: **date from** *or* **date back to** = **come from**, belong to, be made in, be built in, originate in, be created in, originate from, exist from, have existed since, bear a date of • *The palace dates back to the 16th century.*
to date = **up to now**, yet, so far, until now, now, as yet, thus far, up to this point, up to the present • *This is the band's fourth top twenty single to date.*

dated = **old-fashioned**, outdated, out of date, obsolete, archaic, unfashionable, antiquated, outmoded, passé, out, old hat, unhip *(slang)*, untrendy *(Brit. informal)*, démodé *(French)*, out of the ark *(informal)* • *They wore dated clothes.*
OPPOSITES: latest, current, modern

daub AS A VERB = **smear**, dirty, splatter, stain, spatter, sully, deface, smirch, begrime, besmear, bedaub, paint, coat, stain, plaster, slap on *(informal)* • *They daubed his home with slogans.*
▸ AS A NOUN = **smear**, spot, stain, blot, blotch, splodge, splotch, smirch • *Apply an extra daub of colour.*

daughter 1 = **female child**, girl, lass *(informal)* • *a woman with four daughters to marry off*
2 = **descendant**, girl
▸ RELATED ADJECTIVE: filial

QUOTATIONS
As is the mother, so is her daughter
[*Bible: Ezekiel*]
A daughter is an embarrassing and ticklish possession
[Menander *Perinthis*]

daunt = **discourage**, alarm, shake, frighten, scare, terrify, cow, intimidate, deter, dismay, put off, subdue, overawe, frighten off, dishearten, dispirit • *Nothing evil could daunt them.*
OPPOSITES: support, encourage, reassure

daunted = **intimidated**, alarmed, shaken, frightened, overcome, cowed, discouraged, deterred, dismayed, put off, disillusioned, unnerved, demoralized, dispirited, downcast • *I felt a little daunted by the size of the task.*

daunting = **intimidating**, alarming, frightening, discouraging, awesome, unnerving, disconcerting, demoralizing, off-putting *(Brit. informal)*, disheartening • *Occasionally I find the commitment and responsibility daunting.*
OPPOSITES: encouraging, comforting, reassuring

dauntless = **fearless**, brave, daring, bold, heroic, courageous, gritty, resolute, gallant, intrepid, valiant, doughty, undaunted, indomitable, unflinching, lion-hearted, valorous, stouthearted • *Perseverance and dauntless courage brought them to their goal.*

dawdle 1 = **waste time**, potter, trail, lag, idle, loaf, hang about, dally, loiter, dilly-dally *(informal)*, drag your feet *or* heels • *They dawdled arm in arm past the shopfronts.*
OPPOSITES: fly, rush, hurry
2 = **linger**, idle, dally, take your time, procrastinate, drag your feet *or* heels • *I dawdled over a beer.*

dawn AS A NOUN 1 = **daybreak**, morning, sunrise, dawning, daylight, aurora *(poetic)*, crack of dawn, sunup, cockcrow, dayspring *(poetic)* • *She woke at dawn.*
2 = **beginning**, start, birth, rise, origin, dawning, unfolding, emergence, outset, onset, advent, genesis, inception • *the dawn of the radio age*
▸ AS A VERB 1 = **begin**, start, open, rise, develop, emerge, unfold, originate • *A new era seemed about to dawn.*
2 = **grow light**, break, brighten, lighten • *The next day dawned.*
▸ IN PHRASES: **dawn on** *or* **upon someone** = **hit**, strike, occur to, register *(informal)*, become apparent, come to mind, cross your mind, come into your head, flash across your mind • *Then the chilling truth dawned on me.*
▸ RELATED ADJECTIVE: auroral
▸ RELATED PHOBIA: eosophobia

QUOTATIONS
rosy-fingered dawn
[Homer *Iliad*]
For what human ill does not dawn seem to be an alleviation?
[Thornton Wilder *The Bridge of San Luis Rey*]

day AS A NOUN 1 = **twenty-four hours**, working day, twenty-four hour period • *The conference is on for three days.*
2 = **daytime**, daylight, broad daylight, waking hours, daylight hours, hours of light, hours of sunlight • *They sleep during the day.*
3 = **date**, particular day • *What day are you leaving?*
4 = **time**, age, era, prime, period, generation, heyday, epoch • *In my day we treated our elders with more respect.*
▸ IN PHRASES: **call it a day** = **stop**, finish, cease, pack up *(informal)*, leave off, knock off *(informal)*, desist, pack it in *(slang)*, shut up shop, jack it in, chuck it in *(informal)*, give up *or* over • *Faced with such opposition, he had no choice but to call it a day.*
day after day = **continually**, regularly, relentlessly, persistently, incessantly, nonstop, unremittingly, monotonously, twenty-four-seven *(informal)*, unfalteringly • *In this job I just do the same thing day after day.*
day and night = **constantly**, all the time, continually, nonstop, without stopping, twenty-four-seven *(informal)* • *Chantal kept a fire burning day and night.*
day by day = **gradually**, slowly, progressively, daily, steadily, bit by bit, little by little, by degrees • *Day by day, he got weaker.*
day in, day out = **continually**, constantly, all the time, relentlessly, incessantly, nonstop, without stopping, unremittingly, twenty-four-seven *(informal)*, unfalteringly

• *He just sits and watches TV day in, day out.*
have had its day = be obsolete, be dated, be out of date, be old-fashioned, be past its prime • *I think the spy novel has had its day.*
have seen *or* **known better days = be worn out**, be frayed, be ragged, be shabby, be threadbare, be tatty, be tattered, be the worse for wear • *a sports jacket that had seen better days*
in this day and age = nowadays, now, today, these days, at the moment • *diseases which are unknown in this day and age*
make someone's day = make someone happy, delight someone, cheer someone up, hearten someone, enliven someone, gladden someone, perk someone up, gee someone up, buck someone up *(informal)* • *Seeing you has really made my day.*
▸ **RELATED ADJECTIVE:** diurnal

daybreak = dawn, morning, sunrise, first light, crack of dawn, break of day, sunup, cockcrow, dayspring *(poetic)* • *He got up every morning before daybreak.*

daydream AS A NOUN = fantasy, dream, imagining, fancy, reverie, figment of the imagination, wish, pipe dream, fond hope, castle in the air *or* in Spain • *He escaped into daydreams of heroic men and beautiful women.*
▸ **AS A VERB = fantasize**, dream, imagine, envision, stargaze • *He daydreams of being a famous journalist.*

daylight AS A NOUN 1 = sunlight, sunshine, light of day, natural light • *Lack of daylight can make people feel depressed.*
2 = daytime, broad daylight, daylight hours • *It was still daylight but many cars had their headlamps on.*
3 = dawn, dawning, sunrise, aurora *(poetic)*, daybreak, crack of dawn, sunup, cockcrow, dayspring *(poetic)* • *He returned shortly after daylight.*
▸ **IN PHRASES: in broad daylight = in public**, in full view, in the light of day • *The murder happened in broad daylight.*
scare the living daylights out of someone = terrify, shock, frighten, scare, appal, horrify, intimidate, dismay, petrify, terrorize, scare to death, put the fear of God into, make your hair stand on end, fill with terror, make your flesh creep, make your blood run cold, scare the bejesus out of *(informal)*, frighten out of your wits • *This film scared the living daylights out of me.*

day off = holiday, accumulated day off *or* ADO *(Austral.)* • *It was my day off, and he was on duty in my place.*

daytime = day, daylight, waking hours, daylight hours, hours of light, hours of sunlight • *In the daytime he stayed in his room, watching TV.*

day-to-day = everyday, regular, usual, routine, accustomed, customary, habitual, run-of-the-mill, wonted • *I use a lot of lentils in my day-to-day cooking*

daze AS A VERB 1 = stun, shock, paralyse, numb, stupefy, benumb • *The blow caught me on the temple and dazed me.*
2 = confuse, surprise, amaze, blind, astonish, stagger, startle, dazzle, bewilder, astound, perplex, flummox, dumbfound, nonplus, flabbergast *(informal)*, befog • *We were dazed by the sheer size of the spectacle.*
▸ **AS A NOUN = shock**, confusion, distraction, trance, bewilderment, stupor, trancelike state • *I was walking around in a daze.*

dazed = shocked, stunned, confused, staggered, baffled, at sea, bewildered, muddled, numbed, dizzy, bemused, perplexed, disorientated, flabbergasted *(informal)*, dopey *(slang)*, groggy *(informal)*, stupefied, nonplussed, light-headed, flummoxed, punch-drunk, woozy *(informal)*, fuddled • *By the end of the interview I was dazed and exhausted.*

dazzle AS A VERB 1 = impress, amaze, fascinate, overwhelm, astonish, awe, overpower, bowl over *(informal)*, overawe, hypnotize, stupefy, take your breath away, strike dumb • *He dazzled her with his knowledge of the world.*
2 = blind, confuse, daze, bedazzle • *She was dazzled by the lights.*
▸ **AS A NOUN 1 = splendour**, sparkle, glitter, flash, brilliance, magnificence, razzmatazz *(slang)*, razzle-dazzle *(slang)*, éclat • *The dazzle of stardom and status attracts them.*
2 = brilliance, intensity, sparkle, blaze, glitter, gleam, sheen, brightness, lustre, radiance, luminosity, vividness, resplendence, effulgence, refulgence • *The sun's dazzle on the water hurt my eyes.*

dazzling 1 = splendid, brilliant, stunning, superb, divine, glorious, sparkling, glittering, sensational *(informal)*, sublime, virtuoso, drop-dead *(slang)*, ravishing, scintillating • *He gave a dazzling performance.*
OPPOSITES: ordinary, dull, tedious
2 = brilliant, bright, intense, shining, sparkling, glittering, vivid, radiant, luminous, resplendent, scintillating, lustrous, coruscating, refulgent • *He shielded his eyes against the dazzling sun.*

deacon
▸ **RELATED ADJECTIVE:** diaconal

dead AS AN ADJECTIVE 1 = deceased, gone, departed, late, perished, extinct, defunct, passed away, pushing up (the) daisies • *My husband's been dead for a year now.*
OPPOSITES: living, alive, animate
2 = inanimate, still, barren, sterile, stagnant, lifeless, inert, uninhabited • *The polluted and stagnant water seems dead.*
3 = boring, dull, dreary, flat, plain, stale, lifeless, tasteless, humdrum, uninteresting, insipid, ho-hum *(informal)*, vapid, dead-and-alive • *It was a horrible, dead little town.*
4 = not working, broken, useless, defective, dud *(informal)*, malfunctioning, out of order, inactive, conked out, inoperative, kaput *(informal)* • *This battery's dead.*
OPPOSITES: working, effective, active
5 = obsolete, old, forgotten, abandoned, ancient, antique, vanished, discarded, lapsed, extinct, archaic, disused, superseded, antiquated, fossilized • *dead languages*
6 = spiritless, cold, dull, wooden, glazed, indifferent, callous, lukewarm, inhuman, unsympathetic, apathetic, frigid, glassy, unresponsive, unfeeling, torpid • *He watched the procedure with cold, dead eyes.*
OPPOSITES: active, alive, lively
7 = numb, frozen, paralysed, insensitive, inert, deadened, immobilized, unfeeling, torpid, insensible, benumbed • *My arm had gone dead.*
8 = total, complete, perfect, entire, absolute, utter, outright, thorough, downright, unqualified • *They hurried about in dead silence.*
9 = exhausted, tired, worn out, spent, wasted, done in *(informal)*, all in *(slang)*, drained, wiped out *(informal)*, buggered *(slang)*, sapped, knackered *(slang)*, prostrated, clapped out *(Brit., Austral. & N.Z. informal)*, tired out, ready to drop, dog-tired *(informal)*, zonked *(slang)*, dead tired, dead beat *(informal)*, shagged out *(Brit. slang)*, worn to a frazzle *(informal)*, on your last legs *(informal)*, creamcrackered *(Brit. slang)* • *I must get some sleep – I'm absolutely dead.*
▸ **AS A NOUN = middle**, heart, depth, thick, midst • *in the dead of night*
▸ **AS AN ADVERB = exactly**, quite, completely, totally, directly, perfectly, fully, entirely, absolutely, thoroughly, wholly, utterly, consummately, wholeheartedly, unconditionally, to the hilt, one hundred per cent, unmitigatedly • *You're dead right.*

PROVERBS
Dead men tell no tales
Never speak ill of the dead

deadbeat = layabout, bum *(informal)*, waster, lounger, piker *(Austral. & N.Z. slang)*, sponge *(informal)*, parasite, drone, loafer, slacker *(informal)*, scrounger *(informal)*, skiver *(Brit. slang)*, idler, freeloader *(slang)*, good-for-nothing, sponger *(informal)*, wastrel, bludger *(Austral. & N.Z. informal)*, cadger, quandong *(Austral. slang)* • *They're just a bunch of deadbeats.*

deaden 1 = **reduce**, dull, diminish, check, weaken, cushion, damp, suppress, blunt, paralyse, impair, numb, lessen, alleviate, smother, dampen, anaesthetize, benumb • *He needs morphine to deaden the pain in his chest.*
2 = **suppress**, reduce, dull, diminish, cushion, damp, mute, stifle, hush, lessen, smother, dampen, muffle, quieten • *They managed to deaden the sound.*

dead end AS A NOUN 1 = **cul-de-sac**, blind alley • *He stood facing the dead end of the street.*
2 = **impasse**, deadlock, stalemate, standstill, standoff • *We have reached a dead end.*
▸ AS AN ADJECTIVE = **boring**, dull, tedious, dead, flat, stale, monotonous, humdrum, uninteresting, mind-numbing, unexciting, ho-hum *(informal)*, repetitious, wearisome, unvaried • *This is a dead-end job.*

deadline = **time limit**, cutoff point, target date *or* time, limit, finish date *or* time • *The deadline for submission of entries is the end of May.*

deadlock 1 = **impasse**, stalemate, standstill, halt, cessation, gridlock, standoff, full stop • *Peace talks ended in a deadlock last month.*
2 = **tie**, draw, stalemate, impasse, standstill, gridlock, standoff, dead heat • *Larkham broke the deadlock with a late goal.*

deadlocked = **even**, level, equal, parallel, neck and neck, fifty-fifty *(informal)*, equally balanced • *The jury remained deadlocked.*

deadly AS AN ADJECTIVE 1 = **lethal**, fatal, deathly, dangerous, devastating, destructive, mortal, murderous, poisonous, malignant, virulent, pernicious, noxious, venomous, baleful, death-dealing, baneful • *a deadly disease currently affecting dolphins*
2 = **hard**, fierce, harsh, cruel, savage, brutal, grim, stern, ruthless, ferocious, unrelenting, merciless, implacable, barbarous, pitiless, unfeeling, unmerciful, unpitying • *She levelled a deadly look at him.*
3 = **boring**, dull, tedious, flat, monotonous, uninteresting, mind-numbing, unexciting, ho-hum *(informal)*, wearisome, as dry as dust • *She found the party deadly.*
4 = **arch**, savage, mortal, hardline, uncompromising, inflexible, inexorable, implacable, irreconcilable, intransigent, unappeasable • *The two became deadly enemies.*
5 = **accurate**, sure, true, effective, exact, reliable, precise, on target, infallible, unerring, unfailing • *the fastest and most deadly bowlers in the world today*
6 = **deathly**, white, pale, ghostly, ghastly, wan, pasty, colourless, pallid, anaemic, ashen, sallow, whitish, cadaverous, waxen, ashy, deathlike, wheyfaced • *The deadly pallor of her skin.*
7 = **complete**, total, perfect, absolute, utter, outright, thorough, consummate, dyed-in-the-wool, thoroughgoing, deep-dyed *(usually derogatory)* • *He talked about his job with deadly earnestness.*
▸ AS AN ADVERB = **completely**, quite, totally, perfectly, fully, entirely, absolutely, altogether, thoroughly, wholly, utterly, every inch, a hundred per cent, one hundred per cent • *The threat was deadly serious.*

deadpan = **expressionless**, empty, blank, wooden, straight-faced, vacuous, impassive, inscrutable, poker-faced, inexpressive • *his deadpan expression*

deaf 1 = **hard of hearing**, without hearing, stone deaf, deaf as a post *(informal)*, unhearing • *She is now profoundly deaf.*
2 = **oblivious**, indifferent, unmoved, unconcerned, unsympathetic, impervious, unresponsive, heedless, unhearing • *The assembly were deaf to all pleas for financial help.*

PROVERBS
There's none so deaf as those that will not hear

deafen = **make deaf**, deprive of hearing, split *or* burst the eardrums • *He was deafened by the noise from the gun.*

deafening = **ear-splitting**, intense, piercing, ringing, booming, overpowering, resounding, dinning, thunderous, ear-piercing • *the deafening roar of fighter jets taking off*

deal AS A NOUN 1 = **agreement**, understanding, contract, business, negotiation, arrangement, bargain, transaction, pact • *Japan has done a deal with America on rice exports.*
2 = **amount**, quantity, measure, degree, mass, volume, share, portion, bulk • *a great deal of money*
▸ IN PHRASES: **deal in something** = **sell**, trade in, stock, traffic in, buy and sell • *The company deals in antiques.*
deal something out = **distribute**, give, administer, share, divide, assign, allocate, dispense, bestow, allot, mete out, dole out, apportion • *a failure to deal out effective punishments to offenders*
deal with something = **be concerned with**, involve, concern, touch, regard, apply to, bear on, pertain to, be relevant to, treat of • *the parts of the book which deal with events in Florence*
deal with something *or* **someone** 1 = **handle**, manage, treat, cope with, take care of, see to, attend to, get to grips with, come to grips with • *the way in which the company deals with complaints*
2 = **behave towards**, handle, act towards, conduct yourself towards • *He's a hard man to deal with.*

dealer 1 = **trader**, marketer, merchant, supplier, wholesaler, purveyor, tradesman, merchandiser • *She is an antique dealer.*
2 = **pusher**, runner, doper *(slang)*, hawker, peddler • *He was a drug dealer with a dangerous reputation.*

dealings = **business**, selling, trading, trade, traffic, truck, bargaining, commerce, transactions, business relations • *allegations of illegal share dealings*

dean = **faculty head**, director, principal, provost, head of department, department head, head of faculty • *dean of the faculty*
▸ RELATED ADJECTIVE: decanal

dear AS AN ADJECTIVE 1 = **beloved**, close, valued, favourite, respected, prized, dearest, sweet, treasured, precious, darling, intimate, esteemed, cherished, revered • *Mrs Cavendish is a dear friend of mine.*
OPPOSITES: hated, disliked
2 = **expensive**, costly, high-priced, excessive, pricey *(informal)*, at a premium, overpriced, exorbitant • *Don't buy that one – it's too dear.*
OPPOSITES: cheap, inexpensive, worthless
3 = **charming**, appealing, winning, pleasing, attractive, engaging, lovely, pleasant, fetching, delightful, cute, irresistible, captivating, bewitching, winsome, cutesy *(informal, chiefly U.S.)*, likable *or* likeable • *the joy of seeing the looks on their dear little faces*
▸ AS A NOUN = **darling**, love, dearest, sweet, angel, treasure, precious, honey, beloved, loved one, sweetheart, truelove • *Yes, my dear.*

dearest AS A NOUN = **darling** • *What's wrong, my dearest?*
▸ AS AN ADJECTIVE = **most beloved** • *my oldest and dearest friends*

dearly 1 = **very much**, greatly, deeply, extremely, profoundly • *She would dearly love to marry.*
2 = **at great cost**, dear, heavily, at a high price, at a heavy cost, with much suffering • *He is paying dearly for his folly.*
3 = **deeply**, very much, tenderly, fondly, devotedly • *He was a great man and I loved him dearly.*

dearth = **lack**, want, need, absence, poverty, shortage, deficiency, famine, inadequacy, scarcity, paucity, insufficiency, sparsity, scantiness, exiguousness • *a dearth of resources*

death AS A NOUN 1 = **dying**, demise, bereavement, end, passing, release, loss, departure, curtains *(informal)*, cessation, expiration, decease, quietus • *There had been a death in the family.*
OPPOSITES: birth
2 = **destruction**, ending, finish, ruin, wiping out, undoing,

extinction, elimination, downfall, extermination, annihilation, obliteration, ruination • *the death of everything he had ever hoped for*
OPPOSITES: beginning, rise, growth
3 *sometimes capital* = **the Grim Reaper**, the Angel of Death, the Dark Angel • *Carrying a long scythe is the hooded figure of Death.*
▸ **IN PHRASES: at death's door** = **dying**, going, sinking, passing, failing, fading, expiring, perishing, ebbing, moribund, in extremis *(Latin)*, at death's door, not long for this world • *He was at death's door when the disease was finally diagnosed.*
death knell = **doom**, death sentence, beginning of the end, death warrant, near end • *the death knell of the UK motor industry*
put someone to death = **execute**, kill, shoot, murder, slaughter, annihilate, exterminate, send to the electric chair, send to the gas chamber • *The rebels were put to death for treason.*
▸ **RELATED ADJECTIVES:** fatal, lethal, mortal
▸ **RELATED MANIAS:** necromania, thanatomania
▸ **RELATED PHOBIA:** thanatophobia

QUOTATIONS

Dust thou art, and unto dust shalt thou return
[*Bible: Genesis*]

Any man's death diminishes me, because I am involved in Mankind; And therefore never send to know for whom the bell tolls; it tolls for thee
[John Donne *LXXX Sermons*]

To die completely, a person must not only forget but be forgotten, and he who is not forgotten is not dead
[Samuel Butler *Notebooks*]

Death, the most dreaded of evils, is therefore of no concern to us; for while we exist death is not present, and when death is present we no longer exist
[Epicurus *letter to Menoeceus*]

One dies only once, and it's for such a long time
[Molière *Le Dépit Amoureux*]

Anyone can stop a man's life, but no one his death; a thousand doors open on to it
[Seneca *Phoenissae*]

Death hath ten thousand doors
For men to take their exits
[John Webster *The Duchess of Malfi*]

After the first death, there is no other
[Dylan Thomas *A refusal to mourn the death, by fire, of a child in London*]

Revenge triumphs over death; love slights it; honour aspireth to it; grief flieth to it
[Francis Bacon *Essays*]

Fear death? – to feel the fog in my throat,
The mist in my face
[Robert Browning *Prospice*]

Death never takes the wise man by surprise; he is always ready to go
[Jean de la Fontaine *Fables*]

If there wasn't death, I think you couldn't go on
[Stevie Smith]

My name is Death: the last best friend am I
[Robert Southey *The Curse of Kehama*]

O death, where is thy sting? O grave, where is thy victory?
[*Bible: I Corinthians*]

Fear of death is worse than death itself
[William Shakespeare *King Lear*]

I have been half in love with easeful death
[John Keats *Ode to a Nightingale*]

How wonderful is death,
Death and his brother sleep!
[Percy Bysshe Shelley *Queen Mab*]

Though I walk through the valley of the shadow of death, I will fear no evil
[*Bible: Psalm 23*]

Death be not proud, though some have called thee
Mighty and dreadful, for thou art not so
[John Donne *Holy Sonnets*]

We all labour against our own cure, for death is the cure of all diseases
[Thomas Browne *Religio Medici*]

Men fear death as children fear to go in the dark; and as that natural fear in children is increased with tales, so is the other
[Francis Bacon *Essays*]

There is no cure for birth and death save to enjoy the interval
[George Santayana *Soliloquies in England*]

In this world nothing can be said to be certain, except death and taxes
[Benjamin Franklin *letter to Jean Baptiste Le Roy*]

PROVERBS

Death is the great leveller

deathless = **eternal**, timeless, immortal, everlasting, undying, incorruptible, imperishable • *Sara, my love for you is deathless.*
OPPOSITES: passing, mortal, transitory

deathly **1** = **deathlike**, white, pale, ghastly, wan, gaunt, haggard, bloodless, pallid, ashen, sallow, cadaverous, ashy, like death warmed up *(informal)* • *the deathly pallor of her cheeks*
2 = **fatal**, terminal, deadly, terrible, destructive, lethal, mortal, malignant, incurable, pernicious • *a deathly illness*

debacle *or* **débâcle** = **disaster**, catastrophe, fiasco • *the convention was a debacle*

debar = **bar**, exclude, prohibit, black, stop, keep out, preclude, shut out, blackball, interdict, refuse admission to • *She could be debarred from politics for several years.*

debase **1** = **corrupt**, contaminate, devalue, pollute, impair, taint, depreciate, defile, adulterate, vitiate, bastardize • *He claims that advertising debases the English language.*
OPPOSITES: purify
2 = **degrade**, reduce, lower, shame, humble, disgrace, humiliate, demean, drag down, dishonour, cheapen, abase • *I won't debase myself by answering that question.*
OPPOSITES: elevate, uplift, exalt

debased **1** = **corrupt**, devalued, reduced, lowered, mixed, contaminated, polluted, depreciated, impure, adulterated • *a debased form of Buddhism*
2 = **degraded**, corrupt, fallen, low, base, abandoned, perverted, vile, sordid, depraved, debauched, scungy *(Austral. & N.Z.)* • *Such women were seen as morally debased.*
OPPOSITES: good, moral, virtuous

debasement **1** = **contamination**, devaluation, reduction, pollution, depreciation, adulteration • *the progressive debasement of knowledge*
2 = **degradation**, corruption, perversion, abasement, baseness, depravity • *fantasies of domination and debasement*

debatable = **doubtful**, uncertain, dubious, controversial, unsettled, questionable, undecided, borderline, in dispute, moot, arguable, iffy *(informal)*, open to question, disputable • *It is debatable whether or not they were ever properly compensated.*

debate **AS A NOUN** = **discussion**, talk, argument, dispute, analysis, conversation, consideration, controversy, dialogue, contention, deliberation, polemic, altercation, disputation • *There has been a lot of debate about this point.*
▸ **AS A VERB** **1** = **discuss**, question, talk about, argue about, dispute, examine, contest, deliberate, contend, wrangle, thrash out, controvert • *The causes of depression are much debated.*

2 = **consider**, reflect, think about, weigh, contemplate, deliberate, ponder, revolve, mull over, ruminate, give thought to, cogitate, meditate upon • *He debated whether to have yet another double vodka.*

debauch AS A VERB 1 = **corrupt**, seduce, pollute, pervert, subvert, deprave, demoralize, lead astray, vitiate • *a film accused of debauching public morals*
2 = **seduce**, ruin, violate, ravish, lead astray, deflower • *a whorehouse where drunken oafs debauch young women*
▸ AS A NOUN = **orgy**, fling, bout, spree, binge *(informal)*, bender *(informal)*, carouse, saturnalia, bacchanalia, carousal • *The party degenerated into a drunken debauch.*

debauched = **corrupt**, abandoned, perverted, degraded, degenerate, immoral, dissipated, sleazy, depraved, wanton, debased, profligate, dissolute, licentious, pervy *(slang)* • *a debauched circus performer in nineteenth-century Poland*

debauchery = **depravity**, excess, lust, revel, indulgence, orgy, incontinence, gluttony, dissipation, licentiousness, intemperance, overindulgence, lewdness, dissoluteness, carousal • *The police were called to quell scenes of violence and debauchery.*

debilitate = **weaken**, exhaust, wear out, sap, incapacitate, prostrate, enfeeble, enervate, devitalize • *Fear threatened to debilitate me.*
OPPOSITES: stimulate, wake up, invigorate

debilitating = **weakening**, tiring, exhausting, draining, fatiguing, wearing, sapping, incapacitating, enervating, enfeebling, devitalizing • *a debilitating illness*
OPPOSITES: stimulating, animating, invigorating

debility = **weakness**, exhaustion, frailty, incapacity, infirmity, feebleness, faintness, decrepitude, enervation, enfeeblement, sickliness • *Anxiety or general debility can play a part in allergies.*

debit AS A VERB = **pay out from** • *We will confirm with you before debiting your account.*
▸ AS A NOUN = **payout**, debt, payment, commitment, liability • *The total of debits must match the total of credits.*

debonair = **elegant**, charming, dashing, smooth, refined, courteous, affable, suave, urbane, well-bred • *a handsome, debonair, death-defying racing-driver*

debrief = **interrogate**, question, examine, probe, quiz, cross-examine • *The men have been debriefed by officials.*

debris = **remains**, bits, pieces, waste, ruins, wreck, rubbish, fragments, litter, rubble, wreckage, brash, detritus, dross • *People were killed by flying debris.*

debt AS A NOUN 1 = **debit**, bill, score, account, due, duty, commitment, obligation, liability, arrears, money owing • *He is still paying off his debts.*
2 = **indebtedness**, obligation • *I owe a debt of thanks to her*
▸ IN PHRASES: **in debt** = **owing**, liable, accountable, in the red *(informal)*, in arrears, overdrawn, beholden, in hock *(informal, chiefly U.S.)*, behind with payments • *You shouldn't borrow more money if you're already in debt.*
in someone's debt = **indebted to**, grateful to, obliged to, thankful to, appreciative of, obligated to, beholden to, under an obligation to • *I shall be forever in your debt for all your kindness.*

QUOTATIONS
Debt is the worst poverty
[Thomas Fuller *Gnomologia*]

debtor = **borrower**, mortgagor, loanee, drawee • *For every debtor there's a creditor.*

debunk = **expose**, show up, mock, ridicule, puncture, deflate, disparage, lampoon, cut down to size • *The men of the enlightenment who debunked the church and the crown.*

debut 1 = **entrance**, beginning, launch, launching, introduction, first appearance, inauguration • *This young player has his international debut next week.*
2 = **presentation**, coming out, introduction, first appearance, launching, initiation

decadence = **degeneration**, decline, corruption, fall, decay, deterioration, dissolution, perversion, dissipation, debasement, retrogression • *a prime example of the decadence of the age*

decadent = **degenerate**, abandoned, corrupt, degraded, immoral, self-indulgent, depraved, debased, debauched, dissolute • *the excesses of their decadent rock 'n' roll lifestyles*
OPPOSITES: good, principled, moral

decamp = **make off**, fly, escape, desert, flee, bolt, run away, flit *(informal)*, abscond, hook it *(slang)*, sneak off, do a runner *(slang)*, scarper *(Brit. slang)*, steal away, do a bunk *(Brit. slang)*, fly the coop *(U.S. & Canad. informal)*, skedaddle *(informal)*, hightail it *(informal, chiefly U.S.)*, take a powder *(U.S. & Canad. slang)*, take it on the lam *(U.S. & Canad. slang)*, do a Skase *(Austral. informal)* • *Bugsy decided to decamp to Hollywood from New York.*

decant = **transfer**, tap, drain, pour out, draw off, let flow • *She decanted the milk into a jug.*

decapitate = **behead**, execute, guillotine, cut off the head of • *The colonel ordered his men to decapitate the prisoners.*

decay AS A VERB 1 = **rot**, break down, disintegrate, spoil, crumble, deteriorate, perish, degenerate, fester, decompose, mortify, moulder, go bad, putrefy • *The bodies buried in the fine ash slowly decayed.*
2 = **decline**, sink, break down, diminish, dissolve, crumble, deteriorate, fall off, dwindle, lessen, wane, disintegrate, degenerate • *The work ethic in this country has decayed over the past 30 years.*
OPPOSITES: increase, grow, flower
▸ AS A NOUN 1 = **rot**, rotting, deterioration, corruption, mould, blight, perishing, disintegration, corrosion, decomposition, gangrene, mortification, canker, caries, putrefaction, putrescence, cariosity, putridity • *Plaque causes tooth decay and gum disease.*
2 = **decline**, collapse, deterioration, failing, fading, decadence, degeneration, degeneracy • *problems of urban decay and gang violence*
OPPOSITES: growth

decayed = **rotten**, bad, decaying, wasted, spoiled, perished, festering, decomposed, corroded, unsound, putrid, putrefied, putrescent, carrion, carious • *Even young children have teeth so decayed they need to be extracted.*

decaying 1 = **rotting**, deteriorating, disintegrating, crumbling, perishing, wasting away, wearing away, putrefying, gangrenous, putrefacient • *the smell of decaying bodies is all-pervasive*
2 = **declining**, dying, failing, abandoned, neglected, waning, languishing, forsaken • *the problems of decaying inner city areas*

deceased = **dead**, late, departed, lost, gone, expired, defunct, lifeless, pushing up daisies *(informal)* • *his recently deceased mother*

deceit = **lying**, fraud, cheating, deception, hypocrisy, cunning, pretence, treachery, dishonesty, guile, artifice, trickery, misrepresentation, duplicity, subterfuge, feint, double-dealing, chicanery, wile, dissimulation, craftiness, imposture, fraudulence, slyness, deceitfulness, underhandedness • *He was guilty of theft, fraud and deceit on an incredible scale.*
OPPOSITES: honesty, openness, sincerity

deceitful = **dishonest**, false, deceiving, fraudulent, treacherous, deceptive, hypocritical, counterfeit, crafty, sneaky, illusory, two-faced, disingenuous, untrustworthy, underhand, insincere, double-dealing, duplicitous, fallacious, guileful, knavish *(archaic)* • *The ambassador called the report deceitful and misleading.*

deceive AS A VERB = **take in**, trick, fool *(informal)*, cheat, con *(informal)*, kid *(informal)*, stiff *(slang)*, sting *(informal)*, mislead, betray, lead (someone) on *(informal)*, hoax, dupe, beguile, delude, swindle, outwit, ensnare, bamboozle *(informal)*, hoodwink, entrap, double-cross *(informal)*, take for a ride *(informal)*, pull a fast one on *(slang)*, cozen, scam *(slang)*, pull the wool over (someone's) eyes • *He has deceived and disillusioned us all.*

▸ **IN PHRASES: be deceived by something** *or* **someone** = **be taken in by**, fall for, swallow *(informal)*, take the bait, be made a fool of by, be the dupe of, swallow hook, line, and sinker *(informal)* • *I was deceived by her innocent expression.*

deceiver = **liar**, fraud, cheat, fake, betrayer, crook *(informal)*, pretender, deluder, hypocrite, charlatan, trickster, con man *(informal)*, sharper, impostor, fraudster, swindler, dissembler, inveigler, mountebank, snake in the grass, grifter *(slang, chiefly U.S. & Canad.)*, double-dealer, chiseller *(informal)*, cozener, rorter *(Austral. slang)*, rogue trader • *He was condemned as a liar, cheat and deceiver.*

QUOTATIONS

men were deceivers ever

[William Shakespeare *Much Ado About Nothing*]

decelerate 1 = **slow down** *or* **up**, slow, brake, go slower, put the brakes on, reduce speed, hit the brakes • *The driver kept accelerating and decelerating.*

OPPOSITES: accelerate, speed up, pick up speed

2 = **slow**, be checked, slacken (off), be reined in, slow down *or* up • *Inflation has decelerated remarkably.*

OPPOSITES: accelerate, speed up, quicken

decency 1 = **propriety**, correctness, decorum, fitness, good form, respectability, etiquette, appropriateness, seemliness • *His sense of decency forced him to resign.*

2 = **courtesy**, grace, politeness, good manners, civility, good breeding, graciousness, urbanity, courteousness, gallantness • *He did not have the decency to inform me of his plans.*

decent 1 = **satisfactory**, average, fair, all right, reasonable, suitable, sufficient, acceptable, good enough, adequate, competent, ample, tolerable, up to scratch, passable, up to standard, up to the mark • *Nearby there is a village with a decent pub.*

OPPOSITES: unsatisfactory, inept

2 = **proper**, becoming, seemly, fitting, fit, appropriate, suitable, respectable, befitting, decorous, comme il faut *(French)* • *They married after a decent interval.*

OPPOSITES: incorrect, indecent, improper

3 = **good**, kind, friendly, neighbourly, generous, helpful, obliging, accommodating, sympathetic, comradely, benign, gracious, benevolent, courteous, amiable, amicable, sociable, genial, peaceable, companionable, well-disposed • *Most people around here are decent folk.*

4 = **respectable**, nice, pure, proper, modest, polite, chaste, presentable, decorous • *He wanted to marry a decent woman.*

deception 1 = **trickery**, fraud, deceit, hypocrisy, cunning, treachery, guile, duplicity, insincerity, legerdemain, dissimulation, craftiness, fraudulence, deceitfulness, deceptiveness • *He admitted conspiring to obtain property by deception.*

OPPOSITES: honesty, openness, fidelity

2 = **trick**, lie, fraud, cheat, bluff, sham, snare, hoax, decoy, ruse, artifice, subterfuge, canard, feint, stratagem, porky *(Brit. slang)*, pork pie *(Brit. slang)*, wile, hokum *(slang, chiefly U.S. & Canad.)*, leg-pull *(Brit. informal)*, imposture, snow job *(slang, chiefly U.S. & Canad.)*, fastie *(Austral. slang)* • *You've been the victim of a rather cruel deception.*

QUOTATIONS

O what a tangled web we weave,
When first we practise to deceive!

[Walter Scott *Marmion*]

you can fool some of the people all of the time, and all of the people some of the time, but you cannot fool all of the people all of the time

[ascribed to Abraham Lincoln]

One may smile, and smile, and be a villain

[William Shakespeare *Hamlet*]

We are never so easily deceived as when we imagine we are deceiving others

[Duc de la Rochefoucauld *Maxims*]

deceptive 1 = **misleading**, false, fake, mock, ambiguous, unreliable, spurious, illusory, specious, fallacious, delusive • *Appearances can be deceptive.*

2 = **dishonest**, deceiving, fraudulent, treacherous, hypocritical, crafty, sneaky, two-faced, disingenuous, deceitful, untrustworthy, underhand, insincere, duplicitous, guileful • *Her worst fault is a strongly deceptive streak.*

decide 1 = **make a decision**, make up your mind, reach *or* come to a decision, end, choose, determine, purpose, elect, conclude, commit yourself, come to a conclusion • *I can't decide what to do.*

OPPOSITES: hesitate, falter, dither *(chiefly Brit.)*

2 = **resolve**, answer, determine, settle, conclude, decree, clear up, ordain, adjudicate, adjudge, arbitrate • *This is a question that should be decided by government.*

3 = **settle**, determine, conclude, resolve • *The goal that decided the match came just before half-time.*

decided 1 = **definite**, certain, positive, absolute, distinct, pronounced, clear-cut, undisputed, unequivocal, undeniable, unambiguous, indisputable, categorical, unquestionable • *We were at a decided disadvantage.*

OPPOSITES: doubtful, dubious, questionable

2 = **determined**, firm, decisive, assertive, emphatic, resolute, strong-willed, unhesitating, unfaltering • *a man of very decided opinions*

OPPOSITES: weak, hesitant, irresolute

decidedly = **definitely**, clearly, certainly, absolutely, positively, distinctly, downright, decisively, unequivocally, unmistakably • *He was decidedly uncomfortable at what he saw.*

deciding = **determining**, chief, prime, significant, critical, crucial, principal, influential, decisive, conclusive • *Cost was the deciding factor in our final choice.*

decimate 1 = **destroy**, devastate, wipe out, ravage, eradicate, annihilate, put paid to, lay waste, wreak havoc on • *Pollution could decimate the river's population of kingfishers.*

2 = **reduce**, diminish, decrease, weaken, lessen, wind down, downsize, kennet *(Austral. slang)*, jeff *(Austral. slang)* • *The recession decimated the nation's manufacturing industry.*

decipher 1 = **decode**, crack, solve, understand, explain, reveal, figure out *(informal)*, unravel, suss (out) *(slang)* • *I'm still no closer to deciphering the code.*

2 = **figure out**, read, understand, interpret *(informal)*, make out, unravel, deduce, construe, suss (out) *(slang)* • *I can't decipher these notes.*

decision 1 = **judgment**, finding, ruling, order, result, sentence, settlement, resolution, conclusion, outcome, verdict, decree, arbitration • *The judge's decision was greeted with dismay.*

2 = **decisiveness**, purpose, resolution, resolve, determination, firmness, forcefulness, purposefulness, resoluteness, strength of mind *or* will • *He is very much a man of decision and action.*

decisive 1 = **crucial**, significant, critical, final, positive, absolute, influential, definite, definitive, momentous, conclusive, fateful • *his decisive victory in the elections*

OPPOSITES: uncertain, doubtful, undecided

2 = **resolute**, decided, firm, determined, forceful, uncompromising, incisive, trenchant, strong-minded • *Firm decisive action will be taken to end the incident.*

OPPOSITES: uncertain, hesitating, indecisive

deck AS A VERB 1 = **decorate**, dress, trim, clothe, grace, array, garland, adorn, ornament, embellish, apparel *(archaic)*, festoon, attire, bedeck, beautify, bedight *(archaic)*, bedizen *(archaic)*, engarland • *The house was decked with flowers.*

2 = knock over, floor, knock down, prostrate • *He decked his opponent with a single punch.*
▸ **IN PHRASES: deck someone** *or* **something out = dress up**, clothe, attire, fit out, doll up *(slang)*, prettify, trick out, rig out, pretty up, prink, tog up *or* out • *She had decked him out in expensive clothes.*

declaim **AS A VERB = speak**, lecture, proclaim, recite, rant, harangue, hold forth, spiel *(informal)*, orate, perorate • *He used to declaim verse to us with immense energy.*
▸ **IN PHRASES: declaim against something** *or* **someone = protest against**, attack, rail at *or* against, denounce, decry, inveigh against • *He declaimed against the injustice of his treatment.*

d

declamation = speech, address, lecture, rant, tirade, harangue, oration, recitation • *Her warnings and declamations went unheeded.*

declamatory = rhetorical, theatrical, inflated, high-flown, pompous, turgid, bombastic, discursive, grandiloquent, fustian, orotund, stagy, magniloquent • *He has a reputation for making bold, declamatory statements.*

declaration **1 = announcement**, proclamation, decree, notice, manifesto, notification, edict, pronouncement, promulgation, pronunciamento • *The two countries will sign the declaration of peace tomorrow.*
2 = affirmation, profession, assertion, revelation, disclosure, manifestation, acknowledgment, protestation, avowal, attestation, averment • *declarations of undying love*
3 = statement, testimony, deposition, attestation • *I signed a declaration allowing my doctor to disclose my medical details.*

declarative *or* **declaratory = affirmative**, positive, expressive, definite, explanatory, demonstrative, expository, enunciatory • *He spoke in short, declarative sentences.*

declare **1 = state**, claim, announce, voice, express, maintain, confirm, assert, proclaim, pronounce, utter, notify, affirm, profess, avow, aver, asseverate • *He declared his intention to become the best golfer in the world.*
2 = testify, state, witness, swear, assert, affirm, certify, attest, bear witness, vouch, give testimony, asseverate • *They declare that there is no lawful impediment to the marriage.*
3 = make known, tell, reveal, show, broadcast, confess, communicate, disclose, convey, manifest, make public • *Anyone carrying money into or out of the country must declare it.*

decline **AS A VERB 1 = fall**, fail, drop, contract, lower, sink, flag, fade, shrink, diminish, decrease, slow down, fall off, dwindle, lessen, wane, ebb, slacken • *a declining birth rate*
OPPOSITES: rise, increase
2 = deteriorate, fade, weaken, pine, decay, worsen, lapse, languish, degenerate, droop • *Her father's health has declined significantly in recent months.*
OPPOSITES: improve
3 = refuse, reject, turn down, avoid, deny, spurn, abstain, forgo, send your regrets, say 'no' • *He declined their invitation.*
OPPOSITES: agree to, accept, consent
▸ **AS A NOUN 1 = depression**, recession, slump, falling off, downturn, dwindling, lessening, diminution, abatement • *The first signs of economic decline became visible.*
OPPOSITES: rise, upswing
2 = deterioration, fall, failing, slump, weakening, decay, worsening, descent, downturn, disintegration, degeneration, atrophy, decrepitude, retrogression, enfeeblement • *Rome's decline in the fifth century.*
OPPOSITES: improvement
▸ **IN PHRASES: in decline** *or* **on the decline = waning**, dying, failing, collapsing, crumbling, decaying, on the way out, obsolescent • *Thankfully, the popularity of bloodsports is on the decline.*

decode **1 = decipher**, crack, work out, solve, interpret, unscramble, decrypt, descramble • *The secret documents were intercepted and decoded.*
OPPOSITES: scramble, encode, encrypt
2 = understand, explain, interpret, make sense of, construe, decipher, elucidate, throw light on, explicate • *You don't need to be a genius to decode his work.*

décolleté = low-cut, revealing, low-necked • *Many brides wear strapless or décolleté bridal gowns.*

decompose **1 = rot**, spoil, corrupt, crumble, decay, perish, fester, corrode, moulder, go bad, putrefy • *foods which decompose and rot*
2 = break down, break up, crumble, deteriorate, fall apart, disintegrate, degenerate • *Plastics take years to decompose.*

decomposition **1 = rot**, corruption, decay, rotting, perishing, mortification, putrefaction, putrescence, putridity • *The bodies were in an advanced state of decomposition.*
2 = breakdown, disintegration, dissolution, atomization • *a nuclear reactor which gives complete decomposition and no unwanted byproducts*

decontaminate = sterilize, clean, cleanse, purify, make safe, disinfect, fumigate, deodorize, sanitize, disinfest • *procedures for decontaminating people affected by radiation*
OPPOSITES: infect, contaminate, poison

decor *or* **décor = decoration**, look, colour scheme, ornamentation, furnishing style • *The decor is simple but elegant.*

decorate **1 = adorn**, deck, trim, embroider, garnish, ornament, embellish, festoon, bedeck, beautify, grace, engarland • *He decorated the box with glitter and ribbons.*
2 = do up, paper, paint, wallpaper, renovate *(informal)*, furbish • *a small, badly decorated office*
3 = pin a medal on, give a medal to, cite, confer an honour on *or* upon • *He was decorated for his services to the nation.*

decoration **1 = adornment**, trimming, garnishing, enhancement, elaboration, embellishment, ornamentation, beautification • *He played a part in the decoration of the tree.*
2 = ornament, trimmings, garnish, frill, scroll, spangle, festoon, trinket, bauble, flounce, arabesque, curlicue, furbelow, falderal, cartouch(e) • *We were putting the Christmas decorations up.*
3 = medal, award, order, star, colours, ribbon, badge, emblem, garter • *He was awarded several military decorations.*

decorative = ornamental, fancy, pretty, attractive, enhancing, adorning, for show, embellishing, showy, beautifying, nonfunctional, arty-crafty • *highly decorative iron brackets*

decorous = proper, becoming, seemly, fitting, fit, correct, appropriate, mannerly, suitable, decent, polite, sedate, befitting, well-behaved, comely, comme il faut *(French)* • *She was dressed demurely and wearing a suitably decorous expression.*
OPPOSITES: inappropriate, unseemly, undignified

decorum = propriety, decency, etiquette, breeding, protocol, respectability, politeness, good manners, good grace, gentility, deportment, courtliness, politesse, punctilio, seemliness • *I was treated with decorum and respect*
OPPOSITES: impropriety, rudeness, bad manners

decoy **AS A NOUN = lure**, attraction, bait, trap, inducement, enticement, ensnarement • *He acted as a decoy to draw the dogs' attention away from the children.*
▸ **AS A VERB = lure**, tempt, entice, seduce, deceive, allure, ensnare, entrap, inveigle • *They used flares to decoy enemy missiles.*

decrease **AS A VERB 1 = drop**, decline, lessen, contract, lower, ease, shrink, diminish, fall off, dwindle, wane, subside, abate, peter out, slacken • *Population growth is decreasing each year.*
2 = reduce, cut, lower, contract, depress, moderate, weaken, diminish, turn down, slow down, cut down, shorten, dilute, impair, lessen, curtail, wind down, abate, tone down, truncate, abridge, downsize • *Regular doses of aspirin decrease the risk of heart attack.*

OPPOSITES: extend, enlarge, increase, expand
▸ **AS A NOUN = lessening**, decline, reduction, loss, falling off, downturn, dwindling, contraction, ebb, cutback, subsidence, curtailment, shrinkage, diminution, abatement • *There has been a decrease in the number of young unemployed people.*
OPPOSITES: growth, expansion, extension

decree AS A NOUN 1 = law, order, ruling, act, demand, command, regulation, mandate, canon, statute, covenant, ordinance, proclamation, enactment, edict, dictum, precept • *He issued a decree ordering all unofficial armed groups to disband.*
2 = judgment, finding, order, result, ruling, decision, award, conclusion, verdict, arbitration • *court decrees relating to marital property*
▸ **AS A VERB = order**, rule, command, decide, demand, establish, determine, proclaim, dictate, prescribe, pronounce, lay down, enact, ordain • *He got the two men off the hook by decreeing a general amnesty.*

decrepit 1 = ruined, broken-down, battered, crumbling, rundown, deteriorated, decaying, beat-up *(informal)*, shabby, worn-out, ramshackle, dilapidated, antiquated, rickety, weather-beaten, tumbledown • *The film was shot in a decrepit police station.*
2 = weak, aged, frail, wasted, fragile, crippled, feeble, past it, debilitated, incapacitated, infirm, superannuated, doddering • *a decrepit old man*

decrepitude 1 = decay, deterioration, degeneration, dilapidation • *The buildings had been allowed to fall into decrepitude.*
2 = weakness, old age, incapacity, wasting, invalidity, senility, infirmity, dotage, debility, feebleness, eld *(archaic)* • *the boundary between healthy middle age and total decrepitude*

decry = condemn, blame, abuse, blast, flame *(informal)*, denounce, put down, criticize, run down, discredit, censure, detract, denigrate, belittle, disparage, rail against, depreciate, tear into *(informal)*, diss *(slang, chiefly U.S.)*, lambast(e), traduce, excoriate, derogate, cry down, asperse • *He is impatient with those who decry the scheme.*

dedicate 1 = devote, give, apply, commit, concern, occupy, pledge, surrender, give over to • *He dedicated himself to politics.*
2 = offer, address, assign, inscribe • *This book is dedicated to the memory of my sister.*
3 = consecrate, bless, sanctify, set apart, hallow, make sacred • *The church is dedicated to a saint.*

dedicated = committed, devoted, sworn, enthusiastic, single-minded, zealous, purposeful, given over to, wholehearted • *He's quite dedicated to his studies.*
OPPOSITES: indifferent, unconcerned, uncaring

dedication 1 = commitment, loyalty, devotion, allegiance, adherence, single-mindedness, faithfulness, wholeheartedness, devotedness • *To be successful takes hard work and dedication.*
OPPOSITES: indifference, apathy, coolness
2 = inscription, message, address • *His book contains a dedication to his parents.*
3 = consecration, ordaining, sanctification, hallowing • *Some 250 guests attended the dedication ceremony of the church.*

deduce = work out, reason, understand, gather, conclude, derive, infer, glean, extrapolate • *She hoped he hadn't deduced the reason for her visit.*

deduct = subtract, remove, take off, withdraw, take out, take from, take away, reduce by, knock off *(informal)*, decrease by • *Marks will be deducted for spelling mistakes.*
OPPOSITES: add, add to, enlarge

deduction 1 = conclusion, finding, verdict, judgment, assumption, inference, corollary • *It was a pretty astute deduction.*
2 = reasoning, thinking, thought, reason, analysis, logic, cogitation, ratiocination • *'How did you guess?' 'Deduction,' he replied.*
3 = discount, reduction, cut, concession, allowance, decrease, rebate, diminution • *your gross income, before tax and insurance deductions*
4 = subtraction, reduction, allowance, concession • *the deduction of tax at 20%*

deed 1 = action, act, performance, achievement, exploit, feat • *His heroic deeds were celebrated in every corner of the country.*
2 = document, title, contract, title deed, indenture • *He asked if I had the deeds to his father's property.*

deem = consider, think, believe, hold, account, judge, suppose, regard, estimate, imagine, reckon, esteem, conceive • *He said he would used force if he deemed it necessary.*

deep AS AN ADJECTIVE 1 = big, wide, broad, profound, yawning, cavernous, bottomless, unfathomable, fathomless, abyssal • *The workers had dug a deep hole in the centre of the garden.*
OPPOSITES: shallow
2 = intense, great, serious *(informal)*, acute, extreme, grave, profound, heartfelt, unqualified, abject, deeply felt, heartrending • *a period of deep personal crisis*
OPPOSITES: shallow, superficial
3 = sound, peaceful, profound, unbroken, undisturbed, untroubled • *He fell into a deep sleep.*
4 *with* **in = absorbed in**, lost in, gripped by, intent on, preoccupied with, carried away by, immersed in, engrossed in, rapt by • *Before long we were deep in conversation.*
5 = wise, learned, searching, keen, critical, acute, profound, penetrating, discriminating, shrewd, discerning, astute, perceptive, incisive, perspicacious, sagacious • *She gave him a long deep look.*
OPPOSITES: simple
6 = dark, strong, rich, warm, intense, vivid • *rich, deep colours*
OPPOSITES: light, pale, pastel
7 = low, booming, bass, full, mellow, resonant, sonorous, mellifluous, dulcet, low-pitched, full-toned • *His voice was deep and mellow.*
OPPOSITES: high, sharp
8 = astute, knowing, clever, designing, scheming, sharp, smart, intelligent, discriminating, shrewd, cunning, discerning, canny, devious, perceptive, insidious, artful, far-sighted, far-seeing, perspicacious, sagacious • *a very deep individual*
OPPOSITES: simple, shallow
9 = secret, hidden, unknown, mysterious, concealed, obscure, abstract, veiled, esoteric, mystifying, impenetrable, arcane, abstruse, recondite • *a deep, dark secret*
▸ **AS A NOUN = middle**, heart, midst, dead, thick, culmination • *in the deep of night*
▸ **AS AN ADVERB 1 = far**, a long way, a good way, miles, deeply, far down, a great distance • *They travelled deep into the forest.*
2 = far, late, for a long time • *We talked deep into the night.*
3 = inwardly, privately, secretly, within, inside, at heart, to yourself, deep down, in your inmost heart • *Deep in my heart I knew we had no hope.*
▸ **IN PHRASES: the deep = the ocean**, the sea, the waves, the main, the drink *(informal)*, the high seas, the briny *(informal)* • *whales and other creatures of the deep*

PROVERBS
Still waters run deep

deepen 1 = intensify, increase, grow, strengthen, reinforce, escalate, magnify, augment • *Sloane's uneasiness deepened.* • *Further job losses deepened the gloom.*
2 = extend, develop, encourage, promote, foster, stimulate, nurture, cultivate • *an opportunity to deepen your*

understanding of people
3 = **darken**, shade, make dark, make darker • *a spice used in poultry feed to deepen the colour of egg yolks*
4 = **dig out**, excavate, scoop out, hollow out, make deeper, scrape out • *The tunnels have been widened and deepened.*

deeply = **thoroughly**, completely, seriously, sadly, severely, gravely, profoundly, intensely, to the heart, passionately, acutely, to the core, feelingly, movingly, distressingly, to the quick, affectingly • *Our conversation left me deeply depressed.*

deep-rooted *or* **deep-seated** = **fixed**, confirmed, rooted, settled, entrenched, ingrained, inveterate, dyed-in-the-wool, ineradicable • *long-term solutions to a deep-seated problem*
OPPOSITES: surface, slight, superficial

deer
▸ RELATED ADJECTIVE: cervine
▸ NAME OF MALE: hart, stag
▸ NAME OF FEMALE: doe, hind
▸ NAME OF YOUNG: fawn
▸ COLLECTIVE NOUN: herd

deface = **vandalize**, damage, destroy, total *(slang)*, injure, mar, spoil, trash *(slang)*, impair, tarnish, obliterate, mutilate, deform, blemish, disfigure, sully • *It's illegal to deface banknotes.*

de facto AS AN ADVERB = **in fact**, really, actually, in effect, in reality • *Unification has now de facto replaced the signing of such a treaty.*
▸ AS AN ADJECTIVE = **actual**, real, effective, existing • *a de facto recognition of the republic's independence*

defamation = **slander**, smear, libel, scandal, slur, vilification, opprobrium, denigration, calumny, character assassination, disparagement, obloquy, aspersion, traducement • *He was considering suing for defamation.*

defamatory = **slanderous**, insulting, abusive, denigrating, disparaging, vilifying, derogatory, injurious, libellous, vituperative, calumnious, contumelious • *The article was highly defamatory.*

defame = **slander**, smear, libel, discredit, knock *(informal)*, rubbish *(informal)*, disgrace, blacken, slag (off) *(slang)*, detract, malign, denigrate, disparage, vilify, dishonour, stigmatize, bad-mouth *(slang, chiefly U.S. & Canad.)*, besmirch, traduce, cast aspersions on, speak evil of, cast a slur on, calumniate, vituperate, asperse • *He complained that the article defamed him.*

default AS A NOUN 1 = **failure**, want, lack, fault, absence, neglect, defect, deficiency, lapse, omission, dereliction • *The other team failed to turn up so we won by default.*
2 = **nonpayment**, evasion, failure to pay, non-remittance • *The country can't pay its foreign debts and default is inevitable.*
▸ AS A VERB = **fail to pay**, dodge, evade, fall behind, rat *(informal)*, neglect, levant *(Brit.)*, go into arrears, welch *or* welsh *(slang)* • *Many borrowers are defaulting on loans.*

defeat AS A VERB 1 = **beat**, crush, overwhelm, conquer, stuff *(slang)*, master, worst, tank *(slang)*, overthrow, lick *(informal)*, undo, subdue, rout, overpower, quell, trounce, clobber *(slang)*, vanquish, repulse, subjugate, run rings around *(informal)*, wipe the floor with *(informal)*, make mincemeat of *(informal)*, pip at the post, outplay, blow out of the water *(slang)* • *His guerrillas defeated the colonial army.*
OPPOSITES: lose, yield, surrender
2 = **frustrate**, foil, thwart, ruin, baffle, confound, balk, get the better of, forestall, stymie • *The challenges of constructing such a huge novel almost defeated her.*
3 = **overthrow**, destroy, ruin, upset, overturn, demolish, put an end to, subvert, put paid to, bring to ruin • *He swore to defeat the plan.*
▸ AS A NOUN 1 = **conquest**, beating, overthrow, pasting *(slang)*, rout, debacle, trouncing, repulse, vanquishment • *The vote was seen as something of a defeat for the lobbyists.*
OPPOSITES: success, victory, triumph
2 = **frustration**, failure, reverse, disappointment, setback, thwarting • *the final defeat of all his hopes*

QUOTATIONS
Defeat is a thing of weariness, of incoherence, of boredom. And above all futility
[Antoine de Saint-Exupéry *Flight to Arras*]
Victory has a hundred fathers, but defeat is an orphan
[Count Galeazzo Giano *Diary*]

defeated = **beaten**, crushed, conquered, worsted, routed, overcome, overwhelmed, thrashed, licked *(informal)*, thwarted, overpowered, balked, trounced, vanquished, checkmated, bested • *He'll be disinclined to treat a defeated enemy with leniency.*
OPPOSITES: winning, successful, victorious

defeatist AS A NOUN = **pessimist**, sceptic, cynic, misery, scoffer, doubter, killjoy, quitter, prophet of doom, yielder • *a defeatist might give up at this point*
▸ AS AN ADJECTIVE = **pessimistic**, resigned, despairing, hopeless, foreboding, despondent, fatalistic • *Don't go out there with a defeatist attitude.*

defecate = **excrete**, eliminate, shit *(taboo slang)*, discharge, evacuate *(Physiology)*, crap *(taboo slang)*, dump *(slang, chiefly U.S.)*, pass a motion, move the bowels, empty the bowels, open the bowels, egest, void excrement • *Animals defecate after every meal.*

defecation = **excretion**, evacuation *(Physiology)*, elimination, bowel movement, motion, egestion, emptying *or* opening of the bowels, voiding excrement • *Side-effects of the drug include vomiting and involuntary defecation.*

defect AS A NOUN = **deficiency**, want, failing, lack, mistake, fault, error, absence, weakness, flaw, shortcoming, inadequacy, imperfection, frailty, foible • *The report pointed out the defects in the present system.*
▸ AS A VERB = **desert**, rebel, quit, revolt, change sides, apostatize, tergiversate • *a KGB official who defected in 1963*
▸ IN PHRASES: **defect from something** *or* **someone** = **leave**, abandon, desert, quit, resign from, walk out on *(informal)*, break faith with, tergiversate • *He defected from the party twenty years ago.*

defection = **desertion**, revolt, rebellion, abandonment, dereliction, backsliding, apostasy • *the defection of at least sixteen deputies*

defective 1 = **faulty**, broken, not working, flawed, imperfect, out of order, on the blink *(slang)* • *Retailers can return defective merchandise.*
OPPOSITES: working, whole, perfect
2 = **deficient**, lacking, short, inadequate, insufficient, incomplete, scant • *food which is defective in nutritional quality*
OPPOSITES: adequate

defector = **deserter**, renegade, turncoat, apostate, recreant *(archaic)*, runagate *(archaic)*, tergiversator • *Turkey granted asylum to defectors from Communist countries.*

defence *or (U.S.)* **defense** AS A NOUN 1 = **protection**, cover, security, guard, shelter, refuge, resistance, safeguard, immunity • *The land was flat, giving no scope for defence.*
2 = **armaments**, weapons, deterrents, the military, the army, the navy, the air force • *Twenty-eight per cent of the federal budget is spent on defense.*
3 = **argument**, explanation, excuse, plea, apology, justification, vindication, rationalization, apologia, exoneration, exculpation, extenuation • *a spirited defence of the government's economic progress*
4 = **plea** *(Law)*, case, claim, pleading, declaration, testimony, denial, alibi, vindication, rebuttal • *His defence was that records were fabricated by the police.*
▸ AS A PLURAL NOUN = **shield**, barricade, fortification, bastion, buttress, rampart, bulwark, fastness, fortified pa *(N.Z.)* • *Soldiers are beginning to strengthen the city's defences.*

defenceless *or (U.S.)* **defenseless** = **helpless**, exposed, vulnerable, naked, endangered, powerless, wide open, unarmed, unprotected, unguarded • *a leader who would leave the country isolated and defenceless*
OPPOSITES: protected, safe, guarded

defend 1 = **protect**, cover, guard, screen, secure, preserve, look after, shelter, shield, harbour, safeguard, fortify, ward off, watch over, stick up for *(informal)*, keep safe, give sanctuary • *They defended themselves against some racist thugs.*
2 = **support**, champion, justify, maintain, sustain, plead for, endorse, assert, stand by, uphold, vindicate, stand up for, espouse, speak up for, stick up for *(informal)* • *Police chiefs strongly defended police conduct.*

defendant = **accused**, respondent, appellant, litigant, prisoner at the bar • *Charges against the defendant were dismissed.*

defender 1 = **supporter**, champion, advocate, sponsor, follower, patron, apologist, upholder, vindicator • *a strong defender of human rights*
2 = **protector**, guard, guardian, escort, bodyguard, guardian angel • *He proclaims himself a defender of the environment.*

defensible 1 = **justifiable**, right, sound, reasonable, acceptable, sensible, valid, legitimate, plausible, permissible, well-founded, tenable, excusable, pardonable, vindicable • *Her reasons for action are morally defensible.*
OPPOSITES: wrong, untenable, unjustifiable
2 = **secure**, safe, unassailable, impregnable, holdable • *the creation of defensible borders*

defensive 1 = **protective**, guarding, defending, opposing, shielding, safeguarding, watchful, on the defensive, on guard • *hastily organized defensive measures*
2 = **oversensitive**, neurotic, prickly, uptight *(informal)*, thin-skinned, self-justifying, easily offended • *She heard the blustering, defensive note in his voice.*

defensively = **in self-defence**, in defence, suspiciously, on the defensive • *'It's nothing to do with me,' he said defensively.*

defer[1] = **postpone**, delay, put off, suspend, shelve, set aside, adjourn, hold over, procrastinate, put on ice *(informal)*, put on the back burner *(informal)*, protract, take a rain check on *(U.S. & Canad. informal)*, prorogue • *Customers often defer payment for as long as possible.*

defer[2] *with* **to** = **comply with**, give way to, submit to, bow to, give in to, yield to, accede to, capitulate to • *her view that women tend to defer to men*

deference 1 = **respect**, regard, consideration, attention, honour, esteem, courtesy, homage, reverence, politeness, civility, veneration, thoughtfulness • *Out of deference to his feelings, I refrained from commenting.*
OPPOSITES: contempt, disregard, disrespect
2 = **obedience**, yielding, submission, compliance, capitulation, acquiescence, obeisance, complaisance • *a chain of social command linked by deference to authority*
OPPOSITES: disobedience, insubordination, revolt

deferential = **respectful**, civil, polite, courteous, considerate, obedient, submissive, dutiful, ingratiating, reverential, obsequious, complaisant, obeisant, regardful • *stars who like five-star hotels and deferential treatment*

deferment *or* **deferral** = **postponement**, delay, suspension, putting off, stay, moratorium, adjournment • *the deferment of tax payments*

defiance = **resistance**, challenge, opposition, confrontation, contempt, disregard, provocation, disobedience, insolence, insubordination, rebelliousness, recalcitrance, contumacy • *his courageous defiance of the government*
OPPOSITES: regard, respect, obedience

defiant = **resisting**, challenging, rebellious, daring, aggressive, hostile, bold, provocative, audacious, recalcitrant, antagonistic, obstinate, insolent, truculent, uncooperative, mutinous, disobedient, refractory, insubordinate, non-compliant, contumacious • *Despite the risk of suspension, he remained defiant.*
OPPOSITES: cowardly, respectful, obedient

deficiency 1 = **lack**, want, deficit, absence, shortage, deprivation, inadequacy, scarcity, dearth, privation, insufficiency, scantiness • *They did tests for signs of vitamin deficiency.*
OPPOSITES: abundance, sufficiency, adequacy
2 = **failing**, fault, weakness, defect, flaw, drawback, shortcoming, imperfection, frailty, demerit • *the most serious deficiency in their air defence*

deficient 1 = **lacking**, wanting, needing, short, inadequate, insufficient, scarce, scant, meagre, skimpy, scanty, exiguous • *a diet deficient in vitamins*
2 = **unsatisfactory**, poor, inadequate, weak, flawed, inferior, impaired, faulty, incomplete, unsuitable, defective, imperfect, unworthy • *deficient landing systems*

deficit = **shortfall**, shortage, deficiency, loss, default, arrears • *They're ready to cut the budget deficit for the next fiscal year.*

defile 1 = **degrade**, stain, disgrace, sully, debase, dishonour, besmirch, smirch • *He felt his father's memory had been defiled by the article.*
2 = **desecrate**, violate, contaminate, abuse, pollute, profane, dishonour, despoil, treat sacrilegiously • *Who gave you permission to defile this sacred place?*
3 = **dirty**, soil, contaminate, smear, pollute, taint, tarnish, make foul, smirch, befoul • *piles of old clothes defiled with excrement*
4 = **violate**, abuse, rape, seduce, molest, ravish, deflower • *The soldiers brutally defiled her in front of her parents.*

defiled 1 = **unclean**, dirtied, polluted, tainted, impure, besmirched, skanky *(slang)* • *How dirty and defiled he felt.*
OPPOSITES: clean, immaculate, spotless
2 = **desecrated**, violated, contaminate d, abused, polluted, profaned, dishonoured, despoiled, blasphemed • *Their place of worship is regularly defiled by vandals.*
3 = **violated**, abused, raped, assaulted, ravished, dishonoured, debauched • *There lay the victims' bodies, naked and defiled.*
OPPOSITES: innocent, pure, chaste

definable = **specific**, apparent, definite, perceptible, explicable, determinable, describable • *groups broadly definable as conservative*

define 1 = **mark out**, outline, limit, bound, delineate, circumscribe, demarcate, delimit • *Armed forces were deployed to define military zones.*
2 = **describe**, interpret, characterize, explain, spell out, expound, put into words, give the meaning of • *How exactly do you define reasonable behaviour?*
3 = **establish**, decide, detail, determine, fix, specify, designate, stipulate • *The Court must define the limits of its authority.*

defined = **marked**, clear, obvious, prominent, distinct, conspicuous, well-worn, sign-posted • *a clearly defined track down to the valley*

definite 1 = **specific**, exact, precise, clear, particular, express, determined, fixed, black-and-white, explicit, clear-cut, cut-and-dried *(informal)*, clearly defined • *It's too soon to give a definite answer.*
OPPOSITES: general, confused, vague
2 = **clear**, explicit, black-and-white, clear-cut, unequivocal, unambiguous, guaranteed, cut-and-dried *(informal)* • *We didn't have any definite proof.*
3 = **noticeable**, marked, clear, decided, striking, noted, particular, obvious, dramatic, considerable, remarkable, apparent, evident, distinct, notable, manifest, conspicuous • *There has been a definite improvement.*
4 = **certain**, decided, sure, settled, convinced, positive,

confident, assured • *She is very definite about her feelings.*
OPPOSITES: uncertain, undecided

definitely = **certainly**, clearly, obviously, surely, easily, plainly, absolutely, positively, decidedly, needless to say, without doubt, unquestionably, undeniably, categorically, without question, unequivocally, unmistakably, far and away, without fail, beyond any doubt, indubitably, come hell or high water *(informal)* • *Something should definitely be done about him.*

definition 1 = **description**, interpretation, explanation, clarification, exposition, explication, elucidation, statement of meaning • *There is no general agreement on a standard definition of sanity.*
2 = **sharpness**, focus, clarity, contrast, precision, distinctness • *This printer has excellent definition.*

definitive 1 = **final**, convincing, absolute, clinching, decisive, definite, conclusive, irrefutable • *No one has come up with a definitive answer to that question.*
2 = **authoritative**, greatest, ultimate, reliable, most significant, exhaustive, superlative, mother of all *(informal)* • *It is still the definitive book on the islands.*

deflate 1 = **humiliate**, humble, squash, put down *(slang)*, disconcert, chasten, mortify, dispirit • *Her comments deflated him a bit.*
2 = **puncture**, flatten, empty • *The vandals had deflated his car's tyres.*
OPPOSITES: expand, blow up, inflate
3 = **collapse**, go down, contract, empty, shrink, void, flatten • *The balloon began to deflate.*
OPPOSITES: expand, swell, balloon
4 = **reduce**, depress, decrease, diminish, devalue, depreciate • *artificially deflated prices*

deflect 1 = **distract**, divert, sidetrack, draw away, turn aside • *a manoeuvre to deflect our attention from what was happening*
2 = **turn aside**, turn, bend, twist, sidetrack • *His forearm deflected most of the punch.*

deflection = **deviation**, bending, veering, swerving, divergence, turning aside, refraction, declination • *the deflection of light as it passes through the slits in the grating*

deflower 1 = **seduce**, dishonour, deprave • *She was deflowered by a man who worked in the factory.*
2 = **ravish**, rape, violate, assault, molest, force • *marauding invaders who will deflower our womenfolk*

deform 1 = **disfigure**, twist, injure, cripple, ruin, mar, spoil, mutilate, maim, deface • *Severe rheumatoid arthritis deforms limbs.*
2 = **distort**, twist, warp, buckle, mangle, contort, gnarl, misshape, malform • *Plastic deforms when subjected to heat.*

deformation = **distortion**, warping, contortion, malformation, disfiguration, misshapenness • *The deformation of his body was the result of a disease.*

deformed = **distorted**, bent, twisted, crooked, crippled, warped, maimed, marred, mangled, disfigured, misshapen, malformed, misbegotten • *He was born with a deformed right leg.*

deformity 1 = **abnormality**, defect, malformation, disfigurement • *facial deformities in babies*
2 = **distortion**, irregularity, misshapenness, misproportion • *Bones grind against each other, leading to pain and deformity.*

defraud = **cheat**, rob, con *(informal)*, do *(slang)*, skin *(slang)*, stiff *(slang)*, sting *(informal)*, rip off *(slang)*, fleece, swindle, stitch up *(slang)*, rook *(slang)*, diddle *(informal)*, bilk, gyp *(slang)*, pull a fast one on *(informal)*, cozen, scam *(slang)* • *He pleaded guilty to conspiracy to defraud the government.*

defray = **pay**, meet, cover, clear, settle, discharge • *The government has committed billions toward defraying the costs of the war.*

defrost = **thaw**, warm, soften, de-ice, unfreeze • *She uses the microwave mainly for defrosting bread.*
OPPOSITES: freeze (up), frost, ice over *or* up

deft = **skilful**, able, expert, clever, neat, handy, adept, nimble, proficient, agile, adroit, dexterous • *Her movements were neat and deft.*
OPPOSITES: awkward, clumsy, inept

deftness = **skill**, ability, facility, expertise, competence, coordination, finesse, agility, proficiency, dexterity, cleverness, neatness, nimbleness, adroitness, adeptness • *a player who combines deftness of touch with superb technique*
OPPOSITES: incompetence, ineptitude, clumsiness

defunct 1 = **dead**, extinct, gone, departed, expired, deceased, bygone, nonexistent • *the leader of the now defunct Social Democratic Party*
2 = **not functioning**, obsolete, out of commission, inoperative • *He looked at the defunct apparatus and diagnosed the problem.*

defuse 1 = **calm**, settle, cool, contain, smooth, stabilize, damp down, take the heat *or* sting out of • *Officials will hold talks aimed at defusing tensions over trade.*
OPPOSITES: intensify, worsen, aggravate
2 = **deactivate**, disable, disarm, make safe • *Police have defused a bomb.*
OPPOSITES: arm, activate

defy 1 = **resist**, oppose, confront, face, brave, beard, disregard, stand up to, spurn, flout, disobey, hold out against, put up a fight (against), hurl defiance at, contemn • *This was the first time that I had dared to defy her.*
2 = **challenge**, dare, provoke, throw down the gauntlet • *He defied me to come up with a better idea.*
3 = **foil**, defeat, escape, frustrate, be beyond, baffle, thwart, elude, confound • *a fragrance that defies description*

degeneracy = **worsening**, decline, corruption, decrease, decay, deterioration, degradation, decadence, depravity, immorality, debasement, turpitude, depravation, dissoluteness • *the moral degeneracy of society*

degenerate AS A VERB = **decline**, slip, sink, decrease, deteriorate, worsen, rot, decay, lapse, fall off, regress, go to pot, retrogress • *He degenerated into drug and alcohol abuse.*
▸ AS AN ADJECTIVE = **depraved**, base, corrupt, fallen, low, perverted, degraded, degenerated, immoral, decadent, debased, debauched, dissolute, pervy *(slang)* • *the degenerate attitudes he found among some of his fellow officers*
▸ AS A NOUN = **pervert**, deviant, profligate, libertine, reprobate, debauchee • *a degenerate who died from his perverted excesses*

degeneration = **deterioration**, decline, dissolution, descent, regression, dissipation, degeneracy, debasement • *the degeneration of our political system*

degradation 1 = **disgrace**, shame, humiliation, discredit, ignominy, dishonour, mortification • *scenes of misery and degradation*
2 = **deterioration**, decline, decadence, degeneration, perversion, degeneracy, debasement, abasement • *the progressive degradation of the state*
3 = **decay**, deterioration, degeneration, atrophy, wasting away • *land degradation in arid zones*

degrade 1 = **demean**, disgrace, humiliate, injure, shame, corrupt, humble, discredit, pervert, debase, dishonour, cheapen • *Pornography degrades women.*
OPPOSITES: honour, enhance, ennoble
2 = **damage**, injure, harm, mar, undermine, weaken, spoil, impair • *the ability to meet human needs without degrading the environment*
3 = **break down**, decay, degenerate, atrophy • *This substance degrades rapidly in the soil.*
4 = **demote**, reduce, lower, downgrade, depose, cashier, unseat • *He was degraded to a lower rank.*
OPPOSITES: raise, promote, elevate

degraded 1 = **humiliated**, embarrassed, shamed, mortified, debased, discomfited, abased • *I felt cheap and degraded by his actions.*

2 = corrupt, low, base, abandoned, vicious, vile, sordid, decadent, despicable, depraved, debased, profligate, disreputable, debauched, dissolute, scungy *(Austral. & N.Z.)* • *morally degraded individuals*

degrading = demeaning, lowering, humiliating, disgraceful, shameful, unworthy, debasing, undignified, contemptible, cheapening, dishonourable, infra dig *(informal)* • *a degrading experience*

degree AS A NOUN **1 = amount**, measure, rate, level, stage, extent, grade, proportion, gradation • *They achieved varying degrees of success.*
2 = rank, order, standing, level, class, position, station, status, grade, caste, nobility, echelon • *the fall of a man of high degree and noble character*
▸ IN PHRASES: **by degrees = little by little**, slowly, gradually, moderately, gently, piecemeal, bit by bit, imperceptibly, inch by inch, unhurriedly • *The crowd was thinning, but only by degrees.*
give someone the third degree = interrogate, question, examine, ask, pump, grill *(informal)*, quiz, cross-examine, cross-question • *He gave me the third degree on my relationship with you.*
to a degree *or* **to some degree = to some extent**, to a certain extent, up to a point • *These statements are, to some degree, all correct.*
▹ *See panel* Academic degrees

dehydrate = dry, evaporate, parch, desiccate, exsiccate • *The fruits are dehydrated to preserve them.*

deification 1 = worship, adoration, apotheosis, exaltation, glorification • *This book challenges the deification of Christ.*
2 = veneration, hero-worship, glorification, adulation, idolization, elevation, exaltation • *the deification of rock stars*

deify 1 = worship, adore, revere, respect, honour, glorify, exalt, pray to, venerate, adulate, apotheosize • *Apollo's son Asclepius was deified as the god of medicine.*
2 = idolize, elevate, glorify, exalt, extol, idealize, venerate, enthrone, immortalize • *Stalin was to some extent deified during his lifetime.*

deign = condescend, consent, stoop, see fit, think fit, lower yourself, deem it worthy • *He didn't deign to reply.*

deity = god, goddess, immortal, divinity, godhead, divine being, supreme being, celestial being, atua *(N.Z.)* • *an omnipotent, benevolent and omniscient deity*

dejected = downhearted, down, low, blue, sad, depressed, miserable, gloomy, dismal, melancholy, glum, despondent, downcast, morose, disheartened, wretched, disconsolate, crestfallen, doleful, down in the dumps *(informal)*, cast down, sick as a parrot *(informal)*, woebegone, low-spirited • *Everyone has days when they feel dejected or down.*
OPPOSITES: happy, encouraged, cheerful

dejection = low spirits, depression, gloom, blues, dumps *(informal)*, despair, sadness, sorrow, melancholy, unhappiness, doldrums, despondency, the hump *(Brit. informal)*, gloominess, heavy-heartedness, downheartedness • *There was a slight air of dejection about her.*

de jure = legally, by right, rightfully, according to the law • *politicians and kings, de jure leaders of men*
OPPOSITES: de facto

delay AS A VERB **1 = put off**, suspend, postpone, stall, shelve, prolong, defer, hold over, temporize, put on the back burner *(informal)*, protract, take a rain check on *(U.S. & Canad. informal)* • *I delayed my departure until she could join me.*
2 = hold up, detain, hold back, stop, arrest, halt, hinder, obstruct, retard, impede, bog down, set back, slow up • *The passengers were delayed by bad weather.*
OPPOSITES: speed (up), advance, promote
3 = linger, lag, loiter, dawdle, tarry, dilly-dally *(informal)*, drag your feet *or* heels *(informal)* • *If he delayed any longer, the sun would be up.*
▸ AS A NOUN **1 = hold-up**, wait, check, setback, interruption, obstruction, stoppage, impediment, hindrance • *Air restrictions might mean delays for Easter holidaymakers.*
2 = dawdling, lingering, loitering, procrastination, tarrying, dilly-dallying *(informal)* • *We'll send you a quote without delay.*
3 = postponement, suspension, putting off, adjournment, stay, deferment, deferral • *A delay of the federal trial was granted.*

delaying = hindering, obstructive, halting, procrastinating, retardant, temporizing, cunctative *(rare)*, moratory • *Delaying tactics were used to postpone the report.*

delectable 1 = delicious, tasty, luscious, inviting, satisfying, pleasant, delightful, enjoyable, lush, enticing, gratifying, dainty, yummy *(slang)*, scrumptious *(informal)*, appetizing, toothsome, lekker *(S. African slang)*, yummo *(Austral. slang)* • *a delectable dessert*
OPPOSITES: disgusting, terrible, awful
2 = charming, pleasant, delightful, agreeable, adorable • *a delectable young woman in a swimsuit*

delectation = enjoyment, delight, pleasure, entertainment, satisfaction, happiness, relish, amusement, diversion, refreshment, gratification • *She cooks pastries and cakes for the delectation of visitors.*

delegate AS A NOUN **= representative**, agent, deputy, ambassador, commissioner, envoy, proxy, depute *(Scot.)*, legate, spokesman *or* spokeswoman • *The rebels' chief delegate repeated their demands.*
▸ AS A VERB **1 = entrust**, transfer, hand over, give, pass on,

ACADEMIC DEGREES

Degree	Abbreviation	Degree	Abbreviation	Degree	Abbreviation
Bachelor of Agriculture	BAgr	Bachelor of Philosophy	BPhil	Higher National Certificate	HNC
Bachelor of Arts	BA	Bachelor of Science	BSc	Higher National Diploma	HND
Bachelor of Commerce	BCom	Bachelor of Surgery	BS	Master of Arts	MA
Bachelor of Dental Surgery	BDS	Diploma in Education	DipEd	Master of Education	MEd
Bachelor of Divinity	BD	Doctor of Dental Surgery or Science	DDS *or* DDSc	Master of Laws	LLM
Bachelor of Education	BEd			Master of Letters	MLitt
Bachelor of Engineering	BEng	Doctor of Divinity	DD	Master of Music	MMus
Bachelor of Law	BL	Doctor of Laws	LLD	Master of Philosophy	MPhil
Bachelor of Laws	LLB	Doctor of Letters or Literature	DLitt *or* LittD	Master of Science	MSc
Bachelor of Letters	BLitt			Master of Surgery	MCh
Bachelor of Medicine	BM *or* MB	Doctor of Medicine	MD	Master of Technology	MTech
Bachelor of Music	BMus, MusB, *or* MusBac	Doctor of Music	DMus, MusD, *or* MusDoc	Ordinary National Certificate	ONC
				Ordinary National Diploma	OND
Bachelor of Pharmacy	BPharm	Doctor of Philosophy	PhD		

assign, relegate, consign, devolve • *Many employers find it hard to delegate duties.*
2 = appoint, commission, select, contract, engage, nominate, designate, mandate, authorize, empower, accredit, depute • *Officials have been delegated to start work on a settlement.*

delegation 1 = deputation, envoys, contingent, commission, embassy, legation • *They sent a delegation to the talks.*
2 = commissioning, relegation, assignment, devolution, committal, deputizing, entrustment • *the delegation of his responsibilities to his assistant*

d

delete = remove, cancel, cut out, erase, edit, excise, strike out, obliterate, efface, blot out, cross out, expunge, dele, rub out, edit out, blue-pencil • *He deleted files from the computer system.*

deleterious = harmful, bad, damaging, destructive, detrimental, hurtful, pernicious, ruinous, prejudicial, injurious • *Fear of crime is having a deleterious effect on society.*

deliberate AS AN ADJECTIVE 1 = intentional, meant, planned, considered, studied, designed, intended, conscious, calculated, thoughtful, wilful, purposeful, premeditated, prearranged, done on purpose • *The attack was deliberate and unprovoked.*
OPPOSITES: unconscious, accidental, unintended
2 = careful, measured, slow, cautious, wary, thoughtful, prudent, circumspect, methodical, unhurried, heedful • *His movements were gentle and deliberate.*
OPPOSITES: fast, hurried, rash
▸ **AS A VERB = consider**, think, ponder, discuss, debate, reflect, consult, weigh, meditate, mull over, ruminate, cogitate • *The jury deliberated for two hours before returning with the verdict.*

deliberately 1 = intentionally, on purpose, consciously, emphatically, knowingly, resolutely, pointedly, determinedly, wilfully, by design, studiously, in cold blood, wittingly, calculatingly • *The fire was started deliberately.*
2 = carefully, slowly, cautiously, thoughtfully, warily, methodically, prudently, unhurriedly, circumspectly, heedfully • *They have acted calmly and deliberately.*

deliberation 1 = consideration, thought, reflection, study, speculation, calculation, meditation, forethought, circumspection, cogitation • *His decision was the result of great deliberation.*
2 *usually plural* **= discussion**, talk, conference, exchange, debate, analysis, conversation, dialogue, consultation, seminar, symposium, colloquy, confabulation • *The outcome of the deliberations was inconclusive.*

QUOTATIONS
deliberation: the act of examining your bread to determine which side it is buttered on
[Ambrose Bierce *The Devil's Dictionary*]

delicacy 1 = fragility, frailty, brittleness, flimsiness, frailness, frangibility • *the delicacy of the crystal glasses*
2 = daintiness, charm, grace, elegance, neatness, prettiness, slenderness, exquisiteness • *a country where the feminine ideal is delicacy and grace*
3 = difficulty, sensitivity, stickiness *(informal)*, precariousness, critical nature, touchiness, ticklishness • *the delicacy of the political situation*
4 = sensitivity, understanding, consideration, judgment, perception, diplomacy, discretion, skill, finesse, tact, thoughtfulness, savoir-faire, adroitness, sensitiveness • *He's shown considerable delicacy and tact.*
5 = treat, luxury, goody, savoury, dainty, morsel, titbit, choice item, juicy bit, bonne bouche *(French)* • *course after course of mouthwatering delicacies*
6 = lightness, accuracy, precision, elegance, sensibility, purity, subtlety, refinement, finesse, nicety, fineness, exquisiteness • *He played with a superb delicacy of touch.*

delicate 1 = fine, detailed, elegant, exquisite, graceful • *china with a delicate design*
2 = subtle, fine, nice, soft, delicious, faint, refined, muted, subdued, pastel, understated, dainty • *The colours are delicate and tasteful.*
OPPOSITES: strong, bright, rough
3 = fragile, weak, frail, brittle, tender, flimsy, dainty, breakable, frangible • *Although the material looks tough, it is very delicate.*
4 = sickly, weak, ailing, frail, feeble, unhealthy, debilitated, lacklustre, infirm, in poor health, indisposed • *She was physically delicate and psychologically unstable.*
OPPOSITES: strong, healthy
5 = difficult, critical, sensitive, complicated, sticky *(informal)*, problematic, precarious, thorny, touchy, knotty, ticklish • *the delicate issue of adoption*
6 = skilled, accurate, precise, deft • *A cosmetic surgeon performed the delicate operation.*
7 = fastidious, nice, critical, pure, Victorian, proper, refined, discriminating, stuffy, scrupulous, prim, puritanical, squeamish, prudish, prissy *(informal)*, strait-laced, schoolmarmish *(Brit. informal)*, old-maidish *(informal)* • *He didn't want to offend his mother's delicate sensibilities.*
OPPOSITES: rough, crude
8 = diplomatic, sensitive, careful, subtle, thoughtful, discreet, prudent, considerate, judicious, tactful • *a situation which requires delicate handling*
OPPOSITES: rough, harsh, insensitive

delicately 1 = finely, lightly, subtly, softly, carefully, precisely, elegantly, gracefully, deftly, exquisitely, skilfully, daintily • *soup delicately flavoured with nutmeg*
2 = tactfully, carefully, subtly, discreetly, thoughtfully, diplomatically, sensitively, prudently, judiciously, considerately • *a delicately-worded memo*

delicious 1 = delectable, tasty, luscious, choice, savoury, palatable, dainty, mouthwatering, yummy *(slang)*, scrumptious *(informal)*, appetizing, toothsome, ambrosial, lekker *(S. African slang)*, nectareous, yummo *(Austral. slang)* • *a wide selection of delicious meals to choose from*
OPPOSITES: unpleasant, distasteful, disagreeable
2 = delightful, pleasing, charming, heavenly, thrilling, entertaining, pleasant, enjoyable, exquisite, captivating, agreeable, pleasurable, rapturous, delectable • *a delicious feeling of anticipation*
OPPOSITES: unpleasant, distasteful, disagreeable

delight AS A VERB = please, satisfy, content, thrill, charm, cheer, amuse, divert, enchant, rejoice, gratify, ravish, gladden, give pleasure to, tickle pink *(informal)* • *The report has delighted environmentalists.*
OPPOSITES: displease, upset, disgust
▸ **IN PHRASES: delight in** *or* **take a delight in something** *or* **someone = like**, love, enjoy, appreciate, relish, indulge in, savour, revel in, take pleasure in, glory in, luxuriate in • *He delighted in sharing his news.*
▸ **AS A NOUN = pleasure**, joy, satisfaction, comfort, happiness, ecstasy, enjoyment, bliss, felicity, glee, gratification, rapture, gladness • *To my delight, the plan worked perfectly.*
OPPOSITES: dissatisfaction, distaste, displeasure

delighted = pleased, happy, charmed, thrilled, enchanted, ecstatic, captivated, jubilant, joyous, elated, over the moon *(informal)*, overjoyed, rapt, gladdened, cock-a-hoop, blissed out, in seventh heaven, sent, stoked *(Austral. & N.Z. informal)* • *He was delighted with the public response.*

delightful = pleasant, pleasing, charming, engaging, heavenly, thrilling, fascinating, entertaining, amusing, enjoyable, enchanting, captivating, gratifying, agreeable, pleasurable, ravishing, rapturous • *The most delightful garden I had ever seen.*
OPPOSITES: nasty, unpleasant, distasteful

delimit = **define**, mark (out), determine, fix, bound, demarcate • *This is not meant to delimit what approaches social researchers can adopt.*

delineate 1 = **outline**, describe, draw, picture, paint, chart, trace, portray, sketch, render, depict, characterize, map out • *The relationship between Church and State was delineated in a formal agreement.*
2 = **determine**, define, chart, map out • *a settlement to delineate the border*

delineation 1 = **outline**, description, account, drawing, picture, chart, tracing, portrait, representation, diagram, portrayal, depiction • *His razor-sharp delineation of ordinary life.*
2 = **determination**, determining, defining, charting, mapping out • *the delineation of the provincial borders*

delinquency = **crime**, misconduct, wrongdoing, fault, offence, misdemeanour, misdeed, misbehaviour, villainy, lawbreaking • *He had no history of delinquency.*

delinquent AS AN ADJECTIVE 1 = **unruly**, wild, rebellious, anarchic, riotous, insubordinate • *remand homes for delinquent children*
2 = **negligent**, slack, indifferent, careless, thoughtless, neglectful, heedless, inattentive, remiss • *delinquent parents who let their children run wild*
▸ AS A NOUN = **criminal**, offender, villain, culprit, young offender, wrongdoer, juvenile delinquent, miscreant, malefactor, lawbreaker • *a nine-year-old delinquent*

delirious 1 = **mad**, crazy, raving, insane, demented, deranged, incoherent, unhinged, light-headed • *I was delirious and blacked out several times.*
OPPOSITES: calm, sensible, rational
2 = **ecstatic**, wild, excited, frantic, frenzied, hysterical, carried away, blissed out, beside yourself, sent, Corybantic • *He was delirious with joy.*
OPPOSITES: calm, controlled, level-headed

delirium 1 = **madness**, raving, insanity, lunacy, derangement • *In her delirium, she fell to the floor.*
2 = **frenzy**, passion, rage, fever, fury, ecstasy, hysteria • *She was in a delirium of panic.*

deliver 1 = **bring**, take, carry, bear, transport, distribute, convey, cart • *The pizza will be delivered in 20 minutes.*
2 = **fulfil**, provide, give, produce, supply, carry out, discharge, impart • *Don't promise what you can't deliver.*
3 *sometimes with* **over** *or* **up** = **hand over**, present, commit, give up, yield, surrender, turn over, relinquish, make over • *He was led in handcuffs and delivered over to me.*
4 = **give**, read, present, announce, publish, declare, proclaim, pronounce, utter, give forth • *He will deliver a speech about schools.*
5 = **strike**, give, deal, launch, throw, direct, aim, administer, inflict • *A single blow had been delivered to the head.*
6 = **release**, free, save, rescue, loose, discharge, liberate, acquit, redeem, ransom, emancipate • *I thank God for delivering me from that pain.*
7 = **throw**, send, launch, direct, aim, cast, pitch, toss • *Our bowler steamed in to deliver the first ball of the match.*

deliverance = **release**, rescue, liberation, salvation, redemption, ransom, emancipation • *their sudden deliverance from war*

delivery 1 = **handing over**, transfer, distribution, transmission, dispatch, consignment, conveyance, transmittal • *the delivery of goods and resources*
2 = **consignment**, goods, shipment, batch • *a delivery of fresh eggs*
3 = **speech**, speaking, expression, pronunciation, utterance, articulation, intonation, diction, elocution, enunciation, vocalization • *His speeches were magnificent but his delivery was hopeless.*
4 = **childbirth**, labour, confinement, parturition • *She had an easy delivery.*
5 = **throw**, pitch, cast, toss, projection, lob *(informal)* • *a delivery from fast bowler Jason Gillespie*

delude = **deceive**, kid *(informal)*, fool, trick, take in *(informal)*, cheat, con *(informal)*, mislead, impose on, hoax, dupe, beguile, gull *(archaic)*, bamboozle *(informal)*, hoodwink, take for a ride *(informal)*, pull the wool over someone's eyes, lead up the garden path *(informal)*, cozen, misguide, scam *(slang)* • *We delude ourselves that we are in control.*

deluge AS A NOUN 1 = **rush**, flood, avalanche, barrage, spate, torrent • *a deluge of criticism*
2 = **flood**, spate, overflowing, torrent, downpour, cataclysm, inundation • *A dozen homes were damaged in the deluge.*
▸ AS A VERB 1 = **overwhelm**, swamp, engulf, overload, overrun, inundate • *The office was deluged with complaints.*
2 = **flood**, drown, swamp, submerge, soak, drench, inundate, douse • *Torrential rain deluged the capital.*

delusion = **misconception**, mistaken idea, misapprehension, fancy, illusion, deception, hallucination, fallacy, self-deception, false impression, phantasm, misbelief • *I was under the delusion that he intended to marry me.*

deluxe *or* **de luxe** = **luxurious**, grand, select, special, expensive, rich, exclusive, superior, elegant, costly, splendid, gorgeous, sumptuous, plush *(informal)*, opulent, palatial, splendiferous *(facetious)* • *a de luxe hotel in the Victorian Grand style*

delve 1 = **research**, investigate, explore, examine, probe, look into, burrow into, dig into • *She delved into her mother's past.*
2 = **rummage**, search, look, burrow, ransack, forage, dig, fossick *(Austral. & N.Z.)* • *He delved into his rucksack and pulled out a folder.*

demagogue = **agitator**, firebrand, haranguer, rabble-rouser, soapbox orator • *He was dismissed as a radical demagogue.*

demand AS A VERB 1 = **request**, ask (for), order, expect, claim, seek, call for, insist on, exact, appeal for, solicit • *She demanded an immediate apology.*
2 = **challenge**, ask, question, inquire • *'What do you expect me to do about it?' she demanded.*
3 = **require**, take, want, need, involve, call for, entail, necessitate, cry out for • *The task demands much patience and hard work.*
OPPOSITES: give, provide, produce
▸ AS A NOUN 1 = **request**, order, charge, bidding • *He grew ever more fierce in his demands.*
2 = **need**, want, call, market, claim, requirement, necessity • *The demand for coal is down.*
▸ IN PHRASES: **in demand** = **sought after**, needed, popular, favoured, requested, in favour, fashionable, well-liked, in vogue, like gold dust • *He was much in demand as a lecturer.*

demanding 1 = **difficult**, trying, hard, taxing, wearing, challenging, tough, exhausting, exacting, exigent • *It is a demanding job.*
OPPOSITES: easy, simple, straightforward
2 = **trying**, difficult, troublesome, tiresome, imperious, fractious, unmanageable, clamorous, importunate, exigent, high-maintenance • *a very demanding child*

demarcate = **delimit**, mark, separate, determine, fix, define, differentiate, distinguish between • *The police demarcated the city into eighteen geographical divisions.*

demarcation 1 = **limit**, bound, margin, boundary, confine, enclosure, pale • *The demarcation of the border between the two countries.*
2 = **delimitation**, division, distinction, separation, differentiation • *The demarcation of duties became more blurred.*

demean AS A VERB = **degrade**, lower, debase, humble, abase • *Pornography demeans women.*
▸ IN PHRASES: **demean yourself** = **lower yourself**,

humiliate yourself, humble yourself, debase yourself, downgrade yourself, abase yourself, belittle yourself, degrade yourself • *I wasn't going to demean myself by answering him.*

demeaning = **humiliating**, degrading, disgraceful, shameful, unworthy, debasing, undignified, contemptible, cheapening, dishonourable, infra dig *(informal)* • *She was given the most demeaning chores to do.*

demeanour *or (U.S.)* **demeanor** 1 = **behaviour**, conduct, manner • *her calm and cheerful demeanour*
2 = **bearing**, air, manner, carriage, deportment, mien, comportment • *He was nicknamed "the Sergeant Major" for his military demeanour.*

d

demented = **mad**, crazy, foolish, daft *(informal)*, frenzied, distraught, manic, insane, crazed, lunatic, unbalanced, deranged, idiotic, unhinged, dotty *(slang, chiefly Brit.)*, loopy *(informal)*, crackpot *(informal)*, out to lunch *(informal)*, barking mad *(slang)*, barking *(slang)*, maniacal, gonzo *(slang)*, doolally *(slang)*, off your trolley *(slang)*, up the pole *(informal)*, non compos mentis *(Latin)*, not the full shilling *(informal)*, crackbrained, wacko *or* whacko *(slang)*, off the air *(Austral. slang)*, porangi *(N.Z.)* • *Her warnings were dismissed as the ramblings of a demented old woman.*
OPPOSITES: sane, sound, normal

demise 1 = **failure**, end, fall, defeat, collapse, ruin, foundering, breakdown, overthrow, downfall, disintegration, dissolution, termination • *the demise of the reform movement*
2 = **death**, end, dying, passing, departure, expiration, decease • *Smoking was the cause of his early demise.*

demobilize 1 = **discharge**, release, disband, decommission, demob *(Brit. informal)*, deactivate • *demands that they sign a cease-fire and demobilize their troops*
OPPOSITES: draft *(U.S.)*, recruit, call up
2 = **disband**, separate, break up, scatter, disperse, part company, demob *(Brit. informal)*, go (their) separate ways • *It is unlikely that the rebel bands will demobilize.*

democracy = **self-government**, republic, commonwealth, autonomy, representative government, constitutional government, government by the people, elective government • *the spread of democracy in Eastern Europe*

QUOTATIONS

To give victory to the right, not bloody bullets, but peaceful ballots only, are necessary
[Abraham Lincoln *speech*]

My notion of democracy is that under it the weakest should have the same opportunity as the strongest
[Gandhi *Non-Violence in Peace and War*]

Democracy ... is a charming form of government, full of variety and disorder, and dispensing a sort of equality to equals and unequals alike
[Plato *The Republic*]

Democracy is the superior form of government, because it is based on a respect for man as a reasonable being
[John F. Kennedy *Why England Slept*]

Democracy means government by discussion, but it is only effective if you can stop people talking
[Clement Atlee *Anatomy of Britain*]

Democracy is the worst form of Government except all those other forms that have been tried from time to time
[Winston Churchill *speech*]

Democracy is the name we give the people whenever we need them
[Robert, Marquis de Flers and Arman de Caillavet *L'habit vert*]

Democracy substitutes election by the incompetent many for appointment by the corrupt few
[George Bernard Shaw *Man and Superman*]

government of the people, by the people, and for the people
[Abraham Lincoln *Gettysburg Address*]

Democratic nations care but little for what has been, but they are haunted by visions of what will be
[Alexis de Tocqueville *Democracy in America*]

Two Cheers for Democracy: one because it admits variety and two because it permits criticism. Two cheers are quite enough: there is no occasion to give three
[E.M. Forster *Two Cheers for Democracy*]

Democrat ▸ **AS A NOUN** = **left-winger** • *The director of the company has links to the Democrats.*
▸ **AS AN ADJECTIVE** = **left-wing**, Labour • *Al Gore, the Democrat candidate*

democratic = **self-governing**, popular, republican, representative, elected, autonomous, populist, egalitarian • *Bolivia returned to democratic rule in 1982.*

demolish 1 = **knock down**, level, destroy, ruin, overthrow, dismantle, flatten, trash *(slang)*, total *(slang)*, tear down, bulldoze, raze, pulverize • *The building is being demolished to make way for a motorway.*
OPPOSITES: build, create, restore
2 = **destroy**, ruin, wreck, smash, overturn, overthrow, undo, discredit, blow out of the water *(slang)* • *Their intention was to demolish his reputation.*
3 = **defeat**, hammer, tank *(slang)*, massacre, lick *(informal)*, rout, annihilate, wipe the floor with *(informal)*, stuff *(slang)*, run rings round, make mincemeat of • *They demolished the other team 6-0.*
4 = **devour**, eat, consume, swallow, bolt, hoover *(informal)*, gorge, put away, gobble up, guzzle, polish off *(informal)*, gulp down, wolf down, pig out on *(slang)* • *We demolished a six-pack of beer.*

demolition 1 = **knocking down**, levelling, destruction, explosion, wrecking, tearing down, bulldozing, razing • *the total demolition of the old bridge*
2 = **defeat**, beating, overthrow, pasting *(slang)*, conquest, rout, trouncing, vanquishment • *their impressive 6-1 demolition of their rivals*

demon 1 = **evil spirit**, devil, fiend, goblin, ghoul, malignant spirit, atua *(N.Z.)*, wairua *(N.Z.)* • *a woman possessed by evil demons*
2 = **wizard**, master, ace *(informal)*, addict, fanatic, fiend • *He is a demon for discipline.*
3 = **monster**, beast, villain, rogue, barbarian, brute, ogre • *He was a dictator and a demon.*
▸ **RELATED PHOBIA:** demonophobia

demoniac *or* **demonic** *or* **demoniacal** 1 = **devilish**, satanic, diabolical, hellish, infernal, fiendish, diabolic • *demonic forces*
2 = **frenzied**, mad, furious, frantic, hectic, manic, crazed, frenetic, maniacal, like one possessed • *a demonic drive to succeed*

demonstrable = **provable**, obvious, evident, certain, positive, unmistakable, palpable, undeniable, self-evident, verifiable, irrefutable, incontrovertible, axiomatic, indubitable, attestable, evincible • *There is a genuine demonstrable need for change.*

demonstrate 1 = **prove**, show, establish, indicate, make clear, manifest, evidence, testify to, evince, show clearly, flag up • *You have to demonstrate that you are reliable.*
2 = **show**, evidence, express, display, indicate, exhibit, manifest, make clear *or* plain, flag up • *Have they demonstrated a commitment to democracy?*
3 = **march**, protest, rally, object, parade, picket, say no to, remonstrate, take up the cudgels, express disapproval, hikoi *(N.Z.)* • *Vast crowds have been demonstrating against the reforms.*
4 = **describe**, show, explain, teach, illustrate, give a demonstration of • *He demonstrated how to peel and chop garlic.*

demonstration 1 = **march**, protest, rally, sit-in, parade, procession, demo *(informal)*, picket, mass lobby, hikoi *(N.Z.)* • *Riot police broke up the demonstration.*

2 = **display**, show, performance, explanation, description, presentation, demo *(informal)*, exposition • *a cookery demonstration*
3 = **indication**, proof, testimony, confirmation, manifestation, affirmation, validation, substantiation, attestation • *an unprecedented demonstration of people power*
4 = **exhibition**, display, showing, expression, illustration • *physical demonstrations of affection*

demonstrative 1 = **open**, loving, emotional, affectionate, expressive, gushing, expansive, unrestrained, effusive, unreserved • *He was not normally demonstrative but he gave her a hug.*
OPPOSITES: reserved, contained, cold
2 = **indicative**, symptomatic, illustrative, expository, evincive • *His latest paintings were demonstrative of his technical ability.*
3 = **convincing**, powerful, impressive, credible, plausible, persuasive, conclusive, cogent, incontrovertible • *a demonstrative argument for euthanasia*

demonstrator = **protester**, rebel, dissident, dissenter, agitator, protest marcher • *Police tried to break up a crowd of demonstrators.*

demoralize = **dishearten**, undermine, discourage, shake, depress, weaken, rattle *(informal)*, daunt, unnerve, disconcert, psych out *(informal)*, disempower, dispirit, deject • *One of the objectives is to demoralize enemy troops.*
OPPOSITES: encourage, boost, cheer

demoralized = **disheartened**, undermined, discouraged, broken, depressed, crushed, weakened, subdued, unnerved, unmanned, dispirited, downcast, sick as a parrot *(informal)* • *the legitimate grievances of a demoralized workforce*

demoralizing = **disheartening**, discouraging, depressing, crushing, disappointing, daunting, dampening, dispiriting • *Persistent disapproval or criticism can be highly demoralizing.*
OPPOSITES: encouraging, comforting, cheering

demote = **downgrade**, relegate, degrade, kick downstairs *(slang)*, declass, disrate *(Naval)*, lower in rank • *If managers prove inefficient they should be demoted.*
OPPOSITES: raise, advance, promote

demotic 1 = **colloquial**, familiar, informal, everyday, vernacular, conversational, idiomatic • *his command of demotic American speech*
2 = **common**, ordinary, working-class, humble, vulgar, grass-roots, lower-class, proletarian, common or garden, plebeian, lowbrow, lowborn, blue-singlet *(Austral. slang)* • *a populist, demotic politician*
OPPOSITES: elite, noble

demur AS A VERB = **object**, refuse, protest, doubt, dispute, pause, disagree, hesitate, waver, balk, take exception, cavil • *At first I demurred when he asked me to do it.*
▸ AS A NOUN = **objection**, protest, dissent, hesitation, misgiving, qualm, scruple, compunction, demurral, demurrer • *She entered without demur.*

demure 1 = **shy**, reserved, modest, retiring, reticent, unassuming, diffident, decorous • *She's very demure and sweet.*
OPPOSITES: forward, brash, brazen
2 = **coy**, prim, bashful, prudish, prissy *(informal)*, strait-laced, affected, priggish, niminy-piminy • *a demure frumpy middle-aged librarian*

den 1 = **lair**, hole, shelter, tunnel, lodge, cave, haunt, burrow, cavern, hide-out • *The skunk makes its den in burrows and hollow logs.*
2 = **study**, retreat, sanctuary, hideaway, cloister, snug, sanctum, cubbyhole, snuggery • *The walls of his den were covered in posters.*
3 = **haunt**, resort, rendezvous, meeting place, hangout *(informal)*, stamping ground, gathering place • *three illegal drinking dens*

denial 1 = **negation**, dismissal, contradiction, dissent, disclaimer, retraction, repudiation, disavowal, adjuration • *their previous denial that chemical weapons were being used*
OPPOSITES: admission, declaration, profession
2 = **refusal**, veto, rejection, prohibition, rebuff, repulse • *the denial of visas to international workers*
3 = **renunciation**, giving up, rejection, spurning, abstention, abdication, repudiation, forswearing, disavowal, abnegation, relinquishment, eschewal • *This religion teaches denial of the flesh.*

denigrate = **disparage**, run down, slag (off) *(slang)*, knock *(informal)*, rubbish *(informal)*, blacken, malign, belittle, decry, revile, vilify, slander, defame, bad-mouth *(slang, chiefly U.S. & Canad.)*, besmirch, impugn, calumniate, asperse • *She habitually denigrated her husband to other people.*
OPPOSITES: approve, honour, praise

denigration = **disparagement**, defamation, belittling, vilification, besmirching, obloquy, aspersion, detraction • *the denigration of minorities in this country*

denizen = **inhabitant**, resident, citizen, occupant, dweller • *The denizens of New York are used to street violence.*

denomination 1 = **religious group**, belief, sect, persuasion, creed, school, hauhau *(N.Z.)* • *Acceptance of women preachers varies from one denomination to another.*
2 = **unit**, value, size, grade • *a pile of bank notes, mostly in small denominations*

denote 1 = **indicate**, show, mean, mark, express, import, imply, designate, signify, typify, betoken • *Red eyes denote strain and fatigue.*
2 = **represent**, mean, stand for, express, equal, substitute for, correspond to, symbolize, equate with, betoken • *In the table, 'DT' denotes quantity demanded.*
3 = **refer to**, mean, signify, suggest, imply, connote • *In the Middle Ages the term 'drap' denoted a type of woollen cloth.*

denouement or **dénouement** 1 = **climax**, conclusion, finale, termination, culmination • *the book's sentimental denouement*
2 = **outcome**, end, result, consequence, resolution, conclusion, end result, upshot • *an unexpected denouement to the affair*

denounce 1 = **condemn**, attack, censure, decry, castigate, revile, vilify, proscribe, stigmatize, impugn, excoriate, declaim against • *The leaders took the opportunity to denounce the attacks.*
2 = **report**, expose, betray, accuse, implicate, inform on, inculpate, dob in *(Austral. slang)* • *Informers might at any moment denounce them to the authorities.*

dense 1 = **thick**, close, heavy, solid, substantial, compact, compressed, condensed, impenetrable, close-knit, thickset • *a large, dense forest*
OPPOSITES: light, thin, scattered
2 = **heavy**, thick, substantial, opaque, impenetrable, smoggy • *a dense column of smoke*
3 = **obscure**, deep, complex, profound, abstract, enigmatic, esoteric, incomprehensible, arcane, unfathomable, abstruse • *His prose is wordy and dense.*
4 = **stupid** *(Informal)*, slow, thick, dull, dumb *(informal)*, crass, dozy *(Brit. informal)*, stolid, dopey *(informal)*, moronic, obtuse, brainless, blockheaded, braindead *(informal)*, dumb-ass *(informal)*, dead from the neck up *(informal)*, thickheaded, blockish, dim-witted *(informal)*, slow-witted, thick-witted • *He's not a bad man, just a bit dense.*
OPPOSITES: quick, bright, alert

density 1 = **tightness**, closeness, thickness, compactness, impenetrability, denseness, crowdedness • *The region has a high population density.*
2 = **mass**, body, bulk, consistency, solidity • *Jupiter's moon Io has a density of 3.5 grams per cubic centimetre.*

dent AS A NOUN = **hollow**, chip, indentation, depression, impression, pit, dip, crater, ding (*Austral. & N.Z. dated informal*), dimple, concavity • *There was a dent in the bonnet of the car.*
▸ AS A VERB 1 = **make a dent in**, press in, gouge, depress, hollow, imprint, push in, dint, make concave • *The table's brass feet dented the carpet's thick pile.*
2 = **diminish**, reduce, lower, shake, undermine, erode, impair, sap, take the edge off, sap the strength of • *His constant criticisms dented my confidence.*

denude 1 = **strip**, expose, bare, uncover, divest, lay bare • *Many hillsides had been denuded of trees.*
2 = **deprive**, strip, rob, dispossess, divest, expropriate, despoil, bereave • *villages denuded of young people*

denunciation 1 = **condemnation**, criticism, accusation, censure, stick (*slang*), invective, character assassination, stigmatization, castigation, obloquy, denouncement, fulmination • *a stinging denunciation of his critics*
2 = **implication**, accusation, indictment, incrimination, denouncement, inculpation • *Denunciation by family, friends and colleagues inevitably sowed distrust.*

deny 1 = **contradict**, oppose, counter, disagree with, rebuff, negate, rebut, refute, gainsay (*archaic or literary*) • *She denied the accusations.*
OPPOSITES: agree, accept, admit
2 = **renounce**, reject, discard, revoke, retract, repudiate, renege, disown, rebut, disavow, recant, disclaim, abjure, abnegate, refuse to acknowledge *or* recognize • *I denied my parents because I wanted to become someone else.*
3 = **refuse**, decline, forbid, reject, rule out, veto, turn down, prohibit, withhold, preclude, disallow, negate, begrudge, interdict • *His ex-wife denies him access to his children.*
OPPOSITES: let, grant, permit

deodorant 1 = **antiperspirant**, deodorizer • *He took a can of deodorant and sprayed his armpits.*
2 = **deodorizer**, disinfectant, air freshener, fumigant

deodorize = **freshen**, refresh, purify, ventilate, disinfect, aerate, fumigate • *Use an air-freshener to deodorize the room.*

depart 1 = **leave**, go, withdraw, retire, disappear, quit, retreat, exit, go away, vanish, absent (yourself), start out, migrate, set forth, take (your) leave, decamp, hook it (*slang*), slope off, pack your bags (*informal*), make tracks, bog off (*Brit. slang*), rack off (*Austral. & N.Z. slang*) • *In the morning Mr McDonald departed for Sydney.*
OPPOSITES: remain, stay, arrive
2 = **deviate**, vary, differ, stray, veer, swerve, diverge, digress, turn aside • *It takes a brave cook to depart radically from the traditional menu.*
3 = **resign**, leave, quit, step down (*informal*), give in your notice, call it a day *or* night, vacate your post • *A number of staff departed during her reign as manager.*

departed = **dead**, late, deceased, expired, perished • *Departed friends can no longer be replaced at my age.*

department 1 = **section**, office, unit, station, division, branch, bureau, subdivision • *He worked in the sales department.*
2 = **area**, line, responsibility, function, province, sphere, realm, domain, speciality • *Sorry, I don't know – that's not my department.*
3 = **region**, area, division, sector, district, zone, province • *The plan to establish central German administrative departments.*

departure 1 = **leaving**, going, retirement, withdrawal, exit, going away, removal, exodus, leave-taking, setting out *or* off • *The airline has more than 90 scheduled departures from here each day.*
OPPOSITES: coming, return, arrival
2 = **retirement**, going, withdrawal, resignation, retreat, exit, going away, removal • *This would inevitably involve his departure from the post.*
3 = **shift**, change, difference, variation, innovation, novelty, veering, deviation, branching out, divergence, digression • *This album is a considerable departure from her previous work.*

dependable = **reliable**, sure, responsible, steady, faithful, staunch, reputable, trustworthy, trusty, unfailing • *He was a good friend and a dependable companion.*
OPPOSITES: unstable, irresponsible, undependable

dependant = **relative**, rellie (*Austral. slang*), child, minor, subordinate, cohort (*chiefly U.S.*), protégé, henchman, retainer, hanger-on, minion, vassal • *They raise funds to help ex-service personnel and their dependants.*

dependence *or* (*U.S. sometimes*) **dependance** 1 = **reliance**, trust, hope, confidence, belief, faith, expectation, assurance • *the city's traditional dependence on tourism*
2 = **overreliance**, need, addiction, reliance, attachment • *Some doctors regard drug dependence as a psychological disorder.*
3 = **helplessness**, weakness, vulnerability • *the total dependence of her infirm husband*

dependency *or* (*U.S. sometimes*) **dependancy** 1 = **province**, colony, outpost, dominion, protectorate • *a tiny European dependency*
2 = **overreliance**, need, attachment, reliance • *I am concerned by his dependency on his mother.*
3 = **addiction**, dependence, craving, need, habit, obsession, enslavement, overreliance • *He began to show signs of alcohol and drug dependency.*

dependent *or* (*U.S. sometimes*) **dependant** AS AN ADJECTIVE 1 = **reliant**, vulnerable, helpless, incapable, powerless, needy, weak, defenceless • *I refuse to be dependent, despite having a baby to care for.*
OPPOSITES: independent, self-reliant
2 = **determined by**, depending on, subject to, influenced by, relative to, liable to, conditional on, contingent on • *companies whose earnings are largely dependent on foreign economies*
3 = **addicted to**, hooked on (*informal*), over-reliant on • *people who are totally dependent on heroin*
▸ IN PHRASES: **dependent on** *or* **upon** = **reliant on**, relying on, supported by, counting on, leaning on, sustained by • *He was dependent on his parents for everything.*

depend on 1 = **be determined by**, be based on, be subject to, hang on, rest on, be influenced by, revolve around, hinge on, be decided by, be conditional on, be subordinate to, be contingent on • *What happened later would depend on his talk with her.*
2 = **count on**, turn to, trust in, bank on, be sure of, lean on, rely upon, confide in, build upon, calculate on, reckon on • *She assured him that he could depend on her.*

depict 1 = **illustrate**, portray, picture, paint, outline, draw, sketch, render, reproduce, sculpt, delineate, limn • *a gallery of pictures depicting famous battles*
2 = **describe**, present, represent, detail, outline, sketch, characterize • *Children's books often depict animals as gentle creatures.*

depiction 1 = **picture**, drawing, image, outline, illustration, sketch, likeness, delineation • *The vase has a depiction of a man playing a lyre.*
2 = **representation**, description, portrait, illustration, sketch, portrayal • *the depiction of socialists as Utopian dreamers*

deplete = **use up**, reduce, drain, exhaust, consume, empty, decrease, evacuate, lessen, impoverish, expend • *substances that deplete the ozone layer*
OPPOSITES: increase, raise, expand

depleted = **used (up)**, drained, exhausted, consumed, spent, reduced, emptied, weakened, decreased, lessened, worn out, depreciated • *depleted resources*

depletion = **using up**, reduction, drain, consumption, lowering, decrease, expenditure, deficiency, dwindling, lessening, exhaustion, diminution • *the depletion of underground water supplies*

deplorable 1 = **terrible**, distressing, dreadful, sad, unfortunate, disastrous, miserable, dire, melancholy, heartbreaking, grievous, regrettable, lamentable, calamitous, wretched, pitiable • *Many of them work under deplorable conditions.*
OPPOSITES: great *(informal)*, excellent, brilliant
2 = **disgraceful**, shameful, scandalous, reprehensible, disreputable, dishonourable, execrable, blameworthy, opprobrious • *Sexual harassment is deplorable.*
OPPOSITES: notable, admirable, laudable

deplore 1 = **disapprove of**, condemn, object to, denounce, censure, abhor, deprecate, take a dim view of, excoriate • *He says he deplores violence.*
2 = **lament**, regret, mourn, rue, bemoan, grieve for, bewail, sorrow over • *They deplored the heavy loss of life in the earthquake.*

deploy = **use**, station, set up, position, arrange, set out, dispose, utilize, spread out, distribute • *He said he had no intention of deploying ground troops.*

deployment = **use**, stationing, spread, organization, arrangement, positioning, disposition, setup, utilization • *the deployment of troops into townships*

deport AS A VERB = **expel**, exile, throw out, oust, banish, expatriate, extradite, evict, send packing, show you the door • *a government decision to deport all illegal immigrants*
▸ IN PHRASES: **deport yourself** = **behave**, act, conduct yourself, hold yourself, carry yourself, acquit yourself, bear yourself, comport yourself • *Try to deport yourselves like civilized human beings.*

deportation = **expulsion**, exile, removal, transportation, exclusion, extradition, eviction, ejection, banishment, expatriation, debarment • *Thousands of immigrants are now facing deportation.*

deportment = **bearing**, conduct, behaviour, manner, stance, carriage, posture, demeanour, air, mien, comportment • *Deportment and poise were considered important for young ladies.*

depose = **oust**, dismiss, displace, degrade, downgrade, cashier, demote, dethrone, remove from office • *The president was deposed in a coup.*

deposit AS A VERB 1 = **put**, place, lay, drop, settle • *The barman deposited a glass and two bottles of beer in front of him.*
2 = **store**, keep, put, bank, save, lodge, entrust, consign, hoard, stash *(informal)*, lock away, put in storage • *You are advised to deposit valuables in the hotel safe.*
▸ AS A NOUN 1 = **down payment**, security, stake, pledge, warranty, instalment, retainer, part payment • *A deposit of £20 is required when ordering.*
2 = **accumulation**, growth, mass, build-up, layer • *underground deposits of gold and diamonds*
3 = **sediment**, grounds, residue, lees, precipitate, deposition, silt, dregs, alluvium, settlings • *A powdery deposit had settled at the bottom of the glass.*

deposition 1 = **sworn statement** *(Law)*, evidence, testimony, declaration, affidavit • *The material would be checked against depositions from other witnesses.*
2 = **depositing**, build-up, accumulation, settling, precipitation *(technical)* • *This leads to calcium deposition in the blood vessels.*
3 = **removal**, dismissal, ousting, toppling, expulsion, displacement, unseating, dethronement • *It was this issue which led to the deposition of the leader.*

depository = **storehouse**, store, warehouse, depot, repository, safe-deposit box • *They have 2,500 tons of paper stored in their depository.*

depot 1 = **arsenal**, warehouse, storehouse, repository, depository, dump • *a government arms depot*
2 = **bus station**, station, garage, terminus • *She was reunited with her boyfriend in the bus depot.*

deprave = **corrupt**, pervert, degrade, seduce, subvert, debase, demoralize, debauch, brutalize, lead astray, vitiate • *material likely to deprave those who hear or read it*

depraved = **corrupt**, abandoned, perverted, evil, vicious, degraded, vile, degenerate, immoral, wicked, shameless, sinful, lewd, debased, profligate, debauched, lascivious, dissolute, licentious, pervy *(slang)* • *It has been condemned as the most depraved film of its kind.*
OPPOSITES: moral, pure, decent

depravity = **corruption**, vice, evil, criminality, wickedness, immorality, iniquity, profligacy, debauchery, viciousness, degeneracy, sinfulness, debasement, turpitude, baseness, depravation, vitiation • *the absolute depravity that can exist in times of war*

QUOTATIONS
No one ever suddenly became depraved
[Juvenal *Satires*]

deprecate 1 = **disapprove of**, condemn, object to, protest against, deplore, frown on, take exception to • *He deprecated this unseemly behaviour.*
2 = **disparage**, criticize, run down, discredit, scorn, deride, detract, malign, denigrate, belittle, vilify, depreciate, knock *(informal)*, diss *(slang, chiefly U.S.)*, bad-mouth *(slang, chiefly U.S. & Canad.)*, lambast(e), flame *(informal)* • *They deprecate him and refer to him as 'a bit of a red'.*

deprecatory 1 = **disapproving**, censuring, reproachful, condemnatory, opprobrious • *a hollow, self-deprecatory laugh*
2 = **apologetic**, rueful, contrite, remorseful, regretful, penitent • *'Sorry about that,' he said, with a deprecatory grin.*

depreciate 1 = **decrease**, cut, reduce, lessen, devalue, deflate, cheapen, lower in value, devaluate • *The demand for foreign currency depreciates the real value of local currencies.*
OPPOSITES: expand, add to, augment
2 = **lose value**, devalue, fall in price, drop in price, decrease in value, devaluate • *Inflation is rising rapidly and the yuan is depreciating.*
OPPOSITES: appreciate, increase in value, rise in value

depreciation = **devaluation**, fall, drop, depression, slump, deflation • *the depreciation of a currency's value*

depredation = **destruction**, ravaging, devastation, ransacking, pillage, plunder, marauding, laying waste, despoiling, rapine, spoliation • *Crops can be decimated by the unchecked depredations of deer.*

depress 1 = **sadden**, upset, distress, chill, discourage, grieve, daunt, oppress, desolate, weigh down, cast down, bring tears to your eyes, make sad, dishearten, dispirit, make your heart bleed, aggrieve, deject, make despondent, cast a gloom upon • *The state of the country depresses me.*
OPPOSITES: cheer, strengthen, uplift
2 = **lower**, cut, reduce, check, diminish, decrease, curb, slow down, impair, lessen • *The stronger currency depressed sales.*
OPPOSITES: increase, raise, strengthen
3 = **devalue**, cut, reduce, diminish, depreciate, cheapen, devaluate • *A dearth of buyers has depressed prices*
4 = **press down**, push, squeeze, lower, flatten, compress, push down, bear down on • *He depressed the pedal that lowered the chair.*

depressed 1 = **sad**, down, low, blue, unhappy, discouraged, fed up, moody, gloomy, pessimistic, melancholy, sombre, glum, mournful, dejected, despondent, dispirited, downcast, morose, disconsolate, crestfallen, doleful, downhearted, heavy-hearted, down in the dumps *(informal)*, cheerless, woebegone, down in the mouth *(informal)*, low-spirited • *He seemed somewhat depressed.*
2 = **poverty-stricken**, poor, deprived, distressed,

disadvantaged, rundown, impoverished, needy, destitute, down at heel • *attempts to encourage investment in depressed areas*
3 = lowered, devalued, weakened, impaired, depreciated, cheapened • *We need to prevent further falls in already depressed prices.*
4 = sunken, hollow, recessed, set back, indented, concave • *Manual pressure is applied to a depressed point on the body.*

depressing = bleak, black, sad, distressing, discouraging, gloomy, daunting, hopeless, dismal, melancholy, dreary, harrowing, saddening, sombre, heartbreaking, dispiriting, disheartening, funereal, dejecting • *the depressing thought of his mother's death*

d

depression 1 = despair, misery, sadness, dumps *(informal)*, the blues, melancholy, unhappiness, hopelessness, despondency, the hump *(Brit. informal)*, bleakness, melancholia, dejection, wretchedness, low spirits, gloominess, dolefulness, cheerlessness, downheartedness • *I slid into a depression and became morbidly fascinated with death.*
2 = recession, slump, economic decline, stagnation, inactivity, hard *or* bad times • *He never forgot the hardships he witnessed during the depression.*
3 = hollow, pit, dip, bowl, valley, sink, impression, dent, sag, cavity, excavation, indentation, dimple, concavity • *an area pockmarked by rainfilled depressions*

QUOTATIONS
It's a recession when your neighbour loses his job; it's a depression when you lose yours
[Harry S. Truman]

deprivation 1 = lack, denial, deficiency, withholding, robbing, withdrawal, removal, expropriation, divestment, dispossession, deprival • *Millions suffer from sleep deprivation caused by long work hours.*
2 = want, need, hardship, suffering, distress, disadvantage, oppression, detriment, privation, destitution • *Single women with children are likely to suffer financial deprivation.*

deprive = dispossess, rob, strip, divest, expropriate, despoil, bereave • *They've been deprived of the fuel necessary to heat their homes.*

deprived = poor, disadvantaged, needy, in need, lacking, bereft, destitute, in want, denuded, down at heel, necessitous • *the problems associated with life in a deprived inner city area*
OPPOSITES: successful, favoured, prosperous

depth AS A NOUN **1 = deepness**, drop, measure, extent, profundity, profoundness • *The fish were detected at depths of more than a kilometre.*
2 = strength, intensity, seriousness, severity, extremity, keenness, intenseness • *I am well aware of the depth of feeling that exists in the town*
3 = severity, importance, significance, gravity, urgency, moment, weight, danger, seriousness, severeness • *The country's leadership had underestimated the depth of the crisis.*
4 = insight, intelligence, wisdom, penetration, profundity, acuity, discernment, perspicacity, sagacity, astuteness, profoundness, perspicuity • *His writing has a depth that will outlast him.*
OPPOSITES: emptiness, triviality, superficiality
5 = breadth, range, degree, extent, scope, magnitude, amplitude, comprehensiveness, extensiveness • *We were impressed with the depth of her knowledge.*
6 = intensity, strength, warmth, richness, brightness, vibrancy, vividness • *The blue base gives the red paint more depth.*
7 = complexity, intricacy, elaboration, obscurity, abstruseness, reconditeness • *His music lacks depth.*
▸AS A PLURAL NOUN **1 = deepest part**, middle, midst, remotest part, furthest part, innermost part • *A sound came from the depths of the forest.*
2 = most intense part, pit, void, abyss, chasm, deepest part, furthest part, bottomless depth • *a man who had plumbed the depths of despair*
▸IN PHRASES: **in depth = thoroughly**, completely, fully, comprehensively, extensively, inside out, meticulously, intensively, exhaustively, leaving no stone unturned • *We will discuss these three areas in depth.*

deputation = delegation, commission, deputies, embassy, delegates, envoys, legation • *A deputation of elders from the village arrived.*

depute = appoint, choose, commission, select, elect, nominate, assign, charge, mandate, authorize, empower, accredit • *A sub-committee was deputed to investigate the claims.*

deputize = stand in for, act for, take the place of, understudy • *I soon became skilful enough to deputize for him in the kitchen.*

deputy AS A NOUN **= substitute**, representative, stand-in, ambassador, agent, commissioner, delegate, lieutenant, subordinate, proxy, surrogate, second-in-command, nuncio, legate, vicegerent, number two • *France's minister for culture and his deputy attended the meeting.*
▸AS A MODIFIER **= assistant**, acting, supporting, helping, substitute, stand-in, temporary, fill-in, subordinate, depute *(Scot.)* • *the academy's deputy director*

derail = prevent, stop, block, check, frustrate, hamper, foil, inhibit, avert, thwart, obstruct, impede, forestall, nip in the bud • *a fear that any reform could be derailed by hard-liners*

deranged = mad, crazy, insane, distracted, frantic, frenzied, irrational, maddened, crazed, lunatic, demented, unbalanced, berserk, delirious, unhinged, loopy *(informal)*, crackpot *(informal)*, out to lunch *(informal)*, barking mad *(slang)*, barking *(slang)*, gonzo *(slang)*, doolally *(slang)*, off your trolley *(slang)*, up the pole *(informal)*, not the full shilling *(informal)*, wacko *or* whacko *(slang)*, berko *(Austral. slang)*, off the air *(Austral. slang)*, porangi *(N.Z.)* • *A deranged man shot and killed 14 people in the main square.*
OPPOSITES: sane, normal, calm

derangement = madness, mania, insanity, dementia, aberration, lunacy, delirium, loss of reason • *serious evidence of mental derangement*

derby = competition, event, championship, tournament, contest, puzzle, quiz, head-to-head • *He caught a salmon in the annual fishing derby.*

derelict AS AN ADJECTIVE **1 = abandoned**, deserted, ruined, neglected, discarded, forsaken, dilapidated • *His body was found dumped in a derelict warehouse.*
2 = negligent, slack, irresponsible, careless, lax, remiss • *They would be derelict in their duty not to pursue it.*
▸AS A NOUN **= tramp**, bum *(informal)*, outcast, drifter, down-and-out, vagrant, hobo *(chiefly U.S.)*, vagabond, bag lady, dosser *(Brit. slang)*, derro *(Austral. slang)* • *a confused and wizened derelict wandered in off the street*

dereliction 1 = abandonment, desertion, renunciation, relinquishment • *The previous owners had rescued the building from dereliction.*
2 = negligence, failure, neglect, evasion, delinquency, abdication, faithlessness, nonperformance, remissness • *He pleaded guilty to wilful dereliction of duty.*

deride = mock, ridicule, scorn, knock *(informal)*, insult, taunt, sneer, jeer, disdain, scoff, detract, flout, disparage, chaff, gibe, take the piss out of *(taboo slang)*, pooh-pooh, contemn • *This theory is widely derided by conventional scientists.*

de rigueur = necessary, right, required, fitting, correct, done, conventional, decent, proper, decorous, the done thing, comme il faut *(French)* • *T-shirts now seem almost de rigueur in even the smartest places.*

derision = mockery, laughter, contempt, ridicule, scorn, insult, sneering, disdain, scoffing, disrespect, denigration, disparagement, contumely, raillery • *He tried to calm them but was greeted with shouts of derision.*

derisive = mocking, ridiculing, jeering, taunting, scoffing, contemptuous, scornful • *He gave a short, derisive laugh.*

derisory = ridiculous, insulting, outrageous, ludicrous, preposterous, laughable, contemptible • *She was being paid a derisory amount of money.*

derivation = **origin**, source, basis, beginning, root, foundation, descent, ancestry, genealogy, etymology • *The derivation of its name is obscure.*

derivative AS AN ADJECTIVE = **unoriginal**, copied, second-hand, rehashed, imitative, plagiarized, uninventive, plagiaristic • *their dull, derivative debut album*
OPPOSITES: original, first-hand, archetypal
▸ AS A NOUN = **by-product**, spin-off, offshoot, descendant, derivation, outgrowth • *a poppy-seed derivative similar to heroin*

derive AS A VERB = **obtain**, get, receive, draw, gain, collect, gather, extract, elicit, glean, procure • *He is one of those people who derives pleasure from helping others.*
▸ IN PHRASES: **derive from something** = **come from**, stem from, arise from, flow from, spring from, emanate from, proceed from, descend from, issue from, originate from • *The word Druid may derive from 'drus', meaning 'oak tree'.*

derogatory = **disparaging**, damaging, offensive, slighting, detracting, belittling, unfavourable, unflattering, dishonouring, defamatory, injurious, discreditable, uncomplimentary, depreciative • *She refused to withdraw her derogatory remarks.*
OPPOSITES: flattering, complimentary, appreciative

descend AS A VERB 1 = **fall**, drop, sink, go down, plunge, dive, tumble, plummet, subside, move down • *Disaster struck as the plane descended through the mist.*
OPPOSITES: rise, scale, mount
2 = **get off**, alight, disembark, dismount, debus, deplane, detrain • *The bus stopped and three people descended.*
3 = **go down**, come down, walk down, move down, climb down • *Things are cooler and more damp as we descend to the cellar.*
4 = **slope**, decline, sink, dip, incline, slant, fall away, gravitate • *The path descended steeply to the rushing river.*
▸ IN PHRASES: **be descended from** = **originate from**, derive from, spring from, proceed from, issue from, be a descendant of • *He was proud to be descended from tradesmen.*
descend on something *or* **someone** = **attack**, assault, raid, invade, swoop, pounce, assail, arrive, come in force, arrive in hordes • *Drunken mobs descended on their homes.*
descend to something = **lower yourself to**, resort to, stoop to, be reduced to, condescend to, deign to, humble yourself by, debase yourself by, abase yourself by • *She's got too much dignity to descend to writing anonymous letters.*

descendant = **successor**, child, issue, son, daughter, heir, offspring, progeny, scion, inheritor • *They are descendants of the original settlers.*
OPPOSITES: predecessor, ancestor, precursor

descent 1 = **fall**, drop, plunge, coming down, swoop • *The airplane crashed on its descent into the airport.*
2 = **slope**, drop, dip, incline, slant, declination, declivity • *On the descents, cyclists freewheel past cars.*
3 = **decline**, deterioration, degradation, decadence, degeneration, debasement • *his swift descent from respected academic to homeless derelict*
4 = **origin**, extraction, ancestry, lineage, family tree, parentage, heredity, genealogy, derivation • *All the contributors were of foreign descent.*

describe 1 = **relate**, tell, report, present, detail, explain, express, illustrate, set out, specify, chronicle, recount, recite, impart, narrate, set forth, give an account of, put in words • *We asked her to describe what she had seen.*
2 = **portray**, depict, characterize, call, paint, brand, define, dub, sketch • *Even his allies describe him as forceful, aggressive and determined.*
3 = **trace**, draw, outline, sketch, mark out, delineate • *The ball described a perfect arc across the field.*

description 1 = **account**, report, explanation, representation, sketch, narrative, portrayal, depiction, narration, characterization, delineation • *He gave a description of the surgery he was about to perform.*
2 = **calling**, naming, branding, labelling, dubbing, designation • *his description of the country as a 'police state'*
3 = **kind**, sort, type, order, class, variety, brand, species, breed, category, kidney, genre, genus, ilk • *Events of this description occurred daily.*

descriptive = **graphic**, vivid, expressive, picturesque, detailed, explanatory, pictorial, illustrative, depictive • *The group adopted a simpler, more descriptive title.*

descry = **catch sight of**, see, notice, mark, discover, sight, observe, recognize, distinguish, perceive, detect, make out, discern, behold, espy, spy out • *From the top of the hill I descried a solitary rider.*

desecrate = **profane**, dishonour, defile, violate, contaminate, pollute, pervert, despoil, blaspheme, commit sacrilege • *She shouldn't have desecrated the picture of a religious leader*
OPPOSITES: value, respect, revere

desecration = **violation**, blasphemy, sacrilege, debasement, defilement, impiety, profanation • *The whole area has been shocked by the desecration of the cemetery.*

desert[1] AS A NOUN = **wilderness**, waste, wilds, wasteland, dust bowl • *The vehicles have been modified to suit conditions in the desert.*
▸ AS AN ADJECTIVE = **barren**, dry, waste, wild, empty, bare, lonely, solitary, desolate, arid, unproductive, infertile, uninhabited, uncultivated, unfruitful, untilled • *the desert wastes of Mexico*

DESERTS

Arabian	Great Victoria	Rub'al Khali
Atacama	Kalahari	Sahara
Dasht-i-Lut	Kara Kum	Taklimakan
Death Valley	Kyzyl Kum	Shama
Gibson	Libyan	Thar
Gobi	Mojave	
Great Sandy	Nubian	

desert[2] 1 = **abandon**, leave, give up, quit *(informal)*, withdraw from, move out of, relinquish, renounce, vacate, forsake, go away from, leave empty, relinquish possession of • *Poor farmers are deserting their fields and looking for jobs.*
2 = **leave**, abandon, dump *(informal)*, strand, ditch *(informal)*, betray, maroon, walk out on *(informal)*, forsake, jilt, run out on *(informal)*, throw over, leave stranded, leave high and dry, leave (someone) in the lurch • *Her husband deserted her years ago.*
OPPOSITES: maintain, look after, take care of
3 = **abscond**, flee, defect, decamp, go AWOL *(informal)*, go absent without leave, go over the hill *(Military, slang)*, take French leave • *He deserted from the army last month.*

deserted 1 = **empty**, abandoned, desolate, neglected, lonely, vacant, derelict, bereft, unoccupied, godforsaken • *a deserted town*
2 = **abandoned**, neglected, forsaken, lonely, forlorn, cast off, left stranded, left in the lurch, unfriended • *the image of a wronged and deserted wife*

deserter = **defector**, runaway, fugitive, traitor, renegade, truant, escapee, absconder, apostate • *He was a deserter from the army.*

desertion 1 = **abandonment**, betrayal, forsaking, dereliction, relinquishment • *It was a long time since she'd referred to her father's desertion of them.*

2 = defection, betrayal, reneging, repudiation, apostasy, relinquishment, abjuration • *mass desertion by the electorate*
3 = absconding, flight, escape *(informal)*, running away, evasion, defection, truancy, decamping, dereliction, going AWOL, taking French leave • *The high rate of desertion has added to the army's woes.*

deserts IN PHRASES: **just deserts = due**, payment, reward, punishment, right, return, retribution, recompense, come-uppance *(slang)*, meed *(archaic)*, requital, guerdon *(poetic)* • *At the end of the book the bad guys get their just deserts.*

deserve = merit, warrant, be entitled to, have a right to, win, rate, earn, justify, be worthy of, have a claim to • *The young should treat the old with the respect that they deserve.*

d

deserved = well-earned, just, right, meet *(archaic)*, fitting, due, fair, earned, appropriate, justified, suitable, merited, proper, warranted, rightful, justifiable, condign • *his reputation for political skill is well deserved*

deservedly = rightly, fittingly, fairly, appropriately, properly, duly, justifiably, justly, by rights, rightfully, according to your due, condignly • *He deservedly won the Player of the Year award.*
OPPOSITES: wrongly, unfairly, undeservedly

deserving AS AN ADJECTIVE **= worthy**, righteous, commendable, laudable, praiseworthy, meritorious, estimable • *The money saved could be used for more deserving causes.*
OPPOSITES: unworthy, undeserving
▸ IN PHRASES: **deserving of = meriting**, justifying, worthy of, qualified for, warranting, suitable for • *artists deserving of public subsidy*

desiccated 1 = dried, dehydrated, dry, powdered • *desiccated flowers and leaves*
2 = dull, dry, lifeless, passionless, spiritless, dry-as-dust • *a desiccated and boring individual*

design AS A VERB **1 = plan**, describe, draw, draft, trace, outline, invent, devise, sketch, formulate, contrive, think out, delineate • *They have designed a machine that is both attractive and practical.*
2 = create, make, plan, project, fashion, scheme, propose, invent, devise, tailor, draw up, conceive, originate, contrive, fabricate, think up • *We may be able to design a course to suit your particular needs.*
3 = intend, mean, plan, aim, purpose, adjust, adapt, tailor, contrive, destine • *a compromise designed to please everyone*
▸ AS A NOUN **1 = pattern**, form, figure, style, shape, organization, arrangement, construction, motif, configuration • *The pictures are based on simple geometric designs.*
2 = plan, drawing, model, scheme, proposal, draft, outline, representation, sketch, prototype, blueprint, depiction, delineation, scale drawing • *They drew up the design in a week.*
3 = intention, end, point, aim, plan, goal, dream, target, wish, purpose, desire, object, objective, ambition, intent • *Is there some design in having him here?*
▸ IN PHRASES: **by design = deliberately**, intentionally, consciously, knowingly, on purpose, wittingly, calculatedly • *The pair met often – at first by chance but later by design.*

designate 1 = name, call, term, style, label, entitle, dub, nominate, christen • *one man interviewed in our study, whom we shall designate as 'Mr E'*
2 = specify, term, class, describe, indicate, brand, define, pronounce, classify, characterize, stipulate, denote • *I live in Exmoor, which is designated as a national park.*
3 = choose, reserve, select, label, flag, tag, assign, allocate, set aside, earmark, mark out, allot, keep back • *Some of the rooms were designated as offices.*
4 = appoint, name, choose, commission, select, elect, delegate, nominate, assign, depute • *We need to designate someone as our spokesperson.*

designation 1 = name, title, label, description, tag, denomination, epithet, byname • *Level 4 alert is a designation reserved for very serious incidents.*
2 = appointment, classing, labelling, definition, specification, classification, earmarking, stipulation • *the designation of the city as a centre of culture*
3 = election, choice, selection, appointment, nomination • *the designation of Ali as Prophet Muhammad's successor*

designer 1 = couturier, tailor, stylist, dressmaker, costumier • *She is a fashion designer.*
2 = producer, architect, deviser, creator, planner, inventor, artificer, originator • *Designer Harvey Postlethwaite has rejoined Ferrari.*

designing = scheming, plotting, intriguing, crooked *(informal)*, shrewd, conspiring, cunning, sly, astute, treacherous, unscrupulous, devious, wily, crafty, artful, conniving, Machiavellian, deceitful • *He was trapped into marriage by a designing witch.*

desirability 1 = worth, value, benefit, profit, advantage, merit, usefulness • *the desirability of domestic reform*
2 = attractiveness, appeal, beauty, charm, good looks, fairness, allure, magnetism, loveliness, prettiness, seductiveness, gorgeousness, handsomeness, pulchritude *(formal literary)*, winsomeness, comeliness, engagingness, enticingness, glamorousness *or* glamourousness, pleasingness, prepossessingness, takingness, temptingness, winningness • *He had not at all overrated her desirability.*

desirable 1 = advantageous, useful, valuable, helpful, profitable, of service, convenient, worthwhile, beneficial, preferable, advisable • *Prolonged negotiation was not desirable.*
OPPOSITES: disadvantageous, inadvisable
2 = popular, pleasing, appealing, looked-for, in demand, sought-after, enviable, to die for *(informal)*, covetable • *desirable commodities such as coffee and sugar*
OPPOSITES: unacceptable, unpleasant, unpopular
3 = attractive, appealing, beautiful, winning, interesting, pleasing, pretty, fair, inviting, engaging, lovely, charming, fascinating, sexy *(informal)*, handsome, fetching, good-looking, eligible, glamorous, gorgeous, magnetic, cute, enticing, seductive, captivating, alluring, adorable, bonny, winsome, comely, prepossessing • *the young women whom his classmates thought most desirable*
OPPOSITES: undesirable, unattractive, unappealing

desire AS A VERB **1 = want**, long for, crave, fancy, hope for, ache for, covet, aspire to, wish for, yearn for, thirst for, hanker after, set your heart on, desiderate • *He was bored and desired change in his life.*
2 = request, ask, petition, solicit, entreat, importune • *His Majesty desires me to make his wishes known to you.*
▸ AS A NOUN **1 = wish**, want, longing, need, hope, urge, yen *(informal)*, hunger, appetite, aspiration, ache, craving, yearning, inclination, thirst, hankering • *I had a strong desire to help and care for people*
2 = lust, passion, libido, appetite, lechery, carnality, lasciviousness, concupiscence, randiness *(informal, chiefly Brit.)*, lustfulness • *Teenage sex may not always come out of genuine desire.*
▸ RELATED ADJECTIVE: orectic

QUOTATIONS

We do not succeed in changing things according to our desire, but gradually our desire changes
[Marcel Proust *Remembrance of Things Past*]

There are two tragedies in life. One is not to get your heart's desire. The other is to get it
[George Bernard Shaw *Man and Superman*]

Other women cloy
The appetites they feed, but she makes hungry
Where most she satisfies
[William Shakespeare *Antony and Cleopatra*]

If you desire many things, many things will seem but a few
[Benjamin Franklin *Poor Richard's Almanack*]

desired 1 = **intended**, wanted, wished for, needed, longed for, coveted, sought-after • *His warnings have provoked the desired response.*
2 = **required**, necessary, correct, appropriate, right, expected, fitting, particular, express, accurate, proper, exact • *Cut the material to the desired size.*

desirous = **wishing**, wanting, longing for, willing for, hoping for, ready for, desiring, keen on, anxious for, ambitious for, eager for, hopeful for, aspiring towards, craving (for), yearning for, avid for • *The opposition is clearly desirous of peace.*
OPPOSITES: opposed to, reluctant for

desist = **stop**, cease, refrain from, end, kick *(informal)*, give up, suspend, break off, abstain, discontinue, leave off, have done with, give over *(informal)*, forbear, belay *(Nautical)* • *Kindly desist from making so much noise.*

desk = **table**, bureau, work surface, lectern, writing desk, secretaire • *A large portrait hung behind his desk.*
▹ *See panel* **Tables and desks**

desolate AS AN ADJECTIVE 1 = **uninhabited**, deserted, bare, waste, wild, ruined, bleak, solitary, barren, dreary, godforsaken, unfrequented • *a desolate, godforsaken place*
OPPOSITES: inhabited, populous
2 = **miserable**, depressed, lonely, lonesome *(chiefly U.S. & Canad.)*, gloomy, dismal, melancholy, forlorn, bereft, dejected, despondent, downcast, wretched, disconsolate, down in the dumps *(informal)*, cheerless, comfortless, companionless • *He was desolate without her.*
OPPOSITES: happy, cheerful, joyous
▸ AS A VERB 1 = **deject**, depress, distress, discourage, dismay, grieve, daunt, dishearten • *I was desolated by the news.*
OPPOSITES: encourage, cheer, nourish
2 = **destroy**, ruin, devastate, ravage, lay low, lay waste, despoil, depopulate • *A great famine desolated the country.*

desolation 1 = **misery**, distress, despair, gloom, sadness, woe, anguish, melancholy, unhappiness, dejection, wretchedness, gloominess • *He expresses his sense of desolation without self-pity.*
2 = **bleakness**, isolation, loneliness, solitude, wildness, barrenness, solitariness, forlornness, desolateness • *We looked out upon a scene of utter desolation.*
3 = **ruin**, destruction, havoc, devastation, ruination • *The army left a trail of desolation and death in its wake.*

despair AS A VERB = **lose hope**, give up, be discouraged, be pessimistic, lose heart, be despondent, be dejected, be demoralized, resign yourself, look on the black side • *He despairs at much of the press criticism.*
▸ AS A NOUN = **despondency**, depression, misery, gloom, desperation, anguish, melancholy, hopelessness, dejection, wretchedness, disheartenment • *She shook her head in despair at the futility of it all.*

despairing = **hopeless**, desperate, depressed, anxious, miserable, frantic, dismal, suicidal, melancholy, dejected, broken-hearted, despondent, downcast, grief-stricken, wretched, disconsolate, inconsolable, down in the dumps *(informal)*, at the end of your tether • *a despairing middle-aged woman who fell in love with a younger man*

despatch *see* **dispatch**

desperado = **criminal**, thug, outlaw, villain, gangster, gunman, bandit, mugger *(informal)*, cut-throat, hoodlum *(chiefly U.S.)*, ruffian, wise guy *(U.S.)*, face *(Brit. slang)*, heavy *(slang)*, lawbreaker, skelm *(S. African)* • *The judge described him as a 'wicked desperado' and jailed him for life.*

desperate 1 = **hopeless**, despairing, in despair, forlorn, abject, dejected, despondent, demoralized, wretched, disconsolate, inconsolable, downhearted, at the end of your tether • *Her people were poor, desperate and starving.*
2 = **eager**, longing, keen, raring, hungry, enthusiastic, yearning, impatient, up for it *(informal)*, keen as mustard • *She was desperate to start a family.*
3 = **grave**, great, pressing, serious, critical, acute, severe, extreme, urgent, dire, drastic, very grave • *Troops are needed to get food to people in desperate need.*
4 = **last-ditch**, dangerous, daring, determined, wild, violent, furious, last-minute, risky, frantic, rash, hazardous, precipitate, last-resort, hasty, audacious, madcap, foolhardy, eleventh-hour, headstrong, impetuous, death-defying • *a desperate rescue attempt*

desperately 1 = **gravely**, badly, seriously, severely, dangerously, perilously • *a man who was desperately ill with cancer*
2 = **urgently**, intensely, with urgency, pressingly • *He was a boy who desperately needed affection.*

desperation 1 = **misery**, worry, trouble, pain, anxiety, torture, despair, agony, sorrow, distraction, anguish, unhappiness, heartache, hopelessness, despondency • *this feeling of desperation and helplessness*
2 = **recklessness**, madness, defiance, frenzy, impetuosity, rashness, foolhardiness, heedlessness • *It was an act of sheer desperation.*

QUOTATIONS
The mass of men lead lives of quiet desperation
[Henry David Thoreau *Walden*]
PROVERBS
Beggars can't be choosers
A drowning man will clutch at a straw

despicable = **contemptible**, mean, low, base, cheap, infamous, degrading, worthless, disgraceful, shameful, vile, sordid, pitiful, abject, hateful, reprehensible, ignominious, disreputable, wretched, scurvy, detestable, scungy *(Austral. & N.Z.)*, beyond contempt • *He said it was a despicable crime.*
OPPOSITES: good, moral, admirable

despise = **look down on**, loathe, scorn, disdain, spurn, undervalue, deride, detest, revile, abhor, have a down on *(informal)*, contemn • *How I despised myself for my cowardice.*
OPPOSITES: love, take to, admire

despite = **in spite of**, in the face of, regardless of, even with, notwithstanding, in defiance of, in the teeth of, undeterred by, in contempt of • *Despite a thorough investigation, no sign of him has been found.*

despoil = **plunder**, destroy, strip, rob, devastate, wreck, rifle, deprive, loot, trash *(slang)*, total *(slang)*, ravage, dispossess, pillage, divest, denude, vandalize, wreak havoc upon • *the modern day industry which has despoiled the town*

despondency = **dejection**, depression, despair, misery, gloom, sadness, desperation, melancholy, hopelessness, the hump *(Brit. informal)*, discouragement, wretchedness, low spirits, disconsolateness, dispiritedness, downheartedness • *There's a mood of gloom and despondency in the country.*

despondent = **dejected**, sad, depressed, down, low, blue, despairing, discouraged, miserable, gloomy, hopeless, dismal, melancholy, in despair, glum, dispirited, downcast, morose, disheartened, sorrowful, wretched, disconsolate, doleful, downhearted, down in the dumps *(informal)*, sick as a parrot *(informal)*, woebegone, low-spirited • *He often felt despondent after these meetings.*
OPPOSITES: happy, glad, cheerful

despot = **tyrant**, dictator, totalitarian, Big Brother, oppressor, control freak, autocrat, monocrat • *He described the president as a ruthless despot.*

despotic = **tyrannical**, authoritarian, dictatorial, absolute, arrogant, oppressive, autocratic, imperious, domineering, monocratic • *The country was ruled by a despotic tyrant.*

despotism = **tyranny**, dictatorship, oppression,

totalitarianism, autocracy, absolutism, autarchy, monocracy • *a prototypical example of political despotism*

dessert = **pudding**, sweet *(informal)*, afters *(Brit. informal)*, pud, second course, last course, sweet course • *We had homemade ice cream for dessert.*

▹ *See panel* **Desserts and sweet dishes**

destabilize = **undermine**, damage, disable, weaken, sabotage, impair, subvert, disempower • *Their sole aim is to destabilize the government.*

OPPOSITES: sustain, strengthen

destination = **stop**, station, haven, harbour, resting-place, terminus, journey's end, landing-place • *a popular holiday destination*

destined AS AN ADJECTIVE = **fated**, meant, intended, designed, certain, bound, doomed, ordained, predestined, foreordained • *He feels that he was destined to become a musician.*

▸ IN PHRASES: **destined for** = **bound for**, meant for, intended for, booked for, directed towards, scheduled for, routed for, heading for, assigned to, en route to, on the road to • *products destined for the south*

destiny 1 = **fate**, fortune, lot, portion, doom, nemesis, divine decree • *We are masters of our own destiny.*

2 *usually cap.* = **fortune**, stars, chance, karma, providence, kismet, predestination, divine will • *Is it Destiny or accident that brings people together?*

QUOTATIONS

Everything comes gradually and at its appointed hour
[Ovid *The Art of Love*]

Thy lot or portion of life is seeking after thee; therefore be at rest from seeking after it
[Ali Ibn-Abi-Talib]

PROVERBS

What must be, must be

destitute AS AN ADJECTIVE = **penniless**, poor, impoverished, distressed, needy, on the rocks, insolvent, poverty-stricken, down and out, indigent, impecunious, dirt-poor *(informal)*, on the breadline *(informal)*, flat broke *(informal)*, short, penurious, on your uppers, necessitous, in queer street *(informal)*, moneyless, without two pennies to rub together *(informal)* • *destitute children who live on the streets*

▸ IN PHRASES: **destitute of** = **lacking**, wanting, without, in need of, deprived of, devoid of, bereft of, empty of, drained of, deficient in, depleted in • *a country destitute of natural resources*

destitution = **pennilessness**, want, distress, dire straits, privation, penury, neediness, beggary, indigence, pauperism, impecuniousness, utter poverty • *Equality will not relieve destitution but will spread it evenly.*

OPPOSITES: riches, plenty, wealth

destroy 1 = **ruin**, smash, crush, waste, devastate, break down, wreck, shatter, gut, wipe out, dispatch, dismantle, demolish, trash *(slang)*, total *(slang)*, ravage, slay, eradicate, torpedo, extinguish, desolate, annihilate, put paid to, raze, blow to bits, extirpate, blow sky-high • *The building was completely destroyed.*

2 = **devastate**, overwhelm, overpower, floor *(informal)*, take aback, chagrin, nonplus, discompose • *Such criticism would have destroyed a more sensitive person.*

3 = **slaughter**, kill, put down, exterminate, put to sleep • *The horse had to be destroyed.*

4 = **annihilate**, wipe out, obliterate, erase, eradicate, extinguish, liquidate, root out, exterminate, nullify, extirpate, wipe from the face of the earth • *They could destroy the enemy in days rather than weeks.*

5 = **defeat**, beat, master, tank *(slang)*, crush, overwhelm, conquer, overthrow, lick *(informal)*, undo, subdue, rout, overpower, quell, trounce, clobber *(slang)*, stuff *(slang)*, vanquish, subjugate, run rings around *(informal)*, wipe the floor with *(informal)*, make mincemeat of *(informal)*, pip at the post, outplay, blow out of the water *(slang)* • *The team destroyed their opponents in a one-sided game.*

destruction 1 = **ruin**, havoc, wreckage, crushing, wrecking, shattering, undoing, demolition, devastation, annihilation, ruination • *the extensive destruction caused by the rioters*

2 = **massacre**, overwhelming, slaughter, overthrow, extinction, end, downfall, liquidation, obliteration, extermination, annihilation, eradication • *Our objective was the destruction of the enemy forces.*

3 = **slaughter**, slaughtering, putting down, termination, extermination, putting to sleep • *the destruction of animals infected with foot-and-mouth disease*

destructive 1 = **devastating**, fatal, deadly, lethal, harmful, damaging, catastrophic, detrimental, hurtful, pernicious, noxious, ruinous, calamitous, cataclysmic, baleful, deleterious, injurious, baneful, maleficent • *the awesome destructive power of nuclear weapons*

2 = **negative**, hostile, discouraging, undermining, contrary, vicious, adverse, discrediting, disparaging, antagonistic, derogatory • *Try to give constructive rather than destructive criticism.*

desultory = **random**, vague, irregular, loose, rambling, inconsistent, erratic, disconnected, haphazard, cursory, aimless, off and on, fitful, spasmodic, discursive,

DESSERTS AND SWEET DISHES

Atholl Brose
baked Alaska
banana split
bavarois *or* Bavarian cream
Black Forest gateau
blancmange
blintz
bombe
bread and butter pudding
cabinet pudding
cassata
charlotte
charlotte russe
cheesecake
Christmas pudding
cobbler
college pudding
compote
coupe
cranachan
crème brûlée
crème caramel
crêpe
crêpe suzette
crumble
custard
death by chocolate
duff
dumpling
Easter-ledge pudding
Eve's pudding
flummery
fondant
fool
fruit cup
fruit salad *or* cocktail
gâteau
hasty pudding
ice cream
Île Flottante
jelly *or (U.S.)* jello
junket
kissel
knickerbocker glory
kulfi
marrons glacés
milk pudding
Mississippi mud pie
mousse
Neapolitan ice cream
nesselrode
panocha *(U.S.)*
parfait
pashka
pavlova *or (Austral. & N.Z. informal)* pav
peach Melba
plum duff
plum pudding
queen of puddings
rice pudding
roly-poly
sabayon
sago
semolina
shoofly pie *(U.S.)*
shortcake
slump *(U.S.)*
sorbet
soufflé
sponge pudding
spotted dick
spumone *or* spumoni
steamed pudding
strudel
suet pudding
summer pudding
sundae
syllabub
tapioca
tartlet
tiramisu
torte
trifle
tutti-frutti
vacherin
water ice
whip
yogurt
zabaglione

unsystematic, inconstant, maundering, unmethodical • *We made some desultory conversation while we waited for the bus.*

detach AS A VERB 1 = **separate**, free, remove, divide, isolate, cut off, sever, loosen, segregate, disconnect, tear off, disengage, disentangle, unfasten, disunite, uncouple, unhitch, disjoin, unbridle • *Detach the bottom part from the form and keep it for reference.*
OPPOSITES: bind, connect, attach
2 = **free**, remove, separate, isolate, cut off, segregate, disengage • *Gradually my husband detached me from all my friends.*
▸ IN PHRASES: **detach yourself from something** = **distance yourself from**, disengage yourself from, remove yourself from, separate yourself from, liberate yourself from, disconnect yourself from, disentangle yourself from • *Try to detach yourself from the problem and be more objective.*

detached 1 = **objective**, neutral, impartial, reserved, aloof, impersonal, disinterested, unbiased, dispassionate, uncommitted, uninvolved, unprejudiced • *The piece is written in a detached, precise style.*
OPPOSITES: subjective, prejudiced, biased
2 = **separate**, free, severed, disconnected, loosened, discrete, unconnected, undivided, disjoined • *He lost his sight because of a detached retina.*

detachment 1 = **indifference**, fairness, neutrality, objectivity, impartiality, coolness, remoteness, nonchalance, aloofness, unconcern, disinterestedness, nonpartisanship • *her professional detachment*
2 = **unit**, party, force, body, detail, squad, patrol, task force • *a detachment of marines*

detail AS A NOUN 1 = **point**, fact, feature, particular, respect, factor, count, item, instance, element, aspect, specific, component, facet, technicality • *I recall every detail of the party.*
2 = **fine point**, part, particular, trifle, technicality, nicety, minutiae, triviality, unimportant point, matter of no importance *or* consequence • *Only minor details now remain to be settled.*
3 = **party**, force, body, unit, troop, section, duty, squad, crew, assignment, fatigue, detachment • *His personal detail totalled sixty men.*
▸ AS A VERB 1 = **list**, describe, relate, catalogue, portray, specify, depict, recount, rehearse, recite, narrate, delineate, enumerate, itemize, tabulate, particularize • *The report detailed the human rights abuses committed.*
2 = **appoint**, name, choose, commission, select, elect, delegate, nominate, assign, allocate, charge • *He detailed someone to take it to the Incident Room.*
▸ IN PHRASES: **in detail** = **comprehensively**, completely, fully, thoroughly, extensively, inside out, exhaustively, point by point, item by item • *Examine the wording in detail before deciding on the final text.*

detailed 1 = **comprehensive**, full, complete, minute, particular, specific, extensive, exact, thorough, meticulous, exhaustive, all-embracing, itemized, encyclopedic, blow-by-blow, particularized • *a detailed account of the discussions*
OPPOSITES: short, limited, brief
2 = **complicated**, involved, complex, fancy, elaborate, intricate, meticulous, convoluted • *detailed line drawings*

detain 1 = **hold**, arrest, confine, restrain, imprison, intern, take prisoner, take into custody, hold in custody • *He was arrested and detained for questioning.*
2 = **delay**, keep, stop, hold up, hamper, hinder, retard, impede, keep back, slow up *or* down • *We won't detain you any further.*

detainee = **prisoner**, captive, hostage, internee • *The detainee was held without charge.*

detect 1 = **discover**, find, reveal, catch, expose, disclose, uncover, track down, hunt down, unmask, ferret out, smoke out • *equipment used to detect radiation*
2 = **notice**, see, spot, catch, note, identify, observe, remark, recognize, distinguish, perceive, scent, discern, ascertain, descry • *He could detect a certain sadness in her face.*

detection 1 = **diagnosis**, spotting, recognition, observation, perception, identification, discernment • *the early detection of cancer*
2 = **discovery**, arrest, capture, exposure, uncovering, tracking down, unearthing, apprehension, rooting out, unmasking, ferreting out • *These criminals are sophisticated enough to avoid detection.*

detective = **investigator**, cop *(slang)*, copper *(slang)*, dick *(slang, chiefly U.S.)*, constable, tec *(slang)*, private eye, sleuth *(informal)*, private investigator, gumshoe *(U.S. slang)*, bizzy *(slang)*, C.I.D. man • *Detectives are appealing for witnesses.*

détente = **co-operation**, unity, collaboration, teamwork, give-and-take, combined effort, esprit de corps • *their desire to pursue a policy of détente*

detention = **imprisonment**, custody, restraint, keeping in, quarantine, confinement, porridge *(slang)*, incarceration • *the detention without trial of government critics*
OPPOSITES: release, freedom, liberty

deter 1 = **discourage**, inhibit, put off, frighten, intimidate, daunt, hinder, dissuade, talk out of • *Jail sentences have done nothing to deter the offenders.*
2 = **prevent**, stop, check, curb, damp, restrain, prohibit, hinder, debar • *Capital punishment does not deter crime.*

detergent AS A NOUN = **cleaner**, cleanser, washing-up liquid, soap powder, soap flakes • *He squeezed some detergent over the dishes.*
▸ AS AN ADJECTIVE = **cleansing**, cleaning, purifying, abstergent, detersive • *low-lather detergent powders*

deteriorate 1 = **decline**, worsen, degenerate, fall, fail, drop, slip, sink, slide, slump, degrade, depreciate, go downhill, go to the dogs *(informal)*, go down the tubes *(informal)*, go to pot, go to rack and ruin • *There are fears that the situation may deteriorate.*
OPPOSITES: improve, advance, get better
2 = **disintegrate**, rot, decay, spoil, fade, break down, go off, weaken, crumble, fall apart, perish, ebb, degenerate, decompose, go bad, wear away, putrefy, retrogress • *X-rays are used to prevent fresh food from deteriorating.*

deterioration 1 = **decline**, failure, collapse, fall, drop, slump, worsening, downturn, depreciation, degradation, degeneration, debasement, retrogression, vitiation, dégringolade *(French)* • *the rapid deterioration in relations between the two countries*
2 = **disintegration**, decay, rot, breakdown, perishing, degradation, corrosion, degeneration, atrophy, decomposition, putrefaction • *enzymes that cause the deterioration of food*

determinant = **factor**, point, cause, influence, thing, item, element, circumstance, consideration, component • *the types of determinant that are likely to influence trade*

determinate = **definite**, decided, certain, limited, established, express, determined, settled, positive, fixed, defined, absolute, precise, distinct, specified, decisive, explicit, definitive, conclusive, quantified • *the exclusive possession of land for some determinate period*

determination 1 = **resolution**, purpose, resolve, drive, energy, conviction, courage, dedication, backbone, fortitude, persistence, tenacity, perseverance, willpower, boldness, firmness, staying power, stubbornness, strength of character, constancy, single-mindedness, earnestness, obstinacy, steadfastness, doggedness, relentlessness, strength of will, resoluteness, indomitability, staunchness • *They acted with great courage and determination.*
OPPOSITES: doubt, hesitation, indecision
2 = **decision**, ruling, settlement, resolution, resolve, conclusion, verdict, judgment • *A determination will be made as to the future of the treaty.*

PROVERBS
When the going gets tough, the tough get going

d

determine 1 = **affect**, control, decide, rule, condition, direct, influence, shape, govern, regulate, dictate, ordain, have an impact on, have an effect on • *What determines whether you are a success or a failure?*
2 = **settle**, learn, establish, discover, check, confirm, find out, work out, calculate, detect, figure out, certify, verify, ascertain, deduce, fix upon • *The investigation will determine what really happened.*
3 = **decide on**, choose, establish, purpose, fix, elect, arrange, resolve, come to a decision about • *The people have a right to determine their own future.*
4 = **decide**, purpose, conclude, resolve, make a decision, make up your mind, come to a decision • *I determined that I would ask him outright.*

d

determined AS AN ADJECTIVE = **resolute**, firm, dogged, fixed, constant, bold, intent, persistent, relentless, stalwart, persevering, single-minded, purposeful, tenacious, undaunted, strong-willed, steadfast, unwavering, immovable, unflinching, strong-minded • *He is making a determined effort to regain lost ground.*
▸ IN PHRASES: **determined to** *or* **on** = **intent on**, committed to, set on, resolved to, bent on, obsessive about, fixated on, firm about • *His enemies are determined to ruin him.* • *Are you absolutely determined on this course of action?*

determining = **deciding**, important, settling, essential, critical, crucial, decisive, final, definitive, conclusive • *Cost was not a determining factor in my choice.*

deterrence = **prevention**, obstruction, inhibition, hindrance, disincentive, discouragement, dissuasion • *policies of nuclear deterrence*

deterrent AS A NOUN = **discouragement**, obstacle, curb, restraint, impediment, check, hindrance, disincentive, defensive measures, determent • *They seriously believe that capital punishment is a deterrent.*
OPPOSITES: spur, incentive, lure
▸ AS AN ADJECTIVE = **discouraging**, inhibiting, hindering, dissuading • *He believes in the deterrent effect of custodial sentences*

detest = **hate**, loathe, despise, abhor, be hostile to, recoil from, be repelled by, have an aversion to, abominate, dislike intensely, execrate, feel aversion towards, feel disgust towards, feel hostility towards, feel repugnance towards • *My mother detested my ex-husband.*
OPPOSITES: love, relish, adore

detestable = **hateful**, shocking, offensive, disgusting, revolting, obscene, vile, obnoxious, despicable, repulsive, abhorred, heinous, odious, repugnant, loathsome, abominable, accursed, execrable, yucky *or* yukky *(slang)*, yucko *(Austral. slang)* • *I find their racist attitude detestable.*

detestation = **hatred**, disgust, loathing, hostility, dislike, animosity, aversion, revulsion, antipathy, abomination, animus, abhorrence, repugnance, odium, execration • *They were united in their detestation of the government.*

dethrone = **depose**, overthrow, oust, displace, eject, usurp, unseat, supplant, uncrown • *The king was dethroned and went into exile.*

detonate 1 = **set off**, trigger, explode, discharge, blow up, ignite, let off, touch off • *The terrorists planted and detonated the bomb.*
2 = **explode**, blast, discharge, blow up, be set off, fulminate, go bang, go boom, burst apart • *an explosive device which detonated last night*

detonation 1 = **explosion**, blast, bang, report, crack, boom, discharge, fulmination • *a heavy detonation echoed round the housing estate*
2 = **blowing-up**, explosion, discharge • *the accidental detonation of nuclear weapons*

detour = **diversion**, bypass, deviation, circuitous route, roundabout way, indirect course • *He made a detour around the outskirts of the city.*

detract from 1 = **lessen**, reduce, diminish, lower, take away from, derogate, devaluate • *Her faults did not seem to detract from her appeal.*
OPPOSITES: improve, boost, enhance
2 = **divert**, shift, distract, deflect, draw *or* lead away from • *They can only detract attention from the serious issues.*

detractor = **slanderer**, belittler, disparager, defamer, traducer, muckraker, scandalmonger, denigrator, backbiter, derogator *(rare)* • *This performance will silence the majority of his detractors.*

detriment = **damage**, loss, harm, injury, hurt, prejudice, disadvantage, impairment, disservice • *She supported her husband's career to the detriment of her own.*

detrimental = **damaging**, destructive, harmful, adverse, pernicious, unfavourable, prejudicial, baleful, deleterious, injurious, inimical, disadvantageous • *These foods are considered detrimental to health.*
OPPOSITES: good, helpful, beneficial

detritus = **debris**, remains, waste, rubbish, fragments, litter • *burnt-out buildings, littered with the detritus of war*

de trop = **in the way**, surplus, unnecessary, unwanted, redundant, unwelcome, superfluous • *I felt decidedly de trop as they talked shop in front of me.*

devalue = **belittle**, diminish, minimize, underestimate, scorn, downgrade, undervalue, deride, detract, denigrate, scoff at, disparage, decry, sneer at, underrate, deprecate, depreciate, derogate • *They attempted to devalue her work.*

devastate 1 = **destroy**, waste, ruin, sack, wreck, spoil, demolish, trash *(slang)*, level, total *(slang)*, ravage, plunder, desolate, pillage, raze, lay waste, despoil • *A fire devastated large parts of the castle.*
2 = **shatter**, overwhelm, confound, floor *(informal)* • *If word of this gets out, it will devastate his family.*

devastated = **shattered**, shocked, stunned, overcome, crushed, overwhelmed, distressed, gutted *(slang)*, dazed, knocked sideways *(informal)*, knocked for six *(informal)* • *He was devastated by the news of his friend's death.*

devastating 1 = **destructive**, damaging, catastrophic, harmful, detrimental, pernicious, ruinous, calamitous, cataclysmic, deleterious, injurious, maleficent • *the devastating force of the floods*
2 = **traumatic**, shocking, upsetting, disturbing, painful, distressing, scarring • *The diagnosis was devastating. She had cancer.*
3 = **impressive**, moving, striking, touching, affecting, grand, powerful, exciting, dramatic, stirring, awesome, gee-whizz *(slang)* • *the most devastating performance of his career*
4 = **savage**, cutting, overwhelming, withering, overpowering, satirical, incisive, sardonic, caustic, vitriolic, trenchant, mordant • *his devastating criticism of the Prime Minister*

devastation 1 = **destruction**, ruin, havoc, ravages, demolition, plunder, pillage, desolation, depredation, ruination, spoliation • *A huge bomb blast brought devastation to the centre of the city.*
2 = **trauma**, suffering, shock, pain, stress, upset, torture, distress, misery, anguish, upheaval, heartache, heartbreak • *the devastation which sexual abuse causes to the victim*

develop 1 = **grow**, advance, progress, spread, expand, mature, evolve, thrive, flourish, bloom, blossom, burgeon, ripen • *Children develop at different rates.*
2 = **result**, follow, arise, issue, happen, spring, stem, derive, break out, ensue, come about, be a direct result of • *a problem which developed from a leg injury*
3 = **establish**, set up, promote, generate, undertake, initiate, embark on, cultivate, instigate, inaugurate, set in motion • *her dreams of developing her own business*
4 = **form**, start, begin, contract, establish, pick up, breed,

acquire, generate, foster, originate • *She developed a taste for expensive nightclubs.*
5 = fall ill with, get, catch, contract, pick up, succumb to, be infected with, go down with *(Brit. informal)*, come down with, be struck down with, be stricken with, be taken ill with • *He developed pneumonia after a bout of flu.*
6 = produce, make, create, turn out, manufacture, construct, invent, compose, put together, originate, fabricate • *Several countries developed nuclear weapons secretly.*
7 = expand, improve, perfect, extend, work out, polish, reinforce, supplement, elaborate, unfold, enlarge, broaden, amplify, augment, flesh out, dilate upon • *They allowed me to develop their original idea.*

development 1 = growth, increase, growing, advance, progress, spread, expansion, extension, evolution, widening, blooming, maturing, unfolding, unravelling, burgeoning, advancement, progression, thickening, enlargement • *the development of the embryo*
2 = establishment, forming, generation, institution, invention, initiation, inauguration, instigation, origination • *the development of new and innovative services*
3 = event, change, happening, issue, result, situation, incident, circumstance, improvement, outcome, phenomenon, evolution, unfolding, occurrence, upshot, turn of events, evolvement • *There has been a significant development in the case.*

deviant AS AN ADJECTIVE **= perverted**, sick *(informal)*, twisted, bent *(slang)*, abnormal, queer *(informal derogatory)*, warped, perverse, wayward, kinky *(slang)*, devious, deviate, freaky *(slang)*, aberrant, pervy *(slang)*, sicko *(informal)* • *social reactions to deviant and criminal behaviour*
OPPOSITES: straight, normal, conventional
▸ AS A NOUN **= pervert**, freak, queer *(informal derogatory)*, misfit, sicko *(informal)*, odd type • *a dangerous deviant who lived rough*

deviate = differ, vary, depart, part, turn, bend, drift, wander, stray, veer, swerve, meander, diverge, digress, turn aside • *He didn't deviate from his schedule.*

deviation = departure, change, variation, shift, alteration, discrepancy, inconsistency, disparity, aberration, variance, divergence, fluctuation, irregularity, digression • *Deviation from the norm is not tolerated.*

device 1 = gadget, machine, tool, instrument, implement, invention, appliance, apparatus, gimmick, utensil, contraption, widget *(informal)*, contrivance, waldo, gizmo *or* gismo *(slang, chiefly U.S. & Canad.)* • *This device can measure minute quantities of matter.*
2 = ploy, scheme, strategy, plan, design, project, shift, trick, manoeuvre, stunt, dodge, expedient, ruse, artifice, gambit, stratagem, wile • *His actions are obviously a device to buy time.*

devil AS A NOUN **1 = evil spirit**, demon, fiend, ghoul, hellhound, atua *(N.Z.)*, wairua *(N.Z.)* • *the image of devils with horns and cloven hoofs*
2 = brute, monster, savage, beast, villain, rogue, barbarian, fiend, terror, swine, ogre • *the savage devils who mugged a helpless old woman*
3 = person, individual, soul, creature, thing, human being, beggar • *I feel sorry for the poor devil who marries you.*
4 = scamp, monkey *(informal)*, rogue, imp, rascal, tyke *(informal)*, scoundrel, scallywag *(informal)*, mischief-maker, whippersnapper, toerag *(slang)*, pickle *(Brit. informal)*, nointer *(Austral. slang)* • *You cheeky little devil!*
▸ IN PHRASES: **the Devil = Satan**, Lucifer, Prince of Darkness, Old One, Deuce, Old Gentleman *(informal)*, Lord of the Flies, Old Harry *(informal)*, Mephistopheles, Evil One, Beelzebub, Old Nick *(informal)*, Mephisto, Belial, Clootie *(Scot.)*, deil *(Scot.)*, Apollyon, Old Scratch *(informal)*, Foul Fiend, Wicked One, archfiend, Old Hornie *(informal)*, Abbadon • *the eternal conflict between God and the Devil*

QUOTATIONS
If the devil doesn't exist, but man has created him,
he has created him in his own image and likeness
[Fyodor Dostoevsky *The Brothers Karamazov*]
How art thou fallen from heaven, O Lucifer, son of the morning!
[*Bible: Isaiah*]
Be sober, be vigilant; because your adversary the devil, as a roaring lion, walketh about, seeking whom he may devour
[*Bible: I Peter*]
The serpent subtlest beast of all the field,
Of huge extent sometimes, with brazen eyes
And hairy mane terrific
[John Milton *Paradise Lost*]
PROVERBS
Better the devil you know than the devil you don't know
The devil looks after his own
He who sups with the devil should have a long spoon
Talk of the devil, and he shall appear

devilish 1 = fiendish, diabolical, wicked, satanic, atrocious, hellish, infernal, accursed, execrable, detestable, damnable, diabolic • *devilish instruments of torture*
2 = difficult, involved, complex, complicated, baffling, intricate, perplexing, thorny, knotty, problematical, ticklish • *It was a devilish puzzle to solve.*

devil-may-care = happy-go-lucky, casual, careless, easy-going, reckless, unconcerned, flippant, nonchalant, heedless, insouciant • *his reckless, devil-may-care attitude to life*

devilment = mischief, naughtiness, mischievousness, devilry, knavery, roguishness, roguery, rascality • *We sent him a Valentine card out of sheer devilment.*

devious 1 = sly, scheming, calculating, tricky, crooked *(informal)*, indirect, treacherous, dishonest, wily, insidious, evasive, deceitful, underhand, insincere, surreptitious, double-dealing, not straightforward • *She tracked down the other woman by devious means.*
OPPOSITES: direct, straight, straightforward
2 = indirect, roundabout, wandering, crooked, rambling, tortuous, deviating, circuitous, excursive • *He followed a devious route.*
OPPOSITES: direct, straight, straightforward

devise = work out, plan, form, design, imagine, frame, arrange, plot, construct, invent, conceive, formulate, contrive, dream up, concoct, think up • *We devised a scheme to help him.*

devoid *with* **of = lacking in**, without, free from, wanting in, sans *(archaic)*, bereft of, empty of, deficient in, denuded of, barren of • *I have never looked on a face so devoid of feeling.*

devolution = transfer of power, decentralization, distribution of power, surrender of power, relinquishment of power • *We are talking about devolution for Scotland.*

devolve *with* **on, upon, to,** *etc* **= transfer**, surrender, pass on, transmit, relinquish, hand down, entrust, consign, make over, cede, pass down, sign over, depute • *the need to decentralize and devolve power to regional governments*

devote = dedicate, give, commit, apply, reserve, pledge, surrender, assign, allot, give over, consecrate, set apart • *He decided to devote the rest of his life to music.*

devoted = dedicated, loving, committed, concerned, caring, true, constant, loyal, faithful, fond, ardent, staunch, devout, steadfast • *a loving and devoted father*
OPPOSITES: indifferent, unfaithful, disloyal

devotee 1 = enthusiast, fan, supporter, follower, addict, admirer, buff *(informal)*, fanatic, adherent, aficionado • *She is a devotee of Bach's music.*
2 = follower, student, supporter, pupil, convert, believer, partisan, disciple, learner, apostle, adherent, votary,

proselyte, catechumen • *devotees of the Hare Krishna movement*

devotion AS A NOUN 1 = **love**, passion, affection, intensity, attachment, zeal, fondness, fervour, adoration, ardour, earnestness • *She was flattered by his devotion.*
2 = **dedication**, commitment, loyalty, allegiance, fidelity, adherence, constancy, faithfulness • *devotion to the cause*
OPPOSITES: neglect, disregard, indifference
3 = **worship**, reverence, spirituality, holiness, piety, sanctity, adoration, godliness, religiousness, devoutness • *He was kneeling by his bed in an attitude of devotion.*
OPPOSITES: disrespect, irreverence, impiety
▸ AS A PLURAL NOUN = **prayers**, religious observance, church service, prayer meeting, matins, vespers, divine office • *He performs his devotions twice a day.*

devotional = **religious**, spiritual, holy, sacred, devout, pious, reverential • *hymns and devotional songs*

devour 1 = **eat**, consume, swallow, bolt, dispatch, cram, stuff, wolf, hoover *(informal)*, gorge, gulp, gobble, guzzle, polish off *(informal)*, pig out on *(slang)* • *She devoured half an apple pie.*
2 = **enjoy**, go through, absorb, appreciate, take in, relish, drink in, delight in, revel in, be preoccupied with, feast on, be engrossed by, read compulsively *or* voraciously • *He devoured 17 novels during his tour of India.*

devouring = **overwhelming**, powerful, intense, flaming, consuming, excessive, passionate, insatiable • *He has a devouring passion for music.*

devout 1 = **religious**, godly, pious, pure, holy, orthodox, saintly, reverent, prayerful • *She was a devout Christian.*
OPPOSITES: irreverent, sacrilegious, irreligious
2 = **sincere**, serious, deep, earnest, genuine, devoted, intense, passionate, profound, ardent, fervent, heartfelt, zealous, dinkum *(Austral. & N.Z. informal)* • *a devout opponent of racism*
OPPOSITES: passive, indifferent

devoutly = **sincerely**, really, truly, seriously, profoundly, earnestly, wholeheartedly, fervently, heart and soul, in earnest, with all your heart, from the bottom of your heart • *He devoutly hoped it was true.*

dexterity 1 = **skill**, expertise, mastery, touch, facility, craft, knack, finesse, artistry, proficiency, smoothness, neatness, deftness, nimbleness, adroitness, effortlessness, handiness • *He showed great dexterity on the guitar.*
OPPOSITES: inability, incompetence, incapacity
2 = **cleverness**, art, ability, ingenuity, readiness, aptitude, adroitness, aptness, expertness, skilfulness • *the wit and verbal dexterity of the script*

dexterous *or* **dextrous** 1 = **skilful**, able, expert, quick, masterly, active, neat, handy, apt, ingenious, adept, deft, nimble, proficient, agile, adroit, nimble-fingered • *As people grow older they generally become less dexterous.*
2 = **able**, skilled, expert, masterly, clever, practised, accomplished, versed, skilful, adept, masterful, proficient, adroit, tasty *(Brit. informal)* • *the composer's dextrous manipulation of pauses and silence*

diabolic 1 = **satanic**, demonic, hellish, devilish, infernal, fiendish, demoniac • *the diabolic forces which lurk in all violence*
2 = **wicked**, evil, cruel, vicious, monstrous, atrocious, fiendish, villainous, nefarious • *a life of diabolic depravity*

diabolical 1 = **dreadful**, shocking, terrible, appalling, nasty, tricky, unpleasant, outrageous, vile, excruciating, atrocious, abysmal, damnable • *the diabolical treatment of their prisoners*
2 = **wicked**, cruel, savage, monstrous, malicious, satanic, from hell *(informal)*, malignant, unspeakable, inhuman, implacable, malevolent, hellish, devilish, infernal, fiendish, ungodly, black-hearted, demoniac, hellacious *(U.S. slang)* • *sins committed in a spirit of diabolical enjoyment*

diadem = **coronet**, crown, tiara, circlet • *a diadem held the veil firmly in place*

diagnose = **identify**, determine, recognize, distinguish, interpret, pronounce, pinpoint • *The doctor diagnosed schizophrenia.*

diagnosis 1 = **identification**, discovery, recognition, pinpointing, detection • *Diagnosis of this disease can be very difficult.*
2 = **opinion**, result, verdict, conclusion, judgment, interpretation, prognosis, pronouncement • *She needs to have a second test to confirm the diagnosis.*

diagnostic = **symptomatic**, particular, distinguishing, distinctive, peculiar, indicative, idiosyncratic, recognizable, demonstrative • *symptoms diagnostic of cancer*

diagonal = **slanting**, angled, oblique, cross, crosswise, crossways, cater-cornered *(U.S. informal)*, cornerways • *a pattern of diagonal lines*

diagonally = **aslant**, obliquely, on the cross, at an angle, crosswise, on the bias, cornerwise • *He headed diagonally across the field.*

diagram = **plan**, figure, drawing, chart, outline, representation, sketch, layout, graph • *a diagram showing the workings of the engine*

dialect = **language**, speech, tongue, jargon, idiom, vernacular, brogue, lingo *(informal)*, patois, provincialism, localism • *the number of Italians who speak only local dialect*

QUOTATIONS
Dialect words – those terrible marks of the beast to the truly genteel
[Thomas Hardy *The Mayor of Casterbridge*]

dialectic = **debate**, reasoning, discussion, logic, contention, polemics, disputation, argumentation, ratiocination • *He spent much time learning rhetoric and dialectic.*

dialogue 1 = **discussion**, talks, conference, negotiations, exchange, debate, chat, confabulation, interlocution • *He wants to open a dialogue with the protesters.*
2 = **conversation**, discussion, communication, discourse, interchange, converse, colloquy, confabulation, duologue, interlocution • *Those who witnessed their dialogue spoke of high emotion.*
3 = **script**, conversation, lines, words, text, spoken part • *The play's dialogue is sharp and witty.*

diameter = **breadth**, span, width, spread, beam, latitude, broadness, wideness • *the diameter of a human hair*

diametrically = **completely**, totally, entirely, absolutely, utterly • *They came to conclusions diametrically opposed to ours.*

diamond
▸ RELATED ADJECTIVE: diamantine

diaper = **nappy**, terries, training pants • *He never changed the baby's diapers.*

diaphanous = **fine**, light, thin, sheer, delicate, transparent, see-through, translucent, chiffon, gossamer, gauzy, filmy, pellucid, cobwebby • *a diaphanous dress of pale gold chiffon*

diaphragm
▸ RELATED ADJECTIVE: phrenic

diarist

DIARISTS

Marie Bashkirtseff *(Russian)*
Fanny Burney *(English)*
E.M. Delafield *(English)*
John Evelyn *(English)*
Helen Fielding (Bridget Jones) *(English)*
Anne Frank *(Dutch)*
André Gide *(French)*
George and Weedon Grossmith (Charles Pooter) *(English)*
Francis Kilvert *(British)*
Samuel Pepys *(English)*
Marion Rivers-Moore *(English)*
Sue Townsend (Adrian Mole) *(English)*
Anaïs Nin *(French-U.S.)*
Dorothy Wordsworth *(English)*

diarrhoea *or (U.S.)* **diarrhea = the runs**, the trots *(informal)*, dysentery, looseness, the skits *(informal)*, Montezuma's revenge *(informal)*, gippy tummy, holiday tummy, Spanish tummy, the skitters *(informal)* • *One of the chief causes of death from diarrhoea is dehydration.*

diary 1 = journal, log, chronicle, memoir, daily record, logbook, day-to-day account, blog *(informal)* • *the most famous descriptive passage in his diary*
2 = engagement book, schedule, agenda, calendar, timetable, organizer, Filofax *(trademark)*, appointment book, personal organizer • *My diary is pretty full next week.*

QUOTATIONS
Keep a diary and someday it'll keep you
[Mae West *Every Day's a Holiday*]

diatribe = tirade, abuse, criticism, denunciation, reviling, stricture, harangue, invective, vituperation, stream of abuse, verbal onslaught, philippic • *an extended diatribe against academia*

dicey = dangerous, difficult, tricky, risky, hairy *(slang)*, ticklish, chancy *(informal)* • *a dicey moment during a risky climb up the cliff*

dichotomy = division, gulf, split, separation, polarity, disjunction • *a dichotomy between the academic world and the industrial world*

dick = penis, cock *(taboo slang)*, prick *(taboo slang)*, member, tool *(taboo slang)*, organ, wang *(U.S. slang)*, knob *(Brit. taboo slang)*, chopper *(Brit. slang)*, plonker *(slang)*, dong *(slang)*, winkle *(Brit. slang)*, joystick *(slang)*, phallus, pecker *(U.S. & Canad. taboo slang)*, John Thomas *(taboo slang)*, weenie *(U.S. slang)*, whang *(U.S. slang)*, tadger *(Brit. slang)*, schlong *(U.S. slang)*, pizzle *(archaic or dialect)*, willie or willy *(Brit. informal)* • *She remarked that most men think with their dicks, not their heads.*

dicky = weak, poorly, dodgy, queer *(informal)*, shaky, unreliable, sickly, unsteady, unsound, iffy *(informal)*, fluttery • *He always has a dicky stomach after eating curry.*

dictate AS A VERB **1 = speak**, say, utter, read out, read aloud, say aloud • *He dictates his novels to his secretary.*
2 = determine, demand, command, establish, prescribe, pronounce, decree, ordain • *Circumstances dictated that they played a defensive game.*
▸ AS A NOUN **1 = command**, order, decree, word, demand, direction, requirement, bidding, mandate, injunction, statute, fiat, ultimatum, ordinance, edict, behest • *They must abide by the dictates of the new government.*
2 = principle, law, rule, standard, code, criterion, ethic, canon, maxim, dictum, precept, axiom, moral law • *We have followed the dictates of our consciences.*
▸ IN PHRASES: **dictate to someone = order (about)**, direct, dominate, bully, walk (all) over, bulldoze, pressurize, lay down the law, browbeat, give orders to, lord it over, pronounce to, domineer • *What gives them the right to dictate to us?*

dictator = absolute ruler, tyrant, despot, Big Brother, oppressor, control freak, autocrat, absolutist, martinet • *the fall of Haiti's military dictator*

dictatorial 1 = absolute, unlimited, totalitarian, autocratic, unrestricted, tyrannical, despotic • *He suspended the constitution and assumed dictatorial powers.*
OPPOSITES: democratic, restricted, constitutional
2 = domineering, authoritarian, oppressive, bossy *(informal)*, imperious, overbearing, magisterial, iron-handed, dogmatical • *his dictatorial management style*
OPPOSITES: humble, tolerant, servile

dictatorship 1 = absolute rule, tyranny, totalitarianism, authoritarianism, reign of terror, despotism, autocracy, absolutism • *a long period of military dictatorship*
2 = totalitarian state, autocracy, autarchy, monocracy • *every country in the region was a military dictatorship*

diction = pronunciation, speech, articulation, delivery, fluency, inflection, intonation, elocution, enunciation • *Clear diction is important in public speaking.*

dictionary = wordbook, vocabulary, glossary, encyclopedia, lexicon, concordance, word list, vocabulary list • *If you don't know what it means, look it up in the dictionary.*

QUOTATIONS
Dictionaries are like watches; the worst is better than none, and the best cannot be expected to go quite true
[Dr. Johnson]
When I feel inclined to read poetry I take down my Dictionary. The poetry of words is quite as beautiful as that of sentences. The author may arrange the gems effectively, but their shape and lustre have been given by the attrition of the ages
[Oliver Wendell Holmes Sr. *The Autocrat's Autobiography*]
dictionary: a malevolent literary device for cramping the growth of a language and making it hard and inelastic. This dictionary, however, is a most useful work
[Ambrose Bierce *The Devil's Dictionary*]

dictum 1 = saying, saw, maxim, adage, proverb, precept, axiom, gnome • *the dictum that it is preferable to be roughly right than precisely wrong*
2 = decree, order, demand, statement, command, dictate, canon, fiat, edict, pronouncement • *his dictum that the priority of the government must be the health of the people*

didactic 1 = instructive, educational, enlightening, moral, edifying, homiletic, preceptive • *In totalitarian societies, art exists solely for didactic purposes.*
2 = pedantic, academic, formal, pompous, schoolmasterly, erudite, bookish, abstruse, moralizing, priggish, pedagogic • *He adopts a lofty, didactic tone when addressing women.*

die AS A VERB **1 = pass away**, depart, expire, perish, buy it *(U.S. slang)*, check out *(U.S. slang)*, kick it *(slang)*, croak *(slang)*, give up the ghost, go belly-up *(slang)*, snuff it *(slang)*, peg out *(informal)*, kick the bucket *(slang)*, buy the farm *(U.S. slang)*, peg it *(informal)*, decease, cark it *(Austral. & N.Z. slang)*, pop your clogs *(informal)*, breathe your last, hop the twig *(slang)* • *His mother died when he was a child.*
OPPOSITES: live, exist, survive
2 = stop, fail, halt, break down, run down, stop working, peter out, fizzle out, lose power, seize up, conk out *(informal)*, go kaput *(informal)*, go phut, fade out *or* away • *The engine coughed, spluttered, and died.*
3 = dwindle, end, decline, pass, disappear, sink, fade, weaken, diminish, vanish, decrease, decay, lapse, wither, wilt, lessen, wane, subside, ebb, die down, die out, abate, peter out, die away, grow less • *My love for you will never die.*
OPPOSITES: increase, grow, flourish
▸ IN PHRASES: **be dying for something = long for**, want, desire, crave, yearn for, hunger for, pine for, hanker after, be eager for, ache for, swoon over, languish for, set your heart on • *I'm dying for a cigarette.*
be dying of something = be overcome with, succumb to, be overwhelmed by, collapse with • *I'm dying of thirst.*
die away = fade away, decline, disappear, dwindle, subside, ebb, fall away, melt away • *The sound died away.*
die down = decrease, lessen, subside, abate, let up, ease off, slacken off • *The controversy is unlikely to die down.*
die out 1 = vanish, disappear, fade (away), perish, cease to exist, become extinct, disappear from the face of the earth, vanish off the face of the earth, pass into oblivion, cark it *(Austral. & N.Z. slang)* • *We used to believe that capitalism would soon die out.*
2 = go out • *The fire has died out.*

QUOTATIONS
Cowards die many times before their deaths; The valiant never taste of death but once
[William Shakespeare *Julius Caesar*]

Only we die in earnest, that's no jest
[Walter Raleigh *On the Life of Man*]
Die, my dear doctor? That's the last thing I shall do!
[Lord Palmerston]
It's not that I'm afraid to die. I just don't want to be there when it happens
[Woody Allen *Death*]
To die will be an awfully big adventure
[J.M. Barrie *Peter Pan*]
Dying is a very dull, dreary affair. And my advice to you is to have nothing whatever to do with it
[Somerset Maugham]
We shall die alone
[Blaise Pascal *Pensées*]
A man dies still if he has done nothing, as one who has done much
[Homer *Iliad*]
It is as natural to die as to be born; and to a little infant, perhaps, the one is as painful as the other
[Francis Bacon *Of Death*]

die-hard *or* **diehard** AS A NOUN = **reactionary**, fanatic, zealot, intransigent, stick-in-the-mud *(informal)*, old fogey, ultraconservative • *He has links with former Communist diehards.*
▸ AS A MODIFIER = **reactionary**, uncompromising, inflexible, intransigent, immovable, unreconstructed *(chiefly U.S.)*, dyed-in-the-wool, ultraconservative • *Even their die-hard fans can't pretend this was a good game.*

diet[1] AS A NOUN 1 = **food**, provisions, fare, rations, subsistence, kai *(N.Z. informal)*, nourishment, sustenance, victuals, commons, edibles, comestibles, nutriment, viands, aliment • *Watch your diet – you need plenty of fruit and vegetables.*
2 = **fast**, regime, abstinence, regimen, crash diet, dietary regime, dietary programme • *Have you been on a diet? You've lost a lot of weight.*
▸ AS A VERB = **slim**, fast, be on a diet, lose weight, abstain, watch your weight, eat sparingly • *Most of us have dieted at some time in our lives.*
OPPOSITES: indulge, glut, overindulge

QUOTATIONS
all [diets] blur together, leaving you with only one definite piece of information: french-fried potatoes are out
[Jean Kerr *Please Don't Eat the Daisies*]
Diets are like boyfriends – it never really works to go back to them
[Nigella Lawson]

▹ *See panel* **Diets**

diet[2] *often cap.* = **council**, meeting, parliament, sitting, congress, chamber, convention, legislature, legislative assembly • *The Diet has no time to discuss the bill.*

dieter = **slimmer**, weight watcher, calorie counter, faster, reducer • *Dieters can become obsessed with the number of calories in food.*

differ 1 = **be dissimilar**, contradict, contrast with, vary, counter, belie, depart from, diverge, negate, fly in the face of, run counter to, be distinct, stand apart, make a nonsense of, be at variance with • *His story differed from his mother's in several respects.*
OPPOSITES: accord, coincide, harmonize
2 = **be different**, vary, diverge, be distinguishable, be dissimilar, not be alike • *We differ in both approach and views.*
3 = **disagree**, argue, clash, dispute, dissent, quarrel, squabble, quibble, fail to agree • *The two leaders have differed on the issue of sanctions.*
OPPOSITES: agree, accord, concur

difference AS A NOUN 1 = **dissimilarity**, contrast, variation, change, variety, exception, distinction, diversity, alteration, discrepancy, disparity, deviation, differentiation, peculiarity, divergence, singularity, particularity, distinctness, unlikeness • *the vast difference in size*
OPPOSITES: similarity, resemblance, affinity
2 = **remainder**, rest, balance, remains, excess, outstanding amount, remaining amount • *They pledge to refund the difference within 48 hours.*
3 = **disagreement**, conflict, argument, row, clash, dispute, set-to *(informal)*, controversy, contention, quarrel, strife, wrangle, tiff, contretemps, discordance, contrariety • *They are leaning how to resolve their differences.*
OPPOSITES: agreement, concordance, harmony
▸ IN PHRASES: **make a difference to something** *or* **someone** = **change**, transform, alter, modify, metamorphose • *Where you live can make such a difference to the way you feel.*

different 1 = **dissimilar**, opposed, contrasting, changed, clashing, unlike, altered, diverse, at odds, inconsistent, disparate, deviating, divergent, at variance, discrepant, streets apart • *We have totally different views.*
2 = **various**, some, many, several, varied, numerous, diverse, divers *(archaic)*, assorted, miscellaneous, sundry, manifold, multifarious • *Different countries specialise in different products.*
3 = **unusual**, unique, special, strange, rare, extraordinary, bizarre, distinctive, something else, peculiar, uncommon, singular, unconventional, out of the ordinary, left-field *(informal)*, atypical • *Try to think of a menu that is interesting and different.*
4 = **other**, another, separate, individual, distinct, unrelated, discrete • *What you do in the privacy of your own home is a different matter.*

QUOTATIONS
If a man does not keep pace with his companions, perhaps it is because he hears a different drummer
[Henry David Thoreau *Walden*]

DIETS

Atkins diet
breatharian diet *or* inedia
cabbage soup diet
Cambridge diet
CRON-diet
dairy-free diet
detox diet
Diet Smart Plan
DASH diet
fat resistance diet
Feingold diet
Fit for Life diet
flexitarian diet
food combining diet
F-Plan diet
fruitarian diet
gluten-free, casein-free diet
GI diet
Graham diet
grapefruit diet *or* Hollywood diet
hacker's diet
halal diet
hallelujah diet
high protein diet
kosher diet
lacto-vegetarian diet
low-protein diet
macrobiotic diet
Master Cleanse diet
Mediterranean diet
Montignac diet
natural food diet
negative calorie diet
no-grain diet
Okinawa diet
Optimal diet
organic food diet
Ornish diet
ovo-lacto-vegetarian diet
Palaeolithic diet
Perricone Weight-Loss diet
pescetarian diet *or* pesco-vegetarianism
pollotarian diet
Pritikin diet
raw food diet
rice diet
Rosemary Conley diet
Scarsdale Medical diet
sex diet
Shangri-La diet
Slimming World diet
South Beach diet
Stillman diet
Subway diet
veganism
vegetarianism
very low calorie diet *or* VLCD
weigh down diet
Weight Watchers
zone diet

differential AS AN ADJECTIVE = **distinctive**, different, contrasting, distinguishing, discriminatory, dissimilar, divergent, discriminative, diacritical • *They may be forced to eliminate differential voting rights.*
▸ AS A NOUN = **difference**, gulf, gap, distinction, discrepancy, disparity, divergence, amount of difference • *Industrial wage differentials widened.*

differentiate 1 = **distinguish**, separate, discriminate, contrast, discern, mark off, make a distinction, tell apart, set off *or* apart • *He cannot differentiate between his imagination and the real world.*
2 = **make different**, separate, distinguish, characterize, single out, segregate, individualize, mark off, set apart, set off *or* apart • *distinctive policies that differentiate them from the other parties*
3 = **become different**, change, convert, transform, alter, adapt, modify • *These ectodermal cells differentiate into two cell types.*

differentiation = **distinction**, difference, contrast, disparity, divergence, polarity, distinctness • *the differentiation between the two ranges*

differently = **dissimilarly**, otherwise, in another way, in contrary fashion • *He thinks differently from normal people.*
OPPOSITES: similarly, in the same way, likewise

difficult 1 = **hard**, tough, taxing, demanding, challenging, painful, exacting, formidable, uphill, strenuous, problematic, arduous, onerous, laborious, burdensome, wearisome, no picnic *(informal)*, toilsome, like getting blood out of a stone • *It is difficult for single mothers to get jobs.*
OPPOSITES: light, easy, manageable
2 = **problematical**, involved, complex, complicated, delicate, obscure, abstract, baffling, intricate, perplexing, thorny, knotty, abstruse, ticklish, enigmatical • *It was a very difficult decision to make.*
OPPOSITES: simple, obvious, plain
3 = **troublesome**, trying, awkward, demanding, rigid, stubborn, perverse, fussy, tiresome, intractable, fastidious, fractious, unyielding, obstinate, intransigent, unmanageable, unbending, uncooperative, hard to please, refractory, obstreperous, pig-headed, bull-headed, unaccommodating, unamenable • *I had a feeling you were going to be difficult about this.*
OPPOSITES: pleasant, accommodating, cooperative
4 = **tough**, trying, hard, dark, grim, straitened, full of hardship • *These are difficult times.*
OPPOSITES: easy, pleasant

difficulty AS A NOUN 1 = **problem**, trouble, obstacle, hurdle, dilemma, hazard, complication, hassle *(informal)*, snag, uphill *(S. African)*, predicament, pitfall, stumbling block, impediment, hindrance, tribulation, quandary, can of worms *(informal)*, point at issue, disputed point • *There is only one difficulty. The hardest thing is to leave.*
2 = **hardship**, labour, pain, strain, awkwardness, painfulness, strenuousness, arduousness, laboriousness • *The injured man mounted his horse with difficulty.*
3 = **complexity**, involvement, complication, intricacy, hardness, convolution, difficultness, abstruseness • *questions arranged in no particular order of difficulty*
▸ IN PHRASES: **in difficulty** *or* **difficulties** = **in trouble**, in distress, in hot water *(informal)*, in a mess, in deep water, in a spot *(informal)*, in a fix *(informal)*, in a quandary, in a dilemma, in embarrassment, in a jam *(informal)*, in dire straits, in a pickle *(informal)*, in a tight spot, in perplexity, in a predicament • *Rumours spread about banks being in difficulty.*

QUOTATIONS
Difficulties are things that show what men are
[Epictetus *Discourses*]
Difficulty gives all things their estimation
[Montaigne *Essays*]

diffidence = **shyness**, fear, reserve, hesitation, doubt, constraint, reluctance, insecurity, modesty, humility, self-consciousness, timidity, backwardness, hesitancy, meekness, lack of self-confidence, bashfulness, timorousness, unassertiveness, sheepishness, timidness • *He spoke with a certain diffidence.*
OPPOSITES: confidence, courage, assurance

diffident = **shy**, reserved, withdrawn, reluctant, modest, shrinking, doubtful, backward, unsure, insecure, constrained, timid, self-conscious, hesitant, meek, unassuming, unobtrusive, self-effacing, sheepish, aw-shucks, bashful, timorous, unassertive • *She was diffident and reserved in meetings.*

diffuse AS A VERB = **spread**, distribute, scatter, circulate, disperse, dispense, dispel, dissipate, propagate, disseminate • *Our aim is to diffuse new ideas obtained from elsewhere.*
▸ AS AN ADJECTIVE 1 = **spread-out**, scattered, dispersed, unconcentrated • *a diffuse community*
OPPOSITES: concentrated
2 = **rambling**, loose, vague, meandering, waffling *(informal)*, long-winded, wordy, discursive, verbose, prolix, maundering, digressive, diffusive, circumlocutory • *His writing is so diffuse that it is almost impossible to understand.*
OPPOSITES: brief, to the point, concise

diffusion = **spreading**, distribution, scattering, circulation, expansion, propagation, dissemination, dispersal, dispersion, dissipation • *the development and diffusion of ideas*

dig AS A VERB 1 = **hollow out**, mine, bore, cut, pierce, quarry, excavate, gouge, scoop out • *Dig a large hole and bang the stake in.*
2 = **delve**, tunnel, burrow, grub, break up earth *or* soil • *I changed into clothes more suited to digging.*
3 = **turn over**, till, break up, work, hoe • *He was outside digging the garden.*
4 = **search**, hunt, rummage, root, delve, forage, dig down, fossick *(Austral. & N.Z.)* • *He dug around in his pocket for his keys.*
5 = **poke**, drive, push, stick, punch, stab, thrust, shove, prod, jab • *She dug her nails into his flesh.*
6 = **like**, love, enjoy, go for, appreciate, groove *(dated slang)*, delight in, be fond of, be keen on, be partial to • *I really dig this band's energy.*
7 = **understand**, follow, grasp, make out, get the drift of *(informal)* • *Can you dig what I'm trying to say?*
▸ AS A NOUN 1 = **cutting remark**, crack *(slang)*, insult, taunt, sneer, jeer, quip, barb, wisecrack *(informal)*, gibe • *She couldn't resist a dig at him after his unfortunate performance.*
2 = **poke**, thrust, butt, nudge, prod, jab, punch • *She silenced him with a sharp dig in the small of the back.*
▸ AS A PLURAL NOUN = **rented accommodation**, rooms, quarters, lodgings, rented apartments • *He went to the city and lived in digs.*
▸ IN PHRASES: **dig in** = **begin** *or* **start eating**, tuck in *(informal)*, fall to • *Pull up a chair and dig in.*
dig into something = **investigate**, go into, research into, probe into, delve into, inquire into • *Reporters are digging into the history of her family.*
dig something *or* **someone out** 1 = **excavate**, unearth, bring to the surface, disinter, bring out of the ground • *Rescue workers are digging people out of collapsed buildings.*
2 = **find**, locate, track down, unearth, ferret out, lay your hand on, turn up • *I'll try and dig his phone number out for you.*
dig something *or* **someone up** 1 = **unearth**, excavate, bring to the surface, disinter, bring out of the ground • *More bodies have been dug up at the site.*
2 = **discover**, find, expose, come up with, come across, uncover, retrieve, unearth, root out *(informal)*, extricate, bring to light • *His description fits perfectly the evidence dug up by the officer.*

digest AS A VERB **1 = ingest**, absorb, incorporate, dissolve, assimilate • *She couldn't digest food properly.*
2 = take in, master, absorb, grasp, drink in, soak up, devour, assimilate • *She read everything, digesting every fragment of news.*
▸ AS A NOUN **= summary**, résumé, abstract, epitome, condensation, compendium, synopsis, précis, abridgment • *a regular digest of environmental statistics*

digestion = ingestion, absorption, incorporation, assimilation • *Liquids served with meals interfere with digestion.*
▸ RELATED ADJECTIVE: peptic

d

digit 1 = number, figure, numeral, integer • *Her telephone number differs from mine by one digit.*
2 = finger, toe, extremity • *Many animals have five digits.*

dignified = distinguished, august, reserved, imposing, formal, grave, noble, upright, stately, solemn, lofty, exalted, decorous • *He conducted the interview in a dignified and professional manner.*
OPPOSITES: vulgar, crass, undignified

dignify = distinguish, honour, grace, raise, advance, promote, elevate, glorify, exalt, ennoble, aggrandize • *I see no point in dignifying this kind of speculation with a response*

dignitary = public figure, worthy, notable, high-up (*informal*), bigwig (*informal*), celeb (*informal*), personage, pillar of society, pillar of the church, notability, pillar of the state, V.I.P. • *He was a visiting dignitary of great importance.*

dignity 1 = decorum, breeding, gravity, majesty, grandeur, respectability, nobility, propriety, solemnity, gentility, courtliness, loftiness, stateliness • *Everyone admired her extraordinary dignity and composure.*
2 = self-importance, pride, self-esteem, morale, self-respect, self-worth, self-regard, self-possession, amour-propre (*French*) • *Admit that you were wrong. You won't lose dignity.*

QUOTATIONS

Our dignity is not in what we do, but in what we understand
[George Santayana *Winds of Doctrine*]

By dignity, I mean the high place attained only when the heart and mind are lifted, equally at once, by the creative union of perception and grace
[James Thurber *Lanterns and Lances*]

digress = wander, drift, stray, depart, ramble, meander, diverge, deviate, turn aside, be diffuse, expatiate, go off at a tangent, get off the point *or* subject • *She digressed from the matter under discussion.*

digression = departure, aside, diversion, wandering, straying, footnote, deviation, divergence, parenthesis, apostrophe, obiter dictum • *the text is full of digressions*

dilapidated = ruined, fallen in, broken-down, battered, neglected, crumbling, rundown, decayed, decaying, falling apart, beat-up (*informal*), shaky, shabby, worn-out, ramshackle, in ruins, rickety, decrepit, tumbledown, uncared for, gone to rack and ruin • *She lived in a dilapidated old cottage.*

dilate = enlarge, extend, stretch, expand, swell, widen, broaden, puff out, distend • *The pupils dilate to let in more light.*
OPPOSITES: contract, narrow, shrink

dilation = enlargement, increase, spread, expansion, extension, broadening, dilatation, distension • *the constriction and dilation of blood vessels*

dilatory = slow, delaying, lingering, putting off, slack, backward, sluggish, dallying, loitering, time-wasting, laggard, tardy, procrastinating, tarrying, snail-like, behindhand • *They performed their work in a dilatory fashion.*
OPPOSITES: sharp (*informal*), prompt, on-the-ball (*informal*)

dilemma AS A NOUN **= predicament**, problem, difficulty, spot (*informal*), fix (*informal*), mess, puzzle, jam (*informal*), embarrassment, plight, strait, pickle (*informal*), how-do-you-do (*informal*), quandary, perplexity, tight corner *or* spot • *The issue raises a moral dilemma.*
▸ IN PHRASES: **on the horns of a dilemma = between the devil and the deep blue sea**, between a rock and a hard place (*informal*), between Scylla and Charybdis • *I found myself on the horns of a dilemma – whatever I did, it would be wrong.*

dilettante = amateur, aesthete, dabbler, trifler, nonprofessional • *The sailing elite considered him a rank amateur, a dilettante.*

diligence = application, industry, care, activity, attention, perseverance, earnestness, attentiveness, assiduity, intentness, assiduousness, laboriousness, heedfulness, sedulousness • *The police are pursuing their enquiries with great diligence.*

diligent = hard-working, careful, conscientious, earnest, active, busy, persistent, attentive, persevering, tireless, painstaking, laborious, industrious, indefatigable, studious, assiduous, swotty (*Brit. informal*), sedulous • *a diligent student*
OPPOSITES: lazy, indifferent, careless

dilute AS A VERB **1 = water down**, thin (out), weaken, adulterate, add water to, make thinner, cut (*informal*) • *Dilute the syrup well with cooled, boiled water.*
OPPOSITES: concentrate, strengthen, condense
2 = reduce, weaken, diminish, temper, decrease, lessen, diffuse, quell, mitigate, tone down, attenuate, disempower • *It was a clear attempt to dilute black voting power.*
OPPOSITES: strengthen, intensify
▸ AS AN ADJECTIVE **= watered down**, weak, diluted, watery, cut (*informal*) • *a dilute solution of bleach*

diluted = watered down, thinned, weak, weakened, dilute, watery, adulterated, cut (*informal*), wishy-washy (*informal*) • *Encourage your child to drink diluted fruit juice.*

dim AS AN ADJECTIVE **1 = dull**, weak, pale, muted, subdued, feeble, murky, opaque, dingy, subfusc • *She stood waiting in the dim light.*
2 = poorly lit, dark, gloomy, murky, shady, shadowy, dusky, crepuscular, darkish, tenebrous, unilluminated, caliginous (*archaic*) • *The room was dim and cool and quiet.*
3 = cloudy, grey, gloomy, dismal, murky, overcast, leaden • *a dim February day*
OPPOSITES: clear, fair, bright
4 = unclear, obscured, faint, blurred, fuzzy, shadowy, hazy, indistinguishable, bleary, undefined, out of focus, ill-defined, indistinct, indiscernible • *His torch picked out the dim figures.*
OPPOSITES: clear, distinct, sharp
5 = obscure, remote, vague, confused, shadowy, imperfect, hazy, sketchy, intangible, indistinct • *The era of social activism is all but a dim memory.*
6 = unfavourable, bad, black, depressing, discouraging, gloomy, dismal, sombre, unpromising, dispiriting, disheartening • *The prospects for a peaceful solution are dim.*
7 = stupid (*Informal*), slow, thick, dull, dense, dumb (*informal*), daft (*informal*), dozy (*Brit. informal*), obtuse, unintelligent, asinine, slow on the uptake (*informal*), braindead (*informal*), doltish • *She's not as dim as she seems.*
OPPOSITES: bright, aware, sharp
▸ AS A VERB **1 = turn down**, lower, fade, dip, dull, soften, subdue, bedim, make less bright • *Dim the overhead lights.*
2 = grow *or* **become faint**, fade, dull, grow *or* become dim • *The houselights dimmed.*
3 = darken, dull, blacken, cloud over, grow dark, become leaden • *The dusk sky dims to a chilly indigo.*
4 = diminish, decline, dwindle, wane, recede, subside, ebb, die out, fade away, shrivel, peter out, slacken • *Their economic prospects have dimmed.*
5 = fade, fail, disappear, dissolve, melt away, die away • *Their memory of what happened has dimmed.*

dimension AS A NOUN **1** = **aspect**, side, feature, angle, facet • *This adds a new dimension to our work.*
2 = **extent**, size, magnitude, importance, scope, greatness, amplitude, largeness • *She did not understand the dimension of her plight.*
▸ AS A PLURAL NOUN = **proportions**, range, size, scale, measure, volume, capacity, bulk, measurement, amplitude, bigness • *the grandiose dimensions of the room*

diminish **1** = **decrease**, decline, lessen, contract, weaken, shrink, dwindle, wane, recede, subside, ebb, taper, die out, fade away, abate, peter out • *The threat of war has diminished.*
OPPOSITES: increase, grow, expand
2 = **reduce**, cut, decrease, lessen, contract, lower, weaken, curtail, abate, retrench, disempower • *Federalism is intended to diminish the power of the central state.*
OPPOSITES: increase, expand, enhance
3 = **belittle**, scorn, devalue, undervalue, deride, demean, denigrate, scoff at, disparage, decry, sneer at, underrate, deprecate, depreciate, cheapen, derogate • *He never diminished her in front of other people.*

diminution **1** = **decrease**, decline, lessening, weakening, decay, contraction, abatement • *a slight diminution in asset value*
2 = **reduction**, cut, decrease, weakening, deduction, contraction, lessening, cutback, retrenchment, abatement, curtailment • *The president has accepted a diminution of his original powers.*

diminutive = **small**, little, tiny, minute, pocket(-sized), mini, wee, miniature, petite, midget, undersized, teeny-weeny, Lilliputian, bantam, teensy-weensy, pygmy *or* pigmy • *a diminutive figure stood at the entrance*
OPPOSITES: big, great, giant

dimple = **indentation**, pit, hollow, dip, dent, cleft, concavity • *cellulite causes orange peel-like dimples on the skin*

dimwit = **idiot**, bonehead *(slang)*, dunce, dullard, ignoramus, nitwit *(informal)*, blockhead, fathead *(informal)*, booby, dumb-ass *(slang)*, gobshite *(Irish taboo slang)*, dunderhead, numpty *(Scot. informal)*, lamebrain *(informal)*, numbskull *or* numskull • *Frankly, only a dimwit would say that.*

dim-witted *or* **dimwitted** = **stupid**, slow, thick *(informal)*, dull, dim, dense, dumb *(informal)*, dozy *(Brit. informal)*, dopey *(informal)*, obtuse, slow on the uptake, braindead *(informal)*, thick-skulled, dumb-ass *(slang)*, doltish, unperceptive • *He plays a dimwitted Irish priest in the TV series.*
OPPOSITES: bright, smart, sharp

din = **noise**, row, racket, crash, clash, shout, outcry, clamour, clatter, uproar, commotion, pandemonium, babel, hubbub, hullabaloo, clangour • *They tried to make themselves heard over the din of the crowd.*
OPPOSITES: peace, quiet, silence

dine AS A VERB = **eat**, lunch, feast, sup, have supper, chow down *(slang)* • *He dines alone most nights.*
▸ IN PHRASES: **dine on** *or* **off something** = **eat**, consume, feed on, scoff • *I could dine on caviar and champagne for the rest of my life.*

diner **1** = **café**, restaurant, bistro, cafeteria, trattoria, tearoom, eatery *or* eaterie • *I ducked into a diner where I sometimes stop for coffee.*
2 = **customer**, guest, client, eater, feaster, banqueter, gourmand, picnicker • *They sat in a corner, away from the other diners.*

dingy **1** = **dull**, dark, dim, gloomy, murky, dreary, sombre, drab, colourless, dusky, bedimmed • *He took me to his rather dingy office.*
2 = **discoloured**, soiled, dirty, shabby, faded, seedy, grimy • *wallpaper with dingy yellow stripes*

dinkum = **genuine**, honest, natural, frank, sincere, candid, upfront *(informal)*, artless, guileless • *He was a fair dinkum bloke with no pretensions.*

dinky = **cute**, small, neat, mini, trim, miniature, petite, dainty, natty *(informal)*, cutesy *(informal, chiefly U.S.)* • *She drove a dinky little sports car.*

dinner **1** = **meal**, evening meal, main meal, spread *(informal)*, repast, blowout *(slang)*, collation, nosh-up *(informal)*, refection • *Would you like to stay and have dinner?*
2 = **banquet**, feast, blowout *(slang)*, repast, beanfeast *(Brit. informal)*, carousal, hakari *(N.Z.)* • *The annual dinner was held in the spring.*

dinosaur = **fuddy-duddy**, anachronism, dodo *(informal)*, stick-in-the-mud *(informal)*, antique *(informal)*, fossil *(informal)*, relic *(informal)*, fogy *or* fogey, back number *(informal)* • *Such companies are industrial dinosaurs.*
▹ *See panel* **Dinosaurs**

dint
▸ IN PHRASES: **by dint of** = **by means of**, using, due to, as a result of, by virtue of, on the strength of, on account of, as a consequence of, by force of • *He succeeded by dint of sheer hard work.*

diocese = **bishopric**, see • *parishioners of the bishop's diocese*

dip AS A VERB **1** = **plunge**, immerse, bathe, duck, rinse, douse, dunk, souse • *Dip the food into the sauce.*
2 = **drop (down)**, set, fall, lower, disappear, sink, fade, slump, descend, tilt, subside, sag, droop • *The sun dipped below the horizon.*
3 = **slope**, drop (down), descend, fall, decline, pitch, sink, incline, drop away • *a path which suddenly dips down into a tunnel*
4 = **drop**, fall, lower, decline, sink, dive, diminish, tumble, descend • *Unemployment dipped to 6.9 per cent last month.*
5 = **dim**, dull, turn down, darken, bedim • *He dipped the headlights of his car.*
▸ AS A NOUN **1** = **plunge**, ducking, soaking, drenching, immersion, douche, submersion • *Freshen the salad leaves with a quick dip into cold water.*
2 = **nod**, drop, lowering, slump, sag • *She acknowledged me with a slight dip of the head.*
3 = **hollow**, hole, depression, pit, basin, dent, trough, indentation, concavity • *Turn right where the road makes a dip.*
4 = **mixture**, solution, preparation, suspension, infusion, concoction, dilution • *sheep dip*
5 = **drop**, cut, reduction, lowering, decline, slump, decrease, fall-off, downturn • *the current dip in farm spending*
6 = **sauce**, dressing, relish • *prawns with avocado dip*
7 = **bathe**, swim, plunge, dive, splash, paddle • *Let's have a dip in the pool.*
▸ IN PHRASES: **dip into something** **1** = **sample**, try, skim, play at, glance at, run over, browse, dabble, peruse, surf *(Computing)* • *a chance to dip into a wide selection of books*

DINOSAURS

allosaur(us)	ceratosaur(us)	elasmosaur(us)	oviraptor	stegodon	tyrannosaur(us)
ankylosaur(us)	compsognathus	hadrosaur(us)	plesiosaur(us)	stegosaur(us)	velociraptor
apatosaur(us)	dimetrodon	ichthyosaur(us)	pteranodon	theropod	
atlantosaur(us)	diplodocus	iguanodon	pterodactyl *or* pterosaur	titanosaur(us)	
brachiosaur(us)	dolichosaur(us)	megalosaur(us)		trachodon	
brontosaur(us)	dromiosaur(us)	mosasaur(us)	protoceratops	triceratops	

2 = **draw upon**, use, employ, extract, take from, make use of, fall back on, reach into, have recourse to • *She was forced to dip into her savings.*

diploma = **qualification**, degree, certificate • *a diploma in social work*

diplomacy 1 = **statesmanship**, foreign affairs, international relations, statecraft, international negotiation • *Today's resolution is significant for American diplomacy.*
2 = **tact**, skill, sensitivity, craft, discretion, subtlety, delicacy, finesse, savoir-faire, artfulness • *It took all his powers of diplomacy to get her to return.*
OPPOSITES: awkwardness, clumsiness, tactlessness

QUOTATIONS

Diplomacy is to do and say
The nastiest thing in the nicest way
[Isaac Goldberg *The Reflex*]

A soft answer turneth away wrath
[*Bible: Proverbs*]

diplomacy: the patriotic art of lying for one's country
[Ambrose Bierce *The Devil's Dictionary*]

diplomat = **official**, ambassador, envoy, statesman, consul, attaché, emissary, chargé d'affaires • *the senior American diplomat responsible for the Middle East*

QUOTATIONS

A diplomat is a man who remembers a woman's birthday but never remembers her age
[Robert Frost]

A diplomat is a person who can tell you to go to hell in such a way that you actually look forward to the trip
[Caskie Stinnett *Out of the Red*]

diplomatic 1 = **consular**, official, foreign-office, ambassadorial, foreign-politic • *The two countries have resumed full diplomatic relations.*
2 = **tactful**, politic, sensitive, subtle, delicate, polite, discreet, prudent, adept, considerate, judicious, treating with kid gloves • *She is very direct. I tend to be more diplomatic.*
OPPOSITES: rude, insensitive, tactless

dire 1 = **desperate**, pressing, crying, critical, terrible, crucial, alarming, extreme, awful, appalling, urgent, cruel, horrible, disastrous, grim, dreadful, gloomy, fearful, dismal, drastic, catastrophic, ominous, horrid, woeful, ruinous, calamitous, cataclysmic, portentous, godawful *(slang)*, exigent, bodeful • *the dire predicament of the refugees*
2 = **terrible**, awful, appalling, dreadful, abysmal, frightful, godawful *(slang)* • *a book of verse which ranged from the barely tolerable to the utterly dire*

direct AS A VERB 1 = **aim**, point, turn, level, train, focus, fix, cast • *He directed the tiny beam of light at the roof.*
2 = **guide**, show, lead, conduct, steer, usher, point the way, point in the direction of • *A guard directed them to the right.*
3 = **control**, run, manage, lead, rule, guide, handle, conduct, advise, govern, regulate, administer, oversee, supervise, dispose, preside over, mastermind, call the shots, call the tune, superintend • *He will direct day-to-day operations.*
4 = **order**, command, instruct, charge, demand, require, bid, enjoin, adjure • *They have been directed to give special attention to poverty.*
5 = **address**, send, mail, route, label, superscribe • *Please direct your letters to me at this address.*
▸ AS AN ADJECTIVE 1 = **quickest**, shortest • *They took the direct route.*
2 = **straight**, through, unbroken, uninterrupted, straight-through, nonstop • *a direct flight from Glasgow*
OPPOSITES: indirect, circuitous
3 = **first-hand**, personal, immediate • *He has direct experience of the process.*
OPPOSITES: indirect
4 = **clear**, specific, plain, absolute, distinct, definite, explicit, downright, point-blank, unequivocal, unqualified, unambiguous, categorical • *He denied there was a direct connection between the two cases.*
OPPOSITES: indirect, ambiguous, circuitous
5 = **straightforward**, open, straight, frank, blunt, sincere, outspoken, honest, matter-of-fact, downright, candid, forthright, truthful, upfront *(informal)*, man-to-man, plain-spoken • *He avoided giving a direct answer.*
OPPOSITES: subtle, crooked, indirect
6 = **verbatim**, exact, word-for-word, strict, accurate, faithful, letter-for-letter • *It was a direct quotation from his earlier speech.*
▸ AS AN ADVERB = **non-stop**, straight, without stopping • *You can fly there direct from Glasgow.*

direction 1 = **way**, course, line, road, track, bearing, route, path, orientation • *We drove ten miles in the opposite direction.*
2 = **tendency**, attitude, bent, current, trend, leaning, drift, bias, orientation, tack, tenor, proclivity • *They threatened a mass walk-out if the party did not change direction.*
3 = **management**, government, control, charge, administration, leadership, command, guidance, supervision, governance, oversight, superintendence • *The house was built under the direction of his partner.*

directions = **instructions**, rules, information, plan, briefing, regulations, recommendations, indication, guidelines, guidance • *Don't throw away the directions until we've finished cooking.*

directive = **order**, ruling, regulation, charge, notice, command, instruction, dictate, decree, mandate, canon, injunction, imperative, fiat, ordinance, edict • *Thanks to a new directive, labelling will be more specific.*

directly 1 = **straight**, unswervingly, without deviation, by the shortest route, in a beeline • *The plane will fly the hostages directly back home.*
2 = **immediately**, promptly, instantly, right away, straightaway, speedily, instantaneously, pronto *(informal)*, pdq *(slang)* • *Directly after the meeting, an official appealed on television*
3 = **at once**, presently, soon, quickly, as soon as possible, in a second, straightaway, forthwith, posthaste • *He'll be there directly.*
4 = **in person**, personally, at first hand • *We could do nothing directly to help them*
5 = **honestly**, openly, frankly, plainly, face-to-face, overtly, point-blank, unequivocally, truthfully, candidly, unreservedly, straightforwardly, straight from the shoulder *(informal)*, without prevarication • *She explained simply and directly what she hoped to achieve.*

directness = **honesty**, candour, frankness, sincerity, plain speaking, bluntness, outspokenness, forthrightness, straightforwardness • *She spoke with a directness that made him blush.*

director = **controller**, head, leader, manager, chief, executive, chairman, boss *(informal)*, producer, governor, principal, administrator, supervisor, organizer, baas *(S. African)*, helmer, sherang *(Austral. & N.Z.)* • *He is the director of the unit.*
▹ *See panel* **Film directors**

directory = **index**, listing, list, record, register, catalogue, inventory • *a telephone directory*

dirge = **lament**, requiem, elegy, death march, threnody, dead march, funeral song, coronach *(Scot. & Irish)* • *the mournful dirge, 'Erin's Lament'*

dirt 1 = **filth**, muck, grime, dust, mud, stain, crap *(taboo slang)*, tarnish, smudge, mire, impurity, slob *(Irish)*, crud *(slang)*, kak *(S. African taboo slang)*, grot *(slang)* • *I started to scrub off the dirt.*
2 = **soil**, ground, earth, clay, turf, clod, loam, loam • *They all sit on the dirt in the shade of a tree.*
3 = **scandal**, rumours, gossip, goss *(informal)*, slander, tattle,

d

FILM DIRECTORS

Robert Aldrich *(U.S.)*
Woody Allen *(U.S.)*
Pedro Almódovar *(Spanish)*
Robert Altman *(U.S.)*
Lindsay Anderson *(British)*
Wes Anderson *(U.S.)*
Michelangelo Antonioni *(Italian)*
Gillian Armstrong *(Australian)*
Anthony Asquith *(English)*
Richard Attenborough *(British)*
John Badham *(U.S.)*
Warren Beatty *(U.S.)*
Ingmar Bergman *(Swedish)*
Bernardo Bertolucci *(Italian)*
Luc Besson *(French)*
Peter Bogdanovich *(U.S.)*
John Boorman *(English)*
Robert Bresson *(French)*
Peter Brook *(British)*
Mel Brooks *(U.S.)*
Luis Buñuel *(Spanish)*
Tim Burton *(U.S.)*
James Cameron *(U.S.)*
Jane Campion *(New Zealand)*
Frank Capra *(U.S.)*
John Carpenter *(U.S.)*
Marcel Carné *(French)*
Claude Chabrol *(French)*
René Clair *(French)*
Jean Cocteau *(French)*
Ethan Coen *(U.S.)*
Joel Coen *(U.S.)*
Christopher Columbus *(U.S.)*
Francis Ford Coppola *(U.S.)*
Roger Corman *(U.S.)*
David Cronenberg *(Canadian)*
Alfonso Cuarón *(Mexican)*
Michael Curtiz *(American-Hungarian)*
Joe Dante *(U.S.)*
Cecil B de Mille *(U.S.)*
Johnathan Demme *(U.S.)*
Brian de Palma *(U.S.)*
Vittoria De Sica *(Italian)*
Richard Donner *(U.S.)*
Aleksandr Petrovitch Dovzhenko *(Russian)*
Clint Eastwood *(U.S.)*
Blake Edwards *(U.S.)*
Sergei Mikhailovich Eisenstein *(Russian)*
Rainer Werner Fassbinder *(German)*
Federico Fellini *(Italian)*
Victor Fleming *(U.S.)*
Bryan Forbes *(English)*
John Ford *(U.S.)*
Milös Forman *(Czech)*
Bill Forsyth *(Scottish)*
Stephen Frears *(English)*
William Friedkin *(U.S.)*
Abel Gance *(French)*
Terry Gilliam *(U.S.)*
Jean-Luc Godard *(French)*
Peter Greenaway *(English)*
John Grierson *(Scottish)*
D(avid) W(ark) Griffith *(U.S.)*
Sacha Guitry *(French)*
Peter Hall *(English)*
Michael Haneke *(Austrian)*
Howard Hawks *(U.S.)*
Werner Herzog *(German)*
George Roy Hill *(U.S.)*
Alfred Hitchcock *(English)*
John Huston *(U.S.)*
James Ivory *(U.S.)*
Peter Jackson *(New Zealand)*
Derek Jarman *(English)*
Neil Jordan *(Irish)*
Chen Kaige *(Chinese)*
Lawrence Kasdan *(U.S.)*
Philip Kaufman *(U.S.)*
Elia Kazan *(U.S.)*
Buster Keaton *(U.S.)*
Krzysztof Kieslowski *(Polish)*
Stanley Kubrick *(U.S.)*
Akira Kurosawa *(Japanese)*
John Landis *(U.S.)*
Fritz Lang *(Austrian)*
David Lean *(English)*
Ang Lee *(Taiwanese)*
Spike Lee *(U.S.)*
Mike Leigh *(English)*
Sergio Leone *(Italian)*
Richard Lester *(U.S.)*
Barry Levinson *(U.S.)*
Ken Loach *(English)*
George Lucas *(U.S.)*
Sidney Lumet *(U.S.)*
David Lynch *(U.S.)*
Jim McBride *(U.S.)*
Alexander Mackendrick *(Scottish)*
Louis Malle *(French)*
Joseph Mankiewicz *(U.S.)*
Georges Méliès *(French)*
Sam Mendes *(English)*
Ismail Merchant *(Indian)*
George Miller *(Australian)*
Jonathon Wolfe Miller *(English)*
Anthony Minghella *(English)*
Vincente Minnelli *(U.S.)*
Kenji Mizoguchi *(Japanese)*
Mike Nichols *(American-German)*
Laurence Olivier *(English)*
Max Ophüls *(German)*
G(eorge) W(ilhelm) Pabst *(German)*
Marcel Pagnol *(French)*
Alan Parker *(English)*
Pier Paolo Pasolini *(Italian)*
Sam Peckinpah *(U.S.)*
Arthur Penn *(U.S.)*
Roman Polanski *(Polish)*
Sydney Pollack *(U.S.)*
Michael Powell *(English)*
Otto Preminger *(Austrian-U.S.)*
Emeric Pressburger *(Hungarian)*
Vsevolod Pudovkin *(Russian)*
David Puttnam *(English)*
Satyajit Ray *(Indian)*
Robert Redford *(U.S.)*
Carol Reed *(English)*
Carl Reiner *(U.S.)*
Rob Reiner *(U.S.)*
Edgar Reitz *(German)*
Jean Renoir *(French)*
Alain Resnais *(French)*
Leni Riefenstahl *(German)*
Guy Ritchie *(English)*
Hal Roach *(U.S.)*
Tim Robbins *(U.S.)*
Nicholas Roeg *(English)*
Eric Rohmer *(France)*
George Romero *(U.S.)*
Roberto Rossellini *(Italian)*
Ken Russell *(English)*
John Schlesinger *(English)*
Martin Scorsese *(U.S.)*
Ridley Scott *(British)*
Don Siegel *(U.S.)*
Steven Soderbergh *(U.S.)*
Steven Spielberg *(U.S.)*
Robert Stevenson *(English)*
Oliver Stone *(U.S.)*
Preston Sturges *(U.S.)*
Quentin Tarantino *(U.S.)*
Andrei Tarkovsky *(Russian)*
Jacques Tati *(French)*
Bertrand Tavernier *(French)*
François Truffaut *(French)*
Roger Vadim *(French)*
Gus Van Sant *(U.S.)*
Luchino Visconti *(Italian)*
Joseph von Sternberg *(Austrian-U.S.)*
Erich von Stroheim *(Austrian-U.S.)*
Lars von Trier *(Danish)*
Andrei Wajda *(Polish)*
Peter Weir *(Australian)*
Orson Welles *(U.S.)*
Wim Wenders *(German)*
Billy Wilder *(Austrian-U.S.)*
Michael Winner *(English)*
Robert Wise *(U.S.)*
John Woo *(Chinese)*
Zhang Yimou *(Chinese)*
Franco Zeffirelli *(Italian)*
Robert Zemeckis *(U.S.)*
Fred Zinnemann *(Austrian-British)*

dirty linen *(informal)*, aspersion • *Both parties use computers to dig up dirt on their opponents.*

PROVERBS

We must eat a peck of dirt before we die

dirty **AS AN ADJECTIVE** **1 = filthy**, soiled, grubby, nasty, foul, muddy, polluted, messy, sullied, grimy, unclean, mucky, grotty *(slang)*, grungy *(slang, chiefly U.S. & Canad.)*, scuzzy *(slang, chiefly U.S.)*, begrimed, skanky *(slang)*, festy *(Austral. slang)* • *The woman had matted hair and dirty fingernails.*

OPPOSITES: clean, pure, spotless

2 = dishonest, illegal, unfair, cheating, corrupt, crooked, deceiving, fraudulent, treacherous, deceptive, unscrupulous,

crafty, deceitful, double-dealing, unsporting, knavish *(archaic)* • *Their opponents used dirty tactics.*
OPPOSITES: moral, decent, honest
3 = **obscene**, rude, coarse, indecent, blue, offensive, gross, filthy, vulgar, pornographic, sleazy, suggestive, lewd, risqué, X-rated *(informal)*, bawdy, salacious, smutty, off-colour, unwholesome • *He laughed at their dirty jokes.*
OPPOSITES: clean, decent
4 = **despicable**, mean, low, base, cheap, nasty, cowardly, beggarly, worthless, shameful, shabby, vile, sordid, low-down *(informal)*, abject, squalid, ignominious, contemptible, wretched, scurvy, detestable, scungy *(Austral. & N.Z.)* • *That was a dirty trick to play.*
▸ **AS A VERB** = **soil**, foul, stain, spoil, smear, muddy, pollute, blacken, mess up, smudge, sully, defile, smirch, begrime • *He was afraid the dog's hairs might dirty the seats.*
OPPOSITES: clean

disability = **handicap**, affliction, disorder, defect, impairment, disablement, infirmity • *Facilities for people with disabilities are still inadequate.*

disable 1 = **handicap**, weaken, cripple, damage, hamstring, paralyse, impair, debilitate, incapacitate, prostrate, unman, immobilize, put out of action, disempower, enfeeble, render inoperative, render *hors de combat* • *Tendon damage really disabled her.*
2 = **deactivate**, disarm, defuse, make safe • *You need to disable the car alarm.*

disabled = **differently abled**, physically challenged, handicapped, challenged, weakened, crippled, paralysed, impaired, lame, mutilated, maimed, incapacitated, infirm, bedridden • *the practical problems encountered by disabled people in the workplace*
OPPOSITES: strong, sound, able-bodied

disabuse = **enlighten**, correct, set right, open the eyes of, set straight, shatter (someone's) illusions, free from error, undeceive • *I did not disabuse them of this notion*

disadvantage **AS A NOUN** 1 = **drawback**, trouble, burden, weakness, handicap, liability, minus *(informal)*, flaw, hardship, nuisance, snag, inconvenience, downside, impediment, hindrance, privation, weak point, fly in the ointment *(informal)* • *They suffer the disadvantage of having been political exiles.*
OPPOSITES: benefit, advantage, merit
2 = **harm**, loss, damage, injury, hurt, prejudice, detriment, disservice • *An attempt to prevent an election would be to their disadvantage.*
OPPOSITES: help, benefit, aid
▸ **AS A VERB** = **handicap**, limit, restrict, hamstring, hamper, hold back, hinder, retard, impede, hobble, place at a disadvantage • *Competition could reduce liquidity and disadvantage some investors.*
▸ **IN PHRASES:** **at a disadvantage** = **exposed**, vulnerable, wide open, unprotected, defenceless, open to attack, assailable • *Children from poor families were at a distinct disadvantage.*

disadvantaged = **deprived**, struggling, impoverished, discriminated against, underprivileged • *the educational problems of disadvantaged children*

disadvantageous = **unfavourable**, damaging, harmful, adverse, detrimental, inconvenient, hurtful, prejudicial, deleterious, injurious, ill-timed, inopportune, inexpedient • *This policy has proved extremely disadvantageous for us.*

disaffected = **alienated**, resentful, discontented, hostile, estranged, dissatisfied, rebellious, antagonistic, disloyal, seditious, mutinous, uncompliant, unsubmissive • *an attempt to regain the support of disaffected voters*

disaffection = **alienation**, resentment, discontent, hostility, dislike, disagreement, dissatisfaction, animosity, aversion, antagonism, antipathy, disloyalty, estrangement, ill will, repugnance, unfriendliness • *evidence of the people's disaffection with their leaders*

disagree **AS A VERB** 1 = **differ (in opinion)**, argue, debate, clash, dispute, contest, fall out *(informal)*, contend, dissent, quarrel, wrangle, bicker, take issue with, have words *(informal)*, cross swords, be at sixes and sevens • *The two men disagreed about what to do next.*
OPPOSITES: agree, get on (together), concur
2 = **make ill**, upset, sicken, trouble, hurt, bother, distress, discomfort, nauseate, be injurious • *Orange juice seems to disagree with some babies.*
▸ **IN PHRASES:** **disagree with something** *or* **someone** = **oppose**, be against, object to, not support, disapprove of, not believe in, dissent from, think wrong • *I disagree with drug laws in general.*

disagreeable 1 = **nasty**, offensive, disgusting, unpleasant, distasteful, horrid, repellent, unsavoury, obnoxious, unpalatable, displeasing, repulsive, objectionable, repugnant, uninviting, yucky *or* yukky *(slang)*, yucko *(Austral. slang)* • *a disagreeable odour*
OPPOSITES: nice, lovely, pleasant
2 = **ill-natured**, difficult, nasty, cross, contrary, unpleasant, rude, irritable, unfriendly, bad-tempered, surly, churlish, brusque, tetchy, ratty *(Brit. & N.Z. informal)*, peevish, ungracious, disobliging, unlikable *or* unlikeable • *He's a shallow, disagreeable man.*
OPPOSITES: nice, friendly, good-natured

disagreement **AS A NOUN** 1 = **objection**, opposition, doubt, niggle *(informal)*, demur, counter-argument, remonstrance • *They have expressed some disagreement with the proposal.*
2 = **argument**, row, difference, division, debate, conflict, clash, dispute, falling out, misunderstanding, dissent, quarrel, squabble, strife, wrangle, discord, tiff, altercation, turf war *(informal)* • *My instructor and I had a brief disagreement.*
OPPOSITES: accord, agreement, unity
▸ **IN PHRASES:** **in disagreement** = **at odds**, in conflict, at loggerheads, at variance, disunited, at daggers drawn, in disharmony • *The two sides were locked in disagreement.*

QUOTATIONS
The only sin which we never forgive in each other is difference of opinion
[Ralph Waldo Emerson *Clubs*]

disallow = **reject**, refuse, ban, dismiss, cancel, veto, forbid, embargo, prohibit, rebuff, repudiate, disown, proscribe, disavow, disclaim, abjure • *He ruled that my testimony should be disallowed.*

disappear 1 = **vanish**, evaporate, recede, drop out of sight, vanish off the face of the earth, evanesce, be lost to view *or* sight • *The car drove off and disappeared from sight.*
OPPOSITES: appear, arrive, reappear
2 = **pass**, go away, wane, ebb, fade away • *The problem should disappear altogether by the age of five.*
3 = **flee**, bolt, run away, fly, escape, split *(slang)*, retire, withdraw, take off *(informal)*, get away, vanish, depart, go, make off, abscond, take flight, do a runner *(slang)*, scarper *(Brit. slang)*, slope off, cut and run *(informal)*, beat a hasty retreat, make your escape, make your getaway • *The prisoner disappeared after being released on bail.*
4 = **be lost**, be taken, be stolen, go missing, be mislaid • *My wallet seems to have disappeared.*
5 = **cease**, end, fade, vanish, dissolve, expire, evaporate, perish, die out, pass away, cease to exist, melt away, leave no trace, cease to be known • *The immediate threat has disappeared.*

disappearance 1 = **vanishing**, going, passing, disappearing, fading, melting, eclipse, evaporation, evanescence • *the gradual disappearance of the pain*
2 = **flight**, departure, desertion, disappearing trick • *his disappearance while out on bail*

3 = **loss**, losing, theft, mislaying • *Police are investigating the disappearance of confidential files.*
4 = **dying out**, decline, falling off, petering out • *the disappearance of dolphins in recent years*

disappoint 1 = **let down**, dismay, fail, dash, disillusion, sadden, vex, chagrin, dishearten, disenchant, dissatisfy, disgruntle • *He said that he was surprised and disappointed by the decision.*
2 = **frustrate**, foil, thwart, defeat, baffle, balk • *His hopes have been disappointed many times before.*

disappointed 1 = **let down**, upset, distressed, discouraged, depressed, choked, disillusioned, discontented, dejected, disheartened, disgruntled, dissatisfied, downcast, saddened, disenchanted, despondent, downhearted, cast down • *I was disappointed that he was not there.*
OPPOSITES: happy, pleased, satisfied
2 = **frustrated**, foiled, thwarted, balked • *a tale of lost love and disappointed dreams*

disappointing = **unsatisfactory**, inadequate, discouraging, sorry, upsetting, sad, depressing, unhappy, unexpected, pathetic, inferior, insufficient, lame, disconcerting, second-rate, unworthy, not much cop *(Brit. slang)* • *The response to the appeal was disappointing.*

disappointment 1 = **regret**, distress, discontent, dissatisfaction, disillusionment, displeasure, chagrin, disenchantment, dejection, despondency, discouragement, mortification, unfulfilment • *They expressed their disappointment at what had happened.*
2 = **letdown**, blow, disaster, failure, setback, fiasco, misfortune, calamity, whammy *(informal, chiefly U.S.)*, choker *(informal)*, washout *(informal)*, anticlimax • *The defeat was a bitter disappointment.*
3 = **frustration**, failure, dashing, foiling, thwarting, ill-success • *There was resentment among the people at the disappointment of their hopes.*

disapproval = **displeasure**, criticism, objection, condemnation, dissatisfaction, censure, reproach, denunciation, deprecation, disapprobation, stick *(slang)* • *His action had been greeted with almost universal disapproval.*

disapprove 1 = **condemn**, object to, dislike, censure, deplore, deprecate, frown on, take exception to, take a dim view of, find unacceptable, have a down on *(informal)*, discountenance, look down your nose at *(informal)*, raise an *or* your eyebrow • *My mother disapproved of my working in a pub.*
OPPOSITES: like, approve, applaud
2 = **turn down**, reject, veto, set aside, spurn, disallow • *The judge disapproved the adoption because of my criminal record.*
OPPOSITES: approve, endorse, give the go-ahead (to)

disapproving = **critical**, discouraging, frowning, disparaging, censorious, reproachful, deprecatory, condemnatory, denunciatory, disapprobatory • *She gave him a disapproving look.*
OPPOSITES: encouraging, approving, commendatory

disarm 1 = **demilitarize**, disband, demobilize, deactivate, lay down weapons • *The forces in the territory should disarm.*
2 = **win over**, persuade, convert, charm, appease, sweeten, mollify • *She did her best to disarm her critics.*

disarmament = **arms reduction**, demobilization, arms limitation, demilitarization, de-escalation • *The goal is to accelerate the pace of nuclear disarmament.*

disarming = **charming**, winning, irresistible, persuasive, likable *or* likeable • *He approached with a disarming smile.*

disarray 1 = **confusion**, upset, disorder, indiscipline, disunity, disharmony, disorganization, unruliness, discomposure, disorderliness • *The feud has plunged the country into political disarray.*
OPPOSITES: plan, system, order
2 = **untidiness**, state, mess, chaos, tangle, mix-up, muddle, clutter, shambles, jumble, hotchpotch, hodgepodge *(U.S.)*, dishevelment, pig's breakfast *(informal)* • *He found the room in disarray.*
OPPOSITES: tidiness, order, symmetry

disassemble = **take apart**, strike, dismantle, knock down, take down, dismount • *He disassembled the cabin and packed it away.*

disaster 1 = **catastrophe**, trouble, blow, accident, stroke, reverse, tragedy, ruin, misfortune, adversity, calamity, mishap, whammy *(informal, chiefly U.S.)*, misadventure, cataclysm, act of God, bummer *(slang)*, ruination, mischance • *the second air disaster in less than two months*
2 = **failure**, mess, flop *(informal)*, catastrophe, rout, debacle, cock-up *(Brit. slang)*, balls-up *(taboo slang)*, non-starter, fuck-up *(offensive taboo slang)*, washout *(informal)* • *The whole production was a disaster.*

disastrous 1 = **terrible**, devastating, tragic, fatal, unfortunate, dreadful, destructive, unlucky, harmful, adverse, dire, catastrophic, detrimental, untoward, ruinous, calamitous, cataclysmic, ill-starred, unpropitious, ill-fated, cataclysmal • *the recent, disastrous earthquake*
2 = **unsuccessful**, devastating, tragic, abortive, calamitous, cataclysmic • *The team has had another disastrous day.*

disavow = **deny**, reject, contradict, retract, repudiate, disown, rebut, disclaim, forswear, gainsay *(archaic or literary)*, abjure • *He immediately disavowed the newspaper story.*

disavowal = **denial**, rejection, contradiction, disclaimer, renunciation, retraction, repudiation, gainsaying *(archaic or literary)*, recantation, abjuration • *a public disavowal of his beliefs*

disband 1 = **dismiss**, separate, break up, scatter, dissolve, let go, disperse, send home, demobilize • *All the armed groups will be disbanded.*
2 = **break up**, separate, scatter, disperse, part company, go (their) separate ways • *The rebels have agreed to disband by the end of the month.*

disbelief = **scepticism**, doubt, distrust, mistrust, incredulity, unbelief, dubiety • *She looked at him in disbelief.*
OPPOSITES: trust, belief, faith

disbelieve = **doubt**, reject, discount, suspect, discredit, not accept, mistrust, not buy *(slang)*, repudiate, scoff at, not credit, not swallow *(informal)*, give no credence to • *There is no reason to disbelieve his account of the events.*

disbeliever = **sceptic**, scoffer, doubter, atheist, questioner, agnostic, doubting Thomas • *their attempts to convert disbelievers to their faith*
OPPOSITES: supporter, follower

disbelieving = **incredulous**, doubting, sceptical, doubtful, suspicious, dubious, unconvinced, distrustful, mistrustful, unbelieving • *'Is that so?' he asked, in a disbelieving tone.*

disburse = **pay out**, spend, lay out, fork out *(slang)*, expend, shell out *(informal)* • *The aid will not be disbursed until next year.*

disbursement = **payment**, spending, expenditure, disposal, outlay • *We hope to have the funds ready for disbursement by September.*

disc 1 = **circle**, plate, saucer, discus • *a revolving disc with replaceable blades*
2 = **record**, vinyl, gramophone record, phonograph record *(U.S. & Canad.)*, platter *(U.S. slang)* • *This disc includes the piano sonata in C minor.*

discard = **get rid of**, drop, remove, throw away *or* out, reject, abandon, dump *(informal)*, shed, scrap, axe *(informal)*, ditch *(slang)*, junk *(informal)*, chuck *(informal)*, dispose of, relinquish, dispense with, jettison, repudiate, cast aside • *Read the instructions before discarding the box.*
OPPOSITES: keep, save, reserve

discern 1 = **distinguish**, determine, detect, discriminate, pick out, differentiate, make a distinction • *We've been trying to discern a pattern in his behaviour.*
2 = **see**, perceive, make out, notice, observe, recognize, behold, catch sight of, suss (out) *(slang)*, espy, descry • *Under*

the bridge we could just discern a shadowy figure.

discernible = **clear**, obvious, apparent, plain, visible, distinct, noticeable, recognizable, detectable, observable, perceptible, distinguishable, appreciable, discoverable • *There has been no discernible change in his condition.*

discerning = **discriminating**, knowing, sharp, critical, acute, sensitive, wise, intelligent, subtle, piercing, penetrating, shrewd, ingenious, astute, perceptive, judicious, clear-sighted, percipient, perspicacious, sagacious • *tailor-made holidays to suit the more discerning traveller*

discernment = **judgment**, discrimination, perception, understanding, intelligence, awareness, insight, penetration, ingenuity, sharpness, acumen, cleverness, keenness, shrewdness, perspicacity, sagacity, astuteness, acuteness, perceptiveness, clear-sightedness, percipience • *their lack of discernment and acceptance of inferior quality*

discharge AS A VERB 1 = **release**, free, clear, liberate, pardon, let go, acquit, allow to go, set free, exonerate, absolve • *You are being discharged on medical grounds.*
2 = **dismiss**, sack *(informal)*, fire *(informal)*, remove, expel, discard, oust, eject, cashier, give (someone) the boot *(slang)*, give (someone) the sack *(informal)*, give (someone) his *or* her P45 *(informal)*, kennet *(Austral. slang)*, jeff *(Austral. slang)* • *the regulation that gay people should be discharged from the military*
3 = **carry out**, perform, fulfil, accomplish, do, effect, realize, observe, implement, execute, carry through • *the quiet competence with which he discharged his many duties*
4 = **pay**, meet, clear, settle, square (up), honour, satisfy, relieve, liquidate • *The goods will be sold in order to discharge the debt.*
5 = **pour forth**, release, empty, leak, emit, dispense, void, gush, ooze, exude, give off, excrete, disembogue • *The resulting salty water will be discharged at sea.*
6 = **fire**, shoot, set off, explode, activate, let off, detonate, let loose *(informal)* • *He was tried for unlawfully and dangerously discharging a weapon.*
▸ AS A NOUN 1 = **release**, liberation, clearance, pardon, acquittal, remittance, exoneration • *The doctors began to discuss his discharge from hospital.*
2 = **dismissal**, notice, removal, the boot *(slang)*, expulsion, the sack *(informal)*, the push *(slang)*, marching orders *(informal)*, ejection, demobilization, kiss-off *(slang, chiefly U.S. & Canad.)*, the bum's rush *(slang)*, the (old) heave-ho *(informal)*, the order of the boot *(slang)*, congé, your books *or* cards *(informal)* • *They face receiving a dishonourable discharge from the Army.*
3 = **emission**, flow, ooze, secretion, excretion, pus, seepage, suppuration • *They develop a fever and a watery discharge from the eyes.*
4 = **firing**, report, shot, blast, burst, explosion, discharging, volley, salvo, detonation, fusillade • *Where firearms are kept at home, the risk of accidental discharge is high.*
5 = **carrying out**, performance, achievement, execution, accomplishment, fulfilment, observance • *free of any influence which might affect the discharge of his duties*

disciple 1 = **apostle**, follower • *Jesus and his disciples*
2 = **follower**, student, supporter, pupil, convert, believer, partisan, devotee, apostle, adherent, proselyte, votary, catechumen • *a major intellectual figure with disciples throughout Europe*
OPPOSITES: leader, teacher, master

THE DISCIPLES OF JESUS

Andrew	John	Peter
Bartholomew	Judas	Philip
James	Jude	Simon
James	Matthew	Thomas

disciplinarian = **authoritarian**, tyrant, despot, stickler, taskmaster, martinet, drill sergeant, strict teacher, hard master • *He has a reputation for being a hard disciplinarian.*

disciplinary = **punitive**, retaliatory, retaliative, punitory • *She was unhappy that no disciplinary action was being taken.*

discipline AS A NOUN 1 = **control**, rule, authority, direction, regulation, supervision, orderliness, strictness • *the need for strict discipline in military units*
2 = **punishment**, penalty, correction, chastening, chastisement, punitive measures, castigation • *Order and discipline have been placed in the hands of headmasters.*
3 = **self-control**, control, restraint, self-discipline, coolness, cool, willpower, calmness, self-restraint, orderliness, self-mastery, strength of mind *or* will • *His image of calm, control and discipline that appealed to voters.*
4 = **training**, practice, exercise, method, regulation, drill, regimen • *inner disciplines like transcendental meditation*
5 = **field of study**, area, subject, theme, topic, course, curriculum, speciality, subject matter, branch of knowledge, field of inquiry *or* reference • *appropriate topics for the new discipline of political science*
▸ AS A VERB 1 = **punish**, correct, reprimand, castigate, chastise, chasten, penalize, bring to book, reprove • *He was disciplined by his company, but not dismissed.*
2 = **train**, control, govern, check, educate, regulate, instruct, restrain • *I'm very good at disciplining myself.*

PROVERBS
Spare the rod and spoil the child

disclaim 1 = **deny**, decline, reject, disallow, retract, repudiate, renege, rebut, disavow, abnegate, disaffirm • *She disclaims any knowledge of her husband's business activities.*
2 = **renounce**, reject, abandon, relinquish, disown, abdicate, forswear, abjure • *the legislation which enabled him to disclaim his title*

disclaimer = **denial**, rejection, renunciation, retraction, repudiation, disavowal, abjuration • *A disclaimer states that the company will not be held responsible.*

disclose 1 = **make known**, tell, reveal, publish, relate, broadcast, leak, confess, communicate, unveil, utter, make public, impart, divulge, out *(informal)*, let slip, spill the beans about *(informal)*, cough *(slang)*, blow wide open *(slang)*, get off your chest *(informal)*, spill your guts about *(slang)* • *Neither side would disclose details of the transaction.*
OPPOSITES: keep secret, keep dark
2 = **show**, reveal, expose, discover, exhibit, unveil, uncover, lay bare, bring to light, take the wraps off • *clapboard façades that revolve to disclose snug interiors*
OPPOSITES: cover, hide, mask

disclosure 1 = **revelation**, exposé, announcement, publication, leak, admission, declaration, confession, acknowledgment, surprise fact • *unauthorised newspaper disclosures*
2 = **uncovering**, publishing, broadcasting, publication, exposure, revelation, unveiling, divulgence • *The disclosure of his marriage proposal was badly-timed.*

disco = **dance**, ball, hop *(informal)*, knees-up *(Brit. informal)*, discotheque, dancing party, B and S *(Austral. informal)* • *The youth club holds a disco every Friday night.*

discoloration = **stain**, mark, spot, patch, blot, blemish, blotch, splotch • *She has a discoloration just below the lip.*

discolour *or (U.S.)* **discolor** 1 = **mark**, soil, mar, fade, stain, streak, tinge • *Test first as this cleaner may discolour the fabric.*
2 = **stain**, fade, streak, rust, tarnish • *A tooth which has been hit hard may discolour.*

discoloured *or (U.S.)* **discolored** = **stained**, tainted, tarnished, faded, pale, washed out, wan, blotched, besmirched, foxed, etiolated • *Some of the prints were badly discoloured around the edges.*

discomfit = **embarrass**, unsettle, disconcert, confuse, rattle *(informal)*, flurry, ruffle, confound, perplex, unnerve, take aback, fluster, perturb, faze, demoralize, take the wind out of someone's sails, abash, discompose • *He will be discomfited by the dismissal of his plan.*

discomfiture = **embarrassment**, shame, humiliation, confusion, unease, chagrin, demoralization, discomposure, abashment • *He never found pleasure in another's discomfiture.*

discomfort AS A NOUN 1 = **pain**, suffering, hurt, smarting, ache, throbbing, irritation, tenderness, pang, malaise, twinge, soreness • *He suffered some discomfort, but no real pain.*
OPPOSITES: ease, comfort
2 = **uneasiness**, worry, anxiety, doubt, alarm, distress, suspicion, apprehension, misgiving, nervousness, disquiet, agitation, qualms, trepidation, perturbation, apprehensiveness, dubiety, inquietude • *She heard the discomfort in his voice as he reluctantly agreed.*
OPPOSITES: ease, reassurance, solace
3 = **inconvenience**, trouble, difficulty, bother, hardship, irritation, hassle *(informal)*, nuisance, uphill *(S. African)*, annoyance, awkwardness, unpleasantness, vexation • *the hazards and discomforts of primitive continental travel*
▸ AS A VERB = **make uncomfortable**, worry, trouble, shake, alarm, disturb, distress, unsettle, ruffle, unnerve, disquiet, perturb, discomfit, discompose • *World leaders will have been greatly discomforted by these events.*
OPPOSITES: ease, comfort, reassure

disconcert = **disturb**, worry, trouble, upset, confuse, rattle *(informal)*, baffle, put off, unsettle, bewilder, shake up *(informal)*, undo, flurry, agitate, ruffle, perplex, unnerve, unbalance, take aback, fluster, perturb, faze, flummox, throw off balance, nonplus, abash, discompose, put out of countenance • *My lack of response clearly disconcerted him.*

disconcerted = **disturbed**, worried, troubled, thrown *(informal)*, upset, confused, embarrassed, annoyed, rattled *(informal)*, distracted, at sea, unsettled, bewildered, shook up *(informal)*, flurried, ruffled, taken aback, flustered, perturbed, fazed, nonplussed, flummoxed, caught off balance, out of countenance • *He was disconcerted to find his fellow diners already seated.*

disconcerting = **disturbing**, upsetting, alarming, confusing, embarrassing, awkward, distracting, dismaying, baffling, bewildering, perplexing, off-putting *(Brit. informal)*, bothersome • *He has a disconcerting habit of staring at you when he talks to you.*

disconnect 1 = **deactivate**, shut down, turn off, switch off, close *or* shut off • *The device automatically disconnects the ignition.*
2 = **cut off**, stop • *The company has disconnected our electricity for non-payment.*
3 = **detach**, separate, undo, part, divide, sever, disengage, take apart, unhook, unfasten, uncouple, unhitch • *He disconnected the bottle from the overhead hook.*
4 = **break off**, suspend, interrupt, terminate • *The call was disconnected.*

disconnected 1 = **unrelated**, different, dissimilar, not related, unconnected, not kin, not kindred • *a sequence of utterly disconnected events*
2 = **confused**, mixed-up, rambling, irrational, jumbled, unintelligible, illogical, incoherent, disjointed, garbled, uncoordinated • *a meaningless jumble of disconnected words*

disconnection 1 = **cutting off**, suspension, cut-off, interruption, stoppage, cessation, severance, discontinuity, discontinuation • *the disconnection of his phone*
2 = **separation**, cutting off, cut-off, severance, disconnect • *He hopes for a gradual disconnection from the federation.*

disconsolate 1 = **inconsolable**, crushed, despairing, miserable, hopeless, heartbroken, desolate, forlorn, woeful, grief-stricken, wretched • *She was disconsolate when her husband left her.*
2 = **sad**, low, unhappy, miserable, gloomy, dismal, melancholy, forlorn, woeful, dejected, wretched, down in the dumps *(informal)*

discontent = **dissatisfaction**, unhappiness, displeasure, regret, envy, restlessness, uneasiness, vexation, discontentment, fretfulness • *There are reports of widespread discontent in the capital.*

discontented = **dissatisfied**, complaining, unhappy, miserable, fed up, disgruntled, disaffected, vexed, pissed off *(taboo slang)*, displeased, fretful, cheesed off *(Brit. slang)*, brassed off *(Brit. slang)*, with a chip on your shoulder *(informal)* • *The government tried to appease discontented workers.*
OPPOSITES: happy, pleased, satisfied

discontinue = **stop**, end, finish, drop, kick *(informal)*, give up, abandon, suspend, quit, halt, pause, cease, axe *(informal)*, interrupt, terminate, break off, put an end to, refrain from, leave off, pull the plug on, belay *(Nautical)* • *Do not discontinue the treatment without consulting your doctor.*

discontinued = **stopped**, ended, finished, abandoned, halted, terminated, no longer made, given up *or* over • *They have a huge selection of discontinued cookers.*

discontinuity = **lack of unity**, disconnection, incoherence, disunion, lack of coherence, disjointedness, disconnectedness • *The text suffers from discontinuity.*

discontinuous = **intermittent**, interrupted, irregular, disconnected, broken, fitful, spasmodic • *the discontinuous nature of the country's economic development*

discord = **disagreement**, division, conflict, difference, opposition, row, clashing, dispute, contention, friction, strife, wrangling, variance, disunity, dissension, incompatibility, discordance, lack of concord • *He foments discord among the allies.*
OPPOSITES: understanding, accord, agreement

discordant 1 = **disagreeing**, conflicting, clashing, different, opposite, contrary, at odds, contradictory, inconsistent, incompatible, incongruous, divergent • *He displays attitudes and conduct discordant with his culture.*
2 = **harsh**, jarring, grating, strident, shrill, jangling, dissonant, cacophonous, inharmonious, unmelodious • *They produced a discordant sound.*

discount AS A VERB 1 = **mark down**, cut, reduce, lower, slash, lessen, knock down • *Tour prices are being discounted.*
2 = **disregard**, reject, ignore, overlook, discard, set aside, dispel, pass over, repudiate, disbelieve, brush off *(slang)*, lay aside, pooh-pooh • *His theory was discounted immediately.*
▸ AS A NOUN = **deduction**, cut, reduction, concession, allowance, rebate, cut price, lower price, marked-down price • *You often get a discount on discontinued goods.*

discourage 1 = **dishearten**, daunt, deter, crush, put off, depress, cow, dash, intimidate, dismay, unnerve, unman, overawe, demoralize, cast down, put a damper on, psych out *(informal)*, dispirit, deject • *Don't let this setback discourage you.*
OPPOSITES: encourage, inspire, hearten
2 = **put off**, deter, prevent, dissuade, talk out of, discountenance • *a campaign to discourage children from smoking*
OPPOSITES: encourage, bid, urge
3 = **prevent**, check, curb, deter, inhibit, hinder • *We hope that these measures will discourage further unrest.*

discouraged = **put off**, deterred, daunted, dashed, dismayed, pessimistic, dispirited, downcast, disheartened, crestfallen, sick as a parrot *(informal)* • *She was determined not to be too discouraged by his criticism.*

discouragement 1 = **deterrent**, opposition, obstacle, curb, check, setback, restraint, constraint, impediment, hindrance, damper, disincentive • *Uncertainty is one of the major discouragements to investment.*

d

2 = **depression**, disappointment, despair, pessimism, hopelessness, despondency, loss of confidence, dejection, discomfiture, low spirits, downheartedness • *There's a sense of discouragement creeping into the workforce.*

discouraging = **disheartening**, disappointing, depressing, daunting, dampening, unfavourable, off-putting (*Brit. informal*), dispiriting, unpropitious • *We have had a discouraging response to our appeal.*

discourse AS A NOUN 1 = **conversation**, talk, discussion, speech, communication, chat, dialogue, converse • *a tradition of political discourse*

2 = **speech**, talk, address, essay, lecture, sermon, treatise, dissertation, homily, oration, disquisition, whaikorero (*N.Z.*) • *He responds with a lengthy discourse on deployment strategy.*

▸ AS A VERB = **talk**, speak, discuss, debate, confer, converse, declaim, hold forth, expatiate • *He discoursed for several hours on English prose.*

discourteous = **rude**, abrupt, curt, disrespectful, brusque, offhand, boorish, bad-mannered, insolent, impolite, ungentlemanly, ungracious, uncivil, ill-bred, unmannerly, ill-mannered, uncourteous • *Staff are often discourteous and sometimes downright rude.*

OPPOSITES: civil, mannerly, polite

discourtesy 1 = **rudeness**, bad manners, insolence, impertinence, incivility, ill-breeding, impoliteness, disrespectfulness, ungraciousness, unmannerliness • *He was brusque to the point of discourtesy.*

2 = **insult**, slight, snub, rebuff, affront, cold shoulder, kick in the teeth (*slang*) • *To refuse would have been a discourtesy.*

discover 1 = **find out**, see, learn, reveal, spot, determine, notice, realize, recognize, perceive, detect, disclose, uncover, discern, ascertain, suss (out) (*slang*), get wise to (*informal*) • *As he discovered, she had a brilliant mind.*

2 = **find**, come across, uncover, track down, unearth, turn up, dig up, come upon, chance on, stumble on, bring to light, light upon • *His body was discovered on a roadside outside the city.*

3 = **invent**, develop, come up with, design, pioneer, devise, originate, contrive, hit on, conceive of • *Scientists discovered a way of forming the image in a thin layer on the surface.*

discoverer 1 = **explorer**, pioneer • *the myth of the heroic discoverer*

2 = **inventor**, author, creator, originator, initiator • *the discoverer of carbon-dioxide lasers*

discovery 1 = **finding out**, news, announcement, revelation, disclosure, realization • *the discovery that his wife was HIV positive*

2 = **invention**, launch, institution, introduction, pioneering, innovation, initiation, inauguration, induction, coinage, origination • *the discovery of new forensic techniques*

3 = **breakthrough**, find, finding, development, advance, leap, coup, invention, step forward, godsend, quantum leap • *In that year, two momentous discoveries were made.*

4 = **finding**, turning up, locating, revelation, uncovering, disclosure, detection, unearthing, espial • *the discovery of a mass grave in the south-west of the country*

QUOTATIONS

Discovery consists of seeing what everybody has seen and thinking what nobody has thought

[Albert von Szent-Györgyi *The Scientist Speculates*]

discredit AS A VERB 1 = **disgrace**, blame, shame, smear, stain, humiliate, degrade, taint, slur, detract from, disparage, vilify, slander, sully, dishonour, stigmatize, defame, bring into disrepute, bring shame upon • *He says his accusers are trying to discredit him.*

OPPOSITES: honour, praise, acclaim

2 = **dispute**, question, challenge, deny, reject, discount, distrust, mistrust, repudiate, cast doubt on *or* upon, disbelieve, pooh-pooh • *They realized there would be problems in discrediting the evidence.*

▸ AS A NOUN = **disgrace**, scandal, shame, disrepute, smear, stigma, censure, slur, ignominy, dishonour, imputation, odium, ill-repute, aspersion • *His actions have brought discredit on the whole regiment.*

OPPOSITES: credit, honour, praise

discreditable = **disgraceful**, shameful, improper, scandalous, humiliating, infamous, degrading, unworthy, reprehensible, ignominious, unprincipled, dishonourable, blameworthy • *She had been suspended from her job for discreditable behaviour.*

discredited = **rejected**, exposed, exploded, discarded, obsolete, refuted, debunked, outworn • *This theory has now been discredited.*

discreet 1 = **tactful**, diplomatic, politic, reserved, guarded, careful, sensible, cautious, wary, discerning, prudent, considerate, judicious, circumspect, sagacious • *He followed at a discreet distance.*

OPPOSITES: rash, unwise, tactless

2 = **unobtrusive**, modest, subtle, restrained, subdued, low-key, unassuming, unpretentious, inconspicuous, unnoticeable, unostentatious • *She is wearing discreet jewelery.*

discrepancy = **disagreement**, difference, variation, conflict, contradiction, inconsistency, disparity, variance, divergence, dissonance, incongruity, dissimilarity, discordance, contrariety • *the discrepancy between press and radio reports*

discrete = **separate**, individual, distinct, detached, disconnected, unattached, discontinuous • *the process seen as a sequence of discrete phases*

discretion 1 = **tact**, care, consideration, judgment, caution, diplomacy, good sense, prudence, acumen, wariness, discernment, circumspection, sagacity, carefulness, judiciousness, heedfulness • *He conducted the whole affair with the utmost discretion.*

OPPOSITES: indiscretion, carelessness, tactlessness

2 = **choice**, will, wish, liking, mind, option, pleasure, preference, inclination, disposition, predilection, volition • *She was given the money to use at her own discretion.*

PROVERBS

Discretion is the better part of valour

discretionary = **optional**, arbitrary (*Law*), unrestricted, elective, open to choice, nonmandatory • *They were given wider discretionary powers.*

discriminate AS A VERB = **differentiate**, distinguish, discern, separate, assess, evaluate, tell the difference, draw a distinction • *He is incapable of discriminating between a good idea and a bad one.*

▸ IN PHRASES: **discriminate against someone** = **treat differently**, single out, victimize, disfavour, treat as inferior, show bias against, show prejudice against • *They believe the law discriminates against women.*

discriminating = **discerning**, particular, keen, critical, acute, sensitive, refined, cultivated, selective, astute, tasteful, fastidious • *These products are snapped up by more discriminating customers.*

OPPOSITES: careless, indiscriminate, undiscriminating

discrimination 1 = **prejudice**, bias, injustice, intolerance, bigotry, favouritism, unfairness, inequity • *measures to counteract racial discrimination*

2 = **discernment**, taste, judgment, perception, insight, penetration, subtlety, refinement, acumen, keenness, sagacity, acuteness, clearness • *He praised our taste and discrimination.*

3 = **differentiation**, distinction, telling the difference • *the ewe's discrimination between her own and alien lambs*

discriminatory = **prejudiced**, biased, partial, weighted, favouring, one-sided, partisan, unjust, preferential, prejudicial, inequitable • *These reforms will abolish racially discriminatory laws.*

discursive = digressive, loose, rambling, roundabout, diffuse, meandering, desultory, long-winded, circuitous, prolix • *The book is characterized by a reflective, discursive style.*

discuss 1 = talk about, consider, debate, review, go into, examine, argue about, thrash out, ventilate, reason about, exchange views on, deliberate about, weigh up the pros and cons of, converse about, confer about • *They met today to discuss how to respond to the ultimatum.*
2 = **examine**, consider, deal with, treat, go into, tackle, explore, write about, analyze • *I will discuss the role of diet in cancer prevention in Chapter 7.*

discussion 1 = talk, debate, argument, conference, exchange, review, conversation, consideration, dialogue, consultation, seminar, discourse, deliberation, symposium, colloquy, confabulation, korero *(N.Z.)* • *There was a discussion about the wording of the report.*
2 = **examination**, investigation, analysis, scrutiny, dissection • *For a discussion of biology and sexual politics, see chapter 4.*

QUOTATIONS
The aim of argument, or of discussion, should be not victory, but progress
[Joseph Joubert *Pensées*]

disdain AS A NOUN = **contempt**, dislike, scorn, arrogance, indifference, sneering, derision, hauteur, snobbishness, contumely, haughtiness, superciliousness • *She looked at him with disdain.*
▸ AS A VERB = **scorn**, reject, despise, slight, disregard, spurn, undervalue, deride, look down on, belittle, sneer at, pooh-pooh, contemn, look down your nose at *(informal)*, misprize • *a political leader who disdained the compromises of politics*

QUOTATIONS
A little disdain is not amiss; a little scorn is alluring
[William Congreve *The Way of the World*]

disdainful = contemptuous, scornful, arrogant, superior, proud, sneering, aloof, haughty, derisive, supercilious, high and mighty *(informal)*, hoity-toity *(informal)*, turning up your nose (at), on your high horse *(informal)*, looking down your nose (at) • *He gave us a disdainful glance and moved on.*

disease 1 = illness, condition, complaint, upset, infection, disorder, sickness, ailment, affliction, malady, infirmity, indisposition, lurgy *(informal)* • *illnesses such as heart disease*
2 = **evil**, disorder, plague, curse, cancer, blight, contamination, scourge, affliction, bane, contagion, malady, canker • *the disease of racism eating away at the core of our society*
▸ RELATED ADJECTIVE: pathological
▸ RELATED PHOBIAS: nosophobia, pathophobia
▹ *See panel* Diseases

diseased 1 = unhealthy, sick, infected, rotten, ailing, tainted, sickly, unwell, crook *(Austral. & N.Z. informal)*, unsound, unwholesome • *Clear away dead or diseased plants.*
2 = **sick**, evil, twisted, corrupt, vicious, distorted, abnormal, perverted, impaired, warped, unhealthy, unnatural, immoral, deviant, wicked, kinky *(slang)*, depraved, debased, debauched, aberrant, vitiated, pervy *(slang)*, sicko *(slang)* • *the product of a diseased and evil mind*

disembark = land, get off, alight, arrive, step out, go ashore • *Six passengers had already disembarked.*

disembodied = ghostly, phantom, spectral • *A disembodied voice spoke in the darkness.*

disembowel = gut, eviscerate, remove the innards from, draw • *a psychopath who hangs and disembowels his prey*

disenchanted = disillusioned, disappointed, soured, cynical, indifferent, sick, let down, blasé, jaundiced, undeceived • *I'm disenchanted with my marriage at the moment.*

disenchantment = disillusionment, disappointment, disillusion, rude awakening • *There is growing disenchantment with the government.*

disengage 1 = release, free, separate, ease, liberate, loosen, set free, extricate, untie, disentangle, unloose, unbridle • *He gently disengaged himself from his sister's tearful embrace.*
2 = **detach**, withdraw • *More vigorous action is needed to force the army to disengage.*

disengaged = unconnected, separate, apart, detached, unattached • *Diane felt somewhat disengaged from those around her.*

disengagement = disconnection, withdrawal, separation, detachment, disentanglement • *This policy of disengagement from the war had its critics.*

disentangle 1 = resolve, clear (up), work out, sort out, clarify, simplify • *The author brilliantly disentangles complex debates.*
2 = **free**, separate, loose, detach, sever, disconnect, extricate, disengage • *They are looking at ways to disentangle him from this situation.*
3 = **untangle**, unravel, untwist, unsnarl • *The rope could not be disentangled and had to be cut.*

disfavour or *(U.S.)* **disfavor 1 = unpopularity**, shame, disgrace, discredit, doghouse *(informal)*, bad books *(informal)*, disesteem • *He fell into disfavour and had to resign.*
2 = **disapproval**, dislike, displeasure, disapprobation • *She eyed his unruly collar-length hair with disfavour.*

disfigure 1 = damage, scar, mutilate, maim, injure, wound, deform • *These items could be used to injure or disfigure someone.*
2 = **mar**, distort, blemish, deface, make ugly, disfeature • *ugly new houses which disfigure the countryside*

disfigured = damaged, scarred, mutilated, marred, spoilt, ugly, maimed, deformed, blemished • *She tried not to look at his scarred, disfigured face.*

disfigurement = damage, injury, scar, defect, spot, stain, trauma *(Pathology)*, distortion, blemish, mutilation, impairment, deformity, defacement • *He had surgery to correct a facial disfigurement.*

disgorge = emit, discharge, send out, expel, throw out, vent, throw up, eject, spout, spew, belch, send forth • *The ground had opened to disgorge a boiling stream of molten lava.*

disgrace AS A NOUN **1 = shame**, contempt, discredit, degradation, disrepute, ignominy, dishonour, infamy, opprobrium, odium, disfavour, obloquy, disesteem • *I have brought disgrace upon my family.*
OPPOSITES: credit, favour, honour
2 = **scandal**, stain, stigma, blot, blemish • *the disgrace of having an illegitimate child*
▸ AS A VERB = **shame**, stain, humiliate, discredit, degrade, taint, sully, dishonour, stigmatize, defame, abase, bring shame upon • *These soldiers have disgraced their regiment.*
OPPOSITES: credit, honour, grace
▸ IN PHRASES: **in disgrace = out of favour**, unpopular, in the doghouse, in someone's bad books • *He refuses to say why he is in disgrace.*

disgraced = shamed, humiliated, discredited, branded, degraded, mortified, in disgrace, dishonoured, stigmatized, under a cloud, in the doghouse *(informal)* • *the disgraced leader of the coup*

disgraceful = shameful, shocking, scandalous, mean, low, infamous, degrading, unworthy, ignominious, disreputable, contemptible, dishonourable, detestable, discreditable, blameworthy, opprobrious • *I complained about his disgraceful behaviour.*

disgruntled = discontented, dissatisfied, annoyed, irritated, put out, hacked (off) *(U.S. slang)*, grumpy, vexed, pissed off *(taboo slang)*, sullen, displeased, petulant, sulky, peeved, malcontent, testy, peevish, huffy, cheesed off *(Brit. slang)*, hoha *(N.Z.)* • *Disgruntled employees recently called for his resignation.*

DISEASES

HUMAN DISEASES

absinthism
acariasis
acne
acromegaly
actinodermatitis
actinomycosis
Addison's disease
adrenoleukodystrophy *or* ALD
aeroneurosis
agranulocytosis
ague
Aids *or* AIDS
alcoholism
Alzheimer's disease
amoebiasis
ancylostomiasis
angina
anorexia *or* anorexia nervosa
anthracosis
anthrax
aortitis
appendicitis
apraxia
arteriosclerosis
arthritis
asbestosis
ascariasis
asthma
atherosclerosis
athlete's foot
avian flu
avitaminosis
Bell's palsy
beriberi
bilharzia
bilharziasis *or* bilharziosis
bird flu
Black Death
black measles
blackwater fever
Bornholm disease
Bright's disease
bronchiolitis
bronchitis
bronchopneumonia
brucellosis
bubonic plague
bulimia *or* bulimia nervosa
Burkitt lymphoma
bursitis
byssinosis
calenture
cancer
cardiomyopathy
carditis
caries
carpal tunnel syndrome
cellulitis
cerebellar syndrome
Chagas' disease
chickenpox
chin cough
chloracne
chlorosis
cholera
chorea
Christmas disease
chronic fatigue syndrome *or* CFS
cirrhosis
coal miner's lung
coccidioidomycosis
coeliac disease
cold
colitis
common cold
conjunctivitis
constipation
consumption
cor pulmonale
coxalgia
Creutzfeldt-Jakob disease
Crohn's disease
Cushing's disease
cystic fibrosis
cystitis
dead fingers
decompression sickness
dengue
dermatitis
dhobitch
diabetes
diarrhoea
diphtheria
diverticulitis
double pneumonia
dropsy
dysentery
earache
ebola virus disease
Economo's disease
eczema
elephantiasis
emphysema
encephalitis
encephalomyelitis
encephalopathy
endocarditis
enteritis
enterobiasis
enterocolitis
epilepsy
ergotism
erysipelas
erythroblastosis
exophthalmic goitre
farmer's lung
favus
fibrositis
filariasis
fishskin disease
flu
framboesia
furunculosis
gastritis
gastroenteritis
genital herpes
German measles
gingivitis
glandular fever
glaucoma
glomerulonephritis
glossitis
glue ear
goitre
gonorrhoea
gout
grand mal
green monkey disease
greensickness
haemoglobinopathy
haemophilia
Hansen's disease
hebephrenia
hepatitis
hepatitis A
hepatitis B
herpes
herpes simplex
herpes zoster
hidrosis
histoplasmosis
Hodgkin's disease
Huntington's chorea
hypothermia
hypothyroidism
ichthyosis
icterus
impetigo
infectious hepatitis
infectious mononucleosis
influenza
iritis
jaundice
jungle fever
kala-azar
Kaposi's sarcoma
Kawasaki's disease
Korsakoff's psychosis
kuru
labyrinthitis
laryngitis
Lassa fever
lathyrism
legionnaire's disease
leishmaniasis *or* leishmaniosis
leprosy
leptospirosis
leukaemia
listeriosis
lockjaw
lumbago
lupus
lupus erythematosus
lupus vulgaris
Lyme disease
lymphoma
malaria
Marburg disease
mastitis
measles
Ménière's syndrome
meningitis

Human diseases (continued)

metabolic syndrome
milk sickness
motor neurone disease
multiple sclerosis
mumps
muscular dystrophy
myalgic encephalomyelitis *or* ME
myasthenia gravis
myiasis
myopathy
myxoedema
narcolepsy
necrotising fasciitis
nephritis
nephrosis
neuropathy
non-A, non-B hepatitis
non-Hodgkin's lymphoma
onchocerciasis
ornithosis
osteitis
osteitis deformans
osteoarthritis
osteomalacia
osteomyelitis
osteoporosis
otitis
Paget's disease
paratyphoid fever
Parkinson's disease
pellagra
pelvic inflammatory disease
pemphigus
pericarditis
petit mal
pharyngitis
phlebitis
phthisis
pinta
pityriasis
pleurisy
pleuropneumonia
pneumoconiosis
pneumonia
poliomyelitis *or* polio
polycythaemia
porphyria
Pott's disease
pox
presenile dementia
prurigo
psittacosis
psoriasis
purpura
pyorrhoea
Q fever
quinsy
rabies
radiation sickness
ratbite fever *or* ratbite disease
Raynaud's disease
relapsing fever
retinitis
retinopathy
Reye's syndrome
rheumatic fever
rheumatoid arthritis
rhinitis
rickets
rickettsial disease
ringworm
Rocky Mountain spotted fever
rubella
Saint Vitus's dance
salmonella *or* salmonellosis
salpingitis
sapraemia
sarcomatosis
scabies
scarlet fever *or* scarlatina
schistosomiasis
schizophrenia
schizothymia
sciatica
scleroderma
scrofula
scrub typhus
scurvy
seasonal affective disorder
seborrhoea
senile dementia
septicaemia
serpigo
serum sickness
shell shock
shingles
sickle-cell anaemia
siderosis
silicosis
sinusitis
sleeping sickness
smallpox
spina bifida
spirochaetosis
splenitis
splenomegaly
spondylitis
spotted fever
sprue
stomatitis
strongyloidiasis
sunstroke
sweating sickness
swinepox
sycosis
Sydenham's chorea
synovitis
syphilis
syringomyelia
tarantism
Tay-Sachs disease
tetanus
thalassaemia
thrush
tick fever
tinea
tonsillitis
Tourette syndrome
toxic shock syndrome
trachoma
trench fever
trench mouth
trichinosis
trypanosomiasis
tsutsugamushi disease
tuberculosis
typhoid fever
typhus
uncinariasis
uraemia
urethritis
urticaria
utriculitis
uveitis
vaginitis
vagotonia
valvulitis
varicosis
variola
varioloid
venereal disease
Vincent's angina
vulvitis
vulvovaginitis
Weil's disease
whooping cough
yaws
yellow fever

Animal diseases

actinomycosis *or (nontechnical)* lumpy jaw
anbury
anthrax
blackleg
bots
braxy
brucellosis *or* undulant fever
BSE (bovine spongiform encephalopathy) *or (informal)* mad cow disease
bull nose
bush sickness *(N.Z.)*
canker
cowpox
distemper
dourine
foot-and-mouth disease
fowl pest
furunculosis
gallsickness *or* anaplasmosis
gapes
gid
glanders
grapes
hard pad
heaves *or* broken wind
laminitis *or* founder
lampas *or* lampers
loco disease
Lyme disease
malanders
Marburg disease *or* green monkey disease

Animal diseases (continued)

milk fever
moon blindness *or* mooneye
murrain
myxomatosis
nagana
Newcastle disease *or* fowl pest
ornithosis
pinkeye
pip
pityriasis
psittacosis
pullorum disease *or* bacillary white diarrhoea
quarter crack
quittor
red water
rinderpest
ringbone
roaring
rot
roup
sand crack
scab
scrapie
scratches
seedy toe
sheep measles
sitfast
spavin
staggers, blind staggers, *or* megrims
strangles *or* equine distemper
stringhalt *or* springhalt
surra
swamp fever *or* equine infectious anaemia
sweating sickness
sweeny
swine fever *or (U.S.)* hog cholera
swinepox *or* variola porcina
swine vesicular disease
Texas fever
thoroughpin
thrush
toe crack
trembles *or* milk sickness
warble
whistling
windgall

disguise AS A VERB = **hide**, cover, conceal, screen, mask, suppress, withhold, veil, cloak, shroud, camouflage, keep secret, hush up, draw a veil over, keep dark, keep under your hat • *He made no attempt to disguise his contempt.*
▸ IN PHRASES: **disguise something** *or* **someone as something** *or* **someone** = **dress up as**, get up as, camouflage as, fit out as • *He sold cars, stole them back, disguised them as new ones, then sold them again.*
disguise yourself as something *or* **someone** = **dress up as**, masquerade as • *She disguised herself as a man so that she could fight.*
▸ AS A NOUN = **costume**, get-up *(informal)*, mask, camouflage, false appearance • *a ridiculous disguise.*

disguised 1 = **in disguise**, masked, camouflaged, undercover, incognito, unrecognizable • *a disguised bank robber*
2 = **covert**, hidden, concealed, sly, sneaky, furtive, underhand, back-alley • *a disguised tax on immigration*
3 = **false**, assumed, pretend, artificial, forged, fake, mock, imitation, sham, pseudo *(informal)*, counterfeit, feigned, phoney *or* phony *(informal)* • *Their HQ used to be a disguised builders' yard.*

disgust AS A VERB = **sicken**, outrage, offend, revolt, put off, repel, nauseate, gross out *(U.S. slang)*, turn your stomach, fill with loathing, cause aversion • *He disgusted everyone with his boorish behaviour.*
OPPOSITES: please, delight, impress
▸ AS A NOUN 1 = **loathing**, revulsion, hatred, dislike, nausea, distaste, aversion, antipathy, abomination, repulsion, abhorrence, repugnance, odium, detestation, hatefulness • *A look of disgust came over his face.*
OPPOSITES: liking, love, taste
2 = **outrage**, shock, anger, hurt, fury, resentment, wrath, indignation • *Colleagues last night spoke of their disgust at the decision.*

disgusted 1 = **outraged**, appalled, offended, sickened, scandalized • *I'm disgusted with the way that he was treated.*
2 = **sickened**, repelled, repulsed, nauseated • *squeamish men who are disgusted by the idea of menstruation*

disgusting 1 = **sickening**, foul, revolting, gross, nasty, stinking, vulgar, vile, distasteful, repellent, obnoxious, objectionable, nauseating, odious, hateful, repugnant, loathsome, abominable, nauseous, grotty *(slang)*, detestable, cringe-making *(Brit. informal)*, noisome, yucky *or* yukky *(slang)*, festy *(Austral. slang)*, yucko *(Austral. slang)* • *The curry was disgusting.*
2 = **appalling**, shocking, terrible, awful, offensive, dreadful, horrifying, dismaying, dire • *It's a disgusting waste of money*

dish AS A NOUN 1 = **bowl**, plate, platter, salver • *Pile the potatoes into a warm serving dish.*
2 = **food**, meal, fare, course, recipe • *There are plenty of vegetarian dishes to choose from.*
▸ IN PHRASES: **dish something out** = **distribute**, assign, allocate, designate, set aside, hand out, earmark, inflict, mete out, dole out, share out, apportion • *The council wants to dish the money out to specific projects.*
dish something up = **serve up**, serve, produce, present, hand out, ladle out, spoon out • *They dished up the next course.*

disharmony = **discord**, conflict, clash, friction, discordance, disaccord, inharmoniousness • *racial disharmony*

dishearten = **discourage**, depress, crush, dash, deter, dismay, daunt, cast down, dispirit, deject • *These conditions dishearten people and undermine their hope.*
OPPOSITES: encourage, lift, rally

disheartened = **discouraged**, depressed, crushed, dismayed, choked, daunted, dejected, dispirited, downcast, crestfallen, downhearted, sick as a parrot *(informal)* • *He was disheartened by their hostile reaction.*

dishevelled *or (U.S.)* **disheveled** = **untidy**, disordered, messy, ruffled, rumpled, bedraggled, unkempt, tousled, hanging loose, blowsy, uncombed, disarranged, disarrayed, frowzy, daggy *(Austral. & N.Z. informal)* • *She arrived looking flushed and dishevelled.*
OPPOSITES: smart, trim, tidy

dishonest = **deceitful**, corrupt, crooked *(informal)*, designing, lying, bent *(slang)*, false, unfair, cheating, deceiving, shady *(informal)*, fraudulent, treacherous, deceptive, unscrupulous, crafty, swindling, disreputable, untrustworthy, double-dealing, unprincipled, mendacious, perfidious, untruthful, guileful, knavish *(archaic)* • *He had become rich by dishonest means.*
OPPOSITES: true, principled, honest

dishonesty = **deceit**, fraud, corruption, cheating, graft *(informal)*, treachery, trickery, criminality, duplicity, falsehood, chicanery, falsity, sharp practice, perfidy, mendacity, fraudulence, crookedness, wiliness, unscrupulousness, improbity • *She accused the government of dishonesty and incompetence.*

QUOTATIONS

Dishonesty is the raw material not of quacks only, but also in great part of dupes
[Thomas Carlyle *Count Cagliostro*]

dishonour *or (U.S.)* **dishonor** AS A VERB 1 = **disgrace**, shame, discredit, corrupt, degrade, blacken, sully, debase, debauch, defame, abase • *It would dishonour my family if I didn't wear the veil.*
OPPOSITES: respect, worship, esteem

2 = **break**, default on, go back on, retract, repudiate, renege on, back out on, change your mind about • *They claim the company has dishonoured their agreement.*
▸ AS A NOUN = **disgrace**, scandal, shame, discredit, degradation, disrepute, reproach, ignominy, infamy, opprobrium, odium, disfavour, abasement, obloquy • *You have brought dishonour on a fine and venerable institution.*
OPPOSITES: honour, integrity, goodness

dishonourable *or (U.S.)* **dishonorable** = **shameful**, base, corrupt, infamous, disgraceful, treacherous, scandalous, unscrupulous, shameless, despicable, ignominious, disreputable, contemptible, untrustworthy, unprincipled, ignoble, not cricket *(informal)*, discreditable, blackguardly • *He insisted he had done nothing dishonourable.*

disillusion AS A VERB = **shatter the illusions of**, disabuse, bring down to earth, open the eyes of, disenchant, undeceive • *I hate to disillusion you, but he's already married.*
▸ AS A NOUN = **disenchantment**, disappointment, rude awakening • *There is disillusion with established political parties.*

disillusioned = **disenchanted**, disappointed, enlightened, indifferent, disabused, sadder and wiser, undeceived • *I've become very disillusioned with politics.*

disillusionment = **disenchantment**, disappointment, disillusion, enlightenment, rude awakening, lost innocence • *There is a general sense of disillusionment with the government.*

disincentive = **discouragement**, deterrent, impediment, damper, dissuasion, determent • *High tax rates may act as a disincentive to working longer hours.*

disinclination = **reluctance**, aversion, unwillingness, opposition, resistance, dislike, objection, antipathy, demur, lack of enthusiasm, repugnance, lack of desire, hesitance, loathness • *They are showing a disinclination to pursue these opportunities.*

disinclined = **reluctant**, unwilling, averse, opposed, resistant, hesitant, balking, loath, not in the mood, indisposed, antipathetic • *He was disinclined to talk about himself.*

disinfect = **sterilize**, purify, decontaminate, clean, cleanse, fumigate, deodorize, sanitize • *Chlorine is used to disinfect water.*
OPPOSITES: poison, infect, contaminate

disinfectant = **antiseptic**, sterilizer, germicide, sanitizer • *Salt is a natural disinfectant.*

disingenuous = **dishonest**, cunning, sly, designing, wily, insidious, feigned, artful, two-faced, shifty, deceitful, insincere, duplicitous, underhanded, guileful, uncandid • *his disingenuous claims of innocence*

disinherit = **cut off**, dispossess, disown, cut off without a penny • *He threatened to disinherit her if she did not end the relationship.*

disintegrate 1 = **collapse**, fall, fail, fold, founder, give way, subside, cave in, fragment, crumple, go belly-up *(informal)*, fall apart at the seams • *The empire began to disintegrate.*
2 = **break up**, crumble, fall apart, separate, shatter, splinter, break apart, fall to pieces, go to pieces, disunite • *At 420 mph the windscreen disintegrated.*

disinter = **dig up**, unearth, exhume, disentomb • *The bones were disinterred and moved to a burial site.*

disinterest = **indifference**, apathy, lack of interest, disregard, detachment, absence of feeling • *his wife's total disinterest in sex*

disinterested 1 = **impartial**, objective, neutral, detached, equitable, impersonal, unbiased, even-handed, unselfish, uninvolved, unprejudiced, free from self-interest • *Scientists are expected to be impartial and disinterested.*
OPPOSITES: involved, prejudiced, biased
2 = **indifferent**, apathetic, uninterested • *We had become jaded, disinterested and disillusioned.*

disjointed 1 = **incoherent**, confused, disordered, rambling, disconnected, unconnected, loose, aimless, fitful, spasmodic • *his disjointed drunken ramblings*
2 = **disconnected**, separated, divided, split, displaced, dislocated, disunited • *our increasingly fragmented and disjointed society*

dislike AS A VERB = **hate**, object to, loathe, despise, shun, scorn, disapprove of, detest, abhor, recoil from, take a dim view of, be repelled by, be averse to, disfavour, have an aversion to, abominate, have a down on *(informal)*, disrelish, have no taste *or* stomach for, not be able to bear *or* abide *or* stand • *We don't serve liver often because so many people dislike it.*
OPPOSITES: like, favour, esteem
▸ AS A NOUN = **hatred**, disgust, hostility, loathing, disapproval, distaste, animosity, aversion, antagonism, displeasure, antipathy, enmity, animus, disinclination, repugnance, odium, detestation, disapprobation • *The two women viewed each other with dislike and suspicion.*
OPPOSITES: liking, delight, attraction

dislocate 1 = **put out of joint**, disconnect, disengage, unhinge, disunite, disjoint, disarticulate, luxate *(Medical)* • *She had dislocated her shoulder in the fall.*
2 = **disrupt**, confuse, disturb, disorder, disorganize, throw into disarray • *The strike was designed to dislocate the economy.*

dislocation 1 = **disruption**, disorder, disturbance, disarray, disorganization • *The refugees have suffered a total dislocation of their lives.*
2 = **putting out of joint**, unhinging, disengagement, disconnection, disarticulation, luxation *(Medical)* • *He suffered a double dislocation of his left ankle.*

dislodge 1 = **displace**, remove, disturb, dig out, uproot, extricate, disentangle, knock loose • *Use a hoof pick to dislodge stones and dirt from your horse's feet.*
2 = **oust**, remove, expel, throw out, displace, topple, force out, eject, depose, unseat • *The leader cannot dislodge her this time.*

disloyal = **treacherous**, false, unfaithful, subversive, two-faced, faithless, untrustworthy, perfidious, apostate, traitorous • *He proved to be an untrustworthy and disloyal ally.*
OPPOSITES: true, constant, loyal

disloyalty = **treachery**, infidelity, breach of trust, double-dealing, falsity, perfidy, unfaithfulness, falseness, betrayal of trust, inconstancy, deceitfulness, breaking of faith, Punic faith • *Charges of disloyalty had already been made against them.*

dismal 1 = **bad**, awful, dreadful, rotten *(informal)*, terrible, poor, dire, duff *(Brit. informal)*, abysmal, frightful, godawful *(slang)* • *the country's dismal record in the Olympics*
2 = **sad**, gloomy, melancholy, black, dark, depressing, discouraging, bleak, dreary, sombre, forlorn, despondent, lugubrious, sorrowful, wretched, funereal, cheerless, dolorous • *You can't occupy yourself with dismal thoughts all the time.*
OPPOSITES: happy, glad, cheery
3 = **gloomy**, depressing, dull, dreary, lugubrious, cheerless • *The main part of the hospital is pretty dismal.*
OPPOSITES: bright, sunny, cheerful

dismantle 1 = **take apart**, strip, demolish, raze, disassemble, pull to pieces, unrig, take to pieces *or* bits • *He asked for immediate help to dismantle the warheads.*
2 = **abolish**, end, overturn, suppress, overthrow, void, terminate, eradicate, put an end to, quash, do away with, stamp out, obliterate, vitiate • *opposition to the president's policy of dismantling apartheid*

dismay AS A VERB 1 = **alarm**, frighten, scare, panic, distress, terrify, appal, startle, horrify, paralyse, unnerve, put the wind up (someone) *(informal)*, give (someone) a turn *(informal)*, affright, fill with consternation • *The committee was dismayed by what it had been told.*

2 = disappoint, upset, sadden, dash, discourage, put off, daunt, disillusion, let down, vex, chagrin, dishearten, dispirit, disenchant, disgruntle • *He was dismayed to learn that she was already married.*
▸ AS A NOUN **1 = alarm**, fear, horror, panic, anxiety, distress, terror, dread, fright, unease, apprehension, nervousness, agitation, consternation, trepidation, uneasiness • *They reacted to the news with dismay.*
2 = disappointment, upset, distress, frustration, dissatisfaction, disillusionment, chagrin, disenchantment, discouragement, mortification • *Much to her dismay, he did not call.*

dismember = **cut into pieces**, divide, rend, sever, mutilate, dissect, dislocate, amputate, disjoint, anatomize, dislimb • *He dismembered her, hiding parts of her body in the cellar.*

dismiss **1 = reject**, disregard, spurn, repudiate, pooh-pooh • *He dismissed the reports as mere speculation.*
2 = banish, drop, dispel, shelve, discard, set aside, eradicate, cast out, lay aside, put out of your mind • *I dismissed the thought from my mind.*
3 = sack, fire (*informal*), remove (*informal*), axe (*informal*), discharge, oust, lay off, kick out (*informal*), cashier, send packing (*informal*), give notice to, kiss off (*slang, chiefly U.S. & Canad.*), give (someone) their marching orders, give (someone) the push (*informal*), give (someone) the elbow, give the boot to (*slang*), give the bullet to (*Brit. slang*), give someone his *or* her P45 (*informal*), kennet (*Austral. slang*), jeff (*Austral. slang*) • *the power to dismiss civil servants who refuse to work*
4 = let go, free, release, discharge, dissolve, liberate, disperse, disband, send away • *Two more witnesses were called, heard and dismissed.*

dismissal **1 = the sack**, removal, discharge, notice, the boot (*slang*), expulsion (*informal*), the push (*slang*), marching orders (*informal*), kiss-off (*slang, chiefly U.S. & Canad.*), the bum's rush (*slang*), the (old) heave-ho (*informal*), the order of the boot (*slang*), your books *or* cards (*informal*) • *his dismissal from his post*
2 = rejection, refusal, rebuff, knock-back (*slang*), kick in the teeth (*slang*), brushoff (*slang*) • *the high-handed dismissal of public opinion*

dismissive = **contemptuous**, scornful, disdainful, insulting, sneering, derisive • *He was highly dismissive of the report.*

dismount = **get off**, descend, get down, alight, light • *She dismounted and began to lead her horse.*

disobedience = **defiance**, mutiny, indiscipline, revolt, insubordination, waywardness, infraction, recalcitrance, noncompliance, unruliness, nonobservance • *Any further disobedience will be severely punished.*

disobedient = **defiant**, disorderly, contrary, naughty, wayward, mischievous, unruly, intractable, wilful, undisciplined, refractory, obstreperous, insubordinate, noncompliant, contumacious, froward (*archaic*), nonobservant • *Her tone was that of a parent ordering a disobedient child.*
OPPOSITES: manageable, obedient, compliant

disobey **1 = defy**, ignore, rebel, resist, disregard, refuse to obey, dig your heels in (*informal*), go counter to • *a naughty boy who often disobeyed his mother*
2 = infringe, defy, refuse to obey, flout, violate, contravene, overstep, transgress, go counter to • *He was forever disobeying the rules.*

disorder **1 = illness**, disease, complaint, condition, sickness, ailment, affliction, malady, infirmity, indisposition • *a rare nerve disorder that can cause paralysis of the arms*
2 = untidiness, mess, confusion, chaos, muddle, state, clutter, shambles, disarray, jumble, irregularity, disorganization, hotchpotch, derangement, hodgepodge (*U.S.*), pig's breakfast (*informal*), disorderliness • *The emergency room was in disorder.*
3 = disturbance, fight, riot, turmoil, unrest, quarrel, upheaval, brawl, clamour, uproar, turbulence, fracas, commotion, rumpus, tumult, hubbub, shindig (*informal*), hullabaloo, scrimmage, unruliness, shindy (*informal*), bagarre (*French*), biffo (*Austral. slang*) • *He called on the authorities to stop public disorder.*

disordered **1 = untidy**, confused, muddled, all over the place, displaced, out of place, jumbled, misplaced, dislocated, deranged, in a mess, disorganized, in confusion, higgledy-piggledy (*informal*), disarranged, disarrayed, out of kilter, daggy (*Austral. & N.Z. informal*) • *a disordered heap of mossy branches*
2 = disturbed, troubled, unbalanced, neurotic, maladjusted • *agencies working with mentally disordered offenders*

disorderly **1 = untidy**, confused, chaotic, messy, irregular, jumbled, indiscriminate, shambolic (*informal*), disorganized, higgledy-piggledy (*informal*), unsystematic • *The desk was covered in a disorderly jumble of old papers.*
OPPOSITES: neat, tidy, orderly
2 = unruly, disruptive, rowdy, turbulent, unlawful, stormy, rebellious, boisterous, tumultuous, lawless, riotous, unmanageable, ungovernable, refractory, obstreperous, indisciplined • *disorderly conduct*

disorganization = **disorder**, confusion, chaos, disruption, disarray • *The army is suffering from low morale and disorganization.*

disorganized **1 = muddled**, confused, disordered, shuffled, chaotic, jumbled, haphazard, unorganized, unsystematic, unmethodical • *I can't work in a disorganized office.*
2 = unmethodical, careless, inefficient, sloppy, lax, undisciplined, slapdash, remiss • *He is completely disorganized and is always running late.*

disorientate *or* **disorient** = **confuse**, upset, perplex, dislocate, cause to lose your bearings • *techniques used to disorientate and confuse prisoners*

disorientated *or* **disoriented** = **confused**, lost, unsettled, bewildered, mixed up, perplexed, all at sea • *I feel dizzy and disoriented.*

disown = **deny**, reject, abandon, renounce, disallow, retract, repudiate, cast off, rebut, disavow, disclaim, abnegate, refuse to acknowledge *or* recognize • *Those comments were later disowned.*

disparage = **run down**, dismiss, put down, criticize, underestimate, discredit, ridicule, scorn, minimize, disdain, undervalue, deride, slag (off) (*slang*), knock (*informal*), blast, flame (*informal*), rubbish (*informal*), malign, detract from, denigrate, belittle, decry, underrate, vilify, slander, deprecate, depreciate, tear into (*informal*), diss (*slang, chiefly U.S.*), defame, bad-mouth (*slang, chiefly U.S. & Canad.*), lambast(e), traduce, derogate, asperse • *his tendency to disparage literature*

disparagement = **contempt**, criticism, ridicule, discredit, condemnation, scorn, lessening, depreciation, disdain, degradation, denunciation, derision, slander, denigration, debasement, underestimation, derogation, contumely, aspersion, belittlement, detraction • *They were unanimous in their disparagement of the book.*

disparaging = **contemptuous**, damaging, critical, slighting, offensive, insulting, abusive, scathing, dismissive, belittling, unfavourable, derogatory, unflattering, scornful, disdainful, defamatory, derisive, libellous, slanderous, deprecatory, uncomplimentary, fault-finding, contumelious • *He was alleged to have made disparaging remarks.*
OPPOSITES: approving, flattering, complimentary

disparate = **different**, contrasting, unlike, contrary, distinct, diverse, at odds, dissimilar, discordant, at variance, discrepant • *Scientists are trying to pull together disparate ideas.*

disparity = **difference**, gap, inequality, distinction, imbalance, discrepancy, incongruity, unevenness, dissimilarity, disproportion, unlikeness, dissimilitude • *economic disparities between countries*

dispassionate 1 = **unemotional**, cool, collected, calm, moderate, composed, sober, serene, unmoved, temperate, unfazed *(informal)*, unruffled, imperturbable, unexcited, unexcitable • *He spoke in a flat dispassionate tone.*
OPPOSITES: excited, emotional, intense
2 = **objective**, fair, neutral, detached, indifferent, impartial, impersonal, disinterested, unbiased, uninvolved, unprejudiced • *We try to be dispassionate about the cases we bring.*
OPPOSITES: prejudiced, biased, partial

dispatch *or* **despatch** AS A VERB 1 = **send**, transmit, forward, express, communicate, consign, remit • *He dispatched a telegram.*
2 = **kill**, murder, destroy, do in *(slang)*, eliminate *(slang)*, take out *(slang)*, execute, butcher, slaughter, assassinate, slay, finish off, put an end to, do away with, blow away *(slang, chiefly U.S.)*, liquidate, annihilate, exterminate, take (someone's) life, bump off *(slang)* • *They may catch him and dispatch him immediately.*
3 = **carry out**, perform, fulfil, effect, finish, achieve, settle, dismiss, conclude, accomplish, execute, discharge, dispose of, expedite, make short work of *(informal)* • *He dispatched his business.*
▸ AS A NOUN 1 = **sending**, transmission, forwarding, communication, consignment, remittance • *The parcel is ready for dispatch.*
2 = **message**, news, report, story, letter, account, piece, item, document, communication, instruction, bulletin, communiqué, missive • *This dispatch from our West Africa correspondent.*
3 = **speed**, haste, promptness, alacrity, rapidity, quickness, swiftness, briskness, expedition, celerity, promptitude, precipitateness • *He feels we should act with despatch.*

dispel = **drive away**, dismiss, eliminate, resolve, scatter, expel, disperse, banish, rout, allay, dissipate, chase away • *He will hope to dispel their fears.*

dispensable = **expendable**, unnecessary, disposable, superfluous, nonessential, inessential, unrequired • *Those people are dispensable.*
OPPOSITES: important, necessary, indispensable

dispensation 1 = **exemption**, licence, exception, permission, privilege, relaxation, immunity, relief, indulgence, reprieve, remission • *The committee were not prepared to grant special dispensation.*
2 = **distribution**, supplying, dealing out, appointment, endowment, allotment, consignment, disbursement, apportionment, bestowal, conferment • *the dispensation of justice*

dispense AS A VERB 1 = **distribute**, assign, allocate, allot, mete out, dole out, share out, apportion, deal out, disburse • *They had already dispensed £40,000 in grants.*
2 = **prepare**, measure, supply, mix • *a store licensed to dispense prescriptions*
3 = **administer**, direct, operate, carry out, implement, undertake, enforce, execute, apply, discharge • *High Court judges dispensing justice round the country*
4 = **exempt**, except, excuse, release, relieve, reprieve, let off *(informal)*, exonerate • *No-one is dispensed from collaborating in this task.*
▸ IN PHRASES: **dispense with something** *or* **someone**
1 = **do away with**, ignore, give up, cancel, abolish, omit, disregard, pass over, brush aside, forgo, render needless • *We'll dispense with formalities.*
2 = **do without**, get rid of, dispose of, relinquish, shake off • *Up at the lectern he dispensed with his notes.*

dispersal 1 = **scattering**, spread, distribution, dissemination, dissipation • *the plants' mechanisms of dispersal of their spores*
2 = **spread**, broadcast, circulation, diffusion, dissemination • *the dispersal of this notably negative attitude*

disperse 1 = **scatter**, spread, distribute, circulate, strew, diffuse, dissipate, disseminate, throw about • *Intense currents disperse the sewage.*
2 = **break up**, separate, dismiss, disappear, send off, vanish, scatter, dissolve, rout, dispel, disband, part company, demobilize, go (their) separate ways • *The crowd dispersed peacefully.*
OPPOSITES: collect, gather, pool
3 = **dissolve**, disappear, vanish, evaporate, break up, dissipate, melt away, evanesce • *The fog dispersed and I became aware of the sun.*

dispersed = **spread-out**, extensive, scattered, sprawling, expansive, fanned out • *his widely dispersed business*

dispirited = **disheartened**, depressed, discouraged, down, low, sad, gloomy, glum, dejected, in the doldrums, despondent, downcast, morose, crestfallen, sick as a parrot *(informal)* • *I left feeling utterly dispirited.*

dispiriting = **disheartening**, disappointing, depressing, crushing, discouraging, daunting, sickening, saddening, demoralizing • *It's very dispiriting to be out of a job.*
OPPOSITES: encouraging, comforting, reassuring

displace 1 = **replace**, succeed, take over from, supersede, oust, usurp, supplant, take the place of, crowd out, fill *or* step into (someone's) boots • *These factories have displaced tourism.*
2 = **force out**, turn out, expel, throw out, oust, unsettle, kick out *(informal)*, eject, evict, dislodge, boot out *(informal)*, dispossess, turf out *(informal)* • *In Europe alone, 30 million people were displaced.*
3 = **move**, shift, disturb, budge, misplace, disarrange, derange • *A strong wind is all it would take to displace the stones.*
4 = **remove**, fire *(informal)*, dismiss, sack *(informal)*, discharge, oust, depose, cashier, dethrone, remove from office • *They displaced him in a coup.*

displacement 1 = **replacement**, substitution, superseding, ousting, usurping, supplanting • *the displacement of your reason by your emotions*
2 = **dispersal**, spread, scattering, distribution, diffusion, dissemination, dissipation • *the gradual displacement of the American Indian*

display AS A VERB 1 = **show**, present, exhibit, unveil, open to view, take the wraps off, put on view • *The cabinets display seventeenth-century porcelain.*
OPPOSITES: cover, hide, conceal
2 = **expose**, show, reveal, bare, exhibit, uncover, lay bare, expose to view • *She displayed her wound.*
3 = **demonstrate**, show, reveal, register, expose, disclose, betray, manifest, divulge, make known, evidence, evince • *It was unlike him to display his feelings.*
4 = **show off**, parade, exhibit, sport *(informal)*, flash *(informal)*, boast, flourish, brandish, flaunt, vaunt, showboat, make a (great) show of, disport, make an exhibition of • *She does not have to display her charms.*
▸ AS A NOUN 1 = **proof**, exhibition, demonstration, evidence, expression, exposure, illustration, revelation, testimony, confirmation, manifestation, affirmation, substantiation • *an outward display of affection*
2 = **exhibition**, show, demonstration, presentation, showing, array, expo *(informal)*, exposition • *a display of your work*
3 = **ostentation**, show, dash, flourish, fanfare, pomp • *He embraced it with such confidence and display.*
4 = **show**, exhibition, demonstration, parade, spectacle, pageant, pageantry • *a dazzling dance display*

d

displease = **annoy**, upset, anger, provoke, offend, irritate, put out, hassle *(informal)*, aggravate *(informal)*, incense, gall, exasperate, nettle, vex, irk, rile, pique, nark *(Brit., Austral. & N.Z. slang)*, piss you off *(taboo slang)*, dissatisfy, put your back up, hack you off *(informal)* • *He did not wish to displease her.*

displeasure = **annoyance**, anger, resentment, irritation, offence, dislike, wrath, dissatisfaction, disapproval, indignation, distaste, pique, vexation, disgruntlement, disfavour, disapprobation • *displeasure at the slow pace of change*
OPPOSITES: pleasure, approval, satisfaction

d

disposable 1 = **throwaway**, paper, plastic, one-use, expendable, nonreturnable • *disposable nappies for babies up to 8lb*
2 = **available**, expendable, free for use, consumable, spendable, at your service • *He had little disposable income.*

disposal AS A NOUN = **throwing away**, dumping *(informal)*, scrapping, removal, discarding, clearance, jettisoning, ejection, riddance, relinquishment • *the disposal of radioactive waste*
▸ IN PHRASES: **at your disposal** = **available**, ready, to hand, accessible, convenient, handy, on hand, at hand, obtainable, on tap, expendable, at your fingertips, at your service, free for use, ready for use, consumable, spendable • *Do you have this information at your disposal?*

dispose AS A VERB 1 = **arrange**, put, place, group, set, order, stand, range, settle, fix, rank, distribute, array • *He was preparing to dispose his effects about the room.*
2 = **lead**, move, condition, influence, prompt, tempt, adapt, motivate, bias, induce, incline, predispose, actuate • *theologies which dispose their adherents to fanaticism*
▸ IN PHRASES: **dispose of someone** = **kill**, murder, destroy, do in *(slang)*, take out *(slang)*, execute, slaughter, dispatch, assassinate, slay, do away with, knock off *(slang)*, liquidate, neutralize, exterminate, take (someone's) life, bump off *(slang)*, wipe from the face of the earth *(informal)* • *They had hired an assassin to dispose of him.*
dispose of something 1 = **get rid of**, destroy, dump *(informal)*, scrap, bin *(informal)*, junk *(informal)*, chuck *(informal)*, discard, unload, dispense with, jettison, get shot of, throw out *or* away • *Fold up the nappy and dispose of it.*
2 = **deal with**, manage, treat, handle, settle, cope with, take care of, see to, finish with, attend to, get to grips with • *the manner in which you disposed of that problem*
3 = **give**, give up, part with, bestow, transfer, make over, deliver up • *He managed to dispose of more money and goods.*

disposed = **inclined**, given, likely, subject, ready, prone, liable, apt, predisposed, tending towards, of a mind to • *I might be disposed to like him in other circumstances.*

disposition 1 = **character**, nature, spirit, make-up, constitution, temper, temperament • *his friendly and cheerful disposition*
2 = **tendency**, inclination, propensity, habit, leaning, bent, bias, readiness, predisposition, proclivity, proneness • *They show no disposition to take risks.*
3 = **arrangement**, grouping, ordering, organization, distribution, disposal, placement • *the disposition of walls and entrances*
4 = **control**, management, direction, regulation, disposal • *to oversee the disposition of funds*

dispossess = **strip**, deprive • *people who were dispossessed of their land*

dispossessed = **destitute**, landless • *all kinds of displaced and dispossessed people*

disproportion = **inequality**, imbalance, disparity, discrepancy, asymmetry, insufficiency, unevenness, lopsidedness • *There is a disproportion in resources available.*
OPPOSITES: balance, proportion

disproportionate = **excessive**, too much, unreasonable, uneven, unequal, unbalanced, out of proportion, inordinate, incommensurate • *a disproportionate amount of time*

disprove = **prove false**, discredit, refute, contradict, negate, invalidate, rebut, give the lie to, make a nonsense of, blow out of the water *(slang)*, controvert, confute • *The statistics disprove his hypothesis.*
OPPOSITES: show, prove, confirm

disputation = **dispute**, debate, controversy, polemics, dissension, argumentation • *after much legal disputation*

dispute AS A VERB 1 = **contest**, question, challenge, deny, doubt, oppose, object to, contradict, rebut, impugn, controvert, call in *or* into question • *He disputed the allegations.*
2 = **argue**, fight, clash, row, disagree, fall out *(informal)*, contend, feud, quarrel, brawl, squabble, spar, wrangle, bicker, have an argument, cross swords, be at sixes and sevens, fight like cat and dog, go at it hammer and tongs, altercate • *Whole towns disputed with neighboring villages over boundaries.*
▸ AS A NOUN 1 = **disagreement**, conflict, argument, controversy, falling out, contention, dissent, quarreling, friction, strife, antagonism, discord, altercation • *There has been much dispute over the ownership of the lease.*
2 = **argument**, row, clash, controversy, disturbance, contention, feud, quarrel, brawl, squabble, wrangle, difference of opinion, tiff, dissension, turf war *(informal)*, shindig *(informal)*, shindy *(informal)*, bagarre *(French)* • *The dispute between them is settled.*

disqualification = **ban**, exclusion, elimination, rejection, ineligibility, debarment, disenablement, disentitlement • *He faces a four-year disqualification from athletics.*

disqualified = **eliminated**, knocked out, out of the running, debarred, ineligible • *He was disqualified after a drugs test.*

disqualify = **ban**, rule out, prohibit, forbid, preclude, debar, declare ineligible, disentitle • *He has powers to disqualify individuals from public office.*

disquiet AS A NOUN = **uneasiness**, concern, fear, worry, alarm, anxiety, distress, unrest, angst, nervousness, trepidation, foreboding, restlessness, fretfulness, disquietude • *There is growing public disquiet.*
▸ AS A VERB = **make uneasy**, concern, worry, trouble, upset, bother, disturb, distress, annoy, plague, unsettle, harass, hassle *(informal)*, agitate, vex, perturb, discompose, incommode • *He's obviously disquieted by the experience.*

disquieting = **worrying**, troubling, upsetting, disturbing, distressing, annoying, irritating, unsettling, harrowing, unnerving, disconcerting, vexing, perturbing, bothersome • *He found her letter disquieting.*

disquisition = **lecture**, discourse, exposition, dissertation, paper, essay, thesis, treatise • *She launched into an authoritative disquisition.*

disregard AS A VERB = **ignore**, discount, take no notice of, overlook, neglect, pass over, turn a blind eye to, disobey, laugh off, make light of, pay no attention to, pay no heed to, leave out of account, brush aside *or* away • *He disregarded the advice of his executives.*
OPPOSITES: listen to, heed, pay attention to
▸ AS A NOUN = **ignoring**, neglect, contempt, indifference, negligence, disdain, disrespect, heedlessness • *a callous disregard for human life*

disrepair AS A NOUN = **dilapidation**, collapse, decay, deterioration, ruination • *The house was in a bad state of disrepair.*
▸ IN PHRASES: **in disrepair** = **out of order**, broken, decayed, worn-out, decrepit, not functioning, out of commission, on the blink *(slang)*, bust *(informal)*, kaput *(informal)* • *Everything was in disrepair.*

disreputable = **discreditable**, mean, low, base, shocking, disorderly, notorious, vicious, infamous, disgraceful,

shameful, vile, shady *(informal)*, scandalous, ignominious, contemptible, louche, unprincipled, dishonourable, opprobrious • *the noisiest and most disreputable bars*
OPPOSITES: respected, decent, respectable

disrepute = **discredit**, shame, disgrace, unpopularity, ignominy, dishonour, infamy, disfavour, ill repute, obloquy, ill favour, disesteem • *Our profession was brought into disrepute.*

disrespect = **contempt**, cheek, disregard, rudeness, lack of respect, irreverence, insolence, impertinence, impudence, discourtesy, incivility, impoliteness, lese-majesty, unmannerliness • *young people who treated her with complete disrespect*
OPPOSITES: regard, respect, esteem

disrespectful = **contemptuous**, insulting, rude, cheeky, irreverent, bad-mannered, impertinent, insolent, impolite, impudent, discourteous, uncivil, ill-bred • *They shouldn't treat their mothers in this disrespectful way.*

disrobe = **undress**, strip, take off your clothes, remove your clothes, shed your clothes, bare yourself, divest yourself of your clothes, unclothe yourself, uncover yourself • *She stood up and began to disrobe.*

disrupt 1 = **interrupt**, stop, upset, hold up, interfere with, unsettle, obstruct, cut short, intrude on, break up *or* into • *Anti-war protests disrupted the debate.*
2 = **disturb**, upset, confuse, disorder, spoil, unsettle, agitate, disorganize, disarrange, derange, throw into disorder • *The drought has disrupted agricultural production.*

disruption = **disturbance**, disorder, confusion, interference, disarray, interruption, stoppage, disorderliness • *delays and disruption to flights from Britain*

disruptive = **disturbing**, upsetting, disorderly, unsettling, troublesome, unruly, obstreperous, troublemaking • *violent, disruptive behaviour*
OPPOSITES: cooperative, obedient, well-behaved

dissatisfaction = **discontent**, frustration, resentment, regret, distress, disappointment, dismay, irritation, unhappiness, annoyance, displeasure, exasperation, chagrin • *job dissatisfaction among teachers*
PROVERBS
The grass is always greener on the other side of the fence

dissatisfied = **discontented**, frustrated, unhappy, disappointed, fed up, disgruntled, not satisfied, unfulfilled, displeased, unsatisfied, ungratified • *He felt restless and dissatisfied.*
OPPOSITES: pleased, content, satisfied

dissect 1 = **cut up** *or* **apart**, dismember, lay open, anatomize • *We dissected a frog in biology.*
2 = **analyse**, study, investigate, research, explore, break down, inspect, scrutinize • *People want to dissect his work.*

dissection 1 = **cutting up**, anatomy, autopsy, dismemberment, postmortem (examination), necropsy, anatomization • *a growing supply of corpses for dissection*
2 = **analysis**, examination, breakdown, research, investigation, inspection, scrutiny • *the dissection of my proposals*

dissemble = **hide**, act, pretend, bluff, be dishonest, dissimulate, conceal *or* hide *or* mask your feelings • *He was not slow to dissemble when it served his purpose.*

disseminate = **spread**, publish, broadcast, distribute, scatter, proclaim, circulate, sow, disperse, diffuse, publicize, dissipate, propagate, promulgate • *It took years to disseminate information about Aids.*

dissemination = **spread**, publishing, broadcasting, publication, distribution, circulation, diffusion, propagation, promulgation • *the dissemination of scientific ideas*

dissension = **disagreement**, conflict, dissent, dispute, contention, quarreling, friction, strife, discord, discordance, conflict of opinion • *a great deal of dissension within the armed forces*

dissent AS A NOUN = **disagreement**, opposition, protest, resistance, refusal, objection, discord, demur, dissension, dissidence, nonconformity, remonstrance • *He has responded harshly to any dissent.*
OPPOSITES: accord, agreement, assent
▸ AS A VERB = **disagree**, object, disapprove, demur, express disagreement, express objection • *Just one of the 10 members dissented.*
OPPOSITES: accept, agree, assent
▸ IN PHRASES: **dissent from something** = **disagree with**, challenge, dispute, object to, protest against, argue with, refuse to accept, take issue with, quibble with • *No one dissents from the decision to unify.*

dissenter = **objector**, dissident, nonconformist, protestant, disputant • *They do not tolerate dissenters in their ranks.*

dissenting = **disagreeing**, protesting, opposing, conflicting, differing, dissident • *There were dissenting voices.*

dissertation = **thesis**, essay, discourse, critique, exposition, treatise, disquisition • *He is currently writing a dissertation.*

disservice = **wrong**, injury, harm, injustice, disfavour, unkindness, bad turn, ill turn • *You could do yourself a grave disservice.*
OPPOSITES: service, courtesy, good turn

dissidence = **dissent**, dispute, disagreement, feud, rupture, difference of opinion, schism, discordance • *He knew that dissidence could not be crushed.*

dissident AS AN ADJECTIVE = **dissenting**, disagreeing, nonconformist, heterodox, schismatic, dissentient • *links with a dissident group*
▸ AS A NOUN = **protester**, rebel, dissenter, demonstrator, agitator, recusant, protest marcher • *political dissidents*

dissimilar = **different**, contrasting, unlike, various, varied, diverse, assorted, unrelated, disparate, miscellaneous, sundry, divergent, manifold, heterogeneous, mismatched, multifarious, not similar, not alike, not capable of comparison • *Their styles are not so dissimilar.*
OPPOSITES: uniform, alike, resembling

dissipate 1 = **disappear**, fade, vanish, dissolve, disperse, evaporate, diffuse, melt away, evanesce • *The tension in the room had dissipated.*
2 = **squander**, spend, waste, consume, run through, deplete, expend, fritter away, misspend • *Her father had dissipated her inheritance.*

dissipated 1 = **debauched**, abandoned, self-indulgent, profligate, intemperate, dissolute, rakish • *He was still handsome though dissipated.*
2 = **squandered**, spent, wasted, exhausted, consumed, scattered • *A lot of it has simply been dissipated.*

dissipation 1 = **dispersal**, scattering, vanishing, disappearance, disintegration, dissolution, dissemination • *the dissipation of heat*
2 = **waste**, spending, squandering, blowing *(slang)*, consumption, throwing away, misuse, frittering away, misspending • *the dissipation of my wealth*
3 = **debauchery**, excess, indulgence, abandonment, drunkenness, profligacy, intemperance, wantonness, dissoluteness • *Her face was a revelation of age and dissipation.*

dissociate *or* **disassociate** AS A VERB = **separate**, distance, divorce, isolate, detach, segregate, disconnect, set apart • *how to dissociate emotion from reason*
▸ IN PHRASES: **dissociate yourself from something** *or* **someone** = **break away from**, part company with, break off relations with, have nothing more to do with, sever connections with, end relations with • *He dissociated himself from his former friends.*

dissociation = **separation**, break, division, distancing, divorce, isolation, segregation, detachment, severance, disengagement, disconnection, disunion • *a complete dissociation from one another*

d

dissolute = **corrupt**, wild, abandoned, loose, vicious, degenerate, immoral, lax, dissipated, lewd, depraved, wanton, unrestrained, profligate, debauched, rakish, libertine, licentious • *She regretted her dissolute life.*
OPPOSITES: good, moral, virtuous

dissolution 1 = **ending**, end, finish, conclusion, suspension, dismissal, termination, adjournment, disbandment, discontinuation • *He stayed on until the dissolution of the firm.*
OPPOSITES: union, alliance, combination
2 = **breaking up**, parting, divorce, separation, disintegration • *the dissolution of a marriage*
3 = **disintegration**, fall, decline, degradation, degeneration, debasement, retrogression, dégringolade *(French)* • *the dissolution of traditional family life*
4 = **break-up**, ending, conclusion, wind-up, termination, cessation, disbandment, discontinuation • *He called for the dissolution of the government.*
5 = **corruption**, excess, indulgence, depravity, debauchery, gluttony, dissipation, licentiousness, intemperance, overindulgence, wantonness, dissoluteness • *the corruption of manners, and dissolution of life*

dissolve AS A VERB 1 = **melt**, break down, disintegrate, soften, thaw, flux, liquefy, deliquesce • *Heat gently until the sugar dissolves.*
2 = **end**, dismiss, suspend, axe *(informal)*, break up, wind up, overthrow, terminate, discontinue, dismantle, disband, disunite • *The King agreed to dissolve the present commission.*
3 = **disappear**, fade, vanish, break down, crumble, disperse, dwindle, evaporate, disintegrate, perish, diffuse, dissipate, decompose, melt away, waste away, evanesce • *His new-found optimism dissolved.*
▸ IN PHRASES: **dissolve into** *or* **in something** = **break into**, burst into, give way to, launch into • *She dissolved into tears.*

dissonance *or* **dissonancy** 1 = **disagreement**, variance, discord, dissension • *Bring harmony out of dissonance.*
2 = **discordance**, discord, jangle, cacophony, jarring, harshness, lack of harmony, unmelodiousness • *a jumble of silence and dissonance*

dissonant 1 = **disagreeing**, differing, at variance, dissentient • *All but a few dissonant voices agree.*
2 = **discordant**, harsh, jarring, grating, raucous, strident, jangling, out of tune, tuneless, cacophonous, inharmonious, unmelodious • *Guitarists kept strumming wildly dissonant chords.*

dissuade from = **deter from**, put off, warn against, advise against, caution against, discourage from, talk out of, urge not to, persuade not to, disincline, expostulate against • *Doctors tried to dissuade patients from smoking.*
OPPOSITES: persuade to, talk into, convince to

distance AS A NOUN 1 = **space**, length, extent, range, stretch, gap, interval, separation, span, width • *They measured the distance between the island and the shore.*
2 = **remoteness**, farness • *The distance wouldn't be a problem.*
3 = **aloofness**, reserve, detachment, restraint, indifference, stiffness, coolness, coldness, remoteness, frigidity, uninvolvement, standoffishness • *There were periods of distance, of coldness.*
▸ IN PHRASES: **distance yourself from something** *or* **someone** = **disown**, reject, separate yourself from, wash your hands of, dissociate yourself from • *The author distanced himself from some comments in his book.*
go the distance = **finish**, stay the course, complete, see through, bring to an end • *Riders are determined to go the distance.*
in the distance = **far off**, far away, the horizon, afar, yonder • *We suddenly saw her in the distance.*

QUOTATIONS
'Tis distance lends enchantment to the view
[Thomas Campbell *Pleasures of Hope*]

Distance has the same effect on the mind as on the eye
[Dr. Johnson *Rasselas*]

distant 1 = **far-off**, far, remote, removed, abroad, out-of-the-way, far-flung, faraway, outlying, afar • *the war in that distant land*
OPPOSITES: close, near, neighbouring
2 = **faint**, vague, dim, uncertain, obscure, hazy, indistinct • *Last year's drought is a distant memory.*
3 = **remote**, slight, indirect • *He's a distant relative.*
4 = **reserved**, cold, withdrawn, cool, formal, remote, stiff, restrained, detached, indifferent, aloof, unfriendly, reticent, haughty, unapproachable, standoffish • *He's direct and courteous, but distant.*
OPPOSITES: warm, friendly, intimate
5 = **faraway**, blank, abstracted, vague, absorbed, distracted, unaware, musing, vacant, preoccupied, bemused, oblivious, dreamy, daydreaming, absent-minded, inattentive • *There was a distant look in her eyes.*

distaste = **dislike**, horror, disgust, loathing, aversion, revulsion, displeasure, antipathy, abhorrence, disinclination, repugnance, odium, disfavour, detestation, disrelish • *He looked at her with distaste.*

distasteful = **unpleasant**, offensive, obscene, undesirable, unsavoury, obnoxious, unpalatable, displeasing, repulsive, objectionable, disagreeable, repugnant, loathsome, abhorrent, nauseous, uninviting • *an extremely unpleasant and distasteful experience*
OPPOSITES: pleasing, charming, enjoyable

distend = **swell**, stretch, expand, increase, widen, balloon, puff, enlarge, inflate, bulge, dilate, bloat • *The large intestine distends and fills with gas.*

distended = **swollen**, stretched, expanded, enlarged, inflated, bloated, puffy, dilated, tumescent • *an infant with a distended belly*

distil 1 = **ferment**, make, produce, brew • *The whisky had been distilled in 1926.*
2 = **purify**, process, filter, refine, treat, evaporate, condense, sublimate, vaporize • *When water is used it must be distilled*
3 = **extract**, express, squeeze, obtain, take out, draw out, separate out, press out • *The oil is distilled from the berries.*

distillation 1 = **essence**, extract, elixir, spirit, quintessence • *a distillation of the blooms of the Cananga Odorata tree*
2 = **distilling**, processing, refining, purification, filtration • *Stronger beverages are produced by distillation.*

distinct 1 = **different**, individual, separate, disconnected, discrete, dissimilar, unconnected, unattached • *The book is divided into two distinct parts.*
OPPOSITES: similar, connected, identical
2 = **striking**, sharp, dramatic, stunning *(informal)*, outstanding, bold, noticeable, well-defined • *to impart a distinct flavour with a minimum of cooking fat*
3 = **definite**, marked, clear, decided, obvious, sharp, plain, apparent, patent, evident, black-and-white, manifest, noticeable, conspicuous, clear-cut, unmistakable, palpable, recognizable, unambiguous, observable, perceptible, appreciable • *There was a distinct change in her attitude.*
OPPOSITES: obscure, vague, unclear

distinction 1 = **difference**, contrast, variation, differential, discrepancy, disparity, deviation, differentiation, fine line, distinctness, dissimilarity • *There were obvious distinctions between the two.*
2 = **excellence**, note, quality, worth, account, rank, reputation, importance, consequence, fame, celebrity, merit, superiority, prominence, greatness, eminence, renown, repute • *He is a composer of distinction and sensitivity.*
3 = **feature**, quality, characteristic, name, mark, individuality, peculiarity, singularity, distinctiveness, particularity • *He has the distinction of being their greatest living writer.*

4 = merit, credit, honour, integrity, excellence, righteousness, rectitude, uprightness • *She had served her country with distinction and strength.*

distinctive = characteristic, special, individual, specific, unique, typical, extraordinary, distinguishing, signature, peculiar, singular, idiosyncratic • *the distinctive odour of chlorine*
OPPOSITES: common, ordinary, typical

distinctly 1 = definitely, clearly, obviously, sharply, plainly, patently, manifestly, decidedly, markedly, noticeably, unmistakably, palpably • *two distinctly different sectors*
2 = clearly, plainly, precisely • *'If I may speak, gentlemen,' he said distinctly.*

distinguish AS A VERB **1 = differentiate**, determine, separate, discriminate, decide, judge, discern, ascertain, tell the difference, make a distinction, tell apart, tell between • *Could he distinguish right from wrong?*
2 = characterize, mark, separate, single out, individualize, set apart, make different, make distinctive • *one of the things that distinguishes artists from other people*
3 = make out, identify, recognize, perceive, know, see, tell, spot, glimpse, pick out, discern • *He could distinguish voices.*
▸ IN PHRASES: **distinguish yourself = be successful**, become famous, excel yourself, become immortalized, glorify yourself, ennoble yourself • *They distinguished themselves at the Battle of Assaye.*

distinguishable 1 = recognizable, noticeable, conspicuous, discernible, obvious, evident, manifest, perceptible, well-marked • *This port is distinguishable by its colour.*
2 = conspicuous, clear, strong, bright, plain, bold, pronounced, colourful, vivid, eye-catching, salient • *Already shapes were more distinguishable.*

distinguished = eminent, great, important, noted, famous, celebrated, well-known, prominent, esteemed, acclaimed, notable, renowned, prestigious, elevated, big-time *(informal)*, famed, conspicuous, illustrious, major league *(informal)* • *a distinguished academic family*
OPPOSITES: common, unknown, inferior

distinguishing = characteristic, marked, distinctive, typical, signature, peculiar, differentiating, individualistic • *The bird has no distinguishing features.*

distort 1 = misrepresent, twist, bias, disguise, pervert, slant, colour, misinterpret, falsify, garble • *The media distorts reality.*
2 = deform, bend, twist, warp, buckle, mangle, mangulate *(Austral. slang)*, disfigure, contort, gnarl, misshape, malform • *Make sure the image isn't distorted by lumps and bumps.*

distorted 1 = misrepresented, twisted, false, coloured, one-sided, biased, partial, perverted, slanted, garbled • *These figures give a distorted view.*
2 = deformed, bent, twisted, crooked, irregular, warped, buckled, disfigured, contorted, misshapen • *His face was distorted but recognizable.*

distortion 1 = misrepresentation, bias, slant, perversion, falsification, colouring • *He accused reporters of wilful distortion.*
2 = deformity, bend, twist, warp, buckle, contortion, malformation, crookedness, twistedness • *the gargoyle-like distortion of her face*

distract 1 = divert, sidetrack, draw away, turn aside, lead astray, draw or lead away from • *Video games sometimes distract him from his homework.*
2 = amuse, occupy, entertain, beguile, engross • *I took out a book and tried to distract myself.*
3 = agitate, trouble, disturb, confuse, puzzle, torment, bewilder, madden, confound, perplex, disconcert, derange, discompose • *Another story of hers distracts me.*

distracted 1 = agitated, troubled, confused, puzzled, at sea, bewildered, bemused, confounded, perplexed, flustered, in a flap *(informal)* • *At work, he thought about her all day. He was distracted.*
2 = frantic, wild, mad, crazy, desperate, raving, frenzied, distraught, insane, deranged, grief-stricken, overwrought, at the end of your tether • *My father was distracted by grief.*

distracting = disturbing, bothering, confusing, dismaying, bewildering, disconcerting, perturbing, off-putting *(Brit. informal)* • *I find it slightly distracting.*

distraction 1 = disturbance, interference, diversion, interruption • *Total concentration is required with no distractions.*
2 = entertainment, recreation, amusement, diversion, pastime, divertissement, beguilement • *every conceivable distraction from shows to bouncy castles*
3 = frenzy, madness, desperation, hysteria, mania, insanity, delirium, derangement • *A very clingy child can drive a parent to distraction.*

distraught = frantic, wild, desperate, mad, anxious, distressed, raving, distracted, hysterical, worked-up, agitated, crazed, overwrought, out of your mind, at the end of your tether, wrought-up, beside yourself • *Her distraught parents were last night being comforted.*

distress AS A VERB **= upset**, worry, trouble, pain, wound, bother, disturb, dismay, grieve, torment, harass, afflict, harrow, agitate, sadden, perplex, disconcert, agonize, fluster, perturb, faze, throw (someone) off balance • *I did not want to frighten or distress her.*
▸ AS A NOUN **1 = suffering**, pain, worry, anxiety, torture, grief, misery, agony, sadness, discomfort, torment, sorrow, woe, anguish, heartache, affliction, desolation, wretchedness • *Her mouth grew stiff with pain and distress.*
2 = danger, risk, difficulty, peril, jeopardy, endangerment • *The ship might be in distress.*
3 = need, suffering, trouble, trial, difficulties, poverty, misery, hard times, hardship, straits, misfortune, adversity, calamity, affliction, privation, destitution, ill-fortune, ill-luck, indigence • *There was little support to help them in their distress.*

distressed 1 = upset, worried, troubled, anxious, distracted, tormented, distraught, afflicted, agitated, saddened, wretched • *I felt distressed about my problem.*
2 = poverty-stricken, poor, impoverished, needy, destitute, indigent, down at heel, straitened, penurious • *investment in the nation's distressed areas*

distressing = upsetting, worrying, disturbing, painful, affecting, sad, afflicting, harrowing, grievous, hurtful, lamentable, heart-breaking, nerve-racking, gut-wrenching, distressful • *the distressing symptoms of anxiety*

distribute 1 = hand out, dispense, give out, dish out *(informal)*, disseminate, deal out, disburse, pass round • *Students shouted slogans and distributed leaflets.*
2 = circulate, deliver, transmit, convey • *to distribute a national newspaper*
3 = share, give, deal, divide, assign, administer, allocate, dispose, dispense, allot, mete out, dole out, apportion, measure out • *He began to distribute jobs among his friends.*
4 = spread, scatter, disperse, diffuse, disseminate, strew • *Break the exhibition up and distribute it around existing museums.*

distributed = scattered, spread, sprinkled, strewn, diffused, littered • *The cells are distributed throughout the body.*

distribution 1 = delivery, mailing, transport, transportation, handling • *He admitted there had been problems with distribution.*
2 = sharing, division, assignment, rationing, allocation, partition, allotment, dispensation, apportionment • *a more equitable distribution of wealth*
3 = spreading, circulation, diffusion, scattering, propagation, dissemination, dispersal, dispersion • *There will*

be a widespread distribution of leaflets.
4 = spread, organization, arrangement, location, placement, disposition • *those who control the distribution of jobs*

district = **area**, community, region, sector, quarter, ward, parish, neighbourhood, vicinity, locality, locale, neck of the woods *(informal)* • *I drove around the business district.*

distrust AS A VERB = **suspect**, doubt, discredit, be wary of, wonder about, mistrust, disbelieve, be suspicious of, be sceptical of, misbelieve • *I don't have any reason to distrust them.*
OPPOSITES: believe, trust, have faith
▸AS A NOUN = **suspicion**, question, doubt, disbelief, scepticism, mistrust, misgiving, qualm, wariness, lack of faith, dubiety • *an atmosphere of distrust*
OPPOSITES: trust, confidence, faith

QUOTATIONS
Trust him no further than you can throw him
[Thomas Fuller *Gnomologia*]

distrustful = **suspicious**, doubting, wary, cynical, doubtful, sceptical, uneasy, dubious, distrusting, disbelieving, leery *(slang)*, mistrustful, chary • *Voters are distrustful of all politicians.*

disturb 1 = **interrupt**, trouble, bother, startle, plague, disrupt, put out, interfere with, rouse, hassle, inconvenience, pester, intrude on, butt in on • *I didn't want to disturb you.*
2 = upset, concern, worry, trouble, shake, excite, alarm, confuse, distress, distract, dismay, unsettle, agitate, ruffle, confound, unnerve, vex, fluster, perturb, derange, discompose • *He had been disturbed by the news of the attack.*
OPPOSITES: calm, relieve, reassure
3 = muddle, disorder, mix up, mess up, disorganize, jumble up, disarrange, muss *(U.S. & Canad.)* • *His notes had not been disturbed.*
4 = ruffle, stir up, agitate, churn up • *a gentle wave or two disturbing the surface*

disturbance 1 = **disorder**, bother *(informal)*, turmoil, riot, upheaval, fray, brawl, uproar, agitation, fracas, commotion, rumpus, tumult, hubbub, shindig *(informal)*, ruction *(informal)*, ruckus *(informal)*, shindy *(informal)* • *During the disturbance, three men were hurt.*
2 = upset, bother, disorder, confusion, distraction, intrusion, interruption, annoyance, agitation, hindrance, perturbation, derangement • *The home would cause less disturbance than a school.*
3 = disorder, upset, problem, trouble • *Poor educational performance is linked to emotional disturbances.*

disturbed 1 = **unbalanced**, troubled, disordered, unstable, neurotic, upset, deranged, unsound, maladjusted • *The murderer was apparently mentally disturbed.*
OPPOSITES: balanced, untroubled
2 = worried, concerned, troubled, upset, bothered, nervous, anxious, uneasy, agitated, disquieted, apprehensive, antsy *(informal)*, angsty *(informal)* • *I was disturbed to find that the dog was dead.*
OPPOSITES: calm, untroubled, unfazed *(informal)*

disturbing = **worrying**, troubling, upsetting, alarming, frightening, distressing, startling, discouraging, dismaying, unsettling, harrowing, agitating, disconcerting, disquieting, perturbing • *There are disturbing reports of killings.*

disunited = **separated**, split, divided, parted, disrupted, detached, severed, disbanded, segregated, disconnected, disengaged, sundered, disjoined • *an increasingly disunited party*

disunity = **disagreement**, split, breach, dissent, rupture, alienation, variance, discord, schism, estrangement, dissension, discordance • *He was accused of promoting disunity within the armed forces.*

disuse = **neglect**, decay, abandonment, idleness, discontinuance, desuetude, nonuse, non-employment • *a church which had fallen into disuse*
OPPOSITES: use, service

disused = **abandoned**, deserted, neglected, discarded, derelict, forsaken • *a disused airfield*

ditch AS A NOUN = **channel**, drain, trench, gutter, dyke, trough, furrow, gully, conduit, moat, watercourse • *The car went out of control and ended up in a ditch.*
▸AS A VERB 1 = **get rid of**, dump *(informal)*, scrap, bin *(informal)*, junk *(informal)*, chuck *(informal)*, discard, dispose of, dispense with, jettison, cast off, throw out *or* overboard • *I decided to ditch the sofa bed.*
2 = leave, drop, abandon, desert, dump *(informal)*, axe *(informal)*, get rid of, bin *(informal)*, chuck *(informal)*, finish with, walk out on, forsake, jilt, give someone the push, give someone the elbow, give someone the big E *(slang)* • *I can't bring myself to ditch him.*

dither AS A VERB = **vacillate**, hesitate, waver, haver, falter, hum and haw, faff about *(Brit. informal)*, shillyshally *(informal)*, swither *(Scot.)* • *We're still dithering over whether to get married.*
OPPOSITES: decide, settle, resolve
▸AS A NOUN = **flutter**, flap *(informal)*, fluster, bother, stew *(informal)*, twitter *(informal)*, tizzy *(informal)*, pother, tiz-woz *(informal)* • *I am in such a dither I forget to put the water in.*

diurnal 1 = **daytime**, active during the day, non-nocturnal • *Kangaroos are diurnal animals*
2 = daily, regular, everyday, circadian, quotidian • *the diurnal life of monasteries*

diva = **singer**, opera singer, prima donna, songstress, cantatrice • *the Grammy-award winning diva*

divan = **bed**, couch, settee, sofa bed, put-you-up *(Brit.)* • *They went to sit on the divan.*

dive AS A VERB 1 = **plunge**, drop, jump, pitch, leap, duck, dip, descend, plummet • *He tried to escape by diving into a river.*
2 = go underwater, snorkel, scuba-dive, submerge, swim under water • *They are diving to collect marine organisms.*
3 = nose-dive, fall, plunge, crash, pitch, swoop, plummet • *His monoplane stalled and dived into the ground.*
4 = leap, jump, dash, bolt, dart, lunge, scurry, throw yourself • *They dived into a taxi.*
▸AS A NOUN 1 = **plunge**, spring, jump, leap, dash, header *(informal)*, swoop, lunge, nose dive • *He made a sudden dive for his legs.*
2 = sleazy bar, joint *(slang)*, nightclub, honky-tonk *(U.S. slang)*, drinking den, drinking joint • *We've played in all the dives about here.*

diverge 1 = **separate**, part, split, branch, divide, fork, divaricate • *The aims of the partners began to diverge.*
2 = conflict, differ, disagree, dissent, be at odds, be at variance • *Theory and practice sometimes diverged.*
3 = deviate, depart, stray, wander, meander, turn aside • *a course that diverged from the coastline*
4 = digress, stray, deviate, digress, ramble, get sidetracked, go off at a tangent, get off the point • *The manuscripts diverged from the original.*

divergence = **difference**, varying, departure, disparity, deviation, separation • *There's substantial divergence of opinion in the party.*

divergent = **different**, conflicting, differing, disagreeing, diverse, separate, varying, variant, diverging, dissimilar, deviating • *two people who have divergent views*

diverse 1 = **various**, mixed, varied, diversified, assorted, miscellaneous, several, sundry, motley, manifold, heterogeneous, of every description • *shops selling a diverse range of gifts*
2 = different, contrasting, unlike, varying, differing, separate, distinct, disparate, discrete, dissimilar, divergent, discrepant • *Their attitudes were refreshingly diverse.*

diversify = **vary**, change, expand, transform, alter, spread out, branch out • *Manufacturers are encouraged to diversify.*

diversion 1 = **distraction**, deviation, deflection, digression • *The whole argument is a diversion.*
2 = **pastime**, play, game, sport, delight, pleasure, entertainment, hobby, relaxation, recreation, enjoyment, distraction, amusement, gratification, divertissement, beguilement • *Finger-painting is an excellent diversion.*
3 = **detour**, deviation, circuitous route, roundabout way, indirect course • *They turned back because of traffic diversions.*
4 = **deviation**, change, departure, variation, straying, divergence, digression • *a diversion from his fantasy-themed movies*

diversity 1 = **difference**, diversification, variety, divergence, multiplicity, heterogeneity, variegation, diverseness • *the cultural diversity of British society*
2 = **range**, variety, sweep, scope, field, sphere, compass, assortment, medley, amplitude, ambit • *as great a diversity of genetic material as possible*

PROVERBS
It takes all sorts to make a world

divert 1 = **redirect**, switch, avert, deflect, deviate, change the course of, sidetrack, draw away, turn aside, channel away • *A new bypass will divert traffic from the A13.*
2 = **distract**, shift, deflect, detract, sidetrack, draw away, be a distraction, lead astray, draw *or* lead away from • *They want to divert the attention of the people from the real issues.*
3 = **entertain**, delight, amuse, please, charm, gratify, beguile, regale • *diverting her with jokes and fiery arguments*

diverting = **entertaining**, amusing, enjoyable, fun, pleasant, humorous, beguiling • *It was a witty and diverting programme.*

divest 1 = **deprive**, strip, dispossess, despoil • *They were divested of all their personal possessions.*
2 = **strip**, remove, take off, undress, denude, disrobe, unclothe • *the formalities of divesting her of her coat*

divide AS A VERB 1 = **separate**, part, split, cut (up), sever, partition, shear, segregate, cleave, subdivide, bisect, split off, demarcate, sunder • *the artificial line that divided the city*
OPPOSITES: unite, join, combine
2 = **share**, distribute, allocate, portion, dispense, allot, mete, dole out, apportion, deal out, measure out, divvy (up) *(informal)* • *Divide the soup among four bowls.*
3 = **split**, break up, alienate, embroil, come between, disunite, estrange, sow dissension, cause to disagree, set at variance *or* odds, set *or* pit against one another • *She has done more to divide the group than anyone else.*
▸ AS A NOUN = **breach**, gulf, gap, rift, abyss, cleft, hiatus • *the great divide between generations*
▸ IN PHRASES: **divide something up** = **group**, sort, separate, arrange, grade, classify, categorize • *The idea is to divide up the country into four sectors.*

QUOTATIONS
Divide and rule
[Philip of Macedon]

dividend 1 = **bonus**, share, return, cut *(informal)*, gain, extra, plus, portion, payback, divvy *(informal)* • *The first quarter dividend has been increased.*
2 = **benefit**, gain, plus, advantage, bonus, perk *(informal)* • *The confidence that comes from success is sure to pay dividends.*

divination = **prediction**, divining, prophecy, presage, foretelling, clairvoyance, fortune-telling, prognostication, augury, soothsaying, sortilege • *Every method of divination is a philosophy about the world.*
▹ *See panel* **Divination**

divine AS AN ADJECTIVE 1 = **heavenly**, spiritual, holy, immortal, supernatural, celestial, angelic, superhuman, godlike, cherubic, seraphic, supernal *(literary)*, paradisaical • *a gift from divine beings*
2 = **sacred**, religious, holy, spiritual, blessed, revered, venerable, hallowed, consecrated, sanctified • *the message of the Divine Book*
3 = **wonderful**, perfect, beautiful, excellent, lovely, stunning *(informal)*, glorious, marvellous, splendid, gorgeous, delightful, exquisite, radiant, superlative, ravishing • *You look simply divine.*
▸ AS A NOUN = **priest**, minister, vicar, reverend, pastor, cleric, clergyman, curate, churchman, padre *(informal)*, holy man, man of God, man of the cloth, ecclesiastic, father confessor • *He had the air of a divine.*
▸ AS A VERB 1 = **guess**, understand, suppose, suspect, perceive, discern, infer, deduce, apprehend, conjecture, surmise, foretell, intuit, prognosticate • *He had tried to divine her intentions.*
2 = **dowse** *(for water or minerals)*, find through dowsing • *I was divining for water.*

diviner = **psychic**, prophet, visionary, oracle, astrologer, seer, clairvoyant, augur, fortune teller, soothsayer, sibyl, crystal-gazer • *I was called Merlin the diviner.*

divinity 1 = **theology**, religion, religious studies • *He entered university to study arts and divinity*
2 = **godliness**, holiness, sanctity, godhead, divine nature, godhood • *a lasting faith in the divinity of Christ's word*

DIVINATION

METHODS OF DIVINATION

astrology	dice	numerology	scrying	tea leaves
clairvoyance	dowsing	palmistry	sortilege	
crystal gazing	I Ching	runes	tarot	

MEANS OF DIVINATION

ailuromancy	cats	crithomancy	freshly baked bread	necromancy	the dead
alphitomancy	wheat *or* barley cakes	cromniomancy	onions	oneiromancy	dreams
		crystallomancy	crystal ball	ornithomancy	birds
arachnomancy	spiders	dactylomancy	suspended ring	pegomancy	sacred pool
astragalomancy	dice	geomancy	earth, sand, *or* dust	pyromancy	fire *or* flames
bibliomancy	passages from books	hippomancy	horses	radiesthesia	pendulum
		hydromancy	water	rhabdomancy	rod *or* wand
cartomancy	cards	lampadomancy	oil lamps	sciomancy	ghosts
catoptromancy	mirror	lithomancy	precious stones	tasseography	tea leaves
ceromancy	melted wax	lychnomancy	flames of wax candles	theomancy	god
chiromancy	hands			tyromancy	cheese
cleidomancy	suspended key	molybdomancy	molten lead		

3 = **deity**, spirit, genius, guardian spirit, daemon, god *or* goddess, atua *(N.Z.)* • *The three statues are Roman divinities.*

division 1 = **separation**, dividing, splitting up, detaching, partition, cutting up, bisection • *a division into two independent factions*
2 = **sharing**, sharing, distribution, assignment, rationing, allocation, allotment, apportionment • *the division of labour between workers and management*
3 = **disagreement**, split, breach, feud, rift, rupture, abyss, chasm, variance, discord, difference of opinion, estrangement, disunion • *the division between the prosperous west and the impoverished east*
OPPOSITES: union, accord, unity
4 = **dividing line**, border, boundary, divide, partition, demarcation, divider • *the division between North and South Korea*
5 = **department**, group, head, sector, branch, subdivision • *the sales division*
6 = **part**, bit, piece, section, sector, class, category, segment, portion, fraction, compartment • *Each was divided into several divisions.*

QUOTATIONS
If a house be divided against itself, that house cannot stand
[*Bible: St. Mark*]
PROVERBS
He who divides gets the worst share

divisive = **disruptive**, unsettling, alienating, troublesome, controversial, contentious • *Abortion has always been a divisive issue.*

divorce AS A NOUN 1 = **separation**, split, break-up, parting, split-up, rift, dissolution, severance, estrangement, annulment, decree nisi, disunion • *Numerous marriages now end in divorce.*
2 = **breach**, break, split, falling-out *(informal)*, disagreement, feud, rift, bust-up *(informal)*, rupture, abyss, chasm, schism, estrangement • *a divorce between the government and trade unions*
▸ AS A VERB 1 = **separate**, break up, split up, part company, end your marriage, annul your marriage, dissolve your marriage • *My parents divorced when I was young.*
2 = **separate**, divide, isolate, detach, distance, sever, disconnect, dissociate, set apart, disunite, sunder • *We have been able to divorce sex from reproduction.*

divulge = **make known**, tell, reveal, publish, declare, expose, leak, confess, exhibit, communicate, spill *(informal)*, disclose, proclaim, betray, uncover, impart, promulgate, let slip, blow wide open *(slang)*, get off your chest *(informal)*, cough *(slang)*, out *(informal)*, spill your guts about *(slang)* • *He was charged with divulging state secrets.*
OPPOSITES: hide, conceal, keep secret

dizzy 1 = **giddy**, faint, light-headed, swimming, reeling, staggering, shaky, wobbly, off balance, unsteady, vertiginous, woozy *(informal)*, weak at the knees • *She felt slightly dizzy.*
2 = **confused**, dazzled, at sea, bewildered, muddled, bemused, dazed, disorientated, befuddled, light-headed, punch-drunk, fuddled • *Her wonderful dark good looks and wit made me dizzy.*
3 = **scatterbrained**, silly, foolish, frivolous, giddy, capricious, forgetful, flighty, light-headed, scatty *(Brit. informal)*, empty-headed, bird-brained *(informal)*, featherbrained, ditzy *or* ditsy *(slang)* • *a charmingly dizzy grandmother*
4 = **steep**, towering, soaring, lofty, sky-high, vertiginous, dizzy-making, giddy-making • *I escalated to the dizzy heights.*

do AS A VERB 1 = **perform**, work, achieve, carry out, produce, effect, complete, conclude, undertake, accomplish, execute, discharge, pull off, transact • *I was trying to do some work.*
2 = **behave**, act, conduct yourself, deport yourself, bear yourself, acquit yourself • *I go where I will and I do as I please.*
3 = **make**, prepare, fix, arrange, look after, organize, be responsible for, see to, get ready, make ready • *I'll do the dinner, you can help.*
4 = **solve**, work out, resolve, figure out, decode, decipher, puzzle out • *I could have done the crossword.*
5 = **get on**, manage, fare, proceed, make out, prosper, get along • *She did well at school.*
6 = **work as**, be employed at, earn a living at, have as an occupation, have as a profession • *And what does he do for a living?*
7 = **present**, give, show, act, produce, stage, perform, mount, put on • *I've always wanted to do a show on his life.*
8 = **be adequate**, be enough, be sufficient, answer, serve, suit, content, satisfy, suffice, be of use, pass muster, cut the mustard, fill the bill *(informal)*, meet requirements • *A plain old 'I love you' won't do.*
9 = **cheat**, trick, con *(informal)*, skin *(slang)*, stiff *(slang)*, sting *(informal)*, deceive, fleece, hoax, defraud, dupe, swindle, diddle *(informal)*, take (someone) for a ride *(informal)*, pull a fast one on *(informal)*, cozen, scam *(slang)* • *I'll tell you how they did me.*
10 = **produce**, make, create, develop, turn out, manufacture, construct, invent, put together, originate, fabricate • *The company have done a range of tops.*
11 = **decorate**, paper, paint, colour, wallpaper, renovate, do up *(informal)*, furbish • *The bedroom is done in lavenders and pinks.*
12 = **design**, style, dress, arrange, fashion, shape, adapt, tailor • *I did her hair and her make-up.*
13 = **grant**, give, allow, accord, permit, render, confer, bestow • *Would you do me a favour?*
14 = **study**, read, learn, research, investigate, analyse, be taught, read up on, take a course in, take classes in, swot (up) on *(Brit. informal)* • *She's doing English for her Higher Certificate.*
15 = **travel at**, go at, move at, drive at, proceed at • *He was clocked doing 138mph.*
16 = **visit**, tour in *or* around, look at, cover, explore, take in *(informal)*, stop in, journey through *or* around, travel in *or* around • *Families doing Europe can hire one of these motor-homes.*
▸ AS A NOUN = **party**, gathering, function, social, event, affair, at-home, occasion, celebration, reception, bash *(informal)*, rave *(Brit. slang)*, get-together *(informal)*, festivity, knees-up *(Brit. informal)*, beano *(Brit. slang)*, social gathering, shindig *(informal)*, soirée, rave-up *(Brit. slang)*, hooley *or* hoolie *(chiefly Irish & N.Z.)* • *They always have all-night dos there.*
▸ IN PHRASES: **do away with someone** = **kill**, murder, do in *(slang)*, destroy, take out *(slang)*, dispatch, slay, blow away *(slang, chiefly U.S.)*, knock off *(slang)*, liquidate, exterminate, take (someone's) life, bump off *(slang)* • *He tried to do away with her.*
do away with something = **get rid of**, remove, eliminate, axe *(informal)*, abolish, junk *(informal)*, pull, chuck *(informal)*, discard, put an end to, dispense with, discontinue, put paid to, pull the plug on • *They must do away with nuclear weapons altogether.*
do for something *or* **someone** = **destroy**, kill, finish (off), defeat, ruin, shatter, undo, slay, annihilate • *They did for him in the end.*
do's and don'ts = **rules**, code, regulations, standards, instructions, customs, convention, usage, protocol, formalities, etiquette, p's and q's, good *or* proper behaviour • *Please advise me on the do's and dont's.*
do someone in 1 = **kill**, murder, destroy, eliminate *(slang)*, take out *(slang)*, execute, butcher, slaughter, dispatch, assassinate, slay, do away with, blow away *(slang, chiefly U. S.)*, knock off *(slang)*, liquidate, annihilate, neutralize, take (someone's) life, bump off *(slang)* • *Whoever did him in removed a brave man.*

2 = **exhaust**, tire, drain, shatter *(informal)*, weaken, fatigue, weary, fag *(informal)*, sap, wear out, tire out, knacker *(slang)* • *The Christmas thing kind of did me in.*
do someone out of something = **cheat out of**, deprive of, rob of, dispossess of, con out of *(informal)*, swindle out of, trick out of, diddle out of *(informal)*, prevent from having *or* gaining • *He feels I did him out of a profit on some shares.*
do something in = **hurt**, damage, injure, harm, disable, weaken, impair • *I did my back in years ago.*
do something out = **decorate**, paper, paint, wallpaper, renovate, do up *(informal)*, furbish • *a room newly done out in country-house style*
do something up 1 = **fasten**, tie, secure, bind, tighten, knot, lace, tie up, affix, make fast • *Do your coat up.*
2 = **refurbish**, improve, renovate, furbish • *He bought a barn and is doing it up.*
do something *or* **someone down** = **criticize**, dismiss, put down, run down, discredit, ridicule, scorn, disdain, deride, slag (off) *(slang)*, knock *(informal)*, blast, flame *(informal)*, rubbish *(informal)*, malign, detract from, denigrate, belittle, disparage, decry, vilify, slander, deprecate, depreciate, tear into *(informal)*, diss *(slang, chiefly U.S.)*, defame, bad-mouth *(slang, chiefly U.S. & Canad.)*, traduce, derogate, asperse • *He thinks that they did him down.*
do without something *or* **someone** = **manage without**, give up, dispense with, forgo, kick *(informal)*, sacrifice, abstain from, get along without • *This is something we cannot do without.*

PROVERBS

Do unto others what you would they should do unto you

docile = **obedient**, manageable, compliant, amenable, submissive, pliant, tractable, biddable, ductile, teachable *(rare)* • *They were docile, obedient children.*
OPPOSITES: trying, difficult, troublesome

docility = **compliance**, obedience, meekness, submissiveness, manageability, ductility, amenability, pliancy, tractability, biddableness • *The baby's docility had surprised him.*

dock[1] AS A NOUN = **port**, haven, harbour, pier, wharf, quay, waterfront, anchorage • *He brought his boat right into the dock at Southampton.*
▸ AS A VERB 1 = **moor**, land, anchor, put in, tie up, berth, drop anchor • *The vessel is about to dock in Singapore*
2 = **link up**, unite, join, couple, rendezvous, hook up • *The shuttle is scheduled to dock with the space station.*

dock[2] 1 = **cut**, reduce, decrease, diminish, cut back, lessen • *He threatened to dock her fee.*
OPPOSITES: increase, raise, boost
2 = **deduct**, remove, take off, discount, debit, knock off, subtract • *He had a point docked for insulting his opponent.*
3 = **cut off**, crop, clip, shorten, curtail, cut short • *It is an offence for an unqualified person to dock a dog's tail.*

docket 1 = **label**, bill, ticket, certificate, tag, voucher, tab, receipt, tally, chit, chitty, counterfoil • *The clerk asked me to sign the docket.*
2 = **file**, index, register • *The Court has 1,400 appeals on its docket.*

doctor AS A NOUN = **physician**, medic *(informal)*, clinician, general practitioner, medical practitioner, G.P. • *Do not stop the treatment without consulting your doctor.*
▸ AS A VERB 1 = **change**, alter, interfere with, disguise, pervert, fudge, tamper with, tinker with, misrepresent, falsify, meddle with, mess about with • *They doctored the photograph.*
2 = **add to**, spike, cut, mix something with something, dilute, water down, adulterate • *He had doctored her milk.*

QUOTATIONS

God heals, and the doctor takes the fee
[Benjamin Franklin *Poor Richard's Almanack*]

Men who are occupied in the restoration of health to
other men, by the joint exertion of skill and humanity,
are above all the great of the earth
[Voltaire *Philosophical Dictionary*]

The best doctors in the world are Doctor Diet, Doctor
Quiet, and Doctor Merryman
[Jonathan Swift *Polite Conversation*]

God and the doctor we alike adore
But only when in danger, not before;
The danger o'er, both are alike requited,
God is forgotten, and the Doctor slighted
[John Owen *Epigrams*]

doctrinaire 1 = **dogmatic**, rigid, fanatical, inflexible • *forty-five years of doctrinaire Stalinism*
2 = **impractical**, theoretical, speculative, ideological, unrealistic, hypothetical, unpragmatic • *It is a doctrinaire scheme.*

doctrine = **teaching**, principle, belief, opinion, article, concept, conviction, canon, creed, dogma, tenet, precept, article of faith, kaupapa *(N.Z.)* • *the Marxist doctrine of perpetual revolution*

document AS A NOUN = **paper**, form, certificate, report, record, testimonial, authorization, legal form • *The foreign minister signed the document today.*
▸ AS A VERB = **support**, back up, certify, verify, detail, instance, validate, substantiate, corroborate, authenticate, give weight to, particularize • *The effects of smoking have been well documented.*

documentary AS A NOUN = **report**, film, programme, account, broadcast, presentation • *a TV documentary on homelessness*
▸ AS AN ADJECTIVE = **documented**, recorded, registered, archived, chronicled • *The government says it has documentary evidence.*

doddering = **tottering**, aged, weak, shaky, faltering, feeble, shambling, senile, decrepit, unsteady, infirm, doddery, trembly • *a doddering old man*

doddle = **piece of cake**, picnic *(informal)*, child's play *(informal)*, pushover *(slang, informal)*, no sweat *(slang)*, cinch *(slang)*, cakewalk *(informal)*, money for old rope, bludge *(Austral. & N.Z. informal)* • *Running the association should be a doddle.*

dodge AS A VERB 1 = **duck**, dart, swerve, sidestep, shoot, shift, turn aside, body-swerve *(Scot.)* • *We dodged behind a pillar.*
2 = **evade**, avoid, escape, get away from, elude, body-swerve *(Scot.)*, slip through the net of • *Thieves dodged the security system in the shop.*
3 = **avoid**, hedge, parry, get out of, shun, evade, sidestep, circumvent, shirk • *He has repeatedly dodged the question.*
▸ AS A NOUN = **trick**, scheme, ploy, trap, device, fraud, con *(slang)*, manoeuvre, deception, scam *(slang)*, gimmick, hoax, wheeze *(Brit. slang)*, deceit, ruse, artifice, subterfuge, canard, feint, stratagem, contrivance, machination, fastie *(Austral. slang)* • *It was probably just a dodge to stop you going away.*

dodger = **evader**, avoider, abstainer, sidestepper, bilker • *a crackdown on tax dodgers*

dodgy 1 = **nasty**, offensive, unpleasant, revolting, distasteful, repellent, unsavoury, obnoxious, repulsive, objectionable, repugnant, shonky *(Austral. & N.Z. informal)* • *He was a bit of a dodgy character.*
2 = **risky**, difficult, tricky, dangerous, delicate, uncertain, problematic(al), unreliable, dicky *(Brit. informal)*, dicey *(informal, chiefly Brit.)*, ticklish, chancy *(informal)*, shonky *(Austral. & N.Z. informal)* • *Predicting voting trends is a dodgy business.*
3 = **second rate**, poor, inferior, mediocre, shoddy, low-grade, low-quality, substandard, for the birds *(informal)*,

pants *(slang)*, end-of-the-pier *(Brit. informal)*, rubbishy, piss-poor *(slang)*, bush-league *(Austral. & N.Z. informal)*, half-pie *(N.Z. informal)*, bodger *or* bodgie *(Austral. slang)* • *cheap hotels and dodgy food*

doer = **achiever**, organizer, powerhouse *(slang)*, dynamo, live wire *(slang)*, go-getter *(informal)*, active person, wheeler-dealer *(informal)* • *He was a doer, not a thinker.*

doff 1 = **tip**, raise, remove, lift, take off • *The peasants doffed their hats.*
2 = **take off**, remove, shed, discard, throw off, cast off, slip out of, slip off, divest yourself of • *He doffed his shirt and jeans.*

d

dog AS A NOUN 1 = **hound**, canine, bitch, puppy, pup, mongrel, tyke, mutt *(slang)*, pooch *(slang)*, cur, man's best friend, kuri *or* goorie *(N.Z.)*, brak *(S. African)* • *Outside a dog was barking.*
2 = **scoundrel**, villain, cur, heel *(slang)*, knave *(archaic)*, blackguard • *Out of my sight, you dog!*
▸ AS A VERB 1 = **plague**, follow, trouble, haunt, hound, torment, afflict • *His career has been dogged by bad luck.*
2 = **pursue**, follow, track, chase, shadow, harry, tail *(informal)*, trail, hound, stalk, go after, give chase to • *The three creatures had dogged him from hut to hut.*
▸ IN PHRASES: **dog's dinner** = **mess**, state, disorder, confusion, chaos, turmoil, litter, clutter, shambles, disarray, jumble, botch, hash, cock-up *(Brit. slang)*, balls-up *(taboo slang)*, fuck-up *(offensive taboo slang)*, mishmash, disorganization, hotchpotch, bodge *(informal)*, hodgepodge *(U.S.)*, untidiness, pig's breakfast *(informal)* • *A worse dog's dinner it would be hard to imagine.*
dog-eat-dog = **ruthless**, fierce, vicious, ferocious, cut-throat, with no holds barred • *TV is a dog-eat-dog business.*
go to the dogs = **deteriorate**, degenerate, be in decline, go downhill *(informal)*, go down the drain, go to pot, go to ruin • *The country is going to the dogs.*
▸ RELATED ADJECTIVE: canine
▸ NAME OF FEMALE: bitch
▸ NAME OF YOUNG: pup, puppy
▸ RELATED MANIA: cynomania
▸ RELATED PHOBIA: cynophobia

QUOTATIONS

Love me, love my dog
[St. Bernard]

The more one gets to know of men, the more one values dogs
[A. Toussenel]

Dogs live with man as courtiers round a monarch, steeped in the flattery of his notice and enriched with sinecures
[Robert Louis Stevenson *The Character of Dogs*]

The great pleasure of a dog is that you may make a fool of yourself with him and not only will he not scold you, but he will make a fool of himself too
[Samuel Butler *Notebooks*]

PROVERBS

Every dog has its day
Why keep a dog and bark yourself?
If you lie down with dogs, you will get up with fleas
A live dog is better than a dead lion
Let sleeping dogs lie

▹ *See panel* **Breeds of dog**

dogged = **determined**, steady, persistent, stubborn, firm, staunch, persevering, resolute, single-minded, tenacious, steadfast, unyielding, obstinate, indefatigable, immovable, stiff-necked, unshakable, unflagging, pertinacious • *through sheer dogged determination*
OPPOSITES: hesitant, unsteady, irresolute

doggedness = **determination**, resolution, persistence, tenacity, perseverance, endurance, stubbornness, single-mindedness, obstinacy, steadiness, steadfastness, relentlessness, pertinacity, tenaciousness, bulldog tenacity • *the result of doggedness rather than talent*

dogma 1 = **blind faith**, certainty, unquestioning belief, arrogant conviction • *freeing the country from the grip of dogma*
2 = **doctrine**, teachings, principle, opinion, article, belief, creed, tenet, precept, credo, article of faith, code of belief, kaupapa *(N.Z.)* • *the dogma of the Immaculate Conception*

dogmatic 1 = **opinionated**, arrogant, assertive, arbitrary, emphatic, downright, dictatorial, imperious, overbearing, categorical, magisterial, doctrinaire, obdurate, peremptory • *His dogmatic style deflects opposition.*
2 = **doctrinal**, authoritative, categorical, canonical, oracular, ex cathedra • *Dogmatic socialism does not offer a magic formula.*

dogmatism = **arrogance**, presumption, arbitrariness, imperiousness, peremptoriness, dictatorialness, opinionatedness • *Dogmatism cannot stand in the way of progress.*

dogsbody = **drudge**, slave, menial, skivvy *(chiefly Brit.)*, general factotum, maid *or* man of all work • *I turned out to be a general dogsbody.*

doing 1 = **carrying out** *or* **through**, performance, execution, implementation • *Nothing deflates impossibility like the doing of it.*
2 = **handiwork**, act, action, achievement, exploit, deed • *It was all her doing.*

doings 1 = **deeds**, actions, exploits, concerns, events, affairs, happenings, proceedings, transactions, dealings, goings-on *(informal)* • *the everyday doings of a group of schoolchildren*
2 = **gizmo**, thing, whatnot, whatsit, thingummy, doodah, what-d'you-call-it, thingamajig, oojamaflip, thingamabob, what's-it's-name • *all the 'doings' of a modern kitchen*

do-it-yourself = **DIY**, home improvements, painting and decorating • *You can buy the tools at a do-it-yourself store.*

doldrums
▸ IN PHRASES: **in the doldrums** = **slow**, quiet, slack, static, sluggish, stagnant, inactive, inert • *The economy is in the doldrums.*
the doldrums = **blues**, depression, dumps *(informal)*, gloom, boredom, apathy, inertia, stagnation, inactivity, tedium, dullness, the hump *(Brit. informal)*, ennui, torpor, lassitude, listlessness • *He had been through the doldrums.*

dole AS A NOUN = **share**, grant, gift, allowance, portion, donation, quota, parcel, handout, modicum, pittance, alms, gratuity, koha *(N.Z.)* • *They hold out fragile arms for a dole of food.*
▸ IN PHRASES: **dole something out** = **give out**, share, deal out, distribute, divide, assign, administer, allocate, hand out, dispense, allot, mete, apportion • *I began to dole out the money.*
the dole = **benefits**, welfare, social security, unemployment benefit, state benefit, allowance, public assistance, government benefit, Jobseeker's Allowance, JSA, pogey *(Canad.)* • *It's not easy living on the dole.*

doleful = **mournful**, sad, gloomy, depressing, low, painful, distressing, dismal, melancholy, dreary, sombre, pitiful, forlorn, woeful, lugubrious, sorrowful, wretched, funereal, cheerless, woebegone, down in the mouth, dolorous • *He stared over his glasses with a doleful look.*

doll AS A NOUN = **figurine**, model, puppet, dolly *(informal)*, manikin • *Her parents had given her a talking doll for Christmas.*
▸ IN PHRASES: **doll yourself up** *or* **get dolled up** = **dress up** *(Slang)*, get ready, preen, primp, gussy up *(slang)*, tart yourself up *(slang)*, deck yourself out, prink, titivate yourself, trick yourself out, put on your best bib and tucker *(informal)*, put on your glad rags *(informal)* • *We dolled ourselves up and went to town.*

dollop 1 = **lump**, blob
2 = **helping**, serving, portion, scoop, gob • *a dollop of cream*

BREEDS OF DOG

affenpinscher
Afghan hound
Airedale terrier
Akita
Alaskan malamute
Alpine spaniel
Alsatian *or* German shepherd
Australian cattle dog, blue cattle dog, *or* (Queensland) blue heeler
Australian terrier
Australian silky terrier *or* Sydney silky
barb *(Austral.)*
basenji
basset hound
beagle
bearded collie
Bedlington terrier
Belvoir hound
Bichon Frise
Blenheim spaniel
bloodhound, sleuthhound, *or* sleuth
blue Gascon hound
Border collie
Border terrier
borzoi *or* Russian wolfhound
Boston terrier *or* bull terrier
bouvier
boxer
briard
Bruxellois
bulldog
bull mastiff
bull terrier
cairn terrier
chihuahua
chow-chow
clumber spaniel
cocker spaniel
collie
corgi
Cuban bloodhound
dachshund
Dalmatian *or* *(formerly)* carriage dog *or* coach dog
Dandie Dinmont (terrier)
deerhound
Doberman pinscher
Egyptian basset
elkhound *or* Norwegian elkhound
English setter
Eskimo dog
field spaniel
foxhound
fox terrier
French bulldog
golden retriever
Gordon setter
Great Dane
greyhound
griffon
harrier
Highland terrier
husky
Irish setter *or* red setter
Irish terrier
Irish water spaniel
Irish wolfhound
Italian greyhound
Jack Russell (terrier)
Japanese spaniel
Japanese tosa
keeshond
kelpie
Kerry blue terrier
King Charles spaniel
komondor
Labrador retriever, Labrador, *or* lab
Lakeland terrier
Lhasa apso
malamute
Maltese
Manchester terrier *or* black-and-tan terrier
mastiff
Mexican hairless
Newfoundland
Norfolk springer spaniel
Norfolk terrier
Norwich terrier
Old English sheepdog
otterhound
papillon
Pekingese
pit bull terrier
pointer
Pomeranian
poodle
pug
puli
Pyrenean mountain dog
raccoon dog *or* coonhound
retriever
Rhodesian ridgeback
Rottweiler
rough collie
Saint Bernard
Saluki *or* Persian greyhound
Samoyed
schipperke
schnauzer
Scottish, Scotch, *or* *(formerly)* Aberdeen terrier *or* Scottie
Sealyham terrier
setter
Shetland sheepdog *or* sheltie
shih-tzu
Skye terrier
spaniel
spitz
springer spaniel
Staffordshire bull terrier
staghound
Sussex spaniel
talbot
terrier
vizsla
water spaniel
Weimaraner
Welsh terrier
West Highland white terrier
whippet
wire-haired terrier
wolfhound
Yorkshire terrier

dolphin
▸ **COLLECTIVE NOUN:** school
▹ *See panel* **Whales and dolphins**

dolt = **idiot**, fool, dope *(informal)*, jerk *(slang, chiefly U.S. & Canad.)*, ass, clot *(Brit. informal)*, plank *(Brit. slang)*, charlie *(Brit. informal)*, berk *(Brit. slang)*, prick *(derogatory slang)*, wally *(slang)*, booby, prat *(slang)*, plonker *(slang)*, coot, geek *(slang)*, twit *(informal, chiefly Brit.)*, chump *(informal)*, dunce, oaf, simpleton, dullard, dimwit *(informal)*, ignoramus, dipstick *(Brit. slang)*, gonzo *(slang)*, schmuck *(U.S. slang)*, dork *(slang)*, nitwit *(informal)*, blockhead, dweeb *(U.S. slang)*, putz *(U.S. slang)*, fathead *(informal)*, eejit *(Scot. & Irish)*, thicko *(Brit. slang)*, dumb-ass *(slang)*, gobshite *(Irish taboo slang)*, numpty *(Scot. informal)*, doofus *(slang, chiefly U.S.)*, lamebrain *(informal)*, fuckwit *(taboo slang)*, thickhead, dickwit *(slang)*, nerd *or* nurd *(slang)*, numbskull *or* numskull, dorba *or* dorb *(Austral. slang)*, bogan *(Austral. slang)* • *He's a first class dolt.*

domain 1 = **area**, world, field, department, sector, discipline, sphere, realm, speciality • *the great experimenters in the domain of art*
2 = **sphere**, area, field, concern, scene, sector, territory, province, arena, realm • *This sort of information should be in the public domain.*
3 = **kingdom**, lands, region, territory, estate, province, empire, realm, dominion, demesne, policies *(Scot.)* • *the mighty king's domain*
4 = **public park**, park, recreation ground, garden, pleasure garden, forest park *(N.Z.)* • *The domain includes a Victorian gazebo and riverside grotto.*

dome = **arched roof**, hemisphere, vault, rotunda, cupola • *the great golden dome of the mosque*

domestic **AS AN ADJECTIVE** 1 = **home**, state, national, internal, interior, native, indigenous, not foreign • *sales in the domestic market*
2 = **household**, home, family, private, domiciliary • *a plan for sharing domestic chores* • *She described their domestic life as 'normal'*
3 = **home-loving**, homely, housewifely, stay-at-home, domesticated • *She was kind and domestic.*
4 = **domesticated**, trained, tame, house, pet, house-trained • *a domestic cat*
▸ **AS A NOUN** = **servant**, help, maid, woman *(informal)*, daily, char *(informal)*, charwoman, daily help, maid-of-all-work • *She worked for 10 or 15 years as a domestic.*

domesticate *or (U.S. sometimes)* **domesticize** 1 = **tame**, break, train, house-train, gentle • *We domesticated the dog.*
2 = **naturalize**, accustom, familiarize, habituate, acclimatize • *New World peoples domesticated a cornucopia of plants.*

domesticated 1 = **tame**, broken (in), trained, pet, tamed, house-trained *(Brit.)*, house-broken *(U.S.)* • *our domesticated animals and plants*
OPPOSITES: wild, savage, ferocious
2 = **home-loving**, homely, domestic, housewifely, house-trained *(jocular)* • *I have never been very domesticated.*

domesticity = **home life**, housekeeping, domestication, homemaking, housewifery, home-lovingness • *routine and cosy domesticity*

domicile = **dwelling**, home, residence, house, settlement, pad *(slang)*, residency, abode, habitation, legal residence • *They had moved their domicile to Bermuda in 1984.*

dominance = **control**, government, power, rule, authority, command, sway, domination, supremacy, mastery, ascendancy, paramountcy • *They're unpopular for their dominance over the community.*

dominant 1 = **main**, chief, primary, outstanding, principal, prominent, influential, prevailing, paramount, prevalent, predominant, pre-eminent • *She was a dominant figure in the film industry.*
OPPOSITES: junior, minor, secondary

2 = **controlling**, leading, ruling, commanding, supreme, governing, superior, presiding, authoritative, ascendant • *controlled by the dominant class*
3 = **assertive**, confident, forceful, decided, firm, demanding, forward, can-do *(informal)*, positive, decisive, insistent, feisty *(informal, chiefly U.S. & Canad.)*, pushy *(informal)*, in-your-face *(Brit. slang)*, strong-willed, domineering, overbearing, self-assured • *He comes across as such a dominant personality*

dominate 1 = **prevail over**, eclipse, overshadow, cloud, overrule, detract from, outshine • *countries where war dominates life*
2 = **control**, lead, rule, direct, master, govern, monopolize, tyrannize, have the upper hand over, lead by the nose *(informal)*, overbear, have the whip hand over, domineer, keep under your thumb • *He denied that his country wants to dominate Europe.*
3 = **prevail (in)**, predominate (in), be influential (in), have the upper hand (in), rule the roost (in), be pre-eminent (in) • *Usually, one partner dominates.*
4 = **tower above**, overlook, survey, dwarf, stand over, loom over, stand head and shoulders above, bestride • *The building dominates this whole place.*

domination = **control**, power, rule, authority, influence, command, sway, dictatorship, repression, oppression, suppression, supremacy, mastery, tyranny, ascendancy, subordination, despotism, subjection • *They had five centuries of domination by the Romans.*

domineering = **overbearing**, arrogant, authoritarian, oppressive, autocratic, masterful, dictatorial, coercive, bossy *(informal)*, imperious, tyrannical, magisterial, despotic, high-handed, iron-handed • *She is not a domineering mother.*
OPPOSITES: meek, submissive, subservient

dominion 1 = **control**, government, power, rule, authority, command, sovereignty, sway, domination, jurisdiction, supremacy, mastery, ascendancy, mana *(N.Z.)* • *They believe they have dominion over us.*
2 = **kingdom**, territory, province, country, region, empire, patch, turf *(U.S. slang)*, realm, domain • *The Republic is a dominion of the Brazilian people.*

don[1] = **put on**, get into, dress in, pull on, change into, get dressed in, clothe yourself in, slip on *or* into • *The police donned riot gear.*

don[2] = **lecturer**, professor, fellow, academic, acca *(Austral. slang)*, scholar • *The train was full of university dons.*

donate = **give**, present, contribute, grant, commit, gift, hand out, subscribe, endow, chip in *(informal)*, bestow, entrust, impart, bequeath, make a gift of • *He frequently donates large sums to charity.*

donation = **contribution**, gift, subscription, offering, present, grant, hand-out, boon, alms, stipend, gratuity, benefaction, largesse *or* largess, koha *(N.Z.)* • *Employees make regular donations to charity.*

done AS AN INTERJECTION = **agreed**, you're on *(informal)*, O.K. *or* okay *(informal)*, it's a bargain, it's a deal, ka pai *(N.Z.)* • *'You lead and we'll look for it.' – 'Done.'*
▸ AS AN ADJECTIVE 1 = **finished**, completed, accomplished, over, through, ended, perfected, realized, concluded, executed, terminated, consummated, in the can *(informal)* • *By evening the work is done, and just in time.*
2 = **cooked**, ready, cooked enough, cooked to a turn, cooked sufficiently • *When the cake is done, remove it from the oven.*
3 = **acceptable**, proper, polite, conventional, protocol, de rigueur *(French)* • *It simply isn't done.*
4 = **cheated**, tricked, conned *(informal)*, duped, taken for a ride *(informal)* • *If you paid more than a hundred quid for that, you've been done.*
▸ IN PHRASES: **done for** = **finished** *(Informal)*, lost, beaten, defeated, destroyed, ruined, broken, dashed, wrecked, doomed, foiled, undone • *I thought we were all done for.*
done in *or* **up** = **exhausted**, bushed *(informal)*, all in *(slang)*, worn out, dead *(informal)*, knackered *(slang)*, clapped out *(Austral. & N.Z. informal)*, tired out, ready to drop, dog-tired *(informal)*, zonked *(slang)*, dead beat *(informal)*, fagged out *(informal)*, worn to a frazzle *(informal)*, on your last legs, creamcrackered *(Brit. slang)* • *You must be really done in.*
have *or* **be done with something** *or* **someone** = **be through with**, give up, be finished with, throw over, wash your hands of, end relations with • *Let us have done with him.*

Don Juan = **womanizer**, wolf *(informal)*, seducer, rake, Romeo, gallant, Casanova, Prince Charming, philanderer, Lothario, libertine, lady-killer *(informal)*, Lothario, poodle-faker *(slang)*, ladies' man • *the sexual boasting of a Don Juan*

donkey AS A NOUN = **ass**, mule, jackass, neddy • *strange creatures including a wild donkey*
▸ IN PHRASES: **donkey's years** = **a long time**, years, ages, for ever *(informal)*, yonks *(informal)*, an age *or* eternity • *I made them last for donkey's years.*
▸ NAME OF MALE: jack
▸ NAME OF FEMALE: jenny

donnish = **scholarly**, erudite, scholastic, pedantic, bookish, pedagogic, precise, formalistic • *He is precise and mildly donnish in manner.*

donor = **giver**, supporter, contributor, sponsor, patron, backer, benefactor, philanthropist, grantor *(Law)*, donator, almsgiver • *a major donor to UN relief agencies*
OPPOSITES: receiver, recipient, beneficiary

doom AS A NOUN 1 = **destruction**, ruin, catastrophe, death, downfall • *his warnings of impending doom*
2 = **fate**, destiny, fortune, lot • *They are said to have lured sailors to their doom.*
▸ AS A VERB = **condemn**, sentence, consign, foreordain, destine, predestine, preordain • *Some suggest the leisure park is doomed to failure.*

doomed = **hopeless**, condemned, ill-fated, fated, unhappy, unfortunate, cursed, unlucky, blighted, hapless, bedevilled, luckless, ill-starred, star-crossed, ill-omened • *a doomed attempt to rescue the children*

doomsday
QUOTATIONS
This is the way the world ends
Not with a bang but a whimper
[T.S. Eliot *The Hollow Men*]

door AS A NOUN = **opening**, entry, entrance, exit, doorway, ingress, egress • *I was knocking at the front door.*
▸ IN PHRASES: **out of doors** = **in the open air**, outside, outdoors, out, out of the house, alfresco • *The weather was fine for working out of doors.*
show someone the door = **throw out**, remove, eject, evict, turn out, bounce *(slang)*, oust, drive out, boot out *(informal)*, ask to leave, show out, throw out on your ear *(informal)* • *Would they forgive him or show him the door?*

do-or-die = **desperate**, risky, hazardous, going for broke, win-or-bust, death-or-glory, kill-or-cure • *a do-or-die attempt to hold on to power*

dope AS A NOUN 1 = **drugs**, narcotics, illegal drugs, opiates, recreational drugs, addictive drugs, dadah *(Austral. slang)* • *A man asked them if they wanted to buy some dope.*
2 = **idiot**, fool, jerk *(slang, chiefly U.S. & Canad.)*, plank *(Brit. slang)*, charlie *(Brit. informal)*, berk *(Brit. slang)*, prick *(derogatory slang)*, wally *(slang)*, prat *(slang)*, plonker *(slang)*, coot, geek *(slang)*, twit *(informal, chiefly Brit.)*, dunce, oaf, simpleton, dimwit *(informal)*, dipstick *(Brit. slang)*, dickhead *(slang)*, gonzo *(slang)*, schmuck *(U.S. slang)*, dork *(slang)*, nitwit *(informal)*, dolt, blockhead, divvy *(Brit. slang)*, pillock *(Brit. slang)*, dweeb *(U.S. slang)*, putz *(U.S. slang)*, fathead *(informal)*, eejit *(Scot. & Irish)*, thicko *(Brit. slang)*, dumb-ass *(slang)*, gobshite *(Irish taboo slang)*, numpty *(Scot. informal)*,

doofus *(slang, chiefly U.S.)*, lamebrain *(informal)*, fuckwit *(taboo slang)*, dickwit *(slang)*, nerd *or* nurd *(slang)*, numbskull *or* numskull, dorba *or* dorb *(Austral. slang)*, bogan *(Austral. slang)* • *I don't feel I'm such a dope.*
3 = **information**, facts, details, material, news, intelligence, gen *(Brit. informal)*, info *(informal)*, inside information, lowdown *(informal)* • *They had plenty of dope on him.*
▸ **AS A VERB** = **drug**, doctor, knock out, inject, sedate, stupefy, anaesthetize, narcotize • *I'd been doped with Somnolin.*

dopey *or* **dopy** 1 = **drowsy**, dazed, groggy *(informal)*, drugged, muzzy, stupefied, half-asleep, woozy *(informal)* • *The medicine always made him feel dopey.*
2 = **stupid**, simple, slow, thick, silly, foolish, dense, dumb *(informal)*, senseless, goofy *(informal)*, idiotic, dozy *(Brit. informal)*, asinine, dumb-ass *(slang)* • *I was so dopey I believed him.*

dormant 1 = **latent**, inactive, lurking, quiescent, unrealized, unexpressed, inoperative • *The virus remains dormant in nerve tissue.*
2 = **inactive**, sleeping, inert, suspended, asleep, sluggish, slumbering, comatose, hibernating, torpid • *The hamster lapses into a dormant state in cold weather.*
OPPOSITES: active, conscious, alert

dorp = **town**, village, settlement, municipality, kainga *or* kaika *(N.Z.)* • *a South African farm girl born in a dorp called Benoni*

dose 1 = **measure**, amount, allowance, portion, prescription, ration, draught, dosage, potion • *A dose of penicillin can wipe out infection.*
2 = **quantity**, amount, lot, measure, supply, portion • *a healthy dose of self-confidence*
3 = **attack**, spell, bout, stroke, burst, outbreak, flare-up, eruption • *I had a bad dose of flu.*

dossier = **report**, record, file, detail, note, data, intelligence, facts, gen *(Brit. informal)* • *The government kept dossiers on its citizens.*

dot **AS A NOUN** = **spot**, point, mark, circle, atom, dab, mite, fleck, jot, speck, full stop, speckle, mote, iota, pinprick • *a small black dot in the middle*
▸ **IN PHRASES: on the dot** = **on time**, sharp, promptly, precisely, exactly *(informal)*, spot on *(informal)*, bang on, dead on *(informal)*, to the minute, on the button *(informal)*, on the nail, punctually • *At nine o'clock on the dot, they arrived.*
▸ **AS A VERB** = **spot**, cover, spread over, pepper, scatter, stud, litter, strew, fleck, speckle • *Small coastal towns dotted the area.*

dotage = **old age**, senility, advanced years, decrepitude, second childhood, eld *(archaic)*, elderliness, autumn *or* winter of your years, agedness • *He's spending his dotage in a riverside cottage.*

dote *with* **on** *or* **upon** = **adore**, prize, treasure, admire, hold dear, idolize, lavish affection on • *He dotes on his nine-year-old son.*

doting = **adoring**, devoted, fond, foolish, indulgent, lovesick • *his doting parents*

dotty = **crazy**, touched, peculiar, eccentric, batty *(slang)*, off-the-wall *(slang)*, potty *(Brit. informal)*, oddball *(informal)*, loopy *(informal)*, crackpot *(informal)*, out to lunch *(informal)*, out there *(slang)*, outré, doolally *(slang)*, off your trolley *(slang)*, up the pole *(informal)*, wacko *or* whacko *(slang)*, off the air *(Austral. slang)*, porangi *(N.Z.)*, daggy *(Austral. & N.Z. informal)* • *She was obviously going a bit dotty.*

double **AS AN ADJECTIVE** 1 = **matching**, coupled, doubled, paired, twin, dual, complementary, duplicate, in pairs, binate *(Botany)* • *a pair of double doors into the room*
2 = **deceitful**, false, fraudulent, deceiving, treacherous, dishonest, deceptive, hypocritical, counterfeit, two-faced, disingenuous, insincere, double-dealing, duplicitous, perfidious, knavish *(archaic)*, Janus-faced • *a woman who had lived a double life*
3 = **dual**, ambiguous, enigmatic, cryptic, twofold, double-edged, two-edged, Delphic, enigmatical, open to argument *or* debate • *The book has a double meaning.*
▸ **AS A NOUN** = **twin**, lookalike, spitting image, copy, fellow, mate, counterpart, clone, replica, ringer *(slang)*, impersonator *(informal)*, dead ringer *(slang)*, Doppelgänger, duplicate • *Your mother sees you as her double.*
▸ **IN PHRASES: at** *or* **on the double** = **at once**, now, immediately, directly, quickly, promptly, right now, straight away, right away, briskly, without delay, pronto *(informal)*, at full speed, in double-quick time, this instant, this very minute, pdq *(slang)*, posthaste, tout de suite *(French)* • *Come to my office, please, on the double.*
▸ **AS A VERB** 1 = **multiply by two**, duplicate, increase twofold, repeat, enlarge, magnify • *They need to double the number of managers.*
2 = **fold up** *or* **over**, turn up *or* over, tuck back *or* over, bend back *or* over • *He doubled the sheet back upon itself.*
3 *with* **as** = **function as**, serve as, serve the purpose of • *The military greatcoat doubled as a bedroll.*

double back = **backtrack**, circle, reverse, return, loop, dodge, retrace your steps • *Double back for 50 yards.*

double-cross = **betray**, trick, cheat, sting *(informal)*, mislead, two-time *(informal)*, defraud, swindle, hoodwink, sell down the river *(informal)*, cozen • *They were frightened of being double-crossed.*

double-dealing **AS A NOUN** = **treachery**, cheating, betrayal, deception, hypocrisy, two-timing *(informal)*, deceit, dishonesty, trickery, foul play, duplicity, bad faith, perfidy, mendacity • *There has been some double-dealing*
▸ **AS AN ADJECTIVE** = **treacherous**, lying, cheating, tricky, crooked *(informal)*, fraudulent, two-timing *(informal)*, dishonest, hypocritical, wily, swindling, sneaky, two-faced, deceitful, untrustworthy, duplicitous, perfidious, underhanded • *Slimy, double-dealing politicians have betrayed us all.*

double entendre = **double meaning**, ambiguity, pun, innuendo, play on words • *He is a master of the double entendre.*

doubly = **twice as**, in two ways, twofold, as much again, in double measure • *She now felt doubly guilty.*

doubt **AS A NOUN** 1 = **uncertainty**, confusion, hesitation, dilemma, scepticism, misgiving, suspense, indecision, bewilderment, lack of confidence, hesitancy, perplexity, vacillation, lack of conviction, irresolution, dubiety • *They were troubled and full of doubt.*
OPPOSITES: confidence, belief, certainty
2 = **suspicion**, scepticism, distrust, questioning, fear, reservations, cynicism, disbelief, apprehension, mistrust, misgivings, disquiet, qualms, incredulity, lack of faith, misbelief • *Where there is doubt, may we bring faith.*
OPPOSITES: trust, confidence, belief
▸ **AS A VERB** 1 = **be uncertain**, question, query, be sceptical, have reservations about, be dubious • *They doubted whether that could happen.*
2 = **waver**, hesitate, vacillate, sway, fluctuate, dither *(chiefly Brit.)*, haver, oscillate, chop and change, blow hot and cold *(informal)*, keep changing your mind, shillyshally *(informal)*, be irresolute *or* indecisive, swither *(Scot.)* • *Stop doubting and start loving.*
3 = **disbelieve**, question, challenge, suspect, dispute, query, distrust, mistrust, cast doubt on, have doubts about, lack confidence in, have misgivings about, misgive • *I have no reason to doubt his word.*
OPPOSITES: believe, accept, trust
▸ **IN PHRASES: in doubt** = **doubtful**, unsettled, undecided, unconfirmed, up in the air, in limbo, open to question • *The outcome was still in doubt.*

no doubt = certainly, surely, probably, of course, admittedly, doubtless, unquestionably, assuredly, doubtlessly • *No doubt I'm biased.*

QUOTATIONS

There lives more faith in honest doubt,
Believe me, than in half the creeds
[Alfred Tennyson *In Memoriam A.H.H.*]

I show you doubt, to prove that faith exists
[Robert Browning *Balaustion's Adventure*]

If a man will begin with certainties, he shall end in doubts; but if he will be content to begin with doubts, he shall end in certainties
[Francis Bacon *The Advancement of Learning*]

Our doubts are traitors
And make us lose the good we oft might win
By fearing to attempt
[William Shakespeare *Measure for Measure*]

Doubt of the reality of love ends by making us doubt everything
[Henri Frédéric Amiel *Journal*]

doubter = sceptic, questioner, disbeliever, agnostic, unbeliever, doubting Thomas • *Doubters fear this may not be good news.*

doubtful 1 = unlikely, unclear, dubious, unsettled, dodgy (*Brit., Austral. & N.Z. informal*), questionable, ambiguous, improbable, indefinite, unconfirmed, inconclusive, debatable, indeterminate, iffy (*informal*), equivocal, inexact • *It seemed doubtful that he would move at all.*
OPPOSITES: certain, definite, indubitable
2 = unsure, uncertain, hesitant, suspicious, hesitating, sceptical, unsettled, tentative, wavering, unresolved, perplexed, undecided, unconvinced, vacillating, leery (*slang*), distrustful, in two minds (*informal*), irresolute • *Why did he sound so doubtful?*
OPPOSITES: decided, certain, positive
3 = questionable, suspect, suspicious, crooked, dubious, dodgy (*Brit., Austral. & N.Z. informal*), slippery, shady (*informal*), unscrupulous, fishy (*informal*), shifty, disreputable, untrustworthy, shonky (*Austral. & N.Z. informal*) • *They all seemed of very doubtful character.*

doubtless = probably, presumably, most likely • *She took off her shoes, doubtless because her feet hurt.*

doughty = intrepid, brave, daring, bold, hardy, heroic, courageous, gritty, fearless, resolute, gallant, valiant, redoubtable, dauntless, valorous, stouthearted • *doughty campaigns for the underprivileged*

dour = gloomy, forbidding, grim, sour, dismal, dreary, sullen, unfriendly, morose • *a dour, taciturn man*
OPPOSITES: happy, pleasant, cheery

douse *or* **dowse 1 = put out**, smother, blow out, extinguish, snuff (out) • *The crew began to douse the fire.*
2 = drench, soak, steep, saturate, duck, submerge, immerse, dunk, souse, plunge into water • *They doused him in petrol.*

dove
▸ RELATED ADJECTIVE: columbine
▸ COLLECTIVE NOUNS: dule, flight

dovetail 1 = correspond, match, agree, accord, coincide, tally, conform, harmonize • *I'm following up some things that might dovetail.*
2 = fit together, join, fit, unite, link, interlock, tenon, mortise • *The pieces dovetail seamlessly.*

dowdy = frumpy, old-fashioned, shabby, drab, tacky (*U.S. informal*), unfashionable, dingy, unhip (*slang*), frumpish, ill-dressed, frowzy • *Her clothes were clean but dowdy.*
OPPOSITES: smart, trim, chic

dower = dowry, share, portion, legacy, inheritance, provision • *The dower was comprised of royal French lands in Artois.*

down[1] AS A PREPOSITION **1 = along**, to the other end of, throughout the length of, from one end to the other of • *They set off at a jog down the street.*
2 = throughout, over, through, during • *This domination has extended gradually down the years.*
▸ AS AN ADVERB **= downwards**, from top to bottom, towards the bottom, downstairs • *We went down in the lift after the meeting.*
▸ AS AN ADJECTIVE **1 = depressed**, low, sad, blue, unhappy, discouraged, miserable, fed up, dismal, pessimistic, melancholy, glum, dejected, despondent, dispirited, downcast, morose, disheartened, crestfallen, downhearted, down in the dumps (*informal*), sick as a parrot (*informal*), low-spirited • *The old man sounded really down.*
2 = not working, broken, broken down, defective, out of action, out of order, acting up, not functioning, on the blink (*slang*), on its last legs, kaput (*informal*), not in working order • *The computer's down again.*
▸ AS A VERB **1 = swallow**, drink (down), knock back, sink (*informal*), drain, finish off, gulp (down), put away (*informal*), swig (*informal*), guzzle, quaff, polish off, toss off • *We downed several bottles of local wine.*
2 = bring down, fell, knock down, throw, trip, floor, tackle, deck (*slang*), overthrow, prostrate • *A bank guard shot him and downed him.*
▸ IN PHRASES: **have a down on something** *or* **someone = be antagonistic** *or* **hostile to**, be set against, have it in for (*slang*), be anti (*informal*), be prejudiced against, be contra (*informal*), bear a grudge towards, feel ill will towards • *She always had a down on me for some reason.*

down[2] = fluff, nap, fuzz, pile, oose (*Scot.*) • *ducklings covered in soft down*

down-and-out AS AN ADJECTIVE **= destitute**, ruined, impoverished, derelict, penniless, dirt-poor (*informal*), flat broke (*informal*), on your uppers (*informal*), without two pennies to rub together (*informal*) • *He looked unshaven, shabby and down-and-out.*
▸ AS A NOUN **= tramp**, bum (*informal*), beggar, derelict, outcast, pauper, vagrant, vagabond, bag lady, dosser (*Brit. slang*), derro (*Austral. slang*) • *some poor down-and-out in need of a meal*

down-at-heel = poor, impoverished, shabby, badly off, seedy, on the rocks, hard up (*informal*), penniless, poverty-stricken, in need, in want, impecunious, on the breadline, penurious, on your uppers, without two pennies to rub together (*informal*), on your beam-ends, out at elbows • *a down-at-heel waitress in a greasy diner*

downbeat 1 = low-key, muted, subdued, sober, sombre • *The headlines were suitably downbeat.*
2 = gloomy, negative, depressed, pessimistic, unfavourable • *They found him in gloomy, downbeat mood.*
OPPOSITES: encouraging, positive, cheerful

downcast = dejected, sad, depressed, unhappy, disappointed, discouraged, miserable, dismayed, choked, daunted, dismal, despondent, dispirited, disheartened, disconsolate, crestfallen, down in the dumps (*informal*), cheerless, sick as a parrot (*informal*) • *a glum, downcast expression*
OPPOSITES: happy, contented, cheerful

downfall = ruin, fall, destruction, collapse, breakdown, disgrace, overthrow, descent, undoing, comeuppance (*slang*), comedown • *His lack of experience led to his downfall.*

downgrade 1 = demote, degrade, take down a peg (*informal*), lower *or* reduce in rank • *His superiors downgraded him.*
OPPOSITES: raise, advance, promote
2 = run down, denigrate, disparage, detract from, decry • *He was never one to downgrade his talents.*

downhearted = dejected, sad, depressed, unhappy, blue, discouraged, dismayed, despondent, dispirited, downcast, disheartened, sorrowful, crestfallen, sick as a parrot *(informal)*, low-spirited, chapfallen • *Don't be so downhearted.*

down-market = **second-rate**, cheap, inferior, tacky *(informal)*, shoddy, low-grade, tawdry, low-quality, two-bit *(U.S. & Canad. slang)*, cheap and nasty *(informal)*, lowbrow, bush-league *(Austral. & N.Z. informal)*, bodger *or* bodgie *(Austral. slang)* • *downmarket television drama*
OPPOSITES: elite, superior, first-rate

downplay = **soft-pedal**, play down • *The government are trying to downplay the violence which broke out yesterday.*

downpour = **rainstorm**, flood, deluge, torrential rain, cloudburst, inundation • *a sudden downpour of rain*

downright AS AN ADVERB = **totally**, completely, perfectly, extremely, absolutely, thoroughly, wholly, consummately, to the core, one hundred per cent, to the nth degree • *She was often downright rude to him.*
▸ AS AN ADJECTIVE 1 = **complete**, absolute, utter, total, positive, clear, plain, simple, explicit, outright, blatant, unequivocal, unqualified, out-and-out, categorical, undisguised, thoroughgoing, arrant, deep-dyed *(usually derogatory)* • *downright bad manners*
2 = **blunt**, open, frank, plain, straightforward, sincere, outspoken, honest, candid, forthright, upfront *(informal)*, straight-from-the-shoulder • *a simple, downright chap with no rhetorical airs about him*

downside = **drawback**, disadvantage, snag, problem, trouble, minus *(informal)*, flip side, other side of the coin *(informal)*, bad *or* weak point • *There is a downside to this.*
OPPOSITES: benefit, plus *(informal)*, advantage

down-to-earth = **sensible**, practical, realistic, common-sense, matter-of-fact, sane, no-nonsense, hard-headed, unsentimental, plain-spoken, grounded • *She's the most down-to-earth person I've met.*

downtrodden = **oppressed**, abused, exploited, subservient, subjugated, tyrannized • *at the expense of the downtrodden masses*

downward = **descending**, declining, heading down, earthward • *a downward movement*

downy 1 = **fluffy**, woolly, fleecy, feathery, plumate *(Zoology, Botany)* • *the warm downy quilt*
2 = **soft**, smooth, sleek, silky, velvety, silken • *downy head and beautiful skin*

dowry = **portion**, marriage settlement, dot *(archaic)*, lobola *(S. African)* • *The money from her dowry was invested.*

doze AS A VERB = **nap**, sleep, slumber, nod, kip *(Brit. slang)*, snooze *(informal)*, catnap, drowse, sleep lightly, zizz *(Brit. informal)* • *For a while she dozed fitfully.*
▸ AS A NOUN = **nap**, kip *(Brit. slang)*, snooze *(informal)*, siesta, little sleep, catnap, forty winks *(informal)*, shuteye *(slang)*, zizz *(Brit. informal)* • *After lunch I had a doze.*
▸ IN PHRASES: **doze off** = **fall asleep**, nod off, drop off *(informal)*, crash out *(informal)*, drift off, go off, conk out *(informal)* • *I must have dozed off.*

dozy 1 = **drowsy**, sleepy, dozing, nodding, half asleep • *Eating too much makes me dozy.*
2 = **stupid**, simple, slow, silly, daft *(informal)*, senseless, goofy *(informal)*, witless, not all there, slow-witted • *He called me a dozy cow.*

drab = **dull**, grey, gloomy, dismal, dreary, shabby, sombre, lacklustre, flat, dingy, colourless, uninspired, vapid, cheerless • *his drab little office*
OPPOSITES: bright, colourful, vivid

Draconian *sometimes not cap.* = **severe**, hard, harsh, stern, drastic, stringent, punitive, austere, pitiless • *draconian censorship laws*

draft AS A NOUN 1 = **outline**, plan, sketch, version, rough, abstract, blueprint, main points, delineation, preliminary form • *I rewrote his first draft.*
2 = **money order**, bill (of exchange), cheque, postal order • *The money was payable by a draft.*
▸ AS A VERB = **outline**, write, plan, produce, create, design, draw, frame, compose, devise, sketch, draw up, formulate, contrive, delineate • *He drafted a standard letter.*

drag AS A VERB 1 = **pull**, draw, haul, trail, tow, tug, jerk, yank, hale, lug • *He got up and dragged his chair towards the table.*
2 = **lag**, trail, linger, loiter, straggle, dawdle, hang back, tarry, draggle • *I was dragging behind*
3 = **go slowly**, inch, creep, crawl, advance slowly • *The minutes dragged past.*
▸ AS A NOUN = **nuisance**, pain *(informal)*, bore, bother, pest, hassle *(informal)*, inconvenience, annoyance, pain in the neck, pain in the arse *(taboo slang)*, pain in the backside *(informal)*, pain in the butt *(informal)* • *Shopping for clothes is a drag.*
▸ IN PHRASES: **drag on** = **last**, continue, carry on, remain, endure, persist, linger, abide • *The conflict has dragged on for two years.*
drag something in = **mention**, refer to, bring up, point out, allude to, call attention to, touch upon, broach the subject of, speak about *or* of • *They disapproved of my dragging in his wealth.*
drag something out = **prolong**, extend, keep going, stretch out, lengthen, draw out, spin out, protract • *a company that was willing to drag out the proceedings for years*
drag yourself = **go slowly**, creep, crawl, inch, shuffle, shamble, limp along, move at a snail's pace, advance slowly • *I managed to drag myself to the surgery.*

dragoon = **force**, drive, compel, bully, intimidate, railroad *(informal)*, constrain, coerce, impel, strong-arm *(informal)*, browbeat • *He had been dragooned into the excursion.*

drain AS A NOUN 1 = **sewer**, channel, pipe, sink, outlet, ditch, trench, conduit, duct, culvert, watercourse • *He built his own house and laid his own drains.*
2 = **reduction**, strain, drag, expenditure, exhaustion, sapping, depletion • *This has been a big drain on resources.*
▸ IN PHRASES: **down the drain** = **gone**, lost, wasted, ruined, down the tubes, down the pan, gone for good • *His public image is down the drain.*
▸ AS A VERB 1 = **remove**, draw, empty, withdraw, milk, tap, pump, bleed, evacuate • *machines to drain water out of the mines*
2 = **empty**, unload, clear out, remove the contents of • *I didn't know what we would find when we drained the pool.*
3 = **flow out**, leak, discharge, trickle, ooze, seep, exude, well out, effuse • *The water drained away.*
4 = **drink up**, swallow, knock back, finish, sink *(informal)*, put away *(informal)*, swig *(informal)*, guzzle, quaff, polish off, gulp down • *She drained the contents of her glass and refilled it.*
5 = **exhaust**, tire, wear out, strain, weaken, fatigue, weary, debilitate, prostrate, tax, tire out, enfeeble, enervate • *My emotional turmoil has drained me.*
6 = **consume**, waste, exhaust, empty, bleed, deplete, use up, sap, dissipate, expend, swallow up • *Deficits drain resources from the pool of national savings.*

drainage = **sewerage**, waste, sewage • *The drainage system has collapsed.*

dram = **measure**, shot *(informal)*, drop, glass, tot, slug, snort *(slang)*, snifter *(informal)* • *a dram of whisky*

drama 1 = **play**, show, stage show, stage play, dramatization, theatrical piece • *He acted in radio dramas.*
2 = **theatre**, acting, dramatic art, stagecraft, dramaturgy, Thespian art • *He knew nothing of Greek drama.*
3 = **excitement**, crisis, dramatics, spectacle, turmoil, histrionics, theatrics • *the drama of a hostage release*

QUOTATIONS
Drama is life with the dull bits cut out
[Alfred Hitchcock]

d

The drama is make-believe. It does not deal with the truth but with effect
[W. Somerset Maugham *The Summing Up*]
Life is full of internal dramas, instantaneous and sensational, played to an audience of one
[Anthony Powell]

▹ *See panels* **Dramatists; Theatre terms**

DRAMA

TYPES OF DRAMA

comedy	Kathakali	situation comedy
comedy of manners	kitchen sink	*or* sitcom
commedia dell'arte	melodrama	sketch
costume piece *or* costume drama	morality play	soap opera
farce	mystery play	street theatre
Grand Guignol	No *or* Noh	theatre of cruelty
Jacobean	passion play	theatre of the absurd
kabuki	Restoration Comedy	tragedy
	revenge tragedy	tragicomedy
	shadow play	

dramatic 1 = **drastic**, strong, severe, radical, extreme, harsh, dire • *dramatic effects on the economy*
2 = **exciting**, emotional, thrilling, tense, startling, sensational, breathtaking, electrifying, melodramatic, climactic, hair-raising, high-octane *(informal)*, shock-horror *(facetious)*, suspenseful • *He witnessed many dramatic escapes.*
3 = **theatrical**, Thespian, dramaturgical, dramaturgic • *a dramatic arts major in college*
4 = **expressive**, affected, exaggerated, theatrical, melodramatic, showy, ostentatious • *She lifted her hands in a dramatic gesture.*
5 = **powerful**, striking, imposing, stunning *(informal)*, impressive, spectacular, effective, staggering, distinctive, memorable, vivid, jaw-dropping, breath-taking, gee-whizz *(slang)* • *the film's dramatic special effects*
OPPOSITES: ordinary, run-of-the-mill, unexceptional

dramatist = **playwright**, screenwriter, scriptwriter, dramaturge • *the technique of the tragic dramatist*

dramatize *or* **dramatise** 1 = **adapt for the stage**, turn into a play, present as a play, put into dramatic form • *The novel has been dramatized.*
2 = **exaggerate**, overdo, overstate, lay it on (thick) *(slang)*, play-act, play to the gallery, make a performance of • *They have a tendency to dramatize every situation.*
▹ *See panel* **Dramatists**

drape 1 = **lay**, put, place, spread, leave, deposit • *A robe had been draped over a chair.*
2 = **cover**, wrap, fold, array, adorn, cloak, shroud, swathe, envelop, festoon, bedeck, enfold • *He draped himself in the flag.*
3 = **hang**, drop, dangle, suspend, lean, droop, let fall • *She draped her arm over the back of the couch.*

drastic = **extreme**, strong, radical, desperate, severe, harsh, dire, forceful • *Drastic measures are needed.*

draught *or (U.S.)* **draft** 1 = **breeze**, current, wind, movement, flow, puff, influx, gust, current of air • *Block draughts around doors and windows.*
2 = **drink**, swallow, slug, mouthful, swig • *He took a draught of beer.*

draw AS A VERB 1 = **sketch**, design, outline, trace, portray, paint, depict, mark out, map out, delineate, do drawings • *Draw a rough design for a logo.*
2 = **move**, go, come, drive, travel, roll, advance, cruise, proceed, drift, glide • *She had seen the taxi drawing away.*
3 = **pull**, drag, haul, tow, tug • *He drew his chair nearer the fire.*
4 = **close**, shut, pull together, pull shut *or* closed • *After drawing the curtains, she lit a candle.*
5 = **part**, open, raise, pull back, pull open • *He drew the curtains and the sun poured in.*
6 = **take out**, pull out, bring out, draw out, produce, withdraw • *He drew his dagger.*
7 = **inhale**, breathe in, pull, inspire, suck, respire • *He paused, drawing a deep breath.*
8 = **extract**, take, remove, pump, drain, suck • *They still have to draw their water from wells.*
9 = **withdraw**, take out • *Companies could not draw money from bank accounts as cash.*
10 = **choose**, pick, select, take, single out • *We drew the winning name.*
11 = **deduce**, make, gather, get, take, conclude, derive, infer, glean • *He draws two conclusions from this.*
12 = **attract**, capture, engage, grip • *He wanted to draw attention to their plight.*
13 = **entice**, attract, pull in, win, bring in • *The game is currently drawing huge crowds*
14 = **take out**, pull out, extract, extort • *She had gone to Doctor Dougall to have a bad tooth drawn.*
▸ AS A NOUN 1 = **tie**, deadlock, stalemate, impasse, dead heat • *The game ended in a draw.*
2 = **raffle**, lottery, sweepstake, tombola • *I hear you won a case of whisky in the Christmas draw.*
3 = **appeal**, interest, pull *(informal)*, charm, attraction, lure, temptation, fascination, attractiveness, allure, magnetism, enchantment, enticement, captivation, temptingness • *The draw of India lies in its beauty.*
▸ IN PHRASES: **draw back** = **recoil**, withdraw, retreat, shrink, falter, back off, shy away, flinch, retract, quail, start back • *I drew back with a horrified scream.*
draw on *or* **upon something** = **make use of**, use, employ, rely on, exploit, extract, take from, fall back on, have recourse to • *He drew on his experience as a yachtsman.*
draw someone out = **persuade someone to talk**, put someone at their ease • *Her mother tried to draw her out.*
draw something out = **stretch out**, prolong, continue, extend, lengthen, spin out, elongate, drag out, attenuate, protract, keep something going, make something go on • *She drew the speech out interminably.*
draw something up = **draft**, write, produce, create, prepare, frame, compose, devise, formulate, contrive • *They drew up a formal agreement.*
draw up = **halt**, stop, pull up, park, brake, stop short, come to a stop, come to a standstill • *A police car drew up at the gate.*

drawback = **disadvantage**, trouble, difficulty, fault, handicap, obstacle, defect, deficiency, flaw, hitch, nuisance, snag, downside, stumbling block, impediment, detriment, imperfection, hindrance, fly in the ointment *(informal)* • *The only drawback was that the apartment was too small.*
OPPOSITES: help, benefit, advantage

drawing AS A NOUN = **picture**, illustration, representation, cartoon, sketch, portrayal, depiction, study, outline, delineation • *She did a drawing of me.*
▸ IN PHRASES: **go back to the drawing board** = **start (all over) again**, start again from scratch, go back to square one • *We'll have to go back to the drawing board.*

drawl = **speak** *or* **say slowly** • *She grinned and drawled, "Hi, honey".*

drawn = **tense**, worn, strained, stressed, tired, pinched, fatigued, harassed, fraught, sapped, harrowed, haggard • *She looked drawn and tired.*

dread AS A VERB = **fear**, shrink from, be anxious about, flinch from, cringe at the thought of, quail from, shudder to think about, have cold feet about *(informal)*, anticipate with horror, tremble to think about • *I'm dreading Christmas this year.*

Dramatists

Aeschylus *(Greek)*
Edward Albee *(U.S.)*
Robert Amos *(Australian)*
Jean Anouilh *(French)*
Aristophanes *(Greek)*
Alan Ayckbourn *(English)*
Pierre Augustin Caron de Beaumarchais *(French)*
Francis Beaumont *(English)*
Samuel Beckett *(Irish)*
Brendan Behan *(Irish)*
Richard Beynon *(Australian)*
Alan Bleasdale *(English)*
Edward Bond *(English)*
Bertolt Brecht *(German)*
Eugene Brieux *(French)*
Pedro Calderón de la Barca *(Spanish)*
George Chapman *(English)*
Anton Pavlovich Chekhov *(Russian)*
William Congreve *(English)*
Pierre Corneille *(French)*
Noël (Pierce) Coward *(English)*
Thomas Dekker *(English)*
John Dryden *(English)*
T(homas) S(tearns) Eliot *(U.S.-British)*
Louis Esson *(Australian)*
Euripides *(Greek)*
John Fletcher *(English)*
Dario Fo *(Italian)*
John Ford *(English)*
Brian Friel *(Irish)*
John Galsworthy *(English)*
Jean Genet *(French)*
W(illiam) S(chwenk) Gilbert *(English)*
(Hippolyte) Jean Giraudoux *(French)*
Johann Wolfgang von Goethe *(German)*
Nikolai Gogol *(Russian)*
Oliver Goldsmith *(Irish)*
Oriel Gray *(Australian)*
Robert Greene *(English)*
David Hare *(English)*
Gerhart Johann Robert Hauptmann *(German)*
Václav Havel *(Czech)*
Alfred Hayes *(U.S.)*
(Christian) Friedrich Hebbel *(German)*
Dorthy Hewett *(Australian)*
Thomas Heywood *(English)*
Jack Hibberd *(Australian)*
Sidney Howard *(U.S.)*
Henrik Ibsen *(Norwegian)*
William Motter Inge *(U.S.)*
Eugène Ionesco *(Romanian-French)*
Ben Jonson *(English)*
George Kaiser *(German)*
Tony Kushner *(U.S.)*
Thomas Kyd *(English)*
Ray Lawler *(Australian)*
Liz Lochhead *(Scottish)*
Lope de Vega *(Spanish)*
Federico Garcia Lorca *(Spanish)*
Maurice Maeterlinck *(Belgian)*
David Mamet *(U.S.)*
Christopher Marlowe *(English)*
John Marston *(English)*
Menander *(Greek)*
Arthur Miller *(U.S.)*
Molière *(French)*
Barry Oakley *(Australian)*
Sean O'Casey *(Irish)*
Eugene (Gladstone) O'Neill *(U.S.)*
Joe Orton *(English)*
John Osborne *(English)*
Thomas Otway *(English)*
John Patrick *(U.S.)*
Arthur Wing Pinero *(English)*
Harold Pinter *(English)*
Luigi Pirandello *(Italian)*
Titus Maccius Plautus *(Roman)*
Hal Porter *(Australian)*
Aleksander Sergeyevich Pushkin *(Russian)*
Jean Baptiste Racine *(French)*
Terence Mervyn Rattigan *(English)*
John Romeril *(Australian)*
Willy Russell *(English)*
Thomas Sackville *(English)*
Jean-Paul Sartre *(French)*
Johann Christoph Friedrich von Schiller *(German)*
Lucius Annaeus Seneca *(Roman)*
Alan Seymour *(Australian)*
Peter Shaffer *(English)*
William Shakespeare *(English)*
George Bernard Shaw *(Irish)*
Sam Shepard *(U.S.)*
Richard Brinsley Sheridan *(Irish)*
Robert Sherwood *(U.S.)*
Sophocles *(Greek)*
Wole Soyinka *(Nigerian)*
Tom Stoppard *(Czech-English)*
August Strindberg *(Swedish)*
John Millington Synge *(Irish)*
Terence *(Roman)*
John Webster *(English)*
Oscar Wilde *(Irish)*
Thornton Wilder *(U.S.)*
Tennessee Williams *(U.S.)*
David Keith Williamson *(Australian)*
William Wycherly *(English)*

▸ **AS A NOUN** = **fear**, alarm, horror, terror, dismay, fright, apprehension, consternation, trepidation, fearfulness, apprehensiveness, affright • *She thought with dread of the cold winters to come.*

▸ **AS AN ADJECTIVE** = **frightening**, terrible, alarming, awful, terrifying, horrible, dreadful, dreaded, dire, frightful • *the dread phrase 'politically correct'*

dreaded = **feared**, dread, dreadful • *this dreaded disease*

dreadful 1 = **terrible**, shocking, awful, alarming, distressing, appalling, tragic, horrible, formidable, fearful, dire, horrendous, hideous, monstrous, from hell *(informal)*, grievous, atrocious, frightful, godawful *(slang)*, hellacious *(U.S. slang)* • *They told us the dreadful news.*
2 = **serious**, terrible, awful, appalling, horrendous, monstrous, unspeakable, abysmal • *We've made a dreadful mistake*
3 = **awful**, terrible, ghastly, grim, horrendous, frightful, godawful *(slang)*, like death warmed up *(informal)* • *I feel absolutely dreadful*

dreadfully 1 = **extremely**, very, terribly, greatly, badly, deeply, very much, desperately, exceptionally, immensely, tremendously, awfully *(informal)*, exceedingly, excessively • *He looks dreadfully ill.*
2 = **terribly**, badly, horribly, awfully, alarmingly, woefully, appallingly, wickedly, shockingly, frightfully, disgracefully, horrendously, monstrously, wretchedly, abysmally, unforgivably, reprehensibly, disreputably • *She has behaved dreadfully.*

dream **AS A NOUN** 1 = **vision**, nightmare, illusion, delusion, hallucination, reverie • *I had a dream that I was in an old house.*
2 = **ambition**, wish, fantasy, plan, hope, goal, design, aim, desire, objective, aspiration, Holy Grail *(informal)*, pipe dream • *My dream is to have a house in the country.*
3 = **daydream**, trance, daze, reverie, stupor, hypnotic state • *I wandered around in a kind of dream.*
4 = **delight**, pleasure, joy, beauty, treasure, gem, marvel, pearler *(Austral. slang)*, beaut *(Austral. & N.Z. slang)* • *This cart really is a dream to drive.*

▸ **AS A VERB** 1 = **have dreams**, have a dream, have nightmares, have a nightmare, hallucinate • *She dreamt about her baby.*
2 = **daydream**, be preoccupied, stare into space, be in a trance, be lost in thought, be in cloud-cuckoo-land, stargaze, be in a reverie, build castles in the air *or* in Spain • *She spent most of her time looking out of the window and dreaming.*

▸ **AS AN ADJECTIVE** = **fantasy**, perfect, ideal • *a dream holiday in Jamaica*

▸ **IN PHRASES: dream of something** *or* **someone** = **daydream about**, wish to, fantasize about, hope for, desire to, long for, aspire to, hunger for, hanker after, set your heart on • *She dreamed of going to work overseas.*

dream something up = **invent**, create, imagine, devise, hatch, contrive, concoct, think up, cook up *(informal)*, spin • *I dreamed up a plan.*

▸ **RELATED ADJECTIVE:** oneiric

▸ **RELATED PHOBIA:** oneirophobia

QUOTATIONS

We are such stuff
As dreams are made on, and our little life
Is rounded with a sleep
[William Shakespeare *The Tempest*]

I talk of dreams;
Which are the children of an idle brain,
Begot of nothing but vain fantasy
[William Shakespeare *Romeo and Juliet*]

Judge of your natural character by what you do in your dreams
[Ralph Waldo Emerson *Journals*]

I have a dream that one day on the red hills of Georgia the sons of former slaves and the sons of former slave owners will be able to sit down together at the table of brotherhood
[Martin Luther King *speech at 1963 Civil Rights March*]

dreamer = **idealist**, visionary, daydreamer, utopian, theorizer, fantasizer, romancer, Don Quixote, escapist, Walter Mitty, fantasist, fantast • *I was a dreamer, a romancer.*

dreamland = **land of make-believe**, fantasy, illusion, dream world, fairyland, cloud-cuckoo-land, never-never land *(informal)*, land of dreams, cloudland, land of Nod • *In dreamland we play them in the final.*

dreamlike = **unreal**, visionary, surreal, illusory, hallucinatory, trancelike, chimerical, phantasmagorical, phantasmagoric, unsubstantial • *Her paintings have a dreamlike quality.*

dreamy 1 = **vague**, abstracted, absent, musing, preoccupied, daydreaming, faraway, pensive, in a reverie, with your head in the clouds • *His face assumed a dreamy expression.*
2 = **relaxing**, calming, romantic, gentle, soothing, lulling • *a dreamy, delicate song*
3 = **starry-eyed**, romantic, sentimental, utopian, quixotic, over-optimistic • *He's like some dreamy kid*
4 = **impractical**, vague, imaginary, speculative, visionary, fanciful, quixotic, dreamlike, airy-fairy • *full of dreamy ideals*
OPPOSITES: practical, realistic, common-sense

dreary 1 = **dull**, boring, tedious, routine, drab, tiresome, lifeless, monotonous, humdrum, colourless, uneventful, uninteresting, mind-numbing, ho-hum *(informal)*, wearisome, as dry as dust • *They live such dreary lives.*
OPPOSITES: interesting, exciting, fascinating, happy, cheerful
2 = **dismal**, depressing, bleak, sad, lonely, gloomy, solitary, melancholy, sombre, forlorn, glum, mournful, lonesome *(chiefly U.S. & Canad.)*, downcast, sorrowful, wretched, joyless, funereal, doleful, cheerless, drear, comfortless • *A dreary little town in the Midwest*

dredge up = **dig up**, raise, rake up, discover, uncover, draw up, unearth, drag up, fish up • *She dredged up a minor misdemeanour.*

dregs AS A PLURAL NOUN = **sediment**, grounds, lees, waste, deposit, trash, residue, scum, dross, residuum, scourings, draff • *He drained the dregs from his cup.*
▸ **IN PHRASES: the dregs** = **scum**, outcasts, rabble, down-and-outs, good-for-nothings, riffraff, canaille *(French)*, ragtag and bobtail • *the dregs of society*

drench = **soak**, flood, wet, duck, drown, steep, swamp, saturate, inundate, souse, imbrue • *They turned fire hoses on the people and drenched them.*

dress AS A NOUN 1 = **frock**, shift, gown, garment, robe • *She was wearing a black dress.*
2 = **clothing**, clothes, gear *(informal)*, costume, threads *(slang)*, garments, apparel, attire, garb, togs, raiment *(archaic or poetic)*, vestment, schmutter *(slang)*, habiliment • *a well-groomed gent in smart dress and specs*
▸ AS A VERB 1 = **put on clothes**, don clothes, slip on *or* into something • *He told her to wait while he dressed.*
OPPOSITES: undress, strip, disrobe
2 = **clothe**, turn out, get up *(informal)*, attire, fit out, garb, rig out, robe • *We dressed the baby in a warm outfit.*
3 = **bandage**, cover, treat, plaster, swathe, bind up • *I dressed her wounds.*
4 = **decorate**, deck, adorn, trim, array, drape, ornament, embellish, festoon, bedeck, furbish, rig out • *advice on how to dress a Christmas tree*
5 = **arrange**, do (up), groom, set, prepare, comb (out), get ready • *He's so careless about dressing his hair.*
▸ **IN PHRASES: dress down** = **dress casually**, dress informally, be untidy • *She dresses down in baggy clothes.*
dress someone down = **reprimand**, rebuke, scold, berate, castigate, tear into *(informal)*, tell off *(informal)*, read the riot act, reprove, upbraid, slap on the wrist, carpet *(informal)*, bawl out *(informal)*, rap over the knuckles, haul over the coals, chew out *(U.S. & Canad. informal)*, tear (someone) off a strip *(Brit. informal)*, give a rocket *(Brit. & N.Z. informal)* • *He dressed them down in public.*
dress something up = **present**, portray, depict, characterize, gloss, enhance, embroider, embellish, jazz up • *However you dress it up, banks only exist to lend money.*
dress up 1 = **put on fancy dress**, wear a costume, disguise yourself • *She dressed up as a witch.*
2 = **dress formally**, dress for dinner, doll yourself up *(slang)*, put on your best bib and tucker *(informal)*, put on your glad rags *(informal)* • *She did not feel obliged to dress up for the cameras.*

QUOTATIONS

When you're all dressed up and have no place to go
[George Whiting *song title*]

Eat to please thyself, but dress to please others
[Benjamin Franklin *Poor Richard's Almanack*]

▹ *See panels* **Clothing; Dresses**

dressing 1 = **sauce**, dip, relish, condiment • *Mix the salad dressing in a bowl*
2 = **bandage**, plaster, gauze, Band-Aid *(trademark)*, lint, Elastoplast *(trademark)*, ligature, compress • *She'll put a dressing on your thumb.*

DRESSES

ballgown
burka
busuuti
button-through dress
chemise
cheongsam
chiton
coat dress
cocktail dress
dirndl
gymslip
kaftan *or* caftan
kimono
mantua
maxidress
microdress
midi
minidress
Mother Hubbard
muu-muu
negligee *or* negligée
nightdress *or (U.S. & Canad.) (informal)* nightie *or* nighty
nightrobe
nightgown *or*
nightshirt
overdress
peignoir
pinafore dress, pinafore, pinny (informal), *or (U.S. & Canad.)* jumper
riding habit
sack
sari *or* saree
sheath
shift
shirtdress
shirtwaister *or (U.S. & Canad.)* shirtwaist
sundress
sweater dress
tea gown
tunic
wedding dress

dressmaker = **seamstress**, tailor, couturier, sewing woman, modiste • *She used to be a dressmaker.*

dressy = **elegant**, formal, smart, elaborate, stylish, classy *(slang)*, ornate, swish *(informal, chiefly Brit.)*, ritzy *(slang)*, schmick *(Austral. informal)* • *I go to work in quite dressy clothes*

dribble AS A VERB 1 = **run**, drip, trickle, drop, leak, ooze, seep, fall in drops • *Sweat dribbled down his face.*
2 = **drool**, drivel, slaver, slobber, drip saliva • *She's dribbling on her collar.*
▸ AS A NOUN 1 = **trickle**, drop, drizzle, dash, splash, drip • *Apply a dribble of shampoo.*
2 = **saliva**, spit, slaver, spittle • *His top is soaked in dribble.*

dried = **dehydrated**, dry, dried-up, desiccated • *fresh or dried herbs*

drift AS A VERB 1 = **float**, go (aimlessly), bob, coast, slip, sail, slide, glide, meander, waft, be carried along, move gently • *We proceeded to drift along the river.*
2 = **wander**, stroll, stray, roam, meander, rove, range, straggle, traipse *(informal)*, stravaig *(Scot. & Northern English dialect)*, peregrinate • *People drifted around the room.*
3 = **stray**, wander, roam, meander, digress, get sidetracked, go off at a tangent, get off the point • *I let my attention drift.*
4 = **pile up**, gather, accumulate, amass, bank up, heap up, form drifts • *The snow, except where it drifted, was only calf-deep.*
▸ AS A NOUN 1 = **shift**, movement, flow, transfer, relocation, gravitation • *the drift towards the cities*
2 = **pile**, bank, mass, heap, mound, accumulation • *A boy was trapped in a snow drift.*
3 = **meaning**, point, gist, aim, direction, object, import, intention, implication, tendency, significance, thrust, tenor, purport • *She was beginning to get his drift.*
4 = **trend**, course, current, flow, rush, sweep • *their fears at what they see as a drift towards economic chaos*
▸ IN PHRASES: **drift off** = **fall asleep**, go off, drop off *(informal)*, crash out *(informal)*, nod off, conk out *(informal)* • *He finally drifted off.*

drifter = **wanderer**, bum *(informal)*, tramp, itinerant, vagrant, hobo *(U.S.)*, vagabond, rolling stone, bag lady *(chiefly U.S.)*, derro *(Austral. slang)* • *an out-of-work drifter*

drill[1] AS A NOUN 1 = **bit**, borer, brace, gimlet, rotary tool, boring tool • *pneumatic drills*
2 = **training**, exercise, work-out, discipline, instruction, preparation, repetition, square-bashing *(informal)* • *A local army base teaches them military drill.*
3 = **practice**, procedure, routine, system, programme • *a fire drill*
▸ AS A VERB 1 = **bore**, pierce, penetrate, sink in, puncture, perforate • *I drilled five holes at equal distance.*
2 = **train**, coach, teach, exercise, discipline, practise, instruct, rehearse • *He drills the choir to a high standard.*
3 = **drive**, hammer, drum, din, instil, indoctrinate • *These were lessons drilled into him by his Grandpa.*

drink AS A VERB 1 = **swallow**, drain, sip, neck *(slang)*, suck, gulp, sup, swig *(informal)*, swill, guzzle, imbibe, quaff, partake of, toss off • *He drank his cup of tea.*
2 = **booze** *(informal)*, tipple, tope, hit the bottle *(informal)*, bevvy *(dialect)*, bend the elbow *(informal)*, go on a binge *or* bender *(informal)* • *He was smoking and drinking too much.*
▸ AS A NOUN 1 = **glass**, cup, swallow, sip, draught, gulp, swig *(informal)*, taste, tipple, snifter *(informal)*, noggin • *a drink of water.*
2 = **beverage**, refreshment, potion, liquid, thirst quencher • *Can I offer you a drink?*
3 = **alcohol**, booze *(informal)*, liquor, spirits, the bottle *(informal)*, alcoholic drink, Dutch courage, intoxicants, hooch *or* hootch *(informal, chiefly U.S. & Canad.)* • *Too much drink is bad for your health.*
▸ IN PHRASES: **drink something in** = **absorb**, take in, digest, pay attention to, soak up, devour, assimilate, be fascinated by, imbibe • *She stood drinking in the view.*
drink to something = **toast**, salute, propose a toast to, pledge the health of, wish health to • *Let's drink to his memory.*
the drink = **the sea**, the main, the deep, the ocean, the briny *(informal)* • *His plane went down in the drink.*
▸ RELATED MANIA: potomania
▸ RELATED PHOBIA: potophobia

QUOTATIONS

Let us eat and drink; for tomorrow we shall die
[*Bible: Isaiah*]

Take thine ease, eat, drink, and be merry
[*Bible: St. Luke*]

I drink when I have occasion for it, and sometimes when I have not
[Miguel de Cervantes *Don Quixote*]

Drink to me only with thine eyes
[Ben Jonson *To Celia*]

It's all right to drink like a fish – if you drink what a fish drinks
[Mary Pettibone Poole *A Glass Eye at the Keyhole*]

One reason I don't drink is that I want to know when I'm having a good time
[Nancy Astor]

Man wants little drink below,
But wants that little strong
[Oliver Wendell Holmes *A Song of other Days*]

Give strong drink unto him that is ready to perish, and wine unto those that be of heavy hearts
[*Bible: Proverbs*]

Let schoolmasters puzzle their brain,
With grammar, and nonsense, and learning,
Good liquor, I stoutly maintain,
Gives genius a better discerning
[Oliver Goldsmith *She Stoops to Conquer*]

Candy
Is dandy
But liquor
Is quicker
[Ogden Nash *Reflections on Ice-breaking*]

I arrived on the job in what I considered to be a perfect state of equilibrium, half man and half alcohol
[Eddie Condon *We Called it Music*]

Wine is the drink of the gods, milk the drink of babies, tea the drink of women, and water the drink of beasts
[John Stuart Blackie]

Drink moderately, for drunkenness neither keeps a secret, nor observes a promise
[Miguel de Cervantes *Don Quixote*]

We drink one another's healths and spoil our own
[Jerome K. Jerome *The Idle Thoughts of an Idle Fellow*]

Drink! for you know not whence you came, nor why:
Drink! for you know not why you go, nor where
[Omar Khayyám *Rubáiyát*]

I will drink Life to the lees:
all times I have enjoyed greatly, have suffered greatly
[Alfred, Lord Tennyson *Ulysses*]

A little learning is a dangerous thing;
Drink deep, or taste not the Pierian spring:
There shallow draughts intoxicate the brain,
And drinking largely sobers us again
[Alexander Pope *An Essay on Criticism*]

▹ *See panels* **Alcoholic drinks; Beers; Cocktails; Coffees; Liqueurs; Soft drinks; Spirits; Teas; Whiskies; Wines**

drinkable = **fit to drink**, potable, quaffable, gluggable *(informal)* • *The wine was drinkable.*

drinker = **alcoholic**, drunk, boozer *(informal)*, soak *(slang)*, lush *(slang)*, toper, sponge *(informal)*, guzzler, drunkard, sot,

SOFT DRINKS

alcohol-free *or* non-alcoholic beer
apple juice
barley water
bitter lemon
Bovril *(trademark)*
buttermilk
cassis
Coca-Cola *or* Coke *(trademark)*
cocoa
coffee
cola
cordial
cream soda
crush
dandelion and burdock
fruit juice
fruit tea
ginger ale
ginger beer
grapefruit juice
herb tea *or* herbal infusion
hot chocolate
ice-cream soda
iron brew
juice
kumiss
lassi
lemonade
lemon squash
lemon tea *or* Russian tea
limeade
lime cordial
lolly water *(Austral. & N.Z.)*
Lucozade *(trademark)*
maté *or* mate
milk
milk shake
mineral water
nectar
orangeade
orange juice
orgeat
peppermint cordial
Perrier *(trademark)*
prairie oyster
Ribena *(trademark)*
root beer
sarsaparilla
Seltzer
sherbet
smoothie
soapolallie
soda
soda water
spremuta
squash
sweet cider *(U.S., Canad.)*
tea
tisane
Tizer *(trademark)*
tomato juice
tonic
vichy water
Vimto *(trademark)*
water

tippler, wino *(informal)*, inebriate, dipsomaniac, bibber, alko *or* alco *(Austral. slang)* • *I'm not a heavy drinker.*

drip AS A VERB = **drop**, splash, sprinkle, trickle, dribble, exude, drizzle, plop • *a cloth that dripped pink drops upon the floor*
▸ AS A NOUN 1 = **drop**, bead, trickle, dribble, droplet, globule, pearl, driblet • *Drips of water rolled down his uniform.*
2 = **weakling**, wet *(Brit. informal)*, weed *(informal)*, softie *(informal)*, pussycat *(Brit. informal)*, mummy's boy *(informal)*, namby-pamby, ninny, milksop • *The kid is a drip!*

drive AS A VERB 1 = **go (by car)**, ride (by car), motor, travel by car • *I drove into town and went for dinner.*
2 = **operate**, manage, direct, guide, handle, pilot, steer, navigate • *Don't expect to be able to drive a car or operate machinery.*
3 = **run**, take, transport, bring, ferry, convey, chauffeur, give a lift to • *She drove him to the train station.*
4 = **push**, move, power, propel • *pistons that drive the wheels*
5 = **thrust**, push, sink, send, dig, hammer, plunge, stab, ram • *I used the sledgehammer to drive the pegs in.*
6 = **lash**, pound, beat, hammer, drum, dash, buffet • *Rain drove hard against the window.*
7 = **herd**, urge, shepherd, round up, impel • *The shepherds drove the sheep up to pasture.*
8 = **force**, press, prompt, spur, compel, motivate, oblige, railroad *(informal)*, prod, constrain, prick, coerce, goad, impel, dragoon, actuate • *Depression drove him to attempt suicide.*
9 = **work**, push, tax, exert, overwork, overburden • *For the next six years he drove himself mercilessly.*
▸ AS A NOUN 1 = **run**, ride, trip, journey, spin *(informal)*, hurl *(Scot.)*, outing, excursion, jaunt • *We might go for a drive on Sunday.*
2 = **driveway**, avenue, roadway, approach, access road • *I walked back up the drive towards the car.*
3 = **initiative**, push *(informal)*, energy, enterprise, ambition, pep, motivation, zip *(informal)*, vigour, welly *(slang)*, get-up-and-go *(informal)* • *He is best remembered for his drive and enthusiasm.*
4 = **desire**, need, urge, instinct, appetite • *compelling, dynamic sex drives*
5 = **campaign**, push *(informal)*, crusade, action, effort, appeal, advance, surge • *the drive towards democracy*
▸ IN PHRASES: **drive at something** = **mean**, suggest, intend, refer to, imply, intimate, get at, hint at, have in mind, allude to, insinuate • *He wasn't sure what she was driving at.*

drivel AS A VERB = **babble**, ramble, waffle *(informal, chiefly Brit.)*, gab *(informal)*, gas *(informal)*, maunder, blether, prate • *I drivelled on about the big race that day.*
▸ AS A NOUN = **nonsense**, rubbish, garbage, malarkey *(informal)*, balls *(taboo slang)*, bull *(slang)*, shit *(taboo slang)*, rot, crap *(slang)*, trash, bunk *(informal)*, blah *(slang)*, bullshit *(taboo slang)*, hot air *(informal)*, tosh *(slang, chiefly Brit.)*, waffle *(informal, chiefly Brit.)*, prating, pap, cobblers *(Brit. taboo slang)*, bilge *(informal)*, twaddle, tripe *(informal)*, dross, gibberish, guff *(slang)*, moonshine, malarkey, hogwash, hokum *(slang, chiefly U.S. & Canad.)*, piffle *(informal)*, poppycock *(informal)*, balderdash, bosh *(informal)*, eyewash *(informal)*, tommyrot, horsefeathers *(U.S. slang)*, bunkum *or* buncombe *(chiefly U.S.)*, bizzo *(Austral. slang)*, bull's wool *(Austral. & N.Z. slang)* • *What absolute drivel!*

driver = **chauffeur**, pilot, motorist • *a taxi driver*

driving = **forceful**, sweeping, dynamic, compelling, vigorous, energetic, galvanic • *Consumer spending was the driving force behind growth this summer.*

drizzle AS A NOUN = **fine rain**, spray, Scotch mist, mizzle, smir *(Scot.)* • *The drizzle had stopped and the sun was breaking through.*
▸ AS A VERB 1 = **rain**, shower, spit, spray, sprinkle, mizzle *(dialect)*, spot *or* spit with rain • *It was starting to drizzle.*
2 = **trickle**, pour, dribble, splash, drip, sprinkle • *Drizzle the remaining dressing over the duck.*

droll = **amusing**, odd, funny, entertaining, comic, ridiculous, diverting, eccentric, ludicrous, humorous, quaint, off-the-wall *(slang)*, laughable, farcical, whimsical, comical, oddball *(informal)*, risible, jocular, clownish, waggish • *The band have a droll sense of humour.*

drone[1] = **parasite**, skiver *(Brit. slang)*, idler, lounger, piker *(Austral. & N.Z. slang)*, leech, loafer, couch potato *(slang)*, scrounger *(informal)*, sponger *(informal)*, sluggard, bludger *(Austral. & N.Z. informal)*, quandong *(Austral. slang)* • *A few are dim-witted drones, but most are talented.*

drone[2] AS A VERB 1 = **hum**, buzz, vibrate, purr, whirr, thrum • *An invisible plane drones through the night sky.*
2 *often with* **on** = **speak monotonously**, drawl, chant, spout, intone, talk interminably • *Her voice droned on.*
▸ AS A NOUN = **hum**, buzz, purr, vibration, whirr, whirring, thrum • *the constant drone of the motorway*

droning 1 = **humming**, buzzing, vibrating, purring, whirring, thrumming • *the droning sound of a plane overhead*
2 = **monotonous**, boring, tedious, drawling, soporific • *the minister's relentlessly droning voice*

drool 1 = **drivel**, dribble, salivate, slaver, slobber, water at the mouth • *The dog was drooling on my shoulder*
2 *often with* **over** = **gloat over**, pet, gush, make much of, rave about *(informal)*, dote on, slobber over • *Fashion editors drooled over every item.*

droop 1 = **sag**, drop, hang (down), sink, bend, dangle, fall

down • *a young man with a drooping moustache*
2 = flag, decline, fade, slump, diminish, wither, wilt, languish • *Support for him is beginning to droop amongst voters.*

droopy = sagging, limp, wilting, stooped, floppy, drooping, languid, flabby, languorous, pendulous, lassitudinous • *a droopy moustache*

drop AS A VERB **1 = fall**, lower, sink, decline, plunge, slump, diminish, decrease, plummet, dwindle, lessen, slacken • *Temperatures can drop to freezing at night.*
2 *often with* **away = decline**, fall, sink, dip, slope, descend, fall away, slope downwards • *The ground dropped away steeply.*
3 = plunge, fall, dive, tumble, descend, plummet • *Part of an aeroplane had dropped out of the sky and hit me.*
4 = let go of, release, let fall, lose your grip on • *I dropped my glasses and broke them.*
5 = drip, run, flow, leak, trickle, dribble, drizzle, fall in drops • *He felt hot tears dropping onto his fingers.*
6 = deposit, put, place, set, rest, lay, stick, shove, set down, plonk *(informal)* • *He dropped his coat on the floor.*
7 = sink, fall, go down, descend, droop • *She let her head drop.*
8 = collapse, fall, faint, fall down, pass out, black out, lose consciousness, keel over, conk out *(informal)*, flake out *(informal)* • *She looked about to drop.*
9 = set down, leave, deposit, unload, let off • *He dropped me outside the hotel.*
10 = quit, give up, abandon, cease, axe *(informal)*, kick *(informal)*, terminate, shun, relinquish, remit, discontinue, forsake, turn your back on • *He was told to drop the idea.*
11 = abandon, reject, desert, renounce, forsake, repudiate, disown, leave, jilt, throw over, disclaim, turn your back on • *He has dropped those friends who used to drink with him.*
12 = eject, dismiss, throw out, exclude, discharge, discard, oust, evict, send packing, turf out *(informal)*, give the bum's rush *(slang)*, throw out on your ear *(informal)* • *The captain was dropped from the team.*
13 = lose, fail to win, concede, give away, miss out on • *They could drop a match or two, and still make the finals.*
14 = mention, say, introduce, refer to, intimate, hint at, impart • *I dropped a few hints.*
15 = omit, miss (out), exclude, eliminate, leave out, forget, disregard, give (something) a miss *(informal)* • *Drop any reference to socialism.*
▸ AS A NOUN **1 = decrease**, fall, cut, lowering, decline, reduction, slump, fall-off, downturn, deterioration, cutback, diminution, decrement • *He was prepared to take a drop in wages.*
2 = droplet, bead, globule, bubble, pearl, drip, driblet • *a drop of blue ink*
3 = dash, shot *(informal)*, spot, taste, trace, pinch, sip, tot, trickle, nip, dab, mouthful • *I'll have a drop of that milk.*
4 = sweet, candy *(U.S.)*, lozenge, pastille, bonbon • *white or plain chocolate drops*
5 = fall, plunge, descent, abyss, chasm, precipice • *There was a sheer drop just outside my window.*
▸ IN PHRASES: **drop back** *or* **behind = fall back**, hang back • *You're driving too close so drop back a little bit.*
drop in = visit, call, stop, turn up, look up, call in, look in, pop in *(informal)*, swing by *(informal)* • *I'll drop in on my way home.*
drop off 1 = fall asleep, nod (off), doze (off), go off, snooze *(informal)*, drift off, catnap, drowse, have forty winks *(informal)* • *I was just dropping off.*
2 = decrease, lower, decline, shrink, diminish, fall off, dwindle, lessen, wane, subside, slacken • *The toll of casualties has dropped off sharply.*
drop out = leave, stop, give up, withdraw, quit, pull out, back out, renege, throw in the towel, cop out *(slang)*, fall by the wayside • *He went to university, but dropped out after a year.*
drop out of something = discontinue, give up, abandon, quit, cease, terminate, shun, forsake, turn your back on • *She had a troubled childhood and dropped out of high school.*
drop someone off = set down, leave, deliver, let off, allow to alight • *I'm going to drop you off and pick you up myself.*

droppings = excrement, shit *(taboo slang)*, crap *(taboo slang)*, stool, manure, dung, faeces, turds, guano, excreta, doo-doo *(informal)*, ordure, kak *(S. African taboo slang)* • *pigeon droppings*

dross 1 = scum, crust, impurity, scoria, rubbish, remains, refuse, lees, waste, debris, dregs, recrement • *gold nuggets from dross*
2 = nonsense, garbage *(chiefly U.S.)*, drivel, twaddle, balls *(taboo slang)*, bull *(slang)*, shit *(taboo slang)*, pants *(slang)*, rot, crap *(slang)*, trash, bullshit *(taboo slang)*, hot air *(informal)*, tosh *(slang, chiefly Brit.)*, bollocks *(Brit. taboo slang)*, pap, cobblers *(Brit. taboo slang)*, bilge *(informal)*, tripe *(informal)*, gibberish, guff *(slang)*, havers *(Scot.)*, moonshine, claptrap *(informal)*, hogwash, hokum *(slang, chiefly U.S. & Canad.)*, codswallop *(Brit. slang)*, piffle *(informal)*, poppycock *(informal)*, balderdash, bosh *(informal)*, wack *(U.S. slang)*, eyewash *(informal)*, stuff and nonsense, flapdoodle *(slang)*, tommyrot, horsefeathers *(U.S. slang)*, bunkum *or* buncombe *(chiefly U.S.)*, bizzo *(Austral. slang)*, bull's wool *(Austral. & N.Z. slang)* • *Why are you wasting your time reading that dross?*

drought 1 = water shortage, dryness, dry weather, dry spell, aridity, lack of rain, drouth *(Scot.)*, parchedness • *Drought and famines have killed up to two million people.*
OPPOSITES: flood, deluge, downpour
2 = shortage, lack, deficit, deficiency, want, need, shortfall, scarcity, dearth, insufficiency • *The Western world was suffering through the oil drought.*
OPPOSITES: abundance, profusion

drove *often plural* **= herd**, company, crowds, collection, gathering, mob, flocks, swarm, horde, multitude, throng • *Scientists are leaving the country in droves.*

drown 1 = go down, go under, go to a watery grave, go to Davy Jones's locker, die under water • *He drowned during a storm.*
2 = drench, flood, soak, steep, swamp, saturate, engulf, submerge, immerse, inundate, deluge • *The country would be drowned in blood.*
3 *often with* **out = overwhelm**, overcome, wipe out, overpower, obliterate, swallow up, be louder than • *His words were soon drowned by amplified police sirens.*

QUOTATIONS
I was much farther out than you thought
And not waving but drowning
[Stevie Smith *Not Waving But Drowning*]

drowse = sleep, drop off *(informal)*, doze, nap, slumber, kip *(Brit. slang)*, snooze *(informal)*, nod off, get some shut-eye, zizz *(Brit. informal)*, have *or* get forty winks, catch some zeds *(informal)* • *She drowsed for a while.*

drowsiness = sleepiness, tiredness, lethargy, torpor, sluggishness, languor, somnolence, heavy eyelids, doziness, torpidity, oscitancy • *Big meals cause drowsiness.*
OPPOSITES: brightness, alertness, wakefulness

drowsy 1 = sleepy, tired, lethargic, heavy, nodding, dazed, dozy, comatose, dopey *(slang)*, half asleep, somnolent, torpid • *He felt pleasantly drowsy.*
OPPOSITES: alert, lively, awake
2 = peaceful, quiet, sleepy, soothing, lulling, dreamy, restful, soporific • *The drowsy air hummed with bees.*

drubbing = beating, defeat, hammering *(informal)*, pounding, whipping, thrashing, licking *(informal)*, pasting *(slang)*, flogging, trouncing, clobbering *(slang)*, walloping *(informal)*, pummelling • *following their 5-0 drubbing by Holland*

drudge = menial, worker, servant, slave, toiler, dogsbody *(informal)*, plodder, factotum, scullion *(archaic)*, skivvy *(chiefly Brit.)*, maid *or* man of all work • *She felt like a household drudge.*

d

drudgery = **labour**, grind *(informal)*, sweat *(informal)*, hard work, slavery, chore, fag *(informal)*, toil, slog, donkey-work, sweated labour, menial labour, skivvying *(Brit.)* • *the drudgery of everyday life*

drug AS A NOUN 1 = **medication**, medicine, remedy, panacea, elixir, physic, medicament • *The drug will treat those infected*
2 = **dope** *(slang)*, narcotic *(slang)*, stimulant, illegal drug, opiate, recreational drug, addictive drug, hallucinogen, gear *(slang)*, shit, dadah *(Austral. slang)* • *the problem of drug abuse*
▸ AS A VERB 1 = **knock out**, dope *(slang)*, give drugs to, numb, deaden, stupefy, anaesthetize, render unconscious, give narcotics to • *They drugged the guard dog.*
2 = **dope**, lace *(informal)*, spike *(informal)*, tamper with, adulterate, add drugs to • *He had drugged her drink.*
▸ COMBINING FORM: pharmaco-

QUOTATIONS
Sex and drugs and rock and roll
[Ian Dury *song title*]
opiate: an unlocked door in the prison of Identity. It leads into the jail yard
[Ambrose Bierce *The Devil's Dictionary*]
And though she's not really ill,
There's a little yellow pill;
She goes running for the shelter
Of her mother's little helper
[Mick Jagger *Mother's Little Helper*]
Turn on, tune in and drop out
[Timothy Leary *The Politics of Ecstasy*]

▹ *See panel* **Drugs**

drug addict = **junkie** *(informal)*, tripper *(informal)*, crack-head *(informal)*, acid head *(informal)*, dope-fiend *(slang)*, hop-head *(informal)*, head *(informal)* • *His daughter is a drug addict.*

drugged = **stoned**, high *(informal)*, flying *(slang)*, bombed *(slang)*, tripping *(informal)*, wasted *(slang)*, smashed *(slang)*, wrecked *(slang)*, turned on *(slang)*, out of it *(slang)*, doped *(slang)*, under the influence *(informal)*, on a trip *(informal)*, spaced out *(slang)*, comatose, stupefied, out of your mind *(slang)*, off your face *(slang)*, loved-up *(informal)*, zonked *(slang)*, out to it *(Austral. & N.Z. slang)* • *drugged up to the eyeballs.*

drum AS A NOUN 1 = **barrel**, tank, container, cylinder, canister, cask • *a drum of chemical waste*
2 = **pounding**, beat, rhythm, thump, thumping, throb, vibration, patter, pitter-patter • *the drum of heavy feet on the stairs*
▸ AS A VERB = **pound**, beat, tap, rap, lash, thrash, tattoo, throb, pulsate, reverberate • *Rain drummed on the roof of the car.*
▸ IN PHRASES: **drum someone out** = **discharge**, dismiss, expel, throw out, exclude, oust, outlaw, banish, drive out, evict, cashier, send packing, turf out *(informal)* • *They are to be drummed out of the service.*
drum something into someone = **drive**, hammer, instil, din, harp on about • *Examples were drummed into students' heads.*
drum something up = **seek**, attract, request, ask for, obtain, bid for, petition, round up, solicit, canvass • *drumming up business*

drumming = **pounding**, beating, thump, thumping, throb, throbbing, vibration • *He felt a drumming in his temples.*

drunk AS AN ADJECTIVE = **intoxicated**, loaded *(slang, chiefly U.S. & Canad.)*, tight *(informal)*, canned *(slang)*, flying *(slang)*, bombed *(slang)*, stoned *(slang)*, wasted *(slang)*, smashed *(slang)*, hammered *(slang)*, steaming *(slang)*, wrecked *(slang)*, soaked *(informal)*, out of it *(slang)*, plastered *(slang)*, drunken, blitzed *(slang)*, pissed *(Brit., Austral. & N.Z. slang)*, blatted *(Brit. slang)*, boozed-up *(slang)*, lit up *(slang)*, merry *(Brit. informal)*, stewed *(slang)*, pickled *(informal)*, bladdered *(slang)*, under the influence *(informal)*, sloshed *(slang)*, tipsy, maudlin, well-oiled *(slang)*, dronkverdriet *(S. African)*, elephants *(Austral. slang)*, legless *(informal)*, paralytic *(informal)*, tired and emotional *(euphemistic)*, steamboats *(Scot. slang)*, kaylied *(Brit. slang)*, langered *(Irish slang)*, lashed *(Brit. slang)*, mashed *(Brit. slang)*, mullered *(slang)*, ossified *(Irish slang)*, sat *(S. African)*, stukkend *(S. African slang)*, trashed *(slang)*, tiddly *(slang, chiefly Brit.)*, off your face *(slang)*, zonked *(slang)*, blotto *(slang)*, broken *(S. African informal)*, fuddled, inebriated, out to it *(Austral. & N.Z. slang)*, sottish, tanked up *(slang)*, bacchic, rat-arsed *(taboo slang)*, Brahms and Liszt *(slang)*, Adrian Quist *(Austral. slang)*, half seas over *(informal)*, bevvied *(dialect)*, babalas *(S. African)*, fu' *(Scot.)*, pie-eyed *(slang)* • *I got drunk and had to be carried home.*
▸ AS A NOUN = **drunkard**, alcoholic, lush *(slang)*, boozer *(informal)*, toper, sot, soak *(slang)*, wino *(informal)*, inebriate, alko *or* alco *(Austral. slang)* • *A drunk lay in the alley.*

QUOTATIONS
Man, being reasonable, must get drunk;
The best of Life is but intoxication
[Lord Byron *Don Juan*]
It's the wise man who stays home when he's drunk
[Euripides *The Cyclops*]
Two things a man cannot hide: that he is drunk, and that he is in love
[Antiphanes]

drunkard = **drunk**, alcoholic, soak *(slang)*, drinker, lush *(slang)*, carouser, sot, tippler, toper, wino *(informal)*, dipsomaniac, alko *or* alco *(Austral. slang)* • *Although he liked a drink, he was never a drunkard.*

drunken 1 = **intoxicated**, smashed *(slang)*, drunk, flying *(slang)*, bombed *(slang)*, wasted *(slang)*, hammered *(slang)*, steaming *(slang)*, wrecked *(slang)*, out of it *(slang)*, boozing *(informal)*, blitzed *(slang)*, pissed *(Brit., Austral. & N.Z. slang)*, lit up *(slang)*, bladdered *(slang)*, under the influence *(informal)*, tippling, toping, red-nosed, legless *(informal)*, paralytic *(informal)*, steamboats *(Scot. slang)*, off your face *(slang)*, zonked *(slang)*, bibulous, blotto *(slang)*, inebriate, out to it *(Austral. & N.Z. slang)*, sottish, rat-arsed *(taboo slang)*, Brahms and Liszt *(slang)*, bevvied *(dialect)*, boozed-up *(slang)*, dronkverdriet *(S. African)*, elephants *(Austral. slang)*, kaylied *(Brit. slang)*, langered *(Irish slang)*, mashed *(Brit. slang)*, mullered *(slang)*, ossified *(Irish slang)*, sat *(S. African)*, stukkend *(S. African slang)*, trashed *(slang)*, broken *(S. African informal)*, Adrian Quist *(Austral. slang)*, (gin-)sodden • *Drunken yobs smashed shop windows.*
2 = **boozy**, dissipated *(informal)*, riotous, debauched, dionysian, orgiastic, bacchanalian, bacchic, saturnalian • *A loud, drunken party was raging nearby.*

drunkenness = **intoxication**, alcoholism, intemperance, inebriation, dipsomania, tipsiness, insobriety, bibulousness, sottishness • *Even in his drunkenness, he recognized her.*

QUOTATIONS
Drink moderately, for drunkenness neither keeps a secret, nor observes a promise
[Miguel de Cervantes *Don Quixote*]
What does drunkenness not accomplish? It unlocks secrets, confirms our hopes, urges the indolent into battle, lifts the burden from anxious minds, teaches new arts
[Horace *Epistles*]

dry AS AN ADJECTIVE 1 = **dehydrated**, dried-up, baked, arid, scorched, torrid, parched, desiccated, bone dry, waterless, rainless, juiceless, sapless, moistureless • *a hard, dry desert landscape*
OPPOSITES: wet, damp, moist
2 = **dried**, crisp, withered, brittle, shrivelled, crispy, parched, desiccated, sun-baked • *She heard the rustle of dry leaves.*
3 = **thirsty**, dehydrated, parched, dying of thirst, gasping,

longing for a drink • *She was suddenly dry.*
4 = **alcohol-free**, teetotal, abstinent, clean, on the wagon *(informal)*, prohibitionist, non-drinking • *Gujerat is a dry state.*
5 = **sarcastic**, cutting, sharp, keen, cynical, low-key, sly, sardonic, deadpan, droll, ironical, quietly humorous • *He is renowned for his dry wit.*
6 = **unemotional**, cool, impassive, cold, phlegmatic, unfeeling, undemonstrative, unexcitable • *The solicitor's dry voice*
7 = **dull**, boring, tedious, commonplace, dreary, tiresome, monotonous, run-of-the-mill, humdrum, unimaginative, uninteresting, mind-numbing, ho-hum *(informal)* • *The work was very dry and dull*
OPPOSITES: interesting, entertaining, lively
8 = **plain**, simple, bare, basic, pure, stark, unembellished • *an infuriating list of dry facts and dates*
9 = **dried out**, old, hard, stale, dehydrated, overcooked, past its best • *The meat was dry, shrunk on the bone*
▸ **AS A VERB** 1 = **drain**, make dry, remove the water from, wipe, dab dry, rub dry • *Wash and dry the lettuce.*
2 *often with* **out** = **dehydrate**, make dry, desiccate, bake, sear, parch, dehumidify, remove the moisture from • *They bought a machine to dry the wood and cut costs.*
OPPOSITES: wet, moisten
▸ **IN PHRASES: dry out** = **become sober**, give up drinking, give up alcohol, go on the wagon, become teetotal, overcome alcoholism • *He checked into hospital to dry out.*
dry out *or* **up** 1 = **become dry**, harden, wither, mummify, shrivel up, wizen • *The pollen dries up and becomes hard.*
2 = **dwindle**, decline, disappear, run out, diminish, decrease, lessen, wane, subside, ebb, die out, fade away, peter out, taper off • *Credit from foreign banks is drying up.*

dryness 1 = **aridity**, drought, dehydration, aridness, dehumidification, waterlessness, moisturelessness, parchedness • *the parched dryness of the air*
2 = **thirstiness**, thirst, desire for a drink, parchedness • *Symptoms include dryness of the mouth.*

dual = **twofold**, double, twin, matched, coupled, paired, duplicate, binary, duplex • *his dual role as head of party and state*

duality = **dualism**, dichotomy, polarity, doubleness, biformity, duplexity • *We live in a world of duality.*

dub 1 = **name**, call, term, style, label, nickname, designate, christen, denominate • *He dubbed her the most exciting woman in the world.*
2 = **knight**, entitle, confer knighthood upon • *a picture of him being dubbed 'Sir' Frank by a look-alike Queen*

dubious 1 = **suspect**, suspicious, crooked, dodgy *(Brit., Austral. & N.Z. informal)*, questionable, unreliable, shady *(informal)*, unscrupulous, fishy *(informal)*, disreputable, untrustworthy, undependable • *dubious business dealings*
OPPOSITES: reliable, dependable, trustworthy
2 = **unsure**, uncertain, suspicious, hesitating, doubtful, sceptical, tentative, wavering, hesitant, undecided, unconvinced, iffy *(informal)*, leery *(slang)*, distrustful, in two minds *(informal)* • *My parents were a bit dubious about it all.*
OPPOSITES: sure, certain, positive
3 = **doubtful**, questionable, ambiguous, debatable, moot, arguable, equivocal, open to question, disputable • *This is a very dubious honour.*

duck[1] 1 = **bob**, drop, lower, bend, bow, dodge, crouch, stoop • *He ducked in time to save his head from the blow.*
2 = **dodge**, avoid, escape, evade, elude, sidestep, circumvent, shirk, body-swerve *(Scot.)* • *He had ducked the confrontation.*
3 = **dunk**, wet, plunge, dip, submerge, immerse, douse, souse • *She splashed around in the pool trying to duck him.*

duck[2]
▸ **NAME OF MALE:** drake
▸ **NAME OF YOUNG:** duckling
▸ **COLLECTIVE NOUNS:** paddling, team

duct = **pipe**, channel, passage, tube, canal, funnel, conduit • *a big air duct in the ceiling*

dud **AS A NOUN** 1 = **imitation**, copy, reproduction, hoax, forgery, phoney *or* phony *(informal)* • *The mine was a dud.*
2 = **failure**, flop *(informal)*, washout *(informal)*, clinker *(slang, chiefly U.S.)*, clunker *(informal)* • *He's been a dud from day one.*
▸ **AS AN ADJECTIVE** 1 = **faulty**, broken, failed, damaged, bust *(informal)*, not working, useless, flawed, impaired, duff *(Brit. informal)*, worthless, defective, imperfect, malfunctioning, out of order, unsound, not functioning, valueless, on the blink, inoperative, kaput *(informal)* • *He replaced a dud valve.*
2 = **fake**, false, forged, sham, counterfeit, pinchbeck, phoney *or* phony *(informal)* • *He used a dud cheque to pay the bill.*

dudgeon
▸ **IN PHRASES: in high dudgeon** = **indignantly**, angrily, furiously, in a huff, resentfully • *He resigned in high dudgeon.*

due **AS AN ADJECTIVE** 1 = **expected**, scheduled, awaited, expected to arrive • *The results are due at the end of the month.*
2 = **fitting**, deserved, appropriate, just, right, becoming, fit, justified, suitable, merited, proper, obligatory, rightful, requisite, well-earned, bounden • *Treat them with due attention.*
3 = **payable**, outstanding, owed, owing, unsettled, unpaid, in arrears • *I've got a tax rebate due.*
▸ **AS A NOUN** = **right(s)**, privilege, entitlement, deserts, merits, prerogative, comeuppance *(informal)*, fair treatment, just punishment, deserved fate • *No doubt he felt it was his due.*
▸ **IN PHRASES: due to** 1 = **caused by**, attributable to, put down to, traceable to, ascribable to, assignable to, imputable to • *A lot of this will be due to his efforts.*
2 = **because of**, thanks to, as a result of, in view of, owing to, as a consequence of • *Jobs could be lost due to political changes.*
▸ **AS AN ADVERB** = **directly**, dead, straight, exactly, undeviatingly • *They headed due north.*

duel **AS A NOUN** 1 = **single combat**, fight, battle, confrontation, head-to-head, affair of honour • *He killed a man in a duel.*
2 = **contest**, fight, competition, clash, encounter, engagement, rivalry, head-to-head • *sporadic artillery duels*
▸ **AS A VERB** = **fight**, struggle, clash, compete, contest, contend, vie with, lock horns • *We duelled for two years.*

dues = **membership fee**, charges, fee, contribution, levy • *paid for out of membership dues*

duff **AS AN ADJECTIVE** = **bad**, poor, useless, pathetic, inferior, worthless, unsatisfactory, defective, deficient, imperfect, substandard, low-rent *(informal, chiefly U.S.)*, poxy *(slang)*, pants *(informal)*, bodger *or* bodgie *(Austral. slang)* • *A couple of duff tracks prevent this being a masterpiece.*
▸ **IN PHRASES: duff someone up** = **beat (up)**, attack, assault, batter, fill in *(Brit. slang)*, thrash, do over *(Brit., Austral. & N.Z. slang)*, work over *(slang)*, clobber *(slang)*, put the boot in *(slang)*, lambast(e), beat the living daylights out of *(informal)*, knock about *or* around, beat *or* knock seven bells out of *(informal)* • *The kids had duffed up the bus conductor.*

duffer = **clot**, blunderer *(Brit. informal)*, booby, clod, oaf, bungler, galoot *(slang, chiefly U.S.)*, lubber, lummox *(informal)* • *He was a duffer at cricket.*

dulcet = **sweet**, pleasing, musical, charming, pleasant, honeyed, delightful, soothing, agreeable, harmonious, melodious, mellifluous, euphonious, mellifluent • *her beautiful, dulcet voice*

dull **AS AN ADJECTIVE** 1 = **boring**, tedious, dreary, flat, dry, plain, commonplace, tiresome, monotonous, prosaic, run-of-the-mill, humdrum, unimaginative, dozy, uninteresting, mind-numbing, ho-hum *(informal)*, vapid, as dry as dust • *They can both be rather dull.*
OPPOSITES: interesting, exciting

d

d

DRUGS

Drugs

acetanilide *or* acetanilid
acriflavine
allopurinol
aloin
alum *or* potash alum
amitriptyline
amphetamine, Benzedrine *(trademark)*, *or (slang)* speed
ampicillin
amyl nitrite *or (slang)* popper
Amytal *(trademark)*
Antabuse *(trademark)*
antipyrine
apomorphine
araroba *or* Goa powder
Argyrol *(trademark)*
arsphenamine
aspirin *or* acetylsalicylic acid
atropine *or* atropin
azathioprine
azedarach
bacitracin
barbitone *or (U.S.)* barbital
barbiturate
belladonna
Benadryl *(trademark)*
benzocaine
benzodiazepine
berberine
bhang *or* bang
bitter aloes
bromal
bupivacaine
caffeine
calomel
cannabis
cantharides
carbamazepine
carbimazole
cascara sagrada
chlorambucil
chloramphenicol
chlordiazepoxide
chloroquine
chlorothiazide
chlorpromazine
chlorpropamide
chlortetracycline
chlorthalidone
chrysarobin
cinchona
cinchonine
cocaine, cocain, *or (slang)* coke *or* Charlie
codeine
contrayerva
cortisone
co-trimoxazole
crystal methamphetamine *or (informal)* crystal meth
curare *or* curari
cyclopropane
cyclosporin-A
dapsone
DET *or* diethyltryptamine
dextroamphetamine
digitalis
dimenhydrinate *or* Dramamine *(trademark)*
disulfiram
ecstasy
DMT *or* dimethyltryptamine
ephedrin *or* ephedrine
fentanyl
ganja
gemfibrozil
hashish *or* charas
hemlock
hemp
heroin *or* diamorphine
hydrocortisone *or* cortisol
hyoscyamine
ibuprofen
imipramine
indomethacin
ipecac *or* ipecacuanha
ivermectin
kaolin *or* kaoline
ketamine
laudanum
Librium *(trademark)*
LSD, lysergic acid diethylamide, *or (slang)* acid
marijuana *or* marihuana
MDMA
mecamylamine
mepacrine, quinacrine *(U.S.)*, Atebrin *(trademark)*, *or* Atabrine *U.S. trademark*
meperidine *or* meperidene hydrochloride
merbromin
mercaptopurine
mescaline *or* mescalin
methadone *or* methadon
methamphetamine
methicillin
methotrexate
methyldopa
Mogadon *(trademark)*
morphine *or* morphia
neomycin
nepenthe
nicotine
nitrazepam
nitrous oxide, dinitrogen oxide, *or* laughing gas
Novocaine *(trademark) or* procaine hydrochloride
nux vomica
opium
Paludrine *(trademark)*
paracetamol
paraldehyde
paregoric
PCP *(trademark)*, phencyclidine, *or (informal)* angel dust
penicillin
pentamidine
pentaquine
pentazocine
pentobarbitone sodium, sodium pentabarbital *(U.S.)*, *or* Nembutal *(trademark)*
pentylenetetrazol
phenacaine
phenacetin *or* acetophenetidin
phenformin
phenobarbitone
phenolphthalein
phenothiazine
phenylbutazone
phenytoin
poppy
prednisolene
prednisone
primaquine
promethazine
propranolol
Prozac *(trademark)*
psilocybin
quercetin *or* quercitin
quinidine
quinine
reserpine
rhatany *or* krameria
rifampicin *or (U.S.)* rifampin
safflower *or* false saffron
salicin *or* salicine
saloop
salts
sanguinaria
santonin
scammony
scopolamine *or* hyoscine
scopoline
Seidlitz powder, Seidlitz powders, *or* Rochelle powder
senna leaf
senna pods
squill
STP
stramonium
streptomycin
sulphadiazine
sulphadimidine *or (U.S.)* sulfamethazine
sulpha drug
sulphanilamide
sulphathiozole
sulphisoxazole
temazepam
terebene
Terramycin *(trademark)*
tetracycline
thalidomide
thiopentone sodium, thiopental sodium, *or* Sodium Pentothal *(trademark)*
thiouracil
tricyclic
turpeth
valerian
Valium *(trademark) or* diazepam
verapamil
Viagra *(trademark)*
vinblastine

Drugs (continued)

vinca alkaloid
vincristine
witch hazel *or* wych hazel
wormseed
yohimbine
zidovudine *or* Retrovir *(trademark)*

Types of drug

abirritant
abortifacient
ACE inhibitor
adjuvant
agrypnotic
alexipharmic
alkylating agent
alterative
anaesthetic *or (U.S.)* anesthetic
analeptic
analgesic
anaphrodisiac
anodyne
antagonist
antibiotic
anticholinergic
anticonvulsant
antidepressant
antidote
antiemetic
antifebrile
antihistamine
anti-inflammatory
antimalarial
antimetabolite
antimycotic
antiperiodic
antiphlogistic
antipyretic
antispasmodic
antitussive
anxiolytic
aphrodisiac
astringent
ataractic *or* ataraxic
attenuant
beta-blocker
bronchodilator
calcium antagonist *or* blocker
calmative
cardiac
carminative
cathartic
cholagogue
cimetedine
cisplatin
clomiphene
colestipol
contraceptive
convulsant
cytotoxin
decongestant
demulcent
depressant
depressomotor
diaphoretic
diuretic
ecbolic
emetic
emmenagogue
errhine
euphoriant
excitant
expectorant
expellant *or* expellent
febrifuge
general anaesthetic *or (U.S.)* general anesthetic
haemagogue *or (U.S.)* hemagogue *or* hemagog
haemostatic *or (U.S.)* hemostatic
hallucinogen
hepatic
hypnotic
immunosuppressive
inotropic
laxative
lenitive
local anaesthetic *or (U.S.)* local anesthetic
masticatory
miticide
narcotic
nervine
neuroleptic
NSAID *or* nonsteroidal anti-inflammatory drug
opiate
oxytocic
painkiller
palliative
pectoral
preventive
prophylactic
psychedelic *or* psychodelic
psychoactive
psychotomimetic
pulmonic *(rare)*
purgative
radio mimetic
recreational
relaxant
resolvent
restorative
revulsive
roborant
sedative
sialagogue *or* sialogogue
soporific
sorbefacient
spermicide *or (less commonly)* spermatocide
steroid
stimulant
stupefacient
styptic
suppurative
sympatholytic
sympathomimetic
synergist
taeniacide *or (U.S.)* teniacide
taeniafuge *or (U.S.)* teniafuge
tetanic
tonic
tranquillizer, tranquilliser, *or (U.S.)* tranquilizer
tumefacient
vasoconstrictor
vasodilator
vasoinhibitor
vermifuge, anthelminthic, anthelmintic, *or* helminthic
vesicant *or* vesicatory
vomit
vulnerary

General drug terms

absorption
addiction
addictive
adiaphorous
ana
antimonial
aromatic
arsenical
autacoid
bacterin
bioassay
bioavailability
biological
blockade
botanical
chalybeate
chemoprophylaxis
cohobate
confection
contraindicate
control group
decoction
dependency
designer drug
dosage
dose
electuary
elixir
embrocation
emulsion
endermic
ethical
excipient
exhaust
external
extract
fluidextract
galenical
glycoside
hard
hypersensitive
hypodermic
hypodermic needle
hypodermic syringe
idiosyncrasy
incompatible
inhalant
intermediate-acting
intoxicating
lethal dose *or* LD
linctus
liquor
local
long-acting
magistral
mass
median lethal dose *or* mean lethal dose
medication
menstruum
mercurial
mind-expanding
minimum lethal dose *or* MLD
mixture
normal
officinal *(obsolete)*
oleoresin
oral
overdose
over-the-counter
parenteral
pessary
placebo
positive

General drug terms (continued)

potentiate
prescription
proprietary
reaction
reactor
remedy
route
sensitivity
sensitize *or* sensitise
short-acting
side effect
signature *(U.S.)*
soft
spansule
specific
spirit
suppository
tincture
succedaneum
synergism *or* synergy
tachyphylaxis
tolerant
topical
trituration
unit
unofficial
vehicle
venipuncture *or* venepuncture
vinegar
wafer
wine
withdrawal

Drug abuse terms

acid
acidhead
angel dust
blow
blow someone's mind
bombed
bong
bring down
bummer
burned
bust
buzz
Charlie
chillum
coke
cold turkey
comedown
connection
cook up
cop
crack
crackhead
crank up
dadah *(Austral., slang)*
dealer
do
dope
downer
drop
dry out
ecstasy *or* E
fix
freebase
gear
get off
get through *(U.S.)*
glue-sniffing
gone
goof
goofball *(U.S.)*
grass
habit
hash
head
high
hit
hooked
hop *(obsolete)*
hophead *(chiefly U.S.)*
hop up *(dated)*
hype
hyped up
jack up
jag
jellies
joint
joypop
junk
junkie
kick
kif
knockout drops
line
lit up
loaded *(chiefly U.S. & Canad.)*
magic mushroom
mainline
make it
Man *(U.S.)*
Mickey Finn
mind-expanding
monkey *(U.S. & Canad.)*
nail
narc *(U.S.)*
nod out
number
OD *or* overdose
opium den
pep pill
pop
popper
pot
pothead
pusher
reefer
roach
score
shooting gallery
shoot up
skin-pop
skin up
smack
smackhead
smashed
smoke
snort
snowball
solvent abuse
space cadet
spaced out *or* spaced
speed
speedball
speedfreak
spliff
stash
step on
stoned
strung out
stuff
swacked
switch on
tab
toke
toot
trip
turn on
upper
user
wasted
weight
withdrawal
withdrawal symptoms
wrap
wrecked
zonked

2 = lifeless, dead, heavy, slow, indifferent, sluggish, insensitive, apathetic, listless, unresponsive, passionless, insensible • *We all feel dull and sleepy between 1 and 3pm.*
opposites: active, lively, full of beans *(informal)*
3 = drab, faded, muted, subdued, feeble, murky, sombre, toned-down, subfusc • *The stamp was a dull blue colour.*
4 = cloudy, dim, gloomy, dismal, overcast, leaden, turbid • *It's always dull and raining.*
opposites: bright
5 = muted, faint, suppressed, subdued, stifled, muffled, indistinct • *The coffin was closed with a dull thud.*
6 = blunt, dulled, blunted, not keen, not sharp, edgeless, unsharpened • *using the dull edge of her knife*
opposites: sharp, pointed
▸ **as a verb 1 = relieve**, blunt, lessen, moderate, soften, alleviate, allay, mitigate, assuage, take the edge off, palliate • *They gave him morphine to dull the pain.*
2 = cloud over, darken, grow dim, become cloudy • *Her eyes dulled and she gazed blankly.*
3 = dampen, reduce, check, depress, moderate, discourage, stifle, lessen, smother, sadden, dishearten, dispirit, deject • *Her illness failed to dull her optimism.*

dullness 1 = tediousness, monotony, banality, flatness, dreariness, vapidity, insipidity • *the dullness of their routine life*
opposites: interest, colour, liveliness
2 = stupidity, thickness, slowness, dimness, obtuseness, doziness *(Brit. informal)*, dim-wittedness, dopiness *(slang)* • *his dullness of mind*
opposites: intelligence, brightness, sharpness
3 = drabness, greyness, dimness, gloominess, dinginess, colourlessness • *the dullness of an old painting*
opposites: brilliance, brightness, shine

duly 1 = properly, fittingly, correctly, appropriately, accordingly, suitably, deservedly, rightfully, decorously, befittingly • *He duly apologized for his behaviour.*
2 = on time, promptly, in good time, punctually, at the stated time, at the proper time • *The engineer duly arrived, expecting to have to repair the boiler.*

dumb as an adjective 1 = unable to speak, mute, without the power of speech • *a young deaf and dumb man*
opposites: articulate
2 = silent, mute, speechless, inarticulate, tongue-tied, wordless, voiceless, soundless, at a loss for words, mum • *We were all struck dumb for a minute.*
3 = stupid, thick, dull, foolish, dense, dozy *(Brit. informal)*, dim, obtuse, unintelligent, asinine, braindead *(informal)*, dim-witted *(informal)* • *I came up with this dumb idea.*
opposites: bright, smart, clever
▸ **in phrases: dumb something down = trivialize**, sensationalize, make shallow, make superficial, make trivial, make frivolous, make less intelligent • *I know it must be tempting to dumb down news.*

dumbfound = amaze, stun, astonish, confuse, overwhelm, stagger, startle, bewilder, astound, confound, take aback, bowl over *(informal)*, flummox, nonplus, flabbergast *(informal)* • *The question dumbfounded him.*

dumbfounded = amazed, stunned, astonished, confused, overcome, overwhelmed, staggered, thrown, startled, at sea, dumb, bewildered, astounded, breathless, confounded, taken aback, speechless, bowled over *(informal)*, gobsmacked *(Brit. slang)*, flabbergasted *(informal)*, nonplussed, lost for words, flummoxed, thunderstruck, knocked sideways *(informal)*, knocked for six *(informal)* • *I stood there dumbfounded.*

dummy as a noun 1 = model, figure, mannequin, form, manikin, lay figure • *a shop-window dummy*
2 = imitation, copy, duplicate, sham, counterfeit, replica • *The police video camera was a dummy.*

3 = **fool**, jerk *(slang, chiefly U.S. & Canad.)*, idiot, plank *(Brit. slang)*, charlie *(Brit. informal)*, berk *(Brit. slang)*, prick *(slang)*, wally *(slang)*, prat *(slang)*, plonker *(slang)*, coot, geek *(slang)*, dunce, oaf, simpleton, dullard, dimwit *(informal)*, dipstick *(Brit. slang)*, dickhead *(slang)*, gonzo *(slang)*, schmuck *(U.S. slang)*, dork *(slang)*, nitwit *(informal)*, dolt, blockhead, divvy *(Brit. slang)*, pillock *(Brit. slang)*, dweeb *(U.S. slang)*, putz *(U.S. slang)*, fathead *(informal)*, weenie *(U.S. informal)*, eejit *(Scot. & Irish)*, thicko *(Brit. slang)*, dumb-ass *(slang)*, gobshite *(Irish taboo slang)*, numpty *(Scot. informal)*, doofus *(slang, chiefly U. S.)*, lamebrain *(informal)*, fuckwit *(taboo slang)*, dickwit *(slang)*, nerd *or* nurd *(slang)*, numbskull *or* numskull, dorba *or* dorb *(Austral. slang)*, bogan *(Austral. slang)* • *He's no dummy, this guy.*

▸ **AS A MODIFIER** = **imitation**, false, fake, artificial, mock, bogus, simulated, sham, phoney *or* phony *(informal)* • *Soldiers were still using dummy guns.*

dummy run = **practice**, trial, dry run • *They do a dummy run with the brakes.*

dump **AS A VERB** 1 = **drop**, stick *(informal)*, deposit, set down, bung *(informal)*, throw down, park *(informal)*, plonk *(informal)*, let fall, fling down • *We dumped our bags on the table.*

2 = **get rid of**, tip, discharge, discard, dispose of, unload, jettison, empty out, coup *(Scot.)*, throw away *or* out • *Untreated sewage is dumped into the sea.*

3 = **scrap**, axe *(informal)*, get rid of, abolish, junk *(informal)*, put an end to, discontinue, jettison, put paid to • *Ministers believed it was vital to dump the tax.*

4 = **jilt**, drop, abandon, desert, ditch *(slang)*, betray, discard, throw over, leave (someone) in the lurch • *She was dumped by her long-term lover.*

▸ **AS A NOUN** 1 = **rubbish tip**, tip, dumping ground, scrapyard, junkyard, rubbish heap, refuse heap • *The walled garden was used as a dump.*

2 = **pigsty**, hole *(informal)*, joint *(slang)*, slum, shack, shanty, hovel • *'What a dump!' she said.*

dumps **IN PHRASES: down in the dumps** = **down**, low, blue, sad, unhappy, low-spirited, discouraged, fed up, moody, pessimistic, melancholy, glum, dejected, despondent, dispirited, downcast, morose, crestfallen, downhearted • *She's feeling a bit down in the dumps.*

dumpy = **podgy**, homely, short, plump, squat, stout, chunky, chubby, tubby, roly-poly, pudgy, squab, fubsy *(archaic or dialect)* • *She was a dumpy woman, dressed in black.*

dun **AS A NOUN**

▸ **AS AN ADJECTIVE** = **muddy coloured**, khaki, brownish, mousy, greyish-brown • *her dun mare*

▹ *See panel* **Shades of brown**

dunce = **simpleton**, moron, duffer *(informal)*, bonehead *(slang)*, loon *(informal)*, goose *(informal)*, ass, donkey, oaf, dullard, dimwit *(informal)*, ignoramus, nitwit *(informal)*, dolt, blockhead, halfwit, nincompoop, fathead *(informal)*, dunderhead, lamebrain *(informal)*, thickhead, numbskull *or* numskull • *He was a dunce at mathematics.*

dune = **hillock**, down *(archaic)*, mound, mount, drift, elevation, knoll, brae *(Scot.)* • *They climbed a very large dune.*

dung = **manure**, compost, fertilizer, droppings, muck, excrement, ordure • *two ox-carts laden with dung*

dungeon = **prison**, cell, cage, vault, lockup, oubliette, calaboose *(U.S. informal)*, donjon, boob *(Austral. slang)* • *the ceiling of the tiny dungeon*

dunlin

▸ **COLLECTIVE NOUN:** flight

dunny = **toilet**, lavatory, bathroom, loo *(Brit. informal)*, W.C., bog *(slang)*, Gents *or* Ladies, can *(U.S. & Canad. slang)*, john *(slang, chiefly U.S. & Canad.)*, head(s) *(Nautical slang)*, throne *(informal)*, closet, privy, cloakroom *(Brit.)*, urinal, latrine, washroom, powder room, crapper *(taboo slang)*, water closet, khazi *(slang)*, pissoir *(French)*, little boy's room *or* little girl's room *(informal)*, (public) convenience, bogger *(Austral. slang)*, brasco *(Austral. slang)* • *people who don't wash their hands after using the dunny*

duo = **partnership**, couple, pair, duet, twosome • *the famous singing and dancing duo*

dupe **AS A NOUN** 1 = **victim**, mug *(Brit. slang)*, sucker *(slang)*, pigeon *(slang)*, sap *(slang)*, gull, pushover *(slang)*, fall guy *(informal)*, simpleton • *an innocent dupe in a political scandal*

2 = **puppet**, tool, instrument, pawn, stooge *(slang)*, cat's-paw • *He was accused of being a dupe of the communists.*

▸ **AS A VERB** = **deceive**, trick, cheat, con *(informal)*, kid *(informal)*, sting *(informal)*, rip off *(slang)*, hoax, defraud, beguile, gull *(archaic)*, delude, swindle, outwit, bamboozle *(informal)*, hoodwink, take for a ride *(informal)*, pull a fast one on *(informal)*, cozen, scam *(slang)* • *Some of the offenders duped the psychologists.*

duplicate **AS AN ADJECTIVE** = **identical**, matched, matching, twin, corresponding, twofold • *a duplicate copy*

▸ **AS A NOUN** 1 = **copy**, facsimile • *I've lost my card and have to get a duplicate.*

2 = **photocopy**, copy, reproduction, replica, Xerox *(trademark)*, carbon copy, Photostat *(trademark)* • *Enclosed is a duplicate of the invoice we sent you last month.*

▸ **AS A VERB** 1 = **repeat**, reproduce, echo, copy, clone, replicate • *Scientists hope the work done can be duplicated elswhere.*

2 = **copy**, photocopy, Xerox *(trademark)*, Photostat *(trademark)* • *He was duplicating some articles.*

duplication = **copying**, reproduction, photocopying, xeroxing, replication, photostating • *the illegal duplication of documents*

duplicity = **deceit**, fraud, deception, hypocrisy, dishonesty, guile, artifice, falsehood, double-dealing, chicanery, perfidy, dissimulation • *He was guilty of duplicity in his private dealings.*

OPPOSITES: honesty, candour, straightforwardness

durable 1 = **hard-wearing**, strong, tough, sound, substantial, reliable, resistant, sturdy, long-lasting, well made, imperishable, made to last • *Fine bone china is strong and durable.*

OPPOSITES: weak, delicate, fragile

2 = **enduring**, lasting, permanent, continuing, firm, fast, fixed, constant, abiding, dependable, unwavering, unfaltering • *We were unable to establish any durable agreement.*

duration = **length**, time, period, term, stretch, extent, spell, span, time frame, timeline • *the duration of the trial*

duress = **pressure**, threat, constraint, compulsion, coercion • *Her confession had been made under duress.*

during = **throughout**, through, in the course of, throughout the time of • *Plants need to be looked after during bad weather.*

dusk 1 = **twilight**, evening, evo *(Austral. slang)*, nightfall, sunset, dark, sundown, eventide, gloaming *(Scot. poetic)* • *We arrived home at dusk.*

OPPOSITES: morning, dawn, daybreak

2 = **shade**, darkness, gloom, obscurity, murk, shadowiness • *She turned and disappeared into the dusk.*

dusky 1 = **dim**, twilight, shady, shadowy, gloomy, murky, cloudy, overcast, crepuscular, darkish, twilit, tenebrous, caliginous *(archaic)* • *He was walking down the road one dusky evening.*

2 = **dark**, swarthy, dark-complexioned • *I could see dusky girls with flowers about their necks.*

dust **AS A NOUN** 1 = **grime**, grit, powder, powdery dirt • *I could see a thick layer of dust on the stairs.*

2 = **earth**, ground, soil, dirt, clay • *Your trousers will get dirty if you sit down in the dust.*

3 = **particles**, soot, smut, fine fragments • *The air was black with coal dust.*

▸ **AS A VERB** 1 = **remove dust from**, clean, sweep, brush, wipe, mop • *I dusted and polished the living room.*

2 = sprinkle, cover, powder, spread, spray, scatter, sift, dredge • *Lightly dust the fish with flour.*
▸ IN PHRASES: **bite the dust = fail**, flop *(informal)*, fall through, be unsuccessful, go down, founder, fall flat, come to nothing, fizzle out *(informal)*, come unstuck, run aground, come to grief, come a cropper *(informal)*, go up in smoke, go belly-up *(slang)*, come to naught, not make the grade *(informal)*, meet with disaster • *Her first marriage bit the dust because of irreconcilable differences.*
▸ RELATED PHOBIA: amathophobia

dust-up = fight, conflict, argument, set-to *(informal)*, encounter, brush, scrap *(informal)*, quarrel, skirmish, tussle, punch-up *(Brit. informal)*, fracas, shindig *(informal)*, biffo *(Austral. slang)*, boilover *(Austral.)* • *He had a dust-up with the referee.*

d

dusty 1 = dirty, grubby, unclean, unswept, undusted • *The books looked dusty and unused.*
2 = powdery, sandy, chalky, crumbly, granular, friable • *Inside the box was only a dusty substance.*

dutiful = conscientious, devoted, obedient, respectful, compliant, submissive, docile, deferential, reverential, filial, punctilious, duteous *(archaic)* • *The days of the dutiful wife are over.*
OPPOSITES: uncaring, disrespectful, disobedient

duty AS A NOUN **1 = responsibility**, job, task, work, calling, business, service, office, charge, role, function, mission, province, obligation, assignment, pigeon *(informal)*, onus • *My duty is to look after the animals.*
2 = tax, customs, toll, levy, tariff, excise, due, impost • *Duty on imports would also be reduced.*
▸ IN PHRASES: **be the duty of** *or* **be someone's duty = be up to** *(informal)*, rest with, behove *(archaic)*, be (someone's) pigeon *(Brit. informal)*, be incumbent upon, devolve upon • *It is the duty of the state to maintain the educational system.*
off duty = off work, off, free, on holiday, not working, on leave, at leisure • *I'm off duty.*
on duty = at work, working, busy, engaged, on call, on active service • *Extra staff had been put on duty.*

QUOTATIONS

Our duty is to be useful, not according to our desires but according to our powers
[Henri Frédéric Amiel *Journal*]

Without duty, life is soft and boneless; it cannot hold itself together
[Joseph Joubert *Pensées*]

When a stupid man is doing something that he is ashamed of, he always declares that it is his duty
[George Bernard Shaw *Caesar and Cleopatra*]

Do your duty, and leave the outcome to the Gods
[Pierre Corneille *Horace*]

England expects that every man will do his duty
[Horatio Nelson *signal at the Battle of Trafalgar*]

Duty, honour! We make these words say whatever we want, the same as we do with parrots
[Alfred Capus *Mariage Bourgeois*]

dwarf AS A NOUN **= gnome**, midget, Lilliputian, Tom Thumb, munchkin *(informal, chiefly U.S.)*, homunculus, manikin, hop-o'-my-thumb, pygmy *or* pigmy • *With the aid of magic the dwarfs created a wonderful rope.*

SNOW WHITE'S SEVEN DWARFS

Bashful	Dopey	Happy	Sneezy
Doc	Grumpy	Sleepy	

▸ AS A MODIFIER **= miniature**, small, baby, tiny, pocket, dwarfed, diminutive, petite, bonsai, pint-sized, undersized, teeny-weeny, Lilliputian, teensy-weensy • *dwarf shrubs*
▸ AS A VERB **1 = tower above** *or* **over**, dominate, overlook, stand over, loom over, stand head and shoulders above • *The huge sign dwarfed his figure.*
2 = eclipse, tower above *or* over, put in the shade, diminish • *completely dwarfing the achievements of others*

dwell AS A VERB **= live**, stay, reside, rest, quarter, settle, lodge, abide, hang out *(informal)*, sojourn, establish yourself • *He dwells in the mountains.*
▸ IN PHRASES: **dwell on** *or* **upon something = go on about**, emphasize *(informal)*, elaborate on, linger over, harp on about, be engrossed in, expatiate on, continue to think about, tarry over • *I'd rather not dwell on the past.*

dweller = inhabitant, resident, citizen, denizen, indweller • *The number of city dwellers is growing.*

dwelling = home, house, residence, abode, quarters, establishment, lodging, pad *(slang)*, habitation, domicile, dwelling house, whare *(N.Z.)* • *Three thousand new dwellings are planned.*

dwindle = lessen, fall, decline, contract, sink, fade, weaken, shrink, diminish, decrease, decay, wither, wane, subside, ebb, die down, die out, abate, shrivel, peter out, die away, waste away, taper off, grow less • *The factory's workforce has dwindled.*
OPPOSITES: increase, grow, develop

dye AS A NOUN **= colouring**, colour, pigment, wash, stain, tint, tinge, colorant • *bottles of hair dye*
▸ AS A VERB **= colour**, stain, tint, shade, tinge, pigment, tincture, colour-wash • *The woman spun and dyed the wool.*

dyed-in-the-wool = confirmed, complete, established, entrenched, die-hard, deep-rooted, through-and-through, inveterate, deep-dyed *(usually derogatory)* • *He was a dyed-in-the-wool conservative.*

dying 1 = near death, going, failing, fading, doomed, expiring, ebbing, near the end, moribund, fading fast, in extremis *(Latin)*, at death's door, not long for this world, on your deathbed, terminally ill, breathing your last • *He is a dying man.*
2 = final, last, parting, departing • *the dying wishes of her mother*
3 = failing, declining, sinking, foundering, diminishing, decreasing, dwindling, subsiding • *Shipbuilding is a dying business.*

dyke = wall, barrier, dam, enclosure, palisade • *I then slid down the side of the dyke.*

dynamic = energetic, spirited, powerful, active, vital, driving, electric, go-ahead, lively, magnetic, vigorous, animated, high-powered, forceful, go-getting *(informal)*, tireless, indefatigable, high-octane *(informal)*, zippy *(informal)*, full of beans *(informal)* • *He seemed a dynamic and energetic leader.*
OPPOSITES: sluggish, inactive, apathetic

dynamism = energy, go *(informal)*, drive, push *(informal)*, initiative, enterprise, pep, zip *(informal)*, vigour, zap *(slang)*, welly *(slang)*, get-up-and-go *(informal)*, brio, liveliness, forcefulness • *a situation that calls for dynamism and new thinking*

dynasty = empire, house, rule, regime, sovereignty • *The dynasty was founded in 1094.*

Ee

each AS AN ADJECTIVE **= every**, every single • *Each book is beautifully illustrated.*
▸ AS A PRONOUN **= every one**, all, each one, each and every one, one and all • *Three doctors each had a different diagnosis.*
▸ AS AN ADVERB **= apiece**, individually, singly, for each, to each, respectively, per person, from each, per head, per capita • *The children were given one each.*

eager 1 *often with* **to** *or* **for = anxious**, keen, raring, hungry, intent, yearning, impatient, itching, thirsty, zealous • *Robert was eager to talk about life in the Army.*
OPPOSITES: opposed, unconcerned, unenthusiastic
2 **= keen**, interested, earnest, intense, enthusiastic, passionate, ardent, avid *(informal)*, fervent, zealous, fervid, keen as mustard, bright-eyed and bushy-tailed *(informal)* • *He looked at the crowd of eager faces around him.*
OPPOSITES: indifferent, unimpressed, uninterested

eagerness 1 **= longing**, anxiety, hunger, yearning, zeal, impatience, impetuosity, avidity • *an eagerness to learn*
2 **= passion**, interest, enthusiasm, intensity, fervour, ardour, earnestness, keenness, heartiness, thirst, intentness • *the voice of a woman speaking with breathless eagerness*

eagle
▸ RELATED ADJECTIVE: aquiline
▸ NAME OF YOUNG: eaglet
▸ NAME OF HOME: eyrie or aerie

ear AS A NOUN 1 **= sensitivity**, taste, discrimination, appreciation, musical perception • *He has a fine ear for music.*
2 **= attention**, hearing, regard, notice, consideration, observation, awareness, heed • *The lobbyists have the ear of influential western leaders.*
▸ IN PHRASES: **bend someone's ear = nag**, annoy, harass, hassle *(informal)*, badger *(slang)*, pester • *He was fed up with people bending his ear about staying on at school.*
be out on your ear = be dismissed, be removed, be fired *(informal)*, be sacked *(informal)*, be sent packing *(informal)*, get your P45 *(informal)* • *We'd have been out on our ears if we'd complained.*
lend an ear = listen, pay attention, heed, take notice, pay heed, hearken *(archaic)*, give ear • *Please lend an ear for a moment or two.*
play it by ear = improvise, wing it *(informal)*, ad-lib, extemporize • *I don't have a plan for my life. I just play it by ear.*
turn a deaf ear to something = ignore, reject, overlook, neglect, disregard, pass over, take no notice of, be oblivious to, pay no attention to, give the cold shoulder to • *He has resolutely turned a deaf ear to demands for action.*
▸ TECHNICAL NAMES: auricle, pinna
▸ RELATED ADJECTIVES: aural, auricular, otic
▹ *See panel* **Parts of the ear**

earlier AS AN ADVERB **= before**, previously • *For reasons mentioned earlier, I will not be able to attend.*
▸ AS AN ADJECTIVE **= previous**, former, past, prior, preceding • *Earlier reports of gunshots have not been confirmed.*

earliest = first, opening, original, initial • *This is the earliest confirmed case of AIDS in the world.*

early AS AN ADVERB 1 **= in good time**, beforehand, ahead of schedule, in advance, with time to spare, betimes *(archaic)* • *She arrived early to get a good seat.*
OPPOSITES: late, behind
2 **= too soon**, before the usual time, prematurely, ahead of time • *The snow came early that year.*
OPPOSITES: late, behind
▸ AS AN ADJECTIVE 1 **= first**, opening, earliest, initial, introductory • *the book's early chapters*
2 **= premature**, forward, advanced, untimely, unseasonable • *I decided to take early retirement.*
OPPOSITES: overdue, belated, tardy
3 **= primitive**, first, earliest, young, original, undeveloped, primordial, primeval • *early man's cultural development*
OPPOSITES: seasoned, developed, mature

PROVERBS
The early bird catches the worm
Early to bed and early to rise, makes a man healthy, wealthy, and wise

earmark 1 **= set aside**, reserve, label, flag, tag, allocate, designate, mark out, keep back • *Extra money has been earmarked for the new projects.*
2 **= mark out**, identify, designate • *The pit was one of the 31 earmarked for closure by the Trade and Industry Secretary.*

earn 1 **= be paid**, make, get, receive, draw, gain, net, collect, bring in, gross, procure, clear, get paid, take home • *The dancers can earn up to £130 for each session.*
2 **= deserve**, win, gain, attain, justify, merit, warrant, be entitled to, reap, be worthy of • *Companies must earn a reputation for honesty.*

earnest AS AN ADJECTIVE 1 **= serious**, keen, grave, intense,

PARTS OF THE EAR

ancus
auditory nerve
cochlea
eardrum, tympanic membrane, *or* tympanum
ear lobe
Eustachian tube
external auditory canal
incus
malleus
meatus *or* auditory canal
organ of Corti
oval window
pinna
round window
saccule
semicircular canals
stapes
tragus
utricle

steady, dedicated, eager, enthusiastic, passionate, sincere, thoughtful, solemn, ardent, fervent, impassioned, zealous, staid, keen as mustard • *Ella was a pious, earnest young woman.*
OPPOSITES: trifling, frivolous, flippant
2 = **determined**, firm, dogged, constant, urgent, intent, persistent, ardent, persevering, resolute, heartfelt, zealous, vehement, wholehearted • *Despite their earnest efforts, they failed to win support.*
OPPOSITES: indifferent, unconcerned, half-hearted
▸ **IN PHRASES: in earnest** 1 = **seriously**, resolutely, earnestly, wholeheartedly • *Campaigning will begin in earnest tomorrow.*
2 = **genuine**, serious, sincere, honest, dinkum *(Austral. & N.Z. informal)*, not joking • *I can never tell whether he is in earnest or not.*

earnestly 1 = **seriously**, truly, sincerely, in earnest, in all sincerity • *'Do you really mean it?' she asked earnestly.*
2 = **genuinely**, keenly, eagerly, passionately, enthusiastically, fervently, ardently, fanatically, devotedly • *I earnestly hope what I learned will serve me well in my new job.*
3 = **sincerely**, really, truly, honestly, wholeheartedly, in all sincerity, from the bottom of your heart • *He is earnestly pursuing these objectives.*

earnestness 1 = **seriousness**, resolution, passion, enthusiasm, warmth, gravity, urgency, zeal, sincerity, fervour, eagerness, ardour, keenness • *He spoke with intense earnestness.*
2 = **determination**, resolve, urgency, zeal, ardour, vehemence • *the earnestness of their struggle for freedom*

earnings = **income**, pay, wages, revenue, reward, proceeds, salary, receipts, return, remuneration, takings, stipend, take-home pay, emolument, gross pay, net pay • *He was satisfied with his earnings as an accountant.*

earth 1 = **world**, planet, globe, sphere, orb, earthly sphere, terrestrial sphere • *The space shuttle returned safely to earth today.*
2 = **ground**, land, dry land, terra firma • *The earth shook under our feet.*
3 = **soil**, ground, land, dust, mould, clay, dirt, turf, sod, silt, topsoil, clod, loam • *The road winds through parched earth, scrub and cactus.*
▸ **RELATED ADJECTIVES:** tellurian, telluric, terrene, terrestrial

QUOTATIONS

To see the earth as we now see it, small and beautiful in that eternal silence where it floats, is to see ourselves as riders on the earth together, brothers on that bright loveliness in the unending night
[Archibald MacLeish *Riders on Earth*]

LAYERS OF THE EARTH'S CRUST

asthenosphere	lower mantle	sima
basement	Mohorovicíc	sial
continental crust	discontinuity	transition zone
lithosphere	oceanic crust	upper mantle

earthenware = **crockery**, pots, ceramics, pottery, terracotta, crocks, faience, maiolica • *colourful Italian china and earthenware*

earthly 1 = **worldly**, material, physical, secular, mortal, mundane, terrestrial, temporal, human, materialistic, profane, telluric, sublunary, non-spiritual, tellurian, terrene • *They lived in an earthly paradise.*
OPPOSITES: heavenly, spiritual, unearthly
2 = **sensual**, worldly, base, physical, gross, low, fleshly, bodily, vile, sordid, carnal • *He has forsworn all earthly pleasures for the duration of a season.*
3 = **possible**, likely, practical, feasible, conceivable, imaginable • *What earthly reason would they have for lying?*

earthquake = **earth tremor**, quake *(informal)*, tremor, seism • *the catastrophic Mexican earthquake of 1985*
▸ **RELATED ADJECTIVE:** seismic

earth-shattering = **momentous**, shocking, historic, decisive, pivotal, seismic, apocalyptic, fateful, epoch-making, earth-shaking • *the earth-shattering news of his death*

earthworm
▸ **RELATED ADJECTIVE:** lumbricoid

earthy 1 = **direct**, simple, natural, plain, rough, straightforward, robust, down-to-earth, frank, uninhibited, unsophisticated, unrefined • *Denise was a warm, earthy peasant woman with a lively spirit.*
2 = **crude**, coarse, raunchy *(slang)*, lusty, bawdy, ribald • *his extremely earthy brand of humour*
3 = **claylike**, soil-like • *Strong, earthy colours add to the effect.*

ease **AS A NOUN** 1 = **straightforwardness**, simplicity, readiness • *For ease of reference, only the relevant extracts of the regulations are included.*
2 = **comfort**, luxury, leisure, relaxation, prosperity, affluence, rest, repose, restfulness • *She lived a life of ease.*
OPPOSITES: pain, difficulty, hardship
3 = **peace of mind**, peace, content, quiet, comfort, happiness, enjoyment, serenity, tranquillity, contentment, calmness, quietude • *Qigong exercises promote ease of mind and body.*
OPPOSITES: tension, disturbance, agitation
4 = **naturalness**, informality, freedom, liberty, unaffectedness, unconstraint, unreservedness, relaxedness • *Co-stars particularly appreciate his ease on the set.*
OPPOSITES: constraint, formality, awkwardness
▸ **AS A VERB** 1 = **relieve**, calm, moderate, soothe, lessen, alleviate, appease, lighten, lower, allay, relax, still, mitigate, assuage, pacify, mollify, tranquillize, palliate • *I gave him some brandy to ease the pain.*
OPPOSITES: irritate, worsen, aggravate
2 *often with* **off** *or* **up** = **reduce**, moderate, weaken, diminish, decrease, slow down, dwindle, lessen, die down, abate, slacken, grow less, de-escalate • *The heavy snow had eased a little.*
3 = **move carefully**, edge, guide, slip, inch, slide, creep, squeeze, steer, manoeuvre • *I eased my way towards the door.*
4 = **facilitate**, further, aid, forward, smooth, assist, speed up, simplify, fast-track, make easier, expedite, lessen the labour of • *The information pack is designed to ease the process of making a will.*
OPPOSITES: hinder, retard
▸ **IN PHRASES: at ease** = **relaxed**, secure, comfortable, informal, laid-back *(informal)*, easy, free and easy • *It is essential to feel at ease with your therapist.*
ease off = **reduce**, decrease, lessen, curtail, slacken • *Kelly eased off his pace as they reached the elevator*
ease up on someone = **go easy on**, have mercy on, be merciful to, deal leniently with, be less severe with, be less strict with • *The manager does not intend to ease up on his players just yet.*
ease up on something = **reduce**, cut, moderate, decrease, cut down, curtail, cut back on • *Ease up on your training schedule a bit.*
ease up *or* **off** = **die down**, fade, weaken, diminish, decrease, wither, lessen, subside, die out, peter out, die away, taper off, grow less • *The recession may be easing up now.*
with ease = **effortlessly**, simply, easily, readily, without trouble, with no difficulty • *Anne was capable of passing her exams with ease.*

easily 1 = **without a doubt**, clearly, surely, certainly,

obviously, definitely, plainly, absolutely, undoubtedly, unquestionably, undeniably, unequivocally, far and away, indisputably, beyond question, indubitably, doubtlessly • *It could easily be another year before we see any change.*
2 = without difficulty, smoothly, readily, comfortably, effortlessly, simply, with ease, straightforwardly, without trouble, standing on your head, with your eyes closed *or* shut • *Wear clothes you can remove easily.*

east
▸ **RELATED ADJECTIVE:** oriental

Easter
▸ **RELATED ADJECTIVE:** Paschal

easy **1 = simple**, straightforward, no trouble, not difficult, effortless, painless, clear, light, uncomplicated, child's play *(informal)*, plain sailing, undemanding, a pushover *(slang)*, a piece of cake *(informal)*, no bother, a bed of roses, easy-peasy *(slang)*, a piece of piss *(taboo slang)* • *This is not an easy task.*
OPPOSITES: hard, demanding, difficult
2 = untroubled, contented, relaxed, satisfied, calm, peaceful, serene, tranquil, quiet, undisturbed, unworried • *I was not altogether easy in my mind about this decision.*
3 = relaxed, friendly, open, natural, pleasant, casual, informal, laid-back *(informal)*, graceful, gracious, unaffected, easy-going, affable, unpretentious, unforced, undemanding, unconstrained, unceremonious • *She laughed and joked and made easy conversation with everyone.*
OPPOSITES: forced, affected, stiff
4 = carefree, comfortable, pleasant, leisurely, well-to-do, trouble-free, untroubled, cushy *(informal)*, unworried, easeful • *She has had a very easy life.*
OPPOSITES: difficult, worried, uncomfortable
5 = tolerant, light, liberal, soft, flexible, mild, laid-back *(informal)*, indulgent, easy-going, lenient, permissive, unoppressive • *I guess we've always been too easy with our children.*
OPPOSITES: hard, demanding, strict
6 = accommodating, yielding, manageable, easy-going, compliant, amenable, submissive, docile, pliant, tractable, biddable • *'Your father was not an easy child,' she told me.*
OPPOSITES: difficult, impossible, unyielding
7 = vulnerable, soft, naive, susceptible, gullible, exploitable • *She was an easy target for con-men.*
8 = leisurely, relaxed, comfortable, moderate, unhurried, undemanding • *the easy pace set by pilgrims heading to Canterbury*

PROVERBS
Easy come, easy go

easy-going **= relaxed**, easy, liberal, calm, flexible, mild, casual, tolerant, laid-back *(informal)*, indulgent, serene, lenient, carefree, placid, unconcerned, amenable, permissive, happy-go-lucky, unhurried, nonchalant, insouciant, even-tempered, easy-peasy *(slang)*, chilled *(informal)* • *They have a very easy-going attitude to life.*
OPPOSITES: anxious, strict, tense

eat **AS A VERB** **1 = consume**, swallow, chew, hoover *(informal)*, scoff *(slang)*, devour, munch, tuck into *(informal)*, put away, gobble, polish off *(informal)*, wolf down • *She was eating a sandwich.*
2 = have a meal, lunch, breakfast, dine, snack, feed, graze *(informal)*, have lunch, have dinner, have breakfast, nosh *(slang)*, take food, have supper, break bread, chow down *(slang)*, take nourishment • *Let's go out to eat.*
▸ **IN PHRASES: eat into something = use up**, drain, exhaust, consume, deplete, devour, swallow up • *His work responsibilities were eating into his free time.*
eat something away = destroy, dissolve, crumble, rot, decay, erode, wear down, corrode, bite into, waste away, wear away • *The rot is eating away the interior of the house.*
▸ **RELATED MANIA:** phagomania

QUOTATIONS
One should eat to live, and not live to eat
[Molière *L'Avare*]

SPECIFIC EATING HABITS

Habit	Food
anthropophagic *or* anthropophagous	fellow humans
apivorous	bees
cannibalistic	other members of the same species
carnivorous	meat
carpophagous, frugivorous, *or* fruitarian	fruit
carrion	dead and rotting flesh
coprophagous	dung
geophagous	earth
herbivorous	plants
hylophagous	wood
insectivorous	insects
limivorous	mud
macrophagous	relatively large pieces of food
monophagous	only one food
mycetophagous	fungi
myrmecophagous	ants
nectarivorous	nectar
nucivorous	nuts
omnivorous	meat and plants
omophagic *or* omophagous	raw food
piscivorous	fish
theophagous	gods
vegan	no animal products
vegetarian	no flesh
zoophagous	animals

eavesdrop **= listen in**, spy, overhear, bug *(informal)*, pry, tap in, snoop *(informal)*, earwig *(informal)* • *The housemaid eavesdropped from behind the kitchen door.*

ebb **AS A VERB** **1 = flow back**, go out, withdraw, sink, retreat, fall back, wane, recede, fall away • *We hopped from rock to rock as the tide ebbed from the causeway.*
2 = decline, drop, sink, flag, weaken, shrink, diminish, decrease, deteriorate, decay, dwindle, lessen, subside, degenerate, fall away, fade away, abate, peter out, slacken • *There were occasions when my enthusiasm ebbed.*
▸ **AS A NOUN** **1 = flowing back**, going out, withdrawal, retreat, wane, waning, regression, low water, low tide, ebb tide, outgoing tide, falling tide, receding tide • *We decided to leave on the ebb at six o'clock next morning.*
2 = decline, drop, sinking, flagging, weakening, decrease, decay, dwindling, lessening, deterioration, fading away, petering out, slackening, degeneration, subsidence, shrinkage, diminution • *the ebb of her creative powers*
▸ **IN PHRASES: at a low ebb = at a low point**, at rock bottom, not successful, not profitable • *The Government's popularity is at a low ebb.*

ebony **= black**, dark, jet, raven, sable, pitch-black, jet-black, inky, swarthy, coal-black • *He had rich, soft ebony hair.*
▹ *See panel* **Shades from black to white**

ebullience **= exuberance**, enthusiasm, excitement, zest, high spirits, buoyancy, elation, exhilaration, brio, vivacity, effervescence, effusiveness • *His natural ebullience began to return.*

ebullient **= exuberant**, excited, enthusiastic, buoyant, exhilarated, elated, irrepressible, vivacious, effervescent, effusive, in high spirits, zestful • *The Prime Minister was a fiery, ebullient, quick-witted man.*

eccentric AS AN ADJECTIVE = **odd**, strange, bizarre, weird, peculiar, abnormal, queer *(informal)*, irregular, uncommon, quirky, out there *(slang)*, singular, unconventional, idiosyncratic, off-the-wall *(slang)*, outlandish, whimsical, rum *(Brit. slang)*, capricious, anomalous, freakish, aberrant, wacko *(slang)*, outré, daggy *(Austral. & N.Z. informal)* • *an eccentric character who wears a beret and sunglasses*
OPPOSITES: average, normal, regular
▸ AS A NOUN = **crank** *(informal)*, character *(informal)*, nut *(slang)*, freak *(informal)*, flake *(slang, chiefly U.S.)*, oddity, oddball *(informal)*, loose cannon, nonconformist, wacko *(slang)*, case *(informal)*, screwball *(slang, chiefly U.S. & Canad.)*, card *(informal)*, odd fish *(informal)*, kook *(U.S. & Canad. informal)*, queer fish *(Brit. informal)*, rum customer *(Brit. slang)*, weirdo *or* weirdie *(informal)* • *My other friend was a real English eccentric.*

eccentricity 1 = **oddity**, peculiarity, strangeness, irregularity, weirdness, singularity, oddness, waywardness, nonconformity, capriciousness, unconventionality, queerness *(informal)*, bizarreness, whimsicality, freakishness, outlandishness • *She is unusual to the point of eccentricity.*
2 = **foible**, anomaly, abnormality, quirk, oddity, aberration, peculiarity, idiosyncrasy • *We all have our little eccentricities.*

ecclesiastic = **clergyman**, minister, priest, vicar, parson, pastor, cleric, churchman, man of God, divine, man of the cloth, churchwoman, woman of God, clergywoman, woman of the cloth • *He was sent to a school run by ecclesiastics.*

ecclesiastical = **clerical**, religious, church, churchly, priestly, spiritual, holy, divine, pastoral, sacerdotal • *He refused to acknowledge the ecclesiastical supremacy of the monarch.*

echelon = **level**, place, office, position, step, degree, rank, grade, tier, rung • *the lower echelons of society*

echo AS A NOUN 1 = **reverberation**, ringing, repetition, answer, resonance, resounding • *He heard nothing but the echoes of his own voice in the cave.*
2 = **copy**, reflection, clone, reproduction, imitation, duplicate, double, reiteration • *Their cover version is just a pale echo of the real thing.*
3 = **reminder**, suggestion, trace, hint, recollection, vestige, evocation, intimation • *The accident has echoes of past disasters.*
▸ AS A VERB 1 = **reverberate**, repeat, resound, ring, resonate • *The distant crash of bombs echoes through the whole city.*
2 = **recall**, reflect, copy, mirror, resemble, reproduce, parrot, imitate, reiterate, ape • *Many phrases in the last chapter echo earlier passages.*

éclat = **brilliance**, effect, style, success, confidence, show, display, flourish, flair, vigour, splendour, refinement, pomp, lustre, showmanship, ostentation, stylishness • *He performed his piano solo with great éclat.*

eclectic = **diverse**, general, broad, varied, comprehensive, extensive, wide-ranging, selective, diversified, manifold, heterogeneous, catholic, all-embracing, liberal, many-sided, multifarious, dilettantish • *an eclectic collection of exhibits*

eclipse AS A NOUN 1 = **obscuring**, covering, blocking, shading, dimming, extinction, darkening, blotting out, occultation • *a total eclipse of the sun*
2 = **decline**, fall, loss, failure, weakening, deterioration, degeneration, diminution • *the eclipse of the influence of the Republican party in West Germany*
▸ AS A VERB 1 = **surpass**, exceed, overshadow, excel, transcend, outdo, outclass, outshine, leave *or* put in the shade *(informal)* • *The gramophone was eclipsed by the compact disc.*
2 = **obscure**, cover, block, cloud, conceal, dim, veil, darken, shroud, extinguish, blot out • *The sun was eclipsed by the moon.*

ecological = **environmental**, green • *ecological disasters such as the destruction of the rainforest*

ecologist = **environmentalist**, green, friend of the earth, tree-hugger *(informal derogatory)* • *Ecologists say the spread of the algae has been caused by increased pollution.*

ecology = **environment**, conditions, situation, scene, surroundings, context, habitat • *the effects of changes in climate on the coastal ecology*

economic 1 = **financial**, business, trade, industrial, commercial, mercantile • *The pace of economic growth is picking up.*
2 = **monetary**, financial, material, fiscal, budgetary, bread-and-butter *(informal)*, pecuniary • *Their country faces an economic crisis.*
3 = **profitable**, successful, commercial, rewarding, productive, lucrative, worthwhile, viable, solvent, cost-effective, money-making, profit-making, remunerative • *The service will make surfing the Web an economic proposition.*
4 = **economical**, fair, cheap, reasonable, modest, low-priced, inexpensive • *The new process is more economic but less environmentally friendly.*

economical 1 = **economic**, fair, cheap, reasonable, modest, low-priced, inexpensive • *It is more economical to wash a full load.*
OPPOSITES: expensive, unprofitable, exorbitant
2 = **thrifty**, sparing, careful, prudent, provident, frugal, parsimonious, scrimping, economizing • *ideas for economical housekeeping*
OPPOSITES: generous, lavish, extravagant
3 = **efficient**, sparing, cost-effective, money-saving, time-saving, work-saving, unwasteful • *the practical, economical virtues of a small hatchback*
OPPOSITES: extravagant, wasteful

economics = **finance**, commerce, the dismal science • *He gained a first class degree in economics.*

QUOTATIONS
We have always known that heedless self-interest was bad morals; we know now that it is bad economics
[Franklin Delano Roosevelt *First Inaugural Address*]
The Dismal Science
[Thomas Carlyle *Latter-Day Pamphlets*]

▹ *See panel* **Economics**

economist

QUOTATIONS
Economists set themselves too easy, too useless a task if in tempestuous seasons they can only tell us that when the storm is long past the ocean will be flat again
[John Maynard Keynes *A Tract on Monetary Reform*]
If all economists were laid end to end, they would not reach a conclusion
[George Bernard Shaw]

economize = **cut back**, save, save money, be sparing, cut costs, be economical, scrimp, scrimp and save, retrench, be frugal, make economies, cut expenditure, tighten your belt, be on a shoestring, draw in your horns, husband your resources • *We're going to have to economize on our spending from now on.*
OPPOSITES: spend, squander, be extravagant

economy 1 = **financial system**, financial state • *Africa's most industrialized economy*
2 = **thrift**, saving, restraint, prudence, providence, husbandry, retrenchment, frugality, parsimony, thriftiness, sparingness • *They have achieved quite remarkable effects with great economy of means.*

QUOTATIONS
Economy is going without something you do want in case you should, some day, want something you probably won't want
[Anthony Hope *The Dolly Dialogues*]

ECONOMICS

Branches of economics

agronomics
cliometrics
econometrics
economic history
industrial economics
macroeconomics
microeconomics
welfare economics

Economics terms

arbitration
asset
autarky
automation
balanced budget
balance of payments
balance of trade
balance sheet
bank
bankruptcy
barriers to entry
barriers to exit
barter
base rate
bear market
bid
black economy
boom
boycott
bridging loan
budget
budget deficit
building society
bull market
business cycle
buyer's market
capacity
capital
capital good
capitalism
cartel
cash
central bank
Chamber of Commerce
closed shop
collective bargaining
command economy *or* planned economy
commercial bank *or* clearing bank
commission
commodity
common market
comparative advantage
competition
conspicuous consumption
consumer
consumer good
consumption
cooperative
corporation
corporation tax
cost-benefit analysis
cost effectiveness
cost of living
cost-push inflation
credit
credit controls
credit squeeze
currency
current account
customs union
debt
deflation
deindustrialization
demand
demand management *or* stabilization policy
demand-pull inflation
deposit account
depreciation
depression
deregulation
devaluation
diminishing returns
discount
discount house *(Brit.)*
discount rate
disequilibrium
disinflation
disposable income
diversification
divestment
dividend
division of labour
dumping
duopoly
durable good
Dutch disease
duty
earned income
earnings
economic growth
economic policy
economic sanctions
economies of scale
embargo
employee
employer
employment
entrepreneur
environmental audit
exchange
exchange rate
expenditure
export
finance
financial year
fiscal drag
fiscal policy
fiscal year
Five-Year Plan
fixed assets
fixed costs
fixed exchange-rate system
fixed investment
floating exchange-rate system
foreclosure
foreign exchange controls
foreign exchange market
forfaiting
franchise
free-market economy
free rider
free trade
free trade area
free trade zone *or* freeport
freight
friendly society
fringe benefits
full employment
funding
futures market *or* forward exchange market
gains from trade
game theory
gilt-edged security *or* government bond
gold standard
greenfield investment
gross domestic product *or* GDP
gross national product *or* GNP
gross profit
hard currency
hedging
hire
hire purchase *or* HP
hoarding
holding
horizontal integration
hot money
human capital
hyperinflation
imperfect competition
import
import restrictions
income
income support
income tax
index-linked
indirect tax
industrial dispute
industrial estate
industrial policy
industrial relations
industrial sector
inflationary spiral
information agreement
infrastructure
inheritance tax
insolvency
instalment credit
institutional investors
insurance
intangible assets
intangibles
intellectual property right
interest
interest rate
international competitiveness

ECONOMICS TERMS (CONTINUED)

international debt
international reserves
investment
invisible balance
invisible hand
invoice
joint-stock company
joint venture
junk bond
labour
labour market
labour theory of value
laissez faire *or* laisser faire
lease
legal tender
lender
liability
liquidation
liquid asset
liquidity
listed company
loan
lockout
macroeconomic policy
management buy-out
marginal revenue
marginal utility
market
market failure
mass production
means test
mediation
medium of exchange
medium-term financial strategy
mercantilism
merchant bank
merger
microeconomic policy
middleman
mint
mixed economy
monetarism
monetary compensatory amounts, MCAs, *or* green money
monetary policy
money
money supply
monopoly
moonlighting
mortgage
multinational
national debt
national income
national insurance contributions
nationalization
national product
natural rate of unemployment
net profit
nondurable good
offshore
oligopoly
overheads
overheating
overmanning
overtime
patent
pawnbroker
pay
pay-as-you-earn *or* PAYE
payroll
pension
pension fund
per capita income
perfect competition
personal equity plan *or* PEP
picket
piecework
polluter pays principle
portfolio
poverty trap
premium
premium bond
price
prices and incomes policy
primary sector
private enterprise
private property
privatization
producer
production
productivity
profit
profitability
profit-and-loss account
profit margin
profit sharing
progressive taxation
protectionism
public expenditure
public finance
public interest
public-sector borrowing requirement *or* PSBR
public-sector debt repayment
public utility
public works
pump priming
purchasing power
quality control
ratchet effect
rational expectations
rationalization
rationing
recession
recommended retail price
recovery
recycling
redundancy
reflation
regional policy
rent
rent controls
research and development *or* R & D
residual unemployment
restrictive labour practice
retail
retail price index
revaluation
revenue
risk analysis
salary
sales
saving
savings bank
seasonal unemployment
self-employment
self service
self-sufficiency
seller's market
sequestration
service sector
share
shareholder
share issue
share price index
shop
shop steward
simple interest
slump
social costs
socio-economic group
soft currency
specialization
speculation
stagflation
standard of living
stock
stockbroker
stock control
stock exchange, stock market, *or (N.Z.)* share market
stop-go cycle
structural unemployment
subsidiary company
subsidy
supplier
supply
supply-side economics
surplus
synergy
takeover
tangible assets
tariff
tax
taxation
tax avoidance
tax evasion
tax haven
terms of trade
trade
trade barrier
trademark
trade union
trade-weighted index
training
transaction
trust
trustee
underwriter
unearned income
unemployment
unemployment benefit
uniform business rate *or* UBR
unit of account
unit trust
utility
value-added tax *or* VAT
variable costs

ECONOMICS TERMS (CONTINUED)

venture capital
vertical integration
voluntary unemployment
wage
wage restraint
wealth
welfare state
wholesaler
worker participation
working capital
yield

ECONOMICS SCHOOLS AND THEORIES

Austrian school
Chicago school
Classical school
Keynesianism
Marxism
mercantilism
monetarism
neoclassical school
neoKeynesians
Physiocrats
Reaganomics
Rogernomics (N.Z.)
Thatcherism

ECONOMISTS

Norman Angell *(English)*
Walter Bagehot *(British)*
Cesare Bonesana Beccaria *(Italian)*
William Henry Beveridge *(English)*
John Bright *(English)*
Richard Cobden *(English)*
Augustin Cournot *(French)*
Jacques Delors *(French)*
C(lifford) H(ugh) Douglas *(English)*
Milton Friedman *(U.S.)*
Ragnar Frisch *(Norwegian)*
J(ohn) K(enneth) Galbraith *(U.S.)*
Henry George *(U.S.)*
Friedrich August von Hayek *(Austrian-British)*
David Hume *(Scottish)*
William Stanley Jevons *(English)*
John Maynard Keynes *(British)*
Simon Kuznets *(U.S.)*
Arthur Laffer *(U.S.)*
Stephen Butler Leacock *(Canadian)*
Sicco Leendert Mansholt *(Dutch)*
Arthur Lewis West *(Indian)*
Thomas Robert Malthus *(British)*
Alfred Marshall *(British)*
Karl Marx *(German)*
James Mill *(Scottish)*
John Stuart Mill *(English)*
Jean Monnet *(French)*
Nicole d' Oresme *(French)*
Andreas (George) Papandreou *(Greek)*
Vilfredo Pareto *(Italian)*
Frédéric Passy *(French)*
A. W. H. Phillips *(English)*
François Quesnay *(French)*
David Ricardo *(British)*
Ernst Friedrich Schumacher *(British)*
Joseph Schumpeter *(Austrian)*
Jean Charles Léonard Simonde de Sismondi *(Swiss)*
Adam Smith *(British)*
Jan Tinbergen *(Dutch)*
Arnold Toynbee *(English)*
Anne Robert Jacques Turgot *(French)*
Thorstein Veblen *(U.S.)*
Dame Barbara (Mary) Ward *(British)*
Sidney Webb *(British)*
Max Weber *(German)*
Barbara (Frances) Wootton *(English)*

Everybody is always in favour of general economy and particular expenditure
[Anthony Eden]

PROVERBS

Cut your coat according to your cloth

ecstasy = **rapture**, delight, joy, enthusiasm, frenzy, bliss, trance, euphoria, fervour, elation, rhapsody, exaltation, transport, ravishment • *the agony and ecstasy of holiday romance*

OPPOSITES: suffering, pain, agony

QUOTATIONS

To burn always with this hard, gemlike flame, to maintain this ecstasy, is success in life
[Walter Pater *Studies in the History of the Renaissance*]

Take all away from me, but leave me Ecstasy,
And I am richer then than all my Fellow Men
[Emily Dickinson]

To be bewitched is not to be saved, though all the magicians and aesthetes in the world should pronounce it to be so
[George Santayana *The Life of Reason: Reason in Art*]

ecstatic = **rapturous**, entranced, enthusiastic, frenzied, joyous, fervent, joyful, elated, over the moon *(informal)*, overjoyed, blissful, delirious, euphoric, enraptured, on cloud nine *(informal)*, cock-a-hoop, blissed out, transported, rhapsodic, sent, walking on air, in seventh heaven, floating on air, in exaltation, in transports of delight, stoked *(Austral. & N.Z. informal)* • *He was ecstatic about the birth of his first child.*

ecumenical or **oecumenical** or **ecumenic** or **oecumenic** = **unifying**, universal, non-denominational, non-sectarian, general • *ecumenical church services*

eddy AS A NOUN = **swirl**, whirlpool, vortex, undertow, tideway, counter-current, counterflow • *the swirling eddies of the fast-flowing river*

▸ AS A VERB = **swirl**, turn, roll, spin, twist, surge, revolve, whirl, billow • *The dust whirled and eddied in the sunlight.*

edge AS A NOUN 1 = **border**, side, line, limit, bound, lip, margin, outline, boundary, fringe, verge, brink, threshold, rim, brim, perimeter, contour, periphery, flange • *She was standing at the water's edge.*

2 = **verge**, point, brink, threshold • *They have driven the rhino to the edge of extinction.*

3 = **advantage**, lead, dominance, superiority, upper hand, head start, ascendancy, whip hand • *This could give them the edge over their oppponents.*

4 = **power**, interest, force, bite, effectiveness, animation, zest, incisiveness, powerful quality • *Featuring new bands gives the show an edge.*

5 = **sharpness**, point, sting, urgency, bitterness, keenness, pungency, acuteness • *There was an unpleasant edge to her voice.*

▸ AS A VERB 1 = **inch**, ease, creep, worm, slink, steal, sidle, work, move slowly • *He edged closer to the door.*

2 = **border**, shape, bind, trim, fringe, rim, hem, pipe • *a chocolate brown jacket edged with yellow*

▸ IN PHRASES: **on edge** = **tense**, excited, wired *(slang)*, nervous, eager, impatient, irritable, apprehensive, edgy, uptight *(informal)*, ill at ease, twitchy *(informal)*, tetchy, on tenterhooks, keyed up, antsy *(informal)*, adrenalized • *Ever since their arrival she had felt on edge.*

on the edge of your seat = **excited**, moved, stirred, stimulated, roused, worked up • *The final had the spectators on the edge of their seats.*

edging = **border**, trimming, fringe, frill • *the satin edging on the blanket*

edgy = **nervous**, wired *(slang)*, anxious, tense, neurotic, irritable, touchy, uptight *(informal)*, on edge, nervy *(Brit. informal)*, ill at ease, restive, twitchy *(informal)*, irascible, tetchy, chippy *(informal)*, on tenterhooks, keyed up, antsy *(informal)*, on pins and needles, adrenalized • *She was nervous and edgy, still chain-smoking.*

edible = **safe to eat**, harmless, wholesome, palatable, digestible, eatable, comestible *(rare)*, fit to eat, good • *Are these mushrooms edible?*

OPPOSITES: harmful, poisonous, inedible

edict = **decree**, law, act, order, ruling, demand, command, regulation, dictate, mandate, canon, manifesto, injunction, statute, fiat, ordinance, proclamation, enactment, dictum, pronouncement, ukase (*rare*), pronunciamento • *In 1741 Catherine the Great issued an edict of toleration for Buddhism.*

edification = **instruction**, schooling, education, information, teaching, improvement, building up, guidance, nurture, tuition, enlightenment, uplifting, elevation • *the use of Scripture for the edification of believers*

edifice = **building**, house, structure, construction, pile, erection, habitation • *a list of historical edifices she must not fail to visit*

e

edify = **instruct**, school, teach, inform, guide, improve, educate, nurture, elevate, enlighten, uplift • *the ability of comedy to edify as well as to entertain an audience*

edifying = **instructive**, improving, inspiring, elevating, enlightening, uplifting, instructional • *the reading of edifying literature*

edit AS A VERB 1 = **revise**, check, improve, correct, polish, adapt, rewrite, censor, condense, annotate, rephrase, redraft, copy-edit, emend, prepare for publication, redact • *The publisher has the right to edit the book once it has been written.*
2 = **put together**, select, arrange, organize, assemble, compose, rearrange, reorder • *She has edited a collection of essays.*
3 = **be in charge of**, control, direct, be responsible for, be the editor of • *I used to edit the college paper in the old days.*
▸ IN PHRASES: **edit something out** = **remove**, cut, exclude, omit, erase, excise, delete, strike out, expunge, blue-pencil • *This scene was edited out for television.*

QUOTATIONS

Editing is the same as quarreling with writers – same thing exactly
[Harold Ross]

edition 1 = **printing**, publication • *a rare first edition of a Dickens novel*
2 = **copy**, impression, number • *The Christmas edition of the catalogue is out now.*
3 = **version**, volume, issue • *A paperback edition is now available in all good bookshops.*
4 = **programme** (*TV, Radio*) • *We'll be back in our next edition in a week's time.*

editor = **compiler**, writer, journalist, reviser • *the editor of a women's magazine*

educate = **teach**, school, train, coach, develop, improve, exercise, inform, discipline, rear, foster, mature, drill, tutor, instruct, cultivate, enlighten, civilize, edify, indoctrinate • *He was educated at the local grammar school.*

educated 1 = **cultured**, lettered, intellectual, learned, informed, experienced, polished, literary, sophisticated, refined, cultivated, enlightened, knowledgeable, civilized, tasteful, urbane, erudite, well-bred • *He is an educated, amiable and decent man.*
OPPOSITES: philistine, uneducated, uncultured
2 = **taught**, schooled, coached, informed, tutored, instructed, nurtured, well-informed, well-read, well-taught • *The country's workforce is well educated and diligent.*
OPPOSITES: ignorant, illiterate, uneducated

education 1 = **teaching**, schooling, training, development, coaching, improvement, discipline, instruction, drilling, tutoring, nurture, tuition, enlightenment, erudition, indoctrination, edification • *institutions for the care and education of children*
2 = **learning**, schooling, culture, breeding, scholarship, civilization, cultivation, refinement

QUOTATIONS

The roots of education are bitter, but the fruit is sweet
[Aristophanes]

Education makes a people easy to lead, but difficult to drive; easy to govern, but impossible to enslave
[Lord Henry Brougham *speech to the House of Commons*]

To live for a time close to great minds is the best education
[John Buchan *Memory Hold the Door*]

Education is simply the soul of a society as it passes from one generation to another
[G.K. Chesterton]

'Tis education forms the common mind,
Just as the twig is bent, the tree's inclined
[Alexander Pope *Epistles to Several Persons*]

Education is something that tempers the young and consoles the old, gives wealth to the poor and adorns the rich
[Diogenes (The Cynic)]

Education is what survives when what has been learnt has been forgotten
[B.F. Skinner *Education in 1984*]

To me education is a leading out of what is already there in the pupil's soul
[Muriel Spark *The Prime of Miss Jean Brodie*]

When you educate a man you educate an individual; when you educate a woman you educate a whole family
[Charles D. McIver]

education: that which discloses to the wise and disguises from the foolish their lack of understanding
[Ambrose Bierce *The Devil's Dictionary*]

Man is the only creature which must be educated
[Immanuel Kant]

Ask me my three main priorities for government and I tell you: education, education, education
[Tony Blair]

Education is the most powerful weapon which you can use to change the world
[Nelson Mandela]

▷ *See panels* **Academic degrees; Education terms; Schools, colleges and universities**

educational 1 = **academic**, school, learning, teaching, scholastic, pedagogical, pedagogic • *the British educational system*
2 = **instructive**, useful, cultural, illuminating, enlightening, informative, instructional, didactic, edifying, educative, heuristic • *The kids had an enjoyable and educational day.*

educative = **instructive**, educational, useful, helpful, enlightening, informative, didactic, edifying, heuristic • *The exhibition is an educative and emotionally satisfying experience.*

educator = **teacher**, professor, lecturer, don, coach, guide, fellow, trainer, tutor, instructor, mentor, schoolteacher, pedagogue, edifier, educationalist *or* educationist, schoolmaster *or* schoolmistress, master *or* mistress • *As a music educator, I taught in our city schools for many years.*

eel
▸ RELATED ADJECTIVE: anguilliform
▸ NAME OF YOUNG: elver, grig

eerie = **uncanny**, strange, frightening, ghostly, weird, mysterious, scary (*informal*), sinister, uneasy, fearful, awesome, unearthly, supernatural, unnatural, spooky (*informal*), creepy (*informal*), spectral, eldritch (*poetic*), preternatural • *An eerie silence settled over the forest.*

efface AS A VERB = **obliterate**, remove, destroy, cancel, wipe out, erase, eradicate, excise, delete, annihilate, raze, blot out, cross out, expunge, rub out, extirpate • *an attempt to efface the memory of their previous failures*
▸ IN PHRASES: **efface yourself** = **make yourself inconspicuous**, withdraw, be retiring, keep a low profile, be timid, be diffident, be bashful, keep out of the limelight, be modest, keep out of the public eye, be unassertive • *He always wants to efface himself, and hates any kind of ostentation.*

effect AS A NOUN 1 = **result**, consequence, conclusion, outcome, event, issue, aftermath, fruit, end result, upshot

• *the psychological effects of head injuries*
2 = **impression**, feeling, impact, influence • *The whole effect is cool, light and airy*
3 = **purpose**, meaning, impression, sense, import, drift, intent, essence, thread, tenor, purport • *He told me to get lost, or words to that effect.*
4 = **implementation**, force, action, performance, operation, enforcement, execution • *We are now resuming diplomatic relations with Syria with immediate effect.*
▸ **AS A VERB** = **bring about**, make, cause, produce, create, complete, achieve, perform, carry out, fulfil, accomplish, execute, initiate, give rise to, consummate, actuate, effectuate • *Prospects for effecting real political change have taken a step backward.*
▸ **IN PHRASES:** **in effect** = **in fact**, really, actually, essentially, virtually, effectively, in reality, in truth, as good as, in actual fact, to all intents and purposes, in all but name, in actuality, for practical purposes • *The deal would create, in effect, the world's biggest airline.*
put, bring *or* **carry into effect** = **implement**, perform, carry out, fulfil, enforce, execute, bring about, put into action, put into operation, bring into force • *a decree bringing these political reforms into effect*
take effect = **produce results**, work, begin, come into force, become operative • *The ban takes effect from July.*
to good effect = **successfully**, effectively, productively, fruitfully • *Mr Morris feels the museum is using advertising to good effect*
to no effect = **unsuccessfully**, in vain, to no avail, without success, pointlessly, ineffectively, to no purpose, with no use • *Mr Charles made a formal complaint to the manager, to no effect.*

effective 1 = **efficient**, successful, useful, active, capable, valuable, helpful, adequate, productive, operative, competent, serviceable, efficacious, effectual • *Antibiotics are effective against this organism.*
OPPOSITES: inadequate, useless, ineffective
2 = **powerful**, strong, convincing, persuasive, telling, impressive, compelling, potent, forceful, striking, emphatic, weighty, forcible, cogent • *You can't make an effective argument if all you do is stridently voice your opinion.*
OPPOSITES: weak, tame, pathetic
3 = **virtual**, essential, practical, implied, implicit, tacit, unacknowledged • *They have had effective control of the area.*
4 = **in operation**, official, current, legal, real, active, actual, in effect, valid, operative, in force, in execution • *The new rules will become effective in the next few days.*
OPPOSITES: inactive, inoperative

effectively 1 = **virtually**, really, in fact, essentially, in effect, in reality, in truth, as good as, in actual fact, to all intents and purposes, in all but name, in actuality, for practical purposes • *The region was effectively independent.*
2 = **efficiently**, successfully, skilfully, ably, competently, capably, proficiently • *He has the will and ability to govern effectively.*

effectiveness = **power**, effect, efficiency, success, strength, capability, use, validity, usefulness, potency, efficacy, fruitfulness, productiveness • *the effectiveness of computers as an educational tool*

effects = **belongings**, goods, things, property, stuff, gear, furniture, possessions, trappings, paraphernalia, personal property, accoutrements, chattels, movables • *His daughters came to collect his effects.*

effectual 1 = **effective**, successful, efficient, powerful, useful, helpful, productive, potent, constructive, telling, fruitful, advantageous, forcible, serviceable, efficacious • *the most effectual means of preserving peace*
2 = **binding**, legal, in effect, valid, in force, authoritative, contractual, lawful, sound, licit *(rare)* • *an act effectual by law*

effeminate = **womanly**, affected, camp *(informal)*, soft, weak, feminine, unmanly, sissy, effete, foppish, womanish, wussy *(slang)*, womanlike, poofy *(slang)*, wimpish *or* wimpy *(informal)* • *a skinny, effeminate guy in lipstick and earrings*
OPPOSITES: manly, macho, butch *(slang)*

effervescence 1 = **liveliness**, enthusiasm, excitement, vitality, animation, exuberance, high spirits, buoyancy, exhilaration, gaiety, brio, zing *(informal)*, vivacity, ebullience, vim *(slang)*, pizzazz *or* pizazz *(informal)* • *a man of great effervescence and magnetism*
2 = **bubbling**, sparkle, foam, foaming, fizz, ferment, froth, frothing, fermentation • *drink bottled water without natural or added effervescence*

effervescent 1 = **fizzy**, bubbling, sparkling, bubbly, foaming, fizzing, fermenting, frothing, frothy, aerated, carbonated, foamy, gassy • *an effervescent mineral water*
OPPOSITES: still, flat, weak
2 = **lively**, excited, dynamic, enthusiastic, sparkling, energetic, animated, merry, buoyant, exhilarated, bubbly, exuberant, high-spirited, irrepressible, ebullient, chirpy, vital, scintillating, vivacious, zingy *(informal)* • *an effervescent blonde actress*
OPPOSITES: flat, boring, dull

effete = **weak**, cowardly, feeble, ineffectual, decrepit, spineless, enfeebled, weak-kneed *(informal)*, enervated, overrefined, chicken-hearted, wimpish *or* wimpy *(informal)* • *a charming but effete young man*

efficacious = **effective**, successful, efficient, powerful, useful, active, capable, adequate, productive, operative, potent, competent, serviceable, effectual • *The nasal spray was new on the market and highly efficacious.*
OPPOSITES: useless, unsuccessful, ineffective

efficacy = **effectiveness**, efficiency, power, value, success, strength, virtue, vigour, use, usefulness, potency, fruitfulness, productiveness, efficaciousness • *Recent medical studies confirm the efficacy of a healthier lifestyle.*

efficiency 1 = **effectiveness**, power, economy, productivity, organization, efficacy, cost-effectiveness, orderliness • *ways to increase agricultural efficiency*
2 = **competence**, ability, skill, expertise, capability, readiness, professionalism, proficiency, adeptness, skilfulness • *her efficiency as a manager*

efficient 1 = **effective**, successful, structured, productive, powerful, systematic, streamlined, cost-effective, methodical, well-organized, well-planned, labour-saving, effectual • *an efficient form of contraception*
OPPOSITES: inefficient, wasteful, unproductive
2 = **competent**, able, professional, capable, organized, productive, skilful, adept, ready, proficient, businesslike, well-organized, workmanlike • *a highly efficient worker*
OPPOSITES: incompetent, inefficient, sloppy

effigy = **likeness**, figure, image, model, guy, carving, representation, statue, icon, idol, dummy, statuette • *An effigy of her was being burned in the town square.*

effluent = **waste**, discharge, flow, emission, sewage, pollutant, outpouring, outflow, exhalation, issue, emanation, liquid waste, efflux, effluvium, effluence

effort 1 = **attempt**, try, endeavour, shot *(informal)*, bid, essay, go *(informal)*, stab *(informal)* • *He made no effort to hide.*
2 = **exertion**, work, labour, trouble, force, energy, struggle, stress, application, strain, striving, graft, toil, welly *(slang)*, hard graft, travail *(literary)*, elbow grease *(facetious)*, blood, sweat, and tears *(informal)* • *A great deal of effort had been put into the planning.*
3 = **achievement**, act, performance, product, job, production, creation, feat, deed, accomplishment, attainment • *The gallery is showcasing her latest efforts.*

QUOTATIONS

Effort is only effort when it begins to hurt
[José Ortega y Gasset *In Search of Goethe From Within, Letter to a German*]

e

EDUCATION TERMS

A bursary *(N.Z.)*
academic
accredit *(N.Z.)*
accumulation
Advanced level *or* A level *(Brit.)*
adviser *or* advisor *(Brit.)*
advisory teacher *(Brit.)*
aegrotat *(Brit.)*
alumnus *or* alumna *(chiefly U.S. & Canad.)*
assignment
assistant *(U.S. & Canad.)*
associate *(U.S. & Canad.)*
baccalaureate
banding *(Brit.)*
battels *(Brit.)*
B bursary *(N.Z.)*
bedder *(Brit.)*
binary
boarder *(Brit.)*
boarding house *(Austral.)*
bubs grade *(Austral. & N.Z. slang)*
bursar
bursarial
bursary *or* bursarship *(Scot. & N.Z.)*
campus
campus university
catalogue *(U.S. & Canad.)*
catchment *(Brit.)*
Certificate of Pre-vocational Education *or* CPVE *(Brit.)*
Certificate of Proficiency *or* COP *(N.Z.)*
chancellor *(Brit., U.S. & Canad.)*
chapterhouse *(U.S.)*
class
classmate
classroom
co-ed *(U.S.)*
coeducation
collegial
collegian
collegiate
comedown *(Brit.)*
commencement *(U.S. & Canad.)*
commoner *(Brit.)*
Common Entrance *(Brit.)*
conductive education
congregation *(chiefly Brit.)*
continuous assessment
convocation
core subjects *(Brit.)*
coursework
crammer
credit
crib *(Brit.)*
cross-curricular *(Brit.)*
Cuisenaire rod *(trademark)*
curricular
curriculum
dean
deanery
degree
delegacy
department
detention
dissertation
docent *(U.S.)*
dominie *(Scot.)*
don *(Brit.)*
donnish
dropout
dunce
dunce cap
dux
Easter term
educate
education
educational
eleven-plus *(obsolete)*
emeritus
entry
essay
examination *or* exam
exercise
exhibition *(Brit. & Austral.)*
exhibitioner *(Brit.)*
expel
extension
external
extracurricular
extramural
faculty
fail
family grouping *or* vertical grouping
federal
fellow
fellowship
ferule
flunk *(chiefly U.S., Canad. & N.Z. informal)*
fresher *or* freshman
full professor *(U.S. & Canad.)*
further education *(Brit.)*
gaudy *(Brit.)*
General Certificate of Education *or* GCE *(Brit.)*
General Certificate of Secondary Education *or* GCSE *(Brit.)*
gown
grade *(U.S. & Canad.)*
graded post *(Brit.)*
graduand *(chiefly Brit.)*
graduate *(Brit., U.S. & Canad.)*
graduation
grant
grant-in-aid
grant-maintained
Great Public Schools *or* GPS *(Austral.)*
Greats *(Brit.)*
gymnasium
hall
hall of residence
headmaster *or* headmistress
headmastership *or* headmistress-ship
headship *(Brit.)*
higher *(Scot.)*
high school
Hilary term
homework
honours *or* *(U.S.)* honors
hood
hooky *or* hookey *(chiefly U.S., Canad. & N.Z. informal)*
house
housefather
housemaster
housemother
imposition *(Brit.)*
incept *(Brit.)*
infant *(Brit.)*
in residence
instructor *(U.S. & Canad.)*
internal
interscholastic
intramural *(chiefly U.S. & Canad.)*
invigilate *(Brit.)*
invigilator *(Brit.)*
janitor *(Scot.)*
jig *(Austral. slang)*
junior
junior common room
key stage *(Brit.)*
lecture
lecturer
level of attainment *(Brit.)*
liaison officer *(N.Z.)*
lines
literae humaniores *(Brit.)*
LMS *or* local management of schools *(Brit.)*
local examinations
lowerclassman *(U.S.)*
lower school
lycée *(French)*
manciple
marking
master
matriculate
matriculation *or* matric
mature student
Michaelmas term
middle common room
midterm
mistress
mitch *or* mich *(dialect)*
mocks *(informal)*
moderator *(Brit. & N.Z.)*
muck-up day *(Austral. slang)*
National Curriculum *(Brit.)*
Nuffield teaching project *(Brit.)*
open learning
Ordinary grade *or* O grade *(Scot.)*
Ordinary level *or* O level *(Brit.)*
Ordinary National Certificate *or* ONC *(Brit.)*
pandy *(chiefly Scot. & Irish)*
parent teacher association *or* PTA
parietal *(U.S.)*
pass
pedant *(archaic)*
pipe *(U.S. slang)*
porter
postgraduate
prefect *(Brit.)*
prelims *(Scot.)*
prepositor *(Brit., rare)*
primers *(N.Z. informal)*

EDUCATION TERMS (CONTINUED)

principal
Privatdocent
proctor *(U.S.)*
professor
professoriate
prospectus
provost
punishment exercise
reader *(chiefly Brit.)*
readership *(chiefly Brit.)*
reception *(Brit.)*
recess *(U.S. & Canad.)*
record of achievement *(Brit.)*
recreation
rector *(chiefly Brit.)*
redbrick *(Brit.)*
refresher course
regent
registrar
Regius professor *(Brit.)*
remedial
remove *(Brit.)*
report *(Brit.)*
resit
rusticate *(Brit.)*
sabbatical
sandwich course
SCE *or* Scottish Certificate of Education
scholastic
School Certificate *(Brit. & N.Z., old-fashioned)*
schoolleaver
schoolman
schoolmarm
schoolmaster
schoolmistress
schoolteacher
second *(Brit.)*
self-educated
semester *(chiefly U.S. & Canad.)*
seminar
senate
send down
senior
senior common room
session
set
shell *(Brit.)*
sixth form *(Brit.)*
sixth-form college *(Brit.)*
sizar *(Brit.)*
sophomore *(chiefly U.S. & Canad.)*
sorority *(chiefly U.S.)*
speech day *(Brit.)*
sports day *(Brit.)*
stage
Standard Grade *(Scot.)*
standard assessment tasks *or* SATS *(Brit.)*
statement *(Brit.)*
stream *(Brit.)*
student teacher
subject
subprincipal
summa cum laude
summative assessment *(Brit.)*
supervisor
teach-in
term
tertiary bursary *(Brit.)*
test
thesis
transcript *(chiefly U.S. & Canad.)*
transfer
trimester *(chiefly U.S. & Canad.)*
Trinity term
truant
tuition
tutee
tutor
tutorial
tutorial system
union
university entrance (examination) *or* UE *(N.Z.)*
undergraduate
unstreamed *(Brit.)*
upper school
vice chancellor *(Brit.)*
visiting professor
wag *(slang)*
warden *(Brit.)*
wrangler *(Brit.)*
year

Lovely it is, when the winds are churning up the waves on the great sea, to gaze out from the land on the great efforts of someone else
[Lucretius *De Rerum Natura*]

Whatever is worth doing at all is worth doing well
[Lord Chesterfield *Letters to His Son*]

Whatsoever thy hand findeth to do, do it with thy might
[*Bible: Ecclesiastes*]

effortless 1 = **easy**, simple, flowing, smooth, graceful, painless, uncomplicated, trouble-free, facile, undemanding, easy-peasy *(slang)*, untroublesome, unexacting • *In a single effortless motion, he scooped Frannie into his arms.*
OPPOSITES: hard, demanding, difficult
2 = **natural**, simple, spontaneous, instinctive, intuitive • *She liked him above all for his effortless charm.*

effrontery = **insolence**, nerve, arrogance, presumption, face *(informal)*, front, neck *(informal)*, cheek *(informal)*, assurance, brass *(informal)*, gall *(informal)*, disrespect, audacity, boldness, rudeness, temerity, chutzpah *(U.S. & Canad. informal)*, impertinence, impudence, brashness, brass neck *(Brit. informal)*, shamelessness, incivility, cheekiness, brazenness • *He had the effrontery to turn up on my doorstep at 2 in the morning.*

effusive = **demonstrative**, enthusiastic, lavish, extravagant, overflowing, gushing, exuberant, expansive, ebullient, free-flowing, unrestrained, talkative, fulsome, profuse, unreserved • *He was effusive in his praise of the general.*

egalitarian = **equal**, just, fair, equable • *I believe in the notion of an egalitarian society.*

egg[1] **AS A NOUN** = **ovum**, gamete, germ cell • *a baby bird hatching from its egg*
▸ **IN PHRASES: egg someone on** = **incite**, push, encourage, urge, prompt, spur, provoke, prod, goad, exhort • *She was egging him on to fight.*
get *or* **have** *or* **be left with** *or* **end up with egg on your face** = **be humiliated**, be embarrassed, be crushed, be put down, be shamed, look foolish, be taken down a peg *(informal)*, be put in your place • *If they take this game lightly they could end up with egg on their faces.*

QUOTATIONS

A hen's egg is, quite simply, a work of art, a masterpiece of design and construction with, it has to be said, brilliant packaging!
[Delia Smith *How to Cook*]

egghead = **expert**, genius, guru, inventor, wizard, mastermind, intellect, boffin *(Brit. informal)*, rocket scientist *(informal, chiefly U.S.)*, brain(s) *(informal)*, brainbox, bluestocking *(usually disparaging)*, maven *(U.S.)*, fundi *(S. African)* • *The Government was dominated by self-important eggheads.*

ego = **self-esteem**, self-confidence, self-respect, self-image, self-worth, self-assurance, self-importance • *He had a massive ego and would never admit he was wrong.*

QUOTATIONS

The ego is not master in its own house
[Sigmund Freud *A Difficulty in the Path of Psycho-Analysis*]

egocentric = **self-centred**, vain, selfish, narcissistic, self-absorbed, egotistical, inward looking, self-important, self-obsessed, self-seeking, egoistic, egoistical • *a vain and egocentric young woman*

egomaniac = **egotist**, boaster, swaggerer, self-seeker, braggart, braggadocio, narcissist, bighead *(informal)*, blowhard *(informal)*, self-admirer, figjam *(Austral. slang)* • *Adam's clever enough, but he's also something of an egomaniac.*

egotism *or* **egoism** = **self-centredness**, self-esteem, vanity, superiority, self-interest, selfishness, narcissism, self-importance, self-regard, self-love, self-seeking, self-absorption, self-obsession, egocentricity, egomania, self-praise, vainglory, self-conceit, self-admiration, conceitedness • *his amazing blend of egotism, superciliousness and stupidity*

egotist *or* **egoist** = **egomaniac**, boaster, swaggerer, self-seeker, braggart, braggadocio, narcissist, bighead *(informal)*, blowhard *(informal)*, self-admirer, figjam *(Austral. slang)* • *an insufferable egotist with delusions of omnipotence*

QUOTATIONS

egotist: a person of low taste, more interested in himself than in me

[Ambrose Bierce *The Devil's Dictionary*]

egotistic *or* **egotistical** *or* **egoistic** *or* **egoistical** = **self-centred**, superior, vain, conceited, narcissistic, opinionated, self-absorbed, self-important, egocentric, self-seeking, bragging, boasting, vainglorious, egomaniacal, self-admiring • *Susan and Deborah share an intensely selfish, egotistic streak.*

egregious = **grievous**, shocking, appalling, notorious, horrifying, outrageous, glaring, horrific, infamous, intolerable, monstrous, scandalous, frightful, gross, rank, heinous, flagrant, abhorrent, insufferable, arrant • *the most egregious abuses of human rights*

eight

▸ RELATED ADJECTIVE: eighth

▸ RELATED NOUN: octet

▸ RELATED PREFIXES: octa-, octo-

ejaculate 1 = **have an orgasm**, come *(taboo slang)*, climax, emit semen • *a tendency to ejaculate too quickly*

2 = **discharge**, release, emit, shoot out, eject, spurt • *sperm ejaculated by the male during sexual intercourse*

3 = **exclaim**, declare, shout, call out, cry out, burst out, blurt out • *'Good God!' Liz ejaculated.*

ejaculation = **discharge**, release, emission, ejection • *The ejaculation of seminal fluid is neither harmful nor abnormal.*

eject 1 = **throw out**, remove, turn out, expel *(slang)*, exile, oust, banish, deport, drive out, evict, boot out *(informal)*, force to leave, chuck out *(informal)*, bounce, turf out *(informal)*, give the bum's rush *(slang)*, show someone the door, throw someone out on their ear *(informal)* • *He was forcibly ejected from the restaurant.*

2 = **dismiss**, sack *(informal)*, fire *(informal)*, remove, get rid of, discharge, expel, throw out, oust, kick out *(informal)*, give someone their P45 *(informal)*, kennet *(Austral. slang)*, jeff *(Austral. slang)* • *He was ejected from his first job for persistent latecoming.*

3 = **discharge**, expel, emit, give off • *He fired a single shot, then ejected the spent cartridge.*

4 = **bail out**, escape, get out • *The pilot ejected from the plane and escaped injury.*

ejection 1 = **expulsion**, removal, ouster *(Law)*, deportation, eviction, banishment, exile • *the ejection of hecklers at the meeting*

2 = **dismissal**, sacking *(informal)*, firing *(informal)*, removal, discharge, the boot *(slang)*, expulsion, the sack *(informal)*, dislodgement • *These actions led to his ejection from office.*

3 = **emission**, throwing out, expulsion, spouting, casting out, disgorgement • *the ejection of an electron by an atomic nucleus*

eke out AS A VERB = **be sparing with**, stretch out, be economical with, economize on, husband, be frugal with • *I had to eke out my redundancy money for about ten weeks.*

▸ IN PHRASES: **eke out a living** = **support yourself**, survive, get by, make ends meet, scrimp, save, scrimp and save • *people trying to eke out a living in forest areas*

elaborate AS AN ADJECTIVE 1 = **complicated**, detailed, studied, laboured, perfected, complex, careful, exact, precise, thorough, intricate, skilful, painstaking • *an elaborate research project*

2 = **ornate**, detailed, involved, complex, fancy, complicated, decorated, extravagant, intricate, baroque, ornamented, fussy, embellished, showy, ostentatious, florid • *a designer known for his elaborate costumes*

OPPOSITES: simple, basic, plain

▸ AS A VERB 1 = **develop**, improve, enhance, polish, complicate, decorate, refine, garnish, ornament, flesh out • *The plan was elaborated by five members of the council.*

2 *usually with* **on** *or* **upon** = **expand upon**, extend upon, enlarge on, amplify upon, embellish, flesh out, add detail to • *A spokesman declined to elaborate on the statement.*

OPPOSITES: simplify, summarize, streamline

élan = **style**, spirit, dash, flair, animation, vigour, verve, zest, panache, esprit, brio, vivacity, impetuosity • *The part was performed with élan by a promising young tenor.*

elapse = **pass**, go, go by, lapse, pass by, slip away, roll on, slip by, roll by, glide by • *Forty-eight hours have elapsed since his arrest.*

elastic 1 = **flexible**, yielding, supple, rubbery, pliable, plastic, springy, pliant, tensile, stretchy, ductile, stretchable • *Work the dough until it is slightly elastic.*

OPPOSITES: set, firm, rigid

2 = **adaptable**, yielding, variable, flexible, accommodating, tolerant, adjustable, supple, complaisant • *an elastic interpretation of the rules*

OPPOSITES: set, firm, inflexible

elasticity 1 = **flexibility**, suppleness, plasticity, give *(informal)*, pliability, ductility, springiness, pliancy, stretchiness, rubberiness • *Daily facial exercises help to retain the skin's elasticity.*

2 = **adaptability**, accommodation, flexibility, tolerance, variability, suppleness, complaisance, adjustability, compliantness • *the elasticity of demand for this commodity*

elated = **joyful**, excited, delighted, proud, cheered, thrilled, elevated, animated, roused, exhilarated, ecstatic, jubilant, joyous, over the moon *(informal)*, overjoyed, blissful, euphoric, rapt, gleeful, sent, puffed up, exultant, in high spirits, on cloud nine *(informal)*, cock-a-hoop, blissed out, in seventh heaven, floating *or* walking on air, stoked *(Austral. & N.Z. informal)* • *I was elated by my success.*

OPPOSITES: sad, depressed, dejected

elation = **joy**, delight, thrill, excitement, ecstasy, bliss, euphoria, glee, rapture, high spirits, exhilaration, jubilation, exaltation, exultation, joyfulness, joyousness • *His supporters have reacted to the news with elation.*

elbow AS A NOUN = **joint**, turn, corner, bend, angle, curve • *The boat was moored at the elbow of the river.*

▸ AS A VERB = **push**, force, crowd, shoulder, knock, bump, shove, nudge, jostle, hustle • *They elbowed me out of the way.*

▸ IN PHRASES: **at your elbow** = **within reach**, near, to hand, handy, at hand, close by • *the whisky glass that was forever at his elbow*

elbow room = **scope**, room, space, freedom, latitude, leeway • *His speech was designed to give himself more political elbow room.*

elder AS AN ADJECTIVE = **older**, first, senior, first-born, earlier born • *the elder of her two daughters*

▸ AS A NOUN 1 = **older person**, senior • *Nowadays the young have no respect for their elders.*

2 = **church official**, leader, office bearer, presbyter • *He is now an elder of the village church.*

elderly AS AN ADJECTIVE = **old**, aged, ageing, ancient, mature, past it, venerable, patriarchal, grey-haired, geriatric *(derogatory)*, getting on, over the hill *(informal)*, grizzled, decrepit, hoary, superannuated, long in the tooth *(informal)*, grey, doddery, senescent, advanced in years, full of years,

past your prime • *There was an elderly couple on the terrace.*
▸ **AS A PLURAL NOUN** = **old people**, pensioners, senior citizens, geriatrics *(derogatory)*, OAPs, retired people, old age pensioners, wrinklies *(informal derogatory)* • *The elderly are a formidable force in any election.*
▸ **RELATED ADJECTIVE:** geriatric

eldest = **oldest**, first, first-born, earliest born • *David was the eldest of three sons.*

elect **AS A VERB** 1 = **vote for**, choose, pick, determine, select, appoint, opt for, designate, pick out, settle on, decide upon • *The people have voted to elect a new president.*
2 = **choose**, decide, prefer, select, opt • *Those electing to smoke will be seated at the rear.*
▸ **AS AN ADJECTIVE** 1 = **selected**, chosen, picked, choice, preferred, select, elite, of choice, hand-picked • *one of the elect few permitted to enter*
2 = **future**, to-be, coming, next, appointed, designate, prospective • *the date when the president-elect takes office*

election 1 = **vote**, poll, ballot, determination, referendum, franchise, plebiscite, show of hands • *Poland's first fully free elections for more than fifty years*
2 = **appointment**, choosing, picking, choice, selection • *the election of the Labour government in 1964*

QUOTATIONS
Elections are won by men and women chiefly because most people vote against somebody rather than for somebody
[Franklin P. Adams *Nods and Becks*]

elector = **voter**, chooser, selector, constituent, member of the electorate, member of a constituency, enfranchised person • *Each elector is required to list his order of preferences.*

electric 1 = **electric-powered**, powered, cordless, battery-operated, electrically-charged, mains-operated • *her electric guitar*
2 = **charged**, exciting, stirring, thrilling, stimulating, dynamic, tense, rousing, electrifying, adrenalized • *The atmosphere in the hall was electric.*

electricity = **power**, mains, current, energy, power supply, electric power • *The electricity had been cut off.*
▸ **RELATED PHOBIA:** electrophobia

electrify 1 = **thrill**, shock, excite, amaze, stir, stimulate, astonish, startle, arouse, animate, rouse, astound, jolt, fire, galvanize, take your breath away • *The spectators were electrified by his courage.*
OPPOSITES: bore, tire, exhaust
2 = **wire up**, wire, supply electricity to, convert to electricity • *The west-coast line was electrified as long ago as 1974.*

electronic
▸ **RELATED PREFIX:** e-

elegance = **style**, taste, beauty, grace, dignity, sophistication, grandeur, refinement, polish, gentility, sumptuousness, courtliness, gracefulness, tastefulness, exquisiteness • *Princess Grace's understated elegance*

QUOTATIONS
To me, elegance is not to pass unnoticed but to get to the very soul of what one is
[Christian Lacroix]

elegant 1 = **stylish**, fine, beautiful, sophisticated, delicate, artistic, handsome, fashionable, refined, cultivated, chic, luxurious, exquisite, nice, discerning, graceful, polished, sumptuous, genteel, choice, tasteful, urbane, courtly, modish, comely, à la mode, schmick *(Austral. informal)* • *Patricia looked as beautiful and elegant as always.*
OPPOSITES: plain, ugly, inelegant
2 = **ingenious**, simple, effective, appropriate, clever, neat, apt • *The poem impressed me with its elegant simplicity.*

elegiac = **lamenting**, sad, melancholy, nostalgic, mournful, plaintive, melancholic, sorrowful, funereal, valedictory, keening, dirgeful, threnodial, threnodic • *The music has a dreamy, elegiac quality.*

elegy = **lament**, requiem, dirge, plaint *(archaic)*, threnody, keen, funeral song, coronach *(Scot. & Irish)*, funeral poem • *a moving elegy for a lost friend*

element **AS A NOUN** 1 = **component**, part, feature, unit, section, factor, principle, aspect, foundation, ingredient, constituent, subdivision • *one of the key elements of the UN's peace plan*
2 = **group**, faction, clique, set, party, circle • *The government must weed out criminal elements from the security forces.*
3 = **trace**, suggestion, hint, dash, suspicion, tinge, smattering, soupçon • *There is an element of truth in his accusation.*
▸ **AS A PLURAL NOUN** = **weather conditions**, climate, the weather, wind and rain, atmospheric conditions, powers of nature, atmospheric forces • *The area is exposed to the elements.*
▸ **IN PHRASES:** **in your element** = **ina situation you enjoy**, in your natural environment, in familiar surroundings • *My stepmother was in her element, organizing everyone.*

elemental 1 = **basic**, essential, principal, fundamental, elementary • *the elemental theory of music*
2 = **primal**, original, primitive, primordial • *the elemental powers of the universe*
3 = **atmospheric**, natural, meteorological • *the elemental forces that shaped this rugged Atlantic coast*

elementary 1 = **basic**, essential, primary, initial, fundamental, introductory, preparatory, rudimentary, elemental, bog-standard *(informal)* • *Literacy now includes elementary computer skills.*
OPPOSITES: higher, advanced, secondary
2 = **simple**, clear, easy, plain, straightforward, rudimentary, uncomplicated, facile, undemanding, unexacting • *elementary questions designed to test numeracy*
OPPOSITES: complex, complicated, sophisticated

elephant
▸ **RELATED ADJECTIVE:** elephantine
▸ **NAME OF MALE:** bull
▸ **NAME OF FEMALE:** cow
▸ **NAME OF YOUNG:** calf

elephantine = **massive**, great, huge, heavy, giant, enormous, immense, lumbering, gigantic, monstrous, mammoth, bulky, colossal, weighty, hulking, laborious, ponderous, gargantuan, humongous *or* humungous *(U.S. slang)* • *His legs were elephantine, his body obese.*

elevate 1 = **promote**, raise, advance, upgrade, exalt, kick upstairs *(informal)*, aggrandize, give advancement to • *He was elevated to the post of Prime Minister.*
2 = **increase**, lift, raise, step up, intensify, move up, hoist, raise high • *Emotional stress can elevate blood pressure.*
3 = **raise**, lift, heighten, uplift, hoist, lift up, raise up, hike up, upraise • *Jack elevated the gun at the sky.*
4 = **cheer**, raise, excite, boost, animate, rouse, uplift, brighten, exhilarate, hearten, lift up, perk up, buoy up, gladden, elate • *She bought some new clothes, but they failed to elevate her spirits.*

elevated 1 = **exalted**, high, important, august, grand, superior, noble, dignified, high-ranking, lofty • *His new job has given him a certain elevated status.*
2 = **high-minded**, high, fine, grand, noble, inflated, dignified, sublime, lofty, high-flown, pompous, exalted, bombastic • *the magazine's elevated tone*
OPPOSITES: simple, modest, humble
3 = **raised**, high, lifted up, upraised • *an elevated platform on the stage*

elevation 1 = **side**, back, face, front, aspect • *the addition of a two-storey wing on the north elevation*
2 = **altitude**, height • *We're at an elevation of about 13,000 feet above sea level.*

3 = **promotion**, upgrading, advancement, exaltation, preferment, aggrandizement • *celebrating his elevation to the rank of Prime Minister*
4 = **rise**, hill, mountain, height, mound, berg *(S. African)*, high ground, higher ground, eminence, hillock, rising ground, acclivity • *The resort is built on an elevation overlooking the sea.*

elevator = **lift**, hoist, paternoster • *Markham emerged from the guest elevator into the lobby.*

elf = **fairy**, brownie, hob, pixie, puck, imp, sprite, troll, goblin, leprechaun, hobgoblin • *Tolkien's world of dwarves, dragons and elves*

elfin = **elflike**, charming, arch, playful, mischievous, sprightly, impish, puckish, frolicsome, ludic *(literary)*, elvish, prankish, elfish • *Wilfred gave him a mischievous, elfin grin.*

e

elicit 1 = **bring about**, cause, derive, bring out, evoke, give rise to, draw out, bring forth, bring to light, call forth • *He was hopeful that his request would elicit a positive response.*
2 = **obtain**, extract, exact, evoke, wrest, draw out, extort, educe • *the question of how far police should go to elicit a confession*

eligible 1 = **entitled**, fit, qualified, suited, suitable • *You could be eligible for a university scholarship.*
OPPOSITES: unsuitable, ineligible, unqualified
2 = **available**, free, single, unmarried, unattached • *Britain's most eligible bachelor*

eliminate 1 = **remove**, end, stop, withdraw, get rid of, abolish, cut out, dispose of, terminate, banish, eradicate, put an end to, do away with, dispense with, stamp out, exterminate, get shot of, wipe from the face of the earth • *The Act has not eliminated discrimination in employment.*
2 = **knock out**, drop, reject, exclude, axe *(informal)*, get rid of, expel, leave out, throw out, omit, put out, eject • *I was eliminated from the 400 metres in the semifinals.*
3 = **murder**, kill, do in *(slang)*, take out *(slang)*, terminate, slay, blow away *(slang, chiefly U.S.)*, liquidate, annihilate, exterminate, bump off *(slang)*, rub out *(U.S. slang)*, waste *(informal)* • *They claimed that 87,000 'reactionaries' had been eliminated.*

elimination = **removal**, end, withdrawal, taking away, disposal, abolition, purging, termination, eradication, banishment • *the prohibition and elimination of chemical weapons*

elite AS A NOUN = **aristocracy**, best, pick, elect, cream, upper class, nobility, gentry, high society, crème de la crème *(French)*, flower, nonpareil • *a government comprised mainly of the elite*
OPPOSITES: rabble, dregs, hoi polloi
▸ AS AN ADJECTIVE = **leading**, best, finest, pick, choice, selected, elect, crack *(slang)*, supreme, exclusive, privileged, first-class, foremost, first-rate, pre-eminent, most excellent • *the elite troops of the President's bodyguard*

elitist AS AN ADJECTIVE = **snobbish**, exclusive, superior, arrogant, selective, pretentious, stuck-up *(informal)*, patronizing, condescending, snooty *(informal)*, uppity, high and mighty *(informal)*, hoity-toity *(informal)*, high-hat *(informal, chiefly U.S.)*, uppish (*Brit. informal*) • *He described skiing as an elitist sport.*
▸ AS A NOUN = **snob**, highbrow, prig, social climber • *He was an elitist who had no time for the masses.*

elixir 1 = **panacea**, cure-all, nostrum, sovereign remedy • *a magical elixir of eternal youth*
2 = **syrup**, essence, solution, concentrate, mixture, extract, potion, distillation, tincture, distillate • *For severe teething pains, try an infant paracetamol elixir.*

elk
▸ COLLECTIVE NOUN: gang

elliptical 1 = **oval**, egg-shaped, ovoid, ovate, ellipsoidal, oviform • *the moon's elliptical orbit*
2 = **oblique**, concentrated, obscure, compact, indirect, ambiguous, concise, condensed, terse, cryptic, laconic, abstruse, recondite • *elliptical references to matters best not discussed in public*

elocution = **diction**, speech, delivery, rhetoric, pronunciation, utterance, oratory, articulation, public speaking, intonation, modulation, enunciation, declamation, speechmaking, voice production • *He took courses in elocution and acting at the London Academy.*

elongate = **lengthen**, extend, stretch (out), make longer • *Plunge necklines and high heels help to elongate the body.*

elongated = **extended**, long, stretched • *The light from the candle threw his elongated shadow on the walls.*

elope = **run away**, leave, escape, disappear, bolt, run off, slip away, abscond, decamp, sneak off, steal away, do a bunk *(informal)* • *My girlfriend and I eloped to Gretna Green.*

eloquence 1 = **fluency**, effectiveness, oratory, expressiveness, persuasiveness, forcefulness, gracefulness, powerfulness, whaikorero *(N.Z.)* • *the eloquence with which he delivered his message*
2 = **expressiveness**, significance, meaningfulness, pointedness • *the eloquence of his gestures*

eloquent 1 = **silver-tongued**, moving, powerful, effective, stirring, articulate, persuasive, graceful, forceful, fluent, expressive, well-expressed • *He made a very eloquent speech at the dinner.*
OPPOSITES: halting, stumbling, inarticulate
2 = **expressive**, telling, pointed, revealing, significant, pregnant, vivid, meaningful, indicative, suggestive • *Her only reply was an eloquent glance at the clock.*

elsewhere = **in** *or* **to another place**, away, abroad, hence *(archaic)*, somewhere else, not here, in other places, in *or* to a different place • *Almost 80% of the state's residents were born elsewhere.*

elucidate = **clarify**, explain, illustrate, interpret, make clear, unfold, illuminate, spell out, clear up, gloss, expound, make plain, annotate, explicate, shed *or* throw light upon • *He refused to elucidate the reasons for his decision.*

elude 1 = **evade**, escape, lose, avoid, flee, duck *(informal)*, dodge, get away from, shake off, run away from, circumvent, outrun, body-swerve *(Scot.)* • *The thieves managed to elude the police for months.*
2 = **escape**, baffle, frustrate, puzzle, stump, foil, be beyond (someone), thwart, confound • *The appropriate word eluded him.*

elusive 1 = **difficult to catch**, tricky, slippery, difficult to find, evasive, shifty • *I had no luck in tracking down this elusive man.*
2 = **indefinable**, puzzling, fleeting, subtle, baffling, indefinite, transient, intangible, indescribable, transitory, indistinct • *an attempt to recapture an elusive memory*
3 = **evasive**, puzzling, misleading, baffling, ambiguous, fraudulent, deceptive, illusory, equivocal, fallacious, unspecific, oracular, elusory • *an elusive answer*

emaciated = **skeletal**, thin, weak, lean, pinched, skinny, wasted, gaunt, bony, haggard, atrophied, scrawny, attenuate, attenuated, undernourished, scraggy, half-starved, cadaverous, macilent *(rare)* • *horrific television pictures of emaciated prisoners*

e-mail AS A NOUN = **mail, electronic mail**
▸ AS A VERB = **mail**

QUOTATIONS
The e-mail of the species is deadlier than the mail
[Stephen Fry]

emanate 1 = **give out**, send out, emit, radiate, exude, issue, give off, exhale, send forth • *He emanated sympathy.*
2 *often with* **from** = **flow**, emerge, spring, proceed, arise, stem, derive, originate, issue, come forth • *The aroma of burning wood emanated from the stove.*

emanation 1 = **flow**, proceeding, arising, emergence,

derivation, origination • *the emanation of the created order from God*
2 = emission, radiation, discharge, diffusion, effluent, exhalation, effusion, efflux • *The human body is surrounded by an aura of infrared emanations.*

emancipate = free, release, liberate, set free, deliver, discharge, let out, let loose, untie, unchain, enfranchise, unshackle, disencumber, unfetter, unbridle, disenthral, manumit • *the war which preserved the Union and emancipated the slaves*
OPPOSITES: bind, capture, enslave

emancipated = liberated, free, released, independent, unconstrained • *West was the only daughter of an emancipated slave.*

emancipation = liberation, freedom, freeing, release, liberty, discharge, liberating, setting free, letting loose, untying, deliverance, unchaining, manumission, enfranchisement, unshackling, unfettering • *the intellectual emancipation of women*
OPPOSITES: detention, slavery, imprisonment

emasculate = weaken, soften, cripple, impoverish, debilitate, reduce the power of, disempower, enfeeble, make feeble, enervate, deprive of force

embalm = preserve, lay out, mummify

embankment = bank, ridge, mound, causeway, rampart, earthwork • *They climbed a steep railway embankment.*

embargo AS A NOUN **= ban**, bar, block, barrier, restriction, boycott, restraint, check, prohibition, moratorium, stoppage, impediment, blockage, hindrance, interdiction, interdict, proscription, rahui *(N.Z.)* • *The UN has imposed an arms embargo against the country.*
▸ AS A VERB **= block**, stop, bar, ban, restrict, boycott, check, prohibit, impede, blacklist, proscribe, ostracize, debar, interdict • *They embargoed oil shipments to the US.*

embark AS A VERB **= go aboard**, climb aboard, board ship, step aboard, go on board, take ship • *They embarked on the battle cruiser HMS Renown.*
OPPOSITES: land, arrive, get off
▸ IN PHRASES: **embark on something = begin**, start, launch, enter, engage, take up, set out, undertake, initiate, set about, plunge into, commence, broach • *He is embarking on a new career as a writer.*

embarrass = shame, distress, show up *(informal)*, humiliate, disconcert, chagrin, fluster, mortify, faze, discomfit, make uncomfortable, make awkward, discountenance, nonplus, abash, discompose, make ashamed, put out of countenance • *He is always embarrassing me in public.*

embarrassed = ashamed, upset, shamed, uncomfortable, shown-up, awkward, abashed, humiliated, uneasy, unsettled, self-conscious, thrown, disconcerted, red-faced, chagrined, flustered, mortified, sheepish, discomfited, discountenanced, caught with egg on your face, not know where to put yourself, put out of countenance • *He looked a bit embarrassed.*

embarrassing = humiliating, upsetting, compromising, shaming, distressing, delicate, uncomfortable, awkward, tricky, sensitive, troublesome, shameful, disconcerting, touchy, mortifying, discomfiting, toe-curling *(slang)*, cringe-making *(Brit. informal)*, cringeworthy *(Brit. informal)*, barro *(Austral. slang)* • *It was an embarrassing situation for all of us.*

embarrassment AS A NOUN **1 = shame**, distress, showing up *(informal)*, humiliation, discomfort, unease, chagrin, self-consciousness, awkwardness, mortification, discomfiture, bashfulness, discomposure • *We apologise for any embarrassment this statement may have caused.*
2 = problem, difficulty, nuisance, source of trouble, thorn in your flesh • *The poverty figures were an embarrassment to the president.*
3 = predicament, problem, difficulty *(informal)*, mess, jam *(informal)*, plight, scrape *(informal)*, pickle *(informal)* • *He is in a state of temporary financial embarrassment.*
▸ IN PHRASES: **an embarrassment of riches = overabundance**, excess, surplus, glut, profusion, surfeit, superabundance, superfluity • *The art gallery has an embarrassment of riches, with nowhere to put most of them.*

embassy = consulate, ministry, delegation, legation, High Commission • *The American Embassy has already made a formal complaint.*

embed or **imbed** *often with* **in = fix**, set, plant, root, sink, lodge, insert, implant, drive in, dig in, hammer in, ram in • *The fossils are embedded in hard sandstone.*

embellish 1 = decorate, enhance, adorn, dress, grace, deck, trim, dress up, enrich, garnish, ornament, gild, festoon, bedeck, tart up *(slang)*, beautify • *The boat was embellished with red and blue carvings.*
2 = elaborate, colour, exaggerate, dress up, embroider, varnish • *He embellished the story with invented dialogue and extra details.*

embellishment 1 = decoration, garnishing, ornament, gilding, enhancement, enrichment, adornment, ornamentation, trimming, beautification • *Florence is full of buildings with bits of decoration and embellishment.*
2 = elaboration, exaggeration, embroidery • *I lack the story-teller's gift of embellishment.*

ember *usually plural* **= cinders**, ashes, residue, live coals • *We were sitting around the dying embers of the bonfire.*

embezzle = misappropriate, steal, appropriate, rob, pocket, nick *(slang, chiefly Brit.)*, trouser *(slang)*, pinch *(informal)*, rip off *(slang)*, knock off *(slang)*, siphon off, pilfer, purloin, filch, help yourself to, thieve, defalcate *(Law)*, peculate • *The director embezzled $34 million in company funds.*

embezzlement = misappropriation, stealing, robbing, fraud, pocketing, theft, robbery, nicking *(slang, chiefly Brit.)*, pinching *(informal)*, appropriation, siphoning off, thieving, pilfering, larceny, purloining, filching, pilferage, peculation, defalcation *(Law)* • *He was gaoled for six years for embezzlement of government funds.*

embitter = make bitter or **resentful**, anger, poison, sour, alienate, disillusion, antagonize, disaffect, envenom • *He did not let this experience embitter him.*

embittered = resentful, angry, acid, bitter, sour, soured, alienated, disillusioned, disaffected, venomous, rancorous, at daggers drawn *(informal)*, nursing a grudge, with a chip on your shoulder *(informal)* • *He had turned into an embittered, hardened old man.*

emblazon = decorate, show, display, present, colour, paint, illuminate, adorn, ornament, embellish, blazon • *Jackie was sporting a t-shirt with the band's name emblazoned on it.*

emblem 1 = crest, mark, design, image, figure, seal, shield, badge, insignia, coat of arms, heraldic device, sigil *(rare)* • *the emblem of the Red Cross*
2 = representation, symbol, mark, sign, type, token • *The eagle was an emblem of strength and courage.*

emblematic or **emblematical 1 = symbolic**, significant, figurative, allegorical • *Dogs are emblematic of faithfulness.*
2 = characteristic, representative, typical, symptomatic • *This comment is emblematic of his no-nonsense approach to life.*

embodiment = personification, example, model, type, ideal, expression, symbol, representation, manifestation, realization, incarnation, paradigm, epitome, incorporation, paragon, perfect example, exemplar, quintessence, actualization, exemplification, reification • *A baby is the embodiment of vulnerability.*

embody 1 = personify, represent, express, realize, incorporate, stand for, manifest, exemplify, symbolize, typify, incarnate, actualize, reify, concretize • *Jack Kennedy embodied all the hopes of the 1960s.*

2 *often with* **in** = **incorporate**, include, contain, combine, collect, concentrate, organize, take in, integrate, consolidate, bring together, encompass, comprehend, codify, systematize • *The proposal has been embodied in a draft resolution.*

embolden = **encourage**, cheer, stir, strengthen, nerve, stimulate, reassure, fire, animate, rouse, inflame, hearten, invigorate, gee up, make brave, give courage, vitalize, inspirit • *Emboldened by his success, he started on a second novel.*

embrace AS A VERB 1 = **hug**, hold, cuddle, seize, squeeze, grasp, clasp, envelop, encircle, enfold, canoodle *(slang)*, take *or* hold in your arms • *Penelope came forward and embraced her sister.*
2 = **accept**, support, receive, welcome, adopt, grab, take up, seize, make use of, espouse, take on board, welcome with open arms, avail yourself of, receive enthusiastically • *He embraces the new information age.*
3 = **include**, involve, cover, deal with, contain, take in, incorporate, comprise, enclose, provide for, take into account, embody, encompass, comprehend, subsume • *a theory that would embrace the whole field of human endeavour*
▸ AS A NOUN = **hug**, hold, cuddle, squeeze, clinch *(slang)*, clasp, canoodle *(slang)* • *a young couple locked in a passionate embrace*

embroider 1 = **sew**, decorate, stitch, ornament • *I had a pillow with my name embroidered on it.*
2 = **elaborate**, colour, exaggerate, dress up, varnish, embellish • *He said he didn't lie, he just embroidered the truth a little.*

embroidery = **sewing**, tapestry, needlework, needlepoint, needlecraft • *The shirt had embroidery over the pockets.*
▹ *See panel* **Embroidery stitches**

embroil = **involve**, complicate, mix up, implicate, entangle, mire, ensnare, encumber, enmesh • *Any hostilities could further embroil U.N. troops in the fighting.*

embroiled = **involved**, mixed up, implicated, entangled • *the reluctance of the US public to get embroiled in a war*

embryo 1 = **fetus**, unborn child, fertilized egg • *The embryo lives in the amniotic cavity.*
2 = **germ**, beginning, source, root, seed, nucleus, rudiment • *The League of Nations was the embryo of the UN.*

embryonic *or* **embryonal** = **rudimentary**, early, beginning, primary, budding, fledgling, immature, seminal, nascent, undeveloped, incipient, inchoate, unformed, germinal • *Romania's embryonic democracy*
OPPOSITES: developed, advanced, progressive

emerge 1 = **come out**, appear, come up, surface, rise, proceed, arise, turn up, spring up, emanate, materialize, issue, come into view, come forth, become visible, manifest yourself • *He was waiting outside as she emerged from the building.*
OPPOSITES: withdraw, disappear, sink
2 = **become apparent**, develop, come out, turn up, become known, come to light, crop up, transpire, materialize, become evident, come out in the wash • *Several interesting facts emerged from his story.*

emergence 1 = **coming**, development, arrival, surfacing, rise, appearance, arising, turning up, issue, dawn, advent, emanation, materialization • *the emergence of new democracies in Central Europe*
2 = **disclosure**, publishing, broadcasting, broadcast, publication, declaration, revelation, becoming known, becoming apparent, coming to light, becoming evident • *Following the emergence of new facts, the conviction was quashed.*

emergency AS A NOUN = **crisis**, danger, difficulty, accident, disaster, necessity, pinch, plight, scrape *(informal)*, strait, catastrophe, predicament, calamity, extremity, quandary, exigency, critical situation, urgent situation • *He has the ability to deal with emergencies quickly.*
▸ AS AN ADJECTIVE 1 = **urgent**, crisis, immediate • *She made an emergency appointment.*
2 = **alternative**, extra, additional, substitute, replacement, temporary, makeshift, stopgap • *The plane is carrying emergency supplies.*

emergent = **developing**, coming, beginning, rising, appearing, budding, burgeoning, fledgling, nascent, incipient • *an emergent nationalist movement*

emigrate = **move abroad**, move, relocate, migrate, remove, resettle, leave your country • *He emigrated to Belgium.*

emigration = **departure**, removal, migration, exodus, relocation, resettlement • *the huge emigration of workers to the West*

QUOTATIONS

Emigration, forced or chosen, across national frontiers or from village to metropolis, is the quintessential experience of our time
[John Berger *And Our Faces, My Heart, Brief as Photos*]

eminence 1 = **prominence**, reputation, importance, fame, celebrity, distinction, note, esteem, rank, dignity, prestige, superiority, greatness, renown, pre-eminence, repute, notability, illustriousness • *pilots who achieved eminence in the aeronautical world*
2 = **high ground**, bank, rise, hill, summit, height, mound, elevation, knoll, hillock, kopje *or* koppie *(S. African)* • *The house is built on an eminence, and has a pleasing prospect.*

EMBROIDERY STITCHES

Arrowhead stitch
Back stitch
Barb stitch
Basque stitch
Beaded stitch
Berlin stitch
Berwick stitch
Blanket stitch
Briar stitch
Bullion stitch
Buttonhole Bar
Buttonhole Wheel
Buttonhole
Casalguidi
Cast on stitch
Catch stitch
Caterpillar stitch
Chain stitch
Chevron stitch
Chinese stitch
Closed Buttonhole
Closed Feather stitch
Coil stitch
Convent stitch
Coral stitch
Cretan stitch
Crewel stitch
Cross stitch
Crossed Buttonhole
Crossed corners
Crow's-foot
Daisy stitch
Damask stitch
Double Cross
Eyelet stitch
Feather stitch
Feathered Chain
Fern stitch
Fly stitch
French Knot
German Knot stitch
Ghiordes Knot
Greek stitch
Herringbone
Kloster stitch
Ladder stitch
Lazy Daisy stitch
Montenegrin
Open Chain stitch
Outline stitch
Pekinese
Plaited stitch
Porto Rico rose
Portuguese stitch
Post stitch
Quilt Knot stitch
Renaissance
Ribbed Wheel
Rice stitch
Roman Chain stitch
Running stitch
Russian Cross stitch
Russian stitch
Sampler stitch
Satin stitch
Scottish stitch
Scroll stitch
Sham Hem stitch
Split stitch
Stem stitch
Threaded Arrowhead
Threaded Fly stitch
Threaded Running
Twisted Chain
Twisted Lattice Band
Wheatear
Whipped Back
Whipped Chain
Whipped Fly
Whipped Running
Whipped Stem
Woven Spider's Wheel
Zigzag Chain

eminent = **prominent**, high, great, important, noted, respected, grand, famous, celebrated, outstanding, distinguished, well-known, superior, esteemed, notable, renowned, prestigious, elevated, paramount, big-time *(informal)*, foremost, high-ranking, conspicuous, illustrious, major league *(informal)*, exalted, noteworthy, pre-eminent • *an eminent public figure*
OPPOSITES: ordinary, unknown, anonymous

eminently = **extremely**, very, highly, greatly, particularly, seriously *(informal)*, signally, well, notably, remarkably, positively, exceptionally, exceedingly, prominently, strikingly, supremely, conspicuously, outstandingly, surpassingly • *His family was eminently respectable.*

emissary = **envoy**, agent, deputy, representative, ambassador, diplomat, delegate, courier, herald, messenger, consul, attaché, go-between, legate • *the President's special emissary to Hanoi*

emission = **giving off** *or* **out**, release, shedding, leak, radiation, discharge, transmission, venting, issue, diffusion, utterance, ejaculation, outflow, issuance, ejection, exhalation, emanation, exudation • *the emission of gases such as carbon dioxide*

emit 1 = **give off**, release, shed, leak, transmit, discharge, send out, throw out, vent, issue, give out, radiate, eject, pour out, diffuse, emanate, exude, exhale, breathe out, cast out, give vent to, send forth • *The stove emitted a cloud of evil-smelling smoke.*
OPPOSITES: receive, absorb, take in
2 = **utter**, produce, voice, give out, let out • *Polly blinked and emitted a small cry.*

emollient AS A NOUN = **moisturizer**, oil, cream, lotion, balm, ointment, salve, liniment, lenitive • *Grapeseed oil is a gentle emollient.*
▸ AS AN ADJECTIVE 1 = **soothing**, softening, assuaging, palliative, balsamic, mollifying, moisturizing, demulcent, lenitive, assuasive • *an emollient cream which I find invaluable for sunburn*
2 = **conciliatory**, calming, disarming, appeasing, pacifying, pacific, mollifying, peaceable, placatory, irenic, propitiative • *The government's recent tone has been emollient.*

emotion 1 = **feeling**, spirit, soul, passion, excitement, sensation, sentiment, agitation, fervour, ardour, vehemence, perturbation • *Her voice trembled with emotion.*
2 = **instinct**, sentiment, sensibility, intuition, tenderness, gut feeling, soft-heartedness • *the split between reason and emotion*

emotional 1 = **psychological**, private, personal, hidden, spiritual, inner • *Victims are left with emotional problems that can last for life.*
2 = **moving**, touching, affecting, exciting, stirring, thrilling, sentimental, poignant, emotive, heart-rending, heart-warming, tear-jerking *(informal)* • *It was a very emotional moment.*
3 = **emotive**, sensitive, controversial, delicate, contentious, heated, inflammatory, touchy, hot-button *(informal)* • *Selling ivory from elephants is a very emotional issue.*
4 = **passionate**, enthusiastic, sentimental, fiery, feeling, susceptible, responsive, ardent, fervent, zealous, temperamental, excitable, demonstrative, hot-blooded, fervid, touchy-feely *(informal)* • *I don't get as emotional as I once did.*
OPPOSITES: dispassionate, cold, detached

emotionless = **unfeeling**, cold, cool, remote, distant, detached, indifferent, glacial, cold-blooded, frigid, dispassionate, impassive, unemotional, undemonstrative, unexpressive • *He stood emotionless as he heard the judge pass sentence.*

emotive 1 = **sensitive**, controversial, delicate, contentious, inflammatory, touchy, hot-button *(informal)* • *Embryo research is an emotive subject.*
2 = **moving**, touching, affecting, emotional, exciting, stirring, thrilling, sentimental, poignant, heart-rending, heart-warming, tear-jerking *(informal)* • *He made an emotive speech to his fans.*

empathize IN PHRASES: **empathize with** = **identify with**, understand, relate to, feel for, sympathize with, have a rapport with, feel at one with, be on the same wavelength as • *I empathize with anyone who has gone through that trauma.*

empathy AS A NOUN = **understanding**, feeling, appreciation, compassion, rapport, commiseration • *the king's empathy with the suffering of his people*

emperor = **ruler**, king, monarch, sovereign, lord, shah, kaiser, tsar, potentate, khan, mikado, imperator • *the coronation of Japan's new emperor*

emphasis 1 = **importance**, attention, weight, significance, stress, strength, priority, moment, intensity, insistence, prominence, underscoring, pre-eminence • *Too much emphasis is placed on research.*
2 = **stress**, accent, accentuation, force, weight • *The emphasis is on the first syllable of the word.*

emphasize 1 = **highlight**, stress, insist, underline, draw attention to, flag up, dwell on, underscore, weight, play up, make a point of, foreground, give priority to, press home, give prominence to, prioritize • *I should emphasize that nothing has been finally decided as yet.*
OPPOSITES: play down, minimize, make light of
2 = **stress**, accent, accentuate, lay stress on, put the accent on • *'That's up to you,' I said, emphasizing the 'you'.*

emphatic 1 = **forceful**, decided, certain, direct, earnest, positive, absolute, distinct, definite, vigorous, energetic, unmistakable, insistent, unequivocal, vehement, forcible, categorical • *His response was immediate and emphatic.*
OPPOSITES: weak, uncertain, hesitant
2 = **significant**, marked, strong, striking, powerful, telling, storming *(informal)*, impressive, pronounced, decisive, resounding, momentous, conclusive • *Yesterday's emphatic victory was their fifth in succession.*
OPPOSITES: commonplace, insignificant, unremarkable

emphatically 1 = **forcefully**, vigorously, vehemently, earnestly, energetically, insistently • *Mr Davies has emphatically denied the charges.*
2 = **definitely**, certainly, absolutely, positively, categorically • *Hurting her feelings was emphatically not my intention.*

empire 1 = **kingdom**, territory, province, federation, commonwealth, realm, domain, imperium *(rare)* • *the fall of the Roman empire*
2 = **organization**, company, business, firm, concern, corporation, consortium, syndicate, multinational, conglomeration • *control of a huge publishing empire*
▸ RELATED ADJECTIVE: imperial

QUOTATIONS

All empire is no more than power in trust
[John Dryden *Absalom and Achitophel*]

empirical = **first-hand**, direct, observed, practical, actual, experimental, pragmatic, factual, experiential • *There is no empirical evidence to support his theory.*
OPPOSITES: assumed, academic, hypothetical

emplacement 1 = **position**, situation, station, site, platform, lodgment • *Overlooking the terrace was a gun emplacement.*
2 = **positioning**, placing, stationing, setting up, location, placement, putting in place • *the possible emplacement of radioactive waste canisters in the deep sea*

employ AS A VERB 1 = **hire**, commission, appoint, take on, retain, engage, recruit, sign up, enlist, enrol, have on the payroll • *The company employs 18 staff.*
2 = **use**, apply, exercise, exert, make use of, utilize, ply, bring to bear, put to use, bring into play, avail yourself of • *the approaches and methods we employed in this study*

3 = **spend**, fill, occupy, involve, engage, take up, make use of, use up • *Your time could be usefully employed in attending to business matters.*
▸ IN PHRASES: **in the employ of** *or* **in someone's employ** = **in the service of**, employed by, hired by, engaged by, in the payroll of • *They hinted that he was in the employ of the KGB.*

employed 1 = **working**, in work, having a job, in employment, in a job, earning your living • *He was employed on a part-time basis.*
OPPOSITES: redundant, laid off, out of work
2 = **busy**, active, occupied, engaged, hard at work, in harness, rushed off your feet • *You have enough work to keep you fully employed.*
OPPOSITES: idle, unoccupied

e

employee *or (U.S.)* **employe** = **worker**, labourer, workman, staff member, member of staff, hand, wage-earner, white-collar worker, blue-collar worker, hired hand, job-holder, member of the workforce • *Many of the company's employees are women.*

employer 1 = **boss** *(informal)*, manager, head, leader, director, chief, executive, owner, owner, master, chief executive, governor *(informal)*, skipper, managing director, administrator, patron, supervisor, superintendent, gaffer *(informal, chiefly Brit.)*, foreman, proprietor, manageress, overseer, kingpin, honcho *(informal)*, big cheese *(old-fashioned slang)*, baas *(S. African)*, numero uno *(informal)*, Mister Big *(slang, chiefly U.S.)*, sherang *(Austral. & N.Z.)* • *It is a privilege to work for such an excellent employer.*
2 = **company**, business, firm, organization, establishment, outfit *(informal)* • *Shorts is Ulster's biggest private-sector employer*

employment 1 = **job**, work, business, position, trade, post, situation, employ, calling, profession, occupation, pursuit, vocation, métier • *She was unable to find employment in the area.*
2 = **taking on**, commissioning, appointing, hire, hiring, retaining, engaging, appointment, recruiting, engagement, recruitment, enlisting, enrolling, enlistment • *a ban on the employment of children under the age of nine*
3 = **use**, application, exertion, exercise, utilization • *the widespread employment of 'smart' bombs in this war*

emporium = **shop**, market, store, supermarket, outlet, warehouse, department store, mart, boutique, bazaar, retail outlet, superstore, hypermarket • *a famous emporium whose branches grace the capitals of Europe*

empower 1 = **authorize**, allow, commission, qualify, permit, sanction, entitle, delegate, license, warrant, give power to, give authority to, invest with power • *The army is now empowered to operate on a shoot-to-kill basis.*
2 = **enable**, equip, emancipate, give means to, enfranchise • *empowering the underprivileged by means of education*

empowerment = **enabling**, equipping, emancipation, enfranchising • *This government believes strongly in the empowerment of women.*

empress = **ruler**, queen, monarch, sovereign, lady, potentate, tsarina • *the title of Empress of India*

emptiness 1 = **futility**, banality, worthlessness, hollowness, pointlessness, meaninglessness, barrenness, senselessness, aimlessness, purposelessness, unsatisfactoriness, valuelessness • *suffering from feelings of emptiness and depression*
2 = **meaninglessness**, vanity, banality, frivolity, idleness, unreality, silliness, triviality, ineffectiveness, cheapness, insincerity, worthlessness, hollowness, inanity, unsubstantiality, trivialness, vainness • *the unsoundness and emptiness of his beliefs*
3 = **void**, gap, vacuum, empty space, nothingness, blank space, free space, vacuity • *She wanted a man to fill the emptiness in her life.*
4 = **bareness**, waste, desolation, destitution, blankness, barrenness, desertedness, vacantness • *the emptiness of the desert*
5 = **blankness**, vacancy, vacuity, impassivity, vacuousness, expressionlessness, stoniness, unintelligence, absentness, vacantness • *There was an emptiness about her eyes, as if she were in a state of shock.*

empty AS AN ADJECTIVE 1 = **bare**, clear, abandoned, deserted, vacant, free, void, desolate, destitute, uninhabited, unoccupied, waste, unfurnished, untenanted, without contents • *The room was bare and empty.*
OPPOSITES: full, stuffed, packed
2 = **meaningless**, cheap, hollow, vain, idle, trivial, ineffective, futile, insubstantial, insincere • *His father said he was going to beat him, but he knew it was an empty threat.*
3 = **worthless**, meaningless, hollow, pointless, unsatisfactory, futile, unreal, senseless, frivolous, fruitless, aimless, inane, valueless, purposeless, otiose, bootless • *My life was hectic but empty before I met him.*
OPPOSITES: interesting, full, meaningful
4 = **blank**, absent, vacant, stony, deadpan, vacuous, impassive, expressionless, unintelligent • *She saw the empty look in his eyes as he left.*
5 = **hungry**, unfilled, famished, starving *(informal)*, unfed • *Never drink on an empty stomach.*
▸ AS A VERB 1 = **clear**, drain, gut, void, unload, pour out, unpack, unburden, remove the contents of • *I emptied the ashtray.*
OPPOSITES: fill, stuff, pack
2 = **exhaust**, consume the contents of, void, deplete, use up • *Cross emptied his glass with one swallow.*
OPPOSITES: stock, replenish
3 = **evacuate**, clear, vacate • *a bore who could empty a room in two minutes just by talking about his therapy*

empty-handed = **with nothing**, unsuccessful, with empty pockets, unprovided for • *Shirley returned empty-handed from her shopping trip.*

empty-headed = **scatterbrained**, simple, stupid, silly, dizzy *(informal)*, frivolous, giddy, goofy *(informal)*, vacuous, inane, skittish, flighty, brainless, harebrained, featherbrained, ditzy *or* ditsy *(slang)* • *a pretty but empty-headed young woman*

emulate = **imitate**, follow, copy, mirror, echo, mimic, take after, follow in the footsteps of, follow the example of, take a leaf out of someone's book, model yourself on • *Sons are traditionally expected to emulate their fathers.*

emulation = **imitation**, following, copying, mirroring, reproduction, mimicry • *a role model worthy of emulation*

enable 1 = **allow**, permit, facilitate, empower, give someone the opportunity, give someone the means • *The new test should enable doctors to detect the disease early.*
OPPOSITES: stop, prevent, hinder
2 = **authorize**, allow, commission, permit, qualify, sanction, entitle, license, warrant, empower, give someone the right • *The authorities have refused visas to enable them to enter the country.*
OPPOSITES: stop, bar, ban

enact 1 = **establish**, order, pass, command, approve, sanction, proclaim, decree, authorize, ratify, ordain, validate, legislate, make law • *The bill would be submitted for discussion before being enacted as law.*
2 = **perform**, play, act, present, stage, represent, put on, portray, depict, act out, play the part of, appear as *or* in, personate • *She enacted the stories told to her by her father.*

enactment *or* **enaction** 1 = **passing**, legislation, sanction, approval, establishment, proclamation, ratification, authorization, validation, making law • *the enactment of a Bill of Rights*
2 = **decree**, order, law, act, ruling, bill, measure, command,

legislation, regulation, resolution, dictate, canon, statute, ordinance, commandment, edict, bylaw • *enactments which empowered the court to require security to be given*
3 = portrayal, staging, performance, playing, acting, performing, representation, depiction, play-acting, personation • *The building was also used for the enactment of plays.*

enamoured
▸ IN PHRASES: **enamoured with = in love with**, taken with, charmed by, fascinated by, entranced by, fond of, enchanted by, captivated by, enthralled by, smitten with, besotted with, bewitched by, crazy about *(informal)*, infatuated with, enraptured by, wild about *(informal)*, swept off your feet by, nuts on *or* about *(slang)* • *When I was young I was totally enamoured of him.*

encampment = **camp**, base, post, station, quarters, campsite, bivouac, camping ground, cantonment • *a large military encampment*

encapsulate *or* **incapsulate** = **sum up**, digest, summarize, compress, condense, abbreviate, epitomize, abridge, précis • *His ideas were later encapsulated in his book.*

enchant = **fascinate**, delight, charm, entrance, dazzle, captivate, enthral, beguile, bewitch, ravish, mesmerize, hypnotize, cast a spell on, enrapture, enamour, spellbind • *This book will enchant readers.*

enchanted 1 = **bewitched**, magic, possessed, charmed • *fairy stories of enchanted forests*
2 = fascinated, charmed, absorbed, entranced, captivated, enthralled, beguiled, smitten, bewitched, engrossed, spellbound, infatuated, hypnotized, under a spell • *He was enchanted by her youth and love of life.*

enchanting = **delightful**, fascinating, appealing, attractive, lovely, charming, entrancing, pleasant, endearing, captivating, alluring, bewitching, ravishing, winsome, Orphean • *She's an absolutely enchanting child.*

enchantment 1 = **charm**, fascination, delight, beauty, joy, attraction, bliss, allure, transport, rapture, mesmerism, ravishment, captivation, beguilement, allurement • *The campsite had its own peculiar enchantment.*
2 = spell, magic, charm, witchcraft, voodoo, wizardry, sorcery, occultism, incantation, necromancy, conjuration, makutu *(N.Z.)* • *an effective countercharm against enchantment by the faerie folk*

encircle = **surround**, ring, circle, enclose, encompass, compass, envelop, girdle, circumscribe, hem in, enfold, environ, gird in, begird *(poetic)*, enwreath • *A forty-foot-high concrete wall encircles the jail.*

enclave = **area**, community, quarter, haven, region, county, reserve, district, province, reservation, constituency, borough, homeland, precinct • *an Armenian enclave inside Azerbaijan*

enclose *or* **inclose** 1 = **surround**, cover, circle, bound, wrap, fence, pound, pen, hedge, confine, close in, encompass, wall in, encircle, encase, fence in, impound, circumscribe, hem in, shut in, environ • *The land was enclosed by an eight-foot wire fence.*
2 = send with, include, put in, insert • *I enclose a cheque for £10.*

enclosed spaces
▸ RELATED PHOBIA: claustrophobia

enclosure = **compound**, yard, pen, fold, ring, paddock, pound, coop, sty, stockade • *This enclosure was so vast that the outermost wall could hardly be seen.*

encode = **encrypt**, code, scramble, garble, make unintelligible, encipher, put into code • *The sender uses a secret key to encode the message.*

encompass 1 = **include**, hold, involve, cover, admit, deal with, contain, take in, embrace, incorporate, comprise, embody, comprehend, subsume • *His repertoire encompassed everything from Bach to Scott Joplin.*
2 = surround, circle, enclose, close in, envelop, encircle, fence in, ring, girdle, circumscribe, hem in, shut in, environ, enwreath • *Egypt is encompassed by the Mediterranean, Sudan, the Red Sea and Libya.*

encore = **repeat performance**, repetition, rerun, curtain call, extra performance, additional performance • *His final encore was a piece by Ginastera.*

encounter AS A VERB 1 = **experience**, meet, face, suffer, have, go through, sustain, endure, undergo, run into, live through • *Every day we encounter stresses of one kind or another.*
2 = meet, confront, come across, run into *(informal)*, bump into *(informal)*, run across, come upon, chance upon, meet by chance, happen on *or* upon • *Did you encounter anyone on your walk?*
3 = battle with, attack, fight, oppose, engage with, confront, combat, clash with, contend with, strive against, struggle with, grapple with, face off *(slang)*, do battle with, cross swords with, come into conflict with, meet head on • *They were about to cross the border and encounter Iraqi troops.*
▸ AS A NOUN 1 = **meeting**, brush, confrontation, rendezvous, chance meeting • *an encounter with a remarkable man*
2 = battle, fight, action, conflict, clash, dispute, contest, set to *(informal)*, run-in *(informal)*, combat, confrontation, engagement, collision, skirmish, head-to-head, face-off *(slang)* • *They were killed in an encounter with security forces near the border.*

encourage 1 = **inspire**, comfort, rally, cheer, stimulate, reassure, animate, console, rouse, hearten, cheer up, embolden, buoy up, pep up, boost someone's morale, give hope to, buck up *(informal)*, gee up, lift the spirits of, give confidence to, inspirit • *When things aren't going well, he always encourages me.*
OPPOSITES: depress, discourage, dishearten
2 = urge, persuade, prompt, spur, coax, incite, egg on, abet • *He encouraged her to quit her job.*
OPPOSITES: prevent, scare, dissuade
3 = promote, back, help, support, increase, further, aid, forward, advance, favour, boost, strengthen, foster, advocate, stimulate, endorse, commend, succour • *Their task is to encourage private investment in Russia.*
OPPOSITES: prevent, inhibit, hinder

encouragement 1 = **inspiration**, help, support, aid, favour, comfort, comforting, cheer, cheering, consolation, reassurance, morale boosting, succour • *Thanks for all your advice and encouragement.*
2 = urging, prompting, stimulus, persuasion, coaxing, egging on, incitement • *She had needed no encouragement to accept his invitation.*
3 = promotion, backing, support, boost, endorsement, stimulation, advocacy, furtherance • *The encouragement of trade will benefit the process of economic reform in China.*

QUOTATIONS
It's a good thing to shoot an admiral now and then to encourage the others
[Voltaire *Candide*]

encouraging = **promising**, good, bright, comforting, cheering, stimulating, reassuring, hopeful, satisfactory, cheerful, favourable, rosy, heartening, auspicious, propitious • *The results have not been very encouraging.*
OPPOSITES: disappointing, depressing, discouraging

encroach *often with* **on** *or* **upon** = **intrude**, invade, trespass, infringe, usurp, impinge, trench, overstep, make inroads, impose yourself • *He doesn't like people to encroach on his territory.*

encroachment = **intrusion**, invasion, violation, infringement, trespass, incursion, usurpation, inroad, impingement • *This is a sign of the encroachment of commercialism in medicine.*

e

encumber 1 = **burden**, load, embarrass, saddle, oppress, obstruct, retard, weigh down • *The company is still labouring under the debt burden that it was encumbered with in the 1980s.*
2 = **hamper**, restrict, handicap, slow down, cramp, inhibit, clog, hinder, inconvenience, overload, impede, weigh down, trammel, incommode • *fishermen encumbered with bulky clothing and boots*

encumbrance 1 = **burden**, weight, difficulty, load, drag, liability, obstacle, embarrassment, obstruction, albatross, millstone • *She considered the past an irrelevant encumbrance.*
2 = **hindrance**, handicap, restraint, inconvenience, impediment • *the encumbrance of an ankle-length dress*

encyclopedic *or* **encyclopaedic** = **comprehensive**, full, complete, vast, universal, wide-ranging, thorough, in-depth, exhaustive, all-inclusive, all-embracing, all-encompassing, thoroughgoing • *He has an encyclopedic knowledge of 80s popular music.*

e

end AS A NOUN 1 = **close**, ending, finish, expiry, expiration • *The report is expected by the end of the year.*
OPPOSITES: start, beginning, outset, start, opening
2 = **conclusion**, ending, climax, completion, finale, culmination, denouement, consummation • *His big scene comes towards the end of the film.*
OPPOSITES: start, opening, beginning
3 = **finish**, close, stop, resolution, conclusion, closure, wind-up, completion, termination, cessation • *She brought the interview to an abrupt end.*
4 = **extremity**, limit, edge, border, bound, extent, extreme, margin, boundary, terminus • *Surveillance equipment is placed at both ends of the tunnel.*
5 = **tip**, point, head, peak, extremity • *He tapped the ends of his fingers together.*
6 = **purpose**, point, reason, goal, design, target, aim, object, mission, intention, objective, drift, intent, aspiration • *another policy designed to achieve the same end*
7 = **outcome**, result, consequence, resolution, conclusion, completion, issue, sequel, end result, attainment, upshot, consummation • *The end justifies the means.*
8 = **death**, dying, ruin, destruction, passing on, doom, demise, extinction, dissolution, passing away, extermination, annihilation, expiration, ruination • *Soon after we spoke to him, he met a violent end.*
9 = **remnant**, butt, bit, stub, scrap, fragment, stump, remainder, leftover, tail end, oddment, tag end • *an ashtray overflowing with cigarette ends*
▸ AS A VERB 1 = **stop**, finish, complete, resolve, halt, cease, axe *(informal)*, dissolve, wind up, terminate, call off, discontinue, put paid to, bring to an end, pull the plug on, call a halt to, nip in the bud, belay *(Nautical)* • *Talks have resumed to try to end the fighting.*
OPPOSITES: start, launch, initiate
2 = **finish**, close, conclude, wind up, culminate, terminate, come to an end, draw to a close • *The book ends on a lengthy description of Hawaii.*
OPPOSITES: start, begin, kick in
3 = **destroy**, take, kill, abolish, put an end to, do away with, extinguish, annihilate, exterminate, put to death • *I believe you should be free to end your own life.*
▸ IN PHRASES: **end up** 1 = **finish up**, stop, wind up, come to a halt, fetch up *(informal)* • *The car ended up at the bottom of the river.*
2 = **turn out to be**, finish as, finish up, pan out *(informal)*, become eventually • *She could have ended up a millionairess.*
make ends meet = **manage**, cope, make do, scrape by, get along *or* by • *Even with Betty's salary, they could barely make ends meet.*
▸ RELATED ADJECTIVES: final, terminal, ultimate

QUOTATIONS
The end must justify the means
[Matthew Prior *Hans Carvel*]

PROVERBS
All good things must come to an end
All's well that ends well

endanger = **put at risk**, risk, threaten, compromise, hazard, jeopardize, imperil, put in danger, expose to danger • *This debate could endanger the peace talks.*
OPPOSITES: save, protect, guard

endear = **attract**, draw, bind, engage, charm, attach, win, incline, captivate • *Her behaviour did not endear her to her colleagues.*

endearing = **attractive**, winning, pleasing, appealing, sweet, engaging, charming, pleasant, cute, enticing, captivating, lovable, alluring, adorable, winsome, cutesy *(informal, chiefly U.S.)* • *She has such an endearing personality.*

endearment 1 = **loving word**, sweet talk, sweet nothing, term of affection, affectionate utterance • *She was always using endearments like 'darling' and 'sweetheart'.*
2 = **affection**, feeling, love, warmth, attachment, tenderness, fondness • *His favourite term of endearment was 'baby'.*

endeavour AS A VERB = **try**, labour, attempt, aim, struggle, venture, undertake, essay, strive, aspire, have a go, go for it *(informal)*, make an effort, have a shot *(informal)*, have a crack *(informal)*, take pains, bend over backwards *(informal)*, do your best, go for broke *(slang)*, bust a gut *(informal)*, give it your best shot *(informal)*, jump through hoops *(informal)*, have a stab *(informal)*, break your neck *(informal)*, make an all-out effort *(informal)*, knock yourself out *(informal)*, do your damnedest *(informal)*, give it your all *(informal)*, rupture yourself *(informal)* • *I will endeavour to rectify the situation.*
▸ AS A NOUN = **attempt**, try, shot *(informal)*, effort, trial, go *(informal)*, aim, bid, crack *(informal)*, venture, enterprise, undertaking, essay, stab *(informal)* • *His first endeavours in the field were wedding films.*

ended = **finished**, done, over, through, closed, past, complete, done with, settled, all over (bar the shouting), no more, concluded, accomplished, wrapped-up *(informal)*, at an end, finis • *At last our search is ended.*

endemic = **widespread**, common, sweeping, extensive, prevalent, rife, pervasive • *Polio was then endemic among children of my age.*

ending = **finish**, end, close, resolution, conclusion, summing up, wind-up, completion, finale, termination, culmination, cessation, denouement, last part, consummation • *The film has a Hollywood happy ending.*
OPPOSITES: start, opening, source

endless 1 = **eternal**, constant, infinite, perpetual, continual, immortal, unbroken, unlimited, uninterrupted, limitless, interminable, incessant, boundless, everlasting, unending, ceaseless, inexhaustible, undying, unceasing, unbounded, measureless, unfading • *causing over 25,000 deaths in a seemingly endless war*
OPPOSITES: passing, limited, temporary
2 = **interminable**, constant, persistent, perpetual, never-ending, incessant, monotonous, overlong • *I am sick to death of your endless complaints.*
3 = **continuous**, unbroken, uninterrupted, undivided, without end • *an endless conveyor belt*

endorse *or* **indorse** 1 = **approve**, back, support, champion, favour, promote, recommend, sanction, sustain, advocate, warrant, prescribe, uphold, authorize, ratify, affirm, approve of, subscribe to, espouse, vouch for, throw your weight behind • *I can endorse this statement wholeheartedly.*
2 = **sign**, initial, countersign, sign on the back of, superscribe, undersign • *The payee must endorse the cheque.*

endorsement *or* **indorsement** = **approval**, backing, support, championing, favour, promotion, sanction, recommendation, acceptance, agreement, warrant, confirmation, upholding, subscription, fiat, advocacy, affirmation, ratification, authorization, seal of approval, approbation, espousal, O.K. *or* okay *(informal)* • *This is a powerful endorsement of his style of governing.*

endow 1 = **finance**, fund, pay for, award, grant, invest in, confer, settle on, bestow, make over, bequeath, purvey, donate money to • *The ambassador has endowed a public-service fellowship programme.*
2 = **imbue**, steep, bathe, saturate, pervade, instil, infuse, permeate, impregnate, inculcate • *Herbs have been used for centuries to endow a whole range of foods with subtle flavours.*

endowed *usually with* **with** = **provided**, favoured, graced, blessed, supplied, furnished, enriched, endued • *He was endowed with wealth, health and a good intellect.*

endowment 1 = **provision**, fund, funding, award, income, grant, gift, contribution, revenue, subsidy, presentation, donation, legacy, hand-out, boon, bequest, stipend, bestowal, benefaction, largesse *or* largess, koha *(N.Z.)* • *The company gave the Oxford Union a generous £1m endowment.*
2 *usually plural* = **talent**, power, feature, quality, ability, gift, capacity, characteristic, attribute, qualification, genius, faculty, capability, flair, aptitude • *individuals with higher-than-average intellectual endowments*

endurance 1 = **staying power**, strength, resolution, resignation, determination, patience, submission, stamina, fortitude, persistence, tenacity, perseverance, toleration, sufferance, doggedness, stickability *(informal)*, pertinacity • *a test of endurance*
2 = **permanence**, stability, continuity, duration, continuation, longevity, durability, continuance, immutability, lastingness • *The book is about the endurance of the class system in Britain.*

endure 1 = **experience**, suffer, bear, weather, meet, go through, encounter, cope with, sustain, brave, undergo, withstand, live through, thole *(Scot.)* • *He'd endured years of pain and sleepless nights because of arthritis.*
2 = **put up with**, stand, suffer, bear, allow, accept, stick *(slang)*, take *(informal)*, permit, stomach, swallow, brook, tolerate, hack *(slang)*, abide, submit to, countenance, stick out *(informal)*, take patiently • *I simply can't endure another moment of her company.*
3 = **last**, live, continue, remain, stay, hold, stand, go on, survive, live on, prevail, persist, abide, be durable, wear well • *Somehow the language endures and continues to survive to this day.*

PROVERBS
What can't be cured must be endured

enduring = **long-lasting**, lasting, living, continuing, remaining, firm, surviving, permanent, constant, steady, prevailing, persisting, abiding, perennial, durable, immortal, steadfast, unwavering, immovable, imperishable, unfaltering • *Their chance meeting was the start of an enduring friendship.*
OPPOSITES: short, passing, brief

enemy = **foe**, rival, opponent, the opposition, competitor, the other side, adversary, antagonist • *His enemies were quick to take advantage of his weakness.*
OPPOSITES: friend, ally, supporter
▸ RELATED ADJECTIVE: inimical

QUOTATIONS
Pay attention to your enemies, for they are the first to discover your mistakes
[Antisthenes]
You can discover what your enemy fears most by observing the means he uses to frighten you
[Eric Hoffer *The Passionate State of Mind*]
A man cannot be too careful in the choice of his enemies
[Oscar Wilde *Lady Windermere's Fan*]
A very great man once said you should love your enemies, and that's not a bad piece of advice. We can love them, but, by God, that doesn't mean we're not going to fight them
[Norman Schwarzkopf]
The enemy advances, we retreat.
The enemy camps, we harass.
The enemy tires, we attack.
The enemy retreats, we pursue
[Mao Zedong *slogan for his troops*]
We have met the enemy and he is us
[Walt Kelly *Pogo*]
Yet is every man his own greatest enemy, and as it were his own executioner
[Thomas Browne *Religio Medici*]
If we could read the secret history of our enemies, we should find in each man's life sorrow and suffering enough to disarm all hostility
[Henry Wadsworth Longfellow *Driftwood*]

energetic 1 = **forceful**, strong, determined, powerful, storming *(informal)*, active, aggressive, dynamic, vigorous, potent, hard-hitting, high-powered, strenuous, punchy *(informal)*, forcible, high-octane *(informal)* • *an energetic public-relations campaign*
2 = **lively**, spirited, active, dynamic, vigorous, animated, brisk, tireless, bouncy, indefatigable, alive and kicking, zippy *(informal)*, full of beans *(informal)*, bright-eyed and bushy-tailed *(informal)* • *Two-year-olds can be incredibly energetic.*
OPPOSITES: slow, weak, lethargic
3 = **strenuous**, hard, taxing, demanding, tough, exhausting, vigorous, arduous • *an energetic exercise routine*

energize *or* **energise** 1 = **stimulate**, drive, stir, motivate, activate, animate, enthuse, quicken, enliven, galvanize, liven up, pep up, invigorate, vitalize, inspirit • *their ability to energize their followers*
2 = **stimulate**, operate, trigger, turn on, start up, activate, switch on, kick-start, electrify, actuate • *When energized, the coil creates an electromagnetic force.*

energy 1 = **strength**, might, force, power, activity, intensity, stamina, exertion, forcefulness • *He was saving his energy for the big race in Belgium.*
2 = **liveliness**, life, drive, fire, spirit, determination, pep, go *(informal)*, zip *(informal)*, vitality, animation, vigour, verve, zest, resilience, welly *(slang)*, get-up-and-go *(informal)*, élan, brio, vivacity, vim *(slang)* • *At 65 years old, her energy and looks are wonderful.*
3 = **power** • *Oil shortages have brought an energy crisis.*

enervated = **weakened**, spent, done in *(informal)*, weak, tired, drained, undermined, exhausted, fatigued, rundown, limp, feeble, sapped, worn out, debilitated, unnerved, washed out, incapacitated, enfeebled, devitalized • *Warm winds make many people feel enervated and depressed.*

enervating = **weakening**, tiring, draining, exhausting, debilitating • *an appalling and enervating disease*

enfeebled = **weakened**, undermined, exhausted, diminished, fatigued, depleted, sapped, worn out, debilitated, unnerved, unhinged, devitalized, rendered feeble • *in his final years, when Graves was enfeebled by senile dementia*

enfold *or* **infold** 1 = **wrap**, surround, enclose, wrap up, encompass, shroud, immerse, swathe, envelop, sheathe, enwrap • *Wood was comfortably enfolded in a woolly dressing-gown.*
2 = **embrace**, hold, fold, hug, cuddle, clasp • *He enfolded her gently in his arms.*

enforce 1 = **carry out**, apply, implement, fulfil, execute, administer, put into effect, put into action, put into operation, put in force • *The measures are being enforced by Interior Ministry troops.*
2 = **impose**, force, require, urge, insist on, compel, exact, oblige, constrain, coerce • *They tried to limit the cost by enforcing a low-tech specification.*

enforced = **imposed**, required, necessary, compelled, dictated, prescribed, compulsory, mandatory, constrained, ordained, obligatory, unavoidable, involuntary • *the announcement of an enforced air embargo on Iraq*

enforcement 1 = **administration**, carrying out, application, prosecution, execution, implementation, reinforcement, fulfilment • *the adequate enforcement of the law*
2 = **imposition**, requirement, obligation, insistence, exaction • *the stricter enforcement of speed limits for vehicles*

enfranchise = **give the vote to**, give voting rights to, grant suffrage to, grant the franchise to, grant voting rights to • *The city's foreign residents are being enfranchised.*

e

enfranchisement = **giving the vote**, giving voting rights, granting voting rights, granting suffrage *or* the franchise • *Sylvia Pankhurst, who fought for women's enfranchisement*

engage 1 = **participate in**, join in, take part in, undertake, practise, embark on, enter into, become involved in, set about, partake of • *They continue to engage in terrorist activities.*
2 = **captivate**, win, draw, catch, arrest, fix, attract, capture, charm, attach, fascinate, enchant, allure, enamour • *He engaged us with tales of his adventures.*
3 = **occupy**, involve, draw, busy, grip, absorb, tie up, preoccupy, immerse, engross • *He tried to engage me in conversation.*
4 = **employ**, commission, appoint, take on, hire, retain, recruit, enlist, enrol, put on the payroll • *We have been able to engage some staff.*
OPPOSITES: remove, dismiss, sack *(informal)*
5 = **book**, reserve, secure, hire, rent, charter, lease, prearrange • *He managed to engage a room for the night.*
6 = **interlock**, join, interact, mesh, interconnect, dovetail • *Press the lever until you hear the catch engage.*
7 = **set going**, apply, trigger, activate, switch on, energize, bring into operation • *Show me how to engage the four-wheel drive.*
8 = **begin battle with**, attack, take on, encounter, combat, fall on, battle with, meet, fight with, assail, face off *(slang)*, wage war on, join battle with, give battle to, come to close quarters with • *They could engage the enemy beyond the range of the torpedoes.*

engaged 1 = **occupied**, working, involved, committed, employed, busy, absorbed, tied up, preoccupied, engrossed • *the various projects he was engaged on*
2 = **betrothed**, promised, pledged, affianced, promised in marriage • *He was engaged to Miss Julia Boardman.*
OPPOSITES: free, available, unattached
3 = **in use**, busy, tied up, unavailable • *We tried to phone you back but the line was engaged.*
OPPOSITES: free, available

engagement 1 = **appointment**, meeting, interview, date, commitment, arrangement, rendezvous • *He had an engagement at a restaurant in Greek Street at eight.*
2 = **betrothal**, marriage contract, troth *(archaic)*, agreement to marry • *I've broken off my engagement to Arthur.*
3 = **battle**, fight, conflict, action, struggle, clash, contest, encounter, combat, confrontation, skirmish, face-off *(slang)* • *The constitution prevents them from military engagement on foreign soil.*
4 = **participation**, joining, taking part, involvement • *his proactive engagement in the peace process*
5 = **job**, work, post, situation, commission, employment, appointment, gig *(informal)*, stint • *her first official engagement as Miss World*

engaging = **charming**, interesting, pleasing, appealing, attractive, lovely, fascinating, entertaining, winning, pleasant, fetching *(informal)*, delightful, cute, enchanting, captivating, agreeable, lovable, winsome, cutesy *(informal, chiefly U.S.)*, likable *or* likeable • *She was a most engaging child.*
OPPOSITES: offensive, unpleasant, unattractive

engender 1 = **produce**, make, cause, create, lead to, occasion, excite, result in, breed, generate, provoke, induce, bring about, arouse, give rise to, precipitate, incite, instigate, foment, beget • *Insults engender hatred against those who indulge in them.*
2 = **breed**, father, create, generate, conceive, give birth to, spawn, sire, propagate, bring forth, beget, procreate, give life to • *the desire to engender children*

engine = **machine**, motor, mechanism, generator, dynamo • *He got into the driving seat and started the engine.*

engineer AS A NOUN 1 = **designer**, producer, architect, developer, deviser, creator, planner, inventor, stylist, artificer, originator, couturier • *He is a fully qualified civil engineer.*
2 = **worker**, specialist, operator, practitioner, operative, driver, conductor, technician, handler, skilled employee • *They sent a service engineer to repair the disk drive.*
▸ AS A VERB 1 = **design**, plan, create, construct, devise, originate • *Many of Kuwait's freeways were engineered by W. S. Atkins.*
2 = **bring about**, plan, control, cause, effect, manage, set up *(informal)*, scheme, arrange, plot, manoeuvre, encompass, mastermind, orchestrate, contrive, concoct, wangle *(informal)*, finagle *(informal)* • *Some people believe that his murder was engineered by Stalin.*

engineering
▹ *See panel* **Branches of engineering**

England = **Blighty**, Albion • *their first visit to England*
▸ **RELATED PREFIX:** Anglo-
▸ **RELATED MANIA:** Anglomania

Englishman

QUOTATIONS
There is in the Englishman a combination of qualities, a modesty, an independence, a responsibility, a repose, combined with an absence of everything calculated to call a blush into the cheek of a young person, which one would seek in vain among the Nations of the Earth
[Charles Dickens *Our Mutual Friend*]

BRANCHES OF ENGINEERING

aerodynamics
aeronautical engineering
aerospace engineering
agricultural engineering
astronautics
automotive engineering
bioengineering
chemical engineering
civil engineering
computer-aided engineering
cosmonautics
electrical engineering
electronics engineering
environmental engineering
ergonomics
fluid dynamics
genetic engineering
geotechnics
hydraulics
mechanical engineering
mechatronics
military engineering
mining engineering
naval engineering
nuclear engineering
process engineering
production engineering
sanitary engineering
structural engineering
traffic engineering

An Englishman, even if he is alone, forms an orderly queue of one
[George Mikes *How to be an Alien*]
PROVERBS
An Englishman's home is his castle

engorged = **swollen**, filled, enlarged, inflamed, bloated, puffy, puffed up, distended, tumescent, oedematous, tumid • *The tissues in the womb become engorged with blood.*

engrained *see* **ingrained**

engrave = **carve**, cut, etch, inscribe, chisel, incise, chase, enchase *(rare)*, grave *(archaic)* • *Her name was engraved on the goblet.*

engraved = **fixed**, set, printed, impressed, lodged, embedded, imprinted, etched, ingrained, infixed • *Her memory is engraved upon my heart.*

engraving 1 = **print**, block, impression, carving, etching, inscription, plate, woodcut, dry point • *the engraving of Shakespeare at the front of the book*
2 = **cutting**, carving, etching, inscribing, chiselling, inscription, chasing, dry point, enchasing *(rare)* • *Glass engraving has increased in popularity over recent years.*
▸ RELATED ADJECTIVE: glyptic

engrossed = **absorbed**, lost, involved, occupied, deep, engaged, gripped, fascinated, caught up, intrigued, intent, preoccupied, immersed, riveted, captivated, enthralled, rapt • *He didn't notice because he was too engrossed in his work.*

engrossing = **absorbing**, interesting, arresting, engaging, gripping, fascinating, compelling, intriguing, riveting, captivating, enthralling • *an engrossing subject for a documentary*

engulf *or* **ingulf** 1 = **immerse**, bury, flood (out), plunge, consume, drown, swamp, encompass, submerge, overrun, inundate, deluge, envelop, swallow up • *The flat was engulfed in flames.*
2 = **overwhelm**, overcome, crush, absorb, swamp, engross • *He was engulfed by a feeling of emptiness.*

enhance = **improve**, better, increase, raise, lift, boost, add to, strengthen, reinforce, swell, intensify, heighten, elevate, magnify, augment, exalt, embellish, ameliorate • *They want to enhance their reputation abroad.*
OPPOSITES: reduce, lower, spoil

enhancement = **improvement**, strengthening, heightening, enrichment, increment, embellishment, boost, betterment, augmentation, amelioration • *He was concerned with the enhancement of the human condition.*

enigma = **mystery**, problem, puzzle, riddle, paradox, conundrum, teaser • *This country remains an enigma for the outside world.*

enigmatic *or* **enigmatical** = **mysterious**, puzzling, obscure, baffling, ambiguous, perplexing, incomprehensible, mystifying, inexplicable, unintelligible, paradoxical, cryptic, inscrutable, unfathomable, indecipherable, recondite, Delphic, oracular, sphinxlike • *She starred in one of Welles's most enigmatic films.*
OPPOSITES: clear, simple, straightforward

enjoin 1 = **order**, charge, warn, urge, require, direct, bid, command, advise, counsel, prescribe, instruct, call upon • *She enjoined me strictly not to tell anyone else.*
2 = **prohibit**, bar, ban, forbid, restrain, preclude, disallow, proscribe, interdict, place an injunction on • *the government's attempt to enjoin the publication of the book*

enjoy AS A VERB 1 = **take pleasure in** *or* **from**, like, love, appreciate, relish, delight in, revel in, be pleased with, be fond of, be keen on, rejoice in, be entertained by, find pleasure in, find satisfaction in, take joy in • *He enjoys playing cricket.*
OPPOSITES: hate, dislike, loathe
2 = **have**, use, own, experience, possess, have the benefit of, reap the benefits of, have the use of, be blessed *or* favoured with • *The average German will enjoy 40 days' paid holiday this year.*
▸ IN PHRASES: **enjoy yourself** = **have a good time**, be happy, have fun, have a field day *(informal)*, have a ball *(informal)*, live life to the full, make merry, let your hair down • *He's too busy enjoying himself to get much work done.*
PROVERBS
Make hay while the sun shines

enjoyable = **pleasurable**, good, great, fine, pleasing, nice, satisfying, lovely, entertaining, pleasant, amusing, delicious, delightful, gratifying, agreeable, delectable, to your liking • *the most enjoyable part of the holiday*
OPPOSITES: offensive, unpleasant, unsavoury

enjoyment 1 = **pleasure**, liking, fun, delight, entertainment, joy, satisfaction, happiness, relish, recreation, amusement, indulgence, diversion, zest, gratification, gusto, gladness, delectation, beer and skittles *(informal)* • *She ate with great enjoyment.*
2 = **benefit**, use, advantage, favour, possession, blessing • *the enjoyment of equal freedom by all*

enlarge AS A VERB 1 = **expand**, increase, extend, add to, build up, widen, intensify, blow up *(informal)*, heighten, broaden, inflate, lengthen, magnify, amplify, augment, make bigger, elongate, make larger • *plans to enlarge the park into a 30,000 all-seater stadium*
OPPOSITES: reduce, narrow, trim
2 = **grow**, increase, extend, stretch, expand, swell, wax, multiply, inflate, lengthen, diffuse, elongate, dilate, become bigger, puff up, grow larger, grow bigger, become larger, distend, bloat • *The glands in the neck may enlarge.*
▸ IN PHRASES: **enlarge on something** = **expand on**, develop, add to, fill out, elaborate on, flesh out, expatiate on, give further details about • *I wish to enlarge on the statement I made yesterday.*

enlargement 1 = **expansion**, increase, development, growth, spread, inflation, extension, swelling, unfolding, expanse, diffusion, unfurling, opening out, intensification, magnification, multiplication, amplification, elongation, augmentation, dilatation, distension • *There is insufficient space for the enlargement of the buildings.*
2 = **blow-up**, expansion, magnification • *an enlargement of her wedding photo*

enlighten = **inform**, tell, teach, advise, counsel, educate, instruct, illuminate, make aware, edify, apprise, let know, cause to understand • *Their aim is to enlighten the public about the situation.*

enlightened = **informed**, aware, liberal, reasonable, educated, sophisticated, refined, cultivated, open-minded, knowledgeable, literate, broad-minded • *He should be remembered as an enlightened and humane reformer.*
OPPOSITES: unaware, ignorant, short-sighted

enlightenment = **understanding**, information, learning, education, teaching, knowledge, instruction, awareness, wisdom, insight, literacy, sophistication, comprehension, cultivation, refinement, open-mindedness, edification, broad-mindedness • *He'd set off for the East in search of spiritual enlightenment.*

enlist 1 = **join up**, join, enter (into), register, volunteer, sign up, enrol • *He enlisted as a private in the Mexican War.*
2 = **recruit**, secure, gather, take on, hire, sign up, call up, muster, mobilize, conscript • *Three thousand men were enlisted.*
3 = **obtain**, get, gain, secure, engage, procure • *I had to enlist the help of several neighbours to clear the mess.*

enliven = **cheer up**, excite, inspire, cheer, spark, enhance, stimulate, wake up, animate, fire, rouse, brighten, exhilarate, quicken, hearten, perk up, liven up, buoy up, pep up, invigorate, gladden, vitalize, vivify, inspirit, make more exciting, make more lively • *His presence enlivened even the most boring meeting.*

OPPOSITES: depress, chill, subdue

en masse = **all together**, together, as one, as a whole, ensemble, as a group, in a group, all at once, in a mass, as a body, in a body • *The audience left en masse.*

enmeshed = **entangled**, involved, caught, netted, trapped, tangled, implicated, snarled, embroiled, snared, incriminated, ensnared, trammelled • *He was enmeshed in a complex web of personal problems.*

enmity = **hostility**, hate, spite, hatred, bitterness, friction, malice, animosity, aversion, venom, antagonism, antipathy, acrimony, rancour, bad blood, ill will, animus, malevolence, malignity • *The two countries erupted into open enmity during the Gulf war.*

OPPOSITES: love, friendship, affection

ennoble 1 = **dignify**, honour, enhance, elevate, magnify, raise, glorify, exalt, aggrandize • *the fundamental principles of life which ennoble mankind*

2 = **raise to the peerage**, kick upstairs *(informal)*, make noble • *He had been ennobled for arranging a government loan in 1836.*

ennui = **boredom**, dissatisfaction, tiredness, the doldrums, lethargy, tedium, lassitude, listlessness • *He suffered from ennui whenever he was alone.*

enormity 1 = **hugeness**, extent, magnitude, greatness, vastness, immensity, massiveness, enormousness, extensiveness • *He was appalled by the enormity of the task ahead of him.*

2 = **wickedness**, disgrace, atrocity, depravity, viciousness, villainy, turpitude, outrageousness, baseness, vileness, evilness, monstrousness, heinousness, nefariousness, atrociousness • *the enormity of the crime they had committed*

3 = **atrocity**, crime, horror, evil, outrage, disgrace, monstrosity, abomination, barbarity, villainy • *the horrific enormities perpetrated on the islanders*

enormous = **huge**, massive, vast, extensive, tremendous, gross, excessive, immense, titanic, jumbo *(informal)*, gigantic, monstrous, mammoth, colossal, mountainous, stellar *(informal)*, prodigious, gargantuan, fuck-off *(taboo slang)*, elephantine, astronomic, ginormous *(informal)*, Brobdingnagian, humongous *or* humungous *(U.S. slang)*, supersize • *an enormous dust cloud blocking out the sun*

OPPOSITES: little, small, tiny

enormously = **very**, highly, greatly, really, quite, deeply, particularly, seriously *(informal)*, severely, truly, extremely, absolutely, terribly, remarkably, ultra, utterly, unusually, jolly *(Brit.)*, wonderfully, exceptionally, profoundly, extraordinarily, intensely, decidedly, markedly, awfully *(informal)*, acutely, exceedingly, excessively, noticeably, superlatively, inordinately, uncommonly, to a fault, to the nth degree, surpassingly, to *or* in the extreme • *This book was enormously influential.*

enough AS AN ADJECTIVE = **sufficient**, adequate, ample, abundant, as much as you need, as much as is necessary • *They had enough money for a one-way ticket.*

▸ AS A PRONOUN = **sufficiency**, plenty, sufficient, abundance, adequacy, right amount, ample supply • *I hope you brought enough for everyone.*

▸ AS AN ADVERB = **sufficiently**, amply, fairly, moderately, reasonably, adequately, satisfactorily, abundantly, tolerably, passably • *Do you think sentences for criminals are tough enough already?*

PROVERBS

Enough is as good as a feast

en passant = **in passing**, by the way, incidentally, parenthetically, by the bye • *He advised her, en passant, that she should see a doctor.*

enquire see **inquire**

enquiring see **inquiring**

enquiry see **inquiry**

enrage = **anger**, provoke, irritate, infuriate, aggravate *(informal)*, incense, gall, madden, inflame, exasperate, incite, antagonize, make you angry, nark *(Brit., Austral. & N.Z. slang)*, make your blood boil, get your back up, make you see red *(informal)*, put your back up • *Her obstinate refusal enraged him.*

OPPOSITES: calm, soothe, appease

enraged = **furious**, cross, wild, angry, angered, mad *(informal)*, raging, irritated, fuming, choked, pissed *(U.S. slang)*, infuriated, aggravated *(informal)*, incensed, inflamed, exasperated, very angry, pissed off *(taboo slang)*, irate, livid *(informal)*, incandescent, on the warpath, fit to be tied *(slang)*, boiling mad, raging mad, tooshie *(Austral. slang)*, off the air *(Austral. slang)* • *The enraged crowd stoned the car, then set it on fire.*

enraptured = **enchanted**, delighted, charmed, fascinated, absorbed, entranced, captivated, transported, enthralled, beguiled, bewitched, ravished, spellbound, enamoured • *He played to an enraptured audience.*

enrich 1 = **enhance**, develop, improve, boost, supplement, refine, cultivate, heighten, endow, augment, ameliorate, aggrandize • *Vivid fantasies can enrich your sex life.*

2 = **make rich**, make wealthy, make affluent, make prosperous, make well-off • *He enriched himself at the expense of others.*

enrichment = **improvement**, development, advance, progress, rally, amendment, correction, advancement, reformation, enhancement, betterment, furtherance, augmentation, amelioration • *groups contributing to the enrichment of society*

enrol *or (U.S.)* **enroll** 1 = **enlist**, register, be accepted, be admitted, join up, matriculate, put your name down for, sign up *or* on • *To enrol for the conference, fill in the attached form.*

2 = **recruit**, take on, engage, enlist • *I thought I'd enrol you with an art group at the school.*

enrolment *or (U.S.)* **enrollment** = **enlistment**, admission, acceptance, engagement, registration, recruitment, matriculation, signing on *or* up • *The full fee is payable at enrolment.*

en route = **on** *or* **along the way**, travelling, on the road, in transit, on the journey • *a brief stop over en route from Baghdad to Libya*

ensconce = **settle**, establish, install, lodge, nestle, entrench, curl up, snuggle up • *They ensconced themselves on the couch.*

ensconced = **settled**, established, installed, entrenched, well established • *Brian was ensconced behind the bar.*

ensemble 1 = **group**, company, band, troupe, cast, orchestra, chorus, supporting cast • *an ensemble of young musicians*

2 = **collection**, set, body, whole, total, sum, combination, entity, aggregate, entirety, totality, assemblage, conglomeration • *The state is an ensemble of political and social structures.*

3 = **outfit**, suit, get-up *(informal)*, costume • *a dashing ensemble in navy and white*

enshrine = **preserve**, protect, treasure, cherish, revere, exalt, consecrate, embalm, sanctify, hallow, apotheosize • *the apartheid system which enshrined racism*

ensign = **flag**, standard, colours, banner, badge, pennant, streamer, jack, pennon • *a merchant ship flying the blue ensign of a fleet auxiliary*

enslave = **subjugate**, bind, dominate, trap, suppress, enthral, yoke, tyrannize, sell into slavery, reduce to slavery, enchain • *an alien plot to enslave humanity*

enslavement = **subjugation**, slavery, suppression, tyranny, obedience, bondage, thrall, servitude, serfdom, vassalage, thraldom • *The enslavement of the African people is one of the biggest crimes in history.*

ensnare = **trap**, catch, capture, seize, snarl, embroil, net, snare, entangle, entrap, enmesh • *The spider must wait for the prey to be ensnared in its web.*

ensue = **follow**, result, develop, succeed, proceed, arise, stem, derive, come after, roll up, issue, befall, flow, come next, come to pass *(archaic)*, supervene, be consequent on, turn out *or* up • *A brief but violent scuffle ensued.*
OPPOSITES: lead, introduce, come first

ensuing = **following**, resulting, succeeding, subsequent, later, consequent • *In the ensuing violence more than 130 people were injured.*

ensure *or (especially U.S.)* **insure** 1 = **make certain**, guarantee, secure, make sure, confirm, warrant, certify • *Steps must be taken to ensure this never happens again.*
2 = **protect**, defend, secure, safeguard, guard, make safe • *The plan is aimed at ensuring the future of freshwater fish species.*

entail = **involve**, require, cause, produce, demand, lead to, call for, occasion, need, impose, result in, bring about, give rise to, encompass, necessitate • *Such a decision would entail a huge risk.*

entangle 1 = **tangle**, catch, trap, twist, knot, mat, mix up, snag, snarl, snare, jumble, ravel, trammel, enmesh • *The door handle had entangled itself with the strap of her bag.*
OPPOSITES: free, separate, disentangle
2 = **embroil**, involve, complicate, mix up, muddle, implicate, bog down, enmesh • *Bureaucracy can entangle ventures for months.*

entanglement 1 = **affair**, involvement, romance, intrigue, fling, liaison, love affair, amour, illicit romance • *a romantic entanglement*
2 = **difficulty**, mess, confusion, complication, mix-up, muddle, predicament, imbroglio • *trying to do his job without the usual bureaucratic entanglements*
3 = **becoming entangled**, mix-up, becoming enmeshed, becoming ensnared, becoming jumbled, entrapment, snarl-up *(informal, chiefly Brit.)*, ensnarement • *Many dolphins are accidentally killed through entanglement in fishing equipment.*

entente = **agreement**, understanding, accord, contract, arrangement, settlement, deal *(informal)*, treaty, bargain, pact, compact, covenant, friendly agreement • *his attempts to nurture the entente between the two countries*

entente cordiale = **agreement**, understanding, arrangement, treaty, deal *(informal)*, friendship, pact, compact • *holding a conference in an attempt to develop an entente cordiale*

enter AS A VERB 1 = **come** *or* **go in** *or* **into**, arrive, set foot in somewhere, cross the threshold of somewhere, make an entrance • *He entered and stood near the door.*
OPPOSITES: exit, leave, withdraw
2 = **penetrate**, get in, insert into, pierce, pass into, perforate • *The bullet entered his right eye.*
3 = **join**, start work at, begin work at, sign up for, enrol in, become a member of, enlist in, commit yourself to • *He entered the company as a junior trainee.*
OPPOSITES: resign, leave, retire
4 = **participate in**, join (in), be involved in, get involved in, play a part in, partake in, associate yourself with, start to be in • *A million young people enter the labour market each year.*
5 = **begin**, start, take up, move into, set about, commence, set out on, embark upon • *I have entered a new phase in my life.*
6 = **compete in**, contest, take part in, join in, fight, sign up for, go in for • *As a boy he entered many music competitions.*
7 = **record**, note, register, log, list, write down, take down, inscribe, set down, put in writing • *Prue entered the passage in her notebook, then read it aloud again.*
8 = **submit**, offer, present, table, register, lodge, tender, put forward, proffer • *I entered a plea of guilty to the charges.*
▸ IN PHRASES: **enter into something** = **begin**, take part in, undertake, participate in, embark on, get involved with, become involved with • *I have not entered into any financial agreements with them.*

enterprise 1 = **firm**, company, business, concern, operation, organization, establishment, commercial undertaking • *There are plenty of small industrial enterprises.*
2 = **venture**, operation, project, adventure, undertaking, programme, pursuit, endeavour • *Horse breeding is a risky enterprise.*
3 = **initiative**, energy, spirit, resource, daring, enthusiasm, push *(informal)*, imagination, drive, pep, readiness, vigour, zeal, ingenuity, originality, eagerness, audacity, boldness, welly *(slang)*, get-up-and-go *(informal)*, alertness, resourcefulness, gumption *(informal)*, adventurousness, imaginativeness • *His trouble is that he lacks enterprise.*

enterprising = **resourceful**, original, spirited, keen, active, daring, alert, eager, bold, enthusiastic, vigorous, imaginative, energetic, adventurous, ingenious, up-and-coming, audacious, zealous, intrepid, venturesome • *an enterprising and hard-working young woman*

entertain 1 = **amuse**, interest, please, delight, occupy, charm, enthral, cheer, divert, recreate *(rare)*, regale, give pleasure to • *He entertained us with anecdotes about his job.*
2 = **show hospitality to**, receive, accommodate, treat, put up, lodge, be host to, have company of, invite round, ask round, invite to a meal, ask for a meal • *I don't really like to entertain guests any more.*
3 = **consider**, support, maintain, imagine, think about, hold, foster, harbour, contemplate, conceive of, ponder, cherish, bear in mind, keep in mind, think over, muse over, give thought to, cogitate on, allow yourself to consider • *I wouldn't entertain the idea of doing such a job.*

entertainer
▹ *See panel* **Entertainment**

entertaining = **enjoyable**, interesting, pleasing, funny, charming, cheering, pleasant, amusing, diverting, delightful, witty, humorous, pleasurable, recreative *(rare)* • *This is a surprisingly entertaining film.*

entertainment 1 = **enjoyment**, fun, pleasure, leisure, satisfaction, relaxation, recreation, enjoyment, distraction, amusement, diversion • *I play the piano purely for my own entertainment.*
2 = **pastime**, show, sport, performance, play, treat, presentation, leisure activity, beer and skittles • *He organized entertainments and events for elderly people.*

QUOTATIONS
I believe entertainment can aspire to be art, and can become art, but if you set out to make art you're an idiot
[Steve Martin]

▹ *See panel* **Entertainment**

enthral *or (U.S.)* **enthrall** = **engross**, charm, grip, fascinate, absorb, entrance, intrigue, enchant, rivet, captivate, beguile, ravish, mesmerize, hypnotize, enrapture, hold spellbound, spellbind • *Children and adults alike are enthralled by his stories.*

enthralling = **engrossing**, charming, gripping, fascinating, entrancing, compelling, intriguing, compulsive, enchanting, riveting, captivating, beguiling, mesmerizing, hypnotizing, spellbinding • *a film with an enthralling storyline and plenty of action*

enthuse 1 = **rave**, praise, gush, be enthusiastic, be mad *(informal)*, rhapsodize, be wild *(informal)* • *She enthused about her holiday.*
2 = **excite**, inspire, stir, stimulate, rouse • *Find a hobby which enthuses you.*

enthusiasm 1 = **keenness**, interest, passion, excitement, warmth, motivation, relish, devotion, zeal, zest, fervour, eagerness, ardour, vehemence, earnestness, zing *(informal)*, avidity • *Her lack of enthusiasm filled me with disappointment.*
2 = **interest**, passion, rage, hobby, obsession, craze, fad *(informal)*, mania, hobbyhorse • *the current enthusiasm for skateboarding*

enthusiast = **fan**, supporter, lover, follower, addict, freak *(informal)*, admirer, buff *(informal)*, fanatic, devotee, fiend *(informal)*, fan club *(informal)*, adherent, zealot, aficionado

ENTERTAINMENT

Types of entertainment

acrobatics
aerobatics
agon
airshow
all-dayer
all-nighter
antimasque
après-ski
aquashow
ball
ballet
B and S (*Austral., informal*)
banquet
bear-baiting
bullfighting
burlesque show
busking
cabaret
carnival
ceilidh
charade
circus
cockfighting
comedy
command performance
concert
conjuring
cotillion (*U.S. & Canad.*)
dance
escapology
exhibition
fair
farce
fashion show
feast
fête *or* fete
film
fireworks *or* pyrotechnics
floor show
funambulism *or* tightrope-walking
gala
galanty show
garden party
gaudy
gig (*informal*)
ice show
juggling
karaoke
kermis (*U.S. & Canad.*)
levee
light show
magic
masked ball
masque
melodrama
minstrel show
musical
music hall
opera
operetta
pantomime
party
play
puppet show
raree show
rave
reading
reception
recital
recitation
revue *or* review
ridotto
road show
rodeo
shadow play
show
sideshow
singsong
slide show
slot machine
soiree
son et lumière
street theatre
striptease
tragedy
variety
vaudeville
ventriloquism
video game
wall of death
waltzer
warehouse party
whist drive
zarzuela

Types of entertainer

acrobat
actor *or* (*fem.*) actress
artist
artiste
auguste
bareback rider
busker
chorus girl
circus artist
clown
comedian *or* (*fem.*) comedienne
conjurer
contortionist
dancer
diva
equilibrist
escapologist
exotic dancer
fire eater
fool
funambulist *or* tightrope walker
funnyman
go-go dancer
gracioso
guiser
harlequin
illusionist
impersonator
impressionist
jester
jongleur
juggler
lion tamer
magician
merry-andrew
mimic
minstrel
mummer
musician
organ-grinder
performer
prima ballerina
prima donna
puppeteer
quick-change artist
raconteur
ringmaster
show girl
singer
snake charmer
stripteaser *or* stripper
strolling player
strongman
sword swallower
tightrope walker
tragedian *or* (*fem.*) tragedienne
trapeze artist
trouper
tumbler
unicyclist
vaudevillian
ventriloquist

Places of entertainment

amphitheatre
amusement arcade (*Brit.*)
arena
auditorium
ballroom
bandstand
big top
bingo hall
carnival
cinema
circus
coliseum
concert hall
dance hall
disco
fairground
funfair
gallery
hall
leisure centre
lido
marquee
museum
music hall
nightclub
nightspot
niterie (*slang*)
opera house
social club
stadium
theatre
vaudeville
waxworks
zoo

• *He is a great sports enthusiast.*

enthusiastic = **keen**, earnest, spirited, committed, excited, devoted, warm, eager, lively, passionate, vigorous, ardent, hearty, exuberant, avid, fervent, zealous, ebullient, vehement, wholehearted, full of beans (*informal*), fervid, keen as mustard, bright-eyed and bushy-tailed (*informal*) • *The band drew a huge and enthusiastic crowd.*
OPPOSITES: cool, bored, apathetic

entice = **lure**, attract, invite, persuade, draw, tempt, induce, seduce, lead on, coax, beguile, allure, cajole, decoy, wheedle, prevail on, inveigle, dangle a carrot in front of • *Retailers will try almost anything to entice shoppers through their doors.*

enticement = **attraction**, appeal, incentive, invitation, lure, bait, temptation, persuasion, come-on (*informal*), coaxing, seduction, inducement, cajolery, allurement, inveiglement • *The cash bonus is an added enticement for the bank's customers.*

enticing = **attractive**, appealing, inviting, charming, fascinating, tempting, intriguing, irresistible, persuasive, seductive, captivating, beguiling, alluring • *the enticing prospect of a night on the town*
OPPOSITES: unattractive, distasteful, repellent

entire **1 = continuous**, unified, unbroken, uninterrupted, undivided • *He had spent his entire life in China as a doctor.*
2 = whole, full, complete, total • *The entire family was killed in the crash.*
3 = absolute, full, total, utter, outright, thorough, unqualified, unrestricted, undiminished, unmitigated, unreserved • *He assured me of his entire confidence in me.*
4 = intact, whole, perfect, unmarked, unbroken, sound, unharmed, undamaged, without a scratch, unmarred • *No document is entire, and it is often unclear in what order the pieces fit together.*

entirely **1 = completely**, totally, perfectly, absolutely, fully, altogether, thoroughly, wholly, utterly, every inch, without exception, unreservedly, in every respect, without reservation, lock, stock and barrel • *The two cases are entirely different.*

opposites: partly, somewhat, slightly
2 = **only**, exclusively, solely • *The whole episode was entirely my fault.*

entirety **as a noun** = **whole**, total, sum, unity, aggregate, totality • *His own diary forms the entirety of the novel.*
▸ **in phrases: in its entirety** = **completely**, totally, fully, entirely, absolutely, altogether, wholly, every inch, in every respect, lock, stock and barrel • *The peace plan has been accepted in its entirety by all parties.*

entitle 1 = **give the right to**, allow, enable, permit, sanction, license, qualify for, warrant, authorize, empower, enfranchise, make eligible • *Your contract entitles you to a full refund.*
2 = **call**, name, title, term, style, label, dub, designate, characterize, christen, give the title of, denominate • *an instrumental piece entitled 'Changing States'*

entitlement 1 = **right**, claim, due, licence, permission, privilege, prerogative • *You lose your entitlement to benefit when you start work.*
2 = **allowance**, grant, quota, ration, allocation, allotment, apportionment • *such benefits as sick pay, holiday pay and pension entitlement*

entity 1 = **thing**, being, body, individual, object, presence, existence, substance, quantity, creature, organism • *the concept of the earth as a living entity*
2 = **essential nature**, being, existence, essence, quintessence, real nature, quiddity *(Philosophy)* • *key periods of national or cultural entity and development*

entomb = **bury**, inter, lay to rest, sepulchre, place in a tomb, inhume, inurn • *He was entombed here in this crypt alongside his predecessors.*

entourage = **retinue**, company, following, staff, court, train, suite, escort, cortege • *He was surrounded by an entourage of aides.*

entrails = **intestines**, insides *(informal)*, guts, bowels, offal, internal organs, innards *(informal)*, vital organs, viscera • *The ancient soothsayers used to read the entrails of dead animals.*

entrance[1] 1 = **way in**, opening, door, approach, access, entry, gate, passage, avenue, doorway, portal, inlet, ingress, means of access • *He drove in through a side entrance.*
opposites: exit, outlet, way out
2 = **appearance**, coming in, entry, arrival, introduction, ingress • *The audience chanted his name as he made his entrance.*
opposites: departure, exit, exodus
3 = **admission**, access, entry, entrée, admittance, permission to enter, ingress, right of entry • *Hewitt gained entrance to the house by pretending to be a heating engineer.*

entrance[2] 1 = **enchant**, delight, charm, absorb, fascinate, dazzle, captivate, transport, enthral, beguile, bewitch, ravish, gladden, enrapture, spellbind • *She entranced the audience with her classical Indian singing.*
opposites: bore, offend, irritate
2 = **mesmerize**, bewitch, hypnotize, put a spell on, cast a spell on, put in a trance • *The sailors were entranced by the voices of the sirens.*

entrant 1 = **newcomer**, novice, initiate, beginner, trainee, apprentice, convert, new member, fresher, neophyte, tyro, probationer, newbie *(slang)* • *the newest entrant to the political scene*
2 = **competitor**, player, candidate, entry, participant, applicant, contender, contestant • *All items submitted for the competition must be the entrant's own work.*

entrap **as a noun** = **trick**, lure, seduce, entice, deceive, implicate, lead on, embroil, beguile, allure, entangle, ensnare, inveigle, set a trap for, enmesh • *She was trying to entrap him into marriage.*
▸ **as a verb** = **catch**, net, capture, trap, snare, entangle, ensnare • *The whale's mouth contains filters which entrap plankton.*

entreat = **beg**, ask, appeal to, petition, pray to, conjure, request, plead with, exhort, implore, enjoin, beseech, importune, ask earnestly, supplicate • *They entreated the audience to stay calm.*

entreaty = **plea**, appeal, suit, request, prayer, petition, exhortation, solicitation, supplication, importunity, earnest request • *They have resisted all entreaties to pledge their support for the campaign.*

entrée 1 = **entry**, access, way in, introduction, entrance • *She had gained an entrée into the city's cultivated society.*
2 = **starter**, appetizer • *Dinner features an entrée of chicken, veal or lamb.*

entrench *or* **intrench** = **fix**, set, establish, plant, seat, settle, root, install, lodge, anchor, implant, embed, dig in, ensconce, ingrain • *This policy is likely to entrench racial divisions and resentments.*

entrenched *or* **intrenched** = **fixed**, set, firm, rooted, well-established, ingrained, deep-seated, deep-rooted, indelible, unshakeable *or* unshakable, ineradicable • *Japan's entrenched business practices*

entre nous = **between ourselves**, privately, in confidence, off the record, confidentially, between you and me, between the two of us • *He was friendly with me – in fact, entre nous, a little too friendly.*

entrepreneur = **businessman** *or* **businesswoman**, tycoon, director, executive, contractor, industrialist, financier, speculator, magnate, impresario, business executive • *the flamboyant British entrepreneur Richard Branson*

entrepreneurial = **business**, financial, executive, commercial, managerial • *her prodigious entrepreneurial flair*

entrust *or* **intrust** 1 = **give custody of**, trust, deliver, commit, delegate, hand over, turn over, confide, commend, consign • *her reluctance to entrust her children to the care of someone else*
2 *usually with* **with** = **assign**, charge, trust, invest, authorize • *They are prepared to entrust him with the leadership of the party.*

entry 1 = **admission**, access, entrance, admittance, entrée, permission to enter, right of entry • *Entry to the museum is free.*
2 = **coming in**, entering, appearance, arrival, entrance • *He made his triumphal entry into Mexico.*
opposites: departure, withdrawal, exit
3 = **introduction**, presentation, initiation, inauguration, induction, debut, investiture • *The time has come to prepare her for her entry into society.*
4 = **record**, listing, account, note, minute, statement, item, registration, memo, memorandum, jotting • *Her diary entry for that day records his visit.*
5 = **competitor**, player, attempt, effort, candidate, participant, challenger, submission, entrant, contestant • *The winner was selected from hundreds of entries.*
6 = **way in**, opening, door, approach, access, gate, passage, entrance, avenue, doorway, portal, inlet, passageway, ingress, means of access • *A lorry blocked the entry to the school.*

entwine *or* **intwine** = **twist**, surround, embrace, weave, knit, braid, encircle, wind, intertwine, interweave, plait, twine, ravel, interlace, entwist *(archaic)* • *He entwined his fingers with hers.*
opposites: free, separate, disentangle

enumerate 1 = **list**, tell, name, detail, relate, mention, quote, cite, specify, spell out, recount, recite, itemize, recapitulate • *She enumerated all the reasons why she wanted to leave him.*
2 = **count**, calculate, sum up, total, reckon, compute, add up, tally, number • *They enumerated the casualties.*

enunciate 1 = **pronounce**, say, speak, voice, sound, utter, articulate, vocalize, enounce *(formal)* • *She enunciated each word slowly and carefully.*

2 = **state**, declare, proclaim, pronounce, publish, promulgate, propound • *He was always ready to enunciate his views to anyone who would listen.*

envelop = **enclose**, cover, hide, surround, wrap around, embrace, blanket, conceal, obscure, veil, encompass, engulf, cloak, shroud, swathe, encircle, encase, swaddle, sheathe, enfold, enwrap • *the thick black cloud of smoke that enveloped the area*

envelope = **wrapping**, casing, case, covering, cover, skin, shell, coating, jacket, sleeve, sheath, wrapper • *She opened the envelope and withdrew a typed note.*

enveloping = **enclosing**, surrounding, concealing, encompassing, shrouding, encircling, all-embracing, enfolding • *Astronomers are unable to see the planet's surface because of the enveloping clouds.*

e

enviable = **desirable**, favoured, privileged, fortunate, lucky, blessed, advantageous, to die for *(informal)*, win-win, much to be desired, covetable • *an enviable lifestyle*
OPPOSITES: painful, uncomfortable, undesirable

envious = **covetous**, jealous, grudging, malicious, resentful, green-eyed, begrudging, spiteful, jaundiced, green with envy • *I think she is envious of your success.*

environment AS A NOUN 1 = **surroundings**, setting, conditions, situation, medium, scene, circumstances, territory, background, atmosphere, context, habitat, domain, milieu, locale • *The children were brought up in completely different environments.*
2 = **habitat**, home, surroundings, territory, terrain, locality, natural home • *the maintenance of a safe environment for marine mammals*
▸ IN PHRASES: **the environment** = **natural world**, world, nature, creation, living world • *persuading people to respect the environment*

environmental = **ecological**, green, eco-friendly • *Environmental groups plan to stage a protest during the conference.*

ENVIRONMENTAL TERMS

biodegradability *or* biodegradable	carbon offset	recyclables
carbon footprint	green tax	renewable *or* renewables
	recyclable *or*	

environmentalist = **conservationist**, ecologist, green, friend of the earth, tree-hugger *(informal derogatory)* • *Environmentalists argue that drift net fishing should be banned.*

environs = **surrounding area**, surroundings, district, suburbs, neighbourhood, outskirts, precincts, vicinity, locality, purlieus • *From the hill we had a fine view of the village and its environs.*

envisage 1 = **imagine**, contemplate, conceive (of), visualize, picture, fancy, think up, conceptualize • *I can't envisage being married to someone like him.*
2 = **foresee**, see, expect, predict, anticipate, envision • *Scientists envisage a major breakthrough in the next few years.*

envision = **conceive of**, expect, imagine, predict, anticipate, see, contemplate, envisage, foresee, visualize • *trying to envision the outcome of his actions*

envoy 1 = **ambassador**, minister, diplomat, emissary, legate, plenipotentiary • *A French envoy arrived in Beirut on Sunday.*
2 = **messenger**, agent, deputy, representative, delegate, courier, intermediary, emissary • *the Secretary General's personal envoy*

envy AS A NOUN = **covetousness**, spite, hatred, resentment, jealousy, bitterness, malice, ill will, malignity, resentfulness, enviousness *(informal)* • *He admitted his feelings of envy towards his brother.*
▸ AS A VERB 1 = **be jealous (of)**, resent, begrudge, be envious (of) • *I have a famous brother and a lot of people envy me for that.*
2 = **covet**, desire, crave, aspire to, yearn for, hanker after • *He envied Caroline her peace of mind.*

QUOTATIONS
Nothing sharpens sight like envy
[Thomas Fuller *Gnomologia*]
Our envy always lasts much longer than the happiness of those we envy
[Duc de la Rochefoucauld *Maxims*]
Even success softens not the heart of the envious
[Pindar *Odes*]

ephemeral = **transient**, short, passing, brief, temporary, fleeting, short-lived, fugitive, flitting, momentary, transitory, evanescent, impermanent, fugacious • *These paintings are a reminder that earthly pleasures are ephemeral.*
OPPOSITES: lasting, enduring, eternal

epic AS A NOUN = **saga**, legend, adventure, chronicle, long story, long poem • *the Anglo-Saxon epic, 'Beowulf'*
▸ AS AN ADJECTIVE 1 = **long**, great, grand, extended, classic, impressive, noble, elevated, lofty, high-flown, grandiose, exalted • *an epic romance*
2 = **heroic**, long, great, vast, impressive, ambitious • *an epic journey*

epicure = **gourmet**, foodie, glutton, epicurean, hedonist, gourmand, bon vivant *(French)*, gastronome, sensualist, sybarite, voluptuary • *These delicacies will delight gastronomes and epicures.*

epicurean AS AN ADJECTIVE = **hedonistic**, self-indulgent, luxurious, sensual, lush, luscious, voluptuous, libertine, sybaritic, pleasure-seeking, bacchanalian, gluttonous, gourmandizing • *dishes which will send you into transports of epicurean delight*
▸ AS A NOUN = **gourmet**, foodie, bon vivant *(French)*, epicure, gastronome • *I am no great epicurean – give me simple food every time.*

epidemic AS AN ADJECTIVE = **widespread**, wide-ranging, general, sweeping, prevailing, rampant, prevalent, rife, pandemic • *The abuse of crack has reached epidemic proportions in the US in recent years.*
▸ AS A NOUN 1 = **outbreak**, plague, growth, spread, scourge, contagion • *A flu epidemic is sweeping through Britain.*
2 = **spate**, plague, outbreak, wave, rash, eruption, upsurge • *an epidemic of racist crimes*

epigram = **witticism**, quip, aphorism, bon mot, witty saying, witty poem • *Oscar Wilde was famous for his epigrams.*

QUOTATIONS
A thing well said will be wit in all languages
[John Dryden *Essay of Dramatic Poesy*]

epilogue = **conclusion**, postscript, coda, afterword, concluding speech • *the story used by Pasternak in an epilogue to his novel*
OPPOSITES: introduction, prelude, prologue

episode 1 = **event**, experience, happening, matter, affair, incident, circumstance, adventure, business, occurrence, escapade • *an unfortunate and rather sordid episode in my life*
2 = **period**, attack, spell, phase, bout • *He suffered three episodes of depression in two years.*
3 = **instalment**, part, act, scene, section, chapter, passage • *The final episode will be shown next Saturday.*

episodic *or* **episodical** 1 = **irregular**, occasional, sporadic, intermittent • *episodic attacks of fever*
2 = **irregular**, rambling, disconnected, anecdotal, disjointed, wandering, discursive, digressive • *an episodic narrative of unrelated characters*

epistle = **letter**, note, message, communication, missive • *He was deluged by ever more plaintive epistles from his devoted admirer.*

epitaph 1 = **commemoration**, elegy, obituary • *a fitting epitaph for a great man*
2 = **inscription**, engraving • *His words are carved as his epitaph on the headstone of his grave.*

epithet 1 = **name**, title, description, tag, nickname, designation, appellation, sobriquet, moniker *or* monicker *(slang)* • *players who fitted their manager's epithet of 'headless chickens'*
2 = **curse**, obscenity, blasphemy, swear word, imprecation • *a stream of obscene epithets*

epitome = **personification**, essence, embodiment, type, representation, norm, archetype, exemplar, typical example, quintessence • *Maureen was the epitome of sophistication.*

epitomize *or* **epitomise** = **typify**, represent, illustrate, embody, exemplify, symbolize, personify, incarnate • *The goddess Selene epitomized perfect motherhood.*

epoch = **era**, time, age, period, date, aeon • *the beginning of a major epoch in world history*

equable 1 = **even-tempered**, calm, composed, agreeable, serene, easy-going, placid, temperate, level-headed, unfazed *(informal)*, unflappable *(informal)*, unruffled, imperturbable, unexcitable • *He was a man of the most equable temperament.*
OPPOSITES: nervous, temperamental, excitable
2 = **constant**, regular, stable, even, steady, uniform, consistent, tranquil, temperate, unchanging, on an even keel, unvarying • *The climate has grown more equable and the crop yields have risen.*
OPPOSITES: volatile, unstable, changeable

equal AS AN ADJECTIVE 1 *often with* **to** *or* **with** = **identical**, the same, matched, matching, like, equivalent, uniform, alike, corresponding, tantamount, one and the same, proportionate, commensurate • *a population having equal numbers of men and women*
OPPOSITES: different, unlike, unequal
2 = **fair**, just, impartial, egalitarian, unbiased, even-handed, equable • *Women demand equal rights with men.*
OPPOSITES: unfair, biased, partial
3 = **even**, balanced, fifty-fifty *(informal)*, evenly matched, evenly balanced, evenly proportioned • *an equal contest*
OPPOSITES: uneven, unequal, unbalanced, adequate for • *She wanted to show she was equal to any test they gave her.*
▸ AS A NOUN = **match**, equivalent, fellow, twin, mate, peer, parallel, counterpart, compeer • *She was one of the boys, their equal.*
▸ AS A VERB 1 = **amount to**, make, come to, total, balance, agree with, level, parallel, tie with, equate, correspond to, be equal to, square with, be tantamount to, equalize, tally with, be level with, be even with • *The average pay rise equalled 1.41 times inflation.*
OPPOSITES: be different, disagree with, be unequal to
2 = **be equal to**, match, reach, rival, come up to, be level with, be even with • *The victory equalled Scotland's best in history.*
3 = **be as good as**, match, compare with, equate with, measure up to, be as great as • *No amount of money can equal memories like that.*

equality 1 = **fairness**, equal opportunity, equal treatment, egalitarianism, fair treatment, justness • *the principle of racial equality*
OPPOSITES: discrimination, prejudice, inequality
2 = **sameness**, balance, identity, similarity, correspondence, parity, likeness, uniformity, equivalence, evenness, coequality, equatability • *They advocate the unconditional equality of incomes.*
OPPOSITES: disparity, unevenness, lack of balance

QUOTATIONS
We hold these truths to be self-evident, that all men are created equal, that they are endowed by their Creator with certain unalienable rights, that among these are life, liberty, and the pursuit of happiness
[Thomas Jefferson *The Declaration of Independence*]
I have a dream that my four little children will one day live in a nation where they will not be judged by the color of their skin but by the content of their character
[Martin Luther King Jr. *speech at Civil Rights March*]
The defect of equality is that we only desire it with our superiors
[Henry Becque *Querelles littéraires*]
All animals are equal but some animals are more equal than others
[George Orwell *Animal Farm*]
Even the president of the United States sometimes must have to stand naked
[Bob Dylan *It's Alright, Ma (I'm Only Bleeding)*]

equalize *or* **equalise** 1 = **make equal**, match, level, balance, square, equal, smooth, equate, standardize, even out, even up, regularize, make level • *Such measures are needed to equalize wage rates between countries.*
2 = **draw level**, level the score, square the score, make the score level • *Brazil equalized with only 16 minutes remaining.*

equally 1 = **evenly**, regularly, uniformly, identically • *Eat three small meals a day, at equally spaced intervals.*
2 = **similarly**, just as, to the same extent, to the same degree • *All these techniques are equally effective.*
3 = **by the same token**, similarly, in the same way, likewise, correspondingly • *Subscribers should be allowed call-blocking services, but equally they should be able to choose whether to accept calls from blocked numbers.*

equanimity = **composure**, peace, calm, poise, serenity, tranquillity, coolness, aplomb, calmness, phlegm, steadiness, presence of mind, sang-froid, self-possession, placidity, level-headedness, imperturbability • *He faced his defeat with equanimity.*

equate 1 = **identify**, associate, connect, compare, relate, mention in the same breath, think of in connection with, think of together • *I equate suits with power and authority.*
2 = **make equal**, match, balance, square, even up, equalize • *relying on arbitrage to equate prices between the various stock exchanges*
3 = **be equal to**, match, pair, parallel, agree with, compare with, offset, tally, liken, be commensurate with, correspond with *or* to • *the maximum compensation available, equating to six months' wages*

equation = **equating**, match, agreement, balancing, pairing, comparison, parallel, equality, correspondence, likeness, equivalence, equalization • *the equation between higher spending and higher taxes*

equatorial = **tropical**, hot, oppressive, humid, torrid, sultry, sweltering • *the dense forests of the equatorial regions*

equestrian AS AN ADJECTIVE = **riding**, mounted, horse riding • *his equestrian skills*
▸ AS A NOUN = **rider**, jockey *(archaic)*, horseman, horse rider, knight, cavalier • *a record performance yet to be beaten by any other British equestrian*
▹ *See panel* **Equestrianism**

equilibrium 1 = **stability**, balance, symmetry, steadiness, evenness, equipoise, counterpoise • *For the economy to be in equilibrium, income must equal expenditure.*
2 = **composure**, calm, stability, poise, serenity, coolness, calmness, equanimity, steadiness, self-possession, collectedness • *I paused and took deep breaths to restore my equilibrium.*

equip 1 = **supply**, provide, stock, dress, outfit, arm, rig, array, furnish, endow, attire, fit out, deck out, kit out, fit up, accoutre • *The country did not have the funds to equip the reserve army properly.*
2 = **prepare**, qualify, educate, get ready, endow • *Our aim is to provide courses which equip students for future employment.*

e

EQUESTRIANISM

Equestrian events and sports

Ascot
Badminton
buckjumping *(Austral.)*
cavalcade
claiming race *(U.S. & Canad.)*
classic
Derby
dressage
eventing
Grand National
gymkhana
harness racing
horse racing
hunt
joust
jump-off
Kentucky Derby
meeting
nursery stakes
Oaks
One Thousand Guineas
picnic race *(Austral.)*
plate
point-to-point
polo
puissance
race meeting
races, the
Saint Leger
showjumping
steeplechase
sweepstake *or (esp U.S.)* sweepstakes
three-day eventing
Two Thousand Guineas

Classic English horse races

Race	Course	Distance
One Thousand Guineas (fillies)	Newmarket	one mile
Two Thousand Guineas (colts)	Newmarket	one mile
Derby (colts)	Epsom	one and a half miles
the Oaks (fillies)	Epsom	one and a half miles
St. Leger (colts and fillies)	Doncaster	one and three quarter miles

Horse racing terms

accumulator
allowance
also-ran
ante post betting
apprentice
auction plate
away
blanket finish
boring
break
break away
card *or* race card
chaser
claiming race *(U.S. & Canad.)*
classic
clerk of the course
clerk of the scales
colt
come in
course
daily double
dead heat
distance
dope sheet *(slang)*
draw
each way *or (U.S.)* across-the-board
faller
fence
filly
finish
flat
flat jockey
flat racing
flight
furlong
gate
going
green horse
handicap
handicapper
handy
harness race *or (N.Z.)* trotting race
head
home straight *or (U.S.)* home stretch
hurdle
hurdling
impost
jockey
Jockey Club
jump jockey
length
maiden
meeting
milepost
nap
National Hunt
neck
novice
objection
pacemaker *or* pacesetter
pacer
paddock
photo finish
place
plater
point-to-point *(Brit.)*
pole *(chiefly U.S. & Canad.)*
post
roughie
scratch
scurry
selling race *or* plate
short head
silver ring
stakes
starter
starting post
starting price
starting stalls *or (U.S.)* starting gate
stayer
steeplechase *or* chase
steward
stewards' inquiry
straight *or (U.S.)* straightaway
stretch
sweat *(chiefly U.S.)*
sweat up
ticktack
track
trainer
turf
under starter's orders
unplaced
unseated rider
walkover
weigh in
winning post
wire *(U.S. & Canad.)*
yearling

Types of jump

brush and rails
double oxer
gate
hog's back
narrow stile
parallel poles
planks
post and rails
triple bars
wall
water jump

equipment = **apparatus**, stock, supplies, material, stuff, tackle, gear, tools, provisions, kit, rig, baggage, paraphernalia, accoutrements, appurtenances, equipage • *Exports of military equipment to Iraq are banned under British law.*

equitable = **even-handed**, just, right, fair, due, reasonable, proper, honest, impartial, rightful, unbiased, dispassionate, proportionate, unprejudiced, nondiscriminatory • *the equitable distribution of social wealth*

equity = **fairness**, justice, integrity, honesty, fair play, righteousness, impartiality, rectitude, reasonableness, even-handedness, fair-mindedness, uprightness, equitableness • *a system based on social justice and equity*
OPPOSITES: discrimination, preference, unfairness

equivalence *or* **equivalency** = **equality**, correspondence, agreement, similarity, identity, parallel, match, parity, conformity, likeness, sameness, parallelism, evenness, synonymy, alikeness, interchangeableness • *the equivalence of science and rationalism*

equivalent **AS AN ADJECTIVE** = **equal**, even, same, comparable, parallel, identical, alike, corresponding, correspondent, synonymous, of a kind, tantamount, interchangeable, of a piece with, commensurate, homologous • *A unit of alcohol is equivalent to a glass of wine.*
OPPOSITES: different, unlike, unequal
▸ **AS A NOUN** = **equal**, counterpart, correspondent, twin, peer, parallel, match, opposite number • *the civil administrator of the West Bank and his equivalent in Gaza*

equivocal = **ambiguous**, uncertain, misleading, obscure, suspicious, vague, doubtful, dubious, questionable, ambivalent, indefinite, evasive, oblique, indeterminate, prevaricating, oracular • *His equivocal response gave nothing away.*
OPPOSITES: clear, certain, straight

equivocate = **be evasive**, evade, dodge, parry, fence, hedge, shuffle, fudge, flannel *(Brit. informal)*, sidestep, waffle *(informal, chiefly Brit.)*, quibble, prevaricate, pussyfoot *(informal)*, avoid the issue, beat about the bush *(informal)*, tergiversate • *He is equivocating a lot about what is going to happen at the next election.*

equivocation = **ambiguity**, evasion, hedging, waffle *(informal, chiefly Brit.)*, shuffling, quibbling, prevarication, weasel words *(informal, chiefly U.S.)*, double talk, tergiversation, doubtfulness • *Why doesn't he just say what he thinks without equivocation?*

era = **age**, time, period, stage, date, generation, cycle, epoch, aeon, day *or* days • *a custom pre-dating the Christian era*

eradicate = **wipe out**, eliminate, remove, destroy, get rid of, abolish, erase, excise, extinguish, stamp out, obliterate, uproot, weed out, annihilate, put paid to, root out, efface, exterminate, expunge, extirpate, wipe from the face of the earth • *battling to eradicate illnesses such as malaria and tetanus*

eradication = **wiping out**, abolition, destruction, elimination, removal, extinction, extermination, annihilation, erasure, obliteration, effacement, extirpation, expunction • *He is dedicated to the total eradication of apartheid.*

erase 1 = **delete**, cancel out, wipe out, remove, eradicate, excise, obliterate, efface, blot out, expunge • *They are desperate to erase the memory of their defeat.*
2 = **rub out**, remove, wipe out, delete, scratch out • *She erased the words from the blackboard.*

erasure = **deletion**, wiping, wiping out, cancellation, effacing, obliteration, effacement • *the sudden disastrous erasure of my hard drive*

erect AS AN ADJECTIVE = **upright**, raised, straight, standing, stiff, firm, rigid, vertical, elevated, perpendicular, pricked-up • *Her head was erect and her back was straight.*
OPPOSITES: relaxed, leaning, bent
▸ AS A VERB 1 = **build**, raise, set up, lift, pitch, mount, stand up, rear, construct, put up, assemble, put together, elevate • *Demonstrators have erected barricades in the roads.*
OPPOSITES: destroy, dismantle, demolish
2 = **found**, establish, form, create, set up, institute, organize, put up, initiate • *the edifice of free trade which has been erected since the war*

erection 1 = **hard-on** *(slang)*, erect penis • *As he disrobed, his erection became obvious.*
2 = **building**, setting-up, manufacture, construction, assembly, creation, establishment, elevation, fabrication • *the erection of temporary fencing to protect hedges under repair*
3 = **structure**, building, construction, pile, edifice • *The house itself is merely an erection of wooden blocks and ladders.*

QUOTATIONS
Erection: Used only in referring to monuments
[Gustave Flaubert *The Dictionary of Received Ideas*]

ergo = **therefore**, so, then, thus, hence, consequently, accordingly, for that reason, in consequence • *Neither side had an incentive to start a war. Ergo, peace would reign.*

erode 1 = **disintegrate**, crumble, deteriorate, corrode, break up, grind down, waste away, wear down *or* away • *By 1980, Miami beach had all but totally eroded.*
2 = **destroy**, consume, spoil, crumble, eat away, corrode, break up, grind down, abrade, wear down *or* away • *Once exposed, soil is quickly eroded by wind and rain.*
3 = **weaken**, destroy, undermine, diminish, impair, lessen, wear away • *His fumbling of the issue of reform has eroded his authority.*

erosion 1 = **disintegration**, deterioration, corrosion, corrasion, wearing down *or* away, grinding down • *erosion of the river valleys*
2 = **deterioration**, wearing, undermining, destruction, consumption, weakening, spoiling, attrition, eating away, abrasion, grinding down, wearing down *or* away • *an erosion of moral standards*

erotic = **sexual**, sexy *(informal)*, crude, explicit, rousing, sensual, seductive, vulgar, stimulating, steamy *(informal)*, suggestive, aphrodisiac, voluptuous, carnal, titillating, bawdy, lustful, sexually arousing, erogenous, amatory • *photos of naked women in erotic poses*

erotica
▸ RELATED MANIA: eroticomania

err 1 = **make a mistake**, mistake, go wrong, blunder, slip up *(informal)*, misjudge, be incorrect, be inaccurate, miscalculate, go astray, be in error, put your foot in it *(informal)*, misapprehend, blot your copybook *(informal)*, drop a brick *or* clanger *(informal)* • *The contractors seriously erred in their original estimates.*
2 = **sin**, fall, offend, lapse, trespass, do wrong, deviate, misbehave, go astray, transgress, be out of order, blot your copybook *(informal)* • *If he errs again, he will be severely punished.*

QUOTATIONS
To err is human, to forgive divine
[Alexander Pope *An Essay on Criticism*]

errand = **job**, charge, commission, message, task, mission • *Frank ran dodgy errands for a seedy local villain.*

errant = **sinning**, offending, straying, wayward, deviant, erring, aberrant • *His errant son ran up debts of over £3000.*

erratic = **unpredictable**, variable, unstable, irregular, shifting, eccentric, abnormal, inconsistent, uneven, unreliable, wayward, capricious, desultory, changeable, aberrant, fitful, inconstant • *Argentina's erratic inflation rates*
OPPOSITES: certain, natural, regular

erring = **offending**, guilty, transgressive • *photos of the erring politician back in the bosom of his supportive family*

erroneous = **incorrect**, wrong, mistaken, false, flawed, faulty, inaccurate, untrue, invalid, unfounded, spurious, amiss, unsound, wide of the mark, inexact, fallacious • *The conclusions they have come to are completely erroneous.*
OPPOSITES: right, true, correct

erroneously = **incorrectly**, wrongly, falsely, mistakenly, inaccurately, spuriously • *It had been erroneously reported that he had refused to give evidence.*

error AS A NOUN = **mistake**, slip, fault, blunder, flaw, boob *(Brit. slang)*, delusion, oversight, misconception, fallacy, inaccuracy, howler *(informal)*, bloomer *(Brit. informal)*, boner *(slang)*, miscalculation, misapprehension, solecism, erratum, barry *or* Barry Crocker *(Austral. slang)* • *NASA discovered a mathematical error in its calculations.*
▸ IN PHRASES: **in error** = **accidentally**, casually, unexpectedly, incidentally, by accident, by chance, inadvertently, unwittingly, randomly, unconsciously, by mistake, unintentionally, haphazardly, fortuitously, undesignedly • *The plane was shot down in error by a NATO missile.*

QUOTATIONS
Truth lies within a little and certain compass, but error is immense
[Henry St. John, 1st Viscount Bolingbroke *Reflections upon Exile*]

ersatz = **artificial**, substitute, pretend, fake, imitation, synthetic, bogus, simulated, sham, counterfeit, spurious, phoney *or* phony *(informal)* • *an electric fire with ersatz logs*

erstwhile = **former**, old, late, previous, once, past, ex *(informal)*, one-time, sometime, bygone, quondam • *He is suing his erstwhile friend and business partner.*

erudite = **learned**, lettered, cultured, educated, scholarly, cultivated, knowledgeable, literate, well-educated, well-read • *I found him a charming and erudite companion.*
OPPOSITES: shallow, ignorant, uneducated

erudition = **learning**, education, knowledge, scholarship, letters, lore, academic knowledge • *a writer who displays an impressive level of erudition*

erupt 1 = **explode**, blow up, flare up, emit lava • *The volcano erupted in 1980.*
2 = **discharge**, expel, vent, emit, vomit, eject, spout, throw off, spit out, pour forth, spew forth *or* out • *Those volcanoes erupt not lava but liquid sulphur.*
3 = **gush**, burst out, be ejected, burst forth, pour forth, belch forth, spew forth *or* out • *Lava erupted from the volcano and flowed over the ridge.*
4 = **start**, break out, began, explode, flare up, burst out, boil over • *Heavy fighting erupted again two days after the cease-fire.*
5 = **break out**, appear, flare up • *My skin erupted in pimples.*

eruption 1 = **explosion**, discharge, outburst, venting, ejection • *the volcanic eruption of Tambora in 1815*
2 = **flare-up**, outbreak, sally • *the sudden eruption of violence on the streets of the city*
3 = **inflammation**, outbreak, rash, flare-up • *an unpleasant eruption of boils*

escalate 1 = **grow**, increase, extend, intensify, expand, surge, be increased, mount, heighten • *Unions and management fear the dispute could escalate.*
OPPOSITES: contract, diminish, decrease
2 = **increase**, develop, extend, intensify, expand, build up, step up, heighten, enlarge, magnify, amplify • *Defeat could cause one side or the other to escalate the conflict.*
OPPOSITES: limit, lessen, wind down

e

escalation = **increase**, rise, build-up, expansion, heightening, developing, acceleration, upsurge, intensification, amplification • *a sudden escalation of unrest in the south-eastern region*

escapade = **adventure**, fling, stunt, romp, trick, scrape *(informal)*, spree, mischief, lark *(informal)*, caper, prank, antic • *The whole ridiculous escapade was his idea.*

escape AS A VERB 1 = **get away**, flee, take off, fly, bolt, skip, slip away, abscond, decamp, hook it *(slang)*, do a runner *(slang)*, do a bunk *(Brit. slang)*, fly the coop *(U.S. & Canad. informal)*, make a break for it, slip through your fingers, skedaddle *(informal)*, take a powder *(U.S. & Canad. slang)*, make your getaway, take it on the lam *(U.S. & Canad. slang)*, break free *or* out, make *or* effect your escape, run away *or* off, do a Skase *(Austral. informal)* • *A prisoner has escaped from a jail in Northern England.*
2 = **avoid**, miss, evade, dodge, shun, elude, duck, steer clear of, circumvent, body-swerve *(Scot.)* • *He was lucky to escape serious injury.*
3 = **be forgotten by**, be beyond (someone), baffle, elude, puzzle, stump • *an actor whose name escapes me for the moment*
4 *usually with* **from** = **leak out**, flow out, drain away, discharge, gush out, emanate, seep out, exude, spurt out, spill out, pour forth • *Leave a vent open to let some of the moist air escape.*
▸ AS A NOUN 1 = **getaway**, break, flight, break-out, bolt, decampment • *He made his escape from the country.*
2 = **avoidance**, evasion, circumvention, elusion • *his narrow escape from bankruptcy*
3 = **relaxation**, relief, recreation, distraction, diversion, pastime • *For me television is an escape.*
4 = **leak**, emission, discharge, outpouring, gush, spurt, outflow, leakage, drain, seepage, issue, emanation, efflux, effluence, outpour • *You should report any suspected gas escape immediately.*

escapee = **runaway**, escaper, refugee, fugitive, deserter, truant, absconder • *An escapee from Sydney's Long Bay Jail was recaptured today.*

escapism = **fantasy**, dreaming, illusion, delusion, vision, fancy, mirage, hallucination, daydreaming, reverie, flight of fancy, pipe dream, figment of the imagination • *Romantic films are merely harmless escapism from a bleak world.*

eschew = **avoid**, give up, abandon, have nothing to do with, shun, elude, renounce, refrain from, forgo, abstain from, fight shy of, forswear, abjure, kick *(informal)*, swear off, give a wide berth to, keep *or* steer clear of • *He eschewed publicity and avoided nightclubs.*

escort AS A NOUN 1 = **guard**, protection, safeguard, bodyguard, company, train, convoy, entourage, retinue, cortege • *He arrived with a police escort.*
2 = **companion**, partner, attendant, guide, squire *(rare)*, protector, beau, chaperon • *My sister needed an escort for a company dinner.*
▸ AS A VERB = **accompany**, lead, partner, conduct, guide, guard, shepherd, convoy, usher, squire, hold (someone's) hand, chaperon • *I escorted him to the door.*

esoteric = **obscure**, private, secret, hidden, inner, mysterious, mystical, mystic, occult, arcane, cryptic, inscrutable, abstruse, recondite, cabbalistic • *She has published several books on pathworking and other esoteric subjects.*

especial 1 = **exceptional**, marked, special, particular, signal, unusual, extraordinary, outstanding, principal, distinguished, notable, uncommon, noteworthy • *He took especial care not to be seen to show any favouritism.*
2 = **particular**, special, private, individual, personal, express, specific, exclusive, unique, peculiar, singular • *This was Jim's especial foible.*

especially 1 = **notably**, largely, chiefly, mainly, mostly, principally, strikingly, conspicuously, outstandingly • *The group is said to be gaining support, especially in the rural areas.*
2 = **very**, specially, particularly, signally, extremely, remarkably, unusually, exceptionally, extraordinarily, markedly, supremely, uncommonly • *Giving up smoking can be especially difficult.*
3 = **particularly**, expressly, exclusively, precisely, specifically, uniquely, peculiarly, singularly • *The system we design will be especially for you.*

espionage = **spying**, intelligence, surveillance, counter-intelligence, undercover work • *The authorities have arrested several people suspected of espionage.*

espousal = **support**, backing, defence, championing, taking up, promotion, embracing, maintenance, adoption, advocacy • *the leadership's espousal of the causes of reform and nationalism*

espouse = **support**, back, champion, promote, maintain, defend, adopt, take up, advocate, embrace, uphold, stand up for • *She ran away to Mexico and espoused the revolutionary cause.*

esprit = **spirit**, wit, sparkle, vitality, animation, verve, zest, élan, brio, quickness, vivacity, liveliness, sprightliness • *The wonderful esprit of this orchestra is quite unique.*

esprit de corps = **solidarity**, rapport, team spirit, camaraderie, mutual support, common bond, fellow feeling, community of interests, group spirit • *He enjoyed the friendship, comradeship and esprit de corps of the army.*

espy = **catch sight of**, see, discover, spot, notice, sight, observe, spy, perceive, detect, glimpse, make out, discern, behold, catch a glimpse of, descry • *She espied him in the far distance.*

essay AS A NOUN 1 = **composition**, study, paper, article, piece, assignment, discourse, tract, treatise, dissertation, disquisition • *He was asked to write an essay about his home town.*
2 = **attempt**, go *(informal)*, try, effort, shot *(informal)*, trial, struggle, bid, test, experiment, crack *(informal)*, venture, undertaking, stab *(informal)*, endeavour, exertion • *His first essay in running a company was a disaster.*
▸ AS A VERB = **attempt**, try, test, take on, undertake, strive for, endeavour, have a go at, try out, have a shot at *(informal)*, have a crack at *(informal)*, have a bash at *(informal)* • *He essayed a smile, but it was a dismal failure.*

essence AS A NOUN 1 = **fundamental nature**, nature, being, life, meaning, heart, spirit, principle, soul, core, substance, significance, entity, bottom line, essential part, kernel, crux, lifeblood, pith, quintessence, basic characteristic, quiddity • *Some claim that Ireland's very essence is expressed through its language.*
2 = **concentrate**, spirits, extract, elixir, tincture, distillate • *Add a few drops of vanilla essence.*
▸ IN PHRASES: **in essence** = **essentially**, materially, virtually, basically, fundamentally, in effect, substantially, in the main, to all intents and purposes, in substance • *In essence, we share the same ideology.*

of the essence = **vitally important**, essential, vital, critical, crucial, key, indispensable, of the utmost importance • *Time is of the essence with this project.*

essential AS AN ADJECTIVE 1 = **vital**, important, needed, necessary, critical, crucial, key, indispensable, requisite, vitally important, must-have • *It is absolutely essential that we find this man quickly.*
OPPOSITES: unnecessary, trivial, unimportant
2 = **fundamental**, main, basic, radical, key, principal, constitutional, cardinal, inherent, elementary, innate, hard-wired, intrinsic, elemental, immanent • *Two essential elements must be proven: motive and opportunity.*
OPPOSITES: extra, secondary, surplus
3 = **concentrated**, extracted, refined, volatile, rectified, distilled • *essential oils used in aromatherapy*
▸ AS A NOUN = **prerequisite**, principle, fundamental, necessity, must, basic, requisite, vital part, sine qua non *(Latin)*, rudiment, must-have • *the essentials of everyday life, such as food and water*

essentially 1 = **fundamentally**, radically, basically, primarily, at heart, intrinsically, at bottom • *the belief that geniuses are essentially quite different from ordinary people*
2 = **basically**, materially, virtually, fundamentally, in effect, substantially, in the main, to all intents and purposes, in substance • *His analysis is essentially correct.*

establish 1 = **set up**, found, start, create, institute, organize, install, constitute, inaugurate • *They established the school in 1989.*
2 = **prove**, show, confirm, demonstrate, ratify, certify, verify, validate, substantiate, corroborate, authenticate • *An autopsy was being done to establish the cause of death.*
3 = **secure**, form, base, ground, plant, settle, fix, root, implant, entrench, ensconce, put down roots • *He has established himself as a pivotal figure in US politics.*

established 1 = **accepted**, traditional, conventional, historic, customary, time-honoured, officially recognized • *Their religious adherence is not to the established church.*
2 = **famous**, celebrated, distinguished, honoured, noted, remarkable, well-known, prominent, glorious, legendary, acclaimed, notable, renowned, eminent, conspicuous, illustrious, much-publicized, lionized • *the established names of Paris fashion*

establishment 1 = **creation**, founding, setting up, foundation, institution, organization, formation, installation, inauguration, enactment • *discussions to explore the establishment of diplomatic relations*
2 = **organization**, company, business, firm, house, concern, operation, structure, institution, institute, corporation, enterprise, outfit *(informal)*, premises, setup *(informal)* • *Shops and other commercial establishments remained closed today.*
3 = **office**, house, building, plant, quarters, factory • *a scientific research establishment*

Establishment IN PHRASES: **the Establishment** = **the authorities**, the system, the powers that be, the ruling class, the established order, institutionalized authority • *the revolution against the Establishment*

estate 1 = **lands**, property, area, grounds, domain, manor, holdings, demesne, homestead *(U.S. & Canad.)* • *a shooting party on his estate in Yorkshire*
2 = **area**, centre, park, development, site, zone, plot • *an industrial estate*
3 = **property**, capital, assets, fortune, goods, effects, wealth, possessions, belongings • *His estate was valued at £100,000.*

estate agent = **house agent**, real-estate agent, realtor *(U.S.)* • *selling your house through an estate agent*

estate car = **station wagon** *(U.S.)*, shooting brake • *the luggage space of hatchbacks and estate cars*

esteem AS A VERB 1 = **respect**, admire, think highly of, like, love, value, prize, honour, treasure, cherish, revere, reverence, be fond of, venerate, regard highly, take off your hat to • *a scholar whom he highly esteemed*
2 = **consider**, think of, hold, believe in, rate, view, judge, regard, estimate, reckon, calculate, deem • *Nowadays we esteem these paintings as works of art.*
▸ AS A NOUN = **respect**, regard, honour, consideration, admiration, reverence, estimation, veneration • *He is held in high esteem by his colleagues.*

estimable = **respectable**, good, valued, respected, excellent, honoured, valuable, worthy, esteemed, admirable, honourable, reputable, meritorious • *an estimable cricket team with two members holding world records*

estimate AS A VERB 1 = **calculate roughly**, value, guess, judge, reckon, assess, evaluate, gauge, number, appraise • *His personal riches were estimated at over £8 million.*
2 = **think**, believe, consider, rate, judge, hold, rank, guess, reckon, assess, conjecture, surmise • *Officials estimate it will be two days before electricity is restored to the island.*
▸ AS A NOUN 1 = **approximate calculation**, guess, reckoning, assessment, judgment, evaluation, valuation, appraisal, educated guess, guesstimate *(informal)*, rough calculation, ballpark figure *(informal)*, approximate cost, approximate price, ballpark estimate *(informal)*, appraisement • *This figure is five times the original estimate.*
2 = **assessment**, opinion, belief, appraisal, evaluation, conjecture, appraisement, judgment, estimation, surmise • *I was wrong in my estimate of his capabilities.*

estimation 1 = **opinion**, view, regard, belief, honour, credit, consideration, judgment, esteem, evaluation, admiration, reverence, veneration, good opinion, considered opinion • *He has gone down considerably in my estimation.*
2 = **estimate**, reckoning, assessment, appreciation, valuation, appraisal, guesstimate *(informal)*, ballpark figure *(informal)* • *estimations of pre-tax profits of £12.5 million*

estranged = **alienated**, hostile, disaffected, antagonized • *a reunion with his estranged wife*

estrangement = **alienation**, parting, division, split, withdrawal, break-up, breach, hostility, separation, withholding, disaffection, disunity, dissociation, antagonization • *The quarrel marked the beginning of a 20-year estrangement.*

estuary = **inlet**, mouth, creek, firth, fjord • *naval manoeuvres in the Clyde estuary*

et cetera or **etcetera** = **and so on**, and so forth, etc • *people who play cricket, football, rugby, et cetera*

etch 1 = **engrave**, cut, impress, stamp, carve, imprint, inscribe, furrow, incise, ingrain • *a simple band of heavy gold etched with runes*
2 = **corrode**, eat into, burn into • *The acid etched holes in the surface.*

etching = **print**, impression, carving, engraving, imprint, inscription • *There was an old etching of the Thames on the wall opposite the window.*

eternal 1 = **everlasting**, lasting, permanent, enduring, endless, perennial, perpetual, timeless, immortal, unending, unchanging, immutable, indestructible, undying, without end, unceasing, imperishable, deathless, sempiternal *(literary)* • *the quest for eternal youth*
OPPOSITES: changing, transient, transitory
2 = **interminable**, constant, endless, abiding, infinite, continual, immortal, never-ending, everlasting, ceaseless, unremitting, deathless • *In the background was that eternal humming noise.*
OPPOSITES: rare, fleeting, occasional

eternally 1 = **forever**, always, for keeps, for all time, in perpetuity, evermore, for good and all *(informal)*, till the cows come home *(informal)*, world without end, till the end of

time, till Doomsday • *She will be eternally grateful to her family for their support.*
2 = continually, constantly, all the time, endlessly, perpetually, incessantly, interminably, unremittingly, everlastingly, twenty-four-seven *(informal)* • *She complains eternally about how boring her life is.*

eternity **1 = the afterlife**, heaven, paradise, the next world, the hereafter • *I have always found the thought of eternity terrifying.*
2 = perpetuity, immortality, infinity, timelessness, endlessness, infinitude, time without end • *the idea that our species will survive for all eternity*
3 = ages, years, an age, centuries, for ever *(informal)*, aeons, donkey's years *(informal)*, yonks *(informal)*, a month of Sundays *(informal)*, a long time *or* while, an age *or* eternity • *The war went on for an eternity.*

QUOTATIONS
Eternity's a terrible thought. I mean, where's it all going to end?
[Tom Stoppard *Rosencrantz and Guildenstern are Dead*]
Eternity! thou pleasing, dreadful thought!
[Joseph Addison *Cato*]
Every instant of time is a pinprick of eternity
[Marcus Aurelius *Meditations*]
Eternity is in love with the productions of time
[William Blake *The Marriage of Heaven and Hell*]

ethereal **1 = delicate**, light, fine, subtle, refined, exquisite, tenuous, dainty, rarefied • *gorgeous, hauntingly ethereal melodies*
2 = insubstantial, light, fairy, aerial, airy, intangible, rarefied, impalpable • *the ethereal world of romantic fiction*
3 = spiritual, heavenly, unearthly, sublime, celestial, unworldly, empyreal • *the ethereal realm of the divine*

ethical **1 = moral**, behavioural • *the ethical dilemmas of genetic engineering*
2 = right, morally right, morally acceptable, good, just, fitting, fair, responsible, principled, correct, decent, proper, upright, honourable, honest, righteous, virtuous • *Would it be ethical to lie to save a person's life?*
OPPOSITES: unfair, indecent, unethical

ethics **= moral code**, standards, principles, morals, conscience, morality, moral values, moral principles, moral philosophy, rules of conduct, moral beliefs, tikanga *(N.Z.)* • *Such an action was a violation of medical ethics.*

QUOTATIONS
True ethics begin where the use of language ceases
[Albert Schweitzer *Civilization and Ethics*]

ethnic *or* **ethnical** **= cultural**, national, traditional, native, folk, racial, genetic, indigenous • *The country's population of over 40 million people is made up of many ethnic groups.*

ethos **= spirit**, character, attitude, beliefs, ethic, tenor, disposition • *the whole British public school ethos*

etiolated **= pale**, white, faded, bleached, washed out, wan, blanched, colourless, whitened, achromatic • *shrivelled bulbs with long etiolated shoots*

etiquette **= good** *or* **proper behaviour**, manners, rules, code, customs, convention, courtesy, usage, protocol, formalities, propriety, politeness, good manners, decorum, civility, politesse, p's and q's, polite behaviour, kawa *(N.Z.)*, tikanga *(N.Z.)* • *a breach of the rules of diplomatic etiquette*

etymology **= derivation**, word history, development of words, history of words, origin of words • *The etymology of the word 'neon' is the Greek for 'new'.*

eulogize **= praise**, acclaim, applaud, compliment, pay tribute to, commend, magnify *(archaic)*, glorify, exalt, laud, extol, big up *(slang, chiefly Caribbean)*, rhapsodize, panegyrize, sing *or* sound the praises of • *He eulogized Keegan's part in the operation.*

eulogy **= praise**, tribute, acclaim, compliment, applause, accolade, paean, commendation, exaltation, glorification, acclamation, panegyric, encomium, plaudit, laudation • *He added his praise to the glowing eulogies given by her colleagues.*

euphemism **= polite term**, substitute, understatement, alternative word, alternative expression, genteelism • *The term 'early retirement' is often a euphemism for 'redundancy'.*

euphemistic **= polite**, alternative, substitute, genteel • *the many euphemistic terms for death*

euphoria **= elation**, joy, ecstasy, bliss, glee, rapture, high spirits, exhilaration, jubilation, intoxication, transport, exaltation, joyousness • *There was euphoria when the election result was announced.*
OPPOSITES: dumps *(informal)*, depression, despondency

euphoric **= elated**, excited, ecstatic, jubilant, joyful, high-spirited, rapturous, stoked *(Austral. & N.Z. informal)* • *There was an atmosphere of euphoric excitement.*

Europe

EUROPEAN UNION

MEMBER STATES OF THE EU

1958 Belgium
1958 France
1958 Germany
1958 Italy
1958 Luxembourg
1958 The Netherlands
1973 Denmark
1973 Republic of Ireland
1973 United Kingdom
1981 Greece
1986 Portugal
1986 Spain
1995 Finland
1995 Sweden
1995 Austria
2004 Cyprus
2004 Czech Republic
2004 Estonia
2004 Hungary
2004 Latvia
2004 Lithuania
2004 Malta
2004 Poland
2004 Slovakia
2004 Slovenia
2007 Bulgaria
2007 Romania

euthanasia **= mercy killing**, assisted suicide • *the emotive question of whether euthanasia should be legalized*

evacuate **1 = remove**, clear, withdraw, expel, move out, send to a safe place • *18,000 people have been evacuated from the city.*
2 = abandon, leave, clear, desert, quit, depart (from), withdraw from, pull out of, move out of, relinquish, vacate, forsake, decamp from • *The residents have evacuated the area.*

evacuation **1 = removal**, departure, withdrawal, clearance, flight, expulsion, exodus • *an evacuation of the city's four million inhabitants*
2 = abandonment, withdrawal from, pulling out, moving out, clearance from, vacation from • *the mass evacuation of Srebrenica*

evade **1 = avoid**, escape, dodge, get away from, shun, elude, eschew, steer clear of, sidestep, circumvent, duck, shirk, slip through the net of, escape the clutches of, body-swerve *(Scot.)* • *He managed to evade the police for six months.*
OPPOSITES: meet, face, encounter
2 = avoid answering, parry, circumvent, fend off, balk, cop out of *(slang)*, fence, fudge, hedge, prevaricate, flannel *(Brit. informal)*, beat about the bush about, equivocate • *Mr Archer denied that he was evading the question.*

evaluate **= assess**, rate, value, judge, estimate, rank, reckon, weigh, calculate, gauge, weigh up, appraise, size up *(informal)*, assay • *Trained nurses are required to evaluate the patients' individual needs.*

evaluation **= assessment**, rating, judgment, calculation, valuation, appraisal, estimation • *Evaluation is standard practice for the training course.*

evanescent **= ephemeral**, passing, brief, fading, fleeting, vanishing, short-lived, fugitive, transient, momentary, transitory, impermanent, fugacious • *the evanescent effects of light and weather on the landscape*

evangelical = **crusading**, converting, missionary, zealous, revivalist, proselytizing, propagandizing • *He has all the hallmarks of an evangelical preacher.*

evangelism = **preaching**, spreading the word, spreading the gospel, telling the gospel message • *Evangelism can be seen as potentially threatening for other faith communities.*

evangelist = **preacher**, minister, missionary, clergyman, revivalist, clergywoman • *A noted evangelist was preaching to a rather hostile congregation.*

evangelize = **preach to**, exhort, proselytize, spread the gospel to, share the gospel with, tell the gospel to, offer the gospel to • *Irish monks had settled there in the seventh century to evangelize the North.*

evaporate 1 = **disappear**, vaporize, dematerialize, evanesce, melt, vanish, dissolve, disperse, dry up, dispel, dissipate, fade away, melt away • *Moisture is drawn to the surface of the fabric so that it evaporates.*
2 = **dry up**, dry, dehydrate, vaporize, desiccate • *The water is evaporated by the sun.*
3 = **fade away**, disappear, fade, melt, vanish, dissolve, disperse, dissipate, melt away • *My anger evaporated and I wanted to cry.*

evaporation 1 = **vaporization**, vanishing, disappearance, dispelling, dissolution, fading away, melting away, dispersal, dissipation, evanescence, dematerialization • *The cooling effect is caused by the evaporation of sweat on the skin.*
2 = **drying up**, drying, dehydration, desiccation, vaporization • *an increase in evaporation of both lake and ground water*

evasion 1 = **avoidance**, escape, dodging, shirking, cop-out (*slang*), circumvention, elusion • *an evasion of responsibility*
2 = **deception**, shuffling, cunning, fudging, pretext, ruse, artifice, trickery, subterfuge, equivocation, prevarication, sophistry, evasiveness, obliqueness, sophism • *They face accusations from the Opposition Party of evasion and cover-up.*

evasive 1 = **deceptive**, misleading, indirect, cunning, slippery, tricky, shuffling, devious, oblique, shifty, cagey (*informal*), deceitful, dissembling, prevaricating, equivocating, sophistical, casuistic, casuistical • *He was evasive about the circumstances of their first meeting.*
OPPOSITES: open, direct, straightforward
2 = **avoiding**, escaping, circumventing • *Four high-flying warplanes had to take evasive action.*

eve 1 = **night before**, day before, vigil • *the eve of his 27th birthday*
2 = **brink**, point, edge, verge, threshold • *when Europe stood on the eve of war in 1914*

even AS AN ADJECTIVE 1 = **regular**, stable, constant, steady, smooth, uniform, unbroken, uninterrupted, unwavering, unvarying, metrical • *It is important to have an even temperature when you work.*
OPPOSITES: changing, broken, variable
2 = **level**, straight, flat, plane, smooth, true, steady, uniform, parallel, flush, horizontal, plumb • *The tables are fitted with a glass top to provide an even surface.*
OPPOSITES: rough, twisting, uneven
3 = **equal**, like, the same, matching, similar, uniform, parallel, identical, comparable, commensurate, coequal • *Divide the dough into 12 even pieces.*
OPPOSITES: irregular, uneven, unequal
4 = **equally matched**, level, tied, drawn, on a par, neck and neck, fifty-fifty (*informal*), equalized, all square, equally balanced • *It was an even game.*
OPPOSITES: imbalanced, ill-matched
5 = **square**, quits, on the same level, on an equal footing • *You don't owe me anything now. We're even.*
6 = **calm**, stable, steady, composed, peaceful, serene, cool, tranquil, well-balanced, placid, undisturbed, unruffled, imperturbable, equable, even-tempered, unexcitable, equanimous • *Normally Rose had an even temper; she was rarely irritable.*
OPPOSITES: emotional, unpredictable, excitable
7 = **fair**, just, balanced, equitable, impartial, disinterested, unbiased, dispassionate, fair and square, unprejudiced • *We all have an even chance of winning.*
OPPOSITES: unfair, prejudiced, biased
▸ AS AN ADVERB 1 = **despite**, in spite of, disregarding, notwithstanding, in spite of the fact that, regardless of the fact that • *He kept calling me, even though he was married.*
2 = **all the more**, much, still, yet, to a greater extent, to a greater degree • *Stan was speaking even more slowly than usual.*
3 = **so much as**, at all • *He wasn't even listening to me.*
4 = **indeed**, actually, or rather, in truth, in point of fact • *revelations which will make us uncomfortable, angry, even ashamed*
▸ IN PHRASES: **even as** = **while**, just as, whilst, at the time that, at the same time as, exactly as, during the time that • *Even as she said this, she knew it was not quite true.*
even so = **nevertheless**, still, however, yet, despite that, in spite of (that), nonetheless, all the same, notwithstanding that, be that as it may • *The bus was half empty. Even so, he came and sat next to me.*
even something out = **make** *or* **become level**, align, level, square, smooth, steady, flatten, stabilize, balance out, regularize • *Rates of house price inflation have evened out between the North and South of the country.*
even something up = **equalize**, match, balance, equal • *These missiles would help to even up the balance of power.*
even the score = **pay (someone) back**, repay, get even (*informal*), reciprocate, equalize, requite, get your own back, settle the score, take vengeance, take an eye for an eye, give tit for tat, return like for like • *If one partner has an extramarital affair, the other may want to even the score.*
get even (with) = **pay back**, repay, reciprocate, even the score, requite, get your own back, settle the score, take vengeance, take an eye for an eye, be revenged *or* revenge yourself, give tit for tat, pay (someone) back in their own coin, return like for like • *I'm going to get even if it's the last thing I do.*

even-handed = **fair**, just, balanced, equitable, impartial, disinterested, unbiased, fair and square, unprejudiced • *The administration wants to ensure the meetings appear even-handed.*

evening = **dusk** (*archaic*), night, sunset, twilight, sundown, eve, vesper (*archaic*), eventide (*archaic or poetic*), gloaming (*Scot. poetic*), e'en (*archaic or poetic*), close of day, crepuscule, even, evo (*Austral. slang*) • *Finally, towards late evening, the carnival entered its final stage.*

QUOTATIONS

It is a beauteous evening, calm and free,
The holy time is quiet as a nun,
Breathless with adoration
[William Wordsworth *It is a Beauteous Evening*]

The curfew tolls the knell of passing day
[Thomas Gray *Elegy Written in a Country Churchyard*]

Let us go then, you and I
When the evening is spread out against the sky
Like a patient etherized upon a table
[T.S. Eliot *Love Song of J. Alfred Prufrock*]

event AS A NOUN 1 = **incident**, happening, experience, matter, affair, occasion, proceeding, fact, business, circumstance, episode, adventure, milestone, occurrence, escapade • *in the wake of recent events in Europe*
2 = **competition**, game, tournament, contest, bout • *major sporting events*
▸ IN PHRASES: **in any event** *or* **at all events** = **whatever happens**, regardless, in any case, no matter what, at any rate, come what may • *It is not going to be an easy decision, in any event.*

in the event = in the end, as it happened, as it turned out • *In the event, their fears were well founded.*
in the event of = in the eventuality of, in the situation of, in the likelihood of • *The bank will make an immediate refund in the event of any error.*

even-tempered = calm, steady, peaceful, composed, cool, serene, tranquil, placid, level-headed, cool-headed, unruffled, imperturbable, equable, unexcitable • *He was normally a very even-tempered person.*
OPPOSITES: emotional, volatile, temperamental

eventful = exciting, active, busy, dramatic, remarkable, historic, full, lively, memorable, notable, momentous, fateful, noteworthy, consequential • *Our next journey was longer and much more eventful.*
OPPOSITES: ordinary, dull, trivial

eventual = final, later, resulting, future, overall, concluding, ultimate, prospective, ensuing, consequent • *Civil war will be the eventual outcome of the country's racial tensions.*

eventuality = possibility, event, likelihood, probability, case, chance, contingency • *When you go on holiday, try to be prepared for every eventuality.*

eventually = in the end, finally, one day, after all, some time, ultimately, at the end of the day, in the long run, sooner or later, some day, when all is said and done, in the fullness of time, in the course of time • *Eventually your child will leave home to lead her own independent life.*

eventuate = result, follow, ensue, come about, issue, come to pass *(archaic)*, be a consequence, be consequent • *Local interest rate cuts might not eventuate until early next year.*

ever AS AN ADVERB **1 = at any time**, at all, in any case, at any point, by any chance, on any occasion, at any period, • *Don't you ever talk to me like that again!*
2 = always, for ever, at all times, relentlessly, eternally, evermore, unceasingly, to the end of time, everlastingly, unendingly, aye *(Scot.)* • *Mother, ever the peacemaker, told us to stop fighting.*
3 = constantly, continually, endlessly, perpetually, incessantly, unceasingly, unendingly • *They grew ever further apart as time went on.*
▸ IN PHRASES: **ever so = very**, highly, greatly, really, deeply, particularly, truly, extremely, absolutely, terribly, remarkably, unusually, jolly *(Brit.)*, wonderfully, profoundly, awfully *(informal)*, exceedingly, excessively, noticeably, superlatively, uncommonly, surpassingly • *She's ever so kind.*

everlasting 1 = eternal, endless, abiding, infinite, perpetual, timeless, immortal, never-ending, indestructible, undying, imperishable, deathless • *The icon embodies a potent symbol of everlasting life.*
OPPOSITES: passing, brief, transitory
2 = continual, constant, endless, continuous, never-ending, interminable, incessant, ceaseless, unremitting, unceasing • *I'm tired of your everlasting bickering.*

evermore = for ever, always, ever, eternally, to the end of time, in perpetuum *(Latin)* • *Their heroic deeds shall live for evermore.*

every = each, each and every, every single • *I walk to work every day.*

everybody = everyone, each one, the whole world, each person, every person, all and sundry, one and all • *Everybody uses the internet these days.*

everyday 1 = daily, day-to-day, diurnal, quotidian • *opportunities for improving fitness in your everyday routine*
OPPOSITES: occasional, now and then, irregular
2 = ordinary, common, usual, familiar, conventional, routine, dull, stock, accustomed, customary, commonplace, mundane, vanilla *(slang)*, banal, habitual, run-of-the-mill, unimaginative, workaday, unexceptional, bog-standard *(Brit. & Irish slang)*, common or garden *(informal)*, dime-a-dozen *(informal)*, wonted • *an exhilarating escape from the drudgery of everyday life*
OPPOSITES: interesting, special, unusual

everyone = everybody, each one, the whole world, each person, every person, all and sundry, one and all • *Everyone needs some free time for rest and relaxation.*

everything = all, the whole, the total, the lot, the sum, the whole lot, the aggregate, the entirety, each thing, the whole caboodle *(informal)*, the whole kit and caboodle *(informal)* • *Everything in my life seems to be going wrong at the moment.*
▸ RELATED PHOBIAS: panphobia, pantophobia

everywhere 1 = all over, all around, the world over, high and low, in each place, in every nook and cranny, far and wide *or* near, to *or* in every place • *I looked everywhere but I couldn't find him.*
2 = all around, all over, in each place, in every nook and cranny, ubiquitously, far and wide *or* near, to *or* in every place • *There were clothes scattered around everywhere.*

evict = expel, remove, turn out, put out, throw out, oust, kick out *(informal)*, eject, dislodge, boot out *(informal)*, force to leave, dispossess, chuck out *(informal)*, show the door (to), turf out *(informal)*, throw on to the streets • *They were evicted from their apartment.*

eviction = expulsion, removal, clearance, ouster *(Law)*, ejection, dispossession, dislodgement • *He was facing eviction for non-payment of rent.*

evidence AS A NOUN **1 = proof**, grounds, data, demonstration, confirmation, verification, corroboration, authentication, substantiation • *There is no evidence to support this theory.*
2 = sign(s), mark, suggestion, trace, indication, token, manifestation • *Police said there was no evidence of a struggle.*
3 = testimony, statement, witness, declaration, submission, affirmation, deposition, avowal, attestation, averment • *Forensic scientists will be called to give evidence.*
▸ AS A VERB **= show**, prove, reveal, display, indicate, witness, demonstrate, exhibit, manifest, signify, denote, testify to, evince • *He still has a lot to learn, as is evidenced by his recent behaviour.*
▸ IN PHRASES: **in evidence = noticeable**, obvious, visible, manifest, conspicuous, perceptible • *Poverty is still very much in evidence in the city.*

evident = obvious, clear, plain, apparent, visible, patent, manifest, tangible, noticeable, blatant, conspicuous, unmistakable, palpable, salient, indisputable, perceptible, incontrovertible, incontestable, plain as the nose on your face • *He spoke with evident emotion about his ordeal.*
OPPOSITES: secret, hidden, unknown

evidently 1 = obviously, clearly, plainly, patently, undoubtedly, manifestly, doubtless, without question, unmistakably, indisputably, doubtlessly, incontrovertibly, incontestably • *He had evidently just woken up.*
2 = apparently, it seems, seemingly, outwardly, it would seem, ostensibly, so it seems, to all appearances • *Ellis evidently wished to negotiate downwards, after Atkinson had set the guidelines.*

evil AS AN ADJECTIVE **1 = wicked**, bad, wrong, corrupt, vicious, vile, malicious, base, immoral, malignant, sinful, unholy, malevolent, heinous, depraved, villainous, nefarious, iniquitous, reprobate, maleficent • *the country's most evil criminals*
2 = harmful, painful, disastrous, destructive, dire, catastrophic, mischievous, detrimental, hurtful, woeful, pernicious, ruinous, sorrowful, deleterious, injurious, baneful *(archaic)* • *Few people would not condemn slavery as evil.*
3 = demonic, satanic, diabolical, hellish, devilish, infernal, fiendish • *This place is said to be haunted by an evil spirit.*
4 = offensive, nasty, foul, unpleasant, vile, noxious, disagreeable, putrid, pestilential, mephitic • *There was an evil stench in the room.*
5 = unfortunate, unlucky, unfavourable, ruinous,

calamitous, inauspicious • *people of honour who happen to have fallen upon evil times*
▸ **AS A NOUN 1 = wickedness**, bad, wrong, vice, corruption, sin, wrongdoing, depravity, immorality, iniquity, badness, viciousness, villainy, sinfulness, turpitude, baseness, malignity, heinousness, maleficence • *We are being attacked by the forces of evil.*
2 = harm, suffering, pain, hurt, misery, sorrow, woe • *those who see television as the root of all evil*
3 = act of cruelty, crime, ill, horror, outrage, cruelty, brutality, misfortune, mischief, affliction, monstrosity, abomination, barbarity, villainy • *Racism is one of the greatest evils in the world.*

QUOTATIONS

So farewell hope, and with hope farewell fear,
Farewell remorse: all good to me is lost;
Evil be thou my Good
[John Milton *Paradise Lost*]

Evil be to him who evil thinks (Honi soit qui mal y pense)
[*Motto of the Order of the Garter*]

What we call evil is simply ignorance bumping its head in the dark
[Henry Ford]

The evil that men do lives after them
[William Shakespeare *Julius Caesar*]

Evil alone has oil for every wheel
[Edna St. Vincent Millay *Mine the Harvest*]

Sufficient unto the day is the evil thereof
[*Bible: St. Matthew*]

PROVERBS

Choose the lesser of two evils
See no evil, hear no evil, speak no evil

evildoer = sinner, criminal, devil, monster, offender, crook *(informal)*, villain, rogue, culprit, delinquent, fiend, ogre, wrongdoer, reprobate, mischief-maker, miscreant, malefactor, devil incarnate, wrong 'un *(informal)* • *Evildoers deserve God's wrath and punishment.*

evince = show, evidence, reveal, establish, express, display, indicate, demonstrate, exhibit, make clear, manifest, signify, attest, bespeak, betoken, make evident • *He had never, hitherto, evinced any particular interest in economic matters.*

eviscerate = gut, draw, paunch, disembowel, remove the internal organs of • *strangling and eviscerating rabbits for the pot*

evocative = expressive, moving, striking, revealing, pointed, pregnant, vivid, meaningful, poignant, eloquent, indicative, suggestive • *Aaron Copland's beautiful and evocative 'Appalachian Spring'*

evoke 1 = arouse, cause, excite, stimulate, induce, awaken, give rise to, stir up, rekindle, summon up • *The programme has evoked a storm of protest.*
OPPOSITES: contain, suppress, restrain
2 = provoke, produce, elicit, call to mind, call forth, educe *(rare)* • *Hearing these songs can still evoke strong memories and emotions.*

evolution 1 = rise, development, adaptation, natural selection, Darwinism, survival of the fittest, evolvement • *the evolution of plants and animals*
2 = development, growth, advance, progress, working out, expansion, extension, unfolding, progression, enlargement, maturation, unrolling • *a crucial period in the evolution of modern physics*

evolve 1 = develop, metamorphose, adapt yourself • *Modern birds evolved from dinosaurs.*
2 = grow, develop, advance, progress, mature • *Popular music evolved from folk songs.*
3 = work out, develop, progress, expand, elaborate, unfold, enlarge, unroll • *He evolved a working method from which he has never departed.*

exacerbate 1 = make worse, excite, intensify, worsen, provoke, aggravate
2 = irritate, excite, provoke, infuriate, aggravate *(informal)*, enrage, madden, inflame, exasperate, vex, embitter, add insult to injury, fan the flames of, envenom • *Their poverty has been exacerbated by racial divisions.*

exact AS AN ADJECTIVE 1 = accurate, very, correct, true, particular, right, express, specific, careful, precise, identical, authentic, faithful, explicit, definite, orderly, literal, unequivocal, faultless, on the money *(U.S.)*, unerring, veracious • *I can't remember the exact words he used.*
OPPOSITES: rough, loose, approximate
2 = meticulous, severe, careful, strict, exacting, precise, rigorous, painstaking, scrupulous, methodical, punctilious • *She is very punctual and very exact in her duties.*
▸ **AS A VERB 1 = demand**, claim, require, call for, force, impose, command, squeeze, extract, compel, wring, wrest, insist upon, extort • *He has exacted a high price for his co-operation.*
2 = inflict, apply, impose, administer, mete out, deal out • *She exacted a terrible revenge on her attackers.*

exacting 1 = demanding, hard, taxing, difficult, tough, painstaking • *He was not well enough to carry out such an exacting task.*
OPPOSITES: easy, simple, effortless
2 = strict, severe, harsh, stern, rigid, rigorous, stringent, oppressive, imperious, unsparing • *Our new manager has very exacting standards.*

exactitude *or* **exactness = precision**, truth, accuracy, correctness, rigour, regularity, veracity, faithfulness, orderliness, strictness, carefulness, scrupulousness, promptitude, preciseness, faultlessness, rigorousness, painstakingness, unequivocalness • *the care and exactitude with which the research has been executed*
OPPOSITES: inaccuracy, imprecision, incorrectness

exactly AS AN ADVERB 1 = accurately, correctly, definitely, truly, precisely, strictly, literally, faithfully, explicitly, rigorously, unequivocally, scrupulously, truthfully, methodically, unerringly, faultlessly, veraciously • *Can you describe exactly what he looked like?*
2 = precisely, just, expressly, prompt *(informal)*, specifically, bang on *(informal)*, to the letter, on the button *(informal)* • *He arrived at exactly five o'clock.*
▸ **AS A SENTENCE SUBSTITUTE = precisely**, yes, quite, of course, certainly, indeed, truly, that's right, absolutely, spot-on *(Brit. informal)*, just so, quite so, ya *(S. African)*, as you say, you got it *(informal)*, assuredly, yebo *(S. African informal)* • *'We don't know the answer to that.' – 'Exactly. So shut up and stop speculating.'*
▸ **IN PHRASES: not exactly = not at all**, hardly, not really, not quite, certainly not, by no means, in no way, not by any means, in no manner • *Sailing is not exactly a cheap hobby.*

exaggerate = overstate, emphasize, enlarge, inflate, embroider, magnify, overdo, amplify, exalt, embellish, overestimate, overemphasize, pile it on about *(informal)*, blow up out of all proportion, lay it on thick about *(informal)*, lay it on with a trowel about *(informal)*, make a production (out) of *(informal)*, make a federal case of *(U.S. informal)*, hyperbolize • *He tends to exaggerate the importance of his job.*

exaggerated = overstated, extreme, excessive, over the top *(informal)*, inflated, extravagant, overdone, tall *(informal)*, amplified, hyped, pretentious, exalted, overestimated, overblown, fulsome, hyperbolic, highly coloured, O.T.T. *(slang)* • *Be sceptical of exaggerated claims for what these products can do.*

exaggeration = overstatement, inflation, emphasis, excess, enlargement, pretension, extravagance, hyperbole, magnification, amplification, embellishment, exaltation, pretentiousness, overemphasis, overestimation • *Like most of his stories, it smacks of exaggeration.*

OPPOSITES: restraint, understatement, underplaying

QUOTATIONS

An exaggeration is a truth that has lost its temper
[Kahlil Gibran *Sand and Foam*]

exalt 1 = **praise**, acclaim, applaud, pay tribute to, bless, worship, magnify *(archaic)*, glorify, reverence, laud, extol, crack up *(informal)*, pay homage to, idolize, big up *(slang, chiefly Caribbean)*, apotheosize, set on a pedestal • *This book exalts her as a genius.*
2 = **uplift**, raise, lift, excite, delight, inspire, thrill, stimulate, arouse, heighten, elevate, animate, exhilarate, electrify, fire the imagination of, fill with joy, elate, inspirit • *Great music exalts the human spirit.*
3 = **raise**, advance, promote, honour, upgrade, elevate, dignify, ennoble, aggrandize • *God has put down the mighty from their seats, and exalted them of low degree.*

e

exaltation 1 = **elation**, delight, joy, excitement, inspiration, ecstasy, stimulation, bliss, transport, animation, elevation, rapture, exhilaration, jubilation, exultation, joyousness • *The city was swept up in the mood of exaltation.*
2 = **praise**, tribute, worship, acclaim, applause, glory, blessing, homage, reverence, magnification, apotheosis, glorification, acclamation, panegyric, idolization, extolment, lionization, laudation • *The poem is an exaltation of love.*
3 = **rise**, promotion, upgrading, advancement, honour, elevation, eminence, aggrandizement, ennoblement • *his exaltation to supreme power*

exalted 1 = **high-ranking**, high, grand, honoured, intellectual, noble, prestigious, august, elevated, eminent, dignified, lofty • *I seldom move in such exalted circles.*
2 = **noble**, ideal, superior, elevated, intellectual, uplifting, sublime, lofty, high-minded • *I don't think of poetry as an exalted calling, as some poets do.*
3 = **elated**, excited, inspired, stimulated, elevated, animated, uplifted, transported, exhilarated, ecstatic, jubilant, joyous, joyful, over the moon *(informal)*, blissful, rapturous, exultant, in high spirits, on cloud nine *(informal)*, cock-a-hoop, in seventh heaven, inspirited, stoked *(Austral. & N.Z. informal)* • *She had the look of someone exalted by an excess of joy.*

exam 1 = **test**, examination, assessment, evaluation, research, paper, investigation, practical, quiz, oral, appraisal, catechism • *He failed his maths exam and had to retake it.*
2 = **checkup**, analysis, going-over *(informal)*, exploration, health check, once-over *(informal)* • *A full medical exam is usually not required.*

examination 1 = **inspection**, testing, study, research, trial, checking, review, survey, investigation, analysis, consideration, observation, going-over *(informal)*, vetting, scrutiny, appraisal, interrogation, assay, perusal, recce *(slang)* • *They have taken the documents away for examination.*
2 = **checkup**, analysis, going-over *(informal)*, exploration, health check, check, medical, once-over *(informal)* • *a routine medical examination*
3 = **exam**, test, research, paper, investigation, practical, assessment, quiz, evaluation, oral, appraisal, catechism • *accusations of cheating in school examinations*
4 = **questioning**, inquiry, probe, quizzing, cross-examination, inquisition • *the examination of witnesses in this murder case*

QUOTATIONS

In examinations the foolish ask questions that the wise cannot answer
[Oscar Wilde *Phrases and Philosophies for the Use of the Young*]

examine 1 = **inspect**, test, consider, study, check, research, review, survey, investigate, explore, probe, analyse, scan, vet, check out, ponder, look over, look at, sift through, work over, pore over, appraise, scrutinize, peruse, take stock of, assay, recce *(slang)*, look at carefully, go over *or* through • *He examined her passport and stamped it.*
2 = **check**, analyse, check over • *The doctor examined her, but could find nothing wrong.*
3 = **test**, question, assess, quiz, evaluate, appraise, catechize • *the pressures of being judged and examined by our teachers*
4 = **question**, quiz, interrogate, cross-examine, grill *(informal)*, give the third degree to *(informal)* • *I was called and examined as a witness.*

examiner = **inspector**, investigator, interviewer, appraiser, quizmaster • *After she had completed the test, the examiner told her she had passed.*

example AS A NOUN 1 = **instance**, specimen, case, sample, illustration, case in point, particular case, particular instance, typical case, exemplification, representative case • *examples of sexism and racism in the police force*
2 = **illustration**, model, ideal, standard, norm, precedent, pattern, prototype, paradigm, archetype, paragon, exemplar • *This piece is a perfect example of symphonic construction.*
3 = **warning**, lesson, caution, deterrent, admonition • *We were punished as an example to others.*
▸ IN PHRASES: **for example** = **as an illustration**, like, such as, for instance, to illustrate, by way of illustration, exempli gratia *(Latin)*, e.g., to cite an instance • *You could, for example, walk instead of taking the car.*

PROVERBS

Practise what you preach

exasperate = **irritate**, anger, provoke, annoy, rouse, infuriate, hassle *(informal)*, exacerbate, aggravate *(informal)*, incense, enrage, gall, madden, inflame, bug *(informal)*, nettle, get to *(informal)*, vex, embitter, irk, rile *(informal)*, pique, rankle, peeve *(informal)*, needle *(informal)*, get on your nerves *(informal)*, try the patience of, nark *(Brit., Austral. & N.Z. slang)*, piss you off *(taboo slang)*, get in your hair *(informal)*, get on your wick *(Brit. slang)*, hack you off *(informal)* • *The constant interruptions were beginning to exasperate me.*
OPPOSITES: calm, soothe, appease

exasperated = **irritated**, cross, annoyed, infuriated, incensed, enraged, galled, pissed off *(taboo slang)*, mad *(informal)*, irate, riled *(informal)*, up in arms, peeved *(informal)* • *She was clearly exasperated by the delay.*

exasperating = **irritating**, provoking, annoying, infuriating, aggravating *(informal)*, galling, maddening, vexing, irksome, enough to drive you up the wall *(informal)*, enough to try the patience of a saint • *He is a very exasperating man to work with.*

exasperation = **irritation**, anger, rage, fury, wrath, provocation, passion, annoyance, ire *(literary)*, pique, aggravation *(informal)*, vexation, exacerbation • *There was a trace of exasperation in his voice.*

excavate 1 = **dig up**, mine, dig, tunnel, scoop, cut, hollow, trench, burrow, quarry, delve, gouge • *A team of archaeologists is excavating the site.*
2 = **unearth**, expose, uncover, dig out, exhume, lay bare, bring to light, bring to the surface, disinter • *They have excavated the fossil remains of a prehistoric man.*

excavation = **hole**, mine, pit, ditch, shaft, cutting, cut, hollow, trench, burrow, quarry, dig, trough, cavity, dugout, diggings • *excavations in the earth*

exceed 1 = **surpass**, better, pass, eclipse, beat, cap *(informal)*, top, be over, be more than, overtake, go beyond, excel, transcend, be greater than, outstrip, outdo, outreach, be larger than, outshine, surmount, be superior to, outrun, run rings around *(informal)*, outdistance, knock spots off

(informal), put in the shade *(informal)* • *His performance exceeded all expectations.*
2 = **go over the limit of**, go beyond, overstep, go beyond the bounds of • *This programme exceeded the bounds of taste and decency.*

exceeding = **extraordinary**, great, huge, vast, enormous, superior, excessive, exceptional, surpassing, superlative, pre-eminent, streets ahead • *His exceeding politeness masked his annoyance.*

exceedingly = **extremely**, very, highly, greatly, especially, hugely, seriously *(informal)*, vastly, unusually, enormously, exceptionally, extraordinarily, excessively, superlatively, inordinately, to a fault, to the nth degree, surpassingly • *It was an exceedingly difficult decision to make.*

excel AS A VERB = **be superior**, better, pass, eclipse, beat, top, cap *(informal)*, exceed, go beyond, surpass, transcend, outdo, outshine, surmount, run rings around *(informal)*, put in the shade *(informal)*, outrival • *Few dancers have excelled her in virtuosity.*
▸ IN PHRASES: **excel in** *or* **at something** = **be good at**, be master of, predominate in, shine at, be proficient in, show talent in, be skilful at, have (something) down to a fine art, be talented at • *She excelled at outdoor sports.*

excellence = **high quality**, worth, merit, distinction, virtue, goodness, perfection, superiority, purity, greatness, supremacy, eminence, virtuosity, transcendence, pre-eminence, fineness • *a school once noted for its academic excellence*

excellent = **outstanding**, good, great, fine, prime, capital, noted, choice, champion, cool *(informal)*, select, brilliant, very good, cracking *(Brit. informal)*, crucial *(slang)*, mean *(slang)*, superb, distinguished, fantastic, magnificent, superior, sterling, worthy, first-class, marvellous, exceptional, terrific, splendid, notable, mega *(slang)*, topping *(Brit. slang)*, sovereign, dope *(slang)*, world-class, exquisite, admirable, exemplary, wicked *(slang)*, first-rate, def *(slang)*, superlative, top-notch *(informal)*, brill *(informal)*, pre-eminent, meritorious, estimable, tiptop, bodacious *(slang, chiefly U.S.)*, boffo *(slang)*, the dog's bollocks *(taboo slang)*, jim-dandy *(slang)*, A1 *or* A-one *(informal)*, bitchin' *(U.S. slang)*, chillin' *(U.S. slang)*, booshit *(Austral. slang)*, exo *(Austral. slang)*, sik *(Austral. slang)*, rad *(informal)*, phat *(slang)*, schmick *(Austral. informal)*, beaut *(informal)*, barrie *(Scot. slang)*, belting *(Brit. slang)*, pearler *(Austral. slang)* • *We complimented her on doing an excellent job.*
OPPOSITES: bad, poor, terrible, half-pie *(N.Z. informal)*

except AS A PREPOSITION *often with* **for** = **apart from**, but for, saving, bar, barring, excepting, other than, excluding, omitting, with the exception of, aside from, save *(archaic)*, not counting, exclusive of • *I don't drink, except for the occasional glass of wine.*
▸ AS A VERB = **exclude**, rule out, leave out, omit, disregard, pass over • *Men are such swine (present company excepted, of course).*

exception AS A NOUN = **special case**, departure, freak, anomaly, inconsistency, deviation, quirk, oddity, peculiarity, irregularity • *an exception to the usual rule*
▸ IN PHRASES: **take exception** *usually with* **to** = **object to**, disagree with, take offence at, take umbrage at, be resentful of, be offended at, demur at, quibble at • *I take exception to being checked up on like this.*
with the exception of = **apart from**, save, barring, bar, excepting, except, other than, excluding, leaving out, omitting, not counting • *It was a day off for everyone, with the exception of Lawrence.*

QUOTATIONS
The exception proves the rule
[John Wilson *The Cheats*]

exceptional 1 = **remarkable**, special, excellent, extraordinary, outstanding, superior, first-class, marvellous, notable, phenomenal, first-rate, prodigious, unsurpassed, one in a million, bodacious *(slang, chiefly U.S.)*, unexcelled • *His piano playing is exceptional.*
OPPOSITES: bad, average, awful
2 = **unusual**, special, odd, strange, rare, extraordinary, unprecedented, peculiar, abnormal, irregular, uncommon, inconsistent, singular, deviant, anomalous, atypical, aberrant • *The courts hold that this case is exceptional.*
OPPOSITES: common, average, ordinary

exceptionally = **unusually**, very, particularly, surprisingly, strangely, seriously *(informal)*, extremely, remarkably, unexpectedly, peculiarly, to the nth degree • *exceptionally heavy rainfall*

excerpt AS A NOUN = **extract**, part, piece, section, selection, passage, portion, fragment, quotation, citation, pericope • *an excerpt from Tchaikovsky's 'Nutcracker'*
▸ AS A VERB = **extract**, take, select, quote, cite, pick out, cull • *The readings were excerpted from his autobiography.*

excess AS A NOUN 1 = **surfeit**, surplus, overdose, overflow, overload, plethora, glut, overabundance, superabundance, superfluity • *Avoid an excess of sugar in your diet.*
OPPOSITES: want, lack, shortage
2 = **overindulgence**, extravagance, profligacy, debauchery, dissipation, intemperance, indulgence, prodigality, extreme behaviour, immoral behaviour, dissoluteness, immoderation, exorbitance, unrestraint • *He had led a life of excess.*
OPPOSITES: restraint, moderation, self-control
▸ AS AN ADJECTIVE = **spare**, remaining, extra, additional, surplus, unwanted, redundant, residual, leftover, superfluous, unneeded • *After cooking the fish, pour off any excess fat.*
▸ IN PHRASES: **in excess of** = **exceeding**, over, more than, above • *The health club has a membership in excess of five thousand.*

QUOTATIONS
Moderation is a fatal thing.
Nothing succeeds like excess
[Oscar Wilde *A Woman of No Importance*]
Too much of a good thing can be wonderful
[Mae West *Goodness Had Nothing To Do With It*]
In excess, craving and revulsion alternate
[Mason Cooley *City Aphorisms*]
The road of excess leads to the palace of wisdom
[William Blake *The Marriage of Heaven and Hell*]
PROVERBS
Too many cooks spoil the broth
You can have too much of a good thing

excessive 1 = **immoderate**, too much, enormous, extreme, exaggerated, over the top *(slang)*, extravagant, needless, unreasonable, disproportionate, undue, uncontrolled, superfluous, prodigal, unrestrained, profligate, inordinate, fulsome, intemperate, unconscionable, overmuch, O.T.T. *(slang)* • *the alleged use of excessive force by police*
2 = **inordinate**, unfair, unreasonable, disproportionate, undue, unwarranted, exorbitant, over the odds, extortionate, immoderate • *banks which cripple their customers with excessive charges*

excessively 1 = **immoderately**, too much, extravagantly, intemperately • *She had started taking pills and drinking excessively.*
2 = **inordinately**, unnecessarily, unduly, disproportionately, unreasonably • *managers paying themselves excessively high salaries*

exchange AS A VERB = **interchange**, change, trade, switch, swap, truck, barter, reciprocate, bandy, give to each other, give to one another • *We exchanged addresses.*
▸ AS A NOUN 1 = **conversation**, talk, word, discussion, chat,

dialogue, natter, powwow • *I had a brief exchange with him before I left.*
2 = interchange, dealing, trade, switch, swap, traffic, trafficking, truck, swapping, substitution, barter, bartering, reciprocity, tit for tat, quid pro quo • *a free exchange of information*
3 = market, money market, Bourse • *the Stock Exchange*

excise[1] **= tax**, duty, customs, toll, levy, tariff, surcharge, impost • *Smokers will be hit by increases in tax and excise.*

excise[2] **1 = delete**, cut, remove, erase, destroy, eradicate, strike out, exterminate, cross out, expunge, extirpate, wipe from the face of the earth • *a crusade to excise racist and sexist references in newspapers*
2 = cut off *or* **out** *or* **away**, remove, take out, extract • *She has already had one skin cancer excised.*

e

excitability = nervousness, stress, tension, volatility, high spirits, restlessness, restiveness, hot-headedness • *She has always been inclined to excitability and impatience.*

excitable = nervous, emotional, violent, sensitive, tense, passionate, volatile, hasty, edgy, temperamental, touchy, mercurial, uptight *(informal)*, irascible, testy, hot-headed, chippy *(informal)*, hot-tempered, quick-tempered, highly strung, adrenalized • *The patient was in a highly excitable state.*
OPPOSITES: cool, calm, laid-back *(informal)*

excite 1 = thrill, inspire, stir, stimulate, provoke, awaken, animate, move, fire, rouse, exhilarate, agitate, quicken, inflame, enliven, galvanize, foment • *I only take on work that excites me.*
2 = arouse, stimulate, provoke, evoke, rouse, stir up, fire, elicit, work up, incite, instigate, whet, kindle, waken • *The proposal failed to excite our interest.*
3 = titillate, thrill, stimulate, turn on *(slang)*, arouse, get going *(informal)*, electrify • *Try exciting your partner with a little bondage.*

excited 1 = thrilled, stirred, stimulated, enthusiastic, high *(informal)*, moved, wild, aroused, awakened, animated, roused, tumultuous, aflame • *He was so excited he could hardly speak.*
2 = agitated, worried, stressed, alarmed, nervous, disturbed, tense, flurried, worked up, feverish, overwrought, hot and bothered *(informal)*, discomposed, adrenalized • *There's no need to get so excited.*

excitement 1 = exhilaration, action, activity, passion, heat, thrill, adventure, enthusiasm, fever, warmth, flurry, animation, furore, ferment, agitation, commotion, elation, ado, tumult, perturbation, discomposure • *The audience was in a state of great excitement.*
2 = pleasure, thrill, sensation, stimulation, tingle, kick *(informal)* • *The game had its challenges, excitements and rewards.*

exciting 1 = stimulating, inspiring, dramatic, gripping, stirring, thrilling, moving, sensational, rousing, exhilarating, electrifying, intoxicating, rip-roaring *(informal)* • *the most exciting adventure of their lives*
OPPOSITES: flat, boring, dull
2 = titillating, stimulating, sexy *(informal)*, arousing, erotic, provocative • *fantasizing about a sexually exciting scene*

exclaim = cry out, call, declare, cry, shout, proclaim, yell, utter, call out, ejaculate, vociferate • *'I don't believe it!' he exclaimed.*

exclamation = cry, call, shout, yell, outcry, utterance, ejaculation, expletive, interjection, vociferation • *Sue gave an exclamation of surprise.*

exclude 1 = keep out, bar, ban, veto, refuse, forbid, boycott, embargo, prohibit, disallow, shut out, proscribe, black, refuse to admit, ostracize, debar, blackball, interdict, prevent from entering • *The Academy excluded women from its classes.*
OPPOSITES: allow, receive, let in
2 = omit, reject, eliminate, rule out, miss out, leave out, preclude, repudiate • *Vegetarians exclude meat products from their diet.*
OPPOSITES: include, accept, count
3 = eliminate, reject, ignore, rule out, except, leave out, set aside, omit, pass over, not count, repudiate, count out • *We can't exclude the possibility of suicide.*

exclusion 1 = ban, bar, veto, refusal, boycott, embargo, prohibition, disqualification, interdict, proscription, debarment, preclusion, forbiddance, nonadmission • *They demand the exclusion of former communists from political life.*
2 = elimination, exception, missing out, rejection, leaving out, omission, repudiation • *the exclusion of dairy products from your diet*

exclusive AS AN ADJECTIVE **1 = select**, fashionable, stylish, private, limited, choice, narrow, closed, restricted, elegant, posh *(informal, chiefly Brit.)*, chic, selfish, classy *(slang)*, restrictive, aristocratic, high-class, swish *(informal, chiefly Brit.)*, up-market, snobbish, top-drawer, ritzy *(slang)*, high-toned, clannish, discriminative, cliquish • *He is a member of Britain's most exclusive club.*
OPPOSITES: open, public, unrestricted
2 = sole, only, full, whole, single, private, complete, total, entire, unique, absolute, undivided, unshared • *We have exclusive use of a 60-foot boat.*
OPPOSITES: shared, partial, inclusive
3 = entire, full, whole, complete, total, absolute, undivided • *She wants her father's exclusive attention.*
4 = limited, unique, restricted, confined, peculiar • *Infatuations are not exclusive to the very young.*
▸ IN PHRASES: **exclusive of = except for**, excepting, excluding, ruling out, not including, omitting, not counting, leaving aside, debarring • *All charges are exclusive of value added tax.*

exclusively = solely, totally, fully, entirely, wholly, uniquely • *This is still an exclusively male domain.*

excommunicate = expel, ban, remove, exclude, denounce, banish, eject, repudiate, proscribe, cast out, unchurch, anathematize • *In 1656 Spinoza was excommunicated because of his religious views.*

excrement = faeces, shit *(taboo slang)*, crap *(taboo slang)*, dung, stool, droppings, turd *(taboo slang)*, motion, mess *(of a domestic animal)*, defecation, excreta, ordure, kak *(S. African taboo slang)*, night soil • *The tunnel stank of excrement.*

excrescence 1 = protrusion, lump, projection, prominence, knob, blot, outgrowth, protuberance • *The annexe is an architectural excrescence.*
2 = swelling, growth, lump, tumour, wart • *soft excrescences which are attached to the arterial walls*

excrete = defecate, shit *(taboo slang)*, discharge, expel, evacuate, crap *(taboo slang)*, eliminate, void, dump *(slang, chiefly U.S.)*, eject, exude, egest • *the orifice through which the body excretes waste matter*

excruciating = agonizing, acute, severe, extreme, burning, violent, intense, piercing, racking, searing, tormenting, exquisite, harrowing, unbearable, insufferable, torturous, unendurable • *I was in excruciating pain.*

excursion 1 = trip, airing, tour, journey, outing, expedition, ramble, day trip, jaunt, awayday, pleasure trip • *We also recommend a full day excursion to the Upper Douro.*
2 = digression, episode, wandering, deviation, detour, excursus • *All these alarms and excursions diverted attention from the main point of the meeting.*

excusable = forgivable, understandable, justifiable, permissible, minor, slight, allowable, defensible, venial, pardonable, warrantable • *He had made a simple but excusable mistake.*

excuse AS A VERB **1 = justify**, explain, defend, vindicate, condone, mitigate, apologize for, make excuses for • *I know*

you're upset but that doesn't excuse your behaviour.
OPPOSITES: accuse, blame, correct
2 = **forgive**, pardon, overlook, tolerate, indulge, acquit, pass over, turn a blind eye to, exonerate, absolve, bear with, wink at, make allowances for, extenuate, exculpate • *He's a total bastard – excuse me for swearing.*
3 = **free**, relieve, liberate, exempt, release, spare, discharge, let off, absolve • *She was excused from her duties for the day.*
OPPOSITES: charge, sentence, convict
▸ **AS A NOUN** 1 = **justification**, reason, explanation, defence, grounds, plea, apology, pretext, vindication, mitigation, mitigating circumstances, extenuation • *There is no excuse for what he did.*
OPPOSITES: charge, accusation, indictment
2 = **pretext**, evasion, pretence, cover-up, expedient, get-out, cop-out *(slang)*, subterfuge • *It was just an excuse to get out of going to school.*
3 = **poor substitute**, apology, mockery, travesty • *He is a pathetic excuse for a father.*
▸ **IN PHRASES: excuse me** = **I beg your pardon**, sorry, pardon, pardon me • *Excuse me, but could I just squeeze past you?*

QUOTATIONS
And oftentimes excusing of a fault
Doth make the fault the worser by th'excuse
[William Shakespeare *King John*]
Several excuses are always less convincing than one
[Aldous Huxley *Point Counter Point*]
A real failure does not need an excuse. It is an end in itself
[Gertrude Stein *Four in America*]

execrable = **repulsive**, offensive, disgusting, horrible, unpleasant, foul, revolting, obscene, sickening, vile, atrocious, obnoxious, despicable, deplorable, heinous, disagreeable, odious, hateful, loathsome, abhorrent, abominable, nauseous, accursed, detestable, damnable, cringe-making *(Brit. informal)* • *my neighbour's execrable taste in music*

execute 1 = **put to death**, kill, shoot, hang, behead, decapitate, guillotine, electrocute • *His father had been executed for treason.*
2 = **carry out**, effect, finish, complete, achieve, realize, do, implement, fulfil, enforce, accomplish, render, discharge, administer, prosecute, enact, consummate, put into effect, bring off • *We are going to execute our campaign plan to the letter.*
3 = **perform**, do, carry out, accomplish • *The landing was skilfully executed.*
4 = **validate**, sign, serve, deliver, seal • *the procedure for executing a will*

QUOTATIONS
We must execute not only the guilty. Execution of the innocent will impress the masses even more
[Nikolai V. Krylenko]

execution 1 = **killing**, hanging, the death penalty, the rope, capital punishment, beheading, the electric chair, the guillotine, the noose, the scaffold, electrocution, decapitation, the firing squad, necktie party *(informal)* • *He was sentenced to execution by lethal injection.*
2 = **carrying out**, performance, operation, administration, achievement, effect, prosecution, rendering, discharge, enforcement, implementation, completion, accomplishment, realization, enactment, bringing off, consummation • *the unquestioning execution of his orders*
3 = **performance**, style, delivery, manner, technique, mode, presentation, rendition • *his masterly execution of a difficult piece*
4 = **validation**, signing, delivery, sealing • *legislation preventing the due execution of the contracts*

executioner = **hangman**, firing squad, headsman, public executioner, Jack Ketch • *The criminals will be hanged by the official executioner.*

executive **AS A NOUN** 1 = **administrator**, official, director, manager, chairman, managing director, controller, chief executive officer, senior manager, chairwoman, chairperson • *Her husband is a senior bank executive.*
2 = **administration**, government, directors, management, leadership, hierarchy, directorate • *the executive of the National Union of Students*
▸ **AS AN ADJECTIVE** = **administrative**, controlling, directing, governing, regulating, decision-making, managerial • *He sits on the executive committee of the company.*

exegesis = **explanation**, interpretation, clarification, exposition, explication • *a substantial exegesis of his work*

exemplar 1 = **model**, example, standard, ideal, criterion, paradigm, epitome, paragon • *They viewed their new building as an exemplar of taste.*
2 = **example**, instance, illustration, type, specimen, prototype, typical example, representative example, exemplification • *One of the wittiest exemplars of the technique was M.C. Escher.*

exemplary 1 = **ideal**, good, fine, model, excellent, sterling, admirable, honourable, commendable, laudable, praiseworthy, meritorious, estimable, punctilious • *He showed outstanding and exemplary courage in the face of danger.*
2 = **typical**, representative, characteristic, signature, illustrative • *an exemplary case of how issues of this sort can be resolved*
3 = **warning**, harsh, cautionary, admonitory, monitory • *He demanded exemplary sentences for those behind the violence.*

exemplify = **show**, represent, display, demonstrate, instance, illustrate, exhibit, depict, manifest, evidence, embody, serve as an example of • *Her character exemplifies the emotional turmoil of many women.*

exempt **AS A VERB** = **grant immunity**, free, except, excuse, release, spare, relieve, discharge, liberate, let off, exonerate, absolve • *Companies with fewer than 55 employees would be exempted from these requirements.*
▸ **AS AN ADJECTIVE** = **immune**, free, excepted, excused, released, spared, clear, discharged, liberated, not subject to, absolved, not liable to • *Men in college were exempt from military service.*
OPPOSITES: subject, responsible, liable

exemption = **immunity**, freedom, privilege, relief, exception, discharge, release, dispensation, absolution, exoneration • *new exemptions for students and the unwaged*

exercise **AS A VERB** 1 = **put to use**, use, apply, employ, practise, exert, enjoy, wield, utilize, bring to bear, avail yourself of • *They are merely exercising their right to free speech.*
2 = **train**, work out, practise, drill, keep fit, inure, do exercises • *She exercises two or three times a week.*
3 = **worry**, concern, occupy, try, trouble, pain, disturb, burden, distress, preoccupy, agitate, perplex, vex, perturb • *an issue that has long exercised the finest scientific minds*
▸ **AS A NOUN** 1 = **use**, practice, application, operation, employment, discharge, implementation, enjoyment, accomplishment, fulfilment, exertion, utilization • *Leadership does not rest on the exercise of force alone.*
2 = **exertion**, training, activity, action, work, labour, effort, movement, discipline, toil, physical activity • *Lack of exercise can lead to feelings of depression and exhaustion.*
3 = **manoeuvre**, campaign, operation, movement, deployment • *a missile being used in a military exercise*
4 = **task**, problem, lesson, assignment, work, schooling, practice, schoolwork • *Try working through the opening exercises in this chapter.*

exert **AS A VERB** = **apply**, use, exercise, employ, wield, make use of, utilize, expend, bring to bear, put forth, bring into

e

play • *He exerted all his considerable charm to get her to agree.*
▸ **IN PHRASES: exert yourself = make an effort**, work, labour, struggle, strain, strive, endeavour, go for it *(informal)*, try hard, toil, bend over backwards *(informal)*, do your best, go for broke *(slang)*, bust a gut *(informal)*, spare no effort, make a great effort, give it your best shot *(informal)*, break your neck *(informal)*, apply yourself, put yourself out, make an all-out effort *(informal)*, get your finger out *(Brit. informal)*, pull your finger out *(Brit. informal)*, knock yourself out *(informal)*, do your damnedest *(informal)*, give it your all *(informal)*, rupture yourself *(informal)* • *He never exerts himself for other people.*

exertion 1 = effort, action, exercise, struggle, industry, labour, trial, pains, stretch, strain, endeavour, toil, travail *(literary)*, elbow grease *(facetious)* • *panting from the exertion of climbing the stairs*
2 = use, exercise, application, employment, bringing to bear, utilization • *the exertion of legislative power*

e

exhalation 1 = breathing out, breath, blowing out, expiration • *the quick exhalation of breath through the nostrils*
2 = emission, fume, exhaust, smoke, steam, discharge, mist, fog, vapour, evaporation, emanation, effluvium • *These plants give off a poisonous exhalation at night.*

exhale 1 = breathe out, breathe, expel, blow out, respire • *Hold your breath for a moment and exhale.*
2 = give off, emit, steam, discharge, send out, evaporate, issue, eject, emanate • *The craters exhale water, carbon dioxide, and sulphur dioxide.*

exhaust 1 = tire out, tire, fatigue, drain, disable, weaken, cripple, weary, sap, wear out, debilitate, prostrate, enfeeble, make tired, enervate • *The effort of speaking had exhausted him.*
2 = use up, spend, finish, consume, waste, go through, run through, deplete, squander, dissipate, expend • *We have exhausted almost all our food supplies.*

exhausted 1 = worn out, tired, tired out, drained, spent, beat *(slang)*, bushed *(informal)*, dead *(informal)*, wasted, done in *(informal)*, weak, all in *(slang)*, disabled, crippled, fatigued, wiped out *(informal)*, sapped, debilitated, jaded, knackered *(slang)*, prostrated, clapped out *(Brit., Austral. & N.Z. informal)*, effete, enfeebled, enervated, ready to drop, dog-tired *(informal)*, zonked *(slang)*, dead tired, dead beat *(informal)*, shagged out *(Brit. slang)*, fagged out *(informal)*, worn to a frazzle *(informal)*, on your last legs *(informal)*, creamcrackered *(Brit. slang)*, out on your feet *(informal)* • *She was too exhausted even to think clearly.*
OPPOSITES: active, restored, invigorated
2 = used up, consumed, spent, finished, gone, depleted, dissipated, expended, at an end • *Mining companies are shutting down operations as the coal supply is exhausted.*
OPPOSITES: kept, restored, replenished

exhausting = tiring, hard, testing, taxing, difficult, draining, punishing, crippling, fatiguing, wearying, gruelling, sapping, debilitating, strenuous, arduous, laborious, enervating, backbreaking • *She had set herself an exhausting schedule.*

exhaustion 1 = tiredness, fatigue, weariness, lassitude, feebleness, prostration, debilitation, enervation • *He is suffering from nervous exhaustion.*
2 = depletion, emptying, consumption, using up • *the exhaustion of the country's resources*

exhaustive = thorough, detailed, complete, full, total, sweeping, comprehensive, extensive, intensive, full-scale, in-depth, far-reaching, all-inclusive, all-embracing, encyclopedic, thoroughgoing • *The author's treatment of the subject is exhaustive.*
OPPOSITES: casual, superficial, incomplete

exhibit AS A VERB 1 = show, reveal, display, demonstrate, air, evidence, express, indicate, disclose, manifest, evince, make clear *or* plain • *He has exhibited signs of anxiety and stress.*
2 = display, show, present, set out, parade, unveil, flaunt, put on view • *Her work was exhibited in the best galleries in Europe.*
▸ **AS A NOUN 1 = object**, piece, model, article, illustration • *He showed me round the exhibits in the museum.*
2 = exhibition, show, fair, display, spectacle, expo *(informal)*, exposition • *the 8th international exhibit of agricultural technology*

exhibition 1 = show, display, exhibit, showing, fair, representation, presentation, spectacle, showcase, expo *(informal)*, exposition • *an exhibition of expressionist art*
2 = display, show, performance, demonstration, airing, revelation, manifestation • *He treated the fans to an exhibition of power and speed.*

exhibitionist = show-off, boaster, poser, poseur, peacock, hot dog *(chiefly U.S.)*, egotist, braggart, swashbuckler, braggadocio, attitudinizer, swankpot *(informal)* • *She's always been a shameless exhibitionist.*

exhilarate = excite, delight, cheer, thrill, stimulate, animate, exalt, lift, enliven, invigorate, gladden, elate, inspirit, pep *or* perk up • *She felt both exhilarated and disturbed by what had just happened.*

exhilarating = exciting, thrilling, stimulating, breathtaking, cheering, exalting, enlivening, invigorating, gladdening, vitalizing, exhilarant • *It was the most exhilarating experience of my life.*

exhilaration = excitement, delight, joy, happiness, animation, high spirits, elation, mirth, gaiety, hilarity, exaltation, cheerfulness, vivacity, liveliness, gladness, joyfulness, sprightliness, gleefulness • *A wave of exhilaration swept through me.*
OPPOSITES: depression, misery, gloom

exhort = urge, warn, encourage, advise, bid, persuade, prompt, spur, press, counsel, caution, call upon, incite, goad, admonish, enjoin, beseech, entreat • *Kennedy exhorted his listeners to turn away from violence.*

exhortation = urging, warning, advice, counsel, lecture, caution, bidding, encouragement, sermon, persuasion, goading, incitement, admonition, beseeching, entreaty, clarion call, enjoinder *(rare)* • *eve-of-election front-page exhortations to vote Tory*

exhume = dig up, unearth, disinter, unbury, disentomb • *His remains have been exhumed from their resting place.*
OPPOSITES: bury, inter, entomb

exigency *or* **exigence 1 = need**, demand, requirement, necessity, constraint, wont • *The reduction was caused by the exigencies of a wartime economy.*
2 = urgency, pressure, difficulty, emergency, crisis, stress, distress, necessity, constraint, hardship, acuteness, demandingness, criticalness, imperativeness, needfulness, pressingness • *Financial exigency forced him to sell up his business.*

exile AS A NOUN 1 = banishment, expulsion, deportation, eviction, separation, ostracism, proscription, expatriation • *During his exile, he began writing books.*
2 = expatriate, refugee, outcast, émigré, deportee • *the release of all political prisoners and the return of exiles*
▸ **AS A VERB = banish**, expel, throw out, deport, oust, drive out, eject, expatriate, proscribe, cast out, ostracize • *Dante was exiled from Florence in 1302 because of his political activities.*

exiled = banished, deported, expatriate, outcast, refugee, ostracized, expat • *The exiled spiritual leader of Tibet, the Dalai Lama*

exist 1 = live, be present, be living, last, survive, breathe, endure, be in existence, be, be extant, have breath • *Many people believe that the Loch Ness Monster does exist.*
2 = occur, happen, stand, remain, obtain, be present, prevail, abide • *the social climate which existed 20 years ago*

3 = survive, stay alive, make ends meet, subsist, eke out a living, scrape by, scrimp and save, support yourself, keep your head above water, get along *or* by • *the problems of having to exist on unemployment benefit*

existence AS A NOUN **1 = reality**, being, life, survival, duration, endurance, continuation, subsistence, actuality, continuance • *Public worries about accidents are threatening the very existence of the nuclear power industry.*
2 = life, situation, way of life, life style • *the man who rescued her from her wretched existence*
3 = creation, life, the world, reality, the human condition, this mortal coil • *pondering the mysteries of existence*
▸ IN PHRASES: **in existence = surviving**, remaining, functioning, operative, in force, existent, in operation, extant, undestroyed • *It is the only one of its kind that is in existence.*

QUOTATIONS
I think; therefore I am
[René Descartes *Discourse on Method*]
Man is the only animal for whom his own existence is a problem which he has to solve
[Erich Fromm *Man For Himself*]

existent = in existence, living, existing, surviving, around, standing, remaining, present, current, alive, enduring, prevailing, abiding, to the fore *(Scot.)*, extant • *human rights in former and still existent communist states*

existing = in existence, living, present, surviving, remaining, available, alive, in operation, extant, alive and kicking • *the need to improve existing products*
OPPOSITES: lost, gone, dead

exit AS A NOUN **1 = way out**, door, gate, outlet, doorway, vent, gateway, escape route, passage out, egress • *We headed quickly for the fire exit.*
OPPOSITES: entry, way in, entrance
2 = departure, withdrawal, retreat, farewell, going, retirement, goodbye, exodus, evacuation, decamping, leave-taking, adieu • *She made a dignified exit.*
▸ AS A VERB **= depart**, leave, go out, withdraw, retire, quit, retreat, go away, say goodbye, bid farewell, make tracks, take your leave, go offstage *(Theatre)* • *He exited without saying goodbye.*
OPPOSITES: arrive, enter, make an entrance

exodus = departure, withdrawal, retreat, leaving, flight, retirement, exit, migration, evacuation • *The exodus of refugees from the town shows no sign of abating.*

exonerate = acquit, clear, excuse, pardon, justify, discharge, vindicate, absolve, exculpate • *The official report exonerated the school of any blame.*

exoneration = acquittal, discharge, amnesty, justification, pardon, vindication, absolution, exculpation • *the exoneration of an athlete who inadvertently took a banned drug*

exorbitant = excessive, high, expensive, extreme, ridiculous, outrageous, extravagant, unreasonable, undue, preposterous, unwarranted, inordinate, extortionate, unconscionable, immoderate • *exorbitant housing prices*
OPPOSITES: fair, cheap, reasonable

exorcise *or* **exorcize 1 = drive out**, expel, cast out, adjure • *He tried to exorcise the pain of his childhood trauma.*
2 = purify, free, cleanse • *They came to our house and exorcized me.*

exorcism = driving out, cleansing, expulsion, purification, deliverance, casting out, adjuration • *The priest performed a rite of exorcism.*

exotic 1 = unusual, different, striking, strange, extraordinary, bizarre, fascinating, curious, mysterious, colourful, glamorous, peculiar, unfamiliar, outlandish • *his striking and exotic appearance*
OPPOSITES: ordinary, familiar, plain
2 = foreign, alien, tropical, external, extraneous, naturalized, extrinsic, not native • *travelling around the globe to collect rare and exotic plant species*

expand AS A VERB **1 = get bigger**, increase, grow, extend, swell, widen, blow up, wax, heighten, enlarge, multiply, inflate, thicken, fill out, lengthen, fatten, dilate, become bigger, puff up, become larger, distend • *Water expands as it freezes.*
OPPOSITES: contract, shrink, decrease
2 = make bigger, increase, develop, extend, widen, blow up, heighten, enlarge, multiply, broaden, inflate, thicken, fill out, lengthen, magnify, amplify, augment, dilate, make larger, distend, bloat, protract • *We can expand the size of the image.*
OPPOSITES: reduce, decrease, shorten
3 = spread (out), open (out), stretch (out), unfold, unravel, diffuse, unfurl, unroll, outspread • *The flowers fully expand at night.*
▸ IN PHRASES: **expand on something = go into detail about**, embellish, elaborate on, develop, flesh out, expound on, enlarge on, expatiate on, add detail to • *He expanded on some remarks he made in his last speech.*

expanse = area, range, field, space, stretch, sweep, extent, plain, tract, breadth • *a vast expanse of grassland*

expansion 1 = increase, development, growth, spread, diffusion, magnification, multiplication, amplification, augmentation • *the rapid expansion of private health insurance*
2 = enlargement, inflation, increase, growth, swelling, unfolding, expanse, unfurling, opening out, distension • *Slow breathing allows for full expansion of the lungs.*

expansive 1 = wide, broad, extensive, spacious, sweeping • *an expansive grassy play area*
2 = comprehensive, extensive, broad, wide, widespread, wide-ranging, thorough, inclusive, far-reaching, voluminous, all-embracing • *the book's expansive coverage of this period*
3 = talkative, open, friendly, outgoing, free, easy, warm, sociable, genial, affable, communicative, effusive, garrulous, loquacious, unreserved • *He became more expansive as he began to relax.*

expatriate AS AN ADJECTIVE **= exiled**, refugee, banished, emigrant, émigré, expat • *The military is preparing to evacuate women and children of expatriate families.*
▸ AS A NOUN **= exile**, refugee, emigrant, émigré, expat • *British expatriates in Spain*

expect 1 = think, believe, suppose, assume, trust, imagine, reckon, forecast, calculate, presume, foresee, conjecture, surmise, think likely • *We expect the talks will continue until tomorrow.*
2 = anticipate, look forward to, predict, envisage, await, hope for, contemplate, bargain for, look ahead to • *I wasn't expecting to see you today.*
3 = require, demand, want, wish, look for, call for, ask for, hope for, insist on, count on, rely upon • *He expects total obedience and blind loyalty from his staff.*

expectancy 1 = likelihood, prospect, tendency, outlook, probability • *the average life expectancy of the British male*
2 = expectation, hope, anticipation, waiting, belief, looking forward, assumption, prediction, probability, suspense, presumption, conjecture, surmise, supposition • *The atmosphere here at the stadium is one of expectancy.*

expectant 1 = expecting, excited, anticipating, anxious, ready, awaiting, eager, hopeful, apprehensive, watchful, in suspense • *She turned to me with an expectant look on her face.*
2 = pregnant, expecting *(informal)*, gravid, enceinte • *antenatal classes for expectant mothers*

expectation 1 *usually plural* **= projection**, supposition, assumption, calculation, belief, forecast, assurance, likelihood, probability, presumption, conjecture, surmise, presupposition • *Sales of the car have far exceeded expectations.*

2 = **anticipation**, hope, possibility, prospect, chance, fear, promise, looking forward, excitement, prediction, outlook, expectancy, apprehension, suspense • *His nerves tingled with expectation.*
3 *usually plural* = **requirement**, demand, want, wish, insistence, reliance • *Sometimes people have unreasonable expectations of the medical profession.*

QUOTATIONS
Blessed is the man who expects nothing, for he shall never be disappointed
[Alexander Pope *letter to Fortescue*]

expected = **anticipated**, wanted, promised, looked-for, predicted, forecast, awaited, hoped-for, counted on, long-awaited • *Profits last month were well above the expected figure.*

expecting = **pregnant**, with child, expectant, in the club (*Brit. slang*), in the family way (*informal*), gravid, enceinte • *He had just heard that Beverly was expecting again.*

expediency *or* **expedience** = **suitability**, benefit, fitness, utility, effectiveness, convenience, profitability, practicality, usefulness, prudence, pragmatism, propriety, desirability, appropriateness, utilitarianism, helpfulness, advisability, aptness, judiciousness, properness, meetness, advantageousness • *His decision was dictated by expediency rather than morals.*

expedient AS AN ADJECTIVE = **advantageous**, effective, useful, profitable, fit, politic, appropriate, practical, suitable, helpful, proper, convenient, desirable, worthwhile, beneficial, pragmatic, prudent, advisable, utilitarian, judicious, opportune • *It might be expedient to keep this information to yourself.*
OPPOSITES: ineffective, detrimental, unwise
▸ AS A NOUN = **means**, measure, scheme, method, resource, resort, device, manoeuvre, expediency, stratagem, contrivance, stopgap • *I reduced my spending by the simple expedient of destroying my credit cards.*

expedite = **speed (up)**, forward, promote, advance, press, urge, rush, assist, hurry, accelerate, dispatch, facilitate, hasten, precipitate, quicken, fast-track • *We will do all we can to expedite the procedure*
OPPOSITES: restrict, delay, hold up

expedition 1 = **journey**, exploration, mission, voyage, tour, enterprise, undertaking, quest, trek • *Byrd's 1928 expedition to Antarctica*
2 = **team**, crew, party, group, company, travellers, explorers, voyagers, wayfarers • *Forty-three members of the expedition were killed.*
3 = **trip**, tour, outing, excursion, jaunt, awayday • *We went on a shopping expedition.*

expeditious = **quick**, fast, active, prompt, immediate, rapid, ready, alert, efficient, instant, swift, speedy, brisk, hasty, nimble, diligent • *the efficient and expeditious way in which he has conducted this business*

expel 1 = **throw out**, exclude, ban, bar, dismiss, discharge, relegate, kick out (*informal*), ask to leave, send packing, turf out (*informal*), black, debar, drum out, blackball, give the bum's rush (*slang*), show you the door, throw out on your ear (*informal*) • *secondary school students expelled for cheating in exams*
OPPOSITES: admit, let in, give access
2 = **banish**, exile, oust, deport, expatriate, evict, force to leave, proscribe • *An American academic was expelled from the country yesterday.*
OPPOSITES: receive, welcome, take in
3 = **drive out**, discharge, throw out, force out, let out, eject, issue, dislodge, spew, belch, cast out • *Poisonous gas is expelled into the atmosphere.*

expend 1 = **use (up)**, employ, go through (*informal*), exhaust, consume, dissipate • *the number of calories you expend through exercise*
2 = **spend**, pay out, lay out (*informal*), fork out (*slang*), shell out, disburse • *the amount of money expended on this project so far*

expendable = **dispensable**, unnecessary, unimportant, replaceable, nonessential, inessential • *Once we're of no more use to them, we're expendable.*
OPPOSITES: necessary, essential, indispensable

expenditure 1 = **spending**, payment, expense, outgoings, cost, charge, outlay, disbursement • *The government should reduce their expenditure on defence.*
2 = **consumption**, use, using, application, output • *The rewards justified the expenditure of effort.*

QUOTATIONS
Expenditure rises to meet income
[C. Northcote Parkinson *The Law and the Profits*]

expense AS A NOUN = **cost**, charge, expenditure, payment, spending, output, toll, consumption, outlay, disbursement • *She has refurbished the whole place at vast expense.*
▸ AS A PLURAL NOUN = **costs**, expenditure, overheads, outgoings, disbursements, incidentals, incidental expenses • *All her expenses were paid by the company.*
▸ IN PHRASES: **at the expense of** = **with the sacrifice of**, with the loss of, at the cost of, at the price of • *The company has increased productivity at the expense of safety.*

expensive = **costly**, high-priced, lavish, extravagant, rich, dear, stiff, excessive, steep (*informal*), pricey, overpriced, exorbitant • *He has a lot of expensive recording equipment.*
OPPOSITES: budget, cheap, bargain

experience AS A NOUN 1 = **knowledge**, understanding, practice, skill, evidence, trial, contact, expertise, know-how (*informal*), proof, involvement, exposure, observation, participation, familiarity, practical knowledge • *He lacks experience of international rugby.*
2 = **event**, affair, incident, happening, test, trial, encounter, episode, adventure, ordeal, occurrence • *It was an experience I would not like to go through again.*
▸ AS A VERB = **undergo**, have, know, feel, try, meet, face, suffer, taste, go through, observe, sample, encounter, sustain, perceive, endure, participate in, run into, live through, behold, come up against, apprehend, become familiar with • *couples who have experienced the trauma of divorce*

QUOTATIONS
Trust one who has gone through it
[Virgil *Aeneid*]
Experience is not what happens to a man. It is what a man does with what happens to him
[Aldous Huxley *Texts and Pretexts*]
Experience is the name everyone gives to their mistakes
[Oscar Wilde *Lady Windermere's Fan*]
All experience is an arch to build upon
[Henry Brooks Adams *The Education of Henry Adams*]
Nothing ever becomes real till it is experienced -Even a Proverb is no proverb to you till your Life has illustrated it
[John Keats *letter to George and Georgiana Keats*]

PROVERBS
Experience is the mother of wisdom
Experience is the best teacher

experienced 1 = **knowledgeable**, trained, professional, skilled, tried, tested, seasoned, expert, master, qualified, familiar, capable, veteran, practised, accomplished, competent, skilful, adept, well-versed • *a team made up of experienced professionals*
OPPOSITES: new, apprentice, inexperienced
2 = **worldly-wise**, knowing, worldly, wise, mature, sophisticated • *Perhaps I'm a bit more experienced about life than you are.*

experiment AS A NOUN 1 = **test**, trial, investigation, examination, venture, procedure, demonstration, observation, try-out, assay, trial run, scientific test, dummy

run • *a proposed new law banning animal experiments*
2 = **research**, investigation, analysis, observation, research and development, experimentation, trial and error • *The only way to find out is by experiment.*
▸ **AS A VERB** = **test**, investigate, trial, research, try, examine, pilot, sample, verify, put to the test, assay • *Scientists have been experimenting with a new drug.*

experimental 1 = **test**, trial, pilot, preliminary, provisional, tentative, speculative, empirical, exploratory, trial-and-error, fact-finding, probationary • *The technique is still in the experimental stages.*
2 = **innovative**, new, original, radical, creative, ingenious, avant-garde, inventive, ground-breaking • *He writes bizarre and highly experimental music.*

expert **AS A NOUN** = **specialist**, authority, professional, master, pro *(informal)*, ace *(informal)*, genius, guru, pundit, buff *(informal)*, wizard, adept, whizz *(informal)*, maestro, virtuoso, connoisseur, boffin *(Brit. informal)*, hotshot *(informal)*, rocket scientist *(informal, chiefly U.S.)*, past master, dab hand *(Brit. informal)*, wonk *(informal)*, maven *(U.S.)*, fundi *(S. African)* • *an expert in computer graphics*
OPPOSITES: amateur, novice, layman
▸ **AS AN ADJECTIVE** = **skilful**, trained, experienced, able, professional, skilled, master, masterly, qualified, talented, outstanding, clever, practised, accomplished, handy, competent, tasty *(Brit. informal)*, apt, adept, knowledgeable, virtuoso, deft, proficient, facile, adroit, dexterous • *The faces of the waxworks are modelled by expert sculptors.*
OPPOSITES: inexperienced, incompetent, unskilled

QUOTATIONS
An expert is a man who has made all the mistakes which can be made in a very narrow field
[Niels Henrik David Bohr]
An expert is one who knows more and more about less and less
[Nicholas Murray Butler]
An expert is someone who knows some of the worst mistakes that can be made in his subject and who manages to avoid them
[Werner Heisenberg *Der Teil und das Ganze*]

expertise = **skill**, knowledge, know-how *(informal)*, facility, grip, craft, judgment, grasp, mastery, knack, proficiency, dexterity, cleverness, deftness, adroitness, aptness, expertness, knowing inside out, ableness, masterliness, skilfulness • *the lack of management expertise within the company*

expiate = **make amends for**, redeem, redress, atone for, do penance for • *repentant sinners seeking to expiate their wrongdoing*

expiation = **amends**, redemption, redress, atonement, penance, shrift *(archaic)* • *a rite of expiation for their sins*

expiration = **expiry**, end, finish, conclusion, close, termination, cessation • *the expiration of his current passport*

expire 1 = **become invalid**, end, finish, conclude, close, stop, run out, cease, lapse, terminate, come to an end, be no longer valid • *He continued to live in the States after his visa had expired.*
2 = **die**, decease, depart, buy it *(U.S. slang)*, check out *(U.S. slang)*, perish, kick it *(slang)*, croak *(slang)*, go belly-up *(slang)*, snuff it *(informal)*, peg out *(informal)*, kick the bucket *(informal)*, peg it *(informal)*, depart this life, meet your maker, cark it *(Austral. & N.Z. slang)*, pop your clogs *(informal)*, pass away *or* on • *He expired in excruciating agony.*

expiry = **expiration**, ending, end, conclusion, close, demise, lapsing, lapse, termination, cessation • *the expiry of a fixed term contract*

explain 1 = **make clear** *or* **plain**, describe, demonstrate, illustrate, teach, define, solve, resolve, interpret, disclose, unfold, clarify, clear up, simplify, expound, elucidate, put into words, throw light on, explicate *(formal)*, give the details of • *He explained the process to us in simple terms.*
2 = **account for**, excuse, justify, give a reason for, give an explanation for • *Can you explain why you didn't telephone me?*

QUOTATIONS
Never explain – your friends do not need it and your enemies will not believe you anyway
[Elbert Hubbard *The Motto Book*]

explanation 1 = **reason**, meaning, cause, sense, answer, account, excuse, motive, justification, vindication, mitigation, the why and wherefore • *The president has given no explanation for his behaviour.*
2 = **description**, report, definition, demonstration, teaching, resolution, interpretation, illustration, clarification, exposition, simplification, explication, elucidation • *his lucid explanation of the mysteries of cricket*

explanatory *or* **explanative** = **descriptive**, interpretive, illustrative, interpretative, demonstrative, justifying, expository, illuminative, elucidatory, explicative • *The statements are accompanied by a series of explanatory notes.*

expletive = **swear word**, curse, obscenity, oath, four-letter word, cuss *(informal)*, profanity, rude word • *He muttered an expletive under his breath.*

explicable = **definable**, understandable, accountable, intelligible, justifiable, explainable, interpretable, resolvable • *There is no explicable reason for her death.*

explicate = **explain**, interpret, clarify, unfold, clear up, expound, make plain, untangle, elucidate, make clear *or* explicit • *scholars who seek to explicate religious texts*

explication = **explanation**, resolution, demonstration, description, definition, interpretation, illustration, clarification, exposition, simplification, elucidation • *his explication of the major concepts of modern physics*

explicit 1 = **clear**, obvious, specific, direct, certain, express, plain, absolute, exact, precise, straightforward, definite, overt, unequivocal, unqualified, unambiguous, categorical • *He left explicit instructions on how to set the video timer.*
OPPOSITES: uncertain, obscure, vague
2 = **frank**, direct, open, specific, positive, plain, patent, graphic, distinct, outspoken, upfront *(informal)*, unambiguous, unrestricted, unrestrained, uncensored, unreserved • *songs containing explicit references to sexual activity*
OPPOSITES: implied, suggested, indirect

explode 1 = **blow up**, erupt, burst, go off, shatter, shiver • *They were clearing up when the second bomb exploded.*
2 = **detonate**, set off, discharge, let off • *The first test atomic bomb was exploded in the New Mexico desert.*
3 = **lose your temper**, rage, erupt, blow up *(informal)*, lose it *(informal)*, crack up *(informal)*, see red *(informal)*, lose the plot *(informal)*, become angry, have a fit *(informal)*, go ballistic *(slang, chiefly U.S.)*, hit the roof *(informal)*, throw a tantrum, blow a fuse *(slang, chiefly U.S.)*, go berserk *(slang)*, go mad *(slang)*, fly off the handle *(informal)*, go spare *(Brit. slang)*, become enraged, go off the deep end *(informal)*, go up the wall *(slang)*, blow your top *(informal)*, go crook *(Austral. & N.Z. slang)*, fly into a temper, flip your lid *(slang)*, do your nut *(Brit. slang)* • *He exploded with rage at the accusation.*
4 = **increase**, grow, develop, extend, advance, shoot up, soar, boost, expand, build up, swell, step up *(informal)*, escalate, multiply, proliferate, snowball, aggrandize • *The population has exploded in the last twenty years.*
5 = **disprove**, discredit, refute, belie, demolish, repudiate, put paid to, invalidate, debunk, prove impossible, prove wrong, give the lie to, blow out of the water *(slang)* • *an article which explodes the myth that thin equals sexy*

exploit **AS A NOUN** = **feat**, act, achievement, enterprise, adventure, stunt, deed, accomplishment, attainment, escapade • *His wartime exploits were made into a TV series.*

▸ **AS A VERB 1 = take advantage of**, abuse, use, manipulate, milk, misuse, dump on *(slang, chiefly U.S.)*, ill-treat, shit on *(taboo slang)*, play on *or* upon • *Casual workers are being exploited for slave wages.*
2 = make the best use of, use, make use of, utilize, cash in on *(informal)*, capitalize on, put to use, make capital out of, use to advantage, use to good advantage, live off the backs of, turn to account, profit by *or* from • *The opposition are exploiting the situation to their advantage.*

exploitation 1 = misuse, abuse, manipulation, imposition, using, ill-treatment • *the exploitation of working women*
2 = capitalization, utilization, using to good advantage, trading upon • *the exploitation of the famine by local politicians*

exploration 1 = expedition, tour, trip, survey, travel, journey, reconnaissance, recce *(slang)* • *We devoted a week to the exploration of the Mayan sites of Copan.*
2 = investigation, study, research, survey, search, inquiry, analysis, examination, probe, inspection, scrutiny, once-over *(informal)* • *an exploration of Celtic mythology*

exploratory = investigative, trial, searching, probing, experimental, analytic, fact-finding • *Exploratory surgery revealed that she had cancer of the liver.*

explore 1 = travel around, tour, survey, scout, traverse, range over, recce *(slang)*, reconnoitre, case *(slang)*, have *or* take a look around • *We explored the old part of the town.*
2 = investigate, consider, research, survey, search, prospect, examine, probe, analyse, look into, inspect, work over, scrutinize, inquire into • *The film explores the relationship between artist and instrument.*

explorer = traveller, journeyer, adventurer, voyager, globetrotter, discoverer • *the British explorer who discovered the North Magnetic Pole*

explosion 1 = blast, crack, burst, bang, discharge, report, blowing up, outburst, clap, detonation • *Three people were killed in a bomb explosion in London today.*
2 = increase, rise, development, growth, boost, expansion, enlargement, escalation, upturn • *a population explosion*
3 = outburst, fit, storm, attack, surge, flare-up, eruption, paroxysm • *His reaction was an explosion of anger.*
4 = outbreak, flare-up, eruption, upsurge • *an explosion of violence in the country's capital*

explosive AS AN ADJECTIVE 1 = unstable, dangerous, volatile, hazardous, unsafe, perilous, combustible, inflammable • *Highly explosive gas is naturally found in coal mines.*
2 = sudden, rapid, marked, unexpected, startling, swift, abrupt • *the explosive growth of computer networks*
3 = dangerous, worrying, strained, anxious, charged, ugly, tense, hazardous, stressful, perilous, nerve-racking, overwrought • *a potentially explosive situation*
4 = fiery, violent, volatile, stormy, touchy, vehement, chippy *(informal)* • *He inherited his father's explosive temper.*
▸ **AS A NOUN = bomb**, mine, shell, missile, rocket, grenade, charge, torpedo, incendiary • *A large quantity of arms and explosives was seized.*

exponent 1 = advocate, champion, supporter, defender, spokesman, spokeswoman, promoter, backer, spokesperson, proponent, propagandist, upholder • *a leading exponent of genetic engineering*
2 = performer, player, interpreter, presenter, executant • *the great exponent of Bach, Glenn Gould*

export AS A VERB = sell abroad, market, ship, trade in, send abroad, sell overseas, send overseas • *The nation exports beef and coffee.*
▸ **AS A NOUN = foreign trade**, international trade, overseas trade • *A lot of our land is used to grow crops for export.*

exporter = seller, agent, trader, shipper, international trader, foreign trader, overseas trader • *the world's second-biggest exporter of agricultural products*

expose AS A VERB 1 = uncover, show, reveal, display, exhibit, present, unveil, manifest, lay bare, take the wraps off, put on view • *He pulled up his t-shirt, exposing his white belly.*
OPPOSITES: cover, protect, hide
2 = reveal, disclose, uncover, air, detect, betray, show up, denounce, unearth, let out, divulge, unmask, lay bare, make known, bring to light, out *(informal)*, smoke out, blow wide open *(slang)* • *After the scandal was exposed, he committed suicide.*
OPPOSITES: cover, hide, keep secret
3 = make vulnerable, subject, leave open, lay open • *people exposed to high levels of radiation*
▸ **IN PHRASES: expose someone to something = introduce to**, acquaint with, bring into contact with, familiarize with, make familiar with, make conversant with • *when women from these societies become exposed to Western culture*
expose yourself = show your genitals, flash *(informal)*, display your genitals • *Smith admitted indecently exposing himself on Wimbledon Common.*

exposé = exposure, revelation, uncovering, disclosure, divulgence • *The movie is an exposé of prison conditions in the South.*

exposed 1 = unconcealed, revealed, bare, exhibited, unveiled, shown, uncovered, on display, on show, on view, laid bare, made manifest • *Skin cancer is most likely to occur on exposed parts of the body.*
2 = unsheltered, open, unprotected, open to the elements • *This part of the coast is very exposed.*
3 = vulnerable, open, subject, in danger, liable, susceptible, wide open, left open, laid bare, in peril, laid open • *The troops are exposed to attack by the enemy.*

exposition 1 = explanation, account, description, interpretation, illustration, presentation, commentary, critique, exegesis, explication, elucidation • *Her speech was an exposition of her beliefs in freedom and justice.*
2 = exhibition, show, fair, display, demonstration, presentation, expo *(informal)* • *an art exposition*

expository = explanatory, descriptive, interpretive, illustrative, interpretative, hermeneutic, explicatory, explicative, elucidative, exegetic • *A textbook relies heavily on an expository style of writing.*

expostulate = protest, reason (with), argue (with), dissuade, remonstrate (with) • *'Have some sense!' he expostulated.*

exposure 1 = vulnerability, subjection, susceptibility, laying open • *Exposure to lead is known to damage the brains of young children.*
2 = hypothermia, frostbite, extreme cold, intense cold • *Two people died of exposure in Chicago overnight.*
3 = revelation, exposé, uncovering, disclosure, airing, manifestation, detection, divulging, denunciation, unmasking, divulgence • *the exposure of Anthony Blunt as a former Soviet spy*
4 = publicity, promotion, attention, advertising, plugging *(informal)*, propaganda, hype, pushing, media hype • *The candidates have been getting a lot of exposure on TV.*
5 = uncovering, showing, display, exhibition, baring, revelation, presentation, unveiling, manifestation • *a bodice allowing full exposure of the breasts*
6 = contact, experience, awareness, acquaintance, familiarity • *Repeated exposure to the music reveals its hidden depths.*

expound = explain, describe, illustrate, interpret, unfold, spell out, set forth, elucidate, explicate *(formal)* • *Schmidt continued to expound his theories on economics.*

express AS A VERB 1 = state, communicate, convey, articulate, say, tell, put, word, speak, voice, declare, phrase, assert, pronounce, utter, couch, put across, enunciate, put

into words, give voice to, verbalize, asseverate • *He expressed grave concern at their attitude.*
2 = **show**, indicate, exhibit, demonstrate, reveal, disclose, intimate, convey, testify to, depict, designate, manifest, embody, signify, symbolize, denote, divulge, bespeak, make known, evince • *He expressed his anger in a destructive way.*
▸ AS AN ADJECTIVE 1 = **explicit**, clear, direct, precise, pointed, certain, plain, accurate, exact, distinct, definite, outright, unambiguous, categorical • *The ship was sunk on express orders from the Prime Minister.*
2 = **specific**, exclusive, particular, sole, special, deliberate, singular, clear-cut, especial • *I bought the camera with the express purpose of taking nature photos.*
3 = **fast**, direct, quick, rapid, priority, prompt, swift, high-speed, speedy, quickie *(informal)*, nonstop, expeditious • *A special express service is available.*

expression 1 = **statement**, declaration, announcement, communication, mention, assertion, utterance, articulation, pronouncement, enunciation, verbalization, asseveration • *From Cairo came expressions of regret at the attack.*
2 = **indication**, demonstration, exhibition, display, showing, show, sign, symbol, representation, token, manifestation, embodiment • *We attended as an expression of solidarity.*
3 = **look**, countenance, face, air, appearance, aspect, mien *(literary)* • *He sat there with a sad expression on his face.*
4 = **intonation**, style, delivery, phrasing, emphasis, execution, diction • *She puts a lot of expression into her playing.*
5 = **phrase**, saying, word, wording, term, language, speech, remark, maxim, idiom, adage, choice of words, turn of phrase, phraseology, locution, set phrase • *He uses some remarkably coarse expressions.*

expressionless = **blank**, empty, deadpan, straight-faced, wooden, dull, vacuous, inscrutable, poker-faced *(informal)* • *He did his best to keep his face expressionless.*

expressive 1 = **vivid**, strong, striking, telling, moving, lively, sympathetic, energetic, poignant, emphatic, eloquent, forcible • *She had a small, expressive face.*
OPPOSITES: empty, straight-faced, impassive
2 *with* **of** = **meaningful**, indicative, suggestive, demonstrative, revealing, significant, allusive • *All his poems are expressive of his love for nature.*

expressly 1 = **explicitly**, clearly, plainly, absolutely, positively, definitely, outright, manifestly, distinctly, decidedly, categorically, pointedly, unequivocally, unmistakably, in no uncertain terms, unambiguously • *He had expressly forbidden her to go out on her own.*
2 = **specifically**, specially, especially, particularly, purposely, exclusively, precisely, solely, exactly, deliberately, intentionally, on purpose • *Bleasdale had written the role expressly for this actor.*

expropriate = **seize**, take, appropriate, confiscate, assume, take over, take away, commandeer, requisition, arrogate • *The Bolsheviks expropriated the property of the landowners.*

expropriation = **seizure**, takeover, impounding, confiscation, commandeering, requisitioning, sequestration, disseisin *(Law)* • *illegal expropriation of their assets*

expulsion 1 = **ejection**, exclusion, dismissal, removal, exile, discharge, eviction, banishment, extrusion, proscription, expatriation, debarment, dislodgment • *Her behaviour led to her expulsion from school.*
2 = **discharge**, emptying, emission, voiding, spewing, secretion, excretion, ejection, seepage, suppuration • *the expulsion of waste products from the body*

expunge = **erase**, remove, destroy, abolish, cancel, get rid of, wipe out, eradicate, excise, delete, extinguish, strike out, obliterate, annihilate, efface, exterminate, annul, raze, blot out, extirpate • *The experience was something he had tried to expunge from his memory.*

expurgate = **censor**, cut, clean up *(informal)*, purge, purify, blue-pencil, sanitize, bowdlerize • *The work was heavily expurgated for its second edition.*

exquisite 1 = **beautiful**, elegant, graceful, pleasing, attractive, lovely, charming, comely • *She has exquisite manners.*
OPPOSITES: ugly, unattractive, unsightly
2 = **fine**, beautiful, lovely, elegant, precious, delicate, dainty • *The natives brought exquisite beadwork to sell.*
3 = **intense**, acute, severe, sharp, keen, extreme, piercing, poignant, excruciating • *His words gave her exquisite pain.*
4 = **refined**, cultivated, discriminating, sensitive, polished, selective, discerning, impeccable, meticulous, consummate, appreciative, fastidious • *The house was furnished with exquisite taste.*
5 = **excellent**, fine, outstanding, superb, choice, perfect, select, delicious, divine, splendid, admirable, consummate, flawless, superlative, incomparable, peerless, matchless • *The hotel features friendly staff and exquisite cuisine.*
OPPOSITES: flawed, imperfect

extant = **in existence**, existing, remaining, surviving, living, existent, subsisting, undestroyed • *The oldest extant copy is dated 1492.*

extend AS A VERB 1 = **spread out**, reach, stretch, continue, carry on • *The territory extends over one fifth of Canada's land mass.*
2 = **stretch**, stretch out, spread out, unfurl, straighten out, unroll • *Stand straight with your arms extended at your sides.*
3 = **last**, continue, go on, stretch, carry on • *His playing career extended from 1894 to 1920.*
4 = **protrude**, project, stand out, bulge, stick out, hang, overhang, jut out • *His legs extended from the bushes.*
5 = **reach**, spread, go as far as • *His possessiveness extends to people as well as property.*
6 = **widen**, increase, develop, expand, spread, add to, enhance, supplement, enlarge, broaden, diversify, amplify, augment • *They have added three new products to extend their range.*
OPPOSITES: cut, reduce, contract
7 = **make longer**, prolong, lengthen, draw out, spin out, elongate, drag out, protract • *They have extended the deadline by 24 hours.*
OPPOSITES: cut, limit, shorten
8 = **offer**, give, hold out, present, grant, advance, yield, reach out, confer, stretch out, stick out, bestow, impart, proffer, put forth • *'I'm Chuck,' the man said, extending his hand.*
OPPOSITES: withdraw, take back
▸ IN PHRASES: **extend to something** = **include**, cover, affect, take in, embrace, incorporate, encompass • *The service also extends to wrapping gifts.*

extended 1 = **lengthened**, long, prolonged, protracted, stretched out, drawn-out, unfurled, elongated, unrolled • *He and Naomi spent an extended period getting to know one another.*
2 = **broad**, wide, expanded, extensive, widespread, comprehensive, large-scale, enlarged, far-reaching • *a tribal society grouped in huge extended families*
3 = **outstretched**, conferred, stretched out, proffered • *She found herself kissing the old lady's extended hand.*

extension 1 = **annexe**, wing, addition, supplement, branch, appendix, add-on, adjunct, appendage, ell, addendum • *the new extension to London's National Gallery*
2 = **lengthening**, extra time, continuation, postponement, prolongation, additional period of time, protraction • *He has been granted a six-month extension to his visa.*
3 = **development**, expansion, widening, increase, stretching, broadening, continuation, enlargement, diversification, amplification, elongation, augmentation • *Russia is contemplating the extension of its territory*

extensive 1 = **large**, considerable, substantial, spacious, wide, sweeping, broad, expansive, capacious, commodious • *This 18th century manor house is set in extensive grounds.*
OPPOSITES: tight, narrow, confined
2 = **comprehensive**, complete, thorough, lengthy, long, wide, wholesale, pervasive, protracted, all-inclusive • *The story received extensive coverage in the Times.*
OPPOSITES: restricted
3 = **great**, large, huge, extended, vast, widespread, comprehensive, universal, large-scale, far-reaching, prevalent, far-flung, all-inclusive, voluminous, humongous *or* humungous *(U.S. slang)* • *The blast caused extensive damage.*
OPPOSITES: limited

extent 1 = **magnitude**, amount, degree, scale, level, measure, stretch, quantity, bulk, duration, expanse, amplitude • *The full extent of the losses was revealed yesterday.*
2 = **size**, area, range, length, reach, bounds, sweep, sphere, width, compass, breadth, ambit • *an estate about seven or eight acres in extent*

extenuating = **mitigating**, qualifying, justifying, moderating, serving as an excuse • *There were extenuating circumstances for her crime.*

exterior AS A NOUN = **outside**, face, surface, covering, finish, skin, appearance, aspect, shell, coating, façade, outside surface • *The exterior of the building was a masterpiece of architecture.*
▸ AS AN ADJECTIVE = **outer**, outside, external, surface, outward, superficial, outermost • *The exterior walls were made of pre-formed concrete.*
OPPOSITES: inside, interior, inner

exterminate = **destroy**, kill, eliminate, abolish, eradicate, annihilate, extirpate • *A huge effort was made to exterminate the rats.*

extermination = **destruction**, murder, massacre, slaughter, killing, wiping out, genocide, elimination, ethnic cleansing *(euphemistic)*, mass murder, annihilation, eradication, extirpation • *the extermination of thousands of innocent people*

QUOTATIONS
We seem to be in the midst of an era of delirious ferocity, with half of mankind hell bent upon exterminating the other half
[H.L. Mencken]

external 1 = **outer**, outside, surface, apparent, visible, outward, exterior, superficial, outermost • *the external surface of the wall*
OPPOSITES: inside, internal, interior
2 = **foreign**, international, alien, exotic, exterior, extraneous, extrinsic • *the commissioner for external affairs*
OPPOSITES: home, domestic, interior
3 = **outside**, visiting, independent, extramural • *The papers are checked by external examiners.*
OPPOSITES: inside, interior

extinct 1 = **dead**, lost, gone, vanished, defunct • *It is 250 years since the wolf became extinct in Britain.*
OPPOSITES: living, existing, surviving
2 = **obsolete**, abolished, void, terminated, defunct • *Herbalism had become an all but extinct skill in the Western World.*
3 = **inactive**, extinguished, doused, out, snuffed out, quenched • *The island's tallest volcano is long extinct.*

extinction = **dying out**, death, destruction, abolition, oblivion, extermination, annihilation, eradication, obliteration, excision, extirpation • *Many species have been hunted to the point of extinction.*

extinguish 1 = **put out**, stifle, smother, blow out, douse, snuff out, quench • *It took about 50 minutes to extinguish the fire.*
2 = **destroy**, end, kill, remove, eliminate, obscure, abolish, suppress, wipe out, erase, eradicate, annihilate, put paid to, exterminate, expunge, extirpate • *The message extinguished her hopes of Richard's return.*

extirpate = **wipe out**, destroy, eliminate, abolish, erase, remove, eradicate, excise, extinguish, uproot, annihilate, root out, exterminate, expunge, deracinate, pull up by the roots, wipe from the face of the earth • *The Romans wished to extirpate Druidism in Britain.*

extol = **praise**, acclaim, applaud, pay tribute to, celebrate, commend, magnify *(archaic)*, glorify, exalt, laud, crack up *(informal)*, sing the praises of, big up *(slang, chiefly Caribbean)*, eulogize, cry up, panegyrize • *She keeps extolling his managerial skills.*

extort = **extract**, force, squeeze, exact, bully, bleed *(informal)*, blackmail, wring, coerce, wrest • *The kidnappers extorted a £175,000 ransom for his release.*

extortion = **blackmail**, force, oppression, compulsion, coercion, shakedown *(U.S. slang)*, rapacity, exaction • *He has been charged with extortion and abusing his position.*

extortionate 1 = **exorbitant**, excessive, outrageous, unreasonable, inflated, extravagant, preposterous, sky-high, inordinate, immoderate • *the extortionate price of designer clothes*
OPPOSITES: fair, reasonable, moderate
2 = **grasping**, hard, severe, exacting, harsh, rigorous, oppressive, rapacious, blood-sucking *(informal)*, usurious • *people who have entered into extortionate credit transactions*

extra AS AN ADJECTIVE 1 = **additional**, more, new, other, added, further, fresh, accessory, supplementary, auxiliary, add-on, supplemental, ancillary • *Extra staff have been taken on to cover busy periods.*
OPPOSITES: needed, required, vital
2 = **surplus**, excess, reserve, spare, unnecessary, redundant, needless, unused, leftover, superfluous, extraneous, unneeded, inessential, supernumerary, supererogatory • *This exercise will help you burn up any extra calories.*
▸ AS A NOUN = **addition**, bonus, supplement, accessory, complement, add-on, affix, adjunct, appendage, addendum, supernumerary, appurtenance • *Optional extras including cooking tuition.*
OPPOSITES: essential, requirement, necessity
▸ AS AN ADVERB 1 = **in addition**, additionally, over and above, x *(S.M.S.)* • *You may be charged extra for this service.*
2 = **exceptionally**, very, specially, especially, particularly, extremely, remarkably, unusually, extraordinarily, uncommonly • *Try extra hard to be nice to him.*

extract AS A VERB 1 = **obtain**, take out, distil, squeeze out, draw out, express, separate out, press out • *Citric acid can be extracted from the juice of oranges.*
2 = **take out**, draw, pull, remove, withdraw, pull out, bring out • *He extracted a small notebook from his pocket.*
3 = **pull out**, remove, take out, draw, uproot, pluck out, extirpate • *She has to have a tooth extracted at 3 today.*
4 = **elicit**, get, obtain, force, draw, gather, derive, exact, bring out, evoke, reap, wring, glean, coerce, wrest • *He tried to extract further information from the witness.*
5 = **select**, quote, cite, abstract, choose, cut out, reproduce, cull, copy out • *material extracted from a range of texts*
6 = **develop**, obtain, derive, evolve, gather, elicit, glean, deduce, educe • *an idea he had extracted from Theodore Schwenk's 'Sensitive Chaos'*
▸ AS A NOUN 1 = **passage**, selection, excerpt, cutting, clipping, abstract, quotation, citation • *He read us an extract from his latest novel.*
2 = **essence**, solution, concentrate, juice, distillation, decoction, distillate • *fragrances taken from plant extracts*

extraction 1 = **origin**, family, ancestry, descent, race, stock, blood, birth, pedigree, lineage, parentage, derivation • *He married a young lady of Indian extraction.*

2 = **taking out**, drawing, pulling, withdrawal, removal, uprooting, extirpation • *the extraction of wisdom teeth*
3 = **distillation**, separation, derivation • *High temperatures are used during the extraction of cooking oils.*

extradite = **deport**, exile, hand over, expel, banish, send back, expatriate, send for trial • *He was extradited to Britain to face explosive charges.*

extradition = **deportation**, expulsion, banishment, expatriation • *A New York court turned down the British Government's request for his extradition.*

extraneous 1 = **nonessential**, unnecessary, extra, additional, redundant, needless, peripheral, supplementary, incidental, superfluous, unneeded, inessential, adventitious, unessential • *Just give me the basic facts, with no extraneous details.*
2 = **irrelevant**, inappropriate, unrelated, unconnected, immaterial, beside the point, impertinent, inadmissible, off the subject, inapplicable, inapt, inapposite • *Let's not allow ourselves to be sidetracked by extraneous questions.*
3 = **external**, foreign, strange, alien, exotic, out of place, extrinsic, adventitious • *extraneous influences affecting his state of mind*

extraordinary 1 = **remarkable**, special, wonderful, outstanding, rare, amazing, fantastic, astonishing, marvellous, eye-popping *(informal)*, exceptional, notable, serious *(informal)*, phenomenal, singular, wondrous *(archaic or literary)*, out of this world *(informal)*, extremely good • *He is an extraordinary musician.*
OPPOSITES: ordinary, commonplace, unremarkable
2 = **unusual**, surprising, odd, strange, unique, remarkable, bizarre, curious, weird, unprecedented, peculiar, unfamiliar, uncommon, unheard-of, unwonted • *What an extraordinary thing to happen!*
OPPOSITES: common, usual, ordinary

extravagance 1 = **overspending**, squandering, profusion, profligacy, wastefulness, waste, lavishness, prodigality, improvidence • *He was accused of gross mismanagement and financial extravagance.*
2 = **luxury**, treat, indulgence, extra, frill, nonessential • *Her only extravagance was shoes.*
3 = **excess**, folly, exaggeration, absurdity, recklessness, wildness, dissipation, outrageousness, unreasonableness, preposterousness, immoderation, exorbitance, unrestraint • *the ridiculous extravagance of his claims*

extravagant 1 = **wasteful**, excessive, lavish, prodigal, profligate, spendthrift, imprudent, improvident • *his extravagant lifestyle*
OPPOSITES: sparing, careful, economical
2 = **overpriced**, expensive, costly • *Her aunt gave her an uncharacteristically extravagant gift.*
3 = **exorbitant**, excessive, steep *(informal)*, unreasonable, inordinate, extortionate • *hotels charging extravagant prices*
OPPOSITES: reasonable, moderate, economical
4 = **excessive**, exaggerated, outrageous, wild, fantastic, absurd, foolish, over the top *(slang)*, unreasonable, preposterous, fanciful, unrestrained, inordinate, outré, immoderate, O.T.T. *(slang)* • *He was extravagant in his admiration of Lillie.*
OPPOSITES: conservative, reasonable, moderate
5 = **showy**, elaborate, flamboyant, impressive, fancy, flashy, ornate, pretentious, grandiose, gaudy, garish, ostentatious, gee-whizz *(slang)* • *The couple wed in extravagant style in 1995.*
OPPOSITES: conservative, moderate, restrained

extravaganza = **spectacular**, show, spectacle, display, pageant, flight of fancy • *an all-night musical extravaganza*

extreme AS AN ADJECTIVE 1 = **great**, high, highest, greatest, worst, supreme, acute, severe, maximum, intense, ultimate, utmost, mother of all *(informal)*, uttermost • *people living in extreme poverty*
OPPOSITES: common, average, mild
2 = **severe**, radical, strict, harsh, stern, rigid, dire, drastic, uncompromising, unbending • *The scheme was rejected as being too extreme.*
3 = **radical**, unusual, excessive, exceptional, exaggerated, outrageous, over the top *(slang)*, unreasonable, uncommon, unconventional, fanatical, zealous, out-and-out, inordinate, egregious, intemperate, immoderate, O.T.T. *(slang)* • *his extreme political views*
OPPOSITES: moderate
4 = **farthest**, furthest, far, final, last, ultimate, remotest, terminal, utmost, far-off, faraway, outermost, most distant, uttermost • *the room at the extreme end of the corridor*
OPPOSITES: nearest
▸ AS A NOUN = **limit**, end, edge, opposite, pole, ultimate, boundary, antithesis, extremity, acme • *a 'middle way' between the extremes of success and failure*
▸ IN PHRASES: **in the extreme** = **extremely**, very, highly, greatly, particularly, severely, terribly, ultra, utterly, unusually, exceptionally, extraordinarily, intensely, tremendously, markedly, awfully *(informal)*, acutely, exceedingly, excessively, inordinately, uncommonly, to a fault, to the nth degree, to *or* in the extreme • *The television series has proved controversial in the extreme.*

extremely = **very**, highly, greatly, particularly, severely, terribly, ultra, utterly, unusually, exceptionally, extraordinarily, intensely, tremendously, markedly, awfully *(informal)*, acutely, exceedingly, excessively, inordinately, uncommonly, to a fault, to the nth degree, to *or* in the extreme • *Mobile phones are extremely common nowadays.*

extremism = **fanaticism**, enthusiasm, madness, devotion, dedication, zeal, bigotry, infatuation, single-mindedness, zealotry, obsessiveness, monomania, immoderation, overenthusiasm • *an attempt to eliminate racism and right-wing extremism*

QUOTATIONS
Extremism in the defence of liberty is no vice!
[Barry Goldwater]

extremist AS A NOUN = **radical**, activist, militant, enthusiast, fanatic, devotee, die-hard, bigot, zealot, energumen • *Police believe the bombing was the work of left-wing extremists.*
▸ AS AN ADJECTIVE = **extreme**, wild, mad, enthusiastic, passionate, frenzied, obsessive, fanatical, fervent, zealous, bigoted, rabid, immoderate, overenthusiastic • *The riots were organized by extremist groups.*

extremity AS A NOUN 1 = **limit**, end, edge, border, top, tip, bound, minimum, extreme, maximum, pole, margin, boundary, terminal, frontier, verge, brink, rim, brim, pinnacle, termination, nadir, zenith, apex, terminus, apogee, farthest point, furthest point, acme • *a small port on the north-western extremity of the island*
2 = **depth**, height, excess, climax, consummation, acuteness • *his lack of restraint in the extremity of his grief*
3 = **crisis**, trouble, emergency, disaster, setback, pinch, plight, hardship, adversity, dire straits, exigency, extreme suffering • *Even in extremity, she never lost her sense of humour.*
▸ AS A PLURAL NOUN = **hands and feet**, limbs, fingers and toes • *Rheumatoid arthritis affects the extremities and limbs.*

extricate 1 = **withdraw**, relieve, free, clear, deliver, liberate, wriggle out of, get (someone) off the hook *(slang)*, disembarrass • *an attempt to extricate himself from his financial difficulties*
2 = **free**, clear, release, remove, rescue, get out, disengage, disentangle • *Emergency workers tried to extricate the survivors from the wreckage.*

extrinsic = **external**, outside, exterior, foreign, imported, superficial, extraneous • *the extrinsic conditions which affect relationships*

extrovert *or* **extravert** *(Psychology)* AS A NOUN = **outgoing person**, mingler, socializer, mixer, life and soul of the party • *He was a showman, an extrovert who revelled in controversy.*
OPPOSITES: introvert
▸ AS AN ADJECTIVE = **sociable**, social, lively, outgoing, hearty, exuberant, amiable, gregarious • *His extrovert personality won him many friends.*
OPPOSITES: out-going, withdrawn, introverted

extrude = **force out**, expel, eject, squeeze out, thrust out, press out • *The aluminium is melted down and extruded through a die or cast in a mould.*

exuberance 1 = **high spirits**, energy, enthusiasm, vitality, life, spirit, excitement, pep, animation, vigour, zest, eagerness, buoyancy, exhilaration, welly *(slang)*, cheerfulness, brio, vivacity, ebullience, liveliness, effervescence, sprightliness • *Her burst of exuberance overwhelmed me.*
2 = **luxuriance**, abundance, richness, profusion, plenitude, lushness, superabundance, lavishness, rankness, copiousness • *the exuberance of plant life in the region*
QUOTATIONS
Exuberance is Beauty
[William Blake *The Marriage of Heaven and Hell*]
Exuberance is better than taste
[Flaubert *Sentimental Education*]

exuberant 1 = **high-spirited**, spirited, enthusiastic, lively, excited, eager, sparkling, vigorous, cheerful, energetic, animated, upbeat *(informal)*, buoyant, exhilarated, elated, ebullient, chirpy *(informal)*, sprightly, vivacious, effervescent, full of life, full of beans *(informal)*, zestful • *Our son was a highly active and exuberant little person.*
OPPOSITES: dull, subdued, lifeless
2 = **luxuriant**, rich, lavish, abundant, lush, overflowing, plentiful, teeming, copious, profuse, superabundant, plenteous • *hillsides ablaze with exuberant flowers and shrubs*
3 = **fulsome**, excessive, exaggerated, lavish, overdone, superfluous, prodigal, effusive • *exuberant praise*

exude 1 = **radiate**, show, display, exhibit, manifest, emanate • *She exudes an air of confidence.*
2 = **emit**, leak, discharge, ooze, emanate, issue, secrete, excrete • *Nearby was a factory which exuded a pungent smell.*
3 = **seep**, leak, sweat, bleed, weep, trickle, ooze, emanate, issue, filter through, well forth • *the fluid that exudes from the cane toad's back*

exult 1 = **be joyful**, be delighted, rejoice, be overjoyed, celebrate, large it *(Brit. slang)*, be elated, be jubilant, jump for joy, make merry, be in high spirits, jubilate • *He seemed calm, but inwardly he exulted.*
2 *often with* **over** = **revel**, glory in, boast, crow, taunt, brag, vaunt, drool, gloat, take delight in • *He was still exulting over his victory.*

exultant = **joyful**, delighted, flushed, triumphant, revelling, rejoicing, jubilant, joyous, transported, elated, over the moon *(informal)*, overjoyed, rapt, gleeful, exulting, cock-a-hoop, stoked *(Austral. & N.Z. informal)* • *He was exultant over the team's unexpected win.*

exultation 1 = **joy**, delight, celebration, rejoicing, glee, high spirits, elation, transport, jubilation, joyousness, merriness • *I felt a tremendous sense of relief and exultation.*
2 = **triumph**, glory, glorying, boasting, crowing, revelling, bragging, gloating • *He punched the air and waved his bat in exultation.*

eye AS A NOUN 1 = **eyeball**, optic *(informal)*, peeper *(slang)*, orb *(poetic)*, organ of vision, organ of sight • *He is blind in one eye.*
2 *often plural* = **eyesight**, sight, vision, observation, perception, ability to see, range of vision, power of seeing • *her sharp eyes and acute hearing*
3 = **appreciation**, taste, recognition, judgment, discrimination, perception, discernment • *He has an eye for talent.*
4 = **observance**, observation, supervision, surveillance, attention, notice, inspection, heed, vigil, watch, lookout, vigilance, alertness, watchfulness • *He played under his grandmother's watchful eye.*
5 = **centre**, heart, middle, mid, core, nucleus • *the eye of the hurricane*
▸ AS A VERB = **look at**, view, study, watch, check, regard, survey, clock *(Brit. slang)*, observe, stare at, scan, contemplate, check out *(informal)*, inspect, glance at, gaze at, behold *(archaic or literary)*, eyeball *(slang)*, scrutinize, peruse, get a load of *(informal)*, take a dekko at *(Brit. slang)*, have *or* take a look at • *We eyed each other thoughtfully.*
▸ IN PHRASES: **an eye for an eye** = **retaliation**, justice, revenge, vengeance, reprisal, retribution, requital, lex talionis • *His philosophy was an eye for an eye and a tooth for a tooth.*
turn a blind eye to *or* **close your eyes to** = **ignore**, reject, overlook, disregard, pass over, take no notice of, be oblivious to, pay no attention to, turn your back on, turn a deaf ear to, bury your head in the sand • *They just closed their eyes to what was going on.*
eye something *or* **someone up** = **ogle**, leer at, make eyes at, give (someone) the (glad) eye • *My brother is forever eyeing up women in the street.*
in *or* **to someone's eyes** = **in the opinion of**, in the mind of, from someone's viewpoint, in the judgment of, in someone's point of view, in the belief of • *He was, in their eyes, a sensible and reliable man.*
keep an eye *or* **your eye on** = **watch**, supervise, observe, monitor, regard, survey, guard, look after, look out for, pay attention to, watch over, scrutinize, keep tabs on *(informal)*, keep under surveillance, keep in view, watch like a hawk • *You can't keep an eye on your children 24 hours a day.*
see eye to eye (with) = **agree (with)**, accord (with), get on (with), fall in (with), coincide (with), go along (with), subscribe (to), be united (with), concur (with), harmonize (with), speak the same language (as), be on the same wavelength (as), be of the same mind (as), be in unison (with) • *They saw eye to eye on almost every aspect of the production.*
set, clap *or* **lay eyes on someone** = **see**, meet, notice, observe, encounter, come across, run into, behold • *I haven't set eyes on him for years.*
up to your eyes (in) = **very busy (with)**, overwhelmed (with), caught up (in), inundated (by), wrapped up (in), engaged (in), flooded out (by), fully occupied (with), up to here (with), up to your elbows (in) • *I am up to my eyes in work just now.*
▸ RELATED ADJECTIVES: ocular, oculate, ophthalmic, optic
▸ RELATED PHOBIA: ommatophobia
QUOTATIONS
If thy right eye offend thee, pluck it out
[*Bible: St. Matthew*]
The sight of you is good for sore eyes
[Jonathan Swift *Polite Conversation*]
PROVERBS
The eyes are the windows of the soul

PARTS OF THE EYE

aqueous humour	eyeball	retinal vessels
blind spot	fovea	rod
choroid *or* chorioid	iris	sclera
ciliary body	lens	suspensory ligament
cone	ocular muscle	vitreous body
conjunctiva	optic nerve	vitreous humour
cornea	pupil	
	retina	

eyebrow
▸ RELATED ADJECTIVE: superciliary

eye-catching = **striking**, arresting, attractive, dramatic, spectacular, captivating, showy • *skin-tight shorts in bold eye-catching stripes*

eyeful = **look**, view, sight, glance, gaze, butcher's (*Brit. slang*), gander (*informal*), shufti (*Brit. slang*) • *He took his shirt off and gave us an eyeful of his tattoos.*

eyelash
▸ TECHNICAL NAME: cilium
▸ RELATED ADJECTIVE: ciliary

eyelid
▸ TECHNICAL NAME: palpebra
▸ RELATED ADJECTIVE: palpebral
▸ RELATED PREFIXES: blephar- or blepharo-

eyesight = **vision**, sight, observation, perception, ability to see, range of vision, power of seeing, power of sight • *He suffered from poor eyesight and could no longer read properly.*

eyesore = **mess**, blight, blot, blemish, sight (*informal*), horror, disgrace, atrocity, ugliness, monstrosity, disfigurement • *Slums are an eyesore and a health hazard.*

eyewitness = **observer**, witness, spectator, looker-on, viewer, passer-by, watcher, onlooker, bystander • *Eyewitnesses say the police opened fire on the crowd.*

e

f

fab = **wonderful**, great, excellent, fantastic, marvellous, mega *(slang)*, awesome *(slang)*, first-rate, brill *(informal)*, out of this world *(informal)*, mean *(slang)*, booshit *(Austral. slang)*, exo *(Austral. slang)*, sik *(Austral. slang)*, rad *(informal)*, phat *(slang)*, schmick *(Austral. informal)*, beaut *(informal)*, barrie *(Scot. slang)*, belting *(Brit. slang)*, pearler *(Austral. slang)* • *It's a fab place for a holiday.*

fable 1 = **legend**, myth, parable, allegory, story, tale, apologue • *Each tale has the timeless quality of fable.*
2 = **fiction**, lie, fantasy, myth, romance, invention, yarn *(informal)*, fabrication, falsehood, fib, figment, untruth, fairy story *(informal)*, urban myth, white lie, tall story *(informal)*, urban legend • *Is reincarnation fact or fable?*
OPPOSITES: fact, truth, reality
▸ RELATED ADJECTIVE: fabulous

fabled = **legendary**, fictional, famed, mythical, storied, famous, fabulous • *the fabled city of Troy*

fabric 1 = **cloth**, material, stuff, textile, web • *small squares of red cotton fabric*
2 = **framework**, structure, make-up, organization, frame, foundations, construction, constitution, infrastructure • *The fabric of society has been deeply damaged.*
3 = **structure**, foundations, construction, framework, infrastructure • *Condensation will eventually cause the fabric of the building to rot away.*
▹ *See panel* **Fabrics**

fabricate 1 = **make up**, invent, concoct, falsify, form, coin, devise, forge, fake, feign, trump up • *All four claim that officers fabricated evidence against them.*
2 = **manufacture**, make, build, form, fashion, shape, frame, construct, assemble, erect • *All the tools are fabricated from high quality steel.*

fabrication 1 = **forgery**, lie, fiction, myth, fake, invention, fable, concoction, falsehood, figment, untruth, porky *(Brit. slang)*, fairy story *(informal)*, pork pie *(Brit. slang)*, cock-and-bull story *(informal)* • *She described the interview with her as a 'complete fabrication'.*
2 = **manufacture**, production, construction, assembly, erection, assemblage, building • *More than 200 improvements were made in the design and fabrication of the shuttle.*

fabulous 1 = **wonderful**, excellent, brilliant, superb, spectacular, fantastic *(informal)*, marvellous, sensational *(informal)*, first-rate, brill *(informal)*, magic *(informal)*, out-of-this-world *(informal)* • *The scenery and weather were fabulous.*
OPPOSITES: real, common, ordinary
2 = **astounding**, amazing, extraordinary, remarkable, incredible, astonishing, eye-popping *(informal)*, legendary, immense, unbelievable, breathtaking, phenomenal, inconceivable • *You'll be entered in our free draw to win this fabulous prize.*
3 = **legendary**, imaginary, mythical, fictitious, made-up, fantastic, invented, unreal, mythological, apocryphal • *The chimaera of myth is a fabulous beast made up of the parts of other animals.*

façade 1 = **front**, face, exterior, frontage • *the façade of the building*
2 = **show**, front, appearance, mask, exterior, guise, pretence, veneer, semblance • *They hid the troubles plaguing their marriage behind a façade of family togetherness.*

face AS A NOUN 1 = **countenance**, features, kisser *(slang)*, profile, dial *(Brit. slang)*, mug *(slang)*, visage, physiognomy, lineaments, phiz *or* phizog *(slang)* • *She had a beautiful face.*
2 = **expression**, look, air, appearance, aspect, countenance • *He was walking around with a sad face.*
3 = **side**, front, cover, outside, surface, aspect, exterior, right side, elevation, facet, vertical surface • *He climbed 200 feet up the cliff face.*
4 = **dial**, display • *The face of the clock was painted yellow.*
5 = **nature**, image, character, appearance, concept, conception, make-up • *Players like him have changed the face of snooker.*
6 = **self-respect**, respect, reputation, dignity, standing, authority, image, regard, status, honour, esteem, prestige, self-image, mana *(N.Z.)* • *They don't want a war but they don't want to lose face.*
7 = **impudence**, front, confidence, audacity, nerve, neck *(informal)*, sauce *(informal)*, cheek *(informal)*, assurance, gall *(informal)*, presumption, boldness, chutzpah *(U.S. & Canad. informal)*, sass *(U.S. & Canad. informal)*, effrontery, brass neck *(Brit. informal)*, sassiness *(U.S. informal)* • *I haven't the face to borrow off him.*
▸ AS A VERB 1 *often with* **to, towards,** *or* **on** = **look onto**, overlook, be opposite, look out on, front onto, give towards *or* onto • *The garden faces south.*
2 = **confront**, meet, encounter, deal with, oppose, tackle, cope with, experience, brave, defy, come up against, be confronted by, face off *(slang)* • *He looked relaxed and calm as he faced the press.*
3 = **beset**, worry, trouble, bother, distress, plague • *There are two main health risks that face women.*
▸ IN PHRASES: **face someone down** = **intimidate**, defeat, confront, subdue, disconcert • *He's confronted crowds before and faced them down.*
face to face = **facing**, tête-à-tête, opposite, confronting, eyeball to eyeball, in confrontation, à deux *(French)*, vis-à-vis • *It would have been their first face to face encounter.*
fly in the face of something = **defy**, oppose, disregard, go against, flout, rebel against, disobey, act in defiance of • *He said that the decision flew in the face of natural justice.*
make *or* **pull a face at someone** = **scowl**, frown, pout, grimace, smirk, moue *(French)* • *She made a face at him behind his back.*
on the face of it = **to all appearances**, apparently, seemingly, outwardly, at first sight, at face value, to the eye

FABRICS

Acrilan *(trademark)*, alpaca, armure, baize, balbriggan, barathea, barège, batik, batiste, bayadere, beige, bengaline, bird's-eye, bobbinet, bombazine, bouclé, brilliantine, broadcloth, brocade, buckskin, bunting, burlap, calamanco, calico, cambric, camlet, cavalry twill, challis, chambray, Charmeuse *(trademark)*, cheesecloth, chenille, cheviot, chiffon, chintz, cilice, ciré, cloqué, cord, corduroy, cotton, cottonade, cotton flannel, covert cloth, crepe *or* crape, cretonne, Crimplene *(trademark)*, crinoline, cypress, Dacron *(trademark)*, damask, delaine, denim, diamanté, dimity, Donegal tweed, drab, drabbet, Dralon *(trademark)*, drugget, duck, dungaree, duvetyn, etamine, façonné, faille, fearnought, felt, fishnet, flannel, fleece, folk weave, foulard, frieze, frisé, fur, fustian, gaberdine, galatea, georgette, gingham, gloria, Gore-Tex *(trademark)*, gossamer, grogram, gros de Londres, grosgrain, gunny *(chiefly U.S.)*, Harris Tweed *(trademark)*, hessian, honan, hopsack, huckaback *or* huck, India print, jaconet, Jacquard *or* Jacquard weave, jean, jersey, khaki, kincob, knit, lace, lambskin, lamé, lawn, leather, linen, linsey-woolsey, lisle, Lurex *(trademark)*, Lycra *(trademark)*, madras, marabou, marocain, marquisette, marseille, melton, messaline, mohair, moire *or* moiré, moleskin, monk's cloth, moquette, moreen, mousseline, mull, muslin, nainsook, nankeen, needlecord, net, ninon, nun's cloth *or* veiling, oilskin, organdie, organza, organzine, Orlon *(trademark)*, ottoman, Oxford, paduasoy, paisley pattern, panne, paramatta, peau de soie, percale, percaline, petersham, piña cloth, piqué, plush, pongee, poplin, poult *or* poult-de-soie, prunella, prunelle, *or* prunello, rayon, russet, sailcloth, samite, sarcenet, sateen, satin, satinet, saxony, say *(archaic)*, schappe, scrim, seersucker, sendal, serge, shag, shalloon, shantung, sharkskin, sheeting, shirting, shoddy, silesia, silk, silkaline, slipper satin, spandex, spun silk, stockinet, stroud, stuff, suiting, surah, surat, swan's-down, swanskin, swiss muslin, tabaret, tabby, taffeta, tammy, tarlatan, tarpaulin, tartan, tattersall, terry, Terylene *(trademark)*, tick, ticking, tiffany, toile, towelling, tricot, tricotine, tulle, tussore, tweed, twill, velours, velure, velvet, velveteen, Viyella *(trademark)*, voile, wadmal, webbing, whipcord, wild silk, winceyette, wool, worsted

• *On the face of it, that seems to make sense.*

put on a brave face = appear cheerful, air, take courage, grin and bear it *(informal)*, look cheerful, keep your chin up *(informal)*, not show your disappointment • *Friends will see you are putting on a brave face.*

show your face = turn up, come, appear, be seen, show up *(informal)*, put in *or* make an appearance, approach • *I felt I ought to show my face at her father's funeral.*

to your face = directly, openly, straight, in person, in your presence • *Her opponent called her a liar to her face.*

QUOTATIONS

The face is the image of the soul
[Cicero *De Oratore*]

The face is the soul of the body
[Ludwig Wittgenstein *Journal*]

I think your whole life shows in your face and you should be proud of that
[Lauren Bacall]

At 50, everyone has the face he deserves
[George Orwell *last entry in notebook*]

Was this the face that launched a thousand ships
And burnt the topless towers of Ilium?
[Christopher Marlowe *Doctor Faustus*]

faceless = impersonal, remote, unknown, unidentified, anonymous • *Ordinary people are at the mercy of faceless bureaucrats.*

face-lift 1 = renovation, improvement, restoration, refurbishing, modernization, redecoration • *Nothing gives a room a faster facelift than a coat of paint.*
2 = cosmetic surgery, plastic surgery • *She once threw a party to celebrate her facelift.*

facet 1 = aspect, part, face, side, phase, angle • *The caste system shapes nearly every facet of Indian life.*
2 = face, side, surface, plane, slant • *The stones shone back at her, a thousand facets of light in their white-gold settings.*

facetious = flippant, funny, amusing, witty, merry, humorous, playful, pleasant, frivolous, tongue in cheek, comical, jesting, droll, jocular, waggish, unserious, jocose • *Are you going to listen or just make facetious remarks?*
OPPOSITES: serious, earnest, grave

face up to = accept, deal with, tackle, acknowledge, cope with, confront, come to terms with, meet head-on, reconcile yourself to • *You must face the truth that the relationship has ended.*

facile 1 = superficial, shallow, slick, glib, hasty, cursory • *I hated him making facile suggestions when I knew the problem was extremely complex.*
2 = effortless, easy, simple, quick, ready, smooth, skilful,

adept, fluent, uncomplicated, proficient, adroit, dexterous, light • *His facile win tells us he's in form.*
OPPOSITES: difficult, slow, careful

facilitate = **further**, help, forward, promote, ease, speed up, pave the way for, fast-track, make easy, expedite, oil the wheels of, smooth the path of, assist the progress of • *The new airport will facilitate the development of tourism.*
OPPOSITES: prevent, delay, hinder

facility 1 *often plural* = **amenity**, means, aid, opportunity, advantage, resource, equipment, provision, convenience, appliance • *What recreational facilities are now available?*
2 = **opportunity**, possibility, convenience • *The bank will not extend the borrowing facility.*
3 = **ability**, skill, talent, gift, craft, efficiency, knack, fluency, proficiency, dexterity, quickness, adroitness, expertness, skilfulness • *They shared a facility for languages.*
4 = **ease**, readiness, fluency, smoothness, effortlessness • *He had always spoken with facility.*
OPPOSITES: pains, difficulty, hardship
5 = **establishment** • *Some doctors were working all day in one medical facility, then working night shifts in private hospitals.*

facing = **opposite**, fronting, partnering • *The facing page gives a number of questions for you to answer.*

facsimile = **copy**, print, carbon, reproduction, replica, transcript, duplicate, photocopy, Xerox *(trademark)*, carbon copy, Photostat *(trademark)*, fax • *This will be a genuine old copy, not a facsimile.*

fact **AS A NOUN** 1 = **truth**, reality, gospel (truth), certainty, verity, actuality, naked truth • *How much was fact and how much fancy no one knew.*
OPPOSITES: lie, fiction, invention
2 = **detail**, point, feature, particular, item, specific, circumstance • *The lorries always left in the dead of night when there were few witnesses around to record the fact.*
3 = **event**, happening, act, performance, incident, deed, occurrence, fait accompli *(French)* • *He was sure the gun was planted after the fact.*
▸ **AS A PLURAL NOUN** = **information**, details, data, the score *(informal)*, gen *(Brit. informal)*, info *(informal)*, the whole story, ins and outs, the lowdown *(informal)* • *There is so much information you can find the facts for yourself.*
▸ **IN PHRASES: as a matter of fact** *or* **in fact** *or* **in point of fact** = **actually**, really, indeed, truly, in reality, in truth, to tell the truth, in actual fact, in point of fact • *That sounds rather simple, but in fact it's very difficult.*

QUOTATIONS
In this life we want nothing but facts, sir; nothing but facts
[Charles Dickens *Hard Times*]

faction[1] 1 = **group**, set, party, division, section, camp, sector, minority, combination, coalition, gang, lobby, bloc, contingent, pressure group, caucus, junta, clique, coterie, schism, confederacy, splinter group, cabal, ginger group, public-interest group *(U.S. & Canad.)* • *A peace agreement will be signed by the leaders of the country's warring factions.*
2 = **dissension**, division, conflict, rebellion, disagreement, friction, strife, turbulence, variance, discord, infighting, disunity, sedition, tumult, disharmony, divisiveness • *Faction and self-interest appear to be the norm.*
OPPOSITES: accord, peace, agreement

factional = **contentious**, warring, rival, conflicting, dissident, partisan, turbulent, rebellious, sectarian, divisive, tumultuous, malcontent, litigious, seditious, mutinous, refractory, disputatious, insurrectionary, troublemaking • *factional disputes between the various groups*

factor = **element**, thing, point, part, cause, influence, item, aspect, circumstance, characteristic, consideration, component, determinant • *Physical activity is an important factor in maintaining fitness.*

factory = **works**, plant, mill, workshop, assembly line, shop floor, manufactory *(obsolete)* • *He owned furniture factories in New York.*

factotum = **Man Friday** *or* **Girl Friday**, handyman, jack of all trades, odd job man, maid of all work, odd-jobber, man of all work • *I was a sort of office boy and a general factotum.*

factual = **true**, objective, authentic, unbiased, close, real, sure, correct, genuine, accurate, exact, precise, faithful, credible, matter-of-fact, literal, veritable, circumstantial, unadorned, dinkum *(Austral. & N.Z. informal)*, true-to-life • *Any comparison that is not strictly factual runs the risk of being interpreted as subjective.*
OPPOSITES: imaginary, unreal, fictitious

faculty 1 = **power**, ability, capacity, capability, potential • *The severed head still retains the faculty of feeling and thinking during several seconds.*
2 = **ability**, power, skill, facility, talent, gift, capacity, bent, capability, readiness, knack, propensity, aptitude, dexterity, cleverness, adroitness, turn • *A faculty for self-preservation is necessary when you have friends like hers.*
OPPOSITES: failing, weakness, inability
3 = **department**, school, discipline, profession, branch of learning • *the Faculty of Social and Political Sciences*
4 = **teaching staff**, staff, teachers, professors, lecturers *(chiefly U.S.)* • *The faculty agreed on a change in the requirements.*
5 = **power**, reason, sense, intelligence, mental ability, physical ability • *He was drunk and not in control of his faculties.*

fad = **craze**, fashion, trend, fancy, rage, mode, vogue, whim, mania, affectation • *He does not believe that environmental concern is a passing fad.*

faddy = **particular**, choosy *(informal)*, picky *(informal)*, hard to please, exacting, discriminating, fussy, fastidious, nit-picking *(informal)*, finicky, pernickety, overparticular • *My boys have always been faddy eaters.*

fade 1 = **become pale**, dull, dim, bleach, wash out, blanch, discolour, blench, lose colour, lose lustre, decolour • *All colour fades, especially under the impact of direct sunlight.*
2 = **make pale**, dull, dim, bleach, wash out, blanch, discolour, decolour • *Even a soft light fades the carpets in a room.*
3 = **grow dim**, dim, fade away, become less loud • *The sound of the last bomber's engines faded into the distance.*
4 *usually with* **away** *or* **out** = **dwindle**, disappear, vanish, melt away, fall, fail, decline, flag, dissolve, dim, disperse, wither, wilt, wane, perish, ebb, languish, die out, droop, shrivel, die away, waste away, vanish into thin air, become unimportant, evanesce, etiolate • *She had a way of fading into the background when things got rough.*

faded = **discoloured**, pale, bleached, washed out, dull, dim, indistinct, etiolated, lustreless • *a girl in a faded dress*

fading = **declining**, dying, disappearing, vanishing, decreasing, on the decline • *outside in the rapidly fading light*

faeces *or (esp. U.S.)* **feces** = **excrement**, stools, excreta, bodily waste, dung, droppings, ordure • *The faeces contain nitrogen.*

fag[1] = **chore**, bind *(informal)*, bore, drag *(informal)*, bother, irritation, nuisance, inconvenience • *Staff think this form-filling is a bit of a fag.*

fag[2] = **cigarette**, smoke, ciggy *(informal)*, cancer stick *(slang)*, coffin nail *(slang)*, gasper *(slang)* • *A woman on her doorstep asked if he could spare a fag.*

faggot *(Offensive)* = **homosexual**, queen *(slang)*, gay, fairy *(slang)*, queer *(informal derogatory)*, homo *(informal derogatory)*, bender *(slang)*, poof *(Brit. & Austral. derogatory slang)*, nancy boy *(slang)*, poofter *(slang)*, batty boy *(slang)*, catamite, shirt-lifter *(derogatory slang)*, woofter *(derogatory slang)*, auntie or aunty *(Austral. slang)*, lily *(Austral. slang)* • *You didn't tell me your brother was a faggot.*

fail **AS A VERB** 1 = **be unsuccessful**, founder, fall flat, come to

nothing, fall, miss, go down, break down, flop *(informal)*, be defeated, fall short, fall through, fall short of, fizzle out *(informal)*, come unstuck, run aground, miscarry, be in vain, misfire, fall by the wayside, go astray, come to grief, come a cropper *(informal)*, bite the dust, go up in smoke, go belly-up *(slang)*, come to naught, lay an egg *(slang, chiefly U.S. & Canad.)*, go by the board, not make the grade *(informal)*, go down like a lead balloon *(informal)*, turn out badly, fall flat on your face, meet with disaster, be found lacking *or* wanting • *He was afraid the revolution they had started would fail.*
OPPOSITES: grow, pass, succeed
2 = **disappoint**, abandon, desert, neglect, omit, let down, forsake, turn your back on, be disloyal to, break your word, forget • *We waited twenty-one years, don't fail us now.*
3 = **stop working**, stop, die, give up, break down, cease, stall, cut out, malfunction, conk out *(informal)*, go on the blink *(informal)*, go phut • *The lights mysteriously failed.*
4 = **wither**, perish, sag, droop, waste away, shrivel up • *In fact many food crops failed because of the drought.*
5 = **go bankrupt**, crash, collapse, fold *(informal)*, close down, go under, go bust *(informal)*, go out of business, be wound up, go broke *(informal)*, go to the wall, go into receivership, go into liquidation, become insolvent, smash • *So far this year, 104 banks have failed.*
6 = **decline**, fade, weaken, deteriorate, dwindle, sicken, degenerate, fall apart at the seams, be on your last legs *(informal)* • *He was 58 and his health was failing rapidly.*
7 = **give out**, disappear, fade, dim, dwindle, wane, gutter, languish, peter out, die away, grow dim, sink • *Here in the hills, the light failed more quickly.*
8 = **not pass**, be unsuccessful, flunk *(informal)*, screw up *(informal)*, wash out, underperform, not make the grade, not come up to scratch, underachieve, not come up to the mark *(informal)* • *I lived in fear of failing my end-of-term exams.*
▸ **IN PHRASES: without fail = without exception**, regularly, constantly, invariably, religiously, unfailingly, conscientiously, like clockwork, punctually, dependably • *He attended every meeting without fail.*

failing **AS A NOUN** = **shortcoming**, failure, fault, error, weakness, defect, deficiency, lapse, flaw, miscarriage, drawback, misfortune, blemish, imperfection, frailty, foible, blind spot • *He had invented an imaginary son, in order to make up for his real son's failings.*
OPPOSITES: advantage, strength, asset
▸ **AS A PREPOSITION** = **in the absence of**, lacking, in default of • *Find someone who will let you talk things through, or failing that, write down your thoughts.*

failure 1 = **lack of success**, defeat, collapse, abortion, wreck, frustration, breakdown, overthrow, miscarriage, fiasco, downfall • *The policy is doomed to failure.*
OPPOSITES: success, triumph, effectiveness
2 = **catastrophe**, disaster, fiasco, let-down, trouble, tragedy, blunder, misfortune, devastation, calamity, mishap • *The marriage was a failure and they both wanted to be free of it.*
3 = **loser**, disappointment, no-good, flop *(informal)*, write-off, incompetent, no-hoper *(chiefly Austral.)*, dud *(informal)*, clinker *(slang, chiefly U.S.)*, black sheep, washout *(informal)*, clunker *(informal)*, dead duck *(slang)*, ne'er-do-well, saddo *(Brit. slang)*, nonstarter • *I just felt I had been a failure in my personal life.*
4 = **negligence**, neglect, deficiency, default, shortcoming, omission, oversight, dereliction, nonperformance, nonobservance, nonsuccess, remissness • *They didn't prove his case of a failure of duty.*
OPPOSITES: care, observance
5 = **breakdown**, stalling, cutting out, malfunction, crash, disruption, stoppage, mishap, conking out *(informal)* • *There were also several accidents mainly caused by engine failures on take-off.*
6 = **failing**, deterioration, decay, loss, decline • *He was being treated for kidney failure.*
7 = **scarcity**, lack, shortfall, inadequacy, dearth, insufficiency • *displaced by fighting or crop failure*
8 = **bankruptcy**, crash, collapse, ruin, folding *(informal)*, closure, winding up, downfall, going under, liquidation, insolvency • *Business failures rose 16% last month.*
OPPOSITES: fortune, prosperity
▸ **RELATED PHOBIA:** kakorraphiaphobia

QUOTATIONS

A failure is a stranger in his own house
[Eric Hoffer *The Passionate State of Mind*]

There is not a fiercer hell than the failure in a great object
[John Keats *Endymion*]

There is no failure except in no longer trying
[Elbert Hubbard *The Note Book*]

faint **AS AN ADJECTIVE** 1 = **dim**, low, light, soft, thin, faded, whispered, distant, dull, delicate, vague, unclear, muted, subdued, faltering, hushed, bleached, feeble, indefinite, muffled, hazy, ill-defined, indistinct • *He became aware of the soft, faint sounds of water dripping.*
OPPOSITES: clear, strong, powerful
2 = **slight**, weak, feeble, unenthusiastic, remote, slim, vague, slender • *She made a faint attempt at a laugh.*
3 = **timid**, weak, feeble, lame, unconvincing, unenthusiastic, timorous, faint-hearted, spiritless, half-hearted, lily-livered • *He let his arm flail out in a faint attempt to strike her.*
OPPOSITES: brave, bold, courageous
4 = **dizzy**, giddy, light-headed, vertiginous, weak, exhausted, fatigued, faltering, wobbly, drooping, languid, lethargic, muzzy, woozy *(informal)*, weak at the knees, enervated • *Other signs of angina are nausea, feeling faint and shortness of breath.*
OPPOSITES: fresh, vigorous, energetic
▸ **AS A VERB** = **pass out**, black out, lose consciousness, keel over *(informal)*, fail, go out, collapse, fade, weaken, languish, swoon *(literary)*, flake out *(informal)* • *I thought he'd faint when I kissed him.*
▸ **AS A NOUN** = **blackout**, collapse, coma, swoon *(literary)*, unconsciousness, syncope *(Pathology)* • *She slumped on the ground in a faint.*

faint-hearted = **timid**, weak, cowardly, diffident, spineless, boneless, timorous, irresolute, half-arsed *(Brit. slang)*, chickenshit *(U.S. slang)*, half-assed *(U.S. & Canad. slang)*, half-hearted, yellow • *The voters may be ready to punish the politicians who devised a faint-hearted solidarity pact.*
OPPOSITES: brave, daring

faintly 1 = **slightly**, rather, a little, somewhat, dimly • *She felt faintly ridiculous.*
2 = **softly**, weakly, feebly, in a whisper, indistinctly, unclearly • *The voice came faintly back to us across the water.*

fair[1] **AS AN ADJECTIVE** 1 = **unbiased**, impartial, even-handed, unprejudiced, just, clean, square, equal, objective, reasonable, proper, legitimate, upright, honourable, honest, equitable, lawful, trustworthy, on the level *(informal)*, disinterested, dispassionate, above board, according to the rules • *I wanted them to get a fair deal.*
OPPOSITES: unfair, one-sided, prejudiced
2 = **respectable**, middling, average, reasonable, decent, acceptable, moderate, adequate, satisfactory, not bad, mediocre, so-so *(informal)*, tolerable, passable, O.K. *or* okay *(informal)*, all right • *He had a fair command of English.*
3 = **light**, golden, blonde, blond, yellowish, fair-haired, light-coloured, flaxen-haired, towheaded, tow-haired • *She had bright eyes and fair hair.*
4 = **light-complexioned**, white, pale • *It's important to protect my fair skin from the sun.*
5 = **fine**, clear, dry, bright, pleasant, sunny, favourable,

clement, cloudless, unclouded, sunshiny • *Weather conditions were fair.*
6 = **beautiful**, pretty, attractive, lovely, handsome, good-looking, bonny, comely, beauteous, well-favoured, fit *(Brit. informal)* • *Faint heart never won fair lady.*
OPPOSITES: homely, plain, ugly
▸ **IN PHRASES: fair and square = honestly**, straight, legally, on the level *(informal)*, by the book, lawfully, above board, according to the rules, without cheating • *We were beaten fair and square.*

fair² 1 = **carnival**, fête, mela, gala, bazaar • *I used to love going to the fair when I was young.*
2 = **exhibition**, show, market, festival, mart, expo *(informal)*, exposition • *The date for the book fair has been changed.*

fairly 1 = **equitably**, objectively, legitimately, honestly, justly, lawfully, without prejudice, dispassionately, impartially, even-handedly, without bias • *They solved their problems quickly and fairly.*
2 = **moderately**, rather, quite, somewhat, reasonably, adequately, pretty well, tolerably, passably • *We did fairly well.*
3 = **positively**, really, simply, absolutely, in a manner of speaking, veritably • *He fairly flew across the room.*
4 = **deservedly**, objectively, honestly, justifiably, justly, impartially, equitably, without fear or favour, properly • *It can no doubt be fairly argued that he is entitled to every penny.*

fair-minded = **impartial**, just, fair, reasonable, open-minded, disinterested, unbiased, even-handed, unprejudiced • *She is one of the most fair-minded people I know.*

fairness = **impartiality**, justice, equity, legitimacy, decency, disinterestedness, uprightness, rightfulness, equitableness • *concern about the fairness of the election campaign*

QUOTATIONS
One should always play fairly when one has the winning cards
[Oscar Wilde *An Ideal Husband*]

fairy = **sprite**, elf, brownie, hob, pixie, puck, imp, leprechaun, peri, Robin Goodfellow • *The fairy vanished from his sight.*

fairy tale *or* **fairy story** 1 = **folk tale**, romance, traditional story • *She was like a princess in a fairy tale.*
2 = **lie**, fantasy, fiction, invention, fabrication, untruth, porky *(Brit. slang)*, pork pie *(Brit. slang)*, urban myth, tall story, urban legend, cock-and-bull story *(informal)* • *Many of those who write books lie much more than those who tell fairy tales.*

faith **AS A NOUN** 1 = **confidence**, trust, credit, conviction, assurance, dependence, reliance, credence • *She had placed a great deal of faith in him.*
OPPOSITES: doubt, suspicion, distrust
2 = **religion**, church, belief, persuasion, creed, communion, denomination, dogma • *England shifted officially from a Catholic to a Protestant faith in the 16th century.*
OPPOSITES: agnosticism
▸ **IN PHRASES: break faith with someone = be disloyal to**, betray, be unfaithful to, be untrue to, grass *(Brit. slang)*, cheat, stab in the back, sell down the river *(informal)*, break your promise to • *We're breaking faith with our people.*
in good faith = honestly, sincerely, honourably • *This report was published in good faith.*
keep faith with someone = be loyal to, support, defend, stand by, be true to, stick by, be faithful to • *He's expected to keep faith with most of the World Cup team.*

QUOTATIONS
Faith may be defined briefly as an illogical belief in the occurrence of the improbable
[H.L. Mencken *Prejudices: Third Series*]
Faith is the substance of things hoped for, the evidence of things not seen
[*Bible: Hebrews*]
I show you doubt, to prove that faith exists
[Robert Browning *Balaustion's Adventure*]
Faith without works is dead
[*Bible: James*]
The faith that stands on authority is not faith
[Ralph Waldo Emerson *Essays*]

PROVERBS
Faith will move mountains

faithful **AS AN ADJECTIVE** 1 = **loyal**, true, committed, constant, attached, devoted, dedicated, reliable, staunch, truthful, dependable, trusty, steadfast, unwavering, true-blue, immovable, unswerving • *Older Americans are among this country's most faithful voters.* • *She had remained faithful to her husband.*
OPPOSITES: doubting, false, disloyal
2 = **accurate**, just, close, true, strict, exact, precise • *His screenplay is faithful to the novel.*
▸ **IN PHRASES: the faithful = believers**, brethren, followers, congregation, adherents, the elect, communicants • *The faithful revered him then as a prophet.*

faithfully = **loyally**, staunchly, reliably, steadfastly, devotedly, unswervingly, unwaveringly • *He was faithfully followed and supported.*

faithfulness = **loyalty**, devotion, fidelity, constancy, dependability, trustworthiness, fealty, adherence • *She and her husband valued faithfulness as the cornerstone of their marriage.*

faithless = **disloyal**, unreliable, unfaithful, untrustworthy, doubting, false, untrue, treacherous, dishonest, fickle, perfidious, untruthful, traitorous, unbelieving, inconstant, false-hearted, recreant *(archaic)* • *She decided to divorce her increasingly faithless and unreliable husband.*

fake **AS A VERB** 1 = **forge**, copy, reproduce, fabricate, counterfeit, falsify • *Did they fake this evidence?*
2 = **sham**, affect, assume, put on, pretend, simulate, feign, go through the motions of • *He faked nonchalance.*
▸ **AS A NOUN** 1 = **forgery**, copy, fraud, reproduction, dummy, imitation, hoax, counterfeit • *It is filled with famous works of art, and every one of them is a fake.*
2 = **charlatan**, deceiver, sham, quack, mountebank, phoney *or* phony *(informal)* • *She denied claims that she is a fake.*
▸ **AS AN ADJECTIVE** = **artificial**, false, forged, counterfeit, affected, assumed, put-on, pretend *(informal)*, mock, imitation, sham, pseudo *(informal)*, feigned, pinchbeck, phoney *or* phony *(informal)* • *The bank manager is said to have issued fake certificates.*
OPPOSITES: real, true, genuine

falcon
▸ **RELATED ADJECTIVE:** falconine
▸ **NAME OF MALE:** tercel or tiercel
▸ **NAME OF YOUNG:** eyas

fall **AS A VERB** 1 = **drop**, plunge, tumble, plummet, trip, settle, crash, collapse, pitch, sink, go down, come down, dive, stumble, descend, topple, subside, cascade, trip over, drop down, nose-dive, come a cropper *(informal)*, keel over, go head over heels • *Her father fell into the sea after a massive heart attack.*
OPPOSITES: rise, increase, scale
2 = **decrease**, drop, decline, go down, flag, slump, diminish, fall off, dwindle, lessen, subside, ebb, abate, depreciate, become lower • *Her weight fell to under seven stones.*
OPPOSITES: increase, advance, extend
3 = **be overthrown**, be taken, surrender, succumb, yield, submit, give way, capitulate, be conquered, give in *or* up, pass into enemy hands • *The town fell to Croatian forces.*
OPPOSITES: triumph, prevail
4 = **be killed**, die, be lost, perish, be slain, be a casualty, meet your end • *Another wave of troops followed the first, running past those who had fallen.*
OPPOSITES: survive, endure, hold out

5 = become, get, grow • *I am afraid that I might fall ill.*
6 = occur, happen, come about, chance, take place, fall out, befall, come to pass • *Easter falls in early April.*
7 = come, arrive, occur • *When night fell, he sat with his mother.*
▸ **AS A NOUN 1 = drop**, slip, plunge, dive, spill, tumble, descent, plummet, nose dive • *The helmets are designed to withstand impacts equivalent to a fall from a bicycle.*
2 = decrease, drop, lowering, decline, reduction, slump, dip, falling off, dwindling, lessening, diminution, cut • *There was a sharp fall in the value of the pound.*
3 = collapse, defeat, surrender, downfall, death, failure, ruin, resignation, destruction, overthrow, submission, capitulation • *the fall of Rome*
4 = slope, incline, descent, downgrade, slant, declivity • *a fall of 3.5 kilometres*
▸ **AS A PLURAL NOUN = waterfall**, rapids, cascade, cataract, linn *(Scot.)*, force *(Northern English dialect)* • *The falls have always been an insurmountable obstacle for salmon and sea trout.*
▸ **IN PHRASES: fall apart 1 = break up**, crumble, disintegrate, fall to bits, go to seed, come apart at the seams, break into pieces, go *or* come to pieces, shatter • *The work was never finished and bit by bit the building fell apart.*
2 = break down, dissolve, disperse, disband, lose cohesion • *The national coalition fell apart five weeks ago.*
3 = go to pieces, break down, crack up *(informal)*, have a breakdown, crumble • *I was falling apart.*
fall asleep = drop off *(informal)*, go to sleep, doze off, nod off *(informal)*, go out like a light • *I was again able to go to bed and fall asleep.*
fall away 1 = slope, drop, go down, incline, incline downwards • *On either side of the tracks the ground fell away sharply.*
2 = decrease, drop, diminish, fall off, dwindle, lessen • *Demand began to fall away.*
fall back = retreat, retire, withdraw, move back, recede, pull back, back off, recoil, draw back • *The congregation fell back from them as they entered.*
fall back on something *or* **someone = resort to**, have recourse to, employ, turn to, make use of, call upon, press into service • *When necessary, instinct is the most reliable resource you can fall back on.*
fall behind 1 = lag, trail, be left behind, drop back, get left behind, lose your place • *The horse fell behind on the final furlong.*
2 = be in arrears, be late, not keep up • *He faces losing his home after falling behind with the payments.*
fall down *often with* **on = fail**, disappoint, go wrong, fall short, fail to make the grade, prove unsuccessful • *That is where his argument falls down.*
fall for someone = fall in love with, become infatuated with, be smitten by, be swept off your feet by, desire, fancy *(Brit. informal)*, succumb to the charms of, lose your head over • *I just fell for him right away.*
fall for something = be fooled by, be deceived by, be taken in by, be duped by, buy *(slang)*, accept, swallow *(informal)*, take on board, give credence to • *It was just a line to get you out of here, and you fell for it!*
fall foul of something *or* **someone = come into conflict with**, brush with, have trouble with, cross swords with, run foul of, make an enemy of • *Women who fall foul of the law are viewed as wicked.*
fall in 1 = collapse, sink, cave in, crash in, fall to the ground, fall apart at the seams, come down about your ears • *Part of my bedroom ceiling has fallen in.*
2 = get in line, line up, queue, form a crocodile • *He waved them to fall in behind him.*
fall in love with someone = lose your heart (to), fall (for), become infatuated (with), be smitten by, fancy *(Brit. informal)*, become attached to, take a fancy to, become fond of, become enamoured of, be swept off your feet (by), conceive an affection for • *You fall in love with a man for God knows what reasons.*
fall in with someone *often with* **with = make friends with**, go around with, become friendly with, hang about with *(informal)* • *At University he had fallen in with a small clique of literature students.*
fall in with something = go along with, support, accept, agree with, comply with, submit to, yield to, buy into *(informal)*, cooperate with, assent, take on board, concur with • *Her reluctance to fall in with his plans led to trouble.*
fall off 1 = tumble, topple, plummet, be unseated, come a cropper *or* purler *(informal)*, take a fall *or* tumble • *He fell off at the second fence.*
2 = decrease, drop, reduce, decline, fade, slump, weaken, shrink, diminish, dwindle, lessen, wane, subside, fall away, peter out, slacken, tail off *(informal)*, ebb away, go down *or* downhill • *Unemployment is rising again and retail buying has fallen off.*
fall on *or* **upon something** *or* **someone = attack**, assault, snatch, assail, tear into *(informal)*, lay into, descend upon, pitch into *(informal)*, belabour, let fly at, set upon *or* about • *They fell upon the enemy from the rear.*
fall out = argue, fight, row, clash, differ, disagree, quarrel, squabble, have a row, have words, come to blows, cross swords, altercate • *She fell out with her husband.*
fall short *often with* **of = be lacking**, miss, fail, disappoint, be wanting, be inadequate, be deficient, fall down on *(informal)*, prove inadequate, not come up to expectations *or* scratch *(informal)* • *His achievements are bound to fall short of his ambitions.*
fall through = fail, be unsuccessful, come to nothing, fizzle out *(informal)*, miscarry, go awry, go by the board • *The deal fell through.*
fall to someone = be the responsibility of, be up to, come down to, devolve upon • *It fell to me to get rid of them.*
fall to something = begin, start, set to, set about, commence, apply yourself to • *They fell to fighting among themselves.*

fallacious = incorrect, wrong, mistaken, false, misleading, untrue, deceptive, spurious, fictitious, illogical, erroneous, illusory, delusive, delusory, sophistic, sophistical • *Their argument is fallacious.*

QUOTATIONS

The conclusion of your syllogism, I said lightly, is fallacious, being based upon licensed premises
[Flann O'Brien *At Swim-Two-Birds*]

fallacy = error, mistake, illusion, flaw, deception, delusion, inconsistency, misconception, deceit, falsehood, untruth, misapprehension, sophistry, casuistry, sophism, faultiness • *This is the biggest fallacy of all.*

fallen 1 = killed, lost, dead, slaughtered, slain, perished • *Work began on establishing the cemeteries as permanent memorials to our fallen servicemen.*
2 = dishonoured, lost, loose, shamed, ruined, disgraced, immoral, sinful, unchaste • *She would be thought of as a fallen woman.*

fallible = imperfect, weak, uncertain, ignorant, mortal, frail, erring, prone to error • *They are only human and all too fallible.*
OPPOSITES: perfect, divine, infallible

fallout = consequences, results, effects, outcome, repercussions, upshot • *It is the political fallout of the riots which has preoccupied most of the British Press.*

fallow 1 = uncultivated, unused, undeveloped, unplanted, untilled • *The fields lay fallow.*
2 = inactive, resting, idle, dormant, inert • *There followed something of a fallow period.*

f

false AS AN ADJECTIVE 1 = **incorrect**, wrong, mistaken, misleading, faulty, inaccurate, invalid, improper, unfounded, erroneous, inexact • *This resulted in false information being entered.*
OPPOSITES: right, sound, correct
2 = **untrue**, fraudulent, unreal, concocted, fictitious, trumped up, fallacious, untruthful, truthless • *You do not know whether what you are told is true or false.*
OPPOSITES: true, reliable
3 = **artificial**, forged, fake, mock, reproduction, synthetic, replica, imitation, bogus, simulated, sham, pseudo *(informal)*, counterfeit, feigned, spurious, ersatz, pretended • *He paid for a false passport.*
OPPOSITES: real, genuine, authentic
4 = **treacherous**, lying, deceiving, unreliable, two-timing *(informal)*, dishonest, deceptive, hypocritical, unfaithful, two-faced, disloyal, unsound, deceitful, faithless, untrustworthy, insincere, double-dealing, dishonourable, duplicitous, mendacious, perfidious, treasonable, traitorous, inconstant, delusive, false-hearted • *She was a false friend, envious of her lifestyle and her life with her husband.*
OPPOSITES: loyal, faithful, trustworthy
▸ IN PHRASES: **play someone false** = **deceive**, cheat, betray, double-cross, stab in the back, sell down the river *(informal)*, give the Judas kiss to • *I'm afraid he's been playing us all false.*

falsehood 1 = **untruthfulness**, deception, deceit, dishonesty, prevarication, mendacity, dissimulation, perjury, inveracity *(rare)* • *She called the verdict a victory of truth over falsehood.*
2 = **lie**, story, fiction, fabrication, fib, untruth, porky *(Brit. slang)*, pork pie *(Brit. slang)*, misstatement • *He accused them of knowingly spreading falsehoods about him.*

QUOTATIONS
The most dangerous of all falsehoods is a slightly distorted truth
[G.C. Lichtenberg]

falsetto = **high voice**, high-pitched voice • *Even though it's high, it's not a falsetto.*

falsification = **misrepresentation**, distortion, tampering with, forgery, deceit, perversion, adulteration, dissimulation • *recent concern about the falsification of evidence in court*

falsify = **alter**, forge, fake, tamper with, doctor, cook *(slang)*, distort, pervert, belie, counterfeit, misrepresent, garble, misstate • *The charges against him include fraud, bribery, and falsifying business records.*

falsity 1 = **untruth**, deceit, dishonesty, inaccuracy, deception, hypocrisy, treachery, duplicity, unreality, double-dealing, perfidy, mendacity, fraudulence, deceptiveness • *with no clear knowledge of the truth or falsity of the issues involved*
2 = **lie**, fraud, cheating, deception, porky *(Brit. slang)*, pork pie *(Brit. slang)* • *deducing a falsity from two truisms*

falter 1 = **hesitate**, delay, waver, vacillate, break • *I have not faltered in my quest for a new future.*
OPPOSITES: last, continue, persevere
2 = **tumble**, shake, tremble, totter • *As he neared the house, he faltered.*
3 = **stutter**, pause, stumble, hesitate, stammer, speak haltingly • *Her voice faltered and she had to stop a moment to control it.*

faltering = **hesitant**, broken, weak, uncertain, stumbling, tentative, stammering, timid, irresolute • *He spoke in faltering English.*

fame = **prominence**, glory, celebrity, stardom, name, credit, reputation, honour, prestige, stature, eminence, renown, repute, public esteem, illustriousness • *At the height of his fame, his every word was valued.*
OPPOSITES: shame, disgrace, obscurity

QUOTATIONS
If fame is to come only after death, I am in no hurry for it
[Martial *Epigrams*]
In the future everybody will be world famous for fifteen minutes
[Andy Warhol *exhibition catalogue*]
Fame is the spur that the clear spirit doth raise
(That last infirmity of noble mind)
To scorn delights, and live laborious days
[John Milton *Lycidas*]
Fame is like a river, that beareth up things light and swollen, and drowns things heavy and solid
[Francis Bacon *Essays*]
Fame is a food that dead men eat -
I have no stomach for such meat
[Henry Austin Dobson *Fame is a Food*]
Famous men have the whole earth as their memorial
[Pericles]

famed = **renowned**, celebrated, recognized, well-known, acclaimed, widely-known • *The city is famed for its outdoor restaurants.*

familiar AS AN ADJECTIVE 1 = **well-known**, household, everyday, recognized, common, stock, domestic, repeated, ordinary, conventional, routine, frequent, accustomed, customary, mundane, recognizable, common or garden *(informal)* • *They are already familiar faces on our TV screens.*
OPPOSITES: unusual, unknown, unfamiliar
2 = **friendly**, close, dear, intimate, confidential, amicable, chummy *(informal)*, buddy-buddy *(slang, chiefly U.S. & Canad.)*, palsy-walsy *(informal)* • *the old familiar relationship*
OPPOSITES: cold, formal, distant
3 = **relaxed**, open, easy, friendly, free, near, comfortable, intimate, casual, informal, amicable, cordial, free-and-easy, unreserved, unconstrained, unceremonious, hail-fellow-well-met • *the comfortable, familiar atmosphere*
4 = **disrespectful**, forward, bold, presuming, intrusive, presumptuous, impudent, overfamiliar, overfree • *The driver of that taxi-cab seemed to me familiar to the point of impertinence.*
▸ IN PHRASES: **familiar with** = **acquainted with**, aware of, introduced to, conscious of, at home with, no stranger to, informed about, abreast of, knowledgeable about, versed in, well up in, proficient in, conversant with, on speaking terms with, in the know about, *au courant* with, *au fait* with • *only too familiar with the problems*

familiarity 1 = **acquaintance**, experience, understanding, knowledge, awareness, grasp, acquaintanceship • *The enemy would always have the advantage of familiarity with the rugged terrain.*
OPPOSITES: ignorance, inexperience, unfamiliarity
2 = **friendliness**, friendship, intimacy, closeness, freedom, ease, openness, fellowship, informality, sociability, naturalness, absence of reserve, unceremoniousness • *Close personal familiarity between councillors and staff can prove embarrassing.*
OPPOSITES: reserve, distance, formality
3 = **disrespect**, forwardness, overfamiliarity, liberties, liberty, cheek, presumption, boldness • *He had behaved with undue and oily familiarity.*
OPPOSITES: respect, constraint, propriety

PROVERBS
Familiarity breeds contempt

familiarize *or* **familiarise** = **accustom**, instruct, habituate, make used to, school, season, train, prime, coach, get to know (about), inure, bring into common use, make conversant • *The goal of the experiment was to familiarize the people with the new laws.*

family 1 = **relations**, people, children, issue, relatives, household, folk *(informal)*, offspring, descendants, brood, kin, nuclear family, progeny, kindred, next of kin, kinsmen, ménage, kith and kin, your nearest and dearest, kinsfolk,

your own flesh and blood, ainga *(N.Z.)*, rellies *(Austral. slang)* • *His family are completely behind him, whatever he decides.*
2 = children, kids *(informal)*, offspring, little ones, munchkins *(informal, chiefly U.S.)*, littlies *(Austral. informal)* • *Are you going to have a family?*
3 = ancestors, forebears, parentage, forefathers, house, line, race, blood, birth, strain, tribe, sept, clan, descent, dynasty, pedigree, extraction, ancestry, lineage, genealogy, line of descent, stemma, stirps • *Her family came to Los Angeles at the turn of the century.*
4 = species, group, class, system, order, kind, network, genre, classification, subdivision, subclass • *foods in the cabbage family, such as Brussels sprouts*
▸ RELATED ADJECTIVE: familial

QUOTATIONS
You don't choose your family. They are God's gift to you, as you are to them
[Desmond Tutu *address at enthronement as archbishop of Cape Town*]
The family – that dear octopus from whose tentacles we never quite escape
[Dodie Smith *Dear Octopus*]
All happy families are alike, but every unhappy one is unhappy in its own way
[Leo Tolstoy *Anna Karenina*]
PROVERBS
Blood is thicker than water

family tree = lineage, genealogy, line of descent, ancestral tree, line, descent, pedigree, extraction, ancestry, blood line, stemma, stirps, whakapapa *(N.Z.)* • *the difficulties of tracing a complex family tree*

famine = hunger, want, starvation, deprivation, scarcity, dearth, destitution • *refugees trapped by war, drought and famine*

QUOTATIONS
They that die by famine die by inches
[Matthew Henry *Expositions on the Old and New Testament*]

famished = starving, starved, voracious, ravenous, ready to eat a horse *(informal)*, ravening • *Is dinner ready? I'm famished.*

famous = well-known, celebrated, acclaimed, notable, noted, excellent, signal, honoured, remarkable, distinguished, prominent, glorious, legendary, renowned, eminent, conspicuous, illustrious, much-publicized, lionized, far-famed • *England's most famous landscape artist, John Constable*
OPPOSITES: forgotten, unknown, obscure

fan[1] AS A NOUN **= blower**, ventilator, air conditioner, vane, punkah *(in India)*, blade, propeller • *He cools himself with an electric fan.*
▸ AS A VERB **1 = blow**, cool, refresh, air-condition, ventilate, air-cool, winnow *(rare)* • *She fanned herself with a piece of cardboard.*
2 = stimulate, increase, excite, provoke, arouse, rouse, stir up, work up, agitate, whip up, add fuel to the flames, impassion, enkindle • *economic problems which often fan hatred*
3 *often with* **out = spread out**, spread, lay out, disperse, unfurl, open out, space out • *The main body of troops fanned out to the west.*

fan[2] 1 = supporter, lover, follower, enthusiast, admirer, fan club *(informal)*, groupie *(slang)*, rooter *(U.S.)* • *As a boy he was a Manchester United fan.*
2 = devotee, addict, freak *(informal)*, buff *(informal)*, fiend *(informal)*, adherent, zealot, aficionado

fanatic = extremist, activist, militant, addict, enthusiast, buff *(informal)*, visionary, devotee, bigot, zealot, energumen • *I am not a religious fanatic but I am a Christian.*

QUOTATIONS
A fanatic is one who can't change his mind and won't change the subject
[Winston Churchill]

fanatical = obsessive, burning, wild, mad, extreme, enthusiastic, passionate, frenzied, visionary, fervent, zealous, bigoted, rabid, immoderate, overenthusiastic • *As a boy he was a fanatical patriot.*

fanaticism = immoderation, enthusiasm, madness, devotion, dedication, zeal, bigotry, extremism, infatuation, single-mindedness, zealotry, obsessiveness, monomania, overenthusiasm • *a protest against intolerance and religious fanaticism*

QUOTATIONS
Fanaticism is the wisdom of the spirit
[Eva Perón]
Fanaticism consists in redoubling your effort when you have forgotten your aim
[George Santayana *The Life of Reason*]

fancier = expert, amateur, breeder, connoisseur, aficionado • *pigeon fanciers*

fanciful = unreal, wild, ideal, romantic, fantastic, curious, fabulous, imaginative, imaginary, poetic, extravagant, visionary, fairy-tale, mythical, whimsical, capricious, chimerical • *fanciful ideas about Martian life*
OPPOSITES: dry, ordinary, unimaginative

fancy AS AN ADJECTIVE **1 = elaborate**, decorated, decorative, extravagant, intricate, baroque, ornamented, ornamental, ornate, elegant, fanciful, embellished • *It was packaged in a fancy plastic case with attractive graphics.*
OPPOSITES: common, simple, plain
2 = expensive, high-quality, classy, flashy, swish *(informal)*, showy, ostentatious • *They sent me to a fancy private school.*
▸ AS A NOUN **1 = whim**, thought, idea, desire, urge, notion, humour, impulse, inclination, caprice • *His interest was just a passing fancy.*
2 = delusion, dream, vision, fantasy, nightmare, daydream, chimera, phantasm • *His book is a bold surrealist mixture of fact and fancy.*
▸ AS A VERB **1 = wish for**, want, desire, would like, hope for, dream of, relish, long for, crave, be attracted to, yearn for, thirst for, hanker after, have a yen for • *I just fancied a drink.*
2 = be attracted to, find attractive, desire, lust after, like, prefer, favour, take to, go for, be captivated by, have an eye for, have a thing about *(informal)*, have eyes for, take a liking to • *I think he thinks I fancy him.*
3 = suppose, think, believe, imagine, guess *(informal, chiefly U.S. & Canad.)*, reckon, conceive, infer, conjecture, surmise, think likely, be inclined to think • *She fancied he was trying to hide a smile.*
▸ IN PHRASES: **fancy yourself = think you are God's gift**, have a high opinion of yourself, think you are the cat's whiskers • *She really fancies herself in that new outfit.*
take a fancy to something *or* **someone = start liking**, like, want, be fond of, hanker after, have a partiality for • *Sylvia took quite a fancy to him.*

QUOTATIONS
Ever let the fancy roam,
Pleasure never is at home
[John Keats *Fancy*]
Tell me where is fancy bred,
Or in the heart or in the head?
[William Shakespeare *The Merchant of Venice*]

fanfare = trumpet call, flourish, trump *(archaic)*, tucket *(archaic)*, fanfaronade • *a fanfare of trumpets*

fang = tooth, tusk • *the cobra's venomous fangs*

fantasize *or* **fantasise = daydream**, imagine, invent, romance, envision, hallucinate, see visions, live in a dream world, build castles in the air, give free rein to the imagination • *I fantasized about writing music.*

fantastic 1 = wonderful, great, excellent, very good, mean *(slang)*, topping *(Brit. slang)*, cracking *(Brit. informal)*, crucial *(slang)*, smashing *(informal)*, superb, tremendous *(informal)*,

magnificent, marvellous, terrific *(informal)*, sensational *(informal)*, mega *(slang)*, awesome *(slang)*, dope *(slang)*, world-class, first-rate, def *(slang)*, brill *(informal)*, out of this world *(informal)*, boffo *(slang)*, the dog's bollocks *(taboo slang)*, jim-dandy *(slang)*, bitchin' *(U.S. slang)*, chillin' *(U.S. slang)*, booshit *(Austral. slang)*, exo *(Austral. slang)*, sik *(Austral. slang)*, rad *(informal)*, phat *(slang)*, schmick *(Austral. informal)*, beaut *(informal)*, barrie *(Scot. slang)*, belting *(Brit. slang)*, pearler *(Austral. slang)* • *I have a fantastic social life.*
OPPOSITES: common, poor, ordinary
2 = **enormous**, great, huge, vast, severe, extreme, overwhelming, tremendous, immense, fuck-off *(offensive taboo slang)* • *fantastic amounts of money*
3 = **strange**, bizarre, weird, exotic, peculiar, imaginative, queer, grotesque, quaint, unreal, fanciful, outlandish, whimsical, freakish, chimerical, phantasmagorical • *outlandish and fantastic images*
4 = **implausible**, unlikely, incredible, absurd, irrational, preposterous, capricious, cock-and-bull *(informal)*, cockamamie *(slang, chiefly U.S.)*, mad • *He had cooked up some fantastic story about how the ring had come into his possession.*

fantasy *or* **phantasy** 1 = **daydream**, dream, wish, fancy, delusion, reverie, flight of fancy, pipe dream • *Everyone's had a fantasy about winning the lottery*
2 = **fairy tale**, story, romance, fairy story, folk tale • *The film is more a fantasy than a horror story.*
3 = **imagination**, fancy, invention, creativity, originality • *a world of imagination and fantasy*

far AS AN ADVERB 1 = **a long way**, miles, deep, a good way, afar, a great distance • *They came from far away.*
2 = **much**, greatly, very much, extremely, significantly, considerably, decidedly, markedly, incomparably • *He was a far better cook than Amy.*
▸ AS AN ADJECTIVE 1 = **opposite**, farther, farthest, furthest, facing, further • *He wandered to the far end of the room.*
2 *often with* **off** = **remote**, distant, far-flung, faraway, long, removed, out-of-the-way, far-off, far-removed, outlying, off the beaten track • *people in far off lands*
OPPOSITES: close, near, bordering
▸ IN PHRASES: **by far** *or* **far and away** = **very much**, easily, immeasurably, by a long way, incomparably, to a great degree, by a long shot, by a long chalk *(informal)*, by a great amount • *by far the most successful*
far and wide = **extensively**, everywhere, worldwide, far and near, widely, broadly, in all places, in every nook and cranny, here, there and everywhere • *His fame spread far and wide.*
far from = **not at all**, not, by no means, absolutely not • *She is far from happy.*
so far 1 = **up to a point**, to a certain extent, to a limited extent • *Their loyalty only went so far.*
2 = **up to now**, to date, until now, thus far, up to the present • *So far, they have had no success.*

faraway 1 = **distant**, far, remote, far-off, far-removed, far-flung, outlying, beyond the horizon • *They had just returned from faraway places.*
2 = **dreamy**, lost, distant, abstracted, vague, absent • *She smiled with a faraway look in her eyes.*

farce 1 = **comedy**, satire, slapstick, burlesque, buffoonery, broad comedy • *The plot often borders on farce.*
2 = **mockery**, joke, nonsense, parody, shambles, sham, absurdity, malarkey, travesty, ridiculousness • *The election was a farce, as only 22% of voters cast their ballots.*

farcical 1 = **ludicrous**, ridiculous, diverting, absurd, preposterous, laughable, nonsensical, derisory, risible • *a farcical nine months' jail sentence*
2 = **comic**, funny, amusing, slapstick, droll, custard-pie • *from farcical humour to deepest tragedy*

fare AS A NOUN 1 = **charge**, price, ticket price, transport cost, ticket money, passage money • *He could barely afford the railway fare.*
2 = **food**, meals, diet, provisions, board, commons, table, feed, menu, rations, tack *(informal)*, kai *(N.Z. informal)*, nourishment, sustenance, victuals, nosebag *(slang)*, nutriment, vittles *(obsolete or dialect)*, eatables • *traditional Portuguese fare*
3 = **passenger**, customer, pick-up *(informal)*, traveller • *The taxi driver picked up a fare.*
▸ AS A VERB 1 = **get on**, do, manage, make out, prosper, get along • *He was not faring well.*
2 *used impersonally* = **happen**, go, turn out, proceed, pan out *(informal)* • *The show fared quite well.*

farewell AS AN INTERJECTION = **goodbye**, bye *(informal)*, so long, see you, take care, good morning, bye-bye *(informal)*, good day, all the best, good night, good evening, good afternoon, see you later, ciao *(Italian)*, have a nice day *(U.S.)*, adieu *(French)*, au revoir *(French)*, be seeing you, auf Wiedersehen *(German)*, adios *(Spanish)*, mind how you go, haere ra *(N.Z.)* • *'Farewell, lad, and may we meet again soon.'*
▸ AS A NOUN = **goodbye**, parting, departure, leave-taking, adieu, valediction, sendoff *(informal)*, adieux *or* adieus • *a touching farewell*

far-fetched = **unconvincing**, unlikely, strained, fantastic, incredible, doubtful, unbelievable, dubious, unrealistic, improbable, unnatural, preposterous, implausible, hard to swallow *(informal)*, cock-and-bull *(informal)* • *unrealistic characters in far-fetched storylines*
OPPOSITES: possible, likely, believable

farm AS A NOUN = **smallholding**, holding, ranch *(chiefly U.S. & Canad.)*, farmstead, land, station *(Austral. & N.Z.)*, acres, vineyard, plantation, croft *(Scot.)*, grange, homestead, acreage • *We have a small farm.*
▸ AS A VERB = **cultivate**, work, plant, operate, till the soil, grow crops on, bring under cultivation, keep animals on, practise husbandry • *They had farmed the same land for generations.*
▸ IN PHRASES: **farm something out** = **contract out**, hire out, subcontract, outsource • *They farmed out work to contractors.*

farmer = **agriculturist**, yeoman, smallholder, crofter *(Scot.)*, grazier, agriculturalist, rancher, agronomist, husbandman, cockie *or* cocky *(Austral. & N.Z. informal)* • *He was a simple farmer scratching a living from the soil.*

farming = **agriculture**, cultivation, husbandry, land management, agronomy, tilling • *He comes from a farming background.*

far-out = **strange**, wild, unusual, bizarre, weird, avant-garde, unconventional, off-the-wall *(slang)*, outlandish, outré, advanced • *a weird, far-out surrealist*

farrago = **hotchpotch**, mixture, jumble, medley, hash, mixed bag, potpourri, mélange *(French)*, miscellany, mishmash, hodgepodge, salmagundi, gallimaufry • *an intolerable farrago of rubbish*

far-reaching = **extensive**, important, significant, sweeping, broad, widespread, pervasive, momentous • *far-reaching reforms on human rights*

far-sighted = **prudent**, acute, wise, cautious, sage, shrewd, discerning, canny, provident, judicious, prescient, far-seeing, politic • *The decision was described as a far-sighted, significant step.*

fascinate = **entrance**, delight, charm, absorb, intrigue, enchant, rivet, captivate, enthral, beguile, allure, bewitch, ravish, transfix, mesmerize, hypnotize, engross, enrapture, interest greatly, enamour, hold spellbound, spellbind, infatuate • *She fascinated him, on and off stage.*
OPPOSITES: bore, disgust, irritate

fascinated = **entranced**, charmed, absorbed, very

interested, captivated, hooked on, enthralled, beguiled, smitten, bewitched, engrossed, spellbound, infatuated, hypnotized, under a spell • *I sat on the stairs and watched, fascinated.*

fascinating = **captivating**, engaging, gripping, compelling, intriguing, very interesting, irresistible, enticing, enchanting, seductive, riveting, alluring, bewitching, ravishing, engrossing • *Her stories were fascinating.*
OPPOSITES: boring, dull, uninteresting

fascination 1 = **obsession**, interest, complex, enthusiasm, hang-up (*informal*), preoccupation, mania, fetish, fixation, infatuation, ruling passion, idée fixe (*French*), bee in your bonnet (*informal*), thing (*informal*) • *I've had a lifelong fascination with the sea.*
2 = **attraction**, pull, spell, magic, charm, lure, glamour, allure, magnetism, enchantment, sorcery • *She had a charm and fascination all of her own.*

Fascism *sometimes not cap.* = **authoritarianism**, dictatorship, totalitarianism, despotism, autocracy, absolutism, Hitlerism • *The military threat of Fascism had been eliminated.*

Fascist **AS AN ADJECTIVE** *sometimes not cap.* = **totalitarian**, authoritarian, one-party, oppressive, autocratic, dictatorial, undemocratic, monolithic, despotic, tyrannous • *the threatening nature of fascist ideology*
▸ **AS A NOUN** = **Nazi**, dictator, authoritarian, tyrant, Big Brother, totalitarian, control freak, despot, autocrat, absolutist • *He was a fascist and very anti-Semitic.*

fashion **AS A NOUN** 1 = **clothes**, fashion business, clothes industry • *She longed for a career in fashion.*
2 = **style**, look, trend, rage, custom, convention, mode, vogue, usage, craze, fad, latest style, prevailing taste, latest • *I wore short skirts, as was the fashion.*
3 = **method**, way, style, approach, manner, mode • *We must go about this in an organised fashion.*
▸ **AS A VERB** 1 = **make**, shape, cast, construct, work, form, create, design, manufacture, forge, mould, contrive, fabricate • *The desk was fashioned out of oak.*
2 = **fit**, adapt, tailor, suit, adjust, accommodate • *dresses fashioned to hide the bulges*
▸ **IN PHRASES: after a fashion** = **to some extent**, somehow, in a way, moderately, to a certain extent, to a degree, somehow or other, in a manner of speaking • *He knew the way, after a fashion.*
in fashion = **popular**, trendy (*Brit. informal*), all the rage, hip (*slang*), in (*informal*), latest, the new, happening (*informal*), current, modern, cool (*slang*), with it (*informal*), usual, smart, prevailing, fashionable, stylish, chic, up-to-date, customary, genteel, in vogue, up-to-the-minute, modish, du jour (*French*), à la mode, voguish (*informal*), trendsetting, all the go (*informal*), culty, schmick (*Austral. informal*), funky • *That sort of dress is in fashion again.*
out of fashion = **unfashionable**, out, old-fashioned, dated, unpopular, obsolete, out of date, out of fashion, outmoded, passé, old hat, behind the times, unhip (*slang*), out of the ark (*informal*), square (*informal*) • *Marriage seems to be out of fashion.*

QUOTATIONS
Only the minute and the future are interesting in fashion – it exists to be destroyed
[Karl Lagerfeld]
Fashion is made to become unfashionable
[Coco Chanel]

fashionable = **popular**, in fashion, trendy (*Brit. informal*), cool (*slang*), in (*informal*), latest, the new, happening (*informal*), current, modern, with it (*informal*), usual, smart, hip (*slang*), prevailing, stylish, chic, up-to-date, customary, genteel, in vogue, all the rage, up-to-the-minute, modish, du jour (*French*), à la mode, voguish (*informal*), trendsetting, all the go (*informal*), culty, schmick (*Austral. informal*), funky • *It became fashionable to eat certain foods.*
OPPOSITES: old-fashioned, dated, unfashionable

fast[1] **AS AN ADJECTIVE** 1 = **quick**, flying, winged, rapid, fleet, hurried, accelerated, swift, speedy, brisk, hasty, nimble, mercurial, sprightly, nippy (*Brit. informal*) • *She walked at a fast pace.*
OPPOSITES: slow, leisurely, plodding
2 = **fixed**, firm, sound, stuck, secure, tight, jammed, fortified, fastened, impregnable, immovable • *He held the gate fast.*
OPPOSITES: weak, unstable, wavering
3 = **indelible**, lasting, permanent • *The fabric was ironed to make the colours fast.*
4 = **dissipated**, wild, exciting, loose, extravagant, reckless, immoral, promiscuous, giddy, self-indulgent, wanton, profligate, impure, intemperate, dissolute, rakish, licentious, gadabout (*informal*) • *He experimented with drugs and the fast life.*
5 = **close**, lasting, firm, permanent, constant, devoted, loyal, faithful, stalwart, staunch, steadfast, unwavering • *The men had always been fast friends.*
▸ **AS AN ADVERB** 1 = **quickly**, rapidly, swiftly, hastily, hurriedly, speedily, presto, apace, in haste, like a shot (*informal*), at full speed, hell for leather (*informal*), like lightning, hotfoot, like a flash, at a rate of knots, like the clappers (*Brit. informal*), like a bat out of hell (*slang*), pdq (*slang*), like nobody's business (*informal*), posthaste, like greased lightning (*informal*), with all haste • *He drives terrifically fast.*
OPPOSITES: slowly, gradually, steadily
2 = **firmly**, staunchly, resolutely, steadfastly, determinedly, unwaveringly, unchangeably • *We can only try to hold fast to our principles.*
3 = **securely**, firmly, tightly, fixedly • *She held fast to the stair rail.*
4 = **fixedly**, firmly, soundly, deeply, securely, tightly • *The tanker is stuck fast on the rocks.*
5 = **recklessly**, wildly, loosely, extravagantly, promiscuously, rakishly, intemperately • *He lived fast and died young.*
6 = **sound**, soundly, deeply • *When he went to bed, she was already fast asleep.*

fast[2] **AS A VERB** = **go hungry**, abstain, go without food, deny yourself, practise abstention, refrain from food *or* eating • *She had fasted to lose weight.*
▸ **AS A NOUN** = **fasting**, diet, abstinence • *The fast is broken, traditionally with dates and water.*

fasten 1 = **secure**, close, lock, chain, seal, bolt, do up • *He fastened the door behind him.*
2 = **tie**, bind, lace, tie up • *The dress fastens down the back.*
3 = **fix**, join, link, connect, grip, attach, anchor, affix, make firm, make fast • *Use screws to fasten the shelf to the wall.*
4 *often with* **on** *or* **upon** = **concentrate**, focus, fix • *Her thoughts fastened on one event.*
5 = **direct**, aim, focus, fix, concentrate, bend, rivet • *They fastened their gaze on the table and did not look up.*

fastening = **tie**, union, coupling, link, linking, bond, joint, binding, connection, attachment, junction, zip, fusion, clasp, concatenation, ligature, affixation • *His fingers found the fastening and opened it.*

fastidious = **particular**, meticulous, fussy, overdelicate, difficult, nice, critical, discriminating, dainty, squeamish, choosy, picky (*informal*), hard to please, finicky, punctilious, pernickety, hypercritical, overnice, nit-picky (*informal*) • *He was fastidious about his appearance.*
OPPOSITES: disorderly, casual, careless

fat **AS A NOUN** 1 = **fatness**, flesh, bulk, obesity, cellulite, weight problem, flab, blubber, paunch, fatty tissue, adipose tissue, corpulence, beef (*informal*) • *ways of reducing body fat*

2 = oil, cream, cheese, butter, grease, margarine, lard, cooking oil, suet • *Use as little fat as possible when cooking.*
▸ **AS AN ADJECTIVE** **1 = overweight**, large, heavy, plump, gross, stout, obese, fleshy, beefy *(informal)*, tubby, portly, roly-poly, rotund, podgy, corpulent, elephantine, broad in the beam *(informal)*, solid • *I can eat what I like without getting fat.*
OPPOSITES: thin, spare, lean
2 = thick, solid, substantial, bulky • *It was a big, fat book.*
3 = large, rich, substantial, thriving, flourishing, profitable, productive, lucrative, fertile, lush, prosperous, affluent, fruitful, cushy *(slang)*, jammy *(Brit. slang)*, remunerative • *They are set to make a fat profit.*
OPPOSITES: poor, scarce, scanty
4 = fatty, greasy, lipid, adipose, oleaginous, suety, oily • *Most heart cases are the better for cutting out fat meat.*
OPPOSITES: lean
▸ **IN PHRASES:** **a fat chance = no chance**, (a) slim chance, very little chance, not much chance • *You've got a fat chance of getting there on time.*
▸ **RELATED ADJECTIVES:** adipose, lipose, stearic

QUOTATIONS
I'm fat, but I'm thin inside. Has it ever struck you that there's a thin man inside every fat man, just as they say there's a statue inside every block of stone?
[George Orwell *Coming Up for Air*]
Some people are born to fatness. Others have to get there
[Les Murray]
I'm built for comfort, I ain't built for speed
[Willie Dixon *Built for Comfort*]
Fat is a social disease, and fat is a feminist issue
[Susie Orbach *Fat is a Feminist Issue*]

fatal **1 = disastrous**, devastating, crippling, lethal, catastrophic, ruinous, calamitous, baleful, baneful • *It dealt a fatal blow to his chances.*
OPPOSITES: minor, inconsequential
2 = decisive, final, determining, critical, crucial, fateful • *putting off that fatal moment*
3 = lethal, deadly, mortal, causing death, final, killing, terminal, destructive, malignant, incurable, pernicious • *She had suffered a fatal heart attack.*
OPPOSITES: beneficial, harmless, benign

fatalism **= resignation**, acceptance, passivity, determinism, stoicism, necessitarianism, predestinarianism • *Complacent fatalism has become fashionable.*

fatality **= casualty**, death, loss, victim • *the first fatality since the ceasefire began*

fate **1 = destiny**, chance, fortune, luck, the stars, weird *(archaic)*, providence, nemesis, kismet, predestination, divine will • *I see no use quarrelling with fate.*
2 = fortune, destiny, lot, portion, cup, horoscope • *No man chooses his fate.*
3 = outcome, future, destiny, end, issue, upshot • *What will be the fate of the elections?*
4 = downfall, end, death, ruin, destruction, doom, demise • *This new proposal seems doomed to the same fate.*

QUOTATIONS
Fate keeps on happening
[Anita Loos *Gentlemen Prefer Blondes*]
Fate is not an eagle, it creeps like a rat
[Elizabeth Bowen *The House in Paris*]
... to deny fate is arrogance, to declare that we are the sole shapers of our existence is madness
[Oriana Fallaci *A Man*]
Fate and character are the same concept
[Novalis *Heinrich von Ofterdingen*]

PROVERBS
Man proposes, God disposes
What must be, must be (Italian, Che sera, sera)

fated **= destined**, doomed, predestined, preordained, foreordained, pre-elected • *I was fated never to get there.*

fateful **1 = crucial**, important, significant, critical, decisive, momentous, portentous • *What changed for him in that fateful year?*
OPPOSITES: ordinary, insignificant, unimportant
2 = disastrous, fatal, deadly, destructive, lethal, ominous, ruinous • *He had sailed on his third and fateful voyage.*

Fates, the **= the Three Sisters**, Providence, the Norns *(Norse myth)*, the Weird Sisters, the Parcae *(Roman myth)*, the Moirai • *The Fates willed it otherwise.*

THE FATES

Atropos	Clotho	Lachesis

father **AS A NOUN** **1 = daddy** *(informal)*, dad *(informal)*, male parent, patriarch, pop *(U.S. informal)*, governor *(informal)*, old man *(Brit. informal)*, pa *(informal)*, old boy *(informal)*, papa *(old-fashioned informal)*, sire, pater, biological father, foster father, begetter, paterfamilias, birth father • *He was a good father to my children.*
2 = founder, author, maker, architect, creator, inventor, originator, prime mover, initiator • *He was the father of modern photography.*
3 *often plural* **= forefather**, predecessor, ancestor, forebear, progenitor, tupuna *or* tipuna *(N.Z.)* • *land of my fathers*
4 *usually plural* **= leader**, senator, elder, patron, patriarch, guiding light, city father, kaumatua *(N.Z.)* • *City fathers tried to revive the town's economy.*
▸ **AS A VERB** **1 = sire**, parent, conceive, bring to life, beget, procreate, bring into being, give life to, get • *He fathered at least three children.*
2 = originate, found, create, establish, author, institute, invent, engender • *He fathered the modern computer.*
▸ **RELATED ADJECTIVE:** paternal

QUOTATIONS
Honour thy father and thy mother
[*Bible: Exodus*]
'Tis happy for him, that his father was before him
[Jonathan Swift *Polite Conversation*]
No man is responsible for his father. That is entirely his mother's affair
[Margaret Turnbull *Alabaster Lamps*]
No man can know who was his father
[Homer *Odyssey*]
It's all any reasonable child can expect if the dad is present at the conception
[Joe Orton *Entertaining Mr. Sloane*]
It is a wise father that knows his own child
[William Shakespeare *The Merchant of Venice*]

PROVERBS
Like father like son

Father **1 = priest**, minister, vicar, parson, pastor, cleric, churchman, padre *(informal)*, confessor, abbé, curé, man of God • *The prior, Father Alessandro, came over to talk to them.*
2 = God, Lord, Creator, Almighty God, living God, Holy One, eternal God • *Our Father in Heaven*

fatherland **= homeland**, motherland, old country, native land, land of your birth, land of your fathers, whenua *(N.Z.)*, Godzone *(Austral. informal)* • *They served the fatherland in its hour of need.*

fatherly **= paternal**, kind, kindly, tender, protective, supportive, benign, affectionate, indulgent, patriarchal, benevolent, forbearing • *He took my arm in a fatherly way.*

fathom **= understand**, grasp, comprehend, interpret, get to the bottom of • *I couldn't fathom what he was talking about.*

fathomless = **profound**, deep, impenetrable, abysmal, bottomless, unfathomable, immeasurable, unplumbed, incomprehensible • *the fathomless space of the universe*

fatigue AS A NOUN = **tiredness**, lethargy, weariness, ennui, heaviness, debility, languor, listlessness, overtiredness • *Those affected suffer extreme fatigue.*
OPPOSITES: go, life, freshness
▸ AS A PLURAL NOUN = **khakis**, military uniform, combat fatigues, military clothes • *He was wearing combat fatigues.*
▸ AS A VERB = **tire**, exhaust, weaken, weary, drain, fag (out) *(informal)*, whack *(Brit. informal)*, wear out, jade, take it out of *(informal)*, poop *(informal)*, tire out, knacker *(slang)*, drain of energy, overtire • *It fatigues me to list them all.*
OPPOSITES: rest, relieve, refresh
▸ RELATED PHOBIA: kopophobia

fatigued = **tired**, exhausted, weary, tired out, bushed *(informal)*, wasted, all in *(slang)*, fagged (out) *(informal)*, whacked *(Brit. informal)*, jaded, knackered *(slang)*, clapped out *(Austral. & N.Z. informal)*, overtired, zonked *(slang)*, dead beat *(informal)*, jiggered *(informal)*, on your last legs, creamcrackered *(Brit. informal)* • *How long have you been feeling fatigued?*

fatness = **obesity**, corpulence, podginess, flab, size, weight, beef *(informal)*, flesh, overweight, girth, weight problem, heaviness, grossness, embonpoint *(French)*, rotundity, fleshiness, stoutness, bulkiness • *Body weight alone says little about body fatness.*

fatten 1 = **grow fat**, spread, expand, swell, thrive, broaden, thicken, put on weight, gain weight, coarsen, become fat, become fatter • *The creature continued to grow and fatten.*
2 = **feed up**, feed, stuff, build up, cram, nourish, distend, bloat, overfeed • *They fattened up ducks and geese.*

fatty = **greasy**, fat, creamy, oily, adipose, oleaginous, suety, rich • *fatty acids*

fatuous = **foolish**, stupid, silly, dull, absurd, dense, ludicrous, lunatic, mindless, idiotic, vacuous, inane, witless, puerile, moronic, brainless, asinine, weak-minded, dumb-ass *(slang)* • *That is not a fatuous argument, it has to be taken seriously.*

faucet = **tap**, spout, spigot, stopcock, valve

fault AS A NOUN 1 = **responsibility**, liability, guilt, accountability, culpability • *It was all my fault we quarrelled.*
2 = **mistake**, slip, error, offence, blunder, lapse, negligence, omission, boob *(Brit. slang)*, oversight, slip-up, indiscretion, inaccuracy, howler *(informal)*, glitch *(informal)*, error of judgment, boo-boo *(informal)*, barry *or* Barry Crocker *(Austral. slang)* • *It was a genuine fault.*
3 = **failing**, lack, weakness, defect, deficiency, flaw, drawback, shortcoming, snag, blemish, imperfection, Achilles heel, weak point, infirmity, demerit • *His manners always made her blind to his faults.*
OPPOSITES: credit, strength, asset
4 = **misdeed**, failing, wrong, offence, sin, lapse, misconduct, wrongdoing, trespass, frailty, misdemeanour, delinquency, transgression, peccadillo • *Hypocrisy is one fault of which he cannot be accused.*
▸ AS A VERB = **criticize**, blame, complain, condemn, moan about, censure, hold (someone) responsible, hold (someone) accountable, find fault with, call to account, impugn, find lacking, hold (someone) to blame • *You can't fault them for lack of invention.*
▸ IN PHRASES: **at fault** = **guilty**, responsible, to blame, accountable, in the wrong, culpable, answerable, blamable • *He didn't accept that he was at fault.*
find fault with something *or* **someone** = **criticize**, complain about, whinge about *(informal)*, whine about *(informal)*, flame *(informal)*, quibble, diss *(slang, chiefly U.S.)*, carp at, take to task, pick holes in, grouse about *(informal)*, haul over the coals *(informal)*, pull to pieces, nit-pick *(informal)* • *I do tend to find fault with everybody.*
to a fault = **excessively**, overly *(U.S.)*, unduly, ridiculously, in the extreme, needlessly, out of all proportion, preposterously, overmuch, immoderately • *He was generous to a fault.*

QUOTATIONS
The fault, dear Brutus, is not in our stars,
But in ourselves
[William Shakespeare *Julius Caesar*]

faultless = **flawless**, model, perfect, classic, correct, accurate, faithful, impeccable, exemplary, foolproof, unblemished • *His English was faultless.*

faulty 1 = **defective**, damaged, not working, malfunctioning, broken, bad, flawed, impaired, imperfect, blemished, out of order, on the blink • *They will repair the faulty equipment.*
2 = **incorrect**, wrong, flawed, inaccurate, bad, weak, invalid, erroneous, unsound, imprecise, fallacious • *Their interpretation was faulty.*

fauna = **animal lfe**, animals, creatures
▹ *See panel* **National and state fauna**

faux pas = **gaffe**, blunder, indiscretion, impropriety, bloomer *(Brit. informal)*, boob *(Brit. slang)*, clanger *(informal)*, solecism, breach of etiquette, gaucherie • *He made an embarrassing faux pas.*

favour *or (U.S.)* **favor** AS A NOUN 1 = **approval**, grace, esteem, goodwill, kindness, friendliness, commendation, partiality, approbation, kind regard • *They viewed him with favour.*
OPPOSITES: disapproval, animosity, antipathy
2 = **favouritism**, preference, bias, nepotism, preferential treatment, partisanship, jobs for the boys *(informal)*, partiality, one-sidedness • *employers to show favour to women and racial minorities*
3 = **support**, backing, aid, championship, promotion, assistance, patronage, espousal, good opinion • *He wanted to win the favour of the voters.*
4 = **good turn**, service, benefit, courtesy, kindness, indulgence, boon, good deed, kind act, obligement *(Scot. or archaic)* • *I've come to ask for a favour.*
OPPOSITES: wrong, injury, harm
5 = **memento**, present, gift, token, souvenir, keepsake, love-token • *place cards and wedding favours*
▸ AS A VERB 1 = **prefer**, opt for, like better, incline towards, choose, pick, desire, select, elect, adopt, go for, fancy, single out, plump for, be partial to • *She favours community activism over legislation.*
OPPOSITES: dislike, object to, disapprove
2 = **indulge**, reward, spoil, esteem, side with, pamper, befriend, be partial to, smile upon, pull strings for *(informal)*, have in your good books, treat with partiality, value • *There was good reason for favouring him.*
3 = **support**, like, back, choose, champion, encourage, approve, fancy, advocate, opt for, subscribe to, commend, stand up for, espouse, be in favour of, countenance, patronize • *He favours greater protection of the environment.*
OPPOSITES: oppose, thwart
4 = **help**, benefit, aid, advance, promote, assist, accommodate, facilitate, abet, succour, do a kindness to • *Circumstances favoured them.*
5 = **oblige**, please, honour, accommodate, benefit • *The beautiful girls would favour me with a look.*
▸ IN PHRASES: **in favour of** = **for**, backing, supporting, behind, pro, all for *(informal)*, on the side of, right behind • *They were in favour of the decision.*

QUOTATIONS
One good turn deserves another
[John Fletcher & Philip Massinger *The Little French Lawyer*]

favourable *or (U.S.)* **favorable** 1 = **positive**, kind, understanding, encouraging, welcoming, friendly, approving, praising, reassuring, enthusiastic, sympathetic,

NATIONAL AND STATE FAUNA

Creature	Nation or State	Creature	Nation or State
Abyssinian lion	Ethiopia	koala	Queensland
auroch	Moldova	kookaburra	New South Wales
Baird's tapir	Belize	kouprey	Cambodia
bald eagle	United States	Leadbeater's possum	Victoria
Barbary macaque	Gibraltar	leafy sea dragon	South Australia
barn swallow	Estonia	lion	Albania, Banat (Romania), Bulgaria, England, Luxembourg, Netherlands, Sri Lanka, *and* United Kingdom
bear	Russia	llama	Bolivia
beaver	Canada	lynx	Romania
bird of paradise	Papua New Guinea	macaw	Brazil
black swan	Western Australia	markhor	Pakistan
blue groper	New South Wales	merlion	Singapore
blue rock thrush	Malta	moose *or* elk	Norway
brolga	Queensland	mute swan	Denmark
brown bear	Finland *and* Kosovo	numbat	Western Australia
bull	Spain	oryx	Namibia
bulldog	England *and* United Kingdom	ostrich	Grenada
Canje pheasant	Guyana	peafowl	India
carabao	Philippines	piping shrike	South Australia
carp	Japan	platypus	New South Wales
cheetah	Kenya	quetzal	Guatemala
clownfish	Queensland	raven	Muntenia (Romania)
cobra	Israel	red kangaroo	Northern Territory
cougar	Argentina	ring-tailed lemur	Madagascar
cow	Nepal	sheep	Greece
crane	China	springbok	South Africa
dodo	Mauritius	stag	Ireland
dolphin	Dobrogea (Romania)	Steppe eagle	Egypt
dragon	Albania, China, *and* Wales	takin	Bhutan
eagle	Albania, Armenia, Germany, Kosovo, Northern Territory, *and* Transylvania	Tasmanian devil	Tasmania
elephant	Thailand	turpial	Venezuela
falcon	Iceland	unicorn	Scotland
Gallic rooster	France	vervet monkey	St Kitts and Nevis
gang-gang cockatoo	Australian Capital Territory	vicuna	Peru
garuda	Indonesia	water buffalo	Vietnam
giant panda	China	wedge-tailed eagle	Northern Territory
golden eagle	Mexico	weedy sea dragon	Victoria
grey-crowned crane	Uganda	white-tailed deer	Honduras
hairy-nosed wombat	South Australia	white-tailed eagle	Poland
helmeted honeyeater	Victoria	wisent *or* European bison	Belarus
horse	Canada	wolf	Italy, Kosovo, *and* Turkey
jaguar	Guyana	zebra	Botswana
kelb tal-fenek *or* pharoah hound	Malta		
kiwi	New Zealand		

benign, commending, complimentary, agreeable, amicable, well-disposed, commendatory • *He made favourable comments about her work.*
OPPOSITES: disapproving, unfriendly, unfavourable
2 = affirmative, agreeing, confirming, positive, assenting, corroborative • *He expects a favourable reply.*
3 = advantageous, timely, good, promising, fit, encouraging, fair, appropriate, suitable, helpful, hopeful, convenient, beneficial, auspicious, opportune, propitious • *favourable weather conditions*
OPPOSITES: useless, unhelpful, disadvantageous

favourably *or (U.S.)* **favorably** **1 = positively**, well, enthusiastically, helpfully, graciously, approvingly, agreeably, with approval, without prejudice, genially, with approbation, in a kindly manner, with cordiality • *He responded favourably to my suggestions.*
2 = advantageously, well, fortunately, conveniently, profitably, to your advantage, auspiciously, opportunely • *They are far more favourably placed than their opponents.*

favoured **1 = preferred**, special, chosen, favourite, selected, recommended, pet, of choice, singled out, best-liked, fave *(informal)* • *The favoured candidate will emerge soon.*
2 = privileged, advantaged, lucky, blessed, elite, fortunate, jammy *(Brit. slang)* • *They think of us as favoured beings.*

favourite *or (U.S.)* **favorite** **AS AN ADJECTIVE = preferred**, favoured, best-loved, most-liked, special, choice, dearest, pet, esteemed, of choice, fave *(informal)* • *Her favourite writer is Charles Dickens.*
▸ **AS A NOUN 1 = darling**, pet, preference, blue-eyed boy *(informal)*, pick, choice, dear, beloved, idol, fave *(informal)*, teacher's pet, the apple of your eye • *He was a favourite of the King.*
2 = front runner • *The favourite is expected to be the local horse.*

favouritism *or (U.S.)* **favoritism** **= bias**, preference,

nepotism, preferential treatment, partisanship, jobs for the boys *(informal)*, partiality, one-sidedness • *Accusations of political favouritism abound.*
OPPOSITES: equity, equality, impartiality

fawn[1] = **beige**, neutral, buff, yellowish-brown, greyish-brown • *She put on a light fawn coat.*
▷ *See panel* **Shades of brown**

fawn[2] *usually with* **on** *or* **upon** = **ingratiate yourself**, court, flatter, pander to, creep, crawl, kneel, cringe, grovel, curry favour, toady, pay court, kowtow, brown-nose *(taboo slang)*, bow and scrape, dance attendance, truckle, kiss ass *(U.S. & Canad. taboo slang)*, be obsequious, be servile, lick (someone's) boots, lick (someone's) arse *(taboo slang)* • *People fawn on you when you're famous.*

fawning = **obsequious**, crawling, flattering, cringing, abject, grovelling, prostrate, deferential, sycophantic, servile, slavish, bowing and scraping, bootlicking *(informal)* • *flanked on all sides by fawning minions*

fealty = **loyalty**, faith, submission, devotion, allegiance, fidelity, homage, faithfulness, obeisance, troth *(archaic)* • *pledging oaths of homage and fealty*

fear **AS A NOUN** **1** = **dread**, horror, panic, terror, dismay, awe, fright, tremors, qualms, consternation, alarm, trepidation, timidity, fearfulness, blue funk *(informal)*, apprehensiveness, cravenness • *I shivered with fear at the sound of gunfire.*
2 = **bugbear**, bête noire, horror, nightmare, anxiety, terror, dread, spectre, phobia, bogey, thing *(informal)* • *Flying was his greatest fear.*
3 = **anxiety**, concern, worry, doubt, nerves *(informal)*, distress, suspicion, willies *(informal)*, creeps *(informal)*, butterflies *(informal)*, funk *(informal)*, angst, unease, apprehension, misgiving(s), nervousness, agitation, foreboding(s), uneasiness, solicitude, blue funk *(informal)*, heebie-jeebies *(informal)*, collywobbles *(informal)*, disquietude • *His fear might be groundless.*
4 = **possibility**, likelihood • *There was no fear of her weeping.*
5 = **awe**, wonder, respect, worship, dread, reverence, veneration • *There is no fear of God before their eyes.*
▸ **AS A VERB** **1** = **be afraid of**, dread, be scared of, be frightened of, shudder at, be fearful of, be apprehensive about, tremble at, be terrified by, have a horror of, take fright at, have a phobia about, have qualms about, live in dread of, be in a blue funk about *(informal)*, have butterflies in your stomach about *(informal)*, shake in your shoes about • *If people fear you they respect you.*
2 = **worry**, suspect, anticipate, be afraid, expect, foresee, apprehend • *She feared she was coming down with flu.*
3 = **revere**, respect, reverence, venerate, stand in awe of • *They feared God in a way which most modern men can hardly imagine.*
4 = **regret**, feel, suspect, have a feeling, have a hunch, have a sneaking suspicion, have a funny feeling • *I fear that a land war now looks probable.*
▸ **IN PHRASES:** **fear for something** *or* **someone** = **worry about**, be concerned about, be anxious about, tremble for, be distressed about, feel concern for, be disquieted over • *He fled, saying he feared for his life.*
▸ **RELATED PHOBIA:** phobophobia

QUOTATIONS
Let me assert my firm belief that the only thing we have to fear is fear itself
[Franklin D. Roosevelt *Inaugural Address*]
I cannot do this. This is too much for me. I shall ruin myself if I take this risk. I cannot take the leap, it's impossible. All of me will be gone if I do this and I cling to myself
[J.N. Figgis]
Perfect love casteth out fear
[*Bible: 1 John*]
Perfect fear casteth out love
[Cyril Connolly]

fearful **1** = **scared**, afraid, alarmed, frightened, nervous, terrified, apprehensive, petrified, jittery *(informal)* • *They were fearful that the fighting might spread.*
OPPOSITES: confident, undaunted, unafraid
2 = **timid**, afraid, frightened, scared, alarmed, wired *(slang)*, nervous, anxious, shrinking, tense, intimidated, uneasy, neurotic, hesitant, apprehensive, jittery *(informal)*, panicky, nervy *(Brit. informal)*, diffident, jumpy, timorous, pusillanimous, faint-hearted • *I had often been very fearful and isolated.*
OPPOSITES: game *(informal)*, confident, brave
3 = **frightful**, shocking, terrible, awful, distressing, appalling, horrible, grim, dreadful, horrific, dire, horrendous, ghastly, hideous, monstrous, harrowing, gruesome, grievous, unspeakable, atrocious, hair-raising, hellacious *(U.S. slang)* • *The earthquake was a fearful disaster.*

fearfully **1** = **nervously**, uneasily, timidly, apprehensively, diffidently, in fear and trembling, timorously, with bated breath, with many misgivings *or* forebodings, with your heart in your mouth • *Softly, fearfully, he stole from the room.*
2 = **very**, terribly, horribly, tremendously, awfully, exceedingly, excessively, dreadfully, frightfully • *This dress is fearfully expensive.*

fearless = **intrepid**, confident, brave, daring, bold, heroic, courageous, gallant, gutsy *(slang)*, valiant, plucky, game *(informal)*, doughty, undaunted, indomitable, unabashed, unafraid, unflinching, dauntless, ballsy *(taboo slang)*, lion-hearted, valorous, (as) game as Ned Kelly *(Austral. slang)* • *brave and fearless soldiers*

fearsome = **formidable**, alarming, frightening, awful, terrifying, appalling, horrifying, menacing, dismaying, awesome, daunting, horrendous, unnerving, hair-raising, awe-inspiring, baleful, hellacious *(U.S. slang)* • *a fearsome array of weapons*

feasibility = **possibility**, viability, usefulness, expediency, practicability, workability • *He examined the feasibility of the plan.*

feasible = **practicable**, possible, reasonable, viable, workable, achievable, attainable, realizable, likely • *The deal was not economically feasible.*
OPPOSITES: impossible, unreasonable, impracticable

feast **AS A NOUN** **1** = **banquet**, repast, spread *(informal)*, dinner, entertainment, barbecue, revel, junket, beano *(Brit. slang)*, blowout *(slang)*, carouse, slap-up meal *(Brit. informal)*, beanfeast *(Brit. informal)*, jollification, carousal, festive board, treat, hakari *(N.Z.)* • *Lunch was a feast of meat, vegetables, cheese, and wine.*
2 = **festival**, holiday, fête, celebration, holy day, red-letter day, religious festival, saint's day, -fest, gala day • *The feast of passover began last night.*
3 = **treat**, delight, pleasure, enjoyment, gratification, cornucopia • *Chicago provides a feast for the ears of any music lover.*
▸ **AS A VERB** = **eat your fill**, wine and dine, overindulge, eat to your heart's content, stuff yourself, consume, indulge, hoover *(informal)*, gorge, devour, pig out *(slang)*, stuff your face *(slang)*, fare sumptuously, gormandize • *We feasted on cakes and ice cream.*
▸ **IN PHRASES:** **feast your eyes on something** = **look at with delight**, gaze at, devour with your eyes • *She stood feasting her eyes on the view.*

feat = **accomplishment**, act, performance, achievement, enterprise, undertaking, exploit, deed, attainment, feather in your cap • *an incredible feat of agility*

feather **AS A NOUN** = **plume** • *a purple hat with a green feather*
▸ **IN PHRASES:** **a feather in your cap** = **achievement**, success, accomplishment • *It was a feather in his cap to be at a good college.*
▸ **RELATED PHOBIA:** pteronophobia

f

feathers = **plumage**, plumes, down • *black ostrich feathers*
feathery = **downy**, soft, feathered, fluffy, plumed, wispy, plumy, plumate *or* plumose *(Botany, Zoology)*, light • *The foliage was soft and feathery.*
feature AS A NOUN 1 = **aspect**, quality, characteristic, attribute, point, mark, property, factor, trait, hallmark, facet, peculiarity • *The gardens are a special feature of this property.*
2 = **article**, report, story, piece, comment, item, column • *a special feature on breast cancer research*
3 = **highlight**, draw, attraction, innovation, speciality, specialty, main item, honeypot, crowd puller *(informal)*, special attraction, special • *the most striking feature of the whole garden*
4 = **face**, countenance, physiognomy, lineament • *She arranged her features in a bland expression.*
▸ AS A VERB 1 = **spotlight**, present, promote, set off, emphasize, play up, accentuate, foreground, call attention to, give prominence to, give the full works *(slang)* • *This event features a stunning catwalk show.*
2 = **star**, appear, headline, participate, play a part • *She featured in a Hollywood film.*
featured = **headlining**, presented, highlighted, prominent, specially presented • *Our featured speaker will be former Soviet leader Mikhail Gorbachev.*
febrile = **feverish**, hot, fevered, flushed, fiery, inflamed, delirious, pyretic *(Medical)* • *The child was in a febrile condition.*
feckless = **irresponsible**, useless, hopeless, incompetent, feeble, worthless, futile, ineffectual, aimless, good-for-nothing, shiftless, weak • *The young man was feckless and irresponsible.*
fecund 1 = **fertile**, productive, prolific, fruitful, teeming, fructiferous • *a symbol of fecund nature*
2 = **productive**, creative, fertile, inventive, fruitful, generative • *a particularly fecund period of work*
fecundity = **fertility**, creativity, inventiveness, fruitfulness, productiveness, fructiferousness • *an island famous for fecundity and profusion*
federal = **confederate**, combined, federated, in alliance • *Communist deputies in the federal assembly*
federated = **confederated**, united, federal, associated, integrated, unified, amalgamated • *a larger federated Europe*
federation = **union**, league, association, alliance, combination, coalition, partnership, consortium, syndicate, confederation, amalgamation, confederacy, entente, Bund *(German)*, copartnership, federacy • *the British Athletic Federation*
fed up = **cheesed off**, down, depressed, bored, tired, annoyed, hacked (off) *(U.S. slang)*, weary, gloomy, blue, dismal, discontented, dissatisfied, pissed off *(taboo slang)*, glum, sick and tired *(informal)*, browned-off *(informal)*, down in the mouth *(informal)*, brassed off *(Brit. slang)*, hoha *(N.Z.)* • *I'm fed up and don't know what to do.*
fee = **charge**, pay, price, cost, bill, account, payment, wage, reward, hire, salary, compensation, toll, remuneration, recompense, emolument, honorarium, meed *(archaic)* • *How much will the solicitor's fee be?*
feeble 1 = **weak**, failing, exhausted, weakened, delicate, faint, powerless, frail, debilitated, sickly, languid, puny, weedy *(informal)*, infirm, effete, enfeebled, doddering, enervated, etiolated, shilpit *(Scot.)* • *He was old and feeble.*
OPPOSITES: strong, healthy, robust
2 = **inadequate**, weak, pathetic, insufficient, incompetent, ineffective, inefficient, lame, insignificant, ineffectual, indecisive • *He said the Government had been feeble.*
3 = **unconvincing**, poor, thin, weak, slight, tame, pathetic, lame, flimsy, paltry, flat • *This is a feeble argument.*
OPPOSITES: successful, effective, forceful
feed AS A VERB 1 = **cater for**, provide for, nourish, provide with food, supply, sustain, nurture, cook for, wine and dine, victual, provision • *Feeding a hungry family is expensive.*
2 = **graze**, eat, browse, pasture • *The cows stopped feeding.*
3 = **eat**, drink milk, take nourishment • *When a baby is thirsty, it feeds more often.*
4 = **supply**, take, send, carry, convey, impart • *blood vessels that feed blood to the brain*
5 = **disclose**, give, tell, reveal, supply, communicate, pass on, impart, divulge, make known • *He fed information to a rival company.*
6 = **encourage**, boost, fuel, strengthen, foster, minister to, bolster, fortify, augment, make stronger • *Wealth is feeding our obsession with house prices.*
▸ AS A NOUN 1 = **food**, fodder, kai *(N.Z. informal)*, forage, silage, provender, pasturage • *a crop grown for animal feed*
2 = **meal**, spread *(informal)*, dinner, lunch, tea, breakfast, feast, supper, tuck-in *(informal)*, nosh *(slang)*, repast, nosh-up *(Brit. slang)* • *She's had a good feed.*
▸ IN PHRASES: **feed on something** = **live on**, depend on, devour, exist on, partake of, subsist on • *The insects breed and feed on particular cacti.*
feel AS A VERB 1 = **experience**, suffer, bear, go through, endure, undergo, have a sensation of, have • *He was still feeling pain from a stomach injury.*
2 = **touch**, handle, manipulate, run your hands over, finger, stroke, paw, maul, caress, fondle • *The doctor felt his head.*
3 = **be aware of**, have a sensation of, be sensible of, enjoy • *He felt her leg against his.*
4 = **perceive**, sense, detect, discern, know, experience, notice, observe • *He felt something was nearby.*
5 = **grope**, explore, fumble, sound • *He felt his way down the wooden staircase.*
6 = **sense**, be aware, be convinced, have a feeling, have the impression, intuit, have a hunch, feel in your bones • *I feel that he still misses her.*
7 = **believe**, consider, judge, deem, think, hold, be of the opinion that • *They felt that the police could not guarantee their safety.*
8 = **seem**, appear, strike you as • *The air feels wet and cold on these evenings.*
9 = **notice**, note, observe, perceive, detect, discern • *The charity is still feeling the effects of revelations about its former president.*
▸ AS A NOUN 1 = **texture**, finish, touch, surface, surface quality • *a crisp papery feel*
2 = **impression**, feeling, air, sense, quality, atmosphere, mood, aura, ambience, vibes *(slang)* • *He wanted to get the feel of the place.*
▸ IN PHRASES: **feel for someone** = **feel compassion for**, pity, feel sorry for, sympathize with, be moved by, be sorry for, empathize, commiserate with, bleed for, feel sympathy for, condole with • *I really felt for her.*
feel like something = **want**, desire, would like, fancy, wish for, could do with, feel the need for, feel inclined, feel up to, have the inclination for • *I feel like a little exercise.*
feeler
▸ IN PHRASES: **put out feelers** = **approach**, probe, test of the waters, overture, trial, launch a trial balloon • *When vacancies occur, the office puts out feelers to the universities.*
feeling AS A NOUN 1 = **emotion**, sentiment • *Strong feelings of pride welled up in me.*
2 = **opinion**, view, attitude, belief, point of view, instinct, inclination • *She has strong feelings about the growth in violence.*
3 = **passion**, heat, emotion, intensity, warmth, sentimentality • *a voice that trembles with feeling*
4 = **ardour**, love, care, affection, warmth, tenderness, fondness, fervour • *He never lost his feeling for her.*
5 = **sympathy**, understanding, concern, pity, appreciation, sensitivity, compassion, sorrow, sensibility, empathy, fellow feeling • *He felt a rush of feeling for the woman.*

6 = **sensation**, sense, impression, awareness • *Focus on the feeling of relaxation.*
7 = **sense of touch**, sense, perception, sensation, feel, touch • *After the accident he had no feeling in his legs.*
8 = **impression**, idea, sense, notion, suspicion, consciousness, hunch, apprehension, inkling, presentiment • *I have a feeling that everything will come right for us.*
9 = **atmosphere**, mood, aura, ambience, feel, air, quality, vibes *(slang)* • *a feeling of opulence and grandeur*
10 = **flair**, feel, ability, talent, gift, mastery, knack, aptitude • *He had a lovely tenor voice and a real feeling for music.*
▸ **AS A PLURAL NOUN** = **emotions**, ego, self-esteem, sensibilities, susceptibilities, sensitivities • *He was afraid of hurting my feelings.*
▸ **AS AN ADJECTIVE** = **caring**, understanding, soft, sensitive, gentle, tender, sympathetic, compassionate, considerate • *He is a very warm and feeling person.*
▸ **IN PHRASES: bad feeling** = **hostility**, anger, dislike, resentment, bitterness, distrust, enmity, ill feeling, ill will, upset • *There's been some bad feeling between them.*
fellow feeling = **sympathy**, understanding, concern, care, pity, compassion, feeling, empathy • *There is genuine fellow feeling for the victims.*
hard feelings = **resentment**, hostility, hatred, malice, acrimony, ill feeling(s) • *I have no hard feelings towards him.*

feign = **pretend**, affect, assume, put on, devise, forge, fake, imitate, simulate, sham, act, fabricate, counterfeit, give the appearance of, dissemble, make a show of • *You can't feign interest in something you loathe.*

feigned = **pretended**, affected, assumed, false, artificial, fake, imitation, simulated, sham, pseudo *(informal)*, fabricated, counterfeit, spurious, ersatz, insincere • *He answered me with feigned indifference.*

feint = **bluff**, manoeuvre, dodge, mock attack, play, blind, distraction, pretence, expedient, ruse, artifice, gambit, subterfuge, stratagem, wile • *a tiny feint or lunge to one side*

feisty = **fiery**, spirited, active, bold, lively, sparkling, vigorous, energetic, animated, have-a-go *(informal)*, courageous, ardent, game, plucky, high-spirited, sprightly, vivacious, spunky *(informal)*, mettlesome, (as) game as Ned Kelly *(Austral. slang)* • *At 66, she was as feisty as ever.*

felicitous = **fitting**, timely, appropriate, inspired, suitable, neat, apt, well-chosen, well-timed, apposite, apropos, opportune, propitious, happy • *Her speech was not at all felicitous.*

felicity 1 = **happiness**, joy, ecstasy, bliss, delectation, blessedness, blissfulness • *a period of domestic felicity*
2 = **aptness**, grace, effectiveness, suitability, propriety, appropriateness, applicability, becomingness, suitableness • *his felicity of word and phrase*

feline 1 = **catlike**, leonine • *a black, furry, feline creature*
2 = **graceful**, flowing, smooth, elegant, sleek, slinky, sinuous, stealthy • *He moves with feline pace.*

fell 1 = **cut down**, cut, level, demolish, flatten, knock down, hew, raze • *Badly infected trees should be felled.*
2 = **knock down**, floor, flatten, strike down, prostrate, deck *(slang)* • *A blow on the head felled him.*

fellow **AS A NOUN** 1 = **man**, boy, person, individual, customer *(informal)*, character, guy *(informal)*, bloke *(Brit. informal)*, punter *(informal)*, chap *(informal)* • *He appeared to be a fine fellow.*
2 = **associate**, colleague, peer, co-worker, member, friend, partner, equal, companion, comrade, crony, compeer • *He stood out from all his fellows at work.*
▸ **AS A MODIFIER** = **co-**, similar, related, allied, associate, associated, affiliated, akin, like • *My fellow inmates treated me with kindness.*

fellowship 1 = **society**, club, league, association, organization, guild, fraternity, brotherhood, sisterhood, order, sodality • *the National Youth Fellowship*
2 = **camaraderie**, intimacy, communion, familiarity, brotherhood, companionship, sociability, amity, kindliness, fraternization, companionability, intercourse • *a sense of community and fellowship*

QUOTATIONS
Fellowship is heaven, and lack of fellowship is hell
[William Morris *A Dream of John Ball*]

felon = **criminal**, convict, con *(slang)*, offender, crook *(informal)*, villain, culprit, sinner, delinquent, con man *(informal)*, jailbird, malefactor, evildoer, transgressor, lawbreaker, skelm *(S. African)*, lag *(slang)*, rogue trader, perp *(U.S. & Canad. informal)* • *He's a convicted felon.*

felony = **crime**, offence, misdemeanour, transgression, job *(informal)*, wrong, fault, outrage, atrocity, violation, trespass, misdeed, unlawful act, malfeasance • *He pleaded guilty to six felonies.*

female **AS A NOUN** = **woman**, girl, lady, lass, sheila *(Austral. & N.Z. slang)*, charlie *(Austral. slang)*, chook *(Austral. slang)*, wahine *(N.Z.)* • *The average young female is stylish and confident.*
▸ **AS AN ADJECTIVE** = **womanlike**, woman, lady • *Their aim is equal numbers of male and female MPs.*

QUOTATIONS
The female of the species is more deadly than the male
[Rudyard Kipling *The Female of the Species*]

feminine 1 = **womanly**, pretty, soft, gentle, tender, modest, delicate, graceful, girlie, girlish, ladylike • *the ideal of feminine beauty*
OPPOSITES: rough, manly, masculine
2 = **effeminate**, camp *(informal)*, weak, unmanly, effete, womanish, unmasculine • *men with feminine gestures*

femininity = **womanliness**, delicacy, softness, womanhood, gentleness, girlishness, feminineness, muliebrity • *the drudgery behind the ideology of motherhood and femininity*

feminism = **female emancipation**, women's rights, the women's movement, women's liberation, women's lib *(informal)* • *She is a champion of feminism.*

QUOTATIONS
Men their rights and nothing more; women their rights and nothing less
[Susan B. Anthony *Motto of the Revolution*]

feminist

QUOTATIONS
People call me a feminist whenever I express sentiments that differentiate me from a doormat or a prostitute
[Rebecca West]

femme fatale = **seductress**, siren, charmer, vamp *(informal)*, Circe, enchantress • *the allure of the femme fatale*

fen = **marsh**, moss *(Scot.)*, swamp, bog, slough, quagmire, holm *(dialect)*, morass, pakihi *(N.Z.)*, muskeg *(Canad.)* • *Peat is growing in the fen.*

fence **AS A NOUN** 1 = **barrier**, wall, defence, guard, railings, paling, shield, hedge, barricade, hedgerow, rampart, palisade, stockade, barbed wire • *They climbed over the fence into the field.*
2 = **receiver**, dealer, buyer, trader, trafficker, receiver of stolen goods, receiver of stolen property, criminal • *He acted as a fence for a gang of burglars.*
▸ **IN PHRASES: sit on the fence** = **be uncommitted**, be uncertain, be undecided, vacillate, be in two minds, blow hot and cold *(informal)*, be irresolute, avoid committing yourself • *He is sitting on the fence, refusing to commit himself.*
▸ **AS A VERB** *with* **in** *or* **off** = **enclose**, surround, bound, hedge, pound, protect, separate, guard, defend, secure, pen, restrict, confine, fortify, encircle, coop, impound, circumscribe • *He intends to fence in about 100 acres of land.*

fencing
▹ *See panel* **Fencing terms**

FENCING TERMS

backsword	guard	parry	quinte	seconde	terce
bracer	mask	piste	reach	septime	touch
carte	octave	prime	repechage	singlestick	touché
feint	parade	quarte	sabre	sixte	volt

fend IN PHRASES: **fend for yourself = look after yourself**, support yourself, sustain yourself, take care of yourself, provide for yourself, make do, make provision for yourself, shift for yourself • *He was just left to fend for himself.*
fend something *or* **someone off 1 = deflect**, resist, parry, avert, ward off, stave off, turn aside, hold *or* keep at bay • *He fended off questions from the Press.*
2 = beat off, resist, parry, avert, deflect, repel, drive back, ward off, stave off, repulse, keep off, turn aside, hold *or* keep at bay • *He raised his hand to fend off the blow.*

feral 1 = wild, untamed, uncultivated, undomesticated, unbroken • *There are many feral cats roaming the area.*
2 = savage, fierce, brutal, ferocious, fell, wild, vicious, bestial • *the feral scowl of the young street mugger*

ferment AS A NOUN **= commotion**, turmoil, unrest, turbulence, trouble, heat, excitement, glow, fever, disruption, frenzy, stew, furore, uproar, agitation, tumult, hubbub, brouhaha, imbroglio, state of unrest • *The country is in a state of political ferment.*
OPPOSITES: quiet, hush, tranquillity
▸ AS A VERB **1 = brew**, froth, concoct, effervesce, work, rise, heat, boil, bubble, foam, seethe, leaven • *red wine made from grapes left to ferment for three weeks*
2 = stir up, excite, provoke, rouse, agitate, inflame, incite • *They tried to ferment political unrest.*
3 = smoulder, seethe, fester, heat, boil, foment • *His anger still ferments after a decade.*

fermentation
▸ RELATED ADJECTIVE: zymotic

fern
▹ *See panel* **Ferns**

ferocious 1 = fierce, violent, savage, ravening, predatory, feral, rapacious, wild • *By its nature a lion is ferocious.*
OPPOSITES: calm, gentle, mild
2 = cruel, bitter, brutal, vicious, ruthless, relentless, barbaric, merciless, brutish, bloodthirsty, barbarous, pitiless, tigerish • *Fighting has been ferocious.*

ferocity = savagery, violence, cruelty, brutality, ruthlessness, inhumanity, wildness, barbarity, viciousness, fierceness, rapacity, bloodthirstiness, savageness, ferociousness • *surprised by the ferocity of the attack*

ferret AS A VERB **= search**, hunt, sift, scour, rummage, forage, fossick (*Austral. & N.Z.*) • *She ferreted among some papers.*
▸ IN PHRASES: **ferret something** *or* **someone out = track down**, discover, trace, disclose, get at, unearth, drive out, elicit, dig up, root out, search out, bring to light, nose out, smell out, run to earth • *They are trying to ferret out missing details.*
▸ NAME OF MALE: hob
▸ NAME OF FEMALE: gill or jill
▸ NAME OF YOUNG: kit

ferry AS A NOUN **= ferry boat**, boat, ship, passenger boat, packet boat, packet • *They crossed the river by ferry.*
▸ AS A VERB **= transport**, bring, carry, ship, take, run, shuttle, convey, chauffeur • *They ferried in more soldiers to help with the search.*

fertile 1 = productive, rich, flowering, lush, fat, yielding, prolific, abundant, plentiful, fruitful, teeming, luxuriant, generative, fecund, fruit-bearing, flowing with milk and honey, plenteous • *the rolling fertile countryside of Ireland*
OPPOSITES: poor, dry, barren
2 = creative, productive, prolific, inventive, resourceful • *a product of his fertile imagination*
3 = able to conceive, able to reproduce, able to have children, able to have babies, able to have young, potent • *The operation cannot make her fertile again.*

fertility 1 = fruitfulness, abundance, richness, fecundity, luxuriance, productiveness • *He brought large sterile acreages back to fertility.*
2 = ability to conceive, potency, ability to have children, ability to have babies, ability to have young • *Pregnancy is the only sure test for fertility.*

fertilization *or* **fertilisation 1 = insemination**, propagation, procreation, implantation, pollination, impregnation • *From fertilization until birth is about 266 days.*
2 = manuring, mulching, top dressing, dressing • *soil testing and fertilization*

fertilize *or* **fertilise 1 = inseminate**, impregnate, pollinate, make pregnant, fructify, make fruitful, fecundate • *sperm levels needed to fertilize the egg*
2 = enrich, feed, compost, manure, mulch, top-dress, dress, fertigate (*Austral.*) • *grown in recently fertilized soil*

fertilizer *or* **fertiliser = compost**, muck, manure, dung, guano, marl, bone meal, dressing • *Add some fertilizer to the soil.*

fervent = ardent, earnest, enthusiastic, fervid, passionate, warm, excited, emotional, intense, flaming, eager, animated, fiery, ecstatic, devout, heartfelt, impassioned, zealous, vehement, perfervid (*literary*) • *a fervent admirer of her work*
OPPOSITES: cold, cool, apathetic

fervour *or* (*U.S.*) **fervor = ardour**, passion, enthusiasm, excitement, intensity, warmth, animation, zeal, eagerness, vehemence, earnestness, fervency • *an outbreak of religious fervour*

QUOTATIONS
Fervour is the weapon of choice of the impotent
[Frantz Fanon *Black Skins White Masks*]

fester 1 = intensify, gall, smoulder, chafe, irk, rankle, aggravate • *Resentments are starting to fester.*
2 = putrefy, decay, become infected, become inflamed,

FERNS

adder's-tongue	bungwall (*Austral.*)	maidenhair	oak fern	shield fern	walking fern
bladder fern	fishbone fern	male fern	parsley fern	staghorn fern	wall rue
beech fern	hard fern	marsh fern	pillwort	sword fern	woodsia
bracken	hart's-tongue	nardoo (*Austral.*)	rock brake	tree fern	
buckler fern	lady fern	moonwort	royal fern	Venus's-hair	

suppurate, ulcerate, maturate, gather • *The wound is festering and gangrene has set in.*
3 = **rot**, break down, spoil, corrupt, crumble, deteriorate, decay, disintegrate, taint, perish, degenerate, decompose, corrode, moulder, go bad, putrefy • *The food will fester and go to waste.*

festering 1 = **venomous**, vicious, smouldering, virulent, black-hearted • *recrimination and festering resentment*
2 = **septic**, infected, poisonous, inflamed, pussy, suppurating, ulcerated, purulent, maturating, gathering • *afflicted by festering sores*
3 = **rotting**, decaying, decomposing, putrefying • *The cobbles were littered with festering garbage.*

festival 1 = **celebration**, fair, carnival, gala, treat, fête, entertainment, jubilee, fiesta, festivities, jamboree, mela, -fest, field day • *The Festival will provide spectacles like river pageants.*
2 = **holy day**, holiday, feast, commemoration, feast day, red-letter day, saint's day, fiesta, fête, anniversary • *the Jewish festival of the Passover*

festive = **celebratory**, happy, holiday, carnival, jolly, merry, gala, hearty, jubilant, cheery, joyous, joyful, jovial, convivial, gleeful, back-slapping, Christmassy, mirthful, sportive, light-hearted, festal, gay • *The town has a festive holiday atmosphere.*
OPPOSITES: sad, depressing, mournful

festivity 1 = **merrymaking**, fun, pleasure, amusement, mirth, gaiety, merriment, revelry, conviviality, joviality, joyfulness, jollification, sport • *There was a general air of festivity and abandon.*
2 *often plural* = **celebration**, party, festival, entertainment, rave (*Brit. slang*), beano (*Brit. slang*), fun and games, rave-up (*Brit. slang*), jollification, festive event, carousal, festive proceedings, hooley *or* hoolie (*chiefly Irish & N.Z.*) • *The festivities included a firework display.*

festoon AS A NOUN = **decoration**, garland, swathe, wreath, swag, lei, chaplet • *festoons of laurel and magnolia*
▸ AS A VERB = **decorate**, deck, array, drape, garland, swathe, bedeck, wreathe, beribbon, engarland, hang • *The temples are festooned with lights.*

fetch AS A VERB 1 = **bring**, pick up, collect, go and get, get, carry, deliver, conduct, transport, go for, obtain, escort, convey, retrieve • *She fetched a towel from the bathroom.*
2 = **sell for**, make, raise, earn, realize, go for, yield, bring in • *The painting is expected to fetch two million pounds.*
▸ IN PHRASES: **fetch up** = **end up**, reach, arrive, turn up, come, stop, land, halt, finish up • *We eventually fetched up at their house.*

fetching = **attractive**, sweet, charming, enchanting, fascinating, intriguing, cute, enticing, captivating, alluring, winsome • *She wore a fetching outfit in purple and green.*

fête *or* **fete** AS A NOUN = **fair**, festival, gala, bazaar, garden party, sale of work • *The Vicar is organizing a church fete.*
▸ AS A VERB = **entertain**, welcome, honour, make much of, wine and dine, hold a reception for (someone), lionize, bring out the red carpet for (someone), kill the fatted calf for (someone), treat • *The actress was fêted at a special dinner.*

fetid *or* **foetid** = **stinking**, rank, offensive, foul, corrupt, reeking, noxious, rancid, foul-smelling, malodorous, noisome, mephitic, olid, festy (*Austral. slang*) • *the fetid stench of human waste*

fetish 1 = **fixation**, obsession, mania, thing (*informal*), idée fixe (*French*) • *I've got a bit of a shoe fetish.*
2 = **talisman**, amulet, cult object • *Tribal elders carried the sacred fetishes.*

fetter AS A PLURAL NOUN 1 = **restraints**, checks, curbs, constraints, captivity, obstructions, bondage, hindrances • *without the fetters of restrictive rules*
2 = **chains**, bonds, irons, shackles, manacles, leg irons, gyves (*archaic*), bilboes • *He saw a boy in fetters in the dungeon.*
▸ AS A VERB 1 = **restrict**, bind, confine, curb, restrain, hamstring, hamper, encumber, clip someone's wings, trammel, straiten • *He would not be fettered by bureaucracy.*
2 = **chain**, tie, tie up, shackle, hobble, hold captive, manacle, gyve (*archaic*), put a straitjacket on • *My foes fettered me hand and foot.*

fettle = **health**, form, condition, shape, state • *You seem in fine fettle.*

fetus *or* **foetus** = **embryo**, unborn child, fertilized egg • *The fetus can see, hear, experience and taste.*

feud AS A NOUN = **hostility**, row, conflict, argument, faction, falling out, disagreement, rivalry, contention, quarrel, grudge, strife, bickering, vendetta, discord, enmity, broil, bad blood, estrangement, dissension • *a long and bitter feud between families*
▸ AS A VERB = **quarrel**, row, clash, dispute, fall out, contend, brawl, war, squabble, duel, bicker, be at odds, be at daggers drawn • *He feuded with his ex-wife.*

fever 1 = **ague**, high temperature, feverishness, pyrexia (*Medical*) • *Symptoms of the disease include fever and weight loss.*
2 = **excitement**, heat, passion, intensity, flush, turmoil, ecstasy, frenzy, ferment, agitation, fervour, restlessness, delirium • *I got married in a fever of excitement.*
▸ RELATED ADJECTIVES: febrile, pyretic

PROVERBS
Feed a cold and starve a fever

fevered = **frantic**, excited, desperate, distracted, frenzied, impatient, obsessive, restless, agitated, frenetic, overwrought

feverish *or* **fevorous** 1 = **frantic**, excited, desperate, distracted, frenzied, impatient, obsessive, restless, agitated, frenetic, overwrought • *a state of feverish excitement*
OPPOSITES: cool, collected, calm
2 = **hot**, burning, flaming, fevered, flushed, hectic, inflamed, febrile, pyretic (*Medical*) • *She looked feverish, her eyes glistened.*

few AS AN ADJECTIVE = **not many**, one or two, hardly any, scarcely any, rare, thin, scattered, insufficient, scarce, scant, meagre, negligible, sporadic, sparse, infrequent, scanty, inconsiderable • *In some districts there are few survivors.*
OPPOSITES: many, divers (*archaic*), abundant
▸ AS A PRONOUN = **a small number**, a handful, a sprinkling, a scattering, some, scarcely any • *A strict diet is appropriate for only a few.*
▸ IN PHRASES: **few and far between** = **scarce**, rare, unusual, scattered, irregular, uncommon, in short supply, hard to come by, infrequent, thin on the ground, widely spaced, seldom met with • *Successful women politicians were few and far between.*

fiancé *or* **fiancée** = **husband-** *or* **wife-to-be**, intended, betrothed, prospective spouse, future husband *or* wife • *He was intensely attracted to his fiancée.*

fiasco = **flop**, failure, disaster, ruin, mess (*informal*), catastrophe, rout, debacle, cock-up (*Brit. slang*), balls-up (*taboo slang*), fuck-up (*offensive taboo slang*), washout (*informal*) • *The party was a bit of a fiasco.*

fiat = **order**, demand, command, dictate, decree, mandate, canon, ordinance, proclamation, edict, dictum, precept, ukase • *He has imposed solutions by fiat.*

fib AS A NOUN = **lie**, story, fiction, untruth, whopper (*informal*), porky (*Brit. slang*), pork pie (*Brit. slang*), white lie, prevarication • *She told innocent fibs.*
▸ AS A VERB = **lie**, invent, fabricate, misrepresent, falsify, tell a lie, prevaricate, perjure, equivocate, dissimulate, tell untruths, forswear yourself • *He laughed when I accused him of fibbing.*

QUOTATIONS
fib: a lie that has not cut its teeth
[Ambrose Bierce *The Devil's Dictionary*]

fibre *or (U.S.)* **fiber** AS A NOUN **1 = thread**, strand, filament, tendril, pile, texture, staple, wisp, fibril • *a variety of coloured fibres*
2 = cloth, material, stuff, fabric • *Cotton is a natural fibre.*
3 = roughage, bulk • *Eat more fibre, less sugar and less fat.*
▸ IN PHRASES: **moral fibre = strength of character**, strength, resolution, resolve, stamina, backbone, toughness • *They all lacked courage, backbone or moral fibre.*

fickle = capricious, variable, volatile, unpredictable, unstable, unfaithful, temperamental, mercurial, unsteady, faithless, changeable, quicksilver, vacillating, fitful, flighty, blowing hot and cold, mutable, irresolute, inconstant • *They are fickle, faithless and lewd.*
OPPOSITES: predictable, firm, constant

fickleness = inconstancy, volatility, unpredictability, unfaithfulness, capriciousness, mutability, unsteadiness, flightiness, fitfulness • *the fickleness of businessmen and politicians*

f

fiction 1 = tale, story, novel, legend, myth, romance, fable, storytelling, narration, creative writing, work of imagination • *She is a writer of historical fiction.*
2 = imagination, fancy, fantasy, creativity • *a story of truth or fiction*
3 = lie, fancy, fantasy, invention, improvisation, fabrication, concoction, falsehood, untruth, porky *(Brit. slang)*, pork pie *(Brit. slang)*, urban myth, tall story, urban legend, cock and bull story *(informal)*, figment of the imagination • *Total recycling is a fiction.*

QUOTATIONS
'Tis strange – but true; for truth is always strange;
Stranger than fiction
[Lord Byron *Don Juan*]
Truth may be stranger than fiction, but fiction is truer
[Frederic Raphael *Contemporary Novelists*]
Literature is a luxury. Fiction is a necessity
[G.K. Chesterton *The Defendant*]

fictional = imaginary, made-up, invented, legendary, unreal, nonexistent • *a drama featuring fictional characters*

fictitious 1 = false, made-up, bogus, untrue, non-existent, fabricated, counterfeit, feigned, spurious, apocryphal • *a source of fictitious rumours*
OPPOSITES: real, true, actual
2 = imaginary, imagined, made-up, assumed, invented, artificial, improvised, mythical, unreal, fanciful, make-believe • *Persons portrayed in this production are fictitious.*

fiddle AS A NOUN **1 = fraud**, racket, scam *(slang)*, piece of sharp practice, fix, sting *(informal)*, graft *(informal)*, swindle, wangle *(informal)* • *legitimate businesses that act as a cover for tax fiddles*
2 = violin • *He played the fiddle at local dances.*
▸ AS A VERB **1** *often with* **with = fidget**, play, finger, toy, tamper, trifle, mess about *or* around • *She fiddled with a pen on the desk.*
2 *often with* **with = tinker**, adjust, interfere, mess about *or* around • *He fiddled with the radio dial.*
3 = cheat, cook *(informal)*, fix, manoeuvre *(informal)*, graft *(informal)*, diddle *(informal)*, wangle *(informal)*, gerrymander, finagle *(informal)* • *Stop fiddling your expenses account.*

fiddling = trivial, small, petty, trifling, insignificant, unimportant, pettifogging, futile • *There were a thousand fiddling jobs to do.*

fidelity 1 = loyalty, faith, integrity, devotion, allegiance, constancy, faithfulness, dependability, trustworthiness, troth *(archaic)*, fealty, staunchness, devotedness, lealty *(archaic Scot.)*, true-heartedness • *I had to promise fidelity to the Queen.*
OPPOSITES: infidelity, treachery, disloyalty
2 = accuracy, precision, correspondence, closeness, adherence, faithfulness, exactitude, exactness, scrupulousness, preciseness • *the fidelity of these early documents*
OPPOSITES: inaccuracy, inexactness

QUOTATIONS
Histories are more full of examples of the fidelity of dogs than of friends
[Alexander Pope]

fidget = move restlessly, fiddle *(informal)*, bustle, twitch, fret, squirm, chafe, jiggle, jitter *(informal)*, be like a cat on hot bricks *(informal)*, worry • *The children began to fidget.*

fidgety = restless, nervous, uneasy, impatient, jittery *(informal)*, on edge, jerky, restive, jumpy, twitchy *(informal)*, antsy *(informal)* • *I was so fidgety and nervous.*

field AS A NOUN **1 = meadow**, land, green, lea *(poetic)*, pasture, mead *(archaic)*, greensward *(archaic or literary)* • *They went for walks together in the fields.*
2 = pitch, park, ground, arena • *a football field*
3 = speciality, line, area, department, environment, territory, discipline, province, pale, confines, sphere, domain, specialty, sphere of influence, purview, metier, sphere of activity, bailiwick, sphere of interest, sphere of study • *They are both experts in their field.*
4 = line, reach, range, limits, bounds, sweep, scope • *Our field of vision is surprisingly wide.*
5 = competitors, competition, candidates, runners, applicants, entrants, contestants • *The two most experienced athletes led the field.*
▸ AS AN ADJECTIVE **= practical**, applied, empirical • *The field research is headed by two biologists.*
▸ AS A VERB **1 = deal with**, answer, handle, respond to, reply to, deflect, turn aside • *He fielded questions from journalists.*
2 = play, put up • *They intend fielding their strongest team.*
3 = retrieve, return, stop, catch, pick up • *He fielded the ball and threw it at the wicket.*
▸ RELATED ADJECTIVE: campestral

fiend 1 = brute, monster, savage, beast, degenerate, barbarian, ogre, ghoul • *a saint to his parents and a fiend to his children*
2 = enthusiast, fan, addict, freak *(informal)*, fanatic, maniac, energumen • *a strong-tea fiend*
3 = demon, devil, evil spirit, hellhound, atua *(N.Z.)* • *She is a fiend incarnate, leading these people to eternal damnation.*

fiendish 1 = clever, brilliant, imaginative, shrewd, cunning, ingenious • *a fiendish plan*
2 = difficult, involved, complex, puzzling, baffling, intricate, thorny, knotty • *It is a fiendish question without an easy answer.*
3 = wicked, cruel, savage, monstrous, malicious, satanic, malignant, unspeakable, atrocious, inhuman, diabolical, implacable, malevolent, hellish, devilish, infernal, accursed, ungodly, black-hearted, demoniac • *a fiendish act of wickedness*

fierce 1 = ferocious, wild, dangerous, cruel, savage, brutal, aggressive, menacing, vicious, fiery, murderous, uncontrollable, feral, untamed, barbarous, fell *(archaic)*, threatening, baleful, truculent, tigerish, aggers *(Austral. slang)*, biffo *(Austral. slang)* • *the teeth of some fierce animal*
OPPOSITES: kind, cool, gentle
2 = intense, strong, keen, passionate, relentless, cut-throat • *He inspires fierce loyalty in his friends.*
3 = stormy, strong, powerful, violent, intense, raging, furious, howling, uncontrollable, boisterous, tumultuous, tempestuous, blustery, inclement • *Two climbers were trapped by a fierce storm.*
OPPOSITES: tranquil, temperate

fiercely 1 = ferociously, savagely, passionately, furiously, viciously, menacingly, tooth and nail, in a frenzy, like cat and dog, frenziedly, tigerishly, with no holds barred, tempestuously, with bared teeth, uncontrolledly • *They argued fiercely.*

2 = **strongly**, keenly, intensely, passionately, relentlessly • *He has always been fiercely competitive.*

fiery 1 = **burning**, flaming, glowing, blazing, on fire, red-hot, ablaze, in flames, aflame, afire • *People set up fiery barricades.*
2 = **bright**, brilliant, intense, vivid, vibrant • *fiery autumn foliage*
3 = **spicy**, hot, pungent, piquant • *a fiery combination of chillies and rice*
4 = **excitable**, violent, fierce, passionate, irritable, impetuous, irascible, peppery, hot-headed, choleric • *a red-head's fiery temper*

fiesta = **carnival**, party, holiday, fair, fête, festival, celebration, feast, revel, jubilee, festivity, jamboree, Mardi Gras, revelry, mela, Saturnalia, saint's day, merrymaking, carousal, bacchanal *or* bacchanalia, gala • *It was spectacular – a fiesta of music and dance.*

fight AS A VERB 1 = **oppose**, campaign against, dispute, contest, resist, defy, contend, withstand, stand up to, take issue with, make a stand against • *She devoted her life to fighting poverty.*
2 = **strive**, battle, push, struggle, contend • *He had to fight hard for his place in the team.*
3 = **battle**, assault, combat, war with, go to war, do battle, wage war, take up arms, bear arms against, engage in hostilities, carry on war, engage • *The Sioux fought other tribes for territorial rights.*
4 = **engage in**, conduct, wage, pursue, carry on • *They fought a war against injustice.*
5 = **take the field**, cross swords, taste battle • *He fought in the war and was taken prisoner.*
6 = **brawl**, clash, scrap *(informal)*, exchange blows, struggle, row, tilt, wrestle, feud, grapple, tussle, joust, come to blows, lock horns, fight like Kilkenny cats • *a lot of unruly drunks fighting*
7 = **quarrel**, argue, row, dispute, fall out *(informal)*, squabble, wrangle, bicker • *She was always arguing and fighting with him.*
8 = **box**, spar with, exchange blows with • *I'd like to fight him for the title.*
9 = **oppose**, face, take on, resist, stand up to, take issue with, speak against, take a stand against, set your face against • *The newspaper is fighting a damages action.*
10 = **repress**, control, check, master, silence, hold in, overcome, swallow, curb, suppress, restrain, inhibit, hold back, stifle, smother, overpower, muffle, bottle up, keep in check • *I desperately fought the urge to giggle.*
▸ AS A NOUN 1 = **battle**, campaign, movement, struggle • *I will continue the fight for justice.*
2 = **conflict**, war, action, clash, contest, encounter, brush, combat, engagement, hostilities, skirmish, passage of arms • *They used to be allies in the fight against the old Communist regime.*
3 = **brawl**, set-to *(informal)*, riot, scrap *(informal)*, confrontation, rumble *(U.S. & N.Z. slang)*, fray, duel, skirmish, head-to-head, tussle, scuffle, free-for-all *(informal)*, fracas, altercation, dogfight, joust, dissension, affray *(Law)*, shindig *(informal)*, scrimmage, sparring match, exchange of blows, shindy *(informal)*, melee *or* mêlée, biffo *(Austral. slang)*, boilover *(Austral.)* • *He got a bloody nose in a fight.*
4 = **row**, argument, dispute, quarrel, squabble • *He had a big fight with his Dad last night.*
5 = **match**, contest, bout, battle, competition, struggle, set-to, encounter, engagement, head-to-head, boxing match • *The referee stopped the fight in the second round.*
6 = **resistance**, spirit, pluck, militancy, mettle, belligerence, will to resist, gameness, pluckiness • *We had a lot of fight in us.*
▸ IN PHRASES: **fight back** = **retaliate**, reply, resist, hit back, strike back, return fire, put up a fight, defend yourself, give as good as you get, give tit for tat • *The attackers fled when the men fought back.*
fight shy of something = **avoid**, shun, steer clear of, duck out of *(informal)*, keep at arm's length, hang back from, keep aloof from • *It's no use fighting shy of publicity.*
fight something back = **hold back**, control, contain, curb, restrain, repress, muffle, bottle up, hold in check • *She fought back the tears.*
fight something down *or* **off** = **repress**, control, check, master, hold in, overcome, curb, suppress, restrain, inhibit, hold back, stifle, overpower, keep in check • *He fought down the desire to run away.* • *She has fought off her depression by getting back to work.*
fight something *or* **someone off** = **repel**, resist, repress, drive away, fend off, ward off, stave off, beat off, repulse, keep *or* hold at bay • *The woman fought off her attacker.*

fightback = **comeback**, return, rally, recovery, triumph, revival, rebound, resurgence • *The team staged a dramatic fightback.*

fighter 1 = **fighter plane**, military aircraft, armed aircraft • *Royal Air Force's fighters and bombers*
2 = **combatant**, battler, militant, contender, contestant, belligerent, antagonist, disputant • *She's a real fighter and has always defied the odds.*
3 = **boxer**, wrestler, bruiser *(informal)*, pugilist, prize fighter • *a tough little street fighter*
4 = **soldier**, warrior, fighting man, man-at-arms • *His guerrillas are widely accepted as some of the best fighters in the Afghan resistance.*

fighting = **battle**, war, conflict, combat, hostilities, warfare, bloodshed • *More than 900 people have died in the fighting.*

figment = **invention**, production, fancy, creation, fiction, fable, improvisation, fabrication, falsehood • *It wasn't just a figment of my imagination.*

figurative = **symbolical**, representative, abstract, allegorical, typical, tropical *(Rhetoric)*, imaginative, ornate, descriptive, fanciful, pictorial, metaphorical, flowery, florid, poetical, emblematical • *both the literal and figurative sense*
OPPOSITES: true, simple, literal

figure AS A NOUN 1 = **statistic**, amount, total, quantity, number • *No one really knows the true figures.*
2 = **digit**, character, symbol, number, numeral, cipher • *deduct the second figure from the first*
3 = **outline**, form, shape, shadow, profile, silhouette • *A figure appeared in the doorway.*
4 = **representation**, image, likeness • *a life-size bronze figure of a woman*
5 = **shape**, build, body, frame, proportions, chassis *(slang)*, torso, physique • *Take pride in your health and your figure.*
6 = **personage**, force, face *(informal)*, leader, person, individual, character, presence, somebody, personality, celebrity, worthy, notable, big name, dignitary, notability • *The movement is supported by key figures.*
7 = **diagram**, drawing, picture, illustration, representation, sketch, emblem • *Figure 26 shows a small circular garden of herbs.*
8 = **design**, shape, pattern, device, motif, depiction • *The impulsive singer had the figure cut into his shaven hair.*
9 = **price**, cost, value, amount, total, sum • *It's hard to put a figure on the damage.*
▸ AS A VERB 1 = **suppose**, think, believe, expect, guess • *I figure I'll learn from experience.*
2 = **make sense**, follow, be expected, add up, go without saying, seem reasonable • *When I finished, he said, 'Yeah. That figures'.*
3 *usually with* **in** = **feature**, act, appear, contribute to, be included, be mentioned, play a part, be featured, have a place in, be conspicuous • *I didn't figure in his plans.*
4 = **calculate**, work out, compute, tot up, add, total, count, reckon, sum, tally • *Figure the interest rate.*
▸ IN PHRASES: **figure on something** = **plan on**, depend on, rely on, count on, bargain on • *I never figured on that scenario.*

figure something out = **calculate**, reckon, work out, compute • *I want to figure out how much it'll cost.*
figure something *or* **someone out** = **understand**, make out, fathom, make head or tail of *(informal)*, see, solve, resolve, comprehend, make sense of, decipher, think through, suss (out) *(slang)* • *How do you figure that out?* • *I can't figure that guy out at all.*

figurehead = **nominal head**, leader in name only, titular head, front man, name, token, dummy, puppet, mouthpiece, cipher, nonentity, straw man *(chiefly U.S.)*, man of straw • *The President will be little more than a figurehead.*

figure of speech = **expression**, image, turn of phrase, trope • *It was just a figure of speech.*
▹ See panel **Figures of speech**

filament = **strand**, string, wire, fibre, thread, staple, wisp, cilium *(Biology, Zoology)*, fibril, pile • *Some models use a carbon filament.*

filch = **steal**, take, thieve, pinch *(informal)*, lift *(informal)*, nick *(slang, chiefly Brit.)*, trouser *(slang)*, abstract, rip off *(slang)*, cabbage *(Brit. slang)*, swipe *(slang)*, knock off *(slang)*, crib *(informal)*, half-inch *(old-fashioned slang)*, embezzle, pilfer, walk off with, misappropriate, purloin, snaffle *(Brit. informal)* • *I filched some notes from his wallet.*

file[1] AS A NOUN 1 = **folder**, case, portfolio, binder • *a file of insurance papers*
2 = **dossier**, record, information, data, documents, case history, report, case • *We have files on people's tax details.*
3 = **document**, program • *to span a file across more than one disk*
4 = **line**, row, chain, string, column, queue, procession • *A file of soldiers, spaced and on both sides.*
▸ AS A VERB 1 = **arrange**, order, classify, put in place, slot in *(informal)*, categorize, pigeonhole, put in order • *Papers are filed alphabetically.*
2 = **register**, record, enter, log, put on record • *They have filed formal complaints.*
3 = **march**, troop, parade, walk in line, walk behind one another • *They filed into the room and sat down.*

file[2] = **smooth**, shape, polish, rub, refine, scrape, rasp, burnish, rub down, abrade • *shaping and filing nails*

filial = **devoted**, familial, dutiful, respectful • *The son neglected his filial duties.*

filibuster AS A NOUN = **obstruction**, delay, postponement, hindrance, procrastination • *The Senator used a filibuster to stop the bill.*
▸ AS A VERB = **obstruct**, prevent, delay, put off, hinder, play for time, procrastinate • *They threatened to filibuster until senate adjourns.*

filigree = **wirework**, lace, lattice, tracery, lacework • *the filigree inlay of the lock*

fill AS A VERB 1 = **top up**, fill up, make full, become full, brim over • *While the bath was filling, he undressed.*
2 = **swell**, expand, inflate, become bloated, extend, balloon, fatten • *Your lungs fill with air.*
3 = **pack**, crowd, squeeze, cram, throng • *Thousands of people filled the streets.*
4 = **stock**, supply, store, pack, load, furnish, replenish • *I fill the shelves in a supermarket until 12pm.*
5 = **plug**, close, stop, seal, cork, bung, block up, stop up • *Fill the holes with plaster.*
6 = **saturate**, charge, pervade, permeate, imbue, impregnate, suffuse, overspread • *The barn was filled with the smell of hay.*
7 = **fulfil**, hold, perform, carry out, occupy, take up, execute, discharge, officiate • *She filled the role of diplomat's wife for many years.*
8 *often with* **up** = **satisfy**, stuff, gorge, glut, satiate, sate • *They filled themselves with chocolate cake.*
9 = **complete**, carry out, implement, fulfil, execute • *Thank you for filling the order so promptly.*
▸ IN PHRASES: **fill in for someone** = **replace**, represent, substitute for, cover for, take over from, act for, stand in for, sub for, deputize for • *relief employees who fill in for workers while on break*
fill out = **gain weight**, put on weight, gain weight, become fatter • *Shey may fill out before she reaches her full height.*
fill someone in = **inform**, acquaint, advise of, apprise of, bring up to date with, update with, put wise to *(slang)*, give the facts *or* background of • *I'll fill him in on the details.*
fill something in = **complete**, answer, fill up, fill out *(U.S.)* • *Fill in the coupon and send it to the above address.*
fill something out = **complete**, answer, fill in • *Fill out the application carefully.*
your fill = **sufficient**, enough, plenty, ample, all you want, a sufficiency • *We have had our fill of disappointments.*

filling AS A NOUN = **stuffing**, padding, filler, wadding, inside, insides, contents, innards *(informal)* • *Make the filling from down or feathers.*
▸ AS AN ADJECTIVE = **satisfying**, heavy, square, substantial, ample • *a well-spiced and filling meal*

fillip = **boost**, push, spur, spice, incentive, stimulus, prod, zest, goad • *The news gave a tremendous fillip to businesses.*

film AS A NOUN 1 = **movie**, picture, flick *(slang)*, motion picture • *He appeared in the star role of the film.*
2 = **cinema**, the movies • *Film is a business with limited opportunities for actresses.*
3 = **layer**, covering, cover, skin, coating, coat, dusting, tissue, membrane, scum, gauze, integument, pellicle • *The sea is coated with a film of sewage.*
4 = **haze**, cloud, blur, mist, veil, opacity, haziness, mistiness • *There was a sort of film over my eyes.*
▸ AS A VERB 1 = **photograph**, record, shoot, video, videotape, take • *We filmed the scene in one hour.*
2 = **adapt for the screen**, make into a film • *He filmed her life story.*
▸ RELATED ADJECTIVES: cinematic, filmic

film star = **actor**, star, actress, celebrity, performer, superstar, movie star, leading man, Thespian, leading lady,

FIGURES OF SPEECH

alliteration	apophasis	epanorthosis	kenning	periphrasis	spoonerism
allusion	aporia	exclamation	litotes	personification	syllepsis
anacoluthia	aposiopesis	gemination	malapropism	pleonasm	synechdoche
anadiplosis	apostrophe	hendiadys	meiosis	polysyndeton	tmesis
analogy	catachresis	hypallage	metaphor	prolepsis	zeugma
anaphora	chiasmus	hyperbaton	metonymy	prosopopoeia	
anastrophe	circumlocution	hyperbole	onomatopoeia	repetition	
antiphrasis	climax	hysteron proteron	oxymoron	rhetorical question	
antithesis	emphasis	inversion	paralipsis	sarcasm	
antonomasia	epanaphora	irony	parenthesis	simile	

megastar *(informal)*, trouper, thesp *(informal)*, play-actor, dramatic artist, tragedian *or* tragedienne, player • *Perhaps I'll be a famous film star one day.*
▹ *See panels* **Academy award winners; Bafta winners**

filmy = **transparent**, fine, sheer, delicate, fragile, see-through, flimsy, chiffon, insubstantial, floaty, gossamer, diaphanous, gauzy, cobwebby, finespun • *women wearing filmy nightgowns*

filter AS A NOUN = **sieve**, mesh, gauze, strainer, membrane, riddle, sifter • *a paper coffee filter*
▸ AS A VERB 1 = **trickle**, leach, seep, percolate, well, escape, leak, penetrate, ooze, dribble, exude • *Water filtered through the peat.*
2 *with* **through** = **purify**, treat, strain, refine, riddle, sift, sieve, winnow, filtrate, screen • *The best prevention for cholera is to filter water.*
3 = **seep**, trickle, percolate, reach gradually • *The news began to filter through to the politicians.*

filth 1 = **dirt**, refuse, pollution, muck, shit *(taboo slang)*, crap *(taboo slang)*, garbage, sewage, contamination, dung, sludge, squalor, grime, faeces, slime, excrement, nastiness, carrion, excreta, crud *(slang)*, foulness, putrefaction, ordure, defilement, kak *(S. African taboo slang)*, grot *(slang)*, filthiness, uncleanness, putrescence, foul matter • *tons of filth and sewage*
2 = **obscenity**, corruption, pornography, indecency, impurity, vulgarity, smut, vileness, dirty-mindedness • *The dialogue was all filth and innuendo.*

filthy 1 = **dirty**, nasty, foul, polluted, vile, squalid, slimy, unclean, putrid, faecal, scummy, scuzzy *(slang, chiefly U.S.)*, skanky *(slang)*, feculent, festy *(Austral. slang)* • *The water looks stale and filthy.*
2 = **grimy**, black, muddy, smoky, blackened, grubby, sooty, unwashed, mucky, scuzzy *(slang, chiefly U.S.)*, begrimed, skanky *(slang)*, mud-encrusted, miry, festy *(Austral. slang)* • *He always wore a filthy old jacket.*
3 = **obscene**, foul, corrupt, coarse, indecent, pornographic, suggestive, lewd, depraved, foul-mouthed, X-rated *(informal)*, bawdy, impure, smutty, licentious, dirty-minded • *The play was full of filthy foul language.*
4 = **stormy**, bad, wild, rough, wet, horrible, rainy, disagreeable, blustery • *a filthy wet night*
5 = **despicable**, mean, low, base, offensive, vicious, vile, contemptible, scurvy • *'You filthy swine!' Penelope shouted.*
6 = **bad**, angry, grumbling, irritable, sullen, surly, petulant, sulky, ill-tempered, irascible, cantankerous, tetchy, ratty *(Brit. & N.Z. informal)*, cross, testy, grouchy *(informal)*, querulous, peevish, huffy, splenetic, crotchety *(informal)*, liverish • *He was in a filthy temper.*

final AS AN ADJECTIVE 1 = **last**, latest, end, closing, finishing, concluding, ultimate, terminal, last-minute, eventual, terminating • *the final book in the series*
OPPOSITES: first, opening, earliest
2 = **irrevocable**, absolute, decisive, definitive, decided, finished, settled, definite, conclusive, irrefutable, incontrovertible, unalterable, determinate • *The judge's decision is final.*
▸ AS A NOUN = **decider**, Cup final, final match, final game • *The Scottish Cup final*

finale 1 = **climax**, ending, close, conclusion, culmination, denouement, last part, epilogue, last act, crowning glory, finis • *the finale of Shostakovich's Fifth Symphony*
OPPOSITES: opening, lead-in, preliminaries
2 = **end**, ending, close, result, finish, consequence, conclusion, outcome, completion, termination, culmination, end result, denouement, bitter end • *It was a sad finale to a spectacular career.*

finality = **conclusiveness**, resolution, decisiveness, certitude, definiteness, irrevocability, inevitableness, unavoidability, decidedness • *Children have difficulty in grasping the finality of death.*

finalize *or* **finalise** = **complete**, settle, conclude, tie up, decide, agree, work out, clinch, wrap up *(informal)*, shake hands, sew up *(informal)*, complete the arrangements for • *They have not finalized the deal yet.*

finally 1 = **eventually**, at last, in the end, ultimately, at the last, at the end of the day, in the long run, at length, at the last moment, at long last, when all is said and done, in the fullness of time, after a long time • *The food finally arrived at the end of the week.*
2 = **lastly**, in the end, ultimately • *Finally came the dessert trolley.*
3 = **in conclusion**, lastly, in closing, to conclude, to sum up, in summary • *Finally, a word or two of advice.*
4 = **conclusively**, for good, permanently, for ever, completely, definitely, once and for all, decisively, convincingly, inexorably, irrevocably, for all time, inescapably, beyond the shadow of a doubt • *Finally draw a line under the affair.*

finance AS A NOUN 1 = **funds**, backing, money, capital, cash, resources, assets, sponsorship, wonga *(slang)* • *businesses seeking finance*
2 = **economics**, business, money, banking, accounts, investment, commerce, financial affairs, money management • *a major player in the world of high finance*
▸ AS A PLURAL NOUN = **resources**, money, funds, capital, cash, affairs, budgeting, assets, cash flow, financial affairs, money management, wherewithal, financial condition • *Women manage the day-to-day finances.*
▸ AS A VERB = **fund**, back, support, pay for, guarantee, float, invest in, underwrite, endow, subsidize, bankroll *(U.S.)*, set up in business, provide security for, provide money for • *new taxes to finance increased military expenditure*

financial = **economic**, business, money, budgeting, budgetary, commercial, monetary, fiscal, pecuniary • *The company is in financial difficulties.*

financier = **investor**, banker, capitalist, tycoon, stockbroker, industrialist, speculator, magnate, captain of industry • *She was a slick, poised, City financier.*

financing = **funding**, money, support, funds, capital, subsidy, sponsorship, endowment, underwriting, financial support, financial backing, wonga *(slang)* • *The programme needed additional financing.*

finch
▸ RELATED ADJECTIVE: fringilline

find AS A VERB 1 = **discover**, turn up, uncover, unearth, spot, expose, come up with, locate, detect, come across, track down, catch sight of, stumble upon, hit upon, espy, ferret out, chance upon, light upon, put your finger on, lay your hand on, run to ground, run to earth, descry • *The police also found a pistol.*
OPPOSITES: lose, miss, overlook
2 = **regain**, recover, get back, retrieve, repossess • *Luckily she found her bag.*
3 = **obtain**, get, come by, procure, win, gain, achieve, earn, acquire, attain • *Many people here cannot find work.*
4 = **be present**, exist, occur, obtain • *Fibre is found in cereal foods.*
5 = **encounter**, meet, recognize • *They found her walking alone on the beach.*
6 = **observe**, learn, note, discover, notice, realize, remark, come up with, arrive at, perceive, detect, become aware, experience, ascertain • *The study found that heart disease can begin in childhood.*
7 = **judge**, decide, determine, conclude, ascertain, adjudicate, adjudge, arbitrate • *He has been found guilty on all five charges.*
8 = **consider**, think, hold, believe, judge, deem • *I find it ludicrous that nothing has been done.*

ACADEMY AWARD WINNERS

Film	Year of award	Film	Year of award	Film	Year of award
Wings	1929	Marty	1956	Gandhi	1983
The Broadway Melody	1930	Around the World in 80 Days	1957	Terms of Endearment	1984
All Quiet on the Western Front	1931	The Bridge on the River Kwai	1958	Amadeus	1985
Cimarron	1932	Gigi	1959	Out of Africa	1986
Grand Hotel	1933	Ben-Hur	1960	Platoon	1987
Cavalcade	1934	The Apartment	1961	The Last Emperor	1988
It Happened One Night	1935	West-Side Story	1962	Rain Man	1989
Mutiny on the Bounty	1936	Lawrence of Arabia	1963	Driving Miss Daisy	1990
The Great Ziegfeld	1937	Tom Jones	1964	Dances with Wolves	1991
The Life of Emile Zola	1938	My Fair Lady	1965	The Silence of the Lambs	1992
You Can't Take It with You	1939	The Sound of Music	1966	Unforgiven	1993
Gone with the Wind	1940	A Man for All Seasons	1967	Schindler's List	1994
Rebecca	1941	In the Heat of the Night	1968	Forrest Gump	1995
How Green Was My Valley	1942	Oliver!	1969	Braveheart	1996
Mrs Miniver	1943	Midnight Cowboy	1970	The English Patient	1997
Casablanca	1944	Patton	1971	Titanic	1998
Going My Way	1945	The French Connection	1972	Shakespeare in Love	1999
The Lost Weekend	1946	The Godfather	1973	American Beauty	2000
The Best Years of Our Lives	1947	The Sting	1974	Gladiator	2001
Gentleman's Agreement	1948	The Godfather Part II	1975	A Beautiful Mind	2002
Hamlet	1949	One Flew over the Cuckoo's Nest	1976	Chicago	2003
All the King's Men	1950	Rocky	1977	The Lord of the Rings:	
All About Eve	1951	Annie Hall	1978	The Return of the King	2004
An American in Paris	1952	The Deer Hunter	1979	Million Dollar Baby	2005
The Greatest Show on Earth	1953	Kramer vs Kramer	1980	Crash	2006
From Here to Eternity	1954	Ordinary People	1981	The Departed	2007
On the Waterfront	1955	Chariots of Fire	1982	No Country for Old Men	2008

9 = feel, have, experience, sense, obtain, know • *Could anyone find pleasure in killing this creature?*
10 = provide, supply, contribute, furnish, cough up *(informal)*, purvey, be responsible for, bring • *Their parents can usually find the money for them.*
11 = summon (up), gather, muster • *Eventually she found the courage to leave the relationship.*
▸ **AS A NOUN = discovery**, catch, asset, bargain, acquisition, good buy • *Another lucky find was a pair of candle-holders.*
▸ **IN PHRASES: find someone out = detect**, catch, unmask, rumble *(Brit. informal)*, reveal, expose, disclose, uncover, suss (out) *(slang)*, bring to light • *I wondered for a moment if she'd found me out.*
find something out = learn, discover, realize, observe, perceive, detect, become aware, come to know, note • *It was such a relief to find out that the boy was normal.*

PROVERBS
Finders keepers

finding 1 *usually plural* = **result**, decision, conclusion, verdict, recommendation • *the main findings of the survey*
2 = judgment, ruling, decision, award, conclusion, verdict, recommendation, decree, pronouncement • *He said we should accept the findings of the court.*

fine[1] **AS AN ADJECTIVE 1 = excellent**, good, great, striking, choice, beautiful, masterly, select, rare, very good, supreme, impressive, outstanding, magnificent, superior, accomplished, sterling, first-class, divine, exceptional, splendid, world-class, exquisite, admirable, skilful, ornate, first-rate, showy • *This is a fine book.*
OPPOSITES: poor, inferior, indifferent
2 = well, fit, healthy, in good health, strong, sound, robust, hale, hearty, alive and kicking, fighting fit *(informal)*, in fine fettle, up to par, fit as a fiddle, able-bodied • *She is fine and sends her best wishes.*
3 = satisfactory, good, all right, suitable, acceptable, convenient, agreeable, hunky-dory *(informal)*, fair, O.K. *or* okay *(informal)* • *It's fine to ask questions as we go along.*
4 = fine-grained, ground, powdered, powdery, granulated, pulverized • *The ship came to rest on the fine sand.*
5 = thin, small, light, narrow, wispy • *The heat scorched the fine hairs on her arms.*
6 = delicate, light, thin, sheer, lightweight, flimsy, wispy, gossamer, diaphanous, gauzy, chiffony • *Her suit was of a pale grey fine material.*
OPPOSITES: heavy, rough, coarse
7 = stylish, expensive, elegant, refined, tasteful, quality, schmick *(Austral. informal)* • *We waited in our fine clothes.*
8 = exquisite, delicate, fragile, dainty • *She wears fine jewellery wherever she goes.*
9 = intricate, detailed, complex, complicated, exact, meticulous • *Fine detailed work is done with the help of a magnifying glass.*
10 = minute, exact, precise, nice • *They are reserving judgement on the fine detail.*
11 = subtle, narrow, delicate, nice • *a fine distinction between her official and unofficial duties*
12 = keen, minute, nice, quick, sharp, critical, acute, sensitive, subtle, precise, refined, discriminating, tenuous, fastidious, hairsplitting • *She has a fine eye for detail.*
13 = brilliant, quick, keen, alert, clever, intelligent, penetrating, astute • *He had a fine mind and excellent knowledge.*
14 = sharp, keen, polished, honed, razor-sharp, cutting • *tapering to a fine point*
15 = good-looking, striking, pretty, attractive, lovely, smart, handsome, stylish, bonny, well-favoured, fit *(Brit. informal)* • *You're a very fine woman.*
16 = worthy, good, excellent, deserving, valuable, decent, reliable, respectable, upright, admirable, honourable, honest, righteous, reputable, virtuous, dependable, commendable, creditable, laudable, praiseworthy,

BAFTA WINNERS

Film	Year of award	Film	Year of award	Film	Year of award
The Best Years of Our Lives	1948	A Man for All Seasons	1968	Dead Poets Society	1990
Hamlet	1949	The Graduate	1969	GoodFellas	1991
Bicyle Thieves	1950	Midnight Cowboy	1970	The Commitments	1992
All About Eve	1951	Butch Cassidy and the Sundance Kid	1971	Howards End	1993
La Ronde	1952	Sunday Bloody Sunday	1972	Schindler's List	1994
The Sound Barrier	1953	Cabaret	1973	Four Weddings and a Funeral	1995
Forbidden Games	1954	Day for Night	1974	Sense and Sensibility *and* The Usual Suspects (joint winners)	1996
The Wages of Fear	1955	Lacombe Lucien	1975	The English Patient	1997
Richard III	1956	Alice Doesn't Live Here Anymore	1976	The Full Monty	1998
Gervaise	1957	One Flew Over the Cuckoo's Nest	1977	Shakespeare in Love	1999
The Bridge on the River Kwai	1958	Annie Hall	1978	American Beauty	2000
Room at the Top	1959	Julia	1979	Gladiator	2001
Ben-Hur	1960	Manhattan	1980	The Lord of the Rings: The Fellowship of the Ring	2002
The Apartment	1961	The Elephant Man	1981	The Pianist	2003
Ballad of a Soldier *and* The Hustler (joint winners)	1962	Chariots of Fire	1982	The Lord of the Rings: The Return of the King	2004
Lawrence of Arabia	1963	Gandhi	1983	The Aviator	2005
Tom Jones	1964	Educating Rita	1984	Brokeback Mountain	2006
Dr Strangelove: Or How I Learned to Stop Worrying and Love the Bomb	1965	The Killing Fields	1985	The Queen	2007
My Fair Lady	1966	The Purple Rose of Cairo	1986	Atonement	2008
Who's Afraid of Virginis Woolf?	1967	A Room with a View	1987		
		Jean de Florette	1988		
		The Last Emperor	1989		

meritorious, estimable • *He was an excellent journalist and a fine man.*
17 = **sunny**, clear, fair, dry, bright, pleasant, clement, balmy, cloudless • *I'll do the garden if the weather is fine.*
OPPOSITES: dull, unpleasant, cloudy
18 = **pure**, clear, refined, unadulterated, unalloyed, unpolluted, solid, sterling • *a light, fine oil, high in vitamin content*
▸ AS AN ADVERB = **all right**, well, well enough, adequately, not badly, satisfactorily, acceptably, passably, O.K. *or* okay *(informal)* • *After all, we're doing fine now, aren't we?*

fine[2] AS A NOUN = **penalty**, damages, punishment, forfeit, financial penalty, amercement *(obsolete)* • *If convicted he faces a fine of one million dollars.*
▸ AS A VERB = **penalize**, charge, punish • *She was fined £300 and banned from driving.*

finery = **splendour**, trappings, frippery, glad rags *(informal)*, gear *(informal)*, decorations, ornaments, trinkets, Sunday best, gewgaws, showiness, best bib and tucker *(informal)*, bling *(slang)* • *the wedding guests in all their finery*

finesse AS A NOUN 1 = **skill**, style, know-how *(informal)*, polish, craft, sophistication, cleverness, quickness, adroitness, adeptness
2 = **diplomacy**, discretion, subtlety, delicacy, tact, savoir-faire, artfulness, adeptness • *handling diplomatic challenges with finesse*
3 = **stratagem**, trick, manoeuvre, bluff, ruse, artifice, feint, wile • *Declarer was planning to take a finesse in spades.*
▸ AS A VERB = **manoeuvre**, steer, manipulate, bluff • *a typical politician trying to finesse a sticky situation*

finger AS A NOUN 1 = **digit**, thumb, forefinger, little finger, index finger, middle finger, ring finger, third finger, first finger, second finger, fourth finger • *She ran her fingers through her hair.*
2 = **strip**, piece, band, sliver, bit • *a thin finger of land*
▸ AS A VERB 1 = **touch**, feel, handle, play with, manipulate, paw *(informal)*, maul, toy with, fiddle with *(informal)*, meddle with, play about with • *He fingered the few coins in his pocket.*
2 = **inform on**, shop *(slang, chiefly Brit.)*, grass *(Brit. slang)*, rat *(informal)*, betray, notify, peach *(slang)*, tip off, squeal *(slang)*, leak to, incriminate, tell on *(informal)*, blow the whistle on *(informal)*, snitch *(slang)*, blab, nark *(Brit., Austral. & N.Z. slang)*, inculpate, dob in *(Austral. slang)* • *They fingered him to the police.*
▸ IN PHRASES: **put your finger on something** = **identify**, place, remember, discover, indicate, recall, find out, locate, pin down, bring to mind, hit upon, hit the nail on the head • *She couldn't quite put her finger on the reason.*
▸ RELATED ADJECTIVE: digital

fingernail
▸ TECHNICAL NAME: unguis
▸ RELATED ADJECTIVE: ungual, ungular

finicky = **fussy**, difficult, particular, hard to please, critical, scrupulous, fastidious, dainty, squeamish, choosy *(informal)*, picky *(informal)*, nit-picking *(informal)*, finicking, overnice, overparticular, nit-picky *(informal)* • *Even the most finicky eater will find something to eat.*

finish AS A VERB 1 = **stop**, close, complete, achieve, conclude, cease, accomplish, execute, discharge, culminate, wrap up *(informal)*, terminate, round off, bring to a close *or* conclusion • *He was cheered when he finished his speech.*
OPPOSITES: start, begin, create
2 = **get done**, complete, put the finishing touch(es) to, finalize, do, deal with, settle, conclude, fulfil, carry through, get out of the way, make short work of • *They've been working to finish a report this week.*
3 = **end**, stop, conclude, wind up, terminate • *The teaching day finished at around 4pm.*
4 = **leave**, complete, quit, drop out of, pack in *(informal)* • *He had finished school and was waiting to go to university.*
5 = **consume**, dispose of, devour, polish off, drink, eat, neck *(slang)*, drain, get through, dispatch, hoover *(informal)*, deplete • *He finished his dinner and left.*
6 = **use up**, use, spend, empty, exhaust, expend • *Once you have finished all 21 pills, stop for seven days.*
7 = **coat**, polish, stain, texture, wax, varnish, gild, veneer, lacquer, smooth off, face • *The bowl is finished in a pearlised lustre.*
8 *often with* **off** = **destroy**, defeat, overcome, bring down, best, worst, ruin, get rid of, dispose of, rout, put an end to,

overpower, annihilate, put paid to, move in for the kill, drive to the wall, administer *or* give the coup de grâce • *I played well but I didn't finish him off.*
9 *often with* **off** = **kill**, murder, destroy, do in *(slang)*, take out *(slang)*, massacre, butcher, slaughter, dispatch, slay, eradicate, do away with, blow away *(slang, chiefly U.S.)*, knock off *(slang)*, annihilate, exterminate, take (someone's) life, bump off *(slang)* • *She finished him off with an axe.*
▸ **AS A NOUN** 1 = **end**, ending, close, closing, conclusion, run-in, winding up *(informal)*, wind-up, completion, finale, termination, culmination, cessation, last stage(s), denouement, finalization • *I intend to see the job through to the finish.*
OPPOSITES: beginning, birth, conception
2 = **surface**, appearance, polish, shine, grain, texture, glaze, veneer, lacquer, lustre, smoothness, patina • *The finish of the woodwork was excellent.*

QUOTATIONS
To finish a work? To finish a picture? What nonsense! To finish it means to be through with it, to kill it, to rid it of its soul, to give it its final blow ... the *coup de grâce* for the painter as well as for the picture
[Pablo Picasso]

finished 1 = **over**, done, completed, achieved, through, ended, closed, full, final, complete, in the past, concluded, shut, accomplished, executed, tied up, wrapped up *(informal)*, terminated, sewn up *(informal)*, finalized, over and done with • *Finally, last spring, the film was finished.*
OPPOSITES: begun, incomplete
2 = **ruined**, done for *(informal)*, doomed, bankrupt, through, lost, gone, defeated, devastated, wrecked, wiped out, undone, washed up *(informal, chiefly U.S.)*, wound up, liquidated, dead in the water *(informal)* • *'This business is finished,' he said sadly.*
3 = **spent**, drained, exhausted, used up, done, gone, empty, played out *(informal)* • *They got a grant from the government but they claim that's all finished now.*

finite = **limited**, bounded, restricted, demarcated, conditioned, circumscribed, delimited, terminable, subject to limitations • *a finite set of elements*
OPPOSITES: endless, eternal, infinite

fire **AS A NOUN** 1 = **flames**, blaze, combustion, inferno, conflagration, holocaust • *A forest fire is sweeping across the country.*
2 = **heater**, radiator, convector • *She switched on the electric fire.*
3 = **passion**, force, light, energy, heat, spirit, enthusiasm, excitement, dash, intensity, sparkle, life, vitality, animation, vigour, zeal, splendour, verve, fervour, eagerness, dynamism, lustre, radiance, welly *(slang)*, virtuosity, élan, ardour, brio, vivacity, impetuosity, burning passion, scintillation, fervency, pizzazz *or* pizazz *(informal)* • *His punishing schedule seemed to dim his fire at times.*
4 = **bombardment**, shooting, firing, shelling, hail, volley, barrage, gunfire, sniping, flak, salvo, fusillade, cannonade • *His car was raked with fire from automatic weapons.*
5 = **criticism**, condemnation, disapproval, stick *(slang)*, blame, rebuke, reprimand, flak *(informal)*, reproach, dressing down *(informal)*, reproof, sideswipe, castigation, remonstrance, reprehension • *He said they should turn their fire on the opposition.*
▸ **AS A VERB** 1 = **let off**, shoot, launch, shell, loose, set off, discharge, hurl, eject, detonate, let loose *(informal)*, touch off • *a huge gun designed to fire nuclear or chemical shells*
2 = **shoot**, explode, discharge, detonate, pull the trigger • *Soldiers fired rubber bullets to disperse crowds.*
3 = **dismiss**, sack *(informal)*, get rid of, discharge, lay off, make redundant, cashier, give notice, show the door, give the boot *(slang)*, kiss off *(slang, chiefly U.S. & Canad.)*, give the push, give the bullet *(Brit. slang)*, give marching orders, give someone their cards, give the sack to *(informal)*, give someone his *or* her P45 *(informal)*, kennet *(Austral. slang)*, jeff *(Austral. slang)* • *She was sent a letter saying she was fired from her job.*
4 = **inspire**, excite, stir, stimulate, motivate, irritate, arouse, awaken, animate, rouse, stir up, quicken, inflame, incite, electrify, enliven, spur on, galvanize, inspirit, impassion • *They were fired with an enthusiasm for public speaking.*
5 = **set fire to**, torch, ignite, set on fire, kindle, set alight, set ablaze, put a match to, set aflame, enkindle, light • *matches, turpentine and cotton, with which they fired the houses*
▸ **IN PHRASES: catch fire** = **ignite**, flare up, burst into flames, burn • *The aircraft caught fire soon after take-off.*
on fire 1 = **burning**, flaming, blazing, alight, ablaze, in flames, aflame, fiery • *The captain radioed that the ship was on fire.*
2 = **ardent**, excited, inspired, eager, enthusiastic, passionate, fervent • *He was on fire, youthfully impatient.*
▸ **RELATED MANIA:** pyromania
▸ **RELATED PHOBIA:** pyrophobia

PROVERBS
Fight fire with fire
Fire is a good servant but a bad master
If you play with fire you get burnt
Out of the frying pan, into the fire

firearm = **gun**, weapon, handgun, revolver, shooter *(slang)*, piece *(slang)*, rod *(slang)*, pistol, heater *(U.S. slang)* • *He was charged with possession of illegal firearms.*

firebrand = **rabble-rouser**, activist, incendiary, fomenter, instigator, agitator, demagogue, tub-thumper, soapbox orator • *his reputation as a young firebrand*

fireproof = **fire-resistant**, flameproof, flame-retardant, flame-resistant, nonflammable, incombustible • *soldiers wearing fireproof clothing*

fireworks 1 = **pyrotechnics**, illuminations, feux d'artifice • *The rally ended with spectacular fireworks and band music.*
2 = **trouble**, row, storm, rage, temper, wax *(informal, chiefly Brit.)*, uproar, hysterics, paroxysms, fit of rage • *The big media companies will be forced to compete, and we should see some fireworks.*

firm[1] **AS AN ADJECTIVE** 1 = **hard**, solid, compact, dense, set, concentrated, stiff, compacted, rigid, compressed, inflexible, solidified, unyielding, congealed, inelastic, jelled, close-grained, jellified • *Fruit should be firm and excellent in condition.*
OPPOSITES: soft, limp, flabby
2 = **secure**, strong, fixed, secured, rooted, stable, steady, anchored, braced, robust, cemented, fast, sturdy, embedded, fastened, riveted, taut, stationary, motionless, immovable, unmoving, unshakeable, unfluctuating • *use a firm platform or a sturdy ladder*
OPPOSITES: loose, unstable, shaky
3 = **strong**, close, tight, steady • *The quick handshake was firm and cool.*
4 = **strict**, unwavering, unswerving, unshakeable, constant, stalwart, resolute, inflexible, steadfast, unyielding, immovable, unflinching, unbending, obdurate, unalterable, unfaltering • *They needed the guiding hand of a firm father figure.*
5 = **determined**, true, settled, fixed, resolved, strict, definite, set on, adamant, stalwart, staunch, resolute, inflexible, steadfast, unyielding, unwavering, immovable, unflinching, unswerving, unbending, obdurate, unshakeable, unalterable, unshaken, unfaltering • *He held a firm belief in the afterlife.*
OPPOSITES: wavering, irresolute, inconstant
6 = **definite**, hard, clear, confirmed, settled, fixed, hard-and-fast, cut-and-dried *(informal)* • *firm evidence*
7 = **close**, good, devoted, inseparable, loving, dear, familiar,

attached, intimate, confidential • *They met two years ago and soon became firm friends.*

▸ **IN PHRASES: firm something up 1 = tone**, shape up, get in shape, get into condition • *Firm up muscles and tighten the skin.*

2 = confirm, establish, settle, fix, clinch, substantiate • *The government will firm up their plans for a safer Britain.*

firm² = **company**, business, concern, association, organization, house, corporation, venture, enterprise, partnership, establishment, undertaking, outfit *(informal)*, consortium, conglomerate • *The firm's employees were expecting large bonuses.*

firmament 1 = sky, skies, heaven, heavens, the blue, vault, welkin *(archaic)*, empyrean *(poetic)*, vault of heaven, rangi *(N. Z.)* • *There are no stars in the firmament.*

2 = arena, province, sphere, realm, domain • *He was a rising star in the political firmament.*

firmly 1 = securely, safely, tightly • *The door is locked and the windows are firmly shut.*

2 = immovably, securely, steadily, like a rock, unflinchingly, enduringly, motionlessly, unshakeably • *boards firmly fixed to metal posts in the ground*

3 = steadily, securely, tightly, unflinchingly • *She held me firmly by the elbow.*

4 = resolutely, strictly, staunchly, steadfastly, determinedly, through thick and thin, with decision, with a rod of iron, definitely, unwaveringly, unchangeably • *Political opinions are firmly held.*

firmness 1 = hardness, resistance, density, rigidity, stiffness, solidity, inflexibility, compactness, fixedness, inelasticity • *the firmness of the ground*

2 = steadiness, tension, stability, tightness, soundness, tautness, tensile strength, immovability • *testing the firmness of the nearest stakes*

3 = strength, tightness, steadiness • *He was surprised at the firmness of her grip.*

4 = resolve, resolution, constancy, inflexibility, steadfastness, obduracy, strictness, strength of will, fixity, fixedness, staunchness • *There was no denying his considerable firmness of purpose.*

first AS AN ADJECTIVE 1 = earliest, initial, opening, introductory, original, maiden, primitive, primordial, primeval, pristine • *The first men of this race lived like gods.* • *the first few flakes of snow*

2 = top, best, winning, premier • *The first prize is thirty-one thousand pounds.*

3 = elementary, key, basic, primary, fundamental, cardinal, rudimentary, elemental • *It is time to go back to first principles.*

4 = foremost, highest, greatest, leading, head, ruling, chief, prime, supreme, principal, paramount, overriding, pre-eminent • *The first priority for development is to defeat inflation.*

▸ **AS A NOUN = novelty**, innovation, originality, new experience • *It is a first for New York.*

▸ **AS AN ADVERB = to begin with**, firstly, initially, at the beginning, in the first place, beforehand, to start with, at the outset, before all else • *I do not remember who spoke first.*

▸ **IN PHRASES: from the first = start**, beginning, outset, the very beginning, introduction, starting point, inception, commencement, the word 'go' *(informal)* • *You knew about me from the first, didn't you?*

QUOTATIONS

Many that are first shall be last; and the last shall be first

[*Bible: St. Mark*]

PROVERBS

First come, first served

First things first

first class *or* **first-class** = **excellent**, great, very good, superb, topping *(Brit. slang)*, top, tops *(slang)*, bad *(slang)*, prime, capital, choice, champion, cool *(informal)*, brilliant, crack *(slang)*, mean *(slang)*, cracking *(Brit. informal)*, crucial *(slang)*, outstanding, premium, ace *(informal)*, marvellous, exceptional, mega *(slang)*, sovereign, dope *(slang)*, world-class, blue-chip, top-flight, top-class, five-star, exemplary, wicked *(slang)*, first-rate, def *(slang)*, superlative, second to none, top-notch *(informal)*, brill *(informal)*, top-drawer, matchless, tiptop, boffo *(slang)*, the dog's bollocks *(taboo slang)*, jim-dandy *(slang)*, twenty-four carat, A1 *or* A-one *(informal)*, bitchin' *(U.S. slang)*, chillin' *(U.S. slang)*, booshit *(Austral. slang)*, exo *(Austral. slang)*, sik *(Austral. slang)*, rad *(informal)*, phat *(slang)*, schmick *(Austral. informal)*, beaut *(informal)*, barrie *(Scot. slang)*, belting *(Brit. slang)*, pearler *(Austral. slang)* • *The food was first-class.*

OPPOSITES: shocking *(informal)*, terrible, inferior

first-hand AS AN ADJECTIVE = direct, personal, immediate, face-to-face, straight from the horse's mouth • *He'll get a first-hand briefing on the emergency.*

▸ **IN PHRASES: at first hand = directly**, personally, immediately, face-to-face, straight from the horse's mouth • *I heard all about it first-hand.*

firstly = **in the first place**, initially, to begin with, to start with, before all else • *Firstly, vitamin C is needed for hormone production.*

first name = **forename**, Christian name, given name, baptismal name • *Her first name was Mary.*

first-rate = **excellent**, outstanding, first class, exceptional, mean *(slang)*, topping *(Brit. slang)*, top, tops *(slang)*, prime, cool *(informal)*, crack *(slang)*, cracking *(Brit. informal)*, crucial *(slang)*, exclusive, superb, mega *(slang)*, sovereign, dope *(slang)*, world-class, admirable, wicked *(slang)*, def *(slang)*, superlative, second to none, top-notch *(informal)*, brill *(informal)*, tiptop, bodacious *(slang, chiefly U.S.)*, boffo *(slang)*, the dog's bollocks *(taboo slang)*, jim-dandy *(slang)*, A1 *or* A-one *(informal)*, bitchin' *(U.S. slang)*, chillin' *(U.S. slang)*, booshit *(Austral. slang)*, exo *(Austral. slang)*, sik *(Austral. slang)*, rad *(informal)*, phat *(slang)*, schmick *(Austral. informal)* • *They were dealing with a first-rate professional.*

fiscal = **financial**, money, economic, monetary, budgetary, pecuniary, tax • *The government tightened fiscal policy.*

fish AS A VERB 1 = angle, net, cast, trawl • *He learnt to fish in the river Cam.*

2 = look (for), search, delve, ferret, rummage, fossick *(Austral. & N.Z.)* • *He fished in his pocket for the key.*

▸ **IN PHRASES: fish for something = seek**, look for, angle for, try to get, hope for, hunt for, hint at, elicit, solicit, invite, search for • *She may be fishing for a compliment.*

fish something out = pull out, produce, take out, extract, bring out, extricate, haul out, find • *She fished out a pair of his socks.*

▸ **RELATED ADJECTIVES:** piscine, ichthyoid, ichthyic

▸ **NAME OF YOUNG:** fry, fingerling

▸ **COLLECTIVE NOUNS:** shoal, draught, haul, run, catch

▸ **NAME OF HOME:** redd

▸ **RELATED MANIA:** ichthyomania

▹ *See panels* **Fish; Sharks; Shellfish**

fisherman = **angler**, fisher • *Near the coast, a fisherman bobbed in a dinghy.*

fishing = **angling**, trawling • *Despite the weather, the fishing has been good.*

▸ **RELATED ADJECTIVE:** piscatorial

fishy 1 = fishlike, piscine, piscatorial, piscatory • *It hasn't a very strong fishy flavour.*

2 = suspicious, odd, suspect, unlikely, funny *(informal)*, doubtful, dubious, dodgy *(Brit., Austral. & N.Z. informal)*, queer, rum *(Brit. slang)*, questionable, improbable, implausible, cock-and-bull *(informal)*, shonky *(Austral., N.Z. informal)* • *There seems to be something fishy going on.*

fission = **splitting**, parting, breaking, division, rending, rupture, cleavage, schism, scission • *a fission in the earth's crust*

FISH

Types of fish

ahi
ahuru *(N.Z.)*
alewife
albacore
alfonsino
amberjack
anabantid
anabas
anableps
anchoveta
anchovy
angelfish
arapaima
archerfish
argentine
aua *(N.Z.)*
Australian salmon, native salmon, salmon trout, bay trout *or* kahawai *(N.Z. & Austral.)*
barbel
barracouta *or (Austral.)* hake
barracuda
barramunda
barramundi *or (Austral.)* barra, *or* giant perch
bass
batfish
beluga
bib, pout, *or* whiting pout
bigeye
billfish
bitterling
black bass
black bream
black cod *or* Māori chief *(N.Z.)*
blackfish *or (Austral.)* nigger
bleak
blenny
blindfish
bloodfin
blowfish *or (Austral.)* toado
blue cod, rock cod, *or (N.Z.)* rawaru, pakirikiri, *or* patutuki
bluefin tuna
bluefish *or* snapper
bluegill
blue nose *(N.Z.)*
boarfish
bonefish
bonito *or (Austral.)* horse mackerel
bony bream *(Austral.)*
bowfin *or* dogfish
bream *or (Austral.)* brim
brill
brook trout *or* speckled trout
brown trout
buffalo fish
bullhead
bull trout
bully *or (N.Z.)* pakoko, titarakura, *or* toitoi
burbot, eelpout, *or* ling
butterfish
butterfish, greenbone, *or (N.Z.)* koaea *or* marari
butterfly fish
cabezon
cabrilla
callop
candlefish *or* eulachon
capelin
carp
catfish
cavalla *or* cavally
cavefish
cero
characin *or* characid
chimaera
Chinook salmon, quinnat salmon, *or* king salmon
chub
chum
cichlid
cisco *or* lake herring
climbing fish *or* climbing perch
clingfish
coalfish *or (Brit.)* saithe *or* coley
cobia, black kingfish, *or* sergeant fish
cockabully
cod *or* codfish
coelacanth
coho *or* silver salmon
coley
conger
coral trout
crappie
croaker
crucian
dab
dace
damselfish
danio
dart *(Austral.)*
darter
dealfish
dentex
dollarfish
dorado
dory
dragonet
eel *or (N.Z.)* tuna
eelpout
electric eel
fallfish
father lasher *or* short-spined sea scorpion
fighting fish *or* betta
filefish
flatfish *or (N.Z.)* flattie
flathead
flounder *or (N.Z.)* patiki
flying fish
flying gurnard
four-eyed fish
frogfish
garpike, garfish, gar, *or (Austral.)* ballahoo
geelbek
gemfish *or (Austral.)* hake
gilthead
goby
golden perch, freshwater bream, Murray perch, *or* yellow-belly *(Austral.)*
goldeye
goldfish
goldsinny *or* goldfinny
gourami
grayling *or (Austral.)* yarra herring
greenling
grenadier *or* rat-tail
groper *or* grouper
grunion
grunt
gudgeon
guitarfish
gunnel
guppy
gurnard *or* gurnet
gwyniad
haddock
hagfish, hag *or*
blind eel
hairtail *or (U.S.)* cutlass fish
hake
halfbeak
halibut
hapuku *(Austral. & N.Z.)*
herring
hogfish
hoki *(N.Z.)*
horned pout *or* brown bullhead
horse mackerel
houndfish
houting
ice fish
jacksmelt
javelin fish *or* Queensland trumpeter
jewelfish
jewfish *or (Austral. informal)* jewie
John Dory
jurel
kelpfish *or (Austral. informal)* kelpie
killifish
kingfish
kingklip *(S. African)*
kokanee
kokopu *(N.Z.)*
labyrinth fish
lampern *or* river lamprey
lamprey *or* lamper eel
lancet fish
lantern fish
largemouth bass
latimeria
leatherjacket
lemon sole
lepidosiren
ling *or (Austral.)* beardie
lingcod
lionfish
loach
louvar
luderick *or (N.Z.)* parore
lumpfish *or* lumpsucker
lungfish
mackerel *or (colloquial)* shiner
mangrove Jack *(Austral.)*
manta, manta ray, devilfish, *or* devil ray
maomao *(N.Z.)*
marlin *or* spearfish
megrim
menhaden
milkfish
miller's thumb
minnow *or (Scot.)* baggie minnow
mirror carp
moki *or* blue moki *(N.Z.)*
molly
monkfish *or (U.S.)* goosefish
mooneye
moonfish
Moorish idol
moray
morwong, black perch, *or (N.Z.)* porae
mudcat
mudfish
mudskipper
opah, moonfish, *or* kingfish
orange chromide
orange roughy *(Austral.)*
orfe
ouananiche
ox-eye herring *(Austral.)*
paddlefish
panchax
pandora
paradise fish
parore, blackfish, black rockfish *or* mangrove fish *(N.Z.)*
parrotfish
pearl perch *(Austral.)*
perch *or (Austral.)* redfin
pickerel
pigfish *or* hogfish
pike, luce, *or* jackfish
pikeperch
pilchard *or (Austral. informal)* pillie
pilot fish
pinfish *or* sailor's choice
pipefish *or* needlefish
piranha
plaice
platy
pogge *or* armed bullhead
pollack
pollan
pomfret
pompano
porae *(N.Z.)*
porcupine fish *or* globefish
porgy *or* pogy
pout
powan *or* lake herring
puffer *or* globefish
pumpkinseed
Queensland halibut
Queensland lungfish
rabbitfish
rainbow trout
ray
red cod
red emperor
redfin
redfish
red mullet *or (U.S.)* goatfish
red salmon
red snapper
remora
ribbonfish
roach
robalo
rock bass
rock cod
rockfish *or (formerly)* rock salmon
rockling
rosefish
rudd
ruffe *or* pope
runner
salmon
salmon trout
sand dab
sand eel, sand lance, *or* launce
sardine
sauger
saury *or* skipper
sawfish
scabbard fish
scad
scaldfish
scat
scorpion fish
sculpin *(U.S. & Canad.)*
scup *or* northern porgy
sea bass
sea bream
sea horse
sea lamprey
sea perch

TYPES OF FISH (CONTINUED)

sea raven, sea robin, sea scorpion, sea snail *or* snailfish, sea trout, Sergeant Baker, sergeant major, shad, shanny, sheepshead, shiner, shovelnose, Siamese fighting fish, sild, silver belly *(N.Z.)*, silverfish, silverside *or* silversides, skate, skelly, skipjack *or* skipjack tuna, sleeper *or* sleeper goby, smallmouth bass, smelt, smooth hound, snapper, red bream, *or (Austral.)* wollomai, snipefish *or* bellows fish, snoek, snook, sockeye *or* red salmon, sole, solenette, spadefish, Spanish mackerel *or* Queensland kingfish, spotted mackerel *or* school mackerel, sprat, squeteague, squirrelfish, steelhead, sterlet, stickleback, stingray, stone bass *or* wreckfish, stonefish, stone roller, sturgeon, sucker, sunfish, surfperch *or* sea perch, surgeonfish, swordfish, swordtail, tailor, tarakihi *(N.Z.)*, tarpon, tarwhine, tautog *or* blackfish, tench, teraglin, tetra, thornback, threadfin, tilapia, tilefish, toadfish, tommy rough *(Austral.)*, topminnow, torsk *or (U.S. & Canadian)* cusk, trevalla *(Austral.)*, trevally, araara, *or* samson fish *(Austral. & N.Z.)*, triggerfish, tripletail, trout, trunkfish, boxfish, *or* cowfish, tuna *or* tunny, turbot, vendace, wahoo, walleye, walleyed pike, *or* dory, warehou *(N.Z.)*, weakfish, weever, whitebait, whitefish, whiting, wirrah, witch, wobbegong, wolffish *or* catfish, wrasse, yellowfin *(N.Z.)*, yellowfin tuna, yellow jack, yellowtail, zander

EXTINCT FISH

ceratodus, ostracoderm, placoderm

fissure = **crack**, opening, hole, split, gap, rent, fault, breach, break, fracture, rift, slit, rupture, cleavage, cleft, chink, crevice, cranny, interstice • *There was a great crack, and a fissure opened up.*

fit[1] **AS A VERB 1 = be the right size (for)**, be the right shape for • *Always buy clothes that fit you properly.*
2 = adapt, fashion, shape, arrange, alter, tailor, adjust, modify, tweak *(informal)*, customize • *She was having her wedding dress fitted.*
3 = place, position, insert • *She fitted her key in the lock.*
4 = attach, join, connect, interlock • *Fit hinge bolts to give support to the door lock.*
5 = suit, meet, match, belong to, agree with, go with, conform to, correspond to, accord with, be appropriate to, concur with, tally with, dovetail with, be consonant with • *Her daughter doesn't fit the current feminine ideal.*
6 = qualify, train, prepare, equip, empower, make ready • *His experience fits him for the top job.*
7 = equip, provide, arm, prepare, outfit, accommodate, fit out, kit out, rig out, accoutre • *The bombs were fitted with time devices.*
▸ **AS AN ADJECTIVE 1 = appropriate**, qualified, suitable, competent, right, becoming, meet *(archaic)*, seemly, trained, able, prepared, fitting, fitted, ready, skilled, correct, deserving, capable, adapted, proper, equipped, good enough, adequate, worthy, convenient, apt, well-suited, expedient, apposite • *You're not fit to be a mother!*
OPPOSITES: inadequate, inappropriate, unfit
2 = healthy, strong, robust, sturdy, well, trim, strapping, hale, in good shape, in good condition, in good health, toned up, as right as rain, in good trim, able-bodied • *It will take a very fit person to beat me.*
OPPOSITES: unfit, unhealthy, flabby
▸ **IN PHRASES: fit in = conform**, adapt, blend in • *She was great with children and fitted in well.*
fit someone up = entrap, set up, frame, trap • *The police have fitted me up.*
fit something *or* someone in = find time for, accommodate, squeeze in • *I just can't fit in regular domestic work.* • *I'll see if I can fit you in some time this afternoon.*
fit something *or* someone out *or* up = equip, outfit, deck out, kit out, provide, supply, furnish • *We helped to fit him out for his trip.*

fit[2] **AS A NOUN 1 = seizure**, attack, bout, spasm, convulsion, paroxysm • *Once a fit has started there's nothing you can do to stop it.*
2 = bout, burst, outbreak, outburst, spell • *I broke into a fit of giggles.*
▸ **IN PHRASES: have a fit = go mad**, explode, blow up *(informal)*, lose it *(informal)*, see red *(informal)*, lose the plot *(informal)*, throw a tantrum, fly off the handle *(informal)*, go spare *(Brit. slang)*, blow your top *(informal)*, fly into a temper, flip your lid *(slang)*, do your nut *(Brit. slang)* • *He'd have a fit if he knew what we were up to!*
in *or* by fits and starts = spasmodically, sporadically, erratically, fitfully, on and off, irregularly, intermittently, off and on, unsystematically • *Military technology advances by fits and starts.*

fitful = **irregular**, broken, disturbed, erratic, variable, flickering, unstable, uneven, fluctuating, sporadic, intermittent, impulsive, haphazard, desultory, spasmodic, inconstant • *He drifted off into a fitful sleep.*
OPPOSITES: even, regular, constant

fitfully = **irregularly**, on and off, intermittently, sporadically, off and on, erratically, in fits and starts, spasmodically, in snatches, desultorily, by fits and starts, interruptedly • *The sun shone fitfully.*

fitness 1 = appropriateness, qualifications, adaptation, competence, readiness, eligibility, suitability, propriety, preparedness, applicability, aptness, pertinence, seemliness • *There is a debate about his fitness for the job.*
2 = health, strength, good health, vigour, good condition, wellness, robustness • *Squash was thought to offer all-round fitness.*

fitted 1 = tailored, shaped • *baggy trousers with fitted jackets*
2 = built-in, permanent • *I've recarpeted our bedroom and added fitted wardrobes.*
3 = suited • *She was ill fitted to my ideal of a mother.*
4 *often with* **with = equipped**, provided, supplied, set up, appointed, outfitted, furnished, rigged out, accoutred • *Bedrooms are fitted with alarm pull cords.*

fitting AS AN ADJECTIVE = appropriate, suitable, proper, apt, right, becoming, meet *(archaic)*, seemly, correct, decent, desirable, apposite, decorous, comme il faut *(French)* • *The President's address was a fitting end to the campaign.*

OPPOSITES: unfitting, unsuitable, improper
▸ **AS A NOUN** **1 = accessory**, part, piece, unit, connection, component, attachment • *brass light fittings*
2 = installation, placing, putting in • *the fitting of emergency shut-down valves*
▸ **AS A PLURAL NOUN** **= furnishings**, extras, equipment, fixtures, appointments, furniture, trimmings, accessories, conveniences, accoutrements, bells and whistles, fitments, appurtenances • *He has made fittings for antique cars.*

five
▸ **RELATED PREFIXES:** penta-, quinque-

fix **AS A VERB** **1 = place**, join, stick, attach, set, position, couple, plant, link, establish, tie, settle, secure, bind, root, connect, locate, pin, install, anchor, glue, cement, implant, embed, fasten, make fast • *Fix the photo to the card using double-sided tape.*
2 *often with* **up = decide**, set, name, choose, limit, establish, determine, settle, appoint, arrange, define, conclude, resolve, arrive at, specify, agree on • *He's fixed a time when I can see him.*
3 *often with* **up = arrange**, organize, sort out, see to, make arrangements for • *I've fixed it for you to see them.*
4 = repair, mend, service, sort, correct, restore, adjust, regulate, see to, overhaul, patch up, get working, put right, put to rights • *If something is broken, we fix it.*
5 = focus, direct at, level at, fasten on, rivet on • *Attention is fixed on the stock market.*
6 = prepare, make, cook, put together, get ready • *She fixed some food for us.*
7 = neaten, arrange, adjust, tidy, tidy up, put in order • *'I've got to fix my hair,' I said.*
8 = rig, set up *(informal)*, influence, manipulate, bribe, manoeuvre, fiddle *(informal)*, pull strings *(informal)* • *They offered players bribes to fix a league match.*
9 = put paid to, destroy, ruin, get rid of, put an end to, put out of action • *That'll fix him.*
10 = stabilize, set, consolidate, harden, thicken, stiffen, solidify, congeal, rigidify • *Egg yolk is used to fix the pigment.*
▸ **AS A NOUN** **1 = solution**, result, answer, resolution, cure, remedy, antidote • *Those changes could just be a temporary fix.*
2 = dose, hit, shot, injection • *She needed her daily fix of publicity.*
3 = mess, spot *(informal)*, corner, hole *(slang)*, difficulty, jam *(informal)*, dilemma, embarrassment, plight, hot water *(informal)*, pickle *(informal)*, uphill *(S. African)*, predicament, difficult situation, quandary, tight spot, ticklish situation • *The government has got itself in a fix.*
▸ **IN PHRASES:** **fix someone up** *often with* **with = provide**, supply, accommodate, bring about, furnish, lay on, arrange for • *We'll fix him up with a job.*
fix something up = arrange, plan, settle, fix, organize, sort out, agree on, make arrangements for • *I fixed up an appointment to see her.*

PROVERBS
If it ain't broke, don't fix it

fixated **= obsessed**, fascinated, preoccupied, captivated, attached, devoted, absorbed, caught up in, single-minded, smitten, taken up with, besotted, wrapped up in, engrossed, spellbound, infatuated, mesmerized, hypnotized, hung up on *(slang)*, monomaniacal, prepossessed • *As a child, he was fixated with video nasties.*
OPPOSITES: detached, indifferent, uninterested

fixation **= obsession**, complex, addiction, hang-up *(informal)*, preoccupation, mania, infatuation, idée fixe *(French)*, thing *(informal)* • *Somebody has a fixation with you.*

fixed **1 = inflexible**, set, steady, resolute, unwavering, unflinching, unblinking, unbending, undeviating • *people who have fixed ideas about things*
OPPOSITES: varying, wavering, inconstant
2 = immovable, set, established, secure, rooted, permanent, attached, anchored, rigid, made fast • *Nato was concentrating on hitting buildings and other fixed structures.*
OPPOSITES: moving, mobile, bending
3 = false, fake, feigned, insincere • *I had a fixed grin on my face.*
4 = agreed, set, planned, decided, established, settled, arranged, resolved, specified, definite • *The deal was settled at a prearranged fixed price.*
5 = mended, going, sorted, repaired, put right, in working order • *The vehicle was fixed.*
6 = rigged, framed, put-up, manipulated, packed • *Some races are fixed.*

fizz **AS A VERB** **1 = bubble**, froth, fizzle, effervesce, produce bubbles • *She was holding a tray of glasses that fizzed.*
2 = sputter, buzz, sparkle, hiss, crackle • *The engine fizzed and went dead.*
▸ **AS A NOUN** **1 = fizziness**, gas, foam, froth, effervescence, bubbliness • *Is there any fizz left in the lemonade?*
2 = life, spirit, dash, sparkle, zip *(informal)*, vitality, animation, panache, gaiety, élan, brio, vivacity, liveliness, vim *(slang)* • *an ad campaign to put the fizz back in sales*
3 = champagne, sparkling wine • *a bottle of fizz*
4 = crackle, buzzing, hissing, sputter • *the hysterical fizz of the radio*

fizzle *often with* **out = die away**, fail, collapse, fold *(informal)*, abort, fall through, peter out, come to nothing, miss the mark, end in disappointment • *The strike fizzled out on its first day.*

fizzy **= bubbly**, bubbling, sparkling, effervescent, carbonated, gassy • *a can of fizzy drink*

flab **= fat**, flesh, flabbiness, fleshiness, weight, beef *(informal)*, heaviness, slackness, plumpness, loose flesh • *He had a hefty roll of flab over his waistband.*

flabbergasted **= astonished**, amazed, stunned, overcome, overwhelmed, staggered, astounded, dazed, confounded, disconcerted, speechless, bowled over *(informal)*, gobsmacked *(Brit. slang)*, dumbfounded, nonplussed, lost for words, struck dumb, abashed, rendered speechless • *I am amazed and flabbergasted by what happened.*

flabby **1 = limp**, hanging, loose, slack, unfit, sagging, sloppy, baggy, floppy, lax, drooping, flaccid, pendulous, toneless, yielding • *bulging thighs and flabby stomach*
OPPOSITES: hard, strong, firm
2 = weak, ineffective, feeble, impotent, wasteful, ineffectual, disorganized, spineless, effete, boneless, nerveless, enervated, wussy *(slang)*, wimpish *or* wimpy *(informal)* • *Many signs of flabby management remain.*

flaccid **= limp**, soft, weak, loose, slack, lax, drooping, flabby, nerveless • *Her wrist was limp and flaccid.*

flag[1] **AS A NOUN** **= banner**, standard, colours, jack, pennant, ensign, streamer, pennon, banderole, gonfalon • *They raised the white flag in surrender.*
▸ **AS A VERB** **1 = mark**, identify, indicate, label, tab, pick out, note, docket • *I promise to flag these things more clearly.*
2 *often with* **down = hail**, stop, signal, salute, wave down • *They flagged a car down.*
▸ **RELATED ENTHUSIAST:** vexillologist

QUOTATIONS
Then raise the scarlet standard high!
Within its folds we'll live or die
Tho' cowards flinch and traitors sneer
We'll keep the red flag flying here
[James M. Connell *The Red Flag*]

flag[2] **= weaken**, fall, die, fail, decline, sink, fade, slump, pine, faint, weary, fall off, succumb, falter, wilt, wane, ebb, sag, languish, abate, droop, peter out, taper off, feel the pace, lose your strength • *His enthusiasm was in no way flagging.*

flagellation **= whipping**, beating, lashing, thrashing, flogging • *the extreme religious penance of flagellation*

flagging = **weakening**, failing, declining, waning, giving up, tiring, sinking, fading, decreasing, slowing down, deteriorating, wearying, faltering, wilting, ebbing • *The news will boost his flagging reputation.*

flagrant = **outrageous**, open, blatant, barefaced, shocking, crying, enormous, awful, bold, dreadful, notorious, glaring, infamous, scandalous, flaunting, atrocious, brazen, shameless, out-and-out, heinous, ostentatious, egregious, undisguised, immodest, arrant, flagitious • *a flagrant violation of international law*
OPPOSITES: slight, implied, subtle

flagstone = **paving stone**, flag, slab, block • *If we trip over a flagstone, we can sue the council.*

flail = **thrash**, beat, windmill, thresh • *His arms were flailing in all directions.*

flair 1 = **ability**, feel, talent, gift, genius, faculty, accomplishment, mastery, knack, aptitude • *She has a flair for languages.*
2 = **style**, taste, dash, chic, elegance, panache, discernment, stylishness • *the panache and flair you'd expect*

flak = **criticism**, stick *(slang)*, opposition, abuse, complaints, hostility, condemnation, censure, disapproval, bad press, denigration, brickbats *(informal)*, sideswipes, disparagement, fault-finding, disapprobation • *He's getting a lot of flak for that.*

flake AS A NOUN = **chip**, scale, layer, peeling, shaving, disk, wafer, sliver, lamina, squama *(Biology)* • *flakes of paint*
▸ AS A VERB = **chip**, scale (off), peel (off), blister, desquamate • *Some of the shell had flaked away.*

flake out = **collapse**, faint, pass out, swoon *(literary)*, lose consciousness, keel over • *If he flakes out, cover him with a blanket.*

flaky *or* **flakey** = **peeling**, cracking, blistering, desquamative • *remove the dry, flaky skin*

flamboyance = **showiness**, show, style, dash, sparkle, chic, flair, verve, swagger, extravagance, panache, pomp, glitz *(informal)*, élan, bravura, swank *(informal)*, theatricality, exhibitionism, brio, ostentation, stylishness, flashiness, flamboyancy, floridity, pizzazz *or* pizazz *(informal)* • *He was his usual mixture of flamboyance and flair.*
OPPOSITES: restraint, simplicity, dullness

flamboyant 1 = **camp** *(informal)*, dashing, theatrical • *He was a flamboyant personality.*
2 = **showy**, rich, elaborate, over the top *(informal)*, extravagant, baroque, ornate, ostentatious, rococo • *flamboyant architectural paint effects*
3 = **colourful**, striking, exciting, brilliant, glamorous, stylish, dazzling, glitzy *(slang)*, showy, florid, bling *(slang)*, swashbuckling • *He wears flamboyant clothes.*

flame AS A NOUN 1 = **fire**, light, spark, glow, blaze, brightness, inferno • *a huge ball of flame*
2 = **passion**, fire, enthusiasm, intensity, affection, warmth, fervour, ardour, keenness, fervency • *that burning flame of love*
3 = **sweetheart**, partner, lover, girlfriend, boyfriend, squeeze *(informal)*, beloved, heart-throb *(Brit.)*, beau, ladylove • *She kept inviting his old flame round to their house.*
▸ AS A VERB 1 = **burn**, flash, shine, glow, blaze, flare, glare • *His dark eyes flamed with rage.*
2 = **blush**, colour, glow, redden, turn red, go red • *Her face flamed a fiery red.*
3 = **ignite**, set on fire, set ablaze, set light to, kindle • *a medium-rare steak, doused and flamed in cognac*
▸ IN PHRASES: **in flames** = **on fire**, burning, alight, ablaze • *Half the building was in flames.*

flameproof = **nonflammable**, fire-resistant, flame-retardant, incombustible, non-inflammable • *Heat the oil in a flameproof casserole.*

flaming AS AN ADJECTIVE 1 = **burning**, blazing, fiery, ignited, red, brilliant, raging, glowing, red-hot, ablaze, in flames, afire • *A group followed carrying flaming torches.*
2 = **bright**, brilliant, glowing, blazing, dazzling, vivid • *He stroked back the mass of flaming red hair from her face.*
3 = **intense**, angry, raging, impassioned, hot, aroused, vivid, frenzied, ardent, scintillating, vehement • *She had a flaming row with her lover.*
4 = **damned**, bloody *(slang)*, bleeding *(slang)*, blooming *(informal)*, freaking *(slang, chiefly U.S.)*, ruddy *(informal)*, effing *(slang)* • *What the flaming hell do you think you're doing?*
▸ AS AN ADVERB = **damned**, bloody *(slang)*, bleeding *(slang)*, blooming *(informal)*, freaking *(slang, chiefly U.S.)*, ruddy *(informal)*, effing *(slang)* • *I was flaming mad about what happened.*

flammable = **combustible**, incendiary, inflammable, ignitable • *flammable liquids such as petrol or paraffin*

flank AS A NOUN 1 = **side**, quarter, hip, thigh, loin, haunch, ham • *He put his hand on the dog's flank.*
2 = **wing**, side, sector, aspect • *The assault element opened up from their right flank.*
▸ AS A VERB = **border**, line, wall, screen, edge, circle, bound, skirt, fringe, book-end • *The altar was flanked by two Christmas trees.*

flannel AS A NOUN 1 = **cloth**, facecloth • *pass a damp flannel over your forehead*
2 = **waffle** *(Brit. informal)*, flattery, blarney, sweet talk *(U.S. informal)*, baloney *(informal)*, equivocation, hedging, prevarication, weasel words *(informal, chiefly U.S.)*, soft soap *(informal)* • *He gave me a lot of flannel.*
▸ AS A VERB = **prevaricate**, hedge, flatter, waffle *(informal, chiefly Brit.)*, blarney, sweet-talk *(informal)*, soft-soap *(informal)*, equivocate, butter up, pull the wool over (someone's) eyes • *He flannelled and prevaricated.*

flap AS A VERB 1 = **flutter**, wave, swing, swish, flail • *Sheets flapped on the clothes line.*
2 = **beat**, wave, thrash, flutter, agitate, wag, vibrate, shake, thresh • *The bird flapped its wings furiously.*
3 = **panic**, fuss, dither *(chiefly Brit.)* • *There's no point in you flapping around in the kitchen, making your guest feel uneasy.*
▸ AS A NOUN 1 = **cover**, covering, tail, fold, skirt, tab, overlap, fly, apron, lapel, lappet • *He drew back the tent flap and strode out.*
2 = **flutter**, beating, waving, shaking, swinging, bang, banging, swish • *the gunshot flap of a topsail*
3 = **panic**, state *(informal)*, agitation, commotion, sweat *(informal)*, stew *(informal)*, dither *(chiefly Brit.)*, fluster, twitter *(informal)*, tizzy *(informal)*, mind-fuck *(taboo slang)* • *Wherever he goes, there's always a flap.*

flare AS A VERB 1 = **blaze**, flame, dazzle, glare, flicker, flutter, waver, burn up • *Camp fires flared like beacons in the dark.*
2 = **widen**, spread, broaden, spread out, dilate, splay • *a dress cut to flare from the hips*
▸ AS A NOUN 1 = **rocket**, light, signal, beacon • *a ship which had fired a distress flare*
2 = **flame**, burst, flash, blaze, dazzle, glare, flicker • *The flare of fires lights up the blacked-out streets.*
▸ IN PHRASES: **flare up** = **burn**, explode, blaze, be on fire, go up in flames, be alight, flame • *The fire flared up again.*
▸ AS A VERB 1 = **erupt**, break out, fire up, burst out, boil over • *People were injured as fighting flared up. (informal)*
2 = **lose your temper**, explode, lose it *(informal)*, lose control, lose the plot *(informal)*, throw a tantrum, fly off the handle *(informal)*, lose your cool *(informal)*, blow your top *(informal)*, fly into a temper • *She suddenly lost her temper with me and flared up.*
3 = **recur**, come back, reappear, come again • *Old ailments can often flare up again.*

flash AS A NOUN 1 = **blaze**, ray, burst, spark, beam, sparkle, streak, flare, dazzle, shaft, glare, gleam, flicker, shimmer, twinkle, scintillation, coruscation • *a sudden flash of lightning*

f

2 = **burst**, show, sign, touch, display, rush, demonstration, surge, outbreak, outburst, manifestation • *The essay could do with a flash of wit.*

▸ AS A VERB 1 = **blaze**, shine, beam, sparkle, glitter, flare, glare, gleam, light up, flicker, shimmer, twinkle, glint, glisten, scintillate, coruscate • *Lightning flashed among the distant dark clouds.*

2 = **speed**, race, shoot, fly, tear, sweep, dash, barrel (along) *(informal, chiefly U.S. & Canad.)*, whistle, sprint, bolt, streak, dart, zoom, burn rubber *(informal)* • *Cars flashed by every few minutes.*

3 = **show quickly**, display, expose, exhibit, flourish, show off, flaunt • *He flashed his official card.*

4 = **display**, show, present • *The screen flashes a message.*

▸ AS AN ADJECTIVE = **ostentatious**, smart, glamorous, trendy, showy, cheap, bling *(slang)* • *flash jewellery and watches*

▸ IN PHRASES: **in a flash = moment**, second, instant, split second, trice, jiffy *(informal)*, the twinkling of an eye, a twinkling, two shakes of a lamb's tail *(informal)*, the bat of an eye *(informal)* • *The answer came to him in a flash.*

flashy = **showy**, loud, over the top *(informal)*, flamboyant, brash, tacky *(informal)*, flaunting, glitzy *(slang)*, tasteless, naff *(Brit. slang)*, gaudy, garish, jazzy *(informal)*, tawdry, ostentatious, snazzy *(informal)*, glittery, meretricious, cheap and nasty, in poor taste, tinselly, bling *(slang)* • *a flashy sports car*

OPPOSITES: natural, plain, modest

flask = **vessel**, bottle, container, Thermos flask *(trademark)*, hip flask, vacuum flask • *He took out a metal flask from his bag.*

flat[1] AS AN ADJECTIVE 1 = **even**, level, levelled, plane, smooth, uniform, horizontal, unbroken, planar • *Sit the cup on a flat surface while measuring.*

OPPOSITES: broken, rolling, uneven

2 = **horizontal**, prone, outstretched, reclining, prostrate, laid low, supine, recumbent, lying full length • *Two men near him threw themselves flat.*

OPPOSITES: straight, upright, vertical

3 = **shallow**, not deep • *a square flat box*

4 = **low**, low-heeled, with low heels, without heels • *I usually wear flat shoes or boots.*

5 = **punctured**, collapsed, burst, blown out, deflated, empty • *It was impossible to ride with a flat tyre.*

6 = **used up**, finished, empty, drained, expired • *The battery was flat.*

7 = **still**, no longer fizzy • *My hand gripped the glass of flat lemonade.*

8 = **absolute**, firm, direct, straight, positive, fixed, plain, final, explicit, definite, outright, unconditional, downright, unmistakable, unequivocal, unqualified, out-and-out, categorical, peremptory • *She is likely to give you a flat refusal.*

9 = **set**, agreed, settled, fixed, arranged, specified, definite, decided • *You will be charged a flat fee for the connection.*

10 = **sluggish**, slow, stagnant, inactive • *Car sales stayed flat.*

11 = **dull**, dead, empty, boring, depressing, pointless, tedious, stale, lacklustre, tiresome, lifeless, monotonous, uninteresting, insipid, unexciting, spiritless • *The past few days have been flat and empty.*

OPPOSITES: exciting, sparkling, tasty

12 = **without energy**, empty, weak, tired, depressed, drained, weary, worn out, dispirited, downhearted, tired out • *I've been feeling flat at times.*

13 = **monotonous**, boring, uniform, dull, tedious, droning, tiresome, unchanging, colourless, toneless, samey *(informal)*, uninflected, unvaried • *Her voice was flat, with no hope in it.*

▸ AS A NOUN *often plural* = **plain**, strand, shallow, marsh, swamp, shoal, lowland, mud flat • *salt marshes and mud flats*

▸ AS AN ADVERB 1 = **horizontal**, outstretched, lying full length • *Lie down flat on your back.*

2 = **completely**, directly, absolutely, categorically, precisely, exactly, utterly, outright, point blank, unequivocally • *He had turned her down flat.*

▸ IN PHRASES: **flat out = at full speed**, all out, to the full, hell for leather *(informal)*, as hard as possible, at full tilt, at full gallop, posthaste, for all you are worth, under full steam • *Everyone is working flat out.*

flat[2] = **apartment**, rooms, quarters, digs, suite, penthouse, living quarters, duplex *(U.S. & Canad.)*, bachelor apartment *(Canad.)* • *She lives with her husband in a flat.*

flatly = **absolutely**, completely, positively, categorically, unequivocally, unhesitatingly • *He flatly refused to discuss it.*

flatness 1 = **evenness**, uniformity, smoothness, horizontality, levelness • *Notice the flatness and the rich, red earth.*

2 = **dullness**, emptiness, tedium, monotony, staleness, vapidity, insipidity • *He detected a certain flatness in the days that followed.*

flatten 1 *sometimes with* **out** = **level**, roll, plaster, squash, compress, trample, iron out, even out, smooth off • *How do you put enough pressure on to the metal to flatten it?*

2 *sometimes with* **out** = **destroy**, level, ruin, demolish, knock down, pull down, tear down, throw down, bulldoze, raze, remove, kennet *(Austral. slang)*, jeff *(Austral. slang)* • *Bombing raids flattened much of the area.*

3 = **knock down**, fell, floor, deck *(slang)*, bowl over, prostrate, knock off your feet • *I've never seen a woman flatten someone like that!*

4 = **crush**, beat, defeat, trounce, master, worst, overwhelm, conquer, lick *(informal)*, undo, subdue, rout, overpower, quell, clobber *(slang)*, vanquish, run rings around *(informal)*, wipe the floor with *(informal)*, make mincemeat of *(informal)*, blow out of the water *(slang)* • *In the squash court his aim is to flatten me.*

flatter 1 = **praise**, compliment, pander to, sweet-talk *(informal)*, court, humour, puff, flannel *(Brit. informal)*, fawn, cajole, lay it on (thick) *(slang)*, wheedle, inveigle, soft-soap *(informal)*, butter up, blandish • *I knew he was just flattering me.*

2 = **suit**, become, enhance, set off, embellish, do something for, show to advantage • *Orange flatters those with golden skin tones.*

flattered = **pleased**, delighted, honoured, gratified • *I am flattered that they should be so supportive.*

flattering 1 = **becoming**, kind, effective, enhancing, well-chosen • *It wasn't a very flattering photograph.*

OPPOSITES: plain, unattractive, unflattering

2 = **ingratiating**, complimentary, gratifying, fawning, sugary, fulsome, laudatory, adulatory, honeyed, honey-tongued • *The press was flattering.*

OPPOSITES: straight, blunt, uncomplimentary

3 = **pleasing**, satisfying, gratifying, pleasurable • *It is very flattering to be spoken of like that.*

flattery = **obsequiousness**, fawning, adulation, sweet-talk *(informal)*, flannel *(Brit. informal)*, blarney, soft-soap *(informal)*, sycophancy, servility, cajolery, blandishment, fulsomeness, toadyism, false praise, honeyed words • *He is ambitious and susceptible to flattery.*

QUOTATIONS

I suppose flattery hurts no one, that is, if he doesn't inhale

[Adlai Stevenson]

Everyone likes flattery; and when you come to Royalty you should lay it on with a trowel

[Benjamin Disraeli]

flatulence 1 = **wind**, borborygmus *(Medical)*, eructation • *Avoid any food that causes flatulence.*

2 = **pretentiousness**, boasting, hot air *(informal)*, twaddle, pomposity, bombast, claptrap, empty words, fustian,

prolixity, rodomontade, fanfaronade *(rare)* • *so much bloated nationalistic flatulence*

flatulent = **pretentious**, swollen, inflated, tedious, pompous, tiresome, long-winded, turgid, wordy, bombastic, prolix • *flatulent oratory and bar-room barracking*

flaunt = **show off**, display, boast, parade, exhibit, flourish, brandish, vaunt, showboat, make a (great) show of, sport *(informal)*, disport, make an exhibition of, flash about • *openly flaunting their wealth*

flavour *or* **flavor** AS A NOUN **1** = **taste**, seasoning, flavouring, savour, extract, essence, relish, smack, aroma, odour, zest, tang, zing *(informal)*, piquancy, tastiness • *The cheese has a strong flavour.*
OPPOSITES: blandness, flatness, tastelessness
2 = **quality**, feeling, feel, style, property, touch, character, aspect, tone, suggestion, stamp, essence, tinge, soupçon *(French)* • *clothes with a nostalgic Forties flavour*
▸ AS A VERB = **season**, spice, add flavour to, enrich, infuse, imbue, pep up, leaven, ginger up, lace • *Flavour dishes with exotic herbs and spices.*
▸ IN PHRASES: **flavour of the month** = **the latest thing**, fashionable, in vogue, all the rage, the craze, du jour *(French)*, the in thing *(informal)*, culty, the new • *Hats were very much flavour of the month.*

flavouring *or* **flavoring** = **essence**, extract, zest, tincture, spirit • *Our range of herbal teas contains no artificial flavourings.*

flaw **1** = **error**, mistake, fault, blunder, inaccuracy, howler *(informal)*, solecism, barry *or* Barry Crocker *(Austral. slang)* • *Almost all these studies have serious flaws.*
2 = **weakness**, failing, defect, weak spot, spot, fault, scar, blemish, imperfection, speck, disfigurement, chink in your armour • *The only flaw in his character is a short temper.*
3 = **crack**, break, split, breach, tear, rent, fracture, rift, cleft, crevice, fissure, scission • *a flaw in the rock wide enough for a foot*

flawed **1** = **damaged**, defective, imperfect, blemished, broken, cracked, chipped, faulty • *the unique beauty of a flawed object*
2 = **erroneous**, incorrect, inaccurate, invalid, wrong, mistaken, false, faulty, untrue, unfounded, spurious, amiss, unsound, wide of the mark, inexact, fallacious • *The tests were seriously flawed.*

flawless **1** = **perfect**, impeccable, faultless, spotless, unblemished, unsullied • *She has a flawless complexion.*
2 = **intact**, whole, sound, unbroken, undamaged • *Stained glass craftsmen would always use flawless glass.*

flay **1** = **skin**, strip, peel, scrape, excoriate, remove the skin from • *to flay the flesh away from his muscles*
2 = **upbraid**, slam *(slang)*, castigate, revile, tear into *(informal)*, diss *(slang, chiefly U.S.)*, excoriate, tear a strip off, execrate, pull to pieces *(informal)*, give a tongue-lashing, criticize severely, flame *(informal)* • *The critics flayed him with accusations of misanthropy.*

fleck AS A NOUN = **mark**, speck, streak, spot, dot, pinpoint, speckle • *His hair is dark grey with flecks of ginger.*
▸ AS A VERB = **speckle**, mark, spot, dust, dot, streak, dapple, stipple, mottle, variegate, bespeckle, besprinkle • *patches of red paint which flecked her blouse*

fledgling *or* **fledgeling** AS A NOUN = **chick**, nestling, young bird • *The fathers of these fledglings are all dead.*
▸ AS AN ADJECTIVE = **new**, beginning, developing, emerging, amateur, embryonic, probationary • *advice he gave to fledgling writers*

flee = **run away**, leave, escape, bolt, fly, avoid, split *(slang)*, take off *(informal)*, get away, vanish, depart, run off, shun, make off, abscond, decamp, take flight, hook it *(slang)*, do a runner *(slang)*, scarper *(Brit. slang)*, slope off, cut and run *(informal)*, make a run for it, beat a hasty retreat, turn tail, fly the coop *(U.S. & Canad. informal)*, make a quick exit, skedaddle *(informal)*, make yourself scarce *(informal)*, take a powder *(U.S. & Canad. slang)*, make your escape, make your getaway, take it on the lam *(U.S. & Canad. slang)*, take to your heels • *He slammed the bedroom door behind him and fled.*

fleece AS A NOUN = **wool**, hair, coat, fur, coat of wool • *a blanket of lamb's fleece*
▸ AS A VERB = **cheat**, skin *(slang)*, steal, rob, con *(informal)*, rifle, stiff *(slang)*, soak *(U.S. & Canad. slang)*, sting *(informal)*, bleed *(informal)*, rip off *(slang)*, plunder, defraud, overcharge, swindle, rook *(slang)*, diddle *(informal)*, take for a ride *(informal)*, despoil, take to the cleaners *(slang)*, sell a pup, cozen, mulct, scam *(slang)* • *She claims he fleeced her out of thousands of pounds.*

fleecy = **woolly**, soft, fluffy, shaggy, downy • *fleecy walking jackets*

fleet[1] = **navy**, vessels, task force, squadron, warships, flotilla, armada, naval force, sea power, argosy • *damage inflicted up on the British fleet*

fleet[2] = **swift**, flying, fast, quick, winged, rapid, speedy, nimble, mercurial, meteoric, nimble-footed • *He was fleet as a deer.*

fleeting = **momentary**, short, passing, flying, brief, temporary, short-lived, fugitive, transient, flitting, ephemeral, transitory, evanescent, fugacious, here today, gone tomorrow • *They caught only a fleeting glimpse of the driver.*
OPPOSITES: lasting, continuing, permanent

flesh AS A NOUN **1** = **fat**, muscle, beef *(informal)*, tissue, body, brawn • *Illness had wasted the flesh from her body.*
2 = **fatness**, fat, adipose tissue, corpulence, weight • *porcine wrinkles of flesh*
3 = **meat**, food • *the pale pink flesh of trout and salmon*
4 = **physical nature**, sensuality, physicality, carnality, body, human nature, flesh and blood, animality, sinful nature • *the sins of the flesh*
5 = **pulp**, soft part, fleshy part • *Cut the flesh from the olives and discard the stone.*
▸ IN PHRASES: **flesh something out** = **add to**, develop, expand (on), embellish, elaborate on, enlarge on, add detail to • *He has since fleshed out his story.*
in the flesh = **in person**, in real life, really, actually • *He looked smaller in the flesh.*
put flesh on something = **expand**, develop, expand (on), add to, embellish, elaborate on, enlarge on, add detail to • *This is an attempt to put flesh on a very bare plan.*
your own flesh and blood = **family**, blood, relations, relatives, kin, kindred, kith and kin, blood relations, kinsfolk, ainga *(N.Z.)*, rellies *(Austral. slang)* • *The kid was his own flesh and blood.*
▸ RELATED ADJECTIVES: carnal, sarcoid
▸ RELATED PHOBIA: selaphobia

QUOTATIONS

Bone of my bones, and flesh of my flesh
[*Bible: Genesis*]

I saw him now going the way of all flesh
[John Webster *Westward Hoe*]

The spirit indeed is willing, but the flesh is weak
[*Bible: St. Matthew*]

fleshy = **plump**, fat, chubby, obese, hefty, overweight, ample, stout, chunky, meaty, beefy *(informal)*, tubby, podgy, brawny, corpulent, well-padded • *He was well-built, but too fleshy.*

flex = **bend**, contract, stretch, angle, curve, tighten, crook, move • *He slowly flexed his muscles.*

flexibility **1** = **elasticity**, pliability, springiness, pliancy, tensility, give *(informal)* • *The flexibility of the lens decreases with age.*
2 = **adaptability**, openness, versatility, adjustability • *the flexibility of distance learning*

3 = **complaisance**, accommodation, give and take, amenability • *They should be ready to show some flexibility.*

flexible 1 = **pliable**, plastic, yielding, elastic, supple, lithe, limber, springy, willowy, pliant, tensile, stretchy, whippy, lissom(e), ductile, bendable, mouldable • *brushes with long, flexible bristles*
OPPOSITES: tough, fixed, rigid
2 = **adaptable**, open, variable, adjustable, discretionary • *flexible working hours*
OPPOSITES: absolute, inflexible
3 = **compliant**, accommodating, manageable, amenable, docile, tractable, biddable, complaisant, responsive, gentle • *Their boss was flexible and lenient.*
OPPOSITES: determined, staunch, unyielding

flick AS A VERB 1 = **jerk**, pull, tug, lurch, jolt • *The man flicked his gun up from beside his thigh.*
2 = **strike**, tap, jab, remove quickly, hit, touch, stroke, rap, flip, peck, whisk, dab, fillip • *She flicked a speck of fluff from her sleeve.*
3 = **click**, press, snap • *I found some switches and flicked them.*
▸ AS A NOUN = **tap**, touch, sweep, stroke, rap, flip, peck, whisk, jab • *a flick of a paintbrush*
▸ IN PHRASES: **flick through something** = **browse**, glance at, skim, leaf through, flip through, thumb through, skip through • *She flicked through some magazines.*

flicker AS A VERB 1 = **twinkle**, flash, sparkle, flare, shimmer, gutter, glimmer • *Firelight flickered on the faded furnishings.*
2 = **flutter**, waver, quiver, vibrate • *Her eyelids flickered then opened.*
▸ AS A NOUN 1 = **glimmer**, flash, spark, flare, gleam • *I saw the flicker of flames.*
2 = **trace**, drop, breath, spark, atom, glimmer, vestige, iota • *He felt a flicker of regret.*

flickering = **wavering**, guttering, twinkling, unsteady • *flickering candles in the candelabra*

flier see flyer

flight[1] AS A NOUN 1 = **journey**, trip, voyage • *The flight will take four hours.*
2 = **aviation**, flying, air transport, aeronautics, aerial navigation • *Supersonic flight could be come a routine form of travel.*
3 = **flying**, winging, mounting, soaring, ability to fly • *These hawks are magnificent in flight.*
4 = **flock**, group, unit, cloud, formation, squadron, swarm, flying group • *a flight of green parrots*
▸ IN PHRASES: **flight of stairs** = **staircase**, set of stairs • *We walked in silence up a flight of stairs.*

flight[2] AS A NOUN = **escape**, fleeing, departure, retreat, exit, running away, exodus, getaway, absconding • *his secret flight into exile*
▸ IN PHRASES: **put to flight** = **drive off**, scatter, disperse, rout, stampede, scare off, send packing, chase off • *We were put to flight by a herd of bullocks.*
take (to) flight = **run away** *or* **off**, flee, bolt, abscond, decamp, do a runner *(slang)*, turn tail, do a bunk *(Brit. slang)*, fly the coop *(U.S. & Canad. informal)*, beat a retreat, light out *(informal)*, skedaddle *(informal)*, make a hasty retreat, take a powder *(U.S. & Canad. slang)*, withdraw hastily, take it on the lam *(U.S. & Canad. slang)*, do a Skase *(Austral. informal)* • *He decided to take flight immediately.*

flighty = **frivolous**, wild, volatile, unstable, irresponsible, dizzy, fickle, unbalanced, impulsive, mercurial, giddy, capricious, unsteady, thoughtless, changeable, impetuous, skittish, light-headed, harebrained, scatterbrained, ditzy *or* ditsy *(slang)* • *She was a frivolous fool, vain and flighty.*

flimsy 1 = **fragile**, weak, slight, delicate, shallow, shaky, frail, superficial, makeshift, rickety, insubstantial, gimcrack, unsubstantial • *a flimsy wooden door*
OPPOSITES: strong, sound, sturdy
2 = **thin**, light, sheer, transparent, chiffon, gossamer, gauzy • *a flimsy pink chiffon nightgown*
3 = **unconvincing**, poor, thin, weak, inadequate, pathetic, transparent, trivial, feeble, unsatisfactory, frivolous, tenuous, implausible • *The charges were based on flimsy evidence.*

flinch 1 = **wince**, start, duck, shrink, cringe, quail, recoil, cower, blench • *The slightest pressure made her flinch.*
2 *often with* **from** = **shy away**, shrink, withdraw, flee, retreat, back off, swerve, shirk, draw back, baulk • *He has never flinched from harsh decisions.*

fling AS A VERB = **throw**, toss, hurl, chuck *(informal)*, launch, cast, pitch, send, shy, jerk, propel, sling, precipitate, lob *(informal)*, catapult, heave, let fly • *The woman flung the cup at him.*
▸ AS A NOUN 1 = **affair**, relationship, involvement, liaison, flirtation, amour, dalliance • *She had a fling with him 30 years ago.*
2 = **binge**, good time, bash, bit of fun, party, rave *(Brit. slang)*, spree, indulgence *(informal)*, beano *(Brit. slang)*, night on the town, rave-up *(Brit. slang)*, night on the razzle *(informal)*, hooley *or* hoolie *(chiefly Irish & N.Z.)* • *the last fling before you take up a job*
3 = **try**, go *(informal)*, attempt, shot *(informal)*, trial, crack *(informal)*, venture, gamble, stab *(informal)*, bash *(informal)*, whirl *(informal)* • *the England bowler's chance of a fling at South Africa in the second Test today*

flip AS A VERB 1 = **flick**, switch, snap, slick, jerk • *He walked out, flipping off the lights.*
2 *often with* **through** = **thumb**, leaf, glance, thumb, skip, skim, browse • *He flipped the pages of the diary.*
3 = **spin**, turn, overturn, turn over, roll over, twist • *The plane flipped over and burst into flames.*
4 = **toss**, throw, cast, pitch, flick, fling, sling • *I flipped a cigarette butt out of the window.*
▸ AS A NOUN = **toss**, throw, cast, pitch, spin, snap, twist, flick, jerk • *having gambled all on the flip of a coin*

flippancy = **frivolity**, cheek *(informal)*, irreverence, impertinence, levity, glibness, cheekiness, sauciness, pertness, disrespectfulness • *His flippancy subsided rapidly.*

flippant = **frivolous**, rude, cheeky, irreverent, flip *(informal)*, superficial, saucy, glib, pert, disrespectful, offhand, impertinent, impudent • *He dismissed it as a flippant comment.*
OPPOSITES: serious, mannerly, polite

flirt AS A VERB 1 = **chat up**, lead on *(informal)*, dally with, make advances at, make eyes at, coquet, philander, make sheep's eyes at • *He's flirting with all the ladies.*
2 *usually with* **with** = **toy with**, consider, entertain, play with, dabble in, trifle with, give a thought to, expose yourself to • *My mother used to flirt with nationalism.*
▸ AS A NOUN = **tease**, philanderer, coquette, heart-breaker, wanton, trifler • *She's a born flirt.*

flirtation = **teasing**, philandering, dalliance, coquetry, toying, intrigue, trifling • *She was aware of his attempts at flirtation.*

QUOTATIONS

Merely innocent flirtation,
Not quite adultery, but adulteration
[Lord Byron *Don Juan*]

Coquetry whets the appetite; flirtation depraves it. Coquetry is the thorn that guards the rose – easily trimmed off when once plucked. Flirtation is like the slime on water-plants, making them hard to handle, and when caught, only to be cherished in slimy waters
[Donald Grant Mitchell *Reveries of a Bachelor*]

Is that a gun in your pocket, or are you just glad to see me?
[Mae West *Diamond Lil*]

flirtatious = **teasing**, flirty, coquettish, amorous, come-on *(informal)*, arch, enticing, provocative, coy, come-hither, sportive • *He was dashing and flirtatious.*

flit = **fly**, dash, dart, skim, pass, speed, wing, flash, fleet, whisk, flutter • *the bird that flits from tree to tree*

float 1 = **glide**, sail, drift, move gently, bob, coast, slide, be carried, slip along • *barges floating quietly by the grassy river banks*
2 = **be buoyant**, stay afloat, be *or* lie on the surface, rest on water, hang, hover, poise, displace water • *Empty things float.*
OPPOSITES: settle, sink, go down
3 = **waft**, coast, drift • *Sublime music floats on a scented summer breeze.*
4 = **suggest**, present, propose, recommend, put forward, move • *He floated the idea of a new alliance.*
5 = **launch**, offer, sell, set up, promote, get going, push off • *He floated his firm on the Stock Market.*
OPPOSITES: cancel, abolish, dissolve

floating 1 = **buoyant**, drifting, buoyed, resting on water • *Firefighters are unable to use floating booms.*
2 = **uncommitted**, wavering, undecided, indecisive, vacillating, sitting on the fence *(informal)*, unaffiliated, independent • *Floating voters appear to have deserted the party.*
3 = **free**, wandering, variable, fluctuating, unattached, migratory, movable, unfixed • *a house I shared with a floating population of others*

flock AS A NOUN 1 = **herd**, group, flight, drove, colony, gaggle, skein • *They kept a small flock of sheep.*
2 = **crowd**, company, group, host, collection, mass, gathering, assembly, convoy, herd, congregation, horde, multitude, throng, bevy • *his flock of advisors*
▸ AS A VERB 1 = **stream**, crowd, mass, swarm, throng • *The public have flocked to the show.*
2 = **gather**, group, crowd, mass, collect, assemble, herd, huddle, converge, throng, congregate, troop • *The crowds flocked around her.*

flog 1 = **sell**, market, trade, dispose of, put up for sale • *They are trying to flog their house.*
2 = **beat**, whip, lash, thrash, whack, scourge, hit hard, trounce, castigate, chastise, flay, lambast(e), flagellate, punish severely, beat *or* knock seven bells out of *(informal)* • *Flog them soundly!*
3 = **strain**, drive, tax, push, punish, oppress, overtax, overexert • *Don't flog yourself. We've got ages.*

flogging = **beating**, hiding *(informal)*, whipping, lashing, thrashing, caning, scourging, trouncing, flagellation, horsewhipping • *He urged the restoration of flogging and hanging.*
▸ RELATED PHOBIA: mastigophobia

flood AS A NOUN 1 = **deluge**, downpour, flash flood, inundation, tide, overflow, torrent, spate, freshet • *This is the sort of flood dreaded by cavers.*
2 = **torrent**, flow, rush, stream, tide, abundance, multitude, glut, outpouring, profusion • *The administration is trying to stem the flood of refugees.*
3 = **series**, stream, avalanche, barrage, spate, torrent • *He received a flood of complaints.*
4 = **outpouring**, rush, stream, surge, torrent • *She broke into a flood of tears.*
▸ AS A VERB 1 = **immerse**, swamp, submerge, inundate, deluge, drown, cover with water • *The house was flooded.*
2 = **pour over**, swamp, run over, overflow, inundate, brim over • *Many streams have flooded their banks.*
3 = **engulf**, flow into, rush into, sweep into, overwhelm, surge into, swarm into, pour into, gush into • *Large numbers of immigrants flooded the area.*
4 = **saturate**, fill, choke, swamp, glut, oversupply, overfill • *a policy aimed at flooding Europe with exports*
5 = **stream**, flow, rush, pour, surge • *Enquiries flooded in from all over the world.*
▸ RELATED ADJECTIVES: fluvial, diluvial
▸ RELATED PHOBIA: antlophobia

floor AS A NOUN 1 = **ground** • *He's sitting on the floor watching TV.*
2 = **storey**, level, stage, tier • *It's on the fifth floor of the hospital.*
▸ AS A VERB 1 = **disconcert**, stump, baffle, confound, beat, throw *(informal)*, defeat, puzzle, conquer, overthrow, bewilder, perplex, bowl over *(informal)*, faze, discomfit, bring up short, dumbfound, nonplus • *He was floored by the announcement.*
2 = **knock down**, fell, knock over, prostrate, deck *(slang)* • *He was floored twice in the second round.*
▸ IN PHRASES: **wipe the floor with someone** = **beat**, defeat, trounce, run rings around *(informal)*, make mincemeat of *(informal)*, stuff *(slang)*, tank *(slang)*, crush, overwhelm, conquer, overthrow, lick *(informal)*, subdue, rout, overpower, quell, clobber *(slang)*, repulse, outplay, blow out of the water *(slang)* • *I'll wipe the floor with you!*

flop AS A VERB 1 = **slump**, fall, drop, collapse, sink, tumble, topple • *She flopped, exhausted, on to a sofa.*
2 = **hang down**, hang, dangle, sag, droop, hang limply • *His hair flopped over his left eye.*
3 = **fail**, close, bomb *(U.S. & Canad. slang)*, fold *(informal)*, founder, fall short, fall flat, come to nothing, come unstuck, misfire, go belly-up *(slang)*, go down like a lead balloon *(informal)* • *The film flopped badly at the box office.*
OPPOSITES: work, make it *(informal)*, succeed
▸ AS A NOUN = **failure**, disaster, loser, fiasco, debacle, washout *(informal)*, cockup *(Brit. slang)*, nonstarter • *The public decide whether a film is a hit or a flop.*
OPPOSITES: hit, success, triumph

floppy = **droopy**, soft, loose, hanging, limp, flapping, sagging, baggy, flip-flop, flaccid, pendulous • *the girl with the floppy hat*

flora = **plants**, vegetation • *an extraordinary variety of flora and fauna*

floral = **flowery**, flower-patterned • *a bright yellow floral fabric*

florid 1 = **flowery**, high-flown, figurative, grandiloquent, euphuistic • *a liking for florid writing*
2 = **ornate**, busy, flamboyant, baroque, fussy, embellished, flowery, overelaborate • *the cast-iron fireplace and the florid ceiling*
OPPOSITES: plain, bare, dull
3 = **flushed**, ruddy, rubicund, high-coloured, high-complexioned, blowsy • *He was a stout, florid man.*
OPPOSITES: pale, washed out, wan

flotsam 1 = **debris**, rubbish, wreckage, detritus, jetsam
2 = **debris**, sweepings, rubbish, junk, odds and ends • *The water was full of flotsam and refuse.*

flounce[1] *often with* **out, away, out,** *etc* = **bounce**, storm, stamp, go quickly, throw, spring, toss, fling, jerk • *She flounced out of my room in a huff.*

flounce[2] = **ruffle**, gathering, tuck, frill, ruff, furbelow • *a gown with a flounce round the hem*

flounder 1 = **falter**, struggle, stall, slow down, run into trouble, come unstuck *(informal)*, be in difficulties, hit a bad patch • *The economy was floundering.*
2 = **dither**, struggle, blunder, be confused, falter, be in the dark, be out of your depth • *The president is floundering, trying to jump-start his campaign.*
3 = **struggle**, struggle, toss, thrash, plunge, stumble, tumble, muddle, fumble, grope, wallow • *men floundering about in the water*

flourish AS A VERB 1 = **thrive**, increase, develop, advance, progress, boom, bloom, blossom, prosper, burgeon • *Business soon flourished.*
OPPOSITES: fail, decline, fade

2 = **succeed**, do well, be successful, move ahead, get ahead, go places *(informal)*, go great guns *(slang)*, go up in the world • *On graduation he flourished as a journalist.*
3 = **grow**, thrive, develop, flower, succeed, get on, bloom, blossom, prosper, bear fruit, be vigorous, be in your prime • *The plant is flourishing particularly well.*
4 = **wave**, brandish, sweep, swish, display, shake, swing, wield, flutter, wag, flaunt, vaunt, twirl • *He flourished his glass to make the point.*
▸ AS A NOUN 1 = **wave**, sweep, brandish, swish, shaking, swing, dash, brandishing, twirling, twirl, showy gesture • *with a flourish of his hand*
2 = **show**, display, parade, fanfare • *with a flourish of church bells*
3 = **curlicue**, sweep, decoration, swirl, plume, embellishment, ornamentation • *He underlined his name with a showy flourish.*

flourishing = **thriving**, successful, doing well, blooming, mushrooming, prospering, rampant, burgeoning, on a roll, going places, going strong, in the pink, in top form, on the up and up *(informal)* • *London quickly became a flourishing port.*

flout = **defy**, scorn, spurn, scoff at, outrage, insult, mock, scout *(archaic)*, ridicule, taunt, deride, sneer at, jeer at, take the piss out of *(taboo slang)*, laugh in the face of, show contempt for, gibe at, treat with disdain • *illegal campers who persist in flouting the law*
OPPOSITES: mind, value, respect

flow AS A VERB 1 = **run**, course, rush, sweep, move, issue, pass, roll, flood, pour, slide, proceed, stream, run out, surge, spill, go along, circulate, swirl, glide, ripple, cascade, whirl, overflow, gush, inundate, deluge, spurt, teem, spew, squirt, purl, well forth • *A stream flowed down into the valley.*
2 = **pour**, move, sweep, flood, stream, overflow • *Large numbers of refugees continue to flow into the country.*
3 = **issue**, follow, result, emerge, spring, pour, proceed, arise, derive, ensue, emanate • *Undesirable consequences flow from these misconceptions.*
▸ AS A NOUN 1 = **stream**, current, movement, motion, course, issue, flood, drift, tide, spate, gush, flux, outpouring, outflow, undertow, tideway • *watching the quiet flow of the olive-green water*
2 = **outpouring**, flood, stream, succession, train, plenty, abundance, deluge, plethora, outflow, effusion, emanation • *the opportunity to control the flow of information*

flower AS A NOUN 1 = **bloom**, blossom, efflorescence • *Each individual flower is tiny.*
2 = **elite**, best, prime, finest, pick, choice, cream, height, crème de la crème *(French)*, choicest part • *the flower of American manhood*
3 = **height**, prime, peak, vigour, freshness, greatest *or* finest point • *You are hardly in the first flower of youth.*
▸ AS A VERB 1 = **bloom**, open, mature, flourish, unfold, blossom, burgeon, effloresce • *Several of these plants will flower this year.*
2 = **blossom**, grow, develop, progress, mature, thrive, flourish, bloom, bud, prosper • *Their relationship flowered.*
▸ RELATED ADJECTIVE: floral
▸ RELATED PREFIX: antho-
▸ RELATED MANIA: anthomania

QUOTATIONS

There is no 'Why' about the rose, it blossoms because it blossoms
It pays no heed to itself, and does not care whether it is seen
[Angelus Silesius]

The flower is the poetry of reproduction. It is an example of the eternal seductiveness of life
[Jean Giraudoux *The Enchanted*]

When you take a flower in your hand and really look at it, it's your world for the moment
[Georgia O'Keeffe]

▹ *See panel* **Flowers**

flowering AS A NOUN = **development**, developing, thriving, flourishing, blossoming, prospering • *the flowering of multi-party democracy*
▸ AS AN ADJECTIVE = **blooming**, in flower, in bloom, in blossom, out, open, ready, blossoming, florescent, abloom • *pots of flowering shrubs*

FLOWERS

acacia
acanthus
African violet
aloe
alyssum
amaranth
amaryllis
anemone
arbutus
asphodel
aspidistra
aster
aubrietia
azalea
babe-in-a-cradle *(Austral.)*
begonia
betony
bignonia
black-eyed Susan
bluebell
bog asphodel
bougainvillea
burdock
Busy Lizzie
buttercup
cactus
calendula
camellia
camomile
cardinal flower
carnation
celandine
Christmas cactus
chrysanthemum
clematis
clianthus
columbine
Cooktown orchid *(Austral.)*
cornflower
cotoneaster
cowslip
crocus
cyclamen
daffodil
dahlia
daisy
dandelion
deadly nightshade
delphinium
digitalis
dog rose
edelweiss
eglantine
forget-me-not
foxglove
freesia
geranium
gilliflower
gladiolus
godetia
grape hyacinth
groundsel
guelder-rose
gypsophila
harebell
heartsease
heliotrope
hellebore
hemlock
hibiscus
hollyhock
hyacinth
hydrangea
iris
jasmine
jonquil
larkspur
lavender
lily
lily of the valley
lobelia
London pride
lotus
love-in-idleness
love-lies-bleeding
lupin
magnolia
mallow
mandrake
marguerite
marigold
marjoram
meadowsweet
monkshood
Michaelmas daisy
morning-glory
narcissus
nasturtium
old man's beard
orchid
oxeye daisy
oxlip
oxtongue
pansy
passionflower
peony *or* paeony
petunia
phlox
pimpernel
pink
poppy
primrose
primula
ragged robin
ragweed
rose
saffron
samphire
saxifrage
scarlet pimpernel
snapdragon
snowdrop
speedwell
stock
(Sturt's) desert pea *(Austral.)*
sunflower
sweetbrier
sweet pea
sweet william
tiger lily
tulip
valerian
verbena
violet
wallflower
water lily
willowherb
wintergreen
wisteria
wood anemone
woodbine
yarrow
zinnia

flowery 1 = **floral**, flower-patterned • *The baby was dressed in a flowery jumpsuit.*
2 = **ornate**, fancy, rhetorical, high-flown, embellished, figurative, florid, overwrought, euphuistic, baroque • *They were using uncommonly flowery language.*
OPPOSITES: simple, basic, plain

flowing 1 = **streaming**, rushing, gushing, teeming, falling, full, rolling, sweeping, flooded, fluid, prolific, abundant, overrun, brimming over • *fragrance borne by the swiftly flowing stream*
2 = **sleek**, smooth, fluid, unbroken, uninterrupted • *a smooth flowing line against a cloudless sky*
3 = **fluent**, easy, natural, continuous, effortless, uninterrupted, free-flowing, cursive, rich • *his own rhetoric and flowing style of delivery*
4 = **loose**, hanging, floppy, flaccid • *She wore a chic flowing gown.*

fluctuate 1 = **change**, swing, vary, alter, hesitate, alternate, waver, veer, rise and fall, go up and down, ebb and flow, seesaw • *Body temperatures can fluctuate when you are ill.*
2 = **shift**, undulate, oscillate, vacillate • *the constantly fluctuating price of crude oil*

fluctuation = **change**, shift, swing, variation, instability, alteration, wavering, oscillation, alternation, vacillation, unsteadiness, inconstancy • *Don't worry about tiny fluctuations in your weight.*

flue = **chimney**, channel, passage, shaft, vent, conduit, duct • *Cooking smells are vented through the flue.*

fluency 1 = **ability to speak or write**, good command, articulateness • *To work as a translator, you need fluency in at least one language.*
2 = **ease**, control, facility, command, assurance, readiness, smoothness, slickness, glibness, volubility, articulateness • *He was praised for speeches of remarkable fluency.*

fluent 1 = **able to speak or write**, natural, articulate, clear, easy, ready, flowing, smooth • *He is fluent in Arabic, French and English.*
OPPOSITES: halting, stumbling
2 = **effortless**, natural, articulate, well-versed, glib, facile, voluble, smooth-spoken • *He has developed into a fluent debater.*

fluff AS A NOUN = **fuzz**, down, pile, dust, fibre, threads, nap, lint, oose *(Scot.)*, dustball • *bits of fluff on the sleeve of her jumper*
▸ AS A VERB = **mess up**, spoil, bungle, screw up *(informal)*, cock up *(Brit. slang)*, fuck up *(offensive taboo slang)*, foul up *(informal)*, make a nonsense of, be unsuccessful in, make a mess off, muddle, crool or cruel *(Austral. slang)* • *She fluffed her interview at Oxford.*

fluffy = **soft**, fuzzy, feathery, downy, fleecy, flossy • *It's a very fluffy kind of wool.*

fluid AS A NOUN = **liquid**, solution, juice, liquor, sap • *Make sure that you drink plenty of fluids.*
▸ AS AN ADJECTIVE 1 = **flowing**, easy, natural, smooth, elegant, graceful, fluent, effortless, feline, sinuous • *long fluid dresses* • *His painting became more fluid.*
2 = **changeable**, mobile, flexible, volatile, unstable, adjustable, fluctuating, indefinite, shifting, floating, adaptable, mercurial, protean, mutable • *The situation is extremely fluid.*
OPPOSITES: firm, fixed, definite
3 = **liquid**, running, flowing, watery, molten, melted, runny, liquefied, in solution, aqueous • *List the fluid and cellular components of blood.*
OPPOSITES: set, hard, solid

fluke = **stroke of luck**, accident, coincidence, chance occurrence, chance, stroke, blessing, freak, windfall, quirk, lucky break, serendipity, quirk of fate, fortuity, break • *The discovery was something of a fluke.*

flummox = **baffle**, confuse, stump, perplex, defeat, fox, puzzle, bewilder, mystify, stymie, bamboozle *(informal)*, bring up short, nonplus • *This system has the potential to flummox most car thieves.*

flummoxed = **baffled**, confused, puzzled, stumped, foxed, at sea, bewildered, at a loss, mystified, stymied, bamboozled *(informal)*, nonplussed • *The leaders were flummoxed by the suggestion.*

flunk = **fail**, screw up *(informal)*, flop in *(informal)*, plough *(Brit. slang)*, be unsuccessful in, not make the grade at *(informal)*, not come up to scratch in *(informal)*, not come up to the mark in *(informal)* • *He flunked his final exams.*

flurry 1 = **commotion**, stir, bustle, flutter, to-do, excitement, hurry, fuss, disturbance, flap, whirl, furore, ferment, agitation, fluster, ado, tumult • *There was a flurry of excitement.*
2 = **burst**, spell, bout, outbreak, spurt • *a flurry of diplomatic activity*
3 = **gust**, shower, gale, swirl, squall, storm • *A flurry of snowflakes was scudding by the window.*

flush[1] AS A VERB 1 = **blush**, colour, burn, flame, glow, crimson, redden, suffuse, turn red, go red, colour up, go as red as a beetroot • *He turned away, his face flushing.*
2 = **cleanse**, wash out, swab, rinse out, flood, drench, syringe, swill, hose down, douche • *Flush the eye with clean cold water.*
3 = **expel**, drive, eject, dislodge • *Flush the contents down the lavatory.*
▸ AS A NOUN 1 = **blush**, colour, glow, reddening, redness, rosiness • *There was a slight flush on his cheeks.*
2 = **bloom**, glow, vigour, freshness • *the first flush of young love*

flush[2] AS AN ADJECTIVE 1 = **level**, even, true, flat, square, plane • *Make sure the tile is flush with the surrounding tiles.*
2 = **wealthy**, rich, rolling *(slang)*, well-off, in the money *(informal)*, in funds, well-heeled *(informal)*, replete, moneyed, well-supplied, minted *(Brit. slang)* • *Many developing countries were flush with dollars.*
3 = **affluent**, liberal, generous, lavish, abundant, overflowing, plentiful, prodigal, full • *If we're feeling flush we'll give them champagne.*
▸ AS AN ADVERB = **level**, even, touching, squarely, in contact, hard (against) • *The edges fit flush with the walls.*

flush[3] *often with* **out** = **drive out**, force, dislodge, put to flight, start, discover, disturb, uncover, rouse • *They flushed them out of their hiding places.*

flushed 1 *often with* **with** = **exhilarated**, excited, aroused, elated, high *(informal)*, inspired, thrilled, animated, enthused, intoxicated, stoked *(Austral. & N.Z. informal)* • *She was flushed with the success of the venture.*
2 = **blushing**, red, hot, burning, embarrassed, glowing, rosy, crimson, feverish, ruddy, rubicund • *Young girls with flushed faces pass by.*

fluster AS A VERB = **upset**, bother, disturb, ruffle, heat, excite, confuse, hurry, rattle *(informal)*, bustle, hassle *(informal)*, flurry, agitate, confound, unnerve, perturb, throw off balance, make nervous • *She was calm. Nothing could fluster her.*
▸ AS A NOUN = **turmoil**, state *(informal)*, flap *(informal)*, bustle, flutter, flurry, ruffle, furore, agitation, dither *(chiefly Brit.)*, commotion, perturbation, disturbance • *I was in such a fluster that I dropped the lot.*

flute
▸ RELATED PHOBIA: aulophobia

fluted = **grooved**, channelled, furrowed, corrugated • *the fluted wooden post of the porch*

flutter AS A VERB 1 = **beat**, bat, flap, tremble, shiver, flicker, ripple, waver, fluctuate, agitate, ruffle, quiver, vibrate, palpitate • *a butterfly fluttering its wings*

2 = flit, hover, flitter • *The birds were fluttering among the trees.*
3 = flap, fly, wave, shake, swish • *It was silent except for the flags fluttering in the background.*
▸ **AS A NOUN** **1 = bet**, gamble, punt *(chiefly Brit.)*, wager • *I had a flutter on five horses.*
2 = tremor, tremble, shiver, shudder, palpitation • *She felt a flutter of trepidation in her stomach.*
3 = vibration, flapping, twitching, quiver, quivering • *loud twittering and a desperate flutter of wings*
4 = agitation, state *(informal)*, confusion, excitement, flap *(informal)*, tremble, flurry, dither *(chiefly Brit.)*, commotion, fluster, tumult, perturbation, state of nervous excitement • *She was in a flutter.*

flux **1 = instability**, change, transition, unrest, modification, alteration, mutation, fluctuation, mutability • *a period of economic flux*
2 = flow, movement, motion, fluidity • *the flux of cosmic rays*

fly[1] **AS A VERB** **1 = take wing**, soar, glide, take to the air, wing, mount, sail, hover, flutter, flit • *The bird flew away.*
2 = jet, travel by plane, go by air, travel in an aircraft • *He flew back to London.*
3 = pilot, control, operate, steer, manoeuvre, navigate, be at the controls, aviate • *He flew a small plane to Cuba.*
4 = airlift, send by plane, take by plane, take in an aircraft • *The relief supples are being flown from Pisa.*
5 = flutter, wave, float, flap • *A flag was flying on the new HQ.*
6 = display, show, flourish, brandish • *He sailed in a ship flying a red flag.*
7 = rush, race, shoot, career, speed, tear, dash, hurry, barrel (along) *(informal, chiefly U.S. & Canad.)*, sprint, bolt, dart, zoom, hare *(Brit. informal)*, hasten, whizz *(informal)*, scoot, scamper, burn rubber *(informal)*, be off like a shot *(informal)* • *I flew downstairs.*
8 = pass swiftly, pass, glide, slip away, roll on, flit, elapse, run its course, go quickly • *We walked and the time flew by.*
9 = leave, disappear, get away, depart, run, escape, flee, take off, run from, shun, clear out *(informal)*, light out *(informal)*, abscond, decamp, take flight, do a runner *(slang)*, run for it, cut and run *(informal)*, fly the coop *(U.S. & Canad. informal)*, beat a retreat, make a quick exit, make a getaway, show a clean pair of heels, skedaddle *(informal)*, hightail *(informal, chiefly U.S.)*, take a powder *(U.S. & Canad. slang)*, hasten away, make your escape, take it on the lam *(U.S. & Canad. slang)*, take to your heels • *I'll have to fly.*
▸ **IN PHRASES:** **fly at someone = attack**, go for, assault, assail, have a go at *(informal)*, pounce on, fall upon, rush at, get stuck into *(informal)*, pitch into *(informal)*, go for the jugular, lay about, belabour, lash out on • *Both women flew at each other.*
let fly = lose your temper, lash out, burst forth, keep nothing back, give free rein, let (someone) have it • *She let fly with a string of obscenities.*
let something fly = throw, launch, cast, hurl, shoot, fire, fling, chuck *(informal)*, sling, lob *(informal)*, hurtle, let off, heave • *The midfielder let fly a powerful shot.*

fly[2] **IN PHRASES:** **fly in the ointment = problem**, difficulty, rub, flaw, hitch, drawback, snag, small problem
▸ **COLLECTIVE NOUNS:** swarm, grist
▹ *See panel* **Flies**

fly[3] **= cunning**, knowing, sharp, smart, careful, shrewd, astute, on the ball *(informal)*, canny, wide-awake, nobody's fool, not born yesterday • *He is devious and very fly.*

fly-by-night = unreliable, cowboy *(informal)*, dubious, questionable, shady, untrustworthy, undependable • *fly-by-night operators who do shoddy work*

flyer *or* **flier** **1 = pilot**, aeronaut, airman *or* airwoman, aviator *or* aviatrix • *escape lines for shot-down allied flyers*
2 = air traveller, air passenger • *regular business flyers*
3 = handbill, bill, notice, leaf, release, literature *(informal)*, leaflet, advert *(Brit. informal)*, circular, booklet, pamphlet, handout, throwaway *(U.S.)*, promotional material, publicity material • *posters, newsletters and flyers*
4 = jump, spring, bound, leap, hurdle, vault, jeté, flying *or* running jump • *At this point he took a flyer off the front.*
5 = goer, runner, sprinter, racer, scorcher *(informal)*, speed demon *or* merchant *(informal)* • *This horse is a real flyer.*

flying **1 = airborne**, waving, winging, floating, streaming, soaring, in the air, hovering, flapping, gliding, fluttering, wind-borne, volitant • *a species of flying insect*
2 = fast, running, express, speedy, winged, mobile, rapid, fleet, mercurial • *He made a flying start to the final.*
3 = hurried, brief, rushed, fleeting, short-lived, hasty, transitory, fugacious • *I paid a flying visit to the capital.*
▸ **RELATED ADJECTIVE:** volar

foam **AS A NOUN** **= froth**, spray, bubbles, lather, suds, spume, head • *The water curved round the rock in bursts of foam.*
▸ **AS A VERB** **= bubble**, boil, fizz, froth, lather, effervesce • *We watched the water foam and bubble.*
▸ **IN PHRASES:** **foam at the mouth** *or* **be foaming at the mouth = be angry**, rage, fume, be furious, seethe, be in a

FLIES

antlion *or* antlion fly
aphid *or* plant louse
aphis
apple blight *or* American blight
bee fly
beetfly *or* mangold fly
blackfly *or* bean aphid
blowfly, bluebottle, *or* *(Austral. informal)* blowie
botfly
buffalo gnat *or* black fly
bulb fly
bushfly
carrot fly
chalcid *or* chalcid fly
cluster fly
crane fly *or* *(Brit.)* daddy-longlegs
damselfly
dobsonfly
dragonfly *or* *(colloquial)* devil's darning-needle
drosophila, fruit fly, *or* vinegar fly
fly
frit fly
fruit fly
gadfly
gallfly
gnat
grannom
green blowfly *or* *(Austral. informal)* blue-arsed fly
greenbottle
greenfly
horsefly *or* cleg
housefly
hover fly
lacewing
lantern fly
mayfly *or* dayfly
Mediterranean fruit fly *or* Medfly
needle fly
onion fly
robber fly, bee killer, *or* assassin fly
sandfly
scorpion fly
screwworm fly
silverhorn
snake fly
stable fly
stonefly
tachina fly
tsetse fly
vinegar fly
warble fly
whitefly
willow fly

state *(informal)*, see red *(informal)*, be incensed, go berserk, be livid, go ballistic *(slang, chiefly U.S.)*, be incandescent, get hot under the collar *(informal)*, breathe fire and slaughter • *He was foaming at the mouth about the incident.*

foamy = **bubbly**, foaming, frothy, sudsy, lathery, spumescent • *Whisk the egg whites until they are foamy.*

fob IN PHRASES: **fob someone off** = **put off**, deceive, appease, flannel *(Brit. informal)*, give (someone) the run-around *(informal)*, stall, equivocate with • *I've asked her but she fobs me off with excuses.*
fob something off on someone = **pass off**, dump, get rid of, inflict, unload, foist, palm off • *He likes to fob his work off on others.*

focus AS A NOUN 1 = **centre**, focal point, central point, core, bull's eye, centre of attraction, centre of activity, cynosure • *The children are the focus of her life.*
2 = **focal point**, heart, target, headquarters, hub, meeting place • *the focus of the campaign for Black rights*
3 = **attention**, concern, priority, concentration • *IBM has shifted its focus to personal computers.*
4 = **subject**, point, question, issue, matter, object, theme, substance, topic, subject matter, field of inquiry *or* reference • *Food is the main focus of the book.*
▸ AS A VERB 1 *often with* **on** = **concentrate**, centre, spotlight, zero in on *(informal)*, meet, join, direct, aim, pinpoint, converge, rivet, bring to bear, zoom in • *The summit is expected to focus on arms control.*
2 = **fix**, train, direct, aim • *He focused the binoculars on the boat.*
▸ IN PHRASES: **in focus** = **clear**, sharp, distinct, crisp, sharp-edged, sharply defined • *Pictures should be in focus.*
out of focus = **blurred**, obscure, unclear, fuzzy, hazy, muzzy, ill-defined, indistinct • *Some of the pictures are out of focus.*

fodder = **feed**, food, rations, tack *(informal)*, foodstuff, kai *(N.Z. informal)*, forage, victuals, provender, vittles *(obsolete or dialect)* • *fodder for horses*

foe = **enemy**, rival, opponent, adversary, antagonist, foeman *(archaic)* • *support any friend, oppose any foe*
OPPOSITES: friend, partner, ally

fog AS A NOUN 1 = **mist**, gloom, haze, smog, murk, miasma, murkiness, peasouper *(informal)* • *The crash happened in thick fog.*
2 = **stupor**, confusion, trance, daze, haze, disorientation • *He was in a fog when he got up.*
▸ AS A VERB 1 = **mist over** *or* **up**, cloud over, steam up, become misty • *The windows fogged immediately.*
2 = **daze**, cloud, dim, muddle, blind, confuse, obscure, bewilder, darken, perplex, stupefy, befuddle, muddy the waters, obfuscate, blear, becloud, bedim • *His mind was fogged with fatigue.*
▸ RELATED PHOBIA: homichlophobia

fogey *or* **fogy** = **fuddy-duddy**, square *(informal)*, stick-in-the-mud *(informal)*, antique *(informal)*, dinosaur, fossil *(informal)*, relic, anachronism, dodo *(informal)*, back number *(informal)* • *I don't want to sound like I'm some old fogy.*

foggy 1 = **misty**, grey, murky, cloudy, obscure, blurred, dim, hazy, nebulous, indistinct, soupy, smoggy, vaporous, brumous *(rare)* • *Conditions were damp and foggy this morning.*
OPPOSITES: clear, bright
2 = **unclear**, confused, clouded, stupid, obscure, vague, dim, bewildered, muddled, dazed, cloudy, stupefied, indistinct, befuddled, dark • *My foggy brain sifted through the possibilities.*
OPPOSITES: clear, sharp, alert

foible = **idiosyncrasy**, failing, fault, weakness, defect, quirk, imperfection, peculiarity, weak point, infirmity • *human foibles and weaknesses*

foil[1] = **thwart**, stop, check, defeat, disappoint, counter, frustrate, hamper, baffle, elude, balk, circumvent, outwit, nullify, checkmate, nip in the bud, put a spoke in (someone's) wheel *(Brit.)* • *A brave police chief foiled an armed robbery.*

foil[2] = **complement**, setting, relief, contrast, background, antithesis • *A cold beer is the perfect foil for a curry.*

foist IN PHRASES: **foist something on** *or* **upon someone** = **force** • *I don't foist my beliefs on other people.*
foist something *or* **someone off on someone** = **unload**, get rid of, pass off, palm off • *No wonder she was so keen to foist him off on us.*

fold AS A VERB 1 = **bend**, double, gather, tuck, overlap, crease, pleat, intertwine, double over, turn under • *He folded the paper carefully.*
2 *often with* **up** *(Informal)* = **go bankrupt**, close, fail, crash, collapse, founder, shut down, go under, be ruined, go bust *(informal)*, go to the wall, go belly-up *(slang)* • *The company folded in 1990.*
3 *with* **in** = **wrap**, envelop, entwine, enfold • *He folded her in his arms.*
4 *often with* **up** *or* **in** = **wrap up**, wrap, enclose, envelop, do up, enfold • *an object folded neatly in tissue-paper*
▸ AS A NOUN = **crease**, turn, gather, bend, layer, overlap, wrinkle, pleat, ruffle, furrow, knife-edge, double thickness, folded portion • *Make another fold and turn the ends together.*
▸ IN PHRASES: **fold something in** = **stir gently**, introduce, envelop, mix gently • *Fold in the whipped egg whites and cream.*

folder = **file**, portfolio, envelope, dossier, binder • *Inside the folder was a single sheet of paper.*

folk 1 = **people**, persons, humans, individuals, men and women, human beings, humanity, inhabitants, mankind, mortals • *the innate reserve of country folk*
2 *usually plural (Informal)* = **family**, parents, relations, relatives, tribe, clan, kin, kindred, ainga *(N.Z.)*, rellies *(Austral. slang)* • *I've been avoiding my folks lately.*

PROVERBS
There's nowt so queer as folk

follow AS A VERB 1 = **accompany**, attend, escort, come after, go behind, tag along behind, bring up the rear, come behind, come *or* go with, tread on the heels of • *Please follow me, madam.*
2 = **pursue**, track, dog, hunt, chase, shadow, tail *(informal)*, trail, hound, stalk, run after • *I think we're being followed.*
OPPOSITES: avoid, escape from, elude
3 = **come after**, go after, come next • *the rioting and looting that followed the verdict*
OPPOSITES: lead, guide, precede
4 = **result**, issue, develop, spring, flow, proceed, arise, ensue, roll up, emanate, be consequent, supervene • *If the explanation is right, two things will follow.*
5 = **obey**, observe, comply with, adhere to, mind, watch, note, regard, stick to, heed, conform to, keep to, pay attention to, be guided by, toe the line, act according to, act in accordance with, give allegiance to • *Take care to follow the instructions.*
OPPOSITES: reject, ignore, give up
6 = **copy**, imitate, emulate, mimic, model, adopt, live up to, take a leaf out of someone's book, take as an example, pattern yourself upon • *He did not follow his example in taking drugs.*
7 = **succeed**, replace, come after, take over from, come next, supersede, supplant, take the place of, step into the shoes of • *He followed his father and became a surgeon.*
8 = **understand**, get, see, catch, realize, appreciate, take in, grasp, catch on *(informal)*, keep up with, comprehend, fathom, get the hang of *(informal)*, get the picture • *Can you follow the plot so far?*
9 = **keep up with**, support, be interested in, cultivate, be devoted to, be a fan of, keep abreast of, be a devotee *or* supporter of • *the millions of people who follow football*
▸ IN PHRASES: **follow something through** = **complete**, conclude, pursue, see through, consummate, bring to a conclusion • *They have been unwilling to follow through their ideas.*

follow something up 1 = investigate, research, pursue, look into, check out, find out about, make inquiries • *Security police are following up several leads.*
2 = continue, make sure, reinforce, consolidate • *They'll follow it up with a promotional visit in July.*

follower 1 = supporter, fan, representative, convert, believer, admirer, backer, partisan, disciple, protagonist, devotee, worshipper, apostle, pupil, cohort *(chiefly U.S.)*, adherent, henchman, groupie *(slang)*, habitué, votary • *violent clashes between followers of the two organisations*
OPPOSITES: leader, teacher, tutor
2 = attendant, assistant, companion, helper, sidekick *(slang)*, henchman, retainer *(History)*, hanger-on, minion, lackey • *a London gangster and his two thuggish followers*
OPPOSITES: rival, enemy, opponent

f

following AS AN ADJECTIVE **1 = next**, subsequent, successive, ensuing, coming, later, succeeding, specified, consequent, consequential • *We went to dinner the following evening.*
2 = coming, about to be mentioned • *Write down the following information.*
▸ AS A NOUN **= supporters**, backing, public, support, train, fans, audience, circle, suite, patronage, clientele, entourage, coterie, retinue • *Rugby League enjoys a huge following.*

folly = foolishness, bêtise *(rare)*, nonsense, madness, stupidity, absurdity, indiscretion, lunacy, recklessness, silliness, idiocy, irrationality, imprudence, rashness, imbecility, fatuity, preposterousness, daftness *(informal)*, desipience • *a reminder of the follies of war*
OPPOSITES: reason, sense, wisdom

QUOTATIONS
As a dog returneth to his vomit, so a fool returneth to his folly
[*Bible: Proverbs*]

foment = stir up, raise, encourage, promote, excite, spur, foster, stimulate, provoke, brew, arouse, rouse, agitate, quicken, incite, instigate, whip up, goad, abet, sow the seeds of, fan the flames • *They accused strike leaders of fomenting violence.*

fond AS AN ADJECTIVE **1 = loving**, caring, warm, devoted, tender, adoring, affectionate, indulgent, doting, amorous • *She gave him a fond smile.*
OPPOSITES: indifferent, austere, aloof
2 = unrealistic, empty, naive, vain, foolish, deluded, indiscreet, credulous, overoptimistic, delusive, delusory, absurd • *My fond hope is that we'll be ready on time.*
OPPOSITES: sensible, rational
▸ IN PHRASES: **fond of 1 = attached to**, in love with, keen on, attracted to, having a soft spot for, enamoured of • *I am very fond of Michael.*
2 = keen on, into *(informal)*, hooked on, partial to, having a soft spot for, having a taste for, addicted to, having a liking for, predisposed towards, having a fancy for • *He was fond of marmalade.*

fondle = caress, pet, cuddle, touch gently, pat, stroke, dandle • *He tried to kiss and fondle her.*

fondly 1 = lovingly, tenderly, affectionately, amorously, dearly, possessively, with affection, indulgently, adoringly • *Their eyes met fondly across the table.*
2 = unrealistically, stupidly, vainly, foolishly, naively, credulously • *I fondly imagined my life could be better.*

fondness 1 = devotion, love, affection, warmth, attachment, kindness, tenderness, care, aroha *(N.Z.)* • *a great fondness for children*
OPPOSITES: opposition, hostility, dislike
2 = liking, love, taste, fancy, attraction, weakness, preference, attachment, penchant, susceptibility, predisposition, soft spot, predilection, partiality • *I've always had a fondness for jewels.*

food AS A NOUN **= nourishment**, cooking, provisions, fare, board, commons, table, eats *(slang)*, stores, feed, diet, meat, bread, menu, tuck *(informal)*, tucker *(Austral. & N.Z. informal)*, rations, nutrition, cuisine, tack *(informal)*, refreshment, scoff *(slang)*, nibbles, grub *(slang)*, foodstuffs, subsistence, kai *(N.Z. informal)*, larder, chow *(informal)*, sustenance, nosh *(slang)*, daily bread, victuals, edibles, comestibles, provender, nosebag *(slang)*, pabulum *(rare)*, nutriment, vittles *(obsolete or dialect)*, viands, aliment, eatables *(slang)*, survival rations • *Enjoy your food!*
▸ IN PHRASES: **food for thought = mental nourishment**, mental stimulation, food for the mind • *His speech offers much food for thought.*
▸ RELATED ADJECTIVE: alimentary
▸ RELATED NOUN: gastronomy
▸ RELATED MANIA: sitomania
▸ RELATED PHOBIA: sitophobia

QUOTATIONS
We lived for days on nothing but food and water
[W.C. Fields]
Food first, then morality
[Bertolt Brecht *The Threepenny Opera*]
Tell me what you eat and I will tell you what you are
[Anthelme Brillat-Savarin *Physiologie du Gout*]
There is not one kind of food for all men. You must and you will feed those faculties which you exercise. The laborer whose body is weary does not require the same food with the scholar whose brain is weary
[Henry David Thoreau *letter to Harrison Blake*]
After a good dinner one can forgive anybody, even one's own relatives
[Oscar Wilde]
There is no love sincerer than the love of food
[George Bernard Shaw *Man and Superman*]
Sharing food with another human being is an intimate act that should not be indulged in lightly
[M.F.K. Fisher *An Alphabet for Gourmets*]
On the Continent people have good food; in England people have good table manners
[George Mikes *How to be an Alien*]
[If the people have no bread] let them eat cake
[Marie-Antoinette]
Man shall not live by bread alone, but by every word that proceedeth out of the mouth of God
[*Bible: St. Matthew*]

PROVERBS
Half a loaf is better than no bread
You cannot have your cake and eat it
What's sauce for the goose is sauce for the gander
An apple a day keeps the doctor away

▷ *See panels* **Apples; Beans and other pulses; Biscuits; Breads; Cakes and pastries; Cheeses; Desserts and sweet dishes; Herbs, spices and seasonings; Mushrooms and other edible fungi; Nuts; Potatoes; Rice and other cereals; Sauces; Savoury dishes; Seafood; Types of curry; Types and cuts of meat; Types of fruit; Types of meal; Types of pasta; Types of pastry; Vegetables**

foodie = gourmet, connoisseur, bon viveur *(French)*, gourmand, bon vivant *(French)*, epicure, gastronome • *first-class choice for the serious foodie*

fool AS A NOUN **1 = simpleton**, idiot, mug *(Brit. slang)*, berk *(Brit. slang)*, charlie *(Brit. informal)*, silly, goose *(informal)*, dope *(informal)*, jerk *(slang, chiefly U.S. & Canad.)*, dummy *(slang)*, ass *(U.S. & Canad. taboo slang)*, clot *(Brit. informal)*, plank *(Brit. slang)*, sap *(slang)*, prick *(derogatory slang)*, wally *(slang)*, illiterate, prat *(slang)*, plonker *(slang)*, coot, moron, nit *(informal)*, git *(Brit. slang)*, geek *(slang)*, twit *(informal, chiefly Brit.)*, bonehead *(slang)*, chump *(informal)*, dunce, imbecile *(informal)*, loon, clod, cretin, oaf, bozo *(U.S. slang)*,

SAVOURY DISHES

angels-on-horseback, avgolemono, baked beans, beef bourguinon *or* boeuf bourguignonne, beef stroganoff, bhaji, blanquette de veau, blintz, bocconcini, Bombay duck, bouchée, brawn, bredie, bridie *or* Forfar bridie, broth, bruschetta, bubble and squeak, burgoo, burrito, calzone, Caesar salad, canapé, caponata, casserole, cassoulet, cauliflower cheese, cheeseburger, chicken Kiev, chilli con carne, chips, chop suey, chow mein, clam chowder, club sandwich, cock-a-leekie, coddle, consommé, corn chowder, Cornish pasty, cottage pie, coulibiaca, couscous, crêpe, croquette, crostini, croute, crowdie, Cullen skink, curry, curry puff, daube, devils-on-horseback, dolmades, doner kebab, eggs Benedict, enchilada, escargot, faggot, fajitas, falafel, fish and chips *or* *(Scot.)* fish supper, fish cake, fish finger, flan, foo yong, fondue, forcemeat, frankfurter, French toast, fricassee, fry *or* fry-up, gado-gado, galantine, game chips, gefilte fish, goulash, guacamole, haggis, hamburger, hash, hominy grits *or* grits, hotchpotch, hotpot, hummus, houmus, *or* humous, jambalaya, jugged hare, Irish stew, kebab, kedgeree, keftedes, kishke, knish, kofta, kromesky, laksa, Lancashire hotpot, lasagne, laver bread, lobscouse, lobster Newburg, lobster thermidor, macaroni cheese, madrilène, manicotti, matelote, meat loaf, minestrone, mirepoix, mixed grill, mock turtle soup, moussaka, mousse, mulligatawny, nachos, nasi goreng, navarin, olla podrida, omelette, open sandwich, osso bucco, paella, pakora, palm-oil chop, pastitsio, pakora, panini, paté, patty, pease pudding, pepper pot, pie, pilau, pilaf, pilaff, pilao, *or* pilaw, pirogi, pirozhki, pizza, ploughman's lunch, polenta, porridge, pot-au-feu, pot pie, pot roast, pottage, poutine, prairie oyster, prawn cracker, quenelle, quiche, quiche lorraine, Quorn *(trademark)*, ragout, raita, ramekin, ratatouille, ravioli, red pudding, rijsttafel, risotto, rissole, roast, rojak, roulade, salad, salade niçoise, salmagundi *or* salmagundy, salmi *or* salmis, salpicon, samosa, sandwich, sanger *or* sango *(Austral. slang)*, sarmie *(S. African)*, sashimi, satay, sauerbraten, sauerkraut, sausage roll, scaloppine *or* scaloppini, scampi, schnitzel, Scotch broth, Scotch egg, Scotch pie *or* mutton pie, scouse, scrambled eggs, shepherd's pie, shish kebab, skirlie, smorgasbord, smørrebrød, soba, sosatie, soufflé, soup, souvlakia, Spanish rice, spanokopita, spring roll, steak-and-kidney pie, steak-and-kidney pudding, steak pie, steak tartare, stew, stir-fry, stottie, succotash, suet pudding, surf 'n' turf, sukiyaki, sushi, taco, tagine, tamale, taramasalata, tartlet, teriyaki, thali, timbale, toad-in-the-hole, toast, tofu, tomalley, tortilla, tyropitta, tzatziki *or* tsatsiki, udon, veggieburger *or* vegeburger, vichyssoise, vol-au-vent, Waldorf salad, Welsh rabbit *or* rarebit, white pudding, won ton, Yorkshire pudding

dullard, dimwit *(informal)*, ignoramus, dumbo *(slang)*, jackass, dipstick *(Brit. slang)*, dickhead *(slang)*, gonzo *(slang)*, schmuck *(U.S. slang)*, dork *(slang)*, nitwit *(informal)*, dolt, blockhead, ninny, divvy *(Brit. slang)*, bird-brain *(informal)*, pillock *(Brit. slang)*, halfwit, nincompoop, dweeb *(U.S. slang)*, putz *(U.S. slang)*, fathead *(informal)*, weenie *(U.S. informal)*, schlep *(U.S. slang)*, eejit *(Scot. & Irish)*, thicko *(Brit. slang)*, dumb-ass *(slang)*, pea-brain *(slang)*, gobshite *(Irish taboo slang)*, dunderhead, numpty *(Scot. informal)*, doofus *(slang, chiefly U.S.)*, lamebrain *(informal)*, fuckwit *(taboo slang)*, mooncalf, thickhead, clodpate *(archaic)*, dickwit *(slang)*, nerd *or* nurd *(slang)*, numbskull *or* numskull, twerp *or* twirp *(informal)*, dorba *or* dorb *(Austral. slang)*, bogan *(Austral. slang)* • *He'd been a fool to get involved with her.*

OPPOSITES: expert, master, genius

2 = dupe, butt, mug *(Brit. slang)*, sucker *(slang)*, gull *(archaic)*, stooge *(slang)*, laughing stock, pushover *(informal)*, fall guy *(informal)*, chump *(informal)*, greenhorn *(informal)*, easy mark *(informal)* • *He feels she has made a fool of him.*

3 = jester, comic, clown, harlequin, motley, buffoon, pierrot, court jester, punchinello, joculator *or (fem.)* joculatrix, merry-andrew • *Every good court has its resident fool.*

▸ **AS A VERB = deceive**, cheat, mislead, delude, kid *(informal)*, trick, take in, con *(informal)*, stiff *(slang)*, have (someone) on, bluff, hoax, dupe, beguile, gull *(archaic)*, swindle, make a fool of, bamboozle, hoodwink, take for a ride *(informal)*, put one over on *(informal)*, play a trick on, pull a fast one on *(informal)*, scam *(slang)* • *Art dealers fool a lot of people.*

▸ **IN PHRASES: act** *or* **play the fool = mess about**, show off *(informal)*, clown, play (silly) games, be silly, frolic, cavort, act up, lark about *(informal)*, piss about *(taboo slang)*, piss around *(taboo slang)*, act the goat, cut capers, play the goat • *He likes to act the fool.*

fool around with something = play around with, play with, tamper with, toy with, mess around with, meddle with, trifle with, fiddle around with *(informal)*, monkey around with, piss about with *(taboo slang)*, piss around with *(taboo slang)* • *He was fooling around with his cot, and he fell out of bed.*

fool around *or* **about 1 = mess about**, sleep around *(informal)*, womanize *(informal)*, philander, flirt, court, toy, trifle, mess about, mess around, dally, coquet • *Her husband was fooling around.*

2 = **mess about**, hang around, idle, waste time, lark, play about, dawdle, kill time, fool about, play the fool, act the fool, footle *(informal)* • *Stop fooling about.*

QUOTATIONS

Fools rush in where angels fear to tread
[Alexander Pope *An Essay on Criticism*]
A fool and his words are soon parted
[William Shenstone *Works*]
A fool uttereth all his mind
[*Bible: Proverbs*]
I am two fools, I know,
For loving, and for saying so
In whining poetry
[John Donne *Songs and Sonnets*]
Who loves not woman, wine and song
Remains a fool his whole life long
[attributed to Martin Luther]
Be wise with speed;
A fool at forty is a fool indeed
[Edward Young *The Love of Fame*]
There's a sucker born every minute
[Phineas T. Barnum]
You may fool all the people some of the time; you can even fool some of the people all the time; but you can't fool all of the people all the time
[attributed to both Phineas T. Barnum and Abraham Lincoln]
A fool sees not the same tree that a wise man sees
[William Blake *The Marriage of Heaven and Hell*]
A knowledgeable fool is a greater fool than an ignorant fool
[Molière *Les Femmes Savantes*]

PROVERBS

A fool and his money are soon parted
There's no fool like an old fool
Fools build houses and wise men live in them
A fool may give a wise man counsel

foolhardy = **rash**, risky, irresponsible, reckless, precipitate, unwise, impulsive, madcap, impetuous, hot-headed, imprudent, incautious, venturesome, venturous, temerarious • *He had to be restrained from foolhardy action.*
OPPOSITES: careful, alert, cautious

foolish 1 = **unwise**, silly, absurd, rash, unreasonable, senseless, short-sighted, ill-advised, foolhardy, nonsensical, inane, indiscreet, ill-judged, ill-considered, imprudent, unintelligent, asinine, injudicious, incautious • *It would be foolish to raise hopes unnecessarily.*
OPPOSITES: sound, bright, sensible
2 = **silly**, stupid, mad, daft *(informal)*, simple, weak, crazy, ridiculous, dumb *(informal)*, ludicrous, senseless, barmy *(slang)*, potty *(Brit. informal)*, goofy *(informal)*, idiotic, half-baked *(informal)*, dotty *(slang)*, inane, fatuous, loopy *(informal)*, witless, crackpot *(informal)*, moronic, brainless, half-witted, imbecilic, off your head *(informal)*, braindead *(informal)*, harebrained, as daft as a brush *(informal, chiefly Brit.)*, dumb-ass *(slang)*, doltish • *How foolish I was not to have seen my doctor earlier.*

foolishly = **unwisely**, stupidly, mistakenly, absurdly, like a fool, idiotically, incautiously, imprudently, ill-advisedly, indiscreetly, short-sightedly, injudiciously, without due consideration • *He admitted he had acted foolishly.*

foolishness 1 = **stupidity**, irresponsibility, recklessness, idiocy, weakness, absurdity, indiscretion, silliness, inanity, imprudence, rashness, foolhardiness, folly, bêtise *(rare)* • *the foolishness of dangerously squabbling politicians*
2 = **nonsense**, carrying-on *(informal, chiefly Brit.)*, rubbish, trash, bunk, malarkey *(informal)*, claptrap *(informal)*, rigmarole, foolery, bunkum or buncombe *(chiefly U.S.)* • *I don't have time to listen to this foolishness.*

QUOTATIONS

Mix a little foolishness with your prudence; it's good to be silly at the right moment
[Horace *Odes*]

foolproof = **infallible**, certain, safe, guaranteed, never-failing, unassailable, sure-fire *(informal)*, unbreakable • *The system is not 100 per cent foolproof.*

foot AS A PLURAL NOUN = **tootsies** *(informal)* • *his aching arms and sore feet*
▸ AS A NOUN 1 = **paw**, pad, trotter, hoof • *It could trap and hurt an animal's foot.*
2 = **bottom**, end, base, foundation, lowest part • *Friends stood at the foot of the bed.*
▸ IN PHRASES: **drag your feet** = **stall**, procrastinate, block, hold back, obstruct • *They were dragging their feet so as to obstruct political reforms.*
▸ TECHNICAL NAME: pes
▸ RELATED ADJECTIVE: pedal

football = **soccer**, footy *(informal)*, the beautiful game • *a game of football*
▹ *See panel* **Football**

foothold 1 = **basis**, standing, base, position, foundation • *Companies must establish a firm foothold in Europe.*
2 = **toehold**, hold, support, footing, grip • *He had a solid foothold on the rockface beneath him.*

footing 1 = **basis**, foundation, foothold, base position, ground, settlement, establishment, installation, groundwork • *a sounder financial footing for the future*
2 = **relationship**, terms, position, basis, state, standing, condition, relations, rank, status, grade • *They are trying to compete on an equal footing.*
3 = **foothold**, hold, grip, toehold, support • *He lost his footing and slid into the water.*

footnote = **note**, gloss, annotation, marginal note • *At this point a footnote explains.*

footpath = **pavement**, sidewalk *(U.S. & Canad.)* • *A car mounted the footpath and demolished the fence.*

footprint = **impression**, mark, track, trace, outline, imprint, indentation • *I saw a footprint in the snow.*

footstep 1 = **step**, tread, footfall • *I heard footsteps outside.*
2 = **footprint**, mark, track, trace, outline, imprint, indentation, footmark • *people's footsteps in the snow*

footwear = **footgear**, boots, shoes, slippers, sandals • *You can tell a great deal about people from their footwear.*

foppish = **dandyish**, vain, spruce, preening, dapper, natty *(informal)*, dressy *(informal)*, dandified, coxcombical, prinking, finical • *Though not foppish, he appreciated fine clothes.*

for 1 = **intended**, appropriate to, designed to meet the needs of • *a table for two*
2 = **on behalf of**, representing • *the spokesman for the Democrats*
3 = **throughout**, during, over a span of • *They talked for an hour.*
4 = **in favour of**, backing, supporting, pro, in support of • *The case for nuclear power is impressive.*
5 = **towards**, to, in the direction of • *traffic jams heading for the coast*
6 = **because of**, due to, owing to, on account of • *For that reason, I do not think it matters.*

forage AS A NOUN = **fodder**, food, feed, foodstuffs, provender • *forage needed to feed one cow and its calf*
▸ AS A VERB = **search**, hunt, scavenge, cast about, seek, explore, raid, scour, plunder, look round, rummage, ransack, scrounge *(informal)*, fossick *(Austral. & N.Z.)* • *They were forced to forage for clothes and fuel.*

foray = **raid**, sally, incursion, inroad, attack, assault, invasion, swoop, reconnaissance, sortie, irruption • *She made her first forays into politics.*

forbear = **refrain**, avoid, omit, hold back, stop, decline,

FOOTBALL

Terms used in (Association) Football

aggregate (score), back, ballplayer, ballwinner, booking *or* caution, breakaway, cap, catenaccio, centre circle, centre forward, centre half, clearance, cross, crossbar *or* bar, corner (kick), cut out, defender, derby, direct free kick, dribble, dummy, extra time, FA, FIFA, finishing, forward, foul, free kick, fullback, full time, goal, goal area *or* six-yard box, goalkeeper *or* goalie, goal kick *or* bye kick, goal net *or* net, goalpost *or* post, golden goal, half, halfback, half time, half way line, handball, indirect free kick, inside left, inside right, inswinger, international, kick off, lay off, left back, linesman, long ball, mark, midfield, midfielder, nil, non-league, nutmeg, offside, offside trap, onside, one-two, outside left, outside right, own goal, pass, pass-back, penalty (kick) *or* spot kick, penalty area *or* penalty box, penalty shoot-out, penalty spot, playoff, professional foul, promotion, red card, referee, relegation, reserves, right back, Route One, save, score draw, sending-off *or* ordering-off, SFA, shot, silver goal, six-pointer, six-yard line, sliding tackle, stoppage time *or* injury time, striker, square, substitute, sweeper, tackle, target man, technical area, throw in, total football, touchline, transfer, trap, UEFA, wall, wall pass, wing, winger, yellow card

Terms used in Australian Rules Football

Australian Football League *or* AFL, back pocket, behind *or* point, behind line, behind post, boundary, eighteen, the, field umpire, flank, footy, Aussie Rules, *or (jocular)* aerial ping-pong, follower, forward pocket, free kick, goal, goal umpire, guernsey, half-back, half-forward, handball, interchange, mark, nineteenth man, quarter, rove, rover, rub out, ruck, ruckrover, scrimmage, shepherd, shirt front, stab kick, stanza, throw in, twentieth man

Terms used in American football

backfield, blitz, block, center, complete, cornerback, defense, defensive back, defensive end, down, end zone, field goal, football *or* pigskin, fullback, gridiron, guard, halfback, incomplete, interception, kicker, line *or* line of scrimmage, line backer, lineman, offense, overtime, pass, play, point after, punt, punter, quarterback, run *or* rush, running back, sack, safety, scrimmage, secondary, shotgun, snap, special team, Super Bowl, tackle, tight end, touchback, touchdown, turnover, wide receiver

pause, cease, withhold, abstain, eschew, keep from, resist the temptation to, desist, restrain yourself • *I forbore to comment on this.*

forbearance 1 = **patience**, resignation, restraint, tolerance, indulgence, long-suffering, moderation, self-control, leniency, temperance, mildness, lenity, longanimity *(rare)* • *a high degree of tolerance and forbearance*
OPPOSITES: anger, impatience, intolerance
2 = **abstinence**, refraining, avoidance • *forbearance from military action*

forbid = **prohibit**, ban, disallow, proscribe, exclude, rule out, veto, outlaw, inhibit, hinder, preclude, make illegal, debar, interdict, criminalize • *They'll forbid you to marry.*
OPPOSITES: order, let, permit

QUOTATIONS
God forbid
[*Bible: Romans*]

forbidden = **prohibited**, banned, vetoed, outlawed, taboo, out of bounds, proscribed, verboten *(German)* • *Smoking was forbidden everywhere.*

QUOTATIONS
There is a charm about the forbidden that makes it unspeakably desirable
[Mark Twain *Notebook*]

PROVERBS
Stolen fruit is sweet

forbidding = **threatening**, severe, frightening, hostile, grim, menacing, sinister, daunting, ominous, unfriendly, foreboding, baleful, bodeful • *There was something severe and forbidding about her face.*
OPPOSITES: winning, welcoming, inviting

force AS A NOUN 1 = **compulsion**, pressure, violence, enforcement, constraint, oppression, coercion, duress, arm-twisting *(informal)* • *calls for the siege to be ended by force*
2 = **power**, might, pressure, energy, stress, strength, impact, muscle, momentum, impulse, stimulus, vigour, potency, dynamism, welly *(slang)*, life • *slamming the door behind her with all her force*
OPPOSITES: weakness, impotence, frailty
3 = **agency**, means, power, medium, influence, vehicle, instrument, mechanism, instrumentality, operation • *The army was the most powerful political force.*
4 = **influence**, power, effect, authority, weight, strength, punch *(informal)*, significance, effectiveness, validity, efficacy, soundness, persuasiveness, cogency, bite • *He changed our world through the force of his ideas.*
5 = **intensity**, vigour, vehemence, fierceness, drive, emphasis, persistence • *She took a step back from the force of her rage.*

6 = **army**, unit, division, corps, company, body, host, troop, squad, patrol, regiment, battalion, legion, squadron, detachment • *a pan-European peace-keeping force*
▸ **AS A VERB** 1 = **compel**, make, drive, press, pressure, urge, overcome, oblige, railroad *(informal)*, constrain, necessitate, coerce, impel, strong-arm *(informal)*, dragoon, pressurize, press-gang, put the squeeze on *(informal)*, obligate, twist (someone's) arm, put the screws on *(informal)*, bring pressure to bear upon • *They forced him to work for them at gun point.*
2 = **impose**, foist • *To force this agreement on the nation is wrong.*
3 = **push**, thrust, propel • *They forced her head under the icy waters, drowning her.*
4 = **break open**, blast, wrench, prise, open, wrest, use violence on • *The police forced the door of the flat and arrested him.*
5 = **extort**, drag, exact, wring • *using torture to force a confession out of a suspect*
OPPOSITES: convince, persuade, coax
▸ **IN PHRASES: in force** 1 = **valid**, working, current, effective, binding, operative, operational, in operation, on the statute book • *The new tax is already in force.*
2 = **in great numbers**, all together, in full strength • *Voters turned out in force.*

QUOTATIONS
Force without reason falls of its own weight
[Horace *Odes*]
There is no real force without justice
[Napoleon *Maxims*]
Where force is necessary, there it must be applied boldly, decisively and completely. But one must know the limitations of force; one must know when to blend force with a manoeuvre, a blow with an agreement
[Leon Trotsky *What Next?*]
Force is as pitiless to the man who possesses it, or thinks he does, as it is to its victims; the second it crushes, the first it intoxicates. The truth is, nobody really possesses it
[Simone Weil *The Iliad or the Poem of Force*]

forced 1 = **compulsory**, enforced, slave, unwilling, mandatory, obligatory, involuntary, conscripted • *a system of forced labour*
OPPOSITES: voluntary, spontaneous
2 = **false**, affected, strained, wooden, stiff, artificial, contrived, unnatural, insincere, laboured • *a forced smile*
OPPOSITES: easy, simple, natural

forceful 1 = **dynamic**, powerful, vigorous, potent, assertive • *He was a man of forceful character.*
OPPOSITES: weak, exhausted, faint
2 = **powerful**, strong, convincing, effective, compelling, persuasive, weighty, pithy, cogent, telling • *This is a forceful argument for joining them.*

forcible 1 = **violent**, armed, aggressive, compulsory, drastic, coercive • *forcible resettlement of villagers*
2 = **compelling**, strong, powerful, effective, active, impressive, efficient, valid, mighty, potent, energetic, forceful, weighty, cogent • *He is a forcible advocate for the arts.*

forcibly = **by force**, compulsorily, under protest, against your will, under compulsion, by main force, willy-nilly • *They were forcibly removed from his office.*

ford **AS A NOUN** = **crossing**, causeway, crossing place • *They found the ford and waded across.*
▸ **AS A VERB** = **cross**, pass over, traverse, go across, wade across • *We forded the river.*

fore = **front**, head, top, forefront, nearest part, foremost part • *no damage in the fore part of the ship*

forearm
▸ **RELATED ADJECTIVES:** cubital, radial

forebear *or* **forbear** = **ancestor**, father, predecessor, forerunner, forefather, progenitor, tupuna *or* tipuna *(N.Z.)* • *I'll come back to the land of my forebears.*

foreboding 1 = **dread**, fear, anxiety, chill, unease, apprehension, misgiving, premonition, presentiment, apprehensiveness • *an uneasy sense of foreboding*
2 = **omen**, warning, prediction, portent, sign, token, foreshadowing, presage, prognostication, augury, foretoken • *No one paid any attention to their gloomy forebodings.*

forecast **AS A VERB** = **predict**, anticipate, foresee, foretell, call, plan, estimate, calculate, divine, prophesy, augur, forewarn, prognosticate, vaticinate *(rare)* • *They forecast a defeat for the Prime Minister.*
▸ **AS A NOUN** = **prediction**, projection, anticipation, prognosis, planning, guess, outlook, prophecy, foresight, conjecture, forewarning, forethought • *He delivered his election forecast.*

forefather = **ancestor**, father, predecessor, forerunner, forebear, progenitor, procreator, primogenitor, tupuna *or* tipuna *(N.Z.)* • *They went back to the land of their forefathers.*

forefront = **lead**, centre, front, fore, spearhead, prominence, vanguard, foreground, leading position, van • *They are at the forefront of the campaign.*

forego *see* **forgo**

foregoing = **preceding**, former, above, previous, prior, antecedent, anterior, just mentioned, previously stated • *The foregoing discussion has highlighted the difficulties.*

foregone **IN PHRASES: foregone conclusion** = **certainty**, open-and-shut case, sure thing, dead cert *(informal)*, cert *(informal)*, shoo-in *(U.S. & Canad.)* • *The result is a foregone conclusion.*

foreground 1 = **front**, focus, forefront • *the foreground of this boldly painted landscape*
2 = **prominence**, limelight, fore, forefront • *This worry has come to the foreground in recent years.*

forehead = **brow**, temple • *He kissed her forehead.*
▸ **RELATED ADJECTIVE:** frontal

foreign 1 = **alien**, overseas, exotic, unknown, outside, strange, imported, borrowed, remote, distant, external, unfamiliar, far off, outlandish, beyond your ken • *a foreign language*
OPPOSITES: domestic, familiar, native
2 = **unassimilable**, external, extraneous, outside • *rejected the transplanted organ as a foreign object*
3 = **uncharacteristic**, inappropriate, unrelated, incongruous, inapposite, irrelevant • *He fell into a gloomy mood that was usually so foreign to him.*
4 = **unfamiliar**, strange, unknown, alien, undiscovered, uncharted, unexplored, unplumbed • *The whole thing is foreign to us.*

foreigner = **alien**, incomer, immigrant, non-native, stranger, newcomer, settler, outlander • *She was a foreigner and wouldn't understand.*
▸ **RELATED MANIA:** xenomania
▸ **RELATED PHOBIA:** xenophobia

foreknowledge 1 = **prior knowledge**, advance knowledge, previous understanding • *The General had foreknowledge of the plot.*
2 = **precognition**, foresight, forewarning, clairvoyance, prescience, prevision • *the key to the mystery of foreknowledge*

foreman *or* **forewoman** = **supervisor**, steward, controller, superintendent, director, manager, chief, boss *(informal)*, governor, inspector, administrator, gaffer *(informal, chiefly Brit.)*, overseer, baas *(S. African)* • *The foreman called maintenance.*

foremost = **leading**, best, first, top, highest, front, chief, prime, primary, supreme, initial, most important, principal, paramount, inaugural, pre-eminent, headmost • *He was one of the world's foremost scholars.*

forerunner 1 = **omen**, sign, indication, token, premonition,

portent, augury, prognostic, foretoken, harbinger • *Some respiratory symptoms can be the forerunners of asthma.*
2 = **precursor**, predecessor, ancestor, prototype, forebear, progenitor, herald • *the forerunners of those who were to support the Nazis*

foresee = **predict**, forecast, anticipate, envisage, prophesy, foretell, forebode, vaticinate *(rare)*, divine • *He did not foresee any problems.*

foreshadow = **predict**, suggest, promise, indicate, signal, imply, bode, prophesy, augur, presage, prefigure, portend, betoken, adumbrate, forebode • *Sales figures foreshadow more redundancies.*

foresight = **forethought**, prudence, circumspection, far-sightedness, care, provision, caution, precaution, anticipation, preparedness, prescience, premeditation, prevision *(rare)* • *They had the foresight to invest in new technology.*
OPPOSITES: neglect, hindsight, carelessness

foreskin
▸ TECHNICAL NAME: prepuce
▸ RELATED ADJECTIVE: preputial

forest = **wood**, trees, woods, grove, woodland, bushland, plantation, rainforest, thicket, copse, coppice • *Parts of the forest are still dense.*

forestall = **prevent**, stop, frustrate, anticipate, head off, parry, thwart, intercept, hinder, preclude, balk, circumvent, obviate, nip in the bud, provide against • *They had done little to forestall the attack.*

forestry = **woodcraft**, silviculture, arboriculture, dendrology *(Botany)*, woodmanship • *a recognised authority on tropical forestry*

foretaste = **sample**, example, indication, preview, trailer, prelude, whiff, foretoken, warning • *It was a foretaste of things to come.*

foretell = **predict**, forecast, prophesy, portend, call, signify, bode, foreshadow, augur, presage, forewarn, prognosticate, adumbrate, forebode, foreshow, soothsay, vaticinate *(rare)* • *prophets who have foretold the end of the world*

forethought = **anticipation**, foresight, providence, far-sightedness, provision, precaution, prudence • *With a little forethought many accidents could be avoided.*
OPPOSITES: neglect, carelessness, imprudence

forever *or* **for ever** 1 = **evermore**, always, ever, for good, for keeps, for all time, in perpetuity, for good and all *(informal)*, till the cows come home *(informal)*, world without end, till the end of time, till Doomsday • *We will live together forever.*
2 = **constantly**, always, all the time, continually, endlessly, persistently, eternally, perpetually, incessantly, interminably, unremittingly, everlastingly • *He was forever attempting to arrange deals.*

forewarn = **alert**, advise, caution, tip off, apprise, give fair warning, put on guard, put on the qui vive • *The book had forewarned me of what to expect.*

PROVERBS
Forewarned is forearmed

foreword = **introduction**, preliminary, preface, preamble, prologue, prolegomenon • *the foreword to this very special cookery book*

forfeit AS A NOUN = **penalty**, fine, damages, forfeiture, loss, mulct, amercement *(obsolete)* • *That is the forfeit he must pay.*
▸ AS A VERB = **relinquish**, lose, give up, surrender, renounce, be deprived of, say goodbye to, be stripped of • *He was ordered to forfeit more than £1.5m in profits.*

forfeiture = **loss**, giving up, surrender, forfeiting, confiscation, sequestration *(Law)*, relinquishment • *the forfeiture of illegally obtained profits*

forge[1] 1 = **form**, build, create, establish, set up, fashion, shape, frame, construct, invent, devise, mould, contrive, fabricate, hammer out, make, work • *They agreed to forge closer economic ties.*
2 = **fake**, copy, reproduce, imitate, counterfeit, feign, falsify, coin • *They discovered forged dollar notes.*
3 = **create**, make, work, found, form, model, fashion, shape, cast, turn out, construct, devise, mould, contrive, fabricate, hammer out, beat into shape • *To forge a blade takes great skill.*

forge[2] IN PHRASES: **forge ahead** = **progress quickly**, progress, make headway, advance quickly • *He began to forge ahead with his studies.*

forged 1 = **fake**, copy, false, counterfeit, pretend, artificial, mock, pirated, reproduction, synthetic, imitation, bogus, simulated, duplicate, quasi, sham, fraudulent, pseudo, fabricated, copycat *(informal)*, falsified, ersatz, unoriginal, ungenuine, phony *or* phoney *(informal)* • *She was carrying a forged American passport.*
OPPOSITES: real, true, genuine
2 = **formed**, worked, founded, modelled, fashioned, shaped, cast, framed, stamped, crafted, moulded, minted, hammered out, beat out, beaten into shape • *fifteen tons of forged steel parts*

forger = **counterfeiter**, copier, copyist, falsifier, coiner • *the most prolific art forger in the country*

forgery 1 = **falsification**, faking, pirating, counterfeiting, fraudulence, fraudulent imitation, coining • *He was found guilty of forgery.*
2 = **fake**, imitation, sham, counterfeit, falsification, phoney *or* phony *(informal)* • *The letter was a forgery.*

forget AS A VERB 1 = **fail to remember**, not remember, not recollect, let slip from the memory, fail to bring to mind • *She forgot where she left the car.*
OPPOSITES: mind, remember, recall
2 = **neglect**, overlook, omit, not remember, be remiss, fail to remember • *Don't forget that all dogs need a supply of water.*
3 = **leave behind**, lose, lose sight of, mislay • *I forgot my passport.*
4 = **dismiss from your mind**, ignore, overlook, stop thinking about, let bygones be bygones, consign to oblivion, put out of your mind • *I can't forget what happened today.*
▸ IN PHRASES: **forget yourself** = **misbehave**, behave badly, act up *(informal)*, get up to mischief *(informal)*, carry on *(informal)*, be bad, muck about *(Brit. slang)*, be insubordinate • *He was so fascinated by her beauty that he forgot himself.*

PROVERBS
An elephant never forgets

forgetful = **absent-minded**, vague, careless, neglectful, oblivious, lax, negligent, dreamy, slapdash, heedless, slipshod, inattentive, unmindful, apt to forget, having a memory like a sieve • *My mother has become very forgetful recently.*
OPPOSITES: careful, attentive, mindful

forgetfulness = **absent-mindedness**, oblivion, inattention, carelessness, abstraction, laxity, laxness, dreaminess, obliviousness, lapse of memory, heedlessness, woolgathering • *Her forgetfulness is due to advancing age.*

forgivable = **pardonable**, allowable, excusable, condonable, minor, slight, petty, understandable, unimportant, permissible, not serious, venial • *His sense of humour makes all else forgivable.*

forgive = **excuse**, pardon, bear no malice towards, not hold something against, understand, acquit, condone, remit, let off *(informal)*, turn a blind eye to, exonerate, absolve, bury the hatchet, let bygones be bygones, turn a deaf ear to, accept (someone's) apology • *She'll understand and forgive you.*
OPPOSITES: charge, blame, condemn

QUOTATIONS
To err is human, to forgive, divine
[Alexander Pope *An Essay on Criticism*]

forgiveness = **pardon**, mercy, absolution, exoneration, overlooking, amnesty, acquittal, remission, condonation • *I offered up a prayer for forgiveness.*

QUOTATIONS

Resist not evil; but whosoever shall smite thee on thy right cheek, turn to him the other also
[Bible: St. Matthew]

We read that we ought to forgive our enemies; but we do not read that we ought to forgive our friends
[Cosimo de Medici]

Always forgive your enemies; nothing annoys them so much
[Oscar Wilde]

The stupid neither forgive nor forget; the naïve forgive and forget; the wise forgive but do not forget
[Thomas Szasz *The Second Sin*]

God will forgive me; that is His business
[Heinrich Heine]

Father, forgive them; for they know not what they do
[*Bible: St. Luke*]

Lord, how oft shall my brother sin against me, and I forgive him? till seven times? Jesus said unto him, I say not unto thee, Until seven times; but Until seventy times seven
[*Bible: St. Matthew*]

forgiving = **lenient**, tolerant, compassionate, clement, patient, mild, humane, gracious, long-suffering, merciful, magnanimous, forbearing, willing to forgive, soft-hearted • *People are not in a very forgiving mood.*

forgo *or* **forego** = **give up**, sacrifice, surrender, do without, kick *(informal)*, abandon, resign, yield, relinquish, renounce, waive, say goodbye to, cede, abjure, leave alone *or* out • *The men would not forgo the chance of a feast.*

forgotten = **unremembered**, lost, past, buried, left behind, omitted, obliterated, bygone • *a faint whisper of a forgotten world far away*

fork AS A VERB = **branch**, part, separate, split, divide, diverge, subdivide, branch off, go separate ways, bifurcate • *Beyond the village the road forked.*
▸ IN PHRASES: **fork out** = **pay**, pay up, cough up *(informal)*, shell out *(informal)*, remit • *He'll have to fork out for private school fees.*

forked = **branching**, split, branched, divided, angled, pronged, zigzag, tined, Y-shaped, bifurcate(d) • *Jaegers are black birds with long forked tails.*

forlorn 1 = **miserable**, helpless, pathetic, pitiful, lost, forgotten, abandoned, unhappy, lonely, lonesome *(chiefly U.S. & Canad.)*, homeless, forsaken, bereft, destitute, wretched, disconsolate, friendless, down in the dumps *(informal)*, pitiable, cheerless, woebegone, comfortless • *He looked a forlorn figure as he limped off.*
OPPOSITES: happy, optimistic, cheerful
2 = **abandoned**, deserted, ruined, bleak, dreary, desolate, godforsaken, waste • *The once glorious palaces stood empty and forlorn.*
3 = **hopeless**, useless, vain, pointless, futile, no-win, unattainable, impracticable, unachievable, impossible, not having a prayer • *a forlorn effort to keep from losing my mind*

form AS A NOUN 1 = **type**, sort, kind, variety, way, system, order, class, style, practice, method, species, manner, stamp, description • *He contracted a rare form of cancer.*
2 = **shape**, formation, configuration, construction, cut, model, fashion, structure, pattern, cast, appearance, stamp, mould • *Valleys often take the form of deep canyons.*
3 = **structure**, plan, order, organization, arrangement, construction, proportion, format, framework, harmony, symmetry, orderliness • *the sustained narrative form of the novel*
4 = **build**, being, body, figure, shape, frame, outline, anatomy, silhouette, physique, person • *her petite form and delicate features*
5 = **condition**, health, shape, nick *(informal)*, fitness, trim, good condition, good spirits, fettle • *He's now fighting his way back to top form.*
6 = **document**, paper, sheet, questionnaire, application • *You will be asked to fill in an application form.*
7 = **procedure**, behaviour, manners, etiquette, use, rule, conduct, ceremony, custom, convention, ritual, done thing, usage, protocol, formality, wont, right practice, kawa *(N.Z.)*, tikanga *(N.Z.)* • *a frequent broadcaster on correct form and dress*
8 = **class**, year, set, rank, grade, stream • *I was going into the sixth form at school.*
9 = **mode**, character, shape, appearance, arrangement, manifestation, guise, semblance, design • *The rejoicing took the form of exuberant masquerades.*
▸ AS A VERB 1 = **arrange**, combine, line up, organize, assemble, dispose, draw up • *He gave orders for the cadets to form into lines.*
2 = **make**, produce, model, fashion, build, create, shape, manufacture, stamp, construct, assemble, forge, mould, fabricate • *The bowl was formed out of clay.*
3 = **constitute**, make up, compose, comprise, serve as, make • *Children form the majority of dead and injured.*
4 = **establish**, start, found, launch, set up, invent, devise, put together, bring about, contrive • *You may want to form a company to buy a joint freehold.*
5 = **take shape**, grow, develop, materialize, rise, appear, settle, show up *(informal)*, accumulate, come into being, crystallize, become visible • *Stalactites and stalagmites began to form.*
6 = **draw up**, design, devise, formulate, plan, pattern, frame, organize, think up • *She rapidly formed a plan.*
7 = **develop**, pick up, acquire, cultivate, contract, get into *(informal)* • *It is easier to form good habits than to break bad ones.*
8 = **train**, develop, shape, mould, school, teach, guide, discipline, rear, educate, bring up, instruct • *Anger at injustice formed his character.*
▸ IN PHRASES: **good form** = **good manners**, manners, protocol, etiquette, ceremony, courtesy, formalities, refinement, proprieties, politeness, decorum, the done thing, social graces, politesse, p's and q's, kawa *(N.Z.)*, tikanga *(N.Z.)* • *It's not good form to spend lots of money.*
off form = **below par**, unfit, stale, out of condition, under the weather *(informal)*, not up to the mark, not in the pink *(informal)* • *His players were off form and tired.*
on form = **up to the mark**, fit, healthy, in good shape, in good condition, toned up, in good trim • *She was back on form again now.*
take form = **appear**, develop, take shape, materialize, become visible • *Her face took form in the dimness.*

formal 1 = **serious**, stiff, detached, aloof, official, reserved, correct, conventional, remote, exact, precise, starched, prim, unbending, punctilious, ceremonious • *He wrote a very formal letter of apology.*
OPPOSITES: relaxed, casual, informal
2 = **official**, express, explicit, authorized, set, legal, fixed, regular, approved, strict, endorsed, prescribed, rigid, certified, solemn, lawful, methodical, pro forma *(Latin)* • *No formal announcement has been made.*
3 = **ceremonial**, traditional, solemn, ritualistic, dressy • *They arranged a formal dinner after the play.*
4 = **learned**, intellectual, literary, scholarly, highbrow • *an elevated and formal style*
5 = **conventional**, established, traditional • *He didn't have any formal dance training.*
6 = **arranged**, regular, symmetrical • *a formal herb garden*

formality 1 = **correctness**, seriousness, decorum, ceremoniousness, protocol, etiquette, politesse, p's and q's,

punctilio • *Her formality and seriousness amused him.*
2 = **convention**, form, conventionality, matter of form, procedure, ceremony, custom, gesture, ritual, rite • *The will was read, but it was a formality.*

format = **arrangement**, form, style, make-up, look, plan, design, type, appearance, construction, presentation, layout • *They met to discuss the format of future negotiations.*

formation 1 = **establishment**, founding, forming, setting up, starting, production, generation, organization, manufacture, constitution • *the formation of a new government*
2 = **development**, shaping, constitution, evolution, moulding, composition, compilation, accumulation, genesis, crystallization • *The formation of my character and temperament.*
3 = **arrangement**, grouping, figure, design, structure, pattern, rank, organization, array, disposition, configuration • *He was flying in formation with seven other jets.*

formative 1 = **developmental**, sensitive, susceptible, impressionable, malleable, pliant, mouldable • *She spent her formative years growing up in London.*
2 = **influential**, determinative, controlling, important, shaping, significant, moulding, decisive, developmental • *a formative influence on his life*

former 1 = **previous**, one-time, erstwhile, ex-, late, earlier, prior, sometime, foregoing, antecedent, anterior, quondam, whilom *(archaic)*, ci-devant *(French)* • *He pleaded not guilty to murdering his former wife.*
OPPOSITES: coming, following, current
2 = **past**, earlier, long ago, bygone, old, ancient, departed, old-time, long gone, of yore • *Remember him as he was in former years.*
OPPOSITES: future, present, current
3 = **aforementioned**, above, first mentioned, aforesaid, preceding, foregoing • *Most people can be forgiven for choosing the former.*

formerly = **previously**, earlier, in the past, at one time, before, lately, once, already, heretofore, aforetime *(archaic)* • *He had formerly been in the Navy.*

formidable 1 = **difficult**, taxing, challenging, overwhelming, staggering, daunting, mammoth, colossal, arduous, very great, onerous, toilsome • *We have a formidable task ahead of us.*
OPPOSITES: easy
2 = **impressive**, great, powerful, tremendous, mighty, terrific, awesome, invincible, indomitable, redoubtable, puissant • *She looked every bit as formidable as her mother.*
3 = **intimidating**, threatening, dangerous, terrifying, appalling, horrible, dreadful, menacing, dismaying, fearful, daunting, frightful, baleful, shocking • *a formidable, well-trained, well-equipped fighting force*
OPPOSITES: encouraging, comforting, cheering

formless = **shapeless**, amorphous, nebulous, unformed, vague, indefinite, incoherent, disorganized, inchoate • *Large formless images rushed across the screen.*

formula 1 = **method**, plan, policy, rule, principle, procedure, recipe, prescription, blueprint, precept, modus operandi, way • *The new peace formula means hostilities have ended.*
2 = **form of words**, code, phrase, formulary, set expression • *He developed a mathematical formula.*
3 = **mixture**, preparation, compound, composition, concoction, tincture, medicine • *bottles of formula*

formulate 1 = **devise**, plan, develop, prepare, work out, invent, evolve, coin, forge, draw up, originate, map out • *He formulated his plan for escape.*
2 = **express**, detail, frame, define, specify, articulate, set down, codify, put into words, systematize, particularize, give form to • *I was impressed by how he formulated his ideas.*

fornication 1 = **adultery**, infidelity, unfaithfulness, extra-marital congress *or* relations *or* sex, living in sin, extra-curricular sex *(informal)*, pre-marital congress *or* relations *or* sex • *Fornication is a crime in some American states.*
2 = **immorality**, sin, indecency, promiscuity, impurity, incontinence, debauchery, free love, sleeping around, dissipation, looseness, lechery, immodesty, shamelessness, easy virtue, loose morals, salaciousness, lasciviousness, uncleanness, libertinism, unchastity, dissoluteness, indelicacy • *an embarrassing blend of failure, farce and fornication*

forsake 1 = **desert**, leave, abandon, quit, strand, jettison, repudiate, cast off, disown, jilt, throw over, leave in the lurch • *I still love him and would never forsake him.*
2 = **give up**, set aside, relinquish, forgo, kick *(informal)*, yield, surrender, renounce, have done with, stop using, abdicate, stop having, turn your back on, forswear • *She forsook her notebook for new technology.*
3 = **abandon**, leave, go away from, take your leave of • *He has no plans to forsake the hills.*

forsaken 1 = **abandoned**, ignored, lonely, lonesome *(chiefly U.S. & Canad.)*, stranded, ditched, left behind, marooned, outcast, forlorn, cast off, jilted, friendless, left in the lurch • *She felt forsaken and gave up any attempt at order.*
2 = **deserted**, abandoned, isolated, solitary, desolate, forlorn, destitute, disowned, godforsaken • *a forsaken church and a derelict hotel*

forswear 1 = **renounce**, drop *(informal)*, give up, abandon, forsake, forgo, abjure, swear off • *giving up drink or forswearing sex*
2 = **reject**, deny, retract, repudiate, disown, disavow, recant, disclaim • *He forswore the use of trade sanctions.*

fort AS A NOUN = **fortress**, keep, station, camp, tower, castle, garrison, stronghold, citadel, fortification, redoubt, fastness, blockhouse, fortified pa *(N.Z.)* • *Soldiers inside the fort are under sustained attack.*
▸ IN PHRASES: **hold the fort** = **take responsibility**, cover, stand in, carry on, take over the reins, maintain the status quo, deputize, keep things moving, keep things on an even keel • *His partner is holding the fort while he is away.*

forte = **speciality**, strength, talent, strong point, métier, long suit *(informal)*, gift • *Originality was never his forte.*
OPPOSITES: failing, defect, weak point

forth 1 = **forward**, out, away, ahead, onward, outward • *Go forth into the desert.*
2 = **out**, into the open, out of concealment • *He brought forth a small gold amulet.*

forthcoming 1 = **approaching**, coming, expected, future, imminent, prospective, impending, upcoming • *his opponents in the forthcoming election*
2 = **available**, ready, accessible, at hand, in evidence, obtainable, on tap *(informal)* • *They promised that the money would be forthcoming.*
3 = **communicative**, open, free, informative, expansive, sociable, chatty, talkative, unreserved • *He was very forthcoming in court.*

forthright = **outspoken**, open, direct, frank, straightforward, blunt, downright, candid, upfront *(informal)*, plain-spoken, straight from the shoulder *(informal)* • *He was known for his forthright manner.*
OPPOSITES: secret, secretive, dishonest

forthwith = **immediately**, directly, instantly, at once, right away, straightaway, without delay, tout de suite *(French)*, quickly • *I could have you arrested forthwith!*

fortification 1 = **reinforcement**, protecting, securing, protection, strengthening, reinforcing, embattlement • *Europe's fortification of its frontiers*
2 = **defence**, keep, protection, castle, fort, fortress, stronghold, bastion, citadel, bulwark, fastness, fortified pa *(N.Z.)* • *troops stationed just behind the fortification*

3 = **strengthening**, supplementing, reinforcement • *nutrient fortification of food*

fortify 1 = **protect**, defend, secure, strengthen, reinforce, support, brace, garrison, shore up, augment, buttress, make stronger, embattle • *British soldiers working to fortify an airbase*
2 = **strengthen**, add alcohol to • *All sherry is made from wine fortified with brandy.*
3 = **sustain**, encourage, confirm, cheer, strengthen, reassure, brace, stiffen, hearten, embolden, invigorate • *The volunteers were fortified by their patriotic belief.*
OPPOSITES: reduce, weaken, dishearten

fortitude = **courage**, strength, resolution, determination, guts *(informal)*, patience, pluck, grit, endurance, bravery, backbone, perseverance, firmness, staying power, valour, fearlessness, strength of mind, intrepidity, hardihood, dauntlessness, stoutheartedness • *He suffered his illness with dignity and fortitude.*

f

fortress = **castle**, fort, stronghold, citadel, redoubt, fastness, fortified pa *(N.Z.)* • *a 13th-century fortress*

fortuitous 1 = **chance**, lucky, random, casual, contingent, accidental, arbitrary, incidental, unforeseen, unplanned • *a fortuitous quirk of fate*
2 = **lucky**, happy, fortunate, serendipitous, providential, fluky *(informal)* • *It was a fortuitous discovery.*

fortunate 1 = **lucky**, happy, favoured, bright, golden, rosy, on a roll, jammy *(Brit. slang)*, in luck, having a charmed life, born with a silver spoon in your mouth • *He's has had a very fortunate life.*
OPPOSITES: unhappy, unfortunate, miserable
2 = **well-off**, rich, successful, comfortable, wealthy, prosperous, affluent, opulent, well-heeled *(informal)*, well-to-do, sitting pretty *(informal)* • *the economic burdens placed on less fortunate families*
3 = **providential**, auspicious, fortuitous, felicitous, timely, promising, encouraging, helpful, profitable, convenient, favourable, advantageous, expedient, opportune, propitious • *It was fortunate that the water was shallow.*

fortunately = **luckily**, happily, as luck would have it, providentially, by good luck, by a happy chance • *Fortunately the weather was fairly mild.*

fortune 1 = **large sum of money**, bomb *(Brit. slang)*, packet *(slang)*, bundle *(slang)*, big money, big bucks *(informal, chiefly U.S.)*, top dollar *(informal)*, megabucks *(U.S. & Canad. slang)*, an arm and a leg *(informal)*, king's ransom, pretty penny *(informal)*, top whack *(informal)* • *Eating out all the time costs a fortune.*
2 = **wealth**, means, property, riches, resources, assets, pile *(informal)*, possessions, treasure, prosperity, mint, gold mine, wad *(U.S. & Canad. slang)*, affluence, opulence, tidy sum *(informal)* • *He made his fortune in car sales.*
OPPOSITES: poverty, hardship, privation
3 = **luck**, accident, fluke *(informal)*, stroke of luck, serendipity, hap *(archaic)*, twist of fate, run of luck • *Such good fortune must be shared with my friends.*
4 = **chance**, fate, destiny, providence, the stars, Lady Luck, kismet, fortuity • *He is certainly being smiled on by fortune.*
5 *often plural* = **destiny**, life, lot, experiences, history, condition, success, means, circumstances, expectation, adventures • *She kept up with the fortunes of the family.*

QUOTATIONS

Fortune, that favours fools
[Ben Jonson *The Alchemist*]

The slings and arrows of outrageous fortune
[William Shakespeare *Hamlet*]

Base Fortune, now I see, that in thy wheel
There is a point, to which when men aspire,
They tumble headlong down
[Christopher Marlowe *Edward II*]

fortune-teller *or* **fortune teller** = **seer**, diviner, psychic, prophet, visionary, oracle, clairvoyant, augur, predictor, soothsayer, sibyl, prophetess, crystal-gazer, haruspex, telepath, telepathist • *The fortune-teller gazed into her crystal ball.*

forum 1 = **meeting**, conference, assembly, meeting place, court, body, council, parliament, congress, gathering, diet, senate, rally, convention, tribunal *(archaic or literary)*, seminar, get-together *(informal)*, congregation, caucus *(chiefly U.S. & Canad.)*, synod, convergence, symposium, hui *(N.Z.)*, moot, assemblage, conclave, convocation, consistory *(in various Churches)*, ecclesia *(in Church use)*, colloquium, folkmoot *(in medieval England)*, runanga *(N.Z.)* • *a forum where problems could be discussed*
2 = **public square**, court, square, chamber, platform, arena, pulpit, meeting place, amphitheatre, stage, rostrum, agora *(in ancient Greece)* • *Generals appeared before the excited crowds in the Forum.*

forward AS AN ADJECTIVE 1 = **leading**, first, head, front, advance, foremost, fore • *to allow more troops to move to forward positions*
2 = **future**, early, advanced, progressive, premature, prospective, onward, forward-looking • *The University system requires more forward planning.*
3 = **presumptuous**, confident, familiar, bold, fresh *(informal)*, assuming, presuming, cheeky, brash, pushy *(informal)*, brazen, shameless, sassy *(U.S. informal)*, pert, impertinent, impudent, bare-faced, overweening, immodest, brass-necked *(Brit. informal)*, overfamiliar, brazen-faced, overassertive • *He's very forward and confident.*
OPPOSITES: retiring, modest, shy
▸ AS AN ADVERB = **into the open**, out, to light, to the front, to the surface, into consideration, into view, into prominence • *Over the years similar theories have been put forward.*
▸ AS A VERB 1 = **further**, back, help, support, aid, encourage, speed, advance, favour, promote, foster, assist, hurry, hasten, expedite • *He forwarded their cause with courage, skill and humour.*
OPPOSITES: bar, block, retard
2 = **send on**, send, post, pass on, ship, route, transmit, dispatch, freight, redirect • *The document was forwarded to the President.*

forward-looking = **progressive**, modern, reforming, liberal, enterprising, go-ahead, dynamic, enlightened, go-getting *(informal)* • *a need for the party to be forward-looking*

forwardness = **impertinence**, cheek *(informal)*, familiarity, boldness, presumption, chutzpah *(U.S. & Canad. informal)*, impudence, brashness, overconfidence, immodesty, shamelessness, cheekiness, brazenness, pertness, overfamiliarity • *I was taken aback by his forwardness.*

forwards *or* **forward** 1 = **forth**, on, ahead, onwards • *He walked forward into the room.*
OPPOSITES: backward(s)
2 = **frontwards**, towards the front • *The best seats are as far forward as possible.*
3 = **on**, onward, onwards • *His work from that time forward was confined to portraits.*

fossick = **search**, hunt, explore, ferret, check, forage, rummage • *If you fossick around in some specialist music stores, you may be lucky enough to find a copy.*

fossil = **fossilized remains**, remains, petrified remains, impression, relic • *They dissolved the fossil and extracted the DNA.*

fossilized 1 = **petrified**, dead, extinct, prehistoric, ossified, dead as a dodo • *fossilized dinosaur bones*
2 = **obsolete**, antiquated, anachronistic, inflexible, passé, behind the times, superannuated, antediluvian, démodé *(French)*, out of the ark *(informal)*, archaistic • *breathe some new life into these fossilized organisations*

foster 1 = **bring up**, mother, raise, nurse, look after, rear, care for, take care of, nurture • *She has fostered more than 100 children.*
2 = **develop**, support, further, encourage, feed, promote, stimulate, uphold, nurture, cultivate, foment • *They are keen to foster trading links with the West.*
OPPOSITES: oppose, resist, suppress
3 = **cherish**, sustain, entertain, harbour, accommodate, nourish • *She fostered a fierce ambition.*

foul AS AN ADJECTIVE 1 = **dirty**, rank, offensive, nasty, disgusting, unpleasant, revolting, contaminated, rotten, polluted, stinking, filthy, tainted, grubby, repellent, squalid, repulsive, sullied, grimy, nauseating, loathsome, unclean, impure, grotty *(slang)*, fetid, grungy *(slang, chiefly U.S. & Canad.)*, putrid, malodorous, noisome, scuzzy *(slang, chiefly U.S.)*, skanky *(slang)*, mephitic, olid, yucky *or* yukky *(slang)*, festy *(Austral. slang)*, yucko *(Austral. slang)* • *foul, polluted water*
OPPOSITES: clear, clean, pure
2 = **obscene**, crude, indecent, foul-mouthed, low, blue, dirty, gross, abusive, coarse, filthy, vulgar, lewd, profane, blasphemous, scurrilous, smutty, scatological • *He was sent off for using foul language.*
3 = **bad**, nasty, unpleasant, filthy, vile, angry, furious • *He has a foul temper.*
4 = **stormy**, bad, wild, rough, wet, unpleasant, rainy, murky, windy, foggy, disagreeable, blustery • *The weather was foul, with heavy hail and snow.*
5 = **unfair**, illegal, dirty, crooked, shady *(informal)*, fraudulent, unjust, dishonest, unscrupulous, underhand, inequitable, unsportsmanlike • *a foul tackle*
6 = **offensive**, bad, base, wrong, evil, notorious, corrupt, vicious, infamous, disgraceful, shameful, vile, immoral, scandalous, wicked, sinful, despicable, heinous, hateful, abhorrent, egregious, abominable, shitty *(taboo slang)*, dishonourable, nefarious, iniquitous, detestable • *He is accused of all manner of foul deeds.*
OPPOSITES: attractive, decent, admirable
▸ AS A VERB 1 = **dirty**, soil, stain, contaminate, smear, pollute, taint, sully, defile, besmirch, smirch, begrime, besmear • *sea grass fouled with black tar*
OPPOSITES: clear, clean, cleanse
2 = **clog**, block, jam, choke • *The pipe was fouled with grain.*
3 = **entangle**, catch, twist, snarl, ensnare, tangle up • *The freighter fouled its propeller in fishing nets.*

foul-mouthed = **profane**, offensive, obscene, abusive, coarse, blasphemous, Fescennine *(rare)* • *He's a course, foul-mouthed man.*

foul play = **crime**, fraud, corruption, deception, treachery, criminal activity, duplicity, dirty work, double-dealing, skulduggery, chicanery, villainy, sharp practice, perfidy, roguery, dishonest behaviour • *He has been the victim of foul play.*

foul something up = **bungle**, spoil, botch, mess up, cock up *(Brit. slang)*, fuck up *(offensive taboo slang)*, make a mess of, mismanage, make a nonsense of, muck up *(slang)*, bodge *(informal)*, make a pig's ear of *(informal)*, put a spanner in the works *(Brit. informal)*, flub *(U.S. slang)*, crool *or* cruel *(Austral. slang)* • *There are risks that laboratories may foul up these tests.*

found 1 = **establish**, start, set up, begin, create, institute, organize, construct, constitute, originate, endow, inaugurate, bring into being • *He founded the Centre for Journalism Studies.*
2 = **erect**, build, construct, raise, settle • *The town was founded in 1610.*

foundation 1 = **basis**, heart, root, mainstay, beginning, support, ground, rest, key, principle, fundamental, premise, starting point, principal element • *Best friends are the foundation of my life.*
2 *often plural* = **substructure**, underpinning, groundwork, bedrock, base, footing, bottom • *vertical or lateral support for building foundations*
3 = **setting up**, institution, instituting, organization, settlement, establishment, initiating, originating, starting, endowment, inauguration • *the foundation of the modern welfare state*
4 = **justification**, grounds, basis, warrant, reason • *The allegations were without foundation.*

founded IN PHRASES: **founded on** = **based on**, built on, rooted in, grounded on, established on • *His game is founded on power and determination.*

founder[1] = **initiator**, father, establisher, author, maker, framer, designer, architect, builder, creator, beginner, generator, inventor, organizer, patriarch, benefactor, originator, constructor, institutor • *He was the founder of the medical faculty.*

founder[2] 1 = **fail**, collapse, break down, abort, fall through, be unsuccessful, come to nothing, come unstuck, miscarry, misfire, fall by the wayside, come to grief, bite the dust, go belly-up *(slang)*, go down like a lead balloon *(informal)* • *The talks have foundered.*
2 = **sink**, go down, be lost, submerge, capsize, go to the bottom • *Three ships foundered in heavy seas.*

fountain 1 = **font**, spring, reservoir, spout, fount, water feature, well • *In the centre of the courtyard was a round fountain.*
2 = **jet**, stream, spray, gush • *The volcano spewed a fountain of molten rock.*
3 = **source**, fount, wellspring, wellhead, beginning, rise, cause, origin, genesis, commencement, derivation, fountainhead • *You are a fountain of ideas.*

four = **quartet** • *She is married with four children.*
▸ RELATED PREFIXES: quadri-, tetra-

four-square *or* **four square** AS AN ADVERB = **firmly**, squarely, resolutely • *They stood four-square behind their chief.*
▸ AS AN ADJECTIVE = **solid**, strong, firm, steady, resolute, unyielding, immovable, firmly-based • *The old mangle on its four-square iron frame stood ready.*

fowl = **poultry** • *Ducks and many other animals are fowl.*
▸ RELATED ADJECTIVE: gallinaceous
▸ NAME OF MALE: cock
▸ NAME OF FEMALE: hen
▹ *See panel* **Types of fowl**

fox = **reynard** • *footprints of badgers and foxes*
▸ RELATED ADJECTIVE: vulpine
▸ NAME OF MALE: dog
▸ NAME OF FEMALE: vixen
▸ NAME OF YOUNG: cub, kit
▸ COLLECTIVE NOUN: skulk
▸ NAME OF HOME: earth

foxy 1 = **crafty**, knowing, sharp, tricky, shrewd, cunning, sly, astute, canny, devious, wily, artful, guileful • *He had wary, foxy eyes.*
2 = **sexy**, attractive, tempting, provoking, erotic, irresistible, siren, enticing, provocative, sensual, seductive, captivating *(informal)*, beguiling, sensuous, suggestive, alluring, bewitching, ravishing, slinky, specious • *a foxy blonde in a turtleneck sweater*

foyer = **entrance hall**, lobby, reception area, vestibule, anteroom, antechamber • *I went and waited in the foyer.*

fracas = **brawl**, fight, trouble, row, riot, disturbance, quarrel, uproar, skirmish, scuffle, free-for-all *(informal)*, rumpus, aggro *(slang)*, affray *(Law)*, shindig *(informal)*, donnybrook, scrimmage, shindy *(informal)*, bagarre *(French)*, melee *or* mêlée, biffo *(Austral. slang)* • *In the ensuing fracas many were killed.*

fraction 1 = **bit**, little bit, mite, jot, tiny amount, iota, scintilla • *I opened my eyes a fraction.*

f

TYPES OF FOWL

American wigeon *or* baldpate
Ancona chicken
Andalusian chicken
Australorp chicken
bantam chicken
barnacle goose
Bewick's swan
black swan
blue duck
blue goose
Brahma chicken
brush turkey *or* scrub turkey
bufflehead
Campine chicken
Canada goose
canvasback
chicken *or (Austral. slang)* chook
Cochin chicken
cock *or* cockerel
Dorking chicken
duck
eider *or* eider duck
Faverolle chicken
gadwall
goldeneye
goosander
goose
greylag *or* greylag goose
Hamburg chicken
harlequin duck
hen
Houdan chicken
Leghorn chicken
magpie goose
mallard
mallee fowl *or (Austral.)* gnow
mandarin duck
marsh hen
megapode
merganser *or* sawbill
Minorca chicken
moorhen
Muscovy duck *or* musk duck
mute swan
nene
New Hampshire chicken
Orpington chicken
paradise duck
pintail
Plymouth Rock chicken
pochard
redhead
Rhode Island Red chicken
ruddy duck
scaup *or* scaup duck
screamer
sea duck
shelduck
shoveler
smew
snow goose
sultan
Sumatra chicken
Sussex chicken
swan
teal
trumpeter swan
turkey
velvet scoter
whistling swan
whooper *or* whooper swan
wigeon
wood duck
Wyandotte chicken

2 = **percentage**, share, cut, division, section, proportion, slice, ratio, portion, quota, subdivision, moiety • *only a small fraction of the cost*
3 = **fragment**, part, piece, section, sector, selection, segment • *You will find only a fraction of the collection on display.*

fractious = **irritable**, cross, awkward, unruly, touchy, recalcitrant, petulant, tetchy, ratty *(Brit. & N.Z. informal)*, testy, chippy *(informal)*, fretful, grouchy *(informal)*, querulous, peevish, refractory, crabby, captious, froward *(archaic)*, pettish • *The children were predictably fractious.*
OPPOSITES: agreeable, amiable, affable

fracture **AS A NOUN** 1 = **break**, split, crack • *a double fracture of the right arm*
2 = **cleft**, opening, split, crack, gap, rent, breach, rift, rupture, crevice, fissure, schism • *large fractures in the crust creating the valleys*
▸ **AS A VERB** 1 = **break**, split, crack, rupture • *You've fractured a rib.*
2 = **split**, separate, divide, rend, fragment, splinter, rupture • *a society that could fracture along class lines*

fragile 1 = **unstable**, weak, vulnerable, delicate, uncertain, insecure, precarious, flimsy • *The fragile government was on the brink of collapse.*
2 = **fine**, weak, delicate, frail, feeble, brittle, flimsy, dainty, easily broken, breakable, frangible • *Coffee was served to them in cups of fragile china.*
OPPOSITES: lasting, strong, durable
3 = **delicate**, fine, charming, elegant, neat, exquisite, graceful, petite, dainty • *The haircut emphasised her fragile beauty.*
4 = **unwell**, poorly, weak, delicate, crook *(Austral. & N.Z. informal)*, shaky, frail, feeble, sickly, unsteady, infirm • *He felt irritated and strangely fragile.*

fragility 1 = **vulnerability**, weakness, instability, insecurity, precariousness • *the extreme fragility of the Right-wing coalition*
2 = **weakness**, delicacy, frailty, infirmity, feebleness, brittleness, frangibility • *seriously injured because of the fragility of their bones*

fragment **AS A NOUN** = **piece**, part, bit, scrap, particle, portion, fraction, shiver, shred, remnant, speck, sliver, wisp, morsel, oddment, chip • *She read everything, digesting every fragment of news.*
▸ **AS A VERB** 1 = **break**, split, shatter, crumble, shiver, disintegrate, splinter, come apart, break into pieces, come to pieces • *It's an exploded fracture – the bones have fragmented.*
OPPOSITES: link, marry, fuse
2 = **break up**, divide, split up, disunite • *Their country's government has fragmented into disarray.*

fragmentary = **incomplete**, broken, scattered, partial, disconnected, discrete, sketchy, piecemeal, incoherent, scrappy, disjointed, bitty, unsystematic • *The extant volume is fragmentary.*

fragrance *or* **fragrancy** 1 = **scent**, smell, perfume, bouquet, aroma, balm, sweet smell, sweet odour, redolence, fragrancy • *A shrubby plant with a strong fragrance.*
OPPOSITES: smell, stink, whiff *(Brit. slang)*
2 = **perfume**, scent, cologne, eau de toilette, eau de Cologne, toilet water, Cologne water • *The advertisement is for a male fragrance.*

fragrant = **aromatic**, perfumed, balmy, redolent, sweet-smelling, sweet-scented, odorous, ambrosial, odoriferous • *fragrant oils and perfumes*
OPPOSITES: smelling, stinking, smelly

frail 1 = **feeble**, weak, puny, decrepit, infirm • *She lay in bed looking particularly frail.*
OPPOSITES: strong, sound, tough
2 = **flimsy**, weak, vulnerable, delicate, fragile, brittle, unsound, wispy, insubstantial, breakable, frangible, slight • *The frail craft rocked as he clambered in.*

frailty 1 = **weakness**, susceptibility, fallibility, peccability • *a triumph of will over human frailty*
OPPOSITES: might, strength, fortitude
2 = **infirmity**, poor health, feebleness, puniness, frailness • *She died after a long period of increasing frailty.*
3 = **fault**, failing, vice, weakness, defect, deficiency, flaw, shortcoming, blemish, imperfection, foible, weak point, peccadillo, chink in your armour • *She is aware of his faults and frailties.*
OPPOSITES: asset, virtue, strong point

frame **AS A NOUN** 1 = **mounting**, setting, surround, mount • *She kept a picture of her mother in a silver frame.*
2 = **casing**, framework, structure, shell, system, form, construction, fabric, skeleton, chassis • *He supplied housebuilders with modern timber frames.*
3 = **physique**, build, form, body, figure, skeleton, anatomy, carcass, morphology • *belts pulled tight against their bony frames*
▸ **AS A VERB** 1 = **mount**, case, enclose, set • *The picture is now ready to be framed.*
2 = **surround**, ring, enclose, close in, encompass, envelop, encircle, fence in, hem in • *The swimming pool is framed by tropical gardens.*
3 = **devise**, plan, form, shape, institute, draft, compose, sketch, forge, put together, conceive, hatch, draw up, formulate, contrive, map out, concoct, cook up, block out

• *A convention was set up to frame a constitution.*
4 = **express**, word, phrase, couch, put into words • *He framed his question three different ways.*
5 = **falsely incriminate**, set up *(informal)*, fit up *(slang)* • *He claimed he had been framed by the police.*
▸ **IN PHRASES: frame of mind = mood**, state, spirit, attitude, humour, temper, outlook, disposition, mind-set, fettle • *He was not in the right frame of mind to continue.*

frame-up = **false charge**, set-up *(slang)*, fabrication, fit-up *(slang)*, trumped-up charge, put-up job • *He was innocent and the victim of a frame-up.*

framework 1 = **system**, plan, order, scheme, arrangement, fabric, schema, frame of reference, the bare bones • *within the framework of federal regulations*
2 = **structure**, body, frame, foundation, shell, fabric, skeleton • *wooden shelves on a steel framework*

France
▸ **RELATED ADJECTIVES:** French, Gallic
▹ *See panel* **Administrative regions**

franchise 1 = **authorization**, right, permit, licence, charter, privilege, prerogative • *the franchise to build and operate the tunnel*
2 = **vote**, voting rights, suffrage, enfranchisement • *the introduction of universal franchise*

frank **AS AN ADJECTIVE** 1 = **candid**, open, free, round, direct, plain, straightforward, blunt, outright, sincere, outspoken, honest, downright, truthful, forthright, upfront *(informal)*, unrestricted, plain-spoken, unreserved, artless, ingenuous, straight from the shoulder *(informal)* • *They had a frank discussion about the issue.*
OPPOSITES: reserved, shy, secretive
2 = **unconcealed**, open, complete, obvious, genuine, evident, utter, explicit, manifest, transparent, unmistakable, out-and-out, wholehearted, undisguised, dinkum *(Austral. & N.Z. informal)*, thoroughgoing, unfeigned • *with frank admiration on his face*
▸ **AS A VERB** = **postmark**, mark, stamp • *The letter was franked in London.*

frankly 1 = **honestly**, sincerely, in truth, candidly, to tell you the truth, to be frank, to be frank with someone, to be honest • *Quite frankly, I don't care.*
2 = **openly**, freely, directly, straight, plainly, bluntly, overtly, candidly, without reserve, straight from the shoulder • *The leaders have been speaking frankly about their problems.*

frankness = **outspokenness**, openness, candour, truthfulness, plain speaking, bluntness, forthrightness, laying it on the line, ingenuousness, absence of reserve • *The reaction to his frankness was hostile.*

frantic 1 = **frenzied**, wild, mad, raging, furious, raving, distracted, distraught, berserk, uptight *(informal)*, overwrought, at the end of your tether, beside yourself, at your wits' end, berko *(Austral. slang)* • *A bird had been locked in and was now quite frantic.*
OPPOSITES: together *(slang)*, cool, calm
2 = **hectic**, desperate, frenzied, fraught *(informal)*, frenetic • *A busy night in the restaurant is frantic in the kitchen.*

fraternity 1 = **companionship**, fellowship, brotherhood, kinship, camaraderie, comradeship • *He needs the fraternity of others.*
2 = **circle**, company, set, order, clan, guild • *the spread of stolen guns among the criminal fraternity*
3 = **brotherhood**, club, union, society, league, association, sodality • *He joined a college fraternity.*

fraternize = **associate**, mix, socialize, keep company, unite, hang out *(informal)*, mingle, cooperate, concur, consort, sympathize, hang with *(informal, chiefly U.S.)*, hobnob, go around with • *Executives fraternized with the personnel of other banks.*
OPPOSITES: avoid, shun, eschew

fraud 1 = **deception**, deceit, treachery, swindling, guile, trickery, duplicity, double-dealing, chicanery, sharp practice, imposture, fraudulence, spuriousness • *He was jailed for two years for fraud.*
OPPOSITES: virtue, integrity, honesty
2 = **scam**, craft, cheat, sting *(informal)*, deception *(slang)*, artifice, humbug, canard, stratagems, chicane • *a fraud involving pension and social security claims*
3 = **hoax**, trick, cheat, con *(informal)*, deception, sham, spoof *(informal)*, prank, swindle, ruse, practical joke, joke, fast one *(informal)*, imposture, fastie *(Austral. slang)* • *He never wrote the letter; it was a fraud.*
4 = **impostor**, cheat, fake, bluffer, sham, hoax, hoaxer, forgery, counterfeit, pretender, charlatan, quack, fraudster, swindler, mountebank, grifter *(slang, chiefly U.S. & Canad.)*, double-dealer, phoney or phony *(informal)* • *He believes many psychics are frauds.*

fraudulent = **deceitful**, false, crooked *(informal)*, untrue, sham, treacherous, dishonest, deceptive, counterfeit, spurious, crafty, swindling, double-dealing, duplicitous, knavish, phoney or phony *(informal)*, criminal • *fraudulent claims about being a nurse*
OPPOSITES: true, principled, genuine

fraught **AS AN ADJECTIVE** 1 = **tense**, trying, difficult, distressing, tricky, emotionally charged • *It has been a somewhat fraught day.*
2 *usually with* **with** = **agitated**, wired *(slang)*, anxious, distressed, tense, distracted, emotive, uptight *(informal)*, emotionally charged, strung-up, on tenterhooks, hag-ridden, adrenalized • *She's depressed, fraught, and exhausted.*
▸ **IN PHRASES: fraught with** = **filled with**, full of, charged with, accompanied by, attended by, stuffed with, laden with, heavy with, bristling with, replete with, abounding with • *The production has been fraught with problems.*

fray[1] = **fight**, battle, row, conflict, clash, set-to *(informal)*, riot, combat, disturbance, rumble *(U.S. & N.Z. slang)*, quarrel, brawl, skirmish, scuffle, rumpus, broil, affray *(Law)*, shindig *(informal)*, donnybrook, battle royal, ruckus *(informal)*, scrimmage, shindy *(informal)*, bagarre *(French)*, melee or mêlée, biffo *(Austral. slang)*, boilover *(Austral.)* • *Today he entered the fray on the side of the moderates.*

fray[2] 1 = **wear thin**, wear, rub, fret, wear out, chafe, wear away, become threadbare • *The stitching had begun to fray at the edges.*
2 = **strain**, become tense, become stressed, become on edge • *Tempers began to fray as the two teams failed to score.*

frayed 1 = **worn**, ragged, worn out, tattered, threadbare, worn thin, out at elbows • *a shapeless and frayed jumper*
2 = **strained**, stressed, tense, edgy, uptight *(informal)*, frazzled • *Nerves are frayed all round.*

freak **AS A MODIFIER** = **abnormal**, chance, unusual, unexpected, exceptional, unpredictable, queer, erratic, unparalleled, unforeseen, fortuitous, unaccountable, atypical, aberrant, fluky *(informal)*, odd, bizarre • *The ferry was hit by a freak wave off the coast.*
▸ **AS A NOUN** 1 = **enthusiast**, fan, nut *(slang)*, addict, buff *(informal)*, fanatic, devotee, fiend *(informal)*, aficionado • *He's a self-confessed computer freak.*
2 = **aberration**, eccentric, anomaly, abnormality, sport *(Biology)*, monster, mutant, oddity, monstrosity, malformation, rara avis *(Latin)*, queer fish *(Brit. informal)*, teratism • *Not so long ago, transsexuals were regarded as freaks.*
3 = **weirdo** or **weirdie** *(informal)*, eccentric, crank *(informal)*, oddity, case *(informal)*, character *(informal)*, nut *(slang)*, flake *(slang, chiefly U.S.)*, oddball *(informal)*, nonconformist, screwball *(slang, chiefly U.S. & Canad.)*, odd fish *(informal)*, kook *(U.S. & Canad. informal)*, queer fish *(Brit. informal)* • *The cast consisted of a bunch of freaks and social misfits.*
▸ **AS A VERB** *often with* **out** = **go crazy**, snap, flip *(slang)*, go

f

berserk, go bananas *(slang)*, fly off the handle *(informal)*, throw a wobbly *(slang)*, go off the deep end *(informal)*, lose your mind, lose your cool *(informal)*, go out of your mind, flip your lid *(slang)*, go off your rocker *(slang)*, behave in a wild way, go off your head *(slang)* • *I saw five cop cars pull in and I freaked.*

freakish 1 = **odd**, strange, fantastic, weird, abnormal, monstrous, grotesque, unnatural, unconventional, outlandish, freaky *(slang)*, aberrant, outré, malformed, preternatural, teratoid *(Biology)* • *a freakish monstrous thing, something out of a dream*
2 = **whimsical**, odd, unpredictable, arbitrary, humorous, erratic, wayward, fanciful, capricious, changeable, fitful, vagarious *(rare)* • *a freakish, extraordinary incident*

freaky = **weird**, odd, wild, strange, crazy, bizarre, abnormal, queer, rum *(Brit. slang)*, unconventional, far-out *(slang)*, freakish • *This guy bore a really freaky resemblance to Jones.*

free AS AN ADJECTIVE 1 = **complimentary**, for free *(informal)*, for nothing, unpaid, for love, free of charge, on the house, without charge, gratuitous, at no cost, gratis, buckshee *(Brit. slang)* • *The seminars are free, with lunch provided.*
2 = **allowed**, permitted, unrestricted, unimpeded, at liberty, open, clear, able, loose, unattached, unregulated, disengaged, untrammelled, unobstructed, unhampered, unengaged • *The government will be free to pursue its economic policies.*
3 = **at liberty**, loose, liberated, at large, off the hook *(slang)*, on the loose • *All the hostages are free.*
OPPOSITES: secured, bound, confined
4 = **independent**, unfettered, unrestrained, uncommitted, footloose, unconstrained, unengaged, not tied down • *I was young, free and single at the time.*
5 = **non-working**, leisure, unemployed, idle, unoccupied • *She spent her free time shopping.*
6 = **available**, extra, empty, spare, vacant, unused, uninhabited, unoccupied, untaken • *There's only one seat free on the train.*
7 = **unattached**, loose, unsecured, untied, unfastened • *Wrap the free end of the strip over the second length of piping.*
8 *often with* **of** *or* **with** = **generous**, willing, liberal, eager, lavish, charitable, hospitable, prodigal, bountiful, open-handed, unstinting, unsparing, bounteous, munificent, big *(informal)* • *They weren't always so free with their advice.*
OPPOSITES: mean, close, tight
9 = **autonomous**, independent, democratic, sovereign, self-ruling, self-governing, emancipated, self-determining, autarchic • *We cannot survive as a free nation.*
10 = **relaxed**, open, easy, forward, natural, frank, liberal, familiar, loose, casual, informal, spontaneous, laid-back *(informal)*, easy-going *(informal)*, lax, uninhibited, unforced, free and easy, unbidden, unconstrained, unceremonious • *a confidential but free manner*
OPPOSITES: official, formal, stiff
11 = **unencumbered**, open, clear, unrestricted, unobstructed • *They have to ensure the free flow of traffic.*
▸ AS AN ADVERB = **freely**, easily, loosely, smoothly, idly • *Two stubby legs swing free.*
▸ AS A VERB 1 *often with* **of** *or* **from** = **clear**, deliver, disengage, cut loose, release, rescue, rid, relieve, exempt, undo, redeem, ransom, extricate, unburden, unshackle • *It will free us of a whole lot of debt.*
2 = **release**, liberate, let out, set free, deliver, loose, discharge, unleash, let go, untie, emancipate, unchain, turn loose, uncage, set at liberty, unfetter, disenthrall, unbridle, manumit • *They are going to free more prisoners.*
OPPOSITES: limit, restrict, confine
3 = **disentangle**, extricate, disengage, detach, separate, loose, unfold, unravel, disconnect, untangle, untwist, unsnarl • *It took firemen two hours to free him.*
▸ IN PHRASES: **for free** = **without charge**, for nothing, for love, on the house, at no cost, gratis • *He did it for free.*
free and easy = **relaxed**, liberal, casual, informal, tolerant, laid-back *(informal)*, easy-going, lax, lenient, uninhibited, unceremonious • *He had a free and easy approach.*
free of *or* **from** = **unaffected by**, without, above, lacking (in), beyond, clear of, devoid of, exempt from, immune to, sans *(archaic)*, safe from, untouched by, deficient in, unencumbered by, not liable to • *She retains her slim figure and is free of wrinkles.*

QUOTATIONS

Free at last, Free at last
Thank God Almighty
I'm Free at last
[Martin Luther King Jr. *Spiritual, quoted on his tomb*]

The free way of life proposes ends, but it does not prescribe means
[Robert F. Kennedy *The Pursuit of Justice*]

I am condemned to be free
[Jean-Paul Sartre *L'Être et le néant*]

The thoughts of a prisoner – they're not free either. They keep returning to the same things
[Alexander Solzhenitsyn *One Day in the Life of Ivan Denisovich*]

PROVERBS

The best things in life are free
There's no such thing as a free lunch

freedom 1 = **independence**, democracy, sovereignty, autonomy, self-determination, emancipation, self-government, home rule, autarchy, rangatiratanga *(N.Z.)* • *They want greater political freedom.*
2 = **right**, privilege, entitlement, prerogative • *freedom of speech*
3 = **liberty**, release, discharge, emancipation, deliverance, manumission • *All hostages and detainees would gain their freedom.*
OPPOSITES: slavery, imprisonment, captivity
4 *usually with* **from** = **exemption**, release, relief, privilege, immunity, impunity • *freedom from government control*
5 = **licence**, latitude, a free hand, free rein, play, power, range, opportunity, ability, facility, scope, flexibility, discretion, leeway, carte blanche, blank cheque, elbowroom • *freedom to buy and sell at the best price*
OPPOSITES: restriction, limitation
6 = **openness**, ease, directness, naturalness, abandon, familiarity, candour, frankness, informality, casualness, ingenuousness, lack of restraint *or* reserve, unconstraint • *His freedom of manner ran contrary to the norm.*
OPPOSITES: caution, restraint
▸ RELATED MANIA: eleutheromania

QUOTATIONS

Freedom is always and exclusively freedom for the one who thinks differently
[Rosa Luxemburg *Die Russische Revolution*]

We look forward to a world founded upon four essential human freedoms. The first is freedom of speech and expression ... The second is freedom of every person to worship God in his own way ... The third is freedom from want ... The fourth is freedom from fear
[Franklin D. Roosevelt *annual message to Congress*]

Man was born free, and everywhere he is in chains
[Jean Jacques Rousseau *The Social Contract*]

No human being, however great or powerful, was ever so free as a fish
[John Ruskin *The Two Paths*]

Man is a free agent; were it otherwise, the priests would not damn him
[Voltaire *Philosophical Dictionary*]

Perfect freedom is reserved for the man who lives by his own work and in that work does what he wants to do
[R.G. Collingwood *Speculum Mentis*]
Freedom is the freedom to say that two plus two make four. If that is granted, all else follows
[George Orwell *Nineteen Eighty-Four*]

free-for-all = **fight**, row, riot, brawl, fracas, affray *(Law)*, dust-up *(informal)*, shindig *(informal)*, donnybrook, scrimmage, shindy *(informal)*, bagarre *(French)*, melee *or* mêlée, biffo *(Austral. slang)* • *It finished up a shambolic free-for-all.*

freely 1 = **abundantly**, liberally, lavishly, like water, extravagantly, copiously, unstintingly, with a free hand, bountifully, open-handedly, amply • *He was spending very freely.*
2 = **openly**, frankly, plainly, candidly, unreservedly, straightforwardly, without reserve • *He had someone to whom he could talk freely.*
3 = **willingly**, readily, voluntarily, spontaneously, without prompting, of your own free will, of your own accord • *He freely admits he lives for racing.*
4 = **easily**, cleanly, loosely, smoothly, readily • *You must allow the clubhead to swing freely.*
5 = **without restraint**, voluntarily, willingly, unchallenged, as you please, without being forced, without let or hindrance • *They cast their votes freely.*

freeway = **motorway** *(Brit.)*, autobahn *(German)*, autoroute *(French)*, autostrada *(Italian)* • *The speed limit on the freeway is 55mph.*

freewheel = **coast**, drift, glide, relax your efforts, rest on your oars, float • *He freewheeled back down the hill.*

freeze AS A VERB 1 = **ice over** *or* **up**, harden, stiffen, solidify, congeal, become solid, glaciate • *The ground froze solid.*
2 = **deep freeze**, cool, ice, chill, refrigerate, put in the freezer • *You can freeze the soup at this point.*
3 = **chill**, benumb • *The cold morning froze my fingers.*
4 = **stop**, stop dead, stop suddenly, stop in your tracks • *She froze when the beam of the flashlight struck her.*
5 = **fix**, hold, limit, hold up, peg • *Wages have been frozen and workers laid off.*
6 = **suspend**, stop, shelve, curb, cut short, discontinue • *They have already frozen their aid programme.*
▸ AS A NOUN 1 = **cold snap**, frost, freeze-up • *The trees were damaged by a freeze in December.*
2 = **fix**, hold, halt, suspension, standstill • *A wage freeze was imposed on all staff.*
▸ IN PHRASES: **freeze someone out** = **exclude**, leave out, force out, shut out, refuse, remove, reject, ignore, eliminate, rule out, get rid of, boycott, expel, put out, throw out, oust, keep out, drive out, pass over, eject, evict, ostracize, send to Coventry, give the cold-shoulder to • *He's freezing me out because he knows I'm no good.*

freezing 1 = **icy**, biting, bitter, raw, chill, chilled, penetrating, arctic, numbing, polar, Siberian, frosty, glacial, wintry, parky *(Brit. informal)*, cold as ice, frost-bound, cutting • *a freezing January afternoon*
2 = **frozen**, chilled, numb, chilly, very cold, shivery, benumbed, frozen to the marrow • *You must be freezing!*

freight AS A NOUN 1 = **transportation**, traffic, delivery, carriage, shipment, haulage, conveyance, transport • *France derives 16% of revenue from air freight.*
2 = **cargo**, goods, contents, load, lading, delivery, burden, haul, bulk, shipment, merchandise, bales, consignment, payload, tonnage • *26 tonnes of freight*
▸ AS A VERB = **transport**, carry, ship, deliver, convey • *The grain is freighted down to Addis Ababa.*

French = **Gallic** • *All the staff are French.*
▸ RELATED PREFIXES: Franco-, Gallo-

frenetic = **frantic**, wild, excited, crazy, frenzied, distraught, obsessive, fanatical, demented, unbalanced, overwrought, maniacal • *the frenetic pace of life in New York*

frenzied = **uncontrolled**, wild, excited, mad, crazy, furious, frantic, distraught, hysterical, agitated, frenetic, feverish, rabid, maniacal • *the frenzied activity of the general election*

frenzy 1 = **fit**, burst, bout, outburst, spasm, convulsion, paroxysm • *The country was gripped by a frenzy of nationalism.*
2 = **fury**, transport, passion, rage, madness, turmoil, distraction, seizure, hysteria, mania, insanity, agitation, aberration, lunacy, delirium, paroxysm, derangement • *Something like a frenzy enveloped them.*
OPPOSITES: calm, sanity, composure

frequency = **recurrence**, repetition, constancy, periodicity, commonness, frequentness, prevalence • *The cars broke down with increasing frequency.*

frequent AS AN ADJECTIVE = **common**, repeated, usual, familiar, constant, everyday, persistent, reiterated, recurring, customary, continual, recurrent, habitual, incessant • *He is a frequent visitor to the house.*
OPPOSITES: few, rare, infrequent
▸ AS A VERB = **visit**, attend, haunt, be found at, patronize, hang out at *(informal)*, visit often, go to regularly, be a regular customer of • *I hear he frequents that restaurant.*
OPPOSITES: avoid, shun, keep away

frequently = **often**, commonly, repeatedly, many times, very often, oft *(archaic or poetic)*, over and over again, habitually, customarily, oftentimes *(archaic)*, not infrequently, many a time, much • *Iron supplements are frequently given to pregnant women.*
OPPOSITES: rarely, occasionally, infrequently

fresh 1 = **additional**, more, new, other, added, further, extra, renewed, supplementary, auxiliary • *He asked the police to make fresh enquiries.*
2 = **clear**, marked, plain, distinct, noticeable, clear-cut • *fresh footprints in the snow*
3 = **natural**, raw, crude, unsalted, unprocessed, uncured, unpreserved, undried, green • *A meal with fresh ingredients doesn't take long to prepare.*
OPPOSITES: frozen, salted, preserved
4 = **new**, original, novel, unusual, latest, different, recent, modern, up-to-date, this season's, unconventional, unorthodox, ground-breaking, left-field *(informal)*, new-fangled, modernistic • *These designers are full of fresh ideas.*
OPPOSITES: old, ordinary, dull
5 = **invigorating**, clear, clean, bright, sweet, pure, stiff, crisp, sparkling, bracing, refreshing, brisk, spanking, unpolluted • *The air was fresh and she felt revived.*
OPPOSITES: warm, stale, musty
6 = **cool**, cold, refreshing, brisk, chilly, nippy • *The breeze was fresh and from the north.*
7 = **vivid**, bright, verdant, undimmed, unfaded • *a semi-circular mosaic, its colours still fresh*
OPPOSITES: old, weary
8 = **rosy**, clear, fair, bright, healthy, glowing, hardy, blooming, wholesome, ruddy, florid, dewy, good • *His fresh complexion made him look young.*
OPPOSITES: sickly, pallid
9 = **lively**, rested, bright, keen, vital, restored, alert, bouncing, revived, refreshed, vigorous, energetic, sprightly, invigorated, spry, chipper *(informal)*, full of beans *(informal)*, like a new man, full of vim and vigour *(informal)*, unwearied, bright-eyed and bushy-tailed *(informal)* • *I nearly always wake up fresh and rested.*
OPPOSITES: exhausted, weary
10 = **inexperienced**, new, young, green, natural, raw, youthful, unqualified, callow, untrained, untried, artless, uncultivated, wet behind the ears • *The soldiers were fresh recruits.*
OPPOSITES: old, experienced

11 = cheeky *(Informal)*, bold, brazen, impertinent, forward, familiar, flip *(informal)*, saucy, audacious, sassy *(U.S. informal)*, pert, disrespectful, presumptuous, insolent, impudent, smart-alecky *(informal)* • *Don't get fresh with me.*
OPPOSITES: well-mannered

freshen AS A VERB **1 = cool off**, become stronger, become colder, become chilly • *The wind had freshened.*
2 = refresh, restore, rouse, enliven, revitalize, spruce up, liven up, freshen up, titivate • *Cleanse and freshen oily skin.*
3 = ventilate, air, clean, expose, cleanse, aerate • *Try opening windows to freshen the air.*
▸ IN PHRASES: **freshen (yourself) up = have a wash**, wash (yourself), tidy (yourself) up, get washed, spruce yourself up • *After she had freshened up, they went for a walk.*

freshman = undergraduate, fresher *(Brit. informal)*, first-year student • *a freshman at the University of South Carolina*

freshness 1 = novelty, creativity, originality, inventiveness, newness, innovativeness • *They have a freshness and individuality that others lack.*
2 = cleanness, shine, glow, bloom, sparkle, vigour, brightness, wholesomeness, clearness, dewiness • *the freshness of early morning*

fret 1 = worry, anguish, brood, agonize, obsess, lose sleep, upset yourself, distress yourself • *I was constantly fretting about others' problems.*
2 = annoy, trouble, bother, disturb, distress, provoke, irritate, grieve, torment, harass, nag, gall, agitate, ruffle, nettle, vex, goad, chagrin, irk, rile, pique, peeve *(informal)*, rankle with • *The quickening of time frets me.*

fretful = irritable, cross, worried, complaining, anxious, unhappy, uneasy, edgy, touchy, fractious, petulant, out of sorts, tetchy, ratty *(Brit. & N.Z. informal)*, testy, short-tempered, querulous, peevish, splenetic, crotchety *(informal)*, captious • *an extremely fretful four-month old baby*

friar = monk, brother, religious, prior, abbot • *He is a travelling Franciscan friar.*

friction 1 = conflict, opposition, hostility, resentment, disagreement, rivalry, discontent, wrangling, bickering, animosity, antagonism, discord, bad feeling, bad blood, dissension, incompatibility, disharmony, dispute • *There was friction between the children.*
2 = resistance, rubbing, scraping, grating, irritation, erosion, fretting, attrition, rasping, chafing, abrasion, wearing away • *The pistons are graphite-coated to prevent friction.*
3 = rubbing, scraping, grating, fretting, rasping, chafing, abrasion • *the friction of his leg against hers*

friend 1 = companion, pal, mate *(informal)*, buddy *(informal)*, partner, china *(Brit. & S. African informal)*, familiar, best friend, intimate, cock *(Brit. informal)*, close friend, comrade, chum *(informal)*, crony, alter ego, confidant, playmate, confidante, main man *(slang, chiefly U.S.)*, soul mate, homeboy *(slang, chiefly U.S.)*, cobber *(Austral. & N.Z.)*, E hoa *(N.Z. old-fashioned informal)*, bosom friend, boon companion, Achates • *I had a long talk with my best friend.*
OPPOSITES: rival, enemy, foe
2 = supporter, ally, associate, sponsor, advocate, patron, backer, partisan, protagonist, benefactor, adherent, well-wisher • *the Friends of Birmingham Royal Ballet*

QUOTATIONS

A friend should bear his friend's infirmities
[William Shakespeare *Julius Caesar*]

The belongings of friends are common
[Aristotle]

My best friend is the man who in wishing me well wishes it for my sake
[Aristotle *Nicomachean Ethics*]

Friends are born, not made
[Henry Adams *The Education of Henry Adams*]

True happiness
Consists not in the multitude of friends,
But in the worth and choice
[Ben Jonson *Cynthia's Revels*]

Friends are God's apology for relatives
[Hugh Kingsmill]

Old friends are the best. King James used to call for his old shoes; for they were easiest for his feet
[John Seldon *Table Talk*]

Old friends are the blessing of one's later years – half a word conveys one's meaning
[Horace Walpole]

The only way to have a friend is to be one
[Ralph Waldo Emerson *Essays: First Series*]

Of two close friends, one is always the slave of the other
[Mikhail Lermontov *A Hero of Our Time*]

PROVERBS

A friend in need is a friend indeed

friendless = alone, abandoned, deserted, isolated, lonely, cut off, alienated, solitary, shunned, estranged, forsaken, forlorn, unattached, lonesome *(chiefly U.S. & Canad.)*, all alone, ostracized, without ties, with no one to turn to, without a friend in the world • *He was unhappy because he was friendless.*

friendliness = amiability, warmth, sociability, conviviality, neighbourliness, affability, geniality, kindliness, congeniality, companionability, mateyness *or* matiness *(Brit. informal)*, open arms • *She loves the friendliness of the people.*

friendly 1 = amiable, kind, kindly, welcoming, warm, neighbourly, thick *(informal)*, attached, pally *(informal)*, helpful, sympathetic, fond, outgoing, comradely, confiding, affectionate, receptive, benevolent, attentive, sociable, genial, affable, fraternal, good, close, on good terms, chummy *(informal)*, peaceable, companionable, clubby, well-disposed, buddy-buddy *(slang, chiefly U.S. & Canad.)*, palsy-walsy *(informal)*, matey *or* maty *(Brit. informal)*, on visiting terms • *He has been friendly to me.*
2 = amicable, warm, familiar, pleasant, intimate, informal, benign, conciliatory, cordial, congenial, convivial • *a friendly atmosphere*
OPPOSITES: cold, distant, unfriendly

friendship 1 = attachment, relationship, bond, alliance, link, association, tie • *They struck up a close friendship.*
2 = friendliness, affection, harmony, goodwill, intimacy, affinity, familiarity, closeness, rapport, fondness, companionship, concord, benevolence, comradeship, amity, good-fellowship • *a whole new world of friendship and adventure*
OPPOSITES: conflict, hostility, unfriendliness
3 = closeness, love, regard, affection, intimacy, fondness, companionship, comradeship • *He really values your friendship.*

QUOTATIONS

Friendship is a single soul dwelling in two bodies
[Aristotle]

Friendship makes prosperity more brilliant, and lightens adversity by dividing and sharing it
[Cicero *De Amicitia*]

Friendship admits of difference of character, as love does that of sex
[Joseph Roux *Meditations of a Parish Priest*]

fright 1 = fear, shock, alarm, horror, panic, terror, dread, dismay, quaking, apprehension, consternation, trepidation, cold sweat, fear and trembling, (blue) funk *(informal)* • *To hide my fright I asked a question.*
OPPOSITES: courage, pluck, bravery
2 = scare, start, turn, surprise, shock, jolt, the creeps *(informal)*, the shivers, the willies *(slang)*, the heebie-jeebies *(slang)* • *The snake gave everyone a fright.*

3 = **sight** *(informal)*, mess *(informal)*, eyesore, scarecrow, frump • *She looked a fright in a long dark wig.*

frighten AS A VERB = **scare**, shock, alarm, terrify, cow, appal, startle, intimidate, dismay, daunt, unnerve, petrify, unman, terrorize, scare (someone) stiff, put the wind up (someone) *(informal)*, scare the living daylights out of (someone) *(informal)*, make your hair stand on end *(informal)*, get the wind up, make your blood run cold, throw into a panic, scare the bejesus out of *(informal)*, affright *(archaic)*, freeze your blood, make (someone) jump out of his skin *(informal)*, throw into a fright • *Most children are frightened by the sight of blood.*
OPPOSITES: encourage, comfort, reassure
▸ IN PHRASES: **frighten something** *or* **someone off** *or* **away** = **scare off**, startle, put the wind up (someone) *(informal)*, throw into a fright • *He fired into the air to frighten them off.*

frightened = **afraid**, alarmed, scared, terrified, shocked, frozen, cowed, startled, dismayed, unnerved, petrified, flustered, panicky, terrorized, in a panic, scared stiff, in a cold sweat, abashed, scared shitless *(taboo slang)*, terror-stricken, shit-scared *(taboo slang)*, affrighted *(archaic)*, in fear and trepidation, numb with fear • *She was too frightened to tell them what happened.*

frightening = **terrifying**, shocking, alarming, appalling, startling, dreadful, horrifying, menacing, intimidating, dismaying, scary *(informal)*, fearful, daunting, fearsome, unnerving, spooky *(informal)*, hair-raising, baleful, spine-chilling, bloodcurdling • *The number of youngsters involved in crime is frightening.*

frightful 1 = **terrible**, shocking, alarming, awful, appalling, horrible, grim, terrifying, dreadful, dread, fearful, traumatic, dire, horrendous, ghastly, hideous, harrowing, gruesome, unnerving, lurid, from hell *(informal)*, grisly, macabre, petrifying, horrid, unspeakable, godawful *(slang)*, hellacious *(U.S. slang)* • *refugees trapped in frightful conditions*
OPPOSITES: nice, beautiful, pleasant
2 = **dreadful**, great, terrible, extreme, awful, annoying, unpleasant, disagreeable, insufferable • *He got himself into a frightful muddle.*
OPPOSITES: slight, moderate, pleasant

frigid 1 = **freezing**, cold, frozen, icy, chill, arctic, Siberian, frosty, cool, glacial, wintry, gelid, frost-bound, hyperboreal • *The water was too frigid to allow him to remain submerged.*
OPPOSITES: hot, warm, stifling
2 = **sexually unresponsive**, cold, distant, unfeeling, passionless, undemonstrative • *My husband says I am frigid.*
3 = **chilly**, formal, stiff, forbidding, rigid, passive, icy, austere, aloof, lifeless, repellent, unresponsive, unfeeling, unbending, unapproachable, passionless, unloving, cold as ice, cold-hearted • *She replied with a frigid smile.*
OPPOSITES: warm, friendly, passionate

frill AS A NOUN 1 = **ruffle**, gathering, tuck, ruff, flounce, ruche, ruching, furbelow, purfle • *net curtains with frills*
2 *often plural* = **trimmings**, extras, additions, fuss, jazz *(slang)*, dressing up, decoration(s), bits and pieces, icing on the cake, finery, embellishments, affectation(s), ornamentation, ostentation, frippery, bells and whistles, tomfoolery, gewgaws, superfluities, fanciness, frilliness, fandangles • *The booklet restricts itself to facts without frills.*
▸ IN PHRASES: **no frills** = **plain**, ordinary, modest, unpretentious, without extras, unostentatious, without trimmings, with no fancy bits, without bells and whistles, bare-bones • *plain, simple cooking in no-frills surroundings*

frilly = **ruffled**, fancy, lacy, frothy, ruched, flouncy • *maids in frilly aprons*

fringe AS A NOUN 1 = **border**, edging, edge, binding, trimming, hem, frill, tassel, flounce • *The jacket had leather fringes.*
2 = **edge**, limits, border, margin, march, marches, outskirts, perimeter, periphery, borderline • *They lived together on the fringe of the campus.*
▸ AS A MODIFIER = **unofficial**, alternative, radical, innovative, avant-garde, unconventional, unorthodox • *numerous fringe meetings held during the conference*
▸ AS A VERB = **border**, edge, surround, bound, skirt, trim, enclose, flank • *Swampy islands of vegetation fringe the coastline.*

fringe benefit = **added extra**, bonus, allowance, privilege, perk, perquisite *(formal)*, boot money *(informal)*, lagniappe *(U.S.)* • *Fringe benefits need to be incorporated within payment.*

fringed 1 = **bordered**, edged, befringed • *She wore a fringed scarf.*
2 = **edged**, bordered, margined, outlined • *tiny islands fringed with golden sand*

frippery 1 = **frills**, nonsense, finery, ostentation, pretentiousness, fussiness, glad rags *(informal)*, tawdriness, flashiness, foppery, gaudiness, showiness, meretriciousness, fanciness, frilliness • *He despised such frippery.*
2 = **decoration**, toy, ornament, trinket, bauble, adornment, gewgaw, knick-knack, fandangle • *a sombre display, with no frills or fripperies*

frisk 1 = **search**, check, inspect, run over, shake down *(U.S. slang)*, body-search • *He pushed him against the wall and frisked him.*
2 = **frolic**, play, sport, dance, trip, jump, bounce, hop, skip, romp, caper, prance, cavort, gambol, rollick, curvet • *creatures that grunted and frisked about*

frisky = **lively**, spirited, romping, playful, bouncy, high-spirited, rollicking, in high spirits, full of beans *(informal)*, coltish, kittenish, frolicsome, ludic *(literary)*, sportive, full of joie de vivre • *His horse was feeling frisky.*
OPPOSITES: wooden, dull, sedate

fritter *usually with* **away** = **squander**, waste, run through, dissipate, misspend, idle away, fool away, spend like water • *I fritter my time away at coffee mornings.*

frivolous 1 = **flippant**, foolish, dizzy, superficial, silly, flip *(informal)*, juvenile, idle, childish, giddy, puerile, flighty, ill-considered, empty-headed, light-hearted, nonserious, light-minded, ditzy *or* ditsy *(slang)* • *I was a bit too frivolous to be a doctor.*
OPPOSITES: serious, earnest, responsible
2 = **trivial**, petty, trifling, unimportant, light, minor, shallow, pointless, extravagant, peripheral, niggling, paltry, impractical, nickel-and-dime *(U.S. slang)*, footling *(informal)* • *wasting money on frivolous projects*
OPPOSITES: important, serious, vital

frivolousness *or* **frivolity** = **flippancy**, fun, nonsense, folly, trifling, lightness, jest, gaiety, silliness, triviality, superficiality, levity, shallowness, childishness, giddiness, flummery, light-heartedness, puerility, flightiness, frivolousness • *There is a serious message beneath this frivolity.*
OPPOSITES: importance, significance, seriousness

frizzy = **tight-curled**, crisp, corrugated, wiry, crimped, frizzed • *Her hair had a slightly frizzy perm.*

frock = **dress**, suit, get-up *(informal)*, outfit, costume, gown, ensemble, garment, robe, rigout *(informal)* • *She wore a nondescript frock of blue.*

frog
▸ RELATED ADJECTIVE: batrachian
▸ NAME OF YOUNG: tadpole
▹ *See panel* **Amphibians**

frolic AS A NOUN = **merriment**, sport, fun, amusement, gaiety, fun and games, skylarking *(informal)*, high jinks, drollery • *Their relationship is never short on fun and frolic.*
▸ AS A VERB = **play**, romp, lark, caper, cavort, frisk, gambol, make merry, rollick, cut capers, sport • *Tourists sunbathe and frolic in the ocean.*

front AS A NOUN **1 = head**, start, lead, beginning, top, fore, forefront • *Stand at the front of the line.*
2 = exterior, facing, face, façade, frontage, anterior, obverse, forepart • *Attached to the front of the house was a veranda.*
3 = foreground, fore, forefront, nearest part • *the front of the picture*
4 = promenade, parade, boulevard, prom, esplanade • *a stroll on the front*
5 = front line, trenches, vanguard, firing line, van • *Her husband is fighting at the front.*
6 = appearance, look, show, face, air, bearing, aspect, manner, expression, exterior, countenance, demeanour, mien • *He kept up a brave front.*
7 = disguise, cover, screen, blind, mask, cover-up, cloak, façade, pretext • *a front for crime syndicates*
▸ AS AN ADJECTIVE **1 = foremost**, at the front • *She is still missing her front teeth.*
OPPOSITES: back, behind, rear
2 = leading, first, lead, head, foremost, topmost, headmost • *He is the front runner for the star role.*
▸ AS A VERB **1** *often with* **on** *or* **onto = face onto**, overlook, look out on, have a view of, look over *or* onto • *Victorian houses fronting onto the pavement*
2 = lead, head, direct, command, head up • *He fronted a formidable band of guerilla fighters.*
▸ IN PHRASES: **in front = in advance**, first, before, leading, ahead, preceding, in the lead, at the head, to the fore, in the van • *Polls show him out in front in the race.*
in front of 1 = facing, before • *She sat in front of her dressing-table mirror.*
2 = before, preceding • *Something darted out in front of my car.*
3 = in the presence of, before, in the sight of • *They never argued in front of their children.*
up front = in advance, earlier, beforehand, ahead of time • *They'll be prepared to pay cash up front.*

frontier = border, limit, edge, bound, boundary, confines, verge, perimeter, borderline, dividing line, borderland, marches • *It wasn't difficult to cross the frontier.*

frost = hoarfrost, freeze, freeze-up, Jack Frost, rime • *There is a frost in the ground.*

frosty 1 = cold, frozen, icy, chilly, wintry, parky (*Brit. informal*) • *sharp, frosty nights*
2 = icy, ice-capped, icicled, hoar (*rare*), rimy • *a cat lifting its paws off the frosty stones*
3 = unfriendly, cold, discouraging, icy, chilly, frigid, off-putting (*Brit. informal*), unenthusiastic, unwelcoming, standoffish, cold as ice • *He may get a frosty reception.*

froth AS A NOUN **1 = foam**, head, bubbles, lather, suds, spume, effervescence, scum • *the froth on the top of a glass of beer*
2 = trivia, trifles, frivolity, trivialities, pettiness, irrelevancies • *no substance at all, just froth*
▸ AS A VERB **= fizz**, foam, come to a head, lather, bubble over, effervesce • *The sea froths over my feet.*

frothy 1 = foamy, foaming, bubbly, effervescent, sudsy, spumous, spumescent, spumy • *frothy milk shakes*
2 = frilly, fancy, ruffled, lacy, ruched, flouncy • *I'd feel silly in a big white frothy dress.*
3 = trivial, light, empty, slight, unnecessary, vain, petty, trifling, frivolous, frilly, unsubstantial • *the kind of frothy songs one hears*

frown AS A VERB **= glare**, scowl, glower, make a face, look daggers, knit your brows, give a dirty look, lour *or* lower • *He frowned at her anxiously.*
▸ IN PHRASES: **frown on = disapprove of**, dislike, discourage, take a dim view of, look askance at, discountenance, view with disfavour, not take kindly to, show disapproval *or* displeasure • *This practice is frowned upon as being wasteful.*
▸ AS A NOUN **= scowl**, glare, glower, dirty look • *a deep frown on the boy's face*

frozen 1 = icy, hard, solid, frosted, arctic, ice-covered, icebound • *the frozen bleakness of the Far North*
2 = chilled, cold, iced, refrigerated, ice-cold • *frozen desserts like ice cream*
3 = ice-cold, freezing, numb, very cold, frigid, frozen stiff, chilled to the marrow • *I'm frozen out here.*
4 = motionless, rooted, petrified, stock-still, turned to stone, stopped dead in your tracks • *She was frozen in horror.*
5 = fixed, held, stopped, limited, suspended, pegged (*of a price*) • *Prices would be frozen and wages raised.*

frugal 1 = thrifty, sparing, careful, prudent, provident, parsimonious, abstemious, penny-wise, saving, cheeseparing • *She lives a frugal life.*
OPPOSITES: excessive, lavish, wasteful
2 = meagre, economical, niggardly • *Her diet was frugal.*

frugality = thrift, economy, conservation, moderation, providence, good management, husbandry, economizing, carefulness, thriftiness • *We must practise frugality and economy.*

fruit 1 = produce, crop, yield, harvest • *The fruit has got a long storage life.*
2 *often plural* **= result**, reward, outcome, end result, return, effect, benefit, profit, advantage, consequence • *The findings are the fruit of more than three years research.*

QUOTATIONS
A good tree cannot bring forth evil fruit, neither can a corrupt tree bring forth good fruit
[*Bible: St. Matthew*]

PROVERBS
He that would eat the fruit must climb the tree

▹ *See panel* **Fruits**

fruitful 1 = useful, successful, effective, rewarding, profitable, productive, worthwhile, beneficial, advantageous, well-spent, win-win, gainful • *We had a long, fruitful relationship.*
OPPOSITES: useless, vain, pointless
2 = fertile, fecund, fructiferous • *a landscape that was fruitful and lush*
OPPOSITES: barren, sterile, fruitless
3 = productive, prolific, abundant, plentiful, rich, flush, spawning, copious, profuse, plenteous • *blossoms on a fruitful tree*

fruition = fulfilment, maturity, completion, perfection, enjoyment, realization, attainment, maturation, consummation, ripeness, actualization, materialization • *The plans take time to come to fruition.*

fruitless = useless, vain, unsuccessful, in vain, pointless, futile, unproductive, abortive, to no avail, ineffectual, unprofitable, to no effect, unavailing, unfruitful, profitless, bootless • *It was a fruitless search.*
OPPOSITES: effective, useful, fruitful

fruity 1 = rich, full, mellow • *a lovely, fruity wine*
2 = resonant, full, deep, rich, vibrant, mellow • *He had a solid, fruity laugh.*
3 = risqué, indecent, suggestive, racy, blue, hot, sexy, ripe, spicy (*informal*), vulgar, juicy, titillating, bawdy, salacious, smutty, indelicate, near the knuckle (*informal*) • *She clearly enjoyed the fruity joke.*

frumpy *or* **frumpish = dowdy**, dated, dreary, out of date, drab, unfashionable, dingy, mumsy, badly-dressed, unhip (*slang*) • *I looked so frumpy next to those women.*

frustrate 1 = discourage, anger, depress, annoy, infuriate, exasperate, dishearten, dissatisfy • *These questions frustrated me.*
OPPOSITES: encourage, cheer, hearten
2 = thwart, stop, check, block, defeat, disappoint, counter, confront, spoil, foil, baffle, inhibit, hobble, balk, circumvent,

FRUITS

ananas
anchovy pear
apple
apricot
avocado, avocado pear, *or (U.S.)* alligator pear
babaco
banana
Bartlett pear
beach plum
bergamot pear
berry
Beurre Hardy pear
bigarreau cherry
bilberry, blaeberry, huckleberry, whortleberry, *or (Irish)* fraughan
blackberry *or (Scot.)* bramble
black cherry
blackcurrant
blackheart cherry
blood orange
blueberry
Bon Chretien pear
boxberry
boysenberry
breadfruit
calamondin
cantaloup *or* cantaloupe melon
carambola *or* star fruit
casaba *or* cassaba melon
Charentais melon
chayote
chempaduk
cherry
chokecherry
choko
citron
clementine
cloudberry *or (Canad.)* bakeapple
Concord grape
Conference pear
cranberry
custard apple
damson
date
dewberry
durian
elderberry
fig
Galia melon
gooseberry *or (informal)* goosegog
grape
grapefruit
greengage
guava
hackberry
heart cherry
honeydew melon
jackfruit *or* jack
Jaffa orange
kiwano *(trademark)*
Kiwi fruit *or* Chinese gooseberry
kumquat
lemon
lime
lychee
loganberry
longan
loquat *or* Japan plum
mandarin
mango
mangosteen
May apple
medlar
melon
minneola
morello cherry
mulberry
muskmelon
nashi *or* Asian pear
navel orange
nectarine
Ogen melon
olive
orange
ortanique
papaw
papaya
passion fruit *or* granadilla
peach
pear
pepper
physalis, Cape gooseberry, *or* strawberry tomato
pineapple
plantain
plum
pomegranate
pomelo *or* shaddock
prickly pear
prune
pumpkin
Queensland blue
quince
raisin
rambutan
raspberry
redcurrant
rockmelon
salmonberry
sapota
sapodilla, sapodilla plum, *or* naseberry
saskatoon
satsuma
Seville orange
serviceberry
sharon fruit *or* persimmon
sloe
snowberry
sour cherry
sour gourd
soursop
star-apple
strawberry
sultana
sweet cherry
sweetie
sweetsop
tamarillo *or* tree tomato
tamarind
tangelo
tangerine *or (S. African)* naartje
tayberry
tomato *or (archaic)* love apple
UGLI *(trademark)*
victoria *or* victoria plum
watermelon
white currant
Williams pear
wintermelon
youngberry

forestall, neutralize, stymie, nullify, render null and void, crool *or* cruel *(Austral. slang)* • *The government has deliberately frustrated his efforts.*
OPPOSITES: further, forward, encourage

frustrated = **disappointed**, discouraged, infuriated, discontented, exasperated, resentful, embittered, irked, disheartened, carrying a chip on your shoulder *(informal)* • *She felt frustrated and angry.*

frustration 1 = **annoyance**, disappointment, resentment, irritation, grievance, dissatisfaction, exasperation, vexation • *a man fed up with the frustrations of everyday life*
2 = **obstruction**, blocking, curbing, foiling, failure, spoiling, thwarting, contravention, circumvention, nonfulfilment, nonsuccess • *the frustration of their plan*

fuddy-duddy = **conservative**, square *(informal)*, dinosaur, fossil, dodo *(informal)*, museum piece, stick-in-the-mud *(informal)*, stuffed shirt *(informal)*, back number *(informal)*, (old) fogey • *We didn't want all those old fuddy-duddies around.*

fudge = **misrepresent**, avoid, dodge, evade, hedge, stall, fake, flannel *(Brit. informal)*, patch up, falsify, equivocate • *certain issues that can no longer be fudged*

fuel AS A NOUN 1 = **petrol**, oil, gas, gasoline *(U.S.)*, source of energy, propellant, diesel oil • *They ran out of fuel.*
2 = **wood**, coal, logs, firewood, kindling • *I fetched more fuel for the fire.*
3 = **nourishment**, food, kai *(N.Z. informal)*, sustenance • *Babies and toddlers need fuel for growth.*
4 = **incitement**, encouragement, ammunition, provocation, food, material, incentive, fodder • *His comments are bound to add fuel to the debate.*
▸ AS A VERB = **inflame**, power, charge, fire, fan, encourage, feed, boost, sustain, stimulate, nourish, incite, whip up, stoke up • *The economic boom was fuelled by easy credit.*

fug = **stale air**, stink, reek, staleness, fustiness, fetidity, fetor, frowst, frowstiness • *the fug of cigarette smoke*

fugitive AS A NOUN = **runaway**, refugee, deserter, escapee, runagate *(archaic)* • *He was a fugitive from justice.*
▸ AS AN ADJECTIVE = **momentary**, short, passing, brief, fleeing, temporary, fleeting, unstable, short-lived, transient, flitting, ephemeral, transitory, evanescent, fugacious, flying • *Love is as fugitive and insubstantial as smoke, yet we all pursue it.*

fulcrum 1 = **pivot**, centre, heart, hinge, hub, focal point, kingpin • *The decision is the fulcrum of the Budget.*
2 = **axis**, swivel, pivot, axle, spindle • *The metal bar served as a fulcrum.*

fulfil *or (U.S.)* **fullfil** 1 = **carry out**, perform, execute, discharge, keep, effect, finish, complete, achieve, conclude, accomplish, bring to completion • *He is too ill to fulfil his duties.*
OPPOSITES: neglect, fail in, fall short of
2 = **achieve**, realize, satisfy, attain, consummate, bring to fruition, perfect • *He decided to fulfil his dream and go to college.*
3 = **satisfy**, please, content, cheer, refresh, gratify, make happy • *After the war, nothing quite fulfilled her.*
4 = **comply with**, meet, fill, satisfy, observe, obey, conform to, answer • *All the necessary conditions were fulfilled.*

fulfilled = **satisfied**, happy, pleased, content, contented, gratified • *I feel more fulfilled doing this than ever before.*

fulfilment *or (U.S.)* **fullfilment** = **achievement**, effecting, implementation, carrying out *or* through, end, crowning, discharge, discharging, completion, perfection, accomplishment, realization, attainment, observance, consummation • *I will allow no hesitation in the fulfilment of the reforms.*

full AS AN ADJECTIVE 1 = **filled**, stocked, brimming, replete, complete, entire, loaded, sufficient, intact, gorged, saturated, bursting at the seams, brimful • *Repeat the layers until the terrine is full.*
2 = **crammed**, crowded, packed, crushed, jammed, in use, congested, chock-full, chock-a-block • *The centre is full beyond capacity.*
OPPOSITES: empty, blank, vacant

3 = **occupied**, taken, in use, unavailable • *The cheap seats were all full.*
4 = **satiated**, satisfied, having had enough, replete, sated • *It's healthy to stop eating when I'm full.*
5 *often with* **of** *or* **with** = **bursting**, packed, teeming, abounding, jammed, swarming • *A day full of entertainment.*
6 = **extensive**, detailed, complete, broad, generous, adequate, ample, abundant, plentiful, copious, plenary, plenteous • *Full details will be sent to you.*
OPPOSITES: limited, partial, incomplete
7 = **maximum**, highest, greatest, top, utmost • *He revved the engine to full power.*
8 = **comprehensive**, complete, thorough, exhaustive, all-inclusive, all-embracing, unabridged • *They can now publish a full list of candidates.*
9 = **eventful**, exciting, active, busy, lively, energetic • *You will have a very full and interesting life.*
10 = **rounded**, strong, rich, powerful, intense, pungent • *Italian plum tomatoes have a full flavour.*
11 = **plump**, rounded, voluptuous, shapely, well-rounded, buxom, curvaceous • *large sizes for ladies with a fuller figure*
12 = **voluminous**, large, loose, baggy, billowing, puffy, capacious, loose-fitting, balloon-like • *My wedding dress has a very full skirt.*
OPPOSITES: tight, restricted
13 = **rich**, strong, deep, loud, distinct, resonant, sonorous, clear • *She has a full voice, mine is a bit lighter.*
OPPOSITES: thin, faint
▸ **AS AN ADVERB** = **directly**, right, straight, square, squarely, bang *(informal)*, slap bang *(informal)* • *She looked him full in the face.*
▸ **IN PHRASES: full of yourself** = **pleased with yourself**, cocky, self-confident, overconfident, too clever by half • *He's full of himself.*
in full = **completely**, fully, in total, without exception, in its entirety, in toto *(Latin)* • *We will refund your money in full.*
to the full = **thoroughly**, completely, fully, entirely, to the limit, without reservation, to the utmost • *She has a good mind which should be used to the full.*

full-blooded = **wholehearted**, full, complete, sweeping, thorough, uncompromising, exhaustive, all-embracing • *Full-blooded market reform is the only way to save the economy.*

full-blown 1 = **fully developed**, total, full-scale, fully fledged, full, whole, developed, complete, advanced, entire, full-sized, fully grown, fully formed • *You're talking this thing up into a full-blown conspiracy.*
OPPOSITES: potential, dormant, undeveloped
2 = **in full bloom**, full, flowering, unfolded, blossoming, opened out • *the faded hues of full-blown roses*

full-bodied = **rich**, strong, big, heavy, heady, mellow, fruity, redolent, full-flavoured, well-matured • *richly scented, full-bodied wines*

full-grown = **adult**, developed, mature, grown-up, of age, ripe, full-fledged, in your prime • *a full-grown male orang-utan*
OPPOSITES: young, green

fullness *or (U.S.)* **fulness** **AS A NOUN** 1 = **plenty**, glut, saturation, sufficiency, profusion, satiety, repletion, copiousness, ampleness, adequateness • *High fibre diets give the feeling of fullness.*
2 = **completeness**, wealth, entirety, totality, wholeness, vastness, plenitude, comprehensiveness, broadness, extensiveness • *She displayed the fullness of her cycling talent.*
3 = **roundness**, voluptuousness, curvaceousness, swelling, enlargement, dilation, distension, tumescence • *I accept my body with all its womanly fullness.*
4 = **richness**, strength, resonance, loudness, clearness • *with modest riffs and a fullness in sound*
▸ **IN PHRASES: in the fullness of time** = **eventually**, finally, one day, after all, some time, in the end, ultimately, at the end of the day, in the long run, sooner or later, some day, when all is said and done, in the course of time • *a mystery that will be revealed in the fullness of time*

full-scale 1 = **major**, extensive, wide-ranging, all-out, sweeping, comprehensive, proper, thorough, in-depth, exhaustive, all-encompassing, thoroughgoing, full-dress • *the possibility of a full-scale nuclear war*
2 = **full-size**, full-sized, life-size • *working, full-scale prototypes*

fully 1 = **completely**, totally, perfectly, entirely, absolutely, altogether, thoroughly, intimately, wholly, positively, utterly, every inch, heart and soul, to the hilt, one hundred per cent, in all respects, from first to last, lock, stock and barrel • *She was fully aware of my thoughts.*
2 = **in all respects**, completely, totally, entirely, altogether, thoroughly, wholly • *He had still not fully recovered.*
3 = **adequately**, amply, comprehensively, sufficiently, enough, satisfactorily, abundantly, plentifully • *These debates are discussed fully later in the book.*
4 = **at least**, quite, without (any) exaggeration, without a word of a lie *(informal)* • *He set his sights and let fly from fully 35 yards.*

fully-fledged *or* **full-fledged** = **experienced**, trained, senior, professional, qualified, mature, proficient, time-served • *One day I would be a fully-fledged musician.*

fulminate *often with* **against** = **criticize**, rage, curse, denounce, put down, thunder, fume, protest against, censure, berate, castigate, rail against, vilify, tear into *(informal)*, flame *(informal)*, blast, diss *(slang, chiefly U.S.)*, upbraid, inveigh against, reprobate, lambast(e), excoriate, execrate, vituperate, animadvert upon, denunciate • *They all fulminated against the new curriculum.*

fulsome = **extravagant**, excessive, over the top, sickening, overdone, fawning, nauseating, inordinate, ingratiating, cloying, insincere, saccharine, sycophantic, unctuous, smarmy *(Brit. informal)*, immoderate, adulatory, gross • *They have been fulsome in their praise.*

fumble **AS A VERB** 1 *often with* **for** *or* **with** = **grope**, flounder, paw *(informal)*, scrabble, feel around • *She crept from the bed and fumbled for her dressing gown.*
2 = **stumble**, struggle, blunder, flounder, bumble • *I fumbled around like an idiot.*
3 = **bungle**, spoil, botch, mess up, cock up *(Brit. slang)*, mishandle, fuck up *(offensive taboo slang)*, mismanage, muff, make a hash of *(informal)*, make a nonsense of, bodge *(informal)*, misfield, crool *or* cruel *(Austral. slang)* • *I'd hate to fumble a chance like this.*
▸ **AS A NOUN** = **miss**, mistake, slip, fault, error, blunder, botch, cock-up *(slang)*, bodge *(informal)*, barry *or* Barry Crocker *(Austral. slang)* • *Fans cheered a fumble by the home team's star.*

fume **AS A VERB** = **rage**, boil, seethe, see red *(informal)*, storm, rave, rant, smoulder, crack up *(informal)*, go ballistic *(slang, chiefly U.S.)*, champ at the bit *(informal)*, blow a fuse *(slang, chiefly U.S.)*, fly off the handle *(informal)*, get hot under the collar *(informal)*, go off the deep end *(informal)*, wig out *(slang)*, go up the wall *(slang)*, get steamed up about *(slang)* • *I fumed when these women did not respond.*
▸ **AS A NOUN** 1 *often plural* = **smoke**, gas, exhaust, pollution, haze, vapour, smog, miasma, exhalation, effluvium • *car exhaust fumes*
2 = **stench**, stink, whiff *(Brit. slang)*, reek, pong *(Brit. informal)*, foul smell, niff *(Brit. slang)*, malodour, mephitis, fetor, noisomeness • *stale alcohol fumes*

fumigate = **disinfect**, cleanse, purify, sterilize, sanitize, clean out *or* up • *I'm going to fumigate the greenhouse.*

fuming = **furious**, angry, raging, choked, roused, incensed, enraged, seething, pissed off *(taboo slang)*, up in arms, incandescent, in a rage, on the warpath *(informal)*, foaming at the mouth, at boiling point *(informal)*, all steamed up *(slang)*, tooshie *(Austral. slang)* • *He was still fuming over the remark.*

fun AS A NOUN 1 = **amusement**, sport, treat, pleasure, entertainment, cheer, good time, recreation, enjoyment, romp, distraction, diversion, frolic, junketing, merriment, whoopee *(informal)*, high jinks, living it up, jollity, beer and skittles *(informal)*, merrymaking, jollification • *You still have time to join in the fun.*
2 = **joking**, clowning, merriment, playfulness, play, game, sport, nonsense, teasing, jesting, skylarking *(informal)*, horseplay, buffoonery, tomfoolery, jocularity, foolery • *There was lots of fun going on last night.*
3 = **enjoyment**, pleasure, joy, cheer, mirth, gaiety • *She had a great sense of fun.*
OPPOSITES: depression, distress, gloom
4 = **ridicule**, contempt, taunting, scorn, sneering, mockery, derision • *I thought he was a figure of fun.*
▸ AS A MODIFIER = **enjoyable**, entertaining, pleasant, amusing, lively, diverting, witty, convivial • *It was a fun evening.*
▸ IN PHRASES: **for** *or* **in fun** = **for a joke**, tongue in cheek, jokingly, playfully, for a laugh, mischievously, in jest, teasingly, with a straight face, facetiously, light-heartedly, roguishly, with a gleam *or* twinkle in your eye • *Don't say such things, even in fun.*
fun and games = **horseplay**, clowning, romping, pranks, fooling around, rough-and-tumble, junketing, revelry, skylarking *(informal)*, high jinks, jollity, buffoonery, merrymaking • *Their fun and games hurt a lot of people.*
make fun of something *or* **someone** = **mock**, tease, ridicule, poke fun at, take off, rag, rib *(informal)*, laugh at, taunt, mimic, parody, deride, send up *(Brit. informal)*, scoff at, sneer at, lampoon, make a fool of, pour scorn on, take the mickey out of *(Brit. informal)*, take the piss out of *(taboo slang)*, satirize, pull someone's leg, hold up to ridicule, make a monkey of, make sport of, make the butt of, make game of • *Don't make fun of me!*

QUOTATIONS
That [sex] was the most fun I've ever had without laughing
[Woody Allen *Annie Hall*]

function AS A NOUN 1 = **purpose**, business, job, concern, use, part, office, charge, role, post, operation, situation, activity, exercise, responsibility, task, duty, mission, employment, capacity, province, occupation, raison d'être *(French)* • *The main function of merchant banks is to raise capital.*
2 = **result**, effect, consequence, outcome, end result • *Your success will be a function of how well you can work.*
3 = **reception**, party, affair, gathering, bash *(informal)*, lig *(Brit. slang)*, social occasion, soiree, do *(informal)* • *We were going down to a function in London.*
▸ AS A VERB 1 = **work**, run, operate, perform, be in business, be in running order, be in operation *or* action, go • *The authorities say the prison is now functioning properly.*
2 *with* **as** = **act**, serve, operate, perform, behave, officiate, act the part of, do duty, have the role of, be in commission, be in operation *or* action, serve your turn • *On weekdays, one third of the room functions as a workspace.*

functional 1 = **practical**, utility, utilitarian, serviceable, hard-wearing, useful • *The decor is functional.*
2 = **working**, operative, operational, in working order, going, prepared, ready, viable, up and running, workable, usable • *We have fully functional smoke alarms on all staircases.*

functionary = **officer**, official, dignitary, office holder, office bearer, employee • *a properly elected state functionary*

fund AS A NOUN 1 = **reserve**, trust, stock, supply, store, collection, pool, foundation, endowment, tontine • *a scholarship fund for undergraduate students*
2 = **store**, stock, source, supply, mine, reserve, treasury, vein, reservoir, accumulation, hoard, repository • *He has an extraordinary fund of energy.*
▸ AS A VERB = **finance**, back, support, pay for, promote, float, endow, subsidize, stake, capitalize, provide money for, put up the money for • *The foundation has funded a variety of faculty programs.*
▸ IN PHRASES: **in funds** = **finance**, flush *(informal)*, in the black, solvent, well-off, well-supplied • *I'll pay you back as soon as I'm in funds again.*

fundamental 1 = **central**, first, most important, prime, key, necessary, basic, essential, primary, vital, radical, principal, cardinal, integral, indispensable, intrinsic • *the fundamental principles of democracy*
OPPOSITES: extra, advanced, incidental
2 = **basic**, essential, underlying, organic, profound, elementary, rudimentary • *The two leaders have very fundamental differences.*

fundamentally 1 = **basically**, at heart, at bottom • *Fundamentally, women like him for his sensitivity.*
2 = **essentially**, radically, basically, primarily, profoundly, intrinsically • *He disagreed fundamentally with her judgement.*

fundamentals = **basics**, laws, rules, principles, essentials, cornerstones, axioms, first principles, rudiments, sine qua non *(Latin)* • *teaching small children the fundamentals of road safety*

fundi = **expert**, authority, specialist, professional, master, pro *(informal)*, ace *(informal)*, genius, guru, pundit, buff *(informal)*, maestro, virtuoso, boffin *(Brit. informal)*, hotshot *(informal)*, past master, dab hand *(Brit. informal)*, wonk *(informal)*, maven *(U.S.)* • *The local fundi are wonderfully adept and have created a car adapted to hunting.*

funds = **money**, capital, cash, finance, means, savings, necessary *(informal)*, resources, assets, silver, bread *(slang)*, wealth, tin *(slang)*, brass *(Northern English dialect)*, dough *(slang)*, rhino *(Brit. slang)*, the ready *(informal)*, dosh *(Brit. & Austral. slang)*, hard cash, the wherewithal, needful *(informal)*, shekels *(informal)*, dibs *(slang)*, ready money, ackers *(slang)*, spondulicks *(slang)* • *The concert will raise funds for Aids research.*

funeral = **burial**, committal, laying to rest, cremation, interment, obsequies, entombment, inhumation • *He was given a state funeral.*

funereal = **gloomy**, dark, sad, grave, depressing, dismal, lamenting, solemn, dreary, sombre, woeful, mournful, lugubrious, sepulchral, dirge-like, deathlike • *He addressed the group in funereal tones.*

fungus = **mould**, mushroom, decay, mildew, toadstool • *The spores of the fungus are able to germinate in oil.*

FUNGI

agaric	jelly fungus	sickener
bird's-nest fungus	horn of plenty	smut
boletus	liberty cap	stinkhorn
bracket fungus	mildew	sulphur tuft
cramp ball	milk cap	toadstool
death cap	miller	truffle
dry rot	mould	velvet shank
earthstar	mushroom	wax cap
elf-cup	puffball	wet rot
ergot	rust *or* rust fungus	wood hedgehog
funnel cap		wood woollyfoot
ink-cap	shaggy cap	yeast

funk = **chicken out of**, dodge, recoil from, take fright, flinch from, duck out of *(informal)*, turn tail *(informal)* • *When the time came I funked it.*

funnel AS A NOUN **1 = pipe**, tube, pipeline, duct • *Use a funnel to re-fuel.*
2 = chimney, shaft, vent, flue • *a ship with three masts and two funnels*
▸ AS A VERB **1 = conduct**, direct, channel, convey, move, pass, pour, filter • *This device funnels the water from a downpipe into a butt.*
2 = channel, direct, pour, filter, convey • *The centre will funnel money into research.*

funny AS AN ADJECTIVE **1 = humorous**, amusing, comical, entertaining, killing *(informal)*, rich, comic, silly, ridiculous, diverting, absurd, jolly, witty, hilarious, ludicrous, laughable, farcical, slapstick, riotous, droll, risible, facetious, jocular, side-splitting, waggish, jocose • *I'll tell you a funny story.*
OPPOSITES: serious, grave, unfunny
2 = comic, comical, a scream, a card *(informal)*, a caution *(informal)* • *He could be funny when he wanted to be.*
3 = peculiar, odd, strange, unusual, remarkable, bizarre, puzzling, curious, weird, mysterious, suspicious, dubious, queer, rum *(Brit. slang)*, quirky, perplexing • *There's something funny about him.*
4 = ill, poorly *(informal)*, queasy, sick, odd, crook *(Austral. & N.Z. informal)*, ailing, queer, unhealthy, seedy *(informal)*, unwell, out of sorts *(informal)*, off-colour *(informal)*, under the weather *(informal)* • *My head ached and my stomach felt funny.*
▸ AS A NOUN **= joke** *(informal)*, crack *(slang)*, quip, pun, jest, wisecrack, witticism, play on words • *When I played against him, he kept cracking funnies all the time.*

fur = coat, hair, skin, hide, wool, fleece, pelt • *The creature's fur is short and dense.*
▸ RELATED MANIA: doramania
▸ RELATED PHOBIA: doraphobia

furious 1 = angry, mad, raging, boiling, fuming, choked, frantic, pissed *(Brit., Austral. & N.Z. slang)*, frenzied, infuriated, incensed, enraged, maddened, inflamed, very angry, cross, pissed off *(taboo slang)*, livid *(informal)*, up in arms, incandescent, on the warpath *(informal)*, foaming at the mouth, wrathful, in high dudgeon, wroth *(archaic)*, fit to be tied *(slang)*, beside yourself, tooshie *(Austral. slang)* • *He is furious at the way his wife has been treated.*
OPPOSITES: pleased, calm, mild
2 = violent, wild, intense, fierce, savage, turbulent, stormy, agitated, boisterous, tumultuous, vehement, unrestrained, tempestuous, impetuous, ungovernable • *A furious gunbattle ensued.*

furnish 1 = decorate, fit, fit out, appoint, provide, stock, supply, store, provision, outfit, equip, fit up, purvey • *Many proprietors try to furnish their hotels with antiques.*
2 = supply, give, offer, provide, present, reveal, grant, afford, hand out, endow, bestow • *They'll be able to furnish you with the details.*

furniture = household goods, furnishings, fittings, house fittings, goods, things *(informal)*, effects, equipment, appointments, possessions, appliances, chattels, movable property, movables • *Each piece of furniture suited their style of house.*
▹ *See panel* **Furniture**

furore *or (U.S.)* **furor = commotion**, to-do, stir, excitement, fury, disturbance, flap *(informal)*, outburst, frenzy, outcry, uproar, brouhaha, hullabaloo • *an international furore over the plan*

furrow AS A NOUN **1 = groove**, line, channel, hollow, trench, seam, crease, fluting, rut, corrugation • *Bike trails crisscrossed the grassy furrows.*
2 = wrinkle, line, crease, crinkle, crow's-foot, gather, fold, crumple, rumple, pucker, corrugation • *Deep furrows marked the corner of his mouth.*
▸ AS A VERB **= wrinkle**, knit, draw together, crease, seam, flute, corrugate • *My bank manager furrowed his brow.*

furry = hairy, woolly, shaggy, downy, fleecy • *thick furry tails*

further AS AN ADVERB **1 = more distant** • *Now we live further away from the city centre.*
2 = more, to a greater extent, to a greater degree • *These skills are explained further under Key Concept 4.*
3 = in addition, moreover, besides, furthermore, also, yet, on top of, what's more, to boot, additionally, over and above, as well as, into the bargain • *Further, losing one day doesn't mean you won't win the next.*
▸ AS AN ADJECTIVE **1 = additional**, more, new, other, extra, fresh, supplementary • *There was nothing further to be done.*
2 = remote, distant, more distant, more remote • *people from the further reaches of our district*
▸ AS A VERB **= promote**, help, develop, aid, forward, champion,

FURNITURE

TYPES OF FURNITURE

bedpost	coatstand	girandole	hatstand	longcase clock	umbrella stand
bedstead	dumbwaiter	grandfather clock	headboard	screen	vanitory *or* vanity unit
canopy	epergne	grandmother clock	lectern	tester	washstand
cheval glass	footstool	hallstand	litter	trolley	

FURNITURE STYLES

Art Deco	Empire	Louis Quatorze	New Georgian	Restoration	Victorian
Bauhaus	Georgian	Louis Quinze	Norman	Saxon	William and Mary
Cape Dutch	Gothic	Louis Seize	Puritan	Second Empire	
Edwardian	Greek Revival	Louis Treize	Queen Anne	Shaker	
Elizabethan	Jacobean	Medieval	Regency	Tudor	

FURNITURE DESIGNERS

Alvar Aalto *(Finnish)*	Charles Eames *(U.S.)*	Daniel Marot *(French)*
Robert Adam *(Scottish)*	Ambrose Heal *(English)*	William Morris *(English)*
Harry Bertoia *(Italian)*	George Hepplewhite *(English)*	Michael Angelo Pergolesi *(Italian)*
Charles Bevan *(English)*	Inigo Jones *(English)*	Duncan Phyfe *(Scottish-U.S.)*
Marcel Lajos Breuer *(Hungarian-U.S.)*	William Jones *(English)*	Augustus Pugin *(English)*
William Burges *(English)*	William Kent *(English)*	Thomas Sheraton *(English)*
Thomas Chippendale *(English)*	Kaara Klint *(Danish)*	George Smith *(English)*
Donald Deskey *(U.S.)*	Charles Rennie Mackintosh *(Scottish)*	Charles Voysey *(English)*

push, encourage, speed, advance, work for, foster, contribute to, assist, plug *(informal)*, facilitate, pave the way for, hasten, fast-track, patronize, expedite, succour, lend support to • *Education needn't only be about furthering your career.*
OPPOSITES: stop, prevent, hinder
▸ **IN PHRASES: further from = less like**, more unlike • *She thought he was joking but nothing could be further from the truth.*

furtherance = **promotion**, backing, development, championship, carrying-out, boosting, prosecution, pursuit, advancement, advocacy • *The thing that matters is the furtherance of research.*

furthermore = **moreover**, further, in addition, besides, too, as well, not to mention, what's more, to boot, additionally, into the bargain • *Furthermore, I will have to know all the data.*

furthest = **most distant**, extreme, ultimate, remotest, outermost, uttermost, furthermost, outmost • *the furthest point from earth*

furtive = **sly**, secret, hidden, sneaking, covert, cloaked, behind someone's back, secretive, clandestine, sneaky, under-the-table, slinking, conspiratorial, skulking, underhand, surreptitious, stealthy • *a furtive glance over her shoulder*
OPPOSITES: open, public, frank

fury **1 = anger**, passion, rage, madness, frenzy, wrath, ire, red mist *(informal)*, impetuosity • *She screamed, her face distorted with fury.*
OPPOSITES: calm, composure, calmness
2 = violence, force, power, intensity, severity, turbulence, ferocity, savagery, vehemence, fierceness, tempestuousness • *We were lashed by the full fury of the elements.*
OPPOSITES: peace, hush, serenity

fuse **1 = join**, unite, combine, blend, integrate, merge, put together, dissolve, amalgamate, federate, coalesce, intermingle, meld, run together, commingle, intermix, agglutinate • *Conception occurs when a single sperm fuses with an egg.*
OPPOSITES: separate, spread, scatter
2 = bond, join, stick, melt, weld, smelt, solder • *They all fuse into a glassy state.*

fusillade = **barrage**, fire, burst, hail, volley, outburst, salvo, broadside • *Both were killed in a fusillade of bullets.*

fusion = **merging**, uniting, union, merger, federation, mixture, blend, blending, integration, synthesis, amalgamation, coalescence, commingling, commixture

fuss **AS A NOUN** **1 = commotion**, to-do, worry, upset, bother, stir, confusion, excitement, hurry, flap *(informal)*, bustle, flutter, flurry, agitation, fidget, fluster, ado, hue and cry, palaver, storm in a teacup *(Brit.)*, pother • *I don't know what all the fuss is about.*
2 = bother, trouble, struggle, hassle *(informal)*, nuisance, inconvenience, hindrance • *He gets down to work without any fuss.*
3 = complaint, row, protest, objection, trouble, display, argument, difficulty, upset, bother, unrest, hassle *(informal)*, squabble, furore, altercation • *We kicked up a fuss and got an apology.*
▸ **AS A VERB = worry**, flap *(informal)*, bustle, fret, niggle, fidget, chafe, take pains, make a meal of *(informal)*, be agitated, labour over, get worked up, get in a stew *(informal)*, make a thing of *(informal)* • *She fussed about getting me a drink.*
▸ **IN PHRASES: make a fuss of something** *or* **someone = spoil**, indulge, pamper, cosset, coddle, mollycoddle, overindulge, kill with kindness • *My nephews made a big fuss of me.*

fussy **1 = particular**, difficult, exacting, discriminating, fastidious, dainty, squeamish, choosy *(informal)*, picky *(informal)*, nit-picking *(informal)*, hard to please, finicky, pernickety, faddish, faddy, anal retentive, old-maidish, old womanish, overparticular, nit-picky *(informal)* • *She's not fussy about her food.*
2 = overelaborate, busy, cluttered, rococo, overdecorated, overembellished • *We are not keen on floral patterns and fussy designs.*

fusty **1 = old-fashioned**, outdated, out-of-date, archaic, antiquated, passé, antediluvian, out of the ark *(informal)*, old-fogeyish • *What do you give a fusty, old bachelor who's got everything?*
2 = stale, stuffy, musty, frowsty, rank, damp, mouldy, mouldering, airless, malodorous, mildewed, mildewy, ill-smelling • *The bedroom she was given had a fusty grandeur.*

futile **1 = useless**, vain, unsuccessful, pointless, empty, hollow, in vain, worthless, barren, sterile, fruitless, forlorn, unproductive, abortive, to no avail, ineffectual, unprofitable, valueless, unavailing, otiose, profitless, nugatory, without rhyme or reason, bootless • *a futile attempt to ward off the blow*
OPPOSITES: successful, effective, useful
2 = trivial, pointless, trifling, unimportant • *She doesn't want to comment. It's too futile.*
OPPOSITES: important, significant

futility **1 = uselessness**, ineffectiveness, pointlessness, fruitlessness, emptiness, hollowness, spitting in the wind, bootlessness • *the injustice and futility of terrorism*
2 = triviality, vanity, pointlessness, unimportance • *a sense of the emptiness and futility of life*

QUOTATIONS
as futile as a clock in an empty house
[James Thurber]

future **AS A NOUN** **1 = time to come**, hereafter, what lies ahead • *He made plans for the future.*
2 = prospect, expectation, outlook • *She has a splendid future in the police force.*
▸ **AS AN ADJECTIVE = forthcoming**, to be, coming, later, expected, approaching, to come, succeeding, fated, ultimate, subsequent, destined, prospective, eventual, ensuing, impending, unborn, in the offing • *the future King and Queen*
OPPOSITES: late, former, past
▸ **IN PHRASES: in (the) future = after this**, in times to come • *I asked her to be more careful in future.*

QUOTATIONS
I never think of the future. It comes soon enough
[Albert Einstein]

fuzz **AS A NOUN = fluff**, down, hair, pile, fibre, nap, floss, lint • *He had a baby fuzz round his jaw.*
▸ **IN PHRASES: the fuzz = the police**, the law *(informal)*, the police force, the constabulary, the law enforcement agency, the boys in blue *(informal)*, the Old Bill *(slang)* • *The fuzz want to question you.*

fuzzy **1 = frizzy**, fluffy, woolly, downy, flossy, down-covered, linty, napped • *He is a fierce bearded character with fuzzy hair.*
2 = indistinct, faint, blurred, vague, distorted, unclear, shadowy, bleary, unfocused, out of focus, ill-defined • *a couple of fuzzy pictures*
OPPOSITES: clear, detailed, distinct
3 = unclear, confused, blurred, vague, imprecise, nebulous, ill-defined, indistinct • *The border between science fact and science fiction gets a bit fuzzy.*

Gg

gab AS A NOUN
▸ IN PHRASES: **the gift of the gab = eloquence**, fluency, expressiveness, way with words, persuasiveness, forcefulness • *They are naturally good salesmen with the gift of the gab.*

gad *usually with* **about** *or* **around = gallivant**, wander, roam, run around, ramble, rove, range, go walkabout *(Austral.)*, stravaig *(Scot. & Northern English dialect)* • *Don't think I'll just wait here for you while you gad about.*

gadget = device, thing, appliance, machine, tool, implement, invention, instrument, novelty, apparatus, gimmick, utensil, contraption *(informal)*, gizmo *(slang, chiefly U.S. & Canad.)*, contrivance • *a handy gadget for slicing vegetables*

gaffe = blunder, mistake, error, indiscretion, lapse, boob *(Brit. slang)*, slip-up *(informal)*, slip, howler, bloomer *(informal)*, clanger *(informal)*, faux pas, boo-boo *(informal)*, solecism, gaucherie, barry *or* Barry Crocker *(Austral. slang)* • *He made an embarrassing gaffe at the convention last weekend.*

QUOTATIONS
A gaffe is when a politician tells the truth
[Michael Kinsley]

gaffer *(Brit. informal)* **= boss**, manager, supervisor, superintendent, chief *(informal)*, foreman, super *(informal)*, overseer • *The gaffer told me I would playing on Saturday.*

gag[1] AS A NOUN **= muzzle**, tie, restraint • *His captors had put a gag of thick leather in his mouth.*
▸ AS A VERB **1 = silence**, muffle, muzzle, quieten, stifle, stop up • *I gagged him with a towel.*
2 = suppress, silence, subdue, muffle, curb, stifle, muzzle, quieten • *a journalist who claimed he was gagged by his bosses*
3 = retch, choke, heave • *I knelt by the toilet and gagged.*
▸ IN PHRASES: **be gagging for something** *or* **be gagging to do something = crave**, want, desire, long for, yearn for, be desperate for, cry out for *(informal)*, thirst for, hunger for, lust after, be eager for, be dying for, would give your eyeteeth for • *Men everywhere are gagging for a car like this.*

gag[2] **= joke**, crack *(slang)*, funny *(informal)*, quip, pun, jest, wisecrack *(informal)*, sally, witticism • *He made a gag about bald men.*

gaiety 1 = cheerfulness, glee, good humour, buoyancy, happiness, animation, exuberance, high spirits, elation, exhilaration, hilarity, merriment, joie de vivre *(French)*, good cheer, vivacity, jollity, liveliness, gladness, effervescence, light-heartedness, joyousness • *There was a bright, infectious gaiety in the children's laughter.*
OPPOSITES: misery, gloom, sadness
2 = merrymaking, celebration, revels, festivity, fun, mirth, revelry, conviviality, jollification, carousal • *The mood was one of laughter and gaiety.*

gaily 1 = cheerfully, happily, gleefully, brightly, blithely, merrily, joyfully, cheerily, jauntily, light-heartedly, chirpily *(informal)* • *She laughed gaily.*
2 = colourfully, brightly, vividly, flamboyantly, gaudily, brilliantly, flashily, showily • *gaily painted front doors*

gain AS A VERB **1 = acquire**, get, receive, achieve, earn, pick up, win, secure, collect, gather, obtain, build up, attain, glean, procure • *Students can gain valuable experience doing part-time work.*
2 = profit, make, earn, get, win, clear, land, score *(slang)*, achieve, net, bag, secure, collect, gather, realize, obtain, capture, acquire, bring in, harvest, attain, reap, glean, procure • *The company didn't disclose how much it expects to gain from the deal.*
OPPOSITES: lose, forfeit
3 = put on, increase in, gather, build up • *Some people gain weight after they give up smoking.*
4 = attain, earn, get, achieve, win, reach, get to, secure, obtain, acquire, arrive at, procure • *Passing exams is no longer enough to gain a place at university.*
▸ AS A NOUN **1 = rise**, increase, growth, advance, improvement, upsurge, upturn, increment, upswing • *House prices showed a gain of nearly 8% in June.*
2 = increase, rise, growth, addition, accretion • *Heavy consumption of alcohol produces rapid weight gain.*
3 = profit, income, earnings, proceeds, winnings, return, produce, benefit, advantage, yield, dividend, acquisition, attainment, lucre, emolument • *He buys art solely for financial gain.*
OPPOSITES: loss, forfeiture
▸ AS A PLURAL NOUN **= profits**, earnings, revenue, proceeds, winnings, takings, pickings, booty • *Investors will have their gains taxed as income in future.*
▸ IN PHRASES: **gain on something** *or* **someone = get nearer to**, close in on, approach, catch up with, narrow the gap on • *The car began to gain on the van.*
gain time = stall, delay, play for time, procrastinate, temporize, use delaying tactics • *I hoped to gain time by keeping him talking.*

gainful = profitable, rewarding, productive, lucrative, paying, useful, valuable, worthwhile, beneficial, fruitful, advantageous, expedient, win-win, remunerative, moneymaking • *a lack of opportunities for gainful employment*

gainsay = deny, dispute, disagree with, contradict, contravene, rebut, controvert • *There was no-one to gainsay this assertion.*
OPPOSITES: back, support, confirm

gait = walk, step, bearing, pace, stride, carriage, tread, manner of walking • *His gait was peculiarly awkward.*

gal = girl, woman, lady, female, bird *(slang)*, dame *(slang)*, chick *(slang)*, lass, damsel *(archaic)*, colleen *(Irish)*, lassie *(informal)*, wench, charlie *(Austral. slang)*, chook *(Austral. slang)* • *a Southern gal who wanted to make it in the movies*

gala AS A NOUN **= festival**, party, fête, celebration, carnival, festivity, pageant, jamboree • *a gala at the Royal Opera House*

▸ **AS AN ADJECTIVE** = **festive**, merry, joyous, joyful, celebratory, convivial, gay, festal • *I want to make her birthday a gala occasion.*

galaxy 1 = **star system**, solar system, nebula • *Astronomers have discovered a distant galaxy.*
2 = **array**, gathering, assembly, assemblage • *a galaxy of famous movie stars*
▸ **RELATED ADJECTIVE:** galactic

gale 1 = **storm**, hurricane, tornado, cyclone, whirlwind, blast, gust, typhoon, tempest, squall • *forecasts of fierce gales over the next few days*
2 = **outburst**, scream, roar, fit, storm, shout, burst, explosion, outbreak, howl, shriek, eruption, peal, paroxysm • *gales of laughter from the audience*

gall[1] 1 (*Informal*) = **impudence**, audacity, insolence, impertinence, face (*informal*), front, neck (*informal*), nerve (*informal*), sauce (*informal*), cheek (*informal*), brass (*informal*), boldness, chutzpah (*U.S. & Canad. informal*), effrontery, brass neck (*Brit. informal*), sauciness, brazenness, sassiness (*U.S. informal*) • *She had the gall to suggest that I might lend her the money.*
2 = **bitterness**, spite, hostility, malice, animosity, venom, bile, antipathy, spleen, enmity, acrimony, rancour, bad blood, animus, malevolence, sourness, malignity • *all gall and wormwood*

gall = **annoy**, provoke, irritate, aggravate (*informal*), get (*informal*), trouble, bother, disturb, plague, madden, ruffle, exasperate, nettle, vex, displease, irk, rile (*informal*), peeve (*informal*), get under your skin (*informal*), get on your nerves (*informal*), nark (*Brit., Austral. & N.Z. slang*), get up your nose (*informal*), give someone grief (*Brit. & S. African*), make your blood boil, piss you off (*taboo slang*), rub up the wrong way, get on your wick (*Brit. slang*), get your back up, put your back up, hack you off (*informal*) • *It was their smugness that galled her most.*

gall = **growth**, lump, excrescence • *The mites live within the galls that are formed on the plant.*

gallant 1 = **brave**, daring, bold, heroic, courageous, dashing, noble, manly, gritty, fearless, intrepid, valiant, plucky, doughty, dauntless, lion-hearted, valorous, manful, mettlesome • *gallant soldiers who gave their lives*
OPPOSITES: fearful, cowardly, ignoble
2 = **courteous**, mannerly, gentlemanly, polite, gracious, attentive, courtly, chivalrous • *He was a thoughtful, gallant and generous man.*
OPPOSITES: rude, churlish, discourteous

gallantry 1 = **bravery**, spirit, daring, courage, nerve, guts (*informal*), pluck, grit, heroism, mettle, boldness, manliness, valour, derring-do (*archaic*), fearlessness, intrepidity, valiance, courageousness, dauntlessness, doughtiness • *He was awarded a medal for his gallantry.*
OPPOSITES: spinelessness, cowardice
2 = **courtesy**, politeness, chivalry, attentiveness, graciousness, courtliness, gentlemanliness, courteousness • *He kissed her hand with old-fashioned gallantry.*
OPPOSITES: rudeness, discourtesy, churlishness

gallery 1 = **exhibition room**, museum, display room • *an art gallery*
2 = **passage**, hall, lobby, corridor, aisle, hallway, walkway, passageway, vestibule • *A crowd already filled the gallery.*
3 = **upper circle**, gods, balcony • *They had been forced to buy cheap tickets in the gallery.*

galley = **kitchen**, kitchenette, cookhouse • *The bo'sun was in the ship's galley brewing coffee.*

galling = **annoying**, provoking, irritating, aggravating (*informal*), disturbing, humiliating, maddening, exasperating, vexing, displeasing, rankling, irksome, vexatious, nettlesome • *It was especially galling to be criticised by this scoundrel.*

gallivant = **gad about**, wander, roam, run around, ramble, rove, range, go walkabout (*Austral.*), stravaig (*Scot. & Northern English dialect*) • *She shouldn't be gallivanting around filling her head with nonsense.*

gallop **AS A VERB** 1 = **run**, race, shoot, career, speed, bolt, stampede • *The horses galloped away.*
2 = **dash**, run, race, shoot, fly, career, speed, tear, rush, barrel (along) (*informal, chiefly U.S. & Canad.*), sprint, dart, zoom • *They were galloping around the garden playing football.*
3 = **boom**, increase, grow, develop, expand, thrive, flourish • *China's economy galloped ahead.*
▸ **IN PHRASES: at a gallop** = **swiftly**, fast, quickly, rapidly, hastily, briskly, hurriedly, with all speed, posthaste • *I read the book at a gallop.*

gallows = **scaffold**, gibbet • *They were hanged at Smithfield gallows.*

galore = **in abundance**, everywhere, to spare, all over the place, aplenty, in great numbers, in profusion, in great quantity, à gogo (*informal*) • *a popular resort with beaches galore*

galvanize = **stimulate**, encourage, inspire, prompt, move, fire, shock, excite, wake, stir, spur, provoke, startle, arouse, awaken, rouse, prod, jolt, kick-start, electrify, goad, impel, invigorate • *The appeal has galvanized them into taking positive action.*

gambit = **tactic**, move, policy, scheme, strategy, trick, device, manoeuvre, ploy, stratagem • *They said the plan was no more than a clever political gambit.*

gamble **AS A NOUN** 1 = **risk**, chance, venture, lottery, speculation, uncertainty, leap in the dark • *the President's risky gamble in calling an election*
OPPOSITES: certainty, safe bet, foregone conclusion
2 = **bet**, flutter (*informal*), punt (*chiefly Brit.*), wager • *My father-in-law likes a drink and the odd gamble.*
▸ **AS A VERB** 1 *often with* **on** = **take a chance**, back, speculate, take the plunge, stick your neck out (*informal*), put your faith *or* trust in • *Few firms will be prepared to gamble on new products.*
2 = **risk**, chance, stake, venture, hazard, wager • *Are you prepared to gamble your career on this matter?*
3 = **bet**, play, game, stake, speculate, back, punt, wager, put money on, have a flutter (*informal*), try your luck, put your shirt on, lay *or* make a bet • *John gambled heavily on the horses.*

gambler 1 = **better**, punter, backer • *The British are a nation of inveterate gamblers.*
2 = **risk-taker**, speculator • *Never afraid of failure, he was a gambler, ready to try anything.*

gambling = **betting**, gaming, punting, wagering • *The most characteristic form of English gambling is betting through a bookmaker.*

gambol = **frolic**, jump, hop, skip, romp, lark, caper, prance, cavort, frisk • *children gambolling in the fields*

game[1] **AS A NOUN** 1 = **pastime**, sport, activity, entertainment, recreation, distraction, amusement, diversion • *the game of hide-and-seek*
OPPOSITES: work, business, job
2 = **match**, meeting, event, competition, tournament, clash, contest, round, head-to-head • *We won three games against Australia.*
3 = **amusement**, joke, entertainment, diversion, lark • *Some people simply regard life as a game.*
4 = **activity**, business, line, situation, proceeding, enterprise, undertaking, occupation, pursuit • *She's new to this game, so go easy on her.*
5 = **wild animals** *or* **birds**, prey, quarry • *men who shoot game for food*
6 = **scheme**, plan, design, strategy, trick, plot, tactic, manoeuvre, dodge, ploy, scam, stratagem, fastie (*Austral. slang*) • *All right, what's your little game?*

▸ **AS AN ADJECTIVE** 1 = **willing**, prepared, ready, keen, eager, interested, inclined, disposed, up for it *(informal)*, desirous • *He said he's game for a similar challenge next year.*
2 = **brave**, courageous, dogged, spirited, daring, bold, persistent, gritty, fearless, feisty *(informal, chiefly U.S. & Canad.)*, persevering, intrepid, valiant, plucky, unflinching, dauntless, ballsy *(taboo slang)*, (as) game as Ned Kelly *(Austral. slang)* • *They were the only ones game enough to give it a try.*
OPPOSITES: fearful, cowardly, irresolute

QUOTATIONS
Play for more than you can afford to lose, and you will learn the game
[Winston Churchill]
It should be noted that children at play are not playing about; their games should be seen as their most serious-minded activity
[Montaigne *Essais*]
I am sorry I have not learned to play at cards. It is very useful in life; it generates kindness and consolidates society
[Dr. Johnson]
It's just a game – baseball – an amusement, a marginal thing, not an art, not a consequential metaphor for life, not a public trust
[Richard Ford *Stop Blaming Baseball*]
Life is a game in which the rules are constantly changing; nothing spoils a game more than those who take it seriously
[Quentin Crisp *Manners From Heaven*]

▹ *See panel* **Games**

game² = **lame**, injured, disabled, crippled, defective, bad, maimed, deformed, gammy *(Brit. slang)* • *a game leg*
gamut = **range**, series, collection, variety, lot, field, scale, sweep, catalogue, scope, compass, assortment • *I went through the whole gamut of emotions.*
gang 1 = **group**, crowd, pack, company, party, lot, band, crew *(informal)*, bunch, mob, horde • *He was attacked by a gang of youths.*
2 = **ring**, firm *(slang)*, organization, band, cell, mob, syndicate • *an underworld gang*
3 = **circle**, group, crowd, company, set, crew, fellowship, fraternity, posse *(slang)*, clique, coterie • *Come on over; we've got lots of the old gang here.*
4 = **squad**, team, troop, force, shift, dream team, troupe • *a gang of labourers*
gangling *or* **gangly** = **awkward**, skinny, angular, lanky, rangy, rawboned, loose-jointed, unco *(Austral. slang)* • *a gangling teenager dressed in jeans and trainers*
gangster = **hoodlum** *(chiefly U.S.)*, crook *(informal)*, thug, bandit, heavy *(slang)*, tough, hood *(U.S. slang)*, robber, gang member, face *(Brit. slang)*, mobster *(U.S. slang)*, racketeer, desperado, ruffian, brigand, wise guy *(U.S.)*, tsotsi *(S. African)* • *a well-known gangster with convictions for armed robbery*
gaol *see* **jail**
gap 1 = **opening**, space, hole, break, split, divide, crack, rent, breach, slot, vent, rift, aperture, cleft, chink, crevice, fissure, cranny, perforation, interstice • *the wind tearing through gaps in the window frames*
2 = **interval**, pause, recess, interruption, respite, lull, interlude, breathing space, hiatus, intermission, lacuna, entr'acte • *There followed a gap of four years.*
3 = **need**, demand, requirement, necessity • *He identified a gap in the market.*
4 = **difference**, gulf, contrast, disagreement, discrepancy, inconsistency, disparity, divergence • *the gap between the poor and the well-off*
gape 1 = **stare**, wonder, goggle, gawp *(Brit. slang)*, gawk • *She stopped what she was doing and gaped at me.*
2 = **open**, split, crack, yawn • *A hole gaped in the roof.*
gaping = **wide**, great, open, broad, vast, yawning, wide open, cavernous • *a gaping hole*
garage 1 = **lock-up**, car port • *Does the house have a garage?*
2 = **service station**, petrol station • *We'd better stop by at the garage for some petrol.*
garb **AS A NOUN** = **clothes**, dress, clothing, gear *(slang)*, wear, habit, get-up *(informal)*, uniform, outfit, costume, threads *(slang)*, array, ensemble, garments, robes, duds *(informal)*, apparel, clobber *(Brit. slang)*, attire, togs *(informal)*, vestments, raiment *(archaic)*, rigout *(informal)*, bling *(slang)* • *He wore the garb of a general.*
▸ **AS A VERB** = **clothe**, dress, cover, outfit, deck, array, robe, apparel, attire, rig out • *He was garbed from head to toe in black.*
garbage 1 = **junk**, rubbish, litter, trash *(chiefly U.S.)*, refuse, waste, sweepings, scraps, debris, muck, filth, swill, slops, offal, detritus, dross, odds and ends, flotsam and jetsam, grot *(slang)*, leavings, dreck *(slang, chiefly U.S.)*, scourings, offscourings • *rotting piles of garbage*

GAMES

PARTY GAMES

blind man's buff, charades, Chinese whispers, consequences, follow-my-leader, hide-and-seek, I-spy, musical chairs, postman's knock, Simon says, statues

WORD GAMES

acrostic, anagram, crambo, crossword, hangman, logogriph, The Minister's Cat *(Scot.)*, rebus, Scrabble *(trademark)*, twenty questions *or* animal, vegetable, *or* mineral

OTHER GAMES

bar billiards, battleships, beetle, bingo *or* housey-housey, British bulldog, caber tossing, conkers, craps, crown and anchor, deck tennis, dominoes, foosball *or* table football, French cricket, hoopla, hopscotch, horseshoes, jacks, jigsaw puzzle, keno, king of the castle, knur and spell, lansquenet, leapfrog, lotto, mahjong, marbles, nim, noughts and crosses, paintball, pall-mall, pegboard, pinball, pitch-and-toss, quoits, ring taw, roque, roulette, Russian roulette, sack race, scavenger hunt, shuffleboard, skipping, spillikins *or* jackstraws, tag *or* tig, tangram, thimblerig, tiddlywinks, tipcat, trictrac, trugo, wall game, wargame

2 = nonsense, balls *(taboo slang)*, bull *(slang)*, shit *(taboo slang)*, rot, crap *(slang)*, trash, bullshit *(taboo slang)*, hot air *(informal)*, tosh *(informal)*, pap, cobblers *(Brit. taboo slang)*, bilge *(informal)*, drivel, twaddle, tripe *(informal)*, gibberish, malarkey, guff *(slang)*, moonshine, claptrap *(informal)*, hogwash, hokum *(slang, chiefly U.S. & Canad.)*, codswallop *(Brit. slang)*, piffle *(informal)*, poppycock *(informal)*, balderdash, bosh *(informal)*, eyewash *(informal)*, kak *(S. African slang)*, stuff and nonsense, bunkum *or* buncombe *(chiefly U.S.)*, bizzo *(Austral. slang)*, bull's wool *(Austral. & N.Z. slang)* • *I personally think the story is complete garbage.*

garbled = **jumbled**, confused, distorted, mixed up, muddled, incomprehensible, unintelligible • *He gave a garbled version of the story.*

garden = **grounds**, park, plot, patch, lawn, allotment, yard *(U.S. & Canad.)*, forest park *(N.Z.)* • *the most beautiful garden on earth*

▸ **RELATED ADJECTIVE:** horticultural

QUOTATIONS

God Almighty first planted a garden, and, indeed, it is the purest of human pleasures
[Francis Bacon *Essays*]

The kiss of the sun for pardon,
The song of the birds for mirth,
One is nearer God's Heart in a garden
Than anywhere else on earth
[Dorothy Frances Gurney *God's Garden*]

Paradise haunts gardens, and some gardens are paradises
[Derek Jarman *Derek Jarman's Garden*]

If you would be happy for a week, take a wife; if you would be happy for a month, kill your pig; but if you would be happy all your life, plant a garden
[*Chinese proverb*]

gardening

QUOTATIONS

Gardening is not a rational act
[Margaret Atwood *Bluebeard's Egg*]

gargantuan = **huge**, big, large, giant, massive, towering, vast, enormous, extensive, tremendous, immense, mega *(slang)*, titanic, jumbo *(informal)*, gigantic, monumental, monstrous, mammoth, colossal, mountainous, prodigious, stupendous, fuck-off *(offensive taboo slang)*, elephantine, ginormous *(informal)*, Brobdingnagian, humongous *or* humungous *(U.S. slang)* • *a marketing event of gargantuan proportions*

OPPOSITES: little, small, tiny

garish = **gaudy**, bright, glaring, vulgar, brilliant, flash *(informal)*, loud, brash, tacky *(informal)*, flashy, tasteless, naff *(Brit. slang)*, jazzy *(informal)*, tawdry, showy, brassy, raffish • *garish purple curtains*

OPPOSITES: conservative, quiet, dull

garland AS A NOUN = **wreath**, band, bays, crown, honours, loop, laurels, festoon, coronet, coronal, chaplet • *They wore garlands of summer flowers in their hair.*

▸ AS A VERB = **adorn**, crown, deck, festoon, wreathe • *Players were garlanded with flowers.*

garlic

▸ **RELATED ADJECTIVE:** alliaceous

garment *often plural* = **clothes**, wear, dress, clothing, gear *(slang)*, habit, get-up *(informal)*, uniform, outfit, costume, threads *(slang)*, array, robes, duds *(informal)*, apparel, clobber *(Brit. slang)*, attire, garb, togs, vestments, articles of clothing, raiment *(archaic)*, rigout *(informal)*, habiliment • *Put a fancy label on any garment and it gains credibility.*

garner = **collect**, assemble, gather, accumulate, save, husband, store, reserve, treasure, amass, stockpile, hoard, put by, stow away, lay in *or* up • *His priceless collection of Chinese art was garnered over three decades.*

garnish AS A NOUN = **decoration**, ornament, embellishment, adornment, ornamentation, trimming, trim • *Reserve some watercress for garnish.*

▸ AS A VERB = **decorate**, adorn, ornament, embellish, deck, festoon, trim, bedeck • *She had prepared the vegetables and was garnishing the roast.*

OPPOSITES: strip, spoil, denude

garret = **attic**, loft • *a tortured artist living in a garret in Paris*

garrison AS A NOUN **1 = troops**, group, unit, section, command, armed force, detachment • *a five-hundred man garrison*

2 = fort, fortress, camp, base, post, station, stronghold, fortification, encampment, fortified pa *(N.Z.)* • *The approaches to the garrison have been heavily mined.*

▸ AS A VERB **1 = occupy**, protect, guard, defend, man, supply with troops • *British troops still garrisoned the country.*

2 = station, position, post, mount, install, assign, put on duty • *No other soldiers were garrisoned there.*

garrulous 1 = talkative, gossiping, chattering, babbling, gushing, chatty, long-winded, effusive, gabby *(informal)*, prattling, voluble, gossipy, loquacious, verbose, mouthy • *a garrulous old woman*

OPPOSITES: reserved, reticent, taciturn

2 = rambling, lengthy, diffuse, long-winded, wordy, discursive, windy, overlong, verbose, prolix, prosy • *boring, garrulous prose*

OPPOSITES: concise, terse, succinct

gas 1 = fumes, vapour • *Exhaust gases contain many toxins.*

2 = petrol, gasoline • *a tank of gas*

▹ *See panel* **Gases**

gash AS A NOUN = **cut**, tear, split, wound, rent, slash, slit, gouge, incision, laceration • *a long gash just above his right eye*

▸ AS A VERB = **cut**, tear, split, wound, rend, slash, slit, gouge, lacerate • *He gashed his leg while felling trees.*

gasoline *or* **gasolene** = **petrol**, gas • *US gasoline prices have been pushed to their highest level.*

gasp AS A VERB = **pant**, blow, puff, choke, gulp, fight for breath, catch your breath • *He gasped for air before being pulled under again.*

▸ AS A NOUN = **pant**, puff, gulp, intake of breath, sharp intake of breath • *She gave a small gasp of pain.*

gas station = **petrol station** • *I pulled into the gas station and filled up.*

gastric = **stomach**, abdominal, intestinal, duodenal, enteric • *a gastric ulcer*

gate = **barrier**, opening, door, access, port *(Scot.)*, entrance, exit, gateway, portal, egress • *He opened the gate and walked up to the house.*

gather 1 = congregate, assemble, get together, collect, group, meet, mass, rally, flock, come together, muster, convene, converge, rendezvous, foregather • *In the evenings, we gathered round the fire and talked.*

OPPOSITES: separate, scatter, disperse

2 = assemble, group, collect, round up, marshal, bring together, muster, convene, call together • *He called to her to gather the children together.*

OPPOSITES: separate, scatter, disperse

3 = collect, assemble, accumulate, round up, mass, heap, marshal, bring together, muster, pile up, garner, amass, stockpile, hoard, stack up • *She started gathering up her things.*

4 = pick, harvest, pluck, reap, garner, glean • *The people lived by fishing, gathering nuts and fruits, and hunting.*

5 = build up, rise, increase, grow, develop, expand, swell, intensify, wax, heighten, deepen, enlarge, thicken • *Storm clouds were gathering in the distance.*

6 = muster, collect, assemble, summon, call up, marshal, call together • *You must gather your strength for the journey.*

7 = understand, believe, hear, learn, assume, take it, conclude, presume, be informed, infer, deduce, surmise, be

GASES

Types of gas

acetylene, afterdamp, ammonia, argon, arsine, biogas, butadiene, butane, butene, Calor gas *(trademark)*, carbon dioxide *or* carbonic-acid gas, carbon monoxide, chlorine, coal gas, compressed natural gas (CNG), cyanogen, diazomethane, diborane, dichlorodifluoromethane, electrolytic gas, ethane, ethylene, flue gas, fluorine, formaldehyde, helium, hydrogen, hydrogen bromide, hydrogen chloride, hydrogen fluoride, hydrogen iodide, hydrogen sulphide, ketene, krypton, laughing gas *or* nitrous oxide (LNG), liquefied petroleum gas (LPG), marsh gas, methane, methylamine, methyl bromide, methyl chloride, natural gas, neon, nitric oxide, nitrogen, nitrogen dioxide, nitrous oxide, oilgas, oxygen, ozone, phosgene, phosphine, producer gas *or* air gas, propane, radon, sewage gas, stibine, synthetic natural gas (SNG), sulphur dioxide, synthesis gas, tail gas, tetrafluoroethene, tetrafluoroethylene, town gas, vinyl chloride, water gas, xenon

Chemical warfare gases

blister gas, CS gas, lewisite, mustard gas, nerve gas, nitrogen mustard, sarin, soman, tabun, tear gas, VX

led to believe • *I gather his report is highly critical of the project.* **8 = fold**, tuck, pleat, ruffle, pucker, shirr • *Gather the skirt at the waist.*

gathering 1 = assembly, group, crowd, meeting, conference, company, party, congress, mass, rally, convention, knot, flock, get-together *(informal)*, congregation, muster, turnout, multitude, throng, hui *(N.Z.)*, concourse, assemblage, conclave, convocation, runanga *(N.Z.)* • *He spoke today before a large gathering of world leaders.* **2 = collecting**, gaining, collection, obtaining, acquisition, roundup, accumulation, stockpiling, attainment, procuring • *a mission to spearhead the gathering of information*

gauche = awkward, clumsy, inept, unsophisticated, inelegant, graceless, unpolished, uncultured, maladroit, ill-bred, ill-mannered, lacking in social graces • *We're all a bit gauche when we're young.*
OPPOSITES: polished, sophisticated, elegant

gaudy = garish, bright, glaring, vulgar, brilliant, flash *(informal)*, loud, brash, tacky *(informal)*, flashy, tasteless, jazzy *(informal)*, tawdry, showy, gay, ostentatious, raffish • *a gaudy orange-and-purple hat*
OPPOSITES: conservative, quiet, dull

gauge AS A VERB **1 = measure**, calculate, evaluate, value, size, determine, count, weigh, compute, ascertain, quantify • *He gauged the wind at over thirty knots.* **2 = judge**, estimate, guess, assess, evaluate, rate, appraise, reckon, adjudge • *See if you can gauge his reaction to the offer.*
▸ AS A NOUN **1 = meter**, indicator, dial, measuring instrument • *a temperature gauge* **2 = indicator**, test, rule, standard, model, measure, guide, basis, pattern, index, sample, par, guideline, criterion, meter, yardstick, touchstone, exemplar • *The index is the government's chief gauge of future economic activity.* **3 = size**, measure, degree, capacity, bore, extent, height, depth, scope, span, measurement, width, magnitude, thickness • *A narrow gauge steam railway line*

gaunt 1 = thin, lean, skinny, skeletal, wasted, drawn, spare, pinched, angular, bony, lanky, haggard, emaciated, scrawny, skin and bone, scraggy, cadaverous, rawboned • *Looking gaunt and tired, he denied there was anything to worry about.*
OPPOSITES: fat, lush, plump
2 = bleak, bare, harsh, forbidding, grim, stark, dismal, dreary, desolate, forlorn • *a large, gaunt, grey house*
OPPOSITES: inviting, luxurious, lush

gauntlet IN PHRASES: **throw down the gauntlet = issue a challenge**, challenge • *They have thrown down the gauntlet to their competitors.*

gauzy = delicate, light, thin, sheer, transparent, see-through, flimsy, translucent, insubstantial, gossamer, diaphanous, filmy • *thin, gauzy curtains, stirred by the breeze*

gawk = stare, gape, goggle, ogle, gawp *(slang)*, gaze open-mouthed • *He continued to gawk at her and didn't answer.*

gawky = awkward, clumsy, lumbering, ungainly, gauche, uncouth, loutish, graceless, clownish, oafish, maladroit, lumpish, ungraceful, unco *(Austral. slang)* • *a gawky lad with spots*
OPPOSITES: elegant, graceful, self-assured

gay AS AN ADJECTIVE **1 = homosexual**, camp *(informal)*, lesbian, pink *(informal)*, bent *(offensive, slang)*, queer *(informal derogatory)*, same-sex, sapphic, dykey *(slang)*, poofy *(offensive, slang)*, moffie *(S. African slang)* • *The quality of life for gay men has improved over the last decade.* **2 = cheerful**, happy, bright, glad, lively, sparkling, sunny, jolly, animated, merry, upbeat *(informal)*, buoyant, cheery, joyous, joyful, carefree, jaunty, chirpy *(informal)*, vivacious, jovial, gleeful, debonair, blithe, insouciant, full of beans *(informal)*, light-hearted • *I am in good health, gay and cheerful.*
OPPOSITES: serious, sad, grave
3 = colourful, rich, bright, brilliant, vivid, flamboyant, flashy, gaudy, garish, showy • *I like gay, vibrant posters.*
OPPOSITES: conservative, dull, drab
▸ AS A NOUN **= homosexual**, lesbian, fairy *(slang)*, queer *(informal derogatory)*, faggot *(slang, chiefly U.S. & Canad.)*, poof

(Brit. & Austral. derogatory slang), batty boy *(slang)*, bull dyke *(slang)*, shirt-lifter *(derogatory slang)*, dyke *or* dike *(slang)*, auntie *or* aunty *(Austral. slang)*, lily *(Austral. slang)* • *Gays have proved themselves to be style leaders.*
OPPOSITES: straight, heterosexual

gaze AS A VERB = **stare**, look, view, watch, regard, contemplate, gape, eyeball *(slang)*, ogle, look fixedly • *He gazed reflectively at the fire.*
▸ AS A NOUN = **stare**, look, fixed look • *She felt uncomfortable under the woman's steady gaze.*

gazebo = **pavilion**, summer house • *a hilltop gazebo overlooking a deserted beach*

gazette = **newspaper**, paper, journal, organ, periodical, news-sheet • *the Arkansas Gazette*

g'day *or* **gidday** = **hello**, hi *(informal)*, greetings, how do you do?, good morning, good evening, good afternoon, welcome, kia ora *(N.Z.)* • *Gidday, mate!*

gear AS A NOUN 1 = **mechanism**, works, action, gearing, machinery, cogs, cogwheels, gearwheels • *The boat's steering gear failed.*
2 = **equipment**, supplies, tackle, tools, instruments, outfit, rigging, rig, accessories, apparatus, trappings, paraphernalia, accoutrements, appurtenances, equipage • *fishing gear*
3 = **possessions**, things, effects, stuff, kit, luggage, baggage, belongings, paraphernalia, personal property, chattels • *They helped us put our gear in the van.*
4 = **clothing**, wear, dress, clothes, habit, outfit, costume, threads *(slang)*, array, garments, apparel, attire, garb, togs, rigout • *I used to wear trendy gear but it just looked ridiculous.*
▸ AS A VERB *with* **to** *or* **towards** = **equip**, fit, suit, adjust, adapt, rig, tailor • *Colleges are not always geared towards the needs of mature students.*

geezer = **man**, guy *(informal)*, male, gentleman, bloke *(Brit. informal)*, chap *(informal)* • *an old bald geezer in a raincoat*

gel *or* **jell** = **come together**, unite, combine, amalgamate • *The new players have gelled very well with the rest of the team.*

gelatinous = **glutinous**, sticky, viscous, gummy, gluey, jelly-like, mucilaginous, viscid • *Pour a cup of the gelatinous mixture into the blender.*

geld = **castrate**, neuter, emasculate, doctor • *Most male horses are gelded.*

gem 1 = **precious stone**, jewel, stone, semiprecious stone • *The mask is inset with emeralds and other gems.*
2 = **treasure**, pick, prize, jewel, flower, pearl, masterpiece, paragon, humdinger *(slang)*, taonga *(N.Z.)* • *Castel Clara was a gem of a hotel.*
▸ RELATED ADJECTIVE: lapidary

gender = **sex** • *Women are sometimes denied opportunities solely because of their gender.*

genealogy = **ancestry**, descent, pedigree, line, origin, extraction, lineage, family tree, parentage, derivation, blood line • *He had sat and repeated his family's genealogy to her.*

general AS AN ADJECTIVE 1 = **widespread**, accepted, popular, public, common, broad, extensive, universal, prevailing, prevalent • *Contrary to general opinion, Wiccans are not devil-worshippers.*
OPPOSITES: private, individual, personal
2 = **overall**, complete, total, global, comprehensive, blanket, inclusive, all-embracing, overarching • *His firm took over general maintenance of the park last summer.*
OPPOSITES: limited, restricted, partial
3 = **universal**, overall, widespread, collective, across-the-board, all-inclusive • *The figures represent a general decline in unemployment.*
OPPOSITES: special, unusual, exceptional
4 = **vague**, broad, loose, blanket, sweeping, unclear, inaccurate, approximate, woolly, indefinite, hazy, imprecise, ill-defined, inexact, unspecific, undetailed • *chemicals called by the general description 'flavour enhancer'*
OPPOSITES: particular, specific, exact
5 = **ordinary**, regular, usual, typical, conventional, everyday, customary • *This book is intended for the general reader rather than the student.*
OPPOSITES: special, extraordinary, exceptional
▸ IN PHRASES: **in general** 1 = **as a whole**, generally, overall, altogether, across the board • *We need to improve our education system in general.*
2 = **on the whole**, largely, chiefly, mainly, mostly, principally, predominantly, in the main, for the most part • *In general, it was the better educated voters who voted Yes in the referendum.*

generality 1 = **generalization**, abstraction, sweeping statement, vague notion, loose statement • *He avoided this tricky question and talked in generalities.*
2 = **impreciseness**, vagueness, looseness, lack of detail, inexactitude, woolliness, indefiniteness, approximateness, inexactness, lack of preciseness • *There are problems with this definition, given its level of generality.*
3 = **majority**, most, mass, bulk, best part, greater number • *When the generality of the electorate is doing badly, the mood is pessimisitic.*

generalization = **generality**, abstraction, sweeping statement, loose statement • *He was making sweeping generalizations to get his point across.*

generalized = **vague**, obscure, unspecified, hazy, nebulous • *generalized feelings of inadequacy*

generally 1 = **broadly**, mainly, mostly, principally, on the

GEMSTONES

adularia	carnelian	garnet	lapis lazuli	Oriental emerald	spinel
agate	cat's-eye	girasol	liver opal	peridot	spodumene
alexandrite	chalcedony	grossularite	Madagascar aquamarine	plasma	staurolite
almandine	chrysoberyl	hawk's-eye	melanite	pyrope	sunstone
amazonite	chrysolite	helidor	moonstone	quartz	titanite
amethyst	chrysoprase	heliotrope	morganite	rhodolite	topaz
andalusite	citrine	hessonite	morion	rose quartz	topazolite
andradite	Colorado ruby	hiddenite	moss agate	rubellite	tourmaline
aquamarine	Colorado topaz	hyacinth	New Zealand greenstone	ruby	turquoise
aventurine	corundum	indicolite *or* indigolite	odontolite	sapphire	uvarovite
balas	cymophane	jacinth	onyx	sard *or* sardine	vesuvianite
beryl	demantoid	jadeite *or* jade	opal	sardonyx	water sapphire
black opal	diamond	jasper	Oriental almandine	smoky quartz	white sapphire
bloodstone	diopside	jet		Spanish topaz	zircon
bone turquoise	emerald	kunzite		spessartite	
cairngorm	fire opal			sphene	

whole, predominantly, in the main, for the most part • *University teachers generally have admitted a lack of enthusiasm about their subjects.*
2 = usually, commonly, typically, regularly, normally, on average, on the whole, for the most part, almost always, in most cases, by and large, ordinarily, as a rule, habitually, conventionally, customarily • *As women we generally say and feel too much about these things.*
OPPOSITES: rarely, occasionally, unusually
3 = commonly, widely, publicly, universally, extensively, popularly, conventionally, customarily • *It is generally believed that drinking red wine in moderation is beneficial.*
OPPOSITES: individually, particularly

generate = produce, create, make, form, cause, initiate, bring about, originate, give rise to, engender, whip up • *The minister said the reforms would generate new jobs.*
OPPOSITES: end, destroy, crush

g

generation 1 = age group, peer group • *He's the leading American playwright of his generation.*
2 = age, period, era, time, days, lifetime, span, epoch • *Within a generation, flight has become popular with many travellers.*
3 = range, class, series, type, wave, variety, crop, batch • *a new generation of computers*
4 = production, manufacture, manufacturing, creation, formation, origination • *They have announced plans for a sharp rise in nuclear power generation.*

generic = collective, general, common, wide, sweeping, comprehensive, universal, blanket, inclusive, all-encompassing • *Parmesan is a generic term for a family of Italian hard cheeses.*
OPPOSITES: individual, particular, specific

generosity 1 = liberality, charity, bounty, munificence, beneficence, largesse or largess • *There are many stories of his generosity.*
2 = magnanimity, goodness, kindness, benevolence, selflessness, charity, unselfishness, high-mindedness, nobleness • *his moral decency and generosity of spirit*

QUOTATIONS
Generosity knows how to count, but refrains
[Mason Cooley *City Aphorisms*]

generous 1 = liberal, lavish, free, charitable, free-handed, hospitable, prodigal, bountiful, open-handed, unstinting, beneficent, princely, bounteous, munificent, ungrudging • *He's very generous with his money.*
OPPOSITES: mean, selfish, cheap
2 = magnanimous, kind, noble, benevolent, good, big, high-minded, unselfish, big-hearted, ungrudging • *He was not generous enough to congratulate his successor.*
3 = plentiful, lavish, ample, abundant, full, rich, liberal, overflowing, copious, bountiful, unstinting, profuse, bounteous *(literary)*, plenteous • *a room with a generous amount of storage space*
OPPOSITES: small, tiny, meagre

PROVERBS
It is easy to be generous with other people's property

genesis = beginning, source, root, origin, start, generation, birth, creation, dawn, formation, outset, starting point, engendering, inception, commencement, propagation • *The project had its genesis two years earlier.*
OPPOSITES: end, finish, conclusion

genial = friendly, kind, kindly, pleasant, warm, cheerful, jolly, hearty, agreeable, cheery, amiable, cordial, affable, congenial, jovial, convivial, good-natured, warm-hearted • *He was a warm-hearted friend and a genial host.*
OPPOSITES: cool, unpleasant, unfriendly

geniality = friendliness, kindness, cheerfulness, good nature, warmth, good cheer, jollity, conviviality, cordiality, affability, amiability, kindliness, joviality, cheeriness, heartiness, congeniality, pleasantness, warm-heartedness • *He soon recovered his habitual geniality.*

genitals = sex organs, privates, loins, genitalia, private parts, reproductive organs, pudenda • *He was hiding his genitals behind a tray.*
▸ **RELATED ADJECTIVE:** venereal

genius 1 = brilliance, ability, talent, capacity, gift, bent, faculty, excellence, endowment, flair, inclination, knack, propensity, aptitude, cleverness, creative power • *This is the mark of her genius as a designer.*
2 = master, expert, mastermind, brain *(informal)*, buff *(informal)*, intellect *(informal)*, adept, maestro, virtuoso, boffin *(Brit. informal)*, whiz *(informal)*, hotshot *(informal)*, rocket scientist *(informal, chiefly U.S.)*, wonk *(informal)*, brainbox, maven *(U.S.)*, master-hand, fundi *(S. African)* • *a 14-year-old mathematical genius*
OPPOSITES: fool, idiot, dunce

QUOTATIONS
Genius is one per cent inspiration and ninety-nine per cent perspiration
[Thomas Alva Edison *Life*]
When a true genius appears in the world, you may know him by this sign, that the dunces are all in confederacy against him
[Jonathan Swift *Thoughts on Various Subjects*]
The true genius is a mind of large general powers, accidentally determined to some particular direction
[Dr. Johnson *Lives of the English Poets*]
Genius is...the child of imitation
[Joshua Reynolds *Discourses on Art*]
If I have seen further [than other men] it is by standing upon the shoulders of giants
[Isaac Newton *letter to Robert Hooke*]
Genius must be born, and never can be taught
[John Dryden *To Mr. Congreve*]
In every work of genius we recognize our own rejected thoughts
[Ralph Waldo Emerson *Self-Reliance*]
Genius does what it must,
And Talent does what it can
[Owen Meredith *Last Words of a Sensitive Second-rate Poet*]
It takes a lot of time to be a genius, you have to sit around so much doing nothing, really doing nothing
[Gertrude Stein *Everybody's Autobiography*]
Genius is only a greater aptitude for patience
[Comte de Buffon]

genocide = massacre, killing, murder, slaughter, holocaust, ethnic cleansing *(euphemistic)*, carnage, extermination, mass murder, annihilation, pogrom, butchery, mass slaughter • *They have alleged that acts of genocide and torture were carried out.*

genre = type, group, school, form, order, sort, kind, class, style, character, fashion, brand, species, category, stamp, classification, genus, subdivision • *his love of films and novels in the horror genre*

genteel = refined, cultured, mannerly, elegant, formal, gentlemanly, respectable, polite, cultivated, courteous, courtly, well-bred, ladylike, well-mannered • *two maiden ladies with genteel manners and voices*
OPPOSITES: rude, unaffected, unmannerly

gentility 1 = refinement, culture, breeding, courtesy, elegance, formality, respectability, cultivation, politeness, good manners, courtliness • *The old woman had an air of gentility about her.*
2 = blue blood, high birth, rank, good family, good breeding, gentle birth • *He was inordinately proud of his gentility.*

gentle 1 = kind, loving, kindly, peaceful, soft, quiet, pacific, tender, mild, benign, humane, compassionate, amiable, meek, lenient, placid, merciful, kind-hearted, sweet-tempered, tender-hearted • *a quiet and gentle man who liked sports and enjoyed life*
OPPOSITES: hard, rough, unkind

2 = **slow**, easy, slight, deliberate, moderate, gradual, imperceptible • *His movements were gentle and deliberate.*
3 = **moderate**, low, light, easy, soft, calm, slight, mild, soothing, clement, temperate, balmy • *The wind had dropped to a gentle breeze.*
OPPOSITES: strong, powerful, violent
4 = **gradual**, easy, slight • *We first practised our skiing on gentle slopes.*
OPPOSITES: sudden, precipitous
5 = **moderate**, mild • *Cook for 15 minutes over a gentle heat.*

gentleman

QUOTATIONS
It is almost a definition of a gentleman to say that he is one who never inflicts pain
[Cardinal Newman *The Idea of a University*]

gentlemanly = **chivalrous**, mannerly, obliging, refined, polite, civil, cultivated, courteous, gallant, genteel, suave, well-bred, well-mannered • *He was respected for his kind and gentlemanly ways.*

QUOTATIONS
Anyone can be heroic from time to time, but a gentleman is something you have to be all the time
[Luigi Pirandello *The Pleasure of Honesty*]

gentleness = **tenderness**, compassion, kindness, consideration, sympathy, sweetness, softness, mildness, kindliness • *the gentleness with which she treated her pregnant mother*

gentry = **nobility**, lords, elite, nobles, upper class, aristocracy, peerage, ruling class, patricians, upper crust *(informal)*, gentility, gentlefolk • *Most of the country estates were built by the landed gentry during the 19th century.*

genuine 1 = **authentic**, real, original, actual, sound, true, pure, sterling, valid, legitimate, honest, veritable, bona fide, dinkum *(Austral. & N.Z. informal)*, the real McCoy • *They are convinced the painting is genuine.*
OPPOSITES: false, artificial, counterfeit
2 = **heartfelt**, sincere, honest, earnest, real, true, frank, unaffected, wholehearted, unadulterated, unalloyed, unfeigned • *There was genuine joy in the room.*
OPPOSITES: affected, false, phoney
3 = **sincere**, straightforward, honest, natural, frank, candid, upfront *(informal)*, dinkum *(Austral. & N.Z. informal)*, artless, guileless • *She is a very caring and genuine person.*
OPPOSITES: false, hypocritical, phoney

QUOTATIONS
Genuineness only thrives in the dark. Like celery
[Aldous Huxley *Those Barren Leaves*]

genus = **type**, sort, kind, group, set, order, race, class, breed, category, genre, classification • *all the species of a particular genus*

geography
▹ *See panel* **Geography**

geology
▹ *See panel* **Geology; Layers of the Earth's crust**

germ 1 = **microbe**, virus, bug *(informal)*, bacterium, bacillus, microorganism • *a germ that destroyed hundred of millions of lives*
2 = **beginning**, root, seed, origin, spark, bud, embryo, rudiment • *The germ of an idea took root in her mind.*
▸ **RELATED PHOBIAS:** spermaphobia, spermatophobia

German
▸ **RELATED PREFIXES:** Germano-, Teuto-

germane = **relevant**, related, significant, appropriate, fitting, material, allied, connected, suitable, proper, apt, applicable, pertinent, apposite, apropos, cognate, to the point *or* purpose • *the suppression of documents which were germane to the case*
OPPOSITES: foreign, irrelevant, inappropriate

Germany
▸ **RELATED ADJECTIVE:** Teutonic
▹ *See panel* **Administrative regions**

germinate 1 = **sprout**, grow, shoot, develop, generate, swell, bud, vegetate • *Some seed varieties germinate very quickly.*
2 = **develop**, grow, progress, generate, evolve, originate • *He wrote to Eliot about an idea that was germinating in his mind.*

gestation 1 = **incubation**, development, growth, pregnancy, evolution, ripening, maturation • *The gestation period can be anything between 95 and 150 days.*
2 = **development**, progress, evolution, progression, incubation • *the prolonged period of gestation of this design*

gesticulate = **signal**, sign, wave, indicate, motion, gesture, beckon, make a sign • *The man was gesticulating wildly.*

gesticulation = **signalling**, signing, waving, motioning, gestures, beckoning, sign language, arm-waving • *We communicated mainly by signs, gesticulation and mime.*

gesture **AS A NOUN** 1 = **sign**, action, signal, motion, indication, gesticulation • *She made a menacing gesture with her fist.*
2 = **demonstration**, display, exhibition, expression, proof, illustration, testimony, manifestation • *He called on the government to make a gesture of goodwill.*
▸ **AS A VERB** = **signal**, sign, wave, indicate, motion, beckon, gesticulate • *I gestured towards the boathouse and he looked inside.*

get **AS A VERB** 1 = **become**, grow, turn, wax, come to be • *The boys were getting bored.*
2 = **persuade**, convince, win over, induce, influence, sway, entice, coax, incite, impel, talk into, wheedle, prevail upon • *How did you get him to pose for this picture?*
3 = **arrive**, come, reach, make it *(informal)* • *It was dark by the time she got home.*
4 = **manage**, fix, succeed, arrange, contrive, wangle *(informal)* • *How did he get to be the boss of a major company?*
5 = **annoy**, upset, anger, bother, disturb, trouble, bug *(informal)*, irritate, aggravate *(informal)*, gall, madden, exasperate, nettle, vex, irk, rile, pique, get on your nerves *(informal)*, nark *(Brit., Austral. & N.Z. slang)*, get up your nose *(informal)*, give someone grief *(Brit. & S. African)*, make your blood boil, piss you off *(taboo slang)*, get your goat *(slang)*, get on your wick *(Brit. slang)*, get your back up, hack you off *(informal)* • *What gets me is the attitude of these people.*
6 = **obtain**, receive, gain, acquire, win, land, score *(slang)*, achieve, net, pick up, bag, secure, attain, reap, get hold of, come by, glean, procure, get your hands on, come into possession of • *The problem was how to get enough food.*
7 = **inherit**, succeed to, fall heir to • *I get my brains from my mother's side of the family.*
8 = **earn**, receive, make, collect, net, realize, bring in, gross, reap • *He gets a salary of $21,000 a year.*
9 = **fetch**, bring, collect • *Go and get your Daddy for me.*
10 = **prepare**, cook, fix, put together, concoct, fix up • *She was getting a meal for all of us.*
11 = **understand**, follow, catch, see, notice, realize, appreciate, be aware of, take in, perceive, grasp, comprehend, fathom, apprehend, suss (out) *(slang)*, get the hang of *(informal)*, get your head round • *You don't seem to get the point.*
12 = **catch**, develop, contract, succumb to, fall victim to, go down with, come down with, become infected with, be afflicted with, be smitten by • *When I was five I got measles.*
13 = **experience**, suffer from, sustain, undergo • *I keep getting headaches.*
14 = **arrest**, catch, grab, capture, trap, seize, take, nail *(informal)*, collar *(informal)*, nab *(informal)*, apprehend, take prisoner, take into custody, lay hold of • *The police have got the killer.*
15 = **contact**, reach, communicate with, get hold of, get in

GEOGRAPHY

Branches of geography

biogeography, cartography, chorography, chorology, climatology, demography, geology, geomorphology, glaciology, hydrology, human geography, meteorology, oceanography, oceanology, orography *or* orology, pedology, physical geography, political geography *or* geopolitics, seismology, topography, vulcanology

Geography terms and features

afforestation, antipodes, arête, atlas, atmosphere, atoll, basin, bay, beach, canyon, cliff, climate, col, conservation, continent, continental drift, continental shelf, contour, conurbation, coombe, coral reef, core, corrie, cirque, *or* cwm, crag, crater, crevasse, crust, culvert, deforestation, delta, desert, desertification, dormitory, dyke, earthquake, eastings, environment, epicentre, equator, erosion, escarpment, estuary, fault, fell, fjord, flood plain, glaciation, glacier, glade, glen, global warming, green belt, greenhouse effect, grid reference, hanging valley, headland, ice cap, infrastructure, International Date Line, irrigation, isobar, isobath, isohyet, isotherm, isthmus, jungle, lagoon, latitude, levée, loch, longitude, longshore drift, mantle, map, meander, Mercator projection, moraine, new town, northern hemisphere, northings, North Pole, occidental, ocean, Ordnance Survey, oriental, ozone layer, permafrost, plate tectonics, pollution, precipitation, rainforest, rain shadow, reef, relief map, ridge, rift valley, rill, river basin, rivulet, salt flat, salt lake, sandbank, sand bar, sand dune, savanna, scree, sierra, snow line, southern hemisphere, South Pole, spit, spring, spur, stack, steppe, subsoil, suburb, tarn, temperate, Third World, topsoil, tor, tropics, tsunami, tundra, urbanization, veld, volcano, wadi, watercourse, water cycle, waterfall, watershed, water table, weathering, wetland, whirlpool

Geographers

Richard Hakluyt *(English)*
Sir Halford John Mackinder *(British)*
Gerardus Mercator (Gerhard Kremer) *(Flemish)*
Pausanias *(Greek)*
Ptolemy *(Greek)*
Mary Somerville *(British)*
Strabo *(Greek)*

touch with • *We've been trying to get you on the phone all day.*
16 = puzzle, confuse, baffle, bewilder, confound, perplex, mystify, stump, beat *(slang)*, flummox, nonplus • *No, I can't answer that question – you've got me there.*
17 = move, touch, affect, excite, stir, stimulate, arouse, have an impact on, have an effect on, tug at (someone's) heartstrings *(often facetious)* • *I don't know what it is about that song, it just gets me.*
▸ **in phrases: get about** *or* **around 1 = go out**, travel, move around or about • *So you're getting about a bit then? Not shutting yourself away?*
2 = circulate, be reported, be published, become known, be passed around, be put about • *The news got about that he had been suspended.*
get across something = cross, negotiate, pass over, traverse, ford • *When we got across the beach, we saw some Spanish guys waiting for us.*
get ahead = prosper, advance, progress, succeed, get on, do well, thrive, flourish, be successful, make good, cut it *(informal)*, make the grade *(informal)*, turn out well, make your mark • *He wanted safety, security, a home, and a chance to get ahead.*

GEOLOGY

Geological eras

Cenozoic, Mesozoic, Palaeozoic, Precambrian

Geological periods

Quaternary, Tertiary, Cretaceous, Jurassic, Triassic, Permian, Carboniferous, Devonian, Silurian, Ordovician, Cambrian

Epochs of the Cenozoic era

Holocene, Pleistocene, Pliocene, Miocene, Oligocene, Eocene, Palaeocene

get along 1 = **be friendly**, agree, get on, be compatible, hit it off (*informal*), harmonize, be on good terms • *They seem to be getting along.*
2 = **cope**, manage, survive, progress, get on, fare, make out (*informal*), make do, get by (*informal*) • *You can't get along without money.*
3 = **go**, leave, go away, be off, depart, move off, take (your) leave, slope off, make tracks, get on your bike (*Brit. slang*), bog off (*Brit. slang*), sling your hook (*Brit. slang*), rack off (*Austral. & N.Z. slang*) • *Well, I'd better be getting along now.*
get at someone 1 = **criticize**, attack, blame, put down, knock (*informal*), flame (*informal*), carp, have a go (at) (*informal*), taunt, nag, hassle (*informal*), pick on, disparage, diss (*slang, chiefly U.S.*), find fault with, put the boot into (*slang*), nark (*Brit., Austral. & N.Z. slang*), be on your back (*slang*) • *His mother doesn't like me, and she gets at me all the time.*
2 = **corrupt**, influence, bribe, tamper with, buy off, fix (*informal*), suborn • *He claims these government officials have been got at.*
get at something 1 = **reach**, touch, grasp, get (a) hold of, stretch to • *The goat was on its hind legs trying to get at the leaves.*
2 = **find out**, get, learn, reach, reveal, discover, acquire, detect, uncover, attain, get hold of, gain access to, come to grips with • *We're only trying to get at the truth.*
3 = **imply**, mean, suggest, hint, intimate, lead up to, insinuate • *'What are you getting at now?' demanded Rick.*
get away = **escape**, leave, disappear, flee, depart, fly, slip away, abscond, decamp, hook it (*slang*), do a runner (*slang*), slope off, do a bunk (*Brit. slang*), fly the coop (*U.S. & Canad. informal*), skedaddle (*informal*), take a powder (*U.S. & Canad. slang*), make good your escape, make your getaway, take it on the lam (*U.S. & Canad. slang*), break free *or* out, run away *or* off, do a Skase (*Austral. informal*) • *They tried to stop him but he got away.*
get back = **return**, arrive home, come back *or* home • *It was late when we got back from the hospital.*
get back at someone = **retaliate**, pay (someone) back, hit back at, take revenge on, get even with, strike back at, even the score with, exact retribution on, get your own back on, make reprisal with, be avenged on, settle the score with, give (someone) a taste of his *or* her own medicine, give tit for tat, take *or* wreak vengeance on • *My wife had left me and I wanted to get back at her.*
get by = **manage**, survive, cope, fare, get through, exist, make out, get along, make do, subsist, muddle through, keep your head above water, make both ends meet • *I'm a survivor. I'll get by.*
get down = **descend**, get off, step down, alight, climb down, disembark, dismount • *The two ladies got down from the carriage.*
get in = **arrive**, come in, appear, land • *Our flight got in late.*
get off 1 = **be absolved**, be acquitted, escape punishment, walk (*slang, chiefly U.S.*) • *He is likely to get off with a small fine.*
2 = **leave**, go, move, take off (*informal*), depart, slope off, make tracks, set out *or* off • *I'd like to get off before it begins to get dark.*
3 = **descend**, leave, exit, step down, alight, disembark, dismount • *We got off at the next stop.*
get on 1 = **be friendly**, agree, get along, concur, be compatible, hit it off (*informal*), harmonize, be on good terms • *Do you get on with your neighbours?*
2 = **progress**, manage, cope, fare, advance, succeed, make out (*informal*), prosper, cut it (*informal*), get along • *I asked how he was getting on.*
3 = **board**, enter, mount, climb, embark, ascend • *The bus stopped to let the passengers get on.*
get on with something = **continue**, carry on, stick to, pursue, keep up, persist in, keep at, stick at, persevere with, keep on with • *Get on with what you're doing.*
get out 1 = **leave**, escape, withdraw, quit, take off (*informal*), exit, go, break out, go away, depart, evacuate, vacate, clear out (*informal*), abscond, decamp, hook it (*slang*), free yourself, do a bunk (*Brit. slang*), bog off (*Brit. slang*), extricate yourself, sling your hook (*Brit. slang*), rack off (*Austral. & N.Z. slang*), do a Skase (*Austral. informal*) • *I think we should get out while we still can.*
2 = **become known**, emerge, be revealed, be discovered, come to light, be disclosed, leak out • *If word gets out now, there'll be a scandal.*
get out of something = **avoid**, dodge, evade, escape, shirk, wriggle out of, body-swerve (*Scot.*) • *It's amazing what people will do to get out of paying taxes.*
get over something 1 = **recover from**, survive, get better from, come round, bounce back, mend, get well, recuperate, turn the corner, pull through, get back on your feet, feel yourself again, regain your health *or* strength • *It took me a very long time to get over the shock of her death.*
2 = **overcome**, deal with, solve, resolve, defeat, master, lick (*informal*), shake off, rise above, get the better of, surmount • *How would they get over that problem, he wondered?*
3 = **cross**, pass, pass over, traverse, get across, move across, ford, go across • *The travellers were trying to get over the river.*
get round someone = **win over**, persuade, charm, influence, convince, convert, sway, coax, cajole, wheedle, prevail upon, bring round, talk round • *Max could always get round his mother.*
get round something = **overcome**, deal with, solve, resolve, defeat, master, bypass, lick (*informal*), shake off, rise above, get the better of, circumvent, surmount • *No one has found a way of getting round the problem.*
get someone down = **depress**, discourage, bring down, daunt, oppress, weigh down, cast down, dishearten, dispirit, deject, make despondent • *At times my work gets me down.*
get someone up = **dress**, clothe, deck (out), array, attire • *She had got herself up in her mother's best clothes.*
get something across = **communicate**, publish, spread, pass on, transmit, convey, impart, get (something) through, disseminate, bring home, make known, put over, make clear *or* understood • *I need a better way of getting my message across to people.*
get something back = **regain**, recover, retrieve, take back, recoup, repossess • *You have 14 days in which to cancel and get your money back.*
get something over = **communicate**, spread, pass on, convey, impart, make known, get *or* put across, make clear *or* understood • *We have got the message over to young people that smoking isn't cool.*
get something together = **arrange**, set up, organize, put together • *Paul and I were getting a band together, and we needed a record deal.*
get together = **meet**, unite, join, collect, gather, rally, assemble, muster, convene, converge, congregate • *This is the only forum where East and West can get together.*
get up = **arise**, stand (up), rise, get to your feet • *I got up and walked over to the door.*

getaway = **escape**, break, flight, break-out, decampment • *The thieves made their getaway on a stolen motorcycle.*

get-together = **gathering**, party, celebration, reception, meeting, social, function, bash (*informal*), rave (*Brit. slang*), festivity, do (*informal*), knees-up (*Brit. informal*), hui (*N.Z.*), beano (*Brit. slang*), social gathering, shindig (*informal*), soirée, rave-up (*Brit. slang*), hooley *or* hoolie (*chiefly Irish & N.Z.*) • *I arranged a get-together at my home.*

get-up = **outfit**, costume, clothes, gear (*informal*), kit, ensemble, garb, togs (*informal*), rigout (*informal*) • *He couldn't work in such a fancy get-up.*

g

get-up-and-go = **energy**, drive, spirit, life, push *(informal)*, strength, pep, zip *(informal)*, vitality, stamina, vigour, zeal, verve, zest, welly *(slang)*, vivacity, liveliness, vim *(slang)*, forcefulness • *She's got more get-up-and-go than anyone I know.*

ghastly 1 = **horrible**, shocking, terrible, awful, grim, dreadful, horrendous, hideous, from hell *(informal)*, horrid *(informal)*, repulsive, frightful, loathsome, godawful *(slang)* • *This wallpaper is absolutely ghastly.*
OPPOSITES: pleasing, appealing, lovely
2 = **gruesome**, shocking, terrible, terrifying, horrible, grim, horrifying, horrific, fearful, horrendous, hideous, grisly, repellent, repulsive, loathsome • *a particularly ghastly murder*
3 = **pale**, white, washed-out, wan, livid, pasty, pallid, anaemic, ashen, sallow, cadaverous, like death warmed up, deathlike, deathly pale • *She looked ghastly – frail, thin and colourless.*

ghost 1 = **spirit**, soul, phantom, spectre, spook *(informal)*, apparition, wraith, shade *(literary)*, revenant, phantasm, atua *(N.Z.)*, kehua *(N.Z.)*, wairua *(N.Z.)* • *The village is said to be haunted by the ghosts of the dead children.*
2 = **trace**, shadow, suggestion, hint, suspicion, glimmer, semblance • *He gave the ghost of a smile.*
▸ RELATED ADJECTIVE: spectral
▸ RELATED PHOBIA: phasmophobia

QUOTATIONS

Ghost stories appeal to our craving for immortality. If you can be afraid of a ghost, then you have to believe that a ghost may exist. And if a ghost exists then oblivion might not be the end
[Stanley Kubrick]

Even the living were only ghosts in the making
[Pat Barker *The Ghost Road*]

ghostly = **unearthly**, weird, phantom, eerie, supernatural, uncanny, spooky *(informal)*, spectral, eldritch *(poetic)*, ghostlike, phantasmal • *The moon shed a ghostly light on the fields.*

ghoulish = **macabre**, sick *(informal)*, disgusting, hideous, gruesome, grisly, horrid, morbid, unwholesome • *They are there only to satisfy their ghoulish curiosity.*

giant AS AN ADJECTIVE = **huge**, great, large, vast, enormous, extensive, tremendous, immense, titanic, jumbo *(informal)*, gigantic, monumental, monstrous, mammoth, colossal, mountainous, stellar *(informal)*, prodigious, stupendous, gargantuan, fuck-off *(offensive taboo slang)*, elephantine, ginormous *(informal)*, Brobdingnagian, humongous *or* humungous *(U.S. slang)*, supersize • *a giant oak table* • *a giant step towards unification*
OPPOSITES: tiny, miniature, dwarf
▸ AS A NOUN = **ogre**, monster, titan, colossus, leviathan, behemoth • *a Nordic saga of giants and monsters*

gibber = **gabble**, chatter, babble, waffle *(informal, chiefly Brit.)*, prattle, jabber, blab, rabbit on *(Brit. informal)*, blather, blabber, earbash *(Austral. & N.Z. slang)* • *Radio preachers were gibbering about the end of the world.*

gibberish = **nonsense**, balls *(taboo slang)*, bull *(slang)*, shit *(taboo slang)*, crap *(slang)*, garbage *(informal)*, bullshit *(taboo slang)*, hot air *(informal)*, tosh *(slang, chiefly Brit.)*, babble, pap, cobblers *(Brit. taboo slang)*, bilge *(informal)*, drivel, malarkey, twaddle, tripe *(informal)*, guff *(slang)*, prattle, mumbo jumbo, moonshine, jabber, gabble, gobbledegook *(informal)*, hogwash, hokum *(slang, chiefly U.S. & Canad.)*, blather, double talk, piffle *(informal)*, all Greek *(informal)*, poppycock *(informal)*, balderdash, bosh *(informal)*, yammer *(informal)*, eyewash *(informal)*, tommyrot, horsefeathers *(U.S. slang)*, bunkum *or* buncombe *(chiefly U.S.)*, bizzo *(Austral. slang)*, bull's wool *(Austral. & N.Z. slang)* • *When he did speak to her, he spoke gibberish.*

gibe *see* **jibe**

giddiness 1 = **dizziness**, vertigo, faintness, light-headedness • *A wave of giddiness swept over her.*
2 = **flightiness**, dizziness, foolishness, frivolity, silliness, capriciousness, ditziness *or* ditsiness *(slang)* • *I put it down to childish giddiness and high spirits.*

giddy 1 = **dizzy**, reeling, faint, unsteady, light-headed, vertiginous • *He felt giddy and light-headed.*
2 = **flighty**, silly, volatile, irresponsible, reckless, dizzy, careless, frivolous, impulsive, capricious, thoughtless, impetuous, skittish, heedless, scatterbrained, ditzy *or* ditsy *(slang)* • *Man is a giddy creature.*
OPPOSITES: serious, earnest, calm

gift 1 = **donation**, offering, present, contribution, grant, legacy, hand-out, endowment, boon, bequest, gratuity, prezzie *(informal)*, bonsela *(S. African)*, largesse *or* largess, koha *(N.Z.)* • *a gift of $50,000*
2 = **talent**, ability, capacity, genius, power, bent, faculty, capability, forte, flair, knack, aptitude • *As a youth he discovered a gift for teaching.*

gifted = **talented**, able, skilled, expert, masterly, brilliant, capable, clever, accomplished, tasty *(Brit. informal)*, proficient, adroit • *one of the most gifted pianists in the world*
OPPOSITES: amateur, incapable, talentless

gig = **show**, production, appearance, presentation • *The two bands join forces for a gig at the Sheffield Arena.*

gigantic = **huge**, great, large, giant, massive, vast, enormous, extensive, tremendous, immense, titanic, jumbo *(informal)*, monumental, monstrous, mammoth, colossal, mountainous, stellar *(informal)*, prodigious, stupendous, gargantuan, fuck-off *(offensive taboo slang)*, herculean, elephantine, ginormous *(informal)*, Brobdingnagian, humongous *or* humungous *(U.S. slang)*, supersize • *The road is bordered by gigantic rocks.*
OPPOSITES: little, small, tiny

giggle AS A VERB = **laugh**, chuckle, snigger, chortle, titter, twitter, tee-hee • *Both girls began to giggle*
▸ AS A NOUN = **laugh**, chuckle, snigger, chortle, titter, twitter • *She gave a little giggle.*

gill
▸ RELATED ADJECTIVE: branchial

gimcrack = **cheap**, vulgar, tacky *(informal)*, tasteless, naff *(Brit. slang)*, shoddy, gaudy, tawdry, trashy, rubbishy • *a gift shop selling gimcrack badges, keyrings and bottle openers*

gimmick = **stunt**, trick, device, scheme, manoeuvre, dodge, ploy, gambit, stratagem, contrivance • *It's just a public relations gimmick.*

gingerly = **cautiously**, carefully, reluctantly, suspiciously, tentatively, warily, hesitantly, timidly, circumspectly, cagily *(informal)*, charily • *I drove gingerly past the security check points.*
OPPOSITES: boldly, rashly, carelessly

giraffe
▸ COLLECTIVE NOUN: herd

gird 1 = **girdle**, bind, belt • *The other knights urged Galahad to gird on his sword.*
2 = **surround**, ring, pen, enclose, encompass, encircle, hem in, enfold, engird • *a proposal to gird the river with a series of small hydroelectric dams*
3 = **prepare**, ready, steel, brace, fortify, make *or* get ready • *They are girding themselves for battle against a new enemy.*

girdle AS A NOUN = **belt**, band, fillet, sash, waistband, cummerbund • *These muscles hold in the waist like an invisible girdle.*
▸ AS A VERB = **surround**, ring, bound, enclose, encompass, hem, encircle, fence in, gird • *The old town centre is girdled by a boulevard lined with trees.*

girl 1 = **female child**, schoolgirl, lass, lassie *(informal)*, miss, maiden *(archaic)*, maid *(archaic)* • *an eleven-year-old girl*
2 = **daughter**, female child • *My sister has two little girls.*
3 = **young woman**, maiden, chick *(slang)*, maid, lass, damsel *(archaic)*, bird *(slang)*, colleen *(Irish)*, lassie *(informal)*, wench,

charlie *(Austral. slang)*, chook *(Austral. slang)* • *a pretty twenty-year-old girl*
▸ **RELATED PHOBIA:** parthenophobia

girlfriend = **sweetheart**, love, girl, lover, beloved, valentine, truelove, steady *(informal)* • *Has he got a girlfriend?*

girlish = **youthful**, feminine, childish • *a little girlish giggle*

girth = **size**, measure, proportions, dimensions, bulk, measurement(s), circumference • *She had upset him by commenting on his increasing girth.*

gist = **essence**, meaning, point, idea, sense, import, core, substance, drift, significance, nub, pith, quintessence • *He related the gist of his conversation to us.*

give AS A VERB **1** = **perform**, do, carry out, execute • *She stretched her arms out and gave a great yawn.*
2 = **communicate**, announce, publish, transmit, pronounce, utter, emit, issue, be a source of, impart • *He gave no details of his plans.*
3 = **produce**, make, cause, occasion, engender • *Her visit gave great pleasure to the children.*
4 = **organize**, hold, provide, host, throw, lay on • *That evening, I gave a dinner party for a few close friends.*
5 = **present**, contribute, donate, provide, supply, award, grant, deliver, commit, administer, furnish, confer, bestow, entrust, consign, make over, hand over *or* out • *This recipe was given to me years ago.* • *They still give to charity despite hard economic times.*
OPPOSITES: get, take, keep
6 = **pass**, hand, reach, let have • *Could you give me that pencil, please?*
7 = **confer**, allow, accord, award, grant, permit, bestow, vouchsafe • *a citizen's charter giving rights to gays*
8 = **collapse**, fall, break, sink, bend • *My knees gave under me.*
9 = **concede**, allow, grant • *You're a bright enough kid, I'll give you that.*
10 = **surrender**, yield, devote, hand over, relinquish, part with, cede • *a memorial to a man who gave his life for his country*
11 = **demonstrate**, show, offer, provide, evidence, display, indicate, manifest, set forth • *The handout gives all the times of the performances.*
▸ **IN PHRASES: give in** = **admit defeat**, yield, concede, collapse, quit, submit, surrender, comply, succumb, cave in *(informal)*, capitulate • *My parents gave in and let me go to the camp.*
give someone away = **betray**, expose, inform on, shop *(slang, chiefly Brit.)*, grass *(Brit. slang)*, tell on, grass up *(slang)*, put the finger on *(informal)*, dob in *(Austral. slang)* • *I was never tempted for a moment to give her away.*
give something away = **reveal**, expose, leak, disclose, betray, uncover, let out, divulge, let slip, let the cat out of the bag *(informal)* • *They were giving away company secrets.*
give something off *or* **out** = **emit**, produce, release, discharge, send out, throw out, vent, exude, exhale • *Natural gas gives off less carbon dioxide than coal.*
give something out 1 = **distribute**, issue, deliver, circulate, hand out, dispense, dole out, pass round • *There were people at the entrance giving out leaflets.*
2 = **make known**, announce, publish, broadcast, communicate, transmit, utter, notify, impart, disseminate, shout from the rooftops *(informal)* • *He wouldn't give out any information.*
give something up 1 = **abandon**, stop, quit, kick *(informal)*, cease, cut out, renounce, leave off, say goodbye to, desist, kiss (something) goodbye, forswear • *I'm trying to give up smoking.*
2 = **quit**, leave, resign, step down from *(informal)* • *She gave up her job to join her husband's campaign.*
3 = **hand over**, yield, surrender, relinquish, waive • *The government refused to give up any territory.*
give up = **stop trying**, surrender, despair, cave in *(informal)*, capitulate, cede, throw in the towel, fall by the wayside, admit defeat, throw in the sponge, call it a day *or* night • *After a few attempts he gave up.*

QUOTATIONS
It is more blessed to give than to receive
[*Bible: Acts*]

give-and-take = **compromise**, agreement, concession, co-operation, flexibility, reciprocity • *a happy relationship where there's a lot of give-and-take*

giveaway = **sign**, suggestion, hint, indication, evidence, inkling, intimation • *The only giveaway was the look of amusement in her eyes.*

given 1 = **specified**, particular, specific, designated, stated, predetermined • *the number of accidents at this spot in a given period*
2 = **inclined**, addicted, disposed, prone, liable • *I am not very given to emotional displays.*

giver = **donor**, provider, contributor, benefactor, donator • *the largest giver of aid amongst the wealthy counties of the west*

glacial 1 = **icy**, biting, cold, freezing, frozen, bitter, raw, chill, piercing, arctic, polar, chilly, frosty, wintry • *The air from the sea felt glacial.*
2 = **unfriendly**, hostile, cold, icy, frosty, antagonistic, frigid, inimical • *The Duchess gave him a glacial look and moved on.*

glad 1 = **happy**, pleased, delighted, contented, cheerful, gratified, joyful, overjoyed, chuffed *(slang)*, gleeful • *I'm glad I decided to go after all.*
OPPOSITES: sad, depressed, unhappy
2 = **willing**, prepared, happy, pleased, ready, delighted • *I'll be glad to show you round.*
3 = **pleasing**, happy, cheering, pleasant, delightful, cheerful, merry, gratifying, cheery, joyous, felicitous • *the bringer of glad tidings*

gladden = **please**, delight, cheer, exhilarate, gratify, hearten, enliven, elate • *Her visit surprised and gladdened him.*

gladly 1 = **happily**, cheerfully, gleefully, merrily, gaily, joyfully, joyously, jovially • *He gladly accepted my invitation.*
2 = **willingly**, freely, happily, readily, cheerfully, with pleasure, with (a) good grace • *The counsellors will gladly baby-sit during their free time.*
OPPOSITES: sadly, reluctantly, grudgingly

glamorous 1 = **attractive**, beautiful, lovely, charming, entrancing, elegant, dazzling, enchanting, captivating, alluring, bewitching • *some of the world's most beautiful and glamorous women*
OPPOSITES: plain, dull, unglamorous
2 = **exciting**, glittering, prestigious, glossy, glitzy *(slang)*, bling *(slang)* • *his glamorous playboy lifestyle*
OPPOSITES: dull, unglamorous, unexciting

glamour 1 = **charm**, appeal, beauty, attraction, fascination, allure, magnetism, enchantment, bewitchment • *Her air of mystery only added to her glamour.*
2 = **excitement**, magic, thrill, romance, prestige, glitz *(slang)* • *the glamour of show biz*

glance AS A VERB **1** = **peek**, look, view, check, clock *(Brit. informal)*, gaze, glimpse, check out *(informal)*, peep, take a dekko at *(Brit. slang)* • *He glanced at his watch.*
OPPOSITES: study, scrutinize, peruse
2 *with* **over, through**, *etc* = **scan**, browse, dip into, leaf through, flip through, thumb through, skim through, riffle through, run over *or* through, surf *(Computing)* • *I picked up the book and glanced through it.*
▸ **AS A NOUN** = **peek**, look, glimpse, peep, squint, butcher's *(Brit. slang)*, quick look, gander *(informal)*, brief look, dekko *(slang)*, shufti *(Brit. slang)* • *She stole a quick glance at her watch.*
OPPOSITES: examination, inspection, good look
▸ **IN PHRASES: at first glance** = **on the surface**, apparently, seemingly, at first sight, superficially • *At first*

glance, everything looked fine.
glance off = graze, brush, bounce, rebound, skim, ricochet • *My fist glanced off his jaw.*

gland
▸ **RELATED ADJECTIVE:** adenoid

GLANDS

adrenal gland	lacrimal gland	prostate
endocrine gland	liver	salivary gland
exocrine gland	mammary gland	sebaceous gland
hypothalamus	mucus gland	sweat gland
islets of Langerhans *or* islands of Langerhans	ovary	testicle
	pancreas	thyroid gland
	parathyroid gland	
	pituitary gland	

glare AS A VERB 1 = **scowl**, frown, glower, look daggers, stare angrily, give a dirty look, lour *or* lower • *He glared and muttered something.*
2 = **dazzle**, blaze, flare, flame • *The light was glaring straight into my eyes.*
▸ AS A NOUN 1 = **scowl**, frown, glower, dirty look, black look, angry stare, lour *or* lower • *His glasses magnified his irritable glare.*
2 = **dazzle**, glow, blaze, flare, flame, brilliance • *the glare of a car's headlights*

glaring 1 = **obvious**, open, outstanding, patent, visible, gross, outrageous, manifest, blatant, conspicuous, overt, audacious, flagrant, rank, egregious, unconcealed • *I never saw such a glaring example of misrepresentation.*
OPPOSITES: hidden, concealed, inconspicuous
2 = **dazzling**, strong, bright, glowing, blazing • *She was clearly uneasy under the glaring camera lights.*
OPPOSITES: soft, subtle, subdued

glass
▸ **RELATED ADJECTIVES:** vitric, vitreous
▸ **RELATED PHOBIA:** nelophobia

glasses = spectacles, specs *(informal)*, eyeglasses *(U.S.)*

QUOTATIONS
Men seldom make passes
At girls who wear glasses
[Dorothy Parker *Enough Rope*]

glasshouse = greenhouse, conservatory, hothouse • *This kind of plant needs to be grown in a glasshouse.*

glassy 1 = **smooth**, clear, slick, shiny, glossy, transparent, slippery • *glassy green pebbles*
2 = **expressionless**, cold, fixed, empty, dull, blank, glazed, vacant, dazed, lifeless • *There was a remote, glassy look in his eyes.*

glaze AS A NOUN 1 = **coat**, finish, polish, shine, gloss, varnish, enamel, lacquer, lustre, patina • *hand-painted tiles with decorative glazes*
2 = **coating**, topping, icing • *Brush the glaze over the top and sides of the hot cake.*
▸ AS A VERB 1 = **coat**, polish, gloss, varnish, enamel, lacquer, burnish, furbish • *After the pots are fired, they are glazed in a variety of colours.*
2 = **cover**, ice, coat • *Glaze the pie with beaten egg.*

glazed = expressionless, cold, fixed, empty, dull, blank, vacant, dazed, lifeless, glassy • *She sat in front of the television with glazed eyes.*

gleam AS A VERB 1 = **shine**, flash, glow, sparkle, glitter, flare, shimmer, glint, glimmer, glisten, scintillate • *His red sports car gleamed in the sun.*
2 = **glow**, shine • *Neon lights gleamed in the mist.*
▸ AS A NOUN 1 = **glimmer**, flash, beam, glow, sparkle • *the gleam of the headlights*
2 = **brightness**, flash, gloss, brilliance, sheen, lustre • *Her fair hair had a golden gleam.*
3 = **trace**, ray, suggestion, hint, flicker, glimmer, inkling • *There was a gleam of hope for a peaceful settlement.*

gleaming = shining, bright, brilliant, glowing, sparkling, glimmering, glistening, scintillating, burnished, lustrous • *a gleaming new car*
OPPOSITES: dull, unpolished, lustreless

glean = gather, learn, pick up, collect, harvest, accumulate, reap, garner, amass, cull • *At present, we're gleaning information from all sources.*

glee = delight, joy, triumph, exuberance, elation, exhilaration, mirth, hilarity, merriment, exultation, gladness, joyfulness, joyousness • *His victory was greeted with glee.*
OPPOSITES: depression, misery, gloom

gleeful = delighted, happy, pleased, cheerful, merry, triumphant, gratified, exuberant, jubilant, joyous, joyful, elated, overjoyed, chirpy *(informal)*, exultant, cock-a-hoop, mirthful, stoked *(Austral. & N.Z. informal)* • *He took a gleeful delight in proving them all wrong.*

glib = smooth, easy, ready, quick, slick, plausible, slippery, fluent, suave, artful, insincere, fast-talking, smooth-tongued • *He is full of glib excuses for his past mistakes.* • *a glib car salesman*
OPPOSITES: halting, sincere, hesitant

glide 1 = **slip**, sail, slide, ghost, skim • *Waiters glide between tightly packed tables.*
2 = **float**, fly, soar, skim • *the albatross which glides effortlessly behind the yacht*
3 = **sail**, run, coast, skim • *The royal ships glided past fjords and dramatic waterfalls.*

glimmer AS A VERB = **gleam**, shine, glow, sparkle, glitter, blink, flicker, shimmer, twinkle, glisten • *The moon glimmered faintly through the mists.*
▸ AS A NOUN 1 = **glow**, ray, sparkle, gleam, blink, flicker, shimmer, twinkle • *In the east there is the faintest glimmer of light.*
2 = **trace**, ray, suggestion, hint, grain, gleam, flicker, inkling • *Our last glimmer of hope faded.*

glimpse AS A NOUN = **look**, sighting, sight, glance, peep, peek, squint, butcher's *(Brit. slang)*, quick look, gander *(informal)*, brief view, shufti *(Brit. slang)* • *The fans waited outside the hotel to get a glimpse of their heroine.*
▸ AS A VERB = **catch sight of**, spot, sight, view, clock *(Brit. informal)*, spy, espy • *She glimpsed a group of people standing on the bank of a river.*

glint AS A VERB = **gleam**, flash, shine, sparkle, glitter, twinkle, glimmer • *The sea glinted in the sun.*
▸ AS A NOUN = **gleam**, flash, shine, sparkle, glitter, twinkle, twinkling, glimmer • *glints of sunlight*

glisten = gleam, flash, shine, sparkle, glitter, shimmer, twinkle, glint, glimmer, scintillate • *The calm sea glistened in the sunlight.*

glitch = problem, difficulty, fault, flaw, bug *(informal)*, hitch, snag, uphill *(S. African)*, interruption, blip, malfunction, kink, gremlin, fly in the ointment • *Manufacturing glitches have limited the factory's output.*

glitter AS A VERB = **shine**, flash, sparkle, flare, glare, gleam, shimmer, twinkle, glint, glimmer, glisten, scintillate • *The palace glittered with lights.*
▸ AS A NOUN 1 = **glamour**, show, display, gilt, splendour, tinsel, pageantry, gaudiness, showiness • *all the glitter and glamour of a Hollywood premiere*
2 = **sparkle**, flash, shine, beam, glare, gleam, brilliance, sheen, shimmer, brightness, lustre, radiance, scintillation • *the glitter of strobe lights and mirror balls*

glittering = dazzling, brilliant, distinguished, glorious, splendid, glamorous, illustrious • *a glittering academic career*

glitzy = splendid, exciting, impressive, magnificent,

prestigious, plush *(informal)*, opulent, ritzy *(slang)* • *one of the glitziest ski resorts in the world*

gloat = **relish**, triumph, glory, crow, revel in, vaunt, drool, exult, rub your hands • *They are gloating over their rivals' defeat.*

global 1 = **worldwide**, world, international, universal, planetary • *a global ban on nuclear testing*
2 = **comprehensive**, general, total, thorough, unlimited, exhaustive, all-inclusive, all-encompassing, encyclopedic, unbounded • *a global vision of contemporary society*
OPPOSITES: limited, narrow, restricted

globe = **planet**, world, earth, sphere, orb • *delicacies from every corner of the globe*

globular = **spherical**, round • *The globular seed capsule contains numerous small seeds.*

globule = **droplet**, drop, particle, bubble, pearl, bead, pellet • *Bone marrow contains fat in the form of small globules.*

gloom 1 = **darkness**, dark, shadow, cloud, shade, twilight, dusk, obscurity, blackness, dullness, murk, dimness, murkiness, cloudiness, gloominess, duskiness • *the gloom of a foggy November morning*
OPPOSITES: light, daylight, radiance
2 = **depression**, despair, misery, sadness, sorrow, blues, woe, melancholy, unhappiness, desolation, despondency, dejection, low spirits, downheartedness • *the deepening gloom over the economy*
OPPOSITES: delight, joy, happiness

gloomy 1 = **dark**, dull, dim, dismal, black, grey, obscure, murky, dreary, sombre, shadowy, overcast, dusky, crepuscular, Stygian, tenebrous • *Inside it's gloomy after all that sunshine.*
OPPOSITES: light, brilliant, sunny
2 = **miserable**, down, sad, dismal, low, blue, pessimistic, melancholy, glum, dejected, despondent, dispirited, downcast, joyless, downhearted, down in the dumps *(informal)*, cheerless, down in the mouth, in low spirits • *He is gloomy about the fate of the economy.*
OPPOSITES: happy, bright, cheerful
3 = **depressing**, bad, dismal, dreary, black, saddening, sombre, dispiriting, disheartening, funereal, cheerless, comfortless • *Officials say the outlook for next year is gloomy.*

glorify 1 = **praise**, celebrate, magnify, laud, extol, crack up *(informal)*, big up *(slang, chiefly Caribbean)*, eulogize, sing *or* sound the praises of • *the banning of songs glorifying war*
OPPOSITES: condemn, mock, humiliate
2 = **worship**, honour, bless, adore, revere, exalt, pay homage to, venerate, sanctify, immortalize • *We are committed to serving the Lord and glorifying his name.*
OPPOSITES: desecrate, dishonour
3 = **enhance**, raise, elevate, adorn, dignify, magnify, augment, lift up, ennoble, add lustre to, aggrandize • *They've glorified his job with an impressive title, but he's still just a salesman.*
OPPOSITES: degrade, debase, defile

glorious 1 = **splendid**, beautiful, bright, brilliant, shining, superb, divine, gorgeous, dazzling, radiant, resplendent, splendiferous *(facetious)* • *a glorious Edwardian opera house*
OPPOSITES: awful, dull, horrible
2 = **delightful**, fine, wonderful, excellent, heavenly *(informal)*, marvellous, splendid, gorgeous, pleasurable, splendiferous *(facetious)* • *We opened the window and let in the glorious evening air.*
3 = **illustrious**, famous, celebrated, distinguished, noted, grand, excellent, honoured, magnificent, noble, renowned, elevated, eminent, triumphant, majestic, famed, sublime • *He had a glorious career spanning more than six decades.*
OPPOSITES: ordinary, minor, unknown

glory **AS A NOUN** 1 = **honour**, praise, fame, celebrity, distinction, acclaim, prestige, immortality, eminence, kudos, renown, exaltation, illustriousness • *He had his moment of glory when he won the London Marathon.*
OPPOSITES: shame, disgrace, condemnation
2 = **splendour**, majesty, greatness, grandeur, nobility, pomp, magnificence, pageantry, éclat, sublimity • *the glory of the royal court*
3 = **beauty**, brilliance, lustre, radiance, gorgeousness, resplendence • *the glory of an autumn sunset*
4 = **worship**, praise, blessing, gratitude, thanksgiving, homage, adoration, veneration • *Glory be to God.*
▸ **AS A VERB** = **triumph**, boast, relish, revel, crow, drool, gloat, exult, take delight, pride yourself • *The workers were glorying in their new-found freedom.*

QUOTATIONS

We are all motivated by a keen desire for praise, and the better a man is, the more he is inspired by glory. The very philosophers themselves, even in those books which they write on contempt of glory, inscribe their names
[Cicero *Pro Archia*]

The paths of glory lead but to the grave
[Thomas Gray *Elegy Written in a Country Churchyard*]

Not in utter nakedness,
But trailing clouds of glory do we come
[William Wordsworth *Intimations of Immortality*]

gloss[1] **AS A NOUN** 1 = **shine**, gleam, sheen, polish, brilliance, varnish, brightness, veneer, lustre, burnish, patina • *The rain produced a black gloss on the asphalt.*
2 = **façade**, show, front, surface, appearance, mask, semblance • *He tried to put a gloss of respectability on the horrors the regime perpetrated.*
▸ **IN PHRASES:** **gloss over something** = **conceal**, hide, mask, disguise, cover up, veil, camouflage, whitewash *(informal)*, smooth over, sweep under the carpet *(informal)*, airbrush • *Some governments are happy to gloss over continued human rights abuses.*

gloss[2] **AS A NOUN** = **interpretation**, comment, note, explanation, commentary, translation, footnote, elucidation • *A gloss in the margin explains this unfamiliar word.*
▸ **AS A VERB** = **interpret**, explain, comment, translate, construe, annotate, elucidate • *Earlier editors glossed 'drynke' as 'love-potion'.*

glossy 1 = **shiny**, polished, shining, glazed, bright, brilliant, smooth, sleek, silky, burnished, glassy, silken, lustrous • *glossy black hair* • *The leaves were dark and glossy.*
OPPOSITES: dull, drab
2 = **glamorous**, stylish, grand, smart, luxurious, swish *(informal, chiefly Brit.)*, swanky *(informal)*, ritzy *(slang)*, schmick *(Austral. informal)* • *a glossy new office*

glove = **mitten**, gauntlet, mitt • *a pair of white cotton gloves*

glow **AS A NOUN** 1 = **light**, gleam, splendour, glimmer, brilliance, brightness, radiance, luminosity, vividness, incandescence, phosphorescence • *The rising sun cast a golden glow over the fields.*
OPPOSITES: dullness, greyness
2 = **colour**, bloom, flush, blush, reddening, rosiness • *The moisturiser gave my face a healthy glow that lasted all day.*
OPPOSITES: pallor, paleness, wanness
▸ **AS A VERB** 1 = **shine**, burn, gleam, brighten, glimmer, smoulder • *The night lantern glowed softly in the darkness.*
2 = **be pink**, colour, flush, blush • *Her freckled skin glowed with health.*
3 = **be suffused**, thrill, radiate, tingle • *The expectant mothers positively glowed with pride.*

glower **AS A VERB** = **scowl**, glare, frown, look daggers, give a dirty look, lour *or* lower • *He glowered at me but said nothing.*
▸ **AS A NOUN** = **scowl**, glare, frown, dirty look, black look, angry stare, lour *or* lower • *His frown deepened into a glower of resentment.*

glowing 1 = **complimentary**, enthusiastic, rave *(informal)*, ecstatic, rhapsodic, laudatory, adulatory, eulogistic • *The*

premiere of his play received glowing reviews.
OPPOSITES: cruel, scathing, dispassionate
2 = **aglow**, red, bright, beaming, radiant, suffused • *a happy face, glowing with good health*
OPPOSITES: pale, wan, pallid
3 = **flushed**, red, flaming, ruddy, florid, aglow • *Her face was glowing with humiliation.*
4 = **bright**, vivid, vibrant, rich, warm, radiant, luminous • *stained glass in rich, glowing colours*
OPPOSITES: cool, grey, dull

glue AS A NOUN = **adhesive**, cement, gum, paste, mucilage • *a tube of glue*
▸ AS A VERB = **stick**, fix, seal, cement, gum, paste, affix • *Glue the fabric around the window.*

glum = **gloomy**, miserable, dismal, down, low, melancholy, dejected, downcast, morose, doleful, downhearted, down in the dumps *(informal)*, down in the mouth, in low spirits • *What are you looking so glum about?*
OPPOSITES: cheerful, jolly, merry

g

glut AS A NOUN = **surfeit**, excess, surplus, plethora, saturation, oversupply, overabundance, superabundance, superfluity • *There's a glut of agricultural products in Western Europe.*
OPPOSITES: lack, shortage, scarcity
▸ AS A VERB 1 = **saturate**, flood, choke, clog, overload, inundate, deluge, oversupply • *Soldiers returning from war had glutted the job market.*
2 = **overfill**, fill, stuff, cram, satiate • *The pond was glutted with fish.*

glutinous = **sticky**, adhesive, cohesive, gooey, viscous, gummy, gluey, mucilaginous, viscid • *He was covered in soft, glutinous mud.*

glutton = **gourmand**, gorger, gannet *(slang)*, gobbler, pig *(informal)* • *He's a real glutton when it comes to junk food.*

gluttonous = **greedy**, insatiable, voracious, ravenous, rapacious, piggish, hoggish • *a selfish, gluttonous and lazy individual*

gluttony = **greed**, rapacity, voracity, greediness, voraciousness, piggishness • *Gluttony is a deadly sin.*

gnarled 1 = **twisted**, knotted, contorted, knotty, knurled • *a garden full of ancient gnarled trees*
2 = **wrinkled**, rough, rugged, leathery • *an old man with gnarled hands*

gnat
▸ COLLECTIVE NOUNS: swarm, cloud

gnaw 1 = **bite**, chew, nibble, munch • *Woodlice attack living plants and gnaw at the stems.*
2 = **distress**, worry, trouble, harry, haunt, plague, nag, fret • *Doubts were already gnawing away at the back of his mind.*
3 = **erode**, consume, devour, eat away *or* into, wear away *or* down • *This run of bad luck has gnawed away at his usually optimistic character.*

gnawing = **continuous**, constant, endless, persistent, nagging, perpetual, continual, niggling, incessant • *Her exhilaration gave way to gnawing fear.*

go AS A VERB 1 = **move**, travel, advance, journey, proceed, pass, fare *(archaic)*, set off • *It took us an hour to go three miles.*
OPPOSITES: remain, stop, stay
2 = **leave**, withdraw, repair, depart, move out, decamp, slope off, make tracks • *Come on, let's go.*
3 = **lead**, run, reach, spread, extend, stretch, connect, span, give access • *There's a mountain road that goes from Blairstown to Millbrook Village.*
4 = **elapse**, pass, flow, fly by, expire, lapse, slip away • *The week has gone so quickly!*
5 = **be given**, be spent, be awarded, be allotted • *The money goes to projects chosen by the Board.*
6 = **be over**, end, pass, finish, disappear, cease, vanish, pass away • *Those days have gone forever.*
7 = **be dismissed**, be fired, be discharged, be laid off, get the sack, get the chop, get your P45 *(informal)* • *He had made a humiliating tactical error, and had to go.*
8 = **belong**, be kept, be located, be situated • *The shoes go on the shoe shelf.*
9 = **die**, perish, pass away, buy it *(U.S. slang)*, expire, check out *(U.S. slang)*, kick it *(slang)*, croak *(slang)*, give up the ghost, snuff it *(informal)*, peg out *(informal)*, kick the bucket *(slang)*, peg it *(informal)*, cark it *(Austral. & N.Z. slang)*, pop your clogs *(informal)* • *I want you to have my jewellery after I've gone.*
10 = **become**, get, turn • *You'd better serve it up before it goes cold.*
11 = **proceed**, develop, turn out, work out, fare, fall out, roll up, pan out *(informal)* • *She says everything is going smoothly.*
12 = **function**, work, run, move, operate, perform • *My car isn't going very well at the moment.*
OPPOSITES: break (down), stop, fail
13 = **sound**, ring, toll, chime, peal • *The bell went for the break.*
14 = **match**, blend, correspond, fit, suit, chime, harmonize • *That jacket and those trousers don't really go.*
15 = **be used up**, be spent, be exhausted • *After a couple of years, all her money had gone.*
16 = **serve**, help, tend • *It just goes to prove you can't trust anyone.*
▸ AS A NOUN 1 = **attempt**, try, effort, bid, shot *(informal)*, crack *(informal)*, essay, stab *(informal)*, whirl *(informal)*, whack *(informal)* • *It took us two goes to get the colour right.*
2 = **turn**, shot *(informal)*, spell, stint • *Whose go is it next?*
3 = **energy**, life, drive, spirit, pep, vitality, vigour, verve, welly *(slang)*, force, get-up-and-go *(informal)*, oomph *(informal)*, brio, vivacity • *For an old woman she still has a lot of go in her.*
▸ IN PHRASES: **go about something** 1 = **tackle**, begin, approach, undertake, set about • *I want him back, but I just don't know how to go about it.*
2 = **engage in**, perform, conduct, pursue, practise, ply, carry on with, apply yourself to, busy *or* occupy yourself with • *We were simply going about our business when we were pounced on by the police.*
go ahead = **continue**, begin, go on, advance, progress, proceed, go forward • *The board will vote today on whether to go ahead with the plan.*
go along with someone = **accompany**, join, escort • *I went along with my brother to see the match.*
go along with something = **agree**, follow, cooperate, concur, assent, acquiesce • *Whatever the majority decision, I'm prepared to go along with it.*
go around *or* **round** = **circulate**, spread • *There's a nasty rumour going around about him.*
go at something = **set about**, start, begin, tackle, set to, get down to, wade into, get to work on, make a start on, get cracking on *(informal)*, address yourself to, get weaving on *(informal)* • *He went at this unpleasant task with grim determination.*
go away = **leave**, withdraw, exit, depart, move out, go to hell *(informal)*, decamp, hook it *(slang)*, slope off, pack your bags *(informal)*, make tracks, get on your bike *(Brit. slang)*, bog off *(Brit. slang)*, sling your hook *(Brit. slang)*, rack off *(Austral. & N.Z. slang)* • *I wish he'd just go away and leave me alone.*
go back = **return**, revert • *I decided to go back to bed.*
go back on something *often with* **on** = **repudiate**, break, forsake, retract, renege on, desert, back out of, change your mind about • *The budget crisis has forced the President to go back on his word.*
go by = **pass**, proceed, elapse, flow on, move onward • *My grandmother was becoming more and more frail as time went by.*
go by something = **obey**, follow, adopt, observe, comply with, heed, submit to, be guided by, take as guide • *If they*

can prove that I'm wrong, then I'll go by what they say.
go down 1 = fall, drop, decline, slump, decrease, fall off, dwindle, lessen, ebb, depreciate, become lower • *Crime has gone down 70 per cent.*
2 = **lose**, be beaten, go under, suffer defeat • *They went down 2-1 to Australia.*
3 = **set**, sink • *the glow left in the sky after the sun has gone down*
4 = **sink**, founder, go under, be submerged • *The ship went down during a training exercise.*
5 = **be remembered**, be recorded, be recalled, be commemorated • *It will go down as one of the highlights of my career.*
go down with something = fall ill with, catch, get, develop, contract, succumb to • *The whole family have gone down with flu.*
go far = be successful, advance, progress, succeed, get on (*informal*), do well, cut it (*informal*), get ahead (*informal*), make your mark, make a name for yourself • *With your talent, you will go far.*
go for someone 1 = prefer, like, choose, favour, admire, be attracted to, be fond of, hold with • *I tend to go for large dark men.*
2 = **attack**, assault, assail, spring upon, rush upon, launch yourself at, set about *or* upon • *Patrick went for him, grabbing him by the throat.*
3 = **scold**, attack, blast, criticize, flame (*informal*), put down, tear into (*informal*), diss (*slang, chiefly U.S.*), impugn, lambast(e) • *My mum went for me because I hadn't told her where I was going.*
go for something 1 = choose, take, pick, adopt, opt for, decide on, espouse, fix on, plump for, settle upon • *People tried to persuade him to go for a more gradual reform program.*
2 = **try to get**, reach for, clutch at, stretch for • *His opponent impeded him as he went for the ball.*
go in for something *with* **for = participate in**, pursue, take part in, undertake, embrace, practise, engage in, espouse • *They go in for tennis and bowls.*
go into something 1 = investigate, consider, study, research, discuss, review, examine, pursue, probe, analyse, look into, delve into, work over, scrutinize, inquire into • *I'd like to go into this matter in a bit more detail.*
2 = **enter**, begin, participate in • *He has decided to go into the tourism business.*
go off 1 = depart, leave, quit, go away, move out, decamp, hook it (*slang*), slope off, pack your bags (*informal*), bog off (*Brit. slang*), rack off (*Austral. & N.Z. slang*) • *She just went off without saying a word to anyone.*
2 = **explode**, fire, blow up, detonate • *A gun went off somewhere in the distance.*
3 = **sound**, ring, toll, chime, peal • *The fire alarm went off.*
4 = **take place**, happen, occur, come off (*informal*), come about • *The meeting went off all right.*
5 = **go bad**, turn, spoil, rot, go stale • *Don't eat that! It's gone off!*
go on 1 = happen, occur, take place • *I don't know what's going on.*
2 = **continue**, last, stay, proceed, carry on, keep going • *the necessity for the war to go on*
3 *often with* **about = ramble on**, carry on, chatter, waffle (*informal, chiefly Brit.*), witter (on) (*informal*), rabbit on (*Brit. informal*), prattle, blether, earbash (*Austral. & N.Z. slang*) • *They're always going on about choice and market forces.*
go on doing something *or* **go on with something = continue**, pursue, proceed, carry on, stick to, persist, keep on, keep at, persevere, stick at • *Go on with your work.*
go out 1 = see someone, court, date (*informal, chiefly U.S.*), woo, go steady (*informal*), be romantically involved with, step out with (*informal*) • *They've been going out for six weeks now.*
2 = **be extinguished**, die out, fade out • *The bedroom light went out after a moment.*
go over something 1 = examine, study, review, revise, inspect, work over • *An accountant has gone over the books.*
2 = **rehearse**, read, scan, reiterate, skim over, peruse • *We went over our lines together before the show.*
go through = be carried through, be completed, be approved, be concluded • *The bill might have gone through if the economy had been growing.*
go through something 1 = suffer, experience, bear, endure, brave, undergo, tolerate, withstand • *He was going through a very difficult time.*
2 = **search**, look through, rummage through, rifle through, hunt through, fossick through (*Austral. & N.Z.*), ferret about in • *It was evident that someone had been going through my possessions.*
3 = **examine**, check, search, explore, look through, work over • *Going through his list of customers is a massive job.*
4 = **use up**, exhaust, consume, squander • *He goes through around £500 a week.*
go through with something = carry on, continue, pursue, keep on, persevere • *Richard pleaded with Belinda not to go through with the divorce.*
go together 1 = harmonize, match, agree, accord, fit, make a pair • *Red wine and oysters don't really go together.*
2 = **go out**, court, date (*informal, chiefly U.S.*), go steady (*informal*) • *We met a month ago and we've been going together ever since.*
go under 1 = fail, die, sink, go down, fold (*informal*), founder, succumb, go bankrupt • *If one firm goes under it could provoke a cascade of bankruptcies.*
2 = **sink**, go down, founder, submerge • *The ship went under, taking with her all her crew.*
go up = increase, rise, mount, soar, get higher • *Interest rates have gone up again.*
go with something = match, suit, blend, correspond with, agree with, fit, complement, harmonize • *Does this tie go with this shirt?*
go without something = be deprived of, want, lack, be denied, do without, abstain, go short, deny yourself • *I have known what it is like to go without food for days.*
no go = impossible, not on (*informal*), vain, hopeless, futile • *I tried to get him to change his mind, but it was no go.*

goad AS A VERB **1 = provoke**, drive, annoy, sting, irritate, lash, harass, hassle (*informal*), nark (*Brit., Austral. & N.Z. slang*), be on your back (*slang*) • *Charles was forever trying to goad her into losing her temper.*
2 = **urge**, drive, prompt, spur, stimulate, provoke, arouse, propel, prod, prick, incite, instigate, egg on, exhort, impel • *He goaded me into taking direct action.*
▸ AS A NOUN = **incentive**, urge, spur, motivation, pressure, stimulus, stimulation, impetus, incitement • *His distrust only acted as a goad to me to prove him wrong.*

go-ahead AS A NOUN = **permission**, consent, green light, assent, leave, authorization, O.K. *or* okay (*informal*) • *Don't do any major repair work until you get the go-ahead from your insurers.*
▸ AS AN ADJECTIVE = **enterprising**, pioneering, ambitious, progressive, go-getting (*informal*), up-and-coming • *The estate is one of the most go-ahead wine producers in South Africa.*

goal = aim, end, target, purpose, object, intention, objective, ambition, destination, Holy Grail (*informal*) • *The goal is to raise as much money as possible.*

goat
▸ RELATED ADJECTIVES: caprine, hircine
▸ NAME OF MALE: billy, buck
▸ NAME OF FEMALE: nanny
▸ NAME OF YOUNG: kid, yeanling
▸ COLLECTIVE NOUNS: herd, tribe

gob = **piece**, lump, chunk, hunk, nugget, blob, wad, clod, wodge (*Brit. informal*) • *a gob of ice*

gobble = **devour**, swallow, gulp, guzzle, wolf, bolt, cram in, gorge on, pig out on (*slang*), stuff yourself with • *He gobbled all the beef stew.*

gobbledegook = **nonsense**, jargon, babble, cant, twaddle, gibberish, mumbo jumbo, jabber, gabble, rigmarole, malarkey, double talk, Greek (*informal*), officialese, bizzo (*Austral. slang*), bull's wool (*Austral. & N.Z. slang*) • *When he asked questions, all he got back was bureaucratic gobbledegook.*

go-between = **intermediary**, agent, medium, broker, factor, dealer, liaison, mediator, middleman • *He will act as a go-between to try and work out an agenda.*

goblet = **cup**, chalice, beaker, flagon • *a silver brandy goblet*

god = **deity**, immortal, divinity, divine being, supreme being, atua (*N.Z.*) • *Zeus, king of the gods*

QUOTATIONS

As flies to wanton boys are we to the gods;
They kill us for their sport
[William Shakespeare *King Lear*]

Heaven always bears some proportion to earth. The god of the cannibal will be a cannibal, of the crusader a crusader, and of the merchants a merchant
[Ralph Waldo Emerson *The Conduct of Life*]

If the triangles were to make a god, he would have three sides
[Montesquieu *Lettres Persanes*]

▹ *See panels* **Gods and Goddesses; the Fates; the Graces; the Muses**

God

▸ RELATED ADJECTIVE: divine
▸ RELATED PHOBIA: theophobia

QUOTATIONS

God is our refuge and strength, a very present help in trouble
[*Bible: Psalms*]

God is seen God
In the star, in the stone, in the flesh, in the soul and the clod
[Robert Browning *Men and Women*]

You cannot plumb the depths of the human heart, nor find out what a man is thinking; how do you expect to search out God, who made all these things, and find out his mind or comprehend his thoughts?
[*Apocrypha: Judith*]

If God did not exist, man would have to invent him
[Voltaire *Epître CIV à l'auteur du livre des trois imposteurs*]

God moves in a mysterious way
His wonders to perform
[William Cowper *Light Shining Out of Darkness*]

The voice of the people is the voice of God
[Alcuin *Epistles*]

God is but a word invented to explain the world
[Lamartine *Nouvelle harmonies poétiques et religieuses*]

Thou shalt have one God only; who
Would be at the expense of two?
[Arthur Hugh Clough *The Latest Decalogue*]

God is subtle, but he is not malicious
[Albert Einstein]

God, to me, it seems,
is a verb
not a noun,
proper or improper
[R. Buckminster Fuller *No More Secondhand God*]

Theist and Atheist: The fight between them is as to whether God shall be called God or shall have some other name
[Samuel Butler *Notebooks*]

It is an insult to God to believe in God
[Galen Strawson]

God and the doctor we alike adore
But only when in danger, not before;
The danger o'er, both are alike requited,
God is forgotten, and the Doctor slighted
[John Owen *Epigrams*]

Any God I ever felt in church I brought in with me
[Alice Walker *The Color Purple*]

godforsaken = **desolate**, abandoned, deserted, remote, neglected, lonely, bleak, gloomy, backward, dismal, dreary, forlorn, wretched • *I don't want to stay in this God-forsaken country.*

godless = **wicked**, depraved, profane, unprincipled, atheistic, ungodly, irreligious, impious, unrighteous • *a godless and alienated society*

godlike = **divine**, heavenly, celestial, superhuman • *They seemed godlike in their wisdom and nobility.*

godly = **devout**, religious, holy, righteous, pious, good, saintly, god-fearing • *a learned and godly preacher*

godsend = **blessing**, help, benefit, asset, boon • *A microwave is a godsend for busy people.*

gogga = **insect**, bug, creepy-crawly (*Brit. informal*) • *The place was crawling with goggas.*

goggle = **stare**, gape, gawp (*slang*), gawk • *He goggled at her in astonishment.*

going = **current**, accepted, standard, usual, typical • *She says that's the going rate for a house this big.*

going-over 1 = **examination**, study, check, review, survey, investigation, analysis, inspection, scrutiny, perusal • *Michael was given a complete going-over and was diagnosed with hay fever.*
2 = **thrashing**, attack, beating, whipping, thumping, pasting (*slang*), buffeting, drubbing (*informal*) • *The bouncers took him outside and gave him a thorough going-over.*
3 = **dressing-down**, talking-to (*informal*), lecture, rebuke, reprimand, scolding, chiding, tongue-lashing, chastisement, castigation • *Our manager gave us a right going-over in the changing room after the game.*

goings-on = **incidents**, happenings, events, carry-on, shenanigans, hanky-panky, funny business • *She had found out about the goings-on in the factory.*

gold

▸ RELATED ADJECTIVE: auric

golden 1 = **yellow**, bright, brilliant, blonde, blond, flaxen • *She combed and arranged her golden hair.*
OPPOSITES: black, dark, dull
2 = **successful**, glorious, prosperous, best, rich, flourishing, halcyon • *the golden age of American moviemaking*
OPPOSITES: poorest, worst, most unfavourable
3 = **promising**, excellent, valuable, favourable, advantageous, auspicious, opportune, propitious • *There's a golden opportunity for peace which must be seized.*
OPPOSITES: black, dark, unfavourable
4 = **favourite**, favoured, most popular, best-loved, in • *Critics hailed him as the golden boy of British cinema.*
▹ *See panels* **Shades of orange; Shades of yellow**

goldfinch

▸ COLLECTIVE NOUN: charm

golf

▹ *See panel* **Golf terms**

gone 1 = **missing**, lost, away, vanished, absent, astray • *He's already been gone four hours!*
2 = **used up**, spent, finished, consumed • *After two years, all her money was gone.*
3 = **past**, over, ended, finished, elapsed • *Those happy times are gone forever.*
4 = **dead**, no more, departed, extinct, deceased, defunct • *The paramedics tried to revive him, but it was too late – he was gone.*

goo = **gunge**, ooze, sludge, slime, gunk, crud, gloop • *a sticky goo of pineapple and coconut*

GODS AND GODDESSES

Aztec

Acolmiztli	Chicomexochtli	Itzpapalotl	Quetzalcoatl	Tena
Acolnahuacatl	Chiconahui	Ixtlilton	Tecciztecatl	Tzintetol
Amimitl	Cihuacoatl	Macuilxochitl	Techalotl	Tzontemoc
Atl	Coatlicue	Malinalxochi	Techlotl	Uixtociuatl
Atlaua	Cochimetl	Mayahuel	Tepeyollotl	Xilonen
Camaxtli	Coyolxauhqui	Mictlantecihuatl	Teteo	Xipe Totec
Centeotl	Ehecatl	Mictlantecutli	Tezcatlipoca	Xippilli
Centzonuitznaua	Huehueteotl	Mixcoatl	Tlahuixcalpantecuhtli	Xiuhcoatl
Chalchiuhtlatonal	Huitzilopochtli	Nanauatzin	Tlaloc	Xiuhteuctli
Chalchiuhtlicue	Huixtocihuatl	Omacatl	Tlaltecuhtli	Xochipilli
Chalchiutotolin	Ilamatecuhtli	Omecihuatl	Tlazolteotl	Xochiquetzal
Chalmecacihuilt	Innan	Ometecuhtli	Tonacatecuhtli	Xolotl
Chantico	Itzlacoliuhque	Patecatl	Tonatiuh	Yacatecuhtli
Chicomecoatl	Itzli	Paynal	Tzapotla	

Celtic

Áine	Bíle	Danu	Llyr	Nantosuelta	Sequana
Anu	Blodeuedd	Dôn	Lugh	Nechtan	Sirona
Arianhrod	Bóand	Donn	Mabon	Nemain	Sucellus
Artio	Bodb	Epona	Macha	Nemetona	Taranis
Badb	Brigid	Ériu	Manannán	Núadu	Teutates
Balor	Ceridwen	Esus	Manawydan	Ogma	Vagdavercustis
Banba	Cernunnos	Fand	Medb	Óengus Mac Óc	
Bécuma	Dagda	Lir	Midir	Rhiannon	
Belenus	Dana	Lleu Llaw Gyffes	Morrígan	Rosmerta	

Egyptian

Anubis	Horus	Maat	Ptah	Re	Set
Hathor	Isis	Osiris	Ra *or* Amen-Ra	Serapis	Thoth

Greek

Aeolus	winds	Helios	sun
Aphrodite	love and beauty	Hephaestus	fire and metalworking
Apollo	light, youth, and music	Hera	queen of the gods
Ares	war	Hermes	messenger of the gods
Artemis	hunting and the moon	Horae *or* the Hours	seasons
Asclepius	healing	Hymen	marriage
Athene *or* Pallas Athene	wisdom	Hyperion	sun
Bacchus	wine	Hypnos	sleep
Boreas	north wind	Iris	rainbow
Cronos	fertility of the earth	Momus	blame and mockery
Demeter	agriculture	Morpheus	sleep and dreams
Dionysus	wine	Nemesis	vengeance
Eos	dawn	Nike	victory
Eros	love	Pan	woods and shepherds
Fates	destiny	Poseidon	sea and earthquakes
Gaea	the earth	Rhea	fertility
Graces	charm and beauty	Selene	moon
Hades	underworld	Uranus	sky
Hebe	youth and spring	Zephyrus	west wind
Hecate	underworld	Zeus	king of the gods

Hindu

Agni	Durga	Indra	Krishna	Rama	Varuna
Brahma	Ganesa	Kali	Lakshmi	Siva	Vishnu
Devi	Hanuman	Kama	Maya	Ushas	

Incan

Apo	Chasca	Huaca	Mama Oello	Paricia	Zaramama
Apocatequil	Chasca Coyllur	Illapa	Mama Pacha	Punchau	
Apu Illapu	Cocomama	Inti	Mama Quilla	Supay	
Apu Punchau	Coniraya	Ka-Ata-Killa Kon	Manco Capac	Urcaguary	
Catequil	Copacati	Mama Allpa	Pachacamac	Vichama	
Cavillaca	Ekkeko	Mama Cocha	Pariacaca	Viracocha	

GODS AND GODDESSES (CONTINUED)

Mayan

Ac Yanto, Acan, Acat, Ah Bolom Tzacab, Ah Cancum, Ah Chun Caan, Ah Chuy Kak, Ah Ciliz, Ah Cun Can, Ah Cuxtal, Ah Hulneb, Ah Kin, Ah Mun, Ah Muzencab, Ah Peku, Ah Puch, Ah Tabai, Ah Uincir Dz'acab, Ah Uuc Ticab, Ahau-Kin, Ahmakiq, Ahulane, Ajbit, Akhushtal, Alaghom Naom, Alom, Backlum Chaam, Balam, Bitol, Buluc Chabtan, Cabaguil, Cakulha, Camaxtli, Camazotz, Caprakan, Cauac, Chac, Chac Uayab Xoc, Chamer, Chibirias, Cit Bolon Tum, Cizin, Colel Cab, Colop U Uichkin, Coyopa, Cum Hau, Ekchuah, Ghanan, Gucumatz, Hacha'kyum, Hun Came, Hun Hunahpu, Hunab Ku, Hurakan, Itzamna, Itzananohk'u, Ix, Ixchel *or* Ix Chebel Yax, Ixtab, Ixzaluoh, Kan, Kan-u-Uayeyab, Kan-xib-yui, Kianto, K'in, Kinich Ahau, Kukulcan, Mulac, Naum, Nohochacyum, Tlacolotl, Tohil, Tzakol, Votan, Xaman Ek, Yaluk, Yum Caax, Zotz

Norse

Aegir, Aesir, Balder, Bragi, Frey, Freya, Frigg, Hel, Heimdall, Idun, Loki, Njord, Norns, Odin, Thor, Tyr, Vanir

Roman

Aesculapius	medicine
Apollo	light, youth, and music
Aurora	dawn
Bacchus	wine
Bellona	war
Bona Dea	fertility
Ceres	agriculture
Cupid	love
Cybele	nature
Diana	hunting and the moon
Faunus	forests
Flora	flowers
Janus	doors and beginnings
Juno	queen of the gods
Jupiter *or* Jove	king of the gods
Lares	household
Luna	moon
Mars	war
Mercury	messenger of the gods
Minerva	wisdom
Neptune	sea
Penates	storeroom
Phoebus	sun
Pluto	underworld
Quirinus	war
Saturn	agriculture and vegetation
Sol	sun
Somnus	sleep
Trivia	crossroads
Venus	love
Victoria	victory
Vulcan	fire and metalworking

good AS AN ADJECTIVE **1 = excellent**, great, fine, pleasing, capital, choice, crucial *(slang)*, acceptable, pleasant, worthy, first-class, divine, splendid, satisfactory, superb, enjoyable, awesome *(slang)*, dope *(slang)*, world-class, admirable, agreeable, super *(informal)*, pleasurable, wicked *(slang)*, bad *(slang)*, first-rate, tiptop, bitchin' *(U.S. slang)*, booshit *(Austral. slang)*, exo *(Austral. slang)*, sik *(Austral. slang)*, rad *(informal)*, phat *(slang)*, schmick *(Austral. informal)*, beaut *(informal)*, barrie *(Scot. slang)*, belting *(Brit. slang)*, pearler *(Austral. slang)* • *You should read this book – it's really good.*
OPPOSITES: bad, boring, awful
2 = fine, excellent, superior, first-class, first-rate, choice • *He enjoys good food and fine wine.*
OPPOSITES: terrible, inferior
3 = proficient, able, skilled, capable, expert, talented, efficient, clever, accomplished, reliable, first-class, satisfactory, competent, thorough, tasty *(Brit. informal)*, adept, first-rate, adroit, dexterous • *He is very good at his job.*
OPPOSITES: bad, useless, pathetic
4 = positive, beneficial, favourable, advantageous, auspicious, propitious • *Biotechnology should be good news for developing countries.*
OPPOSITES: negative, inauspicious, unpropitious
5 = sensible, useful, wise, valuable, suitable, worthwhile, constructive, shrewd, prudent, sound, commendable, judicious, well-thought-out, well-reasoned • *They thought it was a good idea to make some offenders do community service.*
6 = desirable, pleasing, positive, productive, satisfying, beneficial, constructive, gratifying, advantageous • *I think it's good that some people are going.*
7 = clear, correct, accurate, exact, precise, definite • *I have a fairly good idea of what's going on.*
8 = profitable, fair, reasonable, adequate, lucrative • *I got a good price for the house.*
9 = beneficial, useful, healthy, helpful, favourable, wholesome, advantageous, salutary, salubrious • *Rain water was once considered to be good for the complexion.*
OPPOSITES: damaging, harmful, detrimental
10 = honourable, moral, worthy, ethical, upright, admirable, honest, righteous, exemplary, right, virtuous, trustworthy, altruistic, praiseworthy, estimable • *The president is a good man.*
OPPOSITES: bad, base, evil
11 = well-behaved, seemly, mannerly, proper, polite, orderly, obedient, dutiful, decorous, well-mannered • *The children have been very good all day.*
OPPOSITES: rude, naughty, mischievous
12 = kind, kindly, friendly, obliging, charitable, humane, gracious, benevolent, merciful, beneficent, well-disposed, kind-hearted • *It's very good of you to help out at such short notice.*
OPPOSITES: mean *(informal)*, cruel, unkind
13 = cheerful, happy, pleasant, agreeable, congenial, convivial • *Everyone was in a pretty good mood.*
14 = true, real, genuine, proper, reliable, dependable, sound, trustworthy, dinkum *(Austral. & N.Z. informal)* • *She's been a good friend to me over the years.*
15 = full, long, whole, complete, entire, solid, extensive • *The film lasts a good two and a half hours.*
OPPOSITES: short, scant

GOLF TERMS

ace *(U.S.)*, air shot *or* fresh air shot, albatross, approach, apron, back nine *(chiefly U.S.)*, backswing, bag, ball, bandit, better-ball, birdie, blade, bogey, borrow, bunker, trap, *or (esp U.S. & Canad.)* sand trap, caddie, caddie car, carry, casual water, chip, club, clubhouse, course, cup, cut, divot, dormie, downswing, draw, drive, driver, driving range, duff, eagle, fade, fairway, fluff, foozle, fore, four-ball, foursome, front nine *(chiefly U.S.)*, gimme, green, green fee, green keeper, greensome, grip, half, half shot, handicap, hazard, heel, hole, hole in one, honour, hook, hosel, iron, ladies' tee, lag, lie, links, local rules, loft, long iron, marker, match play, medal play, medal tee, midiron, nine-hole course, nineteenth hole, par, pin, pitch and run, pitching wedge, pitch shot, play through, plus fours, plus twos, practice swing, pull, putt, putter, putting green, rabbit, recovery, rough, round, rub of the green, run, Royal and Ancient *or* R & A, sand wedge, sclaff, score, score card, scratch, shaft, shank, short iron, single, slice, slow play, spoon, Stableford system, stance, stroke, stroke play, stymie, sweetspot, swing, take-away, tee, thin, tiger, threesome, top, trolley, waggle, wedge, wood, yips

16 = considerable, large, substantial, sufficient, adequate, ample • *A good number of people agree with me.*
17 = valid, convincing, compelling, legitimate, authentic, persuasive, sound, bona fide • *Can you think of one good reason why I should tell you?*
OPPOSITES: false, invalid, fraudulent
18 = best, newest, special, finest, nicest, smartest, fancy, most valuable, most precious • *Try not to get paint on your good clothes.*
19 = sunny, clear, fair, bright, calm, mild, clement, balmy, cloudless • *If the weather's good tomorrow, we'll go for a picnic.*
20 = edible, untainted, uncorrupted, eatable, fit to eat • *Is this fish still good, or has it gone off?*
OPPOSITES: off, bad, decayed
21 = convenient, timely, fitting, fit, appropriate, suitable, well-timed, opportune • *Is this a good time for us to discuss our plans?*
OPPOSITES: inappropriate, unfitting, inconvenient
▸ **AS A NOUN 1 = benefit**, interest, gain, advantage, use, service, profit, welfare, behalf, usefulness, wellbeing • *I'm only doing all this for your own good.*
OPPOSITES: harm, loss, disadvantage
2 = virtue, goodness, righteousness, worth, merit, excellence, morality, probity, rectitude, uprightness • *Good and evil may co-exist within one family.*
OPPOSITES: evil, corruption, cruelty
▸ **IN PHRASES: for good = permanently**, finally, for ever, once and for all, irrevocably, never to return, sine die *(Latin)* • *A few shots of this drug cleared up the disease for good.*
in good part = good-naturedly, well, cheerfully, amiably, indulgently, tolerantly, without offence • *He took their teasing in good part.*
make good = make it *(informal)*, succeed, do well, flourish, be successful, prosper, arrive *(informal)*, make the grade *(informal)*, turn out well, make your mark *(informal)*, do all right for yourself *(informal)* • *Both men are poor boys who have made good.*
make good on something = achieve, keep, effect, complete, perform, realise, carry out, fulfil, accomplish, execute, discharge, bring to completion • *He was confident they would make good on their pledges.*

QUOTATIONS

Mostly, we are good when it makes sense. A good society is one that makes sense of being good
[Ian McEwan *Enduring Love*]

Being good is just a matter of temperament in the end
[Iris Murdoch *The Nice and the Good*]

No one can be good for long if goodness is not in demand
[Bertolt Brecht *The Good Woman of Setzuan*]

'For your own good' is a persuasive argument that will eventually make a man agree to his own destruction
[Janet Frame *Faces in the Water*]

goodbye AS A NOUN = farewell, parting, leave-taking • *It was a very emotional goodbye.*
▸ **AS AN INTERJECTION = farewell**, see you, see you later, ciao *(Italian)*, cheerio, adieu, ta-ta, au revoir *(French)*, auf Wiedersehen *(German)*, adios *(Spanish)*, haere ra *(N.Z.)* • *Well, goodbye and good luck.*
good-for-nothing AS AN ADJECTIVE = worthless, useless, idle, irresponsible, feckless • *a good-for-nothing teenager who barely knows how to read*
▸ **AS A NOUN = layabout**, piker *(Austral. & N.Z. slang)*, slacker *(informal)*, profligate, waster, black sheep, skiver *(Brit. slang)*, idler, ne'er-do-well, wastrel, bludger *(Austral. & N.Z. informal)*, scapegrace, rapscallion • *a bunch of lazy good-for-nothings*
good-humoured = genial, happy, pleasant, cheerful, amiable, affable, congenial, good-tempered • *Rose remained good-humoured in spite of all their teasing.*
good-looking = attractive, pretty, fair, beautiful, lovely, handsome, gorgeous, bonny, personable, comely, well-favoured, hot *(informal)*, fit *(Brit. informal)* • *She noticed him because he was good-looking.*
goodly = considerable, large, significant, substantial, tidy *(informal)*, ample, sizable *or* sizeable • *He spent a goodly part of his life in America.*
good-natured = amiable, kind, kindly, friendly, generous, helpful, obliging, tolerant, agreeable, benevolent, good-hearted, magnanimous, well-disposed, warm-hearted • *He was good-natured about it, and didn't make a fuss.*
goodness 1 = virtue, honour, merit, integrity, morality, honesty, righteousness, probity, rectitude, uprightness • *He retains his faith in human goodness.*
OPPOSITES: evil, corruption, badness

2 = **excellence**, value, quality, worth, merit, superiority • *his total belief in the goodness of socialist society*
3 = **nutrition**, benefit, advantage, nourishment, wholesomeness, salubriousness • *drinks full of natural goodness*
4 = **kindness**, charity, humanity, goodwill, mercy, compassion, generosity, friendliness, benevolence, graciousness, beneficence, kindliness, humaneness, kind-heartedness • *performing actions of goodness towards the poor*

QUOTATIONS
Goodness is easier to recognise than to define
[W.H. Auden *I Believe*]
Nobody deserves to be praised for his goodness if he has not the power to be wicked. All other goodness is often only weakness and impotence of the will
[Duc de la Rochefoucauld *Maxims*]
Goodness is not achieved in a vacuum, but in the company of other men, attended by love
[Saul Bellow *Dangling Man*]

g

goods 1 = **merchandise**, stock, products, stuff, commodities, wares • *a wide range of consumer goods*
2 = **property**, things, effects, gear, furniture, movables, possessions, furnishings, belongings, trappings, paraphernalia, chattels, appurtenances • *You can give all your unwanted goods to charity.*

goodwill = **friendliness**, favour, friendship, benevolence, amity, kindliness • *I invited them to dinner as a gesture of goodwill.*

goody-goody AS A NOUN = **prig**, puritan, prude, stuffed shirt *(informal)* • *He's a bit of a goody-goody.*
▸ AS AN ADJECTIVE = **sanctimonious**, pious, pi *(Brit. slang)*, self-righteous, holier-than-thou, priggish • *You're too goody-goody to get into trouble, aren't you?*

gooey 1 = **sticky**, soft, tacky, viscous, glutinous, gummy, icky *(informal)*, gluey, gloopy, mucilaginous, gungy • *a lovely gooey, sticky mess*
2 = **sentimental**, romantic, sloppy, soppy, maudlin, syrupy *(informal)*, slushy *(informal)*, mawkish, tear-jerking *(informal)*, icky *(informal)* • *He wrote me a long, gooey love letter.*

goose
▸ RELATED ADJECTIVES: anserine, anserous
▸ NAME OF MALE: gander
▸ NAME OF YOUNG: gosling
▸ COLLECTIVE NOUNS: gaggle, skein

gore[1] = **blood**, slaughter, bloodshed, carnage, butchery • *video nasties full of blood and gore*

gore[2] = **pierce**, wound, stab, spit, transfix, impale • *He was gored to death by a rhinoceros.*

gorge AS A NOUN = **ravine**, canyon, pass, clough *(dialect)*, chasm, cleft, fissure, defile, gulch *(U.S. & Canad.)* • *a steep path into Crete's Samaria Gorge*
▸ AS A VERB 1 = **overeat**, bolt, devour, gobble, wolf, swallow, gulp, guzzle, pig out *(slang)* • *I could spend all day gorging on chocolate.*
2 *usually reflexive* = **stuff**, fill, feed, cram, glut, surfeit, satiate, sate • *Three men were gorging themselves on grouse and watermelon.*

gorgeous 1 = **magnificent**, grand, beautiful, superb, spectacular, splendid, glittering, dazzling, luxurious, sumptuous, opulent • *Some of these Renaissance buildings are absolutely gorgeous.*
OPPOSITES: cheap, shabby, shoddy
2 = **delightful**, good, great, grand, wonderful, excellent, brilliant, lovely, fantastic, pleasant, terrific, splendid, enjoyable, super, splendiferous *(facetious)* • *I've had a gorgeous time today.*
OPPOSITES: awful, miserable, dismal
3 = **beautiful**, attractive, lovely, stunning *(informal)*, elegant, handsome, good-looking, exquisite, drop-dead *(slang)*, ravishing, hot *(informal)*, fit *(Brit. informal)* • *The cosmetics industry uses gorgeous women to sell its products.*
OPPOSITES: homely, plain, ugly
4 = **dazzling**, bright, brilliant, magnificent, sumptuous, opulent, resplendent, showy • *a red-haired man in the gorgeous uniform of a Marshal of the Empire*
OPPOSITES: dreary, sombre
5 = **fine**, glorious, sunny • *It's a gorgeous day.*
OPPOSITES: dull, gloomy

gory 1 = **grisly**, bloody, murderous, bloodthirsty, sanguinary • *The film is full of gory death scenes.*
2 = **bloody**, bloodstained, blood-soaked • *The ambulanceman carefully stripped off his gory clothes.*

gospel 1 = **doctrine**, news, teachings, message, revelation, creed, credo, tidings • *He visited the sick and preached the gospel.*
2 = **truth**, fact, certainty, the last word, verity • *The results were not to be taken as gospel.*

gossamer = **delicate**, light, fine, thin, sheer, transparent, airy, flimsy, silky, diaphanous, gauzy • *daring gossamer dresses of sheer black lace*

gossip AS A NOUN 1 = **idle talk**, scandal, hearsay, tittle-tattle, buzz, dirt *(U.S. slang)*, goss *(informal)*, jaw *(slang)*, gen *(Brit. informal)*, small talk, chitchat, blether, scuttlebutt *(U.S. slang)*, chinwag *(Brit. informal)* • *There has been a lot of gossip about the reasons for his absence.* • *a magazine packed with celebrity gossip*
2 = **busybody**, babbler, prattler, chatterbox *(informal)*, blether, chatterer, scandalmonger, gossipmonger, tattletale *(chiefly U.S. & Canad.)* • *She was a vicious old gossip.*
▸ AS A VERB = **chat**, chatter, blather, schmooze *(slang)*, jaw *(slang)*, dish the dirt *(informal)*, blether, shoot the breeze *(slang, chiefly U.S.)*, chew the fat *or* rag *(slang)* • *We gossiped well into the night.*

QUOTATIONS
There is only one thing in the world worse than being talked about, and that is not being talked about
[Oscar Wilde *The Picture of Dorian Gray*]
Gossip is a sort of smoke that comes from the dirty tobacco-pipes of those that diffuse it; it proves nothing but the bad taste of the smoker
[George Eliot *Daniel Deronda*]

gouge AS A VERB = **scoop**, cut, score, dig (out), scratch, hollow (out), claw, chisel, gash, incise • *quarries which have gouged great holes in the hills*
▸ AS A NOUN = **gash**, cut, scratch, hollow, score, scoop, notch, groove, trench, furrow, incision • *iron-rimmed wheels digging great gouges into the road's surface*

gourmet AS AN ADJECTIVE = **gastronomic**, epicurean • *They share a love of gourmet cooking.*
▸ AS A NOUN = **connoisseur**, foodie *(informal)*, bon vivant *(French)*, epicure, gastronome • *coquilles Saint-Jacques – a gourmet's delight*

govern 1 = **rule**, lead, control, command, manage, direct, guide, handle, conduct, order, reign over, administer, oversee, supervise, be in power over, call the shots, call the tune, hold sway over, superintend • *They go to the polls on Friday to choose the people they want to govern their country.*
2 = **determine**, decide, guide, rule, influence, underlie, sway • *Marine insurance is governed by a strict series of rules and regulations.*
3 = **restrain**, control, check, contain, master, discipline, regulate, curb, inhibit, tame, subdue, get the better of, bridle, hold in check, keep a tight rein on • *Try to govern your temper.*

governance = **rule**, government, authority, administration, sovereignty, dominion, polity • *A fundamental change in the governance of the country is the key to all other changes.*

governess = **tutor**, teacher • *He studied under the strict tutelage of his English governess.*

governing = **ruling**, controlling, commanding • *The league became the governing body for amateur fencing in the US.*

government 1 = **administration**, executive, ministry, regime, governing body, powers-that-be • *The Government has insisted that confidence is needed before the economy can improve.*

2 = **rule**, state, law, authority, administration, sovereignty, governance, dominion, polity, statecraft • *our system of government*

QUOTATIONS

Government is a contrivance of human wisdom to provide for human wants. Men have a right that these wants should be provided for by this wisdom
[Edmund Burke *Reflections on the Revolution in France*]

As the happiness of the people is the sole end of government, so the consent of the people is the only foundation for it
[John Adams]

The requisites of government are that there be sufficiency of food, sufficiency of military equipment, and the confidence of the people in their ruler
[Confucius *Analects*]

In the long run every government is the exact symbol of its people, with their wisdom and their unwisdom
[Thomas Carlyle *Past and Present*]

Government is either organized benevolence or organized madness
[John Updike *Buchanan Dying*]

All government is evil, and the parent of evil ... The best government is that which governs least
[John L. O'Sullivan]

It is perfectly true that that government is best which governs least. It is equally true that that government is best which provides most
[Walter Lippmann *A Preface to Politics*]

Society in every state is a blessing, but government, even in its best state, is but a necessary evil; in its worst state, an intolerable one
[Thomas Paine *Common Sense*]

Any system of government will work when everything is going well. It's the system that functions in the pinches that survives
[John F. Kennedy *Why England Slept*]

Nothing appears more surprising to those who consider human affairs with a philosophical eye, than the ease with which the many are governed by the few
[David Hume *First Principles of Government*]

The worst thing in this world, next to anarchy, is government
[Henry Ward Beecher *Proverbs from Plymouth Pulpit*]

Government does not solve problems; it subsidizes them
[Ronald Reagan *Speaking My Mind*]

▷ *See panel* **Types of government**

governmental = **administrative**, state, political, official, executive, ministerial, sovereign, bureaucratic • *a governmental agency for providing financial aid to developing countries*

governor = **leader**, administrator, ruler, head, minister, director, manager, chief, officer, executive, boss *(informal)*, commander, controller, supervisor, superintendent, mandarin, comptroller, functionary, overseer, baas *(S. African)* • *He was governor of the province in the late 1970s.*

▸ RELATED ADJECTIVE: gubernatorial

gown = **dress**, costume, garment, robe, frock, garb, habit • *a blue satin ball gown*

▷ *See panel* **Dresses**

grab AS A VERB = **snatch**, catch, seize, capture, bag, grip, grasp, clutch, snap up, pluck, latch on to, catch *or* take hold of • *I managed to grab her hand.*

▸ AS A NOUN = **lunge** • *I made a grab for the knife.*

▸ IN PHRASES: **up for grabs** = **available**, for sale, on the market, to be had, up for sale, obtainable • *The famous Ritz Hotel is up for grabs for £100 million.*

grace AS A NOUN 1 = **elegance**, finesse, poise, ease, polish, refinement, fluency, suppleness, gracefulness • *He moved with the grace of a trained dancer.*

OPPOSITES: stiffness, ugliness, ungainliness

2 = **manners**, decency, cultivation, etiquette, breeding, consideration, propriety, tact, decorum, mannerliness • *He hadn't even the grace to apologize for what he'd done.*

OPPOSITES: bad manners, tactlessness

3 = **indulgence**, mercy, pardon, compassion, quarter,

TYPES OF GOVERNMENT

absolutism	by an absolute ruler	meritocracy	by rulers chosen according to ability
anarchy	absence of government	mobocracy	by the mob
aristocracy	by nobility	monarchy	by monarch
autarchy *or* autocracy	by an unrestricted individual	monocracy	by one ruler
bureaucracy	by officials	nomocracy	by rule of law
communalism	by self-governing communities	ochlocracy	by mob
constitutionalism	according to a constitution	octarchy	by eight rulers
corporatism	by corporate groups	oligarchy	by the few
democracy	by the people	pantisocracy	by all equally
despotism	by a despot or absolute ruler	pentarchy	by five rulers
diarchy	by two rulers	plutocracy	by the rich
dictatorship	by dictator	pornocracy	by whores
ergatocracy	by the workers	ptochocracy	by the poor
gerontocracy	by old people	quangocracy	by quangos
gynaecocracy *or* gynarchy	by women	slavocracy	by slaveholders
hagiocracy *or* hagiarchy	by holy men	squirearchy	by squires
heptarchy	by seven rulers	stratocracy	by the army
hexarchy	by six rulers	technocracy	by experts
hierocracy *or* hierarchy	by priests	tetrarchy	by four rulers
imperialism	by an emperor or empire	theocracy *or* thearchy	by a deity
isocracy	by equals	triarchy	by three rulers
		tyranny	by a tyrant

charity, forgiveness, reprieve, clemency, leniency • *He was granted four days' grace to be with his family.*
4 = benevolence, favour, goodness, goodwill, generosity, kindness, beneficence, kindliness, benefaction • *It was only by the grace of God that no one died.*
OPPOSITES: ill will
5 = prayer, thanks, blessing, thanksgiving, benediction • *Leo, will you say grace?*
6 = favour, regard, respect, approval, esteem, approbation, good opinion • *The reasons for his fall from grace are not clear.*
OPPOSITES: disfavour
▸ **AS A VERB 1 = adorn**, enhance, decorate, enrich, set off, garnish, ornament, deck, embellish, bedeck, beautify • *the beautiful old Welsh dresser that graced this homely room*
2 = honour, favour, distinguish, elevate, dignify, glorify • *He graced our ceremony with his distinguished presence.*
OPPOSITES: ruin, insult, spoil

QUOTATIONS
Some hae meat and canna eat,
Some wad eat that want it;
But we hae meat, and we can eat,
Sae let the Lord be thankit
[Robert Burns *Grace Before Meat*]

graceful 1 = elegant, easy, flowing, smooth, fine, pleasing, beautiful, agile, symmetrical, gracile *(rare)* • *Her movements were so graceful they seemed effortless.*
OPPOSITES: ugly, stiff, inelegant
2 = polite, mannerly, charming, gracious, civil, courteous, well-mannered • *She was calm and graceful under pressure.*

graceless 1 = inelegant, forced, awkward, clumsy, ungainly, unco *(Austral. slang)* • *a graceless pirouette*
2 = ill-mannered, crude, rude, coarse, vulgar, rough, improper, shameless, unsophisticated, gauche, barbarous, boorish, gawky, uncouth, loutish, indecorous, unmannerly • *She couldn't stand his blunt, graceless manner.*

Graces, the = Charities

THE GRACES

Aglaia   Euphrosyne   Thalia

gracious 1 = courteous, polite, civil, accommodating, kind, kindly, pleasing, friendly, obliging, amiable, cordial, hospitable, courtly, chivalrous, well-mannered • *He is always a gracious host.*
OPPOSITES: rude, mean, ungracious
2 = compassionate, charitable, benign, indulgent, benevolent, loving, lenient, considerate, merciful, beneficent • *a sinner saved through God's gracious mercy*
3 = elegant, fine, grand, beautiful, handsome, fashionable, stylish, luxurious, graceful, tasteful • *a gracious old country house*

gradation 1 = degree, level, grade, sequence, succession, series, progression • *TV images require subtle gradations of light and shade.*
2 = stage, level, position, rank, place, point, mark, step, degree, grade, measurement, notch • *gradations of social status* • *small marks like the gradations on a school ruler*

grade AS A VERB = classify, rate, order, class, group, sort, value, range, rank, brand, arrange, evaluate • *The college does not grade the children's work.*
▸ **AS A NOUN 1 = class**, condition, quality, brand • *a good grade of plywood*
2 = mark, degree, place, order • *pressure on students to obtain good grades*
3 = level, position, rank, group, order, class, stage, step, station, category, rung, echelon • *Staff turnover is high among junior grades.*
▸ **IN PHRASES: make the grade = succeed**, measure up, win through, pass muster, come up to scratch *(informal)*, come through with flying colours, prove acceptable, measure up to expectations • *She had a strong desire to be a dancer, but failed to make the grade.*

gradient = slope, hill, rise, grade, incline, bank • *a hill with a gradient of 1 in 3*

gradual = steady, even, slow, regular, gentle, moderate, progressive, piecemeal, unhurried • *Losing weight is a gradual process.*
OPPOSITES: broken, sudden, overnight

gradually = steadily, slowly, moderately, progressively, gently, step by step, evenly, piecemeal, bit by bit, little by little, by degrees, piece by piece, unhurriedly, drop by drop • *Gradually, she began to trust him.*

graduate 1 = qualify, pass, receive a degree • *She graduated in English and Drama from Manchester University.*
2 = progress, advance, proceed, move on or up • *From commercials she quickly graduated to television shows.*
3 = mark off, grade, proportion, regulate, gauge, calibrate, measure out • *The volume control knob is graduated from 1 to 11.*
4 = classify, rank, grade, group, order, sort, range, arrange, sequence • *proposals to introduce an income tax which is graduated*

graduation = calibration, marking, grade, gauge • *medicine bottles with graduations on them*

graft AS A NOUN 1 = transplant, implant • *I am having a skin graft on my arm soon.*
2 = shoot, bud, implant, sprout, splice, scion • *These plants are propagated by grafts, buds or cuttings.*
▸ **AS A VERB 1 = transplant**, implant • *The top layer of skin has to be grafted onto the burns.*
2 = join, insert, transplant, implant, splice, affix • *Pear trees are grafted on quince root-stocks.*

graft AS A NOUN = labour, work, industry, effort, struggle, sweat, toil, slog, exertion, travail, blood, sweat, and tears *(informal)* • *His career has been one of hard graft.*
▸ **AS A VERB = work**, labour, struggle, sweat *(informal)*, grind *(informal)*, slave, strive, toil, drudge • *I really don't enjoy grafting away in a stuffy office all day.*

grain 1 = seed, kernel, grist • *a grain of wheat*
2 = cereal, corn • *a bag of grain*
3 = bit, piece, trace, spark, scrap, suspicion, molecule, particle, fragment, atom, ounce, crumb, mite, jot, speck, morsel, granule, scruple, modicum, mote, whit, iota, scintilla *(rare)* • *a grain of sand*
4 = texture, pattern, surface, fibre, weave, nap • *Brush the paint over the wood in the direction of the grain.*
▹ *See panel* **Rice and other cereals**

grammar = syntax, rules of language • *the basic rules of grammar*
▹ *See panel* **Grammatical cases**

QUOTATIONS
When I split an infinitive, God damn it, I split it so it will stay split
[Raymond Chandler *Letter to Edward Weeks*]
This is the sort of English up with which I will not put
[Winston Churchill]

grammatical = syntactic, linguistic • *grammatical errors*

GRAMMATICAL CASES

ablative	genitive	oblique
accusative	illative	possessive
agentive	instrumental	subjective
dative	locative	vocative
elative	nominative	
ergative	objective	

gramophone records
▸ **RELATED ENTHUSIAST:** discophile

grand 1 = **impressive**, great, large, magnificent, striking, fine, princely, imposing, superb, glorious, noble, splendid, gorgeous, luxurious, eminent, majestic, regal, stately, monumental, sublime, sumptuous, grandiose, opulent, palatial, ostentatious, splendiferous *(facetious)* • *a grand building in the centre of town*
OPPOSITES: undignified, unimposing
2 = **ambitious**, great, glorious, lofty, grandiose, exalted, ostentatious • *He arrived in America full of grand schemes and lofty dreams.*
3 = **superior**, great, lordly, noble, elevated, eminent, majestic, dignified, stately, lofty, august, illustrious, pompous, pretentious, haughty • *She's too busy with her grand new friends to bother with us now.*
4 = **excellent**, great *(informal)*, fine, wonderful, very good, brilliant, outstanding, smashing *(informal)*, superb, first-class, divine, marvellous *(informal)*, terrific *(informal)*, splendid, awesome *(slang)*, world-class, admirable, super *(informal)*, first-rate, splendiferous *(facetious)* • *He was having a grand time meeting new people.*
OPPOSITES: bad, poor, terrible
5 = **chief**, highest, lead, leading, head, main, supreme, principal, big-time *(informal)*, major league *(informal)*, pre-eminent • *the federal grand jury*
OPPOSITES: little, small, inferior

grandeur 1 = **splendour**, glory, majesty, nobility, pomp, state, magnificence, sumptuousness, sublimity, stateliness • *Only once inside do you appreciate the church's true grandeur.*
2 = **importance**, status, prestige, standing, dignity, prominence, greatness, nobility, loftiness • *He is wholly concerned with his own grandeur.*
OPPOSITES: inferiority, insignificance, triviality

grandfather = **grandad**, grandpa, grandaddy, gramps • *My grandfather was a coal miner.*

grandiloquent = **pompous**, inflated, rhetorical, high-flown, pretentious, flowery, bombastic, high-sounding, fustian, orotund • *She attacked her colleagues for indulging in 'grandiloquent' language.*

grandiose 1 = **pretentious**, ambitious, extravagant, flamboyant, high-flown, pompous, showy, ostentatious, bombastic • *Not one of his grandiose plans has ever come to anything.*
OPPOSITES: down-to-earth, unpretentious
2 = **imposing**, grand, impressive, magnificent, majestic, stately, monumental, lofty • *the grandiose building which housed the mayor's offices*
OPPOSITES: modest, humble, small-scale

grandmother = **gran**, granny, grandma, nan • *My grandmothers are both widows.*

grant **AS A NOUN** = **award**, allowance, donation, endowment, gift, concession, subsidy, hand-out, allocation, bounty, allotment, bequest, stipend, benefaction • *My application for a grant has been rejected.*
▸ **AS A VERB** 1 = **give**, allow, present, award, accord, permit, assign, allocate, hand out, confer on, bestow on, impart on, allot, vouchsafe • *France has agreed to grant him political asylum.*
2 = **accept**, allow, admit, acknowledge, concede, cede, accede • *The magistrates granted that the charity was justified in bringing the action.*

granular = **grainy**, rough, sandy, gritty, crumbly, gravelly, granulated • *a granular fertiliser*

granule = **grain**, scrap, molecule, particle, fragment, atom, crumb, jot, speck, iota • *granules of coarse-grain sea salt*

grape
▹ *See panel* **Grapes used in making wine**

grapevine **IN PHRASES:** **hear something on the grapevine** = **hear**, learn, discover, be told of, pick up, find out about, gather, be informed of, get wind of *(informal)*, hear tell *(dialect)* • *He'd doubtless heard rumours on the grapevine.*

graph = **diagram**, figure, table, chart, representation • *As the graph shows, inflation has risen sharply over the last two months.*

graphic 1 = **vivid**, clear, detailed, striking, telling, explicit, picturesque, forceful, expressive, descriptive, illustrative, well-drawn • *graphic descriptions of violence*
OPPOSITES: vague, woolly, generalized
2 = **pictorial**, seen, drawn, visible, visual, representational, illustrative, diagrammatic • *a graphic representation of how the chemical acts on the body*
OPPOSITES: impressionistic

grapple 1 = **deal**, tackle, cope, face, fight, battle, struggle, take on, engage, encounter, confront, combat, contend, wrestle, tussle, get to grips, do battle, address yourself to • *The economy is just one of the problems that the country is grappling with.*
2 = **struggle**, fight, combat, wrestle, battle, clash, contend, strive, tussle, scuffle, come to grips • *He grappled desperately with Holmes for control of the weapon.*

grasp **AS A VERB** 1 = **grip**, hold, catch, grab, seize, snatch, clutch, clinch, clasp, lay *or* take hold of • *He grasped both my hands.*
2 = **understand**, realize, take in, get, see, follow, catch on, comprehend, get the message about, get the picture about, catch *or* get the drift of • *The Government has not yet grasped the seriousness of the crisis.*
▸ **AS A NOUN** 1 = **grip**, hold, possession, embrace, clutches, clasp • *She slipped her hand from his grasp.*
2 = **understanding**, knowledge, grip, perception,

GRAPES USED IN MAKING WINE

WHITE WINE

aligoté
chardonnay
chenin blanc *or* steen
colombard
furmint
gewürztraminer
grüner veltliner
hárslevelü
malvasia
marsanne
müller-thurgau
muscadelle
muscat *or* moscatel
pinot blanc
pinot gris, pinot grigio, ruländer, *or* Tokay-Pinot Gris
riesling *or* rhine riesling
sauvignon blanc
scheurebe
semillon
seyval blanc
silvaner
trebbiano *or* ugni blanc
verdelho
verdicchio
viognier
viura
welschriesling, olasz rizling, *or* laski rizling

RED WINE

barbera
cabernet franc
cabernet sauvignon
cinsault
dolcetto
gamay
grenache *or* garnacha
kékfrankos
malbec
merlot
montepulciano
mourvèdre
nebbiolo *or* spanna
negroamoro
pinotage
pinot noir *or* spätburgunder
sangiovese
shiraz *or* syrah
tempranillo
zinfandel

awareness, realization, mastery, ken, comprehension • *They have a good grasp of foreign languages.*
3 = **reach**, power, control, range, sweep, capacity, scope, sway, compass, mastery • *Peace is now within our grasp.*

grasping = **greedy**, acquisitive, rapacious, mean, selfish, stingy, penny-pinching *(informal)*, venal, miserly, avaricious, niggardly, covetous, tightfisted, close-fisted, tight-arsed *(taboo slang)*, usurious, tight-assed *(U.S. taboo slang)*, snoep *(S. African informal)*, tight as a duck's arse *(taboo slang)* • *She is a grasping and manipulative young woman.*
OPPOSITES: generous, altruistic, unselfish

grass AS A NOUN 1 = **turf**, lawn • *Small creatures stirred in the grass around the tent.*
2 = **cannabis**, blow *(slang)*, pot *(slang)*, weed *(slang)*, dope *(slang)*, hemp, hash *(slang)*, hashish, wacky baccy *(slang)*, dagga *(S. African)* • *I started smoking grass when I was about sixteen.*
3 = **betrayer**, sneak, squealer *(slang)*, Judas, accuser, stool pigeon, nark *(Brit., Austral. & N.Z. slang)* • *He preferred to take the rap rather than be a grass.*
▸ AS A VERB *often with* **on** = **inform on**, shop *(slang, chiefly Brit.)*, betray, denounce, snitch *(slang)*, sing *(slang, chiefly U.S.)*, give away, rat on *(informal)*, sell (someone) down the river *(informal)*, dob in *(Austral. slang)* • *He was repeatedly attacked by other inmates, who accused him of grassing.* • *I'd never grass on a mate.*
▸ RELATED ADJECTIVES: gramineous, verdant
▹ *See panel* **Grasses**

grassland = **grass**, meadow, grazing, lea *(poetic)*, grazing land, pasturage, shieling *(Scot.)* • *areas of open grassland*

grate AS A VERB 1 = **shred**, mince, pulverize • *Grate the cheese into a mixing bowl.*
2 = **scrape**, grind, rub, scratch, creak, rasp • *His chair grated as he got to his feet.*
▸ IN PHRASES: **grate on someone** *or* **grate on someone's nerves** = **annoy**, irritate, aggravate *(informal)*, gall, exasperate, nettle, jar, vex, chafe, irk, rankle, peeve, get under your skin *(informal)*, get up your nose *(informal)*, get on your nerves *(informal)*, nark *(Brit., Austral. & N.Z. slang)*, set your teeth on edge, get on your wick *(Brit. slang)*, rub you up the wrong way, hack you off *(informal)* • *His manner always grated on me.*

grateful = **thankful**, obliged, in (someone's) debt, indebted, appreciative, beholden • *She was grateful to him for all his help.*

gratification 1 = **satisfaction**, delight, pleasure, joy, thrill, relish, enjoyment, glee, kick *or* kicks *(informal)* • *Eventually they recognised him, much to his gratification.*
OPPOSITES: pain, disappointment, frustration
2 = **indulgence**, satisfaction, fulfilment • *the gratification of his every whim*
OPPOSITES: control, discipline, denial

gratify 1 = **please**, delight, satisfy, thrill, give pleasure, gladden • *She was gratified by his response.*
2 = **satisfy**, feed, fulfil, indulge, humour, cater to, pander to, fawn on • *He took advantage of these girls to gratify his own lust.*

grating[1] = **grille**, grid, grate, lattice, trellis, gridiron • *an open grating in the sidewalk*

grating[2] = **irritating**, grinding, harsh, annoying, jarring, unpleasant, scraping, raucous, strident, squeaky, rasping, discordant, disagreeable, irksome • *I can't stand that grating voice of his.*
OPPOSITES: pleasing, soft, musical

gratis = **free**, freely, for nothing, unpaid, free of charge, on the house, buckshee *(Brit. slang)* • *I'll give it you free, gratis and for nothing.*

gratitude = **thankfulness**, thanks, recognition, obligation, appreciation, indebtedness, sense of obligation, gratefulness • *I wish to express my gratitude for everyone's kindness.*
OPPOSITES: ingratitude, ungratefulness, unthankfulness

gratuitous = **unjustified**, unnecessary, needless, unfounded, unwarranted, superfluous, wanton, unprovoked, groundless, baseless, uncalled-for, unmerited, causeless • *The film has been criticized for its gratuitous violence.*
OPPOSITES: relevant, provoked, justifiable

gratuity = **tip**, present, gift, reward, bonus, donation, boon, bounty, recompense, perquisite, baksheesh, benefaction, pourboire *(French)*, bonsela *(S. African)*, largesse *or* largess • *The porter expects a gratuity.*

grave[1] = **tomb**, vault, crypt, mausoleum, sepulchre, pit, last resting place, burying place • *They used to visit her grave twice a year.*
▸ RELATED ADJECTIVE: sepulchral

QUOTATIONS
The grave's a fine and private place,
But none do there, I think, embrace
[Andrew Marvell *To his Coy Mistress*]

grave[2] 1 = **serious**, important, significant, critical, pressing, threatening, dangerous, vital, crucial, acute, severe, urgent, hazardous, life-and-death, momentous, perilous, weighty, leaden, of great consequence • *He says the situation in his country is very grave.*
OPPOSITES: mild, trifling, insignificant
2 = **solemn**, sober, gloomy, dull, thoughtful, subdued, sombre, dour, grim-faced, long-faced, unsmiling • *She could tell by his grave expression that something terrible had happened.*
OPPOSITES: happy, merry, carefree

gravelly = **husky**, rough, harsh, rasping, croaking, hoarse, gruff, throaty, guttural, croaky • *There was a triumphant note in his gravelly voice.*

gravestone = **headstone**, stone, monument, tombstone • *He was buried in the local cemetery, with just a simple gravestone.*

graveyard = **cemetery**, churchyard, burial ground, charnel house, necropolis, boneyard *(informal)*, God's acre *(literary)* • *They made their way to the graveyard to pay their respects to the dead.*

gravitas = **seriousness**, gravity, solemnity • *a man with all the gravitas you might expect of a Booker prize winner*

gravitate *with* **to** *or* **towards** = **be drawn**, move, tend, lean, be pulled, incline, be attracted, be influenced • *Traditionally young Asians in Britain have gravitated towards medicine, law and engineering.*

GRASSES

barley
Bermuda grass
blady grass *or* kunai *(Austral.)*
bluegrass
buffalo grass
buffel grass
cane grass
citronella
corkscrew grass *(Austral.)*
cotton grass
couch grass *or (Austral.)* quack grass, quick grass *or* quitch grass
crab grass
danthonia *or* wallaby grass *(Austral.)*
darnel
elephant grass
esparto
fescue
kangaroo grass *(Austral.)*
maize
marram grass
millet
oat
pampas grass
paspalum
reed
rice
rye
rye-grass
snowgrass *(N.Z.)*
sorghum
spear grass *(Austral.)*
spinifex
sugar cane
wheat
wild oat
wild rye

gravity 1 = **seriousness**, importance, consequence, significance, urgency, severity, acuteness, moment, weightiness, momentousness, perilousness, hazardousness • *You don't seem to appreciate the gravity of this situation.*
OPPOSITES: insignificance, triviality, unimportance
2 = **solemnity**, gloom, seriousness, gravitas, thoughtfulness, grimness • *There was an appealing gravity to everything she said.*
OPPOSITES: joy, happiness, frivolity
▸ RELATED PHOBIA: barophobia

graze[1] = **feed**, crop, browse, pasture • *cows grazing in a field*

graze[2] AS A VERB 1 = **scratch**, skin, bark, scrape, chafe, abrade • *I had grazed my knees a little.*
2 = **touch**, brush, rub, scrape, shave, skim, kiss, glance off • *A bullet had grazed his arm.*
▸ AS A NOUN = **scratch**, scrape, abrasion • *He just has a slight graze.*

greasy 1 = **fatty**, slick, slippery, oily, slimy, oleaginous • *He propped his elbows upon the greasy counter.*
2 = **sycophantic**, fawning, grovelling, ingratiating, smooth, slick, oily, unctuous, smarmy *(Brit. informal)*, toadying • *She called him 'a greasy little Tory sycophant'.*

great 1 = **large**, big, huge, vast, enormous, extensive, tremendous, immense, gigantic, mammoth, bulky, colossal, prodigious, stupendous, voluminous, fuck-off *(offensive taboo slang)*, elephantine, ginormous *(informal)*, humongous *or* humungous *(U.S. slang)*, supersize • *a great hall as long and high as a church*
OPPOSITES: little, small, diminutive
2 = **extreme**, considerable, excessive, high, decided, pronounced, extravagant, prodigious, inordinate • *I'll take great care of it.* • *That must have taken a great effort on his part.*
3 = **major**, lead, leading, chief, main, capital, grand, primary, principal, prominent, superior, paramount, big-time *(informal)*, major league *(informal)* • *the great cultural achievements of the past*
4 = **important**, serious, significant, critical, crucial, heavy, grave, momentous, weighty, consequential • *his pronouncements on the great political matters of the age*
OPPOSITES: petty, trivial, unimportant
5 = **famous**, celebrated, outstanding, excellent, remarkable, distinguished, prominent, glorious, notable, renowned, eminent, famed, illustrious, exalted, noteworthy • *the great American president, Abraham Lincoln*
6 = **expert**, skilled, talented, skilful, good, able, masterly, crack *(slang)*, superb, world-class, adept, stellar *(informal)*, superlative, proficient, adroit • *He was one of the West Indies' greatest cricketers.*
OPPOSITES: inexperienced, unskilled, untrained
7 = **excellent**, good, fine, wonderful, mean *(slang)*, topping *(Brit. slang)*, cracking *(Brit. informal)*, superb, fantastic *(informal)*, tremendous *(informal)*, marvellous *(informal)*, terrific *(informal)*, mega *(slang)*, sovereign, awesome *(slang)*, dope *(slang)*, admirable, first-rate, def *(informal)*, brill *(informal)*, boffo *(slang)*, bitchin', chillin' *(U.S. slang)*, GR8 *(S.M.S.)*, booshit *(Austral. slang)*, exo *(Austral. slang)*, sik *(Austral. slang)*, rad *(informal)*, phat *(slang)*, schmick *(Austral. informal)*, beaut *(informal)*, barrie *(Scot. slang)*, belting *(Brit. slang)*, pearler *(Austral. slang)* • *It's a great film, you must see it.*
OPPOSITES: poor, average, secondary
8 = **very**, really, particularly, truly, extremely, awfully *(informal)*, exceedingly • *He gave me a great big smile.*
9 = **utter**, complete, total, absolute, perfect, positive, downright, consummate, unqualified, out-and-out, flagrant, egregious, unmitigated, thoroughgoing, arrant • *You stupid great git!*
10 = **enthusiastic**, keen, active, devoted, zealous • *I'm not a great fan of football.*

greatly = **very much**, much, hugely, vastly, extremely, highly, seriously *(informal)*, notably, considerably, remarkably, enormously, immensely, tremendously, markedly, powerfully, exceedingly, mightily, abundantly, by much, by leaps and bounds, to the nth degree • *People would benefit greatly from a pollution-free vehicle.*

greatness 1 = **grandeur**, glory, majesty, splendour, power, pomp, magnificence • *the greatness of ancient Rome*
2 = **fame**, glory, celebrity, distinction, eminence, note, lustre, renown, illustriousness • *Abraham Lincoln achieved greatness.*

QUOTATIONS

No really great man ever thought himself so
[William Hazlitt *Whether Genius is Conscious of Its Powers?*]

He is greatest who is most often in men's good thoughts
[Samuel Butler *Notebooks*]

There would be no great ones if there were no little ones
[George Herbert *Outlandish Proverbs*]

The greatest spirits are capable of the greatest vices as well as of the greatest virtues
[René Descartes *Discourse on Method*]

It is the privilege of greatness to confer intense happiness with insignificant gifts
[Friedrich Nietzsche *Human, All Too Human*]

Some are born great, some achieve greatness, and some have greatness thrust upon 'em
[William Shakespeare *Twelfth Night*]

Few great men could pass Personnel
[Paul Goodman *Growing Up Absurd*]

Greece
▸ RELATED ADJECTIVE: Hellenic

greed *or* **greediness** 1 = **gluttony**, voracity, insatiableness, ravenousness • *He ate too much out of sheer greed.*
2 = **avarice**, longing, desire, hunger, craving, eagerness, selfishness, acquisitiveness, rapacity, cupidity, covetousness, insatiableness • *an insatiable greed for power*
OPPOSITES: generosity, altruism, benevolence

QUOTATIONS

There is enough in the world for everyone's need, but not enough for everyone's greed
[Frank Buchman *Remaking the World*]

PROVERBS

The more you get, the more you want
The pitcher will go to the well once too often

greedy 1 = **gluttonous**, insatiable, voracious, ravenous, piggish, hoggish • *a greedy little boy who ate too many sweets*
2 = **avaricious**, grasping, selfish, insatiable, acquisitive, rapacious, materialistic, desirous, covetous • *He attacked greedy bosses for awarding themselves big pay rises.*
OPPOSITES: generous, benevolent, altruistic

Greek AS AN ADJECTIVE = **Hellenic** • *his extensive knowledge of Greek antiquity*
▸ AS A NOUN = **Hellene** • *The ancient Greeks referred to themselves as Hellenes.*

QUOTATIONS

I fear the Greeks, even when they are bearing gifts
[Virgil *Aeneid*]

green AS AN ADJECTIVE 1 = **verdant**, leafy, grassy • *The city has only thirteen square centimetres of green space for each inhabitant.*
2 = **ecological**, conservationist, environment-friendly, ecologically sound, eco-friendly, ozone-friendly, non-polluting • *trying to persuade governments to adopt greener policies*
3 = **unripe**, fresh, raw, immature • *Pick and ripen any green fruits in a warm dark place.*
4 = **inexperienced**, new, innocent, raw, naive, ignorant, immature, gullible, callow, untrained, unsophisticated,

g

credulous, ingenuous, unpolished, wet behind the ears *(informal)* • *He was a young lad, very green and immature.*
5 = **jealous**, grudging, resentful, envious, covetous • *Collectors worldwide will turn green with envy.*
6 = **nauseous**, ill, sick, pale, unhealthy, wan, under the weather • *By the end of the race the runners would be green with sickness.*
▸ AS A NOUN 1 *with capital* = **environmentalist**, conservationist, tree-hugger *(informal derogatory)* • *The Greens see themselves as a radical alternative to the two major parties.*
2 = **lawn**, common, turf, sward, grassplot • *a pageant on the village green*
▸ RELATED ADJECTIVE: verdant

SHADES OF GREEN

almond green	cyan	pea green
apple green	eau de nil	pine green
aqua	emerald green	pistachio
aquamarine	jade	sea green
avocado	lime green	teal
celadon	Lincoln green	turquoise
chartreuse	Nile green	
citron	olive	

greenery = **flora**, plants, foliage, vegetation • *They've ordered a bit of greenery to brighten up the hospital.*

greenhorn = **novice**, newcomer, beginner, apprentice, naïf, learner, ingénue, tyro, raw recruit, newbie *(slang)*, neophyte • *I'm a bit of a greenhorn in the kitchen.*

greenhouse = **glasshouse**, conservatory, hothouse • *Take some cuttings and over-winter them in the greenhouse.*

green light = **authorization**, sanction, approval, go-ahead *(informal)*, blessing, permission, confirmation, clearance, imprimatur, O.K. *or* okay *(informal)* • *The project was given the green light in the Chancellor's autumn budget.*

greet 1 = **salute**, hail, nod to, say hello to, address, accost, tip your hat to • *He greeted us with a smile.*
2 = **welcome**, meet, receive, karanga *(N.Z.)*, mihi *(N.Z.)* • *She was waiting at the door to greet her guests.*
3 = **receive**, take, respond to, react to • *The European Court's decision has been greeted with dismay.*

greeting AS A NOUN = **welcome**, reception, hail, salute, address, salutation, hongi *(N.Z.)*, kia ora *(N.Z.)* • *His greeting was familiar and friendly.*
▸ AS A PLURAL NOUN = **best wishes**, regards, respects, compliments, good wishes, salutations • *They exchanged hearty Christmas greetings.*

gregarious = **outgoing**, friendly, social, cordial, sociable, affable, convivial, companionable • *She's such a gregarious and outgoing person.*
OPPOSITES: reserved, withdrawn, unsociable

grey 1 = **dull**, dark, dim, gloomy, cloudy, murky, drab, misty, foggy, overcast, sunless • *It was a grey, wet April Sunday.*
2 = **bleak**, depressing, grim, discouraging, gloomy, hopeless, dismal, dreary, sombre, unpromising, disheartening, joyless, cheerless, comfortless • *Even the president admits the New Year will be grey and cheerless.*
3 = **boring**, dull, anonymous, faceless, colourless, nondescript, characterless • *little grey men in suits*
4 = **old**, aged, ancient, mature, elderly, venerable, hoary • *a grey old man*
5 = **pale**, wan, livid, bloodless, colourless, pallid, ashen, like death warmed up *(informal)* • *His face was grey with pain.*
6 = **ambiguous**, uncertain, neutral, unclear, debatable • *The whole question of refugees is something of a grey area.*
▹ *See panel* **Shades from black to white**

grid 1 = **grating**, grille, lattice • *a grid of ironwork*
2 = **network** • *a grid of narrow streets*

gridlock 1 = **traffic jam** • *The streets are wedged solid with the traffic gridlock.*
2 = **deadlock**, halt, stalemate, impasse, standstill, full stop • *He agreed that these policies will lead to a gridlock in the future.*

grief AS A NOUN = **sadness**, suffering, pain, regret, distress, misery, agony, mourning, sorrow, woe, anguish, remorse, bereavement, heartache, heartbreak, mournfulness • *Their grief soon gave way to anger.*
OPPOSITES: delight, comfort, joy
▸ IN PHRASES: **come to grief** = **fail**, founder, break down, come unstuck, miscarry, fall flat on your face, meet with disaster • *So many marriages have come to grief over lack of money.*

QUOTATIONS
Grief is a species of idleness
[Dr. Johnson *letter to Mrs Thrale*]

grief-stricken = **heartbroken**, broken, crushed, devastated, overwhelmed, despairing, sorrowing, afflicted, desolate, agonized, sorrowful, wretched, inconsolable, woebegone, brokenhearted • *The Queen was grief-stricken over his death.*

grievance 1 = **complaint**, protest, beef *(slang)*, gripe *(informal)*, axe to grind, chip on your shoulder *(informal)* • *They felt they had a legitimate grievance.*
2 = **injustice**, wrong, injury • *a deep sense of grievance*

grieve 1 = **mourn**, suffer, weep, ache, lament, sorrow, wail • *He's grieving over his dead wife and son.*
2 = **sadden**, hurt, injure, distress, wound, crush, pain, afflict, upset, agonize, break the heart of, make your heart bleed • *It grieved me to see him in such distress.*
OPPOSITES: please, comfort, gladden

grievous 1 = **deplorable**, shocking, appalling, dreadful, outrageous, glaring, intolerable, monstrous, shameful, unbearable, atrocious, heinous, lamentable, egregious • *Their loss would be a grievous blow to our engineering industries.*
OPPOSITES: pleasant, delightful
2 = **severe**, damaging, heavy, wounding, grave, painful, distressing, dreadful, harmful, afflicting, calamitous, injurious • *He survived in spite of suffering grievous injuries.*
OPPOSITES: mild, trivial, insignificant

grim 1 = **terrible**, shocking, severe, harsh, forbidding, horrible, formidable, sinister, ghastly, hideous, gruesome *(slang)*, grisly, horrid, frightful, godawful • *They painted a grim picture of growing crime.*
2 = **dismal**, depressing, bleak, gloomy, hopeless, dreary, sombre, joyless, cheerless, comfortless • *the tower blocks on the city's grim edges*
3 = **stern**, severe, harsh, grave, solemn, forbidding • *Her expression was grim and unpleasant.*
OPPOSITES: kind, happy, benign
4 = **hard**, tough, harsh, unpleasant, bleak • *Things were pretty grim for a time.*
OPPOSITES: easy, pleasant
5 = **merciless**, fierce, cruel, ruthless, ferocious, resolute, unrelenting, implacable, unyielding • *a grim fight to the death*

grimace AS A VERB = **scowl**, frown, sneer, wince, lour *or* lower, make a face *or* faces • *She started to sit up, grimaced with pain, and sank back.*
▸ AS A NOUN = **scowl**, frown, sneer, wince, face, wry face • *He took another drink of his coffee. 'Awful,' he said with a grimace.*

grime = **dirt**, filth, soot, smut, grot *(slang)* • *She washed the grime off her hands.*

grimy = **dirty**, polluted, filthy, soiled, foul, grubby, sooty, unclean, grotty *(slang)*, smutty, scuzzy *(slang)*, begrimed, skanky *(slang)*, festy *(Austral. slang)* • *a grimy industrial city*

grin AS A VERB = **smile**, beam • *He grinned, delighted at the memory.*
▸ AS A NOUN = **smile**, beam • *She had a big grin on her face.*

grind AS A VERB 1 = **crush**, mill, powder, grate, pulverize, pound, kibble, abrade, granulate • *Grind the pepper in a pepper mill.*
2 = **press**, push, crush, jam, mash, force down • *He ground his cigarette under his heel.*
3 = **grate**, scrape, grit, gnash • *If you grind your teeth at night, see your dentist.*
4 = **sharpen**, file, polish, sand, smooth, whet • *The tip can be ground to a much sharper edge.*
▸ AS A NOUN = **hard work** (*Informal*), labour, effort, task, sweat (*informal*), chore, toil, drudgery • *Life continues to be a terrible grind for the ordinary person.*
▸ IN PHRASES: **grind on** = **drag on**, last, persist, keep going, stretch out, draw out, spin out • *The war has been grinding on for seven years.*
grind someone down *with* **down** = **oppress**, suppress, harass, subdue, hound, bring down, plague, persecute, subjugate, trample underfoot, tyrannize (over) • *There will always be some bosses who want to grind you down.*
grind something out = **produce**, turn out, generate, churn out • *He was forced to grind out second-rate out novels in order to support his family.*
grind to a halt = **stop**, halt, stall • *The peace process has ground to a halt.*

grip AS A VERB 1 = **grasp**, hold, catch, seize, clutch, clasp, latch on to, take hold of • *She gripped his hand tightly.*
2 = **afflict**, attack, affect, take over, rack, beset, smite, convulse • *A sudden pain gripped him.*
3 = **engross**, fascinate, absorb, entrance, hold, catch up, compel, rivet, enthral, mesmerize, spellbind • *The whole nation was gripped by the dramatic story.*
▸ AS A NOUN 1 = **clasp**, hold, grasp, handclasp (*U.S.*) • *His strong hand eased the bag from her grip.*
2 = **control**, rule, influence, command, power, possession, sway, dominance, domination, mastery • *The president maintains an iron grip on his country.*
3 = **hold**, purchase, friction, traction • *a new kind of rubber which gives tyres a better grip*
4 = **understanding**, sense, command, perception, awareness, grasp, appreciation, mastery, comprehension, discernment • *He has lost his grip on reality.*
▸ IN PHRASES: **come** *or* **get to grips with something** = **tackle**, deal with, handle, take on, meet, encounter, cope with, confront, undertake, grasp, face up to, grapple with, close with, contend with • *The government's first task is to get to grips with the economy.*

gripe AS A VERB = **complain**, moan, groan, grumble, beef (*slang*), carp, bitch (*slang*), nag, whine, grouse, bleat, grouch (*informal*), bellyache (*slang*), kvetch (*U.S. slang*) • *He started griping about the prices they were charging.*
▸ AS A NOUN = **complaint**, protest, objection, beef (*slang*), moan, grumble, grievance, grouse, grouch (*informal*) • *My only gripe is that just one main course and one dessert were available.*

gripping = **fascinating**, exciting, thrilling, entrancing, compelling, compulsive, riveting, enthralling, engrossing, spellbinding, unputdownable (*informal*) • *a gripping thriller about the hunt for a serial killer*

grisly = **gruesome**, shocking, terrible, awful, terrifying, appalling, horrible, grim, dreadful, sickening, ghastly, hideous, macabre, horrid, frightful, abominable, hellacious (*U.S. slang*) • *a series of grisly murders*
OPPOSITES: nice, attractive, pleasant

grit AS A NOUN 1 = **gravel**, sand, dust, pebbles • *He felt tiny bits of grit and sand peppering his knees.*
2 = **courage**, spirit, resolution, determination, nerve, guts (*informal*), balls (*taboo slang*), pluck, backbone, fortitude, toughness, tenacity, perseverance, mettle, doggedness, hardihood • *He showed grit and determination in his fight back to health.*
▸ AS A VERB = **clench**, grind, grate, gnash • *Gritting my teeth, I did my best to stifle a sharp retort.*

gritty 1 = **rough**, sandy, dusty, abrasive, rasping, grainy, gravelly, granular • *She threw a handful of gritty dust into his eyes.*
2 = **courageous**, game, dogged, determined, tough, spirited, brave, hardy, feisty (*informal, chiefly U.S. & Canad.*), resolute, tenacious, plucky, steadfast, ballsy (*taboo slang*), mettlesome, (as) game as Ned Kelly (*Austral. slang*) • *a gritty determination to get to the top*
3 = **realistic**, hard-hitting, unsentimental, unromantic • *a gritty film about inner-city deprivation*

grizzle = **whine**, fret, whimper, whinge (*informal*), snivel, girn (*Scot.*) • *The children were grizzling and complaining.*

grizzled = **grey**, greying, grey-haired, grizzly, hoary, grey-headed • *an old man with grey, grizzled hair* • *a grizzled old warrior*

groan AS A VERB 1 = **moan**, cry, sigh • *The man on the floor began to groan with pain.*
2 = **complain**, object, moan, grumble, gripe (*informal*), beef (*slang*), carp, bitch (*slang*), lament, whine, grouse, bemoan, whinge (*informal*), grouch (*informal*), bellyache (*slang*) • *His parents were beginning to groan about the cost of it all.*
3 = **creak**, grind, grate, rasp • *The timbers groaned and creaked in the wind.*
▸ AS A NOUN 1 = **moan**, cry, sigh, whine • *She heard him let out a pitiful, muffled groan.*
2 = **complaint**, protest, objection, grumble, beef (*slang*), grouse, gripe (*informal*), grouch (*informal*) • *I don't have time to listen to your moans and groans.*

groggy = **dizzy**, faint, stunned, confused, reeling, shaky, dazed, wobbly, weak, unsteady, muzzy, stupefied, befuddled, punch-drunk, woozy (*informal*) • *She was still feeling a bit groggy when I saw her.*

groin
▸ RELATED ADJECTIVE: inguinal

groom AS A NOUN 1 = **stableman**, stableboy, hostler *or* ostler (*archaic*) • *He worked as a groom at a stables on Dartmoor.*
2 = **newly-wed**, husband, bridegroom, marriage partner • *We toasted the bride and groom.*
▸ AS A VERB 1 = **brush**, clean, tend, rub down, curry • *The horses were exercised and groomed with special care.*
2 = **smarten up**, dress, clean, turn out, get up (*informal*), tidy, preen, spruce up, primp, gussy up (*slang, chiefly U.S.*) • *She always appeared perfectly groomed.*
3 = **train**, prime, prepare, coach, ready, educate, drill, nurture, make ready • *He was already being groomed for a top job.*

groove = **indentation**, cut, hollow, score, channel, trench, rebate, flute, gutter, trough, furrow, rut • *Grooves were made in the shelf to accommodate the back panel.*

grooved = **furrowed**, cut, hollowed, scored, channelled, rutted, indented • *The inscriptions are as deeply grooved as if they had been cut only last week.*

groovy = **fashionable**, stylish, in fashion, in vogue, in (*slang*), now (*informal*), latest, with it (*informal*), trendy, up to the minute, modish, du jour (*French*), voguish, culty, schmick (*Austral. informal*) • *the grooviest club in London*

grope 1 = **feel**, search, fumble, flounder, fish, finger, scrabble, cast about, fossick (*Austral. & N.Z.*) • *He groped in his pocket for his wallet.*
2 = **fondle**, touch, stroke, caress • *He kept trying to grope her breasts.*

gross AS AN ADJECTIVE 1 = **flagrant**, obvious, glaring, blatant, serious, shocking, rank, plain, sheer, utter,

g

outraged, manifest, shameful, downright, grievous, unqualified, heinous, egregious, unmitigated, arrant • *The company were found guilty of gross negligence.*
OPPOSITES: qualified, partial
2 = vulgar, offensive, crude, rude, obscene, low, coarse, indecent, improper, unseemly, lewd, X-rated *(informal)*, impure, smutty, ribald, indelicate • *That's a disgusting thing to say – you're so gross!*
OPPOSITES: pure, decent, proper
3 = coarse, crass, tasteless, unsophisticated, ignorant, insensitive, callous, boorish, unfeeling, unrefined, uncultured, undiscriminating, imperceptive • *He is a gross and boorish individual.*
OPPOSITES: elegant, cultivated
4 = fat, obese, overweight, great, big, large, heavy, massive, dense, bulky, hulking, corpulent, lumpish • *I've put on so much weight I look totally gross.*
OPPOSITES: little, small, slim
5 = total, whole, entire, aggregate, before tax, before deductions • *Gross sales in June totalled 270 million.*
OPPOSITES: net
▸ **AS A VERB = earn**, make, take, bring in, rake in *(informal)* • *So far the films have grossed nearly £290 million.*

grotesque 1 = unnatural, bizarre, weird, odd, strange, fantastic, distorted, fanciful, deformed, outlandish, whimsical, freakish, misshapen, malformed • *statues of grotesque mythical creatures*
OPPOSITES: natural, normal
2 = absurd, ridiculous, ludicrous, preposterous, incongruous • *the grotesque disparities between the rich and the poor*
OPPOSITES: natural, normal

grotto = cave, tunnel, hollow, cavern, underground chamber • *Water trickles through an underground grotto.*

grouch AS A VERB = complain, moan, grumble, beef *(slang)*, carp, bitch *(slang)*, whine, grouse, gripe *(informal)*, whinge *(informal)*, bleat, find fault, bellyache *(slang)*, kvetch *(U.S. slang)* • *They grouched about how hard-up they were.*
▸ **AS A NOUN 1 = moaner**, complainer, grumbler, whiner, grouser, malcontent, curmudgeon, crosspatch *(informal)*, crab *(informal)*, faultfinder • *He's an old grouch but she puts up with him.*
2 = complaint, protest, objection, grievance, moan, grumble, beef *(slang)*, grouse, gripe *(informal)* • *One of their biggest grouches is the new system of payment*

grouchy = bad-tempered, cross, irritable, grumpy, discontented, grumbling, surly, petulant, sulky, ill-tempered, irascible, cantankerous, tetchy, ratty *(Brit. & N.Z. informal)*, testy, querulous, peevish, huffy, liverish • *Grandfather is a grouchy old so-and-so.*

ground AS A NOUN 1 = earth, land, dry land, terra firma • *We slid down the roof and dropped to the ground.*
2 = soil, earth, dust, mould, dirt, terrain, sod, clod, loam • *the marshy ground of the river delta*
3 = land, country, field, turf, terrain, area, tract • *a stretch of waste ground*
4 = arena, pitch, stadium, park *(informal)*, field, enclosure • *the city's football ground*
▸ **AS A PLURAL NOUN 1 = estate**, holding, land, fields, gardens, property, district, territory, domain • *the palace grounds*
2 = reason, cause, basis, argument, call, base, occasion, foundation, excuse, premise, motive, justification, rationale, inducement • *In the interview he gave some grounds for optimism.*
3 = dregs, lees, deposit, sediment • *Place the coffee grounds in the bottom and pour hot water over them.*
▸ **AS A VERB 1 = base**, found, establish, set, settle, fix • *Her argument was grounded in fact.*
2 = instruct, train, prepare, coach, teach, inform, initiate, tutor, acquaint with, familiarize with • *Make sure the children are properly grounded in the basics.*

grounding = coaching, schooling, teaching, instruction, education, guidance, tuition • *The degree provides a thorough grounding in both mathematics and statistics.*

groundless = baseless, false, unfounded, unjustified, unproven, empty, unauthorized, unsubstantiated, unsupported, uncorroborated • *A ministry official described the report as groundless.*
OPPOSITES: proven, supported, well-founded

ground rule = principle, rule, formula, fundamental, standard, criterion, proposition, precept • *The ground rules for the current talks should be maintained.*

groundwork = preliminaries, basis, foundation, base, footing, preparation, fundamentals, cornerstone, underpinnings, spadework • *These courses provide the groundwork of statistical theory.*

group AS A NOUN 1 = crowd, company, party, band, troop, pack, gathering, gang, bunch, congregation, posse *(slang)*, bevy, assemblage • *The trouble involved a small group of football supporters.*
2 = organization, body, association, league, circle • *Members of an environmental group are staging a protest inside a chemical plant.*
3 = faction, set, camp, clique, coterie, schism, cabal • *a radical group within the Communist Party*
4 = category, class, section, grouping, order, sort, type, division, rank, grade, classification • *The recipes are divided into groups according to their main ingredients.*
5 = band, ensemble, combo • *ELP were the progressive rock group par excellence.*
6 = cluster, collection, formation, clump, aggregation • *a small group of islands off northern Japan*
▸ **AS A VERB 1 = arrange**, order, sort, class, range, gather, organize, assemble, put together, classify, dispose, marshal, bracket, assort • *The fact sheets are grouped into seven sections.*
2 = unite, associate, gather, cluster, get together, congregate, band together • *We want to encourage them to group together as one big purchaser.*

grouping = organization, group, body, association, league, circle • *There were two main political groupings pressing for independence.*

grouse[1] AS A VERB = complain, moan, grumble, gripe *(informal)*, beef *(slang)*, carp, bitch *(slang)*, whine, whinge *(informal)*, bleat, find fault, grouch *(informal)*, bellyache *(slang)*, kvetch *(U.S. slang)* • *'How come they never tell us what's going on?' he groused.*
▸ **AS A NOUN = complaint**, protest, objection, moan, grievance, grumble, gripe *(informal)*, beef *(slang)*, grouch *(informal)* • *There have been grouses about the economy, interest rates and house prices.*

grouse[2]
▸ **COLLECTIVE NOUNS:** brood, covey, pack

grove = wood, woodland, plantation, covert, thicket, copse, brake, coppice, spinney • *open fields and groves of trees*

grovel 1 = humble yourself, creep, crawl, flatter, fawn, pander, cower, toady, kowtow, brown-nose *(taboo slang)*, bow and scrape, kiss ass *(taboo slang)*, lick someone's boots, lick someone's arse *(taboo slang)*, demean yourself, abase yourself • *I refuse to grovel to anybody.*
OPPOSITES: be proud, intimidate, hold your head high
2 = crawl, crouch, go on hands and knees, go on all fours • *We grovelled around on our knees, hunting for the key.*

grow AS A VERB 1 = develop, fill out, get bigger, get taller • *We stop growing once we reach maturity.*
OPPOSITES: fail, shrink, diminish
2 = get bigger, spread, swell, extend, stretch, expand, widen, enlarge, multiply, thicken • *An inoperable tumour was growing in his brain.*

3 = spring up, shoot up, develop, flourish, sprout, germinate, vegetate • *The station had roses growing at each end of the platform.*
4 = cultivate, produce, raise, farm, breed, nurture, propagate • *I always grow a few red onions in my allotment.*
5 = become, get, turn, come to be • *He's growing old.*
6 = originate, spring, arise, stem, issue • *The idea for this book grew out of conversations with Philippa Brewster.*
7 = improve, advance, progress, succeed, expand, thrive, flourish, prosper • *The economy continues to grow.*
▸ **IN PHRASES: grow into something** *or* **someone = become**, turn into, develop (into), come to be • *He's grown into a very good-looking young man.*

growl = snarl, show its teeth *(of an animal)* • *The dog was growling and thrashing its tail.*

grown = mature, adult, grown-up, fully-grown • *Dad, I'm a grown woman. I know what I'm doing.*

grown-up AS A NOUN = adult, man, woman • *Tell a grown-up if you're being bullied.*
▸ **AS AN ADJECTIVE = mature**, adult, of age, fully-grown • *Her grown-up children are all doing well in their chosen careers.*

growth 1 = increase, development, expansion, extension, growing, heightening, proliferation, enlargement, multiplication • *the unchecked growth of the country's population*
OPPOSITES: fall, drop, decline
2 = progress, success, improvement, expansion, advance, prosperity, advancement • *enormous economic growth*
OPPOSITES: failure
3 = development, growing • *hormones which control fertility and body growth*
4 = vegetation, development, production, sprouting, germination, shooting • *This helps to encourage new growth and makes the plant flower profusely.*
5 = tumour, cancer, swelling, lump, carcinoma *(Pathology)*, sarcoma *(Medical)*, excrescence • *This type of surgery could even be used to extract cancerous growths.*

PROVERBS
Great oaks from little acorns grow

grub AS A NOUN 1 = larva, maggot, caterpillar • *The grubs do their damage by tunnelling through ripened fruit.*
2 = food, feed, rations, tack *(informal)*, eats *(slang)*, kai *(N.Z. informal)*, sustenance, nosh *(slang)*, victuals, nosebag *(slang)*, vittles *(obsolete or dialect)* • *Get yourself some grub and come and sit down.*
▸ **AS A VERB 1 = search**, hunt, scour, ferret, rummage, forage, fossick *(Austral. & N.Z.)* • *grubbing through piles of paper for his address*
2 = dig, search, root *(informal)*, probe, burrow, rootle *(Brit.)* • *chickens grubbing around in the dirt for food*

grubby = dirty, soiled, filthy, squalid, messy, shabby, seedy, scruffy, sordid, untidy, grimy, unwashed, unkempt, mucky, smutty, grungy *(slang, chiefly U.S. & Canad.)*, slovenly, manky *(Scot., dialect)*, scuzzy *(slang)*, skanky *(slang)*, scungy *(Austral. & N.Z.)*, frowzy, besmeared, festy *(Austral. slang)* • *His white coat was grubby and stained.*

grudge AS A NOUN = resentment, bitterness, grievance, malice, hate, spite, dislike, animosity, aversion, venom, antipathy, enmity, rancour, hard feelings, ill will, animus, malevolence • *It was an accident and I bear him no grudge.*
OPPOSITES: goodwill, liking, appreciation
▸ **AS A VERB = resent**, mind, envy, covet, begrudge • *Few seem to grudge him his good fortune.*
OPPOSITES: welcome, be glad for

grudging = reluctant, unwilling, hesitant, unenthusiastic, half-hearted • *He even earned his opponent's grudging respect.*

gruelling = exhausting, demanding, difficult, tiring, trying, hard, taxing, grinding, severe, crushing, fierce, punishing, harsh, stiff, brutal, fatiguing, strenuous, arduous, laborious, backbreaking • *The flight was more gruelling than I had expected.*
OPPOSITES: light, easy, pleasant

gruesome = horrific, shocking, terrible, awful, horrible, grim, horrifying, fearful, obscene, horrendous, ghastly, hideous, from hell *(informal)*, grisly, macabre, horrid, repulsive, repugnant, loathsome, abominable, spine-chilling, hellacious *(U.S. slang)* • *There has been a series of gruesome murders in the capital.*
OPPOSITES: pleasing, appealing, pleasant

gruff 1 = hoarse, rough, harsh, rasping, husky, low, croaking, throaty, guttural • *He picked up the phone expecting to hear the chairman's gruff voice.*
OPPOSITES: sweet, smooth, mellifluous
2 = surly, rough, rude, grumpy, blunt, crabbed, crusty, sullen, bad-tempered, curt, churlish, bearish, brusque, impolite, grouchy *(informal)*, ungracious, discourteous, uncivil, ill-humoured, unmannerly, ill-natured • *His gruff exterior concealed a kind heart.*
OPPOSITES: kind, pleasant, polite

grumble AS A VERB 1 = complain, moan, gripe *(informal)*, whinge *(informal)*, beef *(slang)*, carp, bitch *(slang)*, whine, grouse, bleat, grouch *(informal)*, bellyache *(slang)*, kvetch *(U.S. slang)*, repine • *'This is very inconvenient,' he grumbled.*
2 = rumble, growl, gurgle • *His stomach grumbled loudly.*
▸ **AS A NOUN 1 = complaint**, protest, objection, moan, grievance, grouse, gripe *(informal)*, grouch *(informal)*, beef *(slang)* • *My grumble is with the structure and organisation of his material.*
2 = rumble, growl, gurgle • *One could hear, far to the east, a grumble of thunder.*

grumpy = irritable, cross, bad-tempered, grumbling, crabbed, edgy, surly, petulant, ill-tempered, cantankerous, tetchy, ratty *(Brit. & N.Z. informal)*, testy, grouchy *(informal)*, querulous, peevish, huffy, crotchety *(informal)*, liverish • *I know people think I'm a grumpy old man.*

grunge = dirt, muck, filth, grime, grot *(slang)* • *cleaning the grunge from under the microwave*

guarantee AS A VERB 1 = ensure, secure, assure, warrant, insure, make certain • *Surplus resources alone do not guarantee growth.*
2 = promise, pledge, undertake, swear • *We guarantee to refund your money if you are not delighted with your purchase.*
▸ **AS A NOUN 1 = promise**, word, pledge, undertaking, assurance, certainty, covenant, word of honour • *We can give no guarantee that their demands will be met.*
2 = warranty, contract, bond, guaranty • *The goods were still under guarantee.*
3 = security, earnest, collateral, surety • *He had to give a personal guarantee on the loan to his company.*

guaranteed = sure, certain, bound • *Reports of this kind are guaranteed to cause anxiety.*

guarantor = underwriter, guarantee, supporter, sponsor, backer, surety, bondsman *(Law)*, warrantor • *They told him he needed to find a guarantor to back him.*

guard AS A VERB 1 = protect, watch, defend, secure, police, mind, cover, screen, preserve, shelter, shield, patrol, oversee, safeguard, watch over • *Gunmen guarded homes near the cemetery.*
2 = watch over, watch, oversee, supervise, keep under surveillance • *He is being guarded by a platoon of police.*
▸ **AS A NOUN 1 = sentry**, warder, warden, custodian, watch, patrol, lookout, watchman, sentinel • *The prisoners overpowered their guards and locked them in a cell.*
2 = escort, patrol, convoy • *a heavily armed guard of police*
3 = shield, security, defence, screen, protection, pad, safeguard, bumper, buffer, rampart, bulwark • *The heater should have a safety guard fitted.*
4 = caution, vigilance, wariness, watchfulness • *It takes me a*

g

long time to drop my guard and get close to people.
▸ **IN PHRASES: off guard = unprepared**, napping, unwary, unready, with your defences down • *His question had caught me off guard.*
on (your) guard = vigilant, cautious, wary, prepared, ready, alert, watchful, on the lookout, circumspect, on the alert, on the qui vive • *Be on your guard against crooked car dealers.*
▸ **RELATED ADJECTIVE:** custodial

guarded = cautious, reserved, careful, suspicious, restrained, wary, discreet, prudent, reticent, circumspect, cagey *(informal)*, leery *(slang)*, noncommittal • *The boy gave him a guarded reply.*

guardian = keeper, champion, defender, guard, trustee, warden, curator, protector, warder, custodian, preserver • *He regards himself as a guardian of traditional values.*

guerrilla = freedom fighter, partisan, irregular, underground fighter, member of the underground *or* resistance • *The guerrillas threatened to kill their hostages.*

guess AS A VERB 1 = estimate, predict, work out, speculate, fathom, conjecture, postulate, surmise, hazard a guess, hypothesize • *I can only guess what it cost him to tell you the truth.*
OPPOSITES: know, show, prove
2 = suppose, think, believe, suspect, judge, imagine, reckon, fancy, conjecture, dare say • *I guess I'm just being paranoid.*
▸ **AS A NOUN 1 = estimate**, reckoning, speculation, judgment, hypothesis, conjecture, surmise, shot in the dark, ballpark figure *(informal)* • *He took her pulse and made a guess at her blood pressure.*
OPPOSITES: fact, certainty
2 = supposition, feeling, idea, theory, notion, suspicion, hypothesis • *My guess is that she's waiting for you to make the first move.*

QUOTATIONS
The shrewd guess, the fertile hypothesis, the courageous leap to a tentative conclusion – these are the most valuable coin of the thinker at work
[Jerome S. Bruner *The Process of Education*]
I never guess. It is a shocking habit – destructive to the logical faculty
[Sir Arthur Conan Doyle *The Sign of Four*]

guesswork = speculation, theory, presumption, conjecture, estimation, surmise, supposition • *He bases his claim on a few facts and a lot of guesswork.*

guest 1 = visitor, company, caller, manu(w)hiri *(N.Z.)* • *The guests sipped drinks on the verandah.*
2 = patron, client, resident, lodger, boarder • *I was the only guest at the hotel.*

QUOTATIONS
Mankind is divisible into two great classes: hosts and guests
[Max Beerbohm *Hosts and Guests*]

guest house = boarding house, motel, bed and breakfast, B & B • *She ran a seaside guest house for 25 years.*

guff = nonsense, rubbish, malarkey, balls *(taboo slang)*, bull *(slang)*, shit *(taboo slang)*, rot, crap *(slang)*, garbage *(informal)*, trash, bullshit *(taboo slang)*, hot air *(informal)*, tosh *(slang, chiefly Brit.)*, pap, cobblers *(Brit. taboo slang)*, bilge *(informal)*, humbug, drivel, tripe *(informal)*, moonshine, hogwash, hokum *(slang, chiefly U.S. & Canad.)*, piffle *(informal)*, poppycock *(informal)*, balderdash, bosh *(informal)*, eyewash *(informal)*, kak *(S. African taboo slang)*, empty talk, tommyrot, horsefeathers *(U.S. slang)*, bunkum *or* buncombe *(chiefly U.S.)*, bizzo *(Austral. slang)*, bull's wool *(Austral. & N.Z slang)* • *These commercials are all guff.*

guffaw AS A NOUN = laugh, roar of laughter, bellow of laughter • *He burst into a loud guffaw.*
▸ **AS A VERB = laugh**, roar with laughter, bellow with laughter • *He stood guffawing at his boss's jokes.*

guidance = advice, direction, leadership, instruction, government, help, control, management, teaching, counsel, counselling, auspices • *They improve their performance under the guidance of professional coaches.*

guide AS A NOUN 1 = handbook, manual, guidebook, instructions, catalogue • *Our 10-page guide will help you change your life for the better.*
2 = directory, street map • *The Rough Guide to Paris lists accommodation for as little as £25 a night.*
3 = escort, leader, controller, attendant, usher, chaperon, cicerone, torchbearer, dragoman • *With guides, the journey can be done in fourteen days.*
4 = adviser, teacher, guru, mentor, director, monitor, counsellor • *He was spiritual guide to a group of young monks.*
5 = pointer, sign, signal, mark, key, clue, landmark, marker, beacon, signpost, guiding light, lodestar • *His only guide was the stars overhead.*
6 = model, example, standard, ideal, master, inspiration, criterion, paradigm, exemplar, lodestar • *The checklist serves as a guide to students, teachers and parents.*
▸ **AS A VERB 1 = lead**, direct, escort, conduct, pilot, accompany, steer, shepherd, convoy, usher, show the way • *He took the bewildered man by the arm and guided him out.*
2 = steer, control, manage, direct, handle, command, manoeuvre • *He guided his plane down the runway and took off.*
3 = supervise, train, rule, teach, influence, advise, counsel, govern, educate, regulate, instruct, oversee, sway, superintend • *He should have let his instinct guide him.*

guidebook 1 = directory, guide, street map • *The guidebook says this is the place where all the Hollywood Westerns were made.*
2 = handbook, guide, manual, instructions, catalogue • *In 1987 they published a series of guidebooks to American politics.*

guideline = recommendation, advice, proposal, direction, suggestion, counsel, specification • *The government should issue clear guidelines on the content of religious education.*

guild = society, union, league, association, company, club, order, organization, corporation, lodge, fellowship, fraternity, brotherhood • *the Writers' Guild of America*

guile = cunning, craft, deception, deceit, trickery, duplicity, cleverness, art, gamesmanship *(informal)*, craftiness, artfulness, slyness, trickiness, wiliness • *I love children's innocence and lack of guile.*
OPPOSITES: honesty, sincerity, candour

guileless = artless, open, genuine, simple, natural, frank, innocent, straightforward, naive, sincere, honest, candid, truthful, upfront *(informal)*, simple-minded, unsophisticated, dinkum *(Austral. & N.Z. informal)*, above-board, ingenuous, undesigning • *She was so guileless that he had no option but to believe her.*

guilt 1 = shame, regret, remorse, contrition, guilty conscience, bad conscience, self-reproach, self-condemnation, guiltiness • *Her emotions went from anger to guilt in the space of a few seconds.*
OPPOSITES: honour, pride, self-respect
2 = culpability, blame, responsibility, misconduct, delinquency, criminality, wickedness, iniquity, sinfulness, blameworthiness, guiltiness • *You were never convinced of his guilt, were you?*
OPPOSITES: virtue, innocence, righteousness

QUOTATIONS
This is his first punishment, that by the verdict of his own heart no guilty man is acquitted
[Juvenal *Satires*]
So full of artless jealousy is guilt
It spills itself in fearing to be spilt
[William Shakespeare *Hamlet*]

guiltless = innocent, pure, blameless, immaculate, spotless, clean *(slang)*, squeaky-clean, untainted, unsullied, unimpeachable, untarnished, irreproachable, sinless • *You are hardly guiltless in this matter yourself, you know.*

guilty 1 = **ashamed**, sorry, rueful, sheepish, contrite, remorseful, regretful, shamefaced, hangdog, conscience-stricken • *When she saw me, she looked extremely guilty.*
OPPOSITES: proud
2 = **culpable**, responsible, convicted, to blame, offending, erring, at fault, reprehensible, iniquitous, felonious, blameworthy • *They were found guilty of manslaughter.* • *The guilty pair were caught red-handed.*
OPPOSITES: moral, innocent, righteous

guise 1 = **form**, appearance, dress, fashion, shape, aspect, mode, semblance • *He claimed the Devil had appeared to him in the guise of a goat.*
2 = **pretence**, show, mask, disguise, face, front, aspect, façade, semblance • *Fascism is on the rise under the guise of conservative politics.*

gulch = **ravine**, canyon, defile, gorge, gully, pass • *A helicopter had crashed in a nearby gulch.*

gulf 1 = **bay**, bight, sea inlet • *Hurricane Andrew was last night heading into the Gulf of Mexico.*
2 = **chasm**, opening, split, gap, rent, breach, separation, void, rift, abyss, cleft • *the gulf between rural and urban life*

gull
▸ RELATED ADJECTIVE: larine
▸ COLLECTIVE NOUN: colony

gullet = **throat**, crop, maw, craw • *He burnt his mouth, throat and gullet.*
▸ TECHNICAL NAME: oesophagus
▸ RELATED ADJECTIVE: oesophageal

gullibility = **credulity**, innocence, naïveté, blind faith, credulousness, simplicity • *She must take part of the blame for her own gullibility.*

gullible = **trusting**, innocent, naive, unsuspecting, green, simple, silly, foolish, unsophisticated, credulous, born yesterday, wet behind the ears *(informal)*, easily taken in, unsceptical, as green as grass • *I'm so gullible I believed him.*
OPPOSITES: worldly, sophisticated, suspicious

gully = **ravine**, canyon, gorge, chasm, channel, fissure, defile, watercourse • *The bodies of the three climbers were located at the bottom of a steep gully.*

gulp AS A VERB 1 = **swallow**, bolt, devour, gobble, knock back *(informal)*, wolf, swig *(informal)*, swill, guzzle, quaff • *She quickly gulped her tea.*
2 = **gasp**, swallow, choke • *He slumped back, gulping for air.*
▸ AS A NOUN = **swallow**, draught, mouthful, swig *(informal)* • *He drank half of his whisky in one gulp.*

gum[1] AS A NOUN = **glue**, adhesive, resin, cement, paste • *a pound note that had been torn in half and stuck together with gum*
▸ AS A VERB = **stick**, glue, affix, cement, paste, clog • *a mild infection in which the baby's eyelashes can become gummed together*

gum[2]
▸ TECHNICAL NAME: gingiva
▸ RELATED ADJECTIVE: gingival

gummy = **sticky**, tacky, adhesive, gluey, viscid • *There was gummy stuff all over the pages of the magazine.*

gumption = **common sense**, sense, ability, spirit, initiative, enterprise, wit(s), savvy *(slang)*, acumen, nous *(Brit. slang)*, get-up-and-go *(informal)*, cleverness, resourcefulness, shrewdness, discernment, sagacity, horse sense, astuteness, mother wit • *He didn't have the gumption to seize the opportunity when it came up.*

gun = **firearm**, shooter *(slang)*, piece *(slang)*, rod *(slang)*, heater *(U.S. slang)*, handgun • *He produced a gun as he came into the room.*

QUOTATIONS

They hesitate
We hesitate.
They have a gun.
We have no gun
[D.H. Lawrence *Mountain Lion*]

▹ *See panel* **Guns**

gunfire = **shots**, shooting, firing, gunshots • *The sound of gunfire grew closer.*

gunman = **armed man**, hit man *(slang)*, gunslinger *(U.S. slang)* • *Two policemen were killed when gunmen opened fire on their patrol vehicle.*

gurgle AS A VERB 1 = **ripple**, lap, bubble, splash, murmur, babble, burble, purl, plash • *a narrow channel along which water gurgles*
2 = **burble**, crow, chuckle, babble • *Henry gurgles happily in his baby chair.*
▸ AS A NOUN 1 = **ripple**, lapping, bubble, splash, murmur, babble, burble, purl, plash • *We could hear the swish and gurgle of water against the hull.*
2 = **burble**, chuckle, ripple, babble • *There was a gurgle of laughter on the other end of the line.*

guru 1 = **authority**, expert, leader, master, pundit, arbiter, Svengali, torchbearer, fundi *(S. African)* • *Fashion gurus dictate crazy ideas such as puffball skirts.*
2 = **teacher**, mentor, sage, master, tutor, mahatma, guiding light, swami, maharishi • *He set himself up as a faith healer and spiritual guru.*

gush AS A VERB 1 = **flow**, run, rush, flood, pour, jet, burst, stream, cascade, issue, spurt, spout • *Piping hot water gushed out of the tap.*
2 = **enthuse**, rave, spout, overstate, rhapsodize, effuse • *'Oh, you were just brilliant,' she gushed.*
▸ AS A NOUN = **stream**, flow, rush, flood, jet, burst, issue, outburst, cascade, torrent, spurt, spout, outflow • *I heard a gush of water.*

gushing = **effusive**, enthusiastic, extravagant, fulsome, over-effusive • *He delivered a gushing speech.*

GUNS

AK-47 *or* Kalashnikov
anti-aircraft gun *or* ack-ack gun
Armalite *(trademark)*
arquebus
BAR
Big Bertha
blunderbuss
Bofors gun
breech-loader
Bren gun
Browning
burp gun
carbine
carronade
chassepot
chokebore
Colt
culverin
derringer
Enfield rifle
firelock
flintlock
forty-five
fusil
Garand rifle
Gatling
howitzer
Lewis gun
Luger *(trademark)*
M-1 rifle
M-14
M-16
machine gun
Magnum *(trademark)*
matchlock
Mauser
Maxim gun
mitrailleuse
musket
muzzle-loader
Owen gun
petronel
pistol
pom-pom
pump gun
Quaker gun
repeater
revolver
rifle
scatter-gun
shotgun
six-shooter
Springfield rifle
Sten gun
stern-chaser
sub-machine-gun
Thompson sub-machine gun *(trademark)*
trench mortar
Uzi *(trademark)*
Winchester rifle
zip gun

gust AS A NOUN 1 = **blast**, blow, rush, breeze, puff, gale, flurry, squall • *A gust of wind drove down the valley.*
2 = **surge**, fit, storm, burst, explosion, gale, outburst, eruption, paroxysm • *A gust of laughter greeted him as he walked into the room.*
▸ AS A VERB = **blow**, blast, puff, squall • *strong winds gusting up to 164 miles an hour*

gusto = **relish**, enthusiasm, appetite, appreciation, liking, delight, pleasure, enjoyment, savour, zeal, verve, zest, fervour, exhilaration, brio, zing *(informal)* • *Hers was a minor part, but she played it with gusto.*
OPPOSITES: apathy, distaste, inertia

gusty = **windy**, stormy, breezy, blustering, tempestuous, blustery, inclement, squally, blowy • *Weather forecasts predict gusty winds and lightning strikes.*

gut AS A NOUN = **paunch** *(Informal)*, belly, spare tyre *(Brit. slang)*, potbelly, puku *(N.Z.)* • *His gut sagged over his belt.*
▸ AS A VERB 1 = **disembowel**, draw, dress, clean, eviscerate • *It is not always necessary to gut the fish prior to freezing.*
2 = **ravage**, strip, empty, sack, rifle, plunder, clean out, ransack, pillage, despoil • *The church had been gutted by vandals.*
▸ AS AN ADJECTIVE = **instinctive**, natural, basic, emotional, spontaneous, innate, intuitive, hard-wired, involuntary, heartfelt, deep-seated, unthinking • *At first my gut reaction was to simply walk out of there.*
▸ TECHNICAL NAME: viscera
▸ RELATED ADJECTIVE: visceral

gutless = **faint-hearted**, weak, cowardly, chicken *(slang)*, craven, feeble, timid, abject, submissive, spineless, boneless, irresolute, chickenshit *(U.S. slang)*, lily-livered • *By attacking his wife, he has proved himself to be a gutless coward.*
OPPOSITES: brave, bold, courageous

guts 1 = **intestines**, insides *(informal)*, stomach, belly, bowels, inwards, innards *(informal)*, entrails • *The crew-men were standing ankle-deep in fish guts.*
2 = **courage**, spirit, nerve, daring, pluck, grit, backbone, willpower, bottle *(slang)*, audacity, mettle, boldness, spunk *(informal)*, forcefulness, hardihood • *The new Chancellor has the guts to push through unpopular tax increases.*

gutsy = **brave**, determined, spirited, bold, have-a-go *(informal)*, courageous, gritty, staunch, feisty *(informal, chiefly U.S. & Canad.)*, game *(informal)*, resolute, gallant, plucky, indomitable, ballsy *(taboo slang)*, mettlesome, (as) game as Ned Kelly *(Austral. slang)* • *They admired his gutsy determination.*

gutter = **drain**, channel, tube, pipe, ditch, trench, trough, conduit, duct, sluice • *The waste washes down the gutter and into the city's sewerage system.*

guttersnipe = **street urchin**, waif, ragamuffin, mudlark *(slang)*, gamin, street Arab *(offensive)* • *An elocution expert plucks a guttersnipe from Covent Garden market and teaches her to talk like a lady.*

guttural = **throaty**, low, deep, thick, rough, rasping, husky, hoarse, gruff, gravelly • *He spoke in a low guttural voice.*

guy = **man**, person, fellow, lad, cat *(dated slang)*, bloke *(Brit. informal)*, chap • *I was working with a guy from Manchester.*

guzzle = **devour**, drink, neck *(slang)*, bolt, wolf, cram, gorge, gobble, knock back *(informal)*, swill, quaff, tope, pig out on *(slang)*, stuff yourself with • *She had been guzzling gin and tonics all evening.*

gymnastics

GYMNASTIC EVENTS

asymmetric bars	horizontal bar	rings
beam	horse vault	rhythmic
floor exercises	parallel bars	gymnastics
high *or*	pommel horse	side horse vault

Gypsy *or* **Gipsy** = **traveller**, roamer, wanderer, Bohemian, rover, rambler, nomad, vagrant, Romany, vagabond • *the largest community of Gypsies of any country*

gyrate 1 = **dance**, move, twist, writhe • *She began to gyrate to the music.*
2 = **rotate**, circle, spin, spiral, revolve, whirl, twirl, pirouette • *The aeroplane was gyrating about in the sky in a most alarming fashion.*

gyration = **rotation**, revolution, spin, spinning, whirl, whirling, pirouette, convolution • *He continued his enthusiastic gyrations on stage.*

Hh

habit AS A NOUN **1 = mannerism**, custom, way, practice, manner, characteristic, tendency, quirk, propensity, foible, proclivity • *He has an endearing habit of licking his lips.*
2 = custom, rule, practice, tradition, routine, convention, mode, usage, wont, second nature • *It had become a habit with her to annoy him.*
3 = addiction, weakness, obsession, dependence, compulsion, fixation • *After twenty years as a chain smoker, he has given up the habit.*
4 = dress, costume, garment, apparel, garb, habiliment, riding dress • *She emerged having changed into her riding habit.*
▸ IN PHRASES: **habit of mind = disposition**, character, nature, make-up, constitution, frame of mind • *In accent, mannerism and habit of mind he appeared East European.*

QUOTATIONS

Habit is a great deadener
[Samuel Beckett *Waiting for Godot*]

It is hard to teach an old dog new tricks
[William Camden *Remains Concerning Britain*]

Habit with him was all the test of truth,
'It must be right; I've done it from my youth.'
[George Crabbe *The Borough*]

The habits of life form the soul, and the soul forms the countenance
[Honoré De Balzac *The Abbé Birotteau*]

The regularity of a habit is generally in proportion to its absurdity
[Marcel Proust *Remembrance of Things Past*]

PROVERBS

Old habits die hard

habitable = fit to live in, in good repair, liveable in, fit to inhabit, fit to occupy • *Making the house habitable was a major undertaking.*
OPPOSITES: inhabitable, unfit to live in

habitat = home, environment, surroundings, element, territory, domain, terrain, locality, home ground, abode, habitation, natural home • *In its natural habitat, the hibiscus will grow up to 25ft.*

habitation 1 = occupation, living in, residence, tenancy, occupancy, residency, inhabitance, inhabitancy • *20 percent of private-rented dwellings are unfit for human habitation.*
2 = dwelling, home, house, residence, quarters, lodging, pad *(slang)*, abode, living quarters, domicile, dwelling house • *Behind the habitations, the sandstone cliffs rose abruptly.*

habit-forming = addictive, compulsive, moreish *(informal)* • *Adventure travel can be habit-forming.*

habitual 1 = customary, normal, usual, common, standard, natural, traditional, fixed, regular, ordinary, familiar, routine, accustomed, wonted • *He soon recovered his habitual geniality.*
OPPOSITES: strange, rare, unusual
2 = persistent, established, confirmed, constant, frequent, chronic, hardened, recurrent, ingrained, inveterate • *three out of four of them would become habitual criminals*
OPPOSITES: occasional, irregular, infrequent

habituate = accustom, train, condition, school, season, discipline, break in, harden, acquaint, familiarize, inure, acclimatize, make used to • *The researchers first habituated each baby to their surroundings.*

habitué = frequent visitor, regular *(informal)*, frequenter, regular patron, constant customer • *They were habitués of this bar.*

hack[1] AS A VERB **1** *sometimes with* **away = cut**, chop, slash, mutilate, mangle, mangulate *(Austral. slang)*, gash, hew, lacerate • *He desperately hacked through the undergrowth.* • *Some were hacked to death with machetes.*
2 = stand, take, bear, handle, cope with, stomach, endure, tolerate, abide, put up with *(informal)* • *I can't hack all the violence*
3 = cough, bark, wheeze, rasp • *The patients splutter and hack.*
▸ AS A NOUN **= cough**, bark, wheeze, rasp • *smoker's hack*
▸ IN PHRASES: **be hacked off = be annoyed**, be fed up, be irked (by), be scunnered *(Scot.)* • *She was jealous, hacked off with the producer, but mostly with herself.*
hack it = cope, manage, handle it, survive, get along, get by • *he couldn't hack it as a solo performer*
hack something off = cut off, chop off, lop off • *a man's arm was hacked off at the elbow*

hack[2] AS A NOUN **1 = reporter**, writer, correspondent, journalist, scribbler, contributor, hackette *(derogatory)*, literary hack, penny-a-liner, Grub Street writer • *tabloid hacks, always eager to find victims*
2 = yes-man, lackey, toady, flunky, brown-noser *(taboo slang)* • *Party hacks from the old days still hold influential jobs.*
▸ AS AN ADJECTIVE **= unoriginal**, pedestrian, mediocre, poor, tired, stereotyped, banal, undistinguished, uninspired • *ill-paid lectureships and hack writing*

hacking = rasping, barking, wheezing • *The quiet was broken by a hacking cough.*

hackles IN PHRASES: **raise someone's hackles** *or* **make someone's hackles rise = anger**, annoy, infuriate, cause resentment, rub someone up the wrong way, make someone see red *(informal)*, get someone's dander up *(slang)*, hack you off *(informal)* • *It made my hackles rise when he got the job.*

hackneyed = clichéd, stock, tired, common, stereotyped, pedestrian, played out *(informal)*, commonplace, worn-out, stale, overworked, banal, run-of-the-mill, threadbare, trite, unoriginal, timeworn • *That's the old hackneyed phrase, but it's true.*
OPPOSITES: new, original, fresh

Hades = underworld, hell, nether regions, lower world, infernal regions, realm of Pluto, (the) inferno • *Zeus finally sent Hermes to Hades with a request to return the maiden.*

haemorrhage AS A NOUN **= drain**, outpouring, rapid loss • *The move would stem the haemorrhage of talent from the area.*

▸ **AS A VERB** = **drain**, bleed, flow rapidly • *cash was haemorrhaging from the conglomerate*

haft = **handle**, butt, shaft, hilt, handgrip, helve • *the small gold and silver inlaid haft of the tiny dagger*

hag = **witch**, virago, shrew, vixen, crone, fury, harridan, beldam *(archaic)*, termagant • *I hope the old hag hasn't come back yet.*

haggard = **gaunt**, wasted, drawn, thin, pinched, wrinkled, ghastly, wan, emaciated, shrunken, careworn, hollow-eyed • *He was pale and a bit haggard.*
OPPOSITES: fresh, robust, vigorous

haggle 1 = **bargain**, barter, beat down, drive a hard bargain, dicker *(chiefly U.S.)*, chaffer, palter, higgle • *Ella taught her how to haggle with used furniture dealers.*
2 = **wrangle**, dispute, quarrel, squabble, bicker • *As the politicians haggle, the violence worsens.*

hail[1] **AS A NOUN** 1 = **hailstones**, sleet, hailstorm, frozen rain • *a short-lived storm with heavy hail*
2 = **shower**, rain, storm, battery, volley, barrage, bombardment, pelting, downpour, salvo, broadside • *The victim was hit by a hail of bullets.*
▸ **AS A VERB** 1 = **rain**, shower, pelt • *It started to hail, huge great stones.*
2 = **batter**, rain, barrage, bombard, pelt, rain down on, beat down upon • *Shellfire was hailing down on the city's edge.*

hail[2] **AS A VERB** 1 = **acclaim**, honour, acknowledge, cheer, applaud, glorify, exalt • *hailed as the greatest American novelist of his generation*
OPPOSITES: condemn, criticize, boo
2 = **salute**, call, greet, address, welcome, speak to, shout to, say hello to, accost, sing out, halloo • *I saw him and hailed him.*
OPPOSITES: cut *(informal)*, avoid, snub
3 = **flag down**, summon, signal to, wave down • *I hurried away to hail a taxi.*
▸ **IN PHRASES:** **hail from somewhere** = **come from**, be born in, originate in, be a native of, have your roots in • *The band hail from Glasgow.*

hair **AS A NOUN** = **locks**, mane, tresses, shock, mop, head of hair • *a girl with long blonde hair*
▸ **IN PHRASES:** **by a hair** = **by a narrow margin**, by a whisker, by a hair's-breadth, by a split second, by a fraction of an inch, by the skin of your teeth
get in someone's hair = **annoy**, plague, irritate, harass, hassle *(informal)*, aggravate *(informal)*, exasperate, pester, be on someone's back *(slang)*, get on someone's nerves *(informal)*, nark *(Brit., Austral. & N.Z. slang)*, get up your nose *(informal)*, piss you off *(taboo slang)*, get on your wick *(Brit. slang)*, hack you off *(informal)*
let your hair down = **let yourself go**, relax, chill out *(slang, chiefly U.S.)*, let off steam *(informal)*, let it all hang out *(informal)*, mellow out *(informal)*, veg out *(slang, chiefly U.S.)*, outspan *(S. African)* • *a time when everyone really lets their hair down*
make someone's hair stand on end = **terrify**, shock, scare, appal, horrify, make someone's hair curl, freeze someone's blood, scare the bejesus out of *(informal)* • *the kind of smile that made your hair stand on end*
not turn a hair = **remain calm**, keep your cool *(slang)*, not bat an eyelid, keep your hair on *(Brit. informal)* • *The man didn't turn a hair.*
split hairs = **quibble**, find fault, cavil, overrefine, pettifog, nit-pick *(informal)* • *Don't split hairs. You know what I'm getting at.*
▸ **RELATED MANIA:** trichomania

QUOTATIONS
Doth not even nature itself teach you, that if a man have long hair, it is a shame unto him? But if a woman have long hair, it is a glory to her
[Bible: I Corinthians]

haircut *or* **hairdo** = **hairstyle**, cut, style, coiffure • *How do you like my new hairdo?*

hairdresser = **stylist**, barber, coiffeur *or* coiffeuse, friseur • *a second year apprentice hairdresser*
▸ **RELATED ADJECTIVE:** tonsorial

hairless = **bare**, bald, clean-shaven, shorn, beardless, tonsured, depilated, baldheaded, glabrous *or* glabrate *(Biology)* • *a smooth and hairless body*

hairpiece = **wig**, toupee, rug *(slang)*, syrup *(slang)*, postiche, switch • *for years he wore a hairpiece both on and off screen*

hair-raising = **frightening**, shocking, alarming, thrilling, exciting, terrifying, startling, horrifying, scary, breathtaking, creepy, petrifying, spine-chilling, bloodcurdling • *hair-raising rides at funfairs*

hair's breadth = **fraction**, jot, hair, whisker, narrow margin • *He did not swerve a hair's breadth from the decision.*

hairstyle = **haircut**, hairdo, coiffure, cut, style • *I think her new short hairstyle looks great.*

HAIRSTYLES

Afro	dreadlocks	perm *or* permanent wave
beehive	duck's arse *or* DA	pigtail
bob	Eton crop	plait
bouffant	feather-cut	pompadour
bun	flat top	ponytail
bunches	French pleat *or* roll	pouf
buzz cut	marcel *or* marcel wave	razor-cut
chignon	mohican	shingle
corn row	mullet	skinhead
crew cut	pageboy	wedge
crop		

hairy 1 = **shaggy**, woolly, furry, stubbly, bushy, bearded, unshaven, hirsute, fleecy, bewhiskered, pileous *(Biology)*, pilose *(Biology)* • *I don't mind having a hairy chest, but the stuff on my back is really thick.*
2 = **dangerous**, scary, risky, unpredictable, hazardous, perilous • *His driving was a bit hairy.*

halcyon 1 = **happy**, golden, flourishing, prosperous, carefree, palmy • *It was all a far cry from those halcyon days in 1990.*
2 = **peaceful**, still, quiet, calm, gentle, mild, serene, tranquil, placid, pacific, undisturbed, unruffled • *The next day dawned sunny with a halcyon blue sky.*

hale = **healthy**, well, strong, sound, fit, flourishing, blooming, robust, vigorous, hearty, in the pink, in fine fettle, right as rain *(Brit. informal)*, able-bodied • *looking hale and hearty*

half **AS A NOUN** = **fifty per cent**, equal part • *A half of the voters have not made up their minds.*
▸ **AS AN ADJECTIVE** = **partial**, limited, fractional, divided, moderate, halved, incomplete • *Children received only a half portion.*
▸ **AS AN ADVERB** = **partially**, partly, incompletely, slightly, all but, barely, in part, inadequately, after a fashion, pretty nearly • *The vegetables are only half cooked.*
▸ **IN PHRASES:** **by half** = **excessively**, very much, considerably • *He's just too clever by half.*
by halves = **incompletely**, inadequately, insufficiently, imperfectly, to a limited extent, skimpily, scrappily • *They rarely do things by halves.*
not half 1 = **not nearly**, nothing like, nowhere near • *not half as clever as he'd thought*
2 = **absolutely**, yes, indeed, ya *(S. African)*, yebo *(S. African informal)* • *'Fancy a top up?' 'Not half.'*
▸ **RELATED PREFIXES:** bi-, hemi-, demi-, semi-

PROVERBS
The half is better than the whole
Half a loaf is better than no bread

half-baked = **stupid**, impractical, crazy, silly, foolish, senseless, short-sighted, inane, loopy *(informal)*, ill-conceived, crackpot *(informal)*, ill-judged, brainless, unformed, poorly planned, harebrained, dumb-ass *(slang)*, unthought out *or* through • *another half-baked scheme that isn't going to work*

half-hearted = **unenthusiastic**, indifferent, apathetic, cool, neutral, passive, lacklustre, lukewarm, uninterested, perfunctory, listless, spiritless, half-arsed *(Brit. slang)*, half-assed *(U.S. & Canad. slang)* • *Joanna had made one or two half-hearted attempts to befriend her.*
OPPOSITES: enthusiastic, energetic, zealous

halfway **AS AN ADVERB** 1 = **midway**, to the midpoint, to *or* in the middle • *He was halfway up the ladder.*
2 = **partially**, partly, moderately, rather, nearly • *You need hard currency to get anything halfway decent.*
▸ **AS AN ADJECTIVE** = **midway**, middle, mid, central, intermediate, equidistant • *He was third fastest at the halfway point.*
▸ **IN PHRASES: meet someone halfway** = **compromise**, accommodate, come to terms, reach a compromise, strike a balance, trade off with, find the middle ground • *The Democrats are willing to meet the president halfway.*

halfwit = **fool**, jerk *(slang, chiefly U.S. & Canad.)*, idiot, plank *(Brit. slang)*, charlie *(Brit. informal)*, berk *(Brit. slang)*, prick *(slang)*, wally *(slang)*, prat *(slang)*, plonker *(slang)*, coot, moron, geek *(slang)*, twit *(informal, chiefly Brit.)*, dunce, imbecile *(informal)*, oaf, simpleton, airhead *(slang)*, dullard, dimwit *(informal)*, dipstick *(Brit. slang)*, dickhead *(slang)*, gonzo *(slang)*, schmuck *(U.S. slang)*, dork *(slang)*, nitwit *(informal)*, dolt, divvy *(Brit. slang)*, pillock *(Brit. slang)*, dweeb *(U.S. slang)*, putz *(U.S. slang)*, fathead *(informal)*, eejit *(Scot. & Irish)*, thicko *(Brit. slang)*, dumb-ass *(slang)*, gobshite *(Irish taboo slang)*, dunderhead, numpty *(Scot. informal)*, doofus *(slang, chiefly U.S.)*, lamebrain *(informal)*, fuckwit *(taboo slang)*, dickwit *(slang)*, nerd *or* nurd *(slang)*, numbskull *or* numskull, dorba *or* dorb *(Austral. slang)*, bogan *(Austral. slang)* • *I'm a mindless optimist, a cheery halfwit.*

hall 1 = **passage**, lobby, corridor, hallway, foyer, entry, passageway, entrance hall, vestibule • *The lights were on in the hall and in the bedroom.*
2 = **meeting place**, chamber, auditorium, concert hall, assembly room • *We filed into the lecture hall.*

hallmark 1 = **trademark**, indication, badge, emblem, sure sign, telltale sign • *a technique that has become the hallmark of their films*
2 = **mark**, sign, device, stamp, seal, symbol, signet, authentication • *He uses a hallmark on the base of his lamps to distinguish them.*

hallowed = **sanctified**, holy, blessed, sacred, honoured, dedicated, revered, consecrated, sacrosanct, inviolable, beatified • *Their resting place is in hallowed ground.*

hallucinate = **imagine**, trip *(informal)*, envision, daydream, fantasize, freak out *(informal)*, have hallucinations • *Miguel stared at him, as if he were hallucinating.*

hallucination = **illusion**, dream, vision, fantasy, delusion, mirage, apparition, smoke and mirrors, phantasmagoria, figment of the imagination • *Perhaps the footprint was a hallucination.*

hallucinogenic = **psychedelic**, mind-blowing *(informal)*, psychoactive, hallucinatory, psychotropic, mind-expanding • *They had not been the first to experiment with hallucinogenic drugs.*

hallway = **corridor**, hall, passageway • *A central hallway leads into the dining and living areas.*

halo = **ring of light**, aura, corona, radiance, nimbus, halation *(Photography)*, aureole *or* aureola • *The sun had a faint halo round it.*

halt **AS A VERB** 1 = **stop**, draw up, pull up, break off, stand still, wait, rest, call it a day, belay *(Nautical)* • *They halted at a short distance from the house.*
OPPOSITES: start, begin, continue
2 = **come to an end**, stop, cease • *The flow of assistance to refugees has virtually halted.*
3 = **hold back**, end, check, block, arrest, stem, curb, terminate, obstruct, staunch, cut short, impede, bring to an end, stem the flow, nip in the bud • *Striking workers halted production at the auto plant yesterday.*
OPPOSITES: encourage, boost, aid
▸ **AS A NOUN** = **stop**, end, close, break, stand, arrest, pause, interruption, impasse, standstill, stoppage, termination • *Air traffic has been brought to a halt.*
OPPOSITES: start, beginning, continuation

halter = **harness**, bridle • *He slipped the halter over Boots, then fed him a handful of grain.*

halting = **faltering**, stumbling, awkward, hesitant, laboured, stammering, imperfect, stuttering • *The officer replied in halting German.*

halve 1 = **cut in half**, reduce by fifty per cent, decrease by fifty per cent, lessen by fifty per cent • *The work force has been halved in two years.*
2 = **split in two**, cut in half, bisect, divide in two, share equally, divide equally • *Halve the pineapple and scoop out the inside.*

ham-fisted = **clumsy** *(Informal)*, awkward, bungling, inept, cack-handed *(informal)*, maladroit, ham-handed *(informal)*, all fingers and thumbs *(informal)*, butterfingered *(informal)*, unhandy, unco *(Austral. slang)* • *They can be made by even the most ham-fisted of cooks.*

hammer **AS A NOUN** = **mallet**, gavel • *He used a hammer and chisel to chip away at the wall.*
▸ **AS A VERB** 1 = **hit**, drive, knock, beat, strike, tap, bang • *Hammer a wooden peg into the hole.*
2 *often with* **into** = **impress upon**, repeat, drive home, drum into, grind into, din into, drub into • *He hammered it into me that I had not become a rotten goalkeeper.*
3 = **criticize**, condemn, censure, rebuke, reprimand, berate, castigate, admonish, chastise, pillory, lambaste • *The report hammers the private motorist.*
4 = **defeat**, beat, thrash, stuff *(slang)*, master, worst, tank *(slang)*, lick *(informal)*, slate *(informal)*, trounce, clobber *(slang)*, run rings around *(informal)*, wipe the floor with *(informal)*, blow out of the water *(slang)*, drub • *He hammered the young left-hander in four straight sets.*
5 = **fashion**, make, form, shape, forge, beat out • *The barrels are hammered from cold steel.*
▸ **IN PHRASES: go at something hammer and tongs** = **do something enthusiastically**, do something with gusto, give something laldy *(Scot.)* • *He loved gardening. He went at it hammer and tongs.*
hammer away at something = **work**, keep on, persevere, grind, persist, stick at, plug away *(informal)*, drudge, pound away, peg away *(chiefly Brit.)*, beaver away *(Brit. informal)* • *Palmer kept hammering away at his report.*
hammer something out = **work out**, produce, finish, complete, settle, negotiate, accomplish, sort out, bring about, make a decision, thrash out, come to a conclusion, form a resolution, excogitate • *I think we can hammer out a solution.*

hamper[1] = **hinder**, handicap, hold up, prevent, restrict, frustrate, curb, slow down, restrain, hamstring, interfere with, cramp, thwart, obstruct, impede, hobble, fetter, encumber, trammel • *I was hampered by a lack of information.*
OPPOSITES: help, further, aid

hamper[2] = **basket**, case, package, flax kit *(N.Z.)*, kete *(N.Z.)* • *a luxury food hamper*

hamstring = **thwart**, stop, block, prevent, ruin, frustrate, handicap, curb, foil, obstruct, impede, balk, fetter • *He could*

h

hamstring a conservative-led coalition.
▸ **RELATED ADJECTIVE:** popliteal

hamstrung = **incapacitated**, disabled, crippled, helpless, paralysed, at a loss, hors de combat *(French)* • *Now he knows what it's like to represent a hamstrung super-power.*

hand **AS A NOUN** 1 = **palm**, fist, paw *(informal)*, mitt *(slang)*, hook, meathook *(slang)* • *I put my hand into my pocket.*
2 = **influence**, part, share, agency, direction, participation • *Did you have a hand in his downfall?*
3 = **assistance**, help, aid, support, helping hand • *Come and give me a hand in the garden.*
4 = **worker**, employee, labourer, workman, operative, craftsman, artisan, hired man, hireling • *He now works as a farm hand.*
5 = **round of applause**, clap, ovation, big hand • *Let's give 'em a big hand.*
6 = **writing**, script, handwriting, calligraphy, longhand, penmanship, chirography • *written in the composer's own hand*
▸ **AS A PLURAL NOUN** = **control**, charge, care, keeping, power, authority, command, possession, custody, disposal, supervision, guardianship • *He is leaving his business in the hands of a colleague.*
▸ **AS A VERB** 1 = **give**, pass, hand over, present to, deliver • *He handed me a little rectangle of white paper.*
2 = **help**, guide, conduct, lead, aid, assist, convey • *He handed her into his old Alfa Romeo sports car.*
▸ **IN PHRASES: at hand** = **approaching**, near, imminent, just round the corner • *His retirement was at hand.*
at *or* **on hand** = **within reach**, nearby, handy, close, available, ready, on tap *(informal)*, at your fingertips • *Having the right equipment on hand is enormously helpful.*
by hand = **manually**, with your hands, freehand • *Her work is painted by hand so every design is unique.*
hand in glove = **in association**, in partnership, in league, in collaboration, in cooperation, in cahoots *(informal)* • *They work hand in glove with the western intelligence agencies.*
hand over fist = **swiftly**, easily, steadily, by leaps and bounds • *Investors would lose money hand over fist if a demerger went ahead.*
hand something around *or* **round** = **pass round**, distribute, circulate, hand out • *John handed round the plate of sandwiches.*
hand something back = **return**, restore, send back, give back • *The management handed back his few possessions.*
hand something down 1 = **pass on** *or* **down**, pass, transfer, bequeath, will, give, grant, gift, endow • *a family heirloom handed down from generation to generation*
2 = **pronounce**, give, decree, deliver • *Tougher sentences are being handed down these days.*
hand something on = **pass on** *or* **down**, pass, transfer, bequeath, will, give, grant, relinquish • *His chauffeur-driven car will be handed on to his successor.*
hand something out = **distribute**, give out, issue, pass out, dish out, dole out, deal out, hand round, pass round, give round • *One of my jobs was to hand out the prizes.*
hand something *or* **someone in** = **give**, turn in, turn over • *Anyone who finds anything is to hand it in to the police.*
hand something *or* **someone over** 1 = **give**, present, deliver, donate • *He handed over a letter of apology.*
2 = **turn over**, release, transfer, deliver, yield, surrender • *The American was formally handed over to the ambassador.*
hands down = **easily**, effortlessly, with ease, comfortably, without difficulty, with no trouble, standing on your head, with one hand tied behind your back, with no contest, with your eyes closed *or* shut • *We should have won hands down.*
in hand 1 = **in reserve**, ready, put by, available for use • *I'll pay now as I have the money in hand.*
2 = **under way**, being dealt with, being attended to • *The business in hand was approaching some kind of climax.*
3 = **under control**, in order, receiving attention • *The organisers say that matters are well in hand.*
lay hands on someone 1 = **attack**, assault, set on, beat up, work over *(slang)*, lay into *(informal)* • *The crowd laid hands on him.*
2 = **bless** *(Christianity)*, confirm, ordain, consecrate • *The bishop laid hands on the sick.*
lay hands on something = **get hold of**, get, obtain, gain, grab, acquire, seize, grasp • *the ease with which prisoners can lay hands on drugs*
lend a hand = **help**, help out, do your bit, be of assistance, lend a helping hand • *I'd be glad to lend a hand.*
try your hand = **attempt**, try, have a go *(informal)*, have a shot *(informal)*, have a crack, have a stab *(informal)* • *I tried my hand at painting*
▸ **TECHNICAL NAME:** manus
▸ **RELATED ADJECTIVE:** manual

PROVERBS
One hand washes the other
Many hands make light work
A bird in the hand is worth two in the bush

handbag = **bag**, purse *(U.S.)*, pocketbook *(U.S.)* • *the foldaway cup that fits into your handbag or pocket*

handbook = **guidebook**, guide, manual, instruction book, Baedeker, vade mecum • *It would be wise to purchase a handbook on the subject.*

handcuff **AS A VERB** = **shackle**, secure, restrain, fetter, manacle • *They tried to handcuff him but he fought his way free.*
▸ **AS A PLURAL NOUN** = **shackles**, cuffs *(informal)*, fetters, manacles, bracelets *(slang)* • *He was led away to jail in handcuffs.*

handful 1 = **few**, sprinkling, small amount, small quantity, smattering, small number • *a handful of potential investors*
OPPOSITES: a lot, scores, loads *(informal)*
2 = **nuisance**, bother, pest, pain in the neck *(informal)*, pain in the backside *(informal)* • *Zara can be a handful sometimes.*

handgun = **pistol**, automatic, revolver, shooter *(informal)*, piece *(U.S. slang)*, rod *(U.S. slang)*, derringer • *A man armed with a small grey handgun escaped with a sum of money.*

hand-held = **portable**, pocket, mini, miniature, palm-top • *keying in the details on a hand-held computer*

handicap **AS A NOUN** 1 = **disability**, defect, impairment, physical abnormality • *a child with a medically recognised handicap*
2 = **disadvantage**, block, barrier, restriction, obstacle, limitation, hazard, drawback, shortcoming, stumbling block, impediment, albatross, hindrance, millstone, encumbrance • *Being a foreigner was not a handicap.*
OPPOSITES: benefit, advantage, asset
3 = **advantage**, penalty, head start • *I see your handicap is down from 16 to 12.*
▸ **AS A VERB** = **hinder**, limit, restrict, burden, hamstring, hamper, hold back, retard, impede, hobble, encumber, place at a disadvantage • *Greater levels of stress may seriously handicap some students.*
OPPOSITES: help, further, benefit

handicapped = **disabled**, impaired, challenged, invalid, incapacitated, infirm • *financial help for visually handicapped workers*

handicraft = **skill**, art, craft, handiwork • *My new handicraft was seashell pictures.*

handily 1 = **conveniently**, readily, suitably, helpfully, advantageously, accessibly • *He was handily placed to slip the ball home at the far post.*
2 = **skilfully**, expertly, cleverly, deftly, adroitly, capably, proficiently, dexterously • *In the November election Nixon won handily.*

handiwork = **creation**, product, production, achievement, result, design, invention, artefact, handicraft, handwork • *The architect stepped back to admire his handiwork.*

handkerchief = **hanky**, tissue *(informal)*, mouchoir, snot rag *(slang)*, nose rag *(slang)* • *She blew her nose on her already damp handkerchief.*

handle AS A NOUN = **grip**, knob, hilt, haft, stock, handgrip, helve • *The handle of a cricket bat protruded from under his arm.*
▸ AS A VERB 1 = **manage**, deal with, tackle, cope with • *I don't know if I can handle the job.*
2 = **deal with**, manage, take care of, administer, conduct, supervise • *She handled travel arrangements for the press corps.*
3 = **control**, manage, direct, operate, guide, use, steer, manipulate, manoeuvre, wield • *One report said the aircraft would become difficult to handle.*
4 = **hold**, feel, touch, pick up, finger, grasp, poke, paw *(informal)*, maul, fondle • *Be careful when handling young animals.*
5 = **deal in**, market, sell, trade in, carry, stock, traffic in • *Japanese dealers won't handle US cars.*
6 = **discuss**, report, treat, review, tackle, examine, discourse on • *I think we should handle the story very sensitively.*
▸ IN PHRASES: **fly off the handle** = **lose your temper**, explode, lose it *(informal)*, lose the plot *(informal)*, let fly *(informal)*, go ballistic *(slang, chiefly U.S.)*, fly into a rage, have a tantrum, wig out *(slang)*, lose your cool *(slang)*, blow your top, flip your lid *(slang)*, hit *or* go through the roof *(informal)* • *He flew off the handle at the slightest thing.*

handling = **management**, running, treatment, approach, administration, conduct, manipulation • *The family has criticized the military's handling of the affair.*

hand-me-down = **cast-off**, used, second-hand, worn, inherited, passed on, handed down, reach-me-down *(informal)*, preloved *(Austral. slang)* • *Most of the children wore hand-me-down clothes.*

hand-out 1 *often plural* = **charity**, dole, alms, pogey *(Canad.)* • *They depended on handouts from the state.*
2 = **press release**, bulletin, circular, mailshot • *Official handouts described the couple as elated.*
3 = **leaflet**, literature *(informal)*, bulletin, flyer, pamphlet, printed matter • *lectures, handouts, slides and videos*
4 = **giveaway**, freebie *(informal)*, free gift, free sample • *advertised with publicity handouts*

handover = **exchange**, trade, transfer, swap • *The handover is supposed to be completed soon.*

hand-picked = **selected**, chosen, choice, select, elect, elite, recherché • *a hand-picked range of timeless classics*
OPPOSITES: random, wholesale, indiscriminate

handsome 1 = **good-looking**, attractive, gorgeous, fine, stunning, elegant, personable, nice-looking, dishy *(informal, chiefly Brit.)*, comely, fanciable, well-proportioned, hot *(informal)*, fit *(Brit. informal)* • *a tall, dark, handsome farmer*
OPPOSITES: ugly, unattractive, unsightly
2 = **generous**, large, princely, liberal, considerable, lavish, ample, abundant, plentiful, bountiful, sizable *or* sizeable • *They will make a handsome profit on the property.*
OPPOSITES: mean, small, base

PROVERBS
Handsome is as handsome does

handsomely = **generously**, amply, richly, liberally, lavishly, abundantly, plentifully, bountifully, munificently • *He was rewarded handsomely for his efforts.*

hands-on = **practical**, interactive, participatory • *People will be able to get involved in the hands-on display.*

hand-to-hand = **face-to-face**, close-up, one to one, mano a mano *(informal)* • *a fierce hand-to-hand battle*

hand-to-mouth AS AN ADJECTIVE = **insecure**, uncertain, unsettled, unsure, precarious • *They live a meaningless hand-to-mouth-existence.*
▸ AS AN ADVERB = **in poverty**, precariously, uncertainly, by necessity, on the breadline *(informal)*, insecurely, improvidently • *I just can't live hand-to-mouth, it's too frightening.*

handwriting = **writing**, hand, script, fist, scrawl, calligraphy, longhand, penmanship, chirography • *The address was in Anna's handwriting.*
▸ RELATED NOUN: graphology

handwritten = **written**, manuscript, ms. • *The papers include a handwritten version of the lyrics.*
OPPOSITES: typed, printed

handy 1 = **useful**, practical, helpful, neat, convenient, easy to use, manageable, user-friendly, serviceable • *handy hints on looking after indoor plants* • *a handy little device*
OPPOSITES: awkward, useless, inconvenient
2 = **convenient**, close, near, available, nearby, accessible, on hand, at hand, within reach, just round the corner, at your fingertips • *This lively town is handy for Londoners.* • *Keep a pencil and paper handy.*
OPPOSITES: awkward, out of the way, inconvenient
3 = **skilful**, skilled, expert, clever, adept, ready, deft, nimble, proficient, adroit, dexterous, tasty *(Brit. informal)* • *Are you handy with a needle?*
OPPOSITES: useless, incompetent, unskilled

handyman = **odd-jobman**, jack-of-all-trades, handy Andy *(informal)*, DIY expert • *a pair of top quality scissors produced with the handyman in mind*

hang AS A VERB 1 = **dangle**, swing, suspend, be pendent • *I was left hanging by my fingertips.*
2 = **lower**, suspend, dangle, let down, let droop • *I hung the sheet out of the window at 6am.*
3 = **lean**, incline, loll, bend forward, bow, bend downward • *He hung over the railing and kicked out with his feet.*
4 = **droop**, drop, dangle, trail, sag • *the shawl hanging loose from her shoulders*
5 = **decorate**, cover, fix, attach, deck, furnish, drape, fasten • *The walls were hung with huge modern paintings.*
6 = **execute**, lynch, string up *(informal)*, gibbet, send to the gallows • *The five were expected to be hanged at 7 am on Tuesday.*
7 = **hover**, float, drift, linger, remain • *A haze of expensive perfume hangs around her.*
▸ IN PHRASES: **get the hang of something** = **grasp**, understand, learn, master, comprehend, catch on to, acquire the technique of, get the knack *or* technique • *It's a bit tricky at first till you get the hang of it.*
hang about *or* **around** = **loiter**, frequent, haunt, linger, roam, loaf, waste time, dally, dawdle, skulk, tarry, doss *(Brit. slang)*, dilly-dally *(informal)* • *On Saturdays we hang about in the park.*
hang around with someone = **associate**, go around with, mix, hang *(informal, chiefly U.S.)*, hang out *(informal)* • *She used to hang around with the boys.*
hang back = **be reluctant**, hesitate, hold back, recoil, demur, be backward • *His closest advisors believe he should hang back no longer.*
hang fire = **put off**, delay, stall, be slow, vacillate, hang back, procrastinate • *I've got to hang fire on that one.*
hang on 1 = **wait**, stop, hold on, hold the line, remain • *Hang on a sec. I'll come with you.*
2 = **continue**, remain, go on, carry on, endure, hold on, persist, hold out, persevere, stay the course • *Manchester United hung on to take the Cup.*
3 = **grasp**, grip, clutch, cling, hold fast • *He hangs on tightly, his arms around my neck.*
hang on *or* **upon something** 1 = **depend on**, turn on, rest on, be subject to, hinge on, be determined by, be dependent on, be conditional on, be contingent on • *Much hangs on the success of the collaboration.*
2 = **listen attentively to**, pay attention to, be rapt, give ear to • *a man who knew his listeners were hanging on his every word*
hang onto something 1 = **retain**, keep, maintain, preserve, hold onto, keep possession of • *The President has been trying hard to hang onto power.*

2 = **grip**, seize, grasp, clutch, hold onto, take hold of, latch onto, hold tightly • *hanging onto his legs*
hang over something *or* **someone** = **loom**, threaten, menace, impend • *A question mark hangs over many of their futures.*

hangdog = **guilty**, defeated, cowed, sneaking, cringing, abject, furtive, downcast, wretched, browbeaten, shamefaced • *a hangdog look*

hanger-on = **parasite**, follower, cohort *(chiefly U.S.)*, leech, dependant, minion, lackey, sycophant, freeloader *(slang)*, sponger *(informal)*, ligger *(slang)*, quandong *(Austral. slang)* • *five thousand delegates, with 30,000 assorted hangers-on*

hanging AS A NOUN = **curtain**, drape, arras • *a giant antique embroidered hanging*
▸ AS AN ADJECTIVE = **suspended**, swinging, dangling, loose, flopping, flapping, floppy, drooping, unattached, unsupported, pendent • *the Old Cutter Inn with a hanging wooden sign out front*

hang-out = **haunt**, joint *(slang)*, resort, dive *(slang)*, den • *He already knew most of London's teenage hangouts.*

hangover 1 = **aftereffects**, morning after *(informal)*, head *(informal)*, crapulence • *I'd go into work with a bad hangover.*
2 = **legacy**, inheritance, throwback, tradition • *a hangover from my childhood*

hang-up = **preoccupation**, thing *(informal)*, problem, block, difficulty, obsession, mania, inhibition, phobia, fixation • *I don't have any hang-ups about my body.*

hank = **coil**, roll, length, bunch, piece, loop, clump, skein • *He twisted up the hank of rope.*

hanker after *or* **hanker for** = **desire**, want, long for, hope for, crave, covet, wish for, yearn for, pine for, lust after, eat your heart out, ache for, yen for *(informal)*, itch for, set your heart on, hunger for *or* after, thirst for *or* after • *In 1969 I hankered after a floor-length suede coat.*

hankering = **desire**, longing, wish, hope, urge, yen *(informal)*, pining, hunger, ache, craving, yearning, itch, thirst • *Have you always had a hankering to be an actress?*

hanky-panky 1 = **sex**, sexual activity, lovemaking, nookie *(slang)*, copulation, fornication, the other *(informal)*, shagging *(Brit. taboo slang)*, coitus, rumpy-pumpy *(slang)*, coition • *Does this mean no hanky-panky after lights out?*
2 = **mischief**, trickery, shenanigans *(informal)*, machinations, subterfuge, chicanery, monkey business *(informal)*, funny business *(informal)*, jiggery-pokery *(informal, chiefly Brit.)*, devilry, knavery • *offering tax credits and other economic hanky-panky*

haphazard 1 = **unsystematic**, disorderly, disorganized, casual, careless, indiscriminate, aimless, slapdash, slipshod, hit or miss *(informal)*, unmethodical • *The investigation does seem haphazard.*
OPPOSITES: organized, systematic, methodical, considered, careful
2 = **random**, chance, accidental, arbitrary, fluky *(informal)* • *She was trying to connect her life's seemingly haphazard events.*
OPPOSITES: planned, arranged, deliberate

hapless = **unlucky**, unfortunate, cursed, unhappy, miserable, jinxed, luckless, wretched, ill-starred, ill-fated • *the hapless victim struggled helplessly*

happen AS A VERB 1 = **occur**, take place, come about, follow, result, appear, develop, arise, come off *(informal)*, ensue, crop up *(informal)*, transpire *(informal)*, materialize, present itself, come to pass, see the light of day, eventuate • *We cannot say for sure what will happen.*
2 = **chance**, turn out *(informal)*, have the fortune to be • *I looked in the nearest paper, which happened to be the Daily Mail.*
3 = **befall**, overtake, become of, betide • *It's the best thing that ever happened to me.*
▸ IN PHRASES: **happen on** *or* **upon something** = **find**, encounter, run into, come upon, turn up, stumble on, hit upon, chance upon, light upon, blunder on, discover unexpectedly • *He just happened upon a charming guest house.*

happening AS A NOUN = **event**, incident, occasion, case, experience, chance, affair, scene, accident, proceeding, episode, adventure, phenomenon, occurrence, escapade • *plans to hire freelance reporters to cover the latest happenings*
▸ AS AN ADJECTIVE = **fashionable**, modern, popular, cool, exciting, hip *(informal)*, up to date, plugged-in *(slang)*, du jour *(French)*, culty, funky • *the most happening place at the moment, the Que Club*

happily 1 = **luckily**, fortunately, providentially, favourably, auspiciously, opportunely, propitiously, seasonably • *Happily, his neck injuries were not serious.*
2 = **joyfully**, cheerfully, gleefully, blithely, merrily, gaily, joyously, delightedly • *Albert leaned back happily and lit a cigarette.*
3 = **willingly**, freely, gladly, enthusiastically, heartily, with pleasure, contentedly, lief *(rare)* • *If I've caused any offence, I will happily apologise.*

happiness = **pleasure**, delight, joy, cheer, satisfaction, prosperity, ecstasy, enjoyment, bliss, felicity, exuberance, contentment, wellbeing, high spirits, elation, gaiety, jubilation, merriment, cheerfulness, gladness, beatitude, cheeriness, blessedness, light-heartedness • *I think she was looking for happiness.*
OPPOSITES: depression, distress, unhappiness

QUOTATIONS

Happiness depends upon ourselves
[Aristotle *Nicomachean Ethics*]

Happiness to me is wine,
Effervescent, superfine.
Full of tang and fiery pleasure,
Far too hot to leave me leisure
For a single thought beyond it
[Amy Lowell *Sword Blades and Poppy Seeds*]

Happiness is a matter of one's most ordinary everyday mode of consciousness being busy and lively and unconcerned with self
[Iris Murdoch *The Nice and the Good*]

To be happy, we must not be too concerned with others
[Albert Camus *The Fall*]

I am happy and content because I think I am
[Alain René Lesage *Histoire de Gil Blas de Santillane*]

Ask yourself whether you are happy, and you cease to be so
[John Stuart Mill *Autobiography*]

Happiness does not lie in happiness, but in the achievement of it
[Fyodor Dostoevsky *A Diary of a Writer*]

In theory there is a possibility of perfect happiness:
To believe in the indestructible element within one, and not to strive towards it
[Franz Kafka *The Collected Aphorisms*]

Happiness is not an ideal of reason but of imagination
[Immanuel Kant *Fundamental Principles of the Metaphysics of Ethics*]

Happiness is in the taste, and not in the things
[La Rochefoucauld *Maxims*]

Shall I give you my recipe for happiness? I find everything useful and nothing indispensable. I find everything wonderful and nothing miraculous.
I reverence the body. I avoid first causes like the plague
[Norman Douglas *South Wind*]

Happiness lies in the fulfilment of the spirit through the body
[Cyril Connolly *The Unquiet Grave*]

We have no more right to consume happiness without producing it than to consume wealth without producing it
[George Bernard Shaw *Candida*]

What we call happiness in the strictest sense comes from the (preferably sudden) satisfaction of needs which have been dammed up to a hi degree
[Sigmund Freud *Civilization and its Discontents*]
Happiness is an imaginary condition, formerly often attributed by the living to the dead, now usually attributed by adults to children, and by children to adults
[Thomas Szasz *The Second Sin*]
Nothing ages like happiness
[Oscar Wilde *An Ideal Husband*]
Happiness is no laughing matter
[Richard Whately *Apophthegms*]
Happiness is enjoyed only in proportion as it is known; and such is the state or folly of man, that it is known only by experience of its contrary
[Samuel Johnson *The Adventurer*]
happiness: an agreeable sensation arising from contemplating the misery of another
[Ambrose Bierce *The Devil's Dictionary*]
Happiness makes up in height for what it lacks in length
[Robert Frost *The Witness Tree*]

happy 1 = **pleased**, delighted, content, contented, thrilled, glad, blessed, blest, sunny, cheerful, jolly, merry, ecstatic, gratified, jubilant, joyous, joyful, elated, over the moon *(informal)*, overjoyed, blissful, rapt, blithe, on cloud nine *(informal)*, cock-a-hoop, walking on air *(informal)*, floating on air, stoked *(Austral. & N.Z. informal)* • *I'm just happy to be back running.*
2 = **contented**, blessed, blest, joyful, blissful, blithe • *We have a very happy marriage.*
OPPOSITES: low, sad, depressed
3 = **willing**, ready, glad, contented, inclined, disposed • *I'm happy to answer any questions.*
OPPOSITES: unwilling, loath
4 = **fortunate**, lucky, timely, appropriate, convenient, favourable, auspicious, propitious, apt, befitting, advantageous, well-timed, opportune, felicitous, seasonable • *a happy coincidence*
OPPOSITES: unhappy, unfortunate, unlucky

QUOTATIONS
Happy the man, and happy he alone
He who can call today his own;
He who, secure within, can say,
Tomorrow, do thy worst, for I have lived today
[John Dryden *Imitation of Horace*]
The happy man is not he who seems thus to others, but who seems thus to himself
[Publilius Syrus *Moral Sayings*]
Call no man happy till he dies, he is at best but fortunate
[Solon]
Happy men are grave. They carry their happiness cautiously, as they would a glass filled to the brim which the slightest movement could cause to spill over, or break
[Jules Barbey D'Aurevilly *Les Diaboliques*]

happy-go-lucky = **carefree**, casual, easy-going, irresponsible, unconcerned, untroubled, nonchalant, blithe, heedless, insouciant, devil-may-care, improvident, light-hearted • *She was a happy-go-lucky girl, always laughing and joking.*
OPPOSITES: serious, sad, unhappy

hara-kiri = **ritual suicide**, suicide, seppuku • *The entire organisation will be compelled to commit hara-kiri.*

harangue **AS A VERB** = **rant at**, address, lecture, exhort, preach to, declaim, hold forth, spout at *(informal)* • *haranguing her furiously in words she didn't understand*
▸ **AS A NOUN** = **rant**, address, speech, lecture, tirade, polemic, broadside, diatribe, homily, exhortation, oration, spiel *(informal)*, declamation, philippic • *a political harangue*

harass = **annoy**, trouble, bother, worry, harry, disturb, devil *(informal)*, plague, bait, hound, torment, hassle *(informal)*, badger, persecute, exasperate, pester, vex, breathe down someone's neck, chivvy *(Brit.)*, give someone grief *(Brit. & S. African)*, be on your back *(slang)*, beleaguer • *We are almost routinely harassed by the police.*

harassed = **hassled**, worried, troubled, strained, harried, under pressure, plagued, tormented, distraught *(informal)*, vexed, under stress, careworn • *Looking harassed and drawn, he tendered his resignation.*

harassment = **hassle**, trouble, bother, grief *(informal)*, torment, irritation, persecution *(informal)*, nuisance, badgering, annoyance, pestering, aggravation *(informal)*, molestation, vexation, bedevilment • *51 percent of women had experienced some form of sexual harassment.*

harbinger = **sign**, indication, herald, messenger, omen, precursor, forerunner, portent, foretoken • *a harbinger of winter*

harbour **AS A NOUN** 1 = **port**, haven, dock, mooring, marina, pier, wharf, anchorage, jetty, pontoon, slipway • *The ship was allowed to tie up in the harbour.*
2 = **sanctuary**, haven, shelter, retreat, asylum, refuge, oasis, covert, safe haven, sanctum • *a safe harbour for music rejected by the mainstream*
▸ **AS A VERB** 1 = **hold**, bear, maintain, nurse, retain, foster, entertain, nurture, cling to, cherish, brood over • *He might have been murdered by someone harbouring a grudge.*
2 = **shelter**, protect, hide, relieve, lodge, shield, conceal, secrete, provide refuge, give asylum to • *harbouring terrorist suspects*

hard **AS AN ADJECTIVE** 1 = **tough**, strong, firm, solid, stiff, compact, rigid, resistant, dense, compressed, stony, impenetrable, inflexible, unyielding, rocklike • *He stamped his feet on the hard floor.*
OPPOSITES: soft, weak, flexible
2 = **difficult**, involved, complex, complicated, puzzling, tangled, baffling, intricate, perplexing, impenetrable, thorny, knotty, unfathomable, ticklish • *That's a very hard question.*
OPPOSITES: easy, simple, straightforward
3 = **exhausting**, tough, exacting, formidable, fatiguing, wearying, rigorous, uphill, gruelling, strenuous, arduous, laborious, burdensome, Herculean, backbreaking, toilsome • *Coping with three babies is very hard work.*
OPPOSITES: light, easy, soft
4 = **forceful**, strong, powerful, driving, heavy, sharp, violent, smart, tremendous, fierce, vigorous, hefty • *He gave her a hard push which toppled her backwards.*
5 = **harsh**, severe, strict, cold, exacting, cruel, grim, stern, ruthless, stubborn, unjust, callous, unkind, unrelenting, implacable, unsympathetic, pitiless, unfeeling, obdurate, unsparing, affectless, hardhearted • *His father was a hard man.*
OPPOSITES: kind, good, gentle
6 = **grim**, dark, painful, distressing, harsh, disastrous, unpleasant, intolerable, grievous, disagreeable, calamitous • *Those were hard times.*
7 = **definite**, reliable, verified, cold, plain, actual, bare, undeniable, indisputable, verifiable, unquestionable, unvarnished • *He wanted more hard evidence.*
8 = **bitter**, angry, hostile, resentful, acrimonious, embittered, antagonistic, rancorous • *I struck him, and dismissed him with hard words.*
▸ **AS AN ADVERB** 1 = **strenuously**, steadily, persistently, earnestly, determinedly, doggedly, diligently, energetically, assiduously, industriously, untiringly • *I'll work hard. I don't want to let him down.*
2 = **intently**, closely, carefully, sharply, keenly • *You had to listen hard to hear him.*

h

3 = **forcefully**, strongly, heavily, sharply, severely, fiercely, vigorously, intensely, violently, powerfully, forcibly, with all your might, with might and main • *I kicked a dustbin very hard and broke my toe.*
OPPOSITES: lightly, softly, weakly
4 = **with difficulty**, painfully, laboriously • *the hard won rights of the working woman*
▸ IN PHRASES: **hard and fast** = **fixed**, strict, rigid, binding, definite, clear-cut, stringent, cast-iron, inflexible, immutable, incontrovertible, invariable, unalterable • *There are no hard and fast rules when it comes to garden design.*
hard by = **right beside**, near, close to, alongside, next to, adjacent to, cheek by jowl with • *The hamper stood hard by the foot of the white iron bed.*

hard-bitten = **tough**, realistic, cynical, practical, shrewd, down-to-earth, matter-of-fact, hard-nosed *(informal)*, hard-headed, unsentimental, hard-boiled *(informal)*, case-hardened, badass *(slang, chiefly U.S.)* • *a cynical hard-bitten journalist*
OPPOSITES: romantic, idealistic, gentle

hard-boiled = **tough**, practical, realistic, cynical, shrewd, down-to-earth, matter-of-fact, hard-nosed *(informal)*, hard-headed, hard-bitten *(informal)*, unsentimental, case-hardened, badass *(slang, chiefly U.S.)* • *fans of hard-boiled crime drama*
OPPOSITES: romantic, idealistic, gentle

hard-core 1 = **dyed-in-the-wool**, extreme, dedicated, rigid, staunch, die-hard, steadfast, obstinate, intransigent • *a hard-core group of right-wing senators*
2 = **explicit**, obscene, pornographic, X-rated *(informal)* • *jailed for peddling hard-core porn videos through the post*

harden 1 = **solidify**, set, freeze, cake, bake, clot, thicken, stiffen, crystallize, congeal, coagulate, anneal • *Mould the mixture into shape before it hardens.*
2 = **accustom**, season, toughen, train, brutalize, inure, habituate, case-harden • *hardened by the rigours of the Siberian steppes*
3 = **reinforce**, strengthen, fortify, steel, nerve, brace, toughen, buttress, gird, indurate • *Their action can only serve to harden the attitude of landowners.*

hardened 1 = **habitual**, set, fixed, chronic, shameless, inveterate, incorrigible, reprobate, irredeemable, badass *(slang, chiefly U.S.)* • *hardened criminals*
OPPOSITES: rare, occasional, irregular
2 = **seasoned**, experienced, accustomed, toughened, inured, habituated • *hardened politicians*
OPPOSITES: green, naive

hard-headed = **shrewd**, tough, practical, cool, sensible, realistic, pragmatic, astute, hard-boiled *(informal)*, hard-bitten, level-headed, unsentimental, badass *(slang, chiefly U.S.)* • *a hard-headed and shrewd businesswoman*
OPPOSITES: sentimental, unrealistic, idealistic

hard-hearted = **unsympathetic**, hard, cold, cruel, indifferent, insensitive, callous, stony, unkind, heartless, inhuman, merciless, intolerant, uncaring, pitiless, unfeeling, unforgiving, hard as nails, affectless • *You would have to be pretty hard-hearted not to feel something.*
OPPOSITES: loving, kind, warm

hard-hitting = **uncompromising**, tough, critical, vigorous, no holds barred, strongly worded, pulling no punches, unsparing • *a hard-hitting account of violence in the home*

hardiness = **resilience**, fortitude, toughness, robustness, ruggedness, sturdiness • *the hardiness, endurance and courage of my companions*

hardline or **hard-line** = **tough**, extreme, strict, definite, uncompromising, single-minded, inflexible, diehard, unyielding, intransigent, immoderate, undeviating • *They've taken a lot of criticism for their hard-line stance.*

hardliner = **extremist**, radical, fanatic, zealot • *Unionist hardliners warned the President he would not be welcome.*

hardly 1 = **barely**, only just, scarcely, just, faintly, with difficulty, infrequently, with effort, at a push *(Brit. informal)*, almost not • *Nick, on the sofa, hardly slept.*
OPPOSITES: really, more than, completely
2 = **only just**, just, only, barely, not quite, scarcely • *I could hardly see the garden for the fog.*
3 = **not at all**, not, no way, by no means • *It's hardly surprising his ideas didn't catch on.*

hardness 1 = **firmness**, toughness, rigidity, stiffness, solidity, inflexibility, denseness • *There was an athletic hardness about his body.*
2 = **severity**, toughness, callousness, strictness, lack of compassion, sternness, cold-heartedness, hard-heartedness • *Her hardness is balanced by a goofy humor.*

hard-nosed = **tough**, practical, realistic, shrewd, pragmatic, down-to-earth, hardline, uncompromising, businesslike, hard-headed, unsentimental, badass *(slang, chiefly U.S.)* • *a hard-nosed government, willing to do unpopular things*

hard-pressed 1 = **under pressure**, pushed *(informal)*, harried, in difficulties, up against it *(informal)*, with your back to the wall • *Hard-pressed consumers are spending less on luxuries.*
2 = **pushed** *(informal)*, in difficulties, up against it *(informal)* • *This year the airline will be hard-pressed to make a profit.*

hardship = **suffering**, want, need, trouble, trial, difficulty, burden, misery, torment, oppression, persecution, grievance, misfortune, austerity, adversity, calamity, affliction, tribulation, privation, destitution • *Many people are suffering economic hardship.*
OPPOSITES: help, aid, ease

hard up = **poor**, broke *(informal)*, short, bust *(informal)*, bankrupt, impoverished, in the red *(informal)*, cleaned out *(slang)*, penniless, out of pocket, down and out, skint *(Brit. slang)*, strapped for cash *(informal)*, impecunious, dirt-poor *(informal)*, on the breadline, flat broke *(informal)*, on your uppers *(informal)*, in queer street, without two pennies to rub together *(informal)*, short of cash or funds • *Her parents were hard up.*
OPPOSITES: rich, loaded *(slang)*, wealthy

hardware 1 = **equipment**, machines, gear, tools, instruments, machinery, apparatus, tackle, paraphernalia • *The General will tour military camps and inspect military hardware.*
2 = **implements**, gadgets, household goods, ironmongery • *household appliances, furnishings and hardware*

hard-wearing = **durable**, strong, tough, rugged, stout, resilient, well-made • *hard-wearing cotton shirts*

hardworking = **industrious**, busy, energetic, conscientious, zealous, diligent, indefatigable, assiduous, sedulous • *He was hardworking and energetic.*
OPPOSITES: lazy, indifferent, careless

hardy 1 = **strong**, tough, robust, sound, fit, healthy, vigorous, rugged, sturdy, hale, stout, stalwart, hearty, lusty, in fine fettle • *They grew up to be farmers, round-faced and hardy.*
OPPOSITES: soft, weak, frail
2 = **courageous**, brave, daring, bold, heroic, manly, gritty, feisty *(informal, chiefly U.S. & Canad.)*, resolute, intrepid, valiant, plucky, valorous, stouthearted • *A few hardy souls leapt into the encircling seas.*
OPPOSITES: soft, weak, feeble

hare
▸ RELATED ADJECTIVE: leporine
▸ NAME OF MALE: buck
▸ NAME OF FEMALE: doe
▸ NAME OF YOUNG: leveret
▸ NAME OF HOME: down, husk
▹ *See panel* **Rabbits and hares**

hare-brained = **foolish**, wild, rash, reckless, careless, mindless, giddy, half-baked *(informal)*, inane, flighty, heedless, empty-headed, asinine, harum-scarum, scatterbrained • *This isn't the first hare-brained scheme he's had.*

harem = **women's quarters**, seraglio, zenana *(in eastern countries)*, gynaeceum *(in ancient Greece)* • *like a sheikh in the midst of his harem*

hark AS A VERB = **listen**, attend, pay attention, hearken *(archaic)*, give ear, hear, mark, notice, give heed • *Hark. I hear the returning footsteps of my love.*
▸ IN PHRASES: **hark back to something** 1 = **recall**, recollect, call to mind, cause you to remember, cause you to recollect • *pitched roofs, which hark back to the Victorian era*
2 = **return to**, remember, recall, revert to, look back to, think back to, recollect, regress to • *The result devastated me at the time. Even now I hark back to it.*

harlequin = **colourful**, rainbow, psychedelic, variegated, chequered, jazzy, multicoloured, kaleidoscopic, many-coloured, polychromatic, varicoloured • *the striking harlequin floor*

harlot = **prostitute**, tart *(informal)*, whore, slag, pro *(slang)*, tramp *(slang)*, call girl, working girl *(facetious slang)*, slapper *(Brit. slang)*, hussy, streetwalker, loose woman, fallen woman, scrubber *(Brit. & Austral. slang)*, strumpet • *At one time, paint was the sign of a harlot or a loose woman.*

harm AS A VERB 1 = **injure**, hurt, wound, abuse, molest, ill-treat, maltreat, lay a finger on, ill-use • *The hijackers seemed anxious not to harm anyone.*
OPPOSITES: heal, cure
2 = **damage**, hurt, ruin, mar, spoil, impair, blemish • *a warning that the product may harm the environment*
▸ AS A NOUN 1 = **injury**, suffering, damage, ill, hurt, distress • *a release of radioactivity which would cause harm*
2 = **damage**, loss, ill, hurt, misfortune, mischief, detriment, impairment, disservice • *It would probably do the economy more harm than good.*
OPPOSITES: good, help, benefit
3 = **sin**, wrong, evil, wickedness, immorality, iniquity, sinfulness, vice • *There was no harm in keeping the money.*
OPPOSITES: good, goodness, righteousness
▸ IN PHRASES: **in** *or* **out of harm's way** = **in** *or* **out of danger**, in *or* out of the firing line • *They were never told how they'd been put in harm's way.*

harmful = **damaging**, dangerous, negative, evil, destructive, hazardous, unhealthy, detrimental, hurtful, pernicious, noxious, baleful, deleterious, injurious, unwholesome, disadvantageous, baneful, maleficent • *the harmful effects of smoking*
OPPOSITES: beneficial, harmless, good

harmless 1 = **safe**, benign, wholesome, innocuous, not dangerous, nontoxic, innoxious • *working at developing harmless substitutes for these gases*
OPPOSITES: dangerous, destructive, harmful
2 = **inoffensive**, innocent, innocuous, gentle, tame, unobjectionable • *He seemed harmless enough.*

harmonious 1 = **friendly**, amicable, cordial, sympathetic, compatible, agreeable, in harmony, in unison, fraternal, congenial, in accord, concordant, of one mind, en rapport *(French)* • *the most harmonious European Community summit for some time*
OPPOSITES: unfriendly, discordant
2 = **compatible**, matching, coordinated, correspondent, agreeable, consistent, consonant, congruous • *a harmonious blend of colours*
OPPOSITES: incompatible, contrasting, unlike
3 = **melodious**, musical, harmonic, harmonizing, tuneful, concordant, mellifluous, dulcet, sweet-sounding, euphonious, euphonic, symphonious *(literary)* • *producing harmonious sounds*
OPPOSITES: harsh, grating, discordant

harmonize 1 = **match**, accord, suit, blend, correspond, tally, chime, coordinate, go together, tone in, cohere, attune, be of one mind, be in unison • *The music had to harmonize with the seasons.*
2 = **coordinate**, match, agree, blend, tally, reconcile, attune • *members have progressed towards harmonizing their economies*

harmony 1 = **accord**, order, understanding, peace, agreement, friendship, unity, sympathy, consensus, cooperation, goodwill, rapport, conformity, compatibility, assent, unanimity, concord, amity, amicability, like-mindedness • *a future in which humans live in harmony with nature*
OPPOSITES: opposition, conflict, hostility
2 = **tune**, melody, unison, tunefulness, euphony, melodiousness • *singing in harmony*
OPPOSITES: cacophony, discord
3 = **balance**, consistency, fitness, correspondence, coordination, symmetry, compatibility, suitability, concord, parallelism, consonance, congruity • *the ordered harmony of the universe*
OPPOSITES: conflict, disagreement, incongruity

harness AS A VERB 1 = **exploit**, control, channel, apply, employ, utilize, mobilize, make productive, turn to account, render useful • *the movement's ability to harness the anger of all Ukrainians*
2 = **put in harness**, couple, saddle, yoke, hitch up • *the horses were harnessed to a heavy wagon*
▸ AS A NOUN = **equipment**, tackle, gear, tack, trappings • *Always check that the straps of the harness are properly adjusted.*
▸ IN PHRASES: **in harness** 1 = **working**, together, in a team • *At Opera North he will be in harness with Paul Daniel.*
2 = **at work**, working, employed, active, busy, in action • *The longing for work will return and you will be right back in harness.*

harp = **go on**, reiterate, dwell on, labour, press, repeat, rub in • *She concentrated on the good parts instead of harping on about the bad.*

harpoon = **spear**, arrow, dart, barb, trident • *harpoon-wielding Japanese fishermen*

harridan = **shrew**, witch, nag, scold, virago, tartar, battle-axe *(informal)*, termagant, Xanthippe, ballbreaker *(slang)* • *She was a mean old harridan.*

harried = **harassed**, worried, troubled, bothered, anxious, distressed, plagued, tormented, hassled *(informal)*, agitated, beset, hard-pressed, hag-ridden • *harried businessmen scurrying from one office to another*

harrowing = **distressing**, disturbing, alarming, frightening, painful, terrifying, chilling, traumatic, tormenting, heartbreaking, excruciating, agonizing, nerve-racking, heart-rending, gut-wrenching • *harrowing pictures of the children who had been murdered*

harry = **pester**, trouble, bother, disturb, worry, annoy, plague, tease, torment, harass, hassle *(informal)*, badger, persecute, molest, vex, bedevil, breathe down someone's neck, chivvy, give someone grief *(Brit. & S. African)*, be on your back *(slang)*, get in your hair *(informal)* • *He would exploit and harry his workers.*

harsh 1 = **severe**, hard, tough, grim, stark, stringent, austere, Spartan, inhospitable, comfortless, bare-bones • *Hundreds of political detainees were held under harsh conditions.*
2 = **bleak**, cold, freezing, severe, bitter, icy • *The weather grew harsh and unpredictable.*
3 = **cruel**, savage, brutal, ruthless, relentless, unrelenting, barbarous, pitiless • *the harsh experience of war*
4 = **hard**, sharp, severe, bitter, cruel, stern, unpleasant, abusive, unkind, pitiless, unfeeling • *He said many harsh and unkind things.*
OPPOSITES: loving, kind, sweet
5 = **drastic**, hard, severe, stringent, punitive, austere, Draconian, punitory • *more harsh laws governing the behaviour, status and even clothes of women*

h

6 = **raucous**, rough, jarring, grating, strident, rasping, discordant, croaking, guttural, dissonant, unmelodious • *It's a pity she has such a loud harsh voice.*
OPPOSITES: soft, sweet, smooth

harshly = **severely**, roughly, cruelly, strictly, grimly, sternly, brutally • *Her husband is being harshly treated in prison.*

harshness 1 = **severity**, brutality, roughness, sternness, hardness • *They treated him with extreme harshness.*
2 = **bitterness**, acrimony, ill-temper, sourness, asperity, acerbity • *a tone of abrupt harshness*

harvest AS A NOUN 1 = **harvesting**, picking, gathering, collecting, reaping, harvest-time • *300 million tons of grain in the fields at the start of the harvest*
2 = **crop**, yield, year's growth, produce • *a bumper potato harvest*
▸ AS A VERB 1 = **gather**, pick, collect, bring in, pluck, reap • *Many farmers are refusing to harvest the sugar cane.*
2 = **collect**, get, gain, earn, obtain, acquire, accumulate, garner, amass • *In his new career he has blossomed and harvested many awards.*

hash IN PHRASES: **make a hash of** = **mess up**, muddle, bungle, botch, cock up (*Brit. slang*), mishandle, fuck up (*taboo slang*), mismanage, make a nonsense of (*informal*), bodge (*informal*), make a pig's ear of (*informal*), flub (*U.S. slang*) • *The government made a total hash of things.*

hassle AS A NOUN = **trouble**, problem, difficulty, upset, bother, grief (*informal*), trial, struggle, uphill (*S. African*), inconvenience • *I don't think it's worth the money or the hassle.*
▸ AS A VERB = **bother**, bug (*informal*), annoy, harry, hound, harass, badger, pester, get on your nerves (*informal*), be on your back (*slang*), get in your hair (*informal*), breath down someone's neck • *My husband started hassling me.*

hassled = **bothered**, pressured, worried, stressed, under pressure, hounded, uptight, browbeaten, hunted, hot and bothered • *I'm feeling tired and hassled.*

haste AS A NOUN = **speed**, rapidity, urgency, expedition, dispatch, velocity, alacrity, quickness, swiftness, briskness, nimbleness, fleetness, celerity, promptitude, rapidness • *Authorities appear to be moving with haste against the three dissidents.*
OPPOSITES: slowness, sluggishness
▸ IN PHRASES: **in haste** = **hastily**, rashly, too quickly, impetuously • *Don't act in haste or be hot-headed.*
make haste = **hurry (up)**, speed up, hasten, get a move on (*informal*), get your skates on (*informal*), crack on (*informal*) • *Simon was under orders to make haste.*

PROVERBS
More haste, less speed
Make haste slowly (Latin *festina lente*)

hasten 1 = **hurry (up)**, speed (up), advance, urge, step up (*informal*), accelerate, press, dispatch, precipitate, quicken, push forward, expedite • *He may hasten the collapse of his own country.*
OPPOSITES: slow, delay, slow down
2 = **rush**, run, race, fly, speed, tear (along), dash, hurry (up), barrel (along) (*informal, chiefly U.S. & Canad.*), sprint, bolt, beetle, scuttle, scurry, haste, burn rubber (*informal*), step on it (*informal*), make haste, get your skates on (*informal*) • *He hastened along the landing to her room.*
OPPOSITES: creep, crawl, dawdle

hastily 1 = **quickly**, fast, rapidly, promptly, straightaway, speedily, apace, pronto (*informal*), double-quick, hotfoot, pdq (*slang*), posthaste • *He said goodnight hastily.*
2 = **hurriedly**, rashly, precipitately, recklessly, too quickly, on the spur of the moment, impulsively, impetuously, heedlessly • *I decided that nothing should be done hastily.*

hasty 1 = **speedy**, fast, quick, prompt, rapid, fleet, hurried, urgent, swift, brisk, expeditious • *They need to make a hasty escape.*
OPPOSITES: slow, leisurely
2 = **brief**, short, quick, passing, rushed, fleeting, superficial, cursory, perfunctory, transitory • *After the hasty meal, they took up their positions.*
OPPOSITES: long, protracted
3 = **rash**, premature, reckless, precipitate, impulsive, headlong, foolhardy, thoughtless, impetuous, indiscreet, imprudent, heedless, incautious, unduly quick • *Let's not be hasty.*
OPPOSITES: detailed, careful, cautious

hat ▹ *See panel* **Hats**

HATS

Hats
Akubra (*Austral. trademark*)
anadem (*poetic*)
babushka
Balaclava
Balmoral *or* bluebonnet
bandanna
bandeau
barret
baseball cap
basinet
beanie *or* beany
bearskin
beaver
beret
billycock (*rare, chiefly Brit.*)
biretta *or* berretta
blackcap
bluebonnet *or* bluecap
boater
bonnet
bowler *or* (*U.S. & Canad.*) derby
broadbrim
busby
calash *or* caleche
calotte
calpac, calpack, *or* kalpak
capuche
castor
chaplet
cheese cutter
circlet
cloche
cloth cap
cocked hat
coif
commode
coonskin
cornet
coronet
cossack hat
crash helmet
crown
curch *or* curchef
deerstalker
diadem
Dolly Varden
dunce cap
earmuff
fascinator (*rare*)
fedora
fez
flat cap
fool's cap
forage cap
frontlet *or* frontal
Gandhi cap
glengarry
hard hat
havelock
headband
headdress
heaume
helmet
homburg
hood
Juliet cap
keffiyeh
kepi
laurels
leghorn
liberty cap
lum-hat (*Scot.*)
mitre
mobcap *or* mob
montero
morion
mortarboard, trencher, *or* trencher cap
mutch
nightcap
opera hat *or* gibus
Panama hat
paper hat
peaked cap
petasus
Phrygian cap
picture hat
pillbox
pinner
pith helmet, topee, *or* topi
poke *or* poke bonnet
porkpie hat
sailor hat
sallet
shako *or* shacko
shovel hat
shower cap
silk hat
skullcap
slouch hat
snood
sombrero
songkok
sou'wester *or* nor'wester
stetson
stocking cap
stovepipe
straw hat
sunbonnet
sunhat
taj
tam-o'-shanter *or* tammy (*Scot.*)
tarboosh
tarpaulin
ten-gallon hat
tiara
tin hat (*informal*)
tricorn
toorie *or* tourie (*Scot.*)
top hat
topper (*informal*)
toque
tricorn
trilby
tuque
turban
veil
visor *or* vizor
watch cap
wimple
yarmulke

hatch 1 = **incubate**, breed, sit on, brood, bring forth • *I transferred the eggs to a hen canary to hatch and rear.*
2 = **devise**, plan, design, project, scheme, manufacture, plot, invent, put together, conceive, brew, formulate, contrive, dream up *(informal)*, concoct, think up, cook up *(informal)*, trump up • *accused of hatching a plot to assassinate the Pope*

hatchet AS A NOUN = **axe**, machete, tomahawk, cleaver • *I have a small hatchet, not near sharp enough.*
▸ IN PHRASES: **bury the hatchet** = **make up**, make peace, cease hostilities • *Can we bury the hatchet?*

hatchet man = **hit man**, heavy *(slang)*, killer, gunman, murderer, thug, assassin, destroyer, cut-throat *(slang)*, hired assassin • *a hatchet man for a famous gangland boss*

hate AS A VERB 1 = **detest**, loathe, despise, dislike, be sick of, abhor, be hostile to, recoil from, be repelled by, have an aversion to, abominate, not be able to bear, execrate • *Most people hate him, but I don't.*
OPPOSITES: like, love, wish
2 = **dislike**, detest, shrink from, recoil from, have no stomach for, not be able to bear • *She hated hospitals and dreaded the operation.*
OPPOSITES: like, enjoy, relish
3 = **be unwilling**, regret, be reluctant, hesitate, be sorry, be loath, feel disinclined • *I hate to admit it, but you were right.*
▸ AS A NOUN = **dislike**, hostility, hatred, loathing, animosity, aversion, antagonism, antipathy, enmity, abomination, animus, abhorrence, odium, detestation, execration • *eyes that held a look of hate*
OPPOSITES: liking, love, affection
▸ IN PHRASES: **pet hate** = **bugbear**, bane of your life, pet aversion, thorn in your side • *My pet hate is aggressive drivers.*

QUOTATIONS
Men love in haste, but they detest at leisure
[Lord Byron *Don Juan*]
If you hate a person, you hate something in him that is part of yourself. What isn't part of ourselves doesn't disturb us
[Hermann Hesse *Demian*]

hateful 1 = **horrible**, despicable, offensive, foul, disgusting, forbidding, revolting, obscene, vile, repellent, obnoxious, repulsive, heinous, odious, repugnant, loathsome, abhorrent, abominable, execrable, detestable • *Society is still a hateful and dysfunctional place.*
2 = **malicious**, malevolent, spiteful, hating, vicious, bitchy *(informal)*, catty *(informal)*, ill-disposed, evil-minded, ill-natured • *They are not necessarily hateful, malicious people.*
OPPOSITES: good, beautiful, pleasant

hatred = **hate**, dislike, animosity, aversion, revulsion, antagonism, antipathy, enmity, abomination, ill will, animus, repugnance, odium, detestation, execration • *He has been accused of inciting racial hatred.*
OPPOSITES: love, liking, affection

QUOTATIONS
Hatred, for the man who is not engaged in it, is a little like the odour of garlic for one who hasn't eaten any
[Jean Rostand *Pensées d'un Biologiste*]

haughtiness = **pride**, arrogance, disdain, airs, contempt, conceit, pomposity, aloofness, hauteur, snobbishness, loftiness, superciliousness, contemptuousness • *She lacks the arrogance and haughtiness of so many musical artists.*

haughty = **proud**, arrogant, lofty, high, stuck-up *(informal)*, contemptuous, conceited, imperious, snooty *(informal)*, scornful, snobbish, disdainful, supercilious, high and mighty *(informal)*, overweening, hoity-toity *(informal)*, on your high horse *(informal)*, uppish *(Brit. informal)* • *He spoke in a haughty tone.*
OPPOSITES: modest, humble, meek

haul AS A VERB 1 = **drag**, draw, pull, hale, heave • *He hauled himself to his feet.*
2 = **pull**, trail, convey, tow, move, carry, transport, tug, cart, hump *(Brit. slang)*, lug • *A crane hauled the car out of the stream.*
▸ AS A NOUN = **yield**, gain, spoils, find, catch, harvest, loot, takings, booty • *The haul was worth £4,000.*
▸ IN PHRASES: **haul someone up** = **indict**, bring before • *He was hauled up before the Board of Trustees.*

haunt AS A VERB 1 = **plague**, trouble, obsess, torment, come back to, possess, stay with, recur, beset, prey on, weigh on • *The decision to leave her children now haunts her.*
2 = **visit**, hang around *or* about, frequent, linger in, resort to, patronize, repair to, spend time in, loiter in, be a regular in • *During the day he haunted the town's cinemas*
3 = **appear in**, materialize in • *His ghost is said to haunt some of the rooms.*
▸ AS A NOUN = **meeting place**, resort, hangout *(informal)*, den, rendezvous, stamping ground, gathering place • *a favourite summer haunt for yachtsmen*

haunted 1 = **possessed**, ghostly, cursed, eerie, spooky *(informal)*, jinxed • *a haunted castle*
2 = **preoccupied**, worried, troubled, plagued, obsessed, tormented • *She looked so haunted, I almost didn't recognise her.*

haunting = **evocative**, poignant, unforgettable, indelible • *the haunting calls of wild birds*

hauteur = **haughtiness**, pride, arrogance, airs, dignity, contempt, disdain, snobbishness, loftiness, stateliness, superciliousness, affectedness • *She had been put off by his hauteur.*

have AS A VERB 1 = **own**, keep, possess, hold, retain, occupy, boast, be the owner of • *I want to have my own business.*
2 = **ask to**, make, compel, direct to, persuade to, induce to, enjoin to • *Have him call me.*
3 = **get**, obtain, take, receive, accept, gain, secure, acquire, procure, take receipt of • *When can I have the new car?*
4 = **suffer**, experience, undergo, sustain, endure, be suffering from • *He might be having a heart attack.*
5 = **give birth to**, bear, deliver, bring forth, beget, bring into the world • *My wife has just had a baby boy.*
6 = **put up with** *(informal)*, allow, permit, consider, think about, entertain, tolerate • *I'm not having any of that nonsense.*
7 = **include**, comprises, contain, consist of, incorporate, be made up of • *The house has 13 rooms.*
8 = **consume**, drink, eat, neck *(slang)*, down *(informal)*, devour, quaff • *They had dinner together.* • *They had sweet wine that day.*
9 = **organize**, plan, hold, arrange, lay on, jack up *(N.Z. informal)* • *We had a party for Christmas.*
10 = **entertain**, receive, invite, wine and dine • *We have had guests for the last week.*
11 = **experience**, go through, undergo, meet with, come across, run into, be faced with • *Did you have some trouble with your neighbours?*
▸ IN PHRASES: **have had it** = **be exhausted**, be knackered *(Brit. informal)*, be finished, be pooped *(U.S. slang)* • *I've had it. Let's call it a day.*
have someone on = **tease**, kid *(informal)*, wind up *(Brit. slang)*, trick, deceive, take the mickey, pull someone's leg, play a joke on, jerk *or* yank someone's chain *(informal)* • *I thought he was just having me on.*
have something on 1 = **wear**, be wearing, be dressed in, be clothed in, be attired in • *She had on new black shoes.*
2 = **have something planned**, be committed to, be engaged to, have something on the agenda • *We have a meeting on that day.*
have to 1 *with* **to** = **must**, should, be forced, ought, be obliged, be bound, have got to, be compelled • *Now, you have to go into town.*
2 = **have got to**, must • *That has to be the biggest lie ever told.*

h

haven 1 = **sanctuary**, shelter, retreat, asylum, refuge, oasis, sanctum • *a real haven at the end of a busy working day*
2 = **harbour**, port, anchorage, road (*Nautical*) • *She lay alongside in Largs Yacht Haven for a few days.*
havoc AS A NOUN 1 = **devastation**, damage, destruction, waste, ruin, wreck, slaughter, ravages, carnage, desolation, rack and ruin, despoliation • *Rioters caused havoc in the centre of the town.*
2 = **disorder**, confusion, chaos, disruption, mayhem, shambles • *A single mare running loose could cause havoc among otherwise reliable stallions.*
▸ IN PHRASES: **play havoc with something** = **wreck**, destroy, devastate, disrupt, demolish, disorganize, bring into chaos • *Drug addiction soon played havoc with his career.*
hawk[1]
▸ RELATED ADJECTIVE: accipitrine
▸ COLLECTIVE NOUN: cast
hawk[2] = **peddle**, market, sell, push, traffic, tout (*informal*), vend • *vendors hawking trinkets*

h

hawker = **pedlar**, tout, vendor, travelling salesman, crier, huckster, barrow boy (*Brit.*), door-to-door salesman • *It was a visitor and not a hawker or tramp at the door.*
hawk-eyed = **sharp-eyed**, vigilant, perceptive, observant, gimlet-eyed, keen-sighted, Argus-eyed, lynx-eyed • *Hawk-eyed readers may also spot mistakes.*
hay = **straw**, fodder, forage, silage, pasturage • *bales of hay*
haywire 1 = **chaotic**, confused, disordered, tangled, mixed up, shambolic (*informal*), topsy-turvy, disorganized, disarranged • *Many Americans think their legal system is haywire.*
2 = **out of order**, out of commission, on the blink (*slang*), on the fritz (*slang*) • *Her pacemaker went haywire near hand dryers.*
3 = **crazy**, wild, mad, potty (*Brit. informal*), berserk, bonkers (*slang, chiefly Brit.*), loopy (*informal*), mad as a hatter, berko (*Austral. slang*), off the air (*Austral. slang*), porangi (*N.Z.*) • *I went haywire in our first few weeks on holiday.*
hazard AS A NOUN = **danger**, risk, threat, problem, menace, peril, jeopardy, pitfall, endangerment, imperilment • *a sole that reduces the hazard of slipping on slick surfaces*
▸ AS A VERB 1 = **jeopardize**, risk, endanger, threaten, expose, imperil, put in jeopardy • *He could not believe that the man would have hazarded his grandson.*
2 = **guess**, suggest, ask • *'Fifteen or sixteen?' Mrs Dearden hazarded.*
▸ IN PHRASES: **hazard a guess** = **guess**, conjecture, suppose, speculate, presume, take a guess • *I would hazard a guess that they'll do fairly well.*
hazardous = **dangerous**, risky, difficult, uncertain, unpredictable, insecure, hairy (*slang*), unsafe, precarious, perilous, parlous (*archaic or humorous*), dicey (*informal, chiefly Brit.*), fraught with danger, chancy (*informal*) • *Below decks was hazardous in very heavy weather.*
OPPOSITES: safe, secure, sure
haze = **mist**, film, cloud, steam, fog, obscurity, vapour, smog, dimness, smokiness • *Dan smiled at him through a haze of smoke and steaming coffee.*
hazy 1 = **misty**, faint, dim, dull, obscure, veiled, smoky, cloudy, foggy, overcast, blurry, nebulous • *The air was filled with hazy sunshine and frost.*
OPPOSITES: clear, light, bright
2 = **vague**, uncertain, unclear, muddled, fuzzy, indefinite, loose, muzzy, nebulous, ill-defined, indistinct • *I have only a hazy memory of what he was like.*
OPPOSITES: clear, detailed, certain
head AS A NOUN 1 = **skull**, crown, pate, bean (*U.S. & Canad. slang*), nut (*slang*), loaf (*slang*), cranium, conk (*slang*), noggin, noddle (*informal, chiefly Brit.*) • *She turned her head away from him.*
2 = **mind**, reasoning, understanding, thought, sense, brain, brains (*informal*), intelligence, wisdom, wits, common sense, loaf (*Brit. informal*), intellect, rationality, grey matter, brainpower, mental capacity • *He was more inclined to use his head.*
3 = **ability**, mind, talent, capacity, faculty, flair, mentality, aptitude • *I don't have a head for business.*
4 = **front**, beginning, top, first place, fore, forefront • *the head of the queue*
5 = **forefront**, cutting edge, vanguard, van • *his familiar position at the head of his field*
6 = **top**, crown, summit, height, peak, crest, pinnacle, apex, vertex • *the head of the stairs*
7 = **head teacher**, principal, headmaster *or* headmistress • *full of admiration for the head and teachers*
8 = **leader**, president, director, manager, chief, boss (*informal*), captain, master, premier, commander, principal, supervisor, superintendent, chieftain, sherang (*Austral. & N.Z.*) • *heads of government from more than 100 countries*
9 = **climax**, crisis, turning point, culmination, end, conclusion, tipping point • *These problems came to a head in September.*
10 = **source**, start, beginning, rise, origin, commencement, well head • *the head of the river*
11 = **headland**, point, cape, promontory, foreland • *a ship off the beach head*
▸ AS AN ADJECTIVE = **chief**, main, leading, first, highest, front, prime, premier, supreme, principal, arch, foremost, pre-eminent, topmost • *I had the head man out from the gas company.*
▸ AS A VERB 1 = **lead**, precede, be the leader of, be *or* go first, be *or* go at the front of, lead the way • *The parson, heading the procession, had just turned right.*
2 = **top**, lead, crown, cap • *Running a business heads the list of ambitions among interviewees.*
3 = **be in charge of**, run, manage, lead, control, rule, direct, guide, command, govern, supervise • *He heads the department's Office of Civil Rights.*
▸ IN PHRASES: **do your head in** = **depress**, dishearten, frustrate, discourage • *Living with my parents is doing my head in.*
from head to foot = **from top to toe**, completely, all over, entirely, thoroughly • *scrubbed from head to foot*
get something into your head = **realise**, understand, get the message, take it in, twig (*informal*) • *Managers have at last got it into their heads.*
go over your head = **be baffling**, be perplexing, be incomprehensible, be impenetrable, be beyond comprehension, be all Greek to you (*informal*), be above your head, be beyond your grasp • *A lot of the ideas went way over my head.*
go to your head 1 = **intoxicate**, befuddle, inebriate, addle, stupefy, fuddle, put (someone) under the table (*informal*) • *That wine was strong, it went to your head.*
2 = **make someone conceited**, puff someone up, make someone full of themselves • *not a man to let a little success go to his head*
head for something *or* **someone** = **make for**, aim for, set off for, go to, turn to, set out for, make a beeline for, start towards, steer for • *He headed for the bus stop.*
head over heels = **completely**, thoroughly, utterly, intensely, wholeheartedly, uncontrollably • *head over heels in love*
head someone off = **intercept**, divert, deflect, cut someone off, interpose, block someone off • *He turned into the hallway and headed her off.*
head something off = **prevent**, stop, avert, parry, fend off, ward off, forestall • *good at spotting trouble on the way and heading it off*
head something up = **lead**, run, head, control, manage, direct, guide, govern, supervise, be in charge of • *Judge Frederick Lacey headed up the investigation.*

keep your head = **stay calm**, stay cool, remain unruffled, keep your shirt on *(informal)*, maintain your equilibrium • *She was able to keep her head and not panic.*
lose your head = **panic**, go to pieces, get hysterical, get flustered, lose your self-control, lose control of yourself, lose your composure • *She lost her head and started screaming at me.*
off your head = **mad**, insane, demented, nuts *(slang)*, barmy *(slang)*, deranged, out of your mind, gaga *(informal)* • *He's gone completely off his head.*
put your heads together = **consult**, confer, discuss, deliberate, talk (something) over, powwow, confab *(informal)*, confabulate • *Everyone put their heads together and reached an arrangement.*
▸ **TECHNICAL NAME:** caput
▸ **RELATED ADJECTIVES:** capital, cephalic

headache 1 = **migraine**, head *(informal)*, neuralgia, cephalalgia *(Medical)* • *I have had a terrible headache for the past two days.*
2 = **problem** *(Informal)*, worry, trouble, bother, nuisance, inconvenience, bane, vexation • *Their biggest headache is the increase in the price of fuel.*

headfirst *or* **head first** 1 = **headlong**, head foremost • *He has apparently fallen head-first down the stairwell.*
2 = **recklessly**, rashly, hastily, precipitately, without thinking, carelessly, heedlessly, without forethought • *On arrival he plunged head first into these problems.*

heading 1 = **title**, name, caption, headline, rubric • *helpful chapter headings*
2 = **category**, class, section, division • *There, under the heading of wholesalers, he found it.*

headland = **promontory**, point, head, cape, cliff, bluff, mull *(Scot.)*, foreland, bill • *The headland south of Coolum has walking trails.*

headline = **heading**, title, caption, headline banner • *I'm sick of reading headlines involving sex scandals.*

headlong AS AN ADVERB 1 = **hastily**, hurriedly, helter-skelter, pell-mell, heedlessly • *He ran headlong for the open door.*
2 = **headfirst**, head-on, headforemost • *She missed her footing and fell headlong down the stairs.*
3 = **rashly**, wildly, hastily, precipitately, head first, thoughtlessly, impetuously, heedlessly, without forethought • *Do not leap headlong into decisions.*
▸ **AS AN ADJECTIVE** = **hasty**, reckless, precipitate, dangerous, impulsive, thoughtless, breakneck, impetuous, inconsiderate • *a headlong rush for the exit*

headman = **chief**, head, leader, lord, master, ruler, chieftain • *the headman of the village*

headmaster *or* **headmistress** = **principal**, head, head teacher, rector • *He was headmaster of Stratford Grammar.*

head-on 1 = **direct**, head-to-head, front-to-front • *a head-on smash*
2 = **face-to-face**, direct, head-to-head, toe-to-toe • *a head-on clash between the president and the assembly*

headquarters = **head office**, base, HQ, command post, nerve centre, mission control • *The building is the headquarters of the family firm.*

head start = **start**, advantage, help, edge, upper hand • *A good education gives your child a head start in life.*

headstone = **gravestone**, monument, tombstone, stone • *He placed two poppies at the base of the headstone.*

headstrong = **stubborn**, wilful, obstinate, contrary, perverse, unruly, intractable, stiff-necked, ungovernable, self-willed, pig-headed, mulish, froward *(archaic)* • *He's very headstrong, but he's a good man underneath.*
OPPOSITES: manageable, impressionable, subservient

head teacher = **principal**, head, headmaster *or* headmistress, dean, rector • *One of the photos must be signed by your head teacher.*

headway = **progress**, ground, inroads, strides • *Police were making little headway in the investigation.*

heady 1 = **exciting**, thrilling, stimulating, exhilarating, overwhelming, intoxicating • *in the heady days just after their marriage*
2 = **intoxicating**, strong, potent, inebriating, spirituous • *The wine is a heady blend of claret and aromatic herbs.*

heal 1 *sometimes with* **up** = **mend**, get better, get well, cure, regenerate, show improvement • *The bruising had gone, but it was six months before it all healed.*
2 = **cure**, restore, mend, make better, remedy, make good, make well • *No doctor has ever healed a broken bone. They just set them.*
OPPOSITES: hurt, injure, wound
3 = **ease**, help, soothe, lessen, alleviate, assuage, salve, ameliorate • *the best way to heal a broken heart*
4 = **patch up**, settle, reconcile, put right, harmonize, conciliate • *Sophie and her sister have healed the family rift.*

healing 1 = **restoring**, medicinal, therapeutic, remedial, restorative, curative, analeptic, sanative • *Get in touch with the body's own healing abilities.*
2 = **soothing**, comforting, gentle, mild, assuaging, palliative, emollient, lenitive, mitigative • *I place my hands on their head in a healing way, and calm them down.*

health 1 = **condition**, state, form, shape, tone, constitution, fettle • *Although he's old, he's in good health.*
2 = **wellbeing**, strength, fitness, vigour, good condition, wellness, soundness, robustness, healthiness, salubrity, haleness • *In hospital they nursed me back to health.*
OPPOSITES: disease, illness, weakness
3 = **state**, condition, shape • *There's no way to predict the future health of the banking industry.*

QUOTATIONS
Health is a state of complete physical, mental and social well-being, and not merely the absence of disease or infirmity
[*Constitution of the World Health Organization*]
PROVERBS
An apple a day keeps the doctor away

healthful = **healthy**, beneficial, good for you, bracing, nourishing, wholesome, nutritious, invigorating, salutary, salubrious, health-giving • *Does the college cafeteria provide a healthful diet?*

healthy 1 = **well**, sound, fit, strong, active, flourishing, hardy, blooming, robust, vigorous, sturdy, hale, hearty, in good shape *(informal)*, in good condition, in the pink, alive and kicking, fighting fit, in fine form, in fine fettle, hale and hearty, fit as a fiddle *(informal)*, right as rain *(Brit. informal)*, physically fit, in fine feather • *She had a normal pregnancy and delivered a healthy child.*
OPPOSITES: ill, sick, poorly *(informal)*
2 = **wholesome**, beneficial, nourishing, good for you, nutritious, salutary, hygienic, healthful, salubrious, health-giving • *a healthy diet*
OPPOSITES: unhealthy, unwholesome
3 = **invigorating**, bracing, beneficial, good for you, salutary, healthful, salubrious • *a healthy outdoor pursuit*

heap AS A NOUN 1 = **pile**, lot, collection, store, mountain, mass, stack, rick, mound, accumulation, stockpile, hoard, aggregation • *a heap of bricks*
2 *often plural (Informal)* = **a lot**, lots *(informal)*, plenty, masses, load(s) *(informal)*, ocean(s), great deal, quantities, tons, stack(s), lashings *(Brit. informal)*, abundance, oodles *(informal)* • *You have heaps of time.*
▸ **AS A VERB** *sometimes with* **up** = **pile**, store, collect, gather, stack, accumulate, mound, amass, stockpile, hoard, bank • *They were heaping up wood for a bonfire.*
▸ **IN PHRASES: heap something on someone** *with* **on** = **load with**, burden with, confer on, assign to, bestow on,

shower upon • *He heaped scorn on both their methods and motives.*

heaped = **piled high**, covered, loaded, overspread • *The large desk was heaped with papers.*

hear 1 = **overhear**, catch, detect • *She heard no further sounds.*
2 = **listen to**, heed, attend to, eavesdrop on, listen in to, give attention to, hearken to *(archaic)*, hark to, be all ears for *(informal)* • *You can hear commentary on the match in about half an hour.*
3 = **try**, judge, examine, investigate • *He had to wait months before his case was heard.*
4 = **learn**, discover, find out, understand, pick up, gather, be informed, ascertain, be told of, get wind of *(informal)*, hear tell *(dialect)* • *He had heard that the trophy had been sold.*

hearing 1 = **sense of hearing**, auditory perception, ear, aural faculty • *His mind still seemed clear and his hearing was excellent.*
2 = **inquiry**, trial, investigation, industrial tribunal • *The judge adjourned the hearing until next Tuesday.*
3 = **chance to speak**, interview, audience, audition • *a means of giving a candidate a fair hearing*
4 = **earshot**, reach, range, hearing distance, auditory range • *No one spoke disparagingly of her father in her hearing.*
▸ **RELATED ADJECTIVE:** audio

hearsay = **rumour**, talk, gossip, report, buzz, dirt *(U.S. slang)*, goss *(informal)*, word of mouth, tittle-tattle, talk of the town, scuttlebutt *(slang, chiefly U.S.)*, idle talk, mere talk, on dit *(French)* • *Much of what was reported to them was hearsay.*

heart AS A NOUN 1 = **emotions**, feelings, sentiments, love, affection • *I phoned him up and poured out my heart.* • *The beauty quickly captured his heart.*
2 = **nature**, character, soul, constitution, essence, temperament, inclination, disposition • *She loved his brilliance and his generous heart.*
3 = **tenderness**, feeling(s), love, understanding, concern, sympathy, pity, humanity, affection, compassion, kindness, empathy, benevolence, concern for others • *They are ruthless, formidable, without heart.*
4 = **root**, core, essence, centre, nucleus, marrow, hub, kernel, crux, gist, central part, nitty-gritty *(informal)*, nub, pith, quintessence • *The heart of the problem is supply and demand.*
5 = **courage**, will, spirit, mind, balls *(taboo slang)*, purpose, bottle *(Brit. informal)*, resolution, resolve, nerve, stomach, enthusiasm, determination, guts *(informal)*, spine, pluck, bravery, backbone, fortitude, mettle, boldness, spunk *(informal)* • *I did not have the heart or spirit left to jog back to my hotel.*
▸ **IN PHRASES: at heart** = **fundamentally**, essentially, basically, really, actually, in fact, truly, in reality, in truth, in essence, deep down, at bottom, au fond *(French)* • *He was a very gentle boy at heart.*
by heart = **from** *or* **by memory**, verbatim, word for word, pat, word-perfect, by rote, off by heart, off pat, parrot-fashion *(informal)* • *Mack knew this passage by heart.*
from (the bottom of) your heart = **deeply**, heartily, fervently, heart and soul, devoutly, with all your heart • *thanking you from the bottom of my heart*
from the heart = **sincerely**, earnestly, in earnest, with all your heart, in all sincerity • *He was clearly speaking from the heart.*
heart and soul = **completely**, entirely, absolutely, wholeheartedly, to the hilt, devotedly • *He is heart and soul a Scot.*
lose heart = **give up**, despair, lose hope, become despondent, give up the ghost *(informal)* • *He appealed to his countrymen not to lose heart.*
set your heart on something = **desire**, long for, yearn for, hunger for, hanker after, want desperately • *He had always set his heart on a career in the theatre.*
take heart = **be encouraged**, be comforted, cheer up, perk up, brighten up, be heartened, buck up *(informal)*, derive comfort • *Investors failed to take heart from the stronger yen.*
▸ **RELATED ADJECTIVES:** cardiac, cardiothoracic

PARTS OF THE HEART

aorta	pulmonary vein	vena cava
atrium *or* auricle	semilunar valve	ventricle
bicuspid valve	septum	
pulmonary artery	tricuspid valve	

heartache = **sorrow**, suffering, pain, torture, distress, despair, grief, agony, torment, bitterness, anguish, remorse, heartbreak, affliction, heartsickness • *He had been the cause of so much heartache.*

heartbreak = **grief**, suffering, pain, despair, misery, sorrow, anguish, desolation • *suffering and heartbreak for those close to the victims*

heartbreaking = **sad**, distressing, tragic, bitter, poignant, harrowing, desolating, grievous, pitiful, agonizing, heart-rending, gut-wrenching • *one of the most heartbreaking letters I have ever received*
OPPOSITES: happy, cheerful, jolly

heartbroken = **brokenhearted**, crushed, miserable, choked, grieved, dismal, desolate, dejected, despondent, dispirited, downcast, disheartened, disconsolate, crestfallen, down in the dumps *(informal)*, sick as a parrot *(informal)*, heartsick • *I was heartbroken when you left.*
OPPOSITES: happy, cheerful, exuberant

heartburn = **indigestion**, upset stomach, dyspepsia, dyspepsy • *There was a burning sensation in his chest – heartburn, no doubt.*

hearten = **encourage**, inspire, cheer, comfort, assure, stimulate, reassure, animate, console, rouse, incite, embolden, buoy up, buck up *(informal)*, raise someone's spirits, revivify, gee up, inspirit • *The news heartened everybody.*

heartfelt = **sincere**, deep, earnest, warm, genuine, profound, honest, ardent, devout, hearty, fervent, cordial, wholehearted, dinkum *(Austral. & N.Z. informal)*, unfeigned • *My heartfelt sympathy goes out to all the relatives.*
OPPOSITES: put on, false, insincere

heartily 1 = **sincerely**, feelingly, deeply, warmly, genuinely, profoundly, cordially, unfeignedly • *He laughed heartily.*
2 = **enthusiastically**, vigorously, eagerly, resolutely, earnestly, zealously • *I heartily agree with her comments.*
3 = **thoroughly**, very, completely, totally, absolutely • *We're all heartily sick of all the aggravation.*

heartland = **centre**, stronghold, bastion • *the industrial heartland of America*

heartless = **cruel**, hard, callous, cold, harsh, brutal, unkind, inhuman, merciless, cold-blooded, uncaring, pitiless, unfeeling, cold-hearted, affectless, hardhearted • *I couldn't believe they were so heartless.*
OPPOSITES: kind, sensitive, compassionate

heart-rending = **moving**, sad, distressing, affecting, tragic, pathetic, poignant, harrowing, heartbreaking, pitiful, gut-wrenching, piteous • *heart-rending pictures of refugees*

heartsick = **despondent**, dejected, dispirited, downcast, heavy-hearted, sick at heart, heartsore • *He groaned – a long, low, heartsick sound.*

heart-throb = **idol**, star, hero, pin-up, dreamboat *(informal)* • *Her ideal co-star would be heart-throb Mel Gibson.*

heart-to-heart AS AN ADJECTIVE = **intimate**, honest, candid, open, personal, sincere, truthful, man-to-man, unreserved, woman-to-woman • *I had a heart-to-heart talk with my mother.*

▸ **AS A NOUN** = **tête-à-tête**, cosy chat, one-to-one, private conversation, private chat • *I've had a heart-to-heart with him.*

heart-warming = **moving**, touching, affecting, pleasing, encouraging, warming, rewarding, satisfying, cheering, gratifying, heartening • *the heart-warming story of enemies who discover a shared humanity*

hearty 1 = **friendly**, genial, warm, generous, eager, enthusiastic, ardent, cordial, affable, ebullient, jovial, effusive, unreserved, back-slapping • *He was a hearty, bluff, athletic sort of guy.*
OPPOSITES: cold, cool, unfriendly
2 = **wholehearted**, sincere, heartfelt, real, true, earnest, genuine, honest, unfeigned • *With the last sentiment, Arnold was in hearty agreement.*
OPPOSITES: mild, insincere, half-hearted
3 = **substantial**, filling, ample, square, solid, nourishing, sizable *or* sizeable • *The men ate a hearty breakfast.*
4 = **healthy**, well, strong, sound, active, hardy, robust, vigorous, energetic, hale, alive and kicking, right as rain *(Brit. informal)* • *She was still hearty and strong at 120 years and married a third husband at 92.*
OPPOSITES: weak, delicate, frail

heat **AS A VERB** 1 *sometimes with* **up** = **warm (up)**, cook, fry, boil, roast, reheat, make hot • *Meanwhile, heat the tomatoes and oil in a pan.*
OPPOSITES: cool, freeze, chill
2 = **intensify**, increase, heighten, deepen, escalate • *The war of words continues to heat up.*
▸ **AS A NOUN** 1 = **warmth**, hotness, temperature, swelter, sultriness, fieriness, torridity, warmness, calefaction • *Leaves drooped in the fierce heat of the sun.*
OPPOSITES: cold, coolness, coldness
2 = **hot weather**, warmth, closeness, high temperature, heatwave, warm weather, hot climate, hot spell, mugginess • *The heat is killing me.*
3 = **passion**, excitement, intensity, violence, fever, fury, warmth, zeal, agitation, fervour, ardour, vehemence, earnestness, impetuosity • *It was all done in the heat of the moment.*
OPPOSITES: composure, coolness, calmness
▸ **IN PHRASES:** **get heated up** = **get excited**, be stimulated, be stirred, become animated, be roused, be inflamed, be inspirited, become impassioned • *I get very heated up when people say that.*
heat up = **warm up**, get hotter, become hot, rise in temperature, become warm, grow hot • *In the summer her mobile home heats up like an oven.*
▸ **RELATED ADJECTIVES:** thermal, calorific
▸ **RELATED PHOBIA:** thermophobia

PROVERBS
If you can't stand the heat get out of the kitchen

heated 1 = **impassioned**, intense, spirited, excited, angry, violent, bitter, raging, furious, fierce, lively, passionate, animated, frenzied, fiery, stormy, vehement, tempestuous • *It was a very heated argument.*
OPPOSITES: calm, peaceful, quiet
2 = **wound up**, worked up, keyed up, het up *(informal)* • *People get a bit heated about issues like these.*

heath = **moorland**, moor, scrub, upland, open country, heathland, common land • *The park contains natural heath, woods and wetland.*

heathen **AS A NOUN** 1 = **pagan**, infidel, unbeliever, idolater, idolatress • *the condescending air of missionaries seeking to convert the heathen*
2 = **barbarian**, savage, philistine, oaf, plebeian, ignoramus, boor • *She called us all heathens and hypocrites.*
▸ **AS AN ADJECTIVE** 1 = **pagan**, infidel, godless, irreligious, idolatrous, heathenish • *a heathen temple*
2 = **uncivilized**, savage, primitive, barbaric, brutish, unenlightened, uncultured • *to disappear into the cold heathen north*

QUOTATIONS
heathen: a benighted creature who has the folly to worship something that he can see and feel
[Ambrose Bierce *The Devil's Dictionary*]

heave 1 = **lift**, raise, pull (up), drag (up), haul (up), tug, lever, hoist, heft *(informal)* • *He heaved Barney to his feet.*
2 = **throw**, fling, toss, send, cast, pitch, hurl, sling • *Heave a brick at the telly.*
3 = **expand**, rise, swell, pant, throb, exhale, dilate, palpitate • *His chest heaved, and he took a deep breath.*
4 = **surge**, rise, swell, billow • *The grey seas heaved.*
5 = **vomit**, be sick, throw up *(informal)*, chuck (up) *(slang, chiefly U.S.)*, chuck *(Austral. & N.Z. informal)*, gag, spew, retch, barf *(U.S. slang)*, chunder *(slang, chiefly Austral.)*, upchuck *(U.S. slang)*, do a technicolour yawn *(slang)*, toss your cookies *(U.S. slang)* • *He gasped and heaved and vomited.*
6 = **breathe**, sigh, puff, groan, sob, breathe heavily, suspire *(archaic)*, utter wearily • *Mr Collier heaved a sigh and got to his feet.*

heaven **AS A NOUN** 1 = **paradise**, next world, hereafter, nirvana *(Buddhism, Hinduism)*, bliss, Zion *(Christianity)*, Valhalla *(Norse myth)*, Happy Valley, happy hunting ground *(Native American legend)*, life to come, life everlasting, abode of God, Elysium *or* Elysian fields *(Greek myth)* • *I believed that when I died I would go to heaven.*
2 = **happiness**, paradise, ecstasy, bliss, felicity, utopia, contentment, rapture, enchantment, dreamland, seventh heaven, transport, sheer bliss • *My idea of heaven is drinking champagne with friends on a sunny day.*
▸ **IN PHRASES:** **in seventh heaven** = **ecstatic**, on a high, over the moon, on top of the world, on cloud nine, tickled pink, walking on air, beside yourself with joy • *He's been in seventh heaven since he met her.*
move heaven and earth = **struggle**, work hard, strive, spare no effort, try very hard, go all out, pull out all the stops, bend over backwards *(informal)*, do your best, put yourself out • *I moved heaven and earth to get you that job!*
the heavens = **sky**, ether, firmament, celestial sphere, welkin *(archaic)*, empyrean *(poetic)* • *a detailed map of the heavens*
▸ **RELATED PHOBIA:** ouranophobia

QUOTATIONS
Work and pray
Live on hay
You'll get pie in the sky when you die
[Joe Hill *The Preacher and the Slave*]
The kingdom of heaven is like to a grain of mustard seed
[*Bible: St. Matthew*]
The kingdom of heaven is like unto a merchant man, seeking goodly pearls; who, when he had found one pearl of great price, went and sold all that he had, and bought it
[*Bible: St. Matthew*]
The heaven of each is but what each desires
[Thomas Moore *Lalla Rookh*]
heaven: a place where the wicked cease from troubling you with talk of their personal affairs, and the good listen with attention while you expound your own
[Ambrose Bierce *The Devil's Dictionary*]

heavenly 1 = **celestial**, holy, divine, blessed, blest, immortal, supernatural, angelic, extraterrestrial, superhuman, godlike, beatific, cherubic, seraphic, supernal *(literary)*, empyrean *(poetic)*, paradisaical • *heavenly beings whose function it is to serve God*
OPPOSITES: worldly, human, earthly
2 = **wonderful**, lovely, delightful, beautiful, entrancing, divine *(informal)*, glorious, exquisite, sublime, alluring,

blissful, ravishing, rapturous • *The idea of spending two weeks with him seems heavenly.*
OPPOSITES: bad, terrible, awful

heaven-sent = **fortunate**, providential, welcome, blessed, opportune, felicitous, serendipitous • *It will be a heaven-sent opportunity to prove himself.*

heavily 1 = **excessively**, to excess, very much, a great deal, frequently, considerably, copiously, without restraint, immoderately, intemperately • *Her husband drank heavily and beat her.*
2 = **densely**, closely, thickly, compactly • *They can be found in grassy and heavily wooded areas.*
3 = **with difficulty**, laboriously, slowly, painfully, sluggishly • *She was breathing heavily with an occasional gasp for air.*
4 = **hard**, clumsily, awkwardly, weightily • *A man stumbled heavily against the car.*

heaviness 1 = **weight**, gravity, ponderousness, heftiness • *the heaviness of earthbound matter*
2 = **sluggishness**, torpor, numbness, dullness, lassitude, languor, deadness • *There was a heaviness in the air that stunned them.*
3 = **sadness**, depression, gloom, seriousness, melancholy, despondency, dejection, gloominess, glumness • *a heaviness in his reply which discouraged further questioning*

h

heavy 1 = **weighty**, large, massive, hefty, bulky, ponderous • *He was carrying a very heavy load.*
OPPOSITES: light, small, compact
2 = **intensive**, severe, serious, concentrated, fierce, excessive, relentless • *Heavy fighting has been going on.*
3 = **considerable**, large, huge, substantial, abundant, copious, profuse • *There was a heavy amount of traffic on the roads.*
OPPOSITES: light, slight, moderate
4 = **solid**, strong, thick, substantial, sturdy • *Put the sugar and water in a heavy pan and heat slowly.*
OPPOSITES: lightweight
5 = **overweight**, fat, plump, obese, stocky, fleshy, portly, corpulent, thickset • *He was short and heavy.*
6 = **viscous**, thick, sticky, gooey *(informal)*, syrupy, glutinous, gummy, gelatinous, icky *(informal)*, gluey, treacly, mucilaginous, viscid • *11 million gallons of heavy crude oil.*
7 = **substantial**, large, filling, generous • *the effects of an unusually heavy meal*
8 = **excessive**, intemperate, immoderate, overindulgent • *He's a smoker and a very heavy drinker.*
9 = **onerous**, hard, difficult, severe, harsh, tedious, intolerable, oppressive, grievous, burdensome, wearisome, vexatious • *They bear a heavy burden of responsibility.*
OPPOSITES: light, easy, soft
10 = **sluggish**, slow, dull, wooden, stupid, inactive, inert, apathetic, drowsy, listless, indolent, torpid • *I struggle to raise eyelids still heavy with sleep.*
OPPOSITES: quick, alert, brisk
11 = **forceful**, hard, powerful, strong, sharp, violent, mighty, vigorous, hefty • *a heavy blow on the back of the skull*
12 = **busy**, full, hectic, tiring • *It's been a heavy day and I'm tired.*
13 = **hard**, demanding, difficult, physical, strenuous, laborious • *They employ two full-timers to do the heavy work.*
14 = **overcast**, dull, gloomy, cloudy, leaden, louring *or* lowering • *The night sky was heavy with rain clouds.*
15 = **humid**, close, sticky, oppressive, clammy, airless, muggy • *The air outside was heavy and moist and sultry.*
16 = **sad**, depressed, gloomy, grieving, melancholy, dejected, despondent, downcast, sorrowful, disconsolate, crestfallen • *My parents' faces were heavy with fallen hope.*
OPPOSITES: happy, calm, cheerful
17 = **sorrowful**, sad, gloomy, melancholy, dejected, downcast, grief-stricken, disconsolate • *He handed over his resignation with a heavy heart.*
18 = **serious**, grave, solemn, difficult, deep, complex, profound, weighty • *I don't want any more of that heavy stuff.*
OPPOSITES: trivial, unimportant, inconsequential
19 = **tempestuous**, wild, rough, stormy, choppy, storm-tossed, squally • *The ship capsized in heavy seas.*

heavy-duty = **durable**, industrial-strength • *a heavy duty polythene bag*

heavy-handed 1 = **oppressive**, harsh, Draconian, autocratic, domineering, overbearing • *heavy-handed police tactics*
2 = **clumsy**, awkward, bungling, inept, graceless, inexpert, maladroit, ham-handed *(informal)*, like a bull in a china shop *(informal)*, ham-fisted *(informal)* • *She tends to be a little heavy-handed.*
OPPOSITES: efficient, gentle, skilful

heavy-hearted = **sad**, depressed, discouraged, miserable, crushed, dismal, melancholy, forlorn, mournful, despondent, downcast, morose, disheartened, sorrowful, downhearted, down in the dumps *(informal)*, sick as a parrot *(informal)*, heartsick • *She looked as heavy-hearted as she felt.*

heckle = **jeer**, interrupt, shout down, disrupt, bait, barrack *(informal)*, boo, taunt, pester • *He was insulted and heckled mercilessly.*

hectic = **frantic**, chaotic, frenzied, heated, wild, excited, furious, fevered, animated, turbulent, flurrying, frenetic, boisterous, feverish, tumultuous, flustering, riotous, rumbustious • *The two days we spent there were enjoyable but hectic.*
OPPOSITES: relaxing, calm, peaceful

hector = **bully**, harass, browbeat, worry, threaten, menace, intimidate, ride roughshod over, bullyrag • *I suppose you'll hector me until I phone him.*

hedge AS A NOUN = **guard**, cover, protection, compensation, shield, safeguard, counterbalance, insurance cover • *Gold is traditionally a hedge against inflation.*
▸ AS A VERB 1 = **prevaricate**, evade, sidestep, duck, dodge, flannel *(Brit. informal)*, waffle *(informal, chiefly Brit.)*, quibble, beg the question, pussyfoot *(informal)*, equivocate, temporize, be noncommittal • *When asked about his involvement, he hedged.*
2 = **enclose**, edge, border, surround, fence • *sweeping lawns hedged with floribundas*
▸ IN PHRASES: **hedge against something** = **protect**, insure, guard, safeguard, shield, cover, fortify • *You can hedge against redundancy or illness with insurance.*
hedge someone in = **hamper**, restrict, handicap, hamstring, hinder, hem in • *He was hedged in by his own shyness.*
hedge something in = **surround**, enclose, encompass, encircle, ring, fence in, girdle, hem in • *a steep and rocky footpath hedged in by the shadowy green forest*
hedge something *or* **someone about** = **restrict**, confine, hinder, hem in, hem around, hem about • *The offer was hedged around by conditions.*

hedgehog
▸ RELATED ADJECTIVE: erinaceous
▸ NAME OF YOUNG: hoglet

hedonism = **pleasure-seeking**, gratification, sensuality, self-indulgence, dolce vita, pursuit of pleasure, luxuriousness, sensualism, sybaritism, epicureanism, epicurism • *the reckless hedonism that life in Las Vegas demands*

hedonist = **pleasure-seeker**, epicurean, bon vivant *(French)*, epicure, sensualist, voluptuary, sybarite • *the world's best-known bachelor and unabashed hedonist*

hedonistic = **pleasure-seeking**, self-indulgent, luxurious, voluptuous, sybaritic, epicurean, bacchanalian • *The cookery course was serious and hedonistic at the same time.*

heed AS A VERB = **pay attention to**, listen to, take notice of, follow, mark, mind, consider, note, regard, attend, observe,

obey, bear in mind, be guided by, take to heart, give ear to • *Few at the conference in London last week heeded his warning.*
OPPOSITES: ignore, disregard, discount
▸ **AS A NOUN** = **thought**, care, mind, note, attention, regard, respect, notice, consideration, watchfulness • *He pays too much heed these days to my nephew Tom.*
OPPOSITES: neglect, disregard, carelessness

heedless = **careless**, reckless, negligent, rash, precipitate, oblivious, foolhardy, thoughtless, unthinking, imprudent, neglectful, inattentive, incautious, unmindful, unobservant • *She scattered the letters about in her heedless haste.*
OPPOSITES: careful, cautious, concerned

heel **AS A NOUN** 1 = **end**, stump, remainder, crust, rump, stub • *the heel of a loaf of bread*
2 = **swine**, cad (*Brit. informal*), scoundrel, scally (*Northwest English dialect*), bounder (*Brit. old-fashioned slang*), rotter (*slang, chiefly Brit.*), scumbag (*slang*), blackguard, cocksucker (*taboo slang*), wrong 'un (*Austral. slang*) • *Suddenly I feel like a total heel.*
▸ **IN PHRASES: bring something** *or* **someone to heel** = **subjugate**, master, suppress, put down, tame, subdue, quell, hold sway over, bring (someone) to their knees, bring under the yoke • *The president will use his power to bring the republics to heel.*
hard on the heels of something *or* **someone** = **straight after**, immediately after, right behind, following on from • *Bad news has come hard on the heels of good.*
take to your heels = **flee**, escape, run away *or* off, take flight, hook it (*slang*), turn tail, show a clean pair of heels, skedaddle (*informal*), vamoose (*slang, chiefly U.S.*) • *He stood, for a moment, then took to his heels.*

heel over = **lean over**, list, incline, tilt, cant, keel over, careen • *The sailing-boat moved on, heeling over under a nice breeze.*

hefty 1 = **big**, strong, massive, strapping, robust, muscular, burly, husky (*informal*), hulking, beefy (*informal*), brawny • *She was quite a hefty woman.*
OPPOSITES: little, small, minute
2 = **forceful**, heavy, powerful, vigorous (*slang*) • *Lambert gave him a hefty shove to send him on his way.*
OPPOSITES: gentle, soft, weak
3 = **heavy**, large, massive, substantial, tremendous, awkward, ample, bulky, colossal, cumbersome, weighty, unwieldy, ponderous • *The gritty foursome took turns shouldering the hefty load every five minutes.*
OPPOSITES: light
4 = **large**, massive, substantial, excessive, inflated, sizeable, astronomical (*informal*), extortionate • *A long-distance romance followed with hefty phone bills.*

hegemony = **domination**, leadership, dominance, sway, supremacy, mastery, upper hand, ascendancy, pre-eminence, predominance • *the economic world hegemony of the West*

height 1 = **tallness**, stature, highness, loftiness • *Her height is intimidating for some men.*
OPPOSITES: shortness, smallness, lowness
2 = **altitude**, measurement, highness, elevation, tallness • *build a wall up to a height of 2 metres*
OPPOSITES: depth
3 = **peak**, top, hill, mountain, crown, summit, crest, pinnacle, elevation, apex, apogee, vertex • *From a height, it looks like a desert.*
OPPOSITES: base, bottom, valley
4 = **culmination**, climax, zenith, limit, maximum, ultimate, extremity, uttermost, ne plus ultra (*Latin*), utmost degree • *He was struck down at the height of his career.*
OPPOSITES: nadir, low point, minimum
▸ **RELATED PHOBIA:** acrophobia

heighten = **intensify**, increase, add to, improve, strengthen, enhance, sharpen, aggravate, magnify, amplify, augment • *The move has heightened tension in the state.*

heinous = **shocking**, evil, monstrous, grave, awful, vicious, outrageous, revolting, infamous, hideous, unspeakable, atrocious, flagrant, odious, hateful, abhorrent, abominable, villainous, nefarious, iniquitous, execrable • *They are capable of the most heinous acts.*

heir = **successor**, beneficiary, inheritor, heiress (*fem.*), scion, next in line, inheritress *or* inheritrix (*fem.*) • *the heir to the throne*

helix = **spiral**, twist, curl, loop, coil, corkscrew, gyre (*literary*), curlicue, volute (*technical*) • *Coil the fibre into a helix.*

hell **AS A NOUN** 1 = **the underworld**, the abyss, Hades (*Greek myth*), hellfire, the inferno, fire and brimstone, the bottomless pit, Gehenna (*New Testament, Judaism*), the nether world, the lower world, Tartarus (*Greek myth*), the infernal regions, the bad fire (*informal*), Acheron (*Greek myth*), Abaddon, the abode of the damned • *Don't worry about going to Hell, just be good.*
2 = **torment**, suffering, agony, trial, nightmare, misery, ordeal, anguish, affliction, martyrdom, wretchedness • *the hell of grief and lost love*
▸ **IN PHRASES: for the hell of it** = **for fun**, meaningless, for a laugh • *It was stupid, just vandalism for the hell of it.*
give someone hell = **scold**, rebuke, reprimand, berate, lecture, be angry at, chastise, slap someone's wrist, bawl out, give someone a rollicking • *My father saw this in the newspaper and gave me absolute hell.*
hell for leather = **headlong**, speedily, quickly, swiftly, hurriedly, at the double, full-tilt, pell-mell, hotfoot, at a rate of knots, like a bat out of hell (*slang*), posthaste • *The first horse often goes hell for leather.*
like hell = **a lot**, very much, a great deal • *It hurts like hell.*
raise hell = **cause a disturbance**, run riot, go wild, raise Cain, be loud and noisy • *Those people will be jabbering and raising hell.*
▸ **RELATED PHOBIAS:** hadephobia, stygiophobia

QUOTATIONS

There is a dreadful Hell,
And everlasting pains;
There sinners must with devils dwell
In darkness, fire, and chains
[Isaac Watts *Divine Songs for Children*]

Hell hath no limits nor is circumscribed
In one self place, where we are is Hell,
And to be short, when all the world dissolves
And every creature shall be purified
All places shall be Hell that are not Heaven
[Christopher Marlowe *Doctor Faustus*]

But wherefore thou alone? Wherefore with thee
Came not all hell broke loose?
[John Milton *Paradise Lost*]

Hell is other people
[Jean-Paul Sartre *Huis Clos*]

A perpetual holiday is a good working definition of hell
[George Bernard Shaw *Parents and Children*]

Hell is a city much like London -
A populous and smoky city
[Percy Bysshe Shelley *Peter Bell the Third*]

Hell is not to love any more, madame. Not to love any more!
[Georges Bernanos *The Diary of a Country Priest*]

What is hell?
Hell is yourself,
Hell is alone, the other figures in it
Merely projections
[T.S. Eliot *The Cocktail Party*]

If there is no Hell, a good many preachers are obtaining money under false pretenses
[William A. Sunday]

hellbent = **intent** *(Informal)*, set, determined, settled, fixed, resolved, bent • *She is hellbent on marrying him.*

hellish AS AN ADJECTIVE 1 = **atrocious**, terrible, dreadful, cruel, vicious, monstrous, wicked, inhuman, barbarous, abominable, nefarious, accursed, execrable, detestable • *He was held for three years in hellish conditions.*
OPPOSITES: fine, wonderful, good
2 = **devilish**, fiendish, diabolical, infernal, damned, damnable, demoniacal • *They began to pray, making devilish gestures with a hellish noise.*
▸ AS AN ADVERB = **very**, extremely, terribly, seriously, incredibly, awfully, exceedingly, excessively • *It's hellish cold up here in winter.*

hello = **hi** *(informal)*, greetings, how do you do?, good morning, good evening, good afternoon, welcome, kia ora *(N.Z.)*, gidday or g'day *(Austral. & N.Z.)* • *Hello. I won't shake hands because they're filthy.*

helm AS A NOUN = **tiller**, wheel, rudder, steering gear • *I got into our dinghy while Willis took the helm.*
▸ IN PHRASES: **at the helm** = **in charge**, in control, in command, directing, at the wheel, in the saddle, in the driving seat • *He has been at the helm of Lonrho for 31 years.*

help AS A VERB 1 *sometimes with* **out** = **aid**, back, support, second, encourage, promote, assist, relieve, stand by, befriend, cooperate with, abet, lend a hand, succour, lend a helping hand, give someone a leg up *(informal)* • *If you're not willing to help me, I'll find somebody who will.*
OPPOSITES: fight, bar, hinder
2 = **improve**, ease, heal, cure, relieve, remedy, facilitate, alleviate, mitigate, ameliorate • *A cosmetic measure which will do nothing to help the situation long term.*
OPPOSITES: aggravate, make worse, hurt
3 = **assist**, aid, support, give a leg up *(informal)* • *Martin helped Tanya over the rail.*
4 = **resist**, refrain from, avoid, control, prevent, withstand, eschew, keep from, abstain from, forbear • *I can't help feeling sorry for the poor man.*
▸ AS A NOUN 1 = **assistance**, aid, support, service, advice, promotion, guidance, cooperation, helping hand • *Thanks very much for your help.*
OPPOSITES: opposition, obstruction, hindrance
2 = **remedy**, cure, relief, corrective, balm, salve, succour, restorative • *There is no help for him and no doctor on this earth could save him.*
3 = **assistant**, hand, worker, employee, helper • *a hired help*
▸ IN PHRASES: **help yourself to something** = **take**, steal, appropriate, pocket, trouser *(slang)*, swipe *(informal)*, knock off *(slang)*, pilfer *(informal)*, purloin, snaffle *(informal)* • *Has somebody helped himself to some film star's diamonds?*

QUOTATIONS
Often we can help each other most by leaving each other alone; at other times we need the hand-grasp and the word of cheer
[Elbert Hubbard *The Note Book*]

PROVERBS
God helps them that help themselves
Many hands make light work

helper = **assistant**, partner, ally, colleague, supporter, mate, deputy, second, subsidiary, aide, aider, attendant, collaborator, auxiliary, henchman, right-hand man, adjutant, helpmate, coadjutor, abettor • *Wheelchair users must be accompanied by a helper.*

helpful 1 = **cooperative**, accommodating, kind, caring, friendly, neighbourly, sympathetic, supportive, benevolent, considerate, beneficent • *The staff in the London office are helpful.*
2 = **useful**, practical, productive, profitable, constructive, serviceable • *The catalog includes helpful information.*
3 = **beneficial**, advantageous, expedient, favourable • *It is often helpful to have someone with you when you get bad news.*

helpfulness 1 = **cooperation**, kindness, support, assistance, sympathy, friendliness, rallying round, neighbourliness, good neighbourliness • *The level of expertise and helpfulness is higher in small shops.*
2 = **usefulness**, benefit, advantage • *the helpfulness of the information pack*

helping = **portion**, serving, ration, piece, dollop *(informal)*, plateful • *extra helpings of ice-cream*

helpless 1 = **vulnerable**, exposed, unprotected, defenceless, abandoned, dependent, stranded, wide open, forlorn, destitute • *The children were left helpless.*
OPPOSITES: safe, secure, invulnerable
2 = **powerless**, weak, disabled, incapable, challenged, paralysed, incompetent, unfit, feeble, debilitated, impotent, infirm • *Since the accident I am completely helpless.*
OPPOSITES: able, strong, powerful

helplessness = **vulnerability**, weakness, impotence, powerlessness, disability, infirmity, feebleness, forlornness, defencelessness • *I remember my feelings of helplessness.*

helter-skelter AS AN ADJECTIVE = **haphazard**, confused, disordered, random, muddled, jumbled, topsy-turvy, hit-or-miss, higgledy-piggledy *(informal)* • *another crisis in his helter-skelter existence*
▸ AS AN ADVERB = **wildly**, rashly, anyhow, headlong, recklessly, carelessly, pell-mell • *a panic-stricken crowd running helter-skelter*

hem AS A NOUN = **edge**, border, margin, trimming, fringe • *Cut a jagged edge along the hem to give a ragged look.*
▸ IN PHRASES: **hem something** *or* **someone in**
1 = **surround**, edge, border, skirt, confine, enclose, shut in, hedge in, environ • *Manchester is hemmed in by greenbelt countryside.*
2 = **restrict**, confine, beset, circumscribe • *hemmed in by rigid, legal contracts*

he-man = **muscle man**, hunk *(slang)*, Hercules, Atlas, Tarzan *(informal)*, bit of beefcake • *Oxford educated he-man offers an insider's view on weightlifting.*

hen
▸ COLLECTIVE NOUN: brood

hence 1 = **therefore**, thus, consequently, for this reason, in consequence, ergo, on that account • *The Socialist Party was profoundly divided and hence very weak.*
2 = **later**, afterwards • *many years hence*

henceforth = **from now on**, in the future, hereafter, hence, hereinafter, from this day forward • *We are henceforth barred from the base.*

henchman = **attendant**, supporter, heavy *(slang)*, associate, aide, follower, subordinate, bodyguard, minder *(slang)*, crony, sidekick *(slang)*, cohort *(chiefly U.S.)*, right-hand man, minion, satellite, myrmidon • *Mad Frankie Fraser, one time henchman of the Krays' arch rivals*

henpecked = **dominated**, subjugated, browbeaten, subject, bullied, timid, cringing, meek, treated like dirt, led by the nose, tied to someone's apron strings, pussy-whipped *(taboo slang)* • *The henpecked husband yielded to her demands.*
OPPOSITES: dominating, aggressive, domineering

herald AS A VERB 1 = **indicate**, promise, precede, pave the way, usher in, harbinger, presage, portend, foretoken • *Their discovery could herald a cure for some forms of impotence.*
2 = **announce**, publish, advertise, proclaim, broadcast, trumpet, publicize • *Tonight's clash is being heralded as the match of the season.*
▸ AS A NOUN 1 = **forerunner**, sign, signal, indication, token, omen, precursor, harbinger • *I welcome the report as the herald of more freedom, not less.*
2 = **messenger**, courier, proclaimer, announcer, crier, town crier, bearer of tidings • *Jill hovered by the hearth while the herald delivered his news.*

heraldry

QUOTATIONS

The science of fools with long memories
[J.R. Planché *The Pursuivant of Arms*]

▹ *See panel* **Heraldry terms**

herb

▹ *See panel* **Herbs, spices and seasonings**

herculean 1 = **arduous**, hard, demanding, difficult, heavy, tough, exhausting, formidable, gruelling, strenuous, prodigious, onerous, laborious, toilsome • *Finding a lawyer may seem like a Herculean task.*
2 = **strong**, muscular, powerful, athletic, strapping, mighty, rugged, sturdy, stalwart, husky *(informal)*, sinewy, brawny • *His shoulders were Herculean with long arms.*

Hercules

▹ *See panel* **Labours of Hercules**

herd AS A NOUN 1 = **flock**, crowd, collection, mass, drove, crush, mob, swarm, horde, multitude, throng, assemblage, press • *large herds of elephant and buffalo*
2 = **mob**, the masses, rabble, populace, the hoi polloi, the plebs, riffraff • *They are individuals; they will not follow the herd.*
▸ AS A VERB 1 = **lead**, drive, force, direct, guide, shepherd • *The group was herded onto a bus.*
2 = **drive**, lead, force, guide, shepherd • *A boy herded sheep down towards the lane.*

herdsman = **stockman**, drover, grazier, cowman, cowherd • *The herdsman came calling the cattle for milking.*

here 1 = **in** *or* **at this place**, on this spot, in *or* at this location • *I'm here all by myself.*
OPPOSITES: there
2 = **at hand**, present, available, in attendance • *I'm here to help you.*
3 = **now**, at this point, at this time, at this moment • *Here is your opportunity to acquire a home.*

hereafter AS AN ADVERB = **in future**, after this, from now on, henceforth, henceforward, hence • *Hereafter for three years my name will not appear at all.*
▸ IN PHRASES: **the hereafter** = **afterlife**, next world, life after death, future life, the beyond • *belief in the hereafter*

hereditary 1 = **genetic**, inborn, inbred, transmissible, inheritable • *In men, hair loss is hereditary.*
2 = **inherited**, handed down, passed down, willed, family, traditional, transmitted, ancestral, bequeathed, patrimonial • *hereditary peerages*

heredity = **genetics**, inheritance, genetic make-up, congenital traits • *Heredity is not a factor in causing the cancer.*

HERALDRY TERMS

annulet	chevron	embattled	heraldic *or* fetial	ordinary	sable
argent	chief	emblazon	impale *or* empale	orle	saltire
armes parlantes	cinquefoil	ermine	inescutcheon	pale	sejant *or* sejeant
armiger	Clarenceux	escutcheon	issuant	pall	scutcheon
armory	coat armour	falcon	king-of-arms	paly	semé (of)
bandeau	coat of arms	fesse *or* fess	label	parted	shield
bar	cockatrice	field	leopard	party	sinister
base	cognizance	fillet	lion	passant	spread eagle
baton	college of arms	fleur-de-lis	lozenge	pean	statant
bearing	compony	flory *or* fleury	lozengy	pile	sun in splendour
bend	coronet	fret	Lyon King of Arms	potent	supporter
bend sinister	couchant	fur	mantling *or*	proper	torse
bezzant *or* byzant	crescent	fusil	lambrequin	purpure	tressure
blazon	crest	garland	mascle *or* voided	pursuivant	urdé *or* urdée
blazonry	cross	giron *or* gyron	lozenge	quarter	urinant
bordure	crosslet	gironny	matriculation	quartered	vair
cadency	crown	griffon	moline	quartering	vert
canting arms	dexter	guardant *or*	naissant	quarterly	voided
canton	difference	gardant	nombril	rampant	volant
chaplet	dimidiate	gules	octofoil	rebus	wreath
charge	dormant	hatchment	officer of arms	regardant	wyvern
checky	eagle	herald	or	roundel	yale

HERBS, SPICES AND SEASONINGS

alligator pepper	cardamom	cumin	lemon grass	peppercorn	star anise
allspice	cassia bark	curry powder	mace	poppy seed	sunflower seed
aniseed	cayenne pepper	dill	marjoram	red pepper	Szechuan
asafoetida	chervil	fennel	mint	rocambole	peppercorns
basil	chilli	fines herbes	miso	rosemary	tansy
bayleaf	chive	five spice	mustard	saffron	tarragon
black pepper	cinnamon	powder	nam pla *or* fish	sage	thyme
borage	clove	galangal	sauce	salt	turmeric
calendula	coconut	garam masala	nutmeg	savory	wasabi
canella	coconut milk	garlic	oregano	sesame seed	white pepper
capers	coriander	ginger	paprika	soy sauce, shoyu,	
caraway seed	cress	Kaffir lime leaf	parsley	*or* tamari	

LABOURS OF HERCULES

the slaying of the Nemean lion
the slaying of the Lernaean hydra
the capture of the hind of Ceryneia
the capture of the wild boar of Erymanthus
the cleansing of the Augean stables
the shooting of the Stymphalian birds
the capture of the Cretan bull
the capture of the horses of Diomedes
the taking of the girdle of Hippolyte
the capture of the cattle of Geryon
the recovery of the golden apples of Hesperides
the taking of Cerberus

heresy = **unorthodoxy**, apostasy, dissidence, impiety, revisionism, iconoclasm, heterodoxy • *It might be considered heresy to suggest such a notion.*

QUOTATIONS

The heresy of one age becomes the orthodoxy of the next
[Helen Keller *Optimism*]

They that approve a private opinion, call it opinion; but they that mislike it, heresy; and yet heresy signifies no more than private opinion
[Thomas Hobbes *Leviathan*]

heretic = **nonconformist**, dissident, separatist, sectarian, renegade, revisionist, dissenter, apostate, schismatic • *He was considered a heretic and was ridiculed for his ideas.*

heretical 1 = **controversial**, unorthodox, revisionist, freethinking • *I made a heretical suggestion.*
2 = **unorthodox**, revisionist, iconoclastic, heterodox, impious, idolatrous, schismatic, freethinking • *The Church regards spirit mediums as heretical.*

heritage = **inheritance**, legacy, birthright, lot, share, estate, tradition, portion, endowment, bequest, patrimony • *The building is part of our heritage.*

hermaphrodite = **bisexual**, androgyne, epicene, ambisexual • *the story of a seventeenth-century French hermaphrodite*

hermetic *or* **hermetical** 1 = **airtight**, sealed, shut • *breaking the hermetic seal of the jar*
2 = **isolated**, solitary, abnormal, anomalous, out on a limb • *Their work is more cosily hermetic than ever.*

hermit = **recluse**, monk, loner *(informal)*, solitary, anchorite, anchoress, stylite, eremite • *He lived like a hermit despite his fortune in shares and property.*

hermitage = **retreat**, refuge, sanctuary, haven, shelter, asylum, hideaway, hideout • *the ancient church where the saint had his hermitage*

hero 1 = **protagonist**, leading man, lead actor, male lead, principal male character • *The hero of Doctor Zhivago dies in 1929.*
2 = **star**, champion, celebrity, victor, superstar, great man, heart-throb *(Brit.)*, conqueror, exemplar, celeb *(informal)*, megastar *(informal)*, popular figure, man of the hour • *the goalscoring hero of the British hockey team*
3 = **idol**, favourite, pin-up *(slang)*, fave *(informal)* • *I still remember my boyhood heroes.*

QUOTATIONS

See, the conquering hero comes!
Sound the trumpets, beat the drums!
[Thomas Morell *Judas Maccabeus*]

Ultimately a hero is a man who would argue with the gods, and so awakens devils to contest his vision
[Norman Mailer *The Presidential Papers*]

heroic 1 = **courageous**, brave, daring, bold, fearless, gallant, intrepid, valiant, doughty, undaunted, dauntless, lion-hearted, valorous, stouthearted • *The heroic sergeant risked his life to rescue 29 fishermen.*
OPPOSITES: cowardly, craven, timid
2 = **legendary**, classical, mythological, Homeric • *another in an endless series of man's heroic myths of his own past*
3 = **epic**, grand, classic, extravagant, exaggerated, elevated, inflated, high-flown, grandiose • *a heroic style, with a touch of antiquarian realism*
OPPOSITES: simple, unadorned, lowbrow

QUOTATIONS

The high sentiments always win in the end, the leaders who offer blood, toil, tears and sweat always get more out of their followers than those who offer safety and a good time. When it comes to the pinch, human beings are heroic
[George Orwell *The Art of Donald McGill*]

heroine 1 = **protagonist**, leading lady, diva, prima donna, female lead, lead actress, principal female character • *The heroine is a senior TV executive.*
2 = **star**, celebrity, goddess, celeb *(informal)*, megastar *(informal)*, woman of the hour • *The heroine of the day was the winner of the Gold medal.*
3 = **idol**, favourite, pin-up *(slang)*, fave *(informal)* • *I still remember my childhood heroines.*

heroism = **bravery**, daring, courage, spirit, fortitude, boldness, gallantry, valour, fearlessness, intrepidity, courageousness • *individual acts of heroism*

heron
▸ COLLECTIVE NOUN: sedge or siege

hero-worship = **admiration**, idolization, adulation, adoration, veneration, idealization, putting on a pedestal • *Their singer inspires old-fashioned hero-worship.*

herring
▸ COLLECTIVE NOUNS: shoal, glean
▸ NAME OF YOUNG: alevin, brit, sparling

hesitancy = **indecision**, doubt, uncertainty, hesitation, vacillation, irresolution, dubiety • *A trace of hesitancy showed in Dr Stockton's eyes.*

hesitant = **uncertain**, reluctant, shy, halting, doubtful, sceptical, unsure, hesitating, wavering, timid, diffident, lacking confidence, vacillating, hanging back, irresolute, half-arsed *(Brit. slang)*, half-assed *(U.S. & Canad. slang)*, half-hearted • *She was hesitant about coming forward with her story.*
OPPOSITES: clear, sure, confident

hesitate 1 = **waver**, delay, pause, haver *(Brit.)*, wait, doubt, falter, be uncertain, dither *(chiefly Brit.)*, vacillate, equivocate, temporize, hum and haw, shillyshally *(informal)*, swither *(Scot. dialect)* • *She hesitated, debating whether to answer the phone.*
OPPOSITES: decide, be confident, be decisive
2 = **be reluctant**, be unwilling, shrink from, think twice, boggle, scruple, demur, hang back, be disinclined, balk *or* baulk • *I will not hesitate to take unpopular decisions.*
OPPOSITES: resolve, be determined

QUOTATIONS

You can hesitate before deciding, but not once the decision is made
[José Bergamín *El cohete y la estrella*]

PROVERBS

He who hesitates is lost

hesitation 1 = **delay**, pausing, uncertainty, stalling, dithering, indecision, hesitancy, doubt, vacillation, temporizing, shilly-shallying, irresolution, hemming and hawing, dubiety • *After some hesitation, he answered her question.*
2 = **reluctance**, reservation(s), misgiving(s), ambivalence, qualm(s), unwillingness, scruple(s), compunction, demurral • *The board said it had no hesitation in rejecting the offer.*

heterodox = **unorthodox**, dissident, heretical, revisionist, unsound, iconoclastic, schismatic • *They were generally treating heterodox ideas as un-American.*

heterogeneous = **varied**, different, mixed, contrasting, unlike, diverse, diversified, assorted, unrelated, disparate, miscellaneous, motley, incongruous, dissimilar, divergent, manifold, discrepant • *the heterogeneous society of today*

heterosexual = **hetero** *(informal)*, straight *(informal)* • *heterosexual couples*

hew 1 = **cut**, chop, axe, hack, split, lop • *He felled, peeled and hewed his own timber.*
2 = **carve**, make, form, fashion, shape, model, sculpture, sculpt • *medieval monasteries hewn out of the rockface*

heyday = **prime**, time, day, flowering, pink, bloom, high point, zenith, salad days, prime of life • *In its heyday, the studio boasted it had more stars than heaven.*

hiatus = **pause**, break, interval, space, gap, breach, blank, lapse, interruption, respite, chasm, discontinuity, lacuna, entr'acte • *Efforts to reach a settlement resume today after a two-week hiatus.*

hibernate = **sleep**, lie dormant, winter, overwinter, vegetate, remain torpid, sleep snug • *Dormice hibernate from October to May.*

hiccup *or* **hiccough** = **setback**, hold-up, hitch, glitch, check, blow, upset, disappointment, bit of trouble • *A recent sales hiccup is nothing to panic about.*

hick = **yokel**, peasant, rustic, redneck, bumpkin, country bumpkin, hayseed *(U.S. & Canad. informal)* • *He is an obnoxious hick.*

hidden 1 = **secret**, veiled, dark, mysterious, obscure, mystical, mystic, shrouded, occult, latent, cryptic, hermetic, ulterior, abstruse, recondite, hermetical • *Uncover hidden meanings and discover special messages.*
2 = **concealed**, covered, secret, covert, unseen, clandestine, secreted, under wraps, unrevealed • *The pictures had obviously been taken by a hidden camera.*

hide[1] 1 = **conceal**, stash *(informal)*, secrete, cache, put out of sight • *He hid the bicycle in the hawthorn hedge.*
OPPOSITES: find, display, exhibit
2 = **go into hiding**, take cover, keep out of sight, hole up, lie low, go underground, go to ground, go to earth • *They hid behind a tree.*
3 = **keep secret**, suppress, withhold, keep quiet about, hush up, draw a veil over, keep dark, keep under your hat • *I have absolutely nothing to hide, I have done nothing wrong.*
OPPOSITES: admit, confess, disclose
4 = **obscure**, cover, screen, bury, shelter, mask, disguise, conceal, eclipse, veil, cloak, shroud, camouflage, blot out • *The compound was hidden by trees and shrubs.*
OPPOSITES: show, reveal, expose

hide[2] = **skin**, fell, leather, pelt • *the process of tanning animal hides*

hideaway = **hiding place**, haven, retreat, refuge, sanctuary, hide-out, nest, sequestered nook • *The bandits fled to a remote mountain hideaway.*

hidebound = **conventional**, set, rigid, narrow, puritan, narrow-minded, strait-laced, brassbound, ultraconservative, set in your ways • *The men are hidebound and reactionary.*
OPPOSITES: open, liberal, broad-minded

hideous 1 = **ugly**, revolting, ghastly, monstrous, grotesque, gruesome, grisly, unsightly, repulsive, fugly *(chiefly U.S. & Austral.)* • *She saw a hideous face at the window and screamed.*
OPPOSITES: beautiful, lovely, pleasing
2 = **terrifying**, shocking, terrible, awful, appalling, disgusting, horrible, dreadful, horrific, obscene, sickening, horrendous, macabre, horrid, odious, loathsome, abominable, detestable, godawful *(slang)* • *His family was subjected to a hideous attack.*

hide-out = **hiding place**, shelter, den, hideaway, lair, secret place • *Police raided a house used as the movement's hideout.*

hiding = **beating**, whipping, thrashing, tanning *(slang)*, caning, licking *(informal)*, flogging, spanking, walloping *(informal)*, drubbing, lathering *(informal)*, whaling, larruping *(Brit. dialect)* • *He was misquoted as saying that the police deserved a bloody good hiding.*

hiding place = **hideout**, shelter, den, hideaway, lair, secret place • *Two days ago he fled from his secret hiding place.*

hierarchical = **graded**, ranked, graduated • *The traditional hierarchical system of military organization*

hierarchy = **grading**, ranking, social order, pecking order, class system, social stratum • *Even in the desert there was a kind of social hierarchy.*

QUOTATIONS

We rank ourselves by the familiar dog system,
a ladderlike social arrangement wherein one individual
outranks all others, the next outranks all but the first,
and so on down the hierarchy

[Elizabeth Marshall Thomas *Strong and Sensitive Cats*]

In a hierarchy every employee tends to rise to his level of
incompetence

[Laurence Peter *The Peter Principle*]

hieroglyphic AS AN ADJECTIVE = **indecipherable**, obscure, figurative, runic, symbolical, enigmatical • *carved funerary vases containing hieroglyphic texts*
▸ AS A PLURAL NOUN = **hieroglyphs**, signs, symbols, code, ciphers, cryptograms, cryptographs • *He could read the ancient Egyptian hieroglyphics.*

hi-fi
▸ RELATED ENTHUSIAST: audiophile

higgledy-piggledy AS AN ADJECTIVE = **haphazard**, muddled, jumbled, indiscriminate, topsy-turvy, helter-skelter, pell-mell • *books stacked in higgledy-piggledy piles on the floor*
▸ AS AN ADVERB = **haphazardly**, all over the place, anyhow, topsy-turvy, helter-skelter, all over the shop *(informal)*, pell-mell, confusedly, any old how • *boulders tossed higgledy-piggledy as though by some giant*

high AS AN ADJECTIVE 1 = **tall**, towering, soaring, steep, elevated, lofty • *A house with a high wall around it.*
OPPOSITES: low, short, dwarfed
2 = **extreme**, great, acute, severe, extraordinary, excessive • *Officials said casualties were high.*
OPPOSITES: low, average, routine
3 = **strong**, violent, extreme, blustery, squally, sharp • *High winds have knocked down trees and power lines.*
4 = **expensive**, dear, steep *(informal)*, costly, stiff, high-priced, exorbitant • *I think it's a good buy overall, despite the high price.*
5 = **important**, leading, ruling, chief, powerful, significant, distinguished, prominent, superior, influential, notable, big-time *(informal)*, eminent, major league *(informal)*, exalted, consequential, skookum *(Canad.)* • *Every one of them is controlled by the families of high officials.*
OPPOSITES: insignificant, lowly, unimportant
6 = **advanced**, complex • *the rise of Japan's high technology industries*
7 = **notable**, leading, important, famous, significant, celebrated, outstanding, distinguished, superior, renowned, eminent, exalted, noteworthy, pre-eminent • *She has always had a high reputation for her excellent stories.*
8 = **high-pitched**, piercing, shrill, penetrating, treble, soprano, strident, sharp, acute, piping • *Her high voice really irritated Maria.*
OPPOSITES: low, deep, low-pitched
9 = **cheerful**, excited, merry, exhilarated, exuberant, joyful, bouncy *(informal)*, boisterous, elated, light-hearted, stoked *(Austral. & N.Z. informal)* • *Her spirits were high with the hope of seeing Nick.*
OPPOSITES: low, sad, dejected

10 = **intoxicated**, stoned *(slang)*, spaced out *(slang)*, tripping *(informal)*, turned on *(slang)*, on a trip *(informal)*, delirious, euphoric, freaked out *(informal)*, hyped up *(slang)*, off your face *(slang)*, loved-up *(informal)*, zonked *(slang)*, inebriated • *He was too high on drugs and alcohol to remember them.*
11 = **luxurious**, rich, grand, lavish, extravagant, opulent, hedonistic, champagne • *an emphatic contrast to his Park Avenue high life*
▸ AS AN ADVERB = **way up**, aloft, far up, to a great height • *on combat patrol flying high above the landing sites*
▸ AS A NOUN 1 = **peak**, height, top, summit, crest, record level, apex • *Sales of Russian vodka have reached an all-time high.*
2 = **intoxication**, trip *(informal)*, euphoria, delirium, ecstasy • *The 'thrill' sought is said to be similar to a drug high.*
▸ IN PHRASES: **high and dry** = **abandoned**, stranded, helpless, forsaken, bereft, destitute, in the lurch • *You could be left high and dry in a strange town.*
high and low = **everywhere**, all over (the place), far and wide, exhaustively, in every nook and cranny • *I have searched high and low for clothes to fit him.*
high and mighty = **self-important**, superior, arrogant, stuck-up *(informal)*, conceited, imperious, overbearing, haughty, snobbish, disdainful • *I think you're a bit too high and mighty yourself.*
high up = **important**, prominent, powerful, significant, distinguished, superior, influential, notable, big-time *(informal)*, eminent, major league *(informal)*, exalted, consequential, skookum *(Canad.)* • *His cousin is somebody quite high up in the navy.*
on a high = **ecstatic**, thrilled, elated, over the moon *(informal)*, delirious, euphoric, on cloud nine, in seventh heaven, stoked *(Austral. & N.Z. informal)* • *For several weeks he was on a high.*

highborn = **noble**, aristocratic, patrician, gentle *(archaic)*, pedigreed, thoroughbred, blue-blooded, well-born • *The girls are always described as 'perfumed' and 'highborn'.*

highbrow AS AN ADJECTIVE = **intellectual**, cultured, sophisticated, deep, cultivated, brainy *(informal)*, highbrowed, bookish • *He presents his own highbrow literary programme.*
OPPOSITES: ignorant, philistine, unintellectual
▸ AS A NOUN = **intellectual**, scholar, egghead *(informal)*, brain *(informal)*, mastermind, Brahmin *(U.S.)*, aesthete, savant, brainbox *(slang)* • *the sniggers of the highbrows*
OPPOSITES: illiterate, moron, philistine

QUOTATIONS
A highbrow is a kind of person who looks at a sausage and thinks of Picasso
[A.P. Herbert *The Highbrow*]

high-class = **high-quality**, top *(slang)*, choice, select, exclusive, elite, superior, posh *(informal, chiefly Brit.)*, classy *(slang)*, top-flight, upper-class, swish *(informal, chiefly Brit.)*, first-rate, up-market, top-drawer, ritzy *(slang)*, tip-top, high-toned, A1 *or* A-one *(informal)* • *a high-class jeweller's*
OPPOSITES: common, cheap, inferior

high-end = **deluxe**, expensive, top-quality, top-notch *(informal)* • *high-end personal computers and workstations*

higher-up = **superior**, senior, manager, director, executive, boss, gaffer *(informal, chiefly Brit.)*, baas *(S. African)*, sherang *(Austral. & N.Z.)* • *Bureau higher-ups have been quoted criticizing the director.*

highfalutin = **pompous**, lofty, high-flown, pretentious, grandiose, swanky *(informal)*, florid, bombastic, supercilious, high-sounding, arty-farty *(informal)*, magniloquent • *This isn't highfalutin art.*

high-flown = **extravagant**, elaborate, pretentious, exaggerated, inflated, lofty, grandiose, overblown, florid, high-falutin *(informal)*, arty-farty *(informal)*, magniloquent • *Many personnel were put off by such high-flown rhetoric.*
OPPOSITES: simple, straightforward, restrained

high ground = **advantage**, lead, edge, dominance, superiority, upper hand, ascendancy, pre-eminence, moral high ground • *The President must seek to regain the high ground in the political debate.*

high-handed = **dictatorial**, domineering, overbearing, arbitrary, oppressive, autocratic, bossy *(informal)*, imperious, tyrannical, despotic, peremptory • *He wants to be seen as less bossy and high-handed.*

high jinks = **fun and games**, sport, spree, junketing, revelry, skylarking *(informal)*, jollity, horseplay, merrymaking • *Their annual parties are notorious for high jinks.*

highlands = **uplands**, hills, heights, hill country, mountainous region • *Uganda's beautiful highlands are host to a wide range of wildlife.*

highlight AS A VERB = **emphasize**, stress, accent, feature, set off, show up, underline, spotlight, play up, accentuate, foreground, focus attention on, call attention to, give prominence to, bring to the fore • *Two events have highlighted the tensions in recent days.*
OPPOSITES: play down, gloss over, overlook
▸ AS A NOUN = **high point**, peak, climax, feature, focus, best part, focal point, main feature, high spot, memorable part • *one of the highlights of the tournament*
OPPOSITES: low point, disappointment, lowlight

highly 1 = **extremely**, very, greatly, seriously *(informal)*, vastly, exceptionally, extraordinarily, immensely, decidedly, tremendously, supremely, eminently • *He was a highly successful salesman.*
2 = **favourably**, well, warmly, enthusiastically, approvingly, appreciatively • *one of the most highly regarded chefs in the French capital*

highly-strung = **nervous**, stressed, tense, sensitive, wired *(slang)*, restless, neurotic, taut, edgy, temperamental, excitable, nervy *(Brit. informal)*, twitchy *(informal)*, on tenterhooks, easily upset, on pins and needles, adrenalized • *He was sensitive and highly-strung.*
OPPOSITES: relaxed, calm, laid-back *(informal)*

high-minded = **principled**, moral, worthy, noble, good, fair, pure, ethical, upright, elevated, honourable, righteous, idealistic, virtuous, magnanimous • *The President's hopes were high-minded, but too vague.*
OPPOSITES: dishonest, unethical, dishonourable

high-pitched = **piercing**, high, sharp, penetrating, shrill, high-frequency, falsetto • *A woman squealed in a high-pitched voice.*

high point = **highlight**, peak, climax, best part, focal point, high spot, memorable part • *The high point of this trip was a day at the races.*

high-powered = **dynamic**, driving, powerful, enterprising, effective, go-ahead, aggressive, vigorous, energetic, forceful, fast-track, go-getting *(informal)*, high-octane *(informal)*, highly capable • *a high-powered lawyer*

high-pressure = **forceful**, aggressive, compelling, intensive, persistent, persuasive, high-powered, insistent, bludgeoning, pushy *(informal)*, in-your-face *(slang)*, coercive, importunate • *They use high-pressure sales tactics.*

high-priced = **expensive**, dear, costly • *high-priced luxuries such as smoked salmon and fillet steak*

high-profile = **famous**, prominent, eminent, celebrated, distinguished, illustrious • *one of football's high profile chairmen*

high-rise = **skyscraper**, multi *(Scot.)*, multi-storey • *That big high-rise above us is where Brian lives.*

high-speed = **fast**, express, quick, rapid, swift, brisk • *It takes a mile and a half to stop a high-speed train.*

high-spirited = **lively**, spirited, vivacious, vital, daring, dashing, bold, energetic, animated, vibrant, exuberant, bouncy, boisterous, fun-loving, ebullient, sparky, effervescent, alive and kicking, full of life, spunky *(informal)*, full of beans *(informal)*, frolicsome, mettlesome • *Her high-spirited demeanour was not ideally suited for palace life.*

high spirits = **exuberance**, abandon, joie de vivre *(French)*, exhilaration, hilarity, good cheer, boisterousness, rare good humour • *This morning he left the house in such high spirits.*

highway = **main road**, motorway, roadway, thoroughfare • *I crossed the highway, dodging the traffic.*

highwayman = **bandit**, robber, brigand, outlaw • *He had a mask tied round his face like a highwayman.*

hijack *or* **highjack** = **seize**, take over, commandeer, expropriate, skyjack • *Two men tried to hijack a plane on a flight from Riga to Murmansk.*

hike AS A NOUN 1 = **walk**, march, trek, ramble, tramp, traipse, journey on foot • *a hike around the cluster of hills*
2 = **increase**, rise, raise • *a hike in taxes and spending cuts*
OPPOSITES: cut, reduction
▸ AS A VERB 1 = **walk**, march, trek, ramble, tramp, leg it *(informal)*, back-pack, hoof it *(slang)* • *You could hike through the Fish River Canyon.*
2 = **increase**, raise, inflate, bump up *(informal)*, up • *It has now been forced to hike its rates by 5.25 per cent.*
OPPOSITES: cut
▸ IN PHRASES: **hike something up** = **hitch up**, raise, lift, pull up, jack up • *He hiked up his trouser legs.*

hiker = **walker**, rambler, backpacker, wayfarer, hillwalker • *There are plenty of public huts to protect hikers from the elements.*

hilarious 1 = **funny**, entertaining, amusing, hysterical, humorous, exhilarating, comical, side-splitting • *He had a fund of hilarious tales.*
2 = **merry**, uproarious, happy, gay, noisy, jolly, joyous, joyful, jovial, rollicking, convivial, mirthful • *Everyone had a hilarious time.*
OPPOSITES: serious, quiet, sad

hilarity = **merriment**, high spirits, mirth, gaiety, laughter, amusement, glee, exuberance, exhilaration, cheerfulness, jollity, levity, conviviality, joviality, boisterousness, joyousness, jollification • *The report in The Times caught the mood of hilarity.*

hill AS A NOUN 1 = **mount**, down *(archaic)*, fell, height, mound, prominence, elevation, eminence, hilltop, tor, knoll, hillock, brae *(Scot.)*, kopje or koppie *(S. African)* • *They climbed to the top of the hill.*
2 = **slope**, incline, gradient, rise, climb, brae *(Scot.)*, acclivity • *the shady street that led up the hill to the office building*
3 = **heap**, pile, mound, hummock • *an ant hill*
▸ IN PHRASES: **over the hill** = **too old**, getting on, ancient, past it *(informal)*, senile, decrepit, past your prime • *He doesn't take kindly to suggestions that he is over the hill.*

hillock = **mound**, knoll, hummock, barrow, knap *(dialect)*, tump *(Western English dialect)*, monticule • *He had spent the night huddled behind a hillock for shelter.*

hilly = **mountainous**, rolling, steep, undulating • *The areas are hilly and densely wooded.*

hilt AS A NOUN = **handle**, grip, haft, handgrip, helve • *the hilt of the small, sharp knife*
▸ IN PHRASES: **to the hilt** = **fully**, completely, totally, entirely, wholly • *James was overdrawn and mortgaged to the hilt.*

hind = **back**, rear, hinder, posterior, caudal *(Anatomy)* • *Suddenly the cow kicked up its hind legs.*

hinder = **obstruct**, stop, check, block, prevent, arrest, delay, oppose, frustrate, handicap, interrupt, slow down, deter, hamstring, hamper, thwart, retard, impede, hobble, stymie, encumber, throw a spanner in the works, trammel, hold up *or* back • *Landslides are continuing to hinder the arrival of relief supplies.*
OPPOSITES: help, aid, speed

hindrance = **obstacle**, check, bar, block, difficulty, drag, barrier, restriction, handicap, limitation, hazard, restraint, hitch, drawback, snag, deterrent, interruption, obstruction, stoppage, stumbling block, impediment, encumbrance, trammel • *Higher rates have been a hindrance to economic recovery.*
OPPOSITES: help, aid, boost

Hinduism

HINDU DENOMINATIONS AND SECTS

Hare Krishna	Saktas
Saivaism	Vaishnavism

hinge on = **depend on**, be subject to, hang on, turn on, rest on, revolve around, be contingent on, pivot on • *The plan hinges on a deal being struck with a new company.*

hint AS A NOUN 1 = **clue**, mention, suggestion, implication, indication, reminder, tip-off, pointer, allusion, innuendo, inkling, intimation, insinuation, word to the wise • *I'd dropped a hint about having an exhibition of his work.*
2 = **advice**, help, tip(s), suggestion(s), pointer(s) • *I'm hoping to get some fashion hints.*
3 = **trace**, touch, suggestion, taste, breath, dash, whisper, suspicion, tinge, whiff, speck, undertone, soupçon *(French)* • *I glanced at her and saw no hint of irony on her face.*
▸ AS A VERB *sometimes with* **at** = **suggest**, mention, indicate, imply, intimate, tip off, let it be known, insinuate, allude to the fact, tip the wink *(informal)* • *The President hinted he might make some changes in the government.*

hinterland = **the wilds**, backwater, remote areas, the backwoods, the back of beyond • *the French Mediterranean coast and its hinterland*

hip = **trendy** *(Brit. informal)*, with it, fashionable, in, aware, informed, wise *(slang)*, switched-on *(informal)*, sussed *(Brit. slang)*, clued-up *(informal)*, funky • *a hip young character with tight-cropped hair*

hipbone
▸ TECHNICAL NAME: innominate bone

hippy *or* **hippie** = **flower child**, bohemian, dropout, free spirit, beatnik, basketweaver *(Austral. derogatory slang)* • *Being a hippie was about 'finding yourself'.*

hire AS A VERB 1 = **employ**, commission, take on, engage, appoint, sign up, enlist • *hired on short-term contracts*
2 = **rent**, charter, lease, let, engage • *To hire a car you must produce a current driving licence.*
▸ AS A NOUN 1 = **rental**, hiring, rent, lease • *Fishing tackle is available for hire.*
2 = **charge**, rental, price, cost, fee • *Surf board hire is $12 per day.*
▸ IN PHRASES: **hire something** *or* **someone out** = **rent out**, lease, let out • *We will be able to hire out the area for various functions.*

hire purchase = **credit**, H.P., finance, easy terms, the never-never, installment plan • *buying a car on hire purchase*

hirsute = **hairy**, bearded, shaggy, unshaven, bristly, bewhiskered, hispid *(Biology)* • *a large, hirsute Scot with an aggressive, blustery personality*

hiss AS A VERB 1 = **whistle**, wheeze, rasp, whiz, whirr, sibilate • *The air hissed out of the pipe.*
2 = **jeer**, mock, ridicule, deride, decry, revile • *The delegates booed and hissed him.*
▸ AS A NOUN = **fizz**, buzz, hissing, fizzing, sibilance, sibilation • *the hiss of a beer bottle opening*

historian = **chronicler**, recorder, biographer, antiquarian, historiographer, annalist, chronologist • *She will become the family historian.*

QUOTATIONS
Historians are left forever chasing shadows, painfully aware of their inability ever to reconstruct a dead world in its completeness
[Simon Schama *Dead Certainties*]
History repeats itself. Historians repeat each other
[Philip Guedalla *Supers and Supermen*]

historic = **significant**, notable, momentous, famous, celebrated, extraordinary, outstanding, remarkable, ground-breaking, consequential, red-letter, epoch-making • *the historic changes in Eastern Europe*
OPPOSITES: ordinary, unknown, unimportant

historical = **factual**, real, documented, actual, authentic, chronicled, attested, archival, verifiable • *a fascinating collection of historical photographs*
OPPOSITES: current, contemporary, fabulous

history 1 = **the past**, the old days, antiquity, yesterday, the good old days, yesteryear, ancient history, olden days, days of old, days of yore, bygone times • *Is history about to repeat itself?*
2 = **chronicle**, record, story, account, relation, narrative, saga, recital, narration, annals, recapitulation • *his magnificent history of broadcasting in Canada*
3 = **life story**, story, biography, autobiography, memoirs • *I studied her history closely.*

QUOTATIONS
The history of all hitherto existing societies is the history of class struggles
[Karl Marx and Friedrich Engels *The Communist Manifesto*]
History is philosophy from examples
[Dionysius of Halicarnassus *Ars Rhetorica*]
There is properly no history; only biography
[Ralph Waldo Emerson *Essays*]
History is more or less bunk. It's tradition. We don't want tradition. We want to live in the present and the only history that is worth a tinker's damn is the history we make today
[Henry Ford]
History is past politics, and politics is present history
[E.A. Freeman *Methods of Historical Study*]
What experience and history teach is this – that people and governments never have learned anything from history, or acted on principles deduced from it
[G.W.F. Hegel *Philosophy of History*]
History is a nightmare from which I am trying to awake
[James Joyce *Ulysses*]
The world's history is the world's judgement
[Friedrich von Schiller]
Indeed, history is nothing more than a tableau of crimes and misfortunes
[Voltaire *L'Ingénu*]
That great dust-heap called 'history'
[Augustine Birrell *Obiter Dicta*]
History [is] a distillation of rumour
[Thomas Carlyle *History of the French Revolution*]
History gets thicker as it approaches recent times
[A.J.P. Taylor *English History 1914-45*]
History repeats itself, first as tragedy, second as farce
[Karl Marx]

PROVERBS
History repeats itself

▹ *See panel* **History**

histrionic AS AN ADJECTIVE = **theatrical**, affected, dramatic, forced, camp *(informal)*, actorly, artificial, unnatural, melodramatic, actressy • *Dorothea let out a histrionic groan.*
▸ AS A PLURAL NOUN = **dramatics**, scene, tantrums, performance, temperament, theatricality, staginess, hissy fit *(informal)* • *When I explained everything, there were no histrionics.*

hit AS A VERB 1 = **strike**, beat, knock, punch, belt *(informal)*, deck *(slang)*, bang, batter, clip *(informal)*, slap, bash *(informal)*, sock *(slang)*, chin *(slang)*, smack, thump, clout *(informal)*, cuff, flog, whack, clobber *(slang)*, smite *(archaic)*, wallop *(informal)*, swat, lay one on *(slang)*, beat *or* knock seven bells out of *(informal)* • *She hit him hard across his left arm.*
2 = **collide with**, run into, bump into, clash with, smash into, crash against, bang into, meet head-on • *The car hit a traffic sign before skidding out of control.*
3 = **affect**, damage, harm, ruin, devastate, overwhelm, touch, impact on, impinge on, leave a mark on, make an impact *or* impression on • *The big cities have been hit by a wave of panic-buying.* • *the earthquake which hit northern Peru*
4 = **strike**, come to, occur to, dawn on, enter your head • *It hit me that I had a choice.*
5 = **reach**, strike, gain, achieve, secure, arrive at, accomplish, attain • *Oil prices hit record levels yesterday.*
▸ AS A NOUN 1 = **shot**, blow, impact, collision • *The house took a direct hit then the rocket exploded.*
2 = **blow**, knock, stroke, belt *(informal)*, rap, slap, bump, smack, clout *(informal)*, cuff, swipe *(informal)*, wallop *(informal)* • *a hit on the head*
3 = **success**, winner, triumph, smash *(informal)*, sensation, sellout, smasheroo *(informal)* • *The song became a massive hit in 1945.*
▸ IN PHRASES: **hit back** = **retaliate**, strike back, take revenge, reciprocate, even the score, get your own back *(informal)*, wreak vengeance, exact retribution, give as good as you get *(informal)*, take an eye for an eye, make reprisal, give tit for tat, return like for like • *They hit back by offering a strong statement denying any involvement.*
hit back at someone = **pay someone back**, get back at, take revenge on, get even with *(informal)*, give someone a taste of his *or* her own medicine • *The President hit back at his detractors.*
hit it off = **get on (well) with**, take to, click *(slang)*, warm to, be on good terms, get on like a house on fire *(informal)* • *How well did you hit it off with one another?*
hit on someone = **make a pass at**, make an indecent proposal to, make an improper suggestion to • *She was hitting on me and I was surprised and flattered.*
hit on *or* **upon something** = **think up**, discover, arrive at, guess, realize, invent, come upon, stumble on, chance upon, light upon, strike upon • *We finally hit on a solution.*
hit out at someone = **attack**, condemn, denounce, lash out, castigate, rail against, assail, inveigh against, strike out at • *The President hit out at what he sees as foreign interference.*

hit-and-miss *or* **hit-or-miss** = **haphazard**, random, uneven, casual, indiscriminate, cursory, perfunctory, aimless, disorganized, undirected, scattershot • *Farming can be very much a hit-and-miss affair.*
OPPOSITES: planned, arranged, systematic

hitch AS A NOUN = **problem**, catch, trouble, check, difficulty, delay, hold-up, obstacle, hazard, drawback, hassle *(informal)*, snag, uphill *(S. African)*, stoppage, mishap, impediment, hindrance • *The five-hour operation went without a hitch.*
▸ AS A VERB 1 = **hitchhike**, thumb a lift • *I hitched a lift into town.*
2 = **fasten**, join, attach, unite, couple, tie, connect, harness, tether, yoke, make fast • *We hitched the horse to the cart.*
▸ IN PHRASES: **get hitched** = **marry**, get married, tie the knot *(informal)* • *The report shows that fewer couples are getting hitched.*
hitch something up = **pull up**, tug, jerk, yank, hoick • *He hitched his trousers up over his potbelly.*

hither AS AN ADVERB = **here**, over here, to this place, close, closer, near, nearer, nigh *(archaic)* • *I came hither to tell you the news.*

HISTORY

HISTORICAL CHARACTERS

Alexander the Great
Alfred the Great
Mark Antony
Attila the Hun
Augustus
Thomas à Becket
Billy the Kid
The Black Prince
Bonnie Prince Charlie (Charles Edward Stuart)
Lucrezia Borgia
Boudicca *or* Boadicea
Brutus
Buddha
Buffalo Bill (William Frederick Cody)
Julius Caesar
Catherine the Great
Charlemagne
Winston Churchill
El Cid
Cleopatra
Clive of India
Christopher Columbus
Captain James Cook
Hernando Cortés
Crazy Horse
Davy Crockett
Oliver Cromwell
George Armstrong Custer
Francis Drake
Guy Fawkes
Yuri Gagarin
Mahatma Gandhi
Giuseppe Garibaldi
Genghis Khan
Geronimo
Gordon of Khartoum
Che Guevara
Haile Selassie
Hannibal
Henry VIII
Hereward the Wake
Hiawatha
Wild Bill (James Butler) Hickok
Adolf Hitler
Ivan the Terrible
Jesse James
Jesus
Joan of Arc
Martin Luther King
Lawrence of Arabia
Robert E(dward) Lee
Vladimir Ilyich Lenin
Abraham Lincoln
Martin Luther
Mary, Queen of Scots
Mao Ze Dong *or* Mao Tse-tung
Marie Antoinette
Mohammed *or* Muhammad
Montezuma
Benito Mussolini
Napoleon Bonaparte
Horatio Nelson
Florence Nightingale
Captain (Lawrence Edward Grace) Oates
Pericles
Marco Polo
Pompey
Walter Raleigh
Grigori Efimovich Rasputin
Richard the Lionheart
Robert the Bruce
Saladin
Robert Falcon Scott
Sitting Bull
Socrates
Joseph Stalin
Tomás de Torquemada
Leon Trotsky
William Wallace
Warwick the Kingmaker
George Washington
Duke of Wellington
William the Conqueror
Orville and Wilbur Wright
Emiliano Zapata

HISTORICAL EVENTS

Agincourt
Alamo
American Civil War
Armistice
Battle of Hastings
Black Death
Bloody Sunday
Boer War
Boston Tea Party
Boxer Rebellion
Charge of the Light Brigade
Civil War
Cold War
Crimean War
Crusades
Cultural Revolution
D-day
Declaration of Independence
Depression
Diet of Worms
Easter Rising
French Revolution
General Strike
Gettysburg Address
Glorious Revolution
Gordon Riots
Great Fire of London
Great Schism
Great Trek
Gunpowder Plot
Hiroshima
Holocaust
Hundred Years War
Hungarian Uprising
Indian Mutiny
Industrial Revolution
Jacobite Rebellion
Korean War
Kristallnacht
Long March
Magna Carta
Munich Agreement
Night of the Long Knives
Napoleonic Wars
Norman Conquest
Pearl Harbor
Peasants' Revolt
Peterloo Massacre
Potato Famine
Reformation
Reign of Terror
Renaissance
Restoration
Risorgimento
Russian Revolution
Saint Valentine's Day Massacre
South Sea Bubble
Spanish Armada
Spanish Civil War
Spanish Inquisition
Suez Crisis
Thirty Years' War
Tiananmen Square Massacre
Trafalgar
Treaty of Versailles
Vietnam War
Wall Street Crash
Wars of the Roses
Watergate
Waterloo

▸ **IN PHRASES: hither and thither = this way and that**, back and forth, hither and yon • *Refugees ran hither and thither in search of safety.*

hitherto = previously, so far, until now, thus far, up to now, till now, heretofore • *The polytechnics have hitherto been at an unfair disadvantage.*

hive 1 = colony, swarm • *the dance performed by honeybees as they returned to the hive*
2 = centre, hub, powerhouse *(slang)* • *In the morning the house was a hive of activity.*

hive off = sell (off), dispose of, put up for sale • *Klockner plans to hive off its loss-making steel business.*

hoard AS A VERB = save, store, collect, gather, treasure, accumulate, garner, amass, stockpile, buy up, put away, hive, cache, lay up, put by, stash away *(informal)* • *They've begun to hoard food and gasoline.*
▸ **AS A NOUN = store**, fund, supply, reserve, mass, pile, heap, fall-back, accumulation, stockpile, stash, cache, treasure-trove • *a hoard of silver and jewels*

hoarder = saver, miser, collector, squirrel *(informal)*, magpie *(Brit.)*, tight-arse *(taboo slang)*, tight-ass *(U.S. taboo slang)*, niggard • *Most hoarders have favourite hiding places.*

hoarse = rough, harsh, husky, grating, growling, raucous, rasping, gruff, throaty, gravelly, guttural, croaky • *Nick's voice was hoarse with screaming.*
OPPOSITES: smooth, harmonious, clear

hoary 1 = old, aged, ancient, antique, venerable, antiquated • *the hoary old myth that women are unpredictable*
2 = white-haired, white, grey, silvery, frosty, grey-haired, grizzled, hoar • *hoary beards*

hoax AS A NOUN = trick, joke, fraud, con *(informal)*, deception, spoof *(informal)*, prank, swindle, ruse, practical joke, canard, fast one *(informal)*, imposture, fastie *(Austral. slang)* • *His claim to have a bomb was a hoax.*
▸ **AS A VERB = deceive**, trick, fool, take in *(informal)*, con *(slang)*, wind up *(Brit. slang)*, kid *(informal)*, bluff, dupe, gull *(archaic)*, delude, swindle, bamboozle *(informal)*, gammon *(Brit. informal)*, hoodwink, take (someone) for a ride *(informal)*, befool, hornswoggle *(slang)*, scam *(slang)* • *He recently hoaxed Nelson Mandela by pretending to be Tony Blair.*

hoaxer = trickster, joker, prankster, spoofer *(informal)*, humbug, bamboozler *(informal)*, hoodwinker, practical joker • *She will enjoy permanent fame as a literary hoaxer.*

hobble 1 = limp, stagger, stumble, shuffle, falter, shamble, totter, dodder, halt • *He got up slowly and hobbled over to the table.*
2 = restrict, hamstring, shackle, fetter • *The poverty of 10 million citizens hobbles our economy.*

hobby = pastime, relaxation, leisure pursuit, sideline, diversion, avocation, favourite occupation, (leisure) activity • *My hobbies are letter-writing, football, music, photography, and tennis.*

hobby-horse = **pet subject**, obsession, preoccupation, fixation, thing *(informal)* • *Honesty is a favourite hobby-horse for him.*

hobnob = **socialize**, mix, associate, hang out *(informal)*, mingle, consort, hang about, keep company, fraternize • *an opportunity to hobnob with the company's president*

hog AS A NOUN = **pig**, swine, porker • *a hog farm in Alabama*
▸ AS A VERB = **monopolize**, dominate, tie up, corner, corner the market in, be a dog in the manger • *Have you done hogging the bathroom?*

hogwash = **nonsense**, rubbish, malarkey, garbage *(informal)*, balls *(taboo slang)*, bull *(slang)*, shit *(taboo slang)*, rot, crap *(slang)*, trash, bunk *(informal)*, bullshit *(taboo slang)*, hot air *(informal)*, tosh *(slang, chiefly Brit.)*, pap, cobblers *(Brit. taboo slang)*, bilge *(informal)*, drivel, twaddle, tripe *(informal)*, guff *(slang)*, moonshine, hokum *(slang, chiefly U.S. & Canad.)*, bunkum *(chiefly U.S.)*, piffle *(informal)*, poppycock *(informal)*, balderdash, bosh *(informal)*, eyewash *(informal)*, kak *(S. African taboo slang)*, hooey *(slang)*, tommyrot, bizzo *(Austral. slang)*, bull's wool *(Austral. & N.Z. slang)* • *That's a oad of hogwash.*

h

hoi polloi = **the common people**, the masses, the (common) herd, the underclass, the populace, the proletariat, the lower orders, the rabble, the great unwashed *(informal, derogatory)*, the plebs, the third estate, riffraff, the proles *(derogatory slang, chiefly Brit.)*, canaille *(French)*, commonalty • *Inflated costs are designed to keep the hoi polloi at bay.*

hoist AS A VERB = **raise**, lift, erect, elevate, heave, upraise • *He hoisted himself to a sitting position.*
▸ AS A NOUN = **lift**, crane, elevator, winch, tackle • *It takes three nurses and a hoist to get me into this chair.*

hoity-toity = **haughty**, proud, arrogant, stuck-up *(informal)*, lofty, conceited, snooty *(informal)*, scornful, snobbish, disdainful, supercilious, high and mighty *(informal)*, overweening, toffee-nosed *(slang, chiefly Brit.)*, uppish *(Brit. informal)* • *My auntie up from the south was trying to be all hoity-toity.*

hold AS A VERB 1 = **carry**, keep, grip, grasp, cling to, clasp • *Hold the baby while I load the car.*
2 = **support**, take, bear, shoulder, sustain, prop, brace • *Hold the weight with a straight arm above your head.*
OPPOSITES: break, give way, loosen
3 = **embrace**, grasp, clutch, hug, squeeze, cradle, clasp, enfold • *If only he would hold her close to him.*
4 = **restrain**, constrain, check, bind, curb, hamper, hinder • *He was held in an arm lock.*
OPPOSITES: free, release, let go
5 = **detain**, arrest, confine, imprison, impound, pound, hold in custody, put in jail • *the return of two seamen held on spying charges*
OPPOSITES: release, free
6 = **accommodate**, take, contain, seat, comprise, have a capacity for • *The small bottles don't seem to hold much.*
7 = **consider**, think, believe, view, judge, regard, maintain, assume, reckon, esteem, deem, presume, entertain the idea • *She holds that it is not admissible to ordain women.*
OPPOSITES: deny, reject, put down
8 = **occupy**, have, fill, maintain, retain, possess, hold down *(informal)* • *She has never held a ministerial post.*
9 = **possess**, have, own, bear, retain, be in possession of • *Applicants should normally hold an Honours degree.*
OPPOSITES: give, offer, give away
10 = **conduct**, convene, have, call, run, celebrate, carry on, assemble, preside over, officiate at, solemnize • *They held frequent consultations concerning technical problems.*
OPPOSITES: cancel, postpone, call off
11 *sometimes with* **up** = **continue**, last, remain, stay, wear, resist, endure, persist, persevere • *Our luck couldn't hold for ever.*
12 = **apply**, exist, be the case, stand up, operate, be in force, remain true, hold good, remain valid • *Today, most people think that argument no longer holds.*
13 = **keep**, catch, maintain, capture, absorb, engross • *Didn't it hold your attention?*
▸ AS A NOUN 1 = **grip**, grasp, clutch, clasp • *He released his hold on the camera.*
2 = **foothold**, footing, purchase, leverage, vantage, anchorage • *The idea didn't really get a hold in this country.*
3 = **control**, authority, influence, pull *(informal)*, sway, dominance, clout *(informal)*, mastery, dominion, ascendancy, mana *(N.Z.)* • *It's always useful to have a hold over people.*
▸ IN PHRASES: **hold back** = **desist**, forbear, hesitate, stop yourself, restrain yourself, refrain from doing something • *She wanted to say something but held back.*
hold forth = **speak**, go on, discourse, lecture, preach, spout *(informal)*, harangue, declaim, spiel *(informal)*, descant, orate, speechify, korero *(N.Z.)* • *He is capable of holding forth with great eloquence.*
hold off = **put off**, delay, postpone, defer, avoid, refrain, keep from • *The hospital staff held off taking him in for an X-ray.*
hold on = **wait (a minute)**, hang on *(informal)*, sit tight *(informal)*, hold your horses *(informal)*, just a moment *or* second • *Hold on while I have a look.*
hold onto something *or* **someone** 1 = **grab**, hold, grip, clutch, cling to • *He was struggling to hold onto the rock above his head.*
2 = **retain**, keep, hang onto, not give away, keep possession of • *to enable Spurs to hold onto their striker*
hold out = **last**, continue, carry on, endure, hang on, persist, persevere, stay the course, stand fast • *He can only hold out for a few more weeks.*
hold out against something *or* **someone** = **withstand**, resist, fend off, keep at bay, fight • *They held out against two companies of troops.*
hold someone back = **hinder**, prevent, restrain, check, hamstring, hamper, inhibit, thwart, obstruct, impede • *Does her illness hold her back from making friends or enjoying life?*
hold someone down = **oppress**, suppress, subdue, dominate, repress, keep down, subjugate, keep under control, tyrannize • *some vast conspiracy to hold down the younger generation*
hold someone up = **delay**, slow down, hinder, stop, detain, retard, impede, set back • *Why were you holding everyone up?* 1 = **restrain**, check, curb, control, suppress, rein (in), repress, stem the flow of • *Stagnation in home sales is holding back economic recovery.*
2 = **withhold**, hold in, suppress, stifle, repress, keep the lid on *(informal)*, keep back • *You seem to be holding something back.*
hold something down 1 = **keep**, hold, maintain, retain • *He could never hold down a job.*
2 = **keep down**, fix, freeze, keep low, peg down • *rates necessary to hold down inflation*
hold something in = **suppress**, repress, smother, hold something back, keep something in, choke something back, fight something back • *Go ahead and cry. Don't hold it in.*
hold something out = **offer**, give, present, extend, proffer • *Max held out his cup for a refill.*
hold something over = **postpone**, delay, suspend, put off, defer, adjourn, waive, take a rain check on *(U.S. & Canad. informal)* • *Further voting might be held over until tomorrow.*
hold something up 1 = **display**, show, exhibit, flourish, show off, hold aloft, present, showboat • *Hold it up so we can see it.*
2 = **support**, prop, brace, bolster, sustain, shore up, buttress, jack up • *Mills have iron pillars holding up the roof.*
3 = **rob**, mug *(informal)*, stick up *(slang, chiefly U.S.)*, waylay

• *A thief ran off with hundreds of pounds after holding up a petrol station.*
hold something *or* **someone dear = revere**, prize, treasure, cherish, appreciate, rate highly, set great store by, value highly, put on a pedestal *(informal)*, care very much for • *Labour has dumped just about all it held dear a decade ago.*
hold something *or* **someone off = fend off**, repel, rebuff, stave off, repulse, keep off • *holding off a tremendous challenge*
hold up 1 = last, survive, endure, bear up, wear • *Children's wear is holding up well in the recession.*
2 = hold water *(informal)*, be valid, be logical, be credible, be consistent • *I'm not sure if the argument holds up, but it's stimulating.*
hold with something = approve of, be in favour of, support, subscribe to, countenance, agree to *or* with, take kindly to • *I don't hold with the way they do things nowadays.*
hold your own = keep up, do well, hold out, keep pace, stay put, stand firm, hold fast, stand your ground, stick to your guns *(informal)*, keep your head above water, maintain your position • *The Frenchman held his own against the challenger.*
lay hold of something *or* **someone = grasp**, grab, seize, grip, snatch, get hold of, get • *They laid hold of him with rough hands.*

holder 1 = owner, bearer, possessor, keeper, purchaser, occupant, proprietor, custodian, incumbent • *the holders of the Championship* • *the club has 73,500 season-ticket holders*
2 = case, cover, container, sheath, receptacle, housing • *a toothbrush holder*

holding *often plural* **= property**, securities, investments, resources, estate, assets, possessions, stocks and shares, land interests

hold-up 1 = robbery, theft, mugging *(informal)*, stick-up *(slang, chiefly U.S.)* • *an armed hold-up at a National Australia bank*
2 = delay, wait, hitch, trouble, difficulty, setback, snag, traffic jam, obstruction, stoppage, bottleneck • *They arrived late due to a motorway hold-up.*

hole **AS A NOUN 1 = cavity**, depression, pit, hollow, pocket, chamber, cave, shaft, cavern, excavation • *He took a shovel, dug a hole, and buried his possessions.*
2 = opening, split, crack, break, tear, gap, rent, breach, outlet, vent, puncture, aperture, fissure, orifice, perforation • *They got in through a hole in the wall.* • *kids with holes in the knees of their jeans*
3 = burrow, nest, den, earth, shelter, retreat, covert, lair • *a rabbit hole*
4 = fault, error, flaw, defect, loophole, discrepancy, inconsistency, fallacy • *There were some holes in that theory.*
5 = hovel, dump *(informal)*, dive *(slang)*, slum, joint *(slang)* • *Why don't you leave this awful hole and come to live with me?*
6 = predicament, spot *(informal)*, fix *(informal)*, mess, jam *(informal)*, dilemma, scrape *(informal)*, tangle, hot water *(informal)*, quandary, tight spot, imbroglio • *He admitted that the government was in 'a dreadful hole'.*
▸ **IN PHRASES: hole up = hide**, shelter, take refuge, go into hiding, take cover, go to earth • *holing up in his Paris flat with the phone off the hook*
pick holes in something = criticize, knock *(informal)*, rubbish *(informal)*, put down, run down, slate *(informal)*, slag (off) *(slang)*, denigrate, disprove, disparage, diss *(slang, chiefly U.S.)*, find fault with, bad-mouth *(slang, chiefly U.S. & Canad.)*, flame *(informal)*, niggle at, cavil at, pull to pieces, asperse, nit-pick *(informal)* • *He then goes on to pick holes in the article.*

hole-and-corner = furtive, secret, secretive, clandestine, sneaky *(informal)*, underhand, surreptitious, stealthy, under the counter *(informal)*, backstairs • *I think we were treated in a rather hole-and-corner fashion.*
OPPOSITES: open, public, frank

holiday 1 = vacation, leave, break, time off, recess, away day, schoolie *(Austral.)*, accumulated day off *or* ADO *(Austral.)* • *I've just come back from a holiday in the United States.*
2 = festival, bank holiday, festivity, public holiday, fête, celebration, anniversary, feast, red-letter day, mela, name day, saint's day, gala • *New Year's Day is a public holiday throughout Britain.*
▸ **RELATED ADJECTIVE:** ferial

QUOTATIONS
He capers, he dances, he has eyes of youth; he writes verses, he speaks of holiday, he smells April and May
[William Shakespeare *The Merry Wives of Windsor*]

holier-than-thou = self-righteous, smug, sanctimonious, self-satisfied, goody-goody *(informal)*, squeaky-clean, priggish, pietistic, religiose, pietistical • *those with holier-than-thou attitudes*

holiness = sanctity, spirituality, sacredness, purity, divinity, righteousness, piety, godliness, saintliness, blessedness, religiousness, devoutness, virtuousness • *We were immediately struck with this city's holiness.*

holler **AS A VERB** *sometimes with* **out = yell**, call, cry, shout, cheer, roar, hail, bellow, whoop, clamour, bawl, hurrah, halloo, huzzah *(archaic)* • *He hollered for help.*
▸ **AS A NOUN = yell**, call, cry, shout, cheer, roar, hail, bellow, whoop, clamour, bawl, hurrah, halloo, huzzah *(archaic)* • *The men were celebrating with drunken whoops and hollers.*

hollow **AS AN ADJECTIVE 1 = empty**, vacant, void, unfilled, not solid • *a hollow cylinder*
OPPOSITES: full, occupied, solid
2 = sunken, depressed, cavernous, indented, concave, deep-set • *hollow cheeks*
OPPOSITES: rounded, convex
3 = worthless, empty, useless, vain, meaningless, pointless, futile, fruitless, specious, Pyrrhic, unavailing • *Any threat to bring in the police is a hollow one.*
OPPOSITES: valuable, worthwhile, meaningful
4 = insincere, false, artificial, cynical, hypocritical, hollow-hearted • *His hollow laugh had no mirth in it.*
5 = dull, low, deep, flat, rumbling, muted, muffled, expressionless, sepulchral, toneless, reverberant • *the hollow sound of a gunshot*
OPPOSITES: vibrant, expressive
▸ **AS A NOUN 1 = cavity**, cup, hole, bowl, depression, pit, cave, den, basin, dent, crater, trough, cavern, excavation, indentation, dimple, concavity • *where water gathers in a hollow and forms a pond*
OPPOSITES: bump, projection, mound
2 = valley, dale, glen, dell, dingle • *Locals in the sleepy hollow peered out of their country cottages.*
OPPOSITES: hill, mountain, height
▸ **AS A VERB** *often followed by* **out = scoop out**, dig out, excavate, gouge out, channel, groove, furrow • *Someone had hollowed out a large block of stone.*

Hollywood

QUOTATIONS
Hollywood has always been a cage ... a cage to catch our dreams
[John Huston]
Hollywood's a place where they'll pay you a thousand dollars for a kiss, and fifty cents for your soul. I know, because I turned down the first offer often enough and held out for the fifty cents
[Marilyn Monroe]
Strip away the phony tinsel of Hollywood and you find the real tinsel underneath
[Oscar Levant *Inquisition in Eden*]

holocaust 1 = devastation, destruction, carnage, genocide, inferno, annihilation, conflagration • *A nuclear holocaust seemed a very real possibility in the '50s.*

2 = **genocide**, massacre, carnage, mass murder, ethnic cleansing *(euphemistic)*, annihilation, pogrom • *a fund for survivors of the holocaust and their families*

holy 1 = **sacred**, blessed, hallowed, dedicated, venerable, consecrated, venerated, sacrosanct, sanctified • *To them, as to all Tibetans, this is a holy place.*
OPPOSITES: unholy, desecrated, unsanctified
2 = **devout**, godly, religious, pure, divine, faithful, righteous, pious, virtuous, hallowed, saintly, god-fearing • *The Indians think of him as a holy man.*
OPPOSITES: worldly, earthly, sinful

QUOTATIONS
Is that which is holy loved by the gods because it is holy, or is it holy because it is loved by the gods?
[Plato *Euthyphro*]

homage 1 = **respect**, honour, worship, esteem, admiration, awe, devotion, reverence, duty, deference, adulation, adoration • *two marvellous films that pay homage to our literary heritage*
OPPOSITES: contempt, disregard, disrespect
2 = **allegiance**, service, tribute, loyalty, devotion, fidelity, faithfulness, obeisance, troth *(archaic)*, fealty • *At his coronation he received the homage of kings.*

home AS A NOUN 1 = **dwelling**, house, residence, abode, habitation, pad *(slang)*, domicile, dwelling place • *the allocation of land for new homes*
2 = **birthplace**, household, homeland, home town, homestead, native land, Godzone *(Austral. informal)* • *She was told to leave home by her father.* • *His father worked away from home for many years.*
3 = **territory**, environment, habitat, range, element, haunt, home ground, abode, habitation, stamping ground • *threatening the home of the famous African mountain gorillas*
▸ AS AN ADJECTIVE = **domestic**, national, local, central, internal, native, inland • *Europe's software companies still have a growing home market.*
▸ IN PHRASES: **at home** 1 = **in**, present, available • *Remember I'm not at home to callers.*
2 = **at ease**, relaxed, comfortable, content, at peace • *We soon felt quite at home.*
at home in, on, *or* **with** = **familiar with**, experienced in, skilled in, proficient in, conversant with, au fait with, knowledgeable of, well-versed in • *Graphic artists will feel at home with Photoshop*
bring something home to someone = **make clear**, emphasize, drive home, press home, impress upon • *It was to bring home to Americans the immediacy of the crisis.*
hit home = **strike home**, get through, sink in, be understood, hit the mark • *Those words of yours really hit home.*
home in on something *or* **someone** = **focus on**, target, concentrate, highlight, underline, spotlight, fix on, focus attention on, zero in on • *The critics immediately homed in on the film's failings.*
▸ RELATED MANIA: oikomania
▸ RELATED PHOBIA: oikophobia

QUOTATIONS
Mid pleasures and palaces though we may roam,
Be it ever so humble, there's no place like home.
Home, home, sweet, sweet home!
There's no place like home! There's no place like home!
[J.H. Payne *Clari, the Maid of Milan*]
Home is where the heart is
[Pliny the Elder]
Home is the place where, when you have to go there,
They have to take you in
[Robert Frost *The Death of the Hired Man*]

PROVERBS
East, west, home's best
An Englishman's home is his castle

▹ *See panel* **Types of home**

homeland = **native land**, birthplace, motherland, fatherland, country of origin, mother country, Godzone *(Austral. informal)* • *Many are planning to return to their homeland.*

homeless = **destitute**, exiled, displaced, dispossessed, unsettled, outcast, abandoned, down-and-out • *the growing number of homeless families*

homely 1 = **comfortable**, welcoming, friendly, domestic, familiar, informal, cosy, comfy *(informal)*, homespun, downhome *(slang, chiefly U.S.)*, homelike, homy • *We try and provide a very homely atmosphere.*
2 = **plain**, simple, natural, ordinary, modest, everyday, down-to-earth, unaffected, unassuming, unpretentious, unfussy • *Scottish baking is homely, comforting and truly good.*
OPPOSITES: affected, grand, elaborate
3 = **unattractive**, plain, ugly, not striking, unprepossessing, not beautiful, no oil painting *(informal)*, ill-favoured, fugly *(chiefly U.S. & Austral.)* • *The man was homely and overweight.*

Homeric = **heroic**, epic, grand, imposing, impressive • *a Homeric epic of movie-making*

homespun = **unsophisticated**, homely, plain, rough, rude, coarse, home-made, rustic, artless, inelegant, unpolished • *The book is simple, homespun philosophy.*

TYPES OF HOME

adobe
apartment
bachelor apartment *(Canadian)*
back-to-back
barrack
bedsitter
black house *(Scot.)*
board-and-shingle *(Caribbean)*
boarding house
booth
bungalow
bunker
but and ben *(Scot.)*
cabin
caboose *(Canad.)*
camboose
Cape Cod cottage
caravan
castle
chalet
chateau
chattel house
consulate
cot *or* cote *(dialect)*
cottage
cottage flat
crannog
croft
dacha *(Russian)*
deanery
digs
doss house
duplex *(U.S. & Canad.)*
embassy
farmhouse
flat
flatlet
flophouse
flotel
garret
grange
guest house
hacienda
hall
hogan
hostel
hotel
house
houseboat
hovel
hut
igloo *or* iglu
inn
lake dwelling
lodge
log cabin
long house
maisonette
manor
manse
mansion
mattamore
mews *(informal)*
mobile home
motel
motor caravan
mud hut
palace
parsonage
penthouse
pied-à-terre
prefab
priory
ranch
rath *(Irish)*
rectory
rest-home
roadhouse
semi
shack
shanty
shooting box
show house
single-end *(Scot. dialect)*
slum
starter home
stately home
studio flat
tavern
tenement
tent
tepee
town house
trailer *(U.S. & Canad.)*
tree house
tupik *(Canad.)*
vicarage
villa
whare *(N.Z.)*
wigwam

homicidal = **murderous**, deadly, lethal, maniacal, death-dealing • *That man is a homicidal maniac.*
homicide = **murder**, killing, manslaughter, slaying, bloodshed • *The police arrived at the scene of the homicide.*
homily = **sermon**, talk, address, speech, lecture, preaching, discourse, oration, declamation • *a receptive audience for his homily on moral values*
homogeneous *or* **homogenous** = **uniform**, similar, consistent, identical, alike, comparable, akin, analogous, kindred, unvarying, cognate • *The unemployed are not a homogeneous group.*
OPPOSITES: different, mixed, diverse
homogenize = **unite**, make uniform, combine, blend, integrate, merge, fuse, synthesize, amalgamate, meld • *Brussels bureaucrats can't homogenize national cultures and tastes.*
homologous = **similar**, like, corresponding, related, correspondent, parallel, comparable, analogous • *The homologous chromosomes remain attached to each other.*
homosexual AS AN ADJECTIVE = **gay**, lesbian, queer *(informal, derogatory)*, camp *(informal)*, pink *(informal)*, bent *(offensive slang)*, same-sex, homoerotic, sapphic, dykey *(derogatory slang)*, moffie *(S. African slang)* • *a homosexual relationship*
▸ AS A NOUN = **gay**, lesbian, queer *(informal, derogatory)*, batty boy *(slang)*, shirt-lifter *(derogatory slang)*, moffie *(S. African slang)*, auntie *or* aunty *(Austral. slang)*, lily *(Austral. slang)* • *You didn't tell me he was a homosexual.*
▸ RELATED PHOBIA: homophobia

QUOTATIONS
I am the Love that dare not speak its name
[Lord Alfred Douglas *Two Loves*]
In homosexual sex you know exactly what the other person is feeling
[William Burroughs]
These names: gay, queer, homosexual, are limiting. I would love to finish with them
[Derek Jarman *At Your Own Risk*]

homy *or* **homey** = **homely**, comfortable, welcoming, domestic, friendly, familiar, cosy, comfy *(informal)*, homespun, downhome *(slang, chiefly U.S.)*, homelike • *a large, homey dining-room*
hone 1 = **improve**, better, polish, enhance, upgrade, refine, sharpen, augment, help • *honing the skills of senior managers*
2 = **sharpen**, point, grind, edge, file, polish, whet, strop • *four grinding wheels for honing fine-edged tools*
honest 1 = **trustworthy**, decent, upright, reliable, ethical, honourable, conscientious, reputable, truthful, virtuous, law-abiding, trusty, scrupulous, high-minded, veracious • *My dad was the most honest man I have ever met.*
OPPOSITES: bad, dishonest, corrupt
2 = **open**, direct, frank, plain, straightforward, outright, sincere, candid, forthright, upfront *(informal)*, undisguised, round, ingenuous, unfeigned • *I was honest about what I was doing.*
OPPOSITES: false, disguised, secretive
3 = **genuine**, real, true, straight, fair, proper, authentic, equitable, impartial, on the level *(informal)*, bona fide, dinkum *(Austral. & N.Z. informal)*, above board, fair and square, on the up and up, honest to goodness • *It was an honest mistake on his part.*
OPPOSITES: false, fraudulent, illegitimate

QUOTATIONS
To be honest, as this world goes, is to be one man picked out of ten thousand
[William Shakespeare *Hamlet*]
An honest man's the noblest work of God
[Alexander Pope *An Essay on Man*]
An honest man's word is as good as his bond
[Cervantes *Don Quixote*]

honestly 1 = **ethically**, legitimately, legally, in good faith, on the level *(informal)*, lawfully, honourably, by fair means, with clean hands • *charged with failing to act honestly in his duties as an officer*
2 = **frankly**, plainly, candidly, straight (out), truthfully, to your face, in plain English, in all sincerity • *It came as a shock to hear him talk so honestly about an old friend.*
3 = **really**, actually, truly, genuinely, assuredly • *Did you honestly think we wouldn't notice?*
honesty 1 = **integrity**, honour, virtue, morality, fidelity, probity, rectitude, veracity, faithfulness, truthfulness, trustworthiness, straightness, incorruptibility, scrupulousness, uprightness, reputability • *It's time for complete honesty from political representatives.*
2 = **frankness**, openness, sincerity, candour, bluntness, outspokenness, genuineness, plainness, straightforwardness • *Good communication encourages honesty in a relationship.*

QUOTATIONS
No legacy is so rich as honesty
[William Shakespeare *All's Well That Ends Well*]
Honesty's a fool
[William Shakespeare *Othello*]
Honesty is a fine jewel, but much out of fashion
[Thomas Fuller *Gnomologia*]
Honesty is praised, then left to shiver
[Juvenal *Satires*]
PROVERBS
Honesty is the best policy

honeyed 1 = **flattering**, sweet, soothing, enticing, mellow, seductive, agreeable, sweetened, cajoling, alluring, melodious, unctuous, dulcet • *His gentle manner and honeyed tones reassured Andrew.*
2 = **sweet**, sweetened, luscious, sugary, syrupy, toothsome • *I could smell the honeyed ripeness of melons and peaches.*
honorary = **nominal**, unofficial, titular, ex officio, honoris causa *(Latin)*, in name *or* title only • *an honorary member of the Golf Club*
honour AS A NOUN 1 = **integrity**, principles, morality, honesty, goodness, fairness, decency, righteousness, probity, rectitude, trustworthiness, uprightness • *I can no longer serve with honour as a member of your government.*
OPPOSITES: degradation, dishonesty, dishonour
2 = **prestige**, credit, reputation, glory, fame, distinction, esteem, dignity, elevation, eminence, renown, repute, high standing • *He brought honour and glory to his country.*
OPPOSITES: shame, disgrace, disrepute
3 = **title**, award, distinction, accolade, decoration, laurel, adornment • *He was showered with honours – among them an Oscar in 1950.*
4 = **reputation**, standing, prestige, image, status, stature, good name, kudos, cachet • *Britain's national honour was at stake.*
5 = **acclaim**, regard, respect, praise, recognition, compliments, homage, accolades, reverence, deference, adoration, commendation, veneration • *One grand old English gentleman at least will be received with honour.*
OPPOSITES: contempt, condemnation, scorn
6 = **privilege**, credit, favour, pleasure, compliment, source of pride *or* satisfaction • *Five other cities had been competing for the honour of staging the Games.*
7 = **virginity**, virtue, innocence, purity, modesty, chastity • *He had fell designs on her honour.*
▸ AS A VERB 1 = **acclaim**, celebrate, praise, decorate, compliment, commemorate, dignify, commend, glorify, exalt, laud, lionize • *Two American surgeons were honoured with the Nobel Prize.*
2 = **respect**, value, esteem, prize, appreciate, admire, worship, adore, revere, glorify, reverence, exalt, venerate,

h

hallow • *Honour your parents, that's what the Bible says.*
OPPOSITES: slight, insult, scorn
3 = **fulfil**, keep, carry out, observe, discharge, live up to, be true to, be as good as *(informal)*, be faithful to • *He had failed to honour his word.*
4 = **pay**, take, accept, clear, pass, cash, credit, acknowledge • *The bank refused to honour his cheque.*
OPPOSITES: refuse

QUOTATIONS
Duty, honour! We make these words say whatever we want, the same as we do with parrots
[Alfred Capus *Mariage Bourgeois*]
If I lose mine honour,
I lose myself
[William Shakespeare *Antony and Cleopatra*]
Remember, you're fighting for this woman's honour.... which is probably more than she ever did
[Groucho Marx *Duck Soup (film)*]
The louder he talked of his honour, the faster we counted our spoons
[Ralph Waldo Emerson *The Conduct of Life*]
PROVERBS
There is no honour among thieves

honourable 1 = **principled**, moral, ethical, just, true, fair, upright, honest, virtuous, trustworthy, trusty, high-minded, upstanding • *I believe he was an honourable man.*
2 = **proper**, right, respectable, righteous, virtuous, creditable • *However, their intentions are honourable.*
3 = **prestigious**, great, noble, noted, distinguished, notable, renowned, eminent, illustrious, venerable • *an honourable profession*

hood 1 = **cowl**, scarf, snood • *The hood zips away into the collar.*
2 = **cap**, cover • *Why aren't all lenses supplied with a lens hood?*

hoodlum = **thug**, hooligan, ruffian, vandal, delinquent, rowdy, lout, tearaway, hoon *(Austral. & N.Z.)*, bruiser *(informal)*, boot boy, yob *or* yobbo *(Brit. informal)*, cougan *(Austral. slang)*, scozza *(Austral. slang)*, bogan *(Austral. slang)* • *Caruso is a small-time hoodlum attempting to go straight.*

hoodoo = **jinx**, curse, bad luck, voodoo, nemesis, hex *(U.S. & Canad. informal)*, evil eye, evil star • *It'll take a football miracle if we are to break that hoodoo.*

hoodwink = **deceive**, trick, fool, cheat, con *(informal)*, kid *(informal)*, mislead, hoax, dupe, gull *(archaic)*, delude, swindle, rook *(slang)*, bamboozle *(informal)*, take (someone) for a ride *(informal)*, lead up the garden path *(informal)*, sell a pup, pull a fast one on *(informal)*, cozen, befool, scam *(slang)* • *Many people are hoodwinked by the so-called beauty industry.*

hoof = **foot**, trotter, cloot • *The horses' hooves could not get a proper grip.*
▸ **TECHNICAL NAME:** ungula
▸ **RELATED ADJECTIVE:** ungular

hook **AS A NOUN** 1 = **fastener**, catch, link, lock, holder, peg, clasp, hasp • *One of his jackets hung from a hook.*
2 = **punch**, hit, blow, smack, thump • *a big left hook*
▸ **AS A VERB** 1 = **fasten**, fix, secure, catch, clasp, hasp • *one of those can openers you hook onto the wall*
2 = **curl**, curve, crook, loop, angle • *I hooked my left arm over the side of the dinghy.*
3 = **catch**, land, trap, entrap • *Whenever one of us hooked a fish, we moved on.*
▸ **IN PHRASES: by hook or by crook** = **by any means**, somehow, somehow or other, someway, by fair means or foul • *They intend to get their way, by hook or by crook.*
hook, line, and sinker = **completely**, totally, entirely, thoroughly, wholly, utterly, through and through, lock, stock and barrel • *We fell for it hook, line, and sinker.*
hook something *or* **someone up** = **connect (up)**, link (up), fix (up) • *technicians who hook up computer systems and networks*
hook up with someone = **get together with**, meet (up) with, join forces with, unite with • *He had just hooked up with Amelia.*
off the hook = **let off**, cleared, acquitted, vindicated, in the clear, exonerated, under no obligation, allowed to walk *(slang, chiefly U.S.)* • *Officials accused of bribery always seem to get off the hook.*

hookah = **water pipe**, hubble-bubble, narghile, kalian • *smoking a hookah*

hooked 1 = **bent**, curved, beaked, aquiline, beaky, hook-shaped, hamate *(rare)*, hooklike, falcate *(Biology)*, unciform *(Anatomy)*, uncinate *(Biology)* • *He was tall and thin, with a hooked nose.*
2 = **obsessed**, addicted, taken, devoted, turned on *(slang)*, enamoured • *Open this book and read a few pages and you will be hooked.*
3 = **addicted**, dependent, using *(informal)*, having a habit • *He spent a number of years hooked on cocaine, heroin and alcohol.*

hooligan = **delinquent**, tough, vandal, casual, ned *(Scot. slang)*, rowdy, hoon *(Austral. & N.Z.)*, hoodlum *(chiefly U.S.)*, ruffian, lager lout, boot boy, yob *or* yobbo *(Brit. slang)*, cougan *(Austral. slang)*, scozza *(Austral. slang)*, bogan *(Austral. slang)*, hoodie *(informal)* • *riots involving football hooligans*

hooliganism = **delinquency**, violence, disorder, vandalism, rowdiness, loutishness, yobbishness • *police investigating football hooliganism*

hoop = **ring**, band, loop, wheel, round, girdle, circlet • *For hand sewing, use an embroidery hoop to keep the fabric taut.*

hoot **AS A NOUN** 1 = **cry**, shout, howl, scream, shriek, whoop • *the hoots of night birds*
2 = **toot**, beep, honk • *He strode on, ignoring the car, in spite of a further warning hoot.*
3 = **jeer**, yell, boo, catcall • *His confession was greeted with derisive hoots.*
4 = **laugh**, scream *(informal)*, caution *(informal)*, card *(informal)* • *He's a hoot, a real character.*
▸ **AS A VERB** 1 = **jeer**, boo, howl, yell, catcall • *The protesters chanted, blew whistles and hooted.*
2 = **cry**, call, screech, tu-whit tu-whoo • *Out in the garden an owl hooted suddenly.*
3 = **toot**, sound, blast, blare, beep, honk • *Somewhere in the distance a siren hooted.*
4 = **shout**, cry, yell, scream, shriek, whoop • *Bev hooted with laughter.*

hop **AS A VERB** = **jump**, spring, bound, leap, skip, vault, caper • *I hopped down three steps.*
▸ **AS A NOUN** 1 = **jump**, step, spring, bound, leap, bounce, skip, vault • *'This is a catchy rhythm,' he added with a few hops.*
2 = **journey**, run, drive, ride, trip, flight, distance, spin *(informal)*, jaunt • *It's only a 20-minute hop in a helicopter.*

hope **AS A VERB** = **believe**, expect, trust, rely, look forward to, anticipate, contemplate, count on, foresee, keep your fingers crossed, cross your fingers • *I hope that the police will take the strongest action against them.*
▸ **AS A NOUN** = **belief**, confidence, expectation, longing, dream, desire, faith, ambition, assumption, anticipation, expectancy, light at the end of the tunnel • *Kevin hasn't given up hope of being fit.*
OPPOSITES: doubt, despair, dread
▸ **IN PHRASES: hope for something** = **expect**, look forward to, anticipate, long for, desire, aspire to, set your heart on • *They had hoped for a greater pay rise.*

QUOTATIONS
Hope springs eternal in the human breast;
Man never Is, but always To be blest
[Alexander Pope *An Essay on Man*]
He that lives in hope danceth without music
[George Herbert *Outlandish Proverbs*]

While there's life, there's hope
[Cicero *Letters to Atticus*]
Hope is the poor man's bread
[George Herbert *Jacula Prudentum*]
What is hope? Nothing but the paint on the face of existence; the least touch of truth rubs it off, and then we see what a hollow-cheeked harlot we have got hold of
[Lord Byron]
Abandon hope, all ye who enter here
[Dante *Divine Comedy*]

PROVERBS

Hope is a good breakfast but a bad supper

hopeful 1 = **optimistic**, confident, assured, looking forward to, anticipating, buoyant, sanguine, expectant • *Surgeons were hopeful of saving her sight.*
OPPOSITES: despairing, hopeless, pessimistic
2 = **promising**, encouraging, bright, reassuring, cheerful, rosy, heartening, auspicious, propitious • *hopeful forecasts that the economy will improve*
OPPOSITES: depressing, discouraging, unpromising

hopefully 1 = **optimistically**, confidently, expectantly, with anticipation, sanguinely • *'Am I welcome?' he smiled hopefully.*
2 = **it is hoped**, probably, all being well, God willing, conceivably, feasibly, expectedly • *Hopefully, you won't have any problems after reading this.*

hopeless 1 = **pessimistic**, desperate, despairing, forlorn, in despair, abject, dejected, despondent, demoralized, defeatist, disconsolate, downhearted • *Even able pupils feel hopeless about job prospects.*
OPPOSITES: optimistic, confident, hopeful
2 = **impossible**, pointless, futile, useless, vain, forlorn, no-win, unattainable, impracticable, unachievable, not having a prayer • *I don't believe your situation is as hopeless as you think.*
3 = **no good**, inadequate, useless *(informal)*, poor, pants *(informal)*, pathetic, inferior, incompetent, ineffectual • *I'd be hopeless at working for somebody else.*
4 = **incurable**, irreversible, irreparable, lost, helpless, irremediable, past remedy, remediless • *a hopeless mess*
OPPOSITES: curable, remediable

hopelessly 1 = **without hope**, desperately, in despair, despairingly, irredeemably, irremediably, beyond all hope • *hopelessly in love*
2 = **completely**, totally, extremely, desperately, terribly, utterly, tremendously, awfully, impossibly, frightfully • *The story is hopelessly confusing.*

horde = **crowd**, mob, swarm, press, host, band, troop, pack, crew, drove, gang, multitude, throng • *A horde of people was screaming for tickets.*

horizon 1 = **skyline**, view, vista, field *or* range of vision • *The sun had already sunk below the horizon.*
2 = **scope**, perspective, range, prospect, stretch, ken, sphere, realm, compass, ambit, purview • *By embracing other cultures, we actually broaden our horizons.*

horizontal = **level**, flat, plane, parallel, supine • *Swing the club back until it is horizontal.*

hormone
▷ *See panel* **Hormones**

horn
▸ **RELATED ADJECTIVES:** corneous, keratoid

horny = **aroused**, excited, turned on *(slang)*, randy *(informal, chiefly Brit.)*, raunchy *(slang)*, amorous, lustful • *horny adolescent boys*

horrendous 1 = **horrific**, shocking, appalling, frightening, awful, terrifying, grim, dreadful, horrifying, ghastly, grisly, frightful, hellacious *(U.S. slang)* • *The violence used was horrendous.*
2 = **enormous**, huge, massive, colossal, astronomic • *horrendous debts*

horrible 1 = **dreadful**, terrible, awful, nasty, cruel, beastly *(informal)*, mean, unpleasant, ghastly *(informal)*, unkind, horrid, disagreeable • *a horrible little boy*
OPPOSITES: appealing, charming, wonderful
2 = **terrible**, awful, appalling, terrifying, shocking, grim, dreadful, revolting, fearful, obscene, ghastly, hideous, shameful, gruesome, from hell *(informal)*, grisly, horrid, repulsive, frightful, heinous, loathsome, abhorrent, abominable, hellacious *(U.S. slang)* • *Still the horrible shrieking came out of his mouth.*
3 = **awful**, terrible, appalling, dire, very bad, deplorable, abysmal • *I've made some horrible mistakes.*

horrid 1 = **unpleasant**, terrible, awful, offensive, nasty, disgusting, horrible, dreadful, obscene, disagreeable, yucky *or* yukky *(slang)*, yucko *(Austral. slang)* • *What a horrid smell!*
2 = **nasty**, dreadful, horrible, mean, unkind, cruel, beastly *(informal)* • *I must have been a horrid little girl.*

horrific = **horrifying**, shocking, appalling, frightening, awful, terrifying, grim, dreadful, horrendous, ghastly, from hell *(informal)*, grisly, frightful, hellacious *(U.S. slang)* • *I have never seen such horrific injuries.*

horrify 1 = **terrify**, alarm, frighten, scare, intimidate, petrify, terrorize, put the wind up *(informal)*, gross out *(U.S. slang)*, make your hair stand on end, scare the bejesus out of *(informal)*, affright • *a crime trend that will horrify all parents*
OPPOSITES: encourage, comfort, reassure
2 = **shock**, appal, disgust, dismay, sicken, outrage • *When I saw these figures I was horrified.*
OPPOSITES: please, delight, enchant

HORMONES

adrenaline *or* epinephrine
adrenocorticotrophic hormone
androsterone
antidiuretic hormone
bursicon
calcitonin
cholecystokinin *or* pancreozymin
chorionic gonadotrophin
corpus luteum hormone *or* progesterone
corticosteroid
corticosterone *or* adrenocorticotrophic hormone
cortisone
deoxycorticosterone
ecdysone
enterogastrone
erythropoietin
florigen
follicle-stimulating hormone
glucagon
gibberellic acid
gastrin
gonadotrophin
growth hormone *or* somatotrophin
insulin
interstitial-cell-stimulating hormone *or* luteinizing hormone
juvenile hormone
lactogenic hormone
luteinizing hormone-releasing hormone
luteotrophin *or* prolactin
noradrenaline
oestradiol
oestriol
oestrone
oxytocin
progesterone
parathyroid hormone
relaxin
secretin
sex hormone
somatomedin
somatostatin
stilboestrol
testosterone
thyroid-stimulating hormone *or* thyrotropin
thyroxine
trichlorophenoxyacetic acid
triiodothyronine
vasopressin

horror **1 = terror**, fear, alarm, panic, dread, dismay, awe, fright, apprehension, consternation, trepidation • *I felt numb with horror.*
2 = hatred, disgust, loathing, aversion, revulsion, antipathy, abomination, abhorrence, repugnance, odium, detestation • *his horror of death*
OPPOSITES: liking, love, delight
3 = atrocity, awfulness, cruelty, outrage, ghastliness, gruesomeness, frightfulness, savageness • *the horror of this most bloody of civil wars*
4 = rascal, terror (*informal*), devil, monkey, monster, perisher (*Brit. informal*), scamp, holy terror (*informal*), nointer (*Austral. slang*) • *They can be little horrors though, little children, can't they?*

QUOTATIONS
Where there is no imagination there is no horror
[Sir Arthur Conan Doyle *A Study in Scarlet*]
Death holds no horrors. It is simply the ultimate horror of life
[Jean Giraudoux *The Enchanted*]
The horror! The horror!
[Joseph Conrad *Heart of Darkness*]

horror-struck *or* **horror-stricken** **= horrified**, shocked, appalled, petrified, aghast, frightened to death, awe-struck, scared out of your wits • *a horror-struck expression*

horse **AS A NOUN** **= nag**, mount, mare, colt, filly, stallion, gelding, jade, pony, yearling, steed (*archaic or literary*), dobbin, moke (*Austral. slang*), hobby (*archaic or dialect*), yarraman *or* yarramin (*Austral.*), gee-gee (*slang*), cuddy *or* cuddie (*dialect, chiefly Scot.*), studhorse *or* stud • *A small man on a grey horse had appeared.*
▸ **IN PHRASES: horse around** *or* **about = play around** *or* **about**, fool about *or* around, clown, misbehave, play the fool, roughhouse (*slang*), play the goat, monkey about *or* around, indulge in horseplay, lark about *or* around • *Later that day I was horsing around with Katie.*
▸ **RELATED ADJECTIVES:** equestrian, equine, horsey
▸ **RELATED NOUN:** equitation
▸ **NAME OF MALE:** stallion
▸ **NAME OF FEMALE:** mare
▸ **NAME OF YOUNG:** foal, colt, filly
▸ **RELATED MANIA:** hippomania
▸ **RELATED PHOBIA:** hippophobia
▹ *See panels* **Equestrianism; Horses**

QUOTATIONS
A horse! a horse! my kingdom for a horse!
[William Shakespeare *Richard III*]
A horse is dangerous at both ends and uncomfortable in the middle
[Ian Fleming]

PROVERBS
Don't change horses in midstream
You can take a horse to water but you cannot make him drink
A nod's as good as a wink to a blind horse
Nothing is so good for the inside of a man as the outside of a horse

horseman **= rider**, equestrian • *Gerald was a fine horseman.*

horseplay **= rough-and-tumble**, clowning, romping, fooling around, skylarking (*informal*), high jinks, pranks, buffoonery, roughhousing (*slang*) • *childish splashing and horseplay*

horticulture **= gardening**, agriculture, cultivation, floriculture, arboriculture • *Available courses are in garden design and practical horticulture.*

hose **= pipe**, tube, hosepipe, tubing, piping, pipeline, conduit, siphon • *The fireman unwrapped their hoses.*

hosiery **= tights**, hose, nylons, pantyhose • *Our lightweight support hosiery relieve tired aching legs.*

hospice **= nursing home**, hospital, sanatorium, convalescent home • *the purpose-built hospice and respite care centre*

hospitable **1 = welcoming**, kind, friendly, liberal, generous, gracious, amicable, cordial, sociable, genial, bountiful • *The locals are hospitable and welcoming.*
OPPOSITES: inhospitable, parsimonious
2 = receptive, tolerant, responsive, open-minded, amenable, accessible • *hospitable political environments*
OPPOSITES: intolerant, inhospitable, unreceptive

hospital **= infirmary**, clinic, nursing home, hospice, medical institution • *a children's hospital with 120 beds*

hospitality **= welcome**, warmth, kindness, friendliness, sociability, conviviality, neighbourliness, cordiality, heartiness, hospitableness • *Every visitor is overwhelmed by the hospitality of the people.*

QUOTATIONS
Be not forgetful to entertain strangers; for thereby some have entertained angels unawares
[*Bible: Hebrews*]
hospitality: the virtue which induces us to feed and lodge certain persons who are not in need of food and lodging
[Ambrose Bierce *The Devil's Dictionary*]
Welcome the coming, speed the going guest
[Alexander Pope *Imitations of Horace*]
When hospitality becomes an art, it loses its very soul
[Max Beerbohm *And Even Now*]

host[1] *or* **hostess** **AS A NOUN** **1 = master of ceremonies**, proprietor, innkeeper, landlord *or* landlady • *We were greeted by our host, a courteous man in a formal suit.*
2 = presenter, compere (*Brit.*), anchorman *or* anchorwoman • *I am host of a live radio programme.*
▸ **AS A VERB** **1 = give**, hold, provide, throw, arrange, lay on, be the host of • *They hosted a dinner for visiting dignitaries.*
2 = present, introduce, compere (*Brit.*), front (*informal*) • *She also hosts a show on St Petersburg Radio.*

QUOTATIONS
A host is like a general; it takes a mishap to reveal his genius
[Horace *Satires*]
Mankind is divisible into two great classes: hosts and guests
[Max Beerbohm *Hosts and Guests*]

host[2] **1 = multitude**, lot, load (*informal*), wealth, array, myriad, great quantity, large number • *a whole host of gadgets*
2 = crowd, army, pack, drove, mob, herd, legion, swarm, horde, throng • *A host of stars from British stage and screen attended the awards ceremony.*

hostage **= captive**, prisoner, pledge, pawn, security, surety • *the man they were holding as a hostage*

hostel **= cheap hotel**, YMCA, YWCA, youth hostel, dormitory • *She spent two years living in a hostel, with no possessions.*

hostile **1 = antagonistic**, anti (*informal*), opposed, opposite, contrary, inimical, ill-disposed • *hostile to the idea of foreign intervention*
2 = unfriendly, belligerent, antagonistic, unkind, malevolent, warlike, bellicose, inimical, rancorous, ill-disposed • *The Governor faced hostile crowds when he visited the town.*
OPPOSITES: warm, friendly, sympathetic
3 = inhospitable, adverse, alien, uncongenial, unsympathetic, unwelcoming, unpropitious • *some of the most hostile climatic conditions in the world*
OPPOSITES: congenial, hospitable

hostility **AS A NOUN** **1 = unfriendliness**, hatred, animosity, spite, bitterness, malice, venom, antagonism, enmity, abhorrence, malevolence, detestation • *She looked at Ron with open hostility.*
OPPOSITES: goodwill, friendliness, amity

HORSES

Breeds of horse

- Akhal-Teke
- American Quarter horse
- American Saddle horse
- Andalusian
- Anglo-Arab
- Anglo-Norman
- Appaloosa
- Arab
- Ardennes
- Balearic
- Barb
- Basuto
- Batak *or* Deli
- boerperd
- Beetewk
- Brabançon
- Breton
- Burmese *or* Shan
- Cleveland Bay
- Clydesdale
- Connemara
- Criollo
- Dales pony
- Danish
- Dartmoor pony
- Don
- Dutch Draught
- Esthonian, Smudish, *or* Zmudzin
- Exmoor
- Fell pony
- Finnish horse
- Fjord pony
- Flemish
- Friesian
- Gelderland
- Gidran
- Groningen
- Gudbrandsdal
- Hackney
- Hafflinger
- Hambletonian
- Hanoverian
- Highland pony
- Holstein
- Huçul
- Iceland pony
- Iomud
- Jutland
- Kabarda
- Karabair
- Karabakh
- Karadagh
- Kathiawari
- Kladruber
- Klepper
- Knabstrup
- Konik
- Kurdistan pony
- Limousin
- Lipizzaner *or* Lippizaner
- Lokai
- Manipur
- Marwari
- Mecklenburg
- Mongolian
- Morgan
- mustang *or* bronco
- New Forest pony
- Nonius
- North Swedish horse
- Oldenburg
- Orlov Trotter
- Palomino
- Percheron
- Persian Arab
- Pinto
- Pinzgauer
- Polish Arab
- Polish Half-bred
- Polish Thoroughbred
- Quarter horse
- racehorse
- Rhenish
- Russian saddle horse *or* Orlov Rostopchin
- Schleswig
- Shagya
- Shetland pony
- Shirazi *or* Gulf Arab
- Shire horse
- Spanish Jennet *or* Genet
- Spiti
- Standard Bred
- Strelet
- Suffolk *or* Suffolk Punch
- Swedish Ardennes
- Tarbenian
- Tarpan
- Tennessee Walking Horse *or* Walking Horse
- Thoroughbred
- Timor pony
- Trakehner
- Turk *or* Turkoman
- Viatka
- Waler
- Welsh Cob
- Welsh Mountain pony
- Welsh pony
- Yamoote
- Yorkshire Coach horse
- Zeeland horse
- Zemaitukas

Types of horse

- carthorse
- cavalry horse
- cayuse (*Western U.S. & Canad.*)
- charger
- cob
- courser (*literary*)
- cow pony
- crock
- destrier (*archaic*)
- drayhorse
- hack
- high-stepper
- hunter
- liberty horse
- nag
- night horse (*Austral.*)
- packhorse
- palfrey (*archaic*)
- pacer
- packhorse
- plug (*chiefly U.S.*)
- polo pony
- pony
- racehorse *or* (*Austral. informal*) neddy
- rip (*informal, archaic*)
- running mate
- saddle horse *or* saddler
- screw (*slang*)
- show jumper
- stalking-horse
- stockhorse
- sumpter (*archaic*)
- trooper
- warhorse
- weed
- workhorse

Wild horses

- brumby (*Austral.*)
- buckjumper (*Austral.*)
- mustang
- Przewalski's horse
- quagga
- tarpan
- warrigal (*Austral.*)
- zebra

Extinct horses

- hyracotherium *or* eohippus
- merychippus
- miohippus
- pliohippus
- quagga
- tarpan

Legendary/fictional/historical horses

- Bayard
- Black Beauty
- Black Bess
- Boxer
- Bucephalus
- Champion
- El Fideldo
- Flicka
- Hercules
- Incitatus
- Mister Ed
- Pegasus
- Rosinante
- Silver
- Sleipnir
- Traveler
- Trigger

Horse colours

- albino
- bay
- black
- blue roan
- chestnut
- claybank
- cream
- dapple
- dapplegrey
- dun
- fleabitten
- grey
- mealy
- palomino
- piebald
- pinto (*U.S. & Canad.*)
- roan
- skewbald
- sorrel
- strawberry roan

Horse markings

- blaze
- coronet
- snip
- sock
- star
- stocking
- stripe
- white face

Horse gaits

- amble
- canter
- extended trot
- gallop
- jog trot
- lope
- pace
- prance
- rising trot
- single-foot *or* rack
- sitting trot
- trot
- walk

HORSES (CONTINUED)

HORSE PARTS

back, coupling, forequarters, mane, shannon *or* shank, bar, croup *or* croupe, frog, muzzle, sheath, barrel, diagonal, gambrel, near-fore, sole, brisket, dock, gaskin *or* second thigh, near-hind, splint bone, buttress, ergot, hamstring, neck, stifle joint, cannon bone, fetlock joint, haunch, off-fore, tail, chestnut, flank, haw, off-hind, toe, chin groove, forearm, heel, pastern, tusk, coffin bone, forehand, hock, poll, wall, coronet band, foreleg, hoof, quarter, white line, counter, forelock, loins, saddle, withers

PEOPLE ASSOCIATED WITH HORSES

broncobuster, coachman, farrier, knacker, roughrider, buster *(U.S. & Canad.)*, coper, groom, knight, rustler *(chiefly U.S. & Canad.)*, caballero *(Southwestern U.S.)*, cowboy, horseman *or (fem.)* horsewoman, lad *(Brit.)*, saddler, cavalier, currier, horse whisperer, ostler, stable lad, cavalry, equerry, hussar, picador, trainer, chevalier *(French history)*, equestrian *or (fem.)* equestrienne, jockey, postilion, wrangler *(Western U.S. & Canad.)*, equites *(Roman history)*, Jockey Club, postrider, rider

TACK AND EQUIPMENT AND THEIR PARTS

anti-sweat rug, curb *or* curb bit, hockboot, rein, swingletree, whippletree, *or (U.S.)* whiffletree, bar, curb chain, hoof pick, roller, tack, bard *or* barde, curb reins, horseshoe, saddle, tail bandage, bearing rein *or (U.S.)* check rein, curry comb, jointed egg-butt snaffle, saddlebag, tail comb, bit, dandy brush, kimblewick, saddlecloth, tailguard, blinkers, day rug, kneecap, saddlery, throatlash *or* throatlatch, body brush, double bridle, lip strap, sidesaddle, trace, boot, double-jointed snaffle, mane comb, skirt, trammel, breastplate, flap, martingale, sliphead, trappings, breeching, front arch, New Zealand rug, snaffle *or* snaffle bit, twisted snaffle, bridle, fulmer snaffle, night rug, split-eared bridle, twitch, bridoon, gag-bit, nosebag, spur, underblanket, browband, gambado, noseband *or* nosepiece, stirrup, water brush, cantle, girth *or (U.S. & Canad.)* cinch, overcheck, stirrup bar, Weymouth curb bit, cavesson, girth strap, pad saddle *or* numnah, stirrup iron, wisp, chamfron, hackamore plate, pelham, stirrup leather, cheek-piece, halter, plain snaffle, summer sheet, crownpiece, harness, plate, surcingle, crupper, headpiece, pommel, sweat scraper

HORSES, RHINOS AND OTHER PERISSODACTYLS

ass, horse, kiang, rhinoceros, chigetai *or* dziggetai, ▷ *See panel* **Breeds of horse**, kulan, tapir, donkey, mule, white elephant, elephant, keitloa, onager, zebra

2 = **opposition**, resentment, antipathy, aversion, antagonism, ill feeling, bad blood, ill-will, animus • *hostility among traditionalists to this method of teaching history*
OPPOSITES: agreement, approval
▸ **AS A PLURAL NOUN** = **warfare**, war, fighting, conflict, combat, armed conflict, state of war • *Military chiefs agreed to cease hostilities throughout the country.*
OPPOSITES: peace, alliance, treaty

hot **AS AN ADJECTIVE** 1 = **heated**, burning, boiling, steaming, flaming, roasting, searing, blistering, fiery, scorching, scalding, piping hot • *Cook the meat quickly on a hot barbecue plate.*
2 = **warm**, close, stifling, humid, torrid, sultry, sweltering, balmy, muggy • *It was too hot even for a gentle stroll.*
OPPOSITES: cold, cool, freezing
3 = **feverish**, burning (up), flushed, febrile • *feeling hot and flushed*
4 = **spicy**, pungent, peppery, piquant, biting, sharp, acrid • *He loved hot curries.*
OPPOSITES: mild, bland
5 = **intense**, passionate, heated, spirited, excited, fierce, lively, animated, ardent, inflamed, fervent, impassioned, fervid • *The nature of Scottishness is a matter of hot debate in Scotland.*
6 = **new**, latest, fresh, recent, up to date, just out, up to the minute, bang up to date *(informal)*, hot off the press • *If you hear any hot news, tell me, won't you?*
OPPOSITES: old, stale, trite
7 = **popular**, hip, fashionable, cool, in demand, sought-after,

must-see, in vogue, the new, du jour *(French)*, culty • *a ticket for the hottest show in town*
OPPOSITES: unpopular, out of favour
8 = fierce, intense, strong, keen, competitive, cut-throat • *hot competition from abroad*
9 = fiery, violent, raging, passionate, stormy, touchy, vehement, impetuous, irascible • *His hot temper was making it difficult for others to work with him.*
OPPOSITES: calm, moderate, mild
10 = stolen, dodgy *(Brit. informal)*, illicit, smuggled, bootleg, contraband, under the counter, knockoff *(informal)*, shonky *(Austral. & N.Z. informal)* • *Buying hot goods is no longer a criminal offence.*
▸ **IN PHRASES: blow hot and cold = dither**, vacillate, hesitate, waver, be unsure, be undecided, hum and haw *(Brit. informal)*, shilly-shally, swither *(Scot. dialect)* • *I blew hot and cold as I weighed up the pros and cons.*
hot on the heels of something *or* **someone = shortly after**, soon after, immediately after, right after, close behind, straight after, hard on the heels of, directly after • *The shock news comes hot on the heels of the company axing its site in Scotland.*
hot under the collar = angry, cross, furious, annoyed, put out, fed up, infuriated, incensed, enraged, aggrieved, irate, hacked off *(informal)*, brassed off *(Brit. informal)*, tooshie *(Austral. slang)*, off the air *(Austral. slang)* • *Some of them were getting very hot under the collar about tax issues.*

hot air = empty talk, rant, guff *(slang)*, bombast, wind, gas *(informal)*, verbiage, claptrap *(informal)*, blather, bunkum *(chiefly U.S.)*, blether, bosh *(informal)*, tall talk *(informal)* • *His justification for the merger was just hot air.*

hotbed = breeding ground, nest, den • *a hotbed of racial intolerance*

hot-blooded = passionate, spirited, wild, rash, fiery, ardent, fervent, temperamental, impulsive, excitable • *His neighbours remembered him as a hot-blooded teenager.*
OPPOSITES: cold, cool, calm

hotch-potch = mixture, mess, jumble, medley, hash, potpourri, mélange *(French)*, miscellany, mishmash, conglomeration, farrago, hodgepodge *(U.S.)*, gallimaufry • *The palace is a complete hotch-potch of architectural styles.*

hotel = inn, motel, bed and breakfast, guest house • *They are staying in a hotel near the airport.*

hotfoot *or* **hot-foot = speedily**, quickly, hastily, hurriedly, helter-skelter, pell-mell, posthaste • *Today's harassed hostess arrives hotfoot from the office.*

hot-headed = volatile, rash, fiery, reckless, precipitate, hasty, unruly, foolhardy, impetuous, hot-tempered, quick-tempered • *a footballer whose fiery temper makes him too hot-headed to handle*

hothouse = greenhouse, conservatory, glasshouse, orangery • *Wilted plants thrive when well tended in a hothouse.*

hotly 1 = fiercely, passionately, angrily, vehemently, indignantly, with indignation, heatedly, impetuously • *The bank hotly denies any wrongdoing.*
2 = closely, enthusiastically, eagerly, with enthusiasm, hotfoot • *He'd snuck out of America hotly pursued by the CIA.*

hound AS A NOUN = dog, pooch *(informal)*, mutt *(informal)*, cur • *my faithful old hound, Bluey*
▸ **AS A VERB 1 = harass**, harry, bother, provoke, annoy, torment, hassle *(informal)*, prod, badger, persecute, pester, goad, keep after • *hounded by the press*
2 = force, drive, pressure, push, chase, railroad *(informal)*, propel, impel, pressurize • *hounded out of office*
▸ **COLLECTIVE NOUNS:** pack, mute, cry

hour
▸ **RELATED ADJECTIVES:** horal, horary

house AS A NOUN 1 = home, residence, dwelling, building, pad *(slang)*, homestead, edifice, abode, habitation, domicile, whare *(N.Z.)* • *her parents' house in Warwickshire*
2 = household, family, ménage • *If he set his alarm clock, it would wake the whole house.*
3 = firm, company, business, concern, organization, partnership, establishment, outfit *(informal)* • *the world's top fashion houses*
4 = assembly, parliament, Commons, legislative body • *the joint sessions of the two parliamentary houses*
5 = restaurant, inn, hotel, pub *(Brit. informal)*, tavern, public house, hostelry • *The house offers a couple of freshly prepared à la carte dishes.*
6 = dynasty, line, race, tribe, clan, ancestry, lineage, family tree, kindred • *the Saudi Royal House*
7 = audience, crowd, gathering, assembly • *They played in front of a packed house.*
▸ **AS A VERB 1 = accommodate**, board, quarter, take in, put up, lodge, harbour, billet, domicile • *Regrettably we have to house families in these inadequate flats.*
2 = contain, keep, hold, cover, store, protect, shelter • *The building houses a collection of motorcycles and cars.*
3 = take, accommodate, sleep, provide shelter for, give a bed to • *The building will house twelve boys and eight girls.*
▸ **IN PHRASES: on the house = free**, for free *(informal)*, for nothing, free of charge, gratis, without expense • *He brought them glasses of champagne on the house.*

QUOTATIONS
A house is a machine for living in
[Le Corbusier *Vers une architecture*]

household AS A NOUN = family, home, house, ménage, family circle, ainga *(N.Z.)* • *growing up in a male-only household*
▸ **AS A MODIFIER = domestic**, family, domiciliary • *I always do the household chores first.*

householder = occupant, resident, tenant, proprietor, homeowner, freeholder, leaseholder • *Millions of householders are eligible to claim the new benefit.*

housekeeping = household management, homemaking *(U.S.)*, home economy, housewifery, housecraft • *I thought that cooking and housekeeping were unimportant tasks.*

houseman = junior doctor, medical officer, house doctor, newly qualified doctor • *My brother was a houseman at a nearby hospital.*

housing 1 = accommodation, homes, houses, dwellings, domiciles • *a shortage of affordable housing*
2 = case, casing, covering, cover, shell, jacket, holder, container, capsule, sheath, encasement • *Both housings are waterproof to a depth of two metres.*

hovel 1 = hut, hole, shed, cabin, den, slum, shack, shanty, whare *(N.Z.)* • *They lived in a squalid hovel for the next five years.*
2 = dump, hole, pigsty • *The room I was given was a hovel.*

hover 1 = float, fly, hang, drift, be suspended, flutter, poise • *Beautiful butterflies hovered above the wild flowers.*
2 = linger, loiter, wait nearby, hang about *or* around *(informal)* • *Judith was hovering in the doorway.*
3 = waver, alternate, fluctuate, haver *(Brit.)*, falter, dither *(chiefly Brit.)*, oscillate, vacillate, seesaw, swither *(Scot. dialect)* • *We hover between great hopes and great fears.*

however 1 = but, nevertheless, still, though, yet, even though, on the other hand, nonetheless, notwithstanding, anyhow, be that as it may • *Some of the food crops failed. However, the cotton did quite well.*
2 = no matter how, regardless of how, in whatever way • *However hard she tried, nothing seemed to work.*
3 = how on earth, how • *However did you find this place in such weather?*

howl AS A VERB 1 = bay, cry, bark, yelp, quest *(of a hound)* • *A dog suddenly howled, baying at the moon.*
2 = cry, shout, scream, roar, weep, yell, cry out, wail, shriek, bellow, bawl, yelp • *The baby was howling for her 3am feed.*

▸ **AS A NOUN** 1 = **baying**, cry, bay, bark, barking, yelp, yelping, yowl • *It was the howl of an animal crying out in hunger.* 2 = **cry**, scream, roar, bay, wail, outcry, shriek, bellow, clamour, hoot, bawl, yelp, yowl • *a howl of rage*

howler = **mistake**, error, blunder, boob *(Brit. slang)*, bloomer *(Brit. informal)*, clanger *(informal)*, malapropism, schoolboy howler, booboo *(informal)*, barry or Barry Crocker *(Austral. slang)* • *I felt as if I had made an outrageous howler.*

hub = **centre**, heart, focus, core, middle, focal point, pivot, nerve centre • *The island's social hub is the Café Sport.*

hubbub 1 = **noise**, racket, din, uproar, cacophony, pandemonium, babel, tumult, hurly-burly • *a hubbub of excited conversation from over a thousand people*
2 = **hue and cry**, confusion, disturbance, riot, disorder, clamour, rumpus, bedlam, brouhaha, ruction *(informal)*, hullabaloo, ruckus *(informal)* • *the hubbub over the election*

hubris = **pride**, vanity, arrogance, conceit, self-importance, haughtiness, conceitedness • *a tale of how an honourable man was afflicted with hubris*

h

huddle **AS A VERB** 1 = **curl up**, crouch, hunch up, nestle, snuggle, make yourself small • *She sat huddled on the side of the bed, weeping.*
2 = **crowd**, press, gather, collect, squeeze, cluster, flock, herd, throng • *strangers huddling together for warmth*
▸ **AS A NOUN** 1 = **crowd**, mass, bunch, cluster, heap, muddle, jumble • *a huddle of bodies, gasping for air*
2 = **discussion**, conference, meeting, hui *(N.Z.)*, powwow, confab *(informal)*, korero *(N.Z.)* • *He went into a huddle with his lawyers to consider an appeal.*

hue 1 = **colour**, tone, shade, dye, tint, tinge, tincture • *The same hue will look different in different lights.*
2 = **aspect**, light, cast, complexion • *a comeback of such theatrical hue*

hue and cry = **outcry**, clamour, furore, uproar, rumpus, brouhaha, ruction *(informal)*, hullabaloo • *He heard a huge hue and cry outside.*

huff **AS A NOUN** = **sulk**, temper, bad mood, passion, rage, pet, pique, foulie *(Austral. slang)* • *He went into a huff because he lost the game.*
▸ **IN PHRASES: in a huff** = **offended**, hurt, angered, provoked, annoyed, put out *(informal)*, hacked (off) *(U.S. slang)*, exasperated, sulking *(informal)*, nettled, vexed, pissed off *(taboo slang)*, miffed *(informal)*, irked, riled, peeved, piqued, in high dudgeon • *She was in a huff about what I'd said.*

huffy = **sulky**, irritable, moody, short, cross, angry, offended, choked, crabbed, disgruntled, resentful, edgy, crusty, snappy, grumpy, sullen, touchy, curt, surly, moping, petulant, tetchy, ratty *(Brit. & N.Z. informal)*, testy, chippy *(informal)*, waspish, querulous, shirty *(slang, chiefly Brit.)*, peevish, crotchety *(informal)*, pettish, tooshie *(Austral. slang)* • *He always seemed so angry or huffy.*
OPPOSITES: happy, gay, good-humoured

hug **AS A VERB** 1 = **embrace**, hold (onto), cuddle, squeeze, cling, clasp, enfold, hold close, take in your arms • *They hugged each other like a couple of lost children.*
2 = **clasp**, hold (onto), grip, nurse, retain • *He trudged towards them, hugging a large box.*
3 = **follow closely**, keep close, stay near, cling to, follow the course of • *The road hugs the coast for hundreds of miles.*
▸ **AS A NOUN** = **embrace**, squeeze, bear hug, clinch *(slang)*, clasp • *She leapt out of the seat, and gave him a hug.*

huge = **enormous**, great, giant, large, massive, vast, extensive, tremendous, immense, mega *(slang)*, titanic, jumbo *(informal)*, gigantic, monumental, mammoth, bulky, colossal, mountainous, stellar *(informal)*, prodigious, stupendous, gargantuan, fuck-off *(taboo slang)*, elephantine, ginormous *(informal)*, Brobdingnagian, humongous or humungous *(U.S. slang)* • *Several painters were working on a huge piece of canvas.*
OPPOSITES: little, small, tiny

hugely = **immensely**, enormously, massively, prodigiously, monumentally, stupendously • *a hugely successful businessman*

hui = **meeting**, gathering, assembly, meet, conference, congress, session, rally, convention, get-together *(informal)*, reunion, congregation, conclave, convocation, powwow • *He arranged a hui which called together a broad span of Māori tribes and opinions.*

hulk = **wreck**, shell, hull, shipwreck, frame • *I could make out the gutted hulk of the tanker.*

hulking = **ungainly**, massive, lumbering, gross, awkward, clumsy, bulky, cumbersome, overgrown, unwieldy, ponderous, clunky *(informal)*, oafish, lumpish, lubberly, unco *(Austral. slang)* • *When I woke up there was a hulking figure staring down at me.*

hull **AS A NOUN** 1 = **framework**, casing, body, covering, frame, skeleton • *The hull had suffered extensive damage to the starboard side.*
2 = **husk**, skin, shell, peel, pod, rind, shuck • *I soaked the hulls off lima beans.*
▸ **AS A VERB** = **trim**, peel, skin, shell, husk, shuck • *Soak them in water with lemon juice for 30 minutes before hulling.*

hullabaloo = **commotion**, to-do, fuss, noise, confusion, turmoil, disturbance, racket, upheaval, outcry, clamour, furore, din, uproar, pandemonium, rumpus, bedlam, babel, tumult, hubbub, hurly-burly, brouhaha, ruction *(informal)*, hue and cry, ruckus *(informal)* • *I was scared by the hullabaloo over my arrival.*

hum **AS A VERB** 1 = **drone**, buzz, murmur, throb, vibrate, purr, croon, thrum, whir • *We could hear a buzz, like a bee humming.*
2 = **be busy**, buzz, bustle, move, stir, pulse, be active, vibrate, pulsate • *On Saturday morning, the town hums with activity.*
▸ **AS A NOUN** = **buzz**, murmur, drone • *There was a general hum of conversation around them.*
▸ **IN PHRASES: hum and haw** *or* **hem and haw** = **hesitate**, waver, dither, vacillate, be indecisive, falter, swither *(Scot. dialect)* • *My mother hummed and hawed at first, then she agreed.*

human **AS AN ADJECTIVE** 1 = **mortal**, anthropoid, manlike • *the human body*
OPPOSITES: animal, nonhuman
2 = **fallible**, imperfect, weak, frail • *We're all human after all.*
3 = **kind**, natural, vulnerable, kindly, understandable, humane, compassionate, considerate, approachable • *Singapore has a human side too, beside the relentless efficiency.*
OPPOSITES: cruel, beastly, inhuman
▸ **AS A NOUN** = **human being**, person, individual, body, creature, mortal, man or woman • *The drug has not yet been tested on humans.*
OPPOSITES: god, animal, nonhuman
▸ **RELATED PREFIX:** anthropo-

QUOTATIONS
Drinking when we are not thirsty and making love all year round, madam; that is all there is to distinguish us from other animals
[Pierre-Augustin Caron de Beaumarchais *The Marriage of Figaro*]
Being human signifies, for each one of us, belonging to a class, a society, a country, a continent and a civilization
[Claude Lévi-Strauss *Tristes Tropiques*]

human being = **human**, man, woman, person, mortal • *not to hear a fellow human being's voice*

humane = **kind**, compassionate, good, kindly, understanding, gentle, forgiving, tender, mild, sympathetic, charitable, benign, clement, benevolent, lenient, merciful, good-natured, forbearing, kind-hearted • *Their aim is for a more just and humane society.*
OPPOSITES: cruel, brutal, ruthless

humanitarian AS AN ADJECTIVE 1 = **compassionate**, charitable, humane, benevolent, altruistic, beneficent • *They will be released as a humanitarian act.*
2 = **charitable**, philanthropic, public-spirited • *a convoy of humanitarian aid from Britain*
▸ AS A NOUN = **philanthropist**, benefactor, Good Samaritan, altruist • *I like to think of myself as a humanitarian.*

humanitarianism = **charity**, philanthropy, benevolence, goodwill, generosity, humanism, beneficence • *notions of humanitarianism and equality*

humanity AS A NOUN 1 = **the human race**, man, mankind, people, men, mortals, humankind, Homo sapiens • *They face charges of committing crimes against humanity.*
2 = **human nature**, mortality, humanness • *It made him feel deprived of his humanity.*
3 = **kindness**, charity, compassion, understanding, sympathy, mercy, tolerance, tenderness, philanthropy, benevolence, fellow feeling, benignity, brotherly love, kind-heartedness • *His speech showed great humility and humanity.*
▸ AS A PLURAL NOUN = **arts**, liberal arts, classics, classical studies, literae humaniores • *The number of students majoring in the humanities has declined.*

QUOTATIONS

Out of the crooked timber of humanity no straight thing can ever be made
[Immanuel Kant *Idee zu einer allgemeinen Geschichte in welt bürgerlicher Absicht*]

We're all of us guinea pigs in the laboratory of God. Humanity is just a work in progress
[Tennessee Williams *Camino Real*]

humanize = **civilize**, improve, refine, polish, educate, soften, cultivate, tame, reclaim, enlighten, mellow • *He used what discretion he could to modify or humanize the system.*

humankind = **humanity**, man, mankind, people, mortals, Homo sapiens • *one of the age-old practices of humankind*

human resources = **personnel**, staff, workers, the workforce • *a drain on financial and human resources*

humble AS AN ADJECTIVE 1 = **modest**, meek, unassuming, unpretentious, submissive, self-effacing, unostentatious • *Andy was a humble, courteous and gentle man.*
OPPOSITES: lordly, proud, superior
2 = **lowly**, common, poor, mean, low, simple, ordinary, modest, obscure, commonplace, insignificant, unimportant, unpretentious, undistinguished, plebeian, low-born • *He came from a fairly humble, poor background.*
OPPOSITES: important, rich, distinguished
3 = **ordinary**, common, commonplace • *He made his own reflector from a strip of humble kitchen foil.*
▸ AS A VERB = **humiliate**, shame, disgrace, break, reduce, lower, sink, crush, put down *(slang)*, bring down, subdue, degrade, demean, chagrin, chasten, mortify, debase, put (someone) in their place, abase, take down a peg *(informal)*, abash • *the little car company that humbled the industry giants*
OPPOSITES: raise, elevate, exalt
▸ IN PHRASES: **humble yourself** = **humiliate yourself**, grovel, eat humble pie, swallow your pride, eat crow *(U.S. informal)*, abase yourself, go on bended knee • *He humbled himself and became obedient.*

humbly = **meekly**, modestly, respectfully, cap in hand, diffidently, deferentially, submissively, unassumingly, obsequiously, subserviently, on bended knee, servilely • *So may I humbly suggest we all do something next time?*

humbug = **nonsense**, rubbish, trash, hypocrisy, cant, malarkey, baloney *(informal)*, claptrap *(informal)*, quackery, eyewash *(informal)*, charlatanry • *Britain's laws on homosexuality are hypocritical humbug.*

humdrum = **dull**, ordinary, boring, routine, commonplace, mundane, tedious, dreary, banal, tiresome, monotonous, uneventful, uninteresting, mind-numbing, ho-hum *(informal)*, repetitious, wearisome, unvaried • *trapped in a humdrum but well-paid job*
OPPOSITES: interesting, exciting, dramatic

humid = **damp**, sticky, moist, wet, steamy, sultry, dank, clammy, muggy • *Visitors can expect hot and humid conditions.*
OPPOSITES: dry, sunny, arid

humidity = **damp**, moisture, dampness, wetness, moistness, sogginess, dankness, clamminess, mugginess, humidness • *The heat and humidity were insufferable.*

humiliate = **embarrass**, shame, humble, crush, disgrace, put down, subdue, degrade, chagrin, chasten, mortify, debase, discomfit, bring low, put (someone) in their place, take the wind out of someone's sails, abase, take down a peg *(informal)*, abash, make (someone) eat humble pie • *His teacher continually humiliates him in maths lessons.*
OPPOSITES: honour, elevate, magnify

humiliating = **embarrassing**, shaming, humbling, mortifying, crushing, disgracing, degrading, ignominious, toe-curling *(slang)*, cringe-making *(Brit. informal)*, cringeworthy *(Brit. informal)*, barro *(Austral. slang)* • *The Conservatives have suffered a humiliating defeat.*

humiliation = **embarrassment**, shame, disgrace, humbling, put-down, degradation, affront, indignity, chagrin, ignominy, dishonour, mortification, loss of face, abasement, self-abasement • *She faced the humiliation of discussing her husband's affair.*

humility = **modesty**, diffidence, meekness, submissiveness, servility, self-abasement, humbleness, lowliness, unpretentiousness, lack of pride • *a deep sense of humility*
OPPOSITES: pride, vanity, superiority

QUOTATIONS

Humility is the first of the virtues – for other people
[Oliver Wendell Holmes *The Professor at the Breakfast Table*]

One may be humble out of pride
[Montaigne *Essais*]

He that humbleth himself wishes to be exalted
[Friedrich Nietzsche *Human, All Too Human*]

The first test of a truly great man is his humility
[John Ruskin *Modern Painters*]

For whosoever exalteth himself shall be abased; and he that humbleth himself shall be exalted
[*Bible: St. Luke*]

humorist = **comedian**, comic, wit, eccentric, wag, joker, card *(informal)*, jester, dag *(N.Z. informal)*, funny man • *a political humorist*

humorous = **funny**, comic, amusing, entertaining, witty, merry, hilarious, ludicrous, laughable, farcical, whimsical, comical, droll, facetious, jocular, side-splitting, waggish, jocose • *a humorous magazine*
OPPOSITES: serious, earnest, sad

humour AS A NOUN 1 = **comedy**, funniness, fun, amusement, funny side, jocularity, facetiousness, ludicrousness, drollery, comical aspect • *She couldn't ignore the humour of the situation.*
OPPOSITES: grief, gravity, seriousness
2 = **mood**, spirits, temper, disposition, frame of mind • *Could that have been the source of his good humour?*
3 = **joking**, jokes, comedy, wit, gags *(informal)*, farce, jesting, jests, wisecracks *(informal)*, witticisms, wittiness • *The film has lots of adult humour.*
▸ AS A VERB = **indulge**, accommodate, go along with, spoil, flatter, pamper, gratify, pander to, mollify, cosset, fawn on • *Most of the time he humoured her for an easy life.*
OPPOSITES: oppose, stand up to, aggravate

QUOTATIONS

Humour is by far the most significant activity of the human brain
[Edward De Bono]

Humor brings insight and tolerance. Irony brings a deeper and less friendly understanding
[Agnes Repplier *In Pursuit of Laughter*]
The secret source of humor itself is not joy but sorrow. There is no humor in heaven
[Mark Twain *Following the Equator*]
There are men so philosophical that they can see humor in their own toothaches. But there has never lived a man so philosophical that he could see the toothache in his own humor
[H.L. Mencken *A Mencken Chrestomathy*]
There seems to be no lengths to which humorless people will not go to analyze humor. It seems to worry them
[Robert Benchley *What Does It Mean?*]

BODILY HUMOURS

black bile	blood
yellow bile	phlegm

humourless = **serious**, intense, solemn, straight, dry, dour, unfunny, po-faced, unsmiling, heavy-going, unamused, unamusing • *He was a straight-faced, humourless character.*

hump AS A NOUN = **lump**, bump, projection, bulge, mound, hunch, knob, protuberance, protrusion • *The path goes over a large hump by a tree.*
▸ AS A VERB = **carry**, lug, heave, hoist, shoulder, humph (*Scot.*) • *Charlie humped his rucksack up the stairs.*
▸ IN PHRASES: **get the hump** = **sulk**, mope, be in the doldrums, get the blues, be down in the dumps (*informal*) • *She's always got the hump about something these days.*

humped = **hunched**, rounded, bent, bowed • *She watched his humped back disappear down a dim corridor.*

hunch AS A NOUN = **feeling**, idea, impression, suspicion, intuition, premonition, inkling, presentiment • *I had a hunch that we would work well together.*
▸ AS A VERB = **crouch**, bend, stoop, curve, arch, huddle, draw in, squat, hump • *He hunched over the map to read the small print.*

hunchback = **humpback**, Quasimodo, crookback (*rare*), crouch-back (*archaic*) • *playing a hunchback in the dark classical epic Jean de Florette*

hundred
▸ RELATED PREFIX: hect- or hecto-

hundredth
▸ RELATED PREFIX: cent-, centi-

hunger AS A NOUN 1 = **appetite**, emptiness, voracity, the munchies (*slang*), hungriness, ravenousness • *Hunger is the body's sign that blood sugar is too low.*
2 = **starvation**, famine, malnutrition, undernourishment • *Three hundred people are dying of hunger every day.*
3 = **desire**, appetite, craving, yen (*informal*), ache, lust, yearning, itch, thirst, greediness • *He has a hunger for success that seems bottomless.*
▸ IN PHRASES: **hunger for** *or* **after something** = **want**, desire, crave, hope for, long for, wish for, yearn for, pine for, hanker after, ache for, thirst after, itch after • *He hungered for adventure.*

QUOTATIONS
There's no sauce in the world like hunger
[Miguel de Cervantes *Don Quixote*]
PROVERBS
Hunger drives the wolf from the wood

hungry AS AN ADJECTIVE 1 = **starving**, ravenous, famished, starved, empty, hollow, voracious, peckish (*informal, chiefly Brit.*), famishing • *My friend was hungry, so we went to get some food.*
2 = **eager**, keen, craving, yearning, greedy, avid, desirous, covetous, athirst • *I left Oxford in 1961 hungry to be a critic.*
▸ IN PHRASES: **go hungry** = **starve**, fast, go *or* do without food • *You've never known what it is to go hungry.*

QUOTATIONS
A hungry stomach has no ears
[Jean de la Fontaine *The Kite and the Nightingale*]

hunk 1 = **lump**, piece, chunk, block, mass, wedge, slab, nugget, wodge (*Brit. informal*), gobbet • *a thick hunk of bread*
2 = **stud** (*informal*), he-man (*informal*), macho man, tough guy (*informal*), strongman, beefcake (*informal*), muscleman • *a blond, blue-eyed hunk*

hunker down = **squat**, crouch (down), hunch • *Betty hunkered down on the floor*

hunt AS A VERB = **stalk**, track, chase, pursue, trail, hound, gun for • *Her irate husband was hunting her lover with a gun.*
▸ AS A NOUN = **search**, hunting, investigation, chase, pursuit, quest • *The couple had helped in the hunt for the toddlers.*
▸ IN PHRASES: **hunt for something** *or* **someone** = **search for**, look for, try to find, seek for, forage for, rummage for, scour for, look high and low, fossick for (*Austral. & N.Z.*), go in quest of, ferret about for • *A forensic team was hunting for clues.*

hunted = **harassed**, desperate, harried, tormented, stricken, distraught, persecuted, terror-stricken • *A hunted look came into her eyes.*

hunter = **huntsman** *or* **huntress**, Diana, Herne, Orion, Nimrod, jaeger (*rare*), Artemis, sportsman *or* sportswoman • *The hunter stalked his prey.*

hunting = **blood sports**, coursing, stalking, field sports • *referendums whether or not to ban hunting in the country*

QUOTATIONS
The English country gentleman galloping after a fox – the unspeakable in full pursuit of the uneatable
[Oscar Wilde]

hurdle AS A NOUN 1 = **obstacle**, block, difficulty, barrier, handicap, hazard, complication, snag, uphill (*S. African*), obstruction, stumbling block, impediment, hindrance • *The weather will be the biggest hurdle.*
2 = **fence**, wall, hedge, block, barrier, barricade • *The horse dived at the hurdle and clipped the top.*
▸ AS A VERB = **overcome**, beat, master, conquer, surmount • *He earns a living helping others hurdle tough challenges.*

hurl 1 = **throw**, fling, chuck (*informal*), send, fire, project, launch, cast, pitch, shy, toss, propel, sling, heave, let fly (with) • *Groups of angry youths hurled stones at police.*
2 = **shout**, scream, yell, roar, bellow • *hurling abuse at one another*

hurly-burly = **commotion**, confusion, chaos, turmoil, disorder, upheaval, furore, uproar, turbulence, pandemonium, bedlam, tumult, hubbub, brouhaha • *the hurly-burly of modern city life*
OPPOSITES: order, organization, composure

hurricane = **storm**, gale, tornado, cyclone, typhoon, tempest, twister (*U.S. informal*), windstorm, willy-willy (*Austral.*) • *People have been killed in the hurricane's destructive path.*

hurried 1 = **hasty**, quick, brief, rushed, short, swift, speedy, precipitate, quickie (*informal*), breakneck • *They had a hurried breakfast, then left.*
2 = **rushed**, perfunctory, hectic, speedy, superficial, hasty, cursory, slapdash • *a hurried overnight redrafting of the text*

hurriedly = **hastily**, quickly, briskly, speedily, in a rush, at the double, hurry-scurry • *students hurriedly taking notes*

hurry AS A VERB 1 = **rush**, fly, dash, barrel (along) (*informal, chiefly U.S. & Canad.*), scurry, scoot, burn rubber (*informal*) • *Claire hurried along the road.*
OPPOSITES: creep, crawl, dawdle

2 = make haste, rush, lose no time, get a move on *(informal)*, step on it *(informal)*, get your skates on *(informal)*, crack on *(informal)* • *There was no longer any reason to hurry.*
3 *sometimes with* **up = speed (up)**, accelerate, hasten, quicken, hustle, urge, push on, goad, expedite • *The President's attempt to hurry the process of independence.*
OPPOSITES: slow, delay, slow down
▸ **AS A NOUN = rush**, haste, speed, urgency, bustle, flurry, commotion, precipitation, quickness, celerity, promptitude • *the hurry of people wanting to get home*
OPPOSITES: slowness
▸ **IN PHRASES: in a hurry = quickly**, hastily, hurriedly, immediately, rapidly, instantly, swiftly, abruptly, briskly, at speed, speedily, expeditiously, at *or* on the double • *Troops had left the area in a hurry.*

hurt AS A VERB 1 = injure, damage, wound, cut, disable, bruise, scrape, impair, gash • *He had hurt his back in an accident.*
OPPOSITES: restore, repair, heal
2 = ache, be sore, be painful, burn, smart, sting, throb, be tender • *His collar bone only hurt when he lifted his arm.*
3 = harm, injure, molest, ill-treat, maltreat, lay a finger on • *Did they hurt you?*
4 = upset, distress, pain, wound, annoy, sting, grieve, afflict, sadden, cut to the quick, aggrieve • *I'll go. I've hurt you enough.*
5 = damage, harm, ruin, mar, undermine, wreck, spoil, sabotage, blight, jeopardize, crool *or* cruel *(Austral. slang)* • *They don't want to hurt their husband's careers.*
▸ **AS A NOUN 1 = distress**, suffering, pain, grief, misery, agony, sadness, sorrow, woe, anguish, heartache, wretchedness • *I was full of jealousy and hurt.*
OPPOSITES: delight, pleasure, happiness
2 = harm, trouble, damage, wrong, loss, injury, misfortune, mischief, affliction • *I am sorry for any hurt that it may have caused.*
▸ **AS AN ADJECTIVE 1 = injured**, wounded, damaged, harmed, cut, scratched, bruised, scarred, scraped, grazed • *They were dazed but did not seem to be badly hurt.*
OPPOSITES: restored, repaired, healed
2 = upset, pained, injured, wounded, sad, crushed, offended, aggrieved, miffed *(informal)*, rueful, piqued, tooshie *(Austral. slang)* • *He gave me a slightly hurt look.*
OPPOSITES: calmed, consoled, placated

hurtful = unkind, upsetting, distressing, mean, cutting, damaging, wounding, nasty, cruel, destructive, harmful, malicious, mischievous, detrimental, pernicious, spiteful, prejudicial, injurious, disadvantageous, maleficent • *Her comments were very hurtful to Mrs Green's family.*

hurtle = rush, charge, race, shoot, fly, speed, tear, crash, plunge, barrel (along) *(informal, chiefly U.S. & Canad.)*, scramble, spurt, stampede, scoot, burn rubber *(informal)*, rush headlong, go hell for leather *(informal)* • *A pretty young girl came hurtling down the stairs.*

husband AS A NOUN = partner, man *(informal)*, spouse, hubby *(informal)*, mate, old man *(informal)*, bridegroom, significant other *(U.S. informal)*, better half *(humorous)*, squeeze *(informal)*, bidie-in *(Scot.)* • *Eva married her husband Jack in 1957.*
▸ **AS A VERB = conserve**, budget, use sparingly, save, store, hoard, economize on, use economically, manage thriftily • *Husbanding precious resources was part of rural life.*
OPPOSITES: spend, squander, splash out *(informal, chiefly Brit.)*

QUOTATIONS

Thy husband is thy lord, thy life, thy keeper,
Thy head, thy sovereign; one that cares for thee,
And for thy maintenance commits his body
To painful labour both by sea and land
[William Shakespeare *The Taming of the Shrew*]

An archaeologist is the best husband any woman can have; the older she gets, the more interested he is in her
[Agatha Christie]

Being a husband is a full-time job. That is why so many husbands fail. They cannot give their entire attention to it
[Arnold Bennett *The Title*]

An early-rising man ... a good spouse but a bad husband
[Gabriel García Márquez *In Evil Hour*]

A husband is what is left of the lover after the nerve has been extracted
[Helen Rowland *A Guide to Men*]

husbandry 1 = farming, agriculture, cultivation, land management, tillage, agronomy • *The current meagre harvest suggests poor husbandry.*
2 = thrift, economy, good housekeeping, frugality, careful management • *These people consider themselves adept at financial husbandry.*

hush AS A VERB = quieten, still, silence, suppress, mute, muzzle, shush • *She tried to hush her noisy father.*
▸ **AS A NOUN = quiet**, silence, calm, still *(poetic)*, peace, tranquillity, stillness, peacefulness • *A hush fell over the crowd.*
▸ **IN PHRASES: hush someone up = silence**, gag *(informal)*, keep quiet, muzzle • *The Conservative Government was only too quick to hush him up.*
hush something up = cover up, conceal, suppress, sit on *(informal)*, squash, smother, keep secret, sweep under the carpet *(informal)*, draw a veil over, keep dark • *The authorities have tried to hush it up.*

hushed = quiet, low, soft, subdued, low-pitched • *At first we spoke in hushed voices.*
OPPOSITES: loud, noisy

hush-hush = secret, confidential, classified, top-secret, restricted, under wraps • *Though these meetings were hush-hush there were sometimes leaks.*

husk = rind, shell, hull, covering, bark, chaff, shuck • *a grey squirrel nibbling on a peanut husk*

husky 1 = hoarse, rough, harsh, raucous, rasping, croaking, gruff, throaty, guttural, croaky • *His voice was husky with grief.*
2 = muscular, powerful, strapping, rugged, hefty, burly, stocky, beefy *(informal)*, brawny, thickset • *a very husky young man, built like a football player*

hussy = slut, tart *(informal)*, strumpet, baggage *(informal, old-fashioned)*, tramp *(slang)*, jade, wanton, minx, wench *(archaic)*, slapper *(Brit. slang)*, scrubber *(Brit. & Austral. slang)*, trollop, floozy *(slang)*, quean *(archaic)*, hornbag *(Austral. slang)* • *Are you going to sunbathe naked? You wanton hussy!*

hustle AS A VERB 1 = jostle, force, push, crowd, rush, hurry, thrust, elbow, shove, jog, bustle, impel • *The guards hustled Harry out of the car.*
2 = hurry, hasten, get a move on *(informal)* • *You'll have to hustle if you're to get home for supper.*
▸ **AS A NOUN = commotion**, bustle, activity, excitement, hubbub, hurly-burly, liveliness • *the perfect retreat from the hustle and bustle of London*

hut 1 = cabin, shack, shanty, hovel, whare *(N.Z.)* • *a mud hut with no electricity, gas, or running water*
2 = shed, outhouse, lean-to, lockup • *Never leave a garage or garden hut unlocked.*

hybrid 1 = crossbreed, cross, mixture, compound, composite, mule, amalgam, mongrel, half-breed, half-blood • *a hybrid between watermint and spearmint* • *best champion Mule or Hybrid*
2 = mixture, compound, composite, amalgam • *a hybrid of solid and liquid fuel*

hydrate = moisten, wet, water, soak, dampen, moisturize, bedew • *Other natural ingredients hydrate and soften skin.*

hydrocarbon
▹ *See panel* **Hydrocarbons**

h

HYDROCARBONS

alkane	cyclopentadiene	octane
alkene	cyclopropane	pentane
alkyne	diene	pyrene
arene	decane	retene
cetane	indene	stilbene
cubane	isooctane	triptane
cycloalkane	naphthalene	xylene

hygiene = **cleanliness**, sanitation, disinfection, sterility, sanitary measures, hygienics • *Be extra careful about personal hygiene.*

hygienic = **clean**, healthy, sanitary, pure, sterile, salutary, disinfected, germ-free, aseptic • *a kitchen that was easy to keep hygienic*
OPPOSITES: dirty, polluted, filthy

h

hymn 1 = **religious song**, song of praise, carol, chant, anthem, psalm, paean, canticle, doxology • *Readings were accompanied by an old Irish hymn.*
2 = **song of praise**, anthem, paean • *a hymn to freedom and rebellion*

hype AS A NOUN = **publicity**, promotion, build-up, plugging *(informal)*, puffing, racket, razzmatazz *(slang)*, brouhaha, ballyhoo *(informal)* • *There was a lot of hype before the film came out.*
▸ AS A VERB *sometimes with* **up** = **publicize**, push, promote, advertise, build up, plug *(informal)*, puff (up), talk up *(informal)* • *We had to hype the film to attract the financiers.*

hyperbole = **exaggeration**, hype *(informal)*, overstatement, enlargement, magnification, amplification • *The debate was carried on with increasing rhetorical hyperbole.*

hyperbolic = **exaggerated**, overstated, enlarged, magnified, amplified • *This kind of hyperbolic writing does him no favours.*

hypercritical = **fault-finding**, carping, fussy, niggling, censorious, finicky, cavilling, pernickety *(informal)*, captious, overcritical, hairsplitting, overscrupulous, overexacting • *women who are hypercritical of their bodies*

hypnotic 1 = **mesmeric**, soothing, narcotic, opiate, soporific, sleep-inducing, somniferous • *The hypnotic state lies between being awake and being asleep.*
2 = **mesmerizing**, spellbinding, mesmeric • *His songs are often both hypnotic and reassurringly pleasant.*

hypnotize 1 = **mesmerize**, put in a trance, put to sleep • *The ability to hypnotize yourself can be learnt in a single session.*
2 = **fascinate**, absorb, entrance, magnetize, spellbind • *He's hypnotized by that black hair and that white face.*

hypochondria = **hypochondriasis**, valetudinarianism • *People with such ruminations often have a tendency towards hypochondria.*

hypochondriac = **neurotic**, valetudinarian • *He was dismissed as a hypochondriac – until tests showed he had thyroid cancer.*

hypocrisy = **insincerity**, pretence, deceit, deception, cant, duplicity, dissembling, falsity, imposture, sanctimoniousness, phoniness *(informal)*, deceitfulness, pharisaism, speciousness, two-facedness, phariseeism • *He accused newspapers of hypocrisy in their treatment of the story.*
OPPOSITES: honesty, sincerity, truthfulness

QUOTATIONS

Hypocrisy is a tribute which vice pays to virtue
[Duc de la Rochefoucauld *Réflexions ou Sentences et Maximes Morales*]

I hope you have not been leading a double life, pretending to be wicked and being really good all the time. That would be hypocrisy
[Oscar Wilde *The Importance of Being Earnest*]

Why beholdest thou the mote that is in thy brother's eye, but considerest not the beam that is in thine own eye?
[*Bible: St. Matthew*]

hypocrisy, the only evil that walks
Invisible, except to God alone
[John Milton *Paradise Lost*]

hypocrite = **fraud**, deceiver, pretender, charlatan, impostor, pharisee, dissembler, Tartuffe, Pecksniff, Holy Willie, whited sepulchre, phoney *or* phony *(informal)* • *The magazine wrongly suggested he was a liar and a hypocrite.*

QUOTATIONS

Their sighan', cantan', grace-proud faces,
Their three-mile prayers, and half-mile graces
[Robert Burns *To the Rev. John M'Math*]

hypocritical = **insincere**, false, fraudulent, hollow, deceptive, spurious, two-faced, deceitful, sanctimonious, specious, duplicitous, dissembling, canting, Janus-faced, pharisaical, phoney *or* phony *(informal)* • *It seems hypocritical to pay someone to do the dirty work for me.*

hypodermic = **syringe**, needle, works *(slang)* • *The hypodermic was properly heat-sterilised.*

hypothesis = **theory**, premise, proposition, assumption, thesis, postulate, supposition, premiss • *Different hypotheses have been put forward.*

hypothetical = **theoretical**, supposed, academic, assumed, imaginary, speculative, putative, conjectural • *a purely hypothetical question*
OPPOSITES: known, real, proven

hysteria = **frenzy**, panic, madness, agitation, delirium, hysterics, unreason • *No one could help getting carried away by the hysteria.*

hysterical 1 = **frenzied**, mad, frantic, raving, distracted, distraught, crazed, uncontrollable, berserk, overwrought, convulsive, beside yourself, berko *(Austral. slang)* • *I slapped her because she became hysterical.*
OPPOSITES: calm, composed, poised
2 = **hilarious**, uproarious, side-splitting, farcical, comical, wildly funny • *a hysterical, satirical revue*
OPPOSITES: serious, sad, grave

I i

ice AS A NOUN 1 = **frozen water** • *Glaciers are moving rivers of ice.*
2 = **ice cream**, water ice • *He's eaten a lot of choc ices.*
▸ AS A VERB = **frost**, coat, glaze • *I've made the cake. I've iced and decorated it.*
▸ IN PHRASES: **break the ice** = **kick off** *(informal)*, lead the way, take the plunge *(informal)*, make a start, begin a relationship, initiate the proceedings, start *or* set the ball rolling *(informal)* • *The main purpose of his trip was to break the ice.*
on ice = **pending**, forthcoming, imminent, awaiting, unsettled, impending, in the balance, undecided, up in the air, in the offing, undetermined, hanging fire • *The $40 million aid package will remain on ice for a month.*
skate on thin ice = **be at risk**, be vulnerable, be unsafe, be in jeopardy, be out on a limb, be open to attack, be sticking your neck out *(informal)* • *I had skated on thin ice for long enough.*
▸ RELATED ADJECTIVE: glacial, related phobia, kristallophobia

ice-cold = **freezing**, biting, frozen, bitter, refrigerated, raw, shivering, arctic, icy, glacial, chilled to the bone *or* marrow • *delicious ice-cold beer*

icing AS A NOUN = **frosting**, glaze • *a birthday cake with yellow icing*
▸ IN PHRASES: **the icing on the cake** = **masterstroke**, accomplishment, stroke of genius, coup de grâce *(French)* • *His two last-minute goals were the icing on the cake.*

icon 1 = **idol**, hero, superstar, favourite, pet, darling, pin-up *(slang)* • *a fashion icon of the nineties*
2 = **representation**, image, figure, statue, idol, likeness, effigy • *He came home with a haul of religious icons.*
▸ RELATED MANIA: iconomania

iconoclast = **rebel**, radical, dissident, heretic • *He was an iconoclast who refused to be bound by tradition.*

iconoclastic = **subversive**, radical, rebellious, questioning, innovative, irreverent, impious, dissentient, denunciatory • *His iconoclastic tendencies can get him into trouble.*

icy 1 = **cold**, freezing, bitter, biting, raw, chill, chilling, arctic, chilly, frosty, glacial, ice-cold, frozen over, frost-bound • *An icy wind blew across the moor.*
OPPOSITES: hot, warm, boiling
2 = **slippery**, glassy, slippy *(informal)*, like a sheet of glass, rimy • *an icy road*
3 = **unfriendly**, cold, distant, hostile, forbidding, indifferent, aloof, stony, steely, frosty, glacial, frigid, unwelcoming • *His response was icy.*
OPPOSITES: warm, friendly, cordial

ID = **identification**, papers, credentials, licence, warrant, identity card, proof of identity, letters of introduction • *He showed his ID to the man.*

idea 1 = **plan**, scheme, proposal, design, theory, strategy, method, solution, suggestion, recommendation, proposition • *It's a good idea to keep a stock of tins in the cupboard.*
2 = **notion**, thought, view, understanding, teaching, opinion, belief, conclusion, hypothesis, impression, conviction, judgment, interpretation, sentiment, doctrine, conception, viewpoint • *Some of his ideas about democracy are entirely his own.*
3 = **impression**, estimate, guess, hint, notion, clue, conjecture, surmise, inkling, approximation, intimation, ballpark figure • *This graph will give you some idea of levels of ability.*
4 = **understanding**, thought, view, sense, opinion, concept, impression, judgment, perception, conception, abstraction, estimation • *By the end of the week you will have a clearer idea of the system.*
5 = **suspicion**, guess, impression, notion, hunch, conjecture, gut feeling *(informal)*, supposition • *I had an idea that he joined the army later.*
6 = **intention**, aim, purpose, object, end, plan, reason, goal, design, objective, motive • *The idea is to help lower-income families to buy their homes.*
▸ RELATED PHOBIA: ideophobia

QUOTATIONS

Nothing is more dangerous than an idea, when you have only one idea
[Alain *Propos sur la religion*]

A stand can be made against invasion by an army; no stand can be made against invasion by an idea
[Victor Hugo *Histoire d'une Crime*]

It is better to entertain an idea than to take it home to live with you for the rest of your life
[Randall Jarrell *Pictures from an Institution*]

Right now it's only a notion, but I think I can get the money to make it into a concept, and later turn it into an idea
[Woody Allen *Annie Hall*]

ideal AS A NOUN 1 *often plural* = **principle**, standard, ideology, morals, conviction, integrity, scruples, probity, moral value, rectitude, sense of duty, sense of honour, uprightness • *The party has drifted too far from its socialist ideals.*
2 = **epitome**, standard, dream, pattern, perfection, last word, paragon, nonpareil, standard of perfection • *Throughout his career she remained his feminine ideal.*
3 = **model**, example, criterion, prototype, paradigm, archetype, exemplar • *the ideal of beauty in those days*
▸ AS AN ADJECTIVE 1 = **perfect**, best, model, classic, supreme, ultimate, archetypal, exemplary, consummate, optimal, quintessential • *She decided I was the ideal person to take over this job.*
OPPOSITES: flawed, deficient, imperfect
2 = **imaginary**, impractical, Utopian, romantic, fantastic, fabulous, poetic, visionary, fairy-tale, mythical, unreal,

fanciful, unattainable, ivory-towered, imagal *(Psychoanalysis)* • *Their ideal society collapsed around them in revolution.*
OPPOSITES: real, ordinary, actual
3 = **hypothetical**, academic, intellectual, abstract, theoretical, speculative, conceptual, metaphysical, transcendental, notional • *an ideal economic world*

> **QUOTATIONS**
> The ideal has many names, and beauty is but one of them
> [W. Somerset Maugham *Cakes and Ale*]

idealism = **romanticism**, Utopianism, quixotism • *She never lost her respect for the idealism of the 1960s.*

> **QUOTATIONS**
> Idealism is the noble toga that political gentlemen drape over their will to power
> [Aldous Huxley]

idealist = **romantic**, visionary, dreamer, Utopian • *He is not such an idealist that he cannot see the problems.*

idealistic = **perfectionist**, romantic, optimistic, visionary, Utopian, quixotic, impracticable, starry-eyed • *She was somewhat idealistic about the pleasures of motherhood.*
OPPOSITES: practical, sensible, realistic

idealization = **glorification**, worship, exaltation, magnification, ennoblement • *her idealization of her dead husband*

idealize = **romanticize**, glorify, exalt, worship, magnify, ennoble, deify, put on a pedestal, apotheosize • *People often idealize the past.*

ideally = **in a perfect world**, in theory, preferably, if possible, all things being equal, under the best of circumstances, if you had your way, in a Utopia • *People should, ideally, eat much less fat and sugar.*

idée fixe = **obsession**, thing *(informal)*, preoccupation, fixation, fixed idea, monomania, hobbyhorse, bee in your bonnet • *It is an idée fixe of mine that women work in a more concentrated way.*

identical AS AN ADJECTIVE = **alike**, like, the same, matching, equal, twin, equivalent, corresponding, duplicate, synonymous, indistinguishable, analogous, interchangeable, a dead ringer *(slang)*, the dead spit *(informal)*, like two peas in a pod • *Nearly all the houses were identical.*
OPPOSITES: different, separate, unlike
▸ IN PHRASES: **the identical** = **the same**, the very same, the selfsame • *She had the identical quirky mannerisms her father used to have.*

> **QUOTATIONS**
> Two things are identical if one can be substituted for the other without affecting the truth
> [Gottfried Wilhelm Leibniz *Table de définitions*]

identifiable = **recognizable**, noticeable, known, unmistakable, discernible, detectable, distinguishable, ascertainable • *He was easily identifiable by his oddly-shaped hat.*

identification **1** = **discovery**, recognition, determining, establishment, diagnosis, confirmation, detection, divination • *Early identification of the disease can prevent death.*
2 = **recognition**, naming, labelling, distinguishing, cataloguing, classifying, confirmation, pinpointing, establishment of identity • *Officials are awaiting positive identification before proceeding.*
3 = **connection**, relationship, link, association, tie, partnership, affinity, familiarity, interconnection, interrelation • *There is a close identification of nationhood with language.*
4 = **understanding**, relationship, involvement, unity, sympathy, empathy, rapport, fellow feeling • *She had an intense identification with animals.*
5 = **ID**, papers, credentials, licence, warrant, identity card, proof of identity, letters of introduction • *I'll need to see some identification.*

identify AS A VERB **1** = **recognize**, place, name, remember, spot, label, flag, catalogue, tag, diagnose, classify, make out, pinpoint, recollect, put your finger on *(informal)* • *I tried to identify her perfume.*
2 = **establish**, spot, confirm, finger *(informal, chiefly U.S.)*, demonstrate, pick out, single out, certify, verify, validate, mark out, substantiate, corroborate, flag up • *Police have already identified around ten suspects.*
3 = **determine**, establish, discover, fix, work out, decide on, settle on, ascertain, deduce, make up your mind on • *Having identified the problem, we now need to overcome it.*
▸ IN PHRASES: **identify something** *or* **someone with something** *or* **someone** = **equate with**, associate with, think of in connection with, put in the same category as • *Audiences identify her with roles depicting sweet, passive women.*
identify with someone = **relate to**, understand, respond to, feel for, ally with, empathize with, speak the same language as, put yourself in the place *or* shoes of, see through another's eyes, be on the same wavelength as • *She would only play the role if she could identify with the character.*

identity **1** = **name**, details, specification • *The police soon established his true identity.*
2 = **individuality**, self, character, personality, existence, distinction, originality, peculiarity, uniqueness, oneness, singularity, separateness, distinctiveness, selfhood, particularity • *I wanted a sense of my own identity.*

ideology = **belief(s)**, ideas, principles, ideals, opinion, philosophy, doctrine, creed, dogma, tenets, world view, credence, articles of faith, Weltanschauung *(German)* • *capitalist ideology*

idiocy = **foolishness**, insanity, lunacy, tomfoolery, inanity, imbecility, senselessness, cretinism, fatuity, abject stupidity, asininity, fatuousness • *the idiocy of subsidies for activities which damage the environment*
OPPOSITES: sense, wisdom, sanity

idiom **1** = **phrase**, expression, turn of phrase, locution, set phrase • *Proverbs and idioms may become worn with over-use.*
2 = **language**, talk, style, usage, jargon, vernacular, parlance, mode of expression • *I was irritated by his use of archaic idiom.*

idiomatic = **vernacular**, native, everyday, conversational, dialectal • *She soon acquired a remarkable command of idiomatic English.*

idiosyncrasy = **peculiarity**, habit, characteristic, quirk, eccentricity, oddity, mannerism, affectation, trick, singularity, personal trait • *One of his idiosyncrasies was to wear orange gloves.*

idiosyncratic = **distinctive**, special, individual, typical, distinguishing, distinct, peculiar, individualistic • *a highly idiosyncratic personality*

idiot AS A NOUN **1** = **fool**, jerk *(slang, chiefly U.S. & Canad.)*, ass, plank *(Brit. slang)*, charlie *(Brit. informal)*, berk *(Brit. slang)*, prick *(slang)*, wally *(slang)*, prat *(slang)*, plonker *(slang)*, moron, geek *(slang)*, twit *(informal, chiefly Brit.)*, chump, imbecile, cretin, oaf, simpleton, airhead *(slang)*, dimwit *(informal)*, dipstick *(Brit. slang)*, dickhead *(slang)*, gonzo *(slang)*, schmuck *(U.S. slang)*, dork *(slang)*, nitwit *(informal)*, blockhead, divvy *(Brit. slang)*, pillock *(Brit. slang)*, halfwit, nincompoop, dweeb *(U.S. slang)*, putz *(U.S. slang)*, eejit *(Scot. & Irish)*, thicko *(Brit. slang)*, dumb-ass *(slang)*, gobshite *(Irish taboo slang)*, dunderhead, numpty *(Scot. informal)*, doofus *(slang, chiefly U.S.)*, lamebrain *(informal)*, fuckwit *(taboo slang)*, mooncalf, nerd *or* nurd *(slang)*, numbskull *or* numskull, galah *(Austral. & N.Z. informal)*, dorba *or* dorb *(Austral. slang)*, bogan *(Austral. slang)* • *I knew I'd been an idiot to stay there.*
2 = **simpleton**, cretin, halfwit • *the village idiot*
▸ AS AN ADJECTIVE = **stupid**, simple, slow, thick, dull, naive,

dim, dense, dumb *(informal)*, deficient, crass, gullible, simple-minded, dozy *(Brit. informal)*, witless, stolid, dopey *(informal)*, moronic, obtuse, brainless, cretinous, unintelligent, half-witted, slow on the uptake *(informal)*, braindead *(informal)*, dumb-ass *(slang)*, doltish, slow-witted, woodenheaded *(informal)* • *a bunch of idiot journalists*

idiotic = **foolish**, crazy, stupid, dumb *(informal)*, daft *(informal)*, insane, lunatic, senseless, foolhardy, inane, fatuous, loopy *(informal)*, crackpot *(informal)*, moronic, imbecile, unintelligent, asinine, imbecilic, braindead *(informal)*, harebrained, dumb-ass *(slang)*, halfwitted • *What an idiotic thing to say!*
OPPOSITES: brilliant, wise, intelligent

idle **AS AN ADJECTIVE** 1 = **unoccupied**, unemployed, redundant, jobless, out of work, out of action, inactive, at leisure, between jobs, unwaged, at a loose end • *Employees have been idle for almost a month now.*
OPPOSITES: working, employed, occupied
2 = **unused**, stationary, inactive, out of order, ticking over, gathering dust, mothballed, out of service, out of action *or* operation • *Now the machine is lying idle.*
3 = **lazy**, slow, slack, sluggish, lax, negligent, inactive, inert, lethargic, indolent, lackadaisical, good-for-nothing, remiss, workshy, slothful, shiftless • *I've never met such an idle bunch of workers!*
OPPOSITES: working, employed, busy
4 = **useless**, vain, pointless, hopeless, unsuccessful, ineffective, worthless, futile, fruitless, unproductive, abortive, ineffectual, groundless, of no use, valueless, disadvantageous, unavailing, otiose, of no avail, profitless, bootless • *It would be idle to pretend the system is worthless.*
OPPOSITES: effective, useful, profitable
5 = **trivial**, superficial, insignificant, frivolous, silly, unnecessary, irrelevant, foolish, unhelpful, flippant, puerile, flighty, ill-considered, empty-headed, nugatory • *He kept up the idle chatter for another five minutes.*
OPPOSITES: important, meaningful
6 = **empty**, useless, hollow, vain, trivial, pointless, worthless, trifling, insignificant, senseless, inconsequential, aimless, insubstantial, valueless, purposeless • *It was more of an idle threat than anything.*
▸ **AS A VERB** 1 *often with* **away** = **fritter**, while, waste, fool, lounge, potter, loaf, dally, loiter, dawdle, laze • *He idled the time away in dreamy thought.*
2 = **do nothing**, slack, hang out *(informal)*, languish, take it easy, shirk, stagnate, mark time, kill time, skive *(Brit. slang)*, vegetate, sit back and do nothing, veg out *(slang)*, kick your heels, bludge *(Austral. & N.Z. informal)* • *We spent many hours idling in cafés.*
3 = **drift**, wander, meander, coast, float, stray, go aimlessly • *They idled along looking at things.*
4 = **tick over**, be in neutral • *Her limo waited with its engine idling.*

QUOTATIONS

As idle as a painted ship
Upon a painted ocean
[Samuel Taylor Coleridge *The Ancient Mariner*]

It is impossible to enjoy idling thoroughly unless one has plenty of work to do
[Jerome K. Jerome *Idle Thoughts of an Idle Fellow*]

Satan finds some mischief still
For idle hands to do
[Isaac Watts *Divine Songs for Children*]

We would all be idle if we could
[Samuel Johnson]

It is better to have loafed and lost than never to have loafed at all
[James Thurber *Fables For Our Time*]

idleness 1 = **inactivity**, unemployment, leisure, inaction, time on your hands • *Idleness is a very bad thing for human nature.*
2 = **loafing**, inertia, sloth, pottering, trifling, laziness, time-wasting, lazing, torpor, sluggishness, skiving *(Brit. slang)*, vegetating, dilly-dallying *(informal)*, shiftlessness • *Idleness and incompetence are not inbred in our workers.*

QUOTATIONS

Idleness is the only refuge of weak minds
[Lord Chesterfield *Letters to his Son*]

idler = **loafer**, lounger, piker *(Austral. & N.Z. slang)*, drone, dodger, slouch *(informal)*, shirker, slacker, couch potato *(slang)*, sloth, dawdler, laggard, time-waster, layabout, deadbeat *(informal, chiefly U.S. & Canad.)*, skiver *(Brit. slang)*, malingerer, sluggard, bludger *(Austral. & N.Z. informal)*, clock-watcher, slugabed, lazybones • *He resents being seen as a moneyed idler.*

idling **AS A NOUN** = **loafing**, resting, drifting, pottering, taking it easy, dawdling • *I'm not very good at idling.*
▸ **AS AN ADJECTIVE** = **failing**, declining, tiring, sinking, flagging, fading, slowing down, deteriorating, faltering, wilting, waning, ebbing • *She attempted to jumpstart her idling singing career.*

idly = **lazily**, casually, passively, languidly, unthinkingly, sluggishly, languorously, lethargically, apathetically, indolently, inertly, lackadaisically, inactively, shiftlessly, slothfully • *We talked idly about magazines and baseball.*
OPPOSITES: actively, busily, energetically

idol 1 = **hero**, superstar, pin-up, favourite, pet, darling, beloved *(slang)*, fave *(informal)* • *They cheered as they caught sight of their idol.*
2 = **graven image**, god, image, deity, pagan symbol • *They shaped the substance into idols that were eaten ceremoniously.*

idolatry 1 = **idol worshipping**, fetishism • *Idolatry was punishable by death.*
2 = **adoration**, adulation, hero worship, apotheosis, exaltation, glorification, idolizing, deification • *Their affection soon increased to almost idolatry.*

idolize = **worship**, love, adore, admire, revere, glorify, exalt, look up to, venerate, hero-worship, deify, bow down before, dote upon, apotheosize, worship to excess • *Naomi idolized her father as she was growing up.*

idyll = **heaven**, ideal, paradise, Eden, Utopia, perfect place, Garden of Eden, Shangri-la, Happy Valley, seventh heaven, Erewhon • *This town was not the rural idyll she had imagined.*

idyllic = **heavenly**, idealized, ideal, charming, peaceful, pastoral, picturesque, rustic, Utopian, halcyon, out of this world, unspoiled, arcadian • *an idyllic setting for a summer romance*

i.e. = **that is**, namely, to wit, id est • *strategic points – i.e. airports or military bases*

if **AS A CONJUNCTION** 1 = **provided**, assuming, given that, providing, allowing, admitting, supposing, granting, in case, presuming, on the assumption that, on condition that, as long as • *If you would like to make a donation, please enclose a cheque.*
2 = **when**, whenever, every time, any time • *She gets very upset if I exclude her from anything.*
3 = **whether** • *He asked if I had left with you, and I said no.*
4 = **though**, but, yet, although, albeit, despite being • *It was beautiful inside, if rather unhomely.*
▸ **AS A NOUN** = **doubt**, condition, uncertainty, provision, constraint, hesitation, vagueness, stipulation • *This business is full of ifs.*

PROVERBS

If ifs and ands were pots and pans there'd be no need for tinkers

iffy 1 = **inferior**, inadequate, unacceptable, imperfect, second-rate, shoddy, substandard, bodger *or* bodgie *(Austral. slang)* • *If your next record's a bit iffy, you're forgotten.*

2 = **uncertain**, doubtful, unpredictable, conditional, undecided, up in the air, problematical, chancy *(informal)*, in the lap of the gods • *His political future is looking iffy.*

ignite 1 = **catch fire**, burn, burst into flames, fire, inflame, flare up, take fire • *The blast was caused by pockets of methane gas which ignited.*
2 = **set fire to**, light, set alight, torch, kindle, touch off, put a match to *(informal)* • *The bombs ignited a fire which destroyed some 60 houses.*

ignoble 1 = **dishonourable**, low, base, mean, petty, infamous, degraded, craven, disgraceful, shabby, vile, degenerate, abject, unworthy, shameless, despicable, heinous, dastardly, contemptible, wretched • *an ignoble episode from their country's past*
2 = **lowly**, mean, low, base, common, peasant, vulgar, plebeian, humble, lowborn *(rare)*, baseborn *(archaic)* • *They wanted to spare him the shame of an ignoble birth.*

ignominious = **humiliating**, disgraceful, shameful, sorry, scandalous, abject, despicable, mortifying, undignified, disreputable, dishonourable, inglorious, discreditable, indecorous • *Many thought that he was doomed to ignominious failure.*
OPPOSITES: worthy, honourable, reputable

ignominy = **disgrace**, shame, humiliation, contempt, discredit, stigma, disrepute, dishonour, infamy, mortification, bad odour • *the ignominy of being made redundant*
OPPOSITES: credit, honour, repute

ignoramus = **dunce**, fool, ass, donkey, bonehead *(slang)*, duffer *(informal)*, simpleton, dullard, dolt, blockhead, lowbrow, putz *(U.S. slang)*, fathead *(informal)*, eejit *(Scot. & Irish)*, thicko *(Brit. slang)*, numpty *(Scot. informal)*, doofus *(slang, chiefly U.S.)*, numbskull *or* numskull, dorba *or* dorb *(Austral. slang)*, bogan *(Austral. slang)* • *I am an ignoramus regarding technical matters.*

ignorance 1 = **lack of education**, stupidity, foolishness, blindness, illiteracy, benightedness, unenlightenment, unintelligence, mental darkness • *In my ignorance, I had never heard of R and B music.*
OPPOSITES: understanding, knowledge, intelligence
2 *with* **of** = **unawareness of**, inexperience of, unfamiliarity with, innocence of, unconsciousness of, greenness about, oblivion about, nescience of *(literary)* • *a complete ignorance of non-European history*

QUOTATIONS

No more; where ignorance is bliss,
'Tis folly to be wise
[Thomas Gray *Ode on a Distant Prospect of Eton College*]

If ignorance is indeed bliss, it is a very low grade of the article
[Tehyi Hsieh *Chinese Epigrams Inside Out and Proverbs*]

Ignorance is not bliss – it is oblivion
[Philip Wylie *Generation of Vipers*]

Ignorance, the stem and root of all evil
[Plato]

What we call evil is simply ignorance bumping its head in the dark
[Henry Ford]

Ignorance is not innocence but sin
[Robert Browning *The Inn Album*]

Ignorance itself is without a doubt a sin for those who do not wish to understand; for those who, however, cannot understand, it is the punishment of sin
[St Augustine]

Ignorance is the curse of God,
Knowledge the wing wherewith we fly to heaven
[William Shakespeare *Henry VI*]

I know nothing except the fact of my ignorance
[Socrates]

If you think education is expensive – try ignorance
[Derek Bok]

PROVERBS

One half of the world does not know how the other half lives

ignorant 1 = **uneducated**, unaware, naive, green, illiterate, inexperienced, innocent, untrained, unlearned, unread, untutored, uncultivated, wet behind the ears *(informal)*, unlettered, untaught, unknowledgeable, uncomprehending, unscholarly, as green as grass • *They don't ask questions for fear of appearing ignorant.*
OPPOSITES: learned, cultured, educated
2 = **insensitive**, gross, crude, rude, shallow, superficial, crass • *Some very ignorant people called me all kinds of names.*
3 *with* **of** = **uninformed of**, unaware of, oblivious to, blind to, innocent of, in the dark about, unconscious of, unschooled in, out of the loop of, inexperienced of, uninitiated about, unknowing of, unenlightened about • *Many people are worryingly ignorant of the facts.*
OPPOSITES: aware, informed, conscious

ignore 1 = **pay no attention to**, neglect, disregard, slight, overlook, scorn, spurn, rebuff, take no notice of, be oblivious to • *She said her husband ignored her.*
OPPOSITES: note, regard, pay attention to
2 = **overlook**, discount, disregard, reject, neglect, shrug off, pass over, brush aside, turn a blind eye to, turn a deaf ear to, shut your eyes to • *Such arguments ignore the important issues.*
3 = **snub**, cut *(informal)*, slight, blank *(slang)*, rebuff, cold-shoulder, turn your back on, give (someone) the cold shoulder, send (someone) to Coventry, give (someone) the brush-off • *I kept sending letters and cards but he just ignored me.*

ilk = **type**, sort, kind, class, style, character, variety, brand, breed, stamp, description, kidney, disposition • *politicians and their ilk*

ill **AS AN ADJECTIVE** 1 = **unwell**, sick, poorly *(informal)*, diseased, funny *(informal)*, weak, crook *(Austral. & N.Z. slang)*, ailing, queer, frail, feeble, unhealthy, seedy *(informal)*, sickly, laid up *(informal)*, queasy, infirm, out of sorts *(informal)*, dicky *(Brit. informal)*, nauseous, off-colour, under the weather *(informal)*, at death's door, indisposed, peaky, on the sick list *(informal)*, valetudinarian, green about the gills, not up to snuff *(informal)* • *He was seriously ill with pneumonia.*
OPPOSITES: well, strong, healthy
2 = **harmful**, bad, damaging, evil, foul, unfortunate, destructive, unlucky, vile, detrimental, hurtful, pernicious, noxious, ruinous, deleterious, injurious, iniquitous, disadvantageous, maleficent • *ill effects from the contamination of the water*
OPPOSITES: good, favourable
3 = **hostile**, malicious, acrimonious, cross, harsh, adverse, belligerent, unkind, hurtful, unfriendly, malevolent, antagonistic, hateful, bellicose, cantankerous, inimical, rancorous, ill-disposed • *He bears no ill feelings towards you.*
OPPOSITES: kind, generous
4 = **bad**, threatening, disturbing, menacing, unlucky, sinister, gloomy, dire, ominous, unhealthy, unfavourable, foreboding, unpromising, inauspicious, unwholesome, unpropitious, bodeful • *His absence preyed on her mind like an ill omen.*
▸ **AS A NOUN** 1 = **problem**, trouble, suffering, worry, trial, injury, pain, hurt, strain, harm, distress, misery, hardship, woe, misfortune, affliction, tribulation, unpleasantness • *He is responsible for many of the country's ills.*
2 = **harm**, suffering, damage, hurt, evil, destruction, grief, trauma, anguish, mischief, malice • *I know it will be difficult for them but I wish them no ill.*
OPPOSITES: good, kindness
▸ **AS AN ADVERB** 1 = **badly**, unfortunately, unfavourably, inauspiciously • *This development may bode ill for the government.*

2 = **hardly**, barely, scarcely, just, only just, by no means, at a push • *We can ill afford another scandal.*
OPPOSITES: well, easily
3 = **illegally**, criminally, unlawfully, fraudulently, dishonestly, illicitly, illegitimately, unscrupulously, foully • *He used his ill-gotten gains to pay for a £360,000 house.*
4 = **insufficiently**, badly, poorly, inadequately, imperfectly, deficiently • *We were ill-prepared for last year's South Africa tour.*
▸ IN PHRASES: **speak ill of someone = malign**, knock *(informal)*, rubbish *(informal)*, run down, blacken, slag (off) *(slang)*, denigrate, belittle, disparage, decry, revile, vilify, slander, defame, bad-mouth *(slang, chiefly U.S. & Canad.)*, besmirch, impugn, calumniate, asperse • *She found it difficult to speak ill of anyone.*

ill-advised = misguided, inappropriate, foolish, rash, reckless, unwise, short-sighted, unseemly, foolhardy, thoughtless, indiscreet, ill-judged, ill-considered, imprudent, wrong-headed, injudicious, incautious, impolitic, overhasty • *She said his remarks had been ill-advised.*
OPPOSITES: seemly, politic, wise

ill-assorted = incompatible, incongruous, unsuited, mismatched, uncongenial, inharmonious • *funny stories about ill-assorted people who had to share cabins*

ill at ease = uncomfortable, nervous, tense, strange, wired *(slang)*, disturbed, anxious, awkward, uneasy, unsettled, faltering, unsure, restless, out of place, neurotic, self-conscious, hesitant, disquieted, edgy, on edge, twitchy *(informal)*, on tenterhooks, fidgety, unquiet, like a fish out of water, antsy *(informal)*, unrelaxed, on pins and needles *(informal)* • *He seemed ill at ease in my company.*
OPPOSITES: easy, at home, comfortable

ill-bred = bad-mannered, rude, coarse, vulgar, crass, churlish, boorish, uncouth, unrefined, impolite, ungentlemanly, uncivilized, discourteous, indelicate, uncivil, unladylike, ungallant, unmannerly, ill-mannered • *They seemed to her rather vulgar and ill-bred.*
OPPOSITES: civil, mannerly, well-bred

ill-considered = unwise, rash, imprudent, careless, precipitate, hasty, heedless, injudicious, improvident, overhasty • *He made some ill-considered remarks about the cost.*

ill-defined = unclear, vague, indistinct, blurred, dim, fuzzy, shadowy, woolly, nebulous • *staff with ill-defined responsibilities*
OPPOSITES: clear, obvious, plain

illegal 1 = **unlawful**, banned, forbidden, prohibited, criminal, outlawed, unofficial, illicit, unconstitutional, illegitimate, lawless, wrongful, off limits, unlicensed, under-the-table, unauthorized, against the law, proscribed, under-the-counter, actionable *(Law)*, felonious • *It is illegal to intercept radio messages.*
OPPOSITES: legal, lawful, permissible
2 = **foul**, dirty, unfair, crooked, shady *(informal)*, fraudulent, unjust, dishonest, unscrupulous, underhand, inequitable, unsportsmanlike • *He was dismissed by the referee for an illegal tackle.*

illegality = crime, wrong, felony, criminality, lawlessness, illegitimacy, wrongness, unlawfulness, illicitness • *There is no evidence of illegality.*

illegible = indecipherable, unreadable, faint, crabbed, scrawled, hieroglyphic, hard to make out, undecipherable, obscure • *Incomplete or illegible applications will not be considered.*
OPPOSITES: clear, readable, legible

illegitimacy 1 = **bastardy**, bastardism • *Divorce and illegitimacy lead to millions of one-parent families.*
2 = **illegality**, unconstitutionality, unlawfulness, illicitness, irregularity • *They denounced the illegitimacy and oppressiveness of the regime.*

illegitimate 1 = **born out of wedlock**, natural, bastard, love, misbegotten *(literary)*, baseborn *(archaic)* • *In 1985 the news of his illegitimate child came out.*
2 = **unlawful**, illegal, illicit, improper, unconstitutional, under-the-table, unauthorized, unsanctioned • *a ruthless and illegitimate regime*
OPPOSITES: legal, legitimate, authorized
3 = **invalid**, incorrect, illogical, spurious, unsound • *It is not illegitimate to seek a parallel between the two events.*

QUOTATIONS
There are no illegitimate children – only illegitimate parents
[Judge Léon R. Yankwich]

ill-fated = doomed, unfortunate, unlucky, unhappy, blighted, hapless, luckless, ill-starred, star-crossed, ill-omened • *They are now home after their ill-fated trip abroad.*

ill feeling = hostility, resentment, bitterness, offence, indignation, animosity, antagonism, enmity, rancour, bad blood, hard feelings, ill will, animus, dudgeon *(archaic)*, chip on your shoulder • *He bears no ill feeling towards you.*
OPPOSITES: favour, friendship, goodwill

ill-founded = groundless, empty, unjustified, idle, unreliable, unproven, unsubstantiated, unsupported, baseless • *Suspicion, however ill-founded, can poison a marriage.*

illiberal = intolerant, prejudiced, bigoted, narrow-minded, small-minded, reactionary, hidebound, uncharitable, ungenerous • *His views are markedly illiberal.*
OPPOSITES: liberal, tolerant, open-minded

illicit 1 = **illegal**, criminal, prohibited, unlawful, black-market, illegitimate, off limits, unlicensed, unauthorized, bootleg, contraband, felonious • *information about the use of illicit drugs*
OPPOSITES: legal, legitimate, lawful
2 = **forbidden**, improper, immoral, wrong, guilty, clandestine, furtive • *He clearly condemns illicit love.*

illiteracy = lack of education, ignorance, benightedness, illiterateness • *The rise in illiteracy is one aspect of the crisis in education.*

illiterate 1 = **uneducated**, ignorant, unlettered, unable to read and write, analphabetic • *A large percentage of the population is illiterate.*
OPPOSITES: lettered, educated, literate
2 = **ignorant**, unaware, inexperienced, blind, innocent, unconscious, in the dark, oblivious, unwitting, uninitiated, uninformed, benighted, untutored, unknowing, out of the loop, unenlightened, unschooled, unlettered, untaught • *Many senior managers are technologically illiterate.*
OPPOSITES: aware, taught, tutored

ill-judged = misguided, foolish, rash, unwise, short-sighted, ill-advised, ill-considered, wrong-headed, injudicious, overhasty • *Critics judged his comments ill-judged and offensive.*

ill-mannered = rude, impolite, discourteous, coarse, churlish, boorish, insolent, uncouth, loutish, uncivil, ill-bred, badly behaved, ill-behaved, unmannerly • *She would have considered it ill-mannered to show surprise.*
OPPOSITES: civil, polite, courteous

illness = sickness, ill health, malaise, attack, disease, complaint, infection, disorder, bug *(informal)*, disability, ailment, affliction, poor health, malady, infirmity, indisposition, lurgy *(informal)* • *She returned to her family home to recover from an illness.*

illogical = irrational, absurd, unreasonable, meaningless, incorrect, faulty, inconsistent, invalid, senseless, spurious, inconclusive, unsound, unscientific, specious, fallacious, sophistical • *his completely illogical arguments*
OPPOSITES: sound, correct, logical

ill-starred = doomed, unfortunate, unlucky, unhappy, hapless, inauspicious, star-crossed, ill-omened, ill-fated • *an ill-starred attempt to create jobs in a deprived area*

ill-tempered = cross, irritable, grumpy, irascible, sharp, annoyed, impatient, touchy, bad-tempered, curt, spiteful,

tetchy, ratty (*Brit. & N.Z. informal*), testy, chippy (*informal*), choleric, ill-humoured, liverish • *He sounded like an ill-tempered child.*
OPPOSITES: cheerful, benign, good-natured

ill-timed = **inopportune**, inappropriate, inconvenient, untimely, unwelcome, unseasonable, awkward • *He argued that the tax cut was ill-timed.*
OPPOSITES: timely, appropriate, well-timed

ill-treat = **abuse**, injure, harm, wrong, damage, harry, harass, misuse, oppress, dump on (*slang, chiefly U.S.*), mishandle, shit on (*taboo*), maltreat, ill-use, handle roughly, knock about *or* around • *The rescued hostages said they had not been ill-treated.*

ill-treatment = **abuse**, harm, mistreatment, damage, injury, misuse, ill-use, rough handling • *Some had died as a result of ill-treatment.*

illuminate 1 = **light up**, light, brighten, irradiate, illumine (*literary*) • *No streetlights illuminate the street.*
OPPOSITES: obscure, dim, darken
2 = **explain**, interpret, make clear, clarify, clear up, enlighten, shed light on, elucidate, explicate, give insight into • *The instructors use games to illuminate the subject.*
OPPOSITES: obscure, cloud, veil
3 = **decorate**, illustrate, adorn, ornament • *medieval illuminated manuscripts*

illuminating = **informative**, revealing, enlightening, helpful, explanatory, instructive • *It's illuminating to compare press coverage of the story.*
OPPOSITES: confusing, puzzling, obscuring

illumination AS A NOUN 1 = **light**, lighting, lights, ray, beam, lighting up, brightening, brightness, radiance • *The only illumination came from a small window above.*
2 = **enlightenment**, understanding, insight, perception, awareness, revelation, inspiration, clarification, edification • *No further illumination can be had from this theory.*
▸ AS A PLURAL NOUN = **lights**, decorations, fairy lights • *the famous Blackpool illuminations*

illusion 1 = **delusion**, misconception, misapprehension, fancy, deception, fallacy, self-deception, false impression, false belief, misbelief • *No one really has any illusions about winning the war.*
2 = **false impression**, feeling, appearance, impression, fancy, deception, imitation, sham, pretence, semblance, fallacy • *Floor-to-ceiling windows give the illusion of extra space.*
OPPOSITES: fact, truth, reality
3 = **fantasy**, vision, hallucination, trick, spectre, mirage, semblance, daydream, apparition, chimera, figment of the imagination, phantasm, ignis fatuus, will-o'-the-wisp • *It creates the illusion of moving around in the computer's graphic environment.*

illusory *or* **illusive** = **unreal**, false, misleading, untrue, seeming, mistaken, apparent, sham, deceptive, deceitful, hallucinatory, fallacious, chimerical, delusive • *the illusory nature of nationhood*
OPPOSITES: real, true, solid

illustrate 1 = **demonstrate**, show, exhibit, emphasize, exemplify, explicate • *The example of the United States illustrates this point.*
2 = **explain**, describe, interpret, sum up, make clear, clarify, summarize, bring home, point up, make plain, elucidate • *She illustrates her analysis with extracts from interviews and discussions.*
3 = **adorn**, ornament, embellish • *He has illustrated the book with black-and-white photographs.*

illustrated = **pictured**, decorated, illuminated, embellished, pictorial, with illustrations • *The book is beautifully illustrated throughout.*

illustration 1 = **example**, case, instance, sample, explanation, demonstration, interpretation, specimen, analogy, clarification, case in point, exemplar, elucidation, exemplification • *These figures are an illustration of the country's dynamism.*
2 = **picture**, drawing, painting, image, print, plate, figure, portrait, representation, sketch, decoration, portrayal, likeness, adornment • *She looked like a princess in a nineteenth century illustration.*

illustrative 1 = **representative**, typical, descriptive, explanatory, interpretive, expository, explicatory, illustrational • *The following excerpt is illustrative of her interaction with students.*
2 = **pictorial**, graphic, diagrammatic, delineative • *an illustrative guide to the daily activities of the football club*

illustrious = **famous**, great, noted, celebrated, signal, brilliant, remarkable, distinguished, prominent, glorious, noble, splendid, notable, renowned, eminent, famed, exalted • *the most illustrious scientists of the century*
OPPOSITES: obscure, notorious, humble

ill will = **hostility**, spite, dislike, hatred, envy, resentment, grudge, malice, animosity, aversion, venom, antagonism, antipathy, enmity, acrimony, rancour, bad blood, hard feelings, animus, malevolence, unfriendliness • *He didn't bear anyone any ill will.*
OPPOSITES: charity, friendship, goodwill

image AS A NOUN 1 = **thought**, idea, vision, concept, impression, perception, conception, mental picture, conceptualization • *The words 'Côte d'Azur' conjure up images of sun, sea and sand.*
2 = **profile**, face, front, role, mask, persona, façade, public face, public impression, assumed role • *The tobacco industry has been trying to improve its image.*
3 = **figure of speech**, metaphor, simile, conceit, trope • *The images in the poem illustrate the poet's frame of mind.*
4 = **reflection**, appearance, likeness, mirror image • *I peered at my image in the mirror.*
5 = **figure**, idol, icon, fetish, talisman • *The polished stone bore the graven image of a snakebird.*
6 = **replica**, copy, reproduction, counterpart, spit (*informal, chiefly Brit.*), clone, facsimile, spitting image (*informal*), similitude, Doppelgänger, (dead) ringer (*slang*), double • *The boy is the image of his father.*
7 = **picture**, photo, photograph, representation, reproduction, snapshot • *A computer creates an image on the screen.*
▸ IN PHRASES: **spitting image** = **replica**, copy, reproduction, counterpart, spit (*informal, chiefly Brit.*), clone, facsimile, similitude, Doppelgänger, (dead) ringer (*slang*), double • *She's the spitting image of her mother.*

imaginable = **possible**, conceivable, likely, credible, plausible, believable, under the sun, comprehensible, thinkable, within the bounds of possibility, supposable • *They encourage every activity imaginable.*
OPPOSITES: impossible, unlikely, unimaginable

imaginary = **fictional**, made-up, invented, supposed, imagined, assumed, ideal, fancied, legendary, visionary, shadowy, unreal, hypothetical, fanciful, fictitious, mythological, illusory, nonexistent, dreamlike, hallucinatory, illusive, chimerical, unsubstantial, phantasmal, suppositious, imagal (*Psychoanalysis*) • *Lots of children have imaginary friends.*
OPPOSITES: true, known, real

imagination 1 = **creativity**, vision, invention, ingenuity, enterprise, insight, inspiration, wit, originality, inventiveness, resourcefulness • *He has a logical mind and a little imagination.*
2 = **mind's eye**, fancy • *Long before I went there, the place was alive in my imagination.*
3 = **interest**, attention, curiosity, fascination • *Italian football captured the imagination of the nation last season.*

QUOTATIONS

The Possible's slow fuse is lit
By the Imagination
[Emily Dickinson]

People can die of mere imagination
[Geoffrey Chaucer *The Miller's Tale*]

Nature uses imagination to lift her work of creation to even higher levels
[Luigi Pirandello *Six Characters in Search of an Author*]

I have imagination, and nothing that is real is alien to me
[George Santayana *Little Essays*]

Only in men's imagination does every truth find an effective and undeniable existence. Imagination, not invention, is the supreme master of art as of life
[Joseph Conrad *A Personal Record*]

My imagination makes me human and makes me a fool; it gives me all the world and exiles me from it
[Ursula Le Guin *Winged: the Creatures on My Mind*]

Imagination, the supreme delight of the immortal and the immature, should be limited. In order to enjoy life, we should not enjoy it too much
[Vladimir Nabokov *Speak, Memory*]

imaginative = **creative**, original, inspired, enterprising, fantastic, clever, stimulating, vivid, ingenious, visionary, inventive, fanciful, dreamy, whimsical, poetical • *hundreds of cooking ideas and imaginative recipes*
OPPOSITES: ordinary, unimaginative, uninspired

imagine 1 = **envisage**, see, picture, plan, create, project, think of, scheme, frame, invent, devise, conjure up, envision, visualize, dream up *(informal)*, think up, conceive of, conceptualize, fantasize about, see in the mind's eye, form a mental picture of • *He could not imagine a more peaceful scene.*
2 = **believe**, think, suppose, assume, suspect, gather, guess *(informal, chiefly U.S. & Canad.)*, realize, take it, reckon, fancy, deem, speculate, presume, take for granted, infer, deduce, apprehend, conjecture, surmise • *I imagine you're referring to me.*
3 = **dream**, fancy, visualize, envisage, conjure up, hallucinate • *Looking back, I think I must have imagined the whole thing.*

imbalance = **unevenness**, bias, inequality, unfairness, partiality, disproportion, lopsidedness, top-heaviness, lack of proportion • *the imbalance between the two sides in this war*

imbecile AS A NOUN = **idiot**, fool, jerk *(slang, chiefly U.S. & Canad.)*, tosser *(Brit. slang)*, plank *(Brit. slang)*, berk *(Brit. slang)*, prick *(derogatory slang)*, wally *(slang)*, charlie *(Brit. informal)*, prat *(slang)*, plonker *(slang)*, coot, moron, geek *(slang)*, twit *(informal, chiefly Brit.)*, chump, cretin, bungler, dipstick *(Brit. slang)*, dickhead *(slang)*, gonzo *(slang)*, schmuck *(U.S. slang)*, dork *(slang)*, dolt, divvy *(Brit. slang)*, pillock *(Brit. slang)*, halfwit, dweeb *(U.S. slang)*, putz *(U.S. slang)*, eejit *(Scot. & Irish)*, thicko *(Brit. slang)*, dumb-ass *(slang)*, gobshite *(Irish taboo slang)*, numpty *(Scot. informal)*, doofus *(slang, chiefly U.S.)*, dotard, fuckwit *(taboo)*, thickhead, dickwit *(slang)*, nerd *or* nurd *(slang)*, numbskull *or* numskull, dorba *or* dorb *(Austral. slang)*, bogan *(Austral. slang)* • *I don't want to deal with these imbeciles any more.*
▸ AS AN ADJECTIVE = **stupid**, foolish, idiotic, simple, thick, ludicrous, simple-minded, inane, fatuous, witless, moronic, asinine, feeble-minded, imbecilic, braindead *(informal)*, dumb-ass *(slang)*, dead from the neck up • *It was an imbecile thing to do.*

imbed *see* embed

imbibe 1 = **drink**, consume, knock back *(informal)*, neck *(slang)*, sink *(informal)*, swallow, suck, hoover *(informal)*, swig *(informal)*, quaff • *They were used to imbibing enormous quantities of alcohol.*
2 = **absorb**, receive, take in, gain, gather, acquire, assimilate, ingest • *He'd imbibed a set of mystical beliefs from the cradle.*

imbroglio = **complication**, involvement, complexity, embarrassment, misunderstanding, quandary, entanglement • *What investor would willingly become involved in this imbroglio?*

imbue = **instil**, infuse, steep, bathe, saturate, pervade, permeate, impregnate, inculcate • *He is able to imbue his listeners with enthusiasm.*

imitate 1 = **copy**, follow, repeat, echo, emulate, ape, simulate, mirror, follow suit, duplicate, counterfeit, follow in the footsteps of, take a leaf out of (someone's) book • *a precedent which may be imitated by other activists*
2 = **do an impression of**, take off *(informal)*, mimic, do *(informal)*, affect, copy, mock, parody, caricature, send up *(Brit. informal)*, spoof *(informal)*, impersonate, burlesque, personate • *He screwed up his face and imitated the Colonel.*

imitation AS A NOUN 1 = **replica**, fake, reproduction, sham, forgery, carbon copy *(informal)*, counterfeit, counterfeiting, likeness, duplication • *the most accurate imitation of Chinese architecture in Europe*
2 = **copying**, echoing, resemblance, aping, simulation, mimicry • *She learned her golf by imitation.*
3 = **impression**, parody, mockery, takeoff *(informal)*, impersonation • *I could do a pretty good imitation of him.*
▸ AS AN ADJECTIVE = **artificial**, mock, reproduction, dummy, synthetic, man-made, simulated, sham, pseudo *(informal)*, ersatz, repro, phoney *or* phony *(informal)* • *a set of Dickens bound in imitation leather*
OPPOSITES: real, genuine, authentic

QUOTATIONS

Imitation is the sincerest flattery
[Charles Colton *Lacon*]

To do the opposite of something is also a form of imitation, namely an imitation of its opposite
[G.C. Lichtenberg *Aphorisms*]

imitative 1 = **copying**, mimicking, derivative, copycat *(informal)*, unoriginal, mimetic, echoic • *Babies of this age are highly imitative.*
2 = **copied**, put-on, mimicking, similar, mock, second-hand, simulated, pseudo *(informal)*, parrot-like, unoriginal, plagiarized, mimetic, onomatopoeic • *This may lead to excitement and to imitative behaviour.*

imitator = **impersonator**, mimic, impressionist, copycat, echo, follower, parrot *(informal)*, copier, carbon copy *(informal)* • *a group of Elvis imitators*

immaculate 1 = **clean**, impeccable, spotless, trim, neat, spruce, squeaky-clean, spick-and-span, neat as a new pin • *Her front room was kept immaculate.*
OPPOSITES: dirty, filthy, unclean
2 = **pure**, perfect, innocent, impeccable, virtuous, flawless, faultless, squeaky-clean, guiltless, above reproach, sinless, incorrupt • *her immaculate reputation*
OPPOSITES: corrupt, impure, impeachable
3 = **perfect**, flawless, impeccable, stainless, faultless, unblemished, unsullied, uncontaminated, unpolluted, untarnished, unexceptionable, undefiled • *My car's in absolutely immaculate condition.*
OPPOSITES: stained, contaminated, tainted

immanent = **inherent**, innate, intrinsic, natural, internal, indigenous, subjective, congenital, inborn, hard-wired, indwelling • *hierarchy as the immanent principle of Western society*

immaterial = **irrelevant**, insignificant, unimportant, unnecessary, trivial, trifling, inconsequential, extraneous, inconsiderable, of no importance, of no consequence, inessential, a matter of indifference, of little account, inapposite • *Whether we like him or not is immaterial.*
OPPOSITES: important, significant, essential

immature 1 = **young**, adolescent, undeveloped, green, raw, premature, unfinished, imperfect, untimely, unripe, unformed, unseasonable, unfledged • *The birds were in immature plumage.*

2 = **childish**, juvenile, infantile, puerile, callow, babyish, wet behind the ears *(informal)*, jejune • *You're just being childish and immature.*
OPPOSITES: developed, adult, mature

immaturity 1 = **rawness**, imperfection, greenness, unpreparedness, unripeness • *In spite of some immaturity of style, it showed real imagination.*
2 = **childishness**, puerility, callowness, juvenility, babyishness • *his immaturity and lack of social skills*

immeasurable = **incalculable**, vast, immense, endless, unlimited, infinite, limitless, boundless, bottomless, inexhaustible, unfathomable, unbounded, inestimable, measureless, illimitable • *I felt an immeasurable love for him.*
OPPOSITES: limited, bounded, finite

immediate 1 = **instant**, prompt, instantaneous, quick, on-the-spot, split-second • *My immediate reaction was one of digust.*
OPPOSITES: late, later, delayed
2 = **current**, present, pressing, existing, actual, urgent, on hand, extant • *The immediate problem is not lack of food, but transportation.*
3 = **nearest**, next, direct, close, near, adjacent, contiguous, proximate • *I was seated at his immediate left.*
OPPOSITES: far, remote, distant
4 = **intimate**, close • *The presence of his immediate family is having a calming influence.*
5 = **recent**, just gone • *jobs and success, which we haven't enjoyed in the immediate past*

immediately 1 = **at once**, now, instantly, straight away, directly, promptly, right now, right away, there and then, speedily, without delay, without hesitation, instantaneously, forthwith, pronto *(informal)*, unhesitatingly, this instant, on the nail, this very minute, posthaste, tout de suite *(French)*, before you could say Jack Robinson *(informal)* • *She answered his letter immediately.*
2 = **directly**, closely, at first hand • *Who is immediately responsible for this misery?*
3 = **exactly**, just, right, closely, nearly, directly, squarely • *She always sits immediately behind the driver.*

immemorial = **age-old**, ancient, long-standing, traditional, fixed, rooted, archaic, time-honoured, of yore, olden *(archaic)* • *a modern version of an immemorial myth*

immense = **huge**, great, massive, vast, large, giant, enormous, extensive, tremendous, mega *(slang)*, titanic, infinite, jumbo *(informal)*, very big, gigantic, monumental, monstrous, mammoth, colossal, mountainous, stellar *(informal)*, prodigious, interminable, stupendous, king-size, king-sized, fuck-off *(taboo)*, immeasurable, elephantine, ginormous *(informal)*, Brobdingnagian, illimitable, humongous *or* humungous *(U.S. slang)*, supersize • *an immense cloud of smoke*
OPPOSITES: little, small, tiny

immensely = **extremely**, very, highly, greatly, quite, severely, terribly, ultra, utterly, unusually, exceptionally, extraordinarily, intensely, markedly, awfully *(informal)*, acutely, exceedingly, excessively, inordinately, uncommonly, to a fault, to the nth degree, to *or* in the extreme • *Wind surfing can be immensely exciting.*

immensity = **size**, extent, magnitude, sweep, bulk, scope, greatness, expanse, enormity, vastness, hugeness, massiveness • *The immensity of the universe is difficult to grasp.*

immerse 1 = **engross**, involve, absorb, busy, occupy, engage • *His commitments did not allow him to immerse himself in family life.*
2 = **plunge**, dip, submerge, sink, duck, bathe, douse, dunk, submerse • *The electrodes are immersed in liquid.*

immersed = **engrossed**, involved, absorbed, deep, busy, occupied, taken up, buried, consumed, wrapped up, bound up, rapt, spellbound, mesmerized, in a brown study • *He's really becoming immersed in his work.*

immersion 1 = **involvement**, concentration, preoccupation, absorption • *long-term assignments that allowed them total immersion in their subjects*
2 = **dipping**, submerging, plunging, ducking, dousing, dunking • *The wood had become swollen from prolonged immersion.*

immigrant = **settler**, incomer, alien, stranger, outsider, newcomer, migrant, emigrant • *an illegal immigrant*

imminent = **near**, coming, close, approaching, threatening, gathering, on the way, in the air, forthcoming, looming, menacing, brewing, impending, at hand, upcoming, on the cards, on the horizon, in the pipeline, nigh *(archaic)*, in the offing, fast-approaching, just round the corner, near-at-hand • *They warned that an attack is imminent.*
OPPOSITES: remote, distant, far-off

immobile 1 = **motionless**, still, stationary, fixed, rooted, frozen, stable, halted, stiff, rigid, static, riveted, lifeless, inert, at rest, inanimate, immovable, immobilized, at a standstill, unmoving, stock-still, like a statue, immotile • *He remained as immobile as if carved out of rock.*
OPPOSITES: mobile, portable, on the move
2 = **crippled**, paralysed, incapacitated, laid up *(informal)*, bedridden, housebound, enfeebled • *A riding accident had left him immobile.*
OPPOSITES: active, vigorous

immobility = **stillness**, firmness, steadiness, stability, fixity, inertness, immovability, motionlessness, absence of movement • *the rigid immobility of his shoulders*

immobilize = **paralyse**, stop, freeze, halt, disable, cripple, lay up *(informal)*, bring to a standstill, put out of action, render inoperative • *a car alarm that immobilizes the engine*

immoderate = **excessive**, extreme, over the top *(slang)*, enormous, steep *(informal)*, exaggerated, extravagant, unreasonable, undue, uncontrolled, unjustified, unwarranted, exorbitant, unrestrained, profligate, inordinate, over the odds *(informal)*, egregious, intemperate, unconscionable, uncalled-for, O.T.T. *(slang)* • *He launched an immoderate tirade on his son.*
OPPOSITES: controlled, reasonable, moderate

immodest 1 = **indecent**, improper, lewd, revealing, obscene, coarse, immoral, depraved, titillating, bawdy, flirtatious, impure, indelicate, indecorous, unchaste, gross • *She was wearing a humiliatingly immodest gown.*
2 = **shameless**, forward, brazen, fresh *(informal)*, bold, pushy *(informal)*, impudent, brass-necked *(Brit. informal)*, bold as brass, unblushing • *He could be ungraciously immodest about his abilities.*

immoral = **wicked**, bad, wrong, abandoned, evil, corrupt, vicious, obscene, indecent, vile, degenerate, dishonest, pornographic, sinful, unethical, lewd, depraved, impure, debauched, unprincipled, nefarious, dissolute, iniquitous, reprobate, licentious, of easy virtue, unchaste • *those who think that birth control is immoral*
OPPOSITES: good, moral, pure

immorality = **wickedness**, wrong, vice, evil, corruption, sin, depravity, iniquity, debauchery, badness, licentiousness, turpitude, dissoluteness • *a reflection of our society's immorality*
OPPOSITES: goodness, morality, honesty

immortal AS AN ADJECTIVE 1 = **timeless**, eternal, everlasting, lasting, traditional, classic, constant, enduring, persistent, abiding, perennial, ageless, unfading • *Wuthering Heights – that immortal love story.*
OPPOSITES: passing, fleeting, ephemeral
2 = **undying**, eternal, perpetual, indestructible, death-defying, imperishable, deathless • *They were considered gods and therefore immortal.*
OPPOSITES: mortal, temporary, fading
▸ AS A NOUN 1 = **hero**, genius, paragon, great • *They had paid £50 a head just to be in the presence of an immortal.*

2 = god, goddess, deity, Olympian, divine being, immortal being, atua *(N.Z.)* • *In the legend, the fire is supposed to turn him into an immortal.*

immortality 1 = eternity, perpetuity, everlasting life, timelessness, incorruptibility, indestructibility, endlessness, deathlessness • *belief in the immortality of the soul*
2 = fame, glory, celebrity, greatness, renown, glorification, gloriousness • *Some people want to achieve immortality through their works.*

QUOTATIONS
I have good hope that there is something after death
[Plato *Phaedo*]
Should this my firm persuasion of the soul's immortality prove to be a mere delusion, it is at least a pleasing delusion, and I will cherish it to my last breath
[Cicero *De Senectute*]
Immortality is health; this life is a long sickness
[St Augustine *Sermons*]
Unable are the Loved to die
For Love is Immortality
[Emily Dickinson]
Children endow their parents with a vicarious immortality
[George Santayana *The Life of Reason: Reason in Society*]
I don't want to achieve immortality through my work ... I want to achieve it through not dying
[Woody Allen]

immortalize = commemorate, celebrate, perpetuate, glorify, enshrine, exalt, memorialize, solemnize, apotheosize, eternalize • *The town was immortalized in the famous story of Dracula.*

immovable 1 = fixed, set, fast, firm, stuck, secure, rooted, stable, jammed, stationary, immutable, unbudgeable • *It was declared unsafe because the support bars were immovable.*
2 = inflexible, adamant, resolute, steadfast, constant, unyielding, unwavering, impassive, obdurate, unshakable, unchangeable, unshaken, stony-hearted, unimpressionable • *On one issue, however, she was immovable.*
OPPOSITES: yielding, flexible, wavering

immune
▸ IN PHRASES: **immune from = exempt from**, free from, let off *(informal)*, not subject to, not liable to • *Members are immune from prosecution for corruption.*
immune to 1 = resistant to, free from, protected from, safe from, not open to, spared from, secure against, invulnerable to, insusceptible to • *The blood test will tell whether you are immune to the disease.*
2 = unaffected by, not affected by, invulnerable to, insusceptible to • *He never became immune to the sight of death.*

immunity 1 = exemption, amnesty, indemnity, release, freedom, liberty, privilege, prerogative, invulnerability, exoneration • *The police are offering immunity to witnesses who can help them.*
2 *with* **to = resistance**, protection, resilience, inoculation, immunization • *immunity to airborne bacteria*
OPPOSITES: exposure, susceptibility, liability

immunize = vaccinate, inoculate, protect, safeguard • *They have decide not to have their child immunized.*

immutable = unchanging, fixed, permanent, stable, constant, enduring, abiding, perpetual, inflexible, steadfast, sacrosanct, immovable, ageless, invariable, unalterable, unchangeable, changeless • *the immutable principles of right and wrong*

imp 1 = demon, devil, sprite • *He sees the devil as a little imp with horns.*
2 = rascal, rogue, brat, urchin, minx, scamp, pickle *(Brit. informal)*, gamin, nointer *(Austral. slang)* • *I didn't say that, you little imp!*

impact AS A NOUN **1 = effect**, influence, consequences, impression, repercussions, ramifications • *They expect the meeting to have a marked impact on the country's future.*
2 = collision, force, contact, shock, crash, knock, stroke, smash, bump, thump, jolt • *The pilot must have died on impact.*
▸ AS A VERB **= hit**, strike, crash, clash, crush, ram, smack, collide • *the sharp tinkle of metal impacting on stone*
▸ IN PHRASES: **impact on something** *or* **someone = affect**, change, involve, interest, concern, influence, transform, alter, modify, act on, sway, bear upon, impinge upon • *Such schemes mean little unless they impact on people.*

impair = worsen, reduce, damage, injure, harm, mar, undermine, weaken, spoil, diminish, decrease, blunt, deteriorate, lessen, hinder, debilitate, vitiate, enfeeble, enervate • *Consumption of alcohol impairs your ability to drive.*
OPPOSITES: better, improve, strengthen

impaired = damaged, flawed, faulty, defective, imperfect, unsound • *The blast left him with permanently impaired vision.*

impairment = disability, disorder, defect, complaint, ailment, affliction, malady, disablement, infirmity • *He has a visual impairment in his right eye.*

impale = pierce, stick, run through, spike, lance, spear, skewer, spit, transfix • *He died after being impaled on railings.*

impart 1 = communicate, pass on, convey, tell, reveal, discover, relate, disclose, divulge, make known • *the ability to impart knowledge and command respect*
2 = give, accord, lend, bestow, offer, grant, afford, contribute, yield, confer • *She managed to impart great elegance to the dress she wore.*

impartial = neutral, objective, detached, just, fair, equal, open-minded, equitable, disinterested, unbiased, even-handed, nonpartisan, unprejudiced, without fear or favour, nondiscriminating • *They offer impartial advice, guidance and information to students.*
OPPOSITES: unfair, prejudiced, biased

impartiality = neutrality, equity, fairness, equality, detachment, objectivity, disinterest, open-mindedness, even-handedness, disinterestedness, dispassion, nonpartisanship, lack of bias • *a justice system lacking impartiality*
OPPOSITES: bias, favouritism, unfairness

impassable = blocked, closed, obstructed, impenetrable, unnavigable • *Many minor roads in the south remained impassable today.*

impasse = deadlock, stalemate, standstill, dead end, standoff, blind alley *(informal)* • *The company has reached an impasse in negotiations.*

impassioned = intense, heated, passionate, warm, excited, inspired, violent, stirring, flaming, furious, glowing, blazing, vivid, animated, rousing, fiery, worked up, ardent, inflamed, fervent, ablaze, vehement, fervid • *He made an impassioned appeal for peace.*
OPPOSITES: cool, objective, indifferent

impassive = unemotional, unmoved, emotionless, reserved, cool, calm, composed, indifferent, self-contained, serene, callous, aloof, stoical, unconcerned, apathetic, dispassionate, unfazed *(informal)*, inscrutable, stolid, unruffled, phlegmatic, unfeeling, poker-faced *(informal)*, imperturbable, insensible, impassible *(rare)*, unexcitable, insusceptible, unimpressible • *He searched the man's impassive face for some indication that he understood.*

impatience 1 = restlessness, frustration, intolerance, agitation, edginess • *There is considerable impatience with the slow pace of political change.*
OPPOSITES: calm, composure, serenity
2 = irritability, shortness, edginess, intolerance, quick temper, snappiness, irritableness • *There was a hint of impatience in his tone.*
OPPOSITES: patience, restraint, tolerance

3 = eagerness, longing, enthusiasm, hunger, yearning, thirst, zeal, fervour, ardour, vehemence, earnestness, keenness, impetuosity, heartiness, avidity, intentness, greediness • *She showed impatience to continue the climb.*
4 = haste, hurry, impetuosity, rashness, hastiness • *They visited a fertility clinic in their impatience to have a child.*

QUOTATIONS
All human errors are impatience, a premature breaking off of methodical procedure, an apparent fencing-in of what is apparently at issue
[Franz Kafka *The Collected Aphorisms*]

impatient 1 = cross, tense, annoyed, irritated, prickly, edgy, touchy, bad-tempered, intolerant, petulant, ill-tempered, cantankerous, ratty *(Brit. & N.Z. informal)*, chippy *(informal)*, hot-tempered, quick-tempered, crotchety *(informal)*, ill-humoured, narky *(Brit. slang)*, out of humour • *He becomes impatient as the hours pass.*
2 = irritable, fiery, abrupt, hasty, snappy, indignant, curt, vehement, brusque, irascible, testy • *Beware of being too impatient with others.*
OPPOSITES: tolerant, easy-going
3 = eager, longing, keen, hot, earnest, raring, anxious, hungry, intent, enthusiastic, yearning, greedy, restless, ardent, avid, fervent, zealous, chafing, vehement, fretful, straining at the leash, fervid, keen as mustard, like a cat on hot bricks *(informal)*, athirst • *They are impatient for jobs and security.*
OPPOSITES: patient, cool, calm

impeach = charge, accuse, prosecute, blame, denounce, indict, censure, bring to trial, arraign • *an opposition move to impeach the President*

impeachment = accusation, prosecution, indictment, arraignment • *Unconstitutional actions would be grounds for impeachment.*

impeccable = faultless, perfect, pure, exact, precise, exquisite, stainless, immaculate, flawless, squeaky-clean, unerring, unblemished, unimpeachable, irreproachable, sinless, incorrupt • *She had impeccable taste in clothes.*
OPPOSITES: corrupt, flawed, faulty

impecunious = poor, broke *(informal)*, penniless, short, strapped *(slang)*, stony *(Brit. slang)*, cleaned out *(slang)*, insolvent, destitute, poverty-stricken, down and out, skint *(Brit. slang)*, indigent, dirt-poor *(informal)*, flat broke *(informal)* • *Back in the eighties he was an impecunious, would-be racing driver.*
OPPOSITES: rich, wealthy, prosperous

impede = hinder, stop, slow (down), check, bar, block, delay, hold up, brake, disrupt, curb, restrain, hamper, thwart, clog, obstruct, retard, encumber, cumber, throw a spanner in the works of *(Brit. informal)* • *Fallen rocks are impeding the progress of rescue workers.*
OPPOSITES: help, further, aid

impediment = obstacle, barrier, check, bar, block, difficulty, hazard, curb, snag, obstruction, stumbling block, hindrance, encumbrance, fly in the ointment, millstone around your neck • *There is no legal impediment to the marriage.*
OPPOSITES: support, benefit, aid

impel = force, move, compel, drive, require, push, influence, urge, inspire, prompt, spur, stimulate, motivate, oblige, induce, prod, constrain, incite, instigate, goad, actuate • *I felt impelled to go on speaking.*
OPPOSITES: check, discourage, restrain

impending = looming, coming, approaching, near, nearing, threatening, forthcoming, brewing, imminent, hovering, upcoming, on the horizon, in the pipeline, in the offing • *He had told us that morning of his impending marriage.*

impenetrable 1 = impassable, solid, impervious, thick, dense, hermetic, impermeable, inviolable, unpierceable • *The range forms an impenetrable barrier between Europe and Asia.*
OPPOSITES: accessible, passable, penetrable
2 = incomprehensible, obscure, baffling, dark, hidden, mysterious, enigmatic, arcane, inexplicable, unintelligible, inscrutable, unfathomable, indiscernible, cabbalistic, enigmatical • *His philosophical work is notoriously impenetrable.*
OPPOSITES: clear, obvious, understandable

imperative = urgent, essential, pressing, vital, crucial, compulsory, indispensable, obligatory, exigent • *It's imperative to know your rights at such a time.*
OPPOSITES: unnecessary, optional, unimportant

imperceptible = undetectable, slight, subtle, small, minute, fine, tiny, faint, invisible, gradual, shadowy, microscopic, indistinguishable, inaudible, infinitesimal, teeny-weeny, unnoticeable, insensible, impalpable, indiscernible, teensy-weensy, inappreciable • *His hesitation was almost imperceptible.*
OPPOSITES: visible, noticeable, perceptible

imperceptibly = invisibly, slowly, subtly, little by little, unobtrusively, unseen, by a hair's-breadth, unnoticeably, indiscernibly, inappreciably • *The disease develops gradually and imperceptibly.*

imperfect = flawed, impaired, faulty, broken, limited, damaged, partial, unfinished, incomplete, defective, patchy, immature, deficient, rudimentary, sketchy, undeveloped, inexact • *We live in an imperfect world.*
OPPOSITES: perfect, finished, complete

imperfection 1 = blemish, fault, defect, flaw, stain • *Scanners locate imperfections in the cloth.*
2 = fault, failing, weakness, defect, deficiency, flaw, shortcoming, inadequacy, frailty, foible, weak point • *He concedes that there are imperfections in the socialist system.*
3 = incompleteness, deficiency, inadequacy, frailty, insufficiency • *It is its imperfection that gives it its beauty.*
OPPOSITES: perfection, sufficiency, adequacy

imperial = royal, regal, kingly, queenly, princely, sovereign, majestic, monarchial, monarchal • *the Imperial Palace in Tokyo*

imperil = endanger, risk, hazard, jeopardize • *You imperilled the lives of other road users with your driving.*
OPPOSITES: protect, guard, safeguard

imperious = domineering, dictatorial, bossy *(informal)*, haughty, lordly, commanding, arrogant, authoritative, autocratic, overbearing, tyrannical, magisterial, despotic, high-handed, overweening, tyrannous • *She gave him a witheringly imperious look.*

imperishable = indestructible, permanent, enduring, eternal, abiding, perennial, perpetual, immortal, unforgettable, everlasting, undying, unfading • *My memories are within me, imperishable.*
OPPOSITES: dying, fading, perishable

impermanent = temporary, passing, brief, fleeting, elusive, mortal, short-lived, flying, fugitive, transient, momentary, ephemeral, transitory, perishable, fly-by-night *(informal)*, evanescent, inconstant, fugacious, here today, gone tomorrow *(informal)* • *Looking at the sky reminds me how impermanent we all are.*

impermeable = impenetrable, resistant, impervious, waterproof, impassable, hermetic, nonporous • *The canoe is made from an impermeable wood.*

impersonal 1 = inhuman, cold, remote, bureaucratic • *a large impersonal orphanage*
2 = detached, neutral, dispassionate, cold, formal, aloof, businesslike • *We must be as impersonal as a surgeon with a knife.*
OPPOSITES: personal, warm, intimate

impersonate 1 = imitate, pose as *(informal)*, masquerade as, enact, ape, act out, pass yourself off as • *He was returned to prison for impersonating a police officer.*

2 = **mimic**, take off *(informal)*, do *(informal)*, ape, parody, caricature, do an impression of, personate • *He was a brilliant mimic who could impersonate most of the staff.*

impersonation = **imitation**, impression, parody, caricature, takeoff *(informal)*, mimicry • *She excelled at impersonations of his teachers.*

impertinence = **rudeness**, nerve *(informal)*, cheek *(informal)*, face *(informal)*, front, neck *(informal)*, sauce *(informal)*, presumption, disrespect, audacity, boldness, chutzpah *(U.S. & Canad. informal)*, insolence, impudence, effrontery, backchat *(informal)*, brass neck *(Brit. informal)*, incivility, brazenness, forwardness, pertness • *The impertinence of the boy is phenomenal!*

impertinent 1 = **rude**, forward, cheeky *(informal)*, saucy *(informal)*, fresh *(informal)*, bold, flip *(informal)*, brazen, sassy *(U.S. informal)*, pert, disrespectful, presumptuous, insolent, impolite, impudent, lippy *(U.S. & Canad. slang)*, discourteous, uncivil, unmannerly • *I don't like strangers who ask impertinent questions.*
OPPOSITES: mannerly, polite, respectful
2 = **inappropriate**, irrelevant, incongruous, inapplicable • *Since we already knew this, to tell us again seemed impertinent.*
OPPOSITES: important, appropriate, relevant

imperturbable = **calm**, cool, collected, composed, complacent, serene, tranquil, sedate, undisturbed, unmoved, stoic, stoical, unfazed *(informal)*, unflappable *(informal)*, unruffled, self-possessed, nerveless, unexcitable, equanimous • *He was cool and aloof, and imperturbable.*
OPPOSITES: upset, nervous, agitated

impervious 1 = **unaffected**, immune, unmoved, closed, untouched, proof, invulnerable, unreceptive, unswayable • *They are impervious to all suggestion of change.*
2 = **resistant**, sealed, impenetrable, invulnerable, impassable, hermetic, impermeable, imperviable • *The floorcovering will need to be impervious to water.*

impetuous = **rash**, hasty, impulsive, violent, furious, fierce, eager, passionate, spontaneous, precipitate, ardent, impassioned, headlong, unplanned, unbridled, vehement, unrestrained, spur-of-the-moment, unthinking, unpremeditated, unreflecting • *He tended to act in a heated and impetuous way.*
OPPOSITES: slow, cautious, wary

impetus 1 = **incentive**, push, spur, motivation, impulse, stimulus, catalyst, goad, impulsion • *She needed a new impetus for her talent.*
2 = **force**, power, energy, momentum • *This decision will give renewed impetus to economic regeneration.*

impinge = **invade**, violate, encroach on, trespass on, infringe on, make inroads on, obtrude on • *If he were at home all the time he would impinge on my space.*
▸ IN PHRASES: **impinge on** *or* **upon something** *or* **someone** = **affect**, influence, relate to, impact on, touch, touch upon, have a bearing on, bear upon • *These cuts have impinged on the region's largest employers.*

impish = **mischievous**, devilish, roguish, rascally, elfin, puckish, waggish, sportive, prankish • *He is known for his impish sense of humour.*

implacable = **ruthless**, cruel, relentless, uncompromising, intractable, inflexible, unrelenting, merciless, unforgiving, inexorable, unyielding, remorseless, pitiless, unbending, unappeasable • *the threat of invasion by a ruthless and implacable enemy*
OPPOSITES: yielding, flexible, merciful

implant AS A VERB 1 = **insert**, place, plant, fix, root, sow, graft, embed, ingraft • *Doctors have implanted an artificial heart into a 46-year-old man.*
2 = **instil**, sow, infuse, inculcate, infix • *His father had implanted in him an ambition to obtain an education.*
▸ AS A NOUN = **implantation**, insert • *They felt a woman had the right to have a breast implant.*

implausible = **improbable**, unlikely, weak, incredible, unbelievable, dubious, suspect, unreasonable, flimsy, unconvincing, far-fetched, cock-and-bull *(informal)* • *It sounded like a convenient and implausible excuse.*

implement AS A VERB = **carry out**, effect, carry through, complete, apply, perform, realize, fulfil, enforce, execute, discharge, bring about, enact, put into action *or* effect • *The government promised to implement a new system to control loan institutions.*
OPPOSITES: delay, hamper, hinder
▸ AS A NOUN = **tool**, machine, device, instrument, appliance, apparatus, gadget, utensil, contraption, contrivance, agent • *writing implements*

implementation = **carrying out**, effecting, execution, performance, performing, discharge, enforcement, accomplishment, realization, fulfilment • *the implementation of the peace agreement*

implicate AS A VERB = **incriminate**, involve, compromise, embroil, entangle, inculpate • *He didn't find anything in the notebooks to implicate her.*
OPPOSITES: eliminate, rule out, dissociate
▸ IN PHRASES: **implicate something** *or* **someone in something** = **involve in**, associate with, connect with, tie up with • *This particular system has been implicated in alcohol effects.*

implicated = **involved**, suspected, incriminated, under suspicion • *Eventually the President was implicated in the cover-up.*

implication 1 = **suggestion**, hint, inference, meaning, conclusion, significance, presumption, overtone, innuendo, intimation, insinuation, signification • *The implication was obvious: vote for us or you'll be sorry.*
2 = **involvement**, association, connection, incrimination, entanglement • *Implication in a murder finally brought him to the gallows.*
3 = **consequence**, result, development, ramification, complication, upshot • *He was acutely aware of the political implications of his decision.*

implicit 1 = **implied**, understood, suggested, hinted at, taken for granted, unspoken, inferred, tacit, undeclared, insinuated, unstated, unsaid, unexpressed • *He wanted to make explicit in the film what was implicit in the play.*
OPPOSITES: stated, spoken, explicit
2 = **inherent**, contained, underlying, intrinsic, latent, ingrained, inbuilt • *Implicit in snobbery is a certain timidity.*
3 = **absolute**, full, complete, total, firm, fixed, entire, constant, utter, outright, consummate, unqualified, out-and-out, steadfast, wholehearted, unadulterated, unreserved, unshakable, unshaken, unhesitating • *He had implicit faith in the noble intentions of the Emperor.*

implicitly = **absolutely**, completely, utterly, unconditionally, unreservedly, firmly, unhesitatingly, without reservation • *I trust him implicitly.*

implied = **suggested**, inherent, indirect, hinted at, implicit, unspoken, tacit, undeclared, insinuated, unstated, unexpressed • *She felt undermined by the implied criticism.*

implore = **beg**, beseech, entreat, conjure, plead with, solicit, pray to, importune, crave of, supplicate, go on bended knee to • *'Tell me what to do!' she implored him.*

imply 1 = **suggest**, hint, insinuate, indicate, signal, intimate, signify, connote, give (someone) to understand • *Are you implying that I had something to do with this?*
2 = **involve**, mean, entail, include, require, indicate, import, point to, signify, denote, presuppose, betoken • *The meeting in no way implies a resumption of contact with the terrorists.*

impolite = **bad-mannered**, rude, disrespectful, rough, churlish, boorish, insolent, uncouth, unrefined, loutish, ungentlemanly, ungracious, discourteous, indelicate, uncivil, unladylike, indecorous, ungallant, ill-bred,

unmannerly, ill-mannered • *It would be most impolite to refuse a simple invitation to supper.*
OPPOSITES: mannerly, polite, courteous

import AS A VERB = **bring in**, buy in, ship in, land, introduce • *We spent $5000 million more on importing food than on selling abroad.*
▸ AS A NOUN 1 = **imported goods**, foreign goods • *farmers protesting about cheap imports*
2 = **significance**, concern, value, worth, weight, consequence, substance, moment, magnitude, usefulness, momentousness • *Such arguments are of little import.*
3 = **meaning**, implication, significance, sense, message, bearing, intention, explanation, substance, drift, interpretation, thrust, purport, upshot, gist, signification • *I have already spoken about the import of his speech.*

importance 1 = **significance**, interest, concern, matter, moment, value, worth, weight, import, consequence, substance, relevance, usefulness, momentousness • *Safety is of paramount importance.*
2 = **prestige**, standing, status, rule, authority, influence, distinction, esteem, prominence, supremacy, mastery, dominion, eminence, ascendancy, pre-eminence, mana *(N.Z.)* • *He was too puffed up with his own importance to accept the verdict.*

important 1 = **significant**, critical, substantial, grave, urgent, serious, material, signal, primary, meaningful, far-reaching, momentous, seminal, weighty, of substance, salient, noteworthy • *an important economic challenge to the government*
OPPOSITES: minor, trivial, unimportant
2 *often with* **to** = **valued**, loved, prized, dear, essential, valuable, of interest, treasured, precious, esteemed, cherished, of concern, highly regarded • *Her sons are the most important thing in her life.*
3 = **powerful**, leading, prominent, commanding, supreme, outstanding, high-level, dominant, influential, notable, big-time *(informal)*, foremost, eminent, high-ranking, authoritative, major league *(informal)*, of note, noteworthy, pre-eminent, skookum *(Canad.)* • *an important figure in the media world*
4 = **main**, major, chief, head, prime, central, necessary, basic, essential, premier, primary, vital, critical, crucial, supreme, principal, paramount, foremost, pre-eminent • *The important thing is that you rest.*

importunate = **persistent**, demanding, pressing, dogged, earnest, troublesome, insistent, solicitous, clamorous, exigent, pertinacious, clamant • *His secretary shielded him from importunate visitors.*

importune = **pester**, press, plague, hound, harass, besiege, badger, beset, solicit, dun, lay siege to, entreat • *beggars importuning passers-by*

impose
▸ IN PHRASES: **impose on someone** = **intrude on**, exploit, take advantage of, use, trouble, abuse, bother, encroach on, horn in *(informal)*, trespass on, gate-crash *(informal)*, take liberties with, butt in on, presume upon, force yourself on, obtrude on • *I was afraid you'd think we were imposing on you.*
impose something on *or* **upon someone** 1 = **levy**, apply, introduce, put, place, set, charge, establish, lay, fix, institute, exact, decree, ordain • *They impose fines on airlines who bring in illegal immigrants.*
2 = **inflict**, force, enforce, visit, press, apply, thrust, dictate, saddle (someone) with, foist • *Beware of imposing your tastes on your children.*

imposing = **impressive**, striking, grand, august, powerful, effective, commanding, awesome, majestic, dignified, stately, forcible • *He was an imposing man.*
OPPOSITES: ordinary, insignificant, unimposing

imposition 1 = **application**, introduction, levying, decree, laying on • *the imposition of VAT on fuel bills*
2 = **intrusion**, liberty, presumption, cheek *(informal)*, encroachment • *I know this is an imposition, but please hear me out.*
3 = **charge**, tax, duty, burden, levy • *the Poll Tax and other local government impositions*

impossibility = **hopelessness**, inability, impracticability, inconceivability • *the impossibility of knowing absolute truth*

impossible 1 = **not possible**, out of the question, impracticable, unfeasible, beyond the bounds of possibility • *It was impossible to get in because no one knew the password.*
2 = **unachievable**, hopeless, out of the question, vain, unthinkable, inconceivable, far-fetched, unworkable, implausible, unattainable, unobtainable, beyond you, not to be thought of • *You shouldn't promise what's impossible.*
OPPOSITES: possible, likely, reasonable
3 = **absurd**, crazy *(informal)*, ridiculous, unacceptable, outrageous, ludicrous, unreasonable, unsuitable, intolerable, preposterous, laughable, farcical, illogical, insoluble, unanswerable, inadmissible, ungovernable • *The Government was now in an impossible situation.*
4 = **intolerable**, unbearable, insufferable, painful, insupportable, unendurable, excruciating, beyond bearing, not to be borne • *This woman is impossible, she thought.*

QUOTATIONS
It is only the impossible that is possible for God. He has given over the possible to the mechanics of matter and the autonomy of his creatures
[Simone Weil *A War of Religions*]
Why, sometimes I've believed as many as six impossible things before breakfast
[Lewis Carroll *Through the Looking-Glass*]
It always seems impossible until it's done
[Nelson Mandela]

impostor = **fraud**, cheat, fake, impersonator, rogue, deceiver, sham, pretender, hypocrite, charlatan, quack, trickster, knave *(archaic)*, phoney *or* phony *(informal)* • *He was an imposter who masqueraded as a doctor.*

impotence = **powerlessness**, inability, helplessness, weakness, disability, incompetence, inadequacy, paralysis, inefficiency, frailty, incapacity, infirmity, ineffectiveness, uselessness, feebleness, enervation, inefficacy • *a sense of impotence in the face of disaster*
OPPOSITES: ability, strength, powerfulness

impotent = **powerless**, weak, helpless, unable, disabled, incapable, paralysed, frail, incompetent, ineffective, feeble, incapacitated, unmanned, infirm, emasculate, nerveless, enervated • *Bullies leave people feeling hurt, angry and impotent.*
OPPOSITES: able, strong, powerful

impound = **confiscate**, appropriate, seize, commandeer, sequester, expropriate, sequestrate • *The police arrested him and impounded the cocaine.*

impoverish 1 = **bankrupt**, ruin, beggar, break, pauperize • *a society impoverished by wartime inflation*
2 = **deplete**, drain, exhaust, diminish, use up, sap, wear out, reduce • *Mint impoverishes the soil quickly.*

impoverished 1 = **poor**, needy, destitute, ruined, distressed, bankrupt, poverty-stricken, indigent, impecunious, straitened, penurious, necessitous, in reduced *or* straitened circumstances • *The goal is to lure businesses into impoverished areas.*
OPPOSITES: rich, wealthy, affluent
2 = **depleted**, spent, reduced, empty, drained, exhausted, played out, worn out, denuded • *Against the impoverished defence, he poached an early goal.*

impracticable = **unfeasible**, impossible, out of the question, unworkable, unattainable, unachievable • *Such measures would be highly impracticable.*
OPPOSITES: possible, feasible, practicable

impractical 1 = **unworkable**, impracticable, unrealistic, inoperable, impossible, unserviceable, nonviable

• *With regularly scheduled airlines, sea travel became impractical.*
OPPOSITES: possible, practical, viable
2 = **unrealistic**, romantic, idealistic, optimistic, visionary, dreamy, Utopian, quixotic, impracticable, starry-eyed • *He was difficult, eccentric and hopelessly impractical.*
3 = **idealistic**, wild, out there *(slang)*, romantic, unrealistic, visionary, unbusinesslike, starry-eyed • *He's full of wacky, weird and impractical ideas.*
OPPOSITES: sensible, realistic, down-to-earth

imprecise = **indefinite**, estimated, rough, vague, loose, careless, ambiguous, inaccurate, sloppy *(informal)*, woolly, hazy, indeterminate, wide of the mark, equivocal, ill-defined, inexact, inexplicit, blurred round the edges • *The charges were vague and imprecise.*
OPPOSITES: accurate, exact, precise

impregnable = **invulnerable**, strong, secure, unbeatable, invincible, impenetrable, unassailable, indestructible, immovable, unshakable, unconquerable • *The old fort with its thick, high walls was virtually impregnable.*
OPPOSITES: open, exposed, vulnerable

impregnate 1 = **saturate**, soak, steep, fill, seep, pervade, infuse, permeate, imbue, suffuse, percolate, imbrue *(rare)* • *plastic impregnated with a light-absorbing dye*
2 = **inseminate**, fertilize, make pregnant, fructify, fecundate, get with child • *War entailed killing the men and impregnating the women.*

impresario = **producer**, director, manager, promoter, organizer, régisseur *(French)* • *He's the actor turned impresario behind the pantomime production.*

impress AS A VERB = **excite**, move, strike, touch, affect, influence, inspire, grab *(informal)*, amaze, overcome, stir, overwhelm, astonish, dazzle, sway, awe, overawe, make an impression on • *What impressed him most was their speed.*
▸ IN PHRASES: **impress something on** *or* **upon someone** = **stress**, bring home to, instil in, drum into, knock into, emphasize to, fix in, inculcate in, ingrain in • *I've impressed on them the need for professionalism.*

impression AS A NOUN 1 = **idea**, feeling, thought, sense, opinion, view, assessment, judgment, reaction, belief, concept, fancy, notion, conviction, suspicion, hunch, apprehension, inkling, funny feeling *(informal)* • *My impression is that they are totally out of control.*
2 = **effect**, influence, impact, sway • *She gave no sign that his charm had made any impression on her.*
3 = **imitation**, parody, impersonation, mockery, send-up *(Brit. informal)*, takeoff *(informal)* • *He amused us doing impressions of film actors.*
4 = **mark**, imprint, stamp, stamping, depression, outline, hollow, dent, impress, indentation • *the world's oldest fossil impressions of plant life*
▸ IN PHRASES: **make an impression** = **cause a stir**, stand out, make an impact, be conspicuous, find favour, make a hit *(informal)*, arouse comment, excite notice • *He's certainly made an impression on the interviewing board.*

PROVERBS
First impressions are the most lasting

impressionable = **suggestible**, vulnerable, susceptible, open, sensitive, responsive, receptive, gullible, ingenuous • *the age at which you are most impressionable*
OPPOSITES: hardened, insensitive, blasé

impressive = **grand**, striking, splendid, good, great *(informal)*, fine, affecting, powerful, exciting, wonderful, excellent, dramatic, outstanding, stirring, superb, first-class, marvellous *(informal)*, terrific *(informal)*, awesome, world-class, admirable, first-rate, forcible, gee-whizz *(slang)* • *The film's special effects are particularly impressive.*
OPPOSITES: ordinary, uninspiring, unimpressive

imprint AS A NOUN 1 = **impact**, effect, impression • *His courage left an imprint on his nation's history.*
2 = **mark**, print, impression, stamp, indentation • *the imprint of his little finger*
▸ AS A VERB 1 = **fix**, establish, place, set, position, plant, print, install, implant, embed • *He repeated the names, as if to imprint them on his mind.*
2 = **engrave**, print, stamp, impress, etch, emboss • *a racket with the club's badge imprinted on the strings*

imprison = **jail**, confine, detain, lock up, constrain, put away, intern, incarcerate, send down *(informal)*, send to prison, impound, put under lock and key, immure • *He was imprisoned for 18 months on charges of anti-state agitation.*
OPPOSITES: free, release, discharge

imprisoned = **jailed**, confined, locked up, inside *(slang)*, in jail, captive, behind bars, put away, interned, incarcerated, in irons, under lock and key, immured • *imprisoned for nonconformist preaching*

imprisonment = **confinement**, custody, detention, captivity, incarceration, internment, duress • *She was sentenced to seven years' imprisonment.*

improbability = **unlikelihood**, uncertainty, dubiety, doubtfulness, unthinkability • *the improbability of such an outcome*

improbable 1 = **doubtful**, unlikely, uncertain, unbelievable, dubious, questionable, fanciful, far-fetched, implausible • *It seems improbable that this year's figure will show a drop.*
OPPOSITES: likely, certain, probable
2 = **unconvincing**, weak, unbelievable, preposterous • *Their marriage seems an improbable alliance.*
OPPOSITES: convincing, plausible

impromptu = **spontaneous**, improvised, unprepared, off-the-cuff *(informal)*, offhand, ad-lib, unscripted, unrehearsed, unpremeditated, extempore, unstudied, extemporaneous, extemporized • *They put on an impromptu concert for the visitors.*
OPPOSITES: planned, prepared, rehearsed

improper 1 = **inappropriate**, unfit, unsuitable, out of place, unwarranted, incongruous, unsuited, ill-timed, uncalled-for, inopportune, inapplicable, unseasonable, inapt, infelicitous, inapposite, malapropos • *He maintained that he had done nothing improper.*
OPPOSITES: appropriate, suitable, apt
2 = **indecent**, vulgar, suggestive, unseemly, untoward, risqué, smutty, unbecoming, unfitting, impolite, off-colour, indelicate, indecorous • *He would never be improper; he is always the perfect gentleman.*
OPPOSITES: decent, becoming, seemly
3 = **incorrect**, wrong, inaccurate, false, irregular, erroneous • *The improper use of medicine can lead to severe adverse reactions.*

impropriety 1 = **indecency**, vulgarity, immodesty, bad taste, incongruity, unsuitability, indecorum • *Inviting him up to your hotel room would smack of impropriety.*
OPPOSITES: decency, delicacy, propriety
2 = **lapse**, mistake, slip, blunder, gaffe, bloomer *(Brit. informal)*, faux pas, solecism, gaucherie • *He resigned amid allegations of financial impropriety.*

QUOTATIONS
Impropriety is the soul of wit
[W. Somerset Maugham *The Moon and Sixpence*]

improve AS A VERB 1 = **enhance**, better, add to, upgrade, amend, mend, augment, embellish, touch up, ameliorate, polish up • *He improved their house.*
OPPOSITES: damage, harm, worsen
2 = **get better**, pick up, look up *(informal)*, develop, advance, perk up, take a turn for the better *(informal)* • *The weather is beginning to improve.*
3 = **make better**, perfect, polish, strengthen, temper, refine, cultivate, elevate, hone • *He said he wanted to improve his football.*
4 = **recuperate**, recover, rally, mend, make progress, turn the corner, gain ground, gain strength, convalesce, be on

the mend, grow better, make strides, take on a new lease of life *(informal)* • *He had improved so much the doctor cut his dosage.*
▸ **IN PHRASES: improve on something = beat**, top, better, cap *(informal)*, exceed, trump, surpass, outstrip, outdo • *We need to improve on our performance against France.*

improvement 1 = enhancement, increase, gain, boost, amendment, correction, heightening, advancement, enrichment, face-lift, embellishment, betterment, rectification, augmentation, amelioration • *the dramatic improvements in conditions*
2 = advance, development, progress, recovery, reformation, upswing, furtherance • *The system we've just introduced has been a great improvement.*

improvisation 1 = invention, spontaneity, ad-libbing, extemporizing • *Funds were not abundant, and clever improvisation was necessary.*
2 = ad-lib • *an improvisation on 'Jingle Bells'*

improvise 1 = devise, contrive, make do, concoct, throw together • *If you don't have a wok, improvise one.*
2 = ad-lib, invent, vamp, busk, wing it *(informal)*, play it by ear *(informal)*, extemporize, speak off the cuff *(informal)* • *Take the story and improvise on it.*

improvised = unprepared, spontaneous, makeshift, spur-of-the-moment, off-the-cuff *(informal)*, ad-lib, unrehearsed, extempore, extemporaneous, extemporized • *He grabbed a script and began an improvised performance.*

imprudent = unwise, foolish, rash, irresponsible, reckless, careless, ill-advised, foolhardy, indiscreet, unthinking, ill-judged, ill-considered, inconsiderate, heedless, injudicious, incautious, improvident, impolitic, overhasty, temerarious • *an imprudent investment he made many years ago*
OPPOSITES: responsible, careful, prudent

impudence = boldness, nerve *(informal)*, cheek *(informal)*, face *(informal)*, front, neck *(informal)*, gall *(informal)*, lip *(slang)*, presumption, audacity, rudeness, chutzpah *(U.S. & Canad. informal)*, insolence, impertinence, effrontery, brass neck *(Brit. informal)*, shamelessness, sauciness, brazenness, sassiness *(U.S. informal)*, pertness, bumptiousness • *One sister had the impudence to wear the other's clothes.*

impudent = bold, rude, cheeky *(informal)*, forward, fresh *(informal)*, saucy *(informal)*, cocky *(informal)*, audacious, brazen, shameless, sassy *(U.S. informal)*, pert, presumptuous, impertinent, insolent, lippy *(U.S. & Canad. slang)*, bumptious, immodest, bold-faced • *Some were well behaved, while others were impudent.*
OPPOSITES: retiring, modest, polite

impugn = challenge, question, attack, dispute, criticize, call into question, assail, gainsay *(archaic or literary)*, traduce, cast doubt upon • *I hope the good name of the company will not be impugned.*

impulse AS A NOUN 1 = urge, longing, desire, drive, wish, fancy, notion, yen *(informal)*, instinct, yearning, inclination, itch, whim, compulsion, caprice • *He resisted an impulse to smile.*
2 = spontaneity, impetuosity, carelessness, irresponsibility, wildness, thoughtlessness, rashness, heedlessness, incautiousness • *He is a creature of impulse.*
3 = force, pressure, push, movement, surge, motive, thrust, momentum, stimulus, catalyst, impetus • *Their impulse of broadcasting was for human rights.*
4 = pulse, beat, current, wave, stroke, rhythm, oscillation • *the electrical impulse which keeps the heart beating*
▸ **IN PHRASES: on impulse = impulsively**, of your own accord, freely, voluntarily, instinctively, spontaneously, impromptu, off the cuff *(informal)*, in the heat of the moment, off your own bat, quite unprompted • *After lunch she decided, on impulse, to take a bath.*

QUOTATIONS
I am the very slave of circumstance
And impulse – borne away with every breath!
[Lord Byron *Sardanapalus*]
To our strongest impulse, to the tyrant in us, not only our reason but also our conscience yields
[Friedrich Nietzsche *Beyond Good and Evil*]
Have no truck with first impulses for they are always generous ones
[Casimir, Comte de Montrond]

impulsive = instinctive, emotional, unpredictable, quick, passionate, rash, spontaneous, precipitate, intuitive, hasty, headlong, impetuous, devil-may-care, unconsidered, unpremeditated • *He is too impulsive to be a responsible prime minister.*
OPPOSITES: planned, considered, cautious

impunity = immunity, freedom, licence, permission, liberty, security, exemption, dispensation, nonliability • *These gangs operate with apparent impunity.*

impure 1 = unrefined, mixed, alloyed, debased, adulterated, admixed • *impure diamonds*
2 = immoral, corrupt, obscene, indecent, gross, coarse, lewd, carnal, X-rated *(informal)*, salacious, unclean, prurient, lascivious, smutty, lustful, ribald, immodest, licentious, indelicate, unchaste • *They say such behaviour might lead to impure temptations.*
OPPOSITES: moral, pure, decent
3 = unclean, dirty, foul, infected, contaminated, polluted, filthy, tainted, sullied, defiled, unwholesome, vitiated, festy *(Austral. slang)* • *They were warned against drinking the impure water from the stream.*
OPPOSITES: clean, immaculate, spotless

impurity 1 *often plural* **= dirt**, pollutant, scum, grime, contaminant, dross, bits, foreign body, foreign matter • *The air is filtered to remove impurities.*
2 = contamination, infection, pollution, taint, filth, foulness, defilement, dirtiness, uncleanness, befoulment • *The soap is boiled to remove all traces of impurity.*
3 = immorality, corruption, obscenity, indecency, vulgarity, prurience, coarseness, licentiousness, immodesty, carnality, lewdness, grossness, salaciousness, lasciviousness, unchastity, smuttiness • *impurity, lust and evil desires*

imputation = blame, charge, accusation, censure, slur, reproach, slander, attribution, insinuation, ascription, aspersion • *They avoided the imputation of criminal negligence.*

impute = attribute, assign, ascribe, credit, refer, accredit • *It is unfair to impute blame to the employees.*

in AS A PREPOSITION 1 = inside, within, in the interior of • *He was in his car.*
2 = into, within, inside • *Put the knives in the kitchen drawer.*
3 = with, by, within • *carrots wrapped in newspaper*
4 = during, in the year of, in the period of • *that early spring day in April 1949*
5 = after, following, subsequent to • *I'll have some breakfast ready in a few minutes.*
6 = per, out of, of • *One in five boys left school without a qualification.*
▸ **AS AN ADVERB 1 = at home** • *My flatmate was in at the time.*
2 = inside, within, indoors, under cover • *They shook hands and went in.*
3 = arrived, here • *The train's in. We'll have to run for it.*
4 = high, rising • *If the tide was in, they went swimming.*
▸ **AS AN ADJECTIVE = fashionable**, current, popular, cool *(slang)*, hip *(slang)*, happening *(informal)*, stylish, trendy *(Brit. informal)*, chic, up-to-date, in vogue, all the rage, up-to-the-minute, modish, à la mode, schmick *(Austral. informal)* • *A few years ago, jogging was in.*
▸ **IN PHRASES: in for = due for**, likely to get, in line for, a candidate for • *When you go outside, you are in for a shock.*

in for it = **in trouble**, for it *(informal)*, in deep water *(informal)*, for the high jump *(informal)* • *He knew he was in for it.*
in on = **aware of**, familiar with, conscious of, wise to *(slang)*, mindful of, acquainted with, alive to, hip to *(slang)*, appreciative of, attentive to, conversant with, apprised of, cognizant of, sensible of • *I wasn't in on that particular discussion.*
in with = **friendly with**, popular with, accepted by, liked by, admired by, intimate with, in favour with • *She seems to have got in with the right crowd.*
the ins and outs of something = **details**, facts, particulars, features, factors, elements, aspects, specifics, components, technicalities • *Experts can advise on the ins and outs of dieting.*

inability = **incapability**, incompetence, inadequacy, impotence, incapacity, ineptitude, powerlessness, ineffectiveness, uselessness, ineptness • *Her inability to concentrate could cause an accident.*
OPPOSITES: power, ability, potential

inaccessible = **out-of-reach**, remote, out-of-the-way, unattainable, impassable, unreachable, unapproachable, un-get-at-able *(informal)* • *people living in remote and inaccessible parts of the country*
OPPOSITES: accessible, approachable, attainable

inaccuracy 1 = **imprecision**, unreliability, incorrectness, unfaithfulness, erroneousness, inexactness • *He was disturbed by the inaccuracy of the answers.*
2 = **error**, mistake, slip, fault, defect, blunder, lapse, boob *(Brit. slang)*, literal *(Printing)*, howler *(informal)*, miscalculation, typo *(informal, Printing)*, erratum, corrigendum, barry *or* Barry Crocker *(Austral. slang)* • *Guard against inaccuracies by checking with a variety of sources.*

inaccurate = **incorrect**, wrong, mistaken, wild, faulty, careless, unreliable, defective, unfaithful, erroneous, unsound, imprecise, wide of the mark, out, inexact, off-base *(U.S. & Canad. informal)*, off-beam *(informal)*, discrepant, way off-beam *(informal)* • *The reports were based on inaccurate information.*
OPPOSITES: sound, correct, accurate

inaccurately = **imprecisely**, carelessly, inexactly, clumsily, unreliably, unfaithfully • *He claimed his remarks had been reported inaccurately.*

inaction = **inactivity**, inertia, idleness, immobility, torpor, dormancy, torpidity • *He is bitter about the inaction of the other political parties.*

QUOTATIONS
The only thing necessary for the triumph of evil is for good men to do nothing
[Edmund Burke]

inactive 1 = **unused**, idle, dormant, latent, inert, immobile, mothballed, out of service, inoperative, abeyant • *The satellite has been inactive since its launch two years ago.*
OPPOSITES: working, used, running
2 = **idle**, unemployed, out of work, jobless, unoccupied, kicking your heels • *He has been inactive since last year.*
OPPOSITES: employed, occupied
3 = **lazy**, passive, slow, quiet, dull, low-key *(informal)*, sluggish, lethargic, sedentary, indolent, somnolent, torpid, slothful • *He certainly was not politically inactive.*
OPPOSITES: active, busy, energetic

inactivity = **immobility**, unemployment, inaction, passivity, hibernation, dormancy • *The players have comparatively long periods of inactivity.*
OPPOSITES: action, movement, mobility

inadequacy = **shortage**, poverty, dearth, paucity, insufficiency, incompleteness, meagreness, skimpiness, scantiness, inadequateness • *the inadequacy of the water supply*
2 = **incompetence**, inability, deficiency, incapacity, ineffectiveness, incompetency, unfitness, inefficacy, defectiveness, inaptness, faultiness, unsuitableness • *his deep-seated sense of inadequacy*
3 = **shortcoming**, failing, lack, weakness, shortage, defect, imperfection • *He drank heavily in an effort to forget his own inadequacies.*

inadequate 1 = **insufficient**, short, scarce, meagre, poor, lacking, incomplete, scant, sparse, skimpy, sketchy, insubstantial, scanty, niggardly, incommensurate • *Supplies of food and medicine are inadequate.*
OPPOSITES: sufficient, adequate, satisfactory
2 = **incapable**, incompetent, ineffective, weak, pathetic, faulty, unfitted, unfit, defective, unequal, inept, deficient, imperfect, unqualified, not up to scratch *(informal)*, inexpert, inapt • *She felt quite painfully inadequate in the crisis.*
OPPOSITES: fit, qualified, capable

inadequately = **insufficiently**, poorly, thinly, sparsely, scantily, imperfectly, sketchily, skimpily, meagrely • *The projects were inadequately funded.*

inadmissible = **unacceptable**, irrelevant, inappropriate, unreasonable, improper, unqualified, immaterial, unallowable • *Evidence presented by the prosecution was judged inadmissible.*

inadvertent = **unintentional**, accidental, unintended, chance, careless, negligent, unwitting, unplanned, thoughtless, unthinking, heedless, unpremeditated, unheeding • *The government has said it was an inadvertent error.*

inadvertently = **unintentionally**, accidentally, by accident, mistakenly, unwittingly, by mistake, involuntarily • *You must have inadvertently pressed the wrong button.*
OPPOSITES: deliberately, consciously, carefully

inadvisable = **unwise**, ill-advised, imprudent, injudicious, impolitic, inexpedient • *For three days it was inadvisable to leave the harbour.*

inalienable = **sacrosanct**, absolute, unassailable, inherent, entailed *(Law)*, non-negotiable, inviolable, nontransferable, untransferable • *respect for the inalienable rights of people and nations*

inane = **senseless**, stupid, silly, empty, daft *(informal)*, worthless, futile, trifling, frivolous, mindless, goofy *(informal)*, idiotic, vacuous, fatuous, puerile, vapid, unintelligent, asinine, imbecilic, devoid of intelligence • *He always had this inane grin.*
OPPOSITES: serious, significant, sensible

inanimate = **lifeless**, inert, dead, cold, extinct, defunct, inactive, soulless, quiescent, spiritless, insensate, insentient • *He thinks that inanimate objects have a life of their own.*
OPPOSITES: living, active, animate

inapplicable = **irrelevant**, inappropriate, unsuitable, unsuited, inapt, inapposite • *His theory was inapplicable to many less developed economies.*
OPPOSITES: fitting, appropriate, applicable

inappropriate 1 = **unsuitable**, unacceptable, unfit, unfitting, incompatible, ineligible, unsuited, ill-fitted, ill-suited • *Some clients had been sold inappropriate polices.*
OPPOSITES: timely, becoming, appropriate
2 = **improper**, unsuitable, out of place, unacceptable, tasteless, unwarranted, incongruous, unseemly, untimely, unsuited, unbecoming, ill-timed, uncalled-for, inapplicable, unbefitting, inapt, malapropos • *That remark was inappropriate for such a serious issue.*

inarticulate 1 = **faltering**, halting, hesitant, tongue-tied • *He was inarticulate and rather shy.*
2 = **incoherent**, incomprehensible, unintelligible, unclear, mumbled, muffled, indistinct, poorly spoken • *He made an inarticulate noise in the back of his throat.*
OPPOSITES: clear, articulate, coherent
3 = **mute**, silent, dumb, unspoken, speechless, wordless, voiceless, unvoiced, unuttered • *extremes of anger, from inarticulate fury to mild irritation*

inattention = **neglect**, disregard, carelessness, indifference, preoccupation, daydreaming, forgetfulness, thoughtlessness, absent-mindedness, inadvertence, inattentiveness, heedlessness, woolgathering • *Evidence had been destroyed as a result of a moment's inattention.*

inattentive = **preoccupied**, distracted, careless, negligent, dreamy, regardless, vague, thoughtless, absent-minded, slapdash, neglectful, heedless, slipshod, remiss, unmindful, unobservant, unheeding, distrait, ditzy *or* ditsy *(slang)* • *These children were more likely to be inattentive at school.*
OPPOSITES: aware, careful, attentive

inaudible = **indistinct**, low, stifled, mumbling, unheard, out of earshot • *His voice was almost inaudible.*
OPPOSITES: clear, distinct, audible

inaugural = **first**, opening, initial, maiden, introductory, dedicatory • *In his inaugural address, he appealed for understanding.*

inaugurate 1 = **invest**, install, induct, instate • *The new president will be inaugurated on January 20.*
2 = **open**, commission, dedicate, ordain • *A new centre for research was inaugurated today.*
3 = **launch**, begin, introduce, institute, set up, kick off *(informal)*, initiate, originate, commence, get under way, usher in, set in motion • *They inaugurated the first ever scheduled flights.*

inauguration 1 = **investiture**, installation, induction • *the inauguration of the new Governor*
2 = **opening**, launch, birth, inception, commencement • *They later attended the inauguration of the University.*
3 = **launch**, launching, setting up, institution, initiation • *the inauguration of monetary union*

inauspicious = **unpromising**, bad, unfortunate, discouraging, unlucky, ominous, unfavourable, black, untoward, ill-omened, unpropitious, bodeful • *The meeting got off to an inauspicious start.*
OPPOSITES: good, promising, auspicious

inborn = **natural**, inherited, inherent, hereditary, instinctive, innate, intuitive, ingrained, congenital, inbred, native, immanent, in your blood, hard-wired, connate • *It is clear that the ability to smile is inborn.*

inbred = **innate**, natural, constitutional, native, ingrained, inherent, deep-seated, immanent, hard-wired • *behaviour patterns that are inbred*

inbuilt = **integral**, built-in, incorporated, component • *the only answering machine with inbuilt fax and printer*

incalculable = **vast**, enormous, immense, countless, infinite, innumerable, untold, limitless, boundless, inestimable, numberless, uncountable, measureless, without number, incomputable • *He has done incalculable damage to his reputation.*

incandescent 1 = **glowing**, brilliant, shining, red-hot, radiant, luminous, white-hot, Day-Glo, phosphorescent • *incandescent light bulbs*
2 = **furious**, angry, mad, raging, boiling, fuming, choked, pissed *(Brit., Austral. & N.Z. slang)*, infuriated, incensed, enraged, maddened, pissed off *(taboo)*, livid *(informal)*, up in arms, on the warpath *(informal)*, foaming at the mouth, wrathful, in high dudgeon, fit to be tied *(slang)*, beside yourself, tooshie *(Austral. slang)*, off the air *(Austral. slang)* • *It makes me incandescent with fury.*

incantation = **chant**, spell, charm, formula, invocation, hex *(U.S. & Canad. informal)*, abracadabra, conjuration • *huddled shapes whispering strange incantations*

incapable **AS AN ADJECTIVE** 1 = **incompetent**, inadequate, insufficient, unfit, unfitted, ineffective, feeble, weak, inept, unqualified, inexpert, not up to something, not equal to something • *He lost his job allegedly for being incapable.*
OPPOSITES: fit, expert, capable
2 = **unable**, helpless, powerless, unfit, impotent • *He argued that he was mentally incapable.*
▸ **IN PHRASES: incapable of** 1 = **not capable of**, unable to carry out • *He seemed to be a man incapable of violence.*
2 = **not susceptible to**, resistant to, impervious to, not admitting of • *The problem of recidivism is not incapable of solution.*

incapacitate = **disable**, cripple, paralyse, scupper *(Brit. slang)*, prostrate, immobilize, put someone out of action *(informal)*, lay someone up *(informal)* • *A serious fall incapacitated him.*

incapacitated = **disabled**, challenged, unfit, out of action *(informal)*, laid up *(informal)*, immobilized, indisposed, hors de combat *(French)* • *He is incapacitated and can't work.*

incapacity = **inability**, weakness, inadequacy, impotence, powerlessness, ineffectiveness, feebleness, incompetency, unfitness, incapability • *patients with mental incapacity*

incapsulate *see* **encapsulate**

incarcerate = **imprison**, confine, detain, lock up, restrict, restrain, intern, send down *(Brit.)*, impound, coop up, throw in jail, put under lock and key, immure, jail *or* gaol • *It can cost $50,000 to incarcerate a prisoner for a year.*

incarceration = **confinement**, restraint, imprisonment, detention, captivity, bondage, internment • *her mother's incarceration in a psychiatric hospital*

incarnate 1 = **personified**, embodied, typified • *He referred to her as evil incarnate.*
2 = **made flesh**, in the flesh, in human form, in bodily form • *Why should God become incarnate as a male?*

incarnation = **embodiment**, manifestation, epitome, type, impersonation, personification, avatar, exemplification, bodily form • *She is a perfect incarnation of glamour.*

incautious = **careless**, rash, reckless, precipitate, hasty, negligent, impulsive, ill-advised, unwary, thoughtless, unguarded, indiscreet, unthinking, ill-judged, imprudent, inconsiderate, heedless, injudicious, improvident • *In case you think I was incautious, take a look at the map.*
OPPOSITES: careful, cautious, wary

incendiary = **inflammatory**, provocative, subversive, seditious, rabble-rousing, dissentious • *making incendiary remarks*

incense[1] = **perfume**, scent, fragrance, bouquet, aroma, balm, redolence • *an atmospheric place, pungent with incense*

incense[2] = **anger**, infuriate, enrage, excite, provoke, irritate, gall, madden, inflame, exasperate, rile *(informal)*, raise the hackles of, nark *(Brit., Austral. & N.Z. slang)*, make your blood boil *(informal)*, rub you up the wrong way, make your hackles rise, get your hackles up, make you see red *(informal)* • *This proposal will incense conservation campaigners.*

incensed = **angry**, mad *(informal)*, furious, cross, fuming, choked, pissed *(Brit., Austral. & N.Z. slang)*, infuriated, enraged, maddened, exasperated, indignant, pissed off *(taboo)*, irate, up in arms, incandescent, steamed up *(slang)*, hot under the collar *(informal)*, on the warpath *(informal)*, wrathful, ireful *(literary)*, tooshie *(Austral. slang)*, off the air *(Austral. slang)* • *She was incensed at his lack of compassion.*

incentive = **inducement**, motive, encouragement, urge, come-on *(informal)*, spur, lure, bait, motivation, carrot *(informal)*, impulse, stimulus, impetus, stimulant, goad, incitement, enticement • *There is little incentive to adopt such measures.*
OPPOSITES: warning, deterrent, disincentive

inception = **beginning**, start, rise, birth, origin, dawn, outset, initiation, inauguration, commencement, kickoff *(informal)* • *Since its inception, the company has produced 53 different designs.*
OPPOSITES: ending, end, finish

incessant = **constant**, endless, continuous, persistent, eternal, relentless, perpetual, continual, unbroken, never-ending, interminable, unrelenting, everlasting, unending,

ceaseless, unremitting, nonstop, unceasing • *Incessant rain made conditions almost intolerable.*
OPPOSITES: rare, occasional, intermittent

incessantly = **all the time**, constantly, continually, endlessly, persistently, eternally, perpetually, nonstop, ceaselessly, without a break, interminably, everlastingly, twenty-four-seven *(informal)* • *She talked about herself incessantly.*

inchoate 1 = **incipient**, beginning, nascent, inceptive • *The dispute threatens to smash the inchoate government to fragments.*
2 = **undeveloped**, elementary, immature, imperfect, embryonic, rudimentary, formless, unformed • *His prose is every bit as inchoate as the wilderness in which he travels.*

incidence = **prevalence**, frequency, occurrence, rate, amount, degree, extent • *The incidence of breast cancer increases with age.*

incident 1 = **disturbance**, scene, clash, disorder, confrontation, brawl, uproar, skirmish, mishap, fracas, commotion, contretemps • *Safety chiefs are investigating the incident.*
2 = **happening**, event, affair, business, fact, matter, occasion, circumstance, episode, occurrence, escapade • *They have not based it on any incident from the past.*
3 = **adventure**, drama, excitement, crisis, spectacle, theatrics • *The birth was not without incident.*

incidental 1 = **secondary**, subsidiary, subordinate, minor, occasional, ancillary, nonessential • *The playing of music proved to be incidental to the main business.*
OPPOSITES: important, necessary, essential
2 = **accompanying**, related, attendant, contingent, contributory, concomitant • *At the bottom of the bill were various incidental expenses.*

incidentally 1 = **by the way**, in passing, en passant, parenthetically, by the bye • *The tower, incidentally, dates from the twelfth century.*
2 = **accidentally**, casually, by chance, coincidentally, fortuitously, by happenstance • *In her denunciation, she incidentally shed some light on another mystery.*

incinerate 1 = **burn up**, carbonize • *The government is trying to stop them incinerating their own waste.*
2 = **cremate**, burn up, reduce to ashes, consume by fire • *Some of the victims were incinerated.*

incipient = **beginning**, starting, developing, originating, commencing, embryonic, nascent, inchoate, inceptive • *There were signs of incipient panic.*

incise = **cut**, carve, etch, engrave, inscribe, chisel • *After polishing, a design is incised or painted.*

incision = **cut**, opening, slash, notch, slit, gash • *It involves making a tiny incision in the skin.*

incisive = **penetrating**, sharp, keen, acute, piercing, trenchant, perspicacious • *a shrewd operator with an incisive mind*
OPPOSITES: dull, vague, dense

incite = **provoke**, encourage, drive, excite, prompt, urge, spur, stimulate, set on, animate, rouse, prod, stir up, inflame, instigate, whip up, egg on, goad, impel, foment, put up to, agitate for *or* against • *He incited his fellow citizens to take revenge.*
OPPOSITES: discourage, deter, dissuade

incitement = **provocation**, prompting, encouragement, spur, motive, motivation, impulse, stimulus, impetus, agitation, inducement, goad, instigation, clarion call • *an incitement to religious hatred*

inclement = **stormy**, severe, rough, foul, harsh, rigorous, boisterous, tempestuous, intemperate, bitter • *Thousands braved the inclement weather last week.*
OPPOSITES: fine, calm, pleasant

inclination 1 = **desire**, longing, wish, need, aspiration, craving, yearning, hankering • *He had neither the time nor the inclination to think about it.*
2 = **tendency**, liking, taste, turn, fancy, leaning, bent, stomach, prejudice, bias, affection, thirst, disposition, penchant, fondness, propensity, aptitude, predisposition, predilection, proclivity, partiality, turn of mind, proneness • *He set out to follow his artistic inclinations.*
OPPOSITES: dislike, aversion, revulsion
3 = **bow**, bending, nod, bowing • *a polite inclination of his head*

incline **AS A VERB** 1 = **predispose**, influence, tend, persuade, prejudice, bias, sway, turn, dispose • *the factors which incline us towards particular beliefs*
2 = **bend**, lower, nod, bow, stoop, nutate *(rare)* • *He inclined his head very slightly.*
▸ **AS A NOUN** = **slope**, rise, dip, grade, descent, ramp, ascent, gradient, declivity, acclivity • *He came to a halt at the edge of a steep incline.*

inclined 1 = **disposed**, given, prone, likely, subject, liable, apt, predisposed, tending towards • *He was inclined to self-pity.*
2 = **willing**, minded, ready, disposed, of a mind *(informal)* • *I am inclined to agree with Alan.*

inclose *see* **enclose**

include 1 = **contain**, involve, incorporate, cover, consist of, take in, embrace, comprise, take into account, embody, encompass, comprehend, subsume • *The trip was extended to include a few other events.*
OPPOSITES: exclude, eliminate, rule out
2 = **count**, introduce, make a part of, number among • *I had worked hard to be included in a project like this.*
3 = **add**, enter, put in, insert • *You should include details of all your benefits.*

including = **containing**, with, counting, plus, together with, as well as, inclusive of • *seventeen Western hostages, including three Britons*

inclusion = **addition**, incorporation, introduction, insertion • *a confident performance which justified his inclusion in the team*
OPPOSITES: exception, rejection, exclusion

inclusive 1 = **comprehensive**, full, overall, general, global, sweeping, all-in, blanket, umbrella, across-the-board, all-together, catch-all *(chiefly U.S.)*, all-embracing, overarching, in toto *(Latin)* • *an inclusive price of £32.90*
OPPOSITES: limited, narrow, exclusive
2 = **incorporating**, including, counting, covering, embracing • *All prices are inclusive of delivery.*

incognito = **in disguise**, unknown, disguised, unrecognized, under an assumed name • *He preferred to travel incognito.*

incoherence = **unintelligibility**, inarticulateness, disconnectedness, disjointedness • *Her incoherence was enough to tell him that something was wrong.*

incoherent = **unintelligible**, wild, confused, disordered, wandering, muddled, rambling, inconsistent, jumbled, stammering, disconnected, stuttering, unconnected, disjointed, inarticulate, uncoordinated • *As the evening progressed he became increasingly incoherent.*
OPPOSITES: rational, logical, coherent

income = **revenue**, gains, earnings, means, pay, interest, returns, profits, wages, rewards, yield, proceeds, salary, receipts, takings • *Over a third of their income is from comedy videos.*

> **QUOTATIONS**
> A large income is the best recipe for happiness I ever heard of. It certainly may secure all the myrtle and turkey part of it
> [Jane Austen *Mansfield Park*]

incoming 1 = **arriving**, landing, approaching, entering, returning, homeward • *The airport was closed to incoming flights.*
OPPOSITES: leaving, exiting, departing
2 = **new**, next, succeeding, elected, elect • *the problems confronting the incoming government*

incomparable = **unequalled**, supreme, unparalleled, paramount, superlative, transcendent, unrivalled, inimitable, unmatched, peerless, matchless, beyond compare • *a performance of incomparable brilliance*

incomparably = **immeasurably**, easily, by far, eminently, far and away, beyond compare • *The country's industry is in incomparably better shape than last year.*

incompatibility = **inconsistency**, conflict, discrepancy, antagonism, incongruity, irreconcilability, disparateness, uncongeniality • *Incompatibility between mother and baby's blood group may cause jaundice.*

incompatible = **inconsistent**, conflicting, contradictory, unsuitable, disparate, incongruous, discordant, antagonistic, irreconcilable, unsuited, mismatched, discrepant, uncongenial, antipathetic, ill-assorted, inconsonant • *Their interests were mutually incompatible.*
OPPOSITES: consistent, compatible, suited

incompetence = **ineptitude**, inability, inadequacy, incapacity, ineffectiveness, uselessness, insufficiency, ineptness, incompetency, unfitness, incapability, skill-lessness • *The incompetence of government officials is appalling.*

incompetent = **inept**, useless, incapable, unable, cowboy *(informal)*, floundering, bungling, unfit, unfitted, ineffectual, incapacitated, inexpert, skill-less, unskilful • *He wants the power to sack incompetent teachers.*
OPPOSITES: able, fit, competent

incomplete = **unfinished**, partial, insufficient, wanting, short, lacking, undone, defective, deficient, imperfect, undeveloped, fragmentary, unaccomplished, unexecuted, half-pie *(N.Z. informal)* • *Some offices had incomplete information on spending.*
OPPOSITES: whole, finished, complete

incomprehensible 1 = **unintelligible**, incoherent, indecipherable, meaningless, muddled, jumbled, inarticulate, unfathomable, indistinct • *Her speech was almost incomprehensible.*
OPPOSITES: understandable, comprehensible, intelligible
2 = **obscure**, puzzling, mysterious, baffling, enigmatic, perplexing, opaque, impenetrable, inscrutable, unfathomable, above your head, beyond comprehension, all Greek to you *(informal)*, beyond your grasp • *incomprehensible mathematics puzzles*
OPPOSITES: clear, obvious, understandable

inconceivable = **unimaginable**, impossible, incredible, staggering *(informal)*, unbelievable, unthinkable, out of the question, incomprehensible, unheard-of, mind-boggling *(informal)*, beyond belief, unknowable, not to be thought of • *It was inconceivable to me that he could have been my attacker.*
OPPOSITES: possible, credible, conceivable

inconclusive = **uncertain**, vague, ambiguous, open, indecisive, unsettled, undecided, unconvincing, up in the air *(informal)*, indeterminate • *Research has so far proved inconclusive.*

incongruity = **inappropriateness**, discrepancy, inconsistency, disparity, incompatibility, unsuitability, inaptness, inharmoniousness • *She smiled at the incongruity of the question.*

incongruous = **inappropriate**, absurd, out of place, conflicting, contrary, contradictory, inconsistent, unsuitable, improper, incompatible, discordant, incoherent, extraneous, unsuited, unbecoming, out of keeping, inapt, disconsonant • *She looked incongruous in an army uniform.*
OPPOSITES: appropriate, becoming, suited

inconsequential = **unimportant**, trivial, insignificant, minor, petty, trifling, negligible, paltry, immaterial, measly, inconsiderable, nickel-and-dime *(U.S. slang)*, of no significance • *a reminder of how inconsequential their lives were*

inconsiderable = **insignificant**, small, slight, light, minor, petty, trivial, trifling, negligible, unimportant, small-time *(informal)*, inconsequential, exiguous • *He was a man of great charm and not inconsiderable wit.*

inconsiderate = **selfish**, rude, insensitive, self-centred, careless, unkind, intolerant, thoughtless, unthinking, tactless, uncharitable, ungracious, indelicate • *his inconsiderate behaviour*
OPPOSITES: kind, sensitive, considerate

inconsistency 1 = **unreliability**, instability, unpredictability, fickleness, unsteadiness • *His worst fault was his inconsistency.*
2 = **incompatibility**, paradox, discrepancy, disparity, disagreement, variance, divergence, incongruity, contrariety, inconsonance • *the alleged inconsistencies in his evidence*

inconsistent 1 = **changeable**, variable, unpredictable, unstable, irregular, erratic, uneven, fickle, capricious, unsteady, inconstant • *You are inconsistent and unpredictable.*
OPPOSITES: stable, constant, consistent
2 = **incompatible**, conflicting, contrary, at odds, contradictory, in conflict, incongruous, discordant, incoherent, out of step, irreconcilable, at variance, discrepant, inconstant • *The outburst was inconsistent with the image he had cultivated.*
OPPOSITES: compatible, uniform, coherent

inconsolable = **heartbroken**, devastated, despairing, desolate, wretched, heartsick, brokenhearted, sick at heart, prostrate with grief • *When my mother died I was inconsolable.*

inconspicuous 1 = **unobtrusive**, hidden, unnoticeable, retiring, quiet, ordinary, plain, muted, camouflaged, insignificant, unassuming, unostentatious • *I'll try to be as inconspicuous as possible.*
OPPOSITES: obvious, visible, noticeable
2 = **plain**, ordinary, modest, unobtrusive, unnoticeable • *The studio is an inconspicuous grey building.*

incontestable = **indisputable**, certain, undeniable, beyond doubt, sure, self-evident, irrefutable, unquestionable, incontrovertible, beyond question, indubitable • *The grandeur of London is unique and incontestable.*

incontrovertible = **indisputable**, sure, certain, established, positive, undeniable, irrefutable, unquestionable, unshakable, beyond dispute, incontestable, indubitable, nailed-on *(slang)* • *incontrovertible evidence that the government is violating the agreement*

inconvenience AS A NOUN 1 = **trouble**, difficulty, bother, upset, fuss, disadvantage, disturbance, disruption, drawback, hassle *(informal)*, nuisance, downside, annoyance, hindrance, awkwardness, vexation, uphill *(S. African)* • *We apologize for any inconvenience caused during the repairs.*
2 = **awkwardness**, unfitness, unwieldiness, cumbersomeness, unhandiness, unsuitableness, untimeliness • *The expense and inconvenience of PCs means that they will be replaced.*
▸ AS A VERB = **trouble**, bother, disturb, upset, disrupt, put out, hassle *(informal)*, irk, discommode, give (someone) bother *or* trouble, make (someone) go out of his way, put to trouble • *He promised not to inconvenience them any further.*

QUOTATIONS
An adventure is only an inconvenience rightly considered. An inconvenience is only an adventure wrongly considered
[G.K. Chesterton *All Things Considered*]

inconvenient 1 = **troublesome**, annoying, awkward, embarrassing, disturbing, unsuitable, tiresome, untimely, bothersome, vexatious, inopportune, disadvantageous, unseasonable • *It's very inconvenient to have to wait so long.*
OPPOSITES: suitable, convenient, handy
2 = **difficult**, awkward, unmanageable, cumbersome, unwieldy, unhandy • *This must be the most inconvenient house ever built.*

incorporate 1 = **include**, contain, take in, embrace, integrate, embody, encompass, assimilate, comprise of • *The new cars will incorporate a number of major improvements.*
2 = **integrate**, include, absorb, unite, merge, accommodate, knit, fuse, assimilate, amalgamate, subsume, coalesce, harmonize, meld • *The agreement allowed the rebels to be incorporated into the police force.*
3 = **blend**, mix, combine, compound, consolidate, fuse, mingle, meld • *Gradually incorporate the olive oil into the dough.*

incorporation = **merger**, federation, blend, integration, unifying, inclusion, fusion, absorption, assimilation, amalgamation, coalescence • *the incorporation of two airlines into one*

incorrect 1 = **false**, wrong, mistaken, flawed, faulty, unfitting, inaccurate, untrue, improper, erroneous, out, wide of the mark *(informal)*, specious, inexact, off-base *(U.S. & Canad. informal)*, off-beam *(informal)*, way off-beam *(informal)* • *He denied that his evidence was incorrect.*
OPPOSITES: right, true, correct
2 = **inappropriate**, wrong, unsuitable, unfit, improper, unseemly, ill-suited, inapt • *injuries caused by incorrect posture*
OPPOSITES: appropriate, right, fitting

incorrigible = **incurable**, hardened, hopeless, intractable, inveterate, unreformed, irredeemable • *Gamblers are incorrigible optimists.*

incorruptible 1 = **honest**, straight, upright, honourable, just, trustworthy, above suspicion, unbribable • *He was a totally reliable and incorruptible businessman.*
2 = **imperishable**, everlasting, undecaying • *Its incorruptible beauty has been prized for millennia.*

increase AS A VERB 1 = **raise**, extend, boost, expand, develop, advance, add to, strengthen, enhance, step up *(informal)*, widen, prolong, intensify, heighten, elevate, enlarge, multiply, inflate, magnify, amplify, augment, aggrandize • *The company has increased the price of its cars.*
OPPOSITES: reduce, diminish, decrease
2 = **grow**, develop, spread, mount, expand, build up, swell, wax, enlarge, escalate, multiply, fill out, get bigger, proliferate, snowball, dilate • *The population continues to increase.*
OPPOSITES: decline, shrink, diminish
▸ AS A NOUN = **growth**, rise, boost, development, gain, addition, expansion, extension, heightening, proliferation, enlargement, escalation, upsurge, upturn, increment, intensification, augmentation, aggrandizement • *a sharp increase in productivity*
▸ IN PHRASES: **on the increase** = **growing**, increasing, spreading, expanding, escalating, multiplying, developing, on the rise, proliferating • *Crime is on the increase.*

increasingly = **progressively**, more and more, to an increasing extent, continuously more • *He was finding it increasingly difficult to make decisions.*

incredible 1 = **amazing**, great, wonderful, brilliant, stunning, extraordinary, overwhelming, ace *(informal)*, astonishing, staggering, marvellous, sensational *(informal)*, mega *(slang)*, breathtaking, astounding, far-out *(slang)*, eye-popping *(informal)*, prodigious, awe-inspiring, superhuman, rad *(informal)* • *Thanks, I had an incredible time.*
2 = **unbelievable**, impossible, absurd, unthinkable, questionable, improbable, inconceivable, preposterous, unconvincing, unimaginable, outlandish, far-fetched, implausible, beyond belief, cock-and-bull *(informal)*, not able to hold water • *Do not dismiss as incredible the stories your children tell you.*

incredulity = **disbelief**, doubt, scepticism, distrust, unbelief • *The announcement has been met with incredulity.*

incredulous = **disbelieving**, doubting, sceptical, suspicious, doubtful, dubious, unconvinced, distrustful, mistrustful, unbelieving • *There was a brief, incredulous silence.*
OPPOSITES: believing, trusting, credulous

increment = **increase**, gain, addition, supplement, step up, advancement, enlargement, accretion, accrual, augmentation, accruement • *Many teachers qualify for an annual increment.*

incriminate = **implicate**, involve, accuse, blame, indict, point the finger at *(informal)*, stigmatize, arraign, blacken the name of, inculpate • *He claimed that the drugs had been planted to incriminate him.*

inculcate = **instil**, impress, implant, infuse, drill, hammer in *(informal)*, drum in, indoctrinate • *Care was taken to inculcate the values of nationhood and family.*

incumbent AS A NOUN = **holder**, keeper, bearer, custodian • *The previous incumbent led the party for eleven years.*
▸ AS AN ADJECTIVE = **obligatory**, required, necessary, essential, binding, compulsory, mandatory, imperative • *It is incumbent upon all of us to make an extra effort.*

incur = **sustain**, experience, suffer, gain, earn, collect, meet with, provoke, run up, induce, arouse, expose yourself to, lay yourself open to, bring upon yourself • *The government has also incurred huge debts.*

incurable 1 = **fatal**, terminal, inoperable, irrecoverable, irremediable, remediless • *He is suffering from an incurable skin disease.*
2 = **incorrigible**, hopeless, inveterate, dyed-in-the-wool • *He's an incurable romantic.*

incursion = **foray**, raid, invasion, penetration, infiltration, inroad, irruption • *armed incursions into border areas by rebel forces*

indebted = **grateful**, obliged, in debt, obligated, beholden, under an obligation • *I am deeply indebted to him for his help.*

indecency = **obscenity**, impurity, lewdness, impropriety, pornography, vulgarity, coarseness, crudity, licentiousness, foulness, outrageousness, immodesty, grossness, vileness, bawdiness, unseemliness, indelicacy, smuttiness, indecorum • *They were found guilty of acts of gross indecency.*
OPPOSITES: purity, decency, delicacy

indecent 1 = **obscene**, lewd, dirty, blue, offensive, outrageous, inappropriate, rude, gross, foul, crude, coarse, filthy, vile, improper, pornographic, salacious, impure, smutty, immodest, licentious, scatological, indelicate • *She accused him of making indecent suggestions.*
OPPOSITES: pure, decent, modest
2 = **unbecoming**, unsuitable, vulgar, improper, tasteless, unseemly, undignified, disreputable, unrefined, discreditable, indelicate, indecorous, unbefitting • *The legislation was drafted with indecent haste.*
OPPOSITES: seemly, decent, proper

indecipherable = **illegible**, unintelligible, indistinguishable, unreadable, crabbed • *Her writing is virtually indecipherable.*

indecision = **hesitation**, doubt, uncertainty, wavering, ambivalence, dithering *(chiefly Brit.)*, hesitancy, indecisiveness, vacillation, shilly-shallying *(informal)*, irresolution • *After months of indecision, they gave the go-ahead on Monday.*

QUOTATIONS
There is no more miserable human being than one in whom nothing is habitual but indecision, and for whom the lighting of every cigar, the drinking of every cup, the time of rising and going to bed every day, and the beginning of every bit of work, are subjects of express volitional deliberation
[William James *Varieties of Religious Experience*]

PROVERBS
The cat would eat fish, but would not wet her feet

indecisive 1 = **hesitating**, uncertain, wavering, doubtful, faltering, tentative, undecided, dithering *(chiefly Brit.)*, vacillating, in two minds *(informal)*, undetermined, pussyfooting *(informal)*, irresolute • *He was criticised as a weak and indecisive leader.*
OPPOSITES: decisive, positive, resolute

2 = **inconclusive**, unclear, undecided, indefinite, indeterminate • *An indecisive vote would force a second round of voting.*
OPPOSITES: final, clear, conclusive

indeed 1 = **certainly**, yes, definitely, surely, truly, absolutely, undoubtedly, positively, decidedly, without doubt, undeniably, without question, unequivocally, indisputably, assuredly, doubtlessly • *'Did you know him?' 'I did indeed.'*
2 = **really**, actually, in fact, certainly, undoubtedly, genuinely, in reality, to be sure, in truth, categorically, verily *(archaic)*, in actuality, in point of fact, veritably • *Later he admitted that the payments had indeed been made.*
3 = **very**, really, truly, greatly, particularly, extremely, terribly, remarkably, unusually, profoundly, decidedly, exceedingly, superlatively, uncommonly, surpassingly • *I am indeed sorry I cannot help you.*

indefatigable = **tireless**, dogged, persevering, patient, relentless, diligent, inexhaustible, unremitting, assiduous, unflagging, untiring, sedulous, pertinacious, unwearying, unwearied • *His indefatigable spirit helped him to cope with the illness.*

indefensible = **unforgivable**, wrong, inexcusable, unjustifiable, untenable, unpardonable, insupportable, unwarrantable • *She described their actions as 'morally indefensible'.*
OPPOSITES: legitimate, justifiable, defensible

indefinable = **inexpressible**, vague, indescribable, obscure, dim, hazy, nameless, indistinct, unrealized, impalpable • *There was something indefinable in her eyes.*

indefinite 1 = **uncertain**, general, vague, unclear, unsettled, loose, unlimited, evasive, indeterminate, imprecise, undefined, equivocal, ill-defined, indistinct, undetermined, inexact, unfixed, oracular • *The trial was adjourned for an indefinite period.*
OPPOSITES: settled
2 = **unclear**, unknown, uncertain, obscure, doubtful, ambiguous, indeterminate, imprecise, undefined, ill-defined, indistinct, undetermined, inexact, unfixed • *a handsome woman of indefinite age*
OPPOSITES: clear, certain, specific

indefinitely = **endlessly**, continually, for ever, ad infinitum, sine die *(Latin)*, till the cows come home *(informal)* • *The visit has now been postponed indefinitely.*

indelible = **permanent**, lasting, enduring, ingrained, indestructible, ineradicable, ineffaceable, inexpungible, inextirpable • *My visit to India left an indelible impression on me.*
OPPOSITES: temporary, short-lived, washable

indelicate = **offensive**, indecent, vulgar, low, blue, embarrassing, gross, crude, rude, obscene, coarse, improper, suggestive, tasteless, unseemly, untoward, risqué, X-rated *(informal)*, unbecoming, off-colour, immodest, near the knuckle *(informal)*, indecorous, barro *(Austral. slang)* • *She could not touch upon such an indelicate subject.*
OPPOSITES: becoming, seemly, decent

indemnify 1 = **insure**, protect, guarantee, secure, endorse, underwrite • *They agreed to indemnify the taxpayers against any loss.*
2 = **compensate**, pay, reimburse, satisfy, repair, repay, requite, remunerate • *They don't have the money to indemnify everybody.*

indemnity 1 = **insurance**, security, guarantee, protection • *They had failed to take out full indemnity cover.*
2 = **compensation**, remuneration, reparation, satisfaction, redress, restitution, reimbursement, requital • *The government paid the family an indemnity for the missing pictures.*
3 = **exemption**, immunity, impunity, privilege • *He was offered indemnity from prosecution in return for his evidence.*

indent 1 = **notch**, cut, score, mark, nick, pink, scallop, dint, serrate • *the country's heavily indented coastline*
2 = **order**, request, ask for, requisition • *We had to indent for hatchets and torches.*

indentation = **notch**, cut, nick, depression, pit, dip, bash *(informal)*, hollow, dent, jag, dimple • *With a knife make slight indentations around the pastry.*

independence 1 = **freedom**, liberty, autonomy, separation, sovereignty, self-determination, self-government, self-rule, self-sufficiency, self-reliance, home rule, autarchy, rangatiratanga *(N.Z.)* • *the country's first elections since independence in 1962*
OPPOSITES: dependence, bondage, subjugation
2 = **self-sufficiency**, self-reliance, self-sustenance • *He was afraid of losing his independence.*
3 = **neutrality**, detachment, objectivity, impartiality, fairness, disinterest, open-mindedness, even-handedness, disinterestedness, dispassion, nonpartisanship, lack of bias • *He stressed the importance of the judge's independence.*

QUOTATIONS

It is easy in the world to live after the world's opinion; it is easy in solitude after our own; but the great man is he who, in the midst of the crowd, keeps with perfect sweetness the independence of solitude
[Ralph Waldo Emerson *'Self-Reliance'*]

He travels the fastest who travels alone
[Rudyard Kipling *The Story of the Gadsbys*]

independent 1 = **separate**, unrelated, unconnected, unattached, uncontrolled, unconstrained • *Two independent studies have been carried out.*
OPPOSITES: controlled
2 = **self-sufficient**, free, liberated, unconventional, self-contained, individualistic, unaided, self-reliant, self-supporting • *There were benefits to being a single, independent woman.*
3 = **self-governing**, free, autonomous, separated, liberated, sovereign, self-determining, nonaligned, decontrolled, autarchic • *a fully independent state*
OPPOSITES: controlled, subject, dependent
4 = **private**, public, private-sector, free-standing • *He taught chemistry at an independent school.*
5 = **neutral**, objective, detached, impartial, just, fair, equal, open-minded, equitable, disinterested, unbiased, even-handed, nonpartisan, unprejudiced, nondiscriminating • *an independent mortgage adviser*

independently = **separately**, alone, solo, on your own, by yourself, unaided, individually, autonomously, under your own steam • *helping disabled students to live and study independently*

indescribable = **unutterable**, indefinable, beyond words, ineffable, inexpressible, beyond description, incommunicable, beggaring description • *The stench from the sewer is indescribable.*

indestructible = **permanent**, durable, unbreakable, lasting, enduring, abiding, immortal, everlasting, indelible, incorruptible, imperishable, indissoluble, unfading, nonperishable • *This type of plastic is almost indestructible.*
OPPOSITES: perishable, breakable, impermanent

indeterminate = **uncertain**, indefinite, unspecified, vague, inconclusive, imprecise, undefined, undetermined, inexact, unfixed, unstipulated • *I hope to carry on for an indeterminate period.*
OPPOSITES: fixed, exact, precise

index 1 = **list**, listing, key, guide, register • *There's even a special subject index.*
2 = **indication**, guide, sign, mark, note, evidence, signal, symptom, hint, clue, token • *Weeds are an index to the character of the soil.*

indicate 1 = **show**, suggest, reveal, display, signal, demonstrate, point to, imply, disclose, manifest, signify,

denote, bespeak, make known, be symptomatic of, evince, betoken, flag up • *The survey indicated that most old people are independent.*
2 = **imply**, suggest, hint, intimate, signify, insinuate, give someone to understand • *He has indicated that he might resign.*
3 = **point to**, point out, specify, gesture towards, designate • *'Sit down,' he said, indicating a chair.*
4 = **register**, show, record, mark, read, express, display, demonstrate • *The gauge indicated that it was boiling.*

indicated = **recommended**, needed, necessary, suggested, called-for, desirable, advisable • *If a hospital stay is indicated, check how much this will cost.*

indication = **sign**, mark, evidence, warning, note, signal, suggestion, symptom, hint, clue, manifestation, omen, inkling, portent, intimation, forewarning, wake-up call • *He gave no indication that he was ready to compromise.*

indicative = **suggestive**, significant, symptomatic, pointing to, exhibitive, indicatory, indicial • *Often physical appearance is indicative of how a person feels.*

indicator = **sign**, mark, measure, guide, display, index, signal, symbol, meter, gauge, marker, benchmark, pointer, signpost, barometer • *The number of wells is a fair indicator of the demand for water.*

indict = **charge**, accuse, prosecute, summon, impeach, arraign, serve with a summons • *He was later indicted on corruption charges.*

indictment = **charge**, allegation, prosecution, accusation, impeachment, summons, arraignment • *Prosecutors may soon seek an indictment on fraud charges.*

indifference 1 = **disregard**, apathy, lack of interest, negligence, detachment, coolness, carelessness, coldness, nonchalance, callousness, aloofness, inattention, unconcern, absence of feeling, heedlessness • *his callous indifference to the plight of his son*
OPPOSITES: interest, concern, care
2 = **irrelevance**, insignificance, triviality, unimportance • *They regard dress as a matter of indifference.*

QUOTATIONS
The worst sin towards our fellow creatures is not to hate them, but to be indifferent to them: that's the essence of inhumanity
[George Bernard Shaw *The Devil's Disciple*]
I regard you with an indifference closely bordering on aversion
[Robert Louis Stevenson *The New Arabian Nights*]

indifferent 1 = **unconcerned**, distant, detached, cold, cool, regardless, careless, callous, aloof, unimpressed, unmoved, unsympathetic, impervious, uncaring, uninterested, apathetic, unresponsive, heedless, inattentive • *People have become indifferent to the suffering of others.*
OPPOSITES: interested, concerned, keen
2 = **mediocre**, middling, average, fair, ordinary, moderate, insignificant, unimportant, so-so (*informal*), immaterial, passable, undistinguished, uninspired, of no consequence, no great shakes (*informal*), half-pie (*N.Z. informal*) • *She had starred in several indifferent movies.*
OPPOSITES: fine, excellent, remarkable

indigenous = **native**, original, aboriginal, home-grown, autochthonous • *the country's indigenous population*

indigent = **destitute**, poor, impoverished, needy, penniless, poverty-stricken, down and out, in want, down at heel (*informal*), impecunious, dirt-poor, straitened, on the breadline, short, flat broke (*informal*), penurious, necessitous • *How can we persuade indigent peasants to stop slaughtering wildlife?*
OPPOSITES: rich, wealthy, prosperous

indigestion = **upset stomach**, heartburn, dyspepsia, dyspepsy, acid reflux • *The symptoms are loss of appetite, indigestion and nausea.*

indignant = **resentful**, angry, mad (*informal*), heated, provoked, furious, annoyed, hacked (off) (*U.S. slang*), sore (*informal*), fuming (*informal*), choked, incensed, disgruntled, exasperated, pissed off (*taboo*), irate, livid (*informal*), seeing red (*informal*), miffed (*informal*), riled, up in arms (*informal*), peeved (*informal*), in a huff, hot under the collar (*informal*), huffy (*informal*), wrathful, narked (*Brit., Austral. & N.Z. slang*), in high dudgeon, tooshie (*Austral. slang*), off the air (*Austral. slang*) • *He is indignant at suggestions that they were secret agents.*

indignation = **resentment**, anger, rage, fury, wrath, ire (*literary*), exasperation, pique, umbrage, righteous anger • *No wonder he could hardly contain his indignation.*

indignity = **humiliation**, abuse, outrage, injury, slight, insult, snub, reproach, affront, disrespect, dishonour, opprobrium, obloquy, contumely • *He suffered the indignity of having to face angry protesters.*

indirect 1 = **related**, accompanying, secondary, subsidiary, contingent, collateral, incidental, unintended, ancillary, concomitant • *They are feeling the indirect effects of the recession elsewhere.*
2 = **circuitous**, winding, roundabout, curving, wandering, rambling, deviant, meandering, tortuous, zigzag, long-drawn-out, circumlocutory • *The goods went by a rather indirect route.*
OPPOSITES: direct, straight, straightforward
3 = **oblique**, implied, roundabout, backhanded, evasive, circuitous, sidelong, circumlocutory, periphrastic • *His remarks amounted to an indirect appeal for aid.*

indirectly 1 = **by implication**, in a roundabout way, circumlocutorily • *Drugs are indirectly responsible for the violence.*
2 = **obliquely**, in a roundabout way, evasively, not in so many words, circuitously, periphrastically • *He referred indirectly to the territorial dispute.*
3 = **second-hand**, on the grapevine (*informal*) • *He'd heard, indirectly, that I was a major opponent of their plan.*

indiscernible = **invisible**, hidden, imperceptible, indistinguishable, indistinct, impalpable, unapparent, undiscernible • *The signs were so concealed as to be almost indiscernible.*
OPPOSITES: clear, apparent, discernible

indiscreet = **tactless**, foolish, rash, reckless, unwise, hasty, ill-advised, unthinking, ill-judged, ill-considered, imprudent, heedless, injudicious, incautious, undiplomatic, impolitic • *He is notoriously indiscreet about his private life.*
OPPOSITES: diplomatic, wise, discreet

indiscretion 1 = **folly**, foolishness, recklessness, imprudence, rashness, tactlessness, gaucherie • *Occasionally they paid for their indiscretion with their lives.*
2 = **mistake**, slip, error, lapse, folly, boob (*Brit. slang*), gaffe, bloomer (*Brit. informal*), faux pas, barry *or* Barry Crocker (*Austral. slang*) • *rumours of his mother's youthful indiscretions*

QUOTATIONS
Careless talk costs lives
[*Second World War security slogan*]

indiscriminate = **random**, general, wholesale, mixed, sweeping, confused, chaotic, careless, mingled, jumbled, miscellaneous, promiscuous, motley, haphazard, uncritical, aimless, desultory, hit or miss (*informal*), higgledy-piggledy (*informal*), undiscriminating, unsystematic, unselective, undistinguishable, unmethodical, scattershot • *the indiscriminate killing of refugees*
OPPOSITES: deliberate, discriminating, systematic

indiscriminately = **at random**, wildly, blindly, madly, instinctively, frantically, randomly, aimlessly, haphazardly, confusedly, purposelessly, unmethodically • *The men opened fire indiscriminately.*

indispensable = **essential**, necessary, needed, key, vital, crucial, imperative, requisite, needful, must-have • *She was becoming indispensable to him.*
OPPOSITES: unnecessary, unimportant, dispensable

indisposed 1 = **ill**, poorly *(informal)*, sick, crook *(Austral. & N.Z. informal)*, ailing, unwell, laid up *(informal)*, under the weather, confined to bed, on the sick list *(informal)* • *The speaker was regrettably indisposed.*
OPPOSITES: well, sound, fit
2 = **unwilling**, reluctant, loath, disinclined, averse • *He seemed indisposed to chat.*

indistinct 1 = **unclear**, confused, obscure, faint, blurred, vague, doubtful, ambiguous, fuzzy, shadowy, indefinite, misty, hazy, unintelligible, indistinguishable, indeterminate, bleary, undefined, out of focus, ill-defined, indiscernible • *The lettering is fuzzy and indistinct.*
OPPOSITES: clear, defined, distinct
2 = **muffled**, confused, faint, dim, weak, indistinguishable, indiscernible • *the indistinct murmur of voices*

indistinguishable = **identical**, the same, cut from the same cloth, like as two peas in a pod *(informal)* • *Replica weapons are indistinguishable from the real thing.*

individual AS AN ADJECTIVE 1 = **separate**, single, independent, isolated, lone, solitary, discrete • *waiting for the group to decide rather than making individual decisions*
OPPOSITES: general, collective
2 = **unique**, different, special, original, fresh, novel, exclusive, distinct, singular, idiosyncratic, unorthodox • *It was all part of her very individual personality.*
OPPOSITES: ordinary, conventional, universal
3 = **distinctive**, special, personal, particular, specific, characteristic, distinguishing, distinct, signature, peculiar, respective, idiosyncratic, personalized • *We develop our own individual style of writing.*
OPPOSITES: general, common, conventional
▸ AS A NOUN = **person**, being, human, party, body *(informal)*, type, unit, character, soul, creature, human being, mortal, personage, living soul • *the rights and responsibilities of the individual*

individualism = **independence**, self-interest, originality, self-reliance, egoism, egocentricity, self-direction, freethinking • *He is stuck with what he calls the individualism of officers.*

individualist = **maverick**, nonconformist, independent, original, loner, lone wolf, freethinker • *Individualists say that you should be able to wear what you want.*

individualistic = **individual**, original, unique, particular, distinctive, special, independent, typical, characteristic, idiosyncratic, self-reliant, egocentric, egoistic • *Most artists are very individualistic.*

individuality = **character**, personality, uniqueness, distinction, distinctiveness, originality, peculiarity, singularity, separateness, discreteness • *People should be free to express their individuality and style.*

individually = **separately**, independently, singly, one by one, one at a time, severally • *cheeses which come in individually wrapped segments*

indoctrinate = **brainwash**, school, train, teach, drill, initiate, instruct, imbue • *They have been completely indoctrinated.*

indoctrination = **brainwashing**, schooling, training, instruction, drilling, inculcation • *political indoctrination classes*

indolence = **idleness**, slacking, laziness, inertia, shirking, lethargy, inactivity, sloth, torpor, skiving *(Brit. slang)*, languor, inertness, torpidity, faineance, faineancy, languidness • *He was noted for his indolence.*

QUOTATIONS
I look upon indolence as a sort of suicide
[Lord Chesterfield]

indolent = **lazy**, slack, idle, slow, sluggish, inactive, inert, languid, lethargic, listless, lackadaisical, torpid, good-for-nothing, workshy, slothful, lumpish, fainéant • *indolent teenagers who won't lift a finger to help*
OPPOSITES: active, busy, industrious

indomitable = **invincible**, resolute, steadfast, set, staunch, unbeatable, unyielding, unflinching, unconquerable, untameable • *a woman of indomitable will*
OPPOSITES: weak, yielding, shrinking

indorse *see* **endorse**

indorsement *see* **endorsement**

indubitable = **certain**, sure, undoubted, obvious, evident, veritable, undeniable, indisputable, irrefutable, unquestionable, open-and-shut, incontrovertible, unarguable, incontestable, nailed-on *(slang)* • *This film is an indubitable classic.*

induce 1 = **cause**, produce, create, begin, effect, lead to, occasion, generate, provoke, motivate, set off, bring about, give rise to, precipitate, incite, instigate, engender, set in motion • *an economic crisis induced by high oil prices*
OPPOSITES: stop, prevent, curb
2 = **persuade**, encourage, influence, get, move, press, draw, convince, urge, prompt, sway, entice, coax, incite, impel, talk someone into, prevail upon, actuate • *I would do anything to induce them to stay.*
OPPOSITES: stop, prevent, dissuade

inducement = **incentive**, motive, cause, influence, reward, come-on *(informal)*, spur, consideration, attraction, lure, bait, carrot *(informal)*, encouragement, impulse, stimulus, incitement, clarion call • *They offer every inducement to encourage investment.*

induct = **install**, admit, introduce, allow, swear, initiate, inaugurate • *Six new members have been inducted into the Cabinet.*

induction = **installation**, institution, introduction, initiation, inauguration, investiture • *an induction course for new members*

indulge AS A VERB 1 = **gratify**, satisfy, fulfil, feed, give way to, yield to, cater to, pander to, regale, gladden, satiate • *His success has let him indulge his love of expensive cars.*
2 = **spoil**, pamper, cosset, baby, favour, humour, give in to, coddle, spoon-feed, mollycoddle, fawn on, overindulge • *He did not agree with indulging children.*
▸ IN PHRASES: **indulge yourself** = **treat yourself**, splash out, spoil yourself, luxuriate in something, overindulge yourself • *You can indulge yourself without spending a fortune.*

indulgence 1 = **luxury**, treat, extravagance, favour, privilege • *The car is one of my few indulgences.*
2 = **leniency**, pampering, spoiling, kindness, fondness, permissiveness, partiality • *The king's indulgence towards his sons angered them.*
3 = **intemperance**, excess, extravagance, debauchery, dissipation, overindulgence, prodigality, immoderation, dissoluteness, intemperateness • *Sadly, constant indulgence can be a costly affair.*
OPPOSITES: moderation, temperance, strictness
4 = **gratification**, satisfaction, fulfilment, appeasement, satiation • *his indulgence of his gross appetites*

indulgent = **lenient**, liberal, kind, kindly, understanding, gentle, tender, mild, fond, favourable, tolerant, gratifying, easy-going, compliant, permissive, forbearing • *His indulgent mother was willing to let him do what he wanted.*
OPPOSITES: strict, harsh, stern

industrial 1 = **manufacturing**, business, commercial • *industrial machinery and equipment*
2 = **industrialized**, developed • *leading western industrial countries*

industrialist = **capitalist**, tycoon, magnate, boss, producer, manufacturer, baron, financier, captain of industry, big businessman • *prominent Japanese industrialists*

industrious = **hard-working**, diligent, active, busy, steady, productive, energetic, conscientious, tireless, zealous, laborious, assiduous, sedulous • *She was an industrious and willing worker*
OPPOSITES: lazy, idle, indolent

industry 1 = **business**, production, manufacturing, trade, trading, commerce, commercial enterprise • *countries where industry is developing rapidly*
2 = **trade**, world, business, service, line, field, craft, profession, occupation • *the textile industry*
3 = **diligence**, effort, labour, hard work, trouble, activity, application, striving, endeavour, toil, vigour, zeal, persistence, assiduity, tirelessness • *No one doubted his industry or his integrity.*

QUOTATIONS
Go to the ant, thou sluggard; consider her ways, and be wise
[*Bible: Proverbs*]
Where there is no desire, there will be no industry
[John Locke *Some Thoughts Concerning Education*]
Avarice, the spur of industry
[David Hume *Essays, Moral and Political: Of Civil Liberty*]

inebriated = **drunk**, wasted *(slang)*, tight *(informal)*, smashed *(slang)*, canned *(slang)*, high *(informal)*, flying *(slang)*, bombed *(slang)*, stoned *(slang)*, hammered *(slang)*, steaming *(slang)*, wrecked *(slang)*, out of it *(slang)*, plastered *(slang)*, blitzed *(slang)*, pissed *(Brit., Austral. & N.Z. slang)*, lit up *(slang)*, merry *(Brit. informal)*, bladdered *(slang)*, under the influence *(informal)*, intoxicated, tipsy, befuddled, legless *(informal)*, under the weather *(informal)*, blatted *(Brit. slang)*, boozed-up *(informal)*, dronkverdriet *(S. African)*, elephants *(Austral. slang)*, broken *(S. African informal)*, boozed-up *(slang)*, kaylied *(Brit. slang)*, langered *(Irish slang)*, lashed *(Brit. slang)*, mashed *(Brit. slang)*, mullered *(slang)*, ossified *(Irish slang)*, sat *(S. African)*, stukkend *(S. African slang)*, trashed *(slang)*, paralytic *(informal)*, sozzled *(informal)*, steamboats *(Scot. slang)*, off your face *(slang)*, half-cut *(informal)*, blind drunk, high as a kite *(informal)*, zonked *(slang)*, blotto *(slang)*, the worse for drink, inebriate, out to it *(Austral. & N.Z. slang)*, drunk as a skunk, bacchic, in your cups, rat-arsed *(taboo)*, Brahms and Liszt *(slang)*, half seas over *(informal)*, bevvied *(dialect)*, three sheets in the wind *(informal)*, babalas *(S. African)*, fou or fu' *(Scot.)*, pie-eyed *(slang)* • *He was obviously inebriated by the time dessert was served.*

inedible = **uneatable**, unpalatable, disagreeable, unpleasant, distasteful, unsavoury, repugnant, unappetizing • *They complained of being given food which was inedible.*

ineffable = **indescribable**, unspeakable, indefinable, beyond words, unutterable, inexpressible, incommunicable • *the ineffable sadness of many of the portraits*

ineffective 1 = **unproductive**, useless, futile, vain, unsuccessful, pointless, fruitless, to no avail, ineffectual, unprofitable, to no effect, unavailing, unfruitful, profitless, bootless, inefficacious • *Reform will continue to be painful and ineffective.*
OPPOSITES: effective, useful, efficient
2 = **inefficient**, inadequate, useless, poor, weak, pathetic, powerless, unfit, feeble, worthless, inept, impotent, ineffectual • *They are burdened with an ineffective leader.*

ineffectual 1 = **unproductive**, useless, ineffective, vain, unsuccessful, pointless, futile, fruitless, to no avail, unprofitable, to no effect, unavailing, unfruitful, profitless, bootless, inefficacious • *the well-meaning but ineffectual jobs programs of the past*
2 = **inefficient**, useless, powerless, poor, weak, inadequate, pathetic, unfit, ineffective, feeble, worthless, inept, impotent • *The mayor had become ineffectual in the war against drugs.*

inefficiency = **incompetence**, slackness, sloppiness, disorganization, carelessness • *the inefficiency of the distribution system*

inefficient 1 = **wasteful**, uneconomical, profligate, ruinous, improvident, unthrifty, inefficacious • *the inefficient use of funds*
2 = **incompetent**, incapable, inept, weak, bungling, feeble, sloppy, ineffectual, disorganized, slipshod, inexpert • *Some people are very inefficient workers.*
OPPOSITES: able, skilled, efficient

inelegant = **clumsy**, awkward, ungainly, rough, crude, coarse, crass, gauche, uncouth, unrefined, clunky *(informal)*, graceless, uncultivated, unpolished, indelicate, ungraceful • *The grand piano has been replaced with a small, inelegant model.* • *She was conscious of how inelegant she looked.*

ineligible = **unqualified**, ruled out, unacceptable, disqualified, incompetent *(Law)*, unfit, unfitted, unsuitable, undesirable, objectionable, unequipped • *They were ineligible to remain there because of criminal records.*

inept 1 = **incompetent**, bungling, clumsy, cowboy *(informal)*, awkward, bumbling, gauche, cack-handed *(informal)*, inexpert, maladroit, unskilful, unhandy, unworkmanlike • *He was inept and lacked the intelligence to govern.*
OPPOSITES: able, qualified, competent
2 = **unsuitable**, inappropriate, out of place, ridiculous, absurd, meaningless, pointless, unfit, improper, inapt, infelicitous, malapropos • *The Government's inept response turned this into a crisis.*
OPPOSITES: appropriate, suitable, sensible

ineptitude = **incompetence**, inefficiency, inability, incapacity, clumsiness, unfitness, gaucheness, inexpertness, unhandiness • *the tactical ineptitude of the commander*

inequality = **disparity**, prejudice, difference, bias, diversity, irregularity, unevenness, lack of balance, disproportion, imparity, preferentiality • *corruption and social inequality*

QUOTATIONS
All animals are equal but some animals are more equal than others
[George Orwell *Animal Farm*]
Whatever may be the general endeavor of a community to render its members equal and alike, the personal pride of individuals will always seek to rise above the line, and to form somewhere an inequality to their own advantage
[Alexis de Tocqueville *Democracy in America*]

inequitable = **unfair**, prejudiced, biased, one-sided, partial, partisan, unjust, discriminatory, preferential • *The system is grossly inequitable and inefficient.*
OPPOSITES: just, fair, unbiased

inequity = **unfairness**, prejudice, bias, injustice, discrimination, one-sidedness, unjustness • *Social imbalance worries him more than inequity of income.*

inert 1 = **inactive**, still, motionless, dead, passive, slack, static, dormant, lifeless, leaden, immobile, inanimate, unresponsive, unmoving, quiescent, torpid, unreactive, slumberous *(chiefly poetic)* • *He covered the inert body with a blanket*
OPPOSITES: moving, active, mobile
2 = **dull**, dry, boring, plain, static, commonplace, tedious, dreary, tiresome, lifeless, monotonous, prosaic, run-of-the-mill, unimaginative, uninteresting, vapid, torpid • *The novel itself remains oddly inert.*

inertia = **inactivity**, apathy, lethargy, passivity, stillness, laziness, sloth, idleness, stupor, drowsiness, dullness, immobility, torpor, sluggishness, indolence, lassitude, languor, listlessness, deadness, unresponsiveness • *He resented her inertia and lack of self-direction.*
OPPOSITES: energy, vitality, activity

inescapable = **unavoidable**, inevitable, certain, sure, fated, destined, inexorable, ineluctable, ineludible *(rare)* • *A sense of imminent doom was inescapable.*

inessential AS AN ADJECTIVE = **unnecessary**, redundant, superfluous, spare, surplus, optional, needless, extraneous, extrinsic, uncalled-for, dispensable • *We judged footnotes inessential to the text.*
▸ AS A NOUN = **luxury**, extra, extravagance, trimming, accessory, makeweight, superfluity • *He could strip away inessentials to reach the core of a problem.* • *Cut down your spending on inessentials.*

inestimable = **incalculable**, invaluable, priceless, precious, prodigious, immeasurable, beyond price • *Human life is of inestimable value.*

inevitability 1 = **certainty**, fate, shoo-in (*U.S. & Canad.*) • *Success is an inevitability for us.*
2 = **sureness**, ineluctability, inexorability *or* inexorableness, unavoidability *or* unavoidableness • *the inevitability of death*

PROVERBS
One does not argue against the sun

inevitable = **unavoidable**, inescapable, inexorable, sure, certain, necessary, settled, fixed, assured, fated, decreed, destined, ordained, predetermined, predestined, preordained, ineluctable, unpreventable • *The defeat had inevitable consequences for policy.*
OPPOSITES: uncertain, preventable, avoidable

inevitably = **unavoidably**, naturally, necessarily, surely, certainly, as a result, automatically, consequently, of necessity, perforce, inescapably, as a necessary consequence • *Inevitably, the proposal is running into difficulties.*

inexact = **imprecise**, inaccurate, indefinite, indeterminate, off, incorrect • *Forecasting was an inexact science.*

QUOTATIONS
It is the nature of all greatness not to be exact
[Edmund Burke]

inexcusable = **unforgivable**, indefensible, unjustifiable, outrageous, unpardonable, unwarrantable, inexpiable • *He said the killing of innocent people was inexcusable.*
OPPOSITES: justifiable, defensible, excusable

inexhaustible 1 = **endless**, infinite, never-ending, limitless, boundless, bottomless, unbounded, measureless, illimitable • *They seem to have an inexhaustible supply of ammunition.*
OPPOSITES: limited, bounded, finite
2 = **tireless**, undaunted, indefatigable, unfailing, unflagging, untiring, unwearying, unwearied • *the sound of his inexhaustible voice, still talking*
OPPOSITES: failing, tiring, flagging

inexorable = **unrelenting**, relentless, implacable, hard, severe, harsh, cruel, adamant, inescapable, inflexible, merciless, unyielding, immovable, remorseless, pitiless, unbending, obdurate, ineluctable, unappeasable • *the seemingly inexorable rise in unemployment*
OPPOSITES: flexible, lenient, relenting

inexorably = **relentlessly**, inevitably, irresistibly, remorselessly, implacably, unrelentingly • *Spending on health is growing inexorably.*

inexpensive = **cheap**, reasonable, low-priced, budget, bargain, modest, low-cost, economical • *a huge variety of good inexpensive restaurants*
OPPOSITES: dear, expensive, costly

inexperience = **unfamiliarity**, ignorance, newness, rawness, greenness, callowness, unexpertness • *the youth and inexperience of his staff*

PROVERBS
You cannot put an old head on young shoulders

inexperienced = **new**, unskilled, untrained, green, fresh, amateur, raw, unfamiliar, unused, callow, immature, unaccustomed, untried, unschooled, wet behind the ears (*informal*), unacquainted, unseasoned, unpractised, unversed, unfledged • *They are inexperienced when it comes to decorating.*
OPPOSITES: seasoned, trained, experienced

inexpert = **amateurish**, awkward, bungling, clumsy, inept, unskilled, unprofessional, cack-handed (*informal*), maladroit, unpractised, skill-less, unskilful, unhandy, unworkmanlike • *He was too inexpert to succeed.*

inexplicable = **unaccountable**, strange, mysterious, baffling, enigmatic, incomprehensible, mystifying, unintelligible, insoluble, inscrutable, unfathomable, beyond comprehension • *His behaviour was extraordinary and inexplicable.*
OPPOSITES: understandable, comprehensible, explicable

inexpressible = **indescribable**, unspeakable, indefinable, ineffable, unutterable, incommunicable • *He felt a sudden inexpressible loneliness.*

inextricably = **inseparably**, totally, intricately, irretrievably, indissolubly, indistinguishably • *Our survival is inextricably linked to survival of the rainforest.*

infallibility 1 = **supremacy**, perfection, omniscience, impeccability, faultlessness, irrefutability, unerringness • *exaggerated views of the infallibility of science*
2 = **reliability**, safety, dependability, trustworthiness, sureness • *The technical infallibility of their systems is without doubt.*

infallible 1 = **perfect**, impeccable, faultless, unerring, omniscient, unimpeachable • *She had an infallible eye for style.*
OPPOSITES: fallible, imperfect, human
2 = **sure**, certain, reliable, unbeatable, dependable, trustworthy, foolproof, sure-fire (*informal*), unfailing • *She hit on an infallible way of staying sober amid a flood of toasts.*
OPPOSITES: unreliable, undependable, uncertain

infamous = **notorious**, base, shocking, outrageous, disgraceful, monstrous, shameful, vile, scandalous, wicked, atrocious, heinous, odious, hateful, loathsome, ignominious, disreputable, egregious, abominable, villainous, dishonourable, nefarious, iniquitous, detestable, opprobrious, ill-famed, flagitious • *He was infamous for his anti-feminist attitudes.*
OPPOSITES: glorious, noble, esteemed

infamy = **notoriety**, scandal, shame, disgrace, atrocity, discredit, stigma, disrepute, ignominy, dishonour, abomination, opprobrium, villainy, odium, outrageousness, obloquy • *one of the greatest acts of infamy in history*

infancy 1 = **early childhood**, babyhood • *the development of the mind from infancy onwards*
2 = **beginnings**, start, birth, roots, seeds, origins, dawn, early stages, emergence, outset, cradle, inception • *the infancy of the electronic revolution*
OPPOSITES: end, close, death

QUOTATIONS
Heaven lies about us in our infancy
[William Wordsworth *Intimations of Immortality*]

infant AS A NOUN = **baby**, child, babe, toddler, tot, wean (*Scot.*), little one, bairn (*Scot.*), suckling, newborn child, babe in arms, sprog (*slang*), munchkin (*informal, chiefly U.S.*), neonate, rug rat (*slang*), littlie (*Austral. informal*), ankle-biter (*Austral. slang*), tacker (*Austral. slang*) • *young mums with infants in prams*
▸ AS AN ADJECTIVE = **early**, new, developing, young, growing, initial, dawning, fledgling, newborn, immature, embryonic, emergent, nascent, unfledged • *The infant company was based in Germany.*

QUOTATIONS
At first the infant,
Mewling and puking in the nurse's arms
[William Shakespeare *As You Like It*]

infantile = **childish**, immature, puerile, babyish, young, weak • *This kind of humour is infantile and boring.*
OPPOSITES: developed, adult, mature

infantry = **infantrymen**, foot soldiers • *The infantry were advancing to attack the ridge.*

infatuated = **obsessed**, fascinated, captivated, possessed, carried away, inflamed, beguiled, smitten *(informal)*, besotted, bewitched, intoxicated, crazy about *(informal)*, spellbound, enamoured, enraptured, under the spell of, head over heels in love with, swept off your feet • *He was utterly infatuated by her.*

infatuation = **obsession**, thing *(informal)*, passion, crush *(informal)*, madness, folly, fixation, foolishness • *Teenagers have their own infatuations.*

infect 1 = **contaminate**, transmit disease to, spread disease to *or* among • *A single mosquito can infect a large number of people.*
2 = **pollute**, dirty, poison, foul, corrupt, contaminate, taint, defile, vitiate • *The birds infect the milk.*
3 = **affect**, move, touch, influence, upset, overcome, stir, disturb • *I was infected by her fear.*

infection = **disease**, condition, complaint, illness, virus, disorder, corruption, poison, pollution, contamination, contagion, defilement, septicity • *Ear infections are common in pre-school children.*

infectious = **catching**, spreading, contagious, communicable, poisoning, corrupting, contaminating, polluting, virulent, defiling, infective, vitiating, pestilential, transmittable • *infectious diseases such as measles*

infer = **deduce**, understand, gather, conclude, derive, presume, conjecture, surmise, read between the lines, put two and two together • *I inferred from what she said that you have not been well.*

inference = **deduction**, conclusion, assumption, reading, consequence, presumption, conjecture, surmise, corollary • *There were two inferences to be drawn from her letter.*

inferior AS AN ADJECTIVE 1 = **lower**, junior, minor, secondary, subsidiary, lesser, humble, subordinate, lowly, less important, menial • *the inferior status of women in many societies*
OPPOSITES: higher, senior, superior
2 = **substandard**, bad, poor, mean, worse, poorer, pants *(informal)*, flawed, rotten, dire, indifferent, duff *(Brit. informal)*, mediocre, second-class, deficient, imperfect, second-rate, shoddy, low-grade, unsound, downmarket, low-rent *(informal, chiefly U.S.)*, for the birds *(informal)*, wretched, two-bit *(U.S. & Canad. slang)*, crappy *(slang)*, no great shakes *(informal)*, poxy *(slang)*, dime-a-dozen *(informal)*, piss-poor *(slang)*, chickenshit *(U.S. slang)*, bush-league *(Austral. & N.Z. informal)*, not much cop *(Brit. slang)*, tinhorn *(U.S. slang)*, half-pie *(N.Z. informal)*, of a sort *or* of sorts, strictly for the birds *(informal)*, bodger *or* bodgie *(Austral. slang)* • *The cassettes were of inferior quality.*
OPPOSITES: fine, excellent, first-class
▸ AS A NOUN = **underling**, junior, subordinate, lesser, menial, minion • *It was a gentleman's duty to be civil, even to his inferiors.*

QUOTATIONS
No-one can make you feel inferior without your consent
[Eleanor Roosevelt]

inferiority = **subservience**, subordination, lowliness, servitude, abasement, inferior status *or* standing • *I found it difficult to shake off a sense of inferiority.*
OPPOSITES: dominance, superiority, ascendancy

infernal 1 = **damned**, malevolent, hellish, devilish, accursed, damnable • *The post office is shut, which is an infernal bore.*
2 = **hellish**, lower, underworld, nether, Stygian, Hadean, Plutonian, chthonian, Tartarean *(literary)* • *the goddess of the infernal regions*
OPPOSITES: heavenly, celestial

inferno = **blaze**, fire, flames, conflagration • *Rescue workers fought to get to victims inside the inferno.*

infertile 1 = **sterile**, barren, infecund • *According to one survey, one woman in eight is infertile.*
2 = **barren**, unproductive, nonproductive, unfruitful, infecund • *The waste is dumped, making the surrounding land infertile.*
OPPOSITES: productive, fertile, fruitful

infertility = **sterility**, barrenness, unproductiveness, unfruitfulness, infecundity • *couples receiving infertility treatment*

infest = **overrun**, flood, invade, penetrate, ravage, swarm, throng, beset, permeate • *Crime and drugs are infesting the inner cities.*

infested = **overrun**, plagued, crawling, swarming, ridden, alive, ravaged, lousy *(slang)*, beset, pervaded, teeming • *The prison is infested with rats.*

infidel = **unbeliever**, sceptic, atheist, heretic, agnostic, heathen, nonconformist, freethinker, nonbeliever • *a holy war to drive the infidels out*

infidelity = **unfaithfulness**, cheating *(informal)*, adultery, betrayal, duplicity, disloyalty, bad faith, perfidy, falseness, faithlessness, false-heartedness • *I divorced him for infidelity.*

infiltrate = **penetrate**, pervade, permeate, creep in, percolate, filter through to, make inroads into, sneak into *(informal)*, insinuate yourself, work *or* worm your way into • *Activists had infiltrated the student movement.*

infinite 1 = **vast**, enormous, immense, wide, countless, innumerable, untold, stupendous, incalculable, immeasurable, inestimable, numberless, uncounted, measureless, uncalculable • *an infinite variety of landscapes*
2 = **enormous**, total, supreme, absolute, all-embracing, unbounded • *With infinite care, he shifted positions.*
3 = **limitless**, endless, unlimited, eternal, perpetual, never-ending, interminable, boundless, everlasting, bottomless, unending, inexhaustible, immeasurable, without end, unbounded, numberless, measureless, illimitable, without number • *There is an infinite number of atoms*
OPPOSITES: limited, finite, measurable

QUOTATIONS
What you see, yet cannot see over, is as good as infinite
[Thomas Carlyle *Sartor Resartus*]

infinitesimal = **microscopic**, minute, tiny, wee, atomic, insignificant, negligible, minuscule, teeny, teeny-weeny, unnoticeable, teensy-weensy, inappreciable • *mineral substances present in infinitesimal amounts in the soil*
OPPOSITES: great, large, huge

infinity = **eternity**, vastness, immensity, perpetuity, endlessness, infinitude, boundlessness • *the darkness of a starless night stretching into infinity*
▸ RELATED PHOBIA: apeirophobia

QUOTATIONS
The eternal silence of these infinite spaces frightens me
[Pascal *Pensées*]
Suffering is permanent, obscure and dark,
And shares the nature of infinity
[William Wordsworth *The Borderers*]

infirm 1 = **frail**, weak, feeble, failing, ailing, debilitated, decrepit, enfeebled, doddery, doddering • *her ageing, infirm husband*
OPPOSITES: strong, sound, robust
2 = **irresolute**, weak, faltering, unstable, shaky, insecure, wavering, wobbly, indecisive, unsound, vacillating • *She has little patience with the 'infirm of purpose'.*

infirmity 1 = **frailty**, ill health, debility, deficiency, imperfection, feebleness, decrepitude, sickliness • *In spite of his age and infirmity, he is still producing plays.*
OPPOSITES: health, strength, vigour
2 = **ailment**, failing, weakness, fault, disorder, defect, sickness, malady • *Older people often try to ignore their infirmities.*

inflame 1 = **enrage**, stimulate, provoke, fire, heat, excite, anger, arouse, rouse, infuriate, ignite, incense, madden, agitate, kindle, rile, foment, intoxicate, make your blood

boil, impassion • *They hold the rebels responsible for inflaming the villagers.*
OPPOSITES: cool, quiet, calm
2 = **aggravate**, increase, intensify, worsen, exacerbate, fan • *The shooting has only inflamed passions further.*

inflamed = **swollen**, sore, red, hot, angry, infected, fevered, festering, chafing, septic • *Her eyes were sore and inflamed.*

inflammable = **flammable**, explosive, volatile, incendiary, combustible • *A highly inflammable liquid escaped into the equipment.*

inflammation = **swelling**, soreness, burning, heat, sore, rash, tenderness, redness, painfulness • *The drug can cause inflammation of the liver.*

inflammatory = **provocative**, incendiary, explosive, fiery, inflaming, insurgent, anarchic, rabid, riotous, intemperate, seditious, rabble-rousing, demagogic, like a red rag to a bull, instigative • *His remarks were irresponsible and inflammatory.*

inflate 1 = **blow up**, pump up, swell, balloon, dilate, distend, aerate, bloat, puff up *or* out • *He jumped into the sea and inflated the liferaft.*
OPPOSITES: deflate, contract, collapse
2 = **increase**, boost, expand, enlarge, escalate, amplify • *Promotion can inflate a film's final cost.*
OPPOSITES: shrink, diminish, lessen
3 = **exaggerate**, embroider, embellish, emphasize, enlarge, magnify, overdo, amplify, exalt, overstate, overestimate, overemphasize, blow out of all proportion, aggrandize, hyperbolize • *Even his war record was fraudulently inflated.*

inflated 1 = **raised**, high, increased, enormous, unfair, excessive, exaggerated, extravagant, unreasonable, sky-high, inordinate, immoderate • *They had to buy everything at inflated prices at the ranch store.*
2 = **blown-up**, pumped-up, filled-up, aerated • *Ninety per cent of vehicles had wrongly inflated tyres.*
3 = **exaggerated**, excessive, swollen, amplified, hyped, exalted, overblown • *They had an inflated idea of how good they were.*
4 = **elaborate**, involved, fancy, detailed, complex, complicated, decorated, extravagant, ornamented, high-flown, ornate, fussy, showy, ostentatious, bombastic, hyperbolic, grandiloquent • *Some of the most inflated prose is held up for ridicule.*

inflation = **increase**, expansion, extension, swelling, escalation, enlargement, intensification • *Such pressure leads to the inflation of course-work marks.*

inflect 1 = **modulate**, intonate, vary, adjust, attune • *a different way of inflecting the line*
2 = **conjugate**, decline • *I shall inflect this word as a Latin noun.*

inflection 1 = **intonation**, stress, emphasis, beat, measure, rhythm, cadence, modulation, accentuation • *His voice was devoid of inflection.*
2 = **conjugation**, declension • *At around 2 years, the child adds many grammatical inflections.*

inflexibility = **obstinacy**, persistence, intransigence, obduracy, fixity, steeliness • *She was irritated by the inflexibility of her colleagues.*

inflexible 1 = **fixed**, set, established, rooted, rigid, immovable, unadaptable • *He was a man of unchanging habits and an inflexible routine.*
2 = **obstinate**, strict, relentless, firm, fixed, iron, adamant, rigorous, stubborn, stringent, uncompromising, resolute, steely, intractable, inexorable, implacable, steadfast, hard and fast, unyielding, immutable, immovable, unbending, obdurate, stiff-necked, dyed-in-the-wool, unchangeable, brassbound, set in your ways • *They viewed him as stubborn, inflexible and dogmatic.*
OPPOSITES: yielding, flexible, movable
3 = **stiff**, hard, rigid, hardened, taut, inelastic, nonflexible • *The boot is too inflexible to be comfortable.*
OPPOSITES: yielding, flexible, pliable

inflict = **impose**, exact, administer, visit, apply, deliver, levy, wreak, mete *or* deal out • *The dog attacked her, inflicting serious injuries.*

infliction = **imposition**, administration, perpetration, exaction • *without the unnecessary or cruel infliction of pain*

influence AS A NOUN 1 = **control**, power, authority, direction, command, domination, supremacy, mastery, ascendancy, mana *(N.Z.)* • *As he grew older, she had less influence and couldn't control him.*
2 = **power**, force, authority, pull *(informal)*, weight, strength, connections, importance, prestige, clout *(informal)*, leverage, good offices • *They should continue to use their influence for the release of all hostages.*
3 = **effect**, impact, impression, sway • *Many other medications have an influence on cholesterol levels.*
4 = **spell**, hold, power, rule, weight, magic, sway, allure, magnetism, enchantment • *I fell under the influence of a history master.*
▸ AS A VERB 1 = **affect**, have an effect on, have an impact on, control, concern, direct, guide, impact on, modify, bear upon, impinge upon, act *or* work upon • *What you eat may influence your risk of getting cancer.*
2 = **persuade**, move, prompt, urge, counsel, induce, incline, dispose, arouse, sway, rouse, entice, coax, incite, instigate, predispose, impel, prevail upon • *The conference influenced us to launch the campaign.*
3 = **carry weight with**, cut any ice with *(informal)*, pull strings with *(informal)*, bring pressure to bear upon, make yourself felt with • *Her attempt to influence the Press rebounded.*
▸ IN PHRASES: **under the influence** = **drunk**, tight *(informal)*, smashed *(slang)*, canned *(slang)*, flying *(slang)*, bombed *(slang)*, stoned *(slang)*, wasted *(slang)*, loaded *(slang, chiefly U.S. & Canad.)*, hammered *(slang)*, steaming *(slang)*, wrecked *(slang)*, soaked *(informal)*, out of it *(slang)*, plastered *(slang)*, drunken, blitzed *(slang)*, pissed *(Brit., Austral. & N.Z. slang)*, lit up *(slang)*, merry *(Brit. informal)*, stewed *(slang)*, pickled *(informal)*, bladdered *(slang)*, sloshed *(slang)*, intoxicated, tipsy, maudlin, well-oiled *(slang)*, legless *(informal)*, paralytic *(informal)*, tired and emotional *(euphemistic)*, steamboats *(Scot. slang)*, tiddly *(slang, chiefly Brit.)*, off your face *(slang)*, zonked *(slang)*, blotto *(slang)*, fuddled, inebriated, out to it *(Austral. & N.Z. slang)*, tanked up *(slang)*, bacchic, rat-arsed *(taboo slang)*, Brahms and Liszt *(slang)*, blatted *(Brit. slang)*, boozed-up *(informal)*, dronkverdriet *(S. African)*, elephants *(Austral. slang)*, broken *(S. African informal)*, boozed-up *(slang)*, kaylied *(Brit. slang)*, langered *(Irish slang)*, lashed *(Brit. slang)*, mashed *(Brit. slang)*, mullered *(slang)*, ossified *(Irish slang)*, sat *(S. African)*, stukkend *(S. African slang)*, trashed *(slang)*, half seas over *(informal)*, bevvied *(dialect)*, babalas *(S. African)*, fu' *(Scot.)*, pie-eyed *(slang)* • *He was charged with driving under the influence.*

influential 1 = **important**, powerful, moving, telling, leading, strong, guiding, inspiring, prestigious, meaningful, potent, persuasive, authoritative, momentous, weighty • *one of the most influential books ever written*
OPPOSITES: powerless, ineffective, unimportant
2 = **instrumental**, important, significant, controlling, guiding, effective, crucial, persuasive, forcible, efficacious • *He had been influential in shaping economic policy.*

influx = **arrival**, flow, rush, invasion, convergence, inflow, incursion, inundation, inrush • *problems caused by the influx of refugees*

infold *see* **enfold**

inform AS A VERB 1 = **tell**, advise, let someone know, notify, brief, instruct, enlighten, acquaint, leak to, communicate to, fill someone in, keep someone posted, apprise, clue someone in *(informal)*, put someone in the picture *(informal)*, tip someone off, send word to, give someone to understand, make someone conversant (with) • *They would inform him of any progress they had made.*

2 = **infuse**, characterize, permeate, animate, saturate, typify, imbue, suffuse • *All great songs are informed by a certain sadness and tension.*
▸ IN PHRASES: **inform on someone** = **betray**, report, denounce, shop *(slang, chiefly Brit.)*, peach *(slang)*, give someone away, incriminate, tell on *(informal)*, blow the whistle on *(informal)*, grass on *(Brit. slang)*, double-cross *(informal)*, rat on *(informal)*, spill the beans on *(informal)*, stab someone in the back, nark *(Brit., Austral. & N.Z. slang)*, blab about, squeal on *(slang)*, snitch on *(slang)*, put the finger on *(informal)*, sell someone down the river *(informal)*, blow the gaff on *(Brit. slang)*, tell all on, inculpate, dob someone in *(Austral. & N.Z. slang)* • *Somebody must have informed on us.*
PROVERBS
Never tell tales out of school

informal 1 = **natural**, relaxed, casual, familiar, unofficial, laid-back, easy-going, colloquial, unconstrained, unceremonious • *She is refreshingly informal.*
2 = **relaxed**, easy, comfortable, simple, natural, casual, cosy, laid-back *(informal)*, mellow, leisurely, easy-going • *The house has an informal atmosphere.*
OPPOSITES: formal, conventional, stiff
3 = **casual**, comfortable, leisure, everyday, simple • *Most of the time she needs informal clothes.*
4 = **unofficial**, irregular, unconstrained, unceremonious • *an informal meeting of EU ministers*
OPPOSITES: official, constrained, ceremonious

informality = **familiarity**, naturalness, casualness, ease, relaxation, simplicity, lack of ceremony • *He was overwhelmed by their cheerfulness and friendly informality.*

informally 1 = **naturally**, casually, normally, simply, genuinely, spontaneously, unpretentiously, unaffectedly • *She was always there, chatting informally to the children.*
2 = **casually**, comfortably, simply • *They dressed informally in shorts or faded jeans.*
3 = **unofficially**, privately, casually • *He began informally to handle my tax affairs for me.*

information = **facts**, details, material, news, latest *(informal)*, report, word, message, notice, advice, knowledge, data, intelligence, instruction, counsel, the score *(informal)*, gen *(Brit. informal)*, dope *(informal)*, info *(informal)*, inside story, blurb, lowdown *(informal)*, tidings, drum *(Austral. informal)*, heads up *(U.S. & Canad.)* • *They refused to give us any information about her.*

informative = **instructive**, revealing, educational, forthcoming, illuminating, enlightening, chatty, communicative, edifying, gossipy, newsy • *This book is a lively, informative read.*

informed = **knowledgeable**, up to date, enlightened, learned, primed, posted, expert, briefed, familiar, versed, acquainted, in the picture, plugged-in *(slang)*, up, abreast, in the know *(informal)*, erudite, well-read, conversant, au fait *(French)*, in the loop, genned up *(Brit. informal)*, au courant *(French)*, keeping your finger on the pulse • *the importance of keeping the public properly informed*

informer = **betrayer**, grass *(Brit. slang)*, sneak, squealer *(slang)*, Judas, accuser, stool pigeon, nark *(Brit., Austral. & N.Z. slang)*, fizgig *(Austral. slang)* • *two men suspected of being police informers*

infraction = **violation**, breach, infringement, breaking, trespass, transgression, contravention, nonfulfilment • *Another infraction would mean a stint in a probation centre.*

infrequent = **occasional**, rare, uncommon, unusual, sporadic, few and far between, once in a blue moon • *He was paying one of his infrequent visits to London.*
OPPOSITES: often, regular, frequent

infringe AS A VERB = **break**, violate, contravene, disobey, transgress • *The film exploited his image and infringed his copyright.*
▸ IN PHRASES: **infringe on** *or* **upon** = **intrude on**, compromise, undermine, limit, weaken, diminish, disrupt, curb, encroach on, trespass on • *It's starting to infringe on our personal liberties.*

infringement = **contravention**, breach, violation, trespass, transgression, infraction, noncompliance, nonobservance • *infringement of privacy*

infuriate = **enrage**, anger, provoke, irritate, incense, gall, madden, exasperate, rile, nark *(Brit., Austral. & N.Z. slang)*, be like a red rag to a bull, make your blood boil, get your goat *(slang)*, make your hackles rise, raise your hackles, get your back up, make you see red *(informal)*, put your back up • *It infuriated her to have to deal with this man.*
OPPOSITES: calm, soothe, appease

infuriated = **angry**, mad *(informal)*, furious, heated, raging, provoked, outraged, annoyed, passionate, irritated, hacked (off) *(U.S. slang)*, choked, pissed *(Brit., Austral. & N.Z. slang)*, incensed, enraged, exasperated, resentful, nettled, indignant, pissed off *(taboo)*, irate, riled, up in arms, incandescent, antagonized, piqued, hot under the collar *(informal)*, on the warpath, foaming at the mouth, choleric, splenetic, wrathful, in high dudgeon, ireful, tooshie *(Austral. slang)*, off the air *(Austral. slang)* • *He realized how infuriated this would make me.*

infuriating = **annoying**, irritating, aggravating *(informal)*, provoking, galling, maddening, exasperating, irksome, vexatious, pestilential • *He accelerated with infuriating slowness.*

infuse 1 = **fill**, charge, inspire, pervade, inundate, imbue, suffuse • *A strange spirit infused the place.*
2 = **instil**, add, introduce, breathe, inject, implant, impart, inculcate • *The only solution was to infuse new blood into all our Courts.*
3 = **brew**, soak, steep, saturate, immerse, macerate • *teas made by infusing the roots of herbs*

infusion 1 = **injection**, introduction, dose, insertion • *He brought a tremendous infusion of hope to the people.*
2 = **brew**, drink, preparation, mixture, blend, beverage, concoction, fermentation, distillation • *a pleasing herbal infusion*

ingenious = **creative**, original, brilliant, clever, masterly, bright, subtle, fertile, shrewd, inventive, skilful, crafty, resourceful, adroit, dexterous • *a truly ingenious invention*
OPPOSITES: clumsy, unimaginative, unoriginal

ingenuity = **originality**, genius, inventiveness, skill, gift, faculty, flair, knack, sharpness, cleverness, resourcefulness, shrewdness, adroitness, ingeniousness • *This task is difficult and may require some ingenuity.*
OPPOSITES: incompetence, ineptitude, dullness

ingenuous = **naive**, open, trusting, simple, frank, plain, innocent, sincere, honest, candid, childlike, unsophisticated, unreserved, artless, guileless, unstudied, trustful • *He seemed too ingenuous for a reporter.*
OPPOSITES: reserved, sophisticated, artful

inglorious = **disgraceful**, dishonourable, humiliating, failed, infamous, unsuccessful, shameful, ignominious, disreputable, ignoble, discreditable, unheroic • *He wouldn't have accepted such an inglorious outcome.*

ingrained *or* **engrained** = **fixed**, rooted, deep-seated, fundamental, constitutional, inherent, hereditary, in the blood, intrinsic, deep-rooted, indelible, inveterate, inborn, inbred, inbuilt, ineradicable, brassbound • *Morals tend to be deeply ingrained.*

ingratiate IN PHRASES: **ingratiate yourself with someone** = **get on the right side of**, court, win over, flatter, pander to, crawl to, play up to, get in with, suck up to *(informal)*, curry favour with, grovel to, keep someone sweet, kiss someone's ass *(U.S. & Canad. taboo)*, lick someone's boots, fawn to, toady to, lick someone's arse *(taboo)*, seek someone's favour, brown-nose to *(taboo)*, rub someone up the right way *(informal)*, be a yes man to, insinuate yourself with • *Many politicians are trying to ingratiate themselves with her.*

ingratiating = **sycophantic**, servile, obsequious, crawling, humble, flattering, fawning, unctuous, toadying, bootlicking *(informal)*, timeserving • *His fellow students had found him too ingratiating.*

ingratitude = **ungratefulness**, thanklessness, lack of recognition, unappreciativeness • *The Government could expect only ingratitude from the electorate.*
OPPOSITES: thanks, appreciation, gratitude

QUOTATIONS

Blow, blow, thou winter wind,
Thou art not so unkind
As man's ingratitude:
Because thou art not seen,
Although thy breath be rude
[William Shakespeare *As You Like It*]

Time hath, my lord, a wallet at his back,
Wherein he puts alms for oblivion,
A great-sized monster of ingratitudes:
Those scraps are good deeds past: which are devoured
As fast as they are made, forgot as soon
As done
[William Shakespeare *Troilus and Cressida*]

ingredient = **component**, part, element, feature, piece, unit, item, aspect, attribute, constituent • *The meeting had all the ingredients of high drama.*

ingress 1 = **entry**, admission, intrusion, leakage, seepage, inundation, inrush • *The wood may have been weakened by the ingress of water.*
2 = **entrance**, access, entry, door, admission, entrée, admittance, right of entry • *A lorry was blocking the ingress.*

ingulf *see* **engulf**

inhabit = **live in**, people, occupy, populate, reside in, tenant, lodge in, dwell in, colonize, take up residence in, abide in, make your home in • *the people who inhabit these islands*

inhabitant = **occupant**, resident, citizen, local, native, tenant, inmate, dweller, occupier, denizen, indigene, indweller • *the inhabitants of Glasgow*
▷ *See panel* **Inhabitants**

inhabited = **populated**, peopled, occupied, held, developed, settled, tenanted, colonized • *a land primarily inhabited by nomads*

inhalation = **breathing**, breath, inspiration, inhaling • *a complete cycle of inhalation and exhalation*

inhale = **breathe in**, gasp, draw in, suck in, respire • *He was treated for the effects of inhaling smoke.*
OPPOSITES: expire, exhale, breathe out

inherent = **intrinsic**, natural, basic, central, essential, native, fundamental, underlying, hereditary, instinctive, innate, ingrained, elemental, congenital, inborn, inbred, inbuilt, immanent, hard-wired, connate • *the dangers inherent in an outbreak of war*
OPPOSITES: imposed, alien, extraneous

inherit 1 = **be left**, come into, be willed, accede to, succeed to, be bequeathed, fall heir to • *He has no son to inherit his land.*
2 = **take over**, take on, acquire, take up, come into, take responsibility for • *The government inherited an impossibly difficult situation.*

inheritance = **legacy**, estate, heritage, provision, endowment, bequest, birthright, patrimony • *She feared losing her inheritance to her stepmother.*

inheritor = **heir**, successor, recipient, beneficiary, legatee • *Two thirds of inheritors promptly sold the houses they were left.*

inhibit 1 = **hinder**, stop, prevent, check, bar, arrest, frustrate, curb, restrain, constrain, obstruct, impede, bridle, stem the flow of, throw a spanner in the works of, hold back *or* in • *Sugary drinks inhibit digestion.*
OPPOSITES: allow, further, encourage
2 = **prevent**, stop, bar, frustrate, forbid, prohibit, debar • *The poor will be inhibited from getting the medical care they need.*
OPPOSITES: support, let, allow

inhibited = **shy**, reserved, guarded, withdrawn, frustrated, subdued, repressed, constrained, self-conscious, reticent, uptight *(informal)* • *Men are more inhibited about touching each other than women are.*
OPPOSITES: free, natural, uninhibited

inhibition 1 = **shyness**, reserve, restraint, hang-up *(informal)*, modesty, nervousness, reticence, self-consciousness, timidity, diffidence, bashfulness, mental blockage, timidness • *They behave with a total lack of inhibition.*
2 = **obstacle**, check, bar, block, barrier, restriction, hazard, restraint, hitch, drawback, snag, deterrent, obstruction, stumbling block, impediment, hindrance, encumbrance, interdict • *They cited security fears as a major inhibition to internet shopping.*

inhospitable 1 = **bleak**, empty, bare, hostile, lonely, forbidding, barren, sterile, desolate, unfavourable, uninhabitable, godforsaken • *the earth's most inhospitable regions*
2 = **unfriendly**, unwelcoming, uncongenial, cool, unkind, xenophobic, ungenerous, unsociable, unreceptive • *He believed the province to be inhabited by a mean, inhospitable people.*
OPPOSITES: welcoming, friendly, hospitable

inhuman = **cruel**, savage, brutal, vicious, ruthless, barbaric, heartless, merciless, diabolical, cold-blooded, remorseless, barbarous, fiendish, pitiless, unfeeling, bestial • *The barbaric slaughter of whales is unnecessary and inhuman.*
OPPOSITES: humane, compassionate, merciful

inhumane = **cruel**, savage, brutal, severe, harsh, grim, unkind, heartless, atrocious, unsympathetic, hellish, depraved, barbarous, pitiless, unfeeling, uncompassionate • *He was kept in inhumane conditions.*

inhumanity = **cruelty**, atrocity, brutality, ruthlessness, barbarism, viciousness, heartlessness, unkindness, brutishness, cold-bloodedness, pitilessness, cold-heartedness, hardheartedness • *the inhumanity of war*

QUOTATIONS

Man's inhumanity to man
Makes countless thousands mourn
[Robert Burns *Man was Made to Mourn*]

The worst sin towards our fellow creatures is not to hate them, but to be indifferent to them: that's the essence of inhumanity
[George Bernard Shaw *The Devil's Disciple*]

inimical = **hostile**, opposed, contrary, destructive, harmful, adverse, hurtful, unfriendly, unfavourable, antagonistic, injurious, unwelcoming, ill-disposed • *a false morality that is inimical to human happiness*
OPPOSITES: good, kindly, helpful

inimitable = **unique**, unparalleled, unrivalled, incomparable, supreme, consummate, unmatched, peerless, unequalled, matchless, unsurpassable, nonpareil, unexampled • *He makes his point in his own inimitable way.*

iniquitous = **wicked**, base, criminal, evil, vicious, infamous, immoral, unjust, atrocious, sinful, heinous, reprehensible, abominable, nefarious, accursed, unrighteous • *an iniquitous fine*

iniquity = **wickedness**, wrong, crime, evil, sin, offence, injustice, wrongdoing, misdeed, infamy, abomination, sinfulness, baseness, unrighteousness, heinousness, evildoing • *He rails against the iniquities of capitalism.*
OPPOSITES: justice, virtue, goodness

INHABITANTS

Place	Inhabitant
Aberdeen	Aberdonian
Afghanistan	Afghan
Alabama	Alabaman
Alaska	Alaskan
Albania	Albanian
Alberta	Albertan
Algeria	Algerian
Alsace	Alsatian
American continent	American
American Samoa	American Samoan
Amsterdam	Amsterdammer
Anatolia	Anatolian
Andorra	Andorran
Angola	Angolan
Anjou	Angevin
Antigua	Antiguan
Argentina	Argentine *or* Argentinian
Arizona	Arizonan
Arkansas	Arkansan
Armenia	Armenian
Asia	Asian
Assam	Assamese
Assyria	Assyrian
Australia	Australian *or (informal)* Aussie
Austria	Austrian
Azerbaijan	Azerbaijani
Babylon	Babylonian
Bahamas	Bahamian
Bahrain	Bahraini
Bangladesh	Bangladeshi
Bali	Balinese
Barbados	Barbadian, Bajan *(informal)*, *or* Bim *(informal)*
Barbuda	Barbudan
Bavaria	Bavarian
Belarus	Belarussian
Belau	Belauan
Belgium	Belgian
Benin	Beninese
Berlin	Berliner
Bhutan	Bhutanese
Birmingham	Brummie
Bohemia	Bohemian
Bolivia	Bolivian
Bordeaux	Bordelais
the Borders	Borderer
Bosnia	Bosnian
Boston	Bostonian *or (U.S. slang)* Bean-eater
Botswana	Botswanan
Brazil	Brazilian
Bristol	Bristolian
Brittany	Breton
British Columbia	British Columbian
Bulgaria	Bulgarian
Burgundy	Burgundian
Burkina-Faso	Burkinabe
Burma	Burmese
Burundi	Burundian
Byzantium	Byzantine
California	Californian
Cambridge	Cantabrigian
Cambodia	Cambodian
Cameroon	Cameroonian
Canada	Canadian *or (informal)* Canuck
Canada, Maritime Provinces	Downeaster
Cape Verde	Cape Verdean
Castile	Castilian
Catalonia	Catalan
the Caucasus	Caucasian
Cayman Islands	Cayman Islander
Chad	Chadian
Chicago	Chicagoan
Chile	Chilean
China	Chinese
Circassia	Circassian
Colombia	Colombian
Colorado	Coloradan
Connecticut	Nutmegger
Cork	Corkonian
Comoros Islands	Comorian
Congo Republic	Congolese
Cornwall	Cornishman, Cornishwoman
Corsica	Corsican
Costa Rica	Costa Rican
Côte d'Ivoire	Ivorian *or* Ivorean
Croatia	Croat *or* Croatian
Cuba	Cuban
Cumbria	Cumbrian
Cyprus	Cypriot
Czech Republic	Czech
Czechoslovakia	Czechoslovak *or* Czechoslovakian
Delaware	Delawarean
Denmark	Dane
Delphi	Pythian
Devon	Devonian
Djibouti	Djiboutian
Dominica	Dominican
Dominican Republic	Dominican
Dublin	Dubliner
Dundee	Dundonian
East Timor	East Timorese
Ecuador	Ecuadorean
Edinburgh	Edinburgher
Egypt	Egyptian
El Salvador	Salvadoran
England	Englishman, Englishwoman
Ephesus	Ephesian
Equatorial Guinea	Equatorian
Eritrea	Eritrean
Estonia	Estonian
Ethiopia	Ethiopian
Europe	European
Euzkadi	Basque
Faeroe Islands	Faeroese
Falkland Islands	Falkland Islander
Fife	Fifer
Fiji	Fijian
Finland	Finn
Flanders	Fleming
Florence	Florentine
Florida	Floridian
France	Frenchman, Frenchwoman
French Guiana	Guianese
Friesland	Frisian
Friuli	Friulian
Gabon	Gabonese
Galicia	Galician
Galilee	Galilean
Galloway	Gallovidian
Galway	Galwegian
Gambia	Gambian
Gascony	Gascon
Genoa	Genoese
Georgia (country)	Georgian
Georgia (U.S. state)	Georgian
Germany	German
Ghana	Ghanaian
Glasgow	Glaswegian
Greece	Greek
Greenland	Greenlander
Grenada	Grenadian
Guam	Guamanian
Guatemala	Guatemalan
Guinea	Guinean
Guyana	Guyanese
Haiti	Haitian
Hawaii	Hawaiian
Havana	Habanero
Hesse	Hessian
Hungary	Hungarian *or* Magyar
Honduras	Honduran
Hyderabad state	Mulki
Ibiza	Ibizan
Iceland	Icelander
Idaho	Idahoan
Illinois	Illinoian *or* Illinoisian
India	Indian
Indiana	Indianan, Indianian, *or (informal)* Hoosier
Indonesia	Indonesian
Iowa	Iowan
Iran	Iranian
Iraq	Iraqi
Ireland	Irishman, Irishwoman
Israel	Israeli
Italy	Italian
Jamaica	Jamaican
Japan	Japanese
Java	Javanese
Jordan	Jordanian
Kansas	Kansan
Karelia	Karelian
Kazakhstan	Kazakh
Kent (East)	Man, Woman of Kent

INHABITANTS (CONTINUED)

Place	Inhabitant
Kent (West)	Kentish Man, Woman
Kentucky	Kentuckian
Kenya	Kenyan
Kirghizia	Kirghiz
Korea	Korean
Kuwait	Kuwaiti
Lancashire	Lancastrian
Lancaster	Lancastrian
Laos	Laotian
Latvia	Latvian *or* Lett
Lebanon	Lebanese
Liberia	Liberian
Libya	Libyan
Liechtenstein	Liechtensteiner
Lincolnshire	yellow belly *(dialect)*
Lithuania	Lithuanian
Liverpool	Liverpudlian *or* *(informal)* Scouse *or* Scouser
Lombardy	Lombard
London	Londoner *or* Cockney
Los Angeles	Angeleno
Louisiana	Louisianan
Luxembourg	Luxembourger
Lyon	Lyonnais
Macao	Macaonese
Macedonia	Macedonian
Madagascar	Madagascan *or* Malagasy
Madrid	Madrileño, Madrileña
Maine	Mainer *or* Downeaster
Majorca	Majorcan
Malawi	Malawian
Malaya	Malayan
Malaysia	Malaysian
Maldive Islands	Maldivian
Malta	Maltese
Man, Isle of	Manxman, Manxwoman
Manchester	Mancunian
Manitoba	Manitoban
Marquesas Islands	Marquesan
Mars	Martian
Marseilles	Marsellais
Marshall Islands	Marshall Islander
Martinique	Martiniquean
Maryland	Marylander
Massachusetts	Bay Stater
Mauritania	Mauritanian
Mauritius	Mauritian
Melanesia	Melanesian
Melbourne	Melburnian
Mexico	Mexican
Michigan	Michigander, Michiganite, *or* Michiganian
Micronesia	Micronesian
Milan	Milanese
Minnesota	Minnesotan

Place	Inhabitant
Mississippi	Mississippian
Missouri	Missourian
Moldavia	Moldavian
Monaco	Monegasque
Mongolia	Mongolian
Montana	Montanan
Montenegro	Montenegrin
Montserrat	Montserratian
Moravia	Moravian
Morocco	Moroccan
Moscow	Muscovite
Mozambique	Mozambican
Namibia	Namibian
Nauru	Nauruan
Naples	Neapolitan
Nebraska	Nebraskan
the Netherlands	Dutchman, Dutchwoman
New Brunswick	New Brunswicker
Newcastle upon Tyne	Geordie
New England	New Englander *or (informal)* Yankee *or* Downeaster
Newfoundland	Newfoundlander *or (informal)* Newfie
Newfoundland fishing village	Outporter
New Hampshire	New Hampshirite
New Jersey	New Jerseyan *or* New Jerseyite
New Mexico	New Mexican
New South Wales	New South Welshman, New South Welshwoman
New York	New Yorker *or* Knickerbocker
New Zealand	New Zealander *or (informal)* Kiwi *or* Enzedder
Nicaragua	Nicaraguan
Niger	Nigerien
Nigeria	Nigerian
Normandy	Norman
North Carolina	North Carolinian *or* Tarheel
North Dakota	North Dakotan
Northern Ireland	Northern Irishman, Northern Irishwoman
Northern Territory	Territorian
Northern Territory, northern part of	Top Ender
North Korea	North Korean
Northumbria	Northumbrian
Norway	Norwegian
Nova Scotia	Nova Scotian *or (informal)* Bluenose
Ohio	Ohioan

Place	Inhabitant
Okinawa	Okinawan
Oklahoma	Oklahoman *or (slang)* Okie
Oman	Omani
Ontario	Ontarian
Oregon	Oregonian
Orkney	Orcadian
Oxford	Oxonian
Pakistan	Pakistani
Palestine	Palestinian
Panama	Panamanian
Papua New Guinea	Papuan
Paraguay	Paraguayan
Paris	Parisian *or* Parisienne
Pennsylvania	Pennsylvanian
Persia	Persian
Perth	Perthite
Peru	Peruvian
the Philippines	Filipino
Poland	Pole
Pomerania	Pomeranian
Portugal	Portuguese
Prince Edward Island	Prince Edward Islander
Provence	Provençal
Prussia	Prussian
Puerto Rico	Puerto Rican
Qatar	Qatari
Quebec	Quebecer, Quebecker, *or* Quebecois
Queensland	Queenslander
Rhode Island	Rhode Islander
Rhodes	Rhodian
Rhodesia	Rhodesian
Rio de Janeiro	Cariocan
Romania	Romanian
Rome	Roman
Russian Federation	Russian
Ruthenia	Ruthenian
Rwanda	Rwandan
Samaria	Samaritan
San Marino	San Marinese *or* Sammarinese
Sardinia	Sardinian
Saskatchewan	Saskatchewanian
Saxony	Saxon
Saudi Arabia	Saudi *or* Saudi Arabian
Savoy	Savoyard
Scandinavia	Scandinavian
Scotland	Scot, Scotsman, Scotswoman, *or* Caledonian
Scottish Highlands	Highlander *or (old-fashioned)* Hielanman
Senegal	Senegalese
Serbia	Serb *or* Serbian
Seychelles	Seychellois
Shetland	Shetlander
Sierra Leone	Sierra Leonean
Sind	Sindhi

INHABITANTS (CONTINUED)

Place	Inhabitant	Place	Inhabitant	Place	Inhabitant
Singapore	Singaporean	Texas	Texan	Venice	Venetian
Slovakia	Slovak	Thailand	Thai	Vermont	Vermonter
Slovenia	Slovene *or*	Thessalonika	Thessalonian	Victoria	Victorian
	Slovenian	Tibet	Tibetan	Vienna	Viennese
Solomon Islands	Solomon Islander	Togo	Togolese	Vietnam	Vietnamese
South Africa	South African	Tonga	Tongan	Virginia	Virginian
South Australia	South Australian	Trinidad	Trinidadian	Wales	Welshman,
	or (informal)	Tobago	Tobagan		Welshwoman
	Croweater	Troy	Trojan	Washington	Washingtonian
South Carolina	South Carolinian	Tuscany	Tuscan	Wearside	Mackem
South Dakota	South Dakota	Tunisia	Tunisian	Wessex	West Saxon
South Korea	South Korean	Turkey	Turk	Western	Western
Spain	Spaniard	Turkmenistan	Turkmen	Australia	Australian,
Sri Lanka	Sri Lankan	Tuvalu	Tuvaluan		Westralian,
Sudan	Sudanese	Tyneside	Geordie		*or (informal)*
Suriname	Surinamese	Tyre	Tyrian		Sandgroper
Swaziland	Swazi	Uganda	Ugandan	Western Sahara	Sahwari
Switzerland	Swiss	Ukraine	Ukrainian	West Virginia	West Virginian
Sweden	Swede	Ulster	Ulsterman,	Winnipeg	Winnipegger
Sydney	Sydneysider		Ulsterwoman	Wisconsin	Wisconsinite
Sydney, Western	Westie *(informal)*	Umbria	Umbrian	Wyoming	Wyomingite
suburbs of		United Kingdom	Briton, Brit	Yemen	Yemeni
Syria	Syrian		*(informal)*,	Yorkshire	Yorkshireman,
Taiwan	Taiwanese		*or* Britisher		Yorkshirewoman
Tajikistan	Tajik	United States	American *or*	the Yukon	Yukoner
Tanzania	Tanzanian	of America	*(informal)* Yank	Zaire	Zairean
Tasmania	Tasmanian		*or* Yankee	Zambia	Zambian
	or (informal)	Uruguay	Uruguayan	Zanzibar	Zanzibari
	Tassie *or* Apple	Utah	Utahan *or* Utahn	Zimbabwe	Zimbabwean
	Islander	Uzbekistan	Uzbek		
Tennessee	Tennessean	Venezuela	Venezuelan		

initial AS AN ADJECTIVE = **opening**, first, early, earliest, beginning, primary, maiden, inaugural, commencing, introductory, embryonic, incipient, inchoate, inceptive • *The initial reaction has been excellent.*
OPPOSITES: last, ending, final
▸ AS A VERB = **sign**, endorse, subscribe, autograph, inscribe, set your hand to • *Would you mind initialling this voucher?*

initially = **at first**, first, firstly, originally, primarily, at the start, in the first place, to begin with, at the outset, in the beginning, in the early stages, at *or* in the beginning • *Initially, they were wary of him.*

initiate AS A VERB 1 = **begin**, start, open, launch, establish, institute, pioneer, kick off *(informal)*, bring about, embark on, originate, set about, get under way, instigate, kick-start, inaugurate, set in motion, trigger off, lay the foundations of, commence on, set going, break the ice on, set the ball rolling on • *They wanted to initiate a discussion on economics.*
2 = **introduce**, admit, enlist, enrol, launch, establish, invest, recruit, induct, instate • *She was initiated as a member of the secret society.*
▸ AS A NOUN = **novice**, member, pupil, convert, amateur, newcomer, beginner, trainee, apprentice, entrant, learner, neophyte, tyro, probationer, novitiate, newbie *(slang)*, proselyte • *He was an initiate of a Chinese spiritual discipline.*
▸ IN PHRASES: **initiate someone into something** = **instruct in**, train in, coach in, acquaint with, drill in, make aware of, teach about, tutor in, indoctrinate, prime in, familiarize with • *I was initiated into the darker side of the work.*

initiation 1 = **introduction**, installation, inauguration, inception, commencement • *They announced the initiation of a rural development programme.*
2 = **entrance**, debut, introduction, admission, inauguration, induction, inception, enrolment, investiture, baptism of fire, instatement • *This was my initiation into the peace movement.*

initiative 1 = **plan**, deal, proposal, act, action, measure, scheme, strategy, technique, suggestion, procedure, gambit • *There's talk of a new peace initiative.*
2 = **advantage**, start, lead, upper hand • *We have the initiative and we intend to keep it.*
3 = **enterprise**, drive, push *(informal)*, energy, spirit, resource, leadership, ambition, daring, enthusiasm, pep, vigour, zeal, originality, eagerness, dynamism, boldness, welly *(slang)*, inventiveness, get-up-and-go *(informal)*, resourcefulness, gumption *(informal)*, adventurousness • *He was disappointed by her lack of initiative.*

inject 1 = **vaccinate**, shoot *(informal)*, administer, jab *(informal)*, shoot up *(informal)*, mainline *(informal)*, inoculate • *His son was injected with strong drugs.*
2 = **introduce**, bring in, insert, instil, infuse, breathe, interject • *She kept trying to inject a little fun into their relationship.*
3 = **invest**, put in, advance, sink, devote, lay out • *He has injected £5.6 billion into the health service.*
4 *often with* **into** = **pump**, force, send, drive, supply, push, pour • *The afterburners inject fuel into the hot gases emitted.*

injection 1 = **vaccination**, shot *(informal)*, jab *(informal)*, dose, vaccine, booster, immunization, inoculation • *They gave me an injection to help me sleep.*
2 = **introduction**, investment, insertion, advancement, dose, infusion, interjection • *An injection of cash is needed to fund some of these projects.*
▸ RELATED PHOBIA: trypanophobia

injudicious = **unwise**, foolish, rash, hasty, ill-advised, indiscreet, unthinking, ill-judged, imprudent, inconsiderate,

ill-timed, incautious, impolitic, inexpedient • *Injudicious remarks by bankers were blamed for the devaluation.*
OPPOSITES: wise, cautious, judicious

injunction = **order**, ruling, command, instruction, dictate, mandate, precept, exhortation, admonition • *He took out a court injunction against the newspaper.*

injure 1 = **hurt**, wound, harm, break, damage, smash, crush, mar, disable, shatter, bruise, impair, mutilate, maim, mangle, mangulate *(Austral. slang)*, incapacitate • *A bomb exploded, seriously injuring five people.*
2 = **damage**, harm, ruin, wreck, weaken, spoil, impair, crool or cruel *(Austral. slang)* • *Too much stress can injure your health.*
3 = **undermine**, damage, mar, blight, tarnish, blacken, besmirch, vitiate • *an attempt to injure another trader's business*

injured 1 = **hurt**, damaged, wounded, broken, cut, crushed, disabled, challenged, weakened, bruised, scarred, crook *(Austral. & N.Z. slang)*, fractured, lamed, mutilated, maimed, mangled • *The injured man had a superficial stomach wound.*
2 = **wronged**, abused, harmed, insulted, offended, tainted, tarnished, blackened, maligned, vilified, mistreated, dishonoured, defamed, ill-treated, maltreated, ill-used • *As yet, there has been no complaint from the injured party.*
3 = **upset**, hurt, wounded, troubled, bothered, undermined, distressed, unhappy, stung, put out, grieved, hassled *(informal)*, disgruntled, displeased, reproachful, cut to the quick • *compensation for injured feelings*

injurious = **harmful**, bad, damaging, corrupting, destructive, adverse, unhealthy, detrimental, hurtful, pernicious, noxious, ruinous, deleterious, iniquitous, disadvantageous, baneful *(archaic)*, maleficent, unconducive • *Stress in itself is not necessarily injurious.*

injury 1 = **wound**, cut, damage, slash, trauma *(Pathology)*, sore, gash, lesion, abrasion, laceration • *Four police officers sustained serious injuries in the explosion.*
2 = **harm**, suffering, damage, ill, hurt, disability, misfortune, affliction, impairment, disfigurement • *The two other passengers escaped serious injury.*
3 = **wrong**, abuse, offence, insult, injustice, grievance, affront, detriment, disservice • *She was awarded £3,500 for injury to her feelings.*

injustice 1 = **unfairness**, discrimination, prejudice, bias, inequality, oppression, intolerance, bigotry, favouritism, inequity, chauvinism, iniquity, partisanship, partiality, narrow-mindedness, one-sidedness, unlawfulness, unjustness • *They will continue to fight injustice.*
OPPOSITES: right, justice, equity
2 = **wrong**, injury, crime, abuse, error, offence, sin, grievance, infringement, trespass, misdeed, transgression, infraction, bad or evil deed • *I don't want to do an injustice to what I've recorded.*

inkling = **suspicion**, idea, hint, suggestion, notion, indication, whisper, clue, conception, glimmering, intimation, faintest or foggiest idea • *We had an inkling that something might be happening.*

inky 1 = **black**, dark, jet, murky, raven, ebony, sable, dusky, pitch-black, stygian, coal-black • *the inky black of night*
▷ See panel **Shades from black to white**
2 = **ink-stained**, stained, ink-covered • *inky fingers and occasional blots*

inlaid = **inset**, set, lined, panelled, graced, adorned, ornamented, embellished, festooned • *a box inlaid with little triangles*

inland = **interior**, internal, upcountry • *a quiet inland town*

inlet 1 = **bay**, creek, cove, passage, entrance, fjord, bight, ingress, sea loch *(Scot.)*, arm of the sea, firth or frith *(Scot.)* • *a sheltered inlet*
2 = **vent**, opening, hole, passage, duct, flue • *a blocked water inlet*

inmate 1 = **patient**, case, sufferer, occupant, invalid, convalescent, sick person • *A fellow inmate said that she was in very good shape.*
2 = **prisoner**, convict, con *(slang)*, lag *(slang)*, captive, detainee, jailbird • *The most touching letter I received was written by a prison inmate.*

inmost = **deepest**, innermost, private, secret, central, personal, deep, basic, essential, buried, intimate • *He knew in his inmost heart that he was behaving badly.*

inn = **tavern**, bar, watering hole *(facetious)*, boozer *(Brit., Austral. & N.Z. informal)*, beer parlour *(Canad.)*, beverage room *(Canad.)*, local *(Brit. informal)*, roadhouse, hostelry *(facetious)*, alehouse *(archaic)*, taproom • *the Waterside inn*

innards 1 = **intestines**, insides *(informal)*, guts, entrails, viscera, vitals • *What happens to the innards of a carcass hung up for butchery?*
2 = **works**, mechanism, guts *(informal)* • *The innards of the PC are built into the desk.*

innate = **inborn**, natural, inherent, essential, native, constitutional, inherited, indigenous, instinctive, intuitive, intrinsic, ingrained, congenital, inbred, immanent, in your blood, hard-wired, connate • *As a race, they have an innate sense of fairness.*
OPPOSITES: learned, assumed, acquired

inner 1 = **inside**, internal, interior, inward • *She got up and went into an inner office.*
OPPOSITES: outside, external, outer
2 = **central**, middle, internal, interior • *I've always taught in inner London.*
3 = **intimate**, close, personal, near, private, friendly, confidential, cherished, bosom • *He was part of the Francoist inner circle.*
4 = **hidden**, deep, secret, underlying, obscure, repressed, esoteric, unrevealed • *He loves studying chess and discovering its inner secrets.*
OPPOSITES: revealed, obvious, visible
5 = **mental**, emotional, intellectual, psychological, spiritual • *All we need to know about his inner life is in his art.*

innermost 1 = **deep**, private, personal, true, hidden, intimate, profound, veiled, sincere, in-depth, heartfelt, deeply felt • *expressing your innermost feelings*
2 = **central**, middle, interior, inner, median • *the innermost part of the eye*

innkeeper = **publican**, hotelier, mine host, host or hostess, landlord or landlady • *He played the part of the innkeeper in the school nativity play.*

innocence 1 = **naiveté**, simplicity, inexperience, freshness, credulity, gullibility, ingenuousness, artlessness, unworldliness, guilelessness, credulousness, simpleness, trustfulness, unsophistication, naiveness • *the sweet innocence of youth*
OPPOSITES: cunning, guile, worldliness
2 = **blamelessness**, righteousness, clean hands, uprightness, sinlessness, irreproachability, guiltlessness • *He claims to have evidence which could prove his innocence.*
OPPOSITES: guilt, sinfulness, corruption
3 = **chastity**, virtue, purity, modesty, virginity, celibacy, continence, maidenhood, stainlessness • *She can still evoke the innocence of 14-year-old Juliet.*
4 = **ignorance**, oblivion, lack of knowledge, inexperience, unfamiliarity, greenness, unawareness, nescience *(literary)* • *'Maybe innocence is bliss,' he suggested.*

QUOTATIONS

He's armed without that's innocent within
[Alexander Pope *Epilogue to the Satires*]

Those who are incapable of committing great crimes do not readily suspect them in others
[La Rochefoucauld *Maxims*]

Whoever blushes is already guilty; true innocence is ashamed of nothing
[Jean Jacques Rousseau *Émile*]

It's innocence when it charms us, ignorance when it doesn't
[Mignon McLaughlin *The Neurotic's Notebook*]

innocent AS AN ADJECTIVE 1 = **not guilty**, in the clear, blameless, clear, clean, honest, faultless, squeaky-clean, uninvolved, irreproachable, guiltless, unoffending • *The police knew from day one that I was innocent.*
OPPOSITES: guilty, responsible, culpable
2 = **naive**, open, trusting, simple, natural, frank, confiding, candid, unaffected, childlike, gullible, unpretentious, unsophisticated, unworldly, credulous, artless, ingenuous, guileless, wet behind the ears (*informal*), unsuspicious • *They seemed so young and innocent.*
OPPOSITES: worldly, sophisticated, artful
3 = **harmless**, innocuous, inoffensive, well-meant, unobjectionable, unmalicious, well-intentioned • *It was probably an innocent question, but he got very flustered.*
OPPOSITES: offensive, harmful, malicious
4 = **pure**, stainless, immaculate, moral, virgin, decent, upright, impeccable, righteous, pristine, wholesome, spotless, demure, chaste, unblemished, virginal, unsullied, sinless, incorrupt • *that innocent virgin, Clarissa*
OPPOSITES: corrupt, immoral, impure
▸ AS A NOUN = **child**, novice, greenhorn (*informal*), babe in arms (*informal*), ingénue *or* (*masc.*) ingénu • *He was a hopeless innocent where women were concerned.*
▸ IN PHRASES: **innocent of** = **free from**, clear of, unaware of, ignorant of, untouched by, unfamiliar with, empty of, lacking, unacquainted with, nescient of • *She was completely natural and innocent of any airs and graces.*

innocuous = **harmless**, safe, innocent, inoffensive, innoxious • *Both mushrooms look innocuous, but are in fact deadly.*

innovation 1 = **change**, revolution, departure, introduction, variation, transformation, upheaval, alteration • *technological innovations of the industrial age*
2 = **newness**, novelty, originality, freshness, modernism, modernization, uniqueness • *We must promote originality and encourage innovation.*

innovative = **novel**, new, original, different, fresh, unusual, unfamiliar, uncommon, inventive, singular, ground-breaking, left-field (*informal*), transformational, variational • *products which are cheaper and more innovative*

innovator = **modernizer**, introducer, inventor, changer, transformer • *He is an innovator in this field.*

innuendo = **insinuation**, suggestion, hint, implication, whisper, overtone, intimation, imputation, aspersion • *The report was based on rumours and innuendo.*

innumerable = **countless**, many, numerous, infinite, myriad, untold, incalculable, numberless, unnumbered, multitudinous, beyond number • *He has invented innumerable excuses and told endless lies.*
OPPOSITES: limited, numbered, finite

inoculation = **injection**, shot (*informal*), jab (*informal*), vaccination, dose, vaccine, booster, immunization • *An inoculation against cholera is recommended.*

inoffensive = **harmless**, mild, innocuous, retiring, quiet, innocent, neutral, humble, unobtrusive, peaceable, unobjectionable, unoffending, innoxious, nonprovocative • *He's a mild, inoffensive man.*
OPPOSITES: offensive, irritating, harmful

inoperative = **out of action**, useless, out of order, broken, broken-down, ineffective, buggered (*slang, chiefly Brit.*), invalid, defective, ineffectual, unworkable, null and void, out of service, out of commission, unserviceable, hors de combat (*French*), on the fritz (*U.S. slang*), inefficacious, nonactive • *The mine has been inoperative since May last year.*

inopportune = **inconvenient**, unfortunate, inappropriate, unsuitable, untimely, unfavourable, mistimed, inauspicious, ill-timed, ill-chosen, unseasonable, unpropitious, malapropos • *The dismissals came at an inopportune time.*
OPPOSITES: timely, appropriate, opportune

inordinate = **excessive**, unreasonable, disproportionate, extravagant, undue, preposterous, unwarranted, exorbitant, unrestrained, intemperate, unconscionable, immoderate • *They spent an inordinate amount of time talking.*
OPPOSITES: reasonable, moderate, sensible

inorganic = **artificial**, chemical, man-made, mineral • *roofing made from organic and inorganic fibres*

input = **information**, facts, material, figures, details, data, documents, statistics, info (*informal*) • *a variety of types of input in the classroom*

inquest = **inquiry**, investigation, probe, inquisition • *The inquest into their deaths opened yesterday.*

inquire *or* **enquire** AS A VERB = **ask**, question, query, quiz, seek information of, request information of • *He inquired whether there had been any messages left for him.*
▸ IN PHRASES: **inquire into** = **investigate**, study, examine, consider, research, search, explore, look into, inspect, probe into, scrutinize, make inquiries into • *Inspectors inquired into the affairs of the company.*

inquiring *or* **enquiring** = **inquisitive**, interested, curious, questioning, wondering, searching, probing, doubtful, analytical, investigative, nosy (*informal*) • *This helps children develop an inquiring attitude to learning.*

inquiry *or* **enquiry** 1 = **question**, query, investigation • *He made some inquiries and discovered she had gone abroad.*
2 = **investigation**, hearing, study, review, search, survey, analysis, examination, probe, inspection, exploration, scrutiny, inquest • *a murder inquiry*
3 = **research**, investigation, analysis, examination, inspection, exploration, scrutiny, interrogation • *The investigation has switched to a new line of inquiry.*

inquisition = **investigation**, questioning, examination, inquiry, grilling (*informal*), quizzing, inquest, cross-examination, third degree (*informal*) • *He suffered a 40-minute inquisition in the press conference.*

inquisitive = **curious**, questioning, inquiring, peering, probing, intrusive, prying, snooping (*informal*), scrutinizing, snoopy (*informal*), nosy (*informal*), nosy-parkering (*informal*) • *Bears are very inquisitive and must be kept constantly stimulated.*
OPPOSITES: indifferent, unconcerned, uninterested

inroad IN PHRASES: **make inroads upon** *or* **into something** = **make advances into**, make forays into, make raids on, make encroachments into • *TV has made great inroads into cinema.*

insane 1 = **mad**, crazy, nuts (*slang*), cracked (*slang*), mental (*slang*), barking (*slang*), crackers (*Brit. slang*), mentally ill, crazed, demented, cuckoo (*informal*), deranged, loopy (*informal*), round the bend (*informal*), barking mad (*slang*), out of your mind, gaga (*informal*), screwy (*informal*), doolally (*slang*), off your trolley (*slang*), round the twist (*informal*), of unsound mind, not right in the head, non compos mentis (*Latin*), off your rocker (*slang*), not the full shilling (*informal*), mentally disordered, off the air (*Austral. slang*), porangi (*N.Z.*) • *Some people simply can't take it and they go insane.*
OPPOSITES: sound, normal, sane
2 = **stupid**, foolish, daft (*informal*), bizarre, irresponsible, irrational, lunatic, senseless, preposterous, impractical, idiotic, inane, fatuous, dumb-ass (*slang*) • *Listen, this is completely insane.*
OPPOSITES: sensible, reasonable, reasoned

insanitary = **unhealthy**, contaminated, polluted, dirtied, dirty, infected, filthy, infested, noxious, unclean, impure, unhygienic, disease-ridden, insalubrious, skanky (*slang*), feculent, festy (*Austral. slang*) • *The prison remains disgracefully crowded and insanitary.*
OPPOSITES: clean, hygienic, healthy

insanity 1 = **madness**, mental illness, dementia, aberration, mental disorder, delirium, craziness, mental derangement • *a powerful study of a woman's descent into insanity*
OPPOSITES: sanity, reason, sense
2 = **stupidity**, folly, lunacy, irresponsibility, senselessness, preposterousness • *the final financial insanity of the decade*
OPPOSITES: sense, wisdom, logic
▸ **RELATED PHOBIAS:** lyssophobia, maniaphobia

insatiable = **unquenchable**, greedy, voracious, ravenous, rapacious, intemperate, gluttonous, unappeasable, insatiate, quenchless, edacious • *an insatiable appetite for stories about the rich and famous*
OPPOSITES: limited, temperate, satiable

inscribe 1 = **carve**, cut, etch, engrave, impress, imprint • *They read the words inscribed on the walls of the monument.*
2 = **dedicate**, sign, address • *The book is inscribed: To John Arlott from Laurie Lee.*

inscription 1 = **engraving**, words, lettering, label, legend, saying • *The medal bears the inscription 'For distinguished service'.*
2 = **dedication**, message, signature, address • *The inscription reads: 'To Emma, with love from Harry'.*

inscrutable 1 = **enigmatic**, blank, impenetrable, deadpan, unreadable, poker-faced *(informal)*, sphinxlike • *It is important to keep a straight face and remain inscrutable.*
OPPOSITES: open, revealing, transparent
2 = **mysterious**, incomprehensible, inexplicable, hidden, unintelligible, unfathomable, unexplainable, undiscoverable • *Even when opened the contents of the package were as inscrutable as ever.*
OPPOSITES: clear, obvious, comprehensible

insect = **bug**, creepy-crawly *(Brit. informal)*, gogga *(S. African informal)*
▸ **RELATED ADJECTIVE:** entomic
▸ **COLLECTIVE NOUN:** swarm
▸ **RELATED MANIA:** entomomania
▸ **RELATED PHOBIA:** entomophobia
▹ *See panels* **Ants, bees and wasps; Beetles; Bugs; Butterflies and moths; Flies; Insects**

insecure 1 = **unconfident**, worried, anxious, afraid, shy, uncertain, unsure, timid, self-conscious, hesitant, meek, self-effacing, diffident, unassertive • *Many women are insecure about their performance as mothers.*
OPPOSITES: secure, confident, assured
2 = **unsafe**, dangerous, exposed, vulnerable, hazardous, wide-open, perilous, unprotected, defenceless, unguarded, open to attack, unshielded, ill-protected • *Mobile phones are inherently insecure, as anyone can listen in.*
OPPOSITES: protected, safe, secure
3 = **unreliable**, unstable, unsafe, precarious, unsteady, unsound • *low-paid, insecure jobs*
OPPOSITES: secure, reliable, stable

insecurity 1 = **anxiety**, fear, worry, uncertainty, unsureness • *She is always assailed by emotional insecurity.*
OPPOSITES: confidence, assurance, security
2 = **vulnerability**, risk, danger, weakness, uncertainty, hazard, peril, defencelessness • *The increase in crime has created feelings of insecurity.*
OPPOSITES: safety
3 = **instability**, uncertainty, unreliability, precariousness, weakness, shakiness, unsteadiness, dubiety, frailness • *the harshness and insecurity of agricultural life*
OPPOSITES: security, stability, reliability

insensitive AS AN ADJECTIVE = **unfeeling**, indifferent, unconcerned, uncaring, tough, hardened, callous, crass, unresponsive, thick-skinned, obtuse, tactless, imperceptive, unsusceptible • *My husband is very insensitive about my problem.*
OPPOSITES: concerned, caring, sensitive
▸ **IN PHRASES: insensitive to** = **unaffected by**, immune to, impervious to, dead to, unmoved by, proof against • *He had become insensitive to cold.*

inseparable 1 = **devoted**, close, intimate, bosom • *The two girls were inseparable.*
2 = **indivisible**, inalienable, conjoined, indissoluble, inseverable • *He believes liberty is inseparable from social justice.*

insert AS A VERB 1 = **put**, place, set, position, work in, slip, slide, slot, thrust, stick in, wedge, tuck in • *He took a key from his pocket and inserted it into the lock.*
2 = **enter**, include, introduce, interject, interpose, interpolate, infix • *They inserted a clause calling for a popular vote on the issue.*
OPPOSITES: remove, withdraw, pull out

INSECTS

TYPES OF INSECT

apple maggot
body louse, cootie *(U.S. & N.Z.)*
bollworm
booklouse
bookworm
bristletail
cabbageworm
caddis worm *or* caseworm
cankerworm
cochineal
cockroach
cotton stainer
crab (louse)
cricket
dust mite
earwig
German cockroach *or (U.S.)* Croton bug
grasshopper
katydid
lac insect
locust
louse *or (N.Z.)* kutu
mantis *or* praying mantis
measuring worm, looper, *or* inchworm
midge
mole cricket
mosquito
nit
phylloxera
scale insect
seventeen-year locust *or* periodical cicada
sheep ked *or* sheep tick
silkworm
silverfish
stick insect
sucking louse
tent caterpillar
thrips
treehopper
wax insect
web spinner
weta *(N.Z.)*
wheel bug
wireworm
woodworm

PARTS OF INSECTS

acetabulum
air sac
antenna
arista
cercus
cirrus
clasper
clypeus
compound eye
corium
coxa
elytron
endocuticle
epicuticle
exocuticle
femur
flagellum
forewing
glossa
gonopod
hamulus
haustellum
hemelytron
ileum
jaw
labium
labrum
ligula
Malpighian tubule
mandible
maxilla
mesothorax
metathorax
notum
ocellus
ovipositor
pedicel
proboscis
proleg
pronotum
prosternum
prothorax
proventriculus
pulvillus
scape
scutellum
scutum
snout
spinneret
spiracle
stigma
tarsus
tegmen
thigh
thorax
tibia
trachea
trochanter
underwing
ventriculus

▸AS A NOUN = **insertion**, addition, inclusion, supplement, implant, inset • *It can be very expensive to place an insert in a newspaper.*

insertion 1 = **inclusion**, introduction, interpolation • *the first experiment involving the insertion of a new gene*
2 = **insert**, addition, inclusion, supplement, implant, inset • *The correction to the text may involve an insertion or a deletion.*

inside AS A NOUN = **interior**, contents, core, nucleus, inner part, inner side • *Cut off the top and scoop out the inside with a teaspoon.*
▸AS A PLURAL NOUN = **stomach**, gut, guts, belly, bowels, internal organs, innards *(informal)*, entrails, viscera, vitals • *My insides ached from eating too much.*
▸AS AN ADJECTIVE 1 = **inner**, internal, interior, inward, innermost • *four-berth inside cabins with en suite bathrooms*
OPPOSITES: outside, external, outer
2 = **confidential**, private, secret, internal, exclusive, restricted, privileged, classified • *The editor denies he had any inside knowledge.*
▸AS AN ADVERB 1 = **indoors**, in, within, under cover • *They chatted briefly on the doorstep before going inside.*
2 = **within**, privately, deep down, secretly, at heart, to yourself, inwardly, in your inmost heart • *Do you get a feeling inside when you write something you like?*
3 = **in prison**, in jail, imprisoned, behind bars *(informal)*, incarcerated, banged up *(Brit. informal)* • *He's been inside three times now.*

insider = **worker**, employee, staff member, workman, job-holder • *a shrewd insider in the music business*

insidious = **stealthy**, subtle, cunning, designing, smooth, tricky, crooked, sneaking, slick, sly, treacherous, deceptive, wily, crafty, artful, disingenuous, Machiavellian, deceitful, surreptitious, duplicitous, guileful • *They focus on overt racism rather than insidious aspects of racism.*
OPPOSITES: open, obvious, straightforward

insight 1 = **understanding**, intelligence, perception, sense, knowledge, vision, judgment, awareness, grasp, appreciation, intuition, penetration, comprehension, acumen, discernment, perspicacity • *He was a man of considerable insight and diplomatic skills.*
2 *with* **into** = **understanding**, perception, awareness, experience, description, introduction, observation, judgment, revelation, comprehension, intuitiveness • *The talk gave us some insight into the work they were doing.*

insightful = **perceptive**, shrewd, discerning, understanding, wise, penetrating, knowledgeable, astute, observant, perspicacious, sagacious • *She offered some really insightful observations.*

insignia = **badge**, symbol, decoration, crest, earmark, emblem, ensign, distinguishing mark • *a tunic bearing the insignia of the captain of the Irish Guards*

insignificance = **unimportance**, irrelevance, triviality, pettiness, worthlessness, meaninglessness, inconsequence, immateriality, paltriness, negligibility • *The event was regarded as of total insignificance.*
OPPOSITES: weight, importance, consequence

insignificant = **unimportant**, minor, irrelevant, petty, trivial, meaningless, trifling, meagre, negligible, flimsy, paltry, immaterial, inconsequential, nondescript, measly, scanty, inconsiderable, of no consequence, nonessential, small potatoes, nickel-and-dime *(U.S. slang)*, of no account, nugatory, unsubstantial, not worth mentioning, of no moment • *In 1949 it was still a small, insignificant city.*
OPPOSITES: important, significant, essential

insincere = **deceitful**, lying, false, pretended, hollow, untrue, dishonest, deceptive, devious, hypocritical, unfaithful, evasive, two-faced, disingenuous, faithless, double-dealing, duplicitous, dissembling, mendacious, perfidious, untruthful, dissimulating, Janus-faced • *He found himself surrounded by insincere flattery.*
OPPOSITES: true, genuine, sincere

insincerity = **deceitfulness**, hypocrisy, pretence, dishonesty, lip service, duplicity, deviousness, perfidy, mendacity, dissimulation, faithlessness, disingenuousness, untruthfulness • *Too many superlatives lend a note of insincerity.*
OPPOSITES: honesty, sincerity, directness

QUOTATIONS

The great enemy of clear language is insincerity. When there is a gap between one's real and one's declared aims, one turns as it were instinctively to long words and exhausted idioms, like a cuttlefish squirting out ink
[George Orwell *Politics and the English Language*]

insinuate = **imply**, suggest, hint, indicate, intimate, allude • *The article insinuated that the President was lying.*

insinuation = **implication**, suggestion, hint, allusion, innuendo • *It isn't right to bring a good man down by rumour and insinuation.*

insipid 1 = **tasteless**, bland, flavourless, watered down, watery, wishy-washy *(informal)*, unappetizing, savourless • *It tasted bland and insipid, like warm cardboard.*
OPPOSITES: tasty, savoury, pungent
2 = **bland**, boring, dull, flat, dry, weak, stupid, limp, tame, pointless, tedious, stale, drab, banal, tiresome, lifeless, prosaic, trite, unimaginative, colourless, uninteresting, anaemic, wishy-washy *(informal)*, ho-hum *(informal)*, vapid, wearisome, characterless, spiritless, jejune, prosy • *On the surface she seemed meek, rather bland and insipid.* • *They gave an insipid opening performance in a nil-nil draw.*
OPPOSITES: interesting, exciting, stimulating

insist 1 = **persist**, press (someone), be firm, stand firm, stand your ground, lay down the law, put your foot down *(informal)*, not take no for an answer, brook no refusal, take *or* make a stand • *I didn't want to join in, but he insisted.*
2 = **demand**, order, urge, require, command, dictate, entreat • *I insisted that the fault be repaired.*
3 = **assert**, state, maintain, hold, claim, declare, repeat, vow, swear, contend, affirm, reiterate, profess, avow, aver, asseverate • *He insisted that he was acting out of compassion.*

insistence 1 = **demand**, urging, command, pressing, dictate, entreaty, importunity, insistency • *She had attended an interview at his insistence.*
2 = **assertion**, claim, statement, declaration, contention, persistence, affirmation, pronouncement, reiteration, avowal, attestation • *her insistence that she wanted to dump her raunchy image*

insistent 1 = **emphatic**, persistent, demanding, pressing, dogged, urgent, forceful, persevering, unrelenting, peremptory, importunate, exigent • *He is most insistent on this point.*
2 = **persistent**, repeated, constant, repetitive, incessant, unremitting • *the insistent rhythms of dance music*

insolence = **rudeness**, cheek *(informal)*, disrespect, front, abuse, sauce *(informal)*, gall *(informal)*, audacity, boldness, chutzpah *(U.S. & Canad. informal)*, insubordination, impertinence, impudence, effrontery, backchat *(informal)*, incivility, sassiness *(U.S. informal)*, pertness, contemptuousness • *The most frequent reason for excluding a pupil was insolence.*
OPPOSITES: respect, esteem, politeness

insolent = **rude**, cheeky, impertinent, fresh *(informal)*, bold, insulting, abusive, saucy, contemptuous, pert, impudent, uncivil, insubordinate, brazen-faced • *Don't be insolent with me, young lady!*
OPPOSITES: respectful, civil, polite

insoluble 1 = **inexplicable**, mysterious, baffling, obscure, mystifying, impenetrable, unaccountable, unfathomable, indecipherable, unsolvable • *an insoluble dilemma that I could do nothing about*
OPPOSITES: comprehensible, explicable, solvable
2 = **indissoluble**, not soluble • *Carotenes are insoluble in water.*

insolvency = **bankruptcy**, failure, ruin, liquidation • *Seven of the eight companies are on the brink of insolvency.*

insolvent = **bankrupt**, ruined, on the rocks *(informal)*, broke *(informal)*, failed, gone bust *(informal)*, in receivership, gone to the wall, in the hands of the receivers, in queer street *(informal)* • *Two years later, the bank was declared insolvent.*

insomnia = **sleeplessness**, restlessness, wakefulness • *For some people, insomnia is a chronic affliction.*
▸ RELATED ADJECTIVE: agrypnotic

insouciance = **nonchalance**, light-heartedness, jauntiness, airiness, breeziness, carefreeness • *He replied with characteristic insouciance, 'So what?'*

insouciant = **nonchalant**, casual, carefree, gay, sunny, buoyant, airy, breezy, unconcerned, jaunty, untroubled, happy-go-lucky, free and easy, unworried, light-hearted • *He worked with insouciant disregard for convention.*

inspect 1 = **examine**, check, look at, view, eye, survey, observe, scan, check out *(informal)*, look over, eyeball *(slang)*, scrutinize, give (something *or* someone) the once-over *(informal)*, take a dekko at *(Brit. slang)*, go over *or* through • *Cut the fruit in half and inspect the pips.*
2 = **check**, examine, investigate, study, look at, research, search, survey, assess, probe, audit, vet, oversee, supervise, check out *(informal)*, look over, work over, superintend, give (something *or* someone) the once-over *(informal)*, go over *or* through • *Each hotel is inspected once a year.*

inspection 1 = **examination**, investigation, scrutiny, scan, look-over, once-over *(informal)* • *Closer inspection reveals that they are banded with yellow.*
2 = **check**, search, investigation, review, survey, examination, scan, scrutiny, supervision, surveillance, look-over, once-over *(informal)*, checkup, recce *(slang)*, superintendence • *A routine inspection of the vessel turned up 50 kg of the drug.*

inspector = **examiner**, investigator, supervisor, monitor, superintendent, auditor, censor, surveyor, scrutinizer, checker, overseer, scrutineer • *The mill was finally closed down by safety inspectors.*

inspiration 1 = **imagination**, creativity, ingenuity, talent, insight, genius, productivity, fertility, stimulation, originality, inventiveness, cleverness, fecundity, imaginativeness • *A good way of getting inspiration is by looking at others' work.*
2 = **motivation**, example, influence, model, boost, spur, incentive, revelation, encouragement, stimulus, catalyst, stimulation, inducement, incitement, instigation, afflatus • *She was very impressive and a great inspiration to all.*
OPPOSITES: deterrent, disenchantment, discouragement
3 = **influence**, spur, stimulus, muse • *India's myths and songs are the inspiration for her books.*
4 = **bright idea**, revelation, brainwave *(informal)* • *She had an inspiration. 'Let's make a tunnel from hardboard'.*

QUOTATIONS
When you do not know what you are doing and what you are doing is the best – that is inspiration
[Robert Bresson *Notes on the Cinematographer*]

inspire 1 = **motivate**, move, cause, stimulate, encourage, influence, persuade, spur, be responsible for, animate, rouse, instil, infuse, hearten, enliven, imbue, spark off, energize, galvanize, gee up, inspirit, fire *or* touch the imagination of • *What inspired you to change your name?*
OPPOSITES: depress, discourage, daunt
2 = **give rise to**, cause, produce, result in, prompt, stir, spawn, engender • *His legend would even inspire a song by Simon and Garfunkel.*
3 = **arouse**, cause, produce, excite, prompt, induce, awaken, give rise to, ignite, kindle, enkindle • *The car's effortless handling inspires confidence.*

inspired 1 = **brilliant**, wonderful, impressive, exciting, outstanding, thrilling, memorable, dazzling, enthralling, superlative, of genius • *She produced an inspired performance.*
2 = **stimulated**, possessed, aroused, uplifted, exhilarated, stirred up, enthused, exalted, elated, galvanized • *Garcia played like a man inspired.*
3 *with* **by** = **based on**, derived from, built around, constructed around • *The book was inspired by a real person.*

inspiring = **uplifting**, encouraging, exciting, moving, affecting, stirring, stimulating, rousing, exhilarating, heartening • *It was not our most inspiring performance of the season.*
OPPOSITES: boring, depressing, uninspiring

instability 1 = **uncertainty**, insecurity, weakness, imbalance, vulnerability, wavering, volatility, unpredictability, restlessness, fluidity, fluctuation, disequilibrium, transience, impermanence, precariousness, mutability, shakiness, unsteadiness, inconstancy • *unpopular policies which resulted in political instability*
OPPOSITES: security, strength, stability
2 = **imbalance**, weakness, volatility, variability, frailty, unpredictability, oscillation, vacillation, capriciousness, unsteadiness, flightiness, fitfulness, changeableness • *Caligula's inherent mental instability*

install 1 = **set up**, put in, place, position, station, establish, lay, fix, locate, lodge • *They had installed a new phone line in the apartment.*
2 = **institute**, establish, introduce, invest, ordain, inaugurate, induct, instate • *A new Catholic bishop was installed yesterday.*
3 = **settle**, position, plant, establish, lodge, ensconce • *Before her husband's death she had installed herself in a modern villa.*

installation 1 = **setting up**, fitting, instalment, placing, positioning, establishment • *Lives could be saved if installation of alarms was stepped up.*
2 = **appointment**, ordination, inauguration, induction, investiture, instatement • *He invited her to attend his installation as chief of his tribe.*
3 = **base**, centre, post, station, camp, settlement, establishment, headquarters • *a secret military installation*

instalment 1 = **payment**, repayment, part payment • *The first instalment is payable on application.*
2 = **part**, section, chapter, episode, portion, division • *The next instalment deals with the social impact of the war*

instance AS A NOUN 1 = **example**, case, occurrence, occasion, sample, illustration, precedent, case in point, exemplification • *a serious instance of corruption*
2 = **insistence**, demand, urging, pressure, stress, application, request, prompting, impulse, behest, incitement, instigation, solicitation, entreaty, importunity • *The meeting was organised at the instance of two senior ministers.*
▸ AS A VERB = **name**, mention, identify, point out, advance, quote, finger *(informal, chiefly U.S.)*, refer to, point to, cite, specify, invoke, allude to, adduce, namecheck, namedrop • *She could have instanced many women who fitted this description.*
▸ IN PHRASES: **for instance** = **for example**, e.g., to illustrate, as an illustration, by way of illustration, exempli gratia *(Latin)*, to cite an instance • *Let your child make his own decisions sometimes. For instance, let him choose which clothes to wear.*
in the first instance = **initially**, at first, to begin with, first, firstly, originally, primarily, at the start, at the outset, in the early stages, at *or* in the beginning • *The post was for one year in the first instance.*

instant AS A NOUN 1 = **moment**, second, minute, shake *(informal)*, flash, tick *(Brit. informal)*, no time, twinkling, split second, jiffy *(informal)*, trice, twinkling of an eye *(informal)*, two shakes *(informal)*, two shakes of a lamb's tail *(informal)*, bat of an eye *(informal)* • *The pain disappeared in an instant.*

2 = **time**, point, hour, moment, stage, occasion, phase, juncture • *At the same instant, he flung open the car door.*

▸ **AS AN ADJECTIVE 1** = **immediate**, prompt, instantaneous, direct, quick, urgent, on-the-spot, split-second • *He had taken an instant dislike to her.*

2 = **ready-made**, fast, convenience, ready-mixed, ready-cooked, precooked • *He was stirring instant coffee into two mugs of hot water.*

instantaneous = **immediate**, prompt, instant, direct, on-the-spot • *Death was not instantaneous.*

instantaneously = **immediately**, instantly, at once, straight away, promptly, on the spot, forthwith, in the same breath, then and there, pronto *(informal)*, in the twinkling of an eye *(informal)*, on the instant, in a fraction of a second, posthaste, quick as lightning, in the bat of an eye *(informal)* • *Airbags inflate instantaneously on impact.*

instantly = **immediately**, at once, straight away, now, directly, on the spot, right away, there and then, without delay, instantaneously, forthwith, this minute, pronto *(informal)*, posthaste, instanter *(Law)*, tout de suite *(French)* • *The man was killed instantly.*

instead **AS AN ADVERB** = **rather**, alternatively, preferably, in preference, in lieu, on second thoughts • *Forget about dieting and eat normally instead.*

▸ **IN PHRASES: instead of** = **in place of**, rather than, in preference to, in lieu of, in contrast with, as an alternative *or* equivalent to • *She had to spend four months away, instead of the usual two.*

instigate = **provoke**, start, encourage, move, influence, prompt, trigger, spur, stimulate, set off, initiate, bring about, rouse, prod, stir up, get going, incite, kick-start, whip up, impel, kindle, foment, actuate • *The violence was instigated by ex-members of the secret police.*

OPPOSITES: stop, discourage, suppress

instigation = **prompting**, urging, bidding, incentive, encouragement, behest, incitement • *The talks are taking place at the instigation of Germany.*

instigator = **ringleader**, inciter, motivator, leader, spur, goad, troublemaker, incendiary, firebrand, prime mover, fomenter, agitator, stirrer *(informal)*, mischief-maker • *the key instigators of reform*

instil *or* **instill** = **introduce**, implant, engender, infuse, imbue, impress, insinuate, sow the seeds, inculcate, engraft, infix • *The work instilled a sense of responsibility in the children.*

instinct 1 = **natural inclination**, feeling, urge, talent, tendency, faculty, inclination, intuition, knack, aptitude, predisposition, sixth sense, proclivity, gut reaction *(informal)*, second sight • *I didn't have a strong maternal instinct.*

2 = **talent**, skill, gift, capacity, bent, genius, faculty, knack, aptitude • *She has a natural instinct to perform.*

3 = **intuition**, feeling, impulse, gut feeling *(informal)*, sixth sense • *I should have gone with my first instinct.*

instinctive = **natural**, inborn, automatic, unconscious, mechanical, native, inherent, spontaneous, reflex, innate, intuitive, subconscious, involuntary, visceral, unthinking, instinctual, unlearned, hard-wired, unpremeditated, intuitional • *It's an instinctive reaction. If a child falls you pick it up.*

OPPOSITES: considered, learned, acquired

instinctively = **intuitively**, naturally, automatically, without thinking, involuntarily, by instinct, in your bones • *She instinctively knew all was not well with her baby.*

institute **AS A NOUN** = **establishment**, body, centre, school, university, society, association, college, institution, organization, foundation, academy, guild, conservatory, fellowship, seminary, seat of learning • *a research institute devoted to software programming*

▸ **AS A VERB** = **establish**, start, begin, found, launch, set up, introduce, settle, fix, invest, organize, install, pioneer, constitute, initiate, originate, enact, commence, inaugurate, set in motion, bring into being, put into operation • *We will institute a number of methods to improve safety.*

OPPOSITES: end, stop, abandon

institution 1 = **establishment**, body, centre, school, university, society, association, college, institute, organization, foundation, academy, guild, conservatory, fellowship, seminary, seat of learning • *Class size varies from one type of institution to another.*

2 = **custom**, practice, tradition, law, rule, procedure, convention, ritual, fixture, rite • *I believe in the institution of marriage.*

3 = **creation**, introduction, establishment, investment, debut, foundation, formation, installation, initiation, inauguration, enactment, inception, commencement, investiture • *the institution of the forty-hour week*

4 = **home**, hostel, residential care home, asylum, prison • *He spent 40 years in an institution before being released last year.*

institutional = **conventional**, accepted, established, formal, establishment *(informal)*, organized, routine, orthodox, bureaucratic, procedural, societal • *social and institutional values*

instruct 1 = **order**, tell, direct, charge, bid, command, mandate, enjoin • *They have instructed solicitors to sue for compensation.*

2 = **teach**, school, train, direct, coach, guide, discipline, educate, drill, tutor, enlighten, give lessons in • *He instructs family members in nursing techniques.*

3 = **tell**, advise, inform, counsel, notify, brief, acquaint, apprise • *Instruct them that they've got three months to get it sorted out.*

instruction **AS A NOUN 1** = **order**, ruling, command, rule, demand, direction, regulation, dictate, decree, mandate, directive, injunction, behest • *No reason for this instruction was given.*

2 = **teaching**, schooling, training, classes, grounding, education, coaching, lesson(s), discipline, preparation, drilling, guidance, tutoring, tuition, enlightenment, apprenticeship, tutorials, tutelage • *Each candidate is given instruction in safety.*

▸ **AS A PLURAL NOUN** = **information**, rules, advice, directions, recommendations, guidance, specifications • *This book gives instructions for making a variety of hand creams.*

instructive = **informative**, revealing, useful, educational, helpful, illuminating, enlightening, instructional, cautionary, didactic, edifying • *an entertaining and instructive documentary*

instructor = **teacher**, coach, guide, adviser, trainer, demonstrator, tutor, guru, mentor, educator, pedagogue, preceptor *(rare)*, master *or* mistress, schoolmaster *or* schoolmistress • *tuition from an approved driving instructor*

instrument 1 = **tool**, device, implement, mechanism, appliance, apparatus, gadget, utensil, contraption *(informal)*, contrivance, waldo • *a thin tube-like optical instrument*

2 = **meter**, display, indicator, dial, gauge • *navigation instruments*

3 = **agent**, means, force, cause, medium, agency, factor, channel, vehicle, mechanism, organ • *The veto is a traditional instrument for diplomacy.*

4 = **puppet**, tool, pawn, toy, creature, dupe, stooge *(slang)*, plaything, cat's-paw • *The Council was an instrument of Government.*

▷ *See panel* **Instruments in a full orchestra; Musical instruments**

instrumental = **active**, involved, influential, useful, helpful, conducive, contributory, of help *or* service • *He was instrumental in the release of some of the hostages.*

insubordinate = **disobedient**, defiant, rebellious, disorderly, turbulent, unruly, insurgent, recalcitrant,

MUSICAL INSTRUMENTS

accordion
aeolian harp
alphorn *or* alpenhorn
althorn
Autoharp *(trademark)*
baby grand
Bach trumpet
bagpipes
balalaika
bandore
banjo
barrel organ
baryton
bass drum
basset horn
bass guitar
bassoon
bass viol
bell
bodhrán
Böhm flute
bombardon
bongo
boudoir grand
bouzouki
bugle
calliope
carillon
castanets
celesta *or* celeste
cello *or* violoncello
cembalo
chamber organ
Chapman stick *(trademark)*
chime
Chinese block
chitarrone
cimbalon
cithara
cittern
clarinet
clarion
clarsach
clave
clavicembalo
clavichord
clavier
concert grand
concertina
conga
contrabass
contrabassoon
cor anglais
cornet
cornett
cottage piano
cowbell
crumhorn
crwth
cymbal
cymbalo
didgeridoo
Dobro *(trademark)*
double bass
double bassoon
drum
drum machine
dulcimer
electric guitar
electronic organ
English horn
euphonium
fiddle
fife
flageolet
flugelhorn
flute
French horn
gittarone
gittern
glass harmonica
glockenspiel
gong
gran cassa
grand piano
guitar
Hammond organ *(trademark)*
handbell
harmonica
harmonium
harp
harpsichord
Hawaiian guitar
helicon
horn
hornpipe
hunting horn
hurdy-gurdy
idiophone
jew's-harp
kazoo
kettledrum
keyboard
kit
kora
koto
lur *or* lure
lute
lyra viol
lyre
mandola
mandolin
maraca
marimba
mbira
mellophone
melodeon
metallophone
Moog *(trademark)*
mouth organ
musette
naker
ngoma
nickelodeon
nose flute
oboe
oboe da caccia
oboe d'amore
ocarina
octachord
ondes Martenot
ophicleide
orchestrina *or* orchestrion
organ
orpharion
oud
panpipes
pedal steel guitar
penny whistle
piano
Pianola *(trademark)*
piccolo
pipe
player piano
portative organ
racket
rebec *or* rebeck
recorder
reco-reco
reed organ
reed pipe
regal
rote
sackbut
samisen
sarangi
sarod
sarrusophone
saxhorn
saxophone
shawm
side drum
sistrum
sitar
slide guitar
snare drum
sousaphone
Spanish guitar
spinet
square piano
steam organ
steel guitar
stylophone
synthesizer
syrinx
tabla
tabor *or* tabour
tambour
tamboura
tambourine
tam-tam
theorbo
Theremin *(trademark)*
timbal
timpani
tom-tom
triangle
trigon
trombone
trumpet
tuba
tubular bells
uillean pipes
ukulele
upright piano
vibraphone
vihuela
vina
viol
viola
viola da braccio
viola da gamba
viola d'amore
violin
violone
virginal
vocoder
washboard
Welsh harp
whip
whistle
wood block
Wurlitzer *(trademark)*
xylophone
xylorimba
zither

fractious, riotous, undisciplined, seditious, mutinous, ungovernable, refractory, contumacious • *Workers who are grossly insubordinate are threatened with discharge.*
OPPOSITES: obedient, compliant, submissive

insubordination = **disobedience**, rebellion, defiance, revolt, mutiny, insurrection, indiscipline, sedition, recalcitrance, ungovernability, riotousness, mutinousness • *The two men were fired for insubordination.*
OPPOSITES: submission, compliance, obedience

insubstantial 1 = **flimsy**, thin, weak, slight, frail, feeble, tenuous • *Her limbs were insubstantial, almost transparent.*
OPPOSITES: strong, solid, substantial
2 = **imaginary**, unreal, fanciful, immaterial, ephemeral, illusory, incorporeal, chimerical • *Their thoughts seemed as insubstantial as smoke.*

insufferable = **unbearable**, impossible, intolerable, dreadful, outrageous, unspeakable, detestable, insupportable, unendurable, past bearing, more than flesh and blood can stand, enough to test the patience of a saint, enough to try the patience of Job • *We all agreed he was the most insufferable bore.*
OPPOSITES: appealing, attractive, bearable

insufficiency = **shortage**, lack, deficiency, want, poverty, inadequacy, short supply, scarcity, dearth, paucity, scantiness, inadequateness • *Late miscarriages are not usually due to hormonal insufficiency.*

insufficient = **inadequate**, incomplete, scant, meagre, short, sparse, deficient, lacking, unqualified, insubstantial, incommensurate • *There was insufficient evidence to proceed.*
OPPOSITES: enough, sufficient, ample

insular = **narrow-minded**, prejudiced, provincial, closed, limited, narrow, petty, parochial, blinkered, circumscribed, inward-looking, illiberal, parish-pump • *The old image of the insular Brit is slowly starting to change.*
OPPOSITES: worldly, experienced, broad-minded

insulate 1 = **isolate**, protect, screen, defend, shelter, shield, cut off, cushion, cocoon, close off, sequester, wrap up in cotton wool • *Their wealthy families had insulated them from reality.*
2 = **cover**, wrap, enclose, swathe, encase, sheathe • *Are your hot and cold water pipes well insulated?*

insult **AS A VERB** = **offend**, abuse, injure, wound, slight, outrage, put down, humiliate, libel, snub, slag (off) *(slang)*, malign, affront, denigrate, disparage, revile, slander, displease, defame, hurt (someone's) feelings, call names, give offence to • *I didn't mean to insult you.*
OPPOSITES: praise, flatter, big up *(slang, chiefly Caribbean)*
▸ **AS A NOUN** 1 = **jibe**, slight, put-down, abuse, snub, barb, affront, indignity, contumely, abusive remark, aspersion • *Some of the officers shouted insults at prisoners on the roof.*
2 = **offence**, slight, outrage, snub, slur, affront, rudeness, slap in the face *(informal)*, kick in the teeth *(informal)*,

insolence, aspersion • *Their behaviour was an insult to the people they represented.*
OPPOSITES: compliment, flattery

QUOTATIONS
This is adding insult to injuries
[Edward Moore *The Foundling*]

▹ *See panel* **Insults and terms of abuse**

insulting = **offensive**, rude, abusive, slighting, degrading, affronting, contemptuous, disparaging, scurrilous, insolent • *One of the workers made an insulting remark to a supervisor.*
OPPOSITES: flattering, complimentary, respectful

insuperable = **insurmountable**, invincible, impassable, unconquerable • *an insuperable obstacle to co-operation*
OPPOSITES: possible, surmountable, conquerable

insupportable 1 = **intolerable**, unbearable, insufferable, unendurable, past bearing • *Life without her was tedious, insupportable.*
2 = **unjustifiable**, untenable, indefensible • *This is an increasingly insupportable argument in these times.*

insurance 1 = **assurance**, cover, security, protection, coverage, safeguard, indemnity, indemnification • *You are advised to take out insurance on your lenses.*
2 = **protection**, security, guarantee, provision, shelter, safeguard, warranty • *Put something away as insurance against failure of the business.*

insure 1 = **assure**, cover, protect, guarantee, warrant, underwrite, indemnify • *We automatically insure your furniture and belongings against fire.*
2 = **protect**, cover, safeguard • *He needs to insure himself against ambitious party rivals.*

insurer = **insurance agent**, insurance company • *The insurer is providing £320 million to cover mortgage losses.*

insurgency = **rebellion**, rising, revolution, resistance, revolt, uprising, mutiny, insurrection, insurgence • *Both countries were threatened with insurgencies in the late 1960s.*

insurgent AS A NOUN = **rebel**, revolutionary, revolter, rioter, resister, mutineer, revolutionist, insurrectionist • *The insurgents took control of the main military air base.*
▸ AS AN ADJECTIVE = **rebellious**, revolutionary, mutinous, revolting, riotous, seditious, disobedient, insubordinate, insurrectionary • *The insurgent leaders were publicly executed.*

insurmountable = **insuperable**, impossible, overwhelming, hopeless, invincible, impassable, unconquerable • *The fiscal crisis does not seem like an insurmountable problem.*

insurrection = **rebellion**, rising, revolution, riot, coup, revolt, uprising, mutiny, insurgency, putsch, sedition • *They were plotting to stage an armed insurrection.*

intact = **undamaged**, whole, complete, sound, perfect, entire, virgin, untouched, unscathed, unbroken, flawless, unhurt, faultless, unharmed, uninjured, unimpaired, undefiled, all in one piece, together, scatheless, unviolated • *After the explosion, most of the cargo was left intact.*
OPPOSITES: broken, damaged, injured

intangible = **abstract**, vague, invisible, dim, elusive, shadowy, airy, unreal, indefinite, ethereal, evanescent, incorporeal, impalpable, unsubstantial • *the intangible dimensions of our existence*

integral 1 = **essential**, basic, fundamental, necessary, component, constituent, indispensable, intrinsic, requisite, elemental • *Rituals form an integral part of any human society.*
OPPOSITES: unnecessary, unimportant, inessential
2 = **whole**, full, complete, entire, intact, undivided • *This is meant to be an integral service.*
OPPOSITES: fractional, partial

integrate AS A VERB = **join**, unite, combine, blend, incorporate, merge, accommodate, knit, fuse, mesh, assimilate, amalgamate, coalesce, harmonize, meld, intermix • *No attempt was made to integrate the parts into a coherent whole.*
OPPOSITES: separate, divide, segregate
▸ IN PHRASES: **integrate into something** = **adapt to**, suit, match with, blend with, correspond with, tally with, reconcile to, chime with, harmonize with, go together with, attune to, tone in with, cohere with, be of one mind with, be in unison with • *He didn't successfully integrate into the Italian way of life.*

integrated 1 = **unified**, united, combined, leagued, allied, pooled, collective, affiliated, banded together • *a fully integrated, supportive society*
2 = **desegregated**, racially mixed, unsegregated, non-segregated • *a black student in Chicago's integrated high school*

integration 1 = **inclusion**, incorporation • *They overwhelmingly support the integration of disabled people into society.*
2 = **combining**, mixing, blending, harmony, unification, fusing, incorporation, assimilation, amalgamation, commingling • *There is little integration of our work and no single focus.*

integrity 1 = **honesty**, principle, honour, virtue, goodness, morality, purity, righteousness, probity, rectitude, truthfulness, trustworthiness, incorruptibility, uprightness, scrupulousness, reputability • *I have always regarded him as a man of integrity.*
OPPOSITES: corruption, dishonesty, immorality
2 = **unity**, unification, cohesion, coherence, wholeness, soundness, completeness • *Separatist movements are a threat to the integrity of the nation.*
OPPOSITES: fragility, flimsiness, unsoundness

QUOTATIONS
This above all: to thine own self be true
[William Shakespeare *Hamlet*]

INSULTS AND TERMS OF ABUSE

airhead, article, berk, bird-brain, bitch, blockhead, bonehead, bozo, bushpig, cabbage, charlie, cheeky monkey, chicken, chuckie, chump, clod, clot, clown, coot, cow, cretin, devil, dimwit, dipstick, divvy, donkey, doofus, dope, dork, doughnut, drip, dumb-ass, dumbo, dummy, dunce, dweeb, eejit, fathead, fool, galah, geek, git, goose, halfwit, heifer, idiot, imbecile, jerk, lamebrain, loon, mincer, minger, mong, moron, mug, muppet, nerd *or* nurd, nincompoop, ninny, nit, nitwit, numbskull *or* numskull, numpty, oaf, ogre, pea-brain, pillock, plank, plonker, prat, rascal, rogue, scab, scoundrel, scrubber, scutter, simpleton, slag, slapper, tart, thickhead, thicko, twerp *or* twirp, twit, wally, whore *or* 'ho, wimp, wretch, wuss

intellect 1 = **intelligence**, mind, reason, understanding, sense, brains *(informal)*, judgment • *Do the emotions develop in parallel with the intellect?*
2 = **thinker**, intellectual, genius, mind, brain *(informal)*, intelligence, rocket scientist *(informal)*, egghead *(informal)* • *My boss isn't a great intellect.*

QUOTATIONS
We should take care not to make the intellect our god; it has, of course, powerful muscles, but no personality
[Albert Einstein *Out of My Later Years*]

intellectual AS AN ADJECTIVE 1 = **mental**, cognitive, cerebral • *High levels of lead could damage intellectual development.*
OPPOSITES: material, physical
2 = **scholarly**, learned, academic, lettered, intelligent, rational, cerebral, erudite, scholastic, highbrow, well-read, studious, bookish • *They were very intellectual and witty.*
OPPOSITES: stupid, ignorant, illiterate
▸ AS A NOUN = **academic**, expert, genius, thinker, master, brain *(informal)*, mastermind, maestro, boffin *(Brit. informal)*, highbrow, rocket scientist *(informal)*, egghead *(informal)*, brainbox, bluestocking *(usually disparaging)*, master-hand, fundi *(S. African)*, acca *(Austral. slang)* • *teachers, artists and other intellectuals*
OPPOSITES: idiot, moron

QUOTATIONS
An intellectual is someone whose mind watches itself
[Albert Camus *Notebooks 1935–42*]
To the man-in-the-street, who, I'm sorry to say
Is a keen observer of life
The word 'Intellectual' suggests straight away
A man who's untrue to his wife
[W.H. Auden *New Year Letter*]

intelligence 1 = **intellect**, understanding, brains *(informal)*, mind, reason, sense, knowledge, capacity, smarts *(slang, chiefly U.S.)*, judgment, wit, perception, awareness, insight, penetration, comprehension, brightness, aptitude, acumen, nous *(Brit. slang)*, alertness, cleverness, quickness, discernment, grey matter *(informal)*, brain power • *She's a woman of exceptional intelligence.*
OPPOSITES: understanding, ignorance, stupidity
2 = **information**, news, facts, report, findings, word, notice, advice, knowledge, data, disclosure, gen *(Brit. informal)*, tip-off, low-down *(informal)*, notification, heads up *(U.S. & Canad.)* • *a senior officer involved in gathering intelligence*
OPPOSITES: misinformation, concealment
3 = **espionage**, spying, surveillance, information gathering, counter-intelligence, undercover work • *Why was military intelligence so lacking?*

QUOTATIONS
Intelligence is characterised by a natural incomprehension of life
[Henri Bergson *L'Évolution Créatrice*]
Intelligence in chains loses in lucidity what it gains in intensity
[Albert Camus *The Rebel*]
The test of a first-rate intelligence is the ability to hold two opposed ideas in the mind at the same time, and still retain the ability to function
[F. Scott Fitzgerald *The Crack-Up*]
Intelligence is quickness in seeing things as they are
[George Santayana *The Life of Reason: Reason in Common Sense*]
Intelligence ... is really a kind of taste: taste in ideas
[Susan Sontag *Notes on Camp*]

intelligent 1 = **clever**, bright, smart, knowing, quick, sharp, acute, alert, rational, penetrating, enlightened, apt, discerning, knowledgeable, astute, well-informed, brainy *(informal)*, perspicacious, quick-witted, sagacious • *She's a very intelligent woman who knows her own mind.*
OPPOSITES: stupid, dull, foolish
2 = **smart** *(informal)*, automatic, automated, robotic, self-regulating • *An intelligent computer will soon be indispensable for every doctor.*
3 = **rational**, cognitive, capable of thought • *the search for intelligent life elsewhere in the universe*

intelligentsia = **intellectuals**, highbrows, literati, masterminds, the learned, eggheads *(informal)*, illuminati • *I was not high enough up in the intelligentsia to be invited.*

intelligibility = **clarity**, precision, simplicity, lucidity, explicitness, plainness, distinctness, clearness, comprehensibility • *the ready intelligibility of her poems*

intelligible = **understandable**, clear, distinct, lucid, comprehensible • *She moaned faintly but made no intelligible response.*
OPPOSITES: unclear, incomprehensible, unintelligible

intemperate = **excessive**, extreme, over the top *(slang)*, wild, violent, severe, passionate, extravagant, uncontrollable, self-indulgent, unbridled, prodigal, unrestrained, tempestuous, profligate, inordinate, incontinent, ungovernable, immoderate, O.T.T. *(slang)* • *the unwisely intemperate language of the party chairman*
OPPOSITES: disciplined, moderate, temperate

intend 1 = **plan**, mean, aim, determine, scheme, propose, purpose, contemplate, envisage, foresee, be resolved *or* determined, have in mind *or* view • *She intends to do A levels and go to university.*
2 *often with* **for** = **destine**, mean, design, earmark, consign, aim, mark out, set apart • *This money is intended for the development of the tourist industry.*

intended AS AN ADJECTIVE = **planned**, proposed • *He hoped the sarcasm would have its intended effect.*
▸ AS A NOUN = **betrothed**, fiancé *or* fiancée, future wife *or* husband, husband- *or* wife-to-be • *Attention is turned to the Queen's youngest son and his intended.*

intense 1 = **extreme**, great, severe, fierce, serious *(informal)*, deep, powerful, concentrated, supreme, acute, harsh, intensive, excessive, profound, exquisite, drastic, forceful, protracted, unqualified, agonizing, mother of all *(informal)* • *He was sweating from the intense heat.*
OPPOSITES: moderate, mild, easy
2 = **fierce**, close, tough • *The battle for third place was intense.*
3 = **passionate**, burning, earnest, emotional, keen, flaming, consuming, fierce, eager, enthusiastic, heightened, energetic, animated, ardent, fanatical, fervent, heartfelt, impassioned, vehement, forcible, fervid • *She is more adult, and more intense than I had imagined.*
OPPOSITES: cool, casual, indifferent

intensely 1 = **very**, highly, extremely, greatly, strongly, severely, terribly, ultra, utterly, unusually, exceptionally, extraordinarily, markedly, awfully *(informal)*, acutely, exceedingly, excessively, inordinately, uncommonly, to the nth degree, to *or* in the extreme • *The fast-food business is intensely competitive.*
2 = **intently**, deeply, seriously *(informal)*, profoundly, passionately • *He sipped his drink, staring intensely at me.*

intensification = **increase**, rise, build-up, expansion, heightening, acceleration, escalation, upsurge, amplification • *the intensification of violent rebel attacks*

intensify 1 = **increase**, boost, raise, extend, concentrate, add to, strengthen, enhance, compound, reinforce, step up *(informal)*, emphasize, widen, heighten, sharpen, magnify, amplify, augment, redouble • *They are intensifying their efforts to secure the release of the hostages.*
OPPOSITES: weaken, lessen, decrease
2 = **escalate**, increase, extend, widen, heighten, deepen, quicken • *The conflict is almost bound to intensify.*

intensity 1 = **force**, power, strength, severity, extremity, fierceness • *The attack was anticipated, but its intensity came as a shock.*

2 = **passion**, emotion, fervour, force, power, fire, energy, strength, depth, concentration, excess, severity, vigour, potency, extremity, welly *(slang)*, fanaticism, ardour, vehemence, earnestness, keenness, fierceness, fervency, intenseness • *His intensity, and the ferocity of his feelings alarmed me.*

intensive = **concentrated**, thorough, exhaustive, full, demanding, detailed, complete, serious, concerted, intense, comprehensive, vigorous, all-out, in-depth, strenuous, painstaking, all-embracing, assiduous, thoroughgoing • *several days and nights of intensive negotiations*

intent AS AN ADJECTIVE = **absorbed**, focused, fixed, earnest, committed, concentrated, occupied, intense, fascinated, steady, alert, wrapped up, preoccupied, enthralled, attentive, watchful, engrossed, steadfast, rapt, enrapt • *She looked from one intent face to another.*
OPPOSITES: casual, indifferent
▸ AS A NOUN = **intention**, aim, purpose, meaning, end, plan, goal, design, target, object, resolution, resolve, objective, ambition, aspiration • *a statement of intent on arms control*
OPPOSITES: chance, fortune
▸ IN PHRASES: **intent on something** = **set on**, committed to, eager to, bent on, fixated on, hellbent on *(informal)*, insistent about, determined about, resolute about, inflexible about, resolved about • *The rebels are obviously intent on stepping up the pressure.*
to all intents and purposes = **in effect**, essentially, effectively, really, actually, in fact, virtually, in reality, in truth, in actuality, for practical purposes • *To all intents and purposes he was my father.*

intention = **aim**, plan, idea, goal, end, design, target, wish, scheme, purpose, desire, object, objective, determination, intent • *He announced his intention of standing for parliament.*

PROVERBS
The road to hell is paved with good intentions

intentional = **deliberate**, meant, planned, studied, designed, purposed, intended, calculated, wilful, premeditated, prearranged, done on purpose, preconcerted • *I can't blame him. It wasn't intentional.*
OPPOSITES: accidental, unintentional, unplanned

intentionally = **deliberately**, on purpose, wilfully, by design, designedly • *I've never intentionally hurt anyone.*

intently = **attentively**, closely, hard, keenly, steadily, fixedly, searchingly, watchfully • *He listened intently, then slammed down the phone.*

inter = **bury**, lay to rest, entomb, sepulchre, consign to the grave, inhume, inurn • *the spot where his bones were originally interred*

intercede = **mediate**, speak, plead, intervene, arbitrate, advocate, interpose • *He had occasionally tried to intercede for me.*

intercept = **catch**, take, stop, check, block, arrest, seize, cut off, interrupt, head off, deflect, obstruct • *Gunmen intercepted him on the way to the airport.*

intercession = **pleading**, prayer, intervention, plea, mediation, advocacy, solicitation, entreaty, good offices, supplication, karakia *(N.Z.)* • *Many claimed to have been cured as a result of her intercessions.*

interchange AS A NOUN = **exchange**, give and take, alternation, reciprocation • *the interchange of ideas from different disciplines*
▸ AS A VERB = **exchange**, switch, swap, alternate, trade, barter, reciprocate, bandy • *She likes to interchange furniture at home with stock from the shop.*

interchangeable = **identical**, the same, equivalent, synonymous, reciprocal, exchangeable, transposable, commutable • *His greatest innovation was the use of interchangeable parts.*

intercourse 1 = **sexual intercourse**, sex *(informal)*, lovemaking, the other *(informal)*, congress, fucking *(taboo)*, screwing *(taboo)*, intimacy, shagging *(Brit. taboo)*, sexual relations, sexual act, nookie *(slang)*, copulation, coitus, carnal knowledge, intimate relations, rumpy-pumpy *(slang)*, legover *(slang)*, coition, poontang *(taboo)*, rumpo *(slang)* • *I did not have intercourse with that woman.*
2 = **contact**, relationships, communication, association, relations, trade, traffic, connection, truck, commerce, dealings, correspondence, communion, converse, intercommunication • *There was social intercourse between the old and the young.*

interdict AS A VERB = **prohibit**, bar, ban, prevent, veto, forbid, outlaw, disallow, proscribe, debar, criminalize • *Troops could be ferried in to interdict drug shipments.*
▸ AS A NOUN = **ban**, veto, prohibition, taboo, disqualification, interdiction, disallowance, restraining order *(U.S. Law)* • *The National Trust has placed an interdict on jet-skis.*

interest AS A NOUN 1 = **importance**, concern, significance, moment, note, weight, import, consequence, substance, relevance, momentousness • *Food was of no interest to her at all.*
OPPOSITES: irrelevance, insignificance, worthlessness
2 = **attention**, regard, curiosity, notice, suspicion, scrutiny, heed, absorption, attentiveness, inquisitiveness, engrossment • *They will follow the political crisis with interest.*
OPPOSITES: disregard, boredom, coolness
3 *often plural* = **hobby**, activity, pursuit, entertainment, relaxation, recreation, amusement, preoccupation, diversion, pastime, leisure activity • *He developed a wide range of sporting interests.*
4 *often plural* = **advantage**, good, benefit, profit, gain, boot *(dialect)* • *Did the Directors act in the best interests of their club?*
5 *often plural* = **business**, concern, matter, affair • *The family controls large dairy interests.*
6 = **stake**, investment • *The West has an interest in promoting democratic forces.*
7 = **returns**, profits, dividends • *Does your current account pay interest?*
▸ AS A VERB 1 = **arouse your curiosity**, engage, appeal to, fascinate, move, involve, touch, affect, attract, grip, entertain, absorb, intrigue, amuse, divert, rivet, captivate, catch your eye, hold the attention of, engross • *This part of the book interests me in particular.*
OPPOSITES: bore, tire, weary
2 *with* **in** = **sell**, persuade to buy • *In the meantime, can I interest you in a new car?*
▸ IN PHRASES: **in the interest(s) of** = **for the sake of**, on behalf of, on the part of, to the advantage of • *We must all work together in the interest of national stability.*

interested 1 = **curious**, into *(informal)*, moved, affected, attracted, excited, drawn, keen, gripped, fascinated, stimulated, intent, responsive, riveted, captivated, attentive • *He did not look interested.*
OPPOSITES: bored, detached, uninterested
2 = **involved**, concerned, affected, prejudiced, biased, partial, partisan, implicated, predisposed • *All the interested parties finally agreed to the idea.*

interesting = **intriguing**, fascinating, absorbing, pleasing, appealing, attractive, engaging, unusual, gripping, stirring, entertaining, entrancing, stimulating, curious, compelling, amusing, compulsive, riveting, captivating, enthralling, beguiling, thought-provoking, engrossing, spellbinding • *It was interesting to be in a different environment.*
OPPOSITES: boring, dull, uninteresting

interface AS A NOUN = **connection**, link, boundary, border, frontier • *the interface between bureaucracy and the working world*

▸ **AS A VERB** = **connect**, couple, link, combine, join together • *the way we interface with the environment*

interfere AS A VERB = **meddle**, intervene, intrude, butt in, get involved, tamper, pry, encroach, intercede, stick your nose in *(informal)*, stick your oar in *(informal)*, poke your nose in *(informal)*, intermeddle, put your two cents in *(U.S. slang)* • *Stop interfering and leave me alone!*
▸ **IN PHRASES: interfere with someone** = **sexually abuse**, abuse, molest, assault, grope, sexually assault • *Will seeing a probation officer stop him interfering with children?*
interfere with something or someone = **conflict with**, affect, get in the way of, check, block, clash, frustrate, handicap, hamper, disrupt, cramp, inhibit, thwart, hinder, obstruct, impede, baulk, trammel, be a drag upon *(informal)* • *Drug problems frequently interfered with his work.*

interference 1 = **intrusion**, intervention, meddling, opposition, conflict, obstruction, prying, impedance, meddlesomeness, intermeddling • *They can now set up cheap fares without interference from the government.*
2 = **static**, feedback, disturbance, disruption, fuzz • *Users complained of interference and background noise.*

i

interfering = **meddling**, intrusive, prying, obtrusive, meddlesome, interruptive • *She regarded her mother as an interfering busybody.*

interim AS AN ADJECTIVE = **temporary**, provisional, makeshift, acting, passing, intervening, caretaker, improvised, transient, stopgap, pro tem • *an interim report*
▸ **AS A NOUN** = **interval**, meanwhile, meantime, respite, interregnum, entr'acte • *He was to remain in jail in the interim.*

interior AS A NOUN 1 = **inside**, centre, heart, middle, contents, depths, core, belly, nucleus, bowels, bosom, innards *(informal)* • *The boat's interior badly needed painting.*
2 = **heartland**, centre, hinterland, upcountry • *a 5-day hike into the interior*
▸ **AS AN ADJECTIVE 1** = **inside**, internal, inner • *He turned on the interior light and examined the map.*
OPPOSITES: outside, exterior, external
2 = **mental**, emotional, psychological, private, personal, secret, hidden, spiritual, intimate, inner, inward, instinctive, impulsive • *the interior life of human beings*
3 = **domestic**, home, national, civil, internal • *The French Interior Minister has intervened over the scandal.*

interject = **interrupt with**, put in, interpose, introduce, throw in, interpolate • *He listened thoughtfully, interjecting only the odd word.*

interjection = **exclamation**, cry, ejaculation, interpolation, interposition • *the insensitive interjections of the disc jockey*

interlaced = **interwoven**, intertwined, interlocked, crossed, knitted, braided, interspersed, plaited, entwined, twined, reticulated, interwreathed • *He sat with his eyes closed and his fingers interlaced.*

interlock 1 = **interweave**, intertwine, interlace, cross, knit, braid, intersperse, plait, entwine, twine, reticulate, interwreathe • *The parts interlock.*
2 = **connect**, unite, link, join, couple, relate, associate, combine, cohere • *The tragedies begin to interlock.*

interloper = **trespasser**, intruder, gate-crasher *(informal)*, uninvited guest, meddler, unwanted visitor, intermeddler • *She had no wish to share her father with any interloper.*

interlude = **interval**, break, spell, stop, rest, halt, episode, pause, respite, stoppage, breathing space, hiatus, intermission, entr'acte • *It was a happy interlude in her life.*

intermediary = **mediator**, agent, middleman, broker, entrepreneur, go-between • *She wanted him to act as an intermediary in the dispute.*

intermediate = **middle**, mid, halfway, in-between *(informal)*, midway, intervening, transitional, intermediary, median, interposed • *Consider breaking the journey with intermediate stopovers.*

interment = **burial**, burying, funeral, committal, entombment, inhumation, sepulture • *As soon as the interment ended she walked over to him.*

interminable = **endless**, long, never-ending, dragging, unlimited, infinite, perpetual, protracted, limitless, boundless, everlasting, ceaseless, long-winded, long-drawn-out, immeasurable, wearisome, unbounded • *an interminable meeting*
OPPOSITES: limited, bounded, restricted

intermingle = **mix**, combine, blend, merge, fuse, amalgamate, interweave, meld, interlace, commingle, intermix, commix • *The two cultures intermingle without losing their identity.*

intermission = **interval**, break, pause, stop, rest, suspension, recess, interruption, respite, lull, stoppage, interlude, cessation, let-up *(informal)*, breathing space, entr'acte • *Drinks were served during the intermission.*

intermittent = **periodic**, broken, occasional, recurring, irregular, punctuated, sporadic, recurrent, stop-go *(informal)*, fitful, spasmodic, discontinuous • *After three hours of intermittent rain, the game was abandoned.*
OPPOSITES: steady, continuous, unceasing

intern AS A VERB = **imprison**, hold, confine, detain, hold in custody • *He was interned as an enemy at the outbreak of the war.*
▸ **AS A NOUN** = **apprentice**, student, pupil, novice, beginner, trainee, learner, tyro, probationer • *She was head nurse at the hospital where I worked as an intern.*

internal 1 = **domestic**, home, national, local, civic, in-house, intramural • *The country stepped up internal security.*
2 = **inner**, inside, interior • *Some of the internal walls are made of plasterboard.*
OPPOSITES: outside, external, outer
3 = **emotional**, mental, private, secret, subjective • *The personal, internal battle is beautifully portrayed.*
OPPOSITES: revealed, exposed, unconcealed

international = **global**, world, worldwide, universal, cosmopolitan, planetary, intercontinental • *an international agreement against exporting arms to that country*

internecine = **destructive**, bloody, deadly, fatal, mortal, exterminating, ruinous, exterminatory • *The episode has turned attention to the internecine strife here.*

internet IN PHRASES: the Internet = **the information superhighway**, the net *(informal)*, the web *(informal)*, the World Wide Web, cyberspace, blogosphere • *He buys most of his books on the Internet.*
▹ *See panels* **Internet domain names; Internet terms**

interplay = **interaction**, give-and-take, reciprocity, reciprocation, meshing • *the interplay between the entertainer and the public*

interpolate = **insert**, add, introduce, intercalate • *He interpolated a lot of spurious matter into the manuscript.*

interpolation = **insertion**, addition, aside, introduction, insert, interjection, intercalation • *The interpolation was inserted soon after the text was finished.*

interpose 1 = **intervene**, step in, interfere, intermediate, mediate, intrude, intercede, come *or* place between • *Police had to interpose themselves between the rival groups.*
2 = **interrupt**, insert, interject, put in, introduce • *'He rang me just now,' she interposed.*

interpret 1 = **take**, understand, read, explain, regard, construe • *The speech might be interpreted as a coded message.*
2 = **translate**, convert, paraphrase, adapt, transliterate • *She spoke little English, so her husband interpreted.*
3 = **explain**, define, clarify, spell out, make sense of, decode, decipher, expound, elucidate, throw light on, explicate • *The judge has to interpret the law as it's being passed.*
4 = **understand**, read, explain, crack, solve, figure out *(informal)*, comprehend, decode, deduce, decipher, suss out *(slang)* • *The pictures are often difficult to interpret.*

INTERNET TERMS

blog, blogger, *or* blogging	eBay *(trademark)*	leetspeak *or* 1337speak	RSS	URL *or* universe resource locator	weblog
bookmark	e-book	lurk	search engine	voip	webmail
broadband	FTP *or* ftp	message board	search engine optimization *or* SEO	VPN	webmaster
browse	Generation C	netiquette	Skype *(trademark)*	Web 2.0	webpage
browser	Google *(trademark)*	newsgroup	spam	web address	website
chatroom	hit	offline	spoofing	WebBoard	Wi-Fi
cookie	home page	online	surf	webcam	Yahoo *(trademark)*
domain name	hotpsot	podcast	upload	webcast	
download	ISP *or* Internet service provider	portal		web directory	

5 = portray, present, perform, render, depict, enact, act out • *Shakespeare, marvellously interpreted by Orson Welles*

interpretation 1 = explanation, meaning, reading, understanding, sense, analysis, construction, exposition, explication, elucidation, signification • *The Opposition put a different interpretation on the figures.*
2 = performance, portrayal, presentation, rendering, reading, execution, rendition, depiction • *her full-bodied interpretation of the role of Micaela*
3 = reading, study, review, version, analysis, explanation, examination, diagnosis, evaluation, exposition, exegesis, explication, elucidation • *the interpretation of the scriptures*
4 = understanding, meaning, reading, conclusion, assumption, inference, presumption, conjecture, supposition • *He was aware of the interpretation many put on his being at her home.*

interpreter 1 = translator, linguist, metaphrast, paraphrast • *Speaking through an interpreter, he said he was disappointed.*
2 = performer, player, presenter, exponent • *Freni is one of the supreme interpreters of Puccini's heroines.*

interrogate = question, ask, examine, investigate, pump, grill *(informal)*, quiz, cross-examine, cross-question, put the screws on *(informal)*, catechize, give (someone) the third degree *(informal)* • *I interrogated everyone who was even slightly involved.*

interrogation = questioning, inquiry, examination, probing, grilling *(informal)*, cross-examination, inquisition, third degree *(informal)*, cross-questioning • *the right to silence in police interrogations*

interrogative = questioning, curious, inquiring, inquisitive, quizzical, inquisitorial • *He cocked an interrogative eye at his companion.*

interrupt 1 = intrude, disturb, intervene, interfere (with), break in, heckle, butt in, barge in *(informal)*, break (someone's) train of thought • *'Sorry to interrupt, Colonel.'*
2 = suspend, break, stop, end, cut, stay, check, delay, cease, cut off, postpone, shelve, put off, defer, break off, adjourn, cut short, discontinue • *He has interrupted his holiday to return to London.*
3 = block, limit, restrict, cut off, obstruct, impede • *Our view was interrupted only by an occasional squall of pigeons.*

interrupted = disturbed, broken, incomplete, cut off, uneven, disconnected, intermittent, discontinuous • *He's had an interrupted training season.*

interruption 1 = disruption, break, halt, obstacle, disturbance, hitch, intrusion, obstruction, impediment, hindrance • *The sudden interruption stopped her in mid-flow.*
2 = stoppage, stop, pause, suspension, cessation, severance, hiatus, disconnection, discontinuance • *interruptions in the supply of food and fuel*

intersect = cross, meet, cut, divide, cut across, bisect, crisscross • *The centre of the city is intersected by the main waterways.*

intersection = junction, crossing, crossroads • *at the intersection of two main canals*

intersperse = scatter, sprinkle, intermix, pepper, interlard, bestrew • *They have interspersed historical scenes with modern ones.*

interspersed = scattered, sprinkled, intermixed, peppered, interlarded, bestrewed • *gunfire interspersed with single shots*

intertwine = interweave, entwine, interlace, cross, link, twist, braid, convolute, reticulate, interwreathe, inweave • *Trees and creepers intertwined, blocking our way.*

interval 1 = period, time, spell, term, season, space, stretch, pause, span • *There was a long interval of silence.*
2 = break, interlude, intermission, rest, gap, pause, respite, lull, entr'acte • *During the interval, wine was served.*
3 = delay, wait, gap, interim, hold-up, meanwhile, meantime, stoppage, hiatus • *the interval between her arrival and lunch*
4 = stretch, area, space, distance, gap • *figures separated by intervals of pattern and colour*

intervene 1 = step in *(informal)*, interfere, mediate, intrude, intercede, arbitrate, interpose, take a hand *(informal)* • *The situation calmed down when police intervened.*
2 = interrupt, involve yourself, put your oar in, interpose yourself, put your two cents in *(U.S. slang)* • *She intervened and told me to stop it.*
3 = happen, occur, take place, follow, succeed, arise, ensue, befall, materialize, come to pass, supervene • *The mailboat comes weekly unless bad weather intervenes.*

intervention = mediation, involvement, interference, intrusion, arbitration, conciliation, intercession, interposition, agency • *the country's intervention in the internal affairs of others*

interventionist = meddling, interfering, intrusive, obtrusive, meddlesome, interruptive • *interventionist industrial policy*

interview ᴀꜱ ᴀ ɴᴏᴜɴ **1 = meeting**, examination, evaluation, oral (examination), interrogation • *When I went for my first job interview I arrived extremely early.*
2 = audience, talk, conference, exchange, dialogue, consultation, press conference • *There'll be an interview with the Chancellor after the break.*
▸ **AS A VERB 1 = examine**, talk to, sound out • *He was among three candidates interviewed for the job.*
2 = question, interrogate, examine, investigate, ask, pump, grill *(informal)*, quiz, cross-examine, cross-question, put the screws on *(informal)*, catechize, give (someone) the third degree *(informal)* • *The police interviewed the driver, but they had no evidence to go on.*

interviewer = questioner, reporter, investigator, examiner, interrogator, interlocutor • *The interviewer did his best to get the truth out of her.*

interweave = intertwine, blend, cross, braid, splice, crisscross, interlace, reticulate, interwreathe, inweave • *The programme successfully interweaves words and pictures.*

interwoven = interconnected, connected, blended, knit, interlocked, entwined, intermingled, interlaced, inmixed • *a necklace of jet interwoven with mother-of-pearl*

INTERNET DOMAIN NAMES

Abbreviation	Top-level domain (TLD)	Abbreviation	Top-level domain (TLD)
.aero	Air-transport industry	.info	General use
.arpa	Internet infrastructure	.int	International organization
.biz	Business	.mil	US military
.co	Commercial company (used with country)	.museum	Museum
.com	Commercial company	.name	Individual user
.coop	Cooperative	.net	Company *or* organization
.edu	Educational establishment	.org	Organization, usually nonprofit
.eu	European Union	.pro	Professionals (accountants, lawyers, etc)
.gov	US government organization		

Abbreviation	Country TLDs	Abbreviation	Country TLDs	Abbreviation	Country TLDs
.ac	Ascension Island	.cr	Costa Rica	.id	Indonesia
.ad	Andorra	.cu	Cuba	.ie	Ireland
.ae	United Arab Emirates	.cv	Cap Verde	.il	Israel
.af	Afghanistan	.cx	Christmas Island	.im	Isle of Man
.ag	Antigua and Barbuda	.cy	Cyprus	.in	India
.ai	Anguilla	.cz	Czech Republic	.io	British Indian Ocean Territory
.al	Albania	.de	Germany	.iq	Iraq
.am	Armenia	.dj	Dijibouti	.ir	Iran (Islamic Republic of)
.an	Netherlands Antilles	.dk	Denmark	.is	Iceland
.ao	Angola	.dm	Dominica	.it	Italy
.aq	Antarctica	.do	Dominican Republic	.je	Jersey
.ar	Argentina	.dz	Algeria	.jm	Jamaica
.as	American Samoa	.ec	Ecuador	.jo	Jordan
.at	Austria	.ee	Estonia	.jp	Japan
.au	Australia	.eg	Egypt	.ke	Kenya
.aw	Aruba	.eh	Western Sahara	.kg	Kyrgyzstan
.az	Azerbaijan	.er	Eritrea	.kh	Cambodia
.ba	Bosnia and Herzegovina	.es	Spain	.ki	Kiribati
.bb	Barbados	.et	Ethiopia	.km	Comoros
.bd	Bangladesh	.fi	Finland	.kn	Saint Kitts and Nevis
.be	Belgium	.fj	Fiji	.kp	Korea, Democratic People's Republic
.bf	Burkina Faso	.fk	Falkland Islands	.kr	Korea, Republic of
.bg	Bulgaria	.fm	Micronesia, Federal State of	.kw	Kuwait
.bh	Bahrain	.fo	Faroe Islands	.ky	Cayman Islands
.bi	Burundi	.fr	France	.kz	Kazakhstan
.bj	Benin	.ga	Gabon	.la	Lao People's Democratic Republic
.bm	Bermuda	.gd	Grenada	.lb	Lebanon
.bn	Brunei Darussalam	.ge	Georgia	.lc	Saint Lucia
.bo	Bolivia	.gf	French Guiana	.li	Liechtenstein
.br	Brazil	.gg	Guernsey	.lk	Sri Lanka
.bs	Bahamas	.gh	Ghana	.lr	Liberia
.bt	Bhutan	.gi	Gibraltar	.ls	Lesotho
.bv	Bouvet Island	.gl	Greenland	.lt	Lithuania
.bw	Botswana	.gm	Gambia	.lu	Luxembourg
.by	Belarus	.gn	Guinea	.lv	Latvia
.bz	Belize	.gp	Equatorial Guinea	.ly	Libyan Arab Jamahiriya
.ca	Canada	.gr	Greece	.ma	Morocco
.cc	Cocos (Keeling) Islands	.gs	South Georgia and the South Sandwich Islands	.mc	Monaco
.cd	Congo, Democratic Republic of the	.gt	Guatemala	.md	Moldova, Republic of
.cf	Central African Republic	.gu	Guam	.mg	Madagascar
.cg	Congo, Republic of	.gw	Guinea-Bissau	.mh	Marshall Islands
.ch	Switzerland	.gy	Guyana	.mk	Macedonia, Former Yugoslav Republic
.ci	Côte d'Ivoire	.hk	Hong Kong	.ml	Mali
.ck	Cook Islands	.hm	Heard and McDonald Islands	.mm	Myanmar
.cl	Chile	.hn	Honduras		
.cm	Cameroon	.hr	Croatia/Hrvatska		
.cn	China	.ht	Haiti		
.co	Colombia	.hu	Hungary		

INTERNET DOMAIN NAMES (CONTINUED)

Abbreviation	Country TLDs	Abbreviation	Country TLDs	Abbreviation	Country TLDs
.mn	Mongolia	.ps	Palestinian	.tk	Tokelau
.mo	Macau		Territories	.tm	Turkmenistan
.mp	Northern Mariana	.pt	Portugal	.tn	Tunisia
	Islands	.pw	Palau	.to	Tongo
.mq	Martinique	.py	Paraguay	.tp	East Timor
.mr	Mauritania	.qa	Qatar	.tr	Turkey
.ms	Montserrat	.re	Reunion Island	.tt	Trinidad and Tobago
.mt	Malta	.ro	Romania	.tv	Tuvalu
.mu	Mauritius	.ru	Russian Federation	.tw	Taiwan
.mv	Maldives	.rw	Rwanda	.tz	Tanzania
.mw	Malawi	.sa	Saudi Arabia	.ua	Ukraine
.mx	Mexico	.sb	Soloman Islands	.ug	Uganda
.my	Malaysia	.sc	Seychelles	.uk	United Kingdom
.mz	Mozambique	.sd	Sudan	.um	US Minor Outlying
.na	Namibia	.se	Sweden		Islands
.nc	New Caledonia	.sg	St. Helena	.us	United States
.ne	Niger	.si	Slovenia	.uy	Uruguay
.nf	Norfolk Island	.sj	Svalbard and Jan	.uz	Uzbekistan
.ng	Nigeria		Mayen Islands	.va	Holy See (City
.ni	Nicaragua	.sk	Slovak Republic		Vatican State)
.nl	Netherlands	.sl	Sierra Leone	.vc	Saint Vincent and
.no	Norway	.sm	San Marino		the Grenadines
.np	Nepal	.sn	Senegal	.ve	Venezuela
.nr	Nauru	.so	Somalia	.vg	Virgin Islands
.nu	Niue	.sr	Suriname		(British)
.nz	New Zealand	.st	Sao Tome and	.vi	Virgin Islands (USA)
.om	Oman		Principe	.vn	Vietnam
.pa	Panama	.sv	El Salvador	.vu	Vanuatu
.pe	Peru	.sy	Syrian Arab Republic	.wf	Wallis and Futuna
.pf	French Polynesia	.sz	Swaziland		Islands
.pg	Papua New Guinea	.tc	Turks and Caicos	.ws	Western Samoa
.ph	Philippines		Islands	.ye	Yemen
.pk	Pakistan	.td	Chad	.yt	Mayotte
.pl	Poland	.tf	French Southern	.yu	Yugoslavia
.pm	St. Pierre and		Territories	.za	South Africa
	Miquelon	.tg	Togo	.zm	Zambia
.pn	Pitcairn Island	.th	Thailand	.zw	Zimbabwe
.pr	Puerto Rico	.tj	Tajikistan		

intestinal = **abdominal**, visceral, duodenal, gut *(informal)*, inner, coeliac, stomachic • *The intestinal tract is examined with a special viewing device.*

intestine *usu pl* = **guts**, insides *(informal)*, bowels, internal organs, innards *(informal)*, entrails, vitals • *This vitamin is absorbed through the walls of the small intestine.*
▸ **TECHNICAL NAME:** viscera
▸ **RELATED ADJECTIVE:** alvine

intimacy 1 = **familiarity**, closeness, understanding, confidence, confidentiality, fraternization • *a means of achieving intimacy with another person*
OPPOSITES: distance, separation, aloofness
2 = **sexual intercourse**, sex *(informal)*, lovemaking, the other *(informal)*, congress, fucking *(taboo)*, screwing *(taboo)*, shagging *(Brit. taboo)*, sexual relations, sexual act, nookie *(slang)*, copulation, coitus, carnal knowledge, intimate relations, rumpy-pumpy *(slang)*, legover *(slang)*, coition, poontang *(taboo)*, rumpo *(slang)* • *The truth was he did not feel like intimacy with any woman.*

intimate[1] **AS AN ADJECTIVE** 1 = **close**, dear, loving, near, warm, friendly, familiar, thick *(informal)*, devoted, confidential, cherished, bosom, inseparable, nearest and dearest • *I discussed this only with my intimate friends.*
OPPOSITES: remote, distant, superficial
2 = **sexual**, romantic, private, sexy, erotic, sensual, carnal, of the flesh, coital • *their intimate moments with their boyfriends*
3 = **private**, personal, confidential, special, individual, particular, secret, exclusive, privy • *He wrote about the intimate details of his family life.*
OPPOSITES: known, open, public
4 = **detailed**, minute, full, experienced, personal, deep, particular, specific, immediate, comprehensive, exact, elaborate, profound, penetrating, thorough, in-depth, intricate, first-hand, exhaustive • *He surprised me with his intimate knowledge of the situation.*
5 = **cosy**, relaxed, friendly, informal, harmonious, snug, comfy *(informal)*, warm • *an intimate candlelit dinner for two*
▸ **AS A NOUN** = **friend**, close friend, buddy *(informal)*, mate *(informal)*, pal, comrade, chum *(informal)*, mucker *(Brit. slang)*, crony, main man *(slang, chiefly U.S.)*, china *(Brit. slang)*, homeboy *(slang, chiefly U.S.)*, cobber *(Austral. & N.Z. old-fashioned informal)*, bosom friend, familiar, confidant or confidante, (constant) companion, E hoa *(N.Z.)* • *They are to have an autumn wedding, an intimate of the couple confides.*
OPPOSITES: enemy, stranger, foe

intimate[2] 1 = **suggest**, indicate, hint, imply, warn, allude, let it be known, insinuate, give (someone) to understand, drop a hint, tip (someone) the wink *(Brit. informal)* • *He intimated that he was contemplating leaving the company.*

2 = **announce**, state, declare, communicate, impart, make known • *He had intimated to them his readiness to come to a settlement.*

intimately 1 = **closely**, very well, personally, warmly, familiarly, tenderly, affectionately, confidentially, confidingly • *You have to be willing to get to know your partner intimately.*
2 = **fully**, very well, thoroughly, in detail, inside out, to the core, through and through • *a golden age of musicians whose work she knew intimately*

intimation 1 = **hint**, warning, suggestion, indication, allusion, inkling, insinuation • *I did not have any intimation that he was going to resign.*
2 = **announcement**, notice, communication, declaration • *their first public intimation of how they will spend the budget*

intimidate = **frighten**, pressure, threaten, alarm, scare, terrify, cow, bully, plague, menace, hound, awe, daunt, harass, subdue, oppress, persecute, lean on *(informal)*, coerce, overawe, scare off *(informal)*, terrorize, pressurize, browbeat, twist someone's arm *(informal)*, tyrannize, dishearten, dispirit, scare the bejesus out of *(informal)*, affright *(archaic)*, domineer • *Attempts to intimidate people into voting for them failed.*

intimidated = **frightened**, afraid, alarmed, scared, terrified, cowed, unnerved, petrified, panicky, terrorized, in a panic, scared stiff, in a cold sweat, abashed, scared shitless *(taboo)*, terror-stricken, shit-scared *(taboo)*, affrighted *(archaic)*, in fear and trepidation, numb with fear • *Women can come in here and not feel intimidated.*

intimidating = **frightening**, alarming, terrifying, menacing, dismaying, scary *(informal)*, daunting, fearsome, unnerving, spooky *(informal)*, hair-raising, baleful, bloodcurdling • *He was a huge, intimidating figure.*

intimidation = **bullying**, pressure, threat(s), menaces, coercion, arm-twisting *(informal)*, browbeating, terrorization • *an inquiry into allegations of intimidation*

intolerable = **unbearable**, insufferable, unendurable, impossible, painful, excruciating, insupportable, beyond bearing, not to be borne, more than flesh and blood can stand • *They felt this would place intolerable pressure on them.*
OPPOSITES: tolerable, bearable, supportable

intolerance 1 = **narrow-mindedness**, discrimination, prejudice, racism, bigotry, xenophobia, chauvinism, fanaticism, narrowness, jingoism, racialism, dogmatism, illiberality • *an act of religious intolerance*
OPPOSITES: tolerance, open-mindedness, liberality
2 = **sensitivity**, allergy, susceptibility, antipathy, hypersensitivity • *a blood test which shows food intolerance*

intolerant 1 = **narrow-minded**, prejudiced, bigoted, narrow, racist, one-sided, fanatical, dictatorial, dogmatic, xenophobic, chauvinistic, small-minded, illiberal, uncharitable, racialist • *intolerant attitudes towards non-Catholics*
OPPOSITES: liberal, tolerant, open-minded
2 = **sensitive**, affected by, susceptible, allergic, sensitized, hypersensitive • *babies who are intolerant to cows' milk*

intonation 1 = **tone**, inflection, cadence, modulation, accentuation • *His voice had a very slight German intonation.*
2 = **incantation**, spell, charm, formula, chant, invocation, hex *(U.S. & Canad. informal)*, conjuration • *They could hear strange music and chanting intonations.*

intone = **chant**, sing, recite, croon, intonate • *He quietly intoned several prayers.*

in toto = **completely**, totally, entirely, as a whole, wholly, uncut, in its entirety, unabridged • *his corpse was interred in toto in a crypt*

intoxicate 1 = **go to your head**, inebriate, stupefy, befuddle, fuddle, put (someone) under the table *(informal)* • *He drank enough lager to intoxicate an army base.*
2 = **exhilarate**, excite, stimulate, inflame, go to your head, make your head spin, elate • *Their power intoxicated them.*

intoxicated 1 = **drunk**, tight *(informal)*, smashed *(slang)*, pissed *(Brit., Austral. & N.Z. slang)*, canned *(slang)*, high *(informal)*, cut *(Brit. slang)*, flying *(slang)*, bombed *(slang)*, stoned *(slang)*, wasted *(slang)*, hammered *(slang)*, steaming *(slang)*, wrecked *(slang)*, stiff *(slang)*, out of it *(slang)*, plastered *(slang)*, drunken, blitzed *(slang)*, lit up *(slang)*, stewed *(slang)*, under the influence, tipsy, legless *(informal)*, paralytic *(informal)*, sozzled *(informal)*, steamboats *(Scot.)*, blatted *(Brit. slang)*, boozed-up *(informal)*, dronkverdriet *(S. African)*, elephants *(Austral. slang)*, broken *(S. African informal)*, boozed-up *(slang)*, kaylied *(Brit. slang)*, langered *(Irish slang)*, lashed *(Brit. slang)*, mashed *(Brit. slang)*, mullered *(slang)*, ossified *(Irish slang)*, sat *(S. African)*, stukkend *(S. African slang)*, trashed *(slang)*, off your face *(slang)*, zonked *(slang)*, blotto *(slang)*, fuddled, the worse for drink, inebriated, out to it *(Austral. & N.Z. slang)*, drunk as a skunk, in your cups *(informal)*, rat-arsed *(taboo)*, Brahms and Liszt *(slang)*, half seas over *(Brit. informal)*, bevvied *(dialect)*, three sheets in the wind *(informal)*, babalas *(S. African)* • *He appeared intoxicated, police said.*
2 = **euphoric**, excited, exhilarated, high *(informal)*, sent *(slang)*, stimulated, dizzy, ecstatic, elated, infatuated, enraptured • *They had become intoxicated by their success.*

intoxicating 1 = **alcoholic**, strong, intoxicant, spirituous, inebriant • *intoxicating liquor*
2 = **exciting**, thrilling, stimulating, sexy *(informal)*, heady, exhilarating • *The music is pulsating and the atmosphere intoxicating.*

intoxication 1 = **drunkenness**, inebriation, tipsiness, inebriety, insobriety • *Intoxication interferes with memory and thinking.*
2 = **excitement**, euphoria, elation, exhilaration, infatuation, delirium, exaltation • *the intoxication of greed and success*

intractable 1 = **difficult**, contrary, awkward, wild, stubborn, perverse, wayward, unruly, uncontrollable, wilful, incurable, fractious, unyielding, obstinate, intransigent, headstrong, unmanageable, undisciplined, cantankerous, unbending, obdurate, uncooperative, stiff-necked, ungovernable, self-willed, refractory, obstreperous, pig-headed, bull-headed • *How can we reduce the influence of intractable opponents?*
2 = **unmanageable**, difficult, insoluble, out of hand, unruly, uncontrollable • *The economy still faces intractable problems.*

intransigent = **uncompromising**, intractable, tough, stubborn, hardline, tenacious, unyielding, obstinate, immovable, unbending, obdurate, stiff-necked, inflexible, unbudgeable • *The worry is that the radicals will grow more intransigent.*
OPPOSITES: compromising, flexible, compliant

intrenched *see* **entrenched**

intrepid = **fearless**, brave, daring, bold, heroic, game *(informal)*, have-a-go *(informal)*, courageous, stalwart, resolute, gallant, audacious, valiant, plucky, doughty, undaunted, unafraid, unflinching, nerveless, dauntless, lion-hearted, valorous, stouthearted, (as) game as Ned Kelly *(Austral. slang)* • *an intrepid space traveller*
OPPOSITES: afraid, fearful, cowardly

intricacy = **complexity**, involvement, complication, elaborateness, obscurity, entanglement, convolutions, involution, intricateness, knottiness • *Garments are priced according to the intricacy of the work.*

intricate = **complicated**, involved, complex, difficult, fancy, sophisticated, elaborate, obscure, tangled, baroque, perplexing, tortuous, Byzantine, convoluted, rococo, knotty, labyrinthine, daedal *(literary)* • *intricate patterns and motifs*
OPPOSITES: simple, plain, straightforward

intrigue AS A NOUN 1 = **plot**, scheme, conspiracy, manoeuvre, manipulation, collusion, ruse, trickery, cabal,

stratagem, double-dealing, chicanery, sharp practice, wile, knavery, machination • *the plots and intrigues in the novel*
2 = **affair**, romance, intimacy, liaison, amour • *She detected her husband in an intrigue with a prostitute.*
▸ **AS A VERB** 1 = **interest**, fascinate, arouse the curiosity of, attract, charm, rivet, titillate, pique, tickle your fancy • *The novelty of the situation intrigued him.*
2 = **plot**, scheme, manoeuvre, conspire, connive, machinate • *The main characters spend their time intriguing for control.*

intrigued = **interested**, keen, fascinated, curious, excited • *I would be intrigued to hear others' views.*

intriguing = **interesting**, fascinating, absorbing, exciting, engaging, gripping, stirring, stimulating, curious, compelling, amusing, diverting, provocative, beguiling, thought-provoking, titillating, engrossing, tantalizing • *This intriguing book is both thoughtful and informative.*

intrinsic = **essential**, real, true, central, natural, basic, radical, native, genuine, fundamental, constitutional, built-in, underlying, inherent, elemental, congenital, inborn, inbred • *Diamonds have little intrinsic value.*
OPPOSITES: added, acquired, extrinsic

intrinsically = **essentially**, basically, fundamentally, constitutionally, as such, in itself, at heart, by definition, per se • *Are people intrinsically good or evil?*

introduce **AS A VERB** 1 = **bring in**, establish, set up, start, begin, found, develop, launch, institute, organize, pioneer, initiate, originate, commence, get going, instigate, phase in, usher in, inaugurate, set in motion, bring into being • *The Government has introduced a number of other money-saving ideas.*
2 = **present**, acquaint, make known, familiarize, do the honours, make the introduction • *Someone introduced us and I sat next to him.*
3 = **announce**, present, open, launch, precede, lead into, preface, lead off • *'Health Matters' is introduced by Dick Oliver on the World Service.*
4 = **suggest**, offer, air, table, advance, propose, recommend, float, submit, bring up, put forward, set forth, ventilate, broach, moot • *She does not abandon her responsibility to introduce new ideas.*
5 = **add**, insert, inject, throw in *(informal)*, infuse, interpose, interpolate • *I wish to introduce a note of cool reason to the discussion.*
6 = **insert**, put in, add, drive, shoot, feed, inject • *An operation can introduce air into the body.*
▸ **IN PHRASES: introduce someone to something** *or* **someone** = **acquaint with**, enlighten to, bring into contact with, familiarize with • *He introduced us to the delights of natural food.*

introduction 1 = **launch**, institution, establishment, start, opening, beginning, pioneering, presentation, initiation, inauguration, induction, commencement, instigation • *He is remembered for the introduction of the moving assembly line.*
OPPOSITES: completion, elimination, termination
2 = **presentation**, meeting, audience, formality • *With considerable shyness she performed the introductions.*
3 = **opening**, prelude, preface, lead-in, preliminaries, overture, preamble, foreword, prologue, intro *(informal)*, commencement, opening remarks, proem, opening passage, prolegomena, prolegomenon, exordium • *In her introduction to the book she provides a summary of the ideas.*
OPPOSITES: end, conclusion, epilogue
4 = **debut**, initiation, inauguration, baptism, first acquaintance • *His introduction to League football could have been easier.*
5 = **description**, report, account, explanation, outline, sketch • *The book is a friendly, helpful introduction to physics.*
6 = **insertion**, addition, injection, interpolation • *the introduction of air bubbles into the veins*
OPPOSITES: withdrawal, removal, extraction

introductory 1 = **preliminary**, elementary, first, early, initial, inaugural, preparatory, initiatory, prefatory, precursory • *an introductory course in religion and theology*
OPPOSITES: last, closing, concluding
2 = **starting**, opening, initial, early • *out on the shelves at an introductory price of £2.99*

introspection = **self-examination**, brooding, self-analysis, navel-gazing *(slang)*, introversion, heart-searching • *He had always had his moments of quiet introspection.*

introspective = **inward-looking**, introverted, brooding, contemplative, meditative, subjective, pensive, inner-directed • *I'm very introspective and shy; terribly so.*

introverted = **introspective**, withdrawn, inward-looking, self-contained, self-centred, indrawn, inner-directed • *He was a lonely, introverted child.*

intrude **AS A VERB** = **butt in**, encroach, push in, obtrude, thrust yourself in *or* forward, put your two cents in *(U.S. slang)* • *He kept intruding with personal questions.*
▸ **IN PHRASES: intrude on something** *or* **someone**
1 = **interfere with**, interrupt, impinge on, encroach on, meddle with, infringe on • *It's annoying when unforeseen events intrude on your day.*
2 = **trespass on**, invade, infringe on, obtrude on • *They intruded on to the field of play.*

intruder = **trespasser**, burglar, invader, squatter, prowler, interloper, infiltrator, gate-crasher *(informal)* • *He disturbed an intruder in the farmhouse.*

intrusion 1 = **interruption**, interference, infringement, trespass, encroachment • *I hope you don't mind this intrusion.*
2 = **invasion**, breach, infringement, infiltration, encroachment, infraction, usurpation • *I felt it was a grotesque intrusion into our lives.*

intrusive 1 = **interfering**, disturbing, invasive, unwanted, presumptuous, uncalled-for, importunate • *The cameras were not an intrusive presence.*
2 = **pushy** *(informal)*, forward, interfering, unwanted, impertinent, nosy *(informal)*, officious, meddlesome • *Her bodyguards were less than gentle with intrusive journalists.*
3 = **personal**, forward, prying, impertinent, offensive, unwanted, nosy *(informal)* • *She faced intrusive questions about her sexual past.*

intrust *see* **entrust**

intuition 1 = **instinct**, perception, insight, sixth sense, discernment • *Her intuition was telling her that something was wrong.*
2 = **feeling**, idea, impression, suspicion, hunch, premonition, inkling, presentiment • *You can't make a case on intuitions, you know.*

intuitive = **instinctive**, spontaneous, innate, involuntary, instinctual, untaught, unreflecting, hard-wired • *A positive pregnancy test soon confirmed her intuitive feelings.*

intuitively = **instinctively**, automatically, spontaneously, involuntarily, innately, instinctually • *He seemed to know intuitively that I must be missing her.*

intwine *see* **entwine**

inundate 1 = **overwhelm**, flood, swamp, engulf, overflow, overrun, glut • *Her office was inundated with requests for tickets.*
2 = **flood**, engulf, submerge, drown, overflow, immerse, deluge • *Their neighbourhood is being inundated by the rising waters.*

inundation 1 = **flood**, overflow, torrent, deluge, tidal wave • *They moved furniture from houses threatened with imminent inundation.*
2 = **onslaught**, flood, torrent, tidal wave, charge, attack, assault, offensive, blitz, onset, onrush • *He was faced with an inundation of lawsuits.*

inured = **accustomed**, hardened, toughened, trained, strengthened, tempered, familiarized, habituated, desensitized, case-hardened, annealed • *Doctors become inured to death.*

invade 1 = **attack**, storm, assault, capture, occupy, seize, raid, overwhelm, violate, conquer, overrun, annex, march into, assail, descend upon, infringe on, burst in on, make inroads on • *In 1944 the allies invaded the Italian mainland.*
2 = **infest**, swarm, overrun, flood, infect, ravage, beset, pervade, permeate, overspread • *Every so often the kitchen would be invaded by ants.*
3 = **intrude on**, disturb, interrupt, violate, disrupt, encroach on, trespass on, infringe on, burst in on, obtrude on • *I don't want to invade your privacy, but this is my job.*
4 = **penetrate**, enter, probe, pervade, permeate • *She felt that he had invaded her whole subconscious.*

invader = **attacker**, raider, plunderer, aggressor, looter, trespasser • *The invaders were finally crushed in June 1719.*

invalid[1] AS A NOUN = **patient**, sufferer, convalescent, valetudinarian • *I hate being treated as an invalid.*
▸ AS AN ADJECTIVE = **disabled**, challenged, ill, sick, poorly (*informal*), weak, ailing, frail, feeble, sickly, infirm, bedridden, valetudinarian • *I have an invalid wife and am labelled as a carer.*

invalid[2] 1 = **null and void**, void, worthless, untrue, null, not binding, inoperative, nugatory • *The trial was stopped and the results declared invalid.*
OPPOSITES: valid, operative, viable
2 = **unfounded**, false, untrue, illogical, irrational, unsound, unscientific, baseless, fallacious, ill-founded • *Those arguments are rendered invalid by the hard facts.*
OPPOSITES: valid, sound, true

invalidate 1 = **nullify**, cancel, annul, undermine, weaken, overthrow, undo, quash, overrule, rescind, abrogate, render null and void • *An official decree invalidated the vote.*
OPPOSITES: validate, sanction, authorize
2 = **disprove**, refute, negate, discredit, contradict, rebut, give the lie to, make a nonsense of, prove false, blow out of the water (*slang*), controvert, confute • *Neither point invalidates my argument.*

invalidity = **falsity**, fallacy, unsoundness, inconsistency, irrationality, illogicality, speciousness, sophism, fallaciousness • *He brushed aside claims about the invalidity of a means test.*

invaluable = **precious**, valuable, priceless, costly, inestimable, beyond price, worth your *or* its weight in gold • *Their advice was invaluable to me at that stage of my work.*
OPPOSITES: cheap, worthless, valueless

invariable = **regular**, set, fixed, constant, uniform, consistent, rigid, inflexible, unchanging, immutable, unwavering, unfailing, unalterable, unchangeable, unvarying, changeless • *It was his invariable custom to have one whisky before supper.*
OPPOSITES: variable, changing, varying

invariably = **always**, regularly, constantly, every time, inevitably, repeatedly, consistently, ever, continually, aye (*Scot.*), eternally, habitually, perpetually, without exception, customarily, unfailingly, on every occasion, unceasingly, twenty-four-seven (*informal*), day in, day out • *They almost invariably get it wrong.*

invasion 1 = **attack**, assault, capture, takeover, raid, offensive, occupation, conquering, seizure, onslaught, foray, appropriation, sortie, annexation, incursion, expropriation, inroad, irruption, arrogation • *seven years after the Roman invasion of Britain*
2 = **flood**, flow, rush, arrival, influx, convergence, inflow, incursion, inundation, inrush • *Seaside resorts are preparing for an invasion of tourists.*
3 = **intrusion**, breach, violation, disturbance, disruption, infringement, overstepping, infiltration, encroachment, infraction, usurpation • *Is reading a child's diary a gross invasion of privacy?*

invective = **abuse**, censure, tirade, reproach, berating, denunciation, diatribe, vilification, tongue-lashing, billingsgate, vituperation, castigation, obloquy, contumely, philippic(s), revilement • *A woman had hurled racist invective at the family.*

inveigh against = **condemn**, denounce, censure, reproach, berate, castigate, rail at, blame, tongue-lash, upbraid, lambast(e), expostulate, excoriate, sound off at, recriminate, vituperate • *A lot of his writings inveigh against luxury and riches.*

inveigle = **coax**, persuade, lure, manipulate, manoeuvre, seduce, entice, lead on, beguile, allure, cajole, ensnare, bamboozle (*informal*), entrap, wheedle, sweet-talk (*informal*) • *She inveigles him into a plot to swindle the old lady.*

invent 1 = **create**, make, produce, develop, design, discover, imagine, manufacture, generate, come up with (*informal*), coin, devise, conceive, originate, formulate, spawn, contrive, improvise, dream up (*informal*), concoct, think up • *He invented the first electric clock.*
2 = **make up**, devise, concoct, forge, fake, fabricate, feign, falsify, cook up (*informal*), trump up • *I stood there, trying to invent a plausible excuse.*

invention 1 = **creation**, machine, device, design, development, instrument, discovery, innovation, gadget, brainchild (*informal*), contraption, contrivance • *It's been tricky marketing his new invention.*
2 = **development**, design, production, setting up, foundation, construction, constitution, creation, discovery, introduction, establishment, pioneering, formation, innovation, conception, masterminding, formulation, inception, contrivance, origination • *fifty years after the invention of the printing press*
3 = **fiction**, story, fantasy, lie, yarn, fabrication, concoction, falsehood, fib (*informal*), untruth, urban myth, prevarication, tall story (*informal*), urban legend, figment *or* product of (someone's) imagination • *The story was undoubtedly pure invention.*
4 = **creativity**, vision, imagination, initiative, enterprise, inspiration, genius, brilliance, ingenuity, originality, inventiveness, resourcefulness, creativeness, ingeniousness, imaginativeness • *powers of invention and mathematical ability*

inventive = **creative**, original, innovative, imaginative, gifted, inspired, fertile, ingenious, ground-breaking, resourceful • *It inspired me to be more inventive with my cooking.*
OPPOSITES: pedestrian, trite, uninspired

inventiveness = **creativity**, vision, initiative, enterprise, imagination, inspiration, genius, invention, brilliance, ingenuity, originality, resourcefulness, creativeness, ingeniousness, imaginativeness • *He has surprised us before with his inventiveness.*

inventor = **creator**, father, maker, author, framer, designer, architect, coiner, originator • *the inventor of the telephone*

inventory = **list**, record, catalogue, listing, account, roll, file, schedule, register, description, log, directory, tally, roster, stock book • *He made an inventory of everything that was to stay.*

inverse AS AN ADJECTIVE 1 = **opposite**, reverse, reversed, contrary, inverted, converse, transposed • *The tension grew in inverse proportion to the distance from their destination.*
2 = **reverse**, opposite, reversed, inverted, transposed • *The hologram can be flipped to show the inverse image.*
▸ AS A NOUN = **converse**, opposite, reverse, contrary, contradiction, antithesis • *There is no sign that you bothered to consider the inverse of your logic.*

inversion = **reversal**, opposite, antithesis, transposition, contrary, contrariety, contraposition, transposal, antipode • *a strange inversion of priorities*

invert = **overturn**, upturn, turn upside down, upset, reverse, capsize, transpose, introvert, turn inside out, turn turtle, invaginate (*Pathology*), overset, intussuscept (*Pathology*) • *Invert the cake onto a cooling rack.*

invertebrate
▷ *See panels* **Crustaceans; Invertebrates; Snails, slugs and other gastropods; Spiders and other arachnids**

invest AS A VERB **1 = spend**, expend, advance, venture, put in, devote, lay out, sink in, use up, plough in • *When people buy houses they're investing a lot of money.*
2 = charge, fill, steep, saturate, endow, pervade, infuse, imbue, suffuse, endue • *The buildings are invested with a nations's history.*
3 = empower, provide, charge, sanction, license, authorize, vest • *The constitution had invested him with certain powers.*
4 = install, establish, ordain, crown, inaugurate, anoint, consecrate, adopt, induct, enthrone, instate • *He was invested as a paramount chief of a district tribe.*
▸ IN PHRASES: **invest in something = buy**, get, purchase, score *(slang)*, pay for, obtain, acquire, procure • *Why don't you invest in an ice cream machine?*

investigate = examine, study, research, consider, go into, explore, search for, analyse, look into, inspect, look over, sift, probe into, work over, scrutinize, inquire into, make inquiries about, enquire into • *Gas officials are investigating the cause of the explosion.*

investigation = examination, study, inquiry, hearing, research, review, search, survey, analysis, probe, inspection, exploration, scrutiny, inquest, fact finding, recce *(slang)* • *He ordered an investigation into the affair.*

investigative = fact-finding, researching, investigating, research, inspecting • *an investigative reporter*

investigator = examiner, researcher, inspector, monitor, detective, analyser, explorer, reviewer, scrutinizer, checker, inquirer, scrutineer • *'She was badly beaten,' said one investigator.*

investiture = installation, ordination, inauguration, investment, investing, admission, induction, enthronement, instatement • *Edward VIII's investiture as Prince of Wales in 1911*

investment 1 = investing, backing, funding, financing, contribution, speculation, transaction, expenditure, outlay • *The government introduced tax incentives to encourage investment.*
2 = stake, interest, share, concern, portion, ante *(informal)* • *an investment of £28 million*
3 = buy, asset, acquisition, venture, risk, speculation, gamble • *A small-screen portable TV can be a good investment.*
4 = sacrifice, surrender, relinquishment • *I worry about this big investment of time and effort not working.* **= sacrifice**

inveterate 1 = chronic, confirmed, incurable, hardened, established, long-standing, hard-core, habitual, obstinate, incorrigible, dyed-in-the-wool, ineradicable, deep-dyed *(usually derogatory)* • *an inveterate gambler*
2 = deep-rooted, entrenched, ingrained, deep-seated, incurable, established • *the inveterate laziness of these boys*
3 = staunch, long-standing, dyed-in-the-wool, deep-dyed *(usually derogatory)* • *the spirit of an inveterate Tory*

invidious 1 = undesirable, unpleasant, hateful, thankless • *He's in the invidious position of having to break the bad news.*
OPPOSITES: pleasant, desirable, pleasing
2 = unfair, unjust, unjustified, inequitable • *It is invidious to make a selection.*

invigorate = refresh, stimulate, brace, strengthen, animate, exhilarate, fortify, quicken, rejuvenate, enliven, perk up, freshen (up), energize, revitalize, galvanize, liven up, pep up, buck up *(informal)*, put new heart into • *Take a deep breath in to invigorate you.*

invigorating = refreshing, stimulating, bracing, fresh, tonic, uplifting, exhilarating, rejuvenating, energizing, healthful, restorative, salubrious, rejuvenative • *the bright sun and invigorating northern air*

invincible = unbeatable, unassailable, indomitable, unyielding, indestructible, impregnable, insuperable, invulnerable, unconquerable, unsurmountable • *When he is on form he is virtually invincible.*
OPPOSITES: weak, vulnerable, powerless

inviolable = sacrosanct, sacred, hallowed, holy, inalienable, unalterable • *The game had a single inviolable rule*

INVERTEBRATES

TYPES OF INVERTEBRATE

amoeba *or (U.S.)* ameba
animalcule
arrowworm
arthropod
Balmain bug
bardy *(Austral.)*
bivalve
bladder worm
blue-ringed octopus *(Austral.)*
Bluff oyster *(N.Z.)*
box jellyfish *or (Austral.)* sea wasp
brachiopod *or* lamp shell
brandling
bryozoan *or (colloquial)* sea mat
catworm, white worm, *or* white cat
centipede
chicken louse
chiton *or* coat-of-mail shell
clam
clappy-doo *or* clabby-doo *(Scot.)*
cockle
cone (shell)
coral
crown-of-thorns (starfish)
ctenophore *or* comb jelly
cunjevoi *(Austral.)*
cuttlefish
daphnia
earthworm
eelworm
gaper
gapeworm
gastropodart
Guinea worm
horseleech
jellyfish *or (Austral. slang)* blubber
kina *(N.Z.)*
lancelet *or* amphioxus
leech
liver fluke
lugworm
lungworm
millipede
mollusc
mussel
octopus *or* devilfish
otter shell
oyster
paddle worm
paper nautilus, nautilus, *or* argonaut
pearly nautilus, nautilus, *or* chambered nautilus
piddock
pipi *or* ugari *(Austral.)*
Portuguese man-of-war *or (Austral.)* bluebottle
quahog, hard-shell clam
ragworm *or (U.S.)* clamworm
razor-shell *or (U.S.)* razor clam
red coral *or* precious coral
roundworm
sandworm *or (Austral.)* pumpworm
scallop
sea anemone
sea cucumber
sea lily
sea mouse
sea pen
sea slater
sea squirt
sea urchin
seed oyster
soft-shell (clam)
sponge
squid
starfish
stomach worm
stony coral
sunstar
tapeworm
tardigrade *or* water bear
tellin
teredo *or* shipworm
trepang *or* bêche-de-mer
tube worm
tubifex
tusk shell *or* tooth shell
Venus's flower basket
Venus's-girdle
Venus shell
vinegar eel, vinegar worm, *or* eelworm
water louse *or* water slater
water measurer
water stick insect
wheatworm
whipworm
woodborer
worm

EXTINCT INVERTEBRATES

ammonite
belemnite
eurypterid
graptolite
trilobite

inviolate = **intact**, whole, untouched, entire, pure, virgin, sacred, stainless, unbroken, unhurt, undisturbed, unsullied, unpolluted, unstained, undefiled • *We believed our love was inviolate.*
OPPOSITES: violated, polluted, sullied

invisible 1 = **unseen**, imperceptible, indiscernible, unseeable, unperceivable • *The lines were so fine as to be nearly invisible.*
OPPOSITES: seen, obvious, visible
2 = **hidden**, concealed, obscured, secret, disguised, inconspicuous, unobserved, unnoticeable, inappreciable • *The problems of the poor are largely invisible.*

invitation 1 = **request**, call, invite *(informal)*, bidding, summons • *He received an invitation to lunch.*
2 = **inducement**, come-on *(informal)*, temptation, challenge, provocation, open door, overture, incitement, enticement, allurement • *Don't leave your bag there – it's an invitation to a thief.*

invite AS A VERB 1 = **ask**, bid, summon, request the pleasure of (someone's) company • *She invited him to her birthday party.*
2 = **request**, seek, look for, call for, ask for, bid for, appeal for, petition, solicit • *The Department is inviting applications from local groups.*
3 = **encourage**, attract, cause, draw, lead to, court, ask for *(informal)*, generate, foster, tempt, provoke, induce, bring on, solicit, engender, allure, call forth, leave the door open to • *Their refusal to compromise will invite more criticism from the UN.*
▸ AS A NOUN = **invitation**, call, request, bidding, summons • *They haven't got an invite to the wedding.*

inviting = **tempting**, appealing, attractive, pleasing, welcoming, warm, engaging, fascinating, intriguing, magnetic, delightful, enticing, seductive, captivating, beguiling, alluring, mouthwatering • *The February air was soft, cool and inviting.*
OPPOSITES: unattractive, repellent, uninviting

invocation 1 = **appeal**, request, petition, beseeching, solicitation, entreaty • *an invocation for divine guidance*
2 = **prayer**, chant, supplication, orison, karakia *(N.Z.)* • *Please stand for the invocation.*
3 = **citation**, mention, appeal to, calling on, reference to, allusion to • *the invocation of 301 legislation*

invoice AS A NOUN = **account**, charge, bill, statement, balance, register, reckoning, tally, inventory, computation • *We will send you an invoice for the total course fees.*
▸ AS A VERB = **charge**, bill, record, figure, reckon, debit • *The agency invoices the client who then pays the full amount.*

invoke 1 = **apply**, use, implement, call in, initiate, resort to, put into effect • *The judge invoked an international law that protects refugees.*
2 = **cite**, mention, refer to, name, evidence, quote, specify, allude to • *He invoked memories of previous disasters to argue against postponement.*
3 = **bring out**, conjure up, summon up • *The work invoked the atmosphere of the open spaces of the prairies.*
4 = **call upon**, appeal to, pray to, petition, conjure, solicit, beseech, entreat, adjure, supplicate • *The great magicians of old invoked their gods with sacrifice.*

involuntary 1 = **unintentional**, automatic, unconscious, spontaneous, reflex, instinctive, uncontrolled, unthinking, instinctual, blind, unconditioned • *A surge of pain caused me to give an involuntary shudder.*
OPPOSITES: voluntary, deliberate, intentional
2 = **compulsory**, forced, mandatory, required, binding, imperative, obligatory, requisite, de rigueur *(French)* • *Involuntary repatriations began this week.*

involve 1 = **entail**, mean, demand, require, call for, occasion, result in, imply, give rise to, encompass, necessitate • *Running a kitchen involves a great deal of discipline and speed.*
2 = **include**, contain, take in, embrace, cover, incorporate, draw in, comprise of, number among • *The cover-up involved people at the very highest level.*
3 = **implicate**, tangle, mix up, embroil, link, entangle, incriminate, mire, stitch up *(slang)*, enmesh, inculpate *(formal)* • *I seem to have involved myself in something I don't understand.*
4 = **concern**, draw in, associate, connect, bear on • *He started involving me in the more confidential aspects of the job.*

involved AS AN ADJECTIVE 1 = **complicated**, complex, intricate, hard, difficult, confused, confusing, sophisticated, elaborate, tangled, bewildering, jumbled, entangled, tortuous, Byzantine, convoluted, knotty, unfathomable, labyrinthine • *The operation can be quite involved, requiring special procedures.*
OPPOSITES: easy, simple, straightforward
2 = **implicated**, taking part, caught up, mixed up, embroiled, entangled, enmeshed, ensnared • *She became involved with the group soon after the Chernobyl disaster.*
▸ IN PHRASES: **involved in something** 1 = **concerned with**, associated with, participating in, connected with, caught up in, occupied by • *It's an organisation for people involved in agriculture.*
2 = **absorbed in**, caught up in, lost in, deep in, fascinated by, immersed in, gripped by, engrossed in, captivated by, enthralled by, preoccupied by, up to your ears in, wrapped up in • *She was so involved in her career she had no time for fun.*

involvement 1 = **collaboration**, implication, participation, hand, association, partnership, cooperation, inclusion, liaison, collusion, complicity, entanglement, connivance, incrimination, inculpation • *You have no proof of my involvement in anything.*
2 = **connection**, interest, relationship, concern, association, commitment, friendship, attachment • *He has always felt a deep involvement with animals.*
3 = **intimacy**, attachment, closeness, familiarity, fraternization • *They were good friends but there was no romantic involvement.*

invulnerable = **safe**, secure, invincible, impenetrable, unassailable, indestructible, insusceptible • *She assumed that her mother was invulnerable and all-powerful.*
OPPOSITES: weak, vulnerable, susceptible

inward 1 = **incoming**, entering, penetrating, inbound, inflowing, ingoing, inpouring • *a sharp, inward breath like a gasp*
2 = **internal**, inner, private, personal, inside, secret, hidden, interior, confidential, privy, innermost, inmost • *a glow of inward satisfaction*
OPPOSITES: external, outer, outward

inwardly = **privately**, secretly, to yourself, within, inside, at heart, deep down, in your head, in your inmost heart • *She smiled inwardly.*

inwards = **inside**, inward • *She pressed against the door until it swung inwards.*

iota = **bit**, particle, atom, trace, hint, scrap, grain, mite, jot, speck, whit, tittle, scintilla *(rare)* • *Our credit standards have not changed one iota.*

irascible = **bad-tempered**, cross, irritable, crabbed, touchy, cantankerous, peppery, tetchy, ratty *(Brit. & N.Z. informal)*, testy, chippy *(informal)*, short-tempered, hot-tempered, quick-tempered, choleric, narky *(Brit. slang)* • *He had an irascible temper.*

irate = **angry**, cross, furious, angered, mad *(informal)*, provoked, annoyed, irritated, fuming *(informal)*, choked, pissed *(Brit., Austral. & N.Z. slang)*, infuriated, incensed, enraged, worked up, exasperated, indignant, pissed off *(taboo)*, livid, riled, up in arms, incandescent, hacked off *(U.S. slang)*, piqued, hot under the collar *(informal)*, wrathful, fit to be tied *(slang)*, as black as thunder, tooshie *(Austral. slang)*, off the air *(Austral. slang)* • *He was so irate he almost threw me out of the place.*

ire *Literary* = **anger**, rage, fury, wrath, passion, indignation, annoyance, displeasure, exasperation, choler • *Their ire was directed mainly at the two instigators.*

Ireland = **Hibernia** *(Latin)* • *I've never visited Ireland, but I'd love to go there.*

iridescent = **shimmering**, pearly, opalescent, shot, opaline, prismatic, rainbow-coloured, polychromatic, nacreous • *iridescent bubbles*

Irish = **Hibernian**, green • *traditional Irish music*

irk = **irritate**, annoy, aggravate *(informal)*, provoke, bug *(informal)*, put out *(informal)*, gall, ruffle, nettle, vex, rile, peeve *(informal)*, get on your nerves *(informal)*, nark *(Brit., Austral. & N.Z. slang)*, miff *(informal)*, be on your back *(slang)*, piss you off *(taboo)*, get in your hair *(informal)*, rub you up the wrong way *(informal)*, put your nose out of joint *(informal)*, get your back up, put your back up, hack you off *(informal)* • *The rehearsal process irked him increasingly.*

irksome = **irritating**, trying, annoying, aggravating, troublesome, unwelcome, exasperating, tiresome, vexing, disagreeable, burdensome, wearisome, bothersome, vexatious • *the irksome regulations*
OPPOSITES: interesting, pleasant, enjoyable

iron **AS A NOUN** **1** = **flat iron**, steam iron, electric iron • *This shirt will never need to see the underside of an iron.*
2 = **tool**, machine, device, instrument, implement, appliance, apparatus, gadget, utensil, contraption, contrivance • *a soldering iron*
▸ **AS A MODIFIER** = **ferrous**, ferric, irony • *The huge iron gate was locked.*
▸ **AS AN ADJECTIVE** = **inflexible**, hard, strong, tough, steel, rigid, adamant, unconditional, steely, implacable, indomitable, unyielding, immovable, unbreakable, unbending, obdurate • *a man of icy nerve and iron will*
OPPOSITES: flexible, soft, weak
▸ **IN PHRASES: iron something out** = **settle**, resolve, sort out, eliminate, get rid of, reconcile, clear up, simplify, unravel, erase, eradicate, put right, straighten out, harmonize, expedite, smooth over • *The various groups had managed to iron out their differences.*
▸ **RELATED ADJECTIVES:** ferric, ferrous
▸ **RELATED PREFIX:** ferro-

ironic *or* **ironical** **1** = **sarcastic**, dry, sharp, acid, bitter, stinging, mocking, sneering, scoffing, wry, scathing, satirical, tongue-in-cheek, sardonic, caustic, double-edged, acerbic, trenchant, mordant, mordacious • *At the most solemn moments he would make an ironic remark.*
2 = **paradoxical**, absurd, contradictory, puzzling, baffling, ambiguous, inconsistent, confounding, enigmatic, illogical, incongruous • *It's ironic that the sort of people this film celebrates would never watch it.*

ironically **1** = **paradoxically**, absurdly, incongruously, ambiguously, illogically, inconsistently, bafflingly • *Ironically, for a man who hated war, he made a superb war reporter.*
2 = **sarcastically**, mockingly, sardonically, acidly, wryly, sneeringly, trenchantly, satirically, acerbically, mordaciously • *His classmates ironically dubbed him 'Beauty'.*

irons = **chains**, shackles, fetters, manacles, bonds • *These people need to be clapped in irons themselves.*

irony **1** = **sarcasm**, mockery, ridicule, bitterness, scorn, satire, cynicism, derision, causticity, mordancy • *She examined his face for a hint of irony, but found none.*
2 = **paradox**, ambiguity, absurdity, incongruity, contrariness • *Opposition parties wasted no time in stressing the irony of the situation.*

irrational **1** = **illogical**, crazy, silly, absurd, foolish, unreasonable, unwise, preposterous, idiotic, nonsensical, unsound, unthinking, injudicious, unreasoning • *an irrational fear of science*
OPPOSITES: sound, wise, rational
2 = **senseless**, wild, crazy, unstable, insane, mindless, demented, aberrant, brainless, off the air *(Austral. slang)* • *They behaved in such a bizarre and irrational manner.*

irrationality = **senselessness**, madness, insanity, absurdity, lunacy, lack of judgment, illogicality, unreasonableness, preposterousness, unsoundness, brainlessness • *the irrationality of his behaviour*

irreconcilable **1** = **implacable**, uncompromising, inflexible, inexorable, intransigent, unappeasable • *an irreconcilable clash of personalities*
2 = **incompatible**, conflicting, opposed, inconsistent, incongruous, diametrically opposed • *their irreconcilable points of view*

irrecoverable = **lost**, irreparable, irretrievable, gone for ever, irredeemable, irremediable, unsalvageable, irreclaimable, unsavable, unregainable • *nostalgic affection for an irrecoverable past*

irrefutable = **undeniable**, sure, certain, irresistible, invincible, unassailable, indisputable, unanswerable, unquestionable, incontrovertible, beyond question, incontestable, indubitable, apodictic, irrefragable • *Her logic was irrefutable.*

irregular **1** = **variable**, inconsistent, erratic, shifting, occasional, random, casual, shaky, wavering, uneven, fluctuating, eccentric, patchy, sporadic, intermittent, haphazard, unsteady, desultory, fitful, spasmodic, unsystematic, inconstant, nonuniform, unmethodical, scattershot • *She was suffering from an irregular heartbeat.*
OPPOSITES: steady, reliable, systematic
2 = **uneven**, broken, rough, twisted, twisting, curving, pitted, ragged, crooked, unequal, jagged, bumpy, lumpy, serpentine, contorted, lopsided, craggy, indented, asymmetrical, serrated, holey, unsymmetrical • *He had bad teeth, irregular and discoloured.*
OPPOSITES: even, regular, symmetrical
3 = **inappropriate**, unconventional, improper, unethical, odd, unusual, extraordinary, disorderly, exceptional, peculiar, unofficial, abnormal, queer, rum *(Brit. slang)*, back-door, unsuitable, unorthodox, out-of-order, unprofessional, anomalous • *The minister was accused of irregular business practices.*
4 = **unofficial**, underground, guerrilla, volunteer, resistance, partisan, rogue, paramilitary, mercenary • *At least 17 irregular units are involved in the war.*
OPPOSITES: standard, conventional

irregularity **1** = **inconsistency**, randomness, disorganization, unsteadiness, unpunctuality, haphazardness, disorderliness, lack of method, desultoriness • *a dangerous irregularity in her heartbeat*
2 = **unevenness**, deformity, asymmetry, crookedness, contortion, patchiness, lopsidedness, raggedness, lack of symmetry, spottiness, jaggedness • *treatment of irregularities of the teeth*
3 = **malpractice**, anomaly, breach, abnormality, deviation, oddity, aberration, malfunction, peculiarity, singularity, unorthodoxy, unconventionality • *charges arising from alleged financial irregularities*

irregularly **1** = **erratically**, occasionally, now and again, intermittently, off and on, anyhow, unevenly, fitfully, haphazardly, eccentrically, spasmodically, jerkily, in snatches, out of sequence, by fits and starts, disconnectedly, unmethodically, unpunctually • *He was eating irregularly and losing weight.*
2 = **asymmetrically**, unevenly, lopsidedly • *an irregularly shaped lake*

irrelevance *or* **irrelevancy** = **inappropriateness**, inapplicability, inaptness, unconnectedness, pointlessness, non sequitur, inconsequence, extraneousness, inappositeness • *the utter irrelevance of the debate*
OPPOSITES: relevance, suitability, appropriateness

irrelevant = **unconnected**, unrelated, unimportant, inappropriate, peripheral, insignificant, negligible, immaterial, extraneous, beside the point, impertinent, neither here nor there, inapplicable, inapt, inapposite, inconsequent • *irrelevant details*
OPPOSITES: related, connected, relevant

irreligious 1 = **atheistic**, sceptical, agnostic, godless, unbelieving, freethinking • *irreligious communities*
2 = **sacrilegious**, irreverent, profane, blasphemous, wicked, sinful, unholy, iconoclastic, ungodly, impious, unrighteous, undevout • *The priest's conversational style was regarded as most irreligious.*

irremediable = **incurable**, hopeless, irreversible, final, terminal, fatal, deadly, mortal, irreparable, irrecoverable, irredeemable, beyond redress • *His memory suffered irremediable damage.*

irreparable = **beyond repair**, irreversible, incurable, irretrievable, irrecoverable, irremediable • *The move would cause irreparable harm to the organization.*

irreplaceable = **indispensable**, unique, invaluable, priceless • *a rare and irreplaceable jewel*

irrepressible = **unstoppable**, buoyant, uncontrollable, boisterous, ebullient, effervescent, unmanageable, unquenchable, bubbling over, uncontainable, unrestrainable, insuppressible • *His exuberance was irrepressible.*

irreproachable = **perfect**, blameless, impeccable, faultless, pure, innocent, squeaky-clean, unblemished, unimpeachable, beyond reproach, guiltless, irreprehensible, inculpable, irreprovable • *a man of irreproachable views*

irresistible 1 = **overwhelming**, compelling, overpowering, urgent, potent, imperative, compulsive, uncontrollable, overmastering • *It proved an irresistible temptation to go back.*
2 = **seductive**, inviting, tempting, enticing, provocative, fascinating, enchanting, captivating, beguiling, alluring, bewitching, ravishing • *The music is irresistible.*
3 = **inescapable**, inevitable, unavoidable, sure, certain, fated, destined, inexorable, ineluctable • *They feel the case for change is irresistible.*

irresolute = **indecisive**, weak, hesitating, doubtful, unsettled, unstable, tentative, wavering, hesitant, undecided, fickle, unsteady, infirm, vacillating, in two minds, undetermined, half-arsed (*Brit. slang*), half-assed (*U.S. & Canad. slang*), half-hearted • *They launched the attack for fear of seeming irresolute.*
OPPOSITES: decisive, strong, resolute

irrespective of = **despite**, in spite of, regardless of, discounting, notwithstanding, without reference to, without regard to • *It's available to all, irrespective of whether they can afford it.*

irresponsible = **thoughtless**, reckless, careless, wild, unreliable, giddy, untrustworthy, flighty, ill-considered, good-for-nothing, shiftless, harebrained, undependable, harum-scarum, scatterbrained, featherbrained • *Is it irresponsible to advocate the legalisation of drugs?*
OPPOSITES: responsible, careful, sensible

irretrievable = **irreversible**, incurable, irrevocable, irreparable, final, unalterable • *a country in irretrievable decline*

irreverence = **disrespect**, cheek (*informal*), impertinence, sauce (*informal*), mockery, derision, lack of respect, impudence, flippancy, cheekiness (*informal*) • *His irreverence for authority marks him out as a troublemaker.*

irreverent = **disrespectful**, cheeky (*informal*), impertinent, fresh (*informal*), mocking, flip (*informal*), saucy, contemptuous, tongue-in-cheek, sassy (*U.S. informal*), flippant, iconoclastic, derisive, impudent • *She's irreverent, fun and hugely popular.*
OPPOSITES: awed, respectful, reverent

irreversible = **irrevocable**, incurable, irreparable, final, unalterable • *She could suffer irreversible brain damage if we don't act fast.*

irrevocable = **fixed**, settled, irreversible, fated, predetermined, immutable, invariable, irretrievable, predestined, unalterable, unchangeable, changeless, irremediable, unreversible • *He said the decision was irrevocable.*

QUOTATIONS

The moving finger writes; and having writ,
Moves on; nor all thy piety nor wit
Shall lure it back to cancel half a line,
Nor all thy tears wash out a word of it.
[Edward Fitzgerald *Rubaiyat of Omar Khayyam*]

One cannot step twice into the same river
[Heraclitus]

irrigate = **water**, wet, moisten, flood, inundate, fertigate (*Austral.*) • *The land is irrigated by a maze of interconnected canals.*

irritability = **bad temper**, impatience, ill humour, prickliness, tetchiness, irascibility, peevishness, testiness, touchiness • *Patients usually suffer from memory loss and irritability.*
OPPOSITES: patience, good humour, cheerfulness

irritable = **bad-tempered**, cross, snappy, hot, tense, crabbed, fiery, snarling, prickly, exasperated, edgy, touchy, petulant, ill-tempered, irascible, cantankerous, tetchy, ratty (*Brit. & N.Z. informal*), testy, chippy (*informal*), fretful, peevish, crabby, dyspeptic, choleric, crotchety (*informal*), oversensitive, snappish, ill-humoured, narky (*Brit. slang*), out of humour • *He had been waiting for an hour and was starting to feel irritable.*
OPPOSITES: calm, cheerful, even-tempered

irritant = **irritation**, nuisance, annoyance, pain (*informal*), drag (*informal*), tease, pest, provocation, gall, goad, aggravation (*informal*), pain in the neck (*informal*), pain in the arse (*taboo*), thorn in your flesh • *He said the issue was not a major irritant.*

irritate 1 = **annoy**, anger, bother, provoke, offend, needle (*informal*), harass, infuriate, aggravate (*informal*), incense, fret, enrage, gall, ruffle, inflame, exasperate, nettle, pester, vex, irk, pique, rankle with, get under your skin (*informal*), get on your nerves (*informal*), nark (*Brit., Austral. & N.Z. slang*), drive you up the wall (*slang*), piss you off (*taboo*), rub you up the wrong way (*informal*), get your goat (*slang*), try your patience, get in your hair (*informal*), get on your wick (*informal*), get your dander up (*informal*), raise your hackles, get your back up, get your hackles up, put your back up, hack you off (*informal*) • *Their attitude irritates me.*
OPPOSITES: calm, soothe, placate
2 = **inflame**, pain, rub, scratch, scrape, grate, graze, fret, gall, chafe, abrade • *Chillies can irritate the skin.*

irritated = **annoyed**, cross, angry, bothered, put out, hacked (off) (*U.S. slang*), pissed (*Brit., Austral. & N.Z. taboo*), harassed, impatient, ruffled, exasperated, irritable, nettled, vexed, pissed off (*taboo*), displeased, flustered, peeved (*informal*), piqued, out of humour, tooshie (*Austral. slang*), hoha (*N.Z.*) • *Not surprisingly, her teacher is getting irritated with her.*

irritating = **annoying**, trying, provoking, infuriating, upsetting, disturbing, nagging, aggravating (*informal*), troublesome, galling, maddening, disquieting, displeasing, worrisome, irksome, vexatious, pestilential • *They have the irritating habit of interrupting you.*
OPPOSITES: calming, soothing, pleasing

irritation 1 = **annoyance**, anger, fury, resentment, wrath, gall, indignation, impatience, displeasure, exasperation, chagrin, irritability, ill temper, shortness, vexation, ill humour, testiness, crossness, snappiness, infuriation • *For the first time he felt irritation at her methods.*
OPPOSITES: ease, calm, pleasure
2 = **nuisance**, annoyance, irritant, pain (*informal*), drag (*informal*), bother, plague, menace, tease, pest, hassle, provocation, gall, goad, aggravation (*informal*), pain in the neck (*informal*), pain in the arse (*taboo slang*), thorn in your flesh • *Don't allow a minor irritation to mar your ambitions.*

Islam

MUSLIM DENOMINATIONS AND SECTS

Alaouites *or* Alawites
Druse *or* Druze
Imami
Ismaili *or* Isma'ili
Nizari
Shiah, Shia *or* Shiite
Sufism
Sunni
Wahhabism *or* Wahabism
Zaidi

island = **isle**, inch *(Scot. & Irish)*, atoll, holm *(dialect)*, islet, ait *or* eyot *(dialect)*, cay *or* key • *a day trip to the island of Gozo*
▸ **RELATED ADJECTIVE:** insular
▹ *See panel* **Islands and island groups**

isolate 1 = separate, break up, cut off, detach, split up, insulate, segregate, disconnect, divorce, sequester, set apart, disunite, estrange • *This policy could isolate members from the UN security council.*
2 = quarantine, separate, exclude, cut off, detach, keep in solitude • *Patients will be isolated for one month after treatment.*

isolated 1 = remote, far, distant, lonely, out-of-the-way, hidden, retired, far-off, secluded, inaccessible, faraway, outlying, in the middle of nowhere, off the beaten track, backwoods, godforsaken, incommunicado, unfrequented • *Many of the refugee areas are in isolated areas.*
2 = single, individual, unique, unusual, sole, random, exceptional, freak, lone, solitary, abnormal, unrelated, anomalous, atypical, untypical • *The allegations related to an isolated case of cheating.*
3 = solitary, withdrawn, lonely, sheltered, segregated, cloistered, reclusive, lonesome *(chiefly U.S. & Canad.)*,

ISLANDS AND ISLAND GROUPS

Achill
Admiralty
Aegean
Aegina
Alcatraz
Aldabra
Alderney
Aleutian
Alexander
Amboina
Andaman
Andaman and Nicobar
Andreanof
Andros
Anglesey
Anguilla
Anticosti
Antigua
Antilles
Antipodes
Aran
Arran
Aru *or* Arru
Aruba
Ascension
Auckland
Azores
Baffin
Bahamas
Balearic
Bali
Banaba
Bangka
Banks
Baranof
Barbados
Barbuda
Bardsey
Barra
Basilan
Basse-Terre
Batan
Belau
Belle
Benbecula
Bermuda
Biak
Billiton
Bioko
Bohol
Bonaire
Bonin
Bora Bora
Borneo
Bornholm
Bougainville
British
Bute
Butung
Caicos
Caldy
Calf of Man
Campobello
Canary
Canna
Canvey
Cape Breton
Capri
Caroline
Cayman
Cebú
Ceylon
Channel
Chatham
Cheju
Chichagof
Chiloé
Chios
Choiseul
Christmas
Cocos
Coll
Colonsay
Coney
Cook
Corfu
Corregidor
Corsica
Crete
Cuba
Curaçao
Cyclades
Cyprus
Cythera
Delos
D'Entrecasteaux
Diomede
Disko
Diu
Djerba *or* Jerba
Dodecanese
Dominica
Dry Tortugas
Easter
Eigg
Elba
Ellesmere
Espíritu Santo
Euboea
Faeroes
Faial *or* Fayal
Fair
Falkland
Falster
Farquhar
Fernando de Noronha
Fiji
Flannan
Flinders
Flores
Florida Keys
Foula
Foulness
Franz Josef Land
French West Indies
Frisian
Fyn
Galápagos
Gambier
Gigha
Gilbert
Gotland
Grand Bahama
Grand Canary
Grande-Terre
Grand Manan
Greater Antilles
Greater Sunda
Greenland
Grenada
Grenadines
Guadalcanal
Guam
Guernsey
Hainan
Handa
Hawaii
Hayling
Heard and McDonald
Hebrides
Heimaey
Heligoland
Herm
Hispaniola
Hokkaido
Holy
Hong Kong
Honshu
Hormuz *or* Ormuz
Howland
Ibiza
Icaria
Iceland
Imbros
Iona
Ionian
Ireland
Ischia
Islay
Isle Royale
Ithaca
Iwo Jima
Jamaica
Jan Mayen
Java
Jersey
Jolo
Juan Fernández
Jura
Kangaroo
Kauai
Keos
Kerrera
Kiritimati
Kodiak
Kos *or* Cos
Kosrae
Krakatoa
Kuril *or* Kurile
Kyushu *or* Kiushu
La Palma
Labuan
Lakshadweep
Lampedusa
Lanai
Lavongai
Leeward
Lemnos
Lesbos
Lesser Antilles
Levkás
Lewis with Harris *or* Lewis and Harris
Leyte
Liberty
Lindisfarne
Line
Lipari
Lismore
Lolland *or* Laaland
Lombok
Long
Longa
Lord Howe
Luing
Lundy
Luzon
Mackinac
Macquarie
Madagascar
Madeira
Madura
Maewo
Mahé
Mainland
Majorca
Maldives
Malé
Malta
Man
Manhattan
Manitoulin
Marajó
Margarita
Marie Galante
Marinduque
Marquesas
Marshall
Martinique
Masbate
Mascarene
Matsu *or* Mazu
Maui
Mauritius
May
Mayotte
Melanesia
Melos
Melville
Mersea
Micronesia
Mindanao
Mindoro
Minorca
Miquelon
Molokai
Moluccas
Montserrat
Mount Desert
Muck
Mull
Mykonos
Nantucket
Nauru
Naxos
Negros
Netherlands Antilles
Nevis
New Britain
New Caledonia
Newfoundland
New Georgia
New Guinea
New Ireland
New Providence
New Siberian
Nicobar
Niue
Norfolk
North
North Uist
Nusa Tenggara

ISLANDS AND ISLAND GROUPS (CONTINUED)

Oahu
Oceania
Okinawa
Orkney
Palawan
Palmyra
Panay
Pantelleria
Páros
Patmos
Pelagian
Pemba
Penang
Pescadores
Philae
Philippines
Phoenix
Pitcairn
Polynesia
Ponape
Pribilof
Prince Edward
Prince of Wales
Principe
Qeshm *or* Qishm
Queen Charlotte
Queen Elizabeth
Quemoy
Raasay
Ramsey
Rarotonga
Rathlin
Réunion
Rhodes
Rhum
Rialto
Roanoke
Robben
Rockall
Rona
Ross
Ryukyu
Saba
Safety
Saipan
Sakhalin
Salamis
Saltee
Samar
Samoa
Samos
Samothrace
San Cristóbal
San Juan
San Salvador
Santa Catalina
Sao Miguel
Sao Tomé
Sardinia
Sark
Savaii
Scalpay
Schouten
Scilly
Sea
Seil
Seram *or* Ceram
Seychelles
Sheppey
Shetland
Sicily
Singapore
Sjælland
Skikoku
Skokholm
Skomer
Skye
Skyros *or* Scyros
Society
Socotra
South
Southampton
South Georgia
South Orkney
South Shetland
South Uist
Spitsbergen
Sporades
Sri Lanka
St. Croix
St. Helena
St. John
St. Kilda
St. Kitts *or* St. Christopher
St. Lucia
St. Martin
St. Tudwal's
St. Vincent
Staffa
Staten
Stewart
Stroma
Stromboli
Sulawesi
Sumatra
Sumba *or* Soemba
Sumbawa *or* Soembawa
Summer
Sunda *or* Soenda
Tahiti
Taiwan
Tasmania
Tenedos
Tenerife
Terceira
Thanet
Thásos
Thera
Thousand
Thursday
Timor
Tiree
Tobago
Tokelau
Tombo
Tonga
Tortola
Tortuga
Trinidad
Tristan da Cunha
Trobriand
Truk
Tsushima
Tuamotu
Tubuai
Turks
Tutuila
Tuvalu
Ulva
Unimak
Upolu
Ushant
Vancouver
Vanua Levu
Vanuatu
Vestmannaeyjar
Victoria
Virgin
Visayan
Viti Levu
Volcano
Walcheren
Walney
West Indies
Western
Wight
Windward
Wrangel
Yap
Youth
Zante
Zanzibar

sequestered, introverted, friendless, companionless • *He now lives an isolated life in the countryside.*

isolation AS A NOUN = **separation**, withdrawal, loneliness, segregation, detachment, quarantine, solitude, exile, self-sufficiency, seclusion, remoteness, disconnection, insularity • *the isolation he endured while he was in captivity*

▸ IN PHRASES: **in isolation 1 = separately**, individually, independently, singly, apart • *Punishment cannot, therefore, be discussed in isolation.*

2 = alone, separately, by yourself, singly, apart, unaided, unassisted, under your own steam, solitarily • *He works in isolation but I have no doubts about his abilities.*

QUOTATIONS
Isolation must precede true society
[Ralph Waldo Emerson *'Self-Reliance'*]
Solitude vivifies;
Isolation kills
[Joseph Roux *Meditations of a Parish Priest*]

issue AS A NOUN **1 = topic**, point, matter, problem, business, case, question, concern, subject, affair, argument, theme, controversy, can of worms *(informal)* • *Is it right for the Church to express a view on political issues?*

2 = point, question, concern, bone of contention, matter of contention, point in question • *I wasn't earning much money, but that was not the issue.*

3 = edition, printing, copy, impression, publication, number, instalment, imprint, version • *The problem is underlined in the latest issue of the Lancet.*

4 = children, young, offspring, babies, kids *(informal)*, seed *(chiefly biblical)*, successors, heirs, descendants, progeny, scions • *He died without issue in 1946.*

OPPOSITES: parent, sire

5 = distribution, issuing, supply, supplying, delivery, publication, circulation, sending out, dissemination, dispersal, issuance • *the issue of supplies to refugees*

▸ AS A VERB **1 = give out**, release, publish, announce, deliver, spread, broadcast, distribute, communicate, proclaim, put out, circulate, emit, impart, disseminate, promulgate, put in circulation • *He issued a statement denying the allegations.*

2 = supply, give, provide, stock, grant, afford, yield, outfit, equip, furnish, endow, purvey • *Staff will be issued with new designer uniforms.*

3 = emerge, came out, proceed, rise, spring, flow, arise, stem, originate, emanate, exude, come forth, be a consequence of • *A tinny voice issued from a speaker.*

OPPOSITES: withdraw, revoke

▸ IN PHRASES: **at issue = under discussion**, in question, in dispute, under consideration, to be decided, for debate • *The problems of immigration were not the question at issue.*

take issue with something *or* **someone = disagree with**, question, challenge, oppose, dispute, object to, argue with, take exception to, raise an objection to • *She might take issue with you on that matter.*

isthmus = strip, spit • *the isthmus of Panama*

Italy

▹ *See panel* **Administrative regions**

itch AS A VERB **1 = prickle**, tickle, tingle, crawl • *When you have hayfever, your eyes and nose stream and itch.*

2 = long, ache, crave, burn, pine, pant, hunger, lust, yearn, hanker • *I was itching to get involved.*

▸ AS A NOUN **1 = irritation**, tingling, prickling, itchiness • *Scratch my back – I've got an itch.*

2 = desire, longing, craving, passion, yen *(informal)*, hunger, lust, yearning, hankering, restlessness • *an insatiable itch to switch from channel to channel*

itching = longing, burning, raring, eager, impatient, avid, inquisitive, spoiling for, agog, mad keen *(informal)*, aquiver, atremble, consumed with curiosity • *She is itching for a fight.*

itchy = impatient, eager, restless, unsettled, edgy, restive, fidgety • *I soon started feeling itchy to get back.*

item AS A NOUN **1 = article**, thing, object, piece, unit, component • *The most valuable item on show will be a Picasso.* **2 = matter**, point, issue, case, question, concern, detail, subject, feature, particular, affair, aspect, entry, theme, consideration, topic • *The other item on the agenda is the tour.* **3 = report**, story, piece, account, note, feature, notice, article, paragraph, bulletin, dispatch, communiqué, write-up • *There was an item in the paper about him.*

▸ IN PHRASES: **an item = a couple**, together, going out (*informal*), attached, partnered • *I hadn't realised Tina and Jim were an item.*

itemize = list, record, detail, count, document, instance, set out, specify, inventory, number, enumerate, particularize • *a fully itemized phone bill*

itinerant = wandering, travelling, journeying, unsettled, Gypsy, roaming, roving, nomadic, migratory, vagrant, peripatetic, vagabond, ambulatory, wayfaring • *the author's experiences as an itinerant musician*

OPPOSITES: established, settled, fixed

itinerary = schedule, line, programme, tour, route, journey, circuit, timetable • *The next place on the itinerary was Silistra.*

ivory tower = seclusion, remoteness, unreality, retreat, refuge, cloister, sanctum, splendid isolation, world of your own • *In their ivory tower they don't realise how pernicious it is.*

jab AS A VERB = **poke**, dig, punch, thrust, tap, stab, nudge, prod, lunge • *a needle was jabbed into the baby's arm*
▸ AS A NOUN 1 = **poke**, dig, punch, thrust, tap, stab, nudge, prod, lunge • *He gave me a jab in the side.*
2 = **injection**, vaccine, vaccination, inoculation, shot *(informal)*, jag *(informal)* • *painful anti-malaria jabs*

jabber = **chatter**, rabbit (on) *(Brit. informal)*, ramble, mumble, babble, waffle *(informal, chiefly Brit.)*, drivel, yap *(informal)*, tattle, gabble, blather, blether, run off at the mouth *(slang)*, prate • *I left them there jabbering away*

jacket 1 = **coat**, blazer • *a black leather jacket*
2 = **covering**, casing, case, cover, skin, shell, coat, wrapping, envelope, capsule, folder, sheath, wrapper, encasement, housing • *potatoes in their jackets*
▹ *See panel* **Jackets**

jack in = **give up**, resign from, quit, stop, kick *(informal)*, abandon, cease, hand over, surrender, cut out, relinquish, renounce, leave off, say goodbye to, cede, step down from *(informal)*, desist, kiss (something) goodbye, forswear • *After she jacked in the teaching, Jane got a job with a shipping line.*

jackpot AS A NOUN = **prize**, winnings, award, pool, reward, pot, kitty, bonanza, pot of gold at the end of the rainbow • *the biggest ever jackpot of more than £5 million*
▸ IN PHRASES: **hit the jackpot** = **strike it lucky**, clean up *(informal)*, hit the big time *(informal)*, strike it rich *(informal)*, make a packet *(informal)*, score *(informal)* • *They hit the jackpot with a million-selling album.*

jack up 1 = **hoist**, raise, elevate, winch up, lift, rear, uplift, lift up, heave, haul up, hike up, upraise • *They jacked up the car.*
2 = **increase**, raise, put up, augment, advance, boost, expand, add to, enhance, step up *(informal)*, intensify, enlarge, escalate, inflate, amplify • *The company would have to jack up its prices.*

jaded 1 = **tired**, bored, weary, worn out, done in *(informal)*, clapped out *(Brit., Austral. & N.Z. informal)*, spent, drained, exhausted, shattered, dulled, fatigued, fed up, wearied, fagged (out) *(informal)*, sapped, uninterested, listless, tired-out, enervated, zonked *(slang)*, over-tired, ennuied, hoha *(N.Z.)* • *We had both become jaded, disinterested and disillusioned.*
OPPOSITES: fresh, keen, eager
2 = **satiated**, sated, surfeited, cloyed, gorged, glutted • *scrumptious little things to tickle my jaded palate*

jagged = **uneven**, pointed, craggy, broken, toothed, rough, ragged, ridged, spiked, notched, barbed, cleft, indented, serrated, snaggy, denticulate • *jagged black cliffs*
OPPOSITES: level, rounded, regular

jail *or* **gaol** AS A NOUN = **prison**, penitentiary *(U.S.)*, jailhouse *(Southern U.S.)*, penal institution, can *(slang)*, inside, cooler *(slang)*, confinement, dungeon, clink *(slang)*, glasshouse *(Military informal)*, brig *(chiefly U.S.)*, borstal, calaboose *(U.S. informal)*, choky *(slang)*, pound, nick *(Brit. slang)*, stir *(slang)*, jug *(slang)*, slammer *(slang)*, lockup, reformatory, quod *(slang)*, poky *or* pokey *(U.S. & Canad. slang)*, boob *(Austral. slang)* • *Three prisoners escaped from a jail.*
▸ AS A VERB = **imprison**, confine, detain, lock up, constrain, put away, intern, incarcerate, send down, send to prison, impound, put under lock and key, immure • *He was jailed for twenty years.*

QUOTATIONS
Go to jail. Go directly to jail. Do not pass go. Do not collect $200.
[Charles Brace Darrow *Instructions for Monopoly*]

jailbird *or* **gaolbird** = **prisoner**, convict, con *(slang)*, lag *(slang)*, trusty, felon, malefactor, ticket-of-leave man *(archaic)* • *He's rubbed shoulders with judges and jailbirds.*

jailer *or* **gaoler** = **guard**, keeper, warden, screw *(slang)*, captor, warder, turnkey *(archaic)* • *The chief said someone slugged the jailer and opened the cell.*

jam[1] AS A NOUN 1 = **tailback**, queue, hold-up, bottleneck, snarl-up, line, chain, congestion, obstruction, stoppage, gridlock • *a nine-mile traffic jam*
2 = **predicament**, tight spot, scrape *(informal)*, corner, state, situation, trouble, spot *(informal)*, hole *(slang)*, fix *(informal)*, bind, emergency, mess, dilemma, pinch, plight, strait, hot

JACKETS

acton
anorak
báinín
banyan
Barbour jacket *(trademark)*
bed jacket
biker jacket
blazer
blouson
body warmer
bolero
bomber jacket
boxy jacket
bush jacket
cagoule *or* cag
cardigan
combat jacket
cymar
denim jacket
dinner jacket *or* *(U.S. & Canad.)* tuxedo *or* tux
dolman
donkey jacket
doublet
duvet *or* duvet jacket
Eton jacket or bumfreezer
flak jacket
fustian jacket
gambeson
gilet
hacking jacket
hug-me-tight
jerkin
leather jacket
life jacket
lumberjacket
Mackinaw coat *or* mackinaw *(chiefly U.S. & Canad.)*
matinée jacket
mess jacket
monkey jacket
Norfolk jacket
pourpoint
reefing jacket
sack *or* sacque
safari jacket
shell jacket
shrug
smoking jacket
spencer
sports jacket *or* coat
tabard
windcheater *or* windjammer

water, pickle *(informal)*, deep water, quandary • *It could get the government out of a jam.*
▸ **AS A VERB** 1 = **pack**, force, press, stuff, squeeze, compact, ram, wedge, cram, compress • *He jammed his hands into his pockets.*
2 = **crowd**, cram, throng, crush, press, mass, surge, flock, swarm, congregate • *In summer, the beach is jammed with day-trippers.*
3 = **congest**, block, clog, stick, halt, stall, obstruct • *The phone lines are jammed. Everybody wants to talk about it.*

jam[2] = **preserve**, jelly *(U.S. & Canad.)*, conserve • *The small fruits are excellent for jam or dessert.*

jamboree = **festival**, party, fête, celebration, blast *(U.S. slang)*, rave *(Brit. slang)*, carnival, spree, jubilee, festivity, beano *(Brit. slang)*, merriment, revelry, carouse, rave-up *(Brit. slang)*, carousal, frolic, hooley *or* hoolie *(chiefly Irish & N.Z.)* • *a fund-raising jamboree in aid of sickle-cell research*

jammy = **lucky**, favoured, charmed, fortunate, blessed, prosperous, serendipitous • *He is seen as lucky. Dead jammy, in fact.*

jam-packed = **crowded**, full, packed, busy, crushed, mobbed, cramped, huddled, swarming, overflowing, thronged, teeming, congested, populous • *His room was jam-packed with fruit, flowers, gifts etc.*

jangle **AS A VERB** 1 = **rattle**, ring, clash, clatter, chime, ping, vibrate, jingle, ding, clank • *Her necklaces and bracelets jangled as she walked.*
2 = **disturb**, worry, trouble, excite, upset, alarm, distress, annoy, distract, unsettle, harass, hassle *(informal)*, agitate, ruffle, confound, shake, unnerve, fluster, perturb, discompose • *The caffeine in coffee can jangle the nerves.*
▸ **AS A NOUN** = **clash**, clang, cacophony, reverberation, rattle, jar, racket, din, dissonance, clangour • *a jangle of bells*
OPPOSITES: quiet, silence, mellifluousness

janitor = **caretaker**, porter, custodian, concierge, doorkeeper • *My mother was the janitor in the town school.*

jar[1] 1 = **pot**, container, flask, receptacle, vessel, drum, vase, jug, pitcher, urn, crock, canister, repository, decanter, carafe, flagon • *We saved each season's harvest in clear glass jars.*
2 = **drink**, cup, glass, taste, swallow, sip, draught, gulp, swig *(informal)*, snifter *(informal)* • *a few jars of their favourite tipple*

jar[2] 1 *usually with* **on** = **irritate**, grind, clash, annoy, offend, rattle, gall, nettle, jangle, irk, grate on, get on your nerves *(informal)*, nark *(Brit., Austral. & N.Z. slang)*, piss you off *(taboo slang)*, discompose • *The least bit of discord seemed to jar on his nerves.*
2 *sometimes with* **with** = **clash**, conflict, contrast, differ, disagree, interfere, contend, collide, oppose • *They had always been complementary and their temperaments seldom jarred.*
3 = **jolt**, rock, shake, disturb, bump, rattle, grate, agitate, vibrate, rasp, convulse • *The impact jarred his arm, right up to the shoulder.*

jargon = **parlance**, slang, idiom, patter, tongue, usage, dialect, cant, lingo *(informal)*, patois, argot • *full of the jargon and slang of self-improvement courses*

jarring = **grating**, grinding, offensive, harsh, annoying, irritating, unpleasant, scraping, raucous, strident, squeaky, rasping, discordant, displeasing, disagreeable, irksome, vexatious • *a jarring, nasal voice*

jaundiced = **cynical**, bitter, hostile, prejudiced, biased, suspicious, partial, jealous, distorted, sceptical, resentful, envious, bigoted, spiteful, preconceived • *The two writers share a jaundiced vision of a tawdry modern Britain.*
OPPOSITES: trusting, optimistic, naive

jaunt = **outing**, tour, trip, stroll, expedition, excursion, ramble, promenade, awayday, airing • *I decided to take a jaunt down to Long Beach.*

jaunty 1 = **sprightly**, buoyant, carefree, high-spirited, gay, lively, airy, breezy, perky, sparky, self-confident • *The novel is altogether jauntier than these quotations imply.*
OPPOSITES: serious, dull, dignified
2 = **smart**, trim, gay, dapper, spruce, showy • *a jaunty little hat*

jaw **AS A PLURAL NOUN** = **opening**, gates, entrance, aperture, mouth, abyss, maw, orifice, ingress • *He opens the jaws of the furnace with the yank of a lever.*
▸ **AS A VERB** = **talk**, chat, rabbit (on) *(Brit. informal)*, gossip, chatter, spout, babble, natter, schmooze *(slang)*, shoot the breeze *(U.S. slang)*, run off at the mouth *(slang)*, chew the fat *or* rag *(slang)* • *jawing for half an hour with the very affable waiter*
▸ **TECHNICAL NAMES:** maxilla *(upper)* mandible *(lower)*
▸ **RELATED ADJECTIVES:** gnathic, gnathal

jazz up = **enliven**, enhance, perk up, brighten up, improve, excite, inspire, cheer, wake up, heighten, animate, hearten, cheer up, buoy up, pep up, invigorate, gladden, inspirit • *She had made an effort at jazzing up the chilly modern interiors.*

jazzy = **flashy**, fancy, snazzy *(informal)*, gaudy, wild, smart, lively, bling *(slang)* • *a check sports jacket, worn with a plain shirt and jazzy tie*

jealous 1 = **suspicious**, suspecting, guarded, protective, wary, doubtful, sceptical, attentive, anxious, apprehensive, vigilant, watchful, zealous, possessive, solicitous, distrustful, mistrustful, unbelieving • *She got insanely jealous and there was a terrible fight.*
OPPOSITES: trusting, indifferent, carefree
2 = **envious**, grudging, resentful, begrudging, green, intolerant, green-eyed, invidious, green with envy, desirous, covetous, emulous • *I have never sought to make my readers jealous of my megastar lifestyle.*
OPPOSITES: satisfied

jealousy 1 = **suspicion**, distrust, mistrust, possessiveness, doubt, spite, resentment, wariness, ill-will, dubiety • *At first his jealousy only showed in small ways – he didn't mind me talking to other guys.*
2 = **envy**, resentment, resentfulness, enviousness, spite, hatred, malice, ill will, covetousness, malignity, the green-eyed monster *(informal)* • *Her beauty causes jealousy.*
▸ **RELATED PHOBIA:** zelophobia

QUOTATIONS

O! Beware, my lord, of jealousy;
It is the green-eyed monster which doth mock
The meat it feeds on
[William Shakespeare *Othello*]

Love is strong as death; jealousy is cruel as the grave
[*Bible: Song of Solomon*]

It is not love that is blind, but jealousy
[Lawrence Durrell *Justine*]

Jealousy is no more than feeling alone against smiling enemies
[Elizabeth Bowen *The House in Paris*]

Jealousy is always born with love, but does not always die with it
[Duc de la Rochefoucauld *Maxims*]

Jealousy is the greatest of all evils, and the one which arouses the least pity in the person who causes it
[Duc de la Rochefoucauld *Maxims*]

Love that is fed by jealousy dies hard
[Ovid *Remedia Amoris*]

To jealousy, nothing is more frightful than laughter
[Françoise Sagan *La Chamade*]

Anger and jealousy can no more bear to lose sight of their objects than love
[George Eliot *The Mill on the Floss*]

the injured lover's hell
[John Milton *Paradise Lost*]

jeans = **denims**, blue jeans, Levis *(trademark)*, blues *(informal)* • *wearing a denim jacket, jeans and a baseball cap*

jeer AS A VERB = **mock**, hector, deride, heckle, knock *(informal)*, barrack, ridicule, taunt, sneer, scoff, banter, flout, gibe, cock a snook at *(Brit.)*, contemn *(formal)* • *His motorcade was jeered by angry residents.*
OPPOSITES: big up *(slang, chiefly Caribbean)*, give it up for *(slang)*, cheer
▸ AS A NOUN = **mockery**, abuse, ridicule, taunt, sneer, hiss, boo, scoff, hoot, derision, gibe, catcall, obloquy, aspersion • *the heckling and jeers of his audience*
OPPOSITES: praise, cheers, applause

jejune 1 = **simple**, silly, juvenile, naive, pointless, childish, immature, senseless, unsophisticated, puerile • *They were of great service in correcting my jejune generalizations.*
2 = **dull**, dry, banal, prosaic, colourless, uninteresting, inane, insipid, wishy-washy *(informal)*, vapid • *We knew we were in for a pretty long, jejune evening.*

jell *see* **gel**

jeopardize = **endanger**, threaten, put at risk, put in jeopardy, risk, expose, gamble, hazard, menace, imperil, put on the line • *The talks may still be jeopardized by disputes.*

jeopardy = **danger**, risk, peril, vulnerability, venture, exposure, liability, hazard, insecurity, pitfall, precariousness, endangerment • *A series of setbacks have put the whole project in jeopardy.*

jerk AS A VERB = **jolt**, bang, bump, lurch, shake • *The car jerked to a halt.*
▸ AS A NOUN 1 = **lurch**, movement, thrust, twitch, jolt, throw • *He indicated the bedroom with a jerk of his head.*
2 = **idiot**, fool, prick *(derogatory slang)*, wally *(slang)*, prat *(slang)*, plonker *(slang)*, coot, moron, geek *(slang)*, twit *(informal, chiefly Brit.)*, plank *(Brit. slang)*, chump, imbecile, cretin, oaf, simpleton, dimwit *(informal)*, dipstick *(Brit. slang)*, dickhead *(slang)*, gonzo *(slang)*, schmuck *(U.S. slang)*, dork *(slang)*, nitwit *(informal)*, divvy *(Brit. slang)*, pillock *(Brit. slang)*, halfwit, nincompoop, dweeb *(U.S. slang)*, putz *(U.S. slang)*, eejit *(Scot. & Irish)*, thicko *(Brit. slang)*, dumb-ass *(slang)*, gobshite *(Irish taboo)*, dunderhead, numpty *(Scot. informal)*, doofus *(slang, chiefly U.S.)*, lamebrain *(informal)*, fuckwit *(taboo)*, mooncalf, dickwit *(slang)*, nerd *or* nurd *(slang)*, numbskull *or* numskull, dorba *or* dorb *(Austral. slang)*, bogan *(Austral. slang)* • *He'd tricked her into walking into the garbage, to make her look like a total jerk!*

jerky = **bumpy**, rough, jolting, jumpy, shaky, bouncy, uncontrolled, twitchy, fitful, spasmodic, convulsive, tremulous • *He stood abruptly and left the room at a fast, jerky walk.*
OPPOSITES: flowing, smooth, gliding

jerry-built = **ramshackle**, cheap, faulty, shabby, defective, flimsy, rickety, thrown together, slipshod, unsubstantial • *Workers at the plant speak of jerry-built equipment.*
OPPOSITES: substantial, sturdy, well-built

jersey = **jumper**, sweater, woolly, pullover • *grey jersey and trousers*

jest AS A NOUN = **joke**, play, crack *(slang)*, sally, gag *(informal)*, quip, josh *(slang, chiefly U.S. & Canad.)*, banter, hoax, prank, wisecrack *(informal)*, pleasantry, witticism, jape, bon mot • *It was a jest rather than a reproach.*
▸ AS A VERB = **joke**, kid *(informal)*, mock, tease, sneer, jeer, quip, josh *(slang, chiefly U.S. & Canad.)*, scoff, banter, deride, chaff, gibe • *He enjoyed drinking and jesting with his cronies.*
▸ IN PHRASES: **in jest** = **as a joke**, tongue in cheek, jokingly, for a laugh, in fun, flippantly, facetiously, light-heartedly, as humour, as a tease • *Many a true word spoken in jest.*

QUOTATIONS
a fellow of infinite jest, of most excellent fancy
[William Shakespeare *Hamlet*]
PROVERBS
Many a truth lie in jest

jester 1 = **fool**, clown, harlequin, zany, madcap, prankster, buffoon, pantaloon, mummer • *a chap dressed as a court jester*
2 = **humorist**, comic, wit, comedian, wag, joker, dag *(N.Z. informal)*, quipster, joculator *or (fem.)* joculatrix • *He is the class jester writ large.*

jet AS A NOUN 1 = **plane**, aircraft, aeroplane, airplane *(U.S. & Canad.)*, jet plane • *He had arrived from Jersey by jet.*
2 = **stream**, current, spring, flow, rush, flood, burst, spray, fountain, cascade, gush, spurt, spout, squirt • *benches equipped with water jets to massage your back and feet*
▸ AS A VERB 1 = **fly**, wing, cruise, soar, zoom • *They spend a great deal of time jetting around the world.*
2 = **stream**, course, issue, shoot, flow, rush, surge, spill, gush, emanated, spout, spew, squirt • *a cloud of white smoke jetted out from the trees*

jet-black AS A NOUN
▸ AS AN ADJECTIVE = **black**, jet, raven, ebony, sable, pitch-black, inky, coal-black • *a woman with large grey eyes and jet-black hair*
▹ *See panel* **Shades of black to white**

jet-setting = **fashionable**, rich, sophisticated, trendy *(Brit. informal)*, cosmopolitan, well-off, high-society, ritzy *(slang)*, trendsetting • *the international jet-setting elite*

jettison 1 = **abandon**, reject, desert, dump, shed, scrap, throw out, discard, throw away, relinquish, forsake, slough off, throw on the scrapheap • *The government seems to have jettisoned the plan.*
2 = **expel**, dump, unload, throw overboard, eject, heave • *The crew jettisoned excess fuel and made an emergency landing.*

jetty = **pier**, dock, wharf, mole, quay, breakwater, groyne • *Schooners are moored off wooden jetties.*

jewel AS A NOUN 1 = **gemstone**, gem, precious stone, brilliant, ornament, trinket, sparkler *(informal)*, rock *(slang)* • *a golden box containing precious jewels*
2 = **treasure**, wonder, prize, darling, pearl, gem, paragon, pride and joy, taonga *(N.Z.)* • *Barbados is a perfect jewel of an island.*
▸ IN PHRASES: **jewel in the crown** = **masterpiece**, classic, jewel, tour de force *(French)*, pièce de résistance *(French)*, magnum opus, master work, chef-d'oeuvre *(French)* • *His achievement is astonishing and this book is the jewel in the crown.*

jeweller = **lapidary**, gemmologist • *He was the son of a jeweller.*

jewellery = **jewels**, treasure, gems, trinkets, precious stones, ornaments, finery, regalia, bling *(slang)* • *beautiful jewellery and silverware*

Jezebel = **harlot**, witch, jade, virago, wanton, hussy, harridan • *'You Jezebel! How could you steal my man from me?'*

jib at = **refuse**, retreat, shrink, stop short, balk, recoil • *Privately, some accused the association of jibbing at its tough line.*

jibe *or* **gibe** AS A NOUN = **jeer**, sneer, dig *(informal)*, crack, taunt, snide remark • *a cruel jibe about her weight*
▸ AS A VERB = **jeer**, mock, sneer, taunt • *'What's the matter, can't you read?' she jibed.*

jiffy = **moment**, second, flash, instant, twinkling, split second, trice, bat of an eye *(informal)* • *I'll have this truck fixed in a jiffy.*

jig = **skip**, bob, prance, jiggle, shake, bounce, twitch, wobble, caper, wiggle, jounce • *Guests bopped and jigged the night away to disco beat.*

jiggle 1 = **shake**, jerk, agitate, joggle • *He jiggled the doorknob noisily.*
2 = **jerk**, bounce, jog, fidget, shake, twitch, wiggle, jig, shimmy, joggle • *He tapped his feet, hummed tunes and jiggled about.*

jilt = **reject**, drop, disappoint, abandon, desert, ditch *(slang)*, betray, discard, deceive, forsake, throw over, coquette, leave (someone) in the lurch • *She was jilted by her first fiancé.*

jingle AS A VERB = **ring**, rattle, clatter, chime, jangle, tinkle, clink, clank, tintinnabulate • *Her bracelets jingled like bells.*

▸ **AS A NOUN** 1 = **rattle**, ringing, tinkle, clang, clink, reverberation, clangour • *the jingle of money in a man's pocket*
2 = **song**, tune, melody, ditty, chorus, slogan, verse, limerick, refrain, doggerel • *advertising jingles*

jingoism = **chauvinism**, bigotry, xenophobia, flag-waving *(informal)*, belligerence, insularity, hawkishness • *an outpouring of militaristic jingoism*

jinx **AS A NOUN** = **curse**, plague, voodoo, nemesis, black magic, hoodoo *(informal)*, hex *(U.S. & Canad. informal)*, evil eye • *Someone had put a jinx on him.*
▸ **AS A VERB** = **curse**, bewitch, hex *(U.S. & Canad. informal)* • *He's trying to rattle me, he said to himself, trying to jinx me so I can't succeed.*

jitters = **nerves**, anxiety, butterflies (in your stomach) *(informal)*, nervousness, the shakes *(informal)*, fidgets, cold feet *(informal)*, the willies *(informal)*, tenseness, heebie-jeebies *(slang)* • *I had a case of the jitters during my first two speeches.*

jittery = **nervous**, anxious, jumpy, twitchy *(informal)*, wired *(slang)*, trembling, shaky, neurotic, agitated, quivering, hyper *(informal)*, fidgety, antsy *(informal)* • *Investors have become jittery about the country's economy.*
OPPOSITES: together *(slang)*, relaxed, calm

job **AS A NOUN** 1 = **position**, post, function, capacity, work, posting, calling, place, business, office, trade, field, career, situation, activity, employment, appointment, craft, profession, occupation, placement, vocation, livelihood, métier • *the pressure of being the first woman in the job*
2 = **task**, concern, duty, charge, work, business, role, operation, affair, responsibility, function, contribution, venture, enterprise, undertaking, pursuit, assignment, stint, chore, errand • *Their main job is to preserve health rather than treat illness.*
3 = **difficulty**, problem, hassle *(informal)*, trouble, hard work • *With all these different pensions, you're going to have a job to keep track.*
▸ **IN PHRASES: jobs for the boys** = **cronyism**, favouritism, nepotism • *a 'jobs for the boys' system of government*
just the job = **perfect**, excellent, ideal, supreme, superb, splendid, sublime, superlative • *This bag is just the job for travelling.*

QUOTATIONS
If you have a job without aggravations, you don't have a job
[Malcolm S. Forbes]
Everyone sees life through their job. To the doctor the world is a hospital, to the broker it is a stock exchange, to the lawyer a vast criminal court
[Alasdair Gray *Janine*]
McJob: A low-pay, low-prestige, low-dignity, low-benefit, no-future job in the service sector
[Douglas Coupland *Generation X*]

jobless = **unemployed**, redundant, out of work, on the dole *(Brit. informal)*, inactive, out of a job, unoccupied, idle • *One in four people are now jobless in inner areas like Tottenham.*

jockey **AS A NOUN** = **horse-rider**, rider, equestrian • *It's a big day for Britain's former top jockey.*
▸ **AS A VERB** 1 = **compete**, fight, struggle, contest, contend, strive, vie, challenge • *The rival political parties are already jockeying for power.*
2 = **manoeuvre**, manage, engineer, negotiate, trim, manipulate, cajole, insinuate, wheedle, finagle *(informal)* • *Neil watched him jockey the craft among the running seas.*

jocose = **humorous**, funny, pleasant, witty, merry, playful, mischievous, joyous, comical, jesting, teasing, jovial, droll, blithe, facetious, jocular, waggish, sportive • *His conversation is carefully maintained at a level of jocose pomposity.*

jocular = **humorous**, joking, funny, amusing, teasing, jolly, witty, playful, whimsical, comical, jesting, jovial, droll, facetious, roguish, frolicsome, ludic *(literary)*, waggish, sportive, jocund, jocose • *He was in a less jocular mood than usual.*
OPPOSITES: serious, earnest, solemn

jog **AS A VERB** 1 = **run**, trot, canter, lope, dogtrot • *He could scarcely jog around the block that first day.*
2 = **nudge**, push, shake, prod • *Avoid jogging the camera.*
3 = **stimulate**, remind, prompt, stir, arouse, activate, nudge, prod • *Keep a card file on the books you have read to jog your memory later.*
▸ **AS A NOUN** = **run**, race, rush, dash, sprint, gallop, spurt • *He went for another early morning jog.*

joie de vivre = **enthusiasm**, zest, gusto, ebullience, joy, relish, enjoyment, gaiety, joyfulness • *He has plenty of joie de vivre.*
OPPOSITES: depression, apathy, distaste

join **AS A VERB** 1 = **enrol in**, enter, sign up for, become a member of, enlist in • *He joined the Army five years ago.*
2 = **become involved in**, associate with, affiliate with, become a part of • *Telephone operators joined the strike.*
3 = **connect**, unite, couple, link, marry, tie, combine, attach, knit, cement, adhere, fasten, annex, add, splice, yoke, append • *The opened link is used to join the two ends of the chain.*
OPPOSITES: separate, detach, sever
4 = **meet**, touch, border, extend, butt, adjoin, conjoin, reach • *Allahabad, where the Ganges and the Yamuna rivers join*
OPPOSITES: leave, part, resign
▸ **IN PHRASES: join in** = **take part**, contribute, participate, pitch in • *Everyone present will join in as she sings.*

PROVERBS
If you can't beat them, join them

joined-up = **sensible**, sound, practical, wise, reasonable, intelligent, realistic, rational, sober, discriminating, discreet, sage, shrewd, down-to-earth, matter-of-fact, prudent, sane, canny, judicious, far-sighted, well-thought-out, sagacious, well-reasoned • *another step towards joined-up government*

joint **AS AN ADJECTIVE** = **shared**, mutual, collective, communal, united, joined, allied, combined, corporate, concerted, consolidated, cooperative, reciprocal, collaborative • *They came to a joint decision as to where they would live.*
▸ **AS A NOUN** 1 = **junction**, union, link, connection, knot, brace, bracket, seam, hinge, weld, linkage, intersection, node, articulation, nexus • *Cut the stem just below a leaf joint.*
▸ **RELATED ADJECTIVE:** articular
2 = **place**, bar, restaurant, establishment, dive *(informal)*, nightclub, club • *I took him to the best 24-hour pizza joint in New York.*
3 = **spliff**, reefer *(informal)*, marijuana cigarette, cannabis cigarette • *She rolled a joint and handed it to me.*

jointly = **collectively**, together, in conjunction, as one, in common, mutually, in partnership, in league, unitedly • *The course is taught jointly with the History Department.*
OPPOSITES: individually, separately, singly

joke **AS A NOUN** 1 = **jest**, gag *(informal)*, wisecrack *(informal)*, witticism, crack *(informal)*, sally, quip, josh *(slang, chiefly U.S. & Canad.)*, pun, quirk, one-liner *(informal)*, jape • *No one told worse jokes than Claus.*
2 = **laugh**, jest, fun, josh *(slang, chiefly U.S. & Canad.)*, lark, sport, frolic, whimsy, jape • *It was probably just a joke to them, but it wasn't funny to me.*
3 = **farce**, nonsense, parody, sham, mockery, absurdity, travesty, ridiculousness • *The police investigation was a joke. A total cover-up.*
4 = **prank**, trick, practical joke, lark *(informal)*, caper, frolic, escapade, antic, jape • *I thought she was playing a joke on me at first but she wasn't.*
5 = **laughing stock**, butt, clown, buffoon, simpleton • *That man is just a complete joke.*

j

▸**AS A VERB** = **jest**, kid *(informal)*, fool, mock, wind up *(Brit. slang)*, tease, ridicule, taunt, quip, josh *(slang, chiefly U.S. & Canad.)*, banter, deride, frolic, chaff, gambol, play the fool, play a trick • *Don't get defensive, Charlie. I was only joking.*

PROVERBS

Many a true word is spoken in jest

joker = **comedian**, comic, wit, clown, wag, kidder *(informal)*, jester, dag *(N.Z. informal)*, prankster, buffoon, trickster, humorist • *He is, by nature, a joker, a witty man with a sense of fun.*

jokey = **playful**, funny, amusing, teasing, humorous, mischievous, jesting, wisecracking, droll, facetious, waggish, prankish, nonserious • *He was still his old jokey self.*
OPPOSITES: dry, grave, humourless

jollity = **fun**, mirth, gaiety, merriment, revelry, liveliness, conviviality, merrymaking • *the singing and jollity of the celebration*

jolly = **happy**, bright, funny, lively, hopeful, sunny, cheerful, merry, vibrant, hilarious, festive, upbeat *(informal)*, bubbly, gay, airy, playful, exuberant, jubilant, cheery, good-humoured, joyous, joyful, carefree, breezy, genial, ebullient, chirpy *(informal)*, sprightly, jovial, convivial, effervescent, frolicsome, ludic *(literary)*, mirthful, sportive, light-hearted, jocund, gladsome *(archaic)*, blithesome • *She was a jolly, kindhearted woman.*
OPPOSITES: serious, grave, miserable

jolt **AS A VERB** 1 = **jerk**, push, shake, knock, jar, shove, jog, jostle • *The train jolted into motion.*
2 = **surprise**, upset, stun, disturb, astonish, stagger, startle, perturb, discompose • *He was momentarily jolted by the news.*
▸**AS A NOUN** 1 = **jerk**, start, jump, shake, bump, jar, jog, lurch, quiver • *One tiny jolt could worsen her injuries.*
2 = **surprise**, blow, shock, setback, reversal, bombshell, thunderbolt, whammy *(informal, chiefly U.S.)*, bolt from the blue • *The campaign came at a time when America needed such a jolt.*

jostle 1 = **push**, press, crowd, shake, squeeze, thrust, butt, elbow, bump, scramble, shove, jog, jolt, throng, hustle, joggle • *We spent an hour jostling with the crowds as we did our shopping.*
2 = **compete**, fight, struggle, contest, contend, strive, vie, be in the running, challenge • *the contenders who have been jostling for the top job*

jot **AS A VERB** *usually with* **down** = **note down**, record, list, note, register, tally, scribble • *Listen carefully to the instructions and jot them down.*
▸**AS A NOUN** = **bit**, detail, ace, scrap, grain, particle, atom, fraction, trifle, mite, tad *(informal, chiefly U.S.)*, speck, morsel, whit, tittle, iota, scintilla, smidgen *or* smidgin *(informal, chiefly U.S. & Canad.)* • *It doesn't affect my judgement one jot.*

journal 1 = **magazine**, record, review, register, publication, bulletin, chronicle, gazette, periodical, zine *(informal)* • *All our results are published in scientific journals.*
2 = **newspaper**, paper, daily, weekly, monthly, tabloid • *He was a spokesperson for The New York Times and some other journals.*
3 = **diary**, record, history, log, notebook, chronicle, annals, yearbook, commonplace book, daybook, blog *(informal)* • *On the plane he wrote in his journal.*

journalism 1 = **the press**, newspapers, the papers, news media, Fleet Street *(Brit.)*, the fourth estate • *He began a career in journalism.*
2 = **reporting**, writing, reportage, article writing, feature writing • *an accomplished piece of investigative journalism*

QUOTATIONS

In America journalism is apt to be regarded as an extension of history: in Britain, as an extension of conversation
[Anthony Sampson *Anatomy of Britain Today*]

Journalism largely consists in saying 'Lord Jones Dead' to people who never knew that Lord Jones was alive
[G.K. Chesterton *The Wisdom of Father Brown*]

Journalism could be described as turning one's enemies into money
[Craig Brown]

Most rock journalism is people who can't write interviewing people who can't talk for people who can't read
[Frank Zappa]

I hope we never see the day when a thing is as bad as some of our newspapers make it
[Will Rogers]

Four hostile newspapers are to be feared more than a thousand bayonets
[Napoleon Bonaparte]

Modern journalism....justifies its own existence by the great Darwinian principle of the survival of the vulgarest
[Oscar Wilde]

The art of newspaper paragraphing is to stroke a platitude until it purrs like an epigram
[Don Marquis]

A good newspaper, I suppose, is a nation talking to itself
[Arthur Miller]

journalist = **reporter**, writer, correspondent, newsman *or* newswoman, stringer, commentator, broadcaster, hack *(derogatory)*, columnist, contributor, scribe *(informal)*, pressman, journo *(slang)*, newshound *(informal)*, hackette *(derogatory)*, newspaperman *or* newspaperwoman • *a freelance journalist with a special interest in the arts*

QUOTATIONS

Journalists say a thing that they know isn't true, in the hope that if they keep on saying it long enough it will be true
[Arnold Bennett *The Title*]

journey **AS A NOUN** 1 = **trip**, drive, tour, flight, excursion, progress, cruise, passage, trek, outing, expedition, voyage, ramble, jaunt, peregrination, travel • *a journey from Manchester to Plymouth*
2 = **progress**, passage, voyage, pilgrimage, odyssey • *My films try to describe a journey of discovery.*
▸**AS A VERB** = **travel**, go, move, walk, fly, range, cross, tour, progress, proceed, fare, wander, trek, voyage, roam, ramble, traverse, rove, wend, go walkabout *(Austral.)*, peregrinate • *She has journeyed on horseback through Africa and Turkey.*

QUOTATIONS

A journey of a thousand miles must begin with a single step
[Lao-tze *Tao Te Ching*]

A journey is like marriage. The certain way to be wrong is to think you control it
[John Steinbeck *Travels With Charley*]

Whenever I prepare for a journey I prepare as though for death. Should I never return, all is in order
[Katherine Mansfield]

joust **AS A VERB** 1 = **compete**, fight, contend, vie, struggle, contest, strive, challenge • *Lawyers joust in the courtroom.*
2 = **cross swords**, fight, engage, tilt, trade blows, enter the lists, break a lance • *Knights joust on the field.*
▸**AS A NOUN** = **duel**, match, lists, tournament, set-to, encounter, combat, engagement, tilt, tourney, passage of arms • *an annual reconstruction of medieval jousts and banquets*

jovial = **cheerful**, happy, jolly, animated, glad, merry, hilarious, buoyant, airy, jubilant, cheery, cordial, convivial, blithe, gay, mirthful, jocund, jocose • *Father Whittaker appeared to be in a jovial mood.*
OPPOSITES: solemn, grumpy, unfriendly

jowl IN PHRASES: **cheek by jowl with something** *or* **someone = near to**, adjacent to, hard by, within striking distance of *(informal)*, nearby to, just round the corner from, within spitting distance of *(informal)*, close by to, within sniffing distance of, proximate to, nigh to, a hop, skip and a jump away from • *She and her family have to live cheek by jowl with these people.*

joy AS A NOUN **1 = delight**, pleasure, triumph, satisfaction, happiness, ecstasy, enjoyment, bliss, transport, euphoria, festivity, felicity, glee, exuberance, rapture, elation, exhilaration, radiance, gaiety, jubilation, hilarity, exaltation, ebullience, exultation, gladness, joyfulness, ravishment • *Salter shouted with joy.*

OPPOSITES: despair, grief, sorrow

2 = treasure, wonder, treat, prize, delight, pride, charm, thrill • *one of the joys of being a chef*

▸ IN PHRASES: **no joy = no luck** *(Informal)*, a negative, no result, no success, no satisfaction • *They expect no joy from the vote itself.*

QUOTATIONS

But headlong joy is ever on the wing
[John Milton *The Passion*]

Things won are done; joy's soul lies in the doing
[William Shakespeare *Troilus and Cressida*]

Joy cometh in the morning
[*Bible: Psalms 5*]

joyful 1 = pleasing, satisfying, engaging, charming, delightful, enjoyable, gratifying, agreeable, pleasurable • *Giving birth to a child is both painful and joyful.*

2 = delighted, happy, satisfied, glad, jolly, merry, gratified, pleased, jubilant, elated, over the moon *(informal)*, jovial, rapt, enraptured, on cloud nine *(informal)*, cock-a-hoop, floating on air, light-hearted, jocund, gladsome *(archaic)*, blithesome, stoked *(Austral. & N.Z. informal)* • *We're a very joyful people.*

joyless = unhappy, sad, depressing, miserable, gloomy, dismal, dreary, dejected, dispirited, downcast, down in the dumps *(informal)*, cheerless • *His work load had become so enormous that life seemed joyless.*

joyous = joyful, cheerful, merry, festive, heartening, rapturous, blithe • *a joyous celebration of life*

jubilant = overjoyed, excited, thrilled, glad, triumphant, rejoicing, exuberant, joyous, elated, over the moon *(informal)*, euphoric, triumphal, enraptured, exultant, cock-a-hoop, rhapsodic, stoked *(Austral. & N.Z. informal)* • *He was jubilant after making an impressive comeback.*

OPPOSITES: sad, melancholy, downcast

jubilation = joy, triumph, celebration, excitement, ecstasy, jubilee, festivity, elation, jamboree, exultation • *His resignation was greeted by jubilation on the streets of Sofia.*

jubilee = celebration, holiday, fête, festival, carnival, festivity, gala • *Queen Victoria's jubilee*

Judaism

JEWISH DENOMINATIONS AND SECTS

Chassidism, Chasidism, Hassidism, *or* Hasidism	Conservative Judaism	Orthodox Judaism
	Liberal Judaism	Reform Judaism
		Zionism

Judas = traitor, betrayer, deceiver, renegade, turncoat • *The first time I left Sheffield Wednesday, they accused me of being a Judas.*

judge AS A NOUN **1 = magistrate**, justice, beak *(Brit. slang)*, His, Her *or* Your Honour • *The judge adjourned the hearing until next Tuesday.*

2 = referee, expert, specialist, umpire, umpie *(Austral. slang)*, mediator, examiner, connoisseur, assessor, arbiter, appraiser, arbitrator, moderator, adjudicator, evaluator, authority • *A panel of judges is now selecting the finalists.*

3 = critic, assessor, arbiter, appraiser, evaluator • *I'm a pretty good judge of character.*

▸ AS A VERB **1 = adjudicate**, referee, umpire, mediate, officiate, adjudge, arbitrate • *Entries will be judged in two age categories.*

2 = evaluate, rate, consider, appreciate, view, class, value, review, rank, examine, esteem, criticize, ascertain, surmise • *It will take a few more years to judge the impact of these ideas.*

3 = estimate, guess, assess, calculate, evaluate, gauge, appraise • *It is important to judge the weight of your washing load.*

4 = find, rule, pass, pronounce, decree, adjudge • *He was judged guilty and burned at the stake.*

▸ RELATED ADJECTIVE: judicial

QUOTATIONS

A judge is not supposed to know anything about the facts of life until they have been presented in evidence and explained to him at least three times
[Lord Parker]

Forbear to judge, for we are sinners all
[William Shakespeare *Henry VI, part II*]

Judge not, that ye be not judged
[*Bible: St. Matthew*]

PROVERBS

No one should be judge in his own cause

judgment AS A NOUN **1 = opinion**, view, estimate, belief, assessment, conviction, diagnosis, valuation, deduction, appraisal • *In your judgement, what has changed over the past few years?*

2 = verdict, finding, result, ruling, decision, sentence, conclusion, determination, decree, order, arbitration, adjudication, pronouncement • *The Court is expected to give its judgement within the next ten days.*

3 = sense, common sense, good sense, judiciousness, reason, understanding, taste, intelligence, smarts *(slang, chiefly U.S.)*, discrimination, perception, awareness, wisdom, wit, penetration, prudence, sharpness, acumen, shrewdness, discernment, perspicacity, sagacity, astuteness, percipience • *Publication of the information was a serious error in judgement.*

▸ IN PHRASES: **against your better judgment = reluctantly**, grudgingly, unwillingly, with reservation, in spite of yourself • *Against my better judgement, I agreed.*

QUOTATIONS

'Tis with our judgments as our watches: none
Go just alike, yet each believes his own
[Alexander Pope *Essay on Criticism*]

judgmental = condemnatory, self-righteous, censorious, pharisaic, critical • *We tried not to seem critical or judgmental.*

judicial = legal, official, judiciary, juridical • *an independent judicial inquiry*

judicious = sensible, considered, reasonable, discerning, sound, politic, acute, informed, diplomatic, careful, wise, cautious, rational, sober, discriminating, thoughtful, discreet, sage, enlightened, shrewd, prudent, sane, skilful, astute, expedient, circumspect, well-advised, well-judged, sagacious, sapient • *The President authorizes the judicious use of military force.*

OPPOSITES: thoughtless, indiscreet, injudicious

jug = container, pitcher, urn, carafe, creamer *(U.S. & Canad.)*, vessel, jar, crock, ewer • *a jug of water*

juggle = manipulate, change, doctor *(informal)*, fix *(informal)*, alter, modify, disguise, manoeuvre, tamper with, misrepresent, falsify • *the expedient juggling of figures for short-term year-end purposes*

juice 1 = **liquid**, extract, fluid, liquor, sap, nectar • *the juice of about six lemons*
2 = **secretion**, serum • *the digestive juices of the human intestinal tract*

juicy 1 = **moist**, lush, watery, succulent, sappy • *a thick, juicy steak*
2 = **interesting**, colourful, sensational, vivid, provocative, spicy *(informal)*, suggestive, racy, risqué • *It provided some juicy gossip for a few days.*

jumble AS A NOUN = **muddle**, mixture, mess, disorder, confusion, chaos, litter, clutter, disarray, medley, mélange *(French)*, miscellany, mishmash, farrago, hotchpotch *(U.S.)*, hodgepodge, gallimaufry, pig's breakfast *(informal)*, disarrangement • *a meaningless jumble of words*
▸ AS A VERB = **mix**, mistake, confuse, disorder, shuffle, tangle, muddle, confound, entangle, ravel, disorganize, disarrange, dishevel • *animals whose remains were jumbled together by scavengers and floods*

jumbo = **giant**, large, huge, immense, mega *(informal)*, gigantic, oversized, fuck-off *(taboo)*, elephantine, ginormous *(informal)*, humongous *or* humungous *(U.S. slang)*, supersize • *a jumbo box of tissues*
OPPOSITES: baby, tiny, pocket

j

jump AS A VERB 1 = **leap**, dance, spring, bound, bounce, hop, skip, caper, prance, gambol • *stamping their boots and jumping up and down to knock the snow off*
2 = **vault**, clear, hurdle, go over, sail over, hop over • *He jumped the first fence beautifully.*
3 = **spring**, bound, leap, bounce • *She jumped to her feet and ran downstairs.*
4 = **recoil**, start, jolt, flinch, shake, jerk, quake, shudder, twitch, wince • *The phone shrilled, making her jump.*
5 = **increase**, rise, climb, escalate, gain, advance, boost, mount, soar, surge, spiral, hike, ascend • *The number of crimes jumped by ten per cent last year.*
6 = **miss**, avoid, skip, omit, evade, digress • *He refused to jump the queue for treatment at the local hospital.*
7 = **attack**, assault, assail, set upon, charge, strike (at), rush, storm, fall upon, lay into *(informal)* • *Two guys jumped me with clubs in the car park.*
▸ AS A NOUN 1 = **leap**, spring, skip, bound, buck, hop, vault, caper • *With a few hops and a jump they launched themselves into the air.*
2 = **rise**, increase, escalation, upswing, advance, boost, elevation, upsurge, upturn, increment, augmentation • *an eleven per cent jump in profits*
3 = **jolt**, start, movement, shock, shake, jar, jerk, lurch, twitch, swerve, spasm • *When Spider tapped on a window, Miguel gave an involuntary jump.*
4 = **hurdle**, gate, barrier, fence, obstacle, barricade, rail • *Hurdlers need to have unnaturally over-flexible knees to clear the jump.*
▸ IN PHRASES: **jump at something** = **seize on**, grab, snatch, snap up, pounce on • *They would jump at the chance to become part owners of the corporation.*
jump in = **dive in**, leap in, plunge in, swoop in, plummet in • *The government had to jump in and purchase millions of dollars' worth of supplies.*
jump out of your skin = **be scared**, be afraid, be frightened, be nervous, be alarmed, be intimidated, be fearful, be timid • *He jumped out of his skin when he saw two rats.*
jump the gun = **act with haste**, be over-hasty, act too soon, act prematurely • *Some booksellers have jumped the gun and decided to sell it early.*

jumped-up = **conceited**, arrogant, pompous, stuck-up, cocky, overbearing, puffed up, presumptuous, insolent, immodest, toffee-nosed, self-opinionated, too big for your boots *or* breeches • *He's nothing better than a jumped-up bank clerk!*

jumper = **sweater**, top, jersey, cardigan, woolly, pullover • *You can't go wrong with a baggy jumper.*

jumpy = **nervous**, anxious, tense, shaky, restless, neurotic, agitated, hyper *(informal)*, apprehensive, jittery *(informal)*, on edge, twitchy *(informal)*, fidgety, timorous, antsy *(informal)*, wired *(slang)* • *I told myself not to be so jumpy.*
OPPOSITES: together *(slang)*, calm, composed

junction = **crossroads**, crossing, intersection, interchange, T-junction • *Follow the road to a junction and turn left.*

juncture = **moment**, time, point, crisis, occasion, emergency, strait, contingency, predicament, crux, exigency, conjuncture • *We're at a critical juncture.*

jungle AS A NOUN 1 = **rainforest**, forest, the bush, bushland, the wilds, wilderness, tropical rainforest • *the mountains and jungles of Papua New Guinea*
2 = **maze**, web, puzzle, confusion, uncertainty, tangle, snarl, mesh, bewilderment, perplexity, imbroglio • *a jungle of stuffed sofas, stuffed birds, knick-knacks, potted plants*
▸ IN PHRASES: **the law of the jungle** = **custom**, form, practice, tradition, procedure, habit, routine, convention, order *or* way of things • *If you make aggression pay, this becomes the law of the jungle.*

junior 1 = **minor**, lower, secondary, lesser, subordinate, inferior • *a junior minister attached to the prime minister's office*
2 = **younger** • *junior pupils*
OPPOSITES: older, senior, superior

junk AS A NOUN = **rubbish**, refuse, waste, scrap, litter, debris, crap *(slang)*, garbage *(chiefly U.S.)*, trash, clutter, rummage, dross, odds and ends, oddments, flotsam and jetsam, leavings, dreck *(slang, chiefly U.S.)* • *What are you going to do with all that junk?*
▸ AS A VERB = **get rid of**, drop, remove, reject, abandon, dump *(informal)*, shed, scrap, axe *(informal)*, ditch *(slang)*, chuck *(informal)*, discard, dispose of, relinquish, dispense with, jettison, repudiate, cast aside, throw away *or* out • *The socialists junked dogma when they came to office.*

junkie *or* **junky** 1 = **addict**, user, drug addict, druggie *(informal)*, head *(slang)*, freak *(informal)*, mainliner *(slang)*, smackhead *(slang)*, pill-popper *(slang)*, pothead *(slang)*, cokehead *(slang)*, acidhead *(slang)*, hashhead *(slang)*, weedhead *(slang)* • *a heroin junkie in a TV drama*
2 = **lover**, fan, supporter, follower, enthusiast, freak *(informal)*, admirer, buff *(informal)*, fanatic, devotee, fiend *(informal)*, zealot, aficionado • *a vinyl junkie*

junta = **cabal**, council, faction, league, set, party, ring, camp, crew, combination, assembly, gang, clique, coterie, schism, confederacy, convocation • *The military junta that had toppled the democratic government was ousted.*

jurisdiction 1 = **authority**, say, power, control, rule, influence, command, sway, dominion, prerogative, mana *(N.Z.)* • *The British police have no jurisdiction over foreign bank accounts.*
2 = **range**, area, field, district, bounds, zone, province, circuit, scope, orbit, sphere, compass, dominion • *matters which lie within his own jurisdiction*

just AS AN ADVERB 1 = **recently**, lately, only now • *The two had only just met.*
2 = **merely**, but, only, simply, solely, no more than, nothing but • *It's just a suggestion.*
3 = **barely**, hardly, only just, scarcely, at most, by a whisker, at a push, by the skin of your teeth • *He could just reach the man's head with his right hand.*
4 = **exactly**, really, quite, completely, totally, perfectly, entirely, truly, absolutely, precisely, altogether, positively • *Kiwi fruit are just the thing for a healthy snack.*
▸ AS AN ADJECTIVE 1 = **fair**, good, legitimate, honourable, right, square, pure, decent, upright, honest, equitable, righteous, conscientious, impartial, virtuous, lawful, blameless, unbiased, fair-minded, unprejudiced • *She fought honestly for a just cause and for freedom.*

OPPOSITES: unfair, prejudiced, corrupt
2 = fitting, due, correct, deserved, appropriate, justified, reasonable, suitable, decent, sensible, merited, proper, legitimate, desirable, apt, rightful, well-deserved, condign • *This cup final is a just reward for all the efforts they have put in.*
OPPOSITES: inappropriate, unreasonable, unfit
▸ **IN PHRASES: just about = practically**, almost, nearly, close to, virtually, all but, not quite, well-nigh • *He is just about the best golfer in the world.*

QUOTATIONS
Thrice is he arm'd that hath his quarrel just
[William Shakespeare *Henry VI, part II*]

justice 1 = fairness, equity, integrity, honesty, decency, impartiality, rectitude, reasonableness, uprightness, justness, rightfulness, right • *There is no justice in this world!*
OPPOSITES: wrong, injustice, dishonesty
2 = justness, fairness, legitimacy, reasonableness, right, integrity, honesty, legality, rectitude, rightfulness • *We must win people round to the justice of our cause.*
3 = law • *A lawyer is part of the machinery of justice.*
4 = judge, magistrate, beak (*Brit. slang*), His, Her *or* Your Honour • *a justice on the Supreme Court*
▸ **RELATED PHOBIA:** dikephobia

QUOTATIONS
It is better that ten guilty persons escape than one innocent suffer
[William Blackstone *Commentaries*]
Justice is conscience, not a personal conscience but the conscience of the whole of humanity
[Alexander Solzhenitsyn *Letter to three students*]
Justice should not only be done, but should manifestly and undoubtedly be seen to be done
[Lord Hewart]
For me, justice is the first condition of humanity
[Wole Soyinka *The Man Died*]

justifiable = reasonable, right, sound, fit, acceptable, sensible, proper, valid, legitimate, understandable, lawful, well-founded, defensible, tenable, excusable, warrantable, vindicable • *the strong and justifiable desire of the Baltic States for independence*
OPPOSITES: unreasonable, arbitrary, indefensible

justification = reason, grounds, defence, basis, excuse, approval, plea, warrant, apology, rationale, vindication, rationalization, absolution, exoneration, explanation, exculpation, extenuation • *I knew there was no justification for what I was doing.*

justified = acceptable, reasonable, understandable, justifiable, natural, normal, legitimate, logical, to be expected • *In my opinion, the decision was wholly justified.*

justify = explain, support, warrant, bear out, legitimize, establish, maintain, confirm, defend, approve, excuse, sustain, uphold, acquit, vindicate, validate, substantiate, exonerate, legalize, absolve, exculpate • *This decision was fully justified by economic conditions.*

justly = justifiably, rightly, correctly, properly, legitimately, rightfully, with good reason, lawfully • *Australians are justly proud of their native wildlife.*

jut = stick out, project, extend, protrude, poke, bulge, overhang, impend • *The northern end of the island juts out.*

juvenile AS A NOUN = child, youth, minor, girl, boy, teenager, infant, adolescent • *The number of juveniles in the general population has fallen.*
OPPOSITES: adult, grown-up
▸ **AS AN ADJECTIVE 1 = young**, junior, adolescent, youthful, immature • *a scheme to lock up persistent juvenile offenders*
OPPOSITES: adult, responsible, mature
2 = immature, childish, infantile, puerile, young, youthful, inexperienced, boyish, callow, undeveloped, unsophisticated, girlish, babyish, jejune • *As he gets older he becomes more juvenile.*

juxtaposition = proximity, adjacency, contact, closeness, vicinity, nearness, contiguity, propinquity • *The setting has an exciting juxtaposition of shapes.*

Kk

k

kai = **food**, grub *(slang)*, provisions, fare, board, commons, eats *(slang)*, feed, diet, meat, bread, tuck *(informal)*, tucker *(Austral. & N.Z. informal)*, rations, nutrition, tack *(informal)*, refreshment, scoff *(slang)*, nibbles, foodstuffs, nourishment, chow *(informal)*, sustenance, nosh *(slang)*, daily bread, victuals, edibles, comestibles, provender, nosebag *(slang)*, pabulum *(rare)*, nutriment, vittles *(obsolete, dialect)*, viands, aliment, eatables *(slang)* • *I'm starving – let's have some kai.*

kak 1 = **faeces**, shit *(taboo)*, excrement, stool, muck, manure, dung, droppings, waste matter • *His shoes were covered in kak.*
2 = **rubbish**, nonsense, malarkey, garbage *(informal)*, balls *(taboo)*, bull *(slang)*, rot, crap *(taboo)*, bullshit *(taboo)*, bollocks *(Brit. taboo)*, cobblers *(Brit. taboo)*, drivel, tripe *(informal)*, claptrap *(informal)*, poppycock *(informal)*, pants, shit *(taboo)*, bizzo *(Austral. slang)*, bull's wool *(Austral. & N.Z. slang)* • *Now you're just talking kak.*

kaleidoscopic 1 = **many-coloured**, multi-coloured, harlequin, psychedelic, motley, variegated, prismatic, varicoloured • *a kaleidoscopic set of bright images*
2 = **changeable**, shifting, varied, mobile, variable, fluid, uncertain, volatile, unpredictable, unstable, fluctuating, indefinite, unsteady, protean, mutable, impermanent, inconstant • *a kaleidoscopic world of complex relationships*
3 = **complicated**, complex, confused, confusing, disordered, puzzling, unclear, baffling, bewildering, chaotic, muddled, intricate, jumbled, convoluted, disorganized, disarranged • *a kaleidoscopic and fractured view of Los Angeles*

kamikaze = **self-destructive**, suicidal, foolhardy • *Tone down your kamikaze tendencies.*

kangaroo
▸ NAME OF MALE: buck, old man
▸ NAME OF YOUNG: joey
▸ COLLECTIVE NOUN: troop

kaput = **broken**, finished, dead, destroyed, ruined, wrecked, undone, extinct, defunct, dead in the water *(informal)* • *His film career was kaput.*

keel over 1 = **collapse**, faint, pass out, black out *(informal)*, swoon *(literary)* • *He keeled over and fell flat on his back.*
2 = **capsize**, list, upset, founder, overturn, turn over, lean over, tip over, topple over, turn turtle • *The vessel keeled over towards the murky water.*

keen[1] AS AN ADJECTIVE 1 = **eager**, earnest, spirited, devoted, intense, fierce, enthusiastic, passionate, ardent, avid, fervent, impassioned, zealous, ebullient, wholehearted, fervid, bright-eyed and bushy-tailed *(informal)* • *a keen amateur photographer*
OPPOSITES: indifferent, lukewarm, unenthusiastic
2 = **earnest**, fierce, intense, vehement, burning, flaming, consuming, eager, passionate, heightened, energetic, ardent, fanatical, fervent, impassioned, fervid • *his keen sense of loyalty*
3 = **faithful**, true, constant, devoted, loyal, patriotic, staunch, dependable, trustworthy, trusty, steadfast, dutiful, unwavering, true-blue, immovable, unswerving, tried and true, true-hearted • *He's been a keen supporter all his life.*
4 = **sharp**, satirical, incisive, trenchant, pointed, cutting, biting, edged, acute, acid, stinging, piercing, penetrating, searing, tart, withering, scathing, pungent, sarcastic, sardonic, caustic, astringent, vitriolic, acerbic, mordant, razor-like, finely honed • *a keen sense of humour*
OPPOSITES: dull, blunt
5 = **perceptive**, quick, sharp, brilliant, acute, smart, wise, clever, subtle, piercing, penetrating, discriminating, shrewd, discerning, ingenious, astute, intuitive, canny, incisive, insightful, observant, perspicacious, sapient • *a man of keen intellect*
OPPOSITES: dull, obtuse, unperceptive
6 = **penetrating**, clear, powerful, sharp, acute, sensitive, piercing, discerning, perceptive, observant • *a keen eye for detail*
7 = **intense**, strong, fierce, relentless, cut-throat • *Competition is keen for these awards.*
▸ IN PHRASES: **keen on** = **attracted to**, fond of, taken with, infatuated with, into *(informal)*, attached to, devoted to, stuck on *(informal)*, enamoured of, sweet on *(informal)*, smitten with • *Mick has always been very keen on Carla.*
keen to = **anxious to**, hoping to, wishing to, determined to, longing to, eager to, dying to, yearning to, itching to, impatient to, ambitious to, desirous to • *We're keen to wrap the matter up within two or three weeks.*

keen[2] = **lament**, cry, weep, sob, mourn, grieve, howl, sorrow, wail, whine, whimper, bewail • *He tossed back his head and keened.*

keenness 1 = **eagerness**, passion, enthusiasm, intensity, zeal, zest, impatience, fervour, diligence, ardour, earnestness, ebullience, avidity, avidness • *the keenness of the students*
2 = **astuteness**, wisdom, insight, sensitivity, cleverness, shrewdness, discernment, sagacity, canniness, sapience • *the keenness of his imagination*

keep AS A VERB 1 = **remain**, stay, continue to be, go on being, carry on being • *Keeping cool out here requires cold drinks plus a hat.*
2 *usually with* **from** = **prevent**, hold back, deter, inhibit, block, stall, restrain, hamstring, hamper, withhold, hinder, retard, impede, shackle, keep back • *Embarrassment has kept me from doing all sorts of things.*
3 *sometimes with* **on** = **continue**, go on, carry on, persist in, persevere in, remain • *I turned back after a while, but he kept walking.*
4 = **hold on to**, maintain, retain, keep possession of, save, preserve, nurture, cherish, conserve • *We want to keep as many players as we can.*
OPPOSITES: retain, lose, give up

5 = **store**, put, place, house, hold, deposit, pile, stack, heap, amass, stow • *She kept her money under the mattress.*
6 = **carry**, stock, have, hold, sell, supply, handle, trade in, deal in • *The shop keeps specialised books on various aspects of the collection.*
7 = **comply with**, carry out, honour, fulfil, hold, follow, mind, respect, observe, respond to, embrace, execute, obey, heed, conform to, adhere to, abide by, act upon • *I'm hoping you'll keep your promise to come for a long visit.*
OPPOSITES: ignore, disregard
8 = **record**, report, write, document, log, chronicle, take down, set down • *Eleanor began to keep a diary.*
9 = **support**, maintain, sustain, provide for, mind, fund, board, finance, feed, look after, foster, shelter, care for, take care of, nurture, safeguard, cherish, nourish, subsidize • *She could just about afford to keep her five kids.*
10 = **raise**, own, maintain, tend, farm, breed, look after, rear, care for, bring up, nurture, nourish • *This mad writer kept a lobster as a pet.*
11 = **manage**, run, administer, be in charge (of), rule, direct, handle, govern, oversee, supervise, preside over, superintend • *His father kept a village shop.*
12 = **delay**, detain, hinder, impede, stop, limit, check, arrest, curb, constrain, obstruct, retard, set back • *'Sorry to keep you, Jack.'*
OPPOSITES: detain, free, release
13 = **stay fresh**, be suitable, be safe to eat, remain flavoursome • *Whatever is left over will keep for 2-3 weeks.*
14 = **associate with**, mix with, mingle with, hang out with (*informal*), hang with (*informal, chiefly U.S.*), be friends with, consort with, run around with (*informal*), hobnob with, socialize with, hang about with, fraternize with • *I don't like the company you keep.*
15 = **honour**, mark, respect, celebrate, observe, acknowledge, recognize, commemorate, ritualize, solemnize, perform • *My father never kept the Sabbath and I never did either.*
▸ **AS A NOUN** 1 = **board**, food, maintenance, upkeep, means, living, support, nurture, livelihood, subsistence, kai (*N.Z. informal*), nourishment, sustenance • *I need to give my parents money for my keep.*
2 = **tower**, castle, stronghold, dungeon, citadel, fastness, donjon • *the parts of the keep open to visitors*
▸ **IN PHRASES: for keeps** = **forever**, permanent, for all time, for always, for evermore, for good and all (*informal*), till the cows come home (*informal*), till the end of time, till Doomsday • *Whatever you gain now will be for keeps.*
keep at it = **persist**, continue, carry on, keep going, stick with it, stay with it, be steadfast, grind it out, persevere, remain with it • *'Keep at it!' Thade encouraged me.*
keep away = **stay away**, hold back, stand back, rest away, wait away • *Keep away from the doors while the train is moving.*
keep off something = **avoid**, steer clear of, dodge, get away from, shun, eschew, sidestep, shirk from • *I managed to stick to the diet and keep off sweet foods.*
keep on about something = **go on about**, go on and on about, ramble on about, rant on about, talk constantly about • *He kept on about me being 'defensive'.*
keep on at someone = **nag**, badger, pester, hassle (*informal*), harry, provoke, plague, harass, berate, bend someone's ear (*informal*), be on your back (*slang*), henpeck • *She kept on at him to get some qualifications.*
keep someone down = **oppress**, burden, depress, harass, dispirit, take the heart out of • *No matter what a woman tries to do, there is some barrier to keep her down.*
keep something back 1 = **hold back**, hold, save, set aside, husband, store, retain, preserve, withhold, hang on to, conserve, stockpile, hoard, lay up, put by • *Roughly chop the vegetables, and keep back a few for decoration.*
2 = **suppress**, hide, reserve, conceal, restrain, cover up, withhold, stifle, censor, repress, smother, muffle, muzzle, keep something under your hat • *Neither of them is telling the whole truth. They're both keeping something back.*
3 = **restrain**, control, limit, check, delay, restrict, curb, prohibit, withhold, hold back, constrain, retard, keep a tight rein on • *I can no longer keep back my tears.*
keep something down = **restrict**, limit, check, curb, fix, specify, restrain, demarcate, delimit • *The prime aim is to keep inflation down.*
keep something from someone = **hide something**, keep someone in the dark, conceal something, mask something, keep something secret, obscure something • *She knew that Gabriel was keeping something from her.*
keep something up 1 = **continue**, make, maintain, carry on, persist in, persevere with • *They can no longer keep up the repayments.*
2 = **maintain**, sustain, uphold, perpetuate, retain, preserve, prolong • *keeping up the pressure against the government*
keep to something = **observe**, follow, obey, stick to, respect, honour, mind, comply with, heed, conform to, adhere to, abide by • *Keep to the speed limit.*
keep up = **keep pace**, match, compete, contend, emulate, persevere • *Things are changing so fast, it's hard to keep up.*

keeper 1 = **goalkeeper**, stopper (*informal*), goalie (*informal*) • *The Portuguese keeper made one of the most remarkable saves*
2 = **curator**, guardian, steward, superintendent, attendant, caretaker, overseer, preserver • *the keeper of the library at the V&A*

keeping **AS A NOUN** = **care**, keep, charge, trust, protection, possession, maintenance, custody, patronage, guardianship, safekeeping • *It has been handed over for safe keeping.*
▸ **IN PHRASES: in keeping with** = **in agreement with**, consistent with, in harmony with, in accord with, in compliance with, in conformity with, in balance with, in correspondence with, in proportion with, in congruity with, in observance with • *His office was in keeping with his station and experience.*

keepsake = **souvenir**, symbol, token, reminder, relic, remembrance, emblem, memento, favour • *a keepsake of their brief encounter*

keg = **barrel**, drum, vat, cask, firkin, tun, hogshead • *a full keg of beer*

ken **IN PHRASES: beyond someone's ken** = **beyond the knowledge of**, beyond the comprehension of, beyond the understanding of, beyond the acquaintance of, beyond the awareness of, beyond the cognizance of • *beyond the ken of the average layman*

kernel = **essence**, core, substance, gist, grain, marrow, germ, nub, pith • *the kernel of his message*

key **AS A NOUN** 1 = **opener**, door key, latchkey • *She reached for her coat and car keys.*
2 = **tone**, sound, pitch, timbre, modulation • *the key of A minor*
3 = **guide**, explanation, interpretation, indicator, translation, glossary • *You will find a key at the start of the book.*
4 = **answer**, means, secret, solution, path, formula, passage, clue, cue, pointer, sign • *The key to success is to be ready from the start.*
▸ **AS A MODIFIER** = **essential**, leading, major, main, important, chief, necessary, basic, vital, crucial, principal, fundamental, decisive, indispensable, pivotal, must-have • *He is expected to be the key witness at the trial.*
OPPOSITES: minor, secondary, subsidiary

keyed up = **nervous**, strained, anxious, tense, under pressure, restless, wound up (*informal*), hyper (*informal*), apprehensive, edgy, jittery (*informal*), wired (*slang*), uptight (*informal*), on edge, jumpy, twitchy (*informal*), overwrought, strung up (*informal*), on tenterhooks, fidgety, antsy (*informal*), wrought up, adrenalized • *I wasn't able to sleep that night, I was so keyed up.*

keynote = **heart**, centre, theme, core, substance, essence, marrow, kernel, gist, pith • *the keynotes of their foreign policy*

keystone = **basis**, principle, core, crux, ground, source, spring, root, motive, cornerstone, lynchpin, mainspring, fundament, quoin • *the keystone of the government's economic policy*

kia ora = **hello**, hi (*informal*), greetings, gidday *or* g'day (*Austral. & N.Z.*), how do you do?, good morning, good evening, good afternoon, welcome • *a postcard bearing the caption 'Kia-Ora: Greetings from Māoriland'*

kick AS A VERB 1 = **boot**, strike, knock, punt, put the boot in(to) (*slang*) • *The fiery actress kicked him in the shins.*
2 = **give up**, break, stop, abandon, quit, cease, eschew, leave off, desist from, end • *She's kicked her drug habit.*
▸ AS A NOUN 1 = **thrill**, glow, buzz (*slang*), tingle, high (*slang*), sensation • *I got a kick out of seeing my name in print.*
2 = **pungency**, force, power, edge, strength, snap (*informal*), punch, intensity, pep, sparkle, vitality, verve, zest, potency, tang, piquancy • *The coffee had more of a kick than it seemed on first tasting.*
▸ IN PHRASES: **a kick in the teeth** = **setback**, defeat, blow, disappointment, hold-up, hitch, misfortune, rebuff, whammy (*informal, chiefly U.S.*), bummer (*slang*) • *It's a real kick in the teeth to see someone make it ahead of us.*
kick against something = **oppose**, resist, complain about, object to, protest against, spurn, rebel against, grumble about, gripe about (*informal*) • *North Sea operators kicked against legislation*
kick someone around = **mistreat**, wrong, abuse, injure, harm, misuse, maul, molest, manhandle, rough up, ill-treat, brutalize, maltreat, ill-use, handle roughly, knock about *or* around • *I'm not going to let anyone kick me around anymore.*
kick someone off something = **dismiss from**, ban from, exclude from, bar from, discharge from, exile from, banish from, evict from, oust from, expatriate from, blackball from, throw you out of, send packing from, turf you out (*informal*), show you the door out of • *We can't just kick them off the team.*
kick someone out = **dismiss**, remove, reject, get rid of, discharge, expel, oust, eject, evict, toss out, give the boot (*slang*), sack (*informal*), kiss off (*slang, chiefly U.S. & Canad.*), give (someone) their marching orders, give the push, give the bum's rush (*slang*), show you the door, throw you out on your ear (*informal*), give someone his *or* her P45 (*informal*), kennet (*Austral. slang*), jeff (*Austral. slang*) • *They kicked five foreign journalists out of the country.*
kick something around = **discuss**, consider, talk about, review, debate, examine, thrash out, exchange views on, weigh up the pros and cons of, converse about • *We kicked a few ideas around.*
kick something off = **begin**, start, open, commence, launch, initiate, get under way, kick-start, get on the road • *We kicked off the meeting with a song.*

kickback = **bribe**, payoff, backhander (*slang*), enticement, share, cut (*informal*), payment, gift, reward, incentive, graft (*informal*), sweetener (*slang*), inducement, sop, recompense, hush money (*slang*), payola (*informal*), allurement • *a nationwide web of alleged kickbacks and illegal party financing*

kick-off = **start**, opening, beginning, commencement, outset, starting point, inception • *people awaiting the kick-off of the parade*

kick-start = **stimulate**, encourage, prompt, spur, provoke, arouse, rouse, quicken, incite, gee up, get something going • *He has chosen to kick-start the economy by slashing interest rates.*

kid[1] AS A NOUN = **child**, girl, boy, baby, lad, teenager, youngster, infant, adolescent, juvenile, toddler, tot, lass, wean, little one, bairn, stripling, sprog (*slang*), munchkin (*informal, chiefly U.S.*), rug rat (*U.S. & Canad. informal*), littlie (*Austral. informal*), ankle-biter (*Austral. slang*), tacker (*Austral. slang*) • *All the kids in my class could read.*
▸ AS AN ADJECTIVE = **younger**, little, baby • *My kid sister woke up and started crying.*

kid[2] AS A VERB = **tease**, joke, trick, fool, pretend, mock, rag (*Brit.*), wind up (*Brit. slang*), ridicule, hoax, beguile, gull (*archaic*), delude, jest, bamboozle, hoodwink, cozen, jerk *or* yank someone's chain (*informal*) • *Are you sure you're not kidding me?* • *I'm just kidding.*
▸ IN PHRASES: **kid yourself** = **fool yourself**, delude yourself, deceive yourself, mislead yourself, con yourself (*informal*), bamboozle yourself, dupe yourself, hoax yourself, trick yourself • *I could kid myself that you did this for me, but it would be a lie.*

kidnap = **abduct**, remove, steal, capture, seize, snatch (*slang*), hijack, run off with, run away with, make off with, hold to ransom • *Police in Brazil uncovered a plot to kidnap him.*

kidney
▸ RELATED ADJECTIVES: renal, nephritic

kill AS A VERB 1 = **slay**, murder, execute, slaughter, destroy, waste (*informal*), do in (*slang*), take out (*slang*), massacre, butcher, wipe out (*informal*), dispatch, cut down, erase, assassinate, eradicate, whack (*informal*), do away with, blow away (*slang, chiefly U.S.*), obliterate, knock off (*slang*), liquidate, decimate, annihilate, neutralize, exterminate, terminate (*slang*), croak, mow down, take (someone's) life, bump off (*slang*), extirpate, wipe from the face of the earth (*informal*) • *More than 1,000 people have been killed by the armed forces.*
2 = **destroy**, defeat, crush, scotch, still, stop, total (*slang*), ruin, halt, cancel, wreck, shatter, veto, suppress, dismantle, stifle, trash (*slang*), ravage, eradicate, smother, quash, quell, extinguish, annihilate, put paid to • *Public opinion may yet kill the proposal.*
3 = **deaden**, reduce, check, dull, diminish, weaken, cushion, suppress, blunt, mute, stifle, paralyse, numb, lessen, alleviate, smother, dampen, muffle, abate, quieten, anaesthetize, benumb • *He was forced to take opium to kill the pain.*
4 = **hurt**, burn, smart, sting, ache, throb, be uncomfortable, be tender, be sore • *My feet are killing me.*
5 = **pass**, spend, fill, waste, occupy, use up, while away • *We've got at least an hour to kill.*
6 = **switch off**, cut, stop, cut off, put out, shut down, turn off, extinguish • *Latovsky killed the lights and motor.*
▸ AS A NOUN = **killing**, murder, massacre, slaughter, execution, dispatch, slaying, bloodshed, carnage, extermination, butchery • *After the kill they collect in an open space.*
▸ IN PHRASES: **kill yourself** = **overexert yourself**, do too much, drive yourself, burn the candle at both ends (*informal*), wear yourself out, strain yourself, knock yourself out, push yourself too hard, work yourself to death, overstrain yourself, overtire yourself, overwork yourself, overtax yourself • *Don't kill yourself trying to get this finished in time.*

QUOTATIONS

Kill one man and you are a murderer. Kill millions and you are a conqueror. Kill all and you are a God
[Jean Rostand *Pensées d'un Biologiste*]

Thou shalt not kill
[*Bible: Exodus*]

Thou shalt not kill; but needst not strive
Officiously, to keep alive
[Arthur Hugh Clough *The Latest Decalogue*]

killer 1 = **murderer**, slaughterer, slayer, hit man (*slang*), butcher, gunman, assassin, destroyer, liquidator, terminator, executioner, exterminator • *The police are searching for his killers.*

2 = **cause of death**, scourge, fatal illness, plague • *Heart disease is the biggest killer of men in most developed countries.*

killing AS A NOUN = **murder**, massacre, slaughter, execution, dispatch, manslaughter, elimination, slaying, homicide, bloodshed, carnage, fatality, liquidation, extermination, annihilation, eradication, butchery, necktie party *(informal)* • *This is a brutal killing.*

▸ AS AN ADJECTIVE 1 = **tiring**, hard, testing, taxing, difficult, draining, exhausting, punishing, crippling, fatiguing, gruelling, sapping, debilitating, strenuous, arduous, laborious, enervating, backbreaking • *He covered the last 300 metres in around 41sec, a killing pace.*

2 = **deadly**, deathly, dangerous, fatal, destructive, lethal, mortal, murderous, death-dealing • *Diphtheria was a killing disease.*

▸ IN PHRASES: **make a killing** = **profit**, gain, clean up *(informal)*, be lucky, be successful, make a fortune, strike it rich *(informal)*, make a bomb *(slang)*, rake it in *(informal)*, had a windfall • *They have made a killing on the deal.*

killjoy = **spoilsport**, dampener, damper, wet blanket *(informal)* • *Don't be such a killjoy!*

kilter IN PHRASES: **out of kilter** = **incompatible**, conflicting, contrary, at odds, contradictory, inconsistent, in conflict, incongruous, discordant, incoherent, out of step, irreconcilable, at variance, discrepant, inconstant • *Her lifestyle was out of kilter with her politics.*

kin = **family**, people, relations, relatives, connections, kindred, kinsmen, kith, kinsfolk, ainga *(N.Z.)*, rellies *(Austral. slang)* • *She has gone to live with her husband's kin.*

kind[1] 1 = **considerate**, good, loving, kindly, understanding, concerned, friendly, neighbourly, gentle, generous, mild, obliging, sympathetic, charitable, thoughtful, benign, humane, affectionate, compassionate, clement, gracious, indulgent, benevolent, attentive, amiable, courteous, amicable, lenient, cordial, congenial, philanthropic, unselfish, propitious, beneficent, kind-hearted, bounteous, tender-hearted • *He was a very kind man, full of common sense.*

OPPOSITES: severe, harsh, unkind

2 = **flattering**, becoming, enhancing • *Summer clothes are invariably less kind to fuller figures.*

kind[2] AS A NOUN 1 = **class**, sort, type, variety, brand, grade, category, genre, classification, league • *They developed a new kind of film-making.*

2 = **sort**, set, type, ilk, family, race, species, breed, genus • *I hate Lewis and his kind just as much as you do.*

3 = **nature**, sort, type, manner, style, quality, character, make-up, habit, stamp, description, mould, essence, temperament, persuasion, calibre, disposition • *Donations came in from all kinds of people.*

▸ IN PHRASES: **kind of** = **rather**, quite, sort of *(informal)*, a little, a bit, pretty *(informal)*, fairly, relatively, somewhat, slightly, moderately, to some extent, to some degree • *It was kind of sad, really.*

of a kind = **of a sort**, of a type • *There is good news of a kind for the Prime Minister.*

kind-hearted = **sympathetic**, kind, generous, helpful, tender, humane, compassionate, gracious, amicable, considerate, altruistic, good-natured, tender-hearted • *He was a warm, generous and kind-hearted man.*

OPPOSITES: cold, severe, hard-hearted

kindle 1 = **arouse**, excite, inspire, stir, thrill, stimulate, provoke, induce, awaken, animate, rouse, sharpen, inflame, incite, foment, bestir, enkindle • *These poems have helped kindle the imagination of generations of children.*

2 = **light**, start, ignite, fire, spark, torch, inflame, set fire to, set a match to • *I came in and kindled a fire in the stove.*

OPPOSITES: quell, extinguish, douse

kindliness = **kindness**, charity, sympathy, humanity, compassion, friendliness, gentleness, benevolence, amiability, beneficence, benignity, kind-heartedness • *His kindliness and warmth made him particularly effective with staff welfare.*

kindly AS AN ADJECTIVE = **benevolent**, kind, caring, nice, warm, gentle, helpful, pleasant, mild, sympathetic, beneficial, polite, favourable, benign, humane, compassionate, hearty, cordial, considerate, genial, affable, good-natured, beneficent, well-disposed, kind-hearted, warm-hearted • *He was a stern critic but an extremely kindly man.*

OPPOSITES: mean, severe, cruel

▸ AS AN ADVERB 1 = **benevolently**, politely, generously, thoughtfully, tenderly, lovingly, cordially, affectionately, helpfully, graciously, obligingly, agreeably, indulgently, selflessly, unselfishly, compassionately, considerately • *He kindly carried our picnic in a rucksack.*

OPPOSITES: meanly, harshly, unkindly

2 = **please**, pray, if you don't mind, if you please, if you'd be so kind • *Will you kindly do as you are told?*

▸ IN PHRASES: **look kindly on** *or* **upon something** *or* **someone** = **help**, back, second, support, aid, forward, champion, encourage, defend, promote, take (someone's) part, strengthen, assist, advocate, uphold, side with, go along with, stand up for, espouse, stand behind, hold (someone's) hand, stick up for *(informal)*, succour, buoy up, boost (someone's) morale, take up the cudgels for, be a source of strength to • *The committee will look kindly on requests to replace injured players.*

not take kindly to something *or* **someone** = **dislike**, object to, resent, take exception to, be offended by, be angry about, be bitter about, take offence at, harbour a grudge against, take as an insult, be in a huff about, take amiss, be pissed (off) about *(taboo slang)*, have hard feelings about • *She did not take kindly to being offered advice on her social life.*

kindness 1 = **goodwill**, understanding, charity, grace, humanity, affection, patience, tolerance, goodness, compassion, hospitality, generosity, indulgence, decency, tenderness, clemency, gentleness, philanthropy, benevolence, magnanimity, fellow-feeling, amiability, beneficence, kindliness • *We have been treated with such kindness by everybody.*

OPPOSITES: cruelty, malice, animosity

2 = **good deed**, help, service, aid, favour, assistance, bounty, benefaction • *It would be a kindness to leave her alone.*

QUOTATIONS

Kindness effects more than severity
[Aesop *Fables: The Wind and the Sun*]

True kindness presupposes the faculty of imagining as one's own the suffering and joys of others
[André Gide *Portraits and Aphorisms*]

That best portion of a good man's life,
His little, nameless, unremembered acts
Of kindness and of love
[William Wordsworth *Lines Composed a Few Miles Above Tintern Abbey*]

Yet I do fear thy nature;
It is too full o' the milk of human kindness
To catch the nearest way
[William Shakespeare *Macbeth*]

kindred AS A NOUN = **family**, relations, relatives, connections, flesh, kin, lineage, kinsmen, kinsfolk, ainga *(N.Z.)*, rellies *(Austral. slang)* • *The offender made proper restitution to the victim's kindred.*

▸ AS AN ADJECTIVE 1 = **similar**, like, related, allied, corresponding, affiliated, akin, kin, cognate, matching • *I recall discussions with her on these and kindred topics.*

2 = **like-minded**, similar, compatible, understanding, similar, friendly, sympathetic, responsive, agreeable, in tune, congenial, like, companionable • *We're sort of kindred spirits.*

k

king AS A NOUN **1 = ruler**, monarch, sovereign, crowned head, leader, lord, prince, Crown, emperor, majesty, head of state, consort, His Majesty, overlord • *In 1154, Henry II became king of England.*
2 = celebrity, star, big name, leading man *or* lady, lead, name, draw, idol, luminary, main attraction, celeb *(informal)*, megastar *(informal)* • *He's the king of unlicensed boxing.*
▸ IN PHRASES: **a king's ransom = fortune**, packet, large sum of money, top dollar *(informal)*, top whack *(informal)* • *clients happy to pay a king's ransom for a haircut*
▸ RELATED ADJECTIVES: royal, regal, monarchical

QUOTATIONS
I know I have the body of a weak and feeble woman, but I have the heart and stomach of a king, and of a king of England too
[Queen Elizabeth I]

kingdom 1 = country, state, nation, land, division, territory, province, empire, commonwealth, realm, domain, tract, dominion, sovereign state • *the Kingdom of Denmark*
2 = domain, territory, province, realm, area, department, field, zone, arena, sphere • *nature study trips to the kingdom of the polar bear*
3 = class, grouping, category, classification, order, sort, department, division, section, rank, grade • *the delicate jewels of the plant and animal kingdoms*

kingly = royal, imperial, sovereign, regal, monarchical • *waving his arms in a kingly manner*

kink 1 = twist, bend, wrinkle, knot, tangle, coil, corkscrew, entanglement, crimp, frizz • *a tiny black kitten with tufted ears and a kink in her tail*
2 = quirk, eccentricity, foible, idiosyncrasy, whim, fetish, vagary, singularity, crotchet • *What kink did he have in his character?*
3 = flaw, difficulty, defect, complication, tangle, knot, hitch, imperfection • *working out the kinks of a potential trade agreement*

kinky 1 = perverted, warped, deviant, unnatural, degenerated, unsavoury, unhealthy, depraved, licentious, pervy *(slang)* • *engaging in some kind of kinky sexual activity*
2 = weird, odd, strange, bizarre, peculiar, eccentric, queer, quirky, unconventional, off-the-wall *(slang)*, outlandish, oddball *(informal)*, wacko *(slang)*, out there *(slang)*, outré • *kinky behaviour*
3 = twisted, curled, curly, frizzy, tangled, coiled, crimped, frizzled • *He had red kinky hair.*

kinsfolk *or* **kinfolk = family**, relations, relatives, connections, kin, kindred, kinsmen, ainga *(N.Z.)*, rellies *(Austral. slang)* • *He honestly liked his kinsfolk.*

kinship 1 = relationship, kin, family ties, consanguinity, ties of blood, blood relationship • *the ties of kinship*
2 = similarity, relationship, association, bearing, connection, alliance, correspondence, affinity • *She evidently felt a sense of kinship with the woman.*

kinsman *or* **kinswoman = relative**, relation, blood relative, fellow tribesman, fellow clansman, rellie *(Austral. slang)* • *Their kinsmen had suffered in silence.*

kiosk = booth, stand, counter, stall, newsstand, bookstall • *I was getting cigarettes at the kiosk.*

kiss AS A VERB **1 = peck** *(informal)*, osculate, snog *(Brit. slang)*, neck *(informal)*, smooch *(informal)*, canoodle *(slang)* • *She kissed me hard on the mouth.*
2 = brush, touch, shave, scrape, graze, caress, glance off, stroke • *The wheels of the aircraft kissed the runway.*
▸ AS A NOUN **= peck** *(informal)*, snog *(Brit. slang)*, smacker *(slang)*, smooch *(informal)*, French kiss, osculation • *I put my arms around her and gave her a kiss.*
▸ RELATED ADJECTIVE: oscular

QUOTATIONS
You must not kiss and tell
[William Congreve *Love for Love*]
When women kiss it always reminds one of prize-fighters shaking hands
[H.L. Mencken *A Mencken Chrestomathy*]
The kiss originated when the first male reptile licked the first female reptile, implying in a subtle, complimentary way that she was as succulent as the small reptile he had for dinner the night before
[F. Scott Fitzgerald *The Crack-Up*]
You must remember this, a kiss is still a kiss,
A sigh is just a sigh;
The fundamental things apply,
As time goes by
[Herman Hupfeld *As Time Goes By*]

kit AS A NOUN **1 = equipment**, supplies, materials, tackle, tools, instruments, provisions, implements, rig, apparatus, trappings, utensils, paraphernalia, accoutrements, appurtenances • *The kit consisted of about twenty cosmetic items.*
2 = gear, things, effects, dress, clothes, clothing, stuff, equipment, uniform, outfit, rig, costume, garments, baggage, equipage • *I forgot my gym kit.*
3 = pack, set, package, flat-pack • *also available in do-it-yourself kits*
▸ IN PHRASES: **get** *or* **take your kit off = strip off**, strip, undress, disrobe, take your clothes off, go naked, unclothe • *I don't like taking my kit off on screen.*
kit something *or* **someone out** *or* **up = equip**, fit, supply, provide with, arm, stock, outfit, costume, furnish, fix up, fit out, deck out, accoutre • *kitted out with winter coat, skirts, jumpers, nylon stockings*

kitchen = cookhouse, galley, kitchenette, scullery • *eating a snack in the kitchen*
▹ *See panel* **Kitchen equipment**

kite IN PHRASES: **high as a kite = excited**, thrilled, worked up, aflame, high *(informal)*, moved, wild, nervous, stirred, disturbed, stimulated, enthusiastic, aroused, awakened, animated, roused, flurried, agitated, hyper *(informal)*, feverish, tumultuous, overwrought, hot and bothered *(informal)*, discomposed • *I was as high as a kite most of the time.*

kitsch = bad taste, vulgarity, coarseness, tastelessness, grossness, tawdriness, gaudiness, lack of refinement • *a hideous ballgown verging on the kitsch*

kittenish = playful, spirited, lively, cheerful, mischievous, coy, joyous, fun-loving, sprightly, vivacious, flirtatious, impish, frisky, coquettish, puckish, frolicsome, ludic *(literary)*, sportive, larkish *(informal)* • *pouting, kittenish waifs*

knack = skill, art, ability, facility, talent, gift, capacity, trick, bent, craft, genius, expertise, forte, flair, competence, ingenuity, propensity, aptitude, dexterity, cleverness, quickness, adroitness, expertness, handiness, skilfulness • *He's got the knack of getting people to listen.*
OPPOSITES: disability, ineptitude, awkwardness

knackered 1 = exhausted, worn out, tired out, drained, beat *(slang)*, done in *(informal)*, all in *(slang)*, buggered *(Brit. slang)*, debilitated, prostrated, enervated, ready to drop, dog-tired *(informal)*, zonked *(slang)*, dead tired, dead beat *(slang)* • *I was absolutely knackered at the end of the match.*
2 = broken, not working, out of order, not functioning, done in *(informal)*, ruined, buggered *(Brit. slang)*, worn out, on the blink *(slang)*, on its last legs • *My tape player's knackered.*

knave = rogue, cheat, villain, rascal, scoundrel, scally *(Northwest English dialect)*, swindler, bounder *(old-fashioned)*, rotter *(slang, chiefly Brit.)*, reprobate, scallywag *(informal)*, scumbag *(slang)*, scamp, blackguard, cocksucker *(taboo)*, scapegrace, rapscallion, varlet *(archaic)*, wrong 'un *(Austral. slang)* • *It is difficult to believe that he is such a knave behind my back.*

KITCHEN EQUIPMENT

Aga *(trademark)*	coffeepot	fork	loaf tin	poacher	tablespoon
bain-marie	colander	frying pan	mandoline	pot	tagine
baking tray	cooker	grater	masher	pot-au-feu	tandoor
barbecue	cooling rack	gravy boat *or* sauce boat	measuring jug	ramekin	teapot
batterie de cuisine	corkscrew	griddle	mezzaluna	ricer *(U.S. & Canad.)*	teaspoon
blender	deep fat fryer	grill	microwave	rolling pin	tenderizer
bottle opener	dessertspoon	ice-cream maker	mixing bowl	rotisserie	timbale
bread knife	double saucepan *or (U.S. & Canad.)* double boiler	icing bag	mortar and pestle	saucepan	tin-opener
cafetiere	egg beater *or* egg whisk	jelly bag	mould	scales	toaster
cake tin	fan-assisted oven	juicer	nutcracker	sieve	toasting fork
carving knife	fish slice	kettle	olla	skillet	whisk
casserole	flan tin	knife	oven	spatula	wok
chip pan	food processor	ladle	pastry cutter	spoon	wooden spoon
chopping board		lemon squeezer	peeler	spurtle	
chopsticks		liquidizer	pepper mill	steamer	
coffee grinder			percolator	strainer	

knavery = **dishonesty**, fraud, corruption, deception, deceit, trickery, duplicity, double-dealing, chicanery, villainy, imposture, roguery, rascality • *a hotbed of intrigue and malicious knavery*

knavish = **dishonest**, tricky, fraudulent, deceptive, unscrupulous, rascally, scoundrelly, deceitful, villainous, unprincipled, dishonourable, roguish • *up to their knavish tricks again*

OPPOSITES: principled, noble, honourable

knead = **squeeze**, work, massage, manipulate, form, press, shape, stroke, blend, rub, mould • *Lightly knead the mixture on a floured surface.*

knee

▸ TECHNICAL NAME: genu

▸ RELATED ADJECTIVE: genal

▸ RELATED PHOBIA: genuphobia

kneecap

▸ TECHNICAL NAME: patella

knee-jerk = **automatic**, unconscious, predictable, spontaneous, reflex, instinctive, involuntary, instinctual, unwilled, natural • *a knee-jerk reaction*

kneel = **genuflect**, bow, stoop, curtsy *or* curtsey, bow down, kowtow, get down on your knees, make obeisance • *She knelt by the bed and prayed.*

knell = **ring**, sound, toll, chime, clang, peal • *the knell of a passing bell*

knickers = **underwear**, smalls, briefs, drawers, panties, bloomers • *She bought Ann two bras and six pairs of knickers.*

knick-knack = **trinket**, trifle, plaything, bauble, bric-a-brac, bagatelle, gimcrack, gewgaw, bibelot, kickshaw • *Her flat is spilling over with knick-knacks.*

knife AS A NOUN = **blade**, carver, cutter, cutting tool • *a knife and fork*

▸ AS A VERB = **cut**, wound, stab, slash, thrust, gore, pierce, spear, jab, bayonet, impale, lacerate • *She was knifed in the back six times.*

knight AS A NOUN = **cavalier**, equestrian, horseman, gallant, chevalier, champion • *I wish I were a fit knight for the sea princess.*

▸ IN PHRASES: **knight in shining armour** = **saviour**, deliverer, hero, defender, guardian, salvation, rescuer, protector, good Samaritan, redeemer, preserver • *believing in happy endings and knights in shining armour*

knightly = **chivalrous**, noble, heroic, courageous, gracious, gallant, valiant, courtly • *the splendour of knightly days, recreated for modern visitors*

knit 1 = **join**, unite, link, tie, bond, ally, combine, secure, bind, connect, merge, weave, fasten, meld • *Sport knits the whole family close together.*

2 = **heal**, unite, join, link, bind, connect, loop, mend, fasten, intertwine, interlace • *broken bones that have failed to knit*

3 = **furrow**, tighten, knot, wrinkle, crease, screw up, pucker, scrunch up • *They knitted their brows and started to grumble.*

KNITTING STITCHES

box stitch	garter rib	rib
cable stitch	garter stitch	roman stripe
diagonal rib	layette	seed stitch
double seed *or* double moss stitch	mistake rib	slip stitch
fisherman's rib	moss panels	stocking stitch
	moss stitch	
	pavilion	

knob 1 = **handle**, grip, door handle, handgrip • *He turned the knob and pushed against the door.*

2 = **ball**, stud, nub, protuberance, boss, bunch, swell, knot, bulk, lump, bump, projection, snag, hump, protrusion, knurl • *a loose brass knob on the bedstead*

3 = **dial**, switch, button, control switch • *the volume knob*

4 = **lump**, ball, piece, wedge, spot, mass, cake, bunch, cluster, chunk, dab, hunk, nugget, gob, clod, gobbet • *a knob of butter*

knock AS A VERB 1 = **bang**, beat, strike, tap, rap, bash *(informal)*, thump, buffet, pummel • *Knock at my window at eight o'clock and I'll be ready.*

2 = **hit**, strike, punch, belt *(informal)*, deck *(slang)*, slap, chin *(slang)*, smack, thump, clap, cuff, smite *(archaic)*, thwack, lay one on *(slang)*, beat *or* knock seven bells out of *(informal)* • *He was mucking around and he knocked her in the stomach.*

3 = **criticize**, condemn, put down, run down, abuse, blast, pan *(informal)*, slam *(slang)*, flame *(informal)*, slate *(informal)*, have a go (at) *(informal)*, censure, slag (off) *(slang)*, denigrate, belittle, disparage, deprecate, diss *(slang, chiefly U.S.)*, find fault with, carp at, lambast(e), pick holes in, cast aspersions on, cavil at, pick to pieces, give (someone *or* something) a bad press, nit-pick *(informal)* • *I'm not knocking them: if they want to do it, it's up to them.*

▸ AS A NOUN 1 = **knocking**, pounding, beating, tap, hammering, bang, banging, rap, thump, thud • *They heard a knock at the front door.*

2 = **bang**, blow, impact, jar, collision, jolt, smash • *The bags have tough exterior materials to protect against knocks.*

3 = **blow**, hit, punch, crack, belt *(informal)*, clip, slap, bash, smack, thump, clout *(informal)*, cuff, box • *He had taken a knock on the head in training.*

4 = **setback**, check, defeat, blow, upset, reverse, disappointment, hold-up, hitch, reversal, misfortune, rebuff, whammy *(informal, chiefly U.S.)*, bummer *(slang)* • *The art market has suffered some severe knocks.*

▸ **IN PHRASES: knock about** *or* **around** = **wander**, travel, roam, rove, range, drift, stray, ramble, straggle, traipse, go walkabout *(Austral.)*, stravaig *(Scot. & Northern English dialect)* • *reporters who knock around in troubled parts of the world*

knock about *or* **around with someone** = **mix with**, associate with, mingle with, hang out with *(informal)*, hang with *(informal, chiefly U.S.)*, be friends with, consort with, run around with *(informal)*, hobnob with, socialize with, accompany, hang about with, fraternize with • *I used to knock about with all the lads.*

knock it off = **stop**, stop it, lay off *(informal)*, cut it *(informal)*, give over *(informal)*, pack it in *(informal)*, cut it out *(informal)*, leave it out *(informal)*, give it a rest *(informal)* • *Will you just knock it off!*

knock off = **stop work**, get out, conclude, shut down, terminate, call it a day *(informal)*, finish work, clock off, clock out • *What time do you knock off?*

knock-on effect = **consequence**, result, repercussion, upshot • *knock-on effects on wages and retail prices*

knock someone about *or* **around** = **hit**, attack, beat, strike, damage, abuse, hurt, injure, wound, assault, harm, batter, slap, bruise, thrash, beat up *(informal)*, buffet, maul, work over *(slang)*, clobber *(slang)*, mistreat, manhandle, maltreat, lambast(e), slap around *(informal)*, beat *or* knock seven bells out of *(informal)* • *He started knocking me around.*

knock someone down = **run over**, hit, run down, knock over, mow down • *He died in hospital after being knocked down by a car.*

knock someone off = **kill**, murder, do in *(slang)*, slaughter, destroy, waste *(informal)*, take out *(slang)*, execute, massacre, butcher, wipe out *(informal)*, dispatch, cut down, erase, assassinate, slay, eradicate, whack *(informal)*, do away with, blow away *(slang, chiefly U.S.)*, obliterate, liquidate, decimate, annihilate, neutralize, exterminate, croak, mow down, take (someone's) life, bump off *(slang)*, extirpate, wipe from the face of the earth *(informal)* • *Several people had a motive to knock him off.*

knock someone out 1 = **floor**, knock unconscious, knock senseless, render unconscious, level, stun, daze • *He had never been knocked out in a professional fight.*

2 = **eliminate**, beat, defeat, trounce, vanquish • *We were knocked out in the quarter-finals.*

3 = **impress**, move, strike, touch, affect, influence, excite, inspire, grab *(informal)*, stir, overwhelm, sway, make an impression on • *That performance knocked me out.*

knock someone up 1 = **wake up**, wake, get up, revive, arouse, awaken, rouse • *He went to knock Rob up at 4.30am.*

2 = **make pregnant**, fertilize, impregnate, inseminate, fructify, fecundate, get with child • *When I got knocked up, the whole town knew about it.*

knock something back = **drink quickly**, down *(informal)*, swallow, swig, guzzle, quaff, drink up, gulp down • *He was knocking back his tenth gin and tonic*

knock something down 1 = **demolish**, destroy, flatten, tear down, level, total *(slang)*, fell, ruin, dismantle, trash *(slang)*, bulldoze, raze, pulverize, kennet *(Austral. slang)*, jeff *(Austral. slang)* • *Why doesn't he just knock the wall down?*

2 = **reduce**, cut, lower, discount, slash, bring down, mark down, cheapen • *The market might abandon the stock, and knock down its price.*

knock something off 1 = **steal**, take, nick *(slang, chiefly Brit.)*, thieve, rob, pinch, cabbage *(Brit. slang)*, blag *(slang)*, pilfer, purloin, filch • *Cars can be stolen almost as easily as knocking off a bike.*

2 = **remove**, take away, deduct, debit, subtract • *I'll knock off another £100 if you pay in cash.*

knock something out = **destroy**, total *(slang)*, waste, ruin, crush, devastate, wreck, shatter, wipe out, dispatch, dismantle, demolish, trash *(slang)*, desolate, raze, blow to bits, blow sky-high, kennet *(Austral. slang)*, jeff *(Austral. slang)* • *A storm has made roads treacherous and knocked out power supplies.*

knock something *or* **someone back** = **set back**, delay, hold up, hinder, retard, impede, slow • *Every time we got rolling something came along to knock us back.*

knockabout = **boisterous**, riotous, rollicking, rough-and-tumble, rumbustious, rambunctious *(informal)*, harum-scarum, farcical, slapstick • *It is all good knockabout fun.*

knockout 1 = **killer blow**, coup de grâce *(French)*, kayo *(slang)*, KO *or* K.O. *(slang)* • *a first-round knockout in Las Vegas*

2 = **success**, hit, winner, triumph, smash, belter *(slang)*, sensation, smash hit, stunner *(informal)*, smasheroo *(informal)* • *The first story is a knockout.*

OPPOSITES: failure, turkey *(informal)*, flop *(informal)*

3 = **beauty**, cracker *(slang)*, stunner *(informal)*, charmer, lovely *(slang)*, good-looker, belle, goddess, Venus, humdinger *(slang)*, pearler *(Austral. slang)*, beaut *(Austral. & N.Z. slang)* • *She was a knockout in navy and scarlet.*

knoll = **hillock**, hill, swell, mound, barrow, hummock • *a grassy knoll*

knot **AS A NOUN** 1 = **connection**, tie, bond, joint, bow, loop, braid, splice, rosette, ligature • *One lace had broken and been tied in a knot.*

2 = **group**, company, set, band, crowd, pack, squad, circle, crew *(informal)*, gang, mob, clique, assemblage • *A little knot of men stood clapping.*

▸ **AS A VERB** 1 = **tie**, secure, bind, complicate, weave, loop, knit, tether, entangle • *He knotted the bandanna around his neck.*

2 = **tighten**, become tense, tauten, stretch • *I felt my stomach knot with apprehension.*

▸ **IN PHRASES: tie the knot** = **get married**, marry, wed, espouse, take the plunge *(informal)*, walk down the aisle *(informal)*, get hitched *(slang)*, get spliced *(informal)*, become man and wife, wive *(archaic)*, take to wife, plight your troth *(old-fashioned)* • *Len tied the knot with Kate five years ago.*

▹ *See panel* **Knots**

knotty 1 = **puzzling**, hard, difficult, complex, complicated, tricky, baffling, intricate, troublesome, perplexing, mystifying, thorny, problematical • *The new management team faces some knotty problems.*

2 = **knotted**, rough, rugged, bumpy, gnarled, knobby, nodular • *the knotty trunk of a hawthorn tree*

know 1 = **have knowledge of**, see, understand, recognize, perceive, be aware of, be conscious of • *I don't know the name of the place.* • *I think I know the answer.*

2 = **be acquainted with**, recognize, associate with, be familiar with, be friends with, be friendly with, have knowledge of, have dealings with, socialize with, fraternize with, be pals with • *Do you two know each other?*

OPPOSITES: be unfamiliar with

3 *sometimes with* **about** *or* **of** = **be familiar with**, experience, understand, ken *(Scot.)*, comprehend, fathom, apprehend, have knowledge of, be acquainted with, feel certain of, have dealings in, be versed in • *Hire someone with experience, someone who knows about real estate.*

OPPOSITES: be ignorant of, be unfamiliar with

4 = **recognize**, remember, identify, recall, place, spot, notice, distinguish, perceive, make out, discern, differentiate, recollect • *Would she know you if she saw you on the street?*

PROVERBS

What you don't know can't hurt you

Know thyself

KNOTS

barrell knot
bend
Blackwall hitch
bow *or* bowknot
bowline
bowstring knot
carrick bend
cat's paw
clinch knot
clove hitch
diamond knot
Englishman's tie
figure of eight
fisherman's bend
fisherman's *or* truelover's knot
girth hitch
granny knot
half hitch
hangman's knot
harness hitch
hawser bend
half-hitch
hitch
loop knot
love knot
magnus hitch
Matthew Walker
monkey fist
overhand knot *or* thumb knot
prusik knot
reef knot, flat knot, *or* square knot
rolling hitch
running bowline
running knot
sailor's knot
sheepshank
sheet bend, becket bend, weaver's hitch, *or* mesh knot
shroud knot
slipknot
slippery hitch
stevedore's knot
surgeon's knot
swab hitch
timber hitch
truelove knot
Turk's-head
wale knot
wall knot
water knot
Windsor knot

know-all = **smart aleck**, wise guy *(informal)*, smarty *(informal)*, clever-clogs *(informal)*, clever Dick *(informal)*, smarty-pants *(informal)*, smartarse *(slang)*, wiseacre, smarty-boots *(informal)* • *She read an article by some cosmopolitan know-all.*

know-how = **expertise**, experience, ability, skill, knowledge, facility, talent, command, craft, grasp, faculty, capability, flair, knack, ingenuity, aptitude, proficiency, dexterity, cleverness, deftness, savoir-faire, adroitness, ableness • *He hasn't got the know-how to run a farm.*

knowing = **meaningful**, significant, expressive, eloquent, enigmatic, suggestive • *Ron gave her a knowing smile.*

knowingly = **deliberately**, purposely, consciously, intentionally, on purpose, wilfully, wittingly • *He repeated that he had never knowingly taken illegal drugs.*

knowledge 1 = **understanding**, sense, intelligence, judgment, perception, awareness, insight, grasp, appreciation, penetration, comprehension, discernment • *the quest for scientific knowledge*
2 = **learning**, schooling, education, science, intelligence, instruction, wisdom, scholarship, tuition, enlightenment, erudition • *She didn't intend to display her knowledge yet.*
OPPOSITES: ignorance, illiteracy
3 = **consciousness**, recognition, awareness, apprehension, cognition, discernment • *taken without my knowledge*
OPPOSITES: misunderstanding, unawareness
4 = **acquaintance**, information, notice, intimacy, familiarity, cognizance • *He has no knowledge of business.*
OPPOSITES: unfamiliarity

QUOTATIONS

Knowledge is power
[Francis Bacon *Meditationes Sacrae*]

Knowledge is power. Unfortunate dupes of this saying will keep on reading, ambitiously, till they have stunned their native initiative, and made their thoughts weak
[Clarence Day *This Simian World*]

Knowledge is power, if you know it about the right person
[Ethel Watts Mumford]

All I know is that I know nothing
[Socrates]

That knowledge which stops at what it does not know, is the highest knowledge
[Chang Tzu *The Music of Heaven and Earth*]

No man's knowledge here can go beyond his experience
[John Locke *Essay concerning Human Understanding*]

Knowledge is not knowledge until someone else knows that one knows
[Lucilius *fragment*]

He that increaseth knowledge increaseth sorrow
[*Bible: Ecclesiastes*]

Knowledge is of two kinds. We know a subject ourselves, or we know where we can find information upon it
[Dr. Johnson]

It is the province of knowledge to speak and it is the privilege of wisdom to listen
[Oliver Wendell Holmes *The Poet at the Breakfast-Table*]

If a little knowledge is dangerous, where is the man who has so much as to be out of danger?
[T.H. Huxley *Collected Essays*]

Owl hasn't exactly got Brain, but he Knows Things
[A.A. Milne *Winnie-the-Pooh*]

Knowledge in the end is based on acknowledgement
[Ludwig Wittgenstein *On Certainty*]

There are known knowns – there are things we know that we know. There are known unknowns – that is to say, there are things that we now know we don't know. But there are also unknown unknowns – there are things we do not know we don't know
[Donald Rumsfeld]

PROVERBS

A little knowledge is a dangerous thing

knowledgeable 1 = **well-informed**, acquainted, conversant, au fait *(French)*, experienced, understanding, aware, familiar, conscious, switched-on *(informal)*, in the know *(informal)*, sussed *(Brit. slang)*, cognizant, in the loop, au courant *(French)*, clued-up *(informal)* • *school-age children who were very knowledgeable about soccer*
2 = **intelligent**, lettered, learned, educated, scholarly, erudite • *He was a knowledgeable and well-read man.*

known = **famous**, well-known, celebrated, popular, common, admitted, noted, published, obvious, familiar, acknowledged, recognized, plain, confessed, patent, manifest, avowed • *He was the best-known actor of his day.*
OPPOSITES: secret, hidden, unknown

knuckle IN PHRASES: **knuckle down** = **apply yourself**, try, study, concentrate, work hard, pay attention, persevere, buckle down *(informal)*, make an effort, commit yourself, be diligent, be industrious, be assiduous, devote yourself, dedicate yourself • *The only thing to do was to knuckle down.*
knuckle under = **give way**, yield, submit, surrender, give in, succumb, cave in *(informal)*, capitulate, accede, acquiesce • *It is arguable whether the rebels will knuckle under.*

koppie *or* **kopje** = **hill**, down *(archaic)*, fell, mount, height, mound, prominence, elevation, eminence, hilltop, tor, knoll, hillock, brae *(Scot.)* • *the rocky kopjes rising like islands*

kosher = **acceptable**, seemly, standard, fitting, correct, appropriate, diplomatic, right, proper, O.K. *or* okay *(informal)* • *I guessed something wasn't quite kosher.*

kowtow = **grovel**, court, flatter, cringe, fawn, pander to, suck up to *(slang)*, toady, kiss someone's ass *(U.S. & Canad. taboo)*, brown-nose *(taboo)*, truckle, lick someone's boots, lick someone's arse *(taboo)* • *Nor did he kowtow to his editors.*

kudos = **prestige**, regard, honour, praise, glory, fame, distinction, esteem, acclaim, applause, plaudits, renown, repute, notability, laudation • *a new hotel chain that has won kudos for the way it treats guests*

label **AS A NOUN** **1 = tag**, ticket, tab, marker, flag, tally, sticker, docket *(chiefly Brit.)* • *He peered at the label on the bottle.*
2 = epithet, description, classification, characterization • *Her treatment of her husband earned her the label of the most hated woman in America.*
3 = brand, company, mark, trademark, brand name, trade name • *designer labels*
▸ **AS A VERB** **1 = tag**, mark, stamp, ticket, flag, tab, tally, sticker, docket *(chiefly Brit.)* • *The produce was labelled 'Made in China'.*
2 = brand, classify, describe, class, call, name, identify, define, designate, characterize, categorize, pigeonhole • *Too often the press are labelled as bad boys.*

laborious **1 = hard**, difficult, tiring, exhausting, wearing, tough, fatiguing, uphill, strenuous, arduous, tiresome, onerous, burdensome, herculean, wearisome, backbreaking, toilsome • *Keeping the garden tidy all year round can be a laborious task.*
OPPOSITES: easy, effortless, light
2 = industrious, hard-working, diligent, tireless, persevering, painstaking, indefatigable, assiduous, unflagging, sedulous • *He was gentle and kindly, living a laborious life in his Paris flat.*
3 = forced, laboured, strained, ponderous, not fluent • *a laborious prose style*
OPPOSITES: simple, natural

labour **AS A NOUN** **1 = toil**, effort, industry, grind *(informal)*, pains, sweat *(informal)*, slog *(informal)*, exertion, drudgery, travail, donkey-work • *the labour of seeding, planting and harvesting*
OPPOSITES: rest, ease, leisure
2 = workers, employees, workforce, labourers, hands, workmen • *The country lacked skilled labour.*
3 = work, effort, employment, toil, industry • *Every man should receive a fair price for the product of his labour.*
4 = childbirth, birth, delivery, contractions, pains, throes, travail, labour pains, parturition • *By the time she realised she was in labour, it was too late.*
5 = chore, job, task, undertaking • *The chef looked up from his labours.*
▸ **AS A VERB** **1 = work**, toil, strive, work hard, grind *(informal)*, sweat *(informal)*, slave, endeavour, plod away, drudge, travail, slog away *(informal)*, exert yourself, peg along *or* away *(chiefly Brit.)*, plug along *or* away *(informal)* • *peasants labouring in the fields*
OPPOSITES: rest, relax
2 = struggle, work, strain, work hard, strive, go for it *(informal)*, grapple, toil, make an effort, make every effort, do your best, exert yourself, work like a Trojan • *For years he laboured to build a religious community.*
3 = overemphasize, stress, elaborate, exaggerate, strain, dwell on, overdo, go on about, make a production (out) of *(informal)*, make a federal case of *(U.S. informal)* • *I don't want to labour the point, but there it is.*
4 *usually with* **under = be disadvantaged by**, suffer from, be a victim of, be burdened by • *She laboured under the illusion that I knew what I was doing.*

Labour Party = left-wing, Democrat *(U.S.)* • *the Labour candidate in the by-election*

laboured **1 = difficult**, forced, strained, heavy, awkward • *From his slow walk and laboured breathing, she realized he was not well.*
2 = contrived, studied, affected, awkward, unnatural, overdone, ponderous, overwrought • *The prose of his official communications was so laboured, pompous and verbose.*

labourer = worker, workman, working man, manual worker, hand, blue-collar worker, drudge, unskilled worker, navvy *(Brit. informal)*, labouring man • *Her husband had been a farm labourer.*

PROVERBS
The labourer is worthy of his hire

labyrinth **1 = maze**, jungle, tangle, coil, snarl, entanglement • *a labyrinth of corridors*
2 = intricacy, puzzle, complexity, riddle, complication, tangle, maze, entanglement, perplexity, convolution, knotty problem • *a labyrinth of conflicting political interpretations*

labyrinthine **1 = mazelike**, winding, tangled, intricate, tortuous, convoluted, mazy • *The streets of the Old City are narrow and labyrinthine.*
2 = complex, puzzling, perplexing, involved, confused, tortuous, Byzantine, convoluted, knotty, Gordian, Daedalian • *his failure to understand the labyrinthine complexities of the situation*

lace **AS A NOUN** **1 = netting**, net, filigree, tatting, meshwork, openwork • *a plain white lace bedspread*
2 = cord, tie, string, lacing, thong, shoelace, bootlace • *He was sitting on the bed, tying the laces of an old pair of running shoes.*
▸ **AS A VERB** **1 = fasten**, tie, tie up, do up, secure, bind, close, attach, thread • *No matter how tightly I lace these shoes, my ankles wobble.*
2 = mix, drug, doctor, add to, spike, contaminate, fortify, adulterate • *She laced his food with sleeping pills.*
3 = enrich, pepper, spice, sprinkle, enliven, liven up • *a speech laced with wry humour*
4 = intertwine, interweave, entwine, twine, interlink • *He took to lacing his fingers together in an attempt to keep his hands still.*

lacerate **1 = tear**, cut, wound, rend, rip, slash, claw, maim, mangle, mangulate *(Austral. slang)*, gash, jag • *Its claws lacerated his thighs.*
2 = hurt, wound, rend, torture, distress, torment, afflict,

harrow • *He was born into a family already lacerated with tensions and divisions.*

laceration = **cut**, injury, tear, wound, rent, rip, slash, trauma *(Pathology)*, gash, mutilation • *He had lacerations on his back and thighs.*

lachrymose = **tearful**, crying, weeping, woeful, sad, mournful, lugubrious, weepy *(informal)*, dolorous • *the tears of lachrymose mourners*

lack AS A NOUN = **shortage**, want, absence, deficiency, need, shortcoming, deprivation, inadequacy, scarcity, dearth, privation, shortness, destitution, insufficiency, scantiness • *Despite his lack of experience, he got the job.*
OPPOSITES: excess, surplus, abundance
▸ AS A VERB = **miss**, want, need, require, not have, be without, be short of, be in need of, be deficient in • *It lacked the power of the Italian cars.*
OPPOSITES: have, own, enjoy

lackadaisical = **lazy**, lethargic, indifferent, idle, abstracted, limp, dreamy, inert, languid, apathetic, listless, indolent, languorous, enervated, spiritless, half-arsed *(Brit. slang)*, half-assed *(U.S. & Canad. slang)*, half-hearted • *Dr. Jonsen seemed a little lackadaisical at times.*
OPPOSITES: spirited, excited, diligent

lackey = **hanger-on**, fawner, pawn, attendant, tool, instrument, parasite, cohort *(chiefly U.S.)*, valet, menial, minion, footman, sycophant, yes-man, manservant, toady, flunky, brown-noser *(taboo)*, flatterer, ass-kisser *(U.S. & Canad. taboo)*, varlet *(archaic)* • *I'm not staying as a paid lackey to act as your yes-man.*

lacking = **deficient**, wanting, needing, missing, inadequate, minus *(informal)*, flawed, impaired, sans *(archaic)* • *Why was military intelligence so lacking?*

lacklustre = **flat**, boring, dull, dim, dry, muted, sombre, drab, lifeless, prosaic, leaden, unimaginative, uninspired, unexciting, vapid, lustreless • *his party's lacklustre performance during the election campaign*

laconic = **terse**, short, brief, clipped, to the point, crisp, compact, concise, curt, succinct, pithy, monosyllabic, sententious • *Usually so laconic in the office, he seemed more relaxed.*
OPPOSITES: rambling, long-winded, wordy

lacquer = **varnish**, wax, glaze, enamel, resin, shellac, japan • *We put on the second coating of lacquer.*

lacy = **filigree**, open, fine, sheer, delicate, frilly, gossamer, gauzy, net-like, lace-like, meshy • *lacy night-gowns*

lad = **boy**, kid *(informal)*, guy *(informal)*, youth, fellow, youngster, chap *(informal)*, juvenile, shaver *(informal)*, nipper *(informal)*, laddie *(Scot.)*, stripling • *a lad of his age*

ladder 1 = **steps**, set of steps • *She broke her arm when she fell off a ladder.*
2 = **hierarchy**, ranking, pecking order • *She admired her sister for climbing up the social ladder.*

laden = **loaded**, burdened, hampered, weighted, full, charged, taxed, oppressed, fraught, weighed down, encumbered • *I came home laden with cardboard boxes.*

la-di-da = **affected**, mannered, posh *(informal, chiefly Brit.)*, pretentious, precious, mincing, stuck-up *(informal)*, conceited, snooty *(informal)*, snobbish, too-too, toffee-nosed *(slang, chiefly Brit.)*, highfalutin *(informal)*, arty-farty *(informal)*, overrefined • *I wouldn't trust them in spite of all their la-di-da manners.*

ladle AS A NOUN = **spoon**, scoop, dipper • *Using a ladle, baste the chicken with the sauce.*
▸ AS A VERB = **serve**, dish out, dish up, scoop out • *She ladled out steaming soup.*

lady 1 = **gentlewoman**, duchess, noble, dame, baroness, countess, aristocrat, viscountess, noblewoman, peeress • *Our governess was told to make sure we knew how to talk like English ladies.*
2 = **woman**, female, girl, miss, maiden *(archaic)*, maid *(archaic)*, lass, damsel, lassie *(informal)*, charlie *(Austral. slang)*, chook *(Austral. slang)*, wahine *(N.Z.)* • *She's a very sweet old lady.*

ladykiller = **womanizer**, heartbreaker, Don Juan, Casanova, rake, philanderer, Lothario, wolf *(informal)*, libertine, roué, ladies' man • *Hollywood's hottest star and a notorious ladykiller*

ladylike = **refined**, cultured, sophisticated, elegant, proper, modest, respectable, polite, genteel, courtly, well-bred, decorous • *She crossed the room with quick, ladylike steps.*
OPPOSITES: rude, unrefined, unladylike

lag 1 = **hang back**, delay, drag (behind), trail, linger, be behind, idle, saunter, loiter, straggle, dawdle, tarry, drag your feet *(informal)* • *The boys crept forward, Roger lagging a little.*
2 = **drop**, fail, diminish, decrease, flag, fall off, wane, ebb, slacken, lose strength • *Trade has lagged since the embargo.*

laggard = **straggler**, lounger, lingerer, piker *(Austral. & N.Z. slang)*, snail, saunterer, loafer, loiterer, dawdler, skiver *(Brit. slang)*, idler, slowcoach *(Brit. informal)*, sluggard, bludger *(Austral. & N.Z. informal)*, slowpoke *(U.S. & Canad. informal)* • *a reputation as a technological laggard in the personal-computer area*

lagoon = **pool**, bay, lake, pond, shallows • *blue sky, blue lagoon and white breakers*

laid-back = **relaxed**, calm, casual, together *(slang)*, at ease, easy-going, unflappable *(informal)*, unhurried, free and easy, easy-peasy *(slang)*, chilled *(informal)* • *Everyone here has a really laid-back attitude.*
OPPOSITES: nervous, tense, wound-up *(informal)*

laid up = **incapacitated**, ill, injured, sick, out of action *(informal)*, bedridden, immobilized, housebound, on the sick list • *I was laid up in bed with acute rheumatism.*

lair 1 = **nest**, den, hole, burrow, resting place • *a fox's lair*
2 = **hide-out** *(Informal)*, retreat, refuge, den, sanctuary • *The village was once a pirate's lair.*

laissez faire or **laisser faire** = **nonintervention**, free trade, individualism, free enterprise, live and let live • *the doctrine of laissez-faire and unbridled individualism*

lake = **pond**, pool, reservoir, loch *(Scot.)*, lagoon, mere, lough *(Irish)*, tarn • *They can go fishing in the lake.*
▸ RELATED ADJECTIVE: lacustrine
▹ *See panel* **Lakes, lochs, and loughs**

lama = **Buddhist priest**, Buddhist monk • *It takes twenty to twenty-five years to qualify as a lama.*

lame 1 = **disabled**, handicapped, crippled, limping, defective, hobbling, game, halt *(archaic)* • *He had to pull out of the Championships when his horse went lame.*
2 = **unconvincing**, poor, pathetic, inadequate, thin, weak, insufficient, feeble, unsatisfactory, flimsy • *He mumbled some lame excuse about having gone to sleep.*

lament AS A VERB = **bemoan**, grieve, mourn, weep over, complain about, regret, wail about, deplore, bewail • *Ken began to lament the death of his only son.*
▸ AS A NOUN 1 = **complaint**, moaning, moan, keening, wail, wailing, lamentation, plaint, ululation • *the professional woman's lament that a woman's judgment is questioned more than a man's*
2 = **dirge**, requiem, elegy, threnody, monody, coronach *(Scot. & Irish)* • *a lament for the late, great Buddy Holly*

lamentable 1 = **regrettable**, distressing, tragic, unfortunate, harrowing, grievous, woeful, deplorable, mournful, sorrowful, gut-wrenching • *This lamentable state of affairs lasted until 1947.*
2 = **disappointing**, poor, miserable, unsatisfactory, mean, low quality, meagre, pitiful, wretched, not much cop *(Brit. slang)* • *He admitted he was partly to blame for England's lamentable performance.*

lamentation = **sorrow**, grief, weeping, mourning, moan, grieving, sobbing, keening, lament, wailing, dirge, plaint, ululation • *It was time for mourning and lamentation.*

LAKES, LOCHS, AND LOUGHS

Allen
Annecy
Aral Sea
Ard
Athabaska
Averno
Awe
Baikal
Bala
Balaton
Balkhash
Bangweulu
Bassenthwaite
Belfast
Biel
Bodensee
Buttermere
Caspian Sea
Chad
Champlain
Como
Coniston Water
Constance
Crummock Water
Dead Sea
Derwentwater
Dongting
Earn
Edward
Ennerdale Water
Erie
Erne
Eyre
Frome
Fyne
Garda
Gatún
Geneva
Grasmere
Great Bear
Great Bitter
Great Lakes
Great Salt
Great Slave
Hawes Water
Huron
Ijsselmeer
Iliamna
Ilmen
Issyk-Kul
Kariba
Katrine
Kivu
Koko Nor
Kootenay
Ladoga
Laggan
Lake of the Woods
Leven
Linnhe
Little Bitter
Lochy
Lomond
Lucerne
Lugano
Léman
Maggiore
Malawi
Managua
Manitoba
Maracaibo
Mead
Meech
Memphremagog
Menteith
Michigan
Miraflores
Mistassini
Mobutu
Morar
Mweru
Nam Co
Nasser
Neagh
Ness
Neuchâtel
Nicaragua
Nipigon
Nipissing
No
Nyasa
Okanagan
Okeechobee
Onega
Oneida
Onondaga
Ontario
Patos
Peipus
Pontchartrain
Poopó
Poyang
Pskov
Rannoch
Reindeer
Rudolf
Saint Clair
Saint John
Sea of Galilee
Sevan
Stanley Pool
Superior
Sween
Taal
Tahoe
Tana
Tanganyika
Taupo
Tay
Thirlmere
Thun
Tien
Titicaca
Tonle Sap
Torrens
Torridon
Trasimene
Tummel
Turkana
Ullswater
Urmia
Van
Victoria
Volta
Waikaremoana
Washington
Wast Water
Windermere
Winnebago
Winnipeg
Zug
Zürich

laminated 1 = **covered**, coated, overlaid, veneered, faced • *laminated work surfaces*
2 = **layered**, stratified, foliated • *Modern windscreens are made from laminated glass.*

lamp

QUOTATIONS
The lamps are going out all over Europe; we shall not see them lit again in our lifetime
[Lord Grey *Twenty-five Years*]

lampoon AS A VERB = **ridicule**, mock, mimic, parody, caricature, send up *(Brit. informal)*, take off *(informal)*, make fun of, squib, burlesque, satirize, pasquinade • *He was lampooned for his short stature and political views.*
▸ AS A NOUN = **satire**, parody, caricature, send-up *(Brit. informal)*, takeoff *(informal)*, skit, squib, burlesque, pasquinade • *his scathing lampoons of consumer culture*

land AS A NOUN 1 = **ground**, earth, dry land, terra firma • *It isn't clear whether the plane went down over land or sea.*
2 = **soil**, ground, earth, clay, dirt, sod, loam • *a small piece of grazing land*
3 = **countryside**, farming, farmland, rural districts • *Living off the land was hard enough at the best of times.*
4 = **property**, grounds, estate, acres, real estate, realty, acreage, real property, homestead *(U.S. & Canad.)* • *Good agricultural land is in short supply.*
5 = **country**, nation, region, state, district, territory, province, kingdom, realm, tract, motherland, fatherland • *America, land of opportunity*
▸ AS A VERB 1 = **come to rest**, come down • *He was sent flying through the air and landed 20 ft away.*
2 = **arrive**, dock, put down, moor, berth, alight, touch down, disembark, come to rest, debark • *The jet landed after a flight of just under three hours.*
3 = **bring down**, dock, moor, take down • *The crew finally landed the plane on its belly.*
4 = **cause to be**, lead, bring • *This is not the first time his exploits have landed him in trouble.*
5 = **saddle**, trouble, burden, encumber • *The other options could simply land him with more expense.*
6 = **gain**, get, win, score *(slang)*, secure, obtain, acquire • *He landed a place on the graduate training scheme.*
7 = **deliver**, hit, apply, impose, administer, inflict • *He landed a punch on his opponent's mouth after the end of the eleventh round.*
▸ IN PHRASES: **land up** = **end up**, arrive, turn up, wind up, finish up, fetch up *(informal)* • *We landed up at the Las Vegas at about 6.30.*
▸ RELATED ADJECTIVE: terrestrial

landing 1 = **coming in**, arrival, touchdown, disembarkation, disembarkment • *I had to make a controlled landing into the sea.*
2 = **platform**, jetty, quayside, landing stage • *Take the bus to the landing.*

landlady 1 = **owner**, landowner, proprietor, freeholder, lessor, landholder • *We had been made homeless by our landlady.*
2 = **inkeeper**, host, hostess, hotelier, hotel-keeper • *Bet, the landlady of the Rovers' Return*

landlord 1 = **owner**, landowner, proprietor, freeholder, lessor, landholder • *His landlord doubled the rent.*
2 = **innkeeper**, host, hotelier, hotel-keeper • *The landlord refused to serve him because he considered him too drunk.*

landmark 1 = **feature**, spectacle, monument • *The Ambassador Hotel is a Los Angeles landmark.*
2 = **milestone**, turning point, watershed, critical point, tipping point • *a landmark in world history*
3 = **boundary marker**, cairn, benchmark, signpost, milepost • *an abandoned landmark on top of Townsville's Castle Hill*

landowner = **owner**, proprietor, freeholder, lessor, landholder • *rural communities involved in conflicts with large landowners*

landscape = **scenery**, country, view, land, scene, prospect, countryside, outlook, terrain, panorama, vista • *Arizona's desert landscape*

landslide 1 = **decisive victory**, triumph, overwhelming majority, walkover • *He won last month's presidential election by a landslide.*
2 = **landslip**, avalanche, rockfall • *The storm caused landslides and flooding.*

lane 1 = **road**, street, track, path, strip, way, passage, trail, pathway, footpath, passageway, thoroughfare • *a quiet country lane*

2 = **track**, way, road, channel, strip, corridor, alley, aisle • *The lorry was travelling at 20 mph in the slow lane.*

language 1 = **tongue**, speech, vocabulary, dialect, idiom, vernacular, patter, lingo *(informal)*, patois, lingua franca • *the English language*
2 = **vocabulary**, tongue, jargon, terminology, idiom, cant, lingo *(informal)*, argot • *the language of business*
3 = **speech**, communication, expression, speaking, talk, talking, conversation, discourse, interchange, utterance, parlance, vocalization, verbalization • *Students examined how children acquire language.*
4 = **style**, wording, expression, phrasing, vocabulary, usage, parlance, diction, phraseology • *a booklet summarising it in plain language*

QUOTATIONS

Language is the dress of thought
[Samuel Johnson *Lives of the English Poets: Cowley*]

After all, when you come right down to it, how many people speak the same language even when they speak the same language?
[Russell Hoban *The Lion of Boaz-Jachin and Jachin-Boaz*]

Languages are the pedigrees of nations
[Samuel Johnson]

A language is a dialect with an army and a navy
[Max Weinrich]

One does not inhabit a country; one inhabits a language. That is our country, our fatherland – and no other
[E.M. Cioran *Anathemas and Admirations*]

Everything can change, but not the language that we carry inside us, like a world more exclusive and final than one's mother's womb
[Italo Calvino *By Way of an Autobiography*]

To God I speak Spanish, to women Italian, to men French, and to my horse – German
[attributed to Emperor Charles V]

In language, the ignorant have prescribed laws to the learned
[Richard Duppa *Maxims*]

Language is fossil poetry
[Ralph Waldo Emerson *Essays: Nominalist and Realist*]

▷ *See panel* **Languages**

languid = **inactive**, lazy, indifferent, lethargic, weary, sluggish, inert, uninterested, listless, unenthusiastic, languorous, lackadaisical, torpid, spiritless • *He's a large languid man with a round and impassive face.*
OPPOSITES: strong, active, energetic

languish 1 = **decline**, waste away, fade away, wither away, flag, weaken, wilt, sicken • *He continues to languish in prison.*
OPPOSITES: thrive, flourish, bloom
2 = **waste away**, suffer, rot, be abandoned, be neglected, be disregarded • *New products languish on the drawing board.*
OPPOSITES: thrive, flourish, bloom
3 *often with* **for** = **pine**, want, long, desire, sigh, hunger, yearn, hanker, eat your heart out over, suspire • *a bride languishing for a kiss that never comes*

languishing = **fading**, failing, declining, flagging, sinking, weakening, deteriorating, withering, wilting, sickening, drooping, droopy, wasting away • *She was instrumental in the revival of his languishing career.*

languor 1 = **lethargy**, weakness, fatigue, apathy, inertia, frailty, weariness, ennui, torpor, heaviness, lassitude, debility, feebleness, listlessness, faintness, enervation • *She, in her languor, had not troubled to eat much.*
2 = **relaxation**, laziness, sloth, drowsiness, sleepiness, indolence, dreaminess, lotus-eating • *She savoured the pleasant languor, the dreamy tranquillity.*
3 = **stillness**, silence, calm, hush, lull, oppressiveness • *a sleepy haven of rural languor*

lank 1 = **limp**, lifeless, long, dull, straggling, lustreless • *She ran her fingers through her hair; it felt lank and dirty.*
2 = **thin**, lean, slim, slender, skinny, spare, gaunt, lanky, emaciated, scrawny, attenuated, scraggy, rawboned • *a lank youth with a ponytail*

lanky = **gangling**, thin, tall, spare, angular, gaunt, bony, weedy *(informal)*, scrawny, rangy, scraggy, rawboned, loose-jointed • *He was six feet four, all lanky and leggy.*
OPPOSITES: rounded, short, chubby

lantern = **lamp**, light, torch, flashlight • *She took out a lantern and struck a match.*

lap[1] AS A NOUN = **circuit**, course, round, tour, leg, distance, stretch, circle, orbit, loop • *the last lap of the race*
▸ AS A VERB = **overtake**, pass, leave behind, go past, get ahead of, outdistance • *He was caught out while lapping a slower rider.*

lap[2] AS A VERB 1 = **ripple**, wash, splash, slap, swish, gurgle, slosh, purl, plash • *the water that lapped against the pillars of the pier*
2 = **drink**, sip, lick, swallow, gulp, sup • *The kitten lapped milk from a dish.*
▸ IN PHRASES: **lap something up** = **relish**, like, enjoy, appreciate, delight in, savour, revel in, wallow in, accept eagerly • *They're eager to learn, so they lap it up.*

lapse AS A NOUN 1 = **decline**, fall, drop, descent, deterioration, relapse, backsliding • *His behaviour showed neither decency or dignity. It was an uncommon lapse.*
2 = **mistake**, failing, fault, failure, error, slip, negligence, omission, oversight, indiscretion • *The incident was being seen as a serious security lapse.*
3 = **interval**, break, gap, passage, pause, interruption, lull, breathing space, intermission • *a time lapse between receipt of new information and its publication*
▸ AS A VERB 1 = **slip**, fall, decline, sink, drop, slide, deteriorate, degenerate • *Teenagers occasionally find it all too much to cope with and lapse into bad behaviour.*
2 = **end**, stop, run out, expire, terminate, become obsolete, become void • *Her membership of the Labour Party has lapsed.*

lapsed 1 = **expired**, ended, finished, run out, invalid, out of date, discontinued, unrenewed • *He returned to the Party after years of lapsed membership.*
2 = **backsliding**, uncommitted, lacking faith, nonpractising • *She calls herself a lapsed Catholic.*

larceny = **theft**, stealing, robbery, burglary, pilfering, misappropriation, purloining • *He now faces two to 20 years in prison on grand larceny charges.*

larder = **pantry**, store, cupboard, storeroom, scullery • *The larder was stocked with tasty home-made jams and chutneys.*

large AS AN ADJECTIVE 1 = **big**, great, huge, heavy, giant, massive, vast, enormous, tall, considerable, substantial, strapping, immense *(informal)*, hefty, gigantic, monumental, bulky, chunky, burly, colossal, hulking, goodly, man-size, brawny, elephantine, thickset, ginormous *(informal)*, humongous *or* humungous *(U.S. slang)*, sizable *or* sizeable, supersize • *He was a large man with a thick square head.*
OPPOSITES: little, small, minute
2 = **massive**, great, big, huge, giant, vast, enormous, considerable, substantial, immense, tidy *(informal)*, jumbo *(informal)*, gigantic, monumental, mammoth, colossal, gargantuan, stellar *(informal)*, king-size, fuck-off *(taboo)*, ginormous *(informal)*, humongous *or* humungous *(U.S. slang)*, sizable *or* sizeable, supersize • *In a large room about a dozen children are sitting on the carpet.*
OPPOSITES: little, small, minute
3 = **plentiful**, full, grand, liberal, sweeping, broad, comprehensive, extensive, generous, lavish, ample, spacious, abundant, grandiose, copious, roomy, bountiful, capacious, profuse • *The gang finally left with a large amount of cash and jewellery.*
OPPOSITES: scarce, sparse, scanty

LANGUAGES

African Languages

- Adamawa
- Afrikaans
- Akan
- Amharic
- Bambara
- Barotse
- Bashkir
- Bemba
- Berber
- Chewa
- Chichewa
- Coptic
- Damara
- Duala
- Dyula
- Edo, Bini, *or* Beni
- Ewe
- Fanagalo *or* Fanakalo
- Fang
- Fanti
- Fula, Fulah, *or* Fulani
- Ga *or* Gã
- Galla
- Ganda
- Griqua *or* Grikwa
- Hausa
- Herero
- Hottentot
- Hutu
- Ibibio *or* Efik
- Ibo *or* Igbo
- Kabyle
- Kikuyu
- Kingwana
- Kirundi
- Kongo
- Krio
- Lozi
- Luba *or* Tshiluba
- Luganda
- Luo
- Malagasy
- Malinke *or* Maninke
- Masai
- Matabele
- Mossi *or* Moore
- Nama *or* Namaqua
- Ndebele
- Nuba
- Nupe
- Nyanja
- Nyoro
- Ovambo
- Pedi *or* Northern Sotho
- Pondo
- Rwanda
- Sango
- Sesotho
- Shona
- Somali
- Songhai
- Sotho
- Susu
- Swahili
- Swazi
- Temne
- Tigré
- Tigrinya
- Tiv
- Tonga
- Tsonga
- Tswana
- Tuareg
- Twi
- Venda
- Wolof
- Xhosa
- Yoruba
- Zulu

Asian Languages

- Abkhaz
- Adygei *or* Adyghe
- Afghan
- Ainu
- Arabic
- Aramaic
- Armenian
- Assamese
- Azerbaijani
- Bahasa Indonesia
- Balinese
- Baluchi *or* Balochi
- Bengali
- Bihari
- Brahui
- Burmese
- Buryat *or* Buriat
- Cantonese
- Chukchee *or* Chukchi
- Chuvash
- Chinese
- Cham
- Circassian
- Dinka
- Divehi
- Dzongka
- Evenki
- Farsi
- Filipino
- Gondi
- Gujarati *or* Gujerati
- Gurkhali
- Hebrew
- Hindi
- Hindustani
- Iranian
- Japanese
- Javanese
- Kabardian
- Kafiri
- Kalmuck *or* Kalmyk
- Kannada *or* Canarese
- Kara-Kalpak
- Karen
- Kashmiri
- Kazakh *or* Kazak
- Kazan Tatar
- Khalkha
- Khmer
- Kirghiz
- Korean
- Kurdish
- Lahnda
- Lao
- Lepcha
- Malay
- Malayalam
- Manchu
- Mandarin
- Marathi
- Mishmi
- Mon
- Mongol
- Mongolian
- Moro
- Naga
- Nepali
- Nuri
- Oriya
- Ossetian *or* Ossetic
- Ostyak
- Pashto
- Punjabi
- Shan
- Sindhi
- Sinhalese
- Sogdian
- Tadzhiki
- Tagalog
- Tamil
- Tatar
- Telugu
- Thai
- Tibetan
- Tungus
- Turkmen
- Turkoman
- Uigur
- Urdu
- Uzbek
- Vietnamese
- Yakut

Australasian Languages

- Aranda
- Beach-la-Mar
- Dinka
- Fijian
- Gurindji
- Hawaiian
- Hiri Motu
- kamilaroi
- Krio
- Māori
- Moriori
- Motu
- Nauruan
- Neo-Melanesian
- Papuan
- Pintubi
- Police Motu
- Samoan
- Solomon Islands Pidgin
- Tongan
- Tuvaluan
- Warlpiri

European Languages

- Albanian
- Alemannic
- Basque
- Bohemian
- Bokmål
- Breton
- Bulgarian
- Byelorussian
- Castilian
- Catalan
- Cheremiss
- Cornish
- Croatian
- Cymric
- Czech
- Danish
- Dutch
- English
- Erse
- Estonian
- Faeroese
- Finnish
- Flemish
- French
- Frisian
- Friulian
- Gaelic
- Gagauzi
- Galician
- Georgian
- German
- Greek
- Hungarian
- Icelandic
- Italian
- Karelian
- Komi
- Ladin
- Ladino
- Lallans *or* Lallan
- Lapp
- Latvian *or* Lettish
- Lithuanian
- Lusatian
- Macedonian
- Magyar
- Maltese
- Manx
- Mingrelian
- Mordvin
- Norwegian
- Nynorsk *or* Landsmål
- Polish
- Portuguese
- Provençal
- Romanian
- Romansch
- Romany
- Russian
- Samoyed
- Sardinian
- Serbo-Croat
- Shelta
- Slovak
- Slovene
- Sorbian
- Spanish
- Swedish
- Turkish
- Udmurt
- Ukrainian
- Vogul
- Votyak
- Welsh
- Yiddish
- Zyrian

North American Languages

- Abnaki
- Aleut
- Algonquin
- Apache
- Arapaho
- Assiniboine
- Blackfoot
- Caddoan
- Catawba
- Cayuga
- Cherokee
- Cheyenne
- Chickasaw
- Chinook
- Choctaw
- Comanche
- Creek
- Crow
- Delaware
- Erie
- Eskimo
- Fox
- Haida
- Hopi
- Huron
- Inuktitut
- Iroquois
- Kwakiutl
- Mohican
- Massachuset
- Menomini
- Micmac
- Mixtec
- Mohave
- Mohawk
- Narraganset
- Navaho
- Nez Percé
- Nootka
- Ojibwa
- Okanagan
- Oneida
- Onondaga
- Osage
- Paiute
- Pawnee
- Pequot
- Sahaptin
- Seminole
- Seneca
- Shawnee
- Shoshone
- Sioux
- Tahltan
- Taino
- Tlingit
- Tuscarora
- Ute
- Winnebago
- Zuñi

LANGUAGES (CONTINUED)

South American Languages

Araucanian	Chibchan	Guarani	Quechua	Zapotec	
Aymara	Galibi	Nahuatl	Tupi		

Ancient Languages

Akkadian	Edomite	Himyaritic	Lycian	Osco-Umbrian	Sumerian
Ancient Greek	Egyptian	Hittite	Lydian	Pahlavi	Syriac
Anglo-Saxon	Elamite	Illyrian	Maya *or* Mayan	Pali	Thracian
Assyrian	Ethiopic	Inca	Messapian	Phoenician	Thraco-Phrygian
Avar	Etruscan	Ionic	Norn	Phrygian	Tocharian
Avestan *or* Avestic	Faliscan	Koine	Old Church	Pictish	Ugaritic
Aztec	Frankish	Langobardic	Slavonic	Punic	Umbrian
Babylonian	Gallo-Romance	langue d'oc	Old High German	Sabaean	Vedic
Canaanite	Ge'ez	langue d'oïl	Old Norse	Sabellian	Venetic
Celtiberian	Gothic	Latin	Old Prussian	Sanskrit	Volscian
Chaldee	Hebrew	Libyan	Oscan	Scythian	Wendish

Artificial Languages

Esperanto	Ido	interlingua	Volapuk

Language Groups

Afro-Asiatic	Carib	Hellenic	Micronesian	Romance	Tungusic
Albanian	Caucasian	Hindustani	Mongolic	Saharan	Tupi-Guarani
Algonquian	Celtic	Indic	Mon-Khmer	Salish	Turkic
Altaic	Chadic	Indo-Aryan	Munda	San	Ugric
Anatolian	Chari-Nile	Indo-European	Muskogean	Sanskritic	Uralic
Athapascan	Cushitic	Indo-Iranian	Na-Dene	Semi-Bantu	Uto-Aztecan
Arawakan	Cymric	Indo-Pacific	Niger-Congo	Semitic	Voltaic
Armenian	Dardic	Iranian	Nilo-Saharan	Semito-Hamitic	Wakashan
Australian	Dravidian	Iroquoian	Nilotic	Shoshonean	West Atlantic
Austro-Asiatic	East Germanic	Italic	Norse	Siouan	West Germanic
Austronesian	East Iranian	Khoisan	North Germanic	Sinitic	West Iranian
Baltic	Eskimo	Kordofanian	Oceanic	Sino-Tibetan	West Slavonic
Bantu	Finnic	Kwa	Pahari	Slavonic	Yuman
Benue-Congo	Germanic	Malayo-Polynesian	Pama-Nyungan	Sudanic	
Brythonic	Gur	Mande	Penutian	Tibeto-Burman	
Caddoan	Hamitic	Mayan	Polynesian	Trans-New Guinea	
Canaanitic	Hamito-Semitic	Melanesian	Rhaetian	phylum	

4 = serious, important, difficult, worrying, pressing, deep, significant, crucial, urgent, far-reaching, momentous, weighty, of moment *or* consequence • *the already large problem of under-age drinking*

▸ **IN PHRASES: at large 1 = in general**, generally, chiefly, mainly, as a whole, in the main • *The public at large does not seem to want any change.*

2 = free, roaming, on the run, fugitive, at liberty, on the loose, unchained, unconfined • *The man who tried to have her killed is still at large.*

by and large = on the whole, generally, mostly, in general, all things considered, predominantly, in the main, for the most part, all in all, as a rule, taking everything into consideration • *By and large, the papers greet the government's new policy with scepticism.*

largely = mainly, generally, chiefly, widely, mostly, principally, primarily, considerably, predominantly, extensively, by and large, as a rule, to a large extent, to a great extent • *I largely work with people who are already motivated.*

large-scale = wide-ranging, global, sweeping, broad, wide, vast, extensive, wholesale, far-reaching • *a large-scale military operation*

largesse *or* **largess 1 = generosity**, charity, bounty, philanthropy, munificence, liberality, alms-giving, benefaction, open-handedness • *his most recent act of largesse*

2 = gift, present, grant, donation, endowment, bounty, bequest • *The president has been travelling around the country distributing largesse.*

lark AS A NOUN = prank, game, fun, fling, romp, spree, revel, mischief, caper, frolic, escapade, skylark, gambol, antic, jape, rollick • *The children thought it was a great lark.*

▸ **IN PHRASES: lark about = fool around**, play around, romp around, have fun, caper, frolic, cavort, gambol, muck around, make mischief, lark around, rollick, cut capers • *They complained about me larking about when they were trying to concentrate.*

larynx

▸ **RELATED ADJECTIVE:** laryngeal

lascivious 1 = lustful, sensual, immoral, randy *(informal, chiefly Brit.)*, horny *(slang)*, voluptuous, lewd, wanton, salacious, prurient, lecherous, libidinous, licentious, unchaste • *The man was lascivious, sexually perverted and insatiable.*

2 = bawdy, dirty, offensive, crude, obscene, coarse, indecent, blue, vulgar, immoral, pornographic, suggestive, X-rated *(informal)*, scurrilous, smutty, ribald • *their lewd and lascivious talk*

lash[1] AS A VERB 1 = pound, beat, strike, hammer, drum, smack *(dialect)* • *The rain was absolutely lashing down.*

2 = censure, attack, blast, put down, criticize, slate *(informal, chiefly Brit.)*, ridicule, scold, berate, flame *(informal)*,

castigate, lampoon, tear into *(informal)*, flay, upbraid, satirize, lambast(e), belabour • *The report lashes into police commanders for failing to act on intelligence information.*
3 = **whip**, beat, thrash, birch, flog, lam *(slang)*, scourge, chastise, lambast(e), flagellate, horsewhip • *They snatched up whips and lashed the backs of those who had fallen.*
▸ AS A NOUN 1 = **whip**, cane, birch, switch, crop, scourge, thong, rawhide, riding crop, horsewhip, bullwhip, knout, cat-o'-nine-tails • *They forced him to run while flogging him with a lash.*
2 = **blow**, hit, strike, stroke, stripe, swipe *(informal)* • *They sentenced him to five lashes for stealing a ham from his neighbour.*
▸ IN PHRASES: **lash out at someone** = **censure**, attack, criticize, slate *(informal, chiefly Brit.)*, berate, flame *(informal)*, castigate, tear into *(informal)*, upbraid, lambast(e) • *As a politician, he frequently lashed out at the press.*

lash[2] = **fasten**, join, tie, secure, bind, rope, strap, make fast • *Secure the anchor by lashing it to the rail.*

lass = **girl**, young woman, miss, bird *(slang)*, maiden, chick *(slang)*, maid, damsel, colleen *(Irish)*, lassie *(informal)*, wench *(facetious)*, charlie *(Austral. slang)*, chook *(Austral. slang)* • *She's a Lancashire lass from Longton, near Preston.*

lassitude = **weariness**, fatigue, exhaustion, apathy, tiredness, inertia, lethargy, drowsiness, dullness, ennui, torpor, heaviness, sluggishness, languor, listlessness, prostration, enervation, sluggardliness • *Symptoms of anaemia include general fatigue and lassitude.*

l

last[1] AS AN ADJECTIVE 1 = **previous**, preceding, most recent • *I got married last July.*
2 = **most recent**, latest, previous • *Much has changed since my last visit.*
3 = **hindmost**, furthest, final, at the end, remotest, furthest behind, most distant, rearmost, aftermost • *She said it was the very last house on the road.*
OPPOSITES: first, foremost
4 = **final**, closing, concluding, ultimate, utmost • *the last three pages of the chapter*
OPPOSITES: first, opening, earliest
5 = **least likely**, most unlikely, most unsuitable, least suitable • *He would be the last person to do such a thing*
▸ AS AN ADVERB = **in** *or* **at the end**, after, behind, in the rear, bringing up the rear • *I testified last.*
▸ AS A NOUN = **end**, ending, close, finish, conclusion, completion, finale, termination • *a thriller with plenty of twists to keep you guessing to the last*
▸ IN PHRASES: **at last** = **finally**, eventually, in the end, ultimately, at the end of the day, at length, at long last, in conclusion, in the fullness of time • *'All right,' he said at last. 'You may go.'*
the last word 1 = **final decision**, final say, final statement, conclusive comment • *She likes to have the last word in any discussion.*
2 = **leading**, best, first, highest, finest, cream, supreme, elite, first-class, foremost, first-rate, superlative, pre-eminent, unsurpassed, crème de la crème *(French)*, most excellent • *a venue that is the last word in trendiness*

QUOTATIONS
Many that are first shall be last; and the last shall be first
[*Bible: St. Mark*]

last[2] AS A VERB = **continue**, keep, remain, survive, wear, carry on, endure, hold on, persist, keep on, hold out, abide • *You only need a very small amount, so the tube lasts for ages.*
OPPOSITES: end, stop, die
▸ IN PHRASES: **last out** = **hold out**, continue, survive • *I don't know if I can last out till then.*
last something out = **get through**, survive, continue throughout, hold out during • *It'll be a miracle if the band lasts out the tour.*

last-ditch = **final**, frantic, desperate, struggling, straining, heroic, all-out *(informal)* • *a last-ditch attempt to prevent civil war*

lasting = **continuing**, long-term, permanent, enduring, remaining, eternal, abiding, long-standing, perennial, lifelong, durable, perpetual, long-lasting, deep-rooted, indelible, unending, undying, unceasing • *She left a lasting impression on him.*
OPPOSITES: passing, fleeting, short-lived

lastly = **finally**, to conclude, at last, in the end, ultimately, all in all, to sum up, in conclusion • *Lastly, I would like to ask you about your future plans.*

last-minute = **late**, final, frantic, last-ditch, last-gasp, deathbed, eleventh-hour • *She was doing some last-minute revision for her exams.*

latch AS A NOUN = **fastening**, catch, bar, lock, hook, bolt, clamp, hasp, sneck *(dialect)* • *You left the latch off the gate and the dog escaped.*
▸ AS A VERB = **fasten**, bar, secure, lock, bolt, make fast, sneck *(dialect)* • *He latched the door, tested it and turned round to speak to us.*
▸ IN PHRASES: **latch on to something** = **understand**, get, see, follow, realize, take in, grasp, comprehend, get the message about, get the hang of *(informal)*, get the picture about, catch *or* get the drift of • *Other trades have been quick to latch on to these methods.*

late AS AN ADJECTIVE 1 = **overdue**, delayed, last-minute, belated, tardy, behind time, unpunctual, behindhand • *A few late arrivals were still straggling in.*
OPPOSITES: timely, early, seasoned
2 = **dead**, deceased, departed, passed on, old, former, previous, preceding, defunct • *my late husband*
OPPOSITES: existing, alive
3 = **recent**, new, advanced, fresh • *some late news just in for the people of Merseyside*
OPPOSITES: old
▸ AS AN ADVERB 1 = **behind time**, belatedly, tardily, behindhand, dilatorily, unpunctually • *The talks began some fifteen minutes late.*
OPPOSITES: early, in advance, beforehand
2 = **late at night**, in the night • *We went to bed late.*
3 = **after hours**, overtime, till all hours • *I was working late at the office.*
▸ IN PHRASES: **of late** = **recently**, just now, in recent times, not long ago, latterly • *He has changed of late.*

PROVERBS
Better late than never
It is never too late

lately = **recently**, of late, just now, in recent times, not long ago, latterly • *His health hasn't been too good lately.*

lateness = **delay**, late date, retardation, tardiness, unpunctuality, belatedness, advanced hour • *A large crowd had gathered despite the lateness of the hour.*

late-night = **late in the evening**, late at night, after-hours • *late-night drinking sessions*

latent = **hidden**, secret, concealed, invisible, lurking, veiled, inherent, unseen, dormant, undeveloped, quiescent, immanent, unrealized, unexpressed • *Advertisements attempt to project a latent meaning behind an overt message.*
OPPOSITES: developed, expressed, obvious

later AS AN ADVERB = **afterwards**, after, next, eventually, in time, subsequently, later on, thereafter, in a while, in due course, at a later date, by and by, at a later time • *I'll join you later.*
▸ AS AN ADJECTIVE = **subsequent**, next, following, ensuing • *at a later news conference*

lateral = **sideways**, side, flanking, edgeways, sideward • *He estimated the lateral movement of the bridge to be about six inches.*

latest = **up-to-date**, current, fresh, newest, the new, happening *(informal)*, modern, most recent, up-to-the-minute • *Latest reports say another five people have been killed.*

lather AS A NOUN 1 = **froth**, soap, bubbles, foam, suds, soapsuds • *He wiped of the lather with a towel.*
2 = **fluster**, state *(informal)*, sweat, fever, fuss, flap *(informal)*, stew *(informal)*, dither *(chiefly Brit.)*, twitter *(informal)*, tizzy *(informal)*, pother • *'I'm not going to get into a lather over this defeat,' said the manager.*
▸ AS A VERB = **froth**, soap, foam • *The shampoo lathers so much it's difficult to rinse it all out.*

latitude = **scope**, liberty, indulgence, freedom, play, room, space, licence, leeway, laxity, elbowroom, unrestrictedness • *He would be given every latitude in forming a new government.*

latter AS A NOUN = **second**, last, last-mentioned, second-mentioned • *He tracked down his cousin and uncle. The latter was sick.*
▸ AS AN ADJECTIVE = **last**, later, latest, ending, closing, final, concluding • *The latter part of the debate concentrated on abortion.*
OPPOSITES: earlier, former, previous

latter-day = **modern**, recent, current, contemporary, up-to-date, present-day, up-to-the-minute • *He holds the belief that he is a latter-day saint.*

latterly = **recently**, lately, of late, hitherto • *Latterly, he has written extensively about alternative medicine.*

lattice = **grid**, network, web, grating, mesh, grille, trellis, fretwork, tracery, latticework, openwork, reticulation • *We were crawling along the narrow steel lattice of the bridge.*

laud = **praise**, celebrate, honour, acclaim, approve, magnify *(archaic)*, glorify, extol, sing *or* sound the praises of • *They lauded the former president as a hero.*

laudable = **praiseworthy**, excellent, worthy, admirable, of note, commendable, creditable, meritorious, estimable • *One of her less laudable characteristics was her jealousy.*
OPPOSITES: lowly, unworthy, blameworthy

laudatory = **eulogistic**, approving, complimentary, adulatory, commendatory, approbatory, panegyrical, acclamatory • *She spoke of the doctor in laudatory terms.*

laugh AS A VERB = **chuckle**, giggle, snigger, crack up *(informal)*, cackle, chortle, guffaw, titter, roar, bust a gut *(informal)*, be convulsed *(informal)*, be in stitches, crease up *(informal)*, split your sides, be rolling in the aisles *(informal)* • *He laughed with pleasure when people said he looked like his Dad.*
▸ AS A NOUN 1 = **chortle**, giggle, chuckle, snigger, guffaw, titter, belly laugh, roar *or* shriek • *He gave a deep rumbling laugh at his own joke.*
2 = **joke**, scream *(informal)*, hoot *(informal)*, lark, prank • *Working there's great. It's quite a good laugh actually.*
3 = **clown**, character *(informal)*, scream *(informal)*, comic, caution *(informal)*, wit, comedian, entertainer, card *(informal)*, wag, joker, hoot *(informal)*, humorist • *He was a good laugh and great to have in the dressing room.*
▸ IN PHRASES: **laugh at something** *or* **someone** = **make fun of**, mock, tease, ridicule, taunt, jeer, deride, scoff at, belittle, lampoon, take the mickey out of *(informal)*, pour scorn on, make a mock of • *I thought people were laughing at me because I was ugly.*
laugh something off = **disregard**, ignore, dismiss, overlook, shrug off, minimize, brush aside, make light of, pooh-pooh • *While I used to laugh it off, I'm now getting irritated by it.*

QUOTATIONS
Laugh and the world laughs with you;
Weep, and you weep alone;
For the sad old earth must borrow its mirth,
But has enough trouble of its own
[Ella Wheeler Wilcox *Solitude*]

One can know a man from his laugh, and if you like a man's laugh before you know anything of him, you may confidently say that he is a good man
[Fyodor Dostoevsky *The House of the Dead*]

PROVERBS
He who laughs last, laughs longest

laughable 1 = **ridiculous**, absurd, ludicrous, preposterous, farcical, nonsensical, derisory, risible, derisive, worthy of scorn • *He claimed that the allegations were 'laughable'.*
2 = **funny**, amusing, hilarious, humorous, diverting, comical, droll, mirthful • *Groucho's laughable view of human pomp*

laughing stock = **figure of fun**, target, victim, butt, fair game, Aunt Sally *(Brit.)*, everybody's fool • *His politics became the laughing stock of the financial community.*

laughter 1 = **chuckling**, laughing, giggling, chortling, guffawing, tittering, cachinnation • *Their laughter filled the corridor.*
2 = **amusement**, entertainment, humour, glee, fun, mirth, hilarity, merriment • *Pantomime is about bringing laughter to thousands.*

QUOTATIONS
If we may believe our logicians, man is distinguished from all other creatures by the faculty of laughter
[Joseph Addison]
The only honest art form is laughter, comedy. You can't fake it ... try to fake three laughs in an hour – ha ha ha ha ha – they'll take you away, man. You can't
[Lenny Bruce *Performing and the Art of Comedy*]
As the crackling of thorns under a pot, so is the laughter of a fool
[*Bible: Ecclesiastes*]

launch AS A VERB 1 = **propel**, fire, dispatch, discharge, project, send off, set in motion, send into orbit • *A Delta II rocket was launched from Cape Canaveral early this morning.*
2 = **set afloat**, cast off, discharge, dispatch, put into water • *There was no time to launch the lifeboats.*
3 = **begin**, start, open, initiate, introduce, found, set up, originate, commence, get under way, instigate, inaugurate, embark upon • *The police have launched an investigation into the incident.*
4 = **throw**, fling, hurtle • *He launched himself into the air.*
▸ AS A NOUN 1 = **propelling**, projection, sendoff • *This morning's launch of the space shuttle Columbia has been delayed.*
2 = **beginning**, start, introduction, initiation, opening, founding, setting-up, inauguration, commencement, instigation • *the launch of a campaign to restore law and order*
▸ IN PHRASES: **launch into something** = **start enthusiastically**, begin, initiate, embark on, instigate, inaugurate, embark upon • *He launched into a speech about the importance of new products.*

launder 1 = **wash**, clean, dry-clean, tub, wash and iron, wash and press • *She wore a freshly laundered and starched white shirt.*
2 = **process**, doctor, manipulate • *The House voted today to crack down on banks that launder drug money.*

laurel IN PHRASES: **rest on your laurels** = **sit back**, relax, take it easy, relax your efforts • *The government shouldn't rest on its laurels, and must press ahead with policy changes.*

lavatory = **toilet**, bathroom, loo *(Brit. informal)*, bog *(slang)*, can *(U.S. & Canad. slang)*, john *(slang, chiefly U.S. & Canad.)*, head(s) *(Nautical slang)*, throne *(informal)*, closet, privy, cloakroom *(Brit.)*, urinal, latrine, washroom, powder room, ablutions *(Military informal)*, crapper *(taboo)*, water closet, khazi *(slang)*, pissoir *(French)*, Gents *or* Ladies, little boy's room *or* little girl's room *(informal)*, (public) convenience, W.C., dunny *(Austral. & N.Z.)*, bogger *(Austral. slang)*, brasco *(Austral. slang)* • *a public lavatory*

lavish AS AN ADJECTIVE 1 = **grand**, magnificent, splendid, lush, abundant, sumptuous, exuberant, opulent, copious, luxuriant, profuse • *a lavish party to celebrate his fiftieth birthday*
OPPOSITES: meagre, frugal, stingy
2 = **extravagant**, wild, excessive, exaggerated, unreasonable, wasteful, prodigal, unrestrained, intemperate, immoderate, improvident, thriftless • *Critics attack his lavish spending and flamboyant style.*
OPPOSITES: sparing, thrifty
3 = **generous**, free, liberal, bountiful, effusive, open-handed, unstinting, munificent • *American reviewers are lavish in their praise of this book.*
OPPOSITES: stingy, parsimonious, miserly
▸ AS A VERB = **shower**, pour, heap, deluge, dissipate • *The emperor promoted the general and lavished him with gifts.*
OPPOSITES: withhold, stint, begrudge

law AS A NOUN 1 = **constitution**, code, legislation, charter, jurisprudence • *Obscene and threatening phone calls are against the law.*
2 = **the police**, constabulary, the police force, law enforcement agency, the boys in blue *(informal)*, the fuzz *(slang)*, the Old Bill *(slang)* • *If you lot don't stop fighting I'll have the law round.*
3 = **statute**, act, bill, rule, demand, order, command, code, regulation, resolution, decree, canon, covenant, ordinance, commandment, enactment, edict • *The law was passed on a second vote.*
4 = **rule**, order, ruling, principle, standard, direction, regulation, guideline, decree, maxim, ordinance, tenet, dictum, precept • *the laws of the Church of England*
5 = **principle**, standard, code, formula, criterion, canon, precept, axiom, kaupapa *(N.Z.)* • *inflexible moral laws*
6 = **the legal profession**, the bar, barristers • *a career in law*
▸ IN PHRASES: **lay down the law** = **be dogmatic**, call the shots *(informal)*, pontificate, rule the roost, crack the whip, boss around, dogmatize, order about *or* around • *traditional parents who believed in laying down the law for their offspring*
▸ RELATED ADJECTIVES: legal, judicial, juridical, jural

QUOTATIONS

The end of the law is, not to abolish or restrain, but to preserve and enlarge freedom
[John Locke *Second Treatise of Civil Government*]

It may be true that the law cannot make a man love me, but it can keep him from lynching me, and I think that's pretty important
[Martin Luther King Jr.]

The law is a causeway upon which so long as he keeps to it a citizen may walk safely
[Robert Bolt *A Man For All Seasons*]

No brilliance is needed in the law. Nothing but common sense, and relatively clean finger nails
[John Mortimer *A Voyage Round My Father*]

Laws were made to be broken
[John Wilson *Noctes Ambrosianae*]

The Common Law of England has been laboriously built about a mythical figure – the figure of "The Reasonable Man"
[A.P. Herbert *Uncommon Law*]

We do not get good laws to restrain bad people. We get good people to restrain bad laws
[G.K. Chesterton *All Things Considered*]

The law is a ass – a idiot
[Charles Dickens *Oliver Twist*]

Written laws are like spider's webs; they will catch, it is true, the weak and poor, but would be torn in pieces by the rich and powerful
[Anacharsis]

Law is a bottomless pit
[Dr. Arbuthnot *The History of John Bull*]

The one great principle of the English law is to make business for itself
[Charles Dickens *Bleak House*]

The laws of most countries are far worse than the people who execute them, and many of them are only able to remain laws by being seldom or never carried into effect
[John Stuart Mill *The Subjection of Women*]

PROVERBS

Hard cases make bad laws

One law for the rich, and another for the poor

▹ *See panel* **Law**

law-abiding = **obedient**, good, peaceful, honourable, orderly, honest, lawful, compliant, dutiful, peaceable • *We want to protect decent law-abiding people and their property.*

lawbreaker = **criminal**, convict, offender, violater, crook *(informal)*, villain, culprit, sinner, delinquent, felon, trespasser, wrongdoer, miscreant, transgressor, skelm *(S. African)*, perp *(U.S. & Canad. informal)* • *The money should be spent on training first-time lawbreakers to earn an honest living.*

law court = **tribunal**, court, the bar, the bench, judiciary, session, court of justice, court of law, assizes • *She would never resort to the law courts to solve her marital problems.*

lawful = **legal**, constitutional, just, proper, valid, warranted, legitimate, authorized, rightful, permissible, legalized, allowable, licit • *lawful for the doctors to treat her in whatever way they considered best*
OPPOSITES: banned, illegal, unlawful

lawless = **disorderly**, wild, unruly, rebellious, chaotic, reckless, insurgent, anarchic, riotous, unrestrained, seditious, mutinous, insubordinate, ungoverned • *They said there could never be an excuse for lawless behaviour.*
OPPOSITES: disciplined, legitimate, law-abiding

lawlessness = **anarchy**, disorder, chaos, reign of terror, mob rule, mobocracy, ochlocracy • *Lawlessness is a major problem.*

lawsuit = **case**, cause, action, trial, suit, argument, proceedings, dispute, contest, prosecution, legal action, indictment, litigation, industrial tribunal, legal proceedings • *The dispute culminated in a lawsuit against the government.*

lawyer = **legal adviser**, attorney, solicitor, counsel, advocate, barrister, counsellor, legal representative • *Prosecution and defense lawyers are expected to deliver closing arguments next week.*

QUOTATIONS

If there were no bad people there would be no good lawyers
[Charles Dickens *The Old Curiosity Shop*]

I'm trusting in the Lord and a good lawyer
[Oliver North]

I don't want a lawyer to tell me what I cannot do; I hire him to tell me how to do what I want to do
[J. Pierpoint Morgan]

Woe unto you, lawyers! For ye have taken away the key of knowledge
[*Bible: St. Luke*]

A lawyer with his briefcase can steal more than a hundred men with guns
[Mario Puzo *The Godfather*]

PROVERBS

A man who is his own lawyer has a fool for a client

lax 1 = **slack**, casual, careless, sloppy *(informal)*, easy-going, negligent, lenient, slapdash, neglectful, slipshod, remiss, easy-peasy *(slang)*, overindulgent • *One of the problems is lax security for airport personnel.*
OPPOSITES: severe, disciplined, strict
2 = **loose**, soft, yielding, slack, flabby, flaccid • *exercises to improve lax muscles*
OPPOSITES: firm, rigid

LAW

Law terms

abandonee
abate
abator
abet
abeyance
able
absente reo
absolute
acceptance *(Contract law)*
accessory *or* accessary
accretion
accrue
accusation
accusatorial
accuse
accused, the
acquit
action
actionable
act of God
adjective
ad litem
adminicle
administration order
admissible
adopt
adult
advocate
advocation
affiant
affidavit
affiliate *or* filiate
affiliation *or* filiation
affiliation order
affiliation proceedings *or* *(U.S.)* paternity suit
affirm
affirmation
affray
agist
alibi
alienable
alienate
alienation
alienee
alienor
alimony
allege
alluvion
ambulatory
a mensa et thoro
amerce *(obsolete)*
amicus curiae
amnesty
ancient
annulment
answer
Anton Piller order
appeal
appearance
appellant
appellate
appellee
appendant
approve
arbitrary
arbitration
arraign
array
arrest judgment
arrest of judgement
articled clerk
assault
assessor
assets
assign
assignee
assignment
assignor
assumpsit
attach
attachment
attainder
attaint *(archaic)*
attorn
attorney
attorney-at-law
attorney general
authentic
authority
automatism
aver
avoid
avoidance
avow *(rare)*
avulsion
award
bail
bailable
bailee *(Contract law)*
bailiff
bailiwick
bailment *(Contract law)*
bailor *(Contract law)*
bailsman *(rare)*
ban
bankrupt
bar
baron *(English law)*
barratry
barrister
bench, the
bencher
beneficial
beneficiary
bequeath
bequest
bigamy
bill of attainder
bill of indictment
bill of sale
blasphemy
body corporate
bona fides
bona vacantia
bond
bondsman
breach of promise
breach of the peace
breach of trust
brief
briefless
bring
burden of proof
capias
capital
caption
carnal knowledge
cartulary *or* chartulary
case
case law
case stated *or* stated case
cassation
cause
caution
CAV, Cur. adv. vult, *or* Curia advisari vult
caveat
caveator
certificate of incorporation *(Company law)*
chamber counsel *or* counsellor
chambers
certification
certiorari
cessor
cessionary
challenge
challenge to the array
challenge to the polls
champerty
chance-medley
chancery
change of venue
charge
chargeable
cheat
chief justice
chose
circuit *(English law)*
citation
cite
civil death
civil marriage
clerk to the justices
close
codicil
codification
coexecutor
cognizable
cognizance
collusion
come on
commitment, committal, *or (especially formerly)* mittimus
common
commonage
common law
commutable
commutation
commute
competence
competency
competent
complainant
complaint *(English law)*
complete *(Land law)*
compound
compliance officer
composition
compurgation
conclusion
condemn
condition
condone
confiscate
connivance
connive
conscience clause
consensual
consideration
consolidation
consortium
constituent
constitute
constructive
contempt
contentious
continuance *(U.S.)*
contraband
contract
contractor
contributory *(Company law)*
contributory negligence
contumacy
convene
conventional
conversion
convert
conveyance
convincing
coparcenary *or* coparceny
coparcener *or* parcener
copyhold
copyholder
co-respondent
coroner
coroner's inquest
coroner's jury
corpus delicti
corpus juris
Corpus Juris Civilis
costs
counsel
counselor
count
countercharge
counterclaim
counterpart
countersign
county court
court
court of first instance
covenant
coverture
covin
criminal conversation
criminate *(rare)*
cross-examine
crown attorney *(Canad.)*
crown court *(English law)*
cruelty
culpa *(Civil law)*
culprit
cumulative evidence
custodian
custody
custom
customary
cy pres
damages
damnify
dead letter
debatable
decedent *(chiefly U.S.)*
declarant
declaration
declaratory
decree
decree absolute
decree nisi
deed
deed poll
defalcate
defamation
default
defeasible
defeat
defence
defendant
deferred sentence
de jure
delict *(Roman law)*
demand
demandant
demisit sine prole
demur
demurrer
denunciation *(obsolete)*
deodand *(English law)*
deponent
depose
deposition
deraign *(obsolete)*
dereliction
descendible *or* descendable
desertion
detainer
determinable
determination
determine
detinue
devil
devisable
devise
devolve
dies non *or* dies non juridicus
digest
diligence
diminished responsibility
direct evidence
disaffirm
disafforest *or* disforest *(English law)*
disannul
disbar
discharge
disclaim
discommon
discontinue
discovert
discovery
disinherit
dismiss
disorderly
disorderly conduct
disorderly house
dissent
distrain *or* distress
distrainee
distraint
distributee *(chiefly U.S.)*

LAW TERMS (CONTINUED)

distribution
distringas
disturbance
dividend
divorce from bed and board *(U.S.)*
docket
documentation
Doe
domain
donee
donor
dot *(Civil law)*
dotation
dowable
dower
droit
due process of law
duress
earnest *or* earnest money *(Contract law)*
effectual
emblements
eminent domain
empanel *or* impanel
encumbrance
encumbrancer
enfranchise *(English law)*
engross
engrossment
enjoin
enter
equitable
equity
escheat
escrow
estop
estoppel
estovers
estray
estreat
evict
evidence
evocation *(French law)*
examination
examine
examine-in-chief
exception
execute
execution
executor *or (fem.)* executrix
executory
exemplary damages
exemplify
exhibit
ex parte
expectancy
expropriate
extend
extent *(U.S.)*
extinguish
extraditable
extradite
extrajudicial
eyre *(English legal history)*
fact
factor *(Commercial law)*
false imprisonment
Family Division
felo de se
feme
feme covert
feme sole
fiction
fideicommissary *(Civil law)*
fideicommissum *(Civil law)*
fiduciary *or* fiducial
fieri facias
file
filiate
filiation
find
finding
first offender
fiscal
flaw
folio
forbearance
force majeure
foreclose
foreign
foreman
forensic
forensic medicine, legal medicine, *or* medical jurisprudence
forest
forfeit
forjudge
fornication
free
fungible
garnish
garnishee
garnishment
gavelkind *(English law)*
gist
goods and chattels
grand jury *(chiefly U.S.)*
grand larceny
grantee
grant
grantor
gratuitous
gravamen
grith *(English legal history)*
ground rent
guarantee
guardian
guilty
habeas corpus
hand down *(U.S. & Canad.)*
handling
hear
hearing
hearsay
heir *or (fem.)* heiress *(Civil law)*
heirship
hereditary
heres *or* haeres *(Civil law)*
heritable
heritage
heritor
holder
homologate
hung jury
hypothec *(Roman law)*
hypothecate
immovable
impartible
impediment
imperfect
implead *(rare)*
imprescriptable
in articles
in banc
in camera
incapacitate
incapacity
in chancery
incompetent
incorporeal
incriminate
indefeasible
indemnity
indenture
indeterminate sentence
inducement
in escrow
infant
in fee
inferior court
infirm
in flagrante delicto
ingoing
inheritance
injunction
injury
innuendo
in personam
in posse
inquest
inquisition
inquisitorial
in rem
insanity
in specie
instanter
institutes
instruct
instructions
instrument
insurable interest
intendment
intent
intention
interdict *(Civil law)*
interlocutory
interplead
interpleader
interrogatories
intervene
inter vivos
intestate
invalidate
in venter
ipso jure
irrepleviable *or* irreplevisable
issuable
issue
jail delivery *(English law)*
jeopardy
joinder
joint
jointress
jointure
judge
judge-made
judges' rules
judgment
judgment by default
judicable
judicative
judicatory
judicature
judicial
judicial separation *(Family law)*
judiciary
junior
jural
jurat
juratory
juridical
jurisconsult
jurisprudence
jurisprudent
jurist
juristic
juror
jury
juryman *or (fem.)* jurywoman
jury process
jus
jus gentium *(Roman law)*
jus naturale *(Roman law)*
jus sanguinis
jus soli
justice
justice court
justice of the peace
justiciable
justices in eyre *(English legal history)*
justify
juvenile court
laches
land
lapse
larceny
Law French
Law Lords
law merchant *(Mercantile law)*
lawsuit
law term
lawyer
leasehold
leaseholder
legist
letters of administration
lex loci
lex non scripta
lex scripta
lex talionis
libel
lien
limit
limitation
lis pendens
litigable
litigant
litigation
locus standi
magistrate
magistrates' court *or* petty sessions
maintenance
malfeasance
malice
manager
mandamus
mandate
manslaughter
manus
mare clausum
mare liberum
material
matter
mayhem
memorandum
mens rea
mental disorder
mental impairment
merger
merits
mesne
ministerial
misadventure
mise
misfeasance
misjoinder
mispleading
mistrial
misuser
mittimus
monopoly
moral
moratorium
morganatic *or* left-handed
mortgagee
mortmain *or (less commonly)* dead hand
motion
moveable
muniments
mute
naked
Napoleonic Code
necessaries
negligence
next friend
nisi
nisi prius *(History, U.S.)*
nolle prosequi, nol. pros., *or* nolle pros.
nolo contendere *(chiefly U.S.)*
nonage
non compos mentis
nonfeasance
nonjoinder
non liquet
non prosequitur *or* non pros.
nonsuit
notary public
not guilty
novation
novel *(Roman law)*
nude
nudum pactum
nuisance
oath
obiter dictum
obligation
oblivion
obreption
obscene
obtaining by deception
occupancy
occupant
offer *(Contract law)*
Official Referee
onerous
onomastic
on, upon *or* under oath
onus probandi
open
opening

LAW TERMS (CONTINUED)

ordinary
overt
owelty
oyer (*English legal history*)
oyer and terminer
panel
paraphernalia
pardon
parol
Particulars of Claim
party
paterfamilias (*Roman law*)
peculium (*Roman law*)
pecuniary
pecuniary advantage
pendente lite
perception
peremptory
persistent cruelty
personal
personal property *or* personalty
petit
petition
petitioner
petit jury *or* petty jury
petit larceny *or* petty larceny
petty
place of safety order
plaint
plaintiff
plea
plea bargaining
plead
pleading
pleadings
portion
port of entry
posse
posse comitatus
possessory
post-obit
prayer
precedent
precept
predispose
pre-emption
prefer
preference
premeditation
premises
prescribe
prescription
presentment (*chiefly U.S.*)
presents
presume
presumption
preterition (*Roman law*)
prima facie
primogeniture
principal
private law
private nuisance
privilege
privileged
privity
privy
prize court
probable cause
probate
proceed
proceeding
process
process-server
procuration
procuratory
prohibition
promisee (*Contract law*)
promisor (*Contract law*)
proof
property centre
proponent
propositus
propound (*English law*)
prosecute
prosecuting attorney (*U.S.*)
prosecution
prosecutor
prothonotary *or* protonotary
prove
provocation (*English criminal law*)
psychopathic disorder
public defender (*U.S.*)
public law
public nuisance
public prosecutor
pupil (*Civil law*)
pupillage
pursuant
purview
quarter sessions
queen's *or* king's evidence
question
question of fact (*English law*)
question of law (*English law*)
quitclaim
quo warranto
real
real property
rebutter
recaption
receivership
recital
recognizance
recognizee
recognizor
recorder
recoup
recover
recovery
recrimination
re-examine
reference
refresher (*English law*)
rejoin
rejoinder
relation
relator
release
relief
remand
remise
remission
remit
repetition (*Civil law*)
replevin
replevy
replication
reply
report
reporter
representation (*Contract law*)
reprieve
rescue
reservation
res gestae
residuary
residue
res ipsa loquitur
res judicata *or* res adjudicata
resolutive
respondent
rest
restitution
restraining order (*U.S.*)
restrictive covenant
retain
retry
return
returnable
reverse
review
right of common
riot
rout
rule
ruling
run
salvo
saving
scandal
schedule
scienter
scire facias (*rare*)
script
secularize
self-defence
self-executing
sentence
separation (*Family law*)
sequester *or* sequestrate
sequestration
serjeant at law, serjeant, sergeant at law, *or* sergeant
servitude
session
settlement
settlor
severable
several
severance
sign
signatory
sine
sine prole
slander
smart money (*U.S.*)
socage (*English law*)
soke (*English legal history*)
solatium (*chiefly U.S.*)
sole
solemnity
solicitor
solution
sound
sound in
special case
special pleading
specialty
specific performance
spinster
spoliation
squat
stale
stand by (*English law*)
stand down
statement
statement of claim
state's evidence (*U.S.*)
statute law
statutory declaration
stillicide
stipulate (*Roman law*)
stranger
stultify
submission
subpoena
subreption (*rare*)
subrogate
subrogation
substantive
succeed
sue
sui juris
suit
suitor
summary
summary jurisdiction
summary offence
summation (*U.S. law*)
summing-up
summons
suo jure
suo loco
surcharge
surety
surplusage
surrebuttal
surrebutter
surrejoinder
surrender
suspension
swear
swear in
swear out (*U.S.*)
tales
tenancy
tenantry
tender
tenor
term
termor *or* termer
territorial court (*U.S.*)
testament
testamentary
testate
testify
testimony
thing
third party
time immemorial
tipstaff
title
tort
tort-feasor
tortious
traffic court
transfer
transitory action
traverse
treasure-trove
trespass
triable
trial
trial court
tribunal
trover
try
udal
ultimogeniture
ultra vires
unalienable
unappealable
unavoidable
uncovenanted
unilateral
unincorporated
unlawful assembly
unreasonable behaviour
unwritten law
use
user
utter barrister
vacant
vacate
variance
vendee
vendor
venire facias
venireman (*U.S.*)
venue
verdict
verification
verify
versus
vesture
vexatious
view
viewer
vindicate (*Roman law*)
vindictive (*English law*)
vitiate
voidable
voir dire
voluntary
voluntary arrangement
volunteer
voucher (*English law, obsolete*)
wager of law (*English legal history*)
waif (*obsolete*)
waive
waiver
ward
ward of court
warrant
warranty (*Contract law, Insurance law*)
waste
will
witness
without prejudice
writ
writ of execution
wrong
year and a day (*English law*)

Criminal law terms

acquittal
actual bodily harm
arson
bailment
battery
burglary (*English law*)
deception *or* (*formerly*) false pretences
embrace
embraceor *or* embracer
embracery
entry
felon
felonious
felony
force
forgery
grievous bodily harm
hard labour
housebreaking
impeach
indictable
indictment
infamous
malice aforethought
misdemeanant
misdemeanour
penal servitude (*English law*)
perjure
perjury
personate
Riot Act
robbery
suborn
theft
thief
true bill (*U.S. law*)
utter

Property law terms

abatement
abstract of title
abuttals
abutter
accession
ademption
administration
administrator
advancement
adverse
amortize
appoint
appointee
appointment
appointor
appurtenance
betterment
chattel
chattel personal
chattel real
convey *or* assure
deforce
demesne
demise
descent
devisee
devisor
dilapidation
disentail
disseise
divest
dominant tenement
dominium
easement
ejectment
enfeoff
entail
entry
equity of redemption
estate
fee
fee simple
fee tail
fixture
freehold
freeholder
heir apparent
heir-at-law
heirdom
heirloom
heriditament
hotchpot
intrusion
messuage
mortgagor
oust
ouster
particular
partition
party wall
perpetuity
power of appointment
reconvert
remainder
remainderman
remitter
result
reversion
reversioner
revert
riparian
seisin *or* (*U.S.*) seizin
servient tenement
severalty
survivor
tail
tenure
transferee
transferor
unity of interest
vested
vested interest
warranty

Scots law terms

advocate
Advocate Depute
agent
aliment
alimentary
approbate
approbate and reprobate
arrestment
assignation
assize
avizandum
condescendence
continue
crown agent
culpable homicide
curator
decern
declarator
decreet
defender
delict
depone
desert
district court *or* (*formerly*) justice of the peace court
feu
feu duty
fire raising
hypothec
interdict
interlocutor
law agent
location
lockfast
mandate
multiplepoinding
notour
notour bankrupt
not proven
poind
poinding
precognition
procurator fiscal *or* fiscal
pupil
repetition
repone
sasine
sequestrate
sheriff officer
thirlage
tradition
tutor
wadset
warrant sale

laxative = **purgative**, salts, purge, cathartic, physic (*rare*), aperient • *Foods that ferment quickly in the stomach are excellent natural laxatives.*

laxity = **slackness**, neglect, negligence, carelessness, leniency, sloppiness (*informal*), unconcern, laxness • *The laxity of expert control authorities has made a significant contribution to the problem.*

lay[1] **as a verb** 1 = **place**, put, set, spread, plant, establish, settle, leave, deposit, put down, set down, posit • *Lay a sheet of newspaper on the floor.*
2 = **devise**, plan, design, prepare, work out, plot, hatch, contrive, concoct • *They were laying a trap for the kidnapper.*
3 = **produce**, bear, deposit • *Freezing weather hampered the hen's ability to lay eggs.*
4 = **arrange**, prepare, make, organize, position, locate, set out, devise, put together, dispose, draw up • *The organisers meet in March to lay plans.*
5 = **attribute**, charge, assign, allocate, allot, ascribe, impute • *She refused to lay the blame on any one party.*
6 = **put forward**, offer, present, advance, lodge, submit, bring forward • *Police have decided not to lay charges over allegations of phone tapping.*
7 = **bet**, stake, venture, gamble, chance, risk, hazard, wager, give odds • *I wouldn't lay bets on his remaining manager after the spring.*
▸ **in phrases: lay into someone** = **attack**, hit, set about, hit out at, assail, tear into, pitch into (*informal*), go for the jugular, lambast(e), belabour, lash into, let fly at • *A mob of women laid into him with handbags and pointed shoes.*
lay it on thick = **exaggerate**, flatter, overdo it, lay it on with a trowel (*informal*), overpraise, soft-soap (*informal*) • *Don't lay it on too thick, but make sure they are flattered.*
lay off = **stop**, give up, quit, cut it out, leave alone, pack in, abstain, leave off, give over (*informal*), let up, get off someone's back (*informal*), give it a rest (*informal*) • *He went on attacking her until other passengers arrived and told him to lay off.*
lay someone off = **dismiss**, fire (*informal*), release, drop, sack (*informal*), pay off, discharge, oust, let go, make redundant, give notice to, give the boot to (*slang*), give the sack to (*informal*), give someone their cards, give someone his *or* her P45 (*informal*), kennet (*Austral. slang*), jeff (*Austral. slang*) • *100,000 federal workers will be laid off to reduce the deficit.*
lay someone out = **knock out**, fell, floor, knock unconscious, knock for six, kayo (*slang*) • *He turned round, marched over to the man, and just laid him out.*
lay someone up = **confine (to bed)**, hospitalize, incapacitate • *He was recovering from a knee injury that laid him up for six months.*
lay something aside = **abandon**, reject, dismiss, postpone, shelve, put off, renounce, put aside, cast aside • *All animosities were laid aside for the moment.*
lay something bare = **reveal**, show, expose, disclose, unveil, divulge • *The clearing out of disused workshops laid bare thousands of glazed tiles.*

lay something down 1 = **stipulate**, state, establish, prescribe, assume, formulate, affirm, ordain, set down, postulate • *The Companies Act lays down a set of minimum requirements.*
2 = **sacrifice**, give up, yield, surrender, turn over, relinquish • *The drug traffickers have offered to lay down their arms.*
lay something in = **store (up)**, collect, build up, accumulate, buy in, amass, stockpile, hoard, stock up, heap up • *They began to lay in extensive stores of food supplies.*
lay something on = **provide**, prepare, supply, organize, give, cater (for), furnish, purvey • *They laid on a superb meal.*
lay something out 1 = **arrange**, order, design, display, exhibit, put out, spread out • *She took a deck of cards and began to lay them out.*
2 = **present**, explain, describe, show, unfold, spell out • *We listened carefully as he laid out his plan.*
3 = **spend**, pay, invest, fork out *(slang)*, expend, shell out *(informal)*, disburse • *You won't have to lay out a fortune for this dining table.*

lay[2] 1 = **nonclerical**, secular, non-ordained, laic, laical • *He is a Methodist lay preacher and social worker.*
2 = **nonspecialist**, amateur, unqualified, untrained, inexpert, nonprofessional • *It is difficult for a lay person to gain access to medical libraries.*

lay[3] = **poem**, song, lyric, ballad, ode • *Yeats used Comyn's 'The Lay of Oisin on the Land of Youth' as a source.*

layabout = **idler**, lounger, piker *(Austral. & N.Z. slang)*, shirker, loafer, couch potato *(slang)*, vagrant, laggard, skiver *(Brit. slang)*, beachcomber, ne'er-do-well, good-for-nothing, wastrel, bludger *(Austral. & N.Z. informal)*, slubberdegullion *(archaic)* • *The plaintiff's sole witness, a gambler and layabout, was easily discredited.*

layer 1 = **covering**, film, cover, sheet, coating, coat, blanket, mantle, dusting • *A fresh layer of snow covered the street.*
2 = **tier**, level, seam, stratum • *Critics and the public puzzle out the layers of meaning in his photos.*

layman = **nonprofessional**, amateur, outsider, lay person, non-expert, nonspecialist • *There are basically two types, called, in layman's terms, blue and white asbestos.*

lay-off = **unemployment**, firing *(informal)*, sacking *(informal)*, dismissal, discharge • *The closure will result in layoffs of an estimated 2000 employees.*

layout = **arrangement**, design, draft, outline, format, plan, formation, geography • *He tried to recall the layout of the farmhouse.*

laze 1 = **idle**, lounge, hang around, loaf, stand around, loll • *Fred lazed in an easy chair.*
2 *often with* **away** = **kill time**, waste time, fritter away, doss *(Brit. slang)*, pass time, while away the hours, veg out *(slang, chiefly U.S.)*, fool away • *She lazed away most of the morning.*

laziness = **idleness**, negligence, inactivity, slowness, sloth, sluggishness, slackness, indolence, tardiness, dilatoriness, slothfulness, do-nothingness, faineance • *Current employment laws will be changed to reward effort and punish laziness.*

lazy 1 = **idle**, inactive, indolent, slack, negligent, inert, remiss, workshy, slothful, shiftless • *I was too lazy to learn how to read music.*
OPPOSITES: active, stimulated, industrious
2 = **lethargic**, languorous, slow-moving, languid, sleepy, sluggish, drowsy, somnolent, torpid • *We would have a lazy lunch and then lie on the beach in the sun.*
OPPOSITES: quick

lazybones = **idler**, lounger, piker *(Austral. & N.Z. slang)*, shirker, loafer, couch potato *(slang)*, skiver *(Brit. slang)*, sleepyhead, sluggard, bludger *(Austral. & N.Z. informal)*, slugabed • *Get this lazybones to school!*

leach = **extract**, strain, drain, filter, seep, percolate, filtrate, lixiviate *(Chemistry)* • *Minerals leach from the soil much faster on cleared land.*

lead[1] AS A VERB 1 = **go in front (of)**, head, be in front, be at the head (of), walk in front (of) • *Tom was leading, a rifle slung over his back.*
2 = **guide**, conduct, steer, escort, precede, usher, pilot, show the way • *He led him into the house.*
3 = **connect to**, link, open onto • *the doors that led to the yard*
4 = **be ahead (of)**, be first, exceed, be winning, excel, surpass, come first, transcend, outstrip, outdo, blaze a trail • *So far he leads by five games to two.*
5 = **command**, rule, govern, preside over, head, control, manage, direct, supervise, be in charge of, head up • *He led the country between 1949 and 1984.*
6 = **live**, have, spend, experience, pass, undergo • *She led a normal happy life with her sister and brother.*
7 = **result in**, cause, produce, contribute, generate, bring about, bring on, give rise to, conduce • *He warned that a pay rise would lead to job cuts.*
8 = **cause**, prompt, persuade, move, draw, influence, motivate, prevail, induce, incline, dispose • *It was not as straightforward as we were led to believe.*
▸ AS A NOUN 1 = **first place**, winning position, primary position, vanguard, van • *Labour are still in the lead in the opinion polls.*
2 = **advantage**, start, advance, edge, margin, winning margin • *He now has a lead of 30 points.*
3 = **example**, direction, leadership, guidance, model, pattern • *the need for the president to give a moral lead*
4 = **clue**, tip, suggestion, trace, hint, guide, indication, pointer, tip-off • *The inquiry team is following up possible leads.*
5 = **leading role**, principal, protagonist, title role, star part, principal part • *Two dancers from the Bolshoi Ballet dance the leads.*
6 = **leash**, line, cord, rein, tether • *He came out with a little dog on a lead.*
▸ AS AN ADJECTIVE = **main**, prime, top, leading, first, head, chief, premier, primary, most important, principal, foremost • *Cossiga's reaction is the lead story in the Italian press.*
▸ IN PHRASES: **lead off** = **begin**, start, open, set out, kick off *(informal)*, initiate, commence, get going, get under way, inaugurate, start the ball rolling *(informal)* • *Whenever there was a dance he and I led off.*
lead someone on = **entice**, tempt, lure, mislead, draw on, seduce, deceive, beguile, delude, hoodwink, inveigle, string along *(informal)* • *I bet she led him on, but how could he be so weak?*
lead up to something = **introduce**, approach, prepare for, intimate, pave the way for, prepare the way, make advances, make overtures, work round to • *I'm leading up to something quite important.*

lead[2]
▸ RELATED ADJECTIVES: plumbeous, plumbic

leaden 1 = **grey**, dingy, overcast, sombre, lacklustre, dark grey, greyish, lustreless, louring *or* lowering • *The weather was bitterly cold, with leaden skies.*
2 = **laboured**, wooden, stiff, sluggish, plodding, stilted, humdrum • *a leaden English translation from the Latin*
3 = **lifeless**, dull, gloomy, dismal, dreary, languid, listless, spiritless • *the leaden boredom of the Victorian marriage*
4 = **heavy**, lead, crushing, oppressive, cumbersome, inert, onerous, burdensome • *The dull, leaden sickly feeling returned.*

leader 1 = **principal**, president, head, chief, boss *(informal)*, director, manager, chairman, captain, chair, premier, governor, commander, superior, ruler, conductor, controller, counsellor, supervisor, superintendent, big name, big gun *(informal)*, chairwoman, chieftain, bigwig *(informal)*, ringleader, chairperson, big shot *(informal)*, overseer, big cheese *(slang, old-fashioned)*, big noise *(informal)*, big hitter *(informal)*, baas *(S. African)*, torchbearer, number one, sherang *(Austral. & N.Z.)* • *the leader of the Conservative Party*
OPPOSITES: supporter, follower, disciple

2 = **front runner**, pioneer, leading light, leading company, trailblazer, trendsetter, best-known company, groundbreaker, primary brand • *the leader in the mass market cosmetics industry*

leadership 1 = **leaders**, directors, chiefs, governors, commanders, rulers, controllers, supervisors, superintendents, overseers • *He is expected to hold talks with the Slovenian leadership.*
2 = **authority**, control, influence, command, premiership, captaincy, governance, headship, superintendency • *He praised her leadership during the crisis.*
3 = **guidance**, government, authority, management, administration, direction, supervision, domination, directorship, superintendency • *What most people want to see is determined, decisive action and firm leadership.*

QUOTATIONS
The art of leadership is saying no, not saying yes. It is very easy to say yes.
[Tony Blair]

leading = **principal**, top, major, main, first, highest, greatest, ruling, chief, prime, key, primary, supreme, most important, outstanding, governing, superior, dominant, foremost, pre-eminent, unsurpassed, number one • *Britain's future as a leading industrial nation depends on investment.*
OPPOSITES: minor, secondary, lesser

lead singer = **star**, lead, leading light • *I was the lead singer in a rock band.*

leaf AS A NOUN 1 = **frond**, flag, needle, pad, blade, bract, cotyledon, foliole • *The leaves of the horse chestnut had already fallen.*
2 = **page**, sheet, folio • *He flattened the wrappers and put them between the leaves of his book.*
▸ IN PHRASES: **leaf through something** = **skim**, glance, scan, browse, look through, dip into, flick through, flip through, thumb through, riffle • *Most patients derive enjoyment from leafing through old picture albums.*
turn over a new leaf = **reform**, change, improve, amend, make a fresh start, begin anew, change your ways, mend your ways • *He realized he was in the wrong and promised to turn over a new leaf.*
▸ RELATED ADJECTIVES: foliar, foliate

leaflet = **booklet**, notice, advert (*Brit. informal*), brochure, bill, circular, flyer, tract, pamphlet, handout, mailshot, handbill • *Campaigners handed out leaflets on passive smoking.*

leafy = **green**, leaved, leafed, shaded, shady, summery, verdant, bosky (*literary*), springlike, in foliage • *His home was surrounded by tall leafy trees.*

league AS A NOUN 1 = **association**, union, alliance, coalition, group, order, band, corporation, combination, partnership, federation, compact, consortium, guild, confederation, fellowship, fraternity, confederacy • *the League of Nations*
2 = **championship**, competition, tournament, contest • *The club are on the brink of promotion to the Premier League.*
3 = **class**, group, level, category, ability group • *Her success has taken her out of my league.*
▸ IN PHRASES: **in league with someone** = **collaborating with**, leagued with, allied with, conspiring with, working together with, in cooperation with, in cahoots with (*informal*), hand in glove with • *He accused the President of being in league with the terrorists.*

leak AS A VERB 1 = **escape**, pass, spill, release, discharge, drip, trickle, ooze, seep, exude, percolate • *The pool's sides had cracked and the water had leaked out.*
2 = **disclose**, tell, reveal, pass on, give away, make public, divulge, let slip, make known, spill the beans (*informal*), blab (*informal*), let the cat out of the bag, blow wide open (*slang*) • *He revealed who had leaked a confidential police report.*
▸ AS A NOUN 1 = **leakage**, leaking, discharge, drip, oozing, seepage, percolation • *It's thought a gas leak may have caused the blast.*
2 = **hole**, opening, crack, puncture, aperture, chink, crevice, fissure, perforation • *a leak in the radiator*
3 = **disclosure**, exposé, exposure, admission, revelation, uncovering, betrayal, unearthing, divulgence • *Serious leaks involving national security are likely to be investigated.*

leaky = **leaking**, split, cracked, punctured, porous, waterlogged, perforated, holey, not watertight • *the cost of repairing the leaky roof*

lean[1] AS A VERB 1 = **bend**, tip, slope, incline, tilt, heel, slant • *He leaned forward to give her a kiss.*
2 = **rest**, prop, be supported, recline, repose • *She was feeling tired and was glad to lean against him.*
3 = **tend**, prefer, favour, incline, be prone to, gravitate, be disposed to, have a propensity to • *Politically, I lean towards the right.*
▸ IN PHRASES: **lean on someone** 1 = **depend on**, trust, rely on, cling to, count on, confide in, have faith in • *She leaned on him to help her solve her problems.*
2 = **pressurize**, intimidate, coerce, breathe down someone's neck, browbeat, twist someone's arm (*informal*), put the screws on (*slang*) • *Colin was being leaned on by his bankers.*

lean[2] 1 = **thin**, slim, slender, skinny, angular, trim, spare, gaunt, bony, lanky, wiry, emaciated, scrawny, svelte, lank, rangy, scraggy, macilent (*rare*) • *She watched the tall, lean figure step into the car.*
OPPOSITES: fat, ample, plump
2 = **poor**, hard, tough, bare, impoverished, barren, meagre, arid, unproductive, unfruitful • *the lean years of the 1930s*
OPPOSITES: rich, abundant, plentiful

leaning = **tendency**, liking for, bias, inclination, taste, bent, disposition, penchant, propensity, aptitude, predilection, proclivity, partiality, proneness • *I always had a leaning towards sport.*

leap AS A VERB 1 = **jump**, spring, bound, bounce, hop, skip, caper, cavort, frisk, gambol • *The newsreels show him leaping into the air.*
2 = **vault**, clear, jump, bound, spring • *He leapt over a wall brandishing a weapon.*
3 = **hurry**, race, rush, hasten, move quickly • *She leapt forward to take control of the situation.*
4 = **rush**, jump, come, reach, arrive at, hurry, hasten, form hastily • *People should not leap to conclusions and blame the pilot.*
5 = **increase**, advance, soar, surge, rocket, escalate, shoot up • *They leapt to third in the table, 31 points behind the leaders.*
▸ AS A NOUN 1 = **jump**, spring, bound, hop, skip, vault, caper, frisk • *He took Britain's fifth medal with a leap of 2.37 metres.*
2 = **rise**, change, increase, soaring, surge, escalation, upsurge, upswing • *The result has been a giant leap in productivity.*
▸ IN PHRASES: **leap at something** = **accept eagerly**, seize on, jump at • *They leapt at the chance of a cheap holiday in Italy.*

learn 1 = **master**, grasp, acquire, pick up, be taught, take in, attain, become able, familiarize yourself with • *Their children were going to learn English.*
2 = **discover**, hear, understand, gain knowledge, find out about, become aware, discern, ascertain, come to know, suss (out) (*slang*) • *It was only after his death that she learned of his affair.*
3 = **memorize**, commit to memory, learn by heart, learn by rote, get (something) word-perfect, learn parrot-fashion, get off pat, con (*archaic*) • *He learned this song as an inmate in a Texas prison.*

learned = **scholarly**, experienced, lettered, cultured, skilled, expert, academic, intellectual, versed, literate, well-informed, erudite, highbrow, well-read • *He is a serious scholar, a genuine learned man.*
OPPOSITES: ignorant, illiterate, uneducated

learner = **student**, pupil, scholar, novice, beginner, trainee, apprentice, disciple, neophyte, tyro • *a new aid for younger children or slow learners*
OPPOSITES: teacher, coach, expert

learning = **knowledge**, study, education, schooling, research, scholarship, tuition, enlightenment • *The library is the focal point of learning on the campus.*

QUOTATIONS

Much learning doth make thee mad
[Bible: Acts]

The further one goes, the less one knows
[Lao-tze *Tao Te Ching*]

Try to learn something about everything and everything about something
[Thomas Henry Huxley *memorial stone*]

Learning without thought is labour lost; thought without learning is perilous
[Confucius *Analects*]

A little learning is a dangerous thing;
Drink deep, or taste not the Pierian spring:
There shallow draughts intoxicate the brain,
And drinking largely sobers us again
[Alexander Pope *An Essay on Criticism*]

That one gets used to everything -
One gets used to that.
The usual name for it is
A learning process
[Hans Magnus Enzensberger *The Force of Habit*]

lease = **hire**, rent, let, loan, charter, rent out, hire out • *He went to Toronto, where he leased an apartment.*

leash **AS A NOUN** 1 = **lead**, line, restraint, cord, rein, tether • *All dogs should be on a leash.*
2 = **restraint**, hold, control, check, curb • *They have kept the company on a tight leash.*
▸ **AS A VERB** = **tether**, control, secure, restrain, tie up, hold back, fasten • *Make sure your dog is leashed and muzzled.*
▸ **IN PHRASES:** **straining at the leash** = **impatient**, eager, restless, chafing • *There are plenty of youngsters straining at the leash to take their place.*

least **AS AN ADJECTIVE** = **smallest**, meanest, fewest, minutest, lowest, tiniest, minimum, slightest, minimal • *If you like cheese, go for the ones with the least fat.*
▸ **IN PHRASES:** **at least** = **at the minimum**, at the very least, not less than • *Aim to have at least half a pint of milk a day.*

leather **AS A NOUN** = **skin**, hide, pelt • *a sleeveless jacket made of leather*
▸ **AS A VERB** = **hit**, beat, strike, belt (*informal*), pound, break, knock, punch, batter, bruise, lash, thrash, lick (*informal*), flog, pelt, clobber, thwack, lambast(e), lay one on (*slang*), drub, beat *or* knock seven bells out of (*informal*) • *They leathered me because they thought I could tell them where she'd gone.*
▸ **RELATED ADJECTIVES:** coriaceous, leathern

leathery = **tough**, hard, rough, hardened, rugged, wrinkled, durable, leathern (*archaic*), coriaceous, leatherlike • *His hair is untidy and his skin is quite leathery.*

leave[1] **AS A VERB** 1 = **depart from**, withdraw from, go from, escape from, desert, quit, flee, exit, pull out of, retire from, move out of, disappear from, run away from, forsake, flit (*informal*), set out from, go away from, hook it (*slang*), pack your bags (*informal*), make tracks, abscond from, bog off (*Brit. slang*), decamp from, sling your hook (*Brit. slang*), slope off from, take your leave of, do a bunk from (*Brit. slang*), take yourself off from (*informal*) • *Just pack your bags and leave.* • *He was not allowed to leave the country.*
OPPOSITES: come, appear, arrive
2 = **quit**, give up, get out of, resign from, drop out of • *He left school with no qualifications.*
3 = **give up**, abandon, desert, dump (*informal*), drop, surrender, ditch (*informal*), chuck (*informal*), discard, relinquish, renounce, jilt (*informal*), cast aside, forbear, leave in the lurch • *He left me for another woman.*
OPPOSITES: stay with, retain, persist with
4 = **entrust**, commit, delegate, refer, hand over, assign, consign, allot, cede, give over • *For the moment, I leave you to make all the decisions.*
5 = **bequeath**, will, transfer, endow, transmit, confer, hand down, devise (*Law*), demise • *He died two years later, leaving everything to his wife.*
6 = **forget**, lay down, leave behind, mislay • *I'd left my raincoat in the restaurant.*
7 = **cause**, produce, result in, generate, deposit • *Abuse always leaves emotional scars.*
▸ **IN PHRASES:** **leave off something** = **stop**, end, finish, give up, cease, halt, break off, refrain from, abstain from, discontinue, knock off (*informal*), give over (*informal*), kick (*informal*), desist, keep off, belay (*Nautical*) • *We all left off eating and stood about with bowed heads.*
leave something *or* **someone out** = **omit**, exclude, miss out, forget, except, reject, ignore, overlook, neglect, skip, disregard, bar, cast aside, count out • *If you prefer mild flavours, leave out the chilli.*

PROVERBS

Let sleeping dogs lie

leave[2] 1 = **holiday**, break, vacation, time off, sabbatical, leave of absence, furlough, schoolie (*Austral.*), accumulated day off *or* ADO (*Austral.*) • *Why don't you take a few days' leave?*
2 = **permission**, freedom, sanction, liberty, concession, consent, allowance, warrant, authorization, dispensation • *an application for leave to appeal against the judge's order*
OPPOSITES: refusal, rejection, denial
3 = **departure**, parting, withdrawal, goodbye, farewell, retirement, leave-taking, adieu, valediction • *He thanked them for the pleasure of their company and took his leave.*
OPPOSITES: arrival, stay

leaven **AS A NOUN** 1 = **yeast**, ferment, leavening, barm • *The ingredients include wholemeal flour, wheat leven, water and salt.*
2 = **catalyst**, influence, inspiration • *The investment will be used as leaven to encourage businesses to do likewise.*
▸ **AS A VERB** 1 = **ferment**, work, raise, lighten • *They used sour dough to leaven their bread.*
2 = **stimulate**, inspire, elevate, quicken, pervade, permeate, imbue, suffuse • *He found congenial officers who knew how to leaven war's rigours with riotous enjoyment.*

leave-taking = **departure**, going, leaving, parting, goodbye, farewell, valediction, sendoff (*informal*) • *For him, the leave-taking was heartbreaking.*

leavings = **leftovers**, remains, bits, pieces, refuse, waste, sweepings, scraps, spoil, fragments, remnants, residue, dregs, orts (*archaic or dialect*) • *She scraped the leavings from plates into a bucket.*

lecher = **womanizer**, seducer, rake, Don Juan, wanton, profligate, Casanova, libertine, dirty old man (*slang*), satyr, roué, sensualist, fornicator, wolf (*informal*), goat (*informal*), debauchee, lech *or* letch (*informal*) • *He's just a sad old lecher.*

lecherous = **lustful**, randy (*informal, chiefly Brit.*), raunchy (*slang*), lewd, wanton, carnal, salacious, prurient, lascivious, libidinous, licentious, lubricious (*literary*), concupiscent, goatish (*archaic or literary*), unchaste, ruttish • *lecherous old men offering sweets at the school gate*
OPPOSITES: proper, virtuous, puritanical

lechery = **lustfulness**, lust, licentiousness, salaciousness, sensuality, profligacy, debauchery, prurience, womanizing, carnality, lewdness, wantonness, lasciviousness, libertinism, concupiscence, randiness (*informal, chiefly Brit.*), leching (*informal*), rakishness, lubricity, libidinousness, lecherousness • *His lechery made him the enemy of every father in the country.*

lecture **AS A NOUN** 1 = **talk**, address, speech, lesson, instruction, presentation, discourse, sermon, exposition, harangue, oration, disquisition • *In his lecture he covered an enormous variety of topics.*
2 = **telling-off** *(informal)*, rebuke, reprimand, talking-to *(informal)*, heat *(slang, chiefly U.S. & Canad.)*, going-over *(informal)*, wigging *(Brit. slang)*, censure, scolding, chiding, dressing-down *(informal)*, reproof, castigation • *Our captain gave us a stern lecture on safety.*
▸ **AS A VERB** 1 = **talk**, speak, teach, address, discourse, spout, expound, harangue, give a talk, hold forth, expatiate • *She has lectured and taught all over the world.*
2 = **tell off** *(informal)*, berate, scold, reprimand, carpet *(informal)*, censure, castigate, chide, admonish, tear into *(informal)*, read the riot act, reprove, bawl out *(informal)*, chew out *(U.S. & Canad. informal)*, tear (someone) off a strip *(Brit. informal)*, give a rocket *(Brit. & N.Z. informal)*, give someone a talking-to *(informal)*, give someone a dressing-down *(informal)*, give someone a telling-off *(informal)* • *He used to lecture me about getting too much sun.*

lecturer = **teacher**, tutor, academic, professor, don, reader, speaker, preacher, public speaker, expositor • *a lecturer in Law at Southampton University*

ledge = **shelf**, step, ridge, projection, mantle, sill • *She had climbed onto the ledge outside his window*

ledger = **account book**, book, record, accounts, register, journal, record book, daybook • *He kept detailed records in an accounts ledger.*

lee = **shelter**, cover, screen, protection, shadow, shade, shield, refuge • *The church nestles in the lee of a hill beneath the town.*

leech = **parasite**, hanger-on, sycophant, freeloader *(slang)*, sponger *(informal)*, ligger *(slang)*, bloodsucker *(informal)*, quandong *(Austral. slang)* • *They're just a bunch of leeches cadging off others!*

leer **AS A VERB** = **grin**, eye, stare, wink, squint, goggle, smirk, drool, gloat, ogle • *men standing around, leering at passing females*
▸ **AS A NOUN** = **grin**, stare, wink, squint, smirk, drool, gloat, ogle • *When I asked the clerk for my room key, he gave it to me with a leer.*

leery = **wary**, cautious, uncertain, suspicious, doubting, careful, shy, sceptical, dubious, unsure, distrustful, on your guard, chary • *They are leery of the proposed system.*

lees = **sediment**, grounds, refuse, deposit, precipitate, dregs, settlings • *a glass-fronted barrel showing the wine resting on its lees.*

leeway = **room**, play, space, margin, scope, latitude, elbowroom • *Schoolteachers rarely have leeway to teach the way they want.*

left 1 = **left-hand**, port, larboard *(Nautical)* • *She had a pain in her chest, on the left side.*
2 = **socialist**, liberal, radical, progressive, left-wing, leftist • *The play offers a new perspective on left politics.*
▸ **RELATED ADJECTIVES:** sinister, sinistral

left-handed = **sinistral**, corrie-fisted *(Scot.)*, sinistromanual, southpaw *(informal)* • *a left-handed boxer*
= **ambiguous**, ironic, indirect, enigmatic, backhanded, sardonic, double-edged, equivocal • *a left-handed compliment*

leftover **AS A NOUN** = **remnant**, leaving, remains, scrap, oddment • *Refrigerate any leftovers.*
▸ **AS AN ADJECTIVE** = **surplus**, remaining, extra, excess, unwanted, unused, uneaten • *Leftover chicken makes a wonderful salad.*

left-wing = **socialist**, communist, red *(informal)*, radical, leftist, liberal, revolutionary, militant, Marxist, Bolshevik, Leninist, collectivist, Trotskyite • *They said they would not be voting for him because he was too left-wing.*

left-winger = **socialist**, communist, red *(informal)*, pinko *(chiefly US, derogatory)*, radical, revolutionary, militant, Marxist, Bolshevik, Leninist, Trotskyite • *We were accused of being militant left-wingers.*

leg **AS A NOUN** 1 = **limb**, member, shank, lower limb, pin *(informal)*, stump *(informal)* • *He was tapping his walking stick against his leg.*
2 = **support**, prop, brace, upright • *His ankles were tied to the legs of the chair.*
3 = **stage**, part, section, stretch, lap, segment, portion • *The first leg of the journey was by boat.*
▸ **IN PHRASES:** **a leg up** = **boost**, help, support, push, assistance, helping hand • *The strong balance sheet should give a leg up to profits.*
leg it = **run**, walk, escape, flee, hurry, run away, make off, make tracks, hotfoot, go on foot, skedaddle *(informal)* • *He was legging it across the field.*
not have a leg to stand on = **have no basis**, be vulnerable, be undermined, be invalid, be illogical, be defenceless, lack support, be full of holes • *It's only my word against his, so I don't have a leg to stand on.*
on its *or* **your last legs** = **worn out**, dying, failing, exhausted, giving up the ghost, at death's door, about to collapse, about to fail, about to break down • *By the mid-1980s the copper industry in the US was on its last legs.*
pull someone's leg = **tease**, joke, trick, fool, kid *(informal)*, have (someone) on, rag, rib *(informal)*, wind up *(Brit. slang)*, deceive, hoax, make fun of, poke fun at, twit, chaff, lead up the garden path, jerk *or* yank someone's chain *(informal)* • *Of course I won't tell them; I was only pulling your leg.*
shake a leg = **hurry**, rush, move it, hasten, get cracking *(informal)*, get a move on *(informal)*, look lively *(informal)*, stir your stumps *(informal)* • *Come on, shake a leg! We've got loads to do today.*
stretch your legs = **take a walk**, exercise, stroll, promenade, move about, go for a walk, take the air • *Take regular breaks to stretch your legs.*
▸ **TECHNICAL NAME:** crus
▸ **RELATED ADJECTIVE:** crural

legacy 1 = **bequest**, inheritance, endowment, gift, estate, devise *(Law)*, heirloom • *You could make a real difference to someone's life by leaving them a generous legacy.*
2 = **heritage**, tradition, inheritance, throwback, birthright, patrimony • *the 'fight or flight syndrome' is a legacy from the days of our ancestors*
3 = **repercussion**, result, fruit, consequences, aftermath • *a programme to overcome the legacy of inequality created by Apartheid*

legal 1 = **judicial**, judiciary, forensic, juridical, jurisdictive • *the British legal system*
2 = **lawful**, allowed, sanctioned, constitutional, proper, valid, legitimate, authorized, rightful, permissible, legalized, allowable, within the law, licit • *What I did was perfectly legal.*

legalistic = **hairsplitting**, narrow, strict, contentious, literal, narrow-minded, polemical, litigious, disputatious • *his fussily legalistic mind*

legality = **lawfulness**, validity, legitimacy, accordance with the law, permissibility, rightfulness, admissibleness • *The auditor has questioned the legality of the contracts.*

legalize *or* **legalise** = **permit**, allow, approve, sanction, license, legitimate, authorize, validate, legitimize, make legal, decriminalize • *Divorce was legalized in 1981.*

legal tender = **currency**, money, medium, payment, specie • *When did the note cease to be legal tender?*

legate = **representative**, deputy, ambassador, delegate, envoy, messenger, emissary, depute *(Scot.)*, nuncio • *Pope Innocent VI's legate*

legatee = **beneficiary**, heir, recipient, inheritor • *He left £500 to a personal legatee.*

legation = **delegation**, ministry, embassy, representation, envoy, consulate, diplomatic mission • *a member of the US legation*

legend 1 = **myth**, story, tale, fiction, narrative, saga, fable, folk tale, urban myth, urban legend, folk story • *the legends of ancient Greece*
2 = **celebrity**, star, phenomenon, genius, spectacle, wonder, big name, marvel, prodigy, luminary, celeb *(informal)*, megastar *(informal)* • *the blues legend, B.B. King*
3 = **inscription**, title, caption, device, device, motto, rubric • *a banner bearing the following legend*

legendary 1 = **famous**, celebrated, well-known, acclaimed, renowned, famed, immortal, illustrious • *His political skill is legendary.*
OPPOSITES: unknown
2 = **mythical**, fabled, traditional, romantic, fabulous, fanciful, fictitious, storybook, apocryphal • *The hill is supposed to be the resting place of the legendary King Lud.*
OPPOSITES: historical, genuine, factual

legerdemain 1 = **sleight of hand**, prestidigitation • *the kind of legerdemain you'd expect from a magician*
2 = **deception**, manoeuvring, manipulation, cunning, artifice, trickery, subterfuge, feint, contrivance, chicanery, hocus-pocus, craftiness, artfulness, footwork *(informal)* • *financial and legal legerdemain*

legibility = **readability**, clarity, neatness, plainness, ease of reading, decipherability, legibleness, readableness • *He checked his notes for spelling and legibility.*

legible = **readable**, clear, plain, bold, neat, distinct, easy to read, easily read, decipherable • *My handwriting isn't very legible.*

legion AS A NOUN 1 = **army**, company, force, division, troop, brigade • *The last of the Roman legions left Britain in AD 410.*
2 = **multitude**, host, mass, drove, number, horde, myriad, throng • *His sense of humour won him a legion of friends.*
▸ AS AN ADJECTIVE = **very many**, numerous, countless, myriad, numberless, multitudinous • *Books on this subject are legion.*

legislate = **make laws**, establish laws, prescribe, enact laws, pass laws, ordain, codify laws, put laws in force • *You cannot legislate to change attitudes.*

legislation 1 = **law**, act, ruling, rule, bill, measure, regulation, charter, statute • *legislation to protect women's rights*
2 = **lawmaking**, regulation, prescription, enactment, codification • *This can be put right through positive legislation.*

legislative = **law-making**, parliamentary, congressional, judicial, ordaining, law-giving, juridical, jurisdictive • *the country's highest legislative body*

legislator = **lawmaker**, parliamentarian, lawgiver • *an attempt to get US legislators to change the system*

legislature = **parliament**, house, congress, diet, senate, assembly, chamber, law-making body • *What are the proposals before the legislature?*

legitimate AS AN ADJECTIVE 1 = **lawful**, real, true, legal, acknowledged, sanctioned, genuine, proper, authentic, statutory, authorized, rightful, kosher *(informal)*, dinkum *(Austral. & N.Z. informal)*, legit *(slang)*, licit • *They have demanded the restoration of the legitimate government.*
OPPOSITES: illegal, false, unlawful
2 = **reasonable**, just, correct, sensible, valid, warranted, logical, justifiable, well-founded, admissible • *That's a perfectly legitimate fear.*
OPPOSITES: unfair, unreasonable, unfounded
▸ AS A VERB = **legitimize**, allow, permit, sanction, authorize, legalize, give the green light to, legitimatize, pronounce lawful • *We want to legitimate this process by passing a law.*

legitimize or **legitimise** = **legalize**, permit, sanction, legitimate, authorize, give the green light to, pronounce lawful • *These images serve to legitimize violence and cruelty.*

leisure AS A NOUN = **spare**, free, rest, holiday, quiet, ease, retirement, relaxation, vacation, recreation, time off, breathing space, spare moments • *I was working constantly, with little or no leisure.*
OPPOSITES: work, business, labour
▸ IN PHRASES: **at one's leisure** = **in your own (good) time**, in due course, at your convenience, unhurriedly, when it suits you, without hurry, at an unhurried pace, when you get round to it *(informal)* • *He could read through all the national papers at his leisure.*

QUOTATIONS
All intellectual improvement arises from leisure
[Dr. Johnson]
Leisure contains the future, it is the new horizon
[Henri Lefebvre *Everyday Life in the Modern World*]

leisurely AS AN ADJECTIVE = **unhurried**, relaxed, slow, easy, comfortable, gentle, lazy, laid-back *(informal)*, restful • *Lunch was a leisurely affair.*
OPPOSITES: rushed, fast, hurried
▸ AS AN ADVERB = **unhurriedly**, slowly, easily, comfortably, lazily, at your leisure, at your convenience, lingeringly, indolently, without haste • *We walked leisurely into the hotel.*
OPPOSITES: quickly, rapidly, hurriedly

leitmotif or **leitmotiv** = **theme**, idea, strain, phrase, melody, motif • *The song's title could serve as a leitmotif for her life.*

lekker = **delicious**, tasty, luscious, choice, savoury, palatable, dainty, delectable, mouthwatering, yummy *(slang)*, scrumptious *(informal)*, appetizing, toothsome, ambrosial, yummo *(Austral. slang)* • *We had a really lekker meal.*

lemon
▸ RELATED ADJECTIVES: citric, citrine, citrous
▹ *See panel* **Shades of yellow**

lend AS A VERB 1 = **loan**, advance, sub *(Brit. informal)*, accommodate one with • *I lent him ten pounds to go to the pictures.*
2 = **give**, provide, add, present, supply, grant, afford, contribute, hand out, furnish, confer, bestow, impart • *He attended the news conference to lend his support.*
▸ IN PHRASES: **lend itself to something** = **be appropriate for**, suit, be suitable for, fit, be appropriate to, be adaptable to, present opportunities of, be serviceable for • *The room itself lends itself well to summer eating with its light airy atmosphere.*

QUOTATIONS
Neither a borrower nor a lender be
[William Shakespeare *Hamlet*]

length AS A NOUN 1 = **distance**, reach, measure, extent, span, longitude • *It is about a metre in length.*
2 = **duration**, term, period, space, stretch, span, expanse • *His film is over two hours in length.*
3 = **piece**, measure, section, segment, portion • *a 30ft length of rope*
4 = **lengthiness**, extent, elongation, wordiness, verbosity, prolixity, long-windedness, extensiveness, protractedness • *I hope the length of this letter will make up for my not having written earlier.*
▸ IN PHRASES: **at length** 1 = **at last**, finally, eventually, in time, in the end, at long last • *At length, my father went into the house.*
2 = **for a long time**, completely, fully, thoroughly, for hours, in detail, for ages, in depth, to the full, exhaustively, interminably • *They spoke at length, reviewing the entire incident.*

lengthen 1 = **extend**, continue, increase, stretch, expand, elongate, make longer • *The runway had to be lengthened.*
OPPOSITES: cut, trim, shorten
2 = **protract**, extend, prolong, draw out, spin out, make longer • *They want to lengthen the school day.*
OPPOSITES: cut, cut down, shorten

lengthy 1 = **protracted**, long, prolonged, very long, tedious, lengthened, diffuse, drawn-out, interminable, long-winded,

long-drawn-out, overlong, verbose, prolix • *the lengthy process of filling out forms*
2 = **very long**, rambling, interminable, long-winded, wordy, discursive, extended, overlong, verbose, prolix • *a lengthy article in the newspaper*
OPPOSITES: short, limited, brief

leniency *or* **lenience** = **mercy**, compassion, clemency, quarter, pity, tolerance, indulgence, tenderness, moderation, gentleness, forbearance, mildness, lenity • *The judge rejected pleas for leniency.*

lenient = **merciful**, sparing, gentle, forgiving, kind, tender, mild, tolerant, compassionate, clement, indulgent, forbearing • *The Professor takes a slightly more lenient view.*
OPPOSITES: severe, strict, harsh

lens
▸ RELATED ADJECTIVE: lenticular

leopard
▸ NAME OF FEMALE: leopardess
▸ COLLECTIVE NOUN: leap

leper = **outcast**, reject, untouchable, pariah, lazar *(archaic)* • *The article branded her a social leper.*

leprechaun = **pixie**, fairy, elf, brownie, hob, puck, imp, sprite • *a wicked, jokey leprechaun*

lesbian AS AN ADJECTIVE = **homosexual**, gay, les *(slang)*, butch *(slang)*, sapphic, dykey *(slang)*, lesbo *(slang)*, tribadic • *Many of her best friends were lesbian.*
▸ AS A NOUN = **lezzie** *(slang)* = **dyke** *(slang)*, les *(slang)*, butch *(slang)*, lesbo *(slang)* • *a youth group for lesbians, gays and bisexuals*

lesion = **injury**, hurt, wound, bruise, trauma *(Pathology)*, sore, impairment, abrasion, contusion • *skin lesions*

less AS AN ADJECTIVE = **smaller**, shorter, slighter, not so much • *Eat less fat to reduce the risk of heart disease.*
▸ AS AN ADVERB = **to a smaller extent**, little, barely, not much, not so much, meagrely • *We are eating more and exercising less.*
▸ AS A PRONOUN = **a smaller amount**, not as much (as) • *Motorways cover less than 0.1 per cent of the countryside.*
▸ AS A PREPOSITION = **minus**, without, lacking, excepting, subtracting • *Company car drivers will pay ten percent, less tax.*

QUOTATIONS
Less is more
[Ludwig Mies van der Rohe]

lessen 1 = **reduce**, lower, diminish, decrease, relax, ease, narrow, moderate, weaken, erode, impair, degrade, minimize, curtail, lighten, wind down, abridge, de-escalate • *Keep immunisations up to date to lessen the risk of serious illness.*
OPPOSITES: increase, raise, boost
2 = **grow less**, diminish, decrease, contract, ease, weaken, shrink, slow down, dwindle, lighten, wind down, die down, abate, slacken • *The attention she gives him will certainly lessen once the baby is born.*

lessening = **reduction**, decline, decrease, weakening, slowing down, dwindling, contraction, erosion, waning, ebbing, moderation, let-up *(informal)*, petering out, slackening, shrinkage, diminution, abatement, curtailment, minimization, de-escalation • *a lessening of tension on the border*

lesser = **lower**, slighter, secondary, subsidiary, subordinate, inferior, less important • *He was feared by other, lesser, men.*
OPPOSITES: higher, greater, major

lesson 1 = **class**, schooling, period, teaching, coaching, session, instruction, lecture, seminar, tutoring, tutorial • *She took piano lessons.*
2 = **example**, warning, model, message, moral, deterrent, precept, exemplar • *There is one lesson to be learned from this crisis.*
3 = **exercise**, reading, practice, task, lecture, drill, assignment, homework, recitation • *Now let's look at lesson one.*
4 = **Bible reading**, reading, text, Bible passage, Scripture passage • *The Rev. Nicola Judd read the lesson.*

lest = **in case**, in order to avoid, for fear that, in order to prevent • *I was afraid to open the door lest he should follow me.*

let[1] AS A VERB 1 = **enable**, make, allow, cause, grant, permit • *They let him talk.*
2 = **allow**, grant, permit, warrant, authorize, give the go-ahead, give permission, suffer *(archaic)*, give the green light, give leave, greenlight, give the O.K. *or* okay *(informal)* • *Mum didn't let us have sweets very often.*
3 = **lease**, hire, rent, rent out, hire out, sublease • *The reasons for letting a house, or part of one, are varied.*
▸ IN PHRASES: **let fly** = **attack**, assault, criticize, assail, tear into *(informal)*, lay into, belabour, lose your temper with, tear someone off a strip, set upon *or* about • *She let fly with a stream of obscenities.*
let on 1 = **reveal**, disclose, say, tell, admit, give away, divulge, let slip, make known, let the cat out of the bag *(informal)* • *He knows who the culprit is, but he is not letting on.*
2 = **pretend**, make out, feign, simulate, affect, profess, counterfeit, make believe, dissemble, dissimulate • *He's been knocking on doors, letting on he's selling encyclopedias.*
let someone down = **disappoint**, fail, abandon, desert, disillusion, fall short, leave stranded, leave in the lurch, disenchant, dissatisfy • *Don't worry, I won't let you down.*
let someone go 1 = **release**, free, let out, allow to leave, set free, allow to escape, turn loose • *They held him for three hours and then let him go.*
2 = **make redundant**, sack *(informal)*, fire *(informal)*, dismiss, discharge, lay off, give someone his *or* her P45 *(informal)*, kennet *(Austral. slang)*, jeff *(Austral. slang)* • *I have no plans to let him go.*
let someone in on something = **allow to know about**, let into, allow to share in • *I'm going to let you in on a little secret.*
let someone loose = **set free**, release, let go, set loose, turn loose • *Trainees go through a four-hour lesson before they are let loose.*
let someone off = **excuse**, release, discharge, pardon, spare, forgive, exempt, dispense, exonerate, absolve, grant an amnesty to • *The police let him off with a warning.*
let someone out = **release**, free, discharge, liberate, let go, set free • *They intend never to let her out of prison.*
let something down = **deflate**, empty, exhaust, flatten, puncture • *I let the tyres down on his car.*
let something go *or* **let go of something** = **stop holding**, release your grip on • *She let go of my hand and took a sip of her drink.*
let something off 1 = **fire**, explode, set off, discharge, detonate • *He had let off fireworks to celebrate the Revolution.*
2 = **emit**, release, leak, exude, give off • *They must do it without letting off any fumes.*
let something out 1 = **release**, discharge • *He let out his breath in a long sigh.*
2 = **emit**, make, produce, give vent to • *When she saw him, she let out a cry of horror.*
3 = **reveal**, tell, make known, let slip, leak, disclose, betray, let fall, take the wraps off • *She let out that she had seen him the night before.*
let something *or* **someone in** = **admit**, include, receive, welcome, greet, take in, incorporate, give access to, allow to enter • *The lattice-work lets in air, but not light.*
let up = **stop**, diminish, decrease, subside, relax, ease (up), moderate, lessen, abate, slacken • *The rain had let up.*

let[2] IN PHRASES: **let or hindrance** = **hindrance**, restriction, obstacle, interference, constraint, prohibition, obstruction, impediment • *Citizens of member states should travel without let or hindrance within the EU.*

letdown = **disappointment**, disillusionment, frustration, anticlimax, setback, washout *(informal)*, comedown *(informal)*, disgruntlement • *There was a great sense of letdown because the doctors had been so confident.*

lethal = **deadly**, terminal, fatal, deathly, dangerous, devastating, destructive, mortal, murderous, poisonous, virulent, pernicious, noxious, baneful • *a lethal dose of sleeping pills*
OPPOSITES: safe, healthy, harmless

lethargic = **sluggish**, slow, lazy, sleepy, heavy, dull, indifferent, debilitated, inactive, inert, languid, apathetic, drowsy, listless, comatose, stupefied, unenthusiastic, somnolent, torpid, slothful, enervated, unenergetic • *He felt too miserable and lethargic to get dressed.*
OPPOSITES: spirited, active, energetic

lethargy = **sluggishness**, inertia, inaction, slowness, indifference, apathy, sloth, stupor, drowsiness, dullness, torpor, sleepiness, lassitude, languor, listlessness, torpidity, hebetude *(rare)* • *Symptoms include tiredness, paleness and lethargy.*
OPPOSITES: energy, spirit, vitality

letter AS A NOUN 1 = **message**, line, answer, note, reply, communication, dispatch, acknowledgment, billet *(archaic)*, missive, epistle, e-mail • *I had received a letter from a very close friend.*
2 = **character**, mark, sign, symbol • *the letters of the alphabet*
▸ IN PHRASES: **to the letter** = **precisely**, strictly, literally, exactly, faithfully, accurately, word for word, punctiliously • *She obeyed his instructions to the letter.*
▸ RELATED ADJECTIVE: epistolatory

QUOTATIONS
Sir, more than kisses, letters mingle souls
[John Donne *To Sir Henry Wotton*]
All letters, methinks, should be free and easy as one's discourse, not studied as an oration, not made up of hard words like a charm
[Dorothy Osborne *Letter to William Temple*]

lettered = **educated**, learned, cultured, informed, accomplished, scholarly, versed, cultivated, switched-on *(informal)*, knowledgeable, literate, well-educated, erudite, well-read • *young and old, lettered and unlettered*

letters = **learning**, education, culture, literature, humanities, scholarship, erudition, belles-lettres • *bon viveur, man of letters and long-time party supporter*

let-up = **lessening**, break, pause, interval, recess, respite, lull, cessation, remission, breathing space, slackening, abatement • *There was no sign of any let-up in the battle on the money markets yesterday.*

level AS A NOUN 1 = **position**, standard, degree, grade, standing, stage, rank, status • *in order according to their level of difficulty*
2 = **height**, altitude, elevation, vertical position • *The water came up to her chin and the bubbles were at eye level.*
3 = **flat surface**, plane, horizontal • *The horse showed good form on the level.*
▸ AS AN ADJECTIVE 1 = **equal**, in line, aligned, balanced, on a line, at the same height • *She knelt down so that their eyes were level.*
2 = **horizontal**, even, flat, plane, smooth, uniform, as flat as a pancake • *a plateau of level ground*
OPPOSITES: uneven, tilted, slanted
3 = **calm**, even, regular, stable, steady, unchanging, equable, even-tempered, unvarying • *He forced his voice to remain level.*
4 = **even**, tied, equal, drawn, neck and neck, all square, level pegging • *The teams were level at the end of extra time.*
▸ AS A VERB 1 = **equalize**, balance, even up • *He got two goals to level the score.*
2 = **destroy**, devastate, wreck, demolish, flatten, knock down, pull down, tear down, bulldoze, raze, lay waste to, kennet *(Austral. slang)*, jeff *(Austral. slang)* • *Further tremors could level yet more buildings.*
OPPOSITES: build, raise, erect
3 = **direct**, point, turn, train, aim, focus, beam • *The soldiers level guns at each other along the border.*
4 = **flatten**, plane, smooth, make flat, even off or out • *He'd been levelling off the ground before putting up the shed.*
▸ IN PHRASES: **level with someone** = **be honest**, be open, be frank, come clean *(informal)*, be straightforward, be up front *(slang)*, be above board, keep nothing back • *Levelling with you, I was in two minds before this happened.*
on the level = **honest**, genuine, sincere, open, straight, fair, square, straightforward, up front *(slang)*, dinkum *(Austral. & N.Z. informal)*, above board • *There were moments where you wondered if anyone was on the level.*

level-headed = **calm**, balanced, reasonable, composed, together *(slang)*, cool, collected, steady, sensible, sane, dependable, unflappable *(informal)*, self-possessed, even-tempered, grounded • *He is level-headed and practical.*

lever AS A NOUN = **handle**, bar, crowbar, jemmy, handspike • *Robert leaned lightly on the lever and the rock groaned.*
▸ AS A VERB = **prise**, move, force, raise, pry *(U.S.)*, jemmy • *Neighbours eventually levered the door open with a crowbar.*

leverage 1 = **influence**, authority, pull *(informal)*, weight, rank, clout *(informal)*, purchasing power, ascendancy • *His position affords him the leverage to get things done through committees.*
2 = **force**, hold, pull, strength, grip, grasp • *The spade and fork have longer shafts, providing better leverage.*

leviathan = **monster**, whale, mammoth, Titan, hulk, colossus, behemoth • *It's a leviathan of a book.*

levity = **light-heartedness**, frivolity, silliness, triviality, fickleness, flippancy, giddiness, skittishness, facetiousness, flightiness, light-mindedness • *At the time, he had disapproved of such levity.*
OPPOSITES: seriousness, gravity, solemnity

levy AS A NOUN = **tax**, fee, toll, tariff, duty, assessment, excise, imposition, impost, exaction • *an annual motorway levy on all drivers*
▸ AS A VERB = **impose**, charge, tax, collect, gather, demand, exact • *Taxes should not be levied without the authority of Parliament.*

lewd = **indecent**, obscene, vulgar, dirty, blue, loose, vile, pornographic, wicked, wanton, X-rated *(informal)*, profligate, bawdy, salacious, impure, lascivious, smutty, lustful, libidinous, licentious, unchaste • *He spends all his day eyeing up women and making lewd comments.*

lewdness = **indecency**, obscenity, impurity, vulgarity, depravity, pornography, smut, profligacy, debauchery, crudity, lechery, licentiousness, carnality, wantonness, salaciousness, lasciviousness, bawdiness, unchastity, smuttiness, lubricity • *The critics condemned the play for lewdness.*

lexicon = **vocabulary**, dictionary, glossary, word list, wordbook • *a lexicon of slang*

liabilities = **debts**, expenditure, debit, arrears, obligations, accounts payable • *The company had liabilities of $250 million.*

liability 1 = **disadvantage**, burden, drawback, inconvenience, drag, handicap, minus *(informal)*, nuisance, impediment, albatross, hindrance, millstone, encumbrance • *What was once a vote-catching policy is now a political liability.*
2 = **responsibility**, accountability, culpability, obligation, onus, answerability • *They admit liability, but dispute the amount of his claim.*
3 = **tendency**, susceptibility, proneness, likelihood, probability • *anyone whose medical history shows a liability to thromboses*

liable 1 = **likely**, tending, inclined, disposed, prone, apt • *Only a small number are liable to harm themselves or others.*
2 = **vulnerable**, subject, exposed, prone, susceptible, open, at risk of • *These women are particularly liable to depression.*
3 = **responsible**, accountable, amenable, answerable,

bound, obligated, chargeable • *The airline's insurer is liable for damages.*

liaise = **communicate**, link up, connect, intermediate, mediate, interchange, hook up, keep contact • *Social services and health workers liaise closely.*

liaison 1 = **contact**, communication, connection, interchange • *Liaison between the police and the art world is vital to combat art crime.*
2 = **intermediary**, contact, hook-up, go-between • *She acts as a liaison between patients and staff.*
3 = **affair**, romance, intrigue, fling, love affair, amour, entanglement, illicit romance • *She embarked on a series of sexual liaisons with society figures.*

liar = **falsifier**, storyteller *(informal)*, perjurer, fibber, fabricator, prevaricator • *He was a liar and a cheat.*

QUOTATIONS
A liar should have a good memory
[Quintilian *Institutio Oratoria*]

libel AS A NOUN = **defamation**, slander, misrepresentation, denigration, smear, calumny, vituperation, obloquy, aspersion • *He sued them for libel over the remarks.*
▸ AS A VERB = **defame**, smear, slur, blacken, malign, denigrate, revile, vilify, slander, traduce, derogate, calumniate, drag (someone's) name through the mud • *The newspaper which libelled him had already offered him compensation.*

libellous = **defamatory**, false, untrue, malicious, maligning, disparaging, vilifying, derogatory, scurrilous, injurious, vituperative, slanderous, traducing, denigratory, calumnious, aspersive, calumniatory • *He claimed the articles were libellous and damaging to the team.*

liberal 1 = **tolerant**, enlightened, open-minded, permissive, advanced, catholic, humanitarian, right-on *(informal)*, indulgent, easy-going, unbiased, high-minded, broad-minded, unprejudiced, unbigoted, politically correct *or* PC • *She is known to have liberal views on abortion and contraception.*
OPPOSITES: intolerant, prejudiced, biased
2 = **progressive**, radical, reformist, libertarian, advanced, right-on *(informal)*, forward-looking, humanistic, free-thinking, latitudinarian, politically correct *or* PC • *a liberal democracy with a multiparty political system*
OPPOSITES: conservative, right-wing, reactionary
3 = **abundant**, generous, handsome, lavish, ample, rich, plentiful, copious, bountiful, profuse, munificent • *She made liberal use of her older sister's make-up and clothes.*
OPPOSITES: small, limited, inadequate
4 = **generous**, kind, charitable, extravagant, free-handed, prodigal, altruistic, open-hearted, bountiful, magnanimous, open-handed, unstinting, beneficent, bounteous • *They thanked him for his liberal generosity.*
OPPOSITES: mean, stingy, cheap
5 = **flexible**, general, broad, rough, free, loose, lenient, not close, inexact, not strict, not literal • *a liberal translation*
OPPOSITES: fixed, strict, literal

QUOTATIONS
conservative: a statesman who is enamoured of existing evils, as distinguished from the Liberal, who wishes to replace them with others
[Ambrose Bierce *The Devil's Dictionary*]

liberalism = **progressivism**, radicalism, humanitarianism, libertarianism, freethinking, latitudinarianism • *He was concerned over growing liberalism in the Church.*

QUOTATIONS
By liberalism I don't mean the creed of any party or any century. I mean a generosity of spirit, a tolerance of others, an attempt to comprehend otherness, a commitment to the rule of law, a high ideal of the worth and dignity of man, a repugnance for authoritarianism and a love of freedom
[Alan Paton *Lecture at Yale University*]

liberalize = **relax**, ease, moderate, modify, stretch, soften, broaden, loosen, mitigate, slacken, ameliorate • *the decision to liberalize travel restrictions*

liberate = **free**, release, rescue, save, deliver, discharge, redeem, let out, set free, let loose, untie, emancipate, unchain, unbind, manumit • *How committed is the leadership to liberating its people from poverty?*
OPPOSITES: jail, detain, imprison

liberation = **freeing**, release, freedom, liberty, liberating, redemption, emancipation, deliverance, manumission, enfranchisement, unshackling, unfettering • *Passover recalls the liberation from slavery in Egypt.*

liberator = **deliverer**, saviour, rescuer, redeemer, freer, emancipator, manumitter • *They were the people's liberators.*

libertarian AS AN ADJECTIVE = **liberal**, radical, progressive, humanitarian, reformist, permissive, humanistic, broad-minded, latitudinarian • *The town's political climate was libertarian.*
▸ AS A NOUN = **liberal**, radical, moderate, humanitarian, reformist • *Libertarians argue that nothing should be censored.*

libertine AS A NOUN = **reprobate**, seducer, profligate, womanizer, rake, swinger *(slang)*, lecher, roué, sensualist, voluptuary, debauchee, lech *or* letch *(informal)*, loose liver • *a self-confessed coward, libertine and scoundrel*
▸ AS AN ADJECTIVE = **promiscuous**, degenerate, immoral, decadent, abandoned, corrupt, voluptuous, depraved, wanton, profligate, debauched, dissolute, rakish, reprobate, licentious • *He was free to explore a libertine lifestyle.*

liberty AS A NOUN 1 = **independence**, sovereignty, liberation, autonomy, immunity, self-determination, emancipation, self-government, self-rule • *Such a system would be a blow to the liberty of the people.*
2 = **freedom**, liberation, redemption, emancipation, deliverance, manumission, enfranchisement, unshackling, unfettering • *Three convictions meant three months' loss of liberty.*
OPPOSITES: restraint, constraint, slavery
▸ IN PHRASES: **at liberty** 1 = **free**, escaped, unlimited, at large, not confined, untied, on the loose, unchained, unbound • *There is no confirmation that he is at liberty.*
2 = **able**, free, allowed, permitted, entitled, authorized • *I'm not at liberty to say where it is, because the deal hasn't gone through yet.*
take liberties *or* **a liberty** = **not show enough respect**, show disrespect, act presumptuously, behave too familiarly, behave impertinently • *She knew she was taking a big liberty in doing this for him without his knowledge.*

QUOTATIONS
I know not what course others may take; but as for me, give me liberty, or give me death!
[Patrick Henry]
Liberty is liberty, not equality or fairness or justice or human happiness or a quiet conscience
[Isaiah Berlin *Two Concepts of Liberty*]
The tree of liberty must be refreshed from time to time with the blood of patriots and tyrants. It is its natural manure
[Thomas Jefferson]
Liberty is precious – so precious that it must be rationed
[Lenin]
Liberty means responsibility. That is why most men dread it
[George Bernard Shaw *Man and Superman*]
Liberty too must be limited in order to be possessed
[Edmund Burke *Letter to the Sheriffs of Bristol*]
The liberty of the individual must be thus far limited; he must not make himself a nuisance to other people
[John Stuart Mill *On Liberty*]

libidinous = **lustful**, sensual, wanton, carnal, loose, randy *(informal, chiefly Brit.)*, wicked, salacious, prurient, impure, debauched, lascivious, incontinent, lecherous, concupiscent, unchaste, ruttish • *He let his libidinous imagination run away with him.*

libido = **sex drive**, passion, sexual desire, sexual appetite, sexual urge, erotic desire, sex instinct, the hots *(informal)*, randiness *(informal, chiefly Brit.)* • *Lack of sleep is a major factor in loss of libido.*

libretto = **words**, book, lines, text, script, lyrics • *the author of one or two opera librettos*

licence AS A NOUN 1 = **certificate**, document, permit, charter, warrant • *The painting was returned on a temporary import licence.*
2 = **permission**, the right, authority, leave, sanction, liberty, privilege, immunity, entitlement, exemption, prerogative, authorization, dispensation, a free hand, carte blanche, blank cheque • *The curfew gave the police licence to hunt people as if they were animals.*
OPPOSITES: restriction, denial, prohibition
3 = **freedom**, creativity, latitude, independence, liberty, deviation, leeway, free rein, looseness • *All that stuff about catching a giant fish was just a bit of poetic licence.*
OPPOSITES: restraint, constraint
4 = **laxity**, abandon, disorder, excess, indulgence, anarchy, lawlessness, impropriety, irresponsibility, profligacy, licentiousness, unruliness, immoderation • *a world of licence and corruption*
OPPOSITES: moderation, strictness
▸ IN PHRASES: **under licence** = **with permission**, under a charter, under warrant, under a permit, with authorization, under a patent • *They made the Mig-21 jet fighter under licence from Russia.*

license = **permit**, commission, enable, sanction, allow, entitle, warrant, authorize, empower, certify, accredit, give a blank cheque to • *the council can license a U.S. company to produce the drug*
OPPOSITES: ban, forbid, prohibit

licensed = **permitted**, allowed, sanctioned, authorized • *a licensed rifle*

licentious = **promiscuous**, immoral, lewd, debauched, abandoned, sensual, uncontrollable, uncontrolled, wanton, profligate, impure, lascivious, lustful, dissolute, libertine, libidinous, lubricious *(literary)*, uncurbed • *alarming stories of licentious behaviour*
OPPOSITES: principled, moral, chaste

lick AS A VERB 1 = **taste**, lap, tongue, touch, wash, brush • *The dog licked the man's hand excitedly.*
2 = **beat**, defeat, overcome, best, top, stuff *(slang)*, tank *(slang)*, undo, rout, excel, surpass, outstrip, outdo, trounce, clobber *(slang)*, vanquish, run rings around *(informal)*, wipe the floor with *(informal)*, blow out of the water *(slang)* • *He might be able to lick us all in a fair fight.*
3 = **flicker**, touch, flick, dart, ripple, ignite, play over, kindle • *The fire sent its red tongues licking into the hallway.*
▸ AS A NOUN 1 = **dab**, little, bit, touch, taste, sample, stroke, brush, speck • *It could do with a lick of paint to brighten up its premises.*
2 = **pace**, rate, speed, clip *(informal)* • *an athletic cyclist travelling at a fair lick*

licking 1 = **defeat**, beating, pasting *(slang)*, trouncing, drubbing • *They gave us a hell of a licking.*
2 = **thrashing**, beating, hiding *(informal)*, whipping, tanning *(slang)*, flogging, spanking, drubbing • *If Dad came home and found us, we could expect a licking.*

lid AS A NOUN = **top**, covering, cover • *I lifted the lid to give it a quick stir.*
▸ IN PHRASES: **put a lid on something** = **stop**, end, limit, control, restrict, put an end to • *The government is keen to put a lid on his scheme.*

lie[1] AS A NOUN = **falsehood**, deceit, fabrication, fib, fiction, invention, deception, untruth, porky *(Brit. slang)*, pork pie *(Brit. slang)*, white lie, falsification, prevarication, falsity, mendacity • *I've had enough of your lies.*
▸ AS A VERB = **fib**, fabricate, invent, misrepresent, falsify, tell a lie, prevaricate, perjure, not tell the truth, equivocate, dissimulate, tell untruths, not speak the truth, say something untrue, forswear yourself • *If asked, he lies about his age.*
▸ IN PHRASES: **give the lie to something** = **disprove**, expose, discredit, contradict, refute, negate, invalidate, rebut, make a nonsense of, prove false, controvert, confute • *This survey gives the lie to the idea that Britain is moving towards economic recovery*
▸ RELATED ADJECTIVE: mendacious
▸ RELATED MANIA: mythomania

QUOTATIONS

There is no worse lie than a truth misunderstood by those who hear it
[William James *Varieties of Religious Experience*]

The lie in the soul is a true lie
[Benjamin Jowett *Introduction to his translation of Plato's Republic*]

I can't tell a lie, Pa; you know I can't tell a lie
[George Washington]

The broad mass of a nation.... will more easily fall victim to a big lie than to a small one
[Adolf Hitler *Mein Kampf*]

Every word she writes is a lie, including 'and' and 'the'
[Mary McCarthy (on Lillian Hellman)]

It contains a misleading impression, not a lie. It was being economical with the truth
[Sir Robert Armstrong (during the 'Spycatcher' trial)]

A lie will easily get you out of a scrape, and yet, strangely and beautifully, rapture possesses you when you have taken the scrape and left out the lie
[C.E. Montague *Disenchantment*]

lie[2] 1 = **recline**, rest, lounge, couch, sprawl, stretch out, be prone, loll, repose, be prostrate, be supine, be recumbent • *He was lying motionless on his back.*
2 = **be placed**, be, rest, exist, extend, be situated • *a newspaper lying on a nearby couch*
3 = **be situated**, sit, be located, be positioned • *The islands lie at the southern end of the mountain range.*
4 *usually with* **in** = **exist**, be present, consist, dwell, reside, pertain, inhere • *The problem lay in the large amounts spent on defence.*
5 = **be buried**, remain, rest, be, be found, belong, be located, be interred, be entombed • *Here lies Catin, son of Magarus.*
6 *usually with* **on** *or* **upon** = **weigh**, press, rest, burden, oppress • *The pain of losing his younger brother still lies heavy on his mind.*

lie-down = **rest**, sleep, nap, doze, relaxation, slumber, kip *(Brit. slang)*, snooze *(informal)*, repose, idleness, siesta, forty winks *(informal)* • *She had gone upstairs for a lie-down*

liege = **feudal lord**, master, superior, sovereign, chieftain, overlord, seigneur, suzerain • *Poachers made truces with their liege lords.*

lieu IN PHRASES: **in lieu of** = **instead of**, in place of • *He left his furniture to his landlord in lieu of rent.*

life AS A NOUN 1 = **being**, existence, living, breath, entity, vitality, animation, viability, sentience • *a newborn baby's first minutes of life*
2 = **living things**, creatures, wildlife, organisms, living beings • *Is there life on Mars?*
3 = **existence**, being, lifetime, time, days, course, span, duration, continuance • *He spent the last fourteen years of his life in retirement.*
4 = **way of life**, situation, conduct, behaviour, life style • *How did you adjust to college life?*

5 = **liveliness**, activity, energy, spirit, go *(informal)*, pep, sparkle, vitality, animation, vigour, verve, zest, high spirits, get-up-and-go *(informal)*, oomph *(informal)*, brio, vivacity • *The town itself was full of life and character.*
6 = **biography**, story, history, career, profile, confessions, autobiography, memoirs, life story • *It was his aim to write a life of John Paul Jones.*
7 = **period of usefulness**, existence, duration • *The repairs did not increase the life of the equipment.*
8 = **spirit**, heart, soul, essence, core, lifeblood, moving spirit, vital spark, animating spirit, élan vital *(French)* • *He's sucked the life out of her.*
9 = **person**, human, individual, soul, human being, mortal • *a war in which thousands of lives were lost*
▸ **IN PHRASES: come to life = rouse**, revive, awaken, become active, become animate, show signs of life • *Poems which had seemed dull suddenly came to life.*
for dear life = desperately, quickly, vigorously, urgently, intensely, for all you are worth • *I made for the raft and clung on for dear life.*
give your life = lay down your life, die, sacrifice yourself • *He gave his life to save his family.*
that's life = that's the way things are, that's it, that's the way the cookie crumbles *(informal)* • *'It might never have happened if she hadn't gone back.' 'That's life.'*
▸ **RELATED ADJECTIVES:** animate, vital

QUOTATIONS

Life's but a walking shadow, a poor player,
That struts and frets his hour upon the stage,
And then is heard no more; it is a tale
Told by an idiot, full of sound and fury,
Signifying nothing
[William Shakespeare *Macbeth*]

The unexamined life is not worth living
[Socrates]

Life can only be understood backwards; but it must be lived forwards
[Søren Kierkegaard]

Life is a comedy to those that think, and a tragedy to those that feel
[Horace Walpole *Letter to Anne, Countess of Upper Ossory*]

Life is a tragedy when seen in close-up, but a comedy in long-shot
[Charlie Chaplin]

Life is long to the miserable, but short to the happy
[Publilius Syrus *Sententiae*]

The essence of life is statistical improbability on a colossal scale
[Richard Dawkins *The Blind Watchmaker*]

Life exists in the universe only because the carbon atom possesses certain exceptional qualities
[James Jeans *The Mysterious Universe*]

Life is an abnormal business
[Eugène Ionesco *The Rhinoceros*]

Life is fired at us point blank
[José Ortega y Gasset]

There is only one minute in which you are alive, *this minute* – here and now. The only way to live is by accepting each minute as an unrepeatable miracle. Which is exactly what it is – a miracle and unrepeatable
[Storm Jameson]

Look to this day
For it is life, the very life of life
[*The Sufi*]

In the time of your life, live – so that in that wondrous time you shall not add to the misery and sorrow of the world – but shall smile at the infinite delight and mystery of it
[William Saroyan]

Man is born to live, not to prepare for life
[Boris Pasternak *Doctor Zhivago*]

What is life? It is the flash of a firefly in the night. It is the breath of a buffalo in the winter time; it is the little shadow which runs across the grass and loses itself in the sunset
[Crowfoot, a great hunter of the Blackfoot *Last words*]

Oh, what a day-to-day business life is
[Jules Laforgue *Complainte sur certains ennuis*]

Believe me! The secret of reaping the greatest fruitfulness and the greatest enjoyment from life is to live dangerously!
[Friedrich Nietzsche *Die fröhliche Wissenschaft*]

Life is just one damned thing after another
[Frank Ward O'Malley]

Life doesn't imitate art, it imitates bad television
[Woody Allen *Husbands and Wives*]

Lift not the painted veil which those who live
Call Life
[Percy Bysshe Shelley *Sonnet*]

Life is one long process of getting tired
[Samuel Butler *Notebooks*]

There is no wealth but life
[John Ruskin *Unto This Last*]

Every man regards his own life as the New Year's Eve of time
[Jean Paul Richter *Levana*]

Life isn't all beer and skittles
[Thomas Hughes *Tom Brown's Schooldays*]

Life is far too important a thing ever to talk seriously about
[Oscar Wilde *Lady Windermere's Fan*]

The meaning of life is that it stops
[Franz Kafka]

It is the essence of life that it exists for its own sake
[A.N. Whitehead *Nature and Life*]

Old and young, we are all on our last cruise
[Robert Louis Stevenson *Virginibus Puerisque*]

Human life is everywhere a state in which much is to be endured, and little to be enjoyed
[Dr. Johnson *Rasselas*]

'Tis all a chequer-board of nights and days
Where Destiny with men for pieces plays;
Hither and thither moves, and mates, and slays,
And one by one back in the closet lays
[Edward Fitzgerald *The Rubáiyát of Omar Khayyám*]

Life is real! Life is earnest!
And the grave is not its goal;
Dust thou art, to dust returnest,
Was not spoken of the soul
[Henry Wadsworth Longfellow *A Psalm of Life*]

PROVERBS

Life begins at forty

life-and-death = **critical**, important, serious, crucial, vital, deciding, pressing, key, significant, dangerous, grave, urgent, decisive, risky, hairy *(slang)*, all-important, pivotal, precarious, high-priority, perilous, momentary, now or never • *We're dealing with a life-and-death situation here.*

lifeblood = **animating force**, life, heart, inspiration, guts *(informal)*, essence, stimulus, driving force, vital spark • *Coal and steel were the region's lifeblood.*

life-giving = **activating**, stimulating, animating, quickening, enlivening, invigorating, livening, vitalizing, inspiriting • *It is here that life-giving oxygen is fed to the cells.*

lifeless 1 = **dead**, unconscious, extinct, deceased, cold, defunct, inert, inanimate, comatose, out cold, out for the count, insensible, in a faint, insensate, dead to the world *(informal)* • *There was no breathing or pulse and he was lifeless.*
OPPOSITES: living, live, alive

2 = **barren**, empty, desert, bare, waste, sterile, unproductive, uninhabited • *They may appear lifeless, but they provide a valuable habitat for plants and animals.*
3 = **dull**, cold, flat, hollow, heavy, slow, wooden, stiff, passive, static, pointless, sluggish, lacklustre, lethargic, colourless, listless, torpid, spiritless • *His novels are shallow and lifeless.*
OPPOSITES: spirited, active, lively

lifelike = **realistic**, faithful, authentic, natural, exact, graphic, vivid, photographic, true-to-life, undistorted • *a lifelike doll*

lifeline = **means of survival**, rescue, safety device, life belt, way of continuing, rescue device • *The orders will throw a lifeline to British shipyards.*

lifelong = **long-lasting**, enduring, lasting, permanent, constant, lifetime, for life, persistent, long-standing, perennial, deep-rooted, for all your life • *her lifelong friendship with the woman*

lifestyle = **way of life**, situation, ways, life, position, condition, conduct, behaviour, habits, customs, civilization, mores • *the change of lifestyle occasioned by the baby's arrival*

life-threatening = **fatal**, deathly, deadly, lethal, dangerous, critical, disastrous, toxic, destructive, harmful, hazardous, poisonous, malignant • *This approach is potentially life-threatening to patients.*

lifetime = **existence**, time, day(s), course, period, span, life span, your natural life, all your born days • *During my lifetime I haven't got round to much travelling.*

lift AS A VERB 1 = **raise**, pick up, hoist, draw up, elevate, uplift, heave up, buoy up, raise high, bear aloft, upheave, upraise • *Curious shoppers lifted their children to take a closer look at the parade.*
OPPOSITES: drop, lower
2 = **revoke**, end, remove, withdraw, stop, relax, cancel, terminate, rescind, annul, countermand • *The Commission has urged them to lift their ban on imports.*
OPPOSITES: establish, impose
3 = **exalt**, raise, improve, advance, promote, boost, enhance, upgrade, elevate, dignify, cheer up, perk up, ameliorate, buoy up • *A brisk walk in the fresh air can lift your mood.*
OPPOSITES: depress
4 = **disappear**, clear, vanish, disperse, dissipate, rise, be dispelled • *The fog had lifted and revealed a warm sunny day.*
5 = **steal**, take, copy, appropriate, nick (*slang, chiefly Brit.*), pocket, trouser (*slang*), pinch (*informal*), pirate, cabbage (*Brit. slang*), knock off (*slang*), crib (*informal*), half-inch (*old-fashioned slang*), blag (*slang*), pilfer, purloin, plagiarize, thieve • *The line could have been lifted from a Woody Allen film.*
▸ AS A NOUN 1 = **boost**, encouragement, stimulus, reassurance, uplift, pick-me-up, fillip, shot in the arm (*informal*), gee-up • *My selection for the team has given me a tremendous lift.*
OPPOSITES: blow, letdown
2 = **elevator** (*chiefly U.S.*), hoist, paternoster • *They took the lift to the fourth floor.*
3 = **ride**, run, drive, transport, hitch (*informal*), car ride • *He had a car and often gave me a lift home.*
▸ IN PHRASES: **lift off** = **take off**, be launched, blast off, take to the air • *The plane lifted off and climbed steeply into the night sky.*

light[1] AS A NOUN 1 = **brightness**, illumination, luminosity, luminescence, ray of light, flash of light, shining, glow, blaze, sparkle, glare, gleam, brilliance, glint, lustre, radiance, incandescence, phosphorescence, scintillation, effulgence, lambency, refulgence • *Cracks of light filtered through the shutters.*
OPPOSITES: dark, shadow, cloud
2 = **lamp**, bulb, torch, candle, flare, beacon, lighthouse, lantern, taper • *You get into the music and lights, and the people around you.*
3 = **match**, spark, flame, lighter • *Have you got a light, anybody?*
4 = **aspect**, approach, attitude, context, angle, point of view, interpretation, viewpoint, slant, standpoint, vantage point • *He has worked hard to portray New York in a better light.*
5 = **understanding**, knowledge, awareness, insight, information, explanation, illustration, enlightenment, comprehension, illumination, elucidation • *At last the light dawned. He was going to get married!*
OPPOSITES: mystery
6 = **daybreak**, morning, dawn, sun, sunrise, sunshine, sunlight, daylight, daytime, sunbeam, morn (*poetic*), cockcrow, broad day • *Three hours before first light, he gave orders for the evacuation of the camp.*
▸ AS AN ADJECTIVE 1 = **bright**, brilliant, shining, glowing, sunny, illuminated, luminous, well-lighted, well-lit, lustrous, aglow, well-illuminated • *Her house is light and airy, crisp and clean.*
OPPOSITES: dark, dim, gloomy
2 = **pale**, fair, faded, blonde, blond, bleached, pastel, light-coloured, whitish, light-toned, light-hued • *The walls are light in colour.*
OPPOSITES: deep, dark
▸ AS A VERB 1 = **illuminate**, light up, brighten, lighten, put on, turn on, clarify, switch on, floodlight, irradiate, illumine, flood with light • *The giant moon lit the road brightly.*
OPPOSITES: cloud, dull, darken
2 = **ignite**, inflame, fire, torch, kindle, touch off, set alight, set a match to • *He hunched down to light a cigarette.*
OPPOSITES: put out, extinguish, douse
▸ IN PHRASES: **bring something to light** = **reveal**, expose, unveil, show, discover, disclose, show up, uncover, unearth, lay bare • *The truth is unlikely to be brought to light by this enquiry.*
come to light = **be revealed**, appear, come out, turn up, be discovered, become known, become apparent, be disclosed, transpire • *Nothing about this sum has come to light.*
in the light of something = **considering**, because of, taking into account, bearing in mind, in view of, taking into consideration, with knowledge of • *In the light of this information, we can now identify a number of issues.*
light something up = **illuminate**, light, brighten, lighten, floodlight, irradiate, make brighter • *Can you light up just one half of the stage?*
light up 1 = **cheer**, shine, blaze, sparkle, animate, brighten, lighten, irradiate • *Sue's face lit up with surprise.*
2 = **shine**, flash, beam, blaze, sparkle, flare, glare, gleam, flicker • *a keypad that lights up when you pick up the handset*
shed or **throw light on something** = **explain**, clarify, make clear, clear up, simplify, make plain, elucidate • *A new approach may shed light on the problem.*
▸ RELATED PREFIX: photo-
▸ RELATED MANIA: photomania
▸ RELATED PHOBIA: photophobia

QUOTATIONS
And God said, Let there be light; and there was light
[*Bible: Genesis*]

light[2] AS AN ADJECTIVE 1 = **insubstantial**, thin, delicate, lightweight, easy, slight, portable, buoyant, airy, flimsy, underweight, not heavy, transportable, lightsome, imponderous • *Try to wear light, loose clothes.*
OPPOSITES: heavy
2 = **weak**, soft, gentle, moderate, slight, mild, faint, indistinct • *a light breeze*
OPPOSITES: strong, forceful
3 = **crumbly**, loose, sandy, porous, spongy, friable • *light, tropical soils*
OPPOSITES: hard, strong

4 = **digestible**, small, restricted, modest, frugal, not rich, not heavy • *wine and cheese or other light refreshment*
OPPOSITES: rich, substantial
5 = **undemanding**, easy, simple, moderate, manageable, effortless, cushy *(informal)*, untaxing, unexacting • *He was on the training field for some light work yesterday.*
OPPOSITES: strenuous, burdensome
6 = **insignificant**, small, minute, tiny, slight, petty, trivial, trifling, inconsequential, inconsiderable, unsubstantial • *She confessed her astonishment at her light sentence.*
OPPOSITES: serious, weighty
7 = **light-hearted**, pleasing, funny, entertaining, amusing, diverting, witty, trivial, superficial, humorous, gay, trifling, frivolous, unserious • *a light entertainment programme*
OPPOSITES: serious, sombre
8 = **carefree**, happy, bright, lively, sunny, cheerful, animated, merry, gay, airy, frivolous, cheery, untroubled, blithe, light-hearted • *to finish on a lighter note*
9 = **nimble**, graceful, airy, deft, agile, sprightly, lithe, limber, lissom, light-footed, sylphlike • *the light steps of a ballet dancer*
OPPOSITES: clumsy
10 = **dizzy**, reeling, faint, volatile, giddy, unsteady, light-headed • *Her head felt light, and a serene confidence came over her.*
▸ **IN PHRASES: light on** *or* **upon something** 1 = **settle**, land, perch, alight • *Her eyes lit on the brandy that he had dropped on the floor.*
2 = **come across**, find, discover, encounter, stumble on, hit upon, happen upon • *the kind of thing that philosophers lighted upon.*
light out = **run away**, escape, depart, make off, abscond, quit, do a runner *(slang)*, scarper *(Brit. slang)*, do a bunk *(Brit. slang)*, fly the coop *(U.S. & Canad. informal)*, skedaddle *(informal)*, take a powder *(U.S. & Canad. slang)*, take it on the lam *(U.S. & Canad. slang)*, do a Skase *(Austral. informal)* • *I lit out of the door and never went back again.*

lighten[3] = **brighten**, flash, shine, illuminate, gleam, light up, irradiate, become light, make bright • *The sky began to lighten.*

lighten[4] 1 = **ease**, relieve, alleviate, allay, reduce, facilitate, lessen, mitigate, assuage • *He felt the need to lighten the atmosphere.*
OPPOSITES: intensify, worsen, heighten
2 = **cheer**, lift, revive, brighten, hearten, perk up, buoy up, gladden, elate • *Here's a little something to lighten your spirits.*
OPPOSITES: depress, sadden, weigh down
3 = **make lighter**, ease, disburden, reduce in weight • *Blending with a food processor lightens the mixture.*

light-fingered = **thieving**, stealing, dishonest, crafty, crooked *(informal)*, pinching *(informal)*, sly, furtive, shifty, underhand, pilfering • *Which goods are most often targeted by light-fingered customers?*

light-footed = **nimble**, tripping, winged, swift, buoyant, graceful, agile, sprightly, lithe, spry • *a new generation of light-footed dancers*

light-headed 1 = **faint**, dizzy, hazy, giddy, delirious, unsteady, vertiginous, woozy *(informal)* • *Your blood pressure will drop and you may feel light-headed.*
2 = **frivolous**, silly, shallow, foolish, superficial, trifling, inane, flippant, flighty, bird-brained *(informal)*, featherbrained, rattlebrained *(slang)* • *a light-headed girl*

light-hearted = **carefree**, happy, bright, glad, sunny, cheerful, jolly, merry, upbeat *(informal)*, playful, joyous, joyful, genial, chirpy *(informal)*, jovial, untroubled, gleeful, happy-go-lucky, gay, effervescent, blithe, insouciant, frolicsome, ludic *(literary)*, jocund, blithesome *(literary)* • *They were light-hearted and prepared to enjoy life.*
OPPOSITES: low, sad, gloomy

lightly 1 = **moderately**, thinly, slightly, sparsely, sparingly • *a small and lightly armed UN contingent*
OPPOSITES: heavily, thickly, abundantly
2 = **gently**, softly, slightly, faintly, delicately, gingerly, airily, timidly • *He kissed her lightly on the mouth.*
OPPOSITES: firmly, heavily, forcefully
3 = **carelessly**, indifferently, breezily, thoughtlessly, flippantly, frivolously, heedlessly, slightingly • *'Once a detective always a detective,' he said lightly.*
OPPOSITES: seriously, carefully, earnestly
4 = **easily**, simply, readily, effortlessly, unthinkingly, without thought, flippantly, heedlessly • *His allegations cannot be dismissed lightly.*
OPPOSITES: awkwardly, with difficulty, arduously

lightning
▸ **RELATED ADJECTIVES:** fulgurous, fulminous
▸ **RELATED PHOBIA:** astraphobia

lightweight 1 = **thin**, fine, delicate, sheer, flimsy, gossamer, diaphanous, filmy, unsubstantial • *lightweight denim*
2 = **unimportant**, shallow, trivial, insignificant, slight, petty, worthless, trifling, flimsy, paltry, inconsequential, undemanding, insubstantial, nickel-and-dime *(U.S. slang)*, of no account • *Some of the discussion in the book is lightweight and unconvincing.*
OPPOSITES: important, serious, significant

likable *or* **likeable** = **pleasant**, appealing, nice, friendly, winning, pleasing, attractive, engaging, charming, sympathetic, agreeable, amiable, genial, winsome • *He was an immensely likable chap.*

like[1] **AS AN ADJECTIVE** = **similar to**, same as, allied to, equivalent to, parallel to, resembling, identical to, alike, corresponding to, comparable to, akin to, approximating, analogous to, cognate to • *She's a great friend; we are like sisters.*
OPPOSITES: different, contrasted, unlike
▸ **AS A NOUN** = **equal**, equivalent, parallel, match, twin, counterpart • *We are dealing with an epidemic the like of which we have never seen.*
OPPOSITES: opposite

PROVERBS
Like breeds like

like[2] **AS A VERB** 1 = **enjoy**, love, adore *(informal)*, delight in, go for, dig *(slang)*, relish, savour, revel in, be fond of, be keen on, be partial to, have a preference for, have a weakness for • *He likes baseball.*
OPPOSITES: hate, dislike, loathe
2 = **admire**, approve of, appreciate, prize, take to, esteem, cherish, hold dear, take a shine to *(informal)*, think well of • *I like the way this book is set out.*
OPPOSITES: hate, dislike, loathe
3 = **wish**, want, choose, prefer, desire, select, fancy, care, feel inclined • *Would you like to come back for coffee?*
4 = **wish**, regard, feel about, consider • *How would you like it if people followed you round all the time?*
▸ **AS A NOUN** *usually plural* = **liking**, favourite, preference, cup of tea *(informal)*, predilection, partiality • *I know all her likes and dislikes, and her political viewpoints.*

likelihood = **probability**, chance, possibility, prospect, liability, good chance, strong possibility, reasonableness, likeliness • *The likelihood is that people would be willing to pay.*

likely AS AN ADJECTIVE 1 = **inclined**, disposed, prone, liable, tending, apt • *People are more likely to accept change if they understand it.*
2 = **probable**, expected, anticipated, odds-on, on the cards, to be expected • *A 'yes' vote is the likely outcome.*
3 = **plausible**, possible, reasonable, credible, feasible, believable, verisimilar • *It's likely that he still loves her.*
4 = **appropriate**, promising, pleasing, fit, fair, favourite, qualified, suitable, acceptable, proper, hopeful, agreeable,

up-and-coming, befitting • *He seemed a likely candidate to becoming Prime Minister.*

▸ AS AN ADVERB = **probably**, no doubt, presumably, in all probability, like enough *(informal)*, doubtlessly, like as not *(informal)* • *Very likely he'd told them of his business interest.*

like-minded = **agreeing**, compatible, harmonious, in harmony, unanimous, in accord, of one mind, of the same mind, en rapport *(French)* • *the opportunity to mix with like-minded people*

liken = **compare**, match, relate, parallel, equate, juxtapose, mention in the same breath, set beside • *The pain is likened to being drilled through the head.*

likeness 1 = **resemblance**, similarity, correspondence, affinity, similitude • *These stories have a startling likeness to one another.*

2 = **portrait**, study, picture, model, image, photograph, copy, counterpart, representation, reproduction, replica, depiction, facsimile, effigy, delineation • *The museum displays wax likenesses of every US president.*

3 = **appearance**, form, guise, semblance • *a disservice in the likeness of a favour*

likewise 1 = **also**, too, as well, further, in addition, moreover, besides, furthermore • *All their attempts were spurned. Similar offers from the right were likewise rejected.*

2 = **similarly**, the same, in the same way, in similar fashion, in like manner • *He made donations and encouraged others to do likewise.*

liking = **fondness**, love, taste, desire, bent, stomach, attraction, weakness, tendency, preference, bias, affection, appreciation, inclination, thirst, affinity, penchant, propensity, soft spot, predilection, partiality, proneness • *She had a liking for good clothes.*

OPPOSITES: dislike, hatred, loathing

lilt = **rhythm**, intonation, cadence, beat, pitch, swing, sway • *Her voice has a West Country lilt.*

lily-white 1 = **pure white**, white, milk-white, white as snow • *Blood stained his lily-white shirt.*

2 = **innocent**, pure, impeccable, virtuous, spotless, squeaky-clean, untainted, unsullied, untarnished, irreproachable • *their lily-white business ethics*

limb AS A NOUN 1 = **part**, member, arm, leg, wing, extension, extremity, appendage • *She stretched out her cramped limbs.*

2 = **branch**, spur, projection, offshoot, bough • *the limb of an enormous leafy tree*

▸ IN PHRASES: **out on a limb** = **independently**, separately, in a dangerous position, sticking your neck out *(informal)* • *They went out on a limb, voting for a controversial energy bill.*

limber AS AN ADJECTIVE = **pliant**, flexible, supple, agile, plastic, graceful, elastic, lithe, pliable, lissom(e), loose-jointed, loose-limbed • *He bent at the waist to show how limber his long back was.*

▸ IN PHRASES: **limber up** = **loosen up**, prepare, exercise, warm up, get ready • *The dancers were limbering up at the back of the hall.* • *some exercises to limber up the legs*

limbo IN PHRASES: **in limbo** = **in a state of uncertainty**, neglected, up in the air, in abeyance, betwixt and between, not knowing whether one is coming or going *(informal)* • *I felt as though I was in limbo.*

limelight = **publicity**, recognition, fame, the spotlight, attention, prominence, stardom, public eye, public notice, glare of publicity • *He has been thrust into the limelight with a high-profile job.*

limit AS A NOUN 1 = **end**, bound, ultimate, deadline, utmost, breaking point, termination, extremity, greatest extent, the bitter end, end point, cutoff point, furthest bound • *Her love for him was being tested to its limits.*

2 = **boundary**, end, edge, border, extent, pale, confines, frontier, precinct, perimeter, periphery • *the city limits*

3 = **limitation**, maximum, restriction, ceiling, restraint • *He outlined the limits of British power.*

▸ AS A VERB = **restrict**, control, check, fix, bound, confine, specify, curb, restrain, ration, hinder, circumscribe, hem in, demarcate, delimit, put a brake on, keep within limits, straiten • *He limited payments on the country's foreign debt.*

▸ IN PHRASES: **the limit** = **the end**, it *(informal)*, enough, the last straw, the straw that broke the camel's back • *Really, Mark, you are the limit!*

limitation 1 = **restriction**, control, check, block, curb, restraint, constraint, obstruction, impediment • *There is to be no limitation on the number of opposition parties.*

2 = **weakness**, failing, qualification, reservation, defect, disadvantage, flaw, drawback, shortcoming, snag, imperfection • *This drug has one important limitation.*

limited 1 = **restricted**, controlled, fixed, defined, checked, bounded, confined, curbed, hampered, constrained, finite, circumscribed • *They have a limited amount of time to get their point across.*

OPPOSITES: unlimited, limitless, boundless

2 = **narrow**, little, small, restricted, slight, inadequate, minimal, insufficient, unsatisfactory, scant • *The shop has a very limited selection.*

limitless = **infinite**, endless, unlimited, never-ending, vast, immense, countless, untold, boundless, unending, inexhaustible, undefined, immeasurable, unbounded, numberless, measureless, illimitable, uncalculable • *a cheap and limitless supply of energy*

limp[1] AS A VERB = **hobble**, stagger, stumble, shuffle, halt *(archaic)*, hop, falter, shamble, totter, dodder, hirple *(Scot.)* • *He limped off with a leg injury.*

▸ AS A NOUN = **lameness**, hobble, hirple *(Scot.)* • *A stiff knee forced her to walk with a limp.*

limp[2] 1 = **floppy**, soft, relaxed, loose, flexible, slack, lax, drooping, flabby, limber, pliable, flaccid • *The residue can leave the hair limp and dull looking.*

OPPOSITES: hard, firm, stiff

2 = **weak**, tired, exhausted, worn out, spent, debilitated, lethargic, enervated • *He carried her limp body into the room and laid her on the bed.*

OPPOSITES: strong, tough, powerful

limpid 1 = **clear**, bright, pure, transparent, translucent, crystal-clear, crystalline, pellucid • *limpid rock-pools*

2 = **understandable**, clear, lucid, unambiguous, comprehensible, intelligible, perspicuous • *The speech was a model of its kind – limpid and unaffected.*

line[1] AS A NOUN 1 = **stroke**, mark, rule, score, bar, band, channel, dash, scratch, slash, underline, streak, stripe, groove • *Draw a line down the centre of the page.*

2 = **wrinkle**, mark, crease, furrow, crow's foot • *He has a large, generous face with deep lines.*

3 = **row**, queue, rank, file, series, column, sequence, convoy, procession, crocodile *(Brit.)* • *Children clutching empty bowls form a line.*

4 = **script**, part, words, dialogue • *Learning lines is easy. Acting is difficult.*

5 = **string**, cable, wire, strand, rope, thread, cord, filament, wisp • *a piece of fishing line*

6 = **trajectory**, way, course, track, channel, direction, route, path, axis • *Walk in a straight line.*

7 = **outline**, shape, figure, style, cut, features, appearance, profile, silhouette, configuration, contour • *a dress that follows the line of the body*

8 = **boundary**, mark, limit, edge, border, frontier, partition, borderline, demarcation • *the California state line*

9 = **formation**, front, position, front line, trenches, firing line • *the fortification they called the Maginot Line*

10 = **approach**, policy, position, way, course, practice, scheme, method, technique, procedure, tactic, avenue,

ideology, course of action • *The government promised to take a hard line on terrorism.*
11 = **course**, way, direction, tendency, drift, tack • *What are the benefits of this line of research?*
12 = **occupation**, work, calling, interest, business, job, area, trade, department, field, career, activity, bag *(slang)*, employment, province, profession, pursuit, forte, vocation, specialization • *What was your father's line of business?*
13 = **brand**, make, sort, kind, product, type, label • *His best selling line is the cheapest lager at £1.99.*
14 = **lineage**, family, breed, succession, race, stock, strain, descent, ancestry, parentage • *We were part of a long line of artists.*
15 = **note**, message, letter, memo, report, word, card, e-mail, postcard, text • *My phone doesn't work, so drop me a line.*
16 = **series**, chain, string, sequence, procession • *the latest in a long line of successes*
17 = **patter**, story, pitch, spiel *(informal)* • *Don't be fooled by that line about having seen you before somewhere.*
18 = **clue**, lead, hint, indication • *No one seems able to pursue a line of inquiry far enough to get an answer.*
▸ AS A VERB 1 = **border**, edge, bound, fringe, rank, skirt, verge, rim • *Thousands of people lined the streets as the procession went by.*
2 = **mark**, draw, crease, furrow, cut, rule, score, trace, underline, inscribe • *Her face was lined with concern.*
▸ IN PHRASES: **draw the line at something** = **object to**, prohibit, stop short at, set a limit at, put your foot down over • *He declared that he would draw the line at hitting a woman.*
in line 1 = **in alignment**, lined, level, true, straight, lined up, in a row, plumb • *Venus, the Sun and Earth were all in line.*
2 = **in accord**, in agreement, in harmony, in step, in conformity • *This is in line with medical opinion.*
3 = **under control**, in order, in check • *All this was just designed to frighten me and keep me in line.*
4 = **in a queue**, in a row, in a column • *I had been standing in line for three hours.*
in line for = **due for**, being considered for, a candidate for, shortlisted for, in the running for, on the short list for, next in succession to • *He must be in line for a place in the Guinness Book of Records.*
line something up 1 = **align**, order, range, arrange, sequence, array, regiment, dispose, marshal, straighten, straighten up, put in a line • *He lined the glasses up behind the bar.*
2 = **prepare**, schedule, organize, secure, obtain, come up with, assemble, get together, lay on, procure, jack up *(N.Z. informal)* • *He's lining up a two-week tour for the New Year.*
line up = **queue up**, file, fall in, form a queue, form ranks • *The senior leaders lined up behind him in orderly rows.*
on the line = **at risk**, in danger, in an endangered position, in jeopardy • *He wouldn't put his career on the line to help a friend.*
toe the line = **conform**, agree, yield, comply, play ball *(informal)*, follow the crowd, run with the pack • *He's one of the politicians who wouldn't toe the party line.*

line² = **fill**, face, cover, reinforce, encase, inlay, interline, ceil • *They line their dens with leaves or grass.*

lineage = **descent**, family, line, succession, house, stock, birth, breed, pedigree, extraction, ancestry, forebears, progeny, heredity, forefathers, genealogy • *They can trace their lineage back to the 18th century.*

lineaments = **features**, face, line, outline, trait, configuration, countenance, visage, physiognomy, phiz *or* phizog *(slang, chiefly Brit.)* • *She recognised the haggard lineaments.*

lined 1 = **wrinkled**, worn, furrowed, wizened • *His lined face was that of an old man.*
2 = **ruled**, feint • *Take a piece of lined paper.*

lines = **principle**, plan, example, model, pattern, procedure, convention • *so-called autonomous republics based on ethnic lines*

line-up = **arrangement**, team, row, selection, array, dream team • *a great line-up of musicians and comedy acts*

linger 1 = **continue**, last, remain, stay, carry on, endure, persist, abide • *The guilty feelings lingered.*
2 = **hang on**, last, survive, cling to life, die slowly • *He lingered for weeks in a coma.*
3 = **stay**, remain, stop, wait, delay, lag, hang around, idle, dally, loiter, take your time, wait around, dawdle, hang in the air, procrastinate, tarry, drag your feet *or* heels • *Customers are welcome to linger over coffee until midnight.*

lingerie = **women's underwear**, undies *(informal)*, frillies *(informal)*, women's undergarments, smalls *(informal)*, women's underclothes, women's nightclothes • *She was clad in satin lingerie.*

lingering = **slow**, prolonged, protracted, long-drawn-out, remaining, dragging, persistent • *He died a lingering death in hospital.*

lingo = **language**, jargon, dialect, talk, speech, tongue, idiom, vernacular, patter, cant, patois, argot • *I don't speak the lingo.*

link AS A NOUN 1 = **connection**, relationship, association, tie-up, affinity, affiliation, vinculum • *the link between smoking and lung cancer*
2 = **relationship**, association, tie, bond, connection, attachment, liaison, affinity, affiliation • *They hope to cement close links with Moscow.*
3 = **joint**, knot • *The metal links had to be sewn to the garment loop ring.*
4 = **component**, part, piece, division, element, constituent • *Seafood is the first link in a chain of contaminations.*
▸ AS A VERB 1 = **associate**, relate, identify, connect, bracket • *Liver cancer is linked to the hepatitis B virus.*
2 = **connect**, join, unite, couple, tie, bind, attach, fasten, yoke • *the Channel Tunnel linking Britain and France*
OPPOSITES: separate, split, divide

link-up = **communication**, connection, transmission, relay • *a live satellite link-up*

lion AS A NOUN 1 = **hero**, champion, fighter, warrior, conqueror, lionheart, brave person • *a frail little man, but with the heart of a lion*
2 = **celebrity**, star, superstar, idol, wonder, notable, big name, prodigy, luminary, celeb *(informal)*, megastar *(informal)*, V.I.P. • *By the 1920s Kahlil Gibran was a social and literary lion.*
▸ IN PHRASES: **lion's share** = **majority part**, most, bulk, greater part, preponderance • *Nuclear research has received the lion's share of public funding.*
▸ RELATED ADJECTIVE: leonine
▸ NAME OF FEMALE: lioness
▸ NAME OF YOUNG: cub
▸ COLLECTIVE NOUNS: pride, troop

lion-hearted = **brave**, daring, bold, heroic, courageous, stalwart, resolute, intrepid, valiant, dauntless, valorous • *He came back to produce a lion-hearted performance in the 200 metres.*
OPPOSITES: cowardly, abject, spineless

lionize = **idolize**, celebrate, honour, acclaim, mob, exalt, make much of, crack up *(informal)*, hero-worship, fête, big up *(slang, chiefly Caribbean)*, eulogize, aggrandize, adulate, glorify, sing *or* sound the praises of • *The press began to lionize him enthusiastically.*

lip AS A NOUN 1 = **edge**, rim, brim, margin, brink, flange • *the lip of the jug*
2 = **impudence**, rudeness, insolence, impertinence, sauce *(informal)*, cheek *(informal)*, effrontery, backchat

(informal), brass neck *(informal)* • *Enough of that lip if you want me to help you!*

▸ **IN PHRASES: pay lip service to something** *or* **someone = pretend to support**, support insincerely, support hypocritically • *He had done no more that pay lip service to their views.*

smack *or* **lick your lips = gloat**, drool, slaver • *They licked their lips in anticipation.*

▸ **RELATED ADJECTIVE:** labial

liquefy = melt, dissolve, thaw, liquidize, run, fuse, flux, deliquesce • *Heat the jam until it liquefies.*

liqueur

▹ *See panel* **Liqueurs**

liquid AS A NOUN = fluid, solution, juice, liquor, sap • *Drink plenty of liquid.*

▸ **AS AN ADJECTIVE 1 = fluid**, running, flowing, wet, melted, thawed, watery, molten, runny, liquefied, aqueous • *Wash in warm water with liquid detergent.*

2 = clear, bright, brilliant, shining, transparent, translucent, limpid • *a mosaic of liquid cobalts and greens*

3 = smooth, clear, soft, flowing, sweet, pure, melting, fluent, melodious, mellifluous, dulcet, mellifluent • *He had a deep liquid voice.*

4 = convertible, disposable, negotiable, realizable • *The bank had sufficient liquid assets to continue operating.*

liquidate 1 = dissolve, cancel, abolish, terminate, annul • *A unanimous vote was taken to liquidate the company.*

2 = convert to cash, cash, realize, sell off, sell up • *The company closed down operations and began liquidating its assets.*

3 = kill, murder, remove, destroy, do in *(slang)*, silence, eliminate, take out *(slang)*, get rid of, wipe out *(informal)*, dispatch, finish off, do away with, blow away *(slang, chiefly U.S.)*, annihilate, exterminate, bump off *(slang)*, rub out *(U.S. slang)* • *They have not hesitated in the past to liquidate their rivals.*

liquor 1 = alcohol, drink, spirits, booze *(informal)*, grog, hard stuff *(informal)*, strong drink, Dutch courage *(informal)*, intoxicant, juice *(informal)*, hooch *or* hootch *(informal, chiefly U.S. & Canad.)* • *The room was filled with cases of liquor.*

2 = juice, stock, liquid, extract, gravy, infusion, broth • *Drain the oysters and retain the liquor.*

lissom *or* **lissome = supple**, light, flexible, graceful, nimble, agile, lithe, limber, pliable, willowy, pliant, loose-jointed, loose-limbed • *a lissom young model*

list[1] **AS A NOUN = inventory**, record, listing, series, roll, file, schedule, index, register, catalogue, directory, tally, invoice, syllabus, tabulation, leet *(Scot.)* • *There were six names on the list.*

▸ **AS A VERB = itemize**, record, note, enter, file, schedule, index, register, catalogue, write down, enrol, set down, enumerate, note down, tabulate • *The students were asked to list their favourite sports.*

list[2] **AS A VERB = lean**, tip, heel, incline, tilt, cant, heel over, careen • *The ship listed again, and she was thrown back across the bunk.*

▸ **AS A NOUN = tilt**, leaning, slant, cant • *The ship's list was so strong that she stumbled.*

listen AS A VERB 1 = hear, attend, pay attention, hark, be attentive, be all ears, lend an ear, hearken *(archaic)*, prick up your ears, give ear, keep your ears open, pin back your ears *(informal)* • *He spent his time listening to the radio.*

2 = pay attention, observe, obey, mind, concentrate, heed, take notice, take note of, take heed of, do as you are told, give heed to • *When I asked him to stop, he wouldn't listen.*

▸ **IN PHRASES: listen in on something = eavesdrop**, monitor, tap, spy, bug *(informal)*, overhear, intrude, pry, snoop *(informal)*, earwig *(informal)* • *He assigned federal agents to listen in on their phone calls.*

QUOTATIONS

Friends, Romans, countrymen, lend me your ears
[William Shakespeare *Julius Caesar*]

We have two ears and only one tongue in order that we may hear more and speak less
[Diogenes Laertius *Lives of the Philosophers*]

listing = list, record, series, roll, file, schedule, index, register, catalogue, directory, tally, inventory, syllabus, tabulation • *A full listing of the companies will be published quarterly.*

listless = languid, sluggish, lifeless, lethargic, heavy, limp, vacant, indifferent, languishing, inert, apathetic, lymphatic, impassive, supine, indolent, torpid, inattentive, enervated, spiritless, mopish • *He was listless and pale and wouldn't eat.*

OPPOSITES: spirited, active, energetic

litany 1 = recital, list, tale, catalogue, account, repetition, refrain, recitation, enumeration • *She listened to the litany of complaints against her client.*

2 = prayer, petition, invocation, supplication, set words • *She recited a litany in an unknown tongue.*

literacy = education, learning, knowledge, scholarship, cultivation, proficiency, articulacy, ability to read and write, articulateness • *Many of them have some problems with literacy and numeracy.*

literal 1 = exact, close, strict, accurate, faithful, verbatim, word for word • *a literal translation*

2 = unimaginative, boring, dull, down-to-earth, matter-of-fact, factual, prosaic, colourless, uninspired, prosy • *He is a very literal person.*

3 = actual, real, true, simple, plain, genuine, gospel, bona fide, unvarnished, unexaggerated • *He was saying no more than the literal truth.*

literally = exactly, really, closely, actually, simply, plainly, truly, precisely, strictly, faithfully, to the letter, verbatim, word for word • *The word 'volk' translates literally as 'folk'.*

literary = well-read, lettered, learned, formal, intellectual, scholarly, literate, erudite, bookish • *a literary masterpiece*

literate = educated, lettered, learned, cultured, informed, scholarly, cultivated, knowledgeable, well-informed, erudite, well-read • *The lyrics are highly literate; they even quote Voltaire.*

LIQUEURS

advocaat
amaretto
Amendoa Amarga
anisette
Bailey's Irish Cream *(trademark)*
Benedictine
chartreuse
cherry brandy
Cointreau *(trademark)*
crème
crème de cacao
crème de menthe
Curaçao
Drambuie *(trademark)*
Frangelico
Galliano *(trademark)*
Glayva *(trademark)*
Grand Marnier *(trademark)*
Kahlua
kümmel
Malibu *(trademark)*
maraschino
Midori
noyau
pastis
peach schnapps
Pernod *(trademark)*
pousse-café
prunelle
ratafia *or* ratafee
sambucca
Southern Comfort *(trademark)*
Tia Maria *(trademark)*
Van der Hum
Veuve Jacquolot

literature 1 = **writings**, letters, compositions, lore, creative writing, written works, belles-lettres • *classic works of literature*
2 = **information**, publicity, leaflet, brochure, circular, pamphlet, handout, mailshot, handbill • *I'm sending you literature from two other companies.*
▷ *See panels* **Figures of speech; Literature; Shakespeare**

QUOTATIONS
It takes a great deal of history to produce a little literature
[Henry James *Hawthorne*]
Remarks are not literature
[Gloria Steinem *Autobiography of Alice B. Toklas*]
Literature is mostly about having sex and not much about children; life is the other way around
[David Lodge *The British Museum is Falling Down*]
Literature is news that STAYS news
[Ezra Pound *ABC of Reading*]
Literature is a luxury. Fiction is a necessity
[G.K. Chesterton *The Defendant*]
Literature is where I go to explore the highest and lowest places in human society and in the human spirit, where I hope to find not absolute truth but the truth of the tale, of the imagination and of the heart
[Salman Rushdie]
When once the itch of literature comes over a man, nothing can cure it but the scratching of a pen
[Samuel Lover *Handy Andy*]

lithe = **supple**, flexible, agile, limber, pliable, pliant, lissom(e), loose-jointed, loose-limbed • *His walk was lithe and graceful.*

litigant = **claimant**, party, plaintiff, contestant, litigator, disputant • *The litigant should first write to the defendant.*

litigation = **lawsuit**, case, action, process, disputing, prosecution, contending • *The settlement ends more than four years of litigation.*

litigious = **contentious**, belligerent, argumentative, quarrelsome, disputatious • *They are probably the most litigious people in the world.*

litter AS A NOUN 1 = **rubbish**, refuse, waste, fragments, junk, debris, shreds, garbage *(chiefly U.S.)*, trash, muck, detritus, grot *(slang)* • *If you see litter in the corridor, pick it up.*
2 = **jumble**, mess, disorder, confusion, scatter, tangle, muddle, clutter, disarray, untidiness • *He pushed aside the litter of books.*
3 = **brood**, family, young, offspring, progeny • *a litter of puppies*
4 = **bedding**, couch, mulch, floor cover, straw-bed • *The birds scratch through leaf litter on the forest floor.*
5 = **stretcher**, palanquin • *The Colonel winced as the porters jolted the litter.*
▸ AS A VERB 1 = **clutter**, mess up, clutter up, be scattered about, disorder, disarrange, derange, muss *(U.S. & Canad.)* • *Glass from broken bottles litters the pavement.*
2 = **scatter**, spread, shower, strew • *Concrete holiday resorts are littered across the mountainside.*

little AS AN ADJECTIVE 1 = **not much**, small, insufficient, scant, meagre, sparse, skimpy, measly, hardly any • *I had little money and little free time.*
OPPOSITES: much, ample, abundant
2 = **small**, minute, short, tiny, mini, wee, compact, miniature, dwarf, slender, diminutive, petite, dainty, elfin, bijou, infinitesimal, teeny-weeny, Lilliputian, munchkin *(informal, chiefly U.S.)*, teensy-weensy, pygmy *or* pigmy • *We sat round a little table.*
OPPOSITES: great, big, large
3 = **young**, small, junior, infant, immature, undeveloped, babyish • *When I was little, I was hyperactive.*
4 = **unimportant**, minor, petty, trivial, trifling, insignificant, negligible, paltry, inconsiderable • *He found himself getting angry over little things.*
OPPOSITES: important, serious, major
5 = **short**, brief, fleeting, short-lived, passing, hasty, momentary • *She stood up quickly, giving a little cry of astonishment.*
OPPOSITES: long
6 = **mean**, base, cheap, petty, narrow-minded, small-minded, illiberal • *I won't play your little mind-games.*
▸ AS AN ADVERB 1 = **hardly**, barely, not quite, not much, only just, scarcely • *On the way back they spoke very little.*
OPPOSITES: much
2 = **rarely**, seldom, scarcely, not often, infrequently, hardly ever • *We go there very little nowadays.*
OPPOSITES: much, always
▸ AS A NOUN = **bit**, touch, spot, trace, hint, dash, particle, fragment, pinch, small amount, dab, trifle, tad *(informal, chiefly U.S.)*, snippet, speck, modicum • *Don't give me too much. Just a little.*
OPPOSITES: much, lot
▸ IN PHRASES: **a little** = **to a small extent**, slightly, to some extent, to a certain extent, to a small degree • *I'm getting a little tired of having to correct your mistakes.*
little by little = **gradually**, slowly, progressively, step by step, piecemeal, bit by bit, imperceptibly, by degrees • *Little by little, he was becoming weaker.*

QUOTATIONS
Little things affect little minds
[Benjamin Disraeli *Sybil*]

liturgical = **ceremonial**, ritual, solemn, sacramental, formal, eucharistic • *a liturgical poem traditionally sung on the Sabbath*

liturgy = **ceremony**, service, ritual, services, celebration, formula, worship, rite, sacrament, form of worship • *A clergyman read the liturgy from the prayer-book.*

livable 1 = **habitable**, fit (for human habitation), comfortable, adequate, satisfactory, inhabitable • *It was voted the most livable city in the US.*
2 = **tolerable**, acceptable, worthwhile, bearable, passable, worth living, supportable, endurable, sufferable • *They were given livable pensions to sustain themselves and their children.*
3 *with* **with** = **congenial**, compatible, easy to live with, harmonious, sociable, companionable, easy • *I wonder if I am livable with.*

live[1] AS A VERB 1 = **dwell**, board, settle, lodge, occupy, abide, inhabit, hang out *(informal)*, stay *(chiefly Scot.)*, reside, have as your home, have your home in • *She has lived here for 10 years.*
2 = **spend your life**, behave, conduct yourself, pass your life • *We lived quite grandly.*
3 = **lead**, have, experience, pass, go through • *We can start living a normal life again now.*
4 = **exist**, last, prevail, be, have being, breathe, persist, be alive, have life, draw breath, remain alive • *He's got a terrible disease and will not live long.*
5 = **survive**, remain alive, feed yourself, get along, make a living, earn a living, make ends meet, subsist, eke out a living, support yourself, maintain yourself • *the last indigenous people to live by hunting*
6 = **thrive**, be happy, flourish, prosper, have fun, enjoy life, enjoy yourself, luxuriate, live life to the full, make the most of life • *My friends told me to get out and live a bit.*
▸ IN PHRASES: **live it up** = **enjoy yourself**, celebrate, have fun, revel, have a ball *(informal)*, large it *(Brit. slang)*, push the boat out *(Brit. informal)*, paint the town red, make whoopee *(informal)*, overindulge yourself • *There's no reason why you couldn't live it up once in a while.*
live on *or* **off something** = **exist on**, depend on, rely on, survive on, keep going on, subsist on, endure on, make ends meet on, stay alive on, keep your head above water, eke out an existence on, sustain yourself on • *He's been living on state benefits.*

PROVERBS
Live and learn
Live and let live
They that live longest see most
He lives long who lives well

LITERATURE

Literature terms

- allegory
- alliteration
- allusion
- amphigory
- Angry Young Men
- anti-hero
- antinovel
- anti-roman
- aphorism
- archaism
- Augustan
- Bakhtinian
- bathos
- Beat Generation
- belles-lettres
- belletrist
- bibliography
- Bildungsroman
- black comedy
- Bloomsbury group
- bodice-ripper
- bombast
- bowdlerization
- Brechtian
- bricolage
- Byronic
- carnivalesque
- campus novel
- causerie
- Celtic Revival
- cento
- chiller
- Ciceronian
- classicism
- coda
- colloquialism
- comedy
- comedy of manners
- commedia dell'arte
- conceit
- courtly love
- cultural materialism
- cut-up technique
- cyberpunk
- death of the author
- decadence
- deconstruction
- denouement
- Derridian
- dialectic
- dialogue
- Dickensian
- discourse
- double entendre
- drama
- epic
- epilogue
- epistle
- epistolary novel
- epitaph
- erasure
- essay
- exegesis
- expressionism
- fable
- fabulist
- faction
- fantastique
- fantasy
- feminist theory
- festschrift
- figure of speech
- fin de siècle
- foreword
- Foucauldian
- Futurism
- gloss
- Gongorism
- Gothic
- hagiography
- Hellenism
- hermeneutics
- historical novel
- historicism
- Homeric
- Horatian
- hudibrastic verse
- imagery
- interior monologue
- intertextuality
- invective
- Jacobean
- Janeite
- Johnsonian
- journalese
- Joycean
- Juvenalian
- Kafkaesque
- kailyard
- kenning
- kiddy lit
- lampoon
- Laurentian *or* Lawrentian
- legend
- literary criticism
- littérateur
- locus classicus
- Lost Generation
- magic realism *or* magical realism
- marxist theory
- maxim
- melodrama
- metafiction
- metalanguage
- metaphor
- mock-heroic
- modernism
- motif
- myth
- mythopoeia
- narrative
- narratology
- narrator
- naturalism
- new criticism
- new historicism
- nom de plume
- nouveau roman
- novel
- novelette
- novella
- onomatopoeia
- oxymoron
- palindrome
- paraphrase
- parody
- pastiche
- pastoral
- pathos
- picaresque
- plagiarism
- plot
- polemic
- pornography
- post-colonialism
- postmodernism
- post-structuralism
- post-theory
- pot-boiler
- queer theory
- realism
- Restoration comedy
- roman
- roman à clef
- Romanticism
- saga
- samizdat
- satire
- science fiction *or* SF
- sentimental novel
- shopping-and-fucking *or* S & F novel
- short story
- signifier and signified
- simile
- sketch
- socialist realism
- splatterpunk
- Spoonerism
- story
- stream of consciousness
- structuralism
- Sturm und Drang
- subplot
- subtext
- Surrealism
- Swiftian
- theme
- theory
- thesis
- tragedy
- tragicomedy
- trope
- verse
- vignette

Literary characters

Character	Book	Author
Captain Ahab	Moby Dick	Herman Melville
Aladdin	The Arabian Nights' Entertainments	Traditional
Alice	Alice's Adventures in Wonderland, Through the Looking-Glass	Lewis Carroll
Bridget Allworthy	Tom Jones	Henry Fielding
Squire Allworthy	Tom Jones	Henry Fielding
Blanch Amory	Pendennis	William Makepeace Thackeray
Harry Angstrom	Rabbit, Run et al.	John Updike
Artful Dodger	Oliver Twist	Charles Dickens
Jack Aubrey	Master and Commander et al.	Patrick O'Brian
Aunt Polly	Tom Sawyer	Mark Twain
Joe Bagstock	Dombey and Son	Charles Dickens
David Balfour	Kidnapped, Catriona	Robert Louis Stevenson
Mrs. Bardell	The Pickwick Papers	Charles Dickens
Barkis	David Copperfield	Charles Dickens
Jake Barnes	The Sun Also Rises	Ernest Hemingway
Adam Bede	Adam Bede	George Eliot
Seth Bede	Adam Bede	George Eliot
Laura Bell	Pendennis	William Makepeace Thackeray
Elizabeth Bennet	Pride and Prejudice	Jane Austen
Jane Bennet	Pride and Prejudice	Jane Austen
Kitty Bennet	Pride and Prejudice	Jane Austen
Lydia Bennet	Pride and Prejudice	Jane Austen
Mary Bennet	Pride and Prejudice	Jane Austen
Mr. Bennet	Pride and Prejudice	Jane Austen
Mrs. Bennet	Pride and Prejudice	Jane Austen
Edmund Bertram	Mansfield Park	Jane Austen

Literary characters (continued)

Character	Book	Author
Julia Bertram	Mansfield Park	Jane Austen
Lady Bertram	Mansfield Park	Jane Austen
Maria Bertram	Mansfield Park	Jane Austen
Sir Thomas Bertram	Mansfield Park	Jane Austen
Tom Bertram	Mansfield Park	Jane Austen
Biddy	Great Expectations	Charles Dickens
Charles Bingley	Pride and Prejudice	Jane Austen
Stephen Blackpool	Hard Times	Charles Dickens
Anthony Blanche	Brideshead Revisited	Evelyn Waugh
Leopold Bloom	Ulysses	James Joyce
Molly Bloom	Ulysses	James Joyce
Mr. Boffin	Our Mutual Friend	Charles Dickens
Mrs. Boffin	Our Mutual Friend	Charles Dickens
Farmer Boldwood	Far from the Madding Crowd	Thomas Hardy
Josiah Bounderby	Hard Times	Charles Dickens
Madeline Bray	Nicholas Nickleby	Charles Dickens
Alan Breck	Kidnapped, Catriona	Robert Louis Stevenson
Sue Bridehead	Jude the Obscure	Thomas Hardy
Miss Briggs	Vanity Fair	William Makepeace Thackeray
Dorothea Brooke	Middlemarch	George Eliot
Mr. Brooke	Middlemarch	George Eliot
Mr. Brownlow	Oliver Twist	Charles Dickens
Daisy Buchanan	The Great Gatsby	F. Scott Fitzgerald
Rosa Bud	Edwin Drood	Charles Dickens
Billy Budd	Billy Budd, Foretopman	Herman Melville
Mr. Bulstrode	Middlemarch	George Eliot
Bumble	Oliver Twist	Charles Dickens
Mrs. Cadwallader	Middlemarch	George Eliot
Carker	Dombey and Son	Charles Dickens
Richard Carstone	Bleak House	Charles Dickens
Sydney Carton	A Tale of Two Cities	Charles Dickens
Mr. Casaubon	Middlemarch	George Eliot
Casby	Little Dorrit	Charles Dickens
Flora Casby	Little Dorrit	Charles Dickens
Dunstan Cass	Silas Marner	George Eliot
Godfrey Cass	Silas Marner	George Eliot
Lady Castlewood	Henry Esmond	William Makepeace Thackeray
Lord Castlewood	Henry Esmond	William Makepeace Thackeray
Holden Caulfield	The Catcher in the Rye	J. D. Salinger
Chadband	Bleak House	Charles Dickens
Constance Chatterley	Lady Chatterley's Lover	D. H. Lawrence
The Cheeryble Brothers	Nicholas Nickleby	Charles Dickens
Edward Chester	Barnaby Rudge	Charles Dickens
Sir James Chettam	Middlemarch	George Eliot
Chuffey	Martin Chuzzlewit	Charles Dickens
Frank Churchill	Emma	Jane Austen
Jonas Chuzzlewit	Martin Chuzzlewit	Charles Dickens
Martin Chuzzlewit	Martin Chuzzlewit	Charles Dickens
Ada Clare	Bleak House	Charles Dickens
Angel Clare	Tess of the D'Urbervilles	Thomas Hardy
Arthur Clennam	Little Dorrit	Charles Dickens
Humphry Clinker	Humphry Clinker	Tobias Smollett
William Collins	Pride and Prejudice	Jane Austen
Benjy Compson	The Sound and the Fury	William Faulkner
David Copperfield	David Copperfield	Charles Dickens
Emily Costigan	Pendennis	William Makepeace Thackeray
Bob Cratchit	A Christmas Carol	Charles Dickens
Henry Crawford	Mansfield Park	Jane Austen
Mary Crawford	Mansfield Park	Jane Austen
Bute Crawley	Vanity Fair	William Makepeace Thackeray
Miss Crawley	Vanity Fair	William Makepeace Thackeray
Mrs. Bute Crawley	Vanity Fair	William Makepeace Thackeray
Pitt Crawley	Vanity Fair	William Makepeace Thackeray
Rawdon Crawley	Vanity Fair	William Makepeace Thackeray
Sir Pitt Crawley	Vanity Fair	William Makepeace Thackeray

LITERARY CHARACTERS (CONTINUED)

Character	Book	Author
Septimus Crisparkle	Edwin Drood	Charles Dickens
Vincent Crummles	Nicholas Nickleby	Charles Dickens
Jerry Cruncher	A Tale of Two Cities	Charles Dickens
Robinson Crusoe	Robinson Crusoe	Daniel Defoe
Captain Cuttle	Dombey and Son	Charles Dickens
Sebastian Dangerfield	The Ginger Man	J. P. Donleavy
Fitzwilliam Darcy	Pride and Prejudice	Jane Austen
Charles Darnay	A Tale of Two Cities	Charles Dickens
Elinor Dashwood	Sense and Sensibility	Jane Austen
John Dashwood	Sense and Sensibility	Jane Austen
Margaret Dashwood	Sense and Sensibility	Jane Austen
Marianne Dashwood	Sense and Sensibility	Jane Austen
Mrs. Henry Dashwood	Sense and Sensibility	Jane Austen
Dick Datchery	Edwin Drood	Charles Dickens
Fancy Day	Under The Greenwood Tree	Thomas Hardy
Lady Catherine de Bourgh	Pride and Prejudice	Jane Austen
Stephen Dedalus	A Portrait of the Artist as a Young Man, Ulysses	James Joyce
Sir Leicester Dedlock	Bleak House	Charles Dickens
Lady Dedlock	Bleak House	Charles Dickens
Madame Defarge	A Tale of Two Cities	Charles Dickens
Dick Dewy	Under The Greenwood Tree	Thomas Hardy
Mr. Dick	David Copperfield	Charles Dickens
Jim Dixon	Lucky Jim	Kingsley Amis
William Dobbin	Vanity Fair	William Makepeace Thackeray
Mr. Dombey	Dombey and Son	Charles Dickens
Florence Dombey	Dombey and Son	Charles Dickens
Don Quixote	Don Quixote de la Mancha	Miguel de Cervantes
Arabella Donn	Jude the Obscure	Thomas Hardy
Lorna Doone	Lorna Doone	R. D. Blackmore
Amy Dorrit *or* Little Dorrit	Little Dorrit	Charles Dickens
Fanny Dorrit	Little Dorrit	Charles Dickens
Tip Dorrit	Little Dorrit	Charles Dickens
William Dorrit	Little Dorrit	Charles Dickens
Edwin Drood	Edwin Drood	Charles Dickens
Bentley Drummle	Great Expectations	Charles Dickens
Catriona Drummond	Catriona	Robert Louis Stevenson
Alec D'Urberville	Tess of the D'Urbervilles	Thomas Hardy
Tess Durbeyfield	Tess of the D'Urbervilles	Thomas Hardy
Catherine Earnshaw	Wuthering Heights	Emily Brontë
Hareton Earnshaw	Wuthering Heights	Emily Brontë
Hindley Earnshaw	Wuthering Heights	Emily Brontë
Anne Elliot	Persuasion	Jane Austen
Elizabeth Elliot	Persuasion	Jane Austen
Sir Walter Elliot	Persuasion	Jane Austen
Em'ly	David Copperfield	Charles Dickens
Eppie	Silas Marner	George Eliot
Esmeralda	Notre Dame de Paris	Victor Hugo
Beatrix Esmond	Henry Esmond	William Makepeace Thackeray
Henry Esmond	Henry Esmond	William Makepeace Thackeray
Estella	Great Expectations	Charles Dickens
Bathsheba Everdene	Far from the Madding Crowd	Thomas Hardy
Jane Eyre	Jane Eyre	Charlotte Brontë
Fagin	Oliver Twist	Charles Dickens
Andrew Fairservice	Rob Roy	Sir Walter Scott
Donald Farfrae	The Mayor of Casterbridge	Thomas Hardy
Jude Fawley	Jude the Obscure	Thomas Hardy
Edward Ferrars	Sense and Sensibility	Jane Austen
Huck *or* Huckleberry Finn	Tom Sawyer, Huckleberry Finn	Mark Twain
Miss Flite	Bleak House	Charles Dickens
Julia Flyte	Brideshead Revisited	Evelyn Waugh
Sebastian Flyte	Brideshead Revisited	Evelyn Waugh
Phileas Fogg	Around the World in Eighty Days	Jules Verne
Man Friday	Robinson Crusoe	Daniel Defoe
Sarah Gamp	Martin Chuzzlewit	Charles Dickens
Joe Gargery	Great Expectations	Charles Dickens

Literary characters (continued)

Character	Book	Author
Jay Gatsby	The Great Gatsby	F. Scott Fitzgerald
Walter Gay	Dombey and Son	Charles Dickens
Solomon Gills	Dombey and Son	Charles Dickens
Louisa Gradgrind	Hard Times	Charles Dickens
Thomas Gradgrind	Hard Times	Charles Dickens
Tom Gradgrind	Hard Times	Charles Dickens
Mary Graham	Martin Chuzzlewit	Charles Dickens
Edith Granger	Dombey and Son	Charles Dickens
Dorian Gray	The Picture of Dorian Gray	Oscar Wilde
Mr. Grewgious	Edwin Drood	Charles Dickens
Mrs. Grundy	Speed the Plough	T. Morton
Ben Gunn	Treasure Island	Robert Louis Stevenson
Chris Guthrie	Sunset Song et al.	Lewis Grassic Gibbon
Ham	David Copperfield	Charles Dickens
Richard Hannay	The Thirty-nine Steps et al.	John Buchan
Emma Haredale	Barnaby Rudge	Charles Dickens
John Harmon	Our Mutual Friend	Charles Dickens
James Harthouse	Hard Times	Charles Dickens
Miss Havisham	Great Expectations	Charles Dickens
Sir Mulberry Hawk	Nicholas Nickleby	Charles Dickens
Jim Hawkins	Treasure Island	Robert Louis Stevenson
Bradley Headstone	Our Mutual Friend	Charles Dickens
Heathcliff	Wuthering Heights	Emily Brontë
Uriah Heep	David Copperfield	Charles Dickens
Michael Henchard	The Mayor of Casterbridge	Thomas Hardy
Lizzy Hexam	Our Mutual Friend	Charles Dickens
Betty Higden	Our Mutual Friend	Charles Dickens
Sherlock Holmes	The Adventures of Sherlock Holmes et al.	Sir Arthur Conan Doyle
Humbert Humbert	Lolita	Vladimir Nabokov
Mr. Hyde	The Strange Case of Dr. Jekyll and Mr. Hyde	Robert Louis Stevenson
Injun Joe	Tom Sawyer	Mark Twain
Ishmael	Moby Dick	Herman Melville
Jaggers	Great Expectations	Charles Dickens
John Jarndyce	Bleak House	Charles Dickens
Bailie Nicol Jarvie	Rob Roy	Sir Walter Scott
John Jasper	Edwin Drood	Charles Dickens
Jeeves	My Man Jeeves et al.	P. G. Wodehouse
Dr. Jekyll	The Strange Case of Dr. Jekyll and Mr. Hyde	Robert Louis Stevenson
Mrs. Jellyby	Bleak House	Charles Dickens
Mrs. Jennings	Sense and Sensibility	Jane Austen
Jim	Huckleberry Finn	Mark Twain
Lord Jim	Lord Jim	Joseph Conrad
Jingle	The Pickwick Papers	Charles Dickens
Jo	Bleak House	Charles Dickens
Cissy Jupe	Hard Times	Charles Dickens
Joseph K.	The Trial	Franz Kafka
George Knightley	Emma	Jane Austen
Krook	Bleak House	Charles Dickens
Kurtz	Heart of Darkness	Joseph Conrad
Will Ladislaw	Middlemarch	George Eliot
Helena Landless	Edwin Drood	Charles Dickens
Neville Landless	Edwin Drood	Charles Dickens
Edgar Linton	Wuthering Heights	Emily Brontë
Isabella Linton	Wuthering Heights	Emily Brontë
Dr. Livesey	Treasure Island	Robert Louis Stevenson
Tertius Lydgate	Middlemarch	George Eliot
Rob Roy Macgregor	Rob Roy	Sir Walter Scott
Randle P. McMurphy	One Flew Over the Cuckoo's Nest	Ken Kesey
Abel Magwitch	Great Expectations	Charles Dickens
Dr. Manette	A Tale of Two Cities	Charles Dickens
Lucie Manette	A Tale of Two Cities	Charles Dickens
Madame Mantalini	Nicholas Nickleby	Charles Dickens
The Marchioness	The Old Curiosity Shop	Charles Dickens
Jacob Marley	A Christmas Carol	Charles Dickens
Philip Marlowe	The Big Sleep et al.	Raymond Chandler

LITERARY CHARACTERS (CONTINUED)

Character	Book	Author
Silas Marner	Silas Marner	George Eliot
Stephen Maturin	Master and Commander et al.	Patrick O'Brian
Oliver Mellors	Lady Chatterley's Lover	D. H. Lawrence
Merdle	Little Dorrit	Charles Dickens
Mrs. Merdle	Little Dorrit	Charles Dickens
Wilkins Micawber	David Copperfield	Charles Dickens
Walter Mitty	The Secret Life of Walter Mitty	James Thurber
Lord Mohun	Henry Esmond	William Makepeace Thackeray
Monks	Oliver Twist	Charles Dickens
Dean Moriarty	On the Road	Jack Kerouac
Professor Moriarty	The Adventures of Sherlock Holmes et al.	Sir Arthur Conan Doyle
Dinah Morris	Adam Bede	George Eliot
Murdstone	David Copperfield	Charles Dickens
Mrs. Grundy	Hard Times	Charles Dickens
Baron Münchhausen	Münchhausen, Baron, Narrative of His Marvellous Travels	R. E. Raspe
Nancy	Oliver Twist	Charles Dickens
Little Nell	The Old Curiosity Shop	Charles Dickens
Captain Nemo	Twenty Thousand Leagues under the Sea	Jules Verne
Kate Nickleby	Nicholas Nickleby	Charles Dickens
Nicholas Nickleby	Nicholas Nickleby	Charles Dickens
Ralph Nickleby	Nicholas Nickleby	Charles Dickens
Newman Noggs	Nicholas Nickleby	Charles Dickens
Susan Nipper	Dombey and Son	Charles Dickens
Kit Nubbles	The Old Curiosity Shop	Charles Dickens
Gabriel Oak	Far from the Madding Crowd	Thomas Hardy
Glorvina O'Dowd	Vanity Fair	William Makepeace Thackeray
Major O'Dowd	Vanity Fair	William Makepeace Thackeray
Mrs. O'Dowd	Vanity Fair	William Makepeace Thackeray
Francis Osbaldistone	Rob Roy	Sir Walter Scott
Rashleigh Osbaldistone	Rob Roy	Sir Walter Scott
George Osborne	Vanity Fair	William Makepeace Thackeray
Pancks	Little Dorrit	Charles Dickens
Sancho Panza	Don Quixote de la Mancha	Miguel de Cervantes
Sal Paradise	On the Road	Jack Kerouac
Passepartout	Around the World in Eighty Days	Jules Verne
Pecksniff	Martin Chuzzlewit	Charles Dickens
Charity Pecksniff	Martin Chuzzlewit	Charles Dickens
Mercy Pecksniff	Martin Chuzzlewit	Charles Dickens
Peggoty	David Copperfield	Charles Dickens
Arthur Pendennis	Pendennis	William Makepeace Thackeray
Helen Pendennis	Pendennis	William Makepeace Thackeray
Pew	Treasure Island	Robert Louis Stevenson
Samuel Pickwick	The Pickwick Papers	Charles Dickens
Ruth Pinch	Martin Chuzzlewit	Charles Dickens
Tom Pinch	Martin Chuzzlewit	Charles Dickens
Pip *or* Philip Pirrip	Great Expectations	Charles Dickens
Herbert Pocket	Great Expectations	Charles Dickens
Charles Pooter	The Diary of a Nobody	G. and W. Grossmith
Martin Poyser	Adam Bede	George Eliot
Mrs. Poyser	Adam Bede	George Eliot
Fanny Price	Mansfield Park	Jane Austen
J. Alfred Prufrock	Prufrock and Other Observations	T. S. Eliot
Pumblechook	Great Expectations	Charles Dickens
Quasimodo	Notre Dame de Paris	Victor Hugo
Queequeg	Moby Dick	Herman Melville
Daniel Quilp	The Old Curiosity Shop	Charles Dickens
Roderick Random	Roderick Random	Tobias Smollett
Riah	Our Mutual Friend	Charles Dickens
Rogue Riderhood	Our Mutual Friend	Charles Dickens
Fanny Robin	Far from the Madding Crowd	Thomas Hardy
Mr. Rochester	Jane Eyre	Charlotte Brontë
Barnaby Rudge	Barnaby Rudge	Charles Dickens
Lady Russell	Persuasion	Jane Austen
Charles Ryder	Brideshead Revisited	Evelyn Waugh

LITERARY CHARACTERS (CONTINUED)

Character	Book	Author
Tom Sawyer	Tom Sawyer	Mark Twain
Scrooge	A Christmas Carol	Charles Dickens
Amelia Sedley	Vanity Fair	William Makepeace Thackeray
Jos Sedley	Vanity Fair	William Makepeace Thackeray
Tristram Shandy	The Life and Opinions of Tristram Shandy	Laurence Sterne
Becky *or* Rebecca Sharp	Vanity Fair	William Makepeace Thackeray
Bill Sikes	Oliver Twist	Charles Dickens
Long John Silver	Treasure Island	Robert Louis Stevenson
Harold Skimpole	Bleak House	Charles Dickens
Sleary	Hard Times	Charles Dickens
Smike	Nicholas Nickleby	Charles Dickens
Harriet Smith	Emma	Jane Austen
Winston Smith	1984	George Orwell
Augustus Snodgrass	The Pickwick Papers	Charles Dickens
Hetty Sorrel	Adam Bede	George Eliot
Lady Southdown	Vanity Fair	William Makepeace Thackeray
Mrs. Sparsit	Hard Times	Charles Dickens
Dora Spenlow	David Copperfield	Charles Dickens
Wackford Squeers	Nicholas Nickleby	Charles Dickens
Starbuck	Moby Dick	Herman Melville
Lucy Steele	Sense and Sensibility	Jane Austen
James Steerforth	David Copperfield	Charles Dickens
Lord Steyne	Vanity Fair	William Makepeace Thackeray
Esther Summerson	Bleak House	Charles Dickens
Dick Swiveller	The Old Curiosity Shop	Charles Dickens
Mark Tapley	Martin Chuzzlewit	Charles Dickens
Tartuffe	Tartuffe	Molière
Mr. Tartar	Edwin Drood	Charles Dickens
Tarzan	Tarzan of the Apes	Edgar Rice Burroughs
Becky Thatcher	Tom Sawyer	Mark Twain
Montague Tigg	Martin Chuzzlewit	Charles Dickens
Tiny Tim	A Christmas Carol	Charles Dickens
Mrs. Todgers	Martin Chuzzlewit	Charles Dickens
Toots	Dombey and Son	Charles Dickens
Traddles	David Copperfield	Charles Dickens
Squire Trelawney	Treasure Island	Robert Louis Stevenson
Fred Trent	The Old Curiosity Shop	Charles Dickens
Job Trotter	The Pickwick Papers	Charles Dickens
Betsey Trotwood	David Copperfield	Charles Dickens
Sergeant Troy	Far from the Madding Crowd	Thomas Hardy
Tulkinghorn	Bleak House	Charles Dickens
Tracy Tupman	The Pickwick Papers	Charles Dickens
Thomas Tusher	Henry Esmond	William Makepeace Thackeray
Oliver Twist	Oliver Twist	Charles Dickens
Gabriel Varden	Barnaby Rudge	Charles Dickens
Dolly Varden	Barnaby Rudge	Charles Dickens
Mr. Veneering	Our Mutual Friend	Charles Dickens
Mrs. Veneering	Our Mutual Friend	Charles Dickens
Diggory Venn	Return of the Native	Thomas Hardy
Diana Vernon	Rob Roy	Sir Walter Scott
Rosamond Vincy	Middlemarch	George Eliot
Johann Voss	Voss	Patrick White
Eustacia Vye	Return of the Native	Thomas Hardy
George Warrington	Pendennis	William Makepeace Thackeray
Dr. Watson	The Adventures of Sherlock Holmes et al.	Sir Arthur Conan Doyle
Silas Wegg	Our Mutual Friend	Charles Dickens
Sam Weller	The Pickwick Papers	Charles Dickens
Wemmick	Great Expectations	Charles Dickens
Frank Wentworth	Persuasion	Jane Austen
Agnes Wickfield	David Copperfield	Charles Dickens
George Wickham	Pride and Prejudice	Jane Austen
Damon Wildeve	Return of the Native	Thomas Hardy
Bella Wilfer	Our Mutual Friend	Charles Dickens
John Willoughby	Sense and Sensibility	Jane Austen
Nathaniel Winkle	The Pickwick Papers	Charles Dickens

LITERARY CHARACTERS (CONTINUED)

Character	Book	Author
Dolly Winthrop	Silas Marner	George Eliot
Allan Woodcourt	Bleak House	Charles Dickens
Emma Woodhouse	Emma	Jane Austen
Mr. Woodhouse	Emma	Jane Austen
Bertie Wooster	My Man Jeeves et al.	P. G. Wodehouse
Eugene Wrayburn	Our Mutual Friend	Charles Dickens
Jenny Wren	Our Mutual Friend	Charles Dickens
Clym Yeobright	Return of the Native	Thomas Hardy
Thomasin Yeobright	Return of the Native	Thomas Hardy
Yossarian	Catch-22	Joseph Heller
Yuri Zhivago	Doctor Zhivago	Boris Pasternak
Zorba *or* Alexis Zorbas	Zorba the Greek	Nikos Kazantzakis

live[2] **AS AN ADJECTIVE 1 = living**, alive, breathing, animate, existent, vital, quick *(archaic)* • *tests on live animals*
2 = not recorded, actual, real-time, unedited • *a live radio show*
3 = active, connected, switched on, unexploded • *A live bomb had earlier been defused.*
4 = burning, hot, glowing, blazing, ignited, alight, red hot, smouldering • *a big pan gurgling over live coals*
5 = topical, important, pressing, current, hot, burning, active, vital, controversial, unsettled, prevalent, pertinent, hot-button *(informal)* • *Directors' remuneration looks set to become a live issue.*
▸ **IN PHRASES: live wire = dynamo**, hustler *(U.S. & Canad. slang)*, ball of fire *(informal)*, life and soul of the party, go-getter *(informal)*, self-starter • *My sister's a real live wire, and full of fun.*

livelihood = occupation, work, employment, means, living, job, maintenance, subsistence, bread and butter *(informal)*, sustenance, (means of) support, (source of) income • *fishermen who depend on the seas for their livelihood.*

liveliness = energy, activity, spirit, vitality, animation, dynamism, gaiety, brio, quickness, vivacity, smartness, briskness, boisterousness, sprightliness • *Some may enjoy the liveliness of such as restaurant.*

lively 1 = animated, spirited, quick, keen, active, alert, dynamic, sparkling, vigorous, cheerful, energetic, outgoing, merry, upbeat *(informal)*, brisk, bubbly, nimble, agile, perky, chirpy *(informal)*, sparky, sprightly, vivacious, frisky, gay, alive and kicking, spry, chipper *(informal)*, blithe, full of beans *(informal)*, frolicsome, full of pep *(informal)*, blithesome, bright-eyed and bushy-tailed • *She had a sweet, lively personality.*
OPPOSITES: slow, dull, lifeless
2 = busy, crowded, stirring, buzzing, bustling, moving, eventful • *lively streets full of bars and cafés*
OPPOSITES: slow, dull
3 = vivid, strong, striking, bright, exciting, stimulating, bold, colourful, refreshing, forceful, racy, invigorating • *toys made with bright and lively colours*
OPPOSITES: dull
4 = enthusiastic, strong, keen, stimulating, eager, formidable, vigorous, animated, weighty • *The newspapers showed a lively interest in European developments.*

liven up 1 = stir, brighten, hot up *(informal)*, cheer up, perk up, buck up *(informal)* • *He livened up after midnight, relaxing a little.*
2 = cheer up, animate, rouse, enliven, perk up, brighten up, pep up, buck up *(informal)*, put life into, vitalize, vivify • *How could we decorate the room to liven it up?*

liver
▸ **RELATED ADJECTIVE:** hepatic

livery = costume, dress, clothing, suit, uniform, attire, garb, regalia, vestments, raiment *(archaic or poetic)* • *She was attended by servants in special livery.*

livestock = farm animals, stock, sheep, cattle • *The heavy rains and flooding killed scores of livestock.*

livid 1 = angry, cross, furious, outraged, mad *(informal)*, boiling, fuming, choked, infuriated, incensed, enraged, exasperated, indignant, pissed off *(taboo)*, incandescent, hot under the collar *(informal)*, fit to be tied *(slang)*, beside yourself, as black as thunder, tooshie *(Austral. slang)*, off the air *(Austral. slang)* • *I am absolutely livid about it.*
OPPOSITES: happy, pleased, delighted
2 = discoloured, angry, purple, bruised, black-and-blue, contused • *The scarred side of his face was a livid red.*

living AS A NOUN 1 = livelihood, work, job, maintenance, occupation, subsistence, bread and butter *(informal)*, sustenance, (means of) support, (source of) income • *He earns his living doing all kinds of things.*
2 = lifestyle, ways, situation, conduct, behaviour, customs, lifestyle, way of life, mode of living • *the stresses of modern living*
▸ **AS AN ADJECTIVE 1 = alive**, existing, moving, active, vital, breathing, lively, vigorous, animated, animate, alive and kicking, in the land of the living *(informal)*, quick *(archaic)* • *All things, whether living or dead, are believed to influence each other.*
OPPOSITES: late, dead, departed
2 = current, continuing, present, developing, active, contemporary, persisting, ongoing, operative, in use, extant • *a living language*
OPPOSITES: vanishing, obsolete, out-of-date

QUOTATIONS
The living are the dead on holiday
[Maurice Maeterlinck]

living room = lounge, parlour, sitting room, drawing room, front room, reception room, television room • *We were sitting in the living room watching TV.*

lizard
▸ **RELATED ADJECTIVES:** lacertilian, saurian
▹ *See panel* **Reptiles**

load AS A VERB 1 = fill, stuff, pack, pile, stack, heap, cram, freight, lade • *The three men had finished loading the truck.*
2 = pack, store, stuff, deposit, stack, put away, stow • *They had loaded all their equipment into the back of the truck.*
3 = make ready, charge, prime, prepare to fire • *I knew how to load and handle a gun.*
4 = insert, place, put in, stick in, pop in *(informal)* • *A technician loads a videotape onto one of the machines.*
▸ **AS A NOUN 1 = cargo**, lading, delivery, haul, shipment, batch, freight, bale, consignment • *He drove by with a big load of hay.*
2 = large amount, a lot, mass, ocean, pile *(informal)*, great deal, quantity, stacks, abundance • *They came up with a load of embarrassing information.*
3 = oppression, charge, pressure, worry, trouble, weight, responsibility, burden, affliction, onus, albatross, millstone,

encumbrance, incubus • *High blood pressure imposes an extra load on the heart.*
▸ **IN PHRASES: load someone down = burden**, worry, trouble, hamper, oppress, weigh down, saddle with, encumber, snow under • *I'm loaded down with work at the moment.*

loaded 1 = laden, full, charged, filled, weighted, burdened, freighted • *shoppers loaded with bags*
2 = charged, armed, primed, at the ready, ready to shoot *or* fire • *He turned up on her doorstep with a loaded gun.*
3 = tricky, charged, sensitive, delicate, manipulative, emotive, insidious, artful, prejudicial, tendentious • *That's a loaded question.*
4 = biased, weighted, rigged, distorted • *The press is loaded in favour of the government.*
5 = rich, wealthy, affluent, well off, rolling (*slang*), flush (*informal*), well-heeled (*informal*), well-to-do, moneyed, minted (*Brit. slang*) • *Her new boyfriend's absolutely loaded.*

loaf[1] **1 = lump**, block, cake, cube, slab • *a loaf of crusty bread*
2 = head, mind, sense, common sense, block (*informal*), nous (*Brit. slang*), chump (*Brit. slang*), gumption (*Brit. informal*), noddle (*informal, chiefly Brit.*) • *You've got to use your loaf in this game.*

loaf[2] **= idle**, hang around, take it easy, lie around, loiter, loll, laze, lounge around, doss (*Brit. slang*), veg out (*slang, chiefly U.S.*), be indolent • *She studied, and I just loafed around.*

loafer = idler, lounger, bum (*informal*), piker (*Austral. & N.Z. slang*), drone (*Brit.*), shirker, couch potato (*slang*), time-waster, layabout, skiver (*Brit. slang*), ne'er-do-well, wastrel, bludger (*Austral. & N.Z. informal*), lazybones (*informal*) • *a lovable loafer with a roving eye*

loan AS A NOUN = advance, credit, mortgage, accommodation, allowance, touch (*slang*), overdraft • *They want to make it easier for people to get a loan.*
▸ **AS A VERB = lend**, allow, credit, advance, accommodate, let out • *They asked us to loan our boat to them.*

loath *or* **loth = unwilling**, against, opposed, counter, resisting, reluctant, backward, averse, disinclined, indisposed • *She is loath to give up her hard-earned liberty.*
OPPOSITES: willing, keen, anxious

loathe = hate, dislike, despise, detest, abhor, abominate, have a strong aversion to, find disgusting, execrate, feel repugnance towards, not be able to bear *or* abide • *The two men loathe each other.*

loathing = hatred, hate, horror, disgust, aversion, revulsion, antipathy, abomination, repulsion, abhorrence, repugnance, odium, detestation, execration • *She looked at him with loathing.*

loathsome = hateful, offensive, nasty, disgusting, horrible, revolting, obscene, vile, obnoxious, repulsive, nauseating, odious, repugnant, abhorrent, abominable, execrable, detestable, yucky *or* yukky (*slang*), yucko (*Austral. slang*) • *the loathsome spectacle we were obliged to witness*
OPPOSITES: attractive, engaging, delightful

lob = throw, launch, toss, hurl, lift, pitch, shy (*informal*), fling, loft • *The protestors were chanting and lobbing firebombs.*

lobby AS A VERB = campaign, press, pressure, push, influence, promote, urge, persuade, appeal, petition, pull strings (*Brit. informal*), exert influence, bring pressure to bear, solicit votes • *Gun control advocates are lobbying hard for new laws.*
▸ **AS A NOUN 1 = pressure group**, group, camp, faction, lobbyists, interest group, special-interest group, ginger group, public-interest group (*U.S. & Canad.*) • *Agricultural interests are some of the most powerful lobbies there.*
2 = corridor, hall, passage, entrance, porch, hallway, foyer, passageway, entrance hall, vestibule • *I met her in the lobby of the museum.*

lobbyist = persuader, manager, influencer, publicist, motivator, pressurizer, press agent • *a parliamentary lobbyist for a disabled rights group*

lobola = dowry, portion, marriage settlement, dot (*archaic*) • *Following the tradition of lobola, the king's family paid 40 head of cattle for his new wife.*

lobster
▸ **NAME OF MALE:** cock
▸ **NAME OF FEMALE:** hen

local AS AN ADJECTIVE 1 = community, district, regional, provincial, parish, neighbourhood, small-town (*chiefly U.S.*), parochial, parish pump • *I was going to pop up to the local library.*
2 = nearby, close, community, near, neighbouring • *We try to support the local shops.*
3 = confined, limited, narrow, restricted • *The blockage caused a local infection.*
▸ **AS A NOUN 1 = resident**, native, inhabitant, character (*informal*), local yokel (*disparaging*) • *That's what the locals call the place.*
2 = pub, bar, inn, tavern, counter, lounge, saloon, canteen, public house, watering hole (*facetious slang*), boozer (*Brit., Austral. & N.Z. informal*), beer parlour (*Canad.*), beverage room (*Canad.*), hostelry (*archaic or facetious*), taproom • *The Black Horse is my local.*

locale = site, place, setting, position, spot, scene, location, venue, locality, locus • *An amusement park is the perfect locale for adventures.*

locality 1 = neighbourhood, area, region, district, vicinity, neck of the woods (*informal*) • *Details of the drinking water quality in your locality can be obtained.*
2 = site, place, setting, position, spot, scene, location, locale • *Such a locality is popularly referred to as a 'hot spot'.*

localize 1 = ascribe, specify, assign, pinpoint, narrow down • *Examine the area carefully in order to localize the most tender point.*
2 = restrict, limit, contain, concentrate, confine, restrain, circumscribe, delimit • *There was an attempt to localize the benefits of the university's output.*

localized = contained, limited, restricted, confined • *localized breast cancer*

locate 1 = find, discover, detect, come across, track down, pinpoint, unearth, pin down, lay your hands on, run to earth *or* ground • *We've simply been unable to locate him.*
2 = place, put, set, position, seat, site, establish, settle, fix, situate • *It was voted the best city to locate a business.*

located = situated, placed, positioned, sited • *The restaurant is located near the cathedral.*

location = place, point, setting, position, situation, spot, venue, whereabouts, locus, locale • *the city's newest luxury hotel has a beautiful location.*

lock[1] **AS A VERB 1 = fasten**, close, secure, shut, bar, seal, bolt, latch, sneck (*dialect*) • *Are you sure you locked the front door?*
2 = unite, join, link, engage, mesh, clench, entangle, interlock, entwine • *He locked his fingers behind his head.*
3 = embrace, press, grasp, clutch, hug, enclose, grapple, clasp, encircle • *He locked her in a passionate clinch.*
▸ **AS A NOUN = fastening**, catch, bolt, clasp, padlock • *He heard her key turning in the lock.*
▸ **IN PHRASES: lock someone out = shut out**, bar, ban, exclude, keep out, debar, refuse admittance to • *My husband's locked me out.*
lock someone up = imprison, jail, confine, cage, detain, shut up, incarcerate, send down (*informal*), send to prison, put behind bars • *You're mad. You should be locked up.*

lock[2] **= strand**, curl, tuft, tress, ringlet • *She brushed a lock of hair off his forehead.*

locker = safe, cabinet, cupboard, compartment • *The stolen items were found in his locker at work.*

locomotion = **movement**, travel, travelling, moving, action, progress, motion, progression, headway • *He specialises in the mechanics of locomotion.*

locution 1 = **manner of speech**, style, phrasing, accent, articulation, inflection, intonation, diction • *The cadence and locution of his voice resonates horribly.*
2 = **expression**, wording, term, phrase, idiom, collocation, turn of speech • *'Sister boy' – that's an odd locution if ever there was one.*

lodestar = **guide**, standard, model, pattern, signal, par, role model, beacon, guiding light • *She was the one lodestar of his life.*

lodge AS A NOUN 1 = **cabin**, house, shelter, cottage, hut, chalet, gatehouse, hunting lodge • *a ski lodge*
2 = **society**, group, club, association, section, wing, chapter, branch, assemblage • *My father would occasionally go to his Masonic lodge.*
▸ AS A VERB 1 = **register**, put, place, set, lay, enter, file, deposit, submit, put on record • *He has four weeks in which to lodge an appeal.*
2 = **stay**, room, stop, board, reside, sojourn • *She lodged with a farming family.*
3 = **accommodate**, house, shelter, put up, entertain, harbour, quarter, billet • *They questioned me, then lodged me in a children's home.*
4 = **stick**, remain, catch, implant, come to rest, become fixed, imbed • *The bullet lodged in the sergeant's leg.*

lodger = **tenant**, roomer, guest, resident, boarder, paying guest • *She took in a lodger to help with the mortgage.*

lodging *often plural* = **accommodation**, rooms, boarding, apartments, quarters, digs *(Brit. informal)*, shelter, residence, dwelling, abode, habitation, bachelor apartment *(Canad.)* • *He was given free meals and lodgings.*

lofty 1 = **noble**, grand, distinguished, superior, imposing, renowned, elevated, majestic, dignified, stately, sublime, illustrious, exalted • *Amid the chaos, he had lofty aims.*
OPPOSITES: mean, low, humble
2 = **high**, raised, towering, tall, soaring, elevated, sky-high • *a light, lofty apartment*
OPPOSITES: low, short, dwarfed
3 = **haughty**, lordly, proud, arrogant, patronizing, condescending, snooty *(informal)*, disdainful, supercilious, high and mighty *(informal)*, toffee-nosed *(slang, chiefly Brit.)* • *the lofty disdain he often expresses for his profession*
OPPOSITES: warm, friendly, modest

log AS A NOUN 1 = **stump**, block, branch, chunk, trunk, bole, piece of timber • *He dumped the logs on the big stone hearth.*
2 = **record**, listing, account, register, journal, chart, diary, tally, logbook, daybook, blog *(informal)* • *The complaint was recorded in the ship's log.*
▸ AS A VERB = **record**, report, enter, book, note, register, chart, put down, tally, set down, make a note of • *Details of the crime are logged in the computer.*

loggerhead IN PHRASES: **at loggerheads** = **quarrelling**, opposed, feuding, at odds, estranged, in dispute, at each other's throats, at daggers drawn, at enmity • *Dentists and the health department have been at loggerheads over fees.*

logic 1 = **science of reasoning**, deduction, dialectics, argumentation, ratiocination, syllogistic reasoning • *Students learn philosophy and logic.*
2 = **connection**, rationale, coherence, relationship, link, chain of thought • *I don't follow the logic of your argument.*
3 = **reason**, reasoning, sense, good reason, good sense, sound judgment • *The plan was based on sound commercial logic.*

logical 1 = **rational**, clear, reasoned, reasonable, sound, relevant, consistent, valid, coherent, pertinent, well-organized, cogent, well-reasoned, deducible • *a logical argument*
OPPOSITES: unreasonable, irrational, illogical
2 = **reasonable**, obvious, sensible, most likely, natural, necessary, wise, plausible, judicious • *There was a logical explanation.*
OPPOSITES: unlikely, unreasonable, illogical

logistics = **organization**, management, strategy, engineering, plans, masterminding, coordination, orchestration • *the logistics of getting such a big show on the road*

logo = **trademark**, figure, design, device, symbol, token, badge, crest, motif, motto, emblem, insignia, colophon • *The letter bore no company name or logo.*

loin
▸ TECHNICAL NAME: lumbus
▸ RELATED ADJECTIVE: lumbar

loiter = **linger**, idle, loaf, saunter, delay, stroll, lag, dally, loll, dawdle, skulk, dilly-dally *(informal)*, hang about *or* around • *unemployed young men loitering at the entrance to the factory.*

loll 1 = **lounge**, relax, lean, slump, flop, sprawl, loaf, slouch, recline, outspan *(S. African)* • *He lolled back in his comfortable chair.*
2 = **droop**, drop, hang, flop, flap, dangle, sag, hang loosely • *his tongue lolling out of the side of his mouth*

London
QUOTATIONS
When a man is tired of London, he is tired of life; for there is in London all that life can afford
[Dr. Johnson]
London: a nation, not a city
[Benjamin Disraeli]
London, that great cesspool into which all the loungers and idlers of the Empire are irresistibly drained
[Sir Arthur Conan Doyle *A Study in Scarlet*]
city of refuge, the mansion-house of liberty
[John Milton *Areopagitica*]

lone 1 = **solitary**, single, separate, one, only, sole, by yourself, unaccompanied • *a lone woman motorist*
2 = **single**, on your own, unmarried, separated, unattached, without a partner • *a lone parent*
3 = **isolated**, deserted, remote, secluded, lonesome *(chiefly U.S. & Canad.)*, godforsaken • *a lone tree on a hill*

loneliness = **solitude**, isolation, desolation, seclusion, aloneness, dreariness, solitariness, forlornness, lonesomeness *(chiefly U.S. & Canad.)*, desertedness • *Deep down I have a fear of loneliness.*
QUOTATIONS
Alone, alone, all, all alone,
Alone on a wide wide sea!
And never a saint took pity on
My soul in agony
[Samuel Taylor Coleridge *The Ancient Mariner*]

lonely 1 = **solitary**, alone, isolated, abandoned, lone, withdrawn, single, estranged, outcast, forsaken, forlorn, destitute, by yourself, lonesome *(chiefly U.S. & Canad.)*, friendless, companionless • *lonely people who just want to talk*
OPPOSITES: together, popular, accompanied
2 = **desolate**, deserted, remote, isolated, solitary, out-of-the-way, secluded, uninhabited, sequestered, off the beaten track *(informal)*, godforsaken, unfrequented • *dark, lonely streets*
OPPOSITES: crowded, frequented, bustling

loner = **individualist**, outsider, solitary, maverick, hermit, recluse, misanthrope, lone wolf • *I'm very much a loner – I never go out.*

lonesome = **lonely**, deserted, isolated, lone, gloomy, dreary, desolate, forlorn, friendless, cheerless, companionless • *I've grown so lonesome, thinking of you.*

long[1] 1 = **elongated**, extended, stretched, expanded, extensive, lengthy, far-reaching, spread out • *Her legs were long and thin.*
OPPOSITES: little, small, short

l

2 = **prolonged**, slow, dragging, sustained, lengthy, lingering, protracted, interminable, spun out, long-drawn-out • *This is a long film, three hours and seven minutes.*
OPPOSITES: short, quick, brief

long² = **desire**, want, wish, burn, dream of, pine, hunger, ache, lust, crave, yearn, covet, itch, hanker, set your heart on, eat your heart out over • *He longed for the good old days.*

long-awaited = **expected**, wanted, promised, looked-for, predicted, forecast, awaited, hoped-for, anticipated, counted on • *the long-awaited signing of a peace agreement*

long-drawn-out = **prolonged**, marathon, lengthy, protracted, interminable, spun out, dragged out, overlong, overextended • *a long-drawn-out election campaign*

longed-for = **sought-after**, wanted, desirable, in demand, coveted, enviable, to-die-for, like gold dust • *the wet weather that prevented our longed-for picnic*

longing AS A NOUN = **desire**, hope, wish, burning, urge, ambition, hunger, yen *(informal)*, hungering, aspiration, ache, craving, yearning, coveting, itch, thirst, hankering • *He felt a longing for the familiar.*
OPPOSITES: disgust, loathing, indifference
▸ AS AN ADJECTIVE = **yearning**, anxious, eager, burning, hungry, pining, craving, languishing, ardent, avid, wishful, wistful, desirous • *sharp intakes of breath and longing looks*
OPPOSITES: cold, disgusted, indifferent

long-lasting = **enduring**, lasting, continuing, remaining, surviving, permanent, prevailing, persisting, persistent, eternal, abiding, perennial, durable, immortal, steadfast • *one of the long-lasting effects of the infection*

long-lived = **long-lasting**, enduring, full of years, old as Methuselah, longevous • *long-lived radioactive material*

long-standing = **established**, fixed, enduring, abiding, long-lasting, long-lived, long-established, time-honoured • *a long-standing dispute*

long-suffering = **uncomplaining**, patient, resigned, forgiving, tolerant, easy-going, stoical, forbearing • *He went back to join his loyal, long-suffering wife.*

long-winded = **rambling**, prolonged, lengthy, tedious, diffuse, tiresome, wordy, long-drawn-out, garrulous, discursive, repetitious, overlong, verbose, prolix • *The manifesto is long-winded and repetitious.*
OPPOSITES: brief, short, to the point

look AS A VERB 1 = **see**, view, consider, watch, eye, study, check, regard, survey, clock *(Brit. slang)*, examine, observe, stare, glance, gaze, scan, check out *(informal)*, inspect, gape, peep, behold *(archaic)*, goggle, eyeball *(slang)*, scrutinize, ogle, gawp *(Brit. slang)*, gawk, recce *(slang)*, get a load of *(informal)*, take a gander at *(informal)*, rubberneck *(slang)*, take a dekko at *(Brit. slang)*, feast your eyes upon • *She turned to look at him.*
2 = **search**, seek, hunt, forage, fossick *(Austral. & N.Z.)* • *Have you looked on the piano?*
3 = **consider**, contemplate, study • *Next term we'll be looking at the Second World War period.*
4 = **face**, overlook, front on, give onto • *The terrace looks onto the sea.*
5 = **hope**, expect, await, anticipate, reckon on • *We're not looking to make a fortune.*
6 = **seem**, appear, display, seem to be, look like, exhibit, manifest, strike you as • *She was looking miserable.*
▸ AS A NOUN 1 = **glimpse**, view, glance, observation, review, survey, sight, examination, gaze, inspection, peek, squint *(informal)*, butcher's *(Brit. slang)*, gander *(informal)*, once-over *(informal)*, recce *(slang)*, eyeful *(informal)*, look-see *(slang)*, shufti *(Brit. slang)* • *She took a last look in the mirror.*
2 = **appearance**, effect, bearing, face, air, style, fashion, cast, aspect, manner, expression, impression, complexion, guise, countenance, semblance, demeanour, mien *(literary)* • *They've opted for a rustic look in the kitchen.*
▸ IN PHRASES: **look after something** *or* **someone** = **take care of**, mind, watch, protect, tend, guard, nurse, care for, supervise, sit with, attend to, keep an eye on, take charge of • *I love looking after the children.*
look back on something = **remember**, reflect on, think about, recall, think back on, bring to mind • *Looking back on it all, I'm amazed how we managed to do it on time.*
look down on *or* **upon someone** = **disdain**, despise, scorn, sneer at, spurn, hold in contempt, treat with contempt, turn your nose up (at) *(informal)*, contemn *(formal)*, look down your nose at *(informal)*, misprize • *I wasn't successful, so they looked down on me.*
look forward to something = **anticipate**, expect, look for, wait for, await, hope for, long for, count on, count the days until, set your heart on • *He was looking forward to working with the new Prime Minister.*
look into something = **investigate**, study, research, go into, examine, explore, probe, follow up, check out, inspect, look over, delve into, scrutinize, inquire about, make inquiries about • *He had once looked into buying an island.*
look like something = **investigate**, echo, take after, remind you of, be the image of, make you think of, put you in mind of • *They look like stars to the naked eye.*
look on *or* **upon something** *or* **someone** = **consider**, believe in, rate, judge, regard, deem, hold to be • *A lot of people looked on him as a healer.*
look out for something = **be careful of**, beware, watch out for, pay attention to, be wary of, be alert to, be vigilant about, keep an eye out for, be on guard for, keep your eyes open for, keep your eyes peeled for, keep your eyes skinned for, be on the qui vive for • *What are the symptoms to look out for?*
look over something = **examine**, view, check, monitor, scan, check out *(informal)*, inspect, look through, eyeball *(slang)*, work over, flick through, peruse, cast an eye over, take a dekko at *(Brit. slang)* • *He could have looked over the papers in less than ten minutes.*
look someone up = **visit**, call on, go to see, pay a visit to, drop in on *(informal)*, look in on • *She looked up some friends of bygone years.*
look something up = **research**, find, search for, hunt for, track down, seek out • *I looked up your name and address in the personnel file.*
look to something = **turn your thoughts to**, consider, think about, contemplate • *Let's look to the future now.*
look to something *or* **someone** = **turn to**, resort to, make use of, fall back on, have recourse to, avail yourself of • *So many of us are looking to alternative therapies.*
look up = **improve**, develop, advance, pick up, progress, come along, get better, shape up *(informal)*, perk up, ameliorate, show improvement • *Things are looking up in the computer industry.*
look up to someone = **respect**, honour, admire, esteem, revere, defer to, have a high opinion of, regard highly, think highly of • *A lot of the younger girls look up to you.*

PROVERBS
Look before you leap

lookalike = **double**, twin, clone, replica, spit *(informal, chiefly Brit.)*, ringer *(slang)*, spitting image *(informal)*, dead ringer *(slang)*, living image, exact match, spit and image *(informal)* • *a Marilyn Monroe lookalike*

lookout 1 = **watchman**, guard, sentry, sentinel, vedette *(Military)* • *One committed the burglary and the other acted as lookout.*
2 = **watch**, guard, vigil, qui vive • *He denied that he had failed to keep a proper lookout during the night.*
3 = **watchtower**, post, tower, beacon, observatory, citadel, observation post • *Troops tried to set up a lookout post inside a refugee camp.*

4 = **concern**, business, worry, funeral *(informal)*, pigeon *(Brit. informal)* • *It was your lookout if you put your life in danger.*
5 = **prospect**, view, future, outlook, likelihood • *If this is true, it's a poor lookout for future generations.*

loom 1 = **appear**, emerge, hover, take shape, threaten, bulk, menace, come into view, become visible • *the bleak mountains that loomed out of the blackness*
2 = **overhang**, rise, mount, dominate, tower, soar, overshadow, hang over, rise up, overtop • *He loomed over me.*
3 = **threaten**, be close, menace, be imminent, impend • *The threat of renewed civil war looms.*

loony AS AN ADJECTIVE = **insane**, strange, mental *(slang)*, mad, out there *(slang)*, crazy *(informal)*, nuts *(slang)*, bananas *(slang)*, barking *(slang)*, raving, distracted, eccentric, frantic, frenzied, unstable, crackers *(Brit. slang)*, batty *(slang)*, crazed, lunatic, psychotic, demented, cuckoo *(informal)*, unbalanced, barmy *(slang)*, nutty *(slang)*, deranged, delirious, rabid, bonkers *(slang, chiefly Brit.)*, flaky *(U.S. slang)*, unhinged, loopy *(informal)*, crackpot *(informal)*, out to lunch *(informal)*, round the bend *(Brit. slang)*, barking mad *(slang)*, out of your mind, gonzo *(slang)*, screwy *(informal)*, doolally *(slang)*, off your head *(slang)*, off your trolley *(slang)*, round the twist *(Brit. slang)*, up the pole *(informal)*, of unsound mind, as daft as a brush *(informal, chiefly Brit.)*, lost your marbles *(informal)*, not right in the head, non compos mentis *(Latin)*, off your rocker *(slang)*, not the full shilling *(informal)*, off your nut *(slang)*, off your chump *(slang)*, wacko *or* whacko *(informal)*, off the air *(Austral. slang)*, daggy *(Austral. & N.Z. informal)* • *She's as loony as her brother!*
▸ AS A NOUN = **mad person**, lunatic, nut *(slang)*, psycho *(slang)*, maniac, psychotic, madman, psychopath, nutter *(Brit. slang)*, basket case *(slang)*, nutcase *(slang)*, madwoman, headcase *(informal)*, mental case *(slang)*, headbanger *(informal)*, crazy *(informal)* • *At first they all though I was a loony.*

loop AS A NOUN = **curve**, ring, circle, bend, twist, curl, spiral, hoop, coil, loophole, twirl, kink, noose, whorl, eyelet, convolution • *She reached for a loop of garden hose.*
▸ AS A VERB 1 = **twist**, turn, join, roll, circle, connect, bend, fold, knot, curl, spiral, coil, braid, encircle, wind round, curve round • *He looped the rope over the wood.*
2 = **turn**, roll, circle, bend, twist, curve • *The helicopter looped west, making for the hills.*

loophole = **let-out**, escape, excuse, plea, avoidance, evasion, pretence, pretext, subterfuge, means of escape • *They exploit some loophole in the law to avoid prosecution.*

loose AS AN ADJECTIVE 1 = **free**, detached, insecure, unfettered, released, floating, wobbly, unsecured, unrestricted, untied, unattached, movable, unfastened, unbound, unconfined • *A page came loose and floated onto the tiles.*
2 = **untethered**, free, roaming, at large, on the run, fugitive, unconfined • *He was chased by a loose dog.*
OPPOSITES: tied, secured, tethered
3 = **slack**, easy, hanging, relaxed, loosened, not fitting, sloppy, baggy, slackened, loose-fitting, not tight • *Wear loose clothes as they're more comfortable.*
OPPOSITES: tight
4 = **promiscuous**, fast, abandoned, immoral, dissipated, lewd, wanton, profligate, disreputable, debauched, dissolute, libertine, licentious, unchaste • *casual sex and loose morals*
OPPOSITES: moral, disciplined, chaste
5 = **vague**, random, inaccurate, disordered, rambling, diffuse, indefinite, disconnected, imprecise, ill-defined, indistinct, inexact • *We came to some sort of loose arrangement before he went home.*
OPPOSITES: clear, accurate, precise
6 = **careless**, rash, lax, negligent, thoughtless, imprudent, heedless, unmindful • *part of a campaign aimed at educating employees on the perils of loose lips*
▸ AS A VERB = **free**, release, ease, liberate, detach, unleash, let go, undo, loosen, disconnect, set free, slacken, untie, disengage, unfasten, unbind, unloose, unbridle • *He loosed his grip on the rifle.*
OPPOSITES: bind, capture, fasten
▸ IN PHRASES: **at a loose end** = **idle**, with nothing to do • *They're most likely to get into trouble when they're at a loose end.*
on the loose = **free**, roaming, at large, on the run, untied, at liberty, unrestrained, unchained, unconfined • *A man-eating lion is on the loose.*

loose-limbed = **limber**, plastic, flexible, graceful, elastic, supple, agile, lithe, pliable, pliant, lissom(e), loose-jointed • *a loose-limbed, feline figure wearing black gloves*

loosen AS A VERB 1 = **untie**, undo, release, separate, detach, let out, unstick, slacken, unbind, work free, work loose, unloose • *He loosened the scarf around his neck.*
2 = **slacken**, ease, work free, work loose • *The ties that bind them are loosening.*
3 = **weaken**, relax, lessen, release, reduce, slacken • *There is no sign that the Party will loosen its grip on the country.*
▸ IN PHRASES: **loosen up** = **relax**, chill *(slang)*, soften, unwind, go easy *(informal)*, lighten up *(slang)*, hang loose, outspan *(S. African)*, ease up *or* off • *Relax, smile; loosen up in mind and body.*

loot AS A VERB = **plunder**, rob, raid, sack, rifle, ravage, ransack, pillage, despoil • *Gangs began breaking windows and looting shops.*
▸ AS A NOUN = **plunder**, goods, prize, haul, spoils, booty, swag *(slang)* • *They steal in order to sell their loot for cash.*

lop = **cut**, crop, chop, trim, clip, dock, hack, detach, prune, shorten, sever, curtail, truncate • *Someone lopped the heads off our tulips.*

lope = **stride**, spring, bound, gallop, canter, lollop • *He was loping across the sand towards me.*

lopsided = **crooked**, one-sided, tilting, warped, uneven, unequal, disproportionate, squint, unbalanced, off balance, awry, askew, out of shape, asymmetrical, cockeyed, out of true, skewwhiff *(Brit. informal)* • *a friendly lopsided grin*

loquacious = **talkative**, chattering, babbling, chatty, wordy, garrulous, gabby *(informal)*, voluble, gossipy, gassy *(informal)*, blathering • *The normally loquacious man said little.*

loquacity = **talkativeness**, chattering, babbling, gabbling, volubility, effusiveness, chattiness, garrulity, gassiness *(informal)* • *The drug induces euphoria, alertness and loquacity.*

lord AS A NOUN 1 = **peer**, nobleman, count, duke, gentleman, earl, noble, baron, aristocrat, viscount, childe *(archaic)* • *She married a lord and lives in a huge house in the country.*
2 = **ruler**, leader, chief, king, prince, master, governor, commander, superior, monarch, sovereign, liege, overlord, potentate, seigneur • *It was the home of the powerful lords of Baux.*
3 = **ruler**, chief, baron, tycoon, heavyweight *(informal)*, bigwig *(informal)*, big shot *(informal)*, big wheel *(slang)*, big noise *(informal)*, heavy hitter *(informal)* • *the lords of the black market*
▸ IN PHRASES: **lord it over someone** = **boss around** *or* **about** *(informal)*, order around, threaten, bully, menace, intimidate, hector, bluster, browbeat, ride roughshod over, pull rank on, tyrannize, put on airs, be overbearing, act big *(slang)*, overbear, play the lord, domineer • *Alex seemed to enjoy lording it over the three girls.*
the Lord *or* **Our Lord** = **Jesus Christ**, God, Christ, Messiah, Jehovah, the Almighty, the Galilean, the Good Shepherd, the Nazarene • *Ask the Lord to help you in your times of trouble.*

lordly 1 = **proud**, arrogant, lofty, stuck-up *(informal)*, patronizing, dictatorial, condescending, imperious, domineering, overbearing, haughty, tyrannical, despotic, disdainful, high-handed, supercilious, high and mighty

(informal), toffee-nosed *(slang, chiefly Brit.)*, hoity-toity *(informal)* • *their lordly indifference to patients*
2 = **noble**, grand, princely, imperial, majestic, dignified, regal, stately, aristocratic, lofty, gracious, exalted • *the site of a lordly mansion*

lore 1 = **traditions**, sayings, experience, saws, teaching, beliefs, wisdom, doctrine, mythos, folk-wisdom, traditional wisdom • *the Book of the Sea, which was stuffed with sailors' lore.*
2 = **learning**, knowledge, know-how *(informal)*, scholarship, letters, erudition • *prophets and diviners, knowledgeable in the lore of the stars*

lorry = **truck**, van, juggernaut, HGV, heavy-goods vehicle, bakkie *(S. African)* • *a seven-ton lorry*

lose AS A VERB 1 = **be defeated**, be beaten, lose out, be worsted, come to grief, come a cropper *(informal)*, be the loser, suffer defeat, get the worst of, take a licking *(informal)* • *The government lost the argument over the pace of reform.*
2 = **mislay**, miss, drop, forget, displace, be deprived of, fail to keep, lose track of, suffer loss, misplace • *I lost my keys.*
3 = **forfeit**, miss, fail, yield, default, be deprived of, pass up *(informal)*, lose out on *(informal)* • *He lost his licence.*
4 = **waste**, consume, squander, drain, exhaust, lavish, deplete, use up, dissipate, expend, misspend • *He stands to lose millions of pounds.*
5 = **miss**, waste, ignore, disregard, squander, forfeit • *The press lost no opportunity to create the impression that she was guilty.*
6 = **stray from**, miss, confuse, wander from • *The men lost their way in a sandstorm.*
7 = **escape from**, pass, leave behind, evade, lap, duck, dodge, shake off, elude, slip away from, outstrip, throw off, outrun, outdistance, give someone the slip • *I couldn't lose him, but he couldn't overtake.*
▸ IN PHRASES: **lose out** = **miss out on**, be defeated, be unsuccessful • *Women have lost out in this new flexible pay system.*

PROVERBS
You cannot lose what you never had

loser = **failure**, flop *(informal)*, underdog, also-ran, no-hoper *(Austral. slang)*, dud *(informal)*, lemon *(slang)*, clinker *(slang, chiefly U.S.)*, washout *(informal)*, non-achiever • *the winners and losers of this year's Super Bowl*

QUOTATIONS
Show me a good loser and I will show you a loser
[Paul Newman]

loss AS A NOUN 1 = **mislaying**, losing, misplacing • *We can help you in case of loss of money or baggage.*
2 = **losing**, waste, disappearance, deprivation, squandering, drain, forfeiture • *The loss of income is about £250 million.*
OPPOSITES: finding, gain
3 = **death**, grief, demise, bereavement, passing away, decease • *Surviving the loss of a loved one has made me feel old.*
4 *sometimes plural* = **deficit**, debt, deficiency, debit, depletion, shrinkage, losings • *The company will cease operating due to continued losses.*
OPPOSITES: gain
5 = **damage**, cost, injury, hurt, harm, disadvantage, detriment, impairment • *His death is a great loss to us.*
OPPOSITES: advantage, recovery, restoration
▸ AS A PLURAL NOUN = **casualties**, dead, victims, death toll, fatalities, number killed, number wounded • *Enemy losses were said to be high.*
▸ IN PHRASES: **at a loss** = **confused**, puzzled, baffled, bewildered, stuck *(informal)*, helpless, stumped, perplexed, mystified, nonplussed, at your wits' end • *I was at a loss for what to do next.*

PROVERBS
One man's loss is another man's gain

lost 1 = **missing**, missed, disappeared, vanished, strayed, wayward, forfeited, misplaced, mislaid • *a lost book*
2 = **off-course**, stray, at sea, adrift, astray, disoriented, disorientated, off-track, gone astray, having lost your bearings • *I think we're lost.*
3 = **bewildered**, confused, puzzled, baffled, helpless, ignorant, perplexed, mystified, clueless *(slang)* • *I feel lost and lonely in a strange town alone.*
4 = **wasted**, consumed, neglected, misused, squandered, forfeited, dissipated, misdirected, frittered away, misspent, misapplied • *a lost opportunity*
5 = **gone**, finished, destroyed, vanished, extinct, defunct, died out • *The sense of community is lost.*
6 = **past**, former, gone, dead, forgotten, lapsed, extinct, obsolete, out-of-date, bygone, unremembered • *the relics of a lost civilization*
7 = **engrossed**, taken up, absorbed, entranced, abstracted, absent, distracted, preoccupied, immersed, dreamy, rapt, spellbound • *She was silent for a while, lost in thought.*
8 = **fallen**, corrupt, depraved, wanton, abandoned, damned, profligate, dissolute, licentious, unchaste, irreclaimable • *without honour, without heart, without religion ... a lost woman*

lot AS A NOUN 1 = **bunch** *(informal)*, group, crowd, crew, set, band, quantity, assortment, consignment • *We've just sacked one lot of builders.*
2 = **destiny**, situation, circumstances, fortune, chance, accident, fate, portion, doom, hazard, plight • *Young people are usually less contented with their lot.*
3 = **share**, group, set, piece, collection, portion, parcel, batch • *The receivers are keen to sell the stores as one lot.*
▸ IN PHRASES: **a lot** *or* **lots** 1 = **plenty**, scores, masses *(informal)*, load(s) *(informal)*, ocean(s), wealth, piles *(informal)*, a great deal, quantities, stack(s), heap(s), a good deal, large amount, abundance, reams *(informal)*, oodles *(informal)* • *A lot of our land is used to grow crops.*
2 = **often**, regularly, a great deal, frequently, a good deal • *They went out a lot when they lived in the city.*
draw lots = **choose**, pick, select, toss up, draw straws *(informal)*, throw dice, spin a coin • *Two names were selected by drawing lots.*
throw in your lot with someone = **join with**, support, join forces with, make common cause with, align yourself with, ally *or* align yourself with, join fortunes with • *He has decided to throw in his lot with the far-right groups.*

lotion = **cream**, solution, balm, salve, liniment, embrocation • *suntan lotion*

lottery 1 = **raffle**, draw, lotto *(Brit., N.Z. & S. African)*, sweepstake • *the national lottery*
2 = **gamble**, chance, risk, venture, hazard, toss-up *(informal)* • *Which judges are assigned to a case is always a bit of a lottery.*

lotto = **lottery**, national lottery, draw, raffle, sweepstake • *If you won the lotto, what would you do with the money?*

loud 1 = **noisy**, strong, booming, roaring, piercing, thundering, forte *(Music)*, turbulent, resounding, deafening, thunderous, rowdy, blaring, strident, boisterous, tumultuous, vociferous, vehement, sonorous, ear-splitting, obstreperous, stentorian, clamorous, ear-piercing, high-sounding • *Suddenly there was a loud bang.*
OPPOSITES: low, soft, quiet
2 = **garish**, bold, glaring, flamboyant, vulgar, brash, tacky *(informal)*, flashy, lurid, tasteless, naff *(Brit. slang)*, gaudy, tawdry, showy, ostentatious, brassy • *He liked to shock with his gold chains and loud clothes.*
OPPOSITES: conservative, dull, sombre
3 = **loud-mouthed**, offensive, crude, coarse, vulgar, brash, crass, raucous, brazen *(informal)* • *I like your manner; loud people are horrible.*
OPPOSITES: reserved, retiring, quiet

loudly = **noisily**, vigorously, vehemently, vociferously, uproariously, lustily, shrilly, fortissimo *(Music)*, at full volume, deafeningly, at the top of your voice, clamorously • *His footsteps echoed loudly in the tiled hall.*

loudmouth = **bigmouth** *(slang)* = **noisily**, swaggerer, brag, blusterer, windbag *(slang)*, braggart, braggadocio, gasbag *(informal)*, blowhard *(informal)*, bullshitter *(taboo)*, bullshit artist *(taboo)*, figjam *(Austral. slang)* • *He is a loudmouth, and very spoilt too.*

lounge AS A VERB = **relax**, pass time, hang out *(informal)*, idle, loaf, potter, sprawl, lie about, waste time, recline, take it easy, saunter, loiter, loll, dawdle, laze, kill time, make yourself at home, veg out *(slang, chiefly U.S.)*, outspan *(S. African)*, fritter time away • *They ate and drank and lounged in the shade.*

▸ AS A NOUN = **sitting room**, living room, parlour, drawing room, front room, reception room, television room • *They sat before a roaring fire in the lounge.*

louring *or* **lowering** 1 = **darkening**, threatening, forbidding, menacing, black, heavy, dark, grey, clouded, gloomy, ominous, cloudy, overcast, foreboding • *a heavy, louring sky*

2 = **glowering**, forbidding, grim, frowning, brooding, scowling, sullen, surly • *We walked in fear of his lowering temperament.*

louse

▸ RELATED ADJECTIVE: pedicular

lousy 1 = **inferior**, bad, poor, terrible, awful, no good, miserable, rotten *(informal)*, duff, second-rate, shoddy, low-rent *(informal, chiefly U.S.)*, for the birds *(informal)*, shitty *(taboo)*, two-bit *(U.S. & Canad. slang)*, slovenly, poxy *(slang)*, dime-a-dozen *(informal)*, piss-poor *(slang)*, chickenshit *(U.S. slang)*, bush-league *(Austral. & N.Z. informal)*, not much cop *(Brit. slang)*, tinhorn *(U.S. slang)*, of a sort *or* of sorts, strictly for the birds *(informal)*, bodger *or* bodgie *(Austral. slang)* • *The menu is limited and the food is lousy.*

2 = **unwell**, poorly *(informal)*, ill, sick, crook *(Austral. & N.Z. informal)*, seedy *(informal)*, queasy, out of sorts *(informal)*, off-colour, under the weather *(informal)* • *I wasn't actually sick but I was feeling lousy.*

3 = **mean**, low, base, dirty, vicious, rotten *(informal)*, vile, despicable, hateful, contemptible, shitty *(taboo)* • *This is just lousy, cheap, fraudulent behaviour from the government.*

4 *with* **with** = **well-supplied with**, rolling in *(slang)*, not short of, amply supplied with • *a hotel lousy with fleas*

lout = **oaf**, thug, hooligan, boor, bear, ned *(Scot. slang)*, yahoo, hoon *(Austral. & N.Z. slang)*, clod, bumpkin, gawk, dolt, churl, lubber, lummox *(informal)*, clumsy idiot, yob *or* yobbo *(Brit. slang)*, cougan *(Austral. slang)*, scozza *(Austral.slang)*, bogan *(Austral. slang)* • *a drunken lout*

loutish = **oafish**, rough, gross, coarse, bungling, churlish, stolid, boorish, gawky, uncouth, lumpen *(informal)*, ill-bred, lumpish, swinish, clodhopping *(informal)*, doltish, unmannerly, ill-mannered, lubberly • *I was appalled by the loutish behaviour.*

lovable *or* **loveable** = **endearing**, attractive, engaging, charming, winning, pleasing, sweet, lovely, fetching *(informal)*, delightful, cute, enchanting, captivating, cuddly, amiable, adorable, winsome, likable *or* likeable • *His vulnerability makes him even more lovable.*

OPPOSITES: offensive, revolting, detestable

love AS A VERB 1 = **adore**, care for, treasure, cherish, prize, worship, be devoted to, be attached to, be in love with, dote on, hold dear, think the world of, idolize, feel affection for, have affection for, adulate • *We love each other, and we want to spend our lives together.*

OPPOSITES: hate, dislike, scorn

2 = **enjoy**, like, desire, fancy, appreciate, relish, delight in, savour, take pleasure in, have a soft spot for, be partial to, have a weakness for • *We loved the food so much, especially the fish dishes.*

OPPOSITES: hate, dislike, scorn

3 = **cuddle**, neck *(informal)*, kiss, pet, embrace, caress, fondle, canoodle *(slang)* • *the loving and talking that marked an earlier stage of the relationship*

▸ AS A NOUN 1 = **passion**, liking, regard, friendship, affection, warmth, attachment, intimacy, devotion, tenderness, fondness, rapture, adulation, adoration, infatuation, ardour, endearment, aroha *(N.Z.)*, amity • *Our love for each other has been increased by what we've been through together.*

OPPOSITES: hate, disgust, hatred

2 = **liking**, taste, delight in, bent for, weakness for, relish for, enjoyment, devotion to, penchant for, inclination for, zest for, fondness for, soft spot for, partiality to • *a love of literature*

3 = **beloved**, dear, dearest, sweet, lover, angel, darling, honey, loved one, sweetheart, truelove, dear one, leman *(archaic)*, inamorata *or* inamorato • *Don't cry, my love.*

OPPOSITES: enemy, foe

4 = **sympathy**, understanding, heart, charity, pity, humanity, warmth, mercy, compassion, sorrow, kindness, tenderness, friendliness, condolence, commiseration, fellow feeling, soft-heartedness, tender-heartedness, aroha *(N.Z.)* • *a manifestation of his love for his fellow men*

5 = **greetings**, regards, compliments, best wishes, good wishes, kind regards • *She's fine and sends her love.*

▸ IN PHRASES: **fall in love with someone** = **lose your heart to**, fall for, be taken with, take a shine to *(informal)*, become infatuated with, fall head over heels in love with, be swept off your feet by, bestow your affections on • *I fell in love with him the moment I saw him.*

for love = **without payment**, freely, for nothing, free of charge, gratis, pleasurably • *She does it for love – not money.*

for love or money = **by any means**, ever, under any conditions • *Replacement parts couldn't be found for love or money.*

in love = **enamoured**, charmed, captivated, smitten, wild *(informal)*, mad *(informal)*, crazy *(informal)*, enthralled, besotted, infatuated, enraptured • *She had never before been in love.*

make love = **have sexual intercourse**, have sex, go to bed, sleep together, do it *(informal)*, mate, have sexual relations, have it off *(slang)*, have it away *(slang)* • *After six months of friendship, one night, they made love.*

▸ RELATED ADJECTIVE: amatory

QUOTATIONS

How do I love thee? Let me count the ways
[Elizabeth Barrett Browning *Sonnets from the Portuguese*]

All that matters is love and work
[attributed to Sigmund Freud]

Love's pleasure lasts but a moment; love's sorrow lasts all through life
[Jean-Pierre Claris de Florian *Celestine*]

What love is, if thou wouldst be taught,
Thy heart must teach alone -
Two souls with but a single thought,
Two hearts that beat as one
[Friedrich Halm *Der Sohn der Wildnis*]

Love is like the measles; we all have to go through it
[Jerome K. Jerome *The Idle Thoughts of an Idle Fellow*]

Love's like the measles – all the worse when it comes late in life
[Douglas Jerrold *Wit and Opinions of Douglas Jerrold*]

No, there's nothing half so sweet in life
As love's young dream
[Thomas Moore *Love's Young Dream*]

'Tis better to have loved and lost

Than never to have loved at all
[Alfred, Lord Tennyson *In Memoriam A.H.H.*]
Love means never having to say you're sorry
[Erich Segal *Love Story*]
In the Spring a livelier iris changes on the burnish'd dove;
In the Spring a young man's fancy lightly turns to thoughts of love
[Alfred, Lord Tennyson *Locksley Hall*]
Love is like any other luxury. You have no right to it unless you can afford it
[Anthony Trollope *The Way we Live Now*]
Love conquers all things; let us too give in to love
[Virgil *Eclogue*]
Love and do what you will
[Saint Augustine of Hippo *In Epistolam Joannis ad Parthos*]
Those have most power to hurt us that we love
[Francis Beaumont and John Fletcher *The Maid's Tragedy*]
My love's a noble madness
[John Dryden *All for Love*]
And love's the noblest frailty of the mind
[John Dryden *The Indian Emperor*]
Love's tongue is in the eyes
[Phineas Fletcher *Piscatory Eclogues*]
Love is only one of many passions
[Dr. Johnson *Plays of William Shakespeare, preface*]
Where both deliberate, the love is slight;
Whoever loved that loved not at first sight?
[Christopher Marlowe *Hero and Leander*]
If love is the answer, could you rephrase the question?
[Lily Tomlin]
Men love in haste, but they detest at leisure
[Lord Byron *Don Juan*]
The course of true love never did run smooth
[William Shakespeare *A Midsummer Night's Dream*]
Love is not love
Which alters when it alteration finds
[William Shakespeare *Sonnets*]
Love is like linen – often changed, the sweeter
[Phineas Fletcher *Sicelides*]
O my love's like a red, red rose
[Robert Burns *A Red, Red Rose*]
Two things a man cannot hide: that he is drunk, and that he is in love
[Antiphanes]
Every man is a poet when he is in love
[Plato *Symposium*]
one that lov'd not wisely but too well
[William Shakespeare *Othello*]
To fall in love is to create a religion that has a fallible god
[Jorge Luis Borges *The Meeting in a Dream*]
Love is like quicksilver in the hand. Leave the fingers open and it stays. Clutch it, and it darts away
[Dorothy Parker]
Love does not consist in gazing at each other, but in looking outward in the same direction
[Antoine de Saint-Exupéry]
Love ceases to be a pleasure, when it ceases to be a secret
[Aphra Behn *The Lover's Watch, Four O'Clock*]
Many waters cannot quench love, neither can the floods drown it
[*Bible: Song of Solomon*]
Greater love hath no man than this, that a man lay down his life for his friends
[*Bible: St. John*]
O lyric Love, half-angel and half-bird
And all a wonder and a wild desire
[Robert Browning *The Ring and the Book*]
Man's love is of man's life a thing apart,
'Tis woman's whole existence
[Lord Byron *Don Juan*]
Whoever loves, if he do not propose
The right true end of love, he's one that goes
To sea for nothing but to make him sick
[John Donne *Love's Progress*]
I am two fools, I know,
For loving, and for saying so
In whining poetry
[John Donne *The Triple Fool*]
How alike are the groans of love to those of the dying
[Malcolm Lowry *Under the Volcano*]
Love is the delusion that one woman differs from another
[H.L. Mencken *Chrestomathy*]
After all, my erstwhile dear,
My no longer cherished,
Need we say it was not love,
Now that love has perished?
[Edna St. Vincent Millay *Passer Mortuus Est*]
If I am pressed to say why I loved him, I feel it can only be explained by replying: 'Because it was he; because it was me.'
[Montaigne *Essais*]
Love built on beauty, soon as beauty, dies
[John Donne *The Anagram*]
Love thy neighbour as thyself
[*Bible: Leviticus*]

PROVERBS

All's fair in love and war
Love is blind
One cannot love and be wise
Love makes the world go round
Love will find a way

love affair 1 = **romance**, relationship, affair, intrigue, liaison, amour, affaire de coeur *(French)* • *a love affair with a married man*
2 = **enthusiasm**, love, passion, appreciation, devotion, mania, zest • *His love affair with France knew no bounds.*

loveless 1 = **unloving**, hard, cold, icy, insensitive, unfriendly, heartless, frigid, unresponsive, unfeeling, cold-hearted • *She is in a loveless relationship.*
2 = **unloved**, disliked, forsaken, lovelorn, friendless, unappreciated, unvalued, uncherished • *A busy professional life had left her loveless at the age of 30.*

lovelorn = **lovesick**, mooning, slighted, pining, yearning, languishing, spurned, jilted, moping, unrequited, crossed in love • *He was acting like a lovelorn teenager.*

lovely 1 = **beautiful**, appealing, attractive, charming, winning, pretty, sweet, handsome, good-looking, exquisite, admirable, enchanting, graceful, captivating, amiable, adorable, comely, fit *(Brit. informal)* • *You look lovely.*
OPPOSITES: ugly, hideous, unattractive
2 = **wonderful**, pleasing, nice, pleasant, engaging, marvellous, delightful, enjoyable, gratifying, agreeable • *What a lovely surprise!*
OPPOSITES: revolting, repellent, horrible

lovemaking = **sexual intercourse**, intercourse, intimacy, sexual relations, the other *(informal)*, mating, nookie *(slang)*, copulation, coitus, act of love, carnal knowledge, rumpy-pumpy *(slang)*, coition, sexual union *or* congress, poontang *(taboo slang)*, rumpo *(slang)* • *Their lovemaking became less and less frequent.*

lover = **sweetheart**, beloved, loved one, beau, flame *(informal)*, mistress, admirer, suitor, swain *(archaic)*, woman friend, lady friend, man friend, toy boy, paramour, leman *(archaic)*, fancy bit *(slang)*, boyfriend *or* girlfriend, fancy man *or* fancy woman *(slang)*, fiancé *or* fiancée, inamorata *or* inamorato, Wag (*Brit. informal*) • *They became lovers soon after they first met.*

QUOTATIONS

All mankind love a lover

[Ralph Waldo Emerson *Spiritual Laws*]

lovesick = **lovelorn**, longing, desiring, pining, yearning, languishing • *a lovesick boy consumed with self pity*

loving 1 = **affectionate**, kind, warm, dear, friendly, devoted, tender, fond, ardent, cordial, doting, amorous, solicitous, demonstrative, warm-hearted • *a loving husband and father*
OPPOSITES: mean, cold, cruel
2 = **tender**, kind, caring, warm, gentle, sympathetic, considerate • *The house has been restored with loving care.*

low[1] AS AN ADJECTIVE 1 = **small**, little, short, stunted, squat, fubsy (*archaic or dialect*) • *She put it down on the low table.*
OPPOSITES: towering, tall
2 = **low-lying**, deep, depressed, shallow, subsided, sunken, ground-level • *The sun was low in the sky.*
OPPOSITES: high, elevated
3 = **inexpensive**, cheap, reasonable, bargain, moderate, modest, cut-price, economical, bargain-basement • *The low prices and friendly service made for a pleasant evening out.*
4 = **meagre**, little, small, reduced, depleted, scant, trifling, insignificant, sparse, paltry, measly • *They are having to live on very low incomes.*
OPPOSITES: significant
5 = **inferior**, bad, poor, inadequate, pathetic, worthless, unsatisfactory, mediocre, deficient, second-rate, shoddy, low-grade, puny, substandard, low-rent (*informal, chiefly U.S.*), half-pie (*N.Z. informal*), bodger *or* bodgie (*Austral. slang*) • *They criticised staff for the low standard of care.*
6 = **unfavourable**, bad, poor, negative, hostile, inimical • *I had an extremely low opinion of the tabloid newspapers.*
7 = **unambitious**, small, limited, ordinary, modest, unexceptional • *People had very low expectations.*
8 = **deep**, rich, bass, resonant, sonorous, low-pitched • *My voice was so low that I was mistaken for a man on the phone.*
9 = **quiet**, soft, gentle, whispered, muted, subdued, hushed, muffled • *Her voice was so low he had to strain to catch it.*
OPPOSITES: loud, noisy
10 = **dejected**, down, blue, sad, depressed, unhappy, miserable, fed up, moody, gloomy, dismal, forlorn, glum, despondent, downcast, morose, disheartened, downhearted, down in the dumps (*informal*), sick as a parrot (*informal*), cheesed off (*informal*), brassed off (*Brit. slang*) • *'I didn't ask for this job, you know,' he tells friends when he is low.*
OPPOSITES: high, happy, cheerful
11 = **scarce**, diminished, inadequate, insufficient, depleted, scant, meagre, sparse, scanty • *World stocks of wheat were getting very low.*
12 = **coarse**, common, rough, gross, crude, rude, obscene, disgraceful, vulgar, undignified, disreputable, unbecoming, unrefined, dishonourable, ill-bred • *stripteases interspersed with bits of ribald low comedy*
13 = **contemptible**, mean, base, nasty, cowardly, degraded, vulgar, vile, sordid, abject, unworthy, despicable, depraved, menial, reprehensible, dastardly, scurvy, servile, unprincipled, dishonourable, ignoble • *That was a really low trick.*
OPPOSITES: fine, grand, honourable
14 = **lowly**, poor, simple, plain, peasant, obscure, humble, meek, unpretentious, plebeian, lowborn • *a man of low birth and no breeding*
15 = **ill**, weak, exhausted, frail, dying, reduced, sinking, stricken, feeble, debilitated, prostrate • *She's still feeling a bit low after having flu.*
OPPOSITES: strong, alert, enthusiastic
▸ AS A NOUN = **lowest level**, nadir, low point, rock bottom • *The dollar fell to a new low.*
▸ IN PHRASES: **lay someone low** = **weaken**, reduce, tire, debilitate, make ill, make weak, sap the strength of, enervate, lower the strength of • *a medical condition that laid him low for 6 months*
lie low = **hide**, lurk, hole up, hide away, keep a low profile, hide out, go underground, skulk, go into hiding, take cover, keep out of sight, go to earth, conceal yourself • *Far from lying low, he became more outspoken than ever.*

low[2] = **moo**, bellow • *Cattle were lowing in the barns.*

lowbrow = **unsophisticated**, popular, shallow, lightweight, tabloid, inferior, easy-to-understand, mass-market, undemanding, insubstantial, unscholarly • *lowbrow novels*

low-down AS A NOUN = **information**, intelligence, info (*informal*), inside story, gen (*Brit. informal*), dope (*informal*) • *We want you to give us the lowdown on your team-mates.*
▸ AS AN ADJECTIVE = **mean**, low, base, cheap (*informal*), nasty, ugly, despicable, reprehensible, contemptible, underhand, scurvy • *They will stoop to every low-down trick.*

lower AS AN ADJECTIVE 1 = **subordinate**, under, smaller, junior, minor, secondary, lesser, low-level, inferior, second-class • *the lower ranks of council officers*
2 = **reduced**, cut, diminished, decreased, lessened, curtailed, pared down • *You may get it at a slightly lower price.*
OPPOSITES: higher, increased, enlarged
▸ AS A VERB 1 = **drop**, sink, depress, let down, submerge, take down, let fall, make lower • *They lowered the coffin into the grave.*
OPPOSITES: raise, lift, elevate
2 = **lessen**, cut, reduce, moderate, diminish, slash, decrease, prune, minimize, curtail, abate • *a drug which lowers cholesterol levels*
OPPOSITES: increase, raise, extend
3 = **demean**, humble, disgrace, humiliate, degrade, devalue, downgrade, belittle, condescend, debase, deign, abase • *Don't lower yourself. Don't be the way they are.*
4 = **quieten**, soften, hush, tone down • *He moved closer, lowering his voice.*

lower[1] *or* **lour** 1 = **darken**, threaten, loom, menace, blacken, be brewing, cloud up *or* over • *a photo of the sea and lowering clouds*
2 = **glower**, glare, frown, scowl, look sullen, look daggers, give a dirty look • *When I came out, he was leaning against the wall, lowering at me.*

lowering
▷ *See* **Louring**

low-grade = **inferior**, bad, poor, duff (*informal*), not good enough, second-rate, substandard, low-rent (*informal, chiefly U.S.*), two-bit (*U.S. & Canad. slang*), poxy (*slang*), dime-a-dozen (*informal*), piss-poor (*slang*), chickenshit (*U.S. slang*), bush-league (*Austral. & N.Z. informal*), not up to snuff (*informal*), tinhorn (*U.S. slang*), of a sort *or* of sorts, bodger *or* bodgie (*Austral. slang*) • *undrinkable low-grade wine*

low-key = **subdued**, quiet, restrained, muted, played down, understated, muffled, toned down, low-pitched • *The wedding will be a very low-key affair.*

lowly 1 = **lowborn**, obscure, subordinate, inferior, mean, proletarian, ignoble, plebeian • *lowly bureaucrats pretending to be senators*
2 = **unpretentious**, common, poor, average, simple, ordinary, plain, modest, homespun • *He started out as a lowly photographer.*

low-spirited = **depressed**, down, sad, unhappy, low, blue, miserable, fed up, moody, gloomy, dismal, dejected, despondent, apathetic, heavy-hearted, down in the dumps (*informal*), down in the mouth, down-hearted, brassed off (*Brit. slang*) • *He was low-spirited, disappointed and out of humour.*

low-tech = **unsophisticated**, simple, basic, elementary • *a simple form of low-tech electric propulsion*
OPPOSITES: scientific, technical, high-tech *or* hi-tech

loyal = **faithful**, true, devoted, dependable, constant, attached, patriotic, staunch, trustworthy, trusty, steadfast, dutiful, unwavering, true-blue, immovable, unswerving, tried and true, true-hearted • *He was always such a loyal friend.*
OPPOSITES: false, treacherous, disloyal

loyalty = **faithfulness**, commitment, devotion, allegiance, reliability, fidelity, homage, patriotism, obedience, constancy, dependability, trustworthiness, steadfastness, troth *(archaic)*, fealty, staunchness, trueness, trustiness, true-heartedness • *I have sworn an oath of loyalty to the monarchy.*
QUOTATIONS
No man can serve two masters
[Bible: St. Matthew]

lozenge = **tablet**, pastille, troche, cough drop, jujube • *throat lozenges*

LP = **album**, record • *his first LP since 1986*

lubricant = **lubricator**, oil, grease • *industrial lubricants*

lubricate = **oil**, grease, smear, smooth the way, oil the wheels, make smooth, make slippery • *Mineral oils are used to lubricate the machinery.*

lucid 1 = **clear**, obvious, plain, evident, distinct, explicit, transparent, clear-cut, crystal clear, comprehensible, intelligible, limpid, pellucid • *His prose is always lucid and compelling.*
OPPOSITES: confused, vague, unclear
2 = **clear-headed**, sound, reasonable, sensible, rational, sober, all there, sane, compos mentis *(Latin)*, in your right mind • *He wasn't very lucid; he didn't quite know where he was.*
OPPOSITES: confused, vague, unclear

luck AS A NOUN 1 = **good fortune**, success, advantage, prosperity, break *(informal)*, stroke of luck, blessing, windfall, good luck, fluke, godsend, serendipity • *I knew I needed a bit of luck to win.*
2 = **fortune**, lot, stars, chance, accident, fate, hazard, destiny, hap *(archaic)*, twist of fate, fortuity • *The goal owed more to luck than good planning.*
▸ IN PHRASES: **in luck** = **fortunate**, successful, favoured, prosperous, rosy, well-off, on a roll, sitting pretty *(informal)*, jammy *(Brit. slang)* • *You're in luck; the doctor's still in.*
out of luck = **unfortunate**, cursed, unlucky, unsuccessful, luckless • *If you want money, you're out of luck.*
QUOTATIONS
The more I practise the luckier I get
[Gary Player]
PROVERBS
You win some, you lose some

luckily = **fortunately**, happily, by chance, as luck would have it, fortuitously, opportunely, as it chanced • *Luckily, we both love football.*

luckless = **unlucky**, unfortunate, unsuccessful, hapless, unhappy, disastrous, cursed, hopeless, jinxed, calamitous, ill-starred, star-crossed, unpropitious, ill-fated • *the luckless parent of an extremely difficult child*

lucky 1 = **fortunate**, successful, favoured, charmed, blessed, prosperous, jammy *(Brit. slang)*, serendipitous • *I consider myself the luckiest man on the face of the earth.*
OPPOSITES: unhappy, unfortunate, unlucky
2 = **fortuitous**, timely, fortunate, auspicious, opportune, propitious, providential, adventitious • *They are now desperate for a lucky break.*
OPPOSITES: unlucky, untimely
PROVERBS
Lucky at cards, unlucky in love
Third time lucky

lucrative = **profitable**, rewarding, productive, fruitful, paying, high-income, well-paid, money-making, advantageous, win-win, gainful, remunerative • *Many of them have found lucrative jobs in private security firms.*

lucre = **money**, profit, gain, riches, wealth, spoils, mammon, pelf • *Now they can feel less guilty about their piles of filthy lucre.*

ludicrous = **ridiculous**, crazy, absurd, preposterous, odd, funny, comic, silly, laughable, farcical, outlandish, incongruous, comical, zany, nonsensical, droll, burlesque, cockamamie *(slang, chiefly U.S.)* • *It's a completely ludicrous idea.*
OPPOSITES: serious, sensible, logical

lug = **drag**, carry, pull, haul, tow, yank, hump *(Brit. slang)*, heave • *Nobody wants to lug around huge heavy suitcases.*

luggage = **baggage**, things, cases, bags, gear, trunks, suitcases, paraphernalia, impedimenta • *Leave your luggage in the hotel.*

lugubrious = **gloomy**, serious, sad, dismal, melancholy, dreary, sombre, woeful, mournful, morose, sorrowful, funereal, doleful, woebegone, dirgelike • *He plays it so slowly that it becomes lugubrious.*

lukewarm 1 = **tepid**, warm, blood-warm • *Wash your face with lukewarm water.*
2 = **half-hearted**, cold, cool, indifferent, unconcerned, uninterested, apathetic, unresponsive, phlegmatic, unenthusiastic, half-arsed *(Brit. slang)*, half-assed *(U.S. & Canad. slang)*, laodicean • *The study received a lukewarm response from the Home Secretary.*

lull AS A NOUN = **respite**, pause, quiet, silence, calm, hush, tranquillity, stillness, let-up *(informal)*, calmness • *a lull in the conversation*
▸ AS A VERB = **calm**, soothe, subdue, still, quiet, compose, hush, quell, allay, pacify, lullaby, tranquillize, rock to sleep • *It is easy to be lulled into a false sense of security.*

lullaby = **cradlesong**, berceuse • *She sang another lullaby and told him how much she loved him.*

lumber[1] AS A VERB = **burden**, land, load, saddle, impose upon, encumber • *She was lumbered with a bill for about £90.*
▸ AS A NOUN = **junk**, refuse, rubbish, discards, trash, clutter, jumble, white elephants, castoffs, trumpery • *The wheels had been consigned to the loft as useless lumber.*

lumber[2] = **plod**, shuffle, shamble, trudge, stump, clump, waddle, trundle, lump along • *He turned and lumbered back to his chair.*

lumbering = **awkward**, heavy, blundering, bumbling, hulking, unwieldy, ponderous, ungainly, elephantine, heavy-footed, lubberly • *He overtook a lumbering lorry.*

luminary = **celebrity**, star, expert, somebody, lion, worthy, notable, big name, dignitary, leading light, celeb *(informal)*, personage, megastar *(informal)*, fundi *(S. African)*, V.I.P. • *the political opinions of such luminaries as Sartre and de Beauvoir*

luminescent = **glowing**, shining, fluorescent, radiant, luminous, Day-Glo, phosphorescent, effulgent • *a ghostly luminescent glow*

luminous 1 = **bright**, lighted, lit, brilliant, shining, glowing, vivid, illuminated, radiant, resplendent, lustrous, luminescent • *The luminous dial on the clock showed five minutes to seven*
2 = **clear**, obvious, plain, evident, transparent, lucid, intelligible, perspicuous • *a remarkable woman with a luminous sense of responsibility.*

lump[1] AS A NOUN 1 = **piece**, group, ball, spot, block, mass, cake, bunch, cluster, chunk, wedge, dab, hunk, nugget, gob, clod, gobbet • *a lump of wood*
2 = **swelling**, growth, bump, tumour, bulge, hump, protuberance, protrusion, tumescence • *I've got a lump on my shoulder.*
▸ AS A VERB = **group**, throw, mass, combine, collect, unite, pool, bunch, consolidate, aggregate, batch, conglomerate, coalesce, agglutinate • *She felt out of place lumped together with alcoholics and hard-drug users.*

lump[2] IN PHRASES: **lump it** = **put up with it**, take it, stand it, bear it, suffer it, hack it *(slang)*, tolerate it, endure it, brook it • *He was going to kick up a fuss, but he realized he'd have to lump it.*

lumpish = **clumsy**, heavy, awkward, bungling, lumbering, lethargic, ungainly, stolid, gawky, obtuse, elephantine, oafish, doltish, puddingy, unco *(Austral. slang)* • *crashing into people with their lumpish rugby players' bodies*

lumpy = **bumpy**, clotted, uneven, knobbly, grainy, curdled, granular, full of lumps • *How do you stop the rice from going lumpy?*

lunacy 1 = **foolishness**, madness, folly, stupidity, absurdity, aberration, idiocy, craziness, tomfoolery, imbecility, foolhardiness, senselessness • *the lunacy of the tax system*
OPPOSITES: reason, sense, prudence
2 = **insanity**, madness, mania, dementia, psychosis, idiocy, derangement • *Lunacy became the official explanation for his actions.*
OPPOSITES: reason, sanity

lunatic AS A NOUN = **madman**, maniac, psychopath, nut *(slang)*, loony *(slang)*, nutter *(Brit. slang)*, basket case *(slang)*, nutcase *(slang)*, headcase *(informal)*, headbanger *(informal)*, crazy *(informal)* • *Her son thinks she's a raving lunatic.*
▸ AS AN ADJECTIVE = **mad**, crazy, insane, irrational, nuts *(slang)*, barking *(slang)*, daft, demented, barmy *(slang)*, deranged, bonkers *(slang, chiefly Brit.)*, unhinged, loopy *(informal)*, crackpot *(informal)*, out to lunch *(informal)*, barking mad *(slang)*, maniacal, gonzo *(slang)*, up the pole *(informal)*, crackbrained, wacko *or* whacko *(informal)*, off the air *(Austral. slang)* • *the operation of the market taken to lunatic extremes*

lunchtime = **dinnertime**, noon, midday • *Could we meet at lunchtime?*

lung
▸ RELATED ADJECTIVES: pulmonary, pulmonic, pneumonic

lunge AS A VERB = **pounce**, charge, bound, dive, leap, plunge, dash, thrust, poke, jab • *I lunged forward to try to hit him.*
▸ AS A NOUN = **thrust**, charge, pounce, pass, spring, swing, jab, swipe *(informal)* • *He knocked on the door and made a lunge for her when she opened it.*

lurch AS A VERB 1 = **tilt**, roll, pitch, list, rock, lean, heel • *As the car sped over a pothole, she lurched forward.*
2 = **stagger**, reel, stumble, weave, sway, totter • *a drunken yob lurching out of a bar, shouting obscenities*
▸ IN PHRASES: **leave someone in the lurch** = **leave**, abandon, desert, strand, leave behind, forsake, jilt • *You wouldn't leave an old friend in the lurch, surely?*

lure AS A VERB = **tempt**, draw, attract, invite, trick, seduce, entice, beckon, lead on, allure, decoy, ensnare, inveigle • *They did not realise that they were being lured into a trap.*
▸ AS A NOUN = **temptation**, attraction, incentive, bait, carrot *(informal)*, magnet, inducement, decoy, enticement, siren song, allurement • *The lure of rural life is proving as strong as ever.*

lurid 1 = **sensational**, shocking, disgusting, graphic, violent, savage, startling, grim, exaggerated, revolting, explicit, vivid, ghastly, gruesome, grisly, macabre, melodramatic, yellow *(of journalism)*, gory, unrestrained, shock-horror *(facetious)* • *lurid accounts of deaths and mutilations*
OPPOSITES: controlled, mild, factual
2 = **glaring**, bright, bloody, intense, flaming, vivid, fiery, livid, sanguine, glowering, overbright • *She always painted her toenails a lurid red or orange.*
OPPOSITES: pale, pastel, watery

lurk = **hide**, sneak, crouch, prowl, snoop, lie in wait, slink, skulk, conceal yourself, move with stealth, go furtively • *He thought he saw someone lurking above the chamber during the address.*

luscious 1 = **sexy**, attractive, arousing, erotic, inviting, provocative, seductive, cuddly, sensuous, alluring, voluptuous, kissable, beddable • *a luscious young blonde*
2 = **delicious**, sweet, juicy, rich, honeyed, savoury, succulent, palatable, mouth-watering, delectable, yummy *(slang)*, scrumptious *(informal)*, appetizing, toothsome, yummo *(Austral. slang)* • *luscious fruit*

lush 1 = **abundant**, green, flourishing, lavish, dense, prolific, rank, teeming, overgrown, verdant • *the lush green meadows*
2 = **luxurious**, grand, elaborate, lavish, extravagant, sumptuous, plush *(informal)*, ornate, opulent, palatial, ritzy *(slang)* • *The hotel is lush, plush and very non-backpacker*
3 = **succulent**, fresh, tender, ripe, juicy • *an unusual combination of vegetables and lush fruits*

lust AS A NOUN 1 = **lechery**, sensuality, licentiousness, carnality, the hots *(slang)*, libido, lewdness, wantonness, salaciousness, lasciviousness, concupiscence, randiness *(informal, chiefly Brit.)*, pruriency • *His lust for her grew until it was overpowering.*
2 = **desire**, longing, passion, appetite, craving, greed, thirst, cupidity, covetousness, avidity, appetence • *It was his lust for glitz and glamour that was driving them apart.*
▸ IN PHRASES: **lust for** *or* **after someone** *or* **something** = **desire**, want, crave, need, yearn for, covet, slaver over, lech after *(informal)*, be consumed with desire for, hunger for *or* after • *Half the campus is lusting after her.* • *She lusted after the Directorship*

QUOTATIONS
Natural freedoms are but just;
There's something generous in mere lust
[John Wilmot, Earl of Rochester *A Ramble in St. James' Park*]

lustful = **lascivious**, sexy *(informal)*, passionate, erotic, craving, sensual, randy *(informal, chiefly Brit.)*, raunchy *(slang)*, horny *(slang)*, hankering, lewd, wanton, carnal, prurient, lecherous, hot-blooded, libidinous, licentious, concupiscent, unchaste • *He can't stop himself from having lustful thoughts.*

lustily = **vigorously**, hard, strongly, loudly, powerfully, forcefully, with all your might, with might and main • *The baby cried lustily when he was hungry.*

lustre 1 = **sparkle**, shine, glow, glitter, dazzle, gleam, gloss, brilliance, sheen, shimmer, glint, brightness, radiance, burnish, resplendence, lambency, luminousness • *Gold retains its lustre for far longer than other metals.*
2 = **excitement**, kick *(informal)*, pleasure, thrill, sensation, tingle • *Is your relationship starting to lose its lustre?*
3 = **glory**, honour, fame, distinction, prestige, renown, illustriousness • *The team is relying too much on names that have lost their lustre.*

lustreless = **dull**, flat, matt, faded, pale, tarnished, drab, lacklustre, washed out, lifeless, dingy, colourless, unpolished • *Her lustreless eyes were sunk deep in her face.*

lustrous = **shining**, bright, glowing, sparkling, dazzling, shiny, gleaming, glossy, shimmering, radiant, luminous, glistening, burnished • *a head of thick, lustrous, wavy brown hair*

lusty = **vigorous**, strong, powerful, healthy, strapping, robust, rugged, energetic, sturdy, hale, stout, stalwart, hearty, virile, red-blooded *(informal)*, brawny • *his lusty singing in the open park*

luxuriant 1 = **lush**, rich, dense, abundant, excessive, thriving, flourishing, rank, productive, lavish, ample, fertile, prolific, overflowing, plentiful, exuberant, fruitful, teeming, copious, prodigal, riotous, profuse, fecund, superabundant, plenteous • *wide spreading branches and luxuriant foliage*
OPPOSITES: sparse, thin, meagre
2 = **elaborate**, fancy, decorated, extravagant, flamboyant, baroque, sumptuous, ornate, festooned, flowery, rococo, florid, corinthian • *luxuriant draperies and soft sofas*
OPPOSITES: simple, plain, unadorned

luxuriate 1 = **enjoy**, delight, indulge, relish, revel, bask, wallow • *Lie back and luxuriate in the scented oil.*
2 = **live in luxury**, take it easy, live the life of Riley, have the time of your life, be in clover • *He retired to luxuriate in Hollywood.*

luxurious 1 = **sumptuous**, expensive, comfortable, magnificent, costly, splendid, lavish, plush (*informal*), opulent, ritzy (*slang*), de luxe, well-appointed • *a luxurious hotel*
2 = **self-indulgent**, pleasure-loving, champagne, sensual, pampered, voluptuous, sybaritic, epicurean • *She had come to enjoy this luxurious lifestyle.*
OPPOSITES: poor, plain, austere

luxury 1 = **opulence**, splendour, richness, extravagance, affluence, hedonism, a bed of roses, voluptuousness, the life of Riley, sumptuousness • *She was brought up in an atmosphere of luxury and wealth.*
OPPOSITES: want, poverty, deprivation
2 = **extravagance**, treat, extra, indulgence, frill, nonessential • *We never had money for little luxuries.*
OPPOSITES: necessity, need
3 = **pleasure**, delight, comfort, satisfaction, enjoyment, bliss, indulgence, gratification, wellbeing • *Relax in the luxury of a Roman-style bath.*
OPPOSITES: difficulty, burden, discomfort

QUOTATIONS
Give us the luxuries of life, and we will dispense with its necessities
[John Lothrop Motley]

lying AS A NOUN = **dishonesty**, perjury, deceit, fabrication, guile, misrepresentation, duplicity, fibbing, double-dealing, prevarication, falsity, mendacity, dissimulation, untruthfulness • *Lying is something that I will not tolerate.*
▸ AS AN ADJECTIVE = **deceitful**, false, deceiving, treacherous, dishonest, two-faced, double-dealing, dissembling, mendacious, perfidious, untruthful, guileful • *that lying hound*
OPPOSITES: straight, frank, reliable, straightforward, sincere, honest, candid, truthful, forthright, veracious

lynch = **hang**, kill, execute, put to death, string up (*informal*), send to the gallows • *They were about to lynch him when reinforcements arrived.*

lynchpin or **linchpin** = **driving force**, director, chief, principal, co-ordinator, cornerstone, mainstay • *He's the lynchpin of our team.*

lynx
▸ RELATED ADJECTIVE: lyncean

lyric AS AN ADJECTIVE 1 = **songlike**, musical, lyrical, expressive, melodic • *His splendid short stories and lyric poetry.*
2 = **melodic**, clear, clear, light, flowing, graceful, mellifluous, dulcet • *her fresh, beautiful, lyric voice*
▸ AS A PLURAL NOUN = **words**, lines, text, libretto, words of a song • *an opera with lyrics by Langston Hughes*

lyrical = **enthusiastic**, emotional, inspired, poetic, carried away, ecstatic, expressive, impassioned, rapturous, effusive, rhapsodic • *His paintings became more lyrical.*

Mm

ma = **mother**, mum *(Brit. informal)*, mater, mom *(U.S. & Canad.)*, mummy *(Brit. informal)* • *Ma was still at work when I got back.*

macabre = **gruesome**, grim, ghastly, frightening, ghostly, weird, dreadful, unearthly, hideous, eerie, grisly, horrid, morbid, frightful, ghoulish • *Police have made a macabre discovery.*
OPPOSITES: appealing, beautiful, delightful

mace = **staff**, club, stick, cosh, cudgel • *a life-size statue of the king holding a golden mace*

macerate = **soften**, soak, steep, squash, pulp, mash, infuse • *I like to macerate the food in liqueur for a few minutes before serving.*

Machiavellian = **scheming**, cynical, shrewd, cunning, designing, intriguing, sly, astute, unscrupulous, wily, opportunist, crafty, artful, amoral, foxy, deceitful, underhand, double-dealing, perfidious • *the Machiavellian and devious way decisions were made*

machination *usually plural* = **plot**, scheme, trick, device, design, intrigue, conspiracy, manoeuvre, dodge, ploy, ruse, artifice, cabal, stratagem • *the political machinations that brought him to power*

machine 1 = **appliance**, device, apparatus, engine, tool, instrument, mechanism, gadget, contraption, gizmo *(informal)*, contrivance • *I put a coin in the machine and pulled the lever.*
2 = **system**, agency, structure, organization, machinery, setup *(informal)* • *He has put the party publicity machine behind another candidate.*

QUOTATIONS
Machines are worshipped because they are beautiful and valued because they confer power; they are hated because they are hideous and loathed because they impose slavery
[Bertrand Russell *Sceptical Essays: Machines and the Emotions*]

machinery 1 = **equipment**, gear, instruments, apparatus, works, technology, tackle, tools, mechanism(s), gadgetry • *Farmers import most of their machinery and materials.*
2 = **administration**, system, organization, agency, machine, structure, channels, procedure • *the government machinery and administrative procedures*
▸ **RELATED PHOBIA:** mechanophobia

QUOTATIONS
The world is dying of machinery
[George Moore *Confessions of a Young Man*]

machismo = **masculinity**, toughness, virility, manliness, laddishness • *He had to prove his machismo by going on the scariest rides.*

QUOTATIONS
The tragedy of machismo is that a man is never quite man enough
[Germaine Greer *The Madwoman's Underclothes: My Mailer Problem*]

macho = **manly**, masculine, butch *(slang)*, two-fisted, tough, chauvinist, virile, he-man • *displays of macho bravado*

mad **AS AN ADJECTIVE** 1 = **insane**, mental *(slang)*, crazy *(informal)*, nuts *(slang)*, bananas *(slang)*, barking *(slang)*, raving, distracted, frantic, frenzied, unstable, crackers *(Brit. slang)*, batty *(slang)*, crazed, lunatic, loony *(slang)*, psychotic, demented, cuckoo *(informal)*, unbalanced, barmy *(slang)*, nutty *(slang)*, deranged, delirious, rabid, bonkers *(slang, chiefly Brit.)*, flaky *(U.S. slang)*, unhinged, loopy *(informal)*, crackpot *(informal)*, out to lunch *(informal)*, round the bend *(Brit. slang)*, aberrant, barking mad *(slang)*, out of your mind, gonzo *(slang)*, screwy *(informal)*, doolally *(slang)*, off your head *(slang)*, off your trolley *(slang)*, round the twist *(Brit. slang)*, up the pole *(informal)*, of unsound mind, as daft as a brush *(informal, chiefly Brit.)*, lost your marbles *(informal)*, not right in the head, non compos mentis *(Latin)*, off your rocker *(slang)*, not the full shilling *(informal)*, off your nut *(slang)*, off your chump *(slang)*, wacko *or* whacko *(informal)*, off the air *(Austral. slang)* • *the mad old lady down the street*
OPPOSITES: rational, sane
2 = **foolish**, absurd, wild, stupid, daft *(informal)*, ludicrous, unreasonable, irrational, unsafe, senseless, preposterous, foolhardy, nonsensical, unsound, inane, imprudent, asinine • *Isn't that a rather mad idea?*
OPPOSITES: sound, sensible
3 = **angry**, cross, furious, irritated, fuming, choked, pissed *(U.S. slang)*, infuriated, raging, ape *(slang)*, incensed, enraged, exasperated, pissed off *(taboo slang)*, irate, livid *(informal)*, berserk, seeing red *(informal)*, incandescent, wrathful, apeshit *(slang)*, fit to be tied *(slang)*, in a wax *(informal, chiefly Brit.)*, berko *(Austral. slang)*, tooshie *(Austral. slang)*, off the air *(Austral. slang)* • *I'm pretty mad about it, I can tell you.*
OPPOSITES: calm, composed, cool
4 *usually with* **about** = **enthusiastic**, wild, crazy *(informal)*, nuts *(slang)*, keen, hooked, devoted, in love with, fond, daft *(informal)*, ardent, fanatical, avid, impassioned, zealous, infatuated, dotty *(slang, chiefly Brit.)*, enamoured • *He's mad about you.*
OPPOSITES: uncaring, nonchalant
5 = **frenzied**, wild, excited, energetic, abandoned, agitated, frenetic, uncontrolled, boisterous, full-on *(informal)*, ebullient, gay, riotous, unrestrained • *The game is a mad dash against the clock.*
▸ **IN PHRASES: go mad** 1 = **become insane**, go crazy, lose your mind, lose your reason, go off your trolley *(informal)* • *She was afraid of going mad.*
2 = **become frenzied**, erupt, lose control, boil over, become uncontrollable • *The audience went mad.*
3 = **go berserk**, rant and rave, lose your temper, go off the deep end *(informal)*, go crazy, flip your lid *(informal)*, do your nut *(Brit. informal)*, go ape *(informal)* • *My dad'll go mad if he finds out.*

like mad 1 = enthusiastically, wildly, madly, furiously, excitedly, fervently, like crazy *(informal)*, ardently, unrestrainedly, with might and main • *He was weight training like mad.*
2 = quickly, rapidly, speedily, hell for leather, like lightning, like the clappers *(Brit. informal)*, like nobody's business *(informal)*, like greased lightning *(informal)* • *If I am in the street and hear them, I run like mad.*

QUOTATIONS
The mad are all in God's keeping
[Rudyard Kipling *Kim*]
The only people for me are the mad ones, the ones who are mad to live
[Jack Kerouac *On the Road*]
I'm mad as hell and I'm not going to take it any more!
[Paddy Chayefsky *Network*]

madcap AS AN ADJECTIVE **= reckless**, rash, impulsive, ill-advised, wild, crazy, foolhardy, thoughtless, crackpot *(informal)*, hot-headed, imprudent, heedless, hare-brained • *They flitted from one madcap scheme to another.*
▸ AS A NOUN **= daredevil**, tearaway, wild man, hothead • *Madcap Mark Roberts can be seen doing dangerous stunts in the countryside.*

madden = infuriate, irritate, incense, enrage, upset, provoke, annoy, aggravate *(informal)*, gall, craze, inflame, exasperate, vex, unhinge, drive you crazy, nark *(Brit., Austral. & N.Z. slang)*, drive you round the bend *(Brit. slang)*, make your blood boil, piss you off *(taboo slang)*, drive you to distraction *(informal)*, get your goat *(slang)*, drive you round the twist *(Brit. slang)*, get your dander up *(informal)*, make your hackles rise, raise your hackles, drive you off your head *(slang)*, drive you out of your mind, get your back up, get your hackles up, make you see red *(informal)*, put your back up, hack you off *(informal)* • *It is close in here and the clock ticks to madden me.*
OPPOSITES: calm, soothe, appease

m

maddening = infuriating, exasperating, annoying, irritating, upsetting, provoking, aggravating *(informal)*, vexing, irksome, bothersome • *Shopping in the sales can be maddening.*

made-up 1 = painted, powdered, rouged, done up • *heavily made-up face*
2 = false, invented, imaginary, fictional, untrue, mythical, unreal, fabricated, make-believe, trumped-up, specious • *It looks like a made-up word to me.*

madhouse 1 = chaos, turmoil, bedlam, Babel • *That place is a madhouse.*
2 = mental hospital, psychiatric hospital, mental institution, lunatic asylum, funny farm *(facetious)*, insane asylum, loony bin *(slang)*, nuthouse *(slang)*, rubber room *(U.S. slang)*, laughing academy *(U.S. slang)* • *It was said that he was 'ripe for the madhouse'.*

madly 1 = passionately, wildly, desperately, intensely, exceedingly, extremely, excessively, to distraction, devotedly • *She has fallen madly in love with him.*
2 = foolishly, wildly, absurdly, ludicrously, unreasonably, irrationally, senselessly, nonsensically • *This seemed madly dangerous.*
3 = energetically, quickly, wildly, rapidly, hastily, furiously, excitedly, hurriedly, recklessly, speedily, like mad *(informal)*, hell for leather, like lightning, hotfoot, like the clappers *(Brit. informal)*, like nobody's business *(informal)*, like greased lightning *(informal)* • *Children ran madly around the tables, shouting and playing.*
4 = insanely, frantically, hysterically, crazily, deliriously, distractedly, rabidly, frenziedly, dementedly • *He would cackle madly to himself in the small hours.*

madman or **madwoman = lunatic**, psycho *(slang)*, maniac, loony *(slang)*, nut *(slang)*, psychotic, psychopath, nutter *(Brit. slang)*, basket case *(slang)*, nutcase *(slang)*, headcase *(informal)*, mental case *(slang)*, headbanger *(informal)*, crazy *(informal)* • *He wanted to run around outside, screaming like a madman.*

QUOTATIONS
There is only one difference between a madman and me. I am not mad
[Salvador Dali *Diary of a Genius*]

madness 1 = insanity, mental illness, delusion, mania, dementia, distraction, aberration, psychosis, lunacy, craziness, derangement, psychopathy • *He was driven to the brink of madness.*
2 = foolishness, nonsense, folly, absurdity, idiocy, wildness, daftness *(informal)*, foolhardiness, preposterousness • *It is political madness.*
3 = frenzy, riot, furore, uproar, abandon, excitement, agitation, intoxication, unrestraint • *The country was in a state of madness.*

QUOTATIONS
We are all born mad. Some remain so
[Samuel Beckett *Waiting for Godot*]
Though this be madness, yet there's method in't
[William Shakespeare *Hamlet*]
O! that way madness lies; let me shun that
[William Shakespeare *King Lear*]
What is a more irrefutable proof of madness than an inability to have a doubt?
[Sir Peter Ustinov *Dear Me*]

maelstrom 1 = whirlpool, swirl, eddy, vortex, Charybdis *(literary)* • *a maelstrom of surf and confused seas*
2 = turmoil, disorder, confusion, chaos, upheaval, uproar, pandemonium, bedlam, tumult • *Inside, she was a maelstrom of churning emotions.*

maestro = master, expert, genius, virtuoso, wonk *(informal)*, fundi *(S. African)* • *the maestro's delightful first show*

magazine = journal, paper, publication, supplement, rag *(informal)*, issue, glossy *(informal)*, pamphlet, periodical, fanzine *(informal)* • *Her face is on the cover of a dozen or more magazines.*

maggot = worm, grub • *fetid, maggot-infested meat*

magic AS A NOUN **1 = sorcery**, wizardry, witchcraft, enchantment, occultism, black art, spells, necromancy, sortilege, theurgy • *Legends say that Merlin raised the stones by magic.*
2 = conjuring, illusion, trickery, sleight of hand, smoke and mirrors, hocus-pocus, jiggery-pokery *(informal, chiefly Brit.)*, legerdemain, prestidigitation, jugglery • *His secret hobby: performing magic.*
3 = charm, power, glamour, fascination, magnetism, enchantment, allurement • *The singer believes he can still regain some of his old magic.*
4 = skill, ability, talent, expertise, brilliance, professionalism, accomplishment, finesse, deftness, adeptness, skilfulness • *He showed some touches of football magic.*
▸ AS AN ADJECTIVE **1 = supernatural**, enchanted, occult, thaumaturgic *(rare)* • *So it's a magic potion?*
2 = miraculous, entrancing, charming, fascinating, marvellous, magical, magnetic, enchanting, bewitching, spellbinding, sorcerous • *Then came those magic moments in the rose-garden.*
3 = marvellous, wonderful, excellent, brilliant *(informal)*, fabulous *(informal)*, terrific *(informal)*, fab *(informal)*, brill *(informal)*, rad *(informal)*, phat *(slang)*, schmick *(Austral. informal)*, beaut *(informal)*, barrie *(Scot. slang)*, belting *(Brit. slang)*, pearler *(Austral. slang)* • *It was magic – one of the best days of my life.*

magical 1 = supernatural, magic, mystical, mystic, occult, other-worldly, paranormal, preternatural • *the story of a little boy who has magical powers*

2 = **enchanting**, wonderful, beautiful, lovely, appealing, attractive, charming, heavenly *(informal)*, superb, fascinating, entrancing, magnificent, divine *(informal)*, glorious, gorgeous *(informal)*, delightful, irresistible, sublime, captivating, idyllic, enthralling, beguiling, alluring, bewitching, spellbinding • *The island is a magical place to get married.*
3 = **extraordinary**, amazing, outstanding, remarkable, wonderful, unique, unusual, incredible, magnificent, astonishing, staggering, marvellous, exceptional, unprecedented, sensational, unbelievable, phenomenal, astounding, miraculous, inconceivable, unheard of, unimaginable, unparalleled • *He is on the brink of a magical breakthrough that could double his money.*

magician 1 = **conjuror**, illusionist, prestidigitator • *It was like watching a magician showing you how he performs a trick.*
2 = **sorcerer**, witch, wizard, illusionist, warlock, necromancer, thaumaturge *(rare)*, theurgist, archimage *(rare)*, enchanter *or* enchantress • *Uther called on Merlin the magician to help him.*
3 = **miracle-worker**, genius, marvel, wizard, virtuoso, wonder-worker, spellbinder • *He was a magician with words.*

magisterial = **authoritative**, lordly, commanding, masterful, imperious • *his magisterial voice and bearing*
OPPOSITES: shy, humble, subservient

magistrate = **judge**, justice, provost *(Scot.)*, bailie *(Scot.)*, justice of the peace, J.P. • *The magistrate ordered them to pay £3000 compensation.*
▸ RELATED ADJECTIVE: magisterial

magnanimity = **generosity**, nobility, benevolence, selflessness, unselfishness, munificence, beneficence, high-mindedness, big-heartedness, charitableness, bountifulness, open-handedness, largesse *or* largess • *We will have to show magnanimity in victory.*

magnanimous = **generous**, kind, noble, selfless, big, free, kindly, handsome, charitable, high-minded, bountiful, unselfish, open-handed, big-hearted, unstinting, beneficent, great-hearted, munificent, ungrudging • *He was a man capable of magnanimous gestures.*
OPPOSITES: petty, selfish, resentful

magnate = **tycoon**, leader, chief, fat cat *(slang, chiefly U.S.)*, baron, notable, mogul, bigwig *(informal)*, grandee, big shot *(informal)*, captain of industry, big wheel *(slang)*, big cheese *(old-fashioned slang)*, plutocrat, big noise *(informal)*, big hitter *(informal)*, magnifico, heavy hitter *(informal)*, nabob *(informal)*, Mister Big *(slang, chiefly U.S.)*, V.I.P. • *a multimillionaire shipping magnate*

magnetic = **attractive**, irresistible, seductive, captivating, charming, fascinating, entrancing, charismatic, enchanting, hypnotic, alluring, mesmerizing • *the magnetic pull of his looks*
OPPOSITES: repellent, repulsive, offensive

magnetism = **charm**, appeal, attraction, power, draw, pull, spell, magic, fascination, charisma, attractiveness, allure, enchantment, hypnotism, drawing power, seductiveness, mesmerism, captivatingness • *There was no doubting the animal magnetism of the man.*

magnification 1 = **enlargement**, increase, inflation, boost, expansion, blow-up *(informal)*, intensification, amplification, dilation, augmentation • *a magnification of the human eye*
2 = **exaggeration**, build-up, heightening, deepening, enhancement, aggrandizement • *the magnification of this character on the screen*

magnificence = **splendour**, glory, majesty, grandeur, brilliance, nobility, gorgeousness, sumptuousness, sublimity, resplendence • *I shall never forget the magnificence of the Swiss mountains.*

magnificent 1 = **splendid**, striking, grand, impressive, august, rich, princely, imposing, elegant, divine *(informal)*, glorious, noble, gorgeous, lavish, elevated, luxurious, majestic, regal, stately, sublime, sumptuous, grandiose, exalted, opulent, transcendent, resplendent, splendiferous *(facetious)* • *a magnificent country house in wooded grounds*
OPPOSITES: ordinary, modest, humble
2 = **brilliant**, fine, excellent, outstanding, superb, superior, splendid • *She is magnificent at making you feel able to talk.*

magnify 1 = **enlarge**, increase, boost, expand, intensify, blow up *(informal)*, heighten, amplify, augment, dilate • *The telescope magnifies images over 11 times.*
OPPOSITES: reduce, shrink, diminish
2 = **make worse**, exaggerate, intensify, worsen, heighten, deepen, exacerbate, aggravate, increase, inflame, fan the flames of • *Poverty and human folly magnify natural disasters.*
3 = **exaggerate**, overdo, overstate, build up, enhance, blow up, inflate, overestimate, dramatize, overrate, overplay, overemphasize, blow up out of all proportion, aggrandize, make a production (out) of *(informal)*, make a federal case of *(U.S. informal)* • *spend their time magnifying ridiculous details*
OPPOSITES: understate, deflate, denigrate

magnitude 1 = **importance**, consequence, significance, mark, moment, note, weight, proportion, dimension, greatness, grandeur, eminence • *An operation of this magnitude is going to be difficult.*
OPPOSITES: insignificance, triviality, unimportance
2 = **immensity**, size, extent, enormity, strength, volume, vastness, bigness, largeness, hugeness • *the magnitude of the task confronting them*
OPPOSITES: meanness, smallness
3 = **intensity**, measure, capacity, amplitude • *a quake with a magnitude exceeding 5*

maid 1 = **servant**, chambermaid, housemaid, menial, handmaiden *(archaic)*, maidservant, female servant, domestic *(archaic)*, parlourmaid, serving-maid • *A maid brought me breakfast at half-past eight.*
2 = **girl**, maiden, lass, miss, nymph *(poetic)*, damsel, lassie *(informal)*, wench • *But can he win back the heart of this fair maid?*

maiden AS A NOUN = **girl**, maid, lass, damsel, miss, virgin, nymph *(poetic)*, lassie *(informal)*, wench • *stories of brave princes and beautiful maidens*
▸ AS A MODIFIER 1 = **first**, initial, inaugural, introductory, initiatory • *The Titanic sank on its maiden voyage.*
2 = **unmarried**, pure, virgin, intact, chaste, virginal, unwed, undefiled • *An elderly maiden aunt had left him £1000.*

maidenly = **modest**, reserved, demure, pure, decent, gentle, virtuous, chaste, girlish, virginal, decorous, unsullied, vestal, undefiled • *She could not avoid a maidenly blush.*
OPPOSITES: indecent, immoral, wanton

mail AS A NOUN 1 = **letters**, post, packages, parcels, correspondence • *She looked through the mail.*
2 = **postal service**, post, postal system • *Your cheque is in the mail.*
▸ AS A VERB 1 = **post**, send, forward, dispatch, send by mail or post • *He mailed me the contract.*
2 = **e-mail**, send, forward • *You can write or mail your CV to us.*

maim = **cripple**, hurt, injure, wound, mar, disable, hamstring, impair, lame, mutilate, mangle, incapacitate, put out of action, mangulate *(Austral. slang)* • *One man has lost his life; another has been maimed.*

main AS AN ADJECTIVE 1 = **chief**, leading, major, prime, head, special, central, particular, necessary, essential, premier, primary, vital, critical, crucial, supreme, outstanding, principal, cardinal, paramount, foremost, predominant, pre-eminent, must-have • *My main concern now is to protect the children.*
OPPOSITES: least, minor, secondary
2 = **sheer**, direct, entire, pure, mere, absolute, utter, utmost,

downright, brute, undisguised • *She had to be held back by main force.*
▸ **AS A PLURAL NOUN 1 = pipeline**, channel, pipe, conduit, duct • *the water supply from the mains*
2 = cable, line, electricity supply, mains supply • *amplifiers which plug into the mains*
▸ **IN PHRASES: in the main = on the whole**, generally, mainly, mostly, in general, for the most part • *In the main, children are taboo in the workplace.*

mainly = chiefly, mostly, largely, generally, usually, principally, in general, primarily, above all, substantially, on the whole, predominantly, in the main, for the most part, most of all, first and foremost, to the greatest extent • *The birds live mainly on nectar.*

main road = highway • *He turned off the main road and into the car park.*

mainspring = cause, inspiration, motivation, source, origin, incentive, motive, impulse, driving force, prime mover • *Music has always been the mainspring of my life.*

mainstay = pillar, backbone, bulwark, prop, anchor, buttress, lynchpin, chief support • *Fish and rice were the mainstays of their diet.*

mainstream = conventional, general, established, received, accepted, central, current, core, prevailing, orthodox • *The show wanted to attract a mainstream audience.*
OPPOSITES: fringe, marginal, unconventional

maintain 1 = continue, retain, preserve, sustain, carry on, keep, keep up, prolong, uphold, nurture, conserve, perpetuate • *You should always maintain your friendships.*
OPPOSITES: end, finish, drop
2 = assert, state, hold, claim, insist, declare, allege, contend, affirm, profess, avow, aver, asseverate • *Prosecutors maintain that no deal was made.*
OPPOSITES: disavow
3 = look after, care for, take care of, finance, conserve, keep in good condition • *The house costs a fortune to maintain.*
4 = support, look after, keep, finance, feed, sustain, take care of, provide for, nurture, nourish • *the basic costs of maintaining a child*

maintenance 1 = upkeep, keeping, care, supply, repairs, provision, conservation, nurture, preservation • *the maintenance of government buildings*
2 = allowance, living, support, keep, food, livelihood, subsistence, upkeep, sustenance, alimony, aliment • *Absent fathers must pay maintenance for their children.*
3 = continuation, carrying-on, continuance, support, perpetuation, prolongation, sustainment, retainment • *the maintenance of peace and stability in Asia*

majestic = grand, magnificent, impressive, superb, kingly, royal, august, princely, imposing, imperial, noble, splendid, elevated, awesome, dignified, regal, stately, monumental, sublime, lofty, pompous, grandiose, exalted, splendiferous *(facetious)* • *a majestic country home*
OPPOSITES: ordinary, modest, humble

majesty = grandeur, glory, splendour, magnificence, dignity, nobility, sublimity, loftiness, impressiveness, awesomeness, exaltedness • *the majesty of the mainland mountains*
OPPOSITES: shame, disgrace, triviality

major 1 = important, vital, critical, significant, great, serious, radical, crucial, outstanding, grave, extensive, notable, weighty, pre-eminent • *Exercise has a major part to play in combating disease.*
2 = main, higher, greater, bigger, lead, leading, head, larger, better, chief, senior, supreme, superior, elder, uppermost • *We heard extracts from three of his major works.*
OPPOSITES: smaller, minor, secondary
3 = significant, big, key, sweeping, substantial • *Drug abuse has long been a major problem here.*
OPPOSITES: trivial, insignificant, unimportant
4 = complicated, difficult, serious, radical • *The removal of a small lump turned out to be major surgery.*

majority 1 = most, more, mass, bulk, best part, better part, lion's share, preponderance, plurality, greater number • *The majority of our customers come from out of town.*
2 = margin, landslide • *They approved the move by a majority of ninety-nine.*
3 = adulthood, maturity, age of consent, seniority, manhood or womanhood • *Once you reach your majority, you can do what you please.*

QUOTATIONS
One, on God's side, is a majority
[Wendell Phillips]

make AS A VERB 1 = produce, cause, create, effect, lead to, occasion, generate, bring about, give rise to, engender, beget • *The crash made a noise like a building coming down.*
2 = perform, do, act out, effect, carry out, engage in, execute, prosecute • *I made a gesture at him and turned away.*
3 = reach, come to, establish, conclude, seal, settle on, determine on • *We've got to make a decision by next week.*
4 = give, deliver, pronounce, utter, recite • *I've been asked to make a speech.*
5 = score, gain, amass, win, notch up *(informal)*, chalk up *(informal)* • *He made 1,972 runs for the county.*
6 = force, cause, press, compel, drive, require, oblige, induce, railroad *(informal)*, constrain, coerce, impel, dragoon, pressurize, prevail upon • *You can't make me do anything.*
7 = appoint, name, select, elect, invest, install, nominate, assign, designate, hire as, cast as, employ as, ordain, vote in as, recruit as, engage as, enlist as • *They made him transport minister.*
8 = create, build, produce, manufacture, form, model, fashion, shape, frame, construct, assemble, compose, forge, mould, put together, originate, fabricate • *They now make cars at two plants in Europe.*
9 = prepare, cook, put together, get ready, whip up, concoct, throw together, dish up, fix *(U.S. informal)*, jack up *(N.Z. informal)* • *You wash while I make some lunch.*
10 = compile, write, produce, draft, pen, compose, draw up, formulate • *Make a list of your questions beforehand.*
11 = enact, form, pass, establish, fix, institute, frame, devise, lay down, draw up • *The only person who makes rules in this house is me.*
12 = earn, get, gain, net, win, clear, secure, realize, obtain, acquire, bring in, take in, fetch • *How much money did we make?*
13 = be, become, form, represent, serve as, come to be, embody, develop into, grow into, act as, function as • *She'll make a good actress, if she gets the training.* • *Your idea will make a good book.*
14 = amount to, total, constitute, add up to, count as, tot up to *(informal)* • *They are adding three aircraft carriers. That makes six in all.*
15 = gain a place in, achieve a place in, get into, attain a place in • *The athletes are just happy to make the British team.*
16 = get to, reach, catch, arrive at, meet, arrive in time for • *We made the train, jumping aboard just as it was pulling out.* • *We have to make New Orleans by nightfall.*
17 = calculate, judge, estimate, determine, think, suppose, reckon, work out, compute, gauge, count up, put a figure on • *I make the total for the year as £69,599.*
▸ **AS A NOUN = brand**, sort, style, model, build, form, mark, kind, type, variety, construction, marque • *What make of car did he rent?*
▸ **IN PHRASES: make as if = pretend**, affect, give the impression that, feign, feint, make a show of, act as if or though • *He made as if to chase me.*

make away *or* **off with something = steal**, nick *(slang, chiefly Brit.)*, pinch *(informal)*, nab *(informal)*, carry off, swipe *(slang)*, knock off *(slang)*, trouser *(slang)*, pilfer, cart off *(slang)*, purloin, filch • *They tied her up and made away with £2000.*

make believe = pretend, play, enact, feign, play-act, act as if *or* though • *He made believe he didn't understand what I was saying.*

make do = manage, cope, improvise, muddle through, get along *or* by, scrape along *or* by • *It's not going to be easy but I can make do.*

make for something 1 = head for, aim for, head towards, set out for, be bound for, make a beeline for, steer (a course) for, proceed towards • *He rose from his seat and made for the door.*

2 = contribute to, produce, further, forward, advance, promote, foster, facilitate, be conducive to • *A happy parent makes for a happy child.*

make it 1 = succeed, be successful, prosper, be a success, arrive *(informal)*, get on, make good, cut it *(informal)*, get ahead, make the grade *(informal)*, crack it *(informal)*, make it big, get somewhere, distinguish yourself • *I have the talent to make it.*

2 = get better, survive, recover, rally, come through, pull through • *The nurses didn't think he was going to make it.*

make off = flee, clear out *(informal)*, abscond, fly, bolt, decamp, hook it *(slang)*, do a runner *(slang)*, run for it *(informal)*, slope off, cut and run *(informal)*, beat a hasty retreat, fly the coop *(U.S. & Canad. informal)*, make away, skedaddle *(informal)*, take a powder *(U.S. & Canad. slang)*, take to your heels, run away *or* off • *They broke free and made off in a stolen car.*

make out 1 = fare, manage, do, succeed, cope, get on, proceed, thrive, prosper • *He wondered how they were making out.*

2 = make love, have sex, fuck *(taboo slang)*, shag *(taboo slang)*, do it *(Brit. informal)*, neck *(informal)*, pet, screw *(taboo slang)*, caress, hump *(taboo slang)*, kiss and cuddle, smooch *(informal)*, bonk *(Brit. informal)*, copulate *(formal)*, canoodle *(informal)*, fornicate *(archaic)* • *pictures of the couple making out on the beach*

make something out 1 = see, observe, distinguish, perceive, recognize, detect, glimpse, pick out, discern, catch sight of, espy, descry • *I could just make out a tall pale figure.*

2 = understand, see, work out, grasp, perceive, follow, realize, comprehend, fathom, decipher, suss (out) *(slang)*, get the drift of • *It's hard to make out what criteria are used.*

3 = write out, complete, draft, draw up, inscribe, fill in *or* out • *I'll make out a receipt for you.*

4 = pretend, claim, suggest, maintain, declare, allege, hint, imply, intimate, assert, insinuate, let on, make as if • *They were trying to make out that I'd done it.*

5 = prove, show, describe, represent, demonstrate, justify • *You could certainly make out a case for this point of view.*

make something up = invent, create, construct, compose, write, frame, manufacture, coin, devise, hatch, originate, formulate, dream up, fabricate, concoct, cook up *(informal)*, trump up • *She made up stories about him.*

make up = settle your differences, shake hands, make peace, bury the hatchet, call it quits, forgive and forget, mend fences, become reconciled, declare a truce, be friends again • *She came back and they made up.*

make up for something 1 = compensate for, redress, make amends for, atone for, balance out, offset, expiate, requite, make reparation for, make recompense for • *The compensation is intended to make up for stress caused.*

2 = offset, balance out, compensate for, redeem, cancel out, neutralize, counterbalance, counterweigh • *His skill makes up for his lack of speed.*

make up something 1 = form, account for, constitute, compose, comprise • *Women officers make up 13 per cent of the police force.*

2 = complete, meet, supply, fill, round off • *Some of the money they receive is in grants; loans make up the rest.*

make up to someone = flirt with, be all over, come on to, chase after, court, pursue, woo, run after, chat up *(informal)*, curry favour with, make overtures to, make eyes at • *She watched as her best friend made up to the man she herself loved.*

make up your mind = decide, choose, determine, settle on, resolve, make a decision about, come to a decision about, reach a decision about • *He had already made up his mind which side he was on.*

QUOTATIONS

God has given you one face, and you make yourselves another

[William Shakespeare *Hamlet*]

Most women are not so young as they are painted

[Max Beerbohm]

make-believe AS A NOUN **= fantasy**, imagination, pretence, charade, unreality, dream, play-acting • *She squandered her millions on a life of make-believe.*

OPPOSITES: fact, reality, actuality

▸ AS AN ADJECTIVE **= imaginary**, dream, imagined, made-up, fantasy, pretend, pretended, mock, sham, unreal, fantasized • *Children withdraw at times into a make-believe world.*

OPPOSITES: real, genuine, authentic

maker = manufacturer, producer, builder, constructor, fabricator • *Japan's two largest car makers*

Maker = God, Creator, Prime Mover • *Let us kneel before the Lord our Maker*

makeshift = temporary, provisional, make-do, substitute, jury *(chiefly Nautical)*, expedient, rough and ready, stopgap • *the makeshift shelters of the homeless*

make-up 1 = cosmetics, paint *(informal)*, powder, face *(informal)*, greasepaint *(Theatre)*, war paint *(informal)*, maquillage *(French)* • *Normally she wore little make-up, but this evening was clearly an exception.*

2 = nature, character, constitution, temperament, make, build, figure, stamp, temper, disposition, frame of mind, cast of mind • *He became convinced that there was some fatal flaw in his make-up.*

3 = structure, organization, arrangement, form, construction, assembly, constitution, format, formation, composition, configuration • *the chemical make-up of the atmosphere*

making AS A NOUN **= creation**, production, manufacture, construction, assembly, forging, composition, fabrication • *a book about the making of the movie*

▸ AS A PLURAL NOUN **= beginnings**, qualities, potential, stuff, basics, materials, capacity, ingredients, essence, capability, potentiality • *He had the makings of a successful journalist.*

▸ IN PHRASES: **in the making = budding**, potential, up and coming, emergent, coming, growing, developing, promising, burgeoning, nascent, incipient • *Her drama teacher says she is a star in the making.*

maladjusted = disturbed, hung-up *(slang)*, alienated, unstable, estranged, neurotic • *a school for maladjusted children*

maladministration = mismanagement, incompetence, inefficiency, misrule, corruption, blundering, bungling, malpractice, dishonesty, malfeasance *(Law)*, misgovernment • *a request to investigate a claim about maladministration*

maladroit = clumsy, awkward, bungling, inept, cack-handed *(informal)*, inexpert, unskilful, unhandy, ham-fisted *or* ham-handed *(informal)* • *Some of his first interviews with the press were rather maladroit.*

malady = **disease**, complaint, illness, disorder, sickness, ailment, affliction, infirmity, ill, indisposition, lurgy *(informal)* • *He was stricken at twenty-one with a crippling malady.*

malaise = **unease**, illness, depression, anxiety, weakness, sickness, discomfort, melancholy, angst, disquiet, doldrums, lassitude, enervation • *He complained of depression, headaches and malaise.*

malcontent AS A NOUN = **troublemaker**, rebel, complainer, grumbler, grouser, agitator, stirrer *(informal)*, mischief-maker, grouch *(informal)*, fault-finder • *Five years ago, a band of malcontents seized power.*

▸ AS AN ADJECTIVE = **discontented**, unhappy, disgruntled, dissatisfied, disgusted, rebellious, resentful, disaffected, restive, unsatisfied, ill-disposed, factious • *The film follows three malcontent teenagers around Paris.*

male = **masculine**, manly, macho, virile, manlike, manful • *a deep male voice*

OPPOSITES: womanly, female, feminine

QUOTATIONS

The male is a domestic animal which, if treated with firmness and kindness, can be trained to do most things
[Jilly Cooper]

A man is as old as he's feeling,
A woman as old as she looks
[Mortimer Collins *The Unknown Quantity*]

malevolence = **malice**, hate, spite, hatred, nastiness, rancour, ill will, vindictiveness, malignity, spitefulness, vengefulness, maliciousness • *His actions betrayed a rare streak of malevolence.*

m

malevolent = **spiteful**, hostile, vicious, malicious, malign, malignant, vindictive, pernicious, vengeful, hateful *(archaic)*, baleful, rancorous, evil-minded, maleficent, ill-natured • *Her stare was malevolent, her mouth a thin line.*

OPPOSITES: kind, friendly, benevolent

malformed = **misshapen**, twisted, crooked, distorted, abnormal, irregular, deformed, contorted • *Her leg had been malformed from birth.*

malfunction AS A VERB = **break down**, fail, go wrong, play up *(Brit. informal)*, stop working, be defective, conk out *(informal)*, develop a fault • *Radiation can cause microprocessors to malfunction.*

▸ AS A NOUN = **fault**, failure, breakdown, defect, flaw, impairment, glitch • *There must have been a computer malfunction.*

malice = **spite**, animosity, enmity, hate, hatred, bitterness, venom, spleen, rancour, bad blood, ill will, animus, malevolence, vindictiveness, evil intent, malignity, spitefulness, vengefulness, maliciousness • *There was no malice on his part.*

QUOTATIONS

Malice is of a low stature, but it hath very long arms
[George Savile, Marquess of Halifax *Political, Moral, and Miscellaneous Thoughts*]

Malice is only another name for mediocrity
[Patrick Kavanagh]

malicious = **spiteful**, malevolent, malignant, vicious, bitter, resentful, pernicious, vengeful, bitchy *(informal)*, hateful, baleful, injurious, rancorous, catty *(informal)*, shrewish, ill-disposed, evil-minded, ill-natured • *She described the charges as malicious.*

OPPOSITES: kind, friendly, benevolent

malign AS A VERB = **disparage**, abuse, run down, libel, knock *(informal)*, injure, rubbish *(informal)*, smear, blacken (someone's name), slag (off) *(slang)*, denigrate, revile, vilify, slander, defame, bad-mouth *(slang, chiefly U.S. & Canad.)*, traduce, speak ill of, derogate, do a hatchet job on *(informal)*, calumniate, asperse • *We maligned him dreadfully, assuming the very worst about him.*

OPPOSITES: praise, compliment, commend

▸ AS AN ADJECTIVE = **evil**, bad, destructive, harmful, hostile, vicious, malignant, wicked, hurtful, pernicious, malevolent, baleful, deleterious, injurious, baneful, maleficent • *the malign influence jealousy had on their lives*

OPPOSITES: good, kind, friendly

malignant 1 = **uncontrollable**, dangerous, evil, fatal, deadly, cancerous, virulent, metastatic, irremediable • *a malignant breast tumour*
2 = **hostile**, harmful, bitter, vicious, destructive, malicious, malign, hurtful, pernicious, malevolent, spiteful, baleful, injurious, inimical, maleficent, of evil intent • *a malignant minority indulging in crime and violence*

OPPOSITES: kind, friendly, benign

mall = **shopping centre**, arcade, shopping mall, shopping precinct, strip mall *(U.S.)* • *I plan to pay a visit to the mall.*

mallard

▸ COLLECTIVE NOUNS: sord, sute

malleable 1 = **manageable**, adaptable, compliant, impressionable, pliable, tractable, biddable, governable, like putty in your hands • *She was young enough to be malleable.*
2 = **workable**, soft, plastic, tensile, ductile • *Silver is the most malleable of all metals.*

malnutrition = **undernourishment**, hunger, famine, starvation, poor diet, lack of food, malnourishment, inadequate diet, inanition • *Infections are more likely in those suffering from malnutrition.*

malodorous = **smelly**, stinking, reeking, nauseating, rank, offensive, fetid, foul-smelling, putrid, evil-smelling, noisome, mephitic, niffy *(Brit. slang)*, olid, festy *(Austral. slang)* • *tons of malodorous garbage bags*

malpractice = **misconduct**, abuse, negligence, mismanagement, misbehaviour, dereliction • *serious allegations of malpractice*

maltreat = **abuse**, damage, hurt, injure, harm, bully, mistreat, ill-treat, handle roughly • *He was not maltreated during his detention.*

maltreatment = **abuse**, bullying, mistreatment, injury, harm, ill-treatment, rough handling, ill-usage • *Two thousand prisoners died as a result of maltreatment.*

mammal

▹ See panels **Anteaters and other edentates; Bats; Carnivores; Cattle and other artiodactyls; Horses, rhinos and other perissodactyls; Marsupials; Monkeys, apes and other primates; Rabbits and hares; Rodents; Sea mammals; Shrews and other insectivores; Whales and dolphins**

PROVERBS

The leopard does not change his spots

EXTINCT MAMMALS

apeman	Irish elk
aurochs	labyrinthodont
australopithecine	mammoth
baluchitherium	mastodon
chalicothere	megathere
creodont	nototherium
dinoceras *or* uintathere	quagga
dinothere	sabre-toothed tiger
dryopithecine	tarpan
eohippus	thylacine
glyptodont	titanothere

mammoth = **colossal**, huge, giant, massive, vast, enormous, mighty, immense, titanic, jumbo *(informal)*, gigantic, monumental, mountainous, stellar *(informal)*, prodigious, stupendous, gargantuan, fuck-off *(offensive*

taboo slang), elephantine, ginormous *(informal)*, Brobdingnagian, humongous *or* humungous *(U.S. slang)*, supersize • *The mammoth undertaking was completed in 18 months.*
OPPOSITES: little, small, tiny

man **AS A NOUN** **1 = male**, guy *(informal)*, fellow *(informal)*, gentleman, bloke *(Brit. informal)*, chap *(Brit. informal)*, dude *(U.S. informal)*, geezer *(informal)*, adult male • *I had not expected the young man to reappear before evening.*
2 = human, human being, body, person, individual, adult, being, somebody, soul, personage • *a possible step to sending a man back to the moon*
3 = mankind, humanity, people, mortals, human race, humankind, Homo sapiens • *Anxiety is modern man's natural state.*
4 = partner, boy, husband, lover, mate, boyfriend, squeeze *(informal)*, old man, groom, spouse, sweetheart, beau, significant other *(U.S.)*, bidie-in *(Scot.)* • *Does your man cuddle you enough?*
5 *usually plural* **= worker**, labourer, workman, hand, employee, subordinate, blue-collar worker, hireling • *The men voted to accept the pay offer.*
▸**AS A VERB** **= staff**, people, fill, crew, occupy, garrison, furnish with men • *Soldiers manned roadblocks in the city.*
▸**IN PHRASES:** **man to man = frankly**, openly, directly, honestly, face to face, candidly, woman to woman, forthrightly • *Confront it face to face. Man to man.*
to a man = without exception, as one, every one, unanimously, each and every one, one and all, bar none • *Economists, almost to a man, were sceptical.*
▸**RELATED ADJECTIVES:** anthropic, anthropoid, anthropoidal
▸**RELATED MANIA:** andromania
▸**RELATED PHOBIA:** androphobia, anthropophobia

QUOTATIONS

Man is only a reed, the weakest thing in nature; but he is a thinking reed
[Blaise Pascal *Pensées*]

Man is the measure of all things
[Protagoras]

Man is heaven's masterpiece
[Francis Quarles *Emblems*]

There are many wonderful things, and nothing is more wonderful than man
[Sophocles *Antigone*]

Man is a noble animal, splendid in ashes, and pompous in the grave
[Thomas Browne *Hydriotaphia*]

Man is an embodied paradox, a bundle of contradictions
[Charles Colton *Lacon*]

Man has but three events in his life: to be born, to live, and to die. He is not conscious of his birth, he suffers at his death and he forgets to live
[Jean de la Bruyère *The Characters, or the Manners of the Age*]

The four stages of man are infancy, childhood, adolescence and obsolescence
[Art Linkletter *A Child's Garden of Misinformation*]

Man is a useless passion
[Jean-Paul Sartre *L'Être et le néant*]

Glory to Man in the highest! for Man is the master of things
[Algernon Charles Swinburne *Atalanta in Calydon: Hymn of Man*]

I sometimes think that God in creating man somewhat overestimated his ability
[Oscar Wilde]

What a piece of work is man! how noble in reason! how infinite in faculty! in form, in moving, how express and admirable! in action how like an angel! in apprehension how like a god! the beauty of the world! the paragon of animals!
[William Shakespeare *Hamlet*]

Man is nature's sole mistake
[W.S. Gilbert *Princess Ida*]

Man is something to be surpassed
[Friedrich Nietzsche *Thus Spake Zarathustra*]

Man was formed for society
[William Blackstone *Commentaries on the Laws of England*]

man: an animal so lost in rapturous contemplation of what he thinks he is as to overlook what he indubitably ought to be
[Ambrose Bierce *The Devil's Dictionary*]

Men are but children of a larger growth
[John Dryden *All for Love*]

Man, became man through work, who stepped out of the animal kingdom as transformer of the natural into the artificial, who became therefore the magician
[Ernst Fischer *The Necessity of Art*]

PROVERBS

The best of men are but men at best

mana **= authority**, influence, power, might, force, weight, strength, domination, sway, standing, status, importance, esteem, stature, eminence • *a leader of great mana and influence*

manacle **AS A NOUN** **= handcuff**, bond, chain, shackle, tie, iron, fetter, gyve *(archaic)* • *He had a steel-reinforced cell with manacles fixed to the walls.*
▸**AS A VERB** **= handcuff**, bind, confine, restrain, check, chain, curb, hamper, inhibit, constrain, shackle, fetter, tie someone's hands, put in chains, clap *or* put in irons • *His hands were manacled behind his back.*

manage **1 = be in charge of**, run, handle, rule, direct, conduct, command, govern, administer, oversee, supervise, preside over, be head of, call the shots in, superintend, call the tune in • *Within two years, he was managing the store.*
2 = organize, use, handle, govern, regulate • *Managing your time is increasingly important.*
3 = cope, survive, shift, succeed, get on, carry on, fare, get through, make out, cut it *(informal)*, get along, make do, get by *(informal)*, crack it *(informal)*, muddle through • *How did your mother manage when he left?*
4 = perform, do, deal with, achieve, carry out, undertake, cope with, accomplish, contrive, finish off, bring about *or* off • *those who can only manage a few hours of work*
5 = control, influence, guide, handle, master, dominate, manipulate • *Her daughter couldn't manage the horse.*
6 = steer, operate, pilot • *managing a car well in bad conditions*

manageable **1 = easy**, convenient, handy, user-friendly, wieldy • *The table folds down into a manageable zipped carrying bag.*
OPPOSITES: hard, demanding, difficult
2 = achievable, possible, reasonable, viable, feasible, practicable, attainable, doable • *It gives the person a manageable goal.*

management **1 = administration**, control, rule, government, running, charge, care, operation, handling, direction, conduct, command, guidance, supervision, manipulation, governance, superintendence • *the responsibility for its day-to-day management*
2 = directors, board, executive(s), bosses *(informal)*, administration, employers, directorate • *The management is doing its best to control the situation.*

manager **= supervisor**, head, director, executive, boss *(informal)*, governor, administrator, conductor, controller, superintendent, gaffer *(informal, chiefly Brit.)*, proprietor, organizer, comptroller, overseer, baas *(S. African)*, sherang *(Austral. & N.Z.)* • *a retired bank manager*

managerial = **supervisory**, executive, administrative, overseeing, superintendent • *He sees his role as essentially managerial.*
mandate = **command**, order, charge, authority, commission, sanction, instruction, warrant, decree, bidding, canon, directive, injunction, fiat, edict, authorization, precept • *The union already has a mandate to ballot for a strike.*
mandatory = **compulsory**, required, binding, obligatory, requisite • *Attendance is mandatory.*
OPPOSITES: voluntary, unnecessary, optional
mane = **head** • *He had a great mane of white hair.*
manfully = **bravely**, boldly, vigorously, stoutly, hard, strongly, desperately, courageously, stalwartly, powerfully, resolutely, determinedly, heroically, valiantly, nobly, gallantly, like the devil, to the best of your ability, like a Trojan, intrepidly, like one possessed, with might and main • *They stuck to their task manfully.*
manger = **trough**, feeder, crib • *All the feed went into one manger.*
mangle 1 = **crush**, mutilate, maim, deform, cut, total *(slang)*, tear, destroy, ruin, mar, rend, wreck, spoil, butcher, cripple, hack, distort, trash *(slang)*, maul, disfigure, lacerate, mangulate *(Austral. slang)* • *His body was mangled beyond recognition.*
2 = **ruin**, murder *(informal)*, mar, spoil, bungle, screw up *(informal)*, mess up, make a hash of *(informal)* • *There is almost no phrase so simple that he cannot mangle it.*
mangy = **scruffy**, mean, dirty, shabby, seedy, shoddy, squalid, grungy *(slang, chiefly U.S.)*, moth-eaten, scabby *(informal)*, scuzzy *(slang, chiefly U.S.)*, skanky *(slang)* • *mangy old dogs*
OPPOSITES: clean, splendid, well-kept
manhandle 1 = **rough up**, pull, push, paw *(informal)*, maul, handle roughly, knock about *or* around • *Foreign journalists were manhandled by the police.*
2 = **haul**, carry, pull, push, lift, manoeuvre, tug, shove, hump *(Brit. slang)*, heave • *The three of us manhandled the dinghy out of the shed.*
manhood 1 = **maturity**, adulthood, sexual maturity • *They were failing to help their sons grow from boyhood to manhood.*
2 = **manliness**, masculinity, spirit, strength, resolution, courage, determination, maturity, bravery, fortitude, mettle, firmness, virility, valour, hardihood, manfulness • *He had never before felt the need to prove his manhood.*
mania 1 = **obsession**, passion, thing *(informal)*, desire, rage, enthusiasm, craving, preoccupation, craze, fad *(informal)*, fetish, fixation, partiality • *They had a mania for travelling.*
2 = **madness**, disorder, frenzy, insanity, dementia, aberration, lunacy, delirium, craziness, derangement • *the treatment of mania*
▷ *See panel* **Types of mania**
maniac 1 = **madman** *or* **madwoman**, psycho *(slang)*, lunatic, loony *(slang)*, psychopath, nutter *(Brit. slang)*, basket case *(slang)*, nutcase *(slang)*, headcase *(informal)*, headbanger *(informal)*, crazy *(informal)* • *a drug-crazed maniac*
2 = **fanatic**, fan, enthusiast, freak *(informal)*, fiend *(informal)* • *big-spending football maniacs*
maniacal *or* **manic** = **crazed**, mad, crazy *(informal)*, insane, wild, raving, frenzied, neurotic, lunatic, psychotic, demented, unbalanced, nutty *(slang)*, deranged, berserk, gonzo *(slang)*, berko *(Austral. slang)*, off the air *(Austral. slang)* • *She is hunched over the wheel with a maniacal expression.*
manic 1 = **frenzied**, intense, hectic, hyper *(informal)*, frenetic, feverish • *He was possessed by an almost manic energy.*
2 = **mad**, crazy *(informal)*, insane, crazed, wild, lunatic, demented, deranged, demonic, maniacal • *His face was frozen in a manic smile.*
manifest AS AN ADJECTIVE = **obvious**, apparent, patent, evident, open, clear, plain, visible, bold, distinct, glaring, noticeable, blatant, conspicuous, unmistakable, palpable, salient • *cases of manifest injustice*
OPPOSITES: masked, disguised, concealed
▸ AS A VERB = **display**, show, reveal, establish, express, prove, declare, demonstrate, expose, exhibit, set forth, make plain, evince • *He's only convincing when that inner fury manifests itself.*
OPPOSITES: hide, cover, conceal
manifestation 1 = **sign**, symptom, indication, mark, example, evidence, instance, proof, token, testimony • *Different animals have different manifestations of the disease.*
2 = **display**, show, exhibition, expression, demonstration, appearance, exposure, revelation, disclosure, materialization • *the manifestation of grief*
manifesto = **policy statement**, publication, declaration, programme, announcement, platform, proclamation, pronouncement • *The Tories are drawing up their election manifesto.*
manifold = **numerous**, many, various, varied, multiple, diverse, multiplied, diversified, abundant, assorted, copious, multifarious, multitudinous, multifold • *The difficulties are manifold.*
manipulate 1 = **influence**, control, direct, guide, conduct, negotiate, exploit, steer, manoeuvre, do a number on *(chiefly U.S.)*, twist around your little finger • *He's a very difficult character. He manipulates people.* • *She was unable, for once, to manipulate events.*
2 = **work**, use, operate, handle, employ, wield • *The technology uses a pen to manipulate a computer.*
3 = **massage**, rub, knead, palpate • *The way he can manipulate my leg has helped my arthritis so much.*
4 = **falsify**, alter, distort, change, doctor, cook *(informal)*, rig, interfere with, fiddle with *(informal)*, juggle, tamper with, tinker with, misrepresent • *The government manipulated the figures.*
manipulative = **scheming**, calculating, cunning, sly, designing, slick, shrewd, slippery, unscrupulous, devious, wily, crafty, artful, disingenuous, conniving, Machiavellian, guileful • *She described him as cold, calculating and manipulative.*
mankind = **people**, man, humanity, human race, humankind, Homo sapiens • *the evolution of mankind*

QUOTATIONS
I hate mankind, for I think myself one of the best of them, and I know how bad I am
[Dr. Johnson]
Mankind have been created for the sake of one another. Either instruct them, therefore, or endure them
[Marcus Aurelius *Meditations*]

manliness = **virility**, masculinity, manhood, machismo, courage, bravery, vigour, heroism, mettle, boldness, firmness, valour, fearlessness, intrepidity, hardihood • *He has no doubts about his manliness.*
manly = **virile**, male, masculine, macho, strong, powerful, brave, daring, bold, strapping, hardy, heroic, robust, vigorous, muscular, courageous, fearless, butch *(slang)*, resolute, gallant, valiant, well-built, red-blooded *(informal)*, dauntless, stout-hearted, valorous, manful • *He set himself manly tasks and expected others to follow him.* • *He was the ideal of manly beauty.*
OPPOSITES: feminine, frail, effeminate
man-made = **artificial**, manufactured, plastic *(slang)*, mock, synthetic, ersatz • *a variety of materials, both natural and man-made*
mannequin 1 = **dummy**, figure, model • *a shop-window mannequin*
2 = **model**, supermodel, fashion model, clothes horse *(informal)*, poster boy *or* girl • *She became a mannequin after being spotted in a hairdresser's.*

TYPES OF MANIA

ablutomania	washing	gamomania	marriage	noctimania	night
agoramania	open spaces	graphomania	writing	nudomania	nudity
ailuromania	cats	gymnomania	nakedness	nymphomania	sex
andromania	men	gynomania	women	ochlomania	crowds
Anglomania	England	hamartiomania	sin	oikomania	home
anthomania	flowers	hedonomania	pleasure	oinomania	wine
apimania	bees	heliomania	sun	ophidiomania	reptiles
arithmomania	counting	hippomania	horses	orchidomania	testicles
automania	solitude	homicidomania	murder	ornithomania	birds
autophonomania	suicide	hydromania	water	phagomania	eating
balletomania	ballet	hylomania	woods	pharmacomania	medicines
ballistomania	bullets	hypnomania	sleep	phonomania	noise
bibliomania	books	ichthyomania	fish	photomania	light
chionomania	snow	iconomania	icons	plutomania	great wealth
choreomania	dancing	kinesomania	movement	potomania	drinking
chrematomania	money	kleptomania	stealing	pyromania	fire
cremnomania	cliffs	logomania	talking	scribomania	writing
cynomania	dogs	macromania	becoming larger	siderodromomania	railway travel
dipsomania	alcohol	megalomania	your own importance	sitomania	food
doramania	fur	melomania	music	sophomania	your own wisdom
dromomania	travelling	mentulomania	penises	thalassomania	the sea
egomania	your self	micromania	becoming smaller	thanatomania	death
eleuthromania	freedom	monomania	one thing	theatromania	theatre
entheomania	religion	musicomania	music	timbromania	stamps
entomomania	insects	musomania	mice	trichomania	hair
ergasiomania	work	mythomania	lies	verbomania	words
eroticomania	erotica	necromania	death	xenomania	foreigners
erotomania	sex			zoomania	animals
florimania	plants				

manner AS A NOUN **1 = style**, way, fashion, method, means, form, process, approach, practice, procedure, habit, custom, routine, mode, genre, tack, tenor, usage, wont • *The manner in which young children are spoken to depends on who is present.*
2 = behaviour, look, air, bearing, conduct, appearance, aspect, presence, tone, demeanour, deportment, mien *(literary)*, comportment • *His manner was self-assured and brusque.*
3 = type, form, sort, kind, nature, variety, brand, breed, category • *What manner of place is this?*
▸ AS A PLURAL NOUN **1 = conduct**, bearing, behaviour, breeding, carriage, demeanour, deportment, comportment • *He dressed well and had impeccable manners.*
2 = politeness, courtesy, etiquette, refinement, polish, decorum, p's and q's • *That should teach you some manners.*
3 = protocol, ceremony, customs, formalities, good form, proprieties, the done thing, social graces, politesse • *the morals and manners of a society*

QUOTATIONS

Manners are love in a cool climate
[Quentin Crisp *Manners From Heaven*]

Manners are the happy ways of doing things; each once a stroke of genius or of love, now repeated and hardened into usage
[Ralph Waldo Emerson *The Conduct of Life*]

Fine manners need the support of fine manners in others
[Ralph Waldo Emerson *The Conduct of Life*]

PROVERBS

Manners maketh man

mannered = affected, put-on, posed, artificial, pseudo *(informal)*, pretentious, stilted, arty-farty *(informal)* • *If you are too careful, the results can look mannered.*
OPPOSITES: real, natural, genuine

mannerism = habit, characteristic, trait, quirk, peculiarity, foible, idiosyncrasy • *His mannerisms are those of a preoccupied professor.*

mannerly = polite, civil, gentlemanly, refined, polished, gracious, civilized, respectful, courteous, genteel, well-behaved, well-bred, ladylike, decorous, well-mannered • *He was gentle of speech, mannerly and concerned about impressions.*
OPPOSITES: rude, disrespectful, impolite

mannish = manlike, masculine, unfeminine, butch *(informal)*, unladylike, unwomanly • *She shook hands in a mannish way.*

manoeuvre AS A VERB **1 = steer**, direct, guide, pilot, work, move, drive, handle, negotiate, jockey, manipulate, navigate • *We attempted to manoeuvre the canoe closer to him.*
2 = scheme, plot, plan, intrigue, wangle *(informal)*, machinate • *He manoeuvred his way to the top.*
3 = manipulate, arrange, organize, devise, manage, set up, engineer, fix, orchestrate, contrive, stage-manage • *You manoeuvred things in similar situations in the past.*
▸ AS A NOUN **1 = stratagem**, move, plan, action, movement, scheme, trick, plot, tactic, intrigue, dodge, ploy, ruse, artifice, subterfuge, machination • *manoeuvres to block the electoral process*
2 *often plural* **= movement**, operation, exercise, deployment, war game • *The camp was used for military manoeuvres.*

manor = manor house, seat, hall, mansion • *Thieves broke into the country manor at night.*

manpower = personnel, people, staff, workers, employees, men and women, workforce, human resources • *There is a shortage of skilled manpower in the industry.*

manse = minister's house, vicarage, rectory, parsonage, deanery • *the dining-room and parlour of the manse*

manservant = attendant, man, butler, valet, steward, retainer, lackey, flunkey, gentleman's gentleman • *They were waited on by a manservant.*

mansion = residence, manor, hall, villa, dwelling, abode, habitation, seat • *an eighteenth-century mansion in Hampshire*

mantle AS A NOUN 1 = **role**, job, position, post, responsibility, task, duty, function, capacity, burden, onus • *She has the intellectual form to take up the mantle of leadership.*
2 = **covering**, cover, screen, cloud, curtain, envelope, blanket, veil, shroud, canopy, pall • *The park looked grim under a mantle of soot and ash.*
3 = **cloak**, wrap, cape, hood, shawl • *flaxen hair that hung round her shoulders like a silken mantle*
▸ AS A VERB = **cover**, hide, blanket, cloud, wrap, screen, mask, disguise, veil, cloak, shroud, envelop, overspread • *Many of the peaks were already mantled with snow.*

manual AS AN ADJECTIVE 1 = **physical**, human, done by hand • *semi-skilled and unskilled manual work*
2 = **hand-operated**, hand, non-automatic • *There is a manual pump to get rid of water.*
▸ AS A NOUN = **handbook**, guide, instructions, bible, guidebook, workbook, enchiridion *(rare)* • *the instruction manual*

manufacture AS A VERB 1 = **make**, build, produce, construct, form, create, process, shape, turn out, assemble, compose, forge, mould, put together, fabricate, mass-produce • *The first three models are being manufactured at our factory in Manchester.*
2 = **concoct**, make up, invent, devise, hatch, fabricate, think up, cook up *(informal)*, trump up • *He said the allegations were manufactured on the flimsiest evidence.*
▸ AS A NOUN = **making**, production, construction, assembly, creation, produce, fabrication, mass-production • *the manufacture of nuclear weapons*

manufacturer = **maker**, producer, builder, creator, industrialist, factory-owner, constructor, fabricator • *the world's largest doll manufacturer*

manumission = **freeing**, release, liberation, emancipation, deliverance, unchaining, enfranchisement • *The country's manumission began in 1762.*

manure = **compost**, muck, fertilizer, dung, droppings, excrement, ordure • *organic manures*

many AS AN ADJECTIVE = **numerous**, various, varied, countless, abundant, myriad, innumerable, sundry, copious, manifold, umpteen *(informal)*, profuse, multifarious, multitudinous, multifold, divers *(archaic)* • *He had many books and papers on the subject.*
▸ AS A PRONOUN = **a lot**, lots *(informal)*, plenty, a mass, scores, piles *(informal)*, tons *(informal)*, heaps *(informal)*, large numbers, a multitude, umpteen *(informal)*, a horde, a thousand and one, a gazillion *(informal)* • *Many had avoided the delays by consulting the tourist office.*
▸ IN PHRASES: **the many** = **the masses**, the people, the crowd, the majority, the rank and file, the multitude, (the) hoi polloi • *It gave power to a few to change the world for the many.*

map AS A NOUN = **chart**, plan, guide, atlas, A to Z, street guide, cartogram • *He unfolded the map and set it on the floor.*
▸ AS A VERB = **chart**, draw, survey, plot, portray, depict, delineate • *a spacecraft using radar to map the surface of Venus*
▸ IN PHRASES: **map something out** = **set out**, plan, detail, plot, draft, organize, outline, draw up, lay out, formulate, think out, think through, sketch out, rough out • *I went home and mapped out my strategy.*

mar 1 = **harm**, damage, hurt, spoil, stain, blight, taint, tarnish, blot, sully, vitiate, put a damper on • *A number of problems marred the smooth running of the event.*
2 = **ruin**, injure, spoil, scar, flaw, impair, mutilate, detract from, maim, deform, blemish, mangle, disfigure, deface • *The scar was discreet enough not to mar his good looks.*
OPPOSITES: better, improve, adorn

maraud = **raid**, loot, plunder, ransack, sack, harry, ravage, foray, forage, pillage, despoil, reive *(dialect)* • *Mobs marauded around the city.*

marauder = **raider**, outlaw, bandit, pirate, robber, ravager, plunderer, pillager, buccaneer, brigand, corsair, sea wolf, freebooter, reiver *(dialect)* • *They were raided by roaming bands of marauders.*

marauding = **predatory**, looting, pillaging, thieving, rapacious, piratical, freebooting • *marauding gangs of armed men*

marble IN PHRASES: **lose your marbles** = **go mad**, go crazy, go insane, take leave of your senses, lose your reason, go off your trolley *(Brit. informal)*, go off your head • *You'll probably think I've lost my marbles.*
▸ RELATED ADJECTIVE: marmoreal

march AS A VERB 1 = **parade**, walk, file, pace, stride, tread, tramp, swagger, footslog • *A Scottish battalion was marching down the street.*
2 = **demonstrate**, protest, rally • *marching for peace and disarmament*
3 = **walk**, strut, storm, sweep, stride, stalk, flounce • *She marched in without even knocking.*
▸ AS A NOUN 1 = **walk**, trek, hike, tramp, slog, yomp *(Brit. informal)*, routemarch • *After a short march, the column entered the village.*
2 = **demonstration**, parade, procession, demo *(informal)* • *Organisers expect up to 3000 people to join the march.*
3 = **progress**, development, advance, evolution, progression • *The relentless march of technology*
▸ IN PHRASES: **on the march** = **advancing**, marching, progressing, proceeding, on the way, under way, en route, afoot, on your way, astir • *Serbian troops and militia on the march*

marches = **borders**, limits, boundaries, confines, frontiers, borderland, marchlands • *the Welsh marches, forming our border with England*

mare
▸ COLLECTIVE NOUN: stud

margin 1 = **gap**, amount, difference, majority • *They could end up with a 50-point winning margin.*
2 = **room**, space, surplus, allowance, scope, play, compass, latitude, leeway, extra room, elbowroom • *There is very little margin for error in the way the money is collected.*
3 = **edge**, side, limit, border, bound, boundary, confine, verge, brink, rim, brim, perimeter, periphery • *These islands are on the margins of human habitation.*

marginal 1 = **insignificant**, small, low, minor, slight, minimal, negligible • *This is a marginal improvement on October.*
2 = **borderline**, bordering, on the edge, peripheral • *The poor are forced to cultivate marginal lands higher up the mountain.*

marginally = **slightly**, a little, somewhat, on a small scale, to some extent or degree • *Sales last year were marginally better.*

marijuana = **cannabis**, pot *(slang)*, weed *(slang)*, dope *(slang)*, black *(slang)*, blow *(slang)*, smoke *(informal)*, stuff *(slang)*, leaf *(slang)*, tea *(U.S. slang)*, grass *(slang)*, chronic *(U.S. slang)*, hemp, hash *(slang)*, gage *(U.S. dated slang)*, hashish, mary jane *(U.S. slang)*, ganja, bhang, kif, wacky baccy *(slang)*, sinsemilla, dagga *(S. African)*, charas • *The minister said he had smoked marijuana once.*

QUOTATIONS
I experimented with marijuana a time or two. And I didn't like it, and I didn't inhale
[Bill Clinton]

marinate or **marinade** = **souse**, soak, steep, immerse • *Marinate the chicken for at least four hours.*

marine = **nautical**, sea, maritime, oceanic, naval, saltwater, seafaring, ocean-going, seagoing, pelagic, thalassic • *breeding grounds for marine life*

mariner = **sailor**, seaman, sea dog, seafarer, hand, salt, tar, navigator, gob *(U.S. slang)*, matelot *(slang, chiefly Brit.)*,

Jack Tar, seafaring man, bluejacket • *He has the weatherbeaten face of a mariner.*

marital = **matrimonial**, married, wedded, nuptial, conjugal, spousal, connubial • *She wanted to make her marital home in the city.*

maritime 1 = **nautical**, marine, naval, sea, oceanic, seafaring • *the largest maritime museum of its kind*
2 = **coastal**, seaside, littoral • *The country has a temperate, maritime climate.*

mark AS A NOUN 1 = **spot**, stain, streak, smudge, line, nick, impression, scratch, bruise, scar, dent, blot, blemish, blotch, pock, splotch, smirch • *The dogs rub against the walls and make dirty marks.*
2 = **symbol**, sign, character, diacritic • *He made marks with a pencil.*
3 = **grade**, rating, score, grading, assessment, percentage, evaluation • *He did well to get such a good mark.*
4 = **point**, level, stage, degree • *Unemployment is fast approaching the one million mark.*
5 = **characteristic**, feature, symptom, standard, quality, measure, stamp, par, attribute, criterion, norm, trait, badge, hallmark, yardstick, peculiarity • *The mark of a civilized society is that it looks after its weakest members.*
6 = **indication**, sign, note, evidence, symbol, proof, token • *Shopkeepers closed their shutters as a mark of respect.*
7 = **brand**, impression, label, stamp, print, device, flag, seal, symbol, token, earmark, emblem, insignia, signet • *Each book was adorned with the publisher's mark at the bottom of the spine.*
8 = **impression**, effect, influence, impact, trace, imprint, vestiges • *A religious upbringing had left its mark on him.*
9 = **target**, goal, aim, purpose, end, object, objective • *The second shot missed its mark completely.*
▸ AS A VERB 1 = **scar**, scratch, dent, imprint, nick, brand, impress, stain, bruise, streak, blot, smudge, blemish, blotch, splotch, smirch • *How do you stop the horses marking the turf?*
2 = **label**, identify, brand, flag, stamp, characterize • *The bank marks the cheque 'certified'.*
3 = **grade**, correct, assess, evaluate, appraise • *He was marking essays in his study.*
4 = **distinguish**, show, illustrate, exemplify, denote, evince, betoken • *the river which marks the border*
5 = **indicate**, represent, herald, denote, betoken • *The announcement marks the end of an extraordinary period.*
6 = **celebrate**, honour, observe, keep, remember, acknowledge, recognize, salute, commemorate, pay tribute to, memorialize, solemnize • *Thousands of people took to the streets to mark the occasion.*
7 = **characterize**, distinguish, identify, typify • *The style is marked by simplicity, clarity and candour.*
8 = **observe**, mind, note, regard, notice, attend to, pay attention to, pay heed to, hearken to *(archaic)* • *Mark my words. He won't last.*
▸ IN PHRASES: **make your mark** = **succeed**, make it *(informal)*, make good, prosper, be a success, achieve recognition, get on in the world, make something of yourself, find a place in the sun, make a success of yourself • *She made her mark in the film industry in the 1960s.*
mark someone off = **distinguish**, identify • *Her clothes marked her off from the other delegates.*
mark something down = **make cheaper**, reduce, lower the price of • *Clothes are the best bargain, with many items marked down.*
mark something *or* **someone out** = **set apart**, single out • *Her independence of spirit marked her out from her colleagues.*
mark something out = **delineate**, outline • *When planting seedlings, I prefer to mark out the rows in advance.*
mark something up 1 = **increase the price of**, raise the price of • *The warehouse marks up its goods by about 10%.*
2 = **edit**, annotate • *Mark up the work on paper, then make the changes electronically.*
up to the mark = **satisfactory**, acceptable, good enough, adequate, up to scratch, passable, up to standard • *They get rid of those whose work isn't up to the mark.*
wide of the mark = **inaccurate**, mistaken, out, wrong, wild, erroneous, off-base *(U.S. & Canad. informal)*, off-beam *(informal)* • *That comparison isn't as wide of the mark as it seems.*

marked = **noticeable**, clear, decided, striking, noted, obvious, signal, dramatic, considerable, outstanding, remarkable, apparent, prominent, patent, evident, distinct, pronounced, notable, manifest, blatant, conspicuous, salient • *There has been a marked increase in crimes against property.*
OPPOSITES: hidden, concealed, imperceptible

markedly = **noticeably**, greatly, clearly, obviously, seriously *(informal)*, signally, patently, notably, considerably, remarkably, evidently, manifestly, distinctly, decidedly, strikingly, conspicuously, to a great extent, outstandingly • *The quality of their relationship improved markedly.*

market AS A NOUN 1 = **fair**, mart, bazaar, souk *(Arabic)* • *Many traders in the market have special offers today.*
2 = **demand**, call, need, desire, requirement • *There's no market for such expensive goods.*
3 = **trade**, business, dealing, commerce, trading, buying and selling • *Two big companies control 72% of the market.*
▸ AS A VERB = **sell**, promote, retail, peddle, vend, offer for sale • *These phones have been marketed here since 1963.*
▸ IN PHRASES: **be in the market for** = **be in need of**, want, seek, lack, wish to buy • *Are you in the market for a new radio?*
on the market = **on offer**, on sale, up for sale • *putting more empty offices on the market*

marketable = **sought after**, wanted, in demand, saleable, merchantable, vendible • *These are marketable skills.*

marketer = **seller**, agent, retailer, promoter, vendor, purveyor • *a leading global marketer of IT products*

marketing = **promotional**, PR • *a marketing campaign*

marksman *or* **markswoman** = **sharpshooter**, good shot, crack shot *(informal)*, dead shot *(informal)*, deadeye *(informal, chiefly U.S.)* • *He was hit in the arm when police marksmen opened fire.*

maroon = **abandon**, leave, desert, strand, leave high and dry *(informal)*, cast away, cast ashore • *marooned on a desert island*

marque = **brand** • *a marque long associated with motor-racing success*

marriage 1 = **wedding**, match, nuptials, wedlock, wedding ceremony, matrimony, espousal, nuptial rites • *When did the marriage take place?*
2 = **union**, coupling, link, association, alliance, merger, confederation, amalgamation • *The merger is an audacious marriage between old and new.*
▸ RELATED ADJECTIVES: conjugal, connubial, hymeneal, marital, nuptial
▸ RELATED MANIA: gamomania

QUOTATIONS

Therefore shall a man leave his father and his mother, and shall cleave unto his wife: and they shall be one flesh

[*Bible: Genesis*]

'Marriage': this I call the will that moves two to create the one which is more than those who created it

[Friedrich Nietzsche *Thus Spake Zarathustra*]

Let me not to the marriage of true minds
Admit impediments. Love is not love
Which alters when it alteration finds,
Or bends with the remover to remove

[William Shakespeare *Sonnet 116*]

A happy marriage perhaps represents the ideal of human relationship – a setting in which each partner,

m

while acknowledging the need of the other, feels free to be what he or she by nature is
[Anthony Storr *The Integrity of the Personality*]
Marriage is an act of will that signifies and involves a mutual gift, which unites the spouses and binds them to their eventual souls, with whom they make up a sole family – a domestic church
[Pope John Paul II]
Marriage is socialism among two people
[Barbara Ehrenreich *The Worst Years of Our Lives*]
The problem with marriage is that it ends every night after making love, and it must be rebuilt every morning before breakfast
[Gabriel García Márquez *Love in the Time of Cholera*]
A journey is like marriage. The certain way to be wrong is to think you control it
[John Steinbeck *Travels With Charley: In Search of America*]
Marriage brings one into fatal connection with custom and tradition, and traditions and customs are like the wind and weather, altogether incalculable
[Søren Kierkegaard *Either/Or*]
Marriage must be a relation either of sympathy or of conquest
[George Eliot *Romola*]
A marriage is no amusement but a solemn act, and generally a sad one
[Queen Victoria *Letter to her daughter*]
Either marriage is a destiny, I believe, or there is no sense in it at all, it's a piece of humbug
[Max Frisch *I'm Not Stiller*]
Happiness in marriage is entirely a matter of chance
[Jane Austen *Pride and Prejudice*]
Every woman should marry – and no man
[Benjamin Disraeli *Lothair*]
There are good marriages, but no delightful ones
[Duc de la Rochefoucauld *Réflexions ou Sentences et Maximes Morales*]
It doesn't much signify whom one marries, for one is sure to find next morning that it was someone else
[Samuel Rogers *Table Talk*]
It is a woman's business to get married as soon as possible, and a man's to keep unmarried as long as he can
[George Bernard Shaw *Man and Superman*]
Marriage is like life in this – that it is a field of battle, and not a bed of roses
[Robert Louis Stevenson *Virginibus Puerisque*]
I married beneath me, all women do
[Nancy Astor]
Single women have a dreadful propensity for being poor – which is one very strong argument in favour of matrimony
[Jane Austen *letter*]
Marriage is the grave or tomb of wit
[Margaret Cavendish, Duchess of Newcastle *Nature's Three Daughters*]
Courtship to marriage, as a very witty prologue to a very dull play
[William Congreve *The Old Bachelor*]
I am to be married within these three days; married past redemption
[John Dryden *Marriage à la Mode*]
Men are April when they woo, December when they wed
[William Shakespeare *As You Like It*]
Marriage is a great institution, but I'm not ready for an institution yet
[Mae West]
Marriage has many pains, but celibacy has no pleasures
[Dr. Johnson]
Marriages are made in Heaven
[John Lyly *Euphues and his England*]
Men marry because they are tired, women because they are curious; both are disappointed
[Oscar Wilde *A Woman of No Importance*]
A happy marriage is a long conversation which always seems too short
[André Maurois *Memories*]
Marriage is three parts love and seven parts forgiveness
[Langdon Mitchell]
Marriage is popular because it combines the maximum of temptation with the maximum of opportunity
[George Bernard Shaw *Maxims for Revolutionists*]
Strange to say what delight we married people have to see these poor fools decoyed into our condition
[Samuel Pepys]
There is not one in a hundred of either sex who is not taken in when they marry ... it is, of all transactions, the one in which people expect most from others, and are least honest themselves
[Jane Austen *Mansfield Park*]
It was very good of God to let Carlyle and Mrs. Carlyle marry one another and so make only two people miserable instead of four
[Samuel Butler]
one fool at least in every married couple
[Henry Fielding *Amelia*]
There once was an old man of Lyme
Who married three wives at a time,
When asked 'Why a third?'
He replied, 'One's absurd!
And bigamy, Sir, is a crime!'
[William Cosmo Monkhouse]
Marriage is based on the theory that when man discovers a brand of beer exactly to his taste he should at once throw up his job and go work in the brewery
[George Jean Nathan]

married 1 = **wedded**, one, united, joined, wed, hitched *(slang)*, spliced *(informal)* • *We have been married for 14 years.*
2 = **marital**, wifely, husbandly, nuptial, matrimonial, conjugal, spousal, connubial • *the first ten years of married life*

marrow = **core**, heart, spirit, quick, soul, cream, substance, essence, kernel, gist, pith, quintessence • *the very marrow of his being*

marry 1 = **tie the knot** *(informal)*, wed, take the plunge *(informal)*, walk down the aisle *(informal)*, get hitched *(slang)*, get spliced *(informal)*, become man and wife, plight your troth *(old-fashioned)* • *They married a month after they met.*
2 = **wed**, espouse, wive *(archaic)*, take to wife, lead to the altar, make an honest woman of *(informal)* • *He wants to marry her.*
3 = **unite**, match, join, link, tie, bond, ally, merge, knit, unify, splice, yoke • *It will be difficult to marry his two interests – cooking and sport.*

QUOTATIONS

There is not one in a hundred of either sex who is not taken in when they marry ... it is, of all transactions, the one in which people expect most from others, and are least honest themselves
[Jane Austen *Mansfield Park*]
It is better to marry than to burn
[*Bible: I Corinthians*]

PROVERBS

Never marry for money, but marry where money is

marsh = **swamp**, moss *(Scot. & Northern English dialect)*, bog, slough, fen, quagmire, morass, muskeg *(Canad.)* • *a recently reclaimed saltwater marsh*
▸ **RELATED ADJECTIVE:** paludal

marshal 1 = **conduct**, take, lead, guide, steer, escort,

shepherd, usher • *He was marshalling the visitors, showing them where to go.*
2 = arrange, group, order, collect, gather, line up, organize, assemble, deploy, array, dispose, draw up, muster, align • *The government marshalled its economic resources.*

marshy = swampy, wet, waterlogged, spongy, boggy, fenny, miry, paludal, quaggy • *the broad, marshy plain of the river*

marsupial
▷ *See panel* **Marsupials**

marten
▸ **COLLECTIVE NOUN:** richesse

martial = military, soldierly, brave, heroic, belligerent, warlike, bellicose • *All three are renowned for martial prowess.*

martial art
▷ *See panel* **Martial arts and terms**

martinet = disciplinarian, authoritarian, stickler, taskmaster, taskmistress, drillmaster • *He's a retired lieutenant and a bit of a martinet.*

martyr AS A VERB = put to death, make a martyr of, martyrize *(rare)* • *St. Pancras was martyred in 304 AD.*
▸ **IN PHRASES: a martyr to something = suffering from**, troubled by, afflicted with, seriously affected by, a sufferer from • *He's still a martyr to that painful right elbow.*

martyrdom = persecution, suffering, torture, agony, ordeal, torment, anguish • *the martyrdom of Bishop Cannio*
OPPOSITES: joy, happiness, bliss

QUOTATIONS
A thing is not necessarily true because a man dies for it
[Oscar Wilde *Sebastian Melmoth*]

marvel AS A VERB = be amazed, wonder, gaze, gape, goggle, be awed, be filled with surprise • *Her fellow workers marvelled at her infinite energy.*
▸ **AS A NOUN 1 = wonder**, phenomenon, miracle, portent • *A new technological marvel was invented there – the electron microscope.*
2 = genius, whizz *(informal)*, prodigy • *Her death is a great tragedy. She really was a marvel.*

marvellous = excellent, great *(informal)*, mean *(slang)*, topping *(Brit. slang)*, wonderful, brilliant, bad *(slang)*, cracking *(Brit. informal)*, amazing, crucial *(slang)*, extraordinary, remarkable, smashing *(informal)*, superb, spectacular, fantastic *(informal)*, magnificent, astonishing, fabulous *(informal)*, divine *(informal)*, glorious, terrific *(informal)*, splendid, sensational *(informal)*, mega *(slang)*, sovereign, awesome *(slang)*, breathtaking, phenomenal, astounding, singular, miraculous, colossal, super *(informal)*, wicked *(informal)*, def *(slang)*, prodigious, wondrous *(archaic*

MARSUPIALS

agile wallaby, river wallaby, sandy wallaby, *or* jungle kangaroo
antechinus
antelope kangaroo *or* antilopine wallaby
bandicoot
barred bandicoot *or* marl
Bennett's tree kangaroo *or* tcharibeena
bettong
bilby, rabbit(-eared) bandicoot, long-eared bandicoot, dalgyte, *or* dalgite
bobuck *or* mountain (brushtail) possum
boodie (rat), burrowing rat-kangaroo, Lesueur's rat-kangaroo, tungoo, *or* tungo
boongary *or* Lumholtz's tree kangaroo
bridled nail-tail wallaby *or* merrin
brindled bandicoot *or* northern brown bandicoot
brush-tail(ed) possum
burramys *or* (mountain) pygmy possum
crest-tailed marsupial mouse, Cannings' little dog, *or* mulgara
crescent nail-tail wallaby *or* wurrung
cuscus
dasyurid, dasyure, native cat, marsupial cat, *or* wild cat
desert bandicoot
desert-rat kangaroo
dibbler
diprotodon
dunnart
eastern grey kangaroo, great grey kangaroo, forest kangaroo, *or* (grey) forester
fluffy glider *or* yellow-bellied glider
flying phalanger, flying squirrel, glider, *or* pongo
green ringtail possum *or* toolah
hairy-nosed wombat
hare-wallaby
honey mouse, honey possum, noolbenger, *or* tait
jerboa, jerboa pouched mouse, jerboa kangaroo, *or* kultarr
kangaroo *or (Austral. informal)* roo
koala (bear) *or (Austral.)* native bear
kowari
larapinta *or* Darling Downs dunnart
Leadbeater's possum *or* fairy possum
lemuroid ringtail possum
long-nosed bandicoot
mardo *or* yellow-footed antechinus
marlu
marsupial mole
marsupial mouse
mongan *or* Herbert River ringtail possum
munning
musky rat-kangaroo
naked-nose wombat
ningaui
northern nail-tail wallaby *or* karrabul
northern native cat *or* satanellus
numbat *or* banded anteater
opossum *or* possum
pademelon *or* paddymelon
parma wallaby
phalanger
pig-footed bandicoot
pitchi-pitchi *or* wuhl-wuhl
platypus, duck-billed platypus, *or* duckbill
potoroo
pretty-face wallaby *or* whiptail wallaby
pygmy glider, feather glider, *or* flying mouse
quenda *or* (southern) brown bandicoot
quokka
quoll
rat kangaroo
red kangaroo *or* plains kangaroo
red(-necked) wallaby, Bennett's wallaby, eastern brush wallaby, rufous wallaby, *or* brush kangaroo
ringtail *or* ringtail(ed) possum
rock wallaby *or* brush-tailed wallaby
rufous rat-kangaroo
scrub wallaby
short-eared bandicoot
short-nosed bandicoot
short-nosed rat kangaroo *or* squeaker
squirrel glider
striped possum
sugar glider
swamp wallaby, black wallaby, *or* black-tailed wallaby
tammar, damar, *or* dama
Tasmanian barred bandicoot *or* Gunn's bandicoot
Tasmanian devil *or* ursine dasyure
thylacine, Tasmanian wolf, *or* Tasmanian tiger
tiger cat *or* spotted native cat
toolache *or* Grey's brush wallaby
tree kangaroo
tuan, phascogale, *or* wambenger
wallaby
wallaroo, uroo, *or* biggada
warabi
western grey kangaroo, black-faced kangaroo, sooty kangaroo, *or* mallee kangaroo
wintarro *or* golden bandicoot
wogoit *or* rock possum
wombat *or (Austral.)* badger
woylie *or* brush-tailed bettong
yapok
yallara
yellow-footed rock wallaby *or* ring-tailed rock wallaby

MARTIAL ARTS AND TERMS

Martial arts

aikido
capoeira
Crane style kung fu
Goju Kai karate
Goju Ryu karate
hapkido
Hung Gar *or* Tiger style kung fu
iai-do
iai-jutsu
Ishin Ryu karate
Jeet Kune Do
judo
ju jitsu, jiu jitsu *or* ju-jutsu
karate *or* karate-do
kendo
kick boxing
kung fu
Kyokushinkai karate
kyudo
naginata-do
ninjitsu *or* ninjutsu
Praying Mantis style kung fu
Sankukai karate
Shito Ryu karate
Shotokai karate
Shotokan karate
Shukokai karate
sumo *or* sumo wrestling
tae kwon-do
tai chi chuan
tai chi qi gong
Ta Sheng Men *or* Monkey style kung fu
Thai boxing *or* Muay Thai
Tomiki aikido
Tukido *(trademark)*
Wado Ryu karate
Wing Chun *or* Wing Tsun kung fu
yari-jutsu

Martial arts terms

Term	Meaning	Term	Meaning	Term	Meaning
basho	sumo turnament	katsu	resuscitation techniques	ozeki	sumo champion
bo	staff	keikogi	kendo jacket	qi gong	breath control
bogu	kendo armour	kesho-mawashi	embroidered sumo apron	randori kyoghi	aikido competition
bokuto	kendo wooden sword	ki, chi *or* qi	inner power	rikishi	sumo wrestler
budo *or* bushido	warrior's way	kiai	yell accompanying movement	rokushakubo	six-foot staff
dan	black belt grade	kihon	repetition of techniques	ryu	martial arts school
do	kendo breastplate	kote	kendo gauntlets	sai	short trident
-do	the way	kyu	student grade	samurai	Japanese warrior caste
dohyo	sumo ring	makiwara	practice block	sensei	teacher
dojo	practice room or mat	mawashi	sumo fighting belt	shinai	kendo bamboo sword
gi	suit	men	kendo mask	sifu	teacher
hachimaki *or* tenugui	kendo headcloth	nage-waza *or* tachi-waza	ju jitsu competition	suneate	naginata shin guards
hakama	divided skirt	naginata	curved-blade spear	tanto randori	aikido competition
ippon	one competition point	ne-waza	ju jitsu competition	tare	kendo apron
jiu-kumite	freestyle karate competition	ninin-dori	aikido competition	te	hand fighting
-jutsu	fighting art	ninja	Japanese trained assassin	ton-fa *or* tui-fa	hardwood weapon
-ka	student	nunchaku	hinged flails	tsuna	sumo grand champion's belt
kama	hand sickle	obi	coloured belt	waza-ari	half competition point
kata	sequence of techniques			yari	spear
katana	kendo sword			yokozuna	sumo grand champion
				zanshin	total awareness
				zha dao	a long knife

or literary), brill *(informal)*, stupendous, jaw-dropping, eye-popping, bodacious *(slang, chiefly U.S.)*, boffo *(slang)*, jim-dandy *(slang)*, chillin' *(U.S. slang)*, booshit *(Austral. slang)*, exo *(Austral. slang)*, sik *(Austral. slang)*, rad *(informal)*, phat *(slang)*, schmick *(Austral. informal)*, beaut *(informal)*, barrie *(Scot. slang)*, belting *(Brit. slang)*, pearler *(Austral. slang)* • *He certainly is a marvellous actor.*
OPPOSITES: bad, ordinary, terrible

Marxism

QUOTATIONS

When asked whether or not we are Marxists, our position is the same as that of a physician or a biologist who is asked if he is a 'Newtonian', or if he is a 'Pasteurian'

['Che' Guevara *'We Are Practical Revolutionaries'*]

masculine 1 = **male**, manly, mannish, manlike, virile, manful • *masculine characteristics such as a deep voice and facial hair*
2 = **strong**, powerful, bold, brave, strapping, hardy, robust, vigorous, muscular, macho, butch *(slang)*, resolute, gallant, well-built, red-blooded *(informal)*, stout-hearted, two-fisted • *an aggressive, masculine image*

masculinity = **virility**, strength, toughness, manliness, maleness, robustness, ruggedness, muscularity • *The old ideas of masculinity do not work for most men.*

mash AS A VERB = **smash**, crush, pulp, pound, beat, whip, soften, squash, mince, purée, liquidize, macerate • *Mash the bananas with a fork.*
▸ AS A NOUN = **pulp**, pâté, paste, purée, mush • *They ate a mash of potatoes, carrot and cabbage.*

mask AS A NOUN 1 = **disguise**, visor, vizard *(archaic)*, stocking mask, false face, domino *(rare)* • *a gunman wearing a mask*
2 = **face mask**, visor, eye mask, surgical mask, safety goggles, protective mask • *She wore a mask and rubber gloves.*
3 = **façade**, disguise, show, front, cover, screen, blind, cover-up, veil, cloak, guise, camouflage, veneer, semblance, concealment • *His mask cracked, and she saw an angry and violent man.*
▸ AS A VERB = **disguise**, hide, conceal, obscure, cover (up), screen, blanket, veil, cloak, mantle, camouflage, enshroud • *A thick grey cloud masked the sun.*

mason = **stonecutter** • *He hired a bulldozer operator and a mason for the job.*

masquerade AS A VERB = **pose**, pretend to be, impersonate, profess to be, pass yourself off, simulate, disguise yourself • *He masqueraded as a doctor and fooled everyone.*
▸ AS A NOUN 1 = **pretence**, disguise, deception, front

(informal), cover, screen, put-on *(slang)*, mask, cover-up, cloak, guise, subterfuge, dissimulation, imposture • *He claimed that the elections would be a masquerade.*

2 = masked ball, masquerade ball, revel, mummery, fancy dress party, costume ball, masked party • *A man was killed at the Christmas masquerade.*

mass AS A NOUN **1 = lot**, collection, load, combination, pile, quantity, bunch, stack, heap, rick, batch, accumulation, stockpile, assemblage, aggregation, conglomeration • *On his desk is a mass of books and papers.*

2 = piece, block, lump, chunk, hunk, concretion • *Cut it up before it cools and sets into a solid mass.*

3 = majority, body, bulk, best part, greater part, almost all, lion's share, preponderance • *The Second World War involved the mass of the population.*

4 = crowd, group, body, pack, lot, army, host, band, troop, drove, crush, bunch *(informal)*, mob, flock, herd, number, horde, multitude, throng, rabble, assemblage • *A mass of excited people clogged the street.*

5 = size, matter, weight, extent, dimensions, bulk, magnitude, greatness • *Pluto and Triton have nearly the same mass and density.*

6 = collection, body, whole, sum, aggregate, entirety, totality, sum total • *The enormous mass of evidence also includes 1,000 witness statements.*

▸ AS AN ADJECTIVE **= large-scale**, general, popular, widespread, extensive, universal, wholesale, indiscriminate, pandemic • *ideas on combating mass unemployment*

▸ AS A VERB **= gather**, assemble, accumulate, collect, rally, mob, muster, swarm, amass, throng, congregate, foregather • *Shortly after the announcement, police began to mass at the shipyard.*

▸ IN PHRASES: **the masses = the multitude**, the crowd, the mob, the common people, the great unwashed *(derogatory)*, the hoi polloi, the commonalty • *His music is commercial. It is aimed at the masses.*

massacre AS A NOUN **= slaughter**, killing, murder, holocaust, carnage, extermination, annihilation, butchery, mass slaughter, blood bath • *She lost her mother in the massacre.*

▸ AS A VERB **= slaughter**, kill, murder, butcher, take out *(slang)*, wipe out, slay, blow away *(slang, chiefly U.S.)*, annihilate, exterminate, mow down, cut to pieces • *Troops indiscriminately massacred the defenceless population.*

massage AS A NOUN **= rub-down**, rubbing, manipulation, kneading, reflexology, shiatsu, acupressure, chiropractic treatment, palpation • *Massage isn't a long-term cure for stress.*

▸ AS A VERB **1 = rub down**, rub, manipulate, knead, pummel, palpate • *She massaged her foot, which was bruised and aching.*

2 = manipulate, alter, distort, doctor, cook *(informal)*, fix *(informal)*, rig, fiddle *(informal)*, tamper with, tinker with, misrepresent, fiddle with, falsify • *efforts to massage the unemployment figures*

massive = huge, great, big, heavy, imposing, vast, enormous, solid, impressive, substantial, extensive, monster, immense, hefty, titanic, gigantic, monumental, whacking *(informal)*, mammoth, bulky, colossal, whopping *(informal)*, weighty, stellar *(informal)*, hulking, ponderous, gargantuan, fuck-off *(offensive taboo slang)*, elephantine, ginormous *(informal)*, humongous *or* humungous *(U.S. slang)*, supersize • *a massive steam boat*

OPPOSITES: little, small, tiny

mast 1 = flagpole, support, post, pole, upright • *the slapping of the flag on the short mast*

2 = aerial, transmitter, pylon • *the closed circuit television mast*

master AS A NOUN **1 = lord**, ruler, commander, chief, director, manager, boss *(informal)*, head, owner, captain, governor, employer, principal, skipper *(informal)*, controller, superintendent, overlord, overseer, baas *(S. African)* • *My master ordered me to deliver the message.*

OPPOSITES: subject, crew, servant

2 = owner, keeper • *The dog yelped excitedly when its master produced a lead.*

3 = expert, maestro, pro *(informal)*, ace *(informal)*, genius, wizard, adept, virtuoso, grandmaster, doyen, past master, dab hand *(Brit. informal)*, wonk *(informal)*, maven *(U.S.)*, fundi *(S. African)* • *He is a master at blocking progress.*

OPPOSITES: amateur

4 = teacher, tutor, instructor, schoolmaster, pedagogue, preceptor • *a retired maths master*

OPPOSITES: student

5 = captain, commander, skipper • *the Royal Pacific's master*

6 = guru, guide, mentor, spiritual leader, swami, torchbearer • *her mission to meet her spiritual master, the Dalai Lama*

▸ AS AN ADJECTIVE **1 = expert**, leading, experienced, skilled, masterly, brilliant, crack *(informal)*, ace *(informal)*, tasty *(Brit. informal)*, skilful, adept, proficient • *a master craftsman*

OPPOSITES: novice, incompetent, unskilled

2 = original, primary, archetypal, prototypical • *Keep one as a master copy for your own reference.*

3 = controlling, ruling, directing, overall, commanding • *We have developed a master plan to address these issues.*

4 = main, principal, chief, prime, grand, great, foremost, predominant • *There's a Georgian four-poster in the master bedroom.*

OPPOSITES: minor, lesser

▸ AS A VERB **1 = learn**, understand, pick up, acquire, grasp, get the hang of *(informal)*, become proficient in, know inside out, know backwards • *Students are expected to master a second language.*

2 = overcome, defeat, suppress, conquer, check, curb, tame, lick *(informal)*, subdue, overpower, quash, quell, triumph over, bridle, vanquish, subjugate • *He wanted to master his fears of becoming ill.*

OPPOSITES: yield to, surrender to, give in to

3 = control, manage, direct, dominate, rule, command, govern, regulate • *His genius alone has mastered every crisis.*

▸ RELATED ADJECTIVE: magistral

masterful 1 = skilful, skilled, expert, finished, fine, masterly, excellent, crack *(informal)*, supreme, clever, superior, world-class, exquisite, tasty *(Brit. informal)*, adept, consummate, first-rate, deft, superlative, adroit, dexterous • *a masterful performance of boxing*

OPPOSITES: incompetent, clumsy, unskilled

2 = domineering, authoritative, dictatorial, bossy *(informal)*, arrogant, imperious, overbearing, tyrannical, magisterial, despotic, high-handed, peremptory, overweening, self-willed • *Successful businesses need bold, masterful managers.*

OPPOSITES: weak, meek, spineless

masterly = skilful, skilled, expert, finished, fine, excellent, crack *(informal)*, supreme, clever, superior, world-class, exquisite, tasty *(Brit. informal)*, adept, consummate, first-rate, superlative, masterful, adroit, dexterous • *He gave a masterly performance.*

mastermind AS A VERB **= plan**, manage, direct, organize, devise, conceive, be the brains behind *(informal)* • *The finance minister will continue to mastermind economic reform.*

▸ AS A NOUN **= organizer**, director, manager, authority, engineer, brain(s) *(informal)*, architect, genius, planner, intellect, virtuoso, rocket scientist *(informal, chiefly U.S.)*, brainbox • *He was the mastermind behind the plan.*

masterpiece = classic, tour de force *(French)*, pièce de résistance *(French)*, magnum opus *(Latin)*, master work, jewel, chef-d'oeuvre *(French)* • *His book is a masterpiece.*

masterstroke = act of genius, victory, triumph, coup, complete success, successful manoeuvre • *To have convinced them that his actions were justified was a masterstroke.*

mastery 1 = **understanding**, knowledge, comprehension, ability, skill, know-how, command, grip, grasp, expertise, prowess, familiarity, attainment, finesse, proficiency, virtuosity, dexterity, cleverness, deftness, acquirement • *He demonstrated his mastery of political manoeuvring.*
2 = **control**, authority, command, rule, victory, triumph, sway, domination, superiority, conquest, supremacy, dominion, upper hand, ascendancy, pre-eminence, mana (*N.Z.*), whip hand • *a region where humans have gained mastery over the major rivers*

masticate = **chew**, eat, champ, crunch, munch • *Her mouth was working, as if she was masticating some tasty titbit.*

masturbate = **practise self-abuse**, wank (*taboo slang*), jerk off (*taboo slang*), touch yourself (*informal*), jack off (*taboo slang*), play with yourself (*informal*), practise onanism (*formal*), toss yourself off (*taboo slang*) • *At the age of 12, he began to masturbate.*

masturbation = **self-abuse**, wanking (*taboo slang*), frigging (*taboo slang*), onanism, playing with yourself (*slang*), autoeroticism, flying solo, beating the meat • *The sperm sample is produced by masturbation.*

QUOTATIONS
Hey, don't knock masturbation! It's sex with someone I love
[Woody Allen *Annie Hall*]

mat 1 = **table mat**, coaster, place mat, doily, beer mat • *The food is served on polished tables with mats.*
2 = **carpet**, runner, rug, doormat, hearthrug • *There was a letter on the mat.*
3 = **mass**, shock, cluster, tangle, knot, mop, thatch, mane • *the thick mat of sandy hair on his chest*

match AS A NOUN 1 = **game**, test, competition, trial, tie, contest, fixture, bout, head-to-head • *He was watching a football match.*
2 = **companion**, mate, equal, equivalent, counterpart, fellow, complement • *Moira was a perfect match for him.*
3 = **replica**, double, copy, twin, equal, spit (*informal, chiefly Brit.*), duplicate, lookalike, ringer (*slang*), spitting image (*informal*), dead ringer (*slang*), spit and image (*informal*) • *He asked his assistant to look for a match of the vase he broke.*
4 = **marriage**, union, couple, pair, pairing, item (*informal*), alliance, combination, partnership, duet, affiliation • *Hollywood's favourite love match foundered on the rocks.*
5 = **equal**, rival, equivalent, peer, competitor, counterpart • *I was no match for a man with such power.*
▸ AS A VERB 1 = **correspond with**, suit, go with, complement, fit with, accompany, team with, blend with, tone with, harmonize with, coordinate with • *These shoes match your dress.*
2 = **tailor**, fit, suit, adapt • *You don't have to match your lipstick to your outfit.*
3 = **go together**, be the same, be a set • *All the chairs matched*
4 = **correspond**, agree, accord, square, coincide, tally, conform, match up, be compatible, harmonize, be consonant • *Their strengths in memory and spatial skills matched.*
5 = **pair**, unite, join, couple, link, marry, ally, combine, mate, yoke • *It can take time and money to match buyers and sellers.*
6 = **rival**, equal, compete with, compare with, emulate, contend with, measure up to • *We matched them in every department of the game.*
▸ IN PHRASES: **match something** *or* **someone against something** *or* **someone** = **pit against**, set against, play off against, put in opposition to • *The finals begin today, matching the United States against France.*
match up to something = **live up to**, satisfy, fulfil, come up to, be equal to, measure up to • *a father's inability to match up to the expectations of his son*

matchbox labels
▸ RELATED ENTHUSIAST: phillumenist

matching = **identical**, like, same, double, paired, equal, toning, twin, equivalent, parallel, corresponding, comparable, duplicate, coordinating, analogous • *She made matching cushion covers.*
OPPOSITES: different, unlike, distinct

matchless = **unequalled**, unique, unparalleled, unrivalled, perfect, supreme, exquisite, consummate, superlative, inimitable, incomparable, unmatched, peerless, unsurpassed • *His simplicity and apparent ease are matchless.*
OPPOSITES: common, average, equalled

matchmaker = **go-between**, marriage broker, pandar • *Some friends played matchmaker and had us both over to dinner.*

mate AS A NOUN 1 = **friend**, pal (*informal*), companion, buddy (*informal*), china (*Brit. slang*), cock (*Brit. informal*), comrade, chum (*informal*), mucker (*Brit. informal*), crony, main man (*slang, chiefly U.S.*), homeboy (*slang, chiefly U.S.*), cobber (*Austral. & N.Z. old-fashioned informal*), E hoa (*N.Z.*), M8 (*S.M.S.*) • *A mate of mine used to play soccer for Liverpool.*
2 = **partner**, lover, companion, spouse, squeeze (*informal*), consort, significant other (*U.S. informal*), better half (*humorous*), helpmeet, husband or wife, bidie-in (*Scot.*) • *He has found his ideal mate.*
3 = **double**, match, fellow, twin, counterpart, companion • *The guest cabin is a mirror image of its mate.*
4 = **assistant**, subordinate, apprentice, helper, accomplice, sidekick (*informal*) • *The electrician's mate ignored the red-lettered warning signs.*
5 = **colleague**, associate, companion, co-worker, fellow-worker, compeer • *He celebrated with work mates in the pub.*
▸ AS A VERB 1 = **pair**, couple, breed, copulate • *They want the males to mate with wild females.*
2 = **marry**, match, wed, get married, shack up (*informal*) • *Women typically seek older men with which to mate.*
3 = **join**, match, couple, pair, yoke • *The film tries very hard to mate modern with old.*

material AS A NOUN 1 = **substance**, body, matter, stuff, elements, constituents • *the decomposition of organic material*
2 = **cloth**, stuff, fabric, textile • *the thick material of her skirt*
3 = **information**, work, details, facts, notes, evidence, particulars, data, info (*informal*), subject matter, documentation • *In my version of the story, I added some new material.*
▸ AS A PLURAL NOUN = **stuff**, things, articles, items, necessaries • *loo rolls, light bulbs, cleaning materials*
▸ AS AN ADJECTIVE 1 = **physical**, worldly, solid, substantial, concrete, fleshly, bodily, tangible, palpable, corporeal, nonspiritual • *the material world*
2 = **sensual**, physical, fleshly, bodily, corporal, materialistic, carnal • *the renunciation of material pleasures*
3 = **relevant**, important, significant, essential, vital, key, serious, grave, meaningful, applicable, indispensable, momentous, weighty, pertinent, consequential, apposite, apropos, germane • *The company failed to disclose material information.*

materialistic = **consumerist**, worldly, grasping, greedy, acquisitive, rapacious, avaricious, capitalistic, money-grubbing, money-orientated • *In the 1980s society became very materialistic.*

materialize 1 = **occur**, happen, take place, turn up, come about, take shape, come into being, come to pass • *None of the anticipated difficulties materialized.*
2 = **appear**, arrive, emerge, surface, turn up, loom, show up (*informal*), pop up (*informal*), put in an appearance • *He materialized at her side, notebook at the ready.*

materially = **significantly**, much, greatly, considerably, essentially, seriously, gravely, substantially • *Profits fell materially below those earned in the previous year.*
OPPOSITES: little, hardly, insignificantly

maternal = **motherly**, protective, nurturing, maternalistic • *Her feelings towards him were maternal.*

maternity = **motherhood**, parenthood, motherliness • *She had experienced maternity herself.*

matey = **friendly**, intimate, comradely, thick *(informal)*, pally *(informal)*, amiable, sociable, chummy *(informal)*, free-and-easy, companionable, clubby, buddy-buddy *(slang, chiefly U.S. & Canad.)*, hail-fellow-well-met, palsy-walsy *(informal)* • *her irritatingly matey tone*

mathematical 1 = **arithmetical**, statistical, numerical, algebraic • *mathematical calculations*
2 = **strict**, careful, exact, precise, scientific, rigorous, pinpoint, meticulous, unerring • *planned with mathematical precision*

mathematics

QUOTATIONS
As far as the laws of mathematics refer to reality, they are not certain; and as far as they are certain, they do not refer to reality
[Albert Einstein]
I have often admired the mystical way of Pythagoras, and the secret magic of numbers
[Thomas Browne *Religio Medici*]
Beauty is the first test; there is no permanent place in the world for ugly mathematics
[Godfrey Harold Hardy *A Mathematician's Apology*]

▹ *See panel* **Mathematics**

mating = **breeding**, sex, pairing, intercourse, procreation, copulating, copulation, coitus *(formal)*, coition *(formal)* • *busy sea lions preparing for mating*

matrimonial = **marital**, married, wedding, wedded, nuptial, conjugal, spousal, connubial, hymeneal • *the matrimonial home*

matrimony = **marriage**, nuptials, wedlock, wedding ceremony, marital rites • *the bonds of matrimony*

matted = **tangled**, knotted, unkempt, knotty, tousled, ratty, uncombed • *She had matted hair and torn dusty clothes.*

matter AS A NOUN 1 = **situation**, thing, issue, concern, business, question, event, subject, affair, incident, proceeding, episode, topic, transaction, occurrence • *It was a private matter.*
2 = **substance**, material, body, stuff • *A proton is an elementary particle of matter.*
3 = **content**, sense, subject, argument, text, substance, burden, thesis, purport, gist, pith • *This conflict forms the matter of the play.*
4 = **pus**, discharge, secretion, suppuration, purulence • *If the wound starts to produce yellow matter, see your doctor.*
5 = **importance**, interest, moment, note, weight, import, consequence, significance • *Forget it; it's of no matter.*
6 = **problem**, worry, trouble, difficulty, upset, bother, distress, complication, uphill *(S. African)* • *What's the matter?*
▸ AS A VERB = **be important**, make a difference, count, be relevant, make any difference, mean anything, have influence, carry weight, cut any ice *(informal)*, be of consequence, be of account • *It doesn't matter how long you take.*
▸ IN PHRASES: **as a matter of fact** = **actually**, in fact, in reality, in truth, as it happens, believe it or not, to tell the truth, in actual fact, in point of fact • *As as matter of fact, you may be wrong.*
no matter = **don't worry about it**, never mind, it doesn't matter, don't apologise, it makes no difference *or* odds • *'I forgot to bring it.' 'No matter.'*

QUOTATIONS
What is matter? – Never mind.
What is mind? – No matter
[*Punch*]

matter-of-fact = **unsentimental**, flat, dry, plain, dull, sober, down-to-earth, mundane, lifeless, prosaic, deadpan, unimaginative, unvarnished, emotionless, unembellished • *He gave her the news in a matter-of-fact way.*

mature AS A VERB 1 = **develop**, grow up, bloom, blossom, come of age, become adult, age, reach adulthood, maturate • *young girls who have not yet matured*
2 = **evolve**, develop, improve, grow, thrive, flourish, bloom, blossom, come to fruition • *Their songwriting has matured.*
3 = **become a responsible adult**, grow up • *Hopefully after university he will have matured.*
4 = **age**, season, perfect, mellow, ripen • *the cellars where the cheeses are matured*
▸ AS AN ADJECTIVE 1 = **sensible**, experienced, adult, responsible, wise, sophisticated, reliable, discriminating, fully-fledged, dependable, level-headed, sagacious • *We are mature, freethinking adults.*
2 = **matured**, seasoned, ripe, mellow, ripened • *Grate some mature cheddar cheese.*
3 = **grown-up**, adult, grown, of age, full-blown, fully fledged, fully-developed, full-grown • *Here is the voice of a mature man, expressing sorrow for a lost ideal.*
OPPOSITES: immature, young, adolescent

maturity 1 = **adulthood**, majority, completion, puberty, coming of age, fullness, full bloom, full growth, pubescence, manhood *or* womanhood • *Humans experience a delayed maturity compared with other mammals.*
OPPOSITES: imperfection, immaturity, youthfulness
2 = **sense of responsibility**, experience, sense, wisdom, sophistication, level-headedness, matureness • *Many teenagers lack self confidence and maturity.*
OPPOSITES: irresponsibility, immaturity, excitability
3 = **ripeness**, perfection, maturation • *the dried seeds of peas that have been picked at maturity*

maudlin = **sentimental**, tearful, mushy *(informal)*, soppy *(Brit. informal)*, weepy *(informal)*, slushy *(informal)*, mawkish, lachrymose, icky *(informal)*, overemotional • *He turned maudlin after three drinks.*

maul 1 = **mangle**, claw, lacerate, tear, mangulate *(Austral. slang)* • *He had been mauled by a bear.*
2 = **ill-treat**, beat, abuse, batter, thrash, beat up *(informal)*, molest, work over *(slang)*, pummel, manhandle, rough up, handle roughly, knock about *or* around, beat *or* knock seven bells out of *(informal)* • *The troops were severely mauled before evacuating the island.*

mausoleum = **crypt**, tomb, vault, catacomb, sepulchre, charnel house, burial chamber • *His tomb lies in the great mausoleum under a slab of jade.*

maverick AS A NOUN = **rebel**, radical, dissenter, individualist, protester, eccentric, heretic, nonconformist, iconoclast, dissentient • *He was too much of a maverick to hold high office.*
OPPOSITES: traditionalist, yes man, Babbitt *(U.S.)*
▸ AS AN ADJECTIVE = **rebel**, radical, dissenting, individualistic, eccentric, heretical, iconoclastic, nonconformist • *Her maverick behaviour precluded any chance of promotion.*

maw = **mouth**, crop, throat, jaws, gullet, craw • *Embed the hook in the shark's gaping maw.*

mawkish = **sentimental**, emotional, feeble, mushy *(informal)*, soppy *(Brit. informal)*, maudlin, slushy *(informal)*, schmaltzy *(slang)*, icky *(informal)*, gushy *(informal)*, three-hankie *(informal)* • *a sentimental plot with an inevitable mawkish ending*

maxim = **saying**, motto, adage, proverb, rule, saw, gnome, dictum, axiom, aphorism, byword, apophthegm • *I believe in the maxim 'if it ain't broke, don't fix it'.*

maximize = **optimize** • *To maximize profit, you need to maximize output.*

maximum AS AN ADJECTIVE = **greatest**, highest, supreme, paramount, utmost, most, maximal, topmost • *The maximum height for a fence here is 2 metres.*
OPPOSITES: lowest, least, minimal

MATHEMATICS

Branches of mathematics

algebra
analysis
analytical geometry *or* coordinate geometry
applied mathematics
arithmetic
Boolean algebra
calculus
chaos geometry
conics
differential calculus
Euclidean geometry
game theory
geometry
group theory
integral calculus
nomography
non-Euclidean geometry
number theory
numerical analysis
probability theory
pure mathematics
set theory
statistics
topology
transformational geometry
trigonometry

Mathematical terms

acute angle
addition
affine
algorithm *or* algorism
amplitude
angle
arc
area
average
axis
base
binary
binomial
cardinal number
Cartesian coordinates
chord
circle
circumference
closed set
coefficient
common denominator
common factor
complex number
concentric
cone
constant
coordinate *or* co-ordinate
cosecant
cosine
cotangent
cube
cube root
cuboid
curve
cusp
cylinder
decagon
decimal
denary
denominator
diagonal
diameter
digit
division
dodecahedron
ellipse
equals
equation
equilateral
even
exponential
factor
factorial
formula
fraction
frequency
function
graph
helix
hemisphere
heptagon
hexagon
hyperbola
hypotenuse
icosahedron
imaginary number
improper fraction
index
infinity
integer
integral
intersection
irrational number
isosceles
locus
logarithm *or* log
lowest common denominator
lowest common multiple
Mandelbrot set
matrix
mean
median
minus
mode
multiplication
natural logarithm
natural number
node
nonagon
number
numerator
oblong
obtuse angle
octagon
octahedron
odd
open set
operation
operator
ordinal number
origin
parabola
parallel
parallelogram
pentagon
percentage
perfect number
pi
plus
polygon
polyhedron
polynomial
power
prime number
prism
probability
product
proof
proper fraction
Pythagoras' theorem
quadrant
quadratic equation
quadrilateral
quotient
radian
radius
ratio
rational number
real number
reciprocal
rectangle
recurring decimal
reflex angle
remainder
rhombus
right angle
right-angled triangle
root
scalar
scalene
secant
sector
semicircle
set
significant figures
simultaneous equations
sine
slide rule
solid
sphere
square
square root
strange attractor
subset
subtraction
sum
surd
tangent
tetrahedron
torus
trapezium
triangle
union
universal set
value
variable
vector
Venn diagram
volume
vulgar fraction
x-axis
y-axis
z-axis
zero

Mathematicians

Maria Gaetana Agnesi *(Italian)*
Howard Hathaway Aiken *(U.S.)*
Jean Le Rond Alembert *(French)*
André Marie Ampère *(French)*
Anaximander *(Greek)*
Apollonius of Perga *(Greek)*
Archimedes *(Greek)*
Charles Babbage *(English)*
Johann Jakob Balmer *(Swiss)*
Daniel Bernoulli *(Swiss)*
Jacques Bernoulli *(Swiss)*
Jean Bernoulli *(Swiss)*
Friedrich Wilhelm Bessel *(German)*
Hermann Bondi *(British)*
George Boole *(English)*
Henry Briggs *(English)*
Augustin Louis Cauchy *(French)*
Arthur Cayley *(English)*
Rudolf Julius Clausius *(German)*
Isidore Auguste Comte *(French)*
George Howard Darwin *(English)*
Julius Wilhelm Richard Dedekind *(German)*
John Dee *(English)*
René Descartes *(French)*
Diophantus *(Greek)*
Peter Gustav Lejeune Dirichlet *(German)*
Albert Einstein *(U.S.)*
Eratosthenes *(Greek)*
Euclid *(Greek)*
Eudoxus of Cnidus *(Greek)*
Leonhard Euler *(Swiss)*
Pierre de Fermat *(French)*
Leonardo Fibonacci *(Italian)*
Jean Baptiste Joseph Fourier *(French)*
Galileo *(Italian)*
Karl Friedrich Gauss *(German)*
Josiah Willard Gibbs *(U.S.)*
Kurt Gödel *(U.S.)*
Edmund Gunter *(English)*
Edmund Halley *(English)*
William Rowan Hamilton *(Irish)*
Hero *(Greek)*
David Hilbert *(German)*
Caius Iacob *(Romanian)*
Karl Gustav Jacob Jacobi *(German)*
Herman Kahn *(U.S.)*
Andrei Nikolaevich Kolmogorov *(Soviet)*
Joseph Louis Lagrange *(French)*
Pierre Simon Laplace *(French)*
Adrien Marie Legendre *(French)*
Gottfried Wilhelm von Leibnitz *(German)*
Nikolai Ivanovich Lobachevsky *(Russian)*
Ada Lovelace *(English)*
Pierre Louis Moreau de Maupertuis *(French)*
Gerardus Mercator *(Flemish)*
Hermann Minkowski *(German)*
John Napier *(Scottish)*
Isaac Newton *(English)*
Omar Khayyám *(Persian)*
Nicole d'Oresme *(French)*
Pappus of Alexandria *(Greek)*
Blaise Pascal *(French)*
Karl Pearson *(English)*
Charles Sanders Peirce *(U.S.)*
William George Penney *(English)*

MATHEMATICIANS (CONTINUED)

Roger Penrose *(English)*
Jules Henri Poincaré *(French)*
Siméon Denis Poisson *(French)*
Ptolemy *(Greek)*
Pythagoras *(Greek)*
Johann Müller Regiomontanus *(German)*
Georg Friedrich Bernhard Riemann *(German)*
Bertrand Russell *(English)*
Claude Shannon *(U.S.)*
Brook Taylor *(English)*
Thales *(Greek)*
Evangelista Torricelli *(Italian)*
Alan Mathison Turing *(English)*
John von Neumann *(U.S.)*
Hermann Weyl *(U.S.)*
Alfred North Whitehead *(English)*
Norbert Wiener *(U.S.)*

▸ **AS A NOUN** = **top**, most, peak, ceiling, crest, utmost, upper limit, uttermost • *The law provides for a maximum of two years in prison.*
OPPOSITES: bottom, minimum

maybe = **perhaps**, possibly, it could be, conceivably, perchance *(archaic)*, mayhap *(archaic)*, peradventure *(archaic)* • *Maybe he sincerely wanted to help.*

mayhem = **chaos**, trouble, violence, disorder, destruction, confusion, havoc, fracas, commotion • *the economic mayhem that this country's going through now*

maze = **web**, puzzle, confusion, tangle, snarl, mesh, labyrinth, imbroglio, convolutions, complex network • *the maze of rules and regulations* • *a maze of dimly-lit corridors*

mazy = **twisting**, winding, twisting and turning, serpentine, labyrinthine • *We ran through mazy backyards towards the hill.*

McCoy **IN PHRASES: the real McCoy** = **real thing**, genuine article • *This isn't just sparkling wine, it's the real McCoy.*

meadow = **field**, pasture, grassland, ley, lea *(poetic)* • *Try turning your lawn into a flower meadow.*

meagre = **insubstantial**, little, small, poor, spare, slight, inadequate, pathetic, slender, scant, sparse, deficient, paltry, skimpy, puny, measly, scanty, exiguous, scrimpy • *a meagre 3% pay rise*

meal **AS A NOUN** = **repast**, board, spread *(informal)*, snack, something to eat, banquet, dinner, feast, bite to eat *(informal)* • *It's rare that I have a meal with my children.*
▸ **IN PHRASES: make a meal of something** = **overdo**, exaggerate, overstate, overplay, do to death *(informal)*, belabour • *He always makes a meal of the simplest little thing.*
▸ **RELATED ADJECTIVE:** prandial

TYPES OF MEAL

afternoon tea	cream tea	lunch *or* luncheon
banquet	dinner	picnic
barbecue	elevenses	smorgasbord
beanfeast	feast	snack
breakfast	fish fry *(U.S.)*	supper
brunch	fondue	tapas
buffet	high tea *or* tea	tiffin

mealy-mouthed = **hesitant**, afraid, doubtful, indirect, mincing, reticent, prim, equivocal, euphemistic, overdelicate • *He did not intend to be mealy-mouthed with the country's leaders.*

mean¹ **1** = **signify**, say, suggest, indicate, represent, express, stand for, convey, spell out, purport, symbolize, denote, connote, betoken • *The red signal means that you can shoot.*
2 = **imply**, suggest, intend, indicate, refer to, intimate, get at *(informal)*, hint at, have in mind, drive at *(informal)*, allude to, insinuate • *What do you think he means by that?*
3 = **presage**, promise, herald, foreshadow, augur, foretell, portend, betoken, adumbrate • *An enlarged prostate does not necessarily mean cancer.*
4 = **result in**, cause, produce, effect, lead to, involve, bring about, give rise to, entail, engender, necessitate • *Trade and product discounts can mean big savings.*
5 = **intend**, want, plan, expect, design, aim, wish, think, propose, purpose, desire, set out, contemplate, aspire, have plans, have in mind • *I didn't mean to hurt you.*
6 = **destine**, make, design, suit, fate, predestine, preordain • *He said that we were meant to be together.*
7 = **matter**, be significant, have significance, have importance • *It doesn't sound much, but it means a lot to me.*

mean² **1** = **miserly**, stingy, parsimonious, niggardly, close *(informal)*, near *(informal)*, tight, selfish, beggarly, mercenary, skimpy, penny-pinching, ungenerous, penurious, tight-fisted, tight-arsed *(taboo slang)*, mingy *(Brit. informal)*, tight-assed *(U.S. taboo slang)*, snoep *(S. African informal)*, tight as a duck's arse *(taboo slang)* • *Don't be mean with the fabric, or the curtains will end up looking skimpy.*
OPPOSITES: generous, prodigal, altruistic
2 = **dishonourable**, base, petty, degraded, disgraceful, shameful, shabby, vile, degenerate, callous, sordid, abject, despicable, narrow-minded, contemptible, wretched, scurvy, ignoble, hard-hearted, scungy *(Austral. & N.Z.)*, low-minded • *Upstaging the bride was a particularly mean trick.*
OPPOSITES: good, honourable, praiseworthy
3 = **malicious**, hostile, nasty, sour, unpleasant, rude, unfriendly, bad-tempered, disagreeable, churlish, ill-tempered, cantankerous • *The prison officer described him as the meanest man he'd ever met.*
OPPOSITES: kind, liberal, gentle
4 = **shabby**, poor, miserable, rundown, beggarly, seedy, scruffy, sordid, paltry, squalid, tawdry, low-rent *(informal, chiefly U.S.)*, contemptible, wretched, down-at-heel, grungy *(slang, chiefly U.S.)*, scuzzy *(slang, chiefly U.S.)* • *He was raised in the mean streets of the central market district.*
OPPOSITES: pleasing, excellent, superb
5 = **excellent**, great *(informal)*, outstanding, superb, bad *(informal)*, fine, masterly, wonderful, brilliant *(Brit. informal)*, smashing *(informal)*, tremendous *(informal)*, ace *(informal)*, magnificent, neat *(U.S. informal)*, fabulous *(informal)*, first-class, marvellous, exceptional, terrific *(informal)*, formidable, sensational *(informal)*, awesome *(informal)*, skilful, A1 *(informal)*, virtuoso, super *(informal)*, wicked *(informal)*, first-rate, bonzer *(Austral. informal)*, badass *(U.S. informal)*, booshit *(Austral. slang)*, exo *(Austral. slang)*, sik *(Austral. slang)*, rad *(informal)*, phat *(slang)*, schmick *(Austral. informal)*, beaut *(informal)*, barrie *(Scot. slang)*, belting *(Brit. slang)*, pearler *(Austral. slang)* • *She plays a mean game of tennis.*
6 = **lowly**, low, common, ordinary, modest, base, obscure, humble, inferior, vulgar, menial, proletarian, undistinguished, servile, ignoble, plebeian, lowborn, baseborn *(archaic)* • *southern opportunists of mean origins*
OPPOSITES: high, important, noble
7 = **inferior**, little, limited, poor, restricted, slender, meagre, sparse, deficient • *a woman of mean understanding*

mean³ **AS A NOUN** = **average**, middle, balance, norm, median, midpoint • *Take a hundred and twenty values and calculate the mean.*
▸ **AS AN ADJECTIVE** = **average**, middle, middling, standard, medium, normal, intermediate, median, medial • *the mean score for 26-year-olds*

meander **AS A VERB** **1** = **wind**, turn, snake, zigzag • *The river meandered in lazy curves.*

m

2 = **wander**, stroll, stray, ramble, stravaig (*Scot. & Northern English dialect*) • *We meandered along the Irish country roads.*
3 = **ramble**, rabbit (*Brit. informal*), rattle, chatter, waffle (*Brit. informal*), witter (*Brit. informal*), prattle, natter (*Brit. informal*), maunder, blether, prate (*rare*), earbash (*Austral. & N.Z. slang*) • *She meandered on, stopping now and again for a breath.*
▸ **AS A NOUN** 1 = **wander**, stroll, amble, saunter, mosey (*informal*) • *a meander round the shops*
2 = **curve**, bend, turn, twist, loop, coil, zigzag • *The outer bank of a meander in the river.*

meandering 1 = **winding**, wandering, snaking, tortuous, convoluted, serpentine, circuitous • *We crossed a meandering stream.*
OPPOSITES: direct, straight, undeviating
2 = **convoluted**, indirect, roundabout, tortuous, digressive • *a rich and meandering novel*
OPPOSITES: straightforward

meaning AS A NOUN 1 = **significance**, message, explanation, substance, value, import, implication, drift, interpretation, essence, purport, connotation, upshot, gist, signification • *I became more aware of the symbols and their meanings.*
2 = **definition**, sense, interpretation, explication, elucidation, denotation • *arguing over the exact meaning of this word or that*
3 = **purpose**, point, end, idea, goal, design, aim, object, intention • *Unsure of the meaning of this remark, he remained silent.*
4 = **force**, use, point, effect, value, worth, consequence, thrust, validity, usefulness, efficacy • *a challenge that gives meaning to life*
▸ **AS AN ADJECTIVE** = **expressive**, meaningful, pointed, revealing, significant, speaking, pregnant, suggestive, telltale • *He nodded and gave me a meaning look.*

m

meaningful 1 = **significant**, important, serious, material, useful, relevant, valid, worthwhile, purposeful • *a meaningful and constructive dialogue*
OPPOSITES: useless, trivial, meaningless
2 = **expressive**, suggestive, meaning, pointed, speaking, pregnant • *The two men expressed a quick, meaningful look.*

meaningless 1 = **nonsensical**, senseless, inconsequential, inane, insubstantial, wanky (*taboo slang*) • *I consider algebra meaningless nonsense.*
OPPOSITES: useful, valuable, worthwhile
2 = **pointless**, empty, useless, hollow, vain, trivial, worthless, futile, trifling, insignificant, aimless, valueless, purposeless, nugatory • *They seek strong sensations to dull their sense of a meaningless existence.*
OPPOSITES: deep, significant, meaningful

meanness 1 = **miserliness**, parsimony, stinginess, tight-fistedness, niggardliness, selfishness, minginess (*Brit. informal*), penuriousness • *This careful attitude to money can border on meanness.*
2 = **pettiness**, degradation, degeneracy, wretchedness, narrow-mindedness, shabbiness, baseness, vileness, sordidness, shamefulness, scurviness, abjectness, low-mindedness, ignobility, despicableness, disgracefulness, dishonourableness • *Their meanness of spirit is embarrassing.*
3 = **malice**, hostility, bad temper, rudeness, nastiness, unpleasantness, ill temper, sourness, unfriendliness, maliciousness, cantankerousness, churlishness, disagreeableness • *There was always a certain amount of cruelty, meanness and villainy.*
4 = **shabbiness**, squalor, insignificance, pettiness, wretchedness, seediness, tawdriness, sordidness, scruffiness, humbleness, poorness, paltriness, beggarliness, contemptibleness • *the meanness of our surroundings*

PROVERBS
Do not spoil the ship for a ha'porth of tar

means AS A PLURAL NOUN 1 = **method**, way, course, process, medium, measure, agency, channel, instrument, avenue, mode, expedient • *We do not have the means to fight such a crimewave.*
2 = **money**, funds, capital, property, riches, income, resources, estate, fortune, wealth, substance, affluence, wherewithal, wonga (*slang*) • *He did not have the means to compensate her.*
▸ **IN PHRASES: by all means** = **certainly**, surely, of course, definitely, absolutely, positively, doubtlessly • *'Can I come and see your house?' 'Yes, by all means.'*
by means of = **by way of**, using, through, via, utilizing, with the aid of, by dint of • *a course taught by means of lectures and seminars*
by no means = **in no way**, no way, not at all, definitely not, not in the least, on no account, not in the slightest, not the least bit, absolutely not • *This is by no means out of the ordinary.*

meant = **supposed**, expected, required, intended • *Parties are meant to be fun.*

meantime or **meanwhile** = **at the same time**, in the meantime, simultaneously, for the present, concurrently, in the meanwhile • *Heat the oil in a heavy pan. Meantime, prepare the aubergines.*

meanwhile or **meantime** = **for now**, in the meantime, for the moment, in the interim, for then, in the interval, in the meanwhile, in the intervening time • *I'll be here when they arrive. Meanwhile I've got some shopping to do.*

measly = **meagre**, miserable, pathetic, paltry, mean, poor, petty, beggarly, pitiful, skimpy, puny, stingy, contemptible, scanty, miserly, niggardly, ungenerous, mingy (*Brit. informal*), snoep (*S. African informal*) • *The average bathroom measures a measly 3.5 metres.*

measurable 1 = **perceptible**, material, significant, distinct, palpable, discernible, detectable • *Both leaders expect measurable progress.*
2 = **quantifiable**, material, quantitative, assessable, determinable, computable, gaugeable, mensurable • *measurable quantities such as the number of jobs*

measure AS A VERB 1 = **monitor**, set, follow, match, test, judge, check, compare, pit, contrast, keep track of • *I continued to measure his progress against the chart.*
2 = **quantify**, rate, judge, determine, value, size, estimate, survey, assess, weigh, calculate, evaluate, compute, gauge, mark out, appraise, calibrate • *Measure the length and width of the gap.*
3 = **choose carefully**, plan, consider, calculate, think carefully about, select with care • *Measure your words before you come to regret them!*
▸ **AS A NOUN** 1 = **quantity**, share, amount, degree, reach, range, size, capacity, extent, proportion, allowance, portion, scope, quota, ration, magnitude, allotment, amplitude • *The colonies were claiming a larger measure of self-government.*
2 = **standard**, example, model, test, par, criterion, norm, benchmark, barometer, yardstick, touchstone, litmus test • *The local elections were seen as a measure of the government's success.*
3 = **action**, act, step, procedure, means, course, control, proceeding, initiative, manoeuvre, legal action, deed, expedient • *He said stern measures would be taken against the rioters.*
4 = **gauge**, rule, scale, metre, ruler, yardstick • *a tape measure*
5 = **law**, act, bill, legislation, resolution, statute, enactment • *They passed a measure that would give small businesses more benefits.*
▸ **IN PHRASES: beyond measure** = **immensely**, deeply, fiercely, profoundly, intensely, excessively • *She irritated him beyond measure.*
for good measure = **in addition**, as well, besides, to boot,

as an extra, into the bargain, as a bonus • *For good measure, a few details of hotels were included.*
get *or* **take the measure of something** *or* **someone** = **assess**, read, judge, evaluate, gauge, weigh up, fathom • *The government had failed to get the measure of the crisis.*
have the measure of someone = be wise to, see through, not fall for, have someone's number *(informal)*, not be deceived by, know someone's little game • *Lili was the only person who had the measure of her brother.*
measure someone up = evaluate, judge, survey, assess, weigh up, rate, appraise, size up • *For a minute, they studied one another, measuring each other up.*
measure something out = dispense, divide, distribute, assign, issue, pour out, allot, mete out, dole out, share out, apportion, deal out, parcel out, divvy up *(informal)* • *I'd already measured out the ingredients.*
measure something up = survey, estimate, count, weigh, meter, appraise, take the measurements of • *I measured up the panels and made copies of them.*
measure up = come up to standard, be fit, be adequate, be capable, be suitable, make the grade *(informal)*, be suited, be satisfactory, come up to scratch *(informal)*, cut the mustard *(U.S. slang)*, fulfil the expectations, fit *or* fill the bill • *I was informed that I didn't measure up.*
measure up to something *or* **someone = achieve**, meet, match, rival, equal, compare to, come up to, be equal to, vie with, be on a level with • *It was tiring, always trying to measure up to her high standards.*

measured 1 = **steady**, even, slow, regular, dignified, stately, solemn, leisurely, sedate, unhurried • *They have to proceed at a measured pace.*
2 = **considered**, planned, reasoned, studied, calculated, deliberate, sober, premeditated, well-thought-out • *Her more measured approach will appeal to voters.*
3 = **quantified**, standard, exact, regulated, precise, gauged, verified, predetermined, modulated • *Is the difference in measured intelligence genetic or environmental?*

measureless = **infinite**, endless, limitless, boundless, vast, immense, incalculable, immeasurable, unbounded, inestimable, beyond measure • *The party is now consigned to measureless years in opposition.*

measurement 1 = **size**, length, dimension, area, amount, weight, volume, capacity, extent, height, depth, width, magnitude, amplitude • *Some of the measurements are doubtless inaccurate.*
2 = **calculation**, assessment, evaluation, estimation, survey, judgment, valuation, appraisal, computation, calibration, mensuration, metage • *Measurement of blood pressure can be undertaken by the practice nurse.*

meat 1 = **food**, provisions, nourishment, sustenance, eats *(slang)*, fare, flesh, rations, grub *(slang)*, subsistence, kai *(N.Z. informal)*, chow *(informal)*, nosh *(slang)*, victuals, comestibles, provender, nutriment, viands • *They gave meat and drink to the poor.*
2 = **gist**, point, heart, core, substance, essence, nucleus, marrow, kernel, nub, pith • *The real meat of the conference was the attempt to agree on minimum standards.*

QUOTATIONS

If you knew how meat was made, you'd probably lose your lunch. I'm from cattle country. That's why I became a vegetarian
[K. D. Lang]

PROVERBS

The nearer the bone, the sweeter the meat

▷ *See panel* **Types and cuts of meat**

meaty 1 = **substantial**, rich, nourishing, hearty • *a lasagne with a meaty sauce*
2 = **brawny**, muscular, heavy, solid, strapping, sturdy, burly, husky *(informal)*, fleshy, beefy *(informal)*, heavily built • *a pleasant lady with meaty arms*
3 = **interesting**, rich, significant, substantial, profound, meaningful, pithy • *This time she has been given a more meaty role in the film.*

mechanic = **engineer**, technician, repairman, grease monkey *(informal)* • *I think you should take the car to your mechanic.*

mechanical 1 = **automatic**, automated, mechanized, power-driven, motor-driven, machine-driven • *a small mechanical device that taps out the numbers*
OPPOSITES: manual
2 = **unthinking**, routine, automatic, matter-of-fact, cold, unconscious, instinctive, lacklustre, involuntary, impersonal, habitual, cursory, perfunctory, unfeeling, machine-like, emotionless, spiritless • *His retort was mechanical.*
OPPOSITES: thinking, warm, conscious

TYPES AND CUTS OF MEAT

bacon
baron of beef
Bath chap
beef
beef-ham
black pudding
bockwurst
boerewors
bratwurst
breast
brisket
cervelat
charqui
Chateaubriand
chicken
chipolata
chitterlings, chitlings, *or* chitlins
chop
chorizo
chuck *or* chuck steak
chump
cold cuts
collar
colonial goose
corned beef
crown roast
Cumberland sausage
cutlet
devon
duck
entrecôte
escalope
fillet
forehock
foreshank
game
gammon
giblets
gigot
goose
gristle
haggis
ham
haslet
hogg *or* hogget
hough or hock
kidney
knackwurst *or* knockwurst
Kobe beef *or* Wagyu
lamb
lamb's fry
leg
lights
liver
liver sausage *or* *(esp U.S.)* liverwurst
loin
Lorne sausage, square sausage, *or* square slice *(Scot.)*
luncheon meat
médaillons
mince
minute steak
mortadella
mutton
noisette
numbles *(archaic)*
offal
oxtail
oxtongue
Parma ham
parson's nose
pastrami
pemmican
pepperoni
pheasant
pigeon
polony
pope's eye
pork
porterhouse steak
prosciutto
rack
rib
rolled lamb
round
rump
saddle
salami
salt beef
salt pork
sausage
saveloy
scrag
shank
shoulder
silverside
sirloin
skirt
Spam *(trademark)*
sparerib
steak
stewing steak
sweetbread
T-bone
tenderloin
tongue
topside
tournedos
tripe
turkey
undercut
veal
venison

mechanism 1 = **workings**, motor, gears, works, action, components, machinery, innards *(informal)* • *the locking mechanism*
2 = **process**, workings, way, means, system, performance, operation, medium, agency, method, functioning, technique, procedure, execution, methodology • *the clumsy mechanism of price controls*
3 = **machine**, system, structure, device, tool, instrument, appliance, apparatus, contrivance • *The heat-producing mechanism will switch itself on automatically.*

medal = **decoration**, order, award, honour, ribbon, gong *(Brit. informal)* • *a gold medal*
▸ **RELATED ENTHUSIAST:** medallist

MEDALS

Bronze Star *(U.S.)*	Iron Cross *(Germany)*
Congressional Medal of Honor *(U.S.)*	Légion d'Honneur *(France)*
	Legion of Merit *(U.S.)*
Croix de Guerre *(France)*	Militaire Willemsorde *(Netherlands)*
Distinguished Service Cross *(U.S.)*	Purple Heart *(U.S.)*
Distinguished Service Order *(Britain)*	Royal Red Cross *(Britain)*
	Silver Star *(U.S.)*
George Cross *(Britain)*	Victoria Cross *(Britain)*

meddle = **interfere**, intervene, tamper, intrude, pry, butt in, interpose, stick your nose in *(informal)*, put your oar in, intermeddle, put your two cents in *(U.S. slang)* • *Do scientists have a right to meddle in these matters?*

meddlesome = **interfering**, meddling, intrusive, intruding, mischievous, prying, officious, intermeddling • *a meddlesome member of the public*

median = **middle**, mid, halfway, medial • *The median mark is 7.*

mediate = **intervene**, moderate, step in *(informal)*, intercede, settle, referee, resolve, umpire, reconcile, arbitrate, interpose, conciliate, make peace, restore harmony, act as middleman, bring to terms, bring to an agreement • *UN officials mediated between the two sides.*

mediation = **arbitration**, intervention, reconciliation, conciliation, good offices, intercession, interposition • *They could reach a compromise through the mediation of a third party.*

mediator = **negotiator**, arbitrator, judge, referee, advocate, umpire, intermediary, middleman, arbiter, peacemaker, go-between, moderator, interceder, honest broker • *He has been acting as a mediator between the rebels and the authorities.*

medic = **doctor**, physician, medical practitioner • *A Navy medic was wounded by sniper fire.*

medication = **medicine**, drug, cure, remedy, prescription, medicament • *She stopped taking the prescribed medication.*

medicinal = **therapeutic**, medical, healing, remedial, restorative, curative, analeptic, roborant, sanative • *medicinal plants*

medicine = **remedy**, drug, cure, prescription, medication, nostrum, physic, medicament • *herbal medicines*
▸ **RELATED ADJECTIVES:** Aesculapian, iatric
▸ **RELATED MANIA:** pharmacomania

QUOTATIONS
Formerly, when religion was strong and science weak, men mistook magic for medicine; now, when science is strong and religion weak, men mistake medicine for magic
[Thomas Szasz *The Second Skin*]

▹ *See panel* **Medicine**

medieval = **old-fashioned**, antique, primitive, obsolete, out-of-date, archaic, prehistoric, antiquated, anachronistic, antediluvian, unenlightened, out of the ark • *There can be no excuse for these medieval methods.*

mediocre = **second-rate**, average, ordinary, indifferent, middling, pedestrian, inferior, commonplace, vanilla *(slang)*, insignificant, so-so *(informal)*, banal, tolerable, run-of-the-mill, passable, undistinguished, uninspired, bog-standard *(Brit. & Irish slang)*, no great shakes *(informal)*, half-pie *(N.Z. informal)*, fair to middling *(informal)* • *His university record was mediocre.*
OPPOSITES: excellent, extraordinary, superb

QUOTATIONS
Some men are born mediocre, some men achieve mediocrity, and some men have mediocrity thrust upon them. With Major it had been all three
[Joseph Heller *Catch-22*]

mediocrity 1 = **insignificance**, indifference, inferiority, meanness, ordinariness, unimportance, poorness • *She lamented the mediocrity of contemporary literature.*
2 = **nonentity**, nobody, lightweight *(informal)*, second-rater, cipher, non-person • *Surrounded by mediocrities, he seemed a towering intellectual.*

QUOTATIONS
Mediocrity knows nothing higher than itself, but talent instantly recognizes genius
[Sir Arthur Conan Doyle *The Valley of Fear*]

meditate AS A VERB = **reflect**, think, consider, contemplate, deliberate, muse, ponder, ruminate, cogitate, be in a brown study • *I was meditating, and reached a higher state of consciousness.*
▸ **IN PHRASES: meditate on something** = **consider**, study, contemplate, ponder, reflect on, mull over, think over, chew over, deliberate on, weigh, turn something over in your mind • *He meditated on the problem.*

meditation = **reflection**, thought, concentration, study, musing, pondering, contemplation, reverie, ruminating, rumination, cogitation, cerebration, a brown study • *Lost in meditation, he walked with slow steps along the shore.*

meditative = **reflective**, thoughtful, contemplative, studious, pensive, deliberative, ruminative, cogitative • *Music can induce a meditative state in the listener.*

medium AS AN ADJECTIVE = **average**, mean, middle, middling, fair, intermediate, midway, mediocre, median, medial • *foods which contain only medium levels of sodium*
OPPOSITES: unique, unusual, extraordinary
▸ AS A NOUN 1 = **means**, way, form, channel, method, vehicle, instrument, avenue, forum, organ, mode • *English is used as a medium of instruction at primary level.*
2 = **spiritualist**, seer, clairvoyant, fortune teller, spiritist, channeller • *Going to see a medium provided a starting point for her.*
3 = **middle**, mean, centre, average, compromise, middle ground, middle way, midpoint, middle course, middle path • *It's difficult to strike a happy medium.*
4 = **environment**, setting, conditions, influences, surroundings, element, atmosphere, habitat, milieu • *Blood is a favourable medium for bacteria to grow in.*

QUOTATIONS
The medium is the message
[Marshall McLuhan *Understanding Media*]

medley = **mixture**, confusion, jumble, assortment, patchwork, pastiche, mixed bag *(informal)*, potpourri, mélange *(French)*, miscellany, mishmash, farrago, hotchpotch, hodgepodge, salmagundi, olio, gallimaufry, omnium-gatherum • *a medley of traditional songs*

meek 1 = **submissive**, soft, yielding, gentle, peaceful, modest, mild, patient, humble, timid, long-suffering, compliant, unassuming, unpretentious, docile, deferential, forbearing, acquiescent • *He was a meek, mild-mannered fellow.*
OPPOSITES: forward, overbearing
2 = **spineless**, weak, tame, boneless, weak-kneed *(informal)*,

spiritless, unresisting, wussy (*slang*), wimpish *or* wimpy (*informal*) • *He may be self-effacing, but he certainly isn't meek.*

QUOTATIONS

Blessed are the meek: for they shall inherit the earth
[*Bible: St. Matthew*]

It's going to be fun to watch and see how long the meek can keep the earth after they inherit it
[Kin Hubbard]

meekness 1 = **submissiveness**, resignation, submission, compliance, modesty, patience, humility, long-suffering, deference, softness, gentleness, acquiescence, timidity, forbearance, peacefulness, docility, mildness, humbleness, lowliness • *She maintained a kind of meekness.*
2 = **spinelessness**, resignation, weakness, tameness, spiritlessness • *She was reduced to an embarrassing posture of meekness and submission.*

meet AS A VERB 1 = **encounter**, come across, run into, happen on, find, contact, confront, bump into (*informal*), run across, chance on, come face to face with • *He's the kindest person I've ever met.*
OPPOSITES: miss, avoid, escape
2 = **be introduced to**, get to know, make the acquaintance of • *Hey Terry, come and meet my Dad.*
3 = **gather**, collect, assemble, get together, rally, come together, muster, convene, congregate, foregather • *The commission met four times between 1988 and 1991.*
OPPOSITES: scatter, disperse, adjourn
4 = **fulfil**, match (up to), answer, perform, handle, carry out, equal, satisfy, cope with, discharge, comply with, come up to, conform to, gratify, measure up to • *The current arrangements are inadequate to meet our needs.*
OPPOSITES: fail, fall short of
5 = **pay for**, clear, settle, square, honour, satisfy, account for, discharge • *The government will help meet some of the costs.*
6 = **experience**, face, suffer, bear, go through, encounter, endure, undergo • *Never had she met such spite and pettiness.*
7 = **converge**, unite, join, cross, touch, connect, come together, link up, adjoin, intersect, abut • *a crossing where four paths meet*
OPPOSITES: diverge
▸ AS A NOUN = **sports event**, competition, tournament, contest • *He pole-vaulted 17ft at a meet in Miami.*
▸ IN PHRASES: **meet someone halfway** = **compromise with**, make a deal with, make concessions to, reach a compromise with, come to an understanding with, split the difference with (*informal*), find a happy medium with, find the middle ground with, go fifty-fifty with • *The Democrats are willing to meet the president halfway.*

meeting 1 = **conference**, gathering, assembly, meet, congress, session, rally, convention, get-together (*informal*), reunion, congregation, hui (*N.Z.*), lekgotal *or* kgotla (*S. African*), conclave, convocation, powwow • *He travels to London regularly for business meetings.*
2 = **encounter**, introduction, confrontation, engagement, rendezvous, tryst, assignation • *Thirty-seven years after our first meeting I was back in his studio.*
3 = **convergence**, union, crossing, conjunction, junction, intersection, concourse, confluence • *the meeting of three streams*

megalomania = **self-importance**, conceit, egotism, delusions of grandeur, grandiosity, folie de grandeur (*French*), conceitedness • *His single-mindedness never veered into megalomania.*

melancholy AS AN ADJECTIVE = **sad**, down, depressed, unhappy, low, blue, miserable, moody, gloomy, dismal, sombre, woeful, glum, mournful, dejected, despondent, dispirited, melancholic, downcast, lugubrious, pensive, sorrowful, disconsolate, joyless, doleful, downhearted, heavy-hearted, down in the dumps (*informal*), woebegone, down in the mouth, low-spirited • *It was at this time of day that he felt most melancholy.*
OPPOSITES: happy, cheerful, bright
▸ AS A NOUN = **sadness**, depression, misery, gloom, sorrow, woe, blues, unhappiness, despondency, the hump (*Brit. informal*), dejection, low spirits, gloominess, pensiveness • *He watched the process with an air of melancholy.*
OPPOSITES: delight, pleasure, happiness

melange *or* **mélange** = **mixture**, mix, jumble, assortment, medley, pastiche, confusion, mixed bag (*informal*), potpourri, miscellany, mishmash, farrago, hotch-potch, hodge-podge, salmagundi, olio, gallimaufry, omnium-gatherum • *a wonderful melange of flavours*

melee *or* **mêlée** = **fight**, fray, brawl, skirmish, tussle, scuffle, free-for-all (*informal*), fracas, set-to (*informal*), rumpus, broil, affray (*Law*), shindig (*informal*), donnybrook, ruction (*informal*), battle royal, ruckus (*informal*), scrimmage, stramash (*Scot.*), shindy (*informal*), bagarre (*French*), biffo (*Austral. slang*) • *Scores of people were injured in the melee.*

mellifluous *or* **mellifluent** = **sweet**, soft, smooth, honeyed, soothing, mellow, silvery, dulcet, sweet-sounding, euphonious • *wonderful mellifluous voices*

mellow AS AN ADJECTIVE 1 = **soft**, deep, rich, warm • *the mellow colours of autumn*
2 = **tuneful**, full, rich, soft, melodious, mellifluous, dulcet, well-tuned, euphonic • *the mellow background music*
3 = **full-flavoured**, rounded, rich, sweet, smooth, delicate, juicy • *a mellow, well-balanced wine*
4 = **ripe**, perfect, mature, ripened, well-matured • *a mellow, creamy Somerset Brie*
OPPOSITES: green, raw, unripe
5 = **easy-going**, warm, gentle, pleasant, sympathetic, tolerant, gracious, amiable, amicable, affable, good-natured, kind-hearted, warm-hearted • *Is she more mellow and tolerant?*
6 = **relaxed**, happy, cheerful, jolly, elevated, merry (*Brit. informal*), expansive, cordial, genial, jovial • *After a few glasses, he was feeling mellow.*
▸ AS A VERB 1 = **relax**, improve, settle, calm, mature, soften, sweeten • *She has mellowed with age.*
2 = **season**, develop, improve, perfect, ripen • *Long cooking mellows the flavour beautifully.*

melodic = **tuneful**, harmonious, catchy, melodious, mellifluous, easy on the ear (*informal*), euphonious, euphonic • *His songs are wonderfully melodic.*

melodious = **musical**, harmonious, melodic, silvery, tuneful, concordant, dulcet, sweet-sounding, euphonious, sweet-toned, euphonic • *She spoke in a quiet melodious voice.*
OPPOSITES: harsh, grating, discordant

melodramatic = **theatrical**, actorly, extravagant, histrionic, sensational, hammy (*informal*), actressy, stagy, overemotional, overdramatic • *She flung herself in a pose of melodramatic exhaustion.*

melody 1 = **tune**, song, theme, refrain, air, music, strain, descant • *a catchy melody with a frenetic beat*
2 = **tunefulness**, music, harmony, musicality, euphony, melodiousness • *Her voice was full of melody.*

melt 1 = **dissolve**, run, soften, fuse, thaw, diffuse, flux, defrost, liquefy, unfreeze, deliquesce • *The snow had melted.*
2 *often with* **away** = **disappear**, fade, vanish, dissolve, disperse, evaporate, evanesce • *When he heard these words, his inner doubts melted away.*
3 = **vanish**, fade (away), go away, evaporate, dissipate • *The youths dispersed and melted into the darkness.*
4 = **soften**, touch, relax, disarm, mollify • *His smile is enough to melt any woman's heart.*

member = **representative**, associate, supporter, fellow, subscriber, comrade, disciple • *The support of our members is of great importance to the Association.*

MEDICINE

Branches of medicine

aetiology *or* etiology, anaesthetics, anaplasty, anatomy, andrology, angiology, audiology, aviation medicine, bacteriology, balneology, bioastronautics, biomedicine, cardiology, chiropody, dental hygiene *or* oral hygiene, dental surgery, dentistry, dermatology, diagnostics, eccrinology, electrophysiology, electrotherapeutics, embryology, encephalography, endocrinology, endodontics, epidemiology, exodontics, forensic *or* legal medicine, gastroenterology, genitourinary medicine, geratology, geriatrics, gerontology, gynaecology *or* (*U.S.*) gynecology, haematology *or* (*U.S.*) hematology, hydrotherapeutics, immunochemistry, immunology, industrial medicine, internal medicine, laryngology, materia medica, midwifery, morbid anatomy, myology, neonatology, nephrology, neuroanatomy, neuroendocrinology, neurology, neuropathology, neurophysiology, neuropsychiatry, neurosurgery, nosology, nostology, nuclear medicine, nutrition, obstetrics, odontology, oncology, ophthalmology, optometry, orthodontics *or* orthodontia, orthopaedics *or* (*U.S.*) orthopedics, orthoptics, orthotics, osteology, osteoplasty, otolaryngology, otology, paediatrics *or* (*U.S.*) pediatrics, pathology, periodontics, pharyngology, physical medicine, physiotherapy *or* (*U.S.*) physiatrics, plastic surgery, posology, preventive medicine, proctology, psychiatry, psychoanalysis, psychology, radiology, rheumatology, rhinology, serology, space medicine, spare-part surgery, speech therapy, sports medicine, stomatology, surgery, symptomatology, syphilology, therapeutics, tocology *or* tokology, toxicology, trichology, urology, venereology, veterinary science *or* medicine, virology

Medical practitioners and specialists

aetiologist *or* etiologist, anaesthetist, anatomist, andrologist, audiologist, bacteriologist, balneologist, barefoot doctor, cardiologist, chiropodist, consultant, dental hygienist *or* oral hygienist, dentist *or* dental surgeon, dermatologist, diagnostician, dietitian, district nurse, doctor, electrophysiologist, embryologist, endocrinologist, endodontist, epidemiologist, exodontist, extern *or* externe (*U.S. & Canad.*), forensic scientist, gastroenterologist, general practitioner *or* GP, geriatrician *or* geriatrist, gerontologist, gynaecologist *or* (*U.S.*) gynecologist, haematologist *or* (*U.S.*) hematologist, health visitor, house physician, houseman, hydrotherapist, immunologist, intern *or* interne (*U.S. & Canad.*), internist, junior doctor, laboratory technician, laryngologist, matron, midwife, myologist, neonatologist, nephrologist, neuroanatomist, neurologist, neuropathologist, neurophysiologist, neuropsychiatrist, neurosurgeon, nosologist, nurse, nursing officer, nutritionist, obstetrician, occupational therapist, odontologist, oncologist, ophthalmologist, optician, optometrist, orderly, orthodontist, orthopaedist *or* (*U.S.*) orthopedist, orthoptist, orthotist, osteologist, otolaryngologist, otologist, paediatrician *or* (*U.S.*) pediatrician, paramedic, pathologist, pharyngologist, physiotherapist *or* physio, plastic surgeon, proctologist, psychiatrist, psychoanalyst, psychologist, radiographer, radiologist, registrar, resident (*U.S. & Canad.*), rheumatologist, rhinologist, serologist, speech therapist, surgeon, syphilologist, therapist, toxicologist, trichologist, urologist, venereologist, veterinary surgeon, vet *or* (*U.S.*) veterinarian, virologist

Medical and surgical instruments and equipment

arthroscope, artificial heart, artificial kidney, aspirator, bandage, bedpan, bistoury, bronchoscope, cannula *or* canula, cardiograph, catheter, catling, clamp, clinical thermometer, colonoscope, colposcope, compressor, CT scanner *or* CAT scanner, curet *or* curette, cystoscope, defibrillator, depressor, dialysis machine, drain, electrocardiograph, electroencephalograph, electromyograph, encephalogram, endoscope, fetoscope, fibrescope *or* (*U.S.*) fiberscope, fluoroscope, forceps, gamma camera, gastroscope, gonioscope, haemostat *or* (*U.S.*) hemostat, heart-lung machine, heat lamp, hypodermic *or* hypodermic needle, hypodermic *or* hypodermic syringe, inhalator

Medical and surgical instruments and equipment (continued)

inspirator
iron lung
kidney machine
kymograph *or* cymograph
lancet *or* lance
laparoscope
laryngoscope
life-support machine
microscope
nebulizer
needle
nephroscope
oesophagoscope *or* (*U.S.*) esophagoscope
ophthalmoscope
orthoscope
otoscope
oxygen mask
oxygen tent
pacemaker
packing
perimeter
pharyngoscope
plaster cast
pneumatometer
pneumograph
probe
proctoscope
Pulmotor (*trademark*)
raspatory
respirator
resuscitator
retinoscope
retractor
rheometer
rhinoscope
roentgenoscope *or* röntgenoscope
scalpel
scanner
skiascope
sling
sound
specimen bottle
speculum
sphygmograph
sphygmomanometer
spirograph
spirometer
splint
stethoscope
stomach pump
stretcher
stupe
stylet
styptic pencil
suture
swab
syringe
thoracoscope
tourniquet
trepan
trephine
trocar
ultrasound scanner
urethroscope
urinometer
ventilator
wet pack
X-ray machine

Branches of alternative medicine

acupressure
acupuncture
Alexander technique
aromatherapy
autogenic training
Bach flower remedy
biofeedback
chiropractic
herbalism
homeopathy *or* homoeopathy
hydrotherapy
hypnosis
hypnotherapy
iridology
kinesiology
massage
moxibustion
naturopathy
osteopathy
radionics
reflexology
shiatsu

membership 1 = **participation**, belonging, fellowship, enrolment • *his membership of the Communist Party*
2 = **members**, body, associates, fellows • *the recent fall in party membership*

membrane = **layer**, film, skin, tissue, veil, diaphragm • *the mucous membrane*

memento = **souvenir**, trophy, memorial, token, reminder, relic, remembrance, keepsake • *He took a camera to provide a memento of the day.*

memo = **memorandum**, minute, note, message, communication, reminder, jotting, e-mail • *A leaked memo to managers identified a dozen danger spots.*

memoir = **account**, life, record, register, journal, essay, biography, narrative, monograph • *He has just published a memoir in honour of his captain.*

memoirs = **autobiography**, diary, life story, life, experiences, memories, journals, recollections, reminiscences • *If you've read my memoirs, you'll know about it.*

QUOTATIONS

To write one's memoirs is to speak ill of everybody except oneself

[Marshal Pétain]

memorabilia = **collectibles** • *Beatles memorabilia*

memorable = **noteworthy**, celebrated, impressive, historic, important, special, striking, famous, significant, signal, extraordinary, remarkable, distinguished, haunting, notable, timeless, unforgettable, momentous, illustrious, catchy, indelible, unfading • *a memorable performance*
OPPOSITES: ordinary, commonplace, forgettable

memorandum 1 = **agreement**, record, note, contract • *The solicitor drew up a memorandum of Ford's financial position.*
2 = **note**, minute, message, communication, reminder, memo, jotting, e-mail • *He sent a memorandum to the members of the board.*

QUOTATIONS

A memorandum is written not to inform the reader but to protect the writer

[Dean Acheson]

memorial AS A NOUN 1 = **monument**, cairn, shrine, plaque, cenotaph • *Every village had its war memorial.*
2 = **remembrance**, tribute, record, souvenir, testimonial, memento • *The museum will serve as a memorial to all those who died.*
3 = **petition**, address, statement, memorandum • *a memorial to the Emperor written in characters of gold*
▸ AS AN ADJECTIVE = **commemorative**, remembrance, monumental • *A memorial service is being held at St Paul's Church.*

memorize = **remember**, learn, commit to memory, learn by heart, learn by rote, get by heart, con (*archaic*) • *He studied the map, trying to memorize the way.*

memory 1 = **recall**, mind, retention, ability to remember, powers of recall, powers of retention • *He had a good memory for faces.*
2 = **recollection**, reminder, reminiscence, impression, echo, remembrance • *He had happy memories of his father.*
3 = **hard disk**, cache • *The data are stored in the computer's memory.*
4 = **commemoration**, respect, honour, recognition, tribute, remembrance, observance • *They held a minute's silence in memory of those who had died.*

QUOTATIONS

The man with a good memory remembers nothing because he forgets nothing

[Augusto Roa Bastos I, *The Supreme*]

The charm, one might say the genius of memory, is that it is choosy, chancy, and temperamental: it rejects the edifying cathedral and indelibly photographs the small boy outside, chewing a hunk of melon in the dust

[Elizabeth Bowen]

Our memories are card-indexes consulted, and then put back in disorder by authorities whom we do not control
[Cyril Connolly *The Unquiet Grave*]
We find a little of everything in our memory; it is a sort of pharmacy, a sort of chemical laboratory, in which our groping hand may come to rest, now on a sedative drug, now on a dangerous poison
[Marcel Proust *Remembrance of Things Past*]

menace AS A NOUN 1 = **danger**, risk, threat, hazard, peril, jeopardy • *In my view you are a menace to the public.*
2 = **nuisance**, plague, pest, annoyance, troublemaker, mischief-maker • *Don't be such a menace!*
3 = **threat**, warning, intimidation, ill-omen, ominousness, commination • *a pervading sense of menace*
▸ AS A VERB 1 = **threaten**, jeopardize, put at risk, loom over, imperil, be a danger to • *The state retained the latent capability to menace people's security.*
2 = **bully**, threaten, intimidate, terrorize, alarm, frighten, scare, browbeat, utter threats to • *She is being menaced by her sister's boyfriend.*

menacing = **threatening**, dangerous, alarming, frightening, forbidding, looming, intimidating, ominous, baleful, intimidatory, minatory, bodeful, louring *or* lowering, minacious • *His dark eyebrows gave his face a menacing look.*
OPPOSITES: promising, encouraging, favourable

mend AS A VERB 1 = **repair**, fix, restore, renew, patch up, renovate, refit, retouch • *They took a long time to mend the roof.*
2 = **darn**, repair, patch, stitch, sew • *cooking their meals, mending their socks*
3 = **heal**, improve, recover, cure, remedy, get better, be all right, be cured, recuperate, pull through, convalesce • *He must have an operation to mend torn knee ligaments.* • *The arm is broken, but you'll mend.*
4 = **put right**, settle, resolve, heal, sort out, remedy, redress, rectify • *I felt that might mend the rift between them.*
5 = **improve**, better, reform, correct, revise, amend, rectify, ameliorate, emend • *There will be disciplinary action if you do not mend your ways.*
▸ IN PHRASES: **on the mend** = **convalescent**, improving, recovering, getting better, recuperating, convalescing • *The baby had been poorly but was on the mend.*

mendacious = **lying**, false, untrue, fraudulent, dishonest, deceptive, deceitful, insincere, duplicitous, perjured, perfidious, fallacious, untruthful • *politicians issuing mendacious claims and counter-claims*
OPPOSITES: true, genuine, truthful

mendacity = **lying**, lie, perjury, deceit, dishonesty, distortion, misrepresentation, duplicity, falsehood, untruth, falsification, insincerity, perfidy, fraudulence, deceitfulness, untruthfulness, mendaciousness, inveracity • *an astonishing display of cowardice and mendacity*

mendicant AS AN ADJECTIVE = **begging**, sponging (*informal*), scrounging (*informal*), mooching (*informal*), cadging • *mendicant religious orders*
▸ AS A NOUN = **beggar**, tramp, vagrant, bum (*U.S. informal*), pauper, hobo (*U.S.*), scrounger (*informal*), vagabond, sponger (*informal*), derro (*Austral. slang*), quandong (*Austral. slang*) • *He had no fear that he would ever become a mendicant.*

menial AS AN ADJECTIVE = **low-status**, degrading, lowly, unskilled, low, base, sorry, boring, routine, dull, humble, mean, vile, demeaning, fawning, abject, grovelling, humdrum, subservient, ignominious, sycophantic, servile, slavish, ignoble, obsequious • *low-paid menial jobs such as cleaning*
OPPOSITES: high, noble, elevated
▸ AS A NOUN = **servant**, domestic, attendant, lackey, labourer, serf, underling, drudge, vassal (*archaic*), dogsbody (*informal*), flunky, skivvy (*chiefly Brit.*), varlet (*archaic*) • *The name 'beef-eater' was aimed at any well-fed menial.*
OPPOSITES: lord, boss, master

menstruation = **period**, menstrual cycle, menses, courses (*Physiology*), flow (*informal*), monthly (*informal*), the curse (*informal*), catamenia (*Physiology*) • *Menstruation may cease when a woman is in her late forties.*

mental 1 = **intellectual**, rational, theoretical, cognitive, brain, conceptual, cerebral • *the mental development of children*
2 = **psychiatric**, psychogenic • *mental health problems*
3 = **insane**, mad, disturbed, unstable, mentally ill, lunatic, psychotic, unbalanced, deranged, round the bend (*Brit. slang*), as daft as a brush (*informal, chiefly Brit.*), not right in the head, a sausage short of a fry-up (*slang*) • *I just said to him 'you must be mental!'*

mentality = **attitude**, character, personality, psychology, make-up, outlook, disposition, way of thinking, frame of mind, turn of mind, cast of mind • *What kind of mentality is required for running a business?*

mentally = **psychologically**, intellectually, rationally, inwardly, subjectively • *This technique will help people mentally organize information.*

mention AS A VERB = **refer to**, point out, acknowledge, bring up, state, report, reveal, declare, cite, communicate, disclose, intimate, tell of, recount, hint at, impart, allude to, divulge, broach, call attention to, make known, touch upon, adduce, speak about *or* of • *She did not mention her mother's absence.*
▸ AS A NOUN 1 *often with* **of** = **reference**, announcement, observation, indication, remark, notification, allusion • *The statement made no mention of government casualties.*
2 = **acknowledgment**, recognition, tribute, citation, honourable mention, namecheck • *Two of the losers deserve special mention.*
▸ IN PHRASES: **don't mention it** = **not at all**, any time, my pleasure • *'Thank you very much.' 'Don't mention it.'*
not to mention = **to say nothing of**, besides, not counting, as well as • *It was both deliberate and malicious, not to mention sick.*

mentor = **guide**, teacher, coach, adviser, tutor, instructor, counsellor, guru • *She has sacked her coach and mentor and is now relying on her father.*

menu = **bill of fare**, tariff (*chiefly Brit.*), set menu, table d'hôte, carte du jour (*French*) • *A waiter offered him the menu.*

mephitic = **foul**, stinking, poisonous, noxious, fetid, foul-smelling, putrid, malodorous, noisome, pestilential, baneful, miasmic, olid, miasmal, miasmatic, baleful, evil- *or* ill-smelling, festy (*Austral. slang*) • *a mephitic stench*

mercantile 1 = **commercial**, business, trade, trading, merchant • *the emergence of a new mercantile class*
2 = **profit-making**, materialistic, capitalistic, money-orientated • *the urban society and its mercantile values*

mercenary AS A NOUN = **hireling**, freelance (*History*), soldier of fortune, condottiere (*History*), free companion (*History*) • *In the film he plays a brutish, trigger-happy mercenary.*
▸ AS AN ADJECTIVE 1 = **greedy**, grasping, acquisitive, venal, avaricious, covetous, money-grubbing (*informal*), bribable • *Despite his mercenary motives, he is not a cynic.*
OPPOSITES: liberal, generous, benevolent
2 = **hired**, paid, bought, venal • *The mercenary soldier is not a valued creature.*

merchandise AS A NOUN = **goods**, produce, stock, products, truck, commodities, staples, wares, stock in trade, vendibles • *25% off selected merchandise*
▸ AS A VERB = **trade**, market, sell, retail, distribute, deal in, buy and sell, traffic in, vend, do business in • *He advises shops on how to merchandise their wares.*

merchandising 1 = **products**, goods, produce, stock, commodities, wares • *We are selling the full range of World Cup merchandising.*
2 = **presentation**, marketing, advertising, distribution • *Revamped merchandising should help profits grow.*

merchant = **tradesman**, dealer, trader, broker, retailer, supplier, seller, salesman, vendor, shopkeeper, trafficker, wholesaler, purveyor • *Any good wine merchant would be able to advise you.*

QUOTATIONS

A merchant shall hardly keep himself from doing wrong
[*Bible: Ecclesiasticus*]

merchantable = **saleable**, marketable, tradable, sellable, vendible, merchandisable • *Goods must reach a high standard of merchantable quality.*

merciful AS AN ADJECTIVE 1 = **compassionate**, forgiving, sympathetic, kind, liberal, soft, sparing, generous, mild, pitying, humane, clement, gracious, lenient, beneficent, forbearing, tender-hearted, benignant • *We can only hope the court is merciful.*
OPPOSITES: cruel, merciless, inhumane
2 = **welcome**, desired, blessed • *Eventually the session came to a merciful end.*
▸ IN PHRASES: **be merciful to** = **show mercy to**, spare, forgive, pardon, let off, go easy on (*informal*), have mercy on, have pity on, be lenient with • *He had always been more merciful to girls than to boys.*

mercifully = **thankfully**, happily, luckily, thank goodness • *Mercifully, a friend came to the rescue.*

merciless = **cruel**, ruthless, hard, severe, harsh, relentless, callous, heartless, unforgiving, fell (*archaic*), inexorable, implacable, unsympathetic, inhumane, barbarous, pitiless, unfeeling, unsparing, hard-hearted, unmerciful, unappeasable, unpitying • *the merciless efficiency of a modern police state*

mercurial = **capricious**, volatile, unpredictable, erratic, variable, unstable, fickle, temperamental, impulsive, irrepressible, changeable, quicksilver, flighty, inconstant • *his mercurial temperament*
OPPOSITES: stable, constant, consistent

mercy AS A NOUN 1 = **compassion**, charity, pity, forgiveness, quarter, favour, grace, kindness, clemency, leniency, benevolence, forbearance • *Neither side showed its prisoners any mercy.*
OPPOSITES: cruelty, brutality, severity
2 = **blessing**, relief, boon, godsend, piece of luck, benison (*archaic*) • *It was a mercy he'd gone so quickly in the end.*
▸ IN PHRASES: **at the mercy of something** or **someone**
1 = **defenceless against**, subject to, open to, exposed to, vulnerable to, threatened by, susceptible to, prey to, an easy target for, naked before, unprotected against • *Buildings are left to decay at the mercy of vandals and bad weather.*
2 = **in the power of**, under the control of, in the clutches of, under the heel of • *Servants or slaves were at the mercy of their masters.*

QUOTATIONS

Yet I shall temper so
Justice with mercy
[John Milton *Paradise Lost*]

mere 1 = **simple**, merely, no more than, nothing more than, just, common, plain, pure, pure and simple, unadulterated, unmitigated, unmixed • *It proved to be a mere trick of fate.*
2 = **bare**, slender, trifling, meagre, just, only, basic, no more than, minimal, scant, paltry, skimpy, scanty • *Cigarettes were a mere 2 cents a packet.*

merely = **only**, but, just, simply, entirely, purely, solely • *He was far from being merely a furniture expert.*

meretricious 1 = **trashy**, flashy, gaudy, garish, tawdry, showy, plastic (*slang*), tinsel, gimcrack • *vulgar, meretricious and shabby souvenirs*
2 = **false**, hollow, bogus, put-on, mock, sham, pseudo (*informal*), counterfeit, spurious, deceitful, insincere, specious, phoney or phony (*informal*) • *meretricious ads that claim their product to be the best around*

merge 1 = **combine**, blend, fuse, amalgamate, unite, join, mix, consolidate, mingle, converge, coalesce, melt into, meld, intermix • *The two countries merged into one.*
OPPOSITES: part, separate, divide
2 = **join**, unite, combine, consolidate, fuse • *He wants to merge the two agencies.*
OPPOSITES: part, separate, divide
3 = **melt**, blend, incorporate, mingle, tone with, be swallowed up by, become lost in • *His features merged into the darkness.*

merger = **union**, fusion, consolidation, amalgamation, combination, coalition, incorporation • *the proposed merger of the two banks*

merit AS A NOUN 1 = **worth**, value, quality, credit, talent, desert, virtue, integrity, excellence, goodness, worthiness • *Box-office success mattered more than artistic merit.*
2 = **advantage**, value, quality, worth, strength, asset, virtue, good point, strong point, worthiness • *They have been persuaded of the merits of the scheme.*
▸ AS A VERB = **deserve**, warrant, be entitled to, earn, incur, have a right to, be worthy of, have a claim to • *Such ideas merit careful consideration.*

QUOTATIONS

What is merit? The opinion one man entertains of another
[Lord Palmerston]

merited = **deserved**, justified, warranted, just, earned, appropriate, entitled, rightful, condign, rightly due • *His selection for the team was a surprise, but a merited one.*

meritorious = **praiseworthy**, admirable, exemplary, good, right, excellent, deserving, worthy, honourable, righteous, virtuous, commendable, creditable, laudable • *I had been promoted for gallant and meritorious service.*
OPPOSITES: dishonourable, unexceptional, unpraiseworthy

merriment = **fun**, amusement, glee, mirth, sport, laughter, festivity, frolic, gaiety, hilarity, revelry, jollity, levity, liveliness, conviviality, joviality, jocularity, merrymaking • *He jokes and ad-libs, to the general merriment of the audience.*

merry AS AN ADJECTIVE 1 = **cheerful**, happy, upbeat (*informal*), carefree, glad, jolly, festive, joyous, joyful, genial, fun-loving, chirpy (*informal*), vivacious, rollicking, convivial, gleeful, blithe, frolicsome, mirthful, sportive, light-hearted, jocund, gay, blithesome • *He was much loved for his merry nature.*
OPPOSITES: sad, unhappy, gloomy
2 = **tipsy**, happy, elevated (*informal*), mellow, tiddly (*slang, chiefly Brit.*), squiffy (*Brit. informal*) • *After a couple of glasses I was feeling a bit merry.*
▸ IN PHRASES: **make merry** = **have fun**, celebrate, revel, have a good time, feast, frolic, enjoy yourself, large it (*Brit. slang*), carouse, make whoopee (*informal*) • *Neighbours went out into the streets and made merry together.*

QUOTATIONS

A merry heart maketh a cheerful countenance
[*Bible: Proverbs*]

merry-go-round 1 = **carousel**, roundabout (*Brit.*) • *a child whooping on a merry-go-round horse*
2 = **whirl**, round, series, succession, bustle, flurry • *a merry-go-round of teas, musical events and the like*

mesh AS A NOUN 1 = **net**, netting, network, web, tracery • *The ground-floor windows are obscured by wire mesh.*
2 = **trap**, web, tangle, toils, snare, entanglement • *He lures young talent into his mesh.*
▸ AS A VERB 1 = **engage**, combine, connect, knit, come together, coordinate, interlock, dovetail, fit together, harmonize • *Their senses of humour meshed perfectly.*
2 = **entangle**, catch, net, trap, tangle, snare, ensnare, enmesh • *Limes and plane trees meshed in unpruned disorder.*

mesmerize = **entrance**, fascinate, absorb, captivate, grip, enthral, hypnotize, magnetize, hold spellbound, spellbind • *There was something about her which mesmerized him.*

m

mess AS A NOUN **1 = untidiness**, disorder, confusion, chaos, turmoil, litter, clutter, disarray, jumble, disorganization, grot *(slang)*, dirtiness • *Linda can't stand mess.*
2 = shambles, botch, hash, cock-up *(Brit. slang)*, state, balls-up *(taboo slang)*, fuck-up *(offensive taboo slang)*, bodge *(informal)*, pig's breakfast *(informal)* • *I've made such a mess of my life.*
3 = difficulty, dilemma, plight, spot *(informal)*, hole *(informal)*, fix *(informal)*, jam *(informal)*, hot water *(informal)*, stew *(informal)*, mix-up, muddle, pickle *(informal)*, uphill *(S. African)*, predicament, deep water, perplexity, tight spot, imbroglio, fine kettle of fish *(informal)* • *I've got myself into a bit of a mess.*
▸ IN PHRASES: **mess about** *or* **around 1 = potter about**, dabble, amuse yourself, footle *(informal)*, fool about *or* around, muck about *or* around *(informal)*, piss about *or* around *(taboo slang)*, play about *or* around • *We were just messing around playing with paint.* • *Stop messing about and get on with your work.*
2 = meddle, play, interfere, toy, fiddle *(informal)*, tamper, tinker, trifle, fool about *or* around, piss about *or* around *(taboo slang)* • *I'd like to know who's been messing about with the pram.*
mess something up 1 = botch, bungle, make a hash of *(informal)*, make a nonsense of, make a pig's ear of *(informal)*, cock something up *(Brit. slang)*, fuck something up *(offensive taboo slang)*, muck something up *(Brit. slang)*, muddle something up • *If I messed it up, I would probably be fired.*
2 = dirty, foul, litter, pollute, clutter, besmirch, disarrange, befoul, dishevel • *I hope they haven't messed up your house.*
mess with something *or* **someone = interfere with**, play with, fiddle with *(informal)*, tamper with, tinker with, meddle with • *You are messing with people's religion and they don't like that.*

message AS A NOUN **1 = communication**, note, bulletin, word, letter, notice, memo, dispatch, memorandum, communiqué, missive, intimation, tidings, e-mail, text • *Would you like to leave a message?*
2 = point, meaning, idea, moral, theme, import, purport • *The report's message was unequivocal.*
3 = errand, job, task, commission, mission • *I was employed to run messages for him in 1957.*
▸ IN PHRASES: **get the message = understand**, see, get it, catch on *(informal)*, comprehend, twig *(Brit. informal)*, get the point, take the hint • *I think they got the message that this attitude is wrong.*

messenger = courier, agent, runner, carrier, herald, envoy, bearer, go-between, emissary, harbinger, delivery boy, errand boy • *The document is to be sent by messenger.*

messy 1 = disorganized, sloppy *(informal)*, untidy, slovenly • *She was a good, if messy, cook.*
2 = dirty, grubby, grimy, scuzzy *(slang, chiefly U.S.)*, skanky *(slang)* • *The work tends to be messy, so wear old clothes.*
3 = untidy, disordered, littered, chaotic, muddled, cluttered, shambolic, disorganized, daggy *(Austral. & N.Z. informal)* • *Mum made me clean up my messy room.*
OPPOSITES: ordered, clean, tidy
4 = dishevelled, ruffled, untidy, rumpled, bedraggled, unkempt, tousled, uncombed, daggy *(Austral. & N.Z. informal)* • *She's just an old woman with very messy hair.*
5 = confusing, difficult, complex, confused, tangled, chaotic, tortuous • *Life is a messy and tangled business*

metal
▹ *See panel* **Metals**

metallic 1 = tinny, jarring, grating, jangling, dissonant, jangly • *There was a metallic click and the gates swung open.*
2 = shiny, polished, burnished, lustrous, pearlescent, metallized • *metallic silver paint*

metamorphose = transform, change, alter, remake, convert, remodel, mutate, reshape, be reborn, transmute, transfigure, transmogrify *(jocular)*, transubstantiate • *She had been metamorphosed by the war.*

metamorphosis = transformation, conversion, alteration, change, mutation, rebirth, changeover, transfiguration, transmutation, transubstantiation, transmogrification *(jocular)* • *his metamorphosis from a republican to a democrat*

metaphor = figure of speech, image, symbol, analogy, emblem, conceit *(literary)*, allegory, trope, figurative expression • *the writer's use of metaphor*

metaphorical = figurative, symbolic, emblematic, allegorical, emblematical, tropical *(Rhetoric)* • *The ship may be heading for the metaphorical rocks unless a buyer can be found.*

metaphysical 1 = abstract, intellectual, theoretical, deep, basic, essential, ideal, fundamental, universal, profound,

METALS

Metal	Symbol	Metal	Symbol	Metal	Symbol	Metal	Symbol
actinium	Ac	europium	Eu	molybdenum	Mo	scandium	Sc
aluminium	Al	fermium	Fm	neodymium	Nd	silver	Ag
americium	Am	francium	Fr	neptunium	Np	sodium	Na
antimony	Sb	gadolinium	Gd	nickel	Ni	strontium	Sr
barium	Ba	gallium	Ga	niobium	Nb	tantalum	Ta
berkelium	Bk	germanium	Ge	nobelium	No	technetium	Tc
beryllium	Be	gold	Au	osmium	Os	terbium	Tb
bismuth	Bi	hafnium	Hf	palladium	Pd	thallium	Tl
cadmium	Cd	holmium	Ho	platinum	Pt	thorium	Th
caesium *or* (*U.S.*) cesium	Cs	indium	In	plutonium	Pu	thulium	Tm
		iridium	Ir	polonium	Po	tin	Sn
calcium	Ca	iron	Fe	potassium	K	titanium	Ti
californium	Cf	lanthanum	La	praseodymium	Pr	tungsten *or* wolfram	W
cerium	Ce	lawrencium	Lr	promethium	Pm		
chromium	Cr	lead	Pb	protactinium	Pa	uranium	U
cobalt	Co	lithium	Li	radium	Ra	vanadium	V
copper	Cu	lutetium	Lu	rhenium	Re	ytterbium	Yb
curium	Cm	magnesium	Mg	rhodium	Rh	yttrium	Y
dysprosium	Dy	manganese	Mn	rubidium	Rb	zinc	Zn
einsteinium	Es	mendelevium	Md	ruthenium	Ru	zirconium	Zr
erbium	Er	mercury	Hg	samarium	Sm		

philosophical, speculative, high-flown, esoteric, transcendental, abstruse, recondite, oversubtle • *metaphysical questions like personal responsibility for violence*
2 = supernatural, spiritual, unreal, intangible, immaterial, incorporeal, impalpable, unsubstantial • *He was moved by a metaphysical sense quite alien to him.*

meteor = falling star, comet, meteorite, fireball, shooting star, bolide • *It takes place in the future after a meteor has landed.*
▸ RELATED PHOBIA: meteorophobia

meteoric = spectacular, sudden, overnight, rapid, fast, brief, brilliant, flashing, fleeting, swift, dazzling, speedy, transient, momentary, ephemeral • *his meteoric rise to fame*
OPPOSITES: long, slow, gradual

meteorological = weather, climatic • *adverse meteorological conditions*

meteorologist = weather forecaster, met man *(informal)*, weather girl *(informal)*, weather man, weather woman • *Meteorologists have predicted mild rains for the next few days.*

mete out = distribute, portion, assign, administer, ration, dispense, allot, dole out, share out, apportion, deal out, measure out, parcel out, divide out • *His father meted out punishment with a slipper.*

method 1 = manner, process, approach, technique, way, plan, course, system, form, rule, programme, style, practice, fashion, scheme, arrangement, procedure, routine, mode, modus operandi • *new teaching methods*
2 = orderliness, planning, order, system, form, design, structure, purpose, pattern, organization, regularity • *They go about their work with method and common sense.*

methodical = orderly, planned, ordered, structured, regular, disciplined, organized, efficient, precise, neat, deliberate, tidy, systematic, meticulous, painstaking, businesslike, well-regulated • *He was methodical in his research.*
OPPOSITES: confused, disordered, haphazard

methodology = practice, style, approach, technique, mode, modus operandi • *Teaching methodologies vary according to the topic.*

meticulous = thorough, detailed, particular, strict, exact, precise, microscopic, fussy, painstaking, perfectionist, scrupulous, fastidious, punctilious, nit-picky *(informal)* • *He was so meticulous about everything.*
OPPOSITES: loose, careless, sloppy

metier 1 = profession, calling, craft, occupation, line, trade, pursuit, vocation • *He found his true métier as the magazine's business manager.*
2 = strong point, forte, speciality, specialty, strong suit, long suit *(informal)* • *This was not his métier, and he was clearly frightened.*

metro = underground, tube, subway • *A bus and metro pass costs about £10.*

metropolis = city, town, capital, big city, municipality, conurbation, megalopolis • *the bustling metropolis*

metropolitan = city, urban, civic, municipal • *a dozen major metropolitan hospitals*

mettle 1 = courage, spirit, resolution, resolve, life, heart, fire, balls *(taboo slang)*, bottle *(Brit. slang)*, nerve, daring, guts *(informal)*, pluck, grit, bravery, fortitude, vigour, boldness, gallantry, ardour, valour, spunk *(informal)*, indomitability, hardihood, gameness • *It's the first real test of his mettle this season.*
2 = character, quality, nature, make-up, stamp, temper, kidney, temperament, calibre, disposition • *He is of a different mettle from the others.*

mettlesome = courageous, daring, dashing, bold, lively, vigorous, fiery, brisk, ardent, game *(informal)*, feisty *(informal, chiefly U.S. & Canad.)*, valiant, plucky, high-spirited, sprightly, frisky, mettled, (as) game as Ned Kelly *(Austral. slang)* • *She was bright and mettlesome – a real go-getter.*

mewl = whimper, cry, whine, whinge *(informal)*, grizzle *(informal, chiefly Brit.)*, blubber, snivel, pule • *Shut up, Steven, you mewling little wimp.*

miasma = unwholesomeness, smell, pollution, odour, stench, reek, effluvium, niff *(Brit. slang)*, mephitis, fetor • *a thick black poisonous miasma which hung over the area*

microbe = microorganism, virus, bug *(informal)*, germ, bacterium, bacillus • *The microbe that poisoned them had got into dental equipment.*
▸ RELATED PHOBIA: bacilliphobia

microscopic = tiny, minute, invisible, negligible, minuscule, imperceptible, infinitesimal, teeny-weeny, teensy-weensy • *microscopic fibres of protein*
OPPOSITES: great, large, huge

midday = noon, twelve o'clock, noonday, noontime, twelve noon, noontide • *At midday everyone would go down to the cafe.*

middle AS A NOUN **1 = centre**, heart, inside, thick, core, midst, nucleus, hub, halfway point, midpoint, midsection • *I was in the middle of the back row.*
2 = waist, gut, belly, tummy *(informal)*, waistline, midriff, paunch, midsection • *At 53, he has a few extra pounds around his middle.*
▸ AS AN ADJECTIVE **1 = central**, medium, inside, mid, intervening, inner, halfway, intermediate, median, medial • *that crucial middle point of the picture*
2 = intermediate, inside, intervening, inner • *the middle level of commanding officers*

middle-class = bourgeois, traditional, conventional, suburban, middle-England, petit-bourgeois • *He is rapidly losing the support of middle-class conservatives.*

middleman = intermediary, broker, entrepreneur, distributor, go-between • *Why don't they cut out the middleman and let us do it ourselves?*

middle-of-the-road 1 = moderate, non-radical, non-extreme, non-reactionary • *an archbishop with middle-of-the-road politics*
2 = ordinary, average, typical, normal, mundane, unremarkable, humdrum, unexciting • *I don't want to be a middle-of-the-road person.*

middling 1 = mediocre, all right, indifferent, so-so *(informal)*, unremarkable, tolerable, run-of-the-mill, passable, serviceable, unexceptional, half-pie *(N.Z. informal)*, O.K. *or* okay *(informal)* • *They enjoyed only middling success until 1963.*
2 = moderate, medium, average, fair, ordinary, modest, adequate, bog-standard *(Brit. & Irish slang)* • *a man of middling height*

midget AS A NOUN **= dwarf**, shrimp *(informal)*, gnome, Tom Thumb, munchkin *(informal, chiefly U.S.)*, homunculus, manikin, homuncule, pygmy *or* pigmy • *They used to call him 'midget' or 'shorty' at work.*
▸ AS AN ADJECTIVE **1 = baby**, small, tiny, miniature, dwarf, teeny-weeny, teensy-weensy • *an accompaniment of midget roast potatoes*
2 = diminutive, little, pocket-sized, Lilliputian, dwarfish, pygmy *or* pigmy • *The part is played by midget actor Warwick Edwards.*

midnight = twelve o'clock, middle of the night, dead of night, twelve o'clock at night, the witching hour • *The entrance gates were locked at midnight.*

midriff
▸ TECHNICAL NAME: diaphragm

midst AS A NOUN **= middle**, centre, heart, interior, thick, depths, core, hub, bosom • *The organisation realised it had a traitor in its midst.*
▸ IN PHRASES: **in the midst of 1 = during**, in the middle of, amidst • *We are in the midst of a recession.*
2 = among, in the middle of, surrounded by, amidst, in the thick of, enveloped by • *I was sitting the midst of a traffic jam.*

midway = halfway, in the middle of, part-way, equidistant, at the midpoint, betwixt and between • *The studio is midway between his house and the station.*

m

mien = **demeanour**, look, air, bearing, appearance, aspect, presence, manner, carriage, aura, countenance, deportment • *his mild manner and aristocratic mien*

miffed = **upset**, hurt, annoyed, offended, irritated, put out, hacked (off) *(U.S. slang)*, pissed *(U.S. slang)*, resentful, nettled, aggrieved, vexed, pissed off *(taboo slang)*, displeased, irked, in a huff, piqued, narked *(Brit., Austral. & N.Z. slang)*, tooshie *(Austral. slang)* • *I was a bit miffed about that.*

might AS A NOUN = **power**, force, energy, ability, strength, capacity, efficiency, capability, sway, clout *(informal)*, vigour, prowess, potency, efficacy, valour, puissance • *The might of the army could prove a decisive factor.*

▸ IN PHRASES: **with all your might** = **forcefully**, vigorously, mightily, full force, manfully, full blast, lustily, as hard as possible, as hard as you can • *She swung the hammer with all her might.*

QUOTATIONS

Might is right

[Thomas Carlyle]

mightily 1 = **very**, highly, greatly, hugely, very much, seriously *(informal)*, extremely, intensely, decidedly, exceedingly • *He had given a mightily impressive performance.*
2 = **powerfully**, vigorously, strongly, forcefully, energetically, with all your strength, with all your might and main • *She strove mightily to put him from her thoughts.*

mighty 1 = **powerful**, strong, strapping, robust, hardy, vigorous, potent, sturdy, stout, forceful, stalwart, doughty, lusty, indomitable, manful, puissant • *a mighty young athlete*
OPPOSITES: weak, feeble, impotent
2 = **great**, large, huge, grand, massive, towering, vast, enormous, tremendous, immense, titanic, gigantic, monumental, bulky, colossal, stellar *(informal)*, prodigious, stupendous, fuck-off *(offensive taboo slang)*, elephantine, ginormous *(informal)*, humongous *or* humungous *(U.S. slang)* • *a land marked with vast lakes and mighty rivers*
OPPOSITES: small, tiny, unimpressive

QUOTATIONS

How are the mighty fallen, and the weapons of war perished

[Bible: II Samuel]

migrant AS A NOUN = **wanderer**, immigrant, traveller, gypsy, tinker, rover, transient, nomad, emigrant, itinerant, drifter, vagrant • *economic migrants and political refugees*
▸ AS AN ADJECTIVE = **itinerant**, wandering, drifting, roving, travelling, shifting, immigrant, gypsy, transient, nomadic, migratory, vagrant • *migrant workers*

migrate = **move**, travel, journey, wander, shift, drift, trek, voyage, roam, emigrate, rove • *The farmers have to migrate if they want to survive.*

migration = **wandering**, journey, voyage, travel, movement, shift, trek, emigration, roving • *the migration of Soviet Jews to Israel*

migratory = **nomadic**, travelling, wandering, migrant, itinerant, unsettled, shifting, gypsy, roving, transient, vagrant, peripatetic • *a migratory farm labourer*

mild 1 = **faint**, slight, vague, minimal, feeble • *He turned to her with a look of mild confusion.*
2 = **gentle**, kind, easy, soft, pacific, calm, moderate, forgiving, tender, pleasant, mellow, compassionate, indulgent, serene, easy-going, amiable, meek, placid, docile, merciful, peaceable, forbearing, equable, easy-oasy *(slang)*, chilled *(informal)* • *He is a mild man, reasonable almost to the point of blandness.*
OPPOSITES: strong, powerful, harsh
3 = **temperate**, warm, calm, moderate, clement, tranquil, balmy • *The area is famous for its mild winters.*
OPPOSITES: cold, wild, violent
4 = **bland**, thin, smooth, tasteless, insipid, flavourless • *The cheese has a soft, mild flavour.*
5 = **soothing**, mollifying, emollient, demulcent, lenitive • *Wash your face thoroughly with a mild soap.*
6 = **light**, humane, compassionate, clement, lenient, merciful • *A mild punishment might be 50 pressups on the spot.*

mildew = **mould**, damp • *The room smelt of mildew.*

mildness = **gentleness**, kindness, indulgence, tenderness, warmth, moderation, tranquillity, softness, clemency, leniency, smoothness, calmness, blandness, forbearance, meekness, docility, placidity, mellowness, lenity, temperateness • *One reason for his success was his mildness and dignity.*

milieu = **surroundings**, setting, scene, environment, element, background, location, sphere, locale, mise en scène *(French)* • *They stayed within their own social milieu.*

militant AS AN ADJECTIVE = **aggressive**, warring, fighting, active, combating, contending, vigorous, two-fisted, assertive, in arms, embattled, belligerent, combative • *one of the most active militant groups*
OPPOSITES: peaceful, pacifist, concessive
▸ AS A NOUN = **activist**, radical, fighter, partisan, belligerent, combatant • *The militants were apparently planning a terrorist attack.*

militaristic = **war-mongering**, martial, aggressive, belligerent, combative, gung-ho *(informal)*, pugnacious, hawkish, warlike, bellicose • *aggressive militaristic governments*

military AS AN ADJECTIVE = **warlike**, armed, soldierly, martial, soldierlike • *Military action may become necessary.*
▸ IN PHRASES: **the military** = **the armed forces**, the forces, the services, the army • *Did you serve in the military?*
▹ *See panel* **Military ranks**

militate AS A VERB
▸ IN PHRASES: **militate against something** = **counteract**, conflict with, contend with, count against, oppose, counter, resist, be detrimental to, weigh against, tell against • *Her background militates against her.*

militia = **reserve(s)**, National Guard *(U.S.)*, Territorial Army *(Brit.)*, yeomanry *(History)*, fencibles *(History)*, trainband *(History)* • *The troops will not attempt to disarm the warring militias.*

milk 1 = **draw milk from**, express milk from • *Farm-workers milked cows by hand.*
2 = **exploit**, use, pump, squeeze, drain, take advantage of, bleed, impose on, wring, fleece, suck dry • *A few people tried to milk the insurance companies.*
▸ RELATED ADJECTIVES: lactic, lacteal

milky = **white**, clouded, opaque, cloudy, alabaster, whitish, milk-white • *A milky mist filled the valley.*

mill AS A NOUN 1 = **grinder**, crusher, quern • *a pepper mill*
2 = **factory**, works, shop, plant, workshop, foundry • *a textile mill*
▸ AS A VERB = **grind**, pound, press, crush, powder, grate, pulverize, granulate, comminute • *freshly-milled black pepper*
▸ IN PHRASES: **mill about** *or* **around** = **swarm**, crowd, stream, surge, seethe, throng • *Quite a few people were milling about.*
run of the mill = **commonplace**, middling, average, fair, ordinary, routine, everyday, unremarkable, unexceptional, bog-standard *(Brit. & Irish slang)* • *I was just a very average run of the mill student.*

millet
▸ RELATED ADJECTIVE: miliary

million
▸ RELATED PREFIX: mega-

millionth
▸ RELATED PREFIX: micro-

millstone 1 = **burden**, weight, load, albatross, drag, affliction, dead weight, encumbrance • *The contract proved to be a millstone around his neck.*

MILITARY RANKS

able rating
able seaman *or* able-bodied seaman (AB)
acting sublieutenant
admiral (Adm)
admiral of the fleet
air chief marshal (ACM)
air commodore (AC)
aircraftmen (AC)
air marshal (AM)
air officer
air vice-marshal (AVM)
branch officer (BO)
brigadier (Brig)
captain (Capt)
chief of staff (COS)
chief petty officer (CPO)
chief technician
colonel (Col)
colour sergeant (Col Sgt)
commander (Cdr)
commander in chief (C-in-C)
commanding officer (CO)
commissioned officer
commodore (Cdre)
company sergeant major (CSM)
corporal (Corp, Cpl)
drum major
field marshal (FM)
field officer (FO)
fleet admiral
fleet chief petty officer
flight engineer
flight lieutenant (Flt Lt)
flight mechanic (FM)
flight sergeant (Flt Sgt)
flying officer (FO)
general (Gen, Genl)
group captain (G Capt)
junior technician
lance corporal (L-Cpl)
leading aircraftman (LAC)
leading rating
lieutenant (Lt)
lieutenant colonel (Lt-Col)
lieutenant commander (Lt-Cdr)
lieutenant general (Lt-Gen)
major (Maj)
major general (Maj-Gen)
marine
marshal
marshal of the Royal Air Force (MRAF)
master aircrew
medical officer (MO)
midshipman
noncommissioned officer (NCO)
ordinary rating
ordinary seaman (OS)
petty officer (PO)
pilot officer (PO)
private (Pte)
quartermaster (QM)
rear admiral (RA)
regimental sergeant major (RSM)
second lieutenant
senior aircraftman
senior medical officer (SMO)
sergeant (Sgt, Sergt)
sergeant major (SM)
squadron leader (Sqn-Ldr)
staff sergeant
subaltern
sublieutenant (Sub Lt)
vice admiral (VA)
warrant officer (WO)
wing commander

2 = **grindstone**, quernstone • *standing in a marketplace, watching a millstone grinding wheat*

mime AS A NOUN = **dumb show**, gesture, pantomime, mummery • *Students presented a mime and a puppet show*
▸ AS A VERB = **act out**, represent, gesture, simulate, pantomime • *She mimed getting up in the morning.*

mimic AS A VERB 1 = **imitate**, do *(informal)*, take off *(informal)*, ape, parody, caricature, impersonate • *He could mimic anybody, reducing his friends to helpless laughter.*
2 = **resemble**, look like, mirror, echo, simulate, take on the appearance of • *Don't try to mimic anybody. Just be yourself.*
▸ AS A NOUN = **imitator**, impressionist, copycat *(informal)*, impersonator, caricaturist, parodist, parrot • *He's a very good mimic.*

mimicry = **imitation**, impression, impersonation, copying, imitating, mimicking, parody, caricature, mockery, burlesque, apery • *One of his strengths was his skill at mimicry.*

mince 1 = **cut**, grind, crumble, dice, hash, chop up • *I'll buy some lean meat and mince it myself.*
2 = **posture**, pose, ponce *(slang)*, attitudinize • *'Ooh, a sailor!' he minced and she laughed aloud.*
3 = **tone down**, spare, moderate, weaken, diminish, soften, hold back, extenuate, palliate, euphemize • *The doctors didn't mince their words, and predicted the worst.*

mincing = **affected**, nice, camp *(informal)*, precious, pretentious, dainty, sissy, effeminate, foppish, poncy *(slang)*, arty-farty *(informal)*, lah-di-dah *(informal)*, niminy-piminy • *He waddled onto the stage with tiny mincing steps.*

mind AS A NOUN 1 = **brain**, head, imagination, psyche, subconscious • *I'm trying to clear my mind of all this.*
2 = **memory**, recollection, remembrance, powers of recollection • *He spent the next hour going over the trial in his mind.*
3 = **attention**, thinking, thoughts, concentration • *My mind was never on my work.*
4 = **intelligence**, reason, reasoning, understanding, sense, spirit, brain(s) *(informal)*, wits, mentality, intellect, grey matter *(informal)*, ratiocination • *an excellent training for the young mind*
5 = **thinker**, academic, intellectual, genius, brain *(informal)*, scholar, sage, intellect, rocket scientist *(informal, chiefly U.S.)*, brainbox, acca *(Austral. slang)* • *She moved to London, meeting some of the best minds of her time.*
6 = **intention**, will, wish, desire, urge, fancy, purpose, leaning, bent, notion, tendency, inclination, disposition • *They could interpret it that way if they'd a mind to.*
7 = **sanity**, reason, senses, judgment, wits, marbles *(informal)*, rationality, mental balance • *Sometimes I feel I'm losing my mind.*
8 = **attitude**, view, opinion, belief, feeling, thoughts, judgment, point of view, outlook, sentiment, way of thinking • *They're all of the same mind.*
▸ AS A VERB 1 = **take offence at**, dislike, care about, object to, resent, disapprove of, be bothered by, look askance at, be affronted by • *I hope you don't mind me calling in like this.*
2 = **be careful**, watch, take care, be wary, be cautious, be on your guard • *Mind you don't burn those sausages.*
3 = **be sure**, ensure, make sure, be careful, make certain • *Mind you don't let the cat out.*
4 = **remember to**, see (that), make sure, don't forget to, take care to • *Mind you take care of him!*
5 = **look after**, watch, protect, tend, guard, take care of, attend to, keep an eye on, have *or* take charge of • *Could you mind the shop while I'm out, please?*
6 = **pay attention to**, follow, mark, watch, note, regard, respect, notice, attend to, listen to, observe, comply with, obey, heed, adhere to, take heed of, pay heed to • *You mind what I say now!*
▸ IN PHRASES: **bear** *or* **keep something** *or* **someone in mind** = **remember**, consider, take into account, take note, do not forget, be mindful, make a mental note, be cognizant • *Bear in mind that petrol stations are scarce in this area.*
cross your mind = **occur to you**, come to mind, spring to mind, strike you, suggest itself, enter your mind • *The possibility of failure did cross my mind.*
have something in mind = **propose**, plan, design, aim for, think, intend • *'Maybe we could celebrate tonight.' 'What did you have in mind?'*
in *or* **of two minds** = **undecided**, uncertain, unsure,

m

wavering, hesitant, dithering *(chiefly Brit.)*, vacillating, swithering *(Scot.)*, shillyshallying *(informal)* • *I am in two minds about going.*
make up your mind = decide, choose, determine, resolve, reach a decision, come to a decision • *Once he made up his mind to do something, there was no stopping him.*
mind out = be careful, watch out, take care, look out, beware, pay attention, keep your eyes open, be on your guard • *Mind out. We're coming in to land!*
never mind 1 = forget, don't worry about, pay no attention to, disregard, don't bother about, don't concern yourself about • *Never mind your shoes. They'll soon dry off.*
2 = forget it, it doesn't matter, don't worry about it, it's unimportant, don't give it a second thought • *'I'm really sorry.' 'Never mind, it happens to me all the time.'*
never you mind = it's none of your business, it's nothing to do with you • *'Where is it?' 'Never you mind.'*
out of your mind 1 = mad, insane, mental *(informal)*, crazy *(informal)*, nuts *(informal)*, demented, deranged, bonkers *(informal)*, raving mad *(informal)*, off your head *(informal)*, off your trolley *(Brit. informal)*, away with the fairies *(informal)*, off your rocker *(informal)*, off your nut *(informal)*, not the full shilling *(Brit. informal)*, not in your right mind, off the air *(Austral. slang)* • *What are you doing? Are you out of your mind?*
2 = frantic, crazy *(informal)*, distraught, berserk, berko *(Austral. slang)*, beside yourself • *I'm out of my mind with worry. I just want him back.*
put *or* **set someone's mind at rest = assure**, comfort, reassure, soothe, hearten • *She could set your mind at rest by giving you the facts*
put someone in mind of something *or* **someone = remind**, recall, evoke, nudge, conjure up, summon up • *This put me in mind of something he said many years ago.*
▸ **RELATED ADJECTIVES:** noetic, mental, phrenic

QUOTATIONS

The mind is at its best about the age of forty-nine
[Aristotle *Rhetoric*]

The mind is its own place, and in itself
Can make a heaven of hell, a hell of heaven
[John Milton *Paradise Lost*]

What is matter? – Never mind.
What is mind? – No matter
[*Punch*]

PROVERBS

Great minds think alike, fools seldom differ

minder = bodyguard • *The two girls and their minder all climbed into the taxi.*
mindful *with* **of = aware**, careful, conscious, alert, sensible, wary, thoughtful, attentive, respectful, watchful, alive to, cognizant, chary, heedful, regardful • *We must be mindful of the consequences of selfishness.*
OPPOSITES: mindless, unaware, heedless
mindless 1 = unthinking, gratuitous, thoughtless, careless, oblivious, brutish, inane, witless, heedless, unmindful, dumb-ass *(slang)* • *blackmail, extortion and mindless violence*
OPPOSITES: thinking, reasoning, aware
2 = unintelligent, stupid, foolish, careless, negligent, idiotic, thoughtless, inane, witless, forgetful, moronic, obtuse, neglectful, asinine, imbecilic, braindead *(informal)*, dumb-ass *(slang)*, dead from the neck up *(informal)* • *She wasn't at all the mindless little wife they perceived her to be.*
3 = mechanical, automatic, monotonous, mind-numbing, brainless • *the mindless repetitiveness of some tasks*
mind-set = attitudes, view, perspective, position, stance, outlook, world view • *Their greatest challenge is understanding their customers' mind-set.*
mind's eye IN PHRASES: in your mind's eye = in your imagination, in your head, in your mind • *In his mind's eye, he can imagine the effect he's having.*

mine AS A NOUN 1 = pit, deposit, shaft, vein, colliery, excavation, coalfield, lode • *an explosion at a coal mine*
2 = source, store, fund, stock, supply, reserve, treasury, wealth, abundance, hoard • *a mine of information*
▸ **AS A VERB 1 = dig up**, extract, quarry, unearth, delve, excavate, hew, dig for • *Not enough coal to be mined economically*
2 = lay mines in *or* **under**, sow with mines • *The approaches to the garrison have been heavily mined.*
minefield = danger zone • *The subject is a political minefield.*
miner = coalminer, pitman *(Brit.)*, collier *(Brit.)* • *a retired Welsh miner*
mineral
▹ *See panel* **Minerals**
mingle 1 = mix, combine, blend, merge, unite, join, marry, compound, alloy, interweave, coalesce, intermingle, meld, commingle, intermix, admix • *Cheers and applause mingled in a single roar.*
OPPOSITES: part, separate, divide
2 = associate, circulate, hang out *(informal)*, consort, socialize, rub shoulders *(informal)*, hobnob, fraternize, hang about *or* around • *Guests ate and mingled.*
OPPOSITES: avoid, dissociate, estrange
miniature = small, little, minute, baby, reduced, tiny, pocket, toy, mini, wee, dwarf, scaled-down, diminutive, minuscule, midget, teeny-weeny, Lilliputian, teensy-weensy, pygmy *or* pigmy • *The farm has been selling miniature roses since 1979.*
OPPOSITES: big, large, giant
minimal = minimum, smallest, least, slightest, token, nominal, negligible, least possible, littlest • *effective defence with minimal expenditure*
minimalist = sparse, simple, basic, plain, bare, discreet, spartan, unadorned, unfussy • *The designers settled on a minimalist approach.*
minimize 1 = reduce, decrease, shrink, diminish, prune, curtail, attenuate, downsize, miniaturize • *You can minimize these problems with sensible planning.*
OPPOSITES: increase, extend, expand
2 = play down, discount, underestimate, belittle, disparage, decry, underrate, deprecate, depreciate, make light *or* little of • *Some have minimized the importance of these factors.*
OPPOSITES: praise, enhance, elevate
minimum AS AN ADJECTIVE = lowest, smallest, least, slightest, minimal, least possible, littlest • *He was only five feet nine, the minimum height for a policeman.*
OPPOSITES: most, highest, maximum
▸ **AS A NOUN = lowest**, least, depth, slightest, lowest level, nadir, bottom level • *She has cut her teaching hours to a minimum.*
minion = follower, henchman, underling, lackey, favourite, pet, creature, darling, parasite, cohort *(chiefly U.S.)*, dependant, hanger-on, sycophant, yes man, toady, hireling, flunky, flatterer, lickspittle, bootlicker *(informal)* • *She delegated the job to one of her minions.*
minister AS A NOUN 1 = member of the government, secretary, politician, secretary of state, cabinet minister, political leader • *He was named minister of culture.*
2 = official, ambassador, diplomat, delegate, executive, administrator, envoy, cabinet member, office-holder, plenipotentiary • *He concluded a deal with the Danish minister in Washington.*
3 = clergyman, priest, divine, vicar, parson, preacher, pastor, chaplain, cleric, rector, curate, churchman, padre *(informal)*, ecclesiastic • *His father was a Baptist minister.*
▸ **IN PHRASES: minister to = attend to**, serve, tend to, answer to, accommodate, take care of, cater to, pander to, administer to, be solicitous of • *For 44 years he had ministered to the poor and the sick.*
ministrations = help, service, support, aid, favour, relief, assistance, patronage, succour • *the tender ministrations of the woman who helped him*

MINERALS

actinolite
agate
albite
allanite
allophane
alunite
amalgam
amblygonite
analcite *or* analcime
anatase
andalusite
andesine
anglesite
anhydrite
ankerite
annabergite
anorthite
apatite
apophyllite
aragonite
argentite
arsenopyrite
augite
autunite
axinite
azurite
baddeleyite
barytes
bastnaesite
bauxite
beryl
biotite
bismuthinite *or* bismuth glance
Boehmite
boracite
borax
bornite
braunite
brookite
calaverite
calcite
carnallite
carnotite
cassiterite
celestite *or* celestine
cerargyrite
chabazite
chalcanthite
chalcocite
chalcopyrite
chlorite
chromite
chrysoberyl
chrysotile
cinnabar
clay mineral
cleveite
clinopyroxene
cobaltite *or* cobaltine
colemanite
columbite
cordierite
corundum
cristobalite
crocidolite
crocoite *or* crocoisite
cryolite
cuprite
cyanite
datolite
diallage
diamond
diaspore
diopside
dioptase
dolomite
dumortierite
emery
enstatite
epidote
erythrite
euxenite
fayalite
feldspar *or* felspar
feldspathoid
fluorapatite
fluorspar, fluor *or* (*U.S. & Canad.*) fluorite
forsterite
franklinite
gahnite
galena *or* galenite
garnet
garnierite
gehlenite
germanite
geyserite
gibbsite
glauconite
goethite
graphite
greenockite
gummite
gypsum
halite
harmotome
hematite
hemimorphite
hessite
heulandite
hiddenite
hornblende
hyacinth
hypersthene
illite
ilmenite
jadeite
jarosite
jasper
kainite
kaolinite
kernite
kieserite
kunzite
labradorite
lapis lazuli
lazulite
lazurite
leucite
limonite
magnesite
magnetite
malachite
manganite
marcasite
margarite
massicot
meerschaum
metamict
mica
microcline
millerite
mimetite
molybdenite
monazite
montmorillonite
monzonite
mullite
muscovite
natrolite
nepheline *or* nephelite
nephrite
niccolite
norite
oligoclase
olivenite
olivine
opal
orpiment
orthoclase
ozocerite *or* ozokerite
pentlandite
periclase
perovskite
petuntse *or* petuntze
phenacite *or* phenakite
phosgenite
phosphorite
piedmontite
pinite
pitchblende
pollucite
polybasite
proustite
psilomelane
pyrargyrite
pyrite
pyrolusite
pyromorphite
pyrophyllite
pyroxene
pyroxenite
pyrrhotite
quartz
realgar
rhodochrosite
rhodonite
rutile
samarskite
saponite
sapphirine
scapolite
scheelite
scolecite
senarmontite
serpentine
siderite
sillimanite
smaltite
smaragdite
smectite
smithsonite
sodalite
sperrylite
sphalerite
sphene
spinel
spodumene
stannite
staurolite
stibnite
stilbite
strontianite
sylvanite
sylvite *or* sylvine
talc
tantalite
tenorite
tetradymite
tetrahedrite
thenardite
thorianite
thorite
tiemannite
topaz
torbernite
tourmaline
tremolite
triphylite
trona
troostite
tungstite
turgite
turquoise
uralite
uraninite
uranite
vanadinite
variscite
vermiculite
vesuvianite
wavellite
willemite
witherite
wolframite
wollastonite
wulfenite
zaratite
zeolite
zincite
zinkenite *or* zinckenite
zircon
zoisite

ministry 1 = **department**, office, bureau, government department • *the Ministry of Justice*
2 = **administration**, government, council, cabinet • *He disclosed that his ministry gave funds to parties in Namibia.*
3 = **the priesthood**, the church, the cloth, the pulpit, holy orders • *So what prompted him to enter the ministry?*

mink
▸ NAME OF FEMALE: sow

minor AS AN ADJECTIVE 1 = **small**, lesser, subordinate, smaller, light, slight, secondary, petty, inferior, trivial, trifling, insignificant, negligible, unimportant, paltry, inconsequential, inconsiderable, nickel-and-dime (*U.S. slang*) • *She is known for a number of minor roles in films.*
OPPOSITES: important, great, major
2 = **unknown**, obscure, little-known, lightweight, insignificant, unimportant, small-time (*informal*), minor-league (*U.S.*), two-bit (*U.S. informal*) • *a minor poet and wannabe actor*
▸ AS A NOUN = **child**, youth, teenager, infant, adolescent, kid (*informal*), teen (*informal*), munchkin (*informal, chiefly U.S.*), littlie (*Austral. informal*), tacker (*Austral. slang*) • *The approach has virtually ended cigarette sales to minors.*

minstrel = **musician**, singer, harper, bard, troubadour, songstress, jongleur • *He was playing a banjo and garbed in a minstrel's outfit.*

mint AS A VERB 1 = **make**, produce, strike, cast, stamp, punch, coin • *the right to mint coins*
2 = **invent**, produce, fashion, make up, construct, coin, devise, forge, fabricate, think up • *The book comprises a lexicon of freshly-minted descriptions.*
▸ AS A NOUN = **fortune**, million, bomb (*Brit. slang*), pile (*informal*), packet (*slang*), bundle (*slang*), heap (*informal*), top dollar (*informal*), King's ransom, top whack (*informal*) • *They were worth a mint.*
▸ AS AN ADJECTIVE = **perfect**, excellent, first-class, brand-new, fresh, unmarked, undamaged, unblemished, untarnished • *a set of Victorian stamps in mint condition*

minus = **without**, lacking, deprived of, bereft of, destitute of • *He was left jobless, and minus his life savings.*

minuscule = **tiny**, little, minute, fine, very small, miniature, microscopic, diminutive, infinitesimal, teeny-weeny,

m

Lilliputian, teensy-weensy • *reducing his handwriting to minuscule proportions*

minute[1] AS A NOUN 1 = **sixty seconds**, sixtieth of an hour • *A minute later she came to the front door.*
2 = **moment**, second, bit, shake *(informal)*, flash, instant, tick *(Brit. informal)*, sec *(informal)*, short time, little while, jiffy *(informal)*, trice • *I'll be with you in a minute.*
3 = **point in time**, time, point, moment, stage, instant, juncture • *What was going on at that very minute?*
▸ IN PHRASES: **any minute = very soon**, any time, at any time, before long, any moment, any second • *It looked as though it might rain any minute.*
at the minute = at present, now, presently, currently, at the moment, this minute • *I can't afford to take any time off at the minute.*
this minute = at once, directly, immediately, right now, instantly, straight away, right away, this second, forthwith, pronto *(informal)*, without further ado, toot sweet *(informal)*, tout de suite *(French)* • *I need to speak to her this minute.*
up to the minute = latest, in, newest, now *(informal)*, with it *(informal)*, smart, stylish, trendiest, trendy *(Brit. informal)*, vogue, up to date, plugged-in *(slang)*, modish, (most) fashionable, schmick *(Austral. informal)* • *a big range of up-to-the-minute appliances*
wait a minute = wait a moment, hold on, hang on *(informal)*, hang about *(Brit. informal)*, hold your horses *(informal)* • *Wait a minute, folks, something is wrong here.*

minute[2] 1 = **small**, little, tiny, miniature, slender, fine, microscopic, diminutive, minuscule, infinitesimal, teeny-weeny, Lilliputian, teensy-weensy • *Only a minute amount is needed.*
OPPOSITES: huge, great, grand
2 = **negligible**, slight, petty, trivial, trifling, unimportant, paltry, puny, piddling *(informal)*, inconsiderable, picayune *(U.S.)* • *gambling large sums on the minute chance of a big win*
OPPOSITES: major, important, significant
3 = **precise**, close, detailed, critical, exact, meticulous, exhaustive, painstaking, punctilious • *We will have to pore over this report in minute detail.*
OPPOSITES: rough, careless, imprecise

m

minutely = precisely, closely, exactly, in detail, critically, meticulously, painstakingly, exhaustively, with a fine-tooth comb • *The metal is minutely examined to ensure there are no cracks.*

minutes = record, notes, proceedings, transactions, transcript, memorandum • *He'd been reading the minutes of the last meeting.*

minutiae = details, particulars, subtleties, trifles, trivia, niceties, finer points, ins and outs • *Much of his early work is concerned with the minutiae of life.*

minx = flirt, tease, madam *(Brit. informal)*, Lolita, wanton, tomboy, hussy, trollop, coquette, jade, hoyden, baggage *(old-fashioned informal)* • *Take that little minx of yours home straight away!*

miracle 1 = **wonder**, phenomenon, sensation, marvel, amazing achievement, astonishing feat • *It's a miracle no one was killed.*
2 = **supernatural phenomenon**, mystery, prodigy, thaumaturgy • *Jesus's ability to perform miracles*

QUOTATIONS
Except ye see signs and wonders, ye will not believe
[Bible: St. John]

PROVERBS
The age of miracles is past

miraculous 1 = **wonderful**, amazing, extraordinary, incredible, astonishing, marvellous, magical, unbelievable, phenomenal, astounding, eye-popping *(informal)*, inexplicable, wondrous *(archaic or literary)*, unaccountable, superhuman • *The horse made a miraculous recovery.*
OPPOSITES: common, normal, ordinary
2 = **supernatural**, magical, phenomenal, prodigious, unaccountable, superhuman, preternatural, thaumaturgic • *She had miraculous powers.*

mirage = illusion, vision, hallucination, pipe dream, chimera, optical illusion, phantasm • *Through my half-closed eyelids I began to see mirages.*

mire AS A NOUN 1 = **mess**, trouble, difficulty, emergency, jam *(informal)*, plight, straits, hot water *(informal)*, predicament, tight spot *or* corner • *The economy is not out of the mire yet.*
2 = **mud**, dirt, muck, ooze, sludge, slime, slob *(Irish)*, gloop *(informal)*, grot *(slang)* • *the muck and mire of farmyards*
3 = **swamp**, marsh, bog, fen, quagmire, morass, wetland, pakihi *(N.Z.)*, muskeg *(Canad.)* • *Many of those killed were buried in the mire.*
▸ AS A VERB 1 = **soil**, dirty, muddy, besmirch, begrime, bespatter • *The party has been mired by allegations of sleaze.*
2 = **entangle**, involve, mix up, catch up, bog down, tangle up, enmesh • *The minister still remains mired in the controversy of the affair.*
▸ IN PHRASES: **in the mire = in trouble**, entangled, in difficulties, encumbered • *We're still in the mire, but I think we're good enough to escape.*

mirror AS A NOUN = **looking-glass**, glass *(Brit.)*, reflector, speculum • *He went into the bathroom and looked in the mirror.*
▸ AS A VERB = **reflect**, show, follow, match, represent, copy, repeat, echo, parallel, depict, reproduce, emulate • *His own shock was mirrored in her face.*
▸ RELATED PHOBIA: eisoptrophobia

mirror image = reflection, double, image, copy, twin, representation, clone, replica, likeness, spitting image *(informal)*, dead ringer *(informal)*, exact likeness • *I saw in him a mirror image of my younger self.*

mirth = merriment, amusement, fun, pleasure, laughter, rejoicing, festivity, glee, frolic, sport, gaiety, hilarity, cheerfulness, revelry, jollity, levity, gladness, joviality, jocularity, merrymaking, joyousness • *That caused considerable mirth amongst the pupils.*

mirthful = merry, happy, funny, glad, amused, amusing, cheerful, jolly, hilarious, festive, playful, cheery, laughable, vivacious, jovial, blithe, uproarious, frolicsome, ludic *(literary)*, sportive, gay, light-hearted, jocund, gladsome *(archaic)* • *She revelled in the mirthful music of her children's laughter.*
OPPOSITES: serious, sad, miserable

misadventure = misfortune, accident, disaster, failure, reverse, setback, catastrophe, debacle, bad luck, calamity, mishap, bad break *(informal)*, ill fortune, ill luck, mischance • *a verdict of death by misadventure*

misanthrope = cynic, sceptic, grouch, grump, misanthropist, mankind-hater • *One myth is that he was a grumbling misanthrope.*

misanthropic = antisocial, suspicious, cynical, sceptical, unfriendly, malevolent, inhumane, jaundiced, grouchy, unsociable • *a misanthropic but successful businessman*

misanthropy = cynicism, scepticism, inhumanity, malevolence, hatred of mankind • *He was known for his outbursts of resentment, and for his misanthropy.*

QUOTATIONS
I wish I loved the human race;
I wish I loved its silly face;
I wish I liked the way it walks;
I wish I liked the way it talks;
And when I'm introduced to one
I wish I thought What Jolly Fun!
[Walter Raleigh *Wishes of an Elderly Man*]

misapply = misuse, abuse, pervert, misappropriate, misemploy • *The law has been misapplied.*

misapprehend = **misunderstand**, mistake, misinterpret, misread, misconstrue, misconceive, get the wrong idea *or* impression about • *To see them as mere stereotypes is to misapprehend their significance.*

misapprehension = **misunderstanding**, mistake, error, delusion, misconception, fallacy, misreading, false impression, misinterpretation, false belief, misconstruction, wrong idea *or* impression • *We were under no misapprehension about the scale of the problem.*

misappropriate = **steal**, embezzle, pocket, misuse, knock off *(slang)*, swindle, misspend, trouser *(slang)*, misapply, defalcate *(Law)* • *I have not misappropriated any funds whatsoever.*

misappropriation = **embezzlement**, stealing, theft, swindling, expropriation, defalcation *(Law)* • *He was accused of misappropriation of bank funds.*

misbegotten = **ill-conceived**, abortive, ill-advised, hare-brained, poorly thought-out • *his grandiose and misbegotten plans*

misbehave = **be naughty**, be bad, act up *(informal)*, muck about *(Brit. slang)*, get up to mischief *(informal)*, carry on *(informal)*, be insubordinate • *When the children misbehaved she was unable to cope.*
OPPOSITES: be good, behave, toe the line

misbehaviour = **misconduct**, mischief, misdemeanour, shenanigans *(informal)*, impropriety, acting up *(informal)*, bad behaviour, misdeeds, rudeness, indiscipline, insubordination, naughtiness, monkey business *(informal)*, incivility • *This child's misbehaviour could have been avoided.*

miscalculate 1 = **misjudge**, get something wrong, underestimate, underrate, overestimate, overrate • *He has badly miscalculated the mood of the people.*
2 = **calculate wrongly**, blunder, make a mistake, get it wrong, err, slip up • *The government seems to have miscalculated and bills are higher.*

miscarriage 1 = **spontaneous abortion**, still birth • *She wanted to get pregnant again after suffering a miscarriage.*
2 = **failure**, error, breakdown, mismanagement, undoing, thwarting, mishap, botch *(informal)*, perversion, misfire, mischance, nonsuccess • *The report concluded that no miscarriage of justice had taken place.*

miscarry 1 = **have a miscarriage**, lose your baby, have a spontaneous abortion • *Many women who miscarry eventually have healthy babies.*
2 = **fail**, go wrong, fall through, come to nothing, misfire, go astray, go awry, come to grief, go amiss, go pear-shaped *(informal)*, gang agley *(Scot.)* • *My career miscarried when I thought I had everything.*

miscellaneous = **mixed**, various, varied, diverse, confused, diversified, mingled, assorted, jumbled, sundry, motley, indiscriminate, manifold, heterogeneous, multifarious, multiform • *a hoard of miscellaneous junk*

miscellany = **assortment**, collection, variety, mixture, diversity, anthology, jumble, medley, mixed bag, potpourri, mélange *(French)*, farrago, hotchpotch, salmagundi, gallimaufry, omnium-gatherum • *glass cases filled with a miscellany of objects*

mischance = **misfortune**, accident, mishap, disaster, bad luck, calamity, misadventure, bummer *(slang)*, contretemps, bad break *(informal)*, ill fortune, ill luck, infelicity, ill chance • *By some mischance, the two letters were lost in the post.*

mischief 1 = **misbehaviour**, trouble, naughtiness, pranks, shenanigans *(informal)*, monkey business *(informal)*, waywardness, devilment, impishness, roguishness, roguery • *The little lad was always up to some mischief.*
2 = **harm**, trouble, damage, injury, hurt, evil, disadvantage, disruption, misfortune, detriment • *The conference was a platform to cause political mischief.*

mischievous 1 = **naughty**, bad, troublesome, wayward, exasperating, playful, rascally, impish, roguish, vexatious, puckish, frolicsome, arch, ludic *(literary)*, sportive, badly behaved • *She rocks back and forth on her chair like a mischievous child.*
2 = **malicious**, damaging, vicious, destructive, harmful, troublesome, malignant, detrimental, hurtful, pernicious, spiteful, deleterious, injurious • *a mischievous campaign by the press*

misconceive = **misunderstand**, mistake, misjudge, fail to understand, misconstrue, get the wrong idea about, misapprehend, get your lines crossed about • *We misconceived their purpose.*

misconception = **delusion**, error, misunderstanding, fallacy, misapprehension, mistaken belief, wrong idea, wrong end of the stick, misconstruction • *There are many fears and misconceptions about cancer.*

misconduct = **immorality**, wrongdoing, mismanagement, malpractice, misdemeanour, delinquency, impropriety, transgression, misbehaviour, dereliction, naughtiness, malfeasance *(Law)*, unethical behaviour, malversation *(rare)* • *He was dismissed from his job for gross misconduct.*

misconstrue = **misinterpret**, misunderstand, misjudge, misread, mistake, misapprehend, get a false impression of, misconceive, mistranslate, get your lines crossed about, make a wrong interpretation of • *An outsider might misconstrue the nature of the relationship.*

miscreant AS A NOUN = **wrongdoer**, criminal, villain, rogue, sinner, rascal, scoundrel, scally *(Northwest English dialect)*, vagabond, knave *(archaic)*, reprobate, malefactor, blackguard, evildoer, caitiff *(archaic)*, skelm *(S. African)*, wrong 'un *(Austral. slang)* • *Local people demanded that the magistrate apprehend the miscreants.*
▸ AS AN ADJECTIVE = **criminal**, corrupt, evil, vicious, wicked, depraved, rascally, reprehensible, scoundrelly, villainous, unprincipled, nefarious, iniquitous, reprobate • *They can force miscreant firms to cease trading.*

misdeed *often plural* = **offence**, wrong, crime, fault, sin, misconduct, trespass, misdemeanour, transgression, villainy • *the alleged financial misdeeds of his government*

misdemeanour = **offence**, misconduct, infringement, trespass, misdeed, transgression, misbehaviour, peccadillo • *She knew nothing about her husband's misdemeanours.*

miser = **hoarder**, Scrooge, penny-pincher *(informal)*, curmudgeon, skinflint, screw *(slang)*, cheapskate *(informal)*, tight-arse *(taboo slang)*, tightwad *(U.S. & Canad. slang)*, churl *(archaic)*, tight-ass *(U.S. taboo slang)*, niggard • *I'm married to a miser.*

miserable 1 = **sad**, down, low, depressed, distressed, gloomy, dismal, afflicted, melancholy, heartbroken, desolate, forlorn, mournful, dejected, broken-hearted, despondent, downcast, sorrowful, wretched, disconsolate, crestfallen, doleful, down in the dumps *(informal)*, woebegone, down in the mouth *(informal)* • *She went to bed, miserable and depressed.*
OPPOSITES: happy, cheerful
2 = **dreary**, bleak, desolate, sorry, depressing, foul, dismal, shabby, vile, unhappy, seedy, sordid, squalid, dilapidated, wretched, cheerless, godforsaken, uninviting, scungy *(Austral. & N.Z.)* • *There was nothing in this miserable place to distract him.*
3 = **unpleasant**, wet, rainy, stormy, rotten *(informal)*, dreich *(Scot.)* • *a grey, wet, miserable day*
4 = **sullen**, sour, moody, grumpy, gloomy, sombre, bad-tempered, glum, surly, sulky, taciturn, ill-tempered, humourless, lugubrious, cantankerous, grouchy, peevish, saturnine • *He always was a miserable man. He never spoke to anyone.*
5 = **pathetic**, low, sorry, disgraceful, mean, shameful, shabby, abject, despicable, deplorable, lamentable,

contemptible, scurvy, pitiable, detestable, piteous • *They have so far accepted a miserable 1,100 refugees from the former Yugoslavia.*
OPPOSITES: respectable, admirable

miserliness = **meanness**, penny-pinching *(informal)*, avarice, parsimony, nearness, stinginess, covetousness, churlishness, cheeseparing, niggardliness, graspingness, close- *or* tightfistedness, penuriousness • *She had always despised miserliness.*

QUOTATIONS
How easy it is for a man to die rich, if he will be contented to live miserable
[Henry Fielding]

miserly = **mean**, stingy, penny-pinching *(informal)*, parsimonious, close, near, grasping, beggarly, illiberal, avaricious, niggardly, ungenerous, covetous, penurious, tightfisted, close-fisted, tight-arsed *(taboo slang)*, mingy *(Brit. informal)*, tight-assed *(U.S. taboo slang)*, snoep *(S. African informal)*, tight as a duck's arse *(taboo slang)* • *He is miserly with both his time and his money.*
OPPOSITES: generous, charitable, extravagant

misery 1 = **unhappiness**, distress, despair, grief, suffering, depression, torture, agony, gloom, sadness, discomfort, torment, hardship, sorrow, woe, anguish, melancholy, desolation, wretchedness • *All that money brought nothing but misery.*
OPPOSITES: ease, pleasure, happiness
2 = **poverty**, want, need, squalor, privation, penury, destitution, wretchedness, sordidness, indigence • *An elite profited from the misery of the poor.*
OPPOSITES: luxury
3 = **moaner**, pessimist, killjoy, spoilsport, grouch *(informal)*, prophet of doom, wet blanket *(informal)*, sourpuss *(informal)*, wowser *(Austral. & N.Z. slang)* • *I'm not such a misery now. I've got things sorted out a bit.*
4 = **misfortune**, trouble, trial, disaster, load, burden, curse, ordeal, hardship, catastrophe, sorrow, woe, calamity, affliction, tribulation, bitter pill *(informal)* • *There is no point dwelling on the miseries of the past.*

misfire = **fail**, go wrong, fall through, miscarry, go pear-shaped *(informal)*, fail to go off, go phut *(informal)* • *Some of their policies had misfired.*

misfit = **nonconformist**, eccentric, flake *(slang, chiefly U.S.)*, oddball *(informal)*, fish out of water *(informal)*, square peg (in a round hole) *(informal)* • *I have been made to feel a social misfit for not wanting children.*

misfortune 1 *often plural* = **bad luck**, adversity, hard luck, ill luck, infelicity, evil fortune, bad trot *(Austral. slang)* • *She seemed to enjoy the misfortunes of others.*
2 = **mishap**, loss, trouble, trial, blow, failure, accident, disaster, reverse, tragedy, harm, misery, setback, hardship, calamity, affliction, tribulation, whammy *(informal, chiefly U.S.)*, misadventure, bummer *(slang)*, mischance, stroke of bad luck, evil chance • *He had had his full share of misfortunes.*
OPPOSITES: relief, fortune, good luck

QUOTATIONS
In the misfortune of our best friends, we always find something which is not displeasing to us
[Duc de la Rochefoucauld *Réflexions ou Maximes Morales*]
misfortune: the kind of fortune which never misses
[Ambrose Bierce *The Devil's Dictionary*]

PROVERBS
Misfortunes never come singly

misgiving = **unease**, worry, doubt, anxiety, suspicion, uncertainty, reservation, hesitation, distrust, apprehension, qualm, trepidation, scruple, dubiety • *She had some misgivings about what she was about to do.*

misguided = **unwise**, mistaken, foolish, misled, misplaced, deluded, ill-advised, imprudent, injudicious, labouring under a delusion *or* misapprehension • *He is misguided in expecting honesty from her.*

mishandle = **mismanage**, bungle, botch, mess up *(informal)*, screw (up) *(informal)*, make a mess of, muff, make a hash of *(informal)*, make a nonsense of, bodge *(informal)*, flub *(U.S. slang)* • *The judge said the police had mishandled the siege.*

mishap = **accident**, disaster, misfortune, stroke of bad luck, adversity, calamity, misadventure, contretemps, mischance, infelicity, evil chance, evil fortune • *After a number of mishaps she finally managed to get back home.*

mishmash = **jumble**, medley, hash, potpourri, farrago, hotchpotch, salmagundi, gallimaufry • *a bizarre mishmash of colours and patterns*

misinform = **mislead**, deceive, misdirect, misguide, give someone a bum steer *(informal, chiefly U.S.)* • *He has been misinformed by members of his own party.*

misinformation = **false information**, gossip, disinformation, misleading information, false rumour, bum steer *(U.S. informal)* • *This was a deliberate piece of misinformation.*

misinterpret = **misunderstand**, mistake, distort, misrepresent, misjudge, falsify, pervert, misread, misconstrue, get wrong, misapprehend, misconceive • *The Prince's words had been misinterpreted.*

misjudge = **miscalculate**, be wrong about, underestimate, underrate, overestimate, overrate, get the wrong idea about • *Perhaps I had misjudged him after all.*

mislay = **lose**, misplace, miss, be unable to find, lose track of, be unable to put *or* lay your hands on, forget the whereabouts of • *I appear to have mislaid my jumper.*

mislead = **deceive**, fool, delude, take someone in *(informal)*, bluff, beguile, misdirect, misinform, hoodwink, lead astray, pull the wool over someone's eyes *(informal)*, take someone for a ride *(informal)*, misguide, give someone a bum steer *(informal, chiefly U.S.)* • *Ministers knowingly misled the public.*

misleading = **confusing**, false, ambiguous, deceptive, spurious, evasive, disingenuous, tricky *(informal)*, deceitful, specious, delusive, delusory, sophistical, casuistical, unstraightforward • *The article contains several misleading statements.*
OPPOSITES: open, clear, straightforward

mismanage = **mishandle**, bungle, botch, mess up, misdirect, misconduct, make a mess of, make a hash of *(informal)*, make a nonsense of, bodge *(informal)*, misgovern, maladminister • *Three-quarters of those surveyed thought the President had mismanaged the economy.*

mismanagement = **maladministration**, inefficiency, mishandling, misdirection, misgovernment • *the Government's economic mismanagement*

mismatch = **inconsistency**, discrepancy, conflict, discord, incongruity, misalliance, incongruousness, mismarriage • *an unfortunate mismatch of styles*

mismatched = **incompatible**, clashing, irregular, disparate, incongruous, discordant, unsuited, ill-assorted, unreconcilable, misallied • *The two opponents are mismatched.*

misogynist **AS AN ADJECTIVE** = **chauvinist**, sexist, patriarchal • *misogynist attitudes*
▸ **AS A NOUN** = **woman-hater**, male chauvinist, anti-feminist, MCP *(informal)*, male chauvinist pig *(informal)*, male supremacist • *Just because he's in the men's movement doesn't mean he's a misogynist.*

misogyny

QUOTATIONS
Nothing makes a man hate a woman more than her constant conversation
[William Wycherley *The Country Wife*]
Sir, a woman preaching is like a dog's walking on his hind legs. It is not done well; but you are surprised to find it done at all.
[Dr. Johnson]

m

misplace = **lose**, mislay, miss, be unable to find, lose track of, put in the wrong place, be unable to put *or* lay your hand(s) on, forget the whereabouts of, misfile • *He misplaces his reading glasses with surprising regularity.*

misplaced 1 = **misguided**, unwise, ill-advised, ill-judged, misconceived, ill-considered • *a telling sign of misplaced priorities*
2 = **lost**, missing, mislaid, nowhere to be found • *a misplaced wallet*

misprint = **mistake**, printing error, typographical error, typo *(informal)*, erratum, literal *(Brit.)*, corrigendum • *He assumed that the figure was a misprint.*

misquote = **misrepresent**, twist, distort, pervert, muddle, mangle, falsify, garble, misreport, misstate, quote *or* take out of context • *His letter was misquoted.*

misrepresent = **distort**, disguise, pervert, belie, twist, misinterpret, falsify, garble, misstate • *The extent of the current strike is being misrepresented.*

misrule 1 = **mismanagement**, maladministration, bad government, misgovernment • *He was accused of corruption and misrule.*
2 = **disorder**, confusion, chaos, turmoil, anarchy, lawlessness, tumult • *gearing up for his role as the lord of misrule*

miss[1] AS A VERB 1 = **fail to hit**, go wide of, fall short of, avoid • *She threw the lampshade across the room, narrowly missing my head.*
2 = **mishit**, fail to score, fumble, fluff • *He scored four goals but missed a penalty.*
3 = **fail to notice**, mistake, overlook, pass over • *It's the first thing you see. You can't miss it.*
4 = **misunderstand**, fail to appreciate • *She seemed to have missed the point.*
5 = **pass up**, skip, disregard, forego, let slip, lose out on • *It was too good an opportunity to miss.*
6 = **long for**, wish for, yearn for, want, need, hunger for, pine for, long to see, ache for, feel the loss of, regret the absence of • *Your mum and I are going to miss you at Christmas.*
7 = **be late for**, fail to catch *or* get • *He missed the last bus home.*
8 = **not go to**, skip, cut, omit, be absent from, fail to attend, skive off *(informal)*, play truant from, bludge *(Austral. & N.Z. informal)*, absent yourself from • *We missed our swimming lesson last week.*
9 = **mishear**, misunderstand, fail to hear, fail to take in • *I'm sorry, I missed what you said.*
10 = **avoid**, beat, escape, skirt, duck, cheat, bypass, dodge, evade, get round, elude, steer clear of, sidestep, circumvent, find a way round, give a wide berth to • *We left early, hoping to miss the worst of the traffic.*
▸ AS A NOUN = **mistake**, failure, fault, error, blunder, omission, oversight • *After several more misses, they finally got two arrows in the lion's chest.*
▸ IN PHRASES: **miss something** *or* **someone out** = **omit**, drop, forget, exclude, overlook, skip, leave out • *You've missed out the word 'men'.*

QUOTATIONS
A miss is as good as a mile
[Walter Scott *Journal*]

PROVERBS
What you've never had you never miss

miss[2] = **girl**, maiden, maid, schoolgirl, young lady, lass, damsel, spinster, lassie *(informal)* • *She didn't always come over as such a shy little miss.*

misshapen = **deformed**, twisted, crippled, distorted, ugly, crooked, warped, grotesque, wry, unsightly, contorted, ungainly, malformed, ill-made, unshapely, ill-proportioned • *Her hands were misshapen because of arthritis.*

missile = **projectile**, weapon, shell, rocket • *nuclear missiles*
▹ *See panel* **Missiles**

missing 1 = **lost**, misplaced, not present, gone, left behind, astray, unaccounted for, mislaid, nowhere to be found • *The playing cards were missing.*
2 = **absent**, lacking, left out, not present, wanting in, not to be found in • *One name was missing from the list.*
OPPOSITES: present, there, here

mission 1 = **assignment**, job, labour, operation, work, commission, trip, message *(Scot.)*, task, undertaking, expedition, chore, errand • *the most crucial stage of his latest peace mission*
2 = **delegation**, ministry, embassy, representation, task force, legation, deputation • *a senior member of a diplomatic mission*
3 = **sortie**, operation, raid • *a bomber that crashed during a training mission*
4 = **task**, work, calling, business, job, office, charge, goal, operation, commission, trust, aim, purpose, duty, undertaking, pursuit, quest, assignment, vocation, errand • *He viewed his mission in life as protecting the weak from evil.*

missionary = **evangelist**, preacher, apostle, converter, propagandist, proselytizer • *He plays the part of a missionary who meets a woman of doubtful morals.*

missive = **letter**, report, note, message, communication, dispatch, memorandum, epistle • *the customary missive from your mother*

misspent = **wasted**, thrown away, squandered, idle, dissipated, prodigal, imprudent, misapplied, profitless • *She recalled getting drunk during her misspent youth.*
OPPOSITES: active, profitable, worthwhile

misstate = **misrepresent**, twist, distort, falsify, pervert, misquote, give a false impression of, garble, misreport • *The reports misstated crucial facts.*

mist AS A NOUN = **fog**, cloud, steam, spray, film, haze, vapour, drizzle, smog, dew, condensation, haar *(Eastern Brit.)*, smirr *(Scot.)* • *Thick mist made flying impossible.*
▸ IN PHRASES: **mist over** *or* **up** = **steam (up)**, cloud, obscure, blur, fog, film, blear, becloud, befog • *The windscreen was misting over.*

mistake AS A NOUN 1 = **error**, blunder, oversight, slip, misunderstanding, boob *(Brit. slang)*, misconception, gaffe *(informal)*, slip-up *(informal)*, bloomer *(Brit. informal)*, clanger *(informal)*, miscalculation, error of judgment, faux pas, false move, boo-boo *(informal)*, barry *or* Barry Crocker *(Austral.*

m

MISSILES

cruise missile	Patriot	SS-18
Exocet	Pershing	SS-20
guided missile	Polaris	Stinger
ICBM *or* intercontinental ballistic missile	rocket	standoff missile
Minuteman	Scud	Trident
MIRV *or* multiple independently targeted re-entry vehicle	SLBM *or* submarine-launched ballistic missile	V-1, doodlebug, buzz bomb, *or* flying bomb
	SLCM *or* sea-launched cruise missile	V-2

slang) • *He says there must have been some mistake.*
2 = **oversight**, error, slip, inaccuracy, fault, slip-up *(informal)*, howler *(informal)*, goof, solecism, erratum, barry *or* Barry Crocker *(Austral. slang)* • *Spelling mistakes are often just the result of haste.*
▸ **AS A VERB** = **misunderstand**, misinterpret, misjudge, misread, misconstrue, get wrong, misapprehend, misconceive • *No one should mistake how serious this issue is.*
▸ **IN PHRASES: make a mistake** = **miscalculate**, be wrong, blunder, err, boob *(Brit. slang)*, slip up *(informal)*, misjudge, goof *(informal)*, drop a clanger *(informal)*, put your foot in it *(informal)*, be wide of *or* be off the mark • *I thought I had made a mistake, so I redid it.*
mistake something *or* **someone for something** *or* **someone** = **confuse with**, accept as, take for, mix up with, misinterpret as, confound with • *Hayfever is often mistaken for a summer cold.*

QUOTATIONS
We are built to make mistakes, coded for error
[Lewis Thomas *The Medusa and the Snail*]
The man who makes no mistakes does not usually make anything
[Edward John Phelps]

mistaken 1 = **wrong**, incorrect, misled, in the wrong, misguided, off the mark, off target, in error, wide of the mark, misinformed, off base *(U.S. & Canad. informal)*, barking up the wrong tree *(informal)*, off beam *(informal)*, getting the wrong end of the stick *(informal)*, way off beam *(informal)*, under a misapprehension, labouring under a misapprehension • *I see I was mistaken about you.*
OPPOSITES: right, correct
2 = **inaccurate**, false, inappropriate, faulty, unfounded, erroneous, unsound, fallacious • *She obviously had a mistaken view.*
OPPOSITES: sound, true, accurate

mistakenly = **incorrectly**, wrongly, falsely, by mistake, inappropriately, erroneously, in error, inaccurately, misguidedly, fallaciously • *They mistakenly believed the licences they held were sufficient.*

mistimed = **inopportune**, badly timed, inconvenient, untimely, ill-timed, unseasonable, unsynchronized • *a certain mistimed comment*

mistreat = **abuse**, injure, harm, molest, misuse, maul, manhandle, wrong, rough up, ill-treat, brutalize, maltreat, ill-use, handle roughly, knock about *or* around • *She has been mistreated by men in the past.*

mistreatment = **abuse**, ill-treatment, maltreatment, injury, harm, misuse, mauling, manhandling, roughing up, molestation, unkindness, rough handling, brutalization, ill-usage • *police brutality and mistreatment of people in prisons*

mistress = **lover**, girlfriend, concubine, kept woman, paramour, floozy *(slang)*, fancy woman *(slang)*, inamorata, doxy *(archaic)*, fancy bit *(slang)*, ladylove *(rare)* • *He has a wife and a mistress.*

mistrust **AS A NOUN** = **suspicion**, scepticism, distrust, doubt, uncertainty, apprehension, misgiving, wariness, dubiety • *There was mutual mistrust between the two men.*
▸ **AS A VERB** = **be wary of**, suspect, beware, distrust, apprehend, have doubts about • *You should mistrust all journalists.*

mistrustful = **suspicious**, nervous, cautious, uncertain, wary, cynical, doubtful, sceptical, dubious, fearful, hesitant, apprehensive, leery *(slang)*, distrustful, chary • *He had always been mistrustful of women.*
OPPOSITES: sure, certain, positive

misty = **foggy**, unclear, murky, fuzzy, obscure, blurred, vague, dim, opaque, cloudy, hazy, overcast, bleary, nebulous, indistinct • *The air was cold and misty.*
OPPOSITES: clear, bright, distinct

misunderstand 1 = **misinterpret**, misread, get the wrong idea (about), mistake, misjudge, misconstrue, mishear, misapprehend, be at cross-purposes with, misconceive • *They simply misunderstood him.*
2 = **miss the point**, get the wrong end of the stick, get your wires crossed, get your lines crossed • *I think he simply misunderstood.*

misunderstanding 1 = **mistake**, error, mix-up, misconception, misreading, misapprehension, false impression, misinterpretation, misjudgment, wrong idea, misconstruction • *Tell them what you want to avoid misunderstandings.*
2 = **disagreement**, difference, conflict, argument, difficulty, breach, falling-out *(informal)*, quarrel, rift, squabble, rupture, variance, discord, dissension • *a misunderstanding between friends*

misunderstood = **misjudged**, misinterpreted, misread, misconstrued, unrecognized, misheard, unappreciated • *He's very badly misunderstood.*

misuse **AS A NOUN** 1 = **waste**, embezzlement, squandering, dissipation, fraudulent use, misemployment, misusage • *the misuse of public funds*
2 = **abuse**, corruption, exploitation • *the misuse of power*
3 = **misapplication**, abuse, illegal use, wrong use • *the misuse of drugs in sport*
4 = **perversion**, distortion, desecration, profanation • *Fundamentalism is a deplorable misuse of a faith.*
5 = **misapplication**, solecism, malapropism, catachresis • *his hilarious misuse of words*
6 = **mistreatment**, abuse, harm, exploitation, injury, manhandling, ill-treatment, maltreatment, rough handling, inhumane treatment, cruel treatment, ill-usage • *the history of the misuse of Aborigines*
▸ **AS A VERB** 1 = **abuse**, misapply, misemploy, prostitute • *She misused her position in the government.*
2 = **waste**, squander, dissipate, embezzle, misappropriate • *The committee has cleared leaders of misusing funds.*
3 = **mistreat**, abuse, injure, harm, exploit, wrong, molest, manhandle, ill-treat, brutalize, maltreat, ill-use, handle roughly • *His parents should not have misused him.*
OPPOSITES: respect, honour, cherish
4 = **profane**, corrupt, desecrate, pervert • *breaking a taboo, misusing a sacred ceremony*

mite[1] = **little**, bit, little bit, jot, whit, iota • *I can't help feeling just a mite uneasy about it.*

mite[2]
▸ **RELATED ADJECTIVE:** acaroid

mitigate = **ease**, moderate, soften, check, quiet, calm, weaken, dull, diminish, temper, blunt, soothe, subdue, lessen, appease, lighten, remit, allay, placate, abate, tone down, assuage, pacify, mollify, take the edge off, extenuate, tranquillize, palliate, reduce the force of • *ways of mitigating the effects of an explosion*
OPPOSITES: increase, strengthen, intensify

mitigating = **extenuating**, qualifying, justifying, moderating, vindicating, palliative, exculpatory, exonerative, vindicatory • *The judge heard that there were mitigating circumstances.*

mitigation 1 = **extenuation**, explanation, excuse • *In mitigation, the offences were at the lower end of the scale.*
2 = **relief**, moderation, allaying, remission, diminution, abatement, alleviation, easement, extenuation, mollification, palliation, assuagement • *the mitigation or cure of a physical or mental condition*

mix **AS A VERB** 1 = **combine**, blend, merge, unite, join, cross, compound, incorporate, put together, fuse, mingle, jumble, alloy, amalgamate, interweave, coalesce, intermingle, meld, commingle, commix • *Oil and water don't mix.* • *Mix the cinnamon with the sugar.*

2 = **go together**, combine, be compatible, fit together, be in harmony • *Politics and sport don't mix.*
3 = **socialize**, associate, hang out *(informal)*, mingle, circulate, come together, consort, hobnob, fraternize, rub elbows *(informal)* • *He mixes with people younger than himself.*
4 *often with* **up** = **combine**, marry, blend, integrate, amalgamate, coalesce, meld, commix • *The plan was to mix up office and residential zones.*
▸ **AS A NOUN** = **mixture**, combination, blend, fusion, compound, jumble, assortment, alloy, medley, concoction, amalgam, mixed bag *(informal)*, meld, melange, miscellany • *a magical mix of fantasy and reality*
▸ **IN PHRASES: mix someone up** = **bewilder**, upset, confuse, disturb, puzzle, muddle, perplex, unnerve, fluster, throw into confusion • *You're not helping at all, you're just mixing me up even more.*
mix someone up in something *usually passive* = **entangle**, involve, implicate, embroil, rope in • *He could have got mixed up in the murder.*
mix something *or* **someone up** = **mistake for**, confuse, take for, muddle someone *or* something up • *People often mix me up with other actors.*
mix something up 1 = **confuse**, scramble, muddle, confound • *Depressed people often mix up their words.*
2 = **blend**, beat, mix, stir, fold • *Mix up the batter in advance.*

mixed 1 = **uncertain**, conflicting, confused, doubtful, unsure, muddled, contradictory, ambivalent, indecisive, equivocal • *I came home from the meeting with mixed feelings.*
2 = **varied**, diverse, different, differing, diversified, cosmopolitan, assorted, jumbled, disparate, miscellaneous, motley, haphazard, manifold, heterogeneous • *I found a very mixed group of individuals.*
OPPOSITES: homogeneous, unmixed
3 = **crossbred**, hybrid, mongrel, impure, cross-breed, half-caste, half-breed, interdenominational, interbred • *a mixed breed dog*
OPPOSITES: pure
4 = **combined**, blended, fused, alloyed, united, compound, incorporated, composite, mingled, amalgamated • *silver jewellery with mixed metals and semi-precious stones*
OPPOSITES: pure, isolated, unmixed

mixed-up = **confused**, disturbed, puzzled, bewildered, at sea, upset, distraught, muddled, perplexed, maladjusted • *I think he's a rather mixed-up kid.*

mixer = **blender**, whisk, churn, food processor, liquidizer • *an electric food mixer*

mixture 1 = **blend**, mix, variety, fusion, assortment, combine, brew, jumble, medley, concoction, amalgam, amalgamation, mixed bag *(informal)*, meld, potpourri, mélange *(French)*, miscellany, conglomeration, hotchpotch, admixture, salmagundi • *a mixture of spiced, grilled vegetables*
2 = **composite**, blend, union, compound, alloy • *a mixture of concrete and resin*
3 = **cross**, combination, blend, association • *a mixture between Reggae, Bhangra, and Soul fusion*
4 = **concoction**, union, compound, blend, brew, composite, amalgam, conglomeration • *Prepare the mixture carefully.*

mix-up = **confusion**, mistake, misunderstanding, mess, tangle, muddle, jumble, fankle *(Scot.)* • *a mix-up over travel arrangements*

moan **AS A VERB** 1 = **groan**, sigh, sob, whine, keen, lament, deplore, bemoan, bewail • *'My head, my head,' she moaned.*
2 = **grumble**, complain, groan, whine, beef *(slang)*, carp, bitch *(slang)*, grouse, gripe *(informal)*, whinge *(informal)*, bleat, moan and groan, grouch *(informal)* • *I used to moan if I didn't get at least 8 hours' sleep.*
3 = **sigh**, whisper, murmur, sough • *The wind moaned through the shattered glass.*
▸ **AS A NOUN** 1 = **groan**, sigh, sob, lament, wail, grunt, whine, lamentation • *She gave a low choking moan and began to tremble violently.*
2 = **complaint**, protest, grumble, beef *(slang)*, bitch *(slang)*, whine, grouse, gripe *(informal)*, grouch *(informal)*, kvetch *(U.S. slang)* • *They have been listening to people's gripes and moans.*
3 = **sigh**, whisper, murmur • *the occasional moan of the wind around the house*

mob **AS A NOUN** 1 = **crowd**, pack, collection, mass, body, press, host, gathering, drove, gang, flock, herd, swarm, horde, multitude, throng, assemblage • *a growing mob of demonstrators*
2 = **masses**, rabble, hoi polloi, scum, great unwashed *(informal derogatory)*, riffraff, canaille *(French)*, commonalty • *If they continue like this, there is a danger of the mob taking over.*
3 = **gang**, company, group, set, lot, troop, crew *(informal)* • *Can you stop your mob tramping all over the place?*
▸ **AS A VERB** 1 = **surround**, besiege, overrun, jostle, fall on, set upon, crowd around, swarm around • *Her car was mobbed by the media.*
2 = **crowd into**, fill, crowd, pack, jam, cram into, fill to overflowing • *Demonstrators mobbed the streets.*

mobile 1 = **movable**, moving, travelling, wandering, portable, locomotive, itinerant, peripatetic, ambulatory, motile • *a four-hundred-seat mobile theatre*
2 = **active**, lively, energetic, able to move, sprightly, spry, motile, ambulant • *I'm still very mobile.*
3 = **adaptable**, flexible, versatile, transplantable • *young, mobile professionals*
4 = **changeable**, meaning, animated, expressive, eloquent, suggestive, ever-changing • *She had a mobile, expressive face.*

mobile home = **caravan** *(Brit.)*, trailer *(U.S.)*, Winnebago *(trademark)* • *The tornado picked up their mobile home and dumped it miles away.*

mobility 1 = **ability to move**, motility, movability, moveableness • *people with mobility difficulties*
2 = **movement**, climbing, progression, upward movement • *no chance of social mobility*

mobilize 1 = **rally**, organize, stimulate, excite, prompt, marshal, activate, awaken, animate, muster, foment, put in motion • *We must try to mobilize international support.*
2 = **deploy**, prepare, ready, rally, assemble, call up, marshal, muster, call to arms, get *or* make ready • *The government has mobilized troops to help.*

mock **AS A VERB** = **laugh at**, insult, tease, ridicule, taunt, scorn, sneer, scoff, deride, flout, make fun of, wind someone up *(Brit. slang)*, poke fun at, chaff, take the mickey out of *(informal)*, jeer at, take the piss out of *(taboo slang)*, show contempt for, make a monkey out of, laugh to scorn • *I thought you were mocking me.*
OPPOSITES: respect, encourage, praise
▸ **AS AN ADJECTIVE** = **imitation**, pretended, artificial, forged, fake, false, faked, dummy, bogus, sham, fraudulent, pseudo *(informal)*, counterfeit, feigned, spurious, ersatz, phoney *or* phony *(informal)* • *'It's tragic,' he swooned in mock horror.*
OPPOSITES: real, true, genuine
▸ **AS A NOUN** = **laughing stock**, mockery, fool, dupe, sport, travesty, jest, Aunt Sally *(Brit.)* • *She found herself made a mock of.*

mockery 1 = **derision**, contempt, ridicule, scorn, jeering, disdain, scoffing, disrespect, gibes, contumely • *Was there a glint of mockery in his eyes?*
2 = **farce**, laughing stock, joke, apology *(informal)*, letdown • *This action makes a mockery of the government's plans.*

mocking = **scornful**, insulting, taunting, scoffing, satirical, contemptuous, irreverent, sarcastic, sardonic, derisory, disrespectful, disdainful, derisive, satiric, contumelious • *She gave a mocking smile.*

m

mode 1 = **method**, way, plan, course, system, form, state, process, condition, style, approach, quality, practice, fashion, technique, manner, procedure, custom, vein • *the capitalist mode of production*
2 = **fashion**, style, trend, rage, vogue, look, craze • *Their designs were exterminated by the mode for uncluttered space.*
3 = **function**, position, role, operation, capacity • *The camera is in manual mode.*

model AS A NOUN 1 = **representation**, image, copy, miniature, dummy, replica, imitation, duplicate, lookalike, facsimile, mock-up • *an architect's model of a wooden house*
2 = **pattern**, example, design, standard, type, original, ideal, mould, norm, gauge, prototype, paradigm, archetype, exemplar, lodestar • *the Chinese model of economic reform*
3 = **paragon**, ideal, embodiment, epitome, perfect example, personification, acme, nonpareil, perfect specimen, beau idéal *(French)* • *a model of good manners*
4 = **version**, form, kind, design, style, type, variety, stamp, mode, configuration • *To keep the cost down, opt for a basic model.*
5 = **sitter**, subject, poser • *an artist's model*
6 = **mannequin**, supermodel, fashion model, clothes horse *(informal)* • *a top photographic model*
▸ AS A MODIFIER 1 = **imitation**, copy, toy, miniature, dummy, duplicate, facsimile • *a model aeroplane*
2 = **ideal**, perfect, impeccable, exemplary, consummate, flawless, faultless • *At school she was a model pupil.*
OPPOSITES: flawed, impaired, imperfect
3 = **archetypal**, standard, typical, illustrative, paradigmatic • *The aim is to develop a model farm from which farmers can learn.*
▸ AS A VERB 1 = **base**, shape, plan, found, pattern, mould • *She asked if he had modelled the hero on anyone in particular.*
2 = **show off** *(informal)*, wear, display, sport, showboat • *Two boys modelled a variety of clothes from Harrods.*
3 = **shape**, form, design, fashion, cast, stamp, carve, mould, sculpt • *Sometimes she carved wood or modelled clay.*

moderate AS AN ADJECTIVE 1 = **mild**, reasonable, controlled, limited, cool, calm, steady, modest, restrained, deliberate, sober, middle-of-the-road, temperate, judicious, peaceable, equable • *He was an easy-going man of very moderate views.*
OPPOSITES: extreme, unreasonable, wild
2 = **reasonable**, average, acceptable, within reason, within limits, non-excessive • *A moderate amount of stress can be beneficial.*
OPPOSITES: unusual, extreme, excessive
3 = **average**, middling, medium, fair, ordinary, indifferent, mediocre, so-so *(informal)*, passable, unexceptional, fairish, half-pie *(N.Z. informal)*, fair to middling *(informal)* • *The drug offered only moderate improvements.*
▸ AS A VERB 1 = **soften**, control, calm, temper, regulate, quiet, diminish, decrease, curb, restrain, tame, subdue, play down, lessen, repress, mitigate, tone down, pacify, modulate, soft-pedal *(informal)* • *They are hoping that he will be persuaded to moderate his views.*
2 = **lessen**, relax, ease, wane, abate • *The crisis has moderated somewhat.*
OPPOSITES: increase, intensify, heighten
3 = **arbitrate**, judge, chair, referee, preside, mediate, take the chair • *trying to moderate a quarrel between the two states*

moderately = **reasonably**, rather, quite, fairly, somewhat, slightly, to some extent, to a degree, in moderation, within reason, tolerably, within limits, passably • *The machine operated moderately well.*

moderation AS A NOUN = **restraint**, justice, fairness, composure, coolness, temperance, calmness, equanimity, reasonableness, mildness, justness, judiciousness, sedateness, moderateness • *He called on all parties to show moderation.*
▸ IN PHRASES: **in moderation** = **moderately**, within reason, within limits, within bounds, in moderate quantities • *Many of us are able to drink in moderation.*

QUOTATIONS
Moderation is a virtue only in those who are thought to have an alternative
[Henry Kissinger]

PROVERBS
Moderation in all things

modern 1 = **current**, present, contemporary, recent, late, present-day, latter-day • *the problem of materialism in modern society*
2 = **up-to-date**, latest, fresh, new, novel, with it *(informal)*, plugged-in *(slang)*, up-to-the-minute, newfangled, neoteric *(rare)* • *a more tailored and modern style*
OPPOSITES: old, former, old-fashioned

modern-day = **present-day**, modern, contemporary • *the by-products of modern-day living*

modernity = **novelty**, currency, innovation, freshness, newness, contemporaneity, recentness • *an office block that astonished the city with its modernity*

modernize = **update**, renew, revamp, remake, renovate, remodel, rejuvenate, make over, face-lift, bring up to date, rebrand • *There is a pressing need to modernize our electoral system.*

modest 1 = **simple**, homely, small, ordinary, plain, humble, low-cost, inexpensive, unpretentious, unostentatious, unimposing • *the modest home of a family who lived off the land*
2 = **moderate**, small, limited, fair, ordinary, middling, meagre, frugal, scanty, unexceptional • *You don't get rich, but you can earn a modest living from it.*
3 = **unpretentious**, simple, reserved, retiring, quiet, shy, humble, discreet, blushing, self-conscious, coy, meek, reticent, unassuming, self-effacing, demure, diffident, bashful, aw-shucks • *He's modest, as well as being a great player.*
4 = **decorous**, seemly, severe, decent, proper, sober, discreet • *She always wore modest clothing.*

modesty 1 = **reserve**, decency, humility, shyness, propriety, reticence, timidity, diffidence, quietness, coyness, self-effacement, meekness, lack of pretension, bashfulness, humbleness, unpretentiousness, demureness, unobtrusiveness, discreetness • *His modesty does him credit.*
OPPOSITES: confidence, pride, conceit
2 = **plainness**, simplicity, ordinariness, unpretentiousness, inexpensiveness • *The modesty of the town itself comes as a surprise.*
3 = **decorum**, virtue, decency, delicacy, propriety, sobriety, coyness, demureness, decorousness, seemliness, chasteness • *There were shrieks as the girls tried to protect their modesty.*

QUOTATIONS
Small is the worth
Of beauty from the light retir'd;
Bid her come forth,
Suffer herself to be desir'd,
And not blush so to be admir'd
[Edmund Waller *Go Lovely Rose!*]

modicum = **little**, bit, drop, touch, inch, scrap, dash, grain, particle, fragment, atom, pinch, ounce, shred, small amount, crumb, tinge, mite, tad *(informal, chiefly U.S.)*, speck, iota • *I like to think I've had a modicum of success.*

modification = **change**, restriction, variation, qualification, adjustment, revision, alteration, mutation, reformation, refinement, makeover, modulation • *Relatively minor modifications were required.*

modify 1 = **change**, reform, vary, convert, transform, alter, adjust, adapt, revise, remodel, rework, tweak *(informal)*, reorganize, recast, reshape, redo, refashion • *They agreed to modify their recruitment policy.*

2 = **tone down**, limit, reduce, lower, qualify, relax, ease, restrict, moderate, temper, soften, restrain, lessen, abate • *He had to modify his language considerably.*

modish = **fashionable**, current, smart, stylish, trendy (*Brit. informal*), in, now (*informal*), with it (*informal*), contemporary, hip (*slang*), vogue, chic, all the rage, up-to-the-minute, du jour (*French*), à la mode (*French*), voguish, culty, schmick (*Austral. informal*), funky • *a short checklist of much that is modish at the moment*

modulate = **adjust**, balance, vary, tone, tune, regulate, harmonize, inflect, attune • *He carefully modulated his voice.*

modus operandi = **procedure**, way, system, process, operation, practice, method, technique, praxis • *We reserve the right to alter our modus operandi.*

mogul = **tycoon**, lord, baron, notable, magnate, big gun (*informal*), big shot (*informal*), personage, nob (*slang, chiefly Brit.*), potentate, big wheel (*slang*), big cheese (*old-fashioned slang*), big noise (*informal*), big hitter (*informal*), heavy hitter (*informal*), nabob (*informal*), bashaw, V.I.P. • *an international media mogul*

moist = **damp**, wet, dripping, rainy, soggy, humid, dank, clammy, dewy, not dry, drizzly, dampish, wettish • *Wipe off any excess with a clean, moist flannel.*

moisten = **dampen**, water, wet, soak, damp, moisturize, humidify, bedew • *She took a sip of water to moisten her dry throat.*

moisture = **damp**, water, liquid, sweat, humidity, dew, perspiration, dampness, wetness, dankness, wateriness • *When the soil is dry, more moisture is lost from the plant.*

moisturizer = **lotion**, cream, balm, lubricant, salve, emollient • *Then I rinse carefully and apply moisturizer.*

mole

▸ **COLLECTIVE NOUN:** labour

molecule = **particle**, atom, mite, jot, speck, mote, iota • *a molecule of sulfur trioxide*

molest **1** = **abuse**, attack, hurt, injure, harm, interfere with, assail, accost, manhandle, ill-treat, maltreat • *He was accused of sexually molesting a colleague.*

2 = **annoy**, worry, upset, harry, bother, disturb, bug (*informal*), plague, irritate, tease, torment, harass, afflict, badger, persecute, beset, hector, pester, vex • *He disguised himself to avoid being molested in the street.*

mollify = **pacify**, quiet, calm, compose, soothe, appease, quell, sweeten, placate, conciliate, propitiate • *The investigation was undertaken to mollify pressure groups.*

mollycoddle = **pamper**, baby, ruin, pet, spoil, indulge, cosset, coddle • *He accused me of mollycoddling the children.*

molten = **melted**, soft, flowing, liquid, fluid, liquefied • *The molten metal is poured into the mould.*

mom = **mum**, mother, ma • *We waited for Mom and Dad to get home.*

moment **1** = **instant**, second, minute, flash, shake (*informal*), tick (*Brit. informal*), no time, twinkling, split second, jiffy (*informal*), trice, two shakes (*informal*), two shakes of a lamb's tail (*informal*), bat of an eye (*informal*) • *In a moment he was gone.*

2 = **time**, point, stage, instant, point in time, hour, juncture • *At this moment a car stopped outside the house.*

3 = **importance**, concern, value, worth, weight, import, consequence, substance, significance, gravity, seriousness, weightiness • *I was glad I had nothing of great moment to do that afternoon.*

QUOTATIONS

in the twinkling of an eye
[*Bible: I Corinthians*]

momentarily = **briefly**, for a moment, temporarily, for a second, for a minute, for a short time, for an instant, for a little while, for a short while, for the nonce • *She paused momentarily when she saw them.*

momentary = **short-lived**, short, brief, temporary, passing, quick, fleeting, hasty, transitory • *a momentary lapse of concentration*

OPPOSITES: lasting, permanent, lengthy

momentous = **significant**, important, serious, vital, critical, crucial, grave, historic, decisive, pivotal, fateful, weighty, consequential, of moment, earth-shaking (*informal*) • *the momentous decision to send in the troops*

OPPOSITES: trivial, trifling, unimportant

momentum = **impetus**, force, power, drive, push, energy, strength, thrust, propulsion, welly (*slang*) • *This campaign is really gaining momentum.*

monarch = **ruler**, king *or* queen, sovereign, tsar, potentate, crowned head, emperor *or* empress, prince *or* princess • *She will never stand down as monarch and we fully support her.*

monarchy **1** = **sovereignty**, despotism, autocracy, kingship, absolutism, royalism, monocracy • *a debate on the future of the monarchy*

2 = **kingdom**, empire, realm, principality • *The country was a monarchy until 1973.*

monastery = **abbey**, house, convent, priory, cloister, religious community, nunnery, friary • *He spent a year in a Buddhist monastery.*

monastic = **monkish**, secluded, cloistered, reclusive, withdrawn, austere, celibate, contemplative, ascetic, sequestered, hermit-like, conventual, cenobitic, coenobitic, cloistral, eremitic, monachal • *He was drawn to the monastic life.*

monetary = **financial**, money, economic, capital, cash, fiscal, budgetary, pecuniary • *They tighten monetary policy to avoid inflation.*

money **AS A NOUN** = **cash**, funds, capital, currency, wealth, hard cash, green (*slang*), readies (*informal*), riches, necessary (*informal*), silver, bread (*slang*), coin, tin (*slang*), brass (*Northern English dialect*), loot (*informal*), dough (*slang*), the ready (*informal*), banknotes, dosh (*Brit. & Austral. slang*), lolly (*Brit. slang*), the wherewithal, legal tender, megabucks (*U.S. & Canad. slang*), needful (*informal*), specie, shekels (*informal*), wonga (*slang*), dibs (*slang*), filthy lucre (*facetious*), moolah (*slang*), ackers (*slang*), gelt (*slang, chiefly U.S.*), spondulicks (*slang*), pelf (*contemptuous*), mazuma (*slang, chiefly U.S.*), kembla (*Austral. slang*) • *A lot of money that you pay goes back to the distributor.*

▸ **IN PHRASES: for my money** = **in my opinion**, in my view, to my mind, in my book, if you ask me, as I see it, in my estimation, from my standpoint • *For my money, it's the best in the world.*

in the money = **rich**, wealthy, prosperous, affluent, rolling (*slang*), loaded (*slang*), flush (*informal*), well-off, well-heeled (*informal*), well-to-do, on Easy Street (*informal*), in clover (*informal*), minted (*Brit. slang*) • *If you are lucky, you could be in the money.*

▸ **RELATED ADJECTIVE:** pecuniary

▸ **RELATED MANIA:** chrematomania

▸ **RELATED PHOBIA:** chrematophobia

▹ *See panel* **Currencies**

QUOTATIONS

Money speaks sense in a language all nations understand
[Aphra Behn *The Lucky Chance*]

When a fellow says, it hain't the money but the principle of the thing, it's the money
[Kin Hubbard *Hoss Sense and Nonsense*]

Money is our madness, our vast collective madness
[D.H. Lawrence]

Wine maketh merry, but money answereth all things
[*Bible: Ecclesiastes*]

Money is coined liberty
[Fyodor Dostoevsky *House of the Dead*]

Money is the sinews of love, as of war
[George Farquhar *Love and a Bottle*]
Better authentic mammon than a bogus god
[Louis MacNiece *Autumn Journal*]
Money is like a sixth sense without which you cannot make a complete use of the other five
[W. Somerset Maugham *Of Human Bondage*]
My boy ... always try to rub up against money, for if you rub up against money long enough, some of it may rub off on you
[Damon Runyon *A Very Honorable Guy*]
If you can actually count your money, then you are not really a rich man
[J. Paul Getty]
Money doesn't make you happy. I now have $50 million but I was just as happy when I had $48 million
[Arnold Schwarzenegger]
Money doesn't talk, it swears
[Bob Dylan *It's Alright, Ma (I'm Only Bleeding)*]
Money is like muck, not good except it be spread
[Francis Bacon *Of Seditions and Troubles*]
Money ... is none of the wheels of trade: it is the oil which renders the motion of the wheels more smooth and easy
[David Hume *Essays: Moral and Political*]
Money couldn't buy friends but you got a better class of enemy
[Spike Milligan *Puckoon*]

PROVERBS
Bad money drives out good
Money isn't everything
Money talks
Money is power
Money makes money
Shrouds have no pockets
You can't take it with you when you go

moneyed *or* **monied** = **rich**, loaded *(slang)*, wealthy, flush *(informal)*, prosperous, affluent, well-off, well-heeled *(informal)*, well-to-do, minted *(Brit. slang)* • *Fear of crime among the new monied classes is rising rapidly.*

money-grubbing = **avaricious**, grasping, greedy, mercenary, acquisitive, rapacious, money-grabbing, grabby *(informal)* • *The main character is portrayed as a money-grubbing parasite.*

moneymaking = **profitable**, successful, lucrative, gainful, paying, thriving, remunerative • *They are trying to attract money-making movies back to Britain.*

mongrel ▸ **AS A NOUN** = **hybrid**, cross, half-breed, crossbreed, mixed breed, bigener *(Biology)* • *They were walking their pet mongrel on the outskirts of the town when it happened.*
▸ **AS AN ADJECTIVE** = **half-breed**, hybrid, crossbred, of mixed breed • *He was determined to save his mongrel puppy.*

monitor ▸ **AS A VERB** = **check**, follow, record, watch, survey, observe, scan, oversee, supervise, keep an eye on, keep track of, keep tabs on • *Officials had not been allowed to monitor the voting.*
▸ **AS A NOUN** 1 = **scanner**, recorder, detector • *The heart monitor shows low levels of consciousness.*
2 = **screen**, VDU, visual display unit • *He was watching tennis on a television monitor.*
3 = **guide**, observer, supervisor, overseer, invigilator • *Government monitors will continue to accompany reporters.*
4 = **prefect** *(Brit.)*, head girl, head boy, senior boy, senior girl • *As a school monitor he set a good example.*

monk = **friar**, brother, religious, novice, monastic, oblate • *saffron-robed Buddhist monks*
▸ **RELATED ADJECTIVE:** monastic

monkey 1 = **simian**, ape, primate, jackanapes *(archaic)* • *He walked on all fours like a monkey.*
2 = **rascal**, horror, devil, rogue, imp, tyke, scallywag, mischief maker, scamp, nointer *(Austral. slang)* • *She's such a little monkey.*
▸ **RELATED ADJECTIVE:** simian
▸ **COLLECTIVE NOUN:** troop

QUOTATIONS
monkey: an arboreal animal which makes itself at home in genealogical trees
[Ambrose Bierce *The Devil's Dictionary*]

▹ *See panel* **Monkeys, apes and other primates**

monkey business 1 = **mischief**, carry-on *(informal, chiefly Brit.)*, clowning, pranks, shenanigans *(informal)*, skylarking *(informal)*, horseplay, tomfoolery, monkey tricks • *In bed by nine, and no monkey business.*
2 = **dishonesty**, trickery, skulduggery *(informal)*, chicanery, hanky-panky *(informal)*, funny business • *cold-blooded expertise and political monkey business*

monolith 1 = **standing stone**, megalith, menhir, sarsen stone • *a fine stone circle surrounding a central monolith*
2 = **multinational**, corporation • *A deal between the two would have created a powerful monolith.*

monolithic 1 = **inflexible**, rigid, impenetrable, intractable, unchanging, immovable, hidebound, unbending, fossilized • *an authoritarian and monolithic system*
2 = **huge**, giant, massive, imposing, solid, substantial, gigantic, monumental, colossal, impenetrable, intractable, immovable • *a monolithic concrete building*

monologue = **speech**, lecture, sermon, harangue, soliloquy, oration, spiel *(informal)* • *He ignored the question and continued his monologue.*

monomania = **obsession**, fanaticism, fixation, one-track mind *(informal)*, hobbyhorse, idée fixe *(French)*, bee in your bonnet *(informal)* • *Over the past two decades, monomania has again gripped the country.*

monopolize 1 = **control**, corner, take over, dominate, exercise *or* have a monopoly of • *They are virtually monopolizing the market.*
2 = **keep to yourself**, corner, hog *(slang)*, engross • *He monopolized her totally, to the exclusion of her brothers and sisters.*

monotonous 1 = **tedious**, boring, dull, repetitive, uniform, all the same, plodding, tiresome, humdrum, unchanging,

MONKEYS, APES AND OTHER PRIMATES

aye-aye
baboon
Barbary ape
bonnet monkey
bushbaby *or* galago
capuchin
chacma
chimpanzee *or* chimp
colobus
douc
douroucouli
drill
flying lemur *or* colugo
gelada
gibbon
gorilla
green monkey
grivet
guenon
guereza
howler monkey
indris *or* indri
langur
lemur
loris
macaco
macaque
mandrill
mangabey
marmoset
mona
monkey *or (archaic)* jackanapes
orang-outang, orang-utan, *or* orang
proboscis monkey
rhesus monkey
saki
siamang
sifaka
spider monkey
squirrel monkey
talapoin
tamarin
tana
tarsier
titi
vervet
wanderoo

colourless, mind-numbing, soporific, ho-hum *(informal)*, repetitious, wearisome, samey *(informal)*, unvaried • *It's monotonous work, like most factory jobs.*
OPPOSITES: interesting, exciting, entertaining
2 = toneless, flat, uniform, droning, unchanging, uninflected • *a monotonous voice*
OPPOSITES: sexy *(informal)*, animated

monotony = tedium, routine, boredom, dullness, sameness, uniformity, flatness, repetitiveness, tediousness, repetitiousness, colourlessness, tiresomeness • *A night out may help break the monotony of the week.*

monster AS A NOUN 1 = giant, mammoth, titan, colossus, monstrosity, leviathan, behemoth, Brobdingnagian • *He said he'd hooked a real monster of a fish.*
2 = brute, devil, savage, beast, demon, villain, barbarian, fiend, ogre, ghoul, bogeyman • *You make me sound like an absolute monster!*
3 = rascal, rogue, horror *(informal)*, devil, monkey *(informal)*, imp, tyke *(informal)*, scallywag *(informal)*, mischief-maker, scamp *(informal)*, nointer *(Austral. slang)* • *I don't think I could be as patient as they are with that little monster!*
4 = freak, mutant, monstrosity, lusus naturae *(Latin)*, miscreation, teratism • *She keeps me hidden like some hideous monster she's ashamed of.*
▸ **AS A MODIFIER = huge**, giant, massive, enormous, tremendous, immense, mega *(slang)*, titanic, jumbo *(informal)*, gigantic, monstrous, mammoth, colossal, stellar *(informal)*, stupendous, gargantuan, fuck-off *(offensive taboo slang)*, elephantine, ginormous *(informal)*, Brobdingnagian, humongous *or* humungous *(U.S. slang)* • *The film will be a monster hit.*

monstrosity 1 = eyesore, horror, carbuncle, blot on the landscape • *Most of the older buildings had been replaced by monstrosities.*
2 = freak, horror, monster, mutant, ogre, lusus naturae *(Latin)*, miscreation, teratism • *The towering figure looked like some monstrosity from a sci-fi movie.*
3 = hideousness, horror, evil, atrocity, abnormality, obscenity, dreadfulness, frightfulness, heinousness, hellishness, loathsomeness • *the monstrosity of globalized commerce*

monstrous 1 = outrageous, shocking, evil, horrifying, vicious, foul, cruel, infamous, intolerable, disgraceful, scandalous, atrocious, inhuman, diabolical, heinous, odious, loathsome, devilish, egregious, fiendish, villainous • *She endured his monstrous behaviour for years.*
OPPOSITES: good, kind, decent
2 = huge, giant, massive, great, towering, vast, enormous, tremendous, immense, titanic, gigantic, mammoth, colossal, stellar *(informal)*, prodigious, stupendous, gargantuan, fuck-off *(offensive taboo slang)*, elephantine, ginormous *(informal)*, humongous *or* humungous *(U.S. slang)* • *They were erecting a monstrous edifice.*
OPPOSITES: little, small, tiny
3 = unnatural, terrible, horrible, dreadful, abnormal, obscene, horrendous, hideous, grotesque, gruesome, frightful, hellish, freakish, fiendish, miscreated, teratoid • *the film's monstrous fantasy figure*
OPPOSITES: appealing, natural, normal

month = four weeks, thirty days, moon • *She was here for a month.*
▸ **RELATED ADJECTIVE:** mensal

monty IN PHRASES: the full monty = the whole lot • *There was everything from simple piano to full orchestral finish. The full monty.*

monument 1 = memorial, cairn, statue, pillar, marker, shrine, tombstone, mausoleum, commemoration, headstone, gravestone, obelisk, cenotaph • *He laid a wreath on a monument near Bayeux.*
2 = testament, record, witness, token, reminder, remembrance, memento • *By his achievements he leaves a fitting monument to his beliefs.*
▷ *See panel* **Buildings and other monuments**

QUOTATIONS
If you seek a monument, look around
(Si monumentum requiris, circumspice)
[son of Sir Christopher Wren *Inscription in St. Paul's Cathedral*]

monumental AS AN ADJECTIVE = important, classic, significant, outstanding, lasting, enormous, historic, enduring, memorable, awesome, majestic, immortal, unforgettable, prodigious, stupendous, awe-inspiring, epoch-making • *his monumental work on Chinese astronomy*
OPPOSITES: ordinary, modest, unimportant
▸ **AS AN INTENSIFIER = immense**, great, massive, terrible, tremendous, horrible, staggering, catastrophic, gigantic, colossal, whopping *(informal)*, indefensible, unforgivable, egregious • *It had been a monumental blunder to give him the assignment.*
OPPOSITES: small, average, tiny
▸ **AS AN ADJECTIVE = commemorative**, memorial, monolithic, statuary, funerary • *monumental architecture*

mood AS A NOUN 1 = state of mind, spirit, humour, temper, vein, tenor, disposition, frame of mind • *He was clearly in a good mood today.*
2 = depression, sulk, bad temper, blues, dumps *(informal)*, wax *(informal, chiefly Brit.)*, melancholy, doldrums, the hump *(Brit. informal)*, bate *(Brit. slang)*, fit of pique, low spirits, the sulks, grumps *(informal)*, foulie *(Austral. slang)* • *She was obviously in a mood.*
3 = atmosphere, feeling, feel, spirit, tone, climate, flavour, tenor, aura, ambience • *First set the mood with some music.*
▸ **IN PHRASES: in the mood = inclined**, willing, interested, minded, keen, eager, disposed towards, in the (right) frame of mind, favourable towards • *After all that activity, we were in the mood for a good meal.*

moody 1 = changeable, volatile, unpredictable, unstable, erratic, fickle, temperamental, impulsive, mercurial, capricious, unsteady, fitful, flighty, faddish, inconstant • *She was unstable and moody.*
OPPOSITES: stable, constant, steady
2 = sulky, cross, wounded, angry, offended, irritable, pissed *(taboo slang)*, crabbed, crusty, temperamental, pissed off *(taboo slang)*, touchy, curt, petulant, ill-tempered, irascible, cantankerous, tetchy, testy, chippy *(informal)*, in a huff, short-tempered, waspish, piqued, crabby, huffy, splenetic, crotchety *(informal)*, ill-humoured, huffish, tooshie *(Austral. slang)* • *He is a moody man behind that jokey front.*
OPPOSITES: happy, gay, cheerful
3 = gloomy, sad, miserable, melancholy, frowning, dismal, dour, sullen, glum, introspective, in the doldrums, out of sorts *(informal)*, downcast, morose, lugubrious, pensive, broody, crestfallen, doleful, down in the dumps *(informal)*, saturnine, down in the mouth *(informal)*, mopish, mopy • *Don't go all moody on me!*
OPPOSITES: happy, gay, cheerful
4 = sad, gloomy, melancholy, sombre • *melancholy guitars and moody lyrics*

moon AS A NOUN = satellite • *Neptune's large moon*
▸ **AS A VERB = idle**, drift, loaf, languish, waste time, daydream, mope, mooch *(Brit. slang)*, doss *(Brit. slang)* • *She was mooning around all morning, doing nothing.*
▸ **IN PHRASES: many moons ago = a long time ago**, years ago, ages ago, donkey's years ago *(Brit. informal)*, yonks ago *(Brit. informal)* • *I saw her once, many moons ago, in a dreadful movie.*
once in a blue moon = rarely, almost never, very seldom, hardly ever, scarcely ever • *Once in a blue moon you get some problems.*

over the moon = **ecstatic**, transported, delighted, thrilled, jubilant, elated, overjoyed, delirious, euphoric, on top of the world *(informal)*, exultant, enraptured, jumping for joy, on cloud nine, cock-a-hoop, in raptures, tickled pink *(informal)*, walking on air, in seventh heaven, as pleased as Punch, beside yourself with joy, stoked *(Austral. & N.Z. informal)* • *We were both over the moon to hear the news.*

▸ **RELATED ADJECTIVE:** lunar

QUOTATIONS

Swear not by the moon, the inconstant moon
[William Shakespeare *Romeo and Juliet*]

moonshine 1 = **bootleg**, poteen *(Scot. & Irish)*, hooch *or* hootch *(informal, chiefly U.S. & Canad.)* • *a bottle of moonshine*
2 = **nonsense**, rubbish, pants *(slang)*, trash, gas *(informal)*, bunk *(informal)*, hot air *(informal)*, tosh *(slang, chiefly Brit.)*, twaddle, tripe *(informal)*, guff *(slang)*, havers *(Scot.)*, claptrap *(informal)*, hogwash, malarkey, blather, piffle *(informal)*, blether, bosh *(informal)*, stuff and nonsense, foolish talk, tarradiddle, bunkum *or* buncombe *(chiefly U.S.)*, bizzo *(Austral. slang)*, bull's wool *(Austral. & N.Z. slang)* • *The story is pure moonshine.*

moor[1] = **moorland**, fell *(Brit.)*, heath, muir *(Scot.)* • *The small town is high up on the moors.*

moor[2] = **tie up**, fix, secure, anchor, dock, lash, berth, fasten, make fast • *She had moored her boat on the right bank of the river.*

moot AS A VERB = **bring up**, propose, suggest, introduce, put forward, ventilate, broach • *When the theatre idea was first mooted, I had my doubts.*

▸ **AS AN ADJECTIVE** = **debatable**, open, controversial, doubtful, unsettled, unresolved, undecided, at issue, arguable, open to debate, contestable, disputable • *How long he'll be able to do so is a moot point.*

mop AS A NOUN 1 = **squeegee**, sponge, swab • *She was standing outside the door with a mop and bucket.*
2 = **mane**, shock, mass, tangle, mat, thatch • *He was dark-eyed with a mop of tight curls.*

▸ **AS A VERB** = **clean**, wash, wipe, sponge, swab, squeegee • *There was a woman mopping the stairs.*

▸ **IN PHRASES: mop something up** 1 = **clean up**, wash, sponge, mop, soak up, swab, wipe up, sop up • *A waiter mopped up the mess as best he could.*
2 = **finish off**, clear, account for, eliminate, round up, clean out, neutralize, pacify • *The infantry divisions mopped up remaining centres of resistance.*

mope = **brood**, moon, pine, hang around, idle, fret, pout, languish, waste time, sulk, be gloomy, eat your heart out, be apathetic, be dejected, be down in the mouth *(informal)*, have a long face, wear a long face, go about like a half-shut knife *(informal)* • *Get on with life; don't sit back and mope.*

moral AS AN ADJECTIVE 1 = **ethical**, social, behavioural • *the moral issues involved in 'playing God'*
2 = **psychological**, emotional, mental • *He showed moral courage in defending his ideas.*
3 = **good**, just, right, principled, pure, decent, innocent, proper, noble, ethical, upright, honourable, honest, righteous, virtuous, blameless, high-minded, chaste, upstanding, meritorious, incorruptible • *The committee members are moral, competent people.*

OPPOSITES: immoral, unfair, improper

▸ **AS A NOUN** = **lesson**, meaning, point, message, teaching, import, significance, precept • *The moral of the story is, let the buyer beware.*

▸ **AS A PLURAL NOUN** = **morality**, standards, conduct, principles, behaviour, manners, habits, ethics, integrity, mores, scruples • *Western ideas and morals*

QUOTATIONS

An Englishman thinks he is moral when he is only uncomfortable
[George Bernard Shaw *Man and Superman*]

Food first, then morals
[Bertolt Brecht *The Threepenny Opera*]

morale = **confidence**, heart, spirit, temper, self-esteem, team spirit, mettle, esprit de corps • *Many pilots are suffering from low morale.*

morality 1 = **virtue**, justice, principles, morals, honour, integrity, goodness, honesty, purity, decency, fair play, righteousness, good behaviour, propriety, chastity, probity, rectitude, rightness, uprightness • *an effort to preserve traditional morality*
2 = **ethics**, conduct, principles, ideals, morals, manners, habits, philosophy, mores, moral code • *aspects of Christian morality*
3 = **rights and wrongs**, ethics, ethicality • *the morality of blood sports*

QUOTATIONS

Morality is the herd-instinct in the individual
[Friedrich Nietzsche *Die fröhliche Wissenschaft*]

Morality is a private and costly luxury
[Henry Brooks Adams *The Education of Henry Adams*]

One becomes moral as soon as one is unhappy
[Marcel Proust *Within a Budding Grove*]

Morality comes with the sad wisdom of age, when the sense of curiosity has withered
[Graham Greene *A Sort of Life*]

morass 1 = **mess**, confusion, chaos, jam *(informal)*, tangle, mix-up, muddle, quagmire • *I tried to drag myself out of the morass of despair.*
2 = **marsh**, swamp, bog, slough, fen, moss *(Scot. & Northern English dialect)*, quagmire, marshland, muskeg *(Canad.)* • *a morass of gooey mud*

moratorium = **postponement**, stay, freeze, halt, suspension, respite, standstill • *a one-year moratorium on nuclear testing*

morbid 1 = **gruesome**, sick, dreadful, ghastly, hideous, unhealthy, grisly, macabre, horrid, ghoulish, unwholesome • *Some people have a morbid fascination with crime.*
2 = **gloomy**, brooding, pessimistic, melancholy, sombre, grim, glum, lugubrious, funereal, low-spirited • *He was in no mood for any morbid introspection.*

OPPOSITES: happy, cheerful, bright

3 = **diseased**, sick, infected, deadly, ailing, unhealthy, malignant, sickly, pathological, unsound • *Uraemia is a morbid condition.*

OPPOSITES: healthy, salubrious

mordant = **sarcastic**, cutting, biting, edged, sharp, acid, harsh, stinging, scathing, acrimonious, pungent, incisive, caustic, venomous, astringent, vitriolic, acerbic, trenchant, waspish, mordacious • *He describes the situation with mordant wit.*

more AS A DETERMINER = **extra**, additional, spare, new, other, added, further, fresh, new-found, supplementary • *Give them a bit more information.*

▸ **AS A NOUN** = **a larger amount**, extra, an increase, a supplement, an addition, a greater amount • *I had four hundred dollars in my pocket. He had more.*

▸ **AS AN ADVERB** 1 = **to a greater extent**, longer, better, further, some more • *When we are tired we feel pain more.*
2 = **moreover**, also, in addition, besides, furthermore, what's more, on top of that, to boot, into the bargain, over and above that • *He was blind, and more, his eyepits were scooped hollows.*

▸ **IN PHRASES: more or less** = **approximately**, about, nearly, close to, roughly, in the region of • *These guys were more or less my own age.*

what's more = **besides**, also, in addition, moreover, furthermore, on top of that, to boot, into the bargain, over and above that • *You should remember. And what's more, you should get it right.*

m

QUOTATIONS
Please, sir, I want some more
[Charles Dickens *Oliver Twist*]
PROVERBS
The more, the merrier

moreover = **furthermore**, also, further, in addition, too, as well, besides, likewise, what is more, to boot, additionally, into the bargain, withal *(literary)* • *There was a man behind her. Moreover he was observing her strangely.*

mores = **customs**, ways, practices, traditions, way of life, conventions, tikanga *(N.Z.)* • *the accepted mores of British society*

moribund = **declining**, weak, waning, standing still, stagnant, stagnating, on the way out, at a standstill, obsolescent, on its last legs, forceless • *the moribund housing market*

morning AS A NOUN 1 = **before noon**, forenoon, morn *(poetic)*, a.m. • *On Sunday morning he was woken by the telephone.*
2 = **dawn**, sunrise, morrow *(archaic)*, first light, daybreak, break of day • *I started to lose hope of ever seeing the morning.*
▸ IN PHRASES: **morning, noon and night** = **all the time**, always, constantly, forever, continually, perpetually, incessantly, without a break, unceasingly, twenty-four-seven *(informal)* • *You get fit by playing the game morning, noon and night.*
▸ RELATED ADJECTIVE: matutinal
QUOTATIONS
Awake! For morning in the bowl of night
Has flung the stone that puts the stars to flight
And lo! the Hunter of the East has caught
The Sultan's turret in a noose of light
[Edward Fitzgerald *The Rubáiyát of Omar Khayyám*]

moron = **fool**, idiot, dummy *(slang)*, berk *(Brit. slang)*, charlie *(Brit. informal)*, tosser *(Brit. slang)*, dope *(informal)*, jerk *(slang, chiefly U.S. & Canad.)*, ass, plank *(Brit. slang)*, prick *(derogatory slang)*, wally *(slang)*, prat *(slang)*, plonker *(slang)*, coot, geek *(slang)*, twit *(informal, chiefly Brit.)*, bonehead *(slang)*, chump, dunce, imbecile, cretin, oaf, simpleton, airhead *(slang)*, dimwit *(informal)*, dipstick *(Brit. slang)*, dickhead *(slang)*, gonzo *(slang)*, schmuck *(U.S. slang)*, dork *(slang)*, nitwit *(informal)*, dolt, blockhead, divvy *(Brit. slang)*, pillock *(Brit. slang)*, halfwit, dweeb *(U.S. slang)*, putz *(U.S. slang)*, fathead *(informal)*, weenie *(U.S. informal)*, eejit *(Scot. & Irish)*, thicko *(Brit. slang)*, dumb-ass *(slang)*, gobshite *(Irish taboo slang)*, dunderhead, numpty *(Scot. informal)*, doofus *(slang, chiefly U.S.)*, lamebrain *(informal)*, mental defective, fuckwit *(taboo slang)*, thickhead, muttonhead *(slang)*, nerd *or* nurd *(slang)*, numbskull *or* numskull, dorba *or* dorb *(Austral. slang)*, bogan *(Austral. slang)* • *I used to think that he was a moron.*

moronic = **idiotic**, simple, foolish, mindless, thick, stupid, daft *(informal)*, retarded, gormless *(Brit. informal)*, brainless, cretinous, unintelligent, dimwitted *(informal)*, asinine, imbecilic, braindead *(informal)*, mentally defective, dumb-ass *(slang)*, doltish, dead from the neck up *(informal)*, halfwitted, Boeotian, muttonheaded *(slang)* • *It was wanton, moronic vandalism.*

morose = **sullen**, miserable, moody, gloomy, down, low, cross, blue, depressed, sour, crabbed, pessimistic, perverse, melancholy, dour, crusty, glum, surly, mournful, gruff, churlish, sulky, taciturn, ill-tempered, in a bad mood, grouchy *(informal)*, down in the dumps *(informal)*, crabby, saturnine, ill-humoured, ill-natured • *She was morose, pale and reticent.*
OPPOSITES: happy, gay, cheerful

morsel = **piece**, bite, bit, slice, scrap, part, grain, taste, segment, fragment, fraction, snack, crumb, nibble, mouthful, tad *(informal, chiefly U.S.)*, titbit, soupçon *(French)* • *a delicious little morsel of meat*

mortal AS AN ADJECTIVE 1 = **human**, worldly, passing, earthly, fleshly, temporal, transient, ephemeral, perishable, corporeal, impermanent, sublunary • *Man is designed to be mortal.*
2 = **fatal**, killing, terminal, deadly, destructive, lethal, murderous, death-dealing • *a mortal blow to terrorism*
3 = **unrelenting**, bitter, sworn, deadly, relentless, to the death, implacable, out-and-out, irreconcilable, remorseless • *Broadcasting was regarded as the mortal enemy of live music.*
4 = **great**, serious, terrible, enormous, severe, extreme, grave, intense, awful, dire, agonizing • *She lived in mortal fear that one day she would be found out.*
5 = **unpardonable**, unforgivable, irremissible • *Masturbation is considered a mortal sin by the church.*
▸ AS A NOUN = **human being**, being, man, woman, body, person, human, individual, earthling • *impossible needs for any mere mortal to meet*
QUOTATIONS
What fools these mortals be!
[William Shakespeare *A Midsummer Night's Dream*]

mortality 1 = **humanity**, transience, impermanence, ephemerality, temporality, corporeality, impermanency • *The event served as a stark reminder of our mortality.*
2 = **death**, dying, fatality, loss of life • *the nation's infant mortality rate*
QUOTATIONS
Dust thou art, and unto dust thou shalt return
[*Bible: Genesis*]
Earth to earth, ashes to ashes, dust to dust
[*Book of Common Prayer*]
Old mortality, the ruins of forgotten times
[Thomas Browne *Hydriotaphia*]
All men think all men mortal but themselves
[Edward Young *Night Thoughts*]
Man that is born of a woman is of few days, and full of trouble. He cometh forth like a flower, and is cut down; he fleeth also as a shadow, and continueth not
[*Bible: Job*]
PROVERBS
Here today and gone tomorrow

mortification 1 = **humiliation**, shame, embarrassment, dissatisfaction, annoyance, chagrin, loss of face, discomfiture, vexation, abasement • *The chairman tried to hide his mortification.*
2 = **discipline**, control, denial, chastening, subjugation, abasement • *ascetism and mortification of the flesh*
3 = **gangrene**, corruption, festering, necrosis, putrescence • *He treated cases of infection, ulceration and mortification.*

mortified = **humiliated**, embarrassed, shamed, crushed, annoyed, humbled, horrified, put down, put out *(informal)*, ashamed, pissed *(U.S. slang)*, confounded, deflated, vexed, affronted, pissed off *(taboo slang)*, displeased, chagrined, chastened, discomfited, abashed, put to shame, rendered speechless, made to eat humble pie *(informal)*, given a showing-up *(informal)* • *I was absolutely mortified about making the mistake.*

mortify 1 = **humiliate**, disappoint, embarrass, shame, crush, annoy, humble, deflate, vex, affront, displease, chagrin, discomfit, abase, put someone to shame, abash • *She mortified her family by leaving her husband.*
2 = **discipline**, control, deny, subdue, chasten, abase • *The most austere of the Christians felt the need to mortify themselves.*

mortuary = **morgue**, funeral home *(U.S.)*, funeral parlour • *The bodies were taken to a mortuary.*

Moslem
▹ *See panel* **Islam**

mosque = **temple** • *We go for prayers at the mosque five times a day.*

most = **nearly all**, the majority, the mass, almost all, the bulk, the lion's share, the preponderance • *By stopping smoking you are undoing most of the damage caused.*

mostly 1 = **mainly**, largely, chiefly, principally, primarily, above all, on the whole, predominantly, for the most part, almost entirely • *I am working with mostly highly motivated people.*
2 = **generally**, usually, on the whole, most often, as a rule, customarily • *We mostly go to clubs, or round to a friend's house.*

mote = **speck**, spot, grain, particle, fragment, atom, mite • *Dust motes swirled in the sunlight.*

moth
▸ NAME OF YOUNG: caterpillar
▸ RELATED ENTHUSIAST: lepidopterist
▹ *See panel* **Butterflies and moths**

moth-eaten = **decayed**, ragged, shabby, worn-out, seedy, dilapidated, tattered, threadbare, decrepit, grungy (*slang, chiefly U.S. & Canad.*), outworn, scuzzy (*slang, chiefly U.S.*) • *a moth-eaten leopardskin jacket*

mother AS A NOUN 1 = **female parent**, mum (*Brit. informal*), ma (*informal*), mater, dam, old woman (*informal*), mom (*U.S. & Canad.*), mummy (*Brit. informal*), old lady (*informal*), foster mother, birth mother, biological mother • *Mother and child form a close attachment.*
2 = **wellspring**, source, origin, inspiration, stimulus, fountain, genesis, fount • *Necessity is the mother of invention.*
▸ AS A VERB 1 = **give birth to**, produce, bear, bring forth, drop • *She had dreamed of mothering a large family.*
2 = **nurture**, raise, protect, tend, nurse, rear, care for, cherish • *She felt a great need to mother him.*
3 = **pamper**, baby, spoil, indulge, fuss over, cosset, mollycoddle, overprotect • *Don't mother me!*
▸ AS A MODIFIER = **native**, natural, innate, inborn, connate • *He looks on Turkey as his mother country.*
▸ RELATED ADJECTIVE: maternal

QUOTATIONS

So for the mother's sake the child was dear
And dearer was the mother for the child
[Samuel Taylor Coleridge *'Sonnet to a Friend Who Asked How I Felt When the Nurse First Presented My Infant Child to Me'*]

Honour thy mother and thy father
[*Bible: Exodus*]

As is the mother, so is her daughter
[*Bible: Ezekiel*]

All women become like their mothers. That is their tragedy. No man does. That is his
[Oscar Wilde *The Importance of Being Earnest*]

motherhood

QUOTATIONS

The hand that rocks the cradle
Is the hand that rules the world
[William Ross Wallace *John O'London's Treasure Trove*]

motherland = **native land**, homeland, fatherland, country of origin, mother country, whenua (*N.Z.*), Godzone (*Austral. informal*) • *Central to our belief is a love for the motherland.*

motherly = **maternal**, loving, kind, caring, warm, comforting, sheltering, gentle, tender, protective, fond, affectionate • *a plump, motherly woman*

mother-of-pearl
▸ RELATED ADJECTIVE: nacreous

motif 1 = **design**, form, shape, decoration, ornament • *wallpaper with a rose motif*
2 = **theme**, idea, subject, concept, leitmotif • *the motif of magical apples in fairytales*

motion AS A NOUN 1 = **movement**, action, mobility, passing, travel, progress, flow, passage, locomotion, motility, kinesics • *the laws governing light, sound and motion*
2 = **gesture**, sign, wave, signal, gesticulation • *He made a neat chopping motion with his hand.*
3 = **proposal**, suggestion, recommendation, proposition, submission • *The conference is now debating the motion.*
▸ AS A VERB = **gesture**, direct, wave, signal, nod, beckon, gesticulate • *She motioned for the doors to be opened.*
▸ IN PHRASES: **in motion** 1 = **in progress**, going on, under way, afoot, on the go (*informal*) • *His job begins in earnest now that the World Cup is in motion.*
2 = **moving**, going, working, travelling, functioning, under way, operational, on the move (*informal*) • *Always stay seated while a bus is in motion.*
set *or* **put something in motion** = **start**, begin, launch, institute, initiate, activate, spark off, trigger off • *Her sharp comments set in motion the events that led to her downfall.*
▸ RELATED ADJECTIVE: kinetic
▸ RELATED MANIA: kinesomania
▸ RELATED PHOBIA: kinesophobia

motionless = **still**, static, stationary, standing, fixed, frozen, calm, halted, paralysed, lifeless, inert, unmoved, transfixed, at rest, immobile, inanimate, at a standstill, unmoving, stock-still • *He stood there motionless.*
OPPOSITES: moving, travelling, active

motion picture = **picture**, film (*Brit.*), movie (*U.S.*), flick (*informal*) • *It was there that I saw my first motion picture.*

motivate 1 = **inspire**, drive, stimulate, provoke, lead, move, cause, prompt, stir, trigger, set off, induce, arouse, prod, get going, instigate, impel, actuate, give incentive to, inspirit • *His hard work was motivated by a need to achieve.*
2 = **stimulate**, drive, inspire, stir, arouse, get going, galvanize, incentivize • *How do you motivate people to work hard and efficiently?*

motivation 1 = **incentive**, inspiration, motive, stimulus, reason, spur, impulse, persuasion, inducement, incitement, instigation, carrot and stick • *Money is my motivation.*
2 = **inspiration**, drive, desire, ambition, hunger, interest • *The team may be lacking motivation for next week's game.*

motive AS A NOUN = **reason**, motivation, cause, ground(s), design, influence, purpose, object, intention, spur, incentive, inspiration, stimulus, rationale, inducement, incitement, mainspring, the why and wherefore • *Police have ruled out robbery as a motive for the killing.*
▸ AS AN ADJECTIVE = **moving**, driving, motivating, operative, activating, impelling • *the motive power behind a boxer's punches*

motley = **miscellaneous**, mixed, varied, diversified, mingled, unlike, assorted, disparate, dissimilar, heterogeneous • *a motley collection of vans and old buses*
OPPOSITES: miscellaneous, uniform, homogeneous

motor = **engine**, machine, mechanism • *She got in and started the motor.*

motor car
▹ *See panel* **Cars**

motor sport

MOTOR SPORTS

air racing	motor-cycle racing	rallycross
autocross	motor racing	scrambling
drag racing	motor rallying *or* rallying	speedway
karting		stock car racing
motocross		truck racing

motorway = **highway** (*U.S.*), A road, main road, freeway (*U.S.*), autobahn (*German*) • *the national motorway network*

mottled = **blotchy**, spotted, pied, streaked, marbled, flecked, variegated, chequered, speckled, freckled, dappled, tabby, stippled, piebald, brindled • *mottled green and yellow leaves*

motto = **saying**, slogan, maxim, rule, cry, formula, gnome, adage, proverb, dictum, precept, byword, watchword, tag-line • *What is your regiment's motto?*

mould[1] **AS A NOUN 1 = cast**, form, die, shape, pattern, stamp, matrix • *the moulds for the foundry*
2 = design, line, style, fashion, build, form, cut, kind, shape, structure, pattern, brand, frame, construction, stamp, format, configuration • *At first sight, he is not cast in the leading man mould.*
3 = nature, character, sort, kind, quality, type, stamp, kidney, calibre, ilk • *every man of heroic mould who struggles up to eminence*
▸ **AS A VERB 1 = shape**, make, work, form, create, model, fashion, cast, stamp, construct, carve, forge, sculpt • *We moulded a statue out of mud.*
2 = influence, make, form, control, direct, affect, shape • *The experience has moulded her personality.*

mould[2] **= fungus**, blight, mildew, mustiness, mouldiness • *jars of jam with mould on them*

mould[3] **= soil**, earth, dirt, humus, loam • *If the soil is very dry or in poor condition, dig in some leaf-mould or compost before planting.*

moulder = decay, waste, break down, crumble, rot, disintegrate, perish, decompose • *the empty, mouldering old house*

mouldy = stale, spoiled, rotting, decaying, bad, rotten, blighted, musty, fusty, mildewed • *mouldy bread*

mound 1 = heap, bing *(Scot.)*, pile, drift, stack, rick • *huge mounds of dirt*
2 = hill, bank, rise, dune, embankment, knoll, hillock, kopje or koppie *(S. African)* • *We sat on a grassy mound and had our picnic.*
3 = barrow, tumulus • *an ancient, man-made burial mound*
4 = earthwork, rampart, bulwark, motte *(History)* • *a rough double-moated mound earmarked as an ancient monument*
▸ **RELATED ADJECTIVE:** tumular

mount AS A VERB 1 = launch, stage, prepare, deliver, set in motion • *a security operation mounted by the army*
2 = increase, build, grow, swell, intensify, escalate, multiply • *For several hours, tension mounted.*
OPPOSITES: reduce, fall, decrease
3 = accumulate, increase, collect, gather, build up, pile up, amass, cumulate • *The uncollected garbage mounts in the streets.*
4 = ascend, scale, climb (up), go up, clamber up, make your way up • *He was mounting the stairs to the tower.*
OPPOSITES: go down, descend, make your way down
5 = climb up on, get on to, jump on to, step aboard, clamber up on • *He mounted the stage and addressed the audience.*
6 = get (up) on, jump on, straddle, climb onto, climb up on, hop on to, bestride, get on the back of, get astride • *He mounted his horse and rode away.*
OPPOSITES: get off, jump off, dismount
7 = display, set, frame, set off • *He mounts the work in a frame.*
8 = fit, place, set, position, set up, fix, secure, attach, install, erect, put in place, put in position, emplace • *The fuel tank is mounted on the side of the truck.*
9 = display, present, stage, prepare, put on, organize, get up *(informal)*, exhibit, put on display • *mounting an exhibition of historical Tiffany jewellery*
▸ **AS A NOUN 1 = horse**, steed *(literary)* • *the number of owners who care for older mounts*
2 = backing, setting, support, stand, base, mounting, frame, fixture, foil • *Even on a solid mount, any movement nearby may shake the image.*

mountain AS A NOUN 1 = peak, mount, height, ben *(Scot.)*, horn, ridge, fell *(Brit.)*, berg *(S. African)*, alp, pinnacle, elevation, Munro, eminence • *Ben Nevis, Britain's highest mountain*
2 = heap, mass, masses, pile, a great deal, ton, stack, abundance, mound, profusion, shedload *(Brit. informal)* • *They are faced with a mountain of bureaucracy.*
3 = surplus, excess, glut, surfeit, oversupply, overabundance • *the weight of the EU butter mountain*
▸ **IN PHRASES: move mountains 1 = perform miracles**, work wonders, do the impossible, achieve the impossible • *If you believe you can move mountains, you are halfway there.*
2 = make every effort, pull out all the stops, bend over backwards *(informal)*, do your utmost *or* best • *We've moved mountains to provide this service.*

PROVERBS
If the mountain will not come to Mahomet, Mahomet must go to the mountain

▹ *See panel* **Mountains**

mountainous 1 = high, towering, soaring, steep, rocky, highland, alpine, upland • *a mountainous region*
2 = huge, great, enormous, mighty, immense, daunting, gigantic, monumental, mammoth, prodigious, hulking, ponderous • *a plan designed to reduce the company's mountainous debt*
OPPOSITES: little, small, tiny

mountainside = mountain face, ridge, hillside, escarpment • *The couple trudged up the dark mountainside.*

mourn 1 *often with* **for = grieve for**, miss, lament, keen for, weep for, sorrow for, wail for, wear black for • *She still mourned her father.*
2 = bemoan, rue, deplore, bewail • *We mourned the loss of our cities.*

mournful 1 = dismal, sad, unhappy, miserable, gloomy, grieving, melancholy, sombre, heartbroken, desolate, woeful, rueful, heavy, downcast, grief-stricken, lugubrious, disconsolate, joyless, funereal, heavy-hearted, down in the dumps *(informal)*, cheerless, brokenhearted • *He looked mournful, even near to tears.*
OPPOSITES: happy, bright, sunny
2 = sad, distressing, unhappy, tragic, painful, afflicting, melancholy, harrowing, grievous, woeful, deplorable, lamentable, plaintive, calamitous, sorrowful, piteous • *the mournful wail of bagpipes*
OPPOSITES: happy, pleasant, cheerful

mourning 1 = grieving, grief, bereavement, weeping, woe, lamentation, keening • *The period of mourning and bereavement may be long.*
2 = black, weeds, sackcloth and ashes, widow's weeds • *Yesterday the whole country was in mourning.*

mouse
▸ **RELATED ADJECTIVE:** murine
▸ **RELATED MANIA:** musomania
▸ **RELATED PHOBIA:** musophobia

moustache = whiskers, face fungus *(informal)*, mustachio, 'tash *(informal)* • *He was short and bald and had a moustache.*

mousy *or* **mousey 1 = brownish**, plain, dull, drab, colourless, indeterminate • *a man of medium build and collar-length mousy hair*
2 = shy, quiet, timid, ineffectual, self-effacing, diffident, timorous, unassertive • *He remembered her as a small, mousy woman, invariably worried.*

mouth AS A NOUN 1 = lips, trap *(slang)*, chops *(slang)*, jaws, gob *(slang, esp. Brit.)*, maw, yap *(slang)*, cakehole *(Brit. slang)* • *She clamped her hand against her mouth.*
2 = entrance, opening, gateway, cavity, door, aperture, crevice, orifice • *the mouth of the tunnel*
3 = opening, lip, rim • *a lit candle stuck in the bottle's mouth*
4 = inlet, outlet, estuary, firth, outfall, debouchment • *the mouth of the river*
5 = boasting, gas *(informal)*, bragging, hot air *(slang)*, braggadocio, idle talk, empty talk • *She is all mouth and no talent.*
6 = insolence, lip *(slang)*, sauce *(informal)*, cheek *(informal)*, rudeness, impudence, backchat *(informal)*

MOUNTAINS

Aconcagua
Adams
Albert Edward
Anai Mudi
Aneto
Annapurna
Apo
Aragats
Aran Fawddwy
Ararat
Arber
Argentera
Belukha
Ben Lomond
Ben Macdhui
Ben Nevis
Blackburn
Blanca Peak
Blue Mountain Peak
Bona
Brocken
Carmarthen Van
Carmel
Carrauntohill
Cerro de Mulhacén
Citlaltépetl
Clingman's Dome
Cook
Corcovado
Corno
Croagh Patrick
Demavend
Dhaulagiri
Eiger
Elbert
Elbrus
El Capitan
Emi Koussi
Estrella
Everest
Finsteraarhorn
Fuji
Gannet Peak
Gerlachovka
Grand Teton
Gran Paradiso
Harney Peak
Helicon
Helvellyn
Hermon
Humphreys Peak
Hymettus
Ida
Illimani
Isto
Jebel Musa
Jungfrau
K2 *or* Godwin Austen
Kamet
Kangchenjunga
Kenya
Kilimanjaro
Kinabalu
Kings Peak
Klínovec
Kommunizma Peak
Kongur Shan
Kosciusko
Lenin Peak
Leone
Logan
Longs Peak
Mansfield
Marcy
Markham
Marmolada
Masharbrum
Matterhorn
McKinley
Mitchell
Mont Blanc
Mount of Olives
Mulhacén
Munku-Sardyk
Musala
Nanda Devi
Nanga Parbat
Narodnaya
Nebo
Negoiu
Olympus
Ossa
Palomar
Parnassus
Pelion
Pentelikon
Perdido
Petermann Peak
Pikes Peak
Pilatus
Piz Bernina
Pobeda Peak
Puy de Dôme
Rainier
Rigi
Robson
Rock Creek
Rosa
Rushmore
Scafell Pike
Schneekoppe
Scopus
Sinai
Siple
Sir Sandford
Sir Wilfrid Laurier
Skalitsy
Slide Mountain
Smólikas
Snowdon
Sorata
Stanley
Sugar Loaf Mountain
Table Mountain
Tabor
Teide
Tengri Khan
Thabana Ntlenyana
Timpanogos
Tirich Mir
Toubkal
Troglav
Ulugh Muztagh
Venusberg
Victoria
Viso
Waddington
Washington
Waun Fach
Weisshorn
White Mountain
Whitney
Wrangell
Zard Kuh
Zugspitze

▸ **AS A VERB** = **utter**, say, speak, voice, express, pronounce, articulate, enunciate, verbalize, vocalize, say insincerely, say for form's sake • *I mouthed some sympathetic platitudes.*
▸ **IN PHRASES: down in** *or* **at the mouth** = **depressed**, down, blue, sad, unhappy, miserable, melancholy, dejected, dispirited, downcast, disheartened, crestfallen, down in the dumps *(informal)*, sick as a parrot *(informal)*, in low spirits
keep your mouth shut = **say nothing**, keep quiet, keep mum *(informal)*, not tell a soul, keep something under your hat • *You'd do well to keep your mouth shut about it.*
mouth off = **rant**, rave, spout, sound off, declaim, jabber • *He received a yellow card for mouthing off to the referee.*
▸ **RELATED ADJECTIVES:** oral, oscular, stomatic

PROVERBS
A shut mouth catches no flies

mouthful = **taste**, little, bite, bit, drop, sample, swallow, sip, sup, spoonful, morsel, forkful • *Could I try a mouthful of that?*

mouthpiece 1 = **spokesperson**, agent, representative, delegate, spokesman *or* spokeswoman • *Their mouthpiece is the vice-president.*
2 = **publication**, journal, organ, periodical • *The newspaper is regarded as a mouthpiece of the ministry.*

movable = **portable**, mobile, transferable, detachable, not fixed, transportable, portative • *The wooden fence is movable.*

move AS A VERB 1 = **transfer**, change, carry, transport, switch, shift, transpose • *She moved the sheaf of papers into position.*
2 = **go**, walk, march, advance, progress, shift, proceed, stir, budge, make a move, change position • *She waited for him to get up, but he didn't move.*
3 = **take action**, act, do something, take steps, take the initiative, make a move, get moving *(informal)*, take measures • *Industrialists must move fast to take advantage of this opportunity.*
4 = **relocate**, leave, remove, quit, go away, migrate, emigrate, move house, flit *(Scot. & Northern English dialect)*, decamp, up sticks *(Brit. informal)*, pack your bags *(informal)*, change residence • *My home is in Yorkshire and I don't want to move.*
5 = **change**, shift, convert, transform, alter, diversify • *He moved from being a researcher to being a lecturer.*
6 = **progress**, develop, advance, make progress, make headway • *Events are moving fast.*
7 = **change your mind**, change, shift, reconsider, budge, climb down, do a U-turn, back-pedal, do an about-turn *(Brit. informal)*, change your tune, do an aboutface • *He made it clear he would not move on this issue.*
8 = **drive**, lead, cause, influence, persuade, push, shift, inspire, prompt, stimulate, motivate, induce, shove, activate, propel, rouse, prod, incite, impel, set going • *The hearings moved him to come up with these suggestions.*
OPPOSITES: stop, prevent, discourage
9 = **touch**, affect, excite, impress, stir, agitate, disquiet, make an impression on, tug at your heartstrings *(often facetious)* • *These stories surprised and moved me.*
10 = **circulate**, mix, associate, go round, hang out *(informal)*, socialize, keep company, fraternize • *She moves in high society circles in London.*
11 = **propose**, suggest, urge, recommend, request, advocate, submit, put forward • *I moved that the case be dismissed.*
▸ **AS A NOUN** 1 = **action**, act, step, movement, shift, motion, manoeuvre, deed • *Daniel's eyes followed her every move.*
2 = **ploy**, action, measure, step, trick, initiative, stroke, tactic, manoeuvre, deed, dodge, tack, ruse, gambit, stratagem • *The cut in interest rates was a wise move.*
3 = **transfer**, posting, shift, removal, migration, relocation, flit *(Scot. & Northern English dialect)*, flitting *(Scot. & Northern English dialect)*, change of address • *He announced his move to Montparnasse in 1909.*
4 = **turn**, go, play, chance, shot *(informal)*, opportunity • *It's your move, chess fans tell Sports Minister.*
▸ **IN PHRASES: get a move on** = **speed up**, hurry (up), get going, get moving, get cracking *(informal)*, step on it *(informal)*, make haste, shake a leg *(informal)*, get your skates on *(informal)*, stir yourself • *I'd better get a move on if I want to finish on time.*
make a move 1 = **leave**, split *(informal)*, be off, set off,

depart, get going, push off *(informal)*, be on your way, shove off *(informal)*, take yourself off, skedaddle *(informal)*, take your leave • *I suppose we'd better make a move.*
2 = **take action**, act, do something, take the initiative, get moving *(informal)*, take measures • *A week before the deal, they made a move to pull out.*
on the move 1 = in transit, moving, travelling, journeying, on the road *(informal)*, under way, voyaging, on the run, in motion, on the wing • *My husband and I were always on the move.*
2 = **active**, moving, developing, advancing, progressing, succeeding, stirring, going forward, astir • *Aviation is on the move, and many airlines are forming alliances.*

movement 1 = **group**, party, organization, grouping, front, camp, faction • *a nationalist movement that's gaining strength*
2 = **campaign**, drive, push, crusade • *He contributed to the Movement for the Ordination of Women.*
3 = **move**, act, action, operation, motion, gesture, manoeuvre • *He could watch her every movement.*
4 = **activity**, moving, stirring, bustle, agitation • *There was movement behind the door.*
5 = **advance**, progress, flow, progression • *the movement of the fish going up river*
6 = **transfer**, transportation, displacement • *the movement of people, goods and services across borders*
7 = **trend**, flow, swing, current, tendency • *the movement towards democracy*
8 = **development**, change, shift, variation, fluctuation • *the meeting seems to have produced no movement on either side*
9 = **progression**, advance, progress, breakthrough • *the participants believed movement forward was possible*
10 = **section**, part, division, passage • *the first movement of Beethoven's 7th symphony*

movie AS A NOUN = **film**, picture, feature, flick *(slang)*, motion picture, moving picture *(U.S.)* • *That was the first movie he ever made.*
▸ IN PHRASES: **the movies = the cinema**, a film, the pictures *(informal)*, the flicks *(slang)*, the silver screen *(informal)* • *He took her to the movies.*

moving 1 = **emotional**, touching, affecting, exciting, inspiring, stirring, arousing, poignant, emotive, impelling • *It was a moving moment for them.*
OPPOSITES: uninspiring, unimpressive, unemotional
2 = **mobile**, running, active, going, operational, in motion, driving, kinetic, movable, motile, unfixed • *the moving parts in the engine*
OPPOSITES: still, fixed, stationary
3 = **motivating**, stimulating, dynamic, propelling, inspirational, impelling, stimulative • *He has been a moving force in the world of art criticism.*

mow AS A VERB = **cut**, crop, trim, shear, scythe • *He mowed the lawn and did other routine chores.*
▸ IN PHRASES: **mow something** *or* **someone down = massacre**, butcher, slaughter, cut down, shoot down, blow away *(slang, chiefly U.S.)*, cut to pieces • *Gunmen mowed down 10 people in the attack.*

much AS AN ADVERB 1 = **greatly**, a lot, considerably, decidedly, exceedingly, appreciably • *My hairstyle has never changed much.*
OPPOSITES: hardly, slightly, barely
2 = **often**, a lot, regularly, routinely, a great deal, frequently, many times, habitually, on many occasions, customarily • *She didn't see her father much.*
▸ AS AN ADJECTIVE = **great**, a lot of, plenty of, considerable, substantial, piles of *(informal)*, ample, abundant, copious, oodles of *(informal)*, plenteous, sizable *or* sizeable amount, shedful *(slang)*, shitload *(taboo slang)* • *They are grown in full sun, without much water.*
OPPOSITES: little, inadequate, insufficient
▸ AS A PRONOUN = **a lot**, plenty, a great deal, lots *(informal)*, masses *(informal)*, loads *(informal)*, tons *(informal)*, heaps *(informal)*, a good deal, an appreciable amount • *There was so much to talk about.*
OPPOSITES: little, very little, not much

QUOTATIONS
much of a muchness
[John Vanburgh & Colley Cibber *The Provok'd Husband*]

muck AS A NOUN 1 = **dirt**, mud, filth, shit *(taboo slang)*, crap *(taboo slang)*, sewage, ooze, scum, sludge, mire, slime, slob *(Irish)*, gunk *(informal)*, gunge *(informal)*, crud *(slang)*, kak *(S. African informal)*, grot *(slang)* • *This congealed muck was interfering with the filter.*
2 = **manure**, shit *(taboo slang)*, crap *(taboo slang)*, dung, ordure • *He could smell muck and clean fresh hay.*
▸ IN PHRASES: **muck about** *or* **around = fool about** *or* **around**, amuse yourself, play about *or* around, fiddle about *or* around, mess about *or* around *(informal)* • *He spent his summers mucking around in boats.*
muck about *or* **around with something = interfere with**, tamper with, tinker with, meddle with, fiddle about *or* around with, mess about *or* around with • *Who's been mucking around with my computer?*
muck something up = ruin, bungle, botch, make a mess of, blow *(slang)*, mar, spoil, muff, make a nonsense of, bodge *(informal)*, make a pig's ear of *(informal)*, flub *(U.S. slang)*, make a muck of *(slang)*, mess something up, screw something up *(informal)*, cock something up *(Brit. slang)*, fuck something up *(offensive taboo slang)*, crool or cruel *(Austral. slang)* • *At the 13th hole, I mucked it up.*

PROVERBS
Where there's muck, there's brass

mucky = **dirty**, soiled, muddy, filthy, messy, grimy, mud-caked, bespattered, begrimed, skanky *(slang)*, festy *(Austral. slang)* • *The design means that you can't see the odd mucky mark.*

mud = **dirt**, clay, ooze, silt, sludge, mire, slime, slob *(Irish)*, gloop *(informal)* • *Their lorry got stuck in the mud.*

muddle AS A NOUN = **confusion**, mess, disorder, chaos, plight, tangle, mix-up, clutter, disarray, daze, predicament, jumble, ravel, perplexity, disorganization, hotchpotch, hodgepodge *(U.S.)*, pig's breakfast *(informal)*, fankle *(Scot.)* • *My thoughts are all in a muddle.*
▸ AS A VERB 1 = **jumble**, confuse, disorder, scramble, tangle, mix up, make a mess of • *Already some people have begun to muddle the two names.*
2 = **confuse**, bewilder, daze, confound, perplex, disorient, stupefy, befuddle • *She felt muddled, and a wave of dizziness swept over her.*
▸ IN PHRASES: **muddle along** *or* **through = scrape by**, make it, manage, cope, get along, get by *(informal)*, manage somehow • *We will muddle through and just play it day by day.*

muddled 1 = **incoherent**, confused, loose, vague, unclear, woolly, muddleheaded • *the muddled thinking of the Government's transport policy*
OPPOSITES: clear, exact, precise
2 = **bewildered**, confused, at sea, dazed, perplexed, disoriented, stupefied, befuddled • *I'm afraid I'm a little muddled. I don't know where to begin.*
3 = **jumbled**, confused, disordered, scrambled, tangled, chaotic, messy, mixed-up, disorganized, higgledy-piggledy *(informal)*, disarrayed • *a muddled pile of historical manuscripts*
OPPOSITES: organized, orderly, cut-and-dried *(informal)*

muddy AS AN ADJECTIVE 1 = **boggy**, swampy, marshy, miry, quaggy • *a muddy track*
2 = **dirty**, soiled, grimy, mucky, mud-caked, bespattered, skanky *(slang)*, clarty *(Scot. & Northern English dialect)* • *muddy boots*
3 = **dull**, flat, blurred, unclear, smoky, washed-out, dingy, lustreless • *The paper has turned a muddy colour.*

4 = **cloudy**, dirty, foul, opaque, impure, turbid • *He was up to his armpits in muddy water.*
5 = **confused**, vague, unclear, muddled, fuzzy, woolly, hazy, indistinct • *Such muddy thinking is typical of those who have always had it easy.*
▸ AS A VERB 1 = **smear**, soil, dirty, smirch, begrime, bespatter • *The clothes he was wearing were all muddied.*
2 = **confuse**, cloud, obscure, blur, mix up, obfuscate, befog, make unclear • *It's difficult enough without muddying the issue with religion.*

muff = **botch**, bungle, fluff *(informal)*, spoil, screw up *(informal)*, mess up, cock up *(Brit. slang)*, fuck up *(offensive taboo slang)*, make a mess of, mismanage, make a nonsense of, bodge *(informal)*, make a pig's ear of *(informal)*, flub *(U.S. slang)*, make a muck of *(informal)*, crool *or* cruel *(Austral. slang)* • *He muffed his opening speech.*

muffle 1 = **deaden**, suppress, gag, stifle, silence, dull, soften, hush, muzzle, quieten • *He held a handkerchief over the mouthpiece to muffle his voice.*
2 *often with* **up** = **wrap up**, cover, disguise, conceal, cloak, shroud, swathe, envelop, swaddle • *All of us were muffled up in several layers of clothing.*

muffled = **indistinct**, suppressed, subdued, dull, faint, dim, muted, strangled, stifled • *She heard a muffled cough behind her.*

mug[1] = **cup**, pot, jug, beaker, tankard, stein, flagon, toby jug • *He had been drinking mugs of coffee to keep himself awake.*

mug[2] AS A NOUN 1 = **face**, features, countenance, visage, clock *(Brit. slang)*, kisser *(slang)*, dial *(slang)*, mush *(Brit. slang)*, puss *(slang)*, phiz *or* phizog *(Brit. slang)* • *He managed to get his ugly mug on telly.*
2 = **fool**, innocent, sucker *(slang)*, charlie *(Brit. informal)*, gull *(archaic)*, chump *(informal)*, simpleton, putz *(U.S. slang)*, weenie *(U.S. informal)*, muggins *(Brit. slang)*, easy *or* soft touch *(slang)*, dorba *or* dorb *(Austral. slang)*, bogan *(Austral. slang)* • *I feel such a mug for signing the agreement.*
▸ AS A VERB = **attack**, assault, beat up, rob, steam *(informal)*, hold up, do over *(Brit., Austral. & N.Z. slang)*, work over *(slang)*, assail, lay into *(informal)*, put the boot in *(slang)*, duff up *(Brit. slang)*, set about *or* upon, beat *or* knock seven bells out of *(informal)* • *I was getting into my car when this guy tried to mug me.*
▸ IN PHRASES: **mug up (on) something** = **study**, cram *(informal)*, bone up on *(informal)*, swot up on *(Brit. informal)*, get up *(informal)* • *It's advisable to mug up on your Spanish before you go.*

muggy = **humid**, close, damp, sticky, moist, oppressive, stuffy, sultry, clammy • *It was muggy and overcast.*

mule
▸ COLLECTIVE NOUN: barren

mulish = **stubborn**, difficult, rigid, unreasonable, perverse, intractable, inflexible, wilful, recalcitrant, obstinate, intransigent, headstrong, stiff-necked, self-willed, refractory, pig-headed, bull-headed, cross-grained • *He had a flushed, mulish look on his heavy face.*

mull over = **ponder**, consider, study, think about, examine, review, weigh, contemplate, reflect on, think over, muse on, meditate on, ruminate on, deliberate on, turn something over in your mind • *He had been mulling over the idea of making a movie.*

multicoloured = **kaleidoscopic**, colourful, rainbow, psychedelic, motley, jazzy, pied, multicolour, many-coloured • *a set of multicoloured umbrellas*

multifarious = **diverse**, many, different, varied, numerous, multiple, legion, diversified, miscellaneous, sundry, variegated, manifold, multitudinous, multiform • *a composite of multifarious religions and people*

multiple = **many**, several, various, numerous, collective, sundry, manifold, multitudinous • *He died in hospital of multiple injuries.*

multiplicity = **number**, lot, host, mass, variety, load *(informal)*, pile *(informal)*, ton, stack, diversity, heap *(informal)*, array, abundance, myriad, profusion • *a writer who uses a multiplicity of styles*

multiply 1 = **increase**, extend, expand, spread, build up, accumulate, augment, proliferate • *Her husband multiplied his demands on her time.*
OPPOSITES: reduce, decline, decrease
2 = **reproduce**, breed, propagate • *These creatures can multiply quickly.*

multitude 1 = **great number**, lot, host, collection, army, sea, mass, assembly, legion, horde, myriad, concourse, assemblage • *Addiction to drugs can bring a multitude of other problems.*
2 = **crowd**, host, mass, mob, congregation, swarm, sea, horde, throng, great number • *the multitudes that surround the Pope*
3 = **public**, mob, herd, populace, rabble, proletariat, common people, hoi polloi, commonalty • *The hideous truth was hidden from the multitude.*

multitudinous = **numerous**, many, considerable, countless, legion, infinite, abounding, abundant, myriad, teeming, innumerable, copious, manifold, profuse • *He was a man of multitudinous talents.*

mum = **silent**, quiet, dumb, mute, secretive, uncommunicative, unforthcoming, tight-lipped, closemouthed • *I'd be in trouble if I let on. So I kept mum.*

mumble AS A VERB = **mutter**, whisper, murmur, drone, speak indistinctly • *He mumbled a few words.*
▸ AS A NOUN = **murmur**, whisper, whispering, buzzing, muttering, rumble, humming, drone, purr, undertone, susurrus *(literary)* • *She could hear the low mumble of his voice.*

mumbo jumbo 1 = **gibberish**, nonsense, jargon, humbug, cant, Greek *(informal)*, claptrap *(informal)*, gobbledegook *(informal)*, rigmarole, double talk • *It's all full of psychoanalytic mumbo jumbo.*
2 = **superstition**, magic, ritual, hocus-pocus • *He dabbled in all sorts of mumbo jumbo.*

munch = **chew**, champ, crunch, chomp, scrunch, masticate • *Sheep were munching their way through a yellow carpet of leaves.*

mundane 1 = **ordinary**, routine, commonplace, banal, everyday, day-to-day, vanilla *(slang)*, prosaic, humdrum, workaday • *Be willing to do mundane tasks with good grace.*
OPPOSITES: interesting, original, extraordinary
2 = **earthly**, worldly, human, material, fleshly, secular, mortal, terrestrial, temporal, sublunary • *spiritual immortals who had transcended the mundane world*
OPPOSITES: heavenly, spiritual, ethereal

municipal = **civic**, city, public, local, community, council, town, district, urban, metropolitan, borough • *the municipal library*

municipality = **town**, city, district, borough, township, burgh *(Scot.)*, urban community, dorp *(S. African)* • *Traffic is the problem of the municipality.*

munificence = **generosity**, bounty, philanthropy, benevolence, beneficence, liberality, big-heartedness, generousness, open-handedness, bounteousness, largesse *or* largess • *Thanks to his munificence, the house has survived.*

munificent = **generous**, liberal, lavish, benevolent, rich, princely, free-handed, philanthropic, bountiful, magnanimous, open-handed, big-hearted, unstinting, beneficent, bounteous • *a munificent donation*
OPPOSITES: mean, small, miserly

munitions = **ammunition**, supplies, weapons, equipment, gear • *the shortage of men and munitions*

murder AS A NOUN 1 = **killing**, homicide, massacre, assassination, slaying, bloodshed, carnage, butchery • *The three accused are charged with attempted murder.*

MUSCLES

accelerator	compressor	elevator	levator	quadriceps	sphincter
accessorius	constrictor	erector	lumbricalis	rectus	supinator
adductor	contractor	evertor	masseter	retractor	suspensory *or* suspensor
agonist	corrugator	extensor	opponent	rhomboideus	tensor
antagonist	deltoid	flexor	pectoral	rotator	trapezius
arytenoid	depressor	gastrocnemius	peroneal muscle	sartorius	triceps
biceps	digrastic	gluteus *or* glutaeus	pronator	scalenus	
buccinator	dilator		psoas	soleus	

2 = agony, misery, hell *(informal)* • *I've taken three aspirins, but this headache's still absolute murder.*
▸ **AS A VERB 1 = kill**, massacre, slaughter, assassinate, hit *(slang)*, destroy, waste *(informal)*, do in *(informal)*, eliminate *(slang)*, take out *(slang)*, terminate *(slang)*, butcher, dispatch, slay, blow away *(slang, chiefly U.S.)*, bump off *(slang)*, rub out *(U.S. slang)*, take the life of, do to death • *a thriller about two men who murder a third*
2 = ruin, destroy, mar, spoil, butcher, mangle • *She murdered the song.*
3 = beat decisively, thrash, stuff *(slang)*, cream *(slang, chiefly U.S.)*, tank *(slang)*, hammer *(informal)*, slaughter, lick *(informal)*, wipe the floor with *(informal)*, make mincemeat of *(informal)*, blow someone out of the water *(slang)*, drub, defeat someone utterly • *The front row murdered the Italians in the scrums.*
▸ **RELATED MANIA:** homicidomania

QUOTATIONS
Thou shalt not kill
[*Bible: Exodus*]
Murder will out
[Geoffrey Chaucer *The Nun's Priest's Tale*]
murder most foul
[William Shakespeare *Hamlet*]

murderer = killer, assassin, slayer, butcher, slaughterer, cut-throat, hit man *(slang)* • *a notorious mass murderer*

QUOTATIONS
Every murderer is probably somebody's old friend
[Agatha Christie *The Mysterious Affair at Styles*]
You can always count on a murderer for a fancy prose style
[Vladimir Nabokov *Lolita*]

murderous 1 = deadly, savage, brutal, destructive, fell *(archaic)*, bloody, devastating, cruel, lethal, withering, ferocious, cut-throat, bloodthirsty, barbarous, internecine, death-dealing, sanguinary • *This murderous lunatic could kill them all.*
2 = unpleasant, difficult, dangerous, exhausting, sapping, harrowing, strenuous, arduous, hellish *(informal)*, killing *(informal)* • *Four games in six days is murderous and most unfair.*

murky 1 = dark, gloomy, dismal, grey, dull, obscure, dim, dreary, cloudy, misty, impenetrable, foggy, overcast, dusky, nebulous, cheerless • *Their plane crashed in murky weather.*
OPPOSITES: clear, bright, sunny
2 = dark, obscure, cloudy, impenetrable • *the deep, murky waters of Loch Ness*
3 = questionable, dark, secret, suspect, mysterious, suspicious, dubious, shady *(informal)* • *There has been a murky conspiracy to keep them out of power.*

murmur AS A VERB = mumble, whisper, mutter, drone, purr, babble, speak in an undertone • *He turned and murmured something to the professor.*
▸ **AS A NOUN 1 = whisper**, whispering, mutter, mumble, drone, purr, babble, undertone • *She spoke in a low murmur.*
2 = drone, buzz, hum, purr, thrum • *The clamour of traffic had receded to a distant murmur.*
3 = complaint, word, moan *(informal)*, grumble, beef *(slang)*, grouse, gripe *(informal)* • *She was so flattered she paid up without a murmur.*

muscle AS A NOUN 1 = tendon, sinew, muscle tissue, thew • *He has a strained thigh muscle.*
2 = strength, might, force, power, weight, stamina, potency, brawn, sturdiness • *The team showed more muscle than mental application.*
3 = power, weight, clout *(informal)*, potency, pull *(informal)*, forcefulness • *He used his muscle to persuade Congress to change the law.*
▸ **IN PHRASES: muscle in = impose yourself**, encroach, butt in, force your way in, elbow your way in • *He complained that they were muscling in on his deal.*
▹ *See panel* **Muscles**

muscular = strong, powerful, athletic, strapping, robust, vigorous, sturdy, stalwart, husky *(informal)*, beefy *(informal)*, lusty, sinewy, muscle-bound, brawny, powerfully built, thickset, well-knit • *tanned muscular legs*

muse = ponder, consider, reflect, contemplate, think, weigh up, deliberate, speculate, brood, meditate, mull over, think over, ruminate, cogitate, be lost in thought, be in a brown study • *Many of the papers mused on the fate of the President.* • *He lay and mused in the warm sunlight.*

Muses, the = goddesses of poetry, Camenae *(Roman myth)*, Pierides *(Greek myth)*

MUSES

Calliope	epic poetry
Clio	history
Erato	love poetry
Euterpe	lyric poetry and music
Melpomene	tragedy
Polyhymnia	singing, mime, and sacred dance
Terpsichore	dance and choral song
Thalia	comedy and pastoral poetry
Urania	astronomy

mush 1 = pulp, paste, mash, purée, pap, slush, goo *(informal)* • *Over-ripe bananas will collapse into a mush in this recipe.*
2 = sentimentality, corn *(informal)*, slush *(informal)*, schmaltz *(slang)*, mawkishness • *The lyrics are mush and the melodies banal.*

mushroom = expand, increase, spread, boom, flourish, sprout, burgeon, spring up, shoot up, proliferate, luxuriate, grow rapidly • *The media training industry has mushroomed over the last decade.*
▹ *See panel* **Mushrooms and other edible fungi**

mushy 1 = soft, squidgy *(informal)*, slushy, squashy, squelchy, pulpy, doughy, pappy, semi-liquid, paste-like, semi-solid • *When the fruit is mushy and cooked, remove from the heat.*
2 = sentimental, emotional, wet *(Brit. informal)*, sloppy *(informal)*, corny *(slang)*, sugary, maudlin, weepy, saccharine, syrupy, slushy *(informal)*, mawkish, schmaltzy *(slang)*, icky *(informal)*, three-hankie *(informal)* • *Don't go getting all mushy and sentimental.*

MUSHROOMS AND OTHER EDIBLE FUNGI

black truffle	champignon	meadow mushroom	shaggy ink cap *or* lawyer's wig	white truffle
blewit	chanterelle	morel	shiitake mushroom	wood ear mushroom
button mushroom	enoki	oyster mushroom	straw mushroom	
cep *or* porcini	horn of plenty	puffball		

music

▸ **RELATED MANIAS:** melomania, musicomania

▸ **RELATED PHOBIA:** musicophobia

QUOTATIONS

Music has charms to soothe a savage breast
[William Congreve *The Mourning Bride*]

There's no passion in the human soul,
But finds its food in music
[George Lillo *The Fatal Curiosity*]

Great music is that which penetrates the ear with facility and leaves the memory with difficulty
[Thomas Beecham]

Bach gave us God's word
Mozart gave us God's laughter
Beethoven gave us God's fire
God gave us music that we might pray without words
[*from a German Opera House poster*]

Music is a beautiful opiate, if you don't take it too seriously
[Henry Miller *The Air-Conditioned Nightmare*]

The opera ain't over till the fat lady sings
[Dan Cook]

It is cruel, you know, that music should be so beautiful. It has the beauty of loneliness and of pain: of strength and freedom. The beauty of disappointment and never-satisfied love. The cruel beauty of nature, and everlasting beauty of monotony
[Benjamin Britten *letter*]

Such sweet compulsion doth in music lie
[John Milton *Arcades*]

The greatest moments of the human spirit may be deduced from the greatest moments in music
[Aaron Copland *Music as an Aspect of the Human Spirit*]

My music is best understood by children and animals
[Igor Stravinsky]

When I get those really intense moments it doesn't feel like it's the violin that's giving them to me, it's like I'm in touch with some realm of consciousness which is much bigger than I am ... It's the music which takes over
[Nigel Kennedy]

Music is your own experience, your own thoughts, your wisdom. If you don't live it, it won't come out of your horn
[Charlie Parker]

Hell is full of musical amateurs; music is the brandy of the damned
[George Bernard Shaw *Man and Superman*]

Music is feeling, then, not sound
[Wallace Stevens *Peter Quince at the Clavier*]

Music is spiritual. The music business is not
[Van Morrison]

If music be the food of love, play on;
Give me excess of it
[William Shakespeare *Twelfth Night*]

Without music life would be a mistake
[Friedrich Nietzsche *The Twilight of the Idols*]

I have been told that Wagner's music is better than it sounds
[Mark Twain]

Music is essentially useless, as life is
[George Santayana *Little Essays*]

Music is a memory bank for finding one's way about the world
[Bruce Chatwin *The Songlines*]

Music is the healing force of the universe
[Albert Ayler]

All music is folk music, I ain't never heard no horse sing a song
[Louis Armstrong]

The only sensual pleasure without vice
[Dr. Johnson]

Classic music is th'kind that we keep thinkin'll turn into a tune
[Kin Hubbard *Comments of Abe Martin and His Neighbors*]

There are two golden rules for an orchestra: start together and finish together. The public doesn't give a damn what goes on in between
[Thomas Beecham]

If the music doesn't say it, how can the words say it for the music?
[John Coltrane]

Extraordinary how potent cheap music is
[Noël Coward *Private Lives*]

What passion cannot music raise and quell?
[John Dryden *A Song for St. Cecilia's Day*]

Music and women I cannot but give way to, whatever my business is
[Samuel Pepys *Diary*]

Music begins to atrophy when it departs too far from the dance... poetry begins to atrophy when it gets too far from music
[Ezra Pound *The ABC of Reading*]

[Rock music] is still only certain elements in the blues isolated, coarsened and amplified. It may affect audiences more strongly but this is only to say that home-distilled hooch is more affecting than château-bottled claret, or a punch on the nose than a reasoned refutation under nineteen headings
[Philip Larkin]

In memory everything seems to happen to music
[Tennessee Williams *The Glass Menagerie*]

You don't need any brains to listen to music
[Luciano Pavarotti]

▹ *See panel* **Music**

musical = **melodious**, lyrical, harmonious, melodic, lilting, tuneful, dulcet, sweet-sounding, euphonious, euphonic • *He had a soft, almost musical voice.*

OPPOSITES: harsh, grating, discordant

musician

QUOTATIONS

I am not a musician. I don't go in too deep. If you have the music in your head, and you sing it with your body, then you'll be alright
[Luciano Pavarotti]

I'm a concert pianist – that's a pretentious way of saying I'm unemployed
[Alan Jay Lerner *An American in Paris*]

musing = **thinking**, reflection, meditation, abstraction, contemplation, introspection, reverie, dreaming, day-dreaming, rumination, navel gazing *(slang)*, absent-

MUSIC

Classical music genres

ars antiqua
ars nova
baroque
classical
expressionist
galant
Gothic
impressionist
minimalist
musique concrète
nationalist
neoclassical
post-romantic
Renaissance
rococo
romantic
salon music
serial music

Types of composition

air
albumblatt
allemande
anthem
aria
bagatelle
ballade
ballet
barcarole
berceuse
bolero
bourrée
canon
cantata
canticle
canzona
canzone
canzonetta
capriccio
cavatina
chaconne
chorale
chorus
concertante
concertino
concerto
concerto grosso
concertstück
contredanse
czardas
dirge
divertimento
divertissement
duet
dumka
duo
ecossaise
elegy
étude
fantasy *or* fantasia
farandole
fugue
galliard
galop
gavotte
gigue
grand opera
hornpipe
humoresque
impromptu
interlude
lament
ländler
lied
madrigal
march
mass
mazurka
medley
minuet
motet
nocturne
nonet
notturno
octet
opera
opera buffa
opera seria
operetta
oratorio
overture
partita
part song
passacaglia
passepied
Passion
pastiche
pastorale
pavane
phantasy
pibroch
polka
polonaise
prelude
psalm
quadrille
quartet
quintet
raga
reel
Requiem
rhapsody
ricercar *or* ricercare
rigadoon
romance
scherzo
schottische
septet
serenade
sextet
sinfonia concertante
sinfonietta
Singspiel
sonata
sonatina
song
song cycle
strathspey
suite
symphonic poem
symphony
toccata
tone poem
trio
trio sonata
waltz

Popular music types

acid house
acid jazz
acid rock
ambient
bebop
bhangra
bluebeat
bluegrass
blues
boogie-woogie
bop
bubblegum
Cajun
calypso
cool jazz
country and western
country blues
country rock
Cu-bop
death metal
disco
Dixieland
doo-wop
dub
folk music
folk rock
free jazz
funk
fusion
gangsta rap
garage
glam rock
gospel
Goth
grunge
hardbop
hardcore
harmolodics
heavy metal
hip-hop
House
Indie
industrial
jazz
jazz-funk
jazz-rock
jungle
mainstream jazz
Merseybeat
modern jazz
Motown *(trademark)*
Muzak *(trademark)*
New Age
New Country
New Orleans jazz
new romantic
New Wave
P-funk
pop
progressive rock
psychobilly
punk
ragga
rap
rave
reggae
rhythm and blues
rock
rockabilly
rock and roll
salsa
ska
skiffle
soul
surf music
swing
swingbeat
techno
thrash metal
trad jazz
world music
zydeco

Musical expressions and tempo instructions

Instruction	Meaning
accelerando	with increasing speed
adagio	slowly
adagietto	fairly slowly
agitato	in an agitated manner
allegretto	fairly quickly or briskly
allegro	quickly, in a brisk, lively manner
amoroso	lovingly
andante	at a moderately slow tempo
andantino	slightly faster than andante
animato	in a lively manner
appassionato	impassioned
assai	(in combination) very
calando	with gradually decreasing tone and speed
cantabile	in a singing style
con	(in combination) with

Instruction	Meaning
con affeto	with tender emotion
con amore	lovingly
con anima	with spirit
con brio	vigorously
con fuoco	with fire
con moto	quickly
crescendo	gradual increase in loudness
diminuendo	gradual decrease in loudness
dolce	gently and sweetly
doloroso	in a sorrowful manner
energico	energetically
espressivo	expressively
forte	loud or loudly
fortissimo	very loud
furioso	frantically rushing
giocoso	merry
grave	solemn and slow
grazioso	graceful

Instruction	Meaning
lacrimoso	sad and mournful
largo	slowly and broadly
larghetto	slowly and broadly, but less so than largo
legato	smoothly and connectedly
leggiero	light
lento	slowly
maestoso	majestically
marziale	martial
mezzo	(in combination) moderately
moderato	at a moderate tempo
molto	(in combination) very
non troppo *or* non tanto	(in combination) not too much
pianissimo	very quietly
piano	softly
più	(in combination) more

Musical expressions and tempo instructions

Instruction	Meaning	Instruction	Meaning	Instruction	Meaning
pizzicato	(in music for stringed instruments) to be plucked with the finger	rubato	with a flexible tempo	strascinando	stretched out
		scherzando	in jocular style	strepitoso	noisy
		sciolto	free and easy	stringendo	with increasing speed
poco *or* un poco	(in combination) a little	semplice	simple and unforced	tanto	(in combination) too much
		sforzando	with strong initial attack		
pomposo	in a pompous manner	smorzando	dying away	tardo	slow
presto	very fast	sospirando	'sighing', plaintive	troppo	(in combination) too much
prestissimo	faster than presto	sostenuto	in a smooth and sustained manner		
quasi	(in combination) almost, as if			vivace	in a brisk lively manner
		sotto voce	extremely quiet		
rallentando	becoming slower	staccato	(of notes) short, clipped	volante	'flying', fast and light

Musical modes

	Final note		Final note		Final note
I Dorian	D	V Lydian	F	IX Aeolian	A
II Hypodorian	A	VI Hypolydian	C	X Hypoaeolian	E
III Phrygian	E	VII Mixolydian	G	XI Ionian	C
IV Hypophrygian	B	VIII Hypomixolydian	D	XII Hypoionian	G

mindedness, cogitation, brown study, cerebration, woolgathering • *She mistook his musing for purposeful loitering.*

muskeg = **swamp**, bog, marsh, quagmire, moss *(Scot. & Northern English dialect)*, slough, fen, mire, morass, everglade(s) *(U.S.)*, pakihi *(N.Z.)*

muss = **mess (up)**, disarrange, dishevel, ruffle, rumple, make untidy, tumble

must[1] AS A NOUN = **necessity**, essential, requirement, duty, fundamental, obligation, imperative, requisite, prerequisite, sine qua non *(Latin)*, necessary thing, must-have • *A visit to the motor museum is a must.*

▸ AS A VERB = **ought to**, have to, should, need to, be required to, have got to, be obliged to, be compelled to, be under an obligation to • *Mr. Allen must pay your legal costs.*

must[2] = **mould**, rot, decay, mildew, mustiness, fustiness, fetor, mouldiness • *The air was heady with the smell of must.*

muster AS A VERB 1 = **summon up**, collect, call up, marshal • *Mustering all her strength, she pulled hard on the oars.*

2 = **rally**, group, gather, assemble, round up, marshal, mobilize, call together • *The general had mustered his troops north of the border.*

3 = **assemble**, meet, come together, convene, congregate, convoke • *They mustered in the open, well wrapped and saying little.*

▸ AS A NOUN = **assembly**, meeting, collection, gathering, rally, convention, congregation, roundup, mobilization, hui *(N.Z.)*, concourse, assemblage, convocation, runanga *(N.Z.)* • *He called a general muster of all soldiers.*

▸ IN PHRASES: **pass muster** = **be acceptable**, qualify, measure up, make the grade, fill the bill *(informal)*, be *or* come up to scratch • *I could not pass muster in this language.*

musty = **stale**, stuffy, airless, decayed, smelly, dank, mouldy, fusty, mildewed, frowsty, mildewy • *He climbed the stairs to a lofty, musty room.*

mutable = **changeable**, changing, variable, flexible, uncertain, volatile, unsettled, unstable, inconsistent, wavering, unreliable, fickle, adaptable, unsteady, vacillating, irresolute, undependable, inconstant, alterable • *Time, space and matter are mutable realities.*

mutant AS A NOUN = **freak**, monster, mutation, deviant, oddity, monstrosity, freak of nature, lusus naturae • *He will play the part of evil mutant, Magneto.*

▸ AS AN ADJECTIVE = **freakish**, crooked, distorted, warped, deformed, misshapen • *stories about strange mutant beasts*

mutate = **change**, convert, transform, evolve, metamorphose, transmute, transfigure • *Overnight, the gossip begins to mutate into headlines.*

mutation 1 = **anomaly**, variation, deviant, freak of nature • *Scientists have found a genetic mutation that causes the disease.*

2 = **change**, variation, evolution, transformation, modification, alteration, deviation, metamorphosis, transfiguration • *I was forced to watch my father's mutation from sober to drunk.*

mute AS AN ADJECTIVE 1 = **close-mouthed**, silent, taciturn, tongue-tied, tight-lipped, unspeaking • *He was mute, distant and indifferent.*

2 = **silent**, dumb, unspoken, tacit, wordless, voiceless, unvoiced • *I threw her a mute look of appeal.*

3 = **dumb**, speechless, voiceless, unspeaking, aphasic, aphonic • *The duke's daughter became mute after a shock.*

▸ AS A VERB 1 = **tone down**, lower, moderate, subdue, dampen, soft-pedal • *Bush muted his racially moderate views.*

2 = **muffle**, subdue, moderate, lower, turn down, soften, dampen, tone down, deaden • *The wooded hillside muted the sounds.*

muted = **subdued**, subtle, faded, delicate, restrained, discreet, low-key, pastel, understated, toned down • *He likes sober muted colours.*

mutilate 1 = **maim**, damage, injure, disable, butcher, cripple, hack, lame, cut up, mangle, mangulate *(Austral. slang)*, dismember, disfigure, lacerate, cut to pieces • *He tortured and mutilated six young men.*

2 = **distort**, cut, damage, mar, spoil, butcher, hack, censor, adulterate, expurgate, bowdlerize • *The writer's verdict was that his screenplay had been mutilated.*

mutilation = **maiming**, injuring, dismembering, disfiguring, disfigurement • *They reported cases of torture and mutilation.*

mutinous = **rebellious**, revolutionary, turbulent, subversive, unruly, insurgent, riotous, unmanageable, seditious, disobedient, ungovernable, refractory, bolshie *(Brit. informal)*, insubordinate, contumacious • *His own army, stung by defeat, is mutinous.*

mutiny AS A NOUN = **rebellion**, revolt, uprising, insurrection, rising, strike, revolution, riot, resistance, disobedience, insubordination, refusal to obey orders • *A series of mutinies in the armed forces destabilized the regime.*

▸ AS A VERB = **rebel**, revolt, rise up, disobey, strike, resist, defy authority, refuse to obey orders, be insubordinate • *Units around the city mutinied after receiving no pay.*

mutt 1 = **mongrel**, dog, hound, tyke, pooch *(informal)*, cur • *He was being harassed by a large, off-the-leash mutt.*
2 = **fool**, idiot, berk *(Brit. slang)*, moron, charlie *(Brit. informal)*, jerk *(slang, chiefly U.S. & Canad.)*, plank *(Brit. slang)*, prick *(derogatory slang)*, wally *(slang)*, prat *(slang)*, plonker *(slang)*, coot, geek *(slang)*, twit *(informal, chiefly Brit.)*, imbecile *(informal)*, ignoramus, dipstick *(Brit. slang)*, dickhead *(slang)*, gonzo *(slang)*, schmuck *(U.S. slang)*, dork *(slang)*, dolt, divvy *(Brit. slang)*, pillock *(Brit. slang)*, dweeb *(U.S. slang)*, putz *(U.S. slang)*, weenie *(U.S. informal)*, eejit *(Scot. & Irish)*, thicko *(Brit. slang)*, dumb-ass *(slang)*, gobshite *(Irish taboo slang)*, dunderhead, numpty *(Scot. informal)*, doofus *(slang, chiefly U.S.)*, fuckwit *(taboo slang)*, thickhead, dickwit *(slang)*, nerd *or* nurd *(slang)*, numbskull *or* numskull, dorba *or* dorb *(Austral. slang)*, bogan *(Austral. slang)* • *'I'm the mutt of my family,' she declares.*

mutter = **grumble**, complain, murmur, rumble, whine, mumble, grouse, bleat, grouch *(informal)*, talk under your breath • *He sat there shaking his head, muttering to himself.*

mutual = **shared**, common, joint, interactive, returned, communal, reciprocal, interchangeable, reciprocated, correlative, requited • *The East and West can work together for mutual benefit.*

muzzle AS A NOUN 1 = **jaws**, mouth, nose, snout • *The dog presented its muzzle for scratching.*
2 = **gag**, guard, restraint • *dogs that have to wear a muzzle*
▸ AS A VERB = **suppress**, silence, curb, restrain, choke, gag, stifle, censor • *He complained of being muzzled by the chairman.*

muzzy 1 = **groggy**, confused, faint, muddled, shaky, dizzy, addled, dopey *(informal)*, befuddled, light-headed, woozy *(informal)*, fuddled, not with it *(informal)*, befogged • *Her ear is still a bit sore and she feels muzzy.*
2 = **blurred**, fuzzy, hazy, foggy, faint, unclear, woolly, unfocused, blurry, ill-defined, indistinct • *that faint, muzzy haze that hangs over many towns*

myopic 1 = **narrow-minded**, short-sighted, narrow, unimaginative, small-minded, unadventurous, near-sighted • *The government still has a myopic attitude to spending.*
2 = **short-sighted**, near-sighted, as blind as a bat *(informal)* • *Rhinos are thick-skinned, myopic and love to wallow in mud.*

myriad AS A NOUN = **multitude**, millions, scores, host, thousands, army, sea, mountain, flood, a million, a thousand, swarm, horde • *They face a myriad of problems bringing up children.*
▸ AS AN ADJECTIVE = **innumerable**, countless, untold, incalculable, immeasurable, a thousand and one, multitudinous • *pop culture in all its myriad forms*

mysterious 1 = **strange**, unknown, puzzling, curious, secret, hidden, weird, concealed, obscure, baffling, veiled, mystical, perplexing, uncanny, incomprehensible, mystifying, impenetrable, arcane, inexplicable, cryptic, insoluble, unfathomable, abstruse, recondite, Delphic • *He died in mysterious circumstances.*
OPPOSITES: clear, plain, apparent
2 = **secretive**, enigmatic, evasive, discreet, covert, reticent, furtive, inscrutable, non-committal, surreptitious, cloak-and-dagger, sphinx-like • *As for his job – well, he was very mysterious about it.*

QUOTATIONS

God moves in a mysterious way
His wonders to perform;
He plants his footsteps in the sea,
And rides upon the storm

[William Cowper *Olney Hymns*]

mystery 1 = **puzzle**, problem, question, secret, riddle, enigma, conundrum, teaser, poser *(informal)*, closed book • *The source of the gunshots still remains a mystery.*
2 = **secrecy**, uncertainty, obscurity, mystique, darkness, ambiguity, ambiguousness • *It is an elaborate ceremony, shrouded in mystery.*

mystical *or* **mystic** = **supernatural**, mysterious, transcendental, spiritual, esoteric, occult, arcane, metaphysical, paranormal, inscrutable, otherworldly, abstruse, cabalistic, preternatural, nonrational • *mystic union with God*

mystify = **puzzle**, confuse, baffle, bewilder, beat *(slang)*, escape, stump, elude, confound, perplex, bamboozle *(informal)*, flummox, be all Greek to *(informal)*, nonplus, befog • *There was something strange in her attitude that mystified me.*

mystique = **fascination**, spell, magic, charm, glamour, awe, charisma • *His book destroyed the mystique of monarchy.*

myth 1 = **legend**, story, tradition, fiction, saga, fable, parable, allegory, fairy story, folk tale, urban myth, urban legend • *a famous Greek myth*
2 = **illusion**, story, fancy, fantasy, imagination, invention, delusion, superstition, fabrication, falsehood, figment, tall story, cock and bull story *(informal)* • *Contrary to popular myth, most women are not spendthrifts.*

mythical 1 = **legendary**, storied, fabulous, imaginary, fairy-tale, fabled, mythological, storybook, allegorical, folkloric, chimerical • *the mythical beast that had seven or more heads*
2 = **imaginary**, made-up, fantasy, invented, pretended, untrue, unreal, fabricated, fanciful, fictitious, make-believe, nonexistent • *They are trying to preserve a mythical sense of nationhood.*

mythological = **legendary**, fabulous, fabled, traditional, invented, heroic, imaginary, mythical, mythic, folkloric • *the mythological beast that was part lion, part goat*

mythology = **legend**, myths, folklore, stories, tradition, lore, folk tales, mythos • *He strips away the pretence and mythology to expose the truth.*
▹ *See panels* **Arthurian legend; Mythology**

m

MYTHOLOGY

CHARACTERS IN CLASSICAL MYTHOLOGY

Achilles	Ariadne	Dido	Hermaphroditus	Midas	Penelope
Actaeon	Atalanta	Echo	Hippolytus	Minos	Persephone
Adonis	Atlas	Electra	Hyacinthus	Muses	Perseus
Aeneas	Callisto	Europa	Icarus	Narcissus	Pleiades
Agamemnon	Calypso	Eurydice	Io	Niobe	Pollux
Ajax	Cassandra	Galatea	Ixion	Odysseus	Polydeuces
Amazons	Cassiopeia	Ganymede	Jason	Oedipus	Polyphemus
Andromache	Castor	Hector	Jocasta	Orestes	Priam
Andromeda	Charon	Hecuba	Leda	Orion	Prometheus
Antigone	Circe	Helen	Medea	Orpheus	Proserpina
Arachne	Clytemnestra	Heracles	Medusa	Pandora	Psyche
Argonauts	Daedalus	Hercules	Menelaus	Paris	Pygmalion

Characters in classical mythology (continued)

Pyramus	Romulus	sibyl	Sisyphus	Theseus	Tiresias
Remus	Semele	Silenus	Tantalus	Thisbe	Ulysses

Places in classical mythology

Acheron	Erebus	Islands of the	Knossos	Parnassus	Tartarus
Colchis	Hades	Blessed	Lethe	Phlegethon	Thebes
Elysium	Helicon	Ithaca	Olympus	Styx	Troy

Mythological creatures

afreet *or* afrit	dragon	goblin	Hydra	Minotaur	salamander
androsphinx	dryad	Gorgon	impundulu	naiad	satyr
banshee	dwarf	gremlin	jinni, jinnee, djinni,	Nereid	Scylla
basilisk	Echidna	Grendel	*or* djinny	nix *or* nixie	Siren
behemoth	elf	griffin, griffon,	kelpie	nymph	Sphinx
bunyip	erlking	*or* gryphon	kraken	Oceanid	sylph
centaur	fairy	hamadryad	kylin	orc	tokoloshe
Cerberus	faun	Harpy	lamia	oread	tricorn
Charybdis	fay	hippocampus	leprechaun	Pegasus	troll
chimera *or*	Fury	hippogriff *or*	leviathan	peri	unicorn
chimaera	genie	hippogryph	Medusa	phoenix	vampire
cockatrice	Geryon	hobbit	mermaid	pixie	water nymph
Cyclops	giant	hobgoblin	merman	roc	wood nymph

Characters in Norse mythology

Andvari	Aurvandil the Bold	Gudrun	Hreidmar	Mimir	Svipdagr
Ask	Brynhild	Gunnar	Lif	Regin	Sigurd
Atli	Fafnir	Gutthorn	Lifthrasir	Sigmund	Wayland

Places in Norse mythology

Asgard *or* Asgarth	Hel *or* Hela	Midgard *or*	Nidhogg	Svartalpheim	Valhalla
Bifrost	Jotunheim	Midgarth	Niflheim	Utgard	Vanaheim

Nn

nab = **catch**, arrest, apprehend, seize, lift *(slang)*, nick *(slang, chiefly Brit.)*, grab, capture, nail *(informal)*, collar *(informal)*, snatch, catch in the act, feel your collar *(slang)* • *He killed 12 people before the authorities nabbed him.*

nadir = **bottom**, depths, lowest point, rock bottom, all-time low • *That period was the nadir of his presidency.*
OPPOSITES: top, summit, height

naff = **bad**, poor, inferior, worthless, pants *(slang)*, duff *(Brit. informal)*, shabby, second-rate, shoddy, low-grade, low-quality, trashy, substandard, for the birds *(informal)*, crappy *(slang)*, valueless, rubbishy, poxy *(slang)*, piss-poor *(slang)*, chickenshit *(U.S. slang)*, strictly for the birds *(informal)*, twopenny-halfpenny, bodger or bodgie *(Austral. slang)* • *This music is really naff.*
OPPOSITES: fine, excellent, superior

nag[1] **AS A VERB 1** = **scold**, harass, badger, pester, worry, harry, plague, hassle *(informal)*, vex, berate, breathe down someone's neck, upbraid, chivvy, bend someone's ear *(informal)*, be on your back *(slang)*, henpeck • *The more Sarah nagged her, the more stubborn Cissie became.*
2 = **worry**, trouble, bother, bug *(informal)*, haunt, annoy, plague, irritate, torment, hang over, niggle, weigh down, irk, gnaw at, weigh heavily on, rankle with, prey on your mind, cause anxiety to, lie heavily on • *the anxiety that had nagged her all through lunch*
▸ **AS A NOUN** = **scold**, complainer, grumbler, virago, shrew, tartar, moaner, harpy, harridan, termagant, fault-finder • *My husband calls me a nag if I complain about anything.*

nag[2] *(often derog.)* = **horse** *(U.S.)*, hack, jade, plug • *a bedraggled knight riding a lame, flea-ridden old nag*

nagging 1 = **continuous**, persistent, continual, niggling, repeated, constant, endless, relentless, perpetual, never-ending, interminable, unrelenting, incessant, unremitting • *He complained about a nagging pain between his shoulders.*
2 = **scolding**, complaining, critical, sharp-tongued, shrewish • *He tried to ignore the screaming, nagging voice of his wife.*

QUOTATIONS
Nagging is the repetition of unpalatable truths
[Edith Summerskill *speech to the Married Women's Association*]

naiad = **water nymph**, nymph, sprite, undine, Oceanid *(Greek myth)* • *The ceiling was covered in paintings of sylphs and naiads, fauns and faeries.*

nail AS A NOUN 1 = **tack**, spike, rivet, hobnail, brad *(technical)* • *A mirror hung on a nail above the washstand.*
2 = **fingernail**, toenail, talon, thumbnail, claw, unguis *(technical)* • *Keep your nails short and your hands clean.*
▸ **AS A VERB 1** = **fasten**, fix, secure, attach, pin, hammer, tack • *Frank put the first plank down and nailed it in place.*
2 = **catch**, arrest, capture, apprehend, lift *(slang)*, trap, nab *(informal)*, snare, ensnare, entrap, feel your collar *(slang)* • *The police have been trying to nail him for years.*
▸ **IN PHRASES: on the nail** = **immediately**, promptly, at once, straight away, without delay, punctually • *She insisted her lodgers pay her every Friday, on the nail.*
▸ **TECHNICAL NAME:** unguis
▸ **RELATED ADJECTIVES:** ungual, ungular

naive or **naïve** or **naïf** = **gullible**, trusting, credulous, unsuspicious, green, simple, innocent, childlike, callow, unsophisticated, unworldly, artless, ingenuous, guileless, wet behind the ears *(informal)*, jejune, as green as grass • *He's so naive he'll believe anything I tell him.*
OPPOSITES: worldly, experienced, sophisticated

naivety or **naiveté** or **naïveté** = **gullibility**, innocence, simplicity, inexperience, credulity, ingenuousness, artlessness, guilelessness, callowness • *She does have a certain girlish naivety about her.*

naked 1 = **nude**, stripped, exposed, bare, uncovered, undressed, divested, in the raw *(informal)*, disrobed, starkers *(informal)*, stark-naked, unclothed, in the buff *(informal)*, in the altogether *(informal)*, buck naked *(slang)*, undraped, in your birthday suit *(informal)*, scuddy *(slang)*, without a stitch on *(informal)*, in the bare scud *(slang)*, naked as the day you were born *(informal)* • *They stripped him naked.* • *A girl was lying on the rug, completely naked.*
OPPOSITES: covered, dressed, clothed
2 = **defenceless**, vulnerable, helpless, wide open, unarmed, unprotected, unguarded • *The deal leaves the authorities virtually naked.*
3 = **undisguised**, open, simple, plain, patent, evident, stark, manifest, blatant, overt, unmistakable, unqualified, unadorned, unvarnished, unconcealed • *Naked aggression could not go unchallenged.*
OPPOSITES: disguised, concealed, secret

nakedness 1 = **nudity**, undress, bareness, deshabille • *He pulled the blanket over his body to hide his nakedness.*
2 = **starkness**, simplicity, openness, plainness • *the nakedness of the emotion expressed in these songs*

namby-pamby = **feeble**, weak, wet, sentimental, mincing, ineffectual, prim, weedy *(informal)*, colourless, effeminate, anaemic, insipid, simpering, spineless, effete, prissy *(informal)*, wishy-washy *(informal)*, vapid, mawkish, wussy *(slang)*, wimpish or wimpy *(informal)* • *I despise his wimpy, namby-pamby attitude.*

name AS A NOUN 1 = **title**, nickname, designation, appellation, term, handle *(slang)*, denomination, epithet, sobriquet, cognomen, moniker or monicker *(slang)* • *I don't even know if Sullivan is his real name.*
2 = **reputation**, character, honour, fame, distinction, esteem, eminence, renown, repute, note • *He had made a name for himself as a musician.* • *I was forced to pursue this litigation to protect my good name.*
▸ **AS A VERB 1** = **call**, christen, baptize, dub, term, style, label, entitle, denominate • *My mother insisted on naming me Horace.*

2 = **nominate**, choose, commission, mention, identify, select, appoint, specify, designate • *The Scots have yet to name their team.*

▸ **RELATED ADJECTIVE:** nominal

QUOTATIONS

What's in a name? That which we call a rose
By any other name would smell as sweet
[William Shakespeare *Romeo and Juliet*]

named 1 = **called**, christened, known as, dubbed, termed, styled, labelled, entitled, denominated, baptized • *He was named John.*

2 = **nominated**, chosen, picked, commissioned, mentioned, identified, selected, appointed, cited, specified, designated, singled out • *She has been named BusinessWoman of the Year.*

nameless 1 = **unnamed**, unknown, obscure, anonymous, unheard-of, undistinguished, untitled • *They had their cases rejected by nameless officials.*

2 = **anonymous**, unknown, unnamed, incognito • *My source of information is a judge who wishes to remain nameless.*

3 = **horrible**, unspeakable, indescribable, abominable, ineffable, unutterable, inexpressible • *He was suddenly seized by a nameless dread.*

namely = **specifically**, that is to say, to wit, i.e., viz. • *One group of people seems to be forgotten, namely pensioners.*

nanny = **childminder**, nurse, au pair, governess, nursemaid, childcarer • *A lot of mothers are against the idea of employing a nanny.*

nap[1] **AS A VERB** = **sleep**, rest, nod, drop off *(informal)*, doze, kip *(Brit. slang)*, snooze *(informal)*, nod off *(informal)*, catnap, drowse, zizz *(Brit. informal)* • *An elderly person may nap during the day.*

▸ **IN PHRASES: catch someone napping** = **catch unawares**, catch out, take by surprise, catch off guard, catch on the hop • *The security services were clearly caught napping.*

▸ **AS A NOUN** = **sleep**, rest, kip *(Brit. slang)*, siesta, catnap, forty winks *(informal)*, shuteye *(slang)*, zizz *(Brit. informal)* • *I think I'll take a little nap for an hour or so.*

nap[2] = **pile**, down, fibre, weave, texture, shag, grain • *She buried her face in the towel's soft nap.*

nape

▸ **TECHNICAL NAME:** nucha

▸ **RELATED ADJECTIVE:** nuchal

napkin = **serviette**, cloth • *She dabbed her lips carefully with a napkin.*

nappy = **diaper**, napkin • *I changed the baby's nappy.*

narcissism or **narcism** = **egotism**, vanity, conceit, self-regard, self-love, self-absorption, egoism, self-obsession, self-centredness, egocentricity, egomania, self-conceit, self-admiration, self-adulation • *Their self-absorption borders on narcissism.*

narcissistic = **self-loving**, conceited, self-centred, self-absorbed, egotistical, egocentric, self-regarding, self-obsessed, egoistic, egotistic, full of yourself, in love with yourself • *I've never met anyone so self-centred and narcissistic.*

narcotic AS A NOUN = **drug**, anaesthetic, downer *(informal)*, painkiller, sedative, opiate, palliative, tranquillizer, anodyne, analgesic • *He appears to be under the influence of some sort of narcotic.*

▸ **AS AN ADJECTIVE** = **sedative**, calming, dulling, numbing, hypnotic, analgesic, stupefying, soporific, somnolent, painkilling • *drugs which have a narcotic effect*

narrate = **tell**, recount, report, detail, describe, relate, unfold, chronicle, recite, set forth • *The film is a story about power, narrated by an old sailor.*

narration 1 = **storytelling**, telling, reading, relation, explanation, description

2 = **account**, explanation, description, recital, voice-over *(in a film)* • *The play is an autobiographical journey with song, dialogue and narration.*

narrative = **story**, report, history, detail, account, statement, tale, chronicle, recital • *He began his narrative with the day of the murder.*

narrator = **storyteller**, writer, author, reporter, commentator, chronicler, reciter, raconteur • *Jules, the story's narrator, is an actress in her late thirties.*

narrow AS AN ADJECTIVE 1 = **thin**, fine, lean, slight, slim, pinched, slender, tapered, tapering, attenuated • *a woman with a full bust and hips and a narrow waist*

OPPOSITES: wide, broad

2 = **limited**, restricted, confined, tight, close, near, squeezed, confining, cramped, meagre, constricted, circumscribed, scanty, straitened, incapacious • *He squeezed his way along the narrow space between the crates.*

OPPOSITES: big, open, wide

3 = **insular**, prejudiced, biased, partial, reactionary, puritan, bigoted, dogmatic, intolerant, narrow-minded, small-minded, illiberal • *a narrow and outdated view of family life*

OPPOSITES: liberal, tolerant, broad-minded

4 = **exclusive**, limited, select, restricted, confined • *She achieved a fame that transcended the narrow world of avant-garde theatre.*

▸ **AS A VERB** 1 *often with* **down** = **restrict**, limit, reduce, diminish, constrict, circumscribe, straiten • *I don't want to narrow my options too early on.*

2 = **get narrower**, taper, shrink, tighten, constrict • *This sign means that the road narrows on both sides.*

narrowly 1 = **just**, barely, only just, scarcely, by the narrowest of margins, by the skin of your teeth, by a whisker or hair's-breadth • *Five firemen narrowly escaped death.*

2 = **closely**, keenly, carefully, intently, intensely, fixedly, searchingly • *He frowned and looked narrowly at his colleague.*

narrow-minded = **intolerant**, conservative, prejudiced, biased, provincial, petty, reactionary, parochial, short-sighted, bigoted, insular, opinionated, small-minded, hidebound, illiberal, strait-laced • *He's just a narrow-minded bigot.*

OPPOSITES: catholic, cosmopolitan, broad-minded

narrowness

▸ **RELATED PHOBIA:** anginophobia

narrows = **channel**, sound, gulf, passage, straits • *The tide was sluicing out through the narrows.*

nascent = **developing**, beginning, dawning, evolving, budding, incipient • *the still nascent science of genomics*

nastiness 1 = **unpleasantness**, ugliness, offensiveness, disagreeableness • *the sheer nastiness of modern urban life*

2 = **spite**, malice, venom, unpleasantness, meanness, bitchiness *(slang)*, offensiveness, spitefulness • *'You're just like your mother,' he said, with a tone of nastiness in his voice.*

3 = **dirt**, pollution, filth, squalor, impurity, foulness, defilement, dirtiness, filthiness, uncleanliness • *Much filth and nastiness is spread amongst the huts.*

4 = **obscenity**, porn *(informal)*, pornography, indecency, impropriety, vulgarity, smut, crudity, licentiousness, offensiveness, ribaldry, lewdness, salaciousness, indelicacy, smuttiness • *Almost every page of the book was filled with this kind of nastiness.*

nasty 1 = **unpleasant**, ugly, disagreeable • *This divorce could turn nasty.*

OPPOSITES: nice, sweet, pleasant

2 = **spiteful**, mean, offensive, annoying, vicious, unpleasant, abusive, vile, malicious, bad-tempered, despicable, disagreeable • *He's only nasty to me when there's no-one around to see it.*

OPPOSITES: kind, nice, pleasant

3 = **disgusting**, unpleasant, dirty, offensive, foul, horrible, polluted, filthy, sickening, vile, distasteful, repellent, obnoxious, objectionable, disagreeable, nauseating, odious, repugnant, loathsome, grotty *(slang)*, malodorous, noisome,

unappetizing, skanky *(slang)*, mephitic, yucky *or* yukky *(slang)*, festy *(Austral. slang)*, yucko *(Austral. slang)* • *It's got a really nasty smell.*
4 = serious, bad, dangerous, critical, terrible, alarming, severe, grave, awful, painful, dreadful, frightful • *Lili had a nasty chest infection.*
5 = foul, unpleasant, filthy, stormy, inclement • *The weather has turned nasty again.*
6 = obscene, blue, sick, dirty, offensive, gross, foul, disgusting, crude, rude, filthy, indecent, vulgar, vile, improper, pornographic, lewd, risqué, profane, x-rated, salacious, impure, lascivious, smutty, ribald, licentious, scatological, indelicate • *There's no need for such nasty language, young man.*
OPPOSITES: clean, decent

nation 1 = **country**, state, nation state, power, land, federation, commonwealth, kingdom, realm, superpower, confederation, sovereign state, polity • *Such policies would require unprecedented cooperation between nations.*
2 = public, people, community, society, population, populace, body politic • *It was a story that touched the nation's heart.*

QUOTATIONS
For nation shall rise against nation, and kingdom against kingdom
[*Bible: St. Matthew*]
No nation is fit to sit in judgement upon any other nation
[Woodrow Wilson *speech*]
A nation is the same people living in the same place
[James Joyce *Ulysses*]

national AS AN ADJECTIVE 1 = **nationwide**, state, public, federal, civil, widespread, governmental, countrywide • *major national and international issues*
2 = ethnic, social, native, racial, indigenous, tribal • *the national characteristics and history of the country*
▸ AS A NOUN = **citizen**, subject, resident, native, inhabitant • *He is in fact a British national and passport holder.*

nationalism 1 = **separatism**, independence, isolationism, xenophobia • *He was jailed on charges of furthering the cause of Albanian nationalism and separatism.*
2 = patriotism, loyalty to your country, chauvinism, jingoism, nationality, allegiance, fealty • *This kind of fierce nationalism is a volatile force.*

QUOTATIONS
Nationalism, that magnificent song that made the people rise against their oppressors, stops short, falters and dies away on the day that independence is proclaimed
[Frantz Fanon *The Wretched of the Earth*]
While it is often the enemy of democracy, nationalism has also been democracy's handmaiden, from the time of the French Revolution
[Francis Fukuyama]

nationalist = **separatist**, isolationist • *Plaid Cymru snatched victory for the nationalists in traditionally Labour constituencies.*

nationalistic = **patriotic**, xenophobic, flag-waving, chauvinistic, jingoistic, loyal to your country • *The violence had an ominously nationalistic character.*

nationality 1 = **citizenship**, birth • *When asked his nationality, he said, 'British'.*
2 = race, nation, tribe, clan, ethnic group • *the many nationalities that comprise Ethopia*

nationwide AS AN ADJECTIVE = **national**, general, widespread, countrywide, coast-to-coast, overall • *The rising number of car crimes is a nationwide problem.*
▸ AS AN ADVERB = **countrywide**, nationally, throughout the country, coast-to-coast, overall • *The programme was shown nationwide.*

native AS AN ADJECTIVE 1 = **home**, national, mother • *It was many years since she had lived in her native country.*
2 = indigenous, local, aboriginal *(often offensive)*, autochthonous • *a spokeswoman for native peoples around the world*
3 = mother, indigenous, vernacular • *French is not my native tongue.*
4 = domestic, local, indigenous, home-made, home-grown, home • *Several native plants also provide edible berries.*
5 = original, natural, built-in, inherited, inherent, hereditary, instinctive, innate, intrinsic, endemic, ingrained, congenital, inveterate, inbred, immanent, hard-wired • *Her conversation revealed no education but much native wit and shrewdness.*
▸ AS A NOUN *usually with* **of** = **inhabitant**, national, resident, citizen, countryman, aborigine *(often offensive)*, dweller • *He was a native of France.*

Nativity = **birth of Christ**, manger scene • *a beautiful painting depicting the Nativity*

natter AS A VERB = **gossip**, talk, rabbit (on) *(Brit. informal)*, jaw *(slang)*, chatter, witter *(informal)*, prattle, jabber, gabble, blather, blether, shoot the breeze *(informal)*, run off at the mouth *(slang)*, prate, talk idly, chew the fat *or* rag *(slang)*, earbash *(Austral. & N.Z. slang)* • *His mother would natter on the phone for hours.*
▸ AS A NOUN = **gossip**, talk, conversation, chat, jaw *(slang)*, craic *(Irish informal)*, gab *(informal)*, prattle, jabber, gabble, palaver, blather, chitchat, blether, chinwag *(Brit. informal)*, gabfest *(informal, chiefly U.S. & Canad.)*, confabulation • *We must get together some time for a good natter.*

natty 1 = **smart**, sharp, dashing, elegant, trim, neat, fashionable, stylish, trendy *(Brit. informal)*, chic, spruce, well-dressed, dapper, debonair, snazzy *(informal)*, modish, well-turned-out, rakish, crucial *(slang)*, schmick *(Austral. informal)* • *He was a natty dresser.* • *a natty pin-stripe suit*
2 = smart, clever, stylish, ingenious, cool, schmick *(Austral. informal)* • *a natty little gadget*

natural 1 = **logical**, normal, reasonable, valid, legitimate • *A period of depression is a natural response to bereavement.*
2 = normal, common, stock, standard, established, regular, usual, ordinary, typical, routine, everyday, accustomed, customary, commonplace, habitual, run-of-the-mill, unexceptional • *It's just not natural behaviour for a child of his age.*
OPPOSITES: strange, abnormal, irregular
3 = innate, native, characteristic, indigenous, inherent, instinctive, intuitive, congenital, inborn, immanent, in your blood, hard-wired, essential • *He has a natural flair for business.*
4 = unaffected, open, frank, genuine, spontaneous, candid, unpretentious, unsophisticated, dinkum *(Austral. & N.Z. informal)*, artless, ingenuous, real, simple, unstudied • *Jan's sister was as natural and friendly as the rest of the family.*
OPPOSITES: affected, assumed, artificial
5 = pure, real, plain, raw, organic, crude, wholesome, whole, unrefined, unbleached, unprocessed, unpolished, unmixed, chemical-free, additive-free, pesticide-free • *He prefers to use high quality natural produce.*
OPPOSITES: processed, manufactured, synthetic

naturalism = **realism**, authenticity, plausibility, verisimilitude, factualism • *the closely observed naturalism of this superbly understated tale*

naturalist = **biologist**, environmentalist, conservationist, ecologist, botanist, zoologist, ornithologist, entomologist, life scientist, preservationist, natural historian, tree-hugger *(informal derogatory)* • *Dr Forsythe is a professional naturalist, author and research entomologist.*

naturalistic 1 = **realistic**, photographic, kitchen sink, representational, lifelike, warts and all *(informal)*, true-to-

life, vérité, factualistic • *These drawings are amongst his most naturalistic.*
2 = **lifelike**, realistic, real-life, true-to-life • *Research is needed under rather more naturalistic conditions.*

naturalize 1 = **domesticate**, establish, introduce, adapt, acclimatize • *The plant has been cultivated and naturalized all over the world.*
2 = **grant citizenship to**, enfranchise, give a passport to • *We are naturalized British citizens.*

naturally 1 = **of course**, certainly, obviously, needless to say, as a matter of course, as might be expected, as anticipated, not unexpectedly • *We are naturally concerned about the future.*
2 = **typically**, simply, normally, spontaneously, customarily • *A study of yoga leads naturally to meditation.*
3 = **inherently**, instinctively, by nature, innately, congenitally, by character • *Some individuals are naturally good communicators.*
4 = **easily**, automatically, instinctively, effortlessly, with ease, without thinking, intuitively, by instinct • *Playing football was just something that came naturally to me.*
5 = **unaffectedly**, normally, genuinely, sincerely, spontaneously, without airs, artlessly, unpretentiously • *Just act naturally and you'll be okay.*

naturalness 1 = **unselfconsciousness**, simplicity, openness, spontaneity, candour, frankness, genuineness, ingenuousness, artlessness, unpretentiousness, simpleness, spontaneousness • *Sidney's naturalness is the key to his charm.*
2 = **realism**, naturalism, verisimilitude, factualism • *The critics praised the naturalness of his acting.*

n

nature 1 = **creation**, world, earth, environment, universe, cosmos, natural world, Mother Nature, natural forces • *man's ancient sense of kinship with nature*
2 = **flora and fauna**, country, landscape, countryside, scenery, natural history • *an organization devoted to the protection of nature*
3 = **quality**, character, make-up, constitution, attributes, essence, traits, complexion, features • *The protests had been non-political in nature.*
4 = **temperament**, character, personality, disposition, outlook, mood, humour, temper • *She trusted people. That was her nature.*
5 = **kind**, sort, style, type, variety, species, category, description • *This – and other books of a similar nature – are urgently needed.*

QUOTATIONS

nature red in tooth and claw
[Alfred, Lord Tennyson *In Memoriam*]

Nature does nothing without purpose or uselessly
[Aristotle *Politics*]

You may drive out nature with a pitchfork, yet she'll be constantly running back
[Horace *Epistles*]

In nature there are neither rewards nor punishments – there are consequences
[Robert G. Ingersoll *Some Reasons Why*]

In her [Nature's] inventions nothing is lacking, and nothing is superfluous
[Leonardo da Vinci]

'I play for seasons; not eternities!'
Says Nature
[George Meredith *Modern Love*]

naturist = **nudist** • *I'm a naturist; I enjoy being naked. It's very liberating after a hard day's work.*

naughty 1 = **disobedient**, bad, mischievous, badly behaved, wayward, playful, wicked, sinful, fractious, impish, roguish, refractory • *You naughty boy, you gave me such a fright.*
OPPOSITES: good, seemly, proper
2 = **obscene**, blue, vulgar, improper, lewd, risqué, X-rated (*informal*), bawdy, smutty, off-colour, ribald • *saucy TV shows crammed with naughty innuendo*
OPPOSITES: clean, proper, polite

nausea 1 = **sickness**, gagging, vomiting, retching, squeamishness, queasiness, biliousness • *I was overcome with a feeling of nausea.*
2 = **disgust**, loathing, distaste, aversion, revulsion, repulsion, abhorrence, repugnance, odium, detestation • *She spoke in a little-girl voice which brought on a palpable feeling of nausea.*

nauseate 1 = **sicken**, make sick, turn your stomach, cause to feel sick • *The smell of frying nauseated her.*
2 = **disgust**, offend, horrify, revolt, repel, repulse, gross out (*U.S. slang*) • *Ugliness nauseates me. I like to have beautiful things around me.*

nauseating 1 = **disgusting**, offensive, appalling, nasty, foul, revolting, sickening, ghastly, vile, obnoxious, repulsive, odious, repugnant, loathsome, abhorrent, abominable, stomach-churning, stomach-turning, repellant, sick-making • *The judge described the offences as nauseating and unspeakable.*
2 = **sickening**, foul, revolting, sickly, odious, stomach-churning, putrid, stomach-turning, emetic, sick-making, yucko (*Austral. slang*) • *the nauseating smell of rotting garbage*

nauseous 1 = **sick**, green, ill, unwell, nauseated, queasy, bilious, crook (*Austral. & N.Z. informal*) • *The drugs make me feel nauseous.*
2 = **sickening**, offensive, disgusting, revolting, distasteful, repulsive, nauseating, repugnant, loathsome, abhorrent, detestable, yucky or yukky (*slang*), yucko (*Austral. slang*) • *The floor was deep with bat dung giving off a nauseous smell.*

nautical = **maritime**, boating, sailing, marine, yachting, naval, seafaring, ocean-going, seagoing • *Jet-skis require no traditional nautical skills.*

naval = **nautical**, marine, maritime • *He was the senior serving naval officer.*

navel 1 = **bellybutton** (*informal*), tummy button (*informal*) • *A small incision is made just below the navel.*
2 = **centre**, eye, heart, middle, focus, core, nucleus, hub, focal point, pivot, nub, central point, midpoint • *The city was once the jewel in the navel of the Gold Coast.*
▸ **TECHNICAL NAME:** umbilicus
▸ **RELATED ADJECTIVE:** umbilical

navigable = **passable**, negotiable, traversable, crossable, open, clear, unobstructed • *the navigable portion of the Nile*

navigate 1 = **steer**, drive, direct, guide, handle, pilot, sail, skipper, con (*Nautical*), manoeuvre • *He was responsible for safely navigating the ship.*
2 = **manoeuvre**, drive, direct, guide, handle, pilot • *He expertly navigated the plane through 45 minutes of fog.*
3 = **plot a course**, sail, find your way, plan a course • *They navigated by the sun and stars.*
4 = **sail**, cruise, manoeuvre, voyage • *Such boats can be built locally and can navigate on the Nile.*
5 = **map-read**, give directions, plan a route • *It is impossible to drive and navigate at the same time.*

navigation = **sailing**, cruising, steering, manoeuvring, voyaging, seamanship, helmsmanship • *Pack ice was becoming a threat to navigation.*

navigator = **helmsman**, guide, pilot, seaman, mariner, steersman • *Which of you is the best navigator?*

navvy = **labourer**, worker, ganger, workman, manual worker, hand • *He spent 18 months doing navvy's work on a building site.*

navy = **fleet**, warships, flotilla, armada, squadron • *He joined the navy at the age of eighteen.*

nay = **indeed**, actually, in fact, and even, or rather, in truth • *Long essays, nay, whole books have been written on this.*

near **AS A PREPOSITION** = **close**, alongside, next to, close by,

not far from, adjacent to • *He drew his chair nearer the fire.*
▸ **AS AN ADVERB 1 = close to**, close by • *As we drew near, I could see that the door was open.*
2 = **almost**, about, nearly, close to, virtually, practically, all but, just about, approximately, as good as, well-nigh • *The picture was near lifesize.*
▸ **AS AN ADJECTIVE 1 = close**, bordering, neighbouring, nearby, beside, adjacent, adjoining, close by, at close quarters, just round the corner, contiguous, proximate, within sniffing distance *(informal)*, a hop, skip and a jump away *(informal)* • *The town is very near.* • *Where's the nearest telephone?*
OPPOSITES: far, removed, remote
2 = **imminent**, forthcoming, approaching, looming, impending, upcoming, on the cards *(informal)*, nigh, in the offing, near-at-hand, next • *Departure time was near.*
OPPOSITES: remote, distant, far-off
3 = **intimate**, close, related, allied, familiar, connected, attached, akin • *I have no near relations.*
OPPOSITES: remote, distant
4 = **mean**, stingy, parsimonious, miserly, niggardly, ungenerous, tightfisted, close-fisted • *They joked about him being so near with his money.*

nearby **AS AN ADJECTIVE = neighbouring**, adjacent, adjoining • *At a nearby table a man was complaining in a loud voice.*
▸ **AS AN ADVERB = close at hand**, within reach, not far away, at close quarters, just round the corner, proximate, within sniffing distance *(informal)* • *He might easily have been seen by someone who lived nearby.*

nearing = **approaching**, coming, advancing, imminent, impending, upcoming • *Harvest time is nearing.*

nearly 1 = **practically**, about, almost, near, close to, virtually, next to, all but, just about, not quite, more or less, pretty well *(informal)*, bordering on, not far from, as good as, verging on, not far off, well-nigh, nigh on, pretty nearly *(informal)* • *The beach was nearly empty.*
2 = **almost**, about, approaching, roughly, just about, approximately, nigh on • *It was already nearly eight o'clock.*

near miss = **close thing**, near thing, close call, close shave, narrow escape • *There was a near miss when the jets' flight paths almost crossed.*

nearness 1 = **closeness**, proximity, juxtaposition, contiguity, availability, vicinity, accessibility, propinquity, handiness • *The nearness of the house to the station is an added bonus.*
2 = **imminence**, closeness, immediacy • *the later years, when we become aware of the nearness of death*

near-sighted *or* **nearsighted** = **short-sighted**, myopic • *She was so nearsighted she didn't even see the sign.*

neat 1 = **tidy**, nice, straight, trim, orderly, immaculate, spruce, well-kept, uncluttered, shipshape, spick-and-span • *Her house was neat and tidy and gleamingly clean.*
OPPOSITES: disorderly, messy, untidy
2 = **methodical**, tidy, systematic, fastidious • *'It's not like Alf to leave a mess like that,' I remarked, 'He's always so neat.'*
OPPOSITES: disorderly, messy, disorganized
3 = **smart**, trim, tidy, spruce, dapper, natty *(informal)*, well-groomed, well-turned out • *She always looked neat and well groomed.*
4 = **dainty**, compact, petite • *a small woman with neat features*
5 = **graceful**, elegant, skilful, adept, deft, nimble, agile, adroit, dexterous, efficient • *He had the neat movements of a dancer.*
OPPOSITES: clumsy, inelegant
6 = **clever**, efficient, handy, apt, nifty *(informal)*, well-judged • *It was a neat solution to the problem.*
OPPOSITES: incompetent, inefficient
7 = **cool**, great *(informal)*, excellent, brilliant, cracking *(Brit. informal)*, smashing *(informal)*, superb, fantastic *(informal)*, tremendous, ace *(informal)*, fabulous *(informal)*, marvellous, terrific, awesome *(slang)*, mean *(slang)*, super *(informal)*, brill *(informal)*, bodacious *(slang, chiefly U.S.)*, boffo *(slang)*, chillin' *(U.S. slang)*, booshit *(Austral. slang)*, exo *(Austral. slang)*, sik *(Austral. slang)*, rad *(informal)*, phat *(slang)*, schmick *(Austral. informal)*, beaut *(informal)*, barrie *(Scot. slang)*, belting *(Brit. slang)*, pearler *(Austral. slang)* • *I've just had a really neat idea.*
OPPOSITES: bad, terrible, awful
8 = **undiluted**, straight, pure, unmixed • *He poured himself a glass of neat brandy and swallowed it in one.*

neaten = **tidy up**, trim, clean up, groom, tidy, spruce up, smarten up, put in order, put to rights, make neat, straighten out *or* up, arrange • *Trim and neaten the edges of the fabric.*

neatly 1 = **tidily**, nicely, smartly, systematically, methodically, fastidiously • *He took off his trousers and folded them neatly.*
2 = **smartly**, elegantly, stylishly, tidily, nattily • *She was neatly dressed, her hair was tidy and she carried a shoulder-bag.*
3 = **gracefully**, expertly, efficiently, adeptly, deftly, skilfully, nimbly, adroitly, dexterously, agilely • *He sent the ball over the bar with a neatly executed header.*
4 = **cleverly**, precisely, accurately, efficiently, aptly, elegantly • *She neatly summed up a common attitude among many teachers and parents.*

neatness 1 = **order**, organization, harmony, tidiness, orderliness • *The grounds were a perfect balance between neatness and natural wildness.*
2 = **tidiness**, niceness, orderliness, smartness, fastidiousness, trimness, spruceness • *He was a paragon of neatness and efficiency.*
3 = **grace**, skill, efficiency, expertise, precision, elegance, agility, dexterity, deftness, nimbleness, adroitness, adeptness, daintiness, gracefulness, preciseness, skilfulness • *neatness of movement*
4 = **cleverness**, efficiency, precision, elegance, aptness • *He appreciated the neatness of their plan.*

nebulous 1 = **vague**, confused, uncertain, obscure, unclear, ambiguous, indefinite, hazy, indeterminate, imprecise, indistinct • *the nebulous concept of 'spirit'*
2 = **obscure**, vague, dim, murky, shadowy, cloudy, misty, hazy, amorphous, indeterminate, shapeless, indistinct, unformed • *We glimpsed a nebulous figure through the mist.*

necessarily 1 = **automatically**, naturally, definitely, undoubtedly, accordingly, by definition, of course, certainly • *A higher price does not necessarily guarantee a better product.*
2 = **inevitably**, of necessity, unavoidably, perforce, incontrovertibly, nolens volens *(Latin)* • *In any policy area, a number of ministries is necessarily involved.*

necessary **AS AN ADJECTIVE 1 = needed**, demanded, required, called for, essential, vital, compulsory, incumbent, mandatory, imperative, indispensable, obligatory, requisite, de rigueur *(French)*, of the essence, needful, must-have • *Is your journey really necessary?* • *Please make all the necessary arrangements.*
OPPOSITES: unnecessary, superfluous, expendable
2 = **inevitable**, sure, certain, unavoidable, inescapable • *Wastage was no doubt a necessary consequence of war.*
OPPOSITES: avoidable, unnecessary
▸ **IN PHRASES: the necessary = money**, means, funds, capital, cash, finances, resources, dough *(informal)*, the readies *(informal)*, dosh *(Brit. informal)*, the wherewithal, wonga *(slang)* • *I could always count on her if I was a bit short of the necessary.*

necessitate = **compel**, force, involve, demand, require, call for, exact, oblige, warrant, entail, constrain, impel, be grounds for, make necessary • *A prolonged drought had necessitated the introduction of water rationing.*

n

necessity AS A NOUN 1 = **need**, demand, requirement, exigency, indispensability, needfulness • *There is agreement on the necessity of reforms.*
2 = **essential**, need, necessary, requirement, fundamental, requisite, prerequisite, sine qua non *(Latin)*, desideratum, want, must-have • *Water is a basic necessity of life.*
3 = **inevitability**, certainty, inexorability, ineluctability, shoo-in *(U.S. & Canad.)* • *the ultimate necessity of death*
4 = **poverty**, need, privation, penury, destitution, extremity, indigence • *They were reduced to begging through economic necessity.*
5 = **essential**, need, requirement, fundamental • *They sometimes had to struggle to pay for necessities.*
▸ IN PHRASES: **of necessity** = **necessarily**, inevitably, unavoidably, perforce, nolens volens *(Latin)* • *The recommendations made in this handbook are, of necessity, fairly general.*

QUOTATIONS

Necessity is the mother of invention
[Jonathan Swift *Gulliver's Travels*]

Necessity never made a good bargain
[Benjamin Franklin *Poor Richard's Almanack*]

Necessity is the plea for every infringement of human freedom; it is the argument of tyrants; it is the creed of slaves
[William Pitt *speech*]

You make a virtue of necessity
[Saint Jerome *Apologeticum adversus Rufinum*]

Give us the luxuries of life, and we will dispense with its necessities
[John Lothrop Motley]

PROVERBS

Necessity knows no law
Needs must when the devil drives

neck AS A NOUN = **nape** • *a short, stocky man with a thick neck*
▸ AS A VERB = **pet**, make out, snog *(Brit. informal)*, kiss and cuddle, smooch, canoodle • *They were necking together on the sofa when I came in.*
▸ IN PHRASES: **neck and neck** = **level**, equal, side by side, close together, nip and tuck, level pegging *(Brit.)*, even-stevens *(informal)* • *The two main parties were almost neck and neck in the polls.*
▸ TECHNICAL NAME: cervix
▸ RELATED ADJECTIVE: cervical

necklace = **chain**, beads, pendant, choker, necklet • *She dropped her pearl necklace on the dressing-table.*

necromancer = **magician**, diviner, witch, wizard, sorcerer, occultist, sorceress, warlock, enchantress, enchanter, black magician • *a necromancer who conjured up the spirits of the dead*

necromancy = **magic**, witchcraft, voodoo, the occult *(rare)*, wizardry, black magic, enchantment, divination, occultism, sorcery, black art, demonology, witchery, voodooism • *They were accused of using necromancy and the black arts.*

necropolis = **cemetery**, graveyard, churchyard, burial ground, burial place, God's acre • *A small Etruscan museum and necropolis are situated 3 km east of the village.*

nee = **born**, previously, formerly • *Linda McCartney, nee Eastman*

need AS A VERB 1 = **want**, miss, require, lack, have to have, demand • *He desperately needed money.*
2 = **require**, want, demand, call for, entail, necessitate, have occasion to *or* for • *The building needs quite a few repairs.*
3 = **have to**, be obliged to • *You needn't bother, I'll do it myself.*
▸ AS A NOUN 1 = **requirement**, demand, essential, necessity, requisite, desideratum, must-have • *the special nutritional needs of children*
2 = **longing**, wish, desire, hunger, want • *The need for revenge kept eating at me.*
3 = **necessity**, call, demand, requirement, obligation • *There's no need to call the police.*
4 = **emergency**, want, necessity, urgency, exigency • *In her moment of need, her mother was nowhere to be seen.*
5 = **poverty**, deprivation, destitution, neediness, distress, extremity, privation, penury, indigence, impecuniousness • *the state of need in Third World countries*
▸ IN PHRASES: **in need** = **poor**, deprived, disadvantaged, impoverished, needy, destitute, poverty-stricken • *Food supplies are being sent to people in need.*

QUOTATIONS

From each according to his abilities, to each according to his needs
[Karl Marx *Critique of the Gotha Programme*]

needed = **necessary**, wanted, required, lacked, lacking, called for, desired • *The relief programme is designed to get much needed food to drought and war-affected areas of the country.*

needful = **necessary**, needed, required, essential, vital, imperative, indispensable, stipulated, requisite • *I will do whatever is needful to obtain the release of my friends.*

needle[1] = **irritate**, anger, provoke, annoy, sting, bait, harass, taunt, infuriate, nag, hassle *(informal)*, aggravate *(informal)*, prod, gall, ruffle, spur, prick, exasperate, nettle, vex, goad, irk, rile, get under your skin *(informal)*, get on your nerves *(informal)*, nark *(Brit., Austral. & N.Z. slang)*, hack you off *(informal)*, piss you off *(taboo slang)*, get in your hair *(informal)*, get your back up *(informal)*, run up the wrong way • *She could see that she had needled him with her constant questions.*

needle[2]
▸ RELATED PHOBIA: belenophobia

needless = **unnecessary**, excessive, pointless, gratuitous, useless, unwanted, redundant, superfluous, groundless, expendable, uncalled-for, dispensable, nonessential, undesired • *Our families thought I was taking a needless risk.*
OPPOSITES: required, essential, useful

needlework = **embroidery**, tailoring, stitching, sewing, needlecraft • *She did beautiful needlework and embroidery.*

needy AS AN ADJECTIVE = **poor**, deprived, disadvantaged, impoverished, penniless, destitute, poverty-stricken, underprivileged, indigent, down at heel *(informal)*, impecunious, dirt-poor, on the breadline *(informal)* • *a project aimed at raising funds for needy children around the world*
OPPOSITES: rich, wealthy, prosperous
▸ IN PHRASES: **the needy** = **the poor**, the disadvantaged, the impoverished, the underprivileged, the deprived, the destitute, trailer trash *(U.S., derogatory)*, the penniless • *They have organised a Christmas collection for the needy of the parish.*

ne'er-do-well = **good-for-nothing**, loser, piker *(Austral. & N.Z. slang)*, loafer, black sheep, layabout, skiver *(Brit. slang)*, idler, wastrel, bludger *(Austral. & N.Z. informal)* • *His father was a spendthrift, an alcoholic and a ne'er-do-well.*

nefarious = **wicked**, base, criminal, evil, foul, horrible, dreadful, vicious, monstrous, shameful, vile, atrocious, sinful, heinous, depraved, odious, abominable, infernal, villainous, iniquitous, execrable, detestable, opprobrious • *He was said to have committed other acts too nefarious to contemplate.*
OPPOSITES: good, just

negate 1 = **invalidate**, reverse, cancel, wipe out, void, repeal, revoke, retract, rescind, neutralize, annul, nullify, obviate, abrogate, countermand • *These environmental protection laws could be negated if the European Community decides they interfere with trade.*
2 = **deny**, oppose, contradict, refute, disallow, disprove, rebut, gainsay *(archaic or literary)* • *I can neither negate nor affirm this claim.*
OPPOSITES: maintain, confirm, testify

negation 1 = **opposite**, reverse, contrary, contradiction, converse, antithesis, inverse, antonym • *He repudiates liberty and equality as the negation of order and government.*
2 = **denial**, refusal, rejection, contradiction, renunciation,

n

repudiation, disavowal, veto • *She shook her head in a gesture of negation.*

negative AS AN ADJECTIVE 1 = **neutralizing**, invalidating, annulling, nullifying, counteractive • *This will have a very serious negative effect on economic recovery.*
2 = **pessimistic**, cynical, unwilling, gloomy, antagonistic, jaundiced, uncooperative, contrary • *There's no point in going along to an interview with a negative attitude.*
OPPOSITES: positive, optimistic, enthusiastic
3 = **dissenting**, contradictory, refusing, denying, rejecting, opposing, resisting, contrary • *Dr. Velayati gave a vague but negative response.*
OPPOSITES: positive, approving, assenting
▸ AS A NOUN = **denial**, no, refusal, rejection, contradiction • *We were fobbed off with a crisp negative.*

negativity = **pessimism**, cynicism, unwillingness, antagonism, contrariness, uncooperativeness, gloom • *I hate negativity – I can't stand people who moan all the time.*

neglect AS A VERB 1 = **disregard**, ignore, leave alone, turn your back on, fail to look after • *The woman denied that she had neglected her child.*
OPPOSITES: remember, look after, take care of
2 = **shirk**, forget, overlook, omit, evade, pass over, skimp, procrastinate over, let slide, be remiss in *or* about • *If you don't keep an eye on them, children tend to neglect their homework.*
3 = **fail**, forget, omit • *She neglected to inform me of her change of plans.*
▸ AS A NOUN 1 = **negligence**, inattention, unconcern • *hundreds of orphans, old and handicapped people, some of whom have since died of neglect*
OPPOSITES: care, attention, consideration
2 = **shirking**, failure, oversight, carelessness, dereliction, forgetfulness, slackness, laxity, laxness, slovenliness, remissness • *her deliberate neglect of her professional duty*

neglected 1 = **uncared-for**, abandoned, underestimated, disregarded, undervalued, unappreciated • *The fact that he is not coming today makes his grandmother feel neglected.*
2 = **run down**, derelict, overgrown, uncared-for • *a neglected house with an overgrown garden*

neglectful = **careless**, indifferent, lax, negligent, uncaring, thoughtless, heedless, inattentive, remiss, unmindful • *Children who are neglected tend to become neglectful parents.*

negligence = **carelessness**, failure, neglect, disregard, indifference, shortcoming, omission, oversight, dereliction, forgetfulness, slackness, inattention, laxity, thoughtlessness, laxness, inadvertence, inattentiveness, heedlessness, remissness • *He was responsible for his patients' deaths through gross negligence.*

negligent 1 = **careless**, slack, thoughtless, inadvertent, unthinking, forgetful, slapdash, neglectful, heedless, slipshod, inattentive, remiss, unmindful, disregardful • *The jury ruled that the Council had acted in a negligent manner.*
OPPOSITES: careful, thorough, thoughtful
2 = **nonchalant**, cool, casual, detached, indifferent, careless, laid-back *(informal)*, airy, unconcerned, dispassionate, offhand, insouciant • *He responded with a negligent wave.*

negligible = **insignificant**, small, minute, minor, petty, trivial, trifling, unimportant, inconsequential, imperceptible, nickel-and-dime *(U.S. slang)* • *Managers are convinced that the strike will have a negligible effect.*
OPPOSITES: important, significant, vital

negotiable 1 = **debatable**, flexible, unsettled, undecided, open to discussion, discussable *or* discussible • *The manor is for sale at a negotiable price.*
2 = **valid**, transferable, transactional • *The bonds may no longer be negotiable*
3 = **passable**, open, clear, navigable, unobstructed, traversable, crossable • *Parts of the road had been washed away, but it was still negotiable.*

negotiate 1 = **bargain**, deal, contract, discuss, debate, consult, confer, mediate, hold talks, arbitrate, cut a deal, conciliate, parley, discuss terms • *The president may be willing to negotiate with the democrats.*
2 = **arrange**, manage, settle, work out, bring about, transact • *The local government and the army have negotiated a truce.*
3 = **get round**, clear, pass, cross, pass through, get over, get past, surmount • *I negotiated the corner on my motorbike.*

negotiation 1 = **bargaining**, debate, discussion, transaction, dialogue, mediation, arbitration, wheeling and dealing *(informal)* • *We have had meaningful negotiations and I believe we are close to a deal.*
2 = **arrangement**, management, settlement, working out, transaction, bringing about • *They intend to take no part in the negotiation of a new treaty of union.*

negotiator = **mediator**, ambassador, diplomat, delegate, intermediary, arbitrator, moderator, honest broker • *He is respected as a strong negotiator.*

neighbourhood *or (U.S.)* **neighborhood** 1 = **district**, community, quarter, region, surroundings, locality, locale • *It seemed like a good neighbourhood to raise my children.*
2 = **vicinity**, confines, proximity, precincts, environs, purlieus • *the loss of woodlands in the neighbourhood of large towns*

QUOTATIONS
The Bible tells us to love our neighbours, and also to love our enemies; probably because they are generally the same people
[G. K. Chesterton]

▸ RELATED ADJECTIVE: vicinal

neighbouring *or (U.S.)* **neighboring** = **nearby**, next, near, bordering, surrounding, connecting, adjacent, adjoining, abutting, contiguous, nearest • *More parents are sending their children to schools in neighbouring areas.*
OPPOSITES: far, remote, distant

neighbourly *or (U.S.)* **neighborly** = **helpful**, kind, social, civil, friendly, obliging, harmonious, amiable, considerate, sociable, genial, hospitable, companionable, well-disposed • *I invited them to dinner as a neighbourly gesture of goodwill.*

Nemesis *sometimes not cap.* = **retribution**, fate, destruction, destiny, vengeance • *So far they had escaped their nemesis, but that afternoon it was to fall heavily on them.*

neologism = **new word**, buzz word *(informal)*, coinage, new phrase, vogue word, nonce word • *The newspaper used the neologism 'dinks', Double Income No Kids*

neophyte = **novice**, student, pupil, recruit, amateur, beginner, trainee, apprentice, disciple, learner, tyro, probationer, novitiate, proselyte, catechumen • *The book is a wonderfully stimulating read for both neophytes and wine buffs.*

ne plus ultra = **ultimate**, extreme, perfection, the last word, culmination, acme, uttermost point • *The new building is the ne plus ultra of theatrical design.*

nepotism = **favouritism**, bias, patronage, preferential treatment, partiality • *They protested at what they described as nepotism and corruption in the government.*

nerd *or* **nurd** 1 = **bore**, obsessive, anorak *(informal)*, geek *(informal)*, trainspotter *(informal)*, dork *(slang)*, wonk *(informal)*, techie *(informal)* • *the outdated notion that users of the Internet are all sad computer nerds*
2 = **fool**, weed, drip *(informal)*, sap *(slang)*, wally *(slang)*, sucker *(slang)*, wimp *(informal)*, booby, prat *(slang)*, plonker *(slang)*, twit *(informal, chiefly Brit.)*, simpleton, dipstick *(Brit. slang)*, schmuck *(U.S. slang)*, divvy *(Brit. slang)*, putz *(U.S. slang)*, wuss *(slang)*, eejit *(Scot. & Irish)*, thicko *(Brit. slang)*, dumb-ass *(slang)*, doofus *(slang, chiefly U.S.)*, dorba *or* dorb

n

(Austral. slang), bogan *(Austral. slang)* • *No woman in her right mind would look twice at such a charmless little nerd.*

nerve AS A NOUN 1 = **bravery**, courage, spirit, bottle *(Brit. slang)*, resolution, daring, determination, guts *(informal)*, pluck, grit, fortitude, vigour, coolness, balls *(taboo slang)*, mettle, firmness, spunk *(informal)*, fearlessness, steadfastness, intrepidity, hardihood, gameness • *I never got up enough nerve to ask her out.* • *If we keep our nerve, we might be able to bluff it out.*
2 = **impudence**, face *(informal)*, front, neck *(informal)*, sauce *(informal)*, cheek *(informal)*, brass *(informal)*, gall, audacity, boldness, temerity, chutzpah *(U.S. & Canad. informal)*, insolence, impertinence, effrontery, brass neck *(Brit. informal)*, brazenness, sassiness *(U.S. slang)* • *He had the nerve to ask me to prove who I was.*
▸ AS A PLURAL NOUN = **tension**, stress, strain, anxiety, butterflies (in your stomach) *(informal)*, nervousness, cold feet *(informal)*, heebie-jeebies *(slang)*, worry • *I just played badly. It wasn't nerves.*
▸ IN PHRASES: **get on someone's nerves** = **annoy**, provoke, bug *(informal)*, needle *(informal)*, plague, irritate, aggravate *(informal)*, madden, ruffle, exasperate, nettle, irk, rile, peeve, get under your skin *(informal)*, nark *(Brit., Austral. & N.Z. slang)*, get up your nose *(informal)*, make your blood boil, piss you off *(taboo slang)*, rub (someone) up the wrong way *(informal)*, get your goat *(slang)*, get in your hair *(informal)*, get on your wick *(Brit. slang)*, put your back up, hack you off *(informal)* • *The kids get on her nerves a bit at times.*
nerve yourself = **brace yourself**, prepare yourself, steel yourself, fortify yourself, gear yourself up, gee yourself up • *I nerved myself to face the pain.*
▸ TECHNICAL NAME: neuron or neurone
▸ RELATED ADJECTIVE: neural

nerveless 1 = **fearless**, cool, collected, calm, brave, daring, composed, courageous, controlled, gutsy *(slang)*, plucky, impassive, unafraid, unemotional, self-possessed, imperturbable • *He's a nerveless player – that's how he won the Open.*
2 = **powerless**, weak, feeble, debilitated, lifeless, enervated • *The phone dropped from his nerveless fingers.*

nerve-racking or **nerve-wracking** = **tense**, trying, difficult, worrying, frightening, distressing, daunting, harassing, stressful, harrowing, gut-wrenching • *The presentation of a speech can be a nerve-racking experience.*

nervous often with **of** = **apprehensive**, anxious, uneasy, edgy, worried, wired *(slang)*, tense, fearful, shaky, hysterical, neurotic, agitated, ruffled, timid, hyper *(informal)*, jittery *(informal)*, uptight *(informal)*, flustered, on edge, excitable, nervy *(Brit. informal)*, jumpy, twitchy *(informal)*, fidgety, timorous, highly strung, antsy *(informal)*, toey *(Austral. slang)*, adrenalized • *I get very nervous when I'm in the house alone at night.*
OPPOSITES: even, together *(slang)*, calm

nervous breakdown = **collapse**, breakdown, crack-up *(informal)*, neurasthenia *(obsolete)*, nervous disorder • *His wife could not cope and suffered a nervous breakdown.*

nervousness = **anxiety**, stress, tension, strain, unease, disquiet, agitation, trepidation, timidity, excitability, perturbation, edginess, worry, jumpiness, antsiness *(informal)* • *I smiled in an attempt to hide my nervousness.*

nervy = **anxious**, nervous, tense, agitated, wired *(slang)*, restless, jittery *(informal)*, on edge, excitable, jumpy, twitchy *(informal)*, fidgety, adrenalized • *Sometimes dad was nice to us, but sometimes he was bad-tempered and nervy.*

nest 1 = **roost**, eyrie • *I can see an eagle's nest on the rocks.*
2 = **lair**, den, burrow • *He discovered a rats' nest built from the remains of cardboard boxes.*
3 = **refuge**, resort, retreat, haunt, den, hideaway • *He moved into a £2,000-a-month love nest with his blonde mistress.*
4 = **hotbed**, den, breeding-ground • *Biarritz was notorious in those days as a nest of spies.*

nest egg = **savings**, fund(s), store, reserve, deposit, fall-back, cache • *They have a little nest egg tucked away for a rainy day.*

nestle often with **up** or **down** = **snuggle**, cuddle, huddle, curl up, nuzzle • *The new puppy nestled in her lap.*

nestling = **chick**, fledgling, baby bird • *The nestlings are six weeks old when they fly for the first time.*

net[1] AS A NOUN = **mesh**, netting, network, web, lattice, reticulum, tracery, lacework, openwork • *the use of a net in greenhouses to protect crops against insects*
▸ AS A VERB = **catch**, bag, capture, trap, nab *(informal)*, entangle, ensnare, enmesh • *Poachers have been netting fish to sell on the black market.*
▸ RELATED ADJECTIVE: retiary

net[2] or **nett** AS AN ADJECTIVE 1 = **after taxes**, final, clear, take-home • *At the year end, net assets were £18 million.*
2 = **final**, closing, ultimate, eventual, conclusive • *The party made a net gain of 210 seats.*
▸ AS A VERB = **earn**, make, clear, gain, realize, bring in, accumulate, reap • *The state government expects to net about 1.46 billion rupees.*

nether = **lower**, bottom, beneath, underground, inferior, basal • *He was escorted back to the nether regions of Main Street.*

netherworld or **nether world** = **hell**, underworld, Hades, nether regions, infernal regions, Avernus • *magic spells which ensured the dead safe passage though the netherworld to paradise*

nettle = **irritate**, provoke, annoy, gall, sting, aggravate *(informal)*, incense, ruffle, exasperate, vex, goad, pique, get on your nerves *(informal)*, nark *(Brit., Austral. & N.Z. slang)*, hack you off *(informal)*, piss you off *(taboo slang)* • *I instantly regretted my remark, because it obviously nettled him.*

nettled = **irritated**, provoked, annoyed, stung, put out, hacked (off) *(U.S. slang)*, pissed *(Brit., Austral. & N.Z. slang)*, incensed, galled, ruffled, exasperated, vexed, pissed off *(taboo slang)*, goaded, riled, peeved, piqued • *He was nettled by her casual manner.*

network 1 = **web**, system, arrangement, grid, mesh, lattice, circuitry, nexus, plexus, interconnection, net • *The uterus is supplied with a network of blood vessels and nerves.*
2 = **maze**, warren, labyrinth • *Strasbourg, with its rambling network of medieval streets*
3 = **system**, structure, complex, organization • *He is keen to point out the benefits which the family network can provide.*

neurosis = **obsession**, instability, mental illness, abnormality, phobia, derangement, mental disturbance, psychological or emotional disorder • *Her mother was over-protective to the point of neurosis.*

neurotic = **unstable**, nervous, disturbed, anxious, abnormal, obsessive, compulsive, manic, unhealthy, hyper *(informal)*, twitchy *(informal)*, overwrought, maladjusted • *He was almost neurotic about being followed.*
OPPOSITES: together *(slang)*, normal, rational

neuter AS A VERB = **castrate**, doctor *(informal)*, emasculate, spay, dress, fix *(informal)*, geld • *Responsible cat owners should have their pets neutered.*
▸ AS AN ADJECTIVE = **sexless**, androgynous, asexual, hermaphrodite, nonsexual, epicene • *I am really neuter, neither male nor female.*

neutral 1 = **unbiased**, impartial, disinterested, even-handed, dispassionate, sitting on the fence, uninvolved, noncommittal, nonpartisan, unprejudiced, nonaligned, unaligned, noncombatant, nonbelligerent • *Those who had decided to remain neutral now found themselves forced to take sides.*
OPPOSITES: active, participating, biased
2 = **expressionless**, dull, blank, deadpan, toneless • *He told her about the death, describing the events in as neutral a manner as he could.*

3 = **uncontroversial** *or* **noncontroversial**, safe, harmless, innocuous, inoffensive, unobjectionable, unprovocative • *Stick to talking about neutral subjects on your first meeting.*
4 = **colourless**, achromatic • *I tend to wear neutral colours like grey and beige.*

neutrality = **impartiality**, detachment, noninterference, disinterestedness, nonpartisanship, noninvolvement, nonalignment, noninterventionism • *He had a reputation for political neutrality and impartiality.*

neutralize *or* **neutralise** = **counteract**, cancel, offset, undo, compensate for, negate, invalidate, counterbalance, nullify • *antibodies that neutralize the toxic effects of soluble antigens*

never 1 = **at no time**, not once, not ever • *She was never really well after that.*
OPPOSITES: always, constantly, every time
2 = **under no circumstances**, no way, not at all, on no account, not on your life *(informal)*, not on your nelly *(Brit. slang)*, not for love nor money *(informal)*, not ever • *I would never do anything to hurt him.*

never-ending = **endless**, constant, continuous, persistent, eternal, relentless, perpetual, continual, unbroken, uninterrupted, interminable, incessant, everlasting, unchanging, ceaseless, unremitting, nonstop, unceasing • *a never-ending round of bombings, shootings and sectarian murder*

never-never = **hire-purchase** *(Brit.)*, H.P. *(Brit.)* • *In Britain we have long considered it socially acceptable to buy on the never-never.*

nevertheless = **even so**, still, however, yet, regardless, nonetheless, notwithstanding, in spite of that, (even) though, but • *She found him physically repugnant, but she nevertheless agreed to marry him.*

new 1 = **modern**, recent, contemporary, up-to-date, latest, happening *(informal)*, different, current, advanced, original, fresh, novel, topical, state-of-the-art, ground-breaking, modish, newfangled, modernistic, ultramodern, all-singing, all-dancing • *a brilliant new invention that puts a world of information at your fingertips*
OPPOSITES: old, aged, old-fashioned
2 = **brand new**, unused • *There are many boats, new and used, for sale.*
3 = **extra**, more, added, new-found, supplementary • *Many are looking for a new source of income by taking on freelance work.*
4 = **unfamiliar**, unaccustomed, strange, unknown • *I had been in my new job only a few days.* • *She was still new to the art of bargaining.*
5 = **renewed**, changed, improved, restored, altered, rejuvenated, revitalized • *The treatment made him feel like a new man.*

QUOTATIONS
There is no new thing under the sun
[*Bible: Ecclesiastes*]

newcomer 1 = **new arrival**, incomer, immigrant, stranger, foreigner, alien, settler • *He must be a newcomer to town.*
2 = **beginner**, stranger, outsider, novice, new arrival, parvenu, newbie *(slang)*, Johnny-come-lately *(informal)* • *The candidates are all relative newcomers to politics.*

newfangled = **new**, recent, modern, contemporary, fashionable, state-of-the-art, new-fashioned, gimmicky, all-singing, all-dancing, novel • *He's just bought one of these new-fangled home cinema systems.*
OPPOSITES: old-fashioned, dated, obsolete

newly = **recently**, just, lately, freshly, anew, latterly • *She was young at the time, and newly married.*

newness = **novelty**, innovation, originality, freshness, strangeness, unfamiliarity • *We all need newness in our lives to stop us from stagnating.*
▸ RELATED PREFIX: neo-
▸ RELATED PHOBIA: neophobia

news = **information**, latest *(informal)*, report, word, story, release, account, statement, advice, exposé, intelligence, scandal, rumour, leak, revelation, buzz, gossip, dirt *(U.S. slang)*, goss *(informal)*, disclosure, bulletin, dispatch, gen *(Brit. informal)*, communiqué, hearsay, tidings, news flash, scuttlebutt *(U.S. slang)* • *They still haven't had any news about the survivors.*

QUOTATIONS
As cold waters to a thirsty soul, so is good news from another country
[*Bible: Proverbs*]
News may be true, but it is not truth, and reporters and officials seldom see it the same way
[James Reston *The Artillery of the Press*]
If people didn't give the news their news, and if everybody kept their news to themselves, the news wouldn't have any news
[Andy Warhol *From A to B and Back Again*]
When a dog bites a man, that is not news, because it happens so often. But if a man bites a dog, that is news
[John B. Bogart]
all the news that's fit to print
[Adolph S. Ochs *motto of the New York Times*]
PROVERBS
No news is good news

newsworthy = **interesting**, important, arresting, significant, remarkable, notable, sensational, noteworthy • *The number of deaths involved makes the story newsworthy.*

next AS AN ADJECTIVE 1 = **following**, later, succeeding, subsequent • *I caught the next available flight.*
2 = **adjacent**, closest, nearest, neighbouring, adjoining • *The man in the next chair was asleep.*
▸ AS AN ADVERB = **afterwards**, then, later, following, subsequently, thereafter • *I don't know what to do next.*
▸ IN PHRASES: **next to** = **beside**, by, near, close to, alongside, next door to, adjacent to, at the side of, abreast of, cheek by jowl with • *The car was parked in the small weedy lot next to the hotel.*

next world = **afterlife**, heaven, paradise, nirvana, hereafter, afterworld • *I believe we shall meet our departed loved ones in the next world.*

nexus = **connection**, link, tie, bond, junction, joining • *The nexus between drugs, prostitution and corruption is universal.*

nibble AS A VERB *often with* **at** = **bite**, eat, peck, pick at, nip, munch, gnaw • *He started to nibble his biscuit.*
▸ AS A NOUN = **snack**, bite, taste, peck, crumb, morsel, titbit, soupçon *(French)* • *We each took a nibble of cheese.*

nice 1 = **pleasant**, delightful, agreeable, good, attractive, charming, pleasurable, enjoyable • *We had a nice meal with a bottle of champagne.*
OPPOSITES: awful, dreadful, unpleasant
2 = **kind**, helpful, obliging, considerate • *It was nice of you to go to so much trouble.*
OPPOSITES: mean, unpleasant, unkind
3 = **likable** *or* **likeable**, friendly, engaging, charming, pleasant, agreeable, amiable, prepossessing • *I've met your father and I think he's really nice.*
4 = **polite**, cultured, refined, courteous, genteel, well-bred, well-mannered • *The kids are very well brought up and have nice manners.*
OPPOSITES: crude, coarse, vulgar
5 = **fine**, clear, fair, dry, bright, pleasant, sunny, clement, balmy • *If the weather stays nice, we'll go for a picnic.*
6 = **precise**, fine, careful, strict, accurate, exact, exacting, subtle, delicate, discriminating, rigorous, meticulous, scrupulous, fastidious • *As a politician, he drew a nice distinction between his own opinions and the wishes of the majority.*
OPPOSITES: rough, vague, careless

n

nicely 1 = **pleasantly**, well, delightfully, attractively, charmingly, agreeably, pleasingly, acceptably, pleasurably • *He's just written a book, nicely illustrated and not too technical.*
OPPOSITES: unpleasantly, unattractively
2 = **kindly**, politely, thoughtfully, amiably, courteously • *He treated you very nicely and acted like a decent guy.*
3 = **precisely**, exactly, accurately, exactingly, finely, carefully, strictly, subtly, delicately, meticulously, rigorously, scrupulously • *I think this sums up the problem very nicely.*
OPPOSITES: carelessly, sloppily *(informal)*
4 = **satisfactorily**, well, adequately, acceptably, passably • *She has a private income, so they manage very nicely.*

niceness = **kindness**, charm, goodness, decency, friendliness, amiability, pleasantness, agreeableness, likableness *or* likeableness • *I think it was Joe's niceness and kindness that attracted me.*

nicety = **fine point**, distinction, subtlety, nuance, refinement, minutiae • *We have dealt with all the legal niceties.*

niche 1 = **recess**, opening, corner, hollow, nook, alcove • *There was a niche in the rock where the path ended.*
2 = **position**, calling, place, slot *(informal)*, vocation, pigeonhole *(informal)* • *Perhaps I will find my niche in a desk job.*

nick AS A NOUN 1 = **cut**, mark, scratch, score, chip, scar, notch, dent, snick • *The barbed wire had left only the tiniest nick below my right eye.*
2 = **prison**, can *(slang)*, jail, clink *(slang)*, stir *(slang)*, cooler *(slang)*, jug *(slang)*, penitentiary *(U.S.)*, slammer *(slang)*, lockup, penal institution, choky *(slang)*, poky *or* pokey *(U.S. & Canad. slang)*, boob *(Austral. slang)* • *He spent a few years in the nick for smuggling.*
▸ AS A VERB 1 = **steal**, pinch *(informal)*, swipe *(slang)*, pilfer, trouser *(slang)*, knock off *(slang)*, snitch *(slang)* • *We used to nick biscuits from the kitchen.*
2 = **arrest**, apprehend, take into custody, nail *(informal)*, lift *(slang)*, seize, run in *(slang)*, bust *(informal)*, collar *(informal)*, pinch *(informal)*, nab *(informal)*, take prisoner, feel your collar *(slang)* • *The police nicked me for carrying an offensive weapon.*
3 = **cut**, mark, score, damage, chip, scratch, scar, notch, dent, snick • *A sharp blade is likely to nick the skin and draw blood.*

nickname = **pet name**, label, diminutive, epithet, sobriquet, familiar name, moniker *or* monicker *(slang)*, handle *(slang)* • *He got the nickname of "Ginger" because of his red hair.*

nifty 1 = **slick**, excellent, sharp, smart, clever, neat, stylish, schmick *(Austral. informal)* • *The film features some nifty special effects.*
2 = **agile**, quick, swift, skilful, deft • *Knight displayed all the nifty legwork of a champion bowler.*

niggardly 1 = **stingy**, mean, avaricious, ungenerous, close, near *(informal)*, sparing, grudging, mercenary, frugal, parsimonious, penurious, tightfisted, Scrooge-like, tight-arse *(taboo slang)*, tight-arsed *(taboo slang)*, tight-ass *(U.S. taboo slang)*, tight-assed *(U.S. taboo slang)*, snoep *(S. African informal)*, tight as a duck's arse *(taboo slang)* • *Officials say the EU is being particularly niggardly with these funds.*
OPPOSITES: liberal, generous, lavish
2 = **paltry**, mean, small, inadequate, miserable, pathetic, insufficient, beggarly, scant, meagre, skimpy, measly, scanty, wretched • *The niggardly compensation for her frightening ordeal amounted to just £6,500.*
OPPOSITES: liberal, generous, handsome

niggle AS A VERB 1 = **bother**, concern, worry, trouble, disturb, rankle • *I realise now that the things which used to niggle me didn't really matter.*
2 = **criticize**, provoke, annoy, plague, irritate, hassle *(informal)*, badger, find fault with, nag at, cavil, be on your back *(slang)* • *I don't react any more when opponents try to niggle me.*
▸ AS A NOUN = **complaint**, moan, grievance, grumble, beef *(slang)*, bitch *(slang)*, lament, grouse, gripe *(informal)*, grouch *(informal)* • *The life we have built together is far more important than any minor niggle either of us might have.*

niggling 1 = **irritating**, troubling, persistent, bothersome • *Both players have been suffering from niggling injuries.*
2 = **petty**, minor, trifling, insignificant, unimportant, fussy, quibbling, picky *(informal)*, piddling *(informal)*, nit-picking *(informal)*, finicky, pettifogging • *They started having tiffs about the most niggling little things.*

nigh AS AN ADVERB = **almost**, about, nearly, close to, practically, approximately • *Accurate earthquake prediction is well nigh impossible.*
▸ AS AN ADJECTIVE = **near**, next, close, imminent, impending, at hand, upcoming • *The end of the world is nigh.*

night AS A NOUN = **darkness**, dark, night-time, dead of night, night watches, hours of darkness • *We spent the night at his house.* • *Finally night fell.*
▸ IN PHRASES: **night and day** = **constantly**, all the time, continually, continuously, endlessly, incessantly, ceaselessly, interminably, unremittingly, twenty-four-seven *(informal)*, day in, day out • *He was at my door night and day, demanding attention.*
▸ RELATED ADJECTIVE: nocturnal
▸ RELATED MANIA: noctimania
▸ RELATED PHOBIA: nyctophobia

QUOTATIONS
Night hath a thousand eyes
[John Lyly *Maides Metamorphose*]
The night has a thousand eyes,
And the day but one
[F.W. Bourdillon *Light*]
Night is the half of life, and the better half
[Johann Wolfgang von Goethe *Wilhelm Meisters Lehrjahre*]
the huge and thoughtful night
[Walt Whitman *When Lilacs Last in the Dooryard Bloom'd*]
sable-vested night, eldest of things
[John Milton *Paradise Lost*]

nightfall = **evening**, sunset, twilight, dusk, sundown, eventide, gloaming *(Scot. poetic)*, eve *(archaic)*, evo *(Austral. slang)* • *We started work at dawn and stopped at nightfall.*
OPPOSITES: morning, dawn, daybreak

nightingale
▸ COLLECTIVE NOUN: watch

nightly AS AN ADJECTIVE = **nocturnal**, night-time • *One of the nurses came by on her nightly rounds.*
▸ AS AN ADVERB = **every night**, nights *(informal)*, each night, night after night • *She had prayed nightly for his safe return.*

nightmare 1 = **bad dream**, hallucination, night terror • *Jane did not eat cheese because it gave her nightmares.*
2 = **ordeal**, trial, hell, horror, torture, torment, tribulation, purgatory, hell on earth • *My years in prison were a nightmare.*

nightmarish = **terrifying**, frightening, disturbing, appalling, horrible, horrific, ghastly, hideous, harrowing, frightful • *She described a nightmarish scene of dead bodies lying in the streets.*

nihilism 1 = **negativity**, rejection, denial, scepticism, cynicism, pessimism, renunciation, atheism, repudiation, agnosticism, unbelief, abnegation • *These disillusioned students embraced agnosticism, atheism, and nihilism.*
2 = **anarchy**, disorder, lawlessness • *This moral nihilism has proved both irresponsible and politically counter-productive.*

nihilist 1 = **cynic**, sceptic, atheist, pessimist, agnostic, unbeliever • *Ripley has become a world-weary nihilist.*
2 = **anarchist**, revolutionary, extremist, agitator • *At heart, he's a revolutionist, an anarchist, a nihilist.*

nil 1 = **nothing**, love, zero, zip *(U.S. slang)* • *The score was 2-nil.*

2 = zero, nothing, none, naught, zilch *(slang)*, zip *(U.S. slang)* • *The chances of success are virtually nil.*

nimble 1 = agile, active, lively, deft, proficient, sprightly, nippy *(Brit. informal)*, spry, dexterous • *Lily, who was light and nimble on her feet, was learning to tap-dance.*
OPPOSITES: heavy, slow, clumsy
2 = alert, ready, bright *(informal)*, sharp, keen, active, smart, quick-witted • *To keep your mind nimble, you must use it.*

nimbleness 1 = agility, skill, grace, lightness, proficiency, dexterity, alacrity, adroitness, sprightliness, nippiness *(Brit. informal)*, spryness • *The friar leapt to his feet with a nimbleness we could scarcely credit.*
2 = smartness, brightness *(informal)*, sharpness, alertness, keenness, quick-wittedness • *One needed all one's nimbleness of wit to answer their questions.*

nimbly 1 = agilely, lightly, easily, smartly, briskly, gracefully, deftly, skilfully, spryly, proficiently, dexterously • *Sabrina jumped nimbly out of the van.*
2 = smartly, sharply, alertly, readily, quick-wittedly • *The head of Quebec's Treasury Board has negotiated nimbly with the trade unions.*

nimbus = halo, atmosphere, glow, aura, ambience, corona, irradiation, aureole • *Kevin was surrounded by a nimbus of sunlight.*

nincompoop = idiot, charlie *(Brit. informal)*, fool, jerk *(slang, chiefly U.S. & Canad.)*, plank *(Brit. slang)*, berk *(Brit. slang)*, prick *(derogatory slang)*, wally *(slang)*, prat *(slang)*, plonker *(slang)*, coot, geek *(slang)*, twit *(informal, chiefly Brit.)*, chump, dunce, oaf, simpleton, dimwit *(informal)*, dipstick *(Brit. slang)*, dickhead *(slang)*, gonzo *(slang)*, schmuck *(U.S. slang)*, dork *(slang)*, nitwit *(informal)*, dolt, blockhead, ninny, divvy *(slang)*, pillock *(Brit. slang)*, dweeb *(U.S. slang)*, putz *(U.S. slang)*, fathead *(informal)*, eejit *(Scot. & Irish)*, thicko *(Brit. slang)*, dumb-ass *(slang)*, gobshite *(Irish taboo slang)*, numpty *(Scot. informal)*, doofus *(slang, chiefly U.S.)*, lamebrain *(informal)*, fuckwit *(taboo slang)*, nerd *or* nurd *(slang)*, numbskull *or* numskull, dorba *or* dorb *(Austral. slang)*, bogan *(Austral. slang)* • *Only a complete nincompoop would believe a story like that.*

nine
▸ **RELATED PREFIX:** nona-

nip[1] AS A VERB 1 *with* **along, up, out,** *(Brit. informal)* **= pop**, go, run, rush, dash • *Could you nip down to the corner shop for some milk?*
2 = bite, snap, nibble • *She was patting the dog when it nipped her finger.*
3 = pinch, catch, grip, squeeze, clip, compress, tweak • *He gave Billy's cheek a nip between two rough fingers.*
▸ **IN PHRASES: nip something in the bud = thwart**, check, frustrate • *It is important to recognize jealousy and to nip it in the bud before it gets out of hand.*

nip[2] = dram, shot *(informal)*, drop, taste, finger, swallow, portion, peg *(Brit.)*, sip, draught, sup, mouthful, snifter *(informal)*, soupçon *(French)* • *She had a habit of taking an occasional nip from a flask of cognac.*

nipper 1 = child, girl, boy, baby, kid *(informal)*, infant, tot, little one, sprog *(slang)*, munchkin *(informal, chiefly U.S.)*, rug rat *(slang)*, littlie *(Austral. informal)*, ankle-biter *(Austral. slang)*, tacker *(Austral. slang)* • *I couldn't have been much more than a nipper when you last saw me.*
2 = pincer, claw • *Just inside the ragworm's mouth is a sharp, powerful pair of nippers.*

nipple = teat, breast, boob *(slang)*, udder, dug, tit, pap, papilla, mamilla • *Most newborn mammals possess an instinctive urge to seek out their mother's nipple.*
▸ **TECHNICAL NAME:** mamilla
▸ **RELATED ADJECTIVE:** mamillary

nippy 1 = chilly, biting, parky *(Brit. informal)* • *It can get quite nippy in the evenings.*
2 = fast *(Informal)*, quick, speedy • *This nippy new car has fold-down rear seats.*
3 = agile, fast, quick, active, lively, nimble, sprightly, spry • *He's nippy, and well suited to badminton.*

nirvana = paradise, peace, joy, bliss, serenity, tranquillity • *They believe in a continuous cycle of births and deaths until the soul is perfected and achieves nirvana.*

nit-picking *or* **nitpicking = fussy**, carping, quibbling, pedantic, finicky, cavilling, pettifogging, anal retentive, captious, hairsplitting • *Perfectionists are fussy, nit-picking types who worry about every little detail.*

nitty-gritty = basics, facts, reality, essentials, core, fundamentals, substance, essence, bottom line, crux, gist, nuts and bolts, heart of the matter, ins and outs, brass tacks *(informal)* • *They are more concerned with matters of principle than with the nitty-gritty of everyday politics.*

nitwit = fool, dummy *(slang)*, plank *(Brit. slang)*, geek *(slang)*, oaf, simpleton, dimwit *(informal)*, dipstick *(Brit. slang)*, dickhead *(slang)*, dork *(slang)*, ninny, divvy *(slang)*, halfwit, nincompoop, putz *(U.S. slang)*, eejit *(Scot. & Irish)*, thicko *(Brit. slang)*, gobshite *(Irish taboo slang)*, numpty *(Scot. informal)*, doofus *(slang, chiefly U.S.)*, lamebrain *(informal)*, fuckwit *(taboo slang)*, dorba *or* dorb *(Austral. slang)*, bogan *(Austral. slang)* • *You great nitwit! What did you do that for?*

no AS A SENTENCE SUBSTITUTE = not at all, certainly not, of course not, absolutely not, never, no way, nay • *'Any problems?' – 'No, everything's fine.'*
OPPOSITES: yes, of course, certainly
▸ **AS A NOUN 1 = refusal**, rejection, denial, negation, veto • *My answer to that is an emphatic no.*
OPPOSITES: acceptance, consent, assent
2 = objector, protester, dissident, dissenter • *According to the latest poll, the noes have 50 per cent and the yeses 35 per cent.*

nob = aristocrat, fat cat *(slang, chiefly U.S.)*, toff *(Brit. slang)*, bigwig *(informal)*, celeb *(informal)*, big shot *(informal)*, big hitter *(informal)*, aristo *(informal)*, heavy hitter *(informal)*, nabob *(informal)*, V.I.P. • *The crook revealed how he mixed with nobs as he pretended to be an aristocrat.*

nobble 1 = influence, square, win over, pay off *(informal)*, corrupt, intimidate, bribe, get at, buy off, suborn, grease the palm *or* hand of *(slang)* • *The trial was stopped after allegations of attempts to nobble the jury.*
2 = disable, handicap, weaken, incapacitate • *the drug used to nobble two horses at Doncaster last week*
3 = thwart, check, defeat, frustrate, snooker, foil, baffle, balk, prevent • *Their plans were nobbled by jealous rivals.*

nobility 1 = aristocracy, lords, elite, nobles, upper class, peerage, ruling class, patricians, high society • *They married into the nobility and entered the highest ranks of society.*
2 = dignity, majesty, greatness, grandeur, magnificence, stateliness, nobleness • *I found Mr. Mandela supremely courteous, with a genuine nobility of bearing.*
3 = integrity, honour, virtue, goodness, honesty, righteousness, probity, rectitude, worthiness, incorruptibility, uprightness • *There can be no doubt about the remarkable strength and nobility of her character.*
▸ **RELATED ADJECTIVE:** nobiliary

QUOTATIONS
New nobility is but the act of power, but ancient nobility is the act of time
[Francis Bacon *Essays*]

▹ *See panel* **Ranks of nobility**

noble AS AN ADJECTIVE 1 = worthy, generous, upright, honourable, virtuous, magnanimous • *He was an upright and noble man.*
OPPOSITES: selfish, dishonest, despicable
2 = dignified, great, august, imposing, impressive, distinguished, magnificent, splendid, stately • *She was described by contemporaries as possessing a noble bearing and excellent manners.*
OPPOSITES: mean, modest, lowly

n

RANKS OF NOBILITY

Ranks of British nobility (in order of precedence)

royal duke *or (fem.)* royal duchess
duke *or (fem.)* duchess
marquess or marquis *or (fem.)* marchioness
earl *or (fem.)* countess
viscount *or (fem.)* viscountess
baron *or (fem.)* baroness
baronet

Ranks of foreign nobility

archduke *or (fem.)* archduchess
boyar
burgrave
count *or (fem.)* countess
grand duke *or (fem.)* grand duchess
grandee
landgrave *or (fem.)* landgravine
marchese *or (fem.)* marchesa
margrave *or (fem.)* margravine
marquis *or (fem.)* marquise
prince *or (fem.)* princess
vicomte *or (fem.)* vicomtesse

3 = **aristocratic**, lordly, titled, gentle *(archaic)*, patrician, blue-blooded, highborn • *Although he was of noble birth he lived as a poor man.*
OPPOSITES: base, peasant, humble
▸ AS A NOUN = **lord**, peer, aristocrat, nobleman, aristo *(informal)* • *In those days, many of the nobles and landowners were a law unto themselves.*
OPPOSITES: peasant, commoner, serf

nobody AS A PRONOUN = **no-one** • *They were shut away in a little room where nobody could overhear*
▸ AS A NOUN = **nonentity**, nothing *(informal)*, lightweight *(informal)*, non-person, zero, cipher • *A man in my position has nothing to fear from a nobody like you.*
OPPOSITES: star, celebrity, superstar

nocturnal = **nightly**, night, of the night, night-time • *These creatures have a predominantly nocturnal lifestyle.*

nod AS A VERB 1 = **agree**, concur, assent, show agreement • *'Are you okay?' I asked. She nodded and smiled.*
2 = **incline**, bob, bow, duck, dip • *She nodded her head in understanding.*
3 = **signal**, indicate, motion, gesture • *He lifted his end of the canoe, nodding to me to take up mine.*
4 = **salute**, acknowledge • *All the girls nodded and said 'Hi'.*
▸ AS A NOUN 1 = **signal**, sign, motion, gesture, indication • *Then, at a nod from their leader, they all sat.*
2 = **salute**, greeting, acknowledgment • *I gave him a quick nod of greeting and slipped into the nearest chair.*
▸ IN PHRASES: **give someone the nod** = **give the go-ahead**, give the green light, give the okay, greenlight • *Keep him outside till I give you the nod.*
nod off = **fall asleep**, sleep, nap, doze, kip *(Brit. slang)*, drowse, slump, droop, drop off • *The judge appeared to nod off while the witness was being cross-examined.*

node = **nodule**, growth, swelling, knot, lump, bump, bud, knob, protuberance • *Cut the branches off cleanly through the stem just below the node.*

noise = **sound**, talk, row, racket, outcry, clamour, din, clatter, uproar, babble, blare, fracas, commotion, pandemonium, rumpus, cry, tumult, hubbub • *There was too much noise in the room and he needed peace.*
OPPOSITES: silence, peace, calm
▸ RELATED MANIA: phonomania

noiseless = **silent**, soundless, quiet, mute, muted, hushed, inaudible, still • *Her soft shoes were noiseless on the marble floor.*

noisome = **disgusting**, offensive, foul, stinking, smelly, reeking, noxious, fetid, putrid, malodorous, mephitic, niffy *(Brit. slang)*, festy *(Austral. slang)*, yucko *(Austral. slang)* • *Noisome vapours arise from the mud left in the docks*

noisy 1 = **rowdy**, chattering, strident, boisterous, vociferous, riotous, uproarious, obstreperous, clamorous • *a noisy group of drunken students*
OPPOSITES: quiet, silent, subdued
2 = **loud**, piercing, deafening, tumultuous, ear-splitting, cacophonous, clamorous • *It may be necessary to ask a neighbour to turn down noisy music.*
OPPOSITES: still, quiet, silent

nomad = **wanderer**, migrant, rover, rambler, itinerant, drifter, vagabond • *The greater part was desert, inhabited by nomads.*

nomadic = **wandering**, travelling, roaming, migrant, roving, itinerant, migratory, vagrant, peripatetic • *the nomadic tribes of the Western Sahara*

nom de plume = **pseudonym**, alias, pen name, assumed name • *Dodgson wrote under the nom de plume of Lewis Carroll.*

nomenclature = **terminology**, vocabulary, classification, taxonomy, phraseology, codification, locution • *We owe the modern system of lunar nomenclature to an Italian astronomer.*

nominal 1 = **titular**, formal, purported, in name only, supposed, so-called, pretended, theoretical, professed, ostensible • *As he was still not allowed to run a company, his wife became its nominal head.*
2 = **token**, small, symbolic, minimal, trivial, trifling, insignificant, inconsiderable • *The ferries carry bicycles for a nominal charge.*

nominate 1 = **propose**, suggest, recommend, submit, put forward • *The public will be able to nominate candidates for the awards.*
2 = **appoint**, name, choose, commission, select, elect, assign, designate, empower • *It is legally possible for an elderly person to nominate someone to act for them.*

nomination 1 = **proposal**, suggestion, recommendation • *a list of nominations for senior lectureships*
2 = **appointment**, election, selection, designation, choice • *On Leo's death there were two main candidates for nomination as his replacement.*

nominee = **candidate**, applicant, entrant, contestant, aspirant, runner • *The President vetoed two Pinochet nominees for the top army rank of major general.*

QUOTATIONS

nominee: a modest gentleman shrinking from the distinction of private life and diligently seeking the honorable obscurity of public office
[Ambrose Bierce *The Devil's Dictionary*]

nonaligned = **neutral**, impartial, uninvolved, nonpartisan, noncombatant, nonbelligerent • *a meeting of foreign ministers from non-aligned countries*

nonchalance = **indifference**, insouciance, detachment, unconcern, cool *(slang)*, calm, apathy, composure, carelessness, equanimity, casualness, sang-froid, self-possession, dispassion, imperturbability • *He walked in with exaggerated nonchalance, his hands in his pockets.*

nonchalant = **indifferent**, cool, calm, casual, detached, careless, laid-back *(informal)*, airy, unconcerned, apathetic, dispassionate, unfazed *(informal)*, unperturbed, blasé, offhand, unemotional, insouciant, imperturbable • *Denis tried unsuccessfully to look nonchalant and uninterested.*
OPPOSITES: involved, concerned, caring

noncommittal = **evasive**, politic, reserved, guarded,

careful, cautious, neutral, vague, wary, discreet, tentative, ambiguous, indefinite, circumspect, tactful, equivocal, temporizing, unrevealing • *I've got a nasty feeling that I shall get a very bland non-committal answer.*

non compos mentis = **insane**, mentally ill, unbalanced, of unsound mind, crazy, deranged, unhinged, a sausage short of a fry-up *(slang)*, off the air *(Austral. slang)* • *No person under guardianship, non compos mentis or insane shall be qualified to vote in any election.*
OPPOSITES: rational, all there *(informal)*, sane

nonconformist AS AN ADJECTIVE = **dissenting**, dissident, heterodox, schismatic • *Their views are nonconformist and their political opinions are extreme.*
▸ AS A NOUN = **dissenter**, rebel, radical, protester, eccentric, maverick, heretic, individualist, iconoclast, dissentient • *Hoover's task was to collect information on radicals and nonconformists.*
OPPOSITES: traditionalist, Babbitt *(U.S.)*, yes man

nondescript = **undistinguished**, ordinary, dull, commonplace, unremarkable, run-of-the-mill, uninspiring, indeterminate, uninteresting, featureless, insipid, unexceptional, common or garden *(informal)*, mousy, characterless, unmemorable, vanilla *(informal)*, nothing to write home about • *a mousy woman as nondescript and lacking in chic as it was possible to be*
OPPOSITES: unique, unusual, distinctive

none AS A PRONOUN 1 = **not any**, nothing, zero, not one, zip *(U.S. slang)*, nil, no part, not a bit, zilch *(slang, chiefly U.S. & Canad.)*, bugger all *(slang)*, fuck all *(Brit. taboo slang)*, diddly *(U.S. slang)*, sweet Fanny Adams *(Brit. slang)*, f.a. *(Brit. slang)*, sweet F.A. *(Brit. slang)* • *I turned to bookshops and libraries seeking information and found none.*
2 = **no-one**, nobody, not one • *None of us knew what to say to her.*
▸ IN PHRASES: **none the** = **not at all**, by no means, not a bit, not the slightest bit • *His lengthy explanation left us none the wiser.*

nonentity = **nobody**, lightweight *(informal)*, mediocrity, cipher, small fry, non-person, unimportant person • *She was written off after that as a political nonentity.*

non-essential or **nonessential** = **unnecessary**, peripheral, unimportant, superfluous, extraneous, expendable, dispensable, inessential • *The crisis has led to the closure of a number of non-essential services.*
OPPOSITES: important, significant, essential

nonetheless = **nevertheless**, however, yet, even so, despite that, in spite of that • *His face was serious, but nonetheless very friendly.*

nonevent = **flop** *(informal)*, failure, disappointment, fiasco, dud *(informal)*, washout, clunker *(informal)* • *Unfortunately, the entire evening was a total non-event.*

nonexistent = **imaginary**, imagined, fancied, fictional, mythical, unreal, hypothetical, illusory, insubstantial, hallucinatory, chimerical • *The paper trail revealed a long history of fraud, with false invoices and sales to nonexistent customers.*
OPPOSITES: real, true, existing

nonpareil AS A NOUN = **ideal**, best, finest, perfection, paragon, ne plus ultra • *In league, if not international football, he remains the nonpareil.*
▸ AS AN ADJECTIVE = **unequalled**, supreme, unique, unparalleled, unrivalled, incomparable, unmatched, peerless, unsurpassed, matchless • *Sinatra is the nonpareil popular vocalist.*

non-partisan or **nonpartisan** = **neutral**, independent, objective, detached, impartial, unbiased, unaffiliated, unprejudiced, nonpolitical • *I went in search of a non-partisan opinion.*

non-payment = **defaulting**, dodging, evasion, failure to pay • *She has received an eviction order for non-payment of rent.*

nonplussed = **taken aback**, stunned, confused, embarrassed, puzzled, astonished, stumped, dismayed, baffled, bewildered, astounded, confounded, perplexed, disconcerted, mystified, fazed, dumbfounded, discomfited, flummoxed, discountenanced • *Patricia was totally nonplussed by Coyne's behaviour.*

nonsense AS A NOUN 1 = **rubbish**, hot air *(informal)*, waffle *(informal, chiefly Brit.)*, twaddle, balls *(taboo slang)*, bull *(slang)*, shit *(taboo slang)*, pants *(slang)*, rot, crap *(slang)*, garbage *(informal)*, trash, bunk *(informal)*, bullshit *(taboo slang)*, tosh *(slang, chiefly Brit.)*, bollocks *(Brit. taboo slang)*, rhubarb, pap, cobblers *(Brit. taboo slang)*, foolishness, bilge *(informal)*, drivel, tripe *(informal)*, gibberish, guff *(slang)*, bombast, moonshine, claptrap *(informal)*, hogwash, hokum *(slang, chiefly U.S. & Canad.)*, blather, double Dutch *(Brit. informal)*, piffle *(informal)*, poppycock *(informal)*, balderdash, bosh *(informal)*, eyewash *(informal)*, stuff and nonsense, tommyrot, horsefeathers *(U.S. slang)*, bunkum or buncombe *(chiefly U.S.)*, bizzo *(Austral. slang)*, bull's wool *(Austral. & N.Z. slang)* • *Most orthodox doctors, however, dismiss this theory as complete nonsense.*
OPPOSITES: fact, reason, sense
2 = **idiocy**, folly, stupidity, absurdity, silliness, inanity, senselessness, ridiculousness, ludicrousness, fatuity • *Surely it is an economic nonsense to deplete the world of natural resources.*
▸ IN PHRASES: **no-nonsense** = **down-to-earth**, practical, sensible, realistic, common-sense, matter-of-fact, hard-headed, grounded • *With his gruff Scottish voice and no-nonsense attitude, he's an imposing figure.*

nonsensical = **senseless**, crazy, silly, ridiculous, absurd, foolish, ludicrous, meaningless, irrational, incomprehensible, inane, asinine, cockamamie *(slang, chiefly U.S.)* • *It seemed to me that Sir Robert's arguments were nonsensical.*

nonstarter = **dead loss**, dud *(informal)*, washout *(informal)*, no-hoper *(informal)*, turkey *(informal)*, lemon *(informal)*, loser, waste of space or time • *The United States is certain to reject the proposal as a non-starter.*

nonstop AS AN ADJECTIVE = **continuous**, constant, relentless, uninterrupted, steady, endless, unbroken, interminable, incessant, unending, ceaseless, unremitting, unfaltering • *The training was non-stop and continued for three days.*
OPPOSITES: broken, occasional, irregular
▸ AS AN ADVERB = **continuously**, constantly, steadily, endlessly, relentlessly, perpetually, incessantly, without stopping, ceaselessly, interminably, unremittingly, uninterruptedly, unendingly, unfalteringly, unbrokenly • *The snow fell non-stop for 24 hours.*

non-violent or **nonviolent** = **peaceful**, pacifist, peaceable, nonbelligerent • *They used only lawful, reasonable and non-violent forms of protest.*

nook = **niche**, corner, recess, cavity, crevice, alcove, cranny, inglenook *(Brit.)*, cubbyhole, opening • *We found a seat in a little nook and had some lunch.*

noon AS A NOUN = **midday**, high noon, noonday, noontime, twelve noon, noontide • *The long day of meetings started at noon.*
▸ AS AN ADJECTIVE = **midday**, noonday, noontime, noontide • *The noon sun was fierce.*

no one or **no-one** = **nobody**, no man, not a soul • *Everyone wants to be a hero, but no one wants to die.*

norm AS A NOUN = **standard**, rule, model, pattern, mean, type, measure, average, par, criterion, benchmark, yardstick • *Their actions departed from what she called the commonly accepted norms of behaviour.*
▸ IN PHRASES: **the norm** = **the rule**, the average, par for the

n

course, the usual thing • *Families of six or seven were the norm in those days.*

normal 1 = **usual**, common, standard, average, natural, regular, ordinary, acknowledged, typical, conventional, routine, accustomed, habitual, run-of-the-mill • *The two countries have resumed normal diplomatic relations.* • *The hospital claimed they were simply following their normal procedure.*
OPPOSITES: rare, unusual, remarkable
2 = **sane**, reasonable, rational, lucid, well-adjusted, compos mentis *(Latin)*, in your right mind, mentally sound, in possession of all your faculties • *Depressed patients are more likely to become ill than normal people.*

normality *or (U.S.)* **normalcy** 1 = **regularity**, order, routine, ordinariness, naturalness, conventionality, typicality, usualness • *A semblance of normality has returned to the city after the attack.*
2 = **sanity**, reason, balance, rationality, lucidity • *Behind the smiling facade of normality lurked a psychopathic serial killer.*

normalize = **standardize**, bring into line, regularize, make normal • *Acupuncture can ease pain and help normalize the menstrual cycle.*

normally 1 = **usually**, generally, commonly, regularly, typically, ordinarily, as a rule, habitually • *Normally, the transportation system in Paris carries 950,000 passengers a day.*
2 = **as usual**, naturally, properly, conventionally, in the usual way • *the failure of the blood to clot normally*

normative = **standardizing**, controlling, regulating, prescriptive, normalizing, regularizing • *Normative sexual behaviour in our society remains heterosexual.*

Norse
▹ *See panel* **Mythology**

north AS AN ADJECTIVE = **northern**, polar, arctic, boreal, northerly • *On the north side of the mountain* • *a bitterly cold north wind*
▸ AS AN ADVERB = **northward(s)**, in a northerly direction • *The hurricane which had destroyed Honolulu was moving north.*

North Star = **Pole Star**, Polaris, lodestar • *I could see the Bear and had identified the North Star.*

nose AS A NOUN 1 = **snout**, bill, beak, hooter *(slang)*, snitch *(slang)*, conk *(slang)*, neb *(archaic or dialect)*, proboscis, schnozzle *(slang, chiefly U.S.)* • *She's got funny eyes and a big nose.*
2 = **instinct**, feeling, intuition, sixth sense • *My mother has always had a nose for a bargain.*
▸ AS A VERB = **ease forward**, push, edge, shove, nudge • *The car nosed forward out of the drive.* • *Ben drove past them, nosing his car into the garage.*
▸ IN PHRASES: **by a nose** = **only just**, just, hardly, barely, scarcely, by the skin of your teeth • *She won her first race by a nose.*
get up someone's nose = **irritate**, annoy, anger, madden, get *(informal)*, bug *(informal)*, aggravate *(informal)*, gall, exasperate, nettle, vex, irk, rile, peeve, get under someone's skin *(informal)*, get someone's back up, piss someone off *(taboo slang)*, put someone's back up, nark *(Brit., Austral. & N.Z. slang)*, get someone's goat *(slang)*, make someone's blood boil, get someone's dander up *(informal)*, hack you off *(informal)* • *What really got up my nose was the way he denied all responsibility.*
look down your nose at something *or* **someone** = **despise**, scorn, disdain, look down on, contemn • *He looks down his nose at those he considers lesser mortals.*
nose around *or* **about** = **search**, examine, investigate, explore, inspect, work over, fossick *(Austral. & N.Z.)* • *Police officers were nosing around for clues.* • *Accountants are nosing around the BBC at the moment, conducting an efficiency study.*
nose something out = **detect**, smell, scent, sniff out • *The dogs nosed out the stash of illegal drugs.*
poke *or* **stick your nose into something** = **pry**, interfere, meddle, intrude, snoop *(informal)*, be inquisitive • *We don't take kindly to strangers who poke their noses into our affairs.*
turn up your nose at *or* **turn your nose up at something** *or* **someone** = **reject**, refuse, turn down, spurn, say no to • *I'm not in a financial position to turn up my nose at such a good offer.*
▸ RELATED ADJECTIVES: nasal, rhinal

QUOTATIONS
Give me a man with a good allowance of nose
[Napoleon Bonaparte]

nose dive AS A NOUN 1 = **drop**, plunge, dive, plummet, sharp fall • *The catamaran sailed over the precipice and plunged into a nosedive.*
2 = **sharp fall**, plunge, drop, dive, plummet • *My career has taken a nosedive in the past year or two.*
▸ AS A VERB 1 = **drop**, plunge, dive, plummet, fall sharply • *The cockpit was submerged as the plane nosedived into the water.*
2 = **fall sharply**, drop, plunge, dive, plummet • *The value of the shares nosedived by £2.6 billion.*

nosegay = **posy**, spray, bouquet, corsage • *In Greece, marjoram is considered to be lucky and is used in bridal garlands and nosegays.*

nosey *or* **nosy** = **inquisitive**, curious, intrusive, prying, eavesdropping, snooping *(informal)*, busybody, interfering, meddlesome • *He whispered to avoid being overheard by their nosey neighbours.*

nosh AS A NOUN 1 = **food**, eats *(slang)*, fare, grub *(slang)*, feed, tack *(informal)*, scoff *(slang)*, kai *(N.Z. informal)*, chow *(informal)*, sustenance, victuals, comestibles, nosebag *(slang)*, vittles *(obsolete dialect)*, viands • *a restaurant which serves fine wines and posh nosh*
2 = **meal**, repast • *We went for a nosh at our local Indian restaurant.*
▸ AS A VERB = **eat**, consume, scoff *(slang)*, devour, feed on, munch, gobble, partake of, wolf down, hoover *(informal)* • *Guests mingled in the gardens, sipped wine, and noshed at cabaret tables.* • *sipping enormous bowls of frothy cappuccino and noshing huge slabs of carrot cake*

nostalgia = **reminiscence**, longing, regret, pining, yearning, remembrance, homesickness, wistfulness • *He felt a wave of nostalgia for the life he had left behind him.*

QUOTATIONS
Nostalgia isn't what it used to be
[Anon.]

nostalgic = **sentimental**, longing, emotional, homesick, wistful, maudlin, regretful • *I got nostalgic the other night and dug out my old photos.*

nostril
▸ TECHNICAL NAME: naris
▸ RELATED ADJECTIVES: narial, narine

nostrum 1 = **remedy**, answer, solution, cure • *They are still peddling yesterday's failed socialist nostrums.*
2 = **medicine**, drug, treatment, cure, remedy, potion, panacea, elixir, cure-all, patent medicine, quack medicine, specific • *Supermarket shelves are lined with nostrums claiming to alleviate flu symptoms.*

notability 1 = **fame**, celebrity, distinction, esteem, eminence, renown • *The book contained 48 charts, each dedicated to a person of notability.*
2 = **celebrity**, worthy, notable, big name, dignitary, celeb *(informal)*, personage, megastar *(informal)*, V.I.P. • *They want to get hold of some minor television notability to open the fete.*

notable AS AN ADJECTIVE 1 = **remarkable**, marked, striking, unusual, extraordinary, outstanding, evident, pronounced, memorable, noticeable, uncommon, conspicuous, salient, noteworthy • *The most notable architectural feature of the town is its castle.*

OPPOSITES: hidden, concealed, imperceptible
2 = prominent, famous, celebrated, distinguished, well-known, notorious, renowned, eminent, pre-eminent • *the notable occultist, Madame Blavatsky*
OPPOSITES: unknown, obscure, anonymous
▸ **AS A NOUN = celebrity**, worthy, big name, dignitary, luminary, celeb (*informal*), personage, megastar (*informal*), notability, V.I.P. • *The notables attending included five Senators, two Supreme Court judges and three State Governors.*

notably 1 = particularly, especially, in particular, principally, primarily, specially • *He said that other countries – notably those of Eastern Europe – were in need of assistance.*
2 = remarkably, unusually, distinctly, extraordinarily, markedly, noticeably, strikingly, conspicuously, singularly, outstandingly, uncommonly, pre-eminently, signally • *a notably brave officer who had served under Wolfe at Quebec*

notation 1 = signs, system, characters, code, symbols, script • *The dot in musical notation symbolizes an abrupt or staccato quality.*
2 = note, record, noting, jotting • *He was checking the readings and making notations on a clipboard.*

notch AS A NOUN 1 = level, step, degree, grade, cut (*informal*) • *Average earnings in the economy moved up another notch in August.*
2 = cut, nick, incision, indentation, mark, score, cleft • *The blade had a hole through the middle and a notch on one side.*
▸ **AS A VERB = cut**, mark, score, nick, scratch, indent • *a bamboo walking stick with a notched handle*
▸ **IN PHRASES: notch something up = achieve**, make, score, gain, register • *He had notched up more than 25 victories worldwide.*

MUSICAL NOTES AND RESTS

British name	American name
breve	double-whole note
semibreve	whole note
minim	half note
crotchet	quarter note
quaver	eighth note
semiquaver	sixteenth note
demisemiquaver	thirty-second note
hemidemisemiquaver	sixty-fourth note

note AS A NOUN 1 = message, letter, communication, memo, memorandum, epistle, e-mail, text • *Stevens wrote him a note asking him to come to his apartment.*
2 = record, reminder, memo, memorandum, jotting, minute • *I made a note of his address.*
3 = annotation, comment, remark, gloss • *See note 16 on page 223.*
4 = document, form, record, certificate • *In the eyes of the law, signing a delivery note is seen as 'accepting' the goods.*
5 = symbol, mark, sign, indication, token • *He has never been able to read or transcribe musical notes.*
6 = tone, touch, trace, hint, sound • *I detected a note of bitterness in his voice.*
▸ **AS A PLURAL NOUN = jottings**, record, impressions, outline, report • *I want to type up my notes from the meeting.*
▸ **AS A VERB 1 = notice**, see, observe, perceive • *Suddenly I noted that the rain had stopped.*
2 = bear in mind, be aware, take into account • *Please note that there are a limited number of tickets.*
3 = mention, record, mark, indicate, register, remark • *The report noted a sharp drop in cases of sexually transmitted diseases.*
4 = write down, record, scribble, take down, set down, jot down, put in writing, put down in black and white • *A policeman was noting the number plates of passing cars.*
▸ **IN PHRASES: of note 1 = famous**, prestigious, eminent, renowned, of standing, of character, of reputation, of consequence, celebrated • *Besides being an artist of great note, he can also be a fascinating conversationalist.*
2 = important, consequential, significant, of distinction • *She has published nothing of note in the last ten years.*
take note of something *or* **someone = notice**, note, regard, observe, heed, pay attention to • *Take note of the weather conditions.*
▹ *See panel* **Music; Musical notes and rests**

notebook = notepad, record book, exercise book, jotter, journal, diary, Filofax (*trademark*), memorandum book • *He brought out a notebook and pen from his pocket.*

noted = famous, celebrated, recognized, distinguished, well-known, prominent, notorious, acclaimed, notable, renowned, eminent, conspicuous, illustrious • *Chomsky's father was a noted Hebrew scholar.* • *The paper has never been noted for its foreign affairs coverage.*
OPPOSITES: unknown, obscure, infamous

noteworthy = remarkable, interesting, important, significant, extraordinary, outstanding, exceptional, notable • *None of these buildings are noteworthy for their architecture.*
OPPOSITES: normal, ordinary, pedestrian

nothing AS A PRONOUN 1 = nought, zero, nil, naught, not a thing, zilch (*slang*), bugger all (*slang*), fuck all (*taboo slang*), sod all (*slang*), damn all (*slang*), zip (*U.S. slang*) • *I know nothing of these matters.*
2 = a trifle, no big deal, a mere bagatelle • *'Thanks for all your help.' 'It was nothing.'*
3 = void, emptiness, nothingness, nullity, nonexistence • *philosophical ideas of the void, the nothing and the 'un-thought'*
▸ **AS A NOUN = nobody**, cipher, nonentity, non-person • *I went from being a complete nothing to all of a sudden having people calling me the new star of the Nineties.*
▸ **IN PHRASES: be** *or* **have nothing to do with something** *or* **someone 1 = be unconnected with**, be irrelevant to, have no connection with, be unrelated to • *Both sides say the deal has nothing to do with the freeing of the hostages.*
2 = avoid, shun, steer clear of, keep away from, cold-shoulder, body-swerve (*Scot.*) • *He's a villain – I'd have nothing to do with him if I were you.*
for nothing = free, for free, without charge, at no cost, gratis • *He said he'd do the repairs for nothing.*
nothing but = just, only, simply, merely • *All that money brought us nothing but misery.*

QUOTATIONS
Nothing, like something, happens anywhere
[Philip Larkin *I Remember, I Remember*]
Nothing can be created out of nothing
[Lucretius *De Rerum Natura*]
Nothing will come of nothing
[William Shakespeare *King Lear*]

nothingness 1 = oblivion, nullity, nonexistence, nonbeing • *There might be something beyond the grave, you know, and not just nothingness.*
2 = insignificance, triviality, worthlessness, meaninglessness, unimportance • *the banal lyrics, clichéd song structures and light, fluffy nothingness of her latest album*

notice AS A NOUN 1 = sign, advertisement, poster, placard, warning, bill • *A few seaside guest houses had 'No Vacancies' notices in their windows.*
2 = notification, warning, advice, intimation, news, communication, intelligence, announcement, instruction, advance warning, wake-up call, heads up (*U.S. & Canad.*) • *Unions are requested to give seven days' notice of industrial action.*
3 = review, comment, criticism, evaluation, critique, critical assessment • *She got some good notices for her performance last night.*

n

4 = **attention**, interest, note, regard, consideration, observation, scrutiny, heed, cognizance • *Nothing that went on in the hospital escaped her notice.*
OPPOSITES: neglect, ignorance, oversight
5 = **the sack** *(informal)*, dismissal, discharge, the boot *(slang)*, the push *(slang)*, marching orders *(informal)*, the (old) heave-ho *(informal)*, your books *or* cards *(informal)* • *They predicted that many teachers would be given their notice by the end of next term.*
▸ **IN PHRASES: take no notice of something** *or* **someone** = **ignore**, pay no attention to, pass over, overlook, cut *(informal)*, discount, neglect, blank *(slang)*, disregard, turn a blind eye to, cold-shoulder, turn your back on, turn a deaf ear to, send (someone) to Coventry, give the cold shoulder to, shut your eyes to • *They took no notice of him.*
▸ **AS A VERB** = **observe**, see, mind, note, spot, remark, distinguish, perceive, detect, heed, discern, behold *(archaic or literary)*, mark, eyeball *(slang)* • *People should not hesitate to contact the police if they notice anything suspicious.*
OPPOSITES: ignore, overlook, neglect

noticeable = **obvious**, clear, striking, plain, bold, evident, distinct, manifest, conspicuous, unmistakable, salient, observable, perceptible, appreciable • *These changes have had no noticeable effect on productivity.*

noticeboard = **pinboard**, bulletin board • *She added her name to the list on the noticeboard.*

notification = **announcement**, declaration, notice, statement, telling, information, warning, message, advice, intelligence, publication, notifying, heads up *(U.S. & Canad.)* • *We require written notification from the person who signed the booking form.*

notify = **inform**, tell, advise, alert to, announce, warn, acquaint with, make known to, apprise of • *The skipper notified the coastguard of the tragedy.*

notion 1 = **idea**, view, opinion, belief, concept, impression, judgment, sentiment, conception, apprehension, inkling, mental image *or* picture, picture • *I disagree with the notion that violence on TV causes acts of violence in society.* • *He has a realistic notion of his capabilities.*
2 = **whim**, wish, desire, fancy, impulse, inclination, caprice • *I had a whimsical notion to fly off to Rio that night.*

notional = **hypothetical**, ideal, abstract, theoretical, imaginary, speculative, conceptual, unreal, fanciful • *the notional value of assets*
OPPOSITES: real, actual, genuine

notoriety = **infamy**, discredit, disrepute, dishonour, bad reputation, opprobrium, ill repute, obloquy • *The team's fans have acquired notoriety as being among the worst hooligans in the country.*

notorious = **infamous**, disreputable, opprobrious • *one of Britain's most notorious serial killers*

notoriously = **infamously**, disreputably • *The company is understaffed and notoriously inefficient.*

notwithstanding **AS A PREPOSITION** = **despite**, in spite of, regardless of • *He despised Pitt, notwithstanding the similar views they both held.*
▸ **AS A SENTENCE CONNECTOR** = **nevertheless**, however, though, nonetheless • *He doesn't want me there, but I'm going, notwithstanding.*

nought *or* **naught** *or* **ought** *or* **aught** 1 = **zero**, nothing, nil • *Properties are graded from nought to ten for energy efficiency.*
2 = **nothing**, zip *(U.S. slang)*, slang, nothingness, nada, zilch, bugger all *(slang)*, fuck all *(taboo slang)*, sod all *(slang)*, damn all *(slang)* • *All our efforts came to nought.*

noun
▸ **RELATED ADJECTIVE:** nominal

nourish 1 = **feed**, supply, sustain, nurture • *The food the mother eats nourishes both her and her baby.*
2 = **encourage**, support, maintain, promote, sustain, foster, cultivate • *This attitude has been carefully nourished by a small group of journalists and scholars.*
3 = **cherish**, have, hold, entertain, harbour, cling to • *They continued to nourish hopes of victory.*

nourishing = **nutritious**, beneficial, wholesome, healthful, health-giving, nutritive • *Eat only sensible, nourishing foods.*

nourishment = **food**, nutrition, sustenance, nutriment, tack *(informal)*, kai *(N.Z. informal)*, victuals, vittles *(obsolete dialect)*, viands • *He was unable to take nourishment for several days.*

nouveau riche **AS A NOUN** = **arriviste**, upstart, new-rich, parvenu • *The nouveau riche have to find a way of being accepted.* • *the gaudy mansions Shaw built for the nouveaux riches in the late 19th century*
▸ **AS AN ADJECTIVE** = **arriviste**, upstart, newly-rich, parvenu • *The countryside is changing and nouveau riche people are moving in.*

novel[1] = **story**, tale, fiction, romance, narrative • *He had all but finished writing a first novel.*

QUOTATIONS
Yes – oh dear yes – the novel tells a story
[E.M. Forster *Aspects of the Novel*]
There are three rules for writing the novel. Unfortunately, no one knows what they are
[W. Somerset Maugham]
novel: a short story padded
[Ambrose Bierce *The Devil's Dictionary*]
If you try to nail anything down in the novel, either it kills the novel, or the novel gets up and walks away with the nail
[D.H. Lawrence *Phoenix*]

novel[2] = **new**, different, original, fresh, unusual, innovative, uncommon, singular, ground-breaking, left-field *(informal)* • *Staging your own murder mystery party is a novel way to entertain a group of friends.*
OPPOSITES: common, traditional, ordinary

novelist = **author**, writer • *The key to success as a romantic novelist is absolute belief in your story.*
▹ *See panel* **Novelists**

novelty 1 = **newness**, originality, freshness, innovation, surprise, uniqueness, strangeness, unfamiliarity • *The radical puritanism of Conceptual art and Minimalism had lost its novelty.*
2 = **curiosity**, marvel, rarity, oddity, wonder • *In those days a motor car was still a novelty.*
3 = **trinket**, souvenir, memento, bauble, bagatelle, gimcrack, trifle, gewgaw, knick-knack • *At Easter, we give them plastic eggs filled with small toys, novelties and coins.*

QUOTATIONS
A "new thinker", when studied closely, is merely a man who does not know what other people have thought
[F.M. Colby]

novice 1 = **beginner**, pupil, amateur, newcomer, trainee, apprentice, learner, neophyte, tyro, probationer, newbie *(slang)*, proselyte • *I'm a novice at these things. You're the professional.*
OPPOSITES: teacher, professional, expert
2 = **novitiate** • *She had entered the monastery as a novice many months previously.*

novitiate 1 = **apprenticeship**, training, probation • *These monks left the monastery without completing their novitiate.*
2 = **novice**, probationer, postulant • *Claudio's sister, Isabella, is a novitiate in a convent.*

now **AS AN ADVERB** 1 = **nowadays**, at the moment, these days • *Beef now costs over 30 roubles a pound.*
2 = **immediately**, presently *(Scot. & U.S.)*, promptly, instantly, at once, straightaway • *Please tell him I need to talk to him now.*
▸ **IN PHRASES: as of now** = **from now on**, henceforth, henceforward, from this time on, from this time forward

NOVELISTS

Peter Abrahams *(South African)*
Chinua Achebe *(Nigerian)*
Peter Ackroyd *(English)*
Douglas Adams *(English)*
Richard Adams *(English)*
Alain-Fournier *(French)*
Brian Aldiss *(English)*
James Aldridge *(Australian)*
Al Alvarez *(English)*
Eric Ambler *(English)*
Kingsley Amis *(English)*
Martin Amis *(English)*
Mulk Raj Anand *(Indian)*
Maya Angelou *(U.S.)*
Lucius Apuleius *(Roman)*
Jeffrey Archer *(English)*
Isaac Asimov *(U.S.)*
Margaret Atwood *(Canadian)*
Louis Auchincloss *(U.S.)*
Jane Austen *(English)*
Beryl Bainbridge *(English)*
R M Ballantyne *(Scottish)*
J G Ballard *(English)*
Honoré de Balzac *(French)*
Iain Banks *(Scottish)*
Lynne Reid Banks *(English)*
Elspeth Barker *(Scottish)*
Pat Barker *(English)*
Julian Barnes *(English)*
Stanley Barstow *(English)*
John Barth *(U.S.)*
H E Bates *(English)*
Nina Bawden *(English)*
Simone de Beauvoir *(French)*
Sybille Bedford *(British)*
Max Beerbohm *(English)*
Aphra Behn *(English)*
Saul Bellow *(Canadian)*
Andrei Bely *(Russian)*
David Benedictus *(English)*
(Enoch) Arnold Bennett *(English)*
John Berger *(English)*
Thomas Berger *(U.S.)*
Maeve Binchy *(Irish)*
R(ichard) D(oddridge) Blackmore *(English)*
Alan Bleasdale *(English)*
Heinrich Böll *(German)*
Elizabeth Bowen *(Irish)*
Paul Bowles *(U.S.)*
William Boyd *(Scottish)*
Malcolm Bradbury *(English)*
Barbara Taylor Bradford *(English)*
Melvin Bragg *(English)*
John Braine *(English)*
André Brink *(South African)*
Vera Brittain *(English)*
Louis Bromfield *(U.S.)*
Anne Brontë *(English)*
Charlotte Brontë *(English)*
Emily (Jane) Brontë *(English)*
Christina Brooke-Rose *(English)*
Anita Brookner *(English)*
Brigid Brophy *(English)*
George Douglas Brown *(Scottish)*
George Mackay Brown *(Scottish)*

John Buchan *(Scottish)*
Pearl Buck *(U.S.)*
Mikhail Afanaseyev Bulgakov *(Russian)*
John Bunyan *(English)*
Anthony Burgess *(British)*
Fanny Burney *(English)*
Edgar Rice Burrows *(U.S.)*
William Burroughs *(U.S.)*
Samuel Butler *(English)*
A S Byatt *(English)*
Italo Calvino *(Italian)*
Albert Camus *(French)*
Elias Canetti *(Bulgarian)*
Truman Capote *(U.S.)*
Peter Carey *(Australian)*
Angela Carter *(English)*
Barbara Cartland *(English)*
Willa Cather *(U.S.)*
Camilo José Cela *(Spanish)*
Miguel de Cervantes *(Spanish)*
Raymond Chandler *(U.S.)*
G K Chesterton *(English)*
Agatha (Mary Clarissa) Christie *(English)*
Arthur C Clarke *(English)*
James Clavell *(U.S.)*
Jon Cleary *(Australian)*
J M Coetzee *(South African)*
Colette *(French)*
(William) Wilkie Collins *(English)*
Ivy Compton-Burnett *(English)*
Richard Condon *(U.S.)*
Evan Connell *(U.S.)*
Joseph Conrad *(Polish-British)*
Catherine Cookson *(English)*
James Fenimore Cooper *(U.S.)*
Jilly Cooper *(English)*
William Cooper *(English)*
Maria Correlli *(English)*
Stephen Crane *(U.S.)*
Lionel Davidson *(English)*
(William) Robertson Davies *(Canadian)*
Daniel Defoe *(English)*
Len Deighton *(English)*
E M Delafield *(English)*
Don DeLillo *(U.S.)*
Thomas de Quincy *(English)*
Anita Desai *(Indian)*
Peter De Vries *(U.S.)*
Charles (John Huffam) Dickens *(English)*
Monica Dickens *(English)*
Joan Didion *(U.S.)*
Isak Dinesen *(Danish)*
Benjamin Disraeli *(English)*
J P Donleavy *(Irish)*
John Roderigo Dos Passos *(U.S.)*
Fyodor Mikhailovich Dostoevsky *(Russian)*
Arthur Conan Doyle *(Scottish)*
Roddy Doyle *(Irish)*
Margaret Drabble *(English)*
Maureen Duffy *(English)*
Alexandre Dumas *(French)*
Daphne Du Maurier *(English)*
Nell Dunn *(English)*
Gerald Durrell *(English)*

Laurence Durrell *(English)*
Umberto Eco *(Italian)*
Maria Edgeworth *(English)*
George Eliot *(English)*
Stanley Elkin *(U.S.)*
Alice Thomas Ellis *(English)*
Ben Elton *(English)*
Zöe Fairbairns *(English)*
Philip José Farmer *(U.S.)*
Howard Fast *(U.S.)*
William Faulkner *(U.S.)*
Elaine Feinstein *(English)*
Helen Fielding *(English)*
Henry Fielding *(English)*
Eva Figes *(British)*
F(rancis) Scott (Key) Fitzgerald *(U.S.)*
Penelope Fitzgerald *(English)*
Gustave Flaubert *(French)*
Ian Fleming *(English)*
Ford Madox Ford *(English)*
Richard Ford *(U.S.)*
C S Forester *(English)*
E M Forster *(English)*
Frederick Forsyth *(English)*
John Fowles *(English)*
Janet Paterson Frame *(New Zealand)*
Dick Francis *(English)*
Antonia Fraser *(English)*
Michael Frayn *(English)*
Nicholas Freeling *(English)*
Marilyn French *(U.S.)*
Roy Fuller *(English)*
William Gaddis *(U.S.)*
Janice Galloway *(Scottish)*
John Galsworthy *(English)*
Gabriel García Márquez *(Colombian)*
Helen Garner *(Australian)*
Elizabeth Gaskell *(English)*
William Alexander Gerhardie *(English)*
Lewis Grassic Gibbon *(Scottish)*
Stella Gibbons *(English)*
André Gide *(French)*
Penelope Gilliat *(English)*
George Gissing *(English)*
Ellen Glasgow *(U.S.)*
(Margaret) Rumer Godden *(English)*
William Godwin *(English)*
Johann Wolfgang von Goethe *(German)*
Nikolai Vasilievich Gogol *(Russian)*
Herbert Gold *(U.S.)*
William (Gerald) Golding *(English)*
William Goldman *(U.S.)*
Oliver Goldsmith *(Anglo-Irish)*
Ivan Aleksandrovich Goncharov *(Russian)*
Nadine Gordimer *(South African)*
Maxim Gorky *(Russian)*
Edmund Gosse *(English)*
Winston Graham *(English)*
Günter (Wilhelm) Grass *(German)*
Robert Graves *(English)*
Alasdair Gray *(Scottish)*
Graham Greene *(English)*
John Grisham *(U.S.)*
George Grossmith *(English)*

NOVELISTS (CONTINUED)

Weedon Grossmith *(English)*
David Guterson *(U.S.)*
Rider Haggard *(English)*
Arthur Hailey *(Anglo-Canadian)*
Thomas Hardy *(English)*
L(eslie) P(oles) Hartley *(English)*
Nathaniel Hawthorne *(U.S.)*
Shirley Hazzard *(U.S.)*
Robert A Heinlein *(U.S.)*
Joseph Heller *(U.S.)*
Ernest Hemingway *(U.S.)*
Hermann Hesse *(German)*
Georgette Heyer *(English)*
Patricia Highsmith *(U.S.)*
Susan Hill *(English)*
James Hilton *(English)*
Barry Hines *(English)*
Russell Hoban *(U.S.)*
James Hogg *(Scottish)*
Winifred Holtby *(English)*
Anthony Hope *(English)*
Paul Horgan *(U.S.)*
Elizabeth Jane Howard *(English)*
Thomas Hughes *(English)*
Victor (Marie) Hugo *(French)*
Keri Hulme *(New Zealand)*
Evan Hunter *(U.S.)*
Zora Neale Hurston *(U.S.)*
Aldous Huxley *(English)*
Hammond Innes *(English)*
John Irving *(U.S.)*
Christopher Isherwood *(English-U.S.)*
Kazuo Ishiguro *(British)*
Henry James *(U.S.-British)*
P D James *(English)*
Ruth Prawer Jhabvala *(Anglo-Polish)*
Erica Jong *(U.S.)*
James Joyce *(Irish)*
Franz Kafka *(Czech)*
Johanna Kaplan *(U.S.)*
Nikos Kazantazakis *(Greek)*
Molly Keane *(Anglo-Irish)*
James Kelman *(Scottish)*
Thomas Keneally *(Australian)*
Margaret Kennedy *(English)*
Jack Kerouac *(U.S.)*
Ken Kesey *(U.S.)*
Francis King *(English)*
Stephen King *(U.S.)*
Charles Kingsley *(English)*
Rudyard Kipling *(English)*
Milan Kundera *(French-Czech)*
Pierre Choderlos de Laclos *(French)*
George Lamming *(Barbadian)*
Guiseppe Tomasi di Lampedusa *(Italian)*
D H Lawrence *(English)*
John Le Carré *(English)*
Harper Lee *(U.S.)*
Laurie Lee *(English)*
Sheridan Le Fanu *(Irish)*
Ursula Le Guin *(U.S.)*
Rosamond Lehmann *(English)*
Mikhail Yurievich Lermontov *(Russian)*
Doris Lessing *(Rhodesian)*
Primo Levi *(Italian)*
(Harry) Sinclair Lewis *(U.S.)*
Penelope Lively *(English)*
David Lodge *(English)*
Jack London *(U.S.)*
(Clarence) Malcolm Lowry *(English)*
Alison Lurie *(U.S.)*
Rose Macauley *(English)*
Carson McCullers *(U.S.)*
George MacDonald *(Scottish)*
Ian McEwan *(English)*
William McIlvanney *(Scottish)*
Colin MacInnes *(English)*
Compton MacKenzie *(English)*
Henry MacKenzie *(Scottish)*
Bernard McLaverty *(Irish)*
Alistair MacLean *(Scottish)*
Naguib Mahfouz *(Egyptian)*
Norman Mailer *(U.S.)*
Bernard Malamud *(U.S.)*
David Malouf *(Australian)*
(Cyril) Wolf Mankowitz *(English)*
Thomas Mann *(German)*
Olivia Manning *(English)*
Kamala Markandaya *(Indian)*
Frederick Marryat *(English)*
Ngaio Marsh *(New Zealand)*
Allan Massie *(Scottish)*
Somerset Maugham *(English)*
Guy de Maupassant *(French)*
Francois Mauriac *(French)*
Herman Melville *(U.S.)*
George Meredith *(English)*
James A Michener *(U.S.)*
Henry Miller *(U.S.)*
Yukio Mishima *(Japanese)*
Julian Mitchell *(English)*
Margaret Mitchell *(U.S.)*
Naomi Mitchison *(Scottish)*
Nancy Mitford *(English)*
Timothy Mo *(British)*
Nicholas Monsarrat *(English)*
Michael Moorcock *(English)*
Brian Moore *(Irish-Canadian)*
Toni Morrison *(U.S.)*
John Mortimer *(English)*
Penelope Mortimer *(Welsh)*
Nicholas Mosley *(English)*
Iris Murdoch *(Irish)*
Vladimir Vladimirovich Nabokov *(Russian-U.S.)*
V S Naipaul *(Trinidadian)*
P H Newby *(English)*
Ngugi wa Thiong'o *(Kenyan)*
Robert Nye *(English)*
Joyce Carol Oates *(U.S.)*
Edna O'Brien *(Irish)*
Flann O'Brien *(Irish)*
Kenzaburo Oë *(Japanese)*
Liam O'Flaherty *(Irish)*
John O'Hara *(U.S.)*
Ben Okri *(Nigerian)*
Margaret Oliphant *(Scottish)*
Michael Ondaatje *(Canadian)*
Baroness Emmuska Orczy *(Hungarian-British)*
George Orwell *(English)*
Ouida *(English)*
Cynthia Ozick *(U.S.)*
Boris Leonidovich Pasternak *(Russian)*
Allan Paton *(South African)*
Thomas Love Peacock *(English)*
Mervyn Peake *(English)*
Harold Porter *(Australian)*
Katherine Anne Porter *(U.S.)*
Anthony Powell *(English)*
John Cowper Powys *(English)*
Terry Pratchett *(English)*
J B Priestley *(English)*
V S Pritchett *(English)*
E Annie Proulx *(U.S.)*
Marcel Proust *(French)*
Mario Puzo *(U.S.)*
Thomas Pynchon *(U.S.)*
Ellery Queen *(U.S.)*
Ann Radcliffe *(English)*
Raja Rao *(Indian)*
Frederic Raphael *(U.S.)*
Piers Paul Read *(English)*
Erich Maria Remarque *(German)*
Mary Renault *(English)*
Ruth Rendell *(English)*
Jean Rhys *(British)*
Dorothy Richardson *(English)*
Samuel Richardson *(English)*
Mordecai Richler *(Canadian)*
Harold Robbins *(U.S.)*
Frederick William Rolfe *(English)*
Henry Roth *(U.S.)*
(Ahmed) Salman Rushdie *(Indian-British)*
Vita Sackville-West *(English)*
Marquis de Sade French
Antoine de Saint-Exupéry *(French)*
Saki *(British)*
J D Salinger *(U.S.)*
George Sand *(French)*
William Saroyan *(U.S.)*
Jean-Paul Sartre *(French)*
Dorothy L Sayers *(English)*
Olive Schreiner *(South African)*
Walter Scott *(Scottish)*
Hubert Selby Jr. *(U.S.)*
Tom Sharpe *(English)*
Mary Shelley *(English)*
Carol Shields *(Canadian-American)*
Mikhail Alexandrovich Sholokhov *(Russian)*
Nevil Shute *(Anglo-Austrian)*
Alan Sillitoe *(English)*
Georges Simenon *(Belgian)*
Claude Simon *(French)*
Isaac Bashevis Singer *(U.S.)*
Iain Crichton Smith *(Scottish)*
Zadie Smith *(British)*
Tobias George Smollett *(Scottish)*
C P Snow *(English)*
Alexander Isayevich Solzhenitsyn *(Russian)*
Muriel Spark *(Scottish)*
Howard Spring *(Welsh)*
C K Stead *(New Zealand)*

NOVELISTS (CONTINUED)

Gertrude Stein *(U.S.)*
John Steinbeck *(U.S.)*
Stendhal *(French)*
Laurence Sterne *(Irish-British)*
Robert Louis Stevenson *(Scottish)*
J I M Stewart *(Scottish)*
Mary Stewart *(English)*
Bram Stoker *(Irish)*
Robert Stone *(U.S.)*
David Storey *(English)*
Harriet Elizabeth Beecher Stowe *(U.S.)*
William Styron *(U.S.)*
Patrick Süskind *(German)*
Graham Swift *(English)*
Jonathan Swift *(Irish)*
Julian Symons *(English)*
Emma Tennant *(English)*
William Makepeace Thackeray *(English)*
Paul Theroux *(U.S.)*
J(ohn) R(onald) R(euel) Tolkien *(English)*
Leo Tolstoy *(Russian)*
John Kennedy Toole *(U.S.)*
Nigel Tranter *(Scottish)*
Rose Tremain *(English)*
William Trevor *(Irish)*
Anthony Trollope *(English)*
Joanna Trollope *(English)*
Frank Tuohy *(English)*
Ivan Sergeyevich Turgenev *(Russian)*
Amos Tutuola *(Nigerian)*
Mark Twain *(U.S.)*
Anne Tyler *(U.S.)*
John Updike *(U.S.)*
Edward (Falaise) Upward *(English)*
Leon Uris *(U.S.)*
Laurens Van der Post *(South African)*
Peter Vansittart *(English)*
Mario Vargos Llosa *(Peruvian)*
Jules Verne *(French)*
Gore Vidal *(U.S.)*
Voltaire *(French)*
Kurt Vonnegut *(U.S.)*
John Wain *(English)*
Alice Walker *(U.S.)*
Horace Walpole *(English)*
Marina Warner *(English)*
Robert Penn Warren *(U.S.)*
Keith Waterhouse *(English)*
Evelyn Waugh *(English)*
Fay Weldon *(English)*
H G Wells *(English)*
Irvine Welsh *(Scottish)*
Eudora Welty *(U.S.)*
Mary Wesley *(English)*
Morris West *(Australian)*
Rebecca West *(Irish)*
Edith Wharton *(U.S.)*
Antonia White *(English)*
Patrick White *(Austrlian)*
T H White *(English)*
Oscar Wilde *(Irish)*
Thornton Wilder *(U.S.)*
Michael Wilding *(Australian)*
A(ndrew) N(orman) Wilson *(English)*
Jeanette Winterson *(English)*
P(elham) G(renville) Wodehouse *(English-U.S.)*
Thomas Clayton Wolfe *(U.S.)*
Tom Wolfe *(U.S.)*
Tobias Wolff *(U.S.)*
Virginia Woolf *(English)*
Herman Wouk *(U.S.)*
Richard Nathaniel Wright *(U.S.)*
Frank Yerby *(U.S.)*
Marguerite Yourcenar *(French)*
Evgeny Ivanovich Zamyatin *(Russian)*
Emile Zola *(French)*

• *As of now there is no longer an East or a West Germany, just Germany.*
for now = for the moment, right now, at present, for the time being, for the present, for the meantime • *That's about all I can tell you for now.*
now and then *or* **again = occasionally**, sometimes, at times, from time to time, on and off, on occasion, once in a while, intermittently, infrequently, sporadically • *Now and then he would pay us a brief visit.*

nowadays = now, today, at the moment, these days, in this day and age • *Economic discontent is widespread in a country which is nowadays one of the poorest in Asia.*

noxious = harmful, deadly, poisonous, unhealthy, hurtful, pernicious, injurious, unwholesome, noisome, pestilential, insalubrious, foul, baneful *(archaic)* • *carbon monoxide and other noxious gases*
OPPOSITES: safe, harmless, innocuous

nuance = subtlety, degree, distinction, graduation, refinement, nicety, gradation • *Our eyes can communicate virtually every subtle nuance of emotion.*

nub = gist, point, heart, core, essence, nucleus, kernel, crux, pith • *That, I think, is the nub of the problem.*

nubile = attractive, sexy *(informal)*, desirable, ripe *(informal)*, marriageable • *He came on stage flanked by two scantily-clad young nubile beauties.*

nucleus = centre, heart, focus, basis, core, pivot, kernel, nub • *The Civic Movement could be the nucleus of a centrist party of the future.*

nude = naked, stripped, exposed, bare, uncovered, undressed, stark-naked, in the raw *(informal)*, disrobed, starkers *(informal)*, unclothed, in the buff *(informal)*, au naturel *(French)*, in the altogether *(informal)*, buck naked *(slang)*, unclad, undraped, in your birthday suit *(informal)*, scuddy *(slang)*, without a stitch on *(informal)*, in the bare scud *(slang)*, naked as the day you were born *(informal)* • *The album contained a dozen or so photographs of nude girls.* • *We are not allowed to perform nude on stage.*
OPPOSITES: covered, dressed, clothed

nudge AS A VERB **1 = push**, touch, dig, jog, prod, elbow, shove, poke • *'Stop it,' he said, and nudged me in the ribs.*
2 = prompt, influence, urge, persuade, spur, prod, coax, prevail upon • *Bit by bit Bob nudged Fritz into selling his controlling interest.*
▸ AS A NOUN **1 = push**, touch, dig, elbow, bump, shove, poke, jog, prod • *She slipped her arm under his and gave him a nudge.*
2 = prompting, push, encouragement, prod • *The challenge appealed to him. All he needed was a little nudge.*

nudity = nakedness, undress, nudism, bareness, deshabille • *I object to the constant nudity and bad language on TV.*
▸ RELATED MANIA: nudomania, gymnomania
▸ RELATED PHOBIA: gymnophobia

nugatory 1 = invalid, ineffectual, null and void, inoperative, useless, vain, futile, unavailing, bootless • *The Stamp Act of 1765 was rendered nugatory by colonial resistance.*
2 = trivial, worthless, trifling, insignificant, valueless • *They wrote for the magazine for fees that were either non-existent or nugatory.*

nugget = lump, piece, mass, chunk, clump, hunk • *Miners sifting gravel from the Yukon River in search of gold nuggets*

nuisance = trouble, problem, trial, bore, drag *(informal)*, bother, plague, pest, irritation, hassle *(informal)*, inconvenience, annoyance, pain *(informal)*, pain in the neck *(informal)*, pain in the arse *(taboo slang)*, pain in the backside *(informal)*, pain in the butt *(informal)* • *He can be a bit of a nuisance when he's drunk.* • *It's a real nuisance having to pick up the kids from school every day.*
OPPOSITES: benefit, delight, pleasure

null IN PHRASES: **null and void = invalid**, useless, void, worthless, ineffectual, valueless, inoperative • *The agreement had been declared null and void.*

nullify 1 = invalidate, quash, revoke, render null and void, abolish, void, repeal, rescind, annul, abrogate • *He used his broad executive powers to nullify decisions by local government.*
OPPOSITES: authorize, confirm, validate
2 = cancel out, counteract, negate, neutralize, obviate,

countervail, bring to naught • *This, of course, would nullify the effect of the move.*

nullity = **invalidity**, voidness, non-legality • *When there has been no legal marriage a judge may pronounce a decree of nullity.*

numb AS AN ADJECTIVE 1 = **unfeeling**, dead, frozen, paralysed, insensitive, deadened, immobilized, torpid, insensible, benumbed • *His legs felt numb and his toes ached.*
OPPOSITES: feeling, sensitive, responsive
2 = **stupefied**, deadened, unfeeling, insensible • *The mother, numb with grief, had trouble speaking.*
▸ AS A VERB 1 = **stun**, knock out, paralyse, daze, stupefy • *For a while the shock of his letter numbed her.*
2 = **deaden**, freeze, dull, paralyse, immobilize, benumb • *The cold numbed my fingers.*

number AS A NOUN 1 = **numeral**, figure, character, digit, integer • *None of the doors have numbers on them.*
2 = **amount**, quantity, collection, total, count, sum, aggregate • *I have had an enormous number of letters from concerned parents.*
OPPOSITES: want, lack, shortage
3 = **crowd**, horde, multitude, throng • *People turned out to vote in huge numbers.*
4 = **group**, company, set, band, crowd, gang, coterie • *We had a stag night for one of our number who had decided to get married.*
5 = **issue**, copy, edition, imprint, printing • *an article which appeared in the summer number of the magazine*
▸ AS A VERB 1 = **amount to**, come to, total, add up to • *They told me that their village numbered 100 or so.*
2 = **calculate**, account, reckon, compute, enumerate • *One widely cited report numbered the dead at over 10,000.*
OPPOSITES: guess, conjecture, theorize
3 = **include**, count • *He numbered several Americans among his friends.*
▸ IN PHRASES: **a number of** = **several**, a few, various • *Artillery fire had been heard in a number of border districts.*

numbered 1 = **reckoned**, totalled, counted • *The Liberian army is officially numbered at eight thousand strong.*
2 = **limited**, restricted, limited in number • *Her days as leader are numbered.*

numberless = **infinite**, endless, countless, myriad, innumerable, untold, unnumbered, multitudinous • *numberless acts of bravery by firefighters and rescue workers*

numbing 1 = **freezing**, biting, bitter, piercing, arctic, icy, glacial • *They huddled together against the numbing cold.*
2 = **deadening**, desensitizing • *We found that television viewing had a numbing effect on emotional states in our participants.*
3 = **stupefying**, paralysing, stultifying • *This was a match of almost numbing boredom.*

numbness 1 = **deadness**, paralysis, insensitivity, dullness, torpor, insensibility • *I have recently been suffering from numbness in my fingers and toes.*
2 = **torpor**, deadness, dullness, stupefaction • *She swung from emotional numbness to overwhelming fear and back again.*

numbskull *or* **numskull** = **fool**, charlie (*Brit. informal*), dope (*informal*), jerk (*slang, chiefly U.S. & Canad.*), dummy (*slang*), clot (*Brit. informal*), plank (*Brit. slang*), berk (*Brit. slang*), prick (*derogatory slang*), wally (*slang*), prat (*slang*), plonker (*slang*), coot, geek (*slang*), twit (*informal*), bonehead (*slang*), buffoon, dunce, oaf, simpleton, dullard, dimwit (*informal*), dipstick (*Brit. slang*), dickhead (*slang*), gonzo (*slang*), schmuck (*U.S. slang*), dork (*slang*), nitwit (*informal*), dolt, blockhead, divvy (*slang*), pillock (*Brit. slang*), dweeb (*U.S. slang*), putz (*U.S. slang*), fathead (*informal*), eejit (*Scot. & Irish*), thicko (*Brit. slang*), gobshite (*Irish taboo slang*), dunderhead, numpty (*Scot. informal*), doofus (*slang, chiefly U.S.*), lamebrain (*informal*), fuckwit (*taboo slang*), thickhead, nerd *or* nurd (*slang*), dorba *or* dorb (*Austral. slang*), bogan (*Austral. slang*) • *What kind of a numbskull would come up with an idea like that?*

numeral = **number**, figure, digit, character, symbol, cipher, integer • *a flat, square wristwatch with roman numerals*

numerous = **many**, several, countless, lots, abundant, plentiful, innumerable, copious, manifold, umpteen (*informal*), profuse, thick on the ground • *Such crimes were just as numerous then as they are today.* • *She made numerous attempts to diet, but her weight still soared.*
OPPOSITES: few, not many, scarcely any

numinous = **holy**, religious, heavenly, spiritual, divine, mysterious, supernatural, awe-inspiring • *the most natural and numinous of human passions*

nun = **sister**, Bride of Christ • *He was taught by the Catholic nuns*

nuncio = **ambassador**, representative, envoy, messenger, legate • *The papal nuncio is expected to arrive in Prague before the end of this month.*

nunnery = **convent**, house, abbey, monastery, cloister • *In monasteries and nunneries, prayers are being offered for him.*

QUOTATIONS
Get thee to a nunnery
[William Shakespeare *Hamlet*]

nuptial = **marital**, wedding, wedded, bridal, matrimonial, conjugal, connubial, hymeneal (*poetic*) • *He had referred to the room as the nuptial chamber.*

nuptials *sometimes singular* = **wedding**, marriage, matrimony, espousal (*archaic*) • *couples who never go near a church but insist on their nuptials being celebrated with a traditional church ceremony*

nurse AS A NOUN 1 = **carer**, caregiver, angel (*informal*) • *Patients are dying because of an acute shortage of nurses.*
2 = **nanny**, nursemaid • *He was brought up by his old nurse.*
▸ AS A VERB 1 = **look after**, treat, tend, care for, take care of, minister to • *All the years he was sick my mother had nursed him.*
2 = **harbour**, have, maintain, preserve, entertain, cherish, keep alive • *He nursed an ambition to lead his own orchestra.*
3 = **breast-feed**, feed, nurture, nourish, suckle, wet-nurse • *She did not have enough milk to nurse the infant.*

nursemaid = **nanny**, nurse, angel (*informal*) • *She worked as nursemaid to the family of a diplomat.*

nursery = **crèche**, kindergarten, playgroup, play-centre (*N.Z.*) • *The company has its own workplace nursery*

nurture AS A NOUN = **upbringing**, training, education, instruction, rearing, development • *The human organism learns partly by nature, partly by nurture.*
▸ AS A VERB 1 = **bring up**, raise, look after, rear, care for, develop • *Parents want to know the best way to nurture and raise their children to adulthood.*
OPPOSITES: ignore, overlook, neglect
2 = **tend**, grow, cultivate • *The modern conservatory is not an environment for nurturing plants.*
3 = **encourage**, support, sustain, cultivate • *Seema's interest in literature was nurtured by her parents.*

nut 1 = **kernel**, stone, seed, pip • *Nuts are a good source of vitamin E.*
2 = **fanatic**, addict, enthusiast, freak, buff (*informal*), devotee • *a football nut who spends thousands of pounds travelling to watch games*
3 = **madman**, eccentric, flake (*slang, chiefly U.S.*), psycho (*slang*), crank (*informal*), lunatic, maniac, loony (*slang*), nutter (*Brit. slang*), oddball (*informal*), crackpot (*informal*), basket case (*slang*), wacko (*slang*), nutcase (*slang*), headcase (*informal*), headbanger (*slang*), crazy (*informal*) • *Some nut with a gun walked in and just opened fire on the diners.*
4 = **head**, skull, noggin • *He took a bottle and smashed me over the nut.*

nutrition = **food**, nourishment, sustenance, nutriment • *There are alternative sources of nutrition to animal flesh.*
▸ RELATED ADJECTIVE: trophic

nutritious = **nourishing**, beneficial, wholesome, healthful, health-giving, nutritive • *It is always important to choose enjoyable, nutritious foods.*

NUTS

almond
beech nut
brazil nut
butternut
cashew
chestnut
chinquapin
coco de mer
dwarf chestnut
earthnut *or* pignut *or* groundnut
hazelnut, filbert, cobnut, *or* cob
macadamia (nut), Queensland nut, *or* bauple nut
marron
peanut, monkey nut,
pecan
pine nut *or* pine kernel
pistachio
quandong
walnut

nuts AS AN ADJECTIVE = **insane**, mad, crazy *(informal)*, bananas *(slang)*, barking *(slang)*, eccentric, batty *(slang)*, psycho *(slang)*, irrational, loony *(slang)*, demented, nutty *(slang)*, deranged, loopy *(informal)*, out to lunch *(informal)*, out there *(slang)*, barking mad *(slang)*, gonzo *(slang)*, doolally *(slang)*, off your trolley *(slang)*, up the pole *(informal)*, as daft as a brush *(informal, chiefly Brit.)*, not the full shilling *(informal)*, wacko *or* whacko *(informal)*, a sausage short of a fry-up *(slang)*, off the air *(Austral. slang)* • *Either he's joking or else he's nuts.* • *A number of the players went nuts, completely out of control.*

▸ IN PHRASES: **nuts and bolts** = **essentials**, basics, fundamentals, nitty-gritty *(informal)*, practicalities, ins and outs, details • *Social skills are the nuts and bolts of social interaction.*

nutty = **mad**, crazy *(informal)*, bananas *(slang)*, barking *(slang)*, mental *(slang)*, crackers *(Brit. slang)*, batty *(slang)*, insane, crazed, loony *(slang)*, demented, cuckoo *(informal)*, unbalanced, barmy *(slang)*, deranged, bonkers *(slang, chiefly Brit.)*, flaky *(U.S. slang)*, unhinged, loopy *(informal)*, crackpot *(informal)*, out to lunch *(informal)*, round the bend *(Brit. slang)*, barking mad *(slang)*, out of your mind, gonzo *(slang)*, screwy *(informal)*, doolally *(slang)*, off your head *(slang)*, off your trolley *(slang)*, round the twist *(Brit. slang)*, up the pole *(informal)*, of unsound mind, as daft as a brush *(informal, chiefly Brit.)*, not right in the head, non compos mentis *(Latin)*, off your rocker *(slang)*, not the full shilling *(informal)*, off your nut *(slang)*, off your chump *(slang)*, wacko *or* whacko *(informal)*, a sausage short of a fry-up *(slang)*, off the air *(Austral. slang)* • *That's a nutty idea.* • *People used to think I was nutty because I talked to my plants.*

nuzzle = **snuggle**, cuddle, nudge, burrow, nestle • *The dog came and nuzzled up against me.*

nymph 1 = **sylph**, dryad, naiad, hamadryad, Oceanid *(Greek myth)*, oread • *In the depths of a river, the three water nymphs – the Rhinemaidens – play and sing.*
2 = **girl**, lass, maiden, maid, damsel • *They had one daughter, an exquisite nymph named Jacqueline.*

n

oaf = **lout**, brute, yob *or* yobbo *(Brit. slang)*, fool, jerk *(slang, chiefly U.S. & Canad.)*, idiot, dummy *(slang)*, plank *(Brit. slang)*, berk *(Brit. slang)*, sap *(slang)*, gorilla *(informal)*, wally *(slang)*, booby, prat *(slang)*, plonker *(slang)*, coot, moron, goon, geek *(slang)*, twit *(informal, chiefly Brit.)*, bonehead *(slang)*, dunce, imbecile, clod, simpleton, gawk, airhead *(slang)*, dullard, dipstick *(Brit. slang)*, dickhead *(slang)*, gonzo *(slang)*, schmuck *(U.S. slang)*, dork *(slang)*, nitwit *(informal)*, dolt, bear, charlie *(Brit. informal)*, blockhead, divvy *(Brit. slang)*, pillock *(Brit. slang)*, halfwit, nincompoop, dweeb *(U.S. slang)*, putz *(U.S. slang)*, fathead *(informal)*, eejit *(Scot. & Irish)*, thicko *(Brit. slang)*, dumb-ass *(slang)*, gobshite *(Irish taboo slang)*, numpty *(Scot. informal)*, doofus *(slang, chiefly U.S.)*, galoot *(slang, chiefly U.S.)*, fuckwit *(taboo slang)*, lummox *(informal)*, dickwit *(slang)*, nerd *or* nurd *(slang)*, numbskull *or* numskull, bumpkin, boor, churl, clumsy idiot, cougan *(Austral. slang)*, scozza *(Austral. slang)*, bogan *(Austral. slang)*, dorba *or* dorb *(Austral. slang)*, bogan *(Austral. slang)* • *Leave the lady alone, you drunken oaf!*
OPPOSITES: brain *(informal)*, genius, intellectual

oafish = **loutish**, stupid, gross, thick, rough, dull, dim, dense, dumb *(informal)*, coarse, lumbering, bovine, churlish, brutish, dozy *(Brit. informal)*, stolid, boorish, moronic, gawky, obtuse, uncouth, lumpen *(informal)*, slow on the uptake *(informal)*, ill-bred, lumpish, swinish, dumb-ass *(slang)*, clodhopping *(informal)*, doltish, unmannerly, boneheaded *(slang)*, ill-mannered, dim-witted *(informal)* • *He's nothing but a bigoted, oafish lout.*
OPPOSITES: bright, sharp, intelligent

oak
▸ RELATED ADJECTIVE: quercine

oar IN PHRASES: **stick your oar in** = **interfere**, intervene, get involved, meddle, butt in, poke your nose in *(informal)*, put your two cents in *(U.S. slang)* • *Keep out of this – nobody asked you to stick your oar in.*

oasis 1 = **watering hole**, spring, water hole, watering place • *The province was largely a wasteland with an occasional oasis.*
2 = **haven**, retreat, refuge, sanctuary, island, resting place, sanctum • *an oasis of peace in a troubled world*

oath 1 = **promise**, bond, pledge, vow, word, compact, covenant, affirmation, sworn statement, avowal, word of honour • *a solemn oath by members to help each other*
2 = **swear word**, curse, obscenity, blasphemy, expletive, four-letter word, cuss *(informal)*, profanity, strong language, imprecation, malediction, vulgarism • *Weller let out a foul oath and hurled himself upon him.*
▸ RELATED ADJECTIVE: juratory

QUOTATIONS
He who cheats with an oath acknowledges that he is afraid of his enemy, but that he thinks little of God
[Plutarch *Lives: Lysander*]
Oaths are but words, and words but wind
[Samuel Butler *Hudibras*]
Let your yea be yea; and your nay, nay
[*Bible: James*]

obdurate = **obstinate**, firm, dogged, determined, fixed, iron, persistent, relentless, adamant, stubborn, intractable, inflexible, wilful, unrelenting, tenacious, inexorable, implacable, steadfast, unyielding, intransigent, immovable, headstrong, strong-minded, unbending, stiff-necked, unshakeable *or* unshakable, refractory, pig-headed, mulish, contumacious, pertinacious, indurate *(rare)*, proof against persuasion, unimpressible • *The administration have been obdurate defenders of the status quo.*
OPPOSITES: yielding, flexible, compliant

obedience = **compliance**, yielding, submission, respect, conformity, reverence, deference, observance, subservience, submissiveness, docility, complaisance, tractability, dutifulness, conformability • *unquestioning obedience to the law*
OPPOSITES: defiance, disobedience, stubbornness

QUOTATIONS
They who know the least obey the best
[George Farquhar]

obedient = **submissive**, yielding, compliant, under control, respectful, law-abiding, well-trained, amenable, docile, dutiful, subservient, deferential, tractable, acquiescent, biddable, accommodating, passive, meek, ingratiating, malleable, pliant, unresisting, bootlicking *(informal)*, obeisant, duteous • *a sweet, obedient little girl*
OPPOSITES: contrary, stubborn, disobedient

obediently = **submissively**, meekly, dutifully, passively, unresistingly • *He walked obediently beside his mother.*

obeisance 1 = **homage**, respect, tribute, loyalty, devotion, fidelity, reverence, deference, faithfulness, fealty • *Everyone paid obeisance to the emperor.*
2 = **bow**, salaam, salutation, kowtow, genuflection, bob, bending of the knee, curtsy *or* curtsey • *He graciously accepted our obeisances.*

obelisk = **column**, shaft, monument, pillar, monolith, needle • *The obelisk was erected in his memory in 1812.*

obese = **fat**, overweight, heavy, solid, gross, plump, stout, fleshy, beefy *(informal)*, tubby, portly, outsize, roly-poly, rotund, podgy, corpulent, elephantine, paunchy, well-upholstered *(informal)*, Falstaffian • *Obese people tend to have higher blood pressure than lean ones.*
OPPOSITES: thin, lean, slender

obesity *or* **obeseness** = **fatness**, flab, heaviness, a weight problem, grossness, corpulence, beef *(informal)*, embonpoint *(French)*, rotundity, fleshiness, stoutness, portliness, bulkiness, podginess, tubbiness • *Excessive consumption of sugar and fat leads to obesity.*
OPPOSITES: thinness, leanness, slenderness

obey 1 = **submit to**, surrender (to), give way to, succumb to, bow to, give in to, yield to, be ruled by, serve, defer to, cave in

to *(informal)*, take orders from, do what you are told by • *Cissie obeyed her mother without question.*
OPPOSITES: rebel, disobey
2 = **submit**, yield, surrender, give in, give way, succumb, cave in, toe the line, knuckle under *(informal)*, do what is expected, come to heel, get into line • *If you love me you will obey.*
3 = **carry out**, follow, perform, respond to, implement, fulfil, execute, discharge, act upon, carry through • *The commander refused to obey an order.*
OPPOSITES: ignore, defy, disregard
4 = **abide by**, keep, follow, comply with, observe, mind, embrace, hold to, heed, conform to, keep to, adhere to, be ruled by • *Most people obey the law.*

obfuscate = **obscure**, confuse, cloud, blur, cover, screen, hide, disguise, conceal, veil, darken, muddy the waters of, befog, throw a veil over • *They are deliberately obfuscating the issue.*

obfuscation = **evasiveness**, shuffling, deception, fudging, waffle *(informal, chiefly Brit.)*, equivocation, prevarication, sophistry, obliqueness, sophism • *His speech was incomprehensible and full of obfuscation.*

obituary = **death notice**, eulogy, obit *(informal)* • *I read your brother's obituary in the Times.*

object[1] AS A NOUN 1 = **thing**, article, device, body, item, implement, entity, gadget, contrivance, thingummyjig *(informal)* • *an object the shape of a coconut*
2 = **purpose**, aim, end, point, plan, idea, reason, goal, design, target, principle, function, intention, objective, intent, motive, end in view, end purpose, the why and wherefore • *The object of the exercise is to raise money for charity.*
3 = **target**, victim, focus, butt, recipient • *She was an object of pity among her friends.*
▸ IN PHRASES: **no object** = **unimportant**, irrelevant, immaterial, of no consequence, of no account, not worth mentioning, of no moment • *Although he was based in Wales, distance was no object.*

object[2] 1 *often with* **to** = **protest against**, oppose, say no to, kick against *(informal)*, argue against, draw the line at, take exception to, raise objections to, cry out against, complain against, take up the cudgels against, expostulate against • *A lot of people objected to the plan.*
OPPOSITES: accept, welcome, approve
2 = **disagree**, demur, remonstrate, expostulate, express disapproval • *We objected strongly.*
OPPOSITES: agree, concur, assent

objection = **protest**, opposition, complaint, doubt, exception, dissent, outcry, censure, disapproval, niggle *(informal)*, protestation, scruple, demur, formal complaint, counter-argument, cavil, remonstrance, demurral • *This objection has obviously been dropped.*
OPPOSITES: support, agreement, acceptance

QUOTATIONS
A technical objection is the first refuge of a scoundrel
[Heywood Broun]

objectionable = **offensive**, annoying, irritating, unacceptable, unpleasant, rude, intolerable, undesirable, distasteful, obnoxious, deplorable, displeasing, unseemly, disagreeable, repugnant, abhorrent, beyond the pale, insufferable, detestable, discourteous, uncivil, unmannerly, exceptionable, dislikable *or* dislikeable • *an objectionable, stuck-up young woman*
OPPOSITES: pleasing, welcome, pleasant

objective AS AN ADJECTIVE 1 = **factual**, real, actual, existing, manifest, empirical, circumstantial, verifiable • *He has no objective evidence to support his claim.*
2 = **unbiased**, neutral, detached, just, fair, judicial, open-minded, equitable, impartial, impersonal, disinterested, even-handed, dispassionate, unemotional, uninvolved, unprejudiced, uncoloured • *I would like your objective opinion on this.*
OPPOSITES: prejudiced, biased, subjective
▸ AS A NOUN = **purpose**, aim, goal, end, plan, hope, idea, design, target, wish, scheme, desire, object, intention, ambition, aspiration, Holy Grail *(informal)*, end in view, why and wherefore • *His objective was to play golf and win.*

objectively = **impartially**, neutrally, fairly, justly, without prejudice, dispassionately, with an open mind, equitably, without fear or favour, even-handedly, without bias, disinterestedly, with objectivity *or* impartiality • *Try to view the situation more objectively.*

objectivity = **impartiality**, detachment, neutrality, equity, fairness, disinterest, open-mindedness, even-handedness, impersonality, disinterestedness, dispassion, nonpartisanship, lack of bias, equitableness • *The analyst must maintain an unusual degree of objectivity.*
OPPOSITES: prejudice, bias, subjectivity

obligated = **obliged**, forced, required, bound, compelled, under an obligation, under compulsion • *He had got her pregnant and felt obligated to marry her.*

obligation AS A NOUN 1 = **duty**, pressure, compulsion • *Students usually feel an obligation to attend lectures.*
2 = **task**, job, duty, work, calling, business, charge, role, function, mission, province, assignment, pigeon *(informal)*, chore • *I feel that's my obligation, to do whatever is possible.*
3 = **responsibility**, duty, liability, accountability, culpability, answerability, accountableness • *I have an ethical and moral obligation to my client.*
4 = **contract**, promise, agreement, understanding, bond, debt, commitment, engagement • *The companies failed to meet their obligation to plant new trees.*
▸ IN PHRASES: **under an obligation** = **in (someone's) debt**, indebted, obliged, grateful, thankful, obligated, beholden, duty-bound, honour-bound, owing a favour • *I'd rather not be under any obligation to him.*
without obligation = **free**, for free *(informal)*, for nothing, unpaid, complimentary, free of charge, on the house, without charge, gratuitous, gratis, buckshee *(Brit. slang)* • *Our advice and quotations are without obligation.*

obligatory 1 = **compulsory**, required, necessary, essential, demanded, binding, enforced, prescribed, statutory, mandatory, imperative, unavoidable, requisite, inescapable, coercive, de rigueur *(French)* • *Third-party insurance is obligatory when driving in Italy.*
OPPOSITES: voluntary, optional, discretionary
2 = **customary**, regular, usual, popular, normal, familiar, conventional, fashionable, bog-standard *(Brit. & Irish slang)* • *This hotel has every facility, including the obligatory swimming-pool.*

oblige 1 = **compel**, make, force, require, bind, railroad *(informal)*, constrain, necessitate, coerce, impel, dragoon, obligate • *This decree obliges unions to delay strikes.*
2 = **help**, assist, serve, benefit, please, favour, humour, accommodate, indulge, gratify, do someone a service, put yourself out for, do (someone) a favour *or* a kindness, meet the wants *or* needs of • *He is always ready to oblige journalists with information.*
OPPOSITES: trouble, bother, put out

obliged AS AN ADJECTIVE 1 = **forced**, required, bound, compelled, obligated, duty-bound, under an obligation, under compulsion, without any option • *I was obliged to answer their questions.*
2 = **grateful**, in (someone's) debt, thankful, indebted, appreciative, beholden • *I am extremely obliged to you.*
▸ IN PHRASES: **much obliged** = **thank you**, thanks, cheers *(informal)*, thanks very much, thanks a lot, many thanks • *Much obliged for your assistance.*

obliging = **accommodating**, kind, helpful, willing, civil, friendly, polite, cooperative, agreeable, amiable, courteous,

considerate, hospitable, unselfish, good-natured, eager to please, complaisant • *He was a most polite and obliging young man.*
OPPOSITES: rude, unhelpful, sullen

oblique 1 = **indirect**, implied, roundabout, backhanded, evasive, elliptical, circuitous, circumlocutory, inexplicit, periphrastic • *It was an oblique reference to his time in prison.*
OPPOSITES: open, direct, frank
2 = **slanting**, angled, sloped, sloping, inclined, tilted, tilting, slanted, diagonal, at an angle, asymmetrical, canted, aslant, slantwise, atilt, cater-cornered *(U.S. informal)* • *The mountain ridge runs at an oblique angle to the coastline.*
3 = **sidelong**, sideways, covert, indirect, furtive, surreptitious • *She gave him an oblique glance.*

obliquely 1 = **indirectly**, evasively, not in so many words, circuitously, in a roundabout manner *or* way • *He referred obliquely to a sordid event in her past.*
2 = **at an angle**, sideways, diagonally, sidelong, aslant, slantwise, aslope • *The muscle runs obliquely downwards inside the abdominal cavity.*

obliterate 1 = **destroy**, eliminate, devastate, waste, wreck, wipe out, demolish, ravage, eradicate, desolate, annihilate, put paid to, raze, blow to bits, extirpate, blow sky-high, destroy root and branch, kennet *(Austral. slang)*, jeff *(Austral. slang)*, wipe from *or* off the face of the earth • *Whole villages were obliterated by the fire.*
OPPOSITES: make, build, create
2 = **eradicate**, remove, eliminate, cancel, get rid of, wipe out, erase, excise, delete, extinguish, root out, efface, blot out, expunge, extirpate • *He drank to obliterate the memory of what had occurred.*

obliteration 1 = **destruction**, ruin, wiping out, elimination, end, demolition, devastation, rooting out, extermination, annihilation, eradication, ruination, extirpation • *the obliteration of an entire city*
OPPOSITES: making, building, creation
2 = **wiping out**, elimination, eradication, blotting out, erasure, deletion, effacement, extirpation, expunction • *the obliteration of the past*

oblivion 1 = **unconsciousness**, forgetfulness, senselessness, obliviousness, unawareness, insensibility, (waters of) Lethe • *He drank himself into oblivion.*
OPPOSITES: perception, awareness, consciousness
2 = **neglect**, anonymity, insignificance, obscurity, limbo, nothingness, unimportance • *Most of these performers will fail and sink into oblivion.*
3 = **extinction**, annihilation, eradication, obliteration • *An entire section of the town was bombed into oblivion.*

oblivious *usually with* **of** *or* **to** = **unaware**, unconscious, ignorant, regardless, careless, negligent, blind to, unaffected by, impervious to, forgetful, deaf to, unconcerned about, neglectful, heedless, inattentive, insensible, unmindful, unobservant, disregardful, incognizant • *He appeared oblivious to his surroundings.*
OPPOSITES: aware, conscious, alert

obnoxious = **loathsome**, offensive, nasty, foul, disgusting, unpleasant, revolting, obscene, sickening, vile, horrid, repellent, repulsive, objectionable, disagreeable, nauseating, odious, hateful, repugnant, reprehensible, abhorrent, abominable, insufferable, execrable, detestable, hateable, dislikable *or* dislikeable, yucky *or* yukky *(slang)*, yucko *(Austral. slang)* • *The people at my table were so obnoxious, I had to leave.*
OPPOSITES: pleasing, charming, pleasant

obscene 1 = **indecent**, dirty, offensive, gross, foul, coarse, filthy, vile, improper, immoral, pornographic, suggestive, blue, loose, shameless, lewd, depraved, X-rated *(informal)*, bawdy, salacious, prurient, impure, lascivious, smutty, ribald, unwholesome, scabrous, immodest, licentious, indelicate, unchaste • *I'm no prude, but I think these photos are obscene.*
OPPOSITES: seemly, pure, decent
2 = **offensive**, shocking, evil, disgusting, outrageous, revolting, sickening, vile, wicked, repellent, atrocious, obnoxious, heinous, nauseating, odious, loathsome, abominable, detestable • *It was obscene to spend millions producing unwanted food.*

obscenity 1 = **indecency**, pornography, impurity, impropriety, vulgarity, smut, prurience, coarseness, crudity, licentiousness, foulness, outrageousness, blueness, immodesty, suggestiveness, lewdness, dirtiness, grossness, vileness, filthiness, bawdiness, unseemliness, indelicacy, smuttiness, salacity • *He justified the use of obscenity on the grounds that it was art.*
OPPOSITES: innocence, purity, decency
2 = **swear word**, curse, oath, expletive, four-letter word, cuss *(informal)*, profanity, vulgarism • *They shouted obscenities at us as we passed.*
3 = **atrocity**, wrong, horror, offence, evil, outrage, cruelty, brutality, abomination, barbarity, vileness • *the obscenities of civil war*

obscure **AS AN ADJECTIVE** 1 = **unknown**, minor, little-known, humble, unfamiliar, out-of-the-way, unseen, lowly, unimportant, unheard-of, unsung, nameless, undistinguished, inconspicuous, unnoted, unhonoured, unrenowned • *The hymn was written by an obscure Greek composer.*
OPPOSITES: major, important, famous
2 = **abstruse**, involved, complex, confusing, puzzling, subtle, mysterious, deep, vague, unclear, doubtful, mystical, intricate, ambiguous, enigmatic, esoteric, perplexing, occult, opaque, incomprehensible, arcane, cryptic, unfathomable, recondite, clear as mud *(informal)* • *The contract is written in obscure language.*
OPPOSITES: clear, obvious, straightforward
3 = **unclear**, hidden, uncertain, confused, mysterious, concealed, doubtful, indefinite, indeterminate • *The word is of obscure origin.*
OPPOSITES: well-known
4 = **indistinct**, vague, blurred, dark, clouded, faint, dim, gloomy, veiled, murky, fuzzy, shadowy, cloudy, misty, hazy, indistinguishable, indeterminate, dusky, undefined, out of focus, ill-defined, obfuscated, indiscernible, tenebrous • *The hills were just an obscure shape in the mist.*
OPPOSITES: clear, sharp
▸ **AS A VERB** 1 = **obstruct**, hinder, block out • *Trees obscured his vision.*
2 = **hide**, cover (up), screen, mask, disguise, conceal, veil, cloak, shroud, camouflage, envelop, encase, enshroud • *The building is almost completely obscured by a huge banner.*
OPPOSITES: show, reveal, expose
3 = **obfuscate**, confuse, cloud, blur, muddy, darken, muddy the waters of, adumbrate, befog, throw a veil over, bedim • *the jargon that frequently obscures legal documents*
OPPOSITES: explain, clarify, interpret

obscurity 1 = **insignificance**, oblivion, unimportance, non-recognition, inconsequence, lowliness, inconspicuousness, namelessness, ingloriousness • *His later life was spent in obscurity and loneliness.*
2 = **vagueness**, complexity, ambiguity, intricacy, incomprehensibility, inexactitude, woolliness, abstruseness, impreciseness, impenetrableness, reconditeness, lack of preciseness • *Hunt was irritated by the obscurity of his reply.*
OPPOSITES: clarity, lucidity, explicitness
3 = **enigma**, mystery, puzzle, problem, difficulty, complexity, riddle, conundrum • *Whatever its obscurities, the poem was clear on one count.*
4 = **darkness**, dark, shadows, shade, gloom, haze,

blackness, murk, dimness, murkiness, haziness, duskiness, shadiness, shadowiness, indistinctness • *the vast branches vanished into deep indigo obscurity above my head*

obsequious = **servile**, flattering, cringing, fawning, abject, submissive, grovelling, menial, subservient, ingratiating, deferential, sycophantic, slavish, unctuous, smarmy *(Brit. informal)*, mealy-mouthed, toadying, bootlicking *(informal)*, toadyish • *She is positively obsequious to anyone with a title.*

observable = **noticeable**, clear, obvious, open, striking, apparent, visible, patent, evident, distinct, manifest, blatant, conspicuous, unmistakable, discernible, salient, recognizable, detectable, perceptible, appreciable, perceivable • *Alcohol can, in some cases, have an observable toxic effect.*

observance 1 *with* **of** = **carrying out of**, attention to, performance of, respect for, notice of, honouring of, observation of, compliance with, adherence to, fulfilment of, discharge of, obedience to, keeping of, heeding of, conformity to • *Councils should ensure strict observance of laws.*
OPPOSITES: neglect of, disregard for, omission of
2 = **ceremony**, rite, procedure, service, form, act, practice, tradition, celebration, custom, ritual, formality, ceremonial, ordinance, liturgy • *Numerous religious observances set the rhythm of the day.*

observant 1 = **attentive**, quick, alert, perceptive, concentrating, careful, vigilant, mindful, watchful, wide-awake, sharp-eyed, eagle-eyed, keen-eyed, on your toes, heedful • *An observant doctor can detect depression from expression and posture.*
OPPOSITES: unobservant, vague, distracted
2 = **devout**, godly, holy, orthodox, pious, obedient, reverent • *This is a profoundly observant Islamic country.*

observation 1 = **watching**, study, survey, review, notice, investigation, monitoring, attention, consideration, examination, inspection, scrutiny, surveillance, contemplation, cognition, perusal • *careful observation of the movement of the planets*
2 = **comment**, finding, thought, note, statement, opinion, remark, explanation, reflection, exposition, utterance, pronouncement, annotation, elucidation, obiter dictum • *This book contains observations about the nature of addiction.*
3 = **remark**, thought, comment, statement, opinion, reflection, assertion, utterance, animadversion • *Is that a criticism or just an observation?*
4 *with* **of** = **observance of**, attention to, compliance with, notice of, honouring of, adherence to, fulfilment of, discharge of, heeding of, carrying out of • *strict observation of oil quotas*

observe 1 = **watch**, study, view, look at, note, check, regard, survey, monitor, contemplate, check out *(informal)*, look on, keep an eye on *(informal)*, gaze at, pay attention to, keep track of, scrutinize, keep tabs on *(informal)*, recce *(slang)*, keep under observation, watch like a hawk, take a dekko at *(Brit. slang)* • *He studies and observes the behaviour of babies.*
2 = **notice**, see, note, mark, discover, spot, regard, witness, clock *(Brit. slang)*, distinguish, perceive, detect, discern, behold *(archaic or literary)*, eye, eyeball *(slang)*, peer at, espy, get a load of *(informal)* • *In 1664 Hooke observed a reddish spot on the surface of the planet.*
3 = **remark**, say, comment, state, note, reflect, mention, declare, opine, pass comment, animadvert • *'I like your hair that way,' he observed.*
4 = **comply with**, keep, follow, mind, respect, perform, carry out, honour, fulfil, discharge, obey, heed, conform to, adhere to, abide by • *Forcing motorists to observe speed restrictions is difficult.*
OPPOSITES: ignore, disregard
5 = **celebrate**, keep, commemorate, mark, remember, participate in, solemnize • *We are observing Christmas quietly this year.*

observer 1 = **witness**, viewer, spectator, looker-on, watcher, onlooker, eyewitness, bystander, spotter, fly on the wall, beholder • *A casual observer would have assumed they were lovers.*
2 = **commentator**, commenter, reporter, special correspondent • *Political observers believe there may be a general election soon.*
3 = **monitor**, inspector, watchdog, supervisor, overseer, scrutineer • *A UN observer should attend the conference.*

QUOTATIONS
I am a camera with its shutter open, quite passive, recording, not thinking
[Christopher Isherwood *Goodbye to Berlin*]

obsess *often with* **with** *or* **by** = **preoccupy**, dominate, grip, absorb, possess, consume, rule, haunt, plague, hound, torment, bedevil, monopolize, be on your mind, engross, prey on your mind, be uppermost in your thoughts • *Thoughts of revenge obsessed him.*

obsessed = **absorbed**, dominated, gripped, caught up, haunted, distracted, hung up *(slang)*, preoccupied, immersed, beset, in the grip, infatuated, fixated, having a one-track mind • *He was obsessed by science fiction films.*
OPPOSITES: detached, indifferent, aloof

obsession = **preoccupation**, thing *(informal)*, complex, enthusiasm, addiction, hang-up *(informal)*, mania, phobia, fetish, fixation, infatuation, ruling passion, pet subject, hobbyhorse, idée fixe *(French)*, bee in your bonnet *(informal)* • *yet another man with an obsession about football*

obsessive = **compulsive**, fixed, gripping, consuming, haunting, tormenting, irresistible, neurotic, besetting, uncontrollable, obsessional • *Eating behaviour is the subject of obsessive, almost phobic interest.*

obsessively = **compulsively**, uncontrollably, neurotically, obsessionally • *worrying obsessively about the future*

obsolescent = **outdated**, passé, old-fashioned, declining, waning, out of date, dying out, unfashionable, antiquated, on the way out, outmoded, on the wane, on the decline, becoming obsolete, behind the times, out of style, past its prime, démodé *(French)*, out of the ark *(informal)*, not with it *(informal)* • *outmoded, obsolescent equipment*

obsolete = **outdated**, old, passé, ancient, antique, old-fashioned, dated, discarded, extinct, past it, out of date, archaic, disused, out of fashion, out, antiquated, anachronistic, outmoded, musty, old hat, behind the times, superannuated, antediluvian, outworn, démodé *(French)*, out of the ark *(informal)*, vieux jeu *(French)* • *The company says the plant is obsolete and does not merit further investment.*
OPPOSITES: new, the new, up-to-date

obstacle 1 = **obstruction**, block, barrier, hurdle, hazard, snag, impediment, blockage, hindrance • *She had to navigate her way round trolleys and other obstacles.*
2 = **hindrance**, check, bar, block, difficulty, barrier, handicap, hurdle, hitch, drawback, snag, deterrent, uphill *(S. African)*, obstruction, stumbling block, impediment • *Overcrowding remains a large obstacle to improving conditions.*
OPPOSITES: help, support, benefit

obstinacy = **stubbornness**, persistence, tenacity, perseverance, resolution, intransigence, firmness, single-mindedness, inflexibility, obduracy, doggedness, relentlessness, wilfulness, resoluteness, pig-headedness, pertinacity, tenaciousness, mulishness • *the obstinacy typical of his thoroughly awkward nature*
OPPOSITES: flexibility, compliance, meekness

QUOTATIONS
Obstinacy in a bad cause, is but constancy in a good
[Thomas Browne *Religio Medici*]

obstinate = **stubborn**, dogged, determined, persistent, firm, perverse, intractable, inflexible, wilful, tenacious, recalcitrant, steadfast, unyielding, opinionated,

intransigent, immovable, headstrong, unmanageable, cussed, strong-minded, unbending, obdurate, stiff-necked, unshakable, self-willed, refractory, pig-headed, bull-headed, mulish, contumacious, pertinacious • *He is obstinate and determined and will not give up.*
OPPOSITES: flexible, wavering, manageable

obstreperous = **unruly**, disorderly, wild, rough, loud, noisy, out of control, turbulent, rampaging, out of hand, wayward, rowdy, raucous, uncontrollable, uncontrolled, boisterous, wilful, lawless, vociferous, fractious, riotous, tempestuous, unmanageable, undisciplined, stroppy *(Brit. slang)*, rip-roaring *(informal)*, mutinous, ungovernable, uproarious, clamorous, rambunctious *(informal)*, rackety, insubordinate, roistering, roisterous • *an awkward and obstreperous customer*
OPPOSITES: controlled, quiet, calm

obstruct 1 = **block**, close, bar, cut off, plug, choke, clog, barricade, shut off, stop up, bung up *(informal)* • *Lorries obstructed the road completely.*
2 = **hold up**, stop, check, bar, block, prevent, arrest, restrict, interrupt, slow down, hamstring, interfere with, hamper, inhibit, clog, hinder, retard, impede, get in the way of, bring to a standstill, cumber • *Drivers who park illegally obstruct the flow of traffic.*
3 = **impede**, prevent, frustrate, hold up, slow down, hamstring, interfere with, hamper, hold back, thwart, hinder, retard, get in the way of, trammel, cumber • *The authorities are obstructing the investigation.*
OPPOSITES: help, support, further
4 = **obscure**, screen, cut off, cover, hide, mask, shield • *She positioned herself so as not to obstruct his view.*

obstruction 1 = **obstacle**, bar, block, difficulty, barrier, hazard, barricade, snag, impediment, hindrance • *drivers parking near his house and causing an obstruction*
2 = **blockage**, stoppage, occlusion • *The boy was suffering from a bowel obstruction.*
3 = **hindrance**, stop, check, bar, block, difficulty, barrier, restriction, handicap, obstacle, restraint, deterrent, stumbling block, impediment, trammel • *Americans viewed the army as an obstruction to legitimate economic development.*
OPPOSITES: help, support, aid

obstructive = **unhelpful**, difficult, awkward, blocking, delaying, contrary, stalling, inhibiting, restrictive, hindering, uncooperative, disobliging, unaccommodating • *Mr Smith was obstructive and refused to co-operate.*
OPPOSITES: encouraging, helpful, obliging

obtain 1 = **get**, gain, acquire, land, net, pick up, bag, secure, get hold of, come by, procure, get your hands on, score *(slang)*, come into possession of • *Evans was trying to obtain a false passport.*
OPPOSITES: lose, give up, hand over
2 = **achieve**, get, gain, realize, accomplish, attain • *The perfect body has always been difficult to obtain.*
3 = **prevail**, hold, stand, exist, be the case, abound, predominate, be in force, be current, be prevalent • *The longer this situation obtains, the bigger the problems will be.*

obtainable 1 = **available**, to be had, procurable • *This herb is obtainable from health food shops.*
2 = **attainable**, accessible, achievable, at your fingertips, at your disposal, reachable, realizable, gettable, accomplishable • *That's new information that isn't obtainable by other means.*

obtrusive 1 = **pushy** *(informal)*, forward, pushing, loud, aggressive, offensive, bold, interfering, assertive, forceful, brash, meddling, intrusive, prying, obnoxious, presumptuous, nosy, officious, bumptious, importunate, self-assertive • *He was a rude and obtrusive man.*
OPPOSITES: reserved, retiring, modest
2 = **noticeable**, striking, obvious, prominent, blatant, conspicuous, sticking out, protruding, observable, perceptible, protuberant • *These heaters are less obtrusive and are easy to store in summer.*
OPPOSITES: hidden, concealed, inconspicuous

obtuse = **stupid**, simple, slow, thick, dull, dim, dense, dumb *(informal)*, sluggish, retarded, simple-minded, dozy *(Brit. informal)*, witless, stolid, dopey *(informal)*, moronic, brainless, uncomprehending, cretinous, unintelligent, half-witted, slow on the uptake *(informal)*, braindead *(informal)*, dumb-ass *(informal)*, doltish, dead from the neck up *(informal)*, boneheaded *(slang)*, thickheaded, dull-witted, imperceptive, slow-witted, muttonheaded *(slang)*, thick as mince *(Scot. informal)*, woodenheaded *(informal)* • *I think you're being deliberately obtuse.*
OPPOSITES: quick, bright, clever

obviate = **avert**, avoid, remove, prevent, counter, do away with, preclude, counteract, ward off, stave off, forestall, render unnecessary • *This would obviate the need for a surgical operation.*

obvious = **clear**, open, plain, apparent, visible, bold, patent, evident, distinct, pronounced, straightforward, explicit, manifest, transparent, noticeable, blatant, conspicuous, overt, unmistakable, palpable, unequivocal, undeniable, salient, recognizable, unambiguous, self-evident, indisputable, perceptible, much in evidence, unquestionable, open-and-shut, cut-and-dried *(informal)*, undisguised, incontrovertible, self-explanatory, unsubtle, unconcealed, clear as a bell, staring you in the face *(informal)*, right under your nose *(informal)*, sticking out a mile *(informal)*, plain as the nose on your face *(informal)* • *It's obvious that he doesn't like me.*
OPPOSITES: hidden, concealed, unclear

obviously 1 = **clearly**, of course, certainly, needless to say, without doubt, assuredly • *There are obviously exceptions to this.*
2 = **plainly**, patently, undoubtedly, evidently, manifestly, markedly, without doubt, unquestionably, undeniably, beyond doubt, palpably, indubitably, incontrovertibly, irrefutably, incontestably • *She's obviously cleverer than I am.*

occasion AS A NOUN 1 = **time**, moment, point, stage, incident, instance, occurrence, juncture • *I often think fondly of an occasion some years ago.*
2 = **function**, event, affair, do *(informal)*, happening, experience, gathering, celebration, occurrence, social occasion • *It will be a unique family occasion.*
3 = **opportunity**, chance, time, opening, window • *It is always an occasion for setting out government policy.*
4 = **reason**, cause, call, ground(s), basis, excuse, incentive, motive, warrant, justification, provocation, inducement • *You had no occasion to speak to him like that.*
▸ AS A VERB = **cause**, begin, produce, create, effect, lead to, inspire, result in, generate, prompt, provoke, induce, bring about, originate, evoke, give rise to, precipitate, elicit, incite, engender • *The incident occasioned a full-scale parliamentary row.*
▸ IN PHRASES: **on occasion** = **occasionally**, sometimes, at times, from time to time, on and off, now and then, now and again, once in a while, every now and then, every so often, off and on • *He was not above breaking the rules on occasion.*

occasional = **infrequent**, odd, rare, casual, irregular, sporadic, intermittent, few and far between, desultory, periodic • *I still get the occasional nightmare about the accident.*
OPPOSITES: regular, usual, constant

occasionally = **sometimes**, at times, from time to time, on and off, now and then, irregularly, on occasion, now and again, periodically, once in a while, every so often, at intervals, off and on, (every) now and then • *I occasionally go to the cinema with a friend.*
OPPOSITES: often, regularly, constantly

occult AS AN ADJECTIVE = **supernatural**, dark, magical, mysterious, psychic, mystical, mystic, unearthly, unnatural,

esoteric, uncanny, arcane, paranormal, abstruse, recondite, preternatural, cabbalistic, supranatural • *organizations which campaign against paganism and occult practices*
▸ **IN PHRASES: the occult = magic**, witchcraft, sorcery, wizardry, enchantment, occultism, black art, necromancy, theurgy • *his unhealthy fascination with the occult*

occultism = black magic, magic, witchcraft, wizardry, sorcery, the black arts, necromancy, diabolism, theurgy, supernaturalism • *the revival of interest in occultism and practical magic*

occupancy = occupation, use, residence, holding, term, possession, tenure, tenancy, habitation, inhabitancy • *Prices given are for a single occupancy of a standard room.*

occupant = occupier, resident, tenant, user, holder, inmate, inhabitant, incumbent, dweller, denizen, addressee, lessee, indweller • *Most of the occupants had left before the fire broke out.*

occupation 1 = job, work, calling, business, line (of work), office, trade, position, post, career, situation, activity, employment, craft, profession, pursuit, vocation, livelihood, walk of life • *I was looking for an occupation which would allow me to travel.*
2 = hobby, pastime, diversion, relaxation, sideline, leisure pursuit, (leisure) activity • *Hang-gliding is a dangerous occupation.*
3 = invasion, seizure, conquest, incursion, subjugation, foreign rule • *the deportation of Jews from Paris during the German occupation*
4 = occupancy, use, residence, holding, control, possession, tenure, tenancy, habitation, inhabitancy • *She is seeking an order for 'sole use and occupation' of the house.*

occupational = job-related, work, professional, vocational, work-related • *Stalking is quickly becoming an occupational hazard of the famous.*

occupied 1 = in use, taken, full, engaged, unavailable • *three beds, two of which were occupied*
2 = inhabited, peopled, lived-in, settled, tenanted • *The house was occupied by successive generations of farmers.*
OPPOSITES: empty, deserted, uninhabited
3 = busy, engaged, employed, working, active, tied up (*informal*), engrossed, hard at work, in harness, hard at it (*informal*), rushed off your feet • *I forgot about it because I was so occupied with other things.*

occupier = tenant, resident, renter, inhabitant, occupant, leaseholder, lessee • *A form will be sent to the current occupier of the address.*

occupy 1 = inhabit, own, live in, stay in (*Scot.*), be established in, dwell in, be in residence in, establish yourself in, ensconce yourself in, tenant, reside in, lodge in, take up residence in, make your home, abide in • *the couple who occupy the flat above mine*
OPPOSITES: abandon, desert, vacate
2 = invade, take over, capture, seize, conquer, keep, hold, garrison, overrun, annex, take possession of, colonize • *Alexandretta had been occupied by the French in 1918.*
OPPOSITES: withdraw, retreat
3 = hold, control, dominate, possess • *Men still occupy more positions of power than women.*
4 = take up, consume, tie up, use up, monopolize, keep busy or occupied • *Her parliamentary career has occupied all of her time.*
5 *often passive* **= engage**, interest, involve, employ, busy, entertain, absorb, amuse, divert, preoccupy, immerse, hold the attention of, engross, keep busy or occupied • *I had other matters to occupy me that day.*
6 = fill, take up, cover, fill up, utilize, pervade, permeate, extend over • *The tombs occupy two thirds of the church*

occur AS A VERB **1 = happen**, take place, come about, follow, result, chance, arise, turn up (*informal*), come off (*informal*), ensue, crop up (*informal*), transpire (*informal*), befall, materialize, come to pass (*archaic*), betide, eventuate • *The deaths occurred when troops tried to disperse the demonstrators.*
2 = exist, appear, be found, develop, obtain, turn up, be present, be met with, manifest itself, present itself, show itself • *The disease occurs throughout Africa.*
▸ **IN PHRASES: occur to someone = come to mind**, strike someone, dawn on someone, come to you, spring to mind, cross someone's mind, present itself to someone, enter someone's head, offer itself to someone, suggest itself to someone • *It didn't occur to me to check my insurance policy.*

occurrence 1 = incident, happening, event, fact, matter, affair, proceeding, circumstance, episode, adventure, phenomenon, transaction • *Traffic jams are now a daily occurrence.*
2 = existence, instance, appearance, manifestation, materialization • *the greatest occurrence of heart disease in the over-65s*

ocean 1 = sea, the deep, the waves, main, the drink (*informal*), the briny (*informal*) • *the beautiful sight of the calm ocean on a warm night*
2 = a lot, a great deal, a mass (*informal*), a load (*informal*), a multitude, a heap, a stack, an abundance, a large amount, a plethora, a quantity, a profusion, a number, a vast number • *He has oceans of loyal fans.*
▹ *See panel* **Seas and oceans**

odd AS AN ADJECTIVE **1 = peculiar**, strange, unusual, different, funny, out there (*slang*), extraordinary, bizarre, weird, exceptional, eccentric, abnormal, queer, rum (*Brit. slang*), deviant, unconventional, far-out (*slang*), quaint, kinky (*informal*), off-the-wall (*slang*), outlandish, whimsical, oddball (*informal*), out of the ordinary, offbeat, left-field (*informal*), freakish, freaky (*slang*), wacko (*slang*), outré, daggy (*Austral. & N.Z. informal*) • *He'd always been odd, but not to this extent.*
2 = unusual, different, strange, rare, funny (*slang*), extraordinary, remarkable, bizarre, fantastic, curious, weird, exceptional, peculiar, abnormal, queer, irregular, uncommon, singular, uncanny, outlandish, out of the ordinary, freakish, atypical, freaky • *Something odd began to happen.*
OPPOSITES: common, natural, normal
3 = occasional, various, varied, random, casual, seasonal, irregular, periodic, miscellaneous, sundry, incidental, intermittent, infrequent • *He did various odd jobs around the place.*
OPPOSITES: regular, permanent, steady
4 = spare, remaining, extra, surplus, single, lone, solitary, uneven, leftover, unmatched, unpaired • *I found an odd sock in the washing machine.*
OPPOSITES: even, matched, paired
▸ **IN PHRASES: odd man** *or* **odd one out = misfit**, exception, outsider, freak, eccentric, maverick, oddball (*informal*), nonconformist, fish out of water (*informal*), square peg in a round hole (*informal*) • *All my family smoke apart from me – I'm the odd man out.*

oddity 1 = misfit, eccentric, crank (*informal*), nut (*slang*), maverick, flake (*slang, chiefly U.S.*), oddball (*informal*), loose cannon, nonconformist, odd man out, wacko (*slang*), screwball (*slang, chiefly U.S. & Canad.*), card (*informal*), fish out of water, square peg (in a round hole) (*informal*), odd fish (*Brit. informal*), odd bird (*informal*), rara avis, weirdo or weirdie (*informal*) • *He's a bit of an oddity, but quite harmless.*
2 = anomaly, exception, curiosity, abnormality, rarity, departure, deviation • *His book remains something of an oddity.*
3 = strangeness, abnormality, peculiarity, eccentricity, weirdness, singularity, incongruity, oddness, unconventionality, queerness, unnaturalness, bizarreness,

O

freakishness, extraordinariness, outlandishness • *I was struck by the oddity of this question.*
4 = **irregularity**, phenomenon, anomaly, freak, abnormality, rarity, quirk, eccentricity, kink, peculiarity, idiosyncrasy, singularity, unorthodoxy, unconventionality • *the oddities of the Welsh legal system*

oddly = **strangely**, remarkably, curiously, extraordinarily, astonishingly, bizarrely, singularly, unaccountably • *He seemed oddly reluctant to talk about it.*

oddment AS A NOUN = **leftover**, bit, scrap, leaving, end, remains, fragment, butt, shred, remnant, stub, snippet, sliver, tail end, fag end, off cut, end of a line • *a blanket crocheted from oddments of wool*
▸ AS A PLURAL NOUN = **items**, things, goods, effects, stuff, possessions, bits and pieces, paraphernalia, odds and ends, impedimenta • *a collection of oddments from his travels*

odds AS A PLURAL NOUN = **probability**, chances, likelihood • *What are the odds of that happening?*
▸ IN PHRASES: **at odds** 1 = **in conflict**, arguing, quarrelling, in opposition to, at loggerheads, in disagreement, at daggers drawn, on bad terms • *He was at odds with his neighbour.*
2 = **at variance**, conflicting, contrary to, at odds, out of line, out of step, at sixes and sevens *(informal)*, not in keeping, out of harmony • *Her inexperience is at odds with the tale she tells.*
it makes no odds = **it makes no difference**, it does not matter, it is all the same • *It makes no odds what I do, it'll be wrong.*
odds and ends = **scraps**, bits, pieces, remains, rubbish, fragments, litter, debris, shreds, remnants, bits and pieces, bric-a-brac, bits and bobs, oddments, odds and sods, leavings, miscellanea, sundry *or* miscellaneous items • *She packed her clothes and a few other odds and ends.*

odds-on = **likely**, expected, anticipated, probable, on the cards • *He was the odds-on favourite to win the contest.*

odious = **offensive**, nasty, foul, disgusting, horrible, unpleasant, revolting, obscene, sickening, vile, horrid, repellent, unsavoury, obnoxious, unpalatable, repulsive, disagreeable, nauseating, hateful, repugnant, loathsome, abhorrent, abominable, execrable, detestable, yucky *or* yukky *(slang)*, yucko *(Austral. slang)* • *He's the most odious man I have ever met.*
OPPOSITES: pleasing, charming, delightful

odium = **hate**, shame, disgust, dislike, disgrace, hatred, discredit, loathing, condemnation, censure, disapproval, animosity, disrepute, antipathy, enmity, dishonour, infamy, opprobrium, abhorrence, disfavour, detestation, obloquy, disapprobation, reprobation, execration • *He has been exposed to public odium and scandal.*

odour *or (U.S.)* **odor** 1 = **smell**, scent, perfume, fragrance, stink, bouquet, aroma, whiff, stench, pong *(Brit. informal)*, niff *(Brit. slang)*, redolence, malodour, fetor • *the faint odour of whisky on his breath*
2 = **atmosphere**, feeling, air, quality, spirit, tone, climate, flavour, aura, vibe *(slang)* • *a tantalising odour of scandal*

odourless = **unscented**, fragrance-free, unperfumed, deodorized, without smell • *a completely odourless, colourless liquid*

Odyssey *often not cap.* = **journey**, tour, trip, passage, quest, trek, expedition, voyage, crusade, excursion, pilgrimage, jaunt, peregrination • *The march to Travnik was the final stretch of a three-week odyssey.*

of = **about**, on, concerning, regarding, with respect to, as regards • *I was thinking of you the other day.*

off AS AN ADVERB 1 = **away**, out, apart, elsewhere, aside, hence, from here • *He went off on his own.*
2 = **absent**, gone, unavailable, not present, inoperative, nonattendant • *She was off sick 27 days last year.*
▸ AS AN ADJECTIVE 1 = **cancelled**, abandoned, postponed, shelved • *Today's game is off.*
2 = **bad**, rotten, rancid, mouldy, high, turned, spoiled, sour, decayed, decomposed, putrid • *Food starts to smell when it goes off.*
3 = **unacceptable**, poor, unsatisfactory, disappointing, inadequate, second-rate, shoddy, displeasing, below par, mortifying, substandard, disheartening • *Coming home drunk like that – it's a bit off, isn't it?*
▸ IN PHRASES: **off and on** = **occasionally**, sometimes, at times, from time to time, on and off, now and then, irregularly, on occasion, now and again, periodically, once in a while, every so often, intermittently, at intervals, sporadically, every once in a while, (every) now and again • *We lived together, off and on, for two years.*

offbeat = **unusual**, odd, strange, novel, out there *(slang)*, extraordinary, bizarre, weird, way-out *(informal)*, eccentric, abnormal, queer, irregular, rum *(Brit. slang)*, uncommon, Bohemian, unconventional, far-out *(slang)*, idiosyncratic, kinky *(informal)*, off-the-wall *(slang)*, unorthodox, oddball *(informal)*, out of the ordinary, left-field *(informal)*, freaky *(slang)*, wacko *(slang)*, outré, boho, daggy *(Austral. & N.Z. informal)* • *his dark, offbeat sense of humour*
OPPOSITES: common, traditional, conventional

off-colour 1 = **ill**, poorly *(informal)*, sick, funny *(informal)*, run down, under par, queer, unhealthy, washed out, unwell, queasy, out of sorts, under the weather *(informal)*, off form, indisposed, peaky, not up to par, green about the gills, peely-wally *(Scot.)* • *He felt off-colour but did not have any dramatic symptoms.*
2 = **smutty**, dirty, crude, obscene, coarse, filthy, indecent, vulgar, blue, improper, pornographic, raunchy *(U.S. slang)*, suggestive, racy, lewd, risqué, X-rated *(informal)*, bawdy, salacious, prurient, off colour, indelicate • *his off-colour jokes about women*

offence *or (U.S.)* **offense** AS A NOUN 1 = **crime**, wrong, sin, lapse, fault, violation, wrongdoing, trespass, felony, misdemeanour, delinquency, misdeed, transgression, peccadillo, unlawful act, breach of conduct • *It is a criminal offence to sell goods which are unsafe.*
2 = **outrage**, shock, anger, trouble, bother, grief *(informal)*, resentment, irritation, hassle *(informal)*, wrath, indignation, annoyance, ire *(literary)*, displeasure, pique, aggravation, hard feelings, umbrage, vexation, wounded feelings • *The book might be published without creating offence.*
3 = **insult**, injury, slight, hurt, harm, outrage, put-down *(slang)*, injustice, snub, affront, indignity, displeasure, rudeness, slap in the face *(informal)*, insolence • *His behaviour was an offence to his hosts.*
▸ IN PHRASES: **take offence** = **be offended**, resent, be upset, be outraged, be put out *(informal)*, be miffed *(informal)*, be displeased, take umbrage, be disgruntled, be affronted, be piqued, take the needle *(informal)*, get riled, take the huff, go into a huff, be huffy • *You're very quick to take offence today.*

offend 1 = **distress**, upset, outrage, pain, wound, slight, provoke, insult, annoy, irritate, put down, dismay, snub, aggravate *(informal)*, gall, agitate, ruffle, disconcert, vex, affront, displease, rile, pique, give offence, hurt (someone's) feelings, nark *(Brit., Austral. & N.Z. slang)*, cut to the quick, miff *(informal)*, tread on (someone's) toes *(informal)*, piss you off *(taboo slang)*, put (someone's) nose out of joint, put (someone's) back up, disgruntle, get (someone's) goat *(slang)*, hack you off *(informal)* • *He had no intention of offending the community.*
OPPOSITES: please, delight, soothe
2 = **disgust**, revolt, turn (someone) off *(informal)*, put off, sicken, repel, repulse, nauseate, gross out *(U.S. slang)*, make (someone) sick, turn your stomach, be disagreeable to, fill with loathing • *The smell of cigar smoke offends me.*
3 = **break the law**, sin, err, do wrong, fall, fall from grace, go astray • *alleged criminals who offend while on bail*

offended = **upset**, pained, hurt, bothered, disturbed, distressed, outraged, stung, put out *(informal)*, grieved, disgruntled, agitated, ruffled, resentful, affronted, miffed *(informal)*, displeased, in a huff, piqued, huffy, tooshie *(Austral. slang)* • *She is terribly offended and hurt by personal remarks.*

offender = **criminal**, convict, con *(slang)*, crook, lag *(slang)*, villain, culprit, sinner, delinquent, felon, jailbird, wrongdoer, miscreant, malefactor, evildoer, transgressor, lawbreaker, perp *(U.S. & Canad. informal)* • *Sex offenders often attack again when they are released.*

offending = **upsetting**, disturbing, offensive, unpleasant, unsavoury, unpalatable, disagreeable • *The book was withdrawn and the offending passages deleted.*

offensive AS AN ADJECTIVE 1 = **insulting**, rude, abusive, embarrassing, slighting, annoying, irritating, degrading, affronting, contemptuous, disparaging, displeasing, objectionable, disrespectful, scurrilous, detestable, discourteous, uncivil, unmannerly • *offensive remarks about minority groups*
OPPOSITES: civil, polite, respectful
2 = **disgusting**, gross, nasty, foul, unpleasant, revolting, stinking, sickening, vile, repellent, unsavoury, obnoxious, unpalatable, objectionable, disagreeable, nauseating, odious, repugnant, loathsome, abominable, grotty *(slang)*, detestable, noisome, yucky *or* yukky *(slang)*, festy *(Austral. slang)*, yucko *(Austral. slang)* • *the offensive smell of manure*
OPPOSITES: attractive, charming, pleasant
3 = **attacking**, threatening, aggressive, striking, hostile, invading, combative • *The troops were in an offensive position.*
OPPOSITES: defensive
▸ AS A NOUN = **attack**, charge, campaign, strike, push *(informal)*, rush, assault, raid, drive, invasion, onslaught, foray, incursion • *The armed forces have launched an offensive to recapture lost ground.*

offer AS A VERB 1 = **present with**, give, hand, hold out to • *Rhys offered him an apple.*
2 = **provide**, present, furnish, make available, afford, place at (someone's) disposal • *Western governments have offered aid.*
OPPOSITES: refuse, withdraw, withhold
3 = **volunteer**, come forward, offer your services, be at (someone's) service • *Peter offered to help us.*
4 = **propose**, suggest, advance, extend, submit, put forward, put forth • *They offered no suggestion as to how it might be done.*
5 = **give**, show, bring, provide, render, impart • *His mother and sister rallied round offering comfort.*
6 = **sacrifice**, give up, offer up • *He will offer the first harvest of rice to the sun goddess.*
7 = **put up for sale**, sell, put on the market, market, put under the hammer • *The house is being offered at 1.5 million pounds.*
8 = **bid**, submit, propose, extend, tender, proffer • *He offered a fair price for the land.*
▸ AS A NOUN 1 = **proposal**, suggestion, proposition, submission, attempt, endeavour, overture • *He has refused all offers of help.*
2 = **bargain**, deal, discount, steal *(informal)*, reduction, good deal, good buy, snip *(informal)*, giveaway, (cheap) purchase • *Today's special offer gives you a choice of three destinations.*
3 = **bid**, tender, bidding price • *We've made an offer for the house.*
▸ IN PHRASES: **on offer** = **available**, for sale, on the market, to be had, purchasable • *country cottages on offer at bargain prices*

QUOTATIONS
He's a businessman ... I'll make him an offer he can't refuse
[Mario Puzo *The Godfather*]

offering 1 = **contribution**, gift, donation, present, subscription, hand-out, stipend, widow's mite • *funds from local church offerings*
2 = **sacrifice**, tribute, libation, burnt offering, oblation *(in religious contexts)* • *a Shinto ritual in which offerings are made to the great Sun*

offhand AS AN ADJECTIVE = **casual**, informal, indifferent, careless, abrupt, cavalier, aloof, unconcerned, curt, uninterested, glib, cursory, couldn't-care-less, apathetic, perfunctory, blasé, brusque, take-it-or-leave-it *(informal)*, nonchalant, lackadaisical, unceremonious, offhanded • *Consumers found the attitude of its staff offhand.*
OPPOSITES: serious, responsible, attentive
▸ AS AN ADVERB = **off the cuff** *(informal)*, spontaneously, impromptu, just like that *(informal)*, ad lib, extempore, off the top of your head *(informal)*, without preparation, extemporaneously • *I couldn't tell you offhand how long he's worked here.*

office AS A NOUN 1 = **place of work**, workplace, base, workroom, place of business • *He had an office just big enough for a desk and chair.*
2 = **branch**, department, division, section, wing, subdivision, subsection • *Downing Street's press office*
3 = **post**, place, role, work, business, service, charge, situation, commission, station, responsibility, duty, function, employment, capacity, appointment, occupation • *the honour and dignity of the office of President*
▸ AS A PLURAL NOUN = **support**, help, backing, aid, favour, assistance, intervention, recommendation, patronage, mediation, advocacy, auspices, aegis, moral support, intercession, espousal • *Thanks to his good offices, a home has been found for the birds.*

officer 1 = **official**, executive, agent, representative, bureaucrat, public servant, appointee, dignitary, functionary, office-holder, office bearer • *a local education authority officer*
2 = **police officer**, detective, PC, police constable, police man, police woman • *an officer in the West Midlands police force*

official AS AN ADJECTIVE 1 = **authorized**, approved, formal, sanctioned, licensed, proper, endorsed, warranted, legitimate, authentic, ratified, certified, authoritative, accredited, bona fide, signed and sealed, ex officio, ex cathedra, straight from the horse's mouth *(informal)* • *An official announcement is expected later today.*
OPPOSITES: casual, informal, unofficial
2 = **formal**, prescribed, bureaucratic, ceremonial, solemn, ritualistic • *his official duties*
▸ AS A NOUN = **officer**, executive, agent, representative, bureaucrat, public servant, appointee, dignitary, functionary, office-holder, office bearer • *a senior UN official*

officiate 1 = **preside**, perform, conduct, celebrate, solemnize • *Bishop Silvester officiated at the funeral.*
2 = **superintend**, supervise, be in charge, run, control, serve, manage, direct, handle, chair, look after, overlook, oversee, preside, take charge, adjudicate, emcee *(informal)* • *He has been chosen to officiate at the cup final.*

officious = **interfering**, bustling, meddling, intrusive, prying, pushy *(informal)*, dictatorial, inquisitive, bossy, overbearing, opinionated, self-important, overzealous, obtrusive, bumptious, meddlesome, overbusy • *An officious little security guard approached us.*
OPPOSITES: reserved, retiring, withdrawn

offing IN PHRASES: **in the offing** = **imminent**, coming, close, near, coming up, gathering, on the way, in the air, forthcoming, looming, brewing, hovering, impending, at hand, upcoming, on the cards, on the horizon, in the wings, in the pipeline, nigh *(archaic)*, in prospect, close at hand, fast-approaching, in the immediate future, just round the corner • *A general amnesty for political prisoners may be in the offing.*

O

off-key = **cacophonous**, harsh, jarring, grating, shrill, jangling, discordant, dissonant, inharmonious, unmelodious • *her wailing, off-key vocals*

off-licence = **offie** *or* **offy** *(Brit. informal)*, liquor store *(U.S. & Canad.)*, bottle shop *(Austral. & N.Z.)*, bottle store *(S. African)*, package store *(U.S. & Canad.)* • *He went into an off-licence to buy a bottle of cider.*

off-load 1 = **get rid of**, shift, dump, dispose of, unload, dispense with, jettison, foist, see the back of, palm off • *Prices have been cut by developers anxious to offload unsold apartments.*
2 = **unload**, take off, transfer, dump, discharge, jettison, unpack, unship, unlade • *The cargo was offloaded in Singapore three days later.*

off-putting = **discouraging**, upsetting, disturbing, frustrating, nasty, formidable, intimidating, dismaying, unsettling, daunting, dampening, unnerving, disconcerting, unfavourable, dispiriting, discomfiting • *Many people find the smell of this product off-putting.*

offset = **cancel out**, balance, set off, make up for, compensate for, redeem, counteract, neutralize, counterbalance, nullify, obviate, balance out, counterpoise, countervail • *The increase in pay costs was more than offset by higher productivity.*

offshoot = **by-product**, development, product, branch, supplement, complement, spin-off, auxiliary, adjunct, appendage, outgrowth, appurtenance • *Psychology began as an offshoot of natural philosophy.*

offspring 1 = **child**, baby, kid *(informal)*, youngster, infant, successor, babe, toddler, heir, issue, tot, descendant, wean *(Scot.)*, little one, brat, bairn *(Scot.)*, nipper *(informal)*, chit, scion, babe in arms *(informal)*, sprog *(slang)*, munchkin *(informal, chiefly U.S.)*, rug rat *(slang)*, littlie *(Austral. informal)*, ankle-biter *(Austral. slang)*, tacker *(Austral. slang)* • *She was less anxious about her offspring than she had been.*
OPPOSITES: parent, predecessor, ancestor
2 = **children**, kids *(informal)*, young, family, issue, stock, seed *(chiefly biblical)*, fry, successors, heirs, spawn, descendants, brood, posterity, lineage, progeny, scions • *Characteristics are often passed from parents to offspring.*

off-the-wall 1 = **weird**, odd, strange, out there *(slang)*, bizarre, extraordinary, fantastic, astonishing, curious, peculiar, eccentric, queer, singular, far-out *(slang)*, outlandish, oddball *(informal)*, left-field *(informal)*, freakish, daggy *(Austral. & N.Z. informal)* • *surreal off-the-wall humour*
2 = **foolish**, silly, unwise, unreasonable, senseless, short-sighted, ill-advised, nonsensical, indiscreet, ill-judged, ill-considered, imprudent, unintelligent, injudicious, incautious • *some absurd, off-the-wall investment strategy*

often = **frequently**, much, generally, commonly, repeatedly, again and again, very often, oft *(archaic or poetic)*, over and over again, time and again, habitually, time after time, customarily, oftentimes *(archaic)*, not infrequently, many a time, ofttimes *(archaic)* • *We often spend our holidays at home.* • *I don't get out often.*
OPPOSITES: never, rarely, occasionally

ogle = **leer at**, stare at, eye up *(informal)*, gawp at *(Brit. slang)*, give the once-over *(informal)*, make sheep's eyes at *(informal)*, give the glad eye *(informal)*, lech or letch after *(informal)* • *She hung round ogling the men at the factory.*

ogre 1 = **fiend**, monster, beast, villain, brute, bogeyman • *Some people think of bank managers as ogres.*
2 = **monster**, giant, devil, beast, demon, bogey, spectre, fiend, ghoul, bogeyman, bugbear • *an ogre in a fairy tale*

oil **AS A NOUN** 1 = **lubricant**, grease, lubrication, fuel oil • *Her car had run out of oil.*
2 = **lotion**, cream, balm, salve, liniment, embrocation, solution • *sun-tan oil*
▸ **AS A VERB** = **lubricate**, grease, make slippery • *A crew of assistants oiled the mechanism until it worked perfectly.*
▹ *See panel* **Oils**

oily 1 = **greasy**, slick, slimy, fatty, slippery, oleaginous, smeary • *traces of an oily substance*
2 = **sycophantic**, smooth, flattering, slick, plausible, hypocritical, fawning, grovelling, glib, ingratiating, fulsome, deferential, servile, unctuous, obsequious, smarmy *(Brit. informal)*, mealy-mouthed, toadying • *He asked in an oily voice what he could do for them today.*

ointment **AS A NOUN** = **salve**, dressing, cream, lotion, balm, lubricant, emollient, liniment, embrocation, unguent, cerate • *a range of ointments for the treatment of eczema*
▸ **IN PHRASES: fly in the ointment** = **problem**, trouble, difficulty, complication, uphill *(S. African)* • *The only fly in the ointment is his ex-wife.*

O.K. *or* **okay** **AS A SENTENCE SUBSTITUTE** = **all right**, right, yes, agreed, very good, roger, very well, fair enough, ya S. African), righto *(Brit. informal)*, okey-dokey *(informal)*, yebo *(S. African informal)*, F.A.B. *(Brit. informal)* • *'Shall I ring you later?' – 'OK.'*
▸ **AS AN ADJECTIVE** 1 = **all right**, fine, fitting, fair, in order, correct, approved, permitted, suitable, acceptable, convenient, allowable • *Is it OK if I bring a friend with me?*

OILS

EDIBLE OILS

benne, gingili, *or* sesame	corn	maize	olive	peppermint	vegetable
butyrin	cottonseed	nut	palm	soya	
	fixed	oleo	peanut	sunflower seed	

INDUSTRIAL OILS

benzaldehyde	Chinese wood *or* tung	drying	heavy	parathion	stand
banana *or* pentyl acetate	coal	fuel	linseed	rapeseed	train
bone	colza	fusel	mineral	rosin	turpentine
crude	diesel	glutaraldehyde	neat's foot	shale	whale oil
		gas	paraffin	sperm	

OILS USED IN PERFUME AND MEDICINE

attar	chaulmoogra	croton	Macassar	patchouli	savin
bergamot	citronella	eucalyptus	musk	peanut	tea tree
cajuput	clove	evening primrose	mustard	rapeseed	wintergreen
camphorated	coconut	jojoba	neroli	sandalwood	ylang-ylang
castor	cod-liver	lavender	palm	sassafras	

OPPOSITES: unacceptable, incorrect, unsatisfactory
2 = fine, good, average, middling, fair, all right, acceptable, adequate, satisfactory, not bad *(informal)*, so-so *(informal)*, tolerable, up to scratch *(informal)*, passable, unobjectionable • *'Did you enjoy the film?' – 'It was okay.'*
OPPOSITES: poor, inadequate, unsatisfactory
3 = well, all right, safe, sound, healthy, hale, unharmed, uninjured, unimpaired • *Would you go and check the baby's ok?*
▸ **AS A VERB = approve**, allow, pass, agree to, permit, sanction, second, endorse, authorize, ratify, go along with, consent to, validate, countenance, give the go-ahead, rubber-stamp *(informal)*, say yes to, give the green light, assent to, give the thumbs up *(informal)*, concur in, greenlight, give your consent to, give your blessing to • *His doctor wouldn't OK the trip.*
▸ **AS A NOUN = authorization**, agreement, sanction, licence, approval, go-ahead *(informal)*, blessing, permission, consent, say-so *(informal)*, confirmation, mandate, endorsement, green light, ratification, assent, seal of approval, approbation • *He gave the okay to issue a new press release.*

old **1 = aged**, elderly, ancient, getting on, grey, mature, past it *(informal)*, venerable, patriarchal, grey-haired, antiquated, over the hill *(informal)*, senile, grizzled, decrepit, hoary, senescent, advanced in years, full of years, past your prime • *He was considered too old for the job.*
OPPOSITES: young, juvenile, youthful
2 = tumbledown, ruined, crumbling, decayed, shaky, disintegrating, worn-out, done, tottering, ramshackle, rickety, decrepit, falling to pieces • *a dilapidated old farmhouse*
3 = worn, ragged, shabby, frayed, cast-off, tattered, tatty, threadbare • *Dress in old clothes for gardening.*
4 = out of date, old-fashioned, dated, passé, antique, outdated, obsolete, archaic, unfashionable, antiquated, outmoded, behind the times, superannuated, out of style, antediluvian, unhip *(slang)*, out of the ark *(informal)*, démodé *(French)* • *They got rid of all their old, outdated office equipment.*
OPPOSITES: new, the new, up-to-date
5 = former, earlier, past, previous, prior, one-time, erstwhile, late, quondam, whilom *(archaic)*, ex- • *Mark was heartbroken when Jane returned to her old boyfriend.*
6 = long-standing, established, fixed, enduring, abiding, long-lasting, long-established, time-honoured • *He is an old enemy of mine.*
7 = early, ancient, original, remote, of old, antique, aboriginal, primitive, archaic, gone by, bygone, undeveloped, primordial, primeval, immemorial, of yore, olden *(archaic)*, pristine • *How did people manage in the old days before electricity?*
8 = stale, common, commonplace, worn-out, banal, threadbare, trite, old hat, insipid, hackneyed, overused, repetitious, unoriginal, platitudinous, cliché-ridden, timeworn • *He trotted out all the same old excuses as before.*
9 = long-established, seasoned, experienced, tried, tested, trained, professional, skilled, expert, master, qualified, familiar, capable, veteran, practised, accomplished, vintage, versed, hardened, competent, skilful, adept, knowledgeable, age-old, of long standing, well-versed • *She's an old campaigner at this game.*
10 = customary, established, traditional, conventional, historic, long-established, time-honoured, of long standing • *They dance, and sing the old songs they sang at home.*

QUOTATIONS

No man is ever so old but he thinks he can live another year
[Cicero *De Senectute*]

PROVERBS

There's many a good tune played on an old fiddle
You can't teach an old dog new tricks

old age = declining years, age, senility, advancing years, dotage, Third Age, senescence, eld *(archaic)*, elderliness, agedness, autumn *or* evening of your life • *They worry about how they will support themselves in their old age.*
OPPOSITES: youth, childhood, adolescence

QUOTATIONS

I am grown peaceful as old age tonight.
I regret a little, would change still less
[Robert Browning *Andrea del Sarto*]

Do not go gentle into that good night,
Old age should burn and rave at close of day;
Rage, rage against the dying of the light
[Dylan Thomas *Do not go gentle into that good night*]

Old age is the most unexpected of all the things that happen to a man
[Leon Trotsky *Diary in Exile*]

sans teeth, sans eyes, sans taste, sans everything
[William Shakespeare *As You Like It*]

old boy *or* **old girl = alumnus** *or* **alumna**, former pupil • *The school boasts a long list of famous old boys.*

old-fashioned **1 = out of date**, ancient, dated, outdated, unfashionable, antiquated, outmoded, passé, old hat, behind the times, fusty, out of style, unhip *(slang)*, démodé *(French)*, out of the ark *(informal)*, not with it *(informal)*, (old-)fogeyish • *She always wears such boring, old-fashioned clothes.*
OPPOSITES: happening *(informal)*, current, up-to-date
2 = oldfangled, square *(informal)*, outdated, old, past, dead, past it *(informal)*, obsolete, old-time, archaic, unfashionable, superannuated, obsolescent, unhip *(slang)*, out of the ark *(informal)* • *She has some old-fashioned values.*

old guard = traditionalists, conservatives, reactionaries • *He belongs to the Nationalist Party's old guard.*

old hand = veteran, expert, master, pro *(informal)*, old-timer, old soldier, past master, trouper, warhorse *(informal)*, old stager, one of the old school • *He is an old hand at organizing training courses.*

old man **1 = senior citizen**, grandfather *(slang)*, patriarch, old age pensioner, old person, old-timer *(U.S.)*, elder, elder statesman, wrinkly *(informal)*, old codger *(informal)*, old stager, greybeard, coffin-dodger *(slang)*, oldster *(informal)*, O.A.P. *(Brit.)*, koro *(N.Z.)* • *a wizened, bent-over old man*
2 = father, pop *(informal)*, dad *(informal)*, daddy *(informal)*, pa *(informal)*, old boy *(informal)*, papa *(old-fashioned informal)*, pater, paterfamilias • *My old man used to work down the mines.*
3 = husband, man *(informal)*, partner, mate, squeeze *(informal)*, spouse, significant other *(U.S. informal)*, better half *(humorous)*, bidie-in *(Scot.)* • *Luckily for me her old man was otherwise engaged.*
4 = manager, boss *(informal)*, supervisor, governor *(informal)*, ganger, superintendent, gaffer *(informal)*, foreman, overseer, baas *(S. African)* • *Why's the old man got it in for you?*

old person = senior citizen, senior, retired person, old age pensioner, elder, pensioner *(slang)*, coffin-dodger *(slang)*, elderly person, O.A.P. *(Brit.)* • *another old person who has frozen to death in an unheated house*

old-style = old-fashioned, traditional, ancient, antique, vintage, old-world, quaint, old-time, bygone, antiquarian • *a proper barber-shop with old-style barber chairs*

old-time = old-fashioned, traditional, vintage, ancient, antique, old-style, bygone • *I love old-time music-hall songs.*

old woman = senior citizen, old lady, pensioner *(slang)*, retired person, old age pensioner, elder, coffin-dodger *(slang)*, elderly person, O.A.P. *(Brit.)*, kuia *(N.Z.)* • *a contemptible thief who mugged an old woman*

old-world = traditional, old-fashioned, picturesque, quaint, archaic, gentlemanly, courteous, gallant, courtly, chivalrous, ceremonious • *his perfect manners and old-world charm*

Olympian 1 = **colossal**, huge, massive, enormous, tremendous, awesome, gigantic, monumental, mammoth, prodigious • *Getting his book into print has been an Olympian task.*
2 = **majestic**, kingly, regal, royal, august, grand, princely, imperial, glorious, noble, splendid, elevated, awesome, dignified, regal, stately, sublime, lofty, pompous, grandiose, exalted, rarefied, godlike • *She affects an Olympian disdain for their opinions.*

omen = **portent**, sign, warning, threat, indication, foreshadowing, foreboding, harbinger, presage, forewarning, writing on the wall, prognostication, augury, prognostic, foretoken • *Her appearance at this moment is an omen of disaster.*

QUOTATIONS
May the gods avert this omen
[Cicero *Third Philippic*]
omen: a sign that something will happen if nothing happens
[Ambrose Bierce *The Devil's Dictionary*]

ominous = **threatening**, menacing, sinister, dark, forbidding, grim, fateful, foreboding, unpromising, portentous, baleful, inauspicious, premonitory, unpropitious, minatory, bodeful • *There was an ominous silence at the other end of the phone.*
OPPOSITES: promising, encouraging, favourable

ominously = **threateningly**, grimly, menacingly, darkly, balefully, sinisterly, forbiddingly • *'I'll be back,' he said ominously.*

omission 1 = **exclusion**, removal, leaving out, elimination, deletion, excision, noninclusion • *her omission from the guest list*
OPPOSITES: addition, inclusion, insertion
2 = **failure**, neglect, default, negligence, oversight, carelessness, dereliction, forgetfulness, slackness, laxity, laxness, slovenliness, neglectfulness, remissness • *an injury occasioned by any omission of the defendant*
3 = **gap**, space, blank, exclusion, lacuna • *There is one noticeable omission in your article.*

omit 1 = **leave out**, miss (out), drop, exclude, eliminate, skip, give (something) a miss *(informal)* • *Our apologies for omitting your name from the article.*
OPPOSITES: include, add, enter
2 = **forget**, fail, overlook, neglect, pass over, lose sight of, leave (something) undone, let (something) slide • *She had omitted to tell him she was married.*

omnipotence = **supremacy**, sovereignty, dominance, domination, mastery, primacy, ascendancy, pre-eminence, predominance, invincibility, supreme power, absolute rule, undisputed sway • *leaders who use violent discipline to assert their omnipotence*
OPPOSITES: weakness, inability, powerlessness

omnipotent = **almighty**, supreme, invincible, all-powerful • *Doug lived in the shadow of his seemingly omnipotent father.*
OPPOSITES: weak, vulnerable, powerless

omnipresent = **ubiquitous**, ever-present, pervasive • *Madonna's omnipresent bodyguards*

omniscient = **all-knowing**, all-seeing, all-wise • *He believes in a benevolent and omniscient deity.*

on AS A PREPOSITION = **on top of**, supported by, resting on, in contact with • *He sat beside her on the sofa.*
▸ AS AN ADVERB 1 = **functioning**, working, operating, in use • *The light had been left on.*
2 = **continuously**, for a long time, at length, ceaselessly, without a break, without end • *She chattered on brightly and aimlessly for several minutes.*
▸ IN PHRASES: **on and off** = **occasionally**, sometimes, at times, from time to time, now and then, irregularly, on occasion, periodically, once in a while, every so often, intermittently, at intervals, sporadically, off and on, fitfully, spasmodically, by fits and starts, discontinuously, (every) now and again, (every) now and then • *They have been fighting on and off throughout their married life.*
on and on = **interminably**, for a long time, for ages, continuously, without a break • *His voice went on and on in her ear.*

once AS AN ADVERB 1 = **on one occasion**, one time, one single time • *I only met her once, very briefly.*
2 = **at one time**, in the past, previously, formerly, long ago, in the old days, once upon a time, in times past, in times gone by • *I lived there once, before I was married.*
▸ AS A CONJUNCTION = **as soon as**, when, after, the moment, immediately, the instant • *Once she got inside the house, she slammed the door.*
▸ IN PHRASES: **all at once** = **suddenly**, unexpectedly, abruptly, all of a sudden, out of the blue *(informal)*, without warning • *All at once there was a knock at the door.*
at once 1 = **immediately**, now, right now, straight away, directly, promptly, instantly, right away, without delay, without hesitation, forthwith, this (very) minute, pronto *(informal)*, this instant, straightway *(archaic)*, posthaste, tout de suite *(French)* • *I must go at once.*
2 = **simultaneously**, together, at the same time, all together, in concert, in unison, concurrently, in the same breath, in chorus, at *or* in one go *(informal)* • *They all started talking at once.*
once and for all = **for the last time**, finally, completely, for good, positively, permanently, for ever, decisively, inexorably, conclusively, irrevocably, for all time, inescapably, with finality, beyond the shadow of a doubt • *We have to resolve this matter once and for all.*
once in a while = **occasionally**, sometimes, at times, from time to time, on and off, irregularly, on occasion, now and again, periodically, every now and then, every so often, at intervals, off and on • *He phones me once in a while.*

oncoming 1 = **approaching**, advancing, looming, onrushing • *He skidded into the path of an oncoming car.*
2 = **forthcoming**, coming, approaching, expected, threatening, advancing, gathering, imminent, impending, upcoming, fast-approaching • *the oncoming storm*

one AS AN ADJECTIVE 1 = **single**, only, sole, particular, distinct, lone, solitary, singular • *My one regret is that I never knew my father.*
2 = **united**, combined, allied, unified, leagued, pooled, concerted, affiliated, in partnership, banded together • *The campaign uses the theme 'Together we are one'.*
▸ IN PHRASES: **get it in one** = **guess immediately**, hit the nail on the head • *'Is he having an affair?' – 'You've got it in one.'*
one by one *or* **one at a time** = **individually**, separately, singly, one after another, in single file • *We went into the room one by one.*
▸ RELATED ADJECTIVE: single
▸ RELATED PREFIXES: mon- or mono- uni-

one and a half
▸ RELATED PREFIX: sesqui-

one-horse = **small**, slow, quiet, minor, obscure, sleepy, unimportant, small-time *(informal)*, backwoods, tinpot *(Brit. informal)* • *I don't want to live in a small, one-horse town all my life.*

onerous = **trying**, hard, taxing, demanding, difficult, heavy, responsible, grave, crushing, exhausting, exacting, formidable, troublesome, oppressive, weighty, laborious, burdensome, irksome, backbreaking, exigent • *parents who have had the onerous task of bringing up a difficult child*
OPPOSITES: light, easy, simple

one-sided 1 = **unequal**, unfair, uneven, unjust, unbalanced, lopsided, inequitable, ill-matched • *It was a totally one-sided competition.*
OPPOSITES: just, fair, equal

2 = **biased**, prejudiced, weighted, twisted, coloured, unfair, partial, distorted, partisan, warped, slanted, unjust, discriminatory, lopsided • *She gave a very one-sided account of the affair.*
OPPOSITES: impartial, just, unbiased

one-time = **former**, previous, prior, sometime, late, erstwhile, quondam, ci-devant *(French)*, ex- • *She is a one-time member of the Ziegfeld Follies.*

one-to-one = **individual**, private, personal, exclusive, intimate, personalized • *one-to-one training*

ongoing 1 = **in progress**, continuing, current, growing, developing, advancing, progressing, proceeding, evolving, unfolding, unfinished, extant • *There is an ongoing debate on this issue.*
2 = **continuous**, continued, constant, sustained, endless, persistent, relentless, perpetual, continual, unbroken, never-ending, uninterrupted, interminable, unrelenting, incessant, ceaseless, unremitting, nonstop, unceasing • *Famine is still an ongoing problem.*

onion
▸ RELATED ADJECTIVE: cepaceous

onlooker = **spectator**, witness, observer, viewer, looker-on, watcher, eyewitness, bystander, sightseer • *A handful of onlookers stood around watching.*

only AS AN ADJECTIVE = **sole**, one, single, individual, exclusive, unique, lone, solitary, one and only • *She was the only applicant for the job.*
▸ AS AN ADVERB 1 = **just**, simply, purely, merely, no more than, nothing but, but, at most, at a push • *At the moment it's only a theory.*
2 = **hardly**, just, barely, only just, scarcely, at most, at a push • *I only have enough money for one ticket.*
3 = **exclusively**, entirely, purely, solely • *Computers are only for use by class members.*

onomatopoeic = **imitative**, mimicking, mimetic, onomatopoetic, echoic • *He spoke the single onomatopoeic word: 'Bang'.*

onset = **beginning**, start, rise, birth, kick-off *(informal)*, outbreak, starting point, inception, commencement • *This drug slows down the onset of the disease.*
OPPOSITES: ending, end, finish

onslaught 1 = **attack**, charge, campaign, strike, rush, assault, raid, invasion, offensive, blitz, onset, foray, incursion, onrush, inroad • *a military onslaught against the rebels*
OPPOSITES: attack, escape, retreat
2 = **surge**, flood, flow, upsurge, outpouring • *the onslaught of cheap second-hand imports*

on-the-spot = **immediate**, instant, instantaneous • *Fare dodgers could face on-the-spot fines.*

onus = **burden**, weight, responsibility, worry, task, stress, duty, load, obligation, liability • *The onus was on the British to find a solution.*

onwards *or* **onward** = **forward**, on, forwards, ahead, beyond, in front, forth • *The bus continued onward.*

ooze[1] AS A VERB 1 = **seep**, well, drop, escape, strain, leak, drain, sweat, filter, bleed, weep, drip, trickle, leach, dribble, percolate • *Blood was still oozing from the wound.*
2 = **emit**, release, leak, sweat, bleed, discharge, drip, leach, give out, dribble, exude, give off, excrete, overflow with, pour forth • *The cut was oozing a clear liquid.*
3 = **exude**, emit, radiate, display, exhibit, manifest, gush, emanate, overflow with • *Graham positively oozed confidence.*
▸ AS A NOUN = **seepage**, leak, leaking, discharge, drip, dripping, trickle, oozing, dribble, leakage, exudation • *His shirt was soaked through with the slow ooze of blood.*

ooze[2] = **mud**, clay, dirt, muck, silt, sludge, mire, slime, slob *(Irish)*, gloop *(informal)*, alluvium • *He thrust his hand into the ooze and brought out a large toad.*

opacity 1 = **opaqueness**, cloudiness, density, obscurity, dullness, murkiness, haziness, impermeability, mistiness, milkiness, filminess • *The opacity of the water is due to its mineral content.*
2 = **obscurity**, complexity, ambiguity, intricacy, vagueness, incomprehensibility, abstruseness, impenetrableness, reconditeness • *the deliberate opacity of his language*

opalescent = **iridescent**, pearly, shimmering, lustrous, opaline, shot, prismatic, rainbow-coloured, polychromatic, rainbow-hued, nacreous • *opalescent blue glass*

opaque 1 = **cloudy**, clouded, dull, dim, muddied, muddy, murky, hazy, filmy, turbid, lustreless, non-transparent • *The bathroom has an opaque glass window.*
OPPOSITES: clear, transparent, bright
2 = **incomprehensible**, obscure, unclear, difficult, puzzling, baffling, enigmatic, perplexing, impenetrable, unintelligible, cryptic, unfathomable, abstruse, obfuscated, beyond comprehension • *the opaque language of the official report*
OPPOSITES: clear, lucid, crystal clear

open AS AN ADJECTIVE 1 = **unclosed**, unlocked, ajar, unfastened, yawning, gaping, unlatched, unbolted, partly open, unbarred, off the latch • *an open door*
OPPOSITES: closed, locked, shut
2 = **unsealed**, unstoppered • *an open bottle of milk*
OPPOSITES: sealed, unopened
3 = **extended**, expanded, unfolded, stretched out, spread out, unfurled, straightened out, unrolled • *A newspaper lay open on the coffee table.*
OPPOSITES: shut, folded
4 = **frank**, direct, natural, plain, innocent, straightforward, sincere, transparent, honest, candid, truthful, upfront *(informal)*, plain-spoken, above board, unreserved, artless, ingenuous, guileless, straight from the shoulder *(informal)* • *She has an open, trusting nature.*
OPPOSITES: reserved, withdrawn, sly
5 = **obvious**, clear, frank, plain, apparent, visible, patent, evident, distinct, pronounced, manifest, transparent, noticeable, blatant, conspicuous, downright, overt, unmistakable, palpable, recognizable, avowed, flagrant, perceptible, much in evidence, undisguised, unsubtle, barefaced, unconcealed • *their open dislike of each other*
OPPOSITES: secret, hidden, disguised
6 = **receptive**, welcoming, sympathetic, responsive, amenable • *He seems open to suggestions.*
7 = **susceptible**, subject, exposed, vulnerable, in danger, disposed, liable, wide open, unprotected, at the mercy of, left open, laid bare, an easy target for, undefended, laid open, defenceless against, unfortified • *They left themselves open to accusations of double standards.*
OPPOSITES: protected, defended
8 = **unresolved**, doubtful, unsettled, unanswered, undecided, debatable, unsolved, up in the air, moot, arguable, yet to be decided • *It is an open question how long his commitment will last.*
9 = **clear**, free, passable, uncluttered, unhindered, unimpeded, navigable, unobstructed, unhampered • *The emergency services will do their best to keep the highway open.*
OPPOSITES: obstructed
10 = **unenclosed**, wide, rolling, sweeping, exposed, extensive, bare, spacious, wide-open, undeveloped, uncrowded, unfenced, not built-up, unsheltered • *Police will continue their search of nearby open ground.*
OPPOSITES: covered, limited, enclosed
11 = **undone**, gaping, unbuttoned, unzipped, agape, unfastened • *Her blouse was open to the waist.*
OPPOSITES: fastened, done up
12 = **available**, to hand, accessible, handy, vacant, on hand, obtainable, attainable, at your fingertips, at your disposal • *There are a wide range of career opportunities open to young people.*

O

13 = **general**, public, free, catholic, broad, universal, blanket, unconditional, across-the-board, unqualified, all-inclusive, unrestricted, overarching, free to all, nondiscriminatory, one-size-fits-all • *an open invitation*
OPPOSITES: private, protected, restricted
14 = **vacant**, free, available, empty, up for grabs *(informal)*, unoccupied, unfilled, unengaged • *The job is still open.*
15 = **generous**, kind, liberal, charitable, benevolent, prodigal, bountiful, open-handed, unstinting, beneficent, bounteous, munificent, ungrudging • *the public's open and generous response to the appeal*
16 = **gappy**, loose, lacy, porous, honeycombed, spongy, filigree, fretted, holey, openwork • *Ciabatta has a distinctive crisp crust and open texture.*
▸ **AS A VERB** 1 = **unfasten**, unlock, unclasp, throw wide, unbolt, unbar, unclose • *He opened the window and looked out.*
OPPOSITES: close, lock, shut
2 = **unwrap**, uncover, undo, unravel, untie, unstrap, unseal, unlace • *The Inspector opened the parcel.*
OPPOSITES: wrap, seal
3 = **uncork**, crack (open), broach • *Let's open another bottle of wine.*
4 = **unfold**, spread (out), expand, stretch out, unfurl, unroll • *When you open the map, you will find it is divided into squares.*
OPPOSITES: fold
5 = **clear**, unblock • *Police have opened the road again after the crash.*
OPPOSITES: block, shut, obstruct
6 = **undo**, loosen, unbutton, unfasten • *He opened his shirt to show me his scar.*
OPPOSITES: fasten, do up
7 = **begin business**, start trading, begin trading, admit customers • *The new shopping complex opens tomorrow.*
8 = **start**, begin, launch, trigger, kick off *(informal)*, initiate, commence, get going, instigate, kick-start, inaugurate, set in motion, get (something) off the ground *(informal)*, enter upon • *They are now ready to open negotiations.*
OPPOSITES: end, close, finish
9 = **begin**, start, commence • *The service opened with a hymn.*
OPPOSITES: end, close, finish
10 = **split**, break, separate, crack, burst, break up, give way, gape, rupture, come apart • *The ground opened beneath his feet.*
11 = **reveal**, bar • *He really opened his heart to me.*

open-air = **outdoor**, outside, out-of-door(s), alfresco • *an open-air concert*

open-and-shut = **straightforward**, simple, obvious, routine, clear-cut, foregone, noncontroversial • *It's an open-and-shut case – the hospital's at fault.*

opening **AS AN ADJECTIVE** = **first**, early, earliest, beginning, premier, primary, initial, maiden, inaugural, commencing, introductory, initiatory • *the season's opening game*
▸ **AS A NOUN** 1 = **beginning**, start, launch, launching, birth, dawn, outset, starting point, onset, overture, initiation, inauguration, inception, commencement, kickoff *(informal)*, opening move • *the opening of peace talks*
OPPOSITES: ending, close, finish
2 = **hole**, break, space, tear, split, crack, gap, rent, breach, slot, outlet, vent, puncture, rupture, aperture, cleft, chink, fissure, orifice, perforation, interstice • *He squeezed through an opening in the fence.*
OPPOSITES: seal, plug, blockage
3 = **opportunity**, chance, break *(informal)*, time, place, moment, window, occasion, look-in *(informal)* • *All she needed was an opening to show her capabilities.*
4 = **job**, position, post, situation, opportunity, vacancy • *We don't have any openings just now, but we'll call you.*
5 = **first night**, debut, premiere, launch, first showing, first performance, opening night • *The play was a triumph from its opening.*

openly 1 = **frankly**, plainly, in public, honestly, face to face, overtly, candidly, unreservedly, unhesitatingly, forthrightly, straight from the shoulder *(informal)* • *We can now talk openly about AIDS.*
OPPOSITES: privately, secretly, quietly
2 = **blatantly**, publicly, brazenly, unashamedly, shamelessly, in full view, flagrantly, unabashedly, wantonly, undisguisedly, without pretence • *He was openly gay.*
OPPOSITES: secretly

open-minded = **unprejudiced**, liberal, free, balanced, catholic, broad, objective, reasonable, enlightened, tolerant, impartial, receptive, unbiased, even-handed, dispassionate, fair-minded, broad-minded, undogmatic • *I have always been open-minded about sex.*
OPPOSITES: prejudiced, biased, narrow-minded

open-mouthed = **astonished**, surprised, shocked, amazed, stunned, staggered, bewildered, astounded, dazed, confounded, perplexed, gobsmacked *(informal)*, dumbfounded, flabbergasted *(informal)*, stupefied • *They watched open-mouthed as he drove off.*

openness = **frankness**, honesty, truthfulness, naturalness, bluntness, forthrightness, ingenuousness, artlessness, guilelessness, candidness, freeness, open-heartedness, absence of reserve, candour *or (U.S.)* candor, sincerity *or* sincereness, unreservedness • *a relationship based on openness and trust*

QUOTATIONS
I will wear my heart upon my sleeve
[William Shakespeare *Othello*]

open spaces
▸ **RELATED MANIA:** agoramania
▸ **RELATED PHOBIA:** agoraphobia

operate 1 = **manage**, run, direct, handle, govern, oversee, supervise, preside over, be in charge of, call the shots in, superintend, call the tune in • *Until his death he owned and operated a huge company.*
2 = **function**, work, act, be in business, be in action • *allowing commercial businesses to operate in the country*
3 = **run**, work, use, control, drive, manoeuvre • *The men were trapped as they operated a tunnelling machine.*
4 = **work**, go, run, perform, function • *the number of fax machines operating around the world*
OPPOSITES: stop, fail, break down
5 = **perform surgery**, carry out surgery, put someone under the knife *(informal)* • *The surgeons had to decide quickly whether or not to operate.*

operation **AS A NOUN** 1 = **undertaking**, process, affair, organization, proceeding, procedure, coordination • *A major rescue operation is under way.*
2 = **manoeuvre**, campaign, movement, exercise, assault, deployment • *a full-scale military operation*
3 = **business**, concern, firm, organization, corporation, venture, enterprise • *The company has converted its mail-order operation into an e-business.*
4 = **surgery**, surgical operation, surgical intervention • *an operation to reduce a bloodclot on the brain*
5 = **performance**, working, running, action, movement, functioning, motion, manipulation • *Dials monitor every aspect of the operation of the aircraft.*
6 = **effect**, force, activity, agency, influence, impact, effectiveness, instrumentality • *This change is due to the operation of several factors.*
▸ **IN PHRASES: in operation** = **in action**, current, effective, going, functioning, active, in effect, in business, operative, in force • *The night-time curfew remains in operation.*

operational = **working**, going, running, ready, functioning, operative, viable, functional, up and running, workable, usable, in working order • *The new space station will be fully operational by next year.*

OPPOSITES: broken, out of order, inoperative

operative AS AN ADJECTIVE 1 = **in force**, current, effective, standing, functioning, active, efficient, in effect, in business, operational, functional, in operation, workable, serviceable • *The scheme was operative by the end of 1983.*
OPPOSITES: powerless, ineffective, inoperative
2 = **working**, going, running, functioning • *Make sure that the safety equipment is operative.*
3 = **relevant**, important, key, fitting, significant, appropriate, crucial, influential, apt, applicable, indicative, pertinent, apposite, germane • *A small whisky may help you sleep – 'small' being the operative word.*
▸ AS A NOUN 1 = **worker**, hand, employee, mechanic, labourer, workman, artisan, machinist, working man *or* working woman • *In an automated car plant there is not a human operative to be seen.*
2 = **spy**, secret agent, double agent, secret service agent, undercover agent, mole, foreign agent, fifth columnist, nark *(Brit., Austral. & N.Z. slang)* • *The CIA wants to protect its operatives.*

operator 1 = **worker**, hand, driver, mechanic, operative, conductor, technician, handler, skilled employee • *He first of all worked as a machine operator.*
2 = **contractor**, dealer, trader, administrator • *the country's largest cable TV operator*
3 = **manipulator**, worker, mover, Machiavellian, mover and shaker, machinator, wheeler-dealer *(informal)*, wirepuller • *one of the shrewdest political operators in the Arab world*

opiate = **narcotic**, drug, downer *(slang)*, painkiller, sedative, tranquillizer, bromide, anodyne, analgesic, soporific, pacifier, nepenthe • *She had to take opiates to control the pain.*

opine = **suggest**, say, think, believe, judge, suppose, declare, conclude, venture, volunteer, imply, intimate, presume, conjecture, surmise, ween *(poetic)*, give as your opinion • *'He's probably just tired,' she opined.*

opinion AS A NOUN 1 = **belief**, feeling, view, idea, theory, notion, conviction, point of view, sentiment, viewpoint, persuasion, conjecture • *Most who expressed an opinion spoke favourably of him.*
2 = **estimation**, view, impression, assessment, judgment, evaluation, conception, appraisal, considered opinion • *That has improved my already favourable opinion of him.*
▸ IN PHRASES: **be of the opinion** = **believe**, think, hold, consider, judge, suppose, maintain, imagine, guess *(informal, chiefly U.S. & Canad.)*, reckon, conclude, be convinced, speculate, presume, conjecture, postulate, surmise, be under the impression • *Frank is of the opinion that there has been a cover-up.*
in your opinion = **in your view**, personally, to your mind, as you see it, (according) to your way of thinking • *He's not making a very good job of it, in my opinion.*
matter of opinion = **debatable point**, debatable, open question, open to question, moot point, open for discussion, matter of judgment • *Whether or not it is a work of art is a matter of opinion.*

QUOTATIONS
There are as many opinions as there are people; each has his own correct way
[Terence *Phormio*]
New opinions are always suspected, and usually opposed, without any other reason but because they are not already common
[John Locke *Essay concerning Human Understanding*]
A man can brave opinion, a woman must submit to it
[Mme de Staël *Delphine*]
Where an opinion is general, it is usually correct
[Jane Austen *Mansfield Park*]
A study of the history of opinion is a necessary preliminary to the emancipation of the mind
[John Maynard Keynes *The End of Laissez-Faire*]
They that approve a private opinion, call it opinion; but they that mislike it, heresy; and yet heresy signifies no more than private opinion
[Thomas Hobbes *Leviathan*]
Opinion in good men is but knowledge in the making
[John Milton *Areopagitica*]

opinionated = **dogmatic**, prejudiced, biased, arrogant, adamant, stubborn, assertive, uncompromising, single-minded, inflexible, bigoted, dictatorial, imperious, overbearing, obstinate, doctrinaire, obdurate, cocksure, pig-headed, self-assertive, bull-headed • *He's an opinionated man who always thinks he knows best.*
OPPOSITES: flexible, tolerant, open-minded

opinion poll = **poll**, survey, ballot, census, Gallup Poll • *75% of people questioned in our opinion poll agreed with the government.*

opponent 1 = **adversary**, rival, enemy, the opposition, competitor, challenger, foe, contestant, antagonist • *Mr Kennedy's opponent in the leadership contest*
OPPOSITES: friend, ally, colleague
2 = **opposer**, dissident, objector, dissentient, disputant • *He became an outspoken opponent of the old Soviet system.*
OPPOSITES: supporter

opportune = **timely**, fitting, fit, welcome, lucky, appropriate, suitable, happy, proper, convenient, fortunate, favourable, apt, advantageous, auspicious, fortuitous, well-timed, propitious, heaven-sent, felicitous, providential, seasonable, falling into your lap • *I have arrived at a very opportune moment.*
OPPOSITES: unfortunate, inappropriate, inopportune

opportunism = **expediency**, convenience, exploitation, realism, manipulation, pragmatism, capitalization, realpolitik, utilitarianism, making hay while the sun shines *(informal)*, striking while the iron is hot *(informal)*, unscrupulousness, Machiavellianism • *The opposition's concern for the environment was mere political opportunism.*

QUOTATIONS
There is a tide in the affairs of men,
Which, taken at the flood, leads on to fortune
[William Shakespeare *Julius Caesar*]

opportunity = **chance**, opening, time, turn, hour, break *(informal)*, moment, window, possibility, occasion, slot, scope, look-in *(informal)* • *I was given an opportunity to bathe and shower.* • *I had the opportunity to go abroad and study.*

PROVERBS
When the cat's away, the mice will play
Never look a gift horse in the mouth
When one door shuts, another door opens
Strike while the iron is hot
There is no time like the present
He who hesitates is lost

oppose = **be against**, fight (against), check, bar, block, prevent, take on, counter, contest, resist, confront, face, combat, defy, thwart, contradict, withstand, stand up to, hinder, struggle against, obstruct, fly in the face of, take issue with, be hostile to, counterattack, speak (out) against, be in opposition to, be in defiance of, strive against, set your face against, take *or* make a stand against • *Mr Taylor was bitter towards those who had opposed him.*
OPPOSITES: back, help, support

opposed AS AN ADJECTIVE 1 *with* **to** = **against**, anti *(informal)*, hostile, adverse, contra *(informal)*, in opposition, averse, antagonistic, inimical, (dead) set against • *I am utterly opposed to any form of terrorism.*
2 = **contrary**, opposite, conflicting, opposing, clashing, counter, adverse, contradictory, in opposition, incompatible, antithetical, antipathetic, dissentient • *people with views almost diametrically opposed to his own*
▸ IN PHRASES: **as opposed to** = **in contrast with**, rather than, as against, as contrasted with • *We ate in the restaurant, as opposed to our rooms.*

O

opposing 1 = **conflicting**, different, opposed, contrasting, opposite, differing, contrary, contradictory, incompatible, irreconcilable • *I have a friend who holds the opposing view.*
2 = **rival**, warring, conflicting, clashing, competing, enemy, opposite, hostile, combatant, antagonistic, antipathetic • *The leader said he still favoured a dialogue between the opposing sides.*

opposite AS AN ADJECTIVE 1 = **facing**, other, opposing • *the opposite side of the room*
2 = **different**, conflicting, opposed, contrasted, contrasting, unlike, differing, contrary, diverse, adverse, at odds, contradictory, inconsistent, dissimilar, divergent, irreconcilable, at variance, poles apart, diametrically opposed, antithetical, streets apart • *Everything he does is opposite to what is considered normal behaviour.*
OPPOSITES: like, same, alike
3 = **rival**, conflicting, opposed, opposing, competing, hostile, antagonistic, inimical • *They fought on opposite sides during the War of Independence.*
▸ AS A PREPOSITION *often with* **to** = **facing**, face to face with, across from, eyeball to eyeball with *(informal)* • *She sat opposite her at breakfast.*
▸ AS A NOUN = **reverse**, contrary, converse, antithesis, the other extreme, contradiction, inverse, the other side of the coin *(informal)*, obverse • *She's very shy, but her sister is quite the opposite.*

PROVERBS
Opposites attract

opposite number = **equivalent**, equal, peer, counterpart, correspondent • *The Defence Minister is to visit Japan for talks with his Japanese opposite number.*

opposition 1 = **hostility**, resistance, resentment, disapproval, obstruction, animosity, aversion, antagonism, antipathy, obstructiveness, counteraction, contrariety • *Much of the opposition to this plan has come from the media.*
OPPOSITES: agreement, approval, support
2 = **opponent(s)**, competition, rival(s), enemy, competitor(s), other side, challenger(s), foe, contestant(s), antagonist(s) • *The team inflicted a crushing defeat on the opposition.*

oppress 1 = **subjugate**, abuse, suppress, wrong, master, overcome, crush, overwhelm, put down, subdue, overpower, persecute, rule over, enslave, maltreat, hold sway over, trample underfoot, bring someone to heel, tyrannize over, rule with an iron hand, bring someone under the yoke • *Men still oppress women both physically and socially.*
OPPOSITES: free, release, liberate
2 = **depress**, burden, discourage, torment, daunt, harass, afflict, sadden, vex, weigh down, dishearten, cast someone down, dispirit, take the heart out of, deject, lie *or* weigh heavy upon, make someone despondent • *The atmosphere in the room oppressed her.*

oppressed = **downtrodden**, abused, exploited, subject, burdened, distressed, slave, disadvantaged, helpless, misused, enslaved, prostrate, underprivileged, subservient, subjugated, browbeaten, maltreated, tyrannized, henpecked • *freedom for the oppressed people of the world*
OPPOSITES: advantaged, favoured, liberated

oppression = **persecution**, control, suffering, abuse, injury, injustice, cruelty, domination, repression, brutality, suppression, severity, tyranny, authoritarianism, harshness, despotism, ill-treatment, subjugation, subjection, maltreatment • *an attempt to escape political oppression*
OPPOSITES: justice, mercy, compassion

QUOTATIONS
the most potent weapon in the hands of the oppressor is the mind of the oppressed
[Steve Biko *'Black Consciousness and the Quest for a True Humanity'*]

oppressive 1 = **tyrannical**, severe, harsh, heavy, overwhelming, cruel, brutal, authoritarian, unjust, repressive, Draconian, autocratic, inhuman, dictatorial, coercive, imperious, domineering, overbearing, burdensome, despotic, high-handed, peremptory, overweening, tyrannous • *The new laws will be as oppressive as those they replace.*
OPPOSITES: just, soft, merciful
2 = **stifling**, close, heavy, sticky, overpowering, suffocating, stuffy, humid, torrid, sultry, airless, muggy • *The oppressive afternoon heat had quite tired him out.*
3 = **overwhelming**, crushing, devastating, towering, intolerable, overpowering, unbearable • *An oppressive sense of sadness weighed upon him.*

oppressor = **persecutor**, tyrant, bully, scourge, tormentor, despot, autocrat, taskmaster, iron hand, slave-driver, harrier, intimidator, subjugator • *The rebels called upon the people to rise up against their oppressors.*

opprobrium 1 = **censure**, criticism, condemnation, discredit, disapproval, reproach, stricture, calumny, odium, sideswipe, disfavour, stick *(slang)*, obloquy, contumely, scurrility • *His political opinions have attracted public opprobrium.*
2 = **disgrace**, scandal, shame, stigma, stain, slur, degradation, disrepute, ignominy, dishonour, infamy, ill repute • *He had to undergo the opprobrium of a public trial.*

opt AS A VERB = **choose**, decide, prefer, select, elect, see fit, make a selection • *Students can opt to stay in residence.*
OPPOSITES: reject, dismiss, exclude
▸ IN PHRASES: **opt for something** *or* **someone** = **choose**, pick, select, take, adopt, go for, designate, decide on, single out, espouse, fix on, plump for, settle upon, exercise your discretion in favour of • *You may wish to opt for one method or the other.*
opt out = **withdraw**, leave, pull out, drop out, back out, secede, cop out *(slang)*, absent yourself • *You may opt out of the scheme at any time.*

optimism = **hope**, confidence, buoyancy, positive attitude, hopefulness, positiveness • *The President has expressed his optimism about the deal.*

QUOTATIONS
To travel hopefully is a better thing than to arrive, and the true success is to labour
[Robert Louis Stevenson *Virginibus Puerisque*]

PROVERBS
Every cloud has a silver lining

optimist

QUOTATIONS
an optimist is a guy
that has never had
much experience
[Don Marquis *archy and mehitabel*]

optimistic 1 = **hopeful**, positive, confident, encouraged, can-do *(informal)*, bright, assured, cheerful, rosy, buoyant, idealistic, Utopian, sanguine, expectant, looking on the bright side, buoyed up, disposed to take a favourable view, seen through rose-coloured spectacles • *Michael was in a jovial and optimistic mood.*
OPPOSITES: resigned, despairing, pessimistic
2 = **encouraging**, promising, bright, good, cheering, reassuring, satisfactory, rosy, heartening, auspicious, propitious • *an optimistic forecast that the economy would pick up by the end of the year*
OPPOSITES: discouraging

optimum = **ideal**, best, highest, finest, choicest, perfect, supreme, peak, outstanding, first-class, foremost, first-rate, flawless, superlative, pre-eminent, most excellent, A1 *or* A-one *(informal)*, most favourable *or* advantageous • *how to make the optimum use of resources*
OPPOSITES: lowest, least, worst

option = **choice**, alternative, selection, preference, freedom of choice, power to choose, election • *He was jailed for thirty days without the option of a fine.*

optional = **voluntary**, open, discretionary, possible, extra, elective, up to the individual, noncompulsory • *Some people feel sex education should remain an optional school subject.*
OPPOSITES: required, compulsory, mandatory

opulence *or* **opulency** 1 = **luxury**, riches, wealth, splendour, prosperity, richness, affluence, voluptuousness, lavishness, sumptuousness, luxuriance • *the opulence of the hotel's sumptuous interior*
2 = **wealth**, means, riches *(informal)*, capital, resources, assets, fortune, substance, prosperity, affluence, easy circumstances, prosperousness • *He is surrounded by possessions which testify to his opulence.*
OPPOSITES: want, lack, poverty

opulent 1 = **luxurious**, expensive, champagne, magnificent, costly, splendid, lavish, sumptuous, plush *(informal)*, ritzy *(slang)*, de luxe, well-appointed • *an opulent lifestyle*
2 = **rich**, wealthy, prosperous, propertied, loaded *(slang)*, flush *(informal)*, affluent, well-off, well-heeled *(informal)*, well-to-do, moneyed, filthy rich, stinking rich *(informal)*, made of money *(informal)*, minted *(Brit. slang)* • *the spoilt child of an opulent father*
OPPOSITES: poor, needy, broke *(informal)*

opus = **work**, piece, production, creation, composition, work of art, brainchild, oeuvre *(French)* • *Emerson, Lake and Palmer have recorded their latest opus in Dolby Surround.*

oracle 1 = **prophet**, diviner, sage, seer, clairvoyant, augur, soothsayer, sibyl, prophesier • *Ancient peoples consulted the oracle and the shaman for advice.*
2 = **prophecy**, vision, revelation, forecast, prediction, divination, prognostication, augury, divine utterance • *Aeneas had begged the Sybil to speak her oracle in words.*
3 = **authority**, judge, expert, source, professional, master, specialist, adviser, scholar, guru, mentor, pundit, wizard, mastermind, connoisseur, arbiter, high priest, horse's mouth, fundi *(S. African)* • *He is the oracle on modern etiquette.*

oral = **spoken**, vocal, verbal, unwritten, viva voce • *All students have to take a written and oral examination.*

orange

SHADES OF ORANGE

amber	grenadine	tangerine
burnt sienna	ochre	terracotta
gold	peach	

oration = **speech**, talk, address, lecture, discourse, harangue, homily, spiel *(informal)*, disquisition, declamation, whaikorero *(N.Z.)* • *a brief funeral oration*

orator = **public speaker**, speaker, lecturer, spokesperson, declaimer, rhetorician, Cicero, spieler *(informal)*, word-spinner, spokesman *or* spokeswoman • *Lenin was the greatest orator of the Russian revolution.*

oratorical = **rhetorical**, verbal, linguistic, eloquent, high-flown, stylistic, bombastic, verbose, grandiloquent, high-sounding, declamatory, silver-tongued, Ciceronian, magniloquent • *He lacks the oratorical brilliance of his opponent.*

oratory = **rhetoric**, eloquence, public speaking, speech-making, expressiveness, fluency, a way with words, declamation, speechifying, grandiloquence, spieling *(informal)*, whaikorero *(N.Z.)* • *Neither candidate is noted for oratory or political skill.*

orb = **sphere**, ball, circle, globe, round • *The moon's orb shone high in the sky.*

orbit AS A NOUN 1 = **path**, course, track, cycle, circle, revolution, passage, rotation, trajectory, sweep, ellipse, circumgyration • *the point at which the planet's orbit is closest to the sun*
2 = **sphere of influence**, reach, range, influence, province, scope, sphere, domain, compass, ambit • *Eisenhower acknowledged that Hungary lay within the Soviet orbit.*
▸ AS A VERB = **circle**, ring, go round, compass, revolve around, encircle, circumscribe, gird, circumnavigate • *the first satellite to orbit the Earth*

orchestra

INSTRUMENTS IN A FULL ORCHESTRA

cello *or* violoncello	oboe	trombone
violin	cor anglais	timpani
viola	contra-bassoon	gong
double bass	bassoon	bass-drum
piano	clarinet	xylophone
harp	french horn	celesta
piccolo	trumpet	snare drum
flute	tuba	tubular bells

orchestrate 1 = **organize**, plan, run, set up, arrange, be responsible for, put together, see to *(informal)*, marshal, coordinate, concert, stage-manage • *The colonel orchestrated the rebellion from inside his army jail.*
2 = **score**, set, arrange, adapt • *He was orchestrating the first act of his opera.*

ordain 1 = **appoint**, call, name, commission, select, elect, invest, install, nominate, anoint, consecrate, frock • *Her brother was ordained as a priest in 1982.*
2 = **order**, will, rule, demand, require, direct, establish, command, dictate, prescribe, pronounce, lay down, decree, instruct, enact, legislate, enjoin • *He ordained that women should be veiled in public.*
3 = **predestine**, fate, intend, mark out, predetermine, foreordain, destine, preordain • *His future seemed ordained right from the start.*

ordeal = **hardship**, trial, difficulty, test, labour, suffering, trouble(s), nightmare, burden, torture, misery, agony, torment, anguish, toil, affliction, tribulation(s), baptism of fire • *the painful ordeal of identifying the body*
OPPOSITES: delight, pleasure, joy

order AS A VERB 1 = **command**, instruct, direct, charge, demand, require, bid, compel, enjoin, adjure • *Williams ordered him to leave.*
OPPOSITES: forbid, ban, prohibit
2 = **decree**, rule, demand, establish, prescribe, pronounce, ordain • *The President has ordered a full investigation.*
OPPOSITES: ban, disallow, proscribe
3 = **request**, ask (for), book, demand, seek, call for, reserve, engage, apply for, contract for, solicit, requisition, put in for, send away for • *I often order goods over the Internet these days.*
4 = **arrange**, group, sort, class, position, range, file, rank, line up, organize, set out, sequence, catalogue, sort out, classify, array, dispose, tidy, marshal, lay out, tabulate, systematize, neaten, put in order, set in order, put to rights • *Entries in the book are ordered alphabetically.*
OPPOSITES: confuse, disturb, disarrange
▸ AS A NOUN 1 = **instruction**, ruling, demand, direction, command, say-so *(informal)*, dictate, decree, mandate, directive, injunction, behest, stipulation • *They were arrested and executed on the orders of Stalin.*
2 = **request**, booking, demand, commission, application, reservation, requisition • *The company say they can't supply our order.*

3 = **sequence**, grouping, ordering, line, series, structure, chain, arrangement, line-up, succession, disposal, array, placement, classification, layout, progression, disposition, setup *(informal)*, categorization, codification • *List the key headings and sort them in a logical order.*
4 = **organization**, system, method, plan, pattern, arrangement, harmony, symmetry, regularity, propriety, neatness, tidiness, orderliness • *The wish to impose order upon confusion is a kind of intellectual instinct.*
OPPOSITES: mess, disorder, chaos
5 = **peace**, control, law, quiet, calm, discipline, law and order, tranquillity, peacefulness, lawfulness • *He has the power to use force to maintain public order.*
6 = **society**, company, group, club, union, community, league, association, institute, organization, circle, corporation, lodge, guild, sect, fellowship, fraternity, brotherhood, sisterhood, sodality • *the Benedictine order of monks*
7 = **class**, set, rank, degree, grade, sphere, caste • *He maintained that the higher orders of society must rule the lower.*
8 = **kind**, group, class, family, form, sort, type, variety, cast, species, breed, strain, category, tribe, genre, classification, genus, ilk, subdivision, subclass, taxonomic group • *the order of insects Coleoptera, better known as beetles*
▸ IN PHRASES: **be the order of the day** = **be obligatory** • *Champagne is the order of the day at weddings.*
in order 1 = **tidy**, ordered, neat, arranged, trim, orderly, spruce, well-kept, well-ordered, shipshape, spick-and-span, trig *(archaic or dialect)*, in apple-pie order *(informal)* • *We tried to keep the room in order.*
2 = **appropriate**, right, fitting, seemly, called for, correct, suitable, acceptable, proper, to the point, apt, applicable, pertinent, befitting, well-suited, well-timed, apposite, germane, to the purpose, meet *(archaic)*, O.K. *or* okay *(informal)* • *I think an apology would be in order.*
order someone about *or* **around** = **dominate**, bully, intimidate, oppress, dictate to, terrorize, put upon, push around *(slang)*, browbeat, ride roughshod over, lord it over, tyrannize, rule with an iron hand • *My big brother's always ordering me about.*
out of order 1 = **not working**, broken, broken-down, ruined, bust *(informal)*, buggered *(slang, chiefly Brit.)*, defective, wonky *(Brit. slang)*, not functioning, out of commission, on the blink *(slang)*, on its last legs, inoperative, kaput *(informal)*, in disrepair, gone haywire *(informal)*, nonfunctional, on the fritz *(U.S. slang)*, gone phut *(informal)*, U.S. *(informal)* • *The phone is out of order.*
2 = **improper**, wrong, unsuitable, not done, not on *(informal)*, unfitting, vulgar, out of place, unseemly, untoward, unbecoming, impolite, off-colour, out of turn, uncalled-for, not cricket *(informal)*, indelicate, indecorous • *Don't you think that remark was a bit out of order?*

PROVERBS
A place for everything, and everything in its place
There's a time and a place for everything

orderly 1 = **well-behaved**, controlled, disciplined, quiet, restrained, law-abiding, obedient, docile, nonviolent, peaceable, decorous • *The organizers guided them in orderly fashion out of the building.*
OPPOSITES: disorderly, uncontrolled, riotous
2 = **well-organized**, ordered, regular, in order, organized, trim, precise, neat, tidy, systematic, businesslike, methodical, well-kept, shipshape, systematized, well-regulated, in apple-pie order *(informal)* • *The vehicles were parked in orderly rows.*
OPPOSITES: disorderly, chaotic, disorganized

ordinance = **rule**, order, law, ruling, standard, guide, direction, principle, command, regulation, guideline, criterion, decree, canon, statute, fiat, edict, dictum, precept • *ordinances that restrict building development*

ordinarily = **usually**, generally, normally, commonly, regularly, routinely, in general, as a rule, habitually, customarily, in the usual way, as is usual, as is the custom, in the general run (of things) • *The streets would ordinarily have been full of people at this time.*
OPPOSITES: rarely, occasionally, seldom

ordinary AS AN ADJECTIVE 1 = **usual**, standard, normal, common, established, settled, regular, familiar, household, typical, conventional, routine, stock, everyday, prevailing, accustomed, customary, habitual, quotidian, wonted • *It was just an ordinary day for us.*
2 = **commonplace**, plain, modest, humble, stereotyped, pedestrian, mundane, vanilla *(slang)*, stale, banal, unremarkable, prosaic, run-of-the-mill, humdrum, homespun, uninteresting, workaday, common or garden *(informal)*, unmemorable • *My life seems pretty ordinary compared to yours.*
3 = **average**, middling, fair, indifferent, not bad, mediocre, so-so *(informal)*, unremarkable, tolerable, run-of-the-mill, passable, undistinguished, uninspired, unexceptional, bog-standard *(Brit. & Irish slang)*, no great shakes *(informal)*, dime-a-dozen *(informal)* • *The food here is cheap, but very ordinary.*
OPPOSITES: special, novel, extraordinary
▸ IN PHRASES: **out of the ordinary** = **unusual**, different, odd, important, special, striking, surprising, significant, strange, exciting, rare, impressive, extraordinary, outstanding, remarkable, bizarre, distinguished, unexpected, curious, exceptional, notable, unfamiliar, abnormal, queer, uncommon, singular, unconventional, noteworthy, atypical • *Have you noticed anything out of the ordinary about him?*

ordnance = **weapons**, arms, guns, artillery, cannon, firearms, weaponry, big guns, armaments, munitions, materiel, instruments of war • *a team clearing an area littered with unexploded ordnance*

organ 1 = **body part**, part of the body, member, element, biological structure • *damage to the muscles and internal organs*
2 = **newspaper**, paper, medium, voice, agency, channel, vehicle, journal, publication, rag *(informal)*, gazette, periodical, mouthpiece • *the People's Daily, the official organ of the Chinese Commmunist Party*

organic 1 = **pesticide-free**, natural, chemical-free, additive-free • *Organic farming is expanding everywhere.*
2 = **natural**, biological, living, live, vital, animate, biotic • *Oxygen is vital to all organic life on Earth.*
3 = **developing**, growing, progressing, maturing, evolving, flourishing, blossoming • *to manage the company and supervise its organic growth*
4 = **systematic**, ordered, structured, organized, integrated, orderly, standardized, methodical, well-ordered, systematized • *City planning treats the city as an organic whole.*
5 = **integral**, fundamental, constitutional, structural, inherent, innate, immanent, hard-wired • *The history of Russia is an organic part of European history.*

organism = **creature**, being, thing, body, animal, structure, beast, entity, living thing, critter *(U.S. dialect)* • *Not all chemicals present in living organisms are harmless.*

organization *or* **organisation** 1 = **group**, company, party, body, concern, league, association, band, institution, gathering, circle, corporation, federation, outfit *(informal)*, faction, consortium, syndicate, combine, congregation, confederation • *Most of the funds are provided by voluntary organizations.*
2 = **management**, running, planning, making, control, operation, handling, structuring, administration, direction, regulation, construction, organizing, supervision, governance, formulation, coordination, methodology,

superintendence • *the work that goes into the organization of this event*
3 = **structure**, grouping, plan, system, form, design, method, pattern, make-up, arrangement, construction, constitution, format, formation, framework, composition, chemistry, configuration, conformation, interrelation of parts • *the internal organization of the department*
▷ *See panel* **Economic organizations and treaties**

organizational = **managerial**, executive, management, administrative, overseeing, governmental, supervisory, directorial, gubernatorial (*chiefly U.S.*) • *Evelyn's organizational skills were soon spotted by her employers*

organize *or* **organise** 1 = **arrange**, run, plan, form, prepare, establish, set up, shape, schedule, frame, look after, be responsible for, construct, constitute, devise, put together, take care of, see to (*informal*), get together, marshal, contrive, get going, coordinate, fix up, straighten out, lay the foundations of, lick into shape, jack up (*N.Z. informal*) • *We need someone to help organize our campaign.*
OPPOSITES: upset, confuse, disrupt
2 = **put in order**, arrange, group, list, file, index, catalogue, classify, codify, pigeonhole, tabulate, inventory, systematize, dispose • *He began to organize his papers.*
OPPOSITES: scramble, mix up, muddle

organized = **methodical**, ordered, efficient, disciplined, precise, neat, tidy, systematic, orderly, meticulous, businesslike • *Such people are very organized and excellent time managers.*

organizer = **planner**, manager, administrator, supervisor, superintendent, overseer • *the organizers of the event*

orgasm = **climax**, coming (*taboo slang*), pleasure, the big O (*informal*), (sexual) satisfaction • *Some women cannot achieve an orgasm during intercourse.*

orgiastic = **wild**, abandoned, riotous, unruly, frenetic, uncontrolled, unbridled, depraved, wanton, unrestrained, debauched, dissolute, Dionysian, uproarious, bacchanalian, bacchic, Saturnalian • *an orgiastic party*

orgy 1 = **party**, celebration, rave (*Brit. slang*), revel, festivity, bender (*informal*), debauch, revelry, carouse, Saturnalia, bacchanal, rave-up (*Brit. slang*), bacchanalia, carousal, hooley *or* hoolie (*chiefly Irish & N.Z.*) • *a drunken orgy*
2 = **spree**, fit, spell, run, session, excess, bout, indulgence, binge (*informal*), splurge, surfeit, overindulgence, sesh (*slang*) • *He blew £43,000 in an 18-month orgy of spending.*

orient *or* **orientate** AS A VERB = **adjust**, settle, adapt, tune, convert, alter, compose, accommodate, accustom, reconcile, align, harmonize, familiarize, acclimatize, find your feet (*informal*) • *It will take some time to orient yourself to this new way of thinking.*
▸ IN PHRASES: **orient yourself** = **get your bearings**, get the lie of the land, establish your location • *She lay still for a few seconds, trying to orient herself.*

orientation 1 = **inclination**, tendency, bias, leaning, bent, disposition, predisposition, predilection, proclivity, partiality, turn of mind • *The party is liberal and democratic in orientation.*
2 = **induction**, introduction, breaking in, adjustment, settling in, adaptation, initiation, assimilation, familiarization, acclimatization • *the company's policy on recruiting and orientation*
3 = **position**, situation, location, site, bearings, direction, arrangement, whereabouts, disposition, coordination • *The orientation of the church is such that the front faces the square.*

-oriented *or* **-orientated** = **aimed**, directed, designed, intended, angled, slanted • *market-oriented economies*

orifice = **opening**, space, hole, split, mouth, gap, rent, breach, vent, pore, rupture, aperture, cleft, chink, fissure, perforation, interstice • *Viruses get into the body via any convenient orifice.*

origin 1 = **beginning**, start, birth, source, launch, foundation, creation, dawning, early stages, emergence, outset, starting point, onset, genesis, initiation, inauguration, inception, font (*poetic*), commencement, fountain, fount, origination, fountainhead, mainspring • *theories about the origin of life*
OPPOSITES: end, death, finish
2 = **root**, source, basis, beginnings, base, cause, spring, roots, seed, foundation, nucleus, germ, provenance, derivation, wellspring, fons et origo (*Latin*) • *What is the origin of the word 'honeymoon'?*
3 = **ancestry**, family, race, beginnings, stock, blood, birth, heritage, ancestors, descent, pedigree, extraction, lineage, forebears, antecedents, parentage, forefathers, genealogy, derivation, progenitors, stirps • *people of Asian origin*

original AS AN ADJECTIVE 1 = **first**, earliest, early, initial, aboriginal, primitive, pristine, primordial, primeval, autochthonous • *The Dayaks were the original inhabitants of Borneo.*

ECONOMIC ORGANIZATIONS AND TREATIES

ACAS *or* Advisory, Conciliation, and Arbitration Service
Bretton Woods System
CACM *or* Central American Common Market
CAP *or* Common Agricultural Policy
CARICOM *or* Caribbean Community and Common Market
CARIFTA *or* Caribbean Free Trade Area
CBI *or* Confederation of British Industry
COMECON *or* Council for Mutual Economic Assistance
ECO *or* European Coal Organization
ECOSOC *or* Economic and Social Council
ECOWAS *or* Economic Community Of West African States
ECSC *or* European Coal and Steel Community
EEA *or* European Economic Area
EFTA *or* European Free Trade association
EMS *or* European Monetary System
EMU *or* European Monetary Union
EU *or* European Union
European Bank for Reconstruction and Development
European Investment Bank
European Monetary Cooperation Fund
European Regional Development Fund
GATT *or* General Agreement on Tariffs and Trade
Group of 7 *or* G7
IFC *or* International Finance Corporation
ILO *or* International Labour Organization
IMF *or* International Monetary Fund
LAFTA *or* Latin American Free Trade Association
Lomé agreements
Maastricht Treaty
Monopolies and Mergers Commission
NAFTA *or* New Zealand and Australia Free Trade Agreement
NAFTA *or* North American Free Trade Agreement
NEDC *or* National Economic Development Council
OECD *or* Organization for Economic Cooperation and Development
Office of Fair Trading
OPEC *or* Organization of Petroleum Exporting Countries
Single European Market Act
Treaty of Rome
TUC *or* Trades Union Congress
UNCTAD *or* United Nations Conference on Trade and Development
UNIDO *or* United Nations Industrial Development Organization
World Bank *or* International Bank for Reconstruction and Development
WTO *or* World Trade Organization

2 = **initial**, first, starting, opening, primary, inaugural, commencing, introductory • *Let's stick to the original plan.*
OPPOSITES: last, latest, final
3 = **authentic**, real, actual, genuine, legitimate, first generation, bona fide, the real McCoy • *The company specializes in selling original movie posters.*
OPPOSITES: copied, borrowed, reproduced
4 = **new**, fresh, novel, different, unusual, unknown, unprecedented, innovative, unfamiliar, unconventional, seminal, ground-breaking, untried, innovatory, newfangled • *an original idea*
OPPOSITES: old, stock, unoriginal
5 = **creative**, inspired, imaginative, artistic, fertile, ingenious, visionary, inventive, resourceful • *a chef with an original touch and a measure of inspiration*
▸ AS A NOUN 1 = **prototype**, master, pattern • *Photocopy the form and send the original to your employer.*
OPPOSITES: copy, reproduction, replica
2 = **character**, eccentric, case *(informal)*, card *(informal)*, nut *(slang)*, flake *(slang, chiefly U.S.)*, anomaly, oddity, oddball *(informal)*, nonconformist, wacko *(slang)*, odd bod *(informal)*, queer fish *(Brit. informal)*, weirdo *or* weirdie *(informal)* • *He's an original, this one, and a good storyteller.*

QUOTATIONS
Original thought is like original sin: both happened before you were born to people you could not have possibly met
[Fran Lebowitz *Social Studies*]

originality = **novelty**, imagination, creativity, innovation, new ideas, individuality, ingenuity, freshness, uniqueness, boldness, inventiveness, cleverness, resourcefulness, break with tradition, newness, unfamiliarity, creative spirit, unorthodoxy, unconventionality, creativeness, innovativeness, imaginativeness • *the startling originality of his writing*
OPPOSITES: orthodoxy, normality, conventionality

originally = **initially**, first, firstly, at first, primarily, at the start, in the first place, to begin with, at the outset, in the beginning, in the early stages • *The castle was originally surrounded by a moat.*

originate 1 = **begin**, start, emerge, come, issue, happen, rise, appear, spring, flow, be born, proceed, arise, dawn, stem, derive, commence, emanate, crop up *(informal)*, come into being, come into existence • *The disease originated in Africa.*
OPPOSITES: end, finish, conclude
2 = **invent**, produce, create, form, develop, design, launch, set up, introduce, imagine, institute, generate, come up with *(informal)*, pioneer, evolve, devise, initiate, conceive, bring about, formulate, give birth to, contrive, improvise, dream up *(informal)*, inaugurate, think up, set in motion • *No-one knows who originated this story.*

originator = **creator**, father *or* mother, founder, author, maker, framer, designer, architect, pioneer, generator, inventor, innovator, prime mover, initiator, begetter • *the originator of the theory of relativity*

ornament AS A NOUN 1 = **decoration**, trimming, accessory, garnish, frill, festoon, trinket, bauble, flounce, gewgaw, knick-knack, furbelow, falderal • *Christmas tree ornaments*
2 = **embellishment**, trimming, decoration, embroidery, elaboration, adornment, ornamentation • *Her dress was plain and without ornament.*
▸ AS A VERB = **decorate**, trim, adorn, enhance, deck, array, dress up, enrich, brighten, garnish, gild, do up *(informal)*, embellish, emblazon, festoon, bedeck, beautify, prettify, bedizen *(archaic)*, engarland • *The Egyptians ornamented their mirrors with carved handles of ivory, gold, or wood.*

ornamental = **decorative**, pretty, attractive, fancy, enhancing, for show, embellishing, showy, beautifying, nonfunctional • *ornamental plaster mouldings*

ornamentation = **decoration**, trimming, frills, garnishing, embroidery, enrichment, elaboration, embellishment, adornment, beautification, ornateness • *The decor was functional and free of ornamentation.*

ornate = **elaborate**, fancy, decorated, detailed, beautiful, complex, busy, complicated, elegant, extravagant, baroque, ornamented, fussy, flowery, showy, ostentatious, rococo, florid, bedecked, overelaborate, high-wrought, aureate • *an ornate gilded staircase*
OPPOSITES: simple, basic, plain

orthodox 1 = **established**, official, accepted, received, common, popular, traditional, normal, regular, usual, ordinary, approved, familiar, acknowledged, conventional, routine, customary, well-established, kosher *(informal)* • *These ideas are now being incorporated into orthodox medical treatment.*
OPPOSITES: original, novel, unorthodox
2 = **conformist**, conservative, traditional, strict, devout, observant, doctrinal • *orthodox Jews*
OPPOSITES: liberal, radical, nonconformist

orthodoxy 1 = **doctrine**, teaching, opinion, principle, belief, convention, canon, creed, dogma, tenet, precept, article of faith • *He departed from prevailing orthodoxies and broke new ground.*
2 = **conformity**, received wisdom, traditionalism, inflexibility, conformism, conventionality • *a return to political orthodoxy*
OPPOSITES: flexibility, heresy, nonconformity

oscillate 1 = **fluctuate**, swing, vary, sway, waver, veer, rise and fall, vibrate, undulate, go up and down, seesaw • *The needle indicating volume was oscillating wildly.*
2 = **waver**, change, swing, shift, vary, sway, alternate, veer, ebb and flow, vacillate, seesaw • *She oscillated between elation and despair.*
OPPOSITES: settle, decide, determine

oscillation 1 = **fluctuation**, swing, variation, instability, imbalance, wavering, volatility, variability, unpredictability, seesawing, disequilibrium, capriciousness, mutability, inconstancy, changeableness • *a slight oscillation in world temperature*
2 = **wavering**, swing, shift, swaying, alteration, veering, seesawing, vacillation • *his oscillation between skepticism and credulity*

ostensible = **apparent**, seeming, supposed, alleged, so-called, pretended, exhibited, manifest, outward, superficial, professed, purported, avowed, specious • *the ostensible reason for his resignation*

ostensibly = **apparently**, seemingly, supposedly, outwardly, on the surface, on the face of it, superficially, to all intents and purposes, professedly, speciously, for the ostensible purpose of • *He came, ostensibly to talk her brother, but really to see her.*

ostentation = **display**, show, parade, boasting, flourish, showing off *(informal)*, pretension, flaunting, vaunting, pomp, window-dressing, flamboyance, affectation, swank *(informal)*, pageantry, exhibitionism, pretentiousness, flashiness, showiness • *Despite her wealth, she lived with a notable lack of ostentation.*
OPPOSITES: reserve, simplicity, modesty

ostentatious = **pretentious**, extravagant, flamboyant, flash *(informal)*, loud, dashing, inflated, conspicuous, vulgar, brash, high-flown, flashy, pompous, flaunted, flaunting, grandiose, crass, gaudy, showy, swanky *(informal)*, snobbish, puffed up, specious, boastful, obtrusive, highfalutin *(informal)*, arty-farty *(informal)*, magniloquent, bling *(slang)* • *the ostentatious lifestyle of the nouveau riche*
OPPOSITES: simple, conservative, modest

ostracism = **exclusion**, boycott, isolation, exile, rejection, expulsion, avoidance, cold-shouldering, renunciation, banishment • *In those days unmarried mothers suffered social ostracism.*
OPPOSITES: welcome, approval, acceptance

ostracize = **exclude**, reject, boycott, avoid, exile, expel, snub, banish, shun, shut out, blacklist, cold-shoulder, cast out, excommunicate, blackball, give (someone) the cold shoulder, send to Coventry • *She is being ostracized by members of her local community.*
OPPOSITES: include, receive, accept

ostrich
▸ RELATED ADJECTIVE: struthious

other 1 = **additional**, more, further, new, added, extra, fresh, spare, supplementary, auxiliary • *No other details are available at the moment.*
2 = **different**, alternative, contrasting, distinct, diverse, dissimilar, separate, alternative, substitute, alternate, unrelated, variant • *Try to find other words and phrases to give variety to your writing.*
3 = **remaining**, left-over, residual, extant • *The other pupils were taken to an exhibition.*

otherwise AS A SENTENCE CONNECTOR = **or else**, or, if not, or then • *Write it down, otherwise you'll forget it.*
▸ AS AN ADVERB 1 = **apart from that**, in other ways, in (all) other respects • *a caravan slightly dented but otherwise in good condition*
2 = **differently**, any other way, in another way, contrarily, contrastingly, in contrary fashion • *I believed he would be home soon – I had no reason to think otherwise.*

other-worldly = **ethereal**, heavenly, spiritual, unearthly, sublime, celestial, unworldly, airy-fairy, empyreal • *stories which encourage an image of the region as an other-worldly sort of place*

otter
▸ NAME OF HOME: holt

ounce = **shred**, bit, drop, trace, scrap, grain, particle, fragment, atom, crumb, snippet, speck, whit, iota • *If only my father had possessed an ounce of business sense.*

oust = **expel**, turn out, dismiss, exclude, exile, discharge, throw out, relegate, displace, topple, banish, eject, depose, evict, dislodge, unseat, dispossess, send packing, turf out *(informal)*, disinherit, drum out, show someone the door, give the bum's rush *(slang)*, throw out on your ear *(informal)* • *The leaders have been ousted from power by nationalists.*

out AS AN ADJECTIVE 1 = **not in**, away, elsewhere, outside, gone, abroad, from home, absent, not here, no there, not at home • *I tried to phone you last night, but you were out.*
2 = **extinguished**, ended, finished, dead, cold, exhausted, expired, used up, doused, at an end • *There was an occasional spark but the fire was out.*
OPPOSITES: burning, blazing, alight
3 = **in bloom**, opening, open, flowering, blooming, in flower, in full bloom • *The daffodils are out now.*
4 = **available**, on sale, in the shops, at hand, to be had, purchasable, procurable • *Their new album is out next week.*
5 = **not allowed**, banned, forbidden, ruled out, vetoed, not on *(informal)*, unacceptable, prohibited, taboo, verboten *(German)* • *Drinking is bad enough, but smoking is right out.*
OPPOSITES: allowed, permitted, acceptable
6 = **out of date**, dead, square *(informal)*, old-fashioned, dated, outdated, unfashionable, antiquated, outmoded, passé, old hat, behind the times, out of style, unhip *(slang)*, démodé *(French)*, not with it *(informal)* • *Romance is making a comeback. Cynicism is out.*
OPPOSITES: in, latest, fashionable
7 = **inaccurate**, wrong, incorrect, faulty, off the mark, erroneous, off target, wide of the mark • *Our calculations were only slightly out.*
OPPOSITES: accurate, correct, right
8 = **revealed**, exposed, common knowledge, public knowledge, (out) in the open • *The secret about his drug addiction is out.*
OPPOSITES: kept secret, concealed, hidden
▸ AS A VERB = **expose**, uncover, unmask • *The New York gay action group recently outed an American Congressman.*
▸ IN PHRASES: **out cold** = **unconscious**, out, knocked out, stunned, numb, senseless, blacked out *(informal)*, comatose, out for the count *(Boxing)*, insensible, dead to the world *(informal)* • *He was lying on the ground nearby, out cold.*

out-and-out = **absolute**, complete, total, perfect, sheer, utter, outright, thorough, downright, consummate, unqualified, unmitigated, dyed-in-the-wool, thoroughgoing, unalloyed, arrant, deep-dyed *(usually derogatory)* • *He's an out-and-out liar.*

outbreak 1 = **eruption**, burst, explosion, epidemic, rash, outburst, flare-up, flash, spasm, upsurge • *an outbreak of violence involving hundreds of youths* • *This outbreak of flu is no worse than normal.*
2 = **onset**, beginning, outset, opening, dawn, commencement • *On the outbreak of war he expected to be called up.*

outburst 1 = **explosion**, surge, outbreak, eruption, flare-up
2 = **fit**, storm, attack, gush, flare-up, eruption, spasm, outpouring, paroxysm • *an outburst of anger*

outcast = **pariah**, exile, outlaw, undesirable, untouchable, leper, vagabond, wretch, persona non grata *(Latin)* • *He had always been an outcast, unwanted and alone.*

outclass = **surpass**, top, beat, cap *(informal)*, exceed, eclipse, overshadow, excel, transcend, outstrip, outdo, outshine, leave standing *(informal)*, tower above, go one better than *(informal)*, be a cut above *(informal)*, run rings around *(informal)*, outdistance, outrank, put in the shade, leave *or* put in the shade • *This story outclasses anything written by his contemporaries.*

outcome = **result**, end, consequence, conclusion, end result, payoff *(informal)*, upshot • *It's too early to predict the outcome of the race.*

outcry = **protest**, complaint, objection, cry, dissent, outburst, disapproval, clamour, uproar, commotion, protestation, exclamation, formal complaint, hue and cry, hullaballoo, demurral • *There was a public outcry from those opposed to abortion.*

outdated = **old-fashioned**, dated, obsolete, out of date, passé, antique, archaic, unfashionable, antiquated, outmoded, behind the times, out of style, obsolescent, unhip *(slang)*, démodé *(French)*, out of the ark *(informal)*, oldfangled • *outdated and inefficient factory equipment*
OPPOSITES: the new, current, modern

outdistance 1 = **leave behind**, lose, escape, get away from, shake off, outstrip, outrun, leave standing *(informal)*, outpace • *He managed to outdistance his pursuers.*
2 = **surpass**, top, beat, cap *(informal)*, eclipse, overshadow, best, outstrip, outdo, outshine, tower above, go one better than *(informal)*, put in the shade • *a businessman who easily outdistanced his rivals for the nomination*

outdo = **surpass**, best, top, beat, overcome, exceed, eclipse, overshadow, excel, transcend, outstrip, get the better of, outclass, outshine, tower above, outsmart *(informal)*, outmanoeuvre, go one better than *(informal)*, run rings around *(informal)*, outfox, outdistance, be one up on, score points off, put in the shade, outjockey • *Both sides have tried to outdo each other.*

outdoor = **open-air**, outside, out-of-door(s), alfresco • *There were outdoor cafés on almost every block.*
OPPOSITES: inside, indoor

outdoors = **outside**, out of doors • *The ceremony was being held outdoors.*

outer 1 = **external**, outside, outward, exterior, exposed, outermost • *Peel away the outer skin of the onion.*
OPPOSITES: central, inside, inner
2 = **surface**, external, outward, exterior, superficial • *Our preoccupation with appearance goes much deeper than the outer image.*
3 = **outlying**, remote, distant, provincial, out-of-the-way, peripheral, far-flung • *the outer suburbs of the city*
OPPOSITES: central, interior, inner

outfit AS A NOUN 1 = **costume**, dress, clothes, clothing, suit, gear *(informal)*, get-up *(informal)*, kit, ensemble, apparel, attire, garb, togs *(informal)*, threads *(slang)*, schmutter *(slang)*, rigout *(informal)* • *She was wearing an outfit we'd bought the previous day.*
2 = **group**, company, team, set, party, firm, association, unit, crowd, squad, organization, crew, gang, corps, dream team, setup *(informal)*, galère *(French)* • *He works for a private security outfit.*
▸ AS A VERB 1 = **equip**, stock, supply, turn out, appoint, provision, furnish, fit out, deck out, kit out, fit up, accoutre • *Homes can be outfitted with security lights for a few hundred dollars.*
2 = **dress**, clothe, attire, deck out, kit out, rig out • *The travel company outfitted their staff in coloured jerseys.*

outfitter = **clothier**, tailor, couturier, dressmaker, seamstress, haberdasher *(U.S.)*, costumier, garment maker, modiste • *J. Hepworth, the men's outfitter*

outflow 1 = **stream**, issue, flow, rush, emergence, spate, deluge, outpouring, effusion, emanation, efflux • *an increasing outflow of refugees from the country*
2 = **discharge**, flow, jet, cascade, ebb, gush, drainage, torrent, deluge, spurt, spout, outpouring, outfall, efflux, effluence, debouchment • *an outflow of fresh water from a river*

outgoing 1 = **leaving**, last, former, past, previous, retiring, withdrawing, prior, departing, erstwhile, late, ex- • *the outgoing director of the Edinburgh International Festival*
OPPOSITES: arriving, entering, incoming
2 = **sociable**, open, social, warm, friendly, accessible, expansive, cordial, genial, affable, extrovert, approachable, gregarious, communicative, convivial, demonstrative, unreserved, companionable • *She is very friendly and outgoing.*
OPPOSITES: cold, reserved, retiring

outgoings = **expenses**, costs, payments, expenditure, overheads, outlay • *Try to keep track of your monthly outgoings.*

outgrowth 1 = **product**, result, development, fruit, consequence, outcome, legacy, emergence, derivative, spin-off, by-product, end result, offshoot, upshot • *Her first book is an outgrowth of an art project she began in 1988.*
2 = **offshoot**, shoot, branch, limb, projection, sprout, node, outcrop, appendage, scion, protuberance, excrescence • *a new organism develops as an outgrowth or bud*

outing = **journey**, run, trip, tour, expedition, excursion, spin *(informal)*, ramble, jaunt, awayday, pleasure trip • *families on a Sunday afternoon outing*

outlandish = **strange**, odd, extraordinary, wonderful, funny, out there *(slang)*, bizarre, fantastic, astonishing, eye-popping *(informal)*, curious, weird, foreign, alien, exotic, exceptional, peculiar, eccentric, abnormal, out-of-the-way, queer, irregular, singular, grotesque, far-out *(slang)*, unheard-of, preposterous, off-the-wall *(slang)*, left-field *(informal)*, freakish, barbarous, outré, daggy *(Austral. & N.Z. informal)* • *This idea is not as outlandish as it seems.*
OPPOSITES: normal, usual, ordinary

outlast = **outlive**, survive, live after, outstay, live on after, endure beyond, outwear, remain alive after • *Naturally dried flowers will outlast a bouquet of fresh blooms.*

outlaw AS A NOUN = **bandit**, criminal, thief, crook, robber, fugitive, outcast, delinquent, felon, highwayman, desperado, marauder, brigand, lawbreaker, footpad *(archaic)* • *a band of desperate outlaws*
▸ AS A VERB 1 = **ban**, bar, veto, forbid, condemn, exclude, embargo, suppress, prohibit, banish, disallow, proscribe, make illegal, interdict, criminalize • *The German government has outlawed some fascist groups.*
OPPOSITES: support, allow, legalise
2 = **banish**, excommunicate, ostracize, put a price on (someone's) head • *He should be outlawed for his crimes against the state.*

outlay = **expenditure**, cost, spending, charge, investment, payment, expense(s), outgoings, disbursement • *Apart from the initial outlay, dishwashers can actually save you money.*

outlet 1 = **shop**, store, supermarket, market, mart, boutique, emporium, hypermarket • *the largest retail outlet in the city*
2 = **channel**, release, medium, avenue, vent, conduit, safety valve, means of expression • *He found an outlet for his emotions in his music.*
3 = **pipe**, opening, channel, passage, tube, exit, canal, way out, funnel, conduit, duct, orifice, egress • *The leak was caused by a fracture in the cooling water outlet.*

outline AS A NOUN 1 = **summary**, review, résumé, abstract, summing-up, digest, rundown, compendium, main features, synopsis, rough idea, précis, bare facts, thumbnail sketch, recapitulation, abridgment • *There follows an outline of the survey findings.*
2 = **draft**, plan, drawing, frame, tracing, rough, framework, sketch, skeleton, layout, delineation, preliminary form • *an outline of a plan to reduce the country's national debt*
3 = **shape**, lines, form, figure, profile, silhouette, configuration, contour(s), delineation, lineament(s) • *He could see only the hazy outline of the trees.*
▸ AS A VERB 1 = **summarize**, review, draft, plan, trace, sketch (in), sum up, encapsulate, delineate, rough out, adumbrate • *The methods outlined in this book are only suggestions.*
2 = **silhouette**, etch, delineate • *The building was a beautiful sight, outlined against the starry sky.*

outlive = **survive**, outlast, live on after, endure beyond, remain alive after • *I'm sure Rose will outlive us all.*

outlook 1 = **attitude**, views, opinion, position, approach, mood, perspective, point of view, stance, viewpoint, disposition, standpoint, frame of mind • *The illness had a profound effect on his outlook.*
2 = **prospect(s)**, future, expectations, forecast, prediction, projection, probability, prognosis • *The economic outlook is one of rising unemployment.*
3 = **view**, prospect, scene, aspect, perspective, panorama, vista • *The house has an expansive southern outlook over the valley.*

outlying = **remote**, isolated, distant, outer, provincial, out-of-the-way, peripheral, far-off, secluded, far-flung, faraway, in the middle of nowhere, off the beaten track, backwoods, godforsaken • *Refugees are making their way into the town from outlying areas.*

outmanoeuvre *or (U.S.)* **outmaneuver** = **outwit**, outdo, get the better of, circumvent, outflank, outsmart *(informal)*, steal a march on *(informal)*, put one over on *(informal)*, outfox, run rings round *(informal)*, outthink, outgeneral, outjockey • *He has shown once again that he is capable of outmanoeuvring his opponents.*

outmoded = **old-fashioned**, passé, dated, out, dead, square *(informal)*, ancient, antique, outdated, obsolete, out-of-date, old-time, archaic, unfashionable, superseded, bygone, antiquated, anachronistic, olden *(archaic)*, behind the times, superannuated, fossilized, out of style, antediluvian, outworn, obsolescent, unhip *(slang)*, démodé *(French)*, out of the ark *(informal)*, not with it *(informal)*, oldfangled • *People in positions of power continue to promote outmoded ideas.*
OPPOSITES: new, latest, modern

O

out of date 1 = **old-fashioned**, ancient, dated, discarded, extinct, outdated, stale, obsolete, démodé *(French)*, archaic, unfashionable, superseded, antiquated, outmoded, passé, old hat, behind the times, superannuated, out of style, outworn, obsolescent, out of the ark *(informal)*, oldfangled • *processes using out-of-date technology and very old equipment*
OPPOSITES: modern, in, new
2 = **invalid**, expired, lapsed, void, superseded, elapsed, null and void • *These tax records are now out of date.*

out of the way 1 = **remote**, far, distant, isolated, lonely, obscure, far-off, secluded, inaccessible, far-flung, faraway, outlying, in the middle of nowhere, off the beaten track, backwoods, godforsaken, unfrequented • *I like travelling to out-of-the-way places.*
OPPOSITES: close, near, nearby
2 = **unusual**, surprising, odd, strange, extraordinary, remarkable, bizarre, unexpected, curious, exceptional, notable, peculiar, abnormal, queer, uncommon, singular, unconventional, outlandish, out of the ordinary, left-field *(informal)*, atypical • *He did not seem to think her behaviour at all out of the way.*

out of work = **unemployed**, redundant, laid off, jobless, idle, on the dole *(Brit.)*, out of a job, resting *(of an actor)*, workless • *a town where half the men are out of work*

outpace = **outdistance**, leave behind, outstrip, lose, shake off, outrun, leave standing *(informal)* • *These hovercraft can easily outpace most boats.*

outperform = **surpass**, top, eclipse, outstrip, outdo, outshine, best, tower above, go one better than *(informal)*, put in the shade • *The Austrian economy has outperformed most other industrial economies.*

outpost = **frontier**, border, borderline, borderland • *a remote mountain outpost*

outpouring = **outburst**, storm, stream, explosion, surge, outbreak, deluge, eruption, spasm, paroxysm, effusion, issue • *The news of his death produced an instant outpouring of grief.*

output = **production**, manufacture, manufacturing, yield, productivity, outturn *(rare)* • *the largest drop in industrial output for ten years*

outrage AS A NOUN 1 = **indignation**, shock, anger, rage, fury, hurt, resentment, scorn, wrath, ire *(literary)*, exasperation, umbrage, righteous anger • *The decision has provoked outrage from human rights groups.*
2 = **atrocity**, crime, horror, evil, cruelty, brutality, enormity, barbarism, inhumanity, abomination, barbarity, villainy, act of cruelty • *The terrorists' latest outrage is a bomb attack on a busy station.*
▸ AS A VERB = **offend**, shock, upset, pain, wound, provoke, insult, infuriate, incense, gall, madden, vex, affront, displease, rile, scandalize, give offence, nark *(Brit., Austral. & N.Z. slang)*, cut to the quick, make your blood boil, piss you off *(taboo slang)*, put (someone's) nose out of joint, put (someone's) back up, disgruntle • *Many people have been outraged by these comments.*

outrageous 1 = **atrocious**, shocking, terrible, violent, offensive, appalling, cruel, savage, horrible, beastly, horrifying, vicious, ruthless, infamous, disgraceful, scandalous, wicked, barbaric, unspeakable, inhuman, diabolical, heinous, flagrant, egregious, abominable, infernal, fiendish, villainous, nefarious, iniquitous, execrable, godawful *(slang)*, hellacious *(U.S. slang)* • *I must apologize for my friend's outrageous behaviour.*
OPPOSITES: minor, mild, trivial
2 = **unreasonable**, unfair, excessive, steep *(informal)*, shocking, over the top *(slang)*, extravagant, too great, scandalous, preposterous, unwarranted, exorbitant, extortionate, immoderate, O.T.T. *(slang)* • *Charges for long-distance telephone calls are absolutely outrageous.*
OPPOSITES: fair, reasonable, just

outré = **eccentric**, odd, strange, out there *(slang)*, bizarre, fantastic, weird, way-out *(informal)*, peculiar, queer *(informal)*, extravagant, rum *(Brit. slang)*, quirky, singular, grotesque, unconventional, idiosyncratic, kinky *(informal)*, off-the-wall *(slang)*, outlandish, whimsical, left-field *(informal)*, freakish, freaky *(slang)*, wacko *(slang)*, daggy *(Austral. & N.Z. informal)* • *outré outfits designed by art students*

outright AS AN ADJECTIVE 1 = **absolute**, complete, total, direct, perfect, pure, sheer, utter, thorough, wholesale, unconditional, downright, consummate, unqualified, undeniable, out-and-out, unadulterated, unmitigated, thoroughgoing, unalloyed, arrant, deep-dyed *(usually derogatory)* • *He told me an outright lie.*
2 = **definite**, clear, certain, straight, flat, absolute, black-and-white, decisive, straightforward, clear-cut, unmistakable, unequivocal, unqualified, unambiguous, cut-and-dried *(informal)*, incontrovertible, uncontestable • *She failed to win an outright victory.*
▸ AS AN ADVERB 1 = **openly**, frankly, plainly, face to face, explicitly, overtly, candidly, unreservedly, unhesitatingly, forthrightly, straight from the shoulder *(informal)* • *Why are you being so mysterious? Why can't you just tell me outright?*
2 = **absolutely**, completely, totally, fully, entirely, thoroughly, wholly, utterly, to the full, without hesitation, to the hilt, one hundred per cent, straightforwardly, without restraint, unmitigatedly, lock, stock and barrel • *His plan was rejected outright.*
3 = **instantly**, immediately, at once, straight away, cleanly, on the spot, right away, there and then, instantaneously • *The driver was killed outright in the crash.*

outrun 1 = **outdistance**, beat, escape, leave behind, get away from, shake off, outstrip, lose, leave standing *(informal)*, outpace • *There are not many sprinters who can outrun him.*
2 = **exceed**, overtake, surpass, top, pass, eclipse, go beyond, outstrip, outdo, outreach • *The population growth will eventually outrun the supply of food.*

outset = **beginning**, start, opening, early days, starting point, onset, inauguration, inception, commencement, kickoff *(informal)* • *Decide at the outset what kind of learning programme will suit you best.*
OPPOSITES: end, finish, conclusion

outshine = **outclass**, beat, eclipse, overshadow, surpass, top, outstrip, upstage, outdo, be superior to, leave standing *(informal)*, be a cut above *(informal)*, be head and shoulders above, run rings around *(informal)*, leave *or* put in the shade • *He outshone all the other contestants.*

outside AS AN ADJECTIVE 1 = **external**, outer, exterior, surface, extreme, outdoor, outward, superficial, extraneous, outermost, extramural • *Cracks are beginning to appear on the outside wall.*
OPPOSITES: inside, internal, inner
2 = **remote**, small, unlikely, slight, slim, poor, distant, faint, marginal, doubtful, dubious, slender, meagre, negligible, inconsiderable • *I thought I had an outside chance of winning.*
▸ AS AN ADVERB = **outdoors**, out, out of the house, out-of-doors • *I went outside and sat on the steps.*
▸ IN PHRASES: **on the outside looking in** = **left out**, excluded, snubbed, shunned, shut out, cold-shouldered, cast out, ostracized, given the cold shoulder • *He was again on the outside looking in.*
▸ AS A NOUN = **exterior**, face, front, covering, skin, surface, shell, coating, finish, façade, topside • *the outside of the building* • *Grill until the outsides are browned.*

outsider = **stranger**, incomer, visitor, foreigner, alien, newcomer, intruder, new arrival, unknown, interloper, odd one out, nonmember, newbie *(slang)*, outlander • *We were made to feel like outsiders.*

outsize *or* **outsized** 1 = **huge**, great, large, giant, massive, enormous, monster, immense, mega *(slang)*, jumbo

(*informal*), gigantic, monumental, mammoth, bulky, colossal, mountainous, oversized, stupendous, gargantuan, fuck-off (*offensive taboo slang*), elephantine, ginormous (*informal*), Brobdingnagian, humongous *or* humungous (*U.S. slang*) • *An outsize teddy bear sat on the bed.*
OPPOSITES: baby, tiny, pocket
2 = extra-large, large, generous, ample, roomy • *Often outsize clothes are made from cheap fabric.*

outskirts = edge, borders, boundary, suburbs, fringe, perimeter, vicinity, periphery, suburbia, environs, purlieus, faubourgs • *The house is on the outskirts of New York.*

outsmart = outwit, trick, take in (*informal*), cheat, sting (*informal*), deceive, defraud, dupe, gull (*archaic*), get the better of, swindle, circumvent, outperform, make a fool of (*informal*), outmanoeuvre, go one better than (*informal*), put one over on (*informal*), outfox, run rings round (*informal*), pull a fast one on (*informal*), outthink, outjockey • *a hoaxer who managed to outsmart the world's top journalists*

outspan = relax, chill out (*slang, chiefly U.S.*), take it easy, loosen up, laze, lighten up (*slang*), put your feet up, hang loose (*slang*), let yourself go (*informal*), let your hair down (*informal*), mellow out (*informal*), make yourself at home • *Let's take a break and just outspan for a while.*

outspoken = forthright, open, free, direct, frank, straightforward, blunt, explicit, downright, candid, upfront (*informal*), unequivocal, undisguised, plain-spoken, unreserved, unconcealed, unceremonious, free-spoken, straight from the shoulder (*informal*), undissembling • *He was an outspoken critic of apartheid.*
OPPOSITES: reserved, diplomatic, gracious

outstanding 1 = excellent, good, great, important, special, fine, noted, champion, celebrated, brilliant, impressive, superb, distinguished, well-known, prominent, superior, first-class, exceptional, notable, world-class, exquisite, admirable, eminent, exemplary, first-rate, stellar (*informal*), superlative, top-notch (*informal*), mean (*slang*), pre-eminent, meritorious, estimable, tiptop, A1 *or* A-one (*informal*), booshit (*Austral. slang*), exo (*Austral. slang*), sik (*Austral. slang*), rad (*informal*), phat (*slang*), schmick (*Austral. informal*), beaut (*informal*), barrie (*Scot. slang*), belting (*Brit. slang*), pearler (*Austral. slang*) • *an outstanding tennis player*
OPPOSITES: ordinary, dull, mediocre
2 = conspicuous, marked, striking, arresting, signal, remarkable, memorable, notable, eye-catching, salient, noteworthy • *an area of outstanding natural beauty*
3 = unpaid, remaining, due, owing, ongoing, pending, payable, unsettled, overdue, unresolved, uncollected, not discharged • *The total debt outstanding is $70 billion.*
4 = undone, left, not done, omitted, unfinished, incomplete, passed over, unfulfilled, not completed, unperformed, unattended to • *Complete any work outstanding from yesterday.*

outstretched = spread, opened (out), extended, stretched, unfolded, sprawled, unfurled, fanned out • *She stepped towards him, her arms outstretched.*

outstrip 1 = exceed, eclipse, overtake, top, cap (*informal*), go beyond, surpass, outdo • *In 1989 and 1990 demand outstripped supply.*
2 = surpass (*informal*), beat, leave behind, eclipse, overtake, best, top, better, overshadow, outdo, outclass, outperform, outshine, leave standing (*informal*), tower above, get ahead of, go one better than (*informal*), run rings around, knock spots off (*informal*), put in the shade • *In pursuing her ambition she outstripped everyone else.*
3 = outdistance, lose, leave behind, shake off, outrun, leave standing (*informal*), outpace • *He soon outstripped the other runners.*

outward = apparent, seeming, outside, surface, external, outer, superficial, ostensible • *In spite of my outward calm, I was very shaken.*
OPPOSITES: inside, internal, inward

outwardly = apparently, externally, seemingly, it seems that, on the surface, it appears that, ostensibly, on the face of it, superficially, to the eye, to all intents and purposes, to all appearances, as far as you can see, professedly • *Outwardly he showed not the faintest sign of concern.*

outweigh = override, cancel (out), eclipse, offset, make up for, compensate for, redeem, supersede, neutralize, counterbalance, nullify, take precedence over, prevail over, obviate, balance out, preponderate, outbalance • *The medical benefits far outweigh the risks involved.*

outwit = outsmart (*informal*), get the better of, circumvent, outperform, outmanoeuvre, go one better than (*informal*), put one over on (*informal*), outfox, run rings round (*informal*), pull a fast one on (*informal*), outthink, outjockey • *To win the presidency he had first to outwit his rivals within the party.*

outworn = outdated, passé, old-fashioned, tired, exhausted, worn-out, stale, obsolete, out-of-date, defunct, archaic, disused, unfashionable, antiquated, outmoded, threadbare, hackneyed, overused, behind the times, superannuated, out of style, unhip (*slang*), démodé (*French*), out of the ark (*informal*) • *stubbornly clinging to outworn traditions*
OPPOSITES: new, the new, recent

oval = elliptical, egg-shaped, ovoid, ovate, ellipsoidal, oviform • *a small oval picture frame*

ovary
▸ **RELATED ADJECTIVE:** ovarian

ovation = applause, hand, cheering, cheers, praise, tribute, acclaim, clapping, accolade, plaudits, big hand, commendation, hand-clapping, acclamation, laudation • *He was pleasantly surprised by the ovation he received.*
OPPOSITES: abuse, booing, derision

oven = stove, range, kiln, kitchen stove, hangi (*N.Z.*), umu (*N.Z.*) • *Put the loaf in the oven and bake for thirty minutes.*

over AS A PREPOSITION 1 = above, on top of, atop • *He looked at himself in the mirror over the fireplace.*
2 = on top of, on, across, upon • *His coat was thrown over a chair.*
3 = across, past, (looking) onto • *a room with a wonderful view over the river*
4 = more than, above, exceeding, in excess of, upwards of • *Smoking kills over 100,000 people in Britain a year.*
5 = about, regarding, relating to, with respect to, re, concerning, apropos of, anent (*Scot.*) • *You're making a lot of fuss over nothing.*
▸ **AS AN ADVERB 1 = above**, overhead, in the sky, on high, aloft, up above • *Planes flew over every 15 minutes or so.*
2 = extra, more, other, further, beyond, additional, in addition, surplus, in excess, left over, unused, supplementary, auxiliary • *There were two for each of us, and one over.*
▸ **AS AN ADJECTIVE = finished**, by, done (with), through, ended, closed, past, completed, complete, gone, in the past, settled, concluded, accomplished, wrapped up (*informal*), bygone, at an end, ancient history (*informal*), over and done with • *I think the worst is over now.*
▸ **IN PHRASES: over and above = in addition to**, added to, on top of, besides, plus, let alone, not to mention, as well as, over and beyond • *Costs have gone up 7% over and above inflation.*
over and done with = finished, done, over, ended, in the past, played out (*informal*) • *We were friends once but that's all over and done with.*
over and over (again) = repeatedly, frequently, again and again, often, many times, time and (time) again, time after time, ad nauseam • *He plays the same song over and over again.*

QUOTATIONS
It ain't over till it's over
[attributed to Yogi Berra]

▸ **RELATED PREFIXES:** hyper-, super-, supra-, sur-

overabundance = **excess**, surplus, glut, plethora, profusion, surfeit, oversupply, embarrassment of riches, superabundance, superfluity • *Dairy farmers produce an overabundance of milk, keeping prices down.*

overact = **exaggerate**, overdo it, go overboard *(informal)*, overplay, overemphasize, lay it on thick *(informal)*, make a production of *(informal)*, ham *or* ham it up *(informal)* • *Sometimes he had overacted in his role as Hamlet.*

overall AS AN ADJECTIVE = **total**, full, whole, general, complete, long-term, entire, global, comprehensive, gross, blanket, umbrella, long-range, inclusive, all-embracing, overarching • *Cut down your overall intake of calories.*

▸ AS AN ADVERB = **in general**, generally, mostly, all things considered, on average, in (the) large, on the whole, predominantly, in the main, in the long term, by and large, all in all, on balance, generally speaking, taking everything into consideration • *Overall, I was disappointed with the result.*

overawed = **intimidated**, threatened, alarmed, frightened, scared, terrified, cowed, put off, daunted, unnerved • *Don't be overawed by people in authority.*

overbalance = **lose your balance**, slip, tumble, tip over, topple over, take a tumble, lose your footing • *He overbalanced and fell headfirst.*

overbearing = **domineering**, lordly, superior, arrogant, authoritarian, oppressive, autocratic, masterful, dictatorial, coercive, bossy *(informal)*, imperious, haughty, tyrannical, magisterial, despotic, high-handed, peremptory, supercilious, officious, overweening, iron-handed • *an arrogant and overbearing man*

OPPOSITES: modest, humble, submissive

overblown 1 = **excessive**, exaggerated, over the top *(slang)*, too much, inflated, extravagant, overdone, disproportionate, undue, fulsome, intemperate, immoderate, O.T.T. *(slang)* • *The reporting of the story was fair, though a little overblown.*

2 = **inflated**, rhetorical, high-flown, pompous, pretentious, flowery, florid, turgid, bombastic, windy, grandiloquent, high-sounding, fustian, orotund, magniloquent, aureate, euphuistic • *The book contains a heavy dose of overblown lyrical description.*

overboard IN PHRASES: **go overboard** = **go too far**, go mad, go over the top • *He doesn't drink often, but when he does, he tends to go a bit overboard.*

throw something *or* **someone overboard** = **give up**, abandon, relinquish, surrender, renounce, waive, say goodbye to, forsake, cede, cast off, kiss (something) goodbye, lay aside • *They had thrown their neutrality overboard in the crisis.*

overcast = **cloudy**, grey, dull, threatening, dark, clouded, dim, gloomy, dismal, murky, dreary, leaden, clouded over, sunless, louring *or* lowering • *It was a cold, wintry, overcast afternoon.*

OPPOSITES: clear, fine, bright

overcharge = **cheat**, con *(informal)*, do *(slang)*, skin *(slang)*, stiff *(slang)*, sting *(informal)*, rip off *(slang)*, fleece, defraud, surcharge, swindle, stitch up *(slang)*, rook *(slang)*, short-change, diddle *(informal)*, take for a ride *(informal)*, cozen • *If you feel a taxi driver has overcharged you, say so.*

overcome 1 = **defeat**, beat, conquer, master, tank *(slang)*, crush, overwhelm, overthrow, lick *(informal)*, undo, subdue, rout, overpower, quell, triumph over, best, get the better of, trounce, worst, clobber *(slang)*, stuff *(slang)*, vanquish, surmount, subjugate, prevail over, wipe the floor with *(informal)*, make mincemeat of *(informal)*, blow (someone) out of the water *(slang)*, come out on top of *(informal)*, bring (someone) to their knees *(informal)*, render incapable, render powerless, be victorious over, render helpless • *the satisfaction of overcoming a rival*

2 = **conquer**, beat, master, survive, weather, curb, suppress, subdue, rise above, quell, triumph over, get the better of, vanquish • *I have fought to overcome my fear of spiders.*

3 = **overwhelm**, move, affect, make emotional, choke, render speechless, bowl over *(informal)*, render unable to continue, sweep off your feet • *I don't know what to say! I'm quite overcome.*

overconfident = **cocky**, arrogant, brash, cocksure, foolhardy, presumptuous, overweening, bumptious, hubristic, riding for a fall *(informal)*, uppish *(Brit. informal)*, full of yourself • *the new generation of noisy, overconfident teenage girls*

OPPOSITES: cautious, uncertain

overcrowded = **packed (out)**, full, crowded, jammed, choked, crammed (full), swarming, overflowing, overloaded, seething, congested, jam-packed, chock-full, bursting at the seams, chock-a-block, overpopulated, packed like sardines, like the Black Hole of Calcutta, hoatching *(Scot.)* • *Obviously our prisons are overcrowded.*

OPPOSITES: abandoned, empty

overdo AS A VERB = **exaggerate**, overstate, overuse, overplay, do to death *(informal)*, belabour, carry *or* take too far, make a production (out) of *(informal)*, lay (something) on thick *(informal)* • *He overdid his usually quite funny vitriol.*

OPPOSITES: play down, minimize, understate

▸ IN PHRASES: **overdo it** 1 = **overwork**, go too far, go overboard, strain *or* overstrain yourself, burn the midnight oil, burn the candle at both ends *(informal)*, wear yourself out, bite off more than you can chew, have too many irons in the fire, overtire yourself, drive yourself too far, overburden yourself, overload yourself, overtax your strength, work your fingers to the bone, practice presenteeism • *When you start your running programme, don't be tempted to overdo it.*

2 = **drink** *or* **eat too much**, go overboard *(informal)*, pig out *(slang)*, live it up *(informal)*, go to extremes, overindulge, have a binge *(informal)*, not know when to stop, make a pig of yourself *(informal)*, go on the piss *(taboo slang)*, be immoderate *or* intemperate • *A drink or two is fine but don't overdo it.*

overdone 1 = **overcooked**, burnt, spoiled, dried up, charred, burnt to a crisp *or* cinder • *The meat was overdone and the vegetables disappointing.*

2 = **excessive**, too much, unfair, unnecessary, exaggerated, over the top *(slang)*, needless, unreasonable, disproportionate, undue, hyped, preposterous, inordinate, fulsome, immoderate, overelaborate, beyond all bounds, O.T.T. *(slang)* • *In fact, all the panic about the drought in Britain was overdone.*

OPPOSITES: moderated, played down, minimized

overdue 1 = **delayed**, belated, late, late in the day, long delayed, behind schedule, tardy, not before time *(informal)*, behind time, unpunctual, behindhand • *I'll go and pay an overdue visit to my mother.*

OPPOSITES: early, in advance, beforehand

2 = **unpaid**, outstanding, owing, due, payable, unsettled • *a strike aimed at forcing the government to pay overdue salaries*

overeat = **gorge**, binge *(informal)*, drink *or* eat too much, guzzle, overdo it, pack away *(slang)*, pig out *(slang)*, overindulge, stuff yourself, eat like a horse *(informal)*, have a binge *(informal)*, make a pig of yourself *(informal)*, pig away *(slang)*, gormandize, be immoderate *or* intemperate • *Many women tend to overeat when depressed.*

overemphasize = **exaggerate**, magnify, inflate, overdo, amplify, overstate, make too much of, belabour, make a big thing of *(informal)*, blow up out of all proportion, overstress, overdramatize, make a production (out) of *(informal)*, lay too much stress on, make a federal case of *(U.S. informal)*, hyperbolize • *Freud overemphasized the role of sexual motivation of behaviour.*

OPPOSITES: play down, minimize, understate

O

overestimate = **exaggerate**, magnify, inflate, amplify, exalt, overstate, overemphasize, blow out of all proportion, make a production (out) of *(informal)*, make a federal case of *(U.S. informal)* • *We must not overestimate the significance of this result.*

overflow AS A VERB 1 = **spill over**, discharge, well over, run over, pour over, pour out, bubble over, brim over, surge over, slop over, teem over • *the sickening stench of raw sewage overflowing from toilets*
2 = **flood**, swamp, submerge, cover, drown, soak, immerse, inundate, deluge, pour over • *The river has overflowed its banks in several places.*
▸ AS A NOUN 1 = **flood**, flooding, spill, discharge, spilling over, inundation • *Carpeting is damaged from the overflow of water from a bathtub.*
2 = **surplus**, extra, excess, overspill, inundation, overabundance, additional people *or* things • *Tents have been set up next to hospitals to handle the overflow.*

overflowing = **full**, filled, abounding, swarming, rife, plentiful, thronged, teeming, copious, replete, bountiful, profuse, brimful, thick on the ground, overfull, superabundant • *The great hall was overflowing with people.*
OPPOSITES: wanting, missing, deficient

overgrown = **covered**, overrun, choked • *a courtyard overgrown with weeds*

overhang = **project (over)**, extend (over), loom (over), stand out (over), bulge (over), stick out (over), protrude (over), jut (over), impend (over) • *The rock wall overhung the path at one point.*

overhaul AS A VERB 1 = **check**, service, maintain, examine, restore, tune (up), repair, go over, inspect, fine tune, do up *(informal)*, re-examine, recondition • *The plumbing was overhauled a year ago.*
2 = **overtake**, pass, leave behind, catch up with, get past, outstrip, get ahead of, draw level with, outdistance • *Beattie led for several laps before he was overhauled by Itoh.*
▸ AS A NOUN = **check**, service, examination, going-over *(informal)*, inspection, once-over *(informal)*, checkup, reconditioning • *The study says there must be a complete overhaul of air traffic control systems.*

overhead AS AN ADJECTIVE = **raised**, suspended, elevated, aerial, overhanging • *people who live under or near overhead cables*
▸ AS AN ADVERB = **above**, in the sky, on high, aloft, up above • *planes passing overhead*
OPPOSITES: below, beneath, underneath

overheads = **running costs**, expenses, outgoings, operating costs, oncosts • *We have to cut costs in order to reduce overheads.*

overhear = **hear**, listen to, eavesdrop on, catch • *I overheard two doctors discussing my case.*

overheated = **angry**, furious, incensed, enraged, pissed *(Brit., Austral. & N.Z. slang)*, worked up, agitated, inflamed, impassioned, pissed off *(taboo slang)*, irate, hot under the collar *(informal)*, hot and bothered *(informal)*, overexcited, tooshie *(Austral. slang)* • *In America, overheated drivers have been known to shoot one another.*
OPPOSITES: cool, collected, calm

overindulge = **drink** *or* **eat too much**, overdo it, live it up *(informal)*, pig out *(slang)*, have a binge *(informal)*, make a pig of yourself *(informal)*, go on the piss *(taboo slang)*, be immoderate *or* intemperate • *We all overindulge occasionally.*

overindulgence = **excess**, overeating, intemperance, immoderation, lack of restraint *or* balance • *His condition is the natural consequence of a lifetime's overindulgence.*

overjoyed = **delighted**, happy, pleased, thrilled, ecstatic, jubilant, joyous, joyful, elated, over the moon *(informal)*, euphoric, rapturous, rapt, only too happy, gladdened, on cloud nine *(informal)*, transported, cock-a-hoop, blissed out, in raptures, tickled pink *(informal)*, deliriously happy, in seventh heaven, floating on air, stoked *(Austral. & N.Z. informal)* • *Shelley was overjoyed to see me.*
OPPOSITES: disappointed, sad, heartbroken

overlay AS A VERB = **cover**, coat, blanket, adorn, mantle, ornament, envelop, veneer, encase, inlay, superimpose, laminate, overspread • *The floor was overlaid with rugs of Oriental design.* • *a very large dark wood table overlaid in glass*
▸ AS A NOUN = **covering**, casing, wrapping, decoration, veneer, adornment, ornamentation, appliqué • *Silver overlay is bonded to the entire surface.*

overload AS A VERB 1 = **weigh down**, burden, encumber, overburden • *Don't overload the boat or it will sink.*
2 = **strain**, tax, burden, saddle, oppress, overwork, overcharge, weigh down, encumber, overtax, overburden, push to the limit • *an effective method that will not overload staff with more paperwork*
▸ AS A NOUN = **excess**, too much, overdose, overburden, overabundance, superabundance • *An overload of stress can hold you back in your career.*

PROVERBS
It is the last straw that breaks the camel's back

overlook 1 = **look over** *or* **out on**, have a view of, command a view of, front on to, give upon, afford a view of • *The rooms overlooked the garden.*
2 = **miss**, forget, neglect, omit, disregard, pass over, fail to notice, leave undone, slip up on, leave out of consideration • *We overlook all sorts of warning signals about our health.*
OPPOSITES: note, spot, notice
3 = **ignore**, excuse, forgive, pardon, disregard, condone, turn a blind eye to, wink at, blink at, make allowances for, let someone off with, let pass, let ride, discount, pass over, take no notice of, be oblivious to, pay no attention to, turn a deaf ear to, shut your eyes to • *satisfying relationships that enable them to overlook each other's faults*

overly = **too**, very, extremely, exceedingly, unduly, excessively, unreasonably, inordinately, immoderately, over- • *Employers may become overly cautious about taking on new staff.*

overpower 1 = **overcome**, master, overwhelm, overthrow, subdue, quell, get the better of, subjugate, prevail over, immobilize, bring (someone) to their knees *(informal)*, render incapable, render powerless, render helpless, get the upper hand over • *It took four policemen to overpower him.*
2 = **beat**, defeat, tank *(slang)*, crush, lick *(informal)*, triumph over, best, clobber *(slang)*, stuff *(slang)*, vanquish, be victorious (over), wipe the floor with *(informal)*, make mincemeat of *(informal)*, worst • *Britain's tennis No.1 yesterday overpowered his American rival.*
3 = **overwhelm**, overcome, bowl over *(informal)*, stagger • *I was so overpowered by shame that I was unable to speak.*

overpowering 1 = **overwhelming**, powerful, extreme, compelling, irresistible, breathtaking, compulsive, invincible, uncontrollable • *The desire for revenge can be overpowering.*
2 = **strong**, marked, powerful, distinct, sickening, unbearable, suffocating, unmistakable, nauseating • *There was an overpowering smell of garlic.*
3 = **forceful**, powerful, overwhelming, dynamic, compelling, persuasive, overbearing • *his overpowering manner*

overrate = **overestimate**, glorify, overvalue, oversell, make too much of, rate too highly, assess too highly, overpraise, exaggerate the worth of, overprize, think *or* expect too much of, think too highly of, attach to much importance to • *I think you're overrating him if you call him a genius.*

overreach AS A VERB
▸ IN PHRASES: **overreach yourself** = **try to be too clever**, go too far, overdo it, bite off more than you can chew, be hoist with your own petard, have too many irons in the fire,

defeat your own ends, have your schemes backfire *or* boomerang *or* rebound on you • *He overreached himself and lost much of his fortune.*

overreact = **get things out of proportion**, go over the top *(Brit. informal)*, blow things out of all proportion, make a mountain out of a molehill, get upset over nothing, react disproportionately • *Am I right to be concerned, or am I overreacting?*

override 1 = **outweigh**, overcome, eclipse, supersede, take precedence over, prevail over, outbalance • *His work frequently overrides all other considerations.*
2 = **overrule**, reverse, cancel, overturn, set aside, repeal, quash, revoke, disallow, rescind, upset, rule against, invalidate, annul, nullify, ride roughshod over, outvote, countermand, trample underfoot, make null and void • *The senate failed by one vote to override the President's veto.*
3 = **ignore**, reject, discount, overlook, set aside, disregard, pass over, take no notice of, take no account of, pay no attention to, turn a deaf ear to • *He overrode all opposition to his plans.*

overriding = **major**, chief, main, prime, predominant, leading, controlling, final, ruling, determining, primary, supreme, principal, ultimate, dominant, compelling, prevailing, cardinal, sovereign, paramount, prevalent, pivotal, top-priority, overruling, preponderant, number one • *Our overriding concern is to raise the standards of state education.*
OPPOSITES: minor, irrelevant, petty

overrule = **reverse**, alter, cancel, recall, discount, overturn, set aside, override, repeal, quash, revoke, disallow, rescind, rule against, invalidate, annul, nullify, outvote, countermand, make null and void • *In 1991, the Court of Appeal overruled this decision.*
OPPOSITES: allow, pass, approve

overrun 1 = **overwhelm**, attack, assault, occupy, raid, invade, penetrate, swamp, rout, assail, descend upon, run riot over • *A group of rebels overran the port.* • *A military group overran them and took four of them off.*
2 = **spread over**, overwhelm, choke, swamp, overflow, infest, inundate, permeate, spread like wildfire, swarm over, surge over, overgrow • *The flower beds were overrun with weeds.*
3 = **exceed**, go beyond, surpass, overshoot, outrun, run over *or* on • *Costs overran the budget by about 30%.*

overseas AS AN ADJECTIVE = **foreign**, international, export, worldwide, intercontinental • *overseas trade figures*
▸ AS AN ADVERB = **abroad**, out of the country, in foreign lands • *Her only relatives live overseas.*

oversee = **supervise**, run, control, manage, direct, handle, conduct, look after, be responsible for, administer, inspect, preside over, keep an eye on, be on duty at, superintend, have *or* be in charge of • *Get a surveyor to oversee and inspect the various stages of the work.*

overseer = **supervisor**, manager, chief, boss *(informal)*, master, inspector, superior, administrator, steward, superintendent, gaffer *(informal, chiefly Brit.)*, foreman, super *(informal)*, baas *(S. African)* • *Officials agreed to appoint a federal overseer to run the agency's daily business.*

overshadow 1 = **spoil**, ruin, mar, wreck, scar, blight, crool *or* cruel *(Austral. slang)*, mess up, take the edge off, put a damper on, cast a gloom upon, take the pleasure *or* enjoyment out of • *Her mother's illness overshadowed her childhood.*
2 = **outshine**, eclipse, surpass, dwarf, rise above, upstage, outclass, take precedence over, be superior to, tower above, be head and shoulders above, steal the limelight from, leave *or* put in the shade, render insignificant by comparison, throw into the shade • *I'm sorry to say that she overshadowed her less attractive sister.*
3 = **shade**, cloud, eclipse, darken, overcast, adumbrate • *one of the towers that overshadow the square*

oversight 1 = **mistake**, error, slip, fault, misunderstanding, blunder, lapse, omission, boob *(Brit. slang)*, gaffe, slip-up *(informal)*, delinquency, inaccuracy, carelessness, howler *(informal)*, goof *(informal)*, bloomer *(Brit. informal)*, clanger *(informal)*, miscalculation, error of judgment, faux pas, inattention, laxity, boo-boo *(informal)*, erratum, barry *or* Barry Crocker *(Austral. slang)* • *By an unfortunate oversight, full instructions do not come with the product.*
2 = **supervision**, keeping, control, charge, care, management, handling, administration, direction, custody, stewardship, superintendence • *I had the oversight of their collection of manuscripts.*

oversized *or* **oversize** = **enormous**, large, giant, massive, vast, immense, jumbo *(informal)*, gigantic, colossal, extra-large, ginormous *(informal)*, humongous *or* humungous *(U.S. slang)* • *An oversized bed dominated the room.*

overstate = **exaggerate**, overdo, overestimate, overemphasize, emphasize too much, hyperbolize • *The importance of health education cannot be overstated.*

overstatement = **exaggeration**, embroidery, hyperbole, magnification, embellishment, overvaluation, over-emphasis, overestimation • *He may be talented, but 'genius' is something of an overstatement.*

overt = **open**, obvious, plain, public, clear, apparent, visible, patent, evident, manifest, noticeable, blatant, downright, avowed, flagrant, observable, undisguised, barefaced, unconcealed • *Although there is no overt hostility, black and white students do not mix much.*
OPPOSITES: secret, hidden, disguised

overtake 1 = **pass**, leave behind, overhaul, catch up with, get past, cut up *(informal)*, leave standing *(informal)*, draw level with, outdistance, go by *or* past • *He overtook the truck and pulled into the inside lane.*
2 = **outdo**, top, exceed, eclipse, surpass, outstrip, get the better of, outclass, outshine, best, go one better than *(informal)*, outdistance, be one up on • *Japan has overtaken Britain as the Mini's biggest market.*
3 = **befall**, hit, happen to, come upon, take by surprise, catch off guard, catch unawares, catch unprepared • *Tragedy was about to overtake him.*
4 = **engulf**, overwhelm, hit, strike, consume, swamp, envelop, swallow up • *A sudden flood of panic overtook me.*

overthrow AS A VERB = **defeat**, beat, master, overcome, crush, overwhelm, conquer, bring down, oust, lick *(informal)*, topple, subdue, rout, overpower, do away with, depose, trounce, unseat, vanquish, subjugate, dethrone • *The government was overthrown in a military coup three years ago.*
OPPOSITES: support, protect, uphold
▸ AS A NOUN = **downfall**, end, fall, defeat, collapse, ruin, destruction, breakdown, ousting, undoing, rout, suppression, displacement, subversion, deposition, unseating, subjugation, dispossession, disestablishment, dethronement • *They were charged with plotting the overthrow of the state.*
OPPOSITES: defence, protection, preservation

overtone *often plural* = **connotation**, association, suggestion, sense, hint, flavour, implication, significance, nuance, colouring, innuendo, undercurrent, intimation • *a powerful story, with religious overtones*

overture = **prelude**, opening, introduction, introductory movement • *the William Tell Overture*
OPPOSITES: finale, coda

overtures AS A PLURAL NOUN = **approach**, offer, advance, proposal, appeal, invitation, tender, proposition, opening move, conciliatory move • *He had begun to make clumsy yet endearing overtures of friendship.*
OPPOSITES: withdrawal, rejection

overturn 1 = **tip over**, spill, topple, upturn, capsize, upend, keel over, overbalance • *The lorry went out of control, overturned and smashed into a wall.* • *Two salmon fishermen died when their boat overturned.*
2 = **knock over** *or* **down**, upset, upturn, tip over, upend • *Alex jumped up so violently that he overturned the table.*
3 = **reverse**, change, alter, cancel, abolish, overthrow, set aside, repeal, quash, revoke, overrule, override, negate, rescind, invalidate, annul, nullify, obviate, countermand, declare null and void, overset • *The Russian parliament overturned his decision.*
4 = **overthrow**, defeat, destroy, overcome, crush, bring down, oust, topple, do away with, depose, unseat, dethrone • *He accused his opponents of wanting to overturn the government.*

overused = **hackneyed**, worn (out), stock, tired, stereotyped, played out, commonplace, stale, overworked, threadbare, trite, clichéd, unoriginal, platitudinous, timeworn • *'Just do it' has become one of the most overused catchphrases in history.*

overview = **survey**, study, review, résumé, outline, summing-up, rundown, synopsis, précis • *The preface to the book is a historical overview of the welfare state.*

overweening 1 = **arrogant**, lordly, proud, vain, swaggering, pompous, cocky, conceited, blustering, imperious, self-confident, overbearing, haughty, opinionated, egotistical, disdainful, presumptuous, high-handed, insolent, supercilious, high and mighty *(informal)*, cocksure, vainglorious, uppish *(Brit. informal)* • *his overweening arrogance and pride*
OPPOSITES: modest, timid
2 = **excessive**, exaggerated, over the top *(slang)*, extravagant, disproportionate, inordinate, intemperate, immoderate, blown up out of all proportion, O.T.T. *(slang)* • *her overweening admiration of her father*

overweight = **fat**, heavy, stout, huge, massive, solid, gross, hefty, ample, plump, bulky, chunky, chubby, obese, fleshy, beefy *(informal)*, tubby *(informal)*, portly, outsize, buxom, roly-poly, rotund, podgy, corpulent, elephantine, well-padded *(informal)*, well-upholstered *(informal)*, broad in the beam *(informal)*, on the plump side • *Being overweight increases your risk of developing high blood presssure.*
OPPOSITES: thin, lean, underweight

overwhelm 1 = **overcome**, overpower, devastate, stagger, get the better of, bowl over *(informal)*, prostrate, knock (someone) for six *(informal)*, render speechless, render incapable, render powerless, render helpless, sweep (someone) off his *or* her feet, take (someone's) breath away • *He was overwhelmed by a longing for times past.*
2 = **destroy**, beat, defeat, overcome, smash, crush, massacre, conquer, wipe out, overthrow, knock out, lick *(informal)*, subdue, rout, eradicate, overpower, quell, annihilate, put paid to, vanquish, subjugate, immobilize, make mincemeat of *(informal)*, cut to pieces • *One massive Allied offensive would overwhelm the weakened enemy.*
3 = **swamp**, bury, flood, crush, engulf, submerge, beset, inundate, deluge, snow under • *The small Pacific island could be overwhelmed by rising sea levels.*

overwhelming 1 = **overpowering**, strong, powerful, towering, vast, stunning, extreme, crushing, devastating, shattering, compelling, irresistible, breathtaking, compulsive, forceful, unbearable, uncontrollable • *She felt an overwhelming desire to have another child.*
OPPOSITES: trivial, commonplace, negligible
2 = **vast**, huge, massive, enormous, tremendous, immense, very large, astronomic, humongous *or* humungous *(U.S. slang)* • *An overwhelming majority of small businesses fail within the first two years.*
OPPOSITES: insignificant, negligible, paltry

overwork 1 = **wear yourself out**, burn the midnight oil, burn the candle at both ends, bite off more than you can chew, strain yourself, overstrain yourself, work your fingers to the bone, overtire yourself, drive yourself too far, overburden yourself, overload yourself, overtax yourself, practise presenteeism • *You've been overworking – you need a holiday.*
2 = **exploit**, exhaust, fatigue, weary, oppress, wear out, prostrate, overtax, drive into the ground, be a slave-driver *or* hard taskmaster to • *He overworks his staff.*

QUOTATIONS
overwork: a dangerous disorder affecting high public functionaries who want to go fishing
[Ambrose Bierce *The Devil's Dictionary*]

overworked 1 = **exhausted**, stressed (out), fatigued, overloaded, overburdened, overtaxed • *an overworked doctor*
2 = **hackneyed**, common, stock, tired, stereotyped, played out *(informal)*, commonplace, worn-out, stale, banal, run-of-the-mill, threadbare, trite, clichéd, unoriginal, timeworn • *'Unique' is one of the most overworked words in advertising.*

overwrought 1 = **distraught**, upset, excited, desperate, wired *(slang)*, anxious, distressed, tense, distracted, frantic, in a state, hysterical, wound up *(informal)*, worked up *(informal)*, agitated, uptight *(informal)*, on edge, strung out *(informal)*, out of your mind, keyed up, overexcited, in a tizzy *(informal)*, at the end of your tether, wrought-up, beside yourself, in a twitter *(informal)*, tooshie *(Austral. slang)*, adrenalized • *When I'm feeling overwrought, I try to take some time out to relax.*
OPPOSITES: controlled, cool, calm
2 = **overelaborate**, contrived, overdone, flamboyant, baroque, high-flown, ornate, fussy, flowery, busy, rococo, florid, grandiloquent, euphuistic, overembellished, overornate • *He writes pretentious, overwrought poetry.*

owe = **be in debt (to)**, be in arrears (to), be overdrawn (by), be beholden to, be under an obligation to, be obligated *or* indebted (to) • *He owes me over £100.*

owing AS AN ADJECTIVE = **unpaid**, due, outstanding, owed, payable, unsettled, overdue, not discharged • *There is still some money owing for the rent.*
▸ IN PHRASES: **owing to** = **because of**, thanks to, as a result of, on account of, by reason of • *He was out of work owing to a physical injury.*

owl
▸ NAME OF YOUNG: owlet
▸ COLLECTIVE NOUN: parliament

own AS A DETERMINER = **personal**, special, private, individual, particular, exclusive • *She insisted on having her own room.*
▸ AS A VERB = **possess**, have, keep, hold, enjoy, retain, be responsible for, be in possession of, have to your name • *His father owns a local pub.*
▸ IN PHRASES: **get your own back** = **get revenge**, pay (someone) back, hit back at, retaliate against, get even with, take revenge against, even the score with • *the bizarre ways in which women have got their own back on former lovers*
hold your own = **keep going**, compete, get on, get along, stand your ground, keep your head above water, keep your end up, maintain your position • *Placed in brilliant company at Eton, he more than held his own.*
on your own 1 = **alone**, by yourself, all alone, unaccompanied, on your tod *(Brit. slang)* • *I need some time on my own.*
2 = **independently**, alone, singly, single-handedly, by yourself, unaided, without help, unassisted, left to your own devices, under your own steam, off your own bat, by your own efforts, (standing) on your own two feet • *I work best on my own.*
own up = **confess**, admit, tell the truth, come clean, come

out of the closet *(informal)*, make a clean breast, own, cough *(slang)*, 'fess up *(U.S.)* • *Last year my husband owned up to having an affair.*

owner = **possessor**, holder, proprietor, freeholder, titleholder, proprietress, proprietrix, landlord *or* landlady, master *or* mistress, deed holder • *The owner of the store was sweeping the floor when I walked in.*

ownership = **possession**, occupation, tenure, dominion, occupancy, proprietorship, proprietary rights, right of possession • *the growth of home ownership in Britain*

ox

▸ **RELATED ADJECTIVE:** bovine
▸ **NAME OF MALE:** bull
▸ **NAME OF FEMALE:** cow
▸ **NAME OF YOUNG:** calf
▸ **COLLECTIVE NOUNS:** yoke, drove, team, herd

pace AS A NOUN 1 = **speed**, rate, momentum, tempo, progress, motion, clip *(informal)*, lick *(informal)*, velocity • *driving at a steady pace*
2 = **step**, walk, stride, tread, gait • *Their pace quickened as they approached their cars.*
3 = **footstep**, step, stride • *I took a pace backwards.*
▸ AS A VERB = **stride**, walk, pound, patrol, walk up and down, march up and down, walk back and forth • *He paced the room nervously.*
▸ IN PHRASES: **pace something out** = **measure**, determine, mark out • *Colin paced out the length of the field.*

pacific 1 = **nonaggressive**, pacifist, nonviolent, friendly, gentle, mild, peace-loving, peaceable, dovish, nonbelligerent, dovelike • *a country with a pacific policy*
OPPOSITES: violent, aggressive, hostile
2 = **peacemaking**, diplomatic, appeasing, conciliatory, placatory, propitiatory, irenic, pacificatory • *He spoke in a pacific voice.*
3 = **peaceful**, still, quiet, calm, serene, tranquil, at peace, placid, halcyon, unruffled • *a pacific scene*

pacifism = **peacemaking**, non-violence, satyagraha, passive resistance • *His work is inspired by ideals of pacifism.*

pacifist = **peace lover**, dove, conscientious objector, peacenik *(informal)*, conchie *(informal)*, peacemonger, satyagrahi *(rare)*, passive resister • *His experiences had made him a pacifist.*

pacify 1 = **calm (down)**, appease, placate, still, content, quiet, moderate, compose, soften, soothe, allay, assuage, make peace with, mollify, ameliorate, conciliate, propitiate, tranquillize, smooth someone's ruffled feathers, clear the air with, restore harmony to • *Is this just something to pacify the critics?*
2 = **quell**, silence, crush, put down, tame, subdue, repress, chasten, impose peace upon • *Government forces have found it difficult to pacify the rebels.*

pack AS A VERB 1 = **package**, load, store, bundle, batch, stow • *They offered me a job packing goods in a warehouse.*
2 = **cram**, charge, crowd, press, fill, stuff, jam, compact, mob, ram, wedge, compress, throng, tamp • *All her possessions were packed into the back of her car.* • *Thousands of people packed into the mosque.*
3 = **parcel**, tie (up), wrap (up), swathe, envelop, encase, swaddle • *Orders come packed in straw-filled boxes.*
▸ AS A NOUN 1 = **packet**, box, package, carton • *a pack of cigarettes*
2 = **bundle**, kit, parcel, load, burden, bale, rucksack, truss, knapsack, back pack, kitbag, fardel *(archaic)* • *I hid the money in my pack.*
3 = **group**, crowd, collection, company, set, lot, band, troop, crew, drove, gang, deck, bunch, mob, flock, herd, assemblage • *a pack of journalists who wanted to interview him*
▸ IN PHRASES: **pack someone in** 1 = **cram**, squeeze in, fill to capacity • *The prisons pack in as many inmates as possible.*
2 = **attract**, draw • *The show is still packing audiences in.*
pack someone off = **send away**, dismiss, send packing *(informal)*, bundle out, hustle out • *The children were packed off to bed.*
pack something in 1 = **resign from**, leave, give up, quit *(informal)*, chuck *(informal)*, jack in *(informal)* • *I've just packed in my job.*
2 = **stop**, give up, kick *(informal)*, cease, chuck *(informal)*, leave off, jack in, desist from • *He's trying to pack in smoking.*
pack something up 1 = **put away**, store, tidy up • *He began packing up his things.*
2 = **stop**, finish, give up, pack in *(Brit. informal)*, call it a day *(informal)*, call it a night *(informal)* • *He's packed up coaching and retired.*
pack up = **break down**, stop, fail, stall, give out, conk out *(informal)* • *Our car packed up.*
send someone packing = **send away**, dismiss, discharge, give someone the bird *(informal)*, give someone the brushoff *(slang)*, send someone about his *or* her business, send someone away with a flea in his *or* her ear *(informal)* • *He was sent packing in disgrace.*

package AS A NOUN 1 = **parcel**, box, container, packet, carton • *I tore open the package.*
2 = **collection**, lot, unit, combination, compilation • *A complete package of teaching aids, course notes and case studies had been drawn up.*
▸ AS A VERB 1 = **pack**, box, wrap up, parcel (up), batch • *The coffee beans are ground and packaged for sale.*
2 = **promote**, advertise, publicize, present, display, plug, hype, put before the public • *A city, like any product, has to be packaged properly for the consumer market.*

packaging = **wrapping**, casing, covering, cover, box, packing, wrapper • *The packaging is made from recycled materials.*

packed = **filled**, full, crowded, jammed, crammed, swarming, overflowing, overloaded, seething, congested, jam-packed, chock-full, bursting at the seams, cram-full, brimful, chock-a-block, packed like sardines, hoatching *(Scot.)*, loaded *or* full to the gunwales • *The streets were packed with people.*
OPPOSITES: empty, deserted, uncrowded

packet 1 = **container**, box, package, wrapping, poke *(dialect)*, carton, wrapper • *He wrote the number on the back of a cigarette packet.*
2 = **package**, parcel • *the cost of sending letters and packets abroad*
3 = **a fortune**, lot(s), pot(s) *(informal)*, a bomb *(Brit. slang)*, a pile *(informal)*, big money, a bundle *(slang)*, big bucks *(informal, chiefly U.S.)*, a small fortune, top dollar *(informal)*, a mint, a wad *(U.S. & Canad. slang)*, megabucks *(U.S. & Canad. slang)*, an arm and a leg *(informal)*, a bob or two *(Brit. informal)*, a tidy sum *(informal)*, a king's ransom *(informal)*,

a pretty penny *(informal)*, top whack *(informal)* • *You could save yourself a packet.*

pact = **agreement**, contract, alliance, treaty, deal, understanding, league, bond, arrangement, bargain, convention, compact, protocol, covenant, concord, concordat • *The two countries signed a non-aggression pact.*

pad[1] AS A NOUN 1 = **wad**, dressing, pack, padding, compress, wadding • *He placed a pad of cotton wool over the cut.*
2 = **cushion**, filling, stuffing, pillow, bolster, upholstery • *Seat-pad covers which tie to the backs of your chairs*
3 = **notepad**, block, tablet, notebook, jotter, writing pad • *Have a pad and pencil ready.*
4 = **home**, flat, apartment, place, room, quarters, hang-out *(informal)*, bachelor apartment *(Canad.)* • *He's bought himself a bachelor pad.*
5 = **paw**, foot, sole • *My cat has an infection in the pad of its foot.*
▸ AS A VERB = **pack**, line, fill, protect, shape, stuff, cushion • *Pad the seat with a pillow.*
▸ IN PHRASES: **pad something out** = **lengthen**, stretch, elaborate, inflate, fill out, amplify, augment, spin out, flesh out, eke out, protract • *He padded out his article with a lot of quotations.*

pad[2] = **sneak**, creep, prowl, steal, ghost, tiptoe, slink, pussyfoot *(informal)*, tread warily, go barefoot, walk quietly • *He padded around in his slippers.*

padding 1 = **filling**, stuffing, packing, wadding • *the chair's foam rubber padding*
2 = **waffle** *(informal, chiefly Brit.)*, hot air *(informal)*, verbiage, wordiness, verbosity, prolixity • *Politicians fill their speeches with a lot of padding.*

paddle[1] AS A NOUN = **oar**, sweep, scull • *He used a piece of driftwood as a paddle.*
▸ AS A VERB = **row**, pull, scull • *paddling around the South Pacific in a kayak*

paddle[2] 1 = **wade**, splash (about), slop, plash • *The children were paddling in the stream.*
2 = **dabble**, wet, stir, dip, splash • *He paddled his hands in the water.*

paddock = **field**, meadow, pasture, pen, corral *(U.S. & Canad.)*, stockade • *The family kept horses in the paddock in front of the house.*

paddy = **temper**, tantrum, bad mood, passion, rage, pet, fit of pique, fit of temper, foulie *(Austral. slang)*, hissy fit *(informal)*, strop *(informal)* • *Don't talk to him just now – he's in a real paddy.*

padlock AS A NOUN = **lock**, fastening, clasp • *They had put a padlock on the door of his flat.*
▸ AS A VERB = **secure**, lock, chain, bolt, lock up, fasten • *The mailbox has been padlocked shut.*

padre = **priest**, vicar, parson, preacher, minister, pastor, chaplain, clergyman, rector, curate, man of the cloth • *Many soldiers found the padre a comforting presence.*

paean or *(U.S. (sometimes))* **pean** 1 = **eulogy**, tribute, panegyric, hymn of praise, encomium • *The film is a paean to adolescent love.*
2 = **hymn**, anthem, thanksgiving, psalm • *The piece is a paean of praise for God and his creation.*

pagan AS A NOUN = **heathen**, infidel, unbeliever, polytheist, idolater • *He has been a practising pagan for years.*
▸ AS AN ADJECTIVE = **heathen**, infidel, irreligious, polytheistic, idolatrous, heathenish • *Britain's ancient pagan heritage*

page[1] 1 = **folio**, side, leaf, sheet • *Turn to page four of your books.*
2 = **period**, chapter, phase, era, episode, time, point, event, stage, incident, epoch • *a new page in the country's history*

page[2] AS A NOUN 1 = **attendant**, bellboy *(U.S.)*, pageboy, footboy • *He worked as a page in a hotel.*
2 = **servant**, attendant, squire, pageboy, footboy • *He served as page to a noble lord.*
▸ AS A VERB = **call**, seek, summon, call out for, send for • *He was paged repeatedly as the flight was boarding.*

pageant 1 = **show**, display, parade, ritual, spectacle, procession, extravaganza, tableau • *a traditional Christmas pageant*
2 = **contest**, competition • *the Miss World beauty pageant*

pageantry = **spectacle**, show, display, drama, parade, splash *(informal)*, state, glitter, glamour, grandeur, splendour, extravagance, pomp, magnificence, theatricality, showiness • *He was greeted with all the pageantry of an official state visit.*

paid = **salaried**, waged, rewarded, remunerated • *a well-paid accountant*

pain AS A NOUN 1 = **suffering**, discomfort, trouble, hurt, irritation, tenderness, soreness • *a disease that causes excruciating pain*
2 = **ache**, smarting, stinging, aching, cramp, throb, throbbing, spasm, pang, twinge, shooting pain • *I felt a sharp pain in my lower back.*
3 = **sorrow**, suffering, torture, distress, despair, grief, misery, agony, sadness, torment, hardship, bitterness, woe, anguish, heartache, affliction, tribulation, desolation, wretchedness • *Her eyes were filled with pain.*
▸ AS A PLURAL NOUN 1 = **trouble**, labour, effort, industry, care, bother, diligence, special attention, assiduousness • *He got little thanks for his pains.*
2 = **contractions**, labour pains, birth-pangs • *Her pains were now about ten minutes apart.*
▸ AS A VERB 1 = **distress**, worry, hurt, wound, torture, grieve, torment, afflict, sadden, disquiet, vex, agonize, cut to the quick, aggrieve • *It pains me to think of an animal being in distress.*
2 = **hurt**, chafe, cause pain to, cause discomfort to • *His ankle still pained him.*
▸ IN PHRASES: **be at pains** = **try hard**, strive, endeavour, make every effort, put yourself out, spare no effort • *He was at pains to deny his involvement in the affair.*
pain in the neck = **nuisance**, pain *(informal)*, bore, drag *(informal)*, bother, headache *(informal)*, pest, irritation, annoyance, aggravation, vexation, pain in the arse *(taboo slang)*, pain in the backside *(informal)* • *She can be an absolute pain in the neck when she's in a scatty mood.*
▸ RELATED PHOBIA: algophobia

pained = **distressed**, worried, hurt, injured, wounded, upset, unhappy, stung, offended, aggrieved, anguished, miffed *(informal)*, reproachful • *He looked at me with a pained expression.*

painful 1 = **sore**, hurting, smarting, aching, raw, tender, throbbing, inflamed, excruciating • *Her glands were swollen and painful.*
OPPOSITES: comforting, relieving, painless
2 = **distressing**, unpleasant, harrowing, saddening, grievous, distasteful, agonizing, disagreeable, afflictive • *His remark brought back painful memories.*
OPPOSITES: satisfying, pleasant, enjoyable
3 = **difficult**, arduous, trying, hard, severe, troublesome, laborious, vexatious • *the long and painful process of getting divorced*
OPPOSITES: easy, simple, straightforward
4 = **terrible**, awful, dreadful, dire, excruciating, abysmal, gut-wrenching, godawful, extremely bad • *The interview was painful to watch.*

painfully = **distressingly**, clearly, sadly, unfortunately, markedly, excessively, alarmingly, woefully, dreadfully, deplorably • *It's painfully obvious that he can't handle the job.*

painkiller = **analgesic**, drug, remedy, anaesthetic, sedative, palliative, anodyne • *Try a painkiller such as paracetamol.*

painless 1 = **pain-free**, without pain • *The operation is a brief, painless procedure.*
2 = **simple**, easy, fast, quick, no trouble, effortless, trouble-free • *There are no painless solutions to the problem.*

painstaking = **thorough**, careful, meticulous, earnest, exacting, strenuous, conscientious, persevering, diligent, scrupulous, industrious, assiduous, thoroughgoing, punctilious, sedulous • *Police carried out a painstaking search of the area.*
OPPOSITES: lazy, careless, negligent

paint AS A NOUN = **colouring**, colour, stain, dye, tint, pigment, emulsion • *a pot of red paint*
▸ AS A VERB 1 = **colour**, cover, coat, decorate, stain, whitewash, daub, distemper, apply paint to • *They painted the walls yellow.*
2 = **depict**, draw, portray, figure, picture, represent, sketch, delineate, catch a likeness • *He was painting a portrait of his wife.*
3 = **describe**, capture, portray, depict, evoke, recount, bring to life, make you see, conjure up a vision, put graphically, tell vividly • *The report paints a grim picture of life in the city.*
▸ IN PHRASES: **paint the town red** = **celebrate**, revel, large it (*Brit. slang*), carouse, live it up (*informal*), make merry, make whoopee (*informal*), go on a binge (*informal*), go on a spree, go on the town • *Thousands of football fans painted the town red after the match.*

QUOTATIONS
And those who paint 'em truest praise 'em most
[Joseph Addison *The Campaign*]
Every time I paint a portrait I lose a friend
[John Singer Sargent]

painter

QUOTATIONS
To me, a painter, if not the most useful, is the least harmful member of our society
[Man Ray *Self-Portrait*]

P

painting = **picture**, portrait, sketch, representation, illustration, image, work of art • *a large oil-painting of Queen Victoria*

pair AS A NOUN 1 = **set**, match, combination, doublet, matched set, two of a kind • *a pair of socks*
2 = **couple**, brace, duo, twosome • *A pair of teenage boys were arrested.*
▸ AS A VERB *often with* **off** = **team**, match (up), join, couple, marry, wed, twin, put together, bracket, yoke, pair off • *Each trainee is paired with an experienced worker.*
▸ IN PHRASES: **pair off** *or* **up** = **get together**, unite, team up, link up, join up, form a couple, make a twosome • *We paired up to dance.* • *She was trying to pair me off with her brother.*

pairing = **collaboration**, partnership, cooperation, linking up • *the pairing of these two fine musicians*

pal = **friend**, companion, mate (*informal*), buddy (*informal*), comrade, chum (*informal*), crony, cock (*Brit. informal*), main man (*slang, chiefly U.S.*), homeboy (*slang, chiefly U.S.*), cobber (*Austral. & N.Z. old-fashioned informal*), boon companion, E hoa (*N.Z.*) • *We've been pals for years.*

palace = **royal residence**, castle, mansion, château (*French*), palazzo (*Italian*), stately home • *the palace courtyard*
▸ RELATED ADJECTIVES: palatial, palatine

palatable 1 = **delicious**, tasty, luscious, savoury, delectable, mouthwatering, appetizing, toothsome, yummo (*Austral. slang*) • *flavourings designed to make the food more palatable*
OPPOSITES: bland, tasteless, unpalatable
2 = **acceptable**, pleasant, agreeable, fair, attractive, satisfactory, enjoyable • *There is no palatable way of sacking someone.*

palate = **taste**, heart, stomach, appetite • *a selection of dishes to tempt every palate*
▸ RELATED ADJECTIVE: palatine

palatial = **magnificent**, grand, imposing, splendid, gorgeous, luxurious, spacious, majestic, regal, stately, sumptuous, plush (*informal*), illustrious, grandiose, opulent, de luxe, splendiferous (*facetious*) • *a palatial Hollywood mansion*

palaver 1 = **fuss**, business (*informal*), to-do, performance (*informal*), procedure, carry-on (*informal, chiefly Brit.*), pantomime (*informal, chiefly Brit.*), song and dance (*Brit. informal*), rigmarole • *We had to go through the whole palaver of changing our flight.*
2 = **prattle**, chatter, babble, yak (*slang*), hubbub, natter (*Brit.*), tongue-wagging, blather, blether • *I had to listen to a lot of palaver about political correctness.*
3 = **conference**, session, discussion, get-together (*informal*), parley, powwow, colloquy, confab (*informal*) • *Have you two finished your little palaver?*

pale[1] AS AN ADJECTIVE 1 = **light**, soft, faded, subtle, muted, bleached, pastel, light-coloured • *a pale blue dress*
2 = **dim**, weak, faint, feeble, thin, wan, watery • *A pale light seeped through the window.*
3 = **white**, pasty, bleached, washed-out, wan, bloodless, colourless, pallid, anaemic, ashen, sallow, whitish, ashy, like death warmed up (*informal*) • *She looked pale and tired.*
OPPOSITES: glowing, blooming, rosy-cheeked
4 = **poor**, weak, inadequate, pathetic, feeble • *a pale imitation of the real thing*
▸ AS A VERB 1 = **fade**, dull, diminish, decrease, dim, lessen, grow dull, lose lustre • *My problems paled in comparison with his.*
2 = **become pale**, blanch, whiten, go white, lose colour • *Her face paled at the news.*

pale[2] AS A NOUN = **post**, stake, paling, upright, picket, slat, palisade • *the pales of the fence*
▸ IN PHRASES: **beyond the pale** = **unacceptable**, not done, forbidden, irregular, indecent, unsuitable, improper, barbaric, unspeakable, out of line, unseemly, inadmissible • *His behaviour was beyond the pale.*

palisade = **fence**, defence, paling, enclosure, bulwark, stockade • *a stout wooden palisade enclosing the yard*

pall[1] 1 = **cloud**, shadow, veil, mantle, shroud • *A pall of black smoke drifted over the cliff-top.*
2 = **gloom**, damp, dismay, melancholy, damper, check • *His depression cast a pall on the proceedings.*

pall[2] *often with* **on** = **become boring**, become dull, become tedious, become tiresome, jade, cloy, become wearisome • *The glamour of her job soon palled.*

palliative AS A NOUN 1 = **drug**, painkiller, sedative, tranquillizer, anodyne, analgesic, demulcent, calmative, lenitive • *Insulin merely acts as a palliative.*
2 = **temporary measure**, stopgap, temporary expedient • *The loan was a palliative, not a cure, for their financial troubles.*
▸ AS AN ADJECTIVE = **soothing**, calming, mollifying, anodyne, demulcent, calmative, lenitive, mitigatory • *the importance of palliative care in hospitals*

pallid 1 = **pale**, wan, pasty, colourless, anaemic, ashen, sallow, whitish, cadaverous, waxen, ashy, like death warmed up (*informal*), wheyfaced • *His thin, pallid face broke into a smile.*
2 = **insipid**, boring, tired, tame, sterile, lifeless, bloodless, colourless, anaemic, uninspired, vapid, spiritless • *pallid romantic fiction*

pallor = **paleness**, whiteness, lack of colour, wanness, bloodlessness, ashen hue, pallidness • *Her face had a deathly pallor.*

pally = **friendly**, intimate, close, familiar, affectionate, chummy (*informal*), buddy-buddy (*slang, chiefly U.S. & Canad.*), thick as thieves (*informal*), palsy-walsy (*informal*) • *Those two seem to be getting very pally.*

palm AS A NOUN = **hand**, hook, paw *(informal)*, mitt *(slang)*, meathook *(slang)* • *He wiped his sweaty palm.*
▸ IN PHRASES: **in the palm of your hand** = **in your power**, in your control, in your clutches, at your mercy • *He had the board of directors in the palm of his hand.*
palm someone off = **fob off**, dismiss, disregard, pooh-pooh *(informal)* • *Mark was palmed off with a series of excuses.*
palm something off on someone = **foist on**, force upon, impose upon, pass off, thrust upon, unload upon • *They palm a lot of junk off on the tourists.*
▸ RELATED ADJECTIVES: thenar, volar

palmistry = **palm-reading**, fortune-telling, chiromancy • *She dabbled in fortune-telling and palmistry.*

palpable = **obvious**, apparent, patent, clear, plain, visible, evident, manifest, open, blatant, conspicuous, unmistakable, salient • *The tension between them is palpable.*

palpitate 1 = **beat**, pound, flutter, pulsate, pitter-patter, pitapat • *Her heart was palpitating wildly.*
2 = **tremble**, pulse, shiver, throb, quiver, vibrate • *His whole body was palpitating with fear.*

paltry 1 = **meagre**, petty, trivial, trifling, beggarly, derisory, measly, piddling *(informal)*, inconsiderable • *He was fined the paltry sum of $50.*
OPPOSITES: considerable, valuable
2 = **insignificant**, trivial, worthless, unimportant, small, low, base, minor, slight, petty, trifling, Mickey Mouse *(slang)*, piddling *(informal)*, toytown *(slang)*, poxy *(slang)*, nickel-and-dime *(U.S. slang)*, picayune *(U.S.)*, chickenshit *(U.S. slang)*, twopenny-halfpenny *(Brit. informal)* • *She had no interest in such paltry concerns.*
OPPOSITES: major, important, grand

pamper = **spoil**, indulge, gratify, baby, pet, humour, pander to, fondle, cosset, coddle, mollycoddle, wait on (someone) hand and foot, cater to your every whim • *Her parents have pampered her since the day she was born.*

pamphlet = **booklet**, leaflet, brochure, circular, tract, folder • *an 80-page long election pamphlet*

pan[1] AS A NOUN = **pot**, vessel, container, saucepan • *Heat the butter in a large pan.*
▸ AS A VERB 1 = **criticize**, knock, blast, hammer *(Brit. informal)*, slam *(slang)*, flame *(informal)*, rubbish *(informal)*, roast *(informal)*, put down, slate *(informal)*, censure, slag (off) *(slang)*, tear into *(informal)*, flay, diss *(slang, chiefly U.S.)*, lambast(e), throw brickbats at *(informal)* • *His first movie was panned by the critics.*
2 = **sift out**, look for, wash, search for • *People came westward in the 1800s to pan for gold in Sierra Nevada.*
▸ IN PHRASES: **pan out** = **work out**, happen, result, come out, turn out, culminate, come to pass *(archaic)*, eventuate • *None of his ideas panned out.*

pan[2] = **move along** *or* **across**, follow, track, sweep, scan, traverse, swing across • *A television camera panned the crowd.*

panacea = **cure-all**, elixir, nostrum, heal-all, sovereign remedy, universal cure • *Western aid will not be a panacea for the country's problems.*

panache = **style**, spirit, dash, flair, verve, swagger, flourish, élan, flamboyance, brio • *The orchestra played with great panache.*

pancake = **crêpe**, drop scone *or* Scotch pancake • *I adore pancakes with maple syrup.*

pandemonium = **uproar**, confusion, chaos, turmoil, racket, clamour, din, commotion, rumpus, bedlam, babel, tumult, hubbub, ruction *(informal)*, hullabaloo, hue and cry, ruckus *(informal)* • *There was pandemonium in the court as the verdict was delivered.*
OPPOSITES: order, peace, arrangement

pander IN PHRASES: **pander to something** *or* **someone** = **indulge**, please, satisfy, gratify, cater to, play up to *(informal)*, fawn on • *The government have pandered to the terrorists for far too long.*

pane = **sheet**, panel, windowpane • *a pane of glass*

panegyric = **tribute**, praise, homage, accolade, eulogy, paean, commendation, encomium • *It is traditional to deliver a panegyric to the departed.*

panel 1 = **committee**, group, team, body, council, board, dream team • *The panel of judges were unanimous in their decision.*
2 = **console**, board, dashboard, fascia • *The equipment was monitored from a central control panel.*

pang 1 = **pain**, stab, sting, stitch, ache, wrench, prick, spasm, twinge, throe *(rare)* • *pangs of hunger*
2 = **twinge**, stab, prick, spasm, qualm, gnawing • *She felt a pang of guilt about the way she was treating him.*

panic AS A NOUN = **fear**, alarm, horror, terror, anxiety, dismay, hysteria, fright, agitation, consternation, trepidation, a flap *(informal)* • *The earthquake has caused panic among the population.*
▸ AS A VERB 1 = **go to pieces**, overreact, become hysterical, have kittens *(informal)*, lose your nerve, be terror-stricken, lose your bottle *(Brit. slang)* • *The guests panicked and screamed when the bomb went off.*
2 = **alarm**, scare, terrify, startle, unnerve • *The dogs were panicked by the noise.*

panicky = **frightened**, worried, afraid, nervous, distressed, fearful, frantic, frenzied, hysterical, worked up, windy *(slang)*, agitated, jittery *(informal)*, in a flap *(informal)*, antsy *(informal)*, in a tizzy *(informal)* • *Many women feel panicky when travelling alone at night.*
OPPOSITES: composed, together *(slang)*, calm

panic-stricken *or* **panic-struck** = **frightened**, alarmed, scared, terrified, startled, horrified, fearful, frenzied, hysterical, agitated, unnerved, petrified, aghast, panicky, scared stiff, in a cold sweat *(informal)*, frightened to death, scared shitless *(taboo slang)*, terror-stricken, shit-scared *(taboo slang)*, horror-stricken, frightened out of your wits • *Thousands of panic-stricken refugees fled the city.*

panoply 1 = **array**, range, display, collection • *The film features a vast panoply of special effects.*
2 = **trappings**, show, dress, get-up *(informal)*, turnout, attire, garb, insignia, regalia, raiment *(archaic or poetic)* • *all the panoply of a royal wedding*

panorama 1 = **view**, prospect, scenery, vista, bird's-eye view, scenic view • *He looked out over a panorama of hills and valleys.*
2 = **survey**, perspective, overview, overall picture • *The play presents a panorama of the history of communism.*

panoramic 1 = **wide**, overall, extensive, scenic, bird's-eye • *I had a panoramic view of the city.*
2 = **comprehensive**, general, extensive, sweeping, inclusive, far-reaching, all-embracing • *the panoramic sweep of his work*

pant AS A VERB = **puff**, blow, breathe, gasp, throb, wheeze, huff, heave, palpitate • *He was panting with the effort of the climb.*
▸ AS A NOUN = **gasp**, puff, wheeze, huff • *His breath was coming in short pants.*
▸ IN PHRASES: **pant for something** = **long for**, want, desire, crave for, covet, yearn for, thirst for, hunger for, pine for, hanker after, ache for, sigh for, set your heart on, eat your heart out over, suspire for *(archaic or poetic)* • *They left the audience panting for more.*

panting 1 = **out of breath**, winded, gasping, puffed, puffing, breathless, puffed out, short of breath, out of puff, out of whack *(informal)* • *She collapsed, panting, at the top of the stairs.*
2 = **eager**, raring, anxious, impatient, champing at the bit *(informal)*, all agog • *He came down here panting to be rescued from the whole ghastly mess.*

pantry = **larder**, store, storecupboard • *Keep your pantry well stocked with pasta.*

P

pants 1 = **underpants**, briefs, drawers, knickers, panties, boxer shorts, Y-fronts *(trademark)*, broekies *(S. African)*, underdaks *(Austral. slang)* • *a matching set of bra and pants*
2 = **trousers**, slacks • *He was wearing brown corduroy pants and a white shirt.*

pap = **rubbish**, trash, trivia, drivel • *All that radio station plays is commercial pap.*

paper AS A NOUN 1 = **newspaper**, news, daily, journal, organ, rag *(informal)*, tabloid, gazette, broadsheet • *The story is in all the papers.*
2 = **essay**, study, article, analysis, script, composition, assignment, thesis, critique, treatise, dissertation, monograph • *He has just written a paper on the subject.*
3 = **examination**, test, exam • *the applied mathematics paper*
4 = **report**, study, survey, inquiry • *a new government paper on European policy*
▸ AS A PLURAL NOUN 1 = **letters**, records, documents, file, diaries, archive, paperwork, dossier • *After her death, her papers were collected and published.*
2 = **documents**, records, certificates, identification, deeds, identity papers, I.D. *(informal)* • *people who were trying to leave the country with forged papers*
▸ AS A VERB = **wallpaper**, line, hang, paste up, cover with paper • *We have papered this room in grey.*
▸ IN PHRASES: **on paper** 1 = **in writing**, written down, on (the) record, in print, in black and white • *It is important to get something down on paper.*
2 = **in theory**, ideally, theoretically, in the abstract • *On paper, he is the best man for the job.*
paper something over *or* **paper over something** = **cover up**, hide, disguise, conceal, camouflage, whitewash, gloss over, airbrush • *Their differences were papered over, but not resolved.*
▸ RELATED ADJECTIVE: papyraceous

papery = **thin**, light, flimsy, fragile, lightweight, frail, insubstantial, wafer-thin, paper-thin, paperlike • *the papery skin of garlic cloves*

par IN PHRASES: **above par** = **excellent**, outstanding, superior, exceptional, first-rate *(informal)* • *Their performance was way above par for an amateur production.*
below *or* **under par** 1 = **inferior**, poor, lacking, imperfect, second-rate, wanting, below average, substandard, two-bit *(U.S. & Canad. slang)*, off form, not up to scratch *(informal)*, dime-a-dozen *(informal)*, bush-league *(Austral. & N.Z. informal)*, not up to snuff *(informal)*, tinhorn *(U.S. slang)*, bodger or bodgie *(Austral. slang)* • *His playing is below par this season.*
2 = **unwell**, sick, poorly *(informal)*, funny *(informal)*, crook *(Austral. & N.Z. informal)*, queer, unfit, unhealthy, queasy, out of sorts *(informal)*, dicky *(Brit. informal)*, off colour *(chiefly Brit.)*, under the weather *(informal)*, off form, indisposed, not yourself, green about the gills • *If you have been feeling below par for a while, consult your doctor.*
on a par with = **equal to**, the same as, much the same as, well-matched with • *Parts of the city are on a par with New York for street crime.*
par for the course = **usual**, expected, standard, average, ordinary, typical, predictable • *Long hours are par for the course in this job.*
up to par = **satisfactory**, acceptable, good enough, adequate, up to scratch *(informal)*, passable, up to the mark • *The service is not up to par here.*

parable = **lesson**, story, fable, allegory, moral tale, exemplum • *the parable of the Good Samaritan*
▸ RELATED ADJECTIVES: parabolic, parabolical

parade AS A NOUN 1 = **procession**, march, ceremony, pageant, train, review, column, spectacle, tattoo, motorcade, cavalcade, cortège • *A military parade marched slowly through the streets.*
2 = **show**, display, exhibition, spectacle, array • *A glittering parade of celebrities attended the event.*
3 = **exhibition**, flaunting, demonstration, display, vaunting • *a parade of military power*
▸ AS A VERB 1 = **march**, process, file, promenade • *More than four thousand people paraded down the Champs Elysées.*
2 = **flaunt**, show, display, exhibit, show off *(informal)*, air, draw attention to, brandish, vaunt, showboat, make a show of • *He was a modest man who never paraded his wealth.*
3 = **strut**, show off *(informal)*, swagger, swank, showboat • *She loves to parade around in designer clothes.*

paradigm = **model**, example, original, pattern, ideal, norm, prototype, archetype, exemplar • *He was the paradigm of the successful man.*

paradise 1 = **heaven**, Promised Land, Zion *(Christianity)*, Happy Valley *(Islam)*, City of God, Elysian fields, garden of delights, divine abode, heavenly kingdom • *They believe they will go to paradise when they die.*
2 = **Garden of Eden**, Eden • *Adam and Eve's expulsion from Paradise*
3 = **bliss**, delight, heaven, felicity, utopia, seventh heaven • *This job is paradise compared to my last one.*

QUOTATIONS
Two paradises 'twere in one
To live in paradise alone
[Andrew Marvell *The Garden*]

paradox = **contradiction**, mystery, puzzle, ambiguity, anomaly, inconsistency, enigma, oddity, absurdity • *Death is a paradox, the end yet the beginning.*

paradoxical = **contradictory**, inconsistent, impossible, puzzling, absurd, baffling, riddling, ambiguous, improbable, confounding, enigmatic, illogical, equivocal, oracular • *It seems paradoxical that some people who claim to be animal lovers still promote fox-hunting.*

paragon = **model**, standard, pattern, ideal, criterion, norm, jewel, masterpiece, prototype, paradigm, archetype, epitome, exemplar, apotheosis, quintessence, nonesuch *(archaic)*, nonpareil, best or greatest thing since sliced bread *(informal)*, cynosure • *She was a paragon of neatness and efficiency.* • *He was not a paragon. He could never be perfect.*

paragraph = **section**, part, notice, item, passage, clause, portion, subdivision • *The length of a paragraph should depend on the information it contains.*

parallel AS A NOUN 1 = **equivalent**, counterpart, match, equal, twin, complement, duplicate, analogue, likeness, corollary • *It is an ecological disaster with no parallel in the modern era.*
OPPOSITES: opposite, reverse
2 = **similarity**, correspondence, correlation, comparison, analogy, resemblance, likeness, parallelism • *Detectives realised there were parallels between the two murders.*
OPPOSITES: difference, divergence, dissimilarity
▸ AS A VERB 1 = **correspond to**, compare with, agree with, complement, conform to, be alike, chime with, correlate to • *His remarks paralleled those of the president.*
OPPOSITES: differ from, diverge from, be unlike
2 = **match**, equal, duplicate, keep pace (with), measure up to • *His achievements have never been paralleled.*
▸ AS AN ADJECTIVE 1 = **matching**, correspondent, corresponding, like, similar, uniform, resembling, complementary, akin, analogous • *He describes the rise in tuberculosis as an epidemic parallel to that of AIDS.*
OPPOSITES: different, unlike, dissimilar
2 = **equidistant**, alongside, aligned, side by side, coextensive • *seventy-two ships, drawn up in two parallel lines*
OPPOSITES: divergent, non-parallel

paralyse 1 = **disable**, cripple, lame, debilitate, incapacitate • *Her sister had been paralysed in a road accident.*
2 = **freeze**, stun, numb, petrify, transfix, stupefy, halt, stop

dead, immobilize, anaesthetize, benumb • *He was paralysed with fear.*
3 = **immobilize**, freeze, halt, disable, cripple, arrest, incapacitate, bring to a standstill • *The strike has virtually paralysed the country.*

paralysed 1 = **disabled**, crippled, handicapped, challenged, helpless, numb, powerless, dead, lame, incapacitated, immobilized, paralytic • *The disease left him with a paralysed right arm.*
2 = **disabled**, crippled, hamstrung, incapacitated • *a period of chaos, with disrupted air services and a paralysed civil service*

paralysis 1 = **immobility**, palsy, paresis (*Pathology*) • *paralysis of the legs*
2 = **standstill**, breakdown, stoppage, shutdown, halt, stagnation, inactivity • *The unions have brought about a total paralysis of trade.*

paralytic 1 = **paralysing**, disabling, crippling, incapacitating, immobilized • *Scientists have managed to reverse paralytic diseases in laboratory animals.*
2 = **drunk**, pissed (*Brit., Austral. & N.Z. slang*), intoxicated, wasted (*slang*), canned (*slang*), flying (*slang*), bombed (*slang*), stoned (*slang*), smashed (*slang*), hammered (*slang*), steaming (*slang*), wrecked (*slang*), out of it (*slang*), plastered (*slang*), blitzed (*slang*), lit up (*slang*), stewed (*slang*), sloshed (*slang*), legless (*informal*), tired and emotional (*euphemistic*), steamboats (*Scot. slang*), off your face (*slang*), zonked (*slang*), blotto (*slang*), inebriated, out to it (*Austral. & N.Z. slang*), rat-arsed (*taboo slang*), blatted (*Brit. slang*), boozed-up (*informal*), dronkverdriet (*S. African*), elephants (*Austral. slang*), blatted (*Brit. slang*), broken (*S. African informal*), boozed-up (*slang*), kaylied (*Brit. slang*), langered (*Irish slang*), lashed (*Brit. slang*), mashed (*Brit. slang*), mullered (*slang*), ossified (*Irish slang*), sat (*S. African*), stukkend (*S. African slang*), trashed (*slang*), Brahms and Liszt (*slang*), bevvied (*dialect*), pie-eyed (*slang*) • *By the end of the evening, we were all totally paralytic.*

parameter *usually plural* = **limit**, constant, restriction, guideline, criterion, framework, limitation, specification • *We have to define the basic parameters within which we want to operate.*

paramount = **principal**, prime, first, chief, main, capital, primary, supreme, outstanding, superior, dominant, cardinal, foremost, eminent, predominant, pre-eminent • *The welfare of the children must be of paramount importance.*
OPPOSITES: least, minor, secondary

paramour = **lover**, mistress, beau, concubine, courtesan, kept woman, fancy man (*slang*), fancy woman (*slang*), inamorata, fancy bit (*slang*), inamorato • *the president's alleged paramour*

paranoia = **obsession**, suspicion, delusion, persecution complex • *The mood is one of paranoia and expectation of war.*

paranoid 1 = **suspicious**, worried, nervous, fearful, apprehensive, antsy (*informal*) • *We live in an increasingly paranoid and fearful society.*
2 = **obsessive**, disturbed, unstable, manic, neurotic, mentally ill, psychotic, deluded, paranoiac • *his increasingly paranoid delusions*

parapet 1 = **balustrade**, wall, railing • *He climbed up on to the parapet of the bridge and sat dangling his legs.*
2 = **battlements**, defence, barricade, rampart, fortification, bulwark, breastwork, castellation • *The soldiers crouched behind the parapet.*

paraphernalia 1 = **equipment**, things, effects, material, stuff, tackle, gear, baggage, apparatus, belongings, clobber (*Brit. slang*), accoutrements, impedimenta, appurtenances, equipage • *a large courtyard full of builders' paraphernalia*
2 = **rigmarole**, procedure, bother, to-do, performance (*informal*), carry-on (*informal, chiefly Brit.*), nonsense, fuss, hassle (*informal*), red tape, pantomime (*informal*), trappings, palaver • *the whole paraphernalia of the legal system*

paraphrase AS A VERB = **reword**, interpret, render, restate, rehash, rephrase, express in other words *or* your own words • *Baxter paraphrased the contents of the press release.*
▸ AS A NOUN = **rewording**, version, interpretation, rendering, translation, rendition, rehash, restatement, rephrasing • *The following is a paraphrase of his remarks.*

parasite = **sponger** (*informal*), sponge (*informal*), drone (*Brit.*), leech, hanger-on, scrounger (*informal*), bloodsucker (*informal*), cadger, quandong (*Austral. slang*) • *parasites living off the state*

parasitic *or* **parasitical** = **scrounging** (*informal*), sponging (*informal*), cadging, bloodsucking (*informal*), leechlike • *They are just parasitic spongers who have no intention of finding work.*

parcel AS A NOUN 1 = **package**, case, box, pack, packet, bundle, carton • *They sent parcels of food and clothing.*
2 = **plot**, area, property, section, patch, tract, allotment, piece of land • *These small parcels of land were sold to the local people.*
3 = **group**, crowd, pack, company, lot, band, collection, crew, gang, bunch, batch • *He described them, quite rightly, as a parcel of rogues.*
▸ AS A VERB *often with* **up** = **wrap**, pack, package, tie up, do up, gift-wrap, box up, fasten together • *We parcelled up our unwanted clothes to take to the charity shop.*
▸ IN PHRASES: **parcel something out** = **distribute**, divide, portion, allocate, split up, dispense, allot, carve up, mete out, dole out, share out, apportion, deal out • *The inheritance was parcelled out equally among the three brothers.*

parched 1 = **dried out** *or* **up**, dry, withered, scorched, arid, torrid, shrivelled, dehydrated, waterless • *Showers poured down upon the parched earth.*
2 = **thirsty**, dry, dehydrated, drouthy (*Scot.*) • *After all that exercise, I was parched.*

pardon AS A VERB = **acquit**, free, release, liberate, reprieve, remit, amnesty, let off (*informal*), exonerate, absolve, exculpate • *Hundreds of political prisoners were pardoned and released.*
OPPOSITES: fine, discipline, punish
▸ AS A NOUN 1 = **forgiveness**, mercy, indulgence, absolution, grace • *He asked God's pardon for his sins.*
OPPOSITES: condemnation
2 = **acquittal**, release, discharge, amnesty, reprieve, remission, exoneration • *They lobbied the government on his behalf and he was granted a pardon.*
OPPOSITES: penalty, punishment, redress
▸ IN PHRASES: **pardon me** = **forgive me**, excuse me • *Pardon me for asking, but what business is it of yours?*

QUOTATIONS
God will pardon me. It is His trade
[Heinrich Heine *on his deathbed*]

pardonable = **forgivable**, understandable, permissible, not serious, allowable, excusable, venial, condonable • *He spoke with pardonable pride.*

pare 1 = **peel**, cut, skin, trim, clip, shave • *Pare the rind thinly from the lemon.*
2 = **cut back**, cut, reduce, crop, decrease, dock, prune, shear, lop, retrench • *Local authorities must pare down their budgets.*

parent AS A NOUN 1 = **father** *or* **mother**, sire, progenitor, begetter, procreator, old (*Austral. & N.Z. informal*), oldie (*Austral. informal*), patriarch • *Both her parents were killed in a car crash.*
2 = **source**, cause, author, root, origin, architect, creator, prototype, forerunner, originator, wellspring • *He is regarded as one of the parents of modern classical music.*
▸ AS A VERB = **bring up**, raise, look after, rear, nurture, be the parent of • *Some people are unwilling to parent a child with special needs.*

QUOTATIONS
Honour thy father and thy mother
[*Bible: Exodus*]

P

Parents love their children more than children love their parents
[Auctoritates Aristotelis]
Children begin by loving their parents; after a time they judge them; rarely, if ever, do they forgive them
[Oscar Wilde *A Woman of No Importance*]
The most difficult job in the world is not being President. It's being a parent
[Bill Clinton]
Parents ... are sometimes a bit of a disappointment to their children. They don't fulfil the promise of their early years
[Anthony Powell *A Buyer's Market*]
They fuck you up, your Mum and Dad.
They may not mean to, but they do.
They fill you with the faults they had
And add some extra, just for you
[Philip Larkin *This Be the Verse*]
The first half of our life is ruined by our parents and the second half by our children
[Clarence Darrow]

parentage = **family**, birth, origin, descent, line, race, stock, pedigree, extraction, ancestry, lineage, paternity, derivation • *She is a Londoner of mixed English and Jamaican parentage.*

QUOTATIONS
Men are generally more careful of the breed of their horses and dogs than of their children
[William Penn *Some Fruits of Solitude*]

parenthetical *or* **parenthetic** = **interposed**, incidental, explanatory, qualifying, inserted, bracketed, extraneous, extrinsic • *He kept interrupting his story with parenthetical remarks.*

parenthetically = **incidentally**, by the way, in passing, by way of explanation, by the bye • *This brings us, parenthetically, to another question.*

parenthood = **fatherhood** *or* **motherhood**, parenting, rearing, bringing up, nurturing, upbringing, child rearing, baby *or* child care, fathering *or* mothering • *She may not feel ready for the responsibilities of parenthood.*

QUOTATIONS
Before I got married I had six theories about bringing up children; now I have six children, and no theories
[John Wilmot, Earl of Rochester]

pariah = **outcast**, exile, outlaw, undesirable, untouchable, leper, unperson • *I was treated like a pariah for the rest of the journey.*

parings = **peelings**, skins, slices, clippings, peel, fragments, shavings, shreds, flakes, rind, snippets, slivers • *You can boil up the vegetable parings to make stock.*

parish 1 = **district**, community • *the vicar of a small parish in a West Country town*
2 = **community**, fold, flock, church, congregation, parishioners, churchgoers • *The whole parish will object if he is appointed as priest.*
▸ RELATED ADJECTIVE: parochial

parity = **equality**, correspondence, consistency, equivalence, quits *(informal)*, par, unity, similarity, likeness, uniformity, equal terms, sameness, parallelism, congruity • *Women have yet to achieve wage parity with men in many fields.*

park AS A NOUN 1 = **recreation ground**, garden, playground, pleasure garden, playpark, domain *(N.Z.)*, forest park *(N.Z.)* • *We went for a brisk walk round the park.*
2 = **parkland**, grounds, estate, lawns, woodland, grassland • *a manor house in six acres of park and woodland*
3 = **field**, pitch, playing field • *Chris was the best player on the park.*
▸ AS A VERB 1 = **leave**, stop, station, position • *He found a place to park the car.*
2 = **put (down)**, leave, place, stick, deposit, dump, shove, plonk *(informal)* • *Just park your bag on the floor.*
▸ IN PHRASES: **park yourself** = **sit (down)**, perch, seat yourself, install yourself • *He parked himself in the corner all night.*

QUOTATIONS
The parks are the lungs of London
[William Pitt, Earl of Chatham]

parlance = **language**, talk, speech, tongue, jargon, idiom, lingo *(informal)*, phraseology, manner of speaking • *He is, in common parlance, a 'sad loser'.*

parley AS A NOUN = **discussion**, conference, meeting, talk(s), council, congress, dialogue, seminar, hui *(N.Z.)*, palaver, powwow, colloquy, confab *(informal)*, korero *(N.Z.)* • *A treaty was reached by a 40-nation parley in Geneva.*
▸ AS A VERB = **discuss**, talk, speak, negotiate, deliberate, confer, palaver, powwow, confabulate • *Both sides indicated their readiness to parley.*

parliament 1 = **assembly**, council, congress, senate, convention, legislature, talking shop *(informal)*, convocation • *The Bangladesh Parliament has approved the policy.*
2 = **sitting**, diet • *The legislation will be passed in the next parliament.*
3 *with cap.* = **Houses of Parliament**, the House, Westminster, Mother of Parliaments, the House of Commons and the House of Lords, House of Representatives *(N.Z.)* • *Questions have been raised in Parliament regarding this issue.*

QUOTATIONS
A parliament can do any thing but make a man a woman, and a woman a man
[2nd Earl of Pembroke]
A Parliament is nothing less than a big meeting of more or less idle people
[Walter Bagehot *The English Constitution*]
England is the mother of Parliaments
[John Bright *speech at Birmingham*]

parliamentary = **governmental**, congressional, legislative, law-making, law-giving, deliberative • *There have been demands for a full parliamentary enquiry.*

parlour *or (U.S.)* **parlor** 1 = **sitting room**, lounge, living room, drawing room, front room, reception room, best room • *The guests were shown into the parlour.*
2 = **establishment**, shop, store, salon • *a funeral parlour*

parlous = **dangerous**, difficult, desperate, risky, dire, hazardous, hairy *(slang)*, perilous, chancy *(informal)* • *Our economy is in a parlous state.*

parochial = **provincial**, narrow, insular, limited, restricted, petty, narrow-minded, inward-looking, small-minded, parish-pump • *the stuffy and parochial atmosphere of a small village*
OPPOSITES: national, international, cosmopolitan

parochialism = **provincialism**, narrowness, insularity, narrow-mindedness, localism, small-mindedness, limitedness, restrictedness • *We have been guilty of parochialism and resistance to change.*

parody AS A NOUN 1 = **takeoff** *(informal)*, imitation, satire, caricature, send-up *(Brit. informal)*, spoof *(informal)*, lampoon, skit, burlesque • *a parody of a well-known soap opera*
2 = **travesty**, farce, caricature, mockery, apology for • *His trial was a parody of justice.*
▸ AS A VERB = **take off** *(informal)*, mimic, caricature, send up *(Brit. informal)*, spoof *(informal)*, travesty, lampoon, poke fun at, burlesque, take the piss out of *(taboo slang)*, satirize, do a takeoff of *(informal)* • *It was easy to parody his rather pompous manner of speaking.*

paroxysm = **outburst**, attack, fit, seizure, flare-up *(informal)*, eruption, spasm, convulsion • *She was overcome by a paroxysm of grief.*

parrot = **repeat**, echo, imitate, copy, reiterate, mimic • *Many politicians simply parrot impressive-sounding phrases.*
▸ RELATED ADJECTIVE: psittacine

parrot-fashion = **by rote**, automatically, without thinking, mechanically, mindlessly • *Pupils had to repeat their verb tables parrot-fashion.*

parry 1 = **evade**, avoid, fence off, dodge, duck *(informal)*, shun, sidestep, circumvent, fight shy of • *He parried questions about his involvement in the affair.*
2 = **ward off**, block, deflect, repel, rebuff, fend off, stave off, repulse, hold at bay • *My opponent parried every blow I got close enough to attempt.*

parsimonious = **mean**, stingy, penny-pinching *(informal)*, miserly, near *(informal)*, saving, sparing, grasping, miserable, stinting, frugal, niggardly, penurious, tightfisted, close-fisted, tight-arse *(taboo slang)*, mingy *(Brit. informal)*, tight-ass *(U.S. taboo slang)*, tight-assed *(U.S. taboo slang)*, cheeseparing, skinflinty, snoep *(S. African informal)*, tight as a duck's arse *(taboo slang)* • *the stereotype of the dour and parsimonious Scotsman*
OPPOSITES: generous, lavish, extravagant

parsimony = **meanness**, tightness, penny-pinching *(informal)*, frugality, nearness *(informal)*, stinginess, miserliness, niggardliness, minginess *(Brit. informal)* • *Due to the parsimony of the local council, only one machine was built.*

parson = **clergyman**, minister, priest, vicar, divine, incumbent, reverend *(informal)*, preacher, pastor, cleric, rector, curate, churchman, man of God, man of the cloth, ecclesiastic • *At that time, the parish did not have a resident parson.*

part AS A NOUN 1 = **piece**, share, proportion, percentage, lot, bit, section, sector, slice, scrap, particle, segment, portion, fragment, lump, fraction, chunk, wedge • *A large part of his earnings went on repaying the bank loan.*
OPPOSITES: mass, bulk, entirety
2 *often plural* = **region**, area, district, territory, neighbourhood, quarter, vicinity, neck of the woods *(informal)*, airt *(Scot.)* • *It's a beautiful part of the country.* • *That kind of behaviour doesn't go down too well round these parts.*
3 = **component**, bit, piece, unit, element, ingredient, constituent, module • *The engine only has three moving parts.*
4 = **branch**, department, division, office, section, wing, subdivision, subsection • *He works in a different part of the company.*
5 = **organ**, member, limb • *hands, feet, and other body parts*
6 = **role**, representation, persona, portrayal, depiction, character part • *the actor who played the part of the doctor in the soap*
7 = **lines**, words, script, dialogue • *She's having a lot of trouble learning her part.*
8 = **duty**, say, place, work, role, hand, business, share, charge, responsibility, task, function, capacity, involvement, participation • *He felt a sense of relief now that his part in this business was over.*
9 = **side**, behalf • *There's no hurry on my part.*
▸ AS A PLURAL NOUN = **talents**, abilities, gifts, attributes, faculties, capabilities, endowments, accomplishments • *He is a man of many parts.*
▸ AS A VERB 1 = **divide**, separate, break, tear, split, rend, detach, sever, disconnect, cleave, come apart, disunite, disjoin • *The clouds parted and a shaft of sunlight broke through.* • *He parted the bushes with his stick.*
OPPOSITES: unite, join, combine
2 = **part company**, separate, break up, split up, say goodbye, go (their) separate ways • *We parted on bad terms.*
OPPOSITES: gather, meet, turn up
▸ IN PHRASES: **for the most part** = **mainly**, largely, generally, chiefly, mostly, principally, on the whole, in the main • *For the most part, they try to keep out of local disputes.*
in good part = **good-naturedly**, well, cheerfully, cordially, without offence • *He took their jokes in good part.*
in part = **partly**, a little, somewhat, slightly, partially, to some degree, to a certain extent, in some measure • *His reaction was due, in part, to his fear of rejection.*
on the part of = **by**, in, from, made by, carried out by • *There was a change of mood on the part of the government.*
part with something = **give up**, abandon, yield, sacrifice, surrender, discard, relinquish, renounce, let go of, forgo • *He was reluctant to part with his money, even in such a good cause.*
take part in = **participate in**, be involved in, join in, play a part in, be instrumental in, have a hand in, partake in, take a hand in, associate yourself with, put your twopence-worth in • *Thousands of students have taken part in the demonstrations.*
take someone's part = **support**, defend, be on someone's side, champion, favour, stand by, side with, stand up for, back someone up, be loyal to, stick up for, take someone's side, give your support to • *Just because she was small, people took her part.*

partake IN PHRASES: **partake in something** = **participate in**, share in, take part in, engage in, enter into • *Do you partake in dangerous sports?*
partake of something 1 = **consume**, take, share, receive, eat • *They were happy to partake of our food and drink.*
2 = **display**, exhibit, evoke, hint at, be characterized by • *These groups generally partake of a common characteristic.*

partial AS AN ADJECTIVE 1 = **incomplete**, limited, unfinished, imperfect, fragmentary, uncompleted • *Their policy only met with partial success.*
OPPOSITES: complete, full, whole
2 = **biased**, prejudiced, discriminatory, partisan, influenced, unfair, one-sided, unjust, predisposed, tendentious • *Some of the umpiring in the tournament was partial.*
OPPOSITES: objective, impartial, unbiased
▸ IN PHRASES: **be partial to** = **have a liking for**, care for, be fond of, be keen on, be taken with, have a soft spot for, have a weakness for • *I am partial to red wine.*

partiality 1 = **liking**, love, taste, weakness, preference, inclination, affinity, penchant, fondness, predisposition, predilection, proclivity • *his partiality for junk food*
OPPOSITES: disgust, dislike, aversion
2 = **bias**, preference, prejudice, favouritism, predisposition, partisanship • *The judge was accused of partiality.*
OPPOSITES: equity, fairness, impartiality

partially = **partly**, somewhat, moderately, in part, halfway, piecemeal, not wholly, fractionally, incompletely, to a certain extent or degree • *He is deaf in one ear and partially blind.*

participant = **participator**, party, member, player, associate, shareholder, contributor, stakeholder, partaker • *He was a reluctant participant in the proceedings.*

participate = **take part**, be involved, engage, perform, join, enter, partake, have a hand, get in on the act, be a party to, be a participant • *Over half the population of the country participate in sport.*
OPPOSITES: boycott, opt out of, refrain from

participation = **taking part**, contribution, partnership, involvement, assistance, sharing in, joining in, partaking • *his reluctant participation in religious activities*

particle = **bit**, piece, scrap, grain, molecule, atom, shred, crumb, mite, jot, speck, mote, whit, tittle, iota • *Particles of food can get stuck between the teeth.*

particular AS AN ADJECTIVE 1 = **specific**, special, express, exact, precise, distinct, peculiar • *What particular aspects of the job are you interested in?*
OPPOSITES: general, vague, indefinite
2 = **special**, exceptional, notable, uncommon, marked, unusual, remarkable, singular, noteworthy, especial • *Stress is a particular problem for women.* • *This is a question of particular importance for us.*
3 = **fussy**, demanding, critical, exacting, discriminating, meticulous, fastidious, dainty, choosy *(informal)*, picky

P

(*informal*), finicky, pernickety (*informal*), anal retentive, overnice, nit-picky (*informal*) • *Ted was very particular about the colours he used.*
OPPOSITES: easy, casual, indiscriminate
4 = **detailed**, minute, precise, thorough, selective, painstaking, circumstantial, itemized, blow-by-blow • *a very particular account of the history of sociology*
▸ AS A NOUN *usually plural* = **detail**, fact, feature, item, circumstance, specification • *The nurses at the admission desk asked for her particulars.*
▸ IN PHRASES: **in particular** = **especially**, particularly, expressly, specifically, exactly, distinctly • *Why should he have noticed me in particular?*

particularity 1 = **individuality**, characteristic, peculiarity, idiosyncrasy, property, singularity, distinctiveness • *different degrees of cultural particularity*
2 *often plural* = **circumstance**, fact, detail, point, item, instance • *Time inevitably glosses over the particularities of each situation.*
3 = **meticulousness**, detail, accuracy, precision, thoroughness, fastidiousness, fussiness, carefulness, choosiness (*informal*) • *The essence of good fiction is its particularity.*

particularly 1 = **specifically**, expressly, explicitly, especially, in particular, distinctly • *I particularly asked for a seat by the window.*
2 = **especially**, surprisingly, notably, unusually, exceptionally, decidedly, markedly, peculiarly, singularly, outstandingly, uncommonly • *The number of fatal road accidents has been particularly high.*

parting AS A NOUN 1 = **farewell**, departure, goodbye, leave-taking, adieu, valediction • *It was a dreadfully emotional parting.*
2 = **division**, breaking, split, separation, rift, partition, detachment, rupture, divergence • *Through a parting in the mist, we saw a huddle of buildings.*
▸ AS A MODIFIER = **farewell**, last, final, departing, valedictory • *Her parting words made him feel empty and alone.*
▸ IN PHRASES: **parting of the ways** = **divorce**, parting, separation, dissolution • *This is the parting of the ways for the three Baltic republics.*

QUOTATIONS
Parting is all we know of heaven,
And all we need of hell
[Emily Dickinson *'My life closed twice before its close'*]
Parting is such sweet sorrow
[William Shakespeare *Romeo and Juliet*]
The king of Babylon stood at the parting of the ways
[*Bible: Ezekiel*]
Since there's no help, come let us kiss and part,
Nay, I have done: you get no more of me,
And I am glad, yea glad with all my heart,
That thus so cleanly, I myself can free,
Shake hands forever, cancel all our vows,
And when we meet at any time again,
Be it not seen in either of our brows,
That we one jot of former love retain
[Michael Drayton *Idea: Sonnet 61*]
In every parting there is an image of death
[George Eliot *Scenes of Clerical Life*]

partisan AS AN ADJECTIVE 1 = **prejudiced**, one-sided, biased, partial, sectarian, factional, tendentious • *He is too partisan to be a referee.*
OPPOSITES: impartial, bipartisan, unbiased
2 = **underground**, resistance, guerrilla, irregular • *the hide-out of a Bulgarian partisan leader*
▸ AS A NOUN 1 = **supporter**, champion, follower, backer, disciple, stalwart, devotee, adherent, upholder, votary • *At first the young poet was a partisan of the Revolution.*
OPPOSITES: leader, rival, opponent
2 = **underground fighter**, guerrilla, irregular, freedom fighter, resistance fighter • *He was rescued by some Italian partisans.*

partisanship = **favouritism**, prejudice, bias, sectarianism, factionalism, one-sidedness • *The Republicans made a rebuttal of the charge of excessive partisanship.*

partition AS A NOUN 1 = **screen**, wall, barrier, divider, room divider • *offices divided only by a glass partition*
2 = **division**, splitting, dividing, separation, segregation, severance • *the fighting which followed the partition of India*
▸ AS A VERB 1 = **separate**, screen, divide, fence off, wall off • *Two rooms have been created by partitioning a single larger room.*
2 = **divide**, separate, segment, split up, share, section, portion, cut up, apportion, subdivide, parcel out • *Korea was partitioned in 1945.*

partly = **partially**, relatively, somewhat, slightly, in part, halfway, not fully, in some measure, incompletely, up to a certain point, to a certain degree *or* extent • *This is partly my fault.*
OPPOSITES: completely, totally, fully

partner 1 = **spouse**, squeeze (*informal*), consort, bedfellow, significant other (*U.S. informal*), mate, better half (*Brit. informal*), helpmate, husband *or* wife, bidie-in (*Scot.*), Wag (*Brit. informal*) • *Wanting other friends doesn't mean you don't love your partner.*
2 = **companion**, collaborator, accomplice, ally, colleague, associate, mate, team-mate, participant, comrade, confederate, bedfellow, copartner • *They were partners in crime.*
3 = **associate**, colleague, collaborator, copartner • *He is a partner in a Chicago law firm.*

partnership 1 = **cooperation**, association, alliance, sharing, union, connection, participation, copartnership • *the partnership between Germany's banks and its businesses*
2 = **company**, firm, corporation, house, interest, society, conglomerate, cooperative • *As the partnership prospered, the employees shared in the benefits.*

partridge
▸ COLLECTIVE NOUN: covey

party AS A NOUN 1 = **faction**, association, alliance, grouping, set, side, league, camp, combination, coalition, clique, coterie, schism, confederacy, cabal • *opposing political parties*
2 = **get-together** (*informal*), celebration, do (*informal*), social, at-home, gathering, function, reception, bash (*informal*), rave (*Brit. slang*), festivity, knees-up (*Brit. informal*), beano (*Brit. slang*), social gathering, shindig (*informal*), soirée, rave-up (*Brit. slang*), hooley *or* hoolie (*chiefly Irish & N.Z.*) • *We threw a huge birthday party.*
3 = **group**, team, band, company, body, unit, squad, gathering, crew, gang, bunch (*informal*), dream team, detachment (*Military*) • *a party of explorers*
4 = **litigant**, defendant, participant, contractor (*Law*), plaintiff • *It has to be proved that he is the guilty party.*
5 = **person**, individual, somebody, someone • *A certain party told me you would be here.*
▸ AS A VERB = **celebrate**, have fun, have a good time, enjoy yourself, have a ball, large it (*Brit. slang*), push the boat out, whoop it up, paint the town red, let your hair down, go on a bender • *Let's party like there's no tomorrow!*
▸ IN PHRASES: **be a party to something** = **get involved in**, be associated with, be a participant in, concern yourself with *or* in • *He insisted he had not been a party to the attack.*

QUOTATIONS
A party is like a marriage ... making itself up while seeming to follow precedent
[Jay McInerney *Brightness Falls*]

Under democracy, one party always devotes its chief energies to trying to prove that the other party is unfit to rule: and both commonly succeed, and are right
[H.L. Mencken]

pass AS A VERB **1 = go by** *or* **past**, overtake, drive past, lap, leave behind, cut up *(informal)*, pull ahead of • *A car passed me going quite fast.*
OPPOSITES: stop, halt, pause
2 = go, move, travel, roll, progress, flow, proceed, move onwards • *He passed through the doorway to ward B.*
3 = run, move, stroke • *He passed a hand through her hair.*
4 = give, hand, send, throw, exchange, transfer, deliver, toss, transmit, convey, chuck *(informal)*, let someone have • *He passed the books to the librarian.*
5 = be left, come, be bequeathed, be inherited by • *His mother's estate passed to him after her death.*
6 = kick, hit, loft, head, lob • *Their team passed the ball better than ours did.*
7 = elapse, progress, go by, lapse, wear on, go past, tick by • *As the years passed, he grew discontented with his marriage.*
8 = end, go, die, disappear, fade, cease, vanish, dissolve, expire, terminate, dwindle, evaporate, wane, ebb, melt away, blow over • *This crisis will pass eventually.* • *Her feelings lightened as the storm passed.*
9 = spend, use (up), kill, fill, waste, employ, occupy, devote, beguile, while away • *The children passed the time playing in the streets.*
10 = exceed, beat, overtake, go beyond, excel, surpass, transcend, outstrip, outdo, surmount • *They were the first company in their field to pass the £2 billion turnover mark.*
11 = be successful in, qualify (in), succeed (in), graduate (in), get through, do, pass muster (in), come up to scratch (in) *(informal)*, gain a pass in • *Kevin has just passed his driving test.*
OPPOSITES: fail, be unsuccessful in, lose
12 = approve, accept, establish, adopt, sanction, decree, enact, authorize, ratify, ordain, validate, legislate (for) • *The Senate passed the bill by a vote of seventy-three to twenty-four.*
OPPOSITES: refuse, ban, reject
13 = pronounce, deliver, issue, set forth • *Passing sentence, the judge described the crime as odious.*
14 = utter, speak, voice, express, declare • *We passed a few remarks about the weather.*
15 = discharge, release, expel, evacuate, emit, let out, eliminate *(rare)* • *The first symptom is extreme pain when passing urine.*
▸ AS A NOUN **1 = licence**, ticket, permit, permission, passport, warrant, identification, identity card, authorization • *Can I see your boarding pass, please?*
2 = gap, route, canyon, col, gorge, ravine, defile • *The monastery is in a remote mountain pass.*
3 = predicament, condition, situation, state, stage, pinch, plight, straits, state of affairs, juncture • *Things have come to a pretty pass when people are afraid to go out after dark.*
▸ IN PHRASES: **come to pass = happen**, develop, occur, take place, come up, fall out, roll up, befall • *Everything I said about the game came to pass that night.*
let something pass = ignore, overlook, neglect, not heed • *I could not let the remark pass.*
make a pass at someone = make advances to, proposition, hit on *(U.S. & Canad. slang)*, come on to *(informal)*, make a play for *(informal)*, make an approach to, make sexual overtures to • *Was he just being friendly, or was he making a pass at her?*
pass as *or* **for something** *or* **someone = be mistaken for**, be taken for, impersonate, be accepted as, be regarded as • *He was trying to pass as one of the locals.*
pass away *or* **on = die**, pass on, depart (this life), buy it *(U.S. slang)*, expire, check out *(U.S. slang)*, pass over, kick it *(slang)*, croak *(slang)*, go belly-up *(slang)*, snuff it *(informal)*, peg out *(informal)*, kick the bucket *(slang)*, buy the farm *(U.S. slang)*, peg it *(informal)*, decease, shuffle off this mortal coil, cark it *(Austral. & N.Z. informal)*, pop your clogs *(informal)* • *He unfortunately passed away last year.*
pass by = go past, pass, move past, walk by *or* past • *He gave me a nod as he passed by.* • *I passed by your house last night.*
pass off 1 = take place, happen, occur, turn out, go down *(U.S. & Canad.)*, be completed, go off, fall out, be finished, pan out • *The event passed off without any major incidents.*
2 = come to an end, disappear, vanish, die away, fade out *or* away • *The effects of the anaesthetic gradually passed off.*
pass out = faint, drop, black out *(informal)*, swoon *(literary)*, lose consciousness, keel over *(informal)*, flake out *(informal)*, become unconscious • *She got drunk and passed out.*
pass someone over = overlook, ignore, discount, pass by, disregard, not consider, take no notice of, not take into consideration, pay not attention to • *She claimed she was repeatedly passed over for promotion.*
pass something out = hand out, distribute, dole out, deal out • *They were passing out leaflets in the street.*
pass something over = disregard, forget, ignore, skip, omit, pass by, not dwell on • *Let's pass over that subject.*
pass something up = miss, ignore, let slip, refuse, decline, reject, neglect, forgo, abstain from, let (something) go by, give (something) a miss *(informal)* • *It's too good a chance to pass up.*
pass something *or* **someone off as something** *or* **someone = misrepresent**, palm something *or* someone off, falsely represent, disguise something *or* someone, dress something *or* someone up • *horse meat being passed off as ground beef*
pass yourself off as someone = pretend to be, fake being, feign being, make a pretence of being • *He tried to pass himself off as a doctor.*

passable 1 = adequate, middling, average, fair, all right, ordinary, acceptable, moderate, fair enough, mediocre, so-so *(informal)*, tolerable, not too bad, allowable, presentable, admissible, unexceptional, half-pie *(N.Z. informal)* • *The meal was passable, but nothing special.*
OPPOSITES: extraordinary, outstanding, unsatisfactory
2 = clear, open, navigable, unobstructed, traversable, crossable • *muddy mountain roads that are barely passable*
OPPOSITES: closed, blocked, impassable

passably = fairly, rather, relatively, somewhat, moderately, pretty, adequately, tolerably, acceptably • *She's always done passably well in school.*

passage 1 = corridor, hallway, passageway, hall, lobby, entrance, exit, doorway, aisle, entrance hall, vestibule • *The toilets are up the stairs and along the passage to your right.*
2 = alley, way, opening, close *(Brit.)*, course, road, channel, route, path, lane, avenue, thoroughfare • *He spotted someone lurking in the passage between the two houses.*
3 = extract, reading, piece, section, sentence, text, clause, excerpt, paragraph, verse, quotation • *He read a passage from the Bible.*
4 = movement, passing, advance, progress, flow, motion, transit, progression • *the passage of troops through Spain*
5 = tube, opening, hole, aperture, inlet, duct, orifice • *cells that line the air passages*
6 = way, route, path, course, way through • *Two men elbowed a passage through the shoppers.*
7 = transit, moving, passing, travelling, crossing, movement, progress, traversal • *the passage of troops through the country*
8 = transition, change, move, development, progress, shift, conversion, progression, metamorphosis • *the passage from school to college*
9 = establishment, passing, legislation, sanction, approval, acceptance, adoption, ratification, enactment,

authorization, validation, legalization • *It has been 200 years since the passage of the Bill of Rights.*
10 = passing, course, march, advance, flow, moving on • *Its value increases with the passage of time.*
11 = journey, crossing, tour, trip, trek, voyage • *We arrived after a 10-hour passage by ship.*
12 = safe-conduct, right to travel, freedom to travel, permission to travel, authorization to travel • *They were granted safe passage to Baghdad.*

passageway = corridor, passage, hallway, hall, lane, lobby, entrance, exit, alley, aisle, wynd *(Scot.)* • *an underground passageway that connects the two buildings*

passé = out-of-date, old-fashioned, dated, outdated, obsolete, unfashionable, antiquated, outmoded, old hat, outworn, unhip *(slang)*, démodé *(French)* • *Punk rock is passé now.*

passenger = traveller, rider, fare, commuter, hitchhiker, pillion rider, fare payer • *a flight from Milan with more than forty passengers aboard* • *the pillion passenger on a motorbike*

passer-by = bystander, witness, observer, viewer, spectator, looker-on, watcher, onlooker, eyewitness • *A passer-by described what had happened.*

passing AS AN ADJECTIVE **1 = momentary**, fleeting, short-lived, transient, ephemeral, short, brief, temporary, transitory, evanescent, fugacious *(rare)* • *people who dismissed mobile phones as a passing fad*
2 = superficial, short, quick, slight, glancing, casual, summary, shallow, hasty, cursory, perfunctory, desultory • *He only gave us a passing glance.*
▸ AS A NOUN **1 = end**, finish, loss, vanishing, disappearance, termination, dying out, expiry, expiration • *the passing of an era*
2 = death, demise, decease, passing on *or* away • *His passing will be mourned by many people.*
3 = passage, course, process, advance, progress, flow • *The passing of time brought a sense of emptiness.*
4 = sanction, approval, passage, adoption, endorsement, enactment, authorization, validation, legalization • *the formal passing of the treaty*
▸ IN PHRASES: **in passing = incidentally**, on the way, by the way, accidentally, en passant, by the bye • *She only mentioned you in passing.*

passion 1 = love, desire, affection, lust, the hots *(slang)*, attachment, itch, fondness, adoration, infatuation, ardour, keenness, concupiscence • *Romeo's passion for Juliet*
2 = emotion, feeling, fire, heat, spirit, transport, joy, excitement, intensity, warmth, animation, zeal, zest, fervour, eagerness, rapture, ardour • *Her eyes were blazing with passion.*
OPPOSITES: hate, indifference, apathy
3 = mania, fancy, enthusiasm, obsession, bug *(informal)*, craving, fascination, craze, infatuation • *She has a passion for gardening.* • *Television is his passion.*
4 = rage, fit, storm, anger, fury, resentment, outburst, frenzy, wrath, indignation, flare-up *(informal)*, ire, vehemence, paroxysm • *Sam flew into a passion at the suggestion.* • *He killed the woman in a fit of passion.*

QUOTATIONS
In passion, the body and the spirit seek expression outside of self
[John Boorman *journal entry*]
A man who has not passed through the inferno of his passions has never overcome them
[Carl Gustav Jung *Memories, Dreams, Reflections*]

passionate 1 = emotional, excited, eager, enthusiastic, animated, strong, warm, wild, intense, flaming, fierce, frenzied, ardent, fervent, heartfelt, impassioned, zealous, impulsive, vehement, impetuous, fervid • *He made a passionate speech about his commitment to peace.*
OPPOSITES: calm, subdued, unemotional
2 = loving, erotic, hot, sexy *(informal)*, aroused, sensual, ardent, steamy *(informal)*, wanton, amorous, lustful, desirous • *a passionate embrace*
OPPOSITES: cold, frigid, unresponsive
3 = quick-tempered, violent, fiery, stormy, irritable, excitable, tempestuous, irascible, peppery, hot-headed, hot-tempered, choleric • *She has a passionate temper.*
OPPOSITES: calm, agreeable, even-tempered

passionately 1 = emotionally, eagerly, enthusiastically, vehemently, excitedly, strongly, warmly, wildly, fiercely, intensely, fervently, impulsively, ardently, zealously, animatedly, with all your heart, frenziedly, impetuously, fervidly • *He spoke passionately about the country's moral crisis.*
OPPOSITES: coldly, calmly, unemotionally
2 = lovingly, with passion, erotically, ardently, sexily *(informal)*, sensually, lustfully, amorously, steamily *(informal)*, libidinously, desirously • *She kissed him passionately.*
OPPOSITES: coldly, frigidly, unresponsively
3 = furiously, angrily, violently, excitably, tempestuously, fierily, stormily, irascibly, hot-headedly • *She burst out passionately, 'Shut up!'*
OPPOSITES: calmly, placidly, unexcitably

passionless 1 = unemotional, calm, neutral, restrained, detached, impartial, dispassionate, impassive, uninvolved • *a passionless academic*
2 = emotionless, cold, indifferent, icy, cold-blooded, uncaring, apathetic, frigid, unresponsive, unfeeling, unloving, cold-hearted • *a self-centred and passionless woman*

passive 1 = submissive, resigned, compliant, receptive, lifeless, docile, nonviolent, quiescent, acquiescent, unassertive, unresisting • *their passive acceptance of the new regime*
OPPOSITES: spirited, violent, lively
2 = inactive, inert, uninvolved, non-participating • *He took a passive role in the interview.*
OPPOSITES: involved, active

Passover
▸ RELATED ADJECTIVE: Paschal

passport 1 = travel document, papers, visa, identity card, travel papers, travel permit, I.D. • *Take your passport with you when changing money.*
2 = key, way, entry, route, path, avenue, means of access • *Qualifications are no automatic passport to a job.*

password = watchword, key word, magic word *(informal)*, open sesame • *No-one can use the computer without a password.*

past AS A NOUN **1 = former times**, history, long ago, antiquity, the good old days, yesteryear *(literary)*, times past, the old times, days gone by, the olden days, days of yore • *In the past, things were very different.*
OPPOSITES: now, today, future
2 = background, life, experience, history, past life, life story, career to date • *shocking revelations about his past*
▸ AS AN ADJECTIVE **1 = former**, late, early, recent, previous, ancient, prior, long-ago, preceding, foregoing, erstwhile, bygone, olden • *a return to the turbulence of past centuries*
OPPOSITES: coming, future, present
2 = previous, former, one-time, sometime, erstwhile, quondam, ex- • *I was still longing for my past lover*
3 = last, recent, previous, preceding • *the events of the past few days*
4 = over, done, ended, spent, finished, completed, gone, forgotten, accomplished, extinct, elapsed, over and done with • *The great age of exploration is past.*
▸ AS A PREPOSITION **1 = after**, beyond, later than, over, outside, farther than, in excess of, subsequent to • *It's well past your bedtime.*
2 = by, across, in front of • *She dashed past me and ran out of the room.*
▸ AS AN ADVERB **= on**, by, along • *The ambulance drove past.*
▸ IN PHRASES: **be past it = be past its** *or* **your sell-by date**, be on the way out, have seen better days • *We could do with a new car – the one we have now is a bit past it.*

P

QUOTATIONS
The past is a foreign country; they do things differently there
[L. P. Hartley *The Go-Between*]
The past is the only dead thing that smells sweet
[Edward Thomas *Early One Morning*]
As all historians know, the past is a great darkness, and filled with echoes
[Margaret Atwood *The Handmaid's Tale*]
The past is never dead, it is not even past
[William Faulkner]
Those who cannot remember the past are condemned to repeat it
[George Santayana *The Life of Reason*]
I think we agree, the past is over
[George Bush]

pasta
▹ *See panel* **Types of pasta**

paste AS A NOUN 1 = **adhesive**, glue, cement, gum, mucilage • *wallpaper paste*
2 = **purée**, pâté, spread • *tomato paste*
▸ AS A VERB = **stick**, fix, glue, cement, gum, fasten • *pasting labels on bottles*

pastel = **pale**, light, soft, delicate, muted, soft-hued • *pretty pastel shades*
OPPOSITES: strong, deep, bright

pastiche 1 = **medley**, mixture, blend, motley, mélange *(French)*, miscellany, farrago, hotchpotch, gallimaufry • *The world menu may be a pastiche of dishes from many countries.*
2 = **parody**, take-off, imitation • *a pastiche of Botticelli's Birth of Venus*

pastille = **lozenge**, tablet, troche *(Medical)*, cough drop, jujube • *a medicated pastille*

pastime = **activity**, game, sport, entertainment, leisure, hobby, relaxation, recreation, distraction, amusement, diversion • *His favourite pastime is golf.*

past master = **expert**, ace *(informal)*, wizard, artist, virtuoso, old hand, dab hand *(Brit. informal)* • *He is a past master at manipulating the media.*

pastor = **clergyman**, minister, priest, vicar, divine, parson, rector, curate, churchman, ecclesiastic • *the pastor of the local Episcopalian church*

pastoral 1 = **ecclesiastical**, priestly, ministerial, clerical • *the pastoral duties of bishops*
2 = **rustic**, country, simple, rural, idyllic, bucolic, Arcadian, georgic *(literary)*, agrestic • *a tranquil pastoral scene*

pastry = **tart**, Danish (pastry), pasty, tartlet • *high fat foods such as cakes and pastries*
▹ *See panel* **Cakes and pastries**

TYPES OF PASTRY

choux pastry	pâte brisée	rough puff pastry
filo pastry	pâte feuilletée	shortcrust pastry
flaky pastry	pâte sucrée	suet pastry
hot water pastry	puff pastry	

pasture = **grassland**, grass, meadow, grazing, lea *(poetic)*, grazing land, pasturage, shieling *(Scot.)* • *The cows are out now, grazing in the pasture.*

pasty = **pale**, unhealthy, wan, sickly, pallid, anaemic, sallow, like death warmed up *(informal)*, wheyfaced • *My complexion remained pale and pasty.*

pat[1] AS A VERB = **stroke**, touch, tap, pet, slap, dab, caress, fondle • *She patted me on the knee.*
▸ AS A NOUN 1 = **tap**, stroke, slap, clap, dab, light blow • *He gave her an encouraging pat on the shoulder.*
2 = **lump**, cake, portion, dab, small piece • *a pat of butter*
▸ IN PHRASES: **pat someone on the back** = **congratulate**, praise, applaud, compliment, commend, sing the praises of, big up *(slang, chiefly Caribbean)* • *industry bigwigs patting each other on the back*
pat yourself on the back = **boast about yourself**, congratulate yourself, blow your own trumpet, talk big *(informal)*, brag about yourself, preen yourself, big yourself up *(slang, chiefly Caribbean)* • *Hollywood patting itself on the back in the annual Academy Awards ceremony*

pat[2] AS AN ADJECTIVE = **glib**, easy, ready, smooth, automatic, slick, simplistic, facile • *There's no pat answer to your question.*
▸ IN PHRASES: **off pat** = **perfectly**, precisely, exactly, flawlessly, faultlessly • *He doesn't have the answer off pat.*

patch AS A NOUN 1 = **spot**, bit, stretch, scrap, shred, small piece • *a damp patch on the carpet*
2 = **plot**, area, ground, land, tract • *the little vegetable patch in her backyard*
3 = **reinforcement**, piece of fabric, piece of cloth, piece of material, piece sewn on • *jackets with patches on the elbows*
4 = **period**, time, spell, phase, spot *(Brit.)*, stretch • *His marriage is going through a rough patch.*
▸ AS A VERB 1 *often with* **up** = **sew (up)**, mend, repair, reinforce, stitch (up) • *elaborately patched blue jeans*
2 *often with* **up** = **mend**, cover, fix, reinforce • *They patched the barn roof.*
▸ IN PHRASES: **not be a patch on something** *or* **someone** = **not be as good as**, not hold a candle to • *He's not a patch on his predecessor.*
patch someone up = **treat**, operate on, mend, perform surgery on • *The surgeons patched him up after the accident.*
patch things up = **settle**, make friends, placate, bury the hatchet, conciliate, settle differences, smooth something over • *He's trying to patch things up with his wife.*

patchwork = **mixture**, confusion, jumble, medley, hash, pastiche, mishmash, hotchpotch • *The republic is a patchwork of cultures, religions and nationalities.*

patchy 1 = **uneven**, irregular, variegated, spotty, mottled, dappled • *Bottle tans can make your legs look a patchy orange colour.*
OPPOSITES: even, regular, unbroken
2 = **irregular**, varying, variable, random, erratic, uneven, sketchy, fitful, bitty, inconstant, scattershot • *The response to the strike call has been patchy.*
OPPOSITES: constant, unbroken, unvarying

patent AS A NOUN = **copyright**, licence, franchise, registered trademark • *He had a number of patents for his inventions.*
▸ AS AN ADJECTIVE = **obvious**, apparent, evident, blatant, open, clear, glaring, manifest, transparent, conspicuous, downright, unmistakable, palpable, unequivocal, flagrant, indisputable, unconcealed • *This was a patent lie.*

paternal 1 = **fatherly**, concerned, protective, benevolent, vigilant, solicitous, fatherlike • *He has always taken a paternal interest in her.*
2 = **patrilineal**, patrimonial • *my paternal grandparents*

paternity = **fatherhood**, fathership *(rare)* • *He was tricked into marriage by a false accusation of paternity.*

path AS A NOUN 1 = **way**, road, walk, track, trail, avenue, pathway, footpath, walkway *(chiefly U.S.)*, towpath, footway, berm *(N.Z.)* • *We followed the path along the clifftops.*
2 = **route**, way, course, direction, passage • *A group of reporters blocked his path.* • *The tornado wrecked everything in its path.*
3 = **course**, way, road, track, route, procedure • *The country is on the path to economic recovery.*
▸ IN PHRASES: **cross someone's path** = **meet**, encounter, run into, run across • *He chats up every presentable female who crosses his path.*

P

TYPES OF PASTA

agnolotti	conchiglie	lasagne	orecchiette	ruote	tortiglioni
bavette	ditali	lasagnette	paglia e fieno	spaghetti	vermicelli
bombolotti	farfalle	linguine	pappardelle	spätzle	zita
bucatini	fettuccine	lumache	penne	tagliatelle	
cannelloni	fusilli	macaroni	pipe	taglioni	
cappelletti	gnocchetti	maultaschen	ravioli	tortellini	
cellentani	gnocchi	noodles	rigatoni	tortelloni	

pathetic 1 = **sad**, moving, touching, affecting, distressing, tender, melting, poignant, harrowing, heartbreaking, plaintive, heart-rending, gut-wrenching, pitiable • *It was a pathetic sight, watching the people queue for food.*
OPPOSITES: funny, entertaining, amusing
2 = **inadequate**, useless, feeble, poor, sorry, wet (*Brit. informal*), pants (*informal*), miserable, petty, worthless, meagre, pitiful, woeful, deplorable, lamentable, trashy, measly, crummy (*slang*), crappy (*slang*), rubbishy, poxy (*slang*), wanky (*taboo slang*), chickenshit (*U.S. slang*) • *That's the most pathetic excuse I've ever heard.*

pathfinder = **pioneer**, guide, scout, explorer, discoverer, trailblazer • *They employed a local guide as pathfinder.*

pathological = **obsessive**, chronic, persistent, compulsive, unreasonable, irrational, habitual, confirmed, illogical, inveterate • *his pathological jealousy*

pathos = **sadness**, poignancy, plaintiveness, pitifulness, pitiableness • *the pathos of his hopeless situation*

patience 1 = **forbearance**, tolerance, composure, serenity, cool (*slang*), restraint, calmness, equanimity, toleration, sufferance, even temper, imperturbability • *She lost her patience and shrieked, 'Just shut up, will you?'*
OPPOSITES: passion, excitement, impatience
2 = **endurance**, resignation, submission, fortitude, persistence, long-suffering, perseverance, stoicism, constancy • *a burden which he has borne with great patience*

QUOTATIONS
Genius is only a greater aptitude for patience
[Comte de Buffon]
Patience is the virtue of an ass
[Lord Lansdowne]
They also serve who only stand and wait
[John Milton *Sonnet on his Blindness*]

PROVERBS
All things come to those who wait
Rome was not built in a day
Patience is a virtue

patient AS A NOUN = **sick person**, case, sufferer, invalid • *He specialized in the treatment of cancer patients.*
▸ AS AN ADJECTIVE 1 = **forbearing**, understanding, forgiving, mild, accommodating, tolerant, indulgent, lenient, even-tempered • *He was endlessly kind and patient with children.*
OPPOSITES: impatient, cross, bad-tempered
2 = **long-suffering**, resigned, calm, enduring, quiet, composed, persistent, philosophical, serene, persevering, stoical, submissive, self-possessed, uncomplaining, untiring • *years of patient devotion to her family*

QUOTATIONS
That patient is not like to recover who makes the doctor his heir
[Thomas Fuller *Gnomologia*]

patio = **terrace**, porch, veranda, loggia, sun deck (*U.S. & Canad.*) • *The door opened on to a mosaic-tiled patio.*

patois 1 = **dialect**, vernacular • *In France patois was spoken in rural regions.*
2 = **jargon**, slang, vernacular, patter, cant, lingo (*informal*), argot • *people from the ghetto who speak street patois*

patriarch = **father**, old man, elder, grandfather, sire, paterfamilias, greybeard • *the patriarch of the clan*

patrician AS A NOUN = **aristocrat**, peer, noble, nobleman, aristo (*informal*) • *He was a patrician, born to wealth.*
▸ AS AN ADJECTIVE = **aristocratic**, noble, lordly, high-class, blue-blooded, highborn • *a member of a patrician German family*

patrimony = **inheritance**, share, heritage, portion, legacy, bequest, birthright • *I relinquished my estate and my patrimony.* • *Britain's patrimony of country houses*

patriot = **nationalist**, loyalist, chauvinist, flag-waver (*informal*), lover of your country • *a passionate patriot steeped in Scottish history*

QUOTATIONS
No man can be a patriot on an empty stomach
[W.C. Brann *Old Glory*]
Patriot: The person who can holler the loudest without knowing what he is hollering about
[Mark Twain]

patriotic = **nationalistic**, loyal, flag-waving (*informal*), chauvinistic, jingoistic • *The crowd chanted patriotic slogans.*

patriotism = **nationalism**, loyalty, flag-waving (*informal*), jingoism, love of your country • *He has joined the army out of a sense of patriotism.*

QUOTATIONS
I only regret that I have but one life to lose for my country
[Nathan Hale *prior to his execution by the British in 1776*]
It is a sweet and honourable thing to die for your country (dulce et decorum est pro patria mori)
[Horace *Odes*]
Patriotism is the last refuge of a scoundrel
[Dr. Johnson]
And so, my fellow Americans; ask not what your country can do for you – ask what you can do for your country. My fellow citizens of the world; ask not what America will do for you, but what together we can do for the freedom of man
[John F. Kennedy *inaugural address*]
England expects that every man will do his duty
[Horatio Nelson *said at the Battle of Trafalgar*]
What do I mean by patriotism in the context of our times? ... a sense of national responsibility ... a patriotism which is not short, frenzied outbursts of emotion, but the tranquil and steady dedication of a lifetime
[Adlai Stevenson *speech to the American Legion Convention*]
Never was patriot yet, but was a fool
[John Dryden *Absalom and Achitophel*]
That kind of patriotism which consists in hating all other nations
[Elizabeth Gaskell *Sylvia's Lovers*]
You'll never have a quiet world until you knock the patriotism out of the human race
[George Bernard Shaw *O'Flaherty V.C.*]

Our country, right or wrong!
[Stephen Decatur *toast*]
If I should die, think only this of me,
That there's some corner of a foreign field
That is for ever England
[Rupert Brooke *The Soldier*]
Patriotism is a lively sense of collective responsibility.
Nationalism is a silly cock crowing on its own dunghill
[Richard Aldington *The Colonel's Daughter*]
patriotism: combustible rubbish ready to the torch of any one ambitious to illuminate his name
[Ambrose Bierce *The Devil's Dictionary*]

patrol AS A VERB = **police**, guard, keep watch (on), pound, range (over), cruise, inspect, safeguard, make the rounds (of), keep guard (on), walk *or* pound the beat (of) • *Prison officers continued to patrol the grounds.*
▸ AS A NOUN = **guard**, watch, garrison, watchman, sentinel, patrolman • *Gunmen opened fire after they were challenged by a patrol.*
▸ IN PHRASES: **on patrol** = **during a vigil**, policing, watching, protecting, guarding, safeguarding, beat-pounding, on your rounds • *a soldier shot while on patrol*

patron 1 = **supporter**, friend, champion, defender, sponsor, guardian, angel *(informal)*, advocate, backer, helper, protagonist, protector, benefactor, philanthropist • *Catherine the Great was a patron of the arts and sciences.*
2 = **customer**, client, buyer, frequenter, shopper, habitué • *Like so many of its patrons, he could not resist the food at the Savoy.*

patronage 1 = **support**, promotion, sponsorship, backing, help, aid, championship, assistance, encouragement, espousal, benefaction • *Japan is moving into international patronage of the arts.*
2 = **nepotism**, bias, favouritism, preferential treatment, partiality • *a system based on corruption and political patronage*
3 = **condescension**, contempt, disdain, snobbery, patronizing, deigning, snobbishness • *exuding all the patronage that was to be expected from a descendant of doges*

patronize 1 = **talk down to**, look down on, treat as inferior, treat like a child, be lofty with, treat condescendingly • *a doctor who does not patronize his patients*
2 = **support**, promote, sponsor, back, help, fund, maintain, foster, assist, subscribe to, befriend • *Some believe it is not the job of the government to patronize the arts.*
3 = **be a customer** *or* **client of**, deal with, frequent, buy from, trade with, shop at, do business with • *the record stores he patronized*

patronizing = **condescending**, superior, stooping, lofty, gracious, contemptuous, haughty, snobbish, disdainful, supercilious, toffee-nosed *(slang, chiefly Brit.)* • *his patronizing attitude to the homeless*
OPPOSITES: humble, respectful, deferential

patter[1] AS A VERB 1 = **tap**, beat, pat, pelt, spatter, rat-a-tat, pitter-patter, pitapat • *All night the sleet pattered on the tin roof.*
2 = **walk lightly**, trip, skip, scuttle, scurry, tiptoe • *He jumped up and pattered across the room.*
▸ AS A NOUN = **tapping**, pattering, pitter-patter, pitapat • *the patter of the driving rain on the window*

patter[2] 1 = **spiel** *(informal)*, line, pitch, monologue • *Don't be taken in by the sales patter.*
2 = **chatter**, prattle, nattering, jabber, gabble, yak *(slang)* • *the cheery patter of DJs*
3 = **jargon**, slang, vernacular, cant, lingo *(informal)*, patois, argot • *the famous Glasgow patter*

pattern 1 = **order**, plan, system, method, arrangement, sequence, orderliness • *All three attacks followed the same pattern.*
2 = **design**, arrangement, motif, figure, device, decoration, ornament, decorative design • *curtains in a light floral pattern*
3 = **plan**, design, original, guide, instructions, diagram, stencil, template • *a sewing pattern*
4 = **model**, example, standard, original, guide, par, criterion, norm, prototype, paradigm, archetype, paragon, exemplar, cynosure • *the ideal pattern of a good society*

patterned 1 = **decorated**, fancy, trimmed, intricate, adorned, mosaic, ornamented, embellished, tessellated • *the elaborately patterned floor of a balcony*
2 = **modelled**, following, ordered, shaped, emulating • *a policy patterned on the federal bill of rights*

paucity = **scarcity**, lack, poverty, shortage, deficiency, rarity, dearth, smallness, insufficiency, slenderness, sparseness, slightness, sparsity, meagreness, paltriness, scantiness • *the paucity of information*

paunch = **belly**, beer-belly *(informal)*, spread *(informal)*, corporation *(informal)*, pot, spare tyre *(Brit. slang)*, middle-age spread *(informal)*, potbelly, large abdomen, puku *(N.Z.)* • *He was developing a paunch.*

pauper = **down-and-out**, have-not, bankrupt, beggar, insolvent, indigent, poor person, mendicant • *Mozart died a pauper.*

pause AS A VERB = **stop briefly**, delay, hesitate, break, wait, rest, halt, cease, interrupt, deliberate, waver, take a break, discontinue, desist, have a breather *(informal)* • *He paused briefly before answering.*
OPPOSITES: continue, advance, progress
▸ AS A NOUN = **stop**, break, delay, interval, hesitation, stay, wait, rest, gap, halt, interruption, respite, lull, stoppage, interlude, cessation, let-up *(informal)*, breathing space, breather *(informal)*, intermission, discontinuance, entr'acte, caesura • *There was a brief pause in the conversation.*
OPPOSITES: advancement, progression, continuance

QUOTATIONS
The right word may be effective, but no word was ever as effective as a rightly timed pause
[Mark Twain]

pave AS A VERB = **cover**, floor, surface, flag, concrete, tile, tar, asphalt, macadamize • *The concourse had been paved with concrete.*
▸ IN PHRASES: **pave the way for something** *or* **someone** = **prepare (the way) for**, introduce, herald, usher in, precede, clear the way for, open the way for, lay the foundations for, set the scene for, be the forerunner of, make preparations for, work round to, do the groundwork for • *It is hoped the meeting will pave the way for peaceful negotiations.*

pavement = **sidewalk** *(U.S. & Canad.)*, footpath *(Austral. & N.Z.)* • *He was hurrying along the pavement.*

paw AS A NOUN = **hand**, palm, mitt *(slang)* • *He shook her hand with his big paw.*
▸ AS A VERB = **manhandle**, grab, maul, molest, handle roughly • *Women do not want to be pawed by the men they work with.*

pawn[1] = **hock** *(informal, chiefly U.S.)*, pop *(Brit. informal)*, stake, mortgage, deposit, pledge, hazard, wager • *He pawned his wedding ring.*

pawn[2] = **tool**, instrument, toy, creature, puppet, dupe, stooge *(slang)*, plaything, cat's-paw • *He is being used as a political pawn by the President.*

pay AS A VERB 1 = **reward**, compensate, reimburse, recompense, requite, remunerate • *They are paid well for doing such a difficult job.*
2 = **spend**, offer, give, fork out *(informal)*, remit, cough up *(informal)*, shell out *(informal)* • *I was prepared to pay anything for that car.*
3 = **settle**, meet, clear, foot, honour, discharge, liquidate, square up • *If you cannot pay your debts, you can file for bankruptcy.*
4 = **bring in**, earn, return, net, yield • *This job pays $500 a week.*

P

5 = be profitable, make money, make a return, provide a living, be remunerative • *She took over her husband's restaurant and made it pay.*
6 = benefit, serve, repay, be worthwhile, be advantageous • *It pays to invest in protective clothing.*
7 = give, extend, present with, grant, render, hand out, bestow, proffer • *My husband never pays me compliments or says he loves me.*
8 = suffer, pay the price, atone, suffer the consequences • *I'll make you pay for this!*
▸ **AS A NOUN = wages**, income, payment, earnings, fee, reward, hire, salary, compensation, allowance, remuneration, takings, reimbursement, hand-outs, recompense, stipend, emolument, meed *(archaic)* • *the workers' complaints about pay and conditions*
▸ **IN PHRASES: pay for something = suffer for**, compensate for, answer for, be punished for, atone for, make amends for, suffer the consequences of, get your just deserts • *Don't you think criminals should pay for their crimes?*
pay off = succeed, work, be successful, be effective, be profitable • *Her persistence paid off in the end.*
pay someone back = get even with *(informal)*, punish, repay, retaliate, hit back at, reciprocate, recompense, get revenge on, settle a score with, get your own back on, revenge yourself on, avenge yourself for • *It was her chance to pay him back for humiliating her.*
pay someone off 1 = bribe, corrupt, oil *(informal)*, get at, buy off, suborn, grease the palm of *(slang)* • *corrupt societies where officials have to be paid off*
2 = dismiss, fire, sack *(informal)*, discharge, let go, lay off, give someone his *or* her P45 *(informal)*, kennet *(Austral. slang)*, jeff *(Austral. slang)* • *Most of the staff are being paid off at the end of the month.*
pay something back = repay, return, square, refund, reimburse, settle up • *I'll pay you back that money tomorrow.*
pay something off = settle, clear, square, discharge, liquidate, pay in full • *It would take him the rest of his life to pay off that loan.*
pay something out = spend, lay out *(informal)*, expend, cough up *(informal)*, shell out *(informal)*, disburse, fork out *or* over *or* up *(slang)* • *football clubs who pay out millions of pounds for players*
pay up = pay, fork out *(informal)*, stump up *(Brit. informal)*, make payment, pay in full, settle up, come up with the money • *We claimed a refund, but the company wouldn't pay up.*

PROVERBS
He who pays the piper calls the tune
You pays your money and you takes your choice

payable = due, outstanding, owed, owing, mature, to be paid, obligatory, receivable • *rates of interest payable on mortgages*
payment 1 = remittance, advance, deposit, premium, portion, instalment • *a deposit of £50, followed by three monthly payments of £15*
2 = settlement, paying, discharge, outlay, remittance, defrayal • *He sought payment of a sum which he claimed was owed to him.*
3 = wages, fee, reward, hire, remuneration • *It is reasonable to expect proper payment for this work.*
payoff 1 = bribe, incentive, cut *(informal)*, payment, sweetener *(informal)*, bung *(Brit. informal)*, inducement, kick-back *(informal)*, backhander *(informal)*, hush money *(informal)* • *payoffs from drugs exporters*
2 = settlement, payment, reward, payout, recompense • *a $1m divorce payoff*
3 = outcome, result, consequence, conclusion, climax, finale, culmination, the crunch *(informal)*, upshot, moment of truth, clincher *(informal)*, punch line • *The payoff of the novel is patently predictable.*

peace AS A NOUN **1 = truce**, ceasefire, treaty, armistice, pacification, conciliation, cessation of hostilities • *They hope the treaty will bring peace to Southeast Asia.*
OPPOSITES: war, warfare, hostilities
2 = stillness, rest, quiet, silence, calm, hush, tranquillity, seclusion, repose, calmness, peacefulness, quietude, restfulness • *All I want is a bit of peace and quiet.*
3 = serenity, calm, relaxation, composure, contentment, repose, equanimity, peacefulness, placidity, harmoniousness • *People always felt a sense of peace in her company.*
4 = harmony, accord, agreement, concord, amity • *a period of relative peace in the country's industrial relations*
▸ **IN PHRASES: hold your peace = say nothing**, be silent, keep quiet, hold your tongue • *He disagreed, but diplomatically held his peace.*
▸ **RELATED ADJECTIVE:** irenic *or* eirenic

QUOTATIONS
Peace hath her victories
No less renowned than war
[John Milton *Sonnet, To the Lord General Cromwell, May 1652*]
Let him who desires peace, prepare for war
[Vegetius *De Re Militari*]
Peace is not the absence of war. Lasting peace is rooted in justice
[David Trimble]
You can't separate peace from freedom because no one can be at peace unless he has his freedom
[Malcolm X *Prospects for Peace in 1965*]
If peace cannot be maintained with honour, it is no longer peace
[Lord John Russell *speech*]
In the arts of peace Man is a bungler
[George Bernard Shaw *Man and Superman*]
the peace of God, which passeth all understanding
[*Bible: Philippians*]
They shall beat their swords into ploughshares, and their spears into pruning-hooks
[*Bible: Isaiah*]
War makes rattling good history; but Peace is poor reading
[Thomas Hardy *The Dynasts*]
peace: in international affairs, a period of cheating between two periods of fighting
[Ambrose Bierce *The Devil's Dictionary*]

peaceable = peace-loving, friendly, gentle, peaceful, mild, conciliatory, amiable, pacific, amicable, placid, inoffensive, dovish, unwarlike, nonbelligerent • *Many normally peaceable people were outraged.*
peaceful 1 = at peace, friendly, harmonious, amicable, cordial, nonviolent, without hostility, free from strife, on friendly *or* good terms • *Their relations with most of these people were peaceful.*
OPPOSITES: warring, violent, hostile
2 = peace-loving, conciliatory, peaceable, placatory, irenic, pacific, unwarlike • *warriors who killed or enslaved the peaceful farmers*
OPPOSITES: belligerent, warlike
3 = calm, still, quiet, gentle, pleasant, soothing, tranquil, placid, restful, chilled *(informal)* • *a peaceful scene*
OPPOSITES: disturbed, loud, agitated
4 = serene, placid, undisturbed, untroubled, unruffled • *I felt relaxed and peaceful.*
peacefully 1 = without violence, cordially, amicably, harmoniously, peaceably, without disturbance • *The rally passed off peacefully.*
2 = quietly, soundly, calmly, serenely, placidly • *The baby was sleeping peacefully.*
peacemaker = mediator, appeaser, arbitrator, conciliator, pacifier, peacemonger • *his reputation as a statesman and peacemaker*

P

QUOTATIONS
Blessed are the peacemakers; for they shall be called the children of God
[*Bible: St. Matthew*]

peafowl
▸ RELATED ADJECTIVE: pavonine
▸ NAME OF MALE: peacock
▸ NAME OF FEMALE: peahen
▸ COLLECTIVE NOUN: muster

peak AS A NOUN 1 = **high point**, crown, climax, culmination, zenith, maximum point, apogee, acme, ne plus ultra *(Latin)* • *His career was at its peak when he died.*
2 = **point**, top, tip, summit, brow, crest, pinnacle, apex, aiguille • *the snow-covered peaks of the Alps*
3 = **mountain**, hill, fell, mount, ben *(Scot.)*, berg *(S. African)*, alp, tor, massif • *He climbed Scafell Pike, the highest peak in England.*
▸ AS A VERB = **culminate**, climax, come to a head, be at its height, reach its highest point, reach the zenith • *Temperatures have peaked at over 30 degrees Celsius.*

peaky = **off colour**, poorly *(informal)*, ill, sick, pale, crook *(Austral. & N.Z. informal)*, pinched, wan, sickly, unwell, emaciated, under the weather *(informal)*, in poor shape, like death warmed up *(informal)*, green about the gills, peelie-wally *(Scot.)* • *Are you feeling all right? You look a little peaky.*

peal AS A VERB = **ring**, sound, toll, resound, chime, resonate, tintinnabulate • *The church bells pealed at the stroke of midnight.*
▸ AS A NOUN 1 = **ring**, sound, ringing, clamour, chime, clang, carillon, tintinnabulation • *the great peals of the Abbey bells*
2 = **clap**, sound, crash, blast, roar, rumble, resounding, reverberation • *great peals of thunder*
3 = **roar**, fit, shout, scream, gale, howl, shriek, hoot • *She burst into peals of laughter.*

pearl
▸ RELATED ADJECTIVES: margaric, margaritic

pearly 1 = **iridescent**, mother-of-pearl, opalescent, nacreous, margaric, margaritic • *a suit covered with pearly buttons*
2 = **ivory**, creamy, milky, silvery • *pearly white teeth*

peasant 1 = **rustic**, countryman, hind *(obsolete)*, swain *(archaic)*, son of the soil, churl *(archaic)* • *land given to peasants for food production*
2 = **boor**, provincial, hick *(informal, chiefly U.S. & Canad.)*, lout, yokel, country bumpkin, hayseed *(U.S. & Canad. informal)*, churl • *Why should I let a lot of peasants traipse over my property?*

peccadillo = **misdeed**, slip, error, lapse, indiscretion, misdemeanour, infraction, petty sin, trifling fault • *extra-marital peccadilloes by public figures*

peck AS A VERB 1 = **pick**, bite, hit, strike, tap, poke, jab, prick, nibble • *The crow pecked his hand.*
2 = **kiss**, plant a kiss, give someone a smacker, give someone a peck *or* kiss • *She walked up to him and pecked him on the cheek.*
▸ AS A NOUN = **kiss**, smacker, osculation *(rare)* • *He gave me a peck on the lips.*

peculiar 1 = **odd**, strange, unusual, bizarre, funny, out-there *(slang)*, extraordinary, curious, weird, exceptional, eccentric, abnormal, out-of-the-way, queer, uncommon, singular, unconventional, far-out *(slang)*, quaint, off-the-wall *(slang)*, outlandish, offbeat, freakish, wacko *(slang)*, outré, daggy *(Austral. & N.Z. informal)* • *He has a very peculiar sense of humour.*
OPPOSITES: expected, usual, ordinary
2 = **special**, private, individual, personal, particular, unique, characteristic, distinguishing, distinct, signature, idiosyncratic • *He has his own peculiar way of doing things.*
OPPOSITES: general, common, unspecific
3 = **ill**, poorly, sick, crook *(Austral. & N.Z. informal)*, run down, washed out, unwell, nauseated, queasy, nauseous, off colour *(Brit.)*, under the weather *(informal)*, indisposed, peaky, wabbit *(Scot. informal)*, green about the gills, peely-wally *(Scot. informal)* • *All this has made me feel a bit peculiar.*
4 *with* **to** = **specific to**, characteristic of, restricted to, appropriate to, special to, unique to, particular to, endemic to, distinctive of • *surnames peculiar to this area*

peculiarity 1 = **oddity**, abnormality, eccentricity, weirdness, queerness, bizarreness, freakishness • *the peculiarity of her behaviour*
2 = **quirk**, caprice, mannerism, whimsy, foible, idiosyncrasy, odd trait • *He had many little peculiarities.*
3 = **characteristic**, mark, feature, quality, property, attribute, trait, speciality, singularity, distinctiveness, particularity • *a strange peculiarity of the Soviet system*

pecuniary = **monetary**, economic, financial, capital, commercial, fiscal, budgetary • *She denies obtaining a pecuniary advantage by deception.*

pedagogue = **teacher**, instructor, educator, pedant, dominie *(Scot.)*, dogmatist, master *or* mistress, schoolmaster *or* schoolmistress • *My grandfather was a born pedagogue; it gave him great pleasure to impart information.*

pedant 1 = **hairsplitter**, quibbler, doctrinaire, literalist, sophist, nit-picker *(informal)*, dogmatist, casuist, pettifogger • *We thought him a pedant and a bore.*
2 = **scholar**, academic, intellectual, scholastic, bookworm, egghead *(informal)*, pedagogue • *a cloistered pedant deeply immersed in the past*

pedantic 1 = **hairsplitting**, particular, formal, precise, fussy, picky *(informal)*, nit-picking *(informal)*, punctilious, priggish, pedagogic, anal retentive, overnice • *all his pedantic quibbles about grammar*
2 = **academic**, pompous, schoolmasterly, stilted, erudite, scholastic, didactic, bookish, abstruse, donnish, sententious • *His lecture was pedantic and uninteresting.*

pedantry 1 = **hairsplitting**, quibbling, pomposity, sophistry, punctiliousness, finickiness, pettifoggery, finicality, overnicety • *The results of the survey are exhaustive to the point of pedantry.*
2 = **stuffiness**, pomposity, intellectualism, pretentiousness, bookishness, donnishness, pedagogism • *The novel suffers from pedantry and dullness.*

QUOTATIONS
Pedantry is the dotage of knowledge
[Holbrook Jackson *Anatomy of Bibliomania*]

peddle 1 = **sell**, trade, push *(informal)*, market, hawk, flog *(slang)*, vend, huckster, sell door to door • *dealers peddling drugs*
2 = **promote**, publish, spread, broadcast, distribute, scatter, circulate, sow, disperse, diffuse, publicize, propagate, disseminate, promulgate • *biased newspapers peddling propaganda*

peddler *or* **pedlar** = **seller**, vendor, hawker, duffer *(dialect)*, huckster, door-to-door salesman, cheap-jack *(informal)*, colporteur • *drug peddlers* • *LA's ban on sidewalk peddlers*

pedestal AS A NOUN = **support**, stand, base, foot, mounting, foundation, pier, plinth, dado *(Architecture)*, socle • *a bronze statue on a granite pedestal*
▸ IN PHRASES: **put someone on a pedestal** = **worship**, dignify, glorify, exalt, idealize, ennoble, deify, apotheosize • *Since childhood, I put my parents on a pedestal.*

pedestrian AS A NOUN = **walker**, foot-traveller, footslogger • *In Los Angeles, a pedestrian is a rare spectacle.*
OPPOSITES: driver, motorist
▸ AS AN ADJECTIVE = **dull**, flat, ordinary, boring, commonplace, mundane, mediocre, plodding, banal, prosaic, run-of-the-mill, humdrum, unimaginative, uninteresting, uninspired, ho-hum *(informal)*, no great

P

shakes *(informal)*, half-pie *(N.Z. informal)* • *His style is so pedestrian that the book is really boring.*
OPPOSITES: interesting, important, exciting

pedigree AS A MODIFIER = **purebred**, thoroughbred, full-blooded • *A pedigree dog will never cost less than a three-figure sum.*
▸ AS A NOUN = **lineage**, family, line, race, stock, blood, breed, heritage, descent, extraction, ancestry, family tree, genealogy, derivation • *a countess of impeccable pedigree*

pedlar *see* **peddler**

pee AS A VERB = **urinate**, wee *(informal)*, piss *(taboo slang)*, tinkle *(Brit. informal)*, piddle *(informal)*, spend a penny *(Brit. informal)*, make water, pass water, wee-wee *(informal)*, take a leak *(slang)*, micturate, take a whizz *(slang, chiefly U.S.)* • *He desperately needed to pee.*
▸ AS A NOUN = **leak** *(informal)*, slash *(slang)*, wee *(informal)*, piss *(taboo slang)* • *The driver was probably having a pee.*

peek AS A VERB = **glance**, look, peer, spy, take a look, peep, eyeball *(slang)*, sneak a look, keek *(Scot.)*, snatch a glimpse, take *or* have a gander *(informal)* • *She peeked at him through a crack in the wall.*
▸ AS A NOUN = **glance**, look, glimpse, blink, peep, butcher's *(Brit. slang)*, gander *(informal)*, look-see *(slang)*, shufti *(Brit. slang)*, keek *(Scot.)* • *I had a quick peek into the bedroom.*

peel AS A NOUN = **rind**, skin, peeling, epicarp, exocarp • *grated lemon peel*
▸ AS A VERB = **skin**, scale, strip, pare, shuck, flake off, decorticate *(rare)*, take the skin *or* rind off • *She sat down and began peeling potatoes.*
▸ IN PHRASES: **peel something off = take off**, remove, discard, strip off, cast off, doff, divest yourself of • *He began to peel off his shirt.*

peep[1] AS A VERB 1 = **peek**, look, peer, spy, eyeball *(slang)*, sneak a look, steal a look, keek *(Scot.)*, look surreptitiously, look from hiding • *Now and then she peeped to see if he was watching her.*
2 = **appear briefly**, emerge, pop up, spring up, issue from, peer out, peek from, show partially • *Purple and yellow flowers peeped between the rocks.*
▸ AS A NOUN = **look**, glimpse, peek, butcher's *(Brit. slang)*, gander *(informal)*, look-see *(slang)*, shufti *(Brit. slang)*, keek *(Scot.)* • *He took a peep at his watch.*

peep[2] = **sound**, word, noise, utterance, cheep *(informal)* • *I don't want to hear another peep out of you tonight.*

peephole = **spyhole**, opening, hole, crack, slit, aperture, keyhole, chink, crevice, fissure, pinhole • *The guards checked at the peephole before entering the cell.*

peer[1] 1 = **noble**, lord, count, duke, earl, baron, aristocrat, viscount, marquess, marquis, nobleman, aristo *(informal)* • *He was made a life peer in 1981.*
2 = **equal**, like, match, fellow, contemporary, coequal, compeer • *His personality made him popular with his peers.*

peer[2] = **squint**, look, spy, gaze, scan, inspect, peep, peek, snoop, scrutinize, look closely • *He peered ahead and saw them on the causeway.* • *She peered at him sleepily over the bedclothes.*

peerage = **aristocracy**, peers, nobility, lords and ladies, titled classes • *the higher echelons of the British peerage*

QUOTATIONS
When I want a peerage, I shall buy it like an honest man
[Lord Northcliffe]

peerless = **unequalled**, excellent, unique, outstanding, unparalleled, superlative, unrivalled, second to none, incomparable, unmatched, unsurpassed, matchless, beyond compare, nonpareil • *a peerless German soprano*
OPPOSITES: poor, ordinary, mediocre

peeved = **irritated**, upset, annoyed, put out, hacked off *(U.S. slang)*, sore, pissed *(U.S. slang)*, galled, exasperated, nettled, vexed, pissed off *(taboo slang)*, irked, riled, piqued, tooshie *(Austral. slang)* • *Susan couldn't help feeling a little peeved.*

peevish = **irritable**, cross, crabbed, childish, acrimonious, crusty, snappy, grumpy, sullen, touchy, whingeing *(informal)*, surly, fractious, petulant, churlish, sulky, ill-tempered, cantankerous, tetchy, ratty *(Brit. & N.Z. informal)*, testy, chippy *(informal)*, fretful, short-tempered, waspish, querulous, huffy, splenetic, crotchety *(informal)*, shrewish, liverish, captious, pettish, ill-natured • *Lack of sleep always made him peevish.*
OPPOSITES: happy, sweet, good-natured

peg AS A NOUN = **pin**, spike, rivet, skewer, dowel, spigot • *He builds furniture using wooden pegs instead of nails.*
▸ AS A VERB 1 = **fasten**, join, fix, secure, attach, make fast • *trying to peg a sheet on to the washing line*
2 = **fix**, set, control, limit, freeze • *The bank wants to peg interest rates at 9%.*
▸ IN PHRASES: **take** *or* **bring someone down a peg (or two) = humble**, humiliate, put down *(slang)*, deflate, chasten, mortify, bring low, take the wind out of (someone's) sails • *It's time she was brought down a peg or two.*

pejorative = **derogatory**, negative, slighting, unpleasant, belittling, disparaging, debasing, deprecatory, uncomplimentary, depreciatory, detractive, detractory • *He used the word in a pejorative sense.*

pellet 1 = **bullet**, shot, buckshot, lead shot • *He was taken to hospital for treatment to pellet wounds.*
2 = **little ball**, little piece • *A beetle was rolling a pellet of dung up the hill.*

pell-mell AS AN ADVERB = **helter-skelter**, rashly, hastily, hurriedly, recklessly, full tilt, precipitously, impetuously, heedlessly, posthaste • *We all rushed pell-mell into the kitchen.*
▸ AS AN ADJECTIVE = **disorderly**, confused, chaotic, tumultuous, haphazard, disorganized • *a pell-mell stampede*

pelt[1] AS A VERB 1 = **shower**, beat, strike, pepper, batter, thrash, bombard, wallop *(informal)*, assail, pummel, hurl at, cast at, belabour, sling at • *Crowds started to pelt police cars with stones.*
2 = **pour**, teem, rain hard, bucket down *(informal)*, rain cats and dogs *(informal)* • *It's pelting down with rain out there.*
3 = **rush**, charge, shoot, career, speed, tear, belt *(slang)*, dash, hurry, barrel (along) *(informal, chiefly U.S. & Canad.)*, whizz *(informal)*, stampede, run fast, burn rubber *(informal)* • *She pelted down the stairs in her nightgown.*
▸ IN PHRASES: **full pelt** *or* **at full pelt = at top speed**, swiftly, very fast, at speed, very quickly, speedily, hell for leather *(informal)*, like lightning, hotfoot, like the clappers *(Brit. informal)*, like nobody's business *(informal)*, with all speed, like greased lightning *(informal)*, at *or* on the double • *Alice ran full pelt towards the emergency room.*

pelt[2] = **coat**, fell, skin, hide • *mink which had been bred for their pelts*

pen[3] = **write (down)**, draft, compose, pencil, draw up, scribble, take down, inscribe, scrawl, jot down, dash off, commit to paper • *She penned a short memo to his private secretary.*

QUOTATIONS
Beneath the rule of men entirely great
The pen is mightier than the sword
[Edward Bulwer-Lytton *Richelieu*]

pen[4] AS A NOUN = **enclosure**, pound, fold, cage, coop, hutch, corral *(chiefly U.S. & Canad.)*, sty • *a holding pen for sheep*
▸ AS A VERB = **enclose**, confine, cage, pound, mew (up), fence in, impound, hem in, coop up, hedge in, shut up *or* in • *The cattle had been milked and penned for the night.*

penal = **disciplinary**, punitive, corrective, penalizing, retributive • *an island that served as a penal colony*

penalize 1 = **punish**, discipline, correct, handicap, award a penalty against *(Sport)*, impose a penalty on • *Players who break the rules will be penalized.*

2 = **put at a disadvantage**, handicap, cause to suffer, unfairly disadvantage, inflict a handicap on • *Old people are being penalized for being pensioners.*

penalty 1 = **punishment**, price, fine, handicap, forfeit, retribution, forfeiture • *The maximum penalty is 7 years' imprisonment.*
2 = **disadvantage**, difficulty, handicap, drawback, snag, uphill *(S. African)*, downside, unpleasant aspect • *the penalty of being a girl*

penance AS A NOUN = **atonement**, punishment, penalty, reparation, expiation, sackcloth and ashes, self-punishment, self-mortification • *carrying out acts of penance for his sins* • *The penance imposed on him proved light.*
▸ IN PHRASES: **do penance** = **atone**, suffer, make amends, make reparation, accept punishment, show contrition, mortify yourself • *He is doing penance for a lifetime of crime.*

penchant = **liking**, taste, tendency, turn, leaning, bent, bias, inclination, affinity, disposition, fondness, propensity, predisposition, predilection, proclivity, partiality, proneness • *He had a penchant for playing jokes on people.*

pencil IN PHRASES: **pencil something** *or* **someone in** = **provisionally arrange**, make a provisional arrangement for, arrange tentatively, arrange subject to confirmation • *The tour was pencilled in for the following March.* • *I'll pencil you in for two this afternoon.*

pendant = **necklace**, medallion, locket • *a jade pendant on a slender gold chain*

pending AS AN ADJECTIVE 1 = **undecided**, unsettled, in the balance, up in the air, undetermined • *The cause of death was listed as pending.*
2 = **forthcoming**, imminent, prospective, impending, in the wind, in the offing • *Customers have been inquiring about the pending price rises.*
▸ AS A PREPOSITION = **awaiting**, until, waiting for, till • *The judge has suspended the ban, pending a full inquiry.*

pendulous = **hanging**, swinging, swaying, dangling, sagging, drooping, pendent • *a pendulous lower lip*

penetrate 1 = **pierce**, enter, go through, bore, probe, stab, prick, perforate, impale • *The needle penetrated the skin.*
2 = **pervade**, enter, permeate, filter through, suffuse, seep through, get in through, percolate through • *A cool breeze penetrated the mosquito netting.*
3 = **infiltrate**, enter, get in to, make inroads into, sneak in to *(informal)*, work *or* worm your way into • *They had managed to penetrate Soviet defences.*
4 = **grasp**, understand, work out, figure out *(informal)*, unravel, discern, comprehend, fathom, decipher, suss (out) *(slang)*, get to the bottom of • *long answers that were often difficult to penetrate*
5 = **be understood by**, touch, affect, impress on, come across to, become clear to, get through to • *His words penetrated her fuddled brain.*

penetrating 1 = **sharp**, harsh, piercing, carrying, piping, loud, intrusive, strident, shrill, high-pitched, ear-splitting • *Her voice was nasal and penetrating.*
OPPOSITES: sweet, dull, mild
2 = **pungent**, biting, strong, powerful, sharp, heady, pervasive, aromatic • *a most wonderful penetrating smell and taste*
3 = **piercing**, cutting, biting, sharp, freezing, fierce, stinging, frosty, bitterly cold, arctic • *A raw, penetrating wind was blowing in off the plain*
4 = **intelligent**, quick, sharp, keen, critical, acute, profound, discriminating, shrewd, discerning, astute, perceptive, incisive, sharp-witted, perspicacious, sagacious • *a penetrating mind*
OPPOSITES: stupid, dull, shallow
5 = **perceptive**, searching, sharp, keen, alert, probing, discerning • *a penetrating stare*
OPPOSITES: unperceptive

penetration 1 = **piercing**, entry, entrance, invasion, puncturing, incision, perforation • *the penetration of eggs by more than one sperm*
2 = **pervasion**, spreading, soaking, diffusion, infiltration, seepage • *the penetration of the ointment into the skin*
3 = **entry**, entrance, inroad • *US penetration of Japanese markets*

peninsula = **cape**, point, head, horn, bluff, mull *(Scot.)*, headland, promontory • *the Korean peninsula*

penis = **phallus**, dick *(taboo slang)*, prick *(derogatory slang)*, member, tool *(taboo slang)*, organ, cock *(taboo slang)*, wang *(U.S. slang)*, knob *(Brit. taboo slang)*, chopper *(Brit. slang)*, plonker *(slang)*, dong *(slang)*, winkle *(Brit. slang)*, joystick *(slang)*, pecker *(U.S. & Canad. taboo slang)*, John Thomas *(taboo slang)*, weenie *(U.S. slang)*, whang *(U.S. slang)*, tadger *(Brit. slang)*, schlong *(U.S. slang)*, willie *or* willy *(Brit. informal)*, tockley *(Austral. slang)* • *She made derogatory remarks about the size of his penis.*
▸ RELATED ADJECTIVE: penile
▸ RELATED MANIA: mentulomania

penitence = **repentance**, shame, regret, sorrow, remorse, contrition, compunction, self-reproach, ruefulness • *She hung her head in mock penitence.*

penitent = **repentant**, sorry, apologetic, abject, atoning, rueful, contrite, sorrowful, remorseful, regretful, conscience-stricken • *a penitent sinner*
OPPOSITES: callous, unrepentant, remorseless

pen name = **pseudonym**, nom de plume, allonym • *Eric Blair, better known by his pen name of George Orwell*

pennant = **flag**, jack, banner, ensign, streamer, burgee *(Nautical)*, pennon, banderole • *The second car was flying the Ghanaian pennant.*

penniless = **poor**, broke *(informal)*, bankrupt, impoverished, short, ruined, strapped *(slang)*, needy, cleaned out *(slang)*, destitute, poverty-stricken, down and out, skint *(Brit. slang)*, indigent, down at heel, impecunious, dirt-poor *(informal)*, on the breadline, flat broke *(informal)*, penurious, on your uppers, stony-broke *(Brit. slang)*, necessitous, in queer street, moneyless, without two pennies to rub together *(informal)*, without a penny to your name • *a penniless refugee*
OPPOSITES: rich, loaded *(slang)*, wealthy

penny IN PHRASES: **two** *or* **ten a penny** = **numerous**, widespread, abundant, ubiquitous, plentiful, very common, copious, numberless, thick on the ground, a dime a dozen *(U.S.)* • *Leggy blondes are two a penny in Hollywood.*

penny-pinching AS A NOUN = **meanness**, selfishness, parsimony, stinginess, miserliness, tight-fistedness, niggardliness, minginess *(Brit. informal)*, penuriousness • *He is well known for his eccentric penny-pinching.*
OPPOSITES: generosity
▸ AS AN ADJECTIVE = **mean**, close, near *(informal)*, frugal, stingy, scrimping, miserly, niggardly, tightfisted, Scrooge-like, tight-arse *(taboo slang)*, tight-arsed *(taboo slang)*, mingy *(Brit. informal)*, tight-ass *(U.S. taboo slang)*, tight-assed *(U.S. taboo slang)*, cheeseparing, snoep *(S. African informal)*, tight as a duck's arse *(taboo slang)* • *small-minded, penny-pinching administrators*
OPPOSITES: kind, liberal, generous

pension = **allowance**, benefit, welfare, annuity, superannuation • *struggling by on a widow's pension*

pensioner = **senior citizen**, retired person, retiree *(U.S.)*, old-age pensioner, O.A.P. • *the pensioners' fuel allowance*

pensive = **thoughtful**, serious, sad, blue *(informal)*, grave, sober, musing, preoccupied, melancholy, solemn, reflective, dreamy, wistful, mournful, contemplative, meditative, sorrowful, ruminative, in a brown study *(informal)*, cogitative • *He looked suddenly sombre and pensive.*
OPPOSITES: happy, active, carefree

pent-up = **suppressed**, checked, curbed, inhibited, held back, stifled, repressed, smothered, constrained, bridled, bottled up • *He still had a lot of pent-up anger to release.*

penury = **poverty**, want, need, privation, destitution, straitened circumstances, beggary, indigence, pauperism

people AS A PLURAL NOUN 1 = **persons**, humans, individuals, folk *(informal)*, men and women, human beings, humanity, mankind, mortals, the human race, Homo sapiens • *People should treat the planet with respect.*
2 = **the public**, the crowd, the masses, the general public, the mob, the herd, the grass roots, the rank and file, the multitude, the populace, the proletariat, the rabble, the plebs, the proles *(derogatory slang, chiefly Brit.)*, the commonalty, (the) hoi polloi • *the will of the people*
3 = **nation**, public, community, subjects, population, residents, citizens, folk, inhabitants, electors, populace, tax payers, citizenry, (general) public • *the people of Rome*
4 = **race**, tribe, ethnic group • *the native peoples of Central and South America*
5 = **family**, parents, relations, relatives, folk, folks *(informal)*, clan, kin, next of kin, kinsmen, nearest and dearest, kith and kin, your own flesh and blood, rellies *(Austral. slang)* • *My people still live in Ireland.*
▸ AS A VERB = **inhabit**, occupy, settle, populate, colonize • *a small town peopled by workers and families*

QUOTATIONS

The voice of the people is the voice of God
[Alcuin *Epistles*]

▹ *See panel* **Peoples**

pep AS A NOUN = **energy**, life, spirit, zip *(informal)*, vitality, animation, vigour, verve, high spirits, gusto, welly *(slang)*, get-up-and-go *(informal)*, brio, vivacity, liveliness, vim *(slang)* • *They need something to put the pep back in their lives.*
▸ IN PHRASES: **pep something** *or* **someone up** = **enliven**, inspire, stimulate, animate, exhilarate, quicken, invigorate, jazz up *(informal)*, vitalize, vivify • *an attempt to pep up your sex life*

pepper AS A NOUN = **seasoning**, flavour, spice • *Season the mixture with salt and pepper.*
▸ AS A VERB 1 = **pelt**, hit, shower, scatter, blitz, riddle, rake, bombard, assail, strafe, rain down on • *He was peppered with shrapnel.*
2 = **sprinkle**, spot, scatter, dot, stud, fleck, intersperse, speck, spatter, freckle, stipple, bespatter • *The road was peppered with glass.*

peppery = **hot**, fiery, spicy, pungent, highly seasoned, piquant • *A crisp green salad with a few peppery radishes.*
OPPOSITES: mild, bland, tasteless

perceive 1 = **see**, notice, note, identify, discover, spot, observe, remark, recognize, distinguish, glimpse, make out, pick out, discern, behold, catch sight of, espy, descry • *I perceived a number of changes*
2 = **understand**, sense, gather, get *(informal)*, know, see, feel, learn, realize, conclude, appreciate, grasp, comprehend, get the message about, deduce, apprehend, suss (out) *(slang)*, get the picture about • *He was beginning to perceive the true nature of their relationship.*
3 = **consider**, believe, judge, suppose, rate, deem, adjudge • *How real do you perceive this threat to be?*

perceptible = **noticeable**, clear, obvious, apparent, visible, evident, distinct, tangible, blatant, conspicuous, palpable, discernible, recognizable, detectable, observable, appreciable, perceivable • *There was a perceptible silence, momentary but definite.*
OPPOSITES: hidden, concealed, imperceptible

perception 1 = **awareness**, understanding, sense, impression, feeling, idea, taste, notion, recognition, observation, consciousness, grasp, sensation, conception, apprehension • *how our perception of death affects the way we live*
2 = **understanding**, intelligence, observation, discrimination, insight, sharpness, cleverness, keenness, shrewdness, acuity, discernment, perspicacity, astuteness, incisiveness, perceptiveness, quick-wittedness, perspicuity • *It did not require a great deal of perception to realise what he meant.*

perceptive = **observant**, acute, intelligent, discerning, quick, aware, sharp, sensitive, alert, penetrating, discriminating, shrewd, responsive, astute, intuitive, insightful, percipient, perspicacious • *a very perceptive critique of Wordsworth*
OPPOSITES: stupid, dull, obtuse

perch[1] AS A VERB 1 = **sit**, rest, balance, settle • *He perched on the corner of the desk.*
2 = **place**, put, rest, balance • *His glasses were perched precariously on his head.*
3 = **land**, alight, roost • *A blackbird perched on the parapet outside the window.*
▸ AS A NOUN = **resting place**, post, branch, pole, roost • *The canary fell off its perch.*

perch[2]
▸ RELATED ADJECTIVE: percoid

perchance = **perhaps**, probably, maybe, possibly, by chance, mayhap *(archaic)*, peradventure *(archaic)*, for all you know, haply *(archaic)* • *Are we, perchance, overlooking one small detail?*

percolate 1 = **penetrate**, filter, seep, pervade, permeate, transfuse • *These truths begin to percolate through our minds.*
2 = **filter**, brew, perk *(informal)* • *the machine I use to percolate my coffee*
3 = **seep**, strain, drain, filter, penetrate, drip, leach, ooze, pervade, permeate, filtrate • *Water cannot percolate through the clay.*

perdition = **damnation**, hell, ruin, destruction, doom, condemnation, downfall, hellfire, everlasting punishment • *He alleged that the film would lead young souls into perdition.*

peregrination 1 = **journey**, tour, trip, exploration, trek, expedition, voyage, odyssey • *their wild peregrinations up and down the Rio Grande*
2 = **travelling**, wandering, trekking, roaming, roving, globetrotting, wayfaring • *De Quincy's intoxicated peregrinations around London*

peremptory 1 = **imperious**, arbitrary, assertive, authoritative, autocratic, dictatorial, dogmatic, bossy *(informal)*, intolerant, domineering, overbearing, high-handed • *He treated his colleagues in a peremptory manner.*
2 = **incontrovertible**, final, binding, commanding, absolute, compelling, decisive, imperative, obligatory, undeniable, categorical, irrefutable • *He had obtained a peremptory court order for his children's return.*

perennial = **continual**, lasting, continuing, permanent, constant, enduring, chronic, persistent, abiding, lifelong, perpetual, recurrent, never-ending, incessant, unchanging, inveterate • *the perennial urban problems of drugs and homelessness*

perfect AS AN ADJECTIVE 1 = **faultless**, correct, pure, accurate, faithful, impeccable, exemplary, flawless, foolproof, blameless • *Nobody's perfect.* • *He spoke perfect English.*
OPPOSITES: flawed, faulty, deficient
2 = **excellent**, ideal, supreme, superb, splendid, sublime, superlative • *This is a perfect time to buy a house.*
3 = **immaculate**, impeccable, flawless, spotless, unblemished, untarnished, unmarred • *The car is in perfect condition.*
OPPOSITES: damaged, ruined, flawed
4 = **complete**, absolute, sheer, utter, consummate, out-and-out, unadulterated, unmitigated, unalloyed • *She behaved like a perfect fool.*
OPPOSITES: partial, unfinished, incomplete

P

PEOPLES

African peoples

- Bantu
- Barotse
- Basotho
- Berber
- Bushman
- Chewa
- Damara
- Dinka
- Duala
- Edo
- Eritrean
- Ethiopian
- Ewe
- Gabonese
- Galla
- Gambian
- Ghanaian
- Griqua
- Hausa
- Herero
- Hottentot
- Hutu
- Ibibio
- Ibo
- Kabyle
- Kikuyu
- Kongo
- Luba
- Luo
- Malinke
- Masai
- Matabele
- Moor
- Mosotho
- Mossi
- Nama
- Ndebele
- Negrillo
- Negro
- Nguni
- Nuba
- Nupe
- Nyanja
- Nyoro
- Ovambo
- Pondo
- Pygmy
- Rif
- Shangaan
- Shluh
- Shona
- Somali
- Songhai
- Sotho
- Strandloper
- Susu
- Swahili
- Swazi
- Temne
- Tiv
- Tsonga
- Tswana
- Tuareg
- Tunisian
- Tutsi
- Venda
- Watusi
- Wolof
- Xhosa
- Yoruba
- Zulu

Asian peoples

- Adivasi
- Ainu
- Akkadian
- Amalekite
- Amorite
- Andamanese
- Arab
- Babylonian
- Bakhtyari
- Baluchi
- Bashkir
- Bedouin
- Bengali
- Bihari
- Burmese
- Buryat
- Chaldean
- Cham
- Chinese
- Chukchee
- Chuvash
- Cossack
- Cumans
- Dani
- Dard
- Dyak
- Elamite
- Ephesian
- Ephraimite
- Essene
- Evenki
- Fulani
- Gond
- Gujarati
- Gurkha
- Hittite
- Hui
- Hun
- Hurrian
- Igorot
- Israeli
- Jat
- Jewish
- Kabardian
- Kalmuck
- Kanarese
- Kara-Kalpak
- Karen
- Kashmiri
- Kassite
- Kazakh
- Khmer
- Kurd
- Lao
- Lepcha
- Lycian
- Lydian
- Malay
- Maratha
- Mede
- Mishmi
- Mon
- Mongol
- Montagnard
- Moro
- Motu
- Munda
- Naga
- Negrito
- Nogay
- Nuri *or* Kafir
- Palestinian
- Pathan *or* Pashto
- Phoenician
- Punjabi
- Sabaean
- Samoyed
- Saracen
- Semite
- Shan
- Sherpa
- Sindhi
- Sinhalese
- Sogdian
- Sumerian
- Tadzhik
- Tagalog
- Talaing
- Tamil
- Tatar
- Thai
- Tocharian
- Tongan
- Tungus
- Turanian
- Turk
- Turkmen
- Uigur
- Uzbek
- Vedda
- Visayan
- Yakut

Australasian peoples

- Aborigine
- Aranda
- Dayak
- Gurindji
- Māori
- Melanesian
- Polynesian
- Tagalog

Central and South American Indian peoples

- Araucanian
- Arawakan
- Aymara
- Aztec
- Carib
- Cashinahua
- Chibca
- Chimú
- Ge
- Guarani
- Inca
- Makuna
- Maya
- Mixtec
- Nahuatl
- Quechua
- Toltec
- Tupi
- Zapotec

Eskimo peoples

- Aleut
- Caribou Eskimo
- Inuit
- Yupik

European peoples

- Achaean
- Aeolian
- Albanian
- Alemanni
- Andalusian
- Angle
- Anglo-Norman
- Anglo-Saxon
- Aragonese
- Armenian
- Aryan
- Ashkenazi
- Austrian
- Azerbaijani *or* Azeri
- Azorean
- Basque
- Bavarian
- Belgae
- Belorussian
- Bosnian Muslim
- Breton
- Briton
- Brython
- Bulgar
- Bulgarian
- Burgundian
- Carinthian
- Castilian
- Catalan
- Celt
- Celtiberi
- Chechen
- Cheremis
- Cimbri
- Cornish
- Corsican
- Croatian
- Cymry
- Czech
- Dane
- Dorian
- Dutch
- English
- Faeroese
- Finn
- Ephesian
- Estonian
- Etruscan
- Fleming
- Frank
- French
- Frisian
- Gaelic
- Galician
- Gascon
- Gaul
- Georgian
- German
- Goidel
- Goth
- Greek
- Gypsy
- Hellenic
- Iberian *or* Celtiberian
- Icelandic
- Iceni
- Illyrian
- Indo-European
- Ingush
- Ionian
- Irish
- Jute
- Karelian
- Komi
- Latin
- Lapp
- Latvian
- Lithuanian
- Lombard *or* Langobard
- Lusatian
- Luxembourger
- Macedonian
- Magyar
- Maltese
- Manx
- Montenegrin
- Mordvin
- Norman
- Norse
- Norwegian
- Ostrogoth
- Ostyak
- Pict
- Pole
- Portuguese
- Provençal
- Prussian
- Romanian
- Russian
- Sabellian
- Sabine
- Salain
- Samnite
- Samoyed
- Sardinian
- Saxon

EUROPEAN PEOPLES (CONTINUED)

Scot	Silures	Swabian	Turk	Viking	Walloon
Scythian	Slav	Swede	Tyrolese	Visigoth	Welsh
Sephardi	Slovak	Swiss	Ugrian	Vlach *or* Walach	Wend
Serbian	Slovene	Teuton	Ukrainian	Volsci	
Sicilian	Sorb	Thracian	Vandal	Votyak	

NATIVE AMERICAN TRIBES

Abnaki	Cayuga	Hupa	Mixtec	Paiute	Sioux
Aguaruna	Cherokee	Huron	Mohawk	Pasamaquoddy	Stonies
Algonquian	Cheyenne	Illinois	Mohegan	Pawnee	Susquehanna
Algonquin	Chickasaw	Inca	Mohican	Penobscot	Teton
Apache	Chilcal	Iowa	Mojave	Pequot	Tlingit
Apalachee	Chinook	Iroquois	Moki	Pericu	Toltec
Arapaho	Chippewa	Kansa	Montagnard	Piegan	Tonkawa
Araucan	Choctaw	Karankawa	Muskogean	Pima	Tuscarora
Arikara	Cocopa	Kichai	Nahuatl	Powhatan	Ute
Ashochimi	Comanche	Kickapoo	Narraganset	Pueblo	Wappo
Assiniboine	Cree	Kiowa	Natchez	Quakaw	Warrau
Athabascan	Creek	Kootenay	Navajo	Quechua	Wichita
Aymara	Crow	Kwakiutl	Nez Percé	Root-digger	Winnebago
Aztec	Dakota	Leni-Lenapé	Nootka	Salish	Wyandot
Bella Coola	Delaware	Lipan	Ojibwa	Santee	Yaqui
Biloxi	Dene	Mandan	Omaha	Sarcee	Yuchi
Blackfoot	Dogrib	Mapuche	Oneida	Sauk	Yuma
Blood	Flathead	Maya	Onondaga	Seminole	Yunca
Caddo	Fox	Menomini	Orejone	Seneca	Zuni
Campa	Haida	Miami	Osage	Shawnee	
Carib	Hidatsa	Micmac	Ostiak	Shoshoni	
Catawba	Hopi	Minnetaree	Ottawa	Shushwap	

5 = **exact**, true, accurate, precise, right, close, correct, strict, faithful, spot-on *(Brit. informal)*, on the money *(U.S.)*, unerring • *She spoke in a perfect imitation of her father's voice.*

6 = **expert**, experienced, finished, skilled, masterly, polished, practised, accomplished, tasty *(Brit. informal)*, skilful, adept • *a perfect performance*

OPPOSITES: bad, poor, inferior

▸ AS A VERB = **improve**, develop, polish, elaborate, refine, cultivate, hone • *He worked hard to perfect his drawing technique.*

OPPOSITES: mar

perfection 1 = **excellence**, integrity, superiority, purity, wholeness, sublimity, exquisiteness, faultlessness, flawlessness, perfectness, immaculateness • *the quest for physical perfection*

2 = **the ideal**, the crown, the last word, one in a million *(informal)*, a paragon, the crème de la crème, the acme, a nonpareil, the beau idéal • *She seems to be perfection itself.*

3 = **accomplishment**, achieving, achievement, polishing, evolution, refining, completion, realization, fulfilment, consummation • *the woman credited with the perfection of this technique*

4 = **exactness**, precision, correctness, exactitude, exactness, meticulousness, preciseness • *the mathematical perfection of a Bach fugue*

QUOTATIONS

Perfection is the child of Time

[Bishop Joseph Hall *Works*]

perfectionist = **stickler**, purist, formalist, precisionist, precisian • *the perfectionist's eye for detail*

perfectly 1 = **completely**, totally, entirely, absolutely, quite, fully, altogether, thoroughly, wholly, utterly, consummately, every inch • *These mushrooms are perfectly safe to eat.*

OPPOSITES: partially, mistakenly, inaccurately

2 = **flawlessly**, ideally, wonderfully, superbly, admirably, supremely, to perfection, exquisitely, superlatively, impeccably, like a dream, faultlessly • *The system worked perfectly.*

OPPOSITES: badly, poorly, imperfectly

perfidious = **treacherous**, dishonest, false, corrupt, unfaithful, two-faced, disloyal, deceitful, faithless, untrustworthy, double-dealing, traitorous, double-faced, treasonous, recreant *(archaic)* • *She says that politicians are a perfidious breed.*

perfidy = **treachery**, betrayal, infidelity, treason, deceit, duplicity, disloyalty, double-dealing, falsity, faithlessness, perfidiousness • *He cited many examples to illustrate the perfidy of his adversaries.*

perforate = **pierce**, hole, bore, punch, drill, penetrate, puncture, honeycomb • *The table was perforated by a series of small holes.*

perforce = **necessarily**, inevitably, of necessity, unavoidably, willy-nilly, by necessity, needs must, without choice, by force of circumstances • *He had, perforce, to be content with being second.*

perform 1 = **do**, achieve, carry out, effect, complete, satisfy, observe, fulfil, accomplish, execute, bring about, pull off, act out, transact • *people who have performed outstanding acts of bravery*

2 = **fulfil**, carry out, execute, discharge • *Each part of the engine performs a different function.*

3 = **present**, act (out), stage, play, produce, represent, put on, render, depict, enact, appear as • *students performing Shakespeare's Macbeth*

4 = **appear on stage**, act • *He began performing in the early fifties.*

5 = **function**, go, work, run, operate, handle, respond, behave • *This car performs well.*

performance 1 = **presentation**, playing, acting (out), staging, production, exhibition, interpretation, representation, rendering, portrayal, rendition • *They are giving a performance of Bizet's Carmen.*

2 = **show**, appearance, concert, gig *(informal)*, recital • *The band did three performances at the Royal Albert Hall.*
3 = **work**, acts, conduct, exploits, feats • *The study looked at the performance of 18 surgeons.*
4 = **functioning**, running, operation, working, action, behaviour, capacity, efficiency, capabilities • *What is the car's performance like?*
5 = **carrying out**, practice, achievement, discharge, execution, completion, accomplishment, fulfilment, consummation • *the performance of his duties*
6 = **carry-on** *(informal, chiefly Brit.)*, business, to-do, act, scene, display, bother, fuss, pantomime *(informal, chiefly Brit.)*, song and dance *(informal)*, palaver, rigmarole, pother • *She made a big performance of cooking the dinner.*

QUOTATIONS
The only true performance is the one which attains madness
[Mick Jagger]

performer = **artiste**, player, Thespian, trouper, play-actor, actor *or* actress • *A performer played classical selections on the violin.*

perfume 1 = **fragrance**, scent, essence, incense, cologne, eau de toilette, eau de cologne, attar • *The room smelled of her mother's perfume.*
2 = **scent**, smell, fragrance, bouquet, aroma, odour, sweetness, niff *(Brit. slang)*, redolence, balminess • *the perfume of roses*

perfumed = **scented**, smelling, fragranced, fragrant, aromatic • *sweetly-perfumed yellow flowers*

perfunctory = **offhand**, routine, wooden, automatic, stereotyped, mechanical, indifferent, careless, superficial, negligent, sketchy, unconcerned, cursory, unthinking, slovenly, heedless, slipshod, inattentive • *She gave the list only a perfunctory glance.*
OPPOSITES: spirited, keen, thorough

perhaps = **maybe**, possibly, it may be, it is possible (that), conceivably, as the case may be, perchance *(archaic)*, feasibly, for all you know, happen *(Northern English dialect)* • *Perhaps you're right.*

peril 1 = **danger**, risk, threat, hazard, menace, jeopardy, perilousness • *sailors in peril on the sea*
2 *often plural* = **pitfall**, problem, risk, hazard • *the perils of starring in a TV commercial*
OPPOSITES: security, safety, certainty

perilous = **dangerous**, threatening, exposed, vulnerable, risky, unsure, hazardous, hairy *(slang)*, unsafe, precarious, parlous *(archaic)*, fraught with danger, chancy *(informal)* • *a perilous journey across the war-zone*

perimeter = **boundary**, edge, border, bounds, limit, margin, confines, periphery, borderline, circumference, ambit • *They walked round the perimeter of the stadium.*
OPPOSITES: centre, heart, middle

period 1 = **time**, term, season, space, run, stretch, spell, phase, patch *(Brit. informal)*, interval, span • *a period of a few months*
2 = **age**, generation, years, time, days, term, stage, date, cycle, era, epoch, aeon • *the Victorian period*
3 = **class**, session, lesson • *a Biology period*

periodic = **recurrent**, regular, repeated, occasional, periodical, seasonal, cyclical, sporadic, intermittent, every so often, infrequent, cyclic, every once in a while, spasmodic, at fixed intervals • *Periodic checks are made to ensure quality.*

periodical AS A NOUN = **publication**, paper, review, magazine, journal, weekly, monthly, organ, serial, quarterly, zine *(informal)* • *The walls were lined with books and periodicals.*
▸ AS AN ADJECTIVE = **recurrent**, regular, repeated, occasional, seasonal, cyclical, sporadic, intermittent, every so often, infrequent, cyclic, every once in a while, spasmodic, at fixed intervals • *periodical fits of depression*

peripatetic = **travelling**, wandering, roaming, migrant, mobile, roving, nomadic, itinerant, vagrant, vagabond, ambulant • *Her father was in the army and the family led a peripatetic existence.*

peripheral 1 = **secondary**, beside the point, minor, marginal, irrelevant, superficial, unimportant, incidental, tangential, inessential • *That information is peripheral to the main story.*
2 = **outermost**, outside, external, outer, exterior, borderline, perimetric • *development in the peripheral areas of large towns*

periphery = **boundary**, edge, border, skirt, fringe, verge, brink, outskirts, rim, hem, brim, perimeter, circumference, outer edge, ambit • *Geographically, the UK is on the periphery of Europe.*

perish 1 = **die**, be killed, be lost, expire, pass away, lose your life, decease, cark it *(Austral. & N.Z. slang)* • *the ferry disaster in which 193 passengers perished*
2 = **be destroyed**, fall, decline, collapse, disappear, vanish, go under • *Civilizations do eventually decline and perish.*
3 = **rot**, waste away, break down, decay, wither, disintegrate, decompose, moulder • *The rubber lining had perished.*

perishable = **short-lived**, biodegradable, easily spoilt, decomposable, liable to rot • *perishable food like fruit and vegetables*
OPPOSITES: lasting, durable, non-perishable

perjure yourself = **commit perjury**, lie under oath, forswear, bear false witness, give false testimony, swear falsely • *Witnesses lied and perjured themselves.*

perjury = **lying under oath**, false statement, forswearing, bearing false witness, giving false testimony, false oath, oath breaking, false swearing, violation of an oath, wilful falsehood • *The witness is now facing charges of perjury.*

perk = **bonus**, benefit, extra, plus, dividend, icing on the cake, fringe benefit, perquisite, boot money *(informal)* • *a company car, private medical insurance and other perks*

perk up AS A VERB = **cheer up**, recover, rally, revive, look up, brighten, take heart, recuperate, buck up *(informal)* • *She perked up and began to laugh.*
▸ IN PHRASES: **perk something** *or* **someone up** = **liven someone up**, revive someone, cheer someone up, pep someone up • *A brisk stroll will perk you up.*

perky = **lively**, spirited, bright, sunny, cheerful, animated, upbeat *(informal)*, buoyant, bubbly, cheery, bouncy, genial, jaunty, chirpy *(informal)*, sprightly, vivacious, in fine fettle, full of beans *(informal)*, gay, bright-eyed and bushy-tailed *(informal)* • *Graham was looking as perky as ever.*

permanence = **continuity**, survival, stability, duration, endurance, immortality, durability, finality, perpetuity, constancy, continuance, dependability, permanency, fixity, indestructibility, fixedness, lastingness, perdurability *(rare)* • *The permanence of the peace treaty has been threatened by their actions.*

permanent 1 = **lasting**, fixed, constant, enduring, persistent, eternal, abiding, perennial, durable, perpetual, everlasting, unchanging, immutable, indestructible, immovable, invariable, imperishable, unfading • *Heavy drinking can cause permanent damage to the brain.*
OPPOSITES: changing, passing, temporary
2 = **long-term**, established, secure, stable, steady, long-lasting • *a permanent job*
OPPOSITES: temporary, casual

permanently = **for ever**, constantly, continually, always, invariably, perennially, persistently, eternally, perpetually, steadfastly, indelibly, in perpetuity, enduringly, unwaveringly, immutably, lastingly, immovably, abidingly, unchangingly, unfadingly • *His face seemed permanently fixed in a scowl.*
OPPOSITES: briefly, temporarily, momentarily

P

permeable = **penetrable**, porous, absorbent, spongy, absorptive, pervious • *materials which are permeable to air and water*

permeate 1 = **infiltrate**, fill, pass through, pervade, filter through, spread through, diffuse throughout • *Bias against women permeates every level of the judicial system.*
2 = **pervade**, saturate, charge, fill, pass through, penetrate, infiltrate, imbue, filter through, spread through, impregnate, seep through, percolate, soak through, diffuse throughout • *The water will eventually permeate through the surrounding concrete.*

permissible = **permitted**, acceptable, legitimate, legal, all right, sanctioned, proper, authorized, lawful, allowable, kosher *(informal)*, admissible, legit *(slang)*, licit, O.K. *or* okay *(informal)* • *He said it was not permissible to postpone the case any longer.*
OPPOSITES: banned, illegal, forbidden

permission = **authorization**, sanction, licence, approval, leave, freedom, permit, go-ahead *(informal)*, liberty, consent, allowance, tolerance, green light, assent, dispensation, carte blanche, blank cheque, sufferance • *They cannot leave the country without permission.* • *Women and children have been given permission to leave.*
OPPOSITES: ban, prohibition, veto

permissive = **tolerant**, liberal, open-minded, indulgent, easy-going, free, lax, lenient, forbearing, acquiescent, latitudinarian, easy-oasy *(slang)* • *Younger people are more likely to be permissive of sex and drugs.*
OPPOSITES: strict, forbidding, rigid

permit **AS A VERB** 1 = **allow**, admit, grant, sanction, let, suffer, agree to, entitle, endure, license, endorse, warrant, tolerate, authorize, empower, consent to, give the green light to, give leave *or* permission • *I was permitted to bring my camera into the concert.* • *The German constitution does not permit the sending of troops.*
OPPOSITES: ban, prohibit, forbid
2 = **enable**, let, allow, cause • *This method of cooking permits the heat to penetrate evenly.*
▸ **AS A NOUN** = **licence**, pass, document, certificate, passport, visa, warrant, authorization • *He has to apply for a permit before looking for a job.*
OPPOSITES: ban, prohibition, veto

permutation = **transformation**, change, shift, variation, modification, alteration, mutation, transmutation, transposition • *an infinite variety of permutations*

pernicious = **wicked**, bad, damaging, dangerous, evil, offensive, fatal, deadly, destructive, harmful, poisonous, malicious, malign, malignant, detrimental, hurtful, malevolent, noxious, venomous, ruinous, baleful, deleterious, injurious, noisome, baneful *(archaic)*, pestilent, maleficent • *the pernicious effects of alcoholism*

pernickety = **fussy**, particular, careful, exacting, carping, painstaking, fastidious, picky *(informal)*, nit-picking *(informal)*, finicky, punctilious, anal retentive, difficult to please, hairsplitting, overprecise, nit-picky *(informal)* • *He's very pernickety about neatness.*
OPPOSITES: slack, careless, sloppy

peroration 1 = **summing-up**, conclusion, recapping *(informal)*, reiteration, recapitulation, closing remarks • *The minister had begun his final peroration.*
2 = **speech**, address, lecture, sermon, diatribe, harangue, spiel *(informal)*, disquisition • *He launched into another peroration against gays.*

perpendicular 1 = **upright**, straight, vertical, plumb, on end • *the perpendicular wall of sandstone*
2 = **steep**, sheer, precipitous, vertiginous • *a narrow, exposed beach and perpendicular cliffs*
3 = **at right angles**, at 90 degrees • *The left wing dipped until it was perpendicular to the ground.*

perpetrate = **commit**, do, perform, carry out, effect, be responsible for, execute, inflict, bring about, enact, wreak • *What kind of person perpetrated this crime?*

perpetual 1 = **everlasting**, permanent, endless, eternal, lasting, enduring, abiding, perennial, infinite, immortal, never-ending, unending, unchanging, undying, sempiternal *(literary)* • *the regions of perpetual night at the lunar poles*
OPPOSITES: passing, brief, temporary
2 = **continual**, repeated, constant, endless, continuous, persistent, perennial, recurrent, never-ending, uninterrupted, interminable, incessant, ceaseless, unremitting, unfailing, unceasing • *her perpetual complaints*
OPPOSITES: passing, brief, temporary

perpetuate = **maintain**, preserve, sustain, keep up, keep going, continue, keep alive, immortalize, eternalize • *This image is a myth perpetuated by the media.*
OPPOSITES: end, forget, destroy

perpetuity **IN PHRASES:** **in perpetuity** = **for ever**, for good, permanently, for keeps *(informal)*, for all time, for eternity, for always • *The US Government gave the land to the tribe in perpetuity.*

perplex = **puzzle**, confuse, stump, baffle, bewilder, muddle, confound, beset, mystify, faze, befuddle, flummox, bemuse, dumbfound, nonplus, mix you up • *problems that perplexed me*

perplexed = **puzzled**, confused, stumped, baffled, bewildered, mixed up, muddled, bemused, confounded, mystified, fazed, dumbfounded, nonplussed, befuddled, flummoxed • *She is perplexed about what to do for her daughter.*

perplexing = **puzzling**, complex, confusing, complicated, involved, hard, taxing, difficult, strange, weird, mysterious, baffling, bewildering, intricate, enigmatic, mystifying, inexplicable, thorny, paradoxical, unaccountable, knotty, labyrinthine • *The procedure is perplexing at the best of times.*

perplexity 1 = **puzzlement**, confusion, bewilderment, incomprehension, bafflement, mystification, stupefaction • *There was utter perplexity in both their expressions.*
2 *usually plural* = **complexity**, difficulty, mystery, involvement, puzzle, paradox, obscurity, enigma, intricacy, inextricability • *the perplexities of quantum mechanics*
3 = **difficulty**, dilemma, snarl, fix *(informal)*, uphill *(S. African)*, how-do-you-do *(informal)*, can of worms *(informal)*, knotty problem • *My chief perplexity was how to interpret the words.*

perquisite = **bonus**, benefit, extra, plus, dividend, perk *(Brit. informal)*, icing on the cake, fringe benefit, boot money *(informal)* • *Free long-distance calls were a perquisite of the job.*

per se = **in itself**, essentially, as such, in essence, by itself, of itself, by definition, intrinsically, by its very nature • *I'm not opposed to capital punishment per se.*

persecute 1 = **victimize**, hunt, injure, pursue, torture, hound, torment, martyr, oppress, pick on, molest, ill-treat, maltreat • *They have been persecuted for their beliefs.*
OPPOSITES: back, support, mollycoddle
2 = **harass**, bother, annoy, bait, tease, worry, hassle *(informal)*, badger, pester, vex, be on your back *(slang)* • *He described his first wife as constantly persecuting him.*
OPPOSITES: let alone, leave alone

persecution = **victimization**, abuse, torture, torment, oppression, tyranny, discrimination against, mistreatment, ill-treatment, maltreatment, tyrannization • *the persecution of minorities*

perseverance = **persistence**, resolution, determination, dedication, stamina, endurance, tenacity, diligence, constancy, steadfastness, doggedness, purposefulness, pertinacity, indefatigability, sedulity • *Perseverance will pay off in the end.*

QUOTATIONS

If at first you don't succeed,
Try, try, try again
[William E. Hickson *Try and Try Again*]

The best way out is always through
[Robert Frost *A Servant to Servants*]

persevere = **keep going**, continue, go on, carry on, endure, hold on *(informal)*, hang on, persist, stand firm, plug away *(informal)*, hold fast, remain firm, stay the course, keep your hand in, pursue your goal, be determined *or* resolved, keep on *or* at, stick at *or* to • *the ability to persevere despite obstacles and setbacks*
OPPOSITES: give up, quit, give in

persist 1 = **continue**, last, remain, carry on, endure, keep up, linger, abide • *Consult your doctor if the symptoms persist.*
2 = **persevere**, continue, go on, carry on, hold on *(informal)*, keep on, keep going, press on, not give up, stand firm, soldier on *(informal)*, stay the course, plough on, be resolute, stick to your guns *(informal)*, show determination, crack on *(informal)* • *He urged them to persist with their efforts to bring about peace.*

persistence = **determination**, resolution, pluck, stamina, grit, endurance, tenacity, diligence, perseverance, constancy, steadfastness, doggedness, pertinacity, indefatigability, tirelessness • *Skill comes only with practice, patience and persistence.*

persistent 1 = **continuous**, constant, relentless, lasting, repeated, endless, perpetual, continual, never-ending, interminable, unrelenting, incessant, unremitting • *flooding caused by persistent rain*
OPPOSITES: occasional, irregular, periodic
2 = **determined**, dogged, fixed, steady, enduring, stubborn, persevering, resolute, tireless, tenacious, steadfast, obstinate, indefatigable, immovable, assiduous, obdurate, stiff-necked, unflagging, pertinacious • *He phoned again this morning – he's very persistent.*
OPPOSITES: yielding, flexible, irresolute

persistently 1 = **continuously**, always, constantly, invariably, continually, twenty-four-seven *(informal)* • *The trains are persistently late.*
2 = **determinedly**, steadily, resolutely, doggedly, single-mindedly • *Rachel gently but persistently imposed her will on her husband.*

person AS A NOUN = **individual**, being, body, human, soul, creature, human being, mortal, living soul, man *or* woman • *He's the only person who can do the job.*
▸ IN PHRASES: **in person** 1 = **personally**, yourself • *She collected the award in person.*
2 = **in the flesh**, actually, physically, bodily • *It was the first time she had seen him in person.*

QUOTATIONS
A person is a person because he recognizes others as persons
[Desmond Tutu *speech at enthronement as Anglican archbishop of Cape Town*]

persona = **personality**, part, face, front, role, character, mask, façade, public face, assumed role • *the contradictions between her private life and her public persona*

personable = **pleasant**, pleasing, nice, attractive, charming, handsome, good-looking, winning, agreeable, amiable, affable, presentable, likable *or* likeable • *an attractive and personable man*
OPPOSITES: ugly, unpleasant, unattractive

personage = **personality**, celebrity, big name, somebody, worthy, notable, public figure, dignitary, luminary, celeb *(informal)*, big shot *(informal)*, megastar *(informal)*, big noise *(informal)*, well-known person, V.I.P. • *MPs, film stars and other important personages*

personal 1 = **own**, special, private, individual, particular, peculiar, privy • *That's my personal property!*
2 = **individual**, special, particular, exclusive • *I'll give it my personal attention.*
3 = **private**, intimate, confidential • *prying into his personal life*
4 = **offensive**, critical, slighting, nasty, insulting, rude, belittling, disparaging, derogatory, disrespectful, pejorative • *a series of personal comments about my family*
5 = **physical**, intimate, bodily, corporal, corporeal • *personal hygiene*
6 = **individual**, original, unique, characteristic, distinctive, idiosyncratic, personalized • *They should cultivate their own personal style rather than always imitating others.*
7 = **direct**, immediate, first-hand, empirical, experiential • *I speak from deep personal knowledge.*
8 = **in person**, live, actual, in the flesh • *I try to keep away from TV interviews and personal appearances.*

personality 1 = **nature**, character, make-up, identity, temper, traits, temperament, psyche, disposition, individuality • *She has such a kind, friendly personality.*
2 = **character**, charm, attraction, charisma, attractiveness, dynamism, magnetism, pleasantness, likableness *or* likeableness • *a woman of great personality and charm*
3 = **celebrity**, star, big name, notable, household name, famous name, celeb *(informal)*, personage, megastar *(informal)*, well-known face, well-known person • *a radio and television personality*

personalize = **customize**, individualize, make to order, make distinctive, give a personal touch to • *We will personalize the gift with the child's name at no extra cost.*

personalized = **customized**, special, private, individual, distinctive, tailor-made, individualized, monogrammed • *a car with a personalized number plate*

personally AS AN ADVERB 1 = **in your opinion**, for yourself, in your book, for your part, from your own viewpoint, in your own view • *Personally, I think it's a waste of time.*
2 = **by yourself**, alone, independently, solely, on your own, in person, in the flesh • *The minister will answer the allegations personally.*
3 = **individually**, specially, subjectively, individualistically • *This topic interests me personally.*
4 = **privately**, in private, off the record • *Personally he was quiet, modest and unobtrusive.*
▸ IN PHRASES: **take something personally** = **be insulted by**, be offended by, take offence at, take umbrage at, feel insulted by, feel hurt by, stake something as an insult • *Don't take this rejection personally.*

personification = **embodiment**, image, representation, recreation, portrayal, incarnation, likeness, semblance, epitome • *Janis Joplin was the personification of the '60s female rock singer.*

personify = **embody**, represent, express, mirror, exemplify, symbolize, typify, incarnate, image *(rare)*, epitomize, body forth • *She seemed to personify goodness and nobility.*

personnel = **employees**, people, members, staff, workers, men and women, workforce, human resources, helpers, liveware • *changes in personnel within the company*

perspective 1 = **outlook**, attitude, context, angle, overview, way of looking, frame of reference, broad view • *The death of my mother gave me a new perspective on life.*
2 = **objectivity**, proportion, relation, relativity, relative importance • *helping her to get her problems into perspective*
3 = **view**, scene, prospect, outlook, panorama, vista • *stretching away along the perspective of a tree-lined, wide avenue*

perspicacious = **perceptive**, aware, sharp, keen, acute, alert, clever, penetrating, shrewd, discerning, astute, observant, clear-sighted, percipient, sharp-witted, sagacious • *a man of perspicacious judgment*

perspicacity = **insight**, discrimination, penetration, acumen, smarts *(slang, chiefly U.S.)*, wit, sharpness, suss *(slang)*, keenness, shrewdness, discernment, sagacity, acuteness, perceptiveness, percipience, perspicuity, perspicaciousness, sagaciousness • *his extraordinary political perspicacity*

perspiration = **sweat**, moisture, wetness, exudation, diaphoresis *(Medical)*, sudor *(Medical)*, hidrosis *(Medical)* • *Her hands were wet with perspiration.*

perspire = **sweat**, glow, swelter, drip with sweat, break out in a sweat, pour with sweat, secrete sweat, be damp *or* wet *or* soaked with sweat, exude sweat • *He began to perspire heavily.*

persuade 1 = **talk (someone) into**, urge, advise, prompt, influence, counsel, win (someone) over, induce, sway, entice, coax, incite, prevail upon, inveigle, bring (someone) round *(informal)*, twist (someone's) arm, argue (someone) into • *My husband persuaded me to come.*
OPPOSITES: forbid, discourage, dissuade
2 = **cause**, prompt, lead, move, influence, motivate, induce, incline, dispose, impel, actuate • *the event which persuaded the United States to enter the war*
3 = **convince**, satisfy, assure, prove to, convert to, cause to believe • *Derek persuaded me of the feasibility of the idea.*

persuasion 1 = **urging**, influencing, conversion, inducement, exhortation, wheedling, enticement, cajolery, blandishment, inveiglement • *It took all her powers of persuasion to induce them to stay.*
2 = **belief**, views, opinion, party, school, side, camp, faith, conviction, faction, cult, sect, creed, denomination, tenet, school of thought, credo, firm belief, certitude, fixed opinion • *people who are of a different political persuasion*

QUOTATIONS
By persuading others, we convince ourselves
[Junius *Public Advertiser*]

persuasive = **convincing**, telling, effective, winning, moving, sound, touching, impressive, compelling, influential, valid, inducing, logical, credible, plausible, forceful, eloquent, weighty, impelling, cogent • *a persuasive argument against reform*
OPPOSITES: weak, incredible, unconvincing

pert = **impudent**, forward, smart, bold, fresh *(informal)*, flip *(informal)*, cheeky, brash, saucy, pushy *(informal)*, sassy *(U.S. informal)*, flippant, presumptuous, impertinent, insolent, lippy *(U.S. & Canad. slang)* • *a pert young hussy*

pertain to = **relate to**, concern, refer to, regard, be part of, belong to, apply to, bear on, befit, be relevant to, be appropriate to, appertain to • *regulations which pertain to your own specific situation*

pertinent = **relevant**, fitting, fit, material, appropriate, pat, suitable, proper, to the point, apt, applicable, apposite, apropos, admissible, germane, to the purpose, ad rem *(Latin)* • *She had asked some pertinent questions.*
OPPOSITES: irrelevant, inappropriate, unfitting

perturb = **disturb**, worry, trouble, upset, alarm, bother, unsettle, agitate, ruffle, unnerve, disconcert, disquiet, vex, fluster, faze, discountenance, discompose • *He didn't seem to be perturbed by the news.*

perturbed = **disturbed**, worried, troubled, shaken, upset, alarmed, nervous, anxious, uncomfortable, uneasy, fearful, restless, flurried, agitated, disconcerted, disquieted, flustered, ill at ease, antsy *(informal)* • *He was not perturbed at the prospect of a policeman coming to call.*
OPPOSITES: relaxed, comfortable, assured

perusal = **read**, study, check, examination, inspection, scrutiny, browse, look through • *a quick perusal of the situations-vacant column*

peruse = **read**, study, scan, check, examine, inspect, browse, look through, eyeball *(slang)*, work over, scrutinize, run your eye over, surf *(Computing)* • *She was perusing a copy of Life magazine.*

pervade = **spread through**, fill, affect, penetrate, infuse, permeate, imbue, suffuse, percolate, extend through, diffuse through, overspread • *the corruption that pervades every stratum of society*

pervasive = **widespread**, general, common, extensive, universal, prevalent, ubiquitous, rife, pervading, permeating, inescapable, omnipresent • *a pervasive and powerful cultural influence*

perverse 1 = **stubborn**, contrary, unreasonable, dogged, contradictory, troublesome, rebellious, wayward, delinquent, intractable, wilful, unyielding, obstinate, intransigent, headstrong, unmanageable, cussed *(informal)*, obdurate, stiff-necked, disobedient, wrong-headed, refractory, pig-headed, miscreant, mulish, cross-grained, contumacious • *You're just being perverse.*
OPPOSITES: cooperative, agreeable, flexible
2 = **ill-natured**, cross, surly, petulant, crabbed, fractious, spiteful, churlish, ill-tempered, stroppy *(Brit. slang)*, cantankerous, peevish, shrewish • *He seems to take a perverse pleasure in being disagreeable.*
OPPOSITES: agreeable, amiable, good-natured
3 = **abnormal**, incorrect, unhealthy, improper, deviant, depraved • *perverse sexual practices*

perversion 1 = **deviation**, vice, abnormality, aberration, kink *(Brit. informal)*, wickedness, depravity, immorality, debauchery, unnaturalness, kinkiness *(slang)*, vitiation • *The most frequent sexual perversion is fetishism.*
2 = **distortion**, twisting, corruption, misuse, misrepresentation, misinterpretation, falsification • *a monstrous perversion of justice*

perversity 1 = **contrariness**, intransigence, obduracy, waywardness, contradictoriness, wrong-headedness, refractoriness, contumacy, contradictiveness, frowardness *(archaic)* • *He refused out of sheer perversity.*
2 = **perversion**, abnormality, deviation, vice, wickedness, depravity, immorality, debauchery, unnaturalness, kinkiness *(slang)*, vitiation • *the public's fascination with sexual perversity*

pervert AS A VERB 1 = **distort**, abuse, twist, misuse, warp, misinterpret, misrepresent, falsify, misconstrue • *officers attempting to pervert the course of justice*
2 = **corrupt**, degrade, subvert, deprave, debase, desecrate, debauch, lead astray • *He was accused of perverting the nation's youth.*
▸ AS A NOUN = **deviant**, degenerate, sicko *(informal)*, sleazeball *(slang)*, debauchee, weirdo *or* weirdie *(informal)* • *You're nothing but a sick pervert.*

perverted = **unnatural**, sick, corrupt, distorted, abnormal, evil, twisted, impaired, warped, misguided, unhealthy, immoral, deviant, wicked, kinky *(slang)*, depraved, debased, debauched, aberrant, vitiated, pervy *(slang)*, sicko *(slang)* • *his perverted desires*

pessimism = **gloominess**, depression, despair, gloom, cynicism, melancholy, hopelessness, despondency, dejection, glumness • *widespread pessimism about the country's political future*

pessimist = **defeatist**, cynic, melancholic, worrier, killjoy, prophet of doom, misanthrope, wet blanket *(informal)*, gloom merchant *(informal)*, doomster • *Unfortunately, the pessimists are being proved right.*

pessimistic = **gloomy**, dark, despairing, bleak, resigned, sad, depressed, cynical, hopeless, melancholy, glum, dejected, foreboding, despondent, morose, fatalistic, distrustful, downhearted, misanthropic • *his excessively pessimistic view of life*
OPPOSITES: optimistic, bright, assured

pest 1 = **infection**, bug, insect, plague, epidemic, blight, scourge, bane, pestilence, gogga *(S. African informal)* • *all kinds of pests like flies and mosquitoes* • *bacterial, fungal, and viral pests of the plants themselves*
2 = **nuisance**, bore, trial, pain *(informal)*, drag *(informal)*, bother, irritation, gall, annoyance, bane, pain in the neck *(informal)*, pain in the arse *(taboo slang)*, vexation, thorn in your flesh • *My neighbour's a real pest.*

pester = **annoy**, worry, bother, disturb, bug *(informal)*, plague, torment, get at, harass, nag, hassle *(informal)*, harry, aggravate *(informal)*, fret, badger, pick on, irk, bedevil, chivvy, get on your nerves *(informal)*, bend someone's ear *(informal)*, drive you up the wall *(slang)*, be on your back *(slang)*, get in your hair *(informal)* • *He's always hanging round and pestering me.*

pestilence = **plague**, epidemic, visitation, pandemic • *areas where the pestilence had broken out*

pestilential 1 = **infectious**, catching, contaminated, poisonous, malignant, contagious, noxious, venomous, disease-ridden, pestiferous • *a pestilential disease*
2 = **deadly**, dangerous, evil, foul, destructive, harmful, hazardous, detrimental, pernicious, ruinous, deleterious, injurious • *the pestilential grey squirrel*

pet AS AN ADJECTIVE 1 = **favourite**, chosen, special, personal, particular, prized, preferred, favoured, dearest, cherished, of choice, fave *(informal)*, dear to your heart • *The proceeds will be split between her pet charities.*
2 = **tame**, trained, domestic, house, domesticated, house-trained *(Brit.)*, house-broken • *One in four households owns a pet dog.*
▸ AS A NOUN = **favourite**, treasure, darling, jewel, idol, fave *(informal)*, apple of your eye, blue-eyed boy or girl *(Brit. informal)* • *They taunted her about being the teacher's pet.*
▸ AS A VERB 1 = **fondle**, pat, stroke, caress • *A woman sat petting a cocker spaniel.*
2 = **pamper**, spoil, indulge, cosset, baby, dote on, coddle, mollycoddle, wrap in cotton wool • *She had petted her son all his life.*
3 = **cuddle**, kiss, snog *(Brit. slang)*, smooch *(informal)*, neck *(informal)*, canoodle *(slang)* • *They were kissing and petting on the couch.*

peter out = **die out**, stop, fail, run out, fade, dwindle, evaporate, wane, give out, ebb, come to nothing, run dry, taper off • *The strike seemed to be petering out.*

petite = **small**, little, slight, delicate, dainty, dinky *(Brit. informal)*, elfin • *a petite young brunette*

petition AS A NOUN 1 = **appeal**, round robin, list of signatures • *We presented the government with a petition signed by 4,500 people.*
2 = **entreaty**, appeal, address, suit, application, request, prayer, plea, invocation, solicitation, supplication • *a humble petition to Saint Anthony*
▸ AS A VERB = **appeal**, press, plead, call (upon), ask, urge, sue, pray, beg, crave, solicit, beseech, entreat, adjure, supplicate • *She is petitioning to regain custody of the child.*

pet name = **nickname**, term of endearment, affectionate name • *Her pet name for me was Scrummy.*

petrified 1 = **terrified**, horrified, shocked, frozen, stunned, appalled, numb, dazed, speechless, aghast, dumbfounded, stupefied, scared stiff, scared shitless *(taboo slang)*, terror-stricken, shit-scared *(taboo slang)* • *He was petrified at the thought of having to make a speech.*
2 = **fossilized**, ossified, rocklike • *a block of petrified wood*

petrify 1 = **terrify**, horrify, amaze, astonish, stun, appal, paralyse, astound, confound, transfix, stupefy, immobilize, dumbfound • *His story petrified me.*
2 = **fossilize**, set, harden, solidify, ossify, turn to stone, calcify • *Bird and bat guano petrifies into a mineral called taranakite.*

petrol = **fuel**, gas *(U.S. & Canad.)*, gasoline *(U.S. & Canad.)*, juice *(informal)* • *Motorists will be rationed to thirty litres of petrol a month.*

petrol station = **garage**, gas station *(U.S. & Canad.)* • *The car was parked in the forecourt of the petrol station.*

petticoat = **underskirt**, slip, undergarment, half-slip, underslip • *a lace-trimmed petticoat*

petty 1 = **trivial**, inferior, insignificant, little, small, slight, trifling, negligible, unimportant, paltry, measly *(informal)*, contemptible, piddling *(informal)*, inconsiderable, inessential, nickel-and-dime *(U.S. slang)* • *Rows would start over petty things.*
OPPOSITES: major, important, significant
2 = **small-minded**, mean, cheap, grudging, shabby, spiteful, stingy, ungenerous, mean-minded • *I think that attitude is a bit petty.*
OPPOSITES: liberal, generous, broad-minded
3 = **minor**, lower, junior, secondary, lesser, subordinate, inferior • *Wilson was not a man who dealt with petty officials.*

petulance = **sulkiness**, bad temper, irritability, spleen, pique, sullenness, ill-humour, peevishness, querulousness, crabbiness, waspishness, pettishness • *an angry display of petulance*

petulant = **sulky**, cross, moody, sour, crabbed, impatient, pouting, perverse, irritable, crusty, sullen, bad-tempered, ratty *(Brit. & N.Z. informal)*, fretful, waspish, querulous, peevish, ungracious, cavilling, huffy, fault-finding, snappish, ill-humoured, captious • *He whined like a petulant child.*
OPPOSITES: happy, patient, good-natured

phalanx
▸ RELATED ADJECTIVE: phalangeal

phallus
▸ RELATED ADJECTIVE: priapic

phantasy *see* **fantasy**

phantom AS A NOUN 1 = **spectre**, ghost, spirit, shade *(literary)*, spook *(informal)*, apparition, wraith, revenant, phantasm • *Many people claimed to have seen the phantom.*
2 = **illusion**, vision, hallucination, figment, chimera, figment of the imagination • *In pressing for an agreement, Mr Kohl may be chasing a phantom.*
▸ AS AN ADJECTIVE = **imaginary**, imagined, fictitious, illusory, nonexistent, hallucinatory • *a phantom pregnancy*

pharynx
▸ RELATED ADJECTIVE: pharyngeal

phase AS A NOUN = **stage**, time, state, point, position, step, development, condition, period, chapter, aspect, juncture • *The crisis is entering a crucial phase.*
▸ IN PHRASES: **phase something in** = **introduce**, incorporate, ease in, start • *Reforms will be phased in over the next three years.*
phase something out = **eliminate**, close, pull, remove, replace, withdraw, pull out, axe *(informal)*, wind up, run down, terminate, wind down, ease off, taper off, deactivate, dispose of gradually • *The present system of military conscription should be phased out.*

pheasant
▸ COLLECTIVE NOUNS: nye, nide

phenomenal = **extraordinary**, outstanding, remarkable, fantastic, unique, unusual, marvellous, exceptional, notable, sensational, uncommon, singular, miraculous, stellar *(informal)*, prodigious, unparalleled, wondrous *(archaic or literary)* • *a phenomenal performance*
OPPOSITES: poor, average, unremarkable

phenomenon 1 = **occurrence**, happening, fact, event, incident, circumstance, episode • *scientific explanations of this natural phenomenon*
2 = **wonder**, sensation, spectacle, sight, exception, miracle, marvel, prodigy, rarity, nonpareil • *The Loch Ness monster is not the only bizarre phenomenon that bookmakers take bets on.*

philanderer = **womanizer** *(informal)*, playboy, Don Juan, Casanova, wolf *(informal)*, stud *(slang)*, flirt, trifler, gallant, Lothario, lady-killer *(informal)*, gay dog, ladies' man • *He was handsome, fun, charming, but a philanderer.*

philanthropic = **humanitarian**, generous, charitable, benevolent, kind, humane, gracious, altruistic, public-spirited, beneficent, kind-hearted, munificent, almsgiving, benignant • *the philanthropic aims of the organization*
OPPOSITES: mean, selfish, stingy

P

philanthropist = **humanitarian**, patron, benefactor, giver, donor, contributor, altruist, almsgiver • *He is a philanthropist and patron of the arts.*

philanthropy = **humanitarianism**, charity, generosity, patronage, bounty, altruism, benevolence, munificence, beneficence, liberality, public-spiritedness, benignity, almsgiving, brotherly love, charitableness, kind-heartedness, generousness, open-handedness, largesse or largess • *a retired banker well known for his philanthropy*

Philistine AS A NOUN = **boor**, barbarian, yahoo, lout, bourgeois, hoon (*Austral. & N.Z.*), ignoramus, lowbrow, vulgarian, cougan (*Austral. slang*), scozza (*Austral. slang*), bogan (*Austral. slang*) • *The man's a total philistine when it comes to the arts.*

▸ AS AN ADJECTIVE *sometimes not cap* = **uncultured**, ignorant, crass, tasteless, bourgeois, uneducated, boorish, unrefined, uncultivated, anti-intellectual, lowbrow, inartistic • *the country's philistine, consumerist mentality*

philosopher = **thinker**, theorist, sage, wise man, logician, metaphysician, dialectician, seeker after truth • *the Greek philosopher Plato*

▹ *See panel* **Philosophy**

QUOTATIONS

It is one of the chief skills of the philosopher not to occupy himself with questions which do not concern him

[Ludwig Wittgenstein *Tractatus Logico-Philosophicus*]

There is no statement so absurd that no philosopher will make it

[Cicero *De Divinatione*]

There was never yet philosopher
That could endure the toothache patiently

[William Shakespeare *Much Ado About Nothing*]

The philosophers have only interpreted the world in various ways; the point, however, is to change it

[Karl Marx *Theses on Feuerbach*]

I have tried too in my time to be a philosopher; but, I don't know how, cheerfulness was always breaking in

[Oliver Edwards]

what I understand by 'philosopher': a terrible explosive in the presence of which everything is in danger

[Friedrich Nietzsche *Ecce Homo*]

philosophical *or* **philosophic** 1 = **theoretical**, abstract, learned, wise, rational, logical, thoughtful, erudite, sagacious • *a philosophical discourse*

OPPOSITES: scientific, practical, pragmatic

2 = **stoical**, calm, composed, patient, cool, collected, resigned, serene, tranquil, sedate, impassive, unruffled, imperturbable • *He was remarkably philosophical about his failure.*

OPPOSITES: emotional, upset, rash

philosophy 1 = **thought**, reason, knowledge, thinking, reasoning, wisdom, logic, metaphysics • *He studied philosophy and psychology at Cambridge.*

2 = **outlook**, values, principles, convictions, thinking, beliefs, doctrine, ideology, viewpoint, tenets, world view, basic idea, attitude to life, Weltanschauung (*German*) • *his philosophy of non-violence*

QUOTATIONS

Philosophy may teach us to bear with equanimity the misfortunes of our neighbours

[Oscar Wilde *The English Renaissance of Art*]

Philosophy is a good horse in the stable, but an arrant jade on a journey

[Oliver Goldsmith *The Good-Natur'd Man*]

All good moral philosophy is but an handmaid to religion

[Francis Bacon *The Advancement of Learning*]

A little philosophy inclineth man's mind to atheism, but depth in philosophy bringeth men's minds about to religion

[Francis Bacon *Essays*]

philosophy: a route of many roads leading from nowhere to nothing

[Ambrose Bierce *The Devil's Dictionary*]

Philosophy will clip an Angel's wings

[John Keats *Lamia*]

How charming is divine philosophy!
Not harsh and crabbèd, as dull fools suppose,
But musical as Apollo's lute

[John Milton *Comus*]

▹ *See panel* **Philosophy**

phlegm 1 = **mucus**, catarrh, sputum, mucous secretion • *Symptoms include vomiting and excess phlegm.*

2 = **self-control**, composure, coolness, cool (*informal*), calm, coldness, calmness, equanimity, self-assurance, self-possession, sangfroid, frostiness, level-headedness,

PHILOSOPHY

Philosophical schools and doctrines

animism
Aristotelianism
atomism
behaviourism
Cartesianism
conceptualism
Confucianism
consequentialism
conventionalism
critical realism
cynicism
deism
determinism
dualism
Eleaticism
empiricism
epicureanism
essentialism
existentialism
fatalism
fideism
hedonism
Hegelianism
humanism
idealism
immaterialism
Kantianism
logical atomism
logical positivism
Marxism
materialism
monism
neo-Platonism
nihilism
nominalism
phenomenalism
Platonism
pluralism
positivism
pragmatism
Pyrrhonism
Pythagoreanism
rationalism
realism
scepticism
scholasticism
sensationalism
Stoicism
structuralism
Taoism
theism
Thomism
utilitarianism
utopianism

Philosophers

Peter Abelard (*French*)
Theodor Wiesengrund Adorno (*German*)
Maria Gaetana Agnesi (*Italian*)
Albertus Magnus (*German*)
Jean Le Rond d'Alembert (*French*)
Mohammed ibn Tarkhan al-Farabi (*Arabian*)
Louis Althusser (*French*)
Anaxagoras (*Greek*)
Anaximander (*Greek*)
Anaximenes (*Greek*)
Antisthenes (*Greek*)
Thomas Aquinas (*Italian*)
Hannah Arendt (*U.S.*)
Aristippus (*Greek*)
Aristotle (*Greek*)
St Augustine of Hippo (*Italian*)
J(ohn) L(angshaw) Austin (*English*)
Averroës (*Arabian*)
Avicenna (*Arabian*)
A(lfred) J(ules) Ayer (*English*)
Francis Bacon (*English*)
Roger Bacon (*English*)
Alexander Gottlieb Baumgarten (*German*)
Pierre Bayle (*French*)
Julien Benda (*French*)
Jeremy Bentham (*English*)
Nikolai Aleksandrovich Berdyayev (*Russian*)
Henri Louis Bergson (*French*)

Philosophers (continued)

George Berkeley *(Irish)*
Isaiah Berlin *(British)*
Anicius Manlius Severinus Boethius *(Roman)*
Bonaventura *(Italian)*
F(rancis) H(erbert) Bradley *(English)*
Giordano Bruno *(Italian)*
Martin Buber *(Austrian-Israeli)*
Jean Buridan *(French)*
Edmund Burke *(Irish)*
Tommaso Campanella *(Italian)*
Rudolf Carnap *(German-U.S.)*
Ernst Cassirer *(German)*
Marcus Porcius Cato *(Roman)*
Paul Churchland *(U.S.)*
Chu Xi *(Chinese)*
Cleanthes *(Greek)*
Auguste Comte *(French)*
Étienne Bonnot de Condillac *(French)*
Marie Jean Antoine Nicholas de Caritat Condorcet *(French)*
Confucius *(Chinese)*
Frederick (Charles) Copleston *(English)*
Victor Cousin *(French)*
Benedetto Croce *(Italian)*
Ralph Cudworth *(English)*
Richard Cumberland *(English)*
Donald Davidson *(U.S.)*
Simone de Beauvoir *(French)*
Democritus *(Greek)*
Jacques Derrida *(French)*
René Descartes *(French)*
John Dewey *(U.S.)*
Denis Diderot *(French)*
Dio Chrysostom *(Greek)*
Diogenes *(Greek)*
John Duns Scotus *(Scottish)*
Johann August Eberhard *(German)*
Empedocles *(Greek)*
Friedrich Engels *(German)*
Epictetus *(Greek)*
Epicurus *(Greek)*
Desiderius Erasmus *(Dutch)*
John Scotus Erigena *(Irish)*
Rudolph Christoph Eucken *(German)*
Gustav Theodor Fechner *(German)*
Ludwig Andreas Feuerbach *(German)*
Johann Gottlieb Fichte *(German)*
Marsilio Ficino *(Italian)*
Bernard le Bovier de Fontenelle *(French)*
Michel Foucault *(French)*
Gottlob Frege *(German)*
Erich Fromm *(German-U.S.)*
Pierre Gassendi *(French)*
Giovanni Gentile *(Italian)*
Kurt Godel *(U.S.)*
Gorgias *(Greek)*
T(homas) H(ill) Green *(English)*
Ernst Heinrich Haeckel *(German)*
William Hamilton *(Scottish)*
Han Fei Zu *(Chinese)*
David Hartley *(English)*
Friedrich August von Hayek *(Austrian-British)*
Georg Wilhelm Friedrich Hegel *(German)*
Martin Heidegger *(German)*
Claude Adrien Helvétius *(French)*
Heracleides *(Greek)*
Heraclitus *(Greek)*
Edward Herbert *(English)*
Johann Gottfried von Herder *(German)*
Aleksandr Ivanovich Herzen *(Russian)*
Thomas Hobbes *(English)*
David Hume *(Scottish)*
Edmund Husserl *(German)*
Francis Hutcheson *(Scottish)*
Hypatia *(Alexandrian)*
Solomon ibn-Gabirol *(Spanish)*
ibn-Khaldun *(Arabian)*
Muhammad Iqbal *(Indian)*
William James *(U.S.)*
Karl Jaspers *(German)*
Judah hah-Levi *(Spanish)*
Immanuel Kant *(German)*
Søren Aabye Kierkegaard *(Danish)*
Suzanne Langer *(U.S.)*
Lao Zi *(Chinese)*
Gottfried Wilhelm von Leibnitz *(German)*
Giacomo Leopardi *(Italian)*
Leucippus *(Greek)*
Lucien Lévy-Bruhl *(French)*
John Locke *(English)*
Lucretius *(Roman)*
Georg Lukács *(Hungarian)*
Ramón Lully *(Spanish)*
Ernst Mach *(Austrian)*
Niccolò Machiavelli *(Italian)*
Maimonides *(Spanish)*
Nicolas Malebranche *(French)*
Gabriel Marcel *(French)*
Herbert Marcuse *(German-U.S.)*
Jacques Maritain *(French)*
Marsilius of Padua *(Italian)*
Karl Marx *(German)*
Tomáš Garrigue Masaryk *(Czech)*
Mencius *(Chinese)*
Maurice Merleau-Ponty *(French)*
James Mill *(Scottish)*
John Stuart Mill *(British)*
Baron de la Brède et de Montesquieu *(French)*
G(eorge) E(dward) Moore *(British)*
Henry More *(English)*
Mo-Zi *(Chinese)*
(Jean) Iris Murdoch *(Irish)*
Isaac Newton *(English)*
Nicholas of Cusa *(German)*
Friedrich Wilhelm Nietzsche *(German)*
William of Ockham *(English)*
José Ortega y Gasset *(Spanish)*
William Paley *(English)*
Parmenides *(Greek)*
Blaise Pascal *(French)*
Charles Sanders Peirce *(U.S.)*
Philo Judaeus *(Alexandrian)*
Giovanni Pico della Mirandola *(Italian)*
Plato *(Greek)*
Plotinus *(Roman)*
Plutarch *(Greek)*
Jules Henri Poincaré *(French)*
Karl Popper *(Austrian-British)*
Porphyry *(Greek)*
Proclus *(Greek)*
Protagoras *(Greek)*
Samuel von Pufendorf *(German)*
Pyrrho *(Greek)*
Pythagoras *(Greek)*
Willard van Orman Quine *(U.S.)*
Ramanuja *(Indian)*
John Rawls *(U.S.)*
Hans Reichenbach *(German)*
Thomas Reid *(Scottish)*
(Joseph) Ernest Renan *(French)*
Paul Ricoeur *(French)*
Jean Jacques Rousseau *(French)*
Josiah Royce *(U.S.)*
Bertrand Russell *(English)*
Gilbert Ryle *(English)*
Comte de Saint-Simon *(French)*
Sankara *(Indian)*
George Santayana *(U.S.)*
Jean-Paul Sartre *(French)*
Friedrich Wilhelm Joseph von Schelling *(German)*
Friedrich von Schlegel *(German)*
Friedrich Ernst Daniel Schleiermacher *(German)*
Moritz Schlick *(German)*
Arthur Schopenhauer *(German)*
Albert Schweitzer *(Franco-German)*
Lucius Annaeus Seneca *(Roman)*
Shankaracharya *or* Shankara *(Indian)*
Adam Smith *(Scottish)*
Socrates *(Greek)*
Georges Sorel *(French)*
Herbert Spencer *(English)*
Oswald Spengler *(German)*
Baruch Spinoza *(Dutch)*
Rudolf Steiner *(Austrian)*
Peter Strawson *(British)*
Francisco de Suárez *(Spanish)*
Rabindranath Tagore *(Indian)*
Alfred Tarski *(Polish)*
Pierre Teilhard de Chardin *(French)*
Thales *(Greek)*
Theophrastus *(Greek)*
Paul Johannes Tillich *(German-U.S.)*
Leo Tolstoy *(Russian)*
Miguel de Unamuno *(Spanish)*
Giovanni Battista Vico *(Italian)*
Voltaire *(French)*
Simone Weil *(French)*
A(lfred) N(orth) Whitehead *(English)*
Bernard Williams *(English)*
Ludwig Josef Johann Wittgenstein *(Austrian-British)*
Xenocrates *(Greek)*
Xun Zi *(Chinese)*
Zeno of Citium *(Greek)*
Zeno of Elea *(Greek)*
Zhuangzi *or* Chuang-tzu *(Chinese)*

unflappability *(informal)*, stolidness • *They're taking it with the apathetic calm which many mistake for British phlegm.*

phlegmatic = **unemotional**, indifferent, cold, heavy, dull, sluggish, matter-of-fact, placid, stoical, lethargic, bovine, apathetic, frigid, lymphatic, listless, impassive, stolid, unfeeling, undemonstrative • *She spoke in a flat, phlegmatic voice.*
OPPOSITES: excited, emotional, active

phobia = **fear**, horror, terror, thing about *(informal)*, obsession, dislike, dread, hatred, loathing, distaste, revulsion, aversion to, repulsion, irrational fear, detestation, overwhelming anxiety about • *She has a phobia of spiders.*
OPPOSITES: liking, love, passion
▹ *See panel* **Phobias**

phone **AS A NOUN** **1** = **telephone**, blower *(informal)*, dog and bone *(slang)* • *I spoke to her on the phone only yesterday.*
2 = **call**, ring *(informal, chiefly Brit.)*, bell *(Brit. slang)*, buzz *(informal)*, tinkle *(Brit. informal)* • *If you need anything, give me a phone.*
▸ **AS A VERB** = **call**, telephone, ring (up) *(informal, chiefly Brit.)*, give someone a call, give someone a ring *(informal, chiefly Brit.)*, make a call, give someone a buzz *(informal)*, give someone a bell *(Brit. slang)*, give someone a tinkle *(Brit. informal)*, get on the blower *(informal)* • *I got more and more angry as I waited for her to phone.*

phonecards
▸ **RELATED ENTHUSIAST:** fusilatelist

phoney **AS AN ADJECTIVE** **1** = **fake**, affected, assumed, trick, put-on, false, forged, imitation, sham, pseudo *(informal)*, counterfeit, feigned, spurious • *He used a phoney accent.*
OPPOSITES: real, original, genuine
2 = **bogus**, false, fake, pseudo *(informal)*, ersatz • *phoney 'experts'*
▸ **AS A NOUN** **1** = **faker**, fraud, fake, pretender, humbug, impostor, pseud *(informal)* • *He was a liar, a cheat, and a phoney.*
2 = **fake**, sham, forgery, counterfeit • *This passport is a phoney.*

photocopy **AS A NOUN** = **copy**, reproduction, duplicate, Xerox *(trademark)*, facsimile, photostat *(trademark)* • *I'll make sure you get a photocopy of the list.*
▸ **AS A VERB** = **copy**, reproduce, duplicate, xerox *(trademark)*, take a photocopy of, make a Xerox of *(trademark)* • *She photocopied the cheque before cashing it.*

photograph **AS A NOUN** = **picture**, photo *(informal)*, shot, image, print, slide, snap *(informal)*, snapshot, transparency, likeness • *He wants to take some photographs of the house.*
▸ **AS A VERB** = **take a picture of**, record, film, shoot, snap *(informal)*, take (someone's) picture, capture on film, get a shot of • *I hate being photographed.*

photographer = **lensman**, cameraman, snapper *(informal)*, paparazzo, documentarian *(rare)* • *a group of TV cameramen and press photographers*

photographic **1** = **pictorial**, visual, graphic, cinematic, filmic • *The bank is able to use photographic evidence of who used the machine.*
2 = **accurate**, minute, detailed, exact, precise, faithful, retentive • *a photographic memory*

phrase **AS A NOUN** = **expression**, saying, remark, motto, construction, tag, quotation, maxim, idiom, utterance, adage, dictum, way of speaking, group of words, locution • *the Latin phrase, 'mens sana in corpore sano'*
▸ **AS A VERB** = **express**, say, word, put, term, present, voice, frame, communicate, convey, utter, couch, formulate, put into words • *The speech was carefully phrased.*

phraseology = **wording**, style, expression, language, speech, phrase, phrasing, idiom, syntax, parlance, diction, choice of words • *The phraseology of his speech was vivid as well as apt.*

physical **1** = **corporal**, fleshly, bodily, carnal, somatic, corporeal • *the physical problems caused by the illness*
2 = **earthly**, fleshly, mortal, incarnate, unspiritual • *They were still aware of the physical world around them.*
3 = **material**, real, substantial, natural, solid, visible, sensible, tangible, palpable • *There is no physical evidence to support the story.*
4 = **manual**, laboring • *They will be unable to cope with the demanding physical work.*
5 = **sexual**, carnal, base, animal, sordid, brutish, bestial • *No unmarried girl would dare to indulge in physical love.*

physician = **doctor**, specialist, doc *(informal)*, healer, medic *(informal)*, general practitioner, medical practitioner, medico *(informal)*, doctor of medicine, sawbones *(slang)*, G.P., M.D. • *the President's personal physician*

QUOTATIONS
Physician, heal thyself
[*Bible: St. Luke*]
Cured yesterday of my disease,
I died last night of my physician
[Matthew Prior *The Remedy Worse than the Disease*]

physics
▹ *See panel* **Physics**

physiognomy = **face**, features, look, clock *(Brit. slang)*, dial *(Brit. slang)*, countenance, visage, phiz *(slang)*, phizog *(slang)* • *his thick black hair and bony Irish physiognomy*

physique = **build**, form, body, figure, shape, structure, make-up, frame, constitution • *He has the physique and energy of a man half his age.*

pick **AS A VERB** **1** = **select**, choose, identify, elect, nominate, sort out, specify, opt for, single out, mark out, plump for, hand-pick, decide upon, cherry-pick, fix upon, settle on *or* upon, sift out, flag up • *He had picked ten people to interview for the jobs.*
OPPOSITES: decline, reject, dismiss
2 = **gather**, cut, pull, collect, take in, harvest, pluck, garner, cull • *He helped his mother pick fruit.*
3 = **provoke**, start, cause, stir up, incite, instigate, foment • *He picked a fight with a waiter and landed in jail.*
4 = **open**, force, crack *(informal)*, break into, break open, prise open, jemmy *(informal)* • *He picked the lock, and rifled the papers in each drawer.*
▸ **AS A NOUN** **1** = **choice**, decision, choosing, option, selection, preference • *We had the pick of winter coats from the shop.*
2 = **best**, prime, finest, tops *(slang)*, choicest, flower, prize, elect, pride, elite, cream, jewel in the crown, crème de la crème *(French)* • *These boys are the pick of the under-15 cricketers in the country.*
▸ **IN PHRASES:** **pick at something** = **nibble (at)**, peck at, have no appetite for, play *or* toy with, push round the plate, eat listlessly • *She picked at her breakfast.*
pick on someone **1** = **torment**, bully, bait, tease, get at *(informal)*, badger, persecute, hector, goad, victimize, have it in for *(informal)*, tyrannize, have a down on *(informal)* • *Bullies pick on smaller children.*
2 = **choose**, select, prefer, elect, single out, fix on, settle upon • *He needed to confess to someone – he just happened to pick on me.*
pick someone up **1** = **arrest**, nick *(slang, chiefly Brit.)*, bust *(informal)*, do *(slang)*, lift *(slang)*, run in *(slang)*, nail *(informal)*, collar *(informal)*, pinch *(informal)*, pull in *(Brit. slang)*, nab *(informal)*, apprehend, take someone into custody, feel your collar *(slang)* • *The police picked him up within the hour.*
2 = **meet**, pull *(informal)*, take up with, get off with *(informal)*, cop off with *(informal)*, make advances to, strike up a casual acquaintance with • *He had picked her up at a nightclub.*
pick something over *or* **pick over something** = **inspect**, examine, go through, look over, sift through, scrutinize • *Pick over the fruit and remove any damaged ones.*

PHOBIAS

Phobia	Meaning	Phobia	Meaning	Phobia	Meaning
acerophobia	sourness	eosophobia	dawn	ochophobia	vehicles
achluophobia	darkness	eremophobia	solitude	odontophobia	teeth
acrophobia	heights	ereuthophobia	blushing	oikophobia	home
aerophobia	air	ergasiophobia	work	olfactophobia	smell
agoraphobia	open spaces	genophobia	sex	ommatophobia	eyes
aichurophobia	points	geumaphobia	taste	oneirophobia	dreams
ailurophobia	cats	graphophobia	writing	ophidiophobia	snakes
akousticophobia	sound	gymnophobia	nudity	ornithophobia	birds
algophobia	pain	gynophobia	women	ouranophobia	heaven
amakaphobia	carriages	hadephobia	hell	panphobia	everything
amathophobia	dust	haematophobia	blood	pantophobia	everything
androphobia	men	hamartiophobia	sin	parthenophobia	girls
anemophobia	wind	haptophobia	touch	pathophobia	disease
anginophobia	narrowness	harpaxophobia	robbers	peniaphobia	poverty
anthropophobia	man	hedonophobia	pleasure	phasmophobia	ghosts
antlophobia	flood	helminthophobia	worms	phobophobia	fears
apeirophobia	infinity	hodophobia	travel	photophobia	light
aquaphobia	water	homichlophobia	fog	pnigerophobia	smothering
arachnophobia	spiders	homophobia	homosexuals	poinephobia	punishment
asthenophobia	weakness	hormephobia	shock	polyphobia	many things
astraphobia	lightning	hydrophobia	water	potophobia	drink
atephobia	ruin	hypegiaphobia	responsibility	pteronophobia	feathers
aulophobia	flute	hypnophobia	sleep	pyrophobia	fire
bacilliphobia	microbes	ideophobia	ideas	Russophobia	Russia
barophobia	gravity	kakorraphiaphobia	failure	rypophobia	soiling
basophobia	walking	katagelophobia	ridicule	Satanophobia	Satan
batrachophobia	reptiles	kenophobia	void	selaphobia	flesh
belonephobia	needles	kinesophobia	motion	siderophobia	stars
bibliophobia	books	kleptophobia	stealing	sitophobia	food
brontophobia	thunder	kopophobia	fatigue	spermaphobia	germs
cancerophobia	cancer	kristallophobia	ice	spermatophobia	germs
cheimaphobia	cold	laliophobia	stuttering	stasiphobia	standing
chionophobia	snow	linonophobia	string	stygiophobia	hell
chrematophobia	money	logophobia	words	taphephobia	being buried alive
chronophobia	duration	lyssophobia	insanity		
chrystallophobia	crystals	maniaphobia	insanity	technophobia	technology
claustrophobia	closed spaces	mastigophobia	flogging	teratophobia	giving birth to a monster
cnidophobia	stings	mechanophobia	machinery		
cometophobia	comets	metallophobia	metals	thaasophobia	sitting
cromophobia	colour	meteorophobia	meteors	thalassophobia	sea
cyberphobia	computers	misophobia	contamination	thanatophobia	death
cynophobia	dogs	monophobia	one thing	theophobia	God
demonophobia	demons	musicophobia	music	thermophobia	heat
demophobia	crowds	musophobia	mice	tonitrophobia	thunder
dermatophobia	skin	necrophobia	corpses	toxiphobia	poison
dikephobia	justice	nelophobia	glass	tremophobia	trembling
doraphobia	fur	neophobia	newness	triskaidekaphobia	thirteen
eisoptrophobia	mirrors	nephophobia	clouds	xenophobia	strangers *or* foreigners
electrophobia	electricity	nosophobia	disease		
enetephobia	pins	nyctophobia	night	zelophobia	jealousy
entomophobia	insects	ochlophobia	crowds	zoophobia	animals

pick something up **1 = learn**, master, acquire, get the hang of *(informal)*, become proficient in • *Where did you pick up your English?*
2 = catch, get, contract, come down with, become infected with, become ill with • *They've picked up a nasty infection.*
3 = receive, get, hear, detect • *The crew picked up a distress signal from the yacht.*
4 = learn, hear, find out, get to know, glean, be informed of • *a snippet of information I'd picked up from some magazine*
5 = develop, advance, expand on, comment on, remark on, dilate upon • *Can I just pick up that gentleman's point?*
6 = obtain, get, find, buy, score *(slang)*, discover, purchase, acquire, locate, come across, come by, unearth, garner, stumble across, chance upon, happen upon • *Auctions can be great places to pick up a bargain.*
7 = continue, resume, begin, go on with, take something up, carry something on • *When she paused, her daughter picked up the story.*
pick something *or* **someone off = shoot**, hit, kill, wound, take out, fire at, gun down, put a bullet in • *Snipers picked people off as they ran out of the church.*
pick something *or* **someone out** **1 = identify**, notice, recognize, distinguish, perceive, discriminate, make someone *or* something out, tell someone *or* something

PHYSICS

Branches of physics

- acoustics
- aerodynamics
- aerostatics
- applied physics
- astrophysics
- atomic physics
- biophysics
- condensed-matter physics *or* solid-state physics
- cosmology
- cryogenics *or* low-temperature physics
- dynamics
- electromagnetism
- electronics
- electrostatics
- geophysics
- harmonics
- high-energy physics *or* particle physics
- kinetics
- macrophysics
- magnetics *or* magnetism
- magnetostatics
- mechanics
- mesoscopics
- microphysics
- nuclear physics
- nucleonics
- optics
- photometry
- pneumatics
- quantum mechanics
- quantum physics
- rheology
- solar physics
- sonics
- spectroscopy
- statistical mechanics
- statics
- superaerodynamics
- theoretical physics
- thermodynamics
- thermometry
- thermostatics
- ultrasonics

Physics terms

- acceleration
- alternating current
- ampere
- amplifier
- angstrom
- anion
- antimatter
- atom
- baryon
- becquerel
- Boyle's law
- Brownian motion
- cacion
- calorie
- capacitance
- cathode ray
- centre of gravity
- centrifugal force
- centripetal force
- charge
- Charles' law
- conductor
- convection
- cosmic ray
- coulomb
- current
- cyclotron
- decibel
- density
- diffraction
- diffusion
- diode
- direct current
- Doppler effect
- earth
- electricity
- electromotive force
- electron
- energy
- farad
- field
- fission
- fluorescence
- force
- frequency
- friction
- fuse
- fusion
- gamma ray
- generator
- gravity
- half-life
- hertz
- hyperon
- impetus
- inductance
- inertia
- infrared
- joule
- kelvin
- kinetic energy
- laser
- lens
- lepton
- luminescence
- mass
- matter
- meson
- microwave
- moment
- momentum
- muon
- neutrino
- neutron
- newton
- nucleon
- nucleus
- ohm
- Ohm's law
- particle
- pascal
- Planck constant
- potential difference
- potential energy
- proton
- quantum
- radiation
- radioactivity
- radio wave
- red shift
- reflection
- refraction
- relativity
- resistance
- rutherford
- semiconductor
- simple harmonic motion
- spectrum
- static electricity
- subatomic particle
- super-conductivity
- superfluidity
- surface tension
- tau particle
- tension
- terminal velocity
- thermostat
- transformer
- transistor
- ultraviolet
- vacuum
- velocity
- viscosity
- volt
- watt
- wave
- wavelength
- x-ray

Physicists

- Ernst Abbe *(German)*
- Jean Le Rond Alembert *(French)*
- Hannes Olaf Gösta Alfvén *(Swedish)*
- Luis Walter Alvarez *(U.S.)*
- André Marie Ampère *(French)*
- Carl David Anderson *(U.S.)*
- Elizabeth Garrett Anderson *(English)*
- Philip Warren Anderson *(U.S.)*
- Anders Jonas Ångström *(Swedish)*
- Edward Appleton *(English)*
- Archimedes *(Greek)*
- Svante August Arrhenius *(Swedish)*
- Francis William Aston *(English)*
- Pierre Auger *(French)*
- Amedeo Avogadro *(Italian)*
- Jacques Babinet *(French)*
- John Bardeen *(U.S.)*
- Heinrich Georg Barkhausen *(German)*
- Charles Glover Barkla *(English)*
- Nikolai Basov *(Russian)*
- Antoine Henri Becquerel *(French)*
- Georg von Békésy *(U.S.)*
- Daniel Bernoulli *(Swiss)*
- Hans Albrecht Bethe *(U.S.)*
- Gerd Binnig *(German)*
- Patrick Maynard Stuart Blackett *(English)*
- Felix Bloch *(U.S.)*
- Aage Niels Bohr *(Danish)*
- Niels (Henrik David) Bohr *(Danish)*
- Ludwig Boltzmann *(Austrian)*
- Max Born *(British)*
- Jagadis Chandra Bose *(Indian)*
- Satyendra Nath Bose *(Indian)*
- Walter Bothe *(German)*
- Robert Boyle *(Irish)*
- Walter Houser Brattain *(U.S.)*
- Karl Ferdinand Braun *(German)*
- Auguste Bravais *(French)*
- David Brewster *(Scottish)*
- Percy Bridgman *(U.S.)*
- Maurice Broglie *(French)*
- Nicolas Leonard Sadi Carnot *(French)*
- Henry Cavendish *(English)*
- James Chadwick *(English)*
- Owen Chamberlain *(U.S.)*
- Jacques Charles *(French)*
- Pavel Alekseyevich Cherenkov *(Soviet)*
- Frederick Alexander Lindemann Cherwell *(English)*
- Rudolf Clausius *(German)*
- John Douglas Cockcroft *(English)*
- Arthur Holly Compton *(U.S.)*
- Leon Cooper *(U.S.)*
- Charles Augustin de Coulomb *(French)*
- James Watson Cronin *(U.S.)*
- William Crookes *(English)*
- Marie Curie *(French)*
- Pierre Curie *(French)*
- John Dalton *(English)*
- Clinton Joseph Davisson *(U.S.)*
- Peter Joseph Wilhelm Debye *(Dutch)*
- James Dewar *(Scottish)*
- Paul Adrien Maurice Dirac *(British)*
- C.J. Doppler *(Austrian)*
- Arthur Stanley Eddington *(English)*
- Albert Einstein *(German-U.S.)*
- Roland von Eötvös *(Hungarian)*
- Charles Fabry *(French)*
- Gabriel Daniel Fahrenheit *(German)*
- Michael Faraday *(British)*
- Gustav Fechner *(German)*
- Enrico Fermi *(Italian)*
- Richard Feynman *(U.S.)*
- Jean Bernard Léon Foucault *(French)*
- William Henry Fox Talbot *(English)*
- James Franck *(U.S.)*
- Joseph von Fraunhofer *(German)*
- Augustin Fresnel *(French)*
- Otto Frisch *(Austrian-British)*
- Klaus Fuchs *(German-British)*
- Galileo (Galilei) *(Italian)*
- William Gilbert *(English)*
- Donald Arthur Glaser *(U.S.)*
- Robert Hutchings Goddard *(U.S.)*
- Joseph Louis Gay-Lussac *(French)*
- Hans Geiger *(German)*
- Murray Gell-Man *(U.S.)*

Physicists (continued)

Josiah Willard Gibbs *(U.S.)*
Pierre Gassendi *(French)*
Thomas Graham *(English)*
Otto von Guericke *(German)*
Otto Hahn *(German)*
Stephen William Hawking *(English)*
Oliver Heaviside *(English)*
Werner Karl Heisenburg *(German)*
Walter Heitler *(German)*
Hermann Ludwig Ferdinand von Helmholtz *(German)*
Joseph Henry *(U.S.)*
Gustav Hertz *(German)*
Heinrich Rudolph Hertz *(German)*
Victor Francis Hess *(U.S.)*
Robert Hooke *(English)*
Christiaan Huygens *(Dutch)*
Vladimir Nikolaievich Ipatieff *(U.S.)*
James Hopwood Jeans *(English)*
Brian David Josephson *(English)*
James Prescott Joule *(English)*
Heike Kamerlingh-Onnes *(Dutch)*
Piotr Leonidovich Kapitza *(Russian)*
William Thomson Kelvin *(English)*
John Kerr *(Scottish)*
Gustav Kirchhoff *(German)*
Willis Eugene Lamb *(U.S.)*
Lev Davidovich Landau *(Soviet)*
Samuel Pierpont Langley *(U.S.)*
Pierre Simon Laplace *(French)*
Max Theodor Felix von Laue *(German)*
Ernest Orlando Lawrence *(U.S.)*
Tsung-Dao Lee *(U.S.)*
Frederick Lindemann *(German-British)*
Gabriel Lippman *(French)*
Oliver Lodge *(English)*
Hendrik Antoon Lorentz *(Dutch)*
Edwin McMillan *(U.S.)*
Guglielmo Marconi *(Italian)*
Ernst Mach *(Austrian)*
James Clerk Maxwell *(Scottish)*
Julius Robert von Mayer *(German)*
Lise Meitner *(Austrian)*
Albert Michelson *(U.S.)*
Robert Milikin *(U.S.)*
Henry Gwyn-Jeffreys Moseley *(English)*
Robert Sanderson Mullikin *(U.S.)*
Louis Néel *(French)*
Isaac Newton *(English)*
Georg Simon Ohm *(German)*
Mark Laurence Elwin Oliphant *(Australian-British)*
J(ulius) Robert Oppenheimer *(U.S.)*
Blaise Pascal *(French)*
Wolfgang Pauli *(U.S.)*
Roger Penrose *(English)*
Jean Baptiste Perrin *(French)*
Auguste Piccard *(Swiss)*
Max (Karl Ernst Ludwig) Planck *(German)*
Jules Henri Poincaré *(French)*
Alexander Stepanovich Popov *(Russian)*
Celic Powell *(English)*
Ludwig Prandtl *(German)*
Edward Mill Purcell *(U.S.)*
Isidor Isaac Rabi *(U.S.)*
John William Strutt Rayleigh *(English)*
Owen Willans Richardson *(English)*
Burton Richter *(U.S.)*
Wilhelm Konrad Roentgen *(German)*
Ernest Rutherford *(British)*
Andrei Sakharov *(Soviet)*
Erwin Schrödinger *(Austrian)*
Glenn Seaborg *(U.S.)*
Emilio Sègre *(U.S.)*
William Bradfield Shockley *(U.S.)*
Kai Siegbahn *(Swedish)*
C.P. Snow *(English)*
Johannes Stark *(German)*
Joseph Wilson Swan *(English)*
Leo Szilard *(U.S.)*
Edward Teller *(U.S.)*
Benjamin Thomson *(Anglo-American)*
George Paget Thomson *(English)*
Joseph John Thomson *(English)*
Samuel Chao Chung Ting *(U.S.)*
Evangelista Torricelli *(Italian)*
Charles Hard Townes *(U.S.)*
John Tyndall *(Irish)*
James Van Allen *(U.S.)*
R.J. Van de Graaff *(U.S.)*
Johannes Diderik van der Waals *(Dutch)*
Alessandro Volta *(Italian)*
Ernest Thomas Sinton Walton *(Irish)*
Robert Alexander Watson-Watt *(Scottish)*
Wilhelm Eduard Weber *(German)*
Steven Weinberg *(U.S.)*
John Archibald Wheeler *(U.S.)*
Wilhelm Wien *(German)*
Eugene Paul Wigner *(U.S.)*
Charles Thomson Rees Wilson *(Scottish)*
Chen Ning Yang *(U.S.)*
Thomas Young *(English)*
Hideki Yukawa *(Japanese)*
Fritz Zwicky *(Swiss)*
Vladimir Kosma Zworykin *(U.S.)*

apart, single someone *or* something out • *He wasn't difficult to pick out when the bus drew in.*
2 = select, choose, decide on, take, sort out, opt for, cull, plump for, hand-pick • *Pick out a painting you think she'd like.*
pick something *or* someone up 1 = lift, raise, gather, take up, grasp, uplift, hoist • *He picked his cap up from the floor.* • *They had to pick him up and carry on.*
2 = collect, get, call for, go for, go to get, fetch, uplift *(Scot.)*, go and get, give someone a lift *or* a ride • *We drove to the airport to pick her up.* • *He went to Miami where he had arranged to pick up the money.*
pick up 1 = improve, recover, rally, get better, bounce back, make progress, make a comeback *(informal)*, perk up, turn the corner, gain ground, take a turn for the better, be on the road to recovery • *Industrial production is beginning to pick up.*
2 = recover, improve, rally, get better, mend, perk up, turn the corner, be on the mend, take a turn for the better • *A good dose of tonic will help you to pick up.*
3 = get stronger, strengthen, blow stronger • *The sheltering trees round about rustled as the wind picked up.*
pick your way = tread carefully, work through, move cautiously, walk tentatively, find *or* make your way • *I picked my way among the rubble.*

picket AS A VERB **= blockade**, boycott, demonstrate outside • *The miners went on strike and picketed the power station.*
▸ AS A NOUN **1 = demonstration**, strike, blockade • *Demonstrators have set up a twenty-four-hour picket.*
2 = protester, demonstrator, picketer, flying picket • *Ten hotels were damaged by pickets in the weekend strike.*
3 = lookout, watch, guard, patrol, scout, spotter, sentry, sentinel, vedette *(Military)* • *Troops are still manning pickets and patrolling the area.*
4 = stake, post, pale, paling, peg, upright, palisade, stanchion • *The area was fenced in with pickets to keep out the animals.*

pickings = profits, returns, rewards, earnings, yield, proceeds, spoils, loot, plunder, gravy *(slang)*, booty, ill-gotten gains • *Sporting events provide rich pickings for unscrupulous touts.*

pickle AS A VERB **= preserve**, marinade, keep, cure, steep • *Herrings can be salted, smoked and pickled.* • *Pickle your favourite vegetables while they're still fresh.*
▸ AS A NOUN **1 = chutney**, relish, piccalilli • *jars of pickle*
2 = predicament, spot *(informal)*, fix *(informal)*, difficulty, bind *(informal)*, jam *(informal)*, dilemma, scrape *(informal)*, hot water *(informal)*, uphill *(S. African)*, quandary, tight spot • *Connie had got herself into a real pickle this time.*

pick-me-up = tonic, drink, pick-up *(slang)*, bracer *(informal)*, refreshment, stimulant, shot in the arm *(informal)*, restorative • *When you need a pick-me-up, try peppermint oil.*

pick-up = improvement, recovery, rise, gain, rally, strengthening, revival, upturn, change for the better, upswing • *a pick-up in the housing market*

pickpocket = thief, bag-snatcher, purse-snatcher, cutpurse *(archaic)* • *Markets are a pickpocket's paradise.*

picky = fussy, particular, critical, carping, fastidious, dainty, choosy, finicky, cavilling, pernickety *(informal)*, fault-finding, captious, nit-picky *(informal)* • *Everyone knows children are picky eaters.*

picnic 1 = **excursion**, fête champêtre *(French)*, barbecue, barbie *(informal)*, cookout *(U.S. & Canad.)*, alfresco meal, déjeuner sur l'herbe *(French)*, clambake *(U.S. & Canad.)*, outdoor meal, outing • *We're going on a picnic tomorrow.*
2 *used in negative constructions* = **walkover** *(informal)*, breeze *(U.S. & Canad. informal)*, pushover *(slang)*, snap *(informal)*, child's play *(informal)*, piece of cake *(Brit. informal)*, cinch *(slang)*, no-brainer *(informal)*, cakewalk *(informal)*, duck soup *(U.S. slang)* • *Emigrating is no picnic.*

pictorial = **graphic**, striking, illustrated, vivid, picturesque, expressive, scenic, representational • *a pictorial history of the Special Air Service*

picture AS A NOUN 1 = **representation**, drawing, painting, portrait, image, print, illustration, sketch, portrayal, engraving, likeness, effigy, delineation, similitude • *drawing a small picture with coloured chalks*
2 = **photograph**, photo, still, shot, image, print, frame, slide, snap, exposure, portrait, snapshot, transparency, enlargement • *I saw his picture in the paper.*
3 = **film**, movie *(U.S. informal)*, flick *(slang)*, feature film, motion picture • *a director of epic pictures*
4 = **idea**, vision, concept, impression, notion, visualization, mental picture, mental image • *I'm trying to get a picture of what kind of person you are.*
5 = **description**, impression, explanation, report, account, image, sketch, depiction, re-creation • *I want to give you a clear picture of what we are trying to do.*
6 = **situation**, case, set of circumstances, scenario, equation, plight, state of affairs, kettle of fish *(informal)* • *It's a similar picture across the border in Ethiopia.*
7 = **personification**, model, embodiment, soul, essence, archetype, epitome, perfect example, exemplar, quintessence, living example • *Six years after the operation, he remains a picture of health.*
▸ AS A VERB 1 = **imagine**, see, envision, visualize, conceive of, fantasize about, conjure up an image of, see in the mind's eye • *She pictured herself working with animals.*
2 = **represent**, show, describe, draw, paint, illustrate, portray, sketch, render, depict, delineate • *The goddess Demeter is pictured holding an ear of wheat.*
3 = **show**, photograph, capture on film • *Betty is pictured here with her award.*
▸ IN PHRASES: **get the picture** = **understand**, follow, catch on *(informal)*, get the message *(informal)*, get the point, see what's going on, see daylight, get the drift *(informal)*, understand what's what *(informal)* • *I think I'm beginning to get the picture.*
put someone in the picture = **inform**, brief, fill someone in, keep someone posted, bring someone up to date, explain the situation to, bring someone up to speed *(informal)*, give details to, explain the circumstances to • *I haven't had time to put him in the picture yet.*
▸ RELATED ADJECTIVE: pictorial

QUOTATIONS
One picture is worth ten thousand words
[Frederick R. Barnard *Printers' Ink*]

PROVERBS
Every picture tells a story

P

pictures = **cinema**, movies, flicks *(informal)* • *I haven't been to the pictures for ages.*

picturesque 1 = **interesting**, pretty, beautiful, attractive, charming, scenic, quaint • *the Algarve's most picturesque village*
OPPOSITES: everyday, commonplace, unattractive
2 = **vivid**, striking, graphic, colourful, memorable • *Every inn had a quaint and picturesque name.*
OPPOSITES: dull, drab

piddling = **trivial**, little, petty, worthless, insignificant, pants *(informal)*, useless, fiddling, trifling, unimportant, paltry, Mickey Mouse *(slang)*, puny, derisory, measly *(informal)*, crappy *(slang)*, toytown *(slang)*, piffling, poxy *(slang)*, nickel-and-dime *(U.S. slang)*, wanky *(taboo slang)*, chickenshit *(U.S. slang)* • *arguing over piddling amounts of money*
OPPOSITES: major, important, significant

pie AS A NOUN = **tart**, pasty, quiche, tartlet • *blueberry pie*
▸ IN PHRASES: **pie in the sky** = **a false hope**, a fantasy, an illusion, a mirage, a delusion, a pipe dream, a daydream, an unrealizable dream, a castle in the sky • *The deadline seemed like pie in the sky.*

piebald = **pied**, spotted, black and white, flecked, speckled, mottled, dappled, brindled • *a piebald pony*

piece AS A NOUN 1 = **bit**, section, slice, part, share, division, block, length, quantity, scrap, segment, portion, fragment, fraction, chunk, wedge, shred, slab, mouthful, morsel, wodge *(Brit. informal)* • *Another piece of cake?* • *a piece of wood*
2 = **component**, part, section, bit, unit, segment, constituent, module • *The equipment was taken down the shaft in pieces.*
3 = **stretch**, area, spread, tract, expanse • *People struggle to get the best piece of land*
4 = **instance**, case, example, sample, specimen, occurrence • *a highly complex piece of legislation*
5 = **item**, report, story, bit *(informal)*, study, production, review, article • *There was a piece about him on television.*
6 = **composition**, work, production, opus • *an orchestral piece*
7 = **work of art**, work, creation • *The cabinets display a wide variety of porcelain pieces.*
8 = **share**, cut *(informal)*, slice, percentage, quantity, portion, quota, fraction, allotment, subdivision • *They got a small piece of the net profits.*
▸ IN PHRASES: **give someone a piece of your mind** = **tell someone off**, rebuke, reprimand, reproach, lecture, carpet *(informal)*, censure, scold, berate, chide, tear into *(informal)*, read the riot act to, reprove, upbraid, take someone to task, tick someone off *(informal)*, bawl someone out *(informal)*, chew someone out *(U.S. & Canad. informal)*, tear someone off a strip *(Brit. informal)*, give someone a piece of your mind, haul someone over the coals *(informal)*, give someone a rocket *(Brit. & N.Z. informal)* • *I'd like to give that man a piece of my mind.*
go *or* **fall to pieces** = **break down**, fall apart, disintegrate, lose control, crumple, crack up *(informal)*, have a breakdown, lose your head • *She went to pieces when her husband died.*
in one piece 1 = **alive**, safe, unscathed, unhurt, uninjured, safe and sound • *We were lucky to get out of there in one piece.*
2 = **intact**, whole, entire, untouched, unmarked, unbroken, unharmed, undamaged, unspoiled • *After the explosion, my house was still in one piece.*
in pieces = **smashed**, broken, shattered, damaged, ruined, bust *(informal)*, disintegrated, in bits, in smithereens • *The bowl was lying in pieces on the floor.*
of a piece (with) = **like**, the same (as), similar (to), consistent (with), identical (to), analogous (to), of the same kind (as) • *These essays are of a piece with his earlier work.* • *Thirties design and architecture was all of a piece.*
piece something together 1 = **work out**, understand, figure out, make out, see, suss out *(slang)*, fathom out • *Frank was beginning to piece together what had happened.*
2 = **mend**, unite, join, fix, restore, repair, patch (together), assemble, compose • *Doctors painstakingly pieced together the broken bones.*
take *or* **tear** *or* **pull something** *or* **someone to pieces** = **criticize**, attack, pan *(informal)*, condemn, slam *(informal)*, flame *(informal)*, rubbish *(Brit. informal)*, savage, slate *(Brit. informal)*, censure, maul, denigrate, pillory, slag off *(Brit. informal)*, diss *(slang, chiefly U.S.)*, find fault with, lambaste, give a bad press to • *Every one of his decisions was pulled to pieces.*

pièce de résistance = **masterpiece**, jewel, showpiece, masterwork, chef-d'oeuvre *(French)* • *The pièce de résistance was a gold evening gown.*

piecemeal AS AN ADJECTIVE = **unsystematic**, interrupted, partial, patchy, intermittent, spotty, fragmentary • *piecemeal changes to the constitution*
▸ AS AN ADVERB = **bit by bit**, slowly, gradually, partially, intermittently, at intervals, little by little, fitfully, by degrees, by fits and starts • *It was built piecemeal over some 130 years.*

pied = **variegated**, spotted, streaked, irregular, flecked, motley, mottled, dappled, multicoloured, piebald, parti-coloured, varicoloured • *a bird with pied markings*

pier 1 = **jetty**, wharf, quay, promenade, landing place • *The lifeboats were moored at the pier.*
2 = **pillar**, support, post, column, pile, piling, upright, buttress • *the cross-beams bracing the piers of the jetty*

pierce 1 = **penetrate**, stab, spike, enter, bore, probe, drill, run through, lance, puncture, prick, transfix, stick into, perforate, impale • *Pierce the skin of the potato with a fork.*
2 = **pass through**, penetrate, light up, cut through, pervade, permeate, filter through, burst through • *A spotlight pierced the darkness.*
3 = **hurt**, cut, wound, strike, touch, affect, pain, move, excite, stir, thrill, sting, rouse, cut to the quick • *Her words pierced Lydia's heart like an arrow.*

piercing 1 = **penetrating**, sharp, loud, shattering, shrill, high-pitched, ear-splitting • *a piercing whistle*
OPPOSITES: low, quiet, inaudible
2 = **perceptive**, searching, aware, bright *(informal)*, sharp, keen, alert, probing, penetrating, shrewd, perspicacious, quick-witted • *He fixes you with a piercing stare.*
OPPOSITES: slow, thick, unperceptive
3 = **sharp**, shooting, powerful, acute, severe, intense, painful, stabbing, fierce, racking, exquisite, excruciating, agonizing • *I felt a piercing pain in my abdomen.*
4 = **cold**, biting, keen, freezing, bitter, raw, arctic, nipping, numbing, frosty, wintry, nippy • *a piercing wind*

piety = **holiness**, duty, faith, religion, grace, devotion, reverence, sanctity, veneration, godliness, devoutness, dutifulness, piousness • *a woman later to be canonized for her piety*

piffle = **nonsense**, rubbish, garbage *(informal)*, malarkey, hot air *(informal)*, balls *(taboo slang)*, bull *(slang)*, shit *(taboo slang)*, pants *(informal)*, rot, crap *(slang)*, trash, bunk *(informal)*, bullshit *(taboo slang)*, tosh *(slang, chiefly Brit.)*, bollocks *(Brit. taboo slang)*, pap, cobblers *(Brit. taboo slang)*, bilge *(informal)*, drivel, twaddle, tripe *(informal)*, guff *(slang)*, moonshine, hogwash, hokum *(slang, chiefly U.S. & Canad.)*, bunkum *(chiefly U.S.)*, codswallop *(Brit. slang)*, poppycock *(informal)*, balderdash, bosh *(informal)*, eyewash *(informal)*, hooey *(slang)*, tommyrot, horsefeathers *(U.S. slang)*, tarradiddle, bizzo *(Austral. slang)*, bull's wool *(Austral. & N.Z. slang)* • *He talks such a load of piffle.*

piffling = **trivial**, petty, trifling, insignificant, little, pants *(informal)*, useless, fiddling, worthless, unimportant, paltry, Mickey Mouse *(slang)*, puny, derisory, measly *(informal)*, piddling *(informal)*, crappy *(slang)*, toytown *(slang)*, poxy *(slang)*, nickel-and-dime *(U.S. slang)*, wanky *(taboo slang)*, chickenshit *(U.S. slang)* • *some piffling dispute regarding visiting rights*

pig AS A NOUN 1 = **hog**, sow, boar, piggy, swine, grunter, piglet, porker, shoat • *He keeps poultry, pigs and goats.*
2 = **slob**, hog *(informal)*, guzzler *(slang)*, glutton, gannet *(informal)*, sloven, greedy guts *(slang)* • *He's just a greedy pig.*
3 = **brute**, monster, scoundrel, animal, beast, rogue, swine, rotter, boor • *Her ex-husband was a real pig to her.*
▸ IN PHRASES: **pig out** = **overindulge**, overdo it, eat too much, have a binge *(informal)*, make a pig of yourself *(informal)*, be immoderate or intemperate • *It's great to pig out on junk food.*
▸ RELATED ADJECTIVE: porcine
▸ NAME OF MALE: boar
▸ NAME OF FEMALE: sow
▸ NAME OF YOUNG: piglet
▸ COLLECTIVE NOUN: litter
▸ NAME OF HOME: sty

BREEDS OF PIG

Berkshire	Hampshire	Saddleback
Cheshire	Landrace	Small White
Chester White	Large Black	Tamworth
Duroc	Large White	Vietnamese
Gloucester Old Spot	Middle White	pot-bellied
	Pietrain	Welsh

pigeon = **squab**, bird, dove, culver *(archaic)* • *A pigeon settled on the window-sill.*
▸ NAME OF YOUNG: squab
▸ COLLECTIVE NOUNS: flock, flight

pigeonhole AS A NOUN 1 = **compartment**, niche, locker, cubicle, cubbyhole • *There was a message waiting for me in the hotel pigeonhole.*
2 = **classification**, class, category, slot *(informal)* • *Most musicians are keen to avoid being put in a pigeonhole.*
▸ AS A VERB = **classify**, label, characterize, categorize, catalogue, codify, compartmentalize, ghettoize • *I don't want to be pigeonholed as a kids' presenter.*

pig-headed = **stubborn**, contrary, perverse, obstinate, stupid, dense, inflexible, wilful, unyielding, stiff-necked, wrong-headed, self-willed, bull-headed, mulish, cross-grained, froward *(archaic)* • *In her pig-headed way, she insisted that she was right.*
OPPOSITES: cooperative, flexible, obliging

pigment = **colour**, colouring, paint, stain, dye, tint, tincture, colouring matter, colorant, dyestuff • *a wide range of natural pigments*

piker = **slacker**, shirker, skiver *(Brit. slang)*, loafer, layabout, idler, passenger, do-nothing, dodger, good-for-nothing, bludger *(Austral. & N.Z. informal)*, gold brick *(U.S. slang)*, scrimshanker *(Brit. military slang)* • *He works so hard he makes the rest of us look like pikers.*

pile[1] AS A NOUN 1 = **heap**, collection, mountain, mass, stack, rick, mound, accumulation, stockpile, hoard, assortment, assemblage • *a pile of books*
2 *often plural* = **lot(s)**, mountain(s), load(s) *(informal)*, oceans, wealth, great deal, stack(s), abundance, large quantity, oodles *(informal)*, shedload *(Brit. informal)* • *I've got piles of questions for you.*
3 = **mansion**, building, residence, manor, country house, seat, big house, stately home, manor house • *a stately pile in the country*
4 = **fortune**, bomb *(Brit. slang)*, pot, packet *(slang)*, mint, big money, wad *(U.S. & Canad. slang)*, big bucks *(informal, chiefly U.S.)*, top dollar *(informal)*, megabucks *(U.S. & Canad. slang)*, tidy sum *(informal)*, pretty penny *(informal)*, top whack *(informal)* • *He made a pile in various business ventures.*
▸ AS A VERB 1 = **load**, stuff, pack, stack, charge, heap, cram, lade • *He was piling clothes into the case.*
2 = **crowd**, pack, charge, rush, climb, flood, stream, crush, squeeze, jam, flock, shove • *They all piled into the car.*
▸ IN PHRASES: **pile something up** 1 = **gather (up)**, collect, assemble, stack (up), mass, heap (up), load up • *Bulldozers piled up huge mounds of dirt.*
2 = **collect**, accumulate, gather in, pull in, amass, hoard, stack up, store up, heap up • *Their aim is to pile up the points and aim for a qualifying place.*

P

pile up = **accumulate**, collect, gather (up), build up, amass • *Her mail had piled up inside the front door.*

pile² = **foundation**, support, post, column, piling, beam, upright, pier, pillar • *wooden houses set on piles along the shore*

pile³ = **nap**, fibre, down, hair, surface, fur, plush, shag, filament • *the carpet's thick pile*

piles = **haemorrhoids** • *More women than men suffer from piles.*

pile-up = **collision**, crash, accident, smash, smash-up (*informal*), multiple collision • *a 54-car pile-up*

pilfer = **steal**, take, rob, lift (*informal*), nick (*slang, chiefly Brit.*), appropriate, trouser (*slang*), rifle, pinch (*informal*), swipe (*slang*), knock off (*slang*), embezzle, blag (*slang*), walk off with, snitch (*slang*), purloin, filch, snaffle (*Brit. informal*), thieve • *Staff were pilfering cash from the bar.*

pilgrim = **traveller**, crusader, wanderer, devotee, palmer, haji (*Islam*), wayfarer • *a pilgrim on the way to Mecca*

QUOTATIONS

pilgrim: a traveler that is taken seriously

[Ambrose Bierce *The Devil's Dictionary*]

pilgrimage = **journey**, tour, trip, mission, expedition, crusade, excursion, hajj (*Islam*) • *a pilgrimage to the Catholic shrine at Lourdes*

pill AS A NOUN = **tablet**, capsule, pellet, bolus, pilule • *a sleeping pill*

▸ IN PHRASES: **a bitter pill (to swallow)** = **trial**, pain (*informal*), bore, drag (*informal*), pest, nuisance, pain in the neck (*informal*) • *You're too old to be given a job. That's a bitter pill to swallow.*

pillage AS A VERB = **plunder**, strip, sack, rob, raid, spoil (*archaic*), rifle, loot, ravage, ransack, despoil, maraud, reive (*dialect*), depredate (*rare*), freeboot, spoliate • *Soldiers went on a rampage, pillaging stores and shooting.*

▸ AS A NOUN = **plundering**, sacking, robbery, plunder, sack, devastation, marauding, depredation, rapine, spoliation • *There were no signs of violence or pillage.*

pillar 1 = **support**, post, column, piling, prop, shaft, upright, pier, obelisk, stanchion, pilaster • *the pillars supporting the roof*

2 = **supporter**, leader, rock, worthy, mainstay, leading light (*informal*), tower of strength, upholder, torchbearer • *My father had been a pillar of the community.*

pillory = **ridicule**, denounce, stigmatize, brand, lash, show someone up, expose someone to ridicule, cast a slur on, heap *or* pour scorn on, hold someone up to shame • *He resigned after being pilloried by the press.*

pillow = **cushion**, bolster, headrest • *I sleep with his photograph under my pillow.*

pilot AS A NOUN 1 = **airman**, captain, flyer, aviator, aeronaut • *He spent seventeen years as an airline pilot.*

2 = **helmsman**, guide, navigator, leader, director, conductor, coxswain, steersman • *The pilot steered the ship safely inside the main channel.*

▸ AS A VERB 1 = **fly**, control, operate, be at the controls of • *the first person to pilot an aircraft across the Pacific*

2 = **navigate**, drive, manage, direct, guide, handle, conduct, steer • *Local fishermen piloted the boats.*

3 = **direct**, lead, manage, conduct, steer • *We are piloting the strategy through Parliament.*

▸ AS A MODIFIER = **trial**, test, model, sample, experimental • *a pilot show for a new TV series*

pimp AS A NOUN = **procurer**, go-between, bawd (*archaic*), white-slaver, pander, panderer, whoremaster (*archaic*) • *Every hooker I ever met had a pimp.*

▸ AS A VERB = **procure**, sell, tout, solicit, live off immoral earnings • *He sold drugs, and also did a bit of pimping on the side.*

pimple = **spot**, boil, swelling, pustule, zit (*slang*), papule (*Pathology*), plook (*Scot.*) • *His face was covered with pimples.*

pin AS A NOUN 1 = **tack**, nail, needle, safety pin • *Use pins to keep the material in place as you work.*

2 = **peg**, rod, brace, bolt • *the steel pin holding his left leg together*

▸ AS A VERB 1 = **fasten**, stick, attach, join, fix, secure, nail, clip, staple, tack, affix • *They pinned a notice to the door.*

2 = **hold fast**, hold down, press, restrain, constrain, immobilize, pinion • *I pinned him against the wall.*

▸ IN PHRASES: **pin someone down** 1 = **force**, pressure, compel, put pressure on, pressurize, nail someone down, make someone commit themselves • *She couldn't pin him down to a decision.*

2 = **trap**, corner, confine, close in on, pen in, hem in, shut in • *The rebels have pinned down government forces.*

pin something down 1 = **determine**, identify, locate, name, specify, designate, pinpoint, home in on • *It has taken until now to pin down its exact location.*

2 = **trap**, confine, constrain, bind, squash, tie down, nail down, immobilize • *The wreckage of the cockpit had pinned down my legs.*

▸ RELATED PHOBIA: enetephobia

pinch AS A VERB 1 = **nip**, press, squeeze, grasp, compress, tweak • *She pinched his arm as hard as she could.*

2 = **hurt**, crush, squeeze, pain, confine, cramp, chafe • *shoes which pinch our toes*

3 = **steal**, rob, snatch, lift (*informal*), nick (*slang, chiefly Brit.*), trouser (*slang*), swipe (*slang*), knock off (*slang*), blag (*slang*), pilfer, snitch (*slang*), purloin, filch, snaffle (*Brit. informal*) • *pickpockets who pinched his wallet*

▸ AS A NOUN 1 = **nip**, squeeze, tweak • *She gave him a little pinch.*

2 = **dash**, bit, taste, mite, jot, speck, small quantity, smidgen (*informal*), soupçon (*French*) • *a pinch of salt*

3 = **emergency**, crisis, difficulty, plight, scrape (*informal*), strait, uphill (*S. African*), predicament, extremity, hardship • *I'd trust her in a pinch.*

▸ IN PHRASES: **at a pinch** = **if necessary**, with difficulty, if need(s) be, just possibly, in a pinch (*U.S. & Canad.*), at a push (*Brit. informal*) • *This recipe serves two, or three at a pinch.*

feel the pinch = **suffer hardship**, be poor, be impoverished, be short of money, have less money, suffer poverty • *The first few months of paying a mortgage is the period when most people feel the pinch.*

pinched = **thin**, starved, worn, drawn, gaunt, haggard, careworn, peaky • *a small, thin woman with pinched features*

OPPOSITES: fat, healthy, plump

pine AS A VERB = **waste**, decline, weaken, sicken, sink, flag, fade, decay, dwindle, wither, wilt, languish, droop • *While away from her children, she pined dreadfully.*

▸ IN PHRASES: **pine for something** *or* **someone**

1 = **long**, ache, crave, yearn, sigh, carry a torch, eat your heart out over, suspire (*archaic or poetic*) • *She was pining for her lost husband.*

2 = **hanker after**, crave, covet, wish for, yearn for, thirst for, hunger for, lust after • *pining for a mythical past*

pinion = **immobilize**, tie, bind, chain, confine, fasten, shackle, pin down, fetter, manacle • *His arms were pinioned against his sides.*

pink AS AN ADJECTIVE = **rosy**, rose, salmon, flushed, reddish, flesh coloured, roseate • *his pink face*

▹ *See panel* **Shades of red**

▸ AS A NOUN = **best**, summit, height, peak, perfection, acme

▸ IN PHRASES: **in the pink** = **in good health**, strong, blooming, very healthy, in fine fettle, in perfect health, in excellent shape, hale and hearty, fit as a fiddle • *A glass of red wine a day will keep you in the pink.*

pinnacle 1 = **summit**, top, height, peak, eminence • *He plunged 80 ft from a rocky pinnacle.*

2 = **height**, top, crown, crest, meridian, zenith, apex, apogee, acme, vertex • *He had reached the pinnacle of his career.*

pinpoint AS A VERB 1 = **identify**, discover, spot, define, distinguish, put your finger on • *It was impossible to pinpoint the cause of death.*
2 = **locate**, find, spot, identify, home in on, zero in on, get a fix on • *trying to pinpoint his precise location*
▸ AS AN ADJECTIVE = **precise**, scientific, careful, strict, accurate, exact, rigorous, meticulous, unerring • *the pinpoint accuracy of the bombing campaign*

pint = **beer**, jar (*Brit. informal*), jug (*Brit. informal*), ale • *Do you fancy a pint?*

pint-sized = **small**, little, tiny, wee, pocket-sized, miniature, diminutive, midget, teeny-weeny, teensy-weensy, pygmy *or* pigmy • *Two pint-sized kids emerged from a doorway.*

pioneer AS A NOUN 1 = **founder**, leader, developer, innovator, founding father, trailblazer • *one of the pioneers in embryology work*
2 = **settler**, explorer, colonist, colonizer, frontiersman • *abandoned settlements of early European pioneers*
▸ AS A VERB = **develop**, create, launch, establish, start, prepare, discover, institute, invent, open up, initiate, originate, take the lead on, instigate, map out, show the way on, lay the groundwork on • *the scientist who invented and pioneered DNA tests*

pious 1 = **religious**, godly, devoted, spiritual, holy, dedicated, righteous, devout, saintly, God-fearing, reverent • *He was brought up by pious female relatives.*
OPPOSITES: irreverent, unholy, irreligious
2 = **self-righteous**, hypocritical, sanctimonious, goody-goody, unctuous, holier-than-thou, pietistic, religiose • *They were derided as pious, self-righteous bores.*
OPPOSITES: humble, sincere, meek

pip = **seed**, stone, pit • *The cape gooseberry has tiny, edible pips.*

pipe AS A NOUN 1 = **tube**, drain, canal, pipeline, line, main, passage, cylinder, hose, conduit, duct, conveyor • *The liquid is conveyed along a pipe.*
2 = **clay (pipe)**, briar, calabash (*rare*), meerschaum, hookah (*rare*) • *He gave up cigarettes and started smoking a pipe.*
3 = **whistle**, horn, recorder, fife, flute, wind instrument, penny whistle • *Pan is often pictured playing a reed pipe.*
▸ AS A VERB = **convey**, channel, supply, conduct, bring in, transmit, siphon • *The gas is piped through a coil surrounded by water.*
▸ IN PHRASES: **pipe down** = **be quiet**, shut up (*informal*), hush, stop talking, quieten down, shush, button it (*slang*), belt up (*slang*), shut your mouth, hold your tongue, put a sock in it (*Brit. slang*), button your lip (*slang*) • *Just pipe down and I'll tell you what I want.*
pipe up = **speak**, volunteer, speak up, have your say, raise your voice, make yourself heard, put your oar in • *'That's right, mister,' another child piped up.*
▹ *See panel* **Tobacco**

pipe dream = **daydream**, dream, notion, fantasy, delusion, vagary, reverie, chimera, castle in the air • *The plan is nothing more than a pipe dream.*

pipeline AS A NOUN = **tube**, passage, pipe, line, conduit, duct, conveyor • *a natural-gas pipeline*
▸ IN PHRASES: **in the pipeline** = **on the way**, expected, coming, close, near, being prepared, anticipated, forthcoming, under way, brewing, imminent, in preparation, in production, in process, in the offing • *A 2.9 per cent pay increase is already in the pipeline.*

piquancy 1 = **spiciness**, bite (*informal*), kick (*informal*), edge, flavour, spice, relish, zest, tang, sharpness, pungency • *a little mustard to add piquancy*
2 = **interest**, pep, zip (*informal*), vitality, colour, spirit, excitement, vigour, zing (*informal*), raciness, pizzazz *or* pizazz (*informal*) • *These facts lent a certain piquancy to the case.*

piquant 1 = **spicy**, biting, sharp, stinging, tart, savoury, pungent, tangy, highly-seasoned, peppery, zesty, with a kick (*informal*), acerb • *a mixed salad with a piquant dressing*
OPPOSITES: mild, bland, insipid
2 = **interesting**, spirited, stimulating, lively, sparkling, provocative, salty, racy, scintillating • *There was a piquant novelty about her books.*
OPPOSITES: boring, dull, tame

pique AS A NOUN = **resentment**, offence, irritation, annoyance, huff, displeasure, umbrage, hurt feelings, vexation, wounded pride • *In a fit of pique, he threw down his bag.*
▸ AS A VERB 1 = **arouse**, excite, stir, spur, stimulate, provoke, rouse, goad, whet, kindle, galvanize • *This phenomenon piqued Dr. Morris' interest.*
2 = **displease**, wound, provoke, annoy, get (*informal*), sting, offend, irritate, put out, incense, gall, nettle, vex, affront, mortify, irk, rile, peeve (*informal*), nark (*Brit., Austral. & N.Z. slang*), put someone's nose out of joint (*informal*), miff (*informal*), hack off (*informal*) • *She was piqued by his lack of enthusiasm.*

piracy 1 = **robbery**, stealing, theft, hijacking, infringement, buccaneering, rapine, freebooting • *Seven of the fishermen have been formally charged with piracy.*
2 = **illegal copying**, bootlegging, plagiarism, copyright infringement, illegal reproduction • *Video piracy is a criminal offence.*

pirate AS A NOUN 1 = **buccaneer**, raider, rover, filibuster, marauder, corsair, sea wolf, freebooter, sea robber, sea rover • *In the nineteenth century, pirates roamed the seas.*
2 = **plagiarist**, plagiarizer, cribber (*informal*), copyright infringer • *software pirates who turn out cheap copies of copyright games*
▸ AS A VERB = **copy**, steal, reproduce, bootleg, lift (*informal*), appropriate, borrow, poach, crib (*informal*), plagiarize • *pirated copies of music tapes*

pirouette AS A NOUN = **spin**, turn, whirl, pivot, twirl • *a ballerina famous for her pirouettes*
▸ AS A VERB = **spin**, turn, whirl, pivot, twirl • *She pirouetted in front of the mirror.*

piss AS A VERB = **urinate**, wee (*informal*), pee (*slang*), tinkle (*Brit. informal*), piddle (*informal*), spend a penny (*Brit. informal*), pass water, wee-wee (*informal*), micturate, take a whizz (*slang, chiefly U.S.*) • *I really need to piss.*
▸ AS A NOUN = **urine**, pee (*slang*), wee-wee (*informal*) • *The hut stank of piss.*
▸ IN PHRASES: **piss off** = **go away**, get lost (*informal*), fuck off (*offensive taboo slang*), bugger off (*taboo slang*), bog off (*Brit. slang*), sling your hook (*slang*), voetsek (*S. African, offensive*), rack off (*Austral. & N.Z. slang*) • *Just piss off and leave me alone!*
piss someone off = **annoy**, get (*informal*), bother, bug (*informal*), irritate, aggravate (*informal*), gall, exasperate, vex, irk, get up someone's nose (*informal*), get someone's back up, get someone's dander up (*informal*), hack someone off (*informal*) • *It pisses me off when they start moaning.*

pissed 1 = **drunk**, wasted (*slang*), wrecked (*slang*), plastered (*slang*), intoxicated, canned (*slang*), bombed (*slang*), loaded (*slang, chiefly U.S. & Canad.*), smashed (*slang*), steaming (*slang*), out of it (*slang*), blitzed (*slang*), hammered (*slang*), pickled (*informal*), bladdered (*slang*), sloshed (*slang*), legless (*informal*), paralytic (*informal*), steamboats (*Scot. slang*), zonked (*slang*), blotto (*slang*), inebriated, rat-arsed (*taboo slang*), blatted (*Brit. slang*), boozed-up (*informal*), dronkverdriet (*S. African*), elephants (*Austral. slang*), broken (*S. African informal*), kaylied (*Brit. slang*), langered (*Irish slang*), lashed (*Brit. slang*), mashed (*Brit. slang*), mullered (*slang*), ossified (*Irish slang*), sat (*S. African*), stukkend (*S. African slang*), trashed (*slang*), Brahms and Liszt (*slang*), bevvied (*dialect*), fu' (*Scot.*), pie-eyed (*slang*) • *He was just lying there completely pissed.*

2 = **angry**, cross, furious, mad *(informal)*, annoyed, pissed off *(taboo slang)*, displeased, irked, tooshie *(Austral. slang)* • *Why is she so pissed at you?*

pistol = **handgun**, shooter, piece *(U.S. & Canad. informal)*, automatic, revolver, side arm • *an unidentified person armed with a pistol*

pit AS A NOUN 1 = **coal mine**, mine, shaft, colliery, mine shaft • *Up to ten pits and ten-thousand jobs could be lost.*
2 = **hole**, gulf, depression, hollow, trench, crater, trough, cavity, abyss, chasm, excavation, pothole • *He lost his footing and began to slide into the pit.*
3 = **pockmark**, depression, hollow, dent, indentation, dimple • *He could see shallow pits in her skin.*
▸ AS A VERB = **scar**, mark, hole, nick, notch, dent, gouge, indent, dint, pockmark • *The plaster was pitted and the paint scuffed.*
▸ IN PHRASES: **pit something** *or* **someone against something** *or* **someone** = **set against**, oppose, match against, measure against, put in competition with, put in opposition to • *You will be pitted against people as good as you are.*
the pits = **terrible**, the worst, awful, dreadful, unspeakable, grotty *(Brit. informal)*, the lowest of the low, extremely bad • *This place is the pits!*

pitch[1] AS A NOUN 1 = **sports field**, ground, stadium, arena, park, field of play • *a cricket pitch*
2 = **tone**, sound, key, frequency, timbre, modulation • *He raised his voice to a higher pitch.*
3 = **level**, point, degree, summit, extent, height, intensity, high point • *Tensions have reached such a pitch in the area that the army have been called in.*
4 = **talk**, line, patter, spiel *(informal)* • *He was impressed with her hard sales pitch.*
5 = **throw**, cast, delivery, toss, hurl, lob • *On the second pitch, Hernandez threw a ball to the backstop.*
▸ AS A VERB 1 = **throw**, launch, cast, toss, hurl, fling, chuck *(informal)*, sling, lob *(informal)*, bung *(Brit. slang)*, heave • *Simon pitched the empty bottle into the lake.*
2 = **aim**, direct, design for, mean for, level • *I think this book is pitched at too high a level for you.*
3 = **fall**, drop, plunge, dive, stagger, tumble, topple, plummet, fall headlong, (take a) nosedive • *He pitched head-first over the low wall.*
4 = **set up**, place, station, locate, raise, plant, settle, fix, put up, erect • *He had pitched his tent in the yard.*
5 = **toss (about)**, roll, plunge, flounder, lurch, wallow, welter, make heavy weather • *The ship was pitching and rolling as if in mid-ocean.*
▸ IN PHRASES: **make a pitch for something** = **promote**, sell, push, plug *(informal)*, puff, hype, publicize, beat the drum for *(informal)* • *The President is making another pitch for his economic program.*
pitch in = **help**, contribute, participate, join in, cooperate, chip in *(informal)*, get stuck in *(Brit. informal)*, lend a hand, muck in *(Brit. informal)*, do your bit, lend a helping hand • *Everyone pitched in to help.*

pitch[2] = **tar**, asphalt, bitumen • *The timbers of the houses were painted with pitch.*
▸ RELATED ADJECTIVE: piceous

pitch-black *or* **pitch-dark** = **dark**, black, jet, raven, ebony, sable, unlit, jet-black, inky, Stygian, pitchy, unilluminated • *a pitch-black winter morning*

pitcher = **jug**, jar, vessel, urn, crock, ewer, carafe • *a pitcher of iced water*

piteous = **pathetic**, moving, affecting, distressing, sad, miserable, dismal, poignant, harrowing, heartbreaking, grievous, pitiful, woeful, deplorable, mournful, lamentable, plaintive, heart-rending, sorrowful, gut-wrenching, wretched, doleful, pitiable • *a piteous sight*

pitfall *usually plural* = **danger**, difficulty, peril, catch, trap, hazard, drawback, snag, uphill *(S. African)*, banana skin *(informal)* • *The pitfalls of working abroad are numerous.*

pithy = **succinct**, pointed, short, brief, to the point, compact, meaningful, forceful, expressive, concise, terse, laconic, trenchant, cogent, epigrammatic, finely honed • *a pithy comment*
OPPOSITES: diffuse, long-winded, wordy

pitiable = **pathetic**, distressing, miserable, poor, sorry, sad, dismal, harrowing, grievous, woeful, deplorable, mournful, lamentable, gut-wrenching, wretched, doleful, piteous • *Her grandmother seemed to her a pitiable figure.*

pitiful 1 = **pathetic**, distressing, miserable, harrowing, heartbreaking, grievous, sad, woeful, deplorable, lamentable, heart-rending, gut-wrenching, wretched, pitiable, piteous • *It was the most pitiful sight I had ever seen.*
OPPOSITES: happy, funny, cheering
2 = **inadequate**, mean, low, miserable, dismal, beggarly, shabby, insignificant, paltry, despicable, measly, contemptible • *Many of them work as farm labourers for pitiful wages.*
OPPOSITES: significant, valuable, adequate
3 = **worthless**, base, sorry, vile, abject, scurvy • *a pitiful performance*
OPPOSITES: significant, admirable, honourable

pitiless = **merciless**, ruthless, heartless, harsh, cruel, brutal, relentless, callous, inhuman, inexorable, implacable, unsympathetic, cold-blooded, uncaring, unfeeling, cold-hearted, unmerciful, hardhearted • *He saw the pitiless eyes of his enemy.*
OPPOSITES: kind, caring, merciful

pittance = **peanuts** *(slang)*, trifle, modicum, drop, mite, chicken feed *(slang)*, slave wages, small allowance • *Her secretaries work tirelessly for a pittance.*

pitted = **scarred**, marked, rough, scratched, dented, riddled, blemished, potholed, indented, eaten away, holey, pockmarked, rutty • *Everywhere building facades are pitted with bullet holes.*

pity AS A NOUN 1 = **compassion**, understanding, charity, sympathy, distress, sadness, sorrow, kindness, tenderness, condolence, commiseration, fellow feeling • *He felt a sudden tender pity for her.*
OPPOSITES: anger, fury, mercilessness
2 = **shame**, crime *(informal)*, sin *(informal)*, misfortune, bad luck, sad thing, bummer *(slang)*, crying shame, source of regret • *It's a pity you couldn't come.*
3 = **mercy**, kindness, clemency, leniency, forbearance, quarter • *a killer who had no pity for his victims*
▸ AS A VERB = **feel sorry for**, feel for, sympathize with, grieve for, weep for, take pity on, empathize with, bleed for, commiserate with, have compassion for, condole with • *I don't know whether to hate him or pity him.*
▸ IN PHRASES: **take pity on something** *or* **someone** = **have mercy on**, spare, forgive, pity, pardon, reprieve, show mercy to, feel compassion for, put out of your misery, relent against • *She took pity on him because he was homeless.*

pivot AS A NOUN 1 = **hub**, centre, heart, hinge, focal point, kingpin • *A large group of watercolours forms the pivot of the exhibition.*
2 = **axis**, swivel, axle, spindle, fulcrum • *The pedal had sheared off at the pivot.*
▸ AS A VERB = **turn**, spin, revolve, rotate, swivel, twirl • *The boat pivoted on its central axis.*
▸ IN PHRASES: **pivot on something** = **rely on**, depend on, hang on, hinge on, be contingent on, revolve round • *the economic problems that pivoted on overseas trade*

pivotal = **crucial**, central, determining, vital, critical, decisive, focal, climactic • *The Court of Appeal has a pivotal role in the English legal system.*

pixie = **elf**, fairy, brownie, sprite, peri • *the fairies, gnomes, elves and pixies of folklore*

placard = **notice**, bill, advertisement, poster, sticker, public notice, affiche *(French)* • *The marchers sang and waved placards.*

placate = **calm**, satisfy, humour, soothe, appease, assuage, pacify, mollify, win someone over, conciliate, propitiate • *He smiled, and made a gesture intended to placate me.*

placatory = **calming**, appeasing, conciliatory, peacemaking, designed to please, pacificatory, propitiative • *He spoke in a placatory tone.*

place AS A NOUN 1 = **spot**, point, position, site, area, situation, station, location, venue, whereabouts, locus • *the place where the temple actually stood*
2 = **region**, city, town, quarter, village, district, neighbourhood, hamlet, vicinity, locality, locale, dorp *(S. African)* • *the opportunity to visit new places*
3 = **position**, point, spot, location • *He returned the album to its place on the shelf.*
4 = **space**, position, seat, chair • *There was a single empty place left at the table.*
▸ IN PHRASES: **know one's place** 1 = **know one's rank**, know one's standing, know one's position, know one's footing, know one's station, know one's status, know one's grade, know one's niche • *a society where everyone knows their place*
2 = **situation**, position, circumstances, shoes *(informal)* • *If I were in your place I'd see a lawyer as soon as possible.*
3 = **job**, position, post, situation, office, employment, appointment, berth *(informal)*, billet *(informal)* • *All the candidates won places on the ruling council.*
4 = **home**, house, room, property, seat, flat, apartment, accommodation, pad *(slang)*, residence, mansion, dwelling, manor, abode, domicile, bachelor apartment *(Canad.)* • *Let's all go back to my place!*
5 *used in negative constructions* = **duty**, right, job, charge, concern, role, affair, responsibility, task, function, prerogative • *It is not my place to comment.*
▸ AS A VERB 1 = **lay (down)**, leave, put (down), set (down), stand, sit, position, rest, plant, station, establish, stick *(informal)*, settle, fix, arrange, lean, deposit, locate, set out, install, prop, dispose, situate, stow, bung *(Brit. slang)*, plonk *(informal)*, array • *Chairs were placed in rows for the parents.*
2 = **put**, lay, set, invest, pin • *Children place their trust in us.*
3 = **classify**, class, group, put, order, sort, rank, arrange, grade, assign, categorize • *The authorities have placed the drug in Class A.*
4 = **entrust to**, give to, assign to, appoint to, allocate to, find a home for • *The twins were placed in a foster home.*
5 = **identify**, remember, recognize, pin someone down, put your finger on, put a name to, set someone in context • *I know we've met, but I can't place you.*

in place 1 = **in position**, positioned, in situ • *The rear plate of the motor was in place.*
2 = **set up**, established, ready, in order, arranged, all set • *Similar legislation is already in place in Wales.*

in place of = **instead of**, rather than, in exchange for, as an alternative to, taking the place of, in lieu of, as a substitute for, as a replacement for • *Cooked kidney beans can be used in place of French beans.*

out of place 1 = **out of position**, messy, out of order, in disarray, in a mess, in disorder, disarranged • *Not a strand of her sleek hair was out of place.*
2 = **incongruous**, uncomfortable, uneasy, ill at ease, like a fish out of water • *I felt out of place in my suit and tie.*
3 = **inappropriate**, wrong, unsuitable, improper, misplaced, unseemly, untoward • *One word out of place may kill the whole peace process.*

put someone in their place = **humble**, humiliate, deflate, crush, mortify, take the wind out of someone's sails, cut someone down to size *(informal)*, take someone down a peg *(informal)*, make someone eat humble pie, bring someone down to size *(informal)*, make someone swallow their pride, settle someone's hash *(informal)* • *She put him in his place with just a few words.*

take place = **happen**, occur, go on, go down *(U.S. & Canad.)*, arise, come about, crop up, transpire *(informal)*, befall, materialize, come to pass *(archaic)*, betide • *Similar demonstrations also took place elsewhere.*

take the place of = **replace**, relieve, substitute for, cover for, take over from, act for, stand in for, fill in for, be a substitute for • *He eventually took Charlie's place in the band.*

P

PLACES AND THEIR NICKNAMES

Place	Nickname
Aberdeen	the Granite City
Adelaide	the City of Churches
Amsterdam	the Venice of the North
Birmingham	Brum *or* the Venice of the North
Boston	Bean Town
Bruges	the Venice of the North
California	the Golden State
Chicago	the Windy City
Dallas	the Big D
Detroit	the Motor City
Dresden	Florence on the Elbe
Dublin	the Fair City
Dumfries	Queen of the South
Edinburgh	Auld Reekie *or* the Athens of the North
Florida	the Sunshine State
Fraserburgh	the Broch
Fremantle	Freo

Place	Nickname
Glasgow	the Dear Green Place
Hamburg	the Venice of the North
Indiana	the Hoosier State
Iowa	the Hawkeye State
Ireland	the Emerald Isle
Jamaica	J.A. *or* the Yard
Jerusalem	the Holy City
Kentucky	the Bluegrass State
Kuala Lumpur	K.L.
London	the Big Smoke *or* the Great Wen
Los Angeles	L.A.
New Jersey	the Garden State
New Orleans	the Crescent City *or* the Big Easy
New South Wales	Ma State
New York (City)	the Big Apple
New York (State)	the Empire State
New Zealand	Pig Island
North Carolina	the Tarheel State

Place	Nickname
Nottingham	Queen of the Midlands
Oklahoma	the Sooner State
Pennsylvania	the Keystone State
Philadelphia	Philly
Portsmouth	Pompey
Prince Edward Island	Spud Island
Queensland	Bananaland *or* the Deep North *(both derogatory)*
Rome	the Eternal City
San Francisco	Frisco
Southeastern U.S.A.	Dixie, Dixieland, *or* the Deep South
Tasmania	Tassie *or* the Apple Isle
Texas	the Lone Star State
Toronto	Hogtown
Utah	the Beehive State
Venice	La Serenissima

placement 1 = **positioning**, stationing, arrangement, location, ordering, distribution, locating, installation, deployment, disposition, emplacement • *The treatment involves the placement of electrodes in the inner ear.*
2 = **appointment**, employment, engagement, assignment • *He had a six-month work placement with the Japanese government.*

placid 1 = **calm**, cool, quiet, peaceful, even, collected, gentle, mild, composed, serene, tranquil, undisturbed, unmoved, untroubled, unfazed (*informal*), unruffled, self-possessed, imperturbable, equable, even-tempered, unexcitable, chilled (*informal*) • *She was a placid child who rarely cried.*
OPPOSITES: emotional, disturbed, excitable
2 = **still**, quiet, calm, peaceful, serene, tranquil, undisturbed, halcyon, unruffled • *the placid waters of Lake Erie*
OPPOSITES: rough, disturbed, agitated

plagiarism = **copying**, borrowing, theft, appropriation, infringement, piracy, lifting (*informal*), cribbing (*informal*) • *He's accused of plagiarism.*

QUOTATIONS
If you steal from one author, it's plagiarism; if you steal from many, it's research
[Wilson Mizner]

plagiarize = **copy**, steal, appropriate, borrow, pirate, infringe, lift (*informal*), crib (*informal*), thieve • *He was accused of plagiarizing copyrighted material.*

plague AS A NOUN 1 = **disease**, infection, epidemic, contagion, pandemic, pestilence, lurgy (*informal*) • *A cholera plague had killed many prisoners of war.*
2 = **infestation**, invasion, epidemic, influx, host, swarm, multitude • *The city is under threat from a plague of rats.*
3 = **bane**, trial, cancer, evil, curse, torment, blight, calamity, scourge, affliction • *the cynicism which is the plague of our generation*
4 = **nuisance**, problem, pain (*informal*), bother, pest, hassle (*informal*), annoyance, irritant, aggravation (*informal*), vexation, thorn in your flesh • *Those children can be a real plague at times.*
▸ AS A VERB 1 = **torment**, trouble, pain, torture, haunt, afflict • *She was plagued by weakness, fatigue, and dizziness.*
2 = **pester**, trouble, bother, disturb, annoy, tease, harry, harass, hassle, fret, badger, persecute, molest, vex, bedevil, get on your nerves (*informal*), give someone grief (*Brit. & S. African*), be on your back (*slang*), get in your hair (*informal*) • *I'm not going to plague you with a lot of questions.*

plain AS AN ADJECTIVE 1 = **unadorned**, simple, basic, severe, pure, bare, modest, stark, restrained, muted, discreet, austere, spartan, unfussy, unvarnished, unembellished, unornamented, unpatterned, bare-bones • *a plain grey stone house, distinguished by its unspoilt simplicity* • *Her dress was plain, but it hung well on her.*
OPPOSITES: adorned, decorated, ornate
2 = **clear**, obvious, patent, evident, apparent, visible, distinct, understandable, manifest, transparent, overt, unmistakable, lucid, unambiguous, comprehensible, legible • *It was plain to me that he was having a nervous breakdown.*
OPPOSITES: hidden, disguised, concealed
3 = **straightforward**, open, direct, frank, bold, blunt, sincere, outspoken, honest, downright, candid, forthright, upfront (*informal*), artless, ingenuous, guileless • *his reputation for plain speaking*
OPPOSITES: indirect, rambling, roundabout
4 = **ugly**, ordinary, unattractive, homely (*U.S. & Canad.*), not striking, unlovely, unprepossessing, not beautiful, no oil painting (*informal*), ill-favoured, unalluring, fugly (*chiefly U.S. & Austral.*) • *a shy, rather plain girl with a pale complexion*
OPPOSITES: beautiful, attractive, handsome
5 = **ordinary**, homely, common, simple, modest, everyday, commonplace, lowly, unaffected, unpretentious, frugal, workaday • *We are just plain people.*
OPPOSITES: worldly, affected, sophisticated
▸ AS A NOUN = **flatland**, plateau, prairie, grassland, mesa, lowland, steppe, open country, pampas, tableland, veld, llano • *Once there were 70 million buffalo on the plains.*

plainly 1 = **clearly**, obviously, undoubtedly, undeniably, beyond doubt, incontrovertibly, incontestably • *The judge's conclusion was plainly wrong.*
2 = **openly**, frankly, publicly, in public, overtly, candidly, unreservedly, forthrightly, straight from the shoulder (*informal*) • *Few of our political leaders are willing to talk plainly about the crisis.*

plain-spoken = **blunt**, direct, frank, straightforward, open, explicit, outright, outspoken, downright, candid, forthright, upfront (*informal*), unequivocal • *a plain-spoken man full of scorn for pomp and pretense*
OPPOSITES: guarded, diplomatic, tactful

plaintive = **sorrowful**, sad, pathetic, melancholy, grievous, pitiful, woeful, wistful, mournful, heart-rending, rueful, grief-stricken, disconsolate, doleful, woebegone, piteous • *Her voice was small and plaintive.*

plan AS A NOUN 1 = **scheme**, system, design, idea, programme, project, proposal, strategy, method, suggestion, procedure, plot, device, scenario, proposition, contrivance • *She met her creditors to propose a plan for making repayments.*
2 = **diagram**, map, drawing, chart, illustration, representation, sketch, blueprint, layout, delineation, scale drawing • *Draw a plan of the garden.*
3 = **intention**, idea, aim, hope, goal, target, object, ambition • *Her plan was to teach the children at home.*
▸ AS A VERB 1 = **devise**, arrange, prepare, scheme, frame, plot, draft, organize, outline, invent, formulate, contrive, think out, concoct • *I had been planning a trip to the West Coast.*
2 = **intend**, aim, mean, propose, purpose, contemplate, envisage, foresee • *The rebel soldiers plan to strike again.*
3 = **design**, outline, draw up a plan of • *The company is planning a theme park on the site.*

plane AS A NOUN 1 = **aeroplane**, aircraft, jet, airliner, jumbo jet • *He had plenty of time to catch his plane.*
2 = **flat surface**, the flat, horizontal, level surface • *a building with angled planes*
3 = **level**, position, stage, footing, condition, standard, degree, rung, stratum, echelon • *life on a higher plane of existence*
▸ AS AN ADJECTIVE = **level**, even, flat, regular, plain, smooth, uniform, flush, horizontal • *a plane surface*
▸ AS A VERB = **skim**, sail, skate, glide • *The boats planed across the lake with the greatest of ease.*

planet

PLANETS

Earth	Mercury	Uranus
Jupiter	Neptune	Venus
Mars	Saturn	

plangent = **resonant**, ringing, loud, resounding, reverberating, mournful, plaintive, sonorous, deep-toned, clangorous • *plangent Celtic music*

plank = **board**, beam, timber, stave • *made of three solid planks of wood*

planning = **arrangement**, organization, setting up, working out, preparation(s), groundwork, forethought • *The trip needs careful planning.*

plant[1] AS A NOUN = **flower**, bush, vegetable, herb, weed, shrub • *Water each plant as often as required.*
▸ AS A VERB 1 = **sow**, scatter, set out, transplant, implant,

put in the ground • *He intends to plant fruit and vegetables.*
2 = seed, sow, implant • *They are going to plant the area with grass and trees.*
3 = place, put, set, settle, fix • *She planted her feet wide and bent her knees slightly.*
4 = hide, put, place, conceal • *So far no-one has admitted to planting the bomb in the hotel.*
5 = place, put, establish, found, fix, institute, root, lodge, insert, sow the seeds of, imbed • *Sir Eric had evidently planted the idea in her mind.*
▸ **RELATED MANIA:** florimania
▹ *See panels* **Algae; Ferns; Flowers; Fungi; Grasses; Parts of plants; Poisons; Shrubs; Trees**

QUOTATIONS
What is a weed? A plant whose virtues have not been discovered
[Ralph Waldo Emerson *Fortune of the Republic*]

plant² **1 = factory**, works, shop, yard, mill, foundry • *The plant provides forty per cent of the country's electricity.*
2 = machinery, equipment, gear, apparatus • *Firms may invest in plant and equipment abroad where costs are cheaper.*

plaque = **plate**, panel, medal, tablet, badge, slab, brooch, medallion, cartouch(e) • *Her Majesty unveiled a commemorative plaque.*

plaster **AS A NOUN 1 = mortar**, stucco, gypsum, plaster of Paris, gesso • *a sculpture in plaster by Rodin*
2 = bandage, dressing, sticking plaster, Elastoplast *(trademark)*, adhesive plaster • *Put a piece of plaster on the graze.*
▸ **AS A VERB = cover**, spread, coat, smear, overlay, daub, besmear, bedaub • *She gets sunburn even when she plasters herself in lotion.*

plastic **1 = false**, artificial, synthetic, superficial, sham, pseudo *(informal)*, spurious, specious, meretricious, phoney or phony *(informal)* • *When girls wear too much make-up, they look plastic.*
OPPOSITES: natural, real, true
2 = pliant, soft, flexible, supple, pliable, tensile, ductile, mouldable, fictile • *The mud is as soft and plastic as butter.*
OPPOSITES: hard, stiff, rigid

plasticity = **pliability**, flexibility, suppleness, malleability, pliableness • *The new insulating compound demonstrated remarkable plasticity.*

plastic surgery = **cosmetic surgery**, face lift *(informal)* • *She had plastic surgery to change the shape of her nose.*

plate **AS A NOUN 1 = platter**, dish, dinner plate, salver, trencher *(archaic)* • *Scott piled his plate with food.*
2 = helping, course, serving, dish, portion, platter, plateful • *a huge plate of bacon and eggs*
3 = layer, panel, sheet, slab • *The beam is strengthened by a steel plate 6 millimetres thick.*
4 = plaque, sign, nameplate, door plate, cartouche • *a brass plate on his office door*
5 = illustration, picture, photograph, print, engraving, lithograph • *The book has 55 colour plates.*
▸ **AS A VERB = coat**, gild, laminate, face, cover, silver, nickel, overlay, electroplate, anodize, platinize • *small steel balls plated with chrome or gold*

plateau **1 = upland**, table, highland, mesa, tableland • *a high, flat plateau of cultivated land*
2 = levelling off, level, stage, stability • *The economy is stuck on a plateau of slow growth.*

platform **1 = stage**, stand, podium, rostrum, dais, soapbox • *Nick finished his speech and jumped down from the platform.*
2 = policy, programme, principle, objective(s), manifesto, tenet(s), party line • *The party has announced a platform of economic reforms.* • *They won a landslide victory on a nationalist platform.*

platitude = **cliché**, stereotype, commonplace, banality, truism, bromide, verbiage, inanity, trite remark, hackneyed saying • *politicians spouting the same old platitudes*

Platonic *often not cap*= **nonphysical**, ideal, intellectual, spiritual, idealistic, transcendent • *Their relationship was purely platonic.*

platoon = **squad**, company, group, team, outfit *(informal)*, patrol, squadron • *a platoon of armed soldiers*

platter = **plate**, dish, tray, charger, salver, trencher *(archaic)* • *The food was served on silver platters.*

plaudits = **approval**, acclaim, applause, praise, clapping, ovation, kudos, congratulation, round of applause, commendation, approbation, acclamation • *They won plaudits and prizes for their films.*

plausible **1 = believable**, possible, likely, reasonable, credible, probable, persuasive, conceivable, tenable, colourable, verisimilar • *That explanation seems entirely plausible to me.*
OPPOSITES: impossible, unlikely, unbelievable
2 = glib, smooth, specious, smooth-talking, smooth-tongued, fair-spoken • *He was so plausible he conned us all.*

play **AS A VERB 1 = amuse yourself**, have fun, frolic, sport, fool, romp, revel, trifle, caper, frisk, gambol, entertain yourself, engage in games • *The children played in the garden.*
2 = take part in, be involved in, engage in, participate in, compete in, be in a team for • *I used to play basketball.*
3 = compete against, challenge, take on, rival, oppose, vie with, contend against • *Northern Ireland will play Latvia tomorrow.*
4 = hit, pass, shoot, kick • *Think before playing the ball*

P

PARTS OF PLANTS

androecium	corolla	gynoecium	nucellus	pollen grain	spathe
anther	corymb	head	offshoot	pollinium	spike
anthophore	costa	hibernaculum	ovary	raceme	spikelet
blossom	cyathium	hypanthium	ovule	rachis	spur
bract	cyme	inflorescence	palea	receptacle, thalamus, *or* torus	stamen
bud	dichasium	internode	panicle		stem
bulbil	epidermis	involucel	pedicel	root	stigma
calyx	filament	involucre	peduncle	root cap	stoma
capitulum	floral envelope	joint	perianth	root hair	style
carpel	floret	leaf	petal	secundine	taproot
carpophore	foliage	lemma	phloem	seed	tassel
catkin	fruit	lip	pistil	seed pod	tepal
caulis	gametophore	micropyle	placenta	sepal	umbel
clinandrium	guard cell	monochasium	pod	sheath	vascular bundle
commissure	glume	nectary	pollen	spadix	xylem

5 = perform, carry out, execute • *Someone had played a trick on her.*
6 = act, portray, represent, perform, impersonate, act the part of, take the part of, personate • *His ambition is to play the part of Dracula.*
7 = perform on, strum, make music on • *Do you play the guitar?*
8 *often with* **about** *or* **around = fool around**, toy, fiddle, trifle, mess around, take something lightly • *He's not working, he's just playing around.*
▸ **AS A NOUN 1 = amusement**, pleasure, leisure, games, sport, fun, entertainment, relaxation, a good time, recreation, enjoyment, romping, larks, capering, frolicking, junketing, fun and games, revelry, skylarking, living it up *(informal)*, gambolling, horseplay, merrymaking, me-time • *Try to strike a balance between work and play.* • *a few hours of play until you go to bed*
2 = drama, show, performance, piece, comedy, entertainment, tragedy, farce, soap opera, soapie *(Austral. slang)*, pantomime, stage show, television drama, radio play, masque, dramatic piece • *The company put on a play about the homeless.*
3 = movement, room, space, give *(informal)*, swing, sweep, margin, slack, latitude, leeway, freedom of movement, elbowroom, free motion • *There should be just enough play to allow the trunk to expand.*
4 = scope, room, range, freedom, licence, liberty, indulgence, latitude, free rein • *a dazzling picture book which allows imaginations full play*
5 = operation, working, action, activity, movement, function, employment • *The play of chance may happen to favour either man.*
▸ **IN PHRASES: in play = in** *or* **for fun**, for sport, for a joke, for a lark *(informal)*, as a prank, for a jest • *It was done only in play, but they got a ticking off from the police.*
play around = philander, have an affair, carry on *(informal)*, fool around, dally, sleep around *(informal)*, womanize, play away from home *(informal)* • *Up to 75 per cent of married men may be playing around.*
play at something = pretend to be, pose as, impersonate, make like *(U.S. & Canad. informal)*, profess to be, assume the role of, give the appearance of, masquerade as, pass yourself off as • *rich people just playing at being farmers*
play ball = cooperate, play the game, show willing, pitch in *(informal)*, play along, go along with the plan • *I was waiting until I knew if you and Jack would play ball.*
play on *or* **upon something = take advantage of**, abuse, exploit, impose on, trade on, misuse, milk, make use of, utilize, profit by, capitalize on, turn to your account • *I felt as if I was playing on her generosity.*
play something down = minimize, make light of, gloss over, talk down, underrate, underplay, pooh-pooh *(informal)*, soft-pedal *(informal)*, make little of, set no store by • *Western diplomats have played down the significance of the reports.*
play something up = emphasize, highlight, underline, magnify, stress, accentuate, foreground, point up, call attention to, turn the spotlight on, bring to the fore • *This increase in crime is definitely being played up by the media.*
play up 1 = hurt, be painful, bother you, trouble you, be sore, pain you, give you trouble, give you gyp *(Brit. & N.Z. slang)* • *My bad back is playing up again.*
2 = malfunction, not work properly, be on the blink *(slang)*, be wonky *(Brit. slang)* • *The engine has started playing up.*
3 = be awkward, misbehave, give trouble, be disobedient, give someone grief *(Brit. & S. African)*, be stroppy *(Brit. slang)*, be bolshie *(Brit. informal)* • *The kids always play up in his class.*
play up to someone = butter up, flatter, pander to, crawl to, get in with, suck up to *(informal)*, curry favour with, toady, fawn over, keep someone sweet, kiss someone's ass *(U.S. & Canad. taboo slang)*, brown-nose *(taboo slang)*, bootlick *(informal)*, ingratiate yourself to • *She plays up to journalists in the media.*
play with something = toy with, wiggle, fiddle with, jiggle, waggle, mess about with, fidget with • *She played idly with the strap of her handbag.*

QUOTATIONS

The play's the thing
Wherein I'll catch the conscience of the king
[William Shakespeare *Hamlet*]

Play it Sam. Play 'As Time Goes By'
[J. Epstein, P. Epstein, H. Koch and M. Curtiz *Casablanca*]

playboy = womanizer, philanderer, rake, socialite, man about town, pleasure seeker, lady-killer *(informal)*, roué, lover boy *(slang)*, ladies' man • *Father was a playboy.*
player 1 = sportsman *or* **sportswoman**, competitor, participant, contestant, team member • *top chess players*
2 = musician, artist, performer, virtuoso, instrumentalist, music maker • *a professional trumpet player*
3 = performer, entertainer, Thespian, trouper, actor *or* actress • *Oscar nominations went to all five leading players*
playful 1 = joking, humorous, jokey, arch, teasing, coy, tongue-in-cheek, jesting, flirtatious, good-natured, roguish, waggish • *She gave her husband a playful slap.*
2 = lively, spirited, cheerful, merry, mischievous, joyous, sprightly, vivacious, rollicking, impish, frisky, puckish, coltish, kittenish, frolicsome, ludic *(literary)*, sportive, gay, larkish *(informal)* • *They tumbled around like playful children.*
OPPOSITES: serious, grave, sedate
playground = play park, play area, recreation ground, adventure playground *(Brit.)* • *a children's zoo with a playground*
playmate = friend, companion, comrade, chum *(informal)*, pal *(informal)*, cobber *(Austral. & N.Z. old-fashioned informal)*, playfellow • *Children benefit from having regular playmates.*
plaything = toy, amusement, game, pastime, trifle, trinket, bauble, gimcrack, gewgaw • *an untidy garden scattered with children's playthings*
playwright = dramatist, scriptwriter, tragedian, dramaturge, dramaturgist • *the German playwright Bertolt Brecht*
plea 1 = appeal, request, suit, prayer, begging, petition, overture, entreaty, intercession, supplication • *an impassioned plea to mankind to act to save the planet*
2 = suit, cause, action, allegation • *We will enter a plea of not guilty.*
3 = excuse, claim, defence, explanation, justification, pretext, vindication, extenuation • *He murdered his wife, but got off on a plea of insanity.*
plead 1 = appeal, ask, request, beg, petition, crave, solicit, implore, beseech, entreat, importune, supplicate • *He was kneeling on the floor pleading for mercy.*
2 = allege, claim, argue, maintain, assert, put forward, adduce, use as an excuse • *The guards pleaded that they were only obeying orders.*
pleasant 1 = pleasing, nice, welcome, satisfying, fine, lovely, acceptable, amusing, refreshing, delightful, enjoyable, gratifying, agreeable, pleasurable, delectable, lekker *(S. African slang)* • *a pleasant surprise*
OPPOSITES: awful, offensive, horrible
2 = friendly, nice, agreeable, likable *or* likeable, engaging, charming, cheerful, cheery, good-humoured, amiable, genial, affable, congenial • *He was most anxious to seem agreeable and pleasant.*
OPPOSITES: offensive, horrible, disagreeable
pleasantry *usually plural* **= comment**, remark, casual remark, polite remark • *They exchanged pleasantries about the weather.*

P

please 1 = **delight**, entertain, humour, amuse, suit, content, satisfy, charm, cheer, indulge, tickle, gratify, gladden, give pleasure to, tickle someone pink *(informal)* • *This comment pleased her immensely.*
OPPOSITES: anger, depress, annoy
2 = **want**, like, choose, wish, will, prefer, desire, opt, be inclined, see fit • *Women should be able to dress as they please.*

pleased = **happy**, delighted, contented, satisfied, thrilled, glad, tickled, gratified, over the moon *(informal)*, chuffed *(Brit. slang)*, euphoric, rapt, in high spirits, tickled pink *(informal)*, pleased as punch *(informal)* • *They're pleased to be going home.*

pleasing 1 = **enjoyable**, satisfying, attractive, charming, entertaining, delightful, gratifying, agreeable, pleasurable • *a pleasing view*
OPPOSITES: boring, dull, unpleasant
2 = **likable** *or* **likeable**, attractive, engaging, charming, winning, entertaining, amusing, delightful, polite, agreeable, amiable • *a pleasing personality*
OPPOSITES: unlikable *or* unlikeable, boring, disagreeable

pleasurable = **enjoyable**, pleasant, diverting, good, nice, welcome, fun, lovely, entertaining, delightful, gratifying, agreeable, congenial • *the most pleasurable experience of the evening*

pleasure AS A NOUN 1 = **happiness**, delight, satisfaction, enjoyment, bliss, gratification, contentment, gladness, delectation • *We exclaimed with pleasure when we saw them.*
OPPOSITES: suffering, pain, displeasure
2 = **amusement**, joy, recreation, diversion, solace, jollies *(slang)*, beer and skittles *(informal)* • *Watching TV is our only pleasure.*
OPPOSITES: labour, duty, obligation
3 = **wish**, choice, desire, will, mind, option, preference, inclination • *Let me get you a drink. What's your pleasure?*
▸ IN PHRASES: **take pleasure in something** = **enjoy**, like, adore, love, relish, delight in, savour, revel in, get a kick out of *(informal)*, be entertained by, be amused by • *He took pleasure in humiliating her.*
with pleasure = **gladly**, of course, happily, readily, cheerfully, willingly, by all means • *'Could you put the advert in the post to us?' – 'With pleasure.'*
▸ RELATED MANIA: hedonomania
▸ RELATED PHOBIA: hedonophobia

QUOTATIONS

Everyone is dragged on by their favourite pleasure
[Virgil *Eclogue*]

Pleasure's a sin, and sometimes sin's a pleasure
[Lord Byron *Don Juan*]

Sweet is pleasure after pain
[John Dryden *Alexander's Feast*]

The rapturous, wild, and ineffable pleasure
Of drinking at somebody else's expense
[Henry Sambrooke Leigh *Carols of Cockayne*]

Pleasure is nothing else but the intermission of pain
[John Selden *Table Talk*]

One half of the world cannot understand the pleasures of the other
[Jane Austen *Emma*]

pleat AS A NOUN = **fold**, crease, gather, tuck, pucker, crimp • *There was a row of starched pleats on her cap.*
▸ AS A VERB = **fold**, crease, gather, tuck, pucker, crimp • *large baggy trousers, pleated at the front*

plebeian AS AN ADJECTIVE 1 = **common**, working-class, lower-class, proletarian, ignoble, lowborn, blue-singlet *(Austral. slang)* • *a man who rose to greatness but never forgot his plebeian past*
OPPOSITES: upper-class, aristocratic, high-class
2 = **uncultivated**, mean, low, base, coarse, vulgar, unrefined, non-U *(Brit. informal)* • *He had a cockney accent and an alarmingly plebeian manner.*
OPPOSITES: polished, refined, well-bred
▸ AS A NOUN = **commoner**, peasant, proletarian, common man, man in the street, pleb, prole *(derogatory slang, chiefly Brit.)* • *the history of class struggles, plebeians against patricians*

plebiscite = **vote**, poll, referendum, ballot • *The future of the country should be decided by plebiscite.*

pledge AS A NOUN 1 = **promise**, vow, assurance, word, undertaking, warrant, oath, covenant, word of honour • *a pledge to step up cooperation between the states*
2 = **guarantee**, security, deposit, bail, bond, collateral, earnest, pawn, gage, surety • *items held in pledge for loans*
3 = **token**, mark, sign, symbol, evidence, proof, testimony • *He gave her the ring as a pledge of his eternal love.*
▸ AS A VERB 1 = **promise**, vow, vouch, swear, contract, engage, undertake, give your word, give your word of honour, give your oath • *I pledge that by next year we will have the problem solved.*
2 = **promise**, contribute, donate, make a gift of, put yourself down for • *He pledged £150 million to build the theatre.*
3 = **bind**, guarantee, mortgage, engage, gage *(archaic)* • *He asked her to pledge the house as security for the loan.*

plenary 1 = **full**, open, general, whole, complete, entire • *a plenary session of the Central Committee*
2 = **complete**, full, sweeping, absolute, thorough, unlimited, unconditional, unqualified, unrestricted • *The president has plenary power in some areas of foreign policy.*

plenitude 1 = **completeness**, fullness, amplitude, repletion • *The music brought him a feeling of plenitude and freedom.*
2 = **abundance**, wealth, excess, bounty, plenty, plethora, profusion, cornucopia, copiousness, plenteousness • *a book with a plenitude of pictures*

plentiful 1 = **abundant**, liberal, generous, lavish, complete, ample, infinite, overflowing, copious, inexhaustible, bountiful, profuse, thick on the ground, bounteous *(literary)*, plenteous • *a plentiful supply*
OPPOSITES: sparing, inadequate, scarce
2 = **productive**, bumper, fertile, prolific, fruitful, luxuriant, plenteous • *a celebration that gives thanks for a plentiful harvest*

plenty 1 = **abundance**, wealth, luxury, prosperity, fertility, profusion, affluence, opulence, plenitude, fruitfulness, copiousness, plenteousness, plentifulness • *You are fortunate to be growing up in a time of peace and plenty.*
2 *usually with* **of** = **lots of** *(informal)*, enough, a great deal of, masses of, quantities of, piles of *(informal)*, mountains of, a good deal of, stacks of, heaps of *(informal)*, a mass of, a volume of, an abundance of, a plethora of, a quantity of, a fund of, oodles of *(informal)*, a store of, a mine of, a sufficiency of • *There was still plenty of time.*

plethora = **excess**, surplus, glut, profusion, surfeit, overabundance, superabundance, superfluity • *A plethora of books have been written on the subject.*
OPPOSITES: lack, shortage, deficiency

pliable 1 = **flexible**, plastic, supple, lithe, limber, malleable, pliant, tensile, bendy, ductile, bendable • *The baskets are made with young, pliable spruce roots.*
OPPOSITES: stiff, rigid
2 = **compliant**, susceptible, responsive, manageable, receptive, yielding, adaptable, docile, impressionable, easily led, pliant, tractable, persuadable, influenceable, like putty in your hands • *His young queen was pliable and easily influenced.*
OPPOSITES: stubborn, intractable, inflexible

pliant 1 = **impressionable**, susceptible, manageable, adaptable, compliant, yielding, pliable, easily led, tractable, biddable, persuadable, influenceable • *She's proud and stubborn under that pliant exterior.*
2 = **flexible**, plastic, supple, lithe, pliable, tensile, bendy, ductile, bendable • *pliant young willows*

plight = **difficulty**, condition, state, situation, trouble, circumstances, dilemma, straits, predicament, extremity, perplexity • *the plight of Third World countries plagued by debts*

plod 1 = **trudge**, drag, tread, clump, lumber, tramp, stomp (*informal*), slog • *He plodded slowly up the hill.*
2 = **slog away**, labour, grind away (*informal*), toil, grub, persevere, soldier on, plough through, plug away (*informal*), drudge, peg away • *He is still plodding away at the same job.*

plot[1] AS A NOUN 1 = **plan**, scheme, intrigue, conspiracy, cabal, stratagem, machination, covin (*Law*) • *a plot to overthrow the government*
2 = **story**, action, subject, theme, outline, scenario, narrative, thread, story line • *the plot of a cheap spy novel*
▸ AS A VERB 1 = **plan**, scheme, conspire, intrigue, manoeuvre, contrive, collude, cabal, hatch a plot, machinate • *They are awaiting trial for plotting against the state.*
2 = **devise**, design, project, lay, imagine, frame, conceive, brew, hatch, contrive, concoct, cook up (*informal*) • *a meeting to plot the survival strategy of the party*
3 = **chart**, mark, draw, map, draft, locate, calculate, outline, compute • *We were trying to plot the course of the submarine.*

QUOTATIONS
Ay, now the plot thickens very much upon us
[George Villiers Buckingham *The Rehearsal*]

plot[2] = **patch**, lot, area, ground, parcel, tract, allotment • *a small plot of land for growing vegetables*

plotter = **conspirator**, architect, intriguer, planner, conspirer, strategist, conniver, Machiavellian, schemer, cabalist • *the chief plotter behind the unsuccessful coup attempt*

plough AS A VERB = **turn over**, dig, till, ridge, cultivate, furrow, break ground • *They ploughed 100,000 acres of virgin moorland.*
▸ IN PHRASES: **plough into something** *or* **someone** = **plunge into**, crash into, smash into, career into, shove into, hurtle into, bulldoze into • *The car veered off the road and ploughed into a culvert.*
plough through something = **forge**, cut, drive, press, push, plunge, surge, stagger, wade, flounder, trudge, plod • *Mr Dambar watched her plough through the grass.*

plover
▸ COLLECTIVE NOUNS: stand, wing

ploy = **tactic**, move, trick, device, game, scheme, manoeuvre, dodge, ruse, gambit, subterfuge, stratagem, contrivance, wile • *a cynical marketing ploy*

pluck AS A VERB 1 = **pull out** *or* **off**, pick, draw, collect, gather, harvest • *I plucked a lemon from the tree.*
2 = **tug**, catch, snatch, clutch, jerk, yank, tweak, pull at • *He plucked the cigarette from his mouth.*
3 = **strum**, pick, finger, twang, thrum, plunk • *Nell was plucking a harp.*
▸ AS A NOUN = **courage**, nerve, heart, spirit, bottle (*Brit. slang*), resolution, determination, guts (*informal*), balls (*taboo slang*), grit, bravery, backbone, mettle, boldness, spunk (*informal*), intrepidity, hardihood, ballsiness (*taboo slang*) • *Cynics might sneer at him but you have to admire his pluck.*

plucky = **courageous**, spirited, brave, daring, bold, game, hardy, heroic, gritty, feisty (*informal, chiefly U.S. & Canad.*), gutsy (*slang*), intrepid, valiant, doughty, undaunted, unflinching, spunky (*informal*), ballsy (*taboo slang*), mettlesome, (as) game as Ned Kelly (*Austral. slang*) • *The plucky schoolgirl amazed doctors by hanging on to life.*
OPPOSITES: yellow (*informal*), afraid, cowardly

plug AS A NOUN 1 = **stopper**, cork, bung, spigot, stopple • *A plug had been inserted in the drill hole.*
2 = **mention**, advertisement, advert (*Brit. informal*), push, promotion, publicity, puff, hype, good word, namecheck • *The show was little more than a plug for her new film.*
▸ AS A VERB 1 = **seal**, close, stop, fill, cover, block, stuff, pack, cork, choke, stopper, bung, stop up, stopple • *Crews are working to plug a major oil leak.*
2 = **mention**, push, promote, publicize, advertise, build up, puff, hype, write up, namecheck • *If I hear another actor plugging his latest book I will scream.*
▸ IN PHRASES: **plug away** = **slog away**, labour, toil away, grind away (*informal*), peg away, plod away, drudge away • *I just keep plugging away at this job, although I hate it.*

plum = **choice**, prize, first-class • *Laura landed a plum job with a smart art gallery.*

plumage = **feathers**, down, plumes • *razorbills with their handsome black and white plumage*

plumb AS A VERB = **delve into**, measure, explore, probe, sound out, search, go into, penetrate, gauge, unravel, fathom • *her attempts to plumb my innermost emotions*
▸ AS AN ADVERB = **exactly**, precisely, bang, slap, spot-on (*Brit. informal*) • *The hotel is set plumb in the middle of the High Street.*
▸ IN PHRASES: **plumb the depths of something** = **find**, reach the nadir, reach the lowest possible level, reach rock bottom of • *questions that plumb the depths of stupidity*

plume = **feather**, crest, quill, pinion, aigrette • *straw hats decorated with ostrich plumes*

plummet 1 = **drop**, fall, crash, nosedive, descend rapidly • *Share prices have plummeted.*
2 = **plunge**, fall, drop, crash, tumble, swoop, stoop, nosedive, descend rapidly • *The car plummeted off a cliff.*

plummy = **deep**, posh (*informal, chiefly Brit.*), refined, upper-class, fruity, resonant • *radio announcers with plummy voices*

plump[1] = **chubby**, fat, stout, full, round, burly, obese, fleshy, beefy (*informal*), tubby, portly, buxom, dumpy, roly-poly, well-covered, rotund, podgy, corpulent, well-upholstered (*informal*) • *Maria was small and plump with a mass of curly hair.*
OPPOSITES: thin, lean, scrawny

plump[2] AS A VERB = **flop**, fall, drop, sink, dump, slump • *Breathlessly, she plumped down next to Katrina.*
▸ IN PHRASES: **plump for something** *or* **someone** = **choose**, favour, go for, back, support, opt for, side with, come down in favour of • *In the end, we plumped for an endowment mortgage.*

plunder AS A VERB 1 = **loot**, strip, sack, rob, raid, devastate, spoil, rifle, ravage, ransack, pillage, despoil • *They plundered and burned the town.*
2 = **steal**, rob, take, nick (*informal*), trouser (*slang*), pinch (*informal*), knock off (*slang*), embezzle, pilfer, thieve • *a settlement to recover money plundered from government coffers*
▸ AS A NOUN 1 = **pillage**, sacking, robbery, marauding, rapine, spoliation • *a guerrilla group infamous for torture and plunder*
2 = **loot**, spoils, prey, booty, swag (*slang*), ill-gotten gains • *Pirates swarmed the seas in search of easy plunder.*

plunge AS A VERB 1 = **descend**, fall, drop, crash, pitch, sink, go down, dive, tumble, plummet, nosedive • *50 people died when a bus plunged into a river.*
2 = **hurtle**, charge, career, jump, tear, rush, dive, dash, swoop, lurch • *I plunged forward, calling her name.*
3 = **stab**, push, stick, sink, thrust, jab • *A soldier plunged a bayonet into his body.*
4 = **submerge**, sink, duck, dip, immerse, douse, dunk • *She plunged her face into a bowl of cold water.*
5 = **throw**, cast, pitch, propel • *conflicts which threaten to plunge the country into chaos*
6 = **fall steeply**, drop, crash (*informal*), go down, slump, plummet, take a nosedive (*informal*) • *Net profits plunged 73% last year.*
▸ AS A NOUN 1 = **fall**, crash (*informal*), slump, drop, tumble • *the stock market plunge*
2 = **dive**, jump, duck, swoop, descent, immersion, submersion • *a refreshing plunge into cold water*
▸ IN PHRASES: **take the plunge** = **commit yourself**, go for it, go all out, throw caution to the wind, jump in at the deep

end *(informal)*, give it your all • *She decided to take the plunge and expand her business.*

plurality = **multiplicity**, variety, diversity, profusion, numerousness • *Federalism implies a plurality of political authorities.*

plus AS A PREPOSITION = **and**, with, added to, coupled with, with the addition of • *Send a cheque for £18.99 plus £2 for postage and packing.*

▸ AS A NOUN = **advantage**, benefit, asset, gain, extra, bonus, perk *(Brit. informal)*, good point, icing on the cake • *A big plus is that the data can be stored on a PC.*

▸ AS AN ADJECTIVE = **additional**, added, extra, positive, supplementary, add-on • *Accessibility is the other plus point of the borough.*

plush = **luxurious**, luxury, costly, lavish, rich, sumptuous, opulent, palatial, ritzy *(slang)*, de luxe • *a plush Georgian house in Mayfair*

OPPOSITES: cheap, ordinary, plain

plutocrat = **rich man**, millionaire, capitalist, tycoon, fat cat *(slang, chiefly U.S.)*, Dives, magnate, moneybags *(slang)*, Croesus • *He denounced plutocrats and the idle rich.*

ply[1] 1 = **provide**, supply, shower, lavish, regale • *Elsie plied her with food and drink.*

2 = **bombard**, press, harass, besiege, beset, assail, importune • *Giovanni plied him with questions.*

3 = **work at**, follow, exercise, pursue, carry on, practise • *streetmarkets with stallholders plying their trade*

4 = **travel**, go, ferry, shuttle • *The brightly-coloured boats ply between the islands.*

5 = **use**, handle, employ, swing, manipulate, wield, utilize • *With startling efficiency, the chef plied his knives.*

ply[2] = **thickness**, leaf, sheet, layer, fold, strand • *The plastic surfaces are covered with teak ply.*

poach 1 = **steal**, rob, plunder, hunt *or* fish illegally • *Many national parks are invaded by people poaching game.*

2 = **take**, steal, appropriate, snatch *(informal)*, nab *(informal)*, purloin • *allegations that it had poached members from other unions*

pochard

▸ COLLECTIVE NOUNS: flight, bunch, rush, knob

pocket AS A NOUN 1 = **pouch**, bag, sack, hollow, compartment, receptacle • *a canvas container with customised pockets for each tool*

2 = **budget**, means, finances, resources • *There are PCs to suit every pocket.*

3 = **area**, centre, island, district, patch, cluster • *There are a few remaining pockets of resistance in the city.*

▸ AS A MODIFIER = **small**, compact, miniature, portable, little, potted *(informal)*, concise, pint-size(d) *(informal)*, abridged • *a pocket dictionary*

▸ AS A VERB = **steal**, take, lift *(informal)*, appropriate, trouser *(slang)*, knock off *(slang)*, pilfer, purloin, filch, help yourself to, snaffle *(Brit. informal)* • *He pocketed a wallet from the bedside of a dead man.*

pockmarked = **scarred**, spotted, pitted, blemished, pocked • *He had a pockmarked face.*

pod = **shell**, case, hull, husk, shuck • *Remove the peas from their pods.*

podgy = **tubby**, fat, plump, chubby, squat, stout, chunky, fleshy, stubby, dumpy, roly-poly, rotund, stumpy, short and fat • *a blond, slightly podgy youngster*

podium = **platform**, stand, stage, rostrum, dais • *A bomb was discovered under the speaker's podium at the conference.*

poem = **verse**, song, lyric, rhyme, sonnet, ode, verse composition • *a tender autobiographical poem set to music*

QUOTATIONS

A poem should not mean
but be
[Archibald McLeish *Ars Poetica*]

poet = **bard**, rhymer, lyricist, lyric poet, versifier, maker *(archaic)*, elegist • *the English poet William Blake*

▹ *See panel* **Poetry**

QUOTATIONS

The poet is the priest of the invisible
[Wallace Stevens *Adagia*]

A poet's hope: to be,
like some valley cheese,
local, but prized elsewhere
[W.H. Auden *Shorts II*]

For that fine madness still he did retain
Which rightly should possess a poet's brain
[Michael Drayton *To Henry Reynolds, of Poets and Poesy*]

Immature poets imitate; mature poets steal
[T.S. Eliot *The Sacred Wood*]

The poet is always indebted to the universe, paying interest and fines on sorrow
[Vladimir Mayakovsky *Conversation with an Inspector of Taxes about Poetry*]

All a poet can do today is warn
[Wilfred Owen *Poems (preface)*]

Sir, I admit your general rule
That every poet is a fool;
But you yourself may serve to show it,
That every fool is not a poet
[Alexander Pope *Epigram from the French*]

poetic 1 = **figurative**, creative, lyric, symbolic, lyrical, rhythmic, rhythmical, songlike • *Heidegger's interest in the poetic, evocative uses of language*

2 = **lyrical**, lyric, rhythmic, elegiac, rhythmical, metrical • *There's a very rich poetic tradition in Gaelic.*

poetry = **verse**, poems, rhyme, rhyming, poesy *(archaic)*, verse composition, metrical composition • *the poetry of Thomas Hardy*

QUOTATIONS

Poetry is a kind of ingenious nonsense
[Isaac Barrow]

Poetry is what gets lost in translation
[Robert Frost]

Poetry is a search for ways of communication; it must be conducted with openness, flexibility, and a constant readiness to listen
[Fleur Adcock]

Poetry is the spontaneous overflow of powerful feelings; it takes its origin from emotion recollected in tranquillity
[William Wordsworth *Lyrical Ballads (preface)*]

Poetry is at bottom a criticism of life
[Matthew Arnold *Essays in Criticism*]

Poetry is a subject as precise as geometry
[Gustave Flaubert *letter*]

Poetry is a way of taking life by the throat
[Robert Frost]

As civilization advances, poetry almost necessarily declines
[Lord Macaulay *Essays*]

Poetry (is) a speaking picture, with this end; to teach and delight
[Sir Philip Sidney *The Defence of Poetry*]

Poetry is truth in its Sunday clothes
[Joseph Roux *Meditations of a Parish Priest*]

Prose = words in their best order; poetry = the best words in their best order
[Samuel Taylor Coleridge *Table Talk*]

Imaginary gardens with real toads in them
[Marianne Moore *Poetry*]

Poetry is something more philosophical and more worthy of serious attention than history
[Aristotle *Poetics*]

POETRY

Poetry and prosody terms

accentual metre
accentual-syllabic metre *or* stress-syllabic metre
Adonic
Alcaic
Alexandrine
alliteration
amoebaean
amphibrach
amphimacer
anacrusis
anapaest
anapaestic
antistrophe
arsis
assonance
bacchius
ballad stanza
blank verse
bob
cadence
caesura
canto
catalectic
choriamb
closed couplet
common measure
common metre
consonance
couplet
cretic *or* amphimacer
dactyl
dactylic
diaeresis
dipody
distich
elision
end-stopped
enjambement
envoy
epode
eye rhyme
feminine ending
feminine rhyme
foot
free verse *or* vers libre
half-rhyme
hemistich
heptameter
heptastich
heroic couplet
hexameter
hypermeter
iamb
iambic
ictus
internal rhyme
ionic
jabberwocky
leonine rhyme
long metre
macaronic
masculine ending
masculine rhyme
metre
octameter
octave *or* octet
onomatopoeia
ottava rima
paeon
paeonic
pararhyme
pentameter
pentastich
perfect rhyme *or* full rhyme
Pindaric
pyhrric
quantitative metre
quatrain
quintain *or* quintet
refrain
rhyme
rhyme royal
rhyme scheme
rhythm
rime riche
Sapphic
scansion
septet
sestet
sestina *or* sextain
short metre
Spenserian stanza
spondaic
spondee
sprung rhythm
stanza
stichic
strophe
syllabic metre
tercet
terza rima
tetrabrach
tetrameter
tetrapody
tetrastich
triplet
trochaic
trochee
unstopped
verse paragraph
wheel

Poetry movements and groupings

Alexandrians
Decadents
Georgian Poets
imagists
Lake Poets
Liverpool Poets
Metaphysical Poets
the Movement
Petrarchans
Romantics
Scottish Chaucerians
symbolists

Poets

Dannie Abse *(Welsh)*
(Karen) Fleur Adcock *(New Zealander)*
Conrad (Potter) Aiken *(U.S.)*
Anna Akhamatova *(Russian)*
Maya Angelou *(U.S.)*
Guillaume Apollinaire *(French)*
Ludovico Ariosto *(Italian)*
Matthew Arnold *(English)*
W(ystan) H(ugh) Auden *(English-U.S.)*
Charles Pierre Baudelaire *(French)*
Patricia Beer *(English)*
Hilaire Belloc *(British)*
John Berryman *(U.S.)*
John Betjeman *(English)*
Elizabeth Bishop *(U.S.)*
William Blake *(English)*
Edmund Blunden *(English)*
Joseph Brodsky *(Russian-American)*
Rupert (Chawner) Brooke *(English)*
Gwendolyn Brooks *(U.S.)*
Elizabeth Barrett Browning *(English)*
Robert Browning *(English)*
Robert Burns *(Scottish)*
(George Gordon) Byron *(British)*
Callimachus *(Greek)*
Luis Vaz de Camoëns *(Portuguese)*
Thomas Campion *(English)*
Raymond Carver *(U.S.)*
Gaius Valerius Catullus *(Roman)*
Charles Causley *(English)*
Geoffrey Chaucer *(English)*
Amy Clampitt *(U.S.)*
John Clare *(English)*
Samuel Taylor Coleridge *(English)*
William Cowper *(English)*
George Crabbe *(English)*
e(dward) e(stlin) cummings *(U.S.)*
Dante (Alighieri) *(Italian)*
Cecil Day Lewis *(Irish)*
Walter de la Mare *(English)*
Emily Dickinson *(U.S.)*
John Donne *(English)*
H D (Hilda Doolittle) *(U.S.)*
John Dryden *(English)*
Carol Ann Duffy *(Scottish)*
William Dunbar *(Scottish)*
Douglas Dunn *(Scottish)*
Geoffrey Dutton *(Australian)*
T(homas) S(tearns) Eliot *(U.S.-British)*
Ebenezer Elliot (the Corn Law Rhymer) *(English)*
Paul Éluard *(French)*
Ralph Waldo Emerson *(U.S.)*
William Empson *(English)*
Edward Fitzgerald *(English)*
Robert Fitzgerald *(Australian)*
Robert (Lee) Frost *(U.S.)*
Allen Ginsberg *(U.S.)*
Johann Wolfgang von Goethe *(German)*
Robert Graves *(English)*
Thomas Gray *(English)*
Thom Gunn *(English)*
Seamus Heaney *(Irish)*
Adrian Henri *(English)*
Robert Henryson *(Scottish)*
George Herbert *(English)*
Robert Herrick *(English)*
Hesiod *(Greek)*
Geoffrey Hill *(English)*
Ralph Hodgson *(English)*
Homer *(Greek)*
Thomas Hood *(English)*
Gerard Manley Hopkins *(English)*
Horace *(Roman)*
A(lfred) E(dward) Housman *(English)*
Ted Hughes *(English)*
Elizabeth Jennings *(English)*
Samuel Johnson *(English)*
Ben Jonson *(English)*
Juvenal *(Roman)*
Patrick Kavanagh *(Irish)*
John Keats *(English)*
Sidney Keyes *(English)*
(Joseph) Rudyard Kipling *(English)*
Jean de La Fontaine *(French)*
Alphonse Marie Louis de Prat de Lamartine *(French)*
Walter Savage Landor *(English)*
William Langland *(English)*
Philip Larkin *(English)*
Tom Leonard *(Scottish)*
Henry Wadsworth Longfellow *(U.S.)*
Amy Lowell *(U.S.)*
Robert Lowell *(U.S.)*
Richard Lovelace *(English)*
Lucretius *(Roman)*
Thomas Macauley *(English)*
Norman MacCaig *(Scottish)*
Hugh MacDiarmid *(Scottish)*
Roger McGough *(English)*
Sorley MacLean *(Scottish)*
Louis MacNeice *(Irish)*
Stéphane Mallarmé *(French)*
Martial *(Roman)*
Andrew Marvell *(English)*
John Masefield *(English)*
Edna St Vincent Millay *(U.S.)*
John Milton *(English)*
Marianne Moore *(U.S.)*
Edwin Morgan *(Scottish)*
Andrew Motion *(English)*

POETS (CONTINUED)

Edwin Muir *(Scottish)*
Ogden Nash *(U.S.)*
Pablo Neruda *(Chilean)*
Frank O'Hara *(U.S.)*
Omar Khayyam *(Persian)*
Ovid *(Roman)*
Wilfred Owen *(British)*
Brian Patten *(English)*
Octavio Paz *(Mexican)*
Petrarch *(Italian)*
Pindar *(Greek)*
Sylvia Plath *(U.S.)*
Alexander Pope *(English)*
Peter Porter *(Australian)*
Ezra (Loomis) Pound *(U.S.)*
Sextus Propertius *(Roman)*
Aleksander Sergeyevich Pushkin *(Russian)*
Kathleen Raine *(English)*
Adrienne Rich *(U.S.)*
Laura Riding *(U.S.)*
Rainer Maria Rilke *(Austro-German)*
Arthur Rimbaud *(French)*
(John Wilmot) Rochester *(English)*
Theodore Huebner Roethke *(U.S.)*
Isaac Rosenberg *(English)*
Christina Georgina Rossetti *(English)*
Dante Gabriel Rossetti *(English)*
Saint-John Perse *(French)*
Sappho *(Greek)*
Siegfried Sassoon *(English)*
Johann Christoph Friedrich von Schiller *(German)*
Delmore Schwarz *(U.S.)*
Sir Walter Scott *(Scottish)*
Jaroslav Seifert *(Czech)*
William Shakespeare *(English)*
Percy Bysshe Shelley *(English)*
Sir Philip Sidney *(English)*
Edith Sitwell *(English)*
John Skelton *(English)*
Christopher Smart *(English)*
Stevie Smith *(English)*
Robert Southey *(English)*
Stephen Spender *(English)*
Edmund Spenser *(English)*
Wallace Stevens *(U.S.)*
Algernon Charles Swinburne *(English)*
Wislawa Szymborska *(Polish)*
Torquato Tasso *(Italian)*
Alfred, Lord Tennyson *(English)*
Dylan (Marlais) Thomas *(Welsh)*
Edward Thomas *(English)*
R(onald) S(tuart) Thomas *(Welsh)*
James Thomson *(Scottish)*
Paul Verlaine *(French)*
Alfred Victor de Vigny *(French)*
François Villon *(French)*
Virgil *(Roman)*
Derek Walcott *(West Indian)*
Francis Charles Webb *(Australian)*
Walt Whitman *(U.S.)*
William Wordsworth *(English)*
Judith Wright *(Australian)*
Thomas Wyatt *(English)*
W(illiam) B(utler) Yeats *(Irish)*

Prose is when all the lines except the last go on to the end. Poetry is when some of them fall short of it
[Jeremy Bentham]

I am two fools, I know,
For loving, and for saying so
In whining poetry
[John Donne *The Triple Fool*]

Poetry's a mere drug, Sir
[George Farquhar *Love and a Battle*]

If poetry comes not as naturally as the leaves to a tree it had better not come at all
[John Keats *letter*]

Writing a book of poetry is like dropping a rose petal down the Grand Canyon and waiting for the echo
[Don Marquis]

Most people ignore most poetry
because
most poetry ignores most people
[Adrian Mitchell *Poems*]

All that is not prose is verse; and all that is not verse is prose
[Molière *Le Bourgeois Gentilhomme*]

it is not poetry, but prose run mad
[Alexander Pope *An Epistle to Dr. Arbuthnot*]

▷ *See panel* **Poetry**

po-faced = **humourless**, disapproving, solemn, prim, puritanical, narrow-minded, stolid, prudish, strait-laced • *a politically-correct bastion of po-faced self-righteousness*

pogey = **benefits**, the dole *(Brit., Austral.)*, welfare, social security, unemployment benefit, state benefit, allowance, public assistance, government benefit, Jobseeker's Allowance, JSA

pogrom = **massacre**, slaughter, holocaust, persecution, genocide, ethnic cleansing *(euphemistic)*, witch-hunt, victimization, bloodbath, extermination, mass murder, annihilation, bloodletting, mass killing, decimation • *a systematic pogrom against southern black Mauritians*

poignancy = **sadness**, emotion, sentiment, intensity, feeling, tenderness, pathos, emotionalism, plaintiveness, evocativeness, piteousness • *the poignancy of their doomed love affair*

poignant = **moving**, touching, affecting, upsetting, sad, bitter, intense, painful, distressing, pathetic, harrowing, heartbreaking, agonizing, heart-rending, gut-wrenching • *a poignant reminder of her sister's death*

point AS A NOUN **1** = **essence**, meaning, subject, question, matter, heart, theme, import, text, core, burden, drift, thrust, proposition, marrow, crux, gist, main idea, nub, pith • *You have missed the main point of my argument.* **2** = **purpose**, aim, object, use, end, reason, goal, design, intention, objective, utility, intent, motive, usefulness • *What's the point of all these questions?* **3** = **aspect**, detail, feature, side, quality, property, particular, respect, item, instance, characteristic, topic, attribute, trait, facet, peculiarity, nicety • *The most interesting point about the village is its religion.* **4** = **place**, area, position, station, site, spot, location, locality, locale • *The town square is a popular meeting point for tourists.* **5** = **moment**, time, stage, period, phase, instant, juncture, moment in time, very minute • *At this point, Diana arrived.* **6** = **stage**, level, position, condition, degree, pitch, circumstance, extent • *It got to the point where he had to leave.* **7** = **end**, tip, sharp end, top, spur, spike, apex, nib, tine, prong • *the point of a knife* **8** = **score**, tally, mark • *Sort the answers out and add up the points.* **9** = **headland**, head, bill, cape, ness *(archaic)*, promontory, foreland • *a long point of land reaching southwards into the sea* **10** = **pinpoint**, mark, spot, dot, fleck, speck • *a point of light in an otherwise dark world*

▸ AS A VERB **1** *usually followed by* **at** *or* **to** = **aim**, level, train, direct • *A man pointed a gun at them and pulled the trigger.* **2** = **face**, look, direct • *He controlled the car until it was pointing forwards again.*

▸ IN PHRASES: **beside the point** = **irrelevant**, inappropriate, pointless, peripheral, unimportant, incidental, unconnected, immaterial, inconsequential, nothing to do with it, extraneous, neither here nor there, off the subject, inapplicable, not to the point, inapposite, without connection, inconsequent, not pertinent, not germane, not to the purpose • *Brian didn't like it, but that was beside the point.*

in point of fact = **in fact**, really, actually, truly, in reality, in truth, as a matter of fact, to tell the truth, in actual fact • *In point of fact, nobody really knows what happened.*

P

on the point of something = on the verge of, ready to, about to, just going to, on the brink of, just about to, all set to • *He was on the point of speaking when the phone rang.*
point at *or* **to something** *or* **someone = indicate**, show, signal, point to, point out, specify, designate, gesture towards • *I pointed at the boy sitting nearest me.*
point of view 1 = opinion, view, attitude, belief, feeling, thought, idea, approach, judgment, sentiment, viewpoint, way of thinking, way of looking at it • *His point of view is that money isn't everything.*
2 = perspective, side, position, stance, stand, angle, outlook, orientation, viewpoint, slant, standpoint, frame of reference • *Try to look at it from my point of view.*
point something up = emphasize, stress, highlight, underline, make clear, accent, spotlight, draw attention to, flag up, underscore, play up, accentuate, foreground, focus attention on, give prominence to, turn the spotlight on, bring to the fore, put emphasis on • *Politicians pointed up the differences between the two countries.*
point something *or* **someone out 1 = identify**, show, point to, indicate, finger *(informal, chiefly U.S.)*, single out, call attention to, draw *or* call attention to, flag up • *She pointed him out to me as we drove past.*
2 = allude to, reveal, mention, identify, indicate, bring up, specify, draw *or* call attention to, flag up • *We all too easily point out other people's failings.*
point to something 1 = denote, reveal, indicate, show, suggest, evidence, signal, signify, be evidence of, bespeak *(literary)* • *All the evidence pointed to his guilt.*
2 = refer to, mention, indicate, specify, single out, touch on, call attention to • *Gooch pointed to their bowling as the key to their success.*
to the point = relevant, appropriate, apt, pointed, short, fitting, material, related, brief, suitable, applicable, pertinent, terse, pithy, apposite, apropos, germane • *The description he gave was brief and to the point.*
up to a point = partly, somewhat, in part, partially, to some extent, to some degree, to a certain extent, to a certain degree • *The plan worked, up to a point.*
▸ **RELATED PHOBIA:** aichurophobia

point-blank AS AN ADJECTIVE = direct, plain, blunt, explicit, abrupt, express, downright, categorical, unreserved, straight-from-the-shoulder • *He gave a point-blank refusal.*
▸ **AS AN ADVERB = directly**, openly, straight, frankly, plainly, bluntly, explicitly, overtly, candidly, brusquely, straightforwardly, forthrightly • *Mr Patterson was asked point-blank if he would resign.*

pointed 1 = sharp, edged, acute, barbed, acicular *(rare)*, acuminate, cuspidate *(rare)*, mucronate *(rare)* • *the pointed end of the chisel*
2 = cutting, telling, biting, sharp, keen, acute, accurate, penetrating, pertinent, incisive, trenchant • *a pointed remark*

pointer 1 = hint, tip, suggestion, warning, recommendation, caution, piece of information, piece of advice • *Here are a few pointers to help you make a choice.*
2 = indication, lead, sign, evidence, signal, suggestion, symptom, hint, implication, clue, indicator, inkling, intimation • *Sunday's elections should be a pointer to the public mood.*
3 = stick, pole, rod, cane • *She tapped on the map with her pointer.*
4 = indicator, hand, guide, needle, arrow • *The pointer indicates the pressure on the dial.*

pointless = senseless, meaningless, futile, fruitless, unproductive, stupid, silly, useless, absurd, irrelevant, in vain, worthless, ineffectual, unprofitable, nonsensical, aimless, inane, unavailing, without rhyme or reason • *Violence is always pointless.*
OPPOSITES: fitting, productive, worthwhile

poise 1 = composure, cool *(slang)*, presence, assurance, dignity, equilibrium, serenity, coolness, aplomb, calmness, equanimity, presence of mind, sang-froid, savoir-faire, self-possession • *It took a moment for Mark to recover his poise.*
2 = grace, balance, equilibrium, elegance • *Ballet classes are important for poise.*

poised 1 = ready, waiting, prepared, standing by, on the brink, in the wings, all set • *US forces are poised for a massive air, land and sea assault.*
2 = composed, calm, together *(informal)*, collected, dignified, graceful, serene, suave, urbane, self-confident, unfazed *(informal)*, debonair, unruffled, nonchalant, self-possessed • *Rachel appeared poised and calm.*
OPPOSITES: excited, disturbed, agitated

poison AS A NOUN 1 = toxin, venom, bane *(archaic)* • *Poison from the weaver fish causes paralysis and swelling.*
2 = contamination, corruption, contagion, cancer, virus, blight, bane, malignancy, miasma, canker • *the poison of crime and violence spreading through the city*
▸ **AS A VERB 1 = murder**, kill, give someone poison, administer poison to • *There were rumours that she had poisoned her husband.*
2 = contaminate, foul, infect, spoil, pollute, blight, taint, adulterate, envenom, befoul • *The land has been completely poisoned by chemicals.*
3 = contaminate, lace, spike, tamper with, doctor, adulterate, put poison in • *He accused them of poisoning his drink*
4 = corrupt, colour, undermine, bias, sour, pervert, warp, taint, subvert, embitter, deprave, defile, jaundice, vitiate, envenom • *ill-feeling that will poison further negotiations*
▸ **AS AN ADJECTIVE = poisonous**, deadly, toxic, lethal, venomous • *a cloud of poison gas*
▸ **RELATED ADJECTIVE:** toxic
▸ **RELATED PHOBIA:** toxiphobia
▹ *See panel* **Poisons**

poisonous 1 = toxic, fatal, deadly, lethal, mortal, virulent, noxious, venomous, baneful *(archaic)*, mephitic • *All parts of the yew tree are poisonous.*
2 = evil, vicious, malicious, corrupting, pernicious, baleful, baneful *(archaic)*, pestiferous • *poisonous attacks on the Church*

poke AS A VERB 1 = jab, hit, push, stick, dig, punch, stab, thrust, butt, elbow, shove, nudge, prod • *Lindy poked him in the ribs.*
2 = protrude, stick, thrust, jut • *His fingers poked through the worn tips of his gloves.*
▸ **AS A NOUN = jab**, hit, dig, punch, thrust, butt, nudge, prod • *John smiled and gave Richard a playful poke.*
▸ **IN PHRASES: poke around** *or* **about = search**, fish, hunt, go through, rifle, comb, scour, grub, ferret, rummage (around), sift through, forage, scavenge, rake through, fossick *(Austral. & N.Z.)*, root about *or* around • *He poked around in the cupboard for the bottle of whisky.*

poky = small, tiny, narrow, confined, cramped, incommodious • *poky little apartments*
OPPOSITES: open, large, spacious

polar 1 = freezing, frozen, extreme, furthest, cold, terminal, Arctic, icy, Antarctic, glacial • *the rigours of life in the polar regions*
2 = opposite, opposed, contrary, contradictory, antagonistic, antithetical, diametric, antipodal • *economists at polar ends of the politico-economic spectrum*

polarity = opposition, contradiction, paradox, ambivalence, dichotomy, duality, contrariety • *the polarities of good and evil*

pole[1] = rod, post, support, staff, standard, bar, stick, stake, paling, shaft, upright, pillar, mast, picket, spar, stave • *The sign hung at the top of a large pole.*

pole[2] AS A NOUN = extremity, limit, terminus, antipode • *The two mayoral candidates represent opposite poles of the political spectrum.*

P

▸ **IN PHRASES: poles apart = at opposite extremes**, incompatible, irreconcilable, worlds apart, miles apart, like chalk and cheese *(Brit.)*, like night and day, widely separated, completely different, at opposite ends of the earth • *Her views on Europe are poles apart from those of her successor.*

polemic = **argument**, attack, debate, dispute, controversy, rant, tirade, diatribe, invective, philippic *(rare)* • *a polemic against the danger of secret societies*

polemical = **controversial**, cutting, biting, critical, acid, bitter, hostile, contentious, scathing, virulent, polemic, sardonic, caustic, venomous, vitriolic, acerbic, trenchant, argumentative, waspish, disputatious • *his biting polemical novel* • *He's best when he's cool and direct, rather than abusive and polemical.*

polemics = **dispute**, debate, argument, discussion, controversy, contention, wrangling, turf war *(informal)*, disputation, argumentation • *She does not want to involve herself in political polemics.*

police AS A NOUN = **the law** *(informal)*, police force, constabulary, fuzz *(slang)*, law enforcement agency, boys in blue *(informal)*, the Old Bill *(slang)*, rozzers *(slang)* • *The police have arrested twenty people following the disturbances.*

▸ AS A VERB **1 = control**, patrol, guard, watch, protect, regulate, keep the peace, keep in order • *the UN force whose job it is to police the border*

2 = monitor, check, observe, oversee, supervise • *the body which polices the investment management business*

police officer = **cop** *(slang)*, officer, pig *(offensive slang)*, bobby *(informal)*, copper *(slang)*, constable, plod *(Brit. slang)*, peeler *(Irish & Brit. obsolete slang)*, gendarme *(slang)*, fuzz *(slang)*, woodentop *(slang)*, bizzy *(informal)*, flatfoot *(slang)*, rozzer *(slang)*, policeman *or* policewoman • *a meeting of senior police officers*

police station = **station**, nick, cop shop *(informal)* • *a mortar attack on a police station in the city*

policy 1 = procedure, plan, action, programme, practice, scheme, theory, code, custom, stratagem • *plans which include changes in foreign policy*

2 = line, rules, approach, guideline, protocol • *significant changes in Britain's policy on global warming*

polish AS A NOUN **1 = varnish**, wax, glaze, lacquer, japan • *The air smelt of furniture polish.*

2 = sheen, finish, sparkle, glaze, gloss, brilliance, brightness, veneer, lustre, smoothness • *I admired the high polish of his boots.*

3 = style, class *(informal)*, finish, breeding, grace, elegance, refinement, finesse, urbanity, suavity, politesse • *She was enormously popular for her charm and polish.*

▸ AS A VERB **1 = shine**, wax, clean, smooth, rub, buff, brighten, burnish, furbish • *Every morning he polished his shoes.*

2 *often with* up **= perfect**, improve, enhance, refine, finish, correct, cultivate, brush up, touch up, emend • *Polish up your writing skills on a one-week course.*

▸ IN PHRASES: **polish someone off = eliminate**, take out *(slang)*, get rid of, dispose of, do away with, blow away *(slang, chiefly U.S.)*, beat someone once and for all • *a chance to polish off their bitter local rivals*

polish something off = finish, down, shift *(informal)*, wolf, consume, hoover *(informal)*, put away, eat up, swill • *He polished off the whole box of truffles on his own.*

polished 1 = elegant, sophisticated, refined, polite, cultivated, civilized, genteel, suave, finished, urbane, courtly, well-bred • *He is polished, charming and articulate.*

OPPOSITES: unsophisticated, unrefined, inelegant

POISONS

Poisonous substances and gases

aconite, acrolein, adamsite, afterdamp, Agent Orange, aldrin, allyl alcohol, aniline, antimony potassium tartrate, arsenic, arsine, atropine *or* atropin, barium hydroxide, benzene, benzidine, brucine, cacodyl, carbon disulphide, carbon monoxide, coniine, curare, cyanic acid, cyanide, cyanogen, digitalin, emetine, formaldehyde, hemlock, hydrastine, hydrogen cyanide, hydrogen fluoride, hydrogen iodide, hydrogen sulphide, hyoscyamine, lead monoxide, lewisite, lindane, mercuric chloride, mercuric oxide, methanol, methyl bromide, muscarine, mustard gas, nerve gas, nitrogen dioxide, osmium tetroxide, ouabain, oxalic acid, Paraquat, Paris green, phenol, phosgene, picrotoxin, poison gas, potassium cyanide, potassium permanganate, prussic acid, ratsbane, red lead, sarin, silver nitrate, sodium cyanide, sodium fluoroacetate, stibine, strychnine, tetramethyldiarsine, thallium, thebaine, tropine, urushiol, veratrine, whitedamp, zinc chloride

Types of poisoning

botulism, bromism, digitalism, ergotism, fluorosis, hydrargyria, iodism, lead poisoning, listeriosis, mercurialism, phosphorism, plumbism, ptomaine poisoning, salmonella, saturnism, strychninism

Poisonous plants

aconite, amanita, baneberry, belladonna, black bryony, black nightshade, castor-oil plant, cowbane, coyotillo, deadly nightshade, death camass, death cap *or* angel, destroying angel, dieffenbachia, dog's mercury, ergot, fly agaric, foxglove, hemlock, henbane, Indian liquorice, laburnum, liberty cap, locoweed, manchineel, monkshood, mountain laurel, Noogoora burr, nux vomica, oleander, poison dogwood *or* elder, poison ivy, poison oak, poison sumach, pokeweed, pokeberry, *or* pokeroot, sassy *or* sasswood, staggerbush, stavesacre, thorn apple, tutu, upas, water hemlock, wolfsbane, woody nightshade

2 = **accomplished**, professional, masterly, fine, expert, outstanding, skilful, adept, impeccable, flawless, superlative, faultless • *a polished performance*
OPPOSITES: inept, unskilled, amateurish
3 = **shining**, bright, smooth, gleaming, glossy, slippery, burnished, glassy, furbished • *a highly polished surface*
OPPOSITES: dark, rough, dull

polite 1 = **mannerly**, civil, courteous, affable, obliging, gracious, respectful, well-behaved, deferential, complaisant, well-mannered • *He was a quiet and very polite young man*
OPPOSITES: insulting, crude, rude
2 = **refined**, cultured, civilized, polished, sophisticated, elegant, genteel, urbane, courtly, well-bred • *Certain words are not acceptable in polite society.*
OPPOSITES: unrefined, uncultured

politeness = **courtesy**, decency, correctness, etiquette, deference, grace, civility, graciousness, common courtesy, complaisance, courteousness, respectfulness, mannerliness, obligingness • *She listened to him, but only out of politeness.*

QUOTATIONS
Politeness is organized indifference
[Paul Valéry *Tel Quel*]

politic = **wise**, diplomatic, sensible, discreet, prudent, advisable, expedient, judicious, tactful, sagacious, in your best interests • *Many people found it politic to change their allegiance.*

political 1 = **governmental**, government, state, parliamentary, constitutional, administrative, legislative, civic, ministerial, policy-making, party political • *a democratic political system*
2 = **factional**, party, militant, partisan • *I'm not political, I take no interest in politics.*

QUOTATIONS
Man is by nature a political animal
[Aristotle *Politics*]

politically correct = **PC**, ideologically sound • *politically correct language about minority groups*

politician = **statesman** *or* **stateswoman**, representative, senator *(U.S.)*, congressman *(U.S.)*, Member of Parliament, legislator, public servant, congresswoman *(U.S.)*, politico *(informal, chiefly U.S.)*, lawmaker, office bearer, M.P., elected offical • *Korea's best-known opposition politician*

QUOTATIONS
A statesman is a politician who has been dead ten or fifteen years
[Harry S. Truman]
A politician is an animal that can sit on a fence and keep both ears to the ground
[H.L. Mencken]
Since a politician never believes what he says, he is always astonished when others do
[Charles de Gaulle]
Well, in politics, I'm a complete neutral; I think they're all scoundrels without exception
[H.L. Mencken]
a politician is an arse upon which everyone has sat except a man
[e e cummings *1 X 1 (no. 10)*]
A statesman is a politician who places himself at the service of the nation. A politician is a statesman who places the nation at his service
[Georges Pompidou]
The politician who never made a mistake never made a decision
[John Major]
Ninety-eight percent of the adults in this country are decent, hard-working, honest Americans. It's the other lousy two percent that get all the publicity. But then – we elected them
[Lily Tomlin]

politics 1 = **affairs of state**, government, government policy, public affairs, civics • *He quickly involved himself in politics.*
2 = **political beliefs**, party politics, political allegiances, political leanings, political sympathies • *My politics are well to the left of centre.*
3 = **political science**, polity, statesmanship, civics, statecraft • *He studied politics and medieval history.*
4 = **power struggle**, machinations, opportunism, realpolitik, Machiavellianism • *He doesn't know how to handle office politics.*

QUOTATIONS
Politics is the art of the possible
[Prince Otto von Bismarck]
A week is a long time in politics
[Harold Wilson]
Politics is not the art of the possible. It consists in choosing between the disastrous and the unpalatable
[John Kenneth Galbraith *Ambassador's Journal*]
Politics...has always been the systematic organisation of hatreds
[Henry Brooks Adams *The Education of Henry Adams*]
Practical politics consists in ignoring facts
[Henry Brooks Adams *The Education of Henry Adams*]
In politics the middle way is none at all
[John Adams]
In politics, what begins in fear usually ends in folly
[Samuel Taylor Coleridge *Table Talk*]
There is a holy mistaken zeal in politics as well as in religion. By persuading others, we convince ourselves
[Junius *Public Advertiser*]
Politics is war without bloodshed while war is politics with bloodshed
[Mao Tse-tung]
Politics is perhaps the only profession for which no preparation is thought necessary
[Robert Louis Stevenson *Familiar Studies of Men and Books*]
Most schemes of political improvement are very laughable things
[Dr. Johnson]
politics: a strife of interests masquerading as a contest of principles. The conduct of public affairs for private advantage
[Ambrose Bierce *The Devil's Dictionary*]

PROVERBS
Politics makes strange bedfellows

▷ *See panel* **Political parties**

poll **AS A NOUN** 1 = **survey**, figures, count, sampling, returns, ballot, tally, census, canvass, Gallup Poll, (public) opinion poll • *Polls show that the party is losing support.*
2 = **election**, vote, voting, referendum, ballot, plebiscite • *In 1945, Churchill was defeated at the polls.*
▸ **AS A VERB** 1 = **question**, interview, survey, sample, ballot, canvass • *More than 18,000 people were polled.*
2 = **gain**, return, record, register, tally • *He had polled enough votes to force a second ballot.*

pollute 1 = **contaminate**, dirty, mar, poison, soil, foul, infect, spoil, stain, taint, adulterate, make filthy, smirch, befoul • *beaches polluted by sewage pumped into the sea*
OPPOSITES: clean, cleanse, decontaminate
2 = **defile**, violate, corrupt, sully, deprave, debase, profane, desecrate, dishonour, debauch, besmirch • *a man accused of polluting the minds of children*
OPPOSITES: honour, esteem

pollution 1 = **contamination**, dirtying, corruption, taint, adulteration, foulness, defilement, uncleanness, vitiation • *environmental pollution*
2 = **waste**, poisons, dirt, impurities • *the level of pollution in the river*

POLITICAL PARTIES

Australia
Australian Labor Party
Liberal Party of Australia
National Party of Australia

Austria
Freedom Party (FPÖ)
People's Party (ÖVP)
Socialist Party (SPÖ)

Belgium
Flemish Bloc (VB)
Flemish Green Party (Agalev)
French Green Party (Ecolo)
Flemish Liberal Party (PVV)
French Liberal Reform Party (PRL)
Flemish Social Christian Party (CVP)
French Social Christian Party (PSC)
Flemish Socialist Party (SP)
French Socialist Party (PS)

Canada
Bloc Quebecois
Liberal Party
New Democratic Party
Progressive Conservative
Reform Party
Social Credit Party

Denmark
Centre Democrats (CD)
Christian People's Party (KrF)
Conservative People's Party (KF)
Left Socialists
Liberals (V)
Progress Party (FP)
Radical Liberals (RV)
Social Democrats (SD)
Socialist People's Party (SF)

Finland
Centre Party (KP)
Democratic Alternative
Finnish People's Democratic League (SKDL)
Finnish Rural Party (SMP)
Green Party
National Coalition Party (KOK)
Social Democratic Party (SD)
Swedish People's Party (SFP)

France
Communist Party (PC)
National Front
Rally for the Republic (RDR)
Republican Party (PR)
Socialist Party (PS)
Union for French Democracy (UDF)

Germany
Christian-Democratic Union (CDU)
Christian-Social Union (CSU)
Free Democratic Party (FDP)
Green Party
Party of Democratic Socialism (PDS)
Social Democratic Party (SPD)

Greece
Greek Communist Party
New Democracy (ND)
Pan-Hellenic Socialist Movement (PASOK)
Political Spring (Politiki Aniksi)

India
Congress (I)
Janata Dal
Bharitiya Janata Party (BJP)

Irish Republic
Democratic Left
Fianna Fáil
Fine Gael
Labour Party
Progressive Democrats

Israel
Labour Party
Likud

Italy
Centre Union
Christian Democrat Party
Democratic Party of the Left (PDS)
Forza Italia
National Alliance
Northern League

Japan
Democratic Socialist Party
Liberal Democratic Party
Komeito
Social Democratic Party

Luxembourg
Communist Party
Democratic Party (PD)
Luxembourg Socialist Workers' Party (POSL)
Christian Social Party (PCS)

Malta
Malta Labour Party
Nationalist Party

Mexico
Institutional Revolutionary Party (PRI)
National Action Party (PAN)
Party of the Democratic Revolution (PRD)
Revolutionary Workers' Party

the Netherlands
Christian Democratic Appeal (CDA)
Labour Party (PvdA)
People's Party for Freedom and Democracy (VVD)

New Zealand
Labour Party
National Party

Northern Ireland
Democratic Unionist Party
Official Ulster Unionist Party
Sinn Féin
Social Democratic and Labour Party (SDLP)

Portugal
Democratic Renewal Party (PRD)
Democratic Social Centre Party (CDS)
Social Democratic Party (PSD)
Socialist Party (PS)

South Africa
African National Congress (ANC)
Inkatha Freedom Party
National Party
Pan-Africanist Congress (PAC)

Spain
Basque Nationalist Party (PNV)
Convergencia i Uni (CiU)
Herri Batasuna (HB)
People's Party (PP)
Socialist Workers' Party (PSOE)
United Left (IU)

Sweden
Centre Party
Christian Democratic Party
Green Party
Left Party
Liberal Party
Moderate Party
Social Democratic Labour Party (SAP)

Turkey
Motherland Party (ANAP)
Kurdish Workers' Party (PKK)
Social Democratic Populist Party
True Path Party

United Kingdom (Mainland)
Conservative and Unionist Party
Labour Party
Liberal Democrats
Plaid Cymru
Scottish National Party

United States of America
Democratic Party
Republican Party

polytechnic = **college**, poly *(informal)* • *a lecturer at the Polytechnic of North London*

pomp 1 = **ceremony**, grandeur, splendour, state, show, display, parade, flourish, pageant, magnificence, solemnity, pageantry, ostentation, éclat • *the pomp and splendour of the English aristocracy*
2 = **show**, pomposity, grandiosity, vainglory • *The band have trawled new depths of pomp and self-indulgence.*

pomposity 1 = **self-importance**, vanity, arrogance, pretension, airs, flaunting, presumption, affectation, pretentiousness, grandiosity, haughtiness, portentousness, vainglory, pompousness • *He was modest and simple, without a trace of pomposity.*
2 = **grandiloquence**, rant, hot air *(informal)*, bombast, fustian, loftiness, turgidity, magniloquence • *She has no time for political jargon and pomposity.*

pompous 1 = **self-important**, affected, arrogant, pretentious, bloated, grandiose, imperious, showy, overbearing, ostentatious, puffed up, portentous, magisterial, supercilious, pontifical, vainglorious • *What a pompous little man he is.*
OPPOSITES: simple, natural, unpretentious
2 = **grandiloquent**, high-flown, inflated, windy, overblown, turgid, bombastic, boastful, flatulent, arty-farty *(informal)*, fustian, orotund, magniloquent • *She winced at his pompous phraseology.*
OPPOSITES: direct, simple, succinct

ponce 1 = **pimp**, procurer, pander, bawd *(archaic)* • *They don't have a 'ponce' – the street name for a pimp.*
2 = **fop**, dandy, swell, beau, popinjay, coxcomb *(archaic)* • *He called him a 'perfumed ponce'.*

pond = **pool**, tarn, small lake, fish pond, duck pond, millpond, lochan *(Scot.)*, dew pond • *youths skating on the frozen village pond*

ponder = **think about**, consider, study, reflect on, examine, weigh up, contemplate, deliberate about, muse on, brood on, meditate on, mull over, puzzle over, ruminate on, give thought to, cogitate on, rack your brains about, excogitate • *He didn't waste time pondering the question.*

ponderous 1 = **dull**, laboured, pedestrian, dreary, heavy, tedious, plodding, tiresome, lifeless, stilted, stodgy, pedantic, long-winded, verbose, prolix • *He had a dense, ponderous writing style.*
2 = **clumsy**, awkward, lumbering, laborious, graceless, elephantine, heavy-footed, unco *(Austral. slang)* • *He strolled about with a ponderous, heavy gait.*
OPPOSITES: light, graceful, light-footed

pontifical 1 = **papal**, ecclesiastical, apostolic, prelatic • *An all-embracing Church, with full pontifical authority, is his ideal.*

pontificate = **expound**, preach, sound off, pronounce, declaim, lay down the law, hold forth, dogmatize, pontify • *Politicians like to pontificate about falling standards.*

pony
▸ COLLECTIVE NOUN: herd

pooh-pooh = **scorn**, dismiss, slight, disregard, play down, sneer at, disdain, spurn, deride, brush aside, scoff at, belittle, sniff at, make little of, turn up your nose at *(informal)* • *The medical profession tends to pooh-pooh colonic irrigation.*
OPPOSITES: praise, glorify, exalt

pool[1] 1 = **swimming pool**, lido, swimming bath(s) *(Brit.)*, bathing pool *(archaic)* • *a heated indoor pool*
2 = **pond**, lake, mere, tarn • *Beautiful gardens filled with pools and fountains.*
3 = **puddle**, drop, patch, splash • *There were pools of water on the gravel drive.*

pool[2] AS A NOUN 1 = **supply**, reserve, fall-back • *the available pool of manpower*
2 = **kitty**, bank, fund, stock, store, pot, jackpot, stockpile, hoard, cache • *a reserve pool of cash*
▸ AS A VERB = **combine**, share, merge, put together, amalgamate, lump together, join forces on • *We pooled our savings to start up a new business.*

poor 1 = **impoverished**, broke *(informal)*, badly off, hard up *(informal)*, short, in need, needy, on the rocks, penniless, destitute, poverty-stricken, down and out, skint *(Brit. slang)*, in want, indigent, down at heel, impecunious, dirt-poor *(informal)*, on the breadline, flat broke *(informal)*, penurious, on your uppers, stony-broke *(Brit. slang)*, necessitous, in queer street, without two pennies to rub together *(informal)*, on your beam-ends • *He was one of thirteen children from a poor family.*
OPPOSITES: rich, wealthy, prosperous
2 = **unfortunate**, pathetic, miserable, unlucky, hapless, pitiful, luckless, wretched, ill-starred, pitiable, ill-fated • *I feel sorry for that poor child.*
OPPOSITES: successful, lucky, fortunate
3 = **inferior**, unsatisfactory, mediocre, second-rate, sorry, weak, pants *(informal)*, rotten *(informal)*, faulty, feeble, worthless, shabby, shoddy, low-grade, below par, substandard, low-rent *(informal)*, crappy *(slang)*, valueless, no great shakes *(informal)*, rubbishy, poxy *(slang)*, piss-poor *(slang)*, chickenshit *(U.S. slang)*, not much cop *(Brit. slang)*, half-pie *(N.Z. informal)*, bodger or bodgie *(Austral. slang)* • *The wine is very poor.* • *He was a poor actor.*
OPPOSITES: excellent, valuable, superior
4 = **meagre**, inadequate, insufficient, reduced, lacking, slight, miserable, pathetic, incomplete, scant, sparse, deficient, skimpy, measly, scanty, pitiable, niggardly, straitened, exiguous • *poor wages and terrible working conditions* • *A poor crop has sent vegetable prices spiralling.*
OPPOSITES: complete, thick, ample
5 = **unproductive**, barren, fruitless, bad, bare, exhausted, depleted, impoverished, sterile, infertile, unfruitful • *Mix in some planting compost to improve poor soil when you dig.*
OPPOSITES: yielding, productive, fertile

QUOTATIONS

The poor man is happy; he expects no change for the worse
[Demetrius]

The poor always ye have with you
[*Bible: St. John*]

Poor and content is rich and rich enough
[William Shakespeare *Othello*]

poorly AS AN ADVERB = **badly**, incompetently, inadequately, crudely, inferiorly, unsuccessfully, insufficiently, shabbily, unsatisfactorily, inexpertly • *poorly built houses*
OPPOSITES: well, expertly, sufficiently
▸ AS AN ADJECTIVE = **ill**, sick, ailing, unwell, crook *(Austral. & N.Z. informal)*, seedy *(informal)*, below par, out of sorts, off colour, under the weather *(informal)*, indisposed, feeling rotten *(informal)* • *I've just phoned Julie and she's still poorly.*
OPPOSITES: well, fit, healthy

pop AS A NOUN 1 = **soft drink**, ginger *(Scot.)*, soda *(U.S. & Canad.)*, fizzy drink, cool drink *(S. African)* • *He still visits the village shop for buns and fizzy pop.*
2 = **bang**, report, crack, noise, burst, explosion • *Each corn kernel will make a loud pop when cooked.*
▸ AS A VERB 1 = **burst**, crack, snap, bang, explode, report, go off (with a bang) • *The champagne cork popped and shot to the ceiling.*
2 = **protrude**, bulge, stick out • *My eyes popped at the sight of so much food.*
3 = **put**, insert, push, stick, slip, thrust, tuck, shove • *He plucked a grape from the bunch and popped it into his mouth.*
4 *often with* **in, out,** *etc* = **call**, visit, appear, drop in *(informal)*, leave quickly, come *or* go suddenly, nip in *or* out *(Brit. informal)* • *Wendy popped in for a quick visit on Monday night.*
▸ IN PHRASES: **pop up** = **appear**, emerge, turn up, show up *(informal)*, crop up, materialize, make an appearance • *You could never be sure where he would pop up next.*

pope = **Holy Father**, pontiff, His Holiness, Bishop of Rome, Vicar of Christ • *The highlight of the Pope's visit will be his message to the people.*
▸ **RELATED ADJECTIVE:** papal
▹ *See panel* **Popes**

poppycock = **nonsense**, rubbish, balls *(taboo slang)*, bull *(slang)*, shit *(taboo slang)*, pants *(informal)*, rot, crap *(slang)*, garbage *(informal)*, trash, bunk *(informal)*, bullshit *(taboo slang)*, hot air *(informal)*, malarkey, tosh *(slang, chiefly Brit.)*, babble, bollocks *(Brit. taboo slang)*, pap, cobblers *(Brit. taboo slang)*, bilge *(informal)*, drivel, twaddle, tripe *(informal)*, gibberish, guff *(slang)*, moonshine, baloney *(informal)*, gobbledegook *(informal)*, hogwash, hokum *(slang, chiefly U.S. & Canad.)*, bunkum *(chiefly U.S.)*, piffle *(informal)*, balderdash, bosh *(informal)*, eyewash *(informal)*, hooey *(slang)*, tommyrot, horsefeathers *(U.S. slang)*, bizzo *(Austral. slang)*, bull's wool *(Austral. & N.Z. slang)* • *Experts dismiss this explanation as poppycock.*

populace = **people**, crowd, masses, mob, inhabitants, general public, multitude, throng, rabble, hoi polloi, Joe Public *(slang)*, Joe Six-Pack *(U.S. slang)*, commonalty • *a large proportion of the populace*

popular 1 = **well-liked**, liked, favoured, celebrated, in, accepted, favourite, famous, approved, in favour, fashionable, in demand, sought-after, fave *(informal)* • *This is the most popular game ever devised.*
OPPOSITES: hated, disliked, unpopular
2 = **mass-market**, general, easy, simple, plain, amateur, accessible, straightforward, simplified, non-specialist, middlebrow, non-technical, lay person's • *the sort of popular science writing that makes the reader feel like a genius*
OPPOSITES: academic, intellectual, highbrow
3 = **common**, general, standard, widespread, prevailing, stock, current, public, conventional, universal, prevalent, ubiquitous • *the popular misconception that dinosaurs were all lumbering giants*
OPPOSITES: rare, unusual, uncommon
4 = **mass**, general, civil, democratic, collective, communal, societal • *He was overthrown by a popular uprising.*

popularity 1 = **favour**, fame, esteem, acclaim, regard, reputation, approval, recognition, celebrity, vogue, adoration, renown, repute, idolization, lionization • *His authority and popularity have declined.*
2 = **currency**, acceptance, circulation, vogue, prevalence • *This theory has enjoyed tremendous popularity among sociologists.*

popularize 1 = **make something popular**, spread the word about, disseminate, universalize, give mass appeal to • *the first person to popularize rock 'n' roll in China*
2 = **simplify**, make available to all, give currency to, give mass appeal to • *a magazine devoted to popularizing science*

popularly = **generally**, commonly, widely, usually, regularly, universally, traditionally, ordinarily, conventionally, customarily • *the infection popularly called mad cow disease*

populate 1 = **inhabit**, people, live in, occupy, reside in, dwell in *(formal)* • *the native people who populate areas around the city*
2 = **settle**, people, occupy, pioneer, colonize • *North America was populated largely by Europeans.*

population = **inhabitants**, people, community, society, residents, natives, folk, occupants, populace, denizens, citizenry • *Bangladesh now has a population of about 100 million.*

QUOTATIONS
Population, when unchecked, increases in a geometrical ratio. Subsistence only increases in an arithmetical ratio
[Thomas Malthus *The Principle of Population*]

populous = **populated**, crowded, packed, swarming, thronged, teeming, heavily populated, overpopulated • *Indonesia is the fourth most populous country in the world.*

porcelain = **china**, ware, fine bone china, porcelain ware • *a priceless collection of English porcelain*

porch = **vestibule**, hall, entry, lobby, entrance, foyer, portal, entrance hall, portico • *She stood framed in the doorway of the porch.*

pore[1] = **opening**, hole, outlet, orifice, stoma • *microscopic pores in the plant's leaves*

pore[2] 1 *followed by* **over** = **study**, read, examine, go over, scrutinize, peruse • *We spent whole afternoons poring over travel brochures.*
2 *followed by* **over, on,** *or* **upon** = **contemplate**, ponder, brood, dwell on, work over • *One day historians will pore over these strange months.*

pornographic = **obscene**, erotic, indecent, blue, dirty, offensive, rude, sexy, filthy, lewd, risqué, X-rated *(informal)*, salacious, prurient, smutty • *I found out he'd been watching pornographic videos.*

pornography = **obscenity**, porn *(informal)*, erotica, dirt, filth, indecency, porno *(informal)*, smut • *a campaign against pornography on television*

QUOTATIONS
Pornography is the attempt to insult sex, to do dirt on it
[D.H. Lawrence *Phoenix*]

porous = **permeable**, absorbent, spongy, absorptive, penetrable, pervious • *The local limestone is extremely porous.*
OPPOSITES: impenetrable, impervious, impermeable

porpoise
▸ **COLLECTIVE NOUNS:** school, gam

port = **harbour**, haven, anchorage, seaport, roadstead • *an attractive little fishing port*

PROVERBS
Any port in a storm

▹ *See panel* **Ports**

portable = **light**, compact, convenient, handy, lightweight, manageable, movable, easily carried, portative • *There was a portable television behind the bar.*

portal = **doorway**, door, entry, way in, entrance, gateway, entrance way • *I entered through the royal portal.*

portend = **foretell**, promise, threaten, indicate, predict, point to, herald, warn of, omen, bode, foreshadow, bespeak, augur, harbinger, presage, forewarn, betoken, prognosticate, adumbrate, foretoken, vaticinate *(rare)* • *Comets, in Western tradition, always portend doom and gloom.*

portent = **omen**, sign, warning, threat, indication, premonition, foreshadowing, foreboding, harbinger, presage, forewarning, prognostication, augury, presentiment, prognostic • *This is a frightening portent for the future.*

portentous 1 = **pompous**, solemn, ponderous, self-important, pontifical • *There was nothing portentous or solemn about him.*
2 = **significant**, alarming, sinister, ominous, important, threatening, crucial, forbidding, menacing, momentous, fateful, minatory, bodeful • *portentous prophecies of doom*

porter[1] = **baggage attendant**, carrier, bearer, baggage-carrier • *A porter slammed the baggage compartment doors.*

porter[2] = **doorman**, caretaker, janitor, concierge, gatekeeper • *a porter at the block of flats*

portion 1 = **part**, bit, piece, section, scrap, segment, fragment, fraction, chunk, wedge, hunk, morsel • *I have spent a large portion of my life here.*
2 = **helping**, serving, piece, plateful • *fish and chips at about £2.70 a portion*
3 = **share**, division, allowance, lot, measure, quantity, quota, ration, allocation, allotment • *his portion of the inheritance*

portly = **stout**, fat, overweight, plump, large, heavy, ample, bulky, burly, obese, fleshy, beefy *(informal)*, tubby *(informal)*, rotund, corpulent • *a portly middle-aged man*

POPES

Pope	Pontificate	Pope	Pontificate	Pope	Pontificate
Peter	until c.64	Sabinianus	604–06	Stephen IX	939–42
Linus	c.64–c.76	Boniface III	607	Marinus II	942–46
Anacletus	c.76–c.90	Boniface IV	608–15	Agapetus II	946–55
Clement I	c.90–c.99	Deusdedit *or* Adeodatus I	615–18	John XII	955–64
Evaristus	c.99–c.105	Boniface V	619–25	Leo VIII	963–65
Alexander I	c.105–c.117	Honorious I	625–38	Benedict V	964–66
Sixtus I	c.117–c.127	Severinus	640	John XIII	965–72
Telesphorus	c.127–c.137	John IV	640–42	Benedict VI	973–74
Hyginus	c.137–c.140	Theodore I	642–49	Benedict VII	974–83
Pius I	c.140–c.154	Martin I	649–54	John XIV	983–84
Anicetus	c.154–c.166	Eugenius I	654–57	John XV	985–96
Soter	c.166–c.175	Vitalian	657–72	Gregory V	996–99
Eleutherius	175–89	Adeotatus II	672–6	Sylvester II	999–1003
Victor I	189–98	Donus	676–78	John XVII	1003
Zephyrinus	198–217	Agatho	678–81	John XVIII	1004–09
Callistus I	217–22	Leo II	682–83	Sergius IV	1009–12
Urban I	222–30	Benedict II	684–85	Benedict VIII	1012–24
Pontian	230–35	John V	685–86	John XIX	1024–32
Anterus	235–36	Cono	686–87	Benedict IX (first reign)	1032–44
Fabian	236–50	Sergius I	687–701	Sylvester III	1045
Cornelius	251–53	John VI	701–05	Benedict IX	1045
Lucius I	253–54	John VII	705–07	(second reign)	
Stephen I	254–57	Sisinnius	708	Gregory VI	1045–46
Sixtus II	257–58	Constantine	708–15	Clement II	1046–47
Dionysius	259–68	Gregory II	715–31	Benedict IX (third reign)	1047–48
Felix I	269–74	Gregory III	731–41	Damasus II	1048
Eutychianus	275–83	Zacharias	741–52	Leo IX	1048–54
Caius	283–96	Stephen II	752	Victor II	1055–57
Marcellinus	296–304	(not consecrated)		Stephen IX (X)	1057–58
Marcellus I	308–09	Stephen II (III)	752–7	Nicholas II	1059–61
Eusebius	310	Paul I	757–67	Alexander II	1061–73
Miltiades	311–14	Stephen III (IV)	768–72	Gregory VII	1073–85
Sylvester I	314–35	Hadrian I	772–95	Victor III	1086–87
Mark	336	Leo III	795–816	Urban II	1088–99
Julius I	337–52	Stephen IV (V)	816–17	Paschal II	1099–1118
Liberius	352–66	Paschal I	817–24	Gelasius II	1118–19
Damasus I	366–84	Eugenius II	824–27	Callistus II	1119–24
Siricius	384–99	Valentine	827	Honorious II	1124–30
Anastasius I	399–401	Gregory IV	827–44	Innocent II	1130–43
Innocent I	402–17	Sergius II	844–47	Celestine II	1143–44
Zosimus	417–18	Leo IV	847–55	Lucius II	1144–45
Boniface I	418–22	Benedict III	855–58	Eugenius III	1145–53
Celestine I	422–32	Nicholas I	858–67	Anastasius IV	1153–54
Sixtus III	432–40	Hadrian II	867–72	Hadrian IV	1154–59
Leo I	440–61	John VIII	872–82	Alexander III	1159–81
Hilarus	461–68	Marinus I	882–84	Lucius III	1181–85
Simplicius	468–83	Hadrian III	884–85	Urban III	1185–87
Felix III (II)	483–92	Stephen V (VI)	885–91	Gregory VIII	1187
Gelasius I	492–96	Formosus	891–96	Clement III	1187–91
Anastasius II	496–98	Boniface VI	896	Celestine III	1191–98
Symmachus	498–514	Stephen VI (VII)	896–97	Innocent III	1198–1216
Hormisdas	514–23	Romanus	897	Honorious III	1216–27
John I	523–26	Theodore II	897	Gregory IX	1227–41
Felix IV (III)	526–30	John IX	898–900	Celestine IV	1241
Boniface II	530–32	Benedict IV	900–03	Innocent IV	1243–54
John II	533–35	Leo V	903	Alexander IV	1254–61
Agapetus I	535–36	Sergius III	904–11	Urban IV	1261–64
Silverius	536–37	Anastasius III	911–13	Clement IV	1265–68
Vigilius	537–55	Lando	913–14	Gregory X	1271–76
Pelagius I	556–61	John X	914–28	Innocent V	1276
John III	561–74	Leo VI	928	Hadrian V	1276
Benedict I	575–79	Stephen VII (VIII)	928–31	John XXI	1276–77
Pelagius II	579–90	John XI	931–35	Nicholas III	1277–80
Gregory I	590–604	Leo VII	936–39	Martin IV	1281–85

POPES (CONTINUED)

Pope	Pontificate	Pope	Pontificate	Pope	Pontificate
Honorious IV	1285–87	Julius II	1503–13	Innocent XII	1691–1700
Nicholas IV	1288–92	Leo X	1513–21	Clement XI	1700–21
Celestine V	1294	Hadrian VI	1522–23	Innocent XIII	1721–24
Boniface VIII	1294–1303	Clement VII	1523–34	Benedict XIII	1724–30
Benedict XI	1303–04	Paul III	1534–49	Clement XII	1730–40
Clement V	1305–14	Julius III	1550–55	Benedict XIV	1740–58
John XXII	1316–34	Marcellus II	1555	Clement XIII	1758–69
Benedict XII	1334–42	Paul IV	1555–59	Clement XIV	1769–74
Clement VI	1342–52	Pius IV	1559–65	Pius VI	1775–99
Innocent VI	1352–62	Pius V	1566–72	Pius VII	1800–23
Urban V	1362–70	Gregory XIII	1572–85	Leo XII	1823–29
Gregory XI	1370–78	Sixtus V	1585–90	Pius VIII	1829–30
Urban VI	1378–89	Urban VII	1590	Gregory XVI	1831–46
Boniface IX	1389–1404	Gregory XIV	1590–91	Pius IX	1846–78
Innocent VII	1404–06	Innocent IX	1591	Leo XIII	1878–1903
Gregory XII	1406–15	Clement VIII	1592–1605	Pius X	1903–14
Martin V	1417–41	Leo XI	1605	Benedict XV	1914–22
Eugenius IV	1431–47	Paul V	1605–21	Pius XI	1922–39
Nicholas V	1447–55	Gregory XV	1621–23	Pius XII	1939–58
Callistus III	1455–58	Urban VIII	1623–44	John XXIII	1958–63
Pius II	1458–64	Innocent X	1644–55	Paul VI	1963–78
Paul II	1464–71	Alexander VII	1655–67	John Paul I	1978
Sixtus IV	1471–84	Clement IX	1667–69	John Paul II	1978–2005
Innocent VIII	1484–92	Clement X	1670–76	Benedictus XVI	2005–
Alexander VI	1492–1503	Innocent XI	1676–89		
Pius III	1503	Alexander VIII	1689–91		

portrait 1 = **picture**, painting, image, photograph, representation, sketch, likeness, portraiture • *Lucian Freud has been asked to paint a portrait of the Queen.*
2 = **description**, account, profile, biography, portrayal, depiction, vignette, characterization, thumbnail sketch • *a beautifully written and sensitive portrait of a great woman*

portray 1 = **play**, take the role of, act the part of, represent, personate *(rare)* • *He portrayed the king in a revival of 'Camelot'.*
2 = **describe**, present, depict, evoke, delineate, put in words • *the novelist accurately portrays provincial domestic life*
3 = **represent**, draw, paint, illustrate, sketch, figure, picture, render, depict, delineate • *the landscape as portrayed by painters such as Poussin*
4 = **characterize**, describe, represent, depict, paint a mental picture of • *complaints about the way women are portrayed in adverts*

portrayal 1 = **performance**, interpretation, enacting, take *(informal, chiefly U.S.)*, acting, impersonation, performance as, characterization, personation *(rare)* • *He is well known for his portrayal of a prison guard in 'The Last Emperor'.*
2 = **depiction**, picture, representation, sketch, rendering, delineation • *a near-monochrome portrayal of a wood infused with silvery light*
3 = **description**, account, representation • *an often funny portrayal of a friendship between two boys*
4 = **characterization**, representation, depiction • *The media persists in its portrayal of us as muggers and dope sellers.*

pose AS A VERB 1 = **present**, cause, produce, create, lead to, result in, constitute, give rise to • *His ill health poses serious problems.*
2 = **ask**, state, advance, put, set, submit, put forward, posit, propound • *When I posed the question 'Why?', he merely shrugged.*
3 = **position yourself**, sit, model, strike a pose, arrange yourself • *The six foreign ministers posed for photographs.*
4 = **put on airs**, affect, posture, show off *(informal)*, showboat, strike an attitude, attitudinize • *He criticized them for posing pretentiously.*
▸ AS A NOUN 1 = **posture**, position, bearing, attitude, stance, mien *(literary)* • *We have had several sittings in various poses.*
2 = **act**, role, façade, air, front, posturing, pretence, masquerade, mannerism, affectation, attitudinizing • *In many writers modesty is a pose, but in him it seems to be genuine.*
▸ IN PHRASES: **pose as something** or **someone** = **impersonate**, pretend to be, sham, feign, profess to be, masquerade as, pass yourself off as • *The team posed as drug dealers to trap the ringleaders.*

poser[1] = **puzzle**, problem, question, riddle, enigma, conundrum, teaser, tough one, vexed question, brain-teaser *(informal)*, knotty point • *Here's a little poser for you.*

poser[2] = **show-off** *(informal)*, poseur, posturer, masquerader, hot dog *(chiefly U.S.)*, impostor, exhibitionist, self-publicist, mannerist, attitudinizer • *He's such a poser.*

posh 1 = **smart**, grand, exclusive, luxury, elegant, fashionable, stylish, luxurious, classy *(slang)*, swish *(informal, chiefly Brit.)*, up-market, swanky *(informal)*, ritzy *(slang)*, schmick *(Austral. informal)* • *I took her to a posh hotel for a cocktail.*
2 = **upper-class**, high-class, top-drawer, plummy, high-toned, la-di-da *(informal)* • *He sounded very posh on the phone.*

posit = **put forward**, advance, submit, state, assume, assert, presume, predicate, postulate, propound • *Several writers have posited the idea of a universal consciousness.*

position AS A NOUN 1 = **location**, place, point, area, post, situation, station, site, spot, bearings, reference, orientation, whereabouts, locality, locale • *The ship's position was reported to the coastguard.*
2 = **posture**, attitude, arrangement, pose, stance, disposition • *He had raised himself into a sitting position.*
3 = **status**, place, standing, class, footing, station, rank, reputation, importance, consequence, prestige, caste, stature, eminence, repute • *their changing role and position in society*
4 = **job**, place, post, opening, office, role, situation, duty, function, employment, capacity, occupation, berth

PORTS

MAJOR PORTS OF THE WORLD

Abidjan
Accra
Aden
Alexandria
Algiers
Alicante
Amsterdam
Anchorage
Antwerp
Apia
Aqaba
Archangel
Ashdod
Auckland
Baku
Baltimore
Bangkok
Barcelona
Basra
Bathurst
Batum
Beira
Beirut
Belize
Benghazi
Bergen
Bilbao
Bissau
Bombay
Bordeaux
Boston
Boulogne
Bridgetown
Brindisi
Brisbane
Bristol
Buenaventura
Buenos Aires
Cádiz
Cagliari
Calais
Calcutta
Callao
Cannes
Canton
Cape Town
Cap-Haitien
Casablanca
Catania
Cebu
Charleston
Cherbourg
Chicago
Chittagong
Colombo
Colón
Conakry
Copenhagen
Corinth
Dakar
Dar es Salaam
Darwin
Dieppe
Djibouti
Dubrovnik
Duluth
Dunedin
Dunkerque
Durban
East London
Eilat
Esbjerg
Europoort
Fray Bentos
Freetown
Fremantle
Gdańsk
Genoa
Georgetown
Gijón
Göteborg
Guayaquil
Haifa
Halifax
Hamburg
Hamilton
Havana
Helsinki
Hobart
Ho Chi Minh City
Honolulu
Hook of Holland
Inchon
Istanbul
Izmir
Jacksonville
Jaffa
Jidda
Juneau
Kaohsiung
Karachi
Kawasaki
Keflavik
Kiel
Kingston
Kobe
Kowloon
Kuwait
La Coruña
Lagos
La Guaira
Las Palmas
Launceston
Le Havre
Limassol
Lisbon
Liverpool
Livorno
Lomé
London
Los Angeles
Luanda
Lübeck
Macao
Madras
Malmo
Manama
Manaus
Manila
Maputo
Mar del Plata
Marseille
Melbourne
Mobile
Mogadiscio
Mombasa
Monrovia
Montego Bay
Montevideo
Montreal
Murmansk
Muscat
Nagasaki
Naples
Nassau
New Orleans
New York
Oakland
Odense
Odessa
Oporto
Osaka
Oslo
Ostend
Phnom Penh
Piraeus
Port Adelaide
Port au Prince
Port Elizabeth
Portland
Port Louis
Port Moresby
Port Said
Portsmouth
Port Sudan
Punta Arenas
Pusan
Recife
Reykjavik
Riga
Rimini
Rio de Janeiro
Rostock
Rotterdam
Saint Petersburg
Salvador
San Diego
San Francisco
San Juan
San Sebastian
Santander
Santo Domingo
Santos
Savannah
Seattle
Sevastopol
Seville
Shanghai
Singapore
Southampton
Split
Stavanger
Stockholm
Suez
Suva
Sydney
Szczecin
Takoradi
Tallinn
Tampa
Tandjungpriok
Tangier
Tokyo
Townsville
Trieste
Tripoli
Trondheim
Tunis
Turku
Tyre
Valencia
Valparaíso
Vancouver
Venice
Veracruz
Vigo
Vishakhapatnam
Vladivostok
Volgograd
Walvis Bay
Wellington
Yangon
Yokohama
Zeebrugge

MAIN BRITISH AND IRISH PORTS

Aberdeen
Arbroath
Ayr
Barry
Belfast
Birkenhead
Bristol
Caernarfon
Cardiff
Cóbh
Cork
Dover
Dundee
Dún Laoghaire
Ellesmere Port
Fishguard
Fleetwood
Folkestone
Galway
Glasgow
Grangemouth
Gravesend
Great Yarmouth
Greenock
Grimsby
Harwich
Holyhead
Hull
Immingham
Kirkcaldy
Larne
Leith
Lerwick
Limerick
Liverpool
London
Londonderry *or* Derry
Lowestoft
Milford Haven
Morecambe
Newcastle upon Tyne
Newhaven
Newport
Newry
Oban
Penzance
Plymouth
Poole
Portsmouth
Port Talbot
Ramsgate
Rosslare
Scarborough
Sheerness
Sligo
Southampton
South Shields
Stornoway
Stranraer
Sunderland
Swansea
Tynemouth
Waterford
Wexford
Weymouth
Whitby
Wicklow

(informal), billet *(informal)* • *He took up a position with the Arts Council.*
5 = place, standing, rank, status • *The players resumed their battle for the no. 1 position.*
6 = situation, state, condition, set of circumstances, plight, strait(s), predicament • *He's going to be in a difficult position if things go badly.*
7 = attitude, view, perspective, point of view, standing, opinion, belief, angle, stance, outlook, posture, viewpoint, slant, way of thinking, standpoint • *He usually takes a moderate position.*
8 = pole position, advantage, the edge, dominance, the upper hand, primacy • *Manufacturers have been jockeying for position in this key sales month.*
▸ **AS A VERB = place**, put, set, stand, stick *(informal)*, settle, fix, arrange, locate, sequence, array, dispose, lay out • *Position trailing plants near the edges of the basket.*

positive 1 = optimistic, confident, hopeful, upbeat *(informal)*, buoyant, sanguine, forward-looking • *a positive frame of mind*
OPPOSITES: negative
2 = beneficial, effective, useful, practical, helpful,

progressive, productive, worthwhile, constructive, pragmatic, efficacious • *Working abroad should be a positive experience.*
OPPOSITES: useless, harmful, detrimental
3 = **favourable**, encouraging, enthusiastic, good, approving, reassuring, supportive, constructive, affirmative, corroborative • *There has been a positive response to the peace efforts.*
OPPOSITES: unfavourable
4 = **certain**, sure, convinced, confident, satisfied, assured, free from doubt • *I'm positive she said she'd be here.*
OPPOSITES: uncertain, unsure, unconvinced
5 = **definite**, real, clear, firm, certain, direct, express, actual, absolute, concrete, decisive, explicit, affirmative, clear-cut, unmistakable, conclusive, unequivocal, indisputable, categorical, incontrovertible, nailed-on *(slang)* • *there was no positive evidence*
OPPOSITES: uncertain, doubtful, inconclusive
6 = **absolute**, complete, perfect, right *(Brit. informal)*, real, total, rank, sheer, utter, thorough, downright, consummate, veritable, unqualified, out-and-out, unmitigated, thoroughgoing, unalloyed • *He was in a positive fury.*
7 = **good**, promising, pleasing, encouraging, welcome, favourable, heartening, auspicious, propitious • *He said that the agreement could be a positive sign*

QUOTATIONS
positive: mistaken at the top of one's voice
[Ambrose Bierce *The Devil's Dictionary*]
You've got to ac-cent-tchu-ate the positive
Elim-my-nate the negative
Latch on to the affirmative
Don't mess with Mister In-Between
[Johnny Mercer *Ac-cent-tchu-ate the Positive*]

positively 1 = **definitely**, surely, firmly, certainly, absolutely, emphatically, unquestionably, undeniably, categorically, unequivocally, unmistakably, with certainty, assuredly, without qualification • *This is positively the worst thing I can imagine.*
2 = **really**, completely, simply, plain *(informal)*, absolutely, thoroughly, utterly, downright • *He was positively furious.*

possess 1 = **own**, have, hold, be in possession of, be the owner of, have in your possession, have to your name • *He is said to possess a huge fortune.*
2 = **be endowed with**, have, enjoy, benefit from, be born with, be blessed with, be possessed of, be gifted with • *individuals who possess the qualities of sense and discretion*
3 = **control**, influence, dominate, consume, obsess, bedevil, mesmerize, eat someone up, fixate, put under a spell • *Absolute terror possessed her.*
4 = **seize**, hold, control, dominate, occupy, haunt, take someone over, bewitch, take possession of, have power over, have mastery over • *It was as if the spirit of his father possessed him.*

possessed = **crazed**, haunted, cursed, obsessed, raving, frenzied, consumed, enchanted, maddened, demented, frenetic, berserk, bewitched, bedevilled, under a spell, hag-ridden • *He behaved like someone possessed.*

possession AS A NOUN 1 = **ownership**, control, custody, hold, hands, tenure, occupancy, proprietorship • *These documents are now in the possession of the authorities.*
2 = **province**, territory, colony, dominion, protectorate • *All of these countries were once French possessions.*
▸ AS A PLURAL NOUN = **property**, things, effects, estate, assets, wealth, belongings, chattels, goods and chattels • *People had lost their homes and all their possessions.*
▸ IN PHRASES: **take possession of** = **seize**, take, appropriate, get hold of, confiscate, impound, commandeer, requisition, sequester, expropriate, help yourself to, sequestrate • *Earl had taken possession of the gun.*

QUOTATIONS
Lay not up for yourselves treasures upon earth, where moth and rust doth corrupt, and where thieves break through and steal
[*Bible: St. Matthew*]

PROVERBS
A bird in the hand is worth two in the bush
Possession is nine points of the law

possessive 1 = **jealous**, controlling, dominating, domineering, proprietorial, overprotective • *Danny could be very jealous and possessive of me.*
2 = **selfish**, grasping, acquisitive • *He's very possessive about his car.*

possibility 1 = **feasibility**, likelihood, plausibility, potentiality, practicability, workableness • *a debate about the possibility of political reform*
2 = **likelihood**, chance, risk, odds, prospect, liability, hazard, probability • *There is still a possibility of unrest in the country.*
3 = **option**, choice, alternative, solution, bet *(informal)*, course of action, recourse • *There were several possibilities open to the manufacturers.*
4 *often plural* = **potential**, promise, prospects, talent, capabilities, potentiality • *This situation has great possibilities.*

QUOTATIONS
Probable impossibilities are to be preferred to improbable possibilities
[Aristotle *Poetics*]

possible 1 = **feasible**, viable, workable, achievable, within reach, on *(informal)*, practicable, attainable, doable, realizable • *Everything is possible if we want it enough.*
OPPOSITES: impossible, unreasonable, unfeasible
2 = **likely**, potential, anticipated, probable, odds-on, on the cards • *One possible solution is to take legal action.*
OPPOSITES: impossible, improbable
3 = **conceivable**, likely, credible, plausible, hypothetical, imaginable, believable, thinkable • *It's just possible that he was trying to put me off the trip.*
OPPOSITES: impossible, unlikely, inconceivable
4 = **aspiring**, would-be, promising, hopeful, prospective, wannabe *(informal)* • *a possible presidential contender*

QUOTATIONS
Everything is possible, including the impossible
[Benito Mussolini]

possibly 1 = **perhaps**, maybe, God willing, perchance *(archaic)*, mayhap *(archaic)*, peradventure *(archaic)*, haply *(archaic)* • *Exercise may possibly protect against heart attacks.*
2 = **at all**, in any way, conceivably, by any means, under any circumstances, by any chance • *I couldn't possibly answer that.*

post[1] AS A NOUN = **support**, stake, pole, stock, standard, column, pale, shaft, upright, pillar, picket, palisade, newel • *Eight wooden posts were driven into the ground.*
▸ AS A VERB = **put up**, announce, publish, display, advertise, proclaim, publicize, promulgate, affix, stick something up, make something known, pin something up • *Officials began posting warning notices.*

post[2] AS A NOUN 1 = **job**, place, office, position, situation, employment, appointment, assignment, berth *(informal)*, billet *(informal)* • *Sir Peter has held several senior military posts.*
2 = **position**, place, base, beat, station • *Quick, men, back to your posts!*
▸ AS A VERB = **station**, assign, put, place, position, establish, locate, situate, put on duty • *After training she was posted to Brixton.*

post[3] AS A NOUN 1 = **mail**, collection, delivery, postal service, snail mail *(informal)* • *You'll receive your book through the post.* • *rushing to catch the post*
2 = **correspondence**, letters, cards, mail • *He flipped through the post without opening any of it.*
▸ AS A VERB = **send (off)**, forward, mail, get off, transmit,

P

dispatch, consign • *I'm posting you a cheque tonight.*
▸ **IN PHRASES: keep someone posted = notify**, brief, advise, inform, report to, keep someone informed, keep someone up to date, apprise, fill someone in on *(informal)*, keep someone plugged-in *(slang)* • *Keep me posted on your progress.*

postcards
▸ **RELATED ENTHUSIAST:** deltiologist

poster = **notice**, bill, announcement, advertisement, sticker, placard, public notice, affiche *(French)* • *Her picture was on wanted posters all over the country.*

posterior AS A NOUN = **bottom**, behind *(informal)*, bum *(Brit. slang)*, seat, rear, tail *(informal)*, butt *(U.S. & Canad. informal)*, ass *(U.S. & Canad. taboo slang)*, buns *(U.S. slang)*, arse *(taboo slang)*, buttocks, backside, rump, rear end, derrière *(euphemistic)*, tush *(U.S. slang)*, fundament, jacksy *(Brit. slang)* • *her curvaceous posterior*
▸ **AS AN ADJECTIVE** = **rear**, back, hinder, hind • *the posterior lobe of the pituitary gland*

posterity 1 = **the future**, future generations, succeeding generations • *A photographer recorded the scene for posterity.*
2 = **descendants**, children, family, issue, seed *(chiefly biblical)*, heirs, offspring, progeny, scions • *the imputation of Adam's sin to all his posterity*

QUOTATIONS
'We are always doing,' says he, 'something for Posterity, but I would fain see Posterity doing something for us.'
[Joseph Addison]

postmortem 1 = **examination**, analysis, autopsy, dissection, necropsy • *A postmortem showed that he had drowned.*
2 = **analysis**, study, review, investigation, assessment, examination, breakdown, evaluation, appraisal • *The postmortem on the presidential campaign is under way.*

postpone = **put off**, delay, suspend, adjourn, table, shelve, defer, put back, hold over, put on ice *(informal)*, put on the back burner *(informal)*, take a rain check on *(U.S. & Canad. informal)* • *He decided to postpone the expedition.*
OPPOSITES: advance, carry out, go ahead with

postponement = **delay**, stay, suspension, moratorium, respite, adjournment, deferment, deferral • *The postponement was due to a dispute over where the talks should be held.*

postscript = **P.S.**, addition, supplement, appendix, afterthought, afterword • *A brief, handwritten postscript lay beneath his signature.*

postulate = **presuppose**, suppose, advance, propose, assume, put forward, take for granted, predicate, theorize, posit, hypothesize • *Freud postulated that we all have a death instinct.*

posture AS A NOUN 1 = **bearing**, set, position, attitude, pose, stance, carriage, disposition, mien *(literary)* • *She walked haltingly and her posture was stooped.*
2 = **attitude**, feeling, mood, point of view, stance, outlook, inclination, disposition, standpoint, frame of mind • *None of the banks changed their posture on the deal as a result of the inquiry.*
▸ **AS A VERB** = **show off** *(informal)*, pose, affect, hot-dog *(chiefly U.S.)*, make a show, showboat, put on airs, try to attract attention, attitudinize, do something for effect • *Rock stars sneered, postured and leaped on the TV screen.*

posy = **bouquet**, spray, buttonhole, corsage, nosegay, boutonniere • *the old-fashioned Victorian posy she carried*

pot AS A NOUN 1 = **container**, bowl, pan, vessel, basin, vase, jug, cauldron, urn, utensil, crock, skillet • *metal cooking pots* • *use a large terracotta pot or a wooden tub.*
2 = **jackpot**, bank, prize, stakes, purse • *The pot for this Saturday's draw stands at over £18 million.*
3 = **kitty**, funds, pool • *If there is more money in the pot, all the members will benefit proportionally.*
4 = **paunch**, beer belly *or* gut *(informal)*, spread *(informal)*, corporation *(informal)*, gut, bulge, spare tyre *(Brit. slang)*, potbelly • *He's already developing a pot from all the beer he drinks.*
▸ **IN PHRASES: go to pot = decline**, slump, deteriorate, worsen, go downhill *(informal)*, go to the dogs *(informal)*, run to seed, go to rack and ruin • *This neighbourhood is really going to pot.*

potato

POTATOES

Arran Comet	Golden Wonder	Pentland Javelin
Arran Pilot	Jersey Royal	Pentland Squire
Arran Victory	Kerr's Pink	Pink Fir Apple
Belle de Fontenay	King Edward	Romano
Cara	Marfona	Roseval
Catriona	Maris Bard	Sharpe's Express
Charlotte	Maris Piper	Ulster Sceptre
Desiree	Pentland Crown	Wilja
Estima	Pentland Dell	

pot-bellied = **fat**, overweight, bloated, obese, distended, corpulent, paunchy • *a podgy-faced, pot-bellied man*

pot belly = **paunch**, beer belly *or* gut *(informal)*, spread *(informal)*, corporation *(informal)*, pot, gut, spare tyre *(Brit. slang)*, middle-age spread *(informal)*, puku *(N.Z.)* • *He wore a tight T-shirt over his pot belly.*

potency 1 = **influence**, might, force, control, authority, energy, potential, strength, capacity, mana *(N.Z.)* • *the extraordinary potency of his personality*
2 = **persuasiveness**, force, strength, muscle, effectiveness, sway, forcefulness, cogency, impressiveness • *His remarks have added potency given the current situation.*
3 = **power**, force, strength, effectiveness, efficacy • *The potency of the wine increases with time.*
4 = **vigour**, puissance • *Alcohol abuse in men can reduce sexual potency.*

potent 1 = **powerful**, commanding, dynamic, dominant, influential, authoritative • *a potent political force*
2 = **persuasive**, telling, convincing, effective, impressive, compelling, forceful, cogent • *a potent electoral message*
OPPOSITES: ineffective, unconvincing
3 = **strong**, powerful, mighty, vigorous, forceful, efficacious, puissant • *The drug is extremely potent, but can have unpleasant side-effects.*
OPPOSITES: weak, impotent

potentate = **ruler**, king, prince, emperor, monarch, sovereign, mogul, overlord • *a rich Eastern potentate*

potential AS AN ADJECTIVE 1 = **possible**, future, likely, promising, budding, embryonic, undeveloped, unrealized, probable • *potential customers*
2 = **hidden**, possible, inherent, dormant, latent • *We are aware of the potential dangers.*
▸ **AS A NOUN** = **ability**, possibilities, capacity, capability, the makings, what it takes *(informal)*, aptitude, wherewithal, potentiality • *The boy has potential.*

potion = **concoction**, mixture, brew, tonic, cup, dose, draught, elixir, philtre • *Socrates killed himself by drinking a potion containing hemlock seeds.*

potpourri = **mixture**, collection, combination, patchwork, medley, motley, pastiche, mixed bag *(informal)*, mélange *(French)*, miscellany, hotchpotch, salmagundi, gallimaufry • *a potpourri of architectural styles from all over the world*

potter *usually with* **around** *or* **about** = **mess about**, fiddle *(informal)*, tinker, dabble, fritter, footle *(informal)*, poke along, fribble • *She was pottering around in the garden.*

pottery = **ceramics**, terracotta, crockery, earthenware, stoneware • *a 17th century piece of pottery*
▸ **RELATED ADJECTIVE:** fictile

potty = **crazy**, eccentric, crackers (*Brit. slang*), barmy (*slang*), touched, soft (*informal*), out there (*slang*), silly, foolish, daft (*informal*), off-the-wall (*slang*), oddball (*informal*), off the rails, dotty (*slang, chiefly Brit.*), loopy (*informal*), crackpot (*informal*), out to lunch (*informal*), dippy (*slang*), gonzo (*slang*), doolally (*slang*), off your trolley (*slang*), up the pole (*informal*), off your chump (*slang*), wacko *or* whacko (*informal*), off the air (*Austral. slang*), porangi (*N.Z.*), daggy (*Austral. & N.Z. informal*) • *I had an old aunt once who went completely potty.*

pouch = **bag**, pocket, sack, container, purse, poke (*dialect*) • *a leather pouch full of tobacco*

poultry
▸ **COLLECTIVE NOUN:** run
▸ **RELATED PHOBIA:** alektorophobia

pounce **AS A VERB** *often followed by* **on** *or* **upon** = **attack**, strike, jump, leap, swoop • *Before I could get to the pigeon, the cat pounced.*
▸ **IN PHRASES: pounce on something** *or* **someone**
1 = **attack**, ambush, leap at, take someone by surprise, take someone unawares • *At that moment, a guard pounced on him.*
2 = **spring on**, attack, snatch, jump on, drop on, swoop on, fall upon, leap at, dash at, bound onto • *like a tiger pouncing on its prey*

pound[1] = **enclosure**, yard, pen, compound, kennels, corral (*chiefly U.S. & Canad.*) • *The dog has been sent to the pound.*

pound[2] 1 *sometimes with* **on** = **beat**, strike, hammer, batter, thrash, thump, pelt, clobber (*slang*), pummel, belabour, beat *or* knock seven bells out of (*informal*), beat the living daylights out of • *He pounded the table with his fist.*
2 = **crush**, powder, bruise, bray (*dialect*), pulverize, comminute (*rare*) • *She paused as she pounded the maize grains.*
3 = **pulsate**, beat, pulse, throb, palpitate, pitapat • *I'm sweating and my heart is pounding.*
4 *often with* **out** = **thump**, beat, hammer, bang • *A group of tribal drummers pounded out an unrelenting beat.*
5 = **stomp**, tramp, march, thunder (*informal*), clomp • *I pounded up the stairs to my room and slammed the door.*

pour **AS A VERB** 1 = **let flow**, spill, splash, dribble, drizzle, slop (*informal*), slosh (*informal*), decant • *Francis poured a generous measure of whisky into the glass.*
2 = **flow**, stream, run, course, rush, emit, cascade, gush, spout, spew • *Blood was pouring from his broken nose.*
3 = **rain**, sheet, pelt (down), teem, bucket down (*informal*), rain cats and dogs (*informal*), come down in torrents, rain hard *or* heavily • *It has been pouring all week.*
4 = **stream**, crowd, flood, swarm, gush, throng, teem • *The northern forces poured across the border.*
▸ **IN PHRASES: pour something out** = **tell**, reveal, relate, divulge, get off your chest • *I've got no-one to come home to and pour out my troubles to.*

pout **AS A VERB** = **sulk**, glower, mope, look sullen, purse your lips, look petulant, pull a long face, lour *or* lower, make a moue, turn down the corners of your mouth • *He whined and pouted like a kid when he didn't get what he wanted.*
▸ **AS A NOUN** = **sullen look**, glower, long face, moue (*French*) • *She jutted her lower lip out in a pout.*

poverty 1 = **pennilessness**, want, need, distress, necessity, hardship, insolvency, privation, penury, destitution, hand-to-mouth existence, beggary, indigence, pauperism, necessitousness • *41 per cent of Brazilians live in absolute poverty.*
OPPOSITES: comfort, wealth, luxury
2 = **scarcity**, lack, absence, want, deficit, shortage, deficiency, inadequacy, dearth, paucity, insufficiency, sparsity • *a poverty of ideas*
OPPOSITES: abundance, plethora, sufficiency
3 = **barrenness**, deficiency, infertility, sterility, aridity, bareness, poorness, meagreness, unfruitfulness • *the poverty of the soil*
OPPOSITES: fertility, fecundity, fruitfulness
▸ **RELATED PHOBIA:** peniaphobia

QUOTATIONS

The greatest of evils and the worst of crimes is poverty
[George Bernard Shaw *Major Barbara*]

Anyone who has ever struggled with poverty knows how extremely expensive it is to be poor
[James Baldwin *Nobody Knows My Name*]

Give me not poverty lest I steal
[Daniel Defoe *Review (later incorporated into Moll Flanders)*]

The want of money is the root of all evil
[Samuel Butler *Erewhon*]

No man should commend poverty unless he is poor
[Saint Bernard]

People don't resent having nothing nearly as much as too little
[Ivy Compton-Burnett *A Family and a Fortune*]

PROVERBS

Poverty is not a crime

poverty-stricken = **penniless**, broke (*informal*), bankrupt, impoverished, short, poor, distressed, beggared, needy, destitute, down and out, skint (*Brit. slang*), indigent, down at heel, impecunious, dirt-poor (*informal*), on the breadline, flat broke (*informal*), penurious, on your uppers, stony-broke (*Brit. slang*), in queer street, without two pennies to rub together (*informal*), on your beam-ends • *two poverty-stricken bag ladies*

powder **AS A NOUN** = **dust**, pounce (*rare*), talc, fine grains, loose particles • *a fine white powder*
▸ **AS A VERB** 1 = **dust**, cover, scatter, sprinkle, strew, dredge • *Powder the puddings with icing sugar.*
2 = **grind**, crush, pound, pestle, pulverize, granulate • *Mix all the powdered ingredients together.*

powdered = **dried**, dehydrated, freeze-dried • *powdered milk*

powder room = **lavatory**, toilet, the Ladies, loo (*Brit. informal*), washroom (*U.S. & Canad.*), ladies room, dunny (*Austral. & N.Z. old-fashioned*), (public) convenience, bogger (*Austral. slang*), brasco (*Austral. slang*) • *To the left of the hall was a powder room.*

powdery = **fine**, dry, sandy, dusty, loose, crumbling, grainy, chalky, crumbly, granular, pulverized, friable • *He scooped up a handful of dry powdery earth.*

power **AS A NOUN** 1 = **control**, authority, influence, command, sovereignty, sway, dominance, domination, supremacy, mastery, dominion, ascendancy, mana (*N.Z.*) • *women who have reached positions of great power and influence*
2 = **ability**, capacity, faculty, property, potential, capability, competence, competency • *He was so drunk that he had lost the power of speech.*
OPPOSITES: inability, incompetence, incapacity
3 = **authority**, right, licence, privilege, warrant, prerogative, authorization • *The Prime Minister has the power to dismiss senior ministers.*
4 = **strength**, might, energy, weight, muscle, vigour, potency, welly (*slang*), brawn • *He had no power in his left arm.*
OPPOSITES: weakness, impotence, feebleness
5 = **forcefulness**, force, strength, punch (*informal*), intensity, potency, eloquence, persuasiveness, cogency, powerfulness • *the power of his rhetoric*
▸ **IN PHRASES: the powers that be** = **the authorities**, the government, the establishment, the people in charge, the men in (grey) suits • *The powers that be banned the advertisement.*

QUOTATIONS

Power tends to corrupt and absolute power corrupts absolutely
[First Baron Acton *letter*]

P

Unlimited power is apt to corrupt the minds of those who possess it
[William Pitt, Earl of Chatham]
Power is the great aphrodisiac
[Henry Kissinger]
Here we may reign secure, and in my choice
To reign is worth ambition though in hell;
Better to reign in hell, than serve in heav'n
[John Milton *Paradise Lost*]
Political power grows out of the barrel of a gun
[Mao Tse-tung]
A friend in power is a friend lost
[Henry Brooks Adams *The Education of Henry Adams*]
The only purpose for which power can be rightfully exercised over any member of a civilized community, against his will, is to prevent harm to others. His own good, either physical or moral, is not a sufficient warrant
[John Stuart Mill *On Liberty*]

powerful 1 = **influential**, dominant, controlling, commanding, supreme, prevailing, sovereign, authoritative, puissant, skookum *(Canad.)* • *You're a powerful woman – people will listen to you.*
OPPOSITES: weak, ineffectual, powerless
2 = **strong**, strapping, mighty, robust, vigorous, potent, energetic, sturdy, stalwart • *a big, powerful man*
OPPOSITES: weak, feeble, frail
3 = **effective**, hard, strong • *a powerful and fast-acting drug*
OPPOSITES: weak, ineffective, inefficacious
4 = **intoxicating**, strong, heady • *tiny flowers with a powerful scent*
5 = **loud**, booming, resounding, sonorous, stentorian • *He had a deep, powerful voice.*
OPPOSITES: weak, quiet, faint, feeble, soft, low, shaky, languid, unsteady, muffled, small
6 = **persuasive**, convincing, effective, telling, moving, striking, storming, dramatic, impressive, compelling, authoritative, forceful, weighty, forcible, cogent, effectual • *a powerful drama about a corrupt city leader*
7 = **intense**, strong, burning, keen, violent, acute, overwhelming, consuming, fierce, passionate, irresistible, overpowering, ardent, fervent, fervid • *in the grip of a powerful emotion*

powerfully = **strongly**, hard, vigorously, forcibly, forcefully, mightily, with might and main • *He shot powerfully from 20 yards and scored.*

powerless 1 = **defenceless**, vulnerable, dependent, subject, tied, ineffective, unarmed, disenfranchised, over a barrel *(informal)*, disfranchised • *political systems that keep women poor and powerless*
2 = **weak**, disabled, helpless, incapable, paralysed, frail, feeble, debilitated, impotent, ineffectual, incapacitated, prostrate, infirm, etiolated • *His leg muscles were powerless with lack of use.*
OPPOSITES: strong, fit, powerful

practicability = **feasibility**, use, value, advantage, possibility, practicality, viability, usefulness, workability, operability • *We discussed the practicability of the idea.*

practicable = **feasible**, possible, viable, workable, achievable, attainable, doable, within the realm of possibility, performable • *Teachers can only be expected to do what is practicable.*
OPPOSITES: impossible, out of the question, unfeasible

practical 1 = **functional**, efficient, realistic, pragmatic • *practical suggestions on how to improve your diet*
OPPOSITES: unrealistic, inefficient, impractical
2 = **empirical**, real, applied, actual, hands-on, in the field, experimental, factual • *theories based on practical knowledge*
OPPOSITES: theoretical, speculative, unpractical
3 = **sensible**, ordinary, realistic, down-to-earth, mundane, matter-of-fact, no-nonsense, businesslike, hard-headed, workaday, grounded • *She is always so practical and full of common sense.*
OPPOSITES: unrealistic, impractical
4 = **feasible**, possible, sound, viable, constructive, workable, practicable, doable • *We do not yet have any practical way to prevent cancer.*
OPPOSITES: impossible, useless, impractical
5 = **useful**, ordinary, appropriate, sensible, everyday, functional, utilitarian, serviceable • *clothes which are practical as well as stylish*
6 = **skilled**, working, seasoned, trained, experienced, qualified, veteran, efficient, accomplished, proficient • *people with practical experience of running businesses*
OPPOSITES: inexperienced, inefficient, unskilled

practicality 1 = **feasibility**, value, use, possibility, utility, viability, usefulness, practicability, workability • *the practicality of the suggestion*
2 = **common sense**, sense, realism, pragmatism, matter-of-factness • *Mr Calder showed commendable practicality in his attitude.*
3 = **functionalism**, utility, usefulness, functionality, serviceability • *The furniture managed to combine practicality with elegance.*
4 = **practical details**, mechanics, nuts and bolts *(informal)*, nitty gritty *(informal)* • *the cost and practicality of the system*

practical joke = **trick**, joke, hoax, prank • *They played a silly practical joke on her.*

practically 1 = **almost**, nearly, close to, essentially, virtually, basically, fundamentally, all but, just about, in effect, very nearly, to all intents and purposes, well-nigh • *He'd known the old man practically all his life.*
2 = **sensibly**, reasonably, matter-of-factly, realistically, rationally, pragmatically, with common sense, unsentimentally • *'Let me help you to bed,' Helen said, practically.*
3 = **empirically**, in the field, experimentally, experientially • *more practically based learning*

practice AS A NOUN 1 = **custom**, use, way, system, rule, method, tradition, habit, routine, mode, usage, wont, praxis, usual procedure, tikanga *(N.Z.)* • *a public inquiry into bank practices*
2 = **training**, study, exercise, work-out, discipline, preparation, drill, rehearsal, repetition • *netball practice*
3 = **profession**, work, business, career, occupation, pursuit, vocation • *improving his skills in the practice of medicine*
4 = **business**, company, office, firm, enterprise, partnership, outfit *(informal)* • *He worked in a small legal practice.*
5 = **use**, experience, action, effect, operation, application, enactment • *attempts to encourage the practice of safe sex*
▸ **IN PHRASES: in practice** = **in reality**, actually, practically, effectively, in real life, realistically • *In practice, this idea has proved very hard to follow up.*
out of practice = **rusty**, not up to scratch, unpractised • *'How's your German?' – 'Not bad, but I'm out of practice.'*
put something into practice = **apply**, use, make use of, exercise, employ, draw on, utilize, put into effect, put to use, bring into play • *a chance to put his new ideas into practice*

PROVERBS
Practice makes perfect

practise 1 = **rehearse**, study, prepare, perfect, repeat, go through, polish, go over, refine, run through • *Lauren practises the concerto every day.*
2 = **do**, train, exercise, work out, drill, warm up, keep your hand in • *practising for a gym display*
3 = **carry out**, follow, apply, perform, observe, engage in, live up to, put into practice • *Astronomy continued to be practised in Byzantium.*

4 = work at, pursue, carry on, undertake, specialize in, ply your trade • *He practised as a lawyer for thirty years.*

practised = skilled, trained, experienced, seasoned, able, expert, qualified, accomplished, versed, proficient • *a practised and experienced surgeon*
OPPOSITES: bungling, inexperienced, incompetent

pragmatic = practical, efficient, sensible, realistic, down-to-earth, matter-of-fact, utilitarian, businesslike, hard-headed • *a pragmatic approach to the problems faced by Latin America*
OPPOSITES: theoretical, unrealistic, idealistic

praise AS A VERB 1 = acclaim, approve of, honour, cheer, admire, applaud, compliment, congratulate, pay tribute to, laud, extol, sing the praises of, pat someone on the back, cry someone up, big up *(slang, chiefly Caribbean)*, eulogize, take your hat off to, crack someone up *(informal)* • *Many praised him for taking a strong stand.*
OPPOSITES: criticize, blame, condemn
2 = give thanks to, bless, worship, adore, magnify *(archaic)*, glorify, exalt, pay homage to • *She asked the congregation to praise God.*
▸ **AS A NOUN 1 = approval**, acclaim, applause, cheering, tribute, compliment, congratulations, ovation, accolade, good word, kudos, eulogy, commendation, approbation, acclamation, panegyric, encomium, plaudit, laudation • *I have nothing but praise for the police.*
OPPOSITES: criticism, blame, condemnation
2 = thanks, glory, worship, devotion, homage, adoration • *Hindus were singing hymns in praise of the god Rama.*
▸ **IN PHRASES: sing something's** *or* **someone's praises = praise**, acclaim, laud, big up *(slang, chiefly Caribbean)* • *I've been singing her praises for years.*

PROVERBS
Self-praise is no recommendation

praiseworthy = creditable, fine, excellent, worthy, admirable, honourable, exemplary, commendable, laudable, meritorious, estimable • *praiseworthy efforts*
OPPOSITES: disgraceful, despicable, discreditable

pram = perambulator, buggy, stroller, baby carriage *(U.S. & Canad.)* • *a woman pushing a pram loaded with both baby and shopping*

prance 1 = dance, bound, leap, trip, spring, jump, skip, romp, caper, cavort, frisk, gambol, cut a rug *(informal)* • *The cheerleaders pranced on the far side of the pitch.*
2 = strut, parade, stalk, show off *(informal)*, swagger, swank *(informal)*, showboat • *models prancing around on the catwalk*

prank = trick, lark *(informal)*, caper, frolic, escapade, practical joke, skylarking *(informal)*, antic, jape • *a stupid schoolboy prank*

prattle AS A VERB = chatter, babble, waffle *(informal, chiefly Brit.)*, run on, rabbit on *(Brit. informal)*, witter on *(informal)*, patter, drivel, clack, twitter, jabber, gabble, rattle on, blather, blether, run off at the mouth *(slang)*, earbash *(Austral. & N.Z. slang)* • *She prattled on until I wanted to scream.*
▸ **AS A NOUN = chatter**, talk, babble, waffle *(informal)*, rambling, wittering *(informal)*, prating, drivel, jabber, gabble, blather, blether • *I had had enough of his mindless prattle.*

pray 1 = say your prayers, offer a prayer, recite the rosary • *He spent his time in prison praying and studying.*
2 = beg, ask, plead, petition, urge, request, sue, crave, invoke, call upon, cry, solicit, implore, beseech, entreat, importune, adjure, supplicate • *They prayed for help.*

QUOTATIONS
pray: to ask that the laws of the universe be annulled in behalf of a single petitioner confessedly unworthy
[Ambrose Bierce *The Devil's Dictionary*]

prayer 1 = supplication, devotion, communion • *The night was spent in prayer and meditation.*
2 = orison, litany, invocation, intercession • *prayers of thanksgiving*
3 = plea, appeal, suit, request, petition, entreaty, supplication • *Say a quick prayer I don't get stopped for speeding.*

QUOTATIONS
More things are wrought by prayer
Than this world dreams of
[Alfred, Lord Tennyson *Morte d'Arthur*]
The wish for prayer is a prayer in itself
[Georges Bernanos *Journal d'un cure de campagne*]
In prayer the lips ne'er act the winning part,
Without the sweet concurrence of the heart
[Robert Herrick *The Heart*]
One single grateful thought raised to heaven is the most perfect prayer
[G.E. Lessing *Minna von Barnhelm*]

preach AS A VERB 1 *often with* **to = deliver a sermon**, address, exhort, evangelize, preach a sermon, orate • *The bishop preached to a huge crowd.*
2 = proclaim, explain, teach, spread, propagate, disseminate, expound, make known • *a humble man who preaches the word of God*
3 = urge, teach, champion, recommend, advise, counsel, advocate, exhort • *the movement preaches revolution*
▸ **IN PHRASES: preach at someone = lecture**, admonish, harangue, sermonize, moralize against, preachify • *I can't stand being preached at.*

preacher = clergyman, minister, parson, missionary, evangelist, revivalist • *a self-educated Methodist lay preacher*

preaching = sermonizing, instruction, sermons, evangelism, religious teaching • *the minister's approach to evangelistic preaching*

preachy = moralizing, self-righteous, didactic, sanctimonious, edifying, holier-than-thou, pontifical, pietistic, canting, pharisaic, religiose, homiletic • *His speech was tinged with a moralistic, preachy tone.*

preamble = introduction, prelude, preface, foreword, overture, opening move, proem, prolegomenon, exordium, opening statement *or* remarks • *the principles contained in the preamble to the Chinese constitution*

prearranged = predetermined, set, agreed, settled, fixed, preplanned, decided beforehand, arranged in advance • *We met at a prearranged time.*

precarious 1 = insecure, dangerous, uncertain, tricky, risky, doubtful, dubious, unsettled, dodgy *(Brit., Austral. & N.Z. informal)*, unstable, unsure, hazardous, shaky, hairy *(slang)*, perilous, touch and go, dicey *(informal, chiefly Brit.)*, chancy *(informal)*, built on sand, shonky *(Austral. & N.Z. informal)* • *Our financial situation had become precarious.*
OPPOSITES: certain, safe, secure
2 = dangerous, unstable, shaky, slippery, insecure, unsafe, unreliable, unsteady • *They crawled up a precarious rope ladder.*
OPPOSITES: secure, stable, steady

precaution 1 = safeguard, insurance, protection, provision, safety measure, preventative measure, belt and braces *(informal)* • *This is purely a safety precaution.*
2 = forethought, care, caution, anticipation, prudence, foresight, providence, wariness, circumspection • *Exercise adequate precaution when out in public.*

precautionary = preventative, safety, protective, preventive • *The curfew is a precautionary measure.*

precede 1 = go before, introduce, herald, pave the way for, usher in, antedate, antecede, forerun • *Intensive negotiations preceded the vote.*
2 = go ahead of, lead, head, go before, take precedence • *Alice preceded them from the room.*
3 = preface, introduce, go before, launch, prefix • *the information that precedes the paragraph in question*

precedence AS A NOUN = priority, lead, rank, preference, superiority, supremacy, seniority, primacy, pre-eminence, antecedence • *the strict order of precedence in which the guests took their place*

▸ **IN PHRASES: take precedence over = take priority over**, outweigh, come before, supersede, prevail over • *Have fun at college, but don't let the fun take precedence over the work.*

precedent = instance, example, authority, standard, model, pattern, criterion, prototype, paradigm, antecedent, exemplar, previous example • *The trial could set an important precedent for similar cases.*

preceding 1 = previous, earlier, former, above, foregoing, aforementioned, anterior, aforesaid • *Please refer back to the preceding chapter.*
2 = past, earlier, former, prior, foregoing • *the student revolution of the preceding years*

precept 1 = rule, order, law, direction, principle, command, regulation, instruction, decree, mandate, canon, statute, ordinance, commandment, behest, dictum • *the precepts of Buddhism*
2 = maxim, saying, rule, principle, guideline, motto, dictum, axiom, byword • *the precept, 'If a job's worth doing, it's worth doing well'*

precinct AS A NOUN = area, quarter, section, sector, district, zone • *a pedestrian precinct*
▸ **AS A PLURAL NOUN = district**, limits, region, borders, bounds, boundaries, confines, neighbourhood, milieu, surrounding area, environs, purlieus • *No-one carrying arms is allowed within the precincts of the temple.*

precious 1 = valuable, expensive, rare, fine, choice, prized, dear, costly, high-priced, exquisite, invaluable, priceless, recherché, inestimable • *jewellery and precious objects belonging to her mother*
OPPOSITES: cheap, worthless, rubbishy
2 = loved, valued, favourite, prized, dear, dearest, treasured, darling, beloved, adored, cherished, fave *(informal)*, idolized, worth your *or* its weight in gold • *her most precious possession*
3 = affected, artificial, fastidious, twee *(Brit. informal)*, chichi, overrefined, overnice • *Actors, he decided, were all precious and neurotic.*

precipice = cliff, crag, rock face, cliff face, height, brink, bluff, sheer drop, steep cliff, scarp • *The path had sheer rock on one side and a precipice on the other.*

precipitate AS A VERB 1 = quicken, trigger, accelerate, further, press, advance, hurry, dispatch, speed up, bring on, hasten, push forward, expedite • *The killings in the city have precipitated the worst crisis yet.*
2 = throw, launch, cast, discharge, hurl, fling, let fly, send forth • *Dust was precipitated into the air.*
▸ **AS AN ADJECTIVE 1 = hasty**, hurried, frantic, rash, reckless, impulsive, madcap, ill-advised, precipitous, impetuous, indiscreet, heedless, harum-scarum • *I don't think we should make any precipitate decisions.*
2 = sudden, quick, brief, rushing, violent, plunging, rapid, unexpected, swift, abrupt, without warning, headlong, breakneck • *the precipitate collapse of European communism*

precipitous 1 = sheer, high, steep, dizzy, abrupt, perpendicular, falling sharply • *a steep, precipitous cliff*
2 = hasty, sudden, hurried, precipitate, abrupt, harum-scarum • *the stock market's precipitous drop*

précis AS A NOUN = summary, résumé, outline, abstract, sketch, digest, rundown, condensation, compendium, synopsis, aperçu *(French)*, abridgment • *a nine-page précis of the manuscript*
▸ **AS A VERB = summarize**, outline, abstract, sum up, shorten, compress, condense, abridge • *a cleverly précised distillation of everything he had written*

precise 1 = exact, specific, actual, particular, express, fixed, correct, absolute, accurate, explicit, definite, clear-cut, literal, unequivocal • *We will never know the precise details of his death.*
OPPOSITES: vague, incorrect, ambiguous
2 = strict, particular, exact, nice, formal, careful, stiff, rigid, meticulous, inflexible, scrupulous, fastidious, prim, puritanical, finicky, punctilious, ceremonious • *They speak very precise English.*
OPPOSITES: relaxed, flexible, inexact

precisely 1 = exactly, bang on, squarely, correctly, absolutely, strictly, accurately, plumb *(informal)*, slap on *(informal)*, square on, on the dot, smack on *(informal)* • *The meeting began at precisely 4.00 p.m.*
2 = just so, yes, absolutely, exactly, quite so, you bet *(informal)*, without a doubt, on the button *(informal)*, indubitably • *'Is that what you meant?' – 'Precisely.'*
3 = just, entirely, absolutely, altogether, exactly, in all respects • *That is precisely what I suggested.*
4 = word for word, literally, exactly, to the letter, neither more nor less • *Please repeat precisely what she said.*

precision = exactness, care, accuracy, fidelity, correctness, rigour, nicety, particularity, exactitude, meticulousness, definiteness, dotting the i's and crossing the t's, preciseness • *The interior is planned with meticulous precision.*

preclude 1 = rule out, put a stop to, obviate, make impossible, make impracticable • *At 84, John feels his age precludes much travelling.*
2 = prevent, stop, check, exclude, restrain, prohibit, inhibit, hinder, forestall, debar • *Poor English precluded them from ever finding a job.*

precocious = advanced, developed, forward, quick, bright, smart • *Lucy was always a precocious child.*
OPPOSITES: slow, dense, backward

preconceived = presumed, premature, predetermined, presupposed, prejudged, forejudged • *preconceived notions about what we want from life*

preconception = preconceived idea *or* **notion**, notion, prejudice, bias, presumption, predisposition, presupposition, prepossession • *his preconceptions about the sort of people who work in computing*

precondition = necessity, essential, requirement, prerequisite, must, sine qua non *(Latin)*, must-have • *The removal of troops is a precondition to any agreement.*

precursor 1 = forerunner, pioneer, predecessor, forebear, antecedent, originator • *Real tennis, a precursor of the modern game, originated in the eleventh century.*
2 = herald, usher, messenger, vanguard, forerunner, harbinger • *The deal should not be seen as a precursor to a merger.*

predatory 1 = hunting, ravening, carnivorous, rapacious, raptorial, predacious • *predatory birds like the eagle*
2 = plundering, ravaging, pillaging, marauding, thieving, despoiling • *predatory gangs*
3 = rapacious, greedy, voracious, vulturous, vulturine • *predatory business practices*

predecessor 1 = previous job holder, precursor, forerunner, antecedent, former job holder, prior job holder • *He learned everything he knew from his predecessor.*
2 = ancestor, forebear, antecedent, forefather, tupuna *or* tipuna *(N.Z.)* • *opportunities our predecessors never had*

predestination = fate, destiny, predetermination, election *(Theology)*, doom, necessity, foreordination, foreordainment • *Her belief in predestination absolved her from personal responsibility.*

predestined = fated, predetermined, preordained, meant, doomed, foreordained, pre-elected, predestinated • *His career was not predestined from birth.*

predetermined 1 = fated, predestined, preordained, meant, doomed, foreordained, pre-elected, predestinated • *our predetermined fate*
2 = prearranged, set, agreed, set up, settled, fixed, cut and dried *(informal)*, preplanned, decided beforehand, arranged in advance • *The capsules release the drug at a predetermined time.*

P

predicament = **fix** *(informal)*, state, situation, spot *(informal)*, corner, hole *(slang)*, emergency, mess, jam *(informal)*, dilemma, pinch, plight, scrape *(informal)*, hot water *(informal)*, pickle *(informal)*, how-do-you-do *(informal)*, quandary, tight spot • *The decision will leave her in a predicament.*

predicate IN PHRASES: **be predicated on** = **be based on**, rest on, be founded on, be built on, be established on, be grounded on • *The whole process of unification is predicated on the hope of economic growth.*

predict = **foretell**, forecast, divine, foresee, prophesy, call, augur, presage, portend, prognosticate, forebode, soothsay, vaticinate *(rare)* • *Nobody can predict what will happen.*

QUOTATIONS
You can only predict things after they happen
[Eugène Ionesco]

predictable = **likely**, expected, sure, certain, anticipated, reliable, foreseen, on the cards, foreseeable, sure-fire *(informal)*, calculable • *This was a predictable reaction.*
OPPOSITES: surprising, unlikely, unpredictable

prediction = **prophecy**, forecast, prognosis, divination, prognostication, augury, soothsaying, sortilege • *He was unwilling to make a prediction for the coming year.*
▷ *See panel* **Divination**

predilection = **liking**, love, taste, weakness, fancy, leaning, tendency, preference, bias, inclination, penchant, fondness, propensity, predisposition, proclivity, partiality, proneness • *his predilection for blondes*

predispose 1 = **incline**, influence, prepare, prompt, lead, prime, affect, prejudice, bias, induce, dispose, sway, make you of a mind to • *Some factors predispose certain individuals to criminal behaviour.*
2 = **make liable to**, lay open to, make susceptible to, make vulnerable to, make prone to, put at a risk of • *people whose lifestyles predispose them to AIDS*

predisposed 1 = **inclined**, willing, given, minded, ready, agreeable, amenable • *Franklin was predisposed to believe him.*
2 = **susceptible**, subject, prone, liable • *Some people are genetically predisposed to diabetes.*

predisposition 1 = **inclination**, tendency, disposition, bent, bias, willingness, likelihood, penchant, propensity, predilection, proclivity, potentiality, proneness • *the predisposition to behave in a certain way*
2 = **susceptibility**, tendency, proneness • *a hereditary predisposition to the disease*

predominance 1 = **prevalence**, weight, preponderance, greater number • *An interesting note was the predominance of London club players.*
2 = **dominance**, hold, control, edge, leadership, sway, supremacy, mastery, dominion, upper hand, ascendancy, paramountcy • *their economic predominance*

predominant 1 = **main**, chief, prevailing, notable, paramount, prevalent, preponderant • *Amanda's predominant emotion was one of confusion.*
2 = **principal**, leading, important, prime, controlling, ruling, chief, capital, primary, supreme, prominent, superior, dominant, sovereign, top-priority, ascendant • *He played a predominant role in shaping French economic policy*
OPPOSITES: minor, secondary, subordinate

predominantly = **mainly**, largely, chiefly, mostly, generally, principally, primarily, on the whole, in the main, for the most part, to a great extent, preponderantly • *The landscape has remained predominantly rural in appearance.*

predominate 1 = **be in the majority**, dominate, prevail, stand out, be predominant, be most noticeable, preponderate • *All nationalities were represented, but the English and American predominated.*
2 = **prevail**, rule, reign, hold sway, get the upper hand, carry weight • *a society where Islamic principles predominate*

pre-eminence = **superiority**, distinction, excellence, supremacy, prestige, prominence, transcendence, renown, predominance, paramountcy • *London's continuing pre-eminence among European financial centres*

pre-eminent = **outstanding**, supreme, paramount, chief, excellent, distinguished, superior, renowned, foremost, consummate, predominant, transcendent, unrivalled, incomparable, peerless, unsurpassed, unequalled, matchless • *He is the pre-eminent political figure in the country.*

pre-eminently = **particularly**, signally, above all, notably, by far, exceptionally, emphatically, strikingly, supremely, eminently, conspicuously, superlatively, singularly, far and away, par excellence *(French)*, incomparably, inimitably, matchlessly • *Britain was depicted as 'pre-eminently a nation of traders and travellers'.*

pre-empt = **forestall**, anticipate, prevent, steal a march on, get in before • *He pre-empted any decision to sack him*

preen AS A VERB 1 *often reflexive* = **smarten**, admire, dress up, doll up *(slang)*, trim, array, deck out, spruce up, prettify, primp, trig *(archaic or dialect)*, titivate, prink • *He spent half an hour preening in front of the mirror.* • *20 minutes preening themselves every morning*
2 = **clean**, smooth, groom, tidy, plume • *The linnet shook herself and preened a few feathers on her breast.*
▸ IN PHRASES: **preen yourself** = **pride yourself**, congratulate yourself, give yourself a pat on the back, pique yourself, plume yourself • *His only negative feature is the desire to brag and preen himself over his abilities.*

preface AS A NOUN = **introduction**, preliminary, prelude, preamble, foreword, prologue, proem, prolegomenon, exordium • *the preface to the English edition of the novel*
▸ AS A VERB = **introduce**, precede, open, begin, launch, lead up to, prefix • *I will preface what I am going to say with a few lines from Shakespeare.*

prefer 1 = **like better**, favour, go for, pick, select, adopt, fancy, opt for, single out, plump for, incline towards, be partial to • *Do you prefer a particular sort of music?*
2 = **choose**, elect, opt for, pick, wish, desire, would rather, would sooner, incline towards • *I prefer to go on self-catering holidays.*

preferable = **better**, best, chosen, choice, preferred, recommended, favoured, superior, worthier, of choice, more suitable, more desirable, more eligible • *Resignation was the preferable option.* • *Goat's milk yogurt is preferable.*
OPPOSITES: undesirable, poor, average

preferably = **ideally**, if possible, rather, sooner, much rather, by choice, much sooner, as a matter of choice, in *or* for preference • *Take exercise, preferably in the fresh air.*

preference AS A NOUN 1 = **liking**, wish, taste, desire, bag *(slang)*, leaning, bent, bias, cup of tea *(informal)*, inclination, penchant, fondness, predisposition, predilection, proclivity, partiality • *Whatever your preference, we have a product to suit you.*
2 = **first choice**, choice, favourite, election, pick, option, selection, top of the list, fave *(informal)* • *He enjoys all styles of music, but his preference is opera.*
3 = **priority**, first place, precedence, advantage, favouritism, pride of place, favoured treatment • *Candidates with the right qualifications should be given preference.*
▸ IN PHRASES: **in preference to** = **rather than**, instead of, in place of, in lieu of • *Sea salt should be used in preference to table salt.*

preferential = **privileged**, favoured, superior, better, special, partial, partisan, advantageous • *Despite her status, the Duchess will not be given preferential treatment.*

preferment = **promotion**, rise, upgrading, dignity, advancement, elevation, exaltation • *He was told by the governors that he could expect no further preferment.*

prefigure = **foreshadow**, suggest, indicate, intimate, presage, portend, shadow forth, adumbrate, foretoken • *The party says his departure did not prefigure a major policy shift.*

P

pregnancy = gestation, gravidity • *It is advisable to cut out all alcohol during pregnancy.*
▸ RELATED ADJECTIVES: antenatal, postnatal, maternity

pregnant 1 = expectant, expecting *(informal)*, with child, in the club *(Brit. slang)*, in the family way *(informal)*, gravid, preggers *(Brit. informal)*, enceinte, in the pudding club *(slang)*, big *or* heavy with child • *Tina was pregnant with their first child.*
2 = meaningful, pointed, charged, significant, telling, loaded, expressive, eloquent, weighty, suggestive • *There was a long, pregnant silence.*
3 *with* **with = full of**, rich in, fraught with, teeming with, replete with, abounding in, abundant in, fecund with • *The songs are pregnant with irony and insight.*

prehistoric 1 = earliest, early, primitive, primordial, primeval • *prehistoric cave painting*
2 = antiquated, ancient, out of date, archaic, antediluvian, out of the ark *(informal)* • *The engine was based on almost prehistoric technology.*

prejudge = jump to conclusions about, anticipate, presume, presuppose, forejudge, make a hasty assessment about • *I don't want to prejudge the commission's findings.*

prejudice AS A NOUN **1 = discrimination**, racism, injustice, sexism, intolerance, bigotry, unfairness, chauvinism, narrow-mindedness • *a victim of racial prejudice*
2 = bias, preconception, partiality, preconceived notion, warp, jaundiced eye, prejudgment • *the male prejudices which Dr Greer identifies*
3 = harm, damage, hurt, disadvantage, loss, mischief, detriment, impairment • *I feel sure it can be done without prejudice to anybody's principles.*
▸ AS A VERB **1 = bias**, influence, colour, poison, distort, sway, warp, slant, predispose, jaundice, prepossess • *I think your upbringing has prejudiced you.*
2 = harm, damage, hurt, injure, mar, undermine, spoil, impair, hinder, crool *or* cruel *(Austral. slang)* • *He claimed that the media coverage had prejudiced his chance of a fair trial.*

QUOTATIONS
Drive out prejudices through the door, and they will return through the window
[Frederick the Great *letter to Voltaire*]

prejudiced = biased, influenced, unfair, one-sided, conditioned, partial, partisan, discriminatory, bigoted, intolerant, opinionated, narrow-minded, jaundiced, prepossessed • *Some landlords and landladies are racially prejudiced.*
OPPOSITES: just, fair, unbiased

prejudicial = harmful, damaging, undermining, detrimental, hurtful, unfavourable, counterproductive, deleterious, injurious, inimical, disadvantageous • *eight years in jail for actions considered prejudicial to security*

preliminary AS AN ADJECTIVE **1 = first**, opening, trial, initial, test, pilot, prior, introductory, preparatory, exploratory, initiatory, prefatory, precursory • *Preliminary talks began yesterday.*
2 = qualifying, eliminating • *the last match of the preliminary rounds*
▸ AS A NOUN **= introduction**, opening, beginning, foundation, start, preparation, first round, prelude, preface, overture, initiation, preamble, groundwork, prelims • *Today's survey is a preliminary to a more detailed one.*

prelude 1 = introduction, beginning, preparation, preliminary, start, commencement, curtain-raiser • *The protests are now seen as the prelude to last year's uprising.*
2 = overture, opening, introduction, introductory movement • *the third-act Prelude of Parsifal*

premature 1 = early, untimely, before time, unseasonable • *a twenty-four-year-old man suffering from premature baldness*
2 = hasty, rash, too soon, precipitate, impulsive, untimely, ill-considered, jumping the gun, ill-timed, inopportune, overhasty • *It now seems their optimism was premature.*
3 = preterm, prem *(informal)*, preemie *(U.S. & Canad. informal)* • *a greater risk of having a premature baby*

prematurely 1 = too early, too soon, before your time, preterm • *Danny was born prematurely.*
2 = overhastily, rashly, too soon, precipitately, too hastily, half-cocked, at half-cock • *He may have spoken just a little prematurely.*

premeditated = planned, calculated, deliberate, considered, studied, intended, conscious, contrived, intentional, wilful, aforethought, prepense • *a case of premeditated murder*
OPPOSITES: accidental, unintentional, unplanned

premeditation = planning, design, purpose, plotting, intention, determination, deliberation, forethought, prearrangement, malice aforethought, predetermination • *The judge concluded that there was insufficient evidence of premeditation.*

premier AS A NOUN **= head of government**, prime minister, chancellor, chief minister, P.M. • *Australia's premier Paul Keating*
▸ AS AN ADJECTIVE **= chief**, leading, top, first, highest, head, main, prime, primary, principal, arch, foremost • *the country's premier opera company*

premiere AS A NOUN **= first night**, opening, debut, first showing, first performance • *The film had its premiere at the Cannes Film Festival.*
▸ AS A VERB **= open**, debut, be shown • *The opera is set to premiere on October 14th.*

premise AS A NOUN **= assumption**, proposition, thesis, ground, argument, hypothesis, assertion, postulate, supposition, presupposition, postulation • *the premise that men and women are on equal terms in this society*
▸ AS A VERB **= predicate**, found, build, ground, establish, posit • *The plan is premised on continuing abundant tax returns.*

premised = based, assumed, postulated, hypothesized • *The plan is premised on continuing abundant tax returns.*

premises = building(s), place, office, property, site, establishment • *The business has moved to new premises.*

premium AS A NOUN **1 = fee**, charge, payment, instalment • *an increase in insurance premiums*
2 = surcharge, extra charge, additional fee *or* charge • *Customers are not willing to pay a premium.*
3 = bonus, reward, prize, percentage *(informal)*, perk *(Brit. informal)*, boon, bounty, remuneration, recompense, perquisite • *Shareholders did not receive a premium on the price of their shares.*
▸ IN PHRASES: **at a premium = in great demand**, valuable, expensive, rare, costly, scarce, in short supply, hard to come by, like gold dust, beyond your means, not to be had for love or money • *Tickets to the game are at a premium.*
put *or* **place a (high) premium on something = hold in high regard**, value, appreciate, set great store by, put a high value on • *I place a high premium on what someone is like as a person.*

premonition 1 = feeling, idea, intuition, suspicion, hunch, apprehension, misgiving, foreboding, funny feeling *(informal)*, presentiment, feeling in your bones • *He had an unshakable premonition that he would die.*
2 = omen, sign, warning, portent, presage, forewarning, wake-up call • *the first premonition of winter*

preoccupation 1 = obsession, concern, hang-up *(informal)*, fixation, pet subject, hobbyhorse, idée fixe *(French)*, bee in your bonnet • *Her main preoccupation from an early age was boys.*
2 = absorption, musing, oblivion, abstraction, daydreaming, immersion, reverie, absent-mindedness, brown study, inattentiveness, absence of mind, pensiveness,

engrossment, prepossession, woolgathering • *He kept sinking back into gloomy preoccupation.*

preoccupied 1 = **absorbed**, taken up, caught up, lost, intent, wrapped up, immersed, engrossed, rapt • *They were preoccupied with their own concerns.*
2 = **lost in thought**, abstracted, distracted, unaware, oblivious, faraway, absent-minded, heedless, distrait, in a brown study • *He was too preoccupied to notice what was going on.*

preoccupy = **absorb**, concern, dominate, occupy, grip, consume, obsess, distract, enthral, engross, become an obsession with • *a question that continues to preoccupy the more serious papers*

preordained = **predetermined**, fated, doomed, destined, predestined, mapped out in advance • *the belief that our actions are governed by a preordained destiny*

preparation 1 = **groundwork**, development, preparing, arranging, devising, getting ready, thinking-up, putting in order • *Behind any successful event lies months of preparation.*
2 = **readiness**, expectation, provision, safeguard, precaution, anticipation, foresight, preparedness, alertness • *a military build-up in preparation for war*
3 *usually plural* = **arrangement**, plan, measure, provision • *Final preparations are under way for the celebration.*
4 = **mixture**, cream, medicine, compound, composition, lotion, concoction, amalgam, ointment, tincture • *a specially formulated natural skin preparation*

preparatory AS AN ADJECTIVE = **introductory**, preliminary, opening, basic, primary, elementary, prefatory, preparative • *At least a year's preparatory work will be needed.*
▸ IN PHRASES: **preparatory to** = **before**, prior to, in preparation for, in advance of, in anticipation of • *Sloan cleared his throat preparatory to speaking.*

prepare 1 = **make** *or* **get ready**, arrange, draw up, form, fashion, get up *(informal)*, construct, assemble, contrive, put together, make provision, put in order, jack up *(N.Z. informal)* • *He said the government must prepare an emergency plan for evacuation.*
2 = **equip**, fit, adapt, adjust, outfit, furnish, fit out, accoutre • *The crew has been preparing the ship for storage.*
3 = **train**, guide, prime, direct, coach, brief, discipline, groom, put someone in the picture • *It is a school's job to prepare students for university studies.*
4 = **make**, cook, put together, get, produce, assemble, muster, concoct, fix up, dish up, rustle up *(informal)* • *She found him in the kitchen, preparing dinner.*
5 = **get ready**, plan, anticipate, make provision, lay the groundwork, make preparations, arrange things, get everything set • *They were not given enough time to prepare for the election battle.*
6 = **practise**, get ready, train, exercise, warm up, get into shape • *giving the players a chance to prepare for the match*
7 *usually reflexive* = **brace**, ready, strengthen, fortify, steel, gird • *I began to prepare myself for the worst.*

prepared 1 = **willing**, minded, able, ready, inclined, disposed, in the mood, predisposed, of a mind • *Are you prepared to take industrial action?*
2 = **ready**, set, all set • *I was prepared for a long wait.*
3 = **fit**, primed, in order, arranged, in readiness, all systems go *(informal)* • *The country is fully prepared for war.*

preparedness = **readiness**, order, preparation, fitness, alertness • *The country has to maintain military preparedness.*

preponderance 1 = **predominance**, instance, dominance, prevalence • *the huge preponderance of males among homeless people*
2 = **greater part**, mass, bulk, weight, lion's share, greater numbers, extensiveness • *The preponderance of the evidence strongly supports his guilt.*
3 = **domination**, power, sway, superiority, supremacy, dominion, ascendancy • *In 1965, the preponderance of West Germany over East had become even greater.*

preposterous = **ridiculous**, bizarre, incredible, outrageous, shocking, impossible, extreme, crazy, excessive, absurd, foolish, ludicrous, extravagant, unthinkable, unreasonable, insane, irrational, monstrous, senseless, out of the question, laughable, exorbitant, nonsensical, risible, asinine, cockamamie *(slang, chiefly U.S.)* • *The whole idea was preposterous.*

prerequisite AS A NOUN = **requirement**, must, essential, necessity, condition, qualification, imperative, precondition, requisite, sine qua non *(Latin)*, must-have • *Good self-esteem is a prerequisite for a happy life.*
▸ AS AN ADJECTIVE = **required**, necessary, essential, called for, vital, mandatory, imperative, indispensable, obligatory, requisite, of the essence, needful • *Young children can be taught the prerequisite skills necessary to learn to read.*

prerogative = **right**, choice, claim, authority, title, due, advantage, sanction, liberty, privilege, immunity, exemption, birthright, droit, perquisite • *I thought it was a woman's prerogative to change her mind?*

presage AS A VERB = **portend**, point to, warn of, signify, omen, bode, foreshadow, augur, betoken, adumbrate, forebode, foretoken • *Diplomats fear the incidents presage a new chapter in the conflict.*
▸ AS A NOUN = **omen**, sign, warning, forecast, prediction, prophecy, portent, harbinger, intimation, forewarning, prognostication, augury, prognostic, auspice • *Soldiers used to believe a raven was a presage of coming battle.*

prescience = **foresight**, clairvoyance, precognition, second sight, foreknowledge, prevision *(rare)* • *his prescience in forecasting the dreadful effects of nuclear weapons*

prescient = **foresighted**, psychic, prophetic, divining, discerning, perceptive, clairvoyant, far-sighted, divinatory, mantic • *an uncannily prescient prediction*

prescribe 1 = **specify**, order, direct, stipulate, write a prescription for • *Our doctor prescribed antibiotics for her throat infection.*
2 = **ordain**, set, order, establish, rule, require, fix, recommend, impose, appoint, command, define, dictate, assign, lay down, decree, stipulate, enjoin • *The judge said he was passing the sentence prescribed by law.*

prescription 1 = **instruction**, direction, formula, script *(informal)*, recipe • *These drugs are freely available without a prescription.*
2 = **medicine**, drug, treatment, preparation, cure, mixture, dose, remedy • *I'm not sleeping, even with that new prescription the doctor gave me.*
3 = **method**, measure, direction, formula, recommendation, recipe • *the prescription for electoral success*

prescriptive = **dictatorial**, rigid, authoritarian, legislating, dogmatic, didactic, preceptive • *prescriptive attitudes to language on the part of teachers*

presence AS A NOUN 1 = **being**, existence, company, residence, attendance, showing up, companionship, occupancy, habitation, inhabitance • *His presence in the village could only stir up trouble.* • *the presence of a carcinogen in the water*
2 = **proximity**, closeness, vicinity, nearness, neighbourhood, immediate circle, propinquity • *conscious of being in the presence of a great man*
3 = **personality**, bearing, appearance, aspect, air, ease, carriage, aura, poise, demeanour, self-assurance, mien *(literary)*, comportment • *Hendrix's stage presence appealed to thousands of teenage rebels.*
4 = **spirit**, ghost, manifestation, spectre, apparition, shade *(literary)*, wraith, supernatural being, revenant, eidolon, atua *(N.Z.)*, wairua *(N.Z.)* • *The house was haunted by shadows and unseen presences.*

▸ IN PHRASES: **presence of mind** = **level-headedness**, assurance, composure, poise, cool *(slang)*, wits, countenance, coolness, aplomb, alertness, calmness, equanimity, self-assurance, phlegm, quickness, sang-froid, self-possession, unflappability *(informal)*, imperturbability, quick-wittedness, self-command, collectedness • *Someone had the presence of mind to call for an ambulance.*

present[1] AS AN ADJECTIVE 1 = **current**, existing, immediate, contemporary, instant, present-day, existent, extant • *the government's present economic difficulties*
2 = **here**, there, near, available, ready, nearby, accounted for, to hand, at hand, in attendance • *The whole family was present.*
OPPOSITES: absent, away, missing
3 = **in existence**, existing, existent, extant • *This vitamin is naturally present in breast milk.*
▸ IN PHRASES: **at present** = **just now**, now, presently, currently, at the moment, right now, nowadays, at this time, at the present time, in this day and age • *At present, children under 14 are not permitted in bars.*
for the present = **for now**, for a while, in the meantime, temporarily, for the moment, for the time being, provisionally, not for long, for the nonce • *The ministers agreed that sanctions should remain in place for the present.*
the present = **now**, today, the time being, here and now, this day and age, the present moment • *His struggle to reconcile the past with the present.*
the present day = **modern times**, today, nowadays, the present age *or* time • *art from the period of Giotto to the present day*

QUOTATIONS
Look to this day
For it is life, the very life of life
[*The Sufi*]
For present joys are more to flesh and blood
Than a dull prospect of a distant good
[John Dryden *The Hindu and the Panther*]
Ah, fill the cup: – what boots it to repeat
How time is slipping underneath our feet;
Unborn tomorrow, and dead yesterday,
Why fret about them if today be sweet!
[Edward Fitzgerald *The Rubáiyát of Omar Khayyám*]
PROVERBS
There is no time like the present

present[2] AS A NOUN = **gift**, offering, grant, favour, donation, hand-out, endowment, boon, bounty, gratuity, prezzie *(informal)*, benefaction, bonsela *(S. African)*, koha *(N.Z.)*, largesse *or* largess • *The vase was a wedding present.*
▸ AS A VERB 1 = **give**, award, hand over, offer, grant, donate, hand out, furnish, confer, bestow, entrust, proffer, put at someone's disposal • *The queen presented the prizes to the winning captain.*
2 = **put forward**, offer, suggest, raise, state, produce, introduce, advance, relate, declare, extend, pose, submit, tender, hold out, recount, expound, proffer, adduce • *We presented three options to the unions for discussion.*
3 = **represent**, portray, describe, depict, characterize • *He was presented as a tragic figure.*
4 = **host**, introduce, announce, anchor, compère, be the presenter of • *She presents a weekly TV fashion programme.*
5 = **put on**, stage, perform, give, show, mount, render, put before the public • *The theatre is presenting a new production of 'Hamlet'.*
6 = **launch**, display, demonstrate, parade, exhibit, unveil • *presenting a new product or service to the market-place*
7 = **introduce**, make known, acquaint someone with • *Fox stepped forward and presented him to Jack.*
▸ IN PHRASES: **present itself** = **occur**, emerge, arise, happen, appear, come up, turn up, come about, pop up, crop up, transpire • *They insulted us whenever the opportunity presented itself.*
present yourself = **arrive**, appear, attend, turn up, be present, make an appearance • *She presented herself at the Town Hall at 11.30 for the ceremony.*

presentable 1 = **tidy**, elegant, well groomed, becoming, trim, spruce, dapper, natty *(informal)*, smartly dressed, fit to be seen • *She managed to make herself presentable in time for work.*
OPPOSITES: unpresentable
2 = **satisfactory**, suitable, decent, acceptable, proper, good enough, respectable, not bad *(informal)*, tolerable, passable, O.K. *or* okay *(informal)* • *His score had reached a presentable total.*
OPPOSITES: unacceptable, unsatisfactory, poor

presentation 1 = **giving**, award, offering, donation, investiture, bestowal, conferral • *at the presentation ceremony*
2 = **demonstration**, show, talk, launch, address, display, speech, exhibition, lecture, unveiling, exposition • *a business presentation*
3 = **appearance**, look, display, packaging, arrangement, layout • *Keep the presentation of the dish simple.*
4 = **submission**, offering, tabling, proposal, delivery, introduction, tendering, proffering • *the presentation of the government's economic report*
5 = **performance**, staging, production, show, arrangement, representation, portrayal, rendition • *Scottish Opera's presentation of Das Rheingold*
6 = **debut**, launch, launching, coming out, introduction, reception • *the white dress she had worn for her presentation at Court*

present-day = **current**, modern, present, recent, contemporary, up-to-date, latter-day, newfangled • *Even by present-day standards, these were huge aircraft.*

presenter = **host**, announcer, compère *(Brit.)*, anchorman *or* anchorwoman • *a television presenter*

presentiment = **premonition**, feeling, expectation, anticipation, fear, forecast, hunch, intuition, apprehension, misgiving, foreboding, presage, forethought • *He had a presentiment of disaster.*

presently 1 = **at present**, currently, now, today, these days, nowadays, at the present time, in this day and age, at the minute *(Brit. informal)* • *The island is presently uninhabited.*
2 = **soon**, shortly, directly, before long, momentarily *(U.S. & Canad.)*, in a moment, in a minute, pretty soon *(informal)*, anon *(archaic)*, by and by, in a short while, in a jiffy *(informal)*, erelong *(archaic or poetic)* • *Just take it easy and you'll feel better presently.*

preservation 1 = **upholding**, keeping, support, security, defence, maintenance, perpetuation • *the preservation of the status quo*
2 = **protection**, safety, maintenance, conservation, salvation, safeguarding, safekeeping • *the preservation of buildings of historic interest*
3 = **storage**, smoking, drying, bottling, freezing, curing, chilling, candying, pickling, conserving, tinning • *the preparation, cooking and preservation of food*

PROVERBS
Self-preservation is the first law of nature

preserve AS A VERB 1 = **maintain**, keep, continue, retain, sustain, keep up, prolong, uphold, conserve, perpetuate, keep alive • *We will do everything we can to preserve peace.*
OPPOSITES: end, drop, give up
2 = **protect**, keep, save, maintain, guard, defend, secure, shelter, shield, care for, safeguard, conserve • *We need to preserve the rainforests.*
OPPOSITES: attack, turn out, assault
3 = **keep**, save, store, can, dry, bottle, salt, cure, candy, pickle, conserve • *ginger preserved in syrup*

▸ **AS A NOUN** 1 *often plural* = **jam**, jelly, conserve, marmalade, confection, sweetmeat, confiture • *jars of pear and blackberry preserves*
2 = **area**, department, field, territory, province, arena, orbit, sphere, realm, domain, specialism • *The conduct of foreign policy is largely the preserve of the president.*
3 = **reserve**, reservation, sanctuary, game reserve • *one of the world's great wildlife preserves*

preside **AS A VERB** = **officiate**, chair, moderate, be chairperson • *He presided at the closing ceremony.*
▸ **IN PHRASES: preside over something** *or* **someone** = **run**, lead, head, control, manage, direct, conduct, govern, administer, supervise, be at the head of, be in authority • *The question of who should preside over the next full commission was being debated.*

president 1 = **head of state**, chief of state • *The White House says the president would veto the bill.*
2 = **chairman**, director, chief executive (officer), managing director, MD, CEO, chairwoman • *the president of the new company*
▹ *See panel* **U.S. Presidents**

press **AS A VERB** 1 = **push (down)**, depress, lean on, bear down, press down, force down • *her hands pressing down on the desk* • *He pressed a button and the door closed.*
2 = **push**, squeeze, jam, thrust, ram, wedge, shove • *He pressed his back against the door.*
3 = **hug**, squeeze, embrace, clasp, crush, encircle, enfold, hold close, fold in your arms • *I pressed my child closer to my heart and shut my eyes.*
4 = **call**, ask, demand, campaign, push, insist on, clamour, make a claim • *Police might now press for changes in the law.*
5 = **urge**, force, beg, petition, sue, enforce, insist on, compel, constrain, exhort, implore, enjoin, pressurize, entreat, importune, supplicate • *The trade unions are pressing him to stand firm.*
6 = **plead**, present, lodge, submit, tender, advance insistently • *mass strikes and demonstrations to press their demands*
7 = **steam**, finish, iron, smooth, flatten, put the creases in • *Vera pressed his shirt.*
8 = **compress**, grind, reduce, mill, crush, pound, squeeze, tread, pulp, mash, trample, condense, pulverize, tamp, macerate • *The grapes are hand-picked and pressed.*
9 = **crowd**, push, gather, rush, surge, mill, hurry, cluster, flock, herd, swarm, hasten, seethe, throng • *As the music stopped, the crowd pressed forward.*
▸ **AS A NOUN** 1 = **publicity**, reports, reviews, articles, coverage, press reporting, write-ups, press treatment • *the bad press that career women get in this country*
2 = **crowd**, host, pack, crush, bunch, mob, flock, herd, push (*informal*), swarm, horde, multitude, throng • *There was still a press of people around the Victoria Memorial.*
▸ **IN PHRASES: be pressed for** = **be short of**, be pushed for, be hard put to, have too little • *I'm pressed for time right now.*
press on 1 = **continue**, proceed, carry on, keep going, move forward, make progress, press ahead, persevere, not give up, soldier on (*informal*), push on, struggle on, forge ahead, go the distance, stay the course, keep at it, stick at it (*informal*), crack on (*informal*) • *Organizers of the strike are determined to press on.*
2 = **trouble**, worry, plague, torment, harass, afflict, besiege, beset, disquiet, vex, assail • *The weight of guilt pressed on her.*
the press 1 = **newspapers**, the papers, journalism, news media, Fleet Street, fourth estate • *Today the British press is full of articles on the subject.*
2 = **journalists**, correspondents, reporters, photographers, columnists, pressmen, newsmen, journos (*slang*), gentlemen of the press • *He looked relaxed and calm as he faced the press.*

QUOTATIONS

The job of the press is to encourage debate, not to supply the public with information
[Christopher Lasch *'Journalism, Publicity, and the Lost Art of Political Argument'*]

Thou god of our idolatry, the press...
Thou fountain, at which drink the good and wise;

U.S. PRESIDENTS

President	Party	Term of office	President	Party	Term of office
1. George Washington	Federalist	1789–97	21. Chester A. Arthur	Republican	1881–85
2. John Adams	Federalist	1797–1801	22. Grover Cleveland	Democrat	1885–89
3. Thomas Jefferson	Democratic Republican	1801–1809	23. Benjamin Harrison	Republican	1889–93
			24. Grover Cleveland	Democrat	1893–97
4. James Madison	Democratic Republican	1809–1817	25. William McKinley	Republican	1897–1901
			26. Theodore Roosevelt	Republican	1901–1909
5. James Monroe	Democratic Republican	1817–25	27. William Howard Taft	Republican	1909–13
			28. Woodrow Wilson	Democrat	1913–21
6. John Quincy Adams	Democratic Republican	1825–29	29. Warren G. Harding	Republican	1921–23
			30. Calvin Coolidge	Republican	1923–29
7. Andrew Jackson	Democrat	1829–37	31. Herbert C. Hoover	Republican	1929–33
8. Martin Van Buren	Democrat	1837–41	32. Franklin D. Roosevelt	Democrat	1933–45
9. William Henry Harrison	Whig	1841	33. Harry S Truman	Democrat	1945–53
10. John Tyler	Whig	1841–45	34. Dwight D. Eisenhower	Republican	1953–61
11. James K. Polk	Democrat	1845–49	35. John F. Kennedy	Democrat	1961–63
12. Zachary Taylor	Whig	1849–50	36. Lyndon B. Johnson	Democrat	1963–69
13. Millard Fillmore	Whig	1850–53	37. Richard M. Nixon	Republican	1969–74
14. Franklin Pierce	Democrat	1853–57	38. Gerald R. Ford	Republican	1974–77
15. James Buchanan	Democrat	1857–61	39. James E. Carter, Jr	Democrat	1977–81
16. Abraham Lincoln	Republican	1861–65	40. Ronald W. Reagan	Republican	1981–89
17. Andrew Johnson	Republican	1865–69	41. George H. W. Bush	Republican	1989–93
18. Ulysses S. Grant	Republican	1869–77	42. William J. Clinton	Democrat	1993–2001
19. Rutherford B. Hayes	Republican	1877–81	43. George W. Bush	Republican	2001–
20. James A. Garfield	Republican	1881			

Thou ever-bubbling spring of endless lies;
Like Eden's dread probationary tree,
Knowledge of good and evil is from thee
[William Cowper *The Progress of Error*]

pressing = **urgent**, serious, burning, vital, crucial, imperative, important, constraining, high-priority, now or never, importunate, exigent • *There is a pressing need for more funds.*
OPPOSITES: regular, routine, unimportant

pressure AS A NOUN 1 = **force**, crushing, squeezing, compressing, weight, compression, heaviness • *The pressure of his fingers had relaxed.*
2 = **power**, influence, force, obligation, constraint, sway, compulsion, coercion • *He may be putting pressure on her to agree.*
3 = **stress**, demands, difficulty, strain, press, heat, load, burden, distress, hurry, urgency, hassle (*informal*), uphill (*S. African*), adversity, affliction, exigency • *The pressures of modern life are great.*
▸ AS A VERB = **force**, influence, persuade, compel, intimidate, drive, badger, coerce, bulldoze, brainwash, dragoon, pressurize, breathe down someone's neck, browbeat, press-gang, prevail on, twist someone's arm (*informal*), turn on the heat (*informal*), put the screws on (*slang*) • *He claimed the police pressured him to change his testimony.*

QUOTATIONS
If you can't stand the heat, get out of the kitchen
[Harry S Truman]

pressurize = **force**, drive, compel, intimidate, coerce, dragoon, breathe down someone's neck, browbeat, press-gang, twist someone's arm (*informal*), turn on the heat (*informal*), put the screws on (*slang*) • *He thought she was trying to pressurize him into marriage.*

prestige = **status**, standing, authority, influence, credit, regard, weight, reputation, honour, importance, fame, celebrity, distinction, esteem, stature, eminence, kudos, cachet, renown, Brownie points, mana (*N.Z.*) • *His work gained him international prestige.*

P

prestigious = **celebrated**, respected, prominent, great, important, imposing, impressive, influential, esteemed, notable, renowned, eminent, illustrious, reputable, exalted • *It's one of the most prestigious schools in the country.*
OPPOSITES: minor, unknown, obscure

presumably = **it would seem**, probably, likely, apparently, most likely, seemingly, doubtless, on the face of it, in all probability, in all likelihood, doubtlessly • *This spear is presumably the murder weapon.*

presume AS A VERB 1 = **believe**, think, suppose, assume, guess (*informal, chiefly U.S. & Canad.*), take it, take for granted, infer, conjecture, postulate, surmise, posit, presuppose • *I presume you're here on business.*
2 = **dare**, venture, undertake, go so far as, have the audacity, take the liberty, make bold, make so bold as • *I wouldn't presume to question your judgement.*
3 = **presuppose**, assume, imply, take as read • *The legal definition of 'know' often presumes mental control.*
▸ IN PHRASES: **presume on something** *or* **someone** = **depend on**, rely on, exploit, take advantage of, count on, bank on, take liberties with, trust in *or* to • *He's presuming on your good nature.*

QUOTATIONS
Dr. Livingstone, I presume?
[Henry Morton Stanley *How I Found Livingstone*]

presumption 1 = **assumption**, opinion, belief, guess, hypothesis, anticipation, conjecture, surmise, supposition, presupposition, premiss • *the presumption that a defendant is innocent until proved guilty*
2 = **cheek** (*informal*), front, neck (*informal*), nerve (*informal*), assurance, brass (*informal*), gall (*informal*), audacity, boldness, temerity, chutzpah (*U.S. & Canad. informal*), insolence, impudence, effrontery, brass neck (*Brit. informal*), sassiness (*U.S. informal*), presumptuousness, forwardness • *He had the presumption to answer me back.*

presumptive 1 = **assumed**, believed, expected, understood, supposed, odds-on, hypothetical, inferred • *the heir presumptive*
2 = **possible**, likely, reasonable, credible, probable, plausible, conceivable, believable, verisimilar • *presumptive cause for dismissal*

presumptuous = **pushy** (*informal*), forward, bold, arrogant, presuming, rash, audacious, conceited, foolhardy, insolent, overweening, overconfident, overfamiliar, bigheaded (*informal*), uppish (*Brit. informal*), too big for your boots • *It would be presumptuous of me to give an opinion.*
OPPOSITES: retiring, modest, shy

presuppose = **presume**, consider, accept, suppose, assume, take it, imply, take for granted, postulate, posit, take as read • *All your arguments presuppose that he is a rational man.*

presupposition = **assumption**, theory, belief, premise, hypothesis, presumption, preconception, supposition, preconceived idea • *the presupposition that human life must be sustained for as long as possible*

pretence 1 = **deception**, invention, sham, fabrication, acting, faking, simulation, deceit, feigning, charade, make-believe, trickery, falsehood, subterfuge, fakery • *struggling to keep up the pretence that all was well*
OPPOSITES: honesty, openness, candour
2 = **show**, posturing, artifice, affectation, display, appearance, posing, façade, veneer, pretentiousness, hokum (*slang, chiefly U.S. & Canad.*) • *She was completely without guile or pretence.*
OPPOSITES: fact, reality, actuality
3 = **pretext**, claim, excuse, show, cover, mask, veil, cloak, guise, façade, masquerade, semblance, ruse, garb, wile • *He claimed the police beat him up under the pretence that he was resisting arrest.*
4 = **claim**, profession, aspiration • *We have never made any pretence to be faithful to each other.*

pretend AS A VERB 1 = **feign**, affect, assume, allege, put on, fake, make out, simulate, profess, sham, counterfeit, falsify, impersonate, dissemble, dissimulate, pass yourself off as • *He pretended to be asleep.*
2 = **make believe**, suppose, imagine, play, act, make up, play the part of • *She can sunbathe and pretend she's in Spain.* • *The children pretended to be animals.*
3 = **lay claim**, claim, allege, aspire, profess, purport • *I cannot pretend to understand the problem.*
▸ AS AN ADJECTIVE = **imaginary**, imagined, made-up, fantasy, invented, pretended, make-believe • *Many children have a pretend playmate.*

pretended = **feigned**, alleged, so-called, phoney *or* phony (*informal*), false, pretend (*informal*), fake, imaginary, bogus, professed, sham, purported, pseudo (*informal*), counterfeit, spurious, fictitious, avowed, ostensible • *Todd shrugged with pretended indifference.*

pretender = **claimant**, claimer, aspirant • *the Comte de Paris, pretender to the French throne*

pretension 1 = **affectation**, hypocrisy, conceit, show, airs, vanity, snobbery, pomposity, self-importance, ostentation, pretentiousness, snobbishness, vainglory, showiness • *We liked him for his honesty and lack of pretension.*
2 *usually plural* = **aspiration**, claim, demand, profession, assumption, assertion, pretence • *one of the few fashion designers who does not have pretensions to be an artist*

pretentious = **affected**, mannered, exaggerated, pompous, assuming, hollow, inflated, extravagant, high-flown, flaunting, grandiose, conceited, showy, ostentatious, snobbish, puffed up, bombastic, specious, grandiloquent,

vainglorious, high-sounding, highfalutin *(informal)*, overambitious, arty-farty *(informal)*, magniloquent • *He talked a lot of pretentious twaddle about modern art.*
OPPOSITES: modest, unaffected, unpretentious

pretext = **guise**, excuse, veil, show, cover, appearance, device, mask, ploy, cloak, simulation, pretence, semblance, ruse, red herring, alleged reason • *They wanted a pretext to restart the war.* • *He excused himself on the pretext of a stomach ache.*

prettify = **adorn**, decorate, garnish, ornament, gild, do up, trim, embellish, deck out, tart up *(Brit. slang)*, doll up *(slang)*, trick out, pretty up, titivate • *an attempt to prettify the town for the tourist trade*

pretty AS AN ADJECTIVE 1 = **attractive**, appealing, beautiful, sweet, lovely, charming, fair, fetching, good-looking, cute, graceful, bonny, personable, comely, prepossessing, fit *(Brit. informal)* • *She's a charming and pretty girl.*
OPPOSITES: unattractive, plain, ugly
2 = **pleasant**, fine, pleasing, nice, elegant, trim, delicate, neat, tasteful, dainty, bijou • *comfortable sofas covered in a pretty floral print*
▸ AS AN ADVERB = **fairly**, rather, quite, kind of *(informal)*, somewhat, moderately, reasonably • *I had a pretty good idea what she was going to do.*

prevail AS A VERB 1 = **win**, succeed, triumph, overcome, overrule, be victorious, carry the day, prove superior, gain mastery • *We hoped that common sense would prevail.*
2 = **be widespread**, abound, predominate, be current, be prevalent, preponderate, exist generally • *A similar situation prevails in America.*
▸ IN PHRASES: **prevail on** *or* **upon someone** = **persuade**, influence, convince, prompt, win over, induce, incline, dispose, sway, talk into, bring round • *Do you think she can be prevailed upon to do it?*

prevailing 1 = **widespread**, general, established, popular, common, set, current, usual, ordinary, fashionable, in style, customary, prevalent, in vogue • *individuals who have gone against the prevailing opinion*
2 = **predominating**, ruling, main, existing, principal • *the prevailing weather conditions in the area*

prevalence = **commonness**, frequency, regularity, currency, universality, ubiquity, common occurrence, pervasiveness, extensiveness, widespread presence, rampancy, rifeness • *the prevalence of asthma in Britain and Western Europe*

prevalent = **common**, accepted, established, popular, general, current, usual, widespread, extensive, universal, frequent, everyday, rampant, customary, commonplace, ubiquitous, rife, habitual • *Smoking is becoming increasingly prevalent among younger women.*
OPPOSITES: rare, unusual, limited

prevaricate = **evade**, lie, shift, hedge, shuffle, dodge, deceive, flannel *(Brit. informal)*, quibble, beg the question, beat about the bush, cavil, equivocate, stretch the truth, palter, give a false colour to • *British ministers continued to prevaricate on the issue.*
OPPOSITES: be direct, be frank, be straightforward

prevarication = **evasion**, lies, deception, pretence, deceit, quibbling, misrepresentation, falsehood, untruth, falsification, equivocation, cavilling • *After months of prevarication, a decision has been made.*

prevent = **stop**, avoid, frustrate, restrain, check, bar, block, anticipate, hamper, foil, inhibit, head off, avert, thwart, intercept, hinder, obstruct, preclude, impede, counteract, ward off, balk, stave off, forestall, defend against, obviate, nip in the bud • *These methods prevent pregnancy.* • *We took steps to prevent it happening.*
OPPOSITES: help, encourage, support

prevention = **elimination**, safeguard, precaution, anticipation, thwarting, avoidance, deterrence, forestalling, prophylaxis, preclusion, obviation • *the prevention of crime*

QUOTATIONS
Prevention is better than cure
[Desiderius Erasmus *Adagia*]

preventive *or* **preventative** AS AN ADJECTIVE
1 = **precautionary**, protective, hampering, hindering, deterrent, impeding, pre-emptive, obstructive, inhibitory • *They accused the police of failing to take adequate preventive measures.*
2 = **prophylactic**, protective, precautionary, counteractive • *preventive medicine*
▸ AS A NOUN 1 = **hindrance**, obstacle, block, impediment, obstruction • *Racial solidarity acts as a preventive of social upheaval.*
2 = **protection**, shield, remedy, prevention, protective, safeguard, deterrent, neutralizer, prophylactic • *Cabbage is a preventive against stomach ulcers.*

preview AS A NOUN = **sample**, sneak preview, trailer, sampler, taster, foretaste, advance showing • *He had gone to see a preview of the play.*
▸ AS A VERB = **sample**, taste, give a foretaste of • *We preview this season's collections from Paris.*

previous 1 = **earlier**, former, past, prior, one-time, preceding, sometime, erstwhile, antecedent, anterior, quondam, ex- • *He had a daughter from a previous marriage.*
OPPOSITES: later, following, succeeding
2 = **preceding**, past, prior, foregoing • *He recalled what Bob had told him the previous night.*
3 *with* **to** = **before**, ahead of, preceding, leading up to, earlier than, in advance of, anterior to *(rare)* • *a six-month period previous to this date*

previously = **before**, earlier, once, in the past, formerly, back then, until now, at one time, hitherto, beforehand, a while ago, heretofore, in days *or* years gone by • *Previously she had no time to work in her own garden.*

prey AS A NOUN 1 = **quarry**, game, kill • *These animals were the prey of hyenas.*
2 = **victim**, target, mark, mug *(Brit. slang)*, dupe, fall guy *(informal)* • *Old people are easy prey for con men.*
▸ IN PHRASES: **prey on something** *or* **someone**
1 = **hunt**, live off, eat, seize, devour, feed upon • *The larvae prey on small aphids.*
2 = **victimize**, bully, intimidate, exploit, take advantage of, bleed *(informal)*, blackmail, terrorize • *unscrupulous men who preyed on young runaways*
3 = **worry**, trouble, burden, distress, haunt, hang over, oppress, weigh down, weigh heavily • *This was the question that preyed on his mind.*
▹ *See panel* **Birds of prey**

price AS A NOUN 1 = **cost**, value, rate, charge, bill, figure, worth, damage *(informal)*, amount, estimate, fee, payment, expense, assessment, expenditure, valuation, face value, outlay, asking price • *a sharp increase in the price of petrol* • *What's the price on that one?*
2 = **consequences**, penalty, cost, result, sacrifice, toll, forfeit • *He's paying the price for pushing his body so hard.*
3 = **reward**, bounty, compensation, premium, recompense • *He is still at large despite the high price on his head.*
▸ AS A VERB = **evaluate**, value, estimate, rate, cost, assess, put a price on • *The shares are priced at 330p.*
▸ IN PHRASES: **at any price** = **whatever the cost**, regardless, no matter what the cost, anyhow, cost what it may, expense no object • *We want the hostages home at any price.*
beyond price = **priceless**, treasured, precious, invaluable, inestimable, without price, of incalculable value • *a treasure that was beyond price*

BIRDS OF PREY

accipiter	goshawk	Montagu's harrier
Australian goshawk *or* chicken hawk	gyrfalcon *or* gerfalcon	mopoke *or (N.Z.)* ruru
bald eagle	harrier	osprey, fish eagle, *or (archaic)* ossifrage
barn owl	hawk	owl
bateleur eagle	hawk owl	peregrine falcon
boobook	hobby	red kite *or (archaic)* gled(e)
brown owl	honey buzzard	rough-legged buzzard
buzzard	hoot owl	saker
caracara	horned owl	screech owl
condor	kestrel	sea eagle, erne, *or* ern
Cooper's hawk	kite	secretary bird
duck hawk	lammergeier, lammergeyer, bearded vulture, *or (archaic)* ossifrage	snowy owl
eagle	lanner	sparrowhawk
eagle-hawk *or* wedge-tailed eagle	little owl	tawny owl
falcon *or (N.Z.)* bush-hawk *or* karearea	long-eared owl	turkey buzzard *or* vulture
falconet	merlin	vulture
golden eagle		

QUOTATIONS
There's no such thing as a free lunch
[Milton Friedman *book title*]
PROVERBS
You don't get something for nothing

priceless = valuable, expensive, precious, invaluable, rich, prized, dear, rare, treasured, costly, cherished, incomparable, irreplaceable, incalculable, inestimable, beyond price, worth a king's ransom, worth your *or* its weight in gold • *priceless works of art*
OPPOSITES: common, cheap, worthless

pricey *or* **pricy = expensive**, dear, steep *(informal)*, costly, high-priced, exorbitant, over the odds *(Brit. informal)*, extortionate • *Medical insurance is very pricey.*

prick AS A VERB **1 = pierce**, stab, puncture, bore, pink, punch, lance, jab, perforate, impale • *She pricked her finger with a needle.*
2 = move, trouble, touch, pain, wound, distress, grieve • *Most were sympathetic once we had pricked their consciences.*
3 = sting, bite, smart, itch, tingle, prickle • *He could feel tears pricking his eyes.*
▸ AS A NOUN **1 = pang**, smart, sting, spasm, gnawing, twinge, prickle • *She felt a prick on the back of her neck.*
2 = puncture, cut, hole, wound, gash, perforation, pinhole • *a tiny hole no bigger than a pin prick*
▸ IN PHRASES: **prick up = raise**, point, rise, stand erect • *The dog's ears pricked up at the sound.*
prick up your ears = listen carefully, attend, pay attention, begin to take notice, be all ears *(informal)*, concentrate on listening, pin your ears back, become attentive • *I pricked up my ears, and said, 'What's that?'*

prickle AS A VERB **1 = tingle**, smart, sting, twitch, itch • *His scalp prickled under his wig.*
2 = prick, stick into, nick, jab • *The pine needles prickled her skin.*
▸ AS A NOUN **1 = tingling**, smart, chill, tickle, tingle, pins and needles *(informal)*, goose bumps, goose flesh, paraesthesia *(Medical)* • *a prickle at the nape of my neck reminds me of my fears*
2 = spike, point, spur, needle, spine, thorn, barb • *an erect stem covered at the base with prickles*

prickly 1 = spiny, barbed, thorny, bristly, brambly, briery • *The grass was prickly and damp.*
2 = itchy, sharp, smarting, stinging, crawling, pricking, tingling, scratchy, prickling • *a hot prickly feeling at the back of her eyes*
3 = irritable, edgy, grumpy, touchy, bad-tempered, fractious, petulant, stroppy *(Brit. slang)*, cantankerous, tetchy, ratty *(Brit. & N.Z. informal)*, chippy *(informal)*, waspish, shirty *(slang, chiefly Brit.)*, arsey *(Brit., Austral. & N.Z. slang)*, peevish, snappish, liverish, pettish • *You know how prickly she can be.*
4 = difficult, complicated, tricky, trying, involved, intricate, troublesome, thorny, knotty, ticklish • *The issue is likely to prove a prickly one.*

pride AS A NOUN **1 = satisfaction**, achievement, fulfilment, delight, content, pleasure, joy, gratification • *the sense of pride in a job well done*
2 = self-respect, honour, ego, dignity, self-esteem, self-image, self-worth, amour-propre *(French)* • *Her rejection was a severe blow to his pride.*
3 = conceit, vanity, arrogance, pretension, presumption, snobbery, morgue *(French)*, hubris, smugness, self-importance, egotism, self-love, hauteur, pretentiousness, haughtiness, loftiness, vainglory, superciliousness, bigheadedness *(informal)* • *His pride may still be his downfall.*
OPPOSITES: modesty, humility, meekness
4 = elite, pick, best, choice, flower, prize, cream, glory, boast, treasure, jewel, gem, pride and joy • *This glittering dress is the pride of her collection.*
▸ IN PHRASES: **pride yourself on something = be proud of**, revel in, boast of, glory in, vaunt, take pride in, brag about, crow about, exult in, congratulate yourself on, flatter yourself, pique yourself, plume yourself • *He prides himself on being able to organise his own life.*

QUOTATIONS
Pride goeth before destruction, and a haughty spirit before a fall
[*Bible: Proverbs*]
And the Devil did grin, for his darling sin
Is pride that apes humility
[Samuel Taylor Coleridge *The Devil's Thoughts*]

priest = clergyman, minister, father, divine, vicar, pastor, cleric, curate, churchman, padre *(informal)*, holy man, man of God, man of the cloth, ecclesiastic, father confessor • *He had trained to be a Catholic priest.*
▸ **RELATED ADJECTIVE:** hieratic

QUOTATIONS
The clergyman is expected to be a kind of human Sunday
[Samuel Butler *The Way of All Flesh*]
A priest,
A piece of mere church furniture at best
[William Cowper *Tirocinium*]

priestly = ecclesiastic, pastoral, clerical, canonical, hieratic, sacerdotal, priestlike • *his priestly duties*

prig = **goody-goody** *(informal)*, puritan, prude, pedant, old maid *(informal)*, stuffed shirt *(informal)*, Holy Joe *(informal)*, Holy Willie *(informal)* • *She was heartily disliked by everyone as a prig and a bore.*

priggish = **self-righteous**, smug, stiff, stuffy, prim, puritanical, narrow-minded, pedantic, starchy *(informal)*, self-satisfied, prudish, goody-goody *(informal)*, holier-than-thou • *He was a priggish, self-righteous little sneak.*

prim = **prudish**, particular, formal, proper, precise, stiff, fussy, fastidious, puritanical, demure, starchy *(informal)*, prissy *(informal)*, strait-laced, priggish, anal retentive, schoolmarmish *(Brit. informal)*, old-maidish *(informal)*, niminy-piminy • *We tend to imagine that the Victorians were very prim and proper.*
OPPOSITES: liberal, relaxed, casual

primacy = **supremacy**, leadership, command, dominance, superiority, dominion, ascendancy, pre-eminence • *He saw this as a challenge to his primacy.*

prima donna = **diva**, star, leading lady, female lead • *her career as prima donna with the opera company*

primal 1 = **basic**, prime, central, first, highest, greatest, major, chief, main, most important, principal, paramount • *the most primal of human fears*
2 = **earliest**, prime, original, primary, first, initial, primitive, pristine, primordial • *Yeats's remarks about folklore and the primal religion*

primarily 1 = **chiefly**, largely, generally, mainly, especially, essentially, mostly, basically, principally, fundamentally, above all, on the whole, for the most part • *Public order is primarily an urban problem.*
2 = **at first**, originally, initially, in the first place, in the beginning, first and foremost, at *or* from the start • *These machines were primarily intended for use in editing.*

primary 1 = **chief**, leading, main, best, first, highest, greatest, top, prime, capital, principal, dominant, cardinal, paramount • *His primary aim in life is to be happy.*
OPPOSITES: lowest, lesser, subordinate
2 = **basic**, essential, radical, fundamental, ultimate, underlying, elemental, bog-standard *(informal)* • *our primary needs of air, food and water*
3 = **major**, chief, main, principal, key, foremost • *the primary cause of the disease*
OPPOSITES: secondary, subsequent, ensuing

primate
▹ *See panel* **Monkeys, apes and other primates**

prime AS AN ADJECTIVE 1 = **main**, leading, chief, central, major, ruling, key, senior, primary, supreme, principal, ultimate, cardinal, paramount, overriding, foremost, predominant, pre-eminent, number-one *(informal)* • *Political stability is a prime concern.*
2 = **best**, top, select, highest, capital, quality, choice, selected, excellent, superior, first-class, first-rate, grade-A • *It was one of the City's prime locations.*
3 = **fundamental**, original, basic, primary, underlying • *A prime cause of deforestation was the burning of charcoal to melt ore into iron.*
4 = **ideal**, standard, classic, typical, stock, excellent, conventional, characteristic, signature, archetypal, quintessential, prototypical • *a prime example of mid-century modernism*
▸ AS A NOUN = **peak**, flower, bloom, maturity, height, perfection, best days, heyday, zenith, full flowering • *She was in her intellectual prime.*
▸ AS A VERB 1 = **inform**, tell, train, coach, brief, fill in *(informal)*, groom *(informal)*, notify, clue in *(informal)*, gen up *(Brit. informal)*, give someone the lowdown, clue up *(informal)* • *The press corps has been primed to avoid this topic.*
2 = **prepare**, set up, load, equip, get ready, make ready • *They had primed the bomb to go off in an hour's time.*

prime minister
▹ *See panel* **Prime Ministers**

primeval *or* **primaeval** 1 = **earliest**, old, original, ancient, primitive, first, early, pristine, primal, prehistoric, primordial • *a vast expanse of primeval swamp*
2 = **primal**, primitive, natural, basic, inherited, inherent, hereditary, instinctive, innate, congenital, primordial, inborn, inbred, hard-wired • *a primeval urge*

primitive 1 = **uncivilized**, savage, barbarian, barbaric, undeveloped, uncultivated • *studies of primitive societies*
OPPOSITES: developed, civilized
2 = **early**, first, earliest, original, primary, elementary, pristine, primordial, primeval • *primitive birds from the dinosaur era*
OPPOSITES: later, modern, advanced
3 = **simple**, naive, childlike, untrained, undeveloped, unsophisticated, untutored • *primitive art*
OPPOSITES: trained, developed, sophisticated
4 = **crude**, simple, rough, rude, rudimentary, unrefined • *primitive tools*
OPPOSITES: elaborate, refined

primordial 1 = **primeval**, primitive, first, earliest, pristine, primal, prehistoric • *Twenty million years ago this was dense primordial forest.*
2 = **fundamental**, original, basic, radical, elemental • *primordial particles generated by the Big Bang*

prince = **ruler**, lord, monarch, sovereign, crown prince, liege, potentate, prince regent, crowned head, dynast • *the prince and other royal guests*

princely 1 = **substantial**, considerable, goodly, large, huge, massive, enormous, tidy *(informal)*, whopping (great) *(informal)*, sizable *or* sizeable • *It cost them the princely sum of seventy-five pounds.*
2 = **regal**, royal, imposing, magnificent, august, grand, imperial, noble, sovereign, majestic, dignified, stately, lofty, high-born • *the embodiment of princely magnificence*

princess = **ruler**, lady, monarch, sovereign, liege, crowned head, crowned princess, dynast, princess regent • *the Princess of Wales*

principal AS AN ADJECTIVE = **main**, leading, chief, prime, first, highest, controlling, strongest, capital, key, essential, primary, most important, dominant, arch, cardinal, paramount, foremost, pre-eminent • *their principal concern is that of winning the next election*
OPPOSITES: minor, subsidiary, subordinate
▸ AS A NOUN 1 = **headmaster** *or* **headmistress**, head *(informal)*, director, dean, head teacher, rector, master *or* mistress • *the principal of the local high school*
2 = **boss**, head, leader, director, chief *(informal)*, master, ruler, superintendent, baas *(S. African)*, sherang *(Austral. & N.Z.)* • *the principal of the company*
3 = **star**, lead, leader, prima ballerina, first violin, leading man *or* lady, coryphée • *soloists and principals of The Scottish Ballet orchestra*
4 = **capital**, money, assets, working capital, capital funds • *Use the higher premiums to pay the interest and principal on the debt.*

principally = **mainly**, largely, chiefly, especially, particularly, mostly, primarily, above all, predominantly, in the main, for the most part, first and foremost • *This is principally because the major export markets are slowing.*

principle AS A NOUN 1 = **morals**, standards, ideals, honour, virtue, ethics, integrity, conscience, morality, decency, scruples, probity, rectitude, moral standards, sense of duty, moral law, sense of honour, uprightness, kaupapa *(N.Z.)* • *He would never compromise his principles.* • *They had great trust in him as a man of principle.*
2 = **belief**, rule, standard, attitude, code, notion, criterion, ethic, doctrine, canon, creed, maxim, dogma, tenet, dictum, credo, axiom • *a violation of the basic principles of Marxism*

PRIME MINISTERS

British Prime Ministers

Prime Minister	Party	Term of office
Robert Walpole	Whig	1721–42
Earl of Wilmington	Whig	1742–43
Henry Pelham	Whig	1743–54
Duke of Newcastle	Whig	1754–56
Duke of Devonshire	Whig	1756–57
Duke of Newcastle	Whig	1757–62
Earl of Bute	Tory	1762–63
George Grenville	Whig	1763–65
Marquess of Rockingham	Whig	1765–66
Duke of Grafton	Whig	1766–70
Lord North	Tory	1770–82
Marquess of Rockingham	Whig	1782
Earl of Shelburne	Whig	1782–83
Duke of Portland	Coalition	1783
William Pitt	Tory	1783–1801
Henry Addington	Tory	1801–04
William Pitt	Tory	1804–06
Lord Grenville	Whig	1806–7
Duke of Portland	Tory	1807–09
Spencer Perceval	Tory	1809–12
Earl of Liverpool	Tory	1812–27
George Canning	Tory	1827
Viscount Goderich	Tory	1827–28
Duke of Wellington	Tory	1828–30
Earl Grey	Whig	1830–34
Viscount Melbourne	Whig	1834
Robert Peel	Conservative	1834–35
Viscount Melbourne	Whig	1835–41
Robert Peel	Conservative	1841–46
Lord John Russell	Liberal	1846–52
Earl of Derby	Conservative	1852
Lord Aberdeen	Peelite	1852–55
Viscount Palmerston	Liberal	1855–58
Earl of Derby	Conservative	1858–59
Viscount Palmerston	Liberal	1859–65
Lord John Russell	Liberal	1865–66
Earl of Derby	Conservative	1866–68
Benjamin Disraeli	Conservative	1868
William Gladstone	Liberal	1868–74
Benjamin Disraeli	Conservative	1874–80
William Gladstone	Liberal	1880–85
Marquess of Salisbury	Conservative	1885–86
William Gladstone	Liberal	1886
Marquess of Salisbury	Conservative	1886–92
William Gladstone	Liberal	1892–94
Earl of Rosebery	Liberal	1894–95
Marquess of Salisbury	Conservative	1895–1902
Arthur James Balfour	Conservative	1902–05
Henry Campbell-Bannerman	Liberal	1905–08
Herbert Henry Asquith	Liberal	1908–15
Herbert Henry Asquith	Coalition	1915–16
David Lloyd George	Coalition	1916–22
Andrew Bonar Law	Conservative	1922–23
Stanley Baldwin	Conservative	1923–24
James Ramsay MacDonald	Labour	1924
Stanley Baldwin	Conservative	1924–29
James Ramsay MacDonald	Labour	1929–31
James Ramsay MacDonald	Nationalist	1931–35
Stanley Baldwin	Nationalist	1935–37
Arthur Neville Chamberlain	Nationalist	1937–40
Winston Churchill	Coalition	1940–45
Clement Attlee	Labour	1945–51
Winston Churchill	Conservative	1951–55
Anthony Eden	Conservative	1955–57
Harold Macmillan	Conservative	1957–63
Alec Douglas-Home	Conservative	1963–64
Harold Wilson	Labour	1964–70
Edward Heath	Conservative	1970–74
Harold Wilson	Labour	1974–76
James Callaghan	Labour	1976–79
Margaret Thatcher	Conservative	1979–90
John Major	Conservative	1990–97
Tony Blair	Labour	1997–2007
Gordon Brown	Labour	2007–

Australian Prime Ministers

Prime Minister	Party	Term of office
Robert Walpole	Whig	1721–42
Edmund Barton	Protectionist	1901–03
Alfred Deakin	Protectionist	1903–04
John Christian Watson	Labor	1904
George Houston Reid	Free Trade	1904–05
Alfred Deakin	Protectionist	1905–08
Andrew Fisher	Labor	1908–09
Alfred Deakin	Fusion	1909–10
Andrew Fisher	Labor	1910–13
Joseph Cook	Liberal	1913–14
Andrew Fisher	Labor	1914–15
William Morris Hughes	National Labor	1915–17
William Morris Hughes	Nationalist	1917–23
Stanley Melbourne Bruce	Nationalist	1923–29
James Henry Scullin	Labor	1929–31
Joseph Aloysius Lyons	United	1931–39
Earle Christmas Page	Country	1939
Robert Gordon Menzies	United	1939–41
Arthur William Fadden	Country	1941
John Joseph Curtin	Labor	1941–45
Joseph Benedict Chifley	Labor	1945–49
Robert Gordon Menzies	Liberal	1949–66
Harold Edward Holt	Liberal	1966–67
John McEwen	Country	1967–68
John Grey Gorton	Liberal	1968–71
William McMahon	Liberal	1971–72
Edward Gough Whitlam	Labor	1972–75
John Malcolm Fraser	Liberal	1975–83
Robert James Lee Hawke	Labor	1983–91
Paul Keating	Labor	1991–96
John Howard	Liberal	1996–2007
Kevin Rudd	Labor	2007–

Canadian Prime Ministers

Prime Minister	Party	Term of office	Prime Minister	Party	Term of office
John A. MacDonald	Conservative	1867–73	William Lyon Mackenzie King	Liberal	1935–48
Alexander Mackenzie	Liberal	1873–78	Louis St. Laurent	Liberal	1948–57
John A. MacDonald	Conservative	1878–91	John George Diefenbaker	Conservative	1957–63
John J.C. Abbot	Conservative	1891–92	Lester Bowles Pearson	Liberal	1963–68
John S.D. Thompson	Conservative	1892–94	Pierre Elliott Trudeau	Liberal	1968–79
Mackenzie Bowell	Conservative	1894–96	Joseph Clark	Conservative	1979–80
Charles Tupper	Conservative	1896	Pierre Elliott Trudeau	Liberal	1980–84
Wilfrid Laurier	Liberal	1896–1911	John Turner	Liberal	1984
Robert Borden	Conservative	1911–20	Brian Mulroney	Conservative	1984–93
Arthur Meighen	Conservative	1920–21	Kim Campbell	Conservative	1993
William Lyon Mackenzie King	Liberal	1921–26	Joseph Jacques Jean Chrétien	Liberal	1993–2003
Arthur Meighen	Conservative	1926	Paul Martin	Liberal	2003–6
William Lyon Mackenzie King	Liberal	1926–30	Stephen Joseph Harper	Conservative	2006–
Richard Bedford Bennet	Conservative	1930–35			

New Zealand Prime Ministers

Prime Minister	Party	Term of office	Prime Minister	Party	Term of office
Henry Sewell	-	1856	William Hall-Jones	Liberal	1906
William Fox	-	1856	Joseph George Ward	Liberal/National	1906–12
Edward William Stafford	-	1856–61	Thomas Mackenzie	National	1912
William Fox	-	1861–62	William Ferguson Massey	Reform	1912–25
Alfred Domett	-	1862–63	Francis Henry Dillon Bell	Reform	1925
Frederick Whitaker	-	1863–64	Joseph Gordon Coates	Reform	1925–28
Frederick Aloysius Weld	-	1864–65	Joseph George Ward	Liberal/National	1928–30
Edward William Stafford	-	1865–69	George William Forbes	United	1930–35
William Fox	-	1869–72	Michael Joseph Savage	Labour	1935–40
Edward William Stafford	-	1872	Peter Fraser	Labour	1940–49
William Fox	-	1873	Sidney George Holland	National	1949–57
Julius Vogel	-	1873–75	Keith Jacka Holyoake	National	1957
Daniel Pollen	-	1875–76	Walter Nash	Labour	1957–60
Julius Vogel	-	1876	Keith Jacka Holyoake	National	1960–72
Harry Albert Atkinson	-	1876–77	John Ross Marshall	National	1972
George Grey	-	1877–79	Norman Eric Kirk	Labour	1972–74
John Hall	-	1879–82	Wallace Edward Rowling	Labour	1974–75
Frederick Whitaker	-	1882–83	Robert David Muldoon	National	1975–84
Harry Albert Atkinson	-	1883–84	David Russell Lange	Labour	1984–89
Robert Stout	-	1884	Geoffrey Palmer	Labour	1989–90
Harry Albert Atkinson	-	1884	Mike Moore	Labour	1990
Robert Stout	-	1884–87	Jim Bolger	National	1990–97
Harry Albert Atkinson	-	1887–91	Jenny Shipley	National	1997–99
John Ballance	-	1891–93	Helen Clark	Labour	1999–
Richard John Seddon	Liberal	1893–1906			

3 = rule, idea, law, theory, basis, truth, concept, formula, fundamental, assumption, essence, proposition, verity, golden rule, precept • *the principles of quantum theory*

▸ **IN PHRASES: in principle 1 = in general**, generally, all things considered, on the whole, in the main, by and large, in essence, all in all, on balance • *I agree with this plan in principle.*

2 = in theory, ideally, on paper, theoretically, in an ideal world, en principe *(French)* • *In principle, it should be possible.*

QUOTATIONS

It is always easier to fight for one's principles than to live up to them

[Alfred Adler]

principled = moral, ethical, upright, honourable, just, correct, decent, righteous, conscientious, virtuous, scrupulous, right-minded, high-minded • *She was a strong, principled woman.*

print AS A VERB **1 = run off**, publish, copy, reproduce, issue, engrave, go to press, put to bed *(informal)* • *It costs far less to press a CD than to print a book.*

2 = publish, release, circulate, issue, disseminate • *a questionnaire printed in the magazine*

3 = mark, impress, stamp, imprint • *printed with a paisley pattern*

4 = record, impress, stamp, imprint, etch, engrave • *indelibly printed on his memory*

▸ **AS A NOUN 1 = photograph**, photo, snap • *a black and white print of the children*

2 = picture, plate, etching, engraving, lithograph, woodcut, linocut • *Hogarth's famous series of prints*

3 = copy, photo *(informal)*, picture, reproduction, replica • *There was a huge print of 'Déjeuner Sur l'Herbe' on the wall.*

4 = type, lettering, letters, characters, face, font *(chiefly U. S.)*, fount, typeface • *columns of tiny print*

5 = mark, impression, fingerprint, footprint • *the unmistakable print of a bare foot in the mud*

▸ **IN PHRASES: in print 1 = published**, printed, on the streets, on paper, in black and white, out • *the appearance of his poems in print*

2 = available, current, on the market, in the shops, on the shelves, obtainable • *The book has been in print for over 40 years.*

out of print = unavailable, unobtainable, no longer published, o.p. • *The book is now out of print, but can be found in libraries.*

prior AS AN ADJECTIVE = **earlier**, previous, former, preceding, foregoing, antecedent, aforementioned, pre-existing, anterior, pre-existent • *He claimed he had no prior knowledge of the protest.*
▸ IN PHRASES: **prior to = before**, preceding, earlier than, in advance of, previous to • *A man was seen in the area prior to the shooting.*

priority 1 = **prime concern**, first concern, primary issue, most pressing matter • *The government's priority should be better health care.*
2 = **precedence**, preference, greater importance, primacy, predominance • *The school gives priority to science and maths.*
3 = **supremacy**, rank, the lead, superiority, precedence, prerogative, seniority, right of way, pre-eminence • *the premise that economic development has priority over the environment*

priory = **monastery**, abbey, convent, cloister, nunnery, religious house • *Lindisfarne priory on Holy Island*

prise *see* **prize**[3]

prison = **jail**, confinement, can (*slang*), pound, nick (*Brit. slang*), stir (*slang*), cooler (*slang*), jug (*slang*), dungeon, clink (*slang*), glasshouse (*Military informal*), gaol, penitentiary (*U.S.*), slammer (*slang*), lockup, quod (*slang*), penal institution, calaboose (*U.S. informal*), choky (*slang*), poky or pokey (*U.S. & Canad. slang*), boob (*Austral. slang*) • *They released him from prison in 1990.*

QUOTATIONS

Prison is a second-by-second assault on the soul, a day-to-day degradation of the self
[Mumia Abu-Jamal *Live From Death Row*]

Stone walls do not a prison make,
Nor iron bars a cage
[Richard Lovelace *To Althea, from Prison*]

Prisons are built with stones of Law, brothels with bricks of Religion
[William Blake *The Marriage of Heaven and Hell*]

prisoner 1 = **convict**, con (*slang*), lag (*slang*), jailbird • *the large number of prisoners sharing cells*
2 = **captive**, hostage, detainee, internee • *wartime hostages and concentration-camp prisoners*

QUOTATIONS

Only free men can negotiate. Prisoners cannot enter into contracts
[Nelson Mandela]

prissy = **prim**, precious, fussy, fastidious, squeamish, prudish, finicky, strait-laced, anal retentive, schoolmarmish (*Brit. informal*), old-maidish (*informal*), niminy-piminy, overnice, prim and proper • *the prissy and puritanical heroine of the novel*

pristine = **new**, pure, virgin, immaculate, untouched, unspoiled, virginal, unsullied, uncorrupted, undefiled • *pristine white shirts*

privacy = **seclusion**, isolation, solitude, retirement, retreat, separateness, sequestration, privateness • *You can try them on in the privacy of your own home.*

PROVERBS

One does not wash one's dirty linen in public

private AS AN ADJECTIVE 1 = **nonpublic**, independent, commercial, privatized, private-enterprise, denationalized • *a joint venture with private industry*
2 = **exclusive**, individual, privately owned, own, special, particular, reserved • *He has had to sell his private plane.*
OPPOSITES: public, general, common
3 = **secret**, confidential, covert, inside, closet, unofficial, privy (*archaic*), clandestine, off the record, hush-hush (*informal*), in camera • *He held a private meeting with the country's political party leaders.*
OPPOSITES: public, known, open
4 = **personal**, individual, secret, hidden, intimate, undisclosed, unspoken, innermost, unvoiced • *I've always kept my private and professional life separate.* • *He hardly ever betrayed his private thoughts.*
5 = **secluded**, secret, separate, isolated, concealed, retired, sequestered, not overlooked • *It was the only reasonably private place they could find to talk.*
OPPOSITES: busy, frequented, bustling
6 = **solitary**, reserved, retiring, withdrawn, discreet, secretive, self-contained, reclusive, reticent, insular, introvert, uncommunicative • *Gould was an intensely private individual.*
OPPOSITES: outgoing, sociable
7 = **unofficial**, personal, non-official • *The President is here on a private visit.*
▸ AS A NOUN = **enlisted man** (*U.S.*), tommy (*Brit. informal*), private soldier, Tommy Atkins (*Brit. informal*), squaddie or squaddy (*Brit. slang*) • *The rest of the gunners in the battery were privates.*
▸ IN PHRASES: **in private = in secret**, privately, personally, behind closed doors, in camera, between ourselves, confidentially • *I think we should discuss this in private.*

private detective = **private investigator**, detective, private eye (*informal*), sleuth (*informal*), gumshoe (*U.S. & Canad.*), private dick (*U.S. & Canad.*) • *She hired a private detective to search for evidence.*

privately 1 = **in private**, alone, discreetly, behind closed doors, in camera, confidentially • *He will see the Prime Minister privately on Thursday.*
2 = **secretly**, personally, deep down, inwardly, unofficially • *He was privately annoyed at the request.*

private parts = **genitals**, privates (*informal*), groin, crotch, genitalia, sexual organs, naughty bits (*informal*), dangly bits (*informal*), pudenda • *He bared his private parts on TV.*

privation = **want**, poverty, need, suffering, loss, lack, distress, misery, necessity, hardship, penury, destitution, neediness, indigence • *They endured years of privation during the war.*

privilege AS A NOUN 1 = **right**, benefit, due, advantage, claim, freedom, sanction, liberty, concession, franchise, entitlement, prerogative, birthright • *The ancient powers and privileges of the House of Commons.*
2 = **advantage**, luxury, indulgence, affluence • *She was born into a life of privilege.*
3 = **honour**, pleasure, source of pleasure or pride or satisfaction • *It's been a privilege to meet you.*
4 = **immunity**, liberty, exemption, dispensation • *He will use parliamentary privilege to make this information public.*
▸ AS A VERB = **favour**, promote, spoil, side with, advance, smile upon, pull strings for, treat with partiality • *They are privileging a tiny number to the disadvantage of the rest.*

privileged 1 = **special**, powerful, advantaged, favoured, ruling, honoured, entitled, elite, indulged • *They were a wealthy and privileged elite.*
2 = **confidential**, special, inside, exceptional, privy, off the record, not for publication • *This data is privileged information.*

privy AS A NOUN = **lavatory**, closet, bog (*slang*), latrine, outside toilet, earth closet, pissoir (*French*), bogger (*Austral. slang*), brasco (*Austral. slang*) • *an outside privy*
▸ AS AN ADJECTIVE *with* **to = informed of**, aware of, in on, wise to (*slang*), hip to (*slang*), switched-on to (*informal*), in the loop, apprised of, cognizant of, in the know about (*informal*), sussed of (*Brit. slang*) • *Only three people were privy to the facts.*

prize[1] AS A NOUN 1 = **reward**, cup, award, honour, premium, medal, trophy, accolade • *He won a prize in the Leeds Piano Competition.*
2 = **winnings**, haul, jackpot, stakes, purse, windfall • *A single winner is in line for a jackpot prize of £8 million.*
3 = **goal**, hope, gain, aim, desire, ambition, conquest, Holy

Grail *(informal)* • *A settlement of the dispute would be a great prize.*
▸ **AS A MODIFIER** = **champion**, best, winning, top, outstanding, award-winning, first-rate, top-notch *(informal)* • *a prize bull*

prize² = **value**, appreciate, treasure, esteem, cherish, hold dear, regard highly, set store by • *These items are greatly prized by collectors.*

prize³ *or* **prise** 1 = **force**, pull, lever • *He tried to prize the dog's jaws open.*
2 = **drag**, force, draw, wring, extort • *We had to prize the story out of him.*

prized = **treasured**, valued, precious, beloved, cherished, much loved • *his most prized possession*

prizewinner = **winner**, champion, victor, champ *(informal)* • *The lucky prizewinner will win a holiday for two.*

probability 1 = **likelihood**, prospect, chance, odds, expectation, liability, presumption, likeliness • *There is a high probability of success.*
2 = **chance**, odds, possibility, likelihood • *the probability of life on other planets*

probable = **likely**, possible, apparent, reasonable to think, most likely, presumed, credible, plausible, feasible, odds-on, on the cards, presumable • *It is probable that food prices will increase.*
OPPOSITES: unlikely, doubtful, not likely

probably = **likely**, perhaps, maybe, possibly, presumably, most likely, doubtless, in all probability, in all likelihood, perchance *(archaic)*, as likely as not • *They probably won't make this plan public until July.*

probation = **trial period**, test, trial, examination, apprenticeship, initiation, novitiate • *The appointment will be subject to a six-month term of probation.*

probationer = **trainee**, novice, beginner, apprentice, rookie *(informal)*, learner, new recruit, neophyte, tyro, greenhorn *(informal)* • *I was a young policeman – a probationer with a training officer.*

probe **AS A VERB** 1 *often with* **into** = **examine**, research, go into, investigate, explore, test, sound, search, look into, query, verify, sift, analyse, dissect, delve into, work over, scrutinize • *The more they probed into his background, the more suspicious they became.*
2 = **explore**, examine, poke, prod, feel around • *A doctor probed deep in his shoulder wound for shrapnel.*
▸ **AS A NOUN** = **investigation**, study, research, inquiry, analysis, examination, exploration, scrutiny, inquest, scrutinization • *a federal grand-jury probe into corruption within the FDA*

probity = **integrity**, worth, justice, honour, equity, virtue, goodness, morality, honesty, fairness, fidelity, sincerity, righteousness, rectitude, truthfulness, trustworthiness, uprightness • *a woman renowned for her moral probity*

problem **AS A NOUN** 1 = **difficulty**, trouble, dispute, plight, obstacle, dilemma, headache *(informal)*, disagreement, complication, predicament, quandary, turf war *(informal)* • *the economic problems of the inner city*
2 = **puzzle**, question, riddle, enigma, conundrum, teaser, poser, brain-teaser *(informal)* • *a mathematical problem*
▸ **AS A MODIFIER** = **difficult**, disturbed, troublesome, unruly, delinquent, uncontrollable, intractable, recalcitrant, intransigent, unmanageable, disobedient, ungovernable, refractory, maladjusted • *Sometimes a problem child is placed in a special school.*

PROVERBS
A problem shared is a problem halved

problematic = **tricky**, puzzling, uncertain, doubtful, dubious, unsettled, questionable, enigmatic, debatable, moot, problematical, chancy *(informal)*, open to doubt • *the problematic business of running an economy*
OPPOSITES: clear, certain, settled

procedure = **method**, policy, process, course, system, form, action, step, performance, operation, practice, scheme, strategy, conduct, formula, custom, routine, transaction, plan of action, modus operandi • *He did not follow the correct procedure in applying for a visa.*

proceed 1 = **begin**, go ahead, get going, make a start, get under way, set something in motion • *I had no idea how to proceed.*
2 = **continue**, go on, progress, carry on, go ahead, get on, press on, crack on *(informal)* • *The defence is not yet ready to proceed with the trial.*
OPPOSITES: end, stop, discontinue
3 = **go on**, continue, advance, progress, carry on, go ahead, move on, move forward, press on, push on, make your way, crack on *(informal)* • *She proceeded along the hallway.*
OPPOSITES: stop, halt, retreat
4 = **arise**, come, follow, issue, result, spring, flow, stem, derive, originate, ensue, emanate • *Does Othello's downfall proceed from a flaw in his character?*

proceeding **AS A NOUN** = **action**, process, procedure, move, act, step, measure, venture, undertaking, deed, occurrence, course of action • *The whole proceeding went very smoothly.*
▸ **AS A PLURAL NOUN** 1 = **legal action**, case, action, suit, lawsuit, litigation, legal proceedings • *criminal proceedings against the former prime minister*
2 = **business**, happenings, matter, events, activities, affair(s), transactions, dealings, goings-on, doings • *He viewed the proceedings with alarm.*
3 = **report(s)**, business, minutes, records, account(s), archives, annals • *The department is to publish the conference proceedings.*

proceeds = **income**, profit, revenue, returns, produce, products, gain, earnings, yield, receipts, takings • *The proceeds from the concert will go towards famine relief.*

process **AS A NOUN** 1 = **procedure**, means, course, system, action, performance, operation, measure, proceeding, manner, transaction, mode, course of action • *The best way to find out is by a process of elimination.*
2 = **development**, growth, progress, course, stage, step, movement, advance, formation, evolution, unfolding, progression • *the evolutionary process of Homo sapiens*
3 = **method**, system, practice, technique, procedure • *the cost of the production process*
4 = **action**, case, trial, suit • *steps in the impeachment process against the president*
▸ **AS A VERB** 1 = **prepare**, treat, convert, transform, alter, refine • *silicon chips process electrical signals* • *facilities to process the beans before export*
2 = **handle**, manage, action, deal with, fulfil, take care of, dispose of • *A number of applications are being processed at the moment.*
▸ **IN PHRASES:** **in the process of** = **in the course of**, in the middle of, in the midst of • *They are in the process of drawing up a peace plan.*

procession 1 = **parade**, train, march, file, column, motorcade, cavalcade, cortege • *a funeral procession*
2 = **sequence**, run, course, train, series, cycle, string, succession • *a seemingly endless procession of corruption cases*

proclaim 1 = **announce**, declare, advertise, show, publish, indicate, blaze (abroad), herald, circulate, trumpet, affirm, give out, profess, promulgate, make known, enunciate, blazon (abroad), shout from the housetops *(informal)* • *He continues to proclaim his innocence.*
OPPOSITES: conceal, suppress, keep secret
2 = **pronounce**, announce, declare • *He launched a coup and proclaimed himself president.*

proclamation 1 = **declaration**, notice, announcement, decree, manifesto, edict, pronouncement, pronunciamento

P

• *A formal proclamation of independence was issued eight days ago.*
2 = publishing, broadcasting, announcement, publication, declaration, notification, pronouncement, promulgation • *his proclamation of the good news*

proclivity = **tendency**, liking, leaning, inclination, bent, weakness, bias, disposition, penchant, propensity, kink, predisposition, predilection, partiality, proneness, liableness • *He was indulging his peculiar sexual proclivities.*

procrastinate = **delay**, stall, postpone, prolong, put off, defer, adjourn, retard, dally, play for time, gain time, temporize, play a waiting game, protract, drag your feet *(informal)*, be dilatory • *We often procrastinate when faced with something we do not want to do.*
OPPOSITES: advance, proceed, hurry (up)

procrastination = **delay**, hesitation, slowness, slackness, dilatoriness, temporization • *He hates delay and procrastination.*

QUOTATIONS
Procrastination is the thief of time
[Edward Young *The Complaint: Night Thoughts*]
Never put off till tomorrow what you can do today
[Lord Chesterfield *letter to his son*]
procrastination is the
art of keeping
up with yesterday
[Don Marquis *archy and mehitabel*]

procreate = **reproduce**, mother, produce, father, breed, generate, sire, engender, propagate, beget, bring into being • *Most people feel a biological need to procreate.*

procure 1 = **obtain**, get, find, buy, win, land, score *(slang)*, gain, earn, pick up, purchase, secure, appropriate, acquire, manage to get, get hold of, come by, lay hands on • *It was difficult to procure food and other daily necessitites.*
2 = bring about, cause, effect, contrive • *They are still trying to procure the release of the hostages.*

prod AS A VERB **1 = poke**, push, dig, shove, propel, nudge, jab, prick • *He prodded Murray with the shotgun.*
2 = prompt, move, urge, motivate, spur, stimulate, rouse, stir up, incite, egg on, goad, impel, put a bomb under *(informal)* • *a tactic to prod the government into spending more on the Health Service*
▸ AS A NOUN **1 = poke**, push, boost, dig, elbow, shove, nudge, jab • *He gave the donkey a prod in the backside.*
2 = prompt, boost, signal, cue, reminder, stimulus • *She won't do it without a prod from you.*
3 = goad, stick, spur, poker • *a cattle prod*

prodigal 1 = **extravagant**, excessive, reckless, squandering, wasteful, wanton, profligate, spendthrift, intemperate, immoderate, improvident • *his prodigal habits*
OPPOSITES: economical, frugal, thrifty
2 *often with* **of = lavish**, bountiful, unstinting, unsparing, bounteous, profuse • *You are prodigal of both your toil and your talent.*
OPPOSITES: generous, free, liberal

prodigious 1 = **huge**, giant, massive, vast, enormous, tremendous, immense, gigantic, monumental, monstrous, mammoth, colossal, stellar *(informal)*, stupendous, inordinate, immeasurable • *This business generates cash in prodigious amounts.*
OPPOSITES: small, tiny, negligible
2 = wonderful, striking, amazing, unusual, dramatic, impressive, extraordinary, remarkable, fantastic *(informal)*, fabulous, staggering, marvellous, startling, exceptional, abnormal, phenomenal, astounding, miraculous, stupendous, flabbergasting *(informal)* • *He impressed everyone with his prodigious memory.*
OPPOSITES: normal, usual, ordinary

prodigy = **genius**, talent, wizard, mastermind, whizz *(informal)*, whizz kid *(informal)*, wunderkind, brainbox, child genius, wonder child, up-and-comer *(informal)* • *an 11-year-old chess prodigy*

produce AS A VERB **1 = cause**, lead to, result in, effect, occasion, generate, trigger, make for, provoke, set off, induce, bring about, give rise to, engender • *The drug is known to produce side-effects.*
2 = make, build, create, develop, turn out, manufacture, construct, invent, assemble, put together, originate, fabricate, mass-produce • *The company produces circuitry for communications systems.*
3 = create, develop, write, turn out, compose, originate, churn out *(informal)* • *So far he has produced only one composition he deems suitable for performance.*
4 = yield, provide, grow, bear, give, supply, afford, render, furnish • *The plant produces sweet fruit with deep red flesh.*
5 = bring forth, bear, deliver, breed, give birth to, beget, bring into the world • *Some species of snake produce live young.*
6 = show, provide, present, advance, demonstrate, offer, come up with, exhibit, put forward, furnish, bring forward, set forth, bring to light • *They challenged him to produce evidence to support his allegations.*
7 = display, show, present, proffer • *You must produce your passport upon re-entering the country.*
8 = present, stage, direct, put on, do, show, mount, exhibit, put before the public • *He produced Broadway's longest show.*
▸ AS A NOUN = **fruit and vegetables**, goods, food, products, crops, yield, harvest, greengrocery *(Brit.)* • *I buy organic produce whenever possible.*

producer 1 = **director**, promoter, impresario, régisseur *(French)* • *a freelance film producer*
2 = maker, manufacturer, builder, creator, fabricator • *producers of precision instruments and electrical equipment*
3 = grower, farmer • *They are producers of high-quality wines.*

product 1 = **goods**, produce, production, creation, commodity, invention, merchandise, artefact, concoction • *Try to get the best products at the lowest price.*
2 = result, fruit, consequence, yield, returns, issue, effect, outcome, legacy, spin-off, end result, offshoot, upshot • *The company is the product of a merger.*

production 1 = **producing**, making, manufacture, manufacturing, construction, assembly, preparation, formation, fabrication, origination • *two companies involved in the production of the steel pipes*
2 = creation, development, fashioning, composition, origination • *the apparent lack of skill in the production of much new modern art*
3 = output, yield, productivity • *We need to increase the volume of production.*
4 = management, administration, direction • *the story behind the show's production*
5 = presentation, staging, mounting • *a critically acclaimed production of Othello*
6 = presentation, showing, display, proffering • *discounts on production of membership cards*

productive 1 = **fertile**, rich, producing, prolific, plentiful, fruitful, teeming, generative, fecund • *fertile and productive soil*
OPPOSITES: poor, barren, sterile
2 = creative, dynamic, vigorous, energetic, inventive • *a highly productive writer of fiction*
3 = useful, rewarding, valuable, profitable, effective, worthwhile, beneficial, constructive, gratifying, fruitful, advantageous, win-win, gainful • *a productive relationship*
OPPOSITES: useless, unproductive, unprofitable

productivity = **output**, production, capacity, yield, efficiency, mass production, work rate, productive capacity, productiveness • *The results reflected a continued improvement in productivity.*

profane AS AN ADJECTIVE **1 = sacrilegious**, wicked, irreverent, sinful, disrespectful, heathen, impure, godless,

ungodly, irreligious, impious, idolatrous • *a hard-drinking, profane Irishman*
OPPOSITES: clean, religious, spiritual
2 = **crude**, foul, obscene, abusive, coarse, filthy, vulgar, blasphemous • *a campaign against suggestive and profane lyrics in country songs*
3 = **secular**, lay, temporal, unholy, worldly, unconsecrated, unhallowed, unsanctified • *Churches should not be used for profane or secular purposes.*
▸ **AS A VERB** = **desecrate**, violate, abuse, prostitute, contaminate, pollute, pervert, misuse, debase, defile, vitiate, commit sacrilege • *They have profaned the traditions of the Church.*

profanity 1 = **sacrilege**, blasphemy, irreverence, impiety, profaneness • *To desecrate a holy spring is considered profanity.*
2 = **swearing**, abuse, curse, cursing, obscenity, four-letter word, foul language, imprecation, malediction, swearword, execration • *Our ears were assailed by curses and profanities.*

profess 1 = **claim**, allege, pretend, fake, make out, sham, purport, feign, act as if, let on, dissemble • *'I don't know,' he replied, professing innocence.*
2 = **state**, admit, announce, maintain, own, confirm, declare, acknowledge, confess, assert, proclaim, affirm, certify, avow, vouch, aver, asseverate • *He professed that he was content with the arrangements.*

professed 1 = **supposed**, would-be, alleged, so-called, apparent, pretended, purported, self-styled, ostensible, soi-disant *(French)* • *their professed concern for justice*
2 = **declared**, confirmed, confessed, proclaimed, certified, self-confessed, avowed, self-acknowledged • *He was a professed anarchist.*

profession 1 = **occupation**, calling, business, career, employment, line, office, position, sphere, vocation, walk of life, line of work, métier • *Harper was a teacher by profession.*
2 = **declaration**, statement, vow, testimony, claim, confession, assertion, affirmation, acknowledgment, avowal, attestation • *a profession of faith*

professional **AS AN ADJECTIVE** 1 = **qualified**, trained, skilled, white-collar • *professional people like doctors and engineers*
2 = **expert**, experienced, finished, skilled, masterly, efficient, crack *(slang)*, polished, practised, ace *(informal)*, accomplished, slick, competent, tasty *(Brit. informal)*, adept, proficient • *She told me we'd done a really professional job.*
OPPOSITES: incapable, inexperienced, amateurish
3 = **full-time**, paid, non-amateur • *He spent several years as a professional football player.*
▸ **AS A NOUN** = **expert**, authority, master, pro *(informal)*, specialist, guru, buff *(informal)*, wizard, adept, whizz *(informal)*, maestro, virtuoso, boffin *(Brit. informal)*, hotshot *(informal)*, past master, dab hand *(Brit. informal)*, wonk *(informal)*, maven *(U.S.)*, fundi *(S. African)* • *a dedicated professional*

professor = **don** *(Brit.)*, fellow *(Brit.)*, prof *(informal)*, head of faculty • *a professor of economics at East Chepstow University*

QUOTATIONS
A professor is one who talks in someone else's sleep
[W.H. Auden]

proffer 1 = **offer**, hand over, present, extend, hold out • *He proffered a box of cigarettes.*
2 = **suggest**, propose, volunteer, submit, tender, propound • *They have not yet proffered an explanation of how the accident happened.*

proficiency = **skill**, ability, know-how *(informal)*, talent, facility, craft, expertise, competence, accomplishment, mastery, knack, aptitude, dexterity, expertness, skilfulness • *Evidence of basic proficiency in English is required.*

proficient = **skilled**, trained, experienced, qualified, able, expert, masterly, talented, gifted, capable, efficient, clever, accomplished, versed, competent, tasty *(Brit. informal)*, apt, skilful, adept, conversant • *Many Egyptians are proficient in foreign languages.*
OPPOSITES: bad, incapable, unskilled

profile **AS A NOUN** 1 = **outline**, lines, form, figure, shape, silhouette, contour, side view • *His handsome profile was turned away from us.*
2 = **biography**, sketch, vignette, characterization, thumbnail sketch, character sketch • *The newspaper published comparative profiles of the candidates.*
3 = **analysis**, study, table, review, survey, chart, examination, diagram, graph • *a profile of the hospital's catchment area*
▸ **AS A VERB** = **describe**, outline, write about, portray, sketch, depict, characterize, give an account of • *He was profiled in a TV documentary about gifted children.*
▸ **IN PHRASES:** **keep a low profile** = **lie low**, keep quiet, keep out of sight, avoid publicity, keep yourself to yourself • *He has kept a low profile throughout this whole affair.*

profit **AS A NOUN** 1 *often plural* = **earnings**, winnings, return, revenue, gain, boot *(dialect)*, yield, proceeds, percentage *(informal)*, surplus, receipts, bottom line, takings, emoluments • *The bank made pre-tax profits of £3.5 million.*
OPPOSITES: loss, debt, deficit
2 = **benefit**, good, use, interest, value, gain, advantage, advancement, mileage *(informal)*, avail • *They saw little profit in risking their lives to capture the militants.*
OPPOSITES: cost, damage, disadvantage
▸ **AS A VERB** 1 = **make money**, clear up, gain, earn, clean up *(informal)*, rake in *(informal)*, make a killing *(informal)*, make a good thing of *(informal)* • *The dealers profited shamelessly at my family's expense.*
2 = **benefit**, help, serve, aid, gain, promote, contribute to, avail, be of advantage to • *So far the French alliance has profited the rebels very little.*
▸ **IN PHRASES:** **profit from something** = **capitalize on**, take advantage of, learn from, use, exploit, make the most of, cash in on *(informal)*, utilize, make good use of, reap the benefit of, put to good use, make capital of, turn to advantage or account • *One can profit from that example and try to follow it.*

profitable 1 = **money-making**, lucrative, paying, commercial, rewarding, worthwhile, cost-effective, fruitful, gainful, remunerative • *Drug manufacturing is the most profitable business in America.*
2 = **beneficial**, useful, rewarding, valuable, productive, worthwhile, fruitful, advantageous, expedient, win-win, serviceable • *a profitable exchange of ideas*
OPPOSITES: useless, vain, worthless

profiteer **AS A NOUN** = **racketeer**, exploiter, extortionist, bloodsucker *(informal)*, black marketeer • *a social class composed largely of war profiteers and gangsters*
▸ **AS A VERB** = **overcharge**, racketeer, make a quick buck *(slang)*, make a quick killing, make someone pay through the nose • *Retailers could profiteer through imposing surcharges.*

profiteering = **extortion**, exploitation, racketeering • *There has been a wave of profiteering and corruption.*

profligacy 1 = **extravagance**, excess, squandering, waste, recklessness, wastefulness, lavishness, prodigality, improvidence • *The country's main problem is fiscal profligacy.*
2 = **immorality**, depravity, debauchery, abandon, corruption, promiscuity, laxity, dissipation, degeneracy, licentiousness, wantonness, libertinism, dissoluteness, unrestraint • *His early warnings about sexual profligacy and AIDS now read as eerily prescient.*

profligate 1 = **extravagant**, reckless, squandering, wasteful, prodigal, spendthrift, immoderate, improvident • *the most profligate consumer of energy in the world*
2 = **depraved**, degenerate, immoral, wild, abandoned,

P

loose, corrupt, dissipated, wicked, promiscuous, shameless, wanton, debauched, unprincipled, dissolute, iniquitous, libertine, vitiated, licentious • *setting his usual profligate and rakish example to society*
OPPOSITES: principled, moral, virtuous

profound 1 = **sincere**, acute, intense, great, keen, extreme, hearty, heartfelt, abject, deeply felt, heartrending • *The overwhelming feeling is profound shock and anger.*
OPPOSITES: shallow, insincere
2 = **wise**, learned, serious, deep, skilled, subtle, penetrating, philosophical, thoughtful, sage, discerning, weighty, insightful, erudite, abstruse, recondite, sagacious • *a book full of profound and challenging insights*
OPPOSITES: stupid, unwise, uninformed
3 = **complete**, intense, absolute, serious *(informal)*, total, extreme, pronounced, utter, consummate, unqualified, out-and-out • *A profound silence fell.*
OPPOSITES: slight, superficial
4 = **radical**, extensive, thorough, far-reaching, exhaustive, thoroughgoing • *the profound changes brought about by World War I*

profoundly = **greatly**, very, deeply, seriously, keenly, extremely, thoroughly, sincerely, intensely, acutely, heartily, to the core, abjectly, to the nth degree, from the bottom of your heart • *I'm profoundly grateful for all the support I've received.*

profundity 1 = **insight**, intelligence, depth, wisdom, learning, penetration, acumen, erudition, acuity, perspicacity, sagacity, perceptiveness, perspicuity • *the profundity of this book*
2 = **intensity**, strength, depth, seriousness, severity, extremity • *the profundity of the problems besetting the country*

profuse 1 = **plentiful**, ample, prolific, abundant, overflowing, teeming, copious, bountiful, luxuriant • *This plant produces profuse bright-blue flowers.*
OPPOSITES: inadequate, scarce, sparse
2 = **extravagant**, liberal, generous, excessive, lavish, exuberant, prodigal, fulsome, open-handed, unstinting, immoderate • *Helena's profuse thanks were met with only a nod.*
OPPOSITES: moderate, provident, frugal

profusion = **abundance**, wealth, excess, quantity, surplus, riot, multitude, bounty, plethora, exuberance, glut, extravagance, cornucopia, oversupply, plenitude, superabundance, superfluity, lavishness, luxuriance, prodigality, copiousness • *a delightful river with a profusion of flowers growing along its banks*

progenitor 1 = **ancestor**, parent, forebear, forefather, begetter, procreator, primogenitor • *the Arabian stallions which were the progenitors of all modern thoroughbreds*
2 = **originator**, source, predecessor, precursor, forerunner, antecedent, instigator • *the man who is considered the progenitor of modern drama*

progeny 1 = **children**, family, young, issue, offspring, descendants • *They set aside funds to ensure the welfare of their progeny.*
2 = **race**, stock, breed, posterity *(archaic)*, seed *(chiefly biblical)*, lineage, scions • *They claimed to be the progeny of Genghis Khan.*

prognosis = **forecast**, prediction, diagnosis, expectation, speculation, projection, surmise, prognostication • *The physiotherapists' prognosis was that he might walk in six months.*

prognostication = **prediction**, expectation, forecast, speculation, projection, prophecy, prognosis, surmise, vaticination • *The country is obsessed with gloomy prognostications about its future.*

programme AS A NOUN 1 = **plan**, scheme, strategy, procedure, project, plan of action • *the programme for reform outlined by the Soviet President*
2 = **schedule**, plan, agenda, timetable, listing, list, line-up, calendar, order • *the programme of events for the forthcoming year*
3 = **course**, curriculum, syllabus • *a detailed ten-step programme of study with attainment targets*
4 = **show**, performance, production, broadcast, episode, presentation, transmission, telecast, podcast • *a series of TV programmes on global warming*
▸ AS A VERB 1 = **schedule**, plan, timetable, book, bill, list, design, arrange, work out, line up, organize, lay on, formulate, map out, itemize, prearrange • *His homework is more manageable now because it is programmed into his schedule.*
2 = **set**, fix • *Most VCRs can be programmed using a remote control handset.*

programming language

PROGRAMMING LANGUAGES

Ada	FORTRAN	Postscript
Algol	Haskell	PROLOG
BASIC	Java	RPG
C	LISP	Simula
C++	LOGO	Smalltalk
C#	Pascal	SNOBOL
COBOL	Perl	SQL
FORTH	PL/1	

progress AS A NOUN 1 = **development**, increase, growth, advance, gain, improvement, promotion, breakthrough, step forward, advancement, progression, headway, betterment, amelioration • *The two sides made little progress towards agreement.* • *The doctors say they are pleased with her progress.*
OPPOSITES: decline, failure, regression
2 = **movement forward**, passage, advancement, progression, course, advance, headway, onward movement • *The road was too rough for further progress in the car.*
OPPOSITES: movement backward, regression, retrogression
▸ AS A VERB 1 = **move on**, continue, travel, advance, proceed, go forward, gain ground, forge ahead, make inroads (into), make headway, make your way, cover ground, make strides, gather way, crack on *(informal)* • *He progressed slowly along the coast in an easterly direction.*
OPPOSITES: move back, recede, get behind
2 = **develop**, improve, advance, better, increase, grow, gain, get on, come on, mature, blossom, roll up, ameliorate • *He came round to see how our work was progressing.*
OPPOSITES: get behind, lose ground, regress
▸ IN PHRASES: **in progress** = **going on**, happening, continuing, being done, occurring, taking place, proceeding, under way, ongoing, being performed, in operation • *The game was already in progress when we took our seats.*

QUOTATIONS

Printing, gunpowder, and the magnet ... these three have changed the whole face and state of things throughout the world
[Francis Bacon *Essays*]

What we call progress is the exchange of one nuisance for another nuisance
[Havelock Ellis *Impressions and Comments*]

Perhaps the best definition of progress would be the continuing efforts of men and women to narrow the gap between the convenience of the powers that be and the unwritten charter
[Nadine Gordimer *Speak Out: The Necessity of Protest*]

Is it progress if a cannibal uses a knife and fork?
[Stanislaw Lec *Unkempt Thoughts*]

That's one small step for a man, one giant leap for mankind
[Neil Armstrong *on his first steps on the moon's surface*]

PROVERBS
one step at a time

progression 1 = **progress**, advance, advancement, gain, headway, furtherance, movement forward • *Both drugs slow the progression of HIV.*
2 = **sequence**, course, order, series, chain, cycle, string, succession • *the steady progression of events in my life*

progressive AS AN ADJECTIVE 1 = **enlightened**, liberal, modern, advanced, radical, enterprising, go-ahead, revolutionary, dynamic, avant-garde, reformist, up-and-coming, forward-looking • *The children go to a progressive school.*
2 = **growing**, continuing, increasing, developing, advancing, accelerating, ongoing, continuous, intensifying, escalating • *One symptom of the disease is a progressive loss of memory.*
▸ AS A NOUN = **reformer**, liberal, reformist, libertarian, innovator, progressivist, progressionist • *The Republicans were split between progressives and conservatives.*

prohibit 1 = **forbid**, ban, rule out, veto, outlaw, disallow, proscribe, debar, interdict, criminalize • *the law which prohibits trading on Sunday*
OPPOSITES: allow, permit, order
2 = **prevent**, restrict, rule out, stop, hamper, hinder, constrain, obstruct, preclude, impede, make impossible • *The contraption prohibited any movement.*
OPPOSITES: let, allow, permit

prohibited = **forbidden**, barred, banned, illegal, not allowed, vetoed, taboo, off limits, proscribed, verboten (*German*) • *Fishing is prohibited here.*

prohibition = **ban**, boycott, embargo, bar, veto, prevention, exclusion, injunction, disqualification, interdiction, interdict, proscription, disallowance, forbiddance, restraining order (*U.S. Law*) • *a comprehensive prohibition of nuclear weapons*

prohibitive 1 = **exorbitant**, excessive, steep (*informal*), high-priced, preposterous, sky-high, extortionate, beyond your means • *The cost of private treatment can be prohibitive.*
2 = **prohibiting**, forbidding, restraining, restrictive, repressive, suppressive, proscriptive • *prohibitive regulations*

project AS A NOUN 1 = **scheme**, plan, job, idea, design, programme, campaign, operation, activity, proposal, venture, enterprise, undertaking, occupation, proposition, plan of action • *a local development project*
2 = **assignment**, task, homework, piece of research • *Students complete their projects at their own pace.*
▸ AS A VERB 1 = **forecast**, expect, estimate, predict, reckon, calculate, gauge, extrapolate, predetermine • *Africa's population is projected to double by 2025.*
2 = **plan**, propose, design, scheme, purpose, frame, draft, outline, devise, contemplate, contrive, map out • *His projected visit to Washington had to be postponed.*
3 = **displace**, move, shift, attribute, assign, transpose, impute, externalize • *He projects his own thoughts and ideas onto her.*
4 = **launch**, shoot, throw, cast, transmit, discharge, hurl, fling, propel • *The hardware can be used for projecting nuclear missiles.*
5 = **stick out**, extend, stand out, bulge, beetle, protrude, overhang, jut • *A piece of metal projected out from the side.*

projectile = **missile**, shell, bullet, rocket • *an enormous artillery gun used to fire a huge projectile*

projecting = **sticking out**, prominent, standing out, bulging, protruding, overhanging, jutting, bulbous, obtrusive • *a piece of projecting metal*

projection = **forecast**, estimate, reckoning, prediction, calculation, estimation, computation, extrapolation • *the company's sales projections for the next year*

proletarian AS AN ADJECTIVE = **working-class**, common, cloth-cap (*informal*), plebeian, blue-singlet (*Austral. slang*) • *the issue of proletarian world solidarity*
▸ AS A NOUN = **worker**, commoner, Joe Bloggs (*Brit. informal*), pleb, plebeian, prole (*derogatory slang, chiefly Brit.*) • *The proletarians have nothing to lose but their chains.*

proletariat = **working class**, the masses, lower classes, commoners, the herd, wage-earners, lower orders, the common people, hoi polloi, plebs, the rabble, the great unwashed (*derogatory*), labouring classes, proles (*derogatory slang, chiefly Brit.*), commonalty • *a struggle between the bourgeoisie and the proletariat*
OPPOSITES: upper class, aristocracy, ruling class

proliferate = **increase**, expand, breed, mushroom, escalate, multiply, burgeon, snowball, run riot, grow rapidly • *the free Internet services that are proliferating across the world*

proliferation = **multiplication**, increase, spread, build-up, concentration, expansion, extension, step-up (*informal*), escalation, intensification • *the proliferation of nuclear weapons*

prolific 1 = **productive**, creative, fertile, inventive, copious • *a prolific writer of novels and short stories*
2 = **fruitful**, fertile, abundant, rich, rank, teeming, bountiful, luxuriant, generative, profuse, fecund • *Closer planting will give you a more prolific crop.*
OPPOSITES: barren, sterile, unproductive

prologue = **introduction**, preliminary, prelude, preface, preamble, foreword, proem, exordium • *The prologue to the novel is written in the form of a newspaper account.*

prolong = **lengthen**, continue, perpetuate, draw out, extend, delay, stretch out, carry on, spin out, drag out, make longer, protract • *He said foreign military aid was prolonging the war.*
OPPOSITES: cut, cut down, shorten

promenade AS A NOUN 1 = **walkway**, parade, boulevard, prom, esplanade, public walk • *a fine promenade running past the boathouses*
2 = **stroll**, walk, turn, airing, constitutional, saunter • *Take a tranquil promenade along a stretch of picturesque coastline.*
▸ AS A VERB 1 = **stroll**, walk, saunter, take a walk, perambulate, stretch your legs • *People came out to promenade along the front.*
2 = **parade**, strut, swagger, flaunt • *attracting attention as he promenaded up and down the street in his flashy clothes*

prominence 1 = **fame**, name, standing, rank, reputation, importance, celebrity, distinction, prestige, greatness, eminence, pre-eminence, notability, outstandingness • *He came to prominence during the World Cup in Italy.*
2 = **conspicuousness**, weight, precedence, top billing, specialness, salience, markedness • *Many papers give prominence to reports of the latest violence.*
3 = **protrusion**, swelling, projection, bulge, jutting, protuberance • *Birds have a prominence on the breast bone called a keel.*

prominent 1 = **famous**, leading, top, chief, important, main, noted, popular, respected, celebrated, outstanding, distinguished, well-known, notable, renowned, big-time (*informal*), foremost, eminent, major league (*informal*), pre-eminent, well-thought-of • *a prominent member of the Law Society*
OPPOSITES: minor, unknown, secondary
2 = **noticeable**, striking, obvious, outstanding, remarkable, pronounced, blatant, conspicuous, to the fore, unmistakable, eye-catching, salient, in the foreground, easily seen, obtrusive • *the lighthouses that are still a prominent feature of the Scottish coast*
OPPOSITES: insignificant, inconspicuous, indistinct
3 = **jutting**, projecting, standing out, bulging, hanging over, protruding, protuberant, protrusive • *a low forehead and prominent eyebrows*
OPPOSITES: receding, indented, concave

promiscuity = **licentiousness**, profligacy, sleeping around (*informal*), permissiveness, abandon, incontinence, depravity, immorality, debauchery, laxity, dissipation, looseness, amorality, lechery, laxness, wantonness, libertinism, promiscuousness • *Precautions against AIDS include wearing condoms and avoiding promiscuity.*

QUOTATIONS

She speaks eighteen languages. And she can't say no in any of them

[Dorothy Parker]

You were born with your legs apart. They'll send you to the grave in a Y-shaped coffin

[Joe Orton *What the Butler Saw*]

promiscuous 1 = **licentious**, wanton, profligate, debauched, fast, wild, abandoned, loose, immoral, lax, dissipated, unbridled, dissolute, libertine, of easy virtue, unchaste • *Everyone nowadays is aware of the risks of promiscuous sex.* • *She is perceived as vain, spoilt and promiscuous.*
OPPOSITES: moral, pure, chaste
2 = **mixed**, confused, disordered, diverse, chaotic, mingled, jumbled, miscellaneous, motley, indiscriminate, heterogeneous, intermingled, intermixed, ill-assorted • *a dazzling, promiscuous display of new styles*
OPPOSITES: ordered, organized, homogeneous

promise AS A VERB 1 = **guarantee**, pledge, vow, swear, contract, assure, undertake, warrant, plight, stipulate, vouch, take an oath, give an undertaking to, cross your heart, give your word • *They promised they would deliver it on Friday.*
2 = **seem likely**, look like, hint at, show signs of, bespeak, augur, betoken, lead you to expect, hold out hopes of, give hope of, bid fair, hold a probability of • *The seminar promises to be most instructive.*
▸ AS A NOUN 1 = **guarantee**, word, bond, vow, commitment, pledge, undertaking, assurance, engagement, compact, oath, covenant, word of honour • *If you make a promise, you should keep it.*
2 = **potential**, ability, talent, capacity, capability, flair, aptitude • *He first showed promise as an athlete in grade school.*

QUOTATIONS

We promise according to our hopes, and perform according to our fears

[La Rochefoucauld *Maxims*]

Promises and pie-crust are made to be broken

[Jonathan Swift *Polite Conversation*]

promising 1 = **encouraging**, likely, bright, reassuring, hopeful, favourable, rosy, auspicious, propitious, full of promise • *a new and promising stage in the negotiations*
OPPOSITES: discouraging, unfavourable, unpromising
2 = **talented**, able, gifted, rising, likely, up-and-coming • *one of the school's brightest and most promising pupils*

promontory = **point**, cape, head, spur, ness *(archaic)*, headland, foreland • *a promontory jutting out into the bay*

promote 1 = **help**, back, support, further, develop, aid, forward, champion, encourage, advance, work for, urge, boost, recommend, sponsor, foster, contribute to, assist, advocate, stimulate, endorse, prescribe, speak for, nurture, push for, espouse, popularize, gee up • *His country will do everything possible to promote peace.*
OPPOSITES: prevent, oppose, impede
2 = **advertise**, sell, hype, publicize, push, plug *(informal)*, puff, call attention to, beat the drum for *(informal)* • *He has announced a full British tour to promote his new album.*
3 = **raise**, upgrade, elevate, honour, dignify, exalt, kick upstairs *(informal)*, aggrandize • *I was promoted to editor and then editorial director.*
OPPOSITES: downgrade, demote, lower *or* reduce in rank

promoter 1 = **organizer**, arranger, entrepreneur, impresario • *one of the top boxing promoters in Britain*
2 = **supporter**, champion, advocate, campaigner, helper, proponent, stalwart, mainstay, upholder • *Aaron Copland was a most energetic promoter of American music.*

promotion 1 = **rise**, upgrading, move up, advancement, elevation, exaltation, preferment, aggrandizement, ennoblement • *rewarding outstanding employees with promotion*
2 = **publicity**, advertising, hype, pushing, plugging *(informal)*, propaganda, advertising campaign, hard sell, media hype, ballyhoo *(informal)*, puffery *(informal)*, boosterism • *The company spent a lot of money on advertising and promotion.*
3 = **encouragement**, backing, support, development, progress, boosting, advancement, advocacy, cultivation, espousal, furtherance, boosterism • *dedicated to the promotion of new ideas and research*

prompt AS A VERB 1 = **cause**, move, inspire, stimulate, occasion, urge, spur, provoke, motivate, induce, evoke, give rise to, elicit, incite, instigate, impel, call forth • *The recession has prompted consumers to cut back on buying cars.*
OPPOSITES: prevent, discourage, restrain
2 = **remind**, assist, cue, help out, prod, jog the memory, refresh the memory • *'What was that you were saying about a guided tour?' he prompted her.*
▸ AS AN ADJECTIVE 1 = **immediate**, quick, rapid, instant, timely, early, swift, on time, speedy, instantaneous, punctual, pdq *(slang)*, unhesitating • *an inflammation of the eyeball which needs prompt treatment*
OPPOSITES: late, slow, hesitating
2 = **quick**, ready, efficient, eager, willing, smart, alert, brisk, responsive, expeditious • *I was impressed by the prompt service I received.*
OPPOSITES: slack, inefficient, inactive
▸ AS AN ADVERB = **exactly**, sharp, promptly, on the dot, punctually • *The invitation specifies eight o'clock prompt.*
▸ AS A NOUN = **reminder**, hint, cue, help, spur, stimulus, jog, prod, jolt • *Her blushes were saved by a prompt from her host.*

prompting = **urging**, pressing, pressure, pushing, influence, reminding, suggestion, hint, assistance, reminder, encouragement, jogging, persuasion, prodding, incitement, clarion call, geeing-up • *The refugees need no prompting to describe what happened to them.*

promptly 1 = **immediately**, instantly, swiftly, directly, quickly, at once, speedily, by return, pronto *(informal)*, unhesitatingly, hotfoot, pdq *(slang)*, posthaste • *She lay down and promptly fell asleep.*
2 = **punctually**, on time, spot on *(informal)*, bang on *(informal)*, on the dot, on the button *(U.S.)*, on the nail • *We left the hotel promptly at seven.*

promptness = **swiftness**, speed, punctuality, willingness, dispatch, readiness, haste, eagerness, alertness, alacrity, quickness, briskness, promptitude • *the company's promptness in settling its debts*

promulgate 1 = **make known**, issue, announce, publish, spread, promote, advertise, broadcast, communicate, proclaim, circulate, notify, make public, disseminate • *Such behaviour promulgates a negative image of the British.*
2 = **make official**, pass, declare, decree • *bills limiting the FDA's authority to promulgate such regulations*

prone 1 = **liable**, given, subject, inclined, tending, bent, disposed, susceptible, apt, predisposed • *For all her experience, she was still prone to nerves.*
OPPOSITES: disinclined, indisposed
2 = **face down**, flat, lying down, horizontal, prostrate, recumbent, procumbent • *Bob slid from his chair and lay prone on the floor.*
OPPOSITES: erect, upright, face up

prong = **point**, tip, spike, tine • *Mark the loaf with the prongs of a fork.*

pronounce 1 = **say**, speak, voice, stress, sound, utter, articulate, enunciate, vocalize • *Have I pronounced your name correctly?*

2 = **declare**, announce, judge, deliver, assert, proclaim, decree, affirm • *A specialist has pronounced him fully fit.* • *They took time to pronounce their verdict.*

pronounced = **noticeable**, clear, decided, strong, marked, striking, obvious, broad, evident, distinct, definite, conspicuous, unmistakable, salient • *Most of the exhibition has a pronounced Scottish theme.*
OPPOSITES: hidden, concealed, imperceptible

pronouncement = **announcement**, statement, declaration, judgment, decree, manifesto, proclamation, notification, edict, dictum, promulgation, pronunciamento • *the President's latest pronouncement about the protection of minorities*

pronunciation = **intonation**, accent, speech, stress, articulation, inflection, diction, elocution, enunciation, accentuation • *You'll have to forgive my bad French pronunciation.*

proof AS A NOUN 1 = **evidence**, demonstration, testimony, confirmation, verification, certification, corroboration, authentication, substantiation, attestation • *You must have proof of residence in the state.*
2 = **trial print**, pull, slip, galley, page proof, galley proof, trial impression • *I'm correcting the proofs of the Spanish edition right now.*
▸ AS AN ADJECTIVE = **impervious**, strong, tight, resistant, impenetrable, repellent • *The fortress was proof against attack.*

PROVERBS
The proof of the pudding is in the eating

prop AS A VERB 1 = **lean**, place, set, stand, position, rest, lay, balance, steady • *He propped his bike against the fence.*
2 *often with* **up** = **support**, maintain, sustain, shore, hold up, brace, uphold, bolster, truss, buttress • *Plaster ceilings are propped with scaffolding.*
▸ AS A NOUN 1 = **support**, stay, brace, mainstay, truss, buttress, stanchion • *The timber is reinforced with three steel props on a concrete foundation.*
2 = **mainstay**, support, sustainer, anchor, backbone, cornerstone, upholder • *The army is one of the main props of the government.*
▸ IN PHRASES: **prop something** *or* **someone up** 1 = **rest**, place, set, stand, lean • *He slouched back and propped his elbows up on the bench behind him.*
2 = **subsidize**, support, fund, finance, maintain, underwrite, shore up, buttress, bolster up • *Investments in the US money markets have propped up the American dollar.*

propaganda = **information**, advertising, promotion, publicity, hype, brainwashing, disinformation, ballyhoo *(informal)*, agitprop, newspeak, boosterism • *He dismissed these reports as mere political propaganda.*

propagandist = **publicist**, advocate, promoter, proponent, evangelist, proselytizer, pamphleteer, indoctrinator • *He was a brilliant propagandist for free trade.*

propagate 1 = **spread**, publish, promote, broadcast, proclaim, transmit, circulate, diffuse, publicize, disseminate, promulgate, make known • *They propagated subversive political doctrines.*
OPPOSITES: suppress, hide, cover up
2 = **produce**, generate, engender, increase • *The easiest way to propagate a vine is to take cuttings.*
3 = **reproduce**, breed, multiply, proliferate, beget, procreate • *Tomatoes rot in order to transmit their seed and propagate the species.*

propagation 1 = **spreading**, spread, promotion, communication, distribution, circulation, transmission, diffusion, dissemination, promulgation • *working towards the propagation of true Buddhism*
2 = **reproduction**, generation, breeding, increase, proliferation, multiplication, procreation • *the successful propagation of a batch of new plants*

propel 1 = **drive**, launch, start, force, send, shoot, push, thrust, shove, set in motion • *The rocket is designed to propel the spacecraft.*
OPPOSITES: stop, pull, check
2 = **impel**, drive, push, prompt, spur, motivate • *He is propelled by the need to avenge his father.*
OPPOSITES: check, delay, hold back

propeller = **prop** *(informal)*, rotor, vane • *an aircraft with a fixed three-blade propeller*

propensity = **tendency**, leaning, weakness, inclination, bent, liability, bias, disposition, penchant, susceptibility, predisposition, proclivity, proneness, aptness • *She hadn't reckoned on his propensity for violence.*

proper 1 = **real**, actual, genuine, true, bona fide, kosher *(informal)*, dinkum *(Austral. & N.Z. informal)* • *Two out of five people do not have a proper job.*
2 = **correct**, accepted, established, appropriate, right, formal, conventional, accurate, exact, precise, legitimate, orthodox, apt • *Please ensure that the proper procedures are followed.*
OPPOSITES: inappropriate, improper, wrong
3 = **polite**, right, becoming, seemly, fitting, fit, mannerly, suitable, decent, gentlemanly, refined, respectable, befitting, genteel, de rigueur *(French)*, ladylike, meet *(archaic)*, decorous, punctilious, comme il faut *(French)* • *In those days it was not thought proper for a woman to be on the stage.*
OPPOSITES: common, crude, unseemly
4 = **characteristic**, own, special, individual, personal, particular, specific, peculiar, respective • *Make sure everything is in its proper place.*

properly 1 = **correctly**, rightly, fittingly, appropriately, legitimately, accurately, suitably, aptly, deservedly, as intended, in the true sense, in the accepted *or* approved manner • *The debate needs to be conducted properly.*
OPPOSITES: wrongly, incorrectly, improperly
2 = **politely**, respectfully, ethically, decently, respectably, decorously, punctiliously • *It's about time that brat learned to behave properly.*
OPPOSITES: badly, improperly, indecently

property 1 = **possessions**, goods, means, effects, holdings, capital, riches, resources, estate, assets, wealth, belongings, chattels • *Security forces confiscated weapons and stolen property.*
2 = **land**, holding, title, estate, acres, real estate, freehold, realty, real property • *He inherited a family property near Stamford.*
3 = **quality**, feature, characteristic, mark, ability, attribute, virtue, trait, hallmark, peculiarity, idiosyncrasy • *A radio signal has both electrical and magnetic properties.*

QUOTATIONS
Property is theft
[Pierre-Joseph Proudhon *Qu'est-ce que la Propriété?*]

prophecy 1 = **prediction**, forecast, revelation, prognosis, foretelling, prognostication, augury, sortilege, vaticination *(rare)* • *Nostradamus's prophecy of the end of the world*
2 = **second sight**, divination, augury, telling the future, soothsaying • *a child born with the gift of prophecy*

prophesy = **predict**, forecast, divine, foresee, augur, presage, foretell, forewarn, prognosticate, soothsay, vaticinate *(rare)* • *She prophesied the Great Fire of London and her own death in 1561.*

prophet *or* **prophetess** AS A NOUN = **soothsayer**, forecaster, diviner, oracle, seer, clairvoyant, augur, sibyl, prognosticator, prophesier • *Merlin, the legendary magician and prophet*
▸ IN PHRASES: **prophet of doom** = **pessimist**, Cassandra, Jeremiah, doom merchant, doom-monger, doomster • *The prophets of doom were predicting that the glory days were over.*
▸ RELATED ADJECTIVE: vatic

P

QUOTATIONS
A prophet is not without honour, but in his own country
[*Bible: St. Mark*]

prophetic = **predictive**, foreshadowing, presaging, prescient, divinatory, oracular, sibylline, prognostic, mantic, vatic *(rare)*, augural, fatidic *(rare)* • *This ominous warning soon proved prophetic.*

prophylactic AS AN ADJECTIVE = **preventative**, protective, preventive, precautionary • *vaccination and other prophylactic measures*
▸ AS A NOUN 1 = **preventative measure**, safeguard, precaution, safety measure, preventative medicine • *The region began to use quinine as a prophylactic.*
2 = **condom**, johnny *(informal)*, rubber *(U.S.)*, sheath, Durex *(Brit. trademark)*, Femidom *(Brit. trademark)*, something for the weekend *(informal)* • *the use of prophylactics for protection against sexually-transmitted disease*

propitiate = **appease**, satisfy, reconcile, placate, pacify, make peace with, mollify, conciliate • *These ancient ceremonies propitiate the spirits of the waters.*

propitious = **favourable**, timely, promising, encouraging, bright, lucky, fortunate, prosperous, rosy, advantageous, auspicious, opportune, full of promise • *the most propitious moment to launch the campaign*

proponent = **supporter**, friend, champion, defender, advocate, patron, enthusiast, subscriber, backer, partisan, exponent, apologist, upholder, vindicator, spokesman *or* spokeswoman • *a leading proponent of the values of progressive education*

proportion AS A NOUN 1 = **part**, share, cut *(informal)*, amount, measure, division, percentage, segment, quota, fraction • *A proportion of the rent is met by the city council.*
2 = **relative amount**, relationship, distribution, ratio • *the proportion of women in the profession* • *the proportion of length to breadth*
3 = **balance**, agreement, harmony, correspondence, symmetry, concord, congruity • *an artist with a special feel for colour and proportion*
▸ AS A PLURAL NOUN = **dimensions**, size, volume, capacity, extent, range, bulk, scope, measurements, magnitude, breadth, expanse, amplitude • *In the tropics, plants grow to huge proportions.*

P

proportional *or* **proportionate** = **correspondent**, equivalent, corresponding, even, balanced, consistent, comparable, compatible, equitable, in proportion, analogous, commensurate • *Loss of weight is directly proportional to the progress of the disease.*
OPPOSITES: different, inconsistent, disproportionate

proposal = **suggestion**, plan, programme, scheme, offer, terms, design, project, bid, motion, recommendation, tender, presentation, proposition, overture • *the government's proposals to abolish free health care*

propose 1 = **put forward**, present, suggest, advance, come up with, submit, tender, proffer, propound • *We are about to propose some changes to the system.*
2 = **intend**, mean, plan, aim, design, scheme, purpose, have in mind, have every intention • *I propose to spend my entire life travelling.*
3 = **nominate**, name, present, introduce, invite, recommend, put up • *He was proposed for renomination as party chairman.*
4 = **offer marriage**, pop the question *(informal)*, ask for someone's hand (in marriage), pay suit • *Merton proposed to her on bended knee.*

proposition AS A NOUN 1 = **task**, problem, activity, job, affair, venture, undertaking • *Designing his own flat was quite a different proposition to designing for clients.*
2 = **theory**, idea, argument, concept, thesis, hypothesis, theorem, premiss, postulation • *the proposition that monarchs derived their authority by divine right*
3 = **proposal**, plan, suggestion, scheme, bid, motion, recommendation • *I want to make you a business proposition.*
4 = **advance**, pass *(informal)*, proposal, overture, improper suggestion, come-on *(informal)* • *unwanted sexual propositions*
▸ AS A VERB = **make a pass at**, solicit, accost, make an indecent proposal to, make an improper suggestion to • *He had allegedly tried to proposition Miss Hawes.*

QUOTATIONS
It is more important that a proposition be interesting than that it be true
[A.N. Whitehead *Adventures of Ideas*]

propound = **put forward**, present, advance, propose, advocate, submit, suggest, lay down, contend, postulate, set forth • *She continues to propound her theories about the supernatural.*

proprietor *or* **proprietress** = **owner**, landowner, freeholder, possessor, titleholder, deed holder, landlord *or* landlady • *the proprietor of a local restaurant*

propriety AS A NOUN 1 = **decorum**, manners, courtesy, protocol, good form, decency, breeding, delicacy, modesty, respectability, etiquette, refinement, politeness, good manners, rectitude, punctilio, seemliness • *Their sense of social propriety is eroded.*
OPPOSITES: indecency, vulgarity, indecorum
2 = **correctness**, fitness, appropriateness, rightness, aptness, seemliness, suitableness • *They questioned the propriety of the corporation's use of public money.*
▸ IN PHRASES: **the proprieties** = **etiquette**, the niceties, the civilities, the amenities, the done thing, the social graces, the rules of conduct, the social conventions, social code, accepted conduct, kawa *(N.Z.)*, tikanga *(N.Z.)* • *respectable couples who observe the proprieties but loathe each other*

propulsion = **power**, pressure, push, thrust, momentum, impulse, impetus, motive power, impulsion, propelling force • *For some time electric propulsion has been seen as a possible answer.*

prosaic = **dull**, ordinary, boring, routine, flat, dry, everyday, tame, pedestrian, commonplace, mundane, matter-of-fact, stale, banal, uninspiring, humdrum, trite, unimaginative, hackneyed, workaday, vapid • *the aimless monotony of our prosaic everyday life*
OPPOSITES: interesting, exciting, unusual

proscribe 1 = **prohibit**, ban, forbid, boycott, embargo, interdict • *They are proscribed by federal law from owning guns.*
OPPOSITES: allow, permit, sanction
2 = **condemn**, reject, damn, denounce, censure • *Slang is reviled and proscribed by pedants and purists.*
3 = **outlaw**, exclude, exile, expel, banish, deport, expatriate, excommunicate, ostracize, blackball, attaint *(archaic)* • *He was proscribed in America, where his estate was put up for sale.*

proscription 1 = **prohibition**, ban, damning, dooming, boycott, embargo, rejection, condemnation, censure, denunciation, interdict • *the proscription of all customs not conforming to religious law*
2 = **banishment**, exile, exclusion, expulsion, deportation, eviction, ejection, ostracism, excommunication, expatriation, attainder *(archaic)*, outlawry • *her proscription by the party's leaders*

prose

QUOTATIONS
Prose = words in their best order; poetry = the best words in their best order
[Samuel Taylor Coleridge *Table Talk*]
Prose is when all the lines except the last go on to the end. Poetry is when some of them fall short of it
[Jeremy Bentham]
All that is not prose is verse; and all that is not verse is prose
[Molière *Le Bourgeois Gentilhomme*]

prosecute 1 = **take someone to court**, try, sue, summon, indict, do *(slang)*, arraign, seek redress, put someone on trial, litigate, bring suit against, bring someone to trial, put someone in the dock, bring action against, prefer charges against • *The police have decided not to prosecute him.*
2 = **conduct**, continue, manage, direct, pursue, work at, carry on, practise, engage in, discharge, persist, see through, follow through, persevere, carry through • *To prosecute this war is costing the country fifteen million pounds a day.*

prosecution = **trial**, trying • *the prosecution of those responsible*

prosecutor = **lawyer**, attorney, counsel, procurator fiscal *(Scot.)*, prosecuting attorney *(U.S.)* • *The public prosecutor modified the charges against him.*

proselytize 1 = **convert**, win over, spread the gospel to, evangelize to, make converts of, bring someone into the fold, bring someone to God • *Christian groups were arrested for trying to proselytize people.*
2 = **promote**, support, champion, back, present, further, suggest, advance, spread, urge, boost, sponsor, foster, advocate, endorse, proclaim, preach, peddle, espouse, propound, propagandize • *a Scottish lawyer who proselytized these ideas*

prospect AS A NOUN 1 = **likelihood**, chance, possibility, plan, hope, promise, proposal, odds, expectation, probability, anticipation, presumption • *There is little prospect of having these questions answered.*
2 = **idea**, thought, outlook, contemplation • *the pleasant prospect of a quiet night in*
3 = **view**, perspective, landscape, scene, sight, vision, outlook, spectacle, panorama, vista • *The windows overlooked the superb prospect of the hills.*
▸ AS A PLURAL NOUN = **possibilities**, openings, chances, future, potential, expectations, outlook, scope • *I chose to work abroad to improve my career prospects.*
▸ AS A VERB = **look**, search, seek, survey, explore, drill, go after, dowse • *The companies are prospecting for oil not far from here.*
▸ IN PHRASES: **in prospect** = **in view**, planned, projected, on the way, in sight, in store, on the cards, in the wind, on the horizon, coming soon, likely to happen, in the offing • *Further defence cuts are now in prospect.*

prospective 1 = **potential**, possible, to come, about to be, upcoming, soon-to-be • *The story is a warning to other prospective buyers.*
2 = **expected**, coming, future, approaching, likely, looked-for, intended, awaited, hoped-for, anticipated, forthcoming, imminent, destined, eventual, on the cards • *The terms of the prospective deal are spelled out clearly.*

prospectus = **catalogue**, plan, list, programme, announcement, outline, brochure, handbook, syllabus, synopsis, conspectus • *Read their prospectus to see what's on offer.*

prosper = **succeed**, advance, progress, thrive, make it *(informal)*, flower, get on, do well, flourish, bloom, make good, be fortunate, grow rich, fare well • *The high street banks continue to prosper.*

prosperity = **success**, riches, plenty, ease, fortune, wealth, boom, luxury, well-being, good times, good fortune, the good life, affluence, top dollar *(informal)*, life of luxury, life of Riley *(informal)*, prosperousness • *a life of peace and prosperity*
OPPOSITES: poverty, want, failure

prosperous 1 = **wealthy**, rich, affluent, well-off, in the money *(informal)*, blooming, opulent, well-heeled *(informal)*, well-to-do, moneyed, in clover *(informal)*, minted *(Brit. slang)* • *the youngest son of a prosperous family*
OPPOSITES: poor, impoverished
2 = **successful**, booming, thriving, flourishing, doing well, prospering, on a roll, on the up and up *(Brit.)*, palmy • *He has developed a prosperous business.*
OPPOSITES: failing, unfortunate, unsuccessful

prostitute AS A NOUN = **whore**, hooker *(U.S. slang)*, pro *(slang)*, brass *(slang)*, tart *(informal)*, hustler *(U.S. & Canad. slang)*, moll *(slang)*, call girl, courtesan, working girl *(facetious slang)*, harlot, streetwalker, camp follower, loose woman, fallen woman, scrubber *(Brit. & Austral. slang)*, strumpet, trollop, white slave, bawd *(archaic)*, cocotte, fille de joie *(French)* • *He admitted that he had paid for sex with a prostitute.*
▸ AS A VERB = **cheapen**, sell out, pervert, degrade, devalue, squander, demean, debase, profane, misapply • *His friends said that he had prostituted his talents.*

prostitution = **harlotry**, the game *(slang)*, vice, the oldest profession, whoredom, streetwalking, harlot's trade, Mrs. Warren's profession • *She eventually drifted into prostitution.*

prostrate AS AN ADJECTIVE 1 = **prone**, fallen, flat, horizontal, abject, bowed low, kowtowing, procumbent • *Percy was lying prostrate with his arms outstretched.*
2 = **exhausted**, overcome, depressed, drained, spent, worn out, desolate, dejected, inconsolable, at a low ebb, fagged out *(informal)* • *After my mother's death, I was prostrate with grief.*
3 = **helpless**, overwhelmed, disarmed, paralysed, powerless, reduced, impotent, defenceless, brought to your knees • *Gaston was prostrate on his sickbed.*
▸ AS A VERB = **exhaust**, tire, drain, fatigue, weary, sap, wear out, fag out *(informal)* • *patients who have been prostrated by fatigue*
▸ IN PHRASES: **prostrate yourself** = **bow down**, submit, kneel, cringe, grovel, fall at someone's feet, bow, kowtow, bend the knee, abase yourself, cast yourself, fall on your knees • *They prostrated themselves before the king in awe and fear.*

protagonist 1 = **supporter**, leader, champion, advocate, exponent, mainstay, prime mover, standard-bearer, moving spirit, torchbearer • *an active protagonist of his country's membership of the EU*
2 = **leading character**, lead, principal, central character, hero *or* heroine • *the protagonist of J.D. Salinger's novel*

protean = **changeable**, variable, volatile, versatile, temperamental, ever-changing, mercurial, many-sided, mutable, polymorphous, multiform • *the protean and complex nature of his work*

protect = **keep someone safe**, defend, keep, support, save, guard, secure, preserve, look after, foster, shelter, shield, care for, harbour, safeguard, watch over, stick up for *(informal)*, cover up for, chaperon, give someone sanctuary, take someone under your wing, mount *or* stand guard over • *He vowed to protect her all the days of her life.*
OPPOSITES: attack, threaten, endanger

protection 1 = **safety**, charge, care, defence, protecting, security, guarding, custody, safeguard, preservation, aegis, guardianship, safekeeping • *The primary duty of parents is the protection of their children.*
2 = **safeguard**, cover, guard, shelter, screen, barrier, shield, refuge, buffer, bulwark • *Innocence is no protection from the evils in our society.*
3 = **armour**, cover, screen, barrier, shelter, shield, bulwark • *Riot shields acted as protection against the attack.*

protective 1 = **protecting**, covering, sheltering, shielding, safeguarding, insulating • *Protective gloves reduce the absorption of chemicals through the skin.*
2 = **caring**, defensive, motherly, fatherly, warm, careful, maternal, vigilant, watchful, paternal, possessive • *He is very protective towards his sisters.*

protector 1 = **defender**, champion, guard, guardian, counsel, advocate, patron, safeguard, bodyguard, benefactor, guardian angel, tower of strength, knight in

shining armour • *Many mothers see their son as a protector and provider.*
2 = guard, screen, protection, shield, pad, cushion, buffer • *Ear protectors must be worn when operating this equipment.*

protégé *or* **protégée = charge**, student, pupil, ward, discovery, dependant • *Klimt's young protégé, Egon Schiele*

protein
▹ *See panel* **Proteins**

protest AS A VERB **1 = object**, demonstrate, oppose, complain, disagree, cry out, disapprove, say no to, demur, take exception, remonstrate, kick against *(informal)*, expostulate, take up the cudgels, express disapproval • *Women took to the streets to protest against the arrests.*
2 = assert, argue, insist, maintain, declare, vow, testify, contend, affirm, profess, attest, avow, asseverate • *'I never said that,' he protested.*
▸ AS A NOUN **1 = demonstration**, march, rally, sit-in, demo *(informal)*, hikoi *(N.Z.)* • *The opposition staged a protest against the government.*
2 = objection, complaint, declaration, dissent, outcry, disapproval, protestation, demur, formal complaint, remonstrance, demurral • *a protest against people's growing economic hardship*

QUOTATIONS
The lady doth protest too much methinks
[William Shakespeare *Hamlet*]

protestation 1 = declaration, pledge, vow, oath, profession, affirmation, avowal, asseveration • *his constant protestations of love and devotion*
2 = objection, protest, complaint, disagreement, dissent, remonstrance, expostulation, remonstration • *Graham's protestation that he has been unjustly treated*

protester 1 = demonstrator, rebel, dissident, dissenter, agitator, picketers, protest marcher • *anti-abortion protesters*
2 = objector, opposer, complainer, opponent, dissident, dissenter • *Protesters say the government is corrupt.*

protocol 1 = code of behaviour, manners, courtesies, conventions, customs, formalities, good form, etiquette, propriety, decorum, rules of conduct, politesse, p's and q's • *He is a stickler for royal protocol.*
2 = agreement, contract, treaty, convention, pact, compact, covenant, concordat • *the Montreal Protocol to phase out use and production of CFCs*

prototype = original, model, precedent, first, example, standard, paradigm, archetype, mock-up • *He has built a prototype of a machine called the wave rotor.* • *the prototype aircraft*

protracted = extended, long, prolonged, lengthy, time-consuming, never-ending, drawn-out, interminable, spun out, dragged out, long-drawn-out, overlong • *The struggle was bitter and protracted.*

protrude = stick out, start (from), point, project, pop *(of an eye)*, extend, come through, stand out, bulge, shoot out, jut, stick out like a sore thumb, obtrude • *A huge round mass of rock protruded from the water.*

protruding = sticking out, projecting, prominent, swollen, standing out, bulging, overhanging, jutting (out), bulbous, distended, obtrusive, protuberant • *protruding ears*

protrusion = protuberance, swelling, lump, bump, projection, bulge, hump, jut, outgrowth • *an ugly protrusion on the ankle where the bone had not set properly*

protuberance = bulge, swelling, lump, bump, tumour, projection, prominence, knob, hump, outgrowth, protrusion, excrescence • *a protuberance on the upper jawbone*

proud 1 = satisfied, pleased, content, contented, honoured, thrilled, glad, gratified, joyful, appreciative, well-pleased • *I am proud to be a Scot.*
OPPOSITES: discontented, dissatisfied, displeased
2 = glorious, rewarding, memorable, pleasing, satisfying, illustrious, gratifying, exalted, red-letter • *My daughter's graduation was a proud moment for me.*
3 = distinguished, great, grand, imposing, magnificent, noble, august, splendid, eminent, majestic, stately, illustrious • *The American Indians were a proud and noble people.*
OPPOSITES: base, humble, lowly
4 = conceited, vain, arrogant, stuck-up *(informal)*, lordly, imperious, narcissistic, overbearing, snooty *(informal)*, haughty, snobbish, egotistical, self-satisfied, disdainful, self-important, presumptuous, boastful, supercilious, high and mighty *(informal)*, toffee-nosed *(slang, chiefly Brit.)*, too big for your boots *or* breeches • *She has a reputation for being proud and arrogant.*
OPPOSITES: modest, humble, ashamed

prove AS A VERB **1 = turn out**, come out, end up, be found to be • *In the past this process has proved difficult.*
2 = verify, establish, determine, show, evidence, confirm, demonstrate, justify, ascertain, bear out, attest, substantiate, corroborate, authenticate, evince, show clearly • *new evidence that could prove their innocence*
OPPOSITES: rule out, discredit, disprove
▸ IN PHRASES: **prove yourself = show yourself**, demonstrate your ability • *Now's your chance to prove yourself.* • *She proved herself to be a good mother.*

proven = established, accepted, proved, confirmed, tried, tested, checked, reliable, valid, definite, authentic, certified, verified, attested, undoubted, dependable, trustworthy • *There is a proven link between smoking and lung cancer.*

provenance = origin, source, birthplace, derivation • *art treasures of indisputably Egyptian provenance*

proverb = saying, saw, maxim, gnome, adage, dictum, aphorism, byword, apophthegm • *the old proverb 'where there's a will, there's a way'*

proverbial = conventional, accepted, traditional, famous, acknowledged, typical, well-known, legendary, notorious, customary, famed, archetypal, time-honoured, self-evident, unquestioned, axiomatic • *He was the proverbial pillar of strength.*

provide AS A VERB **1 = supply**, give, contribute, provision, distribute, outfit, equip, accommodate, donate, furnish, dispense, part with, fork out *(informal)*, stock up, cater to, purvey • *I will be happy to provide you with a copy of the report.* • *They did not provide any food.*
OPPOSITES: refuse, deprive, withhold
2 = give, bring, add, produce, present, serve, afford, yield, lend, render, impart • *The summit will provide an opportunity for discussions on the crisis.*

PROTEINS

actin	calmodulin	fibrinogen	keratin	myosin	sericin
actomyosin	caseinogen	fibroin	lactalbumin	opsin	spongin
aleurone	conchiolin	flagellin	lactoprotein	ossein	thrombogen
alpha-fetoprotein	dystrophin	gliadin	lectin	prion	vitellin
amyloid	factor VIII	globin	legumin	properdin	zein
apoprotein	ferritin	gluten	leptin	ricin	
avidin	fibrin	hordein	lymphokine	sclerotin	

3 = **stipulate**, state, require, determine, specify, lay down • *The treaty provides that, by 2000, the US must have removed its military bases.*
▸ **IN PHRASES: provide for someone = support**, look after, care for, keep, maintain, sustain, take care of, fend for • *He can't even provide for his family.*
provide for or against something = take precautions against, plan for, prepare for, anticipate, arrange for, get ready for, make plans for, make arrangements for, plan ahead for, take measures against, forearm for • *James had provided for just such an emergency.*

providence = fate, fortune, destiny, God's will, divine intervention, predestination • *I regard his death as an act of providence.*

providential = lucky, timely, happy, welcome, fortunate, fortuitous, opportune, heaven-sent • *The bubonic plague was an almost providential killing off of Europe's excess population.*

provider 1 = **supplier**, giver, source, donor, benefactor • *Japan is the largest provider of foreign aid in the world.*
2 = **breadwinner**, supporter, earner, mainstay, wage earner • *A husband's job is to be a good provider.*

providing *or* **provided** *often with* **that = on condition that**, if, subject to, given that, on the assumption that, in the event that, with the proviso that, contingent upon, with the understanding that, as long as, if and only if, upon these terms • *She always believes me, providing I tell her what she wants to hear.*

province 1 = **region**, section, county, district, territory, zone, patch, colony, domain, dependency, tract • *the Algarve, Portugal's southernmost province*
2 = **area**, business, concern, responsibility, part, line, charge, role, post, department, field, duty, function, employment, capacity, orbit, sphere, turf (*U.S. slang*), pigeon (*Brit. informal*) • *Industrial research is the province of the Department of Trade and Industry.*
▹ *See panels* **Canadian provinces; South African provinces and provinicial capitals**

provincial AS AN ADJECTIVE 1 = **regional**, state, local, county, district, territorial, parochial • *The local and provincial elections take place in June.*
2 = **rural**, country, local, home-grown, rustic, homespun, hick (*informal, chiefly U.S. & Canad.*), backwoods • *My accent gave away my provincial roots.*
OPPOSITES: urban
3 = **parochial**, insular, narrow-minded, unsophisticated, limited, narrow, small-town (*chiefly U.S.*), uninformed, inward-looking, small-minded, parish-pump, upcountry • *The audience was dull and very provincial.*
OPPOSITES: sophisticated, refined, cosmopolitan
▸ **AS A NOUN = yokel**, hick (*informal, chiefly U.S. & Canad.*), rustic, country cousin, hayseed (*U.S. & Canad. informal*) • *French provincials looking for work in Paris*

provision AS A NOUN 1 = **supplying**, giving, providing, supply, delivery, distribution, catering, presentation, equipping, furnishing, allocation, fitting out, purveying, accoutrement • *the provision of military supplies to the Khmer Rouge*
2 = **arrangement**, plan, planning, preparation, precaution, contingency, prearrangement • *There is no provision for funding performance-related pay increases.*
3 = **facilities**, services, funds, resources, means, opportunities, arrangements, assistance, concession(s), allowance(s), amenities • *Special provision should be made for single mothers.*
4 = **condition**, term, agreement, requirement, demand, rider, restriction, qualification, clause, reservation, specification, caveat, proviso, stipulation • *a provision that would allow existing regulations to be reviewed*
▸ **AS A PLURAL NOUN = food**, supplies, stores, feed, fare, rations, eats (*slang*), groceries, tack (*informal*), grub (*slang*), foodstuff, kai (*N.Z. informal*), sustenance, victuals, edibles, comestibles, provender, nosebag (*slang*), vittles (*obsolete dialect*), viands, eatables • *On board were enough provisions for two weeks.*

provisional 1 = **temporary**, interim, transitional, stopgap, pro tem • *the possibility of setting up a provisional coalition government*
OPPOSITES: permanent
2 = **conditional**, limited, qualified, contingent, tentative, provisory • *The times stated are provisional and subject to confirmation.*
OPPOSITES: fixed, definite

provisionally = tentatively, conditionally, subject to confirmation • *The EU has provisionally agreed to increase the quotas.*

proviso = condition, requirement, provision, strings, rider, restriction, qualification, clause, reservation, limitation, stipulation • *I accept, with the proviso that Jane agrees.*

provocation 1 = **cause**, reason, grounds, motivation, justification, stimulus, inducement, incitement, instigation, casus belli (*Latin*) • *The soldiers fired without provocation.*
2 = **offence**, challenge, insult, taunt, injury, dare, grievance, annoyance, affront, indignity, red rag, vexation • *They kept their tempers in the face of severe provocation.*

provocative 1 = **offensive**, provoking, insulting, challenging, disturbing, stimulating, annoying, outrageous, aggravating (*informal*), incensing, galling, goading • *Their behaviour was called provocative and antisocial.*

CANADIAN PROVINCES

Province	Abbreviation	Province	Abbreviation	Province	Abbreviation
Alberta	AB	Northwest Territories	NWT	Quebec	PQ
British Columbia	BC	Nova Scotia	NS	Saskatchewan	SK
Manitoba	MB	Nunavut	NU	Yukon Territory	YT
New Brunswick	NB	Ontario	ON		
Newfoundland	NF	Prince Edward Island	PE		

SOUTH AFRICAN PROVINCES AND PROVINCIAL CAPITALS

Province	Capital	Province	Capital	Province	Capital
Eastern Cape	Bisho	KwaZulu-Natal	Pietermaritzburg	North-West	Mafikeng
Free State	Bloemfontein	Limpopo	Pietersburg	Northern Cape	Kimberley
Gauteng	Johannesburg	Mpumalanga	Nelspruit	Western Cape	Cape Town

2 = **suggestive**, tempting, stimulating, exciting, inviting, sexy *(informal)*, arousing, erotic, seductive, alluring, tantalizing • *sexually provocative behaviour*

provoke 1 = **anger**, insult, annoy, offend, irritate, infuriate, hassle *(informal)*, aggravate *(informal)*, incense, enrage, gall, put someone out, madden, exasperate, vex, affront, chafe, irk, rile, pique, get on someone's nerves *(informal)*, get someone's back up, piss someone off *(taboo slang)*, put someone's back up, try someone's patience, nark *(Brit., Austral. & N.Z. slang)*, make someone's blood boil, get in someone's hair *(informal)*, rub someone up the wrong way, hack someone off *(informal)* • *I didn't want to do anything to provoke him.*
OPPOSITES: calm, appease, pacify
2 = **rouse**, cause, produce, lead to, move, fire, promote, occasion, excite, inspire, generate, prompt, stir, stimulate, motivate, induce, bring about, evoke, give rise to, precipitate, elicit, inflame, incite, instigate, kindle, foment, call forth, draw forth, bring on *or* down • *His comments have provoked a shocked reaction.*
OPPOSITES: ease, relieve, curb

QUOTATIONS
No-one provokes me with impunity (Nemo me impune lacessit)
[*Motto of the Crown of Scotland and of all Scottish regiments*]

prow = **bow(s)**, head, front, nose, stem, fore, sharp end *(jocular)*, forepart • *the prow of the ship*

prowess 1 = **skill**, ability, talent, expertise, facility, command, genius, excellence, accomplishment, mastery, attainment, aptitude, dexterity, adroitness, adeptness, expertness • *He's always bragging about his prowess as a cricketer.*
OPPOSITES: inability, incompetence, ineptitude
2 = **bravery**, daring, courage, heroism, mettle, boldness, gallantry, valour, fearlessness, intrepidity, hardihood, valiance, dauntlessness, doughtiness • *a race of people noted for their fighting prowess*
OPPOSITES: fear, cowardice, timidity

prowl = **move stealthily**, hunt, patrol, range, steal, cruise, ghost, stalk, sneak, lurk, roam, rove, scavenge, slink, skulk, nose around • *The stray dogs of the city prowl in packs in search of food.*

proximity = **nearness**, closeness, vicinity, neighbourhood, juxtaposition, contiguity, propinquity, adjacency • *families living in close proximity to one another*

proxy = **representative**, agent, deputy, substitute, factor, attorney, delegate, surrogate • *She sent him as her proxy to board meetings.*

prude = **prig**, puritan, goody-goody *(informal)*, old maid *(informal)*, stuffed shirt *(informal)*, schoolmarm *(Brit. informal)*, Holy Joe *(informal)*, Holy Willie *(informal)* • *I'm no prude but I've never heard such filth.*

prudence 1 = **caution**, care, discretion, vigilance, wariness, circumspection, canniness, heedfulness • *He urged prudence rather than haste on any new resolution.*
2 = **wisdom**, common sense, good sense, good judgment, sagacity, judiciousness • *acting with prudence and judgement*
3 = **thrift**, economy, planning, saving, precaution, foresight, providence, preparedness, good management, husbandry, frugality, forethought, economizing, far-sightedness, careful budgeting • *A lack of prudence may lead to financial problems.*

QUOTATIONS
I would rather worry without need than live without heed
[Beaumarchais *The Barber of Seville*]
Prudence is a rich, ugly, old maid courted by incapacity
[William Blake *Proverbs of Hell*]

PROVERBS
Take care of the pennies and the pounds will look after themselves
A stitch in time saves nine
Waste not, want not

prudent 1 = **cautious**, careful, wary, discreet, canny, vigilant, circumspect • *He is taking a prudent and cautious approach.*
OPPOSITES: rash, careless, thoughtless
2 = **wise**, politic, sensible, sage, shrewd, discerning, judicious, sagacious • *We believed ours was the prudent and responsible course of action.*
OPPOSITES: irrational, unwise, imprudent
3 = **thrifty**, economical, sparing, careful, canny, provident, frugal, far-sighted • *In private, she is prudent and even frugal.*
OPPOSITES: extravagant, careless, wasteful

prudery = **primness**, stuffiness, squeamishness, strictness, prudishness, priggishness, starchiness *(informal)*, old-maidishness *(informal)*, overmodesty, puritanicalness • *the legacy of Victorian prudery that regarded sex as a bestial activity*

prudish = **prim**, formal, proper, stuffy, puritanical, demure, squeamish, narrow-minded, starchy *(informal)*, prissy *(informal)*, strait-laced, Victorian, priggish, schoolmarmish *(Brit. informal)*, old-maidish *(informal)*, niminy-piminy, overmodest, overnice • *His novels are not for prudish readers.*
OPPOSITES: liberal, open-minded, broad-minded

prune 1 = **cut**, trim, clip, dock, shape, cut back, shorten, snip, lop, pare down • *You have to prune the bushes if you want fruit.*
2 = **reduce**, cut, cut back, trim, cut down, pare down, make reductions in • *Economic hard times are forcing the company to prune their budget.*

prurient 1 = **lecherous**, longing, lewd, salacious, lascivious, itching, hankering, voyeuristic, lustful, libidinous, desirous, concupiscent • *our prurient fascination with sexual scandals*
2 = **indecent**, dirty, erotic, obscene, steamy *(informal)*, pornographic, X-rated *(informal)*, salacious, smutty • *the film's harshly prurient and cynical sex scenes*

pry = **be inquisitive**, peer, interfere, poke, peep, meddle, intrude, snoop *(informal)*, nose into, be nosy *(informal)*, be a busybody, ferret about, poke your nose in *or* into *(informal)* • *We do not want people prying into our affairs.*

prying = **inquisitive**, spying, curious, interfering, meddling, intrusive, eavesdropping, snooping *(informal)*, snoopy *(informal)*, impertinent, nosy *(informal)*, meddlesome • *She's a nasty, prying busybody.*

psalm = **hymn**, carol, chant, paean, song of praise • *He recited the twenty-third psalm.*

pseud = **poser** *(informal)*, fraud, phoney *or* phony *(informal)*, trendy *(Brit. informal)*, humbug • *They should be exposed for the snobs and pseuds they truly are.*

pseudo- = **false**, pretended, artificial, fake, phoney *or* phony *(informal)*, mock, imitation, bogus, sham, counterfeit, spurious, ersatz, not genuine, quasi- • *What a load of pompous, pseudo-intellectual rubbish!*
OPPOSITES: genuine, authentic, real

pseudonym = **false name**, alias, incognito, stage name, pen name, assumed name, nom de guerre, nom de plume, professional name • *Both plays were published under the pseudonym of Philip Dayre.*

psych AS A VERB
▸ IN PHRASES: **psych someone out** = **unsettle**, upset, disturb, intimidate, cow, daunt, put someone off, agitate, unnerve, make someone nervous • *his ability to wear you down and psych you out*
psych yourself up = **prepare yourself**, get in the mood, steel yourself, get in the right frame of mind, gear yourself up, nerve yourself, summon up your courage, gird your loins • *After work, it's hard to psych yourself up for an hour at the gym.*

psyche = **soul**, mind, self, spirit, personality, individuality, subconscious, true being, anima, essential nature, pneuma

(Philosophy), innermost self, inner man, wairua *(N.Z.)* • *Knowledge of the human psyche has advanced immeasurably since Freud.*

psychedelic 1 = **hallucinogenic**, mind-blowing *(informal)*, psychoactive, hallucinatory, mind-bending *(informal)*, psychotropic, mind-expanding, consciousness-expanding, psychotomimetic • *experimenting with psychedelic drugs* 2 = **multicoloured**, wild, crazy, freaky *(slang)*, kaleidoscopic • *psychedelic patterns*

psychiatrist = **psychotherapist**, analyst, therapist, psychologist, shrink *(slang)*, psychoanalyst, psychoanalyser, headshrinker *(slang)* • *He has been seeing a psychiatrist for years.*

QUOTATIONS
We believe that civilization has been created under the pressure of the exigencies of life at the cost of satisfaction of the instincts
[Sigmund Freud *Introductory Lectures on Psychoanalysis*]
Anyone who goes to see a psychiatrist needs his head examined
[Samuel Goldwyn]

psychic AS AN ADJECTIVE 1 = **supernatural**, mystic, occult, clairvoyant, telepathic, extrasensory, preternatural, telekinetic • *Trevor helped police by using his psychic powers.* 2 = **mystical**, spiritual, magical, other-worldly, paranormal, preternatural • *He declared his total disbelief in psychic phenomena.* 3 = **psychological**, emotional, mental, spiritual, inner, psychiatric, cognitive, psychogenic • *Childhood mistreatment is the primary cause of every kind of psychic disorder.*
▸ AS A NOUN = **clairvoyant**, prophet, seer, fortune teller, spiritualist, soothsayer • *a natural psychic who used Tarot as a focus for his intuition*

psychological 1 = **mental**, emotional, intellectual, inner, cognitive, cerebral • *the treatment of psychological disorders* 2 = **imaginary**, psychosomatic, unconscious, subconscious, subjective, irrational, unreal, all in the mind • *My GP dismissed my back pains as purely psychological.*

psychology 1 = **behaviourism**, study of personality, science of mind • *He is Professor of Psychology at Bedford Community College.* 2 = **way of thinking**, attitude, behaviour, temperament, mentality, thought processes, mental processes, what makes you tick, mental make-up • *a fascination with the psychology of serial killers*

QUOTATIONS
There is no psychology; there is only biography and autobiography
[Thomas Szasz *The Second Sin*]

▹ *See panel* **Psychology**

psychopath = **madman**, lunatic, maniac, psychotic, nutter *(Brit. slang)*, basket case *(slang)*, nutcase *(slang)*, sociopath, headcase *(informal)*, mental case *(slang)*, headbanger *(informal)*, insane person, crazy *(informal)* • *She was abducted by a dangerous psychopath.*

psychopathic = **mad**, crazy *(informal)*, insane, disturbed, unstable, manic, mentally ill, crazed, lunatic, demented, unbalanced, deranged, unhinged, maniacal, certifiable • *a psychopathic killer*

psychosomatic = **(all) in the mind**, psychological, unconscious, subconscious, subjective, irrational, unreal • *Doctors refused to treat her, saying her problems were psychosomatic.*

psychotic AS AN ADJECTIVE = **mad**, mental *(slang)*, insane, lunatic, demented, unbalanced, deranged, psychopathic, round the bend *(Brit. slang)*, certifiable, off your head *(slang)*, off your trolley *(slang)*, not right in the head, non compos mentis *(Latin)*, off your rocker *(slang)*, off your chump • *He was diagnosed as psychotic and schizophrenic.*
▸ AS A NOUN = **lunatic**, maniac, psychopath, nut *(slang)*, psycho *(slang)*, loony *(slang)*, madman, nutter *(Brit. slang)*, basket case *(slang)*, nutcase *(slang)*, headcase *(informal)*, mental case *(slang)*, headbanger *(informal)*, crazy *(informal)* • *Personality disorder can be found in some psychotics.*

pub *or* **public house** = **tavern**, bar, inn, local *(Brit. informal)*, saloon, watering hole *(facetious slang)*, boozer *(Brit., Austral. & N.Z. informal)*, beer parlour *(Canad.)*, beverage room *(Canad.)*, roadhouse, hostelry *(archaic, facetious)*, alehouse *(archaic)*, taproom • *He was in the pub until closing time.*

QUOTATIONS
There is nothing which has yet been contrived by man, by which so much happiness is produced, as by a good tavern or inn
[Dr. Johnson]

puberty = **adolescence**, teenage, teens, young adulthood, pubescence, awkward age, juvenescence • *Lucy had reached the age of puberty.*
▸ RELATED ADJECTIVE: hebetic

public AS A NOUN 1 = **people**, society, country, population, masses, community, nation, everyone, citizens, voters, electorate, multitude, populace, hoi polloi, Joe Public *(slang)*, Joe Six-Pack *(U.S. slang)*, commonalty • *The poll is a test of the public's confidence in the government.* 2 = **clientele**, fans, supporters, following, followers, audience, buyers, patrons • *She won't do anything that makes her look bad to her public.*
▸ AS AN ADJECTIVE 1 = **civic**, government, state, national, local, official, community, social, federal, civil, constitutional, municipal • *a substantial part of public spending* 2 = **general**, popular, national, shared, common, widespread, universal, collective • *Parliament's decision was in line with public opinion.* 3 = **open**, community, accessible, communal, open to the public, unrestricted, free to all, not private • *a public library*
OPPOSITES: private, closed, personal
4 = **well-known**, leading, important, respected, famous, celebrated, recognized, distinguished, prominent, influential, notable, renowned, eminent, famed, noteworthy, in the public eye • *He hit out at public figures who commit adultery.* 5 = **known**, published, exposed, open, obvious, acknowledged, recognized, plain, patent, notorious, overt, in circulation • *She was reluctant to make her views public.*
OPPOSITES: secret, hidden, unknown
▸ IN PHRASES: **in public** = **openly**, publicly, overtly, for all to see, in full view, coram populo *(Latin)* • *by-laws to make it illegal to smoke in public*

QUOTATIONS
You have to look very carefully at your motives if you become a public figure
[Harold Pinter *One for the Road*]

publication 1 = **pamphlet**, book, newspaper, magazine, issue, title, leaflet, brochure, booklet, paperback, hardback, periodical, zine *(informal)*, handbill, blog *(informal)* • *a renewed campaign against pornographic publications* 2 = **announcement**, publishing, broadcasting, reporting, airing, appearance, declaration, advertisement, disclosure, proclamation, notification, dissemination, promulgation • *We have no comment regarding the publication of these photographs.*

publicist = **PR agent**, spin doctor, public relations man or woman • *He doesn't even have a publicist – almost unheard of for a Hollywood star.*

publicity 1 = **advertising**, press, promotion, hype, boost, build-up, plug *(informal)*, puff, ballyhoo *(informal)*, puffery *(informal)*, boosterism • *Much advance publicity was given to the talks.* 2 = **attention**, exposure, fame, celebrity, fuss, public

PSYCHOLOGY

Branches of psychology

analytic psychology, child psychology, clinical psychology, comparative psychology, developmental psychology, educational psychology, experimental psychology, hedonics, industrial psychology, neuropsychology, organizational psychology, parapsychology, psychiatry, psycholinguistics, psychometrics, psychophysics, psychophysiology, social psychology

Psychology terms

alter ego, anal, analysis, angst, anxiety, complex, compulsion, conditioning, consciousness, death wish, delusion, dementia, depression, ego, Electra complex, extrovert, fixation, Freudian slip, Gestalt therapy, group therapy, hypnosis, hypochondria, hysteria, id, inferiority complex, introvert, mania, mind, neurosis, obsession, Oedipus complex, paranoia, persecution complex, persona, personality, personality disorder, phobia, primal therapy *or* primal scream therapy, psyche, psychoanalysis, psychosis, psychosomatic, regression, repression, Rorschach test *or* inkblot test, schizophrenia, self, stress, subconscious, sublimation, superego, syndrome, trauma, unconscious

Psychologists

Alfred Adler *(Austrian)*
Émile Coué *(French)*
Hermann Ebbinghaus *(German)*
Hans Jürgen Eysenck *(German-British)*
Gustav Theodor Fechner *(German)*
Sigmund Freud *(Austrian)*
Erich Fromm *(U.S.)*
Ewald Hering *(German)*
Karen Horney *(German-U.S.)*
William James *(U.S.)*
Pierre Marie Félix Janet *(French)*
Carl Gustav Jung *(Swiss)*
Wolfgang Köhler *(German)*
Alexander Romanovich Luria *(Russian)*
Johannes Peter Müller *(German)*
Hugo Münsterberg *(German)*
Ivan Petrovich Pavlov *(Russian)*
Jean Piaget *(Swiss)*
Wilhelm Reich *(Austrian)*
B(urrhus) F(rederic) Skinner *(U.S.)*
Edward Lee Thorndike *(U.S.)*
John Watson *(U.S.)*
Wilhelm Max Wundt *(German)*

interest, limelight, notoriety, media attention, renown, public notice • *The case has generated enormous publicity.*

QUOTATIONS
All publicity is good, except an obituary notice
[Brendan Behan]

publicize 1 = **advertise**, promote, plug *(informal)*, hype, push, spotlight, puff, play up, write up, spread about, beat the drum for *(informal)*, give publicity to, bring to public notice • *The author appeared on TV to publicize her latest book.*
2 = **make known**, report, reveal, publish, broadcast, leak, disclose, proclaim, circulate, make public, divulge, blazon • *He never publicized his plans.*
OPPOSITES: conceal, suppress, keep secret

public-spirited = **altruistic**, generous, humanitarian, charitable, philanthropic, unselfish, community-minded • *Thanks to a group of public-spirited citizens, the garden has been preserved.*

publish 1 = **put out**, issue, produce, print, bring out • *His latest book will be published in May.*
2 = **announce**, reveal, declare, spread, advertise, broadcast, leak, distribute, communicate, disclose, proclaim, circulate, impart, publicize, divulge, promulgate, shout from the rooftops *(informal)*, blow wide open *(slang)* • *The paper did not publish his name for legal reasons.*

pucker AS A VERB = **wrinkle**, tighten, purse, pout, contract, gather, knit, crease, compress, crumple, ruffle, furrow, screw up, crinkle, draw together, ruck up, ruckle • *She puckered her lips and kissed him on the nose.*
▸ AS A NOUN = **wrinkle**, fold, crease, crumple, ruck, crinkle, ruckle • *small puckers in the material*

puckish = **mischievous**, teasing, naughty, sly, playful, whimsical, impish, roguish, frolicsome, ludic *(literary)*, waggish, sportive • *He had a puckish sense of humour.*

pudding = **dessert**, afters *(Brit. informal)*, sweet, pud *(informal)*, second course, last course • *I tend to stick to fresh fruit for pudding.*

puddle = **pool**, spill, splash, plash *(literary)* • *puddles of oil in the road*

puerile = **childish**, juvenile, naive, weak, silly, ridiculous, foolish, petty, trivial, irresponsible, immature, infantile, inane, babyish, jejune • *puerile schoolboy humour*
OPPOSITES: adult, mature, responsible

puff AS A VERB 1 = **smoke**, draw, drag *(slang)*, suck, inhale, pull at *or* on • *He gave a wry smile as he puffed on his cigarette.*
2 = **breathe heavily**, pant, exhale, blow, gasp, gulp, wheeze, fight for breath, puff and pant • *I could see he was unfit, because he was puffing.*
3 = **promote**, push, plug *(informal)*, hype, publicize, advertise, praise, crack up *(informal)*, big up *(slang, chiefly Caribbean)*, overpraise • *TV correspondents puffing the new digital channels*
▸ AS A NOUN 1 = **drag**, pull *(slang)*, moke • *She was taking quick puffs at her cigarette.*
2 = **blast**, breath, flurry, whiff, draught, gust, emanation • *an occasional puff of air stirring the brittle leaves*
3 = **advertisement**, ad *(informal)*, promotion, plug *(informal)*, good word, commendation, sales talk, namecheck, favourable mention, piece of publicity • *an elaborate puff for his magazine*
▸ IN PHRASES: **puff out** *or* **up** = **swell**, expand, enlarge, inflate, stick out, dilate, distend, bloat • *His chest puffed out with pride.* • *He puffed out his cheeks and let out his breath*

puffed = **out of breath**, winded, exhausted, spent, done in *(informal)*, panting, gasping, wiped out *(informal)*, breathless, short of breath, out of whack *(informal)*, shagged out *(Brit. taboo slang)* • *Do you get puffed easily when you go up stairs?*

puffed up = **swollen-headed**, proud, high and mighty *(informal)*, bigheaded *(informal)*, full of yourself, too big for your boots • *He was too puffed up with his own importance.*
OPPOSITES: modest, humble, self-effacing

puffin
▸ RELATED ADJECTIVE: alcidine
▸ NAME OF HOME: puffinry

puffy = **swollen**, enlarged, inflated, inflamed, bloated, puffed up, distended • *Her cheeks were puffy with crying.*

pugilist = **boxer**, fighter, bruiser *(informal)*, prizefighter • *He was a noted amateur pugilist.*

pugnacious = **aggressive**, contentious, irritable, belligerent, combative, petulant, antagonistic, argumentative, bellicose, irascible, quarrelsome, hot-tempered, choleric, disputatious, aggers *(Austral. slang)*, biffo *(Austral. slang)* • *He was in a pugnacious mood when he spoke to us.*
OPPOSITES: quiet, calm, peaceful

puke = **vomit**, be sick, throw up *(informal)*, spew, heave, regurgitate, disgorge, retch, be nauseated, chuck *(Austral. & N.Z. informal)*, barf *(U.S. slang)*, chunder *(slang, chiefly Austral.)*, upchuck *(U.S. slang)*, do a technicolour yawn *(slang)*, toss your cookies *(U.S. slang)* • *They got drunk and puked out of the window.*

pukka 1 = **genuine**, official, authentic, real, proper, on the level *(informal)*, bona fide, dinkum *(Austral. & N.Z. informal)*, the real McCoy • *He bought a pukka, rear-drive sports car.*
2 = **proper**, formal, smart, conventional, decent, posh *(Brit. informal)*, respectable, correct, polite, genteel, presentable, decorous • *a pukka English gentleman*

pull **AS A VERB** 1 = **draw**, haul, drag, trail, tow, tug, jerk, yank, prise, wrench, lug, wrest • *I helped pull him out of the water.*
OPPOSITES: drive, push, thrust
2 = **extract**, pick, remove, gather, take out, weed, pluck, cull, uproot, draw out • *Wes was in the yard pulling weeds when we drove up.*
OPPOSITES: plant, insert, implant
3 = **attract**, draw, bring in, tempt, lure, interest, entice, pull in, magnetize • *The organizers have to employ performers to pull a crowd.*
OPPOSITES: discourage, deter, repel
4 = **strain**, tear, stretch, rend, rip, wrench, dislocate, sprain • *Dave pulled a back muscle and could hardly move.*
▸ **AS A NOUN** 1 = **tug**, jerk, yank, twitch, heave • *The tooth must be removed with a firm, straight pull.*
OPPOSITES: push, thrust, shove
2 = **attraction**, appeal, lure, fascination, force, draw, influence, magnetism, enchantment, drawing power, enticement, allurement • *No matter how much you feel the pull of the past, try to look to the future.*
3 = **force**, exertion, magnetism, forcefulness • *the pull of gravity*
4 = **puff**, drag *(slang)*, inhalation • *He took a deep pull of his cigarette.*
5 = **influence**, power, authority, say, standing, weight, advantage, muscle, sway, prestige, clout *(informal)*, leverage, kai *(N.Z. informal)* • *Using all his pull in parliament, he obtained the necessary papers.*
▸ **IN PHRASES: pull a fast one on someone** = **trick**, cheat, con *(informal)*, take advantage of, sting *(informal)*, deceive, defraud, swindle, bamboozle *(informal)*, hoodwink, take for a ride *(informal)*, put one over on *(informal)* • *Someone had pulled a fast one on her over a procedural matter.*
pull back = **withdraw**, pull out, retreat, retire, flee, give way, fall back, back off, draw back, disengage, take flight, turn tail, beat a retreat • *They were asked to pull back from their positions around the city.*
pull in = **draw in**, stop, park, arrive, come in, halt, draw up, pull over, come to a halt • *He pulled in at the side of the road.*
pull it off = **crack it** *(informal)*, cut it *(informal)*, do the trick, score a success, secure your object • *If he had the money, I believe he could pull it off.*
pull out (of) 1 = **withdraw**, retire from, abandon, quit, step down from, back out, bow out, stop participating in • *An injury forced him to pull out of the race.*
2 = **leave**, abandon, get out, quit, retreat from, depart, evacuate • *The militia has agreed to pull out of Beirut.*
pull someone in = **arrest**, nail *(informal)*, bust *(informal)*, lift *(slang)*, run in *(slang)*, collar *(informal)*, pinch *(informal)*, nab *(informal)*, take someone into custody, feel someone's collar *(slang)* • *The police pulled him in for questioning.*
pull someone up = **reprimand**, lecture, rebuke, reproach, carpet *(informal)*, censure, scold, berate, castigate, admonish, chastise, tear into *(informal)*, read the riot act to, tell someone off *(informal)*, reprove, upbraid, take someone to task, tick someone off *(informal)*, read someone the riot act, bawl someone out *(informal)*, dress someone down *(informal)*, lambast(e), give someone an earful, chew someone out *(U.S. & Canad. informal)*, tear someone off a strip *(Brit. informal)*, haul someone over the coals, give someone a dressing down, give someone a rocket *(Brit. & N.Z. informal)*, slap someone on the wrist, rap someone over the knuckles • *My boss pulled me up about my timekeeping.*
pull something apart *or* **to pieces** 1 = **dismantle**, strip down, disassemble, take something apart, break something up, take something to bits • *You'll have to pull it apart and start all over again.*
2 = **criticize**, attack, blast, pan *(informal)*, slam *(slang)*, flame *(informal)*, put down, run down, slate *(informal)*, tear into *(informal)*, lay into *(informal)*, flay, diss *(slang, chiefly U.S.)*, find fault with, lambast(e), pick holes in • *The critics pulled his new book to pieces.*
pull something down = **demolish**, level, destroy, dismantle, remove, flatten, knock down, take down, tear down, bulldoze, raze, lay waste, raze to the ground, kennet *(Austral. slang)*, jeff *(Austral. slang)* • *They'd pulled the school down.*
pull something in 1 = **attract**, draw, pull, bring in, lure • *his ability to pull in a near capacity crowd for a match*
2 = **earn**, make, clear, gain, net, collect, be paid, pocket, bring in, gross, take home, rake in • *I only pull in £15,000 a year as a social worker.*
pull something off 1 = **succeed in**, manage, establish, effect, complete, achieve, engineer, carry out, crack *(informal)*, fulfil, accomplish, execute, discharge, clinch, bring about, carry off, perpetrate, bring off • *Labour might just pull off its third victory in a row.*
2 = **remove**, detach, rip off, tear off, doff, wrench off • *He pulled off his shirt.*
pull something out = **produce**, draw, bring out, draw out • *He pulled out a gun and threatened us.*
pull something up = **uproot**, raise, lift, weed, dig up, dig out, rip up • *Pull up weeds by hand and put them on the compost heap.*
pull through = **survive**, improve, recover, rally, come through, get better, be all right, recuperate, turn the corner, pull round, get well again • *Everyone waited to see whether he would pull through or not.*
pull up = **stop**, park, halt, arrive, brake, draw up, come to a halt, reach a standstill • *The cab pulled up and the driver jumped out.*
pull yourself together = **get a grip on yourself**, recover, get over it, buck up *(informal)*, snap out of it *(informal)*, get your act together, regain your composure • *He pulled himself together and got back to work.*

pulp **AS A NOUN** 1 = **paste**, mash, pap, mush, semisolid, pomace, semiliquid • *The olives are crushed to a pulp by stone rollers.*
2 = **flesh**, meat, marrow, soft part • *Use the whole fruit, including the pulp, which is high in fibre.*
▸ **AS A MODIFIER** = **cheap**, sensational, lurid, mushy *(informal)*, trashy, rubbishy • *lurid '50s pulp fiction*
▸ **AS A VERB** = **crush**, squash, mash, pulverize • *Onions can be boiled and pulped to a puree.*

P

pulpit = **platform**, stand, podium, rostrum, dais, lectern • *The minister took his place at the pulpit and preached a fine sermon.*

pulpy = **soft**, succulent, fleshy, mushy, squashy, pappy • *The chutney should have a thick, pulpy consistency.*

pulsate = **throb**, pound, beat, hammer, pulse, tick, thump, quiver, vibrate, thud, palpitate • *The racing beat of her heart pulsated under my fingertips.*

pulse AS A NOUN = **beat**, rhythm, vibration, beating, stroke, throb, throbbing, oscillation, pulsation • *the repetitive pulse of the music*
▸ AS A VERB = **beat**, tick, throb, vibrate, pulsate • *Her feet pulsed with pain.*

pulverize 1 = **destroy**, wreck, demolish, flatten, raze to the ground, kennet *(Austral. slang)*, jeff *(Austral. slang)* • *A nearby residential area had been pulverized by the bombing.*
2 = **defeat**, stuff *(slang)*, tank *(slang)*, annihilate, vanquish, smash, crush, lick *(informal)*, wipe the floor with *(informal)*, blow out of the water *(slang)* • *He pulverized his opponents in the race for the presidency.*
3 = **crush**, pound, grind, mill, bray, pestle, granulate, comminute, levigate *(Chemistry)* • *Pulverize the bran to a fine powder.*

pummel = **beat**, punch, pound, strike, knock, belt *(informal)*, hammer, bang, batter, thump, clobber *(slang)*, lambast(e), beat the living daylights out of, rain blows upon, beat *or* knock seven bells out of *(informal)* • *He trapped Conn in a corner and pummelled him ferociously.*

pump AS A VERB 1 = **drive out**, empty, drain, force out, bail out, siphon, draw off • *drill rigs that are busy pumping natural gas*
2 = **supply**, send, pour, inject • *The government must pump more money into community care.*
3 = **interrogate**, probe, quiz, cross-examine, grill *(informal)*, worm out of, give someone the third degree, question closely • *He ran in every five minutes to pump me for details.*
4 = **spurt**, run, course, flow, flood, pour, jet, stream, spill, gush, spout, squirt • *blood pumping from a head wound*
5 = **fire**, shoot, discharge, let off • *A gunman burst in and pumped five bullets into her head.*
▸ IN PHRASES: **pump something up** = **inflate**, blow up, fill up, dilate, puff up, aerate • *I was trying to pump up my back tyre.*

pun = **play on words**, quip, double entendre, witticism, paronomasia *(Rhetoric)*, equivoque • *The title of the book is a pun on his name.*

QUOTATIONS
A man who could make so vile a pun would not scruple to pick a pocket
[John Dennis]

punch¹ AS A VERB = **hit**, strike, box, smash, belt *(informal)*, slam, plug *(slang)*, bash *(informal)*, sock *(slang)*, clout *(informal)*, slug, swipe *(informal)*, biff *(slang)*, bop *(informal)*, wallop *(informal)*, pummel • *After punching him on the chin, she hit him over the head.*
▸ AS A NOUN 1 = **blow**, hit, knock, bash *(informal)*, plug *(slang)*, sock *(slang)*, thump, clout *(informal)*, jab, swipe *(informal)*, biff *(slang)*, bop *(informal)*, wallop *(informal)* • *He's asking for a punch on the nose.*
2 = **effectiveness**, force, bite, impact, point, drive, vigour, verve, forcefulness • *The film lacks punch and pace.*

punch² = **pierce**, cut, bore, drill, pink, stamp, puncture, prick, perforate • *I took a pen and punched holes in the carton.*

punch-drunk 1 = **groggy** *(informal)*, confused, reeling, staggering, dazed, unsteady, punchy *(informal)*, in a daze, stupefied, befuddled, woozy *(informal)*, slaphappy *(informal)*, knocked silly • *a punch-drunk boxer, reeling from too many blows*
2 = **groggy**, confused, dazed *(informal)*, in a daze, stupefied, befuddled, woozy *(informal)* • *He was punch-drunk from fatigue.*

punch-up = **fight**, row, argument, set-to *(informal)*, scrap *(informal)*, brawl, free-for-all *(informal)*, dust-up *(informal)*, shindig *(informal)*, battle royal, stand-up fight *(informal)*, dingdong, shindy *(informal)*, bagarre *(French)*, biffo *(Austral. slang)* • *He was involved in a punch-up with Sarah's former lover.*

punchy = **effective**, spirited, dynamic, lively, storming *(informal)*, aggressive, vigorous, forceful, incisive, in-your-face *(slang)* • *A good way to sound confident is to use short, punchy sentences.*

punctilious = **particular**, careful, strict, exact, nice, formal, proper, precise, meticulous, conscientious, fussy, scrupulous, finicky, anal retentive, ceremonious, nit-picky *(informal)* • *He was punctilious about being ready exactly on time.*

punctual = **on time**, timely, early, prompt, strict, exact, precise, in good time, on the dot, seasonable • *He's always very punctual. I'll see if he's here yet.*
OPPOSITES: late, behind, delayed

punctuality = **promptness**, readiness, regularity, promptitude • *Punctuality has never been my strong point.*

QUOTATIONS
Punctuality is the politeness of kings
[Louis XVIII]
Punctuality is the thief of time
[Oscar Wilde]
Punctuality is the virtue of the bored
[Evelyn Waugh *diary*]

punctually = **promptly**, exactly, dead on, sharp, precisely, on time, at the right time, to the minute, bang on (time) *(informal)* • *My guests arrived punctually at eight.*

punctuate 1 = **interrupt**, break, pepper, sprinkle, intersperse, interject • *The silence was punctuated by the distant rumble of traffic.*
2 = **emphasize**, mark, stress, underline, accentuate, foreground, point up, lay stress on • *Moore smiled to punctuate the irony of his comment.*

puncture AS A NOUN 1 = **flat tyre**, flat, flattie *(N.Z.)* • *Someone helped me to mend the puncture.*
2 = **hole**, opening, break, cut, nick, leak, slit, rupture, perforation • *an instrument used to make a puncture in the abdominal wall*
▸ AS A VERB 1 = **pierce**, cut, nick, penetrate, prick, rupture, perforate, impale, bore a hole • *The bullet punctured his stomach.*
2 = **deflate**, go down, go flat • *The tyre is guaranteed never to puncture.*
3 = **humble**, discourage, disillusion, flatten, deflate, take down a peg *(informal)* • *a witty column which punctures celebrity egos*

pundit = **expert**, guru, maestro, buff *(informal)*, boffin *(Brit. informal)*, wonk *(informal)*, fundi *(S. African)*, one of the cognoscenti, (self-appointed) expert *or* authority • *a well-known political pundit*

pungent 1 = **strong**, hot, spicy, seasoned, sharp, acid, bitter, stinging, sour, tart, aromatic, tangy, acrid, peppery, piquant, industrial-strength *(chiefly humorous)*, highly flavoured, acerb • *The more herbs you use, the more pungent the sauce will be.*
OPPOSITES: weak, moderate, mild
2 = **cutting**, pointed, biting, acute, telling, sharp, keen, stinging, piercing, penetrating, poignant, stringent, scathing, acrimonious, barbed, incisive, sarcastic, caustic, vitriolic, trenchant, mordant, mordacious • *He enjoyed the play's shrewd and pungent social analysis.*
OPPOSITES: dull, inane

punish = **discipline**, correct, castigate, chastise, beat, sentence, whip, lash, cane, flog, scourge, chasten, penalize, bring to book, slap someone's wrist, throw the book at, rap someone's knuckles, give someone the works *(slang)*, give a lesson to • *George has never had to punish the children.*

punishable = **culpable**, criminal, chargeable, indictable, blameworthy, convictable • *make slavery a punishable offence*

punishing = **hard**, taxing, demanding, grinding, wearing, tiring, exhausting, uphill, gruelling, strenuous, arduous, burdensome, backbreaking • *his punishing work schedule*
OPPOSITES: light, easy, simple

punishment 1 = **penalizing**, discipline, correction, retribution, what for *(informal)*, chastening, just deserts, chastisement, punitive measures • *The man is guilty and he deserves punishment.*
2 = **penalty**, reward, sanction, penance, comeuppance *(slang)* • *The usual punishment is a fine.*
3 = **beating**, abuse, torture, pain, victimization, manhandling, maltreatment, rough treatment • *He took a lot of punishment in the first few rounds of the fight.*
4 = **rough treatment**, abuse, maltreatment • *This bike isn't designed to take that kind of punishment.*
▸ **RELATED PHOBIA:** poinephobia

QUOTATIONS
Let the punishment fit the crime
[W.S. Gilbert *The Mikado*]
Whoso sheddeth man's blood, by man shall his blood be shed
[*Bible: Genesis*]
They have sown the wind, and they shall reap the whirlwind
[*Bible: Hosea*]
Men are not hanged for stealing horses, but that horses may not be stolen
[George Savile, Marquess of Halifax *Political, Moral, and Miscellaneous Thoughts*]

punitive 1 = **retaliatory**, in retaliation, vindictive, in reprisal, revengeful, retaliative, punitory • *punitive measures against foreign companies*
2 = **severe**, high, harsh, stiff, drastic, stringent, austere, draconian, prohibitive, burdensome • *The Green party wants punitive taxes on petrol.*

punk = **delinquent**, rebel, offender, wrongdoer, juvenile delinquent, miscreant • *He is getting a reputation as a young punk.*

punt AS A VERB = **bet**, back, stake, gamble, lay, wager • *He punted the lot on Little Nell in the third race.*
▸ AS A NOUN = **bet**, stake, gamble, wager • *I like to take the odd punt on the stock exchange.*

punter 1 = **gambler**, better, backer, punt *(chiefly Brit.)* • *Punters are expected to gamble £70m on the Grand National.*
2 = **customer**, guest, client, patron, member of the audience • *The show ended when an irate punter punched one of the performers.*
3 = **person**, guy *(informal)*, fellow, bloke *(Brit. informal)*, man in the street • *Most of these artists are not known to the ordinary punter.*

puny 1 = **feeble**, weak, frail, little, tiny, weakly, stunted, diminutive, sickly, undeveloped, pint-sized *(informal)*, undersized, underfed, dwarfish, pygmy *or* pigmy • *Our Kevin has always been a puny lad.*
OPPOSITES: strong, powerful, healthy
2 = **insignificant**, minor, petty, inferior, trivial, worthless, trifling, paltry, inconsequential, piddling *(informal)* • *the puny resources at our disposal*

pup *or* **puppy** = **whippersnapper**, braggart, whelp, jackanapes, popinjay • *You insolent young pup!*
▸ **COLLECTIVE NOUN:** litter

pupil 1 = **student**, scholar, schoolboy *or* schoolgirl, schoolchild • *a school with over 1,000 pupils*
OPPOSITES: teacher, tutor, schoolteacher
2 = **learner**, student, follower, trainee, novice, beginner, apprentice, disciple, protégé, neophyte, tyro, catechumen • *Goldschmidt became a pupil of the composer Franz Schreker.*
OPPOSITES: coach, trainer, instructor

puppet 1 = **marionette**, doll, glove puppet, finger puppet • *The show features huge inflatable puppets.*
2 = **pawn**, tool, instrument, creature, dupe, gull *(archaic)*, figurehead, mouthpiece, stooge, cat's-paw • *The ministers have denied that they are puppets of a foreign government.*

purchase AS A VERB = **buy**, pay for, obtain, get, score *(slang)*, gain, pick up, secure, acquire, invest in, shop for, get hold of, come by, procure, make a purchase • *She purchased a tuna sandwich and a carton of orange juice.* • *Most of the shares were purchased by brokers.*
OPPOSITES: sell, market, retail
▸ AS A NOUN 1 = **acquisition**, buy, investment, property, gain, asset, possession • *She opened the bag and looked at her purchases.*
2 = **grip**, hold, support, footing, influence, edge, advantage, grasp, lever, leverage, foothold, toehold • *I got a purchase on the rope and pulled.*

purchaser = **buyer**, customer, consumer, vendee *(Law)* • *The broker will get 5% if he finds a purchaser.*
OPPOSITES: dealer, retailer, seller

pure 1 = **unmixed**, real, clear, true, simple, natural, straight, perfect, genuine, neat, authentic, flawless, unalloyed • *The ancient alchemists tried to transmute base metals into pure gold.*
OPPOSITES: mixed, flawed, adulterated
2 = **clean**, immaculate, sterile, wholesome, sanitary, spotless, sterilized, squeaky-clean, unblemished, unadulterated, untainted, disinfected, uncontaminated, unpolluted, pasteurized, germ-free • *Demands for pure and clean river water.*
OPPOSITES: dirty, infected, contaminated
3 = **theoretical**, abstract, philosophical, speculative, academic, conceptual, hypothetical, conjectural, non-practical • *Physics isn't just about pure science with no practical applications.*
OPPOSITES: applied, practical
4 = **complete**, total, perfect, absolute, mere, sheer, patent, utter, outright, thorough, downright, palpable, unqualified, out-and-out, unmitigated • *The old man turned to give her a look of pure surprise.*
OPPOSITES: qualified
5 = **innocent**, virgin, modest, good, true, moral, maidenly, upright, honest, immaculate, impeccable, righteous, virtuous, squeaky-clean, blameless, chaste, virginal, unsullied, guileless, uncorrupted, unstained, undefiled, unspotted • *a pure and chaste maiden*
OPPOSITES: corrupt, spoiled, contaminated

QUOTATIONS
My strength is as the strength of ten
Because my heart is pure
[Alfred, Lord Tennyson *'Sir Galahad'*]
Unto the pure all things are pure
[*Bible: II Timothy*]

pure-bred = **thoroughbred**, blood, pedigree, full-blooded • *a pure-bred Arab horse*

purely = **absolutely**, just, only, completely, simply, totally, entirely, exclusively, plainly, merely, solely, wholly • *It is a racing machine, designed purely for speed.*

purgative AS A NOUN = **purge**, laxative, cathartic, enema, physic *(rare)*, emetic, aperient *(Medical)*, depurative, evacuant • *The doctor tried to reduce his fever by inducing diarrhea with a purgative.*
▸ AS AN ADJECTIVE = **purging**, cleansing, laxative, aperient *(Medical)*, depurative, evacuant • *a purgative tea*

purgatory = **torment**, agony, murder *(informal)*, hell *(informal)*, torture, misery, hell on earth • *Every step of the last three miles was sheer purgatory.*

purge AS A VERB 1 = **rid**, clear, cleanse, strip, empty, void • *They voted to purge the party of 'hostile and anti-party elements'.*
2 = **get rid of**, kill, remove, dismiss, axe *(informal)*, expel, wipe out, oust, eradicate, eject, do away with, liquidate, exterminate, sweep out, rout out, wipe from the face of the earth, rid somewhere of • *They have purged thousands from the*

upper levels of the civil service. • *They purged any individuals suspected of loyalty to the king.*
3 = cleanse, clear, purify, wash, clean out, expiate • *He lay still, trying to purge his mind of anxiety.*
▸ **AS A NOUN = removal**, elimination, crushing, expulsion, suppression, liquidation, cleanup, witch hunt, eradication, ejection • *a thorough purge of people associated with the late ruler*

purify 1 = clean, filter, cleanse, refine, clarify, disinfect, fumigate, decontaminate, sanitize • *Plants can filter and purify the air in your office.*
OPPOSITES: contaminate, pollute, soil
2 = absolve, cleanse, redeem, exonerate, sanctify, exculpate, shrive, lustrate • *They believe that bathing in the Ganges at certain holy places purifies the soul.*
OPPOSITES: stain, taint, sully

purist = stickler, traditionalist, perfectionist, classicist, pedant, formalist, literalist • *Purists say the language is under threat.*

puritan AS A NOUN = moralist, fanatic, zealot, prude, pietist, rigorist • *He delighted in dealing with subjects that enraged puritans.*
▸ **AS AN ADJECTIVE = strict**, austere, puritanical, narrow, severe, intolerant, ascetic, narrow-minded, moralistic, prudish, hidebound, strait-laced • *Paul has always had a puritan streak.*

QUOTATIONS
The Puritan hated bear-baiting, not because it gave pain to the bear, but because it gave pleasure to the spectators
[Lord Macaulay *History of England*]

puritanical = strict, forbidding, puritan, stuffy, narrow, severe, proper, stiff, rigid, disapproving, austere, fanatical, bigoted, prim, ascetic, narrow-minded, prudish, strait-laced • *He has a puritanical attitude towards sex.*
OPPOSITES: liberal, tolerant, indulgent

puritanism = strictness, austerity, severity, zeal, piety, rigidity, fanaticism, narrowness, asceticism, moralism, prudishness, rigorism, piousness • *the tight-lipped puritanism of the Scottish literary world*

QUOTATIONS
Puritanism: The haunting fear that someone, somewhere may be happy
[H.L. Mencken *Chrestomathy*]

purity 1 = cleanness, clarity, cleanliness, brilliance, genuineness, wholesomeness, fineness, clearness, pureness, faultlessness, immaculateness, untaintedness • *the purity of the air in your working environment*
OPPOSITES: contamination, impurity, cloudiness
2 = innocence, virtue, integrity, honesty, decency, sincerity, virginity, piety, chastity, rectitude, guilelessness, virtuousness, chasteness, blamelessness • *The American Female Reform Society promoted sexual purity.*
OPPOSITES: impurity, immorality, vice

purloin = steal, rob, lift *(informal)*, nick *(slang, chiefly Brit.)*, appropriate, trouser *(slang)*, pinch *(informal)*, swipe *(slang)*, knock off *(slang)*, blag *(slang)*, pilfer, walk off with, snitch *(slang)*, filch, prig *(Brit. slang)*, snaffle *(Brit. informal)*, thieve • *He was caught purloining books from the library.*

purple

SHADES OF PURPLE

amethyst	heliotrope	periwinkle
aubergine	indigo	plum
burgundy	lavender	puce
carmine	lilac	royal purple
claret	magenta	Tyrian purple
dubonnet	mauve	violet
gentian	mulberry	wine
gentian blue	pansy	
heather	peach-blow	

purport = claim, allege, proclaim, maintain, declare, pretend, assert, pose as, profess • *a book that purports to tell the whole truth*

purpose AS A NOUN 1 = reason, point, idea, goal, grounds, design, aim, basis, principle, function, object, intention, objective, motive, motivation, justification, impetus, the why and wherefore • *The purpose of the occasion was to raise money for charity.*
2 = aim, end, plan, hope, view, goal, design, project, target, wish, scheme, desire, object, intention, objective, ambition, aspiration, Holy Grail *(informal)* • *They are prepared to go to any lengths to achieve their purpose.*
3 = determination, commitment, resolve, will, resolution, initiative, enterprise, ambition, conviction, motivation, persistence, tenacity, firmness, constancy, single-mindedness, steadfastness • *The teachers are enthusiastic and have a sense of purpose.*
4 = use, good, return, result, effect, value, benefit, profit, worth, gain, advantage, outcome, utility, merit, mileage *(informal)*, avail, behoof *(archaic)* • *Talking about it will serve no purpose.*
▸ **IN PHRASES: on purpose = deliberately**, purposely, consciously, intentionally, knowingly, wilfully, by design, wittingly, calculatedly, designedly • *Was it an accident, or did she do it on purpose?*

purposeful = determined, resolved, resolute, decided, firm, settled, positive, fixed, deliberate, single-minded, tenacious, strong-willed, steadfast, immovable, unfaltering • *She had a purposeful air.*
OPPOSITES: faltering, wavering, undecided

purposely = deliberately, expressly, consciously, intentionally, knowingly, with intent, on purpose, wilfully, by design, calculatedly, designedly • *They are purposely withholding information.*
OPPOSITES: accidentally, by accident, by chance

purse AS A NOUN 1 = pouch, wallet, money-bag • *I dug the money out of my purse.*
2 = handbag, bag, shoulder bag, pocket book, clutch bag • *She reached into her purse for her cigarettes.*
3 = funds, means, money, resources, treasury, wealth, exchequer, coffers, wherewithal • *The money will go into the public purse, helping to lower taxes.*
4 = prize, winnings, award, gift, reward • *She is tipped to win the biggest purse in women's pro volleyball history.*
▸ **AS A VERB = pucker**, close, contract, tighten, knit, wrinkle, pout, press together • *She pursed her lips in disapproval.*

pursuance = carrying out, doing, following, effecting, performance, pursuing, prosecution, discharge, bringing about, execution • *He ordered disclosure of the report in pursuance of a murder investigation.*

pursue 1 = engage in, follow, perform, conduct, wage, tackle, take up, work at, carry on, practise, participate in, prosecute, ply, go in for, apply yourself to • *Japan would continue to pursue the policies laid down at the summit.*
2 = try for, seek, desire, search for, aim for, aspire to, work towards, strive for, have as a goal • *Mr Menendez has aggressively pursued success.*
3 = continue, maintain, carry on, keep on, hold to, see through, adhere to, persist in, proceed in, persevere in • *If your request is denied, don't be afraid to pursue the matter.*
4 = conduct, carry on, undertake, prosecute, devote yourself to • *overseas graduates intending to pursue full-time research*
5 = investigate, study, research, check, review, examine, probe, look into, analyse, delve into, inquire into • *pursuing this line of enquiry*
6 = follow, track, hunt, chase, dog, attend, shadow, accompany, harry, tail *(informal)*, haunt, plague, hound,

stalk, harass, go after, run after, hunt down, give chase to • *She pursued the man who had stolen her bag.*
OPPOSITES: avoid, flee, shun
7 = **court**, woo, pay attention to, make up to *(informal)*, chase after, pay court to, set your cap at • *He had pursued her, and within weeks they had become lovers.*
OPPOSITES: eschew, fight shy of

pursuit 1 = **quest**, seeking, search, aim of, aspiration for, striving towards • *individuals in pursuit of their dreams* • *the pursuit of happiness*
2 = **pursuing**, seeking, tracking, search, hunt, hunting, chase, trail, trailing • *Police had obstructed justice by hindering the pursuit of terrorists.*
3 = **occupation**, activity, interest, line, pleasure, hobby, pastime, vocation • *They both love outdoor pursuits.*

purvey 1 = **communicate**, publish, spread, pass on, transmit, make available • *He accused me of purveying 'silly gossip' about practices in schools.*
2 = **supply**, provide, sell, retail, provision, cater, trade in, deal in, furnish, victual • *two restaurants that purvey Indonesian food*

purveyor = **seller**, trader, retailer, supplier, provider, stockist, vendor • *purveyors of gourmet foods*

purview = **scope**, reach, range, field, limit, extent, province, confine(s), orbit, sphere, compass, ambit • *That, however, was beyond the purview of the court; it was a diplomatic matter.*

pus = **matter**, discharge, secretion, suppuration • *The area of the scar began to discharge pus.*

push **AS A VERB** 1 = **shove**, force, press, thrust, drive, knock, sweep, plunge, elbow, bump, ram, poke, propel, nudge, prod, jostle, hustle, bulldoze, impel, manhandle • *They pushed him into the car.*
OPPOSITES: draw, pull, drag
2 = **press**, operate, depress, squeeze, activate, hold down • *He got into the lift and pushed the button for the second floor.*
3 = **make** *or* **force your way**, move, shoulder, inch, squeeze, thrust, elbow, shove, jostle, work your way, thread your way • *I pushed through the crowds and on to the escalator.*
4 = **advance**, progress, proceed, go on, go ahead, go forward, press on, make inroads, move onward • *The army may push southwards into the Kurdish areas.*
5 = **urge**, encourage, persuade, spur, drive, press, influence, prod, constrain, incite, coerce, egg on, impel, browbeat, exert influence on • *Her parents kept her in school and pushed her to study.*
OPPOSITES: discourage, deter, put off
6 = **promote**, advertise, hype, publicize, boost, plug *(informal)*, puff, make known, propagandize, cry up • *Advertisers often use scientific doublespeak to push their products.*
7 = **sell**, supply, deal in, peddle, traffic in • *She was accused of pushing drugs.*
▸ **AS A NOUN** 1 = **shove**, thrust, butt, elbow, poke, nudge, prod, jolt • *He gave me a sharp push.*
OPPOSITES: pull, tug, jerk
2 = **effort**, charge, attack, campaign, advance, assault, raid, offensive, sally, thrust, blitz, onset • *All that was needed was one final push, and the enemy would be vanquished once and for all.*
3 = **drive**, go *(informal)*, energy, initiative, enterprise, ambition, determination, pep, vitality, vigour, dynamism, welly *(slang)*, get-up-and-go *(informal)*, gumption *(informal)* • *He lacked the push to succeed in his chosen vocation.*
▸ **IN PHRASES:** **push for something** = **demand**, champion, call for, campaign for, urge, request, advocate, insist on, press for, lobby for, espouse, clamour for, drum up support for • *They intend to push for greater political autonomy.*
push off = **go away**, leave, get lost *(informal)*, clear off *(informal)*, take off *(informal)*, depart, beat it *(slang)*, light out *(informal)*, hit the road *(slang)*, hook it *(slang)*, slope off, pack your bags *(informal)*, make tracks, buzz off *(informal)*, hop it *(informal)*, shove off *(informal)*, bog off *(Brit. slang)*, skedaddle *(informal)*, naff off *(informal)*, be off with you, sling your hook *(informal)*, make yourself scarce *(informal)*, voetsek *(S. African, offensive)*, rack off *(Austral. & N.Z. slang)* • *Do me a favour and push off, will you?*
push on = **continue (your journey)**, go on, advance, progress, proceed, carry on, press on, push forward, forge ahead • *Although the journey was a long and lonely one, he pushed on.*
push someone around = **bully**, intimidate, pick on, tread on, trample on, browbeat, ride roughshod over, domineer, boss about *or* around • *He thinks he can just push people around.*
push something forward = **speed (up)**, advance, promote, accelerate, forward, rush, assist, hurry, facilitate, hasten, precipitate, quicken, fast-track, expedite, gee up • *They will use their influence to push forward the peace process.*
the push = **dismissal**, the sack *(informal)*, discharge, the boot *(slang)*, your cards *(informal)*, your books *(informal)*, marching orders *(informal)*, the kiss-off *(slang, chiefly U.S. & Canad.)*, the (old) heave-ho *(informal)*, the order of the boot *(slang)* • *Two cabinet ministers also got the push.*

pushed *often with* **for** = **short of**, pressed, rushed, tight, hurried, under pressure, in difficulty, up against it *(informal)* • *He's going to be a bit pushed for time.*

pushover 1 = **sucker** *(slang)*, mug *(Brit. slang)*, stooge *(slang)*, soft touch *(slang)*, chump *(informal)*, walkover *(informal)*, easy game *(informal)*, easy *or* soft mark *(informal)* • *He's a tough negotiator – you won't find him a pushover.*
2 = **piece of cake** *(Brit. informal)*, breeze *(U.S. & Canad. informal)*, picnic *(informal)*, child's play *(informal)*, plain sailing, doddle *(Brit. slang)*, walkover *(informal)*, cinch *(slang)*, no-brainer *(informal)*, cakewalk *(informal)*, duck soup *(U.S. slang)*, piece of piss *(taboo slang)* • *You might think Hungarian is a pushover to learn, but it isn't.*
OPPOSITES: challenge, test, trial

pushy = **forceful**, aggressive, assertive, brash, loud, offensive, ambitious, bold, obnoxious, presumptuous, obtrusive, officious, bumptious, self-assertive • *She was a confident and pushy young woman.*
OPPOSITES: shy, timid, reserved

pusillanimous = **cowardly**, timid, spineless, craven, yellow *(informal)*, weak, fearful, feeble, abject, gutless *(informal)*, timorous, faint-hearted, recreant *(archaic)*, chicken-hearted, lily-livered • *The authorities are too pusillanimous to deal with this situation.*
OPPOSITES: brave, daring, bold

pussyfoot = **hedge**, sit on the fence, prevaricate, beat about the bush, flannel *(Brit. informal)*, equivocate, be noncommittal, hum and haw, tergiversate • *Stop pussyfooting around and say what you really mean!*

pustule = **boil**, spot, gathering, blister, ulcer, fester, pimple, abscess, zit *(slang)* • *She had a large number of little pimples and pustules on her face.*

put **AS A VERB** 1 = **place**, leave, set, position, rest, park *(informal)*, plant, establish, lay, stick *(informal)*, settle, fix, lean, deposit, dump *(informal)*, prop, lay down, put down, situate, set down, stow, bung *(informal)*, plonk *(informal)* • *She put her bag on the floor.*
2 = **consign to**, place, commit to, doom to, condemn to • *She was put in prison for her beliefs.*
3 = **impose**, subject, levy, inflict • *The government has put a big tax on beer, wine and spirits.*
4 = **lay**, place, set, pin, attach to, attribute to, ascribe to, impute to • *It's no good putting all the blame on me.*
5 = **express**, say, state, word, phrase, set, pose, utter, frame, convey, articulate • *To put it bluntly, he doesn't give a damn.*
6 = **present**, suggest, advance, propose, offer, forward, submit, tender, bring forward, proffer, posit, set before, lay

P

before • *He sat there listening as we put our suggestions to him.*
7 = estimate, value, judge, measure, establish, set, fix, guess, reckon, assess, calculate, evaluate, compute, gauge, guesstimate *(informal)* • *Early estimates put the cost of the damage at millions of pounds.*
8 = assign to, place in, allocate to, consign to, bracket with, classify with, categorize with • *It's impossible to put this band into any category or style of music.*
▸ **IN PHRASES: put in for something = apply for**, try for, seek, request, ask for, put in an application for • *I decided to put in for a job as deputy secretary.*
put one over on someone = outwit, trick, fool, take in, mislead, deceive, dupe, delude, bamboozle *(informal)*, hoodwink, steal a march on, lead astray, pull a fast one on *(informal)*, throw someone off the scent • *It was a chance to put one over on their rivals.*
put someone away = commit, confine, cage *(informal)*, imprison, certify, institutionalize, incarcerate, put in prison, put behind bars, lock up *or* away • *He's insane! He should be put away for life.*
put someone down = humiliate, shame, crush, show up, reject, dismiss, condemn, slight, flame *(informal)*, criticize, snub, have a go at *(informal)*, deflate, denigrate, belittle, disparage, deprecate, mortify, diss *(slang, chiefly U.S.)* • *She's always putting her husband down in public.*
put someone down as something *or* **someone = regard as**, see as, rate (as), consider, judge, deem, view as, value as, esteem as, look upon as • *I would put him down as the most valuable asset this company has.*
put someone off 1 = discourage, intimidate, deter, daunt, dissuade, demoralize, scare off, dishearten • *We tried to visit the abbey but were put off by the queues.*
2 = disconcert, confuse, unsettle, throw *(informal)*, distress, rattle *(informal)*, dismay, perturb, faze, discomfit, take the wind out of someone's sails, nonplus, abash • *All this noise is putting me off.*
put someone out 1 = inconvenience, trouble, upset, bother, disturb, impose upon, discomfit, discommode, incommode • *Thanks for the offer, but I couldn't put you out like that.*
2 = annoy, anger, provoke, irritate, disturb, harass, confound, exasperate, disconcert, nettle, vex, perturb, irk, put on the spot, take the wind out of someone's sails, discountenance, discompose • *They were quite put out to find me in charge.*
put someone up 1 = accommodate, house, board, lodge, quarter, entertain, take someone in, billet, give someone lodging • *She asked if I could put her up for a few days.*
2 = nominate, put forward, offer, present, propose, recommend, float, submit • *The new party is putting up 15 candidates for 22 seats.*
put someone up to something = encourage, urge, persuade, prompt, incite, egg on, goad, put the idea into someone's head • *How do you know he asked me out? Did you put him up to it?*
put something about = spread, circulate, broadcast, pass on, make public, publicize, disseminate, make known, bandy about • *They've been putting rumours about for months.*
put something across *or* **over = communicate**, explain, clarify, express, get through, convey, make clear, spell out, get across, make yourself understood • *The opposition parties were hampered from putting across their message.*
put something aside *or* **by 1 = save**, store, stockpile, deposit, hoard, cache, lay by, stow away, salt away, keep in reserve, squirrel away • *Encourage children to put some money aside each week.*
2 = disregard, forget, ignore, bury, discount, set aside, pay no heed to • *We should put aside our differences and discuss this sensibly.*
put something away 1 = store away, replace, put back, tidy up, clear away, tidy away, return to its place • *She began putting away the dishes.*
2 = save, set aside, put aside, keep, deposit, put by, stash away, store away • *He had been able to put away money, to insure against old age.*
3 = consume, devour, eat up, demolish *(informal)*, hoover *(informal)*, gobble, guzzle, polish off *(informal)*, gulp down, wolf down, pig out on *(informal)* • *The food was superb, and we put away a fair amount of it.*
put something back 1 = postpone, delay, put off, defer, adjourn, hold over, reschedule • *The elections have been put back to October.*
2 = replace, restore, put away, tidy away, return to its place • *He took his wallet out of his pocket and then put it back.*
put something down 1 = record, write down, list, enter, log, take down, inscribe, set down, transcribe, put in black and white • *Never put anything down on paper which might be used in evidence.*
2 = repress, crush, suppress, check, silence, overthrow, squash, subdue, quash, quell, stamp out • *Soldiers went in to put down a rebellion.*
3 = put to sleep, kill, destroy, do away with, put away, put out of its misery • *Magistrates ordered that the dog should be put down at once.*
put something down to something = attribute, blame, ascribe, set down, impute, chalk up • *You may be a sceptic and put it down to coincidence.*
put something forward = recommend, present, suggest, introduce, advance, propose, press, submit, tender, nominate, prescribe, move for, proffer • *He has put forward new peace proposals.*
put something in = submit, present, enter, file, make, lodge • *Players are not allowed to leave unless they put in a transfer request.*
put something off = postpone, delay, defer, adjourn, put back, hold over, reschedule, put on ice, put on the back burner *(informal)*, take a rain check on *(U.S. & Canad. informal)* • *The Association has put the event off until December.*
put something on 1 = don, dress in, slip into, pull on, climb into, change into, throw on, get dressed in, fling on, pour yourself into, doll yourself up in • *She put on her coat and went out.*
2 = present, stage, perform, do, show, produce, mount • *The band are putting on a UK show before the end of the year.*
3 = provide, supply, lay on, run, furnish, make available • *They are putting on an extra flight to London tomorrow.*
4 = add, gain, increase by • *I've put on a stone since I stopped training.*
5 = switch on, turn on, activate, flick on • *I put on the light beside the bed.*
6 = bet, back, place, chance, risk, lay, stake, hazard, wager • *They put £20 on Matthew scoring the first goal.*
7 = fake, affect, assume, simulate, feign, make believe, play-act • *Anything becomes funny if you put on an American accent.*
put something out 1 = issue, release, publish, broadcast, bring out, circulate, make public, make known • *The French news agency put out a statement from the Trade Minister.*
2 = extinguish, smother, blow out, stamp out, douse, snuff out, quench • *Firemen tried to free the injured and put out the blaze.*
put something up 1 = build, raise, set up, construct, erect, fabricate • *He was putting up a new fence round the garden.*
2 = pin up, post, display, hang up, stick up, nail up • *They put up posters about the meeting in the village.*
3 = offer, present, mount, put forward • *In the end they surrendered without putting up any resistance.*
4 = provide, advance, invest, contribute, give, pay up, supply, come up with, pledge, donate, furnish, fork out

(informal), cough up *(informal)*, shell out *(informal)* • *The state agreed to put up the money to start his company.*
5 = **increase**, raise, bump up *(informal)*, jack up *(informal)*, hike up *(informal)* • *They're putting up their prices.*
put up with something *or* **someone** = **stand**, suffer, bear, take, wear *(Brit. informal)*, stomach, endure, swallow, brook, stand for, lump *(informal)*, tolerate, hack *(slang)*, abide, countenance • *I won't put up with this kind of behaviour from you.*
put upon someone = **take advantage of**, trouble, abuse, harry, exploit, saddle, take for granted, put someone out, inconvenience, beset, overwork, impose upon, take for a fool • *Don't allow people to put upon you or take you for granted.*

putative = **supposed**, reported, assumed, alleged, presumed, reputed, imputed, presumptive, commonly believed • *the putative father of the child*

put-down AS A NOUN = **humiliation**, slight, snub, knock *(informal)*, dig, sneer, rebuff, barb, sarcasm, kick in the teeth *(slang)*, gibe, disparagement, one in the eye *(informal)* • *She was getting very sick of his put-downs.*

putrefy = **rot**, break down, spoil, corrupt, deteriorate, decay, stink, decompose, go bad • *the stench of corpses putrefying in the sweltering heat*

putrid = **rotten**, contaminated, stinking, tainted, off, bad, rank, foul, spoiled, corrupt, rotting, decayed, reeking, decomposed, rancid, fetid, putrefied, olid, festy *(Austral. slang)* • *river banks coated with layers of putrid sludge from untreated waste*
OPPOSITES: clean, fresh, sweet

puzzle AS A VERB = **perplex**, beat *(slang)*, confuse, baffle, stump, bewilder, confound, mystify, faze, flummox, bemuse, nonplus • *What puzzles me is why nobody has complained before now.*
▸ AS A NOUN 1 = **problem**, riddle, maze, labyrinth, question, conundrum, teaser, poser, brain-teaser *(informal)* • *a word puzzle*
2 = **mystery**, problem, paradox, enigma, conundrum • *the puzzle of why there are no Stone Age cave paintings in Britain*
▸ IN PHRASES: **puzzle over something** = **think about**, study, wonder about, mull over, muse on, think hard about, ponder on, brood over, ask yourself about, cudgel *or* rack your brains • *puzzling over the complexities of Shakespeare's verse*
puzzle something out = **solve**, work out, figure out, unravel, see, get, crack, resolve, sort out, clear up, decipher, think through, suss (out) *(slang)*, get the answer of, find the key to, crack the code of • *I stared at the symbols, trying to puzzle out their meaning.*

puzzled = **perplexed**, beaten, confused, baffled, lost, stuck, stumped, doubtful, at sea, bewildered, mixed up, at a loss, mystified, clueless, nonplussed, flummoxed, in a fog, without a clue • *Scientists remain puzzled by this phenomenon.*

puzzlement = **perplexity**, questioning, surprise, doubt, wonder, confusion, uncertainty, bewilderment, disorientation, bafflement, mystification, doubtfulness • *He looked at me in puzzlement.*

puzzling = **perplexing**, baffling, bewildering, hard, involved, misleading, unclear, ambiguous, enigmatic, incomprehensible, mystifying, inexplicable, unaccountable, knotty, unfathomable, labyrinthine, full of surprises, abstruse, beyond you, oracular • *His letter poses a number of puzzling questions.*
OPPOSITES: clear, easy, simple

pygmy *or* **pigmy** AS A MODIFIER = **small**, miniature, dwarf, tiny, wee, stunted, diminutive, minuscule, midget, elfin, undersized, teeny-weeny, Lilliputian, dwarfish, teensy-weensy, pygmean • *The pygmy hippopotamus is less than 6 ft long.*
▸ AS A NOUN 1 = **midget**, dwarf, shrimp *(informal)*, Lilliputian, Tom Thumb, munchkin *(informal, chiefly U.S.)*, homunculus, manikin • *an encounter with the Ituri Forest pygmies*
2 = **nonentity**, nobody, lightweight *(informal)*, mediocrity, cipher, small fry, non-person, pipsqueak *(informal)* • *He saw the politicians of his day as pygmies, not as giants.*

Qq

quack AS A NOUN 1 = **doctor**, GP, physician, medical practitioner • *I went everywhere for treatment, tried all sorts of quacks.*
2 = **charlatan**, fraud, fake, pretender, humbug, impostor, mountebank, phoney *or* phony *(informal)* • *The man was a quack after all, just as Rosalinda had warned.*
▸ AS A MODIFIER = **fake**, fraudulent, phoney *or* phony *(informal)*, pretended, sham, counterfeit • *Why do intelligent people find quack remedies so appealing?*

quadrangle = **square**, quad *(informal)*, court, courtyard, plaza, enclosure, precinct, piazza, cloister • *We were in this little room looking out on the quadrangle.*

quaff = **drink**, gulp, swig *(informal)*, have, down, neck *(slang)*, swallow, slug, guzzle, imbibe, partake of • *The older guys quaff their breakfast cappuccinos.*

quagmire 1 = **predicament**, difficulty, quandary, pass, fix *(informal)*, jam *(informal)*, dilemma, pinch, plight, scrape *(informal)*, muddle, pickle *(informal)*, impasse, entanglement, imbroglio • *a political quagmire*
2 = **bog**, marsh, swamp, slough, fen, mire, morass, quicksand, muskeg *(Canad.)* • *Overnight rain had turned the grass airstrip into a quagmire.*

quail[1] = **shrink**, cringe, flinch, shake, faint, tremble, quake, shudder, falter, droop, blanch, recoil, cower, blench, have cold feet *(informal)* • *The very word makes many of us quail.*

quail[2]
▸ COLLECTIVE NOUN: bevy

quaint 1 = **unusual**, odd, curious, original, strange, bizarre, fantastic, old-fashioned, peculiar, eccentric, queer, rum *(Brit. slang)*, singular, fanciful, whimsical, droll • *When visiting restaurants, be prepared for some quaint customs.*
OPPOSITES: normal, ordinary
2 = **old-fashioned**, charming, picturesque, antique, gothic, old-world, antiquated • *Whisky-making is treated as a quaint cottage industry.*
OPPOSITES: new, modern, fashionable

quake AS A NOUN = **earthquake**, tremor, shock • *The quake destroyed mud buildings in many remote villages.*
▸ AS A VERB = **shake**, tremble, quiver, move, rock, shiver, throb, shudder, wobble, waver, vibrate, pulsate, quail, totter, convulse • *Her shoulders quaked.*

qualification 1 = **certificate**, degree, document, diploma • *Mix academic A-levels with vocational qualifications.*
2 = **eligibility**, quality, ability, skill, capacity, fitness, attribute, capability, endowment(s), accomplishment, achievement, aptitude, suitability, suitableness • *That time with him is my qualification to write the book.*
3 = **condition**, restriction, proviso, requirement, rider, exception, criterion, reservation, allowance, objection, limitation, modification, exemption, prerequisite, caveat, stipulation • *The empirical evidence is subject to many qualifications.*

qualified 1 = **capable**, trained, experienced, seasoned, able, fit, expert, talented, chartered, efficient, practised, licensed, certificated, equipped, accomplished, eligible, competent, skilful, adept, knowledgeable, proficient • *Demand has far outstripped supply of qualified teachers.*
OPPOSITES: amateur, unqualified, untrained
2 = **restricted**, limited, provisional, conditional, reserved, guarded, bounded, adjusted, moderated, adapted, confined, modified, tempered, cautious, refined, amended, contingent, tentative, hesitant, circumscribed, equivocal • *He answers both questions with a qualified yes.*
OPPOSITES: outright, unconditional, unequivocal

qualify 1 = **gain qualifications**, pass, graduate, be licensed, make the grade, be authorized, be certified • *I qualified as a doctor over 30 years ago.*
2 = **certify**, equip, empower, train, ground, condition, prepare, fit, commission, ready, permit, sanction, endow, capacitate • *The course does not qualify you to practise as a therapist.*
OPPOSITES: ban, prevent, disqualify
3 = **be described**, count, be considered as, be named, be counted, be eligible, be characterized, be designated, be distinguished • *13 percent of households qualify as poor.*
4 = **restrict**, limit, reduce, vary, ease, moderate, adapt, modify, regulate, diminish, temper, soften, restrain, lessen, mitigate, abate, tone down, assuage, modulate, circumscribe • *I would qualify that by putting it into context.*

quality 1 = **standard**, standing, class, condition, value, rank, grade, merit, classification, calibre • *high quality paper and plywood*
2 = **excellence**, status, merit, position, value, worth, distinction, virtue, superiority, calibre, eminence, pre-eminence • *a college of quality*
3 = **characteristic**, feature, attribute, point, side, mark, property, aspect, streak, trait, facet, quirk, peculiarity, idiosyncrasy • *He wanted to introduce mature people with leadership qualities.*
4 = **nature**, character, constitution, make, sort, kind, worth, description, essence • *The pretentious quality of the poetry.*

qualm = **misgiving**, doubt, uneasiness, regret, anxiety, uncertainty, reluctance, hesitation, remorse, apprehension, disquiet, scruple, compunction, twinge *or* pang of conscience • *I had a sudden qualm that all might not be well.*

quandary = **difficulty**, dilemma, predicament, puzzle, uncertainty, embarrassment, plight, strait, impasse, bewilderment, perplexity, delicate situation, cleft stick • *Young drinkers create a quandary for drinks companies.*

quantity AS A NOUN 1 = **amount**, lot, total, sum, part, portion, quota, aggregate, number, allotment • *a vast quantity of food*
2 = **size**, measure, mass, volume, length, capacity, extent, bulk, magnitude, greatness, expanse • *the sheer quantity of data can cause problems.*

▸ **IN PHRASES: unknown quantity = enigma**, mystery, problem • *He is the unknown quantity who could just upset everything.*

quarantine AS A NOUN = isolation, segregation, solitude • *She was sent home and put in quarantine.*

▸ **AS A VERB = isolate**, separate, segregate, keep apart • *It is sensible to quarantine all new plants for a week or two.*

quarrel AS A NOUN = disagreement, fight, row, difference (of opinion), argument, dispute, controversy, breach, scrap *(informal)*, disturbance, misunderstanding, contention, feud, fray, brawl, spat, squabble, strife, wrangle, skirmish, vendetta, discord, fracas, commotion, tiff, altercation, broil, tumult, dissension, affray, turf war *(informal)*, shindig *(informal)*, disputation, dissidence, shindy *(informal)*, bagarre *(French)*, biffo *(Austral. slang)* • *I had a terrible quarrel with my other brothers.*

OPPOSITES: accord, agreement, concord

▸ **AS A VERB = disagree**, fight, argue, row, clash, dispute, scrap *(informal)*, differ, fall out *(informal)*, brawl, squabble, spar, wrangle, bicker, be at odds, lock horns, cross swords, fight like cat and dog, go at it hammer and tongs, altercate • *My brother quarrelled with my father.*

OPPOSITES: agree, get on *or* along (with)

▸ **IN PHRASES: quarrel with someone** *or* **something = argue with**, oppose, dispute, knock *(informal)*, fault, condemn, be against, complain about, criticize, object to, disapprove of, decry, take issue with, rebut, take exception to, find fault with, carp about, pick holes in, cavil at *or* about *or* over • *I cannot quarrel with the verdict.*

QUOTATIONS

It takes in reality only one to make a quarrel. It is useless for the sheep to pass resolutions in favour of vegetarianism, while the wolf remains of a different opinion

[William Ralph Inge *Outspoken Essays*]

Love-quarrels oft in pleasing concord end

[John Milton *Samson Agonistes*]

quarrelsome = argumentative, belligerent, pugnacious, cross, contentious, irritable, combative, fractious, petulant, ill-tempered, irascible, cantankerous, litigious, querulous, peevish, choleric, disputatious, arsey *(Brit., Austral. & N.Z.)* • *a quarrelsome young man*

OPPOSITES: easy-going, placid, equable

quarry[1] = excavate, mine, dig up, dig out • *The large limestone caves are also quarried for cement.*

quarry[2] = prey, victim, game, goal, aim, prize, objective • *As a journalist he stuck to his quarry like a lamprey.*

quarter AS A NOUN 1 = district, region, neighbourhood, place, point, part, side, area, position, station, spot, territory, zone, location, province, colony, locality • *He wandered through the Chinese quarter.*

2 = source, place, point, person, spot, direction, location • *Help came from an unexpected quarter.*

3 = mercy, pity, compassion, favour, charity, sympathy, tolerance, kindness, forgiveness, indulgence, clemency, leniency, forbearance, lenity • *It is bloody brutal work, with no quarter given.*

▸ **AS A VERB = accommodate**, house, lodge, place, board, post, station, install, put up, billet, give accommodation, provide with accommodation • *Our soldiers are quartered in Peredelkino.*

quarters = lodgings, rooms, accommodation, post, station, chambers, digs *(Brit. informal)*, shelter, lodging, residence, dwelling, barracks, abode, habitation, billet, domicile, cantonment *(Military)* • *Mckinnon went down from the deck to the officers' quarters.*

quash 1 = annul, overturn, reverse, cancel, overthrow, set aside, void, revoke, overrule, rescind, invalidate, nullify, declare null and void • *The Appeal Court has quashed the convictions.*

2 = put an end to, stamp out, put a stop to, end, check, nip in the bud • *He attempted to quash the rumours.*

3 = suppress, crush, put down, beat, destroy, overthrow, squash, subdue, repress, quell, extinguish, quench, extirpate • *an attempt to quash regional violence*

quasi- AS A COMBINING FORM = almost, partly • *The flame is a quasi-religious emblem of immortality.*

▸ **AS AN ADJECTIVE = pseudo-**, so-called, apparent, seeming, would-be, near, pretended, virtual, fake, mock, synthetic, nominal, sham, semi- • *a quasi-biography or mythobiography*

quaver = tremble, shake, quiver, thrill, quake, shudder, flicker, flutter, waver, vibrate, pulsate, oscillate, trill, twitter • *Her voice quavered and she fell silent.*

quay = dock, pier, landing, harbour, berth, wharf, jetty, pontoon, slipway, landing stage • *Jack and Stephen were waiting for them on the quay.*

queasy 1 = sick, ill, nauseous, squeamish, upset, uncomfortable, crook *(Austral. & N.Z. informal)*, queer, unwell, giddy, nauseated, groggy *(informal)*, off colour, bilious, indisposed, green around the gills *(informal)*, sickish • *He was prone to sickness and already felt queasy.*

2 = uneasy, concerned, worried, troubled, disturbed, anxious, uncertain, restless, ill at ease, fidgety • *Some people feel queasy about how their names and addresses have been obtained.*

queen 1 = sovereign, ruler, monarch, leader, Crown, princess, majesty, head of state, Her Majesty, empress, crowned head • *the time she met the Queen*

2 = leading light, star, favourite, celebrity, darling, mistress, idol, big name, doyenne • *the queen of crime writing*

3 = homosexual, gay, queer *(informal, derogatory)*, homo *(informal, derogatory)*, jessie *(slang)*, pansy *(informal, derogatory)*, homosexual man, poof *(Brit. & Austral. derogatory slang)*, effeminate man, diva, prima donna, batty boy *(slang)*, camp man, shirt-lifter *(derogatory slang)*, woofter *(derogatory slang)*, auntie *or* aunty *(Austral. slang)*, lily *(Austral. slang)* • *What a boring old queen he was.*

QUOTATIONS

queen: a woman by whom the realm is ruled when there is a king, and through whom it is ruled when there is not

[Ambrose Bierce *The Devil's Dictionary*]

I'd like to be a queen of people's hearts, in people's hearts, but I don't see myself being Queen of this country

[Diana, Princess of Wales]

queenly = majestic, royal, grand, imperial, noble, regal, stately • *She was a queenly, organizing type.*

queer AS AN ADJECTIVE 1 = strange, odd, funny, unusual, extraordinary, remarkable, curious, weird, peculiar, abnormal, rum *(Brit. slang)*, uncommon, erratic, singular, eerie, unnatural, unconventional, uncanny, disquieting, unorthodox, outlandish, left-field *(informal)*, anomalous, droll, atypical, outré • *If you ask me, there's something queer going on.*

OPPOSITES: normal, regular, ordinary

2 = gay, camp, homosexual, pink *(informal)* • *contemporary queer culture*

3 = faint, dizzy, giddy, queasy, light-headed, reeling • *Wine before beer and you'll feel queer.*

▸ **AS A NOUN = homosexual**, queen *(informal)*, gay, lesbian, homo *(informal derogatory)*, pansy *(informal derogatory)*, poof *(Brit. & Austral. derogatory slang)*, batty boy *(slang)*, shirt-lifter *(derogatory slang)*, woofter *(derogatory slang)*, auntie *or* aunty *(Austral. slang)*, lily *(Austral. slang)* • *She knows more queers than I do.*

quell 1 = suppress, crush, put down, defeat, overcome, conquer, subdue, stifle, overpower, quash, extinguish, stamp out, vanquish, squelch • *Troops eventually quelled the unrest.*

2 = **calm**, quiet, silence, moderate, dull, soothe, alleviate, appease, allay, mitigate, assuage, pacify, mollify, deaden • *He is trying to quell fears of a looming crisis.*

quench 1 = **satisfy**, appease, allay, satiate, slake, sate • *He stopped to quench his thirst at a stream.*
2 = **put out**, extinguish, douse, end, check, destroy, crush, suppress, stifle, smother, snuff out, squelch • *Fire crews struggled to quench the fire.*

querulous = **complaining**, cross, discontented, grumbling, peevish, critical, sour, carping, murmuring, whining, dissatisfied, irritable, touchy, petulant, plaintive, irascible, cantankerous, tetchy, ratty *(Brit. & N.Z. informal)*, testy, chippy *(informal)*, fretful, waspish, censorious, grouchy *(informal)*, hard to please, fault-finding, captious • *a querulous male voice*
OPPOSITES: contented, uncritical, uncomplaining

query AS A NOUN 1 = **question**, inquiry, problem, demand • *If you have any queries, please contact us.*
2 = **doubt**, suspicion, reservation, objection, hesitation, scepticism • *I read the query in the guide's eyes.*
▸ AS A VERB 1 = **question**, challenge, doubt, suspect, dispute, object to, distrust, mistrust, call into question, disbelieve, feel uneasy about, throw doubt on, harbour reservations about • *No one queried my decision.*
2 = **ask**, inquire *or* enquire, question • *'Is there something else?' he queried.*

quest AS A NOUN 1 = **search**, hunt, mission, enterprise, undertaking, exploration, crusade • *his quest to find true love*
2 = **expedition**, journey, adventure, voyage, pilgrimage • *Sir Guy the Seeker came on his quest to Dunstanburgh Castle.*
▸ IN PHRASES: **in quest of** = **searching for**, after, seeking, looking for, in search of, in pursuit of, on the lookout for, chasing after • *The Puritans became fugitives in quest of liberty.*

question AS A NOUN 1 = **inquiry**, enquiry, query, investigation, examination, interrogation • *He refused to answer further questions on the subject.*
OPPOSITES: answer, reply
2 = **difficulty**, problem, doubt, debate, argument, dispute, controversy, confusion, uncertainty, query, contention, misgiving, can of worms *(informal)*, dubiety • *There's no question about their success.*
3 = **issue**, point, matter, subject, problem, debate, proposal, theme, motion, topic, proposition, bone of contention, point at issue • *The whole question of aid is a tricky political one.*
▸ AS A VERB 1 = **interrogate**, cross-examine, interview, examine, investigate, pump *(informal)*, probe, grill *(informal)*, quiz, ask questions, sound out, catechize • *A man is being questioned by police.*
2 = **dispute**, challenge, doubt, suspect, oppose, query, distrust, mistrust, call into question, disbelieve, impugn, cast aspersions on, cast doubt upon, controvert • *It never occurs to them to question the doctor's decisions.*
OPPOSITES: believe, accept, buy *(slang)*
▸ IN PHRASES: **beyond question** 1 = **certain**, undeniable, indisputable, clear, obvious, patent, manifest, without doubt, undoubted, palpable, beyond doubt, irrefutable, unquestionable, incontrovertible, incontestable, indubitable, nailed-on *(slang)* • *That the pair can write is beyond question.*
2 = **irrefutably**, undeniably, beyond doubt, indisputably, clearly, undoubtedly, without doubt, unquestionably, incontrovertibly, incontestably • *Witnesses prove beyond question that contact was made.*
in question = **under discussion**, at issue, under consideration, in doubt, on the agenda, to be discussed, for debate, open to debate • *The film in question detailed allegations about party corruption.*
out of the question = **impossible**, unthinkable, inconceivable, not on *(informal)*, hopeless, unimaginable, unworkable, unattainable, unobtainable, not feasible, impracticable, unachievable, unrealizable, not worth considering, not to be thought of • *Is a tax increase still out of the question?*
pop the question = **propose**, offer marriage • *He got serious quickly and popped the question six months later.*
without question = **undoubtedly**, definitely, undeniably, surely, of course, certainly, doubtless, unquestionably, beyond question, beyond a shadow of (a) doubt • *He was our greatest storyteller, without question.*

PROVERBS
Ask a silly question and you get a silly answer
Ask no questions and hear no lies

questionable = **dubious**, suspect, doubtful, controversial, uncertain, suspicious, dodgy *(Brit., Austral. & N.Z. informal)*, unreliable, shady *(informal)*, debatable, unproven, fishy *(informal)*, moot, arguable, iffy *(informal)*, equivocal, problematical, disputable, controvertible, dubitable, shonky *(Austral. & N.Z. informal)* • *The film is a comedy in highly questionable taste.*
OPPOSITES: certain, straightforward, indisputable

questionnaire = **set of questions**, form, survey form, question sheet • *Headteachers will be asked to fill in a questionnaire.*

queue AS A NOUN 1 = **line**, row, file, train, series, chain, string, column, sequence, succession, procession, crocodile *(Brit. informal)*, progression, cavalcade, concatenation • *A queue of more than sixty people snaked its way down the pavement.*
2 = **tailback**, line, traffic jam, stream • *a long queue of angry motorists*
3 = **wait**, waiting list • *The queue for places at school has never been longer.*
▸ AS A VERB = **wait in line**, line up, stand in a queue, form a queue • *a line of women queueing for bread*

quibble AS A VERB = **split hairs**, carp, cavil, prevaricate, beat about the bush, equivocate, nit-pick *(informal)* • *Let's not quibble.*
▸ AS A NOUN = **objection**, complaint, niggle, protest, criticism, nicety, equivocation, prevarication, cavil, sideswipe, quiddity, sophism • *These are minor quibbles.*

quick AS AN ADJECTIVE 1 = **fast**, swift, speedy, express, active, cracking *(Brit. informal)*, smart, rapid, fleet, brisk, hasty, headlong, nippy *(informal)*, pdq *(slang)* • *Europe has moved a long way at a quick pace.*
OPPOSITES: slow, sluggish
2 = **brief**, passing, hurried, flying, fleeting, summary, lightning, short-lived, hasty, cursory, perfunctory • *I just popped in for a quick chat.*
OPPOSITES: long, gradual
3 = **instant**, immediate, instantaneous, speedy • *These investors feel the need to make quick profits.*
4 = **immediate**, instant, prompt, sudden, abrupt, instantaneous, expeditious • *The President has admitted there is no quick end in sight.*
5 = **excitable**, passionate, impatient, abrupt, hasty, irritable, touchy, curt, petulant, irascible, testy, chippy *(informal)* • *She had inherited her father's quick temper.*
OPPOSITES: patient, calm, restrained
6 = **intelligent**, bright *(informal)*, alert, sharp, acute, smart, clever, all there *(informal)*, shrewd, discerning, astute, receptive, perceptive, quick-witted, quick on the uptake *(informal)*, nimble-witted • *The older adults are not as quick in their thinking.*
OPPOSITES: stupid, unintelligent
▸ AS AN ADVERB = **fast**, soon, quickly, promptly, swiftly, speedily • *I got away as quick as I could.*

quicken 1 = **speed up**, hurry, accelerate, hasten, gee up *(informal)* • *He quickened his pace a little.*

2 = stimulate, inspire, arouse, excite, strengthen, revive, refresh, activate, animate, rouse, incite, resuscitate, energize, revitalize, kindle, galvanize, invigorate, reinvigorate, vitalize, vivify • *Thank you for quickening my spiritual understanding.*

quickly 1 = swiftly, rapidly, hurriedly, speedily, fast, quick, hastily, briskly, at high speed, apace, at full speed, hell for leather *(informal)*, like lightning, at the speed of light, at full tilt, hotfoot, at a rate of knots *(informal)*, like the clappers *(Brit. informal)*, pdq *(slang)*, like nobody's business *(informal)*, with all speed, posthaste, lickety-split *(U.S. informal)*, like greased lightning *(informal)*, at *or* on the double • *She turned and ran quickly up the stairs to the flat above.*
OPPOSITES: slowly
2 = soon, speedily, as soon as possible, momentarily *(U.S.)*, instantaneously, pronto *(informal)*, a.s.a.p. *(informal)* • *You can become fitter quickly and easily.*
3 = immediately, instantly, at once, directly, promptly, abruptly, without delay, expeditiously • *The meeting quickly adjourned.*
4 = briefly, hastily, hurriedly, superficially, fleetingly, in haste, perfunctorily, briskly, desultorily, cursorily • *I quickly looked at her papers while she was out of the room.*

quick-tempered = hot-tempered, fiery, irritable, impatient, impulsive, excitable, petulant, irascible, cantankerous, tetchy, ratty *(Brit. & N.Z. informal)*, testy, quarrelsome, waspish, choleric, splenetic, shrewish • *They are wonderful people, but very quick-tempered.*
OPPOSITES: cool, placid, dispassionate

quick-witted = clever, bright *(informal)*, sharp, keen, smart, alert, shrewd, astute, perceptive • *He is quick-witted and rarely lets an opportunity slip by.*
OPPOSITES: slow, thick *(informal)*, stupid

quid pro quo = exchange, interchange, tit for tat, equivalent, compensation, retaliation, reprisal, substitution • *The statement is emphatic that there must be a quid pro quo.*

quiescent = quiet, still, peaceful, calm, resting, smooth, silent, serene, tranquil, dormant, latent, motionless, placid, undisturbed, inactive, unruffled, unmoving, in abeyance, unagitated • *a quiescent seaside town*

quiet AS AN ADJECTIVE **1 = soft**, low, muted, lowered, whispered, faint, suppressed, stifled, hushed, muffled, inaudible, indistinct, low-pitched • *A quiet murmur passed through the classroom.*
OPPOSITES: loud, noisy, deafening
2 = peaceful, silent, still, hushed, soundless, noiseless • *She was received in a small, quiet office.*
OPPOSITES: loud, noisy, deafening
3 = calm, peaceful, tranquil, contented, gentle, mild, serene, pacific, placid, restful, untroubled, chilled *(informal)* • *She wanted a quiet life.*
OPPOSITES: troubled, exciting, turbulent
4 = still, motionless, calm, peaceful, tranquil, untroubled • *a look of quiet satisfaction*
OPPOSITES: troubled, turbulent, agitated
5 = undisturbed, isolated, secluded, private, secret, retired, sequestered, unfrequented • *a quiet rural backwater*
OPPOSITES: popular, crowded, busy
6 = silent, dumb • *I told them to be quiet and go to sleep.*
7 = discreet, private, confidential, secret, unofficial, off the record • *Can I have a quiet word with you, son?*
8 = reserved, retiring, shy, collected, gentle, mild, composed, serene, sedate, meek, placid, docile, unflappable *(informal)*, phlegmatic, peaceable, imperturbable, equable, even-tempered, unexcitable • *He's a nice quiet man.*
OPPOSITES: excited, passionate, excitable
9 = subdued, conservative, plain, sober, simple, modest, restrained, unassuming, unpretentious, unobtrusive • *They dress in quiet colours.*
OPPOSITES: bright, loud, glaring
▸ AS A NOUN **= peace**, rest, tranquillity, ease, silence, solitude, serenity, stillness, repose, calmness, quietness, peacefulness, restfulness • *He wants some peace and quiet.*
OPPOSITES: noise, disturbance, racket

quieten AS A VERB **1 = silence**, subdue, stifle, still, stop, quiet, mute, hush, quell, muffle, shush *(informal)* • *She tried to quieten her breathing.*
2 = soothe, calm, allay, dull, blunt, alleviate, appease, lull, mitigate, assuage, mollify, deaden, tranquillize, palliate • *a long time to quieten the paranoia of the West*
OPPOSITES: upset, provoke, intensify
▸ IN PHRASES: **quieten someone down = calm someone down**, comfort, soothe, subdue, pacify • *Somehow I managed to quieten her down.*

quietly 1 = noiselessly, silently • *She closed the door quietly.*
2 = softly, in hushed tones, in a low voice *or* whisper, inaudibly, in an undertone, under your breath • *'This is goodbye, isn't it?' she said quietly.*
3 = privately, secretly, discreetly, confidentially • *quietly planning their next move*
4 = calmly, serenely, placidly, patiently, mildly, meekly, contentedly, dispassionately, undemonstratively • *She sat quietly watching all that was going on around her.*
5 = silently, in silence, mutely, without talking, dumbly • *Amy stood quietly in the door watching him.*
6 = modestly, humbly, unobtrusively, diffidently, unpretentiously, unassumingly, unostentatiously • *He is quietly confident about the magazine's chances.*

quietness = peace, still, silence, calm, rest, quiet, hush, serenity, tranquillity, stillness, repose, calmness, quietude, quiescence, placidity • *I miss the quietness of the countryside.*

quilt = bedspread, duvet, comforter *(U.S.)*, downie *(informal)*, coverlet, eiderdown, counterpane, doona *(Austral.)*, continental quilt • *an old patchwork quilt*

quintessence 1 = epitome, representation, embodiment, type, essence, archetype, exemplar, typical example, personification • *He was the quintessence of all Eva most deeply loathed.*
2 = essence, heart, spirit, soul, core, marrow, kernel, gist, distillation, lifeblood, pith • *the quintessence of civilized culture*

quintessential = ultimate, essential, typical, fundamental, definitive, archetypal, prototypical • *Everybody thinks of him as the quintessential New Yorker.*

quip AS A NOUN **= joke**, sally, jest, riposte, wisecrack *(informal)*, retort, counterattack, pleasantry, repartee, gibe, witticism, bon mot, badinage • *a deadpan quip*
▸ AS A VERB **= joke**, jest, wisecrack *(informal)*, pun • *'He'll have to go on a diet,' Ballard quipped.*

quirk 1 = fluke, chance, twist, turn, freak, anomaly • *a tantalising quirk of fate*
2 = peculiarity, eccentricity, mannerism, foible, idiosyncrasy, habit, fancy, characteristic, trait, whim, oddity, caprice, fetish, aberration, kink, vagary, singularity, idée fixe *(French)* • *the quirks and foibles of people in everyday situations*

quirky = odd, unusual, eccentric, idiosyncratic, curious, peculiar, unpredictable, rum *(Brit. slang)*, singular, fanciful, whimsical, capricious, offbeat, out there *(slang)* • *We've developed a reputation for being quite quirky and original.*

quisling = traitor, betrayer, collaborator, renegade, Judas, turncoat, fifth columnist • *They called him a quisling.*

quit 1 = resign (from), leave, retire (from), pull out (of), surrender, chuck *(informal)*, step down (from) *(informal)*, relinquish, renounce, pack in *(informal)*, abdicate • *He figured he would quit his job before he was fired*
2 = stop, give up, cease, end, drop, abandon, suspend, halt, discontinue, belay *(Nautical)* • *I was trying to quit smoking at the time.*
OPPOSITES: continue, finish, see through

3 = leave, depart from, go out of, abandon, desert, exit, withdraw from, forsake, go away from, pull out from, decamp from • *Police were called when he refused to quit the building.*

quite 1 = somewhat, rather, fairly, reasonably, kind of *(informal)*, pretty *(informal)*, relatively, moderately, to some extent, comparatively, to some degree, to a certain extent • *I was doing quite well, but I wasn't earning a lot of money.*
2 = absolutely, perfectly, completely, totally, fully, entirely, precisely, considerably, wholly, in all respects, without reservation • *It is quite clear that we were firing in self-defence.*

quiver AS A VERB **= shake**, tremble, shiver, quake, shudder, agitate, vibrate, pulsate, quaver, convulse, palpitate • *Her bottom lip quivered and big tears rolled down her cheeks.*
▸ AS A NOUN **= shake**, tremble, shiver, throb, shudder, tremor, spasm, vibration, tic, convulsion, palpitation, pulsation • *I felt a quiver of panic.*

quixotic = unrealistic, idealistic, romantic, absurd, imaginary, visionary, fanciful, impractical, dreamy, Utopian, impulsive, fantastical, impracticable, chivalrous, unworldly, chimerical • *He lived his life by a quixotic code of honour.*

quiz AS A NOUN **1 = competition**, test, quiz show, panel game, quiz game, test of knowledge • *We'll have a quiz at the end of the show.*
2 = examination, questioning, interrogation, interview, investigation, grilling *(informal)*, cross-examination, cross-questioning, the third degree *(informal)* • *Man faces quiz over knife death.*
▸ AS A VERB **= question**, ask, interrogate, examine, investigate, pump *(informal)*, grill *(informal)*, catechize • *Sybil quizzed her about life as a working girl.*

quizzical = mocking, questioning, inquiring, curious, arch, teasing, bantering, sardonic, derisive, supercilious • *He gave Robin a mildly quizzical glare.*

quota = share, allowance, ration, allocation, part, cut *(informal)*, limit, proportion, slice, quantity, portion, assignment, whack *(informal)*, dispensation • *The quota of four tickets per person had been reduced to two.*

quotation 1 = passage, quote *(informal)*, excerpt, cutting, selection, reference, extract, citation • *He illustrated his argument with quotations from Pasternak.*
2 = estimate, price, tender, rate, cost, charge, figure, quote *(informal)*, bid price • *Get several written quotations and check exactly what's included in the cost.*

QUOTATIONS

Every quotation contributes something to the stability or enlargement of the language

[Dr. Johnson *Dictionary of the English Language* (preface)]

quote AS A VERB **1 = repeat**, recite, reproduce, recall, echo, extract, excerpt, proclaim, parrot, paraphrase, retell • *Then suddenly he quoted a line from the play.*
2 = refer to, cite, give, name, detail, relate, mention, instance, specify, spell out, recount, recollect, make reference to, adduce • *Most newspapers quote the warning.*
3 = estimate, state, tender, set, offer, bid • *He quoted a price for the repairs.*
▸ AS A NOUN **1 = quotation**, passage, excerpt, reference, extract, citation • *A quote from the Independent article speaks volumes.*
2 = estimate, evaluation, valuation, quotation, guesstimate *(informal)*, ballpark figure *or* estimate *(informal)* • *a quote for insurance*
▸ AS A PLURAL NOUN **= quotation marks**, speech marks • *The word 'remembered' is in quotes.*

quotidian 1 = regular, ordinary, routine, everyday, common, customary, commonplace, habitual • *the minutiae of their quotidian existence*
2 = daily, circadian, diurnal • *the quotidian round of pheasant-rearing*

Rr

rabbit AS A NOUN = **buck**, doe, bunny rabbit *(informal)* • *I caught my first rabbit when I was eight.*
▸ IN PHRASES: **rabbit on** = **go on**, gas, rattle, gossip, chatter, spout, waffle, drivel, drone on, gab, twitter, ramble on, jabber, gabble, blether • *What are you rabbiting on about?*
▸ NAME OF MALE: buck
▸ NAME OF FEMALE: doe
▸ COLLECTIVE NOUN: nest
▸ NAME OF HOME: warren

RABBITS AND HARES

Angora rabbit	hare	cottontail
arctic hare	jack rabbit	snowshoe hare
Belgian hare	pika *or* cony	*or* snowshoe
coney	rabbit *or*	rabbit

rabble 1 = **mob**, crowd, herd, swarm, horde, throng, canaille • *a rabble of gossip columnists*
2 = **commoners**, proletariat, common people, riffraff, crowd, masses, trash *(chiefly U.S. & Canad.)*, scum, lower classes, populace, peasantry, dregs, hoi polloi, the great unwashed *(derogatory)*, canaille, lumpenproletariat, commonalty • *They are forced to socialise with the rabble.*
OPPOSITES: elite, upper classes, aristocracy

rabble-rouser = **agitator**, troublemaker, incendiary, firebrand, demagogue, stirrer *(informal)* • *a loud-mouthed rabble-rouser*

rabid 1 = **fanatical**, extreme, irrational, fervent, zealous, bigoted, intolerant, narrow-minded, intemperate • *the rabid state media*
OPPOSITES: moderate, wishy-washy *(informal)*, half-hearted
2 = **crazed**, wild, violent, mad, raging, furious, frantic, frenzied, infuriated, berserk, maniacal, berko *(Austral. slang)* • *The tablets gave him the look of a rabid dog.*

race[1] AS A NOUN 1 = **competition**, contest, event, chase, dash, pursuit, contention, relay, time-trial • *a running race in a Cambridge quadrangle*
2 = **contest**, competition, quest, rivalry, contention • *the race for the White House*
▸ AS A VERB 1 = **compete against**, run against, try to beat, have a race with • *They may even have raced each other.*
2 = **compete**, run, contend, take part in a race • *He, too, will be racing here again soon.*
3 = **run**, fly, career, speed, tear, dash, hurry, barrel (along) *(informal, chiefly U.S. & Canad.)*, dart, gallop, zoom, hare *(Brit. informal)*, hasten, burn rubber *(informal)*, go like a bomb *(Brit. & N.Z. informal)*, run like mad *(informal)* • *They raced away out of sight.*
4 = **soar**, rise, climb, rocket, escalate, shoot up • *Economic growth raced ahead.*
5 = **pump**, pound, hammer, thump, throb, flutter, thud, pulsate, palpitate, beat rapidly • *Her heart raced uncontrollably.*

race[2] = **people**, ethnic group, nation, blood, house, family, line, issue, stock, type, seed *(chiefly biblical)*, breed, folk, tribe, offspring, clan, kin, lineage, progeny, kindred • *We welcome students of all races, faiths and nationalities.*

QUOTATIONS
No race has the last word on culture and on civilization
[Marcus Garvey *speech*]
There are only two races on this planet – the intelligent and the stupid
[John Fowles]

racecourse = **hippodrome**, course, track, racetrack • *a tragedy on the racecourse*

racehorse = **thoroughbred**, Arab, jumper, sprinter, racer, steeplechaser, bloodstock, purebred • *a very great racehorse*
▸ COLLECTIVE NOUNS: field, string

racer = **competitor**, runner, contender, sprinter • *a former champion powerboat racer*

racial = **ethnic**, ethnological, national, folk, genetic, tribal, genealogical • *the protection of national and racial minorities*

racism = **xenophobia**, bigotry, racial discrimination, racial prejudice, anti-Semitism, intolerance, chauvinism, racialism • *The party is pandering to racism.*

racist AS AN ADJECTIVE = **racially prejudiced**, prejudiced, racialist, racially bigoted, anti-Semitic, intolerant, chauvinist • *a racist society*
▸ AS A NOUN = **racial bigot**, bigot, chauvinist, racialist, anti-Semite • *He has a hard core of support amongst white racists.*

rack AS A NOUN = **frame**, support, stand, structure, holder, shelf, framework, trestle • *a luggage rack*
▸ AS A VERB = **torture**, distress, torment, harass, afflict, oppress, harrow, crucify, agonize, pain, excruciate • *a teenager racked with guilt*
▸ IN PHRASES: **on the rack** = **in difficulties**, suffering, in trouble, having problems, in agony, in distress, racked with pain, going through torture • *on the rack with a heroin addiction*
rack something up = **sustain**, experience, suffer, bear, endure, undergo, withstand, bear up under, feel • *The company continues to rack up huge losses.*
rack your brains = **think hard**, try to remember *(informal)*, scratch your head, give a lot of thought to something, put your mind to something, puzzle over something • *As I ate, I racked my brains in a search for his identity.*

racket 1 = **noise**, row, shouting, fuss, disturbance, outcry, clamour, din, uproar, commotion, pandemonium, rumpus, babel, tumult, hubbub, hullabaloo, ballyhoo *(informal)* • *The racket went on past midnight.*
2 = **fraud**, scheme, criminal activity, fraudulent scheme, illegal enterprise • *a drugs racket*

racketeering = **fraud**, swindling, criminal activity, sharp practice • *He was indicted on racketeering charges.*

raconteur = **storyteller**, relater, recounter, teller of stories, spinner of yarns • *He spoke eight languages and was a noted raconteur*

racy 1 = **risqué**, naughty, indecent, bawdy, blue, broad, spicy *(informal)*, suggestive, smutty, off colour, immodest, indelicate, near the knuckle *(informal)* • *Her novels may be racy but they don't fight shy of larger issues.*
2 = **lively**, spirited, exciting, dramatic, entertaining, stimulating, sexy *(informal)*, sparkling, vigorous, energetic, animated, heady, buoyant, exhilarating, zestful • *very high-quality wines with quite a racy character*

raddled = **rundown**, broken-down, dilapidated, tattered, haggard, dishevelled, unkempt, the worse for wear, coarsened • *He gazed at the raddled streets.*

radiance 1 = **happiness**, delight, pleasure, joy, warmth, rapture, elation, gaiety • *There was a new radiance about her.*
2 = **brightness**, light, shine, glow, glitter, glare, gleam, brilliance, lustre, luminosity, incandescence, resplendence, effulgence • *The dim bulb cast a soft radiance over his face.*

radiant 1 = **happy**, glowing, ecstatic, joyful, sent *(informal)*, gay, delighted, beaming, joyous, blissful, rapturous, rapt, on cloud nine *(informal)*, beatific, blissed out *(informal)*, floating on air • *On her wedding day the bride looked truly radiant.*
OPPOSITES: low, sad, miserable
2 = **bright**, brilliant, shining, glorious, beaming, glowing, sparkling, sunny, glittering, gleaming, luminous, resplendent, incandescent, lustrous, effulgent • *Out on the bay the morning is radiant.*
OPPOSITES: black, dark, dull

radiate 1 = **emit**, spread, send out, disseminate, pour, shed, scatter, glitter, gleam • *Thermal imagery will show up objects radiating heat.*
2 = **shine**, beam, emanate, be diffused • *From here contaminated air radiates out to the open countryside.*
3 = **show**, display, demonstrate, exhibit, emanate, be a picture of, give off *or* out • *She radiates happiness and health.*
4 = **spread out**, issue, extend, diverge, branch out, fan out, split off • *the narrow streets which radiate from the Cathedral Square*

radiation = **emission**, rays, emanation • *They study energy radiation from the most violent stars in the universe.*

radical AS AN ADJECTIVE 1 = **extreme**, complete, entire, sweeping, violent, severe, extensive, wide-ranging, excessive, thorough, drastic, rigorous, far-reaching, draconian • *periods of radical change*
2 = **revolutionary**, reforming, extreme, militant, progressive, left-wing, extremist, reformist, fanatical • *political tension between radical and conservative politicians*
3 = **fundamental**, natural, basic, essential, native, constitutional, organic, profound, innate, deep-seated, thoroughgoing, hard-wired • *the radical differences between them*
OPPOSITES: minor, token, superficial
▸ AS A NOUN = **extremist**, revolutionary, militant, reformer, fanatic, left-winger, zealot, revisionist • *a former left-wing radical who was involved with the civil rights movement*
OPPOSITES: conservative, moderate, reactionary

QUOTATIONS

A radical is a man with both feet firmly planted in the air
[Franklin D. Roosevelt *radio broadcast*]

radicalism = **reformism**, extremism, fanaticism, revisionism, progressivism, socialism, leftism • *a curious mixture of radicalism and conservatism*

raffish = **dashing**, casual, careless, bohemian, sporty, unconventional, jaunty, disreputable, rakish, devil-may-care • *He was handsome in a raffish kind of way.*

raffle = **draw**, lottery, ballot, sweepstake, tombola, sweep • *There will be more great prizes to be won in our latest raffle.*

rag[1] AS A NOUN 1 = **cloth**, piece of cloth • *He was wiping his oily hands on a rag.*
2 = **newspaper**, paper, journal, tabloid, newsletter, periodical, broadsheet • *He works for the local rag.*
▸ AS A PLURAL NOUN = **tatters**, old clothes, tattered clothes, torn clothes, tattered clothing • *There were men, women and children, some dressed in rags.*
OPPOSITES: finery, Sunday best, gladrags
▸ IN PHRASES: **in rags** = **shabby**, ragged, seedy, tattered, down at heel, out at elbow • *Grandma Jana was ashamed to let Cleave see me in rags.*
lose your rag = **become angry**, lose it *(informal)*, fly into a rage, lose your temper, blow a fuse, fly off the handle, throw a wobbly *(informal)*, hit the ceiling, blow a gasket, blow your top, go crook *(Austral. & N.Z. slang)*, blow your stack • *I've only once seen him lose his rag.*

rag[2] AS A VERB = **tease**, provoke, needle *(informal)*, mock, bait, rib *(informal)*, wind up *(Brit. slang)*, torment, ridicule, taunt, goad, take the mickey (out of) *(informal)*, take the piss (out of) *(taboo slang)*, gibe, pull someone's leg *(informal)*, jerk *or* yank someone's chain *(informal)* • *She was ten years older than the youngsters ragging her.*
▸ AS A NOUN = **fundraising event**, charity event, charitable event • *It all feels like a rag week that went on for a few years too long.*

ragamuffin = **urchin**, gamin, guttersnipe, scarecrow *(informal)*, tatterdemalion *(rare)*, street Arab *(offensive)* • *two ragamuffins with a torch*

ragbag = **mixture**, jumble, medley, mixed bag *(informal)*, potpourri, miscellany, hotchpotch, omnium-gatherum, confusion • *a ragbag of right-wing liberals, Flemish nationalists and greens*

rage AS A NOUN 1 = **fury**, temper, frenzy, rampage, tantrum, fit of pique, fit of temper, foulie *(Austral. slang)*, hissy fit *(informal)*, strop *(Brit. informal)* • *I flew into a rage.*
OPPOSITES: pleasure, joy, calmness
2 = **anger**, violence, passion, obsession, madness, raving, wrath, mania, agitation, ire, vehemence, high dudgeon • *The people are full of fear and rage.*
3 = **craze**, fashion, enthusiasm, obsession, vogue, fad *(informal)*, latest thing • *the latest technological rage*
▸ AS A VERB 1 = **be at its height**, surge, rampage, be turbulent, be uncontrollable, storm • *The war rages on and the time has come to take sides.*
2 = **be furious**, rave, blow up *(informal)*, fume, lose it *(informal)*, fret, seethe, crack up *(informal)*, see red *(informal)*, chafe, lose the plot *(informal)*, go ballistic *(slang, chiefly U.S.)*, rant and rave, foam at the mouth, lose your temper, blow a fuse *(slang, chiefly U.S.)*, fly off the handle *(informal)*, be incandescent, go off the deep end *(informal)*, throw a fit *(informal)*, wig out *(slang)*, go up the wall *(slang)*, blow your top, lose your rag *(slang)*, be beside yourself, flip your lid *(slang)* • *He was annoyed, no doubt, but not raging.*
OPPOSITES: accept, stay calm, keep your cool
▸ IN PHRASES: **all the rage** = **in fashion**, fashionable, in style, much sought-after, in great demand, du jour *(French)*, the latest thing, culty, the new • *I was a teenager at the time when platform shoes were all the rage.*

ragged 1 = **tatty**, worn, poor, torn, rent, faded, neglected, rundown, frayed, shabby, worn-out, seedy, scruffy, in tatters, dilapidated, tattered, threadbare, unkempt, in rags, down at heel, the worse for wear, in holes, having seen better days, scraggy • *I am usually happiest in ragged jeans and a t-shirt.*
OPPOSITES: smart, fashionable, well-dressed
2 = **rough**, fragmented, crude, rugged, notched, irregular, unfinished, uneven, jagged, serrated • *She tore her tights on the ragged edge of a desk*

raging 1 = **furious**, mad, raving, fuming, frenzied, infuriated, incensed, enraged, seething, fizzing *(Scot.)*, incandescent,

foaming at the mouth, fit to be tied (*slang*), boiling mad (*informal*), beside yourself, doing your nut (*Brit. slang*), off the air (*Austral. slang*) • *Inside, she was raging.*
2 = **stormy**, strong, wild, violent, turbulent, tempestuous • *raging seas*
3 = **severe**, acute, extreme, excessive, searing, very great • *He felt a raging thirst.*

raid AS A VERB 1 = **steal from**, break into, loot, plunder, ransack, pillage, sack • *The guerrillas raided banks and destroyed a police barracks.*
2 = **attack**, invade, assault, rifle, forage (*Military*), fall upon, swoop down upon, reive (*dialect*) • *8th century Vikings set off to raid the coasts of Europe.*
3 = **make a search of**, search, bust (*informal*), descend on, make a raid on, make a swoop on • *Fraud squad officers raided the firm's offices.*
▸ AS A NOUN 1 = **attack**, invasion, seizure, onset, foray, sortie, incursion, surprise attack, hit-and-run attack, sally, inroad, irruption • *The rebels attempted a surprise raid on a military camp.*
2 = **bust** (*informal*), swoop, descent, surprise search • *a raid on a house by thirty armed police*
3 = **robbery**, sacking, break-in, looting, burglary, ransacking, pillaging, smash-and-grab (*informal*), home invasion (*Austral. & N.Z.*) • *He carried out a series of bank raids.*

raider = **attacker**, thief, robber, plunderer, invader, forager (*Military*), marauder, reiver (*dialect*) • *The raiders escaped with cash and jewellery.*

rail[1] 1 = **handle**, railing, shaft, banister, handrail, balustrade • *She gripped the hand rail in the lift.*
2 = **track**, points • *The train left the rails.*
3 = **train**, locomotive, rolling stock, freightliner • *He travelled by rail.*

rail[2] = **complain**, attack, abuse, blast, flame (*informal*), put down, criticize, censure, scold, castigate, revile, tear into (*informal*), diss (*slang, chiefly U.S.*), fulminate, inveigh, upbraid, lambast(e), vituperate, vociferate • *I'd cursed him and railed at him.*

railing = **fence**, rails, barrier, paling, balustrade • *the iron railings of the convent grounds*

rail travel
▸ RELATED MANIA: siderodromomania

rain AS A NOUN 1 = **rainfall**, fall, showers, deluge, drizzle, downpour, precipitation, raindrops, cloudburst • *You'll get soaked standing out in the rain.*
2 = **shower**, flood, stream, hail, volley, spate, torrent, deluge • *A rain of stones descended on the police.*
▸ AS A VERB 1 = **pour**, pelt (down), teem, bucket down (*informal*), fall, shower, drizzle, rain cats and dogs (*informal*), come down in buckets (*informal*) • *It rained the whole weekend.*
2 = **fall**, shower, be dropped, sprinkle, be deposited • *Rockets, mortars and artillery rained on buildings.*
3 = **bestow**, pour, shower, lavish • *Banks rained money on commercial real estate developers.*
▸ RELATED ADJECTIVES: hyetal, pluvial, pluvious

QUOTATIONS
The rain it raineth every day
[William Shakespeare *Twelfth Night*]

PROVERBS
It never rains but it pours

rainbow
▸ RELATED ADJECTIVE: iridal

rainy = **wet**, damp, inclement, drizzly, showery • *a rainy night*
OPPOSITES: fine, dry, sunny

raise AS A VERB 1 = **lift**, move up, elevate, uplift, heave • *He raised his hand to wave.*
2 = **set upright**, lift, elevate • *She raised herself on one elbow.*
3 = **increase**, reinforce, intensify, heighten, advance, boost, strengthen, enhance, put up, exaggerate, hike (up) (*informal*), enlarge, escalate, inflate, aggravate, magnify, amplify, augment, jack up • *Two incidents in recent days have raised the level of concern.*
OPPOSITES: cut, drop, reduce
4 = **improve**, boost, enhance, upgrade, make better, ameliorate, lift • *a new drive to raise standards of literacy in Britain's schools*
5 = **make louder**, heighten, amplify, louden, increase, turn up, intensify, magnify, augment, make higher • *Don't you raise your voice to me!*
6 = **collect**, get, gather, obtain, acquire, accumulate, amass • *events held to raise money*
7 = **mobilize**, form, mass, rally, recruit, assemble, levy, sign up, muster, enlist, call together • *Landed nobles provided courts of justice and raised troops.*
8 = **cause**, start, produce, create, occasion, provoke, bring about, originate, give rise to, engender • *a joke that raised a smile*
9 = **put forward**, suggest, introduce, advance, bring up, broach, moot • *He had been consulted and had raised no objections.*
10 = **bring up**, develop, rear, foster, educate, care for, provide for, nurture • *the house where she was raised*
11 = **grow**, produce, farm, rear, cultivate, propagate • *He raises 2,000 acres of wheat and hay.*
12 = **breed**, keep, tend, rear, nurture • *She raised chickens and pigs.*
13 = **build**, construct, put up, erect • *They raised a church in the shape of a boat.*
OPPOSITES: level, destroy, demolish
14 = **communicate with**, reach, contact, get hold of, get in touch with, call forth • *the ability to raise the dead*
15 = **promote**, upgrade, elevate, advance, prefer, exalt, aggrandize • *He was to be raised to the rank of ambassador.*
OPPOSITES: reduce, downgrade, demote
▸ AS A NOUN = **rise**, pay increase, increment • *Within two months Kelly got a raise.*

rake[1] AS A VERB 1 = **scrape**, level, smooth, break up, scratch, flatten, scour, harrow, hoe • *The beach is raked and cleaned daily.*
2 = **gather**, collect, scrape together, scrape up, remove • *I watched the men rake leaves into heaps.*
3 = **strafe**, pepper, enfilade • *The caravan was raked with bullets.*
4 = **graze**, scratch, scrape, lacerate, abrade • *Ragged fingernails raked her skin.*
5 with **through** = **search**, hunt, examine, scan, comb, scour, ransack, forage, scrutinize, fossick (*Austral. & N.Z.*) • *Many can only survive by raking through dustbins.*
▸ IN PHRASES: **rake something in** = **earn**, raise, net, acquire, build up, yield, bring in, gross, accumulate, amass, accrue, cumulate • *The privatisation allowed companies to rake in huge profits.*
rake something up = **call to mind**, dig up, dredge up, drag up, revive the memory of • *Do I have to rake up those awful memories?*

rake[2] = **libertine**, playboy, swinger (*slang*), profligate, lecher, roué, sensualist, voluptuary, debauchee, rakehell (*archaic*), dissolute man, lech or letch (*informal*) • *As a young man I was a rake.*
OPPOSITES: monk, puritan, celibate

rakish = **dashing**, smart, sporty, flashy, breezy, jaunty, dapper, natty (*informal*), debonair, snazzy (*informal*), raffish, devil-may-care • *rakish young gentlemen*

rally AS A NOUN 1 = **gathering**, mass meeting, convention, convocation, meeting, conference, congress, assembly, congregation, muster, hui (*N.Z.*) • *They held a rally to mark international human rights day.*
2 = **recovery**, improvement, comeback (*informal*), revival,

renewal, resurgence, recuperation, turn for the better • *After a brief rally, shares returned to 126p.*
OPPOSITES: collapse, deterioration, relapse
▸ **AS A VERB 1 = gather together**, unite, bring together, regroup, reorganize, reassemble, re-form • *He rallied his own supporters for a fight.*
2 = recover, improve, pick up, revive, get better, come round, perk up, recuperate, turn the corner, pull through, take a turn for the better, regain your strength, get your second wind • *He rallied enough to thank his doctor.*
OPPOSITES: fail, deteriorate, get worse
▸ **IN PHRASES: rally around** *or* **round = gather**, unite, collect, organize, assemble, get together, convene, mobilize, bond together, come together • *So many people have rallied round to help the family.*

ram **AS A VERB 1 = hit**, force, drive into, strike, crash, impact, smash, slam, dash, run into, butt, collide with • *They used a lorry to ram the main gate.*
2 = cram, pound, force, stuff, pack, hammer, jam, thrust, tamp • *He rammed the key into the lock and kicked the front door open.*
▸ **IN PHRASES: ram something home = drive home**, stress, emphasize • *We need to ram home the message.*

ramble **AS A NOUN = walk**, tour, trip, stroll, hike, roaming, excursion, roving, saunter, traipse *(informal)*, peregrination, perambulation • *an hour's ramble through the woods*
▸ **AS A VERB 1 = walk**, range, drift, wander, stroll, stray, roam, rove, amble, saunter, straggle, traipse *(informal)*, go walkabout *(Austral.)*, perambulate, stravaig *(Scot. & Northern English dialect)*, peregrinate • *freedom to ramble across the moors*
2 *often with* **on = babble**, go on, gas, wander, rabbit (on) *(Brit. informal)*, rattle, chatter, spout, waffle *(informal, chiefly Brit.)*, drivel, drone on, gab, twitter, digress, jabber, gabble, rattle on, maunder, witter on *(informal)*, blether, expatiate, run off at the mouth *(slang)* • *Sometimes she tended to ramble.*

rambler **= walker**, roamer, wanderer, rover, hiker, drifter, stroller, wayfarer • *A woman rambler was trampled by a herd of cows.*

rambling **1 = sprawling**, spreading, trailing, irregular, straggling • *that rambling house with its bizarre contents*
2 = long-winded, incoherent, disjointed, prolix, irregular, diffuse, disconnected, desultory, wordy, circuitous, discursive, digressive, periphrastic • *He wrote a rambling letter to his wife.*
OPPOSITES: direct, to the point, concise

ramification *usually plural* **= consequences**, results, developments, complications, sequel, upshot • *These issues have powerful personal and political ramifications.*

ramp **= slope**, grade, incline, gradient, inclined plane, rise • *a ramp to facilitate entry into the pool from a wheelchair*

rampage **AS A VERB = go berserk**, tear, storm, rage, run riot, run amok, run wild, go ballistic *(slang)*, go ape *(slang)*, go apeshit *(slang, chiefly U.S.)* • *He used a sword to defend his shop from a rampaging mob.*
▸ **IN PHRASES: on the rampage = berserk**, wild, violent, raging, destructive, out of control, rampant, amok, riotous, berko *(Austral. slang)* • *a bull that went on the rampage*

rampant **1 = widespread**, rank, epidemic, prevalent, rife, exuberant, uncontrolled, unchecked, unrestrained, luxuriant, profuse, spreading like wildfire • *the rampant corruption of the administration*
2 = unrestrained, wild, violent, raging, aggressive, dominant, excessive, outrageous, out of control, rampaging, out of hand, uncontrollable, flagrant, unbridled, vehement, wanton, riotous, on the rampage, ungovernable • *rampant civil and military police atrocities*
3 = lush, rich, luxuriant, profuse • *lush, rampant vegetation writhing out of the grey granite*
4 = upright, standing, rearing, erect • *a shield with a lion rampant*

rampart **= defence**, wall, parapet, fortification, security, guard, fence, fort, barricade, stronghold, bastion, embankment, bulwark, earthwork, breastwork • *a walk along the ramparts of the old city*

ramshackle **= rickety**, broken-down, crumbling, shaky, unsafe, derelict, flimsy, tottering, dilapidated, decrepit, unsteady, tumbledown, jerry-built • *a curious ramshackle building*
OPPOSITES: solid, stable, steady

rancid **= rotten**, sour, foul, bad, off, rank, tainted, stale, musty, fetid, putrid, fusty, strong-smelling, frowsty • *the odour of rancid milk*
OPPOSITES: fresh, pure, undecayed

rancorous **= bitter**, hostile, malicious, malign, resentful, malignant, acrimonious, virulent, vindictive, implacable, malevolent, spiteful, venomous, splenetic • *a series of rancorous disputes*

rancour **= hatred**, hate, spite, hostility, resentment, bitterness, grudge, malice, animosity, venom, antipathy, spleen, enmity, ill feeling, bad blood, ill will, animus, malevolence, malignity, chip on your shoulder *(informal)*, resentfulness • *'That's too bad,' he said without rancour.*

random **AS AN ADJECTIVE 1 = chance**, spot, casual, stray, accidental, arbitrary, incidental, indiscriminate, haphazard, unplanned, fortuitous, aimless, desultory, hit or miss, purposeless, unpremeditated, adventitious • *The competitors will be subject to random drug testing.*
OPPOSITES: planned, intended, specific
2 = casual, arbitrary, indiscriminate, unplanned, aimless, purposeless, unpremeditated • *random violence against innocent children*
▸ **IN PHRASES: at random = haphazardly**, randomly, arbitrarily, casually, accidentally, irregularly, by chance, indiscriminately, aimlessly, willy-nilly, unsystematically, purposelessly, adventitiously • *We received several answers and we picked one at random.*

randy **= lustful**, hot, sexy *(informal)*, turned-on *(slang)*, aroused, raunchy *(slang)*, horny *(slang)*, amorous, lascivious, lecherous, sexually excited, concupiscent, satyric • *It was extremely hot and I was feeling rather randy.*

range **AS A NOUN 1 = series**, variety, selection, assortment, lot, collection, gamut • *The two men discussed a range of issues.*
2 = limits, reach, distance, sweep, extent, pale, confines, parameters *(informal)*, ambit • *The average age range is between 35 and 55.*
3 = scope, area, field, bounds, province, orbit, span, domain, compass, latitude, radius, amplitude, purview, sphere • *The trees on the mountain within my range of vision had all been felled.*
4 = row, series, line, file, rank, chain, string, sequence, tier • *the massive mountain ranges to the north*
5 = pasture, grass, paddock, grassland, grazing land, pastureland • *The job requires workers to attend herds on the range.*
▸ **AS A VERB 1 = vary**, run, reach, extend, go, stretch, fluctuate • *offering merchandise ranging from the everyday to the esoteric*
2 = arrange, order, line up, sequence, array, dispose, draw up, align • *More than 1,500 police are ranged against them.*
3 = roam, explore, wander, rove, sweep, cruise, stroll, ramble, traverse, go walkabout *(Austral.)* • *They range widely in search of carrion.*
4 = group, class, file, rank, arrange, grade, catalogue, classify, bracket, categorize, pigeonhole • *The pots are all ranged in neat rows.*

ranger **= warden**, guard, gamekeeper • *a park ranger*

rangy **= long-limbed**, long-legged, lanky, leggy, gangling • *a tall, rangy, redheaded girl*

rank[1] **AS A NOUN 1 = status**, level, position, grade, order, standing, sort, quality, type, station, division, degree, classification, echelon • *He eventually rose to the rank of captain.*
2 = class, dignity, caste, nobility, stratum • *Each rank of the peerage was respected.*
3 = row, line, file, column, group, range, series, formation, tier • *Ranks of police in riot gear stood nervously by.*
▸ **AS A VERB 1 = be graded**, belong, be placed, be classified, be positioned, be classed, be categorized, have a status • *He does not even rank in the world's top ten.*
2 = order, class, grade, catalogue, classify, dispose, categorize • *Universities were ranked according to marks scored in seven areas.*
3 = arrange, sort, position, range, line up, locate, sequence, array, marshal, align • *Daffodils were ranked along a crazy paving path.*
▸ **IN PHRASES: rank and file 1 = general public**, body, majority, mass, masses, Joe (and Eileen) Public *(slang)*, Joe Six-Pack *(U.S. slang)* • *There was widespread support for him among the rank and file.*
2 = lower ranks, men, troops, soldiers, other ranks, private soldiers • *the rank and file of the Red Army*

rank[2] **1 = absolute**, complete, total, gross, sheer, excessive, utter, glaring, thorough, extravagant, rampant, blatant, downright, flagrant, egregious, unmitigated, undisguised, arrant • *He accused his rival of rank hypocrisy.*
2 = foul, off, bad, offensive, disgusting, revolting, stinking, stale, pungent, noxious, disagreeable, musty, rancid, fetid, putrid, fusty, strong-smelling, gamey, noisome, mephitic, olid, yucky *or* yukky *(slang)*, festy *(Austral. slang)* • *the rank smell of unwashed clothes*
3 = abundant, flourishing, lush, luxuriant, productive, vigorous, dense, exuberant, profuse, strong-growing • *brambles and rank grass*

rankle = annoy, anger, irritate, gall, fester, embitter, chafe, irk, rile, get on your nerves *(informal)*, piss you off *(taboo slang)*, get your goat *(slang)*, hack you off *(informal)* • *The only thing that rankles me is what she says about Ireland.*

ransack 1 = search, go through, rummage through, rake through, explore, comb, scour, forage, turn inside out, fossick *(Austral. & N.Z.)* • *Why should they be allowed to ransack your bag?*
2 = plunder, raid, loot, pillage, strip, sack, gut, rifle, ravage, despoil • *Demonstraters ransacked and burned the house where he was staying.*

ransom AS A NOUN 1 = payment, money, price, payoff • *The demand for the ransom was made by telephone.*
2 = release, rescue, liberation, redemption, deliverance • *the eventual ransom of the victim*
▸ **AS A VERB = buy the freedom of**, release, deliver, rescue, liberate, buy (someone) out *(informal)*, redeem, set free, obtain or pay for the release of • *The same system was used for ransoming or exchanging captives.*

rant AS A VERB = shout, roar, yell, rave, bellow, cry, spout *(informal)*, bluster, declaim, vociferate • *I don't rant and rave or throw tea cups.*
▸ **AS A NOUN = tirade**, rhetoric, bluster, diatribe, harangue, bombast, philippic, vociferation, fanfaronade *(rare)* • *As the boss began his rant, I stood up and went out.*

rap AS A VERB 1 = hit, strike, knock, crack, tap • *A guard raps his stick on a metal hand rail.*
2 = reprimand, knock *(informal)*, blast, pan *(informal)*, carpet *(informal)*, flame *(informal)*, criticize, censure, scold, tick off *(informal)*, castigate, diss *(slang, chiefly U.S.)*, read the riot act, lambast(e), chew out *(U.S. & Canad. informal)*, give a rocket *(Brit. & N.Z. informal)* • *The minister rapped the banks over their treatment of small businesses.*
3 = talk, chat, discourse, converse, shoot the breeze *(slang, chiefly U.S.)*, confabulate • *Today we're going to rap about relationships.*
▸ **AS A NOUN 1 = blow**, knock, crack, tap, clout *(informal)* • *There was a light rap on the door.*
2 = rebuke, sentence, blame, responsibility, punishment, censure, chiding • *You'll be facing a federal rap for aiding and abetting an escaped convict.*
▸ **IN PHRASES: rap someone on the knuckles = scold**, correct, discipline, censure, berate, castigate, chastise, tell off, upbraid • *I joined the workers on strike and was rapped over the knuckles.*
take the rap = take the blame, be blamed, be punished, suffer the consequences, pay for something • *No one is taking the rap for what happened.*

rapacious = greedy, grasping, insatiable, ravenous, preying, plundering, predatory, voracious, marauding, extortionate, avaricious, wolfish, usurious • *He had a rapacious appetite for bird's nest soup.*

rapacity = greed, greediness, voraciousness, insatiableness, avarice, usury, cupidity, avidity, voracity, rapaciousness, predatoriness, graspingness, ravenousness, wolfishness • *their sexual desire and rapacity*

rape AS A VERB 1 = sexually assault, violate, abuse, ravish, force, outrage • *A young woman was brutally raped in her own home.*
2 = pillage, plunder, ransack, despoil, sack, loot, spoliate • *There is no guarantee that companies will not rape the environment.*
▸ **AS A NOUN 1 = sexual assault**, violation, ravishment, outrage • *Ninety per cent of all rapes and violent assaults went unreported.*
2 = plundering, pillage, depredation, despoliation, rapine, spoliation, despoilment, sack • *the rape of the environment*

rapid 1 = sudden, prompt, speedy, precipitate, express, immediate, fleet, swift, quickie *(informal)*, expeditious • *the country's rapid economic growth*
OPPOSITES: gradual, tardy
2 = quick, fast, hurried, swift, brisk, hasty, flying, pdq *(slang)* • *He walked at a rapid pace along Charles Street.*
OPPOSITES: slow, deliberate, leisurely

rapidity = speed, swiftness, promptness, speediness, rush, hurry, expedition, dispatch, velocity, haste, alacrity, quickness, briskness, fleetness, celerity, promptitude, precipitateness • *the rapidity with which the weather can change*

rapidly = quickly, fast, swiftly, briskly, promptly, hastily, precipitately, in a hurry, at speed, hurriedly, speedily, apace, in a rush, in haste, like a shot, pronto *(informal)*, hell for leather, like lightning, expeditiously, hotfoot, like the clappers *(Brit. informal)*, pdq *(slang)*, like nobody's business *(informal)*, posthaste, with dispatch, like greased lightning *(informal)* • *He was moving rapidly around the room.*

rapport = bond, understanding, relationship, link, tie, sympathy, harmony, affinity, empathy, interrelationship • *He said he wanted to establish a rapport with them.*

rapprochement = reconciliation, softening, reunion, détente, reconcilement, restoration of harmony • *the process of political rapprochement between the two former foes*
OPPOSITES: falling-out, quarrel, dissension

rapt 1 = spellbound, entranced, enthralled, engrossed, held, gripped, fascinated, absorbed, intent, preoccupied, carried away • *I noticed that everyone was watching me with rapt attention.*
OPPOSITES: bored, detached, uninterested
2 = rapturous, enchanted, captivated, bewitched, sent, transported, delighted, charmed, ecstatic, blissful, ravished, enraptured, blissed out • *He played to a rapt audience.*

rapture AS A NOUN = ecstasy, delight, enthusiasm, joy, transport, spell, happiness, bliss, euphoria, felicity, rhapsody, exaltation, cloud nine *(informal)*, seventh heaven, delectation, beatitude, ravishment • *His speech was received with rapture by his supporters.*

▸ **IN PHRASES: go into** *or* **be in raptures = wax lyrical**, rave, enthuse, gush, go mad, go crazy, go wild, rhapsodize • *He goes into raptures over the brilliantly coloured paintwork.*

rapturous = ecstatic, delighted, enthusiastic, rapt, sent *(informal)*, happy, transported, joyous, exalted, joyful, over the moon *(informal)*, overjoyed, blissful, ravished, euphoric, on cloud nine *(informal)*, blissed out *(informal)*, rhapsodic, in seventh heaven, floating on air • *The conference greeted the speech with rapturous applause.*

rara avis = oddity, one-off *(informal)*, curiosity, anomaly, rarity, rare thing • *I persuaded this rara avis to tell his story.*

rare[1] 1 = priceless, special, unusual, out of the ordinary, rich, precious, invaluable • *She collects rare plants.*
2 = uncommon, unusual, exceptional, out of the ordinary, few, strange, scarce, singular, sporadic, sparse, infrequent, thin on the ground, recherché • *I think big families are extremely rare nowadays.*
OPPOSITES: many, common, regular
3 = superb, great, fine, excellent, extreme, exquisite, admirable, superlative, choice, incomparable, peerless • *She has a rare ability to record her observations on paper.*

rare[2] = underdone, blue, bloody, undercooked, half-cooked, half-raw • *Waiter, I specifically asked for this steak rare.*

rarefied = exclusive, select, esoteric, cliquish, private, occult, clannish • *the rarefied atmosphere of university*

rarely = seldom, hardly, almost never, hardly ever, little, once in a while, infrequently, on rare occasions, once in a blue moon, only now and then, scarcely ever • *I rarely wear a raincoat because I spend most of my time in a car.*
OPPOSITES: often, commonly, usually

raring IN PHRASES: raring to = eager to, impatient to, longing to, yearning to, willing to, ready to, keen to, desperate to, enthusiastic to, avid to, champing at the bit to *(informal)*, keen as mustard to, athirst to • *Sarah's here and raring to meet you.*

rarity 1 = curio, find, treasure, pearl, one-off, curiosity, gem, collector's item • *Other rarities include an interview with Presley.*
2 = uncommonness, scarcity, infrequency, unusualness, shortage, strangeness, singularity, sparseness • *This indicates the rarity of such attacks.*

rascal = rogue, devil, villain, scoundrel, disgrace, rake, pickle *(Brit. informal)*, imp, scally *(Northwest English dialect)*, wretch, knave *(archaic)*, ne'er-do-well, reprobate, scallywag *(informal)*, good-for-nothing, miscreant, scamp, wastrel, bad egg *(old-fashioned informal)*, blackguard, varmint *(informal)*, rapscallion, caitiff *(archaic)*, wrong 'un *(Austral. slang)*, nointer *(Austral. slang)* • *What's that old rascal been telling you?*

rash[1] = reckless, hasty, impulsive, imprudent, premature, adventurous, careless, precipitate, brash, audacious, headlong, madcap, ill-advised, foolhardy, unwary, thoughtless, unguarded, headstrong, impetuous, indiscreet, unthinking, helter-skelter, ill-considered, hot-headed, heedless, injudicious, incautious, venturesome, harebrained, harum-scarum • *Don't do anything rash until the feelings subside.*
OPPOSITES: considered, careful, cautious

rash[2] 1 = outbreak of spots, spots, hives, urticaria, nettle rash, heat rash, (skin) eruption • *I noticed a rash on my leg.*
2 = spate, series, wave, flood, succession, plague, outbreak, epidemic • *a rash of internet-related companies*

rasp AS A VERB 1 = say hoarsely, croak, squawk • *'Where've you put it?' he rasped.*
2 = scrape, grind, rub, scour, excoriate, abrade • *The blade rasped over his skin.*
▸ **AS A NOUN 1 = hoarse sound**, croak, squawk • *He was still laughing when he heard the rasp of her voice.*
2 = grating, grinding, scratch, scrape • *the rasp of something being drawn across the sand*

rasping *or* **raspy = harsh**, rough, hoarse, gravelly, jarring, grating, creaking, husky, croaking, gruff, croaky • *Both men sang in a deep raspy tone.*

rat AS A NOUN 1 = traitor, grass *(Brit. informal)*, betrayer, deceiver, informer, defector, deserter, double-crosser, quisling, stool pigeon, nark *(Brit., Austral. & N.Z. slang)*, snake in the grass, two-timer *(informal)*, fizgig *(Austral. slang)* • *He was known as 'The Rat', even before the bribes had come to light.*
2 = rogue, scoundrel, heel *(slang)*, shit *(taboo slang)*, bastard *(informal, offensive)*, cad *(Brit. old-fashioned informal)*, bounder *(Brit. old-fashioned slang)*, rotter *(slang, chiefly Brit.)*, bad lot, shyster *(informal, chiefly U.S.)*, ratfink *(slang, chiefly U.S. & Canad.)*, wrong 'un *(Austral. slang)* • *What did you do with the gun you took from that little rat?*
▸ **IN PHRASES: rat on someone = betray**, denounce, tell on, inform on, shop *(slang, chiefly Brit.)*, grass *(Brit. slang)*, peach *(slang)*, squeal *(slang)*, incriminate *(informal)*, blow the whistle on *(informal)*, spill the beans *(informal)*, snitch *(slang)*, blab, let the cat out of the bag, blow the gaff *(Brit. slang)*, nark *(Brit., Austral. & N.Z. slang)*, put the finger on *(informal)*, spill your guts *(slang)*, inculpate, clype *(Scot.)*, dob in *(Austral. slang)* • *They were accused of encouraging children to rat on their parents.*
rat on something = renege on, go back on, repudiate, default on, back out of, break a promise, welsh on *(slang)*, break your word • *She claims he ratted on their divorce settlement.*
smell a rat = suspect something, doubt someone, distrust someone, mistrust someone, harbour suspicions about someone *or* something, have your doubts about someone *or* something • *If I don't send a picture, he will smell a rat.*

rate AS A NOUN 1 = speed, pace, tempo, velocity, time, measure, gait, frequency • *The rate at which hair grows can be agonisingly slow.*
2 = degree, standard, scale, proportion, percentage, ratio • *bank accounts paying above the average rate of interest*
3 = charge, price, cost, fee, tax, figure, dues, duty, hire, toll, tariff • *specially reduced rates*
▸ **AS A VERB 1 = evaluate**, consider, rank, reckon, class, value, measure, regard, estimate, count, grade, assess, weigh, esteem, classify, appraise, adjudge • *The film was rated excellent by 90 per cent of children.*
2 = think highly of, value, respect, admire, esteem • *It's flattering to know other clubs seem to rate me.*
3 = deserve, merit, be entitled to, be worthy of, be deserving of, have a claim to • *Her attire did not rate a second glance.*
▸ **IN PHRASES: at any rate = in any case**, anyway, nevertheless, anyhow, at all events • *Well, at any rate, let me thank you for all you did.*

rather AS A CONJUNCTION = instead of, as opposed to • *She made students think for themselves, rather than telling them what to think.*
▸ **AS AN ADVERB 1 = preferably**, sooner, instead, more readily, more willingly • *I'd rather stay at home than fight against the holiday crowds.*
2 = to some extent, quite, sort of *(informal)*, kind of *(informal)*, a little, a bit, pretty *(informal)*, fairly, relatively, somewhat, slightly, moderately, to some degree • *I'm afraid it's rather a long story.*
3 = more exactly, to be precise, more precisely, to be exact, strictly speaking • *He explained what the Crux is, or rather, what it was.*

ratification = approval, sanction, acceptance, confirmation, endorsement, authorization • *The accord is subject to ratification by the five parliaments.*

ratify = approve, sign, establish, confirm, bind, sanction, endorse, uphold, authorize, affirm, certify, consent to, validate, bear out, corroborate, authenticate • *They have yet to ratify the treaty.*
OPPOSITES: reject, cancel, annul

rating = position, ranking, evaluation, classification, placing, rate, order, standing, class, degree, estimate, rank, status, grade, designation • *a value-for-money rating of ten out of ten*

ratio = **proportion**, rate, relationship, relation, arrangement, percentage, equation, fraction, correspondence, correlation • *The adult to child ratio is 1 to 6.*

ration AS A NOUN = **allowance**, quota, allotment, provision, helping, part, share, measure, dole, portion • *The meat ration was down to one pound per person per week.*
▸ AS A PLURAL NOUN = **supplies**, stores, provisions, necessities, food, commons (*Brit.*), kai (*N.Z. informal*), provender • *emergency food rations*
▸ AS A VERB 1 = **limit**, control, restrict, save, budget, conserve • *Staples such as bread, rice and tea are already being rationed.*
2 = **distribute**, issue, deal, dole, allocate, give out, allot, mete, apportion, measure out, parcel out • *I had a flask so I rationed out cups of tea*

rational 1 = **sensible**, sound, wise, reasonable, intelligent, realistic, logical, enlightened, sane, lucid, judicious, sagacious, grounded • *a rational decision*
2 = **reasoning**, thinking, cognitive, cerebral, ratiocinative • *Man, as a rational being, may act against his impulses.*
3 = **sane**, balanced, normal, all there (*informal*), lucid, of sound mind, compos mentis (*Latin*), in your right mind • *Rachel looked calmer and more rational now.*
OPPOSITES: unreasonable, insane, irrational

rationale = **reason**, grounds, theory, principle, philosophy, logic, motivation, exposition, raison d'être (*French*) • *the rationale for punishment*

rationalize 1 = **justify**, excuse, account for, vindicate, explain away, make allowances for, make excuses for, extenuate • *It's easy to rationalize gambling.*
2 = **reason out**, resolve, think through, elucidate, apply logic to • *an attempt to rationalize my feelings*
3 = **streamline**, trim, slim down, make more efficient, make cuts in, make cutbacks in, reduce wastage in • *They have been unable or unwilling to modernize and rationalize the business.*

rationing = **restriction**, control, regulation, limitation • *The municipal authorities here are preparing for food rationing.*

rattle AS A VERB 1 = **clatter**, bang, jangle, clang, clink • *She slams the kitchen door so hard I hear dishes rattle.*
2 = **shake**, jiggle, jolt, vibrate, bounce, jar, jounce • *He gently rattled the cage and whispered to the canary.*
3 = **fluster**, shake, upset, frighten, scare, disturb, disconcert, perturb, faze, discomfit, discountenance, put (someone) off his stride, discompose, put (someone) out of countenance • *She refused to be rattled by his lawyer.*
▸ AS A NOUN = **clatter**, clattering, jangling, clanging, clink, clinking, clanking • *There was a rattle of rifle fire.*
▸ IN PHRASES: **rattle on** = **prattle**, rabbit (on) (*Brit. informal*), chatter, witter (*informal*), cackle, yak (away) (*slang*), gibber, jabber, gabble, blether, prate, run on, earbash (*Austral. & N.Z. slang*) • *He listened in silence as she rattled on.*
rattle something off = **recite**, list, run through, rehearse, reel off, spiel off (*informal*) • *He could rattle off yards of poetry*

ratty = **irritable**, cross, angry, annoyed, pissed (*U.S. & Canad. slang*), crabbed, impatient, snappy, pissed off (*taboo slang*), touchy, tetchy, testy, chippy (*informal*), short-tempered, tooshie (*Austral. slang*) • *I was beginning to get a bit ratty and fed up.*

raucous = **harsh**, rough, loud, noisy, grating, strident, rasping, husky, hoarse • *the raucous cries of the sea-birds*
OPPOSITES: quiet, sweet, smooth

raunchy = **sexy**, sexual, steamy (*informal*), earthy, suggestive, lewd, lusty, bawdy, salacious, smutty, lustful, lecherous, ribald, coarse • *her raunchy new movie*

ravage AS A VERB = **destroy**, ruin, devastate, wreck, shatter, gut, spoil, loot, demolish, plunder, desolate, sack, ransack, pillage, raze, lay waste, wreak havoc on, despoil, leave in ruins • *The soldiers had ravaged the village.*
▸ AS A NOUN *often plural* = **damage**, destruction, devastation, desolation, waste, ruin, havoc, demolition, plunder, pillage, depredation, ruination, rapine, spoliation • *the ravages of a cold, wet climate*

rave AS A VERB 1 = **rant**, rage, roar, thunder, fume, go mad (*informal*), babble, splutter, storm, be delirious, talk wildly • *She cried and raved for weeks.*
2 = **enthuse**, praise, gush, be delighted by, be mad about (*informal*), big up (*slang, chiefly Caribbean*), rhapsodize, be wild about (*informal*), cry up • *She raved about the new foods she ate while she was there.*
▸ AS A NOUN = **party**, rave-up (*Brit. slang*), do (*informal*), affair, celebration, bash (*informal*), blow-out (*slang*), beano (*Brit. slang*), hooley *or* hoolie (*chiefly Irish & N.Z.*) • *an all-night rave*
▸ AS A MODIFIER = **enthusiastic**, excellent, favourable, ecstatic, laudatory • *The show has drawn rave reviews from the critics.*

raven = **black**, ebony, jet-black, coal-black • *a striking woman with long raven hair*
▸ RELATED ADJECTIVE: corvine
▸ COLLECTIVE NOUN: unkindness
▹ *See panel* **Shades from black to white**

ravenous 1 = **starving**, starved, very hungry, famished, esurient • *a pack of ravenous animals*
OPPOSITES: full, glutted, sated
2 = **greedy**, insatiable, avaricious, covetous, grasping, insatiate • *He had moderated his ravenous appetite.*

ravine = **canyon**, pass, gap (*U.S.*), gorge, clough (*dialect*), gully, defile, linn (*Scot.*), gulch (*U.S. & Canad.*), flume • *The bus is said to have overturned and fallen into a ravine.*

raving = **mad**, wild, raging, crazy, furious, frantic, frenzied, hysterical, insane, irrational, crazed, berserk, delirious, rabid, out of your mind, gonzo (*slang*), berko (*Austral. slang*), off the air (*Austral. slang*) • *Malcolm looked at her as if she were a raving lunatic.*

ravings = **ranting**, rambling, babbling, gibberish, prattle, gabble, incoherent talk • *the lunatic ravings of a mad politician*

ravish 1 = **rape**, sexually assault, violate, abuse, force, outrage • *Her ravished body was found a week later.*
2 = **enchant**, transport, delight, charm, fascinate, entrance, captivate, enrapture, spellbind, overjoy • *an eerie power to ravish the eye and seduce the soul*

QUOTATIONS

He in a few minutes ravished this fair creature, or at least would have ravished her, if she had not, by a timely compliance, prevented him

[Henry Fielding *Jonathan Wild*]

ravishing = **enchanting**, beautiful, lovely, stunning (*informal*), charming, entrancing, gorgeous, dazzling, delightful, radiant, drop-dead (*slang*), bewitching • *She looked ravishing.*

raw AS AN ADJECTIVE 1 = **unrefined**, natural, crude, unprocessed, basic, rough, organic, coarse, unfinished, untreated, unripe • *two ships carrying raw sugar*
OPPOSITES: finished, prepared, refined
2 = **uncooked**, natural, fresh, bloody (*of meat*), undressed, unprepared • *a popular dish made of raw fish*
OPPOSITES: done, cooked, baked
3 = **sore**, open, skinned, sensitive, tender, scratched, grazed, chafed, abraded • *the drag of the rope against the raw flesh of my shoulder*
4 = **frank**, plain, bare, naked, realistic, brutal, blunt, candid, unvarnished, unembellished • *the raw passions of nationalism*
OPPOSITES: gilded, embellished
5 = **simple**, natural, clean, classic, severe, plain, uncluttered, unadorned, unfussy, unembellished • *the raw vitality of his earlier paintings*

r

6 = inexperienced, new, green, ignorant, immature, unskilled, callow, untrained, untried, undisciplined, unseasoned, unpractised • *He is still raw but his potential shows.*
OPPOSITES: trained, experienced, professional
7 = chilly, biting, cold, freezing, bitter, wet, chill, harsh, piercing, damp, unpleasant, bleak, parky (*Brit. informal*) • *a raw December morning*
8 = untreated, crude, unprocessed, in its natural state • *contamination of bathing water by raw sewage*
▸ **IN PHRASES: in the raw = in its natural state**, untouched by human hand, as God intended • *This is nature in the raw.*

ray 1 = beam, bar, flash, shaft, gleam, flicker, glint, glimmer • *The first rays of light spread over the horizon.*
2 = trace, spark, flicker, glimmer, hint, indication, scintilla • *I can offer you a slender ray of hope.*

raze = destroy, level, remove, ruin, demolish, flatten, knock down, pull down, tear down, throw down, bulldoze, kennet (*Austral. slang*), jeff (*Austral. slang*) • *Dozens of villages have been razed.*

re = concerning, about, regarding, respecting, with regard to, on the subject of, in respect of, with reference to, apropos, anent (*Scot.*) • *Re: household insurance.*

reach AS A VERB 1 = arrive at, get to, make it to, get as far as, make, hit, attain, land at, end up at • *He did not stop until he reached the door.*
2 = attain, get to, rise to, amount to, climb to • *We're told the figure could reach 100,000 next year.*
3 = touch, grasp, extend to, get (a) hold of, stretch to, go as far as, contact • *Can you reach your toes with your fingertips?*
4 = contact, get in touch with, get through to, make contact with, get, find, communicate with, get hold of, establish contact with • *I'll tell her you've been trying to reach her.*
5 = come to, move to, rise to, fall to, drop to, sink to • *a nightshirt that reached to his knees*
6 = achieve, come to, negotiate, work out, arrive at, accomplish, put together, draw up, hammer out, thrash out • *They are meeting in Lusaka in an attempt to reach a compromise.*
▸ **AS A NOUN 1 = grasp**, range, distance, stretch, sweep, capacity, extent, extension, scope • *The clothes they model are in easy reach of every woman.*
2 = jurisdiction, power, influence, territory, command, sphere, sway, compass, mastery, ambit • *The elite are no longer beyond the reach of the law.*

react 1 = respond, act, take, proceed, behave, conduct yourself • *They reacted violently to the news.*
2 *with* **against = rebel against**, oppose, revolt against, rise up against • *My father never saved and perhaps I reacted against that.*

reaction 1 = response, acknowledgment, feedback, answer, reply • *He showed no reaction when the judge pronounced his sentence.*
2 = counteraction, compensation, backlash, recoil, counterbalance, counterpoise • *All new fashion starts out as a reaction against existing convention.*
3 = conservatism, the right, the extreme right, counter-revolution, obscurantism • *their victory against the forces of reaction and conservatism*
4 = sensitivity, condition, susceptibility, hypersensitivity, allergic effect • *Common foods which cause this kind of reaction are fish, eggs and shellfish.*

reactionary AS AN ADJECTIVE = conservative, conventional, right-wing, old-fashioned, counter-revolutionary, obscurantist, blimpish, unprogressive • *narrow and reactionary ideas about family life*
OPPOSITES: radical, socialist, revolutionary
▸ **AS A NOUN = conservative**, traditionalist, die-hard, right-winger, rightist, counter-revolutionary, stick-in-the-mud, obscurantist, Colonel Blimp • *Critics viewed him as a reactionary, even a monarchist.*
OPPOSITES: radical, socialist, revolutionary

reactive = apathetic, passive, laissez-faire, inactive, submissive, uninvolved, unassertive, non-participating • *I want our organization to be less reactive and more pro-active.*

read AS A VERB 1 = scan, study, look at, refer to, glance at, pore over, peruse, run your eye over • *He read through the pages slowly and carefully.*
2 = recite, deliver, utter, declaim, speak, announce • *Jay reads poetry so beautifully.*
3 = understand, interpret, comprehend, construe, decipher, perceive the meaning of, see, discover • *He could read words at 18 months.*
4 = register, show, record, display, indicate • *The sign on the bus read 'Private: Not in Service'.*
5 = interpret, take, understand, explain, define, translate, make sense of, decode, construe, decipher, throw light on, explicate • *Now how do you read his remarks on that subject?*
6 = study, take, major in (*U.S.*) • *He is now reading maths at Harvard.*
7 = predict, forecast, divine, foresee, prophecy, foretell • *If I had been able to read the future, I would never have taken this job.*
▸ **AS A NOUN = perusal**, look (through), study, leaf (through), glance (through), scan, flick (through), scrutiny • *I had a read before starting on the washing of the kitchen ceiling.*
▸ **IN PHRASES: read something into something = infer from**, read between the lines, assume from, interpolate from • *It would be wrong to try to read too much into such a light-hearted production.*
read up on something = study, learn, bone up on (*informal*), swot up on (*Brit. informal*), mug up on (*Brit. slang*) • *I've read up on the dangers of all these drugs.*

QUOTATIONS
Read, mark, learn, and inwardly digest
[*Book of Common Prayer*]

readable 1 = enjoyable, interesting, gripping, entertaining, pleasant, enthralling, easy to read, worth reading • *This is an impeccably researched and very readable book.*
OPPOSITES: heavy, boring, dull
2 = legible, clear, plain, understandable, comprehensible, intelligible, decipherable • *a typewritten and readable script*
OPPOSITES: incomprehensible, unintelligible, illegible

reader = book lover, bookworm, bibliophile, book reader, book collector • *Thanks to that job I became an avid reader.*

readership = audience, circulation • *Its readership has grown to over 15,000.*

readily 1 = willingly, freely, quickly, gladly, eagerly, voluntarily, cheerfully, with pleasure, with good grace, lief (*rare*) • *When I was invited to the party, I readily accepted.*
OPPOSITES: reluctantly, unwillingly
2 = promptly, quickly, easily, smoothly, at once, straight away, right away, effortlessly, in no time, speedily, without delay, without hesitation, without difficulty, unhesitatingly, hotfoot, without demur, pdq (*slang*) • *I don't readily make friends.*
OPPOSITES: slowly, with difficulty, hesitatingly

readiness AS A NOUN 1 = willingness, inclination, eagerness, keenness, aptness, gameness (*informal*) • *their readiness to co-operate with the new US envoy*
2 = preparedness, preparation, fitness, maturity, ripeness • *a constant state of readiness for war*
3 = promptness, facility, ease, skill, dexterity, rapidity, quickness, adroitness, handiness, promptitude • *the warmth of his personality and the readiness of his wit*
▸ **IN PHRASES: in readiness = prepared**, set, waiting, primed, ready, all set, waiting in the wings, at the ready, at *or* on hand, fit • *Everything was in readiness for the President's arrival.*

reading 1 = **perusal**, study, review, examination, inspection, scrutiny • *This knowledge makes the second reading as enjoyable as the first.*
2 = **learning**, education, knowledge, scholarship, erudition, edification, book-learning • *a man of great imagination, of wide reading and deep learning*
3 = **recital**, performance, rendering, rendition, lesson, lecture, sermon, homily • *a poetry reading*
4 = **interpretation**, take *(informal, chiefly U.S.)*, understanding, treatment, version, construction, impression, grasp, conception • *There is a reading of this situation which upsets people.*
5 = **measurement**, record, figure, indication • *The gauge must be giving a faulty reading.*

QUOTATIONS
Reading is to the mind what exercise is to the body
[Richard Steele *The Tatler*]
Some people say that life is the thing, but I prefer reading
[Logan Pearsall Smith *Afterthoughts*]
Until I feared I would lose it, I never loved to read. One does not love breathing
[Harper Lee *To Kill a Mockingbird*]

ready AS AN ADJECTIVE 1 = **prepared**, set, primed, organized, all set, in readiness • *It took her a long time to get ready for church.*
OPPOSITES: unfit, immature, unprepared
2 = **completed**, done, prepared, fixed, arranged, organized • *Everything's ready for the family to move in.*
3 = **mature**, ripe, mellow, ripened, fully developed, fully grown, seasoned • *In a few days' time the sprouts will be ready to eat.*
4 = **willing**, happy, glad, disposed, game *(informal)*, minded, keen, eager, inclined, prone, have-a-go *(informal)*, apt, agreeable, predisposed • *She was always ready to give interviews.*
OPPOSITES: reluctant, unwilling, hesitant
5 = **prompt**, smart, quick, bright, sharp, keen, acute, rapid, alert, clever, intelligent, handy, apt, skilful, astute, perceptive, expert, deft, resourceful, adroit, quick-witted, dexterous • *I didn't have a ready answer for this dilemma.*
OPPOSITES: slow
6 = **available**, handy, at the ready, at your fingertips, present, near, accessible, convenient, on call, on tap *(informal)*, close to hand, at *or* on hand • *I'm afraid I don't have much ready cash.*
OPPOSITES: late, distant, unavailable
7 *with* **to** = **on the point of**, close to, about to, on the verge of, likely to, in danger of, liable to, on the brink of • *She looked ready to cry.*
▸ AS A VERB = **prepare**, get set, organize, get ready, order, arrange, equip, fit out, make ready, jack up *(N.Z. informal)* • *John's soldiers were readying themselves for the final assault.*
▸ IN PHRASES: **at the ready** = **poised**, waiting, prepared, in readiness, ready for action, all systems go • *Soldiers came charging through the forest, guns at the ready.*
make ready = **prepare**, get ready, do the necessary • *I'll have a room made ready for him.*

ready-made = **ready-to-wear**, off-the-peg, off-the-rack *(U.S.)* • *local ready-made clothes*

reaffirm = **reiterate**, repeat, restate • *He reaffirmed his commitment to the country's economic reform programme.*

real AS AN ADJECTIVE 1 = **true**, actual, genuine, concrete, sincere, tangible, honest, factual, existent, palpable, dinkum *(Austral. & N.Z. informal)*, unimagined, unfeigned • *No, it wasn't a dream. It was real.*
2 = **genuine**, authentic, bona fide, dinkum *(Austral. & N.Z. informal)* • *the smell of real leather*
OPPOSITES: affected, false, fake
3 = **proper**, true, valid, legitimate • *His first real girlfriend.*
4 = **true**, actual • *This was the real reason for her call.*
5 = **typical**, true, earnest, genuine, sincere, unaffected, heartfelt, wholehearted, untainted, dinkum *(Austral. & N.Z. informal)*, unfeigned, unpretended • *Their expressions of regret did not smack of real sorrow.*
6 = **serious**, pressing, worrying, significant, severe, urgent, weighty • *Global warming is a real problem.*
7 = **complete**, right, total, perfect, positive, absolute, utter, thorough, veritable, out-and-out • *You must think I'm a real idiot.*
▸ AS AN ADVERB = **extremely**, very, really, particularly, seriously *(informal)*, terribly, remarkably, unusually, jolly *(Brit.)*, awfully *(informal)*, uncommonly • *He's been trying real hard.*

realignment = **readjustment**, restructuring, shake-up, reshuffling, reorganization, rationalization, rearrangement • *a realignment of the existing political structure*

realism 1 = **pragmatism**, common sense, practicality, level-headedness, clear-sightedness • *It was the time now to show political realism.*
2 = **authenticity**, naturalism, verisimilitude, fidelity, faithfulness, truthfulness • *Sincere performances and gritty Boston settings add to the film's realism*

realist = **pragmatist**, positivist • *Realists would agree with many of these criticisms.*

realistic 1 = **practical**, real, sensible, rational, common-sense, sober, pragmatic, down-to-earth, matter-of-fact, businesslike, level-headed, hard-headed, unsentimental, unromantic, grounded • *a realistic view of what we can afford*
OPPOSITES: unrealistic, idealistic, impractical
2 = **attainable**, reasonable, sensible, feasible, workable, achievable, practicable, within the bounds of possibility • *Establish deadlines that are more realistic.*
3 = **lifelike**, true to life, authentic, naturalistic, true, natural, genuine, graphic, faithful, truthful, representational, vérité • *The language is foul and the violence horribly realistic.*

realistically = **really**, basically, in truth, if you are honest • *Realistically, there is never one right answer.*

reality AS A NOUN 1 = **fact**, truth, certainty, realism, validity, authenticity, verity, actuality, materiality, genuineness, verisimilitude, corporeality • *Fiction and reality were increasingly blurred.*
2 = **truth**, fact, actuality • *the harsh reality of top international competition*
▸ IN PHRASES: **in reality** = **in fact**, really, actually, in truth, as a matter of fact, in actuality, in point of fact • *He came across as streetwise, but in reality he was not.*

QUOTATIONS
Reality is that which, when you stop believing in it, doesn't go away
[Philip K. Dick *I Hope I Shall Arrive Soon*]
Human kind
Cannot bear very much reality
[T.S. Eliot *East Coker*]

realization 1 = **awareness**, understanding, recognition, perception, imagination, consciousness, grasp, appreciation, conception, comprehension, apprehension, cognizance, aha moment, light bulb moment *(informal)* • *There is a growing realization that things cannot go on like this for much longer.*
2 = **achievement**, carrying-out, completion, accomplishment, fulfilment, consummation, effectuation • *the realization of his worst fears*

realize 1 = **become aware of**, understand, recognize, appreciate, take in, grasp, conceive, catch on *(informal)*, comprehend, twig *(Brit. informal)*, get the message, apprehend, become conscious of, be cognizant of • *As soon as we realized what was going on, we moved the children away.*

r

2 = **fulfil**, achieve, accomplish, bring about, carry through, make real, make concrete, actualize, make happen, make a reality • *Realize your dreams! Pursue your passions!*
3 = **achieve**, do, effect, complete, perform, fulfil, accomplish, bring about, consummate, incarnate, bring off, make concrete, bring to fruition, actualize, make happen, effectuate, reify, carry out *or* through • *The kaleidoscopic quality of the book is brilliantly realized on stage.*
4 = **sell for**, go for, bring *or* take in, make, get, clear, produce, gain, net, earn, obtain, acquire • *A selection of correspondence from P.G. Wodehouse realized £1,232.*

real life = **reality**, actuality, actual existence • *Children use fantasy to explore worrying aspects of real life.*

really 1 = **certainly**, absolutely, undoubtedly, genuinely, positively, categorically, without a doubt, assuredly, verily, surely • *I really do feel that some people are being unfair.*
2 = **very**, particularly, seriously *(informal)*, truly, extremely, terribly, remarkably, unusually, jolly *(Brit.)*, awfully *(informal)*, exceedingly, excessively, eminently, superlatively, uncommonly • *It was really good.*
3 = **truly**, actually, in fact, indeed, in reality, in actuality • *My father didn't really love her.*
4 = **honestly**, actually, truthfully, in all sincerity • *Do you really think he would be that stupid?*

realm 1 = **field**, world, area, province, sphere, department, region, branch, territory, zone, patch, orbit, turf *(U.S. slang)* • *the realm of politics*
2 = **kingdom**, state, country, empire, monarchy, land, province, domain, dominion, principality • *Defence of the realm is crucial.*

reap 1 = **get**, win, gain, obtain, acquire, derive • *We are not in this to reap immense financial rewards.*
2 = **collect**, gather, bring in, harvest, garner, cut • *a group of peasants reaping a harvest of fruit and vegetables*

rear[1] AS A NOUN 1 = **back part**, back, back end, back part, rear part, stern *(Nautical)* • *He settled back in the rear of the taxi.*
OPPOSITES: front, nose, bow
2 = **back**, end, tail, rearguard, tail end, back end • *Musicians played at the front and rear of the procession.*
3 = **behind**, backside *(informal)*, rump, rear end, seat, tail *(informal)*, butt *(U.S. & Canad. informal)*, bum *(Brit. slang)*, ass *(U.S. & Canad. taboo slang)*, buns *(U.S. slang)*, arse *(taboo slang)*, buttocks, posterior, derrière *(euphemistic)*, tush *(U.S. slang)*, fundament, jacksy *(Brit. slang)* • *She blames her rounded rear on her love of butter.*
▸ AS A MODIFIER = **back**, aft, hind, hindmost, after *(Nautical)*, last, following, trailing • *the rear end of a tractor*
OPPOSITES: leading, front, forward

rear[2] 1 = **bring up**, raise, educate, care for, train, nurse, foster, nurture • *I was reared in east Texas.*
2 = **breed**, keep, raise, tend • *She spends a lot of time rearing animals.*
3 *often with* **up** *or* **over** = **rise**, tower, soar, loom • *The exhibition hall reared above me behind a high fence.*

rearrange 1 = **reorganize**, regroup, move round, reposition, change round, switch round • *A waiter was rapidly rearranging tables for the big group.*
2 = **reschedule**, alter, adjust, reshuffle, reorganize, reorder, rejig • *You may cancel or rearrange the appointment.*

reason AS A NOUN 1 = **cause**, grounds, purpose, motive, end, goal, design, target, aim, basis, occasion, object, intention, incentive, warrant, impetus, inducement, why and wherefore *(informal)* • *There is a reason for every important thing that happens.*
2 = **justification**, case, grounds, defence, argument, explanation, excuse, apology, rationale, exposition, vindication, apologia • *I hope you have a good reason for your behaviour.*
3 = **sense**, mind, reasoning, understanding, brains, judgment, logic, mentality, intellect, comprehension, apprehension, sanity, rationality, soundness, sound mind, ratiocination • *a conflict between emotion and reason*
OPPOSITES: feeling, emotion, instinct
▸ AS A VERB = **deduce**, conclude, work out, solve, resolve, make out, infer, draw conclusions, think, ratiocinate, syllogize • *I reasoned that changing my diet would lower my cholesterol level.*
▸ IN PHRASES: **by reason of** = **on account of**, through, because of, due to, as a result of, owing to, by virtue of, as a consequence of • *He pleaded innocent by reason of insanity.*
in *or* **within reason** = **within limits**, within reasonable limits, within bounds • *I will take any job that comes along, within reason.*
reason with someone = **persuade**, debate with, remonstrate with, bring round, urge, win over, argue with, dispute with, dissuade, prevail upon *(informal)*, expostulate with, show (someone) the error of his ways, talk into *or* out of • *All he wanted was to reason with one of them.*
with reason = **justifiably**, rightly, legitimately, justly • *With reason, he feels the mood had changed.*

QUOTATIONS

The heart has reasons that reason knows not of
[Blaise Pascal *Pensées*]

The reason of the strongest is always the best
[Jean de la Fontaine *Fables*]

There is nothing without a reason
[Gottfried Wilhelm Leibniz *Studies in Physics and the Nature of Body*]

Reason is natural revelation
[John Locke *Essay concerning Human Understanding*]

Reason, an ignis fatuus of the mind,
Which leaves the light of nature, sense, behind
[John Wilmot, Earl of Rochester *A Satire against Mankind*]

reasonable 1 = **sensible**, reasoned, sound, practical, wise, intelligent, rational, logical, sober, credible, plausible, sane, judicious, grounded • *He's a reasonable sort of chap.*
OPPOSITES: unreasonable, irrational, unsound
2 = **fair**, just, right, acceptable, moderate, sensible, equitable, justifiable, well-advised, well-thought-out, tenable • *a perfectly reasonable decision*
OPPOSITES: unfair, unreasonable
3 = **within reason**, fitting, fit, appropriate, sensible, proper • *It seems reasonable to expect rapid urban growth.*
OPPOSITES: impossible
4 = **low**, cheap, competitive, moderate, modest, inexpensive, tolerable, within your means • *His fees were quite reasonable.*
5 = **average**, fair, moderate, modest, tolerable, O.K. *or* okay *(informal)* • *The boy answered him in reasonable French.*

reasoned = **sensible**, clear, logical, systematic, judicious, well-thought-out, well-presented, well-expressed • *a reasoned approach*

reasoning 1 = **thinking**, thought, reason, analysis, logic, deduction, cogitation, ratiocination • *the reasoning behind the decision*
2 = **case**, argument, proof, interpretation, hypothesis, exposition, train of thought • *She was not really convinced by their line of reasoning.*

reassess = **reappraise**, reconsider, weigh up again, get a feel for again • *I will reassess the situation when I get home.*

reassure = **encourage**, comfort, bolster, hearten, cheer up, buoy up, gee up, restore confidence to, inspirit, relieve (someone) of anxiety, put *or* set your mind at rest • *She just reassured me and told me that everything was fine.*

reassured = **encouraged**, confident, comforted, relieved, bolstered, heartened, cheered up, buoyed up, inspirited • *I feel much more reassured when I've been for a health check.*

r

reassuring = **encouraging**, comforting, cheering, heartening, inspiriting • *She gave me some reassuring news.*

rebate = **refund**, discount, reduction, bonus, allowance, deduction • *a tax rebate*

rebel AS A NOUN 1 = **revolutionary**, resistance fighter, insurgent, secessionist, mutineer, insurrectionary, revolutionist • *fighting between rebels and government forces*
2 = **nonconformist**, dissident, maverick, dissenter, heretic, apostate, schismatic • *She had been a rebel at school.*
▸ AS A VERB 1 = **revolt**, resist, rise up, mutiny, take to the streets, take up arms, man the barricades • *Poverty-stricken citizens could rise up and rebel.*
2 = **defy**, dissent, disobey, come out against, refuse to obey, dig your heels in (*informal*) • *The child who rebels against his parents is unlikely to be overlooked.*
3 = **recoil**, shrink, shy away, flinch, show repugnance • *His free spirit rebelled at this demand.*
▸ AS A MODIFIER = **rebellious**, revolutionary, insurgent, mutinous, insubordinate, insurrectionary • *Many soldiers in this rebel platoon joined as teenagers.*

QUOTATIONS
What is a rebel? A man who says no
[Albert Camus *The Rebel*]
To be a rebel is not to be a revolutionary. It is more often but a way of spinning one's wheels deeper in the sand
[Kate Millett *Sexual Politics*]
No one can go on being a rebel too long without turning into an autocrat
[Lawrence Durrell *Balthazar*]

rebellion 1 = **resistance**, rising, revolution, revolt, uprising, mutiny, insurrection, insurgency, insurgence • *They soon put down the rebellion.*
2 = **nonconformity**, dissent, defiance, heresy, disobedience, schism, insubordination, apostasy • *He engaged in a small act of rebellion against his heritage.*

QUOTATIONS
Rebellion to tyrants is obedience to God
[John Bradshaw]

rebellious 1 = **defiant**, difficult, resistant, intractable, recalcitrant, obstinate, unmanageable, incorrigible, refractory, contumacious • *a rebellious teenager*
OPPOSITES: obedient, dutiful, subservient
2 = **revolutionary**, rebel, disorderly, unruly, turbulent, disaffected, insurgent, recalcitrant, disloyal, seditious, mutinous, disobedient, ungovernable, insubordinate, insurrectionary • *a rebellious and dissident territory*
OPPOSITES: loyal, subordinate, obedient

rebirth = **revival**, restoration, renaissance, renewal, resurrection, reincarnation, regeneration, resurgence, new beginning, revitalization, renascence • *The hotel is awaiting its rebirth.*

rebound 1 = **bounce**, ricochet, spring back, return, resound, recoil • *His shot rebounded from a post.*
2 = **misfire**, backfire, recoil, boomerang • *Mia realised her trick had rebounded on her.*

rebuff AS A VERB = **reject**, decline, refuse, turn down, cut, check, deny, resist, slight, discourage, put off, snub, spurn, knock back (*slang*), brush off (*slang*), repulse, cold-shoulder • *He wanted to go out with with Julie but she rebuffed him.*
OPPOSITES: encourage, welcome, submit to
▸ AS A NOUN = **rejection**, defeat, snub, knock-back, check, opposition, slight, refusal, denial, brush-off (*slang*), repulse, thumbs down, cold shoulder, slap in the face (*informal*), kick in the teeth (*slang*), discouragement • *The results of the poll dealt a humiliating rebuff to Mr Jones.*
OPPOSITES: welcome, come-on (*informal*), encouragement

rebuild = **reconstruct**, restore, revamp, renovate, remodel, refashion • *The castle was rebuilt by his great grandson in 1859.*

rebuke AS A VERB = **scold**, censure, reprimand, reproach, blame, lecture, carpet (*informal*), berate, tick off (*informal*), castigate, chide, dress down (*informal*), admonish, tear into (*informal*), tell off (*informal*), take to task, read the riot act, reprove, upbraid, bawl out (*informal*), haul (someone) over the coals (*informal*), chew out (*U.S. & Canad. informal*), tear (someone) off a strip (*informal*), give a rocket (*Brit. & N.Z. informal*), reprehend, chew (someone's) ass (*U.S. & Canad. taboo slang*) • *He has been seriously rebuked.*
OPPOSITES: approve, praise, applaud
▸ AS A NOUN = **scolding**, censure, reprimand, reproach, blame, row, lecture, wigging (*Brit. slang*), ticking-off (*informal*), dressing down (*informal*), telling-off (*informal*), admonition, tongue-lashing, reproof, castigation, reproval • *'Silly little boy' was his favourite expression of rebuke.*
OPPOSITES: praise, compliment, commendation

rebut = **disprove**, defeat, overturn, quash, refute, negate, invalidate, prove wrong, confute • *He spent most of his speech rebutting criticisms.*

rebuttal = **disproof**, negation, refutation, invalidation, confutation, defeat • *He is conducting a point-by-point rebuttal of charges from his former colleagues.*

recalcitrant = **disobedient**, contrary, unwilling, defiant, stubborn, wayward, unruly, uncontrollable, intractable, wilful, obstinate, unmanageable, ungovernable, refractory, insubordinate, contumacious • *a recalcitrant child of an unhappy mother*
OPPOSITES: obedient, compliant, amenable

recall AS A VERB 1 = **recollect**, remember, call up, evoke, summon up, reminisce about, call to mind, look *or* think back to, mind (*dialect*) • *I recalled the way they had been dancing together.*
2 = **bring to mind**, call up, evoke, conjure up, call to mind, put you in mind of • *His speech recalled that famous election pledge of his father.*
3 = **call back**, bring back, order back, summon back • *Parliament was recalled from its summer recess.*
4 = **annul**, withdraw, call in, take back, cancel, repeal, call back, revoke, retract, rescind, nullify, countermand, abjure • *The order was recalled.*
▸ AS A NOUN 1 = **recollection**, memory, remembrance • *He had a total recall of her spoken words.*
2 = **calling back**, bringing back, summons, summoning back • *The recall of the ambassador is a public sign of concern.*
3 = **annulment**, withdrawal, repeal, cancellation, retraction, revocation, nullification, rescission, rescindment • *The appellant sought a recall of the order.*

recant = **withdraw**, take back, retract, disclaim, deny, recall, renounce, revoke, repudiate, renege, disown, disavow, forswear, abjure, unsay, apostatize • *a man who refused after torture to recant his heresy*
OPPOSITES: insist, maintain, repeat

recapitulate = **restate**, review, repeat, outline, sum up, recount, reiterate, run over, summarize, epitomize, recap (*informal*), go over again, run through again • *Let's just recapitulate the essential points.*

recapture = **refind**, resurrect, rekindle, resuscitate, reanimate • *He couldn't recapture the form he'd shown in getting to the semi-final.*

recede 1 = **fall back**, withdraw, retreat, draw back, return, go back, retire, back off, regress, retrogress, retrocede • *As she receded into the distance he waved goodbye.*
2 = **lessen**, decline, subside, abate, sink, fade, shrink, diminish, dwindle, wane, ebb • *The illness began to recede.*

receipt AS A NOUN 1 = **sales slip**, proof of purchase, voucher, stub, acknowledgment, counterfoil • *I wrote her a receipt for the money.*
2 = **receiving**, delivery, reception, acceptance, recipience • *the receipt of your order*
▸ AS A PLURAL NOUN = **takings**, return, profits, gains, income, gate, proceeds • *He was tallying the day's receipts.*

receive 1 = **get**, accept, be given, pick up, collect, obtain, acquire, take, derive, be in receipt of, accept delivery of • *I received your letter.*
2 = **experience**, suffer, bear, go through, encounter, meet with, sustain, undergo, be subjected to • *He received a blow to the head.*
3 = **greet**, meet, admit, welcome, entertain, take in, accommodate, be at home to • *The following evening the duchess was again receiving guests.*
4 = **react to**, take, hear, listen to, respond to • *The proposals have been well received by many deputies.*

receiver 1 = **handset**, apparatus • *She held the telephone receiver away from her face.*
2 = **recipient**, beneficiary • *He says he's more a receiver than a giver in the lying stakes.*

recent 1 = **not long past**, just gone, occurring recently • *Sales have fallen by more than 75 per cent in recent years.*
2 = **new**, modern, contemporary, up-to-date, late, young, happening *(informal)*, current, fresh, novel, latter, present-day, latter-day • *a faster, sleeker, more recent model*
OPPOSITES: old, earlier, early

recently = **not long ago**, newly, lately, currently, freshly, of late, latterly • *The bank recently opened a branch in Germany.*

receptacle = **container**, case, box, holder, vessel, drum, basin, crate, canister, repository • *a receptacle for water*

reception 1 = **party**, gathering, get-together, social gathering, do *(informal)*, social, function, entertainment, celebration, bash *(informal)*, festivity, knees-up *(Brit. informal)*, shindig *(informal)*, soirée, levee, rave-up *(Brit. slang)* • *a glittering wedding reception*
2 = **response**, reaction, acknowledgment, recognition, treatment, welcome, greeting • *He received a cool reception to his speech.*
3 = **receiving**, admission, acceptance, receipt, recipience • *the production, distribution and reception of medical knowledge*

receptive 1 = **open**, sympathetic, favourable, amenable, interested, welcoming, friendly, accessible, susceptible, open-minded, hospitable, approachable, open to suggestions • *The voters had seemed receptive to his ideas.*
OPPOSITES: prejudiced, biased, narrow-minded
2 = **responsive**, sensitive • *The patient was not at all receptive to treatment.*
OPPOSITES: unresponsive, unreceptive

r

recess AS A NOUN 1 = **break**, rest, holiday, closure, interval, vacation, respite, intermission, cessation of business, schoolie *(Austral.)* • *Parliament returns to work today after its summer recess.*
2 = **alcove**, corner, bay, depression, hollow, niche, cavity, nook, oriel, indentation • *a discreet recess next to a fireplace*
3 *often plural* = **depths**, reaches, heart, retreats, bowels, innards *(informal)*, secret places, innermost parts, penetralia • *He emerged from the dark recesses of the garage.*
▸ AS A VERB = **adjourn**, break, stop, take a break, take a recess, suspend proceedings • *The hearings have now recessed for dinner.*

recession = **depression**, drop, decline, slump, downturn, slowdown, trough • *The recession caused sales to drop off.*
OPPOSITES: boom, upturn

QUOTATIONS
It's a recession when your neighbour loses his job; it's a depression when you lose yours
[Harry S Truman]

recharge = **repower**, charge up • *He is using your mains electricity to recharge his car battery.*

recherché = **refined**, rare, exotic, esoteric, arcane, far-fetched, choice • *This Valentine's Day, look for something more recherché for your loved one.*

recipe AS A NOUN = **directions**, instructions, ingredients, receipt *(obsolete)* • *I can give you the recipe for these biscuits*
▸ IN PHRASES: **a recipe for something** = **method**, formula, prescription, process, programme, technique, procedure, modus operandi • *Large-scale inflation is a recipe for disaster.*

QUOTATIONS
All recipes are built on the belief that somewhere at the beginning of the chain there is a cook who does not use them
[John Thorne *'Cuisine Mécanique'*]

recipient = **receiver**, beneficiary, donee, legatee • *the largest recipient of foreign aid*

reciprocal = **mutual**, corresponding, reciprocative, reciprocatory, exchanged, equivalent, alternate, complementary, interchangeable, give-and-take, interdependent, correlative • *They expected a reciprocal gesture before more hostages could be freed.*
OPPOSITES: one-way, unilateral, unreciprocated

reciprocate = **return**, requite, feel in return, match, respond, equal, return the compliment • *Their attraction to each other as friends is reciprocated.*

recital 1 = **performance**, rendering, rehearsal, reading • *a solo recital*
2 = **account**, telling, story, detailing, statement, relation, tale, description, narrative, narration, enumeration, recapitulation • *It was a depressing recital of childhood abuse.*
3 = **recitation**, rendering, repetition, reading aloud, declaiming • *The album features a recital of 13th century Latin prayers.*

recitation 1 = **recital**, reading, performance, piece, passage, lecture, rendering, narration, telling • *The transmission began with a recitation from the Koran.*
2 = **account**, story, description, narration, recapitulation • *The letter was a short recitation of their problem.*
3 = **reading**, piece, passage, verse, monologue • *These recitations form an important part of their religion.*

recite 1 = **perform**, relate, deliver, repeat, rehearse, declaim, recapitulate, do your party piece *(informal)* • *They recited poetry to one another.*
2 = **recount**, list, enumerate, itemize, tell, speak, detail, describe, relate, repeat, narrate • *I simply recited the names of a number of Chinese cities I knew.*

reckless = **careless**, wild, rash, irresponsible, precipitate, hasty, mindless, negligent, headlong, madcap, ill-advised, regardless, foolhardy, daredevil, thoughtless, indiscreet, imprudent, heedless, devil-may-care, inattentive, incautious, harebrained, harum-scarum, overventuresome • *He is charged with causing death by reckless driving.*
OPPOSITES: responsible, careful, cautious

reckon AS A VERB 1 = **think**, believe, suppose, imagine, assume, guess *(informal, chiefly U.S. & Canad.)*, fancy, conjecture, surmise, be of the opinion • *He reckoned he was still fond of her.*
2 = **consider**, hold, rate, account, judge, think of, regard, estimate, count, calculate, evaluate, esteem, deem, gauge, look upon, appraise • *The sale has been held up because the price is reckoned to be too high.*
3 = **expect**, hope, anticipate • *Police officers on the case are reckoning to charge someone very shortly.*
4 = **count**, figure, total, calculate, compute, add up, tally, number, enumerate • *The 'normal' by-election swing against a government is reckoned at about 5 per cent.*
▸ IN PHRASES: **reckon on** *or* **upon something** = **rely on**, count on, bank on, depend on, hope for, calculate, trust in, take for granted • *He reckons on being world heavyweight champion.*
reckon with something *or* **someone** *used in negative constructions* = **take into account**, expect, plan for, anticipate, be prepared for, bear in mind, foresee, bargain for, take cognizance of • *He had not reckoned with the strength of her feelings for him.*

reckon without something *or* **someone = overlook**, ignore, disregard, fail to notice, fail to take account of, fail to anticipate • *He reckoned without the strength of his girlfriend.*
to be reckoned with = powerful, important, strong, significant, considerable, influential, weighty, consequential, skookum *(Canad.)* • *This act was a signal that he was someone to be reckoned with.*

reckoning 1 = **count**, working, estimate, calculation, adding, counting, addition, computation, summation • *By my reckoning we were seven or eight kilometers away.*
2 = **retribution**, punishment, revenge, repayment, retaliation, vengeance, reprisal, compensation • *She knew the truce would not last. There would be a reckoning.*
3 = **day of retribution**, fate, doom, Doomsday, judgment day, day of judgment, last judgment • *the day of reckoning*

reclaim 1 = **retrieve**, claim back, get *or* take back, recover, rescue, regain, reinstate, recoup • *I've come to reclaim my property.*
2 = **regain**, rescue, restore, salvage, recapture, regenerate • *The Netherlands has been reclaiming farmland from water.*
3 = **rescue**, save, reform, salvage, redeem, win back • *He set out to fight the drug infestation by reclaiming a youth from the local gangs.*

recline = **lean**, lie (down), stretch out, lie back, rest, lounge, sprawl, loll, repose, be recumbent • *She proceeded to recline on a chaise longue.*
OPPOSITES: stand, rise, stand up

recluse = **hermit**, solitary, ascetic, anchoress, monk, anchorite, eremite • *His widow became a virtual recluse for the remainder of her life.*

reclusive = **solitary**, retiring, withdrawn, isolated, secluded, cloistered, monastic, recluse, ascetic, sequestered, hermit-like, hermitic, eremitic • *She had become increasingly ill and reclusive.*
OPPOSITES: sociable, gregarious

recognition AS A NOUN 1 = **identification**, recall, recollection, discovery, detection, remembrance • *He searched for a sign of recognition on her face.*
2 = **acceptance**, acknowledgment, understanding, admission, perception, awareness, concession, allowance, confession, realization, avowal • *They welcomed his recognition of the recession.*
3 = **acknowledgment**, approval, sanctioning, endorsement, ratification, certification, accreditation, validation • *His government did not receive full recognition until July.*
4 = **approval**, honour, tributes, acclaim, appreciation, applause, salute, gratitude, acknowledgment • *At last, her father's work has received popular recognition.*
▸ IN PHRASES: **in recognition of = in appreciation of**, in respect of, in acknowledgment of, in cognizance of • *He had just received a doctorate in recognition of his contributions to seismology.*

recognizable = **notable**, distinct, noticeable, conspicuous, unmistakable, identifiable, detectable, perceptible, distinguishable • *the world's most recognizable athlete*

recognize 1 = **identify**, know, place, remember, spot, notice, recall, make out, recollect, know again, put your finger on • *The receptionist recognized him at once.*
2 = **acknowledge**, see, allow, understand, accept, admit, grant, realize, concede, perceive, confess, be aware of, take on board, avow • *I recognize my own shortcomings.*
OPPOSITES: forget, ignore, overlook
3 = **approve**, acknowledge, sanction, appreciate, greet, endorse, ratify, accept as valid, honour • *Most doctors appear to recognize homeopathy as a legitimate form of medicine.*
4 = **appreciate**, respect, notice, reward, applaud, salute, give recognition to • *He had the insight to recognize their talents.*

recoil AS A VERB 1 = **jerk back**, pull back, flinch, quail, kick, react, rebound, spring back, resile • *I recoiled in horror.*
2 = **draw back**, shrink, falter, shy away, flinch, quail, balk at • *People used to recoil from the idea of getting into debt.*
▸ AS A NOUN 1 = **jerking back**, reaction, pulling back, flinching, quailing, springing back • *His reaction was as much a rebuff as a physical recoil.*
2 = **kickback**, kick • *The policeman fires again, tensed against the recoil.*

recollect = **remember**, mind *(dialect)*, recall, reminisce, summon up, call to mind, place • *She spoke with warmth when she recollected the doctor who had treated her.*

recollection = **memory**, recall, impression, remembrance, reminiscence, mental image • *He had no recollection of the crash.*

recommend 1 = **advocate**, suggest, propose, approve, endorse, prescribe, commend • *Ask your doctor to recommend a suitable treatment.*
OPPOSITES: reject, veto, disapprove of
2 = **put forward**, approve, put up, endorse, commend, vouch for, praise, big up *(slang, chiefly Caribbean)*, speak well of, put in a good word for • *He recommended me for a promotion.*
3 = **advise**, suggest, advance, propose, urge, counsel, advocate, prescribe, put forward, exhort, enjoin • *I recommend that you consult your doctor.*
4 = **make attractive**, make interesting, make appealing, make acceptable • *These qualities recommended him to Olivier.*

recommendation 1 = **advice**, proposal, suggestion, counsel, guidance, exhortation, urging • *The committee's recommendations are unlikely to be made public.*
2 = **commendation**, reference, praise, sanction, approval, blessing, plug *(informal)*, endorsement, advocacy, testimonial, good word, approbation, favourable mention • *The best way of finding a solicitor is by personal recommendation.*

recompense AS A NOUN = **compensation**, pay, payment, satisfaction, amends, repayment, remuneration, reparation, indemnity, restitution, damages, emolument, indemnification, requital • *He demands no financial recompense for his troubles.*
▸ AS A VERB = **compensate**, reimburse, redress, repay, pay for, satisfy, make good, make up for, make amends for, indemnify, requite, make restitution for • *If they succeed in court, they will be fully recompensed for their loss.*

reconcile AS A VERB 1 = **resolve**, settle, square, adjust, compose, rectify, patch up, harmonize, put to rights • *It is possible to reconcile these apparently opposing perspectives.*
2 = **reunite**, bring back together, make peace between, pacify, conciliate • *He never believed he and Susan would be reconciled.*
3 = **make peace between**, reunite, propitiate, bring to terms, restore harmony between, re-establish friendly relations between • *my attempt to reconcile him and Toby*
▸ IN PHRASES: **reconcile yourself to something** *often passive* = **accept**, come to accept, resign yourself to, get used to, put up with *(informal)*, submit to, yield to, make the best of, accommodate yourself to • *She reconciled herself to never seeing him again.*

reconciliation 1 = **reunion**, conciliation, rapprochement *(French)*, appeasement, détente, pacification, propitiation, understanding, bringing back together, reconcilement • *The couple have separated but he wants a reconciliation.*
OPPOSITES: break-up, separation, falling-out
2 = **harmonizing**, balancing, squaring, adjustment, synthesis, harmonization • *a reconciliation of the values of equality and liberty*
3 = **accommodation**, settlement, resolving, compromise, remedying, rectification • *the reconciliation of our differences*

recondite = **obscure**, involved, difficult, deep, dark, secret, hidden, mysterious, concealed, profound, mystical, esoteric, occult, arcane, abstruse, cabbalistic • *Her poems are recondite in subject matter.*
OPPOSITES: simple, straightforward, exoteric

recondition = **restore**, repair, renew, overhaul, revamp, renovate, remodel, do up *(informal)*, fix up *(informal, chiefly U.S. & Canad.)* • *They sell used and reconditioned motorcycle parts.*

reconnaissance = **inspection**, survey, investigation, observation, patrol, scan, exploration, scouting, scrutiny, recce *(slang)*, reconnoitring • *The airport will be used for reconnaissance rather than combat.*

reconnoitre = **inspect**, investigate, make a reconnaissance (of), see how the land lies, case *(slang)*, survey, observe, explore, patrol, scan, scout, scrutinize, recce *(slang)*, spy out, get the lie of the land • *I left a sergeant in charge and rode forward to reconnoitre.*

reconsider = **rethink**, review, revise, think again, think twice, reassess, re-examine, have second thoughts, change your mind, re-evaluate, think over, think better of, take another look at • *We want you to reconsider your decision to resign.* • *We urge you to reconsider.*

QUOTATIONS
Second thoughts are the wisest
[Euripides *Hippolytus*]

reconsideration = **reappraisal**, review, rethink, re-evaluation, re-examination • *The report urges reconsideration of the decision.*

reconstitute = **reconstruct**, restore, rebuild, overhaul, recreate, regenerate, reassemble • *Slowly Jewish communities were reconstituted and life began anew.*

reconstruct 1 = **rebuild**, reform, restore, recreate, remake, renovate, remodel, re-establish, regenerate, reorganize, reassemble • *The government must reconstruct the shattered economy.*
2 = **build up a picture of**, build up, piece together, deduce, re-enact • *Elaborate efforts were made to reconstruct what had happened.*

reconstruction 1 = **rebuilding**, reform, restoration, remake, remodelling, regeneration, renovation, reorganization, re-creation, re-establishment • *America's part in the post-war reconstruction of Germany.*
2 = **re-enactment**, account, piecing-together • *a reconstruction of her ordeal*

record AS A NOUN 1 = **document**, file, register, log, report, minute, account, entry, journal, diary, memorial, archives, memoir, chronicle, memorandum, annals, blog *(informal)* • *Keep a record of all the payments.*
2 = **evidence**, trace, documentation, testimony, witness, memorial, remembrance • *There's no record of any marriage or children.*
3 = **disc**, recording, single, release, album, waxing *(informal)*, LP, vinyl, EP, forty-five, platter *(U.S. slang)*, seventy-eight, gramophone record, black disc • *This is one of my favourite records.*
4 = **best performance**, best time, fastest time, personal best, highest achievement • *He set the world record.*
5 = **background**, history, performance, career, reputation, track record *(informal)*, curriculum vitae • *His record reveals a tough streak.*
▸ AS A VERB 1 = **set down**, report, minute, note, enter, document, register, preserve, log, put down, chronicle, write down, enrol, take down, inscribe, transcribe, chalk up *(informal)*, put on record, put on file • *In her letters she records the domestic and social details of life in China.*
2 = **make a recording of**, cut, video, tape, lay down *(slang)*, wax *(informal)*, video-tape, tape-record, put on wax *(informal)* • *She recorded a new album in Nashville.*
3 = **register**, show, read, contain, indicate, give evidence of • *The test records the electrical activity of the brain.*
▸ AS AN ADJECTIVE = **record-breaking**, unbeaten, best ever, unparalleled, unsurpassed, unequalled, never previously achieved • *She won the race in record time.*
▸ IN PHRASES: **off the record** 1 = **confidentially**, privately, in private, in confidence, unofficially, sub rosa, under the rose • *May I speak off the record?*
2 = **confidential**, private, secret, classified, unofficial, in confidence, not for publication, not for circulation • *Those remarks were supposed to be off the record.*

recorder 1 = **tape recorder**, video, video recorder, cassette recorder • *He put the recorder on the desk and pressed play.*
2 = **fipple flute**, flute, descant recorder • *She also plays the recorder.*
3 = **chronicler**, archivist, historian, scorer, clerk, registrar, scribe, diarist, scorekeeper, annalist • *I claim to be a recorder of inner conversations.*

recording = **record**, video, tape, disc, gramophone record, cut *(informal)* • *a video recording of a police interview*

recount = **tell**, report, detail, describe, relate, repeat, portray, depict, rehearse, recite, tell the story of, narrate, delineate, enumerate, give an account of • *He then recounted the story.*

recoup = **regain**, recover, get back, make good, retrieve, redeem, win back • *Insurance companies are trying to recount their losses.*

recourse = **option**, choice, alternative, resort, appeal, resource, remedy, way out, refuge, expedient • *The public believes its only recourse is to take to the streets.*

recover 1 = **get better**, improve, get well, recuperate, pick up, heal, revive, come round, bounce back, mend, turn the corner, pull through, convalesce, be on the mend, take a turn for the better, get back on your feet, feel yourself again, regain your health *or* strength • *He is recovering after sustaining a knee injury.*
OPPOSITES: weaken, deteriorate, relapse
2 = **rally**, improve, pick up, bounce back, make a recovery • *The stock market index fell by 80% before it began to recover.*
3 = **save**, rescue, retrieve, salvage, reclaim • *Rescue teams recovered a few more survivors from the rubble.*
OPPOSITES: abandon
4 = **recoup**, restore, repair, get back, regain, make good, retrieve, reclaim, redeem, recapture, win back, take back, repossess, retake, find again • *Legal action is being taken to try and recover the money.*
OPPOSITES: lose, forfeit

recovery AS A NOUN 1 = **improvement**, return to health, rally, healing, revival, mending, recuperation, convalescence, turn for the better • *He made a remarkable recovery from a shin injury.*
2 = **revival**, improvement, rally, restoration, rehabilitation, upturn, betterment, amelioration • *In many sectors of the economy the recovery has started.*
3 = **retrieval**, repossession, reclamation, restoration, repair, redemption, recapture • *the recovery of a painting by Turner*
▸ IN PHRASES: **in recovery** = **in rehabilitation**, in rehab *(informal)*, returning to health, in convalescence, in recuperation • *a compulsive pot smoker and alcoholic in recovery*

recreation 1 = **leisure**, play, sport, exercise, fun, relief, pleasure, entertainment, relaxation, enjoyment, distraction, amusement, diversion, refreshment, beer and skittles *(informal)*, me-time • *Saturday afternoon is for recreation and outings.*
2 = **pastime**, hobby, distraction, leisure activity, sport, entertainment • *She cites one of her recreations as 'picking up litter'.*

recrimination = **bickering**, retaliation, counterattack, mutual accusation, retort, quarrel, squabbling, name-calling, countercharge • *The war sweeps up everything in hatred and recrimination.*

recruit AS A VERB **1 = gather**, take on, obtain, engage, round up, enrol, procure, proselytize • *He helped to recruit volunteers to go to Pakistan.*
2 = assemble, raise, levy, round up, call up, muster, mobilize • *He's managed to recruit an army of crooks.*
3 = enlist, draft, call up, conscript, impress, sign up, round up, enrol • *He had the forlorn job of trying to recruit soldiers.*
OPPOSITES: fire, dismiss, sack *(informal)*
▸ AS A NOUN **= beginner**, trainee, apprentice, novice, convert, initiate, rookie *(informal)*, helper, learner, neophyte, tyro, greenhorn *(informal)*, proselyte • *A new recruit could well arrive later this week.*

rectify = correct, right, improve, reform, square, fix, repair, adjust, remedy, amend, make good, mend, redress, put right, set the record straight, emend • *Only an act of Congress could rectify the situation.*

rectitude 1 = morality, principle, honour, virtue, decency, justice, equity, integrity, goodness, honesty, correctness, righteousness, probity, incorruptibility, scrupulousness, uprightness • *people of the utmost rectitude*
OPPOSITES: corruption, dishonesty, immorality
2 = correctness, justice, accuracy, precision, verity, rightness, soundness, exactness • *Has the rectitude of this principle ever been formally contested?*

rector = priest, minister, vicar, preacher, pastor, chaplain, curate • *He was the rector of the church.*

rectum
▸ RELATED ADJECTIVE: rectal

recumbent = lying down, lying, resting, flat, leaning, prone, horizontal, stretched out, reclining, prostrate, supine, flat on your back • *He stared down at his sister's recumbent form.*

recuperate = recover, improve, pick up, get better, mend, turn the corner, convalesce, be on the mend, get back on your feet, regain your health • *I went away to the country to recuperate.*

recur = happen again, return, come back, repeat, persist, revert, reappear, come and go, come again • *a theme that was to recur frequently in his work*

recurrence = fresh outbreak, repeat, repetition, deterioration, recrudescence • *Police are out in force to prevent a recurrence of the violence.*

recurrent = periodic, continued, regular, repeated, frequent, recurring, repetitive, cyclical, habitual • *buildings in which staff suffer recurrent illness*
OPPOSITES: isolated, one-off

recycle = reprocess, reuse, salvage, reclaim, save, freecycle • *All glass bottles that can't be refilled can be recycled.*

red AS A NOUN **1 = crimson**, scarlet, ruby, vermilion, rose, wine, pink, cherry, cardinal, coral, maroon, claret, carmine • *a deep shade of red*
2 = communist, socialist, revolutionary, militant, Marxist, leftist, left-winger, lefty *(informal)*, Trotskyite • *They're all so terrified of Reds.*
▸ AS AN ADJECTIVE **1 = crimson**, scarlet, ruby, vermilion, rose, wine, pink, cherry, cardinal, coral, maroon, claret, carmine • *a red coat*
2 = flushed, embarrassed, blushing, beetroot, suffused, florid, shamefaced, rubicund • *She was red with shame.*
3 = chestnut, flaming, reddish, flame-coloured, bay, sandy, foxy, Titian, carroty, ginger • *Her red hair flowed out in the wind.*
4 = bloodshot, inflamed, red-rimmed • *He rubbed his red eyes.*
5 = rosy, healthy, glowing, blooming, ruddy, roseate • *rosy red cheeks*
▸ IN PHRASES: **in the red = in debt**, bankrupt, on the rocks, insolvent, in arrears, overdrawn, owing money, in deficit, showing a loss, in debit • *The theatre is in the red.*
see red = lose your temper, boil, lose it *(informal)*, seethe, go mad *(informal)*, crack up *(informal)*, lose the plot *(informal)*, go ballistic *(slang, chiefly U.S.)*, blow a fuse *(slang, chiefly U.S.)*, fly off the handle *(informal)*, become enraged, go off the deep end *(informal)*, wig out *(slang)*, go up the wall *(slang)*, blow your top, lose your rag *(slang)*, be beside yourself with rage *(informal)*, be *or* get pissed (off) *(taboo slang)*, be *or* get very angry, go off your head *(slang)* • *I didn't mean to break his nose. I just saw red.*
▸ RELATED ADJECTIVES: rubicund, ruddy
▹ *See panel* **Shades of red**

red-blooded = vigorous, manly, lusty, virile, strong, vital, robust, hearty • *I am, even if I say so myself, a red-blooded, heterosexual male.*

redden = flush, colour (up), blush, crimson, suffuse, go red, go beetroot *(informal)* • *She reddened instantly.*

redecorate = refurbish, paint, renovate, do up *(informal)*, furbish • *Americans redecorate their houses and offices every few years.*

redeem 1 = reinstate, vindicate, absolve, free from blame, remove the guilt from, restore to favour, rehabilitate • *He had realized the mistake he had made and wanted to redeem himself.*
2 = make up for, offset, make good, compensate for, outweigh, redress, atone for, make amends for, defray • *Work is the way people seek to redeem their sins.*
3 = pay off, clear, square, honour, discharge, pay back • *The amount required to redeem the mortgage was £358,587.*
4 = trade in, cash (in), exchange, convert, turn in, change • *The voucher will be redeemed for one toy.*
5 = buy back, recover, regain, retrieve, reclaim, win back, repossess, repurchase, recover possession of • *the date upon which you plan to redeem the item*
6 = save, free, deliver, rescue, liberate, ransom, set free, extricate, emancipate, buy the freedom of, pay the ransom of • *a new female spiritual force to redeem the world*
7 = fulfil, meet, keep, carry out, satisfy, discharge, make good, hold to, acquit, adhere to, abide by, keep faith with, be faithful to, perform • *They must redeem that pledge.*

SHADES OF RED

auburn	cherry	flame	maroon	puce	scarlet
baby pink	chestnut	flesh	mulberry	raspberry	shell pink
bay	cinnabar	foxy	old rose	rose	strawberry
burgundy	claret	fuchsia	oxblood	roseate	tea rose
burnt sienna	copper	ginger	oyster pink	rosy	terracotta
cardinal red	coral	grenadine	peach	ruby	Titian
carmine	crimson	gules *(Heraldry)*	peach-blow	russet	Turkey red
carnation	cyclamen	henna	pink	rust	vermeil
carroty	damask	liver	plum	salmon pink	vermilion
cerise	dubonnet	magenta	poppy	sandy	wine

r

redemption 1 = **compensation**, saving, amends, reparation, atonement, absolution, expiation • *trying to make some redemption for his actions*
2 = **salvation**, release, rescue, liberation, ransom, emancipation, deliverance • *offering redemption from our sins*
3 = **paying-off**, clearing, squaring, honouring, discharge, paying back • *redemption of the loan*
4 = **trade-in**, return, recovery, retrieval, repurchase, repossession, reclamation, quid pro quo, recoupment • *cash redemptions and quota payments*

redesign = **reorganize**, rearrange, recast, reshape • *The hotel has recently been redesigned.*

red-handed = **in the act**, with your pants down (*U.S. slang*), (in) flagrante delicto, with your fingers *or* hand in the till (*informal*), bang to rights (*slang*) • *My boyfriend and I robbed a store and were caught red-handed.*

red-hot 1 = **very hot**, burning, heated, steaming, searing, scorching, scalding, piping hot • *red-hot iron*
2 = **exciting**, inspiring, sensational (*informal*), electrifying • *the red-hot guitarist*
3 = **passionate**, thrilling, sexy, arousing, titillating • *a red-hot sex life*

rediscover = **discover**, find, turn up, locate, come across, uncover, unearth, dig up, come upon, bring to light, light upon • *Some earlier writings have been rediscovered.*

redistribute = **re-allocate**, divide up, share out, reassign, re-allot, re-apportion • *Taxes could be used to redistribute income.*

redolent 1 = **reminiscent**, evocative, suggestive, remindful • *a sad tale, redolent with regret*
2 = **scented**, perfumed, fragrant, aromatic, sweet-smelling, odorous • *The air was redolent of cinnamon and apple.*

redoubtable = **formidable**, strong, powerful, terrible, awful, mighty, dreadful, fearful, fearsome, resolute, valiant, doughty • *He is a redoubtable fighter.*

redraw = **change**, review, correct, edit, alter, update, modify, amend, rewrite, reconsider, rework, re-examine, redo, emend, remap • *The map of post-war Europe was redrawn.*

r

redress AS A VERB 1 = **make amends for**, pay for, make up for, compensate for, put right, recompense for, make reparation for, make restitution for • *Victims are turning to litigation to redress wrongs done to them.*
2 = **put right**, reform, balance, square, correct, ease, repair, relieve, adjust, regulate, remedy, amend, mend, rectify, even up, restore the balance • *to redress the economic imbalance*
▸ AS A NOUN = **amends**, payment, compensation, reparation, restitution, atonement, recompense, requital, quittance • *a legal battle to seek some redress from the government*

red tape = **bureaucracy**, the government, administration, the system, the authorities, officialdom, the corridors of power • *They are hamstrung to red tape.*

reduce AS A VERB 1 = **lessen**, cut, contract, lower, depress, moderate, weaken, diminish, turn down, decrease, slow down, cut down, shorten, dilute, impair, curtail, wind down, abate, tone down, debase, truncate, abridge, downsize, kennet (*Austral. slang*), jeff (*Austral. slang*) • *Consumption is being reduced by 25 per cent.*
OPPOSITES: increase, extend, enhance
2 = **degrade**, downgrade, demote, lower in rank, break, humble, humiliate, bring low, take down a peg (*informal*), lower the status of • *They wanted the army reduced to a police force.*
OPPOSITES: promote, enhance, elevate
3 = **drive**, force, bring, bring to the point of • *He was reduced to begging for a living.*
4 = **thicken**, set, gel, clot, condense, congeal, jell, coagulate • *Simmer until mixture reduces.*
5 = **cheapen**, cut, lower, discount, slash, knock down, mark down, make cheaper, bring down the price of • *Companies should reduce prices today.*
6 = **impoverish**, ruin, bankrupt, pauperize
▸ IN PHRASES: **in reduced circumstances** = **impoverished**, broke (*informal*), badly off, hard up (*informal*), short, in need, needy, on the rocks, penniless, destitute, poverty-stricken, down and out, skint (*Brit. slang*), in want, indigent, down at heel, impecunious, dirt-poor (*informal*), on the breadline, flat broke (*informal*), penurious, on your uppers, stony-broke (*Brit. slang*), necessitous, in queer street, without two pennies to rub together (*informal*), on your beam-ends • *living in reduced circumstances*

reduction 1 = **decrease**, lowering, lessening, minimizing, diminution • *a future reduction in interest rates*
2 = **cut**, cutting, trimming, pruning, cutback, scaling down, depletion • *a new strategic arms reduction agreement*
3 = **discount**, concession, slash (*informal*), price cut, markdown • *Reductions of 10-15 per cent are common on these package holidays.*

redundancy 1 = **layoff**, sacking, dismissal • *They hope to avoid future redundancies.*
2 = **unemployment**, the sack (*informal*), the axe (*informal*), joblessness • *Thousands of employees are facing redundancy.*
3 = **superfluity**, excess, surplus, surfeit, uselessness, superabundance, expendability • *the redundancy of its two main exhibits*

redundant 1 = **jobless**, dismissed, sacked, unemployed, laid off, out of work • *a redundant miner*
2 = **superfluous**, extra, surplus, excessive, unnecessary, unwanted, inordinate, inessential, supernumerary, de trop (*French*), supererogatory • *the conversion of redundant buildings to residential use*
OPPOSITES: needed, necessary, essential
3 = **tautological**, wordy, repetitious, verbose, padded, diffuse, prolix, iterative, periphrastic, pleonastic • *The last couplet collapses into redundant adjectives.*

reef = **shoal**, key, bar, shelf, spit, ridge, ledge, atoll, barrier reef • *An unspoilt coral reef encloses the bay.*

reek AS A VERB 1 = **stink**, smell, pong (*Brit. informal*), smell to high heaven, hum (*slang*) • *Your breath reeks.*
2 *with* **of** = **be redolent of**, suggest, smack of, testify to, be characterized by, have all the hallmarks of, bear the stamp of, be permeated by, be suggestive *or* indicative of • *The whole thing reeks of hypocrisy.*
▸ AS A NOUN = **stink**, smell, odour, stench, pong (*Brit. informal*), effluvium, niff (*Brit. slang*), malodour, mephitis, fetor • *He smelt the reek of whisky.*

reel AS A VERB 1 = **stagger**, rock, roll, pitch, stumble, sway, falter, lurch, wobble, waver, totter • *He lost his balance and reeled back.*
2 = **be shaken**, be shocked, be stunned, be staggered, be taken aback, be in shock, be numb, be dazed, be dumbstruck • *I'm still reeling from the shock of hearing it.*
3 = **whirl**, swim, spin, revolve, swirl, twirl, go round and round • *The room reeled and he jammed his head down.*
▸ IN PHRASES: **reel something off** = **recite**, list, run through, fire off, rattle off, itemize, detail • *He reeled off the titles of a dozen or so novels.*

re-elect = **re-appoint**, re-select, pick again, choose again, vote in again • *The president will pursue lower taxes if he is re-elected.*

re-examine = **reconsider**, review, take a fresh look at, re-analyse, re-appraise, work over again • *They will also have to re-examine their expectations.*

refer AS A VERB 1 = **pass on**, transfer, deliver, commit, hand over, submit, turn over, consign • *He could refer the matter to the high court.*
2 = **direct**, point, send, guide, recommend • *He referred me to a book on the subject.*

▸ **IN PHRASES: refer to something** *or* **someone**
1 = **allude to**, mention, cite, speak of, bring up, invoke, hint at, touch on, make reference to, make mention of • *He referred to a recent trip to Canada.*
2 = **relate to**, mean, concern, describe, represent, indicate, apply to, stand for, signify, denote, pertain to, be relevant to • *The term 'electronics' refers to electrically-induced action.*
3 = **consult**, go, apply, turn to, look up, have recourse to, seek information from • *He referred briefly to his notebook.*

referee AS A NOUN = **umpire**, umpie *(Austral. slang)*, judge, ref *(informal)*, arbiter, arbitrator, adjudicator • *The referee stopped the fight.*
▸ AS A VERB = **umpire**, judge, mediate, adjudicate, arbitrate • *He has refereed in two World Cups.*

reference AS A NOUN 1 = **allusion**, note, comment, mention, remark, quotation, citation • *He summed up his philosophy, with reference to Calvin.*
2 = **citation**, note, source, credit, footnote, authority • *I would have found a brief list of references useful.*
3 = **passing on**, transfer, handing over, submission, turning over, committal, consignment, deliverance • *The claimants are seeking a reference to the European court of Justice.*
4 = **testimonial**, recommendation, credentials, endorsement, certification, good word, character reference • *The firm offered to give her a reference.*
▸ AS A VERB = **refer to**, mention, cite, speak of, bring up, invoke, touch on, allude to, make reference, make mention of • *It specifically referenced a 1928 book on the subject.*
▸ **IN PHRASES: with reference to** = **concerning**, regarding, relating to, in connection with, with respect to • *I'm calling with reference to your series on prejudice.*

referendum = **public vote**, poll, ballot, popular vote, plebiscite • *a referendum on independence*

refill AS A VERB = **top up**, refresh, replenish, restock • *I refilled our wine glasses.*
▸ AS A NOUN = **top-up** • *Max held out his cup for a refill.*

refinance = **take on a loan**, borrow, remortgage • *It can be costly to refinance.*

refine 1 = **purify**, process, filter, cleanse, clarify, sift, distil, rarefy • *Oil is refined so as to remove naturally occurring impurities.*
2 = **improve**, perfect, polish, temper, elevate, hone, fine-tune • *Surgical techniques are constantly being refined.*

refined 1 = **purified**, processed, pure, filtered, clean, clarified, distilled • *refined sugar*
OPPOSITES: coarse, impure, unrefined
2 = **cultured**, civil, polished, sophisticated, gentlemanly, elegant, polite, cultivated, gracious, civilized, genteel, urbane, courtly, well-bred, ladylike, well-mannered • *His speech and manner are refined.*
OPPOSITES: common, coarse, boorish
3 = **discerning**, fine, nice, sensitive, exact, subtle, delicate, precise, discriminating, sublime, fastidious, punctilious • *refined tastes*

refinement 1 = **subtlety**, nuance, nicety, fine point • *the refinements of the game*
2 = **sophistication**, finish, style, culture, taste, breeding, polish, grace, discrimination, courtesy, civilization, precision, elegance, delicacy, cultivation, finesse, politeness, good manners, civility, gentility, good breeding, graciousness, urbanity, fastidiousness, fineness, courtliness, politesse • *a girl who possessed both dignity and refinement*
3 = **purification**, processing, filtering, cleansing, clarification, distillation, rectification, rarefaction • *the refinement of crude oil*

refit = **repair**, fix, restore, renew, mend, renovate, patch up, put back together, restore to working order • *During the war, navy ships were refitted here.*

reflect 1 = **show**, reveal, express, display, indicate, demonstrate, exhibit, communicate, manifest, bear out, bespeak, evince • *Concern was reflected in the government's budget.*
2 = **throw back**, return, mirror, echo, reproduce, imitate, give back • *The glass appears to reflect light naturally.*
3 *usually followed by* **on** = **consider**, think, contemplate, deliberate, muse, ponder, meditate, mull over, ruminate, cogitate, wonder • *I reflected on the child's future.*

reflection AS A NOUN 1 = **image**, echo, counterpart, likeness, mirror image • *Meg stared at her reflection in the mirror.*
2 = **sending back**, mirroring, throwing back, casting back • *the reflection of a beam of light off a mirror*
3 = **indication**, evidence, display, demonstration, proof, manifestation, attestation • *a reflection of a person's experiences as a child*
4 = **criticism**, censure, slur, reproach, imputation, derogation, aspersion • *Infection with head lice is no reflection on personal hygiene.*
5 = **consideration**, thinking, pondering, deliberation, thought, idea, view, study, opinion, impression, observation, musing, meditation, contemplation, rumination, perusal, cogitation, cerebration • *After days of reflection she decided to write back.*
▸ AS A PLURAL NOUN = **thoughts**, feeling, idea, view, opinion, belief, impression, viewpoint • *a series of reflections on death*

reflective = **thoughtful**, contemplative, meditative, pensive, reasoning, pondering, deliberative, ruminative, cogitating • *Mike is a quiet, reflective man.*

reflex = **automatic**, spontaneous, instinctive, involuntary, impulsive, knee-jerk, unthinking • *I turned to look inside the house in a reflex action.*

reform AS A NOUN = **improvement**, amendment, correction, rehabilitation, renovation, betterment, rectification, amelioration • *a programme of economic reform*
▸ AS A VERB 1 = **improve**, better, correct, restore, repair, rebuild, amend, reclaim, mend, renovate, reconstruct, remodel, rectify, rehabilitate, regenerate, reorganize, reconstitute, revolutionize, ameliorate, emend • *his plans to reform the country's economy*
2 = **mend your ways**, go straight *(informal)*, shape up *(informal)*, get it together *(informal)*, turn over a new leaf, get your act together *(informal)*, clean up your act *(informal)*, pull your socks up *(Brit. informal)*, get back on the straight and narrow *(informal)* • *Under such a system where is the incentive to reform?*

reformation = **advancement**, change, improvement, betterment, amelioration • *the reformation of science*

refractory = **unmanageable**, difficult, stubborn, contentious, perverse, unruly, uncontrollable, intractable, wilful, recalcitrant, obstinate, headstrong, cantankerous, uncooperative, stiff-necked, disobedient, disputatious, mulish, contumacious • *refractory priests who tried to side with the king*

refrain[1] = **stop**, avoid, give up, cease, do without, renounce, abstain, eschew, leave off, desist, forbear, kick *(informal)* • *She refrained from making any comment.*

refrain[2] = **chorus**, song, tune, melody • *a refrain from an old song*

refresh 1 = **revive**, cool, freshen, revitalize, cheer, stimulate, brace, rejuvenate, kick-start *(informal)*, enliven, breathe new life into, invigorate, revivify, reanimate, inspirit • *The lotion cools and refreshes the skin.*
2 = **replenish**, restore, repair, renew, top up, renovate • *She appeared, her make-up refreshed.*
3 = **stimulate**, prompt, renew, jog, prod, brush up *(informal)* • *Allow me to refresh your memory.*

refreshing 1 = **new**, different, original, welcome, novel, unusual, stimulating, innovative • *refreshing new ideas*
2 = **stimulating**, fresh, cooling, bracing, invigorating,

r

revivifying, thirst-quenching, inspiriting • *Herbs have been used for centuries to make refreshing drinks.*
OPPOSITES: tiring, exhausting, soporific

refreshment 1 = **revival**, restoration, renewal, stimulation, renovation, freshening, reanimation, enlivenment, repair • *a place where city dwellers come to find spiritual refreshment*
2 *plural* = **food and drink**, drinks, snacks, nibbles *(informal)*, sustenance, titbits, comestibles, kai *(N.Z. informal)* • *Some refreshments would be nice.*

refrigerate = **cool**, freeze, chill, keep cold • *Refrigerate the dough overnight.*

refrigerator = **fridge**, chiller, cooler, ice-box *(U.S. & Canad.)* • *I expect you've got a refrigerator.*

refuge 1 = **protection**, security, shelter, harbour, asylum, sanctuary • *They took refuge in a bomb shelter.*
2 = **haven**, resort, retreat, harbour, sanctuary, hideaway, hide-out, bolt hole, place of safety • *We climbed up a winding track towards a mountain refuge.*
3 = **solace**, relief, comfort • *Father Rowan took refuge in silence.*

refugee = **exile**, asylum seeker, émigré, displaced person, runaway, fugitive, escapee, stateless person • *an application for refugee status*

refund AS A NOUN = **repayment**, compensation, rebate, reparation, indemnity, reimbursement, return • *They plan to demand a refund.*
▸ AS A VERB = **repay**, return, restore, make good, pay back, reimburse, give back • *She will refund you the purchase price.*

refurbish = **renovate**, restore, repair, clean up, overhaul, revamp, mend, remodel, do up *(informal)*, refit, fix up *(informal, chiefly U.S. & Canad.)*, spruce up, pimp up, pimp out, re-equip, set to rights • *We have spent money on refurbishing the offices.*

refurbishment = **renovation**, cleaning up, restoration, overhaul, revamping, doing up *(informal)*, refitting, sprucing up • *the refurbishment of the estate's housing*

refusal AS A NOUN = **rejection**, denial, defiance, rebuff, knock-back *(slang)*, thumbs down, repudiation, kick in the teeth *(slang)*, negation, no • *a refusal of planning permission*
▸ IN PHRASES: **first refusal** = **option**, choice, opportunity, consideration • *A tenant may have a right of first refusal if a property is offered for sale.*

refuse[1] 1 = **decline**, reject, turn down, scorn, spurn, say no to, repudiate • *I could hardly refuse his invitation.*
2 = **deny**, decline, withhold, not grant, discountenance • *She was refused access to her children.*
OPPOSITES: give, allow, agree

refuse[2] = **rubbish**, waste, sweepings, junk *(informal)*, litter, garbage, trash, sediment, scum, dross, dregs, leavings, dreck *(slang, chiefly U.S.)*, offscourings, lees • *a weekly collection of refuse*

refute = **disprove**, counter, discredit, prove false, silence, overthrow, negate, rebut, give the lie to, blow out of the water *(slang)*, confute • *It was the kind of rumour that is impossible to refute.*
OPPOSITES: prove, confirm, substantiate

regain 1 = **recover**, get back, retrieve, redeem, recapture, win back, take back, recoup, repossess, retake • *Troops have regained control of the city.*
2 = **get back to**, return to, reach again, reattain • *Davis went to regain his carriage.*

regal = **royal**, majestic, kingly *or* queenly, noble, princely, proud, magnificent, sovereign, fit for a king *or* queen • *Never has she looked so regal.*

regale 1 = **entertain**, delight, amuse, divert, gratify • *He was constantly regaled with amusing stories.*
2 = **serve**, refresh, ply, wine and dine, supply lavishly • *On Sunday evenings we were usually regaled with a roast dinner.*

regalia = **trappings**, gear, decorations, finery, apparatus, emblems, paraphernalia, garb, accoutrements, rigout *(informal)*, bling *(slang)* • *a military band in full regalia*

regard AS A VERB 1 = **consider**, see, hold, rate, view, value, account, judge, treat, think of, esteem, deem, look upon, adjudge • *I regard creativity as both a gift and a skill.*
2 = **look at**, view, eye, watch, observe, check, notice, clock *(Brit. slang)*, remark, check out *(informal)*, gaze at, behold, eyeball *(U.S. slang)*, scrutinize, get a load of *(informal)*, take a dekko at *(Brit. slang)* • *She regarded him curiously for a moment.*
▸ AS A NOUN 1 = **respect**, esteem, deference, store, thought, love, concern, care, account, note, reputation, honour, consideration, sympathy, affection, attachment, repute • *I have a very high regard for him and what he has achieved.*
2 = **look**, gaze, scrutiny, stare, glance • *This gave a look of calculated menace to his regard.*
3 *plural* = **good wishes**, respects, greetings, compliments, best wishes, salutations, devoirs • *Give my regards to your family.*
▸ IN PHRASES: **as regards** = **concerning**, regarding, relating to, pertaining to • *As regards the war, he believed in victory at any price.*
in this regard = **on this point**, on this matter, on this detail, in this respect • *In this regard nothing has changed.*
with regard to = **concerning**, regarding, relating to, with respect to, as regards • *The UN has urged sanctions with regard to trade in arms.*

regarding = **concerning**, about, as to, on the subject of, re, respecting, in respect of, as regards, with reference to, in re, in the matter of, apropos, in *or* with regard to • *He refused to divulge any information regarding the man's whereabouts.*

regardless AS AN ADVERB = **in spite of everything**, anyway, nevertheless, nonetheless, in any case, no matter what, for all that, rain or shine, despite everything, come what may • *Despite her recent surgery she has been carrying on regardless.*
▸ AS AN ADJECTIVE *with* **of** = **irrespective of**, without reference to, without regard to, despite, discounting, disregarding, notwithstanding, unconcerned about, heedless of, unmindful of • *It takes in anybody regardless of religion, colour or creed.*

regenerate = **renew**, restore, revive, renovate, change, reproduce, uplift, reconstruct, re-establish, rejuvenate, kick-start *(informal)*, breathe new life into, invigorate, reinvigorate, reawaken, revivify, give a shot in the arm, inspirit • *The government will continue to regenerate inner city areas.*
OPPOSITES: decline, degenerate, stagnate

regime 1 = **government**, rule, authorities, management, administration, leadership, establishment, reign • *the collapse of the fascist regime*
2 = **plan**, course, system, policy, programme, scheme, diet, arrangement, procedure, regimen • *a drastic regime of economic reform*

regiment = **army**, company, force, unit, division, section, corps, brigade, battalion, legion, squadron, detachment, platoon • *a regiment of hungry customers*

regimented = **controlled**, ordered, disciplined, organized, regulated, systematized • *the regimented atmosphere of the orphanage*

region AS A NOUN = **area**, country, place, part, land, quarter, division, section, sector, district, territory, zone, province, patch, turf *(U.S. slang)*, tract, expanse, locality • *a remote mountain region*
▸ IN PHRASES: **in the region of** 1 = **around**, almost, nearing, nearly, approaching, close to, roughly, more or less, approximately • *There are still somewhere in the region of 18 million members.*
2 = **vicinity**, area, range, scope, neighbourhood, sphere • *a series of battles in the region of Matebete*
▹ *See panel* **Administrative regions**

ADMINISTRATIVE REGIONS

French regions
- Alsace
- Aquitaine
- Auvergne
- Basse-Normandie
- Brittany
- Burgundy
- Centre
- Champagne-Ardenne
- Corsica
- Franche-Comté
- Haute-Normandie
- Île-de-France
- Languedoc-Roussillon
- Limousin
- Lorraine
- Midi-Pyrénées
- Nord-Pas-de-Calais
- Pays de Loire
- Picardie
- Poitou-Charentes
- Provence-Alpes-Côte d'Azur
- Rhône-Alpes

French départements
- Ain
- Aisne
- Allier
- Alpes de Haute Provence
- Alpes Maritimes
- Ardèche
- Ardennes
- Ariège
- Aube
- Aude
- Aveyron
- Bas Rhin
- Bouches du Rhône
- Calvados
- Cantal
- Charente
- Charente Maritime
- Cher
- Corrèze
- Corse
- Cote d'Or
- Côtes du Nord
- Creuse
- Deux Sèvres
- Dordogne
- Doubs
- Drôme
- Essone
- Eure
- Eure et Loir
- Finistère
- Gard
- Gayane
- Gers
- Gironde
- Guadeloupe
- Haute Garonne
- Haute Loire
- Haute Marne
- Haute Savoie
- Haute Vienne
- Hautes Alpes
- Hautes Pyrénées
- Haut Rhin
- Hauts de Seine
- Hérault
- Ille et Vilaine
- Indre
- Indre et Loire
- Isère
- Jura
- Landes
- Loire
- Loire Atlantique
- Loiret
- Loir et Cher
- Lot
- Lot et Garonne
- Lozère
- Maine et Loire
- Manche
- Marne
- Martinique
- Mayenne
- Meurthe et Moselle
- Meuse
- Morbihan
- Moselle
- Nièvre
- Nord
- Oise
- Orne
- Paris
- Pas de Calais
- Puy de Dôme
- Pyrénées Atlantiques
- Pyrénées Orientales
- Réunion
- Rhône
- Saône
- Saône et Loire
- Sarthe
- Savoie
- Seine et Marne
- Seine Maritime
- Seine Saint Denis
- Somme
- Tarn
- Tarn et Garonne
- Territoire de Belfort
- Val de Marne
- Val d'Oise
- Var
- Vaucluse
- Vendée
- Vienne
- Vosges
- Yonne
- Yvelines

German states
- Baden-Württemberg
- Bavaria
- Berlin
- Brandenburg
- Bremen
- Hamburg
- Hessen
- Lower Saxony
- Mecklenburg-West Pomerania
- North Rhine-Westphalia
- Rhineland-Palatinate
- Saarland
- Saxony
- Saxony-Anhalt
- Schleswig-Holstein
- Thuringia

Italian regions
- Abruzzo
- Basilicata
- Calabria
- Campania
- Emilia-Romagna
- Friuli-Venezia Giulia
- Lazio
- Liguria
- Lombardy
- Marche
- Molise
- Piedmont
- Puglia
- Sardinia
- Sicily
- Trentino-Alto Adige
- Tuscany
- Umbria
- Valle d'Aosta
- Veneto

Italian provinces
- Agrigento
- Alessandria
- Ancona
- Aosta
- Arezzo
- Ascoli Piceno
- Asti
- Avellino
- Bari
- Belluno
- Benevento
- Bergamo
- Bologna
- Bolzano
- Brescia
- Brindisi
- Cagliari
- Caltanissetta
- Campobasso
- Caserta
- Catania
- Catanzaro
- Chieti
- Como
- Cosenza
- Cremona
- Crotone
- Cuneo
- Enna
- Ferrara
- Firenze
- Foggia
- Forlì
- Frosinone
- Genova
- Gorizia
- Grosseto
- Imperia
- Isernia
- L'Aquila
- La Spezia
- Latina
- Lecce
- Lecco
- Livorno
- Lodi
- Lucca
- Macerata
- Mantova
- Massa Carrara
- Matera
- Messina
- Milano
- Modena
- Napoli
- Novara
- Nuoro
- Oristano
- Padova
- Palermo
- Parma
- Pavia
- Perugia
- Pesaro
- Pescara
- Piacenza
- Pisa
- Pistoia
- Pordenone
- Potenza
- Prato
- Ragusa
- Ravenna
- Reggio di Calabria
- Reggio Emilia
- Repubblica di San Marino
- Rieti
- Rimini
- Roma
- Rovigo
- Salerno
- Sassari
- Savona
- Siena
- Siracusa
- Sondrio
- Taranto
- Teramo
- Terni
- Torino
- Trapani
- Trento
- Treviso
- Trieste
- Udine
- Varese
- Venezia
- Verbania
- Vercelli
- Verona
- Vibo Valentia
- Vicenza
- Viterbo

Spanish regions
- Andalucía
- Aragón
- Asturias
- Balearic Islands
- Basque Country
- Canary Islands
- Cantabria
- Castilla-La Mancha
- Castilla-León
- Catalonia
- Ceuta
- Extremadura
- Galicia
- La Rioja
- Madrid
- Melilla
- Murcia
- Navarra
- Valencian Community

ADMINISTRATIVE REGIONS (CONTINUED)

Spanish provinces

Álava	Burgos	Girona	León	Pontevedra	Valencia
Albacete	Cácares	Granada	Lleida	Salamanca	Valladolid
Alhucemas	Cádiz	Gualalajara	Lugo	Santa Cruz de Tenerife	Vélez de la Gomera
Alicante	Cantabria	Guipúzcoa	Madrid	Segovia	Vizcaya
Almerìa	Castellón	Huelva	Málaga	Sevilla	Zamora
Asturias	Ceuta	Huesca	Melilla	Soria	Zaragoza
Ávila	Chafarinas	Jaén	Murcia	Tarragona	
Badajoz	Ciudad Real	La Coruna	Navarra	Teruel	
Balearics	Cordoba	La Rioja	Orense	Toledo	
Barcelona	Cuenca	Las Palmas	Palencia		

regional = **local**, district, provincial, parochial, sectional, zonal • *concern about regional security*

register AS A NOUN = **list**, record, roll, file, schedule, diary, catalogue, log, archives, chronicle, memorandum, roster, ledger, annals • *registers of births, deaths and marriages*
▸ AS A VERB 1 = **enrol**, sign on *or* up, enlist, list, note, enter, check in, inscribe, set down • *Have you come to register at the school?*
2 = **record**, catalogue, chronicle, take down • *We registered his birth.*
3 = **indicate**, show, record, read, display • *The meter registered loads of 9 and 10 kg.*
4 = **show**, mark, record, reflect, indicate, betray, manifest, bespeak • *Many people registered no symptoms when they became infected.*
5 = **express**, say, show, reveal, display, exhibit • *Workers stopped work to register their protest.*
6 = **have an effect**, get through, sink in, make an impression, tell, impress, come home, dawn on • *What I said sometimes didn't register in her brain.*

regress = **revert**, deteriorate, return, go back, retreat, lapse, fall back, wane, recede, ebb, degenerate, relapse, lose ground, turn the clock back, backslide, retrogress, retrocede, fall away *or* off • *Such countries are not developing at all, but regressing.*
OPPOSITES: improve, advance, progress

regret AS A VERB 1 = **be** *or* **feel sorry about**, feel remorse about, be upset about, rue, deplore, bemoan, repent (of), weep over, bewail, cry over spilt milk • *She regrets having given up her home.*
OPPOSITES: be happy about, be satisfied with, rejoice over
2 = **mourn**, miss, lament, weep over, sigh over, grieve for *or* over, pine for *or* over • *I regret the passing of the old era.*
▸ AS A NOUN 1 = **remorse**, compunction, self-reproach, pang of conscience, bitterness, repentance, contrition, penitence, ruefulness • *He has no regrets about retiring.*
2 = **sorrow**, disappointment, grief, sadness, unhappiness, lamentation, dejection • *He expressed great regret.*
OPPOSITES: pleasure, satisfaction, contentment

regretful = **sorry**, disappointed, sad, ashamed, apologetic, mournful, rueful, contrite, sorrowful, repentant, remorseful, penitent • *He gave a regretful smile.*

regrettable = **unfortunate**, wrong, disappointing, sad, distressing, unhappy, shameful, woeful, deplorable, ill-advised, lamentable, pitiable • *a regrettable incident*

regroup = **reform**, reassemble, reorganize • *The opposition has now regrouped.*

regular 1 = **frequent**, daily, repeated, constant, periodic, continual, recurrent, habitual • *Take regular exercise.*
2 = **normal**, common, established, usual, ordinary, typical, routine, everyday, customary, commonplace, habitual, unvarying • *Children are encouraged to make reading a regular routine.*
OPPOSITES: rare, unusual, infrequent
3 = **steady**, even, constant, uniform, rhythmic, unchanging, unvarying, consistent • *a very regular beat*
4 = **ordinary**, standard, normal, conventional, common or garden *(informal)* • *The product looks and burns like a regular cigarette.*
5 = **even**, level, balanced, straight, flat, fixed, smooth, uniform, symmetrical • *regular rows of wooden huts*
OPPOSITES: irregular, erratic, uneven
6 = **methodical**, set, ordered, formal, steady, efficient, systematic, orderly, standardized, dependable, consistent • *an unfailingly regular procedure*
OPPOSITES: varied, disorderly, inconsistent
7 = **official**, standard, established, traditional, classic, correct, approved, formal, sanctioned, proper, prevailing, orthodox, time-honoured, bona fide • *The regular method is to take your cutting, and insert it into the compost.*

regulate 1 = **control**, run, order, rule, manage, direct, guide, handle, conduct, arrange, monitor, organize, govern, administer, oversee, supervise, systematize, superintend • *a powerful body to regulate the stock market*
2 = **moderate**, control, modulate, settle, fit, balance, tune, adjust • *He breathed deeply, trying to regulate the pound of his heartbeat.*

regulation AS A NOUN 1 = **rule**, order, law, direction, procedure, requirement, dictate, decree, canon, statute, ordinance, commandment, edict, precept, standing order • *new safety regulations*
2 = **control**, government, management, administration, direction, arrangement, supervision, governance, rule • *They also have responsibility for the regulation of nurseries.*
▸ AS A MODIFIER = **conventional**, official, standard, required, normal, usual, prescribed, mandatory, customary • *He wears the regulation dark suit of corporate America.*

regurgitate 1 = **repeat**, echo, reproduce, reiterate, duplicate, restate, retell, recapitulate, iterate • *Many lectures regurgitate old information.*
2 = **disgorge**, throw up *(informal)*, chuck up *(slang, chiefly U. S.)*, puke up *(slang)*, sick up *(informal)*, spew out *or* up • *It was enough to make you regurgitate your plum pudding.*

rehabilitate 1 = **reintegrate**, retrain, restore to health, readapt • *Considerable efforts have been made to rehabilitate patients.*
2 = **reinstate**, restore, re-establish, reinstall, forgive, bring back, pardon, exonerate, absolve, exculpate • *Ten years later, Dreyfus was rehabilitated.*
3 = **restore**, develop, convert, renew, adjust, rebuild, upgrade, make good, overhaul, revamp, mend, refurbish, renovate, reconstruct, reinstate, re-establish, make over, refit, fix up *(informal, chiefly U.S. & Canad.)*, modernize, reconstitute, redecorate, recondition, reinvigorate • *a program for rehabilitating low-income housing*

rehash AS A NOUN = **reworking**, rewrite, new version, rearrangement • *It was a rehash of an old script*

▸ **AS A VERB** = **rework**, rewrite, rearrange, change, alter, reshuffle, make over, reuse, rejig *(informal)*, refashion • *The tour seems to rely heavily on rehashed old favourites.*

rehearsal = **practice**, rehearsing, practice session, run-through, reading, preparation, drill, going-over *(informal)* • *The band was set to begin rehearsals for a concert tour.*

rehearse 1 = **practise**, prepare, run through, go over, train, act, study, ready, repeat, drill, try out, recite • *A group of actors are rehearsing a play about Joan of Arc.*
2 = **recite**, practise, go over, run through, tell, list, detail, describe, review, relate, depict, spell out, recount, narrate, trot out *(informal)*, delineate, enumerate • *Anticipate any tough questions and rehearse your answers.*

reign **AS A VERB** 1 = **be supreme**, prevail, predominate, hold sway, be rife, be rampant • *A relative calm reigned over the city.*
2 = **rule**, govern, be in power, occupy *or* sit on the throne, influence, command, administer, hold sway, wear the crown, wield the sceptre • *Henry II, who reigned from 1154 to 1189*
▸ **AS A NOUN** = **rule**, sovereignty, supremacy, power, control, influence, command, empire, monarchy, sway, dominion, hegemony, ascendancy • *Queen Victoria's reign*
▸ **IN PHRASES: reign of terror** = **tyranny**, dictatorship, oppression, despotism • *They accused him of carrying out a reign of terror.*

QUOTATIONS
Here we may reign secure, and in my choice
To reign is worth ambition though in hell;
Better to reign in hell, than serve in heav'n
[John Milton *Paradise Lost*]

reigning 1 = **current**, presiding, incumbent • *the reigning world champion*
2 = **ruling**, on the throne, regnant • *the reigning monarch*

reimburse = **pay back**, refund, repay, recompense, return, restore, compensate, indemnify, remunerate • *I'll be happy to reimburse you for any expenses.*

reimbursement = **repayment**, compensation, refund, recompense, indemnification • *It can take up to six months before reimbursements are made.*

rein **AS A NOUN** = **control**, harness, bridle, hold, check, restriction, brake, curb, restraint • *He wrapped his horse's reins round his left wrist.*
▸ **IN PHRASES: give (a) free rein to something** *or* **someone** = **give a free hand (to)**, give carte blanche (to), give a blank cheque (to), remove restraints (from), indulge, let go, give way to, give (someone) his *or* her head • *They gave him a free rein with time to mould a decent side.*
rein something in *or* **back** 1 = **check**, control, limit, contain, master, curb, restrain, hold back, constrain, bridle, keep in check • *He promised the government would rein back inflation.*
2 = **bridle**, slow down, restrain, hold back, subdue, keep under control • *Either prices or wage packets had to be reined in*

reincarnation = **rebirth**, metempsychosis, transmigration of souls • *Many African tribes believe in reincarnation.*

reindeer
▸ **NAME OF MALE**: buck

reinforce 1 = **consolidate**, support, increase, further, encourage, promote, boost, sustain, foster, heighten, magnify, amplify, augment • *This sense of privilege tends to be reinforced by the outside world.*
OPPOSITES: undermine, weaken, contradict
2 = **support**, strengthen, fortify, toughen, stress, prop, supplement, emphasize, underline, harden, bolster, stiffen, shore up, buttress • *They had to reinforce the walls with exterior beams.*
3 = **increase**, extend, add to, strengthen, supplement, augment • *Troops and police have been reinforced.*

reinforcement 1 = **strengthening**, increase, supplement, enlargement, fortification, amplification, augmentation • *the reinforcement of peace and security around the world*
2 = **support**, stay, shore, prop, brace, buttress • *There are reinforcements on all doors.*
3 *plural* = **reserves**, support, auxiliaries, additional *or* fresh troops • *troop reinforcements*

reinstate = **restore**, recall, bring back, re-establish, return, rehabilitate • *He has agreed to reinstate five senior workers.*

reinstatement = **restoration**, bringing back, re-establishment, reinstitution, reinstallation, rehabilitation • *Parents campaigned in vain for her reinstatement.*

reissue = **rerelease**, relaunch • *this welcome reissue of a 1955 Ingmar Bergman classic*

reiterate = **repeat**, restate, say again, retell, do again, recapitulate, iterate • *He reiterated his opposition to the creation of a central bank.*

reject **AS A VERB** 1 = **rebuff**, drop, jilt, desert, turn down, ditch *(slang)*, break with, spurn, refuse, say no to, repulse, throw over • *people who have been rejected by their lovers*
OPPOSITES: accept
2 = **deny**, decline, abandon, exclude, veto, discard, relinquish, renounce, spurn, eschew, leave off, throw off, disallow, forsake, retract, repudiate, cast off, disown, forgo, disclaim, forswear, swear off, wash your hands of • *They are rejecting the values on which Thatcherism was built.*
OPPOSITES: allow, agree, approve
3 = **discard**, decline, eliminate, scrap, bin, jettison, cast aside, throw away *or* out • *Seventeen publishers rejected the manuscript.*
OPPOSITES: receive, accept, select
▸ **AS A NOUN** 1 = **castoff**, second, discard, flotsam, clunker *(informal)* • *a hat that looks like a reject from an army patrol*
OPPOSITES: prize, treasure
2 = **failure**, has-been, loser, flop, also-ran, dud, dropout, non-starter, saddo *(Brit. slang)*, castoff • *I'm an outsider, a reject, a social failure.* • *a reject of Real Madrid*

rejection 1 = **refusal**, turning down, declining, dismissal, spurning, rebuff, knock-back *(slang)*, non-acceptance • *a clear rejection of the government's policies*
2 = **denial**, veto, dismissal, exclusion, abandonment, spurning, casting off, disowning, thumbs down, renunciation, repudiation, eschewal • *his rejection of our values*
OPPOSITES: approval, acceptance, affirmation
3 = **rebuff**, refusal, knock-back *(slang)*, kick in the teeth *(slang)*, bum's rush *(slang)*, the (old) heave-ho *(informal)*, brushoff *(slang)* • *These feelings of rejection and hurt remain.*
OPPOSITES: selection, acceptance

rejoice = **be glad**, celebrate, delight, be happy, joy, triumph, glory, revel, be overjoyed, exult, jump for joy, make merry • *We are cold and hungry but we rejoice to have succeeded.*
OPPOSITES: mourn, grieve, lament

rejoicing = **happiness**, delight, joy, triumph, celebration, cheer, festivity, elation, gaiety, jubilation, revelry, exultation, gladness, merrymaking • *There was general rejoicing at the news.*

rejoin[1] 1 = **join again**, return to, come back to, be reunited with, reattain, regain • *She went off to Tunisia to rejoin her father.*
2 = **join again**, return to, regain, come back to, reattain • *In the morning I rejoined highway 127 south.*

rejoin[2] = **reply**, answer, respond, retort, come back with, riposte, return • *'I dare say they do,' rejoined his wife wearily.*

rejoinder = **reply**, answer, response, counter, comeback *(informal)*, retort, riposte, counterattack • *He felt it was an inadequate rejoinder.*

rejuvenate = **revitalize**, restore, renew, refresh, regenerate, breathe new life into, reinvigorate, revivify, give new life to, reanimate, make young again, restore vitality to • *He was advised that the Italian climate would rejuvenate him.*

rekindle = **reawaken**, stimulate, revive, arouse, stir up, revivify, re-activate • *Her interest was rekindled.*

relapse AS A VERB 1 = **lapse**, revert, degenerate, slip back, fail, weaken, fall back, regress, backslide, retrogress • *He was relapsing into his usual gloom.*
2 = **worsen**, deteriorate, sicken, weaken, fail, sink, fade • *In 90 per cent of cases the patient will relapse within six months.*
OPPOSITES: improve, recover, rally
▸ AS A NOUN 1 = **lapse**, regression, fall from grace, reversion, backsliding, recidivism, retrogression • *a relapse into the nationalism of the nineteenth century*
2 = **worsening**, setback, deterioration, recurrence, turn for the worse, weakening • *The sufferer can experience frequent relapses.*
OPPOSITES: improvement, rally, recovery

relate AS A VERB = **tell**, recount, report, present, detail, describe, chronicle, rehearse, recite, impart, narrate, set forth, give an account of • *He was relating a story he had once heard.*
▸ IN PHRASES: **relate to something** *or* **someone**
1 = **concern**, refer to, apply to, have to do with, pertain to, be relevant to, bear upon, appertain to, have reference to • *papers relating to the children*
2 = **connect with**, associate with, link with, couple with, join with, ally with, correlate to, coordinate with • *how language relates to particular cultural codes*
3 = **empathize with**, identify with, associate with, respond to, feel for, ally with, put yourself in the place *or* shoes of • *He is unable to relate to other people.*

related 1 = **associated**, linked, allied, joint, accompanying, connected, affiliated, akin, correlated, interconnected, concomitant, cognate, agnate • *equipment and accessories for diving and related activities*
OPPOSITES: separate, unrelated, unconnected
2 = **akin**, kin, kindred, cognate, consanguineous, agnate • *He is related by marriage to some of the complainants.*
OPPOSITES: unrelated

relation AS A NOUN 1 = **similarity**, link, bearing, bond, application, comparison, tie-in, correlation, interdependence, pertinence, connection • *This theory bears no relation to reality.*
2 = **relative**, kin, kinsman *or* kinswoman, rellie (*Austral. slang*) • *I call him Uncle though he's no relation.*
▸ AS A PLURAL NOUN 1 = **dealings**, relationship, rapport, communications, meetings, terms, associations, affairs, contact, connections, interaction, intercourse, liaison • *The company has a track record of good employee relations.*
2 = **family**, relatives, tribe, clan, kin, kindred, kinsmen, kinsfolk, ainga (*N.Z.*), rellie (*Austral. slang*) • *all my relations come from the place*
▸ IN PHRASES: **in relation to** = **concerning**, regarding, respecting, in connection with, with regard to, on the subject of, in respect of, with reference to, apropos • *He is the sixth person to be arrested in relation to the coup plot.*

relationship 1 = **association**, bond, communications, connection, conjunction, affinity, rapport, kinship • *Money problems place great stress on close family relationships.*
2 = **affair**, romance, fling, liaison, amour, intrigue • *She likes to have a relationship with her leading men.*
3 = **connection**, link, proportion, parallel, ratio, similarity, tie-up, correlation • *the relationship between culture and power*

QUOTATIONS

A relationship, I think, is like a shark, you know? It has to constantly move forward or it dies. And I think what we got on our hands is a dead shark
[Woody Allen *Annie Hall*]

relative AS A NOUN = **relation**, connection, kinsman *or* kinswoman, member of your *or* the family, rellie (*Austral. slang*) • *Do relatives of yours still live in Siberia?*
▸ AS AN ADJECTIVE 1 = **comparative**, considerable, reasonable, moderate, in comparison • *a period of relative calm*
2 = **corresponding**, comparable, respective, comparative, reciprocal, correlative • *the relative importance of education in 50 countries*
3 *with* **to** = **in proportion to**, corresponding to, proportionate to, proportional to • *The satellite remains in one spot relative to the earth's surface.*

QUOTATIONS

Every man sees in his relatives, and especially in his cousins, a series of grotesque caricatures of himself
[H.L. Mencken *Prejudices*]

When you are courting a nice girl an hour seems like a second. When you sit on a red-hot cinder a second seems like an hour. That's relativity
[Albert Einstein]

relatively = **comparatively**, rather, somewhat, to some extent, in *or* by comparison • *The sums needed are relatively small.*

relax 1 = **be** *or* **feel at ease**, chill out (*slang, chiefly U.S.*), take it easy, loosen up, laze, lighten up (*slang*), put your feet up, hang loose (*slang*), let yourself go (*informal*), let your hair down (*informal*), mellow out (*informal*), make yourself at home, outspan (*S. African*), take your ease • *I ought to relax and stop worrying about it.*
OPPOSITES: be alert, be alarmed
2 = **calm down**, calm, soothe, unwind, pacify, loosen up, tranquillize • *Do something that you know relaxes you.*
3 = **make less tense**, soften, loosen up, unbend, unknot, rest • *Massage is used to relax muscles.*
4 = **lessen**, reduce, ease, relieve, weaken, loosen, let up, slacken • *He gradually relaxed his grip on the arms of the chair.*
OPPOSITES: work, increase, tighten
5 = **moderate**, ease, relieve, weaken, diminish, mitigate, slacken • *Rules governing student conduct have been relaxed in recent years.*
OPPOSITES: heighten, tighten up

relaxation 1 = **leisure**, rest, fun, pleasure, entertainment, recreation, enjoyment, amusement, refreshment, beer and skittles (*informal*), me-time • *You should be able to find the odd moment for relaxation.*
2 = **lessening**, easing, reduction, weakening, moderation, let-up (*informal*), slackening, diminution, abatement • *There will be no relaxation of army pressure.*

relaxed 1 = **easy-going**, easy, casual, informal, laid-back (*informal*), mellow, leisurely, downbeat (*informal*), unhurried, nonchalant, free and easy, mild, insouciant, untaxing, chilled (*informal*) • *Try to adopt a more relaxed manner.*
2 = **comfortable**, easy-going, casual, laid-back (*informal*), informal, chilled (*informal*) • *The atmosphere at lunch was relaxed.*

relaxing = **restful**, calming, soothing, tranquillizing • *I find cooking very relaxing.*

relay AS A VERB 1 = **broadcast**, carry, spread, communicate, transmit, send out • *It will be used mainly to relay television programmes.*
2 = **repeat**, transfer, communicate, hand on, pass on, impart • *She relayed the message, then frowned.*
▸ AS A NOUN = **broadcast**, programme, communication, transmission, dispatch, telecast, webcast • *More than a thousand people listened to a relay of the proceedings.*

release AS A VERB 1 = **set free**, free, discharge, liberate, drop, deliver, loose, let go, undo, let out, extricate, untie, disengage, emancipate, unchain, unfasten, turn loose, unshackle, unloose, unfetter, unbridle, manumit • *He was released from custody the next day.*
OPPOSITES: keep, hold, imprison
2 = **acquit**, excuse, exempt, let go, dispense, let off,

exonerate, absolve • *He wants to be released from any promise between us.*
3 = **dissipate**, dissolve, disperse, dispel, drive away • *Humour is wonderful for releasing tension.*
4 = **issue**, publish, make public, make known, break, present, launch, distribute, unveil, put out, circulate, disseminate • *They're not releasing any more details yet.*
OPPOSITES: suppress, withhold
5 = **give off**, discharge, send out, throw out, radiate, diffuse, emanate, exude, cast out, send forth • *a weapon that releases toxic nerve gas*
6 = **launch**, market, unveil, bring out, make available, put on the market, put on sale • *He is releasing an album of love songs.*
▸ **AS A NOUN** 1 = **liberation**, freedom, delivery, liberty, discharge, emancipation, deliverance, manumission, relief • *the secret negotiations necessary to secure the release of the hostages*
OPPOSITES: detention, imprisonment, incarceration
2 = **acquittal**, exemption, let-off *(informal)*, dispensation, absolution, exoneration, acquittance • *a blessed release from the obligation to work*
3 = **issue**, announcement, publication, proclamation, propagation, offering • *a meeting held after the release of the report*
4 = **emission**, issue, shedding, radiation, discharge, transmission, diffusion, ejaculation, issuance, exhalation, emanation, exudation, giving off *or* out • *releases of cancer-causing chemicals*
5 = **publication**, book, CD, record, film, video, album, disc • *this week's new releases*

relegate 1 = **demote**, degrade, downgrade, declass • *Other newspapers relegated the item to the middle pages.*
2 = **banish**, exile, expel, throw out, oust, deport, eject, expatriate • *a team about to be relegated to the second division*

relent 1 = **be merciful**, yield, give in, soften, give way, come round, capitulate, acquiesce, change your mind, unbend, forbear, show mercy, have pity, melt, give quarter • *Finally his mother relented.*
OPPOSITES: remain firm, show no mercy, give no quarter
2 = **ease**, die down, let up, fall, drop, slow, relax, weaken, slacken • *If the bad weather relents the game will be finished today.*
OPPOSITES: increase, strengthen, intensify

relentless 1 = **merciless**, hard, fierce, harsh, cruel, grim, ruthless, uncompromising, unstoppable, inflexible, unrelenting, unforgiving, inexorable, implacable, unyielding, remorseless, pitiless, undeviating • *He was the most relentless enemy I have ever known.*
OPPOSITES: yielding, forgiving, merciful
2 = **unremitting**, sustained, punishing, persistent, unstoppable, unbroken, unrelenting, incessant, unabated, nonstop, unrelieved, unflagging, unfaltering • *The pressure now was relentless.*

relevance = **pertinence**, applicableness, appositeness, appropriateness, aptness, bearing, connection, germaneness • *Their private lives have no relevance to their public roles.*

relevant = **significant**, appropriate, proper, related, fitting, material, suited, relative, to the point, apt, applicable, pertinent, apposite, admissible, germane, to the purpose, appurtenant, ad rem *(Latin)* • *Make sure you enclose all the relevant certificates.*
OPPOSITES: irrelevant, inappropriate, unrelated

reliable 1 = **dependable**, trustworthy, honest, responsible, sure, sound, true, certain, regular, stable, faithful, predictable, upright, staunch, reputable, trusty, unfailing, tried and true • *She was efficient and reliable.*
OPPOSITES: irresponsible, unreliable, untrustworthy
2 = **safe**, dependable, tried and tested, well-built, failsafe, well-engineered • *Japanese cars are so reliable.*
3 = **definitive**, sound, attested, dependable, trustworthy, well-founded • *There is no reliable evidence.*

reliance 1 = **dependency**, dependence, leaning • *the country's increasing reliance on foreign aid*
2 = **trust**, confidence, belief, faith, assurance, credence, credit • *If you respond immediately, you will guarantee people's reliance on you.*

reliant = **dependent**, relying • *These people are not wholly reliant on Western charity.*

relic **AS A NOUN** = **remnant**, vestige, memento, trace, survival, scrap, token, fragment, souvenir, remembrance, keepsake • *a relic from the past*
▸ **AS A PLURAL NOUN** = **remains**, bones, sacred objects, holy objects • *ancient Egyptian relics*

relief 1 = **ease**, release, comfort, cure, remedy, solace, balm, deliverance, mitigation, abatement, alleviation, easement, palliation, assuagement • *The news will come as a great relief.*
2 = **rest**, respite, let-up, relaxation, break, diversion, refreshment *(informal)*, remission, breather *(informal)* • *a self-help programme which can give lasting relief*
3 = **aid**, help, support, assistance, sustenance, succour • *famine relief*
4 = **replacement**, cover, supply, reserve, substitute, stand-in, standby, locum • *No relief drivers were available.*

QUOTATIONS

For this relief much thanks
[William Shakespeare *Hamlet*]

relieve **AS A VERB** 1 = **ease**, soothe, alleviate, allay, relax, comfort, calm, cure, dull, diminish, soften, console, appease, solace, mitigate, abate, assuage, mollify, salve, palliate • *Drugs can relieve much of the pain.*
OPPOSITES: intensify, worsen, heighten
2 = **interrupt**, reduce, break up, alleviate, dispel, brighten, punctuate, lighten, counteract, mitigate, let up on *(informal)*, make bearable • *Television did help to relieve the boredom and isolation.*
3 = **free**, release, deliver, discharge, exempt, unburden, disembarrass, disencumber • *He felt relieved of a burden.*
4 = **take over from**, substitute for, stand in for, take the place of, give (someone) a break or rest • *At seven o'clock the night nurse came in to relieve her.*
5 = **help**, support, aid, sustain, assist, succour, bring aid to • *a programme to relieve poor countries*
▸ **IN PHRASES: relieve yourself** = **pee**, wee *(informal)*, piss *(taboo slang)*, urinate, tinkle *(Brit. informal)*, piddle *(informal)*, spend a penny *(Brit. informal)*, make water, pass water, wee-wee *(informal)*, take a leak *(slang)*, micturate, take a whizz *(slang, chiefly U.S.)* • *She has to relieve herself every ten minutes.*

relieved = **glad**, happy, pleased, comforted, cheered, reassured, grateful, thankful • *We are all relieved to be back home.*

religion = **belief**, faith, doctrine, theology, creed, divinity, teaching • *his understanding of Indian philosophy and religion*
▸ **RELATED MANIA:** entheomania

QUOTATIONS

There is only one religion, though there are a hundred versions of it
[George Bernard Shaw *Plays Unpleasant (preface)*]

Religion enables us to ignore nothingness and get on with the jobs of life
[John Updike *Self-Consciousness*]

I count religion but a childish toy,
And hold there is no sin but ignorance
[Christopher Marlowe *The Jew of Malta*]

Religion ... is the opium of the people
[Karl Marx *Critique of Hegel's Philosophy of Right*]

The true meaning of religion is thus not morality, but morality touched by emotion
[Matthew Arnold *Literature and Dogma*]

r

Science without religion is lame, religion without science is blind
[Albert Einstein *Out of My Later Years*]

Any system of religion that has any thing in it that shocks the mind of a child cannot be a true system
[Thomas Paine *The Age of Reason*]

I am a Millionaire. That is my religion
[George Bernard Shaw *Major Barbara*]

I can't talk religion to a man with bodily hunger in his eyes
[George Bernard Shaw *Major Barbara*]

We have just enough religion to make us hate, but not enough to make us love one another
[Jonathan Swift *Thoughts on Various Subjects*]

I am for religion, against religions
[Victor Hugo *Les Misérables*]

Time consecrates;
And what is grey with age becomes religion
[Friedrich von Schiller *Die Piccolomini*]

One religion is as true as another
[Robert Burton *Anatomy of Melancholy*]

Christians have burnt each other, quite persuaded
That all the apostles would have done as they did
[Lord Byron *Don Juan*]

The nearer the Church the further from God
[Bishop Lancelot Andrews *Of the Nativity*]

To become a popular religion, it is only necessary for a superstition to enslave a philosophy
[Dean Inge *Idea of Progress*]

Religion's in the heart, not in the knees
[Douglas Jerrold *The Devil's Ducat*]

Religion is the frozen thought of men out of which they build temples
[Jiddu Krishnamurti]

▷ *See panel* **Bible; Buddhism; Christianity; Hinduism; Islam; Judaism; Religion**

religious **1 = spiritual**, holy, sacred, divine, theological, righteous, sectarian, sanctified, doctrinal, devotional, scriptural • *different religious beliefs*
2 = devout, believing, godly, committed, holy, practising, faithful, pious, God-fearing, reverent, pure, churchgoing • *They are both very religious.*
OPPOSITES: rational, secular, irreligious
3 = conscientious, exact, faithful, rigid, rigorous,

RELIGION

Religions

animism	druidism	Macumba	Ryobu Shinto	Shango	Yezidis
Babi *or* Babism	heliolatry	Manichaeism	Santeria	Shembe	Zoroastrianism
Baha'ism	Hinduism	Mithraism	Satanism	Shinto	
Buddhism	Islam	Orphism	Scientology (*trademark*)	Sikhism	
Christianity	Jainism	paganism		Taoism	
Confucianism	Judaism	Rastafarianism	shamanism	voodoo	

Religious books

Adi Granth	Bible	Koran	Old Testament	Siddhanta	Tripitaka
Apocrypha	Book of Mormon	Li Chi	Ramayana	Su Ching	Veda
Atharveda	Granth *or* Guru	Lu	Rigveda	Talmud	Yajurveda
Ayurveda	Granth Sahib	Mahabharata	Samaveda	Tipitaka	
Bhagavad-Gita	I Ching	New Testament	Shi Ching	Torah	

Religious buildings

abbey	chapel	gurdwara	monastery	tabernacle
bethel	church	Kaaba	mosque	temple
cathedral	convent	marae	synagogue	

Religious clothing

alb	cassock	cornet	habit	peplos	surcingle
almuce	chasuble	cotta	infulae	pontificals	surplice
amice	chimere	cowl	maniple	rochet	tippet
biretta	clerical collar	dalmatic	mantelletta	scapular	wimple
calotte	clericals	dog collar	mitre	shovel hat	zucchetto
canonicals	coif	gremial	mozzetta	soutane	
capuche	cope	guimpe	pallium	superhumeral	

Religious festivals

Advent	Dhammacakka	Good Friday	Lailat ul-Qadr	Purim	Shrove Tuesday
Al Hijrah	Diwali	Guru Nanak's Birthday	Lent	Quadragesima	Sukkoth
Ascension Day	Dragon Boat Festival	Hanukah	Mahashivaratri	Quinquagesima	Trinity
Ash Wednesday	Dussehra	Hirja	Maundy Thursday	Raksha Bandhan	Wesak
Baisakhi	Easter	Hola Mohalla	Michaelmas	Ramadan	Whitsun
Bodhi Day	Eid ul-Adha	Holi	Moon Festival	Rama Naumi	Winter Festival
Candlemas	Eid ul-Fitr	Janamashtami	Palm Sunday	Rogation	Yom Kippur
Ching Ming	Epiphany	Lailat ul-Barah	Passion Sunday	Rosh Hashanah	Yuan Tan
Christmas	Feast of Tabernacles	Lailat ul-Isra Wal Mi'raj	Passover	Septuagesima	
Corpus Christi			Pentecost	Sexagesima	
Day of Atonement			Pesach	Shavuot	

meticulous, scrupulous, fastidious, unerring, unswerving, punctilious • *The clientele turned up, with religious regularity, every night.*

relinquish = **give up**, leave, release, drop, abandon, resign, desert, quit, yield, hand over, surrender, withdraw from, let go, retire from, renounce, waive, vacate, say goodbye to, forsake, cede, repudiate, cast off, forgo, abdicate, kiss (something) goodbye, lay aside • *He does not intend to relinquish power.*

relish AS A VERB **1** = **enjoy**, like, prefer, taste, appreciate, savour, revel in, luxuriate in • *He ate quietly, relishing his meal.*
OPPOSITES: dislike, loathe, be unenthusiastic about
2 = **look forward to**, fancy, long for, delight in, count the days until, anticipate with pleasure, lick your lips over • *She is not relishing the prospect of another spell in prison.*
▸ AS A NOUN **1** = **enjoyment**, liking, love, taste, fancy, stomach, appetite, appreciation, penchant, zest, fondness, gusto, predilection, zing *(informal)*, partiality • *The three men ate with relish.*
OPPOSITES: dislike, loathing, distaste
2 = **condiment**, seasoning, sauce, appetizer • *pots of spicy relish*

relocate = **move house**, move, change residence, leave, remove, quit, go away, migrate, flit *(Scot. & Northern English dialect)*, pack your bags *(informal)* • *Should they be forced to relocate at the end of the contract?*

reluctance = **unwillingness**, dislike, loathing, distaste, aversion, backwardness, hesitancy, disinclination, repugnance, indisposition, disrelish • *a reluctance to give official approval to the idea*

reluctant = **unwilling**, slow, backward, grudging, hesitant, averse, recalcitrant, loath, disinclined, unenthusiastic, indisposed • *He was reluctant to ask for help.*
OPPOSITES: willing, keen, eager

rely on **1** = **depend on**, lean on, be dependent, fall back on, resort to, be unable to manage without • *They relied heavily on the advice of their advisors.*
2 = **be confident of**, bank on, trust, count on, bet on, reckon on, lean on, be sure of, have confidence in, swear by, repose trust in • *I know I can rely on you to sort it out.*

remain **1** = **stay**, continue, go on, stand, dwell, bide • *The three men remained silent.*
2 = **stay behind**, wait, delay, stay put *(informal)*, tarry • *He remained at home with his family.*
OPPOSITES: go, leave, depart
3 = **continue**, be left, endure, persist, linger, hang in the air, stay • *There remains deep mistrust of his government.*

remainder = **rest**, remains, balance, trace, excess, surplus, butt, remnant, relic, residue, stub, vestige(s), tail end, dregs, oddment, leavings, residuum • *He gulped down the remainder of his coffee.*

remaining **1** = **left-over**, surviving, spare, outstanding, excess, surplus, lingering, unfinished, residual • *Stir in the remaining ingredients.*
2 = **surviving**, lasting, continuing, enduring, persisting, abiding, extant • *They wanted to purge remaining memories of his reign.*

remains **1** = **remnants**, leftovers, remainder, scraps, rest, pieces, balance, traces, fragments, debris, residue, crumbs, vestiges, detritus, dregs, odds and ends, oddments, leavings • *the remains of their picnic*
2 = **relics**, heritage, antiquities • *There are Roman remains all around us.*
3 = **corpse**, body, bones, skeleton, carcass, cadaver • *The remains of a man had been found.*

remark AS A VERB **1** = **comment**, say, state, reflect, mention, declare, observe, pass comment, animadvert • *I remarked that I would go shopping that afternoon.*
2 = **notice**, note, observe, perceive, see, mark, regard, make out, heed, espy, take note *or* notice of • *Everyone has remarked what a lovely lady she is.*
▸ AS A NOUN **1** = **comment**, observation, reflection, statement, thought, word, opinion, declaration, assertion, utterance • *She has made outspoken remarks on the issue.*
2 = **notice**, thought, comment, attention, regard, mention, recognition, consideration, observation, heed, acknowledgment • *He had never found the situation worthy of remark.*

remarkable = **extraordinary**, striking, outstanding, famous, odd, strange, wonderful, signal, rare, unusual, impressive, surprising, distinguished, prominent, notable, phenomenal, uncommon, conspicuous, singular, miraculous, noteworthy, pre-eminent • *He was a remarkable man.*
OPPOSITES: common, usual, ordinary

remedial **1** = **therapeutic**, healing, curing, curative, health-promoting, alleviative • *He is doing remedial exercises.*
2 = **corrective**, preventive, counteracting, reactive, compensatory • *They are having to take remedial action.*
3 = **special needs** • *remedial education*

remedy AS A NOUN **1** = **solution**, relief, redress, antidote, corrective, panacea, countermeasure • *a remedy for economic ills*
2 = **cure**, treatment, specific, medicine, therapy, antidote, panacea, restorative, relief, nostrum, physic *(rare)*, medicament, counteractive • *natural remedies to overcome winter infections*
▸ AS A VERB **1** = **put right**, redress, rectify, reform, fix, correct, solve, repair, relieve, ameliorate, set to rights • *A great deal has been done to remedy the situation.*
2 = **cure**, treat, heal, help, control, ease, restore, relieve, soothe, alleviate, mitigate, assuage, palliate • *He's been remedying a hamstring injury.*

remember AS A VERB **1** = **recall**, think back to, recollect, reminisce about, retain, recognize, call up, look back on, hark back to, summon up, call to mind, cast your mind back to • *He was remembering the old days.*
OPPOSITES: forget, ignore, overlook
2 = **don't forget**, be sure, be certain, make sure that you, mind that you • *Remember to take the present.*
3 = **bear in mind**, not forget, keep in mind, take into account the fact, not lose sight of the fact, take into consideration the fact, be mindful of the fact • *Remember that each person reacts differently.*
4 = **look back (on)**, celebrate, salute, commemorate, pay tribute to • *He is remembered for being bad at games.*
5 = **cherish**, prize, treasure, hold dear • *I'll make it a birthday to remember.*
6 = **memorize**, retain, commit to memory, learn by heart • *I'm good at remembering phone numbers.*
▸ IN PHRASES: **remember someone to someone** = **give your love to**, say hello to, send your love to, send greetings from, send your regards to, send your best wishes to • *Please remember me to my father.*

remembrance **1** = **commemoration**, memorial, testimonial • *They wore black in remembrance of those who had died.*
2 = **souvenir**, token, reminder, monument, relic, remembrancer *(archaic)*, memento, keepsake • *As a remembrance, he left a photo album.*
3 = **memory**, recollection, thought, recall, recognition, retrospect, reminiscence, anamnesis • *He had clung to the remembrance of things past.*

remind AS A VERB = **jog your memory**, prompt, nudge, help you remember, refresh your memory, make you remember • *Can you remind me to buy a bottle of milk?*
▸ IN PHRASES: **remind someone of something** *or* **someone** = **bring to mind**, call to mind, put in mind,

r

awaken memories of, call up, bring back to • *She reminds me of the wife of the pilot.*

reminder = **prompt**, prompting, cue, nudge • *They are about to be given a sharp reminder.*

reminisce = **recall**, remember, look back, hark back, review, think back, recollect, live in the past, go over in the memory • *We reminisced about the trip.*

reminiscence = **recollections**, memories, reflections, retrospections, reviews, recalls, memoirs, anecdotes, remembrances • *Here I am boring you with my reminiscences.*

reminiscent = **suggestive**, evocative, redolent, remindful, similar • *a gesture somehow reminiscent of royalty*

remiss = **careless**, negligent, neglectful, culpable, slow, regardless, slack, indifferent, sloppy *(informal)*, derelict, lax, delinquent, thoughtless, tardy, forgetful, slapdash, heedless, slipshod, lackadaisical, inattentive, dilatory, slothful, unmindful • *I would be remiss if I did not do something about it.*
OPPOSITES: careful, attentive, painstaking

remission 1 = **lessening**, abatement, abeyance, lull, relaxation, ebb, respite, moderation, let-up *(informal)*, alleviation, amelioration • *The disease is in remission.*
2 = **reduction**, easing, lessening, dying down, suspension, decrease, dwindling, waning, ebbing, let-up *(informal)*, slackening, diminution • *It had been raining hard all day, without remission.*
3 = **pardon**, release, discharge, amnesty, forgiveness, indulgence, exemption, reprieve, acquittal, absolution, exoneration, excuse • *I've got 10 years and there's no remission for drug offenders.*

remit AS A NOUN = **instructions**, brief, guidelines, authorization, terms of reference, orders • *That issue is not within the remit of the group.*
▸ AS A VERB 1 = **send**, post, forward, mail, transmit, dispatch • *Many immigrants regularly remit money to their families.*
2 = **refer**, transfer, deliver, commit, hand over, submit, pass on, turn over, consign • *The matter was remitted to the justices for a rehearing.*
3 = **cancel**, stop, halt, repeal, rescind, desist, forbear • *Every creditor shall remit the claim that is held against a neighbour*
4 = **lessen**, diminish, abate, ease up, reduce, relax, moderate, weaken, decrease, soften, dwindle, alleviate, wane, fall away, mitigate, slacken • *an episode of 'baby blues' which eventually remitted*

remittance = **payment**, money, fee, settlement, consideration, cheque, allowance • *Please enclose your remittance.*

remnant = **remainder**, remains, trace, fragment, end, bit, rest, piece, balance, survival, scrap, butt, shred, hangover, residue, rump, leftovers, stub, vestige, tail end, oddment, residuum • *the remnants of Roman flooring*

remonstrate = **protest**, challenge, argue, take issue, object, complain, dispute, dissent, take exception, expostulate • *He remonstrated with the referee.*

remorse = **regret**, shame, guilt, pity, grief, compassion, sorrow, anguish, repentance, contrition, compunction, penitence, self-reproach, pangs of conscience, ruefulness, bad *or* guilty conscience • *He has shown no remorse for his actions.*

QUOTATIONS
remorse, the fatal egg by pleasure laid
[William Cowper *The Progress of Error*]

remorseful = **regretful**, sorry, guilty, sad, ashamed, apologetic, chastened, rueful, contrite, sorrowful, repentant, guilt-ridden, penitent, conscience-stricken, self-reproachful • *He was genuinely remorseful.*

remorseless 1 = **relentless**, unstoppable, unrelenting, inexorable, unremitting • *the remorseless pressure of financial constraint*
2 = **pitiless**, hard, harsh, cruel, savage, ruthless, callous, merciless, unforgiving, implacable, inhumane, unmerciful, hardhearted, uncompassionate • *the capacity for quick, remorseless violence*

remote 1 = **distant**, far, isolated, lonely, out-of-the-way, far-off, secluded, inaccessible, faraway, outlying, in the middle of nowhere, off the beaten track, backwoods, godforsaken • *a remote farm in the hills*
OPPOSITES: close, near, nearby
2 = **far**, distant, obscure, far-off • *particular events in the remote past*
3 = **irrelevant**, foreign, outside, removed, alien, unrelated, unconnected, immaterial, extraneous, extrinsic • *subjects that seem remote from their daily lives*
OPPOSITES: related, relevant, intrinsic
4 = **slight**, small, outside, poor, unlikely, slim, faint, doubtful, dubious, slender, meagre, negligible, implausible, inconsiderable • *The chances of his surviving are pretty remote.*
OPPOSITES: good, strong, likely
5 = **aloof**, cold, removed, reserved, withdrawn, distant, abstracted, detached, indifferent, faraway, introspective, uninterested, introverted, uninvolved, unapproachable, uncommunicative, standoffish • *She looked so remote.*
OPPOSITES: interested, involved, outgoing

remotely = **a bit**, at all, in any way, in the slightest • *We had never seen anything remotely like it.*

removal 1 = **extraction**, stripping, withdrawal, purging, abstraction, uprooting, displacement, eradication, erasure, subtraction, dislodgment, expunction, taking away *or* off *or* out • *the removal of a small lump*
2 = **dismissal**, expulsion, elimination, ejection, dispossession • *His removal from power was illegal.*
3 = **move**, transfer, departure, relocation, flitting *(Scot. & Northern English dialect)* • *Home removals are best done in cool weather.*
4 = **abolition**, ending, end, withdrawal, wiping out, voiding, elimination, cancellation, suppression, termination, stamping out, eradication, annulment, revocation, nullification, rescission • *the removal of limits on foreign ownership*

remove 1 = **take out**, withdraw, get out, extract, abstract • *Remove the cake from the oven.*
OPPOSITES: replace, place in, insert
2 = **take off**, pull off, peel off, slip out of, climb out of, doff, divest yourself of • *He removed his jacket.*
OPPOSITES: don, replace, put on
3 = **erase**, eliminate, take out, wipe off, wash off, clean off, rinse off • *This treatment removes the most stubborn stains.*
4 = **dismiss**, eliminate, get rid of, discharge, abolish, expel, throw out, oust, relegate, purge, eject, do away with, depose, unseat, see the back of, dethrone, show someone the door, give the bum's rush *(slang)*, throw out on your ear *(informal)* • *The senate voted to remove him.*
OPPOSITES: appoint, install
5 = **get rid of**, wipe out, erase, eradicate, blow away *(slang, chiefly U.S.)*, blot out, expunge • *Most of her fears have been removed.*
6 = **take away**, move, pull, transfer, detach, displace, do away with, dislodge, cart off *(slang)*, carry off *or* away • *They tried to remove the barricades which had been erected.*
OPPOSITES: put back
7 = **delete**, shed, get rid of, erase, excise, strike out, efface, expunge • *They intend to remove up to 100 offensive words.*
8 = **amputate**, cut off, excise, chop off, hack off, lop off • *When you remove the branches, cut beyond the trunk ridge.*
OPPOSITES: set, join, link
9 = **move**, transfer, transport, shift, quit, depart, move away, relocate, vacate, flit *(Scot. & Northern English dialect)* • *They removed to America.*

10 = kill, murder, do in *(slang)*, eliminate, take out *(slang)*, get rid of, execute, wipe out, dispose of, assassinate, do away with, liquidate, bump off *(slang)*, wipe from the face of the earth • *If someone irritates you, remove him, destroy him.*

removed = remote, foreign, outside, alien, irrelevant, unrelated, unconnected, immaterial, extraneous, extrinsic • *outlandish rubbish, far removed from reality*

remunerate = pay, reward, compensate, repay, redress, reimburse, recompense, indemnify, requite • *You will be remunerated for your trouble*

remuneration = payment, income, earnings, salary, pay, return, profit, fee, wages, reward, compensation, repayment, reparation, indemnity, retainer, reimbursement, recompense, stipend, emolument, meed *(archaic)* • *$31,000 is a generous remuneration.*

remunerative = profitable, lucrative, paying, gainful, economic, rich, rewarding, worthwhile, recompensing, moneymaking • *seeking remunerative employment*

renaissance *or* **renascence = rebirth**, revival, restoration, renewal, awakening, resurrection, regeneration, resurgence, reappearance, new dawn, re-emergence, reawakening, new birth • *Popular art is experiencing a renaissance.*

rend = tear, break, split, rip, pull, separate, divide, crack, burst, smash, disturb, shatter, pierce, fracture, sever, wrench, splinter, rupture, cleave, lacerate, rive, tear to pieces, sunder *(literary)*, dissever • *pain that rends the heart*

render 1 = make, cause to become, leave • *It has so many errors as to render it useless.*
2 = provide, give, show, pay, present, supply, deliver, contribute, yield, submit, tender, hand out, furnish, turn over, make available • *Any assistance you can render him will be helpful.*
3 = deliver, give, return, announce, bring in, pronounce • *The Board was slow to render its verdict.*
4 = translate, put, explain, interpret, reproduce, transcribe, construe, restate • *150 Psalms rendered into English*
5 *sometimes followed by* **up = give up**, give, deliver, yield, hand over, surrender, turn over, relinquish, cede • *I render up my soul to God.*
6 = represent, interpret, portray, depict, do, give, play, act, present, perform • *a powerful, bizarre, and beautifully rendered story*

rendering = recitation, performance, interpretation, recital, rendition, depiction • *a rendering of Verdi's Requiem*

rendezvous AS A NOUN **1 = appointment**, meeting, date, engagement, tryst *(archaic)*, assignation • *I had decided to keep my rendezvous with him.*
2 = meeting place, venue, gathering point, place of assignation, trysting-place *(archaic)* • *Their rendezvous would be the hotel at the airport.*
▸ AS A VERB **= meet**, assemble, get together, come together, collect, gather, rally, muster, converge, join up, be reunited • *The plan was to rendezvous on Sunday afternoon.*

rendition 1 = performance, arrangement, interpretation, rendering, take *(informal, chiefly U.S.)*, reading, version, delivery, presentation, execution, portrayal, depiction • *The musicians broke into a rousing rendition of the song.*
2 = translation, reading, version, construction, explanation, interpretation, transcription • *a rendition of the works of Conrad*

renegade AS A NOUN **= deserter**, rebel, betrayer, dissident, outlaw, runaway, traitor, defector, mutineer, turncoat, apostate, backslider, recreant *(archaic)* • *He was a renegade – a traitor.*
▸ AS A MODIFIER **= traitorous**, rebel, dissident, outlaw, runaway, rebellious, unfaithful, disloyal, backsliding, mutinous, apostate, recreant *(archaic)* • *The renegade policeman supplied details of the murder.*

renege = break your word, go back, welsh *(slang)*, default, back out, repudiate, break a promise • *He reneged on a promise to leave his wife.*

renew 1 = recommence, continue, extend, repeat, resume, prolong, reopen, recreate, reaffirm, re-establish, rejuvenate, regenerate, restate, begin again, revitalize, bring up to date • *He renewed his attack on government policy.*
2 = reaffirm, confirm, resume, breathe new life into, recommence • *They renewed their friendship.*
3 = replace, refresh, top up, replenish, restock, resupply • *Cells are constantly renewed.*
4 = restore, repair, transform, rebuild, overhaul, mend, refurbish, renovate, refit, redevelop, fix up *(informal, chiefly U.S. & Canad.)*, modernize, recondition • *the cost of renewing the buildings*

renewal 1 = resumption, continuation, re-establishment, recommencement • *the possible renewal of diplomatic relations*
2 = renovation, repair, rebuilding, restoration, transformation, overhaul, redevelopment, refurbishment, renovation, modernization, refitting, reconditioning • *urban renewal and restoration*
3 = restoration, revival, regeneration, rejuvenation, revitalization, reinvigoration • *Now it is spring, a time of renewal.*

renounce 1 = disown, reject, abandon, quit, discard, spurn, eschew, leave off, throw off, forsake, retract, repudiate, cast off, abstain from, recant, forswear, abjure, swear off, wash your hands of • *She renounced terrorism.*
2 = disclaim, deny, decline, give up, resign, relinquish, waive, renege, forgo, abdicate, abjure, abnegate • *He renounced his claim to the throne.*
OPPOSITES: claim, maintain, assert

renovate = restore, repair, refurbish, do up *(informal)*, reform, renew, overhaul, revamp, recreate, remodel, rehabilitate, refit, fix up *(informal, chiefly U.S. & Canad.)*, modernize, reconstitute, recondition • *They spent thousands renovating the house.*

renovation = restoration, repair, overhaul, restoration, renewal, rehabilitation, revamping, refurbishment, doing up *(informal)*, modernization, refitting, fixing up *(informal, chiefly U.S. & Canad.)*, reconditioning • *a property which needs extensive renovation*

renown = fame, note, distinction, repute, mark, reputation, honour, glory, celebrity, acclaim, stardom, eminence, lustre, illustriousness • *She used to be a singer of some renown.*

renowned = famous, noted, celebrated, well-known, distinguished, esteemed, acclaimed, notable, eminent, famed, illustrious • *The area is renowned for its churches.*
OPPOSITES: forgotten, unknown, neglected

rent[1] AS A VERB **1 = hire**, lease • *He rented a car.*
2 = let, lease, sublet, sublease • *She rented rooms to university students.*
▸ AS A NOUN **= hire**, rental, lease, tariff, fee, payment • *She worked to pay the rent.*

rent[2] **1 = tear**, split, rip, slash, slit, gash, perforation, hole • *a small rent in the silk*
2 = opening, break, hole, crack, breach, flaw, chink • *welling up from a rent in the ground*

renunciation 1 = rejection, giving up, denial, abandonment, spurning, abstention, repudiation, forswearing, disavowal, abnegation, eschewal, abjuration • *a renunciation of terrorism*
2 = giving up, resignation, surrender, waiver, disclaimer, abdication, relinquishment, abjuration • *the renunciation of territory*

reopen 1 = open again, resume, restart, begin again, recommence, continue, go on, proceed, carry on, reinstitute, take up *or* pick up where you left off • *There was a call to reopen the investigation*
2 = open again • *The Theatre Royal will reopen in November.*

reorganize = **rearrange**, restructure, shake up, reshuffle, rationalize, spring-clean • *The company has reorganized its sales force of 6,500.*

repair[1] AS A VERB 1 = **mend**, fix, recover, restore, heal, renew, patch, make good, renovate, patch up, put back together, restore to working order • *He has repaired the roof.*
OPPOSITES: damage, destroy, harm
2 = **put right**, make up for, compensate for, rectify, square, retrieve, redress • *They needed to repair the damage done by the interview.*
▸ AS A NOUN 1 = **mend**, restoration, overhaul, adjustment • *Many of the buildings are in need of repair.*
2 = **darn**, mend, patch • *She spotted a couple of obvious repairs in the dress.*
3 = **condition**, state, form, shape *(informal)*, nick *(informal)*, fettle • *The road was in bad repair.*

repair[2] = **go**, retire, withdraw, head for, move, remove, leave for, set off for, betake yourself • *We repaired to the pavilion for lunch.*

reparation = **compensation**, damages, repair, satisfaction, amends, renewal, redress, indemnity, restitution, atonement, recompense, propitiation, requital • *a demand amongst victims for some sort of reparation*

repartee = **wit**, banter, riposte, pleasantry, sally, wordplay, witticism, bon mot, badinage, raillery, persiflage, wittiness • *clever chat-up lines or witty repartee*

repast = **meal**, spread *(informal)*, collation, refection, food, kai *(N.Z. informal)*, nourishment, victuals • *He proclaimed it a splendid repast.*

repay 1 = **pay back**, refund, settle up, return, square, restore, compensate, reimburse, recompense, requite, remunerate • *It will take 30 years to repay the loan.*
2 = **reward**, return, reciprocate, recompense, make restitution • *How can I ever repay such kindness?*

repayment 1 = **refund**, paying back, reimbursement • *the repayment of subsidies made during that period*
2 = **reward**, compensation, reparation, recompense • *as repayment for kindnesses from old friends*

repeal AS A VERB = **abolish**, reverse, revoke, annul, recall, withdraw, cancel, set aside, rescind, invalidate, nullify, obviate, abrogate, countermand, declare null and void • *The government has just repealed that law.*
OPPOSITES: pass, introduce, confirm
▸ AS A NOUN = **abolition**, withdrawal, cancellation, rescinding, annulment, revocation, nullification, abrogation, rescission, invalidation, rescindment • *a repeal of the age of consent law*
OPPOSITES: passing, introduction, confirmation

repeat AS A VERB 1 = **reiterate**, restate, say again, recapitulate, iterate • *He repeated that he had been misquoted.*
2 = **retell**, relate, quote, renew, echo, replay, reproduce, rehearse, recite, duplicate, redo, rerun, reshow • *I repeated the story to a delighted audience.*
▸ AS A NOUN 1 = **repetition**, echo, duplicate, reiteration, recapitulation • *a repeat of Wednesday's massive protests*
2 = **rerun**, replay, reproduction, reshowing • *There's nothing except repeats on TV.*
▸ IN PHRASES: **repeat itself** = **recur**, happen again, occur again • *Is history about to repeat itself, with tragic consequences?*

repeated = **persistent**, constant, relentless, perpetual, continual, unrelenting, incessant, unremitting • *Repeated absence from school is problem behavior.*

repeatedly = **over and over**, often, frequently, many times, again and again, time and (time) again, time after time, many a time and oft *(archaic or poetic)* • *They have repeatedly denied the allegations.*

repel 1 = **drive off**, fight, refuse, check, decline, reject, oppose, resist, confront, parry, hold off, rebuff, ward off, beat off, repulse, keep at arm's length, put to flight • *troops ready to repel an attack*
OPPOSITES: submit to
2 = **disgust**, offend, revolt, sicken, nauseate, put you off, make you sick, gross out *(U.S. slang)*, turn you off *(informal)*, make you shudder, turn your stomach, give you the creeps *(informal)* • *excitement which frightened and repelled her*
OPPOSITES: draw, please, delight

repellent 1 = **disgusting**, offensive, revolting, obscene, sickening, distasteful, horrid, obnoxious, repulsive, noxious, nauseating, odious, hateful, repugnant, off-putting *(Brit. informal)*, loathsome, abhorrent, abominable, cringe-making *(Brit. informal)*, yucky or yukky *(slang)*, yucko *(Austral. slang)*, discouraging • *She still found the place repellent.*
2 = **proof**, resistant, repelling, impermeable • *a shower repellent jacket*

repent = **regret**, lament, rue, sorrow, be sorry about, deplore, be ashamed of, relent, atone for, be contrite about, feel remorse about, reproach yourself for, see the error of your ways, show penitence • *Did he repent of anything in his life?*

repentance = **regret**, guilt, grief, sorrow, remorse, contrition, compunction, penitence, self-reproach, sackcloth and ashes, sorriness • *They showed no repentance during their trial.*

QUOTATIONS

Repentance is the virtue of weak minds
[John Dryden *The Indian Emperor*]

Amendment is repentance
[Thomas Fuller *Gnomologia*]

Joy shall be in heaven over one sinner that repenteth, more than over ninety and nine just persons, which need no repentance
[*Bible: St. Luke*]

repentant = **regretful**, sorry, ashamed, apologetic, chastened, rueful, contrite, remorseful, penitent, self-reproachful • *a repentant criminal*

repercussion *often plural* = **consequences**, result, side effects, backlash, sequel • *It was an incident which had repercussions.*

repertoire = **range**, list, stock, supply, store, collection, repertory, repository • *an impressive repertoire of funny stories*

repertory = **repertoire**, list, range, stock, supply, store, collection, repository • *Her repertory of songs was vast.*

repetition 1 = **recurrence**, repeating, reappearance, duplication, echo • *He wants to avoid repetition of the confusion.*
2 = **repeating**, redundancy, replication, duplication, restatement, iteration, reiteration, tautology, recapitulation, repetitiousness • *He could have cut much of the repetition and saved pages.*

repetitious = **long-winded**, wordy, verbose, prolix, redundant, tedious, windy, tautological, iterative, pleonastic • *The manifesto is repetitious and poorly drafted.*

repetitive = **monotonous**, boring, dull, mechanical, tedious, recurrent, unchanging, samey *(informal)*, unvaried • *factory workers who do repetitive jobs*

rephrase = **reword**, paraphrase, recast, say in other words, put differently • *The executive rephrased the question.*

replace 1 = **take the place of**, follow, succeed, oust, take over from, supersede, supplant, stand in lieu of, fill (someone's) shoes *or* boots, step into (someone's) shoes *or* boots • *the man who deposed and replaced him*
2 = **substitute**, change, exchange, switch, swap, commute • *Replace that liquid with salt, sugar and water.*
3 = **put back**, return, restore, return to its place • *Replace the caps on the bottles.*

replacement 1 = **replacing**, renewal, substitution • *the replacement of damaged or lost books*
2 = **successor**, double, substitute, stand-in, fill-in, proxy, surrogate, understudy • *a replacement for the injured player*

replay 1 = **play again** • *Drawn matches were replayed three days later.*
2 = **play back**, play again, listen to again • *He stopped the machine and replayed the message.*
3 = **go over**, relive • *She lay in bed replaying the fire in her mind.*

replenish 1 = **fill**, top up, refill, replace, renew, furnish • *He went to replenish her glass.*
OPPOSITES: empty, drain, exhaust
2 = **refill**, provide, stock, supply, fill, make up, restore, top up, reload, restock • *stock to replenish the shelves*

replete 1 = **filled**, stuffed, jammed, crammed, abounding, brimming, teeming, glutted, well-stocked, jam-packed, well-provided, chock-full, brimful, full to bursting, charged • *The harbour was replete with boats.*
OPPOSITES: wanting, lacking, empty
2 = **sated**, full, gorged, full up, satiated • *replete after a heavy lunch*
OPPOSITES: empty, hungry, starving

replica 1 = **reproduction**, model, copy, imitation, facsimile, carbon copy • *It was a replica, for display only.*
OPPOSITES: original, master, prototype
2 = **duplicate**, copy, clone, spitting image, dead ringer, carbon copy • *The child was a replica of her mother.*

replicate = **copy**, follow, repeat, reproduce, recreate, ape, mimic, duplicate, reduplicate • *He was not able to replicate this experiment.*

reply AS A VERB = **answer**, respond, retort, return, come back, counter, acknowledge, react, echo, rejoin, retaliate, write back, reciprocate, riposte, make answer • *He replied that this was absolutely impossible.*
▸ AS A NOUN = **answer**, response, reaction, counter, echo, comeback *(informal)*, retort, retaliation, acknowledgment, riposte, counterattack, return, rejoinder, reciprocation • *They went ahead without waiting for a reply.*

report AS A VERB 1 = **inform of**, communicate, announce, mention, declare, recount, give an account of, bring word on • *I reported the theft to the police.*
2 *often with* **on** = **communicate**, publish, record, announce, tell, state, air, detail, describe, note, cover, document, give an account of, relate, broadcast, pass on, proclaim, circulate, relay, recite, narrate, write up • *Several newspapers reported the decision.*
3 = **inform on**, shop *(slang, chiefly Brit.)*, betray, denounce, incriminate, tell on *(informal)*, blow the whistle on *(informal)*, grass on *(Brit. slang)*, rat on *(informal)*, inculpate, dob in *(Austral. slang)* • *His wife reported him to the police.*
4 = **present yourself**, come, appear, arrive, turn up, be present, show up *(informal)*, clock in *or* on • *None of them had reported for duty.*
▸ AS A NOUN 1 = **article**, story, communication, dispatch, piece, message, item, column, communiqué, write-up • *Press reports vary dramatically.*
2 = **account**, record, detail, note, statement, relation, version, communication, tale, description, declaration, narrative, summary, recital • *a full report of what happened here tonight*
3 *often plural* = **news**, word, information, announcement, tidings • *There were no reports of casualties.*
4 = **appraisal**, marks, grades, assessment, evaluation • *She was getting bad school reports.*
5 = **bang**, sound, crash, crack, noise, blast, boom, explosion, discharge, detonation, reverberation • *There was a loud report as the fuel tanks exploded.*
6 = **rumour**, talk, buzz, gossip, goss *(informal)*, hearsay, scuttlebutt *(U.S. slang)* • *According to report, she made an impact at the party.*
7 = **repute**, character, regard, reputation, fame, esteem, eminence • *He is true, manly, and of good report.*

reportedly = **allegedly**, apparently, supposedly, by all accounts, reputedly, purportedly • *They have reportedly agreed.*

reporter = **journalist**, writer, correspondent, newscaster, hack *(derogatory)*, announcer, pressman, journo *(slang)*, newshound *(informal)*, hackette *(derogatory)*, newspaperman or newspaperwoman • *a trainee sports reporter*

reporting = **journalism**, writing, presenting, newscasting • *a reputation for honest and impartial reporting*

repose[1] AS A NOUN 1 = **rest**, relaxation, inactivity, restfulness • *He had a still, almost blank face, in repose.*
2 = **peace**, rest, quiet, ease, relaxation, respite, tranquillity, stillness, inactivity, quietness, quietude, restfulness • *The atmosphere is one of repose.*
3 = **composure**, dignity, peace of mind, poise, serenity, tranquillity, aplomb, calmness, equanimity, self-possession • *She has a great deal of natural repose.*
4 = **sleep**, rest, doze, slumber, kip *(Brit. slang)*, dormancy, beauty sleep *(informal)*, forty winks *(informal)* • *So you'll be ready for a night's repose?*
▸ AS A VERB 1 = **rest**, lie, be set, be placed, be positioned, rest upon • *China soup dishes reposed on silver plates.*
2 = **lie**, rest, sleep, relax, lie down, recline, take it easy, slumber, rest upon, lie upon, drowse, outspan *(S. African)*, take your ease • *They repose on couches.*

repose[2] = **place**, put, store, invest, deposit, lodge, confide, entrust • *Little trust can be reposed in such promises.*

repository 1 = **store**, archive, storehouse, depository, magazine, treasury, warehouse, vault, depot, emporium, receptacle • *The church became a repository for police files.*
2 = **storehouse**, fund, mine, oracle • *He was the repository of all important information.*

reprehensible = **blameworthy**, bad, disgraceful, shameful, delinquent, errant, unworthy, objectionable, culpable, ignoble, discreditable, remiss, erring, opprobrious, condemnable, censurable • *behaving in the most reprehensible manner*
OPPOSITES: acceptable, admirable, praiseworthy

represent AS A VERB 1 = **act for**, speak for, appear for, speak on behalf of, be the representative of • *the lawyers representing the victims*
2 = **stand for**, substitute for, play the part of, assume the role of, serve as • *He will represent the president at ceremonies.*
3 = **play for**, appear for, be a member of the team • *My aim is to represent Britain at the Olympics.*
4 = **constitute**, be, make, comprise • *These developments represent a change.*
5 = **express**, equal, correspond to, symbolize, equate with, mean, betoken • *Circle the letter that represents the sound.*
6 = **exemplify**, embody, symbolize, typify, personify, epitomize • *You represent everything British racing needs.*
7 = **depict**, show, describe, picture, express, illustrate, outline, portray, sketch, render, designate, reproduce, evoke, denote, delineate • *God is represented as male.*
8 = **state**, indicate, point out, put forward • *I represented to him that he had behaved very foolishly.*
▸ IN PHRASES: **represent someone as something** *or* **someone** = **make out to be**, claim to be, describe as • *They tend to represent him as a guru.*
represent yourself as something *or* **someone** = **pass yourself off as**, claim to be, pose as, pretend to be, purport to be, profess to be, present yourself as • *He represented himself as an upright community member.*

representation 1 = **body of representatives**, committee, embassy, delegates, delegation • *They have no representation in congress.*
2 = **picture**, model, image, portrait, illustration, sketch, resemblance, likeness • *a life-like representation of Christ*
3 = **portrayal**, depiction, account, relation, description, narrative, narration, delineation • *the representation of women in film and literature*
4 *often plural* = **statement**, argument, explanation,

exposition, remonstrance, expostulation, account • *We have made representations to ministers.*

representative AS A NOUN **1 = delegate**, member, agent, deputy, commissioner, councillor, proxy, depute *(Scot.)*, spokesman *or* spokeswoman • *trade union representatives*
2 = member, congressman *or* congresswoman *(U.S.)*, member of parliament, Member of Congress *(U.S.)*, M.P. • *the representative for Eastleigh*
3 = agent, salesman, rep, traveller, commercial traveller • *She was a sales representative.*
▸ AS AN ADJECTIVE **1 = chosen**, democratic, elected, appointed, delegated, nominated, elective • *a representative government*
2 = typical, characteristic, archetypal, exemplary, indicative, illustrative • *fairly representative groups of adults*
OPPOSITES: extraordinary, uncharacteristic, atypical
3 = symbolic, evocative, emblematic, typical • *images chosen as representative of English life*

repress 1 = control, suppress, hold back, bottle up, check, master, hold in, overcome, curb, restrain, inhibit, overpower, keep in check • *People who repress their emotions risk having nightmares.*
OPPOSITES: release, encourage, express
2 = hold back, suppress, stifle, smother, silence, swallow, muffle • *I couldn't repress a sigh of admiration.*
3 = subdue, abuse, crush, oppress, quash, wrong, persecute, quell, subjugate, maltreat, trample underfoot, tyrannize over, rule with an iron hand • *They have been repressed for decades.*
OPPOSITES: free, liberate

repressed 1 = inhibited, frustrated, suppressed • *a sexually repressed 30-year-old woman*
2 = suppressed, held in, restrained, inhibited, held back, bottled up • *an effective outlet for repressed emotions*

repression 1 = subjugation, control, constraint, domination, censorship, tyranny, coercion, authoritarianism, despotism • *a society conditioned by violence and repression*
2 = suppression, crushing, prohibition, quashing, dissolution • *extremely violent repression of opposition*
3 = inhibition, control, holding in, restraint, suppression, bottling up • *the repression of intense feelings*

repressive = oppressive, tough, severe, absolute, harsh, authoritarian, dictatorial, coercive, tyrannical, despotic • *The regime was unpopular and repressive.*
OPPOSITES: democratic, liberal, libertarian

reprieve AS A VERB **1 = grant a stay of execution to**, spare, amnesty, pardon, acquit, let off the hook *(slang)*, grant an amnesty to, postpone *or* remit the punishment of • *Fourteen people, waiting to be hanged, have been reprieved.*
2 = save, rescue, give respite to • *Another 21 pits have been reprieved until the New Year at least.*
▸ AS A NOUN **= stay of execution**, suspension, amnesty, pardon, respite, acquittal, remission, abeyance, deferment, postponement of punishment • *a reprieve for eight people waiting to be hanged*

reprimand AS A VERB **= blame**, censure, rebuke, reproach, check, lecture, carpet *(informal)*, scold, tick off *(informal)*, castigate, chide, dress down *(informal)*, admonish, tear into *(informal)*, tell off *(informal)*, take to task, read the riot act, tongue-lash, reprove, upbraid, slap on the wrist *(informal)*, bawl out *(informal)*, rap over the knuckles, haul over the coals *(informal)*, chew out *(U.S. & Canad. informal)*, tear (someone) off a strip *(Brit. informal)*, give a rocket *(Brit. & N.Z. informal)*, reprehend, chew someone's ass *(U.S. & Canad. taboo slang)*, give (someone) a row *(informal)*, send someone away with a flea in his *or* her ear *(informal)* • *He was reprimanded by a teacher.*
OPPOSITES: praise, applaud, compliment
▸ AS A NOUN **= blame**, talking-to *(informal)*, row, lecture, wigging *(Brit. slang)*, censure, rebuke, reproach, ticking-off *(informal)*, dressing-down *(informal)*, telling-off *(informal)*, admonition, tongue-lashing, reproof, castigation, reprehension, flea in your ear *(informal)* • *He has been given a severe reprimand.*
OPPOSITES: praise, compliment, congratulations

reprisal = retaliation, revenge, vengeance, retribution, an eye for an eye, counterstroke, requital • *fear of reprisal or ostracism*

reproach AS A VERB **= blame**, criticize, rebuke, reprimand, abuse, blast, condemn, carpet *(informal)*, flame *(informal)*, discredit, censure, have a go at *(informal)*, scold, disparage, chide, tear into *(informal)*, diss *(slang, chiefly U.S.)*, defame, find fault with, take to task, read the riot act to, reprove, upbraid, lambast(e), bawl out *(informal)*, chew out *(U.S. & Canad. informal)*, tear (someone) off a strip *(Brit. informal)*, give a rocket *(Brit. & N.Z. informal)*, reprehend • *She is quick to reproach anyone.*
▸ AS A NOUN **1 = rebuke**, lecture, wigging *(Brit. slang)*, censure, reprimand, scolding, ticking-off *(informal)*, dressing down *(informal)*, telling-off *(informal)*, admonition, tongue-lashing, reproof, castigation, reproval • *Her reproach was automatic.*
2 = censure, blame, abuse, contempt, condemnation, scorn, disapproval, opprobrium, odium, obloquy • *He looked at her with reproach.*
3 = disgrace, shame, slight, stain, discredit, stigma, slur, disrepute, blemish, indignity, ignominy, dishonour • *The shootings were a reproach to all of us.*

reproachful = critical, disappointed, abusive, disapproving, scolding, contemptuous, censorious, reproving, upbraiding, condemnatory, fault-finding, admonitory, castigatory • *She gave her a reproachful look.*

reprobate AS A NOUN **= scoundrel**, villain, degenerate, profligate, mother *(taboo slang, chiefly U.S.)*, shit *(taboo slang)*, bastard *(informal offensive)*, rake, bugger *(taboo slang)*, sinner, outcast, pariah, rascal, son-of-a-bitch *(slang, chiefly U.S. & Canad.)*, asshole *(U.S. & Canad. taboo slang)*, turd *(taboo slang)*, wretch, wrongdoer, motherfucker *(taboo slang, chiefly U.S.)*, ne'er-do-well, scumbag *(slang)*, miscreant, wastrel, bad egg *(old-fashioned informal)*, blackguard, evildoer, roué, cocksucker *(taboo slang)*, rakehell *(archaic)*, asswipe *(U.S. & Canad. taboo slang)*, skelm *(S. African)*, wrong 'un *(Austral. slang)* • *the drunken reprobate of popular legend*
▸ AS AN ADJECTIVE **= unprincipled**, hardened, depraved, degenerate, bad, base, abandoned, damned, corrupt, vile, immoral, wicked, shameless, sinful, profligate, incorrigible, dissolute • *the most evil-looking gang of reprobate bikers*

reproduce 1 = copy, recreate, replicate, duplicate, match, represent, mirror, echo, parallel, imitate, emulate • *The effect has proved hard to reproduce.*
2 = print, copy, duplicate, photocopy, transcribe, xerox, make a copy of, photostat • *permission to reproduce this article*
3 = breed, produce young, bear young, procreate, generate, multiply, spawn, propagate, proliferate • *Women are defined by their ability to reproduce.*

reproduction 1 = copy, picture, print, replica, imitation, duplicate, reprint, xerox, facsimile, carbon copy • *a reproduction of a religious painting*
OPPOSITES: original, master, prototype
2 = duplication, printing, copying, duplicating, photocopying, xeroxing, photostatting • *I have no problem with the reproduction of old styles.*
3 = breeding, procreation, propagation, multiplying, increase, generation, proliferation, multiplication • *what doctors call 'assisted human reproduction'*

reproductive = procreative, sexual, seminal, life-giving, germinal, spermatic • *reproductive organs*

reproof 1 = **rebuke**, criticism, condemnation, censure, reprimand, reproach, scolding, ticking-off *(informal)*, chiding, dressing-down *(informal)*, admonition, tongue-lashing, upbraiding, sideswipe, castigation, reproval, reprehension, blame • *a reproof that she responded to right away*
OPPOSITES: praise, encouragement, compliment
2 = **disapproval**, stick *(slang)*, criticism, objection, condemnation, dissatisfaction, censure, reproach, denunciation, displeasure, deprecation, disapprobation • *They spoke in tones of gentle reproof.*

reprove = **rebuke**, censure, reprimand, scold, check, blame, abuse, condemn, carpet *(informal)*, berate, tick off *(informal)*, chide, admonish, tear into *(informal)*, tell off *(informal)*, take to task, read the riot act, upbraid, bawl out *(informal)*, chew out *(U.S. & Canad. informal)*, tear (someone) off a strip *(Brit. informal)*, give a rocket *(Brit. & N.Z. informal)*, reprehend • *Women were reproved if they did not wear hats.*
OPPOSITES: encourage, praise, applaud

reptile
▹ *See panel* **Reptiles**

reptilian 1 = **reptile-like**, reptile, cold-blooded, crocodilian, ophidian • *a prehistoric jungle occupied by reptilian creatures*
2 = **nasty**, sly, devious, underhand, horrible, unpleasant, oily, unattractive, creepy *(informal)*, sneaky *(informal)*, disagreeable, off-putting, ingratiating, unappealing, unctuous • *He's a reptilian con man.*

Republican AS AN ADJECTIVE = **right-wing**, Conservative • *Senator John McCain is more moderate than most Republican nominees.*
▸ AS A NOUN = **right-winger**, Conservative • *President Clinton is under pressure from Republicans in Congress.*

repudiate 1 = **reject**, renounce, retract, disown, abandon, desert, reverse, cut off, discard, revoke, forsake, cast off, rescind, disavow, turn your back on, abjure, wash your hands of • *He repudiated any form of nationalism.*
OPPOSITES: own, accept, assert
2 = **deny**, oppose, disagree with, rebuff, refute, disprove, rebut, disclaim, gainsay *(archaic or literary)* • *He repudiated the charges.*
3 = **cancel**, withdraw, reverse, abolish, set aside, repeal, renounce, quash, take back, call back, revoke, retract, negate, renege, rescind, recall, invalidate, annul, nullify, recant, obviate, disclaim, abrogate, countermand, declare null and void • *They had repudiated her contract.*
4 = **divorce**, end your marriage to • *A woman can repudiate her insane husband.*

repudiation = **rejection**, reversal, abandonment, disowning, desertion, retraction, disavowal, renouncement, abjuration • *a public repudiation of the conference decision*

repugnance = **distaste**, disgust, dislike, hatred, reluctance, loathing, aversion, revulsion, antipathy, repulsion, abhorrence, odium, disrelish • *She felt a deep sense of repugnance.*

repugnant 1 = **distasteful**, offensive, foul, disgusting, revolting, sickening, vile, horrid, repellent, obnoxious, objectionable, nauseating, odious, hateful, loathsome, abhorrent, abominable, yucky *or* yukky *(slang)*, yucko *(Austral. slang)* • *His actions were improper and repugnant.*
OPPOSITES: attractive, pleasant, agreeable
2 = **incompatible**, opposed, hostile, adverse, contradictory, inconsistent, averse, antagonistic, inimical, antipathetic • *It is repugnant to the values of our society.*
OPPOSITES: compatible

repulse AS A VERB 1 = **disgust**, offend, revolt, put off, sicken, repel, nauseate, gross out *(U.S. slang)*, turn your stomach, fill with loathing • *The thought of it repulsed me.*
2 = **drive back**, check, defeat, fight off, repel, rebuff, ward off, beat off, throw back • *The army were prepared to repulse any attack.*
3 = **reject**, refuse, turn down, snub, disregard, disdain, spurn, rebuff, give the cold shoulder to • *She repulsed him with undisguised venom.*
▸ AS A NOUN 1 = **defeat**, check • *the repulse of invaders in 1785*
2 = **rejection**, refusal, snub, spurning, rebuff, knock-back *(slang)*, cold shoulder, kick in the teeth *(slang)*, the (old) heave-ho *(informal)* • *If he meets with a repulse he will not be cast down.*

repulsion = **disgust**, hatred, loathing, distaste, aversion, revulsion, abhorrence, repugnance, odium, detestation, disrelish • *She gave a shudder of repulsion.*

repulsive = **disgusting**, offensive, foul, ugly, forbidding, unpleasant, revolting, obscene, sickening, hideous, vile, distasteful, horrid, repellent, obnoxious, objectionable, disagreeable, nauseating, odious, hateful, loathsome, abhorrent, abominable, yucky *or* yukky *(slang)*, yucko *(Austral. slang)*, fugly *(chiefly U.S. & Austral. slang)* • *repulsive, fat, white slugs*
OPPOSITES: appealing, attractive, delightful

REPTILES

adder
agama
agamid
alligator
amphisbaena
anaconda
anole
asp
bandy-bandy
black snake
blind snake
blue racer
blue tongue
boa
boa constrictor
boomslang
box turtle
brown snake
bull snake *or* gopher snake
bushmaster
carpet snake *or* python
cayman
cerastes
chameleon
chuckwalla
cobra
cobra de capello
constrictor
copperhead
coral snake
crocodile
death adder
diamondback
diamond snake
dugite
elapid
fer-de-lance
flying lizard
freshwater crocodile
frill-necked lizard
gaboon viper
galliwasp
garter snake
gavial
gecko
giant tortoise
Gila monster
glass snake
goanna
grass snake
green turtle
habu
harlequin snake
hawksbill
hognose snake *or* puff adder
hoop snake
horned toad
horned viper
iguana
indigo snake
jew lizard, bearded lizard, *or* bearded dragon
kabaragoya
king cobra *or* hamadryad
king snake
Komodo dragon
krait
leatherback
leguan
lizard
loggerhead
mamba
massasauga
milk snake
moloch, thorny devil, thorn lizard, *or* mountain devil
monitor
mud turtle
ngarara *(N.Z.)*
perentie
pit viper
puff adder
python
racer
rat snake
rattlesnake
ringhals
rock snake
saltwater crocodile
sand lizard
sand viper
sea snake
sidewinder
skink
slowworm *or* blindworm
smooth snake
snake
snapping turtle
soft-shelled turtle
swift
taipan
terrapin
tiger snake
tokay
tortoise
tree snake
tuatara
turtle
viper
wall lizard
water moccasin
water snake
whip snake
worm lizard

reputable = **respectable**, good, excellent, reliable, worthy, legitimate, upright, honourable, honoured, trustworthy, creditable, estimable, well-thought-of, of good repute • *Buy your car through a reputable dealer.*
OPPOSITES: cowboy *(informal)*, unreliable, disreputable

reputation = **name**, standing, credit, character, honour, fame, distinction, esteem, stature, eminence, renown, repute • *The stories ruined his reputation.*

repute 1 = **reputation**, standing, fame, celebrity, distinction, esteem, stature, eminence, estimation, renown • *The UN's repute has risen immeasurably.*
2 = **name**, character, reputation • *a house of ill-repute*

reputed 1 = **supposed**, said, seeming, held, believed, thought, considered, accounted, regarded, estimated, alleged, reckoned, rumoured, deemed • *a man reputed to be in his nineties*
2 = **apparent**, supposed, putative, ostensible • *They booked the ballroom for a reputed $15,000 last year.*

reputedly = **supposedly**, apparently, allegedly, seemingly, ostensibly • *He reputedly earns two millions pounds a year.*

request AS A VERB 1 = **ask for**, apply for, appeal for, put in for, demand, desire, pray for, beg for, requisition, beseech • *I requested a copy of the form.*
2 = **invite**, call for, beg, petition, beseech, entreat, supplicate • *They requested him to leave.*
3 = **seek**, ask (for), sue for, solicit • *the right to request a divorce*
▸ AS A NOUN 1 = **appeal**, call, demand, plea, desire, application, prayer, petition, requisition, solicitation, entreaty, supplication, suit • *They agreed to his request for help.*
2 = **asking**, demand, plea, pleading, begging, bidding, petitioning, solicitation, entreaty, supplication • *At his request, they attended some of the meetings.*
3 = **wish**, want, choice, desire, requirement • *A few extra spaces have been made available by special request.*

require 1 = **need**, crave, depend upon, have need of, want, miss, lack, wish, desire, stand in need of • *A baby requires warmth and physical security.*
2 = **demand**, take, involve, call for, entail, necessitate • *This requires thought, effort, and a certain ruthlessness.*
3 = **order**, demand, direct, command, compel, exact, oblige, instruct, call upon, constrain, insist upon • *The rules require employers to provide safety training.*
4 = **ask**, order, bid, command, compel, oblige, instruct, enjoin • *She was required to take to the stage.*

required 1 = **obligatory**, prescribed, compulsory, mandatory, needed, set, demanded, necessary, called for, essential, recommended, vital, unavoidable, requisite, de rigueur *(French)* • *This book is required reading.*
OPPOSITES: voluntary, optional, not necessary
2 = **desired**, right, chosen, preferred, selected, correct, of choice • *Hold the door open, at the required height.*

requirement = **necessity**, demand, specification, stipulation, want, need, must, essential, qualification, precondition, requisite, prerequisite, sine qua non *(Latin)*, desideratum, must-have • *The products met all legal requirements.*

requisite AS AN ADJECTIVE = **necessary**, needed, required, called for, essential, vital, mandatory, indispensable, obligatory, prerequisite, needful • *She filled in the requisite paperwork.*
▸ AS A NOUN = **necessity**, condition, requirement, precondition, need, must, essential, prerequisite, sine qua non *(Latin)*, desideratum, must-have • *a major requisite for the work of the analysts*

requisition AS A VERB 1 = **take over**, appropriate, occupy, seize, confiscate, commandeer, take possession of, sequester • *The vessel was requisitioned by the British Navy.*
2 = **demand**, order, call for, request, apply for, put in for • *the task of requisitioning men and supplies*
▸ AS A NOUN 1 = **demand**, request, call, order, application, summons • *a requisition for a replacement typewriter*
2 = **takeover**, occupation, seizure, appropriation, confiscation, commandeering • *They are against the requisition of common land.*

rescind = **annul**, recall, reverse, cancel, overturn, set aside, void, repeal, quash, revoke, retract, invalidate, obviate, abrogate, countermand, declare null and void • *You will rescind that order immediately.*
OPPOSITES: support, confirm, implement

rescue AS A VERB 1 = **save**, get out, save the life of, extricate, free, release, deliver, recover, liberate, set free, save (someone's) bacon *(Brit. informal)* • *Helicopters rescued nearly 20 people.*
OPPOSITES: leave, lose, desert
2 = **salvage**, save, deliver, redeem, come to the rescue of • *He rescued a 14th century barn from demolition.*
▸ AS A NOUN = **saving**, salvage, deliverance, extrication, release, relief, recovery, liberation, salvation, redemption • *the rescue of the crew of a ship*

research AS A NOUN = **investigation**, study, inquiry, analysis, examination, probe, exploration, scrutiny, experimentation, delving, groundwork, fact-finding • *His groundbreaking research will be vital in future developments.*
▸ AS A VERB = **investigate**, study, examine, experiment, explore, probe, analyse, look into, work over, scrutinize, make inquiries, do tests, consult the archives • *They research the needs of both employers and staff.*

resemblance = **similarity**, correspondence, conformity, semblance, image, comparison, parallel, counterpart, analogy, affinity, closeness, parity, likeness, kinship, facsimile, sameness, comparability, similitude • *There was a remarkable resemblance between them.*
OPPOSITES: difference, variation, dissimilarity

resemble = **be like**, look like, favour *(informal)*, mirror, echo, parallel, be similar to, duplicate, take after, remind you of, bear a resemblance to, put you in mind of • *She so resembles her mother.*

resent = **be bitter about**, dislike, object to, grudge, begrudge, take exception to, be offended by, be angry about, take offence at, take umbrage at, harbour a grudge against, be pissed (off) about *(taboo slang)*, take as an insult, bear a grudge about, be in a huff about, take amiss to, have hard feelings about • *I resent being dependent on her.*
OPPOSITES: like, accept, be content with

resentful = **bitter**, hurt, wounded, angry, offended, put out, jealous, choked, pissed *(Brit., Austral. & N.Z. slang)*, incensed, grudging, exasperated, aggrieved, indignant, pissed off *(taboo slang)*, irate, miffed *(informal)*, embittered, unforgiving, peeved *(informal)*, in a huff, piqued, huffy, in high dudgeon, revengeful, huffish, tooshie *(Austral. slang)* • *He turned away in a resentful silence.*
OPPOSITES: pleased, content, satisfied

resentment = **bitterness**, indignation, ill feeling, ill will, hurt, anger, rage, fury, irritation, grudge, wrath, malice, animosity, huff, ire, displeasure, pique, rancour, bad blood, umbrage, vexation, chip on your shoulder *(informal)* • *Rigid policing can only feed resentment and undermine confidence.*

QUOTATIONS
It is very difficult to get up resentment towards persons whom one has never seen
[Cardinal Newman *Apologia pro Vita Sua*]

reservation AS A NOUN 1 *often plural* = **doubt**, reluctance, scepticism, qualms, scruples, demur, hesitancy • *Their demands were met with some reservations.*
2 = **booking**, advance booking, prior arrangements • *He went to the desk to make a reservation.*
3 = **reserve**, territory, preserve, homeland, sanctuary, tract, enclave • *a Navaho Indian from a North American reservation*

▸ **IN PHRASES: without reservation = unreservedly**, completely, totally, fully, entirely, wholly, implicitly, categorically, unconditionally, in every respect, without reserve, without demur • *men whose work I admire without reservation*

reserve **AS A VERB 1 = book**, arrange in advance, make a reservation for, prearrange, pre-engage, engage, bespeak • *I'll reserve a table for five.*
2 = put by, keep, hold, save, secure, retain, set aside, hold back, put aside, lay aside • *Ask your newsagent to reserve your copy today.*
3 = keep, hold, save, husband, store, retain, preserve, set aside, withhold, hang on to, conserve, stockpile, hoard, lay up, put by, keep back • *Strain and reserve the cooking liquor.*
4 = delay, postpone, withhold, put off, defer, keep back • *The Court has reserved its judgement.*
▸ **AS A NOUN 1 = store**, fund, savings, stock, capital, supply, reservoir, fall-back, stockpile, hoard, backlog, cache • *The country's reserves of petrol are running very low.*
2 = park, reservation, preserve, sanctuary, tract, forest park *(N.Z.)* • *monkeys at the wildlife reserve*
3 = shyness, silence, restraint, constraint, reluctance, formality, modesty, reticence, coolness, aloofness, secretiveness, taciturnity • *I hope you'll overcome your reserve.*
4 = reservation, doubt, delay, uncertainty, hesitation, indecision, hesitancy, vacillation, irresolution, dubiety • *I committed myself without reserve*
5 *often plural* **= reinforcements**, extras, auxiliary, backup • *a squadron leader in the RAF military reserve*
6 = substitute, extra, spare, alternative, fall-back, auxiliary • *In this sport, you always have to have reserves.*
▸ **IN PHRASES: in reserve = in readiness**, ready, spare, to hand, on hand, on call • *This is the vehicle kept in reserve.*

reserved 1 = uncommunicative, cold, cool, retiring, formal, silent, modest, shy, cautious, restrained, secretive, aloof, reticent, prim, demure, taciturn, unresponsive, unapproachable, unsociable, undemonstrative, standoffish, close-mouthed, unforthcoming • *He was unemotional and reserved.*
OPPOSITES: open, forward, uninhibited
2 = set aside, taken, kept, held, booked, retained, engaged, restricted, spoken for • *Three coaches were reserved for us boys.*

reservoir 1 = lake, pond, basin • *Torrents of water gushed into the reservoir.*
2 = repository, store, tank, holder, container, receptacle • *It was on his desk next to the ink reservoir.*
3 = store, stock, source, supply, reserves, fund, pool, accumulation, stockpile • *the body's short-term reservoir of energy*

reshuffle **AS A VERB = reorganize**, restructure, revise, shake up *(informal)*, rearrange, interchange, regroup, redistribute, change around, realign, change the line-up of • *The Prime Minister plans to reshuffle his entire cabinet.*
▸ **AS A NOUN = reorganization**, restructuring, shake-up *(informal)*, revision, interchange, change, redistribution, regrouping, realignment, rearrangement • *a government reshuffle later today*

reside 1 = live, lodge, dwell, have your home, remain, stay, settle, abide, hang out *(informal)*, sojourn • *She resides with her invalid mother.*
OPPOSITES: visit, holiday in
2 = be present, lie, exist, consist, dwell, abide, rest with, be intrinsic to, inhere, be vested • *Happiness does not reside in money.*

residence 1 = home, house, household, dwelling, place, quarters, flat, lodging, pad *(slang)*, abode, habitation, domicile • *There was a stabbing at a residence next door.*
2 = mansion, seat, hall, palace, villa, manor • *She's staying at her country residence.*
3 = stay, tenancy, occupancy, occupation, sojourn • *He returned to his place of residence.*

resident **AS A NOUN 1 = inhabitant**, citizen, native, householder, denizen, indweller, local • *Ten per cent of residents live below the poverty line.*
OPPOSITES: visitor, nonresident
2 = tenant, occupant, lodger • *Council house residents purchasing their own homes*
3 = guest, client, lodger, boarder • *Bar closed on Sunday except to hotel residents.*
▸ **AS AN ADJECTIVE 1 = inhabiting**, living, staying, settled, dwelling, residing • *He had been resident in Brussels since 1967.*
OPPOSITES: visiting, nonresident
2 = incumbent, permanent • *a talk on health by the resident physician*
3 = local, neighbourhood • *The resident population of the inner city has risen.*

residential = suburban, commuter, dormitory • *a smart residential area*

residual = remaining, net, unused, leftover, vestigial, nett, unconsumed • *residual radiation from nuclear weapons*

residue = remainder, remains, remnant, leftovers, rest, extra, balance, excess, surplus, dregs, residuum • *She loaded the residue of lunch onto a tray.*

resign **AS A VERB 1 = quit**, leave, step down *(informal)*, stand down, vacate, abdicate, call it a day *or* night, give *or* hand in your notice • *He has resigned after only ten weeks in office.*
2 = give up, abandon, yield, hand over, surrender, turn over, relinquish, renounce, forsake, cede, forgo • *He has resigned his seat in parliament.*
▸ **IN PHRASES: resign yourself to something = accept**, reconcile yourself to, succumb to, submit to, bow to, give in to, yield to, acquiesce to • *I simply resigned myself to staying indoors.*

resignation 1 = leaving, notice, retirement, departure, surrender, abandonment, abdication, renunciation, relinquishment • *He has withdrawn his letter of resignation.*
2 = acceptance, patience, submission, compliance, endurance, fortitude, passivity, acquiescence, forbearing, sufferance, nonresistance • *He sighed with profound resignation.*
OPPOSITES: protest, resistance, dissent

resigned = stoical, patient, subdued, long-suffering, compliant, submissive, acquiescent, unresisting, unprotesting • *He gave a resigned smile.*

resilience 1 = suppleness, give, spring, flexibility, elasticity, plasticity, pliability, springiness • *the texture of the skin and the resilience of the flesh*
2 = strength, toughness, adaptability, hardiness • *the resilience of human beings*

resilient 1 = flexible, plastic, elastic, supple, bouncy, rubbery, pliable, springy, whippy • *some resilient plastic material*
OPPOSITES: stiff, rigid, limp
2 = tough, strong, hardy, buoyant, feisty *(informal, chiefly U.S. & Canad.)*, bouncy, irrepressible, quick to recover • *I'm a resilient kind of person.*
OPPOSITES: weak, sensitive, delicate

resist **AS A VERB 1 = oppose**, fight, battle against, refuse, check, weather, dispute, confront, combat, defy, curb, thwart, stand up to, hinder, contend with, counteract, hold out against, put up a fight (against), countervail • *They resisted our attempts to modernize distribution.*
OPPOSITES: accept, welcome, yield to
2 = fight against, fight, battle against, struggle against, hold off, fend off, ward off, hold out against, put up a fight (against) • *He tried to resist arrest.*
3 = refrain from, refuse, avoid, turn down, leave alone, keep from, forgo, abstain from, forbear, prevent yourself from • *Try to resist giving him advice.*

r

OPPOSITES: enjoy, indulge in, give in to
4 = withstand, weather, counter, combat, repel, be resistant to, be impervious to, be proof against • *bodies trained to resist the cold*
▸ IN PHRASES: **cannot resist = enjoy**, like, love, relish, adore, delight in, be very keen on, be partial to, take great pleasure in, have a weakness for, be addicted to • *He cannot resist a bit of excitement.*

resistance 1 = opposition, hostility, aversion, refusal to accept, lack of enthusiasm for, reluctance to accept • *In remote villages there is a resistance to change.*
2 = fighting, fight, battle, struggle, combat, contention, defiance, obstruction, impediment, intransigence, hindrance, counteraction • *The protesters offered no resistance.*
3 = immunity from, resilience, ability to withstand, ability to fight off, ability to counteract • *a natural resistance to the disease*

Resistance = freedom fighters, underground, guerrillas, partisans, irregulars, maquis • *The Resistance had captured much of the territory.*

resistant 1 = opposed, hostile, dissident, unwilling, defiant, intractable, combative, recalcitrant, antagonistic, intransigent • *Some people are resistant to the idea of exercise.*
2 = impervious, hard, strong, tough, unaffected, unyielding, insusceptible • *The body may be less resistant if it is cold.*

resolute = determined, set, firm, dogged, fixed, constant, bold, relentless, stubborn, stalwart, staunch, persevering, inflexible, purposeful, tenacious, undaunted, strong-willed, steadfast, obstinate, unwavering, immovable, unflinching, unbending, unshakable, unshaken • *a decisive and resolute international leader*
OPPOSITES: weak, doubtful, irresolute

resolution 1 = declaration, ruling, proposal, motion, verdict, judgment, decree • *The UN had passed two major resolutions.*
2 = decision, commitment, resolve, intention, promise, aim, purpose, object, pledge, determination, intent • *It had been her resolution to lose weight.*
3 = determination, energy, purpose, resolve, courage, dedication, fortitude, sincerity, tenacity, perseverance, willpower, boldness, firmness, staying power, stubbornness, constancy, earnestness, obstinacy, steadfastness, doggedness, relentlessness, resoluteness, staunchness • *He implemented policy with resolution and single-mindedness.*
4 = solution, end, settlement, outcome, finding, answer, working out, solving, sorting out, unravelling, upshot • *a peaceful resolution to the crisis*

resolve AS A VERB **1 = work out**, answer, solve, find the solution to, clear up, crack, fathom, suss (out) *(slang)*, elucidate • *We must find a way to resolve these problems.*
2 = decide, determine, undertake, make up your mind, agree, design, settle, purpose, intend, fix, conclude • *She resolved to report the matter.*
3 = change, convert, transform, alter, metamorphose, transmute • *The spirals of light resolved into points.*
4 = dispel, explain, remove, clear up, banish • *Many years of doubt were finally resolved.*
▸ AS A NOUN **1 = determination**, resolution, courage, willpower, boldness, firmness, earnestness, steadfastness, resoluteness • *He doesn't weaken in his resolve.*
OPPOSITES: wavering, indecision, cowardice
2 = decision, resolution, undertaking, objective, design, project, purpose, conclusion, intention • *the resolve to enforce a settlement using troops*

resolved = determined, intent, set on, bent on, resolute, persistent • *He was resolved to stay till the end.*

resonant 1 = sonorous, full, clear, rich, ringing, booming, vibrant, full-bodied • *He responded with a resonant laugh.*
2 = echoing, filled, resounding, reverberating, reverberant • *a hall, resonant with the sound of violins*
3 = expressive, evocative, indicative, suggestive, demonstrative, allusive • *resonant of the style of traditional Irish music*

resonate = reverberate, echo, resound, vibrate, pulsate • *The bass guitar began to resonate in my head.*

resonating *often with* **with = evoking**, expressive, evocative, indicative, suggestive, demonstrative, allusive • *resonating with the qualities of a civilised city*

resort AS A NOUN **1 = course**, hope, chance, alternative, possibility, expedient • *the option of force as a last resort*
2 = holiday centre, spot, retreat, haunt, refuge, tourist centre, watering place *(Brit.)* • *a genteel resort on the south coast*
3 = recourse to, turning to, the use of, appealing to, reference to, utilizing • *without resort to illegal methods*
▸ IN PHRASES: **resort to something = have recourse to**, turn to, fall back on, bring into play, use, exercise, employ, look to, make use of, utilize, avail yourself of • *We were forced to resort to violence.*

resound 1 = echo, resonate, reverberate, fill the air, re-echo • *The soldiers' boots resounded in the street.*
2 = ring, be filled, vibrate, resonate • *The whole place resounded with music.*

resounding 1 = echoing, full, sounding, rich, ringing, powerful, booming, vibrant, reverberating, resonant, sonorous • *She got a resounding round of applause.*
2 = huge, striking, outstanding, tremendous, terrific, decisive, notable, monumental, conclusive • *The occasion was a resounding success.*

resource AS A NOUN **1 = supply**, fund, source, reserve, pool, reservoir, stockpile, hoard • *a great resource of teaching materials*
2 = facility, help, service, benefit, aid, advantage • *The directory is a valuable resource.*
3 = means, course, resort, device, expedient • *The only resource left to allay her husband's pain was opium.*
▸ AS A PLURAL NOUN **1 = funds**, means, holdings, money, capital, wherewithal, riches, materials, assets, wealth, property • *They do not have the resources to feed themselves properly.*
2 = reserves, supplies, stores, stocks • *We are overpopulated, straining the earth's resources.*

resourceful = ingenious, able, bright, talented, sharp, capable, creative, clever, imaginative, inventive, quick-witted • *Her mother was a resourceful woman.*
OPPOSITES: unimaginative, gormless *(Brit. informal)*, uninventive

respect AS A VERB **1 = think highly of**, value, regard, honour, recognize, appreciate, admire, esteem, adore, revere, reverence, look up to, defer to, venerate, set store by, have a good *or* high opinion of • *I want him to respect me as a career woman.*
2 = show consideration for, regard, notice, honour, observe, heed, attend to, pay attention to • *Trying to respect her wishes, I said I'd leave.*
3 = abide by, follow, observe, comply with, obey, heed, keep to, adhere to • *It's about time they respected the law.*
OPPOSITES: abuse, ignore, disregard
▸ AS A NOUN **1 = regard**, honour, recognition, esteem, appreciation, admiration, reverence, estimation, veneration, approbation • *I have tremendous respect for him.*
OPPOSITES: contempt, disregard, scorn
2 = consideration, kindness, deference, friendliness, tact, thoughtfulness, solicitude, kindliness, considerateness • *They should be treated with respect.*
3 = particular, way, point, matter, sense, detail, feature, aspect, characteristic, facet • *He's simply wonderful in every respect.*

▸ **AS A PLURAL NOUN** = **greetings**, regards, compliments, good wishes, salutations, devoirs • *He visited the hospital to pay his respects to her.*
▸ **IN PHRASES: in respect of** *or* **with respect to** = **concerning**, in relation to, in connection with, with regard to, with reference to, apropos of • *The system is not working in respect of training.*

respectable 1 = **honourable**, good, respected, decent, proper, worthy, upright, admirable, honest, dignified, venerable, reputable, decorous, estimable • *He came from a respectable middle-class family.*
OPPOSITES: indecent, improper, disreputable
2 = **decent**, smart, neat, tidy *(informal)*, spruce • *At last I have something respectable to wear.*
3 = **reasonable**, considerable, substantial, fair, tidy *(informal)*, ample, tolerable, presentable, appreciable, fairly good, sizable *or* sizeable, goodly • *respectable and highly attractive rates of return*
OPPOSITES: small, poor, paltry

respected = **admired**, acclaimed, famous, celebrated, acknowledged, praised, renowned, highly rated, famed, well received, much vaunted, noted, highly esteemed, much touted, well thought of, highly thought of • *a highly respected novelist*

respectful = **polite**, civil, mannerly, humble, gracious, courteous, obedient, submissive, self-effacing, dutiful, courtly, deferential, reverential, solicitous, reverent, regardful, well-mannered • *He was always so polite and respectful.*

respective = **specific**, own, several, individual, personal, particular, various, separate, relevant, corresponding • *They went into their respective bedrooms.*

respite 1 = **pause**, break, rest, relief, halt, interval, relaxation, recess, interruption, lull, cessation, let-up *(informal)*, breathing space, breather *(informal)*, hiatus, intermission • *I rang home during a brief respite at work.*
2 = **reprieve**, stay, delay, suspension, moratorium, postponement, adjournment • *Devaluation would only give the economy brief respite.*

resplendent = **brilliant**, radiant, splendid, glorious, bright, shining, beaming, glittering, dazzling, gleaming, luminous, lustrous, refulgent *(literary)*, effulgent, irradiant • *She was resplendent in royal blue velvet.*

respond 1 = **answer**, return, reply, come back, counter, acknowledge, retort, rejoin • *'Of course,' she responded scornfully.*
OPPOSITES: ignore, turn a blind eye, remain silent
2 *often with* **to** = **reply to**, answer, counter, acknowledge, say something to • *He was quick to respond to questions.*
3 = **react**, retaliate, hit back at, reciprocate, take the bait, rise to the bait, act in response • *He responded to the attacks by exacting suitable retribution.*

response = **answer**, return, reply, reaction, comeback *(informal)*, feedback, retort, acknowledgment, riposte, counterattack, rejoinder, counterblast • *There has been no response to his remarks.*

responsibility 1 = **duty**, business, job, role, task, function, burden, liability, accountability, onus, answerability • *The 600 properties were his responsibility.*
2 = **fault**, blame, liability, guilt, culpability, burden • *They have admitted responsibility for the accident.*
3 = **obligation**, duty, liability, charge, care • *This helps employees balance work and family responsibilities.*
4 = **authority**, power, control, management, leadership, importance, mana *(N.Z.)* • *a better-paying job with more responsibility*
5 = **job**, task, function, role, pigeon *(informal)* • *I'm glad it's not my responsibility to be their guardian*
6 = **level-headedness**, stability, maturity, common sense, reliability, rationality, reasonableness, dependability, trustworthiness, conscientiousness, soberness, sensibleness • *I think she's shown responsibility.*
▸ **RELATED PHOBIA:** hypegiaphobia

QUOTATIONS
Uneasy lies the head that wears a crown
[William Shakespeare *Henry IV, part II*]
The buck stops here
[Harry S Truman *motto on his desk at the White House*]

responsible 1 = **to blame**, guilty, at fault, culpable, behind • *He felt responsible for her death.*
2 = **in charge**, in control, at the helm, in authority, carrying the can *(informal)* • *the minister responsible for the environment*
3 = **accountable**, subject, bound, liable, amenable, answerable, duty-bound, chargeable, under obligation • *I'm responsible to my board of directors.*
OPPOSITES: unaccountable
4 = **sensible**, sound, adult, stable, mature, reliable, rational, sober, conscientious, dependable, trustworthy, level-headed • *He's a very responsible sort of person.*
OPPOSITES: irresponsible, unreliable, untrustworthy
5 = **authoritative**, high, important, executive, decision-making • *demoted to less responsible jobs*

responsive = **sensitive**, open, aware, sharp, alive, forthcoming, sympathetic, awake, susceptible, receptive, reactive, perceptive, impressionable, quick to react • *She was an easy, responsive little girl.*
OPPOSITES: silent, insensitive, unresponsive

rest[1] **AS A VERB** 1 = **relax**, sleep, take it easy, lie down, idle, nap, be calm, doze, sit down, slumber, kip *(Brit. slang)*, snooze *(informal)*, laze, lie still, be at ease, put your feet up, take a nap, drowse, mellow out *(informal)*, have a snooze *(informal)*, refresh yourself, outspan *(S. African)*, zizz *(Brit. informal)*, have forty winks *(informal)*, take your ease • *He has been advised to rest for two weeks.*
OPPOSITES: work, keep going, slog away *(informal)*
2 = **stop**, have a break, break off, take a breather *(informal)*, stay, halt, cease, discontinue, knock off *(informal)*, desist, come to a standstill • *They rested only once that morning.*
OPPOSITES: work, keep going, carry on
3 = **depend**, turn, lie, be founded, hang, be based, rely, hinge, reside • *Such a view rests on incorrect assumptions.*
4 = **place**, lay, repose, stretch out, stand, sit, lean, prop • *He rested his arms on the back of the chair.*
5 = **be placed**, sit, lie, be supported, be positioned, recline, be propped up by • *Matt's elbow rested on the table.*
▸ **AS A NOUN** 1 = **sleep**, snooze *(informal)*, lie-down, nap, doze, slumber, kip *(Brit. slang)*, siesta, forty winks *(informal)*, zizz *(Brit. informal)* • *Go home and have a rest.*
2 = **relaxation**, sleep, time off, repose, ease, leisure, respite, inactivity, idleness, me-time • *I feel in need of some rest.*
OPPOSITES: work, activity, bustle
3 = **pause**, break, breather, time off, stop, holiday, halt, interval, vacation, respite, lull, interlude, cessation, breathing space *(informal)*, intermission • *He took a rest from teaching.*
4 = **refreshment**, release, relief, ease, comfort, cure, remedy, solace, balm, deliverance, mitigation, abatement, alleviation, easement, palliation, assuagement • *some rest from the intense concentration*
5 = **inactivity**, a halt, a stop, a standstill, stationary, motionlessness • *The plane came to rest in a field.*
6 = **support**, stand, base, holder, shelf, prop, trestle • *Keep your elbow on the arm rest.*
7 = **calm**, tranquillity, stillness, somnolence • *a remote part of the valley for those seeking rest and relaxation*
▸ **IN PHRASES: at rest** 1 = **motionless**, still, stopped, at a standstill, unmoving • *When you are at rest you breathe with your tummy muscles.*

r

2 = **calm**, still, cool, quiet, pacific, peaceful, composed, serene, tranquil, at peace, sedate, placid, undisturbed, restful, untroubled, unperturbed, unruffled, unexcited • *with your mind at rest*
3 = **asleep**, resting, sleeping, napping, dormant, crashed out *(slang)*, dozing, slumbering, snoozing *(informal)*, fast asleep, sound asleep, out for the count, dead to the world *(informal)* • *She is at rest; don't disturb her.*

rest² AS A NOUN = **remainder**, remains, excess, remnants, others, balance, surplus, residue, rump, leftovers, residuum • *The rest is thrown away.*
▸ AS A VERB = **continue being**, keep being, remain, stay, be left, go on being • *Of one thing we may rest assured.*

restaurant = **café**, diner *(chiefly U.S. & Canad.)*, bistro, cafeteria, trattoria, tearoom, eatery *or* eaterie • *We had dinner in the hotel's restaurant.*

restful = **relaxing**, quiet, relaxed, comfortable, pacific, calm, calming, peaceful, soothing, sleepy, serene, tranquil, placid, undisturbed, languid, unhurried, tranquillizing, chilled *(informal)* • *a joyous and restful three days*
OPPOSITES: busy, disturbing, uncomfortable

restitution 1 = **compensation**, satisfaction, amends, refund, repayment, redress, remuneration, reparation, indemnity, reimbursement, recompense, indemnification, requital • *The victims are demanding full restitution.*
2 = **return**, replacement, restoration, reinstatement, re-establishment, reinstallation • *the restitution of their equal rights as citizens*

restive = **restless**, nervous, uneasy, impatient, agitated, unruly, edgy, jittery *(informal)*, recalcitrant, on edge, fractious, ill at ease, jumpy, fretful, fidgety, refractory, unquiet, antsy *(informal)* • *The audience grew restive.*
OPPOSITES: content, relaxed, calm

restless 1 = **unsettled**, worried, troubled, nervous, disturbed, anxious, uneasy, agitated, unruly, edgy, fidgeting, on edge, ill at ease, restive, jumpy, fitful, fretful, fidgety, unquiet, antsy *(informal)* • *My father seemed very restless and excited.*
OPPOSITES: easy, quiet, relaxed
2 = **sleepless**, disturbed, wakeful, unsleeping, insomniac, tossing and turning • *He had spent a restless few hours on the plane.*
3 = **moving**, active, wandering, unsettled, unstable, bustling, turbulent, hurried, roving, transient, nomadic, unsteady, changeable, footloose, irresolute, inconstant, having itchy feet • *He led a restless life.*
OPPOSITES: settled, stable, steady

restlessness 1 = **movement**, activity, turmoil, unrest, instability, bustle, turbulence, hurry, transience, inconstancy, hurry-scurry, unsettledness • *increasing sounds of restlessness*
2 = **restiveness**, anxiety, disturbance, nervousness, disquiet, agitation, insomnia, jitters *(informal)*, uneasiness, edginess, heebie-jeebies *(slang)*, jumpiness, fretfulness, ants in your pants *(slang)*, fitfulness, inquietude, worriedness • *She complained of hyperactivity and restlessness.*

restoration 1 = **reinstatement**, return, revival, restitution, re-establishment, reinstallation, replacement • *the restoration of diplomatic relations*
OPPOSITES: overthrow, abolition
2 = **repair**, recovery, reconstruction, renewal, rehabilitation, refurbishing, refreshment, renovation, rejuvenation, revitalization • *I specialized in the restoration of old houses.*
OPPOSITES: scrapping, wrecking, demolition

restore 1 = **reinstate**, re-establish, reintroduce, reimpose, re-enforce, reconstitute • *The army has been brought in to restore order.*
OPPOSITES: abolish, repeal, rescind
2 = **revive**, build up, strengthen, bring back, refresh, rejuvenate, revitalize, revivify, reanimate • *We will restore her to health.*
OPPOSITES: weaken, make worse
3 = **re-establish**, replace, reinstate, give back, reinstall, retrocede • *Civil rights were restored in a matter of days.*
4 = **repair**, refurbish, renovate, reconstruct, fix (up), recover, renew, rebuild, mend, rehabilitate, touch up, recondition, retouch, set to rights • *They partly restored a local castle.*
OPPOSITES: scrap, wreck, demolish
5 = **return**, replace, recover, bring back, send back, hand back • *Their horses and goods were restored.*

restrain 1 = **hold back**, hold, control, check, contain, prevent, restrict, handicap, confine, curb, hamper, rein, harness, subdue, hinder, constrain, curtail, bridle, debar, keep under control, have on a tight leash, straiten • *He grabbed my arm, partly to restrain me.*
OPPOSITES: help, encourage, assist
2 = **control**, keep in, limit, govern, suppress, inhibit, repress, muzzle, keep under control • *She was unable to restrain her desperate anger.*
3 = **imprison**, hold, arrest, jail, bind, chain, confine, detain, tie up, lock up, fetter, manacle, pinion • *Police restrained her on July 28.*
OPPOSITES: free, release, liberate

restrained 1 = **controlled**, reasonable, moderate, self-controlled, soft, calm, steady, mild, muted, reticent, temperate, undemonstrative • *He felt he'd been very restrained.*
OPPOSITES: wild, fiery, hot-headed
2 = **unobtrusive**, subtle, muted, discreet, subdued, understated, tasteful, unostentatious, quiet • *Her black suit was restrained and expensive.*
OPPOSITES: loud, over-the-top, garish

restraint 1 = **limitation**, limit, check, ban, boycott, embargo, curb, rein, taboo, bridle, disqualification, interdict, restraining order *(U.S. Law)* • *Criminals could cross into the country without restraint.*
OPPOSITES: freedom, liberty
2 = **self-control**, self-discipline, self-restraint, self-possession, pulling your punches • *They behaved with more restraint than I'd expected.*
OPPOSITES: licence, excess, self-indulgence
3 = **constraint**, limitation, inhibition, moderation, hold, control, restriction, prevention, suppression, hindrance, curtailment • *A Bill of Rights would act as a restraint on judicial power.*
4 = **confinement**, arrest, detention, imprisonment, captivity, bondage, fetters • *There was a meeting and he was put under restraint.*
5 = **belt**, strap, harness, seat belt, safety belt • *Children are always safer in a restraint or belt.*

restrict 1 = **limit**, fix, regulate, specify, curb, ration, keep within bounds *or* limits • *a move to restrict the number of students on campus at any one time*
OPPOSITES: free, allow, widen
2 = **hamper**, impede, handicap, restrain, cramp, inhibit, straiten • *The shoulder straps restrict movement.*

restricted 1 = **limited**, controlled, reduced, moderate, regulated • *a heavily restricted diet*
2 = **cramped**, small, tight, narrow, confined, inadequate, compact, constricted, poky • *Every inch counts in this restricted space.*
3 = **private**, closed off, off limits, out of bounds • *a restricted area*
4 = **secret**, reserved, exclusive, classified, top secret • *a highly restricted document*

restriction 1 = **control**, rule, condition, check, regulation, curb, restraint, constraint, confinement, containment, demarcation, stipulation • *the relaxation of travel restrictions*

r

2 = **limitation**, limit, handicap, constraint, inhibition • *the restrictions of urban living*

result AS A NOUN 1 = **consequence**, effect, outcome, end result, issue, event, development, product, reaction, fruit, sequel, upshot • *This is the result of eating too much fatty food.*
OPPOSITES: beginning, cause, source
2 = **outcome**, conclusion, verdict, determination, end, decision, judgement, termination • *They were surprised by the result of their trials.*
▸ AS A PLURAL NOUN = **marks**, scores, grades, grading, percentage, evaluation, appraisal • *Her exam results were excellent.*
▸ AS A VERB *often followed by* **from** = **arise**, follow, issue, happen, appear, develop, spring, flow, turn out, stem, derive, ensue, emanate, eventuate • *Many hair problems result from what you eat.*
▸ IN PHRASES: **result in something** = **end in**, bring about, cause, lead to, wind up, finish with, culminate in, terminate in • *Fifty per cent of road accidents result in head injuries.*

resume 1 = **begin again**, continue, go on with, proceed with, carry on, reopen, restart, recommence, reinstitute, take up *or* pick up where you left off • *They are expected to resume the search early today.*
OPPOSITES: stop, cease, discontinue
2 = **take up again**, return to, come back to, assume again • *After the war he resumed his duties at the college.*
3 = **occupy again**, take back, reoccupy • *She resumed her seat.*

résumé 1 = **summary**, synopsis, abstract, précis, review, digest, epitome, rundown, recapitulation • *I will leave you a résumé of his speech.*
2 = **curriculum vitae**, CV, career history, details, biography • *I mailed him my résumé this week.*

resumption = **continuation**, carrying on, reopening, renewal, restart, resurgence, new beginning, re-establishment, fresh outbreak • *a resumption of friendly relations*

resurgence = **revival**, return, renaissance, resurrection, resumption, rebirth, re-emergence, recrudescence, renascence • *a period of economic resurgence*

resurrect 1 = **revive**, renew, bring back, kick-start *(informal)*, reintroduce, breathe new life into • *Attempts to resurrect the ceasefire have failed.*
2 = **restore to life**, bring back to life, raise from the dead • *Only the True Cross was able to resurrect a dead youth.*

resurrection 1 = **revival**, restoration, renewal, resurgence, return, comeback *(informal)*, renaissance, rebirth, reappearance, resuscitation, renascence • *This is a resurrection of an old story.*
OPPOSITES: killing off
2 = **raising** *or* **rising from the dead**, return from the dead, restoration to life • *the Resurrection of Jesus Christ*
OPPOSITES: demise, burial

QUOTATIONS
I am the resurrection, and the life
[Bible: St. John]

resuscitate 1 = **give artificial respiration to**, save, quicken, bring to life, bring round, give the kiss of life to • *A paramedic tried to resuscitate her.*
2 = **revive**, rescue, restore, renew, resurrect, revitalize, breathe new life into, revivify, reanimate • *his promise to resuscitate the failing economy*

retain 1 = **maintain**, keep, reserve, preserve, keep up, uphold, nurture, continue to have, hang *or* hold onto • *He retains a deep respect for the profession.*
2 = **keep**, keep possession of, hang *or* hold onto, save, preserve, cling to, conserve, hold fast to • *They want to retain a strip 33ft wide on the eastern shore.*
OPPOSITES: lose, release, let go
3 = **remember**, learn, recall, bear in mind, keep in mind, memorize, recollect, commit to memory, learn by heart, impress on the memory • *She needs tips on how to retain facts.*
OPPOSITES: forget

retainer 1 = **fee**, advance, deposit, partial payment, retaining fee • *I'll need a five-hundred-dollar retainer.*
2 = **servant**, domestic, attendant, valet, supporter, dependant, henchman, footman, lackey, vassal, flunky • *the ever-faithful family retainer*

retaliate = **pay someone back**, hit back, strike back, reciprocate, take revenge, get back at someone, get even with *(informal)*, even the score, get your own back *(informal)*, wreak vengeance, exact retribution, give as good as you get *(informal)*, take an eye for an eye, make reprisal, give (someone) a taste of his *or* her own medicine, give tit for tat, return like for like • *I was sorely tempted to retaliate.*
OPPOSITES: accept, submit, turn the other cheek

retaliation = **revenge**, repayment, vengeance, reprisal, retribution, tit for tat, an eye for an eye, reciprocation, counterstroke, requital, counterblow, a taste of your own medicine • *They believe the attack was in retaliation for his death.*

QUOTATIONS
The smallest worm will turn, being trodden on
[William Shakespeare *Henry VI, part III*]

retard = **slow down**, check, arrest, delay, handicap, stall, brake, detain, defer, clog, hinder, obstruct, impede, set back, encumber, decelerate, hold back *or* up • *Continuing violence will retard negotiations.*
OPPOSITES: advance, stimulate, speed up

retch = **gag**, be sick, vomit, regurgitate, chuck *(Austral. & N.Z. informal)*, throw up *(informal)*, spew, heave, puke *(slang)*, disgorge, barf *(U.S. slang)*, chunder *(slang, chiefly Austral.)*, upchuck *(U.S. slang)*, do a technicolour yawn *(slang)*, toss your cookies *(U.S. slang)* • *The smell made me retch.*

reticence = **silence**, reserve, restraint, quietness, secretiveness, taciturnity, uncommunicativeness, unforthcomingness • *She didn't mind his reticence.*

reticent = **uncommunicative**, reserved, secretive, unforthcoming, quiet, silent, restrained, taciturn, tight-lipped, unspeaking, close-lipped, mum • *She is so reticent about her achievements.*
OPPOSITES: open, frank, communicative

retinue = **attendants**, entourage, escort, servants, following, train, suite, aides, followers, cortege • *She left, followed by her retinue.*

retire 1 = **stop working**, give up work, reach retirement age, be pensioned off, (be) put out to grass *(informal)* • *In 1974 he retired.*
2 = **withdraw**, leave, remove, exit, go away, depart, absent yourself, betake yourself • *He retired from the room with his colleagues.*
3 = **go to bed**, turn in *(informal)*, go to sleep, hit the sack *(slang)*, go to your room, kip down *(Brit. slang)*, hit the hay *(slang)* • *She retires early most nights.*
4 = **retreat**, withdraw, pull out, give way, recede, pull back, back off, decamp, give ground • *He was wounded, but did not retire from the field.*

retired AS AN ADJECTIVE = **pensioned**, former, in retirement, pensioned off, superannuated, ex- • *a seventy-three-year-old retired teacher*
▸ IN PHRASES: **the retired** = **retired people**, pensioners, old people, the elderly, senior citizens, OAPs • *the skills and energies of the retired*

retirement 1 = **stopping work**, giving up work • *She'll soon be on her way to retirement.*
2 = **retired years**, post-work years • *financial help during retirement*
3 = **withdrawal**, retreat, privacy, loneliness, obscurity, solitude, seclusion • *retirement in the countryside*

r

retiring = **shy**, reserved, quiet, modest, shrinking, humble, timid, coy, meek, reclusive, reticent, unassuming, self-effacing, demure, diffident, bashful, aw-shucks, timorous, unassertive • *I'm still that shy, retiring little girl.*
OPPOSITES: forward, bold, outgoing

retort AS A VERB = **reply**, return, answer, respond, counter, rejoin, retaliate, come back with, riposte, answer back • *'Who do you think you're talking to?' she retorted.*
▸ AS A NOUN = **reply**, return, answer, response, counter, comeback, riposte, rejoinder • *His sharp retort made an impact.*

retract 1 = **withdraw**, take back, revoke, disown, deny, recall, reverse, cancel, repeal, renounce, go back on, repudiate, rescind, renege on, back out of, disavow, recant, disclaim, abjure, eat your words, unsay • *He hurriedly sought to retract the statement.*
2 = **draw in**, pull in, pull back, reel in, sheathe • *A cat in ecstasy will extend and retract his claws.*

retreat AS A VERB 1 = **withdraw**, retire, back off, draw back, leave, go back, shrink, depart, fall back, recede, pull back, back away, recoil, give ground, turn tail • *They were forced to retreat.*
OPPOSITES: advance, engage, move forward
2 = **climb down**, change your decision, backtrack, do a U-turn, reconsider, change your mind, flip-flop *(informal, chiefly U.S.)*, concede defeat, back-pedal, eat your words • *The Government had to retreat on student loans.*
3 = **ebb**, recede, flow out, go down, fall • *The tide retreats up to 500 yards on big springs.*
▸ AS A NOUN 1 = **flight**, retirement, departure, withdrawal, evacuation • *The army was in full retreat.*
OPPOSITES: charge, advance, entrance
2 = **climbdown**, about-turn *(Brit.)*, retraction, backdown, concession • *There will be no retreat from his position.*
3 = **refuge**, haven, resort, retirement, shelter, haunt, asylum, privacy, den, sanctuary, hideaway, seclusion • *He spent yesterday in his country retreat.*

retrench 1 = **economize**, save, cut back, make savings, scrimp and save, be frugal, make economies, make cutbacks, tighten your belt, husband • *Cuts in spending forced them to retrench.*
2 = **cut back**, cut, limit, reduce, trim, diminish, decrease, prune, lessen, curtail, pare • *It promised to retrench its London-based markets.*

retrenchment = **cutback**, cuts, economy, reduction, pruning, contraction, cost-cutting, rundown, curtailment, tightening your belt • *a need for economic retrenchment*
OPPOSITES: investment, expansion

retribution = **punishment**, retaliation, reprisal, redress, justice, reward, reckoning, compensation, satisfaction, revenge, repayment, vengeance, Nemesis, recompense, an eye for an eye, requital • *He decided to get his retribution in first.*

QUOTATIONS
Though the mills of God grind slowly, yet they grind
exceeding small;
Though with patience He stands waiting, with
exactness grinds He all
[Henry Wadsworth Longfellow *Retribution*]

retrieve 1 = **get back**, regain, repossess, fetch back, recall, recover, restore, recapture • *He retrieved his jacket from the seat.*
2 = **redeem**, save, rescue, repair, salvage, win back, recoup • *He could retrieve the situation.*

retro = **old-time**, old, former, past, period, antique, old-fashioned, nostalgia, old-world, bygone, of yesteryear • *original versions of today's retro looks*

retrograde = **deteriorating**, backward, regressive, retrogressive, declining, negative, reverse, retreating, worsening, downward, waning, relapsing, inverse, degenerative • *It would be a retrograde step to revert to the old system.*

retrospect = **hindsight**, review, afterthought, re-examination, survey, recollection, remembrance, reminiscence • *It was a strange feeling in retrospect.*
OPPOSITES: anticipation, foresight

retrospective AS A NOUN = **review**, revision, another look, reassessment, fresh look, second look, reconsideration, re-evaluation, re-examination • *They honoured him with a retrospective of his work.*
▸ AS AN ADJECTIVE = **retroactive**, backdated, backward-looking • *a retrospective fear of the responsibility she had taken on*

return AS A VERB 1 = **come back**, go back, repair, retreat, turn back, revert, reappear • *More than 350,000 people have returned home.*
OPPOSITES: leave, disappear, depart
2 = **put back**, replace, restore, render, transmit, convey, send back, reinstate, take back, give back, carry back, retrocede • *The car was not returned on time.*
OPPOSITES: leave, keep, hold
3 = **give back**, repay, refund, pay back, remit, reimburse, recompense • *They promised to return the money.*
OPPOSITES: leave, keep, hold
4 = **reciprocate**, requite, feel in return, respond to • *Her feelings are not returned.*
5 = **recur**, come back, repeat, persist, revert, happen again, reappear, come and go, come again • *The pain returned in waves.*
6 = **announce**, report, come to, deliver, arrive at, bring in, submit, render • *They returned a verdict of not guilty.*
7 = **earn**, make, net, yield, bring in, repay • *The business returned a handsome profit.*
OPPOSITES: lose
8 = **elect**, choose, pick, vote in • *He has been returned as leader of the party.*
▸ AS A NOUN 1 = **reappearance**, coming back to, homecoming • *his sudden return to London*
OPPOSITES: leaving, departure
2 = **restoration**, replacement, reinstatement, re-establishment • *Their demand was for the return of acres of forest.*
OPPOSITES: removal
3 = **recurrence**, repetition, reappearance, reversion, persistence • *It was like the return of his youth.*
4 = **profit**, interest, benefit, gain, income, advantage, revenue, yield, proceeds, takings, boot *(dialect)* • *They have seen no return on their investment.*
5 = **repayment**, reward, compensation, reparation, reimbursement, recompense, reciprocation, requital, retaliation, meed *(archaic)* • *What do I get in return for taking part in your experiment?*
6 = **statement**, report, form, list, account, summary • *a new analysis of the census returns*

revamp = **renovate**, restore, overhaul, refurbish, rehabilitate, do up *(informal)*, patch up, refit, repair, fix up *(informal, chiefly U.S. & Canad.)*, recondition, give a face-lift to • *It's a good time to revamp your kitchen.*

reveal 1 = **make known**, disclose, give away, make public, tell, announce, publish, broadcast, leak, communicate, proclaim, betray, give out, let out, impart, divulge, let slip, let on, take the wraps off *(informal)*, blow wide open *(slang)*, get off your chest *(informal)* • *She has refused to reveal her daughter's whereabouts.*
OPPOSITES: keep secret, hide, conceal
2 = **show**, display, bare, exhibit, unveil, uncover, manifest, unearth, unmask, lay bare, bring to light, expose to view • *A grey carpet was removed to reveal the pine floor.*
OPPOSITES: hide, conceal, cover up

revel AS A VERB = **celebrate**, rave *(Brit. slang)*, carouse, live it up *(informal)*, push the boat out *(Brit. informal)*, whoop it up (informal), make merry, paint the town red *(informal)*, large it *(Brit. slang)*, go on a spree, roister • *I'm afraid I revelled the night away.*

▸ **AS A NOUN** *often plural* = **merrymaking**, party, celebration, rave *(Brit. slang)*, gala, spree, festivity, beano *(Brit. slang)*, debauch, saturnalia, bacchanal, rave-up *(Brit. slang)*, jollification, carousal, hooley *or* hoolie *(chiefly Irish & N.Z.)*, carouse • *The revels often last until dawn.*

▸ **IN PHRASES: revel in something** = **enjoy**, relish, indulge in, delight in, savour, thrive on, bask in, wallow in, lap up, take pleasure in, drool over, luxuriate in, crow about, rejoice over, gloat about, rub your hands • *She revelled in her freedom.*

revelation 1 = **disclosure**, discovery, news, broadcast, exposé, announcement, publication, exposure, leak, uncovering, confession, divulgence • *revelations about his private life*
2 = **exhibition**, telling, communication, broadcasting, discovery, publication, exposure, leaking, unveiling, uncovering, manifestation, unearthing, giveaway, proclamation, exposition • *the revelation of his private life*
3 = **sign**, warning, omen, portent, presage, forewarning, writing on the wall • *The whole system was based on a divine revelation.*

reveller = **merrymaker**, carouser, pleasure-seeker, partygoer, roisterer, celebrator • *Many of the revellers are tourists.*

revelry = **merrymaking**, partying, fun, celebration, rave *(Brit. slang)*, spree, festivity, beano *(Brit. slang)*, debauch, debauchery, carouse, jollity, saturnalia, roistering, rave-up *(Brit. slang)*, jollification, carousal, hooley *or* hoolie *(chiefly Irish & N.Z.)* • *The sounds of revelry are getting louder.*

revenge **AS A NOUN** = **retaliation**, satisfaction, vengeance, reprisal, retribution, vindictiveness, an eye for an eye, requital • *in revenge for the murder of her lover*

▸ **AS A VERB** = **avenge**, repay, vindicate, pay (someone) back, take revenge for, requite, even the score for, get your own back for *(informal)*, make reprisal for, take an eye for an eye for • *The relatives wanted to revenge the dead man's murder.*

QUOTATIONS

An eye for an eye, a tooth for a tooth
[Bible: Exodus]

Revenge is a kind of wild justice, which the more man's nature runs to, the more ought law to weed it out
[Francis Bacon *Essays*]

Sweet is revenge – especially to women
[Lord Byron *Don Juan*]

PROVERBS

Revenge is a dish best served cold
Don't get mad, get even
Revenge is sweet

revenue = **income**, interest, returns, profits, gain, rewards, yield, proceeds, receipts, takings • *They wanted a big share of the revenue from the mine.*
OPPOSITES: expenses, expenditure, outgoings

reverberate = **echo**, ring, resound, vibrate, re-echo • *A woman's laughter reverberated in the courtyard.*

reverberation 1 *usually plural* = **consequence**, result, effect, event, outcome, repercussion, end result, upshot • *The statement is likely to have strong reverberations.*
2 = **echo**, ringing, resonance, resounding, vibration, re-echoing • *He heard the reverberation of the slammed door.*

revere = **be in awe of**, respect, honour, worship, adore, reverence, exalt, look up to, defer to, venerate, have a high opinion of, put on a pedestal, think highly of • *Those who support him revere him.*
OPPOSITES: despise, scorn, deride

reverence **AS A NOUN** = **respect**, honour, worship, admiration, awe, devotion, homage, deference, adoration, veneration, high esteem • *in mutual support and reverence for the dead*
OPPOSITES: contempt, scorn, disdain

▸ **AS A VERB** = **revere**, respect, honour, admire, worship, adore, pay homage to, venerate, be in awe of, hold in awe • *Some men even seem to reverence them.*

reverent = **respectful**, awed, solemn, deferential, loving, humble, adoring, devout, pious, meek, submissive, reverential • *the reverent hush of a rapt audience*
OPPOSITES: mocking, cheeky, disrespectful

reverie = **daydream**, musing, preoccupation, trance, abstraction, daydreaming, inattention, absent-mindedness, brown study, woolgathering, castles in the air *or* Spain • *The voice brought him out of his reverie.*

reversal 1 = **turnaround**, U-turn, backtracking, turnabout, shift, swing, change of heart, turnround, volte-face, paradigm shift • *the reversal of a steady downward trend*
2 = **change**, overturning, setting aside, undoing, repeal, quashing, overruling, rescinding, retraction, revocation, abrogation, veto • *a striking reversal of policy*
3 = **swap**, change, trading, exchange, swapping, transposition • *a strange role reversal*
4 = **failure**, failing, loss, defeat, frustration, breakdown, downfall, lack of success • *They teach managers to accept reversal.*

reverse **AS A VERB** 1 = **change**, alter, cancel, overturn, overthrow, set aside, undo, repeal, quash, revoke, overrule, retract, negate, rescind, invalidate, annul, obviate, countermand, declare null and void, overset, upset • *They have made it clear they will not reverse the decision.*
OPPOSITES: carry out, implement, enforce
2 = **turn round**, turn over, upturn, turn upside down, upend • *The curve of the spine may be reversed under such circumstances.*
3 = **transpose**, change, move, exchange, transfer, switch, shift, alter, swap, relocate, rearrange, invert, interchange, reorder • *He reversed the position of the two stamps.*
4 = **go backwards**, retreat, back up, turn back, backtrack, move backwards, back • *He reversed and drove away.*
OPPOSITES: advance, move forward, go forward

▸ **AS A NOUN** 1 = **opposite**, contrary, converse, antithesis, inverse, contradiction • *There is absolutely no evidence. Quite the reverse.*
2 = **misfortune**, check, defeat, blow, failure, disappointment, setback, hardship, reversal, adversity, mishap, affliction, repulse, trial, misadventure, vicissitude • *They have suffered a major reverse.*
3 = **back**, rear, other side, wrong side, underside, flip side, verso • *on the reverse of the coin*
OPPOSITES: front, right side, obverse

▸ **AS AN ADJECTIVE** 1 = **opposite**, contrary, converse, inverse • *The wrong attitude will have the reverse effect.*
2 = **backward**, reversed, inverted, transposed, back to front • *We will take them in reverse order.*

revert 1 = **go back**, return, come back, resume, lapse, recur, relapse, regress, backslide, take up where you left off • *He reverted to smoking heavily.*
2 = **return**, go back to, be returned to, be once again in the possession of • *The property reverts to the freeholder.*

review **AS A NOUN** 1 = **re-examination**, revision, rethink, retrospect, another look, reassessment, fresh look, second look, reconsideration, re-evaluation, recapitulation • *She has announced a review of adoption laws.*
2 = **survey**, report, study, analysis, examination, scrutiny, perusal • *a review on the training and education of over-16s*
3 = **critique**, commentary, evaluation, critical assessment, study, notice, criticism, judgment • *We've never had a good review in the press.*
4 = **inspection**, display, parade, procession, march past • *an early morning review of the troops*
5 = **magazine**, journal, periodical, zine *(informal)* • *He was recruited to write for the Edinburgh Review.*

▸ **AS A VERB 1 = reconsider**, revise, rethink, run over, reassess, re-examine, re-evaluate, think over, take another look at, recapitulate, look at again, go over again • *The next day we reviewed the previous day's work.*
2 = assess, write a critique of, study, judge, discuss, weigh, evaluate, criticize, read through, give your opinion of • *I see that no papers have reviewed my book.*
3 = inspect, check, survey, examine, vet, check out (*informal*), scrutinize, give (something *or* someone) the once-over (*informal*) • *He reviewed the troops.*
4 = look back on, remember, recall, reflect on, summon up, recollect, call to mind • *Review all the information you need.*

reviewer = critic, judge, commentator, connoisseur, arbiter, essayist • *the reviewer for the Times Literary Supplement*

revile = malign, abuse, knock (*informal*), rubbish (*informal*), run down, smear, libel, scorn, slag (off) (*slang*), reproach, denigrate, vilify, slander, defame, bad-mouth (*slang, chiefly U.S. & Canad.*), traduce, calumniate, vituperate, asperse • *What right had the crowd to revile them?*

revise 1 = change, review, modify, reconsider, re-examine • *He soon came to revise his opinion.*
2 = edit, correct, alter, update, amend, rewrite, revamp, rework, redo, rebrand, emend • *Three editors handled revising the articles.*
3 = study, go over, run through, cram (*informal*), memorize, reread, swot up on (*Brit. informal*) • *I have to revise maths tonight.*

revision 1 = emendation, editing, updating, correction, rewriting • *The phase of writing that is important is revision.*
2 = change, review, amendment, modification, alteration, re-examination • *The government will make a number of revisions.*
3 = studying, cramming (*informal*), memorizing, swotting (*Brit. informal*), rereading, homework • *They prefer to do their revision at home.*

revitalize = reanimate, restore, renew, refresh, resurrect, rejuvenate, breathe new life into, bring back to life, revivify • *The hot, strong liquid seemed to revitalize her.*

revival 1 = resurgence, picking up, improvement, rallying, comeback, upswing, turn for the better • *There is no chance of a revival in car sales.*
OPPOSITES: decline, falling off, disappearance
2 = reawakening, restoration, renaissance, renewal, awakening, resurrection, refreshment, quickening, rebirth, resuscitation, revitalization, recrudescence, reanimation, renascence, revivification • *a revival of nationalism and the rudiments of democracy*

revive 1 = revitalize, restore, rally, renew, renovate, rekindle, kick-start (*informal*), breathe new life into, invigorate, reanimate • *an attempt to revive the economy*
2 = bring round, awaken, animate, rouse, resuscitate, bring back to life • *They tried in vain to revive him.*
3 = come round, recover, quicken, spring up again • *After three days in a coma, he revived.*
4 = refresh, restore, comfort, cheer, renew, resurrect, rejuvenate, revitalize, reinvigorate, revivify • *Superb food and drink revived our little band.*
OPPOSITES: exhaust, weary, tire out

revoke = cancel, recall, withdraw, reverse, abolish, set aside, repeal, renounce, quash, take back, call back, retract, repudiate, negate, renege, rescind, invalidate, annul, nullify, recant, obviate, disclaim, abrogate, countermand, declare null and void • *The government revoked his licence.*
OPPOSITES: maintain, confirm, endorse

revolt AS A NOUN = uprising, rising, revolution, riot, rebellion, uprising, mutiny, defection, insurrection, subversion, insurgency, putsch, sedition, insurgence • *a revolt by ordinary people against the leaders*
▸ **AS A VERB 1 = rebel**, rise up, resist, defect, mutiny, take to the streets, take up arms (against) • *The townspeople revolted.*
2 = disgust, offend, turn off (*informal*), sicken, repel, repulse, nauseate, gross out (*U.S. slang*), shock, turn your stomach, make your flesh creep, give you the creeps (*informal*) • *He entirely revolts me.*

revolting = disgusting, shocking, offensive, appalling, nasty, foul, horrible, obscene, sickening, distasteful, horrid, repellent, obnoxious, repulsive, nauseating, repugnant, loathsome, abhorrent, abominable, nauseous, cringe-making (*Brit. informal*), noisome, yucky *or* yukky (*slang*), yucko (*Austral. slang*) • *The smell in the cell was revolting.*
OPPOSITES: attractive, pleasant, delightful

revolution 1 = revolt, rising, coup, rebellion, uprising, mutiny, insurgency, coup d'état, putsch • *after the French Revolution*
2 = transformation, shift, innovation, upheaval, reformation, metamorphosis, sea change, drastic *or* radical change • *a revolution in ship design and propulsion*
3 = rotation, turn, cycle, circle, wheel, spin, lap, circuit, orbit, whirl, gyration, round • *The gear drives a wheel 1/10 revolution per cycle.*

revolutionary AS AN ADJECTIVE 1 = rebel, radical, extremist, subversive, insurgent, seditious, mutinous, insurrectionary • *Do you know anything about the revolutionary movement?*
OPPOSITES: loyalist, reactionary, counter-revolutionary
2 = innovative, new, different, novel, radical, fundamental, progressive, experimental, drastic, avant-garde, ground-breaking, thoroughgoing • *His trumpet-playing was quite revolutionary.*
OPPOSITES: conservative, traditional, conventional
▸ **AS A NOUN = rebel**, insurgent, mutineer, insurrectionary, revolutionist, insurrectionist • *The revolutionaries laid down their arms.*
OPPOSITES: loyalist, reactionary, counter-revolutionary

QUOTATIONS
The most radical revolutionary will become a conservative on the day after the revolution
[Hannah Arendt]

revolutionize = transform, reform, restructure, revamp, modernize, reshape, metamorphose, break with the past, remould • *Plastics have revolutionized the way we live.*

revolve 1 = be concerned with, focus on, concentrate on, hang on, centre around, be absorbed in, pivot on • *Her life has revolved around tennis.*
2 = go round, circle, orbit, gyrate • *The satellite revolves around the earth.*
3 = rotate, turn, wheel, spin, twist, whirl • *The entire circle revolved slowly.*
4 = consider, study, reflect, think about, deliberate, ponder, turn over (in your mind), meditate, mull over, think over, ruminate • *He revolved the new notion dizzily in his mind.*

revue = show, production, entertainment, presentation • *the West End success of the revue 'Five Guys Named Moe'*

revulsion = disgust, loathing, distaste, aversion, recoil, abomination, repulsion, abhorrence, repugnance, odium, detestation • *His voice was filled with revulsion.*
OPPOSITES: liking, desire, pleasure

reward AS A NOUN 1 = prize, honour, decoration, recompense, winnings • *He earned his reward for contributions to the struggle.*
2 = punishment, desert, retribution, comeuppance (*slang*), just deserts, requital • *He'll get his reward before long.*
3 = payment, return, benefit, profit, gain, prize, wages, honour, compensation, bonus, premium, merit, repayment, bounty, remuneration, recompense, meed (*archaic*), requital • *They last night offered a £10,000 reward.*
OPPOSITES: fine, penalty, punishment
▸ **AS A VERB = compensate**, pay, honour, repay, recompense, requite, remunerate, make it worth your while • *Their generosity will be rewarded.*
OPPOSITES: fine, punish, penalize

rewarding = **satisfying**, fulfilling, gratifying, edifying, economic, pleasing, valuable, profitable, productive, worthwhile, beneficial, enriching, fruitful, advantageous, gainful, remunerative • *a career which she found rewarding*
OPPOSITES: boring, vain, unrewarding

reword = **put in other words**, paraphrase, recast, rephrase, put another way, express differently • *I'll reword my question.*

rewrite = **revise**, correct, edit, recast, touch up, redraft, emend • *students rewrite their papers and submit them*

rhetoric 1 = **hyperbole**, rant, hot air *(informal)*, pomposity, bombast, wordiness, verbosity, fustian, grandiloquence, magniloquence • *He has continued his warlike rhetoric.*
2 = **oratory**, eloquence, public speaking, speech-making, elocution, declamation, speechifying, grandiloquence, spieling *(informal)*, whaikorero *(N.Z.)* • *the noble institutions, such as political rhetoric*

rhetorical 1 = **oratorical**, verbal, linguistic, stylistic • *a rhetorical device used to emphasize moments in the text*
2 = **high-flown**, flamboyant, windy, flashy, pompous, pretentious, flowery, showy, florid, bombastic, hyperbolic, verbose, oratorical, grandiloquent, high-sounding, declamatory, arty-farty *(informal)*, silver-tongued, magniloquent • *He disgorges a stream of rhetorical flourishes.*

rhyme AS A NOUN = **poem**, song, verse, ode, ditty, piece of poetry, metrical composition • *He has taught her a little rhyme.*
▸ **IN PHRASES: rhyme or reason** *used in negative constructions* = **sense**, meaning, plan, planning, system, method, pattern, logic • *He picked people without rhyme or reason.*

rhythm 1 = **beat**, swing, accent, pulse, tempo, cadence, lilt • *His music fused the rhythms of jazz and classical music.*
2 = **metre**, time, measure *(Prosody)*, stress, flow, cadence • *the rhythm and rhyme inherent in nursery rhymes*
3 = **pattern**, movement, flow, periodicity, recurrent nature • *This is the rhythm of the universe.*

QUOTATIONS
It Don't Mean a Thing if it Ain't Got that Swing
[Duke Ellington *song title*]

rhythmic *or* **rhythmical** = **cadenced**, throbbing, periodic, pulsating, flowing, musical, harmonious, lilting, melodious, metrical • *the rhythmical beat of the drum*

rib
▸ **TECHNICAL NAME:** costa
▸ **RELATED ADJECTIVE:** costal

ribald = **coarse**, rude, indecent, racy, blue, broad, gross, naughty, obscene, filthy, vulgar, raunchy *(slang)*, earthy, risqué, X-rated *(informal)*, bawdy, scurrilous, smutty, off colour, licentious, near the knuckle *(informal)*, Rabelaisian • *her ribald comments about a guest's body language*
OPPOSITES: decent, proper, refined

rice
▹ *See panel* **Rice and other cereals**

rich 1 = **wealthy**, affluent, well-off, opulent, propertied, rolling *(slang)*, loaded *(slang)*, flush *(informal)*, prosperous, well-heeled *(informal)*, well-to-do, moneyed, filthy rich, stinking rich *(informal)*, made of money *(informal)*, minted *(Brit. slang)* • *You're going to be a very rich man.*
OPPOSITES: poor, impoverished, needy
2 = **well-stocked**, full, productive, ample, abundant, plentiful, copious, well-provided, well-supplied, plenteous • *a rich supply of fresh, clean water*
OPPOSITES: wanting, poor, scarce
3 = **full-bodied**, heavy, sweet, delicious, fatty, tasty, creamy, spicy, juicy, luscious, savoury, succulent, flavoursome, highly-flavoured • *the hearty rich foods of Gascony*
OPPOSITES: dull, bland
4 = **fruitful**, productive, fertile, prolific, arable, fecund • *Farmers grow rice in the rich soil.*
OPPOSITES: poor, barren, unproductive
5 = **abounding**, full, packed, crammed, luxurious, lush, abundant, exuberant, replete, well-endowed • *The bees buzzed around a garden rich with flowers.*
6 = **resonant**, full, deep, ringing, mellow, mellifluous, dulcet • *He spoke in that deep rich voice which made them all swoon.*
OPPOSITES: high-pitched
7 = **vivid**, strong, deep, warm, bright, intense, vibrant, gay • *an attractive, glossy rich red colour*
OPPOSITES: weak, dull, insipid
8 = **costly**, fine, expensive, valuable, superb, elegant, precious, elaborate, splendid, gorgeous, lavish, exquisite, sumptuous, priceless, palatial, beyond price • *This is a Baroque church with a rich interior.*
OPPOSITES: cheap, inexpensive, worthless
9 = **funny**, amusing, ridiculous, hilarious, ludicrous, humorous, laughable, comical, risible, side-splitting • *That's rich, coming from him.*

QUOTATIONS
Let me tell you about the very rich. They are different from you and me
[F. Scott Fitzgerald *The Rich Boy*]
I am rich beyond the dreams of avarice
[Edward Moore *The Gamester*]
It is easier for a camel to go through the eye of a needle than for a rich man to enter into the kingdom of God
[*Bible: St. Matthew*]

riches 1 = **wealth**, money, property, gold, assets, plenty, fortune, substance, treasure, abundance, richness, affluence, opulence, top dollar *(informal)*, top whack *(informal)* • *Some people want fame or riches.*
OPPOSITES: want, need, poverty
2 = **resources**, stocks, stores, treasures • *Russia's vast natural riches*

QUOTATIONS
The chief enjoyment of riches consists in the parade of riches
[Adam Smith *Wealth of Nations*]
Riches are a good handmaid, but the worst mistress
[Francis Bacon *De Dignitate et Augmentis Scientiarum*]

richly 1 = **elaborately**, lavishly, elegantly, splendidly, exquisitely, expensively, luxuriously, gorgeously, sumptuously, opulently, palatially • *The rooms are richly decorated.*
2 = **fully**, well, thoroughly, amply, appropriately, properly, suitably, in full measure • *He achieved the success he so richly deserved.*

rickety = **shaky**, broken, weak, broken-down, frail, insecure, feeble, precarious, derelict, flimsy, wobbly, imperfect, tottering, ramshackle, dilapidated, decrepit, unsteady, unsound, infirm, jerry-built • *She climbed the rickety wooden stairway.*

r

RICE AND OTHER CEREALS

arborio rice	bulgur wheat	long grain rice	oats	short grain rice
basmati rice	corn	maize	Patna rice	tapioca
bran	couscous	millet	ragi	wheat
brown rice	Indian rice	oatmeal	sago	wild rice

rid AS A VERB = **free**, clear, deliver, relieve, purge, lighten, unburden, disabuse, make free, disembarrass, disencumber, disburden • *an attempt to rid the country of corruption*
▸ IN PHRASES: **get rid of something** *or* **someone** = **dispose of**, throw away *or* out, dispense with, dump, remove, eliminate, expel, unload, shake off, eject, do away with, jettison, weed out, see the back of, wipe from the face of the earth, give the bum's rush to *(slang)* • *The owner needs to get rid of the car.*

riddle[1] 1 = **puzzle**, problem, conundrum, teaser, poser, rebus, brain-teaser *(informal)*, Chinese puzzle • *Tell me a riddle.*
2 = **enigma**, question, secret, mystery, puzzle, conundrum, teaser, problem • *a riddle of modern architecture*

riddle[2] 1 = **pierce**, pepper, puncture, perforate, honeycomb • *Attackers riddled two homes with gunfire.*
2 = **pervade**, fill, take over, plague, saturate, overrun, beset, imbue, spread through, mar, spoil, corrupt, impair, pervade, infest, permeate • *She was found to be riddled with cancer.* • *The report was riddled with errors.*

ride AS A VERB 1 = **control**, be mounted on, handle, sit on, manage, steer • *I saw a girl riding a horse.*
2 = **travel**, be carried, be supported, be borne, go, move, sit, progress, journey • *I was riding on the back of a friend's bicycle.*
▸ AS A NOUN = **journey**, drive, trip, lift, spin *(informal)*, outing, whirl *(informal)*, jaunt • *Would you like to go for a ride?*
▸ IN PHRASES: **ride something out** = **survive**, last, live through, hold out against • *They managed to ride out the political storm.*

rider = **horse-rider**, jockey, equestrian, horseman, horsewoman • *A rider came towards us.*

ridge = **crest**, bank, rise, fell, scar, escarpment • *In some places the ridge is quite a gentle feature.*

ridicule AS A VERB = **laugh at**, mock, make fun of, make a fool of, humiliate, taunt, sneer at, parody, caricature, jeer at, scoff at, deride, send up *(Brit. informal)*, lampoon, poke fun at, take the piss (out of) *(taboo slang)*, chaff, take the mickey out of *(informal)*, satirize, pooh-pooh, laugh out of court, make a monkey out of, make someone a laughing stock, laugh to scorn • *I admire her for allowing them to ridicule her.*
▸ AS A NOUN = **mockery**, scorn, derision, laughter, irony, rib, taunting, sneer, satire, jeer, banter, sarcasm, chaff, gibe, raillery • *He was subjected to public ridicule.*
▸ RELATED PHOBIA: katagelophobia

r

ridiculous = **laughable**, stupid, incredible, silly, outrageous, absurd, foolish, unbelievable, hilarious, ludicrous, preposterous, farcical, comical, zany, nonsensical, derisory, inane, risible, contemptible, cockamamie *(slang, chiefly U.S.)* • *It was an absolutely ridiculous decision.*
OPPOSITES: serious, bright, sensible

QUOTATIONS

It is only one step from the sublime to the ridiculous
[Napoleon Bonaparte]

The sublime and the ridiculous are often so nearly related, that it is difficult to class them separately. One step above the sublime makes the ridiculous; and one step above the ridiculous makes the sublime again
[Thomas Paine *The Age of Reason*]

rife 1 = **widespread**, abundant, plentiful, rampant, general, common, current, raging, universal, frequent, prevailing, epidemic, prevalent, ubiquitous • *Speculation is rife that he'll be sacked.*
2 *usually with* **with** = **abounding**, full, alive, bursting, swarming, seething, teeming • *Hollywood soon became rife with rumours.*

riff-raff = **rabble**, undesirables, scum, hoi polloi, dregs of society, canaille *(French)*, ragtag and bobtail • *That helps to keep out the riff-raff.*

rifle 1 = **rummage**, go, search, hunt, rake, sift, forage, fossick *(Austral. & N.Z.)* • *The men rifled through his clothing.*
2 = **ransack**, rob, burgle, loot, strip, sack, gut, plunder, pillage, despoil • *The child rifled the till while her mother distracted the postmistress.*

rift 1 = **breach**, difference, division, split, separation, falling out *(informal)*, disagreement, quarrel, alienation, schism, estrangement • *They hope to heal the rift with their father.*
2 = **split**, opening, space, crack, gap, break, fault, breach, fracture, flaw, cleavage, cleft, chink, crevice, fissure, cranny • *In the open bog are many rifts and potholes.*

rig AS A VERB 1 = **fix**, doctor, engineer *(informal)*, arrange, fake, manipulate, juggle, tamper with, fiddle with *(informal)*, falsify, trump up, gerrymander • *She accused her opponents of rigging the vote.*
2 = **equip**, fit out, kit out, outfit, supply, turn out, provision, furnish, accoutre • *He had rigged the dinghy for a sail.*
▸ IN PHRASES: **rig something up** = **set up**, build, construct, put up, arrange, assemble, put together, erect, improvise, fix up, throw together, cobble together • *I rigged up a shelter with a tarpaulin.*

right AS AN ADJECTIVE 1 = **correct**, true, genuine, accurate, exact, precise, valid, authentic, satisfactory, spot-on *(Brit. informal)*, factual, on the money *(U.S.)*, unerring, admissible, dinkum *(Austral. & N.Z. informal)*, veracious, sound • *That's absolutely right!*
OPPOSITES: wrong, mistaken, illegal
2 = **proper**, done, becoming, seemly, fitting, fit, appropriate, suitable, desirable, comme il faut *(French)* • *Make sure you approach it in the right way.*
OPPOSITES: wrong, inappropriate, unfitting
3 = **favourable**, due, ideal, convenient, rightful, advantageous, opportune, propitious • *at the right time in the right place*
OPPOSITES: inconvenient, unfavourable, disadvantageous
4 = **just**, good, fair, moral, proper, ethical, upright, honourable, honest, equitable, righteous, virtuous, lawful • *It's not right, leaving her like this.*
OPPOSITES: bad, wrong, unfair
5 = **sane**, sound, balanced, normal, reasonable, rational, all there *(informal)*, lucid, unimpaired, compos mentis *(Latin)* • *I think he's not right in the head actually.*
6 = **healthy**, well, fine, fit, in good health, in the pink, up to par • *He just didn't look right.*
OPPOSITES: unwell, abnormal, unsound
7 = **complete**, real, pure, absolute, utter, outright, thorough, out-and-out, thoroughgoing • *He gave them a right telling off.*
▸ AS AN ADVERB 1 = **correctly**, truly, precisely, exactly, genuinely, accurately, factually, aright • *He guessed right about some things.*
OPPOSITES: incorrectly, inaccurately, wrongly
2 = **suitably**, fittingly, appropriately, properly, aptly, satisfactorily, befittingly • *They made sure I did everything right.*
OPPOSITES: improperly, incompletely
3 = **exactly**, squarely, precisely, bang, slap-bang *(informal)* • *It caught me right in the middle of the forehead.*
4 = **directly**, straight, precisely, exactly, unswervingly, without deviation, by the shortest route, in a beeline • *It was taken right there on a conveyor belt*
5 = **all the way**, completely, totally, perfectly, entirely, absolutely, altogether, thoroughly, wholly, utterly, quite • *The candle had burned right down.*
6 = **straight**, directly, immediately, quickly, promptly, instantly, straightaway, without delay • *She'll be right down.*
OPPOSITES: slowly, indirectly
7 = **properly**, fittingly, fairly, morally, honestly, justly, ethically, honourably, righteously, virtuously • *If you're not treated right, let us know.*
8 = **favourably**, well, fortunately, for the better, to advantage, beneficially, advantageously • *I hope things will turn out right.*

OPPOSITES: badly, poorly, unfavourably
▸ **AS A NOUN** 1 = **prerogative**, interest, business, power, claim, authority, title, due, freedom, licence, permission, liberty, privilege • *a woman's right to choose*
2 = **justice**, good, reason, truth, honour, equity, virtue, integrity, goodness, morality, fairness, legality, righteousness, propriety, rectitude, lawfulness, uprightness • *a fight between right and wrong*
OPPOSITES: injustice, evil, impropriety
▸ **AS A VERB** 1 = **rectify**, settle, fix, correct, repair, sort out, compensate for, straighten, redress, vindicate, put right • *We've made progress in righting the wrongs of the past.*
2 = **turn up the right way again**, stand upright again, set upright again, turn back over • *He righted the yacht and continued to race.*
OPPOSITES: topple, make crooked
▸ **IN PHRASES: by rights** = **in fairness**, properly, technically, justly, equitably • *Negotiations should, by rights, have been conducted by him.*
in the right = **vindicated**, right, justified, borne out, with the law on your side • *The Foreign Secretary is in the right.*
put something right = **correct**, right, improve, reform, square, fix, repair, adjust, remedy, amend, make good, mend, redress, put right, set the record straight, emend • *If you mess up it's your job to put it right.*
put something to rights = **order**, fix, arrange, solve, resolve, sort out, remedy, make good, retrieve, rectify, put right, straighten out, set right • *He decided to put matters to rights.*
within your rights = **at liberty**, allowed, qualified, entitled, authorized, within the law • *You were quite within your rights to refuse.*
▸ **RELATED ADJECTIVE:** dextral

QUOTATIONS
We hold these truths to be self-evident: that all men are created equal; that they are endowed by their Creator with inalienable rights; that among these are life, liberty, and the pursuit of happiness
[Thomas Jefferson *The Declaration of Independence*]
How forcible are right words
[*Bible: Job*]

right angle
▸ **RELATED ADJECTIVE:** orthogonal

right away = **immediately**, now, directly, promptly, instantly, at once, right off, straightaway, without delay, without hesitation, straight off *(informal)*, forthwith, pronto *(informal)*, this instant, posthaste • *He wants to see you right away.*

righteous 1 = **virtuous**, good, just, fair, moral, pure, ethical, upright, honourable, honest, equitable, law-abiding, squeaky-clean, blameless • *He concluded that it was impossible to find one righteous man.*
OPPOSITES: bad, guilty, wicked
2 = **justified**, just, valid, legitimate, understandable, rightful, well founded, defensible, supportable • *He was full of righteous indignation.*

righteousness = **virtue**, justice, honour, equity, integrity, goodness, morality, honesty, purity, probity, rectitude, faithfulness, uprightness, blamelessness, ethicalness • *adopting a tone of moral righteousness*

rightful = **lawful**, just, real, true, due, legal, suitable, proper, valid, legitimate, authorized, bona fide, de jure • *The car must be returned to its rightful owner.*

right-wing = **conservative**, Tory, traditionalist, reactionary, rightist, unprogressive • *right-wing ideas*
OPPOSITES: left, liberal, left-wing

rigid 1 = **strict**, set, fixed, exact, rigorous, stringent, austere, severe • *Hospital routines for nurses are very rigid.*
OPPOSITES: soft, flexible, tolerant
2 = **inflexible**, harsh, stern, adamant, uncompromising, unrelenting, unyielding, intransigent, unbending, invariable, unalterable, undeviating • *My father is very rigid in his thinking.*
3 = **stiff**, inflexible, hard, firm, taut, unbending, inelastic • *rigid plastic containers*
OPPOSITES: soft, yielding, pliable

rigmarole 1 = **procedure**, to-do, performance *(informal)*, bother, carry-on *(informal, chiefly Brit.)*, nonsense, fuss, hassle *(informal)*, red tape, pantomime *(informal)*, palaver • *Then the whole rigmarole starts over again!*
2 = **twaddle**, story, saga, trash, jargon, yarn, gibberish, spiel *(informal)*, balderdash • *He gave me some rigmarole about the train being late.*

rigorous 1 = **strict**, hard, firm, demanding, challenging, tough, severe, exacting, harsh, stern, rigid, stringent, austere, inflexible • *rigorous military training*
OPPOSITES: kind, easy, soft
2 = **thorough**, meticulous, painstaking, scrupulous, nice, accurate, exact, precise, conscientious, punctilious • *He is rigorous in his control of expenditure.*
OPPOSITES: careless, inaccurate, sloppy

rigour 1 *often plural* = **ordeal**, suffering, trial, hardship, privation • *the rigours of childbirth*
2 = **strictness**, austerity, rigidity, firmness, hardness, harshness, inflexibility, stringency, asperity, sternness • *We need to address such challenging issues with rigour.*
3 = **thoroughness**, accuracy, precision, exactitude, exactness, conscientiousness, meticulousness, punctiliousness, preciseness • *His work is built round academic rigour and years of insight.*

rig-out *or* **rigout** = **outfit**, dress, clothing, gear *(informal)*, get-up *(informal)*, costume, apparel, clobber *(Brit. slang)*, garb, togs, raiment *(archaic or poetic)*, habit • *the regulation punk rigout of leather jacket and torn jeans*

rile = **anger**, upset, provoke, bug *(informal)*, annoy, irritate, aggravate *(informal)*, gall, nettle, vex, irk, pique, peeve *(informal)*, get under your skin *(informal)*, get on your nerves *(informal)*, nark *(Brit., Austral. & N.Z. slang)*, piss you off *(taboo slang)*, get your goat *(slang)*, try your patience, rub you up the wrong way, get *or* put your back up, hack you off *(informal)* • *Cancellations rarely riled him.*

rim 1 = **edge**, lip, brim, flange • *She looked at him over the rim of her glass.*
2 = **border**, edge, trim, circumference • *a round mirror with white metal rim*
3 = **margin**, border, bound, boundary, verge, brink, perimeter, periphery, extremity • *round the eastern rim of the Mediterranean*

rind 1 = **skin**, peel, outer layer, epicarp • *grated lemon rind*
2 = **crust**, covering, shell, husk, integument • *Cut off the rind of the cheese*

ring[1] **AS A VERB** 1 = **phone**, call, telephone, buzz *(informal, chiefly Brit.)*, give someone a call, get on the phone to, give someone a bell *(informal)*, give someone a tinkle *(informal)*, reach • *He rang me at my mother's.*
2 = **chime**, sound, toll, resound, resonate, reverberate, clang, peal • *He heard the school bell ring.*
3 = **reverberate**, echo, resound, resonate • *The whole place was ringing with music.*
▸ **AS A NOUN** 1 = **call**, phone call, buzz *(informal, chiefly Brit.)*, tinkle • *We'll give him a ring as soon as we get back.*
2 = **chime**, toll, jingle, ding, tinkle, knell, peal, dinging • *There was a ring of the bell.*
▸ **IN PHRASES: ring something in** = **celebrate**, announce, introduce, proclaim, herald, usher in • *Ring in the New Year someplace really special!*

ring[2] **AS A NOUN** 1 = **circle**, round, band, circuit, loop, hoop, halo • *a ring of blue smoke*

r

2 = **arena**, enclosure, ground, field, circus, rink • *The fight continued in the ring.*
3 = **gang**, group, firm *(slang)*, association, band, cell, combine, organization, circle, crew *(informal)*, knot, mob, syndicate, cartel, junta, clique, coterie, cabal • *investigation of an international crime ring*
▸ AS A VERB = **encircle**, surround, enclose, encompass, seal off, girdle, circumscribe, hem in, gird • *The area is ringed by troops.*

rinse AS A VERB = **wash**, clean, wet, dip, splash, cleanse, bathe, wash out • *After washing always rinse the hair in clear water.*
▸ AS A NOUN = **wash**, wetting, dip, splash, bath • *plenty of lather followed by a rinse with cold water*

riot AS A NOUN 1 = **disturbance**, row, disorder, confusion, turmoil, quarrel, upheaval, fray, strife, uproar, turbulence, commotion, lawlessness, street fighting, tumult, donnybrook, mob violence • *Twelve inmates have been killed during a riot.*
2 = **display**, show, splash, flourish, extravaganza, profusion • *The garden was a riot of colour.*
3 = **laugh**, joke, scream *(informal)*, blast *(U.S. slang)*, hoot *(informal)*, lark • *It was a riot when I introduced my two cousins!*
▸ AS A VERB = **rampage**, take to the streets, run riot, run amok, run wild, go on the rampage, fight in the streets, cause an affray, raise an uproar • *They rioted in protest against the government.*
▸ IN PHRASES: **run riot** 1 = **rampage**, go wild, be out of control, raise hell, let yourself go, break *or* cut loose, throw off all restraint • *Rampaging prisoners ran riot through the jail.*
2 = **grow profusely**, burgeon, luxuriate, spread like wildfire, grow like weeds • *Virginia creeper ran riot up the walls.*

QUOTATIONS
A riot is at bottom the language of the unheard
[Martin Luther King Jr. *Where Do We Go From Here?*]

riotous 1 = **reckless**, wild, outrageous, lavish, rash, luxurious, extravagant, wanton, unrestrained, intemperate, heedless, immoderate • *They wasted their lives in riotous living.*
2 = **unrestrained**, wild, loud, noisy, boisterous, rollicking, uproarious, orgiastic, side-splitting, rambunctious *(informal)*, saturnalian, roisterous • *Dinner was often a riotous affair.*
3 = **unruly**, violent, disorderly, rebellious, rowdy, anarchic, tumultuous, lawless, mutinous, ungovernable, uproarious, refractory, insubordinate, rampageous • *a riotous mob of hooligans*
OPPOSITES: quiet, calm, orderly

rip AS A VERB 1 = **tear**, cut, score, split, burst, rend, slash, hack, claw, slit, gash, lacerate • *I tried not to rip the paper.*
2 = **be torn**, tear, split, burst, be rent • *I felt the banner rip as we were pushed in opposite directions.*
▸ AS A NOUN = **tear**, cut, hole, split, rent, slash, slit, cleavage, gash, laceration • *She looked at the rip in her new dress.*
▸ IN PHRASES: **rip someone off** = **cheat**, trick, rob, con *(informal)*, skin *(slang)*, stiff *(slang)*, steal from, fleece, defraud, dupe, swindle, diddle *(informal)*, do the dirty on *(Brit. informal)*, gyp *(slang)*, cozen, scam *(slang)* • *Ticket touts ripped them off.*
rip something off = **steal**, pinch *(informal)*, swipe *(slang)*, thieve, lift *(informal)*, trouser *(slang)*, cabbage *(Brit. slang)*, knock off *(slang)*, pilfer, filch • *He ripped off a camera and a Game Boy.*
rip something *or* **someone apart** = **criticize**, condemn, censure, disparage, knock *(informal)*, blast, pan *(informal)*, slam *(slang)*, flame *(informal)*, carp, put down, slate *(informal)*, have a go (at) *(informal)*, disapprove of, tear into *(informal)*, diss *(slang, chiefly U.S.)*, find fault with, nag at, lambast(e), pick holes in, excoriate, pick to pieces, give (someone *or* something) a bad press, animadvert on *or* upon, pass strictures upon • *The audience ripped her apart.*

ripe 1 = **ripened**, seasoned, ready, mature, mellow, fully developed, fully grown • *Always choose firm, but ripe fruit.*
OPPOSITES: green, immature, unripe
2 = **right**, fit, ready, suitable • *Conditions are ripe for an outbreak of cholera.*
3 = **mature**, old, advanced, hoary • *He lived to the ripe old age of 65.*
4 = **suitable**, timely, ideal, favourable, auspicious, opportune • *The time is ripe for high-level dialogue.*
OPPOSITES: inappropriate, unfitting, unsuitable
5 *with* **for** = **ready for**, prepared for, eager for, in readiness for • *Do you think she's ripe for romance again?*

ripen = **mature**, season, develop, get ready, burgeon, come of age, come to fruition, grow ripe, make ripe • *I'm waiting for the apples to ripen.*

rip-off *or* **ripoff** = **cheat**, con *(informal)*, scam *(slang)*, con trick *(informal)*, fraud, theft, sting *(informal)*, robbery, exploitation, swindle, daylight robbery *(informal)* • *Christmas shopping is a rip-off.*

riposte AS A NOUN = **retort**, return, answer, response, reply, sally, comeback *(informal)*, counterattack, repartee, rejoinder • *He glanced at her, expecting a cheeky riposte.*
▸ AS A VERB = **retort**, return, answer, reply, respond, come back, rejoin, reciprocate • *'You look kind of funny,' she riposted blithely.*

ripple AS A NOUN 1 = **wave**, tremor, oscillation, undulation • *the ripples on the sea's calm surface*
2 *usually plural* = **consequence**, result, side effect, backlash, sequel, repercussion, reverberation • *The problem has created economic ripples.*
3 = **flutter**, thrill, tremor, tingle, vibration, frisson • *The news sent a ripple of excitement through the Security Council.*
▸ AS A VERB = **form ripples**, lap, ruffle, babble, undulate • *Throw a pebble in a pool and it ripples.*

rise AS A VERB 1 = **get up**, stand up, spring up, jump up, straighten up, get to your feet • *He rose slowly from his chair.*
2 = **arise**, surface, get out of bed, be up and about, rise and shine, rouse yourself • *He had risen early and gone to work.*
3 = **go up**, climb, soar, move up, ascend • *The sun had risen high in the sky.*
OPPOSITES: fall, drop, descend
4 = **loom**, tower, soar, rise up, stand high • *The building rose before him.*
5 = **get steeper**, mount, climb, ascend, go uphill, slope upwards • *the slope of land that rose from the house*
OPPOSITES: fall, drop, sink
6 = **increase**, mount, go up, rocket, soar, spiral, escalate, shoot up, get higher • *We need to increase our charges in order to meet rising costs.*
OPPOSITES: fall, drop, decrease
7 = **grow**, go up, intensify, get higher, grow louder • *His voice rose almost to a scream.*
8 = **rebel**, resist, revolt, mutiny, take to the streets, take up arms, mount the barricades, stage *or* mount a rebellion • *The people wanted to rise against the oppression.*
9 = **advance**, progress, get on, be promoted, prosper, go places *(informal)*, climb the ladder, work your way up • *She has risen to the top of her organisation.*
10 = **expand**, swell, enlarge, ferment, puff up • *I covered the dough to let it rise.*
▸ AS A NOUN 1 = **upward slope**, incline, elevation, ascent, hillock, rising ground, acclivity, kopje *or* koppie *(S. African)* • *I climbed to the top of the rise.*
2 = **increase**, climb, upturn, upswing, advance, improvement, ascent, upsurge, upward turn • *the prospect of another rise in interest rates*
OPPOSITES: fall, drop, decrease

3 = **pay increase**, raise (*U.S.*), increment • *He will get a rise of nearly £4,000.*

4 = **advancement**, progress, climb, promotion, progression, elevation, aggrandizement • *They celebrated the regime's rise to power.*

▸ **IN PHRASES: give rise to something** = **cause**, produce, effect, result in, provoke, bring about, bring on • *The picture gave rise to speculation.*

risible = **ridiculous**, ludicrous, laughable, farcical, funny, amusing, absurd, hilarious, humorous, comical, droll, side-splitting, rib-tickling (*informal*) • *His claim is risible for its patent untruth.*

risk **AS A NOUN** 1 = **danger**, chance, threat, possibility, prospect, speculation, uncertainty, hazard, likelihood, probability • *There is a small risk of brain damage.*

2 = **gamble**, chance, venture, speculation, leap in the dark • *This was one risk that paid off.*

3 = **peril**, threat, danger, hazard, menace, jeopardy • *He would not put their lives at risk.*

▸ **AS A VERB** 1 = **stand a chance of**, chance, venture, take the risk of • *Those who fail to register risk severe penalties.*

2 = **dare**, endanger, jeopardize, imperil, venture, gamble, hazard, take a chance on, put in jeopardy, expose to danger • *She risked her life to help a woman.*

risky = **dangerous**, hazardous, unsafe, perilous, uncertain, tricky, dodgy (*Brit., Austral. & N.Z. informal*), precarious, touch-and-go, dicey (*informal, chiefly Brit.*), fraught with danger, chancy (*informal*), shonky (*Austral. & N.Z. informal*) • *It is a very risky business.*

OPPOSITES: sure, certain, safe

risqué = **suggestive**, blue, daring, naughty, improper, racy, bawdy, off colour, ribald, immodest, indelicate, near the knuckle (*informal*), Rabelaisian • *a cheeky comment or a risqué suggestion*

rite = **ceremony**, custom, ritual, act, service, form, practice, procedure, mystery, usage, formality, ceremonial, communion, ordinance, observance, sacrament, liturgy, solemnity • *a fertility rite*

ritual **AS A NOUN** 1 = **ceremony**, rite, ceremonial, sacrament, service, mystery, communion, observance, liturgy, solemnity • *This is the most ancient and holiest of the rituals.*

2 = **custom**, tradition, routine, convention, form, practice, procedure, habit, usage, protocol, formality, ordinance, tikanga (*N.Z.*), lockstep (*U.S. & Canad.*) • *Italian culture revolves around the ritual of eating.*

▸ **AS AN ADJECTIVE** = **ceremonial**, formal, conventional, routine, prescribed, stereotyped, customary, procedural, habitual, ceremonious • *Here, the conventions required me to make the ritual noises.*

ritzy = **luxurious**, grand, luxury, elegant, glittering, glamorous, stylish, posh (*informal, chiefly Brit.*), sumptuous, plush (*informal*), high-class, opulent, swanky (*informal*), de luxe, schmick (*Austral. informal*) • *Palm Springs has a lot of ritzy restaurants.*

rival **AS A NOUN** 1 = **opponent**, competitor, contender, challenger, contestant, adversary, antagonist, emulator • *He finished two seconds ahead of his rival.*

OPPOSITES: friend, ally, supporter

2 = **equal**, match, fellow, equivalent, peer, compeer • *He is a pastry chef without rival.*

▸ **AS A VERB** = **compete with**, match, equal, oppose, compare with, contend, come up to, emulate, vie with, measure up to, be a match for, bear comparison with, seek to displace • *Cassettes cannot rival the sound quality of CDs.*

▸ **AS A MODIFIER** = **competing**, conflicting, opposed, opposing, competitive, emulating • *It would be no use having two rival companies.*

rivalry = **competition**, competitiveness, vying, opposition, struggle, conflict, contest, contention, duel, antagonism, emulation • *He had a lot of rivalry with his brother.*

riven = **torn apart**, split, rent, ruptured, ripped apart, torn asunder • *The party was riven with factional fighting.*

river **AS A NOUN** 1 = **stream**, brook, creek, beck, waterway, tributary, rivulet, watercourse, burn (*Scot.*) • *boating on the river*

2 = **flow**, wave, rush, flood, spate, torrent, deluge • *a river of lava was flowing down the mountainside towards the village*

▸ **IN PHRASES: sell someone down the river** = **give up**, betray, sell out (*informal*), deliver up, surrender • *He has been sold down the river by his colleagues*

▸ **RELATED ADJECTIVES:** fluvial, potamic

▹ *See panel* **Rivers**

riveted 1 = **rooted**, fixed, frozen, motionless, immobile, unable to move, stock still • *They stood aghast, riveted to the spot.*

2 = **fascinated**, absorbed, entranced, captivated, enthralled, engrossed, rapt, spellbound, mesmerized, hypnotized • *The Germans and Italians are riveted by his songs.*

riveting = **enthralling**, arresting, gripping, fascinating, absorbing, captivating, hypnotic, engrossing, spellbinding • *I find snooker riveting.*

road 1 = **roadway**, street, highway, motorway, track, direction, route, path, lane, avenue, artery, pathway, carriageway, thoroughfare, course • *There was very little traffic on the roads.*

2 = **way**, course, direction, route, path • *on the road to recovery*

roadblock = **barrier**, block, barricade • *Police set up roadblocks.*

roadside = **kerb**, verge, hard shoulder • *He was forced to leave the car at the roadside.*

roam = **wander**, walk, range, travel, drift, stroll, stray, ramble, prowl, meander, rove, stravaig (*Scot. & Northern English dialect*), peregrinate • *They were encouraged not to let their cattle roam freely.*

roar **AS A VERB** 1 = **thunder**, crash, boom, rumble, roll • *the roaring waters of Niagara Falls*

2 = **guffaw**, laugh heartily, hoot, double up, crack up (*informal*), bust a gut (*informal*), split your sides (*informal*) • *He threw back his head and roared.*

3 = **cry**, shout, yell, howl, bellow, clamour, bawl, bay, vociferate • *'I'll kill you for that,' he roared.*

▸ **AS A NOUN** 1 = **rumble**, boom, booming, thunder, thundering, rumbling • *the roar of traffic*

2 = **guffaw**, gale, howl, shriek, hoot, belly laugh (*informal*) • *There were roars of laughter as he stood up.*

3 = **cry**, crash, shout, yell, howl, outcry, bellow, clamour • *the roar of lions in the distance*

roaring 1 = **blazing**, burning • *There was a roaring fire in the grate.*

2 = **huge**, great, massive, enormous, fantastic, tremendous, terrific, thorough • *The auction was promptly declared a roaring success.*

roast 1 = **cook**, bake, grill, broil (*U.S.*), spit-roast • *I would rather roast a chicken whole.*

2 = **criticize**, condemn, censure, disparage, knock (*informal*), blast, pan (*informal*), slam (*slang*), flame (*informal*), carp, put down, slate (*informal*), have a go (at) (*informal*), disapprove of, tear into (*informal*), diss (*slang, chiefly U.S.*), find fault with, nag at, lambast(e), pick holes in, excoriate, pick to pieces, give (someone *or* something) a bad press, animadvert on *or* upon, pass strictures upon • *She was roasted by the critics.*

roasting **AS A NOUN** = **reprimand**, dressing down (*informal*), chastisement, bawling-out (*informal*), criticism, discipline, condemnation, telling-off, castigation • *He was given a roasting from his boss.*

▸ **AS AN ADJECTIVE** = **blazing**, baking, blistering, scorching,

RIVERS

Adige
Ain
Aire
Aisne
Alabama
Albany
Aldan
Allier
Amazon
Amu Darya
Amur
Anadyr
Anderson
Angara
Apure
Apurimac
Araguaia
Aras
Arkansas
Arno
Aruwimi
Assiniboine
Atbara
Athabaska
Aube
Avon
Back
Barrow
Beni
Benue
Berezina
Bermejo
Bío-Bío
Black Volta
Blue Nile
Bomu
Boyne
Brahmaputra
Bug
Cam
Canadian
Caquetá
Cauca
Cauvery
Chagres
Chao Phraya
Charente
Chari
Chenab
Cher
Chindwin
Churchill
Clutha
Clyde
Colorado
Columbia
Congo
Connecticut
Cooper's Creek
Courantyne
Cuiaba
Damodar
Danube
Darling
Dee
Delaware
Demerara
Derwent
Des Moines
Detroit
Dnieper
Dniester
Don
Donets
Dordogne
Doubs
Douro
Drava
Drin
Durance
Dvina
Ebro
Elbe
Ems
Erne
Essequibo
Euphrates
Fly
Forth
Fraser
Ganges
Garonne
Glomma
Godavari
Gogra
Göta
Granta
Green
Guadalquivir
Guadiana
Guaporé
Han
Havel
Helmand
Hooghly
Hudson
Iguaçú
IJssel
Illinois
Indus
Inn
Irrawaddy
Irtysh
Isar
Isère
Isis
Japurá
Javari
Jhelum
Jordan
Juba
Jumna
Juruá
Kabul
Kagera
Kama
Kasai
Kentucky
Kizil Irmak
Klondike
Kolyma
Komati
Kootenay
Krishna
Kuban
Kura
Kuskokwim
Lachlan
Lech
Lee
Lena
Liao
Liard
Liffey
Limpopo
Lippe
Little Bighorn
Loire
Lot
Lualaba
Mackenzie
Macquarie
Madeira
Madre de Dios
Magdalena
Mahanadi
Main
Mamoré
Marañón
Maritsa
Marne
Medway
Mekong
Menderes
Mersey
Meta
Meuse
Minnesota
Miño
Mississippi
Missouri
Mohawk
Molopo
Monongahela
Morava
Moselle
Moskva
Murray
Murrumbidgee
Narmada
Neckar
Negro
Neisse
Nelson
Neman
Neva
Niagara
Niger
Nile
Ob
Oder
Ogooué
Ohio
Oise
Okanagan
Okavango
Orange
Ord
Orinoco
Orontes
Ottawa
Ouachita
Ouse
Paraguay
Paraíba
Paraná
Parnaíba
Peace
Pearl
Pechora
Pecos
Piave
Pilcomayo
Plate
Po
Potomac
Pripet
Prut
Purús
Putamayo
Red
Rhine
Rhône
Ribble
Richelieu
Rio Branco
Rio Grande
Rubicon
Saar
Sacramento
Safid Rud
Saguenay
Saint Croix
Saint John
Saint Lawrence
Salado
Salambria
Salween
Sambre
San
Santee
Saône
Saskatchewan
Sava
Savannah
Scheldt
Seine
Severn
Shannon
Shatt-al-Arab
Shiré
Siret
Skien
Slave
Snake
Snowy
Somme
Songhua
Spey
Struma
Susquehanna
Sutlej
Suwannee
Swan
Swat
Syr Darya
Tagus
Tana
Tanana
Tapajós
Tarim
Tarn
Tarsus
Tay
Tees
Tennessee
Thames
Tiber
Ticino
Tigris
Tisza
Tobol
Tocantins
Trent
Tugela
Tunguska
Tweed
Tyne
Ubangi
Ucayali
Uele
Ural
Usk
Ussuri
Vaal
Var
Vardar
Vienne
Vistula
Vltava
Volga
Volta
Volturno
Waal
Wabash
Waikato
Warta
Wear
Weser
White Volta
Wisconsin
Xi, Hsi, *or* Si
Xiang, Hsiang, *or* Siang
Xingú
Wye
Yalu
Yangtze
Yaqui
Yarra
Yellow
Yellowstone
Yenisei
Yonne
Yser
Yüan
Yukon
Zambezi
Zhu Jiang

sizzling, sweltering, boiling hot, extremely hot • *Not all of Britain was roasting in the nineties today.*

rob 1 = **steal from**, hold up, rifle, mug *(informal)*, stiff *(slang)* • *Police said he had robbed a man hours earlier.*
2 = **raid**, hold up, break into, sack, loot, plunder, burgle, ransack, pillage • *A man who tried to rob a bank was sentenced yesterday.*
3 = **dispossess**, con *(informal)*, rip off *(slang)*, skin *(slang)*, cheat, defraud, swindle, despoil, gyp *(slang)* • *I was robbed by a used-car dealer.*
4 = **deprive**, deny, strip, divest, do out of *(informal)* • *I can't forgive him for robbing me of an Olympic gold.*

robber = **thief**, raider, burglar, looter, stealer, fraud, cheat, pirate, bandit, plunderer, mugger *(informal)*, highwayman, con man *(informal)*, fraudster, swindler, brigand, grifter *(slang, chiefly U.S. & Canad.)*, footpad *(archaic)*, rogue trader • *Armed robbers broke into a jewellers.*
▸ **RELATED PHOBIA:** harpaxophobia

robbery **1 = burglary**, raid, hold-up, rip-off *(slang)*, stick-up *(slang, chiefly U.S.)*, home invasion *(Austral. & N.Z.)* • *He committed dozens of armed robberies.*
2 = theft, stealing, fraud, steaming *(informal)*, mugging *(informal)*, plunder, swindle, pillage, embezzlement, larceny, depredation, filching, thievery, rapine, spoliation • *He was serving a sentence for robbery.*

robe **1 = gown**, cape, costume, cloak, vestment, habit • *a fur-lined robe of green silk*
2 = dressing gown, wrapper, bathrobe, negligée, housecoat, peignoir • *She put on a robe and went down to the kitchen.*

robed **= dressed**, attired, apparelled, enrobed • *I was sitting robed in the church.*

robot **= machine**, automaton, android, bot *(informal)*, mechanical man • *a working robot assistant for surgeons*

QUOTATIONS

The three fundamental Rules of Robotics ... One, a robot may not injure a human being, or, through inaction, allow a human being to come to harm ... Two ... a robot must obey the orders given it by human beings except where such orders would conflict with the First law ... Three, a robot must protect its own existence as long as such protection does not conflict with the First or Second Laws

[Isaac Asimov *I, Robot*]

robust **1 = strong**, tough, powerful, athletic, well, sound, fit, healthy, strapping, hardy, rude, vigorous, rugged, muscular, sturdy, hale, stout, staunch, hearty, husky *(informal)*, in good health, lusty, alive and kicking, fighting fit, sinewy, brawny, in fine fettle, thickset, fit as a fiddle *(informal)*, able-bodied • *His robust physique counts for much in the modern game.*
OPPOSITES: weak, delicate, slender
2 = rough, raw, rude, coarse, raunchy *(slang)*, earthy, boisterous, rollicking, unsubtle, indecorous, roisterous • *a robust sense of humour*
OPPOSITES: refined
3 = straightforward, practical, sensible, realistic, pragmatic, down-to-earth, hard-headed, common-sensical • *She has a robust attitude to children, and knows how to deal with them.*

rock[1] AS A NOUN **1 = stone**, boulder • *She sat cross-legged on the rock.*
2 = cliff, tor, outcrop, crag • *The tower is built on a rock.*
3 = tower of strength, foundation, cornerstone, mainstay, support, protection, anchor, bulwark • *She was the rock of the family.*
▸ IN PHRASES: **on the rocks = in trouble**, breaking down, falling apart, in tatters • *Why's your marriage on the rocks?*
▹ *See panel* **Types of rock**

rock[2] **1 = sway**, pitch, swing, reel, toss, lurch, wobble, roll • *His body rocked from side to side.*
2 = shock, surprise, shake, stun, astonish, stagger, jar, astound, daze, dumbfound, set you back on your heels *(informal)* • *His death rocked the fashion business.*

rocket AS A NOUN **= missile**, projectile • *There has been a rocket attack on the capital.*
▸ AS A VERB **1 = escalate**, rise, soar, spiral, shoot up, increase dramatically, go through the roof • *Fresh food is so scarce that prices have rocketed sharply.*
2 = zoom, shoot, career, speed, tear, whizz • *A train rocketed by.*

rocky[1] **= rough**, rugged, stony, craggy, pebbly, boulder-strewn, shingly • *The paths are often very rocky.*

rocky[2] **= unstable**, weak, uncertain, doubtful, shaky, unreliable, wobbly, rickety, unsteady, undependable • *Their relationship had gotten off to a rocky start.*

rococo **= extravagant**, fancy, elegant, elaborate, baroque, ornamented, ornate, fussy, convoluted, flowery, florid, overelaborate, high-wrought, highly decorated, aureate • *rococo trimmings and gilt cherubs*

rod **1 = stick**, bar, pole, shaft, switch, crook, cane, birch, dowel • *reinforced with steel rods*
2 = staff, baton, mace, wand, sceptre • *It was a witch-doctor's rod.*

rodent
▹ *See panel* **Rodents**

roe deer
▸ COLLECTIVE NOUN: bevy

rogue **1 = scoundrel**, crook *(informal)*, villain, fraudster, sharper, fraud, cheat, devil, deceiver, charlatan, con man *(informal)*, swindler, knave *(archaic)*, ne'er-do-well, reprobate, scumbag *(slang)*, blackguard, mountebank, grifter *(slang, chiefly U.S. & Canad.)*, skelm *(S. African)*, rorter *(Austral. slang)*, wrong 'un *(Austral. slang)* • *He wasn't a rogue at all.*
2 = scamp, rascal, scally *(Northwest English dialect)*, rapscallion, nointer *(Austral. slang)* • *a loveable rogue*

roguish **1 = mischievous**, arch, cheeky, playful, impish, coquettish, puckish, frolicsome, ludic *(literary)*, waggish, sportive • *She had a roguish grin.*
2 = unprincipled, criminal, crooked, deceiving, shady *(informal)*, fraudulent, dishonest, unscrupulous, swindling, rascally, deceitful, villainous, raffish, knavish • *He was a roguish thief.*

role **1 = job**, part, position, post, task, duty, function, office, capacity • *His role in the events has been pivotal.*
2 = part, character, representation, portrayal, impersonation • *Shakespearean women's roles*

roll AS A VERB **1 = turn**, wheel, spin, reel, go round, revolve, rotate, whirl, swivel, pivot, twirl, gyrate • *The car went off the road and rolled over into a ditch.*
2 = trundle, go, move, pass, travel, cruise • *The lorry slowly rolled forward.*
3 = flow, run, course, pour, slide, stream, trickle, glide, purl • *Tears rolled down her cheeks.*
4 *often with* **up = wind**, bind, wrap, twist, curl, coil, swathe, envelop, entwine, furl, enfold • *He took off his sweater and rolled it into a pillow.*
5 *often with* **out = level**, even, press, spread, smooth, flatten • *Rub in and roll out the pastry.*

TYPES OF ROCK

andesite	coal	gabbro	hornfels	obsidian	rhyolite
anorthosite	conglomerate	gneiss	lamprophyre	pegmatite	sandstone
anthracite	diorite	granite	lava	peridotite	schist
arkose	dolerite	granodiorite	lignite	perknite	shale
basalt	dolomite	gravel	limestone	phyllite	skarn
breccia	dunite	greywacke *or (U.S.)* graywacke	loess	pitchstone	slate
chalk	eclogite		marble	pumice	soapstone
chert	felsite	grit	monzonite	pyroxenite	syenite
clay	flint	hornblendite	mudstone	quartzite	trachyte

RODENTS

acouchi
agouti
African pygmy mouse
beaver
black rat
brown rat *or* Norway rat
cane rat
capybara
cavy
chinchilla
chipmunk
coypu *or* nutria
degu
deer mouse
desert rat
dormouse
fieldmouse
flying squirrel
fox squirrel
gerbil
gopher
grey squirrel
groundhog *or* woodchuck
guinea pig *or* cavy
gundi
hamster
harvest mouse
hedgehog
hopping mouse *or* jerboa rat
house mouse
hutia
jerboa
jumping mouse
kangaroo rat
lemming
Māori rat *or (N.Z.)* kiore
mara
marmot
mole rat
mouse
muskrat *or* musquash
paca
pack rat
pocket mouse
porcupine
rat
red squirrel *or* chickaree
spinifex hopping mouse *or (Austral.)* dargawarra
springhaas
squirrel
suslik *or* souslik
taguan
tucotuco
viscacha *or* vizcacha
vole
water vole *or* water rat
white-footed mouse
white rat

6 = toss, rock, lurch, reel, tumble, sway, wallow, billow, swing, welter • *The ship was still rolling in the troughs.*
7 = rumble, boom, echo, drum, roar, thunder, grumble, resound, reverberate • *guns firing, drums rolling, cymbals clashing*
8 = sway, pitch, reel, stagger, lurch, lumber, waddle, swagger, totter • *They rolled about in hysterics.*
9 = pass, slip by, wear on, go past, elapse • *The years roll by and look at us now.*
▸ **AS A NOUN 1 = reel**, ball, bobbin, cylinder • *a roll of blue insulated wire*
2 = spool, reel, scroll • *a dozen rolls of film*
3 = bun, bagel, bread roll, bap *(Brit.)*, hoagie *(U.S.)*, bridge roll *(Brit.)* • *butter and marmalade on a roll*
4 = rumble, boom, drumming, roar, thunder, grumble, resonance, growl, reverberation • *They heard the roll of drums.*
5 = register, record, list, table, schedule, index, catalogue, directory, inventory, census, chronicle, scroll, roster, annals • *A new electoral roll should be drawn up.*
6 = tossing, rocking, rolling, pitching, swell, lurching, wallowing • *despite the roll of the boat*
7 = turn, run, spin, rotation, cycle, wheel, revolution, reel, whirl, twirl, undulation, gyration • *Control the roll of the ball.*
▸ **IN PHRASES: roll in 1 = flood in**, flow in, stream in, pour in • *I kept the money rolling in.*
2 = turn up, appear, arrive, show up *(informal)*, make an appearance, show your face • *They usually roll in about midday and don't do much when they get there*
roll up = turn up, appear, arrive, show up *(informal)*, make an appearance, show your face • *He rolled up at the front of the hotel.*

rollicking[1] = boisterous, spirited, lively, romping, merry, hearty, playful, exuberant, joyous, carefree, jaunty, cavorting, sprightly, jovial, swashbuckling, frisky, rip-roaring *(informal)*, devil-may-care, full of beans *(informal)*, frolicsome, sportive • *outrageous, and a rollicking good read*
OPPOSITES: serious, sad, sedate

rollicking[2] = scolding, lecture, reprimand, telling-off, roasting *(informal)*, wigging *(Brit. slang)*, ticking off *(informal)*, dressing-down *(informal)*, tongue-lashing *(informal)* • *Whoever was responsible got a rollicking.*

roly-poly = plump, rounded, fat, overweight, chubby, tubby, buxom, rotund, pudgy, podgy • *a short roly-poly man*

romance AS A NOUN 1 = love affair, relationship, affair, intrigue, attachment, liaison, amour, affair of the heart, affaire (du coeur) *(French)* • *a holiday romance*
2 = love, passion, affection, attachment, intimacy, ardour • *He still finds time for romance.*
3 = excitement, colour, charm, mystery, adventure, sentiment, glamour, fascination, nostalgia, exoticness • *We want to recreate the romance of old train journeys.*
4 = story, novel, tale, fantasy, legend, fiction, fairy tale, love story, melodrama, idyll, tear-jerker *(informal)* • *Her taste in fiction was for historical romances.*
▸ **AS A VERB = court**, date, chase, pursue, take out, go (out) with, woo, make love to, run after, serenade, walk out with, keep company with, pay court to, go steady with *(informal)*, set your cap at, pay your addresses to, sue *(archaic)* • *He romanced the world's most eligible women.*

QUOTATIONS

She had been forced into prudence in her youth, she learned romance as she grew older – the natural sequel of an unnatural beginning
[Jane Austen *Persuasion*]

It begins when you sink in his arms. It ends with your arms in his sink
[feminist slogan]

romantic AS AN ADJECTIVE 1 = loving, tender, passionate, fond, sentimental, sloppy *(informal)*, amorous, mushy *(informal)*, soppy *(Brit. informal)*, lovey-dovey, icky *(informal)* • *They enjoyed a romantic dinner for two.*
OPPOSITES: insensitive, unsentimental, unromantic
2 = idealistic, unrealistic, visionary, high-flown, impractical, dreamy, utopian, whimsical, quixotic, starry-eyed • *He has a romantic view of rural society.*
OPPOSITES: practical, realistic
3 = exciting, charming, fascinating, exotic, mysterious, colourful, glamorous, picturesque, nostalgic • *romantic images from travel brochures*
OPPOSITES: unexciting, uninspiring
4 = fictitious, made-up, fantastic, fabulous, legendary, exaggerated, imaginative, imaginary, extravagant, unrealistic, improbable, fairy-tale, idyllic, fanciful, wild, chimerical • *Both figures have become the stuff of romantic legends.*
OPPOSITES: realistic
▸ **AS A NOUN = idealist**, romancer, visionary, dreamer, utopian, Don Quixote, sentimentalist • *You're a hopeless romantic*

QUOTATIONS

Is not this the true romantic feeling – not to desire to escape life, but to prevent life from escaping you?
[Thomas Wolfe]

Rome

THE SEVEN HILLS OF ROME

Aventine
Caelian
Capitoline
Esquiline
Palatine
Quirinal
Viminal

romp AS A VERB = frolic, sport, skip, have fun, revel, caper, cavort, frisk, gambol, make merry, rollick, roister, cut capers • *Dogs romped happily in the garden.*

▸ **AS A NOUN** = **frolic**, lark *(informal)*, caper • *a romp in the snow and slush*
▸ **IN PHRASES: romp home** *or* **in** = **win easily**, walk it *(informal)*, win hands down, run away with it, win by a mile *(informal)* • *He romped home with 141 votes.*

roof **IN PHRASES: hit** *or* **go through the roof** = **be furious**, go mad *(Brit.)*, be very angry, be livid, go ballistic *(informal)*, lose your temper, blow a fuse *(informal)*, go ape *(informal)*, go spare *(Brit. informal)*, go off the deep end *(informal)*, blow a gasket *(informal)*, go into a rage, blow your top *(informal)*, lose your rag *(informal)*, flip your lid *(informal)* • *He will hit the roof when I tell him.*

rook
▸ **COLLECTIVE NOUNS:** building, clamour
▸ **NAME OF HOME:** rookery

room **AS A NOUN** **1** = **chamber**, office, apartment • *He excused himself and left the room.*
2 = **space**, area, territory, volume, capacity, extent, expanse, elbow room • *There wasn't enough room for all the gear.*
3 = **opportunity**, freedom, scope, leeway, play, chance, range, occasion, margin, allowance, compass, latitude • *There's a lot of room for you to express yourself.*
▸ **AS A VERB** = **lodge**, live, stay, board, be housed • *I roomed with him.*

roomy = **spacious**, large, wide, broad, extensive, generous, ample, capacious, commodious, sizable *or* sizeable • *The car is roomy.*
OPPOSITES: small, tiny, cramped

root[1] **AS A NOUN** **1** = **stem**, tuber, rhizome, radix, radicle • *the twisted roots of an apple tree*
2 = **source**, cause, heart, bottom, beginnings, base, seat, occasion, seed, foundation, origin, core, fundamental, essence, nucleus, starting point, germ, crux, nub, derivation, fountainhead, mainspring • *We got to the root of the problem.*
▸ **AS A PLURAL NOUN** = **sense of belonging**, origins, heritage, birthplace, home, family, cradle • *I am proud of my Brazilian roots.*
▸ **IN PHRASES: put down roots** = **settle**, set up home, get established, make your home, establish yourself • *They put down roots in India.*
root and branch **1** = **complete**, total, entire, radical, utter, thorough • *in need of root and branch reform*
2 = **completely**, finally, totally, entirely, radically, thoroughly, wholly, utterly, without exception, to the last man • *They want to deal with the problem root and branch.*
root for someone = **support**, back, encourage, defend, side with, stand up for, stand behind, stick up for *(informal)*, be a source of strength to • *We'll be rooting for you.*
root something *or* **someone out** **1** = **get rid of**, remove, destroy, eliminate, abolish, cut out, erase, eradicate, do away with, uproot, weed out, efface, exterminate, extirpate, wipe from the face of the earth • *The generals have to root out traitors.*
2 = **discover**, find, expose, turn up, uncover, unearth, bring to light, ferret out • *It shouldn't take long to root out the cause of the problem.*
take root **1** = **take hold**, take, develop, establish, become established, become fixed • *Time is needed for democracy to take root.*
2 = **germinate**, take, establish, become established, begin to sprout • *Cover the bulbs with chicken wire, removing it when they take root.*
▸ **RELATED ADJECTIVE:** radical

root[2] = **dig**, hunt, nose, poke, burrow, delve, ferret, pry, rummage, forage, rootle • *She rooted through the bag.*

rooted **1** = **established**, fixed, embedded, entrenched, ingrained, deep-rooted • *powerful songs rooted in tradition*
2 = **deep-seated**, firm, deep, established, confirmed, fixed, radical, rigid, entrenched, ingrained, deeply felt • *a deeply rooted prejudice*

rootless = **footloose**, homeless, roving, transient, itinerant, vagabond • *rootless young people*

rope **AS A NOUN** = **cord**, line, cable, strand, hawser • *He tied the rope around his waist.*
▸ **AS A VERB** = **tie**, bind, moor, lash, hitch, fasten, tether, pinion, lasso • *I roped myself to the chimney.*
▸ **IN PHRASES: know the ropes** = **be experienced**, know the score *(informal)*, be knowledgeable, know what's what, be an old hand, know your way around, know where it's at *(slang)*, know all the ins and outs • *She got to know the ropes.*
rope someone in *or* **into something** = **persuade**, involve, engage, enlist, talk into, drag in, inveigle • *I got roped into helping.*

PROVERBS
Give a man enough rope and he will hang himself

ropey *or* **ropy** *(Brit. informal)* **1** = **inferior**, poor, inadequate, mediocre, deficient, sketchy, substandard, of poor quality, indifferent, no great shakes *(informal)*, half-pie *(N.Z. informal)* • *Your spelling's a bit ropey.*
2 = **unwell**, poorly *(informal)*, rough *(informal)*, crook *(Austral. & N.Z. informal)*, below par, off colour, under the weather *(informal)*, sickish • *He was a bit ropey by all accounts.*

roster = **rota**, listing, list, table, roll, schedule, register, agenda, catalogue, inventory, scroll • *He put himself on the roster for domestic chores.*

rostrum = **stage**, stand, platform, podium, dais • *He stood on the winner's rostrum.*

rosy **1** = **glowing**, fresh, blooming, flushed, blushing, radiant, reddish, ruddy, healthy-looking, roseate, rubicund • *She had bright, rosy cheeks.*
OPPOSITES: white, grey, pale
2 = **promising**, encouraging, bright, reassuring, optimistic, hopeful, sunny, cheerful, favourable, auspicious, rose-coloured, roseate • *Is the future really so rosy?*
OPPOSITES: depressing, unhappy, gloomy
3 = **pink**, red, rose-coloured, roseate • *the rosy brick buildings*
▹ *See panel* **Shades of red**

rot **AS A VERB** **1** = **decay**, break down, spoil, corrupt, deteriorate, taint, perish, degenerate, fester, decompose, corrode, moulder, go bad, putrefy • *The grain will start rotting in the silos.*
2 = **crumble**, decay, disintegrate, perish, decompose, become rotten • *It is not true to say that this wood never rots.*
3 = **deteriorate**, decline, languish, degenerate, wither away, waste away • *I was left to rot nine years for a crime I didn't commit.*
▸ **AS A NOUN** **1** = **decay**, disintegration, corrosion, decomposition, corruption, mould, blight, deterioration, canker, putrefaction, putrescence • *Investigations revealed rot in the beams.*
2 = **nonsense**, rubbish, drivel, twaddle, malarkey, balls *(taboo slang)*, bull *(slang)*, shit *(taboo slang)*, pants *(slang)*, crap *(slang)*, garbage *(chiefly U.S.)*, trash, bunk *(informal)*, bullshit *(taboo slang)*, hot air *(informal)*, tosh *(slang, chiefly Brit.)*, pap, cobblers *(Brit. taboo slang)*, bilge *(informal)*, tripe *(informal)*, guff *(slang)*, moonshine, claptrap *(informal)*, hogwash, hokum *(slang, chiefly U.S. & Canad.)*, codswallop *(Brit. slang)*, piffle *(informal)*, poppycock *(informal)*, balderdash, bosh *(informal)*, eyewash *(informal)*, stuff and nonsense, flapdoodle *(slang)*, tommyrot, horsefeathers *(U.S. slang)*, bunkum or buncombe *(chiefly U.S.)*, bizzo *(Austral. slang)*, bull's wool *(Austral. & N.Z. slang)* • *You do talk rot!*
▸ **RELATED ADJECTIVE:** putrid

rota = **schedule**, list, calendar, timetable, roster • *the washing-up rota*

rotary = **revolving**, turning, spinning, rotating, rotational, gyratory, rotatory • *heavy-duty rotary blades*

rotate 1 = **revolve**, turn, wheel, spin, reel, go round, swivel, pivot, gyrate, pirouette • *The earth rotates round the sun.*
2 = **follow in sequence**, switch, alternate, interchange, take turns • *The members of the club can rotate.*

rotation 1 = **revolution**, turning, turn, wheel, spin, spinning, reel, orbit, pirouette, gyration • *the daily rotation of the earth upon its axis*
2 = **sequence**, switching, cycle, succession, interchanging, alternation • *crop rotation and integration of livestock*

rote IN PHRASES: **by rote** = **automatically**, by heart, parrot-fashion, without thinking, mechanically, mindlessly, unthinkingly • *You are merely reciting facts you learned by rote.*

rotten 1 = **decaying**, bad, rank, foul, corrupt, sour, stinking, tainted, perished, festering, decomposed, decomposing, mouldy, mouldering, fetid, putrid, putrescent, festy *(Austral. slang)* • *The smell is like rotten eggs.*
OPPOSITES: good, fresh, sweet
2 = **crumbling**, decayed, disintegrating, perished, corroded, unsound • *The bay window is rotten.*
3 = **bad**, disappointing, unfortunate, unlucky, regrettable, deplorable • *What rotten luck!*
4 = **despicable**, mean, base, dirty, nasty, unpleasant, filthy, vile, wicked, disagreeable, contemptible, scurrilous, shitty *(taboo slang)* • *You rotten swine!*
5 = **unwell**, poorly *(informal)*, ill, sick, rough *(informal)*, bad, crook *(Austral. & N.Z. informal)*, below par, off colour, under the weather *(informal)*, ropey *or* ropy *(Brit. informal)* • *I felt rotten with the flu.*
6 = **inferior**, poor, sorry, inadequate, unacceptable, punk, duff *(Brit. informal)*, unsatisfactory, lousy *(slang)*, low-grade, substandard, ill-considered, crummy *(slang)*, ill-thought-out, poxy *(slang)*, chickenshit *(U.S. slang)*, of a sort *or* of sorts, ropey *or* ropy *(Brit. informal)*, bodger *or* bodgie *(Austral. slang)* • *I thought it was a rotten idea.*
7 = **corrupt**, immoral, deceitful, untrustworthy, sink, bent *(slang)*, crooked *(informal)*, vicious, degenerate, mercenary, treacherous, dishonest, disloyal, faithless, venal, dishonourable, perfidious • *There was something rotten in our legal system.*
OPPOSITES: moral, decent, honourable
8 = **guilty**, sorry, ashamed, chastened, contrite, guilt-ridden, remorseful, regretful, conscience-stricken • *I feel rotten for having spilt the beans like that.*

rotter = **scoundrel**, rat *(informal)*, stinker *(slang)*, louse *(slang)*, cad *(Brit. informal)*, swine, bounder *(Brit. old-fashioned slang)*, blighter *(Brit. informal)*, cur, scumbag *(slang)*, bad lot, blackguard, cocksucker *(taboo slang)*, scrote *(slang)*, wrong 'un *(Austral. slang)* • *The man's an absolute rotter!*

rotund 1 = **plump**, rounded, heavy, fat, stout, chubby, obese, fleshy, tubby, portly, roly-poly, podgy, corpulent • *A rotund gentleman appeared.*
OPPOSITES: thin, lean, skinny
2 = **pompous**, grandiloquent, orotund, magniloquent, full • *writing rotund passages of purple prose*
3 = **round**, rounded, spherical, bulbous, globular, orbicular • *rotund towers, moats and drawbridges*
4 = **sonorous**, round, deep, rich, mellow, resonant, orotund, reverberant • *the wonderfully rotund tones of the presenter*

rough AS AN ADJECTIVE 1 = **uneven**, broken, rocky, rugged, irregular, jagged, bumpy, stony, craggy • *She made her way across the rough ground.*
OPPOSITES: even, level, regular
2 = **coarse**, disordered, tangled, hairy, fuzzy, bushy, shaggy, dishevelled, uncut, unshaven, tousled, bristly, unshorn • *people who looked rough and stubbly*
OPPOSITES: soft, smooth
3 = **boisterous**, hard, tough, aggressive, two-fisted, brutal, vicious, rugged, arduous, unrestrained • *Rugby's a rough game.*
4 = **ungracious**, blunt, rude, coarse, bluff, curt, churlish, bearish, brusque, uncouth, unrefined, inconsiderate, impolite, loutish, untutored, discourteous, unpolished, indelicate, uncivil, uncultured, unceremonious, ill-bred, unmannerly, ill-mannered • *He was rough and common.*
OPPOSITES: civil, smooth, refined
5 = **unpleasant**, hard, difficult, tough, uncomfortable, drastic, unjust • *Women have a rough time in our society.*
OPPOSITES: easy, soft, comfortable
6 = **unwell**, poorly *(informal)*, ill, upset, sick, crook *(Austral. & N.Z. informal)*, rotten *(informal)*, below par, off colour, under the weather *(informal)*, not a hundred per cent *(informal)*, ropey *or* ropy *(Brit. informal)* • *The lad is still feeling a bit rough.*
7 = **approximate**, estimated, vague, ballpark, imprecise, inexact • *We were only able to make a rough estimate.*
OPPOSITES: perfected, specific, exact
8 = **vague**, general, sketchy, imprecise, hazy, foggy, amorphous, inexact • *I've got a rough idea of what he looks like.*
9 = **basic**, quick, raw, crude, unfinished, incomplete, hasty, imperfect, rudimentary, sketchy, cursory, shapeless, rough-and-ready, unrefined, formless, rough-hewn, untutored, unpolished • *Make a rough plan of the space.*
OPPOSITES: detailed, finished, complete
10 = **rough-hewn**, crude, uncut, unpolished, raw, undressed, unprocessed, unhewn, unwrought • *a rough wooden table*
11 = **stormy**, wild, turbulent, agitated, choppy, tempestuous, inclement, squally • *The ships collided in rough seas.*
OPPOSITES: quiet, calm, smooth
12 = **grating**, harsh, jarring, raucous, rasping, husky, discordant, gruff, cacophonous, unmusical, inharmonious • *'Wait!' a rough voice commanded.*
OPPOSITES: soft, smooth, harmonious
13 = **harsh**, tough, sharp, severe, nasty, cruel, rowdy, curt, unfeeling • *I was a bit rough with you this morning.*
OPPOSITES: just, kind, gentle
▸ AS A NOUN 1 = **outline**, draft, mock-up, preliminary sketch, suggestion • *Editors are always saying that the roughs are better.*
2 = **thug**, tough, casual, rowdy, hoon *(Austral. & N.Z.)*, bully boy, bruiser, ruffian, lager lout, roughneck *(slang)*, ned *(slang)*, cougan *(Austral. slang)*, scozza *(Austral. slang)*, bogan *(Austral. slang)* • *The roughs of the town are out.*
▸ IN PHRASES: **rough and ready** 1 = **makeshift**, adequate, crude, provisional, improvised, sketchy, thrown together, cobbled together, stopgap • *Here is a rough and ready measurement.*
2 = **unrefined**, shabby, untidy, unkempt, unpolished, ungroomed, ill-groomed, daggy *(Austral. & N.Z. informal)* • *The soldiers were a bit rough and ready.*
rough and tumble 1 = **fight**, struggle, scrap *(informal)*, brawl, scuffle, punch-up *(Brit. informal)*, fracas, affray *(Law)*, dust-up *(informal)*, shindig *(informal)*, donnybrook, scrimmage, roughhouse *(slang)*, shindy *(informal)*, melee *or* mêlée, biffo *(Austral. slang)* • *the rough and tumble of political combat*
2 = **disorderly**, rough, scrambled, scrambling, irregular, rowdy, boisterous, haphazard, indisciplined • *He enjoys rough and tumble play.*
rough someone up = **beat up**, batter, thrash, do over *(Brit., Austral. & N.Z. slang)*, work over *(slang)*, mistreat, manhandle, maltreat, bash up *(informal)*, beat the living daylights out of *(informal)*, knock about *or* around, beat *or* knock seven bells out of *(informal)* • *They roughed him up a bit*
rough something out = **outline**, plan, draft, sketch, suggest, block out, delineate, adumbrate • *He roughed out a framework for their story.*

roughly 1 = **forcefully**, abruptly, violently, aggressively, forcibly • *A hand roughly pushed him aside.*
2 = **approximately**, about, around, close to, just about, more or less, in the region of, circa *(of a date)*, in the vicinity of, not far off, in the neighbourhood of • *a period of roughly 30 million years*

roughneck = **thug**, heavy *(slang)*, tough, rough *(informal)*, rowdy, bully boy, bruiser *(informal)*, ruffian • *a rangy lantern-jawed roughneck*

round AS A PREPOSITION 1 = **around**, about, encircling, near • *They were sitting round the kitchen table.*
2 = **throughout**, all over, everywhere in, here and there in • *He has earned respect all round the world.*
▸ AS A NOUN 1 = **series**, session, cycle, sequence, succession, bout • *This is the latest round of job cuts.*
2 = **stage**, turn, level, period, division, session, lap • *in the third round of the cup*
3 = **sphere**, ball, band, ring, circle, disc, globe, orb • *small fresh rounds of goat's cheese*
4 = **course**, turn, tour, circuit, beat, series, schedule, routine, compass, ambit • *The consultant did his morning round.*
5 = **bullet**, shot, shell, discharge, cartridge • *live rounds of ammunition*
▸ AS AN ADJECTIVE 1 = **spherical**, rounded, bowed, curved, circular, cylindrical, bulbous, rotund, globular, curvilinear, ball-shaped, ring-shaped, disc-shaped, annular, discoid, orbicular • *the round church known as The New Temple*
2 = **complete**, full, whole, entire, solid, unbroken, undivided • *a round dozen*
3 = **plump**, full, rounded, ample, fleshy, roly-poly, rotund, full-fleshed • *She was a small, round person in her early sixties.*
4 = **considerable**, large, liberal, substantial, generous, ample, bountiful, bounteous • *She had a nice, round figure.*
▸ AS A VERB = **go round**, circle, skirt, flank, bypass, encircle, turn, circumnavigate • *The boats rounded the Cape.*
▸ IN PHRASES: **round about** = **approximately**, about, around, generally, close to, roughly, loosely, just about, more or less, in the region of, circa *(of a date)*, in the vicinity of, not far off, in the neighbourhood of • *round about one and a half million*
round on someone = **attack**, abuse, turn on, retaliate against, have a go at *(Brit. slang)*, snap at, wade into, lose your temper with, bite (someone's) head off *(informal)* • *He has rounded on his critics.*
round something off 1 = **complete**, close, settle, crown, cap, conclude, finish off, put the finishing touch to, bring to a close • *A fireworks display rounded off the day.*
2 = **smooth off**, level off, plane off, sand off • *Cut just inside the edges, and round off the corners.*
round something *or* **someone up** = **gather**, assemble, bring together, muster, group, drive, collect, rally, herd, marshal • *The police rounded up a number of suspects.*

roundabout 1 = **indirect**, meandering, devious, tortuous, circuitous, evasive, discursive, circumlocutory • *a roundabout route*
OPPOSITES: direct, straight, straightforward
2 = **oblique**, implied, indirect, evasive, circuitous, circumlocutory, periphrastic • *indirect or roundabout language*

rounded = **curbed**, sweeping, curved, arched, bow-shaped • *a low, rounded hill*

roundly = **thoroughly**, sharply, severely, bitterly, fiercely, bluntly, intensely, violently, vehemently, rigorously, outspokenly, frankly • *They have roundly condemned the shooting.*

roundup 1 = **summary**, review, survey, outline, digest, overview, synopsis, collation • *a roundup of the day's news*
2 = **muster**, collection, rally, rallying, assembly, herding, marshalling, mustering, gathering together • *What keeps a cowboy ready for another roundup?*

rouse 1 = **wake up**, call, wake, get up, awaken, knock up *(informal)* • *She roused him at 8.30.*
2 = **excite**, move, arouse, stir, disturb, provoke, anger, startle, animate, prod, exhilarate, get going, agitate, inflame, incite, whip up, galvanize, bestir • *He did more to rouse the crowd than anybody else.*
3 = **stimulate**, provoke, arouse, incite, instigate • *It roused a feeling of rebellion in him.*

rousing = **lively**, moving, spirited, exciting, inspiring, stirring, stimulating, vigorous, brisk, exhilarating, inflammatory, electrifying • *He gave a rousing speech to the convention.*
OPPOSITES: boring, dull, sluggish

rout AS A VERB = **defeat**, beat, overthrow, thrash, stuff *(slang)*, worst, destroy, chase, tank *(slang)*, crush, scatter, conquer, lick *(informal)*, dispel, drive off, overpower, clobber *(slang)*, wipe the floor with *(informal)*, cut to pieces, put to flight, drub, put to rout, throw back in confusion • *The Norman army routed the English opposition.*
▸ AS A NOUN = **defeat**, beating, hiding *(informal)*, ruin, overthrow, thrashing, licking *(informal)*, pasting *(slang)*, shambles, debacle, drubbing, overwhelming defeat, headlong flight, disorderly retreat • *The retreat turned into a rout.*

route AS A NOUN 1 = **way**, course, road, direction, path, journey, passage, avenue, itinerary • *the most direct route to the town centre*
2 = **beat**, run, round, circuit • *They would go out on his route and check him.*
▸ AS A VERB 1 = **direct**, lead, guide, steer, convey, usher • *Approaching cars will be routed into two lanes.*
2 = **send**, forward, dispatch • *plans to route every emergency call through three exchanges*

routine AS A NOUN 1 = **procedure**, programme, way, order, practice, method, pattern, formula, custom, usage, wont, lockstep *(U.S. & Canad.)* • *The players had to change their daily routine.*
2 = **grind** *(informal)*, tedium, monotony, banality, groove, boredom, chore, the doldrums, dullness, sameness, ennui, drabness, deadness, dreariness, tediousness, lifelessness • *the mundane routine of her life*
3 = **performance**, sketch, turn, line, act, bit *(informal)*, piece, spiel *(informal)* • *like a Marx Brothers routine*
▸ AS AN ADJECTIVE 1 = **usual**, standard, normal, customary, ordinary, familiar, typical, conventional, everyday, habitual, workaday, wonted • *a series of routine medical tests*
OPPOSITES: different, special, unusual
2 = **boring**, dull, predictable, tedious, tiresome, run-of-the-mill, humdrum, unimaginative, clichéd, uninspired, mind-numbing, hackneyed, unoriginal, shtick *(slang)* • *So many days are routine and uninteresting.*

rove = **wander**, range, cruise, drift, stroll, stray, roam, ramble, meander, traipse *(informal)*, go walkabout *(Austral.)*, gallivant, gad about, stravaig *(Scot. & Northern English dialect)* • *roving about the town in the dead of night*

rover = **wanderer**, traveller, gypsy, rolling stone, rambler, transient, nomad, itinerant, ranger, drifter, vagrant, stroller, bird of passage, gadabout *(informal)* • *He remained at heart a rover.*

row[1] AS A NOUN = **line**, bank, range, series, file, rank, string, column, sequence, queue, tier • *a row of pretty little cottages*
▸ IN PHRASES: **in a row** = **consecutively**, running, in turn, one after the other, successively, in sequence • *They have won five championships in a row.*

row[2] AS A NOUN 1 = **quarrel**, dispute, argument, squabble, tiff, trouble, controversy, scrap *(informal)*, fuss, falling-out *(informal)*, fray, brawl, fracas, altercation, slanging match *(Brit.)*, shouting match *(informal)*, turf war *(informal)*, shindig *(informal)*, ruction *(informal)*, ruckus *(informal)*, shindy

(informal), bagarre *(French)* • *A man was stabbed to death in a family row.*
2 = **disturbance**, noise, racket, uproar, commotion, pandemonium, rumpus, tumult, hubbub • *'Whatever is that row?' she demanded.*
3 = **telling-off**, talking-to *(informal)*, lecture, reprimand, ticking-off *(informal)*, dressing-down *(informal)*, rollicking *(Brit. informal)*, tongue-lashing, reproof, castigation, flea in your ear *(informal)* • *I can't give you a row for scarpering off.*
▸ AS A VERB = **quarrel**, fight, argue, dispute, scrap *(informal)*, brawl, squabble, spar, wrangle, go at it hammer and tongs • *They rowed all the time.*

rowdy AS AN ADJECTIVE = **disorderly**, rough, loud, noisy, unruly, boisterous, loutish, wild, uproarious, obstreperous • *He has complained about rowdy neighbours.*
OPPOSITES: mannerly, gentle, orderly
▸ AS A NOUN = **hooligan**, tough, rough *(informal)*, casual, ned *(Scot. slang)*, brawler, yahoo, lout, troublemaker, tearaway *(Brit.)*, ruffian, lager lout, boot boy, yob *or* yobbo *(Brit. slang)*, cougan *(Austral. slang)*, scozza *(Austral. slang)*, bogan *(Austral. slang)* • *The owner kept a baseball bat to deal with rowdies.*

royal 1 = **regal**, kingly, queenly, princely, imperial, sovereign, monarchical, kinglike • *an invitation to a royal garden party*
2 = **splendid**, august, grand, impressive, superb, magnificent, superior, majestic, stately • *She was given a royal welcome on her first visit to Britain.*
3 = **total**, complete, perfect, entire, pure, sheer, utter, outright, thorough, downright, unqualified, full-on *(informal)*, out-and-out, unadulterated, unmitigated, unalloyed • *He could be a royal pain in the ass sometimes.*

QUOTATIONS
Royalty is the gold filling in a mouthful of decay
[John Osborne *They Call it Cricket*]

rub AS A VERB 1 = **stroke**, smooth, massage, caress, knead • *He rubbed his arms and stiff legs.*
2 = **polish**, clean, shine, wipe, scour • *She took off her glasses and rubbed them.*
3 = **spread**, put, apply, work in, smear • *He rubbed oil into my aching back.*
4 = **chafe**, scrape, grate, abrade • *Smear cream on to prevent it from rubbing.*
▸ AS A NOUN 1 = **massage**, caress, kneading • *She sometimes asks if I want a back rub.*
2 = **polish**, stroke, shine, wipe • *Give them a rub with a clean, dry cloth.*
▸ IN PHRASES: **rub along** = **cope**, manage, get along, make do, muddle along • *They rubbed along tolerably.*
rub off on someone = **influence**, affect, be transferred to, be passed on to, have an effect on, be transmitted to • *I was hoping some of his genius might rub off on them.*
rub something in = **make an issue of**, stress, highlight, emphasize, underline, dwell on, harp on about • *Officials couldn't resist rubbing it in.*
rub something out = **erase**, remove, cancel, wipe out, excise, delete, obliterate, efface, expunge • *She began rubbing out the pencilled marks.*
rub something *or* **someone down** = **smooth**, clean, dry, wash, sponge • *rub down the whole body with a loofah*
the rub = **difficulty**, problem, catch, trouble, obstacle, hazard, hitch, drawback, snag, uphill *(S. African)*, impediment, hindrance • *And therein lies the rub.*

rubber-stamp = **agree to**, buy *(slang)*, adopt, approve, endorse, consent to, buy into *(slang)*, take on board, accede to • *Nearly 60 banks have rubber-stamped a refinancing deal.*

rubbish AS A NOUN 1 = **waste**, refuse, scrap, junk *(informal)*, litter, debris, crap *(slang)*, garbage *(chiefly U.S.)*, trash, lumber, offal, dross, dregs, flotsam and jetsam, grot *(slang)*, dreck *(slang, chiefly U.S.)*, offscourings • *unwanted household rubbish*
2 = **nonsense**, garbage *(chiefly U.S.)*, drivel, malarkey, twaddle, balls *(taboo slang)*, bull *(slang)*, shit *(taboo slang)*, pants *(slang)*, rot, crap *(slang)*, trash, bullshit *(taboo slang)*, hot air *(informal)*, tosh *(slang, chiefly Brit.)*, bollocks *(Brit. taboo slang)*, pap, cobblers *(Brit. taboo slang)*, bilge *(informal)*, tripe *(informal)*, gibberish, guff *(slang)*, havers *(Scot.)*, moonshine, claptrap *(informal)*, hogwash, hokum *(slang, chiefly U.S. & Canad.)*, codswallop *(Brit. slang)*, piffle *(informal)*, poppycock *(informal)*, balderdash, bosh *(informal)*, wack *(U.S. slang)*, eyewash *(informal)*, stuff and nonsense, flapdoodle *(slang)*, tommyrot, horsefeathers *(U.S. slang)*, bunkum *or* buncombe *(chiefly U.S.)*, bizzo *(Austral. slang)*, bull's wool *(Austral. & N.Z. slang)* • *He's talking rubbish.*
▸ AS AN ADJECTIVE = **hopeless**, incompetent, poor, no good, inadequate, pants *(informal)*, useless *(informal)*, pathetic, inferior, ineffectual • *He was rubbish at his job.*
▸ AS A VERB = **criticize**, condemn, censure, disparage, knock *(informal)*, blast, pan *(informal)*, slam *(slang)*, flame *(informal)*, put down, slate *(informal)*, have a go at *(informal)*, disapprove of, tear into *(informal)*, diss *(slang, chiefly U.S.)*, find fault with, nag at, lambast(e), pick holes in, excoriate, pick to pieces, give (someone *or* something) a bad press, animadvert on *or* upon, pass strictures upon • *devoted to rubbishing her political opponents*

rubbishy = **trashy**, cheap, worthless, paltry, shoddy, tawdry, tatty, throwaway, valueless, gimcrack, twopenny, brummagem, twopenny-halfpenny • *some old rubbishy cop movie*

rubble = **wreckage**, remains, ruins, debris • *Thousands of bodies are still buried under the rubble.*

ruck = **battle**, fight, conflict, clash, set-to *(informal)*, encounter, riot, scrap *(informal)*, fray, brawl, skirmish, head-to-head, tussle, scuffle, free-for-all *(informal)*, fracas, dogfight, affray *(Law)*, scrimmage, exchange of blows, melee *or* mêlée, biffo *(Austral. slang)*, boilover *(Austral.)* • *There'll be a huge ruck with the cops.*

rucksack = **backpack**, pack, knapsack, kitbag, haversack, pikau *(N.Z.)* • *a man carrying a brilliant blue rucksack*

ructions = **row**, to-do, trouble, storm, dispute, scrap *(informal)*, fuss, disturbance, racket, quarrel, brawl, uproar, fracas, commotion, altercation, rumpus, shindig *(informal)*, hue and cry, scrimmage, shindy *(informal)* • *Both activities have caused some ructions.*

ruddy 1 = **rosy**, red, fresh, healthy, glowing, blooming, flushed, blushing, radiant, reddish, sanguine, florid, sunburnt, rosy-cheeked, rubicund • *He had a naturally ruddy complexion.*
OPPOSITES: white, grey, pale
2 = **red**, pink, scarlet, ruby, crimson, reddish, roseate • *barges, with their sails ruddy brown*
▹ *See panel* **Shades of red**
3 = **damn**, blasted, bloody *(Brit. informal)*, blessed, damned, flaming, bleeding *(Brit. informal)*, blooming *(Brit. informal)*, freaking *(slang, chiefly U.S.)*, flipping *(Brit. informal)*, blinking *(Brit. informal)*, confounded, goddam *(U.S. informal)*, effing *(Brit. informal)* • *The ruddy thing wouldn't work.*

rude 1 = **impolite**, insulting, cheeky, abrupt, short, blunt, abusive, curt, churlish, disrespectful, brusque, offhand, impertinent, insolent, inconsiderate, peremptory, impudent, discourteous, uncivil, unmannerly, ill-mannered • *He's rude to her friends.*
OPPOSITES: civil, mannerly, polite
2 = **uncivilized**, low, rough, savage, ignorant, coarse, illiterate, uneducated, brutish, barbarous, scurrilous, boorish, uncouth, unrefined, loutish, untutored, graceless, ungracious, unpolished, oafish, uncultured • *a rude barbarian*
3 = **vulgar**, offensive, gross, crude, obscene, tasteless, lewd, indelicate • *He made a rude gesture with his finger.*
OPPOSITES: learned, cultured, refined

4 = unpleasant, sharp, violent, sudden, harsh, startling, abrupt • *It came as a rude shock.*
5 = roughly-made, simple, rough, raw, crude, primitive, makeshift, rough-hewn, artless, inelegant, inartistic • *He had already constructed a rude cabin.*
OPPOSITES: even, finished, well-made

rudeness = discourtesy, bad manners, insolence, impertinence, incivility, ill-breeding, impoliteness, disrespectfulness, ungraciousness, unmannerliness • *She is cross at his rudeness.*

rudiment *often plural* **= basics**, elements, essentials, fundamentals, beginnings, foundation, nuts and bolts, first principles • *I think I can remember the rudiments of Latin*

rudimentary 1 = primitive, simple, basic, rough, crude, makeshift, undeveloped, unsophisticated, rough and ready • *It had been extended into a kind of rudimentary kitchen.*
2 = basic, fundamental, elementary, early, primary, initial, introductory • *He had only a rudimentary knowledge of French.*
3 = undeveloped, incomplete, immature, embryonic, vestigial • *a rudimentary backbone called a notochord*
OPPOSITES: advanced, mature, complete

rue = regret, mourn, grieve, lament, deplore, bemoan, repent, be sorry for, weep over, sorrow for, bewail, kick yourself for, reproach yourself for • *He was probably ruing his decision.*

rueful = regretful, sad, dismal, melancholy, grievous, pitiful, woeful, sorry, mournful, plaintive, lugubrious, contrite, sorrowful, repentant, doleful, remorseful, penitent, pitiable, woebegone, conscience-stricken, self-reproachful • *He shook his head and gave me a rueful smile.*
OPPOSITES: happy, pleased, unrepentant

ruff
▸ **NAME OF FEMALE:** reeve
▸ **COLLECTIVE NOUN:** hill

ruffian = thug, heavy *(slang)*, tough, rough *(informal)*, bully, casual, villain, ned *(Scot. slang)*, rogue, hooligan, brute, rowdy, rascal, scoundrel, hoodlum, bully boy, bruiser *(informal)*, wretch, yardie, lager lout, roughneck *(slang)*, miscreant, boot boy, tsotsi *(S. African)*, cougan *(Austral. slang)*, scozza *(Austral. slang)*, bogan *(Austral. slang)*, wrong 'un *(Austral. slang)* • *gangs of ruffians who lurk about*

ruffle 1 = disarrange, disorder, wrinkle, mess up, rumple, tousle, derange, discompose, dishevel, muss *(U.S. & Canad.)* • *She let the wind ruffle her hair.*
2 = ripple, riffle, roughen, make ripples in • *The evening breeze ruffled the pond.*
3 = annoy, worry, trouble, upset, confuse, stir, disturb, rattle *(informal)*, irritate, put out, unsettle, shake up *(informal)*, harass, hassle *(informal)*, agitate, unnerve, disconcert, disquiet, nettle, vex, fluster, perturb, faze, peeve *(informal)*, hack off *(informal)* • *My refusal to let him ruffle me infuriated him.*
OPPOSITES: ease, comfort, calm

rug 1 = mat, runner, carpet, hearthrug • *A Persian rug covered the floor.*
2 = blanket, throw, wrap, coverlet • *The old lady had a rug over her knees.*
3 = wig, hairpiece, toupee • *He's either wearing a rug or he's got a hamster on his head.*
▹ *See panel* **Carpets and rugs**

rugby
▹ *See panel* **Rugby terms**

rugged 1 = rocky, broken, rough, craggy, difficult, ragged, stark, irregular, uneven, jagged, bumpy • *a rugged mountainous terrain*
OPPOSITES: even, level, regular
2 = strong-featured, lined, worn, weathered, wrinkled, furrowed, leathery, rough-hewn, weather-beaten • *A look of disbelief crossed his rugged face.*
OPPOSITES: pretty, smooth, delicate
3 = well-built, strong, tough, robust, sturdy • *this rugged all-steel design*
4 = tough, strong, hardy, robust, vigorous, muscular, sturdy, hale, burly, husky *(informal)*, beefy *(informal)*, brawny • *He's rugged and durable, but not the best technical boxer.*
OPPOSITES: soft, weak, delicate
5 = uncompromising, decided, firm, tough, strict, rigid, stubborn, hardline, die-hard, inflexible, inexorable, steadfast, unyielding, obstinate, intransigent, unbending, obdurate, stiff-necked • *Rugged individualism forged America's frontier society.*
6 = difficult, trying, hard, taxing, demanding, tough, exacting, harsh, stern, rigorous, strenuous, arduous, laborious • *enjoying rugged sports like mountain biking*
OPPOSITES: easy, simple, soft
7 = stern, hard, severe, rough, harsh, sour, rude, crabbed, austere, dour, surly, gruff • *a fairly rugged customer*

ruin AS A VERB 1 = destroy, devastate, wreck, trash *(slang)*, break, total *(slang)*, defeat, smash, crush, overwhelm, shatter, overturn, overthrow, bring down, demolish, raze, lay waste, lay in ruins, wreak havoc upon, bring to ruin, bring to nothing, kennet *(Austral. slang)*, jeff *(Austral. slang)* • *Roads have been destroyed and crops ruined.*
OPPOSITES: keep, build, create
2 = bankrupt, break, cripple, impoverish, beggar, make bankrupt, reduce to penury, pauperize, cause to go bankrupt • *She accused him of ruining her financially.*
3 = spoil, damage, mar, mess up, blow *(slang)*, injure, undo, screw up *(informal)*, botch, mangle, cock up *(Brit. slang)*, disfigure, fuck up *(offensive taboo slang)*, make a mess of, bodge *(informal)*, crool or cruel *(Austral. slang)* • *The original decor was all ruined during renovation.*
OPPOSITES: support, improve, restore
▸ **AS A NOUN 1 = bankruptcy**, poverty, insolvency, penury, impoverishment, destitution, financial failure • *Recent inflation has driven them to the brink of ruin.*

RUGBY TERMS

back
back row
ball
centre
conversion
crossbar
drop goal
lock forward
loose forward
loose head
five-eighth *(Austral. & N.Z.)*
flanker *or* wing forward
forward *(Rugby union)*
forward
front row
full back
garryowen *(Rugby union)*
goalpost
half back
hooker
knock on
line-out *(Rugby union)*
mark *(Rugby union)*
maul *(Rugby union)*
number eight forward *(Rugby union)*
scrum
stand-off half, fly half, *or* outside half
pack
pass
penalty
prop forward
punt
referee
ruck *(Rugby union)*
scrum half
second row
tackle
three-quarter
tight head
touch judge
try
up and under *(Rugby league)*
winger

r

2 = **disrepair**, decay, disintegration, ruination, decrepitude, dilapidation, wreckage • *The vineyards were falling into ruin.*
3 = **destruction**, fall, the end, breakdown, damage, defeat, failure, crash, collapse, wreck, overthrow, undoing, havoc, Waterloo, downfall, devastation, dissolution, subversion, nemesis, crackup *(informal)* • *It is the ruin of society.*
OPPOSITES: success, victory, preservation
▸ **AS A PLURAL NOUN** = **wreckage**, wreck, remainder, debris, rubble, remnants, detritus • *the burnt-out ruins of houses*
▸ **IN PHRASES: in ruins** 1 = **ruined**, in tatters *(informal)*, over, finished, destroyed, at an end, in pieces, dead in the water *(informal)* • *The economy is in ruins.*
2 = **derelict**, ruined, broken down, falling apart, ramshackle, dilapidated, falling to pieces, tumbledown • *The building was in ruins.*
▸ **RELATED PHOBIA:** atephobia

ruined = **dilapidated**, broken down, falling apart, derelict, ramshackle, falling to pieces, tumbledown • *a ruined church*

ruinous 1 = **extravagant**, crippling, outrageous, inflated, wasteful, extortionate, excessively high, immoderate • *the ruinous costs of the legal system*
2 = **destructive**, devastating, shattering, fatal, deadly, disastrous, dire, withering, catastrophic, murderous, pernicious, noxious, calamitous, baleful, deleterious, injurious, baneful *(archaic)* • *the ruinous effects of the conflict*
3 = **ruined**, broken-down, derelict, ramshackle, dilapidated, in ruins, decrepit, tumbledown • *They passed by the ruinous building.*

rule **AS A NOUN** 1 = **regulation**, order, law, ruling, guide, direction, guideline, decree, ordinance, dictum • *the rule against retrospective prosecution*
2 = **precept**, principle, criterion, canon, maxim, tenet, axiom • *An important rule is to drink plenty of water.*
3 = **procedure**, policy, standard, method, way, course, formula • *according to the rules of quantum theory*
4 = **custom**, procedure, practice, routine, form, condition, tradition, habit, convention, wont, order *or* way of things • *The usual rule is to start as one group.*
5 = **government**, power, control, authority, influence, administration, direction, leadership, command, regime, empire, reign, sway, domination, jurisdiction, supremacy, mastery, dominion, ascendancy, mana *(N.Z.)* • *the winding-up of British rule over the territory*
▸ **AS A VERB** 1 = **govern**, lead, control, manage, direct, guide, regulate, administer, oversee, preside over, have power over, reign over, command over, have charge of • *the feudal lord who ruled this land*
2 = **reign**, govern, be in power, hold sway, wear the crown, be in authority, be number one *(informal)* • *He ruled for eight years.*
3 = **control**, dominate, monopolize, tyrannize, be pre-eminent, have the upper hand over • *Fear can rule our lives.*
4 = **decree**, find, decide, judge, establish, determine, settle, resolve, pronounce, lay down, adjudge • *The court ruled that laws passed by the assembly remained valid.*
5 = **be prevalent**, prevail, predominate, hold sway, be customary, preponderate, obtain • *A ferocious form of anarchy ruled here.*
▸ **IN PHRASES: as a rule** = **usually**, generally, mainly, normally, on the whole, for the most part, ordinarily, customarily • *As a rule, these tourists take far too many souvenirs with them.*
rule someone out = **exclude**, eliminate, disqualify, ban, prevent, reject, dismiss, forbid, prohibit, leave out, preclude, proscribe, obviate, debar • *a suspension which ruled him out of the grand final*
rule something out = **reject**, dismiss, exclude, eliminate, disregard, preclude, obviate • *Local detectives have ruled out foul play.*

QUOTATIONS

He shall rule them with a rod of iron
[*Bible: Revelation*]

My people and I have come to an agreement which satisfies us both. They are to say what they please, and I am to do what I please
[Frederick the Great]

The hand that rocks the cradle
Is the hand that rules the world
[William Ross Wallace *John O'London's Treasure Trove*]

Rules and models destroy genius and art
[William Hazlitt *Sketches and Essays*]

ruler 1 = **governor**, leader, lord, commander, controller, monarch, sovereign, head of state, potentate, crowned head, emperor *or* empress, king *or* queen, prince *or* princess • *He was an indecisive ruler.*
2 = **measure**, rule, yardstick, straight edge • *taking measurements with a ruler*

RULERS

TITLES OF RULERS

amir, arch duke, Caesar, caliph, chief, Chogyal, Dalai Lama, doge, duke, emir, emperor *or (fem.)* empress, Gaekwar, Great Mogul, hospodar, imam, Inca, kabaka, Kaiser, khan, khedive, king, maharajah, maharani, mikado, nawab, Negus, Nizam, oba, pasha, Pharaoh, podesta, pope, queen, rajah, rani, satrap, shah, sheik, sherif, shogun, stadholder, sultan, tenno, tsar, viceroy *or (fem.)* vicereine

FAMOUS RULERS

Alexander the Great, Alfred the Great, Idi Amin, Augustus, Bismarck, Boudicca, Caligula, Castro, Catherine the Great, Charlemagne, Churchill, Cleopatra, Cromwell, de Gaulle, Edward the Confessor, Elizabeth I, Elizabeth II, Franco, Genghis Khan, Haile Selassie, Herod, Hirohito, Hitler, Ivan the Terrible, Julius Caesar, Kublai Khan, Lenin, Louis XIV, Mao Ze Dong, Montezuma, Mussolini, Napoleon Bonaparte, Nasser, Nero, Nicholas II, Pericles, Peter the Great, Richard the Lionheart, Saladin, Stalin, Suleiman the Magnificent, Tamerlane, Tutankhamen, Victoria, William the Conqueror

ruling AS AN ADJECTIVE 1 = **governing**, upper, reigning, controlling, leading, commanding, dominant, regnant • *the domination of the ruling class*
2 = **predominant**, dominant, prevailing, preponderant, chief, main, current, supreme, principal, prevalent, pre-eminent, regnant • *a ruling passion for liberty and equality*
OPPOSITES: least, minor, secondary
▸ AS A NOUN = **decision**, finding, resolution, verdict, judgment, decree, adjudication, pronouncement • *He tried to have the court ruling overturned.*

rum = **strange**, odd, suspect, funny, unusual, curious, weird, suspicious, peculiar, dodgy *(Brit., Austral. & N.Z. informal)*, queer, singular, shonky *(Austral. & N.Z. informal)* • *It was a rum sort of joke.*

rumble = **roll**, boom, echo, roar, thunder, grumble, resound, reverberate • *Thunder rumbled over the Downs.*

rumbustious = **unruly**, wild, rough, disorderly, loud, noisy, robust, wayward, exuberant, rowdy, boisterous, wilful, unmanageable, uproarious, refractory, obstreperous, clamorous • *the flamboyant and rumbustious prime minister*

ruminate = **ponder**, think, consider, reflect, contemplate, deliberate, muse, brood, meditate, mull over things, chew over things, cogitate, rack your brains, turn over in your mind • *I had time to ruminate as I drove along.*

rummage = **search**, hunt, root, explore, delve, examine, ransack, forage, fossick *(Austral. & N.Z.)*, rootle • *They rummage through piles of second-hand clothes.*

rumour AS A NOUN = **story**, news, report, talk, word, whisper, buzz, gossip, dirt *(U.S. slang)*, goss *(informal)*, hearsay, canard, tidings, scuttlebutt *(U.S. slang)*, bush telegraph, bruit *(archaic)* • *There's a strange rumour going around.*
▸ IN PHRASES: **be rumoured** = **be said**, be told, be reported, be published, be circulated, be whispered, be passed around, be put about, be noised abroad • *It was rumoured that he'd been interned in an asylum.*

rump 1 = **remains**, rest, those left, remaining part • *The rump of the party does still have assets.*
2 = **buttocks**, bottom, rear, backside *(informal)*, tail *(informal)*, seat, butt *(U.S. & Canad. informal)*, bum *(Brit. slang)*, ass *(U.S. & Canad. taboo slang)*, buns *(U.S. slang)*, arse *(taboo slang)*, rear end, posterior, haunch, hindquarters, derrière *(euphemistic)*, croup, jacksy *(Brit. slang)* • *jeans stretching across her rump*

rumple = **ruffle**, crush, disorder, dishevel, wrinkle, crease, crumple, screw up, mess up, pucker, crinkle, scrunch, tousle, derange, muss *(U.S. & Canad.)* • *I leaned forward to rumple his hair.*

rumpus = **commotion**, row, noise, confusion, fuss, disturbance, disruption, furore, uproar, tumult, brouhaha, shindig *(informal)*, hue and cry, kerfuffle *(informal)*, shindy *(informal)* • *He had left before the rumpus started.*

run AS A VERB 1 = **race**, speed, rush, dash, hurry, career, barrel (along) *(informal, chiefly U.S. & Canad.)*, sprint, scramble, bolt, dart, gallop, hare *(Brit. informal)*, jog, scud, hasten, scurry, stampede, scamper, leg it *(informal)*, lope, hie, hotfoot • *I excused myself and ran back to the telephone.*
OPPOSITES: walk, creep, dawdle
2 = **flee**, escape, take off *(informal)*, depart, bolt, clear out, beat it *(slang)*, leg it *(informal)*, make off, abscond, decamp, take flight, do a runner *(slang)*, scarper *(Brit. slang)*, slope off, cut and run *(informal)*, make a run for it, fly the coop *(U.S. & Canad. informal)*, beat a retreat, show a clean pair of heels, skedaddle *(informal)*, take a powder *(U.S. & Canad. slang)*, take it on the lam *(U.S. & Canad. slang)*, take to your heels • *As they closed in on him, he turned and ran.*
OPPOSITES: remain, stay
3 = **take part**, be in, compete, participate, enter • *I was running in the marathon.*
4 = **continue**, go, stretch, last, reach, lie, range, extend, proceed • *the trail which ran through the beech woods*
OPPOSITES: stop, cease
5 = **compete**, stand, contend, be a candidate, put yourself up for, take part, challenge • *He announced he would run for president.*
6 = **manage**, lead, direct, be in charge of, own, head, control, boss *(informal)*, operate, handle, conduct, look after, carry on, regulate, take care of, administer, oversee, supervise, mastermind, coordinate, superintend • *His father ran a prosperous business.*
7 = **go**, work, operate, perform, function, be in business, be in action, tick over • *the staff who have kept the bank running*
8 = **perform**, do, carry out, execute • *He ran a lot of tests.*
9 = **work**, go, operate, function • *The tape recorder was still running.*
10 = **drive**, own, keep, maintain, possess • *I ran a 1960 Rover 100.*
11 = **operate**, go, travel, shuttle • *A shuttle bus runs frequently.*
12 = **give a lift to**, drive, carry, transport, convey, bear, manoeuvre, propel • *Can you run me to work?*
13 = **pass**, go, move, roll, slide, glide, skim • *He winced as he ran his hand over his ribs.*
14 = **flow**, pour, stream, cascade, go, move, issue, proceed, leak, spill, discharge, gush, spout, course • *cisterns to catch rainwater as it ran off the walls*
15 = **spread**, mix, bleed, be diffused, lose colour • *The ink had run on the wet paper.*
16 = **circulate**, spread, creep, go round • *A buzz of excitement ran through the crowd.*
17 = **publish**, carry, feature, display, print • *The paper ran a series of scathing editorials.*
18 = **be staged**, be on, be presented, be produced, be put on, be performed, be mounted • *The play ran for only 3 years in the West End.*
19 = **be valid**, be in force, be legally binding • *The contract was to run from 1992 to 2020.*
20 = **melt**, dissolve, liquefy, go soft, turn to liquid • *The pitch between the planks of the deck melted and ran.*
21 = **unravel**, tear, ladder, come apart, come undone • *ladders in your tights gradually running all the way up your leg*
22 = **smuggle**, deal in, traffic in, bootleg, ship, sneak • *I started running guns again.*
23 = **chase**, drive, hunt, hound • *I was just run out of town.*
▸ AS A NOUN 1 = **race**, rush, dash, sprint, trot, gallop, jog, spurt • *a six mile run*
2 = **ride**, drive, trip, lift, journey, spin *(informal)*, outing, excursion, jaunt, joy ride *(informal)*, awayday • *Take them for a run in the car.*
3 = **round**, route, journey, circuit, course • *doing the morning school run*
4 = **sequence**, period, stretch, spell, course, season, round, series, chain, cycle, string, passage, streak • *Their run of luck is holding.*
5 = **free use**, unrestricted access to, a free hand in, unrestricted use of • *He had the run of the house and the pool.*
6 = **type**, sort, kind, class, variety, category, order • *outside the common run of professional athletes*
7 = **tear**, rip, ladder, snag • *She had a huge run in her tights.*
8 = **enclosure**, pen, coop • *My mother had a little chicken run.*
9 = **direction**, way, course, current, movement, progress, flow, path, trend, motion, passage, stream, tendency, drift, tide, tenor • *The only try came against the run of play.*
10 = **slope**, track, piste • *an alpine ski run*
11 *with* **on** = **sudden demand for**, pressure for, clamour for, rush for • *A run on sterling has killed hopes of a rate cut.*
▸ IN PHRASES: **in the long run** = **in the end**, eventually, in time, ultimately, at the end of the day, in the final analysis, when all is said and done, in the fullness of time • *Things could get worse in the long run.*

on the run 1 = escaping, fugitive, in flight, at liberty, on the loose, on the lam *(U.S. slang)* • *The four men still on the run are Rule 43 prisoners.*
2 = in retreat, defeated, fleeing, retreating, running away, falling back, in flight • *I knew I had him on the run.*
3 = hurrying, hastily, in a hurry, at speed, hurriedly, in a rush, in haste • *We ate lunch on the run.*
run across something *or* **someone = meet**, encounter, meet with, come across, run into, bump into, come upon, chance upon • *We ran across some old friends.*
run after something *or* **someone = pursue**, follow, chase, give chase • *She ran after him and caught him.*
run along = go away, clear off *(informal)*, beat it *(informal)*, on your way, shoo, buzz off *(informal)*, scram *(informal)*, bog off *(Brit. slang)*, skedaddle *(informal)*, be off with you, make yourself scarce • *Run along now and play for a bit.*
run away = flee, escape, take off, bolt, run off, clear out, beat it *(slang)*, abscond, decamp, take flight, hook it *(slang)*, do a runner *(slang)*, scarper *(Brit. slang)*, cut and run *(informal)*, make a run for it, turn tail, do a bunk *(Brit. slang)*, scram *(informal)*, fly the coop *(U.S. & Canad. informal)*, show a clean pair of heels, skedaddle *(informal)*, take a powder *(U.S. & Canad. slang)*, take it on the lam *(U.S. & Canad. slang)*, take to your heels, do a Skase *(Austral. informal)* • *I ran away from home when I was sixteen.*
run away with something *or* **someone 1 = abscond with**, run off with, elope with • *She ran away with a man called Allen.*
2 = win easily, walk it *(informal)*, romp home, win hands down, win by a mile *(informal)* • *She ran away with the gold medal.*
run for it = flee, fly, escape, take off, bolt, make off, abscond, decamp, take flight, do a runner *(slang)*, scarper *(Brit. slang)*, cut and run *(informal)*, do a bunk *(Brit. slang)*, scram *(informal)*, fly the coop *(U.S. & Canad. informal)*, make a break for it, show a clean pair of heels, skedaddle *(informal)*, take a powder *(U.S. & Canad. slang)*, take it on the lam *(U.S. & Canad. slang)*, do a Skase *(Austral. informal)* • *Get out, run for it!*
run high = be intense, be strong, be passionate, be vehement, be impassioned • *Feelings there have been running high.*
run into someone = meet, encounter, bump into, run across, chance upon, come across *or* upon • *He ran into him in the corridor.*
run into something 1 = be beset by, encounter, meet with, come across *or* upon, face, experience, be confronted by, happen on *or* upon • *They ran into financial problems.*
2 = collide with, hit, strike, ram, bump into, crash into, dash against • *The driver ran into a tree.*
run off = flee, escape, bolt, run away, clear out, make off, decamp, take flight, hook it *(slang)*, do a runner *(slang)*, scarper *(Brit. slang)*, cut and run *(informal)*, turn tail, fly the coop *(U.S. & Canad. informal)*, show a clean pair of heels, skedaddle *(informal)*, take a powder *(U.S. & Canad. slang)*, take it on the lam *(U.S. & Canad. slang)*, take to your heels • *He then ran off towards a nearby underground railway station.*
run off with someone = run away with, elope with, abscond with • *He ran off with a younger woman.*
run off with something = steal, take, lift *(informal)*, nick *(slang, chiefly Brit.)*, trouser *(slang)*, pinch *(informal)*, swipe *(slang)*, knock off *(slang)*, run away with, make off with, embezzle, misappropriate, purloin, filch, walk *or* make off with • *Who ran off with the money?*
run on = stretch, reach, cover, spread, extend, unfold • *The sands ran on for five miles before the next town.*
run on something *or* **someone = dwell on**, be dominated by, be concerned with, be preoccupied with, revolve round, centre round, be fixated with • *My thoughts ran on my losses.*
run out 1 = be used up, dry up, give out, peter out, fail, finish, cease, be exhausted • *Supplies are running out.*
2 = expire, end, lapse, terminate, become invalid • *the day my visa ran out*
run out of something = exhaust your supply of, be out of, be cleaned out, have no more, have none left, have no remaining • *The plane ran out of fuel.*
run out on someone = desert, abandon, strand, run away from, forsake, rat on *(informal)*, leave high and dry, leave holding the baby, leave in the lurch • *You can't run out on your wife and children like that.*
run over = overflow, spill over, brim over • *Water ran over the sides and trickled down on to the floor.*
run over something 1 = exceed, overstep, go over the top of, go beyond the bounds of, go over the limit of • *Phase one has run over budget.*
2 = review, check, survey, examine, go through, go over, run through, rehearse, reiterate • *Let's run over the instructions again.*
run over something *or* **someone = knock down**, hit, strike, run down, knock over • *He ran over a six-year-old child.*
run someone in = arrest, apprehend, pull in *(Brit. slang)*, take into custody, lift *(slang)*, pick up, jail, nail *(informal)*, bust *(informal)*, collar *(informal)*, pinch *(informal)*, nab *(informal)*, throw in jail, take to jail, feel your collar *(slang)* • *They had run him in on a petty charge.*
run someone through = pierce, stab, spit, transfix, impale, stick • *He threatened to run him through with his sword.*
run something in = break in gently, run gently • *He hardly had the time to run the car in.*
run something off = produce, print, duplicate, churn out *(informal)* • *They ran off some copies for me.*
run something *or* **someone down 1 = criticize**, denigrate, belittle, revile, knock *(informal)*, flame *(informal)*, rubbish *(informal)*, put down, slag (off) *(slang)*, disparage, decry, vilify, diss *(slang, chiefly U.S.)*, defame, bad-mouth *(slang, chiefly U.S. & Canad.)*, speak ill of, asperse • *He was running down state schools.*
2 = downsize, cut, drop, reduce, trim, decrease, cut back, curtail, pare down, kennet *(Austral. slang)*, jeff *(Austral. slang)* • *The property business could be sold or run down.*
3 = knock down, hit, strike, run into, run over, knock over • *He was in the roadway and I nearly ran him down.*
run through something 1 = review, check, survey, examine, go through, go over, look over, run over • *I ran through the options with him.*
2 = rehearse, read, practise, go over, run over • *I ran through the handover procedure.*
3 = pervade, go through, inform, permeate, suffuse • *themes running through all my novels*
4 = squander, waste, exhaust, throw away, dissipate, fritter away, spend like water, blow *(slang)* • *The country had run through its public food stocks.*

QUOTATIONS
He who fights and runs away
May live to fight another day
[Oliver Goldsmith *The Art of Poetry on a New Plan*]

runaway AS AN ADJECTIVE **1 = easily won**, easy, effortless • *a runaway success*
2 = out of control, uncontrolled, driverless • *The runaway car careered into a bench.*
3 = escaped, wild, fleeing, loose, fugitive • *a runaway horse*
4 = uncontrolled, out of control, rampant, unchecked • *Such a mix of policies would normally lead to runaway inflation.*
▸ AS A NOUN **= fugitive**, escaper, refugee, deserter, truant, escapee, absconder • *a teenage runaway*
rundown *or* **run-down** AS AN ADJECTIVE **1 = exhausted**, weak, tired, drained, fatigued, weary, unhealthy, worn-out, debilitated, below par, under the weather *(informal)*, enervated, out of condition, peaky • *She started to feel rundown last December.*
OPPOSITES: well, fine, fit

2 = **dilapidated**, broken-down, shabby, worn-out, seedy, ramshackle, dingy, decrepit, tumbledown • *a rundown block of flats*
▸ **AS A NOUN** = **summary**, review, briefing, résumé, outline, sketch, run-through, synopsis, recap *(informal)*, précis • *Here's a rundown of the options*
▸ **IN PHRASES: run-in AS A NOUN** = **fight**, row, argument, dispute, set-to *(informal)*, encounter, brush, confrontation, quarrel, skirmish, tussle, altercation, face-off *(slang)*, turf war *(informal)*, dust-up *(informal)*, contretemps, biffo *(Austral. slang)* • *We had a run-in with the Tax people the other day.*

runner AS A NOUN 1 = **athlete**, miler, sprinter, harrier, jogger • *a marathon runner*
2 = **messenger**, courier, errand boy, dispatch bearer • *a bookie's runner*
3 = **stem**, shoot, sprout, sprig, offshoot, tendril, stolon *(Botany)* • *strawberry runners*
▸ **IN PHRASES: do a runner** = **run away**, escape, flee, take off, bolt, run off, clear out, beat it *(slang)*, abscond, decamp, take flight, hook it *(slang)*, scarper *(Brit. slang)*, cut and run *(informal)*, make a run for it, do a bunk *(Brit. slang)*, scram *(informal)*, fly the coop *(U.S. & Canad. informal)*, show a clean pair of heels, skedaddle *(informal)*, take a powder *(U.S. & Canad. slang)*, take it on the lam *(U.S. & Canad. slang)* • *The accountant did a runner.*

running AS A NOUN 1 = **sprinting**, racing, sprint, jogging • *cross-country running*
2 = **management**, control, administration, direction, conduct, charge, leadership, organization, regulation, supervision, coordination, superintendency • *in charge of the day-to-day running of the party*
3 = **working**, performance, operation, functioning, maintenance • *the smooth running of the machine*
▸ **AS AN ADJECTIVE** 1 = **continuous**, constant, perpetual, uninterrupted, incessant, unceasing • *The song turned into a running joke between them.*
2 = **in succession**, together, unbroken, on the trot *(informal)* • *She never seems the same woman two days running.*
3 = **flowing**, moving, rushing, streaming, coursing • *Wash the lentils under cold, running water.*
▸ **IN PHRASES: in the running** = **in contention for**, up for, likely to get, in line for, being considered for, a candidate for, on the shortlist for • *He's in the running for a gold medal.*
out of the running = **out of contention**, out of the competition, out of the contest, no longer a candidate for • *I was out of the running for the title.*
up and running = **operating**, going, working, functioning, in operation *or* action • *We're trying to get the medical facilities up and running.*

runny = **flowing**, liquid, melted, fluid, diluted, watery, streaming, liquefied • *Warm the honey until it becomes runny.*

run-of-the-mill = **ordinary**, middling, average, fair, modest, commonplace, common, vanilla *(informal)*, mediocre, banal, tolerable, passable, undistinguished, unimpressive, unexciting, unexceptional, bog-standard *(Brit. & Irish slang)*, no great shakes *(informal)*, dime-a-dozen *(informal)* • *I was a run-of-the-mill kind of student.*
OPPOSITES: excellent, unusual, exceptional

run-up = **time leading up to**, approach, build-up, preliminaries • *the run-up to the elections*

rupture AS A NOUN 1 = **hernia** *(Medical)* • *a rupture of the abdominal aorta*
2 = **breach**, split, hostility, falling-out *(informal)*, disagreement, contention, feud, disruption, quarrel, rift, break, bust-up *(informal)*, dissolution, altercation, schism, estrangement • *a major rupture between the two countries*
3 = **break**, tear, split, crack, rent, burst, breach, fracture, cleavage, cleft, fissure • *ruptures in a 60-mile pipeline on the island*
▸ **AS A VERB** 1 = **break**, separate, tear, split, crack, burst, rend, fracture, sever, puncture, cleave • *Tanks can rupture and burn in a collision.*
2 = **cause a breach**, split, divide, disrupt, break off, come between, dissever • *an accident which ruptured the bond between them*

rural 1 = **agricultural**, country, farming, agrarian, upcountry, agrestic • *These plants grow in the more rural areas.*
2 = **rustic**, country, hick *(informal, chiefly U.S. & Canad.)*, pastoral, bucolic, sylvan, Arcadian, countrified • *the old rural way of life*
OPPOSITES: city, town, urban

ruse = **trick**, deception, ploy, hoax, device, manoeuvre, dodge, sham, artifice, blind, subterfuge, stratagem, wile, imposture • *This was a ruse to divide them.*

rush AS A VERB 1 = **hurry**, run, race, shoot, fly, career, speed, tear, dash, sprint, scramble, bolt, dart, hasten, scurry, stampede, lose no time, make short work of, burn rubber *(informal)*, make haste, hotfoot • *Someone inside the building rushed out.*
OPPOSITES: wait, delay, dawdle
2 = **push**, hurry, accelerate, dispatch, speed up, quicken, press, hustle, expedite • *The Act was rushed through after a legal loophole was discovered.*
3 = **attack**, storm, capture, overcome, charge at, assail, take by storm • *They rushed the entrance.*
4 = **flow**, run, course, shoot, pour, stream, surge, cascade, gush • *Water rushes out of huge tunnels.*
▸ **AS A NOUN** 1 = **dash**, charge, race, scramble, stampede, expedition, speed, dispatch • *The explosion caused panic and a mad rush for the doors.*
2 = **hurry**, urgency, bustle, haste, hustle, helter-skelter, hastiness • *the rush not to be late for school*
3 = **run (on)**, call, demand, request, clamour • *They are expecting a huge rush for the record.*
4 = **bustle**, commotion, hubbub, hurly-burly, flurry of activity • *the Christmas rush*
5 = **surge**, flow, flood, thrill, flush, gush, spurt • *A rush of affection swept over him.*
6 = **gust**, flurry, draught • *A rush of air on my face woke me.*
7 = **attack**, charge, push, storm, assault, surge, onslaught • *Throw something noisy and feign a rush at him.*
▸ **AS AN ADJECTIVE** = **hasty**, fast, quick, hurried, emergency, prompt, rapid, urgent, swift, brisk, cursory, expeditious • *I guess you could call it a rush job.*
OPPOSITES: detailed, slow, leisurely

rushed 1 = **hasty**, fast, quick, emergency, prompt, rapid, hurried, urgent, swift, brisk, cursory, expeditious • *a rushed job*
2 = **hurried**, frantic, in a hurry, pressed for time, pushed for time • *At no time did I feel rushed.*

rust AS A NOUN 1 = **corrosion**, oxidation • *a decaying tractor, red with rust*
2 = **mildew**, must, mould, rot, blight • *canker, rust, mildew or insect attack*
▸ **AS AN ADJECTIVE** = **reddish-brown**, reddish, russet, coppery • *a pair of rust slacks*
▸ **AS A VERB** 1 = **corrode**, decay, tarnish, oxidize, become rusty • *The bolt on the door had rusted*
2 = **deteriorate**, decline, decay, stagnate, atrophy, go stale • *If you rest, you rust.*

rustic AS AN ADJECTIVE 1 = **rural**, country, pastoral, bucolic, sylvan, Arcadian, countrified, upcountry, agrestic • *the rustic charms of a country lifestyle*
OPPOSITES: urban, cosmopolitan
2 = **simple**, homely, basic, plain, homespun, unsophisticated, unrefined, artless, unpolished • *wonderfully rustic old log cabins*
OPPOSITES: grand, polished, sophisticated

r

▸ **AS A NOUN** = **yokel**, peasant, hick (*informal, chiefly U.S. & Canad.*), bumpkin, Hodge, swain (*archaic*), hillbilly, country boy, clod, boor, country cousin, hayseed (*U.S. & Canad. informal*), clodhopper (*informal*), son of the soil, clown, countryman *or* countrywoman • *rustics in from the country*
OPPOSITES: cosmopolitan, courtier, sophisticate

rustle AS A VERB = **crackle**, whisper, swish, whoosh, crinkle, whish, crepitate, susurrate (*literary*) • *The leaves rustled in the wind.*
▸ **AS A NOUN** = **crackle**, whisper, rustling, crinkling, crepitation, susurration *or* susurrus (*literary*) • *with a rustle of her frilled petticoats*
▸ **IN PHRASES: rustle something up** = **prepare**, make, produce, fix, put together, concoct • *Can you rustle up a cup of coffee for me?*

rusty 1 = **corroded**, rusted, oxidized, rust-covered • *travelling around in a rusty old van*
2 = **out of practice**, weak, impaired, sluggish, stale, deficient, not what it was, unpractised • *Your French is a bit rusty.*
3 = **reddish-brown**, chestnut, reddish, russet, coppery, rust-coloured • *Her hair was rusty brown.*
4 = **croaking**, cracked, creaking, hoarse, croaky • *his mild, rusty voice*
▷ *See panel* **Shades of red**

rut 1 = **habit**, routine, dead end, humdrum existence, system, pattern, groove • *I don't like being in a rut.*
2 = **groove**, score, track, trough, furrow, gouge, pothole, indentation, wheel mark • *deep ruts left by the truck's heavy wheels*

ruthless = **merciless**, hard, severe, fierce, harsh, cruel, savage, brutal, stern, relentless, adamant, ferocious, callous, heartless, unrelenting, inhuman, inexorable, remorseless, barbarous, pitiless, unfeeling, hard-hearted, without pity, unmerciful, unpitying • *a ruthless totalitarian power*
OPPOSITES: kind, sparing, merciful

rutted = **grooved**, cut, marked, scored, holed, furrowed, gouged, indented • *a ride along the deeply rutted roads*

r

Ss

Sabbath

QUOTATIONS

The sabbath was made for man, and not man for the sabbath

[*Bible: St. Mark*]

Remember the sabbath day, to keep it holy

[*Bible: Exodus*]

sable 1 = **black**, jet, raven, jetty, ebony, ebon *(poetic)* • *thick sable lashes*
▹ *See panel* **Shades from black to white**
2 = **dark**, black, dim, gloomy, dismal, dreary, sombre, shadowy, sepulchral, crepuscular, Stygian, tenebrous • *Night enveloped me in its sable mantle.*

sabotage AS A VERB 1 = **damage**, destroy, wreck, undermine, disable, disrupt, cripple, subvert, incapacitate, vandalize, throw a spanner in the works *(Brit. informal)*, sap the foundations of • *The main pipeline was sabotaged by rebels.*
2 = **disrupt**, ruin, wreck, spoil, interrupt, interfere with, obstruct, intrude, crool *or* cruel *(Austral. slang)* • *My ex-wife deliberately sabotages my access to the children.*
▸ AS A NOUN 1 = **damage**, destruction, wrecking, vandalism, deliberate damage • *The bombing was a spectacular act of sabotage.*
2 = **disruption**, ruining, wrecking, spoiling, interference, intrusion, interruption, obstruction • *political sabotage of government policy*

saboteur = **demonstrator**, rebel, dissident, hooligan, vandal, delinquent, dissenter, agitator, protest marcher • *The saboteurs had planned to bomb buses and offices.*

sac = **pouch**, bag, pocket, bladder, pod, cyst, bursa, vesicle • *The lungs consist of millions of tiny air sacs.*

saccharine = **sickly**, honeyed, sentimental, sugary, nauseating, soppy *(Brit. informal)*, cloying, maudlin, syrupy *(informal)*, mawkish, icky *(informal)*, treacly, oversweet • *She smiled with saccharine sweetness.*

sack[1] AS A NOUN = **bag**, pocket, poke *(Scot.)*, sac, pouch, receptacle • *a sack of potatoes*
▸ AS A VERB = **dismiss**, fire *(informal)*, axe *(informal)*, discharge, kick out *(informal)*, give (someone) the boot *(slang)*, give (someone) his marching orders, kiss off *(slang, chiefly U.S. & Canad.)*, give (someone) the push *(informal)*, give (someone) the bullet *(Brit. slang)*, give (someone) his books *(informal)*, give (someone) the elbow, give (someone) his cards, give someone his *or* her P45 *(informal)*, kennet *(Austral. slang)*, jeff *(Austral. slang)* • *He was sacked for slapping a schoolboy.*
▸ IN PHRASES: **hit the sack** = **go to bed**, retire, turn in *(informal)*, bed down, hit the hay *(slang)* • *I hit the sack early.*
the sack = **dismissal**, discharge, the boot *(slang)*, the axe *(informal)*, the chop *(Brit. slang)*, the push *(slang)*, the (old) heave-ho *(informal)*, termination of employment, the order of the boot *(slang)* • *People who make mistakes can be given the sack the same day.*

sack[2] AS A VERB = **plunder**, loot, pillage, destroy, strip, rob, raid, ruin, devastate, spoil, rifle, demolish, ravage, lay waste, despoil, maraud, depredate *(rare)* • *Imperial troops sacked the French ambassador's residence in Rome.*
▸ AS A NOUN = **plundering**, looting, pillage, waste, rape, ruin, destruction, ravage, plunder, devastation, depredation, despoliation, rapine • *the sack of Troy*

sacred 1 = **holy**, hallowed, consecrated, blessed, divine, revered, venerable, sanctified • *shrines and sacred places*
OPPOSITES: worldly, lay, secular
2 = **religious**, holy, ecclesiastical, hallowed, venerated • *the awe-inspiring sacred art of the Renaissance masters*
OPPOSITES: unconsecrated
3 = **inviolable**, protected, sacrosanct, secure, hallowed, inalienable, invulnerable, inviolate, unalterable • *My memories are sacred.*

sacrifice AS A VERB 1 = **offer**, slaughter, offer up, immolate • *The priest sacrificed a chicken.*
2 = **give up**, abandon, relinquish, lose, surrender, let go, do without, renounce, forfeit, forego, say goodbye to • *She sacrificed family life when her career took off.*
▸ AS A NOUN 1 = **offering**, immolation, oblation, hecatomb • *animal sacrifices to the gods*
2 = **surrender**, loss, giving up, resignation, rejection, waiver, abdication, renunciation, repudiation, forswearing, relinquishment, eschewal, self-denial • *They have not suffered any sacrifice of identity.*

QUOTATIONS

Never in the field of human conflict was so much owed by so many to so few

[Winston Churchill *speech to the House of Commons*]

Too long a sacrifice
Can make a stone of the heart

[W.B. Yeats *Easter 1916*]

Greater love hath no man than this, that a man lay down his life for his friends

[*Bible: St. John*]

PROVERBS

You cannot make an omelette without breaking eggs

sacrificial = **propitiatory**, atoning, reparative, expiatory, oblatory • *a sacrificial victim*

sacrilege 1 = **desecration**, violation, blasphemy, mockery, heresy, irreverence, profanity, impiety, profanation, profaneness • *Stealing from a place of worship was considered a sacrilege.*
OPPOSITES: respect, reverence, piety
2 = **disrespect**, contempt, disregard, dishonour, lack of respect, irreverence, impertinence, discourtesy • *It is a sacrilege to offend democracy.*

sacrilegious = **profane**, irreverent, blasphemous, unholy, desecrating, godless, ungodly, irreligious, impious • *Churches were sacked and sacrilegious acts committed.*

sacrosanct = **inviolable**, sacred, inviolate, untouchable, hallowed, sanctified, set apart • *Weekend rest days were considered sacrosanct.*

sad 1 = **unhappy**, down, low, blue, depressed, gloomy, grieved, dismal, melancholy, sombre, glum, wistful, mournful, dejected, downcast, grief-stricken, tearful, lugubrious, pensive, disconsolate, doleful, heavy-hearted, down in the dumps *(informal)*, cheerless, lachrymose, woebegone, down in the mouth *(informal)*, low-spirited, triste *(archaic)*, sick at heart • *The loss left me feeling sad and empty.*
OPPOSITES: happy, pleased, glad
2 = **tragic**, moving, upsetting, dark, sorry, depressing, disastrous, dismal, pathetic, poignant, harrowing, grievous, pitiful, calamitous, heart-rending, pitiable • *the sad news that he had been killed in a motor-cycle accident*
3 = **deplorable**, bad, sorry, terrible, distressing, unfortunate, miserable, dismal, shabby, heartbreaking, regrettable, lamentable, wretched, to be deplored • *It's a sad truth that children are the biggest victims of passive smoking.*
OPPOSITES: good
4 = **ridiculous**, silly, pathetic, sorry, foolish-looking • *sad old bikers*
5 = **regrettable**, disappointing, distressing, unhappy, unfortunate, unsatisfactory, woeful, deplorable, lamentable • *a sad state of affairs*
OPPOSITES: fortunate

sadden = **upset**, depress, distress, grieve, desolate, cast down, bring tears to your eyes, make sad, dispirit, make your heart bleed, aggrieve, deject, cast a gloom upon • *The cruelty in the world saddens me incredibly.*

saddle = **burden**, load, lumber *(Brit. informal)*, charge, tax, task, encumber • *The war saddled the country with huge foreign debt.*

sadism = **cruelty**, savagery, brutality, severity, ferocity, spite, ruthlessness, depravity, harshness, inhumanity, barbarity, callousness, viciousness, bestiality, heartlessness, brutishness, spitefulness, bloodthirstiness, murderousness, mercilessness, fiendishness, hardheartedness • *He was the victim of another's sadism.*

sadistic = **cruel**, savage, brutal, beastly, vicious, ruthless, perverted, perverse, inhuman, barbarous, fiendish • *There was a sadistic streak in him.*

sadness = **unhappiness**, sorrow, grief, tragedy, depression, the blues, misery, melancholy, poignancy, despondency, bleakness, heavy heart, dejection, wretchedness, gloominess, mournfulness, dolour *(poetic)*, dolefulness, cheerlessness, sorrowfulness • *It is with a mixture of sadness and joy that I say farewell.*
OPPOSITES: happiness, delight, pleasure

safe AS AN ADJECTIVE 1 = **protected**, secure, in safety, impregnable, out of danger, safe and sound, in safe hands, out of harm's way, free from harm • *Keep your camera safe from sand.*
OPPOSITES: damaged, threatened, endangered
2 = **all right**, fine, intact, unscathed, unhurt, unharmed, undamaged, out of the woods, O.K. *or* okay *(informal)* • *Where is Sophie? Is she safe?*
3 = **cautious**, prudent, sure, conservative, reliable, realistic, discreet, dependable, trustworthy, circumspect, on the safe side, unadventurous, tried and true • *I shall conceal myself at a safe distance from the battlefield.*
OPPOSITES: risky, reckless, unsafe
4 = **risk-free**, sound, secure, certain, impregnable, riskless • *We are assured by our engineers that the building is safe.*
5 = **boring**, routine, dull, old, dead, flat, tiring, tedious, stale, tiresome, monotonous, humdrum, uninteresting, insipid, mind-numbing, unexciting, ho-hum *(informal)*, repetitious, wearisome, unvaried • *Rock 'n' roll has become so commercialised and safe.*
6 = **harmless**, wholesome, innocuous, pure, tame, unpolluted, nontoxic, nonpoisonous • *a clean, inexpensive and safe fuel*
OPPOSITES: dangerous, harmful, hazardous
▸ AS A NOUN = **strongbox**, vault, coffer, repository, deposit box, safe-deposit box, strongroom • *The files are now in a safe.*
▸ IN PHRASES: **be on the safe side** = **be cautious**, be careful, be prudent, be alert, be tentative, be circumspect, be judicious, be heedful • *Let's say two-thirty to be on the safe side.*

PROVERBS
Better safe than sorry

safeguard AS A VERB = **protect**, guard, defend, save, screen, secure, preserve, look after, shield, watch over, keep safe • *international action to safeguard the ozone layer*
▸ AS A NOUN = **protection**, security, defence, guard, shield, armour, aegis, bulwark, surety • *A system like ours lacks adequate safeguards for civil liberties.*

safe haven = **refuge**, security, haven, protection, resort, shelter, retreat, harbour, asylum, sanctuary, hide-out, bolt hole • *a safe haven for terrorists*

safekeeping = **protection**, keeping, care, charge, trust, ward, custody, supervision, surveillance, tutelage, guardianship • *He had been given the bills for safekeeping by a business partner.*

safely = **in safety**, securely, with impunity, without risk, with safety, safe and sound • *'Drive safely,' he said, and waved goodbye.*

safety 1 = **security**, protection, safeguards, assurance, precautions, immunity, safety measures, impregnability • *The report makes recommendations to improve safety on aircraft.*
OPPOSITES: risk, peril, vulnerability
2 = **shelter**, haven, protection, cover, retreat, asylum, refuge, sanctuary • *the safety of your own home*
3 = **reliability**, security, harmlessness, lack of side effects • *The safety of the drug has not yet been proven.*
4 = **well-being**, security, protection, safeness • *There is grave concern for the safety of witnesses.*

PROVERBS
There is safety in numbers

sag 1 = **sink**, bag, droop, fall, drop, seat *(of a skirt, etc)*, settle, slump, dip, give way, bulge, swag, hang loosely, fall unevenly • *The shirts cuffs won't sag and lose their shape after washing.*
2 = **drop**, sink, slump, flop, droop, loll • *He shrugged and sagged into a chair.*
3 = **decline**, fall, slip, tire, slide, flag, slump, weaken, wilt, wane, cave in, droop • *Some of the tension he builds up begins to sag.*

saga 1 = **carry-on** *(informal)*, to-do, performance *(informal)*, rigmarole, soap opera, pantomime *(informal)*, chain of events, catalogue of disasters • *the whole saga of Hoddle's dismissal*
2 = **epic**, story, tale, legend, adventure, romance, narrative, chronicle, yarn, fairy tale, folk tale, roman-fleuve *(French)* • *a Nordic saga of giants and trolls*

sagacious = **wise**, shrewd, astute, knowing, able, fly *(slang)*, sharp, acute, smart, intelligent, sage, discerning, canny, perceptive, judicious, insightful, far-sighted, clear-sighted, long-headed, sharp-witted, perspicacious • *a wise and sagacious leader*

sagacity = **wisdom**, shrewdness, understanding, sense, insight, penetration, prudence, foresight, sharpness, discernment, perspicacity, knowingness, astuteness, acuteness, canniness, judiciousness, sapience • *a man of great sagacity and immense experience*

sage AS A NOUN = **wise man**, philosopher, guru, authority, expert, master, elder, pundit, Solomon, mahatma, Nestor, savant, Solon, man of learning, tohunga *(N.Z.)* • *ancient Chinese sages*

▸ **AS AN ADJECTIVE** = **wise**, learned, intelligent, sensible, politic, acute, discerning, prudent, canny, judicious, perspicacious, sagacious, sapient • *He was famous for his sage advice to young painters.*

sail **AS A NOUN** = **sheet**, canvas • *The white sails billow with the breezes they catch.*
▸ **AS A VERB** **1** = **go by water**, cruise, voyage, ride the waves, go by sea • *We sailed upstream.*
2 = **set sail**, embark, get under way, put to sea, put off, leave port, hoist sail, cast *or* weigh anchor, hoist the blue peter • *The boat is due to sail tonight.*
3 = **pilot**, steer, helm, navigate, captain, skipper • *I shall get myself a little boat and sail her around the world.*
4 = **glide**, sweep, float, shoot, fly, wing, soar, drift, skim, scud, skirr • *We got into the lift and sailed to the top floor.*
▸ **IN PHRASES:** **sail through something** = **cruise through**, walk through, romp through, pass easily, succeed easily at • *She sailed through her maths exams.*
set sail = **put to sea**, embark, get under way, put off, leave port, hoist sail, cast *or* weigh anchor, hoist the blue peter • *He loaded his vessel with another cargo and set sail.*
under sail = **sailing**, cruising, on the sea, riding the waves • *a big ship under sail*

sailor = **mariner**, marine, seaman, salt, tar *(informal)*, hearty *(informal)*, navigator, sea dog, seafarer, matelot *(slang, chiefly Brit.)*, Jack Tar, seafaring man, lascar, leatherneck *(slang)* • *A navy spokesman said one sailor is still missing.*

saint
▹ See panel **Saints**

saintly = **virtuous**, godly, holy, religious, sainted, blessed, worthy, righteous, devout, pious, angelic, blameless, god-fearing, beatific, sinless, saintlike, full of good works • *I assumed a look of saintly innocence.*

QUOTATIONS
Saintliness is also a temptation
[Jean Anouilh Beckett]

sake **AS A NOUN** = **purpose**, interest, cause, reason, end, aim, principle, objective, motive • *For the sake of historical accuracy, permit us to state the true facts.*
▸ **IN PHRASES:** **for someone's sake** = **in someone's interests**, to someone's advantage, on someone's account, for the benefit of, for the good of, for the welfare of, out of respect for, out of consideration for, out of regard for • *I trust you to do a good job for Stan's sake.*

salacious = **obscene**, indecent, pornographic, blue, erotic, steamy *(informal)*, lewd, X-rated *(informal)*, bawdy, smutty, lustful, ribald, ruttish • *a wildly salacious novel*

salary = **pay**, income, wage, fee, payment, wages, earnings, allowance, remuneration, recompense, stipend, emolument • *The lawyer was paid a huge salary.*

sale **AS A NOUN** **1** = **selling**, marketing, dealing, trading, transaction, disposal, vending • *Efforts were made to limit the sale of alcohol.*
2 = **auction**, fair, mart, bazaar • *The Old Master was bought at the Christie's sale.*
▸ **IN PHRASES:** **for sale** = **available to buy**, on sale, on offer, on the market, in stock, obtainable, purchasable • *His former home is for sale.*
on sale = **going cheap**, reduced, at a discount, at a reduced price • *He bought a sports jacket on sale at the shop.*

salient = **prominent**, outstanding, important, marked, striking, arresting, signal, remarkable, pronounced, noticeable, conspicuous • *He read the salient facts quickly.*

saliva = **spit**, dribble, drool, slaver, spittle, sputum • *A string of saliva looped from his mouth.*
▸ **RELATED ADJECTIVE:** sialoid

sallow = **wan**, pale, sickly, pasty, pallid, unhealthy, yellowish, anaemic, bilious, jaundiced-looking, peely-wally *(Scot.)* • *His face was sallow and shiny with sweat.*
OPPOSITES: glowing, rosy, radiant

sally **AS A NOUN** = **witticism**, joke, quip, crack *(informal)*, retort, jest, riposte, wisecrack *(informal)*, bon mot, smart remark • *He had thus far succeeded in fending off my conversational sallies.*
▸ **AS A VERB** = **go forth**, set out, rush, issue, surge, erupt • *She would sally out on a bitter night to keep her appointments.*

salmon
▸ **NAME OF YOUNG:** alevin, grilse, parr, smolt

salon **1** = **shop**, store, establishment, parlour, boutique • *a beauty salon*
2 = **sitting room**, lounge, living room, parlour, drawing room, front room, reception room, morning room • *His apartment was the most famous literary salon in Russia.*

salt **AS A NOUN** **1** = **seasoning**, sodium chloride, table salt, rock salt • *a pinch of salt*
2 = **sailor**, marine, seaman, mariner, tar *(informal)*, hearty *(informal)*, navigator, sea dog, seafarer, matelot *(slang, chiefly Brit.)*, Jack Tar, seafaring man, lascar, leatherneck *(slang)* • *'Did he look like an old sea salt?' I asked, laughing.*
▸ **AS A VERB** = **add salt to**, flavour with salt • *Salt the stock to your taste.*
▸ **AS AN ADJECTIVE** = **salty**, salted, saline, brackish, briny • *Put a pan of salt water on to boil.*
▸ **IN PHRASES:** **rub salt into the wound** = **make something worse**, add insult to injury, fan the flames, aggravate matters, magnify a problem • *I had no intention of rubbing salt into his wounds.*
with a grain *or* pinch of salt = **sceptically**, suspiciously, cynically, doubtfully, with reservations, disbelievingly, mistrustfully • *You have to take these findings with a pinch of salt.*

salty = **salt**, salted, saline, brackish, briny, over-salted, brak *(S. African)* • *organisms adapted to survive in very salty water*

salubrious **1** = **healthy**, beneficial, good for you, wholesome, invigorating, salutary, healthful, health-giving • *your salubrious lochside hotel*
2 = **agreeable**, respectable, grand, pleasant, nice, posh *(informal)*, luxurious, classy, upmarket, high-class, glitzy, swanky • *London's less salubrious quarters*

salutary = **beneficial**, useful, valuable, helpful, profitable, good, practical, good for you, advantageous, win-win • *It was a new and salutary experience to be in the minority.*

salutation = **greeting**, welcome, salute, address, obeisance • *The old man moved away, raising his hand in salutation.*

salute **AS A VERB** **1** = **greet**, welcome, acknowledge, address, kiss, hail, salaam, accost, pay your respects to, doff your cap to, mihi *(N.Z.)* • *He stepped out and saluted the general.*
2 = **honour**, celebrate, acknowledge, recognize, take your hat off to *(informal)*, pay tribute *or* homage to • *The statement salutes the changes of the past year.*
▸ **AS A NOUN** **1** = **greeting**, recognition, salutation, address, kiss, salaam, obeisance • *He raised his hand in salute.*
2 = **homage**, recognition, tribute, toast, compliment, testimonial, acknowledgment, eulogy • *a special salute to her for her protest*

salvage **AS A VERB** = **save**, recover, rescue, restore, repair, get back, retrieve, redeem, glean, repossess, fetch back • *They studied flight recorders salvaged from the wreckage.*
▸ **AS A NOUN** **1** = **rescue**, saving, recovery, release, relief, liberation, salvation, deliverance, extrication • *The salvage of the ship went on.*
2 = **scrap**, remains, waste, junk, offcuts • *They climbed up on the rock with their salvage.*

salvation **1** = **saving**, help, rescue, recovery, restoration, salvage, redemption, deliverance • *those whose marriages are beyond salvation*
OPPOSITES: loss, ruin, doom

SAINTS

Saint	Feast day
Agatha	5 February
Agnes	31 January
Aidan	31 August
Alban	22 June
Albertus Magnus	15 November
Aloysius (patron saint of youth)	21 June
Ambrose	7 December
Andrew (Scotland)	30 November
Anne	26 July
Anselm	21 April
Anthony	17 January
Anthony of Padua	13 June
Athanasius	2 May
Augustine of Hippo	28 August
Barnabas	11 June
Bartholomew	24 August
Basil	2 January
Bede	25 May
Benedict	11 July
Bernadette of Lourdes	16 April
Bernard of Clairvaux	20 August
Bernard of Menthon	28 May
Bonaventura	15 July
Boniface	5 June
Brendan	16 May
Bridget, Bride *or* Brigid (Ireland)	1 February
Bridget *or* Birgitta (Sweden)	23 July
Catherine of Alexandria	25 November
Catherine of Siena (the Dominican Order)	29 April
Cecilia (music)	22 November
Charles Borromeo	4 November
Christopher (travellers)	25 July
Clare of Assisi	11 August
Clement I	23 November
Clement of Alexandria	5 December
Columba *or* Colmcille	9 June
Crispin (shoemakers)	25 October
Crispinian (shoemakers)	25 October
Cuthbert	20 March
Cyprian	16 September
Cyril	14 February
Cyril of Alexandria	27 June
David (Wales)	1 March
Denis (France)	9 October
Dominic	7 August
Dorothy	6 February
Dunstan	19 May
Edmund	20 November
Edward the Confessor	13 October
Edward the Martyr	18 March
Elizabeth	5 November
Elizabeth of Hungary	17 November
Elmo	2 June
Ethelbert	25 February
Francis of Assisi	4 October
Francis of Sales	24 January
Francis Xavier	3 December
Geneviève (Paris)	3 January
George (England)	23 April
Gertrude	16 November
Gilbert of Sempringham	4 February
Giles (cripples, beggars, and lepers)	1 September
Gregory I (the Great)	3 September
Gregory VII *or* Hildebrand	25 May
Gregory of Nazianzus	2 January
Gregory of Nyssa	9 March
Gregory of Tours	17 November
Hilary of Poitiers	13 January
Hildegard of Bingen	17 September
Helen *or* Helena	18 August
Helier	16 July
Ignatius	17 October
Ignatius of Loyola	31 July
Isidore of Seville	4 April
James	23 October
James the Less	3 May
Jane Frances de Chantal	12 December
Jerome	30 September
Joachim	26 July
Joan of Arc	30 May
John	27 December
John Bosco	31 January
John Chrysostom	13 September
John Ogilvie	10 March
John of Damascus	4 December
John of the Cross	14 December
John the Baptist	24 June
Joseph	19 March
Joseph of Arimathaea	17 March
Joseph of Copertino	18 September
Jude	28 October
Justin	1 June
Kentigern *or* Mungo	14 January
Kevin	3 June
Lawrence	10 August
Lawrence O'Toole	14 November
Leger	2 October
Leo I (the Great)	10 November
Leo II	3 July
Leo III	12 June
Leo IV	17 July
Leonard	6 November
Lucy	13 December
Luke	18 October
Malachy	3 November
Margaret	20 July
Margaret of Scotland (in Scotland)	10 June, 16 November
Maria Goretti	6 July
Mark	25 April
Martha	29 July
Martin de Porres	3 November
Martin of Tours (France)	11 November
Mary	15 August
Mary Magdalene	22 July
Matthew *or* Levi	21 September
Matthias	14 May
Methodius	14 February
Michael	29 September
Neot	31 July
Nicholas (Russia, children, sailors, merchants, and pawnbrokers)	6 December
Nicholas I (the Great)	13 November
Ninian	16 September
Olaf	29 July
Oliver Plunket	1 July
Oswald	28 February
Pachomius	14 May
Patrick (Ireland)	17 March
Paul	29 June
Paulinus	10 October
Paulinus of Nola	22 June
Peter *or* Simon Peter	29 June
Philip	3 May
Philip Neri	26 May
Pius V	30 April
Pius X	21 August
Polycarp	26 January *or* 23 February
Rose of Lima	23 August
Sebastian	20 January
Silas	13 July
Simon Zelotes	28 October
Stanislaw *or* Stanislaus (Poland)	11 April
Stanislaus Kostka	13 November
Stephen	26 *or* 27 December
Stephen of Hungary	16 *or* 20 August
Swithin	15 July
Teresa *or* Theresa of Avila	15 October
Thérèse de Lisieux	1 October
Thomas	3 July
Thomas à Becket	29 December
Thomas Aquinas	28 January
Thomas More	22 June
Timothy	26 January
Titus	26 January
Ursula	21 October
Valentine	14 February
Veronica	12 July
Vincent de Paul	27 September
Vitus	15 June
Vladimir	15 July
Wenceslaus	28 September
Wilfrid	12 October

2 = lifeline, escape, relief, preservation • *I consider books my salvation.*

QUOTATIONS

Work out your own salvation with fear and trembling
[*Bible: Philippians*]

salve AS A VERB = **ease**, soothe, appease, still, allay, pacify, mollify, tranquillize, palliate • *I give myself treats and justify them to salve my conscience.*

▸ AS A NOUN = **balm**, cream, medication, lotion, lubricant, ointment, emollient, liniment, dressing, unguent

• *a soothing salve for sore, dry lips*

salvo = **barrage**, storm, bombardment, strafe, cannonade • *His testimony was only one in a salvo of new attacks.*

same AS AN ADJECTIVE 1 = **identical**, similar, alike, equal, twin, equivalent, corresponding, comparable, duplicate, indistinguishable, interchangeable • *The houses were all the same.*
OPPOSITES: different, diverse, miscellaneous
2 = **the very same**, very, one and the same, selfsame • *Bernard works at the same institution as Arlette.*
3 = **aforementioned**, aforesaid, selfsame • *Wrist watches: £5. Inscription of same: £25.*
4 = **unchanged**, consistent, constant, uniform, unaltered, unfailing, invariable, unvarying, changeless • *Always taking the ingredients from here means the beers stay the same.*
OPPOSITES: altered, variable, inconsistent
▸ IN PHRASES: **all the same** 1 = **nevertheless**, still, regardless, nonetheless, after all, in any case, for all that, notwithstanding, in any event, anyhow, just the same, be that as it may • *She didn't understand the joke but laughed all the same.*
2 = **unimportant**, insignificant, immaterial, inconsequential, of no consequence, of little account, not worth mentioning • *It's all the same to me whether he goes or not.*
same here = **me too**, agreed, so do I, me neither • *'I hate going into stores.' 'Same here,' said William.*

sameness = **similarity**, resemblance, uniformity, likeness, oneness, standardization, indistinguishability, identicalness • *He grew bored by the sameness of the speeches.*

sample AS A NOUN 1 = **specimen**, example, trial, model, pattern, instance, representative, demonstration, indication, illustration, swatch, exemplification • *We're giving away 2000 free samples.*
2 = **cross section**, test, sampling • *We based our analysis on a random sample of more than 200 males.*
▸ AS A VERB = **test**, try, check out *(informal)*, experience, taste, examine, evaluate, inspect, experiment with, appraise, partake of • *We sampled a selection of different bottled waters.*

sanatorium = **clinic** • *I was told I'd be in the sanatorium for two years.*

sanctify 1 = **consecrate**, bless, ordain, anoint, set apart, hallow, beatify, make sacred • *Their marriage has not been sanctified in a Christian church.*
2 = **cleanse**, redeem, purify, absolve, exculpate • *May the God of peace sanctify you entirely.*
3 = **approve**, back, support, sanction, endorse, authorize, ratify, vindicate • *a law that sanctifies changes that have already occurred*

sanctimonious = **pious**, smug, hypocritical, pi *(Brit. slang)*, too good to be true, self-righteous, self-satisfied, goody-goody *(informal)*, unctuous, holier-than-thou, priggish, pietistic, canting, pharisaical, Tartuffian *or* Tartufian • *He writes smug, sanctimonious rubbish.*

sanction AS A VERB 1 = **permit**, back, support, allow, approve, entitle, endorse, authorize, countenance, vouch for, lend your name to • *He may seem ready to sanction the use of force.*
OPPOSITES: refuse, ban, forbid
2 = **punish**, discipline, penalize, chastise, bring to book, slap someone's wrist, throw the book at, rap someone's knuckles • *failure to sanction countries for butchering whales*
▸ AS A NOUN 1 *often plural* = **ban**, restriction, boycott, embargo, exclusion, penalty, deterrent, prohibition, coercive measures • *He expressed his opposition to lifting the sanctions.*
OPPOSITES: authority, licence, permission
2 = **permission**, backing, support, authority, approval, allowance, confirmation, endorsement, countenance, ratification, authorization, approbation, O.K. *or* okay *(informal)*, stamp *or* seal of approval • *The king could not enact laws without the sanction of parliament.*
OPPOSITES: ban, veto, refusal

sanctity = **sacredness**, inviolability, inalienability, hallowedness, sacrosanctness • *the sanctity of human life*

sanctuary 1 = **protection**, shelter, refuge, haven, retreat, asylum • *Some of them have sought sanctuary in the church.*
2 = **reserve**, park, preserve, reservation, national park, tract, nature reserve, conservation area • *a bird sanctuary*

sanctum 1 = **refuge**, retreat, den, hideaway, private room, hide-out • *His bedroom is his inner sanctum.*
2 = **sanctuary**, shrine, altar, holy place, Holy of Holies • *the inner sanctum of the mosque*

sand AS A VERB = **smooth**, file, scrape, scour, wear down, grind down, wear away, abrade • *Sand the surface softly and carefully.*
▸ AS A PLURAL NOUN = **beach**, shore, strand *(literary)*, dunes • *miles of golden sands*

sane 1 = **rational**, normal, all there *(informal)*, lucid, of sound mind, compos mentis *(Latin)*, in your right mind, mentally sound, in possession of all your faculties • *He seemed perfectly sane.*
OPPOSITES: mad, crazy, insane
2 = **sensible**, sound, reasonable, balanced, moderate, sober, judicious, level-headed, grounded • *a sane and safe energy policy*
OPPOSITES: stupid, foolish, unreasonable

sang-froid = **composure**, poise, coolness, aplomb, cool *(slang)*, indifference, calmness, equanimity, nonchalance, phlegm, self-possession, unflappability *(informal)*, imperturbability, cool-headedness • *He behaves throughout with a certain sang-froid.*

sangoma = **witch doctor**, healer, shaman • *They paid a sangoma to cast a spell on their enemies.*

sanguine = **cheerful**, confident, optimistic, assured, hopeful, buoyant, in good heart • *He's remarkably sanguine about the problems involved.*
OPPOSITES: down, gloomy, pessimistic

sanitary = **hygienic**, clean, healthy, wholesome, salubrious, unpolluted, germ-free • *It's not the most sanitary place one could swim.*

sanitation = **hygiene**, cleanliness, sewerage • *the hazards of contaminated water and poor sanitation*

sanitize 1 = **sterilize**, cleanse, disinfect, purge, purify, fumigate, decontaminate, pasteurize • *motels with their sanitized toilet seats and mini bars of soap*
2 = **make acceptable**, clean up, purge, water down, expurgate, make palatable • *the school of crime writers who sanitize violence*

sanity 1 = **mental health**, reason, rationality, stability, normality, right mind *(informal)*, saneness • *He and his wife finally had to move, just to preserve their sanity.*
OPPOSITES: madness, mental illness, insanity
2 = **common sense**, sense, good sense, rationality, level-headedness, judiciousness, soundness of judgment • *He's been looking at ways of introducing some sanity into the market.*
OPPOSITES: folly, stupidity, senselessness

Santa Claus = **Father Christmas**, Kriss Kringle *(chiefly U.S.)*, Saint Nicholas, Old Saint Nick • *the danger that Santa Claus will get stuck down a chimney*

sap[1] 1 = **juice**, essence, vital fluid, secretion, lifeblood, plant fluid • *The leaves, bark and sap are common ingredients of herbal remedies.*
2 = **fool**, jerk *(slang, chiefly U.S. & Canad.)*, idiot, noodle, wally *(slang)*, wet *(Brit. informal)*, charlie *(Brit. informal)*, drip *(informal)*, gull *(archaic)*, prat *(slang)*, plonker *(slang)*, noddy, twit *(informal)*, chump *(informal)*, oaf, simpleton, nitwit *(informal)*, ninny, nincompoop, dweeb *(U.S. slang)*, putz

(U.S. slang), wuss (slang), Simple Simon, weenie (U.S. informal), muggins (Brit. slang), eejit (Scot. & Irish), thicko (Brit. slang), dumb-ass (slang), gobshite (Irish taboo slang), numpty (Scot. informal), doofus (slang, chiefly U.S.), nerd or nurd (slang), numskull or numbskull, dorba or dorb (Austral. slang), bogan (Austral. slang) • *her poor sap of a husband*

sap² = **weaken**, drain, undermine, rob, exhaust, bleed, erode, deplete, wear down, enervate, devitalize • *I was afraid the sickness had sapped my strength.*

sarcasm = **irony**, satire, cynicism, contempt, ridicule, bitterness, scorn, sneering, mockery, venom, derision, vitriol, mordancy, causticness • *His voice was heavy with sarcasm.*

sarcastic = **ironical**, cynical, satirical, cutting, biting, sharp, acid, mocking, taunting, sneering, acrimonious, backhanded, contemptuous, disparaging, sardonic, caustic, bitchy (informal), vitriolic, acerbic, derisive, ironic, mordant, sarky (Brit. informal), mordacious, acerb • *She poked fun at people's shortcomings with sarcastic remarks.*

sardonic = **mocking**, cynical, dry, bitter, sneering, jeering, malicious, wry, sarcastic, derisive, ironical, mordant, mordacious • *a sardonic sense of humour*

sash = **belt**, girdle, waistband, cummerbund • *She wore a white dress with a thin blue sash.*

Satan = **The Devil**, Lucifer, Prince of Darkness, Lord of the Flies, Mephistopheles, Beelzebub, Old Nick (informal), The Evil One, Apollyon, Old Scratch (informal) • *the schemes of Satan*

▸ RELATED PHOBIA: Satanophobia

satanic = **evil**, demonic, hellish, black, malignant, wicked, inhuman, malevolent, devilish, infernal, fiendish, accursed, iniquitous, diabolic, demoniac, demoniacal • *satanic mass murders*

OPPOSITES: godly, holy, divine

sate = **satisfy**, satiate, slake, indulge to the full • *children happily sated with ice cream*

satellite 1 = **spacecraft**, communications satellite, sputnik, space capsule • *The rocket launched two satellites.*
2 = **moon**, secondary planet • *the satellites of Jupiter*
3 = **colony**, dependency, dominion, protectorate • *Russia and its former satellites*

satiate = **glut**, satisfy, surfeit, gorge, jade, nauseate, slake, sate, stuff, overfill, cloy • *There is enough fruit to satiate several children.*

satire 1 = **mockery**, wit, irony, ridicule, sarcasm, raillery, pasquinade • *It's an easy target for satire.*
2 = **parody**, mockery, caricature, send-up (Brit. informal), spoof (informal), travesty, takeoff (informal), lampoon, skit, burlesque • *A sharp satire on the American political process.*

QUOTATIONS

It's hard not to write satire
[Juvenal *Satires*]

Satire is a sort of glass, wherein beholders do generally discover everybody's face but their own
[Jonathan Swift *The Battle of the Books*]

satirical or **satiric** = **mocking**, ironical, cynical, cutting, biting, bitter, taunting, pungent, incisive, sarcastic, sardonic, caustic, vitriolic, burlesque, mordant, Rabelaisian, mordacious • *a satirical novel about London life in the late 80s*

satirize = **ridicule**, parody, send up (Brit. informal), take off (informal), criticize, deride, travesty, pillory, lampoon, burlesque, diss (slang, chiefly U.S.), hold up to ridicule • *The newspaper satirized our political leaders.*

satisfaction 1 = **fulfilment**, pleasure, achievement, joy, triumph, happiness, relish, glee, gratification, pride, complacency • *She felt a small glow of satisfaction.*
OPPOSITES: pain, shame, dissatisfaction
2 = **compensation**, damages, justice, amends, settlement, redress, remuneration, reparation, vindication, restitution, reimbursement, atonement, recompense, indemnification, requital • *Buyers have the right to go to court and demand satifaction.*
OPPOSITES: injury
3 = **contentment**, content, comfort, ease, pleasure, well-being, happiness, enjoyment, peace of mind, gratification, satiety, repletion, contentedness • *a state of satisfaction*
OPPOSITES: discontent, misgivings

satisfactory = **adequate**, acceptable, good enough, average, fair, all right, suitable, sufficient, competent, up to scratch, passable, up to standard, up to the mark • *I never got a satisfactory answer.*
OPPOSITES: inadequate, unacceptable, unsatisfactory

satisfied 1 = **contented**, happy, content, fulfilled, appeased, gratified, pacified, pleased • *our satisfied customers*
OPPOSITES: disappointed, upset, dissatisfied
2 = **smug**, triumphant, complacent, self-satisfied, pleased with yourself, like the cat that swallowed the canary (informal), pleased • *a satisfied look*
3 = **sure**, smug, certain, convinced, positive, free from doubt, easy in your mind • *People must be satisfied that the treatment is safe.*

satisfy 1 = **content**, please, indulge, fill, feed, appease, gratify, pander to, assuage, pacify, quench, mollify, surfeit, satiate, slake, sate • *The pace of change has not been quick enough to satisfy everyone.*
OPPOSITES: frustrate, annoy, dissatisfy
2 = **convince**, persuade, assure, reassure, dispel (someone's) doubts, put (someone's) mind at rest • *He has to satisfy us that real progress will be made.*
OPPOSITES: dissuade, fail to persuade
3 = **comply with**, meet, fulfil, answer, serve, fill, observe, obey, conform to, measure up to, match up to • *The procedures should satisfy certain basic requirements.*
OPPOSITES: fail to meet

satisfying = **satisfactory**, pleasing, enjoyable, gratifying, pleasurable, cheering • *I find wood carving satisfying.*

saturate 1 = **flood**, overwhelm, swamp, overrun, deluge, glut • *Both sides are saturating the airwaves.*
2 = **soak**, steep, drench, seep, imbue, douse, impregnate, suffuse, ret (flax, etc), wet through, waterlog, souse, drouk (Scot.) • *If the filter has been saturated with motor oil, discard it.*

saturated = **soaked**, soaking (wet), drenched, sodden, dripping, waterlogged, sopping (wet), wet through, soaked to the skin, wringing wet, droukit or drookit (Scot.) • *His work clothes were saturated with oil.*

saturnine = **gloomy**, grave, sombre, dour, morose, glum, taciturn, phlegmatic, uncommunicative • *He is a saturnine man who speaks with precision and pedantic care.*

sauce = **dressing**, dip, relish, condiment, jus (French) • *pasta cooked in a sauce of garlic*
▹ *See panel* **Sauces**

saucy = **impudent**, cheeky (informal), impertinent, forward, fresh (informal), flip (informal), rude, sassy (U.S. informal), pert, disrespectful, flippant, presumptuous, insolent, lippy (U.S. & Canad. slang), smart-alecky (informal) • *a saucy joke*

saunter AS A VERB = **stroll**, wander, amble, roam, ramble, meander, rove, take a stroll, mosey (informal), stravaig (Scot. & Northern English dialect) • *We watched our fellow students saunter into the building.*
▸ AS A NOUN = **stroll**, walk, amble, turn, airing, constitutional, ramble, promenade, breather, perambulation • *She began a slow saunter towards the bonfire.*

sausage = **banger** • *sausages and chips*

savage AS AN ADJECTIVE 1 = **cruel**, brutal, vicious, bloody, fierce, harsh, beastly, ruthless, ferocious, murderous, ravening, sadistic, inhuman, merciless, diabolical, brutish, devilish, bloodthirsty, barbarous, pitiless, bestial • *This was a savage attack on a defenceless young girl.*
OPPOSITES: kind, gentle, humane

SAUCES

apple
à la king
barbecue
Béarnaise
béchamel
black bean
bolognese
Bordelaise
brandy butter *or* hard sauce
bread
brown
chasseur
chaudfroid
cheese
chilli
chocolate
chow-chow
coulis
cranberry
cream
creole
cumberland
curry
custard
French dressing
fudge
gravy
hoisin
hollandaise
horseradish
ketchup
mayonnaise
Melba sauce
mint
mornay
mousseline
nam pla *or* fish sauce
orange
oyster
pesto
piccalilli
red pesto
rémoulade
Russian dressing
sabayon
salad cream
salad dressing
salsa
salsa verde
soubise
soy sauce, shoyu, *or* tamari
suprême
sweet-and-sour
Tabasco *(trademark)*
tartare
tomato
velouté
verjuice sauce
vinaigrette
white
wine
Worcester *or* Worcestershire

2 = wild, fierce, ferocious, unbroken, feral, untamed, undomesticated • *a strange and savage animal encountered at the zoo*
OPPOSITES: tame, domesticated
3 = primitive, undeveloped, uncultivated, uncivilized, in a state of nature, nonliterate • *a savage people*
4 = uncultivated, rugged, unspoilt, uninhabited, waste, rough, uncivilized, unfrequented • *stunning images of a wild and savage land*
OPPOSITES: cultivated, civilized
5 = crushing, severe, devastating, tragic, disastrous, crippling, mortal, catastrophic, ruinous, cataclysmic • *The expulsion was a savage blow to her.*
▸ AS A NOUN **1 = native**, barbarian, heathen, indigene, primitive person, autochthon • *a frozen desert peopled by uncouth savages*
2 = lout, yob *(Brit. slang)*, brute, bear, monster, beast, barbarian, fiend, yahoo, hoon *(Austral. & N.Z.)*, yobbo *(Brit. slang)*, roughneck *(slang)*, boor, cougan *(Austral. slang)*, scozza *(Austral. slang)*, bogan *(Austral. slang)* • *Our orchestra is a bunch of savages.*
▸ AS A VERB **1 = maul**, tear, claw, attack, mangle, lacerate, mangulate *(Austral. slang)* • *The animal turned on him and he was savaged to death.*
2 = criticize, attack, knock *(informal)*, blast, pan *(informal)*, slam *(slang)*, put down, slate *(informal)*, have a go (at) *(informal)*, disparage, tear into *(informal)*, diss *(slang, chiefly U.S.)*, flame *(informal)*, find fault with, lambast(e), pick holes in, pick to pieces, give (someone *or* something) a bad press • *The show had already been savaged by the critics.*
OPPOSITES: celebrate, praise, acclaim, big up *(slang, chiefly Caribbean)*

QUOTATIONS
as savage as a bear with a sore head
[Captain Marryat *The King's Own*]

savagery = cruelty, brutality, ferocity, ruthlessness, sadism, inhumanity, barbarity, viciousness, bestiality, fierceness, bloodthirstiness • *the sheer savagery of war*

savant = sage, authority, intellectual, master, philosopher, mastermind, mahatma • *The opinion of the savants on this issue is not united.*

save AS A VERB **1 = rescue**, free, release, deliver, recover, get out, liberate, salvage, redeem, bail out, come to someone's rescue, set free, save the life of, extricate, save someone's bacon *(Brit. informal)* • *She could have saved him from this final disaster.*
OPPOSITES: risk, expose, endanger
2 = keep, reserve, set aside, store, collect, gather, hold, hoard, hide away, lay by, put by, salt away, treasure up, keep up your sleeve *(informal)*, put aside for a rainy day • *I thought we were saving money for a holiday.*
OPPOSITES: use, spend, waste
3 = protect, keep, guard, preserve, look after, take care of, safeguard, salvage, conserve, keep safe • *a final attempt to save 40,000 jobs*
4 = budget, be economical, economize, scrimp and save, retrench, be frugal, make economies, be thrifty, tighten your belt *(informal)*, watch your pennies, draw in your horns • *The majority of people intend to save.*
5 = put aside, keep, reserve, collect, retain, set aside, amass, put by • *Scraps of material were saved, cut up and pieced together for quilts.*
6 = prevent, avoid, spare, rule out, avert, forestall, obviate, make unnecessary • *This will save the expense and trouble of buying two pairs.*
▸ AS A PREPOSITION **= apart from**, but, other than, excluding, besides, except for, aside from, not counting • *There is almost no water, save that brought up from bore holes.*

saving AS A NOUN **= economy**, discount, reduction, bargain, cut • *Use these vouchers for some great savings on holidays.*
▸ AS A PLURAL NOUN **= nest egg**, fund, store, reserves, resources, fall-back, provision for a rainy day • *Many people lost all their savings when the bank collapsed.*

saving grace = redeeming feature, asset, good point, advantage, blessing, boon, ace in the hole, mitigating feature, feather in your cap, ace up your sleeve • *Humour is your saving grace.*

saviour = rescuer, deliverer, defender, guardian, salvation, protector, liberator, Good Samaritan, redeemer, preserver, knight in shining armour, friend in need • *the saviour of his country*

Saviour = Christ, Jesus, Jesus Christ, Emmanuel, the Messiah, the Son of God, the Redeemer, the King of Kings • *the vast Cathedral of Christ the Saviour*

savoir-faire = social graces, diplomacy, discretion, accomplishment, finesse, poise, tact, urbanity, social know-how *(informal)* • *a certain savoir-faire that comes from living with the best*

savour AS A VERB **1 = relish**, like, delight in, revel in, luxuriate in, gloat over • *We won't pretend we savour the prospect of a month in prison.*
2 = enjoy, appreciate, relish, delight in, revel in, partake of, drool over, luxuriate in, enjoy to the full, smack your lips over • *Savour the flavour of each mouthful.*
▸ AS A NOUN **1 = flavour**, taste, smell, relish, smack, zest, tang, zing *(informal)*, piquancy • *The rich savour of the beans give this dish its character.*
2 = zest, interest, spice, excitement, salt, flavour • *Life without Anna had no savour.*

savoury AS AN ADJECTIVE **1 = spicy**, rich, delicious, tasty, luscious, palatable, tangy, dainty, delectable, mouthwatering, piquant, full-flavoured, scrumptious *(informal)*, appetizing, toothsome, yummo *(Austral. slang)* • *Italian cooking is best known for its savoury dishes.*

OPPOSITES: tasteless, unpalatable, insipid
2 = **wholesome**, decent, respectable, honest, reputable, apple-pie *(informal)* • *He does not have a particularly savoury reputation.*
OPPOSITES: nasty, unpleasant, disreputable
▸ **AS A PLURAL NOUN** = **appetizers**, nibbles, apéritifs, canapés, titbits, hors d'oeuvres, amuses-gueules *(French)* • *I'll make some cheese straws or savouries.*

savvy **AS A NOUN** = **understanding**, perception, grasp, ken, comprehension, apprehension • *He is known for his political savvy.*
▸ **AS AN ADJECTIVE** = **shrewd**, sharp, astute, knowing, fly *(slang)*, keen, smart, clever, intelligent, discriminating, discerning, canny, perceptive, artful, far-sighted, far-seeing, long-headed, perspicacious, sagacious • *She was a pretty savvy woman.*

say **AS A VERB** 1 = **state**, declare, remark, add, announce, maintain, mention, assert, affirm, asseverate • *She said she was very impressed.*
2 = **speak**, utter, voice, express, pronounce, come out with *(informal)*, put into words, give voice *or* utterance to • *I hope you didn't say anything about me.*
3 = **make known**, reveal, disclose, divulge, answer, reply, respond, give as your opinion • *I must say that that rather shocked me, too.*
4 = **read**, show, display, indicate • *The clock said four minutes past eleven.*
5 = **suggest**, reveal, express, imply, communicate, disclose, give away, convey, divulge • *That says a lot about the power of their marketing people.*
6 = **suppose**, supposing, imagine, assume, presume, postulate • *Say you lived in Boston, Massachusetts.*
7 = **estimate**, suppose, guess, conjecture, surmise, dare say, hazard a guess • *I'd say she must be at least a size 20.*
8 = **recite**, perform, deliver, do, read, repeat, render, rehearse, orate • *How am I going to go on and say those lines tonight?*
9 = **allege**, report, claim, hold, suggest, insist, maintain, rumour, assert, uphold, profess, put about that • *He says he did it after the police pressured him.*
▸ **AS A NOUN** 1 = **influence**, power, control, authority, weight, sway, clout *(informal)*, predominance, mana *(N.Z.)* • *The students wanted more say in the running of the university.*
2 = **chance to speak**, vote, voice, crack *(informal)*, opportunity to speak, turn to speak • *Let him have his say.*
▸ **IN PHRASES:** **to say the least** = **at the very least**, without any exaggeration, to put it mildly • *The result was, to say the least, fascinating.*

saying **AS A NOUN** = **proverb**, maxim, adage, saw, slogan, gnome, dictum, axiom, aphorism, byword, apophthegm • *that old saying: 'Charity begins at home'*
▸ **IN PHRASES:** **go without saying** = **be obvious**, be understood, be taken for granted, be accepted, be self-evident, be taken as read, be a matter of course • *It should go without saying that you shouldn't smoke.*

say-so = **assertion**, authority, agreement, word, guarantee, sanction, permission, consent, assurance, assent, authorization, dictum, asseveration, O.K. *or* okay *(informal)* • *Nothing happens without their say-so.*

scaffold = **gallows**, block, gibbet • *He ascended the shaky ladder to the scaffold.*

scalding = **burning**, boiling, searing, blistering, piping hot • *scalding hot water*

scale[1] = **flake**, plate, layer, lamina • *a thing with scales all over its body*
▸ **TECHNICAL NAME:** squama
▸ **RELATED ADJECTIVE:** squamous

scale = **weighing machine**, balance, scale, weigh beam • *I step on the scales practically every morning.*

scale[1] **AS A NOUN** 1 = **degree**, size, range, spread, extent, dimensions, scope, magnitude, breadth • *He underestimates the scale of the problem.*
2 = **system of measurement**, register, measuring system, graduated system, calibration, calibrated system • *an earthquake measuring five-point-five on the Richter scale*
3 = **ranking**, ladder, spectrum, hierarchy, series, sequence, progression, pecking order *(informal)*, seniority system • *This has become a reality for increasing numbers across the social scale.*
4 = **ratio**, proportion, relative size • *The map, on a scale of 1:10,000, shows over 5,000 individual paths.*
▸ **AS A VERB** = **climb up**, mount, go up, ascend, surmount, scramble up, clamber up, shin up, escalade • *The men scaled a wall and climbed down scaffolding on the other side.*
▸ **IN PHRASES:** **scale something down** = **reduce**, cut, moderate, slow down, cut down, wind down, tone down, downsize, kennet *(Austral. slang)*, jeff *(Austral. slang)* • *The air rescue operation has now been scaled down.*
scale something up = **expand**, extend, blow up, enlarge, lengthen, magnify, amplify, augment • *Simply scaling up a size 10 garment often leads to disaster.*

scaly 1 = **squamous**, squamate, lamellose, lamelliform • *The brown rat has prominent ears and a long scaly tail.*
2 = **flaky**, scabrous, scurfy, furfuraceous *(Medical)*, squamous *or* squamose *(Biology)*, squamulose • *If your skin becomes red, sore or very scaly, consult your doctor.*

scam = **swindle**, fiddle, racket, stratagem, diddle • *The duo set up a scam to settle their respective debts.*

scamp = **rascal**, devil, monkey, rogue, imp, tyke *(informal)*, wretch, knave *(archaic)*, scallywag *(informal)*, pickle *(Brit. informal)*, mischief-maker, whippersnapper, toerag *(slang)*, scapegrace, nointer *(Austral. slang)* • *Have some respect for me, you scamp!*

scamper = **run**, dash, dart, fly, hurry, sprint, romp, beetle, hasten, scuttle, scurry, scoot, hie *(archaic)* • *The flash sent the foxes scampering away.*

scan **AS A VERB** 1 = **glance over**, skim, look over, eye, check, clock *(Brit. slang)*, examine, check out *(informal)*, run over, eyeball *(slang)*, size up *(informal)*, get a load of *(informal)*, look someone up and down, run your eye over, take a dekko at *(Brit. slang)*, surf *(Computing)* • *She scanned the advertisement pages of the newspaper.*
2 = **survey**, search, investigate, sweep, con *(archaic)*, scour, scrutinize, take stock of, recce *(slang)* • *The officer scanned the room.*
▸ **AS A NOUN** 1 = **look**, glance, skim, browse, flick, squint, butcher's *(Brit. slang)*, brief look, dekko *(Brit. slang)*, shufti *(Brit. slang)* • *I've had a quick scan through your book again.*
2 = **examination**, scanning, ultrasound • *He was rushed to hospital for a brain scan.*

scandal 1 = **disgrace**, crime, offence, sin, embarrassment, misconduct, wrongdoing, skeleton in the cupboard, shocking incident, dishonourable behaviour, discreditable behaviour • *a financial scandal*
2 = **gossip**, goss *(informal)*, talk, rumours, dirt, defamation, slander, tattle, dirty linen *(informal)*, calumny, backbiting, muckraking, aspersion, scandalmongering • *He loved gossip and scandal.*
3 = **shame**, offence, disgrace, stigma, ignominy, infamy, opprobrium, obloquy • *She braved the scandal of her husband's love child*
4 = **outrage**, shame, insult, disgrace, injustice, crying shame • *It is a scandal that a person can be stopped for no reason by the police.*

QUOTATIONS
It is public scandal that constitutes offence, and to sin in secret is not to sin at all
[Molière *Le Tartuffe*]

scandalize = **shock**, outrage, appal, disgust, offend, horrify, affront, raise eyebrows amongst, cause a few raised eyebrows amongst *(informal)* • *She scandalized her family by falling in love with a married man.*

scandalous 1 = **shocking**, disgraceful, outrageous, offensive, appalling, foul, dreadful, horrifying, obscene, monstrous, unspeakable, atrocious, frightful, abominable • *They would be sacked for criminal or scandalous behaviour.*
OPPOSITES: decent, respectable, upright
2 = **slanderous**, gossiping, scurrilous, untrue, defamatory, libellous • *Newspaper columns were full of scandalous tales.*
OPPOSITES: laudatory
3 = **outrageous**, shocking, infamous, disgraceful, monstrous, shameful, atrocious, unseemly, odious, disreputable, opprobrious, highly improper • *a scandalous waste of money*
OPPOSITES: seemly, proper, reputable

scant 1 = **inadequate**, insufficient, meagre, sparse, little, limited, bare, minimal, deficient, barely sufficient • *There is scant evidence of strong economic growth to come.*
OPPOSITES: full, sufficient, adequate
2 = **small**, limited, inadequate, insufficient, meagre, negligible, measly, scanty, inconsiderable • *The hole was a scant 0.23 inches in diameter.*

scanty 1 = **meagre**, sparse, poor, thin, narrow, sparing, restricted, bare, inadequate, pathetic, insufficient, slender, scant, deficient, exiguous • *So far, what scanty evidence we have points to two subjects.*
2 = **skimpy**, short, brief, tight, thin, indecent • *a model in scanty clothing*

scapegoat AS A NOUN = **fall guy**, victim, patsy *(informal)*, whipping boy • *Her supporters see her as a scapegoat for a policy that failed.*
▸ AS A VERB = **blame**, hold responsible, accuse, point a or the finger at • *He has been scapegoated for the lack of jobs and housing problems*

scar AS A NOUN 1 = **mark**, injury, wound, trauma *(Pathology)*, blemish, discoloration, pockmark, naevus, cicatrix • *He had a scar on his forehead.*
2 = **trauma**, suffering, pain, strain, torture, disturbance, anguish • *emotional scars that come from having been abused*
▸ AS A VERB 1 = **mark**, disfigure, damage, brand, mar, mutilate, maim, blemish, deface, traumatize, disfeature • *He was scarred for life during a pub fight.*
2 = **damage**, ruin, mar, spoil, mutilate, deface • *The table top was scarred and dented.*
3 = **traumatize**, distress, afflict, worry, trouble, pain, wound, upset, bother, disturb, torment, harrow, agonize • *This is something that is going to scar him forever.*

scarce 1 = **in short supply**, wanting, insufficient, deficient, at a premium, thin on the ground • *Food was scarce and expensive.*
OPPOSITES: sufficient, ample, plentiful
2 = **rare**, few, unusual, uncommon, few and far between, infrequent, thin on the ground, seldom met with • *I'm unemployed, so luxuries are scarce.*
OPPOSITES: common, numerous, frequent

scarcely 1 = **hardly**, barely, only just, scarce *(archaic)*, almost not • *He could scarcely breathe.*
2 = **by no means**, hardly, not at all, definitely not, under no circumstances, on no account • *It can scarcely be coincidence.*
3 = **rarely**, seldom, not often, infrequently, occasionally, once in a blue moon *(informal)*, hardly ever • *I scarcely ever re-read my published writings.*

scarcity = **shortage**, lack, deficiency, poverty, want, dearth, paucity, insufficiency, infrequency, undersupply, rareness • *an ever-increasing scarcity of water*
OPPOSITES: excess, surplus, abundance

scare AS A VERB = **frighten**, alarm, terrify, panic, shock, startle, intimidate, dismay, daunt, terrorize, put the wind up (someone) *(informal)*, give (someone) a fright, give (someone) a turn *(informal)*, scare the bejesus out of *(informal)*, affright *(archaic)* • *She's just trying to scare me.*
▸ AS A NOUN 1 = **fright**, shock, start, turn • *We got a bit of a scare.*
2 = **panic**, hysteria • *the doctor at the centre of an Aids scare*
3 = **alert**, warning, alarm • *a security scare over a suspect package*

scared = **afraid**, alarmed, frightened, terrified, shaken, cowed, startled, fearful, unnerved, petrified, panicky, terrorized, panic-stricken, scared to death, scared stiff, scared shitless *(taboo slang)*, terror-stricken, shit-scared *(taboo slang)* • *Why are you so scared?*

scarf = **muffler**, stole, headscarf, comforter, cravat, neckerchief, headsquare • *He reached up to loosen the scarf around his neck.*

scarper = **run away**, flee, disappear, go, depart, clear off *(informal)*, beat it *(slang)*, make off, abscond, decamp, take flight, hook it *(slang)*, run for it, slope off, cut and run *(informal)*, beat a hasty retreat, do a bunk *(Brit. slang)*, scram *(informal)*, take yourself off, skedaddle *(informal)*, vamoose *(slang, chiefly U.S.)*, make yourself scarce *(informal)*, take to your heels, do a Skase *(Austral. informal)* • *I've never seen anyone scarper so fast.*

scary = **frightening**, alarming, terrifying, shocking, chilling, horrifying, intimidating, horrendous, hairy *(slang)*, unnerving, spooky *(informal)*, creepy *(informal)*, hair-raising, spine-chilling, bloodcurdling • *I think prison is going to be a scary thing for Harry.*

scathing = **critical**, cutting, biting, harsh, savage, brutal, searing, withering, belittling, sarcastic, caustic, scornful, vitriolic, trenchant, mordant, mordacious • *He then launched a scathing attack on previous leaders.*

scatter 1 = **throw about**, spread, sprinkle, strew, broadcast, shower, fling, litter, sow, diffuse, disseminate • *He began by scattering seed and putting in plants.*
OPPOSITES: collect, gather
2 = **disperse**, separate, break up, dispel, disband, dissipate, go their separate ways, disunite, go in different directions, put to flight • *After dinner, everyone scattered.*
OPPOSITES: assemble, converge, congregate
3 = **dot**, spot, sprinkle, pepper, litter, fleck, stipple • *bays picturesquely scattered with rocky islets*

scatterbrained = **empty-headed**, silly, frivolous, irresponsible, careless, giddy, madcap, goofy *(informal)*, thoughtless, forgetful, scatty *(Brit. informal)*, inattentive, bird-brained *(informal)*, slaphappy *(informal)*, featherbrained • *She plays a scatterbrained blonde.*

scattering = **sprinkling**, few, handful, scatter, smattering, smatter • *the scattering of houses on the east of the village*

scavenge = **search**, hunt, forage, rummage, root about, fossick *(Austral. & N.Z.)*, scratch about, grub about • *The foxes come and scavenge for bones.*

scenario 1 = **situation**, sequence of events, chain of events, course of events, series of developments • *That apocalyptic scenario cannot be ruled out.*
2 = **story line**, résumé, outline, sketch, summary, rundown, synopsis • *I will write an outline of the scenario.*

scene AS A NOUN 1 = **act**, part, division, episode • *the opening scene*
2 = **setting**, set, background, location, backdrop, mise en scène *(French)* • *The lights go up, revealing a scene of chaos.*
3 = **incident**, happening, event, episode • *There were emotional scenes as the refugees enjoyed their first breath of freedom.*
4 = **site**, place, setting, area, position, stage, situation, spot, whereabouts, locality • *Riot vans were on the scene in minutes.*
5 = **world**, business, environment, preserve, arena, realm, domain, milieu, thing, field of interest • *the local music scene* • *Sport just isn't my scene.*

6 = view, prospect, panorama, vista, landscape, tableau, outlook • *James Lynch's country scenes*
7 = fuss, to-do, row, performance, upset, drama, exhibition, carry-on *(informal, chiefly Brit.)*, confrontation, outburst, tantrum, commotion, hue and cry, display of emotion, hissy fit *(informal)* • *I'm sorry I made such a scene.*
8 = section, part, sequence, segment, clip • *She was told to cut some scenes from her new series.*
▸ IN PHRASES: **behind the scenes = secretly**, in private, in secret, behind closed doors, surreptitiously, on the quiet • *But behind the scenes he will be working quietly.*

scenery 1 = landscape, view, surroundings, outlook, terrain, vista • *Sometimes they just drive slowly down the lane enjoying the scenery.*
2 = set, setting, backdrop, flats, décor, stage set, mise en scène *(French)* • *There was a break while the scenery was changed.*

scenic = picturesque, beautiful, spectacular, striking, grand, impressive, breathtaking, panoramic • *A 2-hour drive through scenic country.*

scent AS A NOUN **1 = fragrance**, smell, perfume, bouquet, aroma, odour, niff *(Brit. slang)*, redolence • *She could smell the scent of her mother's lacquer.*
2 = trail, track, spoor • *A police dog picked up the murderer's scent.*
3 = perfume, fragrance, cologne, eau de toilette *(French)*, eau de cologne *(French)*, toilet water • *a bottle of scent*
▸ AS A VERB **= smell**, sense, recognize, detect, sniff, discern, sniff out, nose out, get wind of *(informal)*, be on the track *or* trail of • *dogs which scent the hidden birds*

scented = fragrant, perfumed, aromatic, sweet-smelling, redolent, ambrosial, odoriferous • *scented body lotion*

sceptic 1 = doubter, cynic, scoffer, questioner, disbeliever, Pyrrhonist • *He was a born sceptic.*
2 = agnostic, doubter, unbeliever, doubting Thomas • *a lifelong religious sceptic*

QUOTATIONS
I am too much of a sceptic to deny the possibility of anything
[T.H. Huxley]

sceptical = doubtful, cynical, dubious, questioning, doubting, hesitating, scoffing, hesitant, unconvinced, disbelieving, incredulous, quizzical, mistrustful, unbelieving • *scientists who are sceptical about global warming*
OPPOSITES: believing, trusting, convinced

scepticism = doubt, suspicion, disbelief, cynicism, incredulity, Pyrrhonism • *The report has inevitably been greeted with scepticism.*

schedule AS A NOUN **1 = plan**, programme, agenda, calendar, timetable, itinerary, list of appointments • *He has been forced to adjust his schedule.*
2 = list, catalogue, inventory, syllabus • *a detailed written schedule*
▸ AS A VERB **= plan**, set up, book, programme, arrange, organize, timetable • *No new talks are scheduled.*

schematic = graphic, representational, illustrative, diagrammatic, diagrammatical • *a schematic picture of the solar system*

scheme AS A NOUN **1 = plan**, programme, strategy, system, design, project, theory, proposal, device, tactics, course of action, contrivance • *a private pension scheme*
2 = plot, dodge, ploy, ruse, game *(informal)*, shift, intrigue, conspiracy, manoeuvre, machinations, subterfuge, stratagem • *a quick money-making scheme*
▸ AS A VERB **= plot**, plan, intrigue, manoeuvre, conspire, contrive, collude, wheel and deal, machinate • *Everyone's always scheming and plotting.*

QUOTATIONS
The best laid schemes o' mice an' men
Gang aft a-gley
[Robert Burns *To a Mouse*]

schemer = plotter, intriguer, conniver, Machiavelli, wangler *(informal)*, slyboots *(informal)*, wheeler-dealer *(informal)* • *She is a schemer, my wee sister.*

scheming = calculating, cunning, sly, designing, tricky, slippery, wily, artful, conniving, Machiavellian, foxy, deceitful, underhand, duplicitous • *I'm a cold scheming bitch.*
OPPOSITES: honest, above-board, straightforward

schism = division, break, split, breach, separation, rift, splintering, rupture, discord, disunion • *The church seems to be on the brink of schism.*

schmaltzy = sentimental, sloppy *(informal)*, corny *(slang)*, cheesy *(informal)*, mushy *(informal)*, soppy *(informal)*, gooey *(informal)*, cloying, maudlin, slushy *(informal)*, mawkish, tear-jerking, icky *(informal)*, bathetic, overemotional • *A schmaltzy weep-along if ever there was one!*

schmick 1 = excellent, outstanding, good, great, fine, prime, capital, noted, choice, champion, cool *(informal)*, select, brilliant, very good, cracking *(Brit. informal)*, crucial *(slang)*, mean *(slang)*, superb, distinguished, fantastic, magnificent, superior, sterling, worthy, first-class, marvellous, exceptional, terrific, splendid, notable, mega *(slang)*, topping *(Brit. slang)*, sovereign, dope *(slang)*, world-class, exquisite, admirable, exemplary, wicked *(slang)*, first-rate, def *(slang)*, superlative, top-notch *(informal)*, brill *(informal)*, pre-eminent, meritorious, estimable, tiptop, bodacious *(slang, chiefly U.S.)*, boffo *(slang)*, the dog's bollocks *(taboo slang)*, jim-dandy *(slang)*, A1 *or* A-one *(informal)*, bitchin' *(U.S. slang)*, chillin' *(U.S. slang)*, booshit *(Austral. slang)*, exo *(Austral. slang)*, sik *(Austral. slang)*, rad *(informal)*, phat *(slang)*, beaut *(informal)*, barrie *(Scot. slang)*, belting *(Brit. slang)*, pearler *(Austral. slang)* • *The band launch their schmick new CD next week.*
OPPOSITES: bad, poor, terrible, half-pie *(N.Z. informal)*
2 = stylish, smart, chic, polished, fashionable, trendy *(Brit. informal)*, classy *(slang)*, in fashion, snappy, in vogue, dapper, natty *(informal)*, snazzy *(informal)*, modish, well turned-out, dressy *(informal)*, à la mode, voguish, funky • *the city's schmick new restaurant*
OPPOSITES: shabby, scruffy, unfashionable

scholar 1 = intellectual, academic, man of letters, bookworm, egghead *(informal)*, savant, bluestocking *(usually disparaging)*, acca *(Austral. slang)* • *The library attracts thousands of scholars and researchers.*
2 = student, pupil, learner, schoolboy *or* schoolgirl • *She could be a good scholar if she didn't let her mind wander so much.*

QUOTATIONS
The ink of the scholar is more sacred than the blood of the martyr
[Mohammed]

scholarly = learned, academic, intellectual, lettered, erudite, scholastic, well-read, studious, bookish, swotty *(Brit. informal)* • *He was an intellectual, scholarly man.*
OPPOSITES: philistine, uneducated, middlebrow

scholarship 1 = grant, award, payment, exhibition, endowment, fellowship, bursary • *scholarships for women over 30*
2 = learning, education, culture, knowledge, wisdom, accomplishments, attainments, lore, erudition, academic study, book-learning • *I want to take advantage of your lifetime of scholarship.*

scholastic = learned, academic, scholarly, lettered, literary, bookish • *the values which encouraged her scholastic achievement*

school AS A NOUN **1 = academy**, college, institution, institute, discipline, seminary, educational institution, centre of learning, alma mater • *a boy who was in my class at school*
2 = group, set, circle, following, class, faction, followers, disciples, sect, devotees, denomination, clique, adherents, schism • *the Chicago school of economists*

S

3 = way of life, doctrine, creed, faith, outlook, persuasion, denomination, school of thought • *He was never a member of any school.*

▸ **AS A VERB = train**, prime, coach, prepare, discipline, educate, drill, tutor, instruct, verse, indoctrinate • *He is schooled to spot trouble.*

QUOTATIONS

School is where you go between when your parents can't take you and industry can't take you
[John Updike]

A school is not a factory. Its raison d'être is to provide opportunity for experience
[J.L. Carr *The Harpole Report*]

▹ *See panel* **Schools, colleges and universities**

schooling 1 = teaching, education, tuition, formal education, book-learning • *normal schooling has been severely disrupted* **2 = training**, coaching, instruction, grounding, preparation, drill, guidance • *the schooling of horses*

schoolteacher = schoolmaster *or* **schoolmistress**, instructor, pedagogue, schoolmarm *(informal)*, dominie *(Scot.)* • *His father was a schoolteacher and churchwarden.*

science = discipline, body of knowledge, area of study, branch of knowledge • *the science of microbiology*

QUOTATIONS

Art is meant to disturb. Science reassures
[Georges Braque *Pensées sur l'art*]

Science is the record of dead religions
[Oscar Wilde *Phrases and Philosophies for the Use of the Young*]

Science means simply the aggregate of all the recipes that are always successful. The rest is literature
[Paul Valéry *Moralités*]

Science is nothing but trained and organized common sense
[T.H. Huxley *Biogenesis and Abiogenesis*]

Our scientific power has outrun our spiritual power. We have guided missiles and misguided men
[Martin Luther King]

the great tragedy of Science – the slaying of a beautiful hypothesis by an ugly fact
[T.H. Huxley *Biogenesis and Abiogenesis*]

the essence of science: ask an impertinent question, and you are on the way to a pertinent answer
[Jacob Bronowski *The Ascent of Man*]

In science the credit goes to the man who convinces the world, not to the man to whom the idea first occurs
[Francis Darwin]

Science is an edged tool, with which men play like children, and cut their own fingers
[Arthur Eddington]

Science without religion is lame, religion without science is blind
[Albert Einstein *Science, Philosophy and Religion*]

There are no such things as applied sciences, only applications of science
[Louis Pasteur]

Science is built up of facts, as a house is built of stones; but an accumulation of facts is no more a science than a heap of stones is a house
[Henri Poincaré *Science and Hypothesis*]

Science must begin with myths, and the criticism of myths
[Karl Popper *The Philosophy of Science*]

scientific 1 = technological, technical, chemical, biological, empirical, factual • *scientific research* **2 = systematic**, accurate, exact, precise, ordered, controlled, rational, mathematical, rigorous, analytical, methodical • *the scientific study of capitalist development*

scientist = researcher, inventor, technologist, boffin *(informal)*, technophile • *a dissident scientist*

SCHOOLS, COLLEGES, AND UNIVERSITIES

academe *(literary)*
academy
alma mater
approved school *(Brit.)*
boarding school
choir school *(Brit.)*
city technology college *or* CTC *(Brit.)*
civic university *(Brit.)*
classical college *(Canad.)*
co-ed *(Brit.)*
college
college of advanced technology *or* CAT
college of education
collegiate institute *(Canad.)*
community college
community home
community school *(Brit.)*
composite school *(Canad.)*
comprehensive *or* comprehensive school *(chiefly Brit.)*
convent *or* convent school
correspondence school
council school
dame school *(old-fashioned)*
day school
direct-grant school *(Brit. old-fashioned)*
district high school *(N.Z.)*
elementary school *(Brit. old-fashioned)*
finishing school
first school *(Brit.)*
grade school *(U.S.)*
grammar school *(U.S.)*
Great Public Schools *or* GPS *(Austral.)*
hedge-school *(Irish history)*
hostel *(Canad.)*
independent school
infant school
integrated school *(N.Z.)*
intermediate school *(N.Z.)*
Ivy League
junior college *(U.S. & Canad.)*
junior school
kindergarten
kindy *or* kindie *(Austral. & N.Z.)*
land grant university *(U.S.)*
List D school *(Scot.)*
magnet school
maintained school
middle school *(Brit.)*
mixed school
multiversity *(chiefly U.S. & Canad.)*
National School
night school
normal school
nursery *or* nursery school
Open College
Open University
polytechnic
preparatory school, prep school, *or (chiefly U.S.)* prep
primary school
private school
public school
ragged school *(Brit.)*
reformatory *or* reform school
residential school
Sabbath school *(chiefly U.S.)*
schola cantorum
secondary modern school *(Brit. old-fashioned)*
secondary school
seminary
separate school *(Canad.)*
single-sex school
sixth-form college
special school *(Brit.)*
state school
summer school
Sunday school
technical college *or (informal)* tech *(Brit.)*
technology college
tertiary college *(Brit.)*
trade school
university *or (informal)* uni
varsity *(Brit. & N.Z. informal)*
village college
yeshiva

QUOTATIONS
When a distinguished but elderly scientist states that something is possible, he is almost certainly right. When he states that something is impossible, he is very probably wrong. (Clarke's First Law)
[Arthur C. Clarke *Profile of the Future*]
It is a good morning exercise for a research scientist to discard a pet hypothesis every day before breakfast. It keeps him young
[Konrad Lorenz *On Aggression*]
I don't know what I may seem to the world, but as to myself, I seem to have been only like a boy playing on the sea-shore and diverting myself in now and then finding a smoother pebble or a prettier shell than ordinary, whilst the great ocean of truth lay all undiscovered before me
[Isaac Newton]
Nature, and Nature's laws lay hid in night
God said, Let Newton be! and all was light
[Alexander Pope *Epitaph: Intended for Sir Isaac Newton*]

scintillating = **brilliant**, exciting, stimulating, lively, sparkling, bright, glittering, dazzling, witty, animated • *You can hardly expect scintillating conversation from a kid that age.*

scion = **descendant**, child, offspring, successor, heir • *He was the scion of an aristocratic family that lost its fortune in the revolution.*

scoff[1] = **scorn**, mock, laugh at, ridicule, knock *(informal)*, scout *(archaic)*, taunt, despise, sneer, jeer, deride, slag (off) *(slang)*, flout, belittle, revile, make light of, poke fun at, twit, take the piss (out of) *(taboo slang)*, gibe, pooh-pooh, make sport of • *At first I scoffed at the notion.*

scoff[2] = **gobble (up)**, wolf, devour, bolt, cram, put away, guzzle, gulp down, gorge yourself on, gollop, stuff yourself with, cram yourself on, make a pig of yourself on *(informal)* • *I scoffed the lot!*

scold = **reprimand**, censure, rebuke, rate, blame, lecture, carpet *(informal)*, slate *(informal, chiefly Brit.)*, nag, go on at, reproach, berate, tick off *(informal)*, castigate, chide, tear into *(informal)*, tell off *(informal)*, find fault with, remonstrate with, bring (someone) to book, take (someone) to task, read the riot act, reprove, upbraid, bawl out *(informal)*, give (someone) a talking-to *(informal)*, haul (someone) over the coals *(informal)*, chew out *(U.S. & Canad. informal)*, give (someone) a dressing-down, tear (someone) off a strip *(Brit. informal)*, give a rocket *(Brit. & N.Z. informal)*, vituperate, give (someone) a row, have (someone) on the carpet *(informal)* • *If he finds out, he'll scold me.*
OPPOSITES: approve, praise, acclaim

scolding = **ticking-off**, row, lecture, wigging *(Brit. slang)*, rebuke *(informal)*, dressing-down *(informal)*, telling-off *(informal)*, tongue-lashing, piece of your mind, (good) talking-to *(informal)* • *He was given a scolding for offending his opponents.*

scoop **AS A VERB** = **win**, get, receive, land, gain, achieve, net, earn, pick up, bag *(informal)*, secure, collect, obtain, procure, come away with • *films which scooped awards around the world*
▸ **AS A NOUN** 1 = **ladle**, bailer, spoon, dipper • *a small ice-cream scoop*
2 = **spoonful**, lump, dollop *(informal)*, ball, ladleful • *She gave him an extra scoop of clotted cream.*
3 = **exclusive**, exposé, coup, revelation, sensation, inside story • *one of the biggest scoops in the history of newspapers*
▸ **IN PHRASES:** **scoop something out** 1 = **take out**, empty, dig out, scrape out, spoon out, bail *or* bale out • *Cut a marrow in half and scoop out the seeds.*
2 = **dig**, shovel, excavate, gouge, hollow out • *A hole had been scooped out next to the house.*
scoop something *or* **someone up** = **gather up**, lift, pick up, take up, sweep up *or* away • *He began to scoop his things up frantically.* • *I wanted to scoop him up in my arms and give him a hug.*

scoot = **dash**, run, dart, sprint, bolt, zip, scuttle, scurry, scamper, skitter, skedaddle *(informal)*, skirr • *He scooted up the stairs.*

scope 1 = **opportunity**, room, freedom, play, chance, space, possibility, liberty, latitude, elbowroom, leeway • *He believed in giving his staff scope for initiative.*
2 = **range**, capacity, reach, area, extent, confines, outlook, orbit, span, sphere, compass, remit, terms of reference, ambit, purview, field of reference • *the scope of a novel*

scorch 1 = **burn**, sear, char, roast, blister, wither, blacken, shrivel, parch, singe • *The bomb scorched the side of the building.*
2 = **shrivel**, burn, wither, bake, dry up, parch • *The leaves are inclined to scorch in hot sunshine.*
3 = **tear**, speed, zoom, bomb, belt, barrel *(informal)*, whizz, burn rubber • *Many people dream of scorching around a racetrack.*

scorching = **burning**, boiling, baking, flaming, tropical, roasting, searing, fiery, sizzling, red-hot, torrid, sweltering, broiling, unbearably hot • *It was a scorching day.*

score **AS A VERB** 1 = **gain**, win, achieve, make, get, net, bag, obtain, bring in, attain, amass, notch up *(informal)*, chalk up *(informal)* • *They scored 282 points in their first innings.*
2 = **go down well with (someone)**, impress, triumph, make a hit *(informal)*, make a point, gain an advantage, put yourself across, make an impact *or* impression • *He told them he had scored with the girl.*
3 = **arrange**, set, orchestrate, write, adapt, compose • *He scored a piece for a chamber music ensemble.*
4 = **cut**, scratch, nick, mark, mar, slash, scrape, notch, graze, gash, gouge, deface, indent, crosshatch, make a groove in • *Lightly score the surface of the steaks with a sharp cook's knife.*
5 = **buy**, get, purchase, pay for, obtain, acquire, invest in, procure • *We scored some dope last night.*
▸ **AS A NOUN** 1 = **rating**, mark, grade, percentage • *low maths scores*
2 = **points**, result, total, outcome, tally, number of points *or* goals scored • *The final score was 4-1.*
3 = **composition**, soundtrack, arrangement, orchestration • *the composer of classic film scores*
4 = **twenty** • *three score and ten*
5 = **grievance**, dispute, wrong, injury, complaint, injustice, grudge, bone of contention, axe to grind, turf war *(informal)*, bone to pick • *They had a score to settle with each other.*
6 = **charge**, bill, account, total, debt, reckoning, tab *(U.S. informal)*, tally, amount due • *So what is the score anyway?*
▸ **AS A PLURAL NOUN** = **lots**, loads, many, millions, gazillions *(informal)*, hundreds, hosts, crowds, masses, droves, an army, legions, swarms, multitudes, myriads, very many, a flock, a throng, a great number • *Campaigners lit scores of bonfires.*
▸ **IN PHRASES:** **on this** *or* **that score** = **on this** *or* **that subject**, as far as (something) is concerned, in this *or* that respect, as regards this *or* that, on this *or* that matter • *At least I've had no problems on that score.*
score points off someone = **get the better of**, make a fool of, be one up on *(informal)*, worst, humiliate, have the laugh on, make (someone) look silly • *They kept trying to score points off each other.*
score something out *or* **through** = **cross out**, delete, strike out, cancel, obliterate, expunge, scratch out, put a line through • *Words and sentences had been scored out and underlined.*
settle a score = **get your own back on someone**, retaliate, repay someone, hit back (at someone), pay (someone) back (in their own coin), get even with someone *(informal)*, give (someone) a taste of their own medicine,

S

avenge something, give an eye for an eye, give like for like *or* tit for tat, requite someone's actions • *Attempting to settle the score can provide us with temporary satisfaction.*

the score = **the situation**, the facts, the story, the truth, the picture, the reality, the equation, what's what, the state of play, the lie of the land, the setup *(informal)*, how things stand, the true state of affairs • *He knows the score.*

scorn AS A NOUN = **contempt**, disdain, mockery, derision, despite, slight, sneer, sarcasm, disparagement, contumely, contemptuousness, scornfulness • *They greeted the proposal with scorn.*

OPPOSITES: respect, esteem, admiration

▸ AS A VERB = **despise**, reject, disdain, slight, scout *(archaic)*, snub, shun, be above, spurn, rebuff, deride, flout, look down on, scoff at, make fun of, sneer at, hold in contempt, turn up your nose at *(informal)*, contemn, curl your lip at, consider beneath you • *People scorn me as a single parent.* • *people who scorned traditional methods*

OPPOSITES: respect, admire, esteem

QUOTATIONS

Heav'n has no rage, like love to hatred turn'd,
Nor Hell a fury, like a woman scorn'd
[William Congreve *The Mourning Bride*]

scornful = **contemptuous**, insulting, mocking, defiant, withering, sneering, slighting, jeering, scoffing, scathing, sarcastic, sardonic, haughty, disdainful, insolent, derisive, supercilious, contumelious • *a scornful smile*

scornfully = **contemptuously**, with contempt, dismissively, disdainfully, with disdain, scathingly, witheringly, with a sneer, slightingly, with lip curled • *'I don't think so,' he said scornfully.*

scotch = **put an end to**, destroy, smash, devastate, wreck, thwart, scupper, extinguish, put paid to, nip in the bud, bring to an end, put the lid on, put the kibosh on • *They have scotched rumours that they are planning a special show.*

scot-free = **unpunished**, clear, safe, unscathed, unharmed • *Others who were guilty were being allowed to get off scot-free.*

Scotland = **north of the border**, Caledonia *(Latin)*, the land of the brave • *He inherited a castle in Scotland.*

▸ RELATED ADJECTIVES: Scottish, Caledonian

QUOTATIONS

O Flower of Scotland,
When will we see
Your like again
That fought and died for,
Your wee bit hill and glen,
And stood against him,
Proud Edward's Army,
And sent him homeward,
Tae think again
[Roy Williamson *Flower of Scotland*]

Scots = **Scottish**, Caledonian • *Scots law differs in many respects from English law.*

scoundrel = **rogue**, bastard *(informal offensive)*, villain, mother, heel *(slang)*, cheat, shit *(taboo slang)*, bugger *(taboo slang)*, swine, rascal, son-of-a-bitch *(slang, chiefly U.S. & Canad.)*, asshole *(U.S. & Canad. taboo slang)*, scally *(Northwest English dialect)*, turd *(taboo slang)*, wretch, incorrigible, motherfucker *(taboo slang, chiefly U.S.)*, knave *(archaic)*, rotter *(slang, chiefly Brit.)*, ne'er-do-well, reprobate, scumbag *(slang)*, good-for-nothing, miscreant, scamp, bad egg *(old-fashioned informal)*, blackguard, cocksucker *(taboo slang)*, scapegrace, asswipe *(U.S. & Canad. taboo slang)*, caitiff *(archaic)*, dastard *(archaic)*, skelm *(S. African)*, wrong 'un *(Austral. slang)* • *He is a lying scoundrel.*

scour[1] = **scrub**, clean, polish, rub, cleanse, buff, burnish, whiten, furbish, abrade • *He decided to scour the sink.*

scour[2] = **search**, hunt, comb, ransack, forage, look high and low, go over with a fine-tooth comb • *We scoured the telephone directory for clues.*

scourge AS A NOUN 1 = **affliction**, plague, curse, terror, pest, torment, misfortune, visitation, bane, infliction • *Drugs are a scourge that is devastating our society.*

OPPOSITES: benefit, blessing, boon

2 = **whip**, lash, thong, switch, strap, cat-o'-nine-tails • *a heavy scourge with a piece of iron lashed into its knot*

▸ AS A VERB 1 = **afflict**, plague, curse, torment, harass, terrorize, excoriate • *Economic anarchy scourged the post-war world.*

2 = **whip**, beat, lash, thrash, discipline, belt *(informal)*, leather, punish, whale, cane, flog, trounce, castigate, wallop *(informal)*, chastise, lather *(informal)*, horsewhip, tan (someone's) hide *(slang)*, take a strap to • *They were scourging him severely.*

scout AS A NOUN 1 = **vanguard**, lookout, precursor, outrider, reconnoitrer, advance guard • *They set off, two men out in front as scouts.*

2 = **recruiter**, talent scout, talent spotter • *We've had scouts watching him for some time.*

▸ AS A VERB = **reconnoitre**, investigate, check out, case *(slang)*, watch, survey, observe, spy, probe, recce *(slang)*, spy out, make a reconnaissance, see how the land lies • *I have people scouting the hills already.*

▸ IN PHRASES: **scout around** *or* **round** = **search**, look for, hunt for, fossick *(Austral. & N.Z.)*, cast about *or* around, ferret about *or* around, root about *or* around • *They scouted around for more fuel.*

scout something out = **survey**, investigate, observe, explore, scan, inspect, scrutinize, case *(slang)*, recce *(slang)*, reconnoitre, spy out, make a reconnaissance (of) • *Their mission is to scout out places where helicopters can land.*

scowl AS A VERB = **glower**, frown, look daggers, grimace, lour *or* lower • *She scowled at the two men as they entered the room.*

▸ AS A NOUN = **glower**, frown, dirty look, black look, grimace • *He met the remark with a scowl.*

scrabble 1 = **scrape**, scratch, scramble, dig, claw, paw, grope, clamber • *I hung there, scrabbling with my feet to find a foothold.*

2 = **strive**, rush, hasten, run, push, contend, vie, jostle, jockey for position, make haste • *The banks are now desperately scrabbling to recover their costs.*

scraggy 1 = **scrawny**, lean, skinny, angular, gaunt, bony, lanky, emaciated, undernourished, gangling, rawboned • *a flock of scraggy sheep*

2 = **unkempt**, scruffy, tousled, rough, grotty *(slang)*, lank, draggletailed *(archaic)* • *Their hallmarks are scraggy hair and scruffy clothes.*

scramble AS A VERB 1 = **struggle**, climb, clamber, push, crawl, swarm, scrabble, move with difficulty • *He scrambled up a steep bank.*

2 = **strive**, rush, contend, vie, run, push, hasten, jostle, jockey for position, make haste • *More than a million fans are expected to scramble for tickets.*

3 = **jumble**, mix up, muddle, shuffle, entangle, disarrange • *The latest machines scramble the messages.*

▸ AS A NOUN 1 = **clamber**, ascent • *the scramble to the top of the cliffs*

2 = **race**, competition, struggle, rush, confusion, tussle, hustle, scuffle, free-for-all *(informal)*, commotion, scrimmage, melee *or* mêlée • *the scramble for jobs*

scrap[1] AS A NOUN 1 = **piece**, fragment, bit, trace, grain, particle, portion, snatch, part, atom, remnant, crumb, mite, bite, mouthful, snippet, sliver, morsel, modicum, iota • *a fire fuelled by scraps of wood*

2 = **waste**, refuse, rubbish, junk, litter, debris, garbage, trash, detritus, off cuts • *cut up for scrap*

▸ AS A PLURAL NOUN = **leftovers**, remains, bits, slops, dregs, scrapings, leavings, uneaten food, scourings • *children foraging for scraps of food*

▸ **AS A VERB** = **get rid of**, drop, abandon, shed, break up, ditch *(slang)*, junk *(informal)*, chuck *(informal)*, discard, write off, demolish, trash *(slang)*, dispense with, jettison, toss out, throw on the scrapheap, throw away *or* out • *We should scrap nuclear and chemical weapons.*
OPPOSITES: bring back, reinstate, re-establish

scrap² **AS A NOUN** = **fight**, battle, row, argument, dispute, set-to *(informal)*, disagreement, quarrel, brawl, squabble, wrangle, scuffle, tiff, turf war *(informal)*, dust-up *(informal)*, shindig *(informal)*, scrimmage, shindy *(informal)*, bagarre *(French)*, biffo *(Austral. slang)* • *He has never been one to avoid a scrap.*
▸ **AS A VERB** = **fight**, argue, row, fall out *(informal)*, barney *(informal)*, squabble, spar, wrangle, bicker, have words, come to blows, have a shouting match *(informal)* • *They are always scrapping.*

scrape **AS A VERB** 1 = **rake**, sweep, drag, brush • *She went round the car scraping the frost off the windows.*
2 = **grate**, grind, scratch, screech, squeak, rasp • *The only sound is that of knives and forks scraping against china.*
3 = **graze**, skin, scratch, bark, scuff, rub, abrade • *She stumbled and fell, scraping her palms and knees.*
4 = **clean**, remove, scour • *She scraped food off the plates into the bin.*
▸ **AS A NOUN** = **predicament**, trouble, difficulty, spot *(informal)*, fix *(informal)*, mess, distress, dilemma, plight, tight spot, awkward situation, pretty pickle *(informal)* • *We got into terrible scrapes.*
▸ **IN PHRASES: scrape by** = **manage to live**, make ends meet, scrape a living, scrimp, live from hand to mouth, keep the wolf from the door, keep your head above water, muddle through *or* along • *We're barely scraping by on my salary.*
scrape something together = **collect**, save, muster, get hold of, amass, hoard, glean, dredge up, rake up *or* together • *They only just managed to scrape the money together.*
scrape through = **get by** *(informal)* = **manage to live** *(informal)*, just pass, just make it, have a close shave *(informal)*, pass by a narrow margin, narrowly achieve • *'How did your exams go?' – 'I just scraped through.'*

scrapheap **IN PHRASES: on the scrapheap** = **discarded**, ditched *(slang)*, redundant, written off, jettisoned, put out to grass *(informal)* • *Thousands of miners have suddenly found themselves on the scrapheap.*

S

scrappy = **incomplete**, sketchy, piecemeal, disjointed, perfunctory, thrown together, fragmentary, bitty • *a scrappy affair*

scratch **AS A VERB** 1 = **rub**, scrape, claw at • *The old man lifted his cardigan to scratch his side.*
2 = **mark**, cut, score, damage, grate, graze, etch, lacerate, incise, make a mark on • *Knives will scratch the worktop.*
3 = **cut**, skin, wound, rub, bark, scrape, graze, rasp, chafe, lacerate, abrade • *He had blood on his nose and he had scratched his knees.*
▸ **AS A NOUN** 1 = **mark**, scrape, graze, blemish, gash, laceration, claw mark • *I pointed to a number of scratches on the tile floor.*
2 = **cut**, wound, scrape, graze, abrasion, laceration • *He walked away from the accident without a scratch.*
▸ **IN PHRASES: scratch about** *or* **round** = **search (about** *or* **around)**, hunt (about *or* around), scrabble (about *or* around), rummage (about *or* around), forage (about *or* around), fossick (about *or* around) *(Austral. & N.Z.)*, root about *or* around, ferret about *or* around, cast about *or* around, poke about *or* around, nose about *or* around • *They scratch about in the forest litter.*
scratch something out = **erase**, eliminate, delete, cancel, strike off, annul, cross out • *She scratched out the word 'frightful'.*
not up to scratch = **inadequate**, unacceptable, unsatisfactory, incapable, insufficient, incompetent, not up to standard, not up to snuff *(informal)* • *This work just isn't up to scratch.*

scrawl **AS A VERB** = **scribble**, doodle, squiggle • *graffiti scrawled on school walls*
▸ **AS A NOUN** = **scribble**, doodle, squiggle • *a hasty, barely decipherable scrawl*

scrawny = **thin**, lean, skinny, angular, gaunt, skeletal, bony, lanky, undernourished, skin-and-bones *(informal)*, scraggy, rawboned, macilent *(rare)* • *a scrawny woman with dyed black hair*

scream **AS A VERB** 1 = **cry**, yell, shriek, bellow, screech, squeal, shrill, bawl, howl, holler *(informal)*, yelp, sing out • *If I hear one more joke about my hair, I shall scream.*
2 = **thunder**, rumble, screech • *an airforce jet screamed over the town*
▸ **AS A NOUN** 1 = **cry**, yell, howl, wail, outcry, shriek, screech, yelp • *Hilda let out a scream.*
2 = **screech**, squeal, shriek • *the scream of brakes*
3 = **laugh**, card *(informal)*, riot *(slang)*, comic, character *(informal)*, caution *(informal)*, sensation, wit, comedian, entertainer, wag, joker, hoot *(informal)*, dag *(N.Z. informal)* • *He's a scream, isn't he?*

screech **AS A VERB** 1 = **squeal**, scream, shriek • *The car wheels screeched.*
2 = **shriek**, scream, yell, howl, call out, wail, bellow, squeal, holler, caterwaul • *She was screeching at them.*
3 = **squawk** • *A macaw screeched at him from its perch.*
▸ **AS A NOUN** = **cry**, scream, shriek, squeal, squawk, yelp • *The figure gave a screech.*

screen **AS A NOUN** = **cover**, guard, shade, shelter, shield, hedge, partition, cloak, mantle, shroud, canopy, awning, concealment, room divider • *They put a screen in front of me.*
▸ **AS A VERB** 1 = **broadcast**, show, put on, present, air, cable, beam, transmit, relay, televise, put on the air • *The series is likely to be screened in January.*
2 = **cover**, hide, conceal, shade, mask, disguise, veil, cloak, shroud, camouflage, shut out • *The road is screened by a block of flats.*
3 = **investigate**, test, check, examine, scan • *They need to screen everyone at risk of contracting the illness.*
4 = **process**, sort, examine, grade, filter, scan, evaluate, gauge, sift • *It was their job to screen information for their bosses.*
5 = **vet**, assess, evaluate, check out, scrutinize, check up on, test • *They carefully screen all their candidates.*
6 = **protect**, guard, shield, defend, shelter, safeguard • *They deliberately screened him from knowledge of their operations.*

screw **AS A NOUN** = **nail**, pin, tack, rivet, fastener, spike • *Each bracket is fixed to the wall with just three screws.*
▸ **AS A VERB** 1 = **fasten**, fix, attach, bolt, clamp, rivet • *I like the sort of shelving that you screw on the wall.*
2 = **crumple**, crush, squash, crunch, mash • *She screwed the letter up into a ball and threw it in the bin.*
3 = **turn**, wind, twist, tighten, work in • *Screw down the lid fairly tightly.*
4 = **contort**, twist, distort, contract, wrinkle, warp, crumple, deform, pucker • *He screwed his face into an expression of mock pain.*
5 = **have intercourse with**, fuck *(taboo slang)*, sleep with, have sex with, shag *(Brit. taboo slang)*, hump *(taboo slang)*, bonk *(informal)* • *You mean he was screwing her?*
6 = **cheat**, do *(slang)*, rip (someone) off *(slang)*, skin *(slang)*, trick, con, stiff *(slang)*, sting *(informal)*, deceive, fleece, defraud, dupe, overcharge, swindle, rook *(slang)*, bamboozle *(informal)*, diddle *(informal)*, take (someone) for a ride *(informal)*, put one over on (someone) *(informal)*, pull a fast one (on someone) *(informal)*, take to the cleaners *(informal)*, sell a pup (to) *(slang)*, hornswoggle *(slang)* • *We've been screwed.*

7 *often with* **out of = squeeze**, extort, wring, extract, wrest, bleed someone of something • *rich nations screwing money out of poor nations*

▸ **IN PHRASES: put the screws on someone = coerce**, force, compel, drive, squeeze, intimidate, constrain, oppress, lean on, dragoon, steamroller, pressurize, browbeat, press-gang, twist someone's arm, bring pressure to bear on, put the heat on, hold a knife to someone's throat • *They had to put the screws on Harper to get the information they needed.*

screw something up 1 = contort, contract, wrinkle, knot, knit, distort, crumple, pucker • *She screwed up her eyes.*

2 = bungle, botch, mess up, spoil, bitch (up) *(slang)*, queer *(informal)*, cock up *(Brit. slang)*, mishandle, fuck up *(offensive taboo slang)*, make a mess of *(slang)*, mismanage, make a hash of *(informal)*, make a nonsense of, bodge *(informal)*, flub *(U.S. slang)*, louse up *(slang)*, crool *or* cruel *(Austral. slang)* • *Get out. Haven't you screwed things up enough already!*

screw you *or* **that = sod you** *or* **that** *(taboo slang)*, bugger you *or* that *(taboo slang)*, fuck you *or* that *(taboo slang)* • *'Screw you,' he said bitterly, 'I don't need you.'*

scribble AS A VERB **1 = scrawl**, write, jot, pen, scratch, doodle, dash off • *As I scribbled a note in my diary the light went off.*

2 = draw, write, scrawl, doodle • *When Caroline was five she scribbled on a wall.*

▸ **AS A NOUN = mess**, state, jumble, confusion, hash, mishmash, hotchpotch, hodgepodge *(U.S.)*, pig's *or* dog's breakfast *(informal)* • *I'm sorry what I wrote was such a scribble.*

scribe 1 = secretary, clerk, scrivener *(archaic)*, notary *(archaic)*, amanuensis, copyist • *a temple scribe*

2 = writer, copyist, penman *(rare)* • *another scribe had added the last words*

scrimp *often with* **on = economize**, save, scrape, limit, reduce, pinch, stint, shorten, curtail, skimp, be frugal, pinch pennies, tighten your belt, straiten • *She has to scrimp and save to clothe her son.*

script AS A NOUN **1 = text**, lines, words, book, copy, dialogue, manuscript, libretto • *Jenny's writing a film script.*

2 = handwriting, writing, hand, letters, calligraphy, longhand, penmanship • *She wrote the letter in an elegant script.*

▸ **AS A VERB = write**, draft, pen, compose, author • *I scripted and directed both films.*

scripture = The Bible, The Word, The Gospels, The Scriptures, The Word of God, The Good Book, Holy Scripture, Holy Writ, Holy Bible, The Book of Books • *a quote from scripture*

QUOTATIONS

The devil can cite Scripture for his purpose
[William Shakespeare *The Merchant of Venice*]

scroll AS A NOUN **= roll**, paper, parchment • *Ancient scrolls were found in caves by the Dead Sea.*

▸ **AS A VERB = move**, • *I scrolled down the screen.*

Scrooge = miser, penny-pincher *(informal)*, skinflint, cheapskate *(informal)*, tight-arse *(taboo slang)*, tightwad *(U.S. & Canad. slang)*, tight-ass *(U.S. taboo slang)*, niggard, money-grubber *(informal)*, meanie *or* meany *(informal, chiefly Brit.)* • *What a bunch of Scrooges.*

scrotum

▸ **RELATED ADJECTIVE:** scrotal

scrounge = cadge, beg, sponge *(informal)*, bum *(informal)*, touch (someone) for *(slang)*, blag *(slang)*, wheedle, mooch *(slang)*, forage for, hunt around (for), sorn *(Scot.)*, freeload *(slang)*, bludge *(Austral. & N.Z. informal)* • *She had to scrounge the money.*

scrounger = parasite, freeloader *(slang)*, sponger *(informal)*, bum *(informal)*, cadger, bludger *(Austral. & N.Z. informal)*, sorner *(Scot.)*, quandong *(Austral. slang)* • *They are just scroungers.*

scrub AS A VERB **1 = scour**, clean, polish, rub, wash, cleanse, buff, exfoliate • *The corridors are scrubbed clean.*

2 = cancel, drop, give up, abandon, abolish, forget about, call off, delete, do away with, discontinue • *The whole thing had to be scrubbed.*

▸ **AS A NOUN = undergrowth**, brush, underwood, bracken, brambles, briars, underbrush, brushwood, underbush • *There is an area of scrub and woodland beside the railway.*

scrubby = stunted, meagre, underdeveloped, spindly, scrawny, undersized • *scrubby green bushes*

scruff = nape, scrag *(informal)* • *the scruff of the neck*

scruffy = shabby, untidy, ragged, rundown, messy, sloppy *(informal)*, seedy, squalid, tattered, tatty, unkempt, disreputable, scrubby *(Brit. informal)*, grungy, slovenly, mangy, sluttish, slatternly, ungroomed, frowzy, ill-groomed, draggletailed *(archaic)*, daggy *(Austral. & N.Z. informal)* • *a young man, pale, scruffy and untidy*

OPPOSITES: neat, tidy, spruce

scrum = crowd, group, mob, lot, body, host, band, troop, mass, bunch *(informal)*, number, horde, throng, assemblage • *She pushed through the scrum of photographers.*

scrumptious = delicious, delectable, inviting, magnificent, exquisite, luscious, succulent, mouthwatering, yummy *(slang)*, appetizing, moreish *(informal)*, yummo *(Austral. slang)* • *a scrumptious apple pie*

scrunch 1 = rustle, crackle, whisper • *Her feet scrunched on the ground.*

2 = crumple, crush, squash, crunch, mash, ruck up • *scrunching her white cotton gloves into a ball*

scruple = misgiving, hesitation, qualm, doubt, difficulty, caution, reluctance, second thoughts, uneasiness, perplexity, compunction, squeamishness, twinge of conscience • *a man with no moral scruples*

scrupulous 1 = moral, principled, upright, honourable, conscientious • *I have been scrupulous about telling them the truth.*

OPPOSITES: dishonest, unscrupulous, amoral

2 = careful, strict, precise, minute, nice, exact, rigorous, meticulous, painstaking, fastidious, punctilious • *scrupulous attention to detail*

OPPOSITES: reckless, careless, slapdash

scrutinize = examine, study, inspect, research, search, investigate, explore, probe, analyse, scan, sift, dissect, work over, pore over, peruse, inquire into, go over with a fine-tooth comb • *She scrutinized his features.*

scrutiny = examination, study, investigation, search, inquiry, analysis, inspection, exploration, sifting, once-over *(informal)*, perusal, close study • *His private life came under media scrutiny.*

scud = fly, race, speed, shoot, blow, sail, skim • *heavy, rain-laden clouds scudding across the sky*

scuff = scratch, scrape, graze, chafe, roughen, abrade • *She scuffed her shoes on the pavement.*

scuffle AS A NOUN **= fight**, set-to *(informal)*, scrap *(informal)*, disturbance, fray, brawl, barney *(informal)*, ruck *(slang)*, skirmish, tussle, commotion, rumpus, affray *(Law)*, shindig *(informal)*, ruction *(informal)*, ruckus *(informal)*, scrimmage, shindy *(informal)*, bagarre *(French)*, biffo *(Austral. slang)* • *Violent scuffles broke out.*

▸ **AS A VERB = fight**, struggle, clash, contend, grapple, jostle, tussle, come to blows, exchange blows • *Police scuffled with some of the protesters.*

sculpt = carve, cut, fashion, model, form, shape, cast, sculpture, chisel, hew • *They sculpt the material while it is in the right stage of stickiness.*

sculptor = carver, modeller • *I've been a professional sculptor for a long time.*

sculpture AS A NOUN **= statue**, figure, model, bust, effigy, figurine, statuette • *a collection of 20th-century sculptures*

▸ **AS A VERB** = **carve**, form, cut, model, fashion, shape, mould, sculpt, chisel, hew, sculp • *He sculptured the figure in marble.*

scum 1 = **rabble**, trash (*chiefly U.S. & Canad.*), riffraff, rubbish, dross, lowest of the low, dregs of society, canaille (*French*), ragtag and bobtail • *They're cultureless scum drifted from elsewhere.*
2 = **impurities**, film, crust, froth, scruff, dross, offscourings • *scum around the bath*

scungy = **sordid**, seedy, sleazy, squalid, mean, dirty, foul, filthy, unclean, wretched, seamy, slovenly, skanky (*slang*), slummy, festy (*Austral. slang*) • *He was living in some scungy flat on the outskirts of town.*

scupper = **destroy**, ruin, wreck, defeat, overwhelm, disable, overthrow, demolish, undo, torpedo, put paid to, discomfit • *The entire deal will be scuppered.*

scurrilous = **slanderous**, scandalous, defamatory, low, offensive, gross, foul, insulting, infamous, obscene, abusive, coarse, indecent, vulgar, foul-mouthed, salacious, ribald, vituperative, scabrous, Rabelaisian • *scurrilous rumours*

scurry **AS A VERB** = **hurry**, race, dash, fly, sprint, dart, whisk, skim, beetle, scud, scuttle, scoot, scamper • *The attack began, sending residents scurrying for cover.*
OPPOSITES: wander, stroll, amble
▸ **AS A NOUN** = **flurry**, race, bustle, whirl, scampering • *a mad scurry for a suitable venue*

scurvy = **contemptible**, mean, bad, low, base, rotten, sorry, worthless, shabby, vile, low-down (*informal*), pitiful, abject, despicable, dishonourable, ignoble, scabby (*informal*) • *It was a scurvy trick to play.*
▸ **RELATED ADJECTIVE:** scorbutic

scuttle 1 = **run**, scurry, scamper, rush, hurry, scramble, hare (*Brit. informal*), bustle, beetle, scud, hasten, scoot, scutter (*Brit. informal*) • *Two very small children scuttled away.*
2 = **wreck**, destroy, ruin, overwhelm, disable, overthrow, foil, undo, torpedo, put paid to, discomfit • *Such threats could scuttle the peace conference.*

sea **AS A NOUN 1** = **ocean**, the deep, the waves, the drink (*informal*), the briny (*informal*), main • *Most of the kids have never seen the sea.*
2 = **mass**, lot, lots (*informal*), army, host, crowd, collection, sheet, assembly, mob, congregation, legion, abundance, swarm, horde, multitude, myriad, throng, expanse, plethora, profusion, concourse, assemblage, vast number, great number • *Down below them was the sea of upturned faces.*
▸ **AS A MODIFIER** = **marine**, ocean, maritime, aquatic, oceanic, saltwater, ocean-going, seagoing, pelagic, briny, salt • *a sea vessel*
▸ **IN PHRASES:** **at sea** = **bewildered**, lost, confused, puzzled, uncertain, baffled, adrift, perplexed, disconcerted, at a loss, mystified, disoriented, bamboozled (*informal*), flummoxed, at sixes and sevens • *I'm totally at sea with popular culture.*
▸ **RELATED ADJECTIVES:** marine, maritime, thalassic
▸ **RELATED MANIA:** thalassomania
▸ **RELATED PHOBIA:** thalassophobia

QUOTATIONS

the wine-dark sea
[Homer *Iliad*]

ocean: a body of water occupying about two-thirds of a world made for man – who has no gills
[Ambrose Bierce *The Devil's Dictionary*]

▷ *See panel* **Seas and oceans**

sea bird
▷ *See panel* **Sea birds**

seafaring = **nautical**, marine, naval, maritime, oceanic • *a seafaring vessel*

seafood
▷ *See panel* **Seafood**

seal[1] **AS A VERB 1** = **stick down**, close, secure, shut, fasten • *He sealed the envelope and put on a stamp.*
2 = **shut**, close, seal up, make watertight, make airtight • *A woman picks them up and seals them in plastic bags.*
3 = **cordon off**, shut off, fence off, isolate, segregate, close off • *The soldiers were deployed to help police seal the border.*
4 = **settle**, close, clinch, conclude, wind up, consummate, sew up, finalize, shake hands on (*informal*) • *McLaren are close to sealing a deal with Renault.*
▸ **AS A NOUN 1** = **sealant**, sealer, adhesive • *Wet the edges where the two crusts join, to form a seal.*
2 = **authentication**, stamp, confirmation, assurance, ratification, notification, insignia, imprimatur, attestation • *the President's seal of approval*
3 = **badge**, symbol, crest, emblem, mark, stamp, insignia, monogram • *The eagle almost didn't make it onto the seal of America.*
▸ **IN PHRASES:** **seal something in** = **keep in**, save, retain, maintain, reserve, preserve • *The coffee is freeze-dried to seal in the flavour.*
seal something off = **isolate**, segregate, quarantine, board up, fence off, put out of bounds • *the anti-personnel door that sealed off the chamber*
seal something up = **close up**, fill, plug, stop, block, block up, stop up, bung up • *The paper was used for sealing up holes in walls and roofs.*
set the seal on something = **confirm**, establish, assure, stamp, ratify, validate, attest, authenticate • *Such a visit may set the seal on a new relationship between them.*

seal[2]
▸ **RELATED ADJECTIVES:** phocine, otarid
▸ **NAME OF YOUNG:** pup
▸ **COLLECTIVE NOUNS:** herd, pod
▸ **NAME OF HOME:** sealery

SEAS AND OCEANS

SEAS

Adriatic	Barents	China	Japan	North	Sulu
Aegean	Beaufort	Chukchi	Java	Norwegian	Tasman
Amundsen	Bellingshausen	Coral	Kara	Okhotsk	Timor
Andaman	Bering	East China	Laptev	Philippine	Tyrrhenian
Arabian	Bismarck	East Siberian	Ligurian	Red	Weddell
Arafura	Black *or* Euxine	Flores	Lincoln	Ross	White
Aral	Caribbean	Icarian	Marmara *or* Marmora	Sargasso	Yellow *or* Hwang Hai
Azov	Caspian	Inland	Mediterranean	Scotia	
Baltic	Celebes	Ionian	Nordenskjöld	Solomon	
Banda	Ceram	Irish		South China	

OCEANS

Antarctic *or* Southern	Arctic	Atlantic	Indian	Pacific

SEA BIRDS

albatross *or (informal)* gooney bird
auk
auklet
black-backed gull
black guillemot
black shag *or* kawau *(N.Z.)*
blue penguin, korora *or* little blue penguin *(N.Z.)*
blue shag *(N.Z.)*
booby *(Austral.)*
caspian tern *or* taranui *(N.Z.)*
coot
cormorant
fairy penguin, little penguin, *or (N.Z.)* korora
fish hawk
fulmar
gannet
glaucous gull
guillemot
gull *or (archaic or dialect)* cob(b)
herring gull
ivory gull
kittiwake
man-of-war bird *or* frigate bird
murrelet
old squaw *or* oldwife
oystercatcher
petrel
prion
razorbill *or* razor-billed auk
scoter
sea duck
sea eagle *or* erne
seagull
shearwater
short-tailed shearwater, (Tasmanian) mutton bird, *or (N.Z.)* titi
skua
storm petrel, stormy petrel, *or* Mother Carey's chicken
surf scoter *or* surf duck
takapu *(N.Z.)*
velvet scoter
wandering albatross
white-fronted tern, black cap, kahawai bird, sea swallow *or* tara *(N.Z.)*
Wilson's petrel

seam AS A NOUN **1 = joint**, closure, suture *(Surgery)* • *The seam of her tunic was split from armpit to hem.*
2 = layer, vein, stratum, lode • *The average UK coal seam is one metre thick.*
▸ IN PHRASES: **bursting at the seams = full (to bursting)**, crowded, packed, jammed, crammed, chock-full, chock-a-block • *The hotel was bursting at the seams.*
fall apart at the seams = collapse, fail, stop working, come unstuck, seize up, go kaput *(informal)*, go phut • *The university system is falling apart at the seams.*

sea mammal
▹ *See panel* **Sea mammals**

seaman = sailor, marine, mariner, tar *(informal)*, hearty *(informal)*, navigator, sea dog, seafarer, matelot *(slang, chiefly Brit.)*, Jack Tar, seafaring man, lascar, leatherneck *(slang)*, salt • *The men emigrate to work as seamen.*

seamy = sordid, unpleasant, squalid, low, dark, rough, nasty, corrupt, degraded, disagreeable, disreputable, unwholesome, scungy *(Austral. & N.Z.)* • *the seamier side of life*

sear 1 = wither, burn, blight, brand, scorch, sizzle, shrivel, cauterize, desiccate, dry up *or* out • *Grass fires have seared the land.*
2 = flash fry, brown, fry quickly • *Sear the red pepper strips until they start to blacken.*

search AS A VERB **1 = examine**, check, investigate, explore, probe, inspect, comb, inquire, sift, scour, ferret, pry, ransack, forage, scrutinize, turn upside down, rummage through, frisk *(informal)*, cast around, rifle through, leave no stone unturned, turn inside out, fossick *(Austral. & N.Z.)*, go over with a fine-tooth comb • *Armed troops searched the hospital yesterday.*
2 = inspect, check, examine, frisk, give someone the once over *(informal)* • *His first task was to search them for weapons.*
▸ AS A NOUN **= hunt**, look, inquiry, investigation, examination, pursuit, quest, going-over *(informal)*, inspection, exploration, scrutiny, rummage • *There was no chance of him being found alive and the search was abandoned.*
▸ IN PHRASES: **in search of = seeking**, looking for, hunting for, in pursuit of, on the lookout for, chasing after, on the track

SEAFOOD

abalone
anchovy
Balmain bug *(Austral.)*
banana prawn *(Austral.)*
barramundi
bass
blackfish
bloater
blue cod
blue swimmer, blue manna, *or* sand crab *(Austral.)*
bonito
bream
brill
butterfish
callop
carp
catfish
clam
clappy-doo *(Scot.)*
cockle
coalfish *or* saithe
cockle
cod
codling
crab
crayfish, crawfish, *or (N.Z.)* koura
crayfish, craybob, craydab, crawbob, clawchie, lobster, marron, *or* yabby *(Austral.)*
dab
dogfish
dorado
Dover sole
Dublin Bay prawn
eel
flounder
gemfish
grayling
Greenland halibut
haddock
hake
halibut
herring
huss
jewfish
John Dory
kahawai *or* Australian salmon
kingfish
king prawn
kipper
langoustine
lemon sole
ling
lobster
lumpfish
mackerel
marron
megrim
monkfish
Moreton Bay bug *or* shovel-nosed lobster *(Austral.)*
morwong
mud crab
mullet
mulloway
mussel
nannygai
Norway lobster
octopus
oyster
parrotfish
perch
pike
pilchard *or (Austral. informal)* pillie
pipi
plaice
pollack
pomfret
pout
prawn
queenie *or* queen scallop
rainbow trout
redfish
red snapper
roach
rockfish
salmon
sardine
scallop
school prawn *(Austral.)*
sea cucumber
shad
shark
shrimp
sild
skate
skipjack tuna
snapper
snoek
snook
sockeye *or* red salmon
sole
sprat
squid
swordfish
tarakihi *or* terakihi
teraglin
tiger prawn
tilefish
trevally *(Austral. & N.Z.)*
trout
tuna *or* tunny
turbot
wahoo
whelk
whitebait
whiting
winkle
witch
wolffish
yabby *(Austral.)*
yellow belly *(Austral.)*
zander

SEA MAMMALS

dugong	earless seal	harp seal	manatee	seal	walrus *or (archaic)*
eared seal	elephant seal	hooded seal	sea cow	sea lion	sea horse

of, making inquiries concerning • *She went in search of Jean-Paul.*
search for something *or* **someone = look for**, seek, hunt for, pursue, go in search of, cast around for, go in pursuit of, go in quest of, ferret around for, look high and low for • *The Turkish security forces have started searching for the missing men.*
search me! = I don't know, beats me, I've no idea, I haven't got a clue, how should I know?, I haven't got the faintest *or* foggiest idea • *He shrugged and chuckled: 'Search me!'*

searching = keen, sharp, probing, close, severe, intent, piercing, penetrating, thorough, quizzical • *asking searching questions*
OPPOSITES: superficial, sketchy, cursory

searing 1 = acute, sharp, intense, shooting, violent, severe, painful, distressing, stabbing, fierce, stinging, piercing, sore, excruciating, gut-wrenching • *She woke to a searing pain in her feet.*
2 = cutting, biting, severe, bitter, harsh, scathing, acrimonious, barbed, hurtful, sarcastic, sardonic, caustic, vitriolic, trenchant, mordant, mordacious, acerb • *They have long been subject to searing criticism.*

seaside = coast, sea, beach, sand, shore, beach resort, foreshore, seashore • *I want to spend a few days at the seaside.*

season AS A NOUN = period, time, term, spell, time of year • *birds arriving for the breeding season*
▸ **AS A VERB 1 = flavour**, salt, spice, lace, salt and pepper, enliven, pep up, leaven • *Season the meat with salt and pepper.*
2 = mature, age, condition, prime, prepare, temper, mellow, ripen, acclimatize • *Ensure that the new wood has been seasoned.*
3 = make experienced, train, mature, prepare, discipline, harden, accustom, toughen, inure, habituate, acclimatize, anneal • *Both actors seem to have been seasoned by experience.*
▸ **IN PHRASES: in season = available**, on the market, obtainable, on offer, abundant, plentiful • *Fresh apricots are only available from fruiterers when in season.*

QUOTATIONS

To everything there is a season, and a time to every purpose under the heaven
[*Bible: Ecclesiastes*]

summer afternoon – summer afternoon. the two most beautiful words in the English language
[Henry James]

season of mists and mellow fruitfulness
[John Keats *To Autumn*]

If Winter comes, can Spring be far behind?
[Percy Bysshe Shelley *Ode to the West Wind*]

in the bleak mid-winter
[Christina Rosetti *Mid-Winter*]

In the Spring a young man's fancy lightly turns to thoughts of love
[Alfred, Lord Tennyson *Locksley Hall*]

PROVERBS

One swallow does not make a summer

SEASONS

Season	Related adjective
spring	vernal
summer	aestival *or* estival
autumn	autumnal
winter	hibernal *or* hiemal

seasoned = experienced, veteran, mature, practised, old, weathered, hardened, long-serving, battle-scarred, time-served, well-versed • *The author is a seasoned academic.*
OPPOSITES: novice, inexperienced, new

seasoning = flavouring, spice, salt and pepper, condiment • *seasonings such as cayenne, paprika and ginger*
▹ *See panel* **Herbs, spices and seasonings**

seat AS A NOUN 1 = chair, place, bench, stall, throne, stool, pew, settle • *Stephen returned to his seat.*
2 = bottom, behind *(informal)*, rear, bum *(Brit. slang)*, ass *(U.S. & Canad. taboo slang)*, tail *(informal)*, butt *(U.S. & Canad. informal)*, buns *(U.S. slang)*, arse *(taboo slang)*, buttocks, backside, rump, rear end, posterior, derrière *(euphemistic)*, tush *(U.S. slang)*, fundament, jacksy *(Brit. slang)* • *a kick in the seat of the pants*
3 = membership, place, constituency, chair, incumbency • *He lost his seat to the Tories.*
4 = centre, place, site, heart, capital, situation, source, station, location, headquarters, axis, cradle, hub • *Gunfire broke out around the seat of government.*
5 = mansion, house, residence, abode, ancestral hall • *her family's ancestral seat in Scotland*
▸ **AS A VERB 1 = sit**, place, settle, set, park, station, fix, deposit, locate, install • *He waved towards a chair, and seated himself at the desk.*
2 = hold, take, accommodate, sit, contain, cater for, have room *or* capacity for • *The theatre seats 570.*

seating 1 = accommodation, room, places, seats, chairs • *seating for over eighty thousand spectators*
2 = arrangement of seats, accommodation, places, seats • *She made a mental note to check the seating.*

secede = withdraw, leave, resign, separate, retire, quit, pull out, break with, split from, disaffiliate, apostatize • *On 20 August 1960 Senegal seceded.*

secession = withdrawal, break, split, defection, seceding, apostasy, disaffiliation • *the Ukraine's secession from the Soviet Union*

secluded = private, sheltered, isolated, remote, lonely, cut off, solitary, out-of-the-way, tucked away, cloistered, sequestered, off the beaten track, unfrequented • *We found a secluded beach further on.*
OPPOSITES: public, busy, frequented

seclusion = privacy, isolation, solitude, hiding, retirement, shelter, retreat, remoteness, ivory tower, concealment, purdah • *They love the seclusion of their garden.*

second¹ AS AN ADJECTIVE 1 = next, following, succeeding, subsequent • *the second day of his visit to Delhi*
2 = additional, other, further, extra, alternative, repeated • *Her second attempt proved disastrous.*
3 = spare, duplicate, alternative, additional, relief, twin, substitute, back-up, reproduction • *The suitcase contained clean shirts and a second pair of shoes.*
4 = inferior, secondary, subordinate, supporting, lower, lesser • *They have to rely on their second string strikers.*
▸ **AS A NOUN = supporter**, assistant, aide, partner, colleague, associate, backer, helper, collaborator, henchman, right-hand man, cooperator • *He shouted to his seconds, 'I did it!'*
▸ **AS A PLURAL NOUN 1 = more**, second helpings, a second helping, a further helping • *There's seconds if you want them.*
2 = imperfect goods, rejects, faulty goods, inferior goods, defective goods, flawed goods • *A new shop selling seconds.*

▸ **AS A VERB** = **support**, back, endorse, forward, promote, approve, vote for, go along with, commend, give moral support to • *He seconded the motion against fox hunting.*
▸ **IN PHRASES: second to none** = **the best**, the highest, perfect, outstanding, the finest, first-class, first-rate, superlative, pre-eminent, unsurpassed, the most excellent • *Our scientific research is second to none.*

second² = **moment**, minute, instant, flash, tick *(Brit. informal)*, sec *(informal)*, twinkling, split second, jiffy *(informal)*, trice, twinkling of an eye, two shakes of a lamb's tail *(informal)*, bat of an eye *(informal)*, SEC *(S.M.S.)* • *For a few seconds nobody said anything.*

secondary 1 = **subordinate**, minor, lesser, lower, inferior, unimportant, second-rate • *Refugee problems remained of secondary importance.*
OPPOSITES: head, major, main
2 = **resultant**, resulting, contingent, derived, derivative, indirect, second-hand, consequential • *There was evidence of secondary tumours.*
OPPOSITES: original, preceding

second-class 1 = **inferior**, lesser, second-best, unimportant, second-rate, low-class • *Too many airlines treat our children as second-class citizens.*
2 = **mediocre**, second-rate, mean, middling, ordinary, inferior, indifferent, commonplace, insignificant, so-so *(informal)*, outclassed, uninspiring, undistinguished, uninspired, bog-standard *(Brit. & Irish slang)*, no great shakes *(informal)*, déclassé, half-pie *(N.Z. informal)*, fair to middling *(informal)* • *a second-class education*

second-hand 1 = **used**, old, handed down, hand-me-down *(informal)*, nearly new, pre-owned, reach-me-down *(informal)*, preloved *(Austral. slang)* • *a stack of second-hand books*
2 = **secondary**, derivative, indirect, rehashed, unoriginal • *second-hand information*

second-in-command = **deputy**, assistant, subordinate, understudy, adjutant, depute *(Scot.)*, successor designate, number two, right-hand man *or* woman • *The President was replaced by his second-in-command.*

secondly = **next**, second, moreover, furthermore, also, secondarily, in the second place • *Firstly it's mine, and secondly I don't want to give it away.*

second-rate = **inferior**, mediocre, poor, cheap, pants *(slang)*, commonplace, tacky *(informal)*, shoddy, low-grade, tawdry, low-quality, substandard, low-rent *(informal, chiefly U.S.)*, for the birds *(informal)*, two-bit *(U.S. & Canad. slang)*, end-of-the-pier *(Brit. informal)*, no great shakes *(informal)*, cheap and nasty *(informal)*, rubbishy, dime-a-dozen *(informal)*, piss-poor *(slang)*, bush-league *(Austral. & N.Z. informal)*, not much cop *(Brit. slang)*, tinhorn *(U.S. slang)*, half-pie *(N.Z. informal)*, strictly for the birds *(informal)*, bodger *or* bodgie *(Austral. slang)* • *another second-rate politician*
OPPOSITES: excellent, superior, first-rate

secrecy 1 = **mystery**, stealth, concealment, furtiveness, cloak and dagger, secretiveness, huggermugger *(archaic)*, clandestineness, covertness, surreptitiousness • *He shrouded his business dealings in secrecy.*
2 = **confidentiality**, privacy, private nature, classified nature • *The secrecy of the confessional.*
3 = **privacy**, silence, retirement, solitude, seclusion • *These problems had to be dealt with in the secrecy of your own cell.*

QUOTATIONS
If you would wish another to keep your secret, first keep it yourself
[Seneca *Hippolytus*]

secret **AS AN ADJECTIVE** 1 = **undisclosed**, unknown, confidential, underground, classified, undercover, unpublished, top secret, under wraps, unrevealed • *Soldiers have been training at a secret location.*
2 = **concealed**, hidden, disguised, covered, camouflaged, unseen • *It has a secret compartment hidden behind the magical mirror.*
OPPOSITES: obvious, apparent, unconcealed
3 = **undercover**, covert, furtive, shrouded, behind someone's back, conspiratorial, underhand, hush-hush *(informal)*, surreptitious, cloak-and-dagger, backstairs • *I was heading on a secret mission that made my flesh crawl.*
OPPOSITES: open, public, disclosed
4 = **secretive**, reserved, withdrawn, close, deep, quiet, silent, discreet, enigmatic, reticent, taciturn, cagey *(informal)*, introverted, unforthcoming, tight-lipped • *the secret man behind the masks*
OPPOSITES: open, frank, candid
5 = **mysterious**, cryptic, abstruse, classified, esoteric, occult, clandestine, arcane, recondite, cabbalistic • *a secret code*
OPPOSITES: well-known, straightforward, exoteric
▸ **AS A NOUN** 1 = **private affair**, confidence, skeleton in the cupboard • *I can't tell you; it's a secret.*
2 = **key**, answer, formula, recipe • *The secret of success is honesty and fair dealing.*
3 = **mystery**, question, puzzle, paradox, problem, question mark, enigma, conundrum • *The past is riddled with deep dark secrets.*
▸ **IN PHRASES: in secret** = **secretly**, surreptitiously, slyly, behind closed doors, incognito, by stealth, in camera, huggermugger *(archaic)* • *Dan found out that I'd been meeting my ex-boyfriend in secret.*
▸ **RELATED ADJECTIVE:** cryptic

QUOTATIONS
They have a skeleton in their closet
[William Makepeace Thackeray *The Newcomes*]
I know that's a secret, for it's whispered every where
[William Congreve *Love for Love*]
For secrets are edged tools,
And must be kept from children and from fools
[John Dryden *Sir Martin Mar-All*]

secret agent = **spy**, undercover agent, spook *(U.S. & Canad. informal)*, nark *(Brit., Austral. & N.Z. slang)*, cloak-and-dagger man • *He was blacklisted as a secret agent.*

secrete¹ = **give off**, emit, emanate, exude, extrude, extravasate *(Medical)* • *The sweat glands secrete water.*

secrete² = **hide**, conceal, stash *(informal)*, cover, screen, secure, bury, harbour, disguise, veil, shroud, stow, cache, stash away *(informal)* • *She secreted the gun in the kitchen cabinet.*
OPPOSITES: show, reveal, display

secretion = **discharge**, emission, excretion, exudation, extravasation *(Medical)* • *the secretion of adrenaline*

secretive = **reticent**, reserved, withdrawn, close, deep, enigmatic, cryptic, cagey *(informal)*, uncommunicative, unforthcoming, tight-lipped, playing your cards close to your chest, clamlike • *He was very secretive about his plans.*
OPPOSITES: open, frank, forthcoming

secretly 1 = **in secret**, privately, surreptitiously, quietly, covertly, behind closed doors, in confidence, in your heart, furtively, in camera, confidentially, on the fly *(slang, chiefly Brit.)*, stealthily, under the counter, clandestinely, unobserved, on the sly, in your heart of hearts, behind (someone's) back, in your innermost thoughts, on the q.t. *(informal)* • *secretly organized events*
2 = **privately**, in your heart of hearts, in your innermost thoughts • *I've often secretly wondered if I'd be happier without all this.*

sect = **group**, division, faction, party, school, camp, wing, denomination, school of thought, schism, splinter group • *Do you belong to some religious sect?*

sectarian **AS AN ADJECTIVE** = **narrow-minded**, partisan, fanatic, fanatical, extremist, limited, exclusive, rigid,

S

parochial, factional, bigoted, dogmatic, insular, doctrinaire, hidebound, clannish, cliquish • *sectarian religious groups*
OPPOSITES: liberal, tolerant, open-minded
▸ **AS A NOUN** = **bigot**, extremist, partisan, disciple, fanatic, adherent, zealot, true believer, dogmatist • *He remains a sectarian.*

section **AS A NOUN** 1 = **part**, piece, portion, division, sample, slice, passage, component, segment, fragment, fraction, instalment, cross section, subdivision • *a geological section of a rock*
2 = **district**, area, region, sector, zone • *Kolonarai is a lovely residential section of Athens.*
3 = **department**, part, division, wing, sector, branch • *She was in the dairy section of the supermarket.*
▸ **AS A VERB** = **cut up**, divide, cube, dice, fragment • *It holds vegetables in place while they are being peeled or sectioned.*

sectional = **regional**, local, separate, divided, exclusive, partial, separatist, factional, localized • *a party of sectional interests*

sector 1 = **part**, division, branch, category, arm, sphere, stratum, subdivision • *the nation's manufacturing sector*
2 = **area**, part, region, district, zone, quarter, belt, neighbourhood, tract • *Officers were going to retake sectors of the city.*

secular = **worldly**, state, lay, earthly, civil, temporal, profane, laic, nonspiritual, laical • *secular and religious education*
OPPOSITES: religious, spiritual, holy

secure **AS A VERB** 1 = **obtain**, get, acquire, land *(informal)*, score *(slang)*, gain, pick up, get hold of, come by, procure, make sure of, win possession of • *His achievements helped him to secure the job.*
OPPOSITES: lose, give up, let (something) slip through (your) fingers
2 = **attach**, stick, fix, bind, pin, lash, glue, fasten, rivet • *The frames are secured by horizontal rails to the back wall.*
OPPOSITES: detach, loose, untie
3 = **fasten**, close, lock, shut, seal, bolt, lock up, chain, padlock, batten down, make fast • *With a discreet click he secured the lock.*
4 = **make safe**, strengthen, fortify, make sound, make invulnerable, make impregnable • *We need to teach people how to secure themselves in these areas.*
5 = **moor**, anchor, tie up, lash, berth, hitch, make fast • *He secured the boat and then came to join us.*
6 = **guarantee**, protect, insure, ensure, assure, warrant, indemnify • *The loan is secured against your home.*
OPPOSITES: endanger, imperil, leave unguaranteed
▸ **AS AN ADJECTIVE** 1 = **safe**, protected, shielded, sheltered, immune, unassailable, impregnable • *We shall make sure our home is as secure as possible.*
OPPOSITES: endangered, unsafe, unprotected
2 = **fast**, firm, fixed, tight, stable, steady, fortified, fastened, dependable, immovable • *Shelves are only as secure as their fixings.*
OPPOSITES: loose, insecure, unsafe
3 = **reliable**, definite, solid, absolute, conclusive, in the bag *(informal)* • *demands for secure wages and employment*
4 = **protected**, safe, guarded, sheltered, shielded, in safe hands, out of harm's way, free from danger • *He was determined to give his family a secure and solid base.*
5 = **confident**, relaxed, sure, easy, certain, happy, comfortable, assured, reassured, at ease, unworried • *She felt secure and protected when she was with him.*
OPPOSITES: uncertain, uneasy, unsure

security 1 = **safety**, protection, safekeeping, unassailability, freedom from danger • *Is it worth risking the security of our nation for this?*
2 = **precautions**, defence, safeguards, guards, protection, surveillance, safety measures • *under pressure to tighten airport security*
3 = **assurance**, confidence, safety, comfort, conviction, happiness, certainty, reliance, peace of mind, sureness, positiveness, ease of mind, freedom from doubt, absence of worry • *He loves the security of a happy home life.*
OPPOSITES: uncertainty, insecurity
4 = **pledge**, insurance, guarantee, backing, hostage, collateral, pawn, gage, surety • *The banks will pledge the land as security.*
5 = **protection**, cover, safety, retreat, asylum, custody, refuge, sanctuary, immunity, preservation, safekeeping • *He could not remain long in a place of security.*
OPPOSITES: exposure, vulnerability, jeopardy

sedate **AS AN ADJECTIVE** 1 = **calm**, collected, quiet, seemly, serious, earnest, cool, grave, proper, middle-aged, composed, sober, dignified, solemn, serene, tranquil, placid, staid, demure, unflappable *(informal)*, unruffled, decorous, imperturbable • *She took them to visit her sedate, elderly cousins.*
OPPOSITES: wild, excited, nervous
2 = **unhurried**, easy, relaxed, measured, comfortable, steady, gentle, deliberate, leisurely, plodding, languid, slow-moving, unrushed, chilled *(informal)* • *We set off again at a more sedate pace.*
▸ **AS A VERB** = **drug**, knock out, dope, anaesthetize, tranquillize, put under sedation, give a sedative to • *The patient was sedated.*

sedative **AS AN ADJECTIVE** = **calming**, relaxing, soothing, allaying, anodyne, soporific, sleep-inducing, tranquillizing, calmative, lenitive • *Amber bath oil has a sedative effect.*
▸ **AS A NOUN** = **tranquillizer**, narcotic, sleeping pill, opiate, anodyne, calmative, downer *or* down *(slang)* • *They use opium as a sedative.*

sedentary = **inactive**, sitting, seated, desk, motionless, torpid, desk-bound • *A sedentary lifestyle has been linked with a risk of heart disease.*
OPPOSITES: moving, active, mobile

sediment = **dregs**, grounds, residue, lees, deposit, precipitate, settlings • *ocean sediments*

sedition = **rabble-rousing**, treason, subversion, agitation, disloyalty, incitement to riot • *Government officials charged him with sedition.*

seditious = **revolutionary**, dissident, subversive, rebellious, disloyal, mutinous, refractory, treasonable, insubordinate • *He fell under suspicion for distributing seditious pamphlets.*

seduce 1 = **tempt**, attract, lure, entice, trap, mislead, deceive, beguile, allure, decoy, ensnare, hypnotize, lead astray, inveigle • *The view of the lake and plunging cliffs seduces visitors.*
2 = **corrupt**, take advantage of, have sex with, ruin *(archaic)*, betray, violate, ravish, deprave, dishonour, debauch, deflower, have your wicked way with • *a fifteen-year-old seduced by a man twice her age*

seducer = **charmer**, Don Juan, Casanova, philanderer, wolf *(informal)*, stud *(slang)*, flirt, playboy, trifler, gallant, Lothario, womanizer *(informal)*, lady-killer *(informal)*, gay dog, dallier, ladies' man • *He is proud of his reputation as a seducer.*

seduction 1 = **temptation**, attraction, lure, draw, pull, charm, snare, allure, enticement • *The seduction of the show is the fact that the kids are in it.*
2 = **corruption**, dishonour, ravishment, bedding, ruin *(archaic)*, defloration, taking away someone's innocence • *his seduction of a minor*

seductive 1 = **appealing**, winning, inviting, attractive, engaging, tempting • *It's a seductive argument.*
2 = **tempting**, inviting, attractive, sexy *(informal)*, irresistible, siren, enticing, provocative, captivating, beguiling, alluring, bewitching, ravishing, flirtatious,

come-to-bed *(informal)*, come-hither *(informal)*, hot *(informal)* • *She's a seductive woman.*

seductress = **temptress**, siren, vamp *(informal)*, femme fatale *(French)*, Lorelei, Circe, enchantress • *Few males can resist a self-confident seductress.*

see AS A VERB **1** = **perceive**, note, spot, notice, mark, view, eye, check, regard, identify, sight, witness, clock *(Brit. slang)*, observe, recognize, distinguish, glimpse, check out *(informal)*, make out, heed, discern, behold, eyeball *(slang)*, catch a glimpse of, catch sight of, espy, get a load of *(slang)*, descry, take a dekko at *(Brit. slang)*, lay *or* clap eyes on *(informal)* • *I saw a man making his way towards me.*
2 = **visit**, call on, drop in on *(informal)*, look (someone) up, be the guest of, call in on, pop in on *(informal)*, pay a call on • *I went to see him yesterday.*
3 = **watch**, view, look at, observe • *It was one of the most amazing films I've ever seen.*
4 = **understand**, get, follow, realize, know, appreciate, take in, grasp, make out, catch on *(informal)*, comprehend, fathom, get the hang of *(informal)*, get the drift of • *Oh, I see what you're saying.*
5 = **foresee**, picture, imagine, anticipate, divine, envisage, visualize, foretell • *We can see a day when all people live side by side.*
6 = **witness**, watch, observe, view, note, notice, behold *(archaic or literary)* • *He has seen the economy of his town decline.*
7 = **find out**, learn, discover, establish, determine, investigate, verify, ascertain, make inquiries • *I'd better go and see if she's all right.*
8 = **consider**, decide, think about, judge, reflect, deliberate, mull over, think over, make up your mind, ponder over, give some thought to • *We'll see what we can do, Miss.*
9 = **make sure**, mind, ensure, guarantee, be sure, take care, make certain, see to it • *See that you take care of him.*
10 = **accompany**, show, escort, lead, walk, attend, shepherd, usher • *He didn't offer to see her to her car.*
11 = **speak to**, receive, interview, consult, confer with • *The doctor can see you now.*
12 = **meet**, encounter, come across, run into, happen on, bump into, run across, chance on • *I saw her last night at Monica's.*
13 = **go out with**, court, date *(informal, chiefly U.S.)*, have an affair with, walk out with *(obsolete)*, have a fling with, keep company with, go steady with *(informal)*, consort *or* associate with, step out with *(informal)* • *My husband was still seeing her.*
14 = **refer to** • *See Chapter 7 below.*
▸ IN PHRASES: **I see** = **I understand**, right, uh huh, mmm, I'm with you, I've got you, ah ha • *'He came home in my car.' – 'I see.'*
see about something = **take care of**, deal with, look after, see to, attend to • *I must see about selling the house.*
see someone off = **say goodbye to**, wave goodbye to, wave off • *He saw her off on her plane.*
see someone through = **keep (someone) going**, help, support, aid, encourage, comfort, sustain, assist, help out, keep alive, stick by • *His determination saw him through.*
see something through = **persevere (with)**, keep at, follow through, persist, stick out *(informal)*, carry on with, see out, hang in, continue to the end, stay to the bitter end • *He will not be credited with seeing the project through.*
see through something *or* **someone** = **be undeceived by**, penetrate, be wise to *(informal)*, fathom, get to the bottom of, not fall for, have (someone's) number *(informal)*, read (someone) like a book • *I saw through your little ruse from the start.*
see to something *or* **someone** = **take care of**, manage, arrange, look after, organize, be responsible for, sort out, attend to, take charge of, do • *Franklin saw to the luggage.*
seeing as = **since**, as, in view of the fact that, inasmuch as • *Seeing as he is a doctor, I would assume he has a modicum of intelligence.*

PROVERBS

What the eye doesn't see, the heart doesn't grieve over
What you see is what you get
Seeing is believing

seed AS A NOUN **1** = **grain**, pip, germ, kernel, egg, embryo, spore, ovum, egg cell, ovule • *a packet of cabbage seed*
2 = **beginning**, start, potential (for), suspicion, germ, genesis, inkling • *His questions were meant to plant seeds of doubt in our minds.*
3 = **origin**, source, basis, heart, essence, nucleus, fount, wellspring • *the seed of an idea*
4 = **offspring**, children, descendants, issue, race, successors, heirs, spawn, brood, sons and daughters, progeny, scions • *a curse on my seed*
5 = **semen**, sperm, come *(taboo slang)*, emission, cum *(taboo slang)*, ejaculate, seminal fluid, spermatozoa, jism *(taboo slang)*, spermatic fluid, spunk *(Brit. taboo slang)* • *man's innate tendency to spill his seed as widely as possible*
▸ IN PHRASES: **go** *or* **run to seed** = **decline**, deteriorate, degenerate, decay, go downhill *(informal)*, go to waste, go to pieces, let yourself go, go to pot, go to rack and ruin, retrogress • *If unused, winter radishes run to seed in spring.*
▸ RELATED ADJECTIVE: seminal

seedy 1 = **sleazy**, sordid, squalid, low, nasty • *They suck you into their seedy world.*
2 = **shabby**, rundown, scruffy, old, worn, faded, decaying, grubby, dilapidated, tatty, unkempt, grotty *(slang)*, crummy *(slang)*, down at heel, slovenly, mangy, manky *(Scot. dialect)*, scungy *(Austral. & N.Z.)* • *a seedy hotel close to the red light district*
OPPOSITES: smart, elegant, fashionable
3 = **unwell**, ill, poorly *(informal)*, crook *(Austral. & N.Z. informal)*, ailing, sickly, out of sorts, off colour, under the weather *(informal)*, peely-wally *(Scot.)* • *All right, are you? Not feeling seedy?*

seek 1 = **look for**, pursue, search for, be after, hunt, go in search of, go in pursuit of, go gunning for, go in quest of • *They have had to seek work as labourers.*
2 = **request**, invite, ask for, petition, plead for, solicit, beg for, petition for • *The couple have sought help from marriage guidance counsellors.*
3 = **try**, attempt, aim, strive, endeavour, essay, aspire to, have a go at *(informal)* • *He also denied that he would seek to annex the country.*

QUOTATIONS

Seek, and ye shall find
[*Bible: St. Matthew*]

seem = **appear**, give the impression of being, look, sound, look to be, show signs of being, sound as if you are, look as if you are, come across as being, look like you are, strike you as being, have the *or* every appearance of being • *Everyone seems busy except us.*

seeming = **apparent**, appearing, outward, surface, illusory, ostensible, specious, quasi- • *We'll have peace of mind amidst seeming chaos.*

seemingly = **apparently**, outwardly, on the surface, ostensibly, on the face of it, to all intents and purposes, to all appearances, as far as anyone could tell • *Seemingly he is a man with not an ounce of malice in him.*

seemly = **fitting**, becoming, appropriate, meet *(archaic)*, fit, nice, suited, suitable, decent, proper, befitting, decorous, the done thing, in good taste, comme il faut *(French)* • *It wasn't seemly for a young boy to be courting this woman.*
OPPOSITES: inappropriate, unsuitable, unseemly

seep = **ooze**, well, leak, soak, bleed, weep, trickle, leach, exude, permeate, percolate • *Radioactive water had seeped into underground reservoirs.*

seepage = **leakage**, leak, oozing, percolation, exudation • *The industry's chemical seepage has caused untold damage.*

seer = **prophet**, augur, predictor, soothsayer, sibyl • *the writings of the 16th century French seer, Nostradamus*

seesaw = **alternate**, swing, fluctuate, teeter, oscillate, go from one extreme to the other • *The stock-market see-sawed up and down.*

seethe 1 = **be furious**, storm, rage, fume, simmer, be in a state *(informal)*, see red *(informal)*, be incensed, be livid, be pissed (off) *(taboo slang)*, go ballistic *(slang, chiefly U.S.)*, foam at the mouth, be incandescent, get hot under the collar *(informal)*, wig out *(slang)*, breathe fire and slaughter • *Under the surface she was seething.*
2 = **teem**, be full of, abound, swarm, bristle, brim, be abundant, be alive with, be crawling with • *The forest below him seethed and teemed with life.*
3 = **boil**, bubble, foam, churn, fizz, ferment, froth • *a seething cauldron of broth*

see-through = **transparent**, fine, thin, sheer, flimsy, translucent, gossamer, diaphanous, gauzy, filmy • *She was wearing a white see-through blouse.*

segment AS A NOUN 1 = **section**, part, piece, division, element, slice, portion, wedge, compartment, subdivision • *the poorer segments of society*
2 = **section**, bit, slice, portion, lump, chunk, wedge, slab, hunk • *I handed out segments of orange at half-time.*
▸ AS A VERB = **divide**, split, break up, split up, divide up, subdivide • *As clubs get more organised they'll segment their squads.*

segregate = **set apart**, divide, separate, isolate, single out, discriminate against, dissociate • *They segregate you from the rest of the party.*
OPPOSITES: unite, mix, unify

segregated = **divided**, separate, set apart, isolated, partitioned, kept apart • *racially segregated schools*

segregation = **separation**, discrimination, apartheid, isolation, partitioning, setting apart, keeping apart • *a law which will end compulsory racial segregation in prisons*

seize AS A VERB 1 = **grab**, grip, grasp, take, snatch, clutch, snap up, pluck, fasten, latch on to, lay hands on, catch *or* take hold of • *an otter seizing a fish*
OPPOSITES: let go, loose
2 = **take by storm**, take over, capture, take, acquire, occupy, conquer, overrun, annex, usurp • *Troops have seized the airport and radio terminals.*
3 = **confiscate**, appropriate, commandeer, impound, take possession of, requisition, sequester, expropriate, sequestrate • *Police were reported to have seized all copies of the newspaper.*
OPPOSITES: relinquish, hand back
4 = **capture**, catch, arrest, get, nail *(informal)*, grasp, collar *(informal)*, hijack, abduct, nab *(informal)*, apprehend, take captive • *Men carrying sub-machine guns seized the five soldiers.*
OPPOSITES: free, release, set free
5 = **jump at**, exploit, take advantage of, pounce on, snatch, seize on, leap at • *During the riots people seized the opportunity to steal property.*
▸ IN PHRASES: **seize on something**
6 = **take advantage of**, use, exploit, cash in on *(informal)*
7 = **put to use**, utilize, capitalize on, make capital out of, use to advantage, turn to account, profit by *or* from • *The main fear was that both sides may seize on a ceasefire and rearm.*

seizure 1 = **attack**, fit, spasm, convulsion, paroxysm • *I was prescribed drugs to control seizures.*
2 = **taking**, grabbing, annexation, confiscation, commandeering • *the seizure of territory through force*
3 = **capture**, arrest, apprehension, abduction • *a mass seizure of hostages*
4 = **confiscation**, taking away, appropriation, commandeering, sequestration • *one of the biggest seizures of heroin ever*

seldom = **rarely**, occasionally, not often, once in a while, infrequently, sporadically, once in a blue moon *(informal)*, hardly ever, only now and then, scarcely ever • *They seldom speak.*
OPPOSITES: often, frequently, much

select AS A VERB = **choose**, take, pick, prefer, opt for, decide on, single out, adopt, single out, fix on, cherry-pick, settle upon • *They selected only bright pupils.*
OPPOSITES: reject, eliminate, turn down
▸ AS AN ADJECTIVE 1 = **choice**, special, prime, picked, selected, excellent, rare, superior, first-class, posh *(informal, chiefly Brit.)*, first-rate, hand-picked, top-notch *(informal)*, recherché • *a select group of French cheeses*
OPPOSITES: cheap, ordinary, inferior
2 = **exclusive**, elite, privileged, limited, rarefied, cliquish • *a meeting of a very select club*
OPPOSITES: indiscriminate

selection 1 = **choice**, choosing, pick, option, preference • *Make your selection from the list.*
2 = **anthology**, collection, medley, choice, line-up, mixed bag *(informal)*, potpourri, miscellany • *this selection of popular songs*
3 = **range**, variety, assortment, series, collection, array, repertoire, gamut, lineup • *It offers the widest selection of antiques.*

selective = **particular**, demanding, discriminating, critical, careful, exacting, cautious, discerning, astute, discriminatory, fussy, tasteful, fastidious, choosy, picky *(informal)*, pernickety • *Sales can happen, but buyers are more selective.*
OPPOSITES: careless, indiscriminate, all-embracing

self 1 = **personality**, character, temperament, identity, temper, disposition, individuality • *She was back to her old self again.*
2 = **soul**, spirit, psyche, heart of hearts, innermost feelings, inner person • *I want to explore and get in touch with my inner self.*
▸ RELATED MANIAS: egomania, megalomania

self-assembly = **DIY**, do-it-yourself, self-build, prefabricated, flat-pack, kit-form • *a range of self-assembly bedroom furniture*

self-assurance = **confidence**, self-confidence, poise, nerve, assertiveness, self-possession, positiveness • *They had confidence and self-assurance.*

self-assured = **confident**, assured, can-do *(informal)*, bold, fearless, self-reliant, dauntless • *He's a self-assured negotiator.*

self-centred = **selfish**, narcissistic, self-absorbed, inward looking, self-seeking, egotistic, wrapped up in yourself • *The self-centred ones have little energy for anyone else.*

self-confidence = **self-assurance**, confidence, poise, nerve, self-respect, aplomb, self-reliance, high morale • *Richard's self-confidence is growing steadily.*

self-confident = **self-assured**, confident, assured, secure, poised, fearless, self-reliant, sure of yourself • *She'd blossomed into a self-confident young woman.*

self-conscious = **embarrassed**, nervous, uncomfortable, awkward, insecure, diffident, ill at ease, sheepish, bashful, aw-shucks, shamefaced, like a fish out of water, out of countenance • *I felt a bit self-conscious in my swimming costume.*

self-contained 1 = **self-sufficient**, individualistic, self-reliant, self-supporting • *He seems completely self-contained.*
2 = **independent**, separate, disconnected, discrete, unconnected, free-standing, unattached • *The couple live upstairs in a self-contained flat.*

self-control = **willpower**, restraint, self-discipline, cool, coolness, calmness, self-restraint, self-mastery, strength of mind *or* will • *I began to wish I'd shown more self-control.*

S

QUOTATIONS

He that would govern others, first should be
The master of himself

[Philip Massinger *The Bondman*]

self-denial = **self-sacrifice**, renunciation, asceticism, abstemiousness, selflessness, unselfishness, self-abnegation • *an unprecedented act of self-denial*

QUOTATIONS

Deny yourself! You must deny yourself! That is the song that never ends

[Johann Wolfgang von Goethe *Faust*]

self-determination = **independence**, freedom, autonomy, liberty, separation, sovereignty, self-government, self-rule, self-sufficiency, self-reliance, home rule, autarchy, rangatiratanga (*N.Z.*) • *The principle of self-determination is sacred to us.*

self-discipline = **willpower**, resolve, determination, drive, resolution, grit, self-control, single-mindedness, fixity of purpose, firmness of purpose *or* will, force *or* strength of will • *Exercising at home requires a tremendous amount of self-discipline.*

self-employed = **independent**, temporary, freelance, consulting, out-of-house • *We want more support for self-employed people.*

self-esteem = **self-respect**, confidence, self-confidence, courage, vanity, boldness, self-reliance, self-assurance, self-regard, self-possession, amour-propre (*French*), faith in yourself, pride in yourself • *Poor self-esteem is at the centre of many difficulties.*

self-evident = **obvious**, clear, undeniable, inescapable, written all over (something), cut-and-dried (*informal*), incontrovertible, axiomatic, manifestly *or* patently true • *It is self-evident that we do not have enough resources.*

self-explanatory = **clear**, straightforward, easy to understand, unambiguous, self-evident, readily comprehensible, clearly explained • *I hope the graphs on the following pages are self-explanatory.*

self-governing = **independent**, democratic, sovereign, autonomous, separated, self-determining, nonaligned, decontrolled, autarchic, autarchical • *a self-governing province*

self-government = **independence**, democracy, sovereignty, autonomy, devolution, self-determination, self-rule, home rule • *a campaign for more self-government*

self-important = **conceited**, arrogant, pompous, strutting, swaggering, cocky, pushy (*informal*), overbearing, presumptuous, bumptious, swollen-headed, bigheaded, full of yourself • *He was self-important, vain and ignorant.*

self-imposed = **voluntary**, chosen, unsolicited, unforced, unasked, unprompted • *He returned home after eleven years of self-imposed exile.*

self-indulgence = **extravagance**, excess, incontinence, dissipation, self-gratification, intemperance, sensualism • *Going to the movies is one of my biggest self-indulgences.*

self-indulgent = **extravagant**, excessive, lavish, intemperate, immoderate, self-gratifying • *To buy flowers for myself seems wildly self-indulgent.*

self-interest = **selfishness**, egotism, self-centredness, greed, looking out for number one (*informal*) • *The current protests are motivated purely by self-interest.*

self-interested = **selfish**, self-centred, egotistical, greedy, mercenary, self-seeking, ungenerous, egoistic, egotistic, egotistical, looking out for number one (*informal*) • *Persistently and narrowly self-interested behaviour is ultimately self-defeating.*

selfish = **self-centred**, self-interested, greedy, mercenary, self-seeking, ungenerous, egoistic *or* egoistical, egotistic *or* egotistical, looking out for number one (*informal*) • *the selfish interests of a few people*
OPPOSITES: generous, considerate, unselfish

selfishness = **egotism**, self-interest, self-centredness, greed, looking out for number one (*informal*) • *The selfishness of these people never ceases to amaze me.*

self-knowledge

QUOTATIONS

Know then thyself, presume not God to scan,
The proper study of mankind is man

[Alexander Pope *An Essay on Man*]

Only within yourself exists that other reality for which you long

[Herman Hesse *Steppenwolf*]

All our knowledge is, our selves to know

[Alexander Pope *An Essay on Man*]

The greatest thing in the world is to know how to be oneself

[Montaigne *Essais*]

selfless = **unselfish**, generous, altruistic, self-sacrificing, magnanimous, self-denying, ungrudging • *Her generosity was entirely selfless.*

self-possessed = **self-assured**, confident, poised, together (*slang*), cool, collected, unruffled, cool as a cucumber (*informal*), sure of yourself • *She is the most articulate and self-possessed member of her family.*

self-possession = **self-assurance**, confidence, composure, poise, cool (*slang*), aplomb, sang-froid, unflappability (*informal*), self-command • *She found her customary self-possession had deserted her.*

self-reliant = **independent**, capable, self-sufficient, self-contained, self-sustaining, self-supporting, able to stand on your own two feet (*informal*) • *She is intelligent and self-reliant.*
OPPOSITES: dependent, helpless, reliant

self-respect = **pride**, dignity, self-esteem, morale, amour-propre (*French*), faith in yourself • *Any man with self-respect would have resigned.*

self-restraint = **self-control**, self-discipline, willpower, patience, forbearance, abstemiousness, self-command • *We've been exercising self-restraint in our resistance to occupation.*

self-righteous = **sanctimonious**, smug, pious, superior, complacent, hypocritical, pi (*Brit. slang*), too good to be true, self-satisfied, goody-goody (*informal*), holier-than-thou, priggish, pietistic, pharisaic • *self-righteous reformers*

self-sacrifice = **selflessness**, altruism, self-denial, generosity, self-abnegation • *I thanked my parents for all their self-sacrifice on my behalf.*

self-satisfaction = **smugness**, pride, complacency, contentment, self-approval, flush of success, glow of achievement, ease of mind, self-approbation • *He smiled in smug self-satisfaction.*

self-satisfied = **smug**, complacent, proud of yourself, well-pleased, puffed up, self-congratulatory, flushed with success, pleased with yourself, like a cat that has swallowed the canary, too big for your boots *or* breeches • *You're so bloody self-satisfied.*

self-seeking = **selfish**, self-interested, mercenary, calculating, opportunistic, self-serving, acquisitive, on the make (*slang*), careerist, gold-digging, fortune-hunting, looking out for number one (*informal*), out for what you can get • *Politicians are untrustworthy self-seeking creatures.*

self-styled = **so-called**, would-be, professed, self-appointed, soi-disant (*French*), quasi- • *He fiercely criticised self-styled educational experts.*

self-sufficient = **independent**, self-contained, self-reliant, self-sustaining, self-supporting, able to stand on your own two feet • *He'd created a tiny self-sufficient world for himself.*

self-supporting = **independent**, self-contained, self-sufficient, self-reliant, self-sustaining, able to stand on your own two feet • *The income from visitors makes the museum self-supporting.*

self-willed = **stubborn**, wilful, headstrong, intractable, opinionated, obstinate, cussed *(informal)*, stiff-necked, ungovernable, refractory, pig-headed, stubborn as a mule • *He was very independent and self-willed.*

sell AS A VERB **1** = **trade**, dispose of, offer for sale, exchange, barter, vend, put up for sale, auction off • *I sold everything I owned except for my car and books.*
OPPOSITES: buy, purchase, get
2 = **deal in**, market, trade in, carry, stock, handle, retail, hawk, merchandise, peddle, traffic in, vend, offer for sale, be in the business of • *It sells everything from hair ribbons to oriental rugs.*
OPPOSITES: buy, purchase, get
3 = **be priced at**, cost, go for, sell at, be, be trading at, retail at • *Grain sells at ten times usual prices.*
4 = **be bought**, go, move, be purchased • *The company believes the products will sell well.*
5 = **promote**, get across, put across, win approval for, persuade someone to accept, bring someone round to, gain acceptance for, get acceptance for • *She is hoping she can sell the idea to clients.*
▸ IN PHRASES: **sell out 1** = **be bought up**, be sold out, be gone, be exhausted, be depleted • *Tickets for the show sold out in 70 minutes.*
2 = **betray your ideals**, abandon your principles, demean yourself, degrade yourself • *He will not sell out or be debased by the compromises of politics.*
sell out of something = **run out of**, be fresh out of, be cleaned out of, be out of stock of • *Hardware stores have sold out of water pumps and tarpaulins.*
sell someone out = **double-cross**, fail, give away *(informal)*, stab in the back, rat on *(informal)*, sell down the river *(informal)*, break faith with, play false • *His business partner had sold him out.*
sell someone short 1 = **swindle**, cheat, fleece, defraud, overcharge, short-change, sting *(informal)*, give short measure to • *Selling their fans short in such a way is not acceptable.*
2 = **underestimate**, undervalue, look down on, belittle, disparage, underrate, deprecate, minimize, make light of, set no store by, misprize • *These are boys who were sold short during their schooldays.*

S

seller = **dealer**, merchant, vendor, agent, representative, rep, retailer, traveller, supplier, shopkeeper, purveyor, tradesman, salesman *or* saleswoman • *a flower seller*

semblance = **appearance**, show, form, air, figure, front, image, bearing, aspect, mask, similarity, resemblance, guise, façade, pretence, veneer, likeness, mien • *They had nursed Peter back to some semblance of health.*

semen = **sperm**, seed *(archaic or dialect)*, spunk *(taboo)*, scum *(U.S. slang)*, seminal fluid, come *or* cum *(taboo)*, jism *or* jissom *(taboo)*, spermatic fluid • *semen ejaculated by the male during orgasm*

seminal = **influential**, important, ground-breaking, original, creative, productive, innovative, imaginative, formative • *Those beautiful tracks appear on this seminal album.*

seminar 1 = **meeting**, conference, discussion, summit, convention, forum, symposium, colloquy • *a series of half-day seminars*
2 = **tutorial**, lesson, workshop, study group, session • *Students are asked to prepare material in advance of each weekly seminar.*

seminary = **college**, school, high school, academy, institution, institute • *Nearly all my immediate family were dead, and I went into a seminary.*

send AS A VERB **1** = **dispatch**, post, mail, forward, direct, convey, consign, remit, send on, put in the post *or* mail • *He sent a basket of exotic fruit and a card.*
2 = **transmit**, broadcast, communicate, radio, phone, fax, convey, email, telecast • *The space probe Voyager sent back pictures of Triton.*
3 = **propel**, hurl, fling, shoot, fire, deliver, cast, catapult, let fly • *He let me go with a thrust of his wrist that sent me flying.*
4 = **drive**, make, cause to become • *The constant noise sent him mad.*
▸ IN PHRASES: **send for someone** = **summon**, demand, call for, call in, ask to come • *I've sent for the doctor.*
send for something = **order**, request, ask for, demand • *For full details, send for a brochure.*
send someone down = **imprison**, confine, detain, lock up, put away, intern, incarcerate, bang up *(informal)*, sentence to imprisonment, send to prison *or* jail • *The two rapists were sent down for life.*
send something off = **dispatch**, post, mail, forward, direct, convey, send out, consign, remit, send on, put in the post *or* mail • *He sent off copies to various people.*
send something out 1 = **dispatch**, post, mail, forward, direct, send off, convey, consign, remit, send on, put in the post *or* mail • *She had sent out well over four hundred invitations.*
2 = **emit**, broadcast, discharge, radiate, exude, give off • *The crew did not send out any distress signals.*
3 = **produce**, bear, yield, bring forth • *The plant should send out new side shoots.*
send something *or* **someone up** = **mock**, mimic, parody, spoof *(informal)*, imitate, take off *(informal)*, make fun of, lampoon, burlesque, take the mickey out of *(informal)*, take the piss out of *(taboo slang)*, satirize • *a spoof that sends up the macho world of fighter pilots*

sendoff = **farewell**, departure, leave-taking, valediction, going-away party • *All the people in the buildings came to give me a rousing send-off.*

send-up = **parody**, take-off *(informal)*, satire, mockery, spoof *(informal)*, imitation, skit, mickey-take *(informal)* • *his classic send-up of sixties rock, 'Get Crazy'*

senile = **doddering**, doting, decrepit, failing, imbecile, gaga *(informal)*, in your dotage, in your second childhood • *a senile old man*

senility = **dotage**, Alzheimer's disease, infirmity, senile dementia, decrepitude, senescence, second childhood, caducity, loss of your faculties • *He was showing unmistakable signs of senility.*

senior AS AN ADJECTIVE **1** = **higher ranking**, superior • *Television and radio needed many more women in senior jobs.*
OPPOSITES: lower, subordinate, inferior
2 = **superior**, better • *Williams felt himself to be senior to all of them.*
3 = **the elder**, major *(Brit.)* • *George Bush Senior*
OPPOSITES: younger, junior
▸ IN PHRASES: **senior to** = **older than**, elder than • *She spent her time in the company of girls mostly senior to her.*

senior citizen = **pensioner**, retired person, old age pensioner, O.A.P., elder, old *or* elderly person • *I sat next to her at the Senior Citizens' Club yesterday.*

seniority = **superiority**, rank, priority, precedence, longer service • *he was third or fourth in seniority*

sensation 1 = **feeling**, sense, impression, perception, awareness, consciousness • *A sensation of burning or tingling may be felt in the hands.*
2 = **excitement**, surprise, thrill, stir, scandal, furore, agitation, commotion • *she caused a sensation at the Montreal Olympics*
3 = **hit**, success, wow *(slang, chiefly U.S.)*, crowd puller *(informal)* • *the film that turned her into an overnight sensation*

sensational 1 = **amazing**, dramatic, thrilling, revealing, spectacular, eye-popping *(informal)*, staggering, startling, horrifying, breathtaking, astounding, lurid, electrifying, hair-raising • *The world champions suffered a sensational defeat.*
OPPOSITES: boring, dull, humdrum

2 = **shocking**, scandalous, exciting, yellow *(of the press)*, melodramatic, shock-horror *(facetious)*, sensationalistic • *sensational tabloid newspaper reports*
OPPOSITES: boring, understated, unexciting
3 = **excellent**, brilliant, superb, mean *(slang)*, topping *(Brit. slang)*, cracking *(Brit. informal)*, crucial *(slang)*, impressive, smashing *(informal)*, fabulous *(informal)*, first class, marvellous, exceptional, mega *(slang)*, sovereign, awesome *(slang)*, def *(slang)*, brill *(informal)*, out of this world *(informal)*, mind-blowing *(informal)*, bodacious *(slang, chiefly U.S.)*, gee-whizz *(slang)*, boffo *(slang)*, jim-dandy *(slang)*, chillin' *(U.S. slang)*, booshit *(Austral. slang)*, exo *(Austral. slang)*, sik *(Austral. slang)*, rad *(informal)*, phat *(slang)*, schmick *(Austral. informal)*, beaut *(informal)*, barrie *(Scot. slang)*, belting *(Brit. slang)*, pearler *(Austral. slang)*, funky • *Her voice is sensational.*
OPPOSITES: ordinary, commonplace, mediocre

sense **AS A NOUN** 1 = **faculty**, perception, sensation, feeling, sensibility • *a keen sense of smell*
2 = **feeling**, impression, perception, awareness, consciousness, atmosphere, aura, intuition, premonition, presentiment • *There is no sense of urgency on either side.*
3 = **understanding**, awareness, appreciation, comprehension, discernment • *He has an impeccable sense of timing.*
4 *sometimes plural* = **intelligence**, reason, understanding, brains *(informal)*, smarts *(slang, chiefly U.S.)*, judgment, discrimination, wisdom, wit(s), common sense, sanity, sharpness, tact, nous *(Brit. slang)*, cleverness, quickness, discernment, gumption *(Brit. informal)*, sagacity, clear-headedness, mother wit • *When he was younger he had a bit more sense.*
OPPOSITES: stupidity, foolishness, silliness
5 = **point**, good, use, reason, value, benefit, worth, advantage, purpose, logic • *There's no sense in pretending this doesn't happen.*
6 = **meaning**, definition, interpretation, significance, message, import, substance, implication, drift, purport, nuance, gist, signification, denotation • *a noun which has two senses*
▸ **AS A VERB** = **perceive**, feel, understand, notice, pick up, suspect, realize, observe, appreciate, grasp, be aware of, divine, discern, just know, have a (funny) feeling *(informal)*, get the impression, apprehend, have a hunch • *He had sensed what might happen.*
OPPOSITES: miss, overlook, be unaware of
▸ **IN PHRASES: come to your senses** = **realize**, understand, wake up, catch on *(informal)*, become aware • *Then she came to her senses. She had almost betrayed herself.*
make sense = **be clear**, be understood, come together, have meaning • *It all makes sense now.*
make sense of = **understand**, appreciate, comprehend, get to the bottom of, get your head round • *This is to help her make sense of past experiences.*
take leave of your senses = **go mad**, go crazy *(informal)*, go nuts *(slang)*, go bananas *(slang)*, go bonkers *(slang, chiefly Brit.)*, go barmy *(slang)*, go round the bend *(Brit. slang)*, lose your marbles *(informal)*, go round the twist *(Brit. slang)*, go out of your mind, go off your rocker *(slang)*, go off your head *(slang)* • *They looked at me as though I had taken leave of my senses.*

senseless 1 = **pointless**, mad, crazy, stupid, silly, ridiculous, absurd, foolish, daft *(informal)*, ludicrous, meaningless, unreasonable, irrational, inconsistent, unwise, mindless, illogical, incongruous, idiotic, nonsensical, inane, fatuous, moronic, unintelligent, asinine, imbecilic, dumb-ass *(slang)*, without rhyme or reason, halfwitted • *acts of senseless violence*
OPPOSITES: wise, sensible, rational
2 = **unconscious**, stunned, insensible, out, cold, numb, numbed, deadened, unfeeling, out cold, anaesthetized, insensate • *Then I saw my boy lying senseless on the floor.*
OPPOSITES: conscious, sensible, feeling

sensibility 1 = **awareness**, insight, intuition, taste, appreciation, delicacy, sensitivity, discernment, perceptiveness • *Everything he writes demonstrates the depths of his sensibility.*
OPPOSITES: unconsciousness, lack of awareness, insensibility
2 *often plural* = **feelings**, emotions, sentiments, susceptibilities, moral sense • *The challenge offended their sensibilities.*

sensible 1 = **wise**, practical, prudent, shrewd, well-informed, judicious, well-advised • *It might be sensible to get a solicitor.*
OPPOSITES: stupid, silly, foolish
2 = **intelligent**, practical, reasonable, rational, sound, realistic, sober, discriminating, discreet, sage, shrewd, down-to-earth, matter-of-fact, prudent, sane, canny, judicious, far-sighted, sagacious, grounded • *She was a sensible girl and did not panic.*
OPPOSITES: ignorant, unreasonable, senseless

sensitive 1 = **thoughtful**, kind, understanding, feeling, kindly, concerned, patient, responsive, intuitive, receptive, attentive, perceptive, considerate, tactful, unselfish • *He was always so sensitive and caring.*
2 = **delicate**, tender, fragile, raw, painful, sore, easily damaged • *gentle cosmetics for sensitive skin*
3 = **susceptible**, vulnerable, responsive, reactive, sensitized, easily affected • *My eyes are overly sensitive to bright light.*
4 = **touchy**, defensive, paranoid, neurotic, uptight *(informal)*, twitchy *(informal)*, chippy *(informal)*, thin-skinned, oversensitive, easily upset, easily offended, hyper-sensitive, easily hurt, umbrageous *(rare)* • *Young people are very sensitive about their appearance.*
OPPOSITES: tough, insensitive, callous
5 = **tricky**, difficult, delicate, thorny, touchy, ticklish • *Employment is a very sensitive issue.*
6 = **secret**, private, confidential, classified, hush-hush *(informal)* • *He instructed staff to shred sensitive documents.*
7 = **precise**, fine, acute, keen, responsive, perceptive • *an extremely sensitive microscope*
OPPOSITES: imprecise, inexact, approximate

sensitivity 1 = **susceptibility**, responsiveness, reactivity, receptiveness, sensitiveness, reactiveness • *the sensitivity of cells to chemotherapy*
2 = **consideration**, feeling, understanding, patience, intuition, delicacy, empathy, tact, responsiveness, thoughtfulness, receptiveness • *concern and sensitivity for each other's feelings*
3 = **delicacy**, difficulty, awkwardness, trickiness, ticklishness • *the obvious sensitivity of the issue*
4 = **touchiness**, defensiveness, thin skin, hypersensitivity, twitchiness, oversensitivity • *an atmosphere of extreme sensitivity over the situation*
5 = **responsiveness**, precision, keenness, acuteness • *the sensitivity of the detector*

sensual 1 = **sexual**, sexy *(informal)*, erotic, randy *(informal, chiefly Brit.)*, steamy *(informal)*, raunchy *(slang)*, lewd, voluptuous, lascivious, lustful, lecherous, libidinous, licentious, unchaste • *He was a very sensual person.*
2 = **physical**, bodily, voluptuous, animal, luxurious, fleshly, carnal, epicurean, unspiritual • *sensual pleasure*

sensuality = **eroticism**, sexiness *(informal)*, voluptuousness, prurience, licentiousness, carnality, lewdness, salaciousness, lasciviousness, animalism, libidinousness, lecherousness • *Her blonde hair gave her sensuality and youth.*

sensuous 1 = **pleasurable**, pleasing, sensory, gratifying, aesthetic • *It is a sensuous but demanding car to drive.*

2 = **sexy**, erotic, voluptuous, lush, seductive, luscious • *wide, sensuous lips*
3 = **pleasure-seeking**, hedonistic, sybaritic, epicurean, bacchanalian • *exotic and sensuous scenes follow one after another*
OPPOSITES: Spartan, ascetic, abstemious

sentence AS A NOUN 1 = **punishment**, prison sentence, jail sentence, prison term, condemnation • *He was given a four-year sentence.*
2 = **verdict**, order, ruling, decision, judgment, decree, pronouncement • *When she heard of the sentence, she said: 'Is that all?'*
▸ AS A VERB 1 = **condemn**, doom • *A military court sentenced him to death in his absence.*
2 = **convict**, condemn, penalize, pass judgment on, mete out justice to, impose a sentence on • *They sentenced him for punching a policewoman*

sentient = **feeling**, living, conscious, live, sensitive, reactive • *sentient creatures, human and nonhuman alike*

sentiment 1 = **feeling**, thought, idea, view, opinion, attitude, belief, judgment, persuasion, way of thinking • *The Foreign Secretary echoed this sentiment.*
2 = **sentimentality**, emotion, tenderness, romanticism, sensibility, slush *(informal)*, emotionalism, tender feeling, mawkishness, soft-heartedness, overemotionalism • *Laura kept that letter out of sentiment.*

sentimental = **romantic**, touching, emotional, tender, pathetic, nostalgic, sloppy *(informal)*, tearful, corny *(slang)*, impressionable, mushy *(informal)*, maudlin, simpering, weepy *(informal)*, slushy *(informal)*, mawkish, tear-jerking *(informal)*, drippy *(informal)*, schmaltzy *(slang)*, icky *(informal)*, gushy *(informal)*, soft-hearted, overemotional, dewy-eyed, three-hankie *(informal)* • *It's a very sentimental play.*
OPPOSITES: practical, realistic, unsentimental

sentimentality = **romanticism**, nostalgia, tenderness, gush *(informal)*, pathos, slush *(informal)*, mush *(informal)*, schmaltz *(slang)*, sloppiness *(informal)*, emotionalism, bathos, mawkishness, corniness *(slang)*, play on the emotions, sob stuff *(informal)* • *In this book there is no sentimentality.*

sentinel = **guard**, watch, lookout, sentry, picket, watchman • *a watchful sentinel*

sentry = **guard**, watch, lookout, picket, watchman, sentinel • *The sentry would not let her enter.*

separable = **distinguishable**, detachable, divisible, severable, scissile • *Character is not separable from physical form.*

separate AS AN ADJECTIVE 1 = **unconnected**, individual, particular, divided, divorced, isolated, detached, disconnected, discrete, unattached, disjointed • *The two things are separate and mutually irrelevant.*
OPPOSITES: connected, united, similar
2 = **individual**, independent, apart, isolated, cut off, distinct, autonomous, set apart • *We both live our separate lives.*
OPPOSITES: joined, connected, interdependent
▸ AS A VERB 1 = **divide**, detach, disconnect, come between, disentangle, keep apart, move apart, disjoin • *Police moved in to separate the two groups.*
OPPOSITES: mix, combine, amalgamate
2 = **come apart**, split, break off, come away • *The nose section separates from the fuselage.*
OPPOSITES: unite, join, connect
3 = **sever**, detach, disconnect, disengage, break apart, split in two, disunite, divide in two, disassemble, uncouple, bifurcate, disjoin • *Separate the garlic into cloves.*
OPPOSITES: join, link, connect
4 = **split up**, part, divorce, break up, part company, get divorced, be estranged, go different ways, stop living together • *Her parents separated when she was very young.*
5 = **distinguish**, mark, isolate, single out, set apart, make distinctive, set at variance *or* at odds • *What separates terrorism from other acts of violence?*
OPPOSITES: unite, join, link
6 = **disperse**, split (up), scatter, disband • *Let's separate into smaller groups.*
7 = **part**, part company, wave goodbye, go your separate ways, say goodbye, say your goodbyes • *We separated to inspect different areas of the place.*
▸ IN PHRASES: **separate something out** = **filter (out)**, strain, sift, refine, clarify, purify, sieve, winnow, filtrate • *The water is separated out and ends up back in the ground.*

separated 1 = **estranged**, parted, split up, separate, apart, broken up, disunited, living apart *or* separately • *Most single parents are either separated or divorced.*
2 = **disconnected**, parted, divided, separate, disassociated, disunited, sundered, put asunder • *They're trying their best to bring together separated families.*

separately 1 = **alone**, independently, apart, personally, on your own, by yourself, not together, severally • *Chris had insisted that we went separately to the club.*
OPPOSITES: together, jointly, as one
2 = **individually**, singly, one by one, one at a time • *Cook the stuffing separately.*

separation 1 = **division**, break, segregation, detachment, severance, disengagement, dissociation, disconnection, disjunction, disunion, disconnect • *a permanent separation from his son*
2 = **split-up**, parting, split, divorce, break-up, farewell, rift, estrangement, leave-taking • *They agreed to a trial separation.*

septic = **infected**, poisoned, toxic, festering, pussy, putrid, putrefying, suppurating, putrefactive • *a septic toe*

sepulchral = **gloomy**, sad, sombre, grave, dismal, melancholy, morbid, woeful, mournful, lugubrious, funereal, cheerless, Stygian • *He made his way along the sepulchral corridors.*

sepulchre = **tomb**, grave, vault, mausoleum, sarcophagus, burial place • *Death holds him in his sepulchre.*

sequel 1 = **follow-up**, continuation, development • *She is currently writing a sequel.*
2 = **consequence**, result, outcome, conclusion, end, issue, payoff *(informal)*, upshot • *The arrests were a direct sequel to the investigations.*

sequence 1 = **succession**, course, series, order, chain, cycle, arrangement, procession, progression • *the sequence of events that led to the murder*
2 = **order**, structure, arrangement, ordering, placement, layout, progression • *The chronological sequence gives the book an element of structure.*
3 = **part**, scene, section, episode, extract, excerpt, clip • *the best sequence in the film*

sequester 1 = **take**, seize, confiscate, appropriate, impound, commandeer, take possession of, expropriate, arrogate, sequestrate • *Everything he owned was sequestered.*
2 = **isolate**, cut off, seclude, retire, withdraw, set apart, shut away • *This jury is expected to be sequestered for at least two months.*

serenade = **song**, air, ballad, lay, tune, strain, carol, lyric, anthem, hymn, waiata *(N.Z.)* • *He sang his serenade of love.*

serendipitous = **lucky**, chance, fortuitous, unexpected, random, casual, accidental, spontaneous, unforeseen, unintentional, coincidental, unanticipated, inadvertent, unforeseeable, unlooked-for • *It appears to have been a serendipitous discovery made around the year 200.*

serene = **calm**, peaceful, tranquil, composed, sedate, placid, undisturbed, untroubled, unruffled, imperturbable, chilled *(informal)* • *She looked as calm and serene as always.*
OPPOSITES: troubled, disturbed, anxious

serenity = **calm**, peace, tranquillity, composure, peace of mind, stillness, calmness, quietness, peacefulness, quietude, placidity • *a wonderful feeling of peace and serenity*

serf = **vassal**, servant, slave, thrall, bondsman, varlet *(archaic)*, helot, villein, liegeman • *He was the son of an emancipated serf.*

serial = **drama**, series, soap *(informal)*, sitcom *(informal)*, soap opera, soapie *or* soapie *(Austral. slang)*, situation comedy, set of programmes • *one of BBC television's most popular serials, Eastenders*

series 1 = **sequence**, course, chain, succession, run, set, line, order, train, arrangement, string, progression • *a series of explosions*
2 = **drama**, serial, soap *(informal)*, sitcom *(informal)*, soap opera, soapie *or* soapie *(Austral. slang)*, situation comedy, set of programmes • *Channel 4's 'GBH' won best drama series.*

serious 1 = **grave**, bad, critical, worrying, dangerous, acute, alarming, severe, extreme, grievous • *His condition was serious but stable.*
2 = **important**, crucial, urgent, pressing, difficult, worrying, deep, significant, grim, far-reaching, momentous, fateful, weighty, no laughing matter, of moment *or* consequence • *I regard this as a serious matter.*
OPPOSITES: insignificant, minor, unimportant
3 = **thoughtful**, detailed, careful, deep, profound, in-depth • *It was a question which deserved serious consideration.*
4 = **deep**, cultured, intellectual, literary, sophisticated, scholarly, heavyweight, highbrow, highbrowed • *a serious novel*
5 = **solemn**, earnest, grave, stern, sober, thoughtful, sedate, glum, staid, humourless, long-faced, pensive, unsmiling • *He's quite a serious person.*
OPPOSITES: jolly, frivolous, light-hearted
6 = **sincere**, determined, earnest, resolved, genuine, deliberate, honest, resolute, in earnest • *You really are serious about this, aren't you?*
OPPOSITES: undecided, frivolous, insincere

seriously 1 = **truly**, honestly, sincerely, truthfully, no joking *(informal)*, to be serious, in earnest, all joking aside • *Seriously, though, something must be done about it.*
2 = **really?**, well I never!, truthfully?, honestly?, is that so?, go on!, you don't say!, you're kidding!, well I'll be blowed!, knock me down with a feather! • *'I tried to chat him up at the general store.' He laughed. 'Seriously?'*
3 = **gravely**, solemnly, earnestly, grimly, soberly, thoughtfully, pensively, sombrely, dourly, meditatively, without smiling, humourlessly, ruminatively • *They spoke to me very seriously but politely.*
4 = **badly**, severely, gravely, critically, acutely, sorely, dangerously, distressingly, grievously • *Three people were seriously injured in the blast.*
5 = **very**, really, extremely, particularly, truly, remarkably, unusually, decidedly, exceedingly, excessively, eminently, uncommonly • *one of the first seriously wealthy rock-star landowners*

seriousness 1 = **importance**, gravity, urgency, moment, weight, danger, significance • *the seriousness of the crisis*
2 = **solemnity**, gravity, earnestness, sobriety, gravitas, sternness, humourlessness, staidness, sedateness • *They had shown a commitment and a seriousness of purpose.*

sermon = **homily**, preaching, discourse, talk, address, speech, lesson, exhortation • *his first sermon as bishop*

serpent = **snake** • *the serpent in the Garden of Eden*

serpentine = **twisting**, winding, snaking, crooked, coiling, meandering, tortuous, sinuous, twisty, snaky • *serpentine woodland pathways*

serrated = **notched**, toothed, sawtoothed, serrate, serrulate, sawlike, serriform *(Biology)* • *Bread knives should have a serrated edge.*

serried = **massed**, assembled, dense, close, compact, phalanxed • *the serried ranks of fans*

serum = **antidote**, antihistamine, antitoxin, antiserum, counterirritant, counterpoison • *He had swallowed a serum to ward off ill-effects.*

servant = **attendant**, domestic, slave, maid, help, helper, retainer, menial, drudge, lackey, vassal, skivvy *(chiefly Brit.)*, servitor *(archaic)*, varlet *(archaic)*, liegeman • *She couldn't lift a spoon without a servant.*

serve AS A VERB 1 = **work for**, help, aid, assist, do something for, be of use to, be in the service of, do your bit for • *soldiers who have served their country well*
2 = **perform**, do, complete, go through, fulfil, pass, discharge • *He had served an apprenticeship as a bricklayer.*
3 = **be adequate**, do, suffice, answer, suit, content, satisfy, be good enough, be acceptable, fill the bill *(informal)*, answer the purpose • *This little book should serve.*
4 = **present**, provide, supply, deliver, arrange, set out, distribute, dish up, purvey • *Serve it with French bread.*
5 = **be enough for**, be sufficient for, be adequate for, provide enough for • *Garnish with fresh herbs. Serves 4.*
6 = **attend to**, wait on, deal with, oblige, minister to, be of assistance • *They wouldn't serve me in the pub 'cos I looked too young.*
7 = **deliver to**, give to, present with, hand over to, cause to accept • *Police said they had been unable to serve a summons on him.*
▸ IN PHRASES: **serve as something** *or* **someone** = **act as**, substitute for, function as, do the work of, do duty as • *She ushered me into the front room, which served as her office.*

QUOTATIONS
They also serve who only stand and wait
[John Milton *Sonnet 16*]

PROVERBS
If you would be well served, serve yourself

service AS A NOUN 1 = **facility**, system, resource, utility, amenity • *a campaign for better social services*
2 = **waiting**, attendance, serving of food, waiters *or* waitresses • *clean restaurants with respectable service and fair prices*
3 = **ceremony**, ritual, worship, rite, function, ordinance, observance, sacrament, liturgy • *The President was attending the morning service.*
4 = **work**, labour, employment, business, office, duty, employ • *If a young woman did not have a dowry, she went into domestic service.*
5 = **check**, servicing, routine check, maintenance check • *The car needs a service.*
▸ AS A PLURAL NOUN = **help**, assistance, aid, offices, helping hand, ministrations • *They have offered their services free of charge.*
▸ AS A VERB 1 = **overhaul**, check, maintain, tune (up), repair, go over, fine tune, recondition, keep in good condition, give a maintenance check to • *Make sure that all gas fires are serviced annually.*
2 = **pay off**, clear, settle, square, discharge, liquidate, pay in full • *A quarter of the country's earnings go to service a foreign debt.*
▸ IN PHRASES: **be of service to someone** = **assist**, help, serve, benefit, aid, be helpful, be valuable, be of use, be advantageous, be of assistance, give a helping hand to • *That is, after all, the primary reason we live – to be of service to others.*
in service = **working**, in use, in operation • *Equipment has been kept in service long after it should have been replaced.*
out of service = **out of action**, not working, out of order, not functioning, out of commission, on the blink *(slang)*, inoperative • *The photocopier is out of service today.*
the services = **the armed forces**, the forces, the military,

S

the army, the navy, the marines, the air force, armed services • *the People joined the services entirely on a voluntary basis.*

serviceable = **useful**, practical, efficient, helpful, profitable, convenient, operative, beneficial, functional, durable, usable, dependable, advantageous, utilitarian, hard-wearing • *His Arabic was serviceable enough.*
OPPOSITES: useless, inefficient, impractical

servile = **subservient**, cringing, grovelling, mean, low, base, humble, craven, fawning, abject, submissive, menial, sycophantic, slavish, unctuous, obsequious, toadying, bootlicking *(informal)*, toadyish • *He was subservient and servile.*

servility = **subservience**, fawning, grovelling, meanness, sycophancy, submissiveness, baseness, self-abasement, obsequiousness, abjection, unctuousness, bootlicking *(informal)*, toadyism, slavishness • *She's a curious mixture of stubbornness and servility.*

serving = **portion**, helping, ration, plateful, bowlful • *Each serving contains 240 calories.*

servitude = **slavery**, bondage, enslavement, bonds, chains, obedience, thrall, subjugation, serfdom, vassalage, thraldom • *a life of servitude*

session 1 = **meeting**, hearing, sitting, term, period, conference, congress, discussion, assembly, seminar, get-together *(informal)* • *an emergency session of parliament*
2 = **period**, stretch, spell, time, bout • *Ten players have failed drug tests following a training session.*
3 = **booze up**, binge, bender *(Brit. informal)*, pub crawl *(Brit.)*, piss-up *(Brit. taboo slang)*, sesh *(slang)* • *We had a bit of a session one night.*

set[1] AS A VERB 1 = **put**, place, lay, leave, park *(informal)*, position, rest, plant, station, stick, deposit, locate, lodge, situate, plump, plonk • *He took the case out of her hand and set it on the floor.*
2 = **switch on**, turn on, activate, programme • *I forgot to set my alarm and I overslept.*
3 = **adjust**, regulate, coordinate, rectify, synchronize • *He set his watch, then waited for five minutes.*
4 = **embed**, fix, mount, install, fasten • *a gate set in a high wall*
5 = **arrange**, decide (upon), settle, name, establish, determine, fix, schedule, appoint, specify, allocate, designate, ordain, fix up, agree upon • *A date will be set for a future meeting.*
6 = **assign**, give, allot, prescribe • *We will train you first before we set you a task.*
7 = **create**, provide, establish, set up, institute • *Legal experts said that her case would not set a precedent.*
8 = **harden**, stiffen, condense, solidify, cake, gel, thicken, crystallize, congeal, jell, coagulate, gelatinize • *Lower the heat and allow the omelet to set on the bottom.*
9 = **go down**, sink, dip, decline, disappear, vanish, subside • *The sun sets at about 4pm in winter.*
10 = **prepare**, lay, spread, arrange, make ready • *She had set the table and was drinking coffee at the hearth.*
11 = **impose**, specify, lay down, decree, ordain • *the people who set the rules for the tournament*
▸ AS AN ADJECTIVE 1 = **established**, fixed, specified, planned, decided, agreed, standard, regular, usual, arranged, rigid, definite, customary, inflexible, predetermined, unchanging, hard and fast, immovable, unvarying • *A set period of fasting is supposed to bring us closer to godliness.*
2 = **strict**, firm, rigid, hardened, stubborn, entrenched, inflexible, ingrained, deep-seated, deep-rooted, hidebound • *They have very set ideas about how to get the message across.*
OPPOSITES: open, free, flexible
3 = **compulsory**, required, assigned, recommended, imposed, specified, prescribed, stipulated • *One of the set books is Jane Austen's 'Emma'.*
4 = **conventional**, stock, standard, traditional, formal, routine, artificial, stereotyped, rehearsed, hackneyed, unspontaneous • *Use the subjunctive in some set phrases and idioms.*
5 = **located**, sited, situated, found, perched • *The castle is set in 25 acres of beautiful land.*
▸ AS A NOUN 1 = **scenery**, setting, scene, stage setting, stage set, mise-en-scène *(French)* • *a movie set*
2 = **position**, bearing, attitude, carriage, turn, fit, hang, posture • *the set of his shoulders*
▸ IN PHRASES: **set on** *or* **upon something** = **determined to**, intent on, be resolved to, bent on, insistent on, resolute about • *She was set on going to an all-girls school.*
set about someone = **assault**, attack, mug *(informal)*, assail, sail into *(informal)*, lambast(e), belabour • *Several thugs set about him with clubs.*
set about something = **begin**, start, get down to, attack, tackle, set to, get to work, sail into *(informal)*, take the first step, wade into, get cracking *(informal)*, make a start on, roll up your sleeves, get weaving *(informal)*, address yourself to, put your shoulder to the wheel *(informal)* • *He set about proving she was completely wrong.*
set forth = **embark**, set off, start out, sally forth • *Christopher Columbus set forth on his epic journey of discovery.*
set off = **leave**, set out, depart, embark, start out, sally forth • *I set off, full of optimism.*
set on *or* **upon someone** = **attack**, beat up, assault, turn on, mug *(informal)*, set about, ambush, go for, sic, pounce on, fly at, work over *(slang)*, assail, sail into *(informal)*, fall upon, lay into *(informal)*, put the boot in *(slang)*, pitch into *(informal)*, let fly at, beat *or* knock seven bells out of *(informal)* • *We were set upon by three youths.*
set out 1 = **embark**, set off, start out, begin, get under way, hit the road *(slang)*, take to the road, sally forth • *When setting out on a long walk, always wear suitable boots.*
2 = **determine**, decide, purpose, resolve, make up your mind • *We set out to find the truth behind the story.*
set someone against someone = **alienate**, oppose, divide, drive a wedge between, disunite, estrange, set at odds, make bad blood between, make mischief between, set at cross purposes, set by the ears *(informal)*, sow dissension amongst • *The case has set neighbour against neighbour in the village.*
set someone back = **cost**, knock back *(Brit. informal)* • *The frock is going to set you back thousands.*
set someone off = **upset**, make angry, discompose • *The smallest thing sets him off.*
set someone up 1 = **finance**, back, fund, establish, promote, build up, subsidize • *Grandfather set them up in a liquor business.*
2 = **prepare**, prime, warm up, dispose, make ready, put in order, put in a good position • *The win set us up perfectly for the match in Belgium.*
set something against something = **balance**, compare, contrast, weigh, juxtapose, place side by side with • *a considerable sum when set against the maximum wage*
set something apart = **distinguish**, separate, characterize, single out, individualize, make distinctive, mark as different • *What sets it apart from hundreds of similar French towns is the huge factory.*
set something aside 1 = **reserve**, keep, save, separate, select, single out, earmark, keep back, set apart, put on one side • *£130 million would be set aside for repairs to schools.*
2 = **ignore**, disregard, shrug off, bury, cast aside, put to one side • *He urged them to set aside minor differences.*
3 = **reject**, dismiss, reverse, cancel, overturn, discard, quash, overrule, repudiate, annul, nullify, abrogate, render null and void • *The decision was set aside because one of the judges had links with the defendant.*

set something back = **hold up**, slow, delay, hold back, hinder, obstruct, retard, impede, slow up • *a risk of public protest that could set back reforms*
set something down 1 = **specify**, determine, fix, impose, prescribe, lay down, ordain, stipulate, codify • *It also sets down rules for the maintenance of equipment.*
2 = **write down**, record, jot down, draft, pen, compose, draw up, put in writing, commit to paper, put down in black and white • *Old Walter is setting down his memories of village life.*
set something forth = **present**, describe, explain, detail, advance, relate, define, illustrate, put forward, recount, expound • *He set forth the basis of his approach to teaching students.*
set off 1 = **detonate**, trigger (off), explode, ignite, light, set in motion, touch off • *Who set off the bomb?*
2 = **cause**, start, produce, generate, prompt, trigger (off), provoke, bring about, give rise to, spark off, set in motion • *It set off a storm of speculation.*
3 = **enhance**, show off, complement, throw into relief, bring out the highlights in • *Blue suits you – it sets off the colour of your hair.*
set something out 1 = **arrange**, present, display, lay out, exhibit, array, dispose, set forth, expose to view • *Set out the cakes attractively.*
2 = **explain**, list, describe, detail, elaborate, recount, enumerate, elucidate, itemize, particularize • *He has written a letter setting out his views.*
set something up 1 = **arrange**, organize, prepare, make provision for, prearrange • *an organization that sets up meetings*
2 = **establish**, begin, found, institute, install, initiate, get going, lay the foundations of • *He set up the company four years ago.*
3 = **build**, raise, construct, put up, assemble, put together, erect, elevate • *The activists set up a peace camp at the border.*
4 = **assemble**, put up, put together, fix up, rig up • *I set up the computer so that they could work from home.*

set[2] 1 = **series**, collection, assortment, kit, outfit, batch, compendium, assemblage, coordinated group, ensemble • *Only she and Mr Cohen had complete sets of keys to the shop.*
2 = **group**, company, crowd, circle, class, band, crew (*informal*), gang, outfit, faction, sect, posse (*informal*), clique, coterie, schism • *the popular watering hole for the literary set*
3 = **television**, TV, telly (*Brit. informal*), the box (*Brit. informal*), receiver, the tube (*slang*), TV set, small screen (*informal*), gogglebox (*Brit. slang*), idiot box (*slang*) • *We got our first black-and-white set in 1963.*
4 = **expression**, look • *the steely determination in the set of her face*
5 = **scenery**, backdrop, setting, flats, mise en scène (*French*), stage furniture • *He achieved fame for his stage sets for the Folies Bergères.*

setback = **hold-up**, check, defeat, blow, upset, reverse, disappointment, hitch, misfortune, rebuff, whammy (*informal, chiefly U.S.*), bummer (*slang*), bit of trouble • *He has suffered a serious setback in his political career.*

setting = **surroundings**, site, location, set, scene, surround, background, frame, context, perspective, backdrop, scenery, locale, mise en scène (*French*) • *The house is in a lovely setting in the hills.*

setting up = **creation**, foundation, establishment, development, production, institution, constitution, formation, inception, origination • *The setting up of a special fund.*

settle AS A VERB 1 = **resolve**, work out, remedy, reconcile, clear up, put an end to, iron out, straighten out, set to rights • *They agreed to try and settle their dispute by negotiation.*
2 = **pay**, clear, square (up), discharge, defray • *I settled the bill for my coffee and his two glasses of wine.*
3 = **decide**, close, end, complete, conclude, wind up, dispose of, terminate, round off, draw to a close, bring to an end • *As far as I'm concerned, the matter was settled yesterday.*
4 = **establish**, determine, confirm, fix, appoint, arrange, agree • *Right, that's settled then.*
5 = **move to**, go to live in, take up residence in, live in, dwell in, inhabit, reside in, set up home in, put down roots in, make your home in • *He visited Paris and eventually settled there.*
6 = **colonize**, populate, people, pioneer • *This was one of the first areas to be settled by Europeans.*
7 = **make comfortable**, park (*informal*), install, plonk (*informal*), ensconce, bed down • *Albert settled himself on the sofa.*
8 = **subside**, fall, sink, decline, gravitate • *Once its impurities had settled, the oil could be graded.*
9 = **land**, alight, descend, light, come to rest • *The birds settled less than two hundred paces away.*
10 = **calm**, quiet, relax, relieve, reassure, compose, soothe, lull, quell, allay, sedate, pacify, quieten, tranquillize • *They needed a win to settle their nerves.*
OPPOSITES: trouble, upset, disturb
▸ IN PHRASES: **settle down** 1 = **put down roots**, get married, have a home, stop moving from place to place • *One day I'll want to settle down and have a family.*
2 = **quieten**, be still, relax, wind down, become quiet, stop rushing around • *The children have now settled down.*
3 = **go to bed**, retire, turn in, go to sleep, hit the sack (*slang*), hit the hay (*slang*) • *They put up their tents and settled down for the night.*
settle down to something = **get down to**, focus on, set about, attack, begin to tackle, apply yourself to, address yourself to • *They settled down to some serious work.*
settle for something = **accept**, take, stand for, tolerate, put up with, submit to, yield to, compromise on, suffer • *She was just not prepared to settle for anything mediocre.*
settle in = **get used to something**, adapt, accustom yourself, become acquainted, become acclimatized, familiarize yourself with something • *I enjoyed school once I'd settled in.*
settle on *or* **upon something** *or* **someone** = **decide on**, choose, pick, select, adopt, agree on, opt for, fix on, elect for • *We finally settled on a Mercedes estate.*
settle up = **pay (up)**, pay the bill, square up • *We approached the till to settle up.*

settled 1 = **balanced**, established, permanent, sustained, enduring, long-standing • *His house was the only settled home I had as a child.*
2 = **content**, contented, satisfied, comfortable, fulfilled, at ease, willing to accept • *After a few years of being a diplomat she still didn't feel settled.*

settlement 1 = **agreement**, arrangement, resolution, working out, conclusion, establishment, adjustment, confirmation, completion, disposition, termination • *Our objective must be to secure a peace settlement.*
2 = **ruling**, finding, decision, conclusion, judgment, adjudication • *a libel settlement*
3 = **payment**, clearing, discharge, clearance, defrayal • *ways to delay the settlement of debts*
4 = **colony**, community, outpost, peopling, hamlet, encampment, colonization, kainga *or* kaika (*N.Z.*) • *a Muslim settlement*
5 = **colonization**, settling, peopling, populating • *the settlement of America*

settler = **colonist**, immigrant, pioneer, colonizer, frontiersman • *settlers from the Volga region*

set-to = **fight**, row, argument, brush, scrap (*informal*), disagreement, quarrel, barney (*informal*), spat, squabble,

S

wrangle, fracas, slanging match *(Brit.)*, dust-up *(informal)*, argy-bargy *(Brit. informal)*, biffo *(Austral. slang)* • *a bit of a set-to between Smith and his record company*

setup = **arrangement**, system, structure, organization, conditions, circumstances, regime • *I gradually got rather disillusioned with the whole set-up.*

seven
▸ **RELATED ADJECTIVE:** seventh
▸ **RELATED PREFIXES:** hepta-, septi-

seventh heaven = **ecstasy**, transports, Utopia, raptures, rhapsodies • *After I was given my first camera I was in seventh heaven.*

sever 1 = **cut**, separate, split, part, divide, rend, detach, disconnect, cleave, bisect, disunite, cut in two, sunder, disjoin • *Oil was still gushing from the severed fuel line.*
OPPOSITES: unite, join, link
2 = **discontinue**, terminate, break off, abandon, dissolve, put an end to, dissociate • *He was able to sever all emotional bonds to his family.*
OPPOSITES: continue, maintain, uphold

several AS A PRONOUN = **some**, a few, a number of, a handful of, many, manifold • *I had lived two doors away from his family for several years.*
▸ AS AN ADJECTIVE = **various**, different, diverse, divers *(archaic)*, assorted, disparate, indefinite, sundry • *one of several failed attempts*

severe 1 = **serious**, critical, terrible, desperate, alarming, extreme, grave, awful, distressing, appalling, dire, drastic, very bad, catastrophic, woeful, ruinous • *a business with severe cash flow problems*
2 = **acute**, extreme, intense, burning, violent, piercing, racking, searing, tormenting, exquisite, harrowing, unbearable, excruciating, agonizing, insufferable, torturous, unendurable • *He woke up blinded and in severe pain.*
3 = **tough**, hard, difficult, taxing, demanding, fierce, punishing, exacting, rigorous, stringent, arduous, unrelenting • *He had faced an appallingly severe task in the jungle.*
OPPOSITES: easy, manageable
4 = **strict**, hard, harsh, cruel, rigid, relentless, drastic, oppressive, austere, Draconian, unrelenting, inexorable, pitiless, unbending, iron-handed • *This was a dreadful crime and a severe sentence is necessary.*
OPPOSITES: easy, lax, lenient
5 = **grim**, serious, grave, cold, forbidding, stern, sober, disapproving, dour, unsmiling, flinty, strait-laced, tight-lipped • *He had a severe look that disappeared when he smiled.*
OPPOSITES: genial, affable
6 = **plain**, simple, austere, classic, restrained, functional, Spartan, ascetic, unadorned, unfussy, unembellished, bare-bones • *wearing her felt hats and severe grey suits*
OPPOSITES: fancy, ornate, embellished
7 = **harsh**, cutting, biting, scathing, satirical, caustic, astringent, vitriolic, mordant, unsparing, mordacious • *The team has suffered severe criticism from influential figures.*
OPPOSITES: kind, gentle, compassionate
8 = **cold**, freezing, extreme, bitter, harsh, bleak • *The start of the year brought a very severe winter in Britain.*
9 = **violent**, wild, extreme, intense, dangerous, fierce, turbulent, forceful, tumultuous, inclement • *The fence collapsed during the recent severe weather.*
OPPOSITES: mild, gentle, moderate

severely 1 = **seriously**, badly, extremely, gravely, hard, sorely, dangerously, critically, acutely • *the severely depressed construction industry*
2 = **strictly**, harshly, sternly, rigorously, sharply, like a ton of bricks *(informal)*, with an iron hand, with a rod of iron • *They should punish these drivers more severely.*

severity = **strictness**, seriousness, harshness, austerity, rigour, toughness, hardness, stringency, sternness, severeness • *He was sickened by the severity of the sentence.*

sew AS A VERB = **stitch**, tack, seam, hem, baste • *Anyone can sew a hem, including you.*
▸ IN PHRASES: **sew something up** 1 = **mend**, repair, patch up, darn, stitch up • *Next day, she decided to sew up the rip.*
2 = **secure**, confirm, assure, decide, determine, settle, conclude, seal, clinch • *Why hadn't Shearson tried to sew up the deal before its public disclosure?*

sewage = **waste**, shit *(taboo slang)*, slops, sewerage, effluent, excrement • *the MP's call for more treatment of raw sewage*

sewing = **needlework**, stitching, needlecraft • *Her mother had always done all the sewing.*

sex AS A NOUN 1 = **gender** • *differences between the sexes*
2 = **facts of life**, sexuality, reproduction, the birds and the bees *(informal)* • *a campaign to help parents talk about sex with their children*
3 = **lovemaking**, sexual relations, copulation, the other *(informal)*, fucking *(taboo slang)*, screwing *(taboo slang)*, intimacy, going to bed (with someone), shagging *(Brit. taboo slang)*, nookie *(slang)*, fornication, coitus, rumpy-pumpy *(slang)*, legover *(slang)*, coition, rumpo *(slang)* • *The entire film revolves around sex and drugs.*
▸ IN PHRASES: **have sex** = **have sexual intercourse**, sleep with, make love with, have *(taboo slang)*, lay *(taboo slang)*, roger *(taboo slang)*, bang *(taboo slang)*, fuck *(taboo slang)*, screw *(taboo slang)*, shaft *(taboo slang)*, poke *(taboo slang)*, lie with *(archaic)*, shag *(Brit. taboo slang)*, hump *(taboo slang)*, give someone one *(taboo slang)*, do the business, get it on *(informal)*, go to bed with, fornicate *(archaic)*, get your leg over *(taboo slang)*, have your way with • *I want to have sex, but my girlfriend says no.* • *He was caught having sex with a girl in a public car park.*
▸ **RELATED MANIAS:** erotomania, nymphomania
▸ **RELATED PHOBIA:** genophobia

QUOTATIONS

The pleasure is momentary, the position ridiculous, and the expense damnable
[attributed to Lord Chesterfield]

When I hear his steps outside my door I lie down on my bed, close my eyes, open my legs, and think of England
[Lady Hillingdon]

Sex is what you can get. For some people, most people, it's the most important thing they can get without being born rich or smart or stealing
[Don DeLillo *Underworld*]

Is sex dirty? Only if it's done right
[Woody Allen *Everything You Always Wanted to Know About Sex*]

That [sex] was the most fun I ever had without laughing
[Woody Allen *Annie Hall*]

My mother used to say, Delia, if S-E-X ever rears its ugly head, close your eyes before you see the rest of it
[Alan Ayckbourn *Bedroom Farce*]

While we have sex in the mind, we truly have none in the body
[D.H. Lawrence *Leave Sex Alone*]

There is more difference within the sexes than between them
[Ivy Compton-Burnett]

▹ *See panel* **Sexual practices and terms**

sex appeal = **desirability**, attractiveness, allure, glamour, sensuality, magnetism, sexiness *(informal)*, oomph *(informal)*, it *(informal)*, voluptuousness, seductiveness • *She has the energy and sex appeal of a woman half her age.*

sexism = **sexual discrimination** • *We are committed to eradicating homophobia, racism and sexism.*

S

SEXUAL PRACTICES AND TERMS

adultery
afterplay
algolagnia
anal intercourse, sodomy, *or* buggery
anilingus
autoeroticism
bagpiping
bestiality
bisexuality
bondage
coprophilia
cottaging
cunnilingus
felching
fellatio
fetishism
fisting *or* fist-fucking
flagellation
foreplay
fornication
frottage
heterosexuality
homosexuality
impotence
incest
lesbianism
masochism
masturbation
narcissism
necrophilia
nymphomania
oral sex
paedophilia
paraphilia
pederasty
premature ejaculation
rimming
rough trade
sadism
sadomasochism *or* S&M
safe sex
satyriasis
scopophilia
shrimping
soixante-neuf *or* sixty-nine
tribadism
troilism
voyeurism
water sports, urolagnia, *or* golden shower
zoophilia

sexless = **asexual**, androgynous, neuter, hermaphrodite, nonsexual, parthenogenetic, epicene • *The research team has made a mistake by keeping the robots sexless.*

sexual 1 = **carnal**, erotic, intimate, sensual, of the flesh, coital • *Men's sexual fantasies often have little to do with their sexual desire.*
2 = **reproductive**, sex, genital, venereal, procreative • *the sexual organs*
3 = **sexy**, erotic, sensual, inviting, bedroom, provoking, arousing, naughty, provocative, seductive, sensuous, suggestive, alluring, voluptuous, slinky, titillating, flirtatious, come-hither *(informal)*, kissable, beddable • *exchanging sexual glances*

sexual intercourse = **copulation**, sex *(informal)*, intercourse, the other *(informal)*, union, coupling, congress, mating, commerce *(archaic)*, fucking *(taboo slang)*, screwing *(taboo slang)*, intimacy, penetration, shagging *(Brit. taboo slang)*, nookie *(slang)*, consummation, bonking *(informal)*, coitus, carnal knowledge, rumpy-pumpy *(slang)*, legover *(slang)*, coition, poontang *(taboo slang)* • *various and sometimes improbable positions of sexual intercourse*

sexuality 1 = **desire**, lust, eroticism, sensuality, virility, sexiness *(informal)*, voluptuousness, carnality, bodily appetites • *the growing discussion of human sexuality*
2 = **sexual orientation**, sexual preference, leaning • *He believes he has been discriminated against because of his sexuality.*

sexy = **erotic**, sensual, seductive, inviting, bedroom, provoking, arousing, naughty, provocative, sensuous, suggestive, voluptuous, slinky, titillating, flirtatious, come-hither *(informal)*, kissable, beddable, hot *(informal)* • *a sexy career girl* • *sexy underwear*

shabby 1 = **tatty**, worn, ragged, scruffy, faded, frayed, worn-out, tattered, threadbare, down at heel, the worse for wear, having seen better days • *His clothes were old and shabby.*
OPPOSITES: smart, neat, well-dressed
2 = **rundown**, tatty, seedy, mean, neglected, scruffy, squalid, ramshackle, dilapidated, grotty *(informal)*, tumbledown, insalubrious • *a rather shabby Naples hotel*
3 = **mean**, low, rotten *(informal)*, cheap, dirty, shameful, low-down *(informal)*, shoddy, unworthy, despicable, contemptible, scurvy, dishonourable, ignoble, ungentlemanly • *It was hard to know why the man deserved such shabby treatment.*
OPPOSITES: fair, generous, worthy

shack AS A NOUN = **hut**, cabin, shanty, lean-to, dump *(informal)*, hovel, shiel *(Scot.)*, shieling *(Scot.)*, whare *(N.Z.)* • *a nice shack in shanty town*
▸ IN PHRASES: **shack up with someone** = **move in with**, go to live with, share a house with, live together with • *It turned out she had shacked up with a lawyer in New York.*

shackle AS A VERB 1 = **hamper**, limit, restrict, restrain, hamstring, inhibit, constrain, obstruct, impede, encumber, tie (someone's) hands • *The trade unions are shackled by the law.*
2 = **fetter**, chain, handcuff, secure, bind, hobble, manacle, trammel, put in irons • *She was shackled to a wall.*
▸ AS A NOUN *often plural* = **fetter**, chain, iron, bond, handcuff, hobble, manacle, leg-iron, gyve *(archaic)* • *He unbolted the shackles on Billy's hands.*

shade AS A NOUN 1 = **hue**, tone, colour, tint • *The walls were painted in two shades of green.*
2 = **shadow**, cover, screen, shadows, shelter, coolness, shadiness • *Exotic trees provide welcome shade.*
3 = **dash**, trace, hint, suggestion, suspicion, small amount, semblance • *There was a shade of irony in her voice.*
4 = **nuance**, difference, degree, graduation, subtlety, gradation, modulation • *the capacity to convey subtle shades of meaning*
5 = **screen**, covering, cover, blind, curtain, shield, veil, canopy • *She left the shades down and the lights off.*
6 = **ghost**, spirit, shadow, phantom, spectre, manes, apparition, eidolon, kehua *(N.Z.)* • *His writing benefits from the shade of Lincoln hovering over his shoulder.*
▸ AS A PLURAL NOUN = **sunglasses**, dark glasses, Raybans *(trademark)* • *Wearing shades on the beach allowed them to ogle people undetected.*
▸ AS A VERB 1 = **darken**, shadow, cloud, dim, cast a shadow over, shut out the light • *a health resort whose beaches are shaded by palm trees*
2 = **cover**, protect, screen, hide, shield, conceal, obscure, veil, mute • *You've got to shade your eyes or close them altogether.*
3 = **turn**, transmute, change gradually • *As the dusk shaded into night we drove slowly.*
▸ IN PHRASES: **put something** *or* **someone in the shade** = **outshine**, exceed, eclipse, outdo, overshadow, surpass, transcend, outclass, outshine, make pale by comparison • *a run that put every other hurdler's performance in the shade*

shadow AS A NOUN 1 = **silhouette**, shape, outline, profile, penumbra • *All he could see was his shadow.*
2 = **shade**, dimness, darkness, gloom, cover, protection, shelter, dusk, obscurity, gloaming *(Scot. poetic)*, gathering darkness • *Most of the lake was in shadow.*
3 = **ghost**, apology, remnant, vestige, travesty, poor imitation, poor representation, inferior version, weak image • *He was a shadow of his former self.*
4 = **trace**, suggestion, hint, suspicion, touch, tinge, whiff, jot, soupçon *(French)* • *It was without a shadow of a doubt the best we've played.*
5 = **hint**, suggestion, trace, suspicion, ghost, flicker, glimmer • *The faintest shadow of a frown creased that angelic face.*
▸ AS A VERB 1 = **shade**, screen, shield, darken, overhang, cast a shadow over • *The hood shadowed her face.*
2 = **follow**, track, pursue, dog, tail *(informal)*, trail, stalk, spy on • *shadowed by a large and highly visible body of police*

shadowy 1 = **dark**, shaded, dim, gloomy, shady, obscure, murky, dusky, funereal, crepuscular, tenebrous, tenebrious • *I watched him from a shadowy corner.*

2 = **vague**, indistinct, faint, ghostly, obscure, dim, phantom, imaginary, unreal, intangible, illusory, spectral, undefined, nebulous, dreamlike, impalpable, unsubstantial, wraithlike • *the shadowy shape of a big barge loaded with logs*

shady 1 = **shaded**, cool, shadowy, dim, leafy, bowery, bosky *(literary)*, umbrageous • *After flowering, place the pot in a shady spot.*
OPPOSITES: bright, exposed, sunny
2 = **crooked**, dodgy *(Brit., Austral. & N.Z. informal)*, unethical, suspect, suspicious, dubious, slippery, questionable, unscrupulous, fishy *(informal)*, shifty, disreputable, untrustworthy, shonky *(Austral. & N.Z. informal)* • *Be wary of people who try to talk you into shady deals.*
OPPOSITES: straight, ethical, honest

shaft 1 = **tunnel**, hole, passage, burrow, passageway, channel • *old mine shafts*
2 = **handle**, staff, pole, rod, stem, upright, baton, shank • *a drive shaft*
3 = **ray**, beam, gleam, streak • *A brilliant shaft of sunlight burst through the doorway.*

shag AS A VERB = **have sex with**, sleep with, fuck *(taboo slang)*, screw *(taboo slang)*, have *(taboo slang)*, lay *(taboo slang)*, roger *(taboo slang)*, bang *(taboo slang)*, shaft *(taboo slang)*, poke *(taboo slang)*, lie with *(archaic)*, hump *(taboo slang)*, go to bed with, have sexual intercourse with, get it on with *(informal)*, do the business with, fornicate with *(archaic)*, have your way with • *He'd love to shag her.* • *Moments later, they were shagging in the bathroom.*
▸ AS A NOUN = **screw** *(taboo slang)*, lay *(taboo slang)*, fuck *(taboo slang)*, rogering *(taboo slang)* • *a spy movie with car chases, a murder and a shag*

shaggy = **unkempt**, rough, tousled, hairy, long-haired, hirsute, unshorn • *He has long, shaggy hair.* • *a shaggy dog*
OPPOSITES: cropped, smooth, shorn

shake AS A VERB 1 = **jiggle**, agitate, wave, joggle • *Shake the rugs well and hang them out.*
2 = **tremble**, shiver, quake, shudder, quiver • *I stood there, crying and shaking with fear.*
3 = **rock**, sway, shudder, wobble, waver, totter, oscillate, judder • *The plane shook frighteningly as it hit the high, drenching waves.*
4 = **wave**, wield, flourish, brandish • *They shook clenched fists.*
5 = **upset**, shock, frighten, disturb, distress, move, rattle *(informal)*, intimidate, unnerve, discompose, traumatize • *The news of his escape had shaken them all.*
6 = **undermine**, damage, threaten, disable, weaken, impair, sap, debilitate, subvert, pull the rug out from under *(informal)* • *It won't shake the football world if we beat them.*
▸ AS A NOUN = **vibration**, trembling, quaking, shock, jar, disturbance, jerk, shiver, shudder, jolt, tremor, agitation, convulsion, pulsation, jounce • *blurring of photos caused by camera shake*
▸ IN PHRASES: **no great shakes** = **unexceptional**, mediocre, not very good, rubbish, pedestrian, crap *(slang)*, indifferent, unremarkable, run-of-the-mill, uninspiring, undistinguished, unimpressive, nothing to write home about *(informal)*, half-pie *(N.Z. informal)* • *The album is no great shakes.*
shake someone off = **leave behind**, lose, get rid of, get away from, elude, get rid of, throw off, get shot of *(slang)*, rid yourself of, give the slip • *He had shaken off his pursuers.*
shake someone up = **upset**, shock, frighten, disturb, distress, rattle *(informal)*, unsettle, unnerve, discompose • *He was shaken up when he was thrown from his horse.*
shake something off = **get rid of**, lose, recover from, recuperate from, get shot of *(Brit. informal)*, get better from, free yourself of • *He just couldn't shake off that cough.*
shake something up = **restructure**, reorganize, revolutionize, reform, stir (up), mix, transform, overturn, overhaul, churn (up), turn upside down, alter dramatically • *Directors and shareholders are preparing to shake things up.*

Shakespeare
▹ *See panel* **Shakespeare**

shake-up = **reorganization**, revolution, reformation, shift, innovation, transformation, upheaval, metamorphosis, sea change, drastic *or* radical change • *controversial health service shake-ups*

shaky 1 = **unstable**, weak, precarious, tottering, ramshackle, dilapidated, rickety, unsteady, wonky *(Brit. informal)* • *Our house will remain on shaky foundations unless the architect sorts out the basement.*
OPPOSITES: strong, firm, stable
2 = **unsteady**, faint, trembling, faltering, wobbly, giddy, light-headed, tremulous, weak at the knees, doddery, quivery, all of a quiver *(informal)* • *Even small operations can leave you feeling a bit shaky.*
3 = **uncertain**, suspect, dubious, questionable, unreliable, unsound, iffy *(informal)*, unsupported, undependable • *We knew we may have to charge them on shaky evidence.*
OPPOSITES: dependable, reliable

shallow = **superficial**, surface, empty, slight, foolish, idle, trivial, meaningless, flimsy, frivolous, skin-deep • *I think he is shallow, vain and untrustworthy.*
OPPOSITES: serious, deep, profound

shallows = **bank**, flat, shelf, shoal, sandbank, sand bar • *At dusk more fish come into the shallows.*

sham AS A NOUN = **fraud**, imitation, hoax, pretence, forgery, counterfeit, pretender, humbug, impostor, feint, pseud *(informal)*, wolf in sheep's clothing, imposture, phoney *or* phony *(informal)* • *Their promises were exposed as a hollow sham.*
OPPOSITES: original, the real thing, the genuine article
▸ AS AN ADJECTIVE = **false**, artificial, bogus, pretended, mock, synthetic, imitation, simulated, pseudo *(informal)*, counterfeit, feigned, spurious, ersatz, pseud *(informal)*, phoney *or* phony *(informal)* • *a sham marriage*
OPPOSITES: real, genuine, authentic

shaman = **witch doctor**, medicine man, medicine woman, healer, sorcerer, spirit-raiser, voodooist • *the full control of a shaman*

shamble = **shuffle**, stumble, lurch, limp, lumber, drag your feet • *The conductor shambled to the next carriage.*

shambles 1 = **chaos**, mess, disorder, confusion, muddle, havoc, anarchy, disarray, madhouse, disorganization • *The economy is a shambles.*
2 = **mess**, state, jumble, tip, disaster area, untidiness • *The boat's interior was an utter shambles.*

shambling = **clumsy**, awkward, shuffling, lurching, lumbering, unsteady, ungainly, unco *(Austral. slang)* • *a small dark, shambling figure*

shambolic = **disorganized**, disordered, chaotic, confused, muddled, inefficient, anarchic, topsy-turvy, at sixes and sevens, in total disarray, unsystematic • *a shambolic public relations disaster*

shame AS A NOUN 1 = **embarrassment**, humiliation, chagrin, ignominy, compunction, mortification, loss of face, discomfiture, abashment, shamefacedness • *I was, to my shame, a coward.*
OPPOSITES: cheek, boldness, shamelessness
2 = **disgrace**, scandal, discredit, contempt, smear, degradation, disrepute, reproach, derision, dishonour, infamy, opprobrium, odium, ill repute, obloquy • *I don't want to bring shame on the family name.*
OPPOSITES: credit, honour, glory
3 = **pity** • *What a shame you can't go!*
▸ AS A VERB 1 = **embarrass**, disgrace, humiliate, humble, disconcert, mortify, take (someone) down a peg *(informal)*, abash • *Her son's affair had humiliated and shamed her.*
OPPOSITES: do credit to, make proud

SHAKESPEARE

Characters in Shakespeare	Play
Sir Andrew Aguecheek	Twelfth Night
Antonio	The Merchant of Venice
Antony	Antony and Cleopatra, Julius Caesar
Ariel	The Tempest
Aufidius	Coriolanus
Autolycus	The Winter's Tale
Banquo	Macbeth
Bassanio	The Merchant of Venice
Beatrice	Much Ado About Nothing
Sir Toby Belch	Twelfth Night
Benedick	Much Ado About Nothing
Bolingbroke	Richard II
Bottom	A Midsummer Night's Dream
Brutus	Julius Caesar
Caliban	The Tempest
Casca	Julius Caesar
Cassio	Othello
Cassius	Julius Caesar
Claudio	Much Ado About Nothing, Measure for Measure
Claudius	Hamlet
Cleopatra	Antony and Cleopatra
Cordelia	King Lear
Coriolanus	Coriolanus
Cressida	Troilus and Cressida
Demetrius	A Midsummer Night's Dream
Desdemona	Othello
Dogberry	Much Ado About Nothing
Edmund	King Lear
Enobarbus	Antony and Cleopatra
Falstaff	Henry IV Parts I and II, The Merry Wives of Windsor
Ferdinand	The Tempest
Feste	Twelfth Night
Fluellen	Henry V
Fool	King Lear
Gertrude	Hamlet
Gloucester	King Lear
Goneril	King Lear
Guildenstern	Hamlet
Hamlet	Hamlet
Helena	All's Well that Ends Well, A Midsummer Night's Dream
Hermia	A Midsummer Night's Dream
Hero	Much Ado About Nothing
Hotspur	Henry IV Part I
Iago	Othello

Characters in Shakespeare	Play
Jaques	As You Like It
John of Gaunt	Richard II
Juliet	Romeo and Juliet
Julius Caesar	Julius Caesar
Katharina *or* Kate	The Taming of the Shrew
Kent	King Lear
Laertes	Hamlet
Lear	King Lear
Lysander	A Midsummer Night's Dream
Macbeth	Macbeth
Lady Macbeth	Macbeth
Macduff	Macbeth
Malcolm	Macbeth
Malvolio	Twelfth Night
Mercutio	Romeo and Juliet
Miranda	The Tempest
Oberon	A Midsummer Night's Dream
Octavius	Antony and Cleopatra
Olivia	Twelfth Night
Ophelia	Hamlet
Orlando	As You Like It
Orsino	Twelfth Night
Othello	Othello
Pandarus	Troilus and Cressida
Perdita	The Winter's Tale
Petruchio	The Taming of the Shrew
Pistol	Henry IV Part II, Henry V, The Merry Wives of Windsor
Polonius	Hamlet
Portia	The Merchant of Venice
Prospero	The Tempest
Puck	A Midsummer Night's Dream
Mistress Quickly	The Merry Wives of Windsor
Regan	King Lear
Romeo	Romeo and Juliet
Rosalind	As You Like It
Rosencrantz	Hamlet
Sebastian	The Tempest, Twelfth Night
Shylock	The Merchant of Venice
Thersites	Troilus and Cressida
Timon	Timon of Athens
Titania	A Midsummer Night's Dream
Touchstone	As You Like It
Troilus	Troilus and Cressida
Tybalt	Romeo and Juliet
Viola	Twelfth Night

Plays of Shakespeare

All's Well that Ends Well
Antony and Cleopatra
As You Like It
The Comedy of Errors
Coriolanus
Cymbeline
Hamlet
Henry IV Part I
Henry IV Part II
Henry V
Henry VI Part I
Henry VI Part II
Henry VI Part III
Henry VIII
Julius Caesar
King John
King Lear
Love's Labour's Lost
Macbeth
Measure for Measure
The Merchant of Venice
The Merry Wives of Windsor
A Midsummer Night's Dream
Much Ado About Nothing
Othello
Pericles, Prince of Tyre
Richard II
Richard III
Romeo and Juliet
The Taming of the Shrew
The Tempest
Timon of Athens
Titus Andronicus
Troilus and Cressida
Twelfth Night
The Two Gentlemen of Verona
The Winter's Tale

SHAKESPEARE (CONTINUED)

Poems of Shakespeare

The Passionate Pilgrim
The Phoenix and the Turtle
The Rape of Lucrece
Sonnets
Venus and Adonis

2 = **dishonour**, discredit, degrade, stain, smear, tarnish, blot, blacken, debase, defile, drag through the mud, give a bad name to • *I wouldn't shame my family by trying that.*
opposites: credit, honour, enhance the reputation of
▸ **in phrases: put something *or* someone to shame** = **show up**, disgrace, eclipse, surpass, outstrip, upstage, outdo, outclass, outshine, leave standing, knock spots off, put in the shade *(Brit. informal)* • *His playing really puts me to shame.*

quotations
It is a most miserable thing to feel ashamed of home
[Charles Dickens *Great Expectations*]

shamefaced = **embarrassed**, humiliated, ashamed, red-faced, chagrined, mortified, sheepish, contrite, discomfited, remorseful, abashed, conscience-stricken • *There was a long silence and my father looked shamefaced.*

shameful = **disgraceful**, outrageous, scandalous, mean, low, base, infamous, indecent, degrading, vile, wicked, atrocious, unworthy, reprehensible, ignominious, dastardly, unbecoming, dishonourable • *It is a shameful state of affairs.*
opposites: right, worthy, admirable

shameless = **brazen**, audacious, flagrant, abandoned, corrupt, hardened, indecent, brash, improper, depraved, wanton, unabashed, profligate, unashamed, incorrigible, insolent, unprincipled, impudent, dissolute, reprobate, immodest, barefaced, unblushing • *a shameless hustler and dealer in stolen goods*

shanty[1] = **shack**, shed, cabin, hut, lean-to, hovel, shiel *(Scot.)*, bothy *(Scot.)*, shieling *(Scot.)* • *a young population in urban slums and shanties*

shanty[2] = **song**, song, air, tune, chant, ballad, hymn, ditty, waiata *(N.Z.)* • *one of my father's favourite sea shanties*

shape **as a noun** 1 = **appearance**, form, aspect, guise, likeness, semblance • *The glass bottle is the shape of a woman's torso.*
2 = **form**, profile, outline, lines, build, cut, figure, structure, appearance, silhouette, configuration, contours • *the shapes of the trees against the sky*
3 = **pattern**, model, frame, mould • *Carefully cut round the shape of the design you wish to use.*
4 = **condition**, state, health, nick *(Brit. informal)*, repair, trim, kilter, fettle • *He was still in better shape than many young men.*
▸ **as a verb** 1 = **form**, affect, influence, make, produce, create, model, fashion, mould • *Like it or not, our families shape our lives.*
2 = **mould**, form, make, fashion, model, cast, frame, sculpt • *Cut the dough in half and shape each half into a loaf.*
▸ **in phrases: out of shape** = **unfit**, unhealthy, in poor condition, feeble, debilitated, flabby, decrepit, out of trim • *Physically, Englishmen are out of shape.*
shape up = **progress**, develop, come on, turn out, proceed, look good, be promising • *He is shaping up after being hailed 'the new Paul Gascoigne'.*
take shape = **become clear**, come together, fall into place, crystallize • *The plan started to take shape in his mind.*

shapeless = **formless**, irregular, amorphous, unstructured, misshapen, asymmetrical • *She never wore anything but shapeless black dresses.*
opposites: well-formed, well-turned, well-proportioned

shapely = **well-formed**, elegant, trim, neat, graceful, well-turned, curvaceous, sightly, comely, well-proportioned • *her shapely legs*

shard = **fragment**, bit, piece, chip, scrap, particle, shiver, sliver • *shards of glass flying through the air*

share **as a noun** = **part**, portion, quota, ration, lot, cut *(informal)*, due, division, contribution, proportion, allowance, whack *(informal)*, allotment • *I have had more than my share of adventures.*
▸ **as a verb** 1 = **divide**, split, distribute, assign, apportion, parcel out, divvy up *(informal)* • *the small income he has shared with his brother*
2 = **go halves on**, divide, go fifty-fifty on *(informal)*, go Dutch on *(informal)* • *Share the cost of the flowers.*
▸ **in phrases: share in something** = **take part in**, be involved in, contribute to, participate in, have a hand in, partake in, use in common • *Everybody shares in the cooking chores.*
share something out = **divide up**, distribute, allocate, hand out, ration, apportion, deal out, deal up • *It makes sense to share the work out between you.* • *a formula for sharing out power among the various clans*

shark
▹ *See panel* **Sharks**

sharp **as an adjective** 1 = **keen**, cutting, sharpened, honed, jagged, whetted, knife-edged, razor-sharp, serrated, knifelike • *Using a sharp knife, cut away the pith and peel from both fruits.*
opposites: dull, blunt, rounded
2 = **pointed**, tapering, tapered, spiky, pointy • *sharp-toed cowboy boots*
3 = **quick-witted**, clever, astute, acute, knowing, ready, quick, bright, alert, subtle, penetrating, apt, discerning, on the ball *(informal)*, perceptive, observant, long-headed • *He is very sharp and swift with repartee.*
opposites: slow, stupid, dim

SHARKS

angel shark, angelfish, *or* monkfish
basking shark, sailfish *or (N.Z.)* reremai
blue pointer *or (N.Z.)* blue shark *or* blue whaler
bronze whaler *(Austral.)*
carpet shark *or (Austral.)* wobbegong
cow shark *or* six-gilled shark
dogfish *or (Austral.)* dog shark
grey nurse shark
gummy (shark)
hammerhead
mako
nursehound
nurse shark
porbeagle *or* mackerel shark
requiem shark
school shark *(Austral.)*
seven-gill shark *(Austral.)*
shovelhead
soupfin *or* soupfin shark
thrasher *or* thresher shark
tiger shark
tope
whale shark
whaler shark

4 = **cutting**, biting, severe, bitter, harsh, scathing, acrimonious, barbed, hurtful, sarcastic, sardonic, caustic, vitriolic, trenchant, mordant, mordacious, acerb • *'Don't criticize your mother,' was his sharp reprimand.*
OPPOSITES: kindly, friendly, gentle
5 = **sudden**, marked, abrupt, extreme, distinct • *There's been a sharp rise in the rate of inflation.*
OPPOSITES: gentle, moderate, gradual
6 = **clear**, distinct, clear-cut, well-defined, crisp • *All the footmarks are quite sharp and clear.*
OPPOSITES: blurred, unclear, indistinct
7 = **sour**, strong, tart, pungent, hot, burning, acid, bitter, tangy, acidic, acerbic, acrid, piquant, acetic, vinegary, acerb • *a colourless, almost odourless liquid with a sharp, sweetish taste*
OPPOSITES: mild, bland, tasteless
8 = **cold**, biting, keen, bitter, intense, raw, chill, harsh, piercing, penetrating, icy, brisk, chilly, glacial • *The wind was not as sharp and cruel as it had been.*
9 = **stylish**, smart, fashionable, trendy *(informal)*, chic, classy *(slang)*, snappy, natty *(informal)*, dressy, schmick *(Austral. informal)* • *Now politics is all about the right haircut and a sharp suit.*
10 = **acute**, violent, severe, intense, painful, shooting, distressing, stabbing, fierce, stinging, piercing, sore, excruciating, gut-wrenching • *I felt a sharp pain in my lower back.*
11 = **steep**, sheer, vertical, abrupt, precipitous • *There could be a sharp drop at the entrance to the cave.*
▸ **AS AN ADVERB** 1 = **promptly**, precisely, exactly, on time, on the dot, punctually • *She planned to unlock the store at 8.00 sharp.*
OPPOSITES: roughly, more or less, approximately
2 = **suddenly**, unexpectedly, abruptly, without warning • *Events mid-month should pull you up sharp.*
OPPOSITES: slowly, gradually, gently

sharpen 1 = **improve**, enhance, better, upgrade, hone, brush up, touch up, ameliorate, polish up • *You can sharpen your skills with rehearsal.*
2 = **make sharp**, hone, whet, grind, edge, file, strop, put an edge on • *He started to sharpen his knife.*
3 = **fuel**, fire, stir, arouse, excite, animate, rouse, quicken, inflame, enliven, inspirit • *The case has sharpened the debate over capital punishment.*

sharp-eyed = **keen-sighted**, eagle-eyed, hawk-eyed, Argus-eyed, lynx-eyed • *a sharp-eyed City man*

shatter 1 = **smash**, break, burst, split, crack, crush, explode, demolish, shiver, implode, pulverize, crush to smithereens • *Safety glass won't shatter if it's broken.*
2 = **destroy**, ruin, wreck, blast, disable, overturn, demolish, impair, blight, torpedo, bring to nought • *Something like that really shatters your confidence.*
3 = **devastate**, shock, stun, crush, overwhelm, upset, break (someone's) heart, knock the stuffing out of (someone) *(informal)*, knock sideways, knock for six, traumatize, dumbfound • *the tragedy which had shattered him*

shattered 1 = **devastated**, shocked, stunned, crushed, upset, overwhelmed, gutted *(slang)*, traumatized, knocked sideways, knocked for six • *I am absolutely shattered to hear the news.*
2 = **exhausted**, drained, worn out, spent, done in *(informal)*, all in *(slang)*, wiped out *(informal)*, weary, knackered *(slang)*, clapped out *(Brit., Austral. & N.Z. informal)*, tired out, ready to drop, dog-tired *(informal)*, zonked *(slang)*, dead tired *(informal)*, dead beat *(informal)*, shagged out *(Brit. slang)*, jiggered *(informal)* • *He was shattered and too tired to concentrate.*

shattering = **devastating**, stunning, severe, crushing, overwhelming, paralysing • *Yesterday's news was another shattering blow.*

shave **AS A VERB** 1 = **trim**, cut, crop, barber, snip • *It's a pity you shaved your moustache off.*
2 = **scrape**, plane, trim, shear, whittle, pare • *I set the log on the ground and shaved off the bark.*
3 = **reduce**, lower, slash, decrease, discount, cut down, mark down • *Supermarket chains have shaved prices.*
4 = **cut**, take, remove, lop • *She's already shaved four seconds off the national record.*
5 = **brush past**, touch, graze, kiss, glance off • *The ball shaved the goalpost.*
▸ **IN PHRASES:** **close shave** = **lucky escape**, close call, narrow escape • *I can't quite believe the close shaves I've had recently.*

shaving = **flake**, strip, slice, wafer, lamella • *The floor was covered with shavings from his wood carvings.*

sheaf = **bundle**, mass, pile, bunch, stack, heap, wodge *(informal)* • *He took out a sheaf of papers and leafed through them.*

shear **AS A VERB** = **shave**, fleece • *In the Hebrides they shear their sheep later than everyone else.*
▸ **AS A PLURAL NOUN** = **blades**, cutters, clippers, trimmers • *Trim the shrubs with shears.*

sheath 1 = **scabbard**, case • *She drew a combat knife from its sheath.*
2 = **condom**, rubber *(U.S. informal)*, contraceptive, Durex *(Brit., trademark)*, johnny *(Brit. informal)*, prophylactic *(U.S.)*, French letter *(Brit. archaic)* • *A rubber sheath placed over the erect penis stops sperm entering the vagina.*
3 = **covering**, casing, case, cover, sleeve • *It grows on a nerve sheath within the spinal column.*

shed[1] = **hut**, shack, lean-to, outhouse, potting shed, lockup, bothy *(chiefly Scot.)*, whare *(N.Z.)* • *a garden shed*

shed[2] 1 = **drop**, spill, scatter, let drop • *Some of the trees were already beginning to shed their leaves.*
2 = **cast off**, discard, moult, slough off, exuviate • *a snake who has shed its skin*
3 = **give out**, cast, emit, give, throw, afford, radiate, diffuse, pour forth • *as dawn sheds its first light*
4 = **spill**, let flow • *He refused to shed the blood of a fellow creature.*
5 = **sack**, fire *(informal)*, dismiss *(informal)*, axe *(informal)*, discharge, remove, oust, lay off, make redundant, cashier, send packing *(informal)*, give notice to, kiss off *(slang, chiefly U.S. & Canad.)*, give (someone) their marching orders, give the boot to *(slang)*, give the bullet to *(Brit. slang)*, give someone his *or* her P45 *(informal)* • *He has called on employers not to shed workers.*

sheen = **shine**, gleam, gloss, polish, brightness, lustre, burnish, patina, shininess • *The carpet has a silvery sheen to it.*

sheep
▸ **RELATED ADJECTIVE:** ovine
▸ **NAME OF MALE:** ram, tup
▸ **NAME OF FEMALE:** ewe
▸ **NAME OF YOUNG:** lamb, yeanling
▸ **COLLECTIVE NOUN:** flock

QUOTATIONS
He is brought as a lamb to the slaughter
[Bible: Isaiah]

▹ *See panel* **Breeds of sheep**

sheepish = **embarrassed**, uncomfortable, ashamed, silly, foolish, self-conscious, chagrined, mortified, abashed, shamefaced • *He looked a little sheepish when he answered.*
OPPOSITES: confident, bold, unembarrassed

sheer 1 = **total**, complete, absolute, utter, rank, pure, downright, unqualified, out-and-out, unadulterated, unmitigated, thoroughgoing, unalloyed, arrant • *acts of sheer desperation*
OPPOSITES: moderate
2 = **steep**, abrupt, perpendicular, precipitous • *There was a sheer drop just outside my window.*
OPPOSITES: gentle, gradual, horizontal

S

BREEDS OF SHEEP

Beulah Speckled-face
bighorn *or* mountain sheep
Blackface
Black Welsh Mountain
Blue-faced *or* Hexham Leicester
Border Leicester
Boreray
Brecknock Hill Cheviot
British Bleu du Maine
British Charollais
British Friesland
British Milksheep
British Oldenburg
British Texel
British Vendéen
Cambridge
Cheviot
Clun Forest
Colbred
Corriedale
Cotswold
Dalesbred
Dartmoor
Derbyshire Gritstone
Devon and Cornwall Longwool
Devon Closewool
Dorset Down
Dorset Horn
East Friesland
English Halfbred
Exmoor Horn
Hampshire Down
Hebridian *or* St. Kilda
Herdwick
Hill Radnor
Île de France
Jacob
karakul, caracul, *or* broadtail
Kerry Hill
Leicester Longwool
Lincoln Longwool
Llanwenog
Lleyn
Lonk
Manx Loghtan
Masham
Merino
Mule
Norfolk Horn
North Country Cheviot
Orkney *or* North Ronaldsay
Oxford *or* Oxfordshire Down
Polwarth
Portland
Rambouillet
Romney Marsh
Rouge de l'Ouest
Rough Fell
Ryeland
Scottish Blackface
Scottish Halfbred
Shetland
Shropshire
Soay
Southdown
South Wales Mountain
Suffolk
Swaledale
Teeswater
Texel
Welsh Halfbred
Welsh Hill Speckled
Welsh Mountain
Welsh Mountain Badger Faced
Welsh Mule
Wensleydale Longwool
White Face Dartmoor
Whitefaced Woodland
Wiltshire Horn

3 = **fine**, thin, transparent, see-through, gossamer, diaphanous, gauzy • *sheer black tights*
OPPOSITES: heavy, thick, coarse

sheet 1 = **bedding**, bed linen, bed clothes • *the luxury of silk sheets*
2 = **page**, leaf, folio, piece of paper • *I was able to fit it all on one sheet.*
3 = **plate**, piece, panel, slab, pane • *a cracked sheet of glass*
4 = **coat**, film, layer, membrane, surface, stratum, veneer, overlay, lamina • *a sheet of ice*
5 = **expanse**, area, stretch, sweep, covering, blanket • *Sheets of rain slanted across the road.*

sheldrake
▸ **COLLECTIVE NOUN:** dopping

shelf **AS A NOUN** = **shelving**, rack, bookshelf, mantelpiece • *He took a book from the shelf.*
▸ **IN PHRASES: on the shelf** = **unmarried**, single, unwed, unwedded, spouseless • *I was afraid of getting left on the shelf.*

shell **AS A NOUN** 1 = **husk**, case, pod, shuck • *They cracked the nuts and removed their shells.*
2 = **carapace**, armour • *The baby tortoise tucked his head in his shell.*
3 = **shyness**, modesty, lack of confidence, self-consciousness, nervousness, reticence, timidity, diffidence, bashfulness, timorousness, mousiness, timidness • *a lonely boy struggling to emerge from his shell*
4 = **frame**, structure, hull, framework, skeleton, chassis • *The solid feel of the car's shell is impressive.*
5 = **missile**, shot, bullet, slug, cartridge, pellet, projectile • *the whistling screech of an enemy shell*
▸ **AS A VERB** 1 = **remove the shells from**, pod, husk, shuck *(U.S.)* • *She shelled and ate a few nuts.*
2 = **bomb**, barrage, bombard, attack, strike, blitz, strafe • *The rebels shelled the densely-populated suburbs near the port.*
▸ **IN PHRASES: shell something out** = **pay out**, fork out *(slang)*, expend, give, hand over, lay out *(informal)*, disburse, ante up *(informal, chiefly U.S.)* • *You won't have to shell out a fortune for it.*

shellfish = **mollusc**, crustacean, bivalve • *Fish and shellfish are the specialities.*
▸ *See panel* **Shellfish**

shelter **AS A NOUN** 1 = **cover**, screen, awning, shiel *(Scot.)* • *a bus shelter*
2 = **protection**, safety, refuge, cover, security, defence, safeguarding, sanctuary, roof over your head • *the hut where they were given food and shelter*

SHELLFISH

banana prawn *(Austral.)*
blue swimmer, blue manna, *or* sand crab *(Austral.)*
clam
clappy-doo *(Scot.)*
cockle
crab
crayfish, crawfish, *or (N.Z.)* koura
crayfish, craybob, craydab, crawbob, clawchie, lobster, marron, *or* yabby *(Austral.)*
Dublin Bay prawn
freshwater shrimp
king prawn
langoustine
lobster
Moreton Bay bug *or* shovel-nosed lobster *(Austral.)*
mud crab
mussel
Norway lobster
oyster
prawn
scallop *or* scollop
school prawn *(Austral.)*
soldier crab *(Austral.)*

3 = **refuge**, haven, sanctuary, retreat, asylum, safe haven, safe house • *a shelter for homeless women*
▸ **AS A VERB** 1 = **take shelter**, hide, seek refuge, take cover, seek protection • *a man sheltering in a doorway*
2 = **protect**, shield, harbour, safeguard, cover, save, hide, guard, defend, take in, keep safe, keep from harm • *A neighbour sheltered the boy for seven days.*
OPPOSITES: risk, expose, endanger

sheltered 1 = **screened**, covered, protected, shielded, secluded • *a shallow-sloping beach next to a sheltered bay*
OPPOSITES: open, exposed, unprotected
2 = **protected**, screened, shielded, quiet, withdrawn, isolated, secluded, cloistered, reclusive, ensconced, hermitic, conventual • *She had a sheltered upbringing.*

shelve 1 = **postpone**, put off, defer, table *(U.S.)*, dismiss, freeze, suspend, put aside, hold over, mothball, pigeonhole, lay aside, put on ice, put on the back burner *(informal)*, hold in abeyance, take a rain check on *(U.S. & Canad. informal)* • *Sadly, the project has now been shelved.*
2 = **fall**, drop, plunge, descend, plummet • *The shoreline shelves away steeply.*

shepherd **AS A NOUN** = **drover**, stockman, herdsman, grazier • *The shepherd was filled with terror.*
▸ **AS A VERB** = **guide**, conduct, lead, steer, convoy, herd, marshal, usher • *She was shepherded by her guards up the rear ramp of the aircraft.*
▸ **RELATED ADJECTIVES:** pastoral, bucolic

QUOTATIONS
The Lord is my shepherd; I shall not want
[*Bible: Psalm 23*]

sherang = **boss**, manager, head, leader, director, chief, executive, owner, master, governor *(informal)*, employer, administrator, supervisor, superintendent, gaffer *(informal, chiefly Brit.)*, foreman, overseer, kingpin, big cheese *(old-fashioned slang)*, baas *(S. African)*, numero uno *(informal)*, Mister Big *(slang, chiefly U.S.)* • *I am in touch with the head sherang at both sites*

sheriff
▸ **RELATED ADJECTIVE:** shrieval

shield **AS A NOUN** 1 = **protection**, cover, defence, screen, guard, ward *(archaic)*, shelter, safeguard, aegis, rampart, bulwark • *innocents used as a human shield against attack*
2 = **buckler**, escutcheon *(Heraldry)*, targe *(archaic)* • *a warrior with sword and shield*
▸ **AS A VERB** = **protect**, cover, screen, guard, defend, shelter, safeguard • *He shielded his head from the sun with an old sack.*

shift **AS A VERB** 1 = **move**, drift, move around, veer, budge, swerve, change position • *The entire pile shifted and slid, thumping onto the floor.*
2 = **remove**, move, transfer, displace, relocate, rearrange, transpose, reposition • *We shifted the vans and used the area for skateboarding.*
3 = **change**, vary, alter, adjust, adapt, revise, modify, amend, recast • *The computer senses when you shift position.*
4 = **change direction**, change, switch, vary, alter, fluctuate • *The wind shifted and the helicopter lurched.*
▸ **AS A NOUN** 1 = **change**, switch, shifting, modification, alteration, displacement, about-turn, permutation, fluctuation • *a shift in policy*
2 = **move**, transfer, removal, veering, relocation, rearrangement, conveyance, repositioning • *There has been a shift of the elderly to this state.*
3 = **stint**, stretch, spell, work period • *His father worked shifts in a steel mill.*
4 = **team**, squad, crew, gang, patrol • *The night shift should have been safely down the mine long ago.*

shiftless = **lazy**, idle, indolent, irresponsible, incompetent, inefficient, inept, aimless, unambitious, lackadaisical, good-for-nothing, slothful, unenterprising • *a shiftless husband*

shifty = **untrustworthy**, sly, devious, scheming, tricky, slippery, contriving, wily, crafty, evasive, furtive, deceitful, underhand, unprincipled, duplicitous, fly-by-night *(informal)* • *He had a shifty face and previous convictions.*
OPPOSITES: honest, trustworthy, open

shimmer **AS A VERB** = **gleam**, twinkle, glimmer, dance, glisten, scintillate • *The lights shimmered on the water.*
▸ **AS A NOUN** = **gleam**, glimmer, iridescence, unsteady light • *a shimmer of starlight*

shinbone
▸ **TECHNICAL NAME:** tibia

shine **AS A VERB** 1 = **gleam**, flash, beam, glow, sparkle, glitter, glare, shimmer, radiate, twinkle, glimmer, glisten, emit light, give off light, scintillate • *It is a mild morning and the sun is shining.*
2 = **polish**, buff, burnish, brush, wax, gloss, rub up • *Let him dust and shine the furniture.*
3 = **be outstanding**, stand out, excel, star, be successful, be distinguished, steal the show, be conspicuous, be pre-eminent, stand out in a crowd • *He conspicuously failed to shine academically.*
▸ **AS A NOUN** 1 = **polish**, gloss, sheen, glaze, lustre, patina • *The wood has been recently polished to bring back the shine.*
2 = **brightness**, light, sparkle, radiance • *There was a sparkle about her, a shine of anticipation.*
▸ **IN PHRASES: take a shine to something** *or* **someone** = **take a fancy to**, be captivated by, have a crush on, find attractive, have a thing about, start to like, start to fancy, grow attracted to • *Seems to me you've taken quite a shine to her.*

shining 1 = **outstanding**, glorious, splendid, leading, celebrated, brilliant, distinguished, eminent, conspicuous, illustrious • *She is a shining example to us all.*
2 = **bright**, brilliant, gleaming, beaming, sparkling, glittering, shimmering, radiant, luminous, glistening, resplendent, aglow, effulgent, incandescent • *shining brass buttons*

shin up = **climb**, scale, ascend, scramble up, clamber up, swarm up • *Nancy shinned up the tree.*

shiny = **bright**, gleaming, glossy, glistening, polished, burnished, lustrous, satiny, sheeny, agleam, nitid *(poetic)* • *a shiny new sports car*

ship **AS A NOUN** = **vessel**, boat, craft, liner • *We went by ship over to America.*
▸ **AS A VERB** = **send**, take, run, bring, carry, bear, transfer, ferry, convey • *Food is being shipped to drought-stricken countries.*
▹ *See panel* **Boats and ships**

QUOTATIONS
Ships that pass in the night, and speak each other in passing;
Only a signal shown and a distant voice in the darkness
[Henry Wadsworth Longfellow *Tales of a Wayside Inn*]

shipshape = **tidy**, neat, orderly, trim, businesslike, well-organized, uncluttered, well-ordered, well-regulated, spick-and-span, trig *(archaic or dialect)*, Bristol fashion • *We moved in and soon had the place shipshape.*

shirk 1 = **dodge**, avoid, evade, get out of, duck (out of) *(informal)*, shun, sidestep, body-swerve *(Scot.)*, bob off *(Brit. slang)*, scrimshank *(Brit. Military slang)* • *We will not shirk the task of considering the need for further action.*
2 = **skive** *(Brit. slang)*, slack, idle, malinger, swing the lead, gold-brick *(U.S. slang)*, bob off *(Brit. slang)*, bludge *(Austral. & N.Z. informal)*, scrimshank *(Brit. Military slang)* • *He was sacked for shirking.*

shirt
▹ *See panel* **Shirts**

shit **AS A NOUN** 1 = **dung**, faeces, excrement, stool, muck, manure, droppings, kak *(S. African)*, waste matter • *I feel like throwing a pile of dog shit over the fence.*

SHIRTS

banyan
blouse
boiled shirt
bush shirt
camise
chemise
cover-shoulder
dashiki
dress shirt
garibaldi
grandad shirt
guimpe
Jacky Howe
(*Austral. informal*)
hair shirt
kerbaya
kurta *or* khurta
lava-lava
middy blouse
overblouse
polo shirt
sark (*Scot.*)
skivvy
sports shirt
Swanndri
(*trademark N.Z.*)
T-shirt *or* tee shirt

2 = rubbish, nonsense, garbage (*informal*), malarkey, balls (*taboo slang*), bull (*slang*), rot, crap (*taboo slang*), bullshit (*taboo slang*), bollocks (*Brit. taboo slang*), cobblers (*Brit. taboo slang*), drivel, twaddle, tripe (*informal*), claptrap (*informal*), poppycock (*informal*), kak (*S. African*), pants (*slang*), bizzo (*Austral. slang*), bull's wool (*Austral. & N.Z. slang*) • *This is a load of shit.*
3 = bastard (*informal offensive*), villain, rogue, scoundrel, wretch, knave (*archaic*), blackguard, evildoer, wrong 'un (*Austral. slang*) • *As I said, in many ways he was a shit.*
▸ AS AN INTERJECTION **= dash it**, damn (*informal*), fuck (*taboo slang*), bugger (*taboo slang*) • *I said, 'Oh, shit!' and threw something, then walked off-stage.*
▸ IN PHRASES: **beat** *or* **kick the shit out of someone = beat up**, assault, set about, assail, fall upon, set upon, lay into (*informal*), beat *or* knock seven bells out of (*informal*) • *You have to beat the shit out of him to get an answer.*
not give a shit = not care, not mind, not be interested, not be concerned, not be bothered, not give a damn (*informal*), not give a monkey's (*informal*) • *I don't give a shit what others think.*
the shits = diarrhoea, the runs, the trots, the skits, Delhi belly, Montezuma's revenge, gutrot, the squits (*Brit. informal*) • *'No olive oil,' he mimicked. 'Remember it gives you the shits.'*

shiver AS A VERB **= shudder**, shake, tremble, quake, quiver, palpitate • *He shivered in the cold.*
▸ AS A NOUN **= tremble**, shake, shudder, quiver, thrill, trembling, flutter, tremor, frisson (*French*) • *Alice gave a shiver of delight.*
▸ IN PHRASES: **the shivers = the shakes**, a chill (*informal*), goose pimples, goose flesh, chattering teeth • *My boss gives me the shivers.*

shivery = shaky, cold, chilled, quaking, chilly, trembly, shuddery, quivery • *She felt shivery and a little sick.*

shock AS A NOUN **1 = upset**, blow, trauma, bombshell, turn (*informal*), distress, disturbance, consternation, whammy (*informal, chiefly U.S.*), state of shock, rude awakening, bolt from the blue, prostration • *The extent of the violence came as a shock.*
2 = trauma, collapse, breakdown, daze, stupor, stupefaction • *He was found beaten and in shock.*
3 = impact, blow, jolt, clash, encounter, bump, jarring, collision, jerk • *Steel barriers can bend and absorb the shock.*
4 = start, scare, fright, turn, jolt • *It gave me quite a shock to see his face on the screen.*
5 = mass, head, mop, tangle, cascade, thatch, mane • *a very old priest with a shock of white hair*
▸ AS A VERB **1 = shake**, stun, stagger, jar, shake up (*informal*), paralyse, numb, jolt, stupefy, shake out of your complacency • *Relief workers were shocked by what they saw.*
2 = horrify, appal, disgust, outrage, offend, revolt, unsettle, sicken, agitate, disquiet, nauseate, raise someone's eyebrows, scandalize, gross out (*U.S. slang*), traumatize, give (someone) a turn (*informal*) • *They were easily shocked in those days.*
▸ AS AN ADJECTIVE **= surprise**, surprising, unexpected, startling, unusual, extraordinary, remarkable, incredible, astonishing, astounding, jaw-dropping • *a shock defeat*
▸ RELATED PHOBIA: hormephobia

shocking 1 = terrible, appalling, dreadful, bad, fearful, dire, horrendous, ghastly, from hell (*informal*), deplorable, abysmal, frightful, godawful (*slang*) • *I must have been in a shocking state last night.*
2 = appalling, outrageous, disgraceful, offensive, distressing, disgusting, horrible, dreadful, horrifying, revolting, obscene, sickening, ghastly, hideous, monstrous, scandalous, disquieting, unspeakable, atrocious, repulsive, nauseating, odious, loathsome, abominable, stupefying, hellacious (*U.S. slang*) • *This was a shocking invasion of privacy.*
OPPOSITES: fine, wonderful, excellent

shoddy = inferior, poor, second-rate, cheap, tacky (*informal*), tawdry, tatty, trashy, low-rent (*informal, chiefly U.S.*), slipshod, cheapo (*informal*), rubbishy, junky (*informal*), cheap-jack (*informal*), bodger *or* bodgie (*Austral. slang*) • *I'm normally quick to complain about shoddy service.*
OPPOSITES: fine, quality, excellent

shoe

SHOES AND BOOTS

ankle boot
arctic (*U.S.*)
Balmoral
biker boot
blucher (*obsolete*)
bootee
bottine
bovver boot (*Brit. slang*)
brogan
brogue
brothel creeper (*informal*)
buskin
chopine
chukka boot
clog
co-respondent
cothurnus *or* cothurn
court shoe
cowboy boot
creeper (*informal*)
crowboot
deck shoe
Doc Marten (*trademark*)
espadrille
field boot
flat *or* flatty
flip-flop
football boot
gaiter *or* spat
galosh
ghillie (*Scot.*)
golf shoe
gumboot
gumshoe
gym shoe
half boot
Hessian boot
high heel
hobnail boot
jackboot
Jandal (*N.Z., trademark*)
kitten heel
lace-up
larrigan
loafer
moccasin
moonboot
mukluk
mule
overshoe
Oxford
pantofle (*archaic*)
platform
plimsoll
pump
racket *or* racquet
running shoe
rock boot
sabot
sandal
sandshoe
scuff
slingback
slip-on
slipper
sneaker
snowshoe
spike
stiletto
surgical boot
tennis shoe
thigh boot
top boot
track shoe
training shoe *or* trainer
veldskoen
wader
wedge *or* wedge heel
welly
Wellington boot
winkle-picker

S

shoemaker = **cobbler**, bootmaker, souter *(Scot.)* • *I'm a shoemaker by trade.*

shoot AS A VERB **1** = **open fire on**, blast *(slang)*, hit, kill, bag, plug *(slang)*, bring down, blow away *(slang, chiefly U.S.)*, zap *(slang)*, pick off, pump full of lead *(slang)* • *The police had orders to shoot anyone who attacked them.*
2 = **fire**, launch, discharge, project, hurl, fling, propel, emit, let fly • *He shot an arrow into the air.*
3 = **speed**, race, rush, charge, fly, spring, tear, flash, dash, barrel (along) *(informal, chiefly U.S. & Canad.)*, bolt, streak, dart, whisk, whizz *(informal)*, hurtle, scoot, burn rubber *(informal)* • *They had almost reached the boat when a figure shot past them.*
4 = **film**, video, photograph, capture on film, make a film of • *He'd love to shoot his film in Cuba.*
▸ AS A NOUN = **sprout**, branch, bud, twig, sprig, offshoot, scion, slip • *This week saw the first pink shoots of the new season's crop.*
▸ IN PHRASES: **shoot someone down** = **gun down**, blow away *(slang, chiefly U.S.)*, put a bullet into *(informal)*, fell, take out *(slang)*, execute, pump full of lead *(informal)* • *They shot him down in cold blood.*
shoot something down = **bring down**, gun down • *His plane was shot down.*
shoot something *or* **someone down in flames** = **put down**, dismiss, dispel, reject, banish, spurn, repudiate, lay aside, pooh-pooh • *She was able to shoot the rumour down in flames.*
shoot up = **increase**, grow, expand, go up, mount, multiply, snowball • *Sales shot up by 9% last month.*

shooter = **gunman**, gunner, sniper, marksman, rifleman, musketeer, artilleryman, markswoman • *An eyewitness identified him as the shooter.*

shop AS A NOUN = **store**, market, supermarket, mart, boutique, emporium, hypermarket, dairy *(N.Z.)* • *It's not available in the shops.*
▸ AS A VERB **1** = **go shopping**, buy things, do the shopping, go to the shops • *customers who shop once a week*
2 = **betray**, grass on *(Brit. slang)*, inform on *or* against, sell out *(informal)*, double-cross *(informal)*, stab in the back, sell down the river *(informal)*, grass up *(slang)*, put the finger on *(informal)*, dob in *(Austral. slang)* • *Fraudsters are often shopped by honest friends and neighbours.*
▸ IN PHRASES: **all over the shop** = **everywhere**, all over, all around, the world over, high and low, in each place, in every nook and cranny, ubiquitously, far and wide *or* near, to *or* in every place • *This gave him the freedom to make trouble all over the shop.*
shop around = **search**, look, hunt, cast around, leave no stone unturned, scout about, look high and low • *He shopped around for a firm that would be flexible.*
shut up shop = **close down**, shut down, cease trading, wind up a business, discontinue trading • *They shut up shop and fled the country.*

shopkeeper = **retailer**, trader, tradesman, dealer, seller, salesman, vendor, shop owner, saleswoman • *a struggling shopkeeper unable to pay his rent*

shopper = **buyer**, customer, client, purchaser • *crowds of Christmas shoppers*

shopping = **purchases**, buys, acquisitions • *We put the shopping away.*

shopping centre = **shopping complex**, shopping mall, shopping precinct, shopping arcade, gallery, parade of shops • *The new shopping centre was built at a cost of 1.1 million.*

shore = **beach**, coast, sands, strand *(poetic)*, lakeside, waterside, seaboard *(chiefly U.S.)*, foreshore, seashore • *He made it to the shore after leaving the boat.*
▸ RELATED ADJECTIVE: littoral

shore up = **support**, strengthen, reinforce, prop, brace, underpin, augment, buttress • *They may find it hard to shore up their defences.*

short AS AN ADJECTIVE **1** = **brief**, quick, fleeting, short-term, lightning, short-lived, momentary, cursory • *We had a short meeting.*
OPPOSITES: long, extended, long-term
2 = **concise**, brief, succinct, contracted, clipped, compact, summary, compressed, curtailed, terse, laconic, pithy, abridged, compendious, sententious • *This is a short note to say thank you.*
OPPOSITES: long, prolonged, lengthy
3 = **small**, little, wee, tiny, squat, diminutive, petite, pint-sized *(informal)*, dumpy, dwarfish, knee high to a grasshopper, fubsy *(archaic or dialect)*, knee high to a gnat • *I'm tall and thin and he's short and fat.*
OPPOSITES: big, tall, lofty
4 = **abrupt**, sharp, terse, curt, blunt, crusty, gruff, brusque, offhand, testy, impolite, discourteous, uncivil • *She was definitely short with me.*
OPPOSITES: civil, polite, courteous
5 = **crumbly**, crisp, brittle, friable • *a crisp short pastry*
6 = **direct**, straight, undeviating, through • *a short route through the town*
7 = **scarce**, wanting, low, missing, limited, lacking, tight, slim, inadequate, insufficient, slender, scant, meagre, sparse, deficient, scanty • *Money was short in those days.*
OPPOSITES: sufficient, adequate, plentiful
▸ AS AN ADVERB = **abruptly**, suddenly, unaware, by surprise, without warning • *He had no insurance and was caught short when his house was burgled.*
OPPOSITES: slowly, gradually, gently
▸ IN PHRASES: **cut someone short** = **stop**, interrupt, cut in on, butt in on • *His father cut him short.*
cut something short = **curtail**, stop, reduce, halt, dock, terminate, abbreviate • *They had to cut short their holiday.*
in short = **briefly**, in essence, in a word, in a nutshell, to cut a long story short, to come to the point, to put it briefly • *In short, it is a treaty that everyone should be pleased with.*
short of 1 = **except for**, apart from, other than, besides, save • *They have no means, short of civil war, to enforce their will.*
2 = **lacking**, wanting, low on, in need of, deficient in, strapped for *(slang)* • *Her father's illness left the family short of money.*

shortage = **deficiency**, want, lack, failure, deficit, poverty, shortfall, inadequacy, scarcity, dearth, paucity, insufficiency • *There's no shortage of ideas.*
OPPOSITES: excess, surplus, abundance

shortcoming = **failing**, fault, weakness, defect, flaw, drawback, imperfection, frailty, foible, weak point • *His book has its shortcomings.*

shorten 1 = **cut**, reduce, decrease, cut down, trim, diminish, dock, cut back, prune, lessen, curtail, abbreviate, truncate, abridge, downsize • *The day surgery will help to shorten waiting lists.*
OPPOSITES: increase, extend, expand
2 = **turn up**, trim • *It's a simple matter to shorten trouser legs.*
3 = **get shorter**, contract, diminish, dwindle, shrink • *When the days shorten, some people suffer from depression.*

shortfall = **deficit**, shortage, deficiency, loss, default, arrears • *The government has refused to make up a shortfall in funding.*

short-lived = **brief**, short, temporary, fleeting, passing, transient, ephemeral, transitory, impermanent • *Any hope that the speech would end the war was short-lived.*

shortly 1 = **soon**, presently, before long, anon *(archaic)*, in a little while, any minute now, erelong *(archaic or poetic)* • *Their trial will begin shortly.*
2 = **curtly**, sharply, abruptly, tartly, tersely, succinctly, briefly, concisely, in a few words • *'I don't know you,' he said shortly, 'and I'm in a hurry.'*

short-sighted 1 = **near-sighted**, myopic, blind as a bat • *Testing showed her to be very short-sighted.*

S

2 = imprudent, injudicious, ill-advised, unthinking, careless, impractical, ill-considered, improvident, impolitic, seeing no further than (the end of) your nose • *I think we're being very short-sighted.*

short-staffed = undermanned, understaffed, short-handed, below strength • *The hospital is desperately short-staffed.*

short-tempered = quick-tempered, impatient, touchy, irascible, fiery, peppery, ratty (*Brit. & N.Z. informal*), testy, chippy (*informal*), hot-tempered, choleric • *I'm a bit short-tempered sometimes.*

shot AS A NOUN **1 = discharge**, report, gunfire, crack, blast, explosion, bang • *Guards at the training base heard the shots.*
2 = ammunition, bullet, slug, pellet, projectile, lead, ball • *These guns are lighter and take more shot for their size.*
3 = marksman, shooter, rifleman, markswoman • *He was not a particularly good shot because of his eyesight.*
4 = strike, hit, throw, kick, pitch, stroke, lob • *He had only one shot at goal.*
5 = photograph, photo, picture, still, print, slide, snap, proof, snapshot, transparency • *He received praise for the monochrome shots in the film.*
6 = attempt, go (*informal*), try, turn, chance, effort, opportunity, crack (*informal*), essay, stab (*informal*), endeavour • *He will be given a shot at the world title.*
7 = injection, jab, dose, measure, quantity, draught, booster, dosage, vaccination, immunization, inoculation • *a shot of the drug Nembutal*
▸ IN PHRASES: **a shot in the arm = boost**, lift, encouragement, push, stimulus, tonic, impetus, pick-me-up, fillip, geeing-up • *A win would provide a much-needed shot in the arm for the team.*
a shot in the dark = guess, speculation, conjecture, surmise, wild guess • *It was a shot in the dark but I decided to write to him.*
by a long shot 1 = by far, undoubtedly, without doubt, far and away, indubitably • *He's missed the mark by a long shot.*
2 = by any means, in any circumstances, on any account • *This isn't over by a long shot.*
call the shots = have control, rule, have the power, call the tune, hold the purse strings, dominate • *The directors call the shots.*
have a shot = make an attempt, have a go, try, have a crack (*informal*), try your luck, have a stab (*informal*), have a bash (*informal*), tackle • *Why don't you have a shot at it?*
like a shot = at once, immediately, in a flash, quickly, eagerly, unhesitatingly, like a bat out of hell (*slang*) • *I heard the key in the front door and I was out of bed like a shot.*
long shot = outsider, outside chance, slim chance, fat chance (*informal*), remote possibility, chance in a million • *The prospect of them being freed is not such a long shot.*

shoulder AS A VERB **1 = bear**, carry, take on, accept, assume, be responsible for, take upon yourself • *He has to shoulder the responsibilities of his father's mistakes.*
2 = push, thrust, elbow, shove, jostle, press • *He shouldered past her and opened the door.*
▸ IN PHRASES: **a shoulder to cry on = comfort**, help, support, relief, encouragement, consolation, succour • *He sometimes saw me as a shoulder to cry on.*
give someone the cold shoulder = snub, ignore, blank (*slang*), put down, shun, rebuff, kick in the teeth (*slang*), ostracize, send someone to Coventry, cut (*informal*) • *He was given the cold shoulder by his former friends.*
rub shoulders with someone = mix with, associate with, consort with, hobnob with, socialize with, fraternize with • *I was destined to rub shoulders with the most unexpected people.*
shoulder to shoulder 1 = side by side, abreast, next to each other • *walking shoulder to shoulder with their heads bent against the rain*
2 = together, united, jointly, as one, in partnership, in cooperation, in unity • *My party will stand shoulder to shoulder with the Prime Minister and his Government.*
straight from the shoulder = frankly, directly, straight, plainly, candidly, outright, unequivocally, man to man, pulling no punches (*informal*), with no holds barred • *I want you to give me the truth, straight from the shoulder.*

shoulder blade
▸ TECHNICAL NAME: scapula

shout AS A VERB **= cry (out)**, call (out), yell, scream, roar, wail, shriek, bellow, bawl, holler (*informal*), raise your voice, hollo • *We began to shout for help.*
▸ AS A NOUN **= cry**, call, yell, scream, roar, wail, shriek, bellow • *I heard a distant shout.*
▸ IN PHRASES: **shout someone down = drown out**, overwhelm, drown, silence • *The hecklers began to shout down the speakers.*

shove AS A VERB **1 = push**, shoulder, thrust, elbow, drive, press, crowd, propel, jostle, impel • *He shoved her out of the way.*
2 = stick, push, thrust, ram, plonk, park • *He shoved a cloth into my hand.*
▸ AS A NOUN **= push**, knock, thrust, elbow, bump, nudge, jostle • *She gave Gracie a shove in the back.*
▸ IN PHRASES: **shove off = go away**, leave, clear off (*informal*), depart, go to hell (*informal*), push off (*informal*), fuck off (*offensive taboo slang*), bugger off (*taboo slang*), slope off, pack your bags (*informal*), scram (*informal*), get on your bike (*Brit. slang*), bog off (*Brit. slang*), take yourself off, vamoose (*slang, chiefly U.S.*), sling your hook (*Brit. slang*), rack off (*Austral. & N.Z. slang*) • *Why don't you just shove off and leave me alone?*

shovel AS A NOUN **= spade**, scoop • *She dug the foundation with a pick and shovel.*
▸ AS A VERB **1 = move**, scoop, dredge, shift, load, heap • *He had to get out and shovel snow.*
2 = stuff, spoon, ladle • *shovelling food into his mouth*

show AS A VERB **1 = indicate**, demonstrate, prove, reveal, display, evidence, point out, manifest, testify to, evince, flag up • *These figures show an increase in unemployment.*
OPPOSITES: refute, disprove, deny
2 = display, exhibit, put on display, present, disclose, unveil, put on show, expose to view, put before the public • *What made you decide to show your paintings?*
3 = guide, lead, conduct, accompany, direct, steer, escort, usher • *Let me show you to my study.*
4 = demonstrate, describe, explain, teach, illustrate, instruct • *Claire showed us how to make a chocolate roulade.*
5 = be visible, be seen, be obvious, be in view, be revealed • *I'd driven both ways down this road, but the tracks didn't show.*
OPPOSITES: be invisible
6 = express, display, reveal, indicate, register, demonstrate, disclose, convey, manifest, divulge, make plain, make known, evince • *She had enough time to show her gratitude.*
OPPOSITES: hide, mask, conceal
7 = turn up, come, appear, arrive, attend, show up (*informal*), get here, materialize, put in *or* make an appearance • *There was always a chance he wouldn't show.*
8 = broadcast, transmit, air, beam, relay, televise, put on the air, podcast • *The drama will be shown on American TV.*
▸ AS A NOUN **1 = display**, view, sight, spectacle, array • *Spring brings a lovely show of green and yellow striped leaves.*
2 = exhibition, fair, display, parade, expo (*informal*), extravaganza, exposition, pageant, pageantry • *the Chelsea flower show*
3 = appearance, display, impression, pose, profession, parade, ostentation • *The change in government is more for show than for real.*
4 = pretence, appearance, semblance, illusion, pretext, likeness, affectation • *We need to make a show of acknowledging their expertise.*

5 = programme, broadcast, presentation, production • *I had my own TV show.*
6 = entertainment, performance, play, production, drama, musical, presentation, theatrical performance • *How about going to see a show in London?*
▸ **IN PHRASES: show off = boast**, brag, blow your own trumpet, swagger, hot-dog *(chiefly U.S.)*, showboat, strut your stuff *(chiefly U.S.)*, make a spectacle of yourself • *He had been showing off at the poker table.*
show someone up = embarrass, shame, let down, mortify, put to shame, show in a bad light • *He wanted to teach her a lesson for showing him up.*
show something off = exhibit, display, parade, advertise, demonstrate, spread out, flaunt • *She was showing off her engagement ring.*
show something up = reveal, expose, highlight, pinpoint, unmask, lay bare, put the spotlight on • *The awards showed up the fact that TV has been a washout this year.*
show up 1 = stand out, be visible, be conspicuous, appear, catch the eye, leap to the eye • *The orange tip shows up well against most backgrounds.*
2 = arrive, come, turn up, appear, make an appearance, put in an appearance, show your face • *Many workers failed to show up for work today.*

showcase = display, model, ideal, showpiece, paragon, perfect example, exemplar • *The country sees itself as a showcase for capitalism.*

showdown = confrontation, crisis, clash, moment of truth, face-off *(slang)* • *They may be pushing him towards a final showdown with his party.*

shower AS A NOUN 1 = deluge, fall, sprinkling, flurry, downpour, light fall • *a shower of rain*
2 = storm, rain, volley, barrage, stream, torrent, fusillade • *a shower of meteorites*
3 = profusion, abundance, plethora, inundation • *They were reunited in a shower of kisses and tears.*
▸ **AS A VERB 1 = cover**, dust, spray, sprinkle • *They were showered with rice in the traditional manner.*
2 = inundate, load, heap, lavish, pour, deluge • *He showered her with emeralds and furs.* • *She showered gifts on us.*

showing 1 = display, staging, presentation, exhibition, demonstration • *a private showing of the hit film*
2 = performance, demonstration, track record, show, appearance, impression, account of yourself • *On this showing he has a big job ahead of him.*

showman = performer, entertainer, artiste, player, show-off, extrovert, Thespian, trouper, play-actor, actor *or* actress • *I think Kasparov's a bit of a showman.*

show-off = exhibitionist, boaster, swaggerer, hot dog *(chiefly U.S.)*, poseur, egotist, braggart, braggadocio, peacock, figjam *(Austral. slang)* • *He's outgoing, but not a show-off.*

showpiece = display, model, ideal, showcase, paragon, perfect example, exemplar • *The factory is a showpiece of Western investment in the East.*

showy = ostentatious, flamboyant, flashy, flash *(informal)*, loud, over the top *(informal)*, brash, pompous, pretentious, gaudy, garish, tawdry, splashy *(informal)*, tinselly • *They were smart but not showy.*
OPPOSITES: quiet, restrained, tasteful

shred AS A VERB = tear up, rip up, cut up, mince, chop finely • *They may be shredding the documents.*
▸ **AS A NOUN 1 = strip**, bit, piece, scrap, fragment, rag, ribbon, snippet, sliver, tatter • *Cut the cabbage into fine long shreds.*
2 = particle, trace, scrap, grain, atom, jot, whit, iota • *There is not a shred of truth in this story.*

shrew[1] = nag, fury, dragon *(informal)*, spitfire, virago, vixen, harpy, harridan, termagant *(rare)*, scold, Xanthippe, ballbreaker *(slang)* • *After the first visit he announced that his stepmother was a shrew.*

shrew[2]
▸ **RELATED ADJECTIVE:** soricine

SHREWS AND OTHER INSECTIVORES

desman	shrew *or* shrewmouse	star-nosed mole
elephant shrew	shrew mole	tenrec
mole	solenodon	tree shrew
moon rat		water shrew

shrewd = astute, clever, sharp, knowing, fly *(slang)*, keen, acute, smart, calculated, calculating, intelligent, discriminating, cunning, discerning, sly, canny, perceptive, wily, crafty, artful, far-sighted, far-seeing, long-headed, perspicacious, sagacious • *She's a shrewd businesswoman.* • *a shrewd guess*
OPPOSITES: stupid, naive, gullible

shrewdly = astutely, perceptively, cleverly, knowingly, artfully, cannily, with consummate skill, sagaciously, far-sightedly, perspicaciously, with all your wits about you • *'I don't see you offering to help', he observed shrewdly.*

shrewdness = astuteness, cleverness, sharpness, judgment, grasp, penetration, acumen, suss *(slang)*, discernment, perspicacity, sagacity, smartness, quick wits, acuteness, canniness • *His natural shrewdness tells him what is needed to succeed.*

shriek AS A VERB = scream, cry, yell, howl, wail, whoop, screech, squeal, holler • *She shrieked and leapt from the bed.*
▸ **AS A NOUN = scream**, cry, yell, howl, wail, whoop, screech, squeal, holler • *a shriek of joy*

shrill AS AN ADJECTIVE = piercing, high, sharp, acute, piping, penetrating, screeching, high-pitched, ear-splitting, ear-piercing • *the shrill whistle of the engine*
OPPOSITES: deep, soft, soothing
▸ **AS A VERB = ring**, buzz, trill • *The phone shrilled nearby, making her jump.*

shrine 1 = holy place, temple, sanctuary, altar, church, tabernacle, Holy City, place of pilgrimage • *the holy shrine of Mecca*
2 = memorial, tribute, cairn, monument • *a shrine to the dead and the missing*
3 = vault, crypt, catacomb, sepulchre • *He was given his ceremonial shave in front of the family shrine.*

shrink AS A VERB = decrease, dwindle, lessen, grow *or* get smaller, contract, narrow, diminish, fall off, shorten, wrinkle, wither, drop off, deflate, shrivel, downsize • *The vast forests have shrunk.*
OPPOSITES: increase, expand, grow
▸ **AS A NOUN = psychiatrist**, psychologist, psychotherapist, psychoanalyst, head shrinker *(informal)* • *I've seen a shrink already.*
▸ **IN PHRASES: shrink back = recoil**, cringe, draw back, withdraw, wince, shy away, flinch, quail, cower, hang back • *She shrank back with an involuntary gasp.*
shrink from something *or* **someone = shy away from**, recoil from, flinch from, think twice about, fight shy of, baulk at, be averse to, have qualms about, have scruples about • *They didn't shrink from danger.*

shrivel = wither, dry (up), wilt, shrink, wrinkle, dwindle, dehydrate, desiccate, wizen • *The plant shrivels and dies.*

shrivelled = withered, dry, dried up, wrinkled, shrunken, wizened, desiccated, sere *(archaic)* • *It looked old and shrivelled.*

shroud AS A NOUN 1 = winding sheet, grave clothes, cerecloth, cerement • *a burial shroud*

2 = **covering**, veil, mantle, screen, cloud, pall • *a parked car huddled under a shroud of grey snow*
▸ **AS A VERB** = **conceal**, cover, screen, hide, surround, blanket, veil, cloak, swathe, envelop • *Mist shrouded the outline of the palace.*

shrub
▹ *See panel* **Shrubs**

shrug off = **disregard**, reject, dispel, spurn, repudiate, brush off, pooh-pooh, put out of your mind • *He shrugged off the criticism.*

shudder **AS A VERB** = **shiver**, shake, tremble, quake, quiver, convulse • *She shuddered with cold.*
▸ **AS A NOUN** = **shiver**, trembling, tremor, quiver, spasm, convulsion • *She recoiled with a shudder.*

shuffle 1 = **shamble**, stagger, stumble, lumber, dodder • *She shuffled across the kitchen.*
2 = **scuffle**, drag, scrape, scuff • *He shuffled his feet along the gravel path.*
3 = **rearrange**, jumble, reorganize, mix, shift, disorder, disarrange, intermix • *The silence lengthened as he unnecessarily shuffled some papers.*

shun = **avoid**, steer clear of, keep away from, snub, evade, eschew, shy away from, brush off, cold-shoulder, have no part in, fight shy of, give (someone *or* something) a wide berth, body-swerve (*Scot.*), give (someone) the brush-off, keep your distance from • *From that time forward everybody shunned him.*

shut **AS A VERB** = **close**, secure, fasten, bar, seal, slam, push to, draw to, padlock • *Just make sure you shut the gate after you.*
OPPOSITES: open, unlock, unfasten
▸ **AS AN ADJECTIVE** = **closed**, fastened, sealed, locked • *A smell of burning came from behind the shut door.*
OPPOSITES: open, ajar, unfastened
▸ **IN PHRASES: shut down** = **stop work**, halt work, cease operating, close down, cease trading, discontinue, wind up business • *Smaller constructors had been forced to shut down.*
shut someone off = **cut off**, isolate, detach, separate, divorce, segregate, sequester, set apart • *She shut herself off from all the social aspects of life.*
shut someone out = **exclude**, bar, keep out, black, lock out, ostracize, debar, blackball • *I was set to shut out anyone else who came knocking.*
shut someone up 1 = **silence**, gag, hush, muzzle, fall silent, button it (*slang*), pipe down (*slang*), hold your tongue, put a sock in it (*Brit. slang*), keep your trap shut (*slang*), cut the cackle (*informal*), button your lip (*slang*) • *A sharp put-down was the only way he knew of shutting her up.*
2 = **confine**, cage, imprison, keep in, box in, intern, incarcerate, coop up, immure • *They shut him up in a windowless tower.*
shut something down 1 = **switch off**, close down • *The rollercoaster was shut down yesterday.*
2 = **close down**, shut up, put into receivership, discontinue, liquidate • *They've begun action to have the business shut down.*
shut something in = **confine**, cage, enclose, imprison, impound, pound, wall off *or* up • *The door enables us to shut the birds in in bad weather.*
shut something off = **block off**, stop, halt, arrest, obstruct, impede • *They have shut off all supplies to farmers.*
shut something out = **block out**, screen, hide, cover, mask, veil • *I shut out the memory that was too painful to dwell on.*
shut up = **be quiet**, hush, fall silent, button it (*slang*), pipe down (*slang*), hold your tongue, put a sock in it (*Brit. slang*), keep your trap shut (*slang*), cut the cackle (*informal*), button your lip (*slang*) • *Why don't you just shut up for a minute?*
shut yourself away = **hide away**, hole up, lie low, go into hiding, go underground, take cover, go to ground • *He had again shut himself away in his darkened studio.*

shutter = **blind**, screen, shade, curtain, canopy, louvre • *She opened the shutters and gazed out over roofs.*

shuttle = **go back and forth**, commute, go to and fro, alternate, ply, shunt, seesaw • *They have shuttled back and forth between the three capitals.*

shy[1] **AS AN ADJECTIVE** 1 = **timid**, self-conscious, bashful, reserved, retiring, nervous, modest, aw-shucks, shrinking, backward, coy, reticent, self-effacing, diffident, mousy • *He is painfully shy when it comes to talking to women.*
OPPOSITES: forward, confident, assured
2 = **cautious**, wary, hesitant, suspicious, reticent, distrustful, chary • *You should not be shy of having your say.*
OPPOSITES: rash, reckless, unsuspecting
▸ **AS A VERB** *sometimes with* **off** *or* **away** = **recoil**, flinch, draw back, start, rear, buck, wince, swerve, balk, quail, take fright • *The horse shied as the wind sent sparks flying.*
▸ **IN PHRASES: fight shy of something** = **avoid**, dodge, duck (out of) (*informal*), eschew, shirk • *Dermatologists fight shy of any question about hormones.*
shy away from something = **shrink from**, flinch from, fight shy of, baulk at, think twice about, recoil from, be averse to, have misgivings about • *We frequently shy away from making decisions.*

shy[2] = **throw**, send, cast, pitch, toss, hurl, fling, chuck (*informal*), propel, sling, lob (*informal*)

shyness = **timidity**, self-consciousness, bashfulness, modesty, nervousness, lack of confidence, reticence,

SHRUBS

acacia
acanthus
arbutus
banksia
bauera
bilberry
black boy *or* yacca (bush) (*Austral.*)
blackcurrant
blackthorn
blueberry
bluebush
boronia
bottlebrush (*Austral.*)
box
bramble
briar
broom
buckthorn
buddleia
camellia
caper
Christmas bush (*Austral.*)
clematis
coca
correa
cotton
cottonbush (*Austral.*)
cottonwood,
blanket bush, tawine, *or* tauhinu (*Austral.*)
cranberry
crowea
crown-of-thorns
daphne
dogwood
emu bush (*Austral.*)
eriostemon
forsythia
frangipani
fuchsia
gardenia
geebung (*Austral.*)
Geraldton waxflower (*Austral.*)
gooseberry
gorse
grevillea
hakea (*Austral.*)
hawthorn
heath
heather
honeysuckle
hydrangea
jasmine
juniper
kerrawang (*Austral.*)
laburnum
laurel
lilac
liquorice
magnolia
mistletoe
mock orange
myrtle
oleander
olearia *or* daisy bush (*Austral.*)
pittosporum
pituri (*Austral.*)
poinsettia
poison ivy
poison oak
potentilla
privet
pyracantha
raspberry
redcurrant
rhododendron
rose
rosemary
rue
saltbush (*Austral.*)
strawberry
tea
thyme
waratah (*Austral.*)
wax(flower) (*Austral.*)

diffidence, timorousness, mousiness, timidness • *Eventually he overcame his shyness.*

sibling = **brother** *or* **sister** • *His siblings are mostly in their early twenties.*

sick AS AN ADJECTIVE 1 = **unwell**, ill, poorly *(informal)*, diseased, weak, crook *(Austral. & N.Z. informal)*, under par *(informal)*, ailing, feeble, laid up *(informal)*, under the weather, indisposed, on the sick list *(informal)* • *He's very sick.*
OPPOSITES: well, fit, healthy
2 = **nauseous**, ill, queasy, nauseated, bilious, green about the gills *(informal)*, qualmish • *The very thought of food made him feel sick.*
3 = **tired**, bored, fed up, weary, glutted, jaded, blasé, satiated • *I am sick of hearing all these people moaning.*
4 = **disappointed**, upset, depressed, gutted, disgusted, discouraged, choked, disillusioned, discontented, disgruntled, saddened, disenchanted, displeased, despondent, downhearted • *We were sick to concede that third goal.*
5 = **morbid**, cruel, sadistic, black, offensive, gruesome, macabre, ghoulish • *a sick joke about a cat*
▸ AS A NOUN = **vomit**, puke *(slang)* • *a dog examining a pile of sick*
▸ IN PHRASES: **be sick** = **vomit**, throw up *(informal)*, puke *(slang)*, chuck *(Austral. & N.Z. informal)*, heave, retch, barf *(U.S. slang)*, chunder *(slang, chiefly Austral.)*, upchuck *(U.S. slang)*, do a technicolour yawn *(slang)*, spew out *or* up, toss your cookies *(U.S. slang)* • *It was distressing to see her being sick all the time.*

sicken AS A VERB 1 = **disgust**, revolt, nauseate, repel, gross out *(U.S. slang)*, turn your stomach, make your gorge rise • *What he saw there sickened him, despite years of police work.*
2 = **fall ill**, take sick, ail, go down with something, contract something, be stricken by something • *Many of them sickened and died.*
▸ IN PHRASES: **sicken for something** = **fall ill with**, get, go down with, contract, be stricken with, show symptoms of, take ill with • *I think he must be sickening for something.*
sicken of something *or* **someone** = **grow tired of**, tire of, weary of, have had enough of, become bored with, become jaded by • *They sickened of their image as the hippies of hip-hop.*

sickening = **disgusting**, revolting, vile, offensive, foul, distasteful, repulsive, nauseating, loathsome, nauseous, gut-wrenching, putrid, stomach-turning *(informal)*, cringe-making *(Brit. informal)*, noisome, yucky *or* yukky *(slang)*, yucko *(Austral. slang)* • *This was a sickening attack on a defenceless woman.*
OPPOSITES: delightful, pleasant, wholesome

sickly 1 = **unhealthy**, weak, delicate, ailing, feeble, infirm, in poor health, indisposed • *He had been a sickly child.*
2 = **pale**, washed out, wan, pasty, bloodless, pallid, sallow, ashen-faced, waxen, peaky • *his pale, sickly face and woebegone expression*
3 = **nauseating**, revolting *(informal)*, cloying, icky *(informal)* • *the sickly smell of rum*
4 = **sentimental**, romantic, sloppy *(informal)*, corny *(slang)*, cheesy *(informal)*, mushy *(informal)*, weepy *(informal)*, slushy *(informal)*, mawkish, tear-jerking *(informal)*, schmaltzy *(slang)*, gushy *(informal)* • *a sickly sequel to the flimsy series*
5 = **insipid**, pale, washed out, colourless, faint, milky, light-coloured, whitish • *Wallpapers are too often designed in sickly pastel shades.*

sickness 1 = **illness**, disorder, ailment, disease, complaint, bug *(informal)*, affliction, malady, infirmity, indisposition, lurgy *(informal)* • *a sickness that affects children*
2 = **nausea**, queasiness, biliousness • *He felt a great rush of sickness.*
3 = **vomiting**, nausea, upset stomach, throwing up, puking *(slang)*, retching, barfing *(U.S. slang)* • *Symptoms include sickness and diarrhoea.*

side AS A NOUN 1 = **border**, margin, boundary, verge, flank, rim, perimeter, periphery, extremity, edge • *Park at the side of the road.*
OPPOSITES: centre, heart, middle
2 = **face**, surface, plane, facet • *The copier only copies onto one side of the paper.*
3 = **half**, part • *the right side of your face*
4 = **district**, area, region, quarter, sector, neighbourhood, vicinity, locality, locale, neck of the woods *(informal)* • *He lives on the south side of Edinburgh.*
5 = **party**, camp, faction, cause • *Both sides appealed for a new ceasefire.*
6 = **point of view**, viewpoint, position, opinion, angle, slant, way of thinking, standpoint • *those with the ability to see all sides of a question*
7 = **team**, squad, crew, line-up • *Italy were the better side.*
8 = **aspect**, feature, angle, facet • *He is in charge of the civilian side of the UN mission.*
▸ AS AN ADJECTIVE = **subordinate**, minor, secondary, subsidiary, lesser, marginal, irrelevant, indirect, peripheral, incidental, ancillary, extraneous, non-essential • *The refugees were treated as a side issue.*
OPPOSITES: main, middle, central
▸ IN PHRASES: **side by side** = **shoulder to shoulder**, abreast, alongside each other, cheek by jowl • *We're usually working side by side with the men.*
side with someone = **support**, back, champion, agree with, stand up for, second, prefer, favour, defend, team up with *(informal)*, go along with, befriend, join with, sympathize with, be loyal to, take the part of, associate yourself with, ally yourself with • *They side with the forces of evil.*
▸ RELATED ADJECTIVE: lateral

PROVERBS
There are two sides to every question

side-effect = **spin-off**, result, consequence, outcome, legacy, aftermath, repercussion • *One side-effect of modern life is stress.*

sideline
▸ IN PHRASES: **stand on the sidelines** = **not get involved**, not take part, not participate, be passive • *They have just stood on the sidelines and let the situation get worse.*

sidelong = **sideways**, indirect, oblique, covert, surreptitious, sideward • *She gave him a quick sidelong glance.*

side-splitting = **hilarious**, hysterical, uproarious, farcical, rollicking • *a side-splitting joke*

sidestep = **avoid**, dodge, evade, duck *(informal)*, skirt, skip, bypass, elude, circumvent, find a way round, body-swerve *(Scot.)* • *He was trying to sidestep responsibility.*

sidetrack = **distract**, divert, lead off the subject, deflect, lead away, draw away • *They have a tendency to try to sidetrack you.*

sidewalk = **pavement**, footpath *(Austral. & N.Z.)* • *She stepped off a New York sidewalk into the path of oncoming traffic.*

sideways AS AN ADVERB 1 = **indirectly**, covertly, obliquely, surreptitiously, furtively • *He glanced sideways at her.*
2 = **to the side**, laterally, crabwise • *They moved sideways, their arms still locked together.*
▸ AS AN ADJECTIVE = **sidelong**, side, covert, slanted, oblique, furtive, surreptitious • *Alfred shot him a sideways glance.*

sidle = **edge**, steal, slink, inch, ghost, creep, sneak • *A young man sidled up to me and said, 'May I help you?'*

siege = **blockade**, encirclement, besiegement • *We must do everything possible to lift the siege.*

siesta = **nap**, rest, sleep, doze, kip *(Brit. slang)*, snooze *(informal)*, catnap, forty winks *(informal)*, zizz *(Brit. informal)* • *Many cultures have a siesta during the hottest part of the day.*

S

sieve AS A NOUN = **strainer**, sifter, colander, screen, riddle, tammy cloth • *Press the raspberries through a fine sieve to form a puree.*

▸ AS A VERB = **sift**, part, filter, strain, separate, pan, bolt, riddle • *Sieve the icing sugar into the bowl.*

sift 1 = **part**, filter, strain, separate, pan, bolt, riddle, sieve • *Sift the flour and baking powder into a medium-sized mixing bowl.*

2 = **examine**, investigate, go through, research, screen, probe, analyse, work over, pore over, scrutinize • *He has sifted the evidence and summarised it clearly.*

sigh AS A VERB 1 = **breathe out**, exhale, moan, suspire (archaic) • *Dad sighed and stood up.*

2 = **moan**, complain, groan, mourn, grieve, lament, sorrow • *'Everyone forgets,' she sighed.*

3 = **rustle**, whisper, murmur, sough • *The wind sighed through the valley.*

▸ AS A NOUN = **exhalation**, moan, groan • *She heaved a weary sigh.*

▸ IN PHRASES: **sigh for something** *or* **someone** = **long for**, yearn for, pine for, mourn for, languish over, eat your heart out over • *sighing for the good old days*

sight AS A NOUN 1 = **vision**, eyes, eyesight, seeing, eye • *My sight is failing and I can't see to read any more.*

2 = **appearance**, view, sighting, glimpse • *I faint at the sight of blood.*

3 = **spectacle**, show, scene, display, exhibition, vista, pageant • *Among the most spectacular sights are the great sea-bird colonies.*

4 = **attraction**, place of interest, view, wonder, landmark, monument, curiosity, marvel • *I am going to show you the sights of our wonderful city.*

5 = **view**, field of vision, range of vision, eyeshot, viewing, ken, visibility • *The Queen's carriage came into sight.*

6 = **perception**, opinion, judgment, thinking, belief, point of view, outlook, viewpoint, standpoint • *reasons which will justify it in the sight of God and Man*

7 = **eyesore**, mess, spectacle, fright (informal), monstrosity, blot on the landscape (informal) • *She looked a sight in the street-lamps.*

▸ AS A VERB = **spot**, see, observe, notice, distinguish, perceive, make out, discern, behold • *A fleet of ships was sighted in the North Sea.*

▸ IN PHRASES: **catch sight of something** *or* **someone** = **see**, spot, glimpse, view, clock (Brit. informal), recognize, spy, espy, descry • *Every time I catch sight of myself in the mirror, I feel so disappointed.*

set your sights on something *or* **someone** = **aim for**, want, aspire to, try for, strive for, have designs on • *They have set their sights on the world record.*

▸ RELATED ADJECTIVES: optical, visual

PROVERBS

Out of sight, out of mind

sign AS A NOUN 1 = **symbol**, mark, character, figure, device, representation, logo, badge, emblem, ensign, cipher • *Equations are generally written with a two-bar equals sign.*

2 = **figure**, form, shape, outline • *The priest made the sign of the cross over him.*

3 = **gesture**, signal, motion, indication, cue, gesticulation • *They gave him the thumbs-up sign.*

4 = **notice**, board, warning, signpost, placard, road sign, traffic sign • *a sign saying that the highway was closed*

5 = **indication**, evidence, trace, mark, note, signal, suggestion, symptom, hint, proof, gesture, clue, token, manifestation, giveaway, vestige, spoor • *His face and movements rarely betrayed any sign of nerves.*

6 = **omen**, warning, portent, foreboding, presage, forewarning, writing on the wall, augury, auspice, wake-up call • *It is a sign of things to come.*

▸ AS A VERB 1 = **gesture**, indicate, signal, wave, beckon, gesticulate, use sign language • *She signed to me to go out.*

2 = **autograph**, initial, inscribe, subscribe, set your hand to • *I got him to sign my copy of his book.*

▸ IN PHRASES: **sign on** = **get unemployment benefit**, draw benefit, get income support, get jobseekers' allowance • *I had to accept that I was unemployed and that I would have to sign on.*

sign someone up = **engage**, recruit, employ, take on, hire, contract, take on board (informal), put on the payroll, take into service • *Spalding wants to sign you up.*

sign something away = **give up**, relinquish, renounce, lose, transfer, abandon, surrender, dispose of, waive, forgo • *The Duke signed away his inheritance.*

sign up = **enlist**, join, volunteer, register, enrol, join up • *He signed up as a steward.*

signal AS A NOUN 1 = **flare**, rocket, beam, beacon, smoke signal, signal fire • *They fired three distress signals.*

2 = **cue**, sign, nod, prompting, go-ahead (informal), reminder, green light • *You mustn't fire without my signal.*

3 = **sign**, gesture, indication, mark, note, evidence, expression, proof, token, indicator, manifestation • *The event was seen as a signal of support.*

▸ AS A VERB 1 = **gesture**, sign, wave, indicate, nod, motion, beckon, gesticulate, give a sign to • *She signalled a passing taxi.*

2 = **show**, express, display, indicate, make known, announce, declare, register, communicate, proclaim, flag up • *The country was signalling its readiness to have the embargo lifted.*

3 = **mark**, announce, signify, be a sign of, identify, flag • *The siren signalled the end of play.*

significance = **importance**, import, consequence, matter, moment, weight, consideration, gravity, relevance, magnitude, seriousness, impressiveness, noteworthiness • *ideas about the social significance of religion*

significant 1 = **important**, marked, notable, striking, serious, material, vital, critical, considerable, impressive, pronounced, conspicuous, momentous, weighty, noteworthy • *It is the first drug that seems to have a significant effect on this disease.*

OPPOSITES: insignificant, unimportant, inconsequential

2 = **meaningful**, expressive, eloquent, knowing, telling, meaning, expressing, pregnant, indicative, suggestive • *The old woman gave her a significant glance.*

OPPOSITES: meaningless

significantly 1 = **very much**, greatly, hugely, vastly, notably, considerably, remarkably, enormously, immensely, tremendously, markedly, by much • *The number supporting him had increased significantly.*

2 = **meaningfully**, eloquently, expressively, knowingly, suggestively, in a telling manner • *She looked up at me significantly, raising an eyebrow.*

signify 1 = **indicate**, show, mean, matter, suggest, announce, evidence, represent, express, imply, exhibit, communicate, intimate, stand for, proclaim, convey, be a sign of, symbolize, denote, connote, portend, betoken, flag up • *The two approaches signified a sharp difference between the men.*

2 = **make known**, show, express, indicate, announce, display, declare, signal, register, communicate, proclaim, flag up • *Two jurors signified their dissent.*

silence AS A NOUN 1 = **quiet**, peace, calm, hush, lull, stillness, quiescence, noiselessness • *They stood in silence.*

OPPOSITES: sound, noise, racket

2 = **reticence**, dumbness, taciturnity, speechlessness, muteness, uncommunicativeness, voicelessness • *The court ruled that his silence should be entered as a plea of not guilty.*

OPPOSITES: talk, talking, speech

S

▸ **AS A VERB** 1 = **quieten**, still, quiet, cut off, subdue, stifle, cut short, quell, muffle, deaden, strike dumb • *The shock silenced him completely.*
OPPOSITES: rouse, amplify, make louder
2 = **suppress**, gag, muzzle, censor, stifle • *He tried to silence anyone who spoke out against him.*
OPPOSITES: support, encourage
3 = **kill**, do in *(informal)*, eliminate *(slang)*, take out *(slang)*, dispatch, bump off *(slang)*, rub out *(U.S. slang)* • *A hit man had been sent to silence her.*

QUOTATIONS
Silence is the virtue of fools
[Francis Bacon *Advancement of Learning*]
Silence is more eloquent than words
[Thomas Carlyle *Heroes and Hero-Worship*]

PROVERBS
Silence is golden
Silence means consent

silent 1 = **mute**, dumb, speechless, wordless, mum, struck dumb, voiceless, unspeaking • *They both fell silent.*
OPPOSITES: noisy, chattering, rowdy
2 = **uncommunicative**, quiet, taciturn, tongue-tied, unspeaking, nonvocal, not talkative • *He was a serious, silent man.*
3 = **quiet**, still, hushed, soundless, noiseless, muted, stilly *(poetic)* • *The heavy guns have again fallen silent.*
OPPOSITES: noisy, loud, piercing
4 = **unspoken**, implied, implicit, tacit, understood, unexpressed • *He watched with silent contempt.*

silently 1 = **quietly**, in silence, soundlessly, noiselessly, inaudibly, without a sound • *as silently as a mouse*
2 = **mutely**, dumbly, in silence, wordlessly, speechlessly, reticently, uncommunicatively, unspeakingly • *He could no longer stand by silently while these rumours persisted.*

silhouette **AS A NOUN** = **outline**, form, shape, profile, delineation • *The dark silhouette of the castle ruins.*
▸ **AS A VERB** = **outline**, define, delineate, etch, demarcate, delimit • *firefighters silhouetted against the burning wreckage*

silky = **smooth**, soft, sleek, velvety, silken, lustrous, satiny • *I stroked her silky hair.*

silly **AS AN ADJECTIVE** 1 = **stupid**, ridiculous, absurd, daft, inane, childish, immature, senseless, frivolous, preposterous, giddy, goofy *(informal)*, idiotic, dozy *(Brit. informal)*, fatuous, witless, puerile, brainless, asinine, dumb-ass *(slang)*, cockamamie *(slang, chiefly U.S.)*, dopy *(slang)* • *That's a silly thing to say.*
OPPOSITES: smart, clever, intelligent
2 = **foolish**, stupid, unwise, inappropriate, rash, irresponsible, reckless, foolhardy, idiotic, thoughtless, imprudent, inadvisable • *Don't go doing anything silly, now, will you?*
OPPOSITES: wise, sensible, prudent
3 = **senseless**, stupid, numb, into oblivion, groggy, stupefied, into a stupor • *Right now the poor old devil's drinking himself silly.*
▸ **AS A NOUN** = **fool**, idiot, twit *(informal)*, goose *(informal)*, clot *(Brit. informal)*, wally *(slang)*, prat *(slang)*, plonker *(slang)*, duffer *(informal)*, simpleton, ignoramus, nitwit *(informal)*, ninny, silly-billy *(informal)*, dweeb *(U.S. slang)*, putz *(U.S. slang)*, eejit *(Scot. & Irish)*, thicko *(Brit. slang)*, doofus *(slang, chiefly U.S.)*, nerd *or* nurd *(slang)*, dorba *or* dorb *(Austral. slang)*, bogan *(Austral. slang)* • *Come on, silly, we'll miss all the fun.*

silt **AS A NOUN** = **sediment**, deposit, residue, ooze, sludge, alluvium • *The lake was almost solid with silt and vegetation.*
▸ **IN PHRASES:** **silt something up** = **clog up**, block up, choke up, obstruct, stop up, jam up, dam up, bung up, occlude, congest • *The soil washed from the hills is silting up the dams.*

silver **AS A NOUN** 1 = **silverware**, silver plate • *He beat the rugs and polished the silver.*
2 = **silver coins**, coins, loose change, (small) change • *the basement where £150,000 in silver was buried*
3 = **second prize**, silver medal • *They followed it up by winning silver in the World Cup.*
▸ **AS AN ADJECTIVE** = **snowy**, white, grey, silvery, greyish-white, whitish-grey • *He had thick silver hair which needed cutting.*
▸ **RELATED ADJECTIVE:** argent

similar 1 = **alike**, uniform, resembling, corresponding, comparable, much the same, akin, indistinguishable, homogeneous, of a piece, homogenous, cut from the same cloth, congruous • *The sisters looked very similar.*
OPPOSITES: different, opposite, dissimilar
2 *with* **to** = **like**, much the same as, comparable to, analogous to, close to, cut from the same cloth as • *The accident was similar to one that happened in 1973.*

similarity = **resemblance**, likeness, sameness, agreement, relation, correspondence, analogy, affinity, closeness, kinship, concordance, congruence, comparability, point of comparison, similitude, indistinguishability • *the astonishing similarity between my brother and my eldest son*
OPPOSITES: difference, dissimilarity, disparity

PROVERBS
Birds of a feather flock together

similarly 1 = **in the same way**, the same, identically, in a similar fashion, uniformly, homogeneously, undistinguishably • *Most of the men who now gathered round him were similarly dressed.*
2 = **likewise**, in the same way, by the same token, correspondingly, in like manner • *Similarly a baby's cry is instantly identified by the mother.*

simmer **AS A VERB** 1 = **bubble**, stew, boil gently, seethe, cook gently • *Turn the heat down so the sauce simmers gently.*
2 = **fume**, seethe, smoulder, burn, smart, rage, boil, be angry, see red *(informal)*, be tense, be pissed (off) *(taboo slang)*, be agitated, be uptight *(informal)* • *He simmered with rage.*
▸ **IN PHRASES:** **simmer down** = **calm down**, grow quieter, control yourself, unwind *(informal)*, contain yourself, collect yourself, cool off *or* down, get down off your high horse *(informal)* • *After an hour or so, she finally managed to simmer down.*

simper = **smile coyly**, smirk, smile self-consciously, smile affectedly • *The maid lowered her chin and simpered.*

simpering = **coy**, affected, flirtatious, coquettish, kittenish • *a simpering little ninny*

simple 1 = **uncomplicated**, clear, plain, understandable, coherent, lucid, recognizable, unambiguous, comprehensible, intelligible, uninvolved • *simple pictures and diagrams*
OPPOSITES: involved, difficult, complicated
2 = **easy**, straightforward, not difficult, light, elementary, manageable, effortless, painless, uncomplicated, undemanding, easy-peasy *(slang)* • *The job itself had been simple enough.*
3 = **plain**, natural, basic, classic, severe, Spartan, uncluttered, unadorned, unfussy, unembellished, bare-bones • *She's shunned Armani for a simple blouse and jeans.*
OPPOSITES: elaborate, intricate, ornate
4 = **pure**, mere, sheer, unalloyed • *His refusal to talk was simple stubbornness.*
5 = **artless**, innocent, naive, natural, frank, green, sincere, simplistic, unaffected, childlike, unpretentious, unsophisticated, ingenuous, guileless • *He was as simple as a child.*
OPPOSITES: worldly, smart, sophisticated
6 = **unpretentious**, modest, humble, homely, lowly, rustic, uncluttered, unfussy, unembellished • *It was a simple home.*
OPPOSITES: fancy, extravagant, flashy

simple-minded = **stupid**, simple, foolish, backward, idiot, retarded, idiotic, moronic, brainless, feeble-minded, addle-brained, dead from the neck up *(informal)*, a bit lacking *(informal)*, dim-witted • *She was a simple-minded romantic.*

simpleton = **halfwit**, fool, idiot, charlie *(Brit. informal)*, goose *(informal)*, dope *(informal)*, jerk *(slang, chiefly U.S. & Canad.)*, plank *(Brit. slang)*, berk *(Brit. slang)*, wally *(slang)*, booby, coot, moron, geek *(slang)*, twit *(informal, chiefly Brit.)*, chump, dunce, imbecile *(informal)*, oaf, dullard, jackass, dipstick *(Brit. slang)*, dickhead *(slang)*, gonzo *(slang)*, schmuck *(U.S. slang)*, dork *(slang)*, nitwit *(informal)*, dolt, blockhead, greenhorn *(informal)*, ninny, divvy *(Brit. slang)*, nincompoop, dweeb *(U.S. slang)*, putz *(U.S. slang)*, fathead *(informal)*, Simple Simon, weenie *(U.S. informal)*, eejit *(Scot. & Irish)*, thicko *(Brit. slang)*, dumb-ass *(slang)*, gobshite *(Irish taboo slang)*, numpty *(Scot. informal)*, doofus *(slang, chiefly U.S.)*, fuckwit *(taboo slang)*, dickwit *(slang)*, nerd *or* nurd *(slang)*, numskull *or* numbskull, twerp *or* twirp *(informal)*, dorba *or* dorb *(Austral. slang)*, bogan *(Austral. slang)* • *He was a lightweight, a political simpleton.*

simplicity 1 = **straightforwardness**, ease, clarity, obviousness, easiness, clearness, absence of complications, elementariness • *The apparent simplicity of his plot is deceptive.*
OPPOSITES: difficulty, complexity, intricacy
2 = **plainness**, restraint, purity, clean lines, naturalness, lack of adornment • *fussy details that ruin the simplicity of the design*
OPPOSITES: decoration, embellishment, elaborateness

simplify = **make simpler**, facilitate, streamline, disentangle, dumb down, make intelligible, reduce to essentials, declutter • *The aim of the scheme is to simplify the system.*

simplistic = **oversimplified**, shallow, facile, naive, oversimple • *The logic behind the questions is too simplistic.*

simply 1 = **just**, only, merely, purely, solely • *The table is simply a chip-board circle on a base.*
2 = **totally**, really, completely, absolutely, altogether, wholly, utterly, unreservedly • *He's simply wonderful in every respect.*
3 = **clearly**, straightforwardly, directly, plainly, intelligibly, unaffectedly • *The book is clearly and simply written.*
4 = **plainly**, naturally, severely, starkly, modestly, with restraint, unpretentiously, without decoration, unelaborately, without any elaboration • *He dressed simply and led a quiet family life.*
5 = **without doubt**, surely, certainly, definitely, unquestionably, undeniably, unmistakably, beyond question, come hell or high water *(informal)*, beyond a shadow of (a) doubt • *It was simply the greatest night any of us ever had.*

simulate 1 = **pretend**, act, feign, affect, assume, put on, reproduce, imitate, sham, fabricate, counterfeit, make believe • *They rolled about, simulating a bloodthirsty fight.*
2 = **look like**, imitate • *The wood had been painted to simulate stone.*

simulated 1 = **pretended**, put-on, feigned, assumed, artificial, make-believe, insincere, phoney *or* phony *(informal)* • *He performed a simulated striptease.*
2 = **synthetic**, artificial, fake, substitute, mock, imitation, man-made, sham, pseudo *(informal)* • *a necklace of simulated pearls*

simulation = **copy**, reproduction, replica, imitation, duplicate, facsimile • *a simulation of the greenhouse effect*

simultaneous = **coinciding**, parallel, concurrent, synchronized, concomitant, contemporaneous, coincident, synchronous, happening at the same time • *The film will provide simultaneous translation in both English and Chinese.*

simultaneously = **at the same time**, together, all together, in concert, in unison, in parallel, concurrently, in the same breath, in chorus • *The two guns fired almost simultaneously.*

sin AS A NOUN 1 = **wickedness**, wrong, evil, crime, error, trespass, blasphemy, immorality, transgression, iniquity, irreverence, sinfulness, impiety, unrighteousness, ungodliness • *Sin can be forgiven, but never condoned.*
2 = **crime**, offence, misdemeanour, error, lapse, wrongdoing, misdeed, transgression, act of evil, guilt • *Was it a sin to have believed too much in themselves?*
▸ AS A VERB = **transgress**, offend, lapse, err, trespass *(archaic)*, fall from grace, go astray, commit a sin, do wrong • *They charged him with sinning against God and man.*
▸ RELATED MANIA: hamartiomania
▸ RELATED PHOBIA: hamartiophobia

QUOTATIONS

I count religion but a childish toy
And hold there is no sin but ignorance
[Christopher Marlowe *The Jew of Malta*]

The wages of sin is death
[*Bible: Romans*]

more sinn'd against than sinning
[William Shakespeare *King Lear*]

All good biography, as all good fiction, comes down to the study of original sin, of our inherent disposition to choose death when we ought to choose life
[Rebecca West *Time and Tide*]

There's no such thing as an original sin
[Elvis Costello *I'm not Angry*]

Though your sins be as scarlet, they shall be as white as snow
[*Bible: Isaiah*]

He that toucheth pitch shall be defiled therewith
[*Bible: Ecclesiasticus*]

If we say that we have no sin, we deceive ourselves, and the truth is not in us
[*Bible: I John*]

It is public scandal that constitutes offence, and to sin in secret is not to sin at all
[Molière *Le Tartuffe*]

PROVERBS

Old sins cast long shadows

SEVEN DEADLY SINS

anger	envy	pride
covetousness *or* avarice	gluttony	sloth
	lust	

sincere = **honest**, genuine, real, true, serious, natural, earnest, frank, open, straightforward, candid, unaffected, no-nonsense, heartfelt, upfront *(informal)*, bona fide, wholehearted, dinkum *(Austral. & N.Z. informal)*, artless, guileless, unfeigned • *He accepted her apologies as sincere.*
OPPOSITES: put on, false, pretended

sincerely = **honestly**, really, truly, genuinely, seriously, earnestly, wholeheartedly, in good faith, in earnest, in all sincerity, from the bottom of your heart • *He sincerely believed that she was acting in his interest.*

sincerity = **honesty**, truth, candour, frankness, seriousness, good faith, probity, bona fides, genuineness, straightforwardness, artlessness, guilelessness, wholeheartedness • *The film is made with sincerity.*

sinecure = **cushy number** *(informal)* = **honesty**, gravy train *(slang)*, soft option, soft job *(informal)*, money for jam *or* old rope *(informal)* • *a lucrative sinecure with a big law firm*

sinewy = **muscular**, strong, powerful, athletic, robust, wiry, brawny • *a short, sinewy young man*

sinful = **wicked**, bad, criminal, guilty, corrupt, immoral, erring, unholy, depraved, iniquitous, ungodly, irreligious,

unrighteous, morally wrong • *He reminded us that such behaviour was sinful in the eyes of God.*
OPPOSITES: godly, moral, virtuous

sing **AS A VERB** **1 = croon**, carol, chant, trill, warble, yodel, pipe, vocalize • *Go on, then, sing us a song!*
2 = trill, chirp, warble, make melody • *Birds were already singing in the garden.*
▸ **IN PHRASES: sing out = call (out)**, cry (out), shout, yell, holler *(informal)*, halloo • *'See you,' Jeff sang out.*

singe = burn, sear, scorch, char, blacken • *Her hair was singed and her anorak was burnt.*

singer = vocalist, crooner, minstrel, soloist, cantor, troubadour, chorister, chanteuse *fem.*, balladeer, songster *or* songstress • *My mother was a singer in a dance band.*

single **AS AN ADJECTIVE** **1 = one**, sole, lone, solitary, only, only one, unique, isolated, singular • *A single shot rang out.*
2 = individual, particular, separate, distinct • *Every single house had been damaged.*
3 = unmarried, free, unattached, on the shelf, a bachelor, unwed, a spinster, partnerless, spouseless • *The last I heard she was still single, still out there.*
4 = separate, individual, exclusive, undivided, unshared • *A single room at the hotel costs £36 a night.*
5 = simple, unmixed, unblended, uncompounded • *single malt whisky*
▸ **IN PHRASES: single something** *or* **someone out = pick**, choose, select, separate, distinguish, fix on, set apart, winnow, put on one side, pick on *or* out, flag up • *He singled me out for special attention.*

single-handed = unaided, on your own, by yourself, alone, independently, solo, without help, unassisted, under your own steam • *I brought up my seven children single-handed.*

single-minded = determined, dogged, fixed, dedicated, stubborn, tireless, steadfast, unwavering, unswerving, hellbent *(informal)*, undeviating, monomaniacal • *a single-minded determination to win*

singly = one by one, individually, one at a time, separately, one after the other • *Patients went singly into the consultation room.*

sing-song = droning, repetitive, monotonous, boring, uniform, unchanging, monotone, soporific, repetitious, toneless, samey *(informal)*, uninflected • *He started to speak in a nasal sing-song voice.*

singular **1 = single**, individual • *The pronoun 'you' can be singular or plural.*
2 = remarkable, unique, extraordinary, outstanding, exceptional, rare, notable, eminent, uncommon, conspicuous, prodigious, unparalleled, noteworthy • *a smile of singular sweetness*
OPPOSITES: common, normal, ordinary
3 = unusual, odd, strange, extraordinary, puzzling, curious, peculiar, eccentric, out-of-the-way, queer, oddball *(informal)*, atypical, wacko *(slang)*, outré, out there *(slang)*, daggy *(Austral. & N.Z. informal)* • *He was without doubt a singular character.*
OPPOSITES: common, normal, conventional

singularity = oddity, abnormality, eccentricity, peculiarity, strangeness, idiosyncrasy, irregularity, particularity, oddness, queerness, extraordinariness, curiousness • *his abrupt, turbulent style and the singularity of his appearance*

singularly = remarkably, particularly, exceptionally, especially, seriously *(informal)*, surprisingly, notably, unusually, extraordinarily, conspicuously, outstandingly, uncommonly, prodigiously • *a singularly ill-judged enterprise*

sinister = threatening, evil, menacing, forbidding, dire, ominous, malign, disquieting, malignant, malevolent, baleful, injurious, bodeful • *There was something sinister about him that she found disturbing.*
OPPOSITES: good, encouraging, reassuring

sink **AS A NOUN** **= basin**, washbasin, hand basin, wash-hand basin • *The sink was full of dirty dishes.*
▸ **AS A VERB** **1 = scupper**, scuttle • *In a naval battle your aim is to sink the enemy's ship.*
2 = go down, founder, go under, submerge, capsize • *The boat was beginning to sink fast.*
3 = descend, lower, go down, dip, fall, disappear • *Far off to the west the sun was sinking.*
OPPOSITES: arise, ascend
4 = slump, drop, flop, collapse, droop, plonk yourself *(informal)*, plump yourself • *Kate laughed, and sank down again to her seat.*
5 = fall, drop, decline, slip, plunge, plummet, subside, relapse, abate, retrogress • *Pay increases have sunk to around seven per cent.*
6 = drop, fall, get lower, get softer, get quieter • *Her voice had sunk to a whisper.*
7 = stoop, descend, be reduced to, succumb, lower yourself, debase yourself, demean yourself • *You know who you are, be proud of it and don't sink to his level.*
8 = decline, die, fade, fail, flag, weaken, diminish, decrease, deteriorate, decay, worsen, dwindle, lessen, degenerate, depreciate, go downhill *(informal)* • *He's still alive, but sinking fast.*
OPPOSITES: rise, increase, improve
9 = dig, bore, drill, drive, lay, put down, excavate • *the site where Stephenson sank his first mineshaft*
10 = invest, put in, plough, risk, lay out • *He has already sunk $25 million into the project.*
11 = drink, down, knock back, neck *(slang)*, swill, quaff, polish off, gulp down • *She sank two glasses of white wine.*
▸ **IN PHRASES: sink in = be understood**, register *(informal)*, penetrate, get through to, make an impression, be taken hold of • *The implication took a while to sink in.*

sinner = wrongdoer, offender, evildoer, trespasser *(archaic)*, reprobate, miscreant, malefactor, transgressor • *I was shown that I was a sinner, that I needed to repent.*

sinuous **1 = supple**, flexible, lithe, graceful, agile, slinky, limber, pliable, pliant, lissom(e), loose-jointed, loose-limbed • *the sinuous approach of a snake*
2 = curving, winding, meandering, crooked, coiling, tortuous, undulating, serpentine, curvy, lithe, twisty, mazy • *I drove along sinuous mountain roads.*

sip **AS A VERB** **= drink**, taste, sample, sup • *Jessica sipped her drink thoughtfully.*
▸ **AS A NOUN** **= swallow**, mouthful, swig, drop, taste, slurp, thimbleful • *Harry took a sip of bourbon.*

siren **1 = alert**, warning, signal, alarm • *It sounds like an air raid siren.*
2 = seductress, vamp *(informal)*, femme fatale *(French)*, witch, charmer, temptress, Lorelei, Circe • *She's a voluptuous siren with a husky voice.*

sissy *or* **cissy** **AS A NOUN** **= wimp**, softie *(informal)*, weakling, baby, wet *(Brit. informal)*, coward *(informal)*, jessie *(Scot. slang)*, pansy, pussy *(slang, chiefly U.S.)*, pussycat *(Brit. informal)*, mummy's boy, mollycoddle, namby-pamby, wuss *(slang)*, milksop, milquetoast *(U.S.)*, sisspot *(informal)* • *They were rough kids and thought we were sissies.*
▸ **AS AN ADJECTIVE** **= wimpish** *or* **wimpy** *(informal)*, soft *(informal)*, weak, wet *(Brit. informal)*, cowardly, feeble, unmanly, effeminate, namby-pamby, wussy *(slang)*, sissified *(informal)* • *Far from being sissy, it takes a real man to admit he's not perfect.*

sister **AS A NOUN** **1 = sibling**, relation, relative, kin, kinswoman • *The two sisters look nothing like one another.*
2 = fellow woman, colleague, associate, comrade, compatriot • *Modern woman has been freed from many of the duties that befell her sisters in times past.*
▸ **AS AN ADJECTIVE** **= affiliated**, allied, associated, joined,

S

linked, connected, incorporated, confederated, federated • *a sister organization*

sit AS A VERB 1 = **take a seat**, perch, settle down, be seated, take a pew, plant yourself, park yourself, plonk yourself, take the weight off your feet, install yourself, ensconce yourself • *Eva pulled up a chair and sat beside her husband.*
2 = **place**, set, put, park, position, rest, lay, settle, deposit, dump, situate, plonk • *She found her chair and sat it in the usual spot.*
3 = **pose**, model • *She was sitting for the artist for 8 hours.*
4 = **be a member of**, serve on, have a seat on, preside on • *He was asked to sit on numerous committees.*
5 = **convene**, meet, assemble, officiate, be in session • *Parliament sits for only 28 weeks out of 52.*
6 = **be situated**, stand, lie, be placed, be positioned • *Our new house sat next to a stream.*
7 = **babysit**, childmind • *I've asked Mum to sit for us next Saturday.*
▸ IN PHRASES: **sit about** *or* **around** = **laze about** *or* **around**, hang about *or* around, loaf about *or* around, loll about *or* around, lounge about *or* around, stand about *or* around, idle about *or* around • *She isn't the type to sit around doing nothing.*
sit in on something = **attend**, watch, observe, be present at • *Perhaps ministers could sit in on the classes.*
sit up = **stay up**, stay awake, not go to bed • *I didn't feel like sitting up all night.*

site AS A NOUN 1 = **area**, ground, plot, patch, tract • *He became a hod carrier on a building site.*
2 = **location**, place, setting, point, position, situation, spot, whereabouts, locus • *the site of Moses' tomb*
3 = **website** • *This is a fun and cool site.*
▸ AS A VERB = **locate**, put, place, set, position, establish, install, situate • *He said chemical weapons had never been sited in Germany.*

sitting 1 = **session**, period • *Dinner was in two sittings.*
2 = **meeting**, hearing, session, congress, consultation, get-together *(informal)* • *the recent emergency sittings*

sitting room = **living room**, lounge, drawing room, front room, family room • *I went into the sitting room and turned on the television.*

situate = **locate**, set, base, position, site • *The pain was situated above and below the eyes.*

situation 1 = **position**, state, case, condition, circumstances, equation, plight, status quo, state of affairs, ball game *(informal)*, kettle of fish *(informal)* • *We are in a difficult financial situation.*
2 = **scenario**, the picture *(informal)*, the score *(informal)*, state of affairs, equation, state of play, lie of the land • *They looked at each other and weighed up the situation.*
3 = **location**, place, setting, position, seat, site, spot, locality, locale • *The garden is in a beautiful situation.*

six
▸ RELATED ADJECTIVE: sixth
▸ RELATED PREFIXES: sex-, hexa-

sixth sense = **intuition**, second sight, clairvoyance, feyness • *He has a sixth sense for finding people who have good ideas.*

size AS A NOUN = **dimensions**, extent, measurement(s), range, amount, mass, length, volume, capacity, proportions, bulk, width, magnitude, greatness, vastness, immensity, bigness, largeness, hugeness • *books of various sizes*
▸ IN PHRASES: **cut someone down to size** = **weaken**, crush, disable, silence, suppress, sabotage, impair, repress, sap, quash, debilitate, quell, stamp out, subvert, disempower • *The once powerful unions have been cut down to size.*
size something *or* **someone up** = **assess**, evaluate, appraise, take stock of, eye up, get the measure of, get (something) taped *(Brit. informal)* • *He spent the evening sizing me up intellectually.*

sizeable *or* **sizable** = **large**, considerable, substantial, goodly, decent, respectable, tidy *(informal)*, decent-sized, largish • *These polls give the candidate a very sizeable vote.*

sizzle = **hiss**, spit, crackle, sputter, fry, frizzle • *The sausages and the burgers sizzled on the barbecue.*

skeletal 1 = **emaciated**, wasted, gaunt, skin-and-bone *(informal)*, cadaverous, hollow-cheeked, lantern-jawed, fleshless, worn to a shadow • *a hospital filled with skeletal children*
2 = **incomplete**, inadequate, insufficient, wanting, lacking, partial, patchy, deficient, scrappy, fragmentary, bitty • *Passenger services can best be described as skeletal.*

skeleton AS A NOUN 1 = **bones**, bare bones • *a human skeleton*
2 = **frame**, shell, framework, basic structure • *Only skeletons of buildings remained in the area.*
3 = **plan**, structure, frame, draft, outline, framework, sketch, abstract, blueprint, main points • *a skeleton of policy guidelines*
▸ AS A MODIFIER = **minimum**, reduced, minimal, essential • *Only a skeleton staff remains to see anyone interested around the site.*

sketch AS A NOUN 1 = **drawing**, design, representation, draft, delineation • *a sketch of a soldier*
2 = **draft**, outline, framework, plan, frame, rough, skeleton, blueprint, layout, lineament(s) • *I had a basic sketch of a plan.*
3 = **skit**, piece, scene, turn, act, performance, item, routine, number • *a five-minute humorous sketch*
▸ AS A VERB 1 = **draw**, paint, outline, represent, draft, portray, depict, delineate, rough out • *I sketched the scene with my pen and paper.*
2 = **summarize**, give a summary of, give a resume of, go through the main points of • *He sketched the story briefly.*
▸ IN PHRASES: **sketch something out** = **outline**, describe, map out, plot, block out, give an idea of, rough out • *A settlement was sketched out at a meeting of Russian ministers.*

sketchily = **incompletely**, roughly, imperfectly, hastily, perfunctorily, patchily, cursorily • *The ideas seem sketchily developed and the images vague.*

sketchy = **incomplete**, rough, vague, slight, outline, inadequate, crude, superficial, unfinished, skimpy, scrappy, cursory, perfunctory, cobbled together, bitty • *Details of what actually happened are still sketchy.*
OPPOSITES: full, detailed, complete

skew = **distort**, slant, misrepresent, colour, twist, weigh, bias, falsify • *This figure is skewed because much of the work still hasn't been done.*

skewer = **pierce**, gore, impale, spike, spear, bayonet • *He skewered his victim through the neck.*

skid AS A VERB = **slide**, slip, slither, coast, glide, skim, veer, toboggan • *The car pulled up too fast and skidded on the shoulder of the road.*
▸ IN PHRASES: **on the skids** = **in trouble**, breaking down, on the rocks, going downhill, be on its last legs, falling apart at the seams • *My marriage was on the skids.*

skilful = **expert**, skilled, masterly, trained, experienced, able, professional, quick, clever, practised, accomplished, handy, competent, tasty *(Brit. informal)*, apt, adept, proficient, adroit, dexterous • *his skilful use of light and shade*
OPPOSITES: awkward, bungling, clumsy

skill = **expertise**, ability, proficiency, experience, art, technique, facility, talent, intelligence, craft, competence, readiness, accomplishment, knack, ingenuity, finesse, aptitude, dexterity, cleverness, quickness, adroitness, expertness, handiness, skilfulness • *The cut of a diamond depends on the skill of its craftsman.*
OPPOSITES: inability, incompetence, clumsiness

skilled = **expert**, professional, accomplished, trained, experienced, able, masterly, practised, tasty *(Brit. informal)*, skilful, proficient, a dab hand at *(Brit. informal)* • *skilled workers, such as plumbers*
OPPOSITES: inexperienced, unskilled, unqualified

skim AS A VERB **1** = **remove**, separate, cream, take off, spoon off, ladle off • *Skim off the fat.*
2 = **glide**, fly, coast, plane, sail, float, brush, dart, scud • *seagulls skimming over the waves*
3 *usually with* **over** *or* **through** = **scan**, glance, run your eye over, thumb *or* leaf through • *I only had time to skim over the script before I came here.*
▸ **IN PHRASES: skim something off** = **embezzle**, steal, misappropriate, trouser *(slang)*, defraud, knock off *(slang)*, spirit away • *If I read this right, he skimmed off about thirty million.*

skimp = **stint**, scrimp, be sparing with, pinch, withhold, scant, cut corners, scamp, be mean with, be niggardly, tighten your belt • *Many families must skimp on their food and other necessities.*
OPPOSITES: squander, fritter away, be extravagant

skimpy = **inadequate**, insufficient, scant, meagre, short, tight, thin, sparse, scanty, miserly, niggardly, exiguous • *skimpy underwear*

skin AS A NOUN **1** = **complexion**, colouring, skin tone, cuticle, epidermis, dermis • *His skin is clear and smooth.*
2 = **hide**, fleece, pelt, fell, integument, tegument • *That was real crocodile skin.*
3 = **peel**, rind, husk, casing, outside, crust • *banana skins*
4 = **film**, coating, coat, membrane • *Stir the custard occasionally to prevent a skin forming.*
▸ **AS A VERB 1** = **peel**, pare, hull • *two tomatoes, skinned, peeled and chopped*
2 = **scrape**, graze, bark, flay, excoriate, abrade • *He fell down and skinned his knee.*
▸ **IN PHRASES: by the skin of one's teeth** = **narrowly**, only just, by a whisker *(informal)*, by a narrow margin, by a hair's-breadth • *He won, but only by the skin of his teeth.*
get under your skin = **annoy**, irritate, aggravate *(informal)*, needle *(informal)*, nettle, irk, grate on, get on your nerves *(informal)*, piss you off *(taboo slang)*, get in your hair *(informal)*, rub you up the wrong way, hack you off *(informal)* • *Her mannerisms can just get under your skin and needle you.*
▸ **TECHNICAL NAME:** cutis
▸ **RELATED ADJECTIVES:** cutaneous, dermatoid
▸ **RELATED PHOBIA:** dermatophobia

skin-deep = **superficial**, surface, external, artificial, shallow, on the surface, meaningless • *He denies that racism is just skin-deep.*

skinny = **thin**, lean, scrawny, skeletal, emaciated, twiggy, undernourished, skin-and-bone *(informal)*, scraggy, macilent *(rare)* • *He was quite a skinny little boy.*
OPPOSITES: fat, plump, stout

skip 1 = **hop**, dance, bob, trip, bounce, caper, prance, cavort, frisk, gambol • *She was skipping along the pavement.*
2 = **miss out**, omit, leave out, overlook, pass over, eschew, forego, skim over, give (something) a miss • *It is important not to skip meals.*
3 = **miss**, cut *(informal)*, bunk off *(slang)*, play truant from, wag *(dialect)*, skive off, play hookey from *(U.S. informal)*, dog it *or* dog off *(dialect)* • *Her daughter started skipping school.*

skipper = **captain**, master • *the skipper of a fishing boat*

skirmish AS A NOUN **1** = **fight**, battle, conflict, incident, clash, contest, set-to *(informal)*, encounter, brush, combat, scrap *(informal)*, engagement, spat, tussle, fracas, affray *(Law)*, dust-up *(informal)*, scrimmage, biffo *(Austral. slang)*, boilover *(Austral.)* • *Border skirmishes are common.*
2 = **argument**, fight, row, clash, dispute, falling out *(informal)*, disagreement, feud, quarrel, barney *(informal)*, squabble, wrangle, bickering, difference of opinion, altercation, turf war *(informal)* • *This difference has led to several political skirmishes.*
▸ **AS A VERB** = **fight**, clash, come to blows, scrap *(informal)*, collide, grapple, wrangle, tussle, lock horns, cross swords • *Police skirmished with youths on a council estate last Friday.*

skirt AS A VERB **1** = **border**, edge, lie alongside, line, fringe, flank • *We raced across a large field that skirted the slope of the hill.*
2 *often with* **around** *or* **round** = **go round**, bypass, walk round, circumvent • *She skirted around the edge of the room to the door.*
3 *often with* **around** *or* **round** = **avoid**, dodge, evade, steer clear of, sidestep, circumvent, detour, fail to mention, body-swerve *(Scot.)* • *They have, until now, skirted around the issue.*
▸ **AS A NOUN** *often plural* = **border**, edge, margin, fringe, outskirts, rim, hem, periphery, purlieus • *the skirts of the hill*
▹ *See panel* **Skirts**

skit = **parody**, spoof *(informal)*, travesty, takeoff *(informal)*, burlesque, turn, sketch • *clever skits on popular songs*

skittish 1 = **nervous**, lively, excitable, jumpy, restive, fidgety, highly strung, antsy *(informal)* • *The declining dollar gave heart to skittish investors.*
OPPOSITES: relaxed, calm, steady
2 = **offbeat**, bizarre, weird, way-out *(informal)*, eccentric, novel, strange, unusual, rum *(Brit. slang)*, uncommon, Bohemian, unconventional, far-out *(slang)*, idiosyncratic, kinky *(informal)*, off-the-wall *(slang)*, unorthodox, oddball *(informal)*, left-field *(informal)*, freaky *(slang)*, wacko *(slang)*, outré, out there *(slang)* • *a fertile talent at war with a skittish sense of humour*

skive = **slack**, idle, shirk, dodge, skulk, malinger, swing the lead, gold-brick *(U.S. slang)*, bob off *(Brit. slang)*, bludge *(Austral. & N.Z. informal)*, scrimshank *(Brit. Military slang)* • *The company treated me as though I were skiving.*

skiver = **slacker**, loafer, idler, do-nothing, piker *(Austral. & N.Z. slang)*, dodger, shirker, bludger *(Austral. & N.Z. informal)*, gold brick *(U.S. slang)*, scrimshanker *(Brit. Military slang)* • *He was a skiver and a thief.*

skookum = **powerful**, influential, big, dominant, controlling, commanding, supreme, prevailing, sovereign, authoritative, puissant

skulduggery = **trickery**, swindling, machinations, duplicity, double-dealing, fraudulence, shenanigan(s) *(informal)*, unscrupulousness, underhandedness • *accusations of intimidation and political skulduggery*

skulk 1 = **creep**, sneak, slink, pad, slope, prowl, sidle • *He skulked off.*
2 = **lurk**, hide, lie in wait, loiter • *skulking in the safety of the car*

SKIRTS

A-line	filibeg	half-slip *or* waist-slip	maxiskirt	petticoat	underskirt
button-through	full skirt	hobble skirt	microskirt	puffball skirt	wrapover *or* wrapround
crinoline	fustanella *or* fustanelle	hoop skirt	midiskirt	ra-ra skirt	
dirndl	gaberdine	kilt	miniskirt	riding skirt	
divided skirt	grass skirt	lava-lava	overskirt	sarong	
drop-waisted			pencil skirt	tutu	

skull
▸ **TECHNICAL NAME:** cranium
▸ **RELATED ADJECTIVE:** cranial

sky = **heavens**, firmament, upper atmosphere, azure *(poetic)*, welkin *(archaic)*, vault of heaven, rangi *(N.Z.)* • *The sun is already high in the sky.*
▸ **RELATED ADJECTIVES:** celestial, empyrean

slab = **piece**, slice, lump, chunk, wedge, hunk, portion, nugget, wodge *(Brit. informal)* • *slabs of stone*

slack AS AN ADJECTIVE **1** = **limp**, relaxed, loose, lax, flaccid, not tight, not taut • *The electronic pads work slack muscles to astounding effect.*
2 = **loose**, hanging, flapping, baggy • *The wind had gone, leaving the sails slack.*
OPPOSITES: stretched, tight, taut
3 = **slow**, quiet, inactive, dull, sluggish, slow-moving • *busy times and slack periods*
OPPOSITES: active, busy, hectic
4 = **negligent**, lazy, lax, idle, easy-going, inactive, tardy, slapdash, neglectful, slipshod, inattentive, remiss, asleep on the job *(informal)* • *Many publishers have simply become far too slack.*
OPPOSITES: strict, exacting, meticulous
▸ AS A NOUN **1** = **surplus**, excess, overflow, leftover, glut, surfeit, overabundance, superabundance, superfluity • *Buying-to-let could stimulate the housing market by reducing the slack.*
2 = **room**, excess, leeway, give *(informal)*, play, looseness • *He cranked in the slack, and the ship was moored.*
▸ AS A VERB **1** = **shirk**, idle, relax, flag, neglect, dodge, skive *(Brit. slang)*, bob off *(Brit. slang)*, bludge *(Austral. & N.Z. informal)* • *He had never let a foreman see him slacking.*
2 = **idle**, waste time, take it easy, be lazy, doss *(Brit. slang)*, lounge about, bunk off *(informal)* • *If someone slacks, he comes down hard on them.*

slacken **1** *often with* **off** = **lessen**, reduce, decrease, ease (off), moderate, diminish, slow down, drop off, abate, let up, slack off • *Inflationary pressures continued to slacken last month.*
2 = **loosen**, release, relax, weaken, lessen, become looser • *Her grip slackened on his arm.*

slacker = **layabout**, shirker, loafer, skiver *(Brit. slang)*, idler, passenger, do-nothing, piker *(Austral. & N.Z. slang)*, dodger, good-for-nothing, bludger *(Austral. & N.Z. informal)*, gold brick *(U.S. slang)*, scrimshanker *(Brit. Military slang)* • *He's not a slacker, he's the best worker they've got.*

slag AS A NOUN = **tart** *(informal)*, scrubber *(Brit. & Austral. slang)*, whore, pro *(slang)*, brass *(slang)*, prostitute, hooker *(U.S. slang)*, hustler *(U.S. & Canad. slang)*, moll *(slang)*, call girl, courtesan, working girl *(facetious slang)*, harlot, slapper *(Brit. informal)*, streetwalker, camp follower, loose woman, fallen woman, strumpet, trollop, white slave, bawd *(archaic)*, cocotte, fille de joie *(French)* • *She became a slag, a tart, a hustler, a lost girl.*
▸ IN PHRASES: **slag something** *or* **someone off** = **criticize**, abuse, malign, slam, insult, mock, slate, slang, deride, berate, slander, diss *(slang, chiefly U.S.)*, lambast(e), flame *(informal)* • *People keep slagging me off.*

slake = **satisfy**, gratify, assuage, quench, satiate, sate • *They had to melt snow to slake their thirst.*

slam **1** = **bang**, crash, smash, thump, shut with a bang, shut noisily • *She slammed the door and locked it behind her.*
2 = **throw**, dash, hurl, fling • *They slammed him up against a wall.*
3 = **criticize**, attack, blast, pan *(informal)*, damn, slate *(informal)*, shoot down *(informal)*, castigate, vilify, pillory, tear into *(informal)*, diss *(slang, chiefly U.S.)*, lambast(e), excoriate • *The director slammed the claims as an outrageous lie.*

slander AS A NOUN = **defamation**, smear, libel, scandal, misrepresentation, calumny, backbiting, muckraking, obloquy, aspersion, detraction • *He is now suing the company for slander.*
OPPOSITES: praise, approval, acclaim
▸ AS A VERB = **defame**, smear, libel, slur, malign, detract, disparage, decry, vilify, traduce, backbite, blacken (someone's) name, calumniate, muckrake • *He has been questioned on suspicion of slandering the politician.*
OPPOSITES: approve, praise, acclaim

> **PROVERBS**
> Throw enough dirt and some will stick
> Give a dog a bad name and hang him

slanderous = **defamatory**, libellous, abusive, malicious, damaging, calumnious • *He wanted an explanation for what he described as 'slanderous' remarks.*

slang = **colloquialisms**, jargon, idioms, argot, informal language • *He liked to think he kept up with current slang.*

slanging match = **quarrel**, row, argument, set-to *(informal)*, barney *(informal)*, spat, altercation, ding-dong, argy-bargy *(Brit. informal)*, battle of words • *They conducted a public slanging match on television.*

slant AS A VERB **1** = **slope**, incline, tilt, list, bend, lean, heel, shelve, skew, cant, bevel, angle off • *The morning sun slanted through the glass roof.*
2 = **bias**, colour, weight, twist, angle, distort • *The coverage was deliberately slanted to make the home team look good.*
▸ AS A NOUN **1** = **slope**, incline, tilt, gradient, pitch, ramp, diagonal, camber, declination • *The house is on a slant.*
2 = **bias**, emphasis, prejudice, angle, leaning, point of view, viewpoint, one-sidedness • *They give a slant to every single news item that's put on the air.*

slanting = **sloping**, angled, inclined, tilted, tilting, sideways, slanted, bent, diagonal, oblique, at an angle, canted, on the bias, aslant, slantwise, atilt, cater-cornered *(U.S. informal)* • *those slanting cheekbones*

slap AS A VERB **1** = **smack**, hit, strike, beat, bang, clap, clout *(informal)*, cuff, whack, swipe, spank, clobber *(slang)*, wallop *(informal)*, lay one on *(slang)* • *He would push and slap her once in a while.*
2 = **throw**, fling, sling, stick, bung *(informal)*, plonk *(informal)* • *He slapped the cup onto the waiting saucer.*
3 = **impose**, put, place, lay, introduce, institute • *The government slapped a ban on the export of processed logs.*
4 = **plaster**, apply, spread, daub • *We now routinely slap sun screen on ourselves before venturing out.*
▸ AS A NOUN = **smack**, blow, whack, wallop *(informal)*, bang, clout *(informal)*, cuff, swipe, spank • *He reached forward and gave her a slap.*
▸ IN PHRASES: **a slap in the face** = **insult**, humiliation, snub, affront, blow, rejection, put-down, rebuke, rebuff, repulse • *They treated any pay rise of less than 5% as a slap in the face.*
a slap on the wrist = **reprimand**, row, rebuke, ticking-off *(informal)*, dressing-down *(informal)*, telling-off *(informal)*, wigging *(Brit. slang)*, censure, reproach, admonition, chastisement, reproof, castigation, rap on the knuckles, reprehension • *We got a slap on the wrist for misuse of the company equipment.*

slap-bang *or* **slap bang** = **exactly**, directly, precisely, bang, slap *(informal)*, smack *(informal)*, plumb *(informal)* • *Of course, slap-bang in the middle of town, rents are high.*

slapdash = **careless**, sloppy *(informal)*, hasty, disorderly, hurried, last-minute, messy, clumsy, negligent, untidy, haphazard, perfunctory, thoughtless, thrown-together, slovenly, slipshod • *a slapdash piece of work*
OPPOSITES: careful, meticulous, painstaking

slapstick = **farce**, horseplay, buffoonery, knockabout comedy • *inspired bursts of slapstick*

slap-up = **luxurious**, lavish, sumptuous, princely, excellent, superb, magnificent, elaborate, splendid, first-rate, no-expense-spared, fit for a king • *We usually had one slap-up meal a day.*

S

slash AS A VERB 1 = **cut**, slit, gash, lacerate, score, rend, rip, hack • *He nearly bled to death after slashing his wrists.*
2 = **reduce**, cut, decrease, drop, lower, moderate, diminish, cut down, lessen, curtail • *Everyone agrees that subsidies have to be slashed.*
3 = **cut**, lose, shed, get rid of • *They decided to slash jobs, close down plants and downsize.*
▸ AS A NOUN = **cut**, slit, gash, rent, rip, incision, laceration • *deep slashes in the meat*

slate AS A VERB 1 = **schedule**, plan, book, programme, appoint, arrange • *The meeting is slated for next Thursday.*
2 = **criticize**, blast, pan *(informal)*, slam *(slang)*, blame, roast *(informal)*, censure, rebuke, slang, scold, berate, castigate, rail against, tear into *(informal)*, lay into *(informal)*, pitch into *(informal)*, take to task, lambast(e), flame *(informal)*, excoriate, haul over the coals *(informal)*, tear (someone) off a strip *(informal)*, rap (someone's) knuckles • *Slated by critics at the time, the film has since become a classic.*
▸ IN PHRASES: **with a clean slate = afresh**, over, anew, with a clear conscience • *Try to pay everything you owe, so that you can start with a clean slate.*

slaughter AS A VERB 1 = **kill**, murder, massacre, destroy, do in *(slang)*, execute, dispatch, assassinate, blow away *(slang, chiefly U.S.)*, annihilate, bump off *(slang)* • *Thirty-four people were slaughtered while queueing up to cast their votes.*
2 = **butcher**, kill, slay, destroy, massacre, exterminate • *Whales and dolphins are still being slaughtered for commercial gain.*
3 = **defeat**, thrash, vanquish, stuff *(slang)*, tank *(slang)*, hammer *(informal)*, crush, overwhelm, lick *(informal)*, undo, rout, trounce, wipe the floor with *(informal)*, blow out of the water *(slang)* • *He slaughtered his opponent in three sets.*
▸ AS A NOUN 1 = **slaying**, killing, murder, massacre, holocaust, bloodshed, carnage, liquidation, extermination, butchery, blood bath • *The annual slaughter of wildlife is horrific.*
2 = **butchery**, killing • *sheep exported for slaughter*

slaughterhouse = **abattoir**, butchery, shambles • *horses en route to the slaughterhouse*

slave AS A NOUN 1 = **servant**, serf, vassal, bondsman, slavey *(Brit. informal)*, varlet *(archaic)*, villein, bondservant • *still living as slaves in the desert*
2 = **drudge**, skivvy *(chiefly Brit.)*, scullion *(archaic)* • *Mum says to Dad, 'I'm not your slave, you know!'*
▸ AS A VERB = **toil**, labour, grind *(informal)*, drudge, sweat, graft, slog, sweat blood, skivvy *(Brit.)*, work your fingers to the bone, work your guts out, keep your nose to the grindstone • *slaving over a hot stove*

slaver 1 = **dribble**, drool, salivate, slobber • *the wolf's slavering jaws*
2 = **drool**, salivate, slobber, dribble, drivel, water at the mouth • *No doubt many readers will slaver over these bits.*

slavery = **enslavement**, servitude, subjugation, captivity, bondage, thrall, serfdom, vassalage, thraldom • *My people have survived 300 years of slavery.*
OPPOSITES: freedom, liberty, emancipation

QUOTATIONS
There're two people in the world that are not likeable: a master and a slave
[Nikki Giovanni *A Dialogue [with James Baldwin]*]
Slavery they can have anywhere. It is a weed that grows on every soil
[Edmund Burke *On Conciliation with America*]

slavish 1 = **imitative**, unimaginative, unoriginal, conventional, second-hand, uninspired • *a slavish follower of fashion*
OPPOSITES: independent, original, imaginative
2 = **servile**, cringing, abject, submissive, grovelling, mean, low, base, fawning, despicable, menial, sycophantic, obsequious • *slavish devotion*
OPPOSITES: assertive, rebellious, wilful

slay 1 = **kill**, destroy, slaughter, eliminate, massacre, butcher, dispatch, annihilate, exterminate • *the hill where he slew the dragon*
2 = **murder**, kill, assassinate, do in *(slang)*, eliminate, massacre, slaughter, do away with, exterminate, mow down, rub out *(U.S. slang)* • *Two Australian tourists were slain.*

slaying = **killing**, murder, massacre, assassination, manslaughter, homicide, bloodshed, carnage, butchery • *a trail of motiveless slayings*

sleaze = **corruption**, fraud, dishonesty, fiddling *(informal)*, bribery, extortion, venality, shady dealings *(informal)*, crookedness *(informal)*, unscrupulousness • *porn movies and sleaze*

sleazy = **squalid**, seedy, sordid, low, rundown, tacky *(informal)*, disreputable, crummy, scungy *(Austral. & N.Z.)* • *sleazy bars*

sledge AS A NOUN = **bobsleigh**, sled *(U.S. & Canad.)*, sleigh, toboggan • *She travelled 14,000 miles by sledge.*
▸ AS A VERB = **bobsleigh**, sled (U.S.), sleigh, toboggan • *We spent the afternoon making snowmen and sledging down the hill.*

sleek 1 = **glossy**, shiny, lustrous, smooth, silky, velvety, well-groomed • *sleek black hair*
OPPOSITES: rough, shaggy, dishevelled
2 = **elegant**, stylish, chic, beautiful, fashionable, refined, graceful, tasteful • *sleek modern furniture*

sleep AS A NOUN = **slumber(s)**, rest, nap, doze, kip *(Brit. slang)*, snooze *(informal)*, repose, hibernation, siesta, dormancy, beauty sleep *(informal)*, forty winks *(informal)*, shuteye *(slang)*, zizz *(Brit. informal)* • *Try and get some sleep.*
▸ AS A VERB 1 = **slumber**, drop off *(informal)*, doze, kip *(Brit. slang)*, snooze *(informal)*, snore, hibernate, nod off *(informal)*, take a nap, catnap, drowse, go out like a light, take forty winks *(informal)*, zizz *(Brit. informal)*, be in the land of Nod, rest in the arms of Morpheus • *I've not been able to sleep for the last few nights.*
2 = **accommodate**, take, house, hold, lodge, cater for, have space for, have beds for • *The villa sleeps 10.*
▸ IN PHRASES: **get to sleep = fall asleep**, drop off, nod off • *I can't get to sleep with all that noise.*
lose any *or* **much sleep about** *or* **over something** = **worry**, brood, fret, obsess, be anxious, agonize, feel uneasy, get distressed • *I didn't lose any sleep over that investigation.*
put something to sleep = put down, destroy, put out of its misery • *We took the dog down to the vet's and had her put to sleep.*
sleep over = stay the night, stay over • *She said his friends could sleep over.*
sleep together = have sex, have sexual intercourse, make love, fuck *(taboo slang)*, screw *(taboo slang)*, shag *(taboo slang)*, do the business, get it on *(informal)*, fornicate *(archaic)*, go to bed together • *I'm pretty sure they slept together.*
sleep with someone = have sex with, make love with, fuck *(taboo slang)*, screw *(taboo slang)*, shag *(taboo slang)*, go to bed with, have sexual intercourse with, get it on with *(informal)*, do the business with, fornicate with *(archaic)* • *He was old enough to sleep with a girl and make her pregnant.*
▸ RELATED MANIA: hypnomania
▸ RELATED PHOBIA: hypnophobia

QUOTATIONS
Oh Sleep! it is a gentle thing,
Beloved from pole to pole,
To Mary Queen the praise be given!
She sent the gentle sleep from Heaven,
That slid into my soul
[Samuel Taylor Coleridge *The Ancient Mariner*]

Come, sleep, O sleep, the certain knot of peace,
The baiting place of wit, the balm of woe
[Philip Sidney *Astrophil and Stella*]
to sleep: perchance to dream
[William Shakespeare *Hamlet*]
sleep the twin of death
[Homer *Iliad*]
The sleep of a labouring man is sweet
[*Bible: Ecclesiastes*]
Care-charmer Sleep, son of the sable Night,
Brother to Death, in silent darkness born
[Samuel Daniel *Delia*]
Care-charming Sleep, thou easer of all woes,
Brother to Death
[John Fletcher *Wit Without Money*]
I sleep like a baby. I wake up every 10 minutes screaming
[Boris Jordan]

PROVERBS

One hour's sleep before midnight is worth two after

sleepiness = **drowsiness**, lethargy, torpor, heaviness, somnolence, doziness • *I was doomed to sleepiness for the remainder of the morning.*

sleepless 1 = **wakeful**, disturbed, restless, insomniac, unsleeping • *I have sleepless nights worrying about her.*
2 = **alert**, vigilant, watchful, wide awake, unsleeping • *his sleepless vigilance*

sleeplessness = **insomnia**, wakefulness • *Sleeplessness is sometimes the side effect of certain medications.*

sleepwalker = **somnambulist**, noctambulist • *Don't awaken sleepwalkers suddenly; you may frighten them into a mishap.*

sleepwalking = **somnambulism**, noctambulation, noctambulism, somnambulation • *When she was stressed, her sleepwalking started up again.*

sleepy 1 = **drowsy**, sluggish, lethargic, heavy, dull, inactive, somnolent, torpid, slumbersome • *I was beginning to feel amazingly sleepy.*
OPPOSITES: active, alert, wide-awake
2 = **soporific**, hypnotic, somnolent, sleep-inducing, slumberous • *How long we spent there in that sleepy heat, I don't know.*
3 = **quiet**, peaceful, dull, tranquil, inactive • *a sleepy little town*
OPPOSITES: active, busy, lively

sleight of hand = **trickery**, fraud, deception, cunning, deceit, treachery, guile, duplicity, legerdemain, dissimulation, craftiness, fraudulence, deceitfulness, deceptiveness • *financial sleight of hand*

slender 1 = **slim**, narrow, slight, lean, svelte, willowy, sylphlike • *He gazed at her slender neck.*
OPPOSITES: fat, stout, chubby
2 = **faint**, slight, remote, slim, thin, weak, fragile, feeble, flimsy, tenuous • *the first slender hope of peace*
OPPOSITES: good, strong, solid
3 = **meagre**, little, small, inadequate, insufficient, scant, scanty, inconsiderable • *the Government's slender 21-seat majority*
OPPOSITES: large, considerable, substantial

sleuth = **detective**, private eye (*informal*), (private) investigator, tail (*informal*), dick (*slang, chiefly U.S.*), gumshoe (*U.S. slang*), sleuthhound (*informal*) • *a tenacious sleuth*

slice AS A NOUN 1 = **piece**, segment, portion, wedge, sliver, helping, share, cut • *water flavoured with a slice of lemon*
2 = **part**, share, piece, proportion, allocation, allotment, tranche • *Fiction takes up a large slice of the publishing market.*
▸ AS A VERB = **cut**, divide, carve, segment, sever, dissect, cleave, bisect • *She sliced the cake.*
▸ IN PHRASES: **slice something off** = **cut off**, sever, chop off, hack off, shear off • *Slice off the stalks and bases of the courgettes.*

slick AS AN ADJECTIVE 1 = **efficient**, professional, smart, smooth, streamlined, masterly, sharp, deft, well-organized, adroit • *His style is slick and visually exciting.*
2 = **skilful**, deft, adroit, dextrous, dexterous, professional, polished • *a slick gear change*
OPPOSITES: amateur, crude, clumsy
3 = **glib**, smooth, sophisticated, plausible, polished, specious, meretricious • *a slick, suit-wearing detective*
4 = **glossy**, smooth, shiny, greasy, oily, silky, lustrous • *his greasy, slick hair-do*
▸ AS A VERB = **smooth**, oil, grease, sleek, plaster down, make glossy, smarm down (*Brit. informal*) • *She had slicked her hair.*

slide AS A VERB 1 = **slip**, slither, glide, skim, coast, toboggan, glissade • *She slipped and slid downhill on her backside.*
2 = **fall**, drop, descend, decline, deteriorate, degenerate, slip • *She had slid into depression.*
▸ AS A NOUN = **reduction**, fall, decrease, cut, drop, lowering, decline, slump, falling off, dwindling, lessening, diminution • *the slide in oil prices*
▸ IN PHRASES: **let something slide** = **neglect**, forget, ignore, pass over, turn a blind eye to, gloss over, push to the back of your mind, let ride • *The company had let environmental standards slide.*

slight AS AN ADJECTIVE 1 = **small**, minor, insignificant, negligible, weak, modest, trivial, superficial, feeble, trifling, meagre, unimportant, paltry, measly, insubstantial, scanty, inconsiderable • *It's only made a slight difference.*
OPPOSITES: great, large, important
2 = **slim**, small, delicate, spare, fragile, lightly-built • *a man of slight build*
OPPOSITES: solid, muscular, sturdy
▸ AS A VERB = **snub**, insult, ignore, rebuff, affront, neglect, put down, despise, scorn, disdain, disparage, cold-shoulder, treat with contempt, show disrespect for, give offence *or* umbrage to • *They felt slighted by not being adequately consulted.*
OPPOSITES: praise, flatter, compliment
▸ AS A NOUN = **insult**, snub, affront, contempt, disregard, indifference, disdain, rebuff, disrespect, slap in the face (*informal*), inattention, discourtesy, (the) cold shoulder • *a child weeping over an imagined slight*
OPPOSITES: praise, compliment, flattery

slighting = **insulting**, offensive, disparaging, derogatory, belittling, scornful, disrespectful, disdainful, supercilious, uncomplimentary • *slighting references to her age*

slightly = **a little**, a bit, somewhat, moderately, marginally, a shade, to some degree, on a small scale, to some extent *or* degree • *The house they moved to was slightly larger.*

slim AS AN ADJECTIVE 1 = **slender**, slight, trim, thin, narrow, lean, skinny, svelte, willowy, rangy, sylphlike • *She is pretty, of slim build, with blue eyes.*
OPPOSITES: wide, heavy, chubby
2 = **slight**, remote, faint, distant, fragile, slender, improbable, negligible, flimsy • *a slim chance*
OPPOSITES: good, strong
▸ AS A VERB 1 = **lose weight**, diet, get thinner, get into shape, lose some pounds, lose some inches, slenderize (*chiefly U.S.*) • *Some people will gain weight no matter how hard they try to slim.*
OPPOSITES: put on weight, build yourself up
2 = **reduce**, cut, cut down, trim, diminish, decrease, scale down, rationalize, pare down, downsize, make cutbacks in, kennet (*Austral. slang*), jeff (*Austral. slang*) • *The company recently slimmed down its product line.*

slime = **sludge**, ooze, gunge (*informal*), mud, muck, mire, gunk (*informal*), gloop (*informal*) • *the muck and slime at the bottom of the pond*

slimy 1 = **viscous**, clammy, glutinous, muddy, mucous,

gloopy *(informal)*, oozy, miry • *Her hand touched something cold and slimy.*
2 = obsequious, creepy, unctuous, smarmy *(Brit. informal)*, oily, grovelling, soapy *(slang)*, sycophantic, servile, toadying • *his slimy business partner*

sling AS A VERB **1 = throw**, cast, toss, hurl, fling, chuck *(informal)*, lob *(informal)*, heave, shy • *She slung her coat over the desk chair.*
2 = hang, swing, suspend, string, drape, dangle • *We slept in hammocks slung beneath the roof.*
▸ AS A NOUN **= harness**, support, bandage, strap • *She was back at work with her arm in a sling.*

slink = creep, steal, sneak, slip, ghost, prowl, skulk, pussyfoot *(informal)* • *He couldn't just slink away.*

slinky = figure-hugging, clinging, sleek, close-fitting, skintight • *She's wearing a slinky black mini-skirt.*

slip[1] AS A VERB **1 = fall**, trip (over), slide, skid, lose your balance, miss *or* lose your footing • *Be careful not to slip.*
2 = slide, fall, drop, slither • *The hammer slipped out of her grasp.*
3 = sneak, creep, steal, slope, sidle, move stealthily, ghost, insinuate yourself • *She slipped downstairs and out of the house.*
4 = drop, sink, plunge, slump, tumble, nosedive • *The club has slipped to the bottom of division four.*
5 = decline, fall, deteriorate, drop, worsen, wane, degenerate • *There is a general public belief that standards have slipped.*
6 = pass, elapse, roll by, wear on, tick by • *Time slipped by in silence.*
▸ AS A NOUN **= mistake**, failure, error, blunder, lapse, omission, boob *(Brit. slang)*, oversight, slip-up *(informal)*, indiscretion, bloomer *(Brit. informal)*, faux pas, slip of the tongue, imprudence, barry *or* Barry Crocker *(Austral. slang)* • *There must be no slips.*
▸ IN PHRASES: **give someone the slip = escape from**, get away from, evade, shake (someone) off, elude, lose (someone), flee, dodge, outwit, slip through someone's fingers • *He gave reporters the slip by leaving by the back door at midnight.*
let something slip = give away, reveal, disclose, divulge, leak, come out with *(informal)*, let out *(informal)*, blurt out, let the cat out of the bag • *I bet he'd let slip that I'd gone to America.*
slip away 1 = get away, escape, disappear, break away, break free, get clear of, take French leave • *He slipped away in the early hours to exile in France.*
2 = die, expire, pass away, buy it *(U.S. slang)*, check out *(U.S. slang)*, perish, kick it *(slang)*, croak *(slang)*, give up the ghost, go belly-up *(slang)*, snuff it *(slang)*, peg out *(informal)*, kick the bucket *(slang)*, buy the farm *(U.S. slang)*, peg it *(informal)*, decease, cark it *(Austral. & N.Z. slang)*, pop your clogs *(informal)*, breathe your last, hop the twig *(slang)* • *He just slipped away in my arms.*
slip something off = take off, remove, pull off, strip off, shed, discard, peel off, doff, divest yourself of • *I slipped off my woollen gloves.*
slip something on = put on, don, dress in, pull on, climb into, change into, get dressed in • *I slipped on something more comfortable and went downstairs.*
slip up = make a mistake, go wrong, blunder, mistake, boob *(Brit. slang)*, err, misjudge, miscalculate, drop a brick *or* clanger *(informal)* • *You will see exactly where you are slipping up.*

slip[2] AS A NOUN **= strip**, piece, scrap, sliver, sheet • *little slips of paper*
▸ IN PHRASES: **a slip of a = small**, little, tiny, slight, slim, delicate, slender, frail, petite, slightly built • *She was just a slip of a girl.*

slipper = carpet slipper, mule, moccasin, bedroom slipper, house-shoe • *She rushed from the scene in dressing gown and slippers.*

slippery 1 = smooth, icy, greasy, glassy, slippy *(informal or dialect)*, unsafe, lubricious *(rare)*, skiddy *(informal)* • *The floor was wet and slippery.*
2 = untrustworthy, tricky, cunning, false, treacherous, dishonest, devious, crafty, evasive, sneaky, two-faced, shifty, foxy, duplicitous • *a slippery customer*

slipshod = careless, sloppy *(informal)*, loose, slapdash, casual, untidy, slovenly, unsystematic • *The hotel had always been run in a slipshod way.*

slip-up = mistake, slip, error, misunderstanding, blunder, boob *(Brit. slang)*, oversight, misconception, gaffe, inaccuracy, howler *(informal)*, goof *(informal)*, bloomer *(Brit. informal)*, clanger *(informal)*, miscalculation, error of judgment, false move, misstep, solecism, barry *or* Barry Crocker *(Austral. slang)* • *The girls had made three crucial slip-ups.*

slit AS A VERB **= cut (open)**, rip, slash, knife, pierce, lance, gash, split open • *They say somebody slit her throat.*
▸ AS A NOUN **1 = cut**, gash, incision, tear, rent, fissure • *Make a slit in the stem.*
2 = opening, split, crack, aperture, chink, space • *She watched them through a slit in the curtain.*

slither = slide, slip, glide, snake, undulate, slink, skitter • *He slithered down the bank.*

sliver = shred, fragment, splinter, slip, shaving, flake, paring • *A sliver of glass was embedded in the skin.*

slob = layabout, lounger, loafer, couch potato *(slang)*, idler, good-for-nothing • *My boyfriend used to call me a fat slob.*

slobber = drool, dribble, drivel, salivate, slaver, slabber *(dialect)*, water at the mouth • *slobbering on his eternal cigarette end*

slog AS A VERB **1 = work**, labour, toil, slave, plod, persevere, plough through, sweat blood *(informal)*, apply yourself to, work your fingers to the bone, peg away at, keep your nose to the grindstone • *While slogging at your work, have you neglected your marriage?*
2 = trudge, tramp, plod, trek, hike, traipse *(informal)*, yomp, walk heavily, footslog • *The men had to slog up a muddy incline.*
▸ AS A NOUN **1 = work**, labour, toil, industry, grind *(informal)*, effort, struggle, pains, sweat *(informal)*, painstaking, exertion, donkey-work, blood, sweat, and tears *(informal)* • *There is little to show for two years of hard slog.*
2 = trudge, tramp, trek, hike, traipse *(informal)*, yomp, footslog • *a slog through heather and bracken*

slogan = catch phrase, motto, jingle, mantra, rallying cry, watchword, tag-line, catchword, catchcry *(Austral.)* • *a group of angry demonstrators shouting slogans*

slop AS A VERB **= spill**, splash, overflow, splatter, spatter, slosh *(informal)* • *A little cognac slopped over the edge of the glass.*
▸ AS A PLURAL NOUN **= scraps**, leftovers, dregs, debris, crumbs, detritus, leavings • *Breakfast plates were collected and the slops emptied.*

slope AS A NOUN **= inclination**, rise, incline, tilt, descent, downgrade *(chiefly U.S.)*, slant, ramp, gradient, brae *(Scot.)*, scarp, declination, declivity • *a mountain slope*
▸ AS A VERB **1 = incline**, rise, gradient, dip, descent, ramp, ascent, declivity, acclivity • *The street must have been on a slope.*
2 = slant, incline, drop away, fall, rise, pitch, lean, tilt • *The garden sloped quite steeply.*
▸ IN PHRASES: **slope off = slink away**, slip away, sneak off, steal away, make off, skulk, creep away, make yourself scarce • *She sloped off quietly on Saturday afternoon.*

sloping = slanting, leaning, inclined, inclining, oblique, atilt • *the gently sloping beach*

sloppy 1 = careless, slovenly, slipshod, messy, clumsy, untidy, amateurish, hit-or-miss *(informal)*, inattentive • *I won't accept sloppy work from my students.*

2 = **sentimental**, mushy *(informal)*, soppy *(Brit. informal)*, slushy *(informal)*, wet *(Brit. informal)*, gushing, banal, trite, mawkish, icky *(informal)*, overemotional, three-hankie *(informal)* • *some sloppy love-story*
3 = **wet**, watery, slushy, splashy, sludgy • *sloppy foods*

slosh 1 = **splash**, wash, slop, break, plash • *The water sloshed around the bridge.*
2 = **wade**, splash, flounder, paddle, dabble, wallow, swash • *We sloshed through the mud together.*

slot AS A NOUN 1 = **opening**, hole, groove, vent, slit, aperture, channel • *He dropped a coin in the slot and dialled.*
2 = **place**, time, space, spot, opening, position, window, vacancy, niche • *Visitors can book a time slot a week or more in advance.*
▸ AS A VERB = **fit**, slide, insert, put, place • *She slotted a fresh filter into the machine.*

sloth = **laziness**, inactivity, idleness, inertia, torpor, sluggishness, slackness, indolence, slothfulness, faineance • *I judged him guilty of sloth.*

slothful = **lazy**, idle, inactive, indolent, do-nothing *(informal)*, slack, sluggish, inert, skiving *(Brit. slang)*, torpid, good-for-nothing, workshy, fainéant • *He was not slothful: he had been busy all night.*

slouch = **lounge**, slump, flop, sprawl, stoop, droop, loll, lean • *She had recently begun to slouch over her typewriter.*

slouching = **shambling**, lumbering, ungainly, awkward, uncouth, loutish • *It has to be him. That slouching frame, those long arms.*

slough off = **shed**, discard, throw off, cast off, divest yourself of • *She tried to slough off her old habits.*

slovenly 1 = **untidy**, disorderly, unkempt, slatternly, daggy *(Austral. & N.Z. informal)* • *He was gruff, slovenly, and given to brooding.*
OPPOSITES: smart, trim, tidy
2 = **careless**, sloppy *(informal)*, negligent, slapdash, loose, slack, heedless, slipshod • *Such slovenly work is simply unacceptable.*
OPPOSITES: careful, meticulous, conscientious

slow AS AN ADJECTIVE 1 = **unhurried**, sluggish, leisurely, easy, measured, creeping, deliberate, lagging, lazy, plodding, slow-moving, loitering, ponderous, leaden, dawdling, laggard, lackadaisical, tortoise-like, sluggardly • *He moved in a slow, unhurried way.*
OPPOSITES: fast, quick, hurried
2 = **prolonged**, time-consuming, protracted, long-drawn-out, lingering, gradual • *The distribution of passports has been a slow process.*
3 = **unwilling**, reluctant, loath, averse, hesitant, disinclined, indisposed • *He was not slow to take up the offer.*
4 = **late**, unpunctual, behindhand, behind, tardy • *My watch is slow.*
5 = **tardy**, dilatory, late, behindhand, backward • *They have been slow in responding.*
6 = **stupid**, dim, dense, thick, dull, dumb *(informal)*, retarded, bovine, dozy *(Brit. informal)*, unresponsive, obtuse, slow on the uptake *(informal)*, braindead *(informal)*, dull-witted, blockish, slow-witted, intellectually handicapped *(Austral.)* • *He got hit in the head and he's been a bit slow since.*
OPPOSITES: quick, bright, smart
7 = **dull**, quiet, boring, dead, tame, slack, sleepy, sluggish, tedious, stagnant, unproductive, inactive, one-horse *(informal)*, uneventful, uninteresting, wearisome, dead-and-alive *(Brit.)*, unprogressive • *Island life is too slow for her liking.*
OPPOSITES: interesting, exciting, stimulating
▸ AS A VERB 1 *often with* **down** = **decelerate**, brake, lag • *The car slowed down as they passed customs.*
2 *often with* **down** = **delay**, hold up, hinder, check, restrict, handicap, detain, curb, retard, rein in • *Damage to the turbine slowed the work down.*
OPPOSITES: accelerate, speed up, quicken
▸ IN PHRASES: **slow down** = **relax**, rest, calm down, unwind, chill out *(slang, chiefly U.S.)*, take it easy, slacken (off), lighten up *(slang)*, put your feet up, hang loose *(slang)*, mellow out *(informal)*, outspan *(S. African)* • *You will need to slow down for a while.*

slowly = **gradually**, steadily, by degrees, unhurriedly, taking your time, at your leisure, at a snail's pace, in your own (good) time, ploddingly, inchmeal • *My resentment of her slowly began to fade.*
OPPOSITES: quickly, at a rate of knots *(informal)*, briskly

sludge = **sediment**, ooze, silt, mud, muck, residue, slop, mire, slime, slush, slob *(Irish)*, dregs, gloop *(informal)* • *All dumping of sludge will be banned.*

slug
▸ RELATED ADJECTIVE: limacine
▹ *See panel* **Snails, slugs and other gastropods**

sluggish = **inactive**, slow, lethargic, listless, heavy, dull, lifeless, inert, slow-moving, unresponsive, phlegmatic, indolent, torpid, slothful • *feeling sluggish and lethargic after a big meal*
OPPOSITES: lively, vigorous, energetic

sluggishness = **inactivity**, lethargy, drowsiness, apathy, inertia, stagnation, dullness, torpor, heaviness, indolence, lassitude, languor, listlessness, somnolence, slothfulness • *a medical condition which causes sluggishness and bad breath*

sluice = **drain**, cleanse, flush, drench, wash out, wash down • *sluicing off dust at the town fountain*

slum = **hovel**, ghetto, shanty • *I grew up in a slum in the East End.*

slumber AS A NOUN = **sleep**, nap, doze, rest, kip *(Brit. informal)*, snooze *(informal)*, siesta, catnap, forty winks *(informal)*, zizz *(Brit. informal)* • *He had fallen into exhausted slumber.*
▸ AS A VERB = **sleep**, nap, doze, kip *(Brit. slang)*, snooze *(informal)*, lie dormant, drowse, zizz *(Brit. informal)* • *The older three girls are still slumbering peacefully.*

slump AS A VERB 1 = **fall**, decline, sink, plunge, crash, collapse, slip, deteriorate, fall off, plummet, go downhill *(informal)*, reach a new low • *Net profits slumped.*
OPPOSITES: increase, grow, expand
2 = **sag**, collapse, sink, flop, fall, bend, hunch, droop, slouch, loll, plonk yourself • *I closed the door and slumped into a chair.*
▸ AS A NOUN 1 = **fall**, drop, decline, crash, collapse, reverse, lapse, falling-off, downturn, depreciation, trough, meltdown *(informal)* • *a slump in property prices*
OPPOSITES: increase, growth, boom
2 = **recession**, depression, stagnation, inactivity, hard *or* bad times • *the slump of the early 1980s*

slur AS A NOUN = **insult**, stain, smear, stigma, disgrace, discredit, blot, affront, innuendo, calumny, insinuation, aspersion, blot on your escutcheon • *yet another slur on the integrity of the police*
▸ AS A VERB = **mumble**, stammer, stutter, stumble over, falter, mispronounce, garble, speak unclearly • *He repeated himself and slurred his words more than usual.*

slush = **sentimentality**, emotion, romanticism, emotionalism, tenderness, tender feeling, mawkishness, soft-heartedness, overemotionalism • *sentimental slush*

slut = **tart**, slag *(Brit. slang)*, slapper *(Brit. slang)*, scrubber *(Brit. & Austral. slang)*, trollop, drab *(archaic)*, sloven, slattern, hornbag *(Austral. slang)* • *You look like a slut, dressed like that.*

sly AS AN ADJECTIVE 1 = **roguish**, knowing, arch, teasing, naughty, mischievous, wicked, impish • *His lips were spread in a sly smile.*
2 = **cunning**, scheming, devious, secret, clever, subtle, tricky, covert, astute, wily, insidious, crafty, artful, furtive, conniving, Machiavellian, shifty, foxy, underhand, stealthy, guileful • *She is devious, sly and manipulative.*
OPPOSITES: open, direct, frank

3 = **secret**, furtive, surreptitious, stealthy, sneaking, covert, clandestine • *They were giving each other sly looks across the room.*

▸ **IN PHRASES: on the sly = secretly**, privately, covertly, surreptitiously, under the counter *(informal)*, on the quiet, behind (someone's) back, like a thief in the night, underhandedly, on the q.t. *(informal)* • *Was she meeting some guy on the sly?*

smack AS A VERB 1 = slap, hit, strike, pat, tap, sock *(slang)*, clap, cuff, swipe, box, spank • *She smacked me on the side of the head.*

2 = **drive**, hit, strike, thrust, impel • *He smacked the ball against the post.*

▸ **AS A NOUN = slap**, blow, whack, clout *(informal)*, cuff, crack, swipe, spank, wallop *(informal)* • *I end up shouting at him or giving him a smack.*

▸ **AS AN ADVERB = directly**, right, straight, squarely, precisely, exactly, slap *(informal)*, plumb, point-blank • *smack in the middle of the city*

▸ **IN PHRASES: smack of something = be suggestive** *or* **indicative of**, suggest, smell of, testify to, reek of, have all the hallmarks of, betoken, be redolent of, bear the stamp of • *His comments smacked of racism.*

small 1 = little, minute, tiny, slight, mini, miniature, minuscule, diminutive, petite, teeny, puny, pint-sized *(informal)*, pocket-sized, undersized, teeny-weeny, Lilliputian, teensy-weensy, pygmy *or* pigmy • *She is small for her age.*

OPPOSITES: great, big, large

2 = **intimate**, close, private • *a small select group of friends*

3 = **young**, little, growing up, junior, wee, juvenile, youthful, immature, unfledged, in the springtime of life • *What were you like when you were small?*

4 = **unimportant**, minor, trivial, insignificant, little, lesser, petty, trifling, negligible, paltry, piddling *(informal)* • *No detail was too small to escape her attention.*

OPPOSITES: major, important, significant

5 = **modest**, small-scale, humble, unpretentious, small-time • *shops, restaurants and other small businesses*

OPPOSITES: grand, large-scale

6 = **soft**, low, quiet, inaudible, low-pitched, noiseless • *a very small voice*

7 = **foolish**, uncomfortable, humiliated, crushed, stupid, ashamed, deflated, mortified • *This may be just another of her schemes to make me feel small.*

8 = **meagre**, inadequate, insufficient, scant, measly, scanty, limited, inconsiderable • *a diet of one small meal a day*

OPPOSITES: substantial, generous, ample

QUOTATIONS

Small is beautiful

[Professor E.F. Schumacher *title of book*]

PROVERBS

The best things come in small packages

small-minded = petty, mean, rigid, grudging, envious, bigoted, intolerant, blinkered, narrow-minded, hidebound, dyed-in-the-wool, ungenerous • *their small-minded preoccupation with making money*

OPPOSITES: open, liberal, broad-minded

smallpox

▸ **RELATED ADJECTIVE:** variolous

small-time = minor, insignificant, unimportant, petty, no-account *(U.S. informal)*, piddling *(informal)*, of no consequence, of no account • *a small-time actress and model*

smarmy = obsequious, slimy, ingratiating, unctuous, smooth, crawling, greasy, oily, fawning, suave, soapy *(slang)*, fulsome, sycophantic, servile, toadying, bowing and scraping, bootlicking *(informal)* • *He is slightly smarmy and eager to impress.*

smart AS AN ADJECTIVE 1 = chic, trim, neat, fashionable, stylish, fine, elegant, trendy *(Brit. informal)*, spruce, snappy, natty *(informal)*, modish, well turned-out, schmick *(Austral. informal)* • *I was dressed in a smart navy-blue suit.*

OPPOSITES: scruffy, dowdy, unfashionable

2 = **clever**, bright, intelligent, quick, sharp, keen, acute, shrewd, apt, ingenious, astute, canny, quick-witted • *He thinks he's much smarter than Sarah.*

OPPOSITES: thick, stupid, dull

3 = **fashionable**, stylish, chic, genteel, in vogue, voguish *(informal)* • *smart dinner parties*

4 = **brisk**, quick, lively, vigorous, spirited, cracking *(informal)*, spanking, jaunty • *We set off at a smart pace.*

▸ **AS A VERB 1 = sting**, burn, tingle, pain, hurt, throb • *My eyes smarted from the smoke.*

2 = **feel resentful**, feel annoyed, feel offended, feel wounded, feel indignant • *He is still smarting over criticism of his clumsy performance.*

smart alec, smart aleck *or* **smart arse** *(informal)*

AS A NOUN = know-all *(informal)*, wise guy *(informal)*, clever-clogs *(informal)*, clever Dick *(informal)*, smarty pants *(informal)*, smartarse *(slang)*, smarty boots *(informal)* • *Don't be such a smart alec.* • *All right then, if you're such a smart arse, have you got any better ideas?*

▸ **AS AN ADJECTIVE = cocky**, arrogant, conceited, brash, swaggering, egotistical, cocksure, overconfident, swollen-headed, full of yourself • *a fortyish smart-alec TV reporter* • *I can do without your smart-arse comments, thank you.*

smarten AS A VERB *often with* **up = tidy**, spruce up, groom, beautify, put in order, put to rights, gussy up *(slang, chiefly U.S.)* • *The reason for the uniform was to smarten up their image.*

▸ **IN PHRASES: smarten yourself up = spruce yourself up**, freshen yourself up, titivate yourself *(informal)*, tart yourself up *(Brit. informal)*, beautify yourself • *The rest of us must smarten ourselves up immediately.*

smash AS A VERB 1 = break, crush, shatter, crack, demolish, shiver, disintegrate, pulverize, crush to smithereens • *A crowd of youths started smashing windows.*

2 = **shatter**, break, disintegrate, split, crack, explode, splinter • *The bottle smashed against a wall.*

3 = **collide**, crash, meet head-on, clash, come into collision • *The train smashed into the car at 40 mph.*

4 = **destroy**, ruin, wreck, total *(slang)*, defeat, overthrow, trash *(slang)*, lay waste • *Police staged a raid to smash one of Britain's biggest crack factories.*

▸ **AS A NOUN 1 = success**, hit, winner, triumph *(informal)*, belter *(slang)*, sensation, smash hit, sellout, smasheroo *(informal)* • *It is the public who decide if a film is a smash or a flop.*

2 = **collision**, crash, accident, pile-up *(informal)*, smash-up *(informal)* • *He was near to death after a car smash.*

3 = **crash**, smashing, clatter, clash, bang, thunder, racket, din, clattering, clang • *the smash of falling crockery*

smashing = excellent, mean *(slang)*, great *(informal)*, wonderful, topping *(Brit. slang)*, brilliant *(informal)*, cracking *(Brit. informal)*, crucial *(slang)*, superb, fantastic *(informal)*, magnificent, fabulous *(informal)*, first-class, marvellous, terrific *(informal)*, sensational *(informal)*, mega *(slang)*, sovereign, awesome *(slang)*, world-class, exhilarating, fab *(informal, chiefly Brit.)*, super *(informal)*, first-rate, def *(slang)*, superlative, brill *(informal)*, stupendous, out of this world *(informal)*, bodacious *(slang, chiefly U.S.)*, boffo *(slang)*, jim-dandy *(slang)*, chillin' *(U.S. slang)*, booshit *(Austral. slang)*, exo *(Austral. slang)*, sik *(Austral. slang)*, rad *(informal)*, phat *(slang)*, schmick *(Austral. informal)* • *It was a smashing success.*

OPPOSITES: bad, terrible, awful

smattering = modicum, dash, rudiments, bit, elements, sprinkling, passing acquaintance, nodding acquaintance, smatter • *a smattering of Greek grammar*

smear AS A VERB 1 = spread over, daub, rub on, cover, coat, plaster, bedaub • *Smear a little olive oil over the inside of the salad bowl.*

2 = **slander**, tarnish, malign, vilify, blacken, sully, besmirch, traduce, calumniate, asperse, drag (someone's) name through the mud • *a crude attempt to smear her*
3 = **smudge**, soil, dirty, stain, sully, besmirch, smirch • *a face covered by a heavy beard, smeared with dirt*
▸ **AS A NOUN** 1 = **smudge**, daub, streak, blot, blotch, splotch, smirch • *a smear of gravy*
2 = **slander**, libel, defamation, vilification, whispering campaign, calumny, mudslinging • *a smear by his rivals*

smeared = **filthy**, soiled, dirty, muddy, messy, grubby, sullied, grimy, unclean, mucky, grotty *(slang)*, grungy *(slang, chiefly U.S. & Canad.)*, scuzzy *(slang, chiefly U.S.)*, begrimed, skanky *(slang)* • *long, smeared windows*

smell **AS A NOUN** 1 = **odour**, scent, fragrance, perfume, bouquet, savour, aroma, whiff, niff *(Brit. slang)*, redolence • *the smell of freshly baked bread*
2 = **stink**, stench, reek, pong *(Brit. informal)*, niff *(Brit. slang)*, malodour, fetor • *horrible smells*
▸ **AS A VERB** 1 = **reek**, stink, have the fragrance of, whiff • *The room smelled of lemons.*
2 = **stink**, reek, pong *(Brit. informal)*, hum *(slang)*, whiff *(Brit. slang)*, stink to high heaven *(informal)*, niff *(Brit. slang)*, be malodorous • *Do my feet smell?*
3 = **sniff**, scent, get a whiff of, detect the smell of, nose • *We could smell the gas.*
▸ **IN PHRASES: smell of something** = **smack of**, suggest, seem like, have the hallmarks of, have all the signs of • *The lawyer's solution smells of quackery.*
▸ **RELATED ADJECTIVE:** olfactory
▸ **RELATED PHOBIA:** olfactophobia

smelly = **stinking**, reeking, fetid, foul-smelling, high, strong, foul, putrid, strong-smelling, stinky *(informal)*, malodorous, evil-smelling, noisome, whiffy *(Brit. slang)*, pongy *(Brit. informal)*, mephitic, niffy *(Brit. slang)*, olid, festy *(Austral. slang)* • *a chunk of smelly cheese*
OPPOSITES: fragrant, perfumed, aromatic

smile **AS A VERB** = **grin**, beam, smirk, twinkle, grin from ear to ear • *He smiled and waved.*
▸ **AS A NOUN** = **grin**, beam, smirk • *She gave a wry smile.*
▸ **IN PHRASES: all smiles** = **smiling**, beaming, grinning, grinning like a Cheshire cat • *As soon as I said yes, he was all smiles.*

smirk **AS A NOUN** = **smug smile**, grin, simper • *Wipe that smirk off your face!*
▸ **AS A VERB** = **give a smug look**, grin, simper • *They nudged each other and smirked.*

smitten 1 = **infatuated**, charmed, captivated, beguiled, bewitched, bowled over *(informal)*, enamoured, swept off your feet • *They were totally smitten with each other.*
2 = **afflicted**, struck, beset, laid low, plagued • *smitten with yellow fever*

smog = **exhaust fumes**, pollution, fog, haze, vapour, pea-souper *(Brit. informal)* • *Cars cause pollution, and both smog and acid rain.*

smoke **AS A NOUN** 1 = **fumes** • *The air was thick with cigarette smoke.*
2 = **cigarette**, fag *(Brit. informal)*, ciggie *(Brit. informal)* • *Someone went out for a smoke.*
▸ **AS A VERB** 1 = **smoulder**, fume, emit smoke • *The rubble was still smoking.*
2 = **puff on**, draw on, inhale, drag on *(informal)* • *He didn't argue, he just quietly smoked a cigarette.*
3 = **preserve** • *The fish was being smoked.*
▸ **IN PHRASES: go up in smoke** = **come to nothing**, vanish, be shattered, be ruined • *Their dreams had gone up in smoke.*
smoke something *or* **someone out** = **detect**, find, catch, reveal, discover, expose, disclose, uncover, track down, unmask • *new technology to smoke out tax evaders*

QUOTATIONS
As an example to others, and not that I care for moderation myself, it has always been my rule never to smoke when asleep, and never to refrain from smoking when awake
[Mark Twain *70th birthday speech*]

smoky 1 = **thick**, murky, hazy, reeky • *the extremely smoky atmosphere at work*
2 = **grey**, dark grey, slate-grey, dark • *He had smoky grey-blue eyes.*

smooth **AS AN ADJECTIVE** 1 = **even**, level, flat, plane, plain, flush, horizontal, unwrinkled • *a smooth surface*
OPPOSITES: rough, irregular, uneven
2 = **sleek**, polished, shiny, glossy, silky, velvety, glassy, mirror-like • *The flagstones were worn smooth by centuries of use.*
OPPOSITES: rough, coarse, abrasive
3 = **hairless**, clean-shaven, smooth-shaven • *His baby-smooth skin might never have felt a razor.*
4 = **creamy**, velvety, whipped • *Continue whisking until the mixture looks smooth and creamy.*
5 = **mellow**, pleasant, mild, soothing, bland, agreeable • *This makes the flavour much smoother.*
6 = **flowing**, steady, fluent, regular, uniform, rhythmic • *This exercise is done in one smooth motion.*
7 = **calm**, peaceful, serene, tranquil, undisturbed, unruffled, equable • *This was only a brief upset in their smooth lives.*
OPPOSITES: troubled, nervous, disturbed
8 = **easy**, straightforward, trouble-free, effortless, untroubled, well-ordered • *A number of problems marred the smooth running of this event.*
9 = **suave**, slick, persuasive, urbane, silky, glib, facile, ingratiating, debonair, unctuous, smarmy *(Brit. informal)* • *Twelve extremely good-looking, smooth young men have been picked as finalists.*
▸ **AS A VERB** 1 = **flatten**, level, press, plane, iron • *She stood up and smoothed down her frock.*
2 = **spread**, rub, smear • *She smoothed the lotion across his shoulder blades.*
3 = **ease**, aid, assist, facilitate, pave the way, make easier, help along, iron out the difficulties of • *smoothing the path towards a treaty*
OPPOSITES: hamper, exacerbate, hinder
▸ **IN PHRASES: smooth something over** *or* **out** = **calm**, ease, soothe, soften, alleviate, appease, allay, mitigate, assuage, mollify, extenuate, palliate • *an attempt to smooth over the violent splits that have occurred*

smoothness 1 = **evenness**, regularity, levelness, flushness, unbrokenness • *The lawn was rich, weed-free, and trimmed to smoothness.*
2 = **fluency**, finish, flow, ease, polish, rhythm, efficiency, felicity, smooth running, slickness, effortlessness • *the strength and smoothness of his movements*
3 = **ease**, simplicity, straightforwardness, effortlessness, easiness • *the smoothness of the procedure*
4 = **sleekness**, softness, smooth texture, silkiness, velvetiness • *the smoothness of her skin*
5 = **suavity**, urbanity, oiliness, glibness, smarminess *(Brit. informal)* • *His cleverness, smoothness even, made his relationships uneasy.*

smooth-talking = **slick**, suave, glib, ingratiating, sycophantic, unctuous, obsequious, smarmy *(informal)*, smooth-tongued, smooth-spoken • *the smooth-talking cameraman*

smother 1 = **extinguish**, put out, stifle, snuff • *They tried to smother the flames.*
2 = **suffocate**, choke, strangle, stifle • *He had attempted to smother his sixteen-week-old son.*
3 = **suppress**, stifle, repress, hide, conceal, muffle, keep back • *She tried to smother her feelings of panic.*

S

4 = overwhelm, cover, shower, surround, heap, shroud, inundate, envelop, cocoon • *He smothered her with kisses.*
5 = stifle, suppress, hold in, restrain, hold back, repress, muffle, bottle up, keep in check • *trying to smother our giggles*
6 = smear, cover, spread • *Luckily, it wasn't smothered in creamy sauce.*

smothering
▸ **RELATED PHOBIA:** pnigerophobia

smoulder **1 = smoke**, burn slowly • *Whole blocks had been turned into smouldering rubble.*
2 = seethe, rage, fume, burn, boil, simmer, fester, be resentful, smart • *He smouldered as he drove home for lunch.*

smudge **AS A NOUN = smear**, blot, smut, smutch • *smudges of blood*
▸ **AS A VERB 1 = smear**, blur, blot • *Smudge the outline using a cotton-wool bud.*
2 = mark, soil, dirty, daub, smirch • *She kissed me, careful not to smudge me with her fresh lipstick.*

smug **= self-satisfied**, superior, complacent, conceited, self-righteous, holier-than-thou, priggish, self-opinionated • *smug satisfaction*

smuggle **= sneak**, spirit, slip, bring illegally • *Had it really been impossible to find someone who could smuggle out a letter?*

smuggler **= trafficker**, runner, bootlegger, moonshiner (*U.S.*), rum-runner, contrabandist • *drug smugglers*

smutty **= obscene**, dirty, crude, coarse, filthy, indecent, vulgar, improper, blue, pornographic, raunchy (*U.S. slang*), suggestive, racy, lewd, risqué, X-rated (*informal*), bawdy, salacious, prurient, off colour, indelicate • *She said she detested smutty jokes.*

snack **AS A NOUN = light meal**, bite, refreshment(s), nibble, titbit, bite to eat, elevenses (*Brit. informal*) • *Lunch was a snack in the fields.*
▸ **AS A VERB = eat between meals**, graze (*informal*), nibble • *She would improve her diet if she snacked less.*

snag **AS A NOUN = difficulty**, hitch, problem, obstacle, catch, hazard, disadvantage, complication, drawback, inconvenience, downside, stumbling block, the rub • *A police crackdown hit a snag when villains stole one of their cars.*
▸ **AS A VERB = catch**, tear, rip, hole • *He snagged his suit.*

snail

SNAILS, SLUGS AND OTHER GASTROPODS

abalone *or* ear shell	slug	slug
conch	ormer *or* sea-ear	snail
cowrie *or* cowry	periwinkle *or* winkle	top-shell
limpet	ramshorn snail	triton
murex	Roman snail	wentletrap
nudibranch *or* sea	sea hare	whelk

snake **AS A NOUN = serpent** • *He was caught with his pet snake in his pocket.*
▸ **AS A VERB = wind**, twist, curve, turn, bend, ramble, meander, deviate, zigzag • *The road snaked through the forested mountains.*
▸ **RELATED ADJECTIVES:** serpentine, anguine, ophidian, colubrine
▸ **RELATED MANIA:** ophidiomania
▸ **RELATED PHOBIA:** ophidiophobia
▹ *See panel* **Reptiles**

snap **AS A VERB 1 = break**, split, crack, separate, fracture, give way, come apart • *The brake pedal had just snapped.*
2 = pop, click, crackle • *He snapped the cap on his ballpoint.*
3 = speak sharply, bark, lash out at, flash, retort, snarl, growl, fly off the handle at (*informal*), jump down (someone's) throat (*informal*) • *I'm sorry, I didn't mean to snap at you.*
4 = lose your temper, crack, lose it (*informal*), freak (*informal*), crack up, freak out (*informal*), fly off the handle, lose your cool, blow your top • *He finally snapped when she prevented their children from visiting one weekend.*
5 = bite at, bite, nip • *The poodle yapped and snapped at our legs.*
6 = photograph, capture on film, take a photograph of, get a photograph of • *the paparazzi's repeated attempts to snap a royal*
▸ **AS A NOUN 1 = crack**, pop, crash, report, burst, explosion, clap • *Every minute or so I could hear a snap, a crack and a crash as another tree went down.*
2 = pop, crack, smack, whack • *He shut the book with a snap and stood up.*
3 = photograph, photo, picture, shot, print, slide, snapshot • *a snap my mother took last year*
4 = spell, period, interval, run, stretch, patch • *a cold snap in the middle of spring*
▸ **AS A MODIFIER = instant**, immediate, hurried, sudden, quick, abrupt, spur-of-the-moment, unpremeditated • *I think this is too important for a snap decision.*
▸ **IN PHRASES: snap out of it = get over it**, recover, cheer up, perk up, liven up, pull yourself together (*informal*), get a grip on yourself • *Come on, snap out of it!*
snap something up = grab, seize, take advantage of, swoop down on, pounce upon, avail yourself of • *a queue of people waiting to snap up the bargains*

snappy **AS AN ADJECTIVE 1 = succinct**, brief, concise, to the point, crisp, witty, condensed, incisive, pithy, short and sweet, in a few well-chosen words • *Each film gets a snappy two-line summary.*
2 = smart, fashionable, stylish, trendy (*Brit. informal*), chic, dapper, up-to-the-minute, natty (*informal*), modish, voguish, schmick (*Austral. informal*) • *snappy sports jackets*
3 = irritable, cross, bad-tempered, pissed (*U.S. slang*), tart, impatient, edgy, pissed off (*taboo slang*), touchy, tetchy, ratty (*Brit. & N.Z. informal*), testy, chippy (*informal*), waspish, quick-tempered, snappish, like a bear with a sore head (*informal*), apt to fly off the handle (*informal*) • *He wasn't irritable or snappy.*
▸ **IN PHRASES: make it snappy = hurry (up)**, be quick, get a move on (*informal*), buck up (*informal*), make haste, look lively, get your skates on • *Look at the pamphlets, and make it snappy.*

snare **AS A NOUN = trap**, net, wire, gin, pitfall, noose, springe • *an animal caught in a snare*
▸ **AS A VERB = trap**, catch, net, wire, seize, entrap, springe • *He'd snared a rabbit earlier in the day.*

snarl[1] **1 = growl**, show its teeth (*of an animal*) • *The dogs snarled at the intruders.*
2 = snap, bark, lash out, speak angrily, jump down someone's throat, speak roughly • *'Call that a good performance?' he snarled.*

snarl[2] **AS A NOUN = tangle**, mass, twist, web, knot, jungle, mat, coil, mesh, ravel, entanglement • *a snarl of logs and branches*
▸ **IN PHRASES: snarl something up = tangle**, complicate, muddle, embroil, entangle, entwine, ravel, enmesh • *The row snarled up the work of the commission.* • *The group had succeeded in snarling up rush-hour traffic throughout the country.*

snarl-up **= tangle**, confusion, muddle, entanglement • *What idiot has caused this snarl-up?*

snatch **AS A VERB 1 = grab**, seize, wrench, wrest, take, grip, grasp, clutch, take hold of • *He snatched the telephone from me.*
2 = steal, take, nick (*slang, chiefly Brit.*), pinch (*informal*), swipe (*slang*), lift (*informal*), pilfer, filch, shoplift, thieve, walk

S

or make off with • *He snatched her bag and threw her to the ground.*
3 = **win**, take, score, gain, secure, obtain • *They snatched a third goal.*
4 = **save**, free, rescue, pull, recover, get out, salvage, extricate • *He was snatched from the jaws of death at the last minute.*
▸ **AS A NOUN** = **bit**, part, fragment, piece, spell, snippet, smattering • *I heard snatches of the conversation.*

snazzy = **stylish**, smart, dashing, with it *(informal)*, attractive, sophisticated, flamboyant, sporty, flashy, jazzy *(informal)*, showy, ritzy *(slang)*, raffish, schmick *(Austral. informal)* • *snazzy swimsuits*

sneak **AS A VERB** 1 = **slink**, slip, steal, creep, ghost, pad, tiptoe, sidle, skulk • *Don't sneak away and hide.*
2 = **slip**, smuggle, spirit • *He snuck me a cigarette.*
3 = **snatch**, steal, do something furtively *or* stealthily • *She sneaked a look at her watch.*
▸ **AS A NOUN** = **informer**, grass *(Brit. slang)*, betrayer, telltale, squealer *(slang)*, Judas, accuser, stool pigeon, snake in the grass, nark *(Brit., Austral. & N.Z. slang)*, fizgig *(Austral. slang)* • *He is disloyal, distrustful and a sneak.*
▸ **AS A MODIFIER** = **secret**, quick, clandestine, furtive, stealthy • *We can give you this exclusive sneak preview.*
▸ **IN PHRASES: sneak on someone** = **inform on**, shop *(slang, chiefly Brit.)*, peach on *(slang)*, tell on *(informal)*, grass on *(Brit. slang)*, dob in *(Austral. slang)* • *I'd never sneak on a friend.*
sneak up on something *or* **someone** = **creep up on**, take by surprise, tiptoe up on • *I managed to sneak up on him.*

sneakers = **trainers**, running shoes, tennis shoes, plimsolls, gym shoes • *The motto is written on their sneakers.*

sneaking 1 = **nagging**, worrying, persistent, niggling, uncomfortable • *a sneaking suspicion*
2 = **secret**, private, hidden, suppressed, unexpressed, unvoiced, unavowed, unconfessed, undivulged • *a sneaking admiration*

sneaky = **sly**, dishonest, devious, mean, low, base, nasty, cowardly, slippery, unreliable, malicious, unscrupulous, furtive, disingenuous, shifty, snide, deceitful, contemptible, untrustworthy, double-dealing • *One kid can generally tell when another kid is sneaky.*

S

sneer **AS A VERB** 1 = **scorn**, mock, ridicule, laugh, jeer, disdain, scoff, deride, look down on, snigger, sniff at, gibe, hold in contempt, hold up to ridicule, turn up your nose *(informal)* • *There is too great a readiness to sneer at anything they do.*
2 = **say contemptuously**, snigger • *'I wonder what you people do with your lives,' he sneered.*
▸ **AS A NOUN** 1 = **scorn**, ridicule, mockery, derision, jeer, disdain, snigger, gibe, snidery • *Best-selling authors may have to face the sneers of the literati.*
2 = **contemptuous smile**, snigger, curl of the lip • *His mouth twisted in a contemptous sneer.*

QUOTATIONS
Who can refute a sneer?
[Revd. William Paley *Principles of Moral and Political Philosophy*]
Damn with faint praise, assent with civil leer,
And, without sneering, teach the rest to sneer
[Alexander Pope *Epistle to Dr. Arbuthnot*]

sneeze **IN PHRASES: not to be sneezed at** = **considerable**, great, large, substantial, reasonable, tidy, lavish, plentiful, tolerable, appreciable, sizable *or* sizeable • *The money's not to be sneezed at.*

snicker **AS A VERB** = **snigger**, laugh, giggle, smirk, titter • *We all snickered at her.*
▸ **AS A NOUN** = **snigger**, laugh, giggle, titter • *a chorus of jeers and snickers*

snide *or* **snidey** = **nasty**, sneering, malicious, mean, cynical, unkind, hurtful, sarcastic, disparaging, spiteful, insinuating, scornful, shrewish, ill-natured, snarky *(informal)* • *He made a snide comment about her weight.*

sniff **AS A VERB** 1 = **breathe in**, inhale, snuffle, snuff • *She wiped her face and sniffed loudly.*
2 = **smell**, nose, breathe in, scent, get a whiff of, catch the scent of, detect the smell of • *Suddenly, he stopped and sniffed the air.*
3 = **inhale**, breathe in, suck in, draw in • *He'd been sniffing glue.*
▸ **AS A NOUN** 1 = **snuffle**, intake of breath, quick inhalation • *At last the sobs ceased, to be replaced by sniffs.*
2 = **hint**, clue, inkling, sign, wind, suggestion, whiff, intimation • *Have the Press got a sniff of this story yet?*
▸ **IN PHRASES: not to be sniffed at** = **considerable**, great, large, substantial, reasonable, tidy, lavish, plentiful, tolerable, appreciable, sizable *or* sizeable • *The salary was not to be sniffed at either.*
sniff around = **nose around**, hunt around, see what you can find, search for clues • *Pop down there and just sniff around.*
sniff something out 1 = **find**, discover, spot, recognize, detect, scent, track down • *those who like sniffing out bargains*
2 = **discover**, find, reveal, spot, expose, recognize, disclose, scent, uncover, track down, unmask • *a police dog trained to sniff out explosives*

sniffy = **contemptuous**, superior, condescending, haughty, scornful, disdainful, supercilious • *sniffy art critics*

snigger **AS A VERB** = **laugh**, giggle, sneer, snicker, titter • *The tourists snigger at the locals' outdated ways and dress.*
▸ **AS A NOUN** = **laugh**, giggle, sneer, snicker, titter • *trying to suppress a snigger*

snip **AS A VERB** = **cut**, nick, clip, crop, trim, dock, notch, nip off • *Snip the corners off the card.*
▸ **AS A NOUN** = **bargain**, steal *(informal)*, good buy, giveaway • *a snip at £74.25*

snipe[1] 1 = **criticize**, knock *(informal)*, put down, carp, bitch, have a go (at) *(informal)*, jeer, denigrate, disparage, flame *(informal)* • *She kept sniping at her husband all through dinner.*
2 = **shoot at**, open fire on, hit at, blast at *(slang)* • *Gunmen have reportedly sniped at army positions.*

snipe[2]
▸ **COLLECTIVE NOUNS:** walk, wisp

snippet = **piece**, scrap, fragment, part, particle, snatch, shred • *I read a snippet she had cut from a magazine.*

snivel = **whine**, cry, whinge *(informal)*, weep, moan, gripe *(informal)*, whimper, grizzle *(informal, chiefly Brit.)*, blubber, sniffle, snuffle, mewl, girn *(Scot. & Northern English dialect)* • *a snivelling child*

snob = **elitist**, highbrow, social climber • *She was an intellectual snob.*

snobbery = **arrogance**, airs, pride, pretension, condescension, snobbishness, snootiness *(informal)*, side *(Brit. slang)*, uppishness *(Brit. informal)* • *social and educational snobbery*

snobbish = **superior**, arrogant, stuck-up *(informal)*, patronizing, condescending, snooty *(informal)*, pretentious, uppity, high and mighty *(informal)*, toffee-nosed *(slang, chiefly Brit.)*, hoity-toity *(informal)*, high-hat *(informal, chiefly U.S.)*, uppish *(Brit. informal)* • *I'd expected her to be snobbish but she was warm and friendly.*
OPPOSITES: modest, humble, down to earth

snooker
▹ *See panel* **Snooker and billiards terms**

snoop **AS A VERB** 1 = **investigate**, explore, have a good look at, prowl around, nose around, peer into • *He's been snooping around her hotel.*
2 = **spy**, poke your nose in, nose, interfere, pry *(informal)* • *Governments have been known to snoop into innocent citizens' lives.*
▸ **AS A NOUN** 1 = **look**, search, nose, prowl, investigation • *He had a snoop around.*

SNOOKER AND BILLIARDS TERMS

baize
ball
baulk
baulkline
black
blue
bouclée
break
bricole
bridge
brown
cannon
carom *(chiefly U.S. & Canad.)*
chalk
clearance
cue ball
cue extension
cue tip
cushion
D *or* d
double
draw
drop cannon
fluke
foul
frame
free ball
green
half-butt
hazard
headrail
in-off
jenny
kick
kiss
lag
long jenny
massé
maximum break *or* 147
miscue
nurse
nursery cannon
object ball
pink
plain ball
plant
pocket
pot
red
rest
safety
scratch
screw
short jenny
side *or (U.S. & Canad.)* English
snooker
spider
spot
spot ball
stun
top
triangle *or (U.S. & Canad.)* rack
white
Whitechapel
yellow

2 = **spy**, secret agent, double agent, secret service agent, undercover agent, mole, foreign agent, fifth columnist, nark *(Brit., Austral. & N.Z. slang)* • *its own organization of snoops*

snooper = **nosy parker**, snoop *(informal)*, busybody, meddler, pry, stickybeak *(Austral. informal)*, Paul Pry *(informal)* • *We're naturally a nation of snoopers.*

snooty = **snobbish**, superior, aloof, pretentious, stuck-up *(informal)*, condescending, proud, haughty, disdainful, snotty, uppity, supercilious, high and mighty *(informal)*, toffee-nosed *(slang, chiefly Brit.)*, hoity-toity *(informal)*, high-hat *(informal, chiefly U.S.)*, uppish *(Brit. informal)*, toplofty *(informal)* • *snooty intellectuals*
OPPOSITES: modest, humble, down to earth

snooze AS A NOUN = **doze**, nap, kip *(Brit. slang)*, siesta, catnap, forty winks *(informal)* • *The bird is enjoying a snooze.*
▸ AS A VERB = **doze**, drop off *(informal)*, nap, kip *(Brit. slang)*, nod off *(informal)*, catnap, drowse, take forty winks *(informal)* • *He snoozed in front of the television.*

snout = **proboscis**, nose, jaws, trunk, beak, mouth, muzzle • *Two alligators rest their snouts on the water's surface.*

snow = **snowflakes**, blizzard, snowfall, snowstorm, sleet, snowdrift • *They tramped through the falling snow.*
▸ RELATED ADJECTIVE: niveous
▸ RELATED MANIA: chionomania
▸ RELATED PHOBIA: chionophobia

snowy = **snow-covered**, frosty, wintry, ice-capped • *the snowy peaks*

snub AS A VERB = **insult**, slight, put down, humiliate, cut *(informal)*, shame, humble, rebuff, mortify, cold-shoulder, blank *(informal)*, kick in the teeth *(slang)*, give (someone) the cold shoulder, give (someone) the brush-off *(slang)*, cut dead *(informal)* • *He snubbed her in public and made her feel an idiot.*
▸ AS A NOUN = **insult**, put-down, humiliation, affront, slap in the face, brush-off *(slang)* • *He took it as a snub.*

snuff IN PHRASES: **snuff it** = **die**, expire, perish, pass away, depart, buy it *(U.S. slang)*, check out *(U.S. slang)*, kick it *(slang)*, croak *(slang)*, give up the ghost, go belly-up *(slang)*, peg out *(informal)*, kick the bucket *(slang)*, buy the farm *(U.S. slang)*, peg it *(informal)*, decease, cark it *(Austral. & N.Z. slang)*, pop your clogs *(informal)*, breathe your last, hop the twig *(slang)* • *Perhaps he thought he was about to snuff it.*
snuff someone out = **kill**, murder, slay, destroy, waste *(informal)*, do in *(slang)*, take out *(slang)*, execute, massacre, butcher, slaughter, dispatch, assassinate, eradicate, do away with, blow away *(slang, chiefly U.S.)*, obliterate, knock off *(slang)*, liquidate, annihilate, neutralize, exterminate, take (someone's) life, bump off *(slang)*, extirpate, wipe from the face of the earth *(informal)* • *a bright, articulate young man who was snuffed out by the racism of a few white thugs*
snuff something out = **blow out**, put out, extinguish, douse, snuff out, quench, stifle, smother • *She snuffed out the candle.*

snug 1 = **cosy**, warm, comfortable, homely, sheltered, intimate, comfy *(informal)* • *a snug log cabin*
2 = **tight**, close, trim, neat • *a snug black T-shirt and skin-tight black jeans*

snuggle = **nestle**, curl up, cuddle up, huddle • *I snuggled down in the big, comfortable seat.*

so = **therefore**, thus, hence, consequently, then, as a result, accordingly, for that reason, whence, thence, ergo • *Everyone joked about us, so we had to show them we were serious.*

soak AS A VERB 1 = **steep**, immerse, submerge, infuse, marinate *(Cookery)*, dunk, submerse • *Soak the beans for two hours.*
2 = **wet**, damp, saturate, drench, douse, moisten, suffuse, wet through, waterlog, souse, drouk *(Scot.)* • *Soak the soil around each bush with at least 4 gallons of water.*
3 = **penetrate**, pervade, permeate, enter, get in, infiltrate, diffuse, seep, suffuse, make inroads (into) • *Rain had soaked into the sand.*
▸ IN PHRASES: **soak something up** = **absorb**, suck up, take in *or* up, drink in, assimilate • *Wrap in absorbent paper after frying to soak up excess oil.*

soaked = **drenched**, saturated, sodden, sopping, dripping wet, wet through, soaked to the skin, wringing wet, like a drowned rat, droukit *or* drookit *(Scot.)* • *We got soaked walking home.*

soaking = **soaked**, dripping, saturated, drenched, sodden, waterlogged, streaming, sopping, wet through, soaked to the skin, wringing wet, like a drowned rat, droukit *or* drookit *(Scot.)* • *My face and raincoat were soaking.*

so-and-so 1 = **what's-his-name** *or* **what's-her-name**, X, what-d'you-call-him *or* what-d'you-call-her, whatsit, thingummy, thingamajig • *If Mrs So-and-so was ill, then someone down the street would come in and clean for her.*
2 = **demon**, devil, rogue, imp, rascal, scoundrel, scamp, thing, nointer *(Austral. slang)* • *It was all her fault, the wicked little so-and-so.*

soap
▸ RELATED ADJECTIVE: saponaceous

soar 1 = **rise**, increase, grow, mount, climb, go up, rocket, swell, escalate, shoot up • *soaring unemployment*
2 = **fly**, rise, wing, climb, ascend, fly up • *Buzzards soar overhead at a great height.*
OPPOSITES: fall, drop, plunge
3 = **tower**, rise, climb, go up • *The steeple soars skyward.*

sob AS A VERB = **cry**, weep, blubber, greet *(Scot. or archaic)*, howl, bawl, snivel, shed tears, boohoo • *She began to sob again, burying her face in the pillow.*
▸ AS A NOUN = **cry**, whimper, howl • *Her body was racked by violent sobs.*

sober AS AN ADJECTIVE 1 = **abstinent**, temperate, abstemious, moderate, on the wagon *(informal)* • *He was dour and uncommunicative when stone sober.*

OPPOSITES: drunk, intoxicated, tight *(informal)*
2 = **serious**, practical, realistic, sound, cool, calm, grave, reasonable, steady, composed, rational, solemn, lucid, sedate, staid, level-headed, dispassionate, unruffled, clear-headed, unexcited, grounded • *We are now far more sober and realistic.*
OPPOSITES: unrealistic, irrational, frivolous
3 = **plain**, dark, sombre, quiet, severe, subdued, drab • *He dresses in sober grey suits.*
OPPOSITES: bright, flamboyant, flashy
▸ AS A VERB 1 = **calm down**, steady, cool down, become more serious • *After they had sobered, he was able to reassert his authority.*
2 *usually with* **up** = **come to your senses** • *He was left to sober up in a police cell.*
OPPOSITES: get drunk, become intoxicated, get hammered *(slang)*
3 *usually with* **up** = **clear your head**, dry you out • *These events sobered him up considerably*

sobering = **depressing**, discouraging, daunting, saddening, dispiriting, disheartening • *a sobering thought*

sobriety 1 = **abstinence**, temperance, abstemiousness, moderation, self-restraint, soberness, nonindulgence • *the boredom of a lifetime of sobriety*
2 = **seriousness**, gravity, steadiness, restraint, composure, coolness, calmness, solemnity, reasonableness, level-headedness, staidness, sedateness • *the values society depends upon, such as honesty, sobriety and trust*

so-called = **alleged**, supposed, professed, pretended, self-styled, ostensible, soi-disant *(French)* • *their so-called economic miracle*

soccer = **football** *(Brit.)*, Association Football • *There were reports of violence involving soccer fans.*

sociability = **friendliness**, conviviality, cordiality, congeniality, neighbourliness, affability, gregariousness, companionability • *Enthusiasm, adaptability, sociability, and good health are essential.*

sociable = **friendly**, social, outgoing, warm, neighbourly, accessible, cordial, genial, affable, approachable, gregarious, convivial, companionable, conversable • *Some children have more sociable personalities than others.*
OPPOSITES: cold, withdrawn, unsociable

S

social AS AN ADJECTIVE 1 = **communal**, community, collective, group, public, general, common, societal • *the tightly woven social fabric of small towns*
2 = **sociable**, friendly, companionable, neighbourly • *We ought to organize more social events.*
3 = **organized**, gregarious, interactional • *social insects like bees and ants*
▸ AS A NOUN = **get-together** *(informal)*, party, gathering, function, do *(informal)*, reception, bash *(informal)*, social gathering • *church socials*

socialism = **Marxism**, communism, leftism, social democracy, Leninism, progressivism, syndicalism, labourism, Trotskyism, Fabianism • *the steady rise of socialism in this country*

QUOTATIONS

If Socialism can only be realized when the intellectual development of all the people permits it, then we shall not see Socialism for at least five hundred years
[Vladimir Ilyich Lenin *speech at Peasants' Congress*]

The worst advertisement for Socialism is its adherents
[George Orwell]

The language of priorities is the religion of Socialism
[Aneurin Bevan]

To the ordinary working man, the sort you would meet in any pub on Saturday night, Socialism does not mean much more than better wages and shorter hours and nobody bossing you about
[George Orwell *The Road to Wigan Pier*]

Idleness, selfishness, fecklessness, envy and irresponsibility are the vices upon which socialism in any form flourishes and which it in turn encourages. But socialism's devilishly clever tactic is to play up to all those human failings, while making those who practise them feel good about it
[Margaret Thatcher *Nicholas Ridley Memorial Lecture*]

Socialism can only arrive by bicycle
[José Antonio Viera Gallo]

socialist AS AN ADJECTIVE = **left-wing**, communist, Marxist, Labour, red, progressive, social democratic, leftist, Fabian, Leninist, Trotskyist, syndicalist • *members of the ruling Socialist party*
▸ AS A NOUN = **left-winger**, communist, Marxist, red, social democrat, leftist, Fabian, Leninist, Trotskyist, syndicalist, Labourite, progressivist • *His views have always been popular among socialists.*

socialize 1 = **mix**, interact, mingle, be sociable, meet, go out, entertain, get together, fraternize, have people round, be a good mixer, get about *or* around • *They no longer socialized as they used to.*
2 = **condition**, train, teach, rear, educate, brainwash • *You may have been socialized to do as you are told.*

society 1 = **the community**, social order, people, the public, the population, humanity, civilization, mankind, the general public, the world at large • *This reflects attitudes and values prevailing in society.*
2 = **culture**, community, population • *those responsible for destroying our African heritage and the fabric of our society*
3 = **organization**, group, club, union, league, association, institute, circle, corporation, guild, fellowship, fraternity, brotherhood *or* sisterhood • *the historical society*
4 = **upper classes**, gentry, upper crust *(informal)*, elite, the swells *(informal)*, high society, the top drawer, polite society, the toffs *(Brit. slang)*, the smart set, beau monde, the nobs *(slang)*, the country set, haut monde *(French)* • *The couple tried to secure themselves a position in society.*
5 = **companionship**, company, fellowship, friendship, camaraderie • *I largely withdrew from the society of others.*

QUOTATIONS

Human life in common is only made possible when a majority comes together which is stronger than any separate individual and which remains united against all separate individuals
[Sigmund Freud *Civilization and its Discontents*]

Man did not enter into society to become worse than he was before, nor to have fewer rights than he had before, but to have those rights better secured
[Thomas Paine *The Rights of Man*]

There is no such thing as society
[Margaret Thatcher]

He who is unable to live in society, or who has no need because he is sufficient for himself, must be either a beast or a god
[Aristotle *Politics*]

sock

SOCKS AND TIGHTS

ankle sock *or* *(U.S.)* anklet	legwarmer	pantyhose
argyle	lisle stocking	sock
bed sock	maillot	slouch sock
bobby sock	nylons	stay-up
half-hose	pop sock	stock *(archaic)*
hose *(History)*	puttee *or* putty	stocking
knee-high sock	tights *or* *(esp U.S. & Austral.)*	

sod = **rogue**, bastard *(offensive)*, scoundrel, devil, villain, imp, scally *(Northwest English dialect)*, wretch, knave *(archaic)*, ne'er-do-well, reprobate, scallywag *(informal)*, good-for-nothing, miscreant, varmint *(informal)*, wrong 'un *(Austral. slang)* • *some rotten stinking sod*

sodden = **soaked**, saturated, sopping, drenched, soggy, waterlogged, marshy, boggy, miry, droukit *or* drookit *(Scot.)* • *We stripped off our sodden clothes.*

sodomy = **anal intercourse**, anal sex, buggery • *Half of the states still have laws against sodomy.*

sofa = **couch**, settee, divan, chaise longue, chesterfield, ottoman • *That night the Major had slept on the sofa.*

TYPES OF SOFA

bergère	day bed	sofa bed
canapé	divan	squab
chaise longue *or* chaise	futon	studio couch
	lounge	tête-à-tête
chesterfield	love seat	vis-à-vis
couch	settee	
davenport *(U.S.)*	settle	

soft 1 = **velvety**, smooth, silky, furry, feathery, downy, fleecy, like a baby's bottom *(informal)* • *Regular use of a body lotion will keep the skin soft and supple.*
OPPOSITES: rough, grating, coarse
2 = **yielding**, flexible, pliable, cushioned, elastic, malleable, spongy, springy, cushiony • *She lay down on the soft, comfortable bed.*
OPPOSITES: hard, firm, rigid
3 = **soggy**, swampy, marshy, boggy, squelchy, quaggy • *The horse didn't handle the soft ground very well.*
4 = **squashy**, sloppy, mushy, spongy, squidgy *(Brit. informal)*, squishy, gelatinous, squelchy, pulpy, doughy, gloopy *(informal)*, semi-liquid • *a simple bread made with a soft dough*
5 = **pliable**, flexible, supple, malleable, plastic, elastic, tensile, ductile *(of a metal)*, bendable, mouldable, impressible • *Aluminium is a soft metal.*
6 = **quiet**, low, gentle, sweet, whispered, soothing, murmured, muted, subdued, mellow, understated, melodious, mellifluous, dulcet, soft-toned • *When he woke again he could hear soft music.* • *She spoke in a soft whisper.*
OPPOSITES: loud, harsh, noisy
7 = **lenient**, easy-going, lax, liberal, weak, indulgent, permissive, spineless, boneless, overindulgent • *He says the measure is soft and weak on criminals.*
OPPOSITES: strict, harsh, stern
8 = **kind**, tender, sentimental, compassionate, sensitive, gentle, pitying, sympathetic, tenderhearted, touchy-feely *(informal)* • *a very soft and sensitive heart*
9 = **easy**, comfortable, undemanding, cushy *(informal)*, easy-peasy *(slang)* • *a soft option*
10 = **pale**, light, subdued, pastel, pleasing, bland, mellow • *The room was tempered by the soft colours.*
OPPOSITES: bright, gaudy, garish
11 = **dim**, faint, dimmed • *His skin looked golden in the soft light.*
OPPOSITES: bright, harsh, glaring
12 = **mild**, delicate, caressing, temperate, balmy • *a soft breeze*
13 = **feeble-minded**, simple, silly, foolish, daft *(informal)*, soft in the head *(informal)*, a bit lacking *(informal)* • *They were wary of him, thinking he was soft in the head.*

soften AS A VERB 1 = **melt**, tenderize • *Soften the butter mixture in a small saucepan.*
2 = **lessen**, moderate, diminish, temper, lower, relax, ease, calm, modify, cushion, soothe, subdue, alleviate, lighten, quell, muffle, allay, mitigate, abate, tone down, assuage • *He could not think how to soften the blow of what he had to tell her.*
▸ IN PHRASES: **soften someone up** = **win over**, weaken, disarm, soft-soap *(informal)*, work on, melt, conciliate • *If they'd treated you well it was only to soften you up.*

softly-softly = **cautious**, careful, wary, guarded, tentative, prudent, judicious, circumspect, chary, belt-and-braces • *the government's softly-softly approach to prison reform*

soggy = **sodden**, saturated, moist, heavy, soaked, dripping, waterlogged, sopping, mushy, spongy, pulpy • *soggy cheese and tomato sandwiches*

soil[1] 1 = **earth**, ground, clay, dust, dirt, loam • *regions with sandy soils*
2 = **territory**, country, land, region, turf *(U.S. slang)*, terrain • *The issue of foreign troops on Turkish soil is a sensitive one.*
▸ RELATED ADJECTIVE: telluric

soil[2] = **dirty**, foul, stain, smear, muddy, pollute, tarnish, spatter, sully, defile, besmirch, smirch, maculate *(literary)*, bedraggle, befoul, begrime • *Young people don't want to do things that soil their hands.*
OPPOSITES: clean, wash, bath

sojourn = **stay**, visit, stop, rest, stopover • *my first sojourn in Lhasa*

solace AS A NOUN = **comfort**, consolation, help, support, relief, succour, alleviation, assuagement • *I found solace in writing when my father died.*
▸ AS A VERB = **comfort**, console, soothe • *They solaced themselves with their fan mail.*

soldier AS A NOUN = **fighter**, serviceman, trooper, warrior, Tommy *(Brit. informal)*, GI *(U.S. informal)*, military man, redcoat, enlisted man *(U.S.)*, man-at-arms, squaddie *or* squaddy *(Brit. slang)* • *an attack on an off-duty soldier*
▸ IN PHRASES: **soldier on** = **carry on**, continue, keep going, press on, persevere, battle on, stick it out *(informal)*, plug away *(informal)*, stay the course, plod on • *The government has soldiered on as if nothing were wrong.*

sole[1] = **only**, one, single, individual, alone, exclusive, solitary, singular, one and only • *Their sole aim is to enjoy life.*

sole[2]
▸ RELATED ADJECTIVES: plantar, volar

solely = **only**, completely, entirely, exclusively, alone, singly, merely, single-handedly • *Too often we make decisions based solely on what we see in magazines.*

solemn 1 = **serious**, earnest, grave, sober, thoughtful, sedate, glum, staid, portentous • *His solemn little face broke into smiles.*
OPPOSITES: bright, cheerful, merry
2 = **formal**, august, grand, imposing, impressive, grave, majestic, dignified, ceremonial, stately, momentous, awe-inspiring, ceremonious • *This is a solemn occasion.*
OPPOSITES: informal, relaxed, unceremonious
3 = **sacred**, religious, holy, ritual, venerable, hallowed, sanctified, devotional, reverential • *a solemn religious ceremony*
OPPOSITES: unholy, irreligious, irreverent

solemnity 1 = **seriousness**, gravity, formality, grandeur, gravitas, earnestness, portentousness, momentousness, impressiveness • *the solemnity of the occasion*
2 *often plural* = **ritual**, proceedings, ceremony, rite, formalities, ceremonial, observance, celebration • *the constitutional solemnities*

solicit 1 = **request**, seek, ask for, petition, crave, pray for, plead for, canvass, beg for • *He's already solicited their support on health care reform.*
2 = **appeal to**, ask, call on, lobby, press, beg, petition, plead with, implore, beseech, entreat, importune, supplicate • *They were soliciting Nader's supporters to re-register as Republicans.*

3 = work as a prostitute, tout for business, make sexual advances, engage in prostitution • *Prostitutes were forbidden to solicit on public roads and in public places.*

solicitor = lawyer, attorney, counsel, advocate, barrister, counsellor, legal adviser • *I was a solicitor before I retired.*

solicitous = concerned, caring, attentive, careful • *He was so solicitous of his guests.*

solicitude = concern, care, consideration, attentiveness, worry, regard, anxiety, considerateness • *He is full of tender solicitude towards my sister.*

solid 1 = firm, hard, compact, dense, massed, concrete • *a tunnel carved through 50ft of solid rock*
OPPOSITES: unsubstantial, liquid, hollow
2 = strong, stable, sturdy, sound, substantial, durable, well-built, well-constructed, unshakable • *I stared up at the square, solid house.*
OPPOSITES: unstable, precarious, flimsy
3 = pure, unalloyed, unmixed, complete, genuine • *The taps appeared to be made of solid gold.*
4 = continuous, unbroken, uninterrupted • *a solid line*
5 = reliable, decent, dependable, upstanding, serious, constant, sensible, worthy, upright, sober, law-abiding, trusty, level-headed, estimable • *a good, solid member of the community*
OPPOSITES: unstable, irresponsible, unreliable
6 = sound, real, reliable, good, genuine, dinkum *(Austral. & N.Z. informal)* • *Some solid evidence was what was required.*
OPPOSITES: unreliable, unsound
7 = firm, united, unanimous, consistent, undivided, of one mind • *an attempt to build a solid international coalition*

solidarity = unity, harmony, unification, accord, stability, cohesion, team spirit, camaraderie, unanimity, soundness, concordance, esprit de corps, community of interest, singleness of purpose, like-mindedness, kotahitanga *(N.Z.)* • *Supporters want to march tomorrow to show solidarity with their leaders.*

solidify = harden, set, congeal, cake, jell, coagulate, cohere • *The thicker lava would have taken two weeks to solidify.*

soliloquy = monologue, address, speech, aside, oration, dramatic monologue • *On stage Hamlet is delivering his soliloquy.*

S

solitary 1 = unsociable, retiring, reclusive, unsocial, isolated, lonely, cloistered, lonesome, friendless, companionless, hermitical • *Paul was a shy, pleasant, solitary man.*
OPPOSITES: social, outgoing, sociable
2 = lone, alone • *His evenings were spent in solitary drinking.*
3 = isolated, remote, out-of-the-way, desolate, hidden, sequestered, unvisited, unfrequented • *a boy of eighteen in a solitary house in the Ohio countryside*
OPPOSITES: public, busy, frequented

QUOTATIONS
If you are idle, be not solitary; if you are solitary, be not idle
[Dr. Johnson]

solitude 1 = isolation, privacy, seclusion, retirement, loneliness, ivory tower, reclusiveness • *Imagine long golden beaches where you can wander in solitude.*
2 = wilderness, waste, desert, emptiness, wasteland • *travelling by yourself in these vast solitudes*
▸ RELATED MANIA: automania
▸ RELATED PHOBIA: eremophobia

QUOTATIONS
far from the madding crowd's ignoble strife
[Thomas Gray *Elegy Written in a Country Churchyard*]
Solitude should teach us how to die
[Lord Byron *Childe Harold*]
That inward eye
Which is the bliss of solitude
[William Wordsworth *I Wandered Lonely as a Cloud*]
Two paradises 'twere in one
To live in paradise alone
[Andrew Marvell *The Garden*]

solo AS AN ADJECTIVE **= unaccompanied**, independent, single-handed, lonely, solitary, unattended, unescorted, unchaperoned • *He completed a solo flight around the world in 1933.*
▸ AS AN ADVERB **= unaccompanied**, independently, single-handedly, alone, unattended, unescorted, unchaperoned, under your own steam, by your own efforts, companionless • *He became the very first person to fly solo across the Atlantic.*

solution 1 = answer, resolution, key, result, solving, explanation, unfolding, unravelling, clarification, explication, elucidation • *the ability to sort out effective solutions to practical problems*
2 = mixture, mix, compound, blend, suspension, solvent, emulsion • *a warm solution of liquid detergent*

solve = answer, work out, resolve, explain, crack, interpret, unfold, clarify, clear up, unravel, decipher, expound, suss (out) *(slang)*, get to the bottom of, disentangle, elucidate • *Their domestic reforms did nothing to solve unemployment.*

solvent AS AN ADJECTIVE **= financially sound**, secure, in the black, solid, profit-making, in credit, debt-free, unindebted • *They're going to have to show that the company is now solvent.*
▸ AS A NOUN **= resolvent**, dissolvent *(rare)* • *a small amount of cleaning solvent*

sombre 1 = gloomy, sad, sober, grave, dismal, melancholy, mournful, lugubrious, joyless, funereal, doleful, sepulchral • *The pair were in sombre mood.*
OPPOSITES: happy, bright, cheerful
2 = dark, dull, gloomy, sober, drab • *a worried official in sombre black*
OPPOSITES: bright, colourful, dazzling

somebody = celebrity, big name, public figure, name, star, heavyweight *(informal)*, notable, superstar, household name, dignitary, luminary, bigwig *(informal)*, celeb *(informal)*, big shot *(informal)*, personage, megastar *(informal)*, big wheel *(slang)*, big noise *(informal)*, big hitter *(informal)*, heavy hitter *(informal)*, person of note, V.I.P., someone • *He suddenly became a somebody.*
OPPOSITES: nothing *(informal)*, nobody, nonentity

someday = one day, eventually, ultimately, sooner or later, one of these (fine) days, in the fullness of time • *Someday I'll be a pilot.*

somehow = one way or another, come what may, come hell or high water *(informal)*, by fair means or foul, by hook or (by) crook, by some means or other • *I managed, somehow, to scrape a living.*

someone = somebody • *There's someone at the door.*

sometime AS AN ADVERB **= some day**, one day, at some point in the future, sooner or later, one of these days, by and by • *Why don't you come and see me sometime?*
▸ AS AN ADJECTIVE **= former**, one-time, erstwhile, ex-, late, past, previous • *She was in her early thirties, a sometime actress, dancer and singer.*

sometimes = occasionally, at times, now and then, from time to time, on occasion, now and again, once in a while, every now and then, every so often, off and on • *During the summer, my skin sometimes gets greasy.*
OPPOSITES: constantly, continually, always

somewhat = rather, quite, a little, sort of *(informal)*, kind of *(informal)*, a bit, pretty *(informal)*, fairly, relatively, slightly, moderately, to some extent, to some degree • *He concluded that Oswald was somewhat abnormal.*

somnolent 1 = sleepy, drowsy, dozy, comatose, nodding off *(informal)*, torpid, half-awake, heavy-eyed • *The sedative makes people very somnolent.*
2 = quiet, peaceful, dull, sleepy, tranquil, inactive • *the somnolent villages of Sicily*

son = **male child**, boy, lad *(informal)*, descendant, son and heir • *He shared a pizza with his son, Laurence.*
▸ **RELATED ADJECTIVE:** filial

QUOTATIONS
A wise son maketh a glad father; but a foolish son is the heaviness of his mother
[*Bible: Proverbs*]

PROVERBS
Like father like son

song **AS A NOUN** 1 = **ballad**, air, tune, lay, strain, carol, lyric, chant, chorus, melody, anthem, number, hymn, psalm, shanty, pop song, ditty, canticle, canzonet, waiata *(N.Z.)* • *a voice singing a Spanish song*
2 = **birdsong**, call, warbling, chirp, chirping, warble, twitter, twittering, cheep, chirrup, chirruping, cheeping • *It's been a long time since I heard a blackbird's song in the evening.*
▸ **IN PHRASES:** **on song** = **on form**, fit, in good shape, in good condition, toned up, in good trim • *When he is on song he is a world beater.*

song and dance = **fuss**, to-do, flap *(informal)*, performance *(informal)*, stir, pantomime *(informal)*, commotion, ado, shindig *(informal)*, kerfuffle *(informal)*, hoo-ha, pother, shindy *(informal)* • *He used his money to help others – but he never made a song and dance about it.*

songbird
▸ **RELATED ADJECTIVE:** oscine

sonorous 1 = **rich**, deep, ringing, resonant, full, rounded, sounding, loud, resounding, plangent • *'Doctor McKee?' the man called in an even, sonorous voice.*
2 = **high-flown**, grandiloquent, high-sounding, orotund • *a clutch of children with sonorous Old Testament names*

soon = **before long**, shortly, in the near future, in a minute, anon *(archaic)*, in a short time, in a little while, any minute now, betimes *(archaic)*, in two shakes of a lamb's tail, erelong *(archaic or poetic)*, in a couple of shakes • *You'll be hearing from us very soon.*

sooner 1 = **earlier**, before, already, beforehand, ahead of time • *I thought she would have recovered sooner.*
2 = **rather**, more readily, by preference, more willingly • *They would sooner die than stay in London.*

soothe 1 = **calm**, still, quiet, hush, settle, calm down, appease, lull, mitigate, pacify, mollify, smooth down, tranquillize • *He would take her in his arms and soothe her.*
OPPOSITES: worry, excite, upset
2 = **relieve**, ease, alleviate, dull, diminish, soften, assuage, deaden, take the edge off • *Lemon tisanes with honey can soothe sore throats.*
OPPOSITES: irritate, exacerbate, increase

soothing 1 = **calming**, relaxing, peaceful, quiet, calm, restful • *Put on some nice soothing music.*
2 = **emollient**, palliative, balsamic, demulcent, easeful, lenitive • *Cold tea is very soothing for burns.*

soothsayer = **prophet**, diviner, oracle, fortune-teller, forecaster, Cassandra, seer, clairvoyant, augur, sibyl, prognosticator, prophesier • *You don't have to be a soothsayer to predict his likely tactics.*

sophisticated 1 = **complex**, advanced, complicated, subtle, delicate, elaborate, refined, intricate, multifaceted, highly-developed • *a large and sophisticated new telescope*
OPPOSITES: simple, basic, uncomplicated
2 = **cultured**, refined, cultivated, worldly, cosmopolitan, urbane, jet-set, world-weary, citified, worldly-wise • *Recently her tastes have become more sophisticated.*
OPPOSITES: unsophisticated, unrefined, unworldly

sophistication = **poise**, worldliness, savoir-faire, urbanity, finesse, savoir-vivre *(French)*, worldly wisdom • *They now have the sophistication attained by performing in public.*

sophistry = **fallacy**, quibble, casuistry, sophism, specious reasoning • *a triumph of sophistry*

soporific = **sleep-inducing**, hypnotic, sedative, sleepy, somnolent, tranquillizing, somniferous *(rare)* • *the soporific effects of alcohol*

QUOTATIONS
It is said that the effect of eating too much lettuce is 'soporific'
[Beatrix Potter *The Tale of the Flopsy Bunnies*]

soppy = **sentimental**, corny *(slang)*, slushy *(informal)*, soft *(informal)*, silly, daft *(informal)*, weepy *(informal)*, mawkish, drippy *(informal)*, lovey-dovey, schmaltzy *(slang)*, icky *(informal)*, gushy *(informal)*, overemotional, three-hankie *(informal)* • *She loves soppy love stories.*

sorcerer *or* **sorceress** = **magician**, witch, wizard, magus, warlock, mage *(archaic)*, enchanter, necromancer • *In voodoo the sorcerer manipulates the victim's symbolic image.*

sorcery = **black magic**, witchcraft, black art, necromancy, spell, magic, charm, wizardry, enchantment, divination, incantation, witchery • *The man swore never to practise sorcery again, and was released.*

sordid 1 = **base**, degraded, shameful, low, vicious, shabby, vile, degenerate, despicable, disreputable, debauched • *He put his head in his hands as his sordid life was exposed.*
OPPOSITES: pure, decent, honourable
2 = **dirty**, seedy, sleazy, squalid, mean, foul, filthy, unclean, wretched, seamy, slovenly, skanky *(slang)*, slummy, scungy *(Austral. & N.Z.)*, festy *(Austral. slang)* • *the attic windows of their sordid little rooms*
OPPOSITES: clean, spotless, fresh

sore **AS AN ADJECTIVE** 1 = **painful**, smarting, raw, tender, burning, angry, sensitive, irritated, inflamed, chafed, reddened • *My chest is still sore from the surgery.*
2 = **annoyed**, cross, angry, pained, hurt, upset, stung, irritated, grieved, pissed *(U.S. slang)*, pissed (off) *(taboo slang)*, resentful, aggrieved, vexed, irked, peeved *(informal)*, tooshie *(Austral. slang)*, hoha *(N.Z.)* • *The result of it is that they are all feeling very sore at you.*
3 = **annoying**, distressing, troublesome, harrowing, grievous • *Timing is frequently a sore point.*
4 = **urgent**, desperate, extreme, dire, pressing, critical, acute • *The prime minister is in sore need of friends.*
▸ **AS A NOUN** = **abscess**, boil, ulcer, inflammation, gathering • *All of us had long sores on our backs.*

sorrow **AS A NOUN** 1 = **grief**, sadness, woe, regret, distress, misery, mourning, anguish, unhappiness, heartache, heartbreak, affliction • *It was a time of great sorrow.*
OPPOSITES: joy, happiness, delight
2 = **hardship**, trial, tribulation, affliction, worry, trouble, blow, grief, woe, misfortune, bummer *(slang)* • *the joys and sorrows of family life*
OPPOSITES: good fortune, lucky break
▸ **AS A VERB** = **grieve**, mourn, lament, weep, moan, be sad, bemoan, agonize, eat your heart out, bewail • *She was lamented by a large circle of sorrowing friends and acquaintances.*
OPPOSITES: celebrate, rejoice, exult

QUOTATIONS
There is no greater sorrow than to recall a time of happiness in misery
[Dante *Divine Comedy*]
Into each life some rain must fall
[Henry Wadsworth Longfellow]
Sorrow makes us wise
[Alfred Tennyson *In Memoriam*]
Sorrow is tranquillity remembered in emotion
[Dorothy Parker *Here Lies*]

sorrowful = **sad**, unhappy, miserable, sorry, depressed, painful, distressed, grieving, dismal, afflicted, melancholy, tearful, heartbroken, woeful, mournful, dejected, rueful, lugubrious, wretched, disconsolate, doleful, heavy-hearted, down in the dumps *(informal)*, woebegone, piteous, sick at

S

heart • *His father's face looked suddenly soft and sorrowful.*

sorry 1 = **regretful**, apologetic, contrite, repentant, guilt-ridden, remorseful, penitent, shamefaced, conscience-stricken, in sackcloth and ashes, self-reproachful • *She was very sorry about all the trouble she'd caused.*
OPPOSITES: unrepentant, unashamed, unapologetic
2 = **sympathetic**, moved, full of pity, pitying, compassionate, commiserative • *I am very sorry for the family.*
OPPOSITES: indifferent, unmoved, unsympathetic
3 = **sad**, distressed, unhappy, grieved, melancholy, mournful, sorrowful, disconsolate • *What he must not do is sit around at home feeling sorry for himself.*
OPPOSITES: happy, delighted, cheerful
4 = **wretched**, miserable, pathetic, mean, base, poor, sad, distressing, dismal, shabby, vile, paltry, pitiful, abject, deplorable, pitiable, piteous • *She is in a sorry state.*

sort **AS A NOUN** 1 = **kind**, type, class, make, group, family, order, race, style, quality, character, nature, variety, brand, species, breed, category, stamp, description, denomination, genus, ilk • *What sort of person is he?*
2 = **person**, individual, type, customer *(informal)*, soul, creature, human being, bloke *(informal)*, chap *(informal)* • *He seemed to be just the right sort for the job.*
▸ **AS A VERB** 1 = **arrange**, group, order, class, separate, file, rank, divide, grade, sequence, distribute, catalogue, classify, categorize, tabulate, systematize, put in order, assort • *He sorted the materials into their folders.*
2 = **resolve**, answer, work out, clear up, crack, fathom, suss (out) *(slang)*, find the solution to • *These problems have now been sorted.*
▸ **IN PHRASES: all sorts of** = **various**, varied, diverse, divers *(archaic)*, assorted, miscellaneous, sundry • *It was used by all sorts of people.*
of sorts = **of a kind** • *He has made a living of sorts selling pancakes from a van.*
out of sorts 1 = **irritable**, cross, edgy, tense, crabbed, snarling, prickly, snappy, touchy, bad-tempered, petulant, ill-tempered, irascible, cantankerous, tetchy, ratty *(Brit. & N.Z. informal)*, testy, chippy *(informal)*, fretful, grouchy *(informal)*, peevish, crabby, dyspeptic, choleric, crotchety, oversensitive, snappish, ill-humoured, narky *(Brit. slang)*, out of humour • *Lack of sleep can leave us feeling jaded and out of sorts.*
2 = **depressed**, miserable, in low spirits, down, low, blue, sad, unhappy, gloomy, melancholy, mournful, dejected, despondent, dispirited, downcast, long-faced, sorrowful, disconsolate, crestfallen, down in the dumps *(informal)*, down in the mouth *(informal)*, mopy • *You are feeling out of sorts and unable to see the wood for the trees.*
3 = **unwell**, ill, sick, poorly *(informal)*, funny *(informal)*, crook *(Austral. & N.Z. informal)*, ailing, queer, unhealthy, seedy *(informal)*, laid up *(informal)*, queasy, infirm, dicky *(Brit. informal)*, off colour, under the weather *(informal)*, at death's door, indisposed, on the sick list *(informal)*, not up to par, valetudinarian, green about the gills, not up to snuff *(informal)* • *At times, he has seemed lifeless and out of sorts.*
sort of = **rather**, somewhat, as it were, slightly, moderately, in part, reasonably • *I sort of made my own happiness.*
sort someone out = **deal with**, handle, cope with, take care of, see to, attend to • *The crucial skill you need to develop is sorting out the parents.*
sort something out 1 = **resolve**, work out, clear up, clarify, tidy up, put *or* get straight • *They have sorted out their trade and security dispute.*
2 = **organize**, tidy, straighten out, put in order, arrange, catalogue, classify, categorize • *He carried out the usual checks and sorted out the paperwork.*
sort something out from something 1 = **separate**, determine, distinguish, differentiate, tell apart • *How do we sort out fact from fiction?*
2 = **sift**, separate, pick out, select, segregate • *We need to sort out the genuine cases from the layabouts.*

sortie 1 = **outing**, trip, expedition, excursion, jaunt, spin *(informal)*, awayday, pleasure trip • *From here we plan several sorties into the countryside.*
2 = **raid**, operation, mission, flight • *They flew 2,700 sorties in a day and didn't lose a single plane.*

so-so = **average**, middling, fair, ordinary, moderate, adequate, respectable, indifferent, not bad *(informal)*, tolerable, run-of-the-mill, passable, undistinguished, fair to middling *(informal)*, O.K. *or* okay *(informal)* • *Their lunch was only so-so.*

sought-after = **in demand**, wanted, desirable, longed-for, coveted, enviable, to-die-for, like gold dust • *An Olympic gold medal is the most sought-after prize in sport.*

soul 1 = **spirit**, essence, psyche, life, mind, reason, intellect, vital force, animating principle, wairua *(N.Z.)* • *Such memories stirred in his soul.*
2 = **embodiment**, essence, incarnation, epitome, personification, quintessence, type • *With such celebrated clients, she necessarily remains the soul of discretion.*
3 = **person**, being, human, individual, body, creature, mortal, man *or* woman • *a tiny village of only 100 souls*
4 = **feeling**, force, energy, vitality, animation, fervour, ardour, vivacity • *an ice goddess without soul*
▸ **RELATED ADJECTIVE:** pneumatic

soul-destroying = **mind-numbing**, dull, tedious, dreary, tiresome, treadmill, monotonous, humdrum, wearisome, unvarying • *an utterly soul-destroying job*

soulful = **expressive**, sensitive, eloquent, moving, profound, meaningful, heartfelt, mournful • *his great, soulful, brown eyes*

soulless 1 = **characterless**, dull, bland, mundane, ordinary, grey, commonplace, dreary, mediocre, drab, uninspiring, colourless, featureless, unexceptional • *a clean but soulless hotel*
2 = **unfeeling**, dead, cold, lifeless, inhuman, harsh, cruel, callous, unkind, unsympathetic, spiritless • *He was big and brawny with soulless eyes.*

sound[1] **AS A NOUN** 1 = **noise**, racket, din, report, tone, bang, resonance, hubbub, reverberation • *Peter heard the sound of gunfire.*
2 = **idea**, prospect, impression, implication(s), drift • *Here's a new idea we like the sound of.*
3 = **cry**, noise, peep, squeak • *She didn't make a sound.*
4 = **tone**, music, note, chord, tenor • *the soulful sound of the violin*
5 = **earshot**, hearing, hearing distance • *I was born and bred within the sound of the cathedral bells.*
▸ **AS A VERB** 1 = **toll**, set off • *A young man sounds the bell to start the Sunday service.*
2 = **resound**, echo, go off, toll, set off, chime, resonate, reverberate, ding, clang, peal • *A silvery bell sounded somewhere.*
3 = **express**, declare, utter, announce, signal, pronounce, articulate, enunciate • *Others consider the move premature and have sounded a note of caution.*
4 = **seem**, seem to be, appear to be, give the impression of being, strike you as being, give every indication of being • *She sounded a bit worried.*
▸ **RELATED ADJECTIVES:** sonic, acoustic
▸ **RELATED PHOBIA:** akousticophobia

sound[2] 1 = **fit**, healthy, robust, firm, perfect, intact, vigorous, hale, unhurt, undamaged, uninjured, unimpaired, hale and hearty • *His body was still sound.*
OPPOSITES: weak, ailing, frail
2 = **sturdy**, strong, solid, stable, substantial, durable, stout, well-constructed • *a perfectly sound building*
3 = **safe**, secure, reliable, proven, established, recognized,

S

solid, stable, solvent, reputable, tried-and-true • *a sound financial proposition*
OPPOSITES: unreliable, unsound, unstable
4 = **sensible**, wise, reasonable, right, true, responsible, correct, proper, reliable, valid, orthodox, rational, logical, prudent, trustworthy, well-founded, level-headed, right-thinking, well-grounded, grounded • *They are trained nutritionists who can give sound advice on diets.*
OPPOSITES: irresponsible, faulty, irrational
5 = **deep**, peaceful, unbroken, undisturbed, untroubled • *She has woken me out of a sound sleep.*
OPPOSITES: broken, troubled, fitful
6 = **thorough**, complete, total, severe, absolute, downright, unqualified, out-and-out, unmitigated • *a sound beating*

QUOTATIONS
a sound mind in a sound body
[Juvenal *Satires*]

sound[3] **IN PHRASES: sound someone out = question**, interview, survey, poll, examine, investigate, pump *(informal)*, inspect, canvass, test the opinion of • *Sound him out gradually.*
sound something out = investigate, research, examine, probe, look into, test the water, put out feelers to, see how the land lies, carry out an investigation of • *They are discreetly sounding out blue-chip American banks.*

sound[4] = **channel**, passage, strait, inlet, fjord, voe, arm of the sea • *a blizzard blasting great drifts of snow across the sound*

soundly 1 = **thoroughly**, completely, absolutely • *They were soundly beaten.*
2 = **sensibly**, wisely, prudently, correctly, properly, reasonably, logically, rationally, responsibly • *Changes must be soundly based in economic reality.*
3 = **deeply**, peacefully, without waking • *How can he sleep soundly at night?*

soup = **broth**, bisque, chowder, consommé, bouillon, goulash, pot au feu • *home-made chicken soup*

sour **AS AN ADJECTIVE** 1 = **sharp**, acid, tart, bitter, unpleasant, pungent, acetic, acidulated, acerb • *The stewed apple was sour even with honey.*
OPPOSITES: sweet, sugary, pleasant
2 = **rancid**, turned, gone off, fermented, unsavoury, curdled, unwholesome, gone bad, off • *tiny fridges full of sour milk*
OPPOSITES: fresh, unspoiled, unimpaired
3 = **bitter**, cynical, crabbed, tart, discontented, grudging, acrimonious, embittered, disagreeable, churlish, ill-tempered, jaundiced, waspish, grouchy *(informal)*, ungenerous, peevish, ill-natured • *He became a sour, lonely old man.*
OPPOSITES: pleasant, good-humoured, good-natured
▸ **AS A VERB = embitter**, disenchant, alienate, envenom • *The experience, she says, has soured her.*

source **AS A NOUN** 1 = **cause**, origin, derivation, beginning, author, commencement, begetter • *This gave me a clue as to the source of the problem.*
2 = **informant**, authority, documentation • *a major source of information about the arts*
3 = **origin**, spring, fount, fountainhead, wellspring, rise • *the source of the Tiber*
▸ **AS A VERB = obtain**, get, acquire, score *(slang)*, secure, get hold of, come by, procure • *furniture sourced from all over the world*

sourness
▸ **RELATED PHOBIA:** acerophobia

south
▸ **RELATED ADJECTIVES:** austral, meridional

souvenir = **keepsake**, token, reminder, relic, remembrancer *(archaic)*, memento • *a souvenir of the summer of 1992*

sovereign **AS AN ADJECTIVE** 1 = **independent**, autonomous, self-governing, free, non-aligned, self-determining • *The Russian Federation declared itself to be a sovereign republic.*
2 = **supreme**, ruling, absolute, chief, royal, principal, dominant, imperial, unlimited, paramount, regal, predominant, monarchal, kingly *or* queenly • *No contract can absolutely restrain a sovereign power.*
3 = **excellent**, valuable, efficient, helpful, reliable, worthwhile, unfailing, efficacious, effectual • *wild garlic, a sovereign remedy in any healer's chest*
▸ **AS A NOUN = monarch**, ruler, king *or* queen, chief, shah, potentate, supreme ruler, emperor *or* empress, prince *or* princess, tsar *or* tsarina • *the first British sovereign to set foot on Spanish soil*

sovereignty = **supreme power**, domination, supremacy, primacy, sway, ascendancy, kingship, suzerainty, rangatiratanga *(N.Z.)* • *Britain's concern to protect national sovereignty is far from new.*

sow **AS A VERB** 1 = **scatter**, plant, seed, lodge, implant, disseminate, broadcast, inseminate • *Yesterday the field opposite was sown with maize.*
2 = **produce**, cause, create, occasion, generate, provoke, induce, bring about, give rise to, precipitate, incite, engender • *He sowed doubt into the minds of his rivals.*
▸ **IN PHRASES: sow the seeds of something = set in motion**, trigger, initiate, originate, activate, get going, engender, instigate, kick-start • *Rich industrialised countries have sowed the seeds of global warming.*

space **AS A NOUN** 1 = **room**, volume, capacity, extent, margin, extension, scope, play, expanse, leeway, amplitude, spaciousness, elbowroom • *The furniture proved impractical because it took up too much space.*
2 = **gap**, opening, interval, gulf, cavity, aperture • *The space underneath could be used as a storage area.*
3 = **period**, interval, time, while, stretch, span, duration, time frame, timeline • *They've come a long way in a short space of time.*
4 = **outer space**, the universe, the galaxy, the solar system, the cosmos • *launching satellites into space*
5 = **blank**, gap, interval • *Affix your stamps on the space provided.*
▸ **IN PHRASES: space something** *or* **someone out = place**, set, position, order, stand, station, settle, arrange, locate, deploy, array, dispose • *Space them out so that they don't overlap at any point.*
▸ **RELATED ADJECTIVE:** spatial

spacecraft = **spaceship**, space shuttle, space probe, space capsule, space rocket, lunar module • *We turned the spacecraft so the sun fell more fully on the antenna.*

spaceman *or* **spacewoman** = **astronaut**, cosmonaut, space cadet, space traveller • *He wants to give up acting to become a spaceman.*

spacious = **roomy**, large, huge, broad, vast, extensive, ample, expansive, capacious, uncrowded, commodious, comfortable, sizable *or* sizeable • *The house has a spacious kitchen and dining area.*
OPPOSITES: limited, narrow, restricted

Spain
▸ **RELATED ADJECTIVE:** Spanish
▹ *See panel* **Administrative regions**

span **AS A NOUN** 1 = **period**, term, duration, course, stretch, spell • *The batteries had a life span of six hours.*
2 = **extent**, reach, spread, length, distance, stretch • *With a span of 6ft, her wings dominated the stage.*
▸ **AS A VERB** 1 = **extend over**, cover, encompass, last, comprise, spread over, stretch across, range over • *a man whose interests spanned almost every aspect of nature* • *His professional career spanned 16 years.*
2 = **extend across**, cross, bridge, cover, link, vault, traverse, range over, arch across • *the humped iron bridge spanning the railway*

S

spank = **smack**, slap, whack, belt *(informal)*, tan *(slang)*, slipper *(informal)*, cuff, wallop *(informal)*, give (someone) a hiding *(informal)*, put (someone) over your knee • *She saw him spank the girl several times.*

spanking = **smacking**, hiding *(informal)*, whacking, slapping, walloping *(informal)* • *Andrea gave her son a sound spanking.*

spanking 1 = **smart**, brand-new, fine, gleaming • *a spanking new car*
2 = **fast**, quick, brisk, lively, smart, vigorous, energetic, snappy • *The film moves along at a spanking pace.*

spar = **argue**, row, squabble, dispute, scrap *(informal)*, fall out *(informal)*, spat *(U.S.)*, wrangle, skirmish, bicker, have a tiff • *The sparring couple have declared a truce in public.*

spare AS AN ADJECTIVE 1 = **back-up**, reserve, second, extra, relief, emergency, additional, substitute, fall-back, auxiliary, in reserve • *He could have taken a spare key.*
2 = **extra**, surplus, leftover, over, free, odd, unwanted, in excess, unused, superfluous, going begging, supernumerary • *They don't have a lot of spare cash.*
OPPOSITES: needed, necessary, spoken for
3 = **free**, leisure, unoccupied, own • *In her spare time she raises funds for charity.*
4 = **thin**, lean, slim, slender, slight, meagre, gaunt, wiry, lank, macilent *(rare)* • *She was thin and spare, with a shapely intelligent face.*
OPPOSITES: heavy, fat, plump
5 = **meagre**, sparing, modest, economical, frugal, scanty • *The two rooms were spare and neat, stripped bare of ornaments.*
▸ AS A VERB 1 = **afford**, give, grant, do without, relinquish, part with, allow, bestow, dispense with, manage without, let someone have • *He suggested that his country could not spare the troops.*
2 = **have mercy on**, pardon, have pity on, leave, release, excuse, let off *(informal)*, not harm, go easy on *(informal)*, leave unharmed, be merciful to, grant pardon to, deal leniently with, leave uninjured, refrain from hurting, save (from harm) • *Not a man was spared.*
OPPOSITES: show no mercy to, condemn, punish
▸ IN PHRASES: **go spare** = **become angry**, become upset, go mental *(slang)*, become distracted, become enraged, become mad *(informal)*, go up the wall *(slang)*, become distraught, blow your top *(informal)*, be *or* get pissed (off) *(taboo slang)*, do your nut *(Brit. slang)*, have *or* throw a fit *(informal)* • *She went spare when we told her what had happened.*
to spare = **left**, remaining, extra, surplus, left over, superfluous, unused • *You got here with ninety seconds to spare.*

spare time = **leisure time**, free time, odd moments, time to kill, time on your hands • *I spend a lot of my spare time watching videos.*

sparing = **economical**, frugal, thrifty, saving, careful, prudent, cost-conscious, chary, money-conscious • *I've not been sparing with the garlic.*
OPPOSITES: liberal, lavish, extravagant

spark AS A NOUN 1 = **flicker**, flash, gleam, glint, spit, flare, scintillation • *Sparks flew in all directions.*
2 = **trace**, hint, scrap, atom, jot, vestige, scintilla • *Even Oliver felt a tiny spark of excitement.*
▸ AS A VERB *often with* **off** = **start**, stimulate, provoke, excite, inspire, stir, trigger (off), set off, animate, rouse, prod, precipitate, kick-start, set in motion, kindle, touch off • *What was it that sparked your interest in motoring?*

sparkle AS A VERB 1 = **glitter**, flash, spark, shine, beam, glow, gleam, wink, shimmer, twinkle, dance, glint, glisten, glister *(archaic)*, scintillate, coruscate • *His bright eyes sparkled.*
2 = **be lively**, be full of life, be bubbly, be ebullient, be vivacious, be effervescent • *She sparkles, and has as much zest as a person half her age.*
▸ AS A NOUN 1 = **glitter**, flash, gleam, spark, dazzle, flicker, brilliance, twinkle, glint, radiance, coruscation • *There was a sparkle in her eye that could not be hidden.*
2 = **vivacity**, life, spirit, dash, zip *(informal)*, vitality, animation, panache, gaiety, élan, brio, liveliness, vim *(slang)* • *There was little sparkle in their performance.*

sparkling 1 = **fizzy**, bubbly, effervescent, frothy, carbonated, foamy, gassy • *a glass of sparkling wine*
2 = **vibrant**, lively, animated, vivacious, bright, brilliant, ebullient, effervescent • *He is sparkling and versatile in front of the camera.*
3 = **glittering**, bright, glistening, flashing, shining, gleaming, shimmering, twinkling, glinting, scintillating, lustrous • *jellies that look like sparkling jewels in the fall sunshine*

sparrow
▸ RELATED ADJECTIVE: passerine
▸ COLLECTIVE NOUN: host

sparse = **scattered**, scarce, meagre, sporadic, few and far between, scanty • *Many slopes are rock fields with sparse vegetation.*
OPPOSITES: thick, lavish, dense

Spartan = **austere**, severe, frugal, ascetic, plain, disciplined, extreme, strict, stern, bleak, rigorous, stringent, abstemious, self-denying, bare-bones • *Their spartan lifestyle prohibits a fridge or a phone.*

spasm 1 = **convulsion**, contraction, paroxysm, twitch, throe *(rare)* • *A lack of magnesium causes muscles to go into spasm.*
2 = **burst**, fit, outburst, seizure, frenzy, eruption, access • *He felt a spasm of fear.*

spasmodic = **sporadic**, irregular, erratic, intermittent, jerky, fitful, convulsive • *My husband's work was so spasmodic.*

spat = **quarrel**, dispute, squabble, controversy, contention, bickering, tiff, altercation, turf war *(informal)* • *a spat over interest rates and currencies*

spate 1 = **flood**, flow, torrent, rush, deluge, outpouring • *an incomprehensible spate of words*
2 = **series**, sequence, course, chain, succession, run, train, string • *the current spate of scandals*

spatter = **splash**, spray, sprinkle, soil, dirty, scatter, daub, speckle, splodge, bespatter, bestrew • *Blood spattered the dark concrete.*

spawn AS A NOUN = **offspring**, issue, product, seed *(chiefly biblical)*, progeny, yield • *They are the spawn of Bible-belting repression.*
▸ AS A VERB = **generate**, produce, give rise to, start, prompt, provoke, set off, bring about, spark off, set in motion • *His novels spawned both movies and television shows.*

speak AS A VERB 1 = **talk**, say something • *The President spoke of the need for territorial compromise.*
2 = **articulate**, say, voice, pronounce, utter, tell, state, talk, express, communicate, make known, enunciate • *The very act of speaking the words gave him comfort.*
3 = **converse**, talk, chat, discourse, confer, commune, have a word, have a talk, natter *(Brit. informal)*, exchange views, shoot the breeze *(slang, chiefly U.S. & Canad.)*, korero *(N.Z.)* • *It was very emotional when we spoke again.*
4 = **lecture**, talk, discourse, spout *(informal)*, make a speech, pontificate, give a speech, declaim, hold forth, spiel *(informal)*, address an audience, deliver an address, orate, speechify • *Last month I spoke in front of two thousand people in Birmingham.*
▸ IN PHRASES: **speak for something** *or* **someone** 1 = **represent**, act for *or* on behalf of, appear for, hold a brief for, hold a mandate for • *It was the job of the church to speak for the underprivileged.*
2 = **support**, back, champion, defend, promote, advocate, fight for, uphold, commend, espouse, stick up for *(informal)* • *a role in which he would be seen as speaking for the Government*
speak of something 1 = **deal with**, discuss, go into, write about, be concerned with, touch upon, discourse upon • *Throughout the book Liu speaks of the abuse of Party power.*

2 = **indicate**, show, reveal, display, suggest, signal, point to, imply, manifest, signify, denote, bespeak, be symptomatic of, betoken • *His behaviour spoke of an early maturity.*
speak out *or* **up** 1 = **speak publicly**, have your say, speak your mind, sound off, stand up and be counted, speak openly, speak frankly, make your position plain • *She continued to speak out at rallies around the country.*
2 = **speak loudly**, raise your voice, make yourself heard, say it loud and clear • *I'm quite deaf – you'll have to speak up.*
speak to someone 1 = **reprimand**, rebuke, scold, check, lecture, censure, reproach, tick off *(informal)*, castigate, chide, dress down *(informal)*, admonish, tell off *(informal)*, take to task, read the riot act, tongue-lash, reprove, upbraid, slap on the wrist *(informal)*, bawl out *(informal)*, rap over the knuckles, haul over the coals *(informal)*, tear (someone) off a strip *(Brit. informal)*, reprehend, give (someone) a row *(informal)*, send someone away with a flea in his *or* her ear *(informal)* • *This is not the first time I have had to speak to you about your timekeeping.*
2 = **address**, talk to, accost, direct your words at, apostrophize • *Are you speaking to me?*

speaker = **orator**, public speaker, lecturer, spokesperson, mouthpiece, spieler *(informal)*, word-spinner, spokesman *or* spokeswoman • *He was not a good speaker.*

spear = **gore**, pierce, lance, bayonet, impale • *A police officer was speared to death.*

spearhead AS A VERB = **lead**, head, pioneer, launch, set off, initiate, lead the way, set in motion, blaze the trail, be in the van, lay the first stone • *She's spearheading a national campaign against bullying.*
▸ AS A NOUN = **leader**, front runner, driving force, front line • *He will be their attacking spearhead.*

special 1 = **exceptional**, important, significant, particular, unique, unusual, extraordinary, distinguished, memorable, gala, festive, uncommon, momentous, out of the ordinary, one in a million, red-letter, especial • *I usually reserve these outfits for special occasions.*
OPPOSITES: common, ordinary, normal
2 = **major**, chief, main, primary • *He is a special correspondent for Newsweek magazine.*
3 = **specific**, particular, distinctive, certain, individual, appropriate, characteristic, precise, signature, peculiar, specialized, especial • *It requires a very special brand of courage to fight dictators.*
OPPOSITES: general, unspecialized, undistinctive

specialist = **expert**, authority, professional, master, consultant, guru, buff *(informal)*, whizz *(informal)*, connoisseur, boffin *(Brit. informal)*, hotshot *(informal)*, wonk *(informal)*, maven *(U.S.)*, fundi *(S. African)* • *a specialist in diseases of the nervous system*

speciality 1 = **forte**, strength, special talent, métier, specialty, bag *(slang)*, claim to fame, pièce de résistance *(French)*, distinctive *or* distinguishing feature • *His speciality was creating rich, creamy sauces.*
2 = **special subject**, specialty, field of study, branch of knowledge, area of specialization • *His speciality was the history of Germany.*

specialized = **in-depth**, comprehensive, extensive, detailed, complete, concentrated, intensive, thorough, far-reaching, exhaustive, all-embracing, encyclopedic • *a specialized knowledge of American History*

specialize in = **concentrate on**, focus on, centre on, zero in on *(informal)* • *a Portuguese restaurant which specializes in seafood*

specially 1 = **specifically**, especially, particularly, exclusively • *a soap specially designed for those with sensitive skins*
2 = **particularly**, especially, notably, exceptionally, markedly, outstandingly • *What was specially enjoyable about that job?*

species = **kind**, sort, type, group, class, variety, breed, category, description, genus • *There are several thousand species of trees here.*

specific AS AN ADJECTIVE 1 = **particular**, special, characteristic, distinguishing, signature, peculiar, definite, especial • *the specific needs of the individual*
OPPOSITES: general, common
2 = **precise**, exact, explicit, definite, limited, express, clear-cut, unequivocal, unambiguous • *I asked him to be more specific.*
OPPOSITES: general, vague, unclear
3 = **peculiar**, appropriate, individual, particular, personal, unique, restricted, idiosyncratic, endemic • *Send your resume with a covering letter that is specific to that particular job.*
▸ AS A PLURAL NOUN = **fine points**, particulars, niceties, minutiae, trivialities • *Things improved when we got down to the specifics.*

specifically 1 = **particularly**, peculiarly, uniquely, individually, idiosyncratically • *the only book specifically about that event*
2 = **precisely**, exactly, explicitly, unambiguously • *brain cells, or more specifically, neurons*
3 = **solely**, completely, entirely, exclusively, only • *a specifically female audience*

specification 1 = **requirement**, detail, particular, stipulation, condition, qualification • *I'd like to have a house built to my specifications.*
2 = **statement**, description, definition, setting out, instancing, citing, prescription, identification, itemizing • *such difficulties as the unclear specification of measures*

specify = **state**, designate, spell out, stipulate, name, detail, mention, indicate, define, cite, individualize, enumerate, itemize, be specific about, particularize • *He has not specified what action he would like them to take.*

specimen 1 = **sample**, example, individual, model, type, pattern, instance, representative, exemplar, exemplification • *a perfect specimen of a dinosaur fossil*
2 = **example**, model, exhibit, embodiment, type • *a fine specimen of manhood*

specious = **fallacious**, misleading, deceptive, plausible, unsound, sophistic, sophistical, casuistic • *The Duke was not convinced by such specious arguments.*

speck 1 = **mark**, spot, dot, stain, blot, fleck, speckle, mote • *There is a speck of blood by his ear.*
2 = **particle**, bit, grain, dot, atom, shred, mite, jot, modicum, whit, tittle, iota • *He leaned forward and brushed a speck of dust off his shoes.*

speckled = **flecked**, spotted, dotted, sprinkled, spotty, freckled, mottled, dappled, stippled, brindled, speckledy • *The sky was speckled with stars.*

spectacle 1 = **show**, display, exhibition, event, performance, sight, parade, extravaganza, pageant • *a director passionate about music and spectacle*
2 = **sight**, wonder, scene, phenomenon, curiosity, marvel, laughing stock • *the bizarre spectacle of an actor desperately demanding an encore*

spectacles = **glasses**, specs *(informal)*, eyeglasses *(U.S.)*, eyewear • *He looked at me over the tops of his spectacles.*

spectacular AS AN ADJECTIVE = **impressive**, striking, dramatic, stunning *(informal)*, marked, grand, remarkable, fantastic *(informal)*, magnificent, staggering, splendid, dazzling, sensational, breathtaking, eye-catching, gee-whizz *(slang)* • *The results have been spectacular.*
OPPOSITES: ordinary, unimpressive, unspectacular
▸ AS A NOUN = **show**, display, spectacle, extravaganza • *a television spectacular*

spectator = **onlooker**, observer, viewer, witness, looker-on, watcher, eyewitness, bystander, beholder • *Thirty thousand spectators watched the final game.*
OPPOSITES: participant, contributor, party

S

spectral = **ghostly**, unearthly, eerie, supernatural, weird, phantom, shadowy, uncanny, spooky *(informal)*, insubstantial, incorporeal, wraithlike • *the spectral quality of the light*

spectre = **ghost**, spirit, phantom, presence, vision, shadow, shade *(literary)*, apparition, wraith, eidolon, kehua *(N.Z.)* • *His spectre is said to walk the castle battlements.*

spectrum = **range**, variety, assortment, series, selection, gamut • *a wide spectrum of problems*

speculate 1 = **conjecture**, consider, wonder, guess, suppose, contemplate, deliberate, muse, meditate, surmise, theorize, hypothesize, cogitate • *The reader can speculate about what will happen next.*
2 = **gamble**, risk, venture, hazard, have a flutter *(informal)*, take a chance with, play the market • *They speculated in property whose value has now dropped.*

speculation 1 = **theory**, opinion, hypothesis, conjecture, guess, consideration, deliberation, contemplation, surmise, guesswork, supposition • *I had published my speculations about the future of the universe.*
2 = **gamble**, risk, gambling, hazard • *speculation on the Stock Exchange*

speculative 1 = **hypothetical**, academic, theoretical, abstract, tentative, notional, conjectural, suppositional • *He has written a speculative biography of Christopher Marlowe.*
2 = **risky**, uncertain, hazardous, unpredictable, dicey *(informal, chiefly Brit.)*, chancy *(informal)* • *a speculative venture*

speculator = **venturer**, trader, entrepreneur, bear, bull, stag, manipulator, merchant venturer • *a City speculator*

speech 1 = **communication**, talk, conversation, articulation, discussion, dialogue, intercourse, verbal communication, verbal expression • *the development of speech in children*
2 = **diction**, pronunciation, articulation, delivery, fluency, inflection, intonation, elocution, enunciation • *His speech became increasingly thick and nasal.*
3 = **language**, tongue, utterance, jargon, dialect, idiom, parlance, articulation, diction, lingo *(informal)*, enunciation • *the way common letter clusters are pronounced in speech*
4 = **talk**, address, lecture, discourse, harangue, homily, oration, spiel *(informal)*, disquisition, whaikorero *(N.Z.)* • *He delivered his speech in French.*

QUOTATIONS

A speech is poetry: cadence, rhythm, imagery, sweep! A speech reminds us that words, like children, have the power to make dance the dullest beanbag of a heart
[Peggy Noonan *What I Saw at the Revolution*]

A speech is like a love-affair. Any fool can start it, but to end it requires considerable skill
[Lord Mancroft]

Speech is the small-change of silence
[George Meredith *The Ordeal of Richard Feverel*]

Human speech is like a cracked kettle on which we tap crude rhythms for bears to dance to, while we long to make music that will melt the stars
[Gustave Flaubert *Madame Bovary*]

speechless = **dumb**, dumbfounded, lost for words, dumbstruck, astounded, shocked, mum, amazed, silent, mute, dazed, aghast, inarticulate, tongue-tied, wordless, thunderstruck, unable to get a word out *(informal)* • *Alex was speechless with rage and despair.*

speed AS A NOUN 1 = **rate**, pace, momentum, tempo, velocity • *He drove off at high speed.*
2 = **velocity**, swiftness, acceleration, precipitation, rapidity, quickness, fastness, briskness, speediness, precipitateness • *Speed is the essential ingredient of all athletics.*
3 = **swiftness**, rush, hurry, expedition, haste, rapidity, quickness, fleetness, celerity • *I was amazed at his speed of working.*
OPPOSITES: slowness, sluggishness, tardiness
▸ AS A VERB 1 = **race**, rush, hurry, zoom, career, bomb (along), tear, flash, belt (along) *(slang)*, barrel (along) *(informal, chiefly U.S. & Canad.)*, sprint, gallop, hasten, press on, quicken, lose no time, get a move on *(informal)*, burn rubber *(informal)*, bowl along, put your foot down *(informal)*, step on it *(informal)*, make haste, go hell for leather *(informal)*, exceed the speed limit, go like a bomb *(Brit. & N.Z. informal)*, go like the wind, go like a bat out of hell • *The engine noise rises only slightly as I speed along.*
OPPOSITES: creep, crawl, take your time
2 = **exceed the speed limit**, drive too fast, break the speed limit • *This man was not qualified to drive and was speeding.*
3 = **help**, further, advance, aid, promote, boost, assist, facilitate, fast-track, impel, expedite • *Invest in low-cost language courses to speed your progress.*
OPPOSITES: slow, delay, hinder
▸ IN PHRASES: **speed something up** = **accelerate**, promote, hasten, help along, further, forward, advance • *Excessive drinking will speed up the ageing process.*
speed up = **accelerate**, increase, speed, gather momentum, get moving, put your foot down *(informal)*, increase the tempo, open up the throttle, put on speed • *I woke when we started to speed up.*

speedily = **quickly**, rapidly, swiftly, fast, promptly, hastily, briskly, expeditiously • *This review is being conducted as speedily as possible.*

speedy = **quick**, fast, rapid, swift, express, winged, immediate, prompt, fleet, hurried, summary, precipitate, hasty, headlong, quickie *(informal)*, expeditious, fleet of foot, pdq *(slang)* • *We wish Bill a speedy recovery.*
OPPOSITES: slow, leisurely, unhurried

spell[1] AS A VERB = **indicate**, mean, signify, suggest, promise, point to, imply, amount to, herald, augur, presage, portend • *The report spells more trouble.*
▸ IN PHRASES: **spell something out** = **make clear** *or* **plain**, specify, make explicit, clarify, elucidate, explicate • *How many times do I have to spell it out?*

spell[2] AS A NOUN 1 = **incantation**, charm, sorcery, exorcism, abracadabra, witchery, conjuration, makutu *(N.Z.)* • *Vile witch! She cast a spell on me!*
2 = **enchantment**, magic, fascination, glamour, allure, bewitchment • *The King also falls under her spell.*
▸ IN PHRASES: **cast a spell on someone** = **enchant**, charm, fascinate, captivate, delight, enthral, beguile, bewitch, ravish, mesmerize, hypnotize, enrapture, enamour, spellbind • *People said he was able to cast a spell on the public.*

spell[3] = **period**, time, term, stretch, turn, course, season, patch, interval, bout, stint • *There has been a spell of dry weather.*

spellbinding = **fascinating**, exciting, gripping, thrilling, entrancing, compelling, compulsive, riveting, enthralling, engrossing, unputdownable *(informal)* • *He describes these ladies in spellbinding detail.*

spellbound = **entranced**, gripped, fascinated, transported, charmed, hooked, possessed, bemused, captivated, enthralled, bewitched, transfixed, rapt, mesmerized, under a spell • *He was in awe of her; she held him spellbound.*

spelling = **orthography** • *I had to correct several mistakes in her spelling.*

QUOTATIONS

My spelling is Wobbly. It's good spelling but it Wobbles, and the letters get in the wrong place
[A.A. Milne *Winnie-the-Pooh*]

'Do you spell it with a "V" or a "W"?'. 'That depends upon the taste and fancy of the speller, my Lord.'
[Charles Dickens *Pickwick Papers*]

orthography: the science of spelling by the eye instead of the ear
[Ambrose Bierce *The Devil's Dictionary*]

spend 1 = **pay out**, fork out *(slang)*, expend, lay out, splash out *(Brit. informal)*, shell out *(informal)*, disburse • *They have spent £23m on new players.*
OPPOSITES: keep, save, store
2 = **apply**, use, employ, concentrate, invest, put in, devote, lavish, exert, bestow • *This energy could be much better spent taking some positive action.*
3 = **pass**, fill, occupy, while away • *We spent the night in a hotel.*
4 = **use up**, waste, squander, blow *(slang)*, empty, drain, exhaust, consume, run through, deplete, dissipate, fritter away • *My stepson was spending money like it grew on trees.*
OPPOSITES: keep, save, store

spendthrift **AS A NOUN** = **squanderer**, spender, profligate, prodigal, big spender, waster, wastrel • *I was a natural spendthrift when I was single.*
OPPOSITES: penny-pincher *(informal)*, miser, skinflint
▸ **AS AN ADJECTIVE** = **wasteful**, extravagant, prodigal, profligate, improvident • *his father's spendthrift ways*
OPPOSITES: careful, prudent, economical

spent 1 = **used up**, finished, gone, consumed, expended • *The money was spent.*
2 = **exhausted**, drained, worn out, bushed *(informal)*, all in *(slang)*, shattered *(informal)*, weakened, wiped out *(informal)*, wearied, weary, played out *(informal)*, burnt out, fagged (out) *(informal)*, whacked *(Brit. informal)*, debilitated, knackered *(slang)*, prostrate, clapped out *(Brit., Austral. & N.Z. informal)*, tired out, ready to drop *(informal)*, dog-tired *(informal)*, zonked *(informal)*, dead beat *(informal)*, shagged out *(Brit. slang)*, done in or up *(informal)* • *After all that exertion, we were completely spent.*

sperm 1 = **spermatozoon**, reproductive cell, male gamete • *Conception occurs when a single sperm fuses with an egg.*
2 = **semen**, seed *(archaic or dialect)*, spermatozoa, scum *(U.S. slang)*, come or cum *(taboo)*, jism or jissom *(taboo)* • *the ejaculation of sperm*

spew 1 = **shed**, discharge, send out, issue, throw out, eject, diffuse, emanate, exude, cast out • *An oil tanker spewed its cargo into the sea.*
2 = **vomit**, throw up *(informal)*, puke *(slang)*, chuck *(Austral. & N.Z. informal)*, spit out, regurgitate, disgorge, barf *(U.S. slang)*, chunder *(slang, chiefly Austral.)*, belch forth, upchuck *(U.S. slang)*, do a technicolour yawn *(slang)*, toss your cookies *(U.S. slang)* • *Let's get out of his way before he starts spewing.*

sphere **AS A NOUN** 1 = **ball**, globe, orb, globule, circle • *The cactus will form a large sphere crested with golden thorns.*
2 = **field**, range, area, department, function, territory, capacity, province, patch, scope, turf *(U.S. slang)*, realm, domain, compass, walk of life • *the sphere of international politics*
3 = **rank**, class, station, status, stratum • *life outside academic spheres of society*
▸ **IN PHRASES: sphere of influence** = **area**, range, scope, field, extent, orbit, jurisdiction, compass, remit • *the British or American spheres of influence*

spherical = **round**, globular, globe-shaped, rotund, orbicular • *purple and gold spherical earrings*

spice **AS A NOUN** 1 = **seasoning**, condiment • *herbs and spices*
2 = **excitement**, kick *(informal)*, zest, colour, pep, zip *(informal)*, tang, zap *(slang)*, gusto, zing *(informal)*, piquancy • *The spice of danger will add to the lure.*
▸ **IN PHRASES: spice something up** = **make more interesting**, enliven, liven up, animate, perk up, pep up, invigorate, vitalize, vivify, make more exciting • *Her publishers wants her to spice the stories up with sex.*
▹ *See panel* **Herbs, spices and seasonings**

spick and span = **neat**, trim, tidy, clean, immaculate, impeccable, spruce, spotless, shipshape, fresh as paint, in apple-pie order *(informal)* • *The apartment was spick and span.*

spicy 1 = **hot**, seasoned, pungent, aromatic, savoury, tangy, piquant, flavoursome • *Thai food is hot and spicy.*
2 = **risqué**, racy, off-colour, ribald, hot *(informal)*, broad, improper, suggestive, unseemly, titillating, indelicate, indecorous • *spicy anecdotes about his sexual adventures*

spider
▸ **RELATED ADJECTIVE:** arachnoid
▸ **RELATED PHOBIA:** arachnophobia
▹ *See panel* **Spiders and other arachnids**

spiel = **patter**, speech, pitch, recital, harangue, sales talk, sales patter • *She had been hearing this kind of spiel for thirty years now.*

spike **AS A NOUN** 1 = **point**, stake, spur, pin, nail, spine, barb, tine, prong • *a 15-foot wall topped with iron spikes*
2 = **prickle**, spine, bristle, thorn • *Its skin is covered with spikes.*
▸ **AS A VERB** 1 = **drug**, lace, dope, cut, contaminate, adulterate • *drinks spiked with tranquillizers*
2 = **impale**, spit, spear, stick • *She was spiked on a railing after a 20ft plunge.*

spiky = **prickly**, barbed, spiny, bristly, thorny, brambly, briery • *tall, spiky evergreen trees*

spill **AS A VERB** 1 = **tip over**, upset, overturn, capsize, knock over, topple over • *He always spilled the drinks.*
2 = **shed**, scatter, discharge, throw off, disgorge, spill or run over • *A number of bags had split and were spilling their contents.*
3 = **slop**, flow, pour, run, overflow, slosh, splosh • *It doesn't matter if red wine spills on this floor.*
4 = **emerge**, flood, pour, mill, stream, surge, swarm, crowd, teem • *When the bell rings, more than 1,000 children spill from the classrooms.*
▸ **AS A NOUN** = **spillage**, flood, leak, leakage, overspill • *An oil spill could be devastating for wildlife.*
▸ **IN PHRASES: spill someone's blood** = **slay**, kill, murder, destroy, waste *(informal)*, do in *(slang)*, take out *(slang)*, execute, massacre, butcher, slaughter, dispatch, assassinate, eradicate, do away with, blow away *(slang, chiefly U.S.)*, obliterate, knock off *(slang)*, liquidate, annihilate, neutralize, exterminate, take (someone's) life, bump off *(slang)*, extirpate, wipe from the face of the earth *(informal)* • *He is prepared to spill the blood of a million people.*

SPIDERS AND OTHER ARACHNIDS

bird spider
black widow
book scorpion
cardinal spider
cheese mite
chigger, chigoe, or *(U.S. & Canad.)* redbug
chigoe, chigger, jigger, or sand flea
false scorpion
funnel-web
harvestman or *(U.S. & Canad.)* daddy-longlegs
house spider
itch mite
jockey spider
jumping spider
katipo *(N.Z.)*
mite
money spider
red-back (spider) *(Austral.)*
spider
spider mite
tarantula
tick
trap-door spider
vinegarroon
water spider
whip scorpion
wolf spider or hunting spider

S

spill the beans = **blab**, inform, squeal *(slang)*, tell all, shop *(slang, chiefly Brit.)*, sing *(slang, chiefly U.S.)*, split *(slang)*, grass *(Brit. slang)*, give the game away, tattle, let the cat out of the bag, blow the gaff *(Brit. slang)*, talk out of turn, spill your guts *(slang)*, betray a secret • *He was ready to spill the beans about the whole affair.*

spin AS A VERB 1 = **revolve**, turn, rotate, wheel, twist, reel, whirl, twirl, gyrate, pirouette, birl *(Scot.)* • *The Earth spins on its own axis.*
2 = **reel**, swim, whirl, be giddy, be in a whirl, grow dizzy • *My head was spinning from the wine.*
3 = **tell**, relate, recount, develop, invent, unfold, concoct, narrate • *She had spun a story that was too good to be true.*
▸ AS A NOUN 1 = **bias**, prejudice, slant, turn, leaning, bent, partiality, one-sidedness • *the wholly improper political spin given to the report*
2 = **drive**, ride, turn, hurl *(Scot.)*, whirl, joy ride *(informal)* • *Think twice about going for a spin by the light of the silvery moon.*
3 = **revolution**, roll, whirl, twist, gyration • *a spin of the roulette wheel*
▸ IN PHRASES: **flat spin** = **panic**, state *(informal)*, flap *(informal)*, agitation, commotion, tizzy *(informal)*, tiz-woz *(informal)* • *She was in a flat spin about the party.*
spin something out = **prolong**, extend, lengthen, draw out, drag out, delay, amplify, pad out, protract, prolongate • *They will try to spin out the conference into next autumn.*

spindle = **pivot**, pin, rod, axle • *Magnetic fields pull and push the spindle of the motor.*

spindly = **lanky**, gangly, spidery, leggy, twiggy, attenuated, gangling, spindle-shanked • *I did have rather spindly legs.*

spin doctor = **PR person**, publicist, propagandist, PRO, PR man, public relations officer, press agent, PR woman • *a spin doctor-turned-minister*

spine 1 = **backbone**, vertebrae, spinal column, vertebral column • *fractures of the hip and spine*
2 = **barb**, spur, needle, spike, ray, quill, rachis • *Carry a pair of thick gloves to protect you from hedgehog spines.*
3 = **determination**, resolution, backbone, resolve, drive, conviction, fortitude, persistence, tenacity, perseverance, willpower, firmness, constancy, single-mindedness, steadfastness, doggedness, resoluteness, indomitability • *If you had any spine, you wouldn't let her walk all over you like that.*

S

spine-chilling = **frightening**, terrifying, horrifying, scary *(informal)*, eerie, spooky *(informal)*, hair-raising, bloodcurdling • *There was a spine-chilling scream.*

spineless = **weak**, soft, cowardly, ineffective, feeble, yellow *(informal)*, inadequate, pathetic, submissive, squeamish, vacillating, boneless, gutless *(informal)*, weak-willed, weak-kneed *(informal)*, faint-hearted, irresolute, spiritless, chickenshit *(U.S. slang)*, lily-livered, without a will of your own • *bureaucrats and spineless politicians*
OPPOSITES: strong, brave, bold

spinney = **copse**, thicket, coppice, holt • *A spinney of thorn hung on the craggy edge of the hill.*

spiny = **prickly**, barbed, thorny, bristly, brambly, briery • *low spiny bushes of sage*

spiral AS AN ADJECTIVE = **coiled**, winding, corkscrew, circular, scrolled, whorled, helical, cochlear, voluted, cochleate *(Biology)* • *a spiral staircase*
▸ AS A NOUN = **coil**, helix, corkscrew, whorl, screw, gyre *(literary)*, curlicue, volute • *Larks were rising in spirals from the ridge.*
▸ AS A VERB 1 = **coil**, wind, twist, snake, twirl • *Smoke spiralled from a joss stick.*
2 = **soar**, rise, escalate, climb, rocket, shoot up • *a spiralling trend of violence*
▸ IN PHRASES: **spiral downwards** = **decline**, fall, drop, sink, shrink, decrease, deteriorate, fall off, dwindle, wane, ebb • *House prices will continue to spiral downwards.*

spire = **steeple**, turret, pillar, column, skyscraper, belfry, obelisk • *He saw the spire ahead through the trees.*

spirit AS A NOUN 1 = **soul**, life, psyche, ego, essential being, inner self, wairua *(N.Z.)* • *The human spirit is virtually indestructable.*
2 = **life force**, vital spark, breath, mauri *(N.Z.)* • *His spirit left him during the night.*
3 = **ghost**, phantom, spectre, vision, shadow, shade *(literary)*, spook *(informal)*, apparition, sprite, eidolon, atua *(N.Z.)*, kehua *(N.Z.)* • *Do you believe in the existence of evil spirits?*
4 = **courage**, guts *(informal)*, grit, balls *(taboo slang)*, backbone, spunk *(informal)*, gameness, ballsiness *(taboo slang)*, dauntlessness, stoutheartedness • *She was a very brave girl and everyone admired her spirit.*
5 = **liveliness**, energy, vigour, life, force, fire, resolution, enterprise, enthusiasm, sparkle, warmth, animation, zest, mettle, welly *(slang)*, ardour, earnestness, brio • *They played with spirit.*
6 = **attitude**, character, quality, humour, temper, outlook, temperament, complexion, disposition • *They approached the talks in a conciliatory spirit.*
7 = **team spirit**, loyalty, togetherness • *There is a great sense of spirit among the squad.*
8 = **heart**, sense, nature, soul, core, substance, essence, lifeblood, quintessence, fundamental nature • *the real spirit of the Labour movement*
9 = **intention**, meaning, purpose, substance, intent, essence, purport, gist • *the spirit of the treaty*
10 = **feeling**, atmosphere, character, feel, quality, tone, mood, flavour, tenor, ambience, vibes *(slang)* • *I appreciate the sounds, smells and the spirit of the place.*
11 = **resolve**, will, drive, resolution, conviction, determination, motivation, dedication, backbone, fortitude, persistence, tenacity, perseverance, willpower, firmness, constancy, single-mindedness, steadfastness, doggedness, resoluteness, indomitability • *It takes a lot of spirit to win with 10 men.*
12 *plural* = **mood**, feelings, morale, humour, temper, tenor, disposition, state of mind, frame of mind • *A bit of exercise will help lift his spirits.*
▸ IN PHRASES: **spirit something** *or* **someone away** = **remove**, steal, carry off, seize, trouser *(slang)*, abstract, whisk, abduct, knock off *(slang)*, purloin, snaffle *(Brit. informal)*, make away with • *The urn containing the ashes was spirited away.*

spirit *often plural* = **strong alcohol**, liquor, the hard stuff *(informal)*, firewater, strong liquor • *He's stopped drinking spirits these days.*
▹ *See panel* **Spirits**

spirited = **lively**, vigorous, energetic, animated, game, active, bold, sparkling, have-a-go *(informal)*, courageous, ardent, feisty *(informal, chiefly U.S. & Canad.)*, plucky, high-spirited, sprightly, vivacious, spunky *(informal)*, mettlesome, (as) game as Ned Kelly *(Austral. slang)* • *He wanted merely to provoke a spirited debate.*
OPPOSITES: calm, dull, lifeless

spiritless = **apathetic**, lacklustre, dispirited, listless, low *(informal)*, depressed, dull, melancholy, lifeless, unmoved, languid, dejected, despondent, melancholic, droopy, unenthusiastic, torpid, mopy • *The crowds were too spiritless to resist.*

spiritual 1 = **nonmaterial**, metaphysical, other-worldly, ethereal, intangible, immaterial, incorporeal • *She lived entirely by spiritual values.*
OPPOSITES: material, physical, corporeal
2 = **sacred**, religious, holy, divine, ethereal, devotional, otherworldly • *A man in priestly clothes offered spiritual guidance.*

SPIRITS

absinth	Armagnac	dark rum	hooch	palinka	taffia
aguardiente	arrack	eau de vie	Kirsch *or* Kirschwasser	poteen	tequila
applejack, applejack brandy, *or* apple brandy	Bacardi *(trademark)*	firewater	korn	raki	triple sec
aquavit	brandy	framboise	marc	rum	vodka
aqua vitae *(archaic)*	bitters	gin	mescal	schnapps	whisky
	Calvados	grappa	ouzo	slivovitz	white rum
	Cognac	Hollands		sloe gin	

spit[1] AS A VERB 1 = **expectorate**, gob *(Brit. informal)*, sputter, hoick *(Brit. informal)* • *They spat at me and taunted me.*
2 = **eject**, discharge, throw out • *I spat it on to my plate.*
3 = **sizzle**, hiss, crackle, sputter • *the fire where pork chops were sizzling and spitting*
4 = **snap**, bark, snarl, say angrily, sputter, speak sharply • *'Get out of here,' he spat angrily.*
5 = **rain lightly**, drizzle, spot • *It will stop in a minute – it's only spitting.*
▸ AS A NOUN = **saliva**, dribble, spittle, drool, slaver, sputum • *When he took a corner kick he was showered with spit.*
▸ IN PHRASES: **within spitting distance** = **close**, near, beside, alongside, close by, just round the corner, within sniffing distance *(informal)*, a hop, skip and a jump away *(informal)* • *a restaurant within spitting distance of the Tower of London*

spit[2] = **rotisserie**, skewer, brochette • *She roasted the meat on a spit.*

spite AS A NOUN = **malice**, malevolence, ill will, hate, hatred, gall, animosity, venom, spleen, pique, rancour, bitchiness *(slang)*, malignity, spitefulness • *Never had she met such spite and pettiness.*
OPPOSITES: kindness, benevolence, love
▸ AS A VERB = **annoy**, hurt, injure, harm, provoke, offend, needle *(informal)*, put out, gall, nettle, vex, pique, discomfit, put someone's nose out of joint *(informal)*, hack someone off *(informal)* • *He was giving his art collection away for nothing, to spite them.*
OPPOSITES: help, benefit, please
▸ IN PHRASES: **in spite of** = **despite**, regardless of, notwithstanding, in defiance of, (even) though • *Their love of life comes in spite of considerable hardship.*

PROVERBS
Don't cut off your nose to spite your face

spiteful = **malicious**, nasty, vindictive, cruel, malignant, barbed, malevolent, venomous, bitchy *(informal)*, snide, rancorous, catty *(informal)*, splenetic, shrewish, ill-disposed, ill-natured • *He could be spiteful.*

spitting image = **double**, lookalike, (dead) ringer *(slang)*, picture, spit *(informal, chiefly Brit.)*, clone, replica, likeness, living image, spit and image *(informal)* • *Nina looks the spitting image of Sissy Spacek.*

splash AS A VERB 1 = **paddle**, plunge, bathe, dabble, wade, wallow • *A lot of people were in the water, splashing about.*
2 = **scatter**, shower, spray, sprinkle, spread, wet, strew, squirt, spatter, slop, slosh *(informal)* • *He closed his eyes tight, and splashed the water on his face.*
3 = **spatter**, mark, stain, smear, speck, speckle, blotch, splodge, bespatter • *The carpet was splashed with beer stains.*
4 = **dash**, break, strike, wash, batter, surge, smack, buffet, plop, plash • *waves splashing against the side of the boat*
5 = **broadcast**, plaster, headline, trumpet, tout, flaunt, publicize, blazon • *The newspapers splashed the story all over their front pages.*
▸ AS A NOUN 1 = **splashing**, dashing, plash, beating, battering, swashing • *I would sit alone and listen to the splash of water on the rocks.*
2 = **dash**, touch, spattering, splodge • *Add a splash of lemon juice to flavour the butter.*
3 = **spot**, burst, patch, stretch, spurt • *splashes of colour*
4 = **feature**, story, piece, article • *On their first day, they handed their editor a front-page splash.*
5 = **blob**, spot, smudge, stain, smear, fleck, speck • *splashes of ink over a glowing white surface*
▸ IN PHRASES: **make a splash** = **cause a stir**, make an impact, cause a sensation, cut a dash, be ostentatious • *He knows how to make a splash in the House of Lords.*
splash out = **spend**, splurge, be extravagant, push the boat out *(Brit. informal)*, lash out *(informal)*, spare no expense • *Can you afford to splash out a little?*

splatter = **stain**, spatter, mark, smear, speckle, blotch, splodge, bespatter • *a mud-splattered white suit*

spleen = **spite**, anger, bitterness, hostility, hatred, resentment, wrath, gall, malice, animosity, venom, bile, bad temper, acrimony, pique, rancour, ill will, animus, malevolence, vindictiveness, malignity, spitefulness, ill humour, peevishness • *There were other targets for his spleen.*
▸ RELATED ADJECTIVES: splenetic, splenic, lienal

splendid 1 = **excellent**, wonderful, marvellous, mean *(slang)*, great *(informal)*, topping *(Brit. slang)*, fine, cracking *(Brit. informal)*, crucial *(slang)*, fantastic *(informal)*, first-class, glorious, mega *(slang)*, sovereign, awesome *(slang)*, def *(slang)*, brill *(informal)*, bodacious *(slang, chiefly U.S.)*, boffo *(slang)*, chillin' *(U.S. slang)*, booshit *(Austral. slang)*, exo *(Austral. slang)*, sik *(Austral. slang)*, rad *(informal)*, phat *(slang)*, schmick *(Austral. informal)*, beaut *(informal)*, barrie *(Scot. slang)*, belting *(Brit. slang)*, pearler *(Austral. slang)* • *The book includes a wealth of splendid photographs.*
OPPOSITES: poor, ordinary, mediocre
2 = **magnificent**, grand, imposing, impressive, rich, superb, costly, gorgeous, dazzling, lavish, luxurious, sumptuous, ornate, resplendent, splendiferous *(facetious)* • *a splendid Victorian mansion*
OPPOSITES: drab, sordid, squalid
3 = **glorious**, superb, magnificent, grand, brilliant, rare, supreme, outstanding, remarkable, sterling, exceptional, renowned, admirable, sublime, illustrious • *a splendid career in publishing*
OPPOSITES: ignominious, ignoble

splendour 1 = **magnificence**, glory, grandeur, show, display, ceremony, luxury, spectacle, majesty, richness, nobility, pomp, opulence, solemnity, éclat, gorgeousness, sumptuousness, stateliness, resplendence, luxuriousness • *They met in the splendour of the hotel.*
OPPOSITES: squalor, meanness, poverty
2 = **brilliance**, brightness, radiance, dazzle, lustre, effulgence, refulgence • *We were led through the fairy-lit splendour of the centre.*
OPPOSITES: dullness

splenetic = **irritable**, cross, bad-tempered, acid, sour, crabbed, sullen, touchy, petulant, spiteful, bitchy *(informal)*, churlish, morose, irascible, tetchy, ratty *(Brit. & N.Z. informal)*, testy, chippy *(informal)*, fretful, rancorous, peevish, crabby, choleric, envenomed • *retired military men with splenetic opinions*

S

splice = **join**, unite, graft, marry, wed, knit, mesh, braid, intertwine, interweave, yoke, plait, entwine, interlace, intertwist • *He taught me to edit and splice film.*

splinter AS A NOUN = **sliver**, fragment, chip, needle, shaving, flake, paring • *a splinter in the finger*
▸ AS A VERB = **shatter**, split, fracture, shiver, disintegrate, break into fragments, smash into smithereens • *The ruler cracked and splintered into pieces.*

split AS A VERB 1 = **break**, crack, burst, snap, break up, open, give way, splinter, gape, come apart, come undone • *In a severe gale the ship split in two.*
2 = **cut**, break, crack, snap, chop, cleave, hew • *He started on the main course while she split the avocados.*
3 = **divide**, separate, disunite, disrupt, disband, cleave, pull apart, set at odds, set at variance • *It is feared they could split the government.*
4 = **diverge**, separate, branch, fork, part, go separate ways • *that place where the road split in two*
5 = **tear**, rend, rip, slash, slit • *The seat of his short grey trousers split.*
6 = **share out**, divide, distribute, halve, allocate, partition, allot, carve up, dole out, apportion, slice up, parcel out, divvy up *(informal)* • *Split the wages between you.*
▸ AS A NOUN 1 = **division**, break, breach, rift, difference, disruption, rupture, discord, divergence, schism, estrangement, dissension, disunion • *a split in the party*
2 = **separation**, break, divorce, break-up, split-up, disunion • *The split from her husband was acrimonious.*
3 = **crack**, tear, rip, damage, gap, rent, breach, slash, slit, fissure • *The seat had a few small splits around the corners.*
▸ AS AN ADJECTIVE 1 = **divided**, ambivalent, disunited, bisected, torn asunder, factionalized • *The Kremlin is deeply split in its approach to foreign policy.*
2 = **broken**, cracked, snapped, fractured, splintered, ruptured, cleft • *a split finger nail*
▸ IN PHRASES: **split on someone** = **betray**, tell on, shop *(slang, chiefly Brit.)*, sing *(slang, chiefly U.S.)*, grass *(Brit. slang)*, give away, peach *(slang)*, squeal *(slang)*, inform on, spill your guts *(slang)*, dob in *(Austral. slang)* • *If I wanted to tell, I'd have split on you before now.*
split something up = **separate**, divide, disband, pull apart, disunite, bifurcate • *Any thought of splitting up the company was unthinkable, they said.*
split up = **break up**, part, separate, divorce, disband, part company, go separate ways • *I was beginning to think that we would never split up.*

S

spoil AS A VERB 1 = **ruin**, destroy, wreck, damage, total *(slang)*, blow *(slang)*, injure, upset, harm, mar, scar, undo, trash *(slang)*, impair, mess up, blemish, disfigure, debase, deface, put a damper on, crool *or* cruel *(Austral. slang)* • *It is important not to let mistakes spoil your life.*
OPPOSITES: save, preserve, improve
2 = **overindulge**, indulge, pamper, baby, cocker *(rare)*, cosset, coddle, spoon-feed, mollycoddle, kill with kindness • *Grandparents are often tempted to spoil their grandchildren.*
OPPOSITES: deprive, be strict with, treat harshly
3 = **indulge**, treat, pamper, satisfy, gratify, pander to, regale • *Spoil yourself with a new perfume this summer.*
4 = **go bad**, turn, go off *(Brit. informal)*, rot, decay, decompose, curdle, mildew, addle, putrefy, become tainted • *Fats spoil by becoming tainted.*
▸ IN PHRASES: **spoiling for** = **eager for**, looking for, keen to, enthusiastic about, out to get *(informal)*, raring to, desirous of, bent upon • *A mob armed with guns was at the border, spoiling for a fight.*

spoils = **booty**, loot, plunder, gain, prizes, prey, pickings, pillage, swag *(slang)*, boodle *(slang, chiefly U.S.)*, rapine • *Competing warlords and foreign powers scrambled for political spoils.*

spoilsport = **killjoy**, misery *(Brit. informal)*, wet blanket *(informal)*, damper, dog in the manger, party-pooper *(U.S. slang)*, wowser *(Austral. slang)* • *a jealous spoilsport who can't take a joke*

spoken AS AN ADJECTIVE = **verbal**, voiced, expressed, uttered, oral, said, told, unwritten, phonetic, by word of mouth, put into words, viva voce • *written and spoken communication skills*
▸ IN PHRASES: **spoken for** 1 = **reserved**, booked, claimed, chosen, selected, set aside • *The top jobs in the party are already spoken for.*
2 = **engaged**, taken, going out with someone, betrothed *(archaic)*, going steady • *Both girls, I remind him, are spoken for.*

spokesperson = **speaker**, official, spokesman *or* spokeswoman, voice, spin doctor *(informal)*, mouthpiece • *The Opposition spokesperson struggled gamely on.*

sponge AS A VERB = **swab**, wipe, mop, clean, wash, rinse, sluice • *Gently sponge your face and body.*
▸ IN PHRASES: **sponge off someone** = **scrounge**, cadge, freeload *(slang)*, beg, bum *(informal)*, touch (someone) for *(slang)*, blag *(slang)*, wheedle, sorn *(Scot.)*, bludge *(Austral. & N.Z. informal)* • *He should just get an honest job and stop sponging off the rest of us!*

sponger = **scrounger**, parasite, leech, hanger-on *(informal)*, cadge *(Brit.)*, freeloader *(slang)*, bloodsucker *(informal)*, bludger *(Austral. & N.Z. informal)*, cadger, quandong *(Austral. slang)* • *Is he an aggressive sponger or does he have a case?*

spongy = **porous**, light, absorbent, springy, cushioned, elastic, cushiony • *The earth was spongy from rain.*

sponsor AS A VERB = **back**, fund, finance, promote, subsidize, patronize, put up the money for, act as a guarantor for, lend your name to • *They are sponsoring a major pop art exhibition.*
▸ AS A NOUN = **backer**, patron, promoter, angel *(informal)*, guarantor • *the new sponsors of the League Cup*

spontaneous 1 = **unplanned**, impromptu, unprompted, willing, free, natural, voluntary, instinctive, impulsive, unforced, unbidden, unconstrained, unpremeditated, extempore, uncompelled • *I joined in the spontaneous applause.*
OPPOSITES: planned, arranged, calculated
2 = **reflex**, natural, instinctive, unconscious, mechanical, involuntary, instinctual, unwilled • *a spontaneous reaction*

spontaneously 1 = **voluntarily**, freely, instinctively, impromptu, off the cuff *(informal)*, on impulse, impulsively, in the heat of the moment, extempore, off your own bat, of your own accord, quite unprompted • *Her husband was never spontaneously warm or friendly towards us.*
2 = **automatically**, instinctively, involuntarily, unthinkingly • *These images surface spontaneously in dreams.*

spoof = **parody**, take-off *(informal)*, satire, caricature, mockery, send-up *(Brit. informal)*, travesty, lampoon, burlesque • *a spoof on Hollywood life*

spook AS A NOUN 1 = **ghost**, spirit, phantom, spectre, soul, shade *(literary)*, manes, apparition, wraith, revenant, phantasm, eidolon, kehua *(N.Z.)* • *She woke up to see a spook hovering over her bed.*
2 = **spy**, secret agent, double agent, secret service agent, undercover agent, mole, foreign agent, fifth columnist, nark *(Brit., Austral. & N.Z. slang)* • *a U.S. intelligence spook*
▸ AS A VERB = **frighten**, alarm, scare, terrify, startle, intimidate, daunt, unnerve, petrify, scare (someone) stiff, put the wind up (someone) *(informal)*, scare the living daylights out of (someone) *(informal)*, make your hair stand on end *(informal)*, get the wind up, make your blood run cold, throw into a panic, scare the bejesus out of *(informal)*, affright *(archaic)*, freeze your blood, make (someone) jump out of his skin *(informal)*, throw into a fright • *But was it the wind that spooked her?*

spooky = **eerie**, frightening, chilling, ghostly, weird, mysterious, scary *(informal)*, unearthly, supernatural, uncanny, creepy *(informal)*, spine-chilling • *The whole place had a slightly spooky atmosphere.*

spoon-feed = **mollycoddle**, spoil, cosset, baby, featherbed, overindulge, overprotect, wrap up in cotton wool *(informal)* • *He spoon-fed me and did everything around the house.*

sporadic = **intermittent**, occasional, scattered, isolated, random, on and off, irregular, infrequent, spasmodic, scattershot • *The sound of sporadic shooting could still be heard.*
OPPOSITES: regular, steady, consistent

sport **AS A NOUN** 1 = **game**, exercise, recreation, play, entertainment, amusement, diversion, pastime, physical activity • *I'd say football is my favourite sport.*
2 = **fun**, kidding *(informal)*, joking, teasing, ridicule, joshing *(slang, chiefly U.S. & Canad.)*, banter, frolic, jest, mirth, merriment, badinage, raillery • *Had themselves a bit of sport first, didn't they?*
▸ **AS A VERB** = **wear**, display, flaunt, boast, exhibit, flourish, show off, vaunt • *He was fat-faced, heavily-built and sported a red moustache.*
▹ *See panels* **Athletic events; Ball games; Boxing weights; Cricket terms; Equestrianism; Fencing terms; Football; Golf terms; Gymnastic events; Martial arts and terms; Motor sports; Rugby terms; Snooker and billiards terms; Tennis terms; Water sports; Winter sports**

QUOTATIONS

I'm fanatical about sport: there seems to me something almost religious about the fact that human beings can organize play, the spirit of play
[Simon Gray]

When a man wants to murder a tiger he calls it sport; when the tiger wants to murder him he calls it ferocity
[George Bernard Shaw *Maxims for Revolutionists*]

The flannelled fools at the wicket or the muddied oafs at the goals
[Rudyard Kipling *The Islanders*]

To be No. 1 in sport you have to have a narrow tunnel vision. Dedication. You want to call it selfishness, arrogance, whatever. It's dog eat dog. There are no prisoners taken; there's none expected
[Ian Botham]

▹ *See panel* **Sports**

sporting **AS AN ADJECTIVE** = **fair**, sportsmanlike, game *(informal)*, gentlemanly • *a sporting gesture in the highest traditions*
OPPOSITES: unfair, unsporting, unsportsmanlike
▸ **IN PHRASES: a sporting chance** = **probability**, good chance, fair chance, fighting chance, reasonable likelihood • *There was a sporting chance that they would meet.*

sporty 1 = **fast**, speedy, nippy, zippy • *a sporty car*
2 = **athletic**, active, sports-loving, outdoor, energetic, hearty • *He would go to the ballgames with his sporty friends.*
3 = **casual**, stylish, jazzy *(informal)*, loud, informal, trendy *(Brit. informal)*, flashy, jaunty, showy, snazzy *(informal)*, raffish, rakish, gay, schmick *(Austral. informal)* • *The moustache gave him a certain sporty air.*

spot **AS A NOUN** 1 = **mark**, stain, speck, scar, flaw, taint, blot, smudge, blemish, daub, speckle, blotch, discoloration • *The floorboards were covered with white spots.*
2 = **pimple**, blackhead, pustule, zit *(slang)*, plook *(Scot.)*, swelling, acne • *Never squeeze blackheads, spots or pimples.*
3 = **bit**, little, drop, bite, splash, small amount, tad, morsel, modicum • *We've given all the club members tea, coffee and a spot of lunch.*
4 = **place**, situation, site, point, position, scene, location, locality • *They returned to the remote spot where they had left him.*
5 = **predicament**, trouble, difficulty, mess, plight, hot water *(informal)*, quandary, tight spot • *In a tight spot there is no one I would sooner see than Frank.*
▸ **AS A VERB** 1 = **see**, observe, catch sight of, identify, sight, recognize, detect, make out, pick out, discern, behold *(archaic or literary)*, espy, descry • *He left the party seconds before smoke was spotted coming up the stairs.*
2 = **mark**, stain, dot, soil, dirty, scar, taint, tarnish, blot, fleck, spatter, sully, speckle, besmirch, splodge, splotch, mottle, smirch • *a brown shoe spotted with paint*

SPORTS

TEAM SPORTS

American football	bandy	football	kabbadi	rugby *or* rugby	tug-of-war
association	basketball	Gaelic football	korfball	football	volleyball
football *or* soccer	camogie	goalball	lacrosse	rugby league	water polo
Australian Rules *or*	Canadian football	handball	netball	rugby union	
Australian Rules	cricket	hockey	polo	shinty	
football	curling	hurling *or* hurley	roller hockey	softball	
baseball	five-a-side football	ice hockey	rounders	stool ball	

COMBAT SPORTS

boxing	fencing	sambo *or* sambo	savate	wrestling	
		wrestling			

OTHER SPORTS

angling *or* fishing	shooting	fox-hunting	paddleball	rackets	squash *or*
archery	cockfighting	gliding	parachuting	real tennis	squash rackets
badminton	coursing	golf	paragliding	rhythmic	table tennis
ballooning	croquet	greyhound racing	parascending	gymnastics	tennis
billiards	cycling	gymnastics	paraskiing	rock climbing	tenpin bowling
boules	cyclo-cross	hang gliding	pelota	roller skating	trampolining
bowls	darts	jai alai	pétanque	shooting	trapshooting
bullfighting	decathlon	lawn tennis	pigeon racing	skeet	triathlon
candlepins	falconry	modern	pool	skittles	weightlifting
canyoning	fives	pentathlon	potholing	skydiving	
clay pigeon	fly-fishing	mountaineering	quoits	snooker	

3 = **spit**, drizzle, rain lightly • *It starts to spot with rain.*
▸ IN PHRASES: **a soft spot for** = **fondness for**, liking for, attachment to, love of, taste for, preference for, penchant for, weakness for, predilection for, fancy for, partiality for • *You've still got a soft spot for red-haired colleens.*
on the spot = **immediately**, instantly, at once, straight away, directly, without delay, without hesitation, forthwith, unhesitatingly, before you could say Jack Robinson *(informal)* • *He went to see the producer and they offered him the job on the spot.*

QUOTATIONS
Out, damned spot!
[William Shakespeare *Macbeth*]

spotless 1 = **clean**, immaculate, impeccable, white, pure, virgin, shining, gleaming, snowy, flawless, faultless, unblemished, virginal, unsullied, untarnished, unstained • *Every morning cleaners make sure everything is spotless.*
OPPOSITES: spotted, soiled, dirty
2 = **blameless**, squeaky-clean, unimpeachable, innocent, chaste, irreproachable, above reproach • *He was determined to leave a spotless record behind him.*
OPPOSITES: notorious, reprehensible

spotlight AS A NOUN 1 = **search light**, headlight, floodlight, headlamp, foglamp • *the light of a powerful spotlight from a police helicopter*
2 = **attention**, limelight, public eye, interest, fame, notoriety, media attention, public attention, glare of publicity • *Webb is back in the spotlight.*
▸ AS A VERB = **highlight**, feature, draw attention to, focus attention on, accentuate, point up, give prominence to, throw into relief • *a new book spotlighting female entrepreneurs*

spot-on = **accurate**, exact, precise, right, correct, on the money *(U.S.)*, unerring, punctual (to the minute), hitting the nail on the head *(informal)*, on the bull's-eye *(informal)* • *Schools were told their exam information had to be spot-on.*

spotted = **speckled**, dotted, flecked, pied, specked, mottled, dappled, polka-dot • *hand-painted spotted cups*

spotty 1 = **pimply**, pimpled, blotchy, poor-complexioned, plooky-faced *(Scot.)* • *She was rather fat, and her complexion was muddy and spotty.*
2 = **inconsistent**, irregular, erratic, uneven, fluctuating, patchy, sporadic • *His attendance record was spotty.*

S

spouse = **partner**, mate, husband *or* wife, companion, consort, significant other *(U.S. informal)*, better half *(humorous)*, her indoors *(Brit. slang)*, helpmate, bidie-in *(Scot.)*, squeeze *(informal)* • *living with someone other than a spouse*
▸ RELATED ADJECTIVE: spousal

spout AS A VERB 1 = **stream**, shoot, gush, spurt, jet, spray, surge, discharge, erupt, emit, squirt • *In a storm, water spouts out of the blowhole just like a whale.*
2 = **hold forth**, talk, rant, go on *(informal)*, rabbit (on) *(Brit. informal)*, ramble (on), pontificate, declaim, spiel *(informal)*, expatiate, orate, speechify • *She would go red in the face and start to spout.*
▸ AS A NOUN 1 = **jet**, fountain, gush, outpouring, geyser • *Experts later blew it up – sending a spout of water soaring 30ft into the sky.*
2 = **nozzle**, lip, rose • *a pot with a broken spout*

sprain = **twist**, turn, wrench, dislocate, pull, rick • *He fell and sprained his ankle.*

sprat
▸ NAME OF YOUNG: brit

sprawl = **loll**, slump, lounge, flop, lie down, slouch, recline, drape yourself • *She sprawled on the bed, not even moving to cover herself up.*

spray[1] AS A NOUN 1 = **droplets**, moisture, fine mist, drizzle, spindrift, spoondrift • *The moon was casting a rainbow through the spray of the waterfall.*
2 = **aerosol**, sprinkler, nebulizer, atomizer • *an insect-repellent spray*
▸ AS A VERB = **scatter**, shower, sprinkle, diffuse • *A shower of seeds sprayed into the air and fell on the grass.* • *We sprayed the area with weedkiller.*

spray[2] = **sprig**, buttonhole, floral arrangement, branch, bough, shoot, corsage, boutonniere *(French)* • *a small spray of freesias*

spread AS A VERB 1 = **open (out)**, extend, stretch, unfold, sprawl, unfurl, fan out, unroll • *He spread his coat over the bed.*
2 = **extend**, open, stretch • *He stepped back and spread his hands wide.*
3 = **coat**, cover, butter, smear, smother • *Spread the bread with the cream cheese.*
4 = **smear**, apply, rub, put, smooth, plaster, daub • *Spread the cream over the skin and allow it to remain for 12 hours.*
5 = **grow**, increase, develop, expand, widen, mushroom, escalate, proliferate, multiply, broaden • *The sense of fear is spreading in residential neighbourhoods.*
6 = **space out**, stagger • *The course is spread over a five-week period.*
7 = **circulate**, publish, broadcast, advertise, distribute, scatter, proclaim, transmit, make public, publicize, propagate, disseminate, promulgate, make known, blazon, bruit • *Someone has been spreading rumours about us.*
OPPOSITES: hold back, stifle, suppress
8 = **diffuse**, cast, shed, radiate • *The overall flaring tends to spread light.* = **diffuse**
▸ AS A NOUN 1 = **increase**, development, advance, spreading, expansion, transmission, proliferation, advancement, escalation, diffusion, dissemination, dispersal, suffusion • *The greatest hope for reform is the gradual spread of information.*
2 = **extent**, reach, span, stretch, sweep, width, compass • *The rhododendron grows to 18 inches with a spread of 24 inches.*
3 = **feast**, banquet, blowout *(slang)*, repast, array • *They put on a spread of sandwiches for us.*
4 = **feature**, report, story, piece, article, item • *There was a double-page spread on a dinner for 46 people.*
5 = **range**, variety, selection, assortment, gamut • *We have an enormous spread of industries in the area.*
▸ IN PHRASES: **spread out** = **disperse**, spread, dissipate, be dispersed, thin out, diffract • *A crude-oil slick quickly spreads out over the water.*
spread something out = **lay out**, stretch out, unfurl, unroll • *I spread out my groundsheet and my sleeping bag.*

spree 1 = **fling**, binge *(informal)*, orgy, splurge • *They went on a spending spree.*
2 = **binge**, bender *(informal)*, orgy, revel *(informal)*, jag *(slang)*, junketing, beano *(Brit. slang)*, debauch, carouse, drinking bout, bacchanalia, carousal, a night on the piss *(taboo slang)*, a night on the razzle *(informal)* • *They attacked two London shops after a drinking spree.*

sprig = **spray**, stem, twig • *Chop the watercress, reserving a sprig or two for garnish.*

sprightly = **lively**, spirited, active, energetic, animated, brisk, nimble, agile, jaunty, gay, perky, vivacious, spry, bright-eyed and bushy-tailed • *the sprightly 85-year-old president*
OPPOSITES: dull, sluggish, inactive

spring AS A NOUN 1 = **springtime**, springtide *(literary)* • *We met again in the spring of 1977.*
2 = **source**, root, origin, well, beginning, cause, fount, fountainhead, wellspring • *the hidden springs of consciousness*
3 = **flexibility**, give *(informal)*, bounce, resilience, elasticity, recoil, buoyancy, springiness, bounciness • *Put some spring back into your old sofa.*
4 = **vigour**, energy, vitality, life, spirit, verve, welly *(slang)*, brio, vivacity, liveliness, jauntiness • *The sky was blue and we walked with a spring in our step.*
▸ AS A VERB 1 = **jump**, bound, leap, bounce, hop, rebound, vault, recoil • *The lion roared once and sprang.*

2 *usually followed by* **from = originate**, come, derive, start, issue, grow, emerge, proceed, arise, stem, descend, be derived, emanate, be descended • *The art springs from the country's Muslim heritage.*
3 = **announce suddenly**, present suddenly, introduce suddenly, reveal suddenly • *McLaren sprang a new idea on him.*
▸ **AS A MODIFIER = vernal**, springlike • *Walking carefree through the fresh spring rain.*
▸ **AS A NOUN = geyser**, hot spring, fount *(literary)*, well head, thermal spring • *To the north are the hot springs.*
▸ **IN PHRASES: spring up = appear**, develop, come into existence *or* being, mushroom, burgeon, shoot up • *New theatres and arts centres sprang up all over the country.*
▸ **RELATED ADJECTIVE:** vernal

QUOTATIONS
April is the cruellest month, breeding
Lilacs out of the dead land, mixing
Memory and desire, stirring
Dull roots with spring rain
[T.S. Eliot *The Waste Land*]

springy = flexible, elastic, resilient, bouncy, rubbery, spongy • *Knead the dough until smooth and springy.*

sprinkle 1 = scatter, dust, strew, pepper, shower, spray, powder, dredge • *Cheese can be sprinkled on egg and vegetable dishes.*
2 = **litter**, clutter, mess up • *Unfortunately, the text is sprinkled with errors.*

sprinkling = scattering, dusting, scatter, few, dash, handful, sprinkle, smattering, admixture • *a light sprinkling of snow*

sprint = run, race, shoot, tear, dash, barrel (along) *(informal, chiefly U.S. & Canad.)*, dart, hare *(Brit. informal)*, whizz *(informal)*, scamper, hotfoot, go like a bomb *(Brit. & N.Z. informal)*, put on a burst of speed, go at top speed • *He sprinted to the car.*

sprite = spirit, fairy, elf, nymph, brownie, pixie, apparition, imp, goblin, leprechaun, peri, dryad, naiad, sylph, Oceanid *(Greek myth)*, atua *(N.Z.)* • *a scampering puckish sprite*

sprout 1 = germinate, bud, shoot, push, spring, vegetate • *It only takes a few days for beans to sprout.*
2 = **grow**, develop, blossom, ripen • *Leaf-shoots were beginning to sprout on the hawthorn.*
3 = **appear**, emerge, turn up, show up *(informal)*, materialize, surface, come into sight • *More than a million satellite dishes have sprouted across the country.*

spruce AS AN ADJECTIVE = smart, trim, neat, elegant, dainty, dapper, natty *(informal)*, well-groomed, well turned out, trig *(archaic or dialect)*, as if you had just stepped out of a bandbox, soigné *or* soignée • *Chris was looking spruce in his black shirt.*
OPPOSITES: messy, untidy, dishevelled
▸ **IN PHRASES: spruce something** *or* **someone up**
1 = **smarten up**, groom, tidy, titivate, gussy up *(slang, chiefly U.S.)*, have a wash and brush-up *(Brit.)* • *In the evening we spruced ourselves up and went out for dinner*
2 = **do up**, clean up *(informal)*, tidy up, smarten up, tart up *(informal)*, put in order, make smarter, neaten up • *Many buildings have been spruced up.*

spry = active, sprightly, lively, quick, brisk, supple, nimble, agile, nippy *(Brit. informal)* • *a spry old lady*
OPPOSITES: slow, stiff, inactive

spunk = courage, spirit, nerve, balls *(taboo slang)*, bottle *(Brit. slang)*, resolution, guts *(informal)*, pluck, grit, backbone, toughness, mettle, gumption *(informal)*, gameness, ballsiness *(taboo slang)* • *I admired her independence and her spunk.*

spur AS A VERB = incite, drive, prompt, press, urge, stimulate, animate, prod, prick, goad, impel • *His friend's plight had spurred him into taking part.*
▸ **AS A NOUN 1 = stimulus**, incentive, impetus, motive, impulse, inducement, incitement, kick up the backside *(informal)* • *Redundancy is the spur for many to embark on new careers.*
2 = **projection**, spike, protuberance, protrusion • *An X-ray might show a small spur of bone at the site of your pain.*
▸ **IN PHRASES: on the spur of the moment = on impulse**, without thinking, impulsively, on the spot, impromptu, unthinkingly, without planning, impetuously, unpremeditatedly • *They admitted they had taken a vehicle on the spur of the moment.*

spurious = false, bogus, sham, pretended, artificial, forged, fake, mock, imitation, simulated, contrived, pseudo *(informal)*, counterfeit, feigned, ersatz, specious, unauthentic, phoney *or* phony *(informal)* • *a spurious framework for analysis*
OPPOSITES: real, genuine, valid

spurn = reject, slight, scorn, rebuff, put down, snub, disregard, despise, disdain, repulse, cold-shoulder, kick in the teeth *(slang)*, turn your nose up at *(informal)*, contemn *(formal)* • *a spurned lover*
OPPOSITES: accept, welcome, take up

spurt AS A VERB 1 = gush, shoot, burst, spring, jet, spray, surge, erupt, spew, squirt • *I saw flames spurt from the roof.*
2 = **shoot**, race, fly, speed, tear, barrel (along) *(informal, chiefly U.S. & Canad.)*, bolt, streak, whizz *(informal)*, scoot, burn rubber *(informal)* • *The back wheel spun and the van spurted up the last few feet.*
▸ **AS A NOUN 1 = gush**, jet, burst, spray, surge, eruption, squirt • *A spurt of diesel came from one valve and none from the other.*
2 = **burst**, rush, surge, fit, access, spate • *I flushed bright red as a spurt of anger flashed through me.*

spy AS A NOUN = undercover agent, secret agent, double agent, secret service agent, foreign agent, mole, fifth columnist, nark *(Brit., Austral. & N.Z. slang)* • *He was jailed for five years as an alleged British spy.*
▸ **AS A VERB 1 = be a spy**, snoop *(informal)*, gather intelligence, be engaged in spying, work for the secret service • *I never agreed to spy for the United States.*
2 *usually followed by* **on = watch**, follow, shadow, tail *(informal)*, trail, keep watch on, keep under surveillance • *He had his wife spied on for evidence in a divorce case.*
3 = **catch sight of**, see, spot, notice, sight, observe, glimpse, behold *(archaic or literary)*, set eyes on, espy, descry • *He was walking down the street when he spied an old friend.*

spying = espionage, reconnaissance, infiltration, undercover work • *a ten-year sentence for spying*

squabble AS A VERB = quarrel, fight, argue, row, clash, dispute, scrap *(informal)*, fall out *(informal)*, brawl, spar, wrangle, bicker, have words, fight like cat and dog, go at it hammer and tongs • *Mother is devoted to Dad although they squabble all the time.*
▸ **AS A NOUN = quarrel**, fight, row, argument, dispute, set-to *(informal)*, scrap *(informal)*, disagreement, barney *(informal)*, spat, difference of opinion, tiff, turf war *(informal)*, bagarre *(French)* • *There have been minor squabbles about phone bills.*

squad = team, group, band, company, force, troop, crew, gang, dream team • *The club is under investigation by the fraud squad.*

squalid 1 = dirty, filthy, seedy, sleazy, sordid, low, nasty, foul, disgusting, rundown, decayed, repulsive, poverty-stricken, unclean, fetid, slovenly, skanky *(slang)*, slummy, yucky *or* yukky *(slang)*, yucko *(Austral. slang)*, festy *(Austral. slang)* • *The migrants have been living in squalid conditions.*
OPPOSITES: clean, spotless, hygienic
2 = **unseemly**, sordid, inappropriate, unsuitable, out of place, improper, undignified, disreputable, unbecoming,

S

unrefined, out of keeping, discreditable, indelicate, in poor taste, indecorous, unbefitting • *the squalid pursuit of profit*

squall AS A NOUN = **storm**, gale, flurry, blow, rush, blast, breeze, puff, gust • *The boat was hit by a squall north of the island.*
▸ AS A VERB = **wail**, cry, howl, bawl, weep, yowl • *There was an infant squalling at the back of the church.*

squally = **stormy**, wild, rough, turbulent, windy, tempestuous, blustery, gusty, inclement • *The competitors had to contend with squally weather conditions.*

squalor = **filth**, wretchedness, sleaziness, decay, foulness, slumminess, squalidness, meanness • *He was out of work and living in squalor.*
OPPOSITES: luxury, splendour, cleanliness

squander = **waste**, spend, fritter away, blow (*slang*), consume, scatter, run through, lavish, throw away, misuse, dissipate, expend, misspend, be prodigal with, frivol away, spend like water • *He had squandered his chances to win.*
OPPOSITES: keep, save, be frugal

square AS A NOUN 1 = **town square**, close, quad, market square, quadrangle, village square • *The house is located in one of Pimlico's prettiest squares.*
2 = **conservative**, dinosaur, traditionalist, die-hard, stick-in-the-mud (*informal*), fuddy-duddy (*informal*), old buffer (*Brit. informal*), antediluvian, back number (*informal*), (old) fogey • *I'm a square, man. I adore Steely Dan.*
▸ AS AN ADJECTIVE 1 = **straight**, rectangular, oblong, at right angles, quadrilateral • *His fingernails were square and cut neatly across.*
2 = **fair**, just, straight, genuine, decent, ethical, straightforward, upright, honest, equitable, upfront (*informal*), on the level (*informal*), kosher (*informal*), dinkum (*Austral. & N.Z. informal*), above board, fair and square, on the up and up • *We are asking for a square deal.*
3 = **old-fashioned**, straight (*slang*), conservative, conventional, dated, bourgeois, out of date, stuffy, behind the times, strait-laced, out of the ark (*informal*), Pooterish • *I felt so square in my three-piece suit.*
OPPOSITES: modern, fashionable, stylish
4 = **level**, even, equal, evenly, matched, balanced, drawn, on a par, neck and neck, level pegging, even stevens (*informal*) • *The sides finished all square in the first leg.*
▸ AS A VERB 1 *often followed by* **with** = **agree**, match, fit, accord, correspond, tally, conform, reconcile, harmonize • *His dreams did not square with reality.*
2 = **even up**, make equal • *They came from three down to square the match.*
▸ IN PHRASES: **square up to something** *or* **someone** = **confront**, face, challenge, oppose, encounter, brave, face up to, stand up to, come face to face with, face off (*slang*) • *Yesterday, the two men squared up to each other again.*

squarely 1 = **directly**, straight, exactly, precisely, unswervingly, without deviation • *I kept the gun aimed squarely at his eyes.*
2 = **fully**, completely, totally, entirely, absolutely, wholly, every inch, one hundred per cent, lock, stock and barrel • *The president put the blame squarely on his opponent.*
3 = **resolutely**, firmly, directly, boldly, unswervingly, unwaveringly, unfalteringly, unshrinkingly • *The management committee have faced the situation squarely.*

squash 1 = **crush**, press, flatten, mash, pound, smash, distort, pulp, compress, stamp on, trample down • *She made clay models and squashed them flat again.*
2 = **suppress**, put down (*slang*), quell, silence, sit on (*informal*), crush, quash, annihilate • *The troops would stay in position to squash the first murmur of trouble.*
3 = **embarrass**, put down, humiliate, shame, disgrace, degrade, mortify, debase, discomfit, take the wind out of someone's sails, put (someone) in his (*or* her) place, take down a peg (*informal*) • *Worried managers would be sacked or simply squashed.*

squashy = **soft**, yielding, mushy, spongy, pulpy, pappy • *deep, squashy sofas*

squat AS A VERB = **crouch down**, sit on your heels, hunker down, sit on your haunches • *He came over and squatted on his heels, looking up at the boys.*
▸ AS AN ADJECTIVE = **low**, short, stunted, stumpy, small • *squat stone houses*

squawk AS A VERB 1 = **cry**, crow, screech, hoot, yelp, cackle • *I threw pebbles at the hens, and that made them jump and squawk.*
2 = **complain**, protest, squeal (*informal, chiefly Brit.*), kick up a fuss (*informal*), raise Cain (*slang*) • *He squawked that the deal was a double cross.*
▸ AS A NOUN 1 = **cry**, crow, screech, hoot, yelp, cackle • *rising steeply into the air with an angry squawk*
2 = **scream**, cry, yell, wail, shriek, screech, squeal, yelp, yowl • *She gave a loud squawk when the water was poured on her.*

squeak AS A VERB = **squeal**, pipe, peep, shrill, whine, yelp • *In the darkness, a bat squeaked.*
▸ AS A NOUN = **squeal**, pipe, peep, shrill, yelp, whine • *He gave an outraged squeak.*

squeal AS A VERB 1 = **scream**, yell, shriek, screech, yelp, wail, yowl • *Jennifer squealed with delight and hugged me.*
2 = **complain**, protest, moan, squawk (*informal*), kick up a fuss (*informal*) • *They went squealing to the European Commission.*
3 = **inform on**, grass (*Brit. slang*), betray, shop (*slang, chiefly Brit.*), sing (*slang, chiefly U.S.*), peach (*slang*), tell all, spill the beans (*informal*), snitch (*slang*), blab, rat on (*informal*), sell (someone) down the river (*informal*), blow the gaff (*Brit. slang*), spill your guts (*slang*), dob in (*Austral. slang*) • *There was no question of squealing to the police.*
▸ AS A NOUN = **scream**, shriek, screech, yell, scream, shriek, wail, yelp, yowl • *At that moment there was a squeal of brakes.* • *the squeal of piglets*

squeamish 1 = **queasy**, sick, nauseous, queer, sickish, qualmish • *I feel squeamish at the sight of blood.*
OPPOSITES: strong-stomached
2 = **fastidious**, particular, delicate, nice (*rare*), scrupulous, prudish, prissy (*informal*), finicky, strait-laced, punctilious • *A meeting with this man is not for the socially squeamish.*
OPPOSITES: tough, bold, coarse

squeeze AS A VERB 1 = **press**, crush, squash, grip, grasp, pinch, flatten, nip • *Dip the bread in the water and squeeze it dry.*
2 = **clutch**, press, grip, crush, pinch, cling to, squash, nip, compress, clasp, wring, hold tight, enclasp • *He squeezed her arm reassuringly.*
3 = **extract**, force, press, express • *Joe squeezed some juice from the oranges.*
4 = **cram**, press, crowd, force, stuff, pack, jam, thrust, ram, wedge, jostle • *Somehow they managed to squeeze into the tight space.*
5 = **pressurize**, lean on (*informal*), bring pressure to bear on, milk, bleed (*informal*), oppress, wrest, extort, put the squeeze on (*informal*), put the screws on (*informal*) • *The investigators are accused of squeezing the residents for information.*
6 = **hug**, embrace, cuddle, clasp, enfold, hold tight • *He longed to just scoop her up and squeeze her.*
▸ AS A NOUN 1 = **press**, grip, clasp, crush, pinch, squash, nip, wring • *I like her way of reassuring you with a squeeze of the hand.*
2 = **crush**, jam, squash, press, crowd, congestion • *The lift holds six people, but it's a bit of a squeeze.*
3 = **drop**, dash, trickle, bit, shot (*informal*), touch, taste, trace, hint, nip • *a teaspoon or two of olive oil, followed by a squeeze of lemon juice*

S

4 = hug, embrace, cuddle, hold, clasp, handclasp • *She gave her teddy bear a squeeze.*
▸ IN PHRASES: **squeeze something out = leave out**, exclude, eliminate, omit, preclude • *Latin and Greek will be squeezed out of school timetables.*

squint AS A VERB **= peer**, screw up your eyes, narrow your eyes, look through narrowed eyes • *The girl squinted at the photograph.*
▸ AS A NOUN **1 = cross eyes**, strabismus • *She had a bad squint in her right eye.*
2 = look, glimpse, peek, glance, butcher's *(Brit. slang)*, gander *(informal)*, look-see *(slang)*, shufti *(Brit. slang or informal)* • *They have waited a long time to have a squint inside my lovely shed.*

squirm **1 = wriggle**, twist, writhe, shift, flounder, wiggle, fidget • *He gave a feeble shrug and tried to squirm free.*
2 = feel uncomfortable, worry, writhe, agonize • *Mentioning religion is a sure way to make him squirm.*

squirrel AS A VERB
▸ IN PHRASES: **squirrel something away = save**, reserve, set aside, hoard, keep, hold, store, collect, gather, put aside, hide away, lay by, put by, salt away, treasure up, keep up your sleeve *(informal)*, put aside for a rainy day • *Arlott squirrelled away books, pictures and porcelain plates.*
▸ AS A NOUN
▸ RELATED ADJECTIVE: sciurine
▸ NAME OF HOME: drey or dray

squirt AS A VERB **1 = spurt**, shoot, gush, burst, jet, surge, erupt, spew • *The water squirted from its throat.*
2 = spray, wet, sprinkle, shower, scatter, diffuse, spatter, atomize • *Its linings were simply squirted with oil.*
▸ AS A NOUN **1 = spurt**, jet, burst, gush, surge, eruption • *a squirt of air freshener*
2 = pipsqueak, twerp *(Brit. informal)*, whippersnapper, squit *(Brit. informal)*, nerd or nurd *(Brit. informal)* • *He was, by his own admission, 'a bit of a squirt' as a kid.*

stab AS A VERB **1 = pierce**, cut, gore, run through, stick, injure, wound, knife, thrust, spear, jab, puncture, bayonet, transfix, impale, spill blood • *Somebody stabbed him in the stomach.*
2 = jab, poke, prod, thrust, lunge • *Bess stabbed at a slice of cucumber.*
▸ AS A NOUN **1 = attempt**, go, try, shot *(informal)*, crack *(informal)*, essay *(informal)*, endeavour • *Several times tennis stars have had a stab at acting.*
2 = twinge, prick, pang, ache • *a stab of pain just above his eye*
▸ IN PHRASES: **stab someone in the back = betray**, double-cross *(informal)*, sell out *(informal)*, sell, let down, inform on, do the dirty on *(Brit. slang)*, break faith with, play false, give the Judas kiss to, dob in *(Austral. slang)* • *She has been stabbed in the back by her supposed 'friends'.*

stabbing = sharp, shooting, violent, acute, severe, fierce, piercing, excruciating, gut-wrenching • *He was struck by a stabbing pain in his midriff.*

stability = firmness, strength, soundness, durability, permanence, solidity, constancy, steadiness, steadfastness • *It was a time of political stability and progress.*
OPPOSITES: instability, frailty, fragility

stabilize = make stable, support, balance, root, keep steady • *Officials hope the move will stabilize exchange rates.*

stable **1 = secure**, lasting, strong, sound, fast, sure, established, permanent, constant, steady, enduring, reliable, abiding, durable, deep-rooted, well-founded, steadfast, immutable, unwavering, invariable, unalterable, unchangeable • *a stable marriage*
OPPOSITES: uncertain, shaky, insecure
2 = well-balanced, balanced, sensible, reasonable, rational, clear-headed, sound of mind, mentally sound • *Their characters are fully formed and they are both very stable children.*
3 = solid, firm, secure, fixed, substantial, sturdy, durable, well-made, well-built, immovable, built to last • *This structure must be stable.*
OPPOSITES: unstable, rickety

stack AS A NOUN **1 = pile**, heap, mountain, mass, load, cock, rick, clamp *(Brit., Agriculture)*, mound • *There were stacks of books on the bedside table and floor.*
2 = lot, mass, load *(informal)*, ton *(informal)*, heap *(informal)*, large quantity, great amount • *If the job's that good, you'll have stacks of money.*
3 = chimney, funnel, smoke stack, factory chimney • *the black chimney stack*
4 = pillar, column, dome, tor, plug • *the tallest sea stack in Britain*
▸ AS A VERB **1 = pile**, heap up, load, assemble, accumulate, amass, stockpile, bank up • *They are stacked neatly in piles of three.*
2 = pack, fill, crowd, stuff, mob, cram, throng • *The committee is stacked with members from energy-producing states.*

stadium = arena, stand, ground, field, track, bowl, pitch, racecourse, grandstand, racetrack, hippodrome, velodrome, running track • *a baseball stadium*

staff AS A NOUN **1 = workers**, employees, personnel, workforce, team, organization • *The staff were very good.*
2 = stick, pole, rod, prop, crook, cane, stave, wand, sceptre • *We carried a staff that was notched at various lengths*
▸ AS A VERB **= man**, work, operate, crew, people • *They are staffed by volunteers.*

stage AS A NOUN **1 = step**, leg, phase, point, level, period, division, length, lap, juncture • *the final stage of the tour*
2 = platform, stand, podium, rostrum, dais, soapbox • *I went on stage and did my show.*
3 = scene, area, field, theatre, sector, territory, province, arena, scope, sphere, realm, domain • *He was finally forced off the political stage last year.*
▸ AS A VERB **1 = present**, produce, perform, put on, do, give, play • *She staged her first play in the late 1970s.*
2 = organize, mount, arrange, lay on, orchestrate, engineer • *At the middle of this year the government staged a huge military parade.*
▸ IN PHRASES: **the stage = the theatre**, show business, the boards, the footlights, the dramatic arts • *Madge did not want to put her daughter on the stage.*

stagger **1 = totter**, reel, sway, falter, lurch, wobble, waver, teeter • *He was staggering and had to lean on the bar.*
2 = lurch, reel, stumble, sway, totter • *a government that staggered from crisis to crisis*
3 = astound, amaze, stun, surprise, shock, shake, overwhelm, astonish, confound, take (someone) aback, bowl over *(informal)*, stupefy, strike (someone) dumb, throw off balance, give (someone) a shock, dumbfound, nonplus, flabbergast, take (someone's) breath away • *The whole thing staggers me.*

staggered = astounded, amazed, stunned, surprised, shocked, shaken, overwhelmed, astonished, confounded, taken aback, bowled over *(informal)*, dumbfounded, flabbergasted, stupefied, nonplussed, struck dumb, throw off balance • *I was simply staggered by the heat of the Argentine high-summer.*

staggering = astounding, amazing, stunning, surprising, overwhelming, astonishing, breathtaking, stupefying, jaw-dropping, eye-popping *(informal)* • *The results have been quite staggering.*

stagnant **1 = stale**, still, standing, quiet, sluggish, motionless, brackish • *Mosquitoes have been thriving in stagnant water on building sites.*
OPPOSITES: clear, fresh, flowing
2 = inactive, declining, stagnating, flat, slow, depressed,

sluggish, slow-moving • *Mass movements are often a factor in the awakening of stagnant societies.*

stagnate 1 = **vegetate**, decline, deteriorate, rot, decay, idle, rust, languish, stand still, fester, go to seed, lie fallow • *His career had stagnated.*
2 = **fester**, become stale, become stagnant, become trapped, putrefy, stop flowing, become foul • *They do not like water gathering round their roots and stagnating.*

staid = **sedate**, serious, sober, quiet, calm, grave, steady, composed, solemn, demure, decorous, self-restrained, set in your ways • *a staid country doctor*
OPPOSITES: wild, lively, exuberant

stain AS A NOUN 1 = **mark**, spot, blot, blemish, discoloration, smirch • *a black stain*
2 = **stigma**, shame, disgrace, slur, reproach, blemish, dishonour, infamy, blot on the escutcheon • *a stain on the honour of its war dead*
3 = **dye**, colour, tint • *Give each surface two coats of stain.*
▸ AS A VERB 1 = **mark**, soil, discolour, dirty, tarnish, tinge, spot, blot, blemish, smirch • *Some foods can stain teeth, as of course can smoking.*
2 = **dye**, colour, tint • *a technique biologists use to stain proteins*
3 = **disgrace**, taint, blacken, sully, corrupt, contaminate, deprave, defile, besmirch, drag through the mud • *It was too late. Their reputation had been stained.*

stake[1] AS A NOUN = **pole**, post, spike, stick, pale, paling, picket, stave, palisade • *Drive in a stake before planting the tree.*
▸ AS A VERB = **support**, secure, prop, brace, tie up, tether • *The plants are susceptible to wind, and should be well staked.*
▸ IN PHRASES: **stake something out** = **lay claim to**, define, outline, mark out, demarcate, delimit • *The time has come for Hindus to stake out their claim to their own homeland.*

stake[2] AS A NOUN 1 = **bet**, ante, wager, chance, risk, venture, hazard • *The game was usually played for high stakes between two large groups.*
2 = **contest**, race, challenge, battle, competition, running, scramble, rivalry • *Britain lags behind in the European childcare stakes.*
3 = **interest**, share, involvement, claim, concern, investment • *a stake in the plot*
▸ AS A VERB = **bet**, gamble, wager, chance, risk, venture, hazard, jeopardize, imperil, put on the line • *He has staked his reputation on the outcome.*
▸ IN PHRASES: **at stake** = **to lose**, at risk, being risked • *The tension was naturally high for a game with so much at stake.*
stake a claim *or* **stake your claim as something** = **make your mark as**, make it as, be successful as, get ahead as, achieve recognition as, distinguish yourself as • *Joyce is determined to stake her claim as an actress.*

stale 1 = **old**, hard, dry, decayed, fetid • *a lump of stale bread*
OPPOSITES: fresh, crisp
2 = **musty**, stagnant, fusty • *the smell of stale sweat*
3 = **tasteless**, flat, sour, insipid • *The place smelled of stale beer and dusty carpets.*
4 = **unoriginal**, banal, trite, common, flat, stereotyped, commonplace, worn-out, antiquated, threadbare, old hat, insipid, hackneyed, overused, repetitious, platitudinous, cliché-ridden • *repeating stale jokes to kill the time*
OPPOSITES: new, original, novel

stalemate = **deadlock**, draw, tie, impasse, standstill • *He said the war had reached a stalemate.*

stalk[1] = **stem**, shoot, branch, stock, trunk, peduncle • *A single pale blue flower grows up from each joint on a long stalk.*

stalk[2] 1 = **pursue**, follow, track, hunt, shadow, tail *(informal)*, haunt, creep up on • *He stalks his victims like a hunter after a deer.*
2 = **march**, pace, stride, strut, flounce • *If his patience is tried at meetings he has been known to stalk out.*

stall AS A VERB = **stop dead**, jam, seize up, catch, stick, stop short • *The engine stalled.*
▸ AS A NOUN 1 = **stand**, table, counter, booth, kiosk • *market stalls selling local fruits*
2 = **enclosure**, pen, coop, corral, sty • *mucking out the animal stalls*

stall 1 = **hinder**, obstruct, impede, block, check, arrest, halt, slow down, hamper, thwart, sabotage • *an attempt to stall the negotiations*
2 = **play for time**, delay, hedge, procrastinate, stonewall, beat about the bush *(informal)*, temporize, drag your feet • *Thomas had spent all week stalling over a decision.*
3 = **hold up**, delay, detain, divert, distract • *Shop manager Brian Steel stalled the man until the police arrived.*

stalwart AS A NOUN = **adherent**, supporter, fan, follower, attendant, groupie *(informal)*, hanger-on *(informal)* • *a stalwart of the revered Kurt Edelhagen Orchestra*
▸ AS AN ADJECTIVE 1 = **loyal**, faithful, staunch, strong, firm, true, constant, resolute, dependable, steadfast, true-blue, tried and true • *a stalwart supporter of the colonial government*
2 = **strong**, strapping, robust, athletic, vigorous, rugged, manly, hefty *(informal)*, muscular, sturdy, stout, husky *(informal)*, beefy *(informal)*, lusty, sinewy, brawny • *I was never in any danger with my stalwart bodyguard around me.*
OPPOSITES: feeble, puny, weak

stamina = **staying power**, endurance, resilience, force, power, energy, strength, resistance, grit, vigour, tenacity, welly *(slang)*, power of endurance, indefatigability, lustiness • *You have to have a lot of stamina to be a top-class dancer.*

stammer AS A VERB = **stutter**, falter, splutter, pause, hesitate, hem and haw, stumble over your words • *She stammered her way through an introduction.*
▸ AS A NOUN = **speech impediment**, stutter, speech defect • *A speech-therapist cured his stammer.*

stamp AS A NOUN 1 = **imprint**, mark, brand, cast, mould, signature, earmark, hallmark • *You may live only where the stamp in your passport says you may.*
2 = **stomp**, stump, clump, tramp, clomp • *the stamp of feet on the stairs*
3 = **type**, sort, kind, form, cut, character, fashion, cast, breed, description • *Montgomerie's style is of a different stamp.*
4 = **mark**, indication, hallmark, badge, emblem, sure sign, telltale sign • *lawns and flowerbeds that bear the stamp of years of confident care*
▸ AS A VERB 1 = **print**, mark, fix, impress, mould, imprint, engrave, inscribe • *'Eat before July 14' was stamped on the label.*
2 = **stomp**, stump, clump, tramp, clomp • *She stamped her feet on the pavement to keep out the cold.*
3 = **trample**, step, tread, crush • *He received a ban last week after stamping on the referee's foot.*
4 = **identify**, mark, brand, label, reveal, exhibit, betray, pronounce, show to be, categorize, typecast • *They had stamped me as a bad woman.*
▸ IN PHRASES: **stamp on something** = **suppress**, eliminate, eradicate, cut out, beat, squash, quash, do away with, quell, stamp out • *The government's first duty is to stamp on inflation.*
stamp something out = **eliminate**, destroy, eradicate, crush, suppress, put down, put out, scotch, quell, extinguish, quench, extirpate • *on-the-spot fines to stamp the problems out*

stamp collecting = **philately** • *Are you interested in stamp collecting, train spotting and bird watching?*
▸ RELATED MANIA: timbromania
▸ RELATED ENTHUSIAST: philatelist

stampede AS A NOUN = **rush**, charge, flight, scattering, rout • *There was a stampede for the exit.*
▸ AS A VERB = **bolt**, run, charge, race, career, rush, dash • *The crowd stampeded and many were crushed or trampled underfoot.*

stance 1 = **attitude**, stand, position, viewpoint, standpoint • *They have maintained a consistently neutral stance.*

2 = **posture**, carriage, bearing, deportment • *The woman detective shifted her stance from one foot to another.*

stand AS A VERB 1 = **be upright**, be erect, be vertical, be on your feet • *She was standing beside my bed staring down at me.*
2 = **get to your feet**, rise, stand up, straighten up, pick yourself up, find your feet • *Becker stood and shook hands with Ben.*
3 = **be located**, be, sit, be found, perch, nestle, be positioned, be sited, be perched, be situated *or* located • *The house stands alone on top of a small hill.*
4 = **be valid**, apply, be in force, hold good, continue, stay, exist, prevail, remain valid, remain effective, remain in operation • *The supreme court says the convictions still stand.*
5 = **put**, place, position, set, mount, lean, prop • *Stand the plant in the open in a sunny, sheltered place.*
6 = **sit**, rest, mellow, maturate • *The salad improves if made in the open and left to stand.*
7 = **resist**, endure, withstand, wear (*Brit. slang*), weather, undergo, defy, tolerate, stand up to, hold out against, stand firm against • *Ancient wisdom has stood the test of time.*
8 = **tolerate**, bear, abide, suffer, stomach, endure, brook, hack (*slang*), submit to, thole (*dialect*) • *He hates vegetables and can't stand curry.*
9 = **take**, bear, handle, cope with, experience, sustain, endure, undergo, put up with (*informal*), withstand, countenance • *I can't stand any more. I'm going to run away.*
▸ AS A NOUN 1 = **position**, attitude, stance, opinion, determination, standpoint, firm stand • *His tough stand won some grudging admiration.*
2 = **stall**, booth, kiosk, table • *She bought a hot dog from a stand on a street corner.*
3 = **grandstand** • *The people in the stands are cheering with all their might.*
4 = **support**, base, platform, place, stage, frame, rack, bracket, tripod, dais, trivet • *The teapot came with a stand to catch the drips.*
5 = **rank**, station, bay, place, park • *Luckily there was a taxi stand near-by.*
▸ IN PHRASES: **stand aside** = **not participate**, stand by, sit tight, sit on the fence, watch, look on, turn a blind eye, bide your time, let well alone • *Ireland stood aside and refused to get involved in this conflict.*
stand by 1 = **be prepared**, wait, stand ready, prepare yourself, wait in the wings • *Stand by for details.*
2 = **look on**, watch, not lift a finger, wait, turn a blind eye, procrastinate, not stir, let things take their course, let well alone • *The police just stood by and watched as the missiles rained down on us.*
stand by something = **support**, maintain, defend, champion, justify, sustain, endorse, assert, uphold, vindicate, stand up for, espouse, speak up for, stick up for (*informal*) • *The decision has been made and I have got to stand by it.*
stand by someone = **support**, back, champion, defend, take (someone's) part, uphold, befriend, be loyal to, stick up for (*informal*) • *I wouldn't break the law for a friend, but I would stand by her if she did.*
stand down = **resign**, leave, quit, abdicate, give in your notice, call it a day *or* night • *Profits plunged and he stood down as chairman last January.*
stand for something 1 = **represent**, mean, signify, denote, indicate, exemplify, symbolize, betoken • *What does EEC stand for?*
2 = **support**, champion, propose, promote, recommend, advocate, campaign for, prescribe, speak for, uphold, press for, argue for, espouse • *He hates us and everything we stand for.*
▸ AS A VERB = **tolerate**, suffer, bear, endure, put up with, wear (*Brit. informal*), brook, lie down under (*informal*) • *It's outrageous, and we won't stand for it any more.*
stand in for someone = **be a substitute for**, represent, cover for, take the place of, replace, understudy, hold the fort for, do duty for, deputize for • *I had to stand in for her on Tuesday when she didn't show up.*
stand out 1 = **be conspicuous**, be striking, be prominent, be obvious, be highlighted, attract attention, catch the eye, be distinct, stick out like a sore thumb (*informal*), stare you in the face (*informal*), be thrown into relief, bulk large, stick out a mile (*informal*), leap to the eye • *Every tree, wall and fence stood out against dazzling white fields.*
2 = **be better**, eclipse, overshadow, be superior, steal the show, outshine • *He played the violin, and he stood out from all the other musicians.*
3 = **project**, protrude, bristle • *Her hair stood out in spikes.*
stand someone up = **let down**, leave stranded, leave in the lurch • *We were to have dinner yesterday evening, but he stood me up.*
stand up = **be plausible**, be convincing, hold up, hold water, carry weight, wash (*informal*), bear scrutiny • *He made wild accusations that did not stand up in court.*
stand up for something *or* **someone** = **support**, champion, defend, uphold, side with, stick up for (*informal*), come to the defence of • *They stood up for what they believed to be right.*
stand up to something *or* **someone** 1 = **withstand**, take, bear, weather, cope with, resist, endure, tolerate, hold out against, stand firm against • *Is this building going to stand up to the strongest gales?*
2 = **resist**, oppose, confront, tackle, brave, defy • *Women are now aware of their rights and are prepared to stand up to their employers.*

standard AS A NOUN 1 = **level**, grade, calibre, quality • *There will be new standards of hospital cleanliness.*
2 = **criterion**, measure, guideline, example, model, average, guide, pattern, sample, par, norm, gauge, benchmark, yardstick, touchstone • *systems that were by later standards absurdly primitive*
3 *often plural* = **principles**, ideals, morals, rule, ethics, canon, moral principles, code of honour • *My father has always had high moral standards.*
4 = **flag**, banner, pennant, colours, ensign, pennon • *a gleaming limousine bearing the royal standard*
▸ AS AN ADJECTIVE 1 = **usual**, normal, customary, set, stock, average, popular, basic, regular, typical, prevailing, orthodox, staple, one-size-fits-all • *It was standard practice for them to advise in cases of murder.*
OPPOSITES: strange, unusual, extraordinary
2 = **accepted**, official, established, classic, approved, recognized, definitive, authoritative • *a standard text in several languages*
OPPOSITES: unofficial, unconventional, unauthorised

QUOTATIONS
Standards are always out of date. That's what makes them standards
[Alan Bennett *Forty Years On*]

standardize = **bring into line**, regularize, stereotype, regiment, assimilate, mass-produce, institutionalize • *His new dictionary helped standardize the national language.*

stand-in = **substitute**, deputy, replacement, reserve, surrogate, understudy, locum, stopgap • *He was a stand-in for my regular doctor.*

standing AS A NOUN 1 = **status**, position, station, footing, condition, credit, rank, reputation, eminence, estimation, repute • *He has improved his country's standing abroad.*
2 = **duration**, existence, length of time, experience, continuance • *My girlfriend of long standing left me.*
▸ AS AN ADJECTIVE 1 = **permanent**, lasting, fixed, regular, repeated, perpetual • *a standing offer*

S

2 = **upright**, erect, vertical, rampant *(Heraldry)*, perpendicular, upended • *standing stones*
3 = **stagnant**, still, sluggish, quiet, stale, motionless, brackish • *Mosquito larvae require standing water in which to complete their development.*
▸ RELATED PHOBIA: stasiphobia

stand-off = **deadlock**, stalemate, impasse, draw, tie, standstill, gridlock, dead heat • *This could lead to another diplomatic stand-off.*

stand-offish = **reserved**, remote, distant, aloof, avoidant, cold, haughty, unapproachable, unsociable • *He can be quite stand-offish and rude, even to his friends.*
OPPOSITES: open, warm

standpoint = **point of view**, position, angle, viewpoint, stance, vantage point • *From my standpoint, you know, this thing is just ridiculous.*

standstill = **halt**, stop, stand • *Production is more or less at a standstill.*

staple AS AN ADJECTIVE = **principal**, chief, main, key, basic, essential, primary, fundamental, predominant • *Staple goods are disappearing from the shops.*
▸ AS A NOUN = **essential**, basic, necessity, must, requisite, must-have • *boutiques selling such staples as jeans and T-shirts*

star AS A NOUN 1 = **heavenly body**, sun, celestial body • *The nights were pure with cold air and lit with stars.*
2 = **celebrity**, big name, celeb *(informal)*, megastar *(informal)*, name, draw, idol, luminary, leading man *or* lady, lead, hero *or* heroine, principal, main attraction • *Not all football stars are ill-behaved louts.*
▸ AS A PLURAL NOUN = **horoscope**, forecast, astrological chart • *There was nothing in my stars to say I'd have problems.*
▸ AS A VERB = **play the lead**, appear, feature, perform • *He's starred in dozens of films.*
▸ AS A MODIFIER = **leading**, major, principal, celebrated, brilliant, well-known, prominent, paramount, illustrious • *He was the school's star pupil.*
▸ RELATED ADJECTIVES: astral, sidereal, stellar
▸ RELATED PHOBIA: siderophobia
▹ *See panel* **Stars and constellations**

starch
▸ RELATED ADJECTIVE: amylaceous

starchy = **formal**, stiff, stuffy, conventional, precise, prim, punctilious, ceremonious • *The poses were starchy, the smiles a shade false.*

stardom = **fame**, celebrity, prominence, glory, renown, repute, illustriousness • *In 1929 she shot to stardom on Broadway.*

stare AS A VERB = **gaze**, look, goggle, watch, gape, eyeball *(slang)*, ogle, gawp *(Brit. slang)*, gawk, rubberneck *(slang)* • *Mahoney tried not to stare.*
▸ IN PHRASES: **stare someone in the face** = **be obvious**, be clear, be evident, be apparent, be blinding, be plain, be patent, be unmistakable, be self-evident, be crystal clear, be as plain as the nose on your face, be right under your nose • *The answer had been staring me in the face.*

stark AS AN ADJECTIVE 1 = **plain**, simple, harsh, basic, bare, grim, straightforward, blunt, bald • *The stark truth is that we are paying more now than we ever were.*
2 = **sharp**, clear, striking, graphic, distinct, clear-cut, clearly delineated • *in stark contrast*
3 = **austere**, severe, plain, bare, harsh, unadorned, bare-bones • *the stark, white, characterless fireplace in the drawing room*
4 = **bleak**, grim, barren, hard, cold, depressing, dreary, desolate, forsaken, godforsaken, drear *(literary)* • *a stark landscape of concrete, wire and utility equipment*
5 = **absolute**, pure, sheer, utter, downright, patent, consummate, palpable, out-and-out, flagrant, unmitigated, unalloyed, arrant • *They are motivated, he said, by stark fear.*
▸ AS AN ADVERB = **absolutely**, quite, completely, clean, entirely, altogether, wholly, utterly • *I gasped again. He must have gone stark staring mad.*

stark naked = **nude**, stripped, naked, stark, undressed, in the raw *(informal)*, starkers *(informal)*, in the buff *(informal)*, in the altogether *(informal)*, buck naked *(slang)*, unclad, in a state of nature, in your birthday suit *(informal)*, scuddy *(slang)*, without a stitch on *(informal)*, in the bare scud *(slang)*, naked as the day you were born *(informal)* • *All contestants were completely stark naked.*

starling
▸ COLLECTIVE NOUN: murmuration

start AS A VERB 1 = **set about**, begin, proceed, embark upon, take the plunge *(informal)*, take the first step, make a beginning, put your hand to the plough *(informal)* • *She started cleaning the kitchen.*
OPPOSITES: stop, finish, delay
2 = **begin**, arise, originate, issue, appear, kick in, commence, get under way, come into being, come into existence, first see the light of day • *The fire is thought to have started in an upstairs room.*
OPPOSITES: end, stop, finish
3 = **set in motion**, initiate, instigate, open, trigger, kick off *(informal)*, originate, get going, engender, kick-start, get (something) off the ground *(informal)*, enter upon, get *or* set *or* start the ball rolling • *Who started the fight?*
OPPOSITES: end, stop, finish
4 = **establish**, begin, found, father, create, launch, set up, introduce, institute, pioneer, initiate, inaugurate, lay the foundations of • *Now is probably as good a time as any to start a business.*
OPPOSITES: end, finish, terminate
5 = **start up**, activate, get something going, fire up, set in motion, start something functioning *or* operating • *He started the car, which hummed smoothly.*
OPPOSITES: stop, turn off, switch off
6 = **jump**, shy, jerk, twitch, flinch, recoil • *Rachel started at his touch.*
▸ AS A NOUN 1 = **beginning**, outset, opening, birth, foundation, dawn, first step(s), onset, initiation, inauguration, inception, commencement, kickoff *(informal)*, opening move • *She demanded to know why she had not been told from the start.*
OPPOSITES: end, finish, conclusion
2 = **jump**, jerk, twitch, spasm, convulsion • *He gave a start of surprise and astonishment.*
▸ IN PHRASES: **start something off** = **set off**, start, cause, produce, generate, prompt, provoke, bring about, activate, give rise to, spark off, set in motion • *He became more aware of the things that started that tension off.*

starting point 1 = **first step**, opening, foundation, introduction, first move, opening gambit • *These proposals represent a realistic starting point for negotiation.*
2 = **point of departure**, starting post • *They had already walked a couple of miles or more from their starting point.*

startle = **surprise**, shock, alarm, frighten, scare, agitate, take (someone) aback, make (someone) jump, give (someone) a turn *(informal)*, scare the bejesus out of *(informal)* • *The telephone startled him.*

startling = **surprising**, shocking, alarming, extraordinary, sudden, unexpected, staggering, unforeseen, jaw-dropping • *His hair was dyed a startling black.*

starvation = **lack of food**, famine, malnourishment, food deprivation • *Over three hundred people had died of starvation.*

starve 1 = **die from lack of food**, die from malnourishment • *A number of the prisoners we saw are starving.*
2 = **deprive**, strip, rob, dispossess, divest • *The electricity industry is not the only one to be starved of investment.*

starving = **hungry**, starved, ravenous, famished, hungering, sharp-set, esurient, faint from lack of food,

STARS AND CONSTELLATIONS

Stars

Aldebaran
Betelgeuse
Polaris, the Pole Star, *or* the North Star
Sirius, the Dog Star, Canicula, *or* Sothis
the Sun

Constellations

Latin name	English name
Andromeda	Andromeda
Antila	Air Pump
Apus	Bird of Paradise
Aquarius	Water Bearer
Aquila	Eagle
Ara	Altar
Aries	Ram
Auriga	Charioteer
Boötes	Herdsman
Caelum	Chisel
Camelopardalis	Giraffe
Cancer	Crab
Canes Venatici	Hunting Dogs
Canis Major	Great Dog
Canis Minor	Little Dog
Capricornus	Sea Goat
Carina	Keel
Cassiopeia	Cassiopeia
Centaurus	Centaur
Cepheus	Cepheus
Cetus	Whale
Chamaeleon	Chameleon
Circinus	Compasses
Columba	Dove
Coma Bernices	Bernice's Hair
Corona Australis	Southern Crown
Corona Borealis	Northern Crown
Corvus	Crow
Crater	Cup
Crux	Southern Cross
Cygnus	Swan
Delphinus	Dolphin
Dorado	Swordfish
Draco	Dragon
Equuleus	Little Horse
Eridanus	River Eridanus
Fornax	Furnace
Gemini	Twins
Grus	Crane
Hercules	Hercules
Horologium	Clock
Hydra	Sea Serpent
Hydrus	Water Snake
Indus	Indian
Lacerta	Lizard
Leo	Lion
Leo Minor	Little Lion
Lepus	Hare
Libra	Scales
Lupus	Wolf
Lynx	Lynx
Lyra	Harp
Mensa	Table
Microscopium	Microscope
Monoceros	Unicorn
Musca	Fly
Norma	Level
Octans	Octant
Ophiuchus	Serpent Bearer
Orion	Orion
Pavo	Peacock
Pegasus	Winged Horse
Perseus	Perseus
Phoenix	Phoenix
Pictor	Easel
Pisces	Fishes
Piscis Austrinus	Southern Fish
Puppis	Ship's Stern
Pyxis	Mariner's Compass
Reticulum	Net
Sagitta	Arrow
Sagittarius	Archer
Scorpius	Scorpion
Sculptor	Sculptor
Scutum	Shield
Serpens	Serpent
Sextans	Sextant
Taurus	Bull
Telescopium	Telescope
Triangulum	Triangle
Triangulum Australe	Southern Triangle
Tucana	Toucan
Ursa Major	Great Bear (contains the Plough *or (U.S.)* Big Dipper)
Ursa Minor	Little Bear *or (U.S.)* Little Dipper
Vela	Sails
Virgo	Virgin
Volans	Flying Fish
Vulpecula	Fox

ready to eat a horse *(informal)* • *Apart from anything else, I was starving.*

stash AS A VERB = **store**, stockpile, save up, hoard, hide, secrete, stow, cache, lay up, salt away, put aside for a rainy day • *He had stashed money away in secret offshore bank accounts.*
▸ AS A NOUN = **hoard**, supply, store, stockpile, cache, collection • *A large stash of drugs had been found aboard the yacht.*

state AS A NOUN 1 = **country**, nation, land, republic, territory, federation, commonwealth, kingdom, body politic • *Mexico is a secular state.*
2 = **province**, region, district, area, territory, federal state • *Leaders of the Southern States are meeting in Louisville.*
3 = **government**, ministry, administration, executive, regime, powers-that-be • *The state does not collect enough revenue to cover its expenditure.*
4 = **condition**, shape, state of affairs • *When we moved here the walls and ceiling were in an awful state.*
5 = **frame of mind**, condition, spirits, attitude, mood, humour • *When you left our place, you weren't in a fit state to drive.*
6 = **ceremony**, glory, grandeur, splendour, dignity, majesty, pomp • *Nelson's body lay in state in the Painted Hall after the battle of Trafalgar.*

7 = **circumstances**, situation, position, case, pass, mode, plight, predicament • *You shouldn't be lifting heavy things in your state.*

▸ **AS A VERB** = **say**, report, declare, specify, put, present, explain, voice, express, assert, utter, articulate, affirm, expound, enumerate, propound, aver, asseverate • *Clearly state your address and telephone number.*

▸ **AS AN ADJECTIVE** = **official**, public, ceremonial, governmental • *a state visit to Moscow*

▸ **IN PHRASES: in a state 1** = **distressed**, upset, agitated, disturbed, anxious, ruffled, uptight *(informal)*, flustered, panic-stricken, het up, all steamed up *(slang)* • *I was in a terrible state because nobody could understand why I had this illness.*

2 = **untidy**, disordered, messy, muddled, cluttered, jumbled, in disarray, shambolic, topsy-turvy, higgledy-piggledy *(informal)* • *The living room was in a dreadful state.*

▹ *See panel* **States**

stately = **grand**, majestic, dignified, royal, august, imposing, impressive, elegant, imperial, noble, regal, solemn, lofty, pompous, ceremonious • *Instead of moving at his usual stately pace, he was almost running.*

OPPOSITES: common, humble, lowly

stately home = **mansion**, hall, palace, château, manor house • *It's a nice, smallish, comfortable stately home.*

statement 1 = **announcement**, declaration, communication, explanation, communiqué, proclamation, utterance • *He now disowns that statement, saying he was depressed when he made it.*

2 = **account**, report, testimony, evidence • *statements from witnesses to the event*

state of affairs = **situation**, state, circumstances, scenario, equation, plight, status quo • *This state of affairs cannot continue for too long.*

state of mind = **attitude**, perspective, outlook, approach, mood, disposition, frame of mind, mindset, way of looking at things • *I want you to get into a whole new state of mind.*

state-of-the-art = **latest**, newest, up-to-date, up-to-the-minute • *state-of-the-art technology*

OPPOSITES: old-fashioned, outdated, obsolete

statesman *or* **stateswoman** = **political figure**, leader, politician, political leader • *He is a great statesman and political figure.*

STATES

Indian states

Andhra Pradesh	Goa	Kashmir	Maharashtra	Orissa	Tripura
Arunachal Pradesh	Gujarat	Jharkand	Manipur	Punjab	Uttaranchal
Assam	Haryana	Karnataka	Meghalaya	Rajasthan	Uttar Pradesh
Bihar	Himachal Pradesh	Kerala	Mizoram	Sikkim	West Bengal
Chhattisgarh	Jammu and	Madhya Pradesh	Nagaland	Tamil Nadu	

Indian Union territories

Andaman and Nicobar Islands	Dadra and Nagar Haveli	Delhi	Pondicherry
Chandigarh	Daman and Diu	Lakshadweep	

US States

State	Abbreviation	Zip code	State	Abbreviation	Zip code
Alabama	Ala.	AL	Montana	Mont.	MT
Alaska	Alas.	AK	Nebraska	Neb.	NE
Arizona	Ariz.	AZ	Nevada	Nev.	NV
Arkansas	Ark.	AR	New Hampshire	N.H.	NH
California	Cal.	CA	New Jersey	N.J.	NJ
Colorado	Colo.	CO	New Mexico	N.M. *or* N.Mex.	NM
Connecticut	Conn.	CT	New York	N.Y.	NY
Delaware	Del.	DE	North Carolina	N.C.	NC
District of Columbia	D.C.	DC	North Dakota	N.D. *or* N.Dak.	ND
Florida	Fla.	FL	Ohio	O.	OH
Georgia	Ga.	GA	Oklahoma	Okla.	OK
Hawaii	Haw.	HI	Oregon	Oreg.	OR
Idaho	Id. *or* Ida.	ID	Pennsylvania	Pa., Penn., *or* Penna.	PA
Illinois	Ill.	IL	Rhode Island	R.I.	RI
Indiana	Ind.	IN	South Carolina	S.C.	SC
Iowa	Ia. *or* Io.	IA	South Dakota	S.Dak.	SD
Kansas	Kan. *or* Kans.	KS	Tennessee	Tenn.	TN
Kentucky	Ken.	KY	Texas	Tex.	TX
Louisiana	La.	LA	Utah	Ut.	UT
Maine	Me.	ME	Vermont	Vt.	VT
Maryland	Md.	MD	Virginia	Va.	VA
Massachusetts	Mass.	MA	Washington	Wash.	WA
Michigan	Mich.	MI	West Virginia	W.Va.	WV
Minnesota	Minn.	MN	Wisconsin	Wis.	WI
Mississippi	Miss.	MS	Wyoming	Wyo.	WY
Missouri	Mo.	MO			

Australian States and Territories

Australian Capital Territory	Northern Territory	South Australia	Victoria
New South Wales	Queensland	Tasmania	Western Australia

static = **stationary**, still, motionless, fixed, constant, stagnant, inert, immobile, unmoving, stock-still, unvarying, changeless • *Both your pictures are of static subjects.*
OPPOSITES: moving, active, mobile

station AS A NOUN 1 = **railway station**, stop, stage, halt, terminal, train station, terminus • *She went with him to the station to see him off.*
2 = **headquarters**, base, depot • *He was taken to the police station for questioning.*
3 = **channel**, wavelength, broadcasting company • *Which radio station do you usually listen to?*
4 = **position**, rank, status, standing, post, situation, grade, sphere • *The vast majority knew their station in life and kept to it.*
5 = **post**, place, location, position, situation, seat • *Police said the bomb was buried in the sand near a lifeguard station.*
▸ AS A VERB = **assign**, post, locate, set, establish, fix, install, garrison • *I was stationed there just after the war.*

stationary = **motionless**, standing, at a standstill, parked, fixed, moored, static, inert, unmoving, stock-still • *The train was stationary for 90 minutes.*
OPPOSITES: moving, travelling, mobile

statistics

QUOTATIONS

There are three kinds of lies: lies, damned lies, and statistics
[Benjamin Disraeli]

He uses statistics like a drunken man uses lamp-posts – for support rather than illumination
[Andrew Lang]

statue = **sculpture**, figure, carving, bronze, effigy, figurine, statuette • *a huge white statue of Chairman Mao*

statuesque = **well-proportioned**, stately, Junoesque, imposing, majestic, dignified, regal • *She was a statuesque brunette of thirty-eight.*

stature 1 = **height**, build, size, tallness • *She was a little short in stature.*
2 = **importance**, standing, prestige, size, rank, consequence, prominence, eminence, high station • *This club has grown in stature over the last 20 years.*

status 1 = **position**, rank, grade, degree, ranking • *promoted to the status of foreman*
2 = **prestige**, standing, authority, note, influence, weight, reputation, honour, importance, consequence, fame, distinction, eminence, renown, mana *(N.Z.)* • *She cheated banks to satisfy her desire for money and status.*
3 = **state of play**, development, progress, condition, evolution, progression • *Please keep us informed of the status of this project.*

statute = **law**, act, rule, regulation, decree, ordinance, enactment, edict • *a new statute to take in both pay and discrimination laws*

staunch[1] *or* **stanch** = **stop**, stay, check, arrest, halt, stem, plug, dam • *The pilot managed to staunch the fuel leak using tape.*

staunch = **loyal**, faithful, stalwart, sure, strong, firm, sound, true, constant, reliable, stout, resolute, dependable, trustworthy, trusty, steadfast, true-blue, immovable, tried and true • *He's a staunch supporter of controls on government spending.*

stave off = **hold off**, avert, ward off, parry, evade, fend off, keep at bay, keep at arm's length • *a desperate attempt to stave off defeat*

stay AS A VERB 1 = **remain**, continue to be, linger, stand, stop, wait, settle, delay, halt, pause, hover, abide, hang around *(informal)*, reside, stay put, bide, loiter, hang in the air, tarry, put down roots, establish yourself • *Hundreds of people defied army orders to stay at home.*
OPPOSITES: go, leave, depart
2 *often with* **at** = **lodge**, visit, sojourn, put up at, be accommodated at • *He tried to stay at the hotel a few days every year.*
3 = **continue**, remain, go on, survive, endure • *Nothing stays the same for long.*
4 = **suspend**, put off, defer, adjourn, hold over, hold in abeyance, prorogue • *The finance ministry stayed the execution to avoid upsetting a nervous market.*
▸ AS A NOUN 1 = **visit**, stop, holiday, stopover, sojourn • *An experienced Italian guide is provided during your stay.*
2 = **postponement**, delay, suspension, stopping, halt, pause, reprieve, remission, deferment • *The court dismissed defence appeals for a permanent stay of execution.*
▸ IN PHRASES: **stay in** = **stay at home**, stop in *(informal)*, not go out • *Let's just stay in tonight and watch TV.*
stay out of something = **not get involved in**, steer clear of, keep away from, duck (out of) *(informal)*, dodge, shun, eschew, sidestep, fight shy of, give a wide berth to, keep aloof from • *In the past, the UN has stayed out of international affairs.*

staying power = **endurance**, strength, stamina, toughness • *Someone who lacks staying power is unlikely to make a good researcher.*

steadfast 1 = **loyal**, faithful, stalwart, staunch, constant, steady, dedicated, reliable, persevering, dependable • *a steadfast friend*
OPPOSITES: unreliable, undependable, fickle
2 = **resolute**, firm, fast, fixed, stable, intent, single-minded, unwavering, immovable, unflinching, unswerving, unfaltering • *He remained steadfast in his belief that he had done the right thing.*
OPPOSITES: faltering, wavering, irresolute

steady AS AN ADJECTIVE 1 = **continuous**, even, regular, constant, consistent, persistent, rhythmic, unbroken, habitual, uninterrupted, incessant, ceaseless, unremitting, unwavering, nonstop, unvarying, unfaltering, unfluctuating • *the steady beat of the drums*
OPPOSITES: occasional, irregular, sporadic
2 = **stable**, fixed, secure, still, firm, fast, safe, anchored, moored, immovable, unshaking, on an even keel • *Make sure the camera is steady.*
OPPOSITES: unstable, insecure, unsteady
3 = **regular**, established, settled, usual, customary • *a steady boyfriend*
4 = **dependable**, sensible, reliable, balanced, settled, secure, calm, supportive, sober, staunch, serene, sedate, staid, steadfast, level-headed, serious-minded, imperturbable, equable, unchangeable, having both feet on the ground • *He was firm and steady, unlike other men she knew.*
OPPOSITES: unpredictable, unreliable, undependable
▸ AS A VERB 1 = **make steady**, stabilize, hold steady, make fast • *He eased back the throttles to steady the ship.*
OPPOSITES: shake, upset
2 = **settle**, get control of, compose, calm down, quieten, make calm • *She breathed in to steady her voice.*
▸ IN PHRASES: **go steady** = **go out**, court, be seeing someone, be in a relationship • *She and Randolph have been going steady for almost a year now.*

PROVERBS

slow but sure

steal AS A VERB 1 = **take**, nick *(slang, chiefly Brit.)*, pinch *(informal)*, lift *(informal)*, trouser *(slang)*, cabbage *(Brit. slang)*, swipe *(slang)*, knock off *(slang)*, half-inch *(old-fashioned slang)*, heist *(U.S. slang)*, embezzle, blag *(slang)*, pilfer, misappropriate, snitch *(slang)*, purloin, filch, prig *(Brit. slang)*, shoplift, thieve, be light-fingered, peculate, walk *or* make off with • *People who are drug addicts come in and steal stuff.*
2 = **copy**, take, plagiarize, appropriate, pinch *(informal)*, pirate, poach • *They solved the problem by stealing an idea from nature.*

S

3 = **sneak**, slip, creep, flit, tiptoe, slink, insinuate yourself • *They can steal away at night and join us.*
▸ **AS A NOUN** 1 = **bargain**, good deal, good value, good buy, snip *(informal)*, giveaway, (cheap) purchase • *This champagne is a steal.*
2 = **rip-off**, theft *(slang)*, thieving, pilfering, misappropriation, purloining, thievery • *His favourite joke is a steal from Billy Connolly.*

stealing = **theft**, robbery, shoplifting, embezzlement, plagiarism, thieving, pilfering, larceny, misappropriation, thievery, pilferage • *You can't just help yourself – that's stealing!*
▸ **RELATED MANIA:** kleptomania
▸ **RELATED PHOBIA:** kleptophobia

stealth = **secrecy**, furtiveness, slyness, sneakiness, unobtrusiveness, stealthiness, surreptitiousness • *Both sides advanced by stealth.*

stealthy = **secret**, secretive, furtive, sneaking, covert, sly, clandestine, sneaky, skulking, underhand, surreptitious • *It was a stealthy sound made by someone anxious not to be heard.*

steam **AS A NOUN** 1 = **vapour**, mist, condensation, moisture • *The heat converts water into high-pressure steam.*
2 = **energy**, drive, stamina, go *(informal)*, power, strength, pep, zip *(informal)*, vitality, vigour, zeal, verve, zest, welly *(slang)*, get-up-and-go *(informal)*, élan, vivacity, liveliness, vim *(slang)*, forcefulness • *Socialists everywhere had run out of steam and ideas.*
▸ **IN PHRASES: get steamed up** = **get worked up**, get angry, go mad, go crazy, see red, go ballistic, blow a fuse, get uptight, go off the deep end, get flustered, go up the wall, blow your top, lose your rag, go crook *(Austral. & N.Z. slang)*, get in a stew, get overwrought, flip your lid, hit *or* go through the roof • *I think you're getting steamed up over nothing.*
let off steam 1 = **use up energy**, let yourself go, release surplus energy • *a place where children can rush around to let off steam*
2 = **speak your mind**, sound off, give vent to your feelings • *I just phoned to let off steam.*
under your own steam = **without help**, independently, on your own, by yourself, unaided, by your own efforts • *The most reliable form of transport is provided by moving under your own steam.*

steamy 1 = **erotic**, hot *(slang)*, sexy *(informal)*, sensual, raunchy *(slang)*, lewd, carnal, titillating, prurient, lascivious, lustful, lubricious *(formal or literary)* • *He'd had a steamy affair with an office colleague.*
2 = **muggy**, damp, humid, sweaty, like a sauna • *a steamy café*

steely 1 = **determined**, firm, dogged, persevering, resolute, purposeful, tenacious, undaunted, steadfast, obstinate, unwavering, unflinching, unbending, unshakable, unshaken • *Their indecision had been replaced by steely determination.*
2 = **blue-grey**, grey, steel-grey, iron-grey • *steely grey hair*

steel yourself = **brace yourself**, make up your mind, grit your teeth, fortify yourself, harden yourself • *I was steeling myself to call round when Simon arrived.*

steep[1] 1 = **sheer**, precipitous, perpendicular, abrupt, headlong, vertical • *a narrow, steep-sided valley*
OPPOSITES: gentle, moderate, gradual
2 = **sharp**, sudden, abrupt, marked, extreme, distinct • *Unemployment has shown a steep rise.*
3 = **high**, excessive, exorbitant, extreme, stiff, unreasonable, overpriced, extortionate, uncalled-for • *The annual premium can be a little steep.*
OPPOSITES: fair, reasonable, moderate

steep[2] = **soak**, immerse, marinate *(Cookery)*, damp, submerge, drench, moisten, macerate, souse, imbrue *(rare)* • *green beans steeped in olive oil*

steeped = **saturated**, pervaded, permeated, filled, infused, imbued, suffused • *The castle is steeped in history and legend.*

steeple = **spire**, tower, belfry • *The church had a steeple, a bell tower and a clock.*

steer **AS A VERB** 1 = **drive**, control, direct, handle, conduct, pilot, govern, be in the driver's seat • *What is it like to steer a ship of this size?*
2 = **direct**, lead, guide, conduct, escort, usher, show in *or* out • *Nick steered them into the nearest seats.*
▸ **IN PHRASES: steer clear of something** *or* **someone** = **avoid**, evade, fight shy of, shun, eschew, circumvent, body-swerve *(Scot.)*, give a wide berth to, sheer off • *A lot of people steer clear of these sensitive issues.*

stem[1] **AS A NOUN** = **stalk**, branch, trunk, shoot, stock, axis, peduncle • *He cut the stem for her with his knife and handed her the flower.*
▸ **IN PHRASES: stem from something** = **originate from**, be caused by, derive from, arise from, flow from, emanate from, develop from, be generated by, be brought about by, be bred by, issue forth from • *Much of the instability stems from the economic effects of the war.*

stem[2] = **stop**, hold back, staunch, stay *(archaic)*, check, contain, dam, curb, restrain, bring to a standstill, stanch • *He was still conscious, trying to stem the bleeding with his right hand.*

stench = **stink**, whiff *(Brit. slang)*, reek, pong *(Brit. informal)*, foul smell, niff *(Brit. slang)*, malodour, mephitis, noisomeness • *The stench of burning rubber was overpowering.*

stentorian = **loud**, powerful, booming, full, carrying, strong, ringing, thundering, resounding, blaring, strident, resonant, sonorous • *He bellowed in a stentorian voice.*
OPPOSITES: low, soft

step **AS A NOUN** 1 = **pace**, stride, footstep • *I took a step towards him.*
2 = **footfall** • *He heard steps in the corridor.*
3 = **stair**, tread, rung • *He slowly climbed the steps.*
4 = **doorstep**, sill • *Leave empty milk bottles on the step.*
5 = **move**, measure, action, means, act, proceeding, procedure, manoeuvre, deed, expedient • *He greeted the agreement as the first step towards peace.*
6 = **stage**, point, phase • *Aristotle took the scientific approach a step further.*
7 = **gait**, walk • *He quickened his step.*
8 = **level**, rank, remove, degree • *This is the final step in the career ladder.*
▸ **AS A VERB** 1 = **walk**, pace, tread, move • *the first man to step on the moon*
2 = **stand**, stamp, tread, walk • *One of them accidentally stepped on my hand.*
▸ **IN PHRASES: in step** = **in agreement**, in harmony, in unison, in line, coinciding, conforming, in conformity • *Now they are more in step and more in love with each other.*
mind *or* **watch your step** = **be careful**, take care, look out, be cautious, be discreet, take heed, tread carefully, be canny, be on your guard, mind how you go, have your wits about you, mind your p's and q's • *Hey! she thought. Watch your step, girl!*
out of step = **in disagreement**, out of line, out of phase, out of harmony, incongruous, pulling different ways • *They jogged in silence a while, faces lowered, out of step.*
step by step = **gradually**, bit by bit, one step at a time, slowly but surely • *I am not rushing things and I'm taking it step by step.*
step down *or* **aside** = **resign**, retire, quit, leave, give up, pull out, bow out, abdicate • *Many would prefer to see him step aside in favour of a younger man.*
step in = **intervene**, take action, become involved, chip in *(informal)*, intercede, take a hand • *If no agreement was reached, the army would step in.*
step on it = **go faster**, speed up, hurry up *(informal)*, get moving, accelerate, get cracking, get a move on, get your

S

skates on, rattle your dags (*N.Z. informal*) • *We've only got thirty-five minutes, so step on it.*
step something up = increase, boost, intensify, up, raise, accelerate, speed up, escalate, augment • *Security is being stepped up to deal with the increase in violence.*
take steps = take action, act, intervene, move in, take the initiative, take measures • *They agreed to take steps to avoid confrontation.*

PROVERBS
one step at a time

stereotype AS A NOUN **= formula**, cliché, pattern, mould, received idea • *Accents can reinforce a stereotype.*
▸ AS A VERB **= categorize**, typecast, pigeonhole, dub, standardize, take to be, ghettoize, conventionalize • *He was stereotyped by some as a renegade.*

stereotyped = unoriginal, stock, standard, tired, conventional, played out, stale, banal, standardized, mass-produced, corny (*slang*), threadbare, trite, hackneyed, overused, platitudinous, cliché-ridden • *Listeners seem to have stereotyped ideas.*

sterile 1 **= germ-free**, antiseptic, sterilized, disinfected, aseptic • *He always made sure that any cuts were protected by sterile dressings.*
OPPOSITES: dirty, infected, unhygienic
2 **= barren**, infertile, unproductive, childless, infecund • *a sterile male*
OPPOSITES: productive, fertile, prolific
3 **= unproductive**, fruitless, unprofitable, empty, unfruitful, unprolific • *Too much time has been wasted in sterile debate.*
4 **= bare**, dry, unproductive, waste, empty, desert, barren, desolate, arid, infertile, unfruitful • *a sterile and barren wasteland*

sterility 1 **= infertility**, childlessness, infecundity (*technical*) • *This disease causes sterility in both males and females.*
2 **= emptiness**, futility, banality, worthlessness, hollowness, meaninglessness, barrenness, senselessness, aimlessness, purposelessness, valuelessness • *the sterility of Dorothea's life in industry*

sterilize 1 **= disinfect**, clean, purify, fumigate, decontaminate, autoclave, sanitize • *Sulphur is also used to sterilize equipment.*
2 **= make infertile**, hysterectomize, vasectomize • *Just after a birth may seem a logical time to be sterilized.*

sterling = excellent, sound, fine, first-class, superlative • *his years of sterling service*

stern 1 **= strict**, harsh, rigorous, hard, cruel, grim, rigid, relentless, drastic, authoritarian, austere, inflexible, unrelenting, unyielding, unsparing • *He said stern measures would be taken against the killers.*
OPPOSITES: kind, liberal, lenient
2 **= severe**, serious, forbidding, steely, flinty • *Her father was stern and hard to please.*
OPPOSITES: warm, friendly, approachable

stew AS A NOUN **= hash**, goulash, ragout, olla, olio, olla podrida • *She served him a bowl of beef stew.*
▸ AS A VERB 1 **= braise**, boil, simmer, casserole • *Stew the apple and blackberries to make a thick pulp.*
2 **= worry**, suffer, be anxious, obsess, brood, fret, agonize, feel uneasy, go through the mill, be in anguish • *I'd rather let him stew.*
▸ IN PHRASES: **in a stew = troubled**, concerned, anxious, worried, fretting, in a panic, in a lather (*informal*) • *Highly charged emotions have you in a stew.*

steward 1 **= flight attendant**, stewardess, air hostess, air stewardess, cabin attendant • *a former airline steward who joined the police*
2 **= custodian**, warden, caretaker, curator, keeper, guardian, watchdog, superintendent, protector, warder, watchman, overseer • *a steward to manage the place*

stick[1] AS A NOUN 1 **= twig**, branch, birch, offshoot • *people carrying bundles of dry sticks to sell for firewood*
2 **= cane**, staff, pole, rod, stake, switch, crook, baton, wand, sceptre • *Crowds armed with sticks and stones took to the streets.*
3 **= abuse**, criticism, flak (*informal*), blame, knocking (*informal*), hostility, slagging (*slang*), denigration, critical remarks, fault-finding • *It's not motorists who give you the most stick, it's the general public.*
▸ IN PHRASES: **the sticks = the middle of nowhere**, the countryside, a backwater, the back of beyond, a godforsaken place • *He lived out in the sticks somewhere.*

stick[2] AS A VERB 1 **= put**, place, set, position, drop, plant, store, lay, stuff, fix, deposit, install, plonk • *He folded the papers and stuck them in a drawer.*
2 **= poke**, dig, stab, insert, thrust, pierce, penetrate, spear, prod, jab, transfix • *They stuck a needle in my back.* • *The knife stuck in his chest.*
3 **= fasten**, fix, bind, hold, bond, attach, hold on, glue, fuse, paste, adhere, affix • *Stick down any loose bits of flooring.*
4 **= adhere**, cling, cleave, become joined, become cemented, become welded • *The soil sticks to the blade and blocks the plough.*
5 **= stay**, remain, linger, persist • *That song has stuck in my head for years.*
6 **= catch**, lodge, jam, stop, clog, snag, be embedded, be bogged down, come to a standstill, become immobilized • *The dagger stuck tightly in the silver scabbard.*
7 **= tolerate**, take, stand, stomach, endure, hack (*slang*), abide, bear up under • *How long did you stick that abuse for?*
▸ IN PHRASES: **stick at something = keep at**, continue, persist, see through, persevere in, plug away at (*informal*) • *You will find the diet hard at first, but stick at it.*
stick out = protrude, stand out, jut out, show, project, bulge, obtrude • *Your label's sticking out.*
stick something out 1 **= offer**, present, extend, hold out, advance, reach out, stretch out, proffer • *He stuck his hand out in welcome.*
2 **= endure**, bear, put up with (*informal*), weather, take it (*informal*), see through, soldier on, last out, grin and bear it (*informal*) • *I know the job's tough, but try to stick it out a bit longer.*
stick to someone = remain faithful, remain true, remain loyal • *He stuck to me through thick and thin.*
stick to something 1 **= keep to**, persevere in, cleave to • *Stick to well-lit roads.*
2 **= stand by**, fulfil, make good, continue in, hold to • *They are waiting to see if he sticks to his word.*
3 **= adhere to**, honour, hold to, keep to, abide by, stand by • *We must stick to the rules.*
stick up for someone = defend, support, champion, stand by, uphold, stand up for, be supportive of, come to the defence of, take the part or side of • *Thanks for sticking up for me.*

stick-in-the-mud = (old) fogey, conservative, reactionary, stick (*informal*), dinosaur, die-hard, fuddy-duddy (*informal*), Colonel Blimp, sobersides • *a stick-in-the-mud who prefers the old, tried and tested methods*

stickler = fanatic, nut (*slang*), maniac (*informal*), purist, perfectionist, pedant, martinet, hard taskmaster, fusspot (*Brit. informal*) • *I'm a bit of a stickler for accuracy.*

sticky 1 **= adhesive**, gummed, adherent • *Peel away the sticky paper.*
2 **= gooey**, tacky (*informal*), syrupy, viscous, glutinous, gummy, icky (*informal*), gluey, clinging, claggy (*dialect*), viscid • *a weakness for rich meat dishes and sticky puddings*
3 **= difficult**, awkward, tricky, embarrassing, painful, nasty, delicate, unpleasant, discomforting, hairy (*slang*), thorny, barro (*Austral. slang*) • *He found himself in a not inconsiderably sticky situation.*

S

4 = **humid**, close, sultry, oppressive, sweltering, clammy, muggy • *sticky days in the middle of August*

stiff 1 = **inflexible**, rigid, unyielding, hard, firm, tight, solid, tense, hardened, brittle, taut, solidified, unbending, inelastic • *The film is crammed with corsets, bustles and stiff collars.*
OPPOSITES: flexible, elastic, pliable
2 = **unsupple**, arthritic, creaky *(informal)*, rheumaticky • *I'm stiff all over right now.*
OPPOSITES: flexible, supple, lithe
3 = **formal**, constrained, reserved, forced, laboured, cold, mannered, wooden, artificial, uneasy, chilly, unnatural, austere, pompous, prim, stilted, starchy *(informal)*, punctilious, priggish, standoffish, ceremonious, unrelaxed • *They always seemed a little awkward with each other, a bit stiff and formal.*
OPPOSITES: easy, natural, informal
4 = **vigorous**, great, strong, determined, spirited, resolute, steely, unyielding, unflagging • *The film faces stiff competition for the nomination.*
5 = **severe**, strict, harsh, hard, heavy, sharp, extreme, cruel, drastic, rigorous, stringent, oppressive, austere, inexorable, pitiless • *stiff anti-drugs laws*
6 = **strong**, fresh, powerful, vigorous, brisk • *a stiff breeze rustling the trees*
7 = **difficult**, hard, tough, exacting, formidable, trying, fatiguing, uphill, arduous, laborious • *the stiff climb to the finish*
8 = **potent**, strong, powerful, alcoholic, intoxicating • *a stiff whisky*

stiffen 1 = **become stiff**, set, harden, gel, thicken, solidify, crystallize, congeal, coagulate, become solid • *The fine-tuning lens in the eye stiffens with age.*
2 = **tighten**, tense (up), tauten, become stiff • *The blood supply to the skin is reduced when muscles stiffen.*
3 = **strengthen**, reinforce, harden, toughen • *Canada has recently stiffened its immigration rules.*

stifle 1 = **suppress**, repress, prevent, stop, check, silence, curb, restrain, cover up, gag, hush, smother, extinguish, muffle, choke back • *Critics have accused them of trying to stifle debate.*
2 = **restrain**, suppress, repress, smother • *She makes no attempt to stifle a yawn.*

S

stifling 1 = **suffocating**, close, oppressive, airless, sticky, muggy • *The stifling heat of the little room was beginning to make me nauseous.*
2 = **oppressive**, severe, overwhelming, repressive, cruel, brutal, unjust, overbearing, tyrannical, despotic • *a stifling bureaucracy*

stigma = **disgrace**, shame, dishonour, mark, spot, brand, stain, slur, blot, reproach, imputation, smirch • *There is very little stigma attached to crime and criminals.*

stigmatize = **brand**, label, denounce, mark, discredit, pillory, defame, cast a slur upon • *They are often stigmatized by the rest of society as lazy and dirty.*

still AS AN ADJECTIVE 1 = **motionless**, stationary, at rest, calm, smooth, peaceful, serene, tranquil, lifeless, placid, undisturbed, inert, restful, unruffled, unstirring • *He sat very still for several minutes.*
OPPOSITES: moving, active, restless
2 = **silent**, quiet, hushed, noiseless, stilly *(poetic)* • *The night air was very still.*
OPPOSITES: noisy
▸ AS A VERB = **quieten**, calm, subdue, settle, quiet, silence, soothe, hush, alleviate, lull, tranquillize • *Her crying slowly stilled.* • *The people's voice has been stilled.*
OPPOSITES: get louder, increase, get worse
▸ AS A NOUN = **stillness**, peace, quiet, silence, hush, tranquillity • *It was the only noise in the still of the night.*
OPPOSITES: noise, clamour, uproar
▸ AS AN ADVERB = **yet**, even now, up until now, up to this time • *I still dream of home.*
▸ AS A SENTENCE CONNECTOR = **however**, but, yet, nevertheless, for all that, notwithstanding • *Despite the ruling, he was still found guilty.* • *It won't be easy. Still, I'll do my best.*

stilted = **stiff**, forced, wooden, laboured, artificial, inflated, constrained, unnatural, high-flown, pompous, pretentious, pedantic, bombastic, grandiloquent, high-sounding, arty-farty *(informal)*, fustian • *His delivery was stilted and occasionally stumbling.*
OPPOSITES: free, natural, spontaneous

stimulant = **pick-me-up**, tonic, restorative, upper *(slang)*, reviver, bracer *(informal)*, energizer, pep pill *(informal)*, excitant, analeptic • *the use of a banned stimulant*
OPPOSITES: downer *(slang)*, sedative, depressant

stimulate = **encourage**, inspire, prompt, fire, fan, urge, spur, provoke, turn on *(slang)*, arouse, animate, rouse, prod, quicken, inflame, incite, instigate, goad, whet, impel, foment, gee up • *I was stimulated to examine my deepest thoughts.*

stimulating 1 = **exciting**, inspiring, stirring, provoking, intriguing, rousing, provocative, exhilarating, thought-provoking, galvanic • *The atmosphere was always stimulating.*
OPPOSITES: boring, dull, uninteresting
2 = **invigorating**, bracing, revitalizing, revivifying • *the stimulating effect of adrenaline*

stimulus = **incentive**, spur, encouragement, impetus, provocation, inducement, goad, incitement, fillip, shot in the arm *(informal)*, clarion call, geeing-up • *Falling interest rates could be a stimulus to the economy.*

sting AS A VERB 1 = **hurt**, burn, wound, nip, prick, bite • *The nettles stung their legs.*
2 = **smart**, burn, pain, hurt, tingle • *His cheeks were stinging from the icy wind.*
3 = **anger**, provoke, infuriate, incense, gall, inflame, nettle, rile, pique • *Some of the criticism has really stung him.*
▸ AS A NOUN 1 = **prick**, injury, wound, puncture • *Remove the bee sting with tweezers.*
2 = **smarting**, pain, stinging, pricking, soreness, prickling • *This won't hurt – you will just feel a little sting.*
3 = **fraud**, swindle, cheat, trickery, sharp practice, piece of deception • *a sting set by the FBI*
4 = **sharpness**, spite, bite, punch, severity, sarcasm, acrimony, mordancy • *The sting of those words had festered in Roderick's mind.*
▸ RELATED PHOBIA: cnidophobia

stingy 1 = **mean**, penny-pinching *(informal)*, miserly, near, parsimonious, scrimping, illiberal, avaricious, niggardly, ungenerous, penurious, tightfisted, close-fisted, tight-arse *(taboo slang)*, tight-arsed *(taboo slang)*, mingy *(Brit. informal)*, tight-ass *(U.S. taboo slang)*, tight-assed *(U.S. taboo slang)*, cheeseparing, snoep *(S. African informal)*, tight as a duck's arse *(taboo slang)* • *The West is stingy with aid.*
2 = **insufficient**, inadequate, meagre, small, pathetic, scant, skimpy, measly *(informal)*, scanty, on the small side • *Many people may consider this a rather stingy amount.*

stink AS A VERB 1 = **reek**, pong *(Brit. informal)*, whiff *(Brit. slang)*, stink to high heaven *(informal)*, offend the nostrils • *We all stank and nobody minded.*
2 = **be bad**, be no good, be rotten, be offensive, be abhorrent, have a bad name, be detestable, be held in disrepute • *I think their methods stink.*
▸ AS A NOUN 1 = **stench**, pong *(Brit. informal)*, foul smell, foulness, malodour, fetor, noisomeness • *The stink was overpowering.*
2 = **fuss**, to-do, row, upset, scandal, stir, disturbance, uproar, commotion, rumpus, hubbub, brouhaha, deal of trouble *(informal)* • *The family's making a hell of a stink.*

stinker = **scoundrel**, heel, sod *(slang)*, cad *(Brit. informal)*, swine, bounder *(Brit. old-fashioned slang)*, cur, rotter *(slang, chiefly Brit.)*, nasty piece of work *(informal)*, cocksucker *(taboo slang)*, scrote *(slang)*, dastard *(archaic)*, wrong 'un *(Austral. slang)* • *I think he's an absolute stinker to do that to her.*

stinking 1 = **rotten**, disgusting, unpleasant, vile, contemptible, shitty *(taboo slang)*, wretched • *I had a stinking cold.*
2 = **foul-smelling**, smelly, reeking, fetid, malodorous, noisome, whiffy *(Brit. slang)*, pongy *(Brit. informal)*, mephitic, ill-smelling, niffy *(Brit. slang)*, olid, festy *(Austral. slang)*, yucko *(Austral. slang)* • *They were locked up in a stinking cell.*

stint AS A NOUN = **term**, time, turn, bit, period, share, tour, shift, stretch, spell, quota, assignment • *a five-year stint in Hong Kong*
▸ AS A VERB = **be mean**, hold back, be sparing, scrimp, skimp on, save, withhold, begrudge, economize, be frugal, be parsimonious, be mingy *(Brit. informal)*, spoil the ship for a ha'porth of tar • *He didn't stint on the special effects.*

stipend = **grant**, award, subsidy, allowance, donation, endowment, allocation, benefaction • *Olympic probables receive a stipend of £6000 of lottery money a year.*

stipulate = **specify**, state, agree, require, promise, contract, settle, guarantee, engage, pledge, lay down, covenant, postulate, insist upon, lay down *or* impose conditions • *International rules stipulate the number of foreign entrants.*

stipulation = **condition**, requirement, provision, term, contract, agreement, settlement, rider, restriction, qualification, clause, engagement, specification, precondition, prerequisite, proviso, sine qua non *(Latin)* • *His only stipulation is that his clients follow his advice.*

stir AS A VERB 1 = **mix**, blend, whisk, beat, agitate • *Stir the soup for a few seconds.*
2 = **move**, change position • *The two women lay on their backs, not stirring.*
3 = **flutter**, tremble, quiver, shake, rustle • *The long white curtains stirred in the breeze.*
4 = **get moving**, move, get a move on *(informal)*, hasten, budge, make an effort, be up and about *(informal)*, look lively *(informal)*, shake a leg *(informal)*, exert yourself, bestir yourself • *Stir yourself! We've got a visitor.*
5 = **stimulate**, move, excite, fire, raise, touch, affect, urge, inspire, prompt, spur, thrill, provoke, arouse, awaken, animate, rouse, prod, quicken, inflame, incite, instigate, electrify, kindle • *I was intrigued by him, stirred by his intellect.*
OPPOSITES: curb, restrain, inhibit
6 = **spur**, drive, prompt, stimulate, prod, press, urge, animate, prick, incite, goad, impel • *The sight of them stirred him into action.*
7 = **awaken**, activate, animate, stir up, fan, excite, stimulate, provoke, kick-start *(informal)*, kindle, call forth • *Beneath my antipathy, a powerful curiosity was stirred.*
▸ AS A NOUN = **commotion**, to-do, excitement, sensation, activity, movement, disorder, fuss, disturbance, bustle, flurry, uproar, ferment, agitation, ado, tumult • *His film has caused a stir in America.*
▸ IN PHRASES: **stir something up** = **produce**, make, cause, create, generate, trigger, initiate, bring about, originate, give rise to, whip up • *They saw first a cloud of dust and then the car that was stirring it up.*

stirring = **exciting**, dramatic, thrilling, moving, spirited, inspiring, stimulating, lively, animating, rousing, heady, exhilarating, impassioned, emotive, intoxicating • *a stirring account of the final months of the old regime*

stitch AS A VERB = **sew**, tack, seam, hem, baste • *Fold the fabric and stitch the two layers together.*
▸ AS A NOUN = **pain**, spasm, pang, twinge • *If you do get a stitch, try to run bent forward.*
▸ IN PHRASES: **stitch someone up** = **deceive**, trick, cheat, betray, stab in the back • *He claimed that a police officer had threatened to stitch him up.*
stitch something up = **clinch**, settle, secure, seal, conclude, assure, set the seal on • *He has stitched up major deals all over the world to boost sales.*

stock AS A NOUN 1 = **shares**, holdings, securities, investments, bonds, equities • *Stock prices have dropped.*
2 = **property**, capital, assets, funds • *The Fisher family holds 40% of the stock.*
3 = **goods**, merchandise, wares, range, choice, variety, selection, commodities, array, assortment • *We took a decision to withdraw a quantity of stock from sale.*
4 = **supply**, store, reserve, fund, reservoir, stockpile, hoard, cache • *a stock of ammunition*
5 = **lineage**, descent, extraction, ancestry, house, family, line, race, type, variety, background, breed, strain, pedigree, forebears, parentage, line of descent • *We are both from working-class stock.*
6 = **livestock**, cattle, beasts, domestic animals • *I am carefully selecting the breeding stock.*
7 = **rolling stock**, carriages, wagons, locomotives, equipment • *a firm with considerable experience of transporting railway stock by road*
▸ AS A VERB 1 = **sell**, supply, handle, keep, trade in, deal in, carry • *The shop stocks everything from cigarettes to recycled loo paper.*
2 = **fill**, supply, provide with, provision, equip, furnish, fit out, kit out • *I worked stocking shelves in a grocery store.*
▸ AS AN ADJECTIVE 1 = **hackneyed**, standard, usual, set, routine, stereotyped, staple, commonplace, worn-out, banal, run-of-the-mill, trite, overused • *National security is the stock excuse for keeping things confidential.*
2 = **regular**, traditional, usual, basic, ordinary, conventional, staple, customary • *They supply stock sizes outside the middle range.*
▸ IN PHRASES: **in stock** = **available**, for sale • *Check that your size is in stock.*
stock something up = **fill**, pack, load, cram, freight, lade • *I had to stock up the boat with food.*
stock up with something = **store (up)**, lay in, hoard, save, gather, accumulate, amass, buy up, put away, replenish supplies of • *New Yorkers have been stocking up with bottled water.*
take stock = **review the situation**, weigh up, appraise, estimate, size up *(informal)*, see how the land lies • *It was time to take stock of my life.*

stockings = **hosiery**, tights, nylons, pantyhose *(U.S.)*, stay-ups • *a pair of nylon stockings*

stockist = **store**, shop, supplier, retail outlet, boutique • *The name of your nearest stockist is available from the company.*

stockpile AS A VERB = **store up**, hoard, put away, save, collect, gather, accumulate, garner, amass, buy up, cache, lay up, put by, stash away *(informal)* • *People are stockpiling food for the coming winter.*
▸ AS A NOUN = **stock**, store, reserve, bank, supply, collection, pool, arsenal, accumulation, hoard, cache • *stockpiles of chemical weapons*

stock-still = **motionless**, still, stationary, fixed, frozen, halted, static, paralysed, lifeless, inert, transfixed, immobile, at a standstill, unmoving • *The lieutenant stopped and stood stock-still.*

stocky = **thickset**, solid, sturdy, chunky, stubby, dumpy, stumpy, mesomorphic • *She had been quite a stocky girl.*

stodgy 1 = **heavy**, filling, substantial, leaden, starchy • *He was disgusted by the stodgy pizzas on sale in London.*
OPPOSITES: light, fluffy, insubstantial
2 = **dull**, boring, stuffy, formal, tedious, tiresome, staid, unimaginative, turgid, uninspired, unexciting, ho-hum, heavy going, fuddy-duddy *(informal)*, dull as ditchwater • *stodgy old fogies*

S

opposites: interesting, exciting, stimulating

stoical = **resigned**, long-suffering, phlegmatic, philosophic, cool, calm, indifferent, stoic, dispassionate, impassive, stolid, imperturbable • *He had been stoical at their parting.*

stoicism = **resignation**, acceptance, patience, indifference, fortitude, long-suffering, calmness, fatalism, forbearance, stolidity, dispassion, impassivity, imperturbability • *They bore their plight with stoicism and fortitude.*

stoke = **fuel**, rekindle, add fuel to, tend, keep burning • *She was stoking the fire with sticks of maple.*

stole = **wrap**, cape, mantle, shawl, poncho, pelerine • *fur stoles*

stolen = **hot** *(slang)*, bent *(slang)*, knockoff *(informal)*, hooky *(slang)*, off the back of a lorry *(Brit. informal)* • *dealing in stolen goods*

stolid = **apathetic**, unemotional, dull, heavy, slow, wooden, stupid, bovine, dozy *(Brit. informal)*, obtuse, lumpish, doltish • *the stolid faces of the two detectives*

opposites: interested, bright, lively

stomach **as a noun** 1 = **belly**, inside(s) *(informal)*, gut *(informal)*, abdomen, tummy *(informal)*, puku *(N.Z.)* • *My stomach is completely full.*

2 = **tummy**, pot, spare tyre *(informal)*, paunch, belly, breadbasket *(slang)*, potbelly • *This exercise strengthens the stomach, buttocks and thighs.*

3 = **inclination**, taste, desire, appetite, relish, mind • *They have no stomach for a fight.*

▸ **as a verb** 1 = **bear**, take, tolerate, suffer, endure, swallow, hack *(slang)*, abide, put up with *(informal)*, submit to, reconcile *or* resign yourself to • *I could never stomach the cruelty involved in the wounding of animals.*

2 = **keep down**, swallow, digest, manage to eat, find palatable • *It's specially developed for those who can't stomach natural fish oil.*

▸ **in phrases:** **sick to your stomach** = **distressed**, upset, disturbed, worried, troubled, dismayed, grieved, frantic, hassled *(informal)*, agitated, disquieted, overwrought • *She felt sick to her stomach just thinking about it.*

turn your stomach = **sicken**, disgust, revolt, repel, nauseate, gross out *(U.S. slang)*, make your gorge rise • *The true facts will turn your stomach.*

▸ **related adjective:** gastric

proverbs

An army marches on its stomach

The way to a man's heart is through his stomach

stomach ache = **indigestion**, colic, dyspepsia, tummy ache *(informal)*, belly ache *(informal)*, stomach gripes • *tiredness, stomach ache and chest pains*

stone **as a noun** 1 = **masonry**, rock • *He could not tell if the floor was wood or stone.*

2 = **rock**, pebble • *The crowd began throwing stones.*

3 = **gem**, jewel, precious stone, gemstone, rock *(informal)* • *a diamond ring with three stones*

4 = **pip**, seed, pit, kernel • *Old men sat beneath the plane trees and spat cherry stones at my feet.*

▸ **in phrases:** **cast in stone** = **fixed**, decided, definite, established, settled, arranged • *The idea is not cast in stone.*

▸ **related adjective:** lithic

stony 1 = **rocky**, rough, gritty, gravelly, rock-strewn, pebble • *a stony track*

2 = **cold**, icy, hostile, hard, harsh, blank, adamant, indifferent, chilly, callous, heartless, merciless, unforgiving, inexorable, frigid, expressionless, unresponsive, pitiless, unfeeling, obdurate • *The stony look he was giving her made it hard to think.*

stooge = **pawn**, puppet, fall guy *(informal)*, butt, foil, patsy *(slang, chiefly U.S. & Canad.)*, dupe, henchman, lackey • *He has vehemently rejected claims that he is a government stooge.*

stoop **as a verb** 1 = **hunch**, walk with a stoop, be bowed *or* round-shouldered • *She was taller than he was and stooped slightly.*

2 = **bend**, lean, bow, duck, descend, incline, kneel, crouch, squat • *He stooped to pick up the carrier bag of groceries.*

▸ **as a noun** = **slouch**, slump, droop, sag, bad posture, round-shoulderedness • *He was a tall, thin fellow with a slight stoop.*

▸ **in phrases:** **stoop to something** = **resort to**, sink to, descend to, deign to, condescend to, demean yourself by, lower yourself by • *How could anyone stoop to doing such a thing?*

stop **as a verb** 1 = **quit**, cease, refrain, break off, put an end to, pack in *(Brit. informal)*, discontinue, leave off, call it a day *(informal)*, desist, belay *(Nautical)*, bring *or* come to a halt *or* standstill • *I've been told to lose weight and stop smoking.*

opposites: start, begin, continue

2 = **prevent**, suspend, cut short, close, break, check, bar, arrest, silence, frustrate, axe *(informal)*, interrupt, restrain, hold back, intercept, hinder, repress, impede, rein in, forestall, nip (something) in the bud • *I think she really would have liked to stop everything right there.*

opposites: further, push, facilitate

3 = **end**, conclude, finish, be over, cut out *(informal)*, terminate, come to an end, peter out • *The music stopped and the lights were turned up.*

opposites: start, begin, continue

4 = **cease**, shut down, discontinue, desist • *His heart stopped three times.*

opposites: start, begin, continue

5 = **halt**, pause, stall, draw up, pull up • *The car failed to stop at an army checkpoint.*

opposites: continue, keep on, keep going

6 = **pause**, wait, rest, hesitate, deliberate, take a break, have a breather *(informal)*, stop briefly • *She doesn't stop to think about what she's saying.*

7 = **stay**, rest, put up, lodge, sojourn, tarry, break your journey • *He insisted we stop at a small restaurant just outside Atlanta.*

▸ **as a noun** 1 = **halt**, standstill • *He slowed the car almost to a stop.*

2 = **station**, stage, halt, destination, depot, termination, terminus • *They waited at a bus stop.*

3 = **stay**, break, visit, rest, stopover, sojourn • *The last stop in his lengthy tour was Paris.*

▸ **in phrases:** **put a stop to something** *or* **someone** = **check**, silence, nip (something) in the bud, arrest, intercept, repress, cut short, forestall • *His daughter should have stood up and put a stop to all these rumours.* • *Someone should put a stop to him before he does any more damage.*

stop by = **call in**, drop in, look in, drop by • *I'll stop by to see you before going home.*

stop off = **break your journey**, stay, rest, stop over, sojourn, tarry • *The president stopped off in Munich for the economic summit.*

stop something up = **plug**, block, seal, stem, obstruct, staunch, bung • *They stopped up leaks with chewing gum.*

stopgap **as a noun** = **makeshift**, improvisation, temporary expedient, shift, resort, substitute • *It is not an acceptable long term solution, just a stopgap.*

▸ **as a modifier** = **makeshift**, emergency, temporary, provisional, improvised, impromptu, rough-and-ready • *It was only ever intended as a stopgap solution.*

stopover = **stop**, break, stop-off, stay, visit, sojourn • *The Sunday flights will make a stopover in Paris.*

stoppage 1 = **stopping**, halt, standstill, close, arrest, lay-off, shutdown, cutoff, abeyance, discontinuance • *a seven-hour stoppage by air-traffic controllers*

2 = **strike**, industrial action, walkout, closure, shutdown • *Mineworkers have voted for a one-day stoppage next month.*

3 = **blockage**, obstruction, stopping up, occlusion • *The small traffic disturbance will soon grow into a complete stoppage.*

stopper = **cork**, top, cap, plug, lid, bung • *a bottle of colourless liquid sealed with a cork stopper*

store AS A NOUN 1 = **shop**, outlet, department store, market, supermarket, mart, emporium, chain store, hypermarket • *Bombs were planted in stores in Manchester and Blackpool.*
2 = **supply**, stock, reserve, lot, fund, mine, plenty, provision, wealth, quantity, reservoir, abundance, accumulation, stockpile, hoard, plethora, cache • *I handed over my store of chocolate biscuits.*
3 = **repository**, warehouse, depot, storehouse, depository, storeroom • *a grain store*
▸ AS A VERB 1 *often with* **away** *or* **up** = **put by**, save, hoard, keep, stock, husband, reserve, deposit, accumulate, garner, stockpile, put aside, stash *(informal)*, salt away, keep in reserve, put aside for a rainy day, lay by *or* in • *storing away cash that will come in useful later on*
2 = **put away**, put in storage, put in store, lock away • *Some types of garden furniture must be stored inside in the winter.*
3 = **keep**, hold, preserve, maintain, retain, conserve • *chips for storing data*
▸ IN PHRASES: **set great store by something** = **value**, prize, esteem, appreciate, hold in high regard, think highly of • *a retail group that sets great store by traditional values*

storehouse = **warehouse**, store, depot, depository, stockroom, pataka *(N.Z.)* • *barns and storehouses*

storey = **floor**, level, flight, deck, tier • *Houses must not be more than two storeys high.*

storm AS A NOUN 1 = **tempest**, blast, hurricane, gale, tornado, cyclone, blizzard, whirlwind, gust, squall • *the violent storms which whipped America's East Coast*
2 = **outburst**, row, stir, outcry, furore, violence, anger, passion, outbreak, turmoil, disturbance, strife, clamour, agitation, commotion, rumpus, tumult, hubbub • *The photos caused a storm when they were first published.*
3 = **roar**, thunder, clamour, din • *His speech was greeted with a storm of applause.*
4 = **attack**, rush, assault, offensive, blitz, onset, onslaught, blitzkrieg • *The attack was code-named Desert Storm.*
5 = **barrage**, volley, salvo, rain, shower, spray, discharge, fusillade • *a storm of missiles*
▸ AS A VERB 1 = **rush**, stamp, flounce, fly, stalk, stomp *(informal)* • *After a bit of an argument, he stormed out.*
2 = **rage**, fume, rant, complain, thunder, rave, scold, bluster, go ballistic *(slang, chiefly U.S.)*, fly off the handle *(informal)*, wig out *(slang)* • *'It's a fiasco,' he stormed.*
3 = **attack**, charge, rush, assault, beset, assail, take by storm • *The refugees decided to storm the embassy.*

stormy 1 = **wild**, rough, tempestuous, raging, dirty, foul, turbulent, windy, blustering, blustery, gusty, inclement, squally • *the long stormy winter of 1942*
2 = **rough**, wild, turbulent, tempestuous, raging • *the stormy waters that surround the British Isles*
3 = **angry**, heated, fierce, passionate, fiery, impassioned, tumultuous • *The letter was read at a stormy meeting.*

story 1 = **tale**, romance, narrative, record, history, version, novel, legend, chronicle, yarn, recital, narration, urban myth, urban legend, fictional account • *a popular love story with a happy ending*
2 = **anecdote**, account, tale, report, detail, relation, testimony • *The parents all shared interesting stories about their children.*
3 = **lie**, falsehood, fib, fiction, untruth, porky *(Brit. slang)*, pork pie *(Brit. slang)*, white lie • *He invented some story about a cousin.*
4 = **report**, news, article, feature, scoop, news item • *Those are some of the top stories in the news.*

storyline = **narrative**, plot • *The surprise twists in the storyline are the film's greatest strength.*

storyteller = **raconteur**, author, narrator, romancer, novelist, chronicler, bard, fabulist, spinner of yarns, anecdotist • *Celtic storytellers*

stout 1 = **fat**, big, heavy, overweight, plump, bulky, substantial, burly, obese, fleshy, tubby, portly, rotund, corpulent, on the large *or* heavy side • *exercises ideal for stout women of maturer years*
OPPOSITES: lean, slim, slender
2 = **strong**, strapping, muscular, tough, substantial, athletic, hardy, robust, vigorous, sturdy, stalwart, husky *(informal)*, hulking, beefy *(informal)*, lusty, brawny, thickset, able-bodied • *a great stout fellow, big in brawn and bone*
OPPOSITES: frail, feeble, puny
3 = **brave**, bold, courageous, fearless, resolute, gallant, intrepid, valiant, plucky, doughty, indomitable, dauntless, lion-hearted, valorous • *The invasion was held up by unexpectedly stout resistance.*
OPPOSITES: fearful, cowardly, timid

stove = **hob**, range, cooker, burner, oven • *She put the kettle on the gas stove.*

stow AS A VERB = **pack**, load, put away, store, stuff, deposit, jam, tuck, bundle, cram, stash *(informal)*, secrete • *I helped her stow her bags in the boot of the car.*
▸ IN PHRASES: **stow away** = **travel secretly**, hide, conceal yourself, secrete yourself • *He stowed away on a ferry and landed in North Shields.*

straddle 1 = **sit astride**, bestride, mount, sit with legs either side of • *He looked at her with a grin and sat down, straddling the chair.*
2 = **span**, cross, bridge, vault, traverse, range over, extend across, arch across • *A small wooden bridge straddled the dike.*
3 = **cover**, bridge, span, range over • *He straddles two cultures, having been brought up in Britain and later converted to Islam.*

straggle 1 = **trail**, drift, wander, range, lag, stray, roam, ramble, rove, loiter, string out • *They came straggling up the cliff road.*
2 = **hang (down)**, trail, dangle, sag, droop • *Her grey hair straggled in wisps about her face.*

straggly = **spread out**, spreading, rambling, untidy, loose, drifting, random, straying, irregular, aimless, disorganized, straggling • *The yard held a few straggly bushes.*

straight AS AN ADJECTIVE 1 = **direct**, unswerving, undeviating • *Keep the boat in a straight line.*
OPPOSITES: winding, indirect, roundabout
2 = **level**, even, right, square, true, smooth, in line, aligned, horizontal • *There wasn't a single straight wall in the building.*
OPPOSITES: bent, crooked, uneven
3 = **frank**, plain, straightforward, blunt, outright, honest, downright, candid, forthright, bold, point-blank, upfront *(informal)*, unqualified • *a straight answer to a straight question*
OPPOSITES: vague, indirect, evasive
4 = **successive**, consecutive, continuous, through, running, solid, sustained, uninterrupted, nonstop, unrelieved • *They'd won twelve straight games before they lost.*
OPPOSITES: broken, interrupted, discontinuous
5 = **straightforward**, clear, simple, routine, clear-cut, uncomplicated • *It's a straight choice between low-paid jobs and no jobs.*
6 = **conventional**, conservative, orthodox, traditional, square *(informal)*, bourgeois, Pooterish • *Dorothy was described as a very straight woman.*
OPPOSITES: fashionable, trendy *(Brit. informal)*, voguish
7 = **honest**, just, fair, decent, reliable, respectable, upright, honourable, equitable, law-abiding, trustworthy, above board, fair and square • *You need to be straight with them to gain their respect.*
OPPOSITES: bent *(slang)*, crooked *(informal)*, dishonest

S

8 = undiluted, pure, neat, unadulterated, unmixed • *a large straight whisky, with ice*
9 = in order, organized, arranged, sorted out, neat, tidy, orderly, shipshape, put to rights • *We need to get the house straight again before they come home.*
OPPOSITES: disorderly, messy, untidy
▸ AS AN ADVERB **1 = upright**, erect, vertical, tall • *Stand straight and stretch the left hand to the right foot.*
2 = directly, precisely, exactly, as the crow flies, unswervingly, by the shortest route, in a beeline • *Straight ahead were the low cabins of the motel.*
3 = immediately, directly, promptly, instantly, at once, straight away, without delay, without hesitation, forthwith, unhesitatingly, before you could say Jack Robinson *(informal)* • *As always, we went straight to the experts for advice.*
4 = frankly, honestly, point-blank, candidly, pulling no punches *(informal)*, in plain English, with no holds barred • *I told him straight that I had been looking for another job.*
▸ IN PHRASES: **go straight = reform**, turn over a new leaf, make a new start, get back on the straight and narrow • *I thought you were going straight after that last robbery?*

straightaway = immediately, now, at once, directly, instantly, on the spot, right away, there and then, this minute, straightway *(archaic)*, without more ado, without any delay • *I should go and see a doctor straight away.*

straighten AS A VERB **= neaten**, arrange, tidy (up), order, spruce up, smarten up, put in order, set *or* put to rights • *She looked in the mirror and straightened her hair.*
▸ IN PHRASES: **straighten something out = sort out**, resolve, put right, settle, correct, work out, clear up, rectify, disentangle, unsnarl • *My sister had come in with her common sense and straightened things out.*
straighten up = stand upright, stand up, stand up straight, straighten your back • *He straightened up and slipped his hands in his pockets.*

straightforward 1 = simple, easy, uncomplicated, routine, elementary, clear-cut, undemanding, easy-peasy *(slang)* • *The question seemed straightforward enough.*
OPPOSITES: complex, confused, complicated
2 = honest, open, direct, genuine, sincere, candid, truthful, forthright, upfront *(informal)*, dinkum *(Austral. & N.Z. informal)*, above board, guileless • *I was impressed by his straightforward intelligent manner.*
OPPOSITES: sharp, shady, devious

S

strain[1] AS A NOUN **1 = pressure**, stress, difficulty, demands, burden, adversity • *The prison service is already under considerable strain.*
2 = stress, pressure, anxiety, difficulty, distress, exhaustion, weariness, nervous tension • *She was tired and under great strain.*
3 = worry, effort, struggle, tension, hassle • *the strain of being responsible for the mortgage*
OPPOSITES: ease, relaxation, effortlessness
4 = burden, tension, tightness, tautness • *Place your hands under your buttocks to take some of the strain off your back.*
5 = injury, wrench, sprain, pull, tension, tautness, tensity *(rare)* • *a groin strain*
6 = tune, air, melody, measure *(poetic)*, lay, song, theme • *She could hear the tinny strains of a chamber orchestra.*
▸ AS A VERB **1 = stretch**, test, tax, overtax, push to the limit • *Resources will be further strained by new demands for housing.*
2 = injure, wrench, sprain, damage, pull, tear, hurt, twist, rick, impair, overexert • *He strained his back during a practice session.*
3 = strive, struggle, endeavour, labour, go for it *(informal)*, bend over backwards *(informal)*, go for broke *(slang)*, go all out for *(informal)*, bust a gut *(informal)*, give it your best shot *(informal)*, make an all-out effort *(informal)*, knock yourself out *(informal)*, do your damnedest *(informal)*, give it your all *(informal)*, break your back *or* neck *(informal)*, rupture yourself *(informal)* • *Several thousand supporters strained to catch a glimpse of the new president.*
OPPOSITES: rest, relax, idle
4 = sieve, filter, sift, screen, separate, riddle, purify • *Strain the stock and put it back in the pan.*

strain[2] 1 = trace, suggestion, suspicion, tendency, streak, trait • *There was a strain of bitterness in his voice.*
2 = breed, type, stock, family, race, blood, descent, pedigree, extraction, ancestry, lineage • *a particularly beautiful strain of Swiss pansies*

strained 1 = tense, difficult, uncomfortable, awkward, embarrassed, stiff, uneasy, constrained, self-conscious, unrelaxed • *a period of strained relations*
OPPOSITES: relaxed, comfortable
2 = forced, put on, false, artificial, unnatural, laboured • *His laughter seemed a little strained.*
OPPOSITES: natural

strainer = sieve, filter, colander, riddle, sifter • *a tea strainer*

strait AS A NOUN *often plural* **= channel**, sound, narrows, stretch of water, sea passage • *Thousands of vessels pass through the straits annually.*
▸ AS A PLURAL NOUN **= difficulty**, crisis, mess, pass, hole *(slang)*, emergency, distress, dilemma, embarrassment, plight, hardship, uphill *(S. African)*, predicament, extremity, perplexity, panic stations *(informal)*, pretty *or* fine kettle of fish *(informal)* • *If we had a child, we'd be in really dire straits.*

strait-laced *or* **straight-laced = puritanical**, proper, prim, narrow, Victorian, strict, narrow-minded, moralistic, of the old school, prudish, old-maidish *(informal)*, overscrupulous, niminy-piminy • *He was criticized for being boring, strait-laced and narrow-minded.*
OPPOSITES: relaxed, uninhibited, broad-minded

strand 1 = filament, fibre, thread, length, lock, string, twist, rope, wisp, tress • *high fences, topped by strands of barbed wire*
2 = component, part, element, ingredient, constituent, feature • *There have been two strands to his tactics.*

stranded 1 = beached, grounded, marooned, ashore, shipwrecked, aground, cast away • *He returned to his stranded vessel yesterday afternoon.*
2 = helpless, abandoned, high and dry, left in the lurch • *He left me stranded by the side of the road.*

strange 1 = odd, unusual, curious, weird, wonderful, rare, funny, extraordinary, remarkable, bizarre, fantastic, astonishing, marvellous, exceptional, peculiar, eccentric, abnormal, out-of-the-way, queer, irregular, rum *(Brit. slang)*, uncommon, singular, perplexing, uncanny, mystifying, unheard-of, off-the-wall *(slang)*, oddball *(informal)*, unaccountable, left-field *(informal)*, outré, curiouser and curiouser, out there *(slang)*, daggy *(Austral. & N.Z. informal)* • *There was something strange about the flickering blue light.*
OPPOSITES: usual, ordinary, common
2 = out of place, lost, uncomfortable, awkward, bewildered, disoriented, ill at ease, like a fish out of water • *I felt strange in his office, realizing how absurd it was.*
OPPOSITES: at home, relaxed, comfortable
3 = unfamiliar, new, unknown, foreign, novel, alien, exotic, untried, unexplored, outside your experience • *I ended up alone in a strange city.*
OPPOSITES: familiar, accustomed, habitual
4 = unwell, ill, sick, poorly *(informal)*, funny *(informal)*, crook *(Austral. & N.Z. informal)*, ailing, queer, queasy, out of sorts *(informal)*, dicky *(Brit. informal)*, off-colour, under the weather *(informal)*, indisposed, green about the gills, not up to snuff *(informal)* • *I felt all dizzy and strange.*

strangely = paradoxically, oddly, unexpectedly, bizarrely, funnily, puzzlingly • *No, strangely enough, this is not the case.*

strangeness = oddity, abnormality, peculiarity, weirdness, unfamiliarity, unexpectedness, bizarreness, unusualness, freakishness, outlandishness, curiousness • *the breathy strangeness of the music*

stranger AS A NOUN **1 = unknown person** • *Sometimes I feel like I'm living with a stranger.*
2 = newcomer, incomer, foreigner, guest, visitor, unknown, alien, new arrival, newbie *(slang)*, outlander • *Being a stranger in town can be a painful experience.*
▸ IN PHRASES: **a stranger to something = unaccustomed to**, new to, unused to, ignorant of, inexperienced in, unversed in, unpractised in, unseasoned in • *He is no stranger to controversy.*
▸ RELATED PHOBIA: xenophobia

QUOTATIONS
a stranger in a strange land
[*Bible: Exodus*]

strangle 1 = throttle, choke, asphyxiate, garrotte, strangulate, smother, suffocate • *He was almost strangled by his parachute harness straps.*
2 = suppress, inhibit, subdue, stifle, gag, repress, overpower, quash, quell, quench • *His creative drive has been strangled by his sense of guilt.*

stranglehold = grip, hold, grasp, clutches, iron grip • *The troops are tightening their stranglehold on the city.*

strap AS A NOUN **= tie**, thong, leash, belt • *Nancy gripped the strap of her beach bag.*
▸ AS A VERB **= fasten**, tie, secure, bind, lash, buckle, truss • *She strapped the gun belt around the middle.*

strapped IN PHRASES: **strapped for** *(slang)* **= short of**, in need of, stuck for • *I'm a little strapped for cash at the moment.*

strapping = well-built, big, powerful, robust, hefty *(informal)*, sturdy, stalwart, burly, husky *(informal)*, hulking, beefy *(informal)*, brawny, well set-up • *He was a bricklayer – a big, strapping fellow.*

stratagem = trick, scheme, manoeuvre, plan, plot, device, intrigue, dodge, ploy, ruse, artifice, subterfuge, feint, wile • *a competitive stratagem to secure customer loyalty*

strategic 1 = tactical, calculated, deliberate, planned, politic, diplomatic • *a strategic plan for reducing the rate of infant mortality*
2 = crucial, important, key, vital, critical, decisive, cardinal • *an operation to take the strategic island*

strategist = planner, tactician, schemer, intriguer, manoeuvrer, diplomatist, wheeler-dealer • *a clever political strategist*

strategy 1 = policy, procedure, planning, programme, approach, scheme, manoeuvring, grand design • *Community involvement is now integral to company strategy.*
2 = plan, approach, scheme, manoeuvring, grand design • *the basic principles of my strategy*

stratum 1 = class, group, level, station, estate, rank, grade, category, bracket, caste • *It was an enormous task that affected every stratum of society.*
2 = layer, level, seam, table, bed, vein, tier, stratification, lode • *The rock strata shows that the region was intensely dry 15,000 years ago.*

stray AS A VERB **1 = wander**, roam, go astray, range, drift, meander, rove, straggle, lose your way, be abandoned *or* lost • *A railway line crosses the park so children must not be allowed to stray.*
2 = drift, wander, roam, meander, rove • *She could not keep her eyes from straying towards him.*
3 = digress, diverge, deviate, ramble, get sidetracked, go off at a tangent, get off the point • *Anyway, as usual, we seem to have strayed from the point.*
4 = be unfaithful, play around *(informal)*, have affairs, play the field *(informal)*, philander • *Some men are womanizers, others would never stray.*
▸ AS A MODIFIER **= lost**, abandoned, homeless, roaming, vagrant • *A stray dog came up to him.*
▸ AS AN ADJECTIVE **= random**, chance, freak, accidental, odd, scattered, erratic, scattershot • *An 8-year-old boy was killed by a stray bullet.*
▸ AS A NOUN **= homeless animal**, waif, foundling, abandoned dog *or* cat • *The dog was a stray which had been adopted.*

streak AS A NOUN **1 = band**, line, strip, stroke, layer, slash, vein, stripe, smear • *There are these dark streaks on the surface of the moon.*
2 = trace, touch, element, strain, dash, vein • *He's still got a mean streak.*
▸ AS A VERB **1 = fleck**, smear, daub, band, slash, stripe, striate • *Rain had begun to streak the window pains.*
2 = speed, fly, tear, sweep, flash, barrel (along) *(informal, chiefly U.S. & Canad.)*, whistle, sprint, dart, zoom, whizz *(informal)*, hurtle, burn rubber *(informal)*, move like greased lightning *(informal)* • *A meteorite streaked across the sky.*

streaky = streaked, striped, banded, veined • *three rashers of streaky bacon*

stream AS A NOUN **1 = river**, brook, creek *(U.S.)*, burn *(Scot.)*, beck, tributary, bayou, rivulet, rill, freshet • *a mountain stream*
2 = flow, current, rush, run, course, drift, surge, tide, torrent, outpouring, tideway • *a continuous stream of lava*
3 = succession, series, flood, chain, battery, volley, avalanche, barrage, torrent • *a never-ending stream of jokes*
4 = group, grouping, set, class, division, grade, category • *Examinations are used to choose which pupils will move into the top streams.*
▸ AS A VERB **1 = flow**, run, pour, course, issue, flood, shed, spill, emit, glide, cascade, gush, spout • *Tears streamed down their faces.*
2 = rush, fly, speed, tear, flood, pour • *The traffic streamed past him.*
3 = float, fly, flap, flutter, waft, swing • *She was wearing a flimsy pink dress that streamed out behind her.*

streamer = banner, flag, pennant, standard, colours, ribbon, ensign, pennon • *a red streamer with white lettering*

streamline = rationalize, restructure, reorganize, modernize, bring up to date, make more efficient • *They're making efforts to streamline their bureaucracy.*

streamlined = efficient, organized, modernized, rationalized, smooth, slick, sleek, well-run, time-saving, smooth-running • *streamlined companies using cheap freelance staff*

street AS A NOUN **= road**, lane, avenue, terrace, row, boulevard, roadway, thoroughfare • *a small, quaint town with narrow streets*
▸ IN PHRASES: **on the streets = homeless**, down and out, sleeping rough, living rough, of no fixed abode • *youngsters who are on the streets*
streets ahead of something *or* **someone = much better than**, a cut above, head and shoulders above, more than a match for, in a different class from • *He was streets ahead of the other contestants.*
the man *or* **woman in the street = Joe Public**, John Doe *(U.S. informal)*, Joe Bloggs *(Brit. informal)*, the man on the Clapham omnibus *(Brit. informal)*, Mr *or* Mrs Average • *the average man or woman in the street*
up one's street = to one's liking, to one's taste, one's cup of tea *(informal)*, pleasing, familiar, suitable, acceptable, compatible, congenial • *She loved it, this was right up her street.*

strength AS A NOUN **1 = might**, muscle, brawn, sinew, brawniness • *He threw it forward with all his strength.*
OPPOSITES: weakness, frailty, powerlessness
2 = will, spirit, resolution, resolve, courage, character, nerve, determination, pluck, stamina, grit, backbone, fortitude, toughness, tenacity, willpower, mettle, firmness, strength of

character, steadfastness, moral fibre • *Something gave me the strength to overcome the difficulty.*
3 = **health**, fitness, vigour, wellness, healthiness, lustiness • *It'll take a while before you regain full strength.*
4 = **mainstay**, anchor, tower of strength, security, rock, succour • *He was my strength during that terrible time.*
5 = **toughness**, soundness, robustness, sturdiness, stoutness, resistance • *He checked the strength of the cables.*
6 = **power**, influence, dominance, clout *(informal)*, supremacy, ascendancy • *They have their own independence movement which is gathering strength.*
7 = **force**, power, intensity, energy, depth, vehemence, intenseness • *He was surprised at the strength of his own feeling.*
OPPOSITES: weakness, feebleness
8 = **potency**, effectiveness, concentration, efficacy • *maximum strength migraine tablets*
9 = **strong point**, skill, asset, advantage, talent, forte, speciality, aptitude • *Take into account your own strengths and weaknesses.*
OPPOSITES: failing, weakness, defect
10 = **size**, extent, magnitude, greatness, largeness • *the strength of the army*
▸ **IN PHRASES: on the strength of something = because of**, due to, based on, on the basis of, by virtue of, on account of • *He was elected on the strength of his charisma.*
under *or* **below strength = depleted**, reduced, exhausted, weakened, used (up), spent, short, decreased, lessened, worn out, depreciated • *He was hampered by his regular troops being so much under strength.*

QUOTATIONS
Out of the mouths of very babes and sucklings hast thou ordained strength
[*Bible: Psalm 8*]

strengthen 1 = **fortify**, encourage, harden, toughen, fuel, steel, consolidate, stiffen, hearten, buoy up, gee up, brace up, vitalize, give new energy to • *Such antagonism, he has asserted, strengthened his resolve.*
OPPOSITES: undermine, weaken, dilute
2 = **reinforce**, support, confirm, establish, justify, enhance, intensify, bolster, substantiate, buttress, corroborate, give a boost to • *Research would strengthen the case for socialist reform.*
3 = **increase in value**, become stronger • *The dollar strengthened against other currencies.*
4 = **step up**, reinforce, increase, heighten, escalate, crank up *(informal)*, scale up • *Community leaders want to strengthen controls at external frontiers.*
5 = **bolster**, harden, reinforce, give a boost to • *Any experience can teach and strengthen you.*
6 = **heighten**, intensify, reinforce • *Every day of sunshine strengthens the feeling of optimism.*
7 = **make stronger**, build up, invigorate, restore, nourish, rejuvenate, make healthy, give strength to • *Yoga can be used to strengthen the immune system.*
8 = **support**, brace, steel, reinforce, consolidate, harden, bolster, augment, buttress • *The builders will have to strengthen the existing joists with additional timber.*
9 = **become stronger**, pick up, intensify, heighten, gain strength • *As it strengthened, the wind was veering southerly.*

strenuous 1 = **demanding**, hard, tough, exhausting, taxing, uphill, arduous, laborious, Herculean, tough going, toilsome, unrelaxing • *Avoid strenuous exercise in the evening.*
OPPOSITES: easy, effortless, undemanding
2 = **tireless**, determined, zealous, strong, earnest, spirited, active, eager, bold, persistent, vigorous, energetic, resolute • *Strenuous efforts have been made to improve conditions in the jail.*

stress **AS A VERB** 1 = **emphasize**, highlight, underline, repeat, draw attention to, dwell on, underscore, accentuate, point up, rub in, flag up, impress on someone, harp on, press home, bring to the fore, belabour • *He stressed the need for new measures.*
2 = **place the emphasis on**, emphasize, give emphasis to, place the accent on, lay emphasis upon • *She stresses the syllables as though teaching a child.*
▸ **AS A NOUN** 1 = **emphasis**, importance, significance, force, weight, urgency • *Japanese car makers are laying ever more stress on European sales.*
2 = **strain**, pressure, worry, tension, burden, anxiety, trauma, oppression, hassle *(informal)*, nervous tension • *Katy could not think clearly when under stress.*
3 = **accent**, beat, emphasis, accentuation, ictus • *the misplaced stress on the first syllable*

QUOTATIONS
I don't have ulcers, I give them
[Harry Cohn]

stressed = **anxious**, worried, tense, upset, distressed, under pressure, harassed, pressurized • *Work out what situations or people make you feel stressed and avoid them.*

stressful = **worrying**, anxious, tense, trying, hard, taxing, demanding, wearing, tough, draining, exhausting, exacting, traumatic, agitating, nerve-racking • *I think I've got one of the most stressful jobs there is.*

stretch **AS A VERB** 1 = **extend**, cover, spread, reach, unfold, put forth, unroll • *an artificial reef stretching the length of the coast*
2 = **straighten out**, extend, unbend • *She arched her back and stretched herself.*
3 = **last**, continue, go on, extend, carry on, reach • *Protests stretched into their second week.*
4 = **range**, go, run, extend, vary • *interests that stretched from chemicals to sugar*
5 = **expand**, lengthen, be elastic, be stretchy, be tensile • *The cables are designed not to stretch.*
6 = **pull**, distend, pull out of shape, strain, swell, tighten, rack, inflate, lengthen, draw out, elongate • *Make sure you don't stretch the pastry as you ease it into the corners.*
7 = **put demands on**, put a strain on, overextend • *They're used to stretching their budgets.*
8 = **afford**, have enough money for • *I don't know whether I can stretch to that.*
9 = **test**, challenge, push, tax, stimulate • *I'm trying to move on and stretch myself with something different.*
10 = **hold out**, offer, present, extend, proffer • *She stretched out her hand and slowly led him upstairs.*
▸ **AS A NOUN** 1 = **expanse**, area, tract, spread, distance, sweep, extent • *It's a very dangerous stretch of road.*
2 = **period**, time, spell, stint, run, term, bit, space • *He would study for eight to ten hour stretches.*
▸ **IN PHRASES: stretch out = lie down**, lounge, lean back, recline, loll • *The jacuzzi was too small to stretch out in.*

strew = **scatter**, spread, litter, toss, sprinkle, disperse, bestrew • *By the end, bodies were strewn all around the headquarters building.*

stricken = **affected**, hit, afflicted, struck, injured, struck down, smitten, laid low • *Foreign aid workers will not be allowed into the stricken areas.* • *a family stricken by genetically inherited cancer*

strict 1 = **severe**, harsh, stern, firm, rigid, rigorous, stringent, austere • *French privacy laws are very strict.*
OPPOSITES: soft, moderate, easy-going
2 = **stern**, firm, severe, harsh, authoritarian, austere, no-nonsense • *My parents were very strict.*
3 = **exact**, accurate, precise, close, true, particular, religious, faithful, meticulous, scrupulous • *the strictest sense of the word*
4 = **devout**, religious, orthodox, pious, pure, reverent, prayerful • *a strict Catholic*

5 = **absolute**, complete, total, perfect, utter • *Your enquiry will be handled in strict confidence.*

strictly = **particularly**, only, especially, exclusively • *This session was strictly for the boys.*

stricture 1 = **criticism**, disapproval, censure, stick *(slang)*, blame, rebuke, flak *(informal)*, bad press, sideswipe, animadversion • *a thinly disguised stricture against the rights of man*
2 = **limitation**, restriction, constraint, condition, handicap, restraint, demarcation • *Your goals are hindered by financial strictures.*

stride AS A VERB = **march**, walk, stalk, pace, tread, strut • *He turned abruptly and strode off down the corridor.*
▸ AS A NOUN = **step**, pace, footstep • *He walked with long strides.*
▸ IN PHRASES: **take something in your stride** = **deal** *or* **cope with easily**, think nothing of, not bat an eyelid, not be fazed by • *I was struck by how she took the mistake in her stride.*

strident 1 = **forceful**, offensive, hostile, belligerent, pugnacious, destructive, quarrelsome • *the unnecessarily strident tone of the President's remarks*
2 = **harsh**, jarring, grating, clashing, screeching, raucous, shrill, rasping, jangling, discordant, clamorous, unmusical, stridulant, stridulous • *She tried to laugh, and the sound was harsh and strident.*
OPPOSITES: soft, quiet, sweet

strife = **conflict**, battle, struggle, row, clash, clashes, contest, controversy, combat, warfare, rivalry, contention, quarrel, friction, squabbling, wrangling, bickering, animosity, discord, dissension • *The boardroom strife at the company is far from over.*

strike AS A NOUN 1 = **walkout**, industrial action, mutiny, revolt • *a call for a strike*
2 = **attack**, bombing, assault, air strike, blitz • *a nuclear strike*
3 = **find**, discovery, uncovering, unearthing • *an oil strike off the Shetland Islands*
▸ AS A VERB 1 = **walk out**, take industrial action, down tools, revolt, mutiny • *their recognition of the worker's right to strike*
2 = **hit**, smack, thump, pound, beat, box, knock, punch, hammer, deck *(slang)*, slap, sock *(slang)*, chin *(slang)*, buffet, clout *(informal)*, cuff, clump *(slang)*, swipe, clobber *(slang)*, smite, wallop *(informal)*, lambast(e), lay a finger on *(informal)*, lay one on *(slang)*, beat *or* knock seven bells out of *(informal)* • *She took two steps forward and struck him across the mouth.*
3 = **drive**, propel, force, hit, smack, wallop *(informal)* • *He struck the ball straight into the hospitality tents.*
4 = **collide with**, hit, run into, bump into, touch, smash into, come into contact with, knock into, be in collision with • *He was killed when a car struck him.*
5 = **knock**, bang, smack, thump, beat, smite • *He fell and struck his head on the stone floor.*
6 = **affect**, move, hit, touch, devastate, overwhelm, leave a mark on, make an impact *or* impression on • *He was suddenly struck with a sense of loss.*
7 = **attack**, assault someone, fall upon someone, set upon someone, lay into someone *(informal)* • *The killer says he will strike again.*
8 = **occur to**, hit, come to, register *(informal)*, come to the mind of, dawn on *or* upon • *At this point, it suddenly struck me that I was wasting my time.*
9 = **seem to**, appear to, look to, give the impression to • *He struck me as a very serious but friendly person.*
10 = **move**, touch, impress, hit, affect, overcome, stir, disturb, perturb, make an impact on • *She was struck by his simple, spellbinding eloquence.*
11 = **agree on**, settle on, come to an agreement on, sign, sanction, endorse, clinch *(informal)*, ratify • *He insists he has struck no bargains for their release.*
12 = **achieve**, arrive at, attain, reach, effect, arrange • *You have to strike a balance between sleep and homework.*
13 = **assume**, adopt, affect, take on, take up, feign • *She struck a pose, one hand on her hip.*
14 = **make**, render, cause to become, leave • *For this revelation he was struck blind by the goddess Hera.*
15 = **ring**, sound, toll, dong, peal, boom • *The clock struck nine.*
16 = **delete**, remove, erase, pull, eliminate, extract, get rid of, strike out, expunge, take away *or* off *or* out • *Strike that from the minutes.*
17 = **ignite**, light, set alight, touch off • *She struck a match and held it to the crumpled newspaper in the grate.*
18 *sometimes with* **upon** = **discover**, find, come upon *or* across, reach, encounter, turn up, uncover, unearth, hit upon, light upon, happen *or* chance upon, stumble upon *or* across • *He realized he had just struck oil.*
▸ IN PHRASES: **strike back** = **retaliate**, hit back, pay (someone) back, reciprocate, take revenge, even the score, get your own back *(informal)*, wreak vengeance, exact retribution, give as good as you get *(informal)*, take an eye for an eye, make reprisal, give (someone) a taste of his *or* her own medicine, give tit for tat, return like for like • *Our instinctive reaction when someone causes us pain is to strike back.*
strike out = **set out**, set off, start out, sally forth • *They left the car and struck out along the muddy track.*
strike someone down = **kill**, destroy, slay, ruin, afflict, smite, bring low, deal a deathblow to • *a great sporting hero, struck down at 49*
strike something out *or* **off** *or* **through** = **score out**, delete, cross out, remove, cancel, erase, excise, efface, expunge • *The censor struck out the next two lines.*
strike something up 1 = **establish**, start, begin, initiate, embark on, commence, get under way • *He struck up a friendship with a small boy who owned a pony on the island.*
2 = **start to play**, start playing, embark on • *The band struck up a tune, and riders paraded around the ring.*

striking 1 = **distinct**, noticeable, conspicuous, clear, obvious, evident, manifest, unmistakable, observable, perceptible, appreciable • *He bears a striking resemblance to Lenin.*
2 = **impressive**, dramatic, stunning *(informal)*, wonderful, extraordinary, outstanding, astonishing, memorable, dazzling, noticeable, conspicuous, drop-dead *(slang)*, out of the ordinary, forcible, jaw-dropping, eye-popping *(informal)*, gee-whizz *(slang)* • *She was a striking woman with long blonde hair.*
OPPOSITES: average, unimpressive, unexceptional

string AS A NOUN 1 = **cord**, yarn, twine, wire, strand, rope, fibre, thread, hawser, ligature • *He held out a small bag tied with string.*
2 = **necklace**, strand, rope, rosary, chaplet • *She wore a string of pearls around her neck.*
3 = **series**, line, row, file, sequence, queue, succession, procession • *The landscape is broken only by a string of villages.*
4 = **sequence**, run, series, chain, succession, streak • *The incident was the latest in a string of attacks.*
▸ AS A PLURAL NOUN 1 = **stringed instruments** • *The strings provided a melodic background.*
2 = **conditions**, catches *(informal)*, provisos, stipulations, requirements, riders, obligations, qualifications, complications, prerequisites • *an offer made in good faith, with no strings attached*
▸ AS A VERB = **hang**, stretch, suspend, sling, thread, loop, festoon • *He had strung a banner across the wall.*
▸ IN PHRASES: **string along with someone** = **accompany**, go with, go along with, chaperon • *Can I string along with you for a while?*
string someone along = **deceive**, fool, take (someone) for

a ride *(informal)*, kid *(informal)*, bluff, hoax, dupe, put one over on (someone) *(informal)*, play fast and loose with (someone) *(informal)*, play (someone) false • *She was stringing him along even after they were divorced.*
string someone up = hang, lynch, gibbet • *Guards rushed into his cell and strung him up.*
string something out = prolong, extend, lengthen, protract • *Do you want to get it over with, or do you want to string it out?*
▸ **RELATED PHOBIA:** linonophobia

stringent = strict, tough, rigorous, demanding, binding, tight, severe, exacting, rigid, inflexible • *Its drug-testing procedures are the most stringent in the world.*
OPPOSITES: relaxed, slack, lax

stringy 1 = fibrous, tough, chewy, sinewy, gristly, wiry • *The meat was stringy.*
2 = straggly, thin, straggling, lank • *an enormously fat man with long, stringy gray hair*

strip[1] 1 = undress, disrobe, expose yourself, take your clothes off, unclothe, uncover yourself • *Women residents stripped naked in protest.*
2 = peel, clean, clear, rub, shave, scrape, abrade • *The floorboards have been stripped and sanded.*
3 = dismantle, take apart, disassemble, take to pieces, take to bits • *They stripped the car.*
4 = plunder, rob, loot, empty, sack, deprive, ransack, pillage, divest, denude • *The soldiers have stripped the civilians of their passports.*

strip[2] AS A NOUN 1 = piece, shred, bit, band, slip, belt, tongue, ribbon, fillet, swathe • *Serve with strips of fresh raw vegetables.*
2 = stretch, area, tract, expanse, extent • *a short boat ride across a narrow strip of water*
3 = street, road, avenue, row, lane, terrace, boulevard, roadway, thoroughfare • *a busy commercial strip in North Dallas*
▸ **IN PHRASES: tear someone off a strip = tell off**, rebuke, reprimand, lecture, carpet *(informal)*, censure, reproach, scold, berate, tick off *(informal)*, chide, tear into *(informal)*, take to task, read the riot act, reprove, upbraid, bawl out *(informal)*, haul over the coals *(informal)*, chew out *(U.S. & Canad. informal)*, give (someone) a rocket *(Brit. & N.Z. informal)*, give (someone) a piece of your mind • *He heard Nora tear an orderly off a strip.*

stripe = band, line, streak, marking, mark, rule, score, bar, flash, blaze • *a white stripe down the sides*

striped = banded, stripy, barred, streaky, striated • *striped wallpaper*

stripling = boy, youth, lad, youngster, adolescent, fledgling, shaver *(informal)*, young fellow, hobbledehoy *(archaic)* • *a stripling of 20*

stripy *or* **stripey = banded**, striped, barred, streaky, striated • *He was wearing a stripy shirt and baggy blue trousers.*

strive = try, labour, struggle, fight, attempt, compete, strain, contend, endeavour, go for it *(informal)*, try hard, toil, make every effort, go all out *(informal)*, bend over backwards *(informal)*, do your best, go for broke *(slang)*, leave no stone unturned, bust a gut *(informal)*, do all you can, give it your best shot *(informal)*, jump through hoops *(informal)*, break your neck *(informal)*, exert yourself, make an all-out effort *(informal)*, knock yourself out *(informal)*, do your utmost, do your damnedest *(informal)*, give it your all *(informal)*, rupture yourself *(informal)* • *He strives hard to keep himself very fit.*

stroke AS A VERB = caress, rub, fondle, pat, pet • *She was smoking a cigarette and stroking her cat.*
▸ **AS A NOUN 1 = apoplexy**, fit, seizure, attack, shock, collapse • *He had a minor stroke in 1987, which left him partly paralysed.*
2 = mark, line, slash • *Fill in gaps by using short, upward strokes of the pencil.*
3 = movement, action, motion • *I turned and swam a few strokes further out to sea.*
4 = chime, striking, ring, knell, peal, ding dong • *On the stroke of 12, fireworks suddenly exploded into the night.*
5 = blow, hit, knock, pat, rap, thump, swipe • *He was sending the ball into the net with each stroke.*
6 = feat, move, achievement, accomplishment, movement • *At the time, his appointment seemed a stroke of genius.*
▸ **IN PHRASES: at a stroke = in one go**, at the same time, simultaneously, synchronously • *The disease knocked out 40 million rabbits at a stroke.*

stroll AS A VERB = walk, ramble, amble, wander, promenade, saunter, stooge *(slang)*, take a turn, toddle, make your way, mooch *(slang)*, mosey *(informal)*, stretch your legs • *We strolled back, put the kettle on and settled down.*
▸ **AS A NOUN = walk**, promenade, turn, airing, constitutional, excursion, ramble, breath of air • *After dinner, I took a stroll around the city.*

strong 1 = powerful, muscular, tough, capable, athletic, strapping, hardy, sturdy, stout, stalwart, burly, beefy *(informal)*, virile, Herculean, sinewy, brawny • *I'm not strong enough to carry him.*
OPPOSITES: weak, feeble, puny
2 = fit, sound, healthy, thriving, blooming, robust, hale, in good shape, in good condition, lusty, fighting fit, in fine fettle, hale and hearty, fit as a fiddle • *It took me a long while to feel well and strong again.*
3 = self-confident, determined, tough, brave, aggressive, courageous, high-powered, forceful, resilient, feisty *(informal, chiefly U.S. & Canad.)*, resolute, resourceful, tenacious, plucky, hard-nosed *(informal)*, steadfast, unyielding, hard as nails, self-assertive, stout-hearted, two-fisted, firm in spirit • *Eventually I felt strong enough to look at him.*
OPPOSITES: timid, spineless, unassertive
4 = durable, substantial, sturdy, reinforced, heavy-duty, well-built, well-armed, hard-wearing, well-protected, on a firm foundation • *Around its summit, a strong wall had been built.*
OPPOSITES: fragile, delicate, flimsy
5 = forceful, powerful, intense, vigorous • *A strong current seemed to be moving the whole boat.*
6 = convincing, persuasive, powerful, effective, compelling, potent, plausible, forceful, weighty • *There will be a strong incentive to enter into negotiations.*
7 = extreme, radical, drastic, strict, harsh, rigid, forceful, uncompromising, Draconian, unbending • *She is known to hold strong views on Cuba.*
8 = decisive, firm, forceful, decided, determined, severe, resolute, incisive • *The government will take strong action against any further strikes.*
9 = persuasive, convincing, compelling, telling, great, clear, sound, effective, urgent, formidable, potent, well-established, clear-cut, overpowering, weighty, well-founded, redoubtable, trenchant, cogent • *The evidence that such investment promotes growth is strong.*
10 = secure, established, solid, stable, reliable, tried-and-true • *He felt he had a relationship strong enough to talk frankly to Sarah.*
11 = stable, secure, safe, solid, robust, solvent • *The local economy is strong and the population is growing.*
12 = pungent, powerful, concentrated, pure, undiluted, industrial-strength *(chiefly humorous)* • *strong aftershave*
OPPOSITES: weak, mild, bland
13 = highly-flavoured, hot, spicy, piquant, biting, sharp, heady, overpowering, intoxicating, highly-seasoned • *It's a good strong flavour, without being overpowering.*
14 = keen, deep, acute, eager, fervent, zealous, vehement • *He has a strong interest in paintings and owns a fine collection.*

15 = intense, deep, passionate, ardent, fierce, profound, forceful, fervent, deep-rooted, vehement, fervid • *Having strong unrequited feelings for someone is hard.*
16 = staunch, firm, earnest, keen, dedicated, fierce, ardent, eager, loyal, enthusiastic, passionate, fervent, steadfast • *The Deputy Prime Minister is a strong supporter of the plan.*
17 = distinct, marked, clear, unmistakable • *'Good, Mr Royle,' he said in English with a strong French accent.*
OPPOSITES: slight, delicate, faint
18 = bright, brilliant, dazzling, loud, bold, stark, glaring • *strong colours*
OPPOSITES: pale, dull, insipid

strong-arm = bullying, threatening, aggressive, violent, terror, forceful, high-pressure, coercive, terrorizing, thuggish, aggers *(Austral. slang)* • *The paper is openly critical of his strong-arm tactics.*

stronghold 1 = bastion, fortress, bulwark, fastness • *The seat was a stronghold of the labour party.*
2 = refuge, haven, retreat, sanctuary, hide-out, bolt hole • *Shetland is the last stronghold of otters in the British Isles.*

strong-minded = determined, resolute, strong-willed, firm, independent, uncompromising, iron-willed, unbending • *She is a strong-minded, independent woman.*

strong point = forte, strength, speciality, advantage, asset, strong suit, métier, long suit *(informal)* • *Discretion is not his strong point.*

strong-willed = resolute, firm, single-minded, purposeful, fixed, intent, persistent, stalwart, persevering, tenacious, steadfast, unwavering, immovable, headstrong, unflinching, strong-minded, self-willed • *He is a very determined and strong-willed person.*

stroppy = awkward, difficult, obstreperous, destructive, perverse, unhelpful, cantankerous, bloody-minded *(Brit. informal)*, quarrelsome, litigious, uncooperative, arsey *(Brit., Austral. & N.Z. slang)* • *I shall have to get stroppy with them.*

structural = constructional, constitutional, configurational, formational • *structural reform of the tax system*

structure AS A NOUN **1 = arrangement**, form, make-up, make, design, organization, construction, fabric, formation, configuration, conformation, interrelation of parts • *The chemical structure of this particular molecule is very unusual.*
2 = building, construction, erection, edifice, pile • *The house was a handsome four-storey brick structure.*
▸ AS A VERB **= arrange**, organize, design, shape, build up, assemble, put together • *You have begun to structure your time.*

struggle AS A VERB **1 = strive**, labour, toil, work, strain, go for it *(informal)*, make every effort, go all out *(informal)*, bend over backwards *(informal)*, go for broke *(slang)*, bust a gut *(informal)*, give it your best shot *(informal)*, break your neck *(informal)*, exert yourself, make an all-out effort *(informal)*, work like a Trojan, knock yourself out *(informal)*, do your damnedest *(informal)*, give it your all *(informal)*, rupture yourself *(informal)* • *They had to struggle against all kinds of adversity.*
2 = fight, battle, wrestle, grapple, compete, contend, scuffle, lock horns • *We were struggling for the gun when it went off.*
3 = have trouble, have problems, have difficulties, fight, come unstuck • *The company is struggling to find visitors.*
▸ AS A NOUN **1 = problem**, battle, effort, trial, strain • *Life became a struggle.*
2 = effort, labour, toil, work, grind *(informal)*, pains, scramble, long haul, exertion • *a young lad's struggle to support his poverty-stricken family*
3 = fight, battle, conflict, clash, contest, encounter, brush, combat, hostilities, strife, skirmish, tussle, biffo *(Austral. slang)* • *He died in a struggle with prison officers.*
4 = ordeal, test, suffering, trouble(s), trial, nightmare, torture, agony, hardship, anguish, tribulation(s) • *Losing weight was a terrible struggle.*

strum = pluck, twang, thrum, strike • *Vaska strummed away on his guitar.*

strung up = tense, wired *(slang)*, nervous, edgy, jittery *(informal)*, uptight *(informal)*, on edge, twitchy *(informal)*, on tenterhooks, keyed up, antsy *(informal)*, a bundle of nerves *(informal)*, under a strain, adrenalized • *Those who saw him at the Olympics will recall just how strung up he was.*

strut = swagger, parade, stalk, peacock, prance • *He struts around the town as though he owns the place.*

stub 1 = butt, end, stump, tail, remnant, tail end, fag end *(informal)*, dog-end *(informal)* • *an ashtray of cigarette stubs*
2 = counterfoil, tab, receipt, coupon • *Those who still have their ticket stubs, please contact the arena.*

stubble 1 = straw, stalks • *The stubble was burning in the fields.*
2 = bristles, hair, whiskers, beard, facial hair, designer stubble, five o'clock shadow • *His face was covered with the stubble of several nights.*

stubborn 1 = obstinate, dogged, inflexible, fixed, persistent, intractable, wilful, tenacious, recalcitrant, unyielding, headstrong, unmanageable, unbending, obdurate, stiff-necked, unshakeable, self-willed, refractory, pig-headed, bull-headed, mulish, cross-grained, contumacious • *He is a stubborn character used to getting his own way.*
OPPOSITES: yielding, flexible, compliant
2 = persistent, tenacious, indelible, fast, permanent, resistant, obstinate • *The treatment removes the most stubborn stains.*

stubby = stumpy, short, squat, stocky, chunky, dumpy, thickset, fubsy *(archaic or dialect)* • *He pointed a stubby finger at the wooden chair opposite him.*

stuck AS AN ADJECTIVE **1 = fastened**, fast, fixed, joined, glued, cemented • *She had got something stuck between her teeth.*
2 = trapped, caught, ensnared • *I don't want to get stuck in another job like that.*
3 = burdened, saddled, lumbered, landed, loaded, encumbered • *Many people are now stuck with fixed-rate mortgages.*
4 = baffled, stumped, at a loss, beaten, nonplussed, at a standstill, bereft of ideas, up against a brick wall *(informal)*, at your wits' end • *They will be there to help if you're stuck.*
▸ IN PHRASES: **be stuck on something** *or* **someone = infatuated with**, obsessed with, keen on, enthusiastic about, mad about, wild about *(informal)*, hung up on *(slang)*, crazy about, for, *or* over *(informal)* • *She's stuck on him because he was her first lover.*
get stuck into something = set about, tackle, get down to, make a start on, take the bit between your teeth • *The sooner we get stuck into this, the sooner we'll finish.*

stuck-up = snobbish, arrogant, conceited, proud, patronizing, condescending, snooty *(informal)*, haughty, uppity *(informal)*, high and mighty *(informal)*, toffee-nosed *(slang, chiefly Brit.)*, hoity-toity *(informal)*, swollen-headed, bigheaded *(informal)*, uppish *(Brit. informal)* • *She was a famous actress but she wasn't a bit stuck-up.*

stud = rivet, tack, press-stud, tintack • *You see studs on lots of London front doors.*

studded = covered, dotted, scattered, spotted, peppered, sprinkled, spangled • *a metal panel studded with small microphones*

student 1 = undergraduate, scholar, postgraduate, fresher *(Brit. informal)*, tutee • *a 23-year-old medical student*
2 = pupil, scholar, schoolchild, schoolboy *or* schoolgirl • *She's a former student of the school.*
3 = learner, observer, trainee, apprentice, disciple • *a passionate student of history*

studied = **planned**, calculated, deliberate, conscious, intentional, wilful, purposeful, premeditated, well-considered • *a studied understatement*
OPPOSITES: spontaneous, impulsive, unplanned

studio = **workshop**, shop, workroom, office, study, atelier • *She was in her studio again, painting onto a large canvas.*

studious 1 = **scholarly**, academic, intellectual, serious, earnest, hard-working, thoughtful, reflective, diligent, meditative, bookish, assiduous, swotty *(Brit. informal)*, sedulous • *I was a very quiet, studious little girl.*
OPPOSITES: lazy, idle, unacademic
2 = **intent**, attentive, watchful, listening, concentrating, careful, regardful • *He had a look of studious concentration on his face.*
OPPOSITES: indifferent, careless, negligent
3 = **deliberate**, planned, conscious, calculated, considered, studied, designed, thoughtful, intentional, wilful, purposeful, premeditated, prearranged • *the studious refusal of most of these firms to get involved in politics*

study AS A VERB 1 = **learn**, cram *(informal)*, swot (up) *(Brit. informal)*, read up, hammer away at, bone up on *(informal)*, burn the midnight oil, mug up *(Brit. slang)*, lucubrate *(rare)* • *The rehearsals make it difficult for her to study for her law exams.*
2 = **examine**, survey, look at, scrutinize, peruse • *Debbie studied her friend's face for a moment.*
3 = **contemplate**, read, examine, consider, go into, con *(archaic)*, pore over, scrutinize, peruse, apply yourself (to) • *I invite every citizen to carefully study the document.*
▸ AS A NOUN 1 = **examination**, investigation, analysis, consideration, inspection, scrutiny, contemplation, perusal, cogitation • *the use of maps and visual evidence in the study of local history*
2 = **piece of research**, survey, report, paper, review, article, inquiry, investigation, essay, commentary, critique • *the first study of English children's attitudes*
3 = **learning**, lessons, school work, academic work, reading, research, cramming *(informal)*, swotting *(Brit. informal)*, book work • *She gave up her studies to have a family.*
4 = **office**, room, studio, workplace, den, place of work, workroom • *I went through the papers in his study.*

QUOTATIONS
Of making many books there is no end; and much study is a weariness of the flesh
[*Bible: Ecclesiastes*]

S

stuff AS A NOUN 1 = **things**, gear, possessions, effects, materials, equipment, objects, tackle, kit, junk, luggage, belongings, trappings, bits and pieces, paraphernalia, clobber *(Brit. slang)*, impedimenta, goods and chattels • *He pointed to a duffle bag. 'That's my stuff.'*
2 = **nonsense**, rubbish, rot, trash, bunk *(informal)*, foolishness, humbug, twaddle, tripe *(informal)*, baloney *(informal)*, verbiage, claptrap, malarkey *(informal)*, bunkum, poppycock *(informal)*, balderdash, pants *(slang)*, bosh *(informal)*, stuff and nonsense, tommyrot, bizzo *(Austral. slang)*, bull's wool *(Austral. & N.Z. slang)* • *Don't tell me you believe in all that stuff.*
3 = **substance**, material, essence, matter, staple, pith, quintessence • *The idea that we can be what we want has become the stuff of TV commercials.*
4 = **facts**, information, subject, data • *These chaps know their stuff after seven years of war.*
▸ AS A VERB 1 = **shove**, force, push, squeeze, jam, ram, wedge, compress, stow • *His trousers were stuffed inside the tops of his boots.*
2 = **cram**, fill, pack, load, crowd • *wallets stuffed with dollars*
▸ IN PHRASES: **stuff yourself** = **gorge**, gobble, guzzle, satiate, pig out *(slang)*, sate, overindulge, make a pig of yourself *(informal)*, gormandize • *I could stuff myself with ten chocolate bars and still feel hungry.*

stuffing 1 = **filling**, farce, forcemeat, farcemeat • *a stuffing for turkey, guinea fowl or chicken*
2 = **wadding**, filling, packing, quilting, kapok • *She made a wig from pillow stuffing.*

stuffy 1 = **staid**, conventional, dull, old-fashioned, deadly, dreary, pompous, formal, prim, stilted, musty, stodgy, uninteresting, humourless, fusty, strait-laced, priggish, as dry as dust, old-fogeyish, niminy-piminy, prim and proper • *stuffy attitudes*
2 = **airless**, stifling, oppressive, close, heavy, stale, suffocating, sultry, fetid, muggy, unventilated, fuggy, frowsty • *It was hot and stuffy in the classroom.*
OPPOSITES: fresh, cool, airy
3 = **blocked**, congested, stuffed up, bunged up • *Aromatic capsules are great for easing the discomfort of a stuffy nose.*

stumble AS A VERB 1 = **trip**, fall, slip, reel, stagger, falter, flounder, lurch, come a cropper *(informal)*, lose your balance, blunder about • *The smoke was so thick that I stumbled on the first step.*
2 = **totter**, reel, stagger, blunder, falter, flounder, lurch, wobble, teeter, move clumsily • *I stumbled into the telephone box and dialled 999.*
3 = **falter**, hesitate, stammer, stutter, fluff *(informal)* • *His voiced wavered and he stumbled over his words.*
▸ IN PHRASES: **stumble across** *or* **on** *or* **upon something** *or* **someone** = **discover**, find, come across, encounter, run across, chance upon, happen upon, light upon, blunder upon • *History relates that they stumbled on a magnificent waterfall.*

stumbling block = **obstacle**, difficulty, problem, bar, barrier, hurdle, hazard, snag, uphill *(S. African)*, obstruction, impediment, hindrance • *Perhaps the major stumbling block is the military presence.*

stump AS A NOUN = **tail end**, end, remnant, remainder • *The tramp produced a stump of candle from his pocket.*
▸ AS A VERB 1 = **baffle**, confuse, puzzle, snooker, foil, bewilder, confound, perplex, mystify, outwit, stymie, flummox, bring (someone) up short, dumbfound, nonplus • *Well, maybe I stumped you on that one.*
2 = **stamp**, clump, stomp *(informal)*, trudge, plod, clomp • *The marshal stumped out of the room.*
▸ IN PHRASES: **stump something up** = **pay**, fork out *(slang)*, shell out *(informal)*, contribute, hand over, donate, chip in *(informal)*, cough up *(informal)*, come across with *(informal)* • *Customers do not have to stump up cash for at least four weeks.*

stumped = **baffled**, perplexed, at a loss, floored *(informal)*, at sea, stymied, nonplussed, flummoxed, brought to a standstill, uncertain which way to turn, at your wits' end • *I must confess I was stumped for a moment.*

stumpy = **chunky**, short, heavy, thick, squat, stocky, stubby, dumpy, thickset, fubsy *(archaic or dialect)* • *Does this dress make my legs look stumpy?*

stun 1 = **overcome**, shock, amaze, confuse, astonish, stagger, bewilder, astound, overpower, confound, stupefy, strike (someone) dumb, knock (someone) for six *(informal)*, dumbfound, flabbergast *(informal)*, hit (someone) like a ton of bricks *(informal)*, take (someone's) breath away • *Many cinema-goers were stunned by the film's violent and tragic end.*
2 = **daze**, knock out, stupefy, numb, knock unconscious, benumb • *He stood his ground and took a heavy blow that stunned him.*

stung = **hurt**, wounded, angered, roused, incensed, exasperated, resentful, nettled, goaded, piqued • *I was stung by her attitude.*

stunned = **staggered**, shocked, devastated, numb, astounded, bowled over *(informal)*, gobsmacked *(Brit. slang)*, dumbfounded, flabbergasted *(informal)*, struck dumb, at a loss for words • *When they told me she had gone missing I was totally stunned.*

stunner = **beauty**, looker *(informal, chiefly U.S.)*, lovely *(slang)*, dish *(informal)*, sensation, honey *(informal)*, good-looker, dazzler, peach *(informal)*, wow *(slang, chiefly U.S.)*, dolly *(slang)*, knockout *(informal)*, heart-throb, charmer, eyeful *(informal)*, smasher *(informal)*, humdinger *(slang)*, glamour puss, beaut *(Austral. & N.Z. slang)* • *One of the girls was an absolute stunner.*

stunning 1 = **wonderful**, beautiful, impressive, great *(informal)*, striking, brilliant, dramatic, lovely, remarkable, smashing *(informal)*, heavenly, devastating *(informal)*, spectacular, marvellous, splendid, gorgeous, dazzling, sensational *(informal)*, drop-dead *(slang)*, ravishing, out of this world *(informal)*, jaw-dropping, eye-popping *(informal)*, gee-whizz *(slang)* • *A stunning display of fireworks lit up the sky.*
OPPOSITES: average, ordinary, unimpressive
2 = **staggering**, surprising, shocking, astonishing, extraordinary, unexpected, startling, sensational, astounding, jaw-dropping • *The announcement was a stunning piece of news.*

stunt[1] = **hamper**, restrict, curb, slow down, hold up, interfere with, hinder, impede • *The heart condition has stunted his growth a bit.*

stunt[2] = **feat**, act, trick, exploit, deed, tour de force *(French)*, gest *(archaic)* • *a bold promotional stunt*

stunted = **undersized**, dwarfed, little, small, tiny, diminutive, dwarfish • *low, stunted trees*

stupefaction = **astonishment**, wonder, amazement, awe, wonderment • *He stared at her in stupefaction.*

stupefy = **astound**, shock, amaze, stun, stagger, bewilder, numb, daze, confound, knock senseless, dumbfound • *The aim is to shock, upset, stupefy, or just plain scare them.*

stupendous 1 = **wonderful**, brilliant, amazing, stunning *(informal)*, superb, overwhelming, fantastic *(informal)*, tremendous *(informal)*, fabulous *(informal)*, surprising, staggering, marvellous, sensational *(informal)*, breathtaking, phenomenal, astounding, prodigious, wondrous *(archaic or literary)*, mind-boggling *(informal)*, out of this world *(informal)*, mind-blowing *(informal)*, jaw-dropping, surpassing belief • *This stupendous novel keeps you gripped to the end.*
OPPOSITES: average, ordinary, unremarkable
2 = **huge**, vast, enormous, mega *(slang)*, gigantic, colossal • *a stupendous amount of money*
OPPOSITES: tiny, diminutive, puny

stupid 1 = **unintelligent**, thick, dumb *(informal)*, simple, slow, dull, dim, dense, sluggish, deficient, crass, gullible, simple-minded, dozy *(Brit. informal)*, witless, stolid, dopey *(informal)*, moronic, obtuse, brainless, cretinous, half-witted, slow on the uptake *(informal)*, braindead *(informal)*, dumb-ass *(slang)*, doltish, dead from the neck up, thickheaded, slow-witted, Boeotian, thick as mince *(Scot. informal)*, woodenheaded *(informal)* • *I'm not stupid, you know.*
OPPOSITES: bright, smart, intelligent
2 = **silly**, foolish, daft *(informal)*, rash, trivial, ludicrous, meaningless, irresponsible, pointless, futile, senseless, mindless, laughable, short-sighted, ill-advised, idiotic, fatuous, nonsensical, half-baked *(informal)*, inane, crackpot *(informal)*, unthinking, puerile, unintelligent, asinine, imbecilic, crackbrained • *I wouldn't call it art. It's just stupid and tasteless.* • *You won't go and do anything stupid, will you?*
OPPOSITES: wise, sensible, shrewd
3 = **senseless**, dazed, groggy, into oblivion, punch-drunk, insensate, semiconscious, into a daze • *She would drink herself stupid.*

QUOTATIONS
He that reads and grows no wiser seldom suspects his own deficiency, but complains of hard words and obscure sentences, and asks why books are written which cannot be understood
[Dr. Johnson *The Idler*]

Nothing sways the stupid more than arguments they can't understand
[Cardinal De Retz *Mémoirs*]

stupidity 1 = **lack of intelligence**, imbecility, obtuseness, simplicity, thickness, slowness, dullness, dimness, dumbness *(informal)*, feeble-mindedness, lack of brain, denseness, brainlessness, doziness *(Brit. informal)*, asininity, dopiness *(slang)*, thickheadedness • *I stared at him, astonished by his stupidity.*
2 = **silliness**, folly, foolishness, idiocy, madness, absurdity, futility, lunacy, irresponsibility, pointlessness, inanity, rashness, impracticality, foolhardiness, senselessness, bêtise *(rare)*, ludicrousness, puerility, fatuousness, fatuity • *I can't get over the stupidity of their decision.*

stupor = **daze**, numbness, unconsciousness, trance, coma, inertia, lethargy, torpor, stupefaction, insensibility • *He was drinking himself into a stupor every night.*

sturdy 1 = **robust**, hardy, vigorous, powerful, athletic, muscular, stalwart, staunch, hearty, lusty, brawny, thickset • *She was a short, sturdy woman in her early sixties.*
OPPOSITES: weak, feeble, puny
2 = **substantial**, secure, solid, durable, well-made, well-built, built to last • *The camera was mounted on a sturdy tripod.*
OPPOSITES: frail, flimsy, rickety

stutter AS A NOUN = **stammer**, faltering, speech impediment, speech defect, hesitance • *He spoke with a pronounced stutter.*
▸ AS A VERB = **stammer**, stumble, falter, hesitate, splutter, speak haltingly • *I was trembling so hard, I though I would stutter when I spoke.*

stuttering
▸ RELATED PHOBIA: laliophobia

style AS A NOUN 1 = **manner**, way, method, approach, technique, custom, mode • *Our children's different learning styles created many problems.*
2 = **elegance**, taste, chic, flair, polish, grace, dash, sophistication, refinement, panache, élan, cosmopolitanism, savoir-faire, smartness, urbanity, stylishness, bon ton *(French)*, fashionableness, dressiness *(informal)* • *She has not lost her grace and style.*
3 = **design**, form, cut • *Several styles of hat were available.*
4 = **type**, sort, kind, spirit, pattern, variety, appearance, tone, strain, category, characteristic, genre, tenor • *six scenes in the style of a classical Greek tragedy*
5 = **fashion**, trend, mode, vogue, rage • *The longer length of skirt is the style at the moment.*
6 = **luxury**, ease, comfort, elegance, grandeur, affluence, gracious living • *The £17 million settlement allowed her to live in style to the end.*
7 = **mode of expression**, phrasing, turn of phrase, wording, treatment, expression, vein, diction, phraseology • *The author's style is wonderfully anecdotal.*
▸ AS A VERB 1 = **design**, cut, tailor, fashion, shape, arrange, adapt • *classically styled clothes*
2 = **call**, name, term, address, label, entitle, dub, designate, christen, denominate • *people who would like to style themselves as arms dealers*

stylish = **smart**, chic, polished, fashionable, trendy *(Brit. informal)*, classy *(slang)*, in fashion, snappy, in vogue, dapper, natty *(informal)*, snazzy *(informal)*, modish, well turned-out, dressy *(informal)*, à la mode, voguish, schmick *(Austral. informal)*, bling *(slang)*, funky • *a very attractive and stylish woman of 27*
OPPOSITES: shabby, scruffy, unfashionable

stylus = **needle**, pen, probe, pointer • *the stylus on a record player*

stymie = **frustrate**, defeat, foil, thwart, puzzle, stump, snooker, hinder, confound, mystify, balk, flummox, throw a spanner in the works *(Brit. informal)*, nonplus, spike (someone's) guns • *Relief efforts have been stymied in recent weeks by armed gunmen.*

suave = **smooth**, charming, urbane, debonair, worldly, cool *(informal)*, sophisticated, polite, gracious, agreeable, courteous, affable, smooth-tongued • *He is a suave, cool and cultured man.*

subconscious AS A NOUN = **mind**, psyche, essential being, imagination, inner self • *the hidden power of the subconscious*
▸ AS AN ADJECTIVE = **hidden**, inner, suppressed, repressed, intuitive, latent, innermost, subliminal • *a subconscious cry for affection*
OPPOSITES: knowing, aware, conscious

subdue 1 = **overcome**, defeat, master, break, control, discipline, crush, humble, put down, conquer, tame, overpower, overrun, trample, quell, triumph over, get the better of, vanquish, beat down, get under control, get the upper hand over, gain ascendancy over • *They admit they have not been able to subdue the rebels.*
2 = **moderate**, control, check, suppress, soften, repress, mellow, tone down, quieten down • *He forced himself to subdue and overcome his fears.*
OPPOSITES: provoke, arouse, stir up

subdued 1 = **quiet**, serious, sober, sad, grave, restrained, repressed, solemn, chastened, dejected, downcast, crestfallen, repentant, down in the mouth, sadder and wiser, out of spirits • *He faced the press, initially, in a somewhat subdued mood.*
OPPOSITES: happy, lively, cheerful
2 = **hushed**, soft, quiet, whispered, murmured, muted, muffled, inaudible, indistinct • *The conversation around them was resumed, but in subdued tones.*
OPPOSITES: loud, strident
3 = **dim**, soft, subtle, muted, shaded, low-key, understated, toned down, unobtrusive • *The lighting was subdued.*
OPPOSITES: bright

subject AS A NOUN 1 = **topic**, question, issue, matter, point, business, affair, object, theme, substance, subject matter, field of inquiry or reference • *It was I who first raised the subject of plastic surgery.*
2 = **branch of study**, area, field, discipline, speciality, branch of knowledge • *a tutor in maths and science subjects*
3 = **participant**, case, patient, victim, client, guinea pig *(informal)* • *Subjects in the study were forced to follow a modified diet.*
4 = **citizen**, resident, native, inhabitant, national • *Roughly half of them are British subjects.*
5 = **dependant**, subordinate, underling, follower, vassal, liegeman • *His subjects regard him as a great and wise monarch.*
▸ AS AN ADJECTIVE = **subordinate**, dependent, satellite, inferior, captive, obedient, enslaved, submissive, subservient, subjugated • *colonies and other subject territories*
▸ AS A VERB = **put through**, expose, submit, lay open, make liable • *He had subjected her to four years of beatings and abuse.*
▸ IN PHRASES: **subject to** 1 = **liable to**, open to, exposed to, vulnerable to, prone to, susceptible to, disposed to • *Prices may be subject to alteration.*
2 = **bound by**, under the control of, accountable to, constrained by • *It could not be subject to another country's laws.*
3 = **dependent on**, hanging on, contingent on, controlled by, hinging on, conditional on • *The merger is subject to certain conditions.*

subjection = **oppression**, domination, subjugation, exploitation, persecution, suppression, enslavement • *the complete subjection of the prisoners to their captors*

subjective = **personal**, emotional, prejudiced, biased, instinctive, intuitive, idiosyncratic, nonobjective • *We know that taste in art is a subjective matter.*
OPPOSITES: objective, detached, impartial

subjugate = **conquer**, master, overcome, defeat, crush, suppress, put down, overthrow, tame, lick *(informal)*, subdue, overpower, quell, rule over, enslave, vanquish, hold sway over, bring to heel, bring (someone) to his knees, bring under the yoke • *Their costly attempt to subjugate the citizens lasted 10 years.*

sublimate = **channel**, transfer, convert, divert, redirect, turn • *The erotic impulse is sublimated into art.*

sublime 1 = **noble**, magnificent, glorious, high, great, grand, imposing, elevated, eminent, majestic, lofty, exalted, transcendent • *the sublime beauty of nature*
OPPOSITES: ordinary, commonplace, lowly
2 = **total**, complete, utter, supreme, extreme, consummate • *The administration's sublime incompetence is probably temporary.*

QUOTATIONS

It is only one step from the sublime to the ridiculous
[Napoleon Bonaparte]

The sublime and the ridiculous are often so nearly related, that it is difficult to class them separately. One step above the sublime, makes the ridiculous; and one step above the ridiculous, makes the sublime again
[Thomas Paine *The Age of Reason*]

subliminal = **subconscious**, hidden, concealed, unconscious • *subliminal advertising*

submerge 1 = **flood**, swamp, engulf, drown, overflow, inundate, deluge • *The river burst its banks, submerging an entire village.*
2 = **immerse**, plunge, dip, duck, dunk • *Submerge the pieces of fish in the poaching liquid and simmer.*
3 = **sink**, drop, go down, plunge, go under water • *Just as I shot at it, the crocodile submerged again.*
4 = **overwhelm**, swamp, engulf, overload, inundate, deluge, snow under, overburden • *He was suddenly submerged in an avalanche of scripts and offers.*

submerged = **immersed**, sunk, underwater, drowned, submarine, sunken, undersea, subaqueous, submersed, subaquatic • *Most of the mouth of the cave was submerged in the lake.*

submission 1 = **surrender**, yielding, giving in, cave-in *(informal)*, capitulation, acquiescence • *The army intends to take the city or force it into submission.*
2 = **presentation**, submitting, handing in, entry, tendering • *the submission of a dissertation*
3 = **proposal**, offer, proposition, argument, suggestion, motion, recommendation, contention • *A written submission has to be prepared.*
4 = **compliance**, obedience, submissiveness, meekness, resignation, deference, passivity, docility, tractability, unassertiveness • *She nodded her head in submission.*

submissive = **meek**, passive, obedient, compliant, patient, resigned, yielding, accommodating, humble, subdued, lowly, abject, amenable, docile, dutiful, ingratiating, malleable, deferential, pliant, obsequious, uncomplaining, tractable, acquiescent, biddable, unresisting, bootlicking *(informal)*, obeisant • *Most doctors want their patients to be submissive.*
OPPOSITES: difficult, awkward, obstinate

submit 1 = **surrender**, yield, give in, agree, bend, bow, endure, tolerate, comply, put up with *(informal)*, succumb, defer, stoop, cave in *(informal)*, capitulate, accede, acquiesce, toe the line, knuckle under, resign yourself, lay down arms, hoist the white flag, throw in the sponge • *If I submitted to their demands, they would not press the allegations.*
2 = **present**, hand in, tender, put forward, table, commit, refer, proffer • *They submitted their reports to the Chancellor yesterday.*
3 = **suggest**, claim, argue, propose, state, put, move, advance, volunteer, assert, contend, propound • *I submit that you knew exactly what you were doing.*

subnormal = **retarded**, simple, slow, moronic, cretinous, feeble-minded, imbecilic, mentally defective, E.S.N., intellectually handicapped *(Austral.)* • *educationally subnormal children*

subordinate AS A NOUN = **inferior**, junior, assistant, aide, second, attendant, dependant, underling, subaltern • *Nearly all her subordinates adored her.*
OPPOSITES: head, leader, superior
▸ AS AN ADJECTIVE 1 = **inferior**, lesser, lower, junior, subject, minor, secondary, dependent, subservient • *Sixty of his subordinate officers followed his example.*
OPPOSITES: senior, superior, higher
2 = **subsidiary**, supplementary, auxiliary, ancillary • *It was an art in which words were subordinate to images.*

subordination = **inferiority**, servitude, subjection, inferior or secondary status • *the social subordination of women*

subscribe to 1 = **support**, agree with, advocate, consent to, endorse, countenance, acquiesce with • *I've personally never subscribed to the view.*
2 = **pay a subscription to**, read regularly, buy regularly, take, take regularly • *You can also subscribe to the newspaper.*
3 = **contribute to**, give to, donate to, chip in to *(informal)* • *I subscribe to a few favourable charities.*

subscriber = **reader**, customer, regular reader • *I have been a subscriber to Railway Magazine for many years.*

subscription = **membership fee**, charge, dues, annual payment, retainer • *You can become a member by paying the yearly subscription.*

subsequent AS AN ADJECTIVE = **following**, later, succeeding, after, successive, ensuing, consequent • *the increase of population in subsequent years*
OPPOSITES: earlier, former, previous
▸ IN PHRASES: **subsequent to** = **after**, following, succeeding • *They won only one more game subsequent to their Cup semi-final win.*

subsequently = **later**, afterwards, in the end, consequently, in the aftermath (of), at a later date • *Subsequently the arrangement was terminated.*

subservient 1 = **servile**, submissive, deferential, subject, inferior, abject, sycophantic, slavish, obsequious, truckling, bootlicking *(informal)* • *Her willingness to be subservient to her children isolated her.*
OPPOSITES: bossy, domineering, overbearing
2 = **subordinate**, subsidiary, accessory, auxiliary, conducive, ancillary • *The individual's needs are seen as subservient to the group's.*

subside 1 = **decrease**, diminish, lessen, ease, moderate, dwindle, wane, recede, ebb, abate, let up, peter out, slacken, melt away, quieten, level off, de-escalate • *The pain had subsided during the night.*
OPPOSITES: rise, increase, grow
2 = **collapse**, sink, cave in, drop, lower, settle • *Does that mean that the whole house is subsiding?*
3 = **drop**, fall, decline, ebb, descend • *Local officials say the flood waters have subsided.*

subsidence = **sinking**, settling, collapse, settlement • *The problems were caused by subsidence.*

subsidiary AS A NOUN = **branch**, division, section, office, department, wing, satellite, subdivision, subsection, local office • *a subsidiary of the American multinational*
▸ AS AN ADJECTIVE = **secondary**, lesser, subordinate, minor, supplementary, auxiliary, supplemental, contributory, ancillary, subservient • *a subsidiary position*
OPPOSITES: leading, major, main

subsidize = **fund**, finance, support, promote, sponsor, underwrite, put up the money for • *a government decision to subsidize coal mining*

subsidy = **aid**, help, support, grant, contribution, assistance, allowance, financial aid, stipend, subvention • *They've slashed state subsidies.*

subsist = **stay alive**, survive, keep going, make ends meet, last, live, continue, exist, endure, eke out an existence, keep your head above water, sustain yourself • *Almost every employee must moonlight simply to subsist.*

subsistence = **living**, maintenance, upkeep, keep, support, board, existence, survival, livelihood, board and lodging • *Up to £350,000 has been spent on travel and subsistence.*

substance 1 = **material**, body, stuff, element, fabric, texture • *The substance that causes the problem comes from the barley.*
2 = **importance**, significance, moment, meaningfulness, concreteness • *It is questionable whether anything of substance has been achieved.*
3 = **meaning**, main point, gist, matter, subject, theme, import, significance, essence, pith, burden, sum and substance, gravamen *(Law)* • *The substance of his discussions doesn't really matter.*
4 = **truth**, fact, reality, certainty, validity, authenticity, verity, verisimilitude • *There is no substance in any of these allegations.*
5 = **wealth**, means, property, assets, resources, estate, affluence • *mature men of substance*

substandard = **inferior**, inadequate, unacceptable, damaged, imperfect, second-rate, shoddy • *a policy of clearing substandard housing*

substantial 1 = **big**, significant, considerable, goodly, large, important, generous, worthwhile, tidy *(informal)*, ample, sizable or sizeable • *That is a very substantial improvement in the current situation.*
OPPOSITES: small, insignificant, inadequate
2 = **solid**, sound, sturdy, strong, firm, massive, hefty, durable, bulky, well-built • *those fortunate enough to have a fairly substantial property to sell*
OPPOSITES: weak, rickety, insubstantial
3 = **real**, true, positive, material, actual, valid, weighty • *talk of imminent and substantial progress*
OPPOSITES: imagined, imaginary

substantially 1 = **considerably**, significantly, very much, greatly, seriously *(informal)*, remarkably, markedly, noticeably, appreciably • *The price was substantially higher than had been expected.*
2 = **essentially**, largely, mainly, materially, in the main, in essence, to a large extent, in substance, in essentials • *He checked the details given and found them substantially correct.*

substantiate = **support**, prove, confirm, establish, affirm, verify, validate, bear out, corroborate, attest to, authenticate • *There is little scientific evidence to substantiate the claims.*
OPPOSITES: contradict, refute, disprove

substitute AS A VERB 1 = **replace**, exchange, swap, change, switch, commute, interchange • *They were substituting violence for dialogue.*
2 *with* **for** = **stand in for**, take the place of, cover for, take over from, relieve, act for, double for, fill in for, hold the fort for, be in place of, deputize for • *Her parents are trying to be supportive but they can't substitute for Jackie as a mother.*
▸ AS A NOUN = **replacement**, reserve, equivalent, surrogate, deputy, relief, representative, sub, temporary, stand-by, makeshift, proxy, temp *(informal)*, expedient, locum, depute *(Scot.)*, stopgap, locum tenens • *She is seeking a substitute for the man who broke her heart.*
▸ AS AN ADJECTIVE = **replacement**, reserve, temporary, surrogate, second, acting, alternative, additional, fall-back, proxy • *They had fallen for their substitute teacher.*

substitution = **replacement**, exchange, switch, swap, change, interchange • *last-minute substitutions*

subterfuge = **trick**, dodge, ploy, shift, manoeuvre, deception, evasion, pretence, pretext, ruse, artifice, duplicity, stratagem, deviousness, machination • *Most people can see right through that type of subterfuge.*

S

subtle 1 = **faint**, slight, implied, delicate, indirect, understated, insinuated • *a subtle hint*
OPPOSITES: blatant, obvious
2 = **crafty**, cunning, sly, designing, scheming, intriguing, shrewd, ingenious, astute, devious, wily, artful, Machiavellian • *He is a subtle character, you know.*
OPPOSITES: straightforward, blunt, downright
3 = **muted**, soft, faint, subdued, low-key, toned down • *subtle shades of brown*
4 = **fine**, minute, narrow, tenuous, hair-splitting • *There was, however, a subtle distinction between the two lawsuits.*

subtlety 1 = **fine point**, refinement, nicety, sophistication, delicacy, intricacy, discernment • *All those linguistic subtleties get lost when a book goes into translation.*
2 = **delicacy**, softness, delicateness, subtleness • *Many of the resulting wines lack the subtlety of the original model.*
3 = **skill**, acumen, astuteness, ingenuity, guile, cleverness, deviousness, sagacity, acuteness, craftiness, artfulness, slyness, wiliness • *She analyses herself with great subtlety.*
4 = **sensitivity**, diplomacy, discretion, delicacy, understanding, skill, consideration, judgment, perception, finesse, tact, thoughtfulness, discernment, savoir-faire, adroitness • *They had obviously been hoping to approach the topic with more subtlety.*

subtract = **take away**, take off, deduct, remove, withdraw, diminish, take from, detract • *Subtract the date of birth from the date of death.*
OPPOSITES: add, add to, supplement

suburb = **residential area**, neighbourhood, outskirts, precincts, suburbia, environs, purlieus, dormitory area (*Brit.*), faubourgs • *a suburb of Manchester*

suburban 1 = **residential**, commuter, dormitory • *a comfortable suburban area*
2 = **conventional**, boring, conservative, dull, ordinary, small-town, bourgeois, parochial • *ghastly good taste and suburban gentility*

subversion = **trouble-making**, rebellion, insurrection, revolution, mutiny, rabble-rousing, insurgence • *He was arrested on charges of subversion.*

subversive AS AN ADJECTIVE = **seditious**, inflammatory, incendiary, underground, undermining, destructive, overthrowing, riotous, insurrectionary, treasonous, perversive • *The play was promptly banned as subversive and possibly treasonous.*
▸ AS A NOUN = **dissident**, terrorist, saboteur, insurrectionary, quisling, fifth columnist, deviationist, seditionary, seditionist • *Agents regularly rounded up suspected subversives.*

subvert 1 = **overturn**, destroy, undermine, upset, ruin, wreck, demolish, sabotage • *an alleged plot to subvert the state*
2 = **corrupt**, pervert, deprave, poison, contaminate, confound, debase, demoralize, vitiate • *an attempt to subvert culture from within*

subway 1 = **underground**, tube (*Brit. informal*), metro, underground railway • *I don't ride the subway late at night.*
2 = **underpass**, tunnel, underground passage, pedestrian tunnel • *The majority of us feel worried if we walk through a subway.*

succeed 1 = **triumph**, win, prevail • *Some people will succeed in their efforts to stop smoking.*
2 = **work out**, work, be successful, come off (*informal*), be effective, do the trick (*informal*), get results, have legs (*informal*), turn out well, go as planned, go like a bomb (*Brit. & N.Z. informal*), go down a bomb (*informal, chiefly Brit.*), do the business (*informal*) • *a move which would make any future talks even more unlikely to succeed*
3 = **make it** (*informal*), do well, be successful, arrive (*informal*), triumph, thrive, flourish, make good, prosper, cut it (*informal*), make the grade (*informal*), get to the top, crack it (*informal*), hit the jackpot (*informal*), bring home the bacon (*informal*), make your mark (*informal*), gain your end, carry all before you, do all right for yourself • *the skills and qualities needed to succeed*
OPPOSITES: fail, flop (*informal*), be unsuccessful
4 = **take over from**, replace, oust, supersede, usurp, unseat, supplant, assume the office of, fill (someone's) boots, step into (someone's) boots • *He is almost certain to succeed him as chairman.*
5 *with* **to** = **take over**, assume, attain, acquire, come into, inherit, accede to, come into possession of • *He eventually succeeded to the post in 1998.*
6 = **follow**, come after, follow after, replace, be subsequent to, supervene • *He succeeded Trajan as emperor in AD 117.*
OPPOSITES: precede, pave the way for, go before

success 1 = **victory**, triumph, positive result, favourable outcome, successfulness • *the success of European business in building a stronger partnership*
OPPOSITES: failure, collapse, disaster
2 = **prosperity**, riches, fortune, luck, wealth, fame, eminence, ascendancy, affluence, opulence • *Nearly all of them believed work was the key to success.*
3 = **hit** (*informal*), winner, smash (*informal*), triumph, belter (*slang*), sensation, sell-out, wow (*slang*), best seller, market leader, smash hit (*informal*), box office success • *We hope it will be a commercial success.*
OPPOSITES: flop (*informal*), fiasco, washout
4 = **big name**, star, hit (*informal*), somebody, celebrity, sensation, megastar (*informal*), V.I.P. • *Everyone who knows her says she will be a great success.*
OPPOSITES: nobody, loser, no-hoper

QUOTATIONS

Eighty percent of success is showing up
[Woody Allen]

It is not enough to succeed. Others must fail
[Gore Vidal]

Failure is inevitable. Success is elusive
[Steven Spielberg]

Getting on is the opium of the middle classes
[Walter James]

To succeed in the world we must look foolish but be wise
[C.L. de Montesquieu *Pensées*]

Success has ruin'd many a man
[Benjamin Franklin *Poor Richard's Almanack*]

The secret of business success is honesty and sincerity. If you can fake those, you've got it made
[attributed to Groucho Marx]

If A is success in life, then A equals x plus y plus z. Work is x; y is play; and z is keeping your mouth shut
[Albert Einstein]

Success is relative;
It is what we can make of the mess we have made of things
[T.S. Eliot *The Family Reunion*]

success: the one unpardonable sin against one's fellows
[Ambrose Bierce *The Devil's Dictionary*]

Be nice to people on your way up because you'll meet 'em on your way down
[Wilson Mizner]

PROVERBS

Nothing succeeds like success
There is always room at the top

successful 1 = **triumphant**, victorious, lucky, fortunate • *The successful candidate will be announced in June.*
2 = **thriving**, profitable, productive, paying, effective, rewarding, booming, efficient, flourishing, unbeaten, lucrative, favourable, buoyant, fruitful, profit-making, efficacious, moneymaking • *One of the keys to successful business is careful planning.*
OPPOSITES: failed, unsuccessful, unprofitable

3 = top, prosperous, eminent, acknowledged, wealthy, out in front *(informal)*, going places, at the top of the tree • *She is a successful lawyer.*

successfully = well, favourably, in triumph, with flying colours, famously *(informal)*, swimmingly, victoriously • *The doctors have concluded preliminary tests successfully.*

succession AS A NOUN **1 = series**, run, sequence, course, order, train, flow, chain, cycle, procession, continuation, progression • *He took a succession of jobs which have stood him in good stead.*

2 = taking over, assumption, inheritance, elevation, accession, entering upon • *She is now seventh in line of succession to the throne.*

▸ IN PHRASES: **in succession = one after the other**, running, successively, consecutively, on the trot *(informal)*, one behind the other • *They needed to reach the World Cup final for the third time in succession.*

successive = consecutive, following, succeeding, in a row, in succession, sequent • *He was the winner for the second successive year.*

successor = heir, beneficiary, inheritor, next-in-line, descendant • *He set out several principles that he hopes will guide his successors.*

succinct = brief, to the point, concise, compact, summary, condensed, terse, laconic, pithy, gnomic, compendious, in a few well-chosen words • *Make sure your work is accurate, succinct and to the point.*

OPPOSITES: rambling, long-winded, wordy

succour AS A NOUN **= help**, support, aid, relief, comfort, assistance • *Have you offered comfort and succour to your friend?*

▸ AS A VERB **= help**, support, aid, encourage, nurse, comfort, foster, assist, relieve, minister to, befriend, render assistance to, give aid and encouragement to • *They had left nothing to succour a dung beetle, let alone a human.*

succulent = juicy, moist, luscious, rich, lush, mellow, mouthwatering • *succulent early vegetables*

succumb 1 *often with* **to = surrender (to)**, yield (to), submit (to), give in (to), give way (to), go under (to), cave in (to) *(informal)*, capitulate (to), knuckle under (to) • *Don't succumb to the temptation to have just one cigarette.*

OPPOSITES: beat, master, overcome

2 *with* **to** *(an illness)* **= catch**, contract, fall victim to, die from, get, develop, pick up, die of, fall ill with, become infected by, come *or* go down with, cark it from *(Austral. & N.Z. slang)* • *I was determined not to succumb to the virus.*

suck AS A VERB **1 = drink**, sip, draw, sup, siphon, quaff, slurp • *They waited in silence and sucked their drinks through straws.*

2 = take, draw, pull, extract • *The air is sucked out by a high-powered fan.*

3 = be very bad, be terrible, be awful, be dreadful, be foul, be very unpleasant • *The system sucks.*

▸ IN PHRASES: **suck someone in** *or* **into something = involve in**, mix up in, draw into, implicate in • *the extent to which they have been sucked into a cycle of violence*

suck up to someone = ingratiate yourself with, play up to *(informal)*, curry favour with, flatter, pander to, toady, butter up, kiss someone's ass *(U.S. & Canad. taboo slang)*, brown-nose *(taboo slang)*, keep in with *(informal)*, fawn on, truckle, lick someone's boots, dance attendance on, get on the right side of, worm yourself into (someone's) favour • *She kept sucking up to the teachers.*

sucker = fool, mug *(Brit. slang)*, dupe, victim, butt, sap *(slang)*, pushover *(slang)*, sitting duck *(informal)*, sitting target, putz *(U.S. slang)*, cat's paw, easy game *or* mark *(informal)*, nerd *or* nurd *(slang)*, dorba *or* dorb *(Austral. slang)*, bogan *(Austral. slang)* • *Keep giving us your money, sucker!*

sudden = quick, rapid, unexpected, swift, hurried, abrupt, hasty, impulsive, unforeseen • *It was all very sudden.*

OPPOSITES: expected, slow, gradual

suddenly = abruptly, all of a sudden, all at once, unexpectedly, straight away, out of the blue *(informal)*, without warning, in an instant, without notice, on the spur of the moment, like a shot • *Suddenly, she looked ten years older.*

suds = lather, bubbles, foam, froth, soap, soapsuds • *He had soap suds in his ears.*

sue 1 = take (someone) to court, prosecute, bring an action against (someone), charge, summon, indict, have the law on (someone) *(informal)*, prefer charges against (someone), institute legal proceedings against (someone) • *The company could be sued for damages.*

2 = appeal for, plead, beg, petition, solicit, beseech, entreat, supplicate • *He realized that suing for peace was the only option.*

suffer 1 = be in pain, hurt, ache, be racked, have a bad time, go through a lot *(informal)*, go through the mill *(informal)*, feel wretched • *Can you assure me that my father is not suffering?*

2 = be affected, have trouble with, be afflicted, be troubled with • *I realized he was suffering from shock.*

3 = undergo, experience, sustain, feel, bear, go through, endure • *The peace process has suffered a serious blow now.*

4 = deteriorate, decline, get worse, fall off, be impaired • *I'm not surprised that your studies are suffering.*

5 = tolerate, stand, put up with *(informal)*, support, bear, endure, brook, hack *(Brit. informal)*, abide • *She doesn't suffer fools gladly and, in her view, most people are fools.*

suffering = pain, torture, distress, agony, misery, ordeal, discomfort, torment, hardship, anguish, affliction, martyrdom • *It has caused terrible suffering to animals.*

suffice = be enough, do, be sufficient, be adequate, answer, serve, content, satisfy, fill the bill *(informal)*, meet requirements • *A far shorter letter will suffice.*

sufficiency = abundance, adequacy, adequate supply, amplitude, copiousness, ample store • *There's a sufficiency of drama here to sustain your interest.*

sufficient = adequate, enough, ample, satisfactory, enow *(archaic)* • *There was not sufficient evidence to secure a conviction.*

OPPOSITES: not enough, inadequate, insufficient

suffocate 1 = choke, stifle, smother, asphyxiate • *They were suffocated as they slept.*

2 = be choked, be stifled, be smothered, be asphyxiated • *He either suffocated, or froze to death.*

3 = be short of air, boil *(informal)*, swelter, be too hot, struggle for air • *That's better. I was suffocating in that cell of a room.*

suffrage = right to vote, vote, franchise, voice, ballot, consent, enfranchisement • *the women's suffrage movement*

suffuse = spread through *or* **over**, flood, infuse, cover, steep, bathe, mantle, pervade, permeate, imbue, overspread, transfuse • *A dull red flash suffused Selby's face.*

sugar

▸ RELATED ADJECTIVE: saccharine

▹ *See panel* **Sugars**

sugary 1 = sweet, oversweet, sugared, sickly, too sweet • *sugary tea*

2 = sentimental, sloppy *(informal)*, mushy *(informal)*, touching, emotional, romantic, tender, pathetic, nostalgic, tearful, corny *(slang)*, maudlin, simpering, weepy *(informal)*, slushy *(informal)*, mawkish, tear-jerking *(informal)*, drippy *(informal)*, schmaltzy *(slang)*, icky *(informal)*, gushy *(informal)*, soft-hearted, overemotional, dewy-eyed, three-hankie *(informal)* • *The programme seemed false and sugary.*

suggest 1 = recommend, propose, advise, move, table, counsel, advocate, prescribe, put forward, propound, offer a suggestion • *I suggest you ask him some specific questions about his past.*

2 = indicate, show, demonstrate, give the impression, lead you to believe • *The figures suggest that their success is conditional on this restriction.*

SUGARS

EDIBLE SUGARS

beet sugar, caster sugar, granulated sugar, maple sugar, powdered sugar, white sugar, brown sugar, crystallized sugar, icing sugar, muscovado sugar, panocha, cane sugar, demerara sugar, jaggery, palm sugar, refined sugar

BIOCHEMICAL SUGARS

aldose, grape sugar, glucose, maltose, ribose, xylose *or* wood sugar, arabinose, fructose *or* laevulose, invert sugar, mannose, sorbose, deoxyribose, lactose *or* milk sugar, raffinose, trehalose, dextrose *or* galactose, rhamnose, triose

3 = **hint at**, imply, insinuate, intimate, get at, drive at *(informal)* • *What exactly are you suggesting?*
4 = **bring to mind**, evoke, remind you of, smack of, connote, make you think of, put you in mind of • *Its hairy body suggests a mammal.*

suggestion 1 = **recommendation**, proposal, proposition, plan, motion, submission • *I have lots of suggestions for the park's future.*
2 = **hint**, implication, insinuation, intimation • *There is absolutely no suggestion of any mainstream political party involvement.*
3 = **trace**, touch, hint, shadow, impression, breath, indication, whisper, suspicion, ghost, intimation • *that fashionably faint suggestion of a tan*

suggestive AS AN ADJECTIVE = **smutty**, rude, indecent, improper, blue, provocative, spicy *(informal)*, racy, unseemly, titillating, risqué, bawdy, prurient, off colour, ribald, immodest, indelicate • *A female employee claimed he made suggestive remarks to her.*
▸ IN PHRASES: **suggestive of** = **reminiscent of**, indicative of, redolent of, evocative of • *These headaches were most suggestive of raised blood pressure.*

suicide = **taking your own life**, self-destruction, ending it all *(informal)*, self-immolation, self-murder, self-slaughter, topping yourself *(informal)* • *a case of attempted suicide*
▸ RELATED MANIA: autophonomania

QUOTATIONS

Suicide is confession
[Daniel Webster]

It is cowardice to commit suicide
[Napoleon Bonaparte]

A suicide kills two people, Maggie, that's what it's for!
[Arthur Miller *After the Fall*]

suit AS A NOUN 1 = **outfit**, costume, ensemble, dress, clothing, habit • *a smart suit and tie*
2 = **lawsuit**, case, trial, proceeding, cause, action, prosecution, industrial tribunal • *The judge dismissed the suit.*
▸ AS A VERB 1 = **be acceptable to**, please, satisfy, do, answer, gratify • *They will only release information if it suits them.*
2 = **agree with**, become, match, go with, correspond with, conform to, befit, harmonize with • *I don't think a sedentary life would altogether suit me.*
3 = **look attractive on**, become, flatter, look good on, enhance the appearance of, show to advantage • *Green suits you.*
4 = **adjust**, adapt, modify, fit, fashion, proportion, accommodate, tailor, customize • *'I'm off.' He suited the action to the word and left.*
▸ IN PHRASES: **follow suit** = **copy someone**, emulate someone, accord with someone, take your cue from someone, run with the herd • *The Dutch seem set to follow suit.*
▹ *See panel* **Suits**

suitability = **appropriateness**, fitness, rightness, aptness • *information on the suitability of a product for use in the home*

suitable 1 = **appropriate**, right, fitting, fit, suited, acceptable, becoming, correct, satisfactory, apt, befitting • *She had no other dress suitable for the occasion.*
OPPOSITES: inappropriate, incorrect, unfitting
2 = **seemly**, fitting, becoming, due, proper, correct • *Was it really suitable behaviour for someone who wants to be taken seriously?*
OPPOSITES: jarring, unseemly, discordant
3 = **suited**, appropriate, in keeping with, in character, cut out for • *a resort where the slopes are more suitable for young children*
OPPOSITES: out of character, out of keeping
4 = **pertinent**, relevant, applicable, fitting, appropriate, to the point, apt, apposite, germane • *Give a few people an idea of suitable questions to ask.*
OPPOSITES: irrelevant, inapposite
5 = **convenient**, timely, appropriate, well-timed, opportune, commodious • *He could think of no less suitable moment to mention the idea.*
OPPOSITES: inopportune

suitably 1 = **appropriately**, properly, satisfactorily, acceptably • *Unfortunately I'm not suitably dressed for gardening.*
2 = **fittingly**, aptly • *Her exit seemed suitably dramatic.*

suitcase = **case**, bag, trunk, holdall, travel bag, valise • *It did not take Andrew long to pack a suitcase.*

suite 1 = **rooms**, apartment, set of rooms, living quarters • *a suite at the Paris Hilton*
2 = **set**, series, collection • *We will run a suite of checks.*
3 = **attendants**, escorts, entourage, train, followers, retainers, retinue • *Fox and his suite sat there, looking uncertain.*

SUITS

boiler suit, judogi, pyjamas *or (U.S.)* pajamas, single-breasted suit, three-piece suit, buckskins, jump suit, ski suit, tracksuit, catsuit, lounge suit, romper suit, slack suit, trouser suit *or (U.S. & Canad.)* pant suit, double-breasted suit, Mao suit, safari suit, sunsuit, dress suit, morning dress, sailor suit, spacesuit, evening dress, penguin suit, scrubs, sweat suit *or* sweats, wet suit, G-suit *or* anti-G suit, playsuit, shell suit, swimsuit, zoot suit

suitor 1 = **admirer**, young man, beau, follower *(obsolete)*, swain *(archaic)*, wooer • *My mother had a suitor who adored her.*
2 = **bidder**, customer, candidate, applicant • *The company was making little progress in trying to find a suitor.*

sulk = **be sullen**, brood, be in a huff, pout, be put out, have the hump *(Brit. informal)* • *He turned his back and sulked.*

sulky = **huffy**, sullen, petulant, cross, put out, moody, perverse, disgruntled, aloof, resentful, vexed, churlish, morose, querulous, ill-humoured, in the sulks • *a sulky adolescent*

sullen = **morose**, cross, moody, sour, gloomy, brooding, dour, surly, glowering, sulky, unsociable, out of humour • *The offenders lapsed into a sullen silence.*
OPPOSITES: cheerful, cheery, good-humoured

sully 1 = **dishonour**, ruin, disgrace, besmirch, smirch • *Reputations are easily sullied and business lost.*
2 = **defile**, dirty, stain, spot, spoil, contaminate, pollute, taint, tarnish, blemish, befoul • *I felt loath to sully the gleaming brass knocker by handling it.*

sulphur
▸ RELATED ADJECTIVE: thionic

sultry 1 = **humid**, close, hot, sticky, stifling, oppressive, stuffy, sweltering, muggy • *The climax came one sultry August evening.*
OPPOSITES: fresh, cool, refreshing
2 = **seductive**, sexy *(informal)*, sensual, voluptuous, passionate, erotic, provocative, amorous, come-hither *(informal)* • *a dark-haired sultry woman*

sum AS A NOUN 1 = **amount**, quantity, volume • *Large sums of money were lost.*
2 = **calculation**, figures, arithmetic, problem, numbers, reckonings, mathematics, maths *(Brit. informal)*, tally, math *(U.S. informal)*, arithmetical problem • *I can't do my sums.*
3 = **total**, aggregate, tally, entirety, sum total • *The sum of all the angles of a triangle is 180 degrees.*
4 = **totality**, whole, aggregate, entirety, beginning and end, summation • *The sum of evidence points to the crime resting on them.*
▸ IN PHRASES: **in sum** = **in brief**, in short, in a word, in a nutshell • *It is a situation, in sum, devoid of logic.*
sum something *or* **someone up** = **size up**, estimate *(informal)*, get the measure of, form an opinion of • *My mother probably summed her up better than I ever could.*
sum something up = **summarize**, express concisely, express pithily, express in a word • *He summed his weakness up in one word: 'Disastrous.'*
sum up = **summarize**, review, recapitulate, close, conclude, put something in a nutshell • *When the judge summed up it was clear he wanted a guilty verdict.*

summarily = **immediately**, promptly, swiftly, on the spot, speedily, without delay, arbitrarily, at short notice, forthwith, expeditiously, peremptorily, without wasting words • *Several detainees had been summarily executed.*

summarize = **sum up**, recap, review, outline, condense, encapsulate, epitomize, abridge, précis, recapitulate, give a rundown of, put in a nutshell, give the main points of • *To summarize, this is a clever approach to a common problem.*

summary AS A NOUN = **synopsis**, résumé, précis, recapitulation, review, outline, extract, essence, abstract, summing-up, digest, epitome, rundown, compendium, abridgment • *Here's a summary of the day's news.*
▸ AS AN ADJECTIVE 1 = **hasty**, cursory, perfunctory, arbitrary • *The four men were killed after a summary trial.*
2 = **concise**, brief, compact, condensed, laconic, succinct, pithy, compendious • *a summary profit and loss statement*

summer
▸ RELATED ADJECTIVE: aestival or estival

summit 1 = **meeting**, talks, conference, discussion, negotiation, dialogue • *a NATO summit held in Rome*
2 = **peak**, top, tip, pinnacle, apex, head, crown, crest • *the first man to reach the summit of Mount Everest*
OPPOSITES: base, foot, bottom
3 = **height**, pinnacle, culmination, peak, high point, zenith, acme, crowning point • *This is just a molehill on the way to the summit of her ambitions.*
OPPOSITES: depths, nadir, lowest point

summon 1 = **send for**, call, bid, invite, rally, assemble, convene, call together, convoke • *Howe summoned a doctor and hurried over.*
2 *often with* **up** = **gather**, muster, draw on, invoke, mobilize, call into action • *We couldn't even summon up the energy to open the envelope.*

summons AS A NOUN 1 = **order**, call, command, request, instruction, invitation, directive, edict, dictum • *a summons to the palace*
2 = **court order**, warrant, writ, subpoena, arraignment • *She had received a summons to appear in court.*
▸ AS A VERB = **serve with a writ**, summon, subpoena, cite, serve with a summons • *The men were summonsed to appear before Hove magistrates.*

sumptuous = **luxurious**, rich, grand, expensive, superb, magnificent, costly, splendid, posh *(informal, chiefly Brit.)*, gorgeous, lavish, extravagant, plush *(informal)*, opulent, palatial, ritzy *(slang)*, de luxe, splendiferous *(facetious)* • *a sumptuous feast*
OPPOSITES: mean, basic, plain

sun AS A NOUN 1 = **Sol** *(Roman myth)*, Helios *(Greek myth)*, Phoebus *(Greek myth)*, daystar *(poetic)*, eye of heaven, Phoebus Apollo *(Greek myth)* • *The sun was now high in the southern sky.*
2 = **sunshine**, sunlight, daylight, light, rays, warmth • *They were trying to soak up the sun.*
▸ IN PHRASES: **sun yourself** = **sunbathe**, tan, bask • *She was last seen sunning herself in a riverside park.*
▸ RELATED ADJECTIVE: solar
▸ RELATED MANIA: heliomania

sunbathe = **sun yourself**, tan, bask, get a tan • *Franklin swam and sunbathed at the pool every morning.*

sunburnt 1 = **burnt**, red, peeling, scarlet, ruddy, burnt to a crisp, like a lobster • *A badly sunburnt face or back is extremely painful.*
2 = **tanned**, brown, bronzed, brown as a berry • *Mr Cooper looked fit and sunburnt*

Sunday = **the Sabbath**, the Lord's day • *I thought we might go for a drive on Sunday.*

sundry = **various**, several, varied, assorted, some, different, divers *(archaic)*, miscellaneous • *She could ring for food and drink, laundry and sundry services.*

sunk = **ruined**, lost, finished, done for *(informal)*, on the rocks, dead in the water *(informal)*, all washed up *(informal)*, up the creek without a paddle *(informal)* • *Without him we'd all be well and truly sunk.*

sunken 1 = **submerged**, immersed, submersed • *Try diving for sunken treasure.*
2 = **lowered**, buried, depressed, recessed, below ground, at a lower level • *Steps led down to the sunken bath.*
3 = **hollow**, drawn, haggard, hollowed, concave • *an elderly man with sunken cheeks*

sunless = **cloudy**, grey, gloomy, hazy, overcast, dark • *The day dawned sunless and with a low cloud base.*

sunlight = **sunshine**, light, sun, daylight, natural light, sun's rays • *I saw her sitting at a window table, bathed in sunlight.*

sunny 1 = **bright**, clear, fine, brilliant, radiant, luminous, sunlit, summery, unclouded, sunshiny, without a cloud in the sky • *The weather was surprisingly warm and sunny.*
OPPOSITES: wet, dull, gloomy
2 = **cheerful**, happy, cheery, smiling, beaming, pleasant, optimistic, buoyant, joyful, genial, chirpy *(informal)*, blithe,

light-hearted • *The staff wear big sunny smiles.*
OPPOSITES: miserable, gloomy, morbid

sunrise = **dawn**, daybreak, break of day, daylight, aurora *(poetic)*, sunup, cockcrow, dayspring *(poetic)* • *The rain began towards sunrise.*

sunset = **nightfall**, dusk, sundown, eventide, gloaming *(Scot. poetic)*, close of (the) day • *The dance ends at sunset.*
▸ **RELATED ADJECTIVE:** acronychal or acronycal or acronical *(US)*

super = **excellent**, wonderful, marvellous, mean *(slang)*, topping *(Brit. slang)*, cracking *(Brit. informal)*, crucial *(slang)*, outstanding, smashing *(informal)*, superb, magnificent, glorious, terrific *(informal)*, sensational *(informal)*, mega *(slang)*, sovereign, awesome *(slang)*, def *(slang)*, top-notch *(informal)*, brill *(informal)*, incomparable, out of this world *(informal)*, peerless, matchless, boffo *(slang)*, jim-dandy *(slang)*, chillin' *(U.S. slang)*, booshit *(Austral. slang)*, exo *(Austral. slang)*, sik *(Austral. slang)*, rad *(informal)*, phat *(slang)*, schmick *(Austral. informal)* • *We had a super time.*

superannuated = **obsolete**, antiquated, outmoded, old, aged, past it *(informal)*, defunct, decrepit • *the superannuated idealism of the sixties*

superb 1 = **splendid**, excellent, magnificent, topping *(Brit. slang)*, fine, choice, grand, superior, divine, marvellous, gorgeous, mega *(slang)*, awesome *(slang)*, world-class, exquisite, breathtaking, first-rate, superlative, unrivalled, brill *(informal)*, bodacious *(slang, chiefly U.S.)*, boffo *(slang)*, splendiferous *(facetious)*, of the first water, chillin' *(U.S. slang)*, booshit *(Austral. slang)*, exo *(Austral. slang)*, sik *(Austral. slang)*, rad *(informal)*, phat *(slang)*, schmick *(Austral. informal)*, beaut *(informal)*, barrie *(Scot. slang)*, belting *(Brit. slang)*, pearler *(Austral. slang)* • *a superb 18-hole golf course*
OPPOSITES: bad, terrible, inferior
2 = **magnificent**, superior, marvellous, exquisite, breathtaking, admirable, superlative, unrivalled, splendiferous *(facetious)* • *With superb skill he managed to make a perfect landing.*
OPPOSITES: bad, terrible, awful

supercilious = **scornful**, arrogant, contemptuous, disdainful, lordly, proud, lofty, stuck-up *(informal)*, patronizing, condescending, imperious, overbearing, snooty *(informal)*, haughty, high and mighty *(informal)*, vainglorious, toffee-nosed *(slang, chiefly Brit.)*, hoity-toity *(informal)*, uppish *(Brit. informal)* • *His manner is supercilious and arrogant.*
OPPOSITES: modest, humble

superficial 1 = **shallow**, frivolous, empty-headed, empty, silly, lightweight, trivial • *a superficial yuppie with no intellect whatsoever*
OPPOSITES: serious, earnest
2 = **hasty**, cursory, perfunctory, passing, nodding, hurried, casual, sketchy, facile, desultory, slapdash, inattentive • *He only gave it a superficial glance through.*
OPPOSITES: detailed, comprehensive, thorough
3 = **slight**, surface, external, cosmetic, on the surface, exterior, peripheral, skin-deep • *It may well look different but the changes are only superficial.*
OPPOSITES: deep, profound

superficiality = **shallowness**, lack of depth, lack of substance, emptiness, triviality • *the superficiality of the judgements we make when we first meet people*

superficially = **at first glance**, apparently, on the surface, ostensibly, externally, at face value, to the casual eye • *Many of these killers are glib and superficially charming.*

superfluity = **excess**, surplus, surfeit, redundancy, plethora, exuberance, glut, superabundance • *a superfluity of five-star hotels*

superfluous = **excess**, surplus, redundant, remaining, extra, spare, excessive, unnecessary, in excess, needless, left over, on your hands, surplus to requirements, uncalled-for, unneeded, residuary, supernumerary, superabundant, pleonastic *(Rhetoric)*, unrequired, supererogatory • *My presence at the afternoon's proceedings was superflous.*
OPPOSITES: necessary, essential, vital

superhuman = **heroic**, phenomenal, prodigious, stupendous, herculean • *Officers were terrified of his superhuman strength.*

superintend = **supervise**, run, oversee, control, manage, direct, handle, look after, overlook, administer, inspect • *During the interval, he superintended a prize draw.*

superintendent 1 = **supervisor**, director, manager, chief, governor, inspector, administrator, conductor, controller, overseer • *He became superintendent of the bank's East African branches.*
2 = **warden**, caretaker, curator, keeper, porter, custodian, watchman, janitor, concierge • *He lost his job as a building superintendent.*

superior **AS AN ADJECTIVE** 1 = **better**, higher, greater, grander, preferred, prevailing, paramount, surpassing, more advanced, predominant, unrivalled, more extensive, more skilful, more expert, a cut above *(informal)*, streets ahead *(informal)*, running rings around *(informal)* • *a woman greatly superior to her husband in education*
OPPOSITES: worse, inferior, not as good
2 = **first-class**, excellent, first-rate, good, fine, choice, exclusive, distinguished, exceptional, world-class, good quality, admirable, high-class, high calibre, de luxe, of the first order, booshit *(Austral. slang)*, exo *(Austral. slang)*, sik *(Austral. slang)*, rad *(informal)*, phat *(slang)*, schmick *(Austral. informal)* • *He's got a superior car, and it's easy to win races that way.*
OPPOSITES: average, ordinary, inferior
3 = **higher-ranking**, senior, higher-level, upper-level • *negotiations between mutineers and their superior officers*
4 = **supercilious**, patronizing, condescending, haughty, disdainful, lordly, lofty, airy, pretentious, stuck-up *(informal)*, snobbish, on your high horse *(informal)* • *Finch gave a superior smile.*
▸ **AS A NOUN** = **boss**, senior, director, manager, chief *(informal)*, principal, supervisor, baas *(S. African)*, sherang *(Austral. & N.Z.)* • *my immediate superior*
OPPOSITES: junior, subordinate, inferior

superiority = **supremacy**, lead, advantage, excellence, prevalence, ascendancy, pre-eminence, preponderance, predominance • *Our army has air superiority.*

> **QUOTATIONS**
> Superiority is always detested
> [Baltasar Gracián *The Art of Worldly Wisdom*]

superlative = **supreme**, excellent, outstanding, highest, greatest, crack *(slang)*, magnificent, surpassing, consummate, stellar *(informal)*, unparalleled, transcendent, unrivalled, peerless, unsurpassed, matchless, of the highest order, of the first water • *Some superlative wines are made in this region.*
OPPOSITES: poor, average, ordinary

supermarket = **hypermarket**, superstore, cash and carry • *Most of us do our food shopping in the supermarket.*

supernatural = **paranormal**, mysterious, unearthly, uncanny, dark, hidden, ghostly, psychic, phantom, abnormal, mystic, miraculous, unnatural, occult, spectral, preternatural, supranatural • *evil spirits who looked like humans and possessed supernatural powers*

> **QUOTATIONS**
> There are more things in Heaven and earth, Horatio,
> Than are dreamt of in your philosophy
> [William Shakespeare *Hamlet*]

▹ *See panel* **The supernatural**

supersede = **replace**, displace, usurp, supplant, remove, take over, oust, take the place of, fill *or* step into (someone's) boots

THE SUPERNATURAL

People with supernatural powers

archimage, channeller, clairaudient, clairvoyant, conjurer, diviner, dowser, enchanter, enchantress, exorcist, fortune-teller, hag, hex, mage, magician, magus, medium, necromancer, rainmaker, seer, shaman, siren, sorcerer, sorceress, spaewife *(Scot.)*, superhero, thaumaturge, warlock, water diviner, water witch, white witch, witch, witch doctor, witch master, wizard

Supernatural creatures

angel, banshee, brownie, demon, devil, dwarf, dybbuk, elf, fairy, fairy godmother, familiar, fay, genie, ghost, ghoul, giant, gnome, goblin, god *or* goddess, golem, gremlin, guardian angel, hobgoblin, imp, incubus, jinni, kachina, kelpie, lamia, leprechaun, little people *or* folk, monster, ogre, peri, phantom, pixie, poltergeist, sandman, selkie *(Scot.)*, spectre, sprite, succubus, sylph, troll, vampire, werewolf *or* lycanthrope, wraith, zombie

Supernatural terms

abracadabra, amulet, apport, aura, black magic *or* the Black Art, charm, clairaudience, clairvoyance, cryptaesthesia, curse, divination, ectoplasm, evil eye, exorcism, extrasensory perception *or* ESP, fate, fetish, grigri, grimoire, hex, hoodoo, incantation, invultuation, Indian sign, jinx, juju, kismet, levitation, magic circle, magic spell, magic wand, mojo, necromancy, obi *or* obeah, Ouija *(trademark)*, parapsychology, pentagram, philtre, portent, possession, premonition, reincarnation, rune, seance, second sight, sigil, sixth sense, spell, talisman, talking in tongues, xenoglossia, *or* xenoglossy, telaesthesia, telegnosis, telekinesis *or* psychokinesis, telepathy, voodoo, wand, white magic, witching hour

• *Madness follows, and the birth of a son who will supersede him.*

superstar = **celebrity**, star, big name, face *(informal)*, name, personality, lion, dignitary, luminary, bigwig *(informal)*, celeb *(informal)*, big shot *(informal)*, personage, megastar *(informal)*, V.I.P. • *a Hollywood superstar*

superstition 1 = **unfounded belief** • *Fortune-telling is an art surrounded by superstition.*
2 = **myth**, story, belief, legend, old wives' tale, notion • *The phantom of the merry-go-round is just a local superstition.*

QUOTATIONS
Superstition is the religion of feeble minds
[Edmund Burke *Reflections on the Revolution in France*]
Superstition is the poetry of life
[Johann Wolfgang von Goethe *Maximen und Reflexionen*]

superstitious 1 = **prone to superstition**, naive, gullible • *Jean was superstitious and believed that green brought bad luck.*
2 = **irrational**, unfounded, groundless, unprovable, mythical • *A wave of superstitious fear spread among the townspeople.*

supervise 1 = **observe**, guide, monitor, oversee, keep an eye on • *He supervised and trained more than 400 volunteers.*
2 = **oversee**, run, manage, control, direct, handle, conduct, look after, be responsible for, administer, inspect, preside over, keep an eye on, be on duty at, superintend, have *or* be in charge of • *One of his jobs was supervising the dining room.*

supervision = **superintendence**, direction, instruction, control, charge, care, management, administration, guidance, surveillance, oversight, auspices, stewardship • *First-time licence holders have to work under supervision.*

supervisor = **boss** *(informal)*, manager, superintendent, chief, inspector, administrator, steward, gaffer *(informal, chiefly Brit.)*, foreman, overseer, baas *(S. African)* • *a full-time job as a supervisor at a factory*

supervisory = **managerial**, administrative, overseeing, superintendent, executive • *staff with a minor supervisory role*

supine 1 = **flat on your back**, flat, horizontal, recumbent • *a statue of a supine dog*
OPPOSITES: prone, prostrate, lying on your face
2 = **lethargic**, passive, lazy, idle, indifferent, careless, sluggish, negligent, inert, languid, uninterested, apathetic, lymphatic, listless, indolent, heedless, torpid, slothful, spiritless • *a willing and supine executive*

supper 1 = **dinner**, evening meal, main meal • *Some guests like to dress for supper.*
2 = **evening snack**, bite, bite to eat • *We can have a light supper later on.*

supplant = **replace**, oust, displace, supersede, remove, take over, undermine, overthrow, unseat, take the place of • *He may be supplanted by a younger man.*

supple 1 = **pliant**, flexible, pliable, plastic, bending, elastic, rubbery, bendable, stretchable • *The leather is supple and sturdy enough to last for years.*
OPPOSITES: firm, stiff, rigid
2 = **flexible**, lithe, limber, lissom(e), loose-limbed • *Paul was incredibly supple and strong.*
OPPOSITES: stiff, awkward, inflexible

supplement AS A VERB = **add to**, reinforce, complement, augment, extend, top up, fill out • *I suggest supplementing your diet with vitamins E and A.*
▸ AS A NOUN 1 = **pull-out**, insert, magazine section, added feature, special feature section • *a special supplement to a monthly financial magazine*
2 = **appendix**, sequel, add-on, complement, postscript, addendum, codicil • *the supplement to the Encyclopedia Britannica*
3 = **addition**, extra, surcharge • *The single room supplement is £11 a night.*

supplementary = **additional**, extra, complementary, accompanying, secondary, auxiliary, add-on, supplemental, ancillary • *the question of whether or not we need to take supplementary vitamins*

supplication = **plea**, appeal, prayer, pleading, request, petition, invocation, solicitation, entreaty • *He raised his arms in a gesture of supplication.*

supply AS A VERB 1 = **provide**, give, furnish, produce, stock, store, grant, afford, contribute, yield, come up with, outfit, endow, purvey, victual • *an agreement not to supply chemical weapons to these countries*

2 = **furnish**, provide, equip, serve, endow • *a pipeline which will supply the city with natural gas*

3 = **meet**, provide for, fill, satisfy, fulfil, be adequate for, cater to *or* for • *a society that looks to the government to supply their needs*

▸ AS A NOUN 1 = **store**, fund, stock, source, reserve, quantity, reservoir, stockpile, hoard, cache • *The brain requires a constant supply of oxygen.*

2 = **supplying**, provision, distribution, sending out, furnishing, dissemination • *Prices have changed according to supply and demand.*

▸ AS A PLURAL NOUN = **provisions**, necessities, stores, food, materials, items, equipment, rations, foodstuff, provender • *The country's only supplies are those it can import by lorry.*

support AS A VERB 1 = **help**, back, champion, second, aid, forward, encourage, defend, promote, take (someone's) part, strengthen, assist, advocate, uphold, side with, go along with, stand up for, espouse, stand behind, hold (someone's) hand, stick up for *(informal)*, succour, buoy up, boost (someone's) morale, take up the cudgels for, be a source of strength to • *He supported the hardworking people.*
OPPOSITES: oppose, undermine, hinder

2 = **provide for**, maintain, look after, keep, fund, finance, sustain, foster, take care of, subsidize • *I have children to support, and a home to be maintained.*
OPPOSITES: live off, sponge off

3 = **bear out**, confirm, verify, substantiate, corroborate, document, endorse, attest to, authenticate, lend credence to • *The evidence does not support the argument.*
OPPOSITES: deny, contradict, refute

4 = **bear**, hold up, carry, sustain, prop (up), reinforce, hold, brace, uphold, bolster, underpin, shore up, buttress • *the thick wooden posts that supported the ceiling*

5 = **follow**, back, champion, encourage, favour, advocate, side with, espouse • *I've supported Newcastle all my miserable life.*

▸ AS A NOUN 1 = **furtherance**, backing, promotion, championship, approval, assistance, encouragement, espousal • *They are prepared to resort to violence in support of their views.*

2 = **help**, protection, comfort, friendship, assistance, blessing, loyalty, patronage, moral support, succour • *We hope to continue to have her close support and friendship.*
OPPOSITES: opposition, undermining, rejection

3 = **aid**, help, benefits, relief, assistance • *the EC's proposal to cut agricultural support*

4 = **prop**, post, foundation, back, lining, stay, shore, brace, pillar, underpinning, stanchion, stiffener, abutment • *Rats had been gnawing at the supports of the house.*

5 = **supporter**, prop, mainstay, tower of strength, second, stay, backer, backbone, comforter • *Andrew is terrific. He's been such a support to me.*
OPPOSITES: antagonist

6 = **upkeep**, maintenance, keep, livelihood, subsistence, sustenance • *He failed to send child support.*

supporter = **follower**, fan, advocate, friend, champion, ally, defender, sponsor, patron, helper, protagonist, adherent, henchman, apologist, upholder, well-wisher • *a major supporter of the 1986 tax reform plan*
OPPOSITES: rival, opponent, adversary

supportive = **helpful**, caring, encouraging, understanding, reassuring, sympathetic • *They were always supportive of each other.*
▸ RELATED PREFIX: pro-

suppose 1 = **imagine**, believe, consider, conclude, fancy, conceive, conjecture, postulate, hypothesize • *Where do you suppose he's got to?*

2 = **think**, imagine, expect, judge, assume, guess *(informal, chiefly U.S. & Canad.)*, calculate *(U.S. dialect)*, presume, take for granted, infer, conjecture, surmise, dare say, opine, presuppose, take as read • *The problem was more complex than he supposed.*

supposed 1 *usually with* **to** = **meant**, expected, required, obliged • *He produced a handwritten note of nine men he was supposed to kill.*

2 = **presumed**, alleged, professed, reputed, accepted, assumed, rumoured, hypothetical, putative, presupposed • *What is it his son is supposed to have said?*

supposedly = **presumably**, allegedly, ostensibly, theoretically, by all accounts, purportedly, avowedly, hypothetically, at a guess, professedly • *He was more of a victim than any of the women he supposedly offended.*
OPPOSITES: really, actually, in fact

supposition = **belief**, idea, notion, view, theory, speculation, assumption, hypothesis, presumption, conjecture, postulate, surmise, guesswork • *There's a popular supposition that we're publicly funded.*

suppress 1 = **stamp out**, stop, check, crush, conquer, overthrow, subdue, put an end to, overpower, quash, crack down on, quell, extinguish, clamp down on, snuff out, quench, beat down, trample on, drive underground • *drug traffickers who flourish despite attempts to suppress them*
OPPOSITES: encourage, promote, stimulate

2 = **check**, inhibit, subdue, stop, quell, quench • *strong evidence that ultraviolet light can suppress immune responses*

3 = **restrain**, cover up, withhold, stifle, contain, silence, conceal, curb, repress, smother, keep secret, muffle, muzzle, hold in check, hold in *or* back • *Liz thought of Barry and suppressed a smile.*

4 = **conceal**, hide, keep secret, hush up, censor, stonewall, sweep under the carpet, draw a veil over, keep silent about, keep dark, keep under your hat *(informal)* • *At no time did they try to persuade me to suppress the information.*

suppression 1 = **elimination**, crushing, crackdown, check, extinction, prohibition, quashing, dissolution, termination, clampdown • *They were imprisoned after the suppression of pro-democracy protests.*

2 = **inhibition**, blocking, checking, restriction, restraint, smothering • *suppression of the immune system*

3 = **concealment**, covering, hiding, disguising, camouflage • *A mother's suppression of her own feelings can cause problems.*

4 = **hiding**, censorship, hushing up, stonewalling • *suppression of official documents*

QUOTATIONS

Everybody knows there is no fineness or accuracy of suppression: if you hold down one thing, you hold down the adjoining

[Saul Bellow *The Adventures of Augie March*]

supremacy = **domination**, dominance, ascendancy, sovereignty, sway, lordship, mastery, dominion, primacy, pre-eminence, predominance, supreme power, absolute rule, paramountcy • *The president asserted his supremacy over the prime minister.*

supreme 1 = **paramount**, surpassing, superlative, prevailing, sovereign, predominant, incomparable, mother of all *(informal)*, unsurpassed, matchless • *The lady conspired to seize supreme power.*
OPPOSITES: lowest, least, poorest

2 = **chief**, leading, principal, first, highest, head, top, prime, cardinal, foremost, pre-eminent, peerless • *He proposes to make himself the supreme overlord.*
OPPOSITES: lowest, most minor, most inferior
3 = **ultimate**, highest, greatest, utmost, final, crowning, extreme, culminating • *My oldest son made the supreme sacrifice in Vietnam*

supremo = **head**, leader, boss *(informal)*, director, master, governor, commander, principal, ruler, baas *(S. African)* • *an economics supremo*

sure AS AN ADJECTIVE 1 = **certain**, positive, clear, decided, convinced, persuaded, confident, satisfied, assured, definite, free from doubt • *She was no longer sure how she felt about him.*
OPPOSITES: uncertain, doubtful, unsure
2 = **inevitable**, guaranteed, bound, assured, in the bag *(slang)*, inescapable, irrevocable, ineluctable, nailed-on *(slang)* • *Another victory is now sure.*
OPPOSITES: unsure, touch-and-go
3 = **reliable**, accurate, dependable, effective, precise, honest, unmistakable, undoubted, undeniable, trustworthy, never-failing, trusty, foolproof, infallible, indisputable, sure-fire *(informal)*, unerring, well-proven, unfailing, tried and true • *a sure sign of rain*
OPPOSITES: unreliable, untrustworthy, undependable
4 = **secure**, firm, steady, fast, safe, confident, solid, stable, unhesitating, unfaltering • *A doctor's sure hands may perform surgery.*
▸ AS AN INTERJECTION = **certainly**, of course, OK *or* okay *(informal)*, absolutely, you bet *(informal)*, sure thing *(informal)*, yes, all right • *Yeah, sure, you can have the key.*
▸ IN PHRASES: **be sure to** = **remember to**, take care to, see that you, be careful to, don't forget to, make sure to, mind that you • *Be sure to read about how mozzarella is made.*
for sure = **definitely**, absolutely, without question, surely, certainly, beyond any doubt • *We still don't know what happened for sure.*
make sure = **check**, ensure, confirm, make certain, verify • *Before you cut the cloth, make sure the pattern matches up.*
sure enough = **as expected**, as anticipated • *Sure enough, it was delicious.*
sure of yourself = **confident**, self-confident, self-assured, can-do *(informal)*, assured, bold, fearless, self-reliant, dauntless • *I'd never seen him like this, so sure of himself, so in command.*

surely 1 = **it must be the case that**, without question, assuredly • *If I can accept this situation, surely you can?*
2 = **undoubtedly**, certainly, definitely, inevitably, doubtless, for certain, without doubt, unquestionably, inexorably, come what may, without fail, indubitably, doubtlessly, beyond the shadow of a doubt • *He knew that under the surgeon's knife he would surely die.*
3 = **steadily**, determinedly, doggedly, assuredly, unswervingly, unfalteringly • *He's recovering, slowly but surely.*

surety 1 = **security**, guarantee, deposit, insurance, bond, safety, pledge, bail, warranty, indemnity • *a surety of £2,500*
2 = **guarantor**, sponsor, hostage, bondsman, mortgagor • *I agreed to stand surety for Arthur to be bailed out.*

surface AS A NOUN 1 = **covering**, face, exterior, side, top, skin, plane, facet, veneer, superficies *(rare)* • *The road surface had started breaking up.*
2 = **worktop**, top, table, counter, working top • *It can simply be left on the work surface.*
3 = **façade**, outward appearance, superficial appearance • *A much wider controversy was bubbling under the surface.*
▸ AS A MODIFIER = **superficial**, external, outward, cosmetic, exterior, skin-deep • *Doctors believed it was just a surface wound.*
▸ AS A VERB 1 = **emerge**, rise, appear, come up, come to the surface • *He surfaced, gasping for air.*
2 = **appear**, emerge, arise, come to light, crop up *(informal)*, transpire, materialize • *The emotions will surface at some point in life.*
3 = **get up**, rise, awaken, get out of bed, waken, emerge • *What time do you surface?*
▸ IN PHRASES: **on the surface** = **at first glance**, apparently, outwardly, seemingly, ostensibly, superficially, to all appearances, to the casual eye • *On the surface the elections appear to be democratic.*

surfeit = **excess**, plethora, glut, satiety, overindulgence, superabundance, superfluity • *Rationing had put an end to a surfeit of biscuits long ago.*
OPPOSITES: want, lack, shortage

surge AS A NOUN 1 = **rush**, rise, growth, boost, flood, escalation, upsurge, upswing, sudden increase, uprush • *a new surge of interest in Dylan's work*
2 = **flow**, wave, rush, stream, roller, breaker, gush, upsurge, outpouring, efflux, uprush • *The bridge was destroyed in a tidal surge during a storm.*
3 = **tide**, roll, rolling, swell, swirling, billowing • *the beating and surge of the sea*
4 = **rush**, wave, storm, outburst, torrent, eruption • *He was overcome by a sudden surge of jealousy.*
▸ AS A VERB 1 = **increase**, rise, grow, jump, boost, leap, escalate • *Surging imports will add to the demand for hard currency.*
2 = **rush**, pour, stream, rise, crowd, swell, spill, swarm, seethe, gush, well forth • *The crowd surged out from the church.*
3 = **roll**, rush, billow, heave, swirl, eddy, undulate • *Fish and seaweed rose, caught motionless in the surging water.*
4 = **sweep**, rush, storm, blaze, erupt • *Panic surged through her.*

surgery = **operation**, treatment • *His father had just recovered from heart surgery.*

surly = **ill-tempered**, cross, churlish, crabbed, perverse, crusty, sullen, gruff, bearish, sulky, morose, brusque, testy, grouchy *(informal)*, curmudgeonly, ungracious, uncivil, shrewish • *He behaves in a surly and rude manner towards me.*
OPPOSITES: happy, pleasant, cheerful

surmise AS A VERB = **guess**, suppose, imagine, presume, consider, suspect, conclude, fancy, speculate, infer, deduce, come to the conclusion, conjecture, opine, hazard a guess • *He surmised that he had discovered one of the illegal streets.*
▸ AS A NOUN = **guess**, speculation, assumption, thought, idea, conclusion, notion, suspicion, hypothesis, deduction, inference, presumption, conjecture, supposition • *His surmise proved correct.*

surmount 1 = **overcome**, master, conquer, pass, exceed, surpass, overpower, triumph over, vanquish, prevail over • *I realised I had to surmount the language barrier.*
2 = **cap**, top, crown, tip • *The mountain is surmounted by a huge black castle.*

surname = **family name**, last name, patronymic, matronymic • *She'd never known his surname.*

surpass = **outdo**, top, beat, best, cap *(informal)*, exceed, eclipse, overshadow, excel, transcend, outstrip, outshine, tower above, go one better than *(informal)*, put in the shade • *He was determined to surpass the achievements of his older brothers.*

surpassing = **supreme**, extraordinary, outstanding, exceptional, rare, phenomenal, stellar *(informal)*, transcendent, unrivalled, incomparable, matchless • *The flower has large, hanging blooms of surpassing beauty.*

surplus AS A NOUN = **excess**, surfeit, superabundance, superfluity • *Germany suffers from a surplus of teachers.*
OPPOSITES: lack, deficit, shortage
▸ AS AN ADJECTIVE = **extra**, spare, excess, remaining, odd, in excess, left over, unused, superfluous • *Few people have large sums of surplus cash.*

OPPOSITES: lacking, inadequate, insufficient

surprise AS A NOUN 1 = **shock**, start *(informal)*, revelation, jolt, bombshell, eye-opener *(informal)*, bolt from the blue, turn-up for the books *(informal)* • *It is perhaps no surprise to see her attempting a comeback.*
2 = **amazement**, astonishment, wonder, disbelief, incredulity, stupefaction • *To my surprise I am in a room where I see one of my mother's sisters.*
▸ AS A VERB 1 = **amaze**, astonish, astound, stun, startle, stagger, disconcert, take aback, bowl over *(informal)*, leave open-mouthed, nonplus, flabbergast *(informal)*, take (someone's) breath away • *We'll solve the case ourselves and surprise everyone.*
2 = **catch unawares** *or* **off-guard**, catch napping, catch on the hop *(informal)*, burst in on, spring upon, catch in the act *or* red-handed, come down on like a bolt from the blue • *The army surprised their enemy near the village of Blenheim.*

QUOTATIONS
Surprises are foolish things. The pleasure is not enhanced, and the inconvenience is often considerable
[Jane Austen *Emma*]

surprised = **amazed**, astonished, startled, disconcerted, at a loss, taken aback, speechless, incredulous, open-mouthed, nonplussed, thunderstruck, unable to believe your eyes • *He seemed surprised to find the big living room empty.*

surprising = **amazing**, remarkable, incredible, astonishing, wonderful, unusual, extraordinary, unexpected, staggering, marvellous, startling, astounding, jaw-dropping, eye-popping *(informal)*, unlooked-for • *A surprising number of customers order the same sandwich each day.*

surrender AS A VERB 1 = **give in**, yield, submit, give way, quit, succumb, cave in *(informal)*, capitulate, throw in the towel, lay down arms, give yourself up, show the white flag • *We'll never surrender to the terrorists.*
OPPOSITES: fight (on), oppose, resist
2 = **give up**, abandon, relinquish, resign, yield, concede, part with, renounce, waive, forego, cede, deliver up • *She had to surrender all rights to her property.*
▸ AS A NOUN 1 = **submission**, yielding, cave-in *(informal)*, capitulation, resignation, renunciation, relinquishment • *the unconditional surrender of the rebels*
2 = **relinquishment**, giving up, handing over, transfer, surrendering, forsaking, ceding, abdication, renunciation, yielding up, forgoing • *a complete surrender of weapons*

surreptitious = **secret**, clandestine, furtive, sneaking, veiled, covert, sly, fraudulent, unauthorized, underhand, stealthy • *They had several surreptitious conversations.*
OPPOSITES: open, frank, obvious

surrogate = **substitute**, deputy, representative, stand-in, proxy • *Leningrad was the third alien city to offer him a surrogate home.*

surround AS A VERB 1 = **enclose**, ring, encircle, encompass, envelop, close in on, fence in, girdle, hem in, environ, enwreath • *The church was surrounded by a rusted wrought-iron fence.*
2 = **besiege**, beset, lay siege to, invest *(rare)* • *When the car stopped it was surrounded by police and militiamen.*
▸ AS A NOUN = **border**, edging, skirting, boundary, fringe, perimeter • *a small fireplace with a cast-iron surround*

surrounding = **nearby**, neighbouring, adjacent, local, bordering, adjoining, abutting • *Aerial bombing of the surrounding area is continuing.*

surroundings = **environment**, setting, background, location, neighbourhood, milieu, environs • *a peaceful holiday home in beautiful surroundings*

surveillance = **observation**, watch, scrutiny, supervision, control, care, direction, inspection, vigilance, superintendence • *He was arrested after being kept under constant surveillance.*

QUOTATIONS
Big Brother is watching you
[George Orwell *1984*]

survey AS A NOUN 1 = **poll**, study, research, review, inquiry, investigation, sampling, opinion poll, questionnaire, census • *According to the survey, overall world trade has also slackened.*
2 = **examination**, inspection, scrutiny, overview, once-over *(informal)*, perusal • *He sniffed the perfume she wore, then gave her a quick survey.*
3 = **valuation**, pricing, estimate, assessment, appraisal • *a structural survey undertaken by a qualified surveyor*
▸ AS A VERB 1 = **interview**, question, poll, study, research, investigate, sample, canvass, cross-examine • *Only 18 percent of those surveyed opposed the idea.*
2 = **look over**, view, scan, examine, observe, contemplate, supervise, inspect, eyeball *(slang)*, scrutinize, size up, take stock of, eye up, recce *(slang)*, reconnoitre • *He pushed himself to his feet and surveyed the room.*
3 = **measure**, estimate, prospect, assess, appraise, triangulate • *Geological experts were commissioned to survey the land.*

survival = **staying alive**, existence, being alive, viability, life span, holding on to life • *An animal's sense of smell is crucial to its survival.*

survive 1 = **remain alive**, live, pull through, last, exist, live on, endure, hold out, subsist, keep body and soul together *(informal)*, be extant, fight for your life, keep your head above water • *Drugs that dissolve blood clots can help heart-attack victims survive.*
2 = **continue**, last, exist, live on, endure, persist, abide, pull through • *Rejected by the people, can the organization survive at all?*
3 = **live longer than**, outlive, outlast, live on after, remain alive after • *Most women will survive their spouses.*

susceptibility 1 = **vulnerability**, weakness, liability, propensity, predisposition, proneness • *his increased susceptibility to infections*
2 = **sensitivity**, responsiveness, receptiveness, suggestibility, vulnerability, openness, defenselessness • *She has difficulty dining out because of her susceptibility to smells.*

susceptible 1 = **responsive**, sensitive, receptive, alive to, impressionable, easily moved, suggestible • *He was unusually susceptible to flattery.*
OPPOSITES: unresponsive, unaffected, insensitive
2 *usually with* **to** = **liable**, inclined, prone, given, open, subject, vulnerable, disposed, predisposed • *Walking with weights makes the shoulders susceptible to injury.*
OPPOSITES: immune, resistant, unaffected by

suspect AS A VERB 1 = **believe**, feel, guess, consider, suppose, conclude, fancy, speculate, conjecture, surmise, hazard a guess, have a sneaking suspicion, think probable • *I suspect they were right.*
OPPOSITES: be certain, be confident of, know
2 = **distrust**, doubt, mistrust, smell a rat *(informal)*, harbour suspicions about, have your doubts about • *You don't really think he suspects you, do you?*
OPPOSITES: trust, have faith in, think innocent
▸ AS A NOUN = **accused**, defendant, suspected person • *Police have arrested a suspect in a series of killings in the city.*
▸ AS AN ADJECTIVE = **dubious**, doubtful, dodgy *(Brit., Austral. & N.Z. informal)*, questionable, fishy *(informal)*, iffy *(informal)*, open to suspicion, shonky *(Austral. & N.Z. informal)* • *Delegates evacuated the building when a suspect package was found.*
OPPOSITES: innocent, above suspicion

suspend 1 = **postpone**, delay, put off, arrest, cease, interrupt, shelve, withhold, defer, adjourn, hold off, cut short, discontinue, lay aside, put in cold storage • *The union suspended strike action this week.*
OPPOSITES: continue, carry on, resume

2 = remove, expel, eject, debar • *Julie was suspended from her job shortly after the incident.*
OPPOSITES: restore, reinstate
3 = hang, attach, dangle, swing, append • *chandeliers suspended on heavy chains from the ceiling*

suspense AS A NOUN **= uncertainty**, doubt, tension, anticipation, expectation, anxiety, insecurity, expectancy, apprehension • *a writer who holds the suspense throughout her tale*
▸ IN PHRASES: **in suspense = on tenterhooks**, anxious, on edge, keyed up, in an agony of doubt, with bated breath • *'Go on, don't leave us in suspense,' Dennis said.*

suspenseful = thrilling, exciting, gripping, Hitchcockian, cliffhanging • *a suspenseful and sinister tale*

suspension 1 = postponement, delay, stopping, break, stay, breaking off, interruption, moratorium, respite, remission, adjournment, abeyance, deferment, discontinuation, disbarment • *the suspension of flights between London and Manchester*
2 = removal, expulsion, rejection, exclusion, elimination, ejection, gardening leave (*Brit. informal*), debarment • *The athlete received a two-year suspension.*

suspicion AS A NOUN **1 = feeling**, theory, impression, intuition, conjecture, surmise, funny feeling (*informal*), presentiment • *Police had suspicions that it was not a natural death.*
2 = distrust, scepticism, mistrust, doubt, misgiving, qualm, lack of confidence, wariness, bad vibes (*slang*), dubiety, chariness • *Our culture harbours deep suspicions of big-time industry.*
3 = idea, notion, hunch, guess, impression, conjecture, surmise, gut feeling (*informal*), supposition • *I have a sneaking suspicion that they are going to succeed.*
4 = trace, touch, hint, shadow, suggestion, strain, shade, streak, tinge, glimmer, soupçon (*French*) • *large blooms of white with a suspicion of pale pink*
▸ IN PHRASES: **above suspicion = blameless**, unimpeachable, above reproach, pure, honourable, virtuous, sinless, like Caesar's wife • *He was a respected academic and above suspicion.*

QUOTATIONS
Caesar's wife should be above suspicion
[Julius Caesar]

suspicious 1 = distrustful, suspecting, sceptical, doubtful, apprehensive, leery (*slang*), mistrustful, unbelieving, wary • *He has his father's suspicious nature.*
OPPOSITES: trusting, gullible, credulous
2 = suspect, dubious, questionable, funny, doubtful, dodgy (*Brit., Austral. & N.Z. informal*), queer, irregular, shady (*informal*), fishy (*informal*), of doubtful honesty, open to doubt *or* misconstruction, shonky (*Austral. & N.Z. informal*) • *two suspicious-looking characters*
OPPOSITES: straight, above board, beyond suspicion
3 = odd, strange, mysterious, dark, dubious, irregular, questionable, murky (*informal*), shady (*informal*), fishy • *Four people have died in suspicious circumstances.*

suspiciously = strangely, worryingly, disturbingly • *The tan-coloured dog looks suspiciously like an American pit bull terrier.*

suss out = work out, figure out, puzzle out, find out, solve, resolve, calculate, clear up • *If you can't suss out the codes, you won't be seen as part of the team.*

sustain 1 = maintain, continue, keep up, prolong, keep going, keep alive, protract • *He has sustained his fierce social conscience.*
2 = suffer, experience, undergo, feel, bear, endure, withstand, bear up under • *Every aircraft in there has sustained some damage.*
3 = help, aid, comfort, foster, assist, relieve, nurture • *I am sustained by letters of support.*
4 = keep alive, nourish, provide for • *not enough food to sustain a mouse*
5 = support, carry, bear, keep up, uphold, keep from falling • *The magnets have lost the capacity to sustain the weight.*
6 = uphold, confirm, endorse, approve, ratify, verify, validate • *The court sustained his objection.*

sustained = continuous, constant, steady, prolonged, perpetual, unremitting, nonstop • *The proposals follow sustained criticism from teachers.*
OPPOSITES: periodic, sporadic, intermittent

sustenance 1 = nourishment, food, provisions, rations, refreshments, kai (*N.Z. informal*), daily bread, victuals, edibles, comestibles, provender, aliment, eatables, refection • *The state provided a basic quantity of food for daily sustenance.*
2 = support, maintenance, livelihood, subsistence • *everything that is necessary for the sustenance of the offspring*

svelte = slender, lithe, willowy, graceful, slinky, lissom(e), sylphlike • *She's svelte and smart.*

swagger AS A VERB **1 = stride**, parade, strut, prance, walk confidently, walk arrogantly • *The burly brute swaggered forward, towering over me, and shouted.*
2 = show off, boast, brag, hot-dog (*chiefly U.S.*), bluster, swank (*informal*), showboat, gasconade (*rare*) • *It's bad manners to swagger about how rich you are.*
▸ AS A NOUN **1 = strut**, roll, parading, prancing • *He walked with something of a swagger.*
2 = ostentation, show, display, showing off (*informal*), bluster, swashbuckling, swank (*informal*), braggadocio, gasconade (*rare*) • *What he needed was confidence and a bit of swagger.*

swallow[1] AS A VERB **1 = eat**, down (*informal*), consume, devour, absorb, hoover (*informal*), put away (*informal*), eat up, swig (*informal*), swill, wash down, ingest, bolt down (*informal*) • *Polly took a bite of the apple, chewed and swallowed it.*
2 = gulp, drink, sip, sup, swig (*informal*), guzzle, imbibe, quaff, neck (*slang*), slurp • *He took a glass of Scotch and swallowed it down.*
3 = believe, accept, buy (*slang*), fall for, take (something) as gospel • *I too found this story a little hard to swallow.*
4 = suppress, hold in, restrain, contain, overcome, hold back, stifle, repress, smother, muffle, bottle up, bite back, choke back • *Gordon swallowed the anger he felt.*
▸ IN PHRASES: **swallow something** *or* **someone up**
1 = engulf, overwhelmed, overrun, consume • *Weeds had swallowed up the garden.*
2 = absorb, assimilate, envelop • *Wage costs swallow up two-thirds of the turnover.*

swallow[2]
▸ RELATED ADJECTIVE: hirundine
▸ COLLECTIVE NOUN: flight

swamp AS A NOUN **= bog**, marsh, quagmire, moss (*Scot. & Northern English dialect*), slough, fen, mire, morass, everglade(s) (*U.S.*), pakihi (*N.Z.*), muskeg (*Canad.*) • *Much of the land is desert or swamp.*
▸ AS A VERB **1 = flood**, engulf, submerge, inundate, deluge • *The Ventura river burst its banks, swamping a mobile home park.*
2 = overload, overwhelm, inundate, besiege, beset, snow under • *We swamp them with praise, make them think that they are important.*

swampy = boggy, waterlogged, marshy, wet, fenny, miry, quaggy, marish (*obsolete*) • *the swampy lowlands of southern Tuscany*

swan
▸ NAME OF MALE: cob
▸ NAME OF FEMALE: pen
▸ NAME OF YOUNG: cygnet
▸ COLLECTIVE NOUNS: herd, bevy

S

swank AS A VERB = **show off**, swagger, give yourself airs, posture *(informal)*, hot-dog *(chiefly U.S.)*, put on side *(Brit. slang)* • *I never swank about the things I have been lucky enough to win.*

▸ AS A NOUN = **boastfulness**, show, ostentation, display, swagger, vainglory • *There was no swank in Martin.*

swanky = **ostentatious**, grand, posh *(informal, chiefly Brit.)*, rich, expensive, exclusive, smart, fancy, flash, fashionable, glamorous, stylish, gorgeous, lavish, luxurious, sumptuous, plush *(informal)*, flashy, swish *(informal, chiefly Brit.)*, glitzy *(slang)*, showy, ritzy *(slang)*, de luxe, swank *(informal)*, plushy *(informal)*, schmick *(Austral. informal)* • *They were put up in a swanky hotel in Kensington.*

OPPOSITES: modest, humble, unpretentious

swap *or* **swop** AS A VERB **1** = **exchange**, trade, switch, traffic, interchange, barter, trade off • *Some hostages were swapped for convicted prisoners.*

2 = **trade**, exchange, reciprocate, bandy, pass back and forth • *They all sat together at a table, laughing and swapping stories.*

▸ AS A NOUN = **exchange**, trade, switch, interchange, barter, trade-off • *If she ever fancies a job swap, I could be interested.*

swarm AS A NOUN = **multitude**, crowd, mass, army, host, drove, flock, herd, horde, myriad, throng, shoal, concourse, bevy • *A swarm of people encircled the hotel.*

▸ AS A VERB **1** = **crowd**, flock, throng, mass, stream, congregate • *People swarmed to the shops, buying up everything in sight.*

2 = **teem**, crawl, be alive, abound, bristle, be overrun, be infested • *Within minutes the area was swarming with officers.*

swarthy = **dark-skinned**, black, brown, dark, tawny, dusky, swart *(archaic)*, dark-complexioned • *He had a broad swarthy face.*

swashbuckling = **dashing**, spirited, bold, flamboyant, swaggering, gallant, daredevil, mettlesome, roisterous • *a swashbuckling adventurer*

swastika = **crooked cross**, fylfot • *On her new brown passport was a black eagle with a swastika.*

swath *or* **swathe** = **area**, section, stretch, patch, tract • *On May 1st the army took over another swathe of territory.*

swathe = **wrap**, drape, envelop, bind, lap, fold, bandage, cloak, shroud, swaddle, bedeck, furl, sheathe, enfold, bundle up, muffle up, enwrap • *She swathed her enormous body in thin black fabrics.*

S

sway AS A VERB **1** = **move from side to side**, rock, wave, roll, swing, bend, lean, incline, lurch, oscillate, move to and fro • *The people swayed back and forth with arms linked.*

2 = **influence**, control, direct, affect, guide, dominate, persuade, govern, win over, induce, prevail on • *Don't ever be swayed by fashion.*

▸ AS A NOUN = **power**, control, influence, government, rule, authority, command, sovereignty, jurisdiction, clout *(informal)*, dominion, predominance, ascendency • *How can mothers keep daughters under their sway?*

▸ IN PHRASES: **hold sway** = **prevail**, rule, predominate, reign, be in power, hold power, exercise power, wield power, have the greatest influence, be most powerful, have the ascendancy • *Here, a completely different approach seems to hold sway.*

swear AS A VERB **1** = **curse**, cuss *(informal)*, blaspheme, turn the air blue *(informal)*, be foul-mouthed, take the Lord's name in vain, utter profanities, imprecate • *It is wrong to swear and shout.*

2 = **vow**, promise, take an oath, warrant, testify, depose, attest, avow, give your word, state under oath, pledge yourself • *Alan swore that he would do everything in his power to help us.*

3 = **declare**, assert, affirm, swear blind, asseverate • *I swear I've told you all I know.*

▸ IN PHRASES: **swear by something** = **believe in**, trust, depend on, rely on, have confidence in, have faith in, put your faith in, set store by, rate • *Many people swear by vitamin C's ability to ward off colds.*

swear someone in = **install**, inaugurate, establish, adopt, invest, ordain, consecrate, induct, enthrone • *She has been formally sworn in as Ireland's first woman president.*

QUOTATIONS

Swear not by the moon, the inconstant moon
[William Shakespeare *Romeo and Juliet*]

As he knew not what to say, he swore
[Lord Byron *The Island*]

swearing = **bad language**, cursing, profanity, blasphemy, cussing *(informal)*, foul language, imprecations, malediction • *a stream of swearing and abuse*

QUOTATIONS

Expletive deleted
[editor of Nixon's Watergate tapes]

swearword = **oath**, curse, obscenity, expletive, four-letter word, cuss *(informal)*, profanity • *I'd never heard a swear word in my life.*

sweat AS A NOUN **1** = **perspiration**, moisture, dampness, exudation, diaphoresis *(Medical)*, sudor *(Medical)* • *He wiped the sweat off his face and looked around.*

2 = **panic**, anxiety, state *(informal)*, worry, distress, flap *(informal)*, frenzy, agitation, fluster, lather *(informal)*, tizzy *(informal)*, state of anxiety • *She was in a sweat about the exam.*

▸ AS A VERB **1** = **perspire**, swelter, sweat like a pig *(informal)*, sweat buckets *(informal)*, break out in a sweat, exude moisture, be pouring with sweat, glow • *Already they were sweating as the sun beat down upon them.*

2 = **worry**, fret, agonize, lose sleep over, be on tenterhooks, torture yourself, be on pins and needles *(informal)* • *It gives sales chiefs something to sweat about.*

▸ IN PHRASES: **no sweat** = **no problem** *(informal)*, it's nothing, you're welcome, it's a pleasure • *'Many thanks.' 'No sweat.'*

sweat something out = **endure**, see (something) through, stick it out *(informal)*, stay the course • *I just had to sweat it out and hope.*

▸ RELATED ADJECTIVE: sudorific

sweater

SWEATERS

Aran sweater	crew-necked sweater	pullover
cardigan	Fairisle	rollneck
Cowichan sweater, Indian sweater, siwash, *or* siwash sweater *(Canad.)*	Guernsey *(Austral.)*	skivvy *(Austral. & N.Z.)*
cowl-necked sweater	hoodie *(informal)*	slipover
crew-neck *or*	Icelandic	sloppy joe
	jersey	sweatshirt
	jumper	turtleneck
	polo *or* polo neck	V-neck *or* V-necked sweater

sweaty = **perspiring**, sweating, sticky, clammy, bathed *or* drenched *or* soaked in perspiration, glowing • *She was hot and sweaty.*

sweep AS A VERB **1** = **brush**, clean, wipe, vacuum, scrub, hoover, scour • *She was in the kitchen sweeping the floor.*

2 = **clear**, remove, brush, clean, get rid of, dispose of • *I swept rainwater off the flat top of a gravestone.*

3 = **carry**, pull, drag, drive • *Suddenly, she was swept along by the crowd.*

4 = **sail**, pass, fly, tear, zoom, glide, skim, scud, hurtle • *The car swept past the gate house.*

5 = spread through, flood, overwhelm, engulf, flow across, surge over • *A flu epidemic is sweeping the city.*
6 = swagger, sail, breeze, stride, stroll, glide, flounce • *She swept into the conference room.*
7 = scan, run over, skim, eye, check, examine, eyeball *(slang)*, glance over, run your eye over • *Her gaze sweeps rapidly around the room.*
▸ **AS A NOUN** **1 = movement**, move, swing, stroke, gesture • *She indicated the garden with a sweep of her hand.*
2 = arc, bend, curve • *the great sweep of the bay*
3 = search, check, examination, look, hunt, investigation, going-over *(informal)*, inspection, exploration, combing • *Two of the soldiers swiftly began making a sweep of the premises.*
4 = extent, range, span, stretch, scope, compass • *the whole sweep of German social and political history*
▸ **IN PHRASES: sweep something aside = dismiss**, reject, set aside, disregard, drop, shelve, discard, relegate, banish, dispel, spurn, repudiate, lay aside, pooh-pooh, put out of your mind • *His original diagnosis has now been swept aside by experts.*
sweep something under the carpet = conceal, hide, suppress, keep secret, ignore, stonewall, hush up, draw a veil over, keep silent about, keep dark, keep under your hat *(informal)* • *For a long time this problem has been swept under the carpet.*

sweeping **1 = extensive**, broad, vast, expansive, panoramic, spacious • *the long sweeping curve of Rio's Guanabara Bay*
2 = indiscriminate, blanket, across-the-board, wholesale, exaggerated, overstated, unqualified, overdrawn, oversimplified • *sweeping generalizations about ability based on gender*
3 = wide-ranging, global, comprehensive, wide, broad, radical, extensive, all-inclusive, all-embracing, overarching, thoroughgoing • *sweeping economic reforms*
OPPOSITES: limited, narrow, minor
4 = decisive, complete, total, overwhelming, unconditional, unqualified, out-and-out • *The election was a sweeping victory for the secular centre left.*

sweet **AS AN ADJECTIVE** **1 = sugary**, sweetened, cloying, honeyed, saccharine, syrupy, icky *(informal)*, treacly • *a mug of sweet tea*
OPPOSITES: sharp, sour, tart
2 = fragrant, perfumed, aromatic, redolent, sweet-smelling • *the sweet smell of a summer garden*
OPPOSITES: rank, foul, stinking
3 = fresh, clean, pure, wholesome • *I gulped a breath of sweet air.*
4 = melodious, musical, harmonious, soft, mellow, silvery, tuneful, dulcet, sweet-sounding, euphonious, silver-toned, euphonic • *the sweet sounds of Mozart*
OPPOSITES: harsh, unpleasant, grating
5 = charming, kind, gentle, tender, affectionate, agreeable, amiable, sweet-tempered • *He was a sweet man but when he drank he tended to quarrel.*
OPPOSITES: nasty, obnoxious, disagreeable
6 = delightful, appealing, cute, taking, winning, fair, beautiful, attractive, engaging, lovable, winsome, cutesy *(informal, chiefly U.S.)*, likable *or* likeable • *a sweet little baby girl*
OPPOSITES: nasty, unpleasant, unattractive
7 = beloved, dear, darling, dearest, pet, treasured, precious, cherished • *my dear, sweet mother*
▸ **AS A NOUN** **1** *usually plural* **= confectionery**, candy *(U.S.)*, sweetie, lolly *(Austral. & N.Z.)*, sweetmeat, fondant, bonbon • *They've always enjoyed fish and chips – and sweets and cakes.*
2 = dessert, pudding, afters *(Brit. informal)*, last course, sweet course • *The sweet was a mousse flavoured with whisky.*
3 = darling, sweetheart, beloved, dearest, angel, treasure, honey • *'Welcome home, my sweet!' he said.*
▸ **IN PHRASES: sweet on = in love with**, keen on, infatuated with, gone on *(slang)*, fond of, taken with, enamoured of, head over heels in love with, obsessed *or* bewitched by, wild *or* mad about *(informal)* • *It was rumoured that she was sweet on him.*
▹ *See panel* **Desserts and sweet dishes**

sweeten **1 = sugar**, honey, sugar-coat • *He liberally sweetened his coffee.*
2 = soften, ease, alleviate, relieve, temper, cushion, mellow, make less painful • *They sweetened the deal with a rather generous cash payment.*
3 = mollify, appease, placate, soothe, pacify, soften up, sugar the pill • *He is likely to try to sweeten them with pledges of fresh aid.*

sweetheart **1 = dearest**, beloved, sweet, angel, treasure, honey, dear, sweetie *(informal)* • *Happy birthday, sweetheart!*
2 = love, boyfriend *or* girlfriend, beloved, lover, steady *(informal)*, flame *(informal)*, darling, follower *(obsolete)*, valentine, admirer, suitor, beau, swain *(archaic)*, truelove, leman *(archaic)*, inamorata *or* inamorato • *I married my childhood sweetheart, in Liverpool.*

sweet-talk **= persuade**, coax, beguile, flatter, tempt, mislead, manoeuvre, seduce, entice, dupe, cajole, chat up, wheedle, palaver, inveigle, soft-soap *(informal)*, blandish • *He even tried to sweet-talk the policewoman who arrested him.*

swell **AS A VERB** **1 = increase**, rise, grow, mount, expand, surge, step up, accelerate, escalate, multiply, grow larger • *The human population swelled as migrants moved south.*
OPPOSITES: fall, decrease, lessen
2 = expand, increase, grow, rise, extend, balloon, belly, enlarge, bulge, protrude, well up, billow, fatten, dilate, puff up, round out, be inflated, become larger, distend, bloat, tumefy, become bloated *or* distended • *The limbs swell to an enormous size.*
OPPOSITES: contract, shrink, become smaller
3 = be filled, be full, be overcome, brim, overflow, be bursting • *She could see her two sons swell with pride.*
4 = become louder, intensify, amplify, become loud, heighten • *Heavenly music swelled from nowhere.*
▸ **AS A NOUN** **= wave**, rise, surge, billow, undulation • *the swell of the incoming tide*
▸ **AS AN ADJECTIVE** **= wonderful**, excellent, superb, marvellous, topping *(Brit. slang)*, sensational *(informal)*, sovereign, awesome *(slang)*, first-rate, brill *(informal)*, out of this world *(informal)*, the dog's bollocks *(taboo slang)*, booshit *(Austral. slang)*, exo *(Austral. slang)*, sik *(Austral. slang)*, rad *(informal)*, phat *(slang)*, schmick *(Austral. informal)* • *I've had a swell time.*

swelling **= enlargement**, lump, puffiness, bump, blister, bulge, inflammation, dilation, protuberance, distension, tumescence • *There is some swelling and he is being detained for observation.*
▸ **RELATED ADJECTIVE:** tumescent

sweltering **= hot**, burning, boiling, steaming, baking, roasting, stifling, scorching, oppressive, humid, torrid, sultry, airless • *It was an unimpressive contest in sweltering heat.*

swerve **AS A VERB** **= veer**, turn, swing, shift, bend, incline, deflect, depart from, skew, diverge, deviate, turn aside, sheer off • *Drivers swerved to avoid the debris.*
▸ **AS A NOUN** **= change of direction**, bend, twist, deviation • *He swung the car to the left and that swerve saved Malone's life.*

swift[1] **1 = quick**, immediate, prompt, rapid, instant, abrupt, ready, expeditious • *We need to make a swift decision.*
2 = fast, quick, rapid, flying, express, winged, sudden, fleet, hurried, speedy, spanking, nimble, quickie *(informal)*, nippy *(Brit. informal)*, fleet-footed, pdq *(slang)* • *a swift runner*
OPPOSITES: slow, sluggish, plodding

swift²
▸ COLLECTIVE NOUN: flock

swiftly 1 = **quickly**, rapidly, speedily, without losing time • *They have acted swiftly and decisively.*
2 = **fast**, promptly, hurriedly, apace, pronto *(informal)*, double-quick, hell for leather, like lightning, hotfoot, like the clappers *(Brit. informal)*, posthaste, like greased lightning *(informal)*, nippily *(Brit. informal)*, in less than no time, as fast as your legs can carry you, (at) full tilt • *Lenny moved swiftly and silently across the front lawn.*

swiftness 1 = **rapidity**, speed, quickness, promptness • *The secrecy and swiftness of the invasion shocked and amazed army officers.*
2 = **speed**, velocity, alacrity, expedition, dispatch, fleetness, celerity, speediness • *With incredible swiftness she ran down the passage.*

swill AS A VERB 1 = **drink**, gulp, swig *(informal)*, guzzle, neck *(slang)*, drain, consume, swallow, hoover *(informal)*, imbibe, quaff, bevvy *(dialect)*, toss off, bend the elbow *(informal)*, pour down your gullet • *A crowd of men were standing around swilling beer.*
2 *often with* **out** = **rinse**, wash out, sluice, flush, drench, clean out, wash down • *He swilled out the mug and left it on the draining board.*
▸ AS A NOUN = **waste**, slops, mash, mush, hogwash, pigswill, scourings • *The porker ate swill from a trough.*

swim AS A VERB 1 = **go swimming**, bathe, take a dip, dip • *They loved the outdoors, and swam in the sea in all weathers.*
2 = **reel**, spin, swirl, revolve, whirl, twirl, go round and round • *The musty aroma of the incense made her head swim.*
3 = **be covered in**, be immersed in, be soaked in, be drenched in, be saturated in • *broccoli swimming in thick sauce*
▸ AS A NOUN = **dip**, plunge, bathe, paddle, dive • *When can we go for a swim, Mam?*

swimmingly = **successfully**, very well, smoothly, effortlessly, as planned, like a dream, without a hitch, cosily, like clockwork, with no trouble • *The work has been going swimmingly.*

swimming pool = **swimming baths**, pool, baths, lido • *They had been drinking water from the swimming pool.*

swimsuit = **swimming costume**, swimwear, bathing suit, bikini, swimming trunks • *She came out to meet him in her swimsuit.*

swindle AS A VERB = **cheat**, do *(slang)*, con, skin *(slang)*, trick, stiff *(slang)*, sting *(informal)*, rip (someone) off *(slang)*, deceive, fleece, defraud, dupe, overcharge, rook *(slang)*, bamboozle *(informal)*, diddle *(informal)*, take (someone) for a ride *(informal)*, put one over on (someone) *(informal)*, pull a fast one (on someone) *(informal)*, bilk (of), take to the cleaners *(informal)*, sell a pup (to) *(slang)*, cozen, hornswoggle *(slang)*, scam *(slang)* • *He swindled investors out of millions of pounds.*
▸ AS A NOUN = **fraud**, fiddle *(Brit. informal)*, rip-off *(slang)*, racket, scam *(slang)*, sting *(informal)*, deception, imposition, deceit, trickery, double-dealing, con trick *(informal)*, sharp practice, swizzle *(Brit. informal)*, knavery, swizz *(Brit. informal)*, roguery, fastie *(Austral. slang)* • *He fled to Switzerland rather than face trial for a tax swindle.*

swindler = **cheat**, fraud, hustler *(U.S. informal)*, con man *(informal)*, sharper, shark, rogue, charlatan, rook *(slang)*, rascal, trickster, impostor, fraudster, knave *(archaic)*, confidence trickster, mountebank, grifter *(slang, chiefly U.S. & Canad.)*, chiseller *(informal)*, rorter *(Austral. slang)*, rogue trader • *Swindlers have cheated investors out of £12 million.*

swine
▸ COLLECTIVE NOUNS: herd, sounder, drift

swing AS A VERB 1 = **brandish**, wave, shake, flourish, wield, dangle • *She was swinging a bottle of wine by its neck.*
2 = **sway**, rock, wave, veer, vibrate, oscillate, move back and forth, move to and fro • *The sail of the little boat swung from one side to the other.*
3 *usually with* **round** = **turn**, veer, swivel, bear, bend, twist, curve, rotate, pivot, deviate, sheer off, turn on your heel • *The canoe found the current and swung around.*
4 = **hit out**, strike, swipe, lash out at, slap • *I picked up his baseball bat and swung at the man's head.*
5 = **change**, shift, vary, waver, fluctuate, oscillate, see-saw • *The vote could swing again.*
6 = **hang**, dangle, be suspended, suspend, move back and forth, be pendent • *He looks cute swinging from a branch.*
▸ AS A NOUN 1 = **swaying**, sway • *a woman walking with a slight swing to her hips*
2 = **fluctuation**, change, shift, switch, variation • *Dieters can suffer from violent mood swings.*
3 = **change**, move, reversal, turnaround, U-turn, change of heart, sea change, about-face, volte face • *The statistics show a swing towards Labour.*
▸ IN PHRASES: **in full swing** = **at its height**, under way, on the go *(informal)* • *The international rugby season was in full swing.*

swingeing = **severe**, heavy, drastic, huge, punishing, harsh, excessive, daunting, stringent, oppressive, Draconian, exorbitant • *swingeing cuts in the workforce*

swinging = **trendy**, happening *(informal)*, with it *(informal)*, hip *(slang)*, fashionable *(Brit. informal)*, up-to-date, groovy *(dated slang)*, up to the minute, in the swim *(informal)*, full of go or pep *(informal)* • *The stuffy '50s gave way to the swinging '60s.*

swipe AS A VERB 1 = **hit out**, strike, slap, lash out at • *She swiped at him as though he were a fly.*
2 = **steal**, nick *(slang, chiefly Brit.)*, pinch *(informal)*, lift *(informal)*, appropriate, trouser *(slang)*, cabbage *(Brit. slang)*, knock off *(slang)*, make off with, pilfer, purloin, filch, snaffle *(Brit. informal)* • *People kept trying to swipe my copy of the New York Times.*
▸ AS A NOUN 1 = **blow**, slap, smack, clip *(informal)*, thump, clout *(informal)*, cuff, clump *(slang)*, wallop *(informal)* • *He gave Andrew a swipe on the ear.*
2 = **criticism**, knocking *(informal)*, verbal attack, character assassination, critical remark • *a swipe at the president*

swirl = **whirl**, churn, spin, twist, boil, surge, agitate, eddy, twirl • *She smiled, swirling the wine in her glass.* • *The water swirled around his legs.*

swish = **smart**, grand, posh *(informal, chiefly Brit.)*, exclusive, elegant, swell *(informal)*, fashionable, sumptuous, ritzy *(slang)*, de luxe, plush or plushy *(informal)* • *a swish cocktail bar*

switch AS A NOUN 1 = **control**, button, lever, on/off device • *a light switch*
2 = **change**, shift, transition, conversion, reversal, alteration, about-turn, change of direction • *New technology made the switch to oil possible.*
▸ AS A VERB 1 = **change**, shift, convert, divert, deviate, change course • *I'm switching to a new gas supplier.*
2 = **exchange**, trade, swap, replace, substitute, rearrange, interchange • *The ballot boxes have been switched.*
▸ IN PHRASES: **switch something off** = **turn off**, shut off, deactivate, cut • *She switched off the coffee-machine.*
switch something on = **turn on**, put on, set off, activate, initiate, get going, set in motion, trigger off, initialize • *He pointed the light at his feet and tried to switch it on.*

swivel AS A VERB = **turn**, spin, revolve, rotate, pivot, pirouette, swing round • *He swivelled round to face Sarah.*
▸ AS A NOUN = **turn**, rotation, pirouette, swinging round • *a slight swivel of the hips*

swollen = **enlarged**, bloated, puffy, inflamed, puffed up, distended, tumescent, oedematous, dropsical, tumid, edematous • *My eyes were so swollen I could hardly see.*

swoop AS A VERB 1 = **pounce**, attack, charge, rush, raid, descend, assail, make a raid • *The terror ended when armed police swooped on the car.*

2 = **drop**, plunge, dive, rush, sweep, descend, plummet, pounce, stoop, nosedive • *The hawk swooped and soared away carrying something.*
▸ AS A NOUN = **raid**, attack, assault, surprise search • *a swoop on a German lorry*

swop *see* **swap**

sword AS A NOUN = **blade**, brand *(archaic)*, trusty steel • *The stubby sword used by ancient Roman gladiators.*
▸ IN PHRASES: **cross swords** = **fight**, argue, dispute, disagree, spar, wrangle, be at loggerheads, come to blows, have a dispute, engage in conflict • *The last time they crossed swords was during the 1980s.*
put someone to the sword = **kill**, murder, slaughter, execute, massacre, put to death, mow down • *Seventy thousand people were put to the sword.*

QUOTATIONS
The pen is mightier than the sword
[E.G. Bulwer-Lytton *Richelieu*]
All they that take the sword shall perish with the sword
[*Bible: St. Matthew*]

▹ *See panel* **Swords and other weapons with blades**

swot AS A VERB = **study**, revise, cram *(informal)*, work, get up *(informal)*, pore over, bone up on *(informal)*, burn the midnight oil, mug up *(Brit. slang)*, toil over, apply yourself to, lucubrate *(rare)* • *They swotted for their A levels.*
▸ AS A NOUN = **academic**, intellectual, bookworm, egghead *(informal)*, savant, bluestocking *(usually disparaging)*, acca *(Austral. slang)* • *He was a bit of a swot and excelled at school and university.*

sybaritic = **pleasure-loving**, self-indulgent, hedonistic, champagne, luxurious, sensual, voluptuous, epicurean, bacchanalian, luxury-loving, Lucullan • *They have always lived a very sybaritic life.*

sycophancy = **obsequiousness**, grovelling, servility, cringing, fawning, adulation, flattery, kowtowing, truckling, bootlicking *(informal)*, toadyism, slavishness • *snobbery, sycophancy and nepotism*

sycophant = **crawler**, yes man, toady, slave, parasite, cringer, fawner, hanger-on, sponger, brown-noser *(taboo slang)*, flatterer, truckler, lickspittle, ass-kisser *(U.S. & Canad. taboo slang)*, apple polisher *(U.S. slang)*, bootlicker *(informal)*, toadeater *(rare)* • *a dictator surrounded by sycophants*

sycophantic = **obsequious**, grovelling, ingratiating, servile, crawling, flattering, cringing, fawning, slimy, slavish, unctuous, smarmy *(Brit. informal)*, toadying, parasitical, arse-licking *(taboo slang)*, bootlicking *(informal)*, timeserving • *his clique of sycophantic friends*

syllabus = **course of study**, course, curriculum, educational programme, programme of study, course outline • *the history syllabus*

symbol 1 = **metaphor**, image, allegory, sign, representation, token • *To them the monarchy is a special symbol of nationhood.*
2 = **representation**, sign, figure, mark, type, image, token, logo, badge, emblem, glyph • *I frequently use sunflowers as symbols of strength.*
3 = **sign**, mark, letter, character, hieroglyph, ideogram • *What's the chemical symbol for mercury?*

symbolic 1 = **representative**, token, emblematic, allegorical • *The move today was largely symbolic.*
2 = **representative**, figurative, allegorical, illustrative, allusive, connotative • *symbolic representations of landscape*

symbolize = **represent**, signify, stand for, mean, exemplify, denote, typify, personify, connote, betoken, body forth • *The fall of the Berlin Wall symbolized the end of the Cold War.*

symmetrical = **balanced**, regular, proportional, in proportion, well-proportioned • *the neat rows of perfectly symmetrical windows*
OPPOSITES: irregular, unbalanced, asymmetrical

symmetry 1 = **balance**, proportion, regularity, form, order, harmony, correspondence, evenness • *the incredible beauty and symmetry of a snowflake*
2 = **equality**, agreement, balance, proportion, coordination, concord • *The superpowers pledged to maintain symmetry in their arms shipments.*

sympathetic 1 = **caring**, kind, understanding, concerned, feeling, interested, kindly, warm, tender, pitying, supportive, responsive, affectionate, compassionate, commiserating, warm-hearted, condoling • *It may be that he sees you only as a sympathetic friend.*
OPPOSITES: indifferent, insensitive, uncaring
2 = **supportive**, encouraging, pro, approving of, friendly to, in sympathy with, well-disposed towards, favourably disposed towards • *They were sympathetic to our cause.*
3 = **like-minded**, compatible, agreeable, friendly, responsive, appreciative, congenial, companionable, well-intentioned • *She sounds a most sympathetic character.*
OPPOSITES: unresponsive, uncongenial

sympathetically = **feelingly**, kindly, understandingly, warmly, with interest, with feeling, sensitively, with compassion, appreciatively, perceptively, responsively, warm-heartedly • *She nodded sympathetically.*

sympathize with 1 = **feel for**, pity, empathize with, commiserate with, bleed for, have compassion for, grieve with, offer consolation for, condole with, share another's sorrow, feel your heart go out to • *I must tell you how much I sympathize with you for your loss.*
OPPOSITES: mock, disregard, have no feelings for
2 = **agree with**, support, side with, understand, identify with, go along with, be in accord with, be in sympathy with • *Some Europeans sympathize with the Americans over the issue.*
OPPOSITES: reject, oppose, disagree with

sympathizer = **supporter**, partisan, protagonist, fellow traveller, well-wisher • *a well-known playwright and Communist sympathizer*

sympathy 1 = **compassion**, understanding, pity, empathy, tenderness, condolence(s), thoughtfulness, commiseration, aroha *(N.Z.)* • *We expressed our sympathy for her loss.*
OPPOSITES: indifference, scorn, disdain
2 = **affinity**, agreement, rapport, union, harmony, warmth, correspondence, fellow feeling, congeniality • *I still have sympathy with this point of view.*
OPPOSITES: opposition, resistance, hostility

S

SWORDS AND OTHER WEAPONS WITH BLADES

assegai
backsword
battle-axe
bayonet
bill
bowie knife
broadsword
claymore
cutlass
dagger
dirk
épée
falchion
foil
halberd
hatchet
jackknife
jerid
knife *or (slang)* chiv
kris
kukri
machete
parang
partisan
pike
poleaxe
poniard
rapier
sabre
scimitar
sgian-dhu
sheath knife
skean
smallsword
snickersnee
spear
spontoon
stiletto
stone axe
sword *or (archaic)* glaive
sword bayonet
swordstick
tomahawk
trench knife
yataghan

3 = **agreement**, support, favour, approval, encouragement, affiliation, partiality, approbation • *Several hundred workers struck in sympathy with their colleagues.*

QUOTATIONS
A fellow-feeling makes one wond'rous kind
[David Garrick *An Occasional Prologue on Quitting the Theatre*]

symposium = **congress**, meeting, conference, convention, seminar, caucus *(chiefly U.S. & Canad.)*, colloquium • *He had been taking part in an international symposium on population.*

symptom 1 = **sign**, mark, indication, warning • *patients with flu symptoms*
2 = **manifestation**, sign, indication, mark, warning, evidence, expression, proof, token, portent, augury • *Your problem with sleep is just a symptom of a larger problem.*

symptomatic = **indicative**, representative, typical, characteristic, suggestive • *The city's problems are symptomatic of the crisis.*

syndicate AS A NOUN = **group**, league, association, company, body, concern, institution, organization, corporation, federation, outfit *(informal)*, consortium, confederation • *They formed a syndicate to buy the car.*
‣ AS A VERB = **network**, distribute • *Today his programme is syndicated to 500 stations.*

syndrome = **condition**, complaint, illness, symptoms, disorder, ailment, affliction • *The syndrome strikes those whose immune systems are below par.*

synonymous with = **equivalent to**, the same as, identical to, similar to, identified with, equal to, tantamount to, interchangeable with, one and the same as • *Going grey is not necessarily synonymous with growing old.*

synopsis = **summary**, review, résumé, outline, abstract, digest, epitome, rundown, condensation, compendium, précis, aperçu *(French)*, abridgment, conspectus, outline sketch • *For each title there is a brief synopsis of the book.*

synthesis = **combining**, integration, amalgamation, unification, welding, coalescence • *His novels are a rich synthesis of Balkan history and mythology.*

synthetic = **artificial**, manufactured, fake, man-made, mock, simulated, sham, pseudo *(informal)*, ersatz • *synthetic rubber*
OPPOSITES: real, natural, genuine

syrupy = **romantic**, emotional, sloppy *(informal)*, touching, tender, pathetic, sentimental, nostalgic, tearful, corny *(slang)*, cheesy *(informal)*, mushy *(informal)*, maudlin, simpering, weepy *(informal)*, slushy *(informal)*, mawkish, tear-jerking *(informal)*, drippy *(informal)*, schmaltzy *(slang)*, icky *(informal)*, gushy *(informal)*, soft-hearted, overemotional, dewy-eyed, three-hankie *(informal)* • *this syrupy film version of Conroy's novel*

system AS A NOUN 1 = **arrangement**, structure, organization, scheme, combination, classification, coordination, setup *(informal)* • *a multi-party system of government*
2 = **network**, organization, web, grid, set of channels • *a news channel on a local cable system*
3 = **method**, practice, technique, procedure, routine, theory, usage, methodology, frame of reference, modus operandi, fixed order • *the decimal system of metric weights and measures*
‣ IN PHRASES: **the system** = **the establishment**, the authorities, the established order, the system, the ruling class, the powers that be, institutionalized authority • *He wants to be a tough rebel who bucks the system.*

systematic = **methodical**, organized, efficient, precise, orderly, standardized, businesslike, well-ordered, systematized • *They went about their business in a systematic way.*
OPPOSITES: disorderly, random, unmethodical

systematize = **arrange**, organize, rationalize, sequence, regulate, classify, dispose, standardize, tabulate, put in order, make uniform, schematize, methodize • *The way to stay on top is to systematize your approach.*

tab = **flap**, tag, label, ticket, flag, marker, sticker • *a small red tab sewn on to the side of the pocket*

tabby = **striped**, banded, streaked, stripy, brindled • *A tabby cat shot out beside her feet.*

table AS A NOUN **1** = **counter**, bench, stand, board, surface, slab, work surface • *I placed his drink on the small table.*
2 = **list**, chart, tabulation, record, roll, index, register, digest, diagram, inventory, graph, synopsis, itemization • *Consult the table on page 104.*
3 = **food**, spread *(informal)*, board, diet, fare, kai *(N.Z. informal)*, victuals • *She always sets a marvellous table.*
▸ AS A VERB = **submit**, propose, put forward, move, suggest, enter, file, lodge, moot • *They've tabled a motion criticising the government for inaction.*
▸ RELATED ADJECTIVE: mensal
▹ *See panel* **Tables and desks**

tableau = **picture**, scene, representation, arrangement, spectacle • *a nativity tableau*

tablet **1** = **pill**, capsule, pellet, tab, pastille, caplet • *It's not a good idea to take sleeping tablets regularly.*
2 = **plaque**, slab, panel, stone, plate, memorial, gravestone • *ancient stone tablets from the pyramids*

taboo *or* **tabu** AS AN ADJECTIVE = **forbidden**, banned, prohibited, ruled out, not allowed, unacceptable, outlawed, unthinkable, not permitted, disapproved of, anathema, off limits, frowned on, proscribed, beyond the pale, unmentionable • *Cancer is a taboo subject.*
OPPOSITES: allowed, permitted, sanctioned
▸ AS A NOUN = **prohibition**, ban, restriction, disapproval, anathema, interdict, proscription, tapu *(N.Z.)* • *Not all men respect the taboo against bedding a friend's woman.*

tabulate = **arrange**, order, list, range, index, chart, catalogue, classify, categorize, codify, systematize, tabularize • *Results for the test program haven't been tabulated yet.*

tacit = **implied**, understood, implicit, silent, taken for granted, unspoken, inferred, undeclared, wordless, unstated, unexpressed • *a tacit admission that a mistake had been made*
OPPOSITES: stated, spoken, explicit

taciturn = **uncommunicative**, reserved, reticent, unforthcoming, quiet, withdrawn, silent, distant, dumb, mute, aloof, antisocial, tight-lipped, close-lipped • *A taciturn man, he replied to my questions in monosyllables.*
OPPOSITES: open, forthcoming, communicative

tack AS A NOUN **1** = **nail**, pin, stud, staple, rivet, drawing pin, thumbtack *(U.S.)*, tintack • *Use a staple gun or upholstery tacks.*
2 = **course**, approach, direction, tactic, way, plan, heading, line, bearing, method, path, procedure, tenor • *In desperation I changed tack.*
3 = **direction**, course, bearing, heading, line, track, path • *The forecast was bad. If only we'd kept on the other tack!*
▸ AS A VERB **1** = **fasten**, fix, attach, pin, nail, staple, affix • *He had tacked this note to the door.*
2 = **change course**, swerve, change direction, go about, come about, zigzag, change heading, sail into the wind • *We were tacking fairly close inshore.*
3 = **stitch**, sew, hem, bind, baste • *Tack the cord around the cushion.*
▸ IN PHRASES: **tack something on to something** = **append**, add, attach, tag, annex • *The child-care bill is to be tacked on to the budget plan.*

tackle AS A NOUN **1** = **block**, stop, challenge • *a tackle by a full-back*
2 = **gear**, equipment, kit, apparatus, tools, implements, outfit, trappings, paraphernalia, accoutrements • *fishing tackle*
3 = **rig**, rigging, apparatus • *I finally hoisted him up with a block and tackle.*
▸ AS A VERB **1** = **deal with**, take on, set about, wade into, get stuck into *(informal)*, sink your teeth into, apply yourself to, come *or* get to grips with, step up to the plate *(informal)* • *We need to tackle these problems and save people's lives.*
2 = **undertake**, deal with, attempt, try, begin, essay, engage in, embark upon, get stuck into *(informal)*, turn your hand to, have a go *or* stab at *(informal)* • *My husband is quite good at DIY and wants to tackle the job himself.*

TABLES AND DESKS

bar
bedside table
billiard table
breakfast bar
breakfast table
buffet
bureau
card table
carrel
coffee table
console table
counter
davenport *(Brit.)*
desk
dining table
dressing table
drop-leaf table
drum table
escritoire
folding table
gate-leg *or* gate-legged table
kitchen table
lapboard
lowboy *(U.S. & Canad.)*
nest of tables
occasional table
pedestal desk
Pembroke table
piecrust table
reading desk
refectory table
roll-top desk
secretaire
side table
snooker table
teapoy
tea table
tea trolley
traymobile *(Austral.)*
trestle table
wool table
workbench
worktable
writing desk
writing table

3 = **confront**, speak to, face up to, question, cross-examine, accost, remonstrate with, waylay • *I tackled him about how he could tolerate such behaviour.*
4 = **intercept**, block, bring down, stop, challenge • *He tackled the quarter-back.*
5 = **grab**, stop, throw, seize, halt, grasp, clutch, take hold of • *The man tackled him, pushing him into the dirt.*

tacky[1] = **sticky**, wet, adhesive, gummy, icky *(informal)*, gluey • *If the finish is still tacky, leave to harden.*

tacky[2] 1 = **vulgar**, cheap, tasteless, nasty, sleazy, naff *(Brit. slang)* • *tacky red sunglasses*
2 = **seedy**, shabby, shoddy • *The whole thing is dreadfully tacky.*

tact = **diplomacy**, understanding, consideration, sensitivity, delicacy, skill, judgment, perception, discretion, finesse, thoughtfulness, savoir-faire, adroitness • *Her tact and intuition never failed.*
OPPOSITES: indiscretion, insensitivity, tactlessness

PROVERBS
Least said, soonest mended

tactful = **diplomatic**, politic, discreet, prudent, understanding, sensitive, polished, careful, subtle, delicate, polite, thoughtful, perceptive, considerate, judicious • *I decided it wouldn't be tactful to order another beer.*
OPPOSITES: insensitive, thoughtless, tactless

tactic = **policy**, approach, course, way, means, move, line, scheme, plans, method, trick, device, manoeuvre, tack, ploy, stratagem • *His tactic to press on paid off.*

tactical = **strategic**, politic, shrewd, smart, diplomatic, clever, cunning, skilful, artful, foxy, adroit • *The security forces had made a tactical withdrawal from the area.*
OPPOSITES: impolitic, blundering, clumsy

tactician = **strategist**, campaigner, planner, mastermind, general, director, brain *(informal)*, coordinator, schemer • *He is an extremely astute political tactician.*

tactics = **strategy**, campaigning, manoeuvres, generalship • *guerrilla tactics*

tactless = **insensitive**, thoughtless, inconsiderate, sharp, rough, harsh, rude, blundering, careless, clumsy, inept, unkind, gauche, indiscreet, boorish, unfeeling, imprudent, impolite, unsubtle, discourteous, injudicious, indelicate, undiplomatic, uncivil, maladroit, impolitic • *He had alienated many people with his tactless remarks.*
OPPOSITES: diplomatic, discreet, tactful

t

tag AS A NOUN 1 = **label**, tab, sticker, note, ticket, slip, flag, identification, marker, flap, docket • *Staff wore name tags and called inmates by their first names.*
2 = **identity**, name, label, description, denomination, characterization • *Jazz is starting to lose its elitist tag.*
▸ AS A VERB 1 = **label**, mark, flag, ticket, identify, earmark • *Important trees were tagged to protect them from machinery.*
2 = **name**, call, label, term, style, dub, nickname, christen • *The critics still tagged him with his old name.*
▸ IN PHRASES: **tag along with** *or* **behind someone** = **accompany**, follow, shadow, dog, attend, tail *(informal)*, trail • *She seemed happy to tag along with us.*
tag something on = **add**, tack on, append, adjoin, fasten, annex, affix • *It's worth tagging on an extra day or two to see the capital.*

tail AS A NOUN 1 = **extremity**, appendage, brush, rear end, hindquarters, hind part, empennage • *The cattle were swinging their tails to disperse the flies.*
2 = **train**, end, trail, tailpiece • *a comet tail*
3 = **shadow**, detective, private eye *(informal)*, sleuth *(informal)*, private investigator • *The police had already put a tail on a couple of suspects.*
4 = **close**, end, conclusion, termination, tail end • *We still have the tail of the outbreak to deal with.*
5 = **buttocks**, behind *(informal)*, bottom, butt *(U.S. & Canad. informal)*, bum *(Brit. slang)*, ass *(U.S. & Canad. taboo slang)*, rear *(informal)*, buns *(U.S. slang)*, arse *(taboo slang)*, backside *(informal)*, rump, rear end, posterior, derrière *(euphemistic)*, jacksy *(Brit. slang)* • *He desperately needs a kick in the tail.*
6 = **ponytail**, braid, plait, tress, pigtail • *She wore bleached denims with her golden tail of hair swinging.*
▸ AS A VERB = **follow**, track, shadow, trail, stalk, keep an eye on, dog the footsteps of • *Officers had tailed the gang in an undercover inquiry.*
▸ IN PHRASES: **on someone's tail** = **close behind someone**, hard on someone's heels, following someone closely, tailing someone • *He knew that the journalists were on his tail.*
tail away *or* **off** = **decrease**, fade, die out, fail, drop, dwindle, wane, fall away, peter out • *His voice tailed away in the bitter cold air.*
turn tail = **run away**, flee, run off, escape, take off *(informal)*, retreat, make off, hook it *(slang)*, run for it *(informal)*, scarper *(Brit. slang)*, cut and run, show a clean pair of heels, skedaddle *(informal)*, take to your heels • *I turned tail and fled in the direction of the house.*
▸ RELATED ADJECTIVE: caudal

tailor AS A NOUN = **outfitter**, couturier, dressmaker, seamstress, clothier, costumier, garment maker • *He's the grandson of an East End tailor.*
▸ AS A VERB = **adapt**, adjust, modify, cut, style, fit, fashion, shape, suit, convert, alter, accommodate, mould, customize • *scripts tailored to American comedy audiences*
▸ RELATED ADJECTIVE: sartorial

tailor-made 1 = **custom-made**, personalized, customized • *Each client's portfolio is tailor-made.*
2 = **perfect**, right, ideal, suitable, just right, right up your street *(informal)*, up your alley • *This job was tailor-made for me.*
3 = **made-to-measure**, fitted, cut to fit, made to order • *his expensive tailor-made shirt*

taint AS A VERB 1 = **disgrace**, shame, dishonour, brand, ruin, blacken, stigmatize • *They said that the elections had been tainted by corruption.*
2 = **spoil**, ruin, contaminate, damage, soil, dirty, poison, foul, infect, stain, corrupt, smear, muddy, pollute, blight, tarnish, blot, blemish, sully, defile, adulterate, besmirch, vitiate, smirch • *Rancid oil will taint the flavour.*
OPPOSITES: clean, cleanse, purify
▸ AS A NOUN = **disgrace**, shame, stigma, dishonour • *Her government never really shook off the taint of corruption.*

take AS A VERB 1 = **grip**, grab, seize, catch, grasp, clutch, get hold of, clasp, take hold of, lay hold of • *He took her by the shoulders and shook her.*
2 = **carry**, bring, bear, transport, ferry, haul, convey, fetch, cart, tote *(informal)* • *I'll take these papers home and read them.*
OPPOSITES: send
3 = **accompany**, lead, bring, guide, conduct, escort, convoy, usher • *She was taken to hospital.*
4 = **remove**, draw, pull, fish, withdraw, extract, abstract • *He took a handkerchief from his pocket.*
5 = **steal**, nick *(slang, chiefly Brit.)*, appropriate, pocket, trouser *(slang)*, pinch *(informal)*, carry off, swipe *(slang)*, knock off *(slang)*, run off with, blag *(slang)*, walk off with, misappropriate, cart off *(slang)*, purloin, filch, help yourself to, gain possession of • *The burglars took just about anything they could carry.*
OPPOSITES: give, return, restore
6 = **capture**, arrest, seize, abduct, take into custody, ensnare, entrap, lay hold of • *Marines went in and took 15 prisoners.*
OPPOSITES: free, release, let go
7 = **tolerate**, stand, bear, suffer, weather, go through, brave, stomach, endure, undergo, swallow, brook, hack *(slang)*, abide, put up with *(informal)*, withstand, submit to,

countenance, pocket, thole *(Scot.)* • *His rudeness was becoming hard to take.*
OPPOSITES: avoid, dodge
8 = last, go on for, continue for, carry on for, endure for, run on for, keep on for • *The journey took a long time.*
9 = require, need, involve, demand, call for, entail, necessitate • *Walking across the room took all her strength.*
10 = accept, assume, take on, undertake, adopt, take up, enter upon • *When I took the job, I thought I could change the system.*
OPPOSITES: refuse, decline, reject
11 = draw, derive, feel, know, experience, undergo • *The government will take comfort from the latest opinion poll.*
12 = earn, make, net, collect, realize, bring in, gross • *The firm took £100,000 in bookings.*
13 = win, get, be awarded, receive, land *(informal)*, be given, pick up, bag *(informal)*, secure, collect, obtain, scoop *(informal)*, be presented with, carry off, walk away *or* off with • *He took the gold medal in the 100 metres.*
14 = receive, get, accept, be given, gain, obtain • *She was reluctant to take all the credit.*
15 = respond to, meet, deal with, receive, cope with, greet, react to • *He had taken the news badly.*
16 = consider, study, think about, examine, contemplate, ponder, weigh up, mull over, chew over, ruminate on, give thought to, deliberate over, cogitate on • *Taken in isolation, these statements can be dangerous.*
17 = understand, follow, comprehend, get, see, grasp, apprehend • *They've turned sensible, if you take my meaning.*
18 = have, choose, pick, prefer, select, opt for, settle on • *I'll take the grilled tuna sandwich, please.*
19 = travel, go, journey, walk, progress, proceed, trek, voyage, traverse, make your way • *He had to take a different route home.*
20 = hire, book, rent, lease, reserve, pay for, engage, make a reservation for • *My wife and I have taken the cottage for a month.*
21 = subscribe to, buy, read regularly, purchase, buy regularly • *Before the Chronicle I used to take the Guardian.*
22 = travel by, travel on, make use of, journey on • *We'll take a train home.*
23 = study, learn, be taught, do *(informal)*, read *(Brit.)*, pursue, work at, read up on, have lessons in • *Students may take European and American history.*
24 = perform, have, do, make, effect, accomplish, execute • *She took her driving test last week.*
25 = ingest, consume, swallow, inhale • *She's been taking sleeping pills.*
26 = consume, have, drink, eat, imbibe • *She took tea with Nanny every day.*
27 = write, record, jot (down), note (down), scribble, set down, scrawl, make a note of • *She sat expressionless, carefully taking notes.*
28 = measure, establish, determine, find out, assess, calculate, evaluate, gauge, ascertain, appraise • *If he feels hotter than normal, take his temperature.*
29 = have room for, hold, contain, accommodate, accept • *The place could just about take 2000 people.*
30 = wear, need, require, fit • *Half of all women take a size 16 or above.*
31 = work, succeed, do the trick *(informal)*, have effect, be efficacious • *If the cortisone doesn't take, I may have to have surgery.*
OPPOSITES: fail, flop *(informal)*
32 = extract, quote, cite, excerpt, reproduce, abstract, cull • *a passage taken from a talk she gave in 1988*
33 = occupy, use, engage, hold, fill, reserve, bag *(informal)* • *Ninety-five per cent of business-class seats were taken.*
34 = derive, get, obtain, acquire, come by • *Do you know where cappuccino coffee takes its name from?*
35 = take advantage of, grab, seize (on), exploit, grasp, act on, make the most of, jump on, pounce on, capitalize on, leap at, turn to account, put to advantage • *He took the opportunity to show off his new car.*
▸ AS A NOUN **1 = takings**, profits, revenue, return, gate, yield, proceeds, haul, receipts • *It added another $11.8 million to the take.*
2 = scene, sequence, filmed sequence • *She didn't know her lines and we had to do several takes.*
3 = view, opinion, understanding of, analysis of, interpretation of, reading of, explanation of • *That sort of thing gives you a different take on who you are.*
▸ IN PHRASES: **take after someone = resemble**, be like, be similar to, look like, favour *(informal)*, remind you of, be the spitting image of *(informal)*, bear a resemblance to, put you in mind of • *He's always been like that – he takes after his dad.*
take against something *or* **someone = take a dislike to**, feel hostile to, view with disfavour, look askance on, become unfriendly towards • *He's taken against me for some reason.*
take it = assume, suppose, presume, expect, imagine, guess *(informal, chiefly U.S. & Canad.)* • *I take it you're a friend of theirs.*
take it out of someone = exhaust, tire, drain, fatigue, weary, bush *(informal)*, whack *(informal)*, wear out, debilitate, knacker *(informal)*, enervate • *That last race really took it out of me.*
take off 1 = lift off, leave the ground, take to the air, become airborne • *We eventually took off at 11am and arrived in Venice at 1.30pm.*
2 = depart, go, leave, split *(slang)*, disappear, set out, strike out, beat it *(slang)*, hit the road *(slang)*, abscond, decamp, hook it *(slang)*, slope off, pack your bags *(informal)* • *He took off at once and headed home.*
3 = do well, succeed, thrive, flourish, progress, boom, prosper, have legs *(informal)*, turn out well • *He met her in 1944, and his career took off.*
take on = get upset, get excited, make a fuss, break down, give way • *Please don't take on so. I'll help you.*
take someone back 1 = be reconciled with, forgive, pardon, welcome someone back, accept someone back • *Why did she take him back?*
2 = evoke, remind you of, awaken your memories of, call up, summon up • *It took me back to my childhood.*
take someone for something = regard as, see as, believe to be, consider to be, think of as, deem to be, perceive to be, hold to be, judge to be, reckon to be, presume to be, look on as • *Do you take me for an idiot?*
take someone in 1 = let in, receive, admit, board, welcome, harbour, accommodate, take care of, put up, billet • *The monastery has taken in 26 refugees.*
2 = deceive, fool, con *(informal)*, do *(slang)*, trick, cheat, mislead, dupe, gull *(archaic)*, swindle, hoodwink, pull the wool over someone's eyes *(informal)*, bilk, cozen, scam *(slang)* • *He was a real charmer who totally took me in.*
take someone off = parody, imitate, mimic, mock, ridicule, ape, caricature, send up *(Brit. informal)*, spoof *(informal)*, travesty, impersonate, lampoon, burlesque, satirize • *He can take off his father to perfection.*
take someone on 1 = compete against, face, contend with, fight, oppose, vie with, pit yourself against, enter the lists against, match yourself against • *I knew I couldn't take him on if it came to a fight.*
2 = engage, employ, hire, retain, enlist, enrol • *A publishing firm agreed to take him on.*
take someone out 1 = escort, accompany, go out with • *Her grandparents took her out for the day.*
2 = kill, murder, execute, assassinate, top *(informal)*, eliminate, do someone in *(informal)*, get rid of, dispatch, put an end to, do away with, exterminate, finish someone off,

put someone to death, bump someone off *(informal)*, rub someone out *(informal)* • *The local dealers would have taken him out years ago.*
take something apart 1 = dismantle, break up, pull apart, disassemble, pull *or* take to pieces *or* bits • *He took the clock apart to find out what was wrong with it.*
2 = dissect, study, analyse, scrutinize, research, explore, break down • *They took the problem apart and discussed it in detail.*
take something away = subtract, deduct, take something off • *Take one number away from the other and you get the answer.*
take something back 1 = return, bring back, send back, hand back • *I'm going to take it back and ask for a refund.*
2 = give a refund for, exchange, accept something back • *The store wouldn't take damaged goods back.*
3 = retract, withdraw, renounce, renege on, disavow, recant, disclaim, unsay • *Take back what you said about Jeremy!*
4 = regain, get back, reclaim, recapture, repossess, retake, reconquer • *The government took back control of the city.*
take something down 1 = remove, take off, extract • *He went to the bookcase and took down a volume.*
2 = lower, drop, let down, pull down, haul down • *The flag was taken down from the flag pole.*
3 = dismantle, demolish, take apart, disassemble, level, tear down, raze, take to pieces • *They took down the barricades that had been erected.*
4 = make a note of, record, write down, minute, note, set down, transcribe, put on record • *I took down his comments in shorthand.*
take something in 1 = understand, absorb, grasp, digest, comprehend, assimilate, get the hang of *(informal)* • *She seemed to take in all he said.*
2 = include, contain, comprise, cover, embrace, encompass • *The constituency takes in a population of more than 4 million people.*
take something off 1 = remove, discard, strip off, drop, peel off, doff, divest yourself of • *She took off her spectacles.*
2 = detach, remove, separate, cut off, pull off, chop off, hack off, clip off, prune off • *Take off the first few layers of wallpaper.*
3 = subtract, deduct, take something away, remove, eliminate • *Take off the price of the house; that's another thirty thousand.*
take something on 1 = accept, tackle, undertake, shoulder, have a go at *(informal)*, agree to do, address yourself to, step up to the plate *(informal)* • *No one was able or willing to take on the job.*
2 = acquire, assume, come to have • *His writing took on a feverish intensity.*
take something *or* **someone apart = attack**, pan *(informal)*, condemn, slam *(informal)*, savage, censure, maul, pillory, flay, diss *(slang, chiefly U.S.)*, flame *(informal)*, lambaste, criticize harshly • *The critics had taken her apart.*
take something out = extract, remove, pull out, draw, yank out • *I got an abscess so he took the tooth out.*
take something over = gain control of, take command of, assume control of, come to power in, become leader of • *They took over Rwanda under a League of Nations mandate.*
take something up 1 = start, begin, engage in, assume, adopt, become involved in • *He didn't want to take up a competitive sport.*
2 = accept, agree to, say yes to, accede to • *Most of the employees took up the offer.*
3 = occupy, absorb, consume, use up, cover, fill, waste, squander, extend over • *I don't want to take up too much of your time.*
4 = resume, continue, go on with, pick up, proceed with, restart, carry on with, recommence, follow on with, begin something again • *His wife takes up the story.*
take to someone = like, get on with, warm to, be taken with, be pleased by, become friendly with, conceive an affection for • *Did the children take to him?*
take to something 1 = start, resort to, make a habit of, have recourse to • *They had taken to aimlessly wandering through the streets.*
2 = become good at, like, enjoy, become interested in, develop an aptitude for • *She took to the piano immediately.*
3 = head for, make for, run for, flee to • *He took to the roof of his home when police officers came round.*
take up with someone = become friendly with, get involved with, start seeing, fall in with, go around with, become friends with, hang about with *(Brit. informal)*, knock about *or* around with *(informal)* • *He took up with a woman 21 years his junior.*
take yourself off = go away, withdraw, depart, retire, exit, clear out *(informal)*, clear off *(informal)*, bog off *(Brit. slang)*, take your leave, rack off *(Austral. & N.Z. slang)* • *He took himself off to Mexico.*

take aback = surprise, stun, astonish, floor *(informal)*, stagger, startle, bewilder, astound, disconcert, nonplus, flabbergast *(informal)* • *He was taken aback when a man answered the phone.*

taken = charmed, pleased, delighted, fascinated, entertained, attracted to, enchanted, captivated, beguiled, bewitched • *I was much taken with their new TV ad.*

takeoff 1 = departure, launch, liftoff • *The aircraft crashed soon after takeoff.*
2 = parody, imitation, send-up *(Brit. informal)*, mocking, satire, caricature, spoof *(informal)*, travesty, lampoon • *an inspired takeoff of the two sisters*

takeover = merger, coup, change of leadership, incorporation • *the proposed takeover of the company*

taking AS AN ADJECTIVE **= charming**, winning, pleasing, attractive, engaging, fascinating, compelling, intriguing, fetching *(informal)*, delightful, cute, enchanting, captivating, beguiling, prepossessing, likable *or* likeable • *He looked clean, childish, and very taking.*
OPPOSITES: offensive, unpleasant, unattractive
▸ AS A PLURAL NOUN **= revenue**, take, returns, profits, gain, income, gate, earnings, yield, proceeds, receipts, pickings • *Their takings were fifteen to twenty thousand pounds a month.*

tale 1 = story, narrative, anecdote, account, relation, novel, legend, fiction, romance, saga, short story, yarn *(informal)*, fable, narration, conte *(French)*, spiel *(informal)*, urban myth, urban legend • *a collection of poems and folk tales*
2 = lie, fabrication, falsehood, fib, untruth, spiel *(informal)*, tall story *(informal)*, rigmarole, cock-and-bull story *(informal)* • *He's always ready to spin a tall tale about the one that got away.*

QUOTATIONS
And so from hour to hour we ripe and ripe,
And then from hour to hour we rot and rot;
And thereby hangs a tale
[William Shakespeare *As You Like It*]

PROVERBS
A tale never loses in the telling

talent = ability, gift, aptitude, power, skill, facility, capacity, bent, genius, expertise, faculty, endowment, forte, flair, knack • *Both her children have a talent for music.*

QUOTATIONS
Talent is like electricity. We don't understand electricity. We use it
[Maya Angelou]
Genius does what it must, and talent does what it can
[E.G. Bulwer-Lytton]
Mediocrity knows nothing higher than itself, but talent instantly recognizes genius
[Sir Arthur Conan Doyle *The Valley of Fear*]

talented = gifted, able, expert, master, masterly, brilliant, ace *(informal)*, artistic, consummate, first-rate, top-notch *(informal)*, adroit • *He is a talented pianist.*

talisman = **charm**, mascot, amulet, lucky charm, fetish, juju, periapt *(rare)* • *a talisman with protective powers*

talk AS A VERB **1** = **speak**, chat, chatter, converse, communicate, rap *(slang)*, articulate, witter *(informal)*, gab *(informal)*, express yourself, prattle, natter, shoot the breeze *(U.S. slang)*, prate, run off at the mouth *(slang)*, earbash *(Austral. & N.Z. slang)* • *The boys all began to talk at once.*
2 = **discuss**, confer, hold discussions, negotiate, palaver, parley, confabulate, have a confab *(informal)*, chew the rag *or* fat *(slang)*, korero *(N.Z.)* • *Let's talk about these new ideas of yours.*
3 = **gossip**, criticize, make remarks, tattle, dish the dirt *(informal)* • *People will talk, but you have to get on with your life.*
4 = **inform**, shop *(slang, chiefly Brit.)*, grass *(Brit. slang)*, sing *(slang, chiefly U.S.)*, squeal *(slang)*, squeak *(informal)*, tell all, spill the beans *(informal)*, give the game away, blab, let the cat out of the bag, reveal information, spill your guts *(slang)* • *They'll talk; they'll implicate me.*
5 = **speak**, speak in, communicate in, use, discourse in, converse in, express yourself in • *You don't sound like a foreigner talking English.*
6 = **utter**, say, express, spout, give voice to, verbalize, vocalize • *Come on; you're talking rubbish.*
▸ AS A NOUN **1** = **speech**, lecture, presentation, report, address, seminar, discourse, sermon, symposium, dissertation, harangue, oration, disquisition, whaikorero *(N.Z.)* • *The guide gave us a brief talk on the history of the site.*
2 = **discussion**, tête-à-tête, conference, dialogue, consultation, heart-to-heart, confabulation, confab *(informal)*, powwow, korero *(N.Z.)* • *I think it's time we had a talk.*
3 = **conversation**, chat, natter, crack *(Scot. & Irish)*, rap *(slang)*, jaw *(slang)*, chatter, craic *(Irish informal)*, gab *(informal)*, chitchat, blether, blather, korero *(N.Z.)* • *We had a long talk about her father.*
4 = **gossip**, rumour, hearsay, tittle-tattle, goss *(informal)* • *There has been a lot of talk about me getting married.*
5 = **language**, words, speech, jargon, slang, dialect, lingo *(informal)*, patois, argot • *children babbling on in baby talk*
6 *often plural* = **meeting**, conference, discussions, negotiations, congress, summit, mediation, arbitration, conciliation, conclave, palaver, parley, hui *(N.Z.)* • *Talks between strikers and government have broken down.*
▸ IN PHRASES: **talk about** *or* **of something** *or* **someone** = **mention**, discuss, refer to, speak about, make reference to, make mention of, namecheck • *They didn't talk of meeting again.*
talk back = **answer back**, argue, be rude, be cheeky, be impertinent, disagree • *How dare you talk back like that!*
talk big = **boast**, exaggerate, brag, crow, vaunt, bluster, blow your own trumpet • *men who talk big and drive fast cars*
talk down to someone = **condescend to**, patronize, look down on, put down, look down your nose at, be snobbish to, speak condescendingly to • *She never talked down to her students.*
talk someone into something = **persuade**, convince, win someone over, sway, bring round *(informal)*, sweet-talk someone into, prevail on *or* upon • *He talked me into marrying him.*
talk someone out of something = **dissuade someone from**, put someone off, discourage someone from, stop someone from, deter someone from, advise someone against, argue someone out of, persuade someone against, urge someone against • *She tried to talk me out of getting a divorce.*
talk something *or* **someone down** **1** = **help to land**, bring to land, give landing instructions to • *They began to talk the plane down over the radio.*
2 = **criticize**, belittle, disparage, knock *(informal)*, pan *(informal)*, diminish, put down *(informal)*, denigrate, deprecate, depreciate, diss *(slang, chiefly U.S.)* • *They're tired of politicians talking the economy down.*

QUOTATIONS
A fool may talk, but a wise man speaks
[Ben Jonson *Discoveries*]

PROVERBS
Fine words butter no parsnips
Talk is cheap

talkative = **loquacious**, chatty, garrulous, long-winded, big-mouthed *(slang)*, wordy, effusive, gabby *(informal)*, voluble, gossipy, verbose, mouthy, prolix • *He suddenly became very talkative, his face slightly flushed.*
OPPOSITES: reserved, quiet, silent

talker = **speaker**, lecturer, orator, conversationalist, chatterbox, speechmaker • *She was a fluent talker.*

talking
▸ RELATED MANIA: logomania

talking-to = **reprimand**, lecture, rebuke, scolding, row, criticism, wigging *(Brit. slang)*, slating *(informal)*, reproach, ticking-off *(informal)*, dressing-down *(informal)*, telling-off *(informal)*, reproof, rap on the knuckles • *He has had a good talking-to and regrets his actions.*
OPPOSITES: praise, acclaim, commendation

tall **1** = **lofty**, big, giant, long-legged, lanky, leggy, Brobdingnagian • *Being tall can make you incredibly self-confident.*
2 = **high**, towering, soaring, steep, elevated, lofty • *a lawn of tall, waving grass*
OPPOSITES: small, short, tiny
3 = **implausible**, incredible, far-fetched, steep *(Brit. informal)*, exaggerated, absurd, unbelievable, preposterous, embellished, overblown, cock-and-bull *(informal)* • *a tall story*
OPPOSITES: true, plausible, believable
4 = **difficult**, hard, demanding, unreasonable, exorbitant, well-nigh impossible • *Financing your studies can be a tall order.*

tally AS A VERB **1** = **agree**, match, accord, fit, suit, square, parallel, coincide, correspond, conform, concur, harmonize • *The figures didn't seem to tally.*
OPPOSITES: conflict, clash, disagree
2 = **count up**, total, compute, keep score • *When the final numbers are tallied, sales will probably have fallen.*
▸ AS A NOUN = **record**, score, total, count, reckoning, running total • *They do not keep a tally of visitors to the palace.*

tame AS AN ADJECTIVE **1** = **domesticated**, unafraid, docile, broken, gentle, fearless, obedient, amenable, tractable, used to human contact • *tame animals at a children's zoo or farm*
OPPOSITES: wild, savage, ferocious
2 = **submissive**, meek, compliant, subdued, manageable, obedient, docile, spiritless, unresisting • *a tame and gullible newspaper journalist*
OPPOSITES: aggressive, stubborn, strong-willed
3 = **unexciting**, boring, dull, bland, tedious, flat, tiresome, lifeless, prosaic, uninspiring, humdrum, uninteresting, insipid, vapid, wearisome • *The report was pretty tame stuff.*
OPPOSITES: interesting, exciting, stimulating
▸ AS A VERB **1** = **domesticate**, train, break in, gentle, pacify, house-train, make tame • *They were the first to tame horses.*
OPPOSITES: make fiercer
2 = **subdue**, suppress, master, discipline, curb, humble, conquer, repress, bridle, enslave, subjugate, bring to heel, break the spirit of • *Two regiments were called out to tame the crowds.*
OPPOSITES: arouse, incite, intensify

tamper *usually with* **with** **1** = **interfere with**, tinker with, meddle with, alter, fiddle with *(informal)*, mess about with, muck about with *(Brit. slang)*, monkey around with, fool about with *(informal)* • *He found his computer had been tampered with.*

t

2 = **influence**, fix *(informal)*, rig, corrupt, manipulate • *I don't want to be accused of tampering with the evidence.*

tan AS A VERB 1 = **brown**, bronze, go brown, become suntanned, take a suntan *or* tan • *I have very pale skin that never tans.*
2 = **thrash**, belt, leather, whip, strap, smack, cane, flog, spank, wallop, flay, horsewhip • *I'll tan his backside for him.*
▸ AS AN ADJECTIVE = **tawny**, light brown, pale brown, yellowish-brown • *a tan leather jacket*
▹ *See panel* **Shades of brown**

tang 1 = **scent**, smell, odour, perfume, fragrance, aroma, reek, redolence • *She could smell the salty tang of the sea.*
2 = **taste**, bite, flavour, edge, relish, smack, savour, zest, sharpness, piquancy, spiciness, zestiness • *Some liked its strong, fruity tang.*
3 = **trace**, touch, tinge, suggestion, hint, whiff, smattering • *His criticism seemed to have acquired a tang of friendliness.*

tangible = **definite**, real, positive, solid, material, physical, actual, substantial, objective, concrete, evident, manifest, palpable, discernible, tactile, perceptible, corporeal, touchable • *There is tangible evidence that the economy is starting to recover.*
OPPOSITES: abstract, theoretical, intangible

tangle AS A NOUN 1 = **knot**, mass, twist, web, jungle, mat, coil, snarl, mesh, ravel, entanglement • *a tangle of wires*
2 = **mess**, jam, fix *(informal)*, confusion, complication, maze, mix-up, shambles, labyrinth, entanglement, imbroglio • *I was thinking what a tangle we had got ourselves into.*
▸ AS A VERB 1 = **twist**, knot, mat, coil, snarl, mesh, entangle, interlock, kink, interweave, ravel, interlace, enmesh, intertwist • *a huge mass of hair, all tangled together*
OPPOSITES: unravel, disentangle, untangle
2 *sometimes with* **up** = **entangle**, catch, ensnare, entrap • *Animals get tangled in fishing nets and drown.*
3 = **confuse**, mix up, muddle, jumble, scramble • *Themes get tangled in his elliptical storytelling.*
▸ IN PHRASES: **tangle something** *or* **someone up** *usually passive* 1 = **entangle**, catch, trap, snare, ensnare • *Sheep keep getting tangled up in the wire.*
2 = **mix up**, involve, implicate, embroil, drag into, mire • *He tried to avoid getting tangled up in any awkward situations.*
tangle with someone = **come into conflict with**, come up against, cross swords with, dispute with, contend with, contest with, lock horns with • *They are not the first bank to tangle with the taxman recently.*

tangled 1 = **knotted**, twisted, matted, messy, snarled, jumbled, entangled, knotty, tousled • *tugging a comb through her tangled hair*
2 = **complicated**, involved, complex, confused, messy, mixed-up, convoluted, knotty • *His personal life has become more tangled than ever.*

tangy = **sharp**, tart, piquant, biting, fresh, spicy, pungent, briny, acerb • *smoked salmon, tangy cheeses and oysters*

tank 1 = **container**, barrel, vat, reservoir, cistern, receptacle • *an empty fuel tank*
2 = **aquarium**, bowl • *a tank full of goldfish*
3 = **armoured vehicle**, Panzer *(German)*, armoured car, combat vehicle • *soldiers backed up by tanks*

tantalize *or* **tantalise** = **torment**, tease, taunt, torture, provoke, entice, lead on, titillate, make someone's mouth water, keep someone hanging on • *He would tantalize the dog with food.*

tantamount IN PHRASES: **tantamount to** = **equivalent to**, equal to, as good as, synonymous with, the same as, commensurate with • *What he was saying was tantamount to heresy.*

tantrum = **outburst**, temper, hysterics, fit, storm, paddy *(Brit. informal)*, wax *(informal, chiefly Brit.)*, flare-up, paroxysm, bate *(Brit. slang)*, ill humour, foulie *(Austral. slang)*, hissy fit *(informal)*, strop *(Brit. informal)* • *My son had a tantrum and banged his fist on the ground.*

tap[1] AS A VERB = **knock**, strike, pat, rap, beat, touch, drum • *Tap the egg lightly with a teaspoon.*
▸ AS A NOUN = **knock**, pat, rap, beat, touch, drumming, light blow • *A tap on the door interrupted him.*

tap[2] AS A NOUN 1 = **valve**, spout, faucet *(U.S. & Canad.)*, spigot, stopcock • *She turned on the taps.*
2 = **bug** *(informal)*, listening device, wiretap, bugging device, hidden microphone • *Ministers are not subject to phone taps.*
▸ AS A VERB 1 = **listen in on**, monitor, bug *(informal)*, spy on, eavesdrop on, wiretap • *laws allowing the police to tap telephones*
2 = **use**, draw on, make use of, mine, milk, exploit, utilize, put to use, turn to account • *She tapped her own experiences for her novels.*
▸ IN PHRASES: **on tap** 1 = **available**, ready, standing by, to hand, on hand, at hand, in reserve • *He's already got surveyors on tap to measure for the road.*
2 = **on draught**, cask-conditioned, from barrels, not bottled or canned • *They only have one beer on tap.*

tape AS A NOUN 1 = **binding**, strip, band, string, ribbon • *The books were all tied up with tape.*
2 = **sticky tape**, Sellotape *(trademark)*, masking tape, adhesive tape • *His steel spectacles had been repaired with tape.*
3 = **recording**, cassette, tape recording • *She still listens to the tapes I made her.*
▸ AS A VERB 1 = **record**, video, tape-record, make a recording of • *She has just taped an interview.*
2 *sometimes with* **up** = **bind**, secure, stick, seal, wrap • *I taped the base of the feather onto the velvet.*
▸ IN PHRASES: **have something** *or* **someone taped** = **understand fully**, know all about, know the ins and outs of, have someone's number *(informal)*, have all the details of • *Dave has life taped.*
tape something off = **cordon off**, close (off), shut (off), isolate, segregate, quarantine, seal off, fence off, form a ring round, put a cordon around • *The whole of the West End was taped off by police.*

taper AS A VERB = **narrow**, thin, attenuate, come to a point, become thinner, become narrow • *The trunk doesn't taper very much.*
OPPOSITES: widen, grow, swell
▸ AS A NOUN = **candle**, spill, wick, glim *(old-fashioned)* • *Singe the stems slightly with a lighted taper.*
▸ IN PHRASES: **taper off** = **decrease**, dwindle, lessen, reduce, fade, weaken, wane, subside, wind down, die out, die away, thin out • *Immigration is beginning to taper off.*

tardiness 1 = **lateness**, dilatoriness, unpunctuality • *His legendary tardiness left audiences waiting for hours.*
2 = **delay**, slowness, procrastination, belatedness • *his tardiness in giving talented players international experience*

tardy 1 = **late**, overdue, unpunctual, belated, dilatory, behindhand • *He was as tardy as ever for our appointment.*
2 = **slow**, belated, delayed • *the agency's tardy response to the hurricane*

target AS A NOUN 1 = **mark**, goal, bull's-eye • *We threw knives at targets.*
2 = **goal**, aim, objective, end, mark, object, intention, ambition, Holy Grail *(informal)* • *school leavers who fail to reach their targets*
3 = **victim**, butt, prey, quarry, scapegoat • *In the past they have been the targets of racist abuse.*
▸ AS A VERB 1 = **attack**, aim at, pick out, single out, fire at • *The terrorists targeted military bases.*
2 = **choose**, select, single out, earmark, fix on • *The company has targeted adults as its primary customers.*
▸ IN PHRASES: **on target** 1 = **accurate**, precise, spot on *(informal)*, on the mark • *He was dead on target when he took the penalty.*

t

2 = on schedule, on time, on course, on track • *We were still right on target for our deadline.*
target something at something *or* **someone = aim at**, focus on, direct at, intend for, level at, position for • *marketing activities targeted at export markets*

tariff 1 = tax, rate, duty, toll, levy, excise, impost, assessment • *America wants to eliminate tariffs on items such as electronics.*
2 = price list, charges, schedule • *electricity tariffs and telephone charges*

tarnish AS A VERB 1 = stain, dull, discolour, spot, soil, dim, rust, darken, blot, blemish, befoul, lose lustre *or* shine • *It never rusts or tarnishes.*
OPPOSITES: shine, brighten, polish up
2 = damage, taint, blacken, sully, drag through the mud, smirch • *His image was tarnished by the savings and loans scandal.*
OPPOSITES: enhance
▸ **AS A NOUN = stain**, taint, discoloration, spot, rust, blot, blemish • *The tarnish lay thick on the inside of the ring.*

tarry = linger, remain, loiter, wait, delay, pause, hang around (*informal*), lose time, bide, dally, take your time, dawdle, drag your feet *or* heels • *Two old boys tarried on the street corner discussing cattle.*
OPPOSITES: rush, move on, hurry

tart[1] = pie, pastry, pasty, tartlet, patty • *a slice of home-made tart*

tart[2] 1 = sharp, acid, sour, bitter, pungent, tangy, astringent, piquant, vinegary, acidulous, acerb • *a slightly tart wine*
OPPOSITES: sweet, sugary, honeyed
2 = cutting, biting, sharp, short, wounding, nasty, harsh, scathing, acrimonious, barbed, hurtful, caustic, astringent, vitriolic, trenchant, testy, mordant, snappish, mordacious • *The words were more tart than she had intended.*
OPPOSITES: kind, gentle, pleasant

tart[3] AS A NOUN = slut, prostitute, hooker (*U.S. slang*), whore, slag (*Brit. slang*), call girl, working girl (*facetious slang*), harlot, streetwalker, loose woman, fallen woman, scrubber (*Brit. & Austral. slang*), strumpet, trollop, floozy (*slang*), woman of easy virtue, fille de joie (*French*), hornbag (*Austral. slang*) • *He said I looked like a tart.*
▸ **IN PHRASES: tart something up = do up**, decorate, refurbish, renovate (*informal*), do over (*Brit., Austral. & N.Z. slang*), fix up (*informal*), modernize, smarten up, give something a facelift (*informal*) • *They prefer to tart up their stations than improve their services.*
tart yourself up = do yourself up, doll yourself up (*informal*), smarten yourself up, beautify yourself, make yourself up, preen yourself, titivate yourself (*informal*) • *She ran to the loo to tart herself up.*

task AS A NOUN = job, duty, assignment, work, business, charge, labour, exercise, mission, employment, enterprise, undertaking, occupation, chore, toil • *He had the unenviable task of breaking the bad news.*
▸ **AS A VERB = charge**, assign to, entrust • *The minister was tasked with checking that aid was spent wisely.*
▸ **IN PHRASES: take someone to task = criticize**, blame, blast, lecture, carpet (*informal*), flame (*informal*), censure, rebuke, reprimand, reproach, scold, tear into (*informal*), tell off (*informal*), diss (*slang, chiefly U.S.*), read the riot act, reprove, upbraid, lambast(e), bawl out (*informal*), chew out (*U.S. & Canad. informal*), tear (someone) off a strip (*Brit. informal*), give a rocket (*Brit. & N.Z. informal*) • *The country's intellectuals are being taken to task.*

taste AS A NOUN 1 = flavour, savour, relish, smack, tang • *Nettles have a surprisingly sweet taste.*
OPPOSITES: blandness, tastelessness, insipidity
2 = bit, bite, drop, swallow, sip, mouthful, touch, sample, dash, nip, spoonful, morsel, titbit, soupçon (*French*) • *He took another small taste.*
3 = experience, contact with, exposure to, impression, participation in, involvement with, familiarity with • *This voyage was his first taste of freedom.*
4 = liking, preference, penchant, fondness, partiality, desire, fancy, leaning, bent, appetite, relish, inclination, palate, predilection • *She developed a taste for journeys to hazardous regions.*
OPPOSITES: dislike, hatred, loathing
5 = refinement, style, judgment, culture, polish, grace, discrimination, perception, appreciation, elegance, sophistication, cultivation, discernment • *She has very good taste in clothes.*
OPPOSITES: lack of judgment, tastelessness, tackiness
6 = propriety, discretion, correctness, delicacy, tact, politeness, nicety, decorum, tactfulness • *I do not feel your actions were in good taste.*
OPPOSITES: impropriety, crudeness, tactlessness
▸ **AS A VERB 1** *often with* **of = have a flavour of**, smack of, savour of • *The drink tastes like chocolate.*
2 = sample, try, test, relish, sip, savour, nibble • *Cut off a small piece of meat and taste it.*
3 = distinguish, perceive, discern, differentiate • *You can taste the chilli in the dish.*
4 = experience, know, undergo, partake of, feel, encounter, meet with, come up against, have knowledge of • *He had tasted outdoor life, and didn't want to come home.*
OPPOSITES: miss, fail to experience, remain ignorant of
▸ **RELATED NOUN:** gustation
▸ **RELATED PHOBIA:** geumaphobia

QUOTATIONS
Taste is the only morality. Tell me what you like, and I'll tell you who you are
[John Ruskin]
Taste is the enemy of creativeness
[Pablo Picasso]

PROVERBS
There's no accounting for tastes
Beauty is in the eye of the beholder
One man's meat is another man's poison

tasteful = refined, stylish, elegant, cultured, beautiful, smart, charming, polished, delicate, artistic, handsome, cultivated, discriminating, exquisite, graceful, harmonious, urbane, fastidious, aesthetically pleasing, in good taste • *The decor is tasteful and restrained.*
OPPOSITES: vulgar, tacky (*informal*), tasteless

tasteless 1 = gaudy, cheap, vulgar, tacky (*informal*), flashy, naff (*Brit. slang*), garish, inelegant, tawdry • *spectacularly tasteless objets d'art*
OPPOSITES: elegant, refined, tasteful
2 = vulgar, crude, improper, low, gross, rude, coarse, crass, unseemly, indiscreet, tactless, uncouth, impolite, graceless, indelicate, indecorous • *a tasteless remark*
3 = insipid, bland, flat, boring, thin, weak, dull, mild, tame, watered-down, uninteresting, uninspired, vapid, flavourless • *The fish was mushy and tasteless.*
OPPOSITES: delicious, tasty, delectable

tasty = delicious, luscious, palatable, delectable, good-tasting, savoury, full-flavoured, yummy (*slang*), flavoursome, scrumptious (*informal*), appetizing, toothsome, flavourful, sapid, lekker (*S. African slang*), yummo (*Austral. slang*) • *I thought the food was very tasty.*
OPPOSITES: bland, tasteless, insipid

tattered = torn, ripped, ragged, frayed, threadbare • *He fled wearing a sarong and a tattered shirt.*

tatters AS A PLURAL NOUN = rags, scraps, shreds, bits, pieces, fragments • *The walls are bare with a few tatters of wallpaper here and there.*
▸ **IN PHRASES: in tatters 1 = ragged**, torn, ripped, tattered, in rags, in shreds • *His jersey was left in tatters.*

t

2 = **in ruins**, ruined, devastated, finished, destroyed, shattered, in disarray, dead in the water *(informal)* • *The economy was in tatters.*

tattle AS A VERB 1 = **gossip**, talk idly • *I make it a rule not to tattle.*
2 = **tell tales**, report, inform, squeal *(informal)*, spill the beans • *He encourages people to tattle on one another.*
▸AS A NOUN = **gossip**, goss *(informal)*, hearsay, tittle-tattle, idle talk • *This was not just idle newspaper tattle.*

tattletale = **gossip**, busybody, babbler, prattler, chatterbox *(informal)*, blether, chatterer, bigmouth *(slang)*, scandalmonger, gossipmonger

tatty = **shabby**, seedy, scruffy, worn, poor, neglected, ragged, rundown, frayed, worn out, dilapidated, tattered, tawdry, threadbare, rumpled, bedraggled, unkempt, down at heel, the worse for wear, having seen better days • *A lot of the houses in the street were very tatty.*
OPPOSITES: new, good, smart

taunt AS A VERB = **jeer**, mock, tease, ridicule, provoke, insult, torment, sneer, deride, revile, twit, take the piss (out of) *(taboo slang)*, guy *(informal)*, gibe • *Other youths taunted him about his clothes.*
▸AS A NOUN = **jeer**, dig, insult, ridicule, cut, teasing, provocation, barb, derision, sarcasm, gibe • *For years they suffered racist taunts.*

taut 1 = **tense**, rigid, tight, stressed, stretched, strained, flexed • *When muscles are taut or cold, there is more chance of injury.*
OPPOSITES: relaxed, loose, slack
2 = **tight**, stretched, rigid, tightly stretched • *The clothes line is pulled taut and secured.*
OPPOSITES: relaxed, loose, slack
3 = **strained**, stressed, tense, fraught, drawn, drained, sapped, uptight *(informal)*, adrenalized • *She started to lose the taut air of anxiety.*
4 = **concise**, terse, succinct, sharp, crisp, compact, pithy • *a taut thriller about the hijacking of a school bus*

tautology = **repetition**, redundancy, verbiage, iteration, verbosity, repetitiveness, prolixity, repetitiousness, pleonasm • *The tautology and circularity of this argument were swept aside.*

tavern = **inn**, bar, pub *(informal, chiefly Brit.)*, public house, watering hole *(facetious slang)*, boozer *(Brit., Austral. & N.Z. informal)*, beer parlour *(Canad.)*, beverage room *(Canad.)*, hostelry, alehouse *(archaic)*, taproom • *The tavern was packed with about 120 drinkers.*

QUOTATIONS
There is nothing which has yet been contrived by man, by which so much happiness is produced as by a good tavern or inn
[Dr. Johnson]

tawdry = **vulgar**, cheap, tacky *(informal)*, flashy, tasteless, plastic *(slang)*, glittering, naff *(Brit. slang)*, gaudy, tatty, showy, tinsel, raffish, gimcrack, meretricious, tinselly, cheap-jack *(informal)* • *tawdry jewellery*
OPPOSITES: elegant, stylish, tasteful

tax AS A NOUN 1 = **charge**, rate, duty, toll, levy, tariff, excise, contribution, assessment, customs, tribute, imposition, tithe, impost • *a cut in tax on new cars*
2 = **strain**, demand, burden, pressure, weight, load, drain • *less of a tax on her bodily resources*
▸AS A VERB 1 = **charge**, impose a tax on, levy a tax on, rate, demand, assess, extract, exact, tithe • *The government taxes profits of corporations at a high rate.*
2 = **strain**, push, stretch, try, test, task, load, burden, drain, exhaust, weaken, weary, put pressure on, sap, wear out, weigh heavily on, overburden, make heavy demands on, enervate • *Overcrowding has taxed the city's ability to deal with waste.*
3 = **accuse**, charge, blame, confront, impeach, incriminate, arraign, impugn, lay at your door • *Writers to the letters column taxed me with shallowness.*
OPPOSITES: clear, acquit, vindicate

QUOTATIONS
In this world nothing can be said to be certain, except death and taxes
[Benjamin Franklin *letter to Jean Baptiste Le Roy*]
The Chancellor of the Exchequer is a man whose duties make him more or less of a taxing machine. He is entrusted with a certain amount of misery which it is his duty to distribute as fairly as he can
[Robert Lowe, Viscount Sherbrooke *speech*]
To tax and to please, no more than to love and to be wise, is not given to men
[Edmund Burke *On American Taxation*]
If you tax too high, the revenue will yield nothing
[Ralph Waldo Emerson]
Only the little people pay taxes
[Leona Helmsley]
Read my lips: no new taxes
[George Bush *speech during election campaign – later, he raised taxes*]
Taxation without representation is tyranny
[James Otis]
What is the difference between a taxidermist and a tax collector? The taxidermist takes only your skin
[Mark Twain]

taxing = **demanding**, trying, wearing, heavy, tough, tiring, punishing, exacting, stressful, sapping, onerous, burdensome, wearisome, enervating • *You won't be asked to do anything too taxing.*
OPPOSITES: light, easy, effortless

tea

QUOTATIONS
Tea to the English is really a picnic indoors
[Alice Walker *The Color Purple*]

TEAS

Assam	English breakfast	lemon tea
bohea	green tea	mint tea
camomile tea	gunpowder tea	oolong
Ceylon	herbal tea	orange pekoe
Chinese tea	Indian tea	post-and-rail tea *(archaic)*
congou	jasmine tea	Russian tea
Darjeeling	Lapsang Souchong	
Earl Grey		

teach 1 = **instruct**, train, coach, school, direct, advise, inform, discipline, educate, drill, tutor, enlighten, impart, instil, inculcate, edify, give lessons in • *a programme to teach educational skills* • *She taught me to read.*
2 *often with* **how** = **show**, train, demonstrate • *George had taught him how to ride a horse.*
3 = **give lessons in**, lecture in, give instruction in, tutor, explain, expound, inculcate, inform someone about • *She teaches English to Japanese business people.*

teacher = **instructor**, coach, tutor, don, guide, professor, trainer, lecturer, guru, mentor, educator, handler, schoolteacher, pedagogue, dominie *(Scot.)*, master *or* mistress, schoolmaster *or* schoolmistress • *I'm a teacher with 21 years' experience.*

QUOTATIONS
We teachers can only help the work going on, as servants wait upon a master
[Maria Montessori *The Absorbent Mind*]

A teacher affects eternity; he can never tell where his influence stops
[Henry Brooks Adams *The Education of Henry Adams*]
The true teacher defends his pupils against his own personal influence
[A. Bronson Alcot]
He who can, does. He who cannot, teaches
[George Bernard Shaw *Maxims for Revolutionists*]
I owe a lot to my teachers and mean to pay them back some day
[Stephen Leacock]
It is when the gods hate a man with uncommon abhorrence that they drive him into the profession of a schoolmaster
[Seneca]

teal
▸ COLLECTIVE NOUNS: bunch, knob, spring

team AS A NOUN **1 = side**, squad, dream team, troupe • *The team failed to qualify for the final.*
2 = group, company, set, body, band, crew, gang, line-up, bunch, dream team, posse *(informal)* • *Mr Hunter and his management team*
3 = pair, span, yoke • *Ploughing is no longer done with a team of oxen.*
▸ AS A VERB **= match**, coordinate, pair up, complement • *It just doesn't do to team a couture frock with undressed hair.*
▸ IN PHRASES: **team up = join**, unite, work together, cooperate, couple, link up, get together, yoke, band together, collaborate, join forces • *He suggested that we team up for a working holiday in France.*

teamwork = cooperation, collaboration, unity, concert, harmony, fellowship, coordination, joint action, esprit de corps • *The buildings require close teamwork between the architect and the builders.*

tear AS A VERB **1 = rip**, split, rend, shred, rupture, sunder • *She very nearly tore my overcoat.*
2 = run, rip, ladder, snag • *Too fine a material may tear.*
3 = scratch, cut (open), gash, lacerate, injure, mangle, cut to pieces, cut to ribbons, mangulate *(Austral. slang)* • *He'd torn his skin trying to do it barehanded.*
4 = pull apart, claw, lacerate, sever, mutilate, mangle, mangulate *(Austral. slang)* • *Canine teeth are for tearing flesh.*
5 = rush, run, charge, race, shoot, fly, career, speed, belt *(slang)*, dash, hurry, barrel (along) *(informal, chiefly U.S. & Canad.)*, sprint, bolt, dart, gallop, zoom, burn rubber *(informal)* • *The door flew open and she tore into the room.*
6 *often with* **away** *or* **from = pull**, seize, rip, grab, snatch, pluck, yank, wrench, wrest • *She tore the windscreen wipers from his car.*
7 *often with* **apart = divide**, split, break apart, rupture, split down the middle, disunite • *a country that has been torn by civil war*
8 = torment, torture, rack, wring • *Torn by guilt, they gave a mandate to protect civilians.*
▸ AS A NOUN **= hole**, split, rip, run, rent, snag, rupture • *I peered through a tear in the van's curtains.*
▸ IN PHRASES: **tear something down = demolish**, knock down, pull down, level, dismantle, flatten, take down, bulldoze, raze, raze to the ground, disassemble • *They'll be tearing down those buildings sooner or later.*

tearaway = hooligan, delinquent, tough, rough *(informal)*, rowdy, ruffian, roughneck *(slang)*, good-for-nothing • *He blamed the parents for the tearaways' behaviour.*

tearful 1 = weeping, crying, sobbing, in tears, whimpering, blubbering, weepy *(informal)*, lachrymose • *She was tearful when asked to talk about it.*
2 = sad, pathetic, poignant, upsetting, distressing, harrowing, pitiful, woeful, mournful, lamentable, sorrowful, pitiable, dolorous • *a tearful farewell*

tears AS A PLURAL NOUN **= crying**, weeping, sobbing, wailing, whimpering, blubbering, lamentation • *She was very near to tears.*
▸ IN PHRASES: **in tears = weeping**, crying, sobbing, whimpering, blubbering, visibly moved • *He was in tears at the funeral.*
▸ RELATED ADJECTIVES: lacrimal or lachrymal or lacrymal

tease 1 = mock, bait, wind up *(Brit. slang)*, worry, bother, provoke, annoy, needle *(informal)*, plague *(informal)*, rag, rib *(informal)*, torment, ridicule, taunt, aggravate *(informal)*, badger, pester, vex, goad, bedevil, take the mickey out of *(informal)*, twit, take the piss out of *(taboo slang)*, chaff, guy *(informal)*, gibe, pull someone's leg *(informal)*, make fun of • *He teased me mercilessly about going there.*
2 = tantalize, lead on, flirt with, titillate • *When did you last flirt with him or tease him?*

technical 1 = scientific, technological, skilled, specialist, specialized, hi-tech *or* high-tech • *jobs that require technical knowledge*
2 = specialist, scientific, specialized, esoteric, complex, complicated • *I hadn't realized how technical our language was.*
3 = mechanical • *a technical fault*

technique 1 = method, way, system, approach, means, course, style, fashion, manner, procedure, mode, MO, modus operandi • *tests performed using a new technique*
2 = skill, art, performance, craft, touch, know-how *(informal)*, facility, delivery, execution, knack, artistry, craftsmanship, proficiency, adroitness • *He went abroad to improve his tennis technique.*

technology
▸ RELATED PHOBIA: technophobia

teddy bear
▸ RELATED ENTHUSIAST: arctophile

tedious = boring, dull, dreary, monotonous, tiring, annoying, fatiguing, drab, banal, tiresome, lifeless, prosaic, laborious, humdrum, uninteresting, long-drawn-out, mind-numbing, irksome, unexciting, soporific, ho-hum *(informal)*, vapid, wearisome, deadly dull, prosy, dreich *(Scot.)* • *the tedious business of line-by-line programming*
OPPOSITES: interesting, exciting, inspiring

tedium = boredom, monotony, dullness, routine, the doldrums, banality, sameness, ennui, drabness, deadness, dreariness, tediousness, lifelessness • *She felt she would go mad with the tedium of the job.*
OPPOSITES: interest, excitement, stimulation

teem[1] **= be full of**, abound, swarm, bristle, brim, overflow, be abundant, burst at the seams, be prolific, be crawling, pullulate • *The forest below him seethed and teemed with life.*

teem[2] *often with* **down** *or* **with rain = pour**, lash, pelt (down), sheet, stream, belt *(slang)*, bucket down *(informal)*, rain cats and dogs *(informal)* • *The wedding was supposed to be outside but it teemed with rain.*

teeming[1] **= full**, packed, crowded, alive, thick, bursting, numerous, crawling, swarming, abundant, bristling, brimming, overflowing, fruitful, replete, chock-full, brimful, chock-a-block • *The area is usually teeming with tourists.*
OPPOSITES: wanting, short, lacking

teeming[2] **= pouring**, lashing, pelting, sheeting, streaming, belting *(slang)*, bucketing down *(informal)* • *I arrived early to find it teeming with rain.*

teenage = youthful, adolescent, juvenile, immature • *One in four teenage girls now smoke.*

teenager = youth, minor, adolescent, juvenile, girl, boy • *As a teenager he attended the local high school.*

teeny = tiny, minute, wee, miniature, microscopic, diminutive, minuscule, teeny-weeny, teensy-weensy • *The people on the ground looked like little, teeny bugs.*

teeter 1 = wobble, rock, totter, balance, stagger, sway, tremble, waver, pivot, seesaw • *He watched the cup teeter on*

the edge before it fell.
2 = waver, wobble, seesaw, veer • *They are teetering on the edge of bankruptcy.*

teetotal = abstinent, on the wagon *(informal)*, abstemious, dry *(informal)*, off the booze *(informal)*, off the sauce *(informal)* • *He won't be having a drink as he's teetotal.*

teetotaller = abstainer, wowser *(Austral. & N.Z. slang)*, nondrinker • *He's a strict teetotaller.*

telecommunications

TELECOMMUNICATION TERMS

Blackberry	messaging	pager
Bluetooth	MMS	Skype
e-mail	mobile phone	SMS *or* text
IM *or* instant	MSN	messaging

telegram = cable, wire *(informal)*, telegraph, telex, radiogram • *The President received a briefing by telegram.*

telegraph = cable, wire *(informal)*, transmit, telex, send • *He telegraphed me an urgent message.*

telepathic = psychic, clairvoyant, having sixth sense, having second sight • *I couldn't know that. I'm not telepathic.*

telepathy = mind-reading, ESP, sixth sense, clairvoyance, extra sensory perception, psychometry, thought transference • *We expect people to know by telepathy what we are thinking.*

telephone AS A NOUN **= phone**, blower *(informal)*, mobile, mobile phone *or (informal)* moby, cellphone *or* cellular phone *(U.S.)*, handset, dog and bone *(slang)* • *They usually exchanged messages by telephone.*
▸ AS A VERB **= call**, phone, ring *(chiefly Brit.)*, buzz *(informal)*, dial, call up, give someone a call, give someone a ring *(informal, chiefly Brit.)*, give someone a buzz *(informal)*, give someone a bell *(Brit. slang)*, put a call through to, give someone a tinkle *(Brit. informal)*, get on the blower to *(informal)* • *I had to telephone him to say I was sorry.*

QUOTATIONS
The telephone gives us the happiness of being together yet safely apart
[Mason Cooley *City Aphorisms*]
The telephone, which interrupts the most serious conversations and cuts short the most weighty observations, has a romance of its own
[Virginia Woolf *The Common Reader*]

telescope AS A NOUN **= glass**, scope *(informal)*, spyglass • *The telescope enables us to see deeper into the universe than ever.*
▸ AS A VERB **= shorten**, contract, compress, cut, trim, shrink, tighten, condense, abbreviate, abridge, capsulize • *Film naturally tends to telescope time.*
OPPOSITES: extend, spread out, lengthen

televise = broadcast, show, transmit, air, put on air • *The Grand Prix will be televised by the BBC.*

television = TV, telly *(Brit. informal)*, small screen *(informal)*, the box *(Brit. informal)*, receiver, the tube *(slang)*, TV set, gogglebox *(Brit. slang)*, idiot box *(slang)* • *She turned the television on and flicked around the channels.*

QUOTATIONS
Television tells a story in a way that requires no imagination
[Witold Rybczynski]
I find television very educational. Every time someone switches it on I go into another room and read a good book
[Groucho Marx]

tell AS A VERB **1 = inform**, notify, make aware, say to, state to, warn, reveal to, express to, brief, advise, disclose to, proclaim to, fill in, speak about to, confess to, impart, alert to, divulge, announce to, acquaint with, communicate to, mention to, make known to, apprise, utter to, get off your chest *(informal)*, let know, flag up • *I called her to tell her how spectacular it looked.*
2 = describe, relate, recount, report, portray, depict, chronicle, rehearse, narrate, give an account of • *He told his story to the Sunday Times.*
3 = instruct, order, command, direct, bid, enjoin • *She told me to come and help clean the house.*
4 = see, make out, discern, understand, discover, be certain, comprehend • *It was impossible to tell where the bullet had entered.*
5 = distinguish, discriminate, discern, differentiate, identify • *I can't really tell the difference between their policies and ours.*
6 = talk, tell tales, spill the beans *(informal)*, give the game away, blab *(informal)*, let the cat out of the bag *(informal)* • *The children know who they are, but they are not telling.*
7 = reveal, show, indicate, disclose, signify, be evidence of • *The facts tell a very different story.*
8 = have *or* **take effect**, register, weigh, have force, count, take its toll, carry weight, make its presence felt • *The pressure began to tell as rain closed in after 20 laps.*
9 = assure, promise, guarantee, swear, give someone your word • *I tell you, I will not rest until that day has come.*
▸ IN PHRASES: **tell on someone = inform on**, shop *(Brit. informal)*, give someone away, denounce, split on *(informal)*, grass on *(Brit. informal)*, sell someone out, stab someone in the back, tell tales on, dob in *(Austral. slang)* • *Don't worry; I won't tell on you.*
tell someone off = reprimand, rebuke, scold, lecture, carpet *(informal)*, censure, reproach, berate, chide, tear into *(informal)*, read the riot act, reprove, upbraid, take to task, tick off *(informal)*, bawl out *(informal)*, chew out *(U.S. & Canad. informal)*, tear off a strip *(Brit. informal)*, give a piece of your mind to, haul over the coals *(informal)*, give a rocket to *(Brit. & N.Z. informal)* • *He never listened to us when we told him off.*
tell something apart = differentiate between, distinguish between, discriminate between, make a distinction between, separate, set apart • *It is difficult to tell the two products apart.*

telling = effective, significant, considerable, marked, striking, powerful, solid, impressive, influential, decisive, potent, forceful, weighty, forcible, trenchant, effectual • *How a man shaves is a telling clue to his age.*
OPPOSITES: minor, slight, unimportant

telling-off = reprimand, talking-to, row, criticism, lecture, rocket *(Brit. & N.Z. informal)*, wigging *(Brit. slang)*, slating *(informal)*, censure, rebuke, reproach, scolding, ticking-off *(informal)*, dressing-down *(informal)*, reproof, rap on the knuckles • *I got a severe telling-off for not phoning him.*

telltale AS AN ADJECTIVE **= revealing**, significant, meaningful, giveaway *(informal)*, unmistakable, suggestive, revelatory • *the telltale redness around his eyes*
▸ AS A NOUN **= blabbermouth** *(informal)*, sneak *(Brit. informal)*, squealer *(informal)*, snitch *(informal)*, tattletale *(U.S. informal)*, clype *(Scot. informal)* • *I didn't want to be a telltale so I kept quiet.*

temerity = audacity, nerve *(informal)*, cheek, gall *(informal)*, front, assurance, pluck, boldness, recklessness, chutzpah *(U.S. & Canad. informal)*, impudence, effrontery, impulsiveness, rashness, brass neck *(Brit. informal)*, foolhardiness, sassiness *(U.S. informal)*, forwardness, heedlessness • *patients who have the temerity to challenge their doctor*

temper AS A NOUN **1 = irritability**, anger, irascibility, passion, resentment, irritation, annoyance, petulance, surliness, ill humour, peevishness, hot-headedness • *I hope he can control his temper.*
OPPOSITES: goodwill, contentment, good humour

t

2 = **frame of mind**, character, nature, attitude, mind, mood, constitution, humour, vein, temperament, tenor, disposition • *He's known for his placid temper.*
3 = **rage**, fury, bad mood, passion, paddy *(Brit. informal)*, wax *(informal, chiefly Brit.)*, tantrum, bate *(Brit. slang)*, fit of pique, foulie *(Austral. slang)*, hissy fit *(informal)*, strop *(Brit. informal)* • *She was still in a temper when I arrived.*
4 = **self-control**, composure, cool *(slang)*, calm, good humour, tranquillity, coolness, calmness, equanimity • *I've never seen him lose his temper.*
OPPOSITES: anger, fury, wrath
▸ **AS A VERB** 1 = **moderate**, restrain, tone down, calm, soften, soothe, lessen, allay, mitigate, abate, assuage, mollify, soft-pedal *(informal)*, palliate, admix • *He had to learn to temper his enthusiasm.*
OPPOSITES: intensify, arouse, heighten
2 = **strengthen**, harden, toughen, anneal • *a new way of tempering glass*
OPPOSITES: soften

temperament 1 = **nature**, character, personality, quality, spirit, make-up, soul, constitution, bent, stamp, humour, tendencies, tendency, temper, outlook, complexion, disposition, frame of mind, mettle, cast of mind • *His impulsive temperament regularly got him into difficulties.*
2 = **moods**, anger, volatility, impatience, petulance, excitability, moodiness, explosiveness, hot-headedness, mercurialness • *Some of the models were given to fits of temperament.*

temperamental 1 = **moody**, emotional, touchy, sensitive, explosive, passionate, volatile, fiery, impatient, erratic, neurotic, irritable, mercurial, excitable, capricious, petulant, hot-headed, chippy *(informal)*, hypersensitive, highly strung, easily upset, unstable • *a man given to temperamental outbursts and paranoia*
OPPOSITES: calm, level-headed, even-tempered
2 = **unreliable**, unpredictable, undependable, inconsistent, erratic, inconstant, unstable • *The machine guns could be temperamental.*
OPPOSITES: reliable, dependable, stable
3 = **natural**, inherent, innate, constitutional, ingrained, congenital, inborn, hard-wired • *Some temperamental qualities are not easily detected by parents.*

temperance 1 = **teetotalism**, abstinence, sobriety, abstemiousness • *a reformed alcoholic extolling the joys of temperance*
2 = **moderation**, restraint, self-control, self-discipline, continence, self-restraint, forbearance • *The age of hedonism was replaced by a new era of temperance.*
OPPOSITES: excess, intemperance, overindulgence

QUOTATIONS
Temperance is the greatest of all the virtues
[Plutarch *Moralia*]

temperate 1 = **mild**, moderate, balmy, fair, cool, soft, calm, gentle, pleasant, clement, agreeable • *The valley keeps a temperate climate throughout the year.*
OPPOSITES: severe, extreme, harsh
2 = **moderate**, dispassionate, self-controlled, calm, stable, reasonable, sensible, mild, composed, equable, even-tempered, self-restrained • *His final report was more temperate than earlier ones.*
OPPOSITES: wild, uncontrolled, unrestrained
3 = **abstemious**, continent, sober, abstinent, moderate • *He lived a temperate and contented life with his wife.*
OPPOSITES: intemperate, immoderate, excessive

tempest 1 = **storm**, hurricane, gale, tornado, cyclone, typhoon, squall • *torrential rain and howling tempest*
2 = **uproar**, storm, furore, disturbance, upheaval, ferment, commotion, tumult • *I hadn't foreseen the tempest my request would cause.*
OPPOSITES: peace, quiet, calm

tempestuous 1 = **passionate**, intense, turbulent, heated, wild, excited, emotional, violent, flaming, hysterical, stormy, impassioned, uncontrolled, boisterous, feverish • *the couple's tempestuous relationship*
OPPOSITES: serene, quiet, peaceful
2 = **stormy**, turbulent, inclement, raging, windy, boisterous, blustery, gusty, squally • *adverse winds and tempestuous weather*

temple[1] = **shrine**, church, sanctuary, holy place, place of worship, house of God • *a small Hindu temple*

temple[2]
▸ **RELATED ADJECTIVE:** temporal

tempo 1 = **speed**, pace, velocity • *Both teams played with quality, pace and tempo.*
2 = **pace**, time, rate, beat, measure *(Prosody)*, speed, metre, rhythm, cadence, pulse • *Elgar supplied his work with precise indications of tempo.*

temporal 1 = **secular**, worldly, lay, earthly, mundane, material, civil, fleshly, mortal, terrestrial, carnal, profane, sublunary • *Clergy should not be preoccupied with temporal matters.*
2 = **time-related**, of time, relating to time • *Specific acts are related to a temporal and spatial context.*
3 = **temporary**, passing, transitory, fleeting, short-lived, fugitive, transient, momentary, evanescent, impermanent, fugacious • *The temporal gifts that Fortune grants in this world are finally worthless.*

temporarily = **briefly**, for the moment, for the time being, momentarily, for a moment, for a short time, for a little while, fleetingly, for a short while, pro tem, for the nonce • *The agreement has at least temporarily halted the civil war.*

temporary 1 = **impermanent**, passing, transitory, brief, fleeting, interim, short-lived, fugitive, transient, momentary, ephemeral, evanescent, pro tem, here today and gone tomorrow, pro tempore *(Latin)*, fugacious • *a temporary loss of memory*
OPPOSITES: long-term, permanent, enduring
2 = **short-term**, acting, interim, supply, stand-in, fill-in, caretaker, provisional, stopgap • *She was working as a temporary teacher at a Belfast school.*

temporize = **play for time**, delay, stall, procrastinate, be evasive, beat about the bush, gain time, equivocate, play a waiting game, hum and haw, tergiversate • *'Not exactly, sir,' he temporized.*

tempt 1 = **attract**, draw, appeal to, allure, whet the appetite of, make your mouth water • *Can I tempt you with a little puff pastry?*
2 = **entice**, lure, lead on, invite, woo, seduce, coax, decoy, inveigle • *Don't let credit tempt you to buy something you can't afford.*
OPPOSITES: discourage, deter, put off
3 = **provoke**, try, test, risk, dare, bait, fly in the face of • *As soon as you talk about never losing, it's tempting fate.*

temptation 1 = **enticement**, lure, inducement, pull, come-on *(informal)*, invitation, bait, coaxing, snare, seduction, decoy, allurement, tantalization • *the many temptations to which they will be exposed*
2 = **urge**, desire, impulse, inclination, itch • *Will they be able to resist the temptation to buy?*
3 = **appeal**, draw, attraction, attractiveness • *The thrill and the temptation of crime is very strong.*

QUOTATIONS
I can resist everything except temptation
[Oscar Wilde *Lady Windermere's Fan*]
No temptation can ever be measured by the value of its object
[Colette]
The serpent beguiled me, and I did eat
[Bible: Genesis]

t

Watch and pray, that ye enter not into temptation;
the spirit indeed is willing but the flesh is weak
[*Bible: St. Matthew*]
The last temptation is the greatest treason: To do the
right deed for the wrong reason
[T.S. Eliot *Murder in the Cathedral*]

tempting = **inviting**, enticing, seductive, alluring, attractive, mouthwatering, appetizing • *Resisting tempting goodies becomes a measure of your success.*
OPPOSITES: off-putting (*Brit. informal*), uninviting, undesirable

ten
▸ RELATED ADJECTIVE: decimal
▸ RELATED PREFIX: deca-

tenable = **sound**, justifiable, arguable, defensible, reasonable, rational, viable, plausible, believable, defendable, maintainable • *This argument is simply not tenable.*
OPPOSITES: untenable, indefensible, unjustifiable

tenacious 1 = **stubborn**, dogged, determined, persistent, sure, firm, adamant, staunch, resolute, inflexible, strong-willed, steadfast, unyielding, obstinate, intransigent, immovable, unswerving, obdurate, stiff-necked, pertinacious • *He is regarded as a persistent and tenacious interviewer.*
OPPOSITES: wavering, changeable, irresolute
2 = **firm**, dogged, persistent, unyielding, unswerving • *a tenacious belief*
3 = **strong**, firm, fast, iron, tight, clinging, forceful, immovable, unshakeable • *He has a particularly tenacious grip on life.*
4 = **retentive**, good, photographic, unforgetful • *her analytical mind and tenacious memory*
5 = **adhesive**, clinging, sticky, glutinous, gluey, mucilaginous • *tenacious catarrh in the nasal passages and lungs*

tenacity = **perseverance**, resolution, determination, application, resolve, persistence, diligence, intransigence, firmness, stubbornness, inflexibility, obstinacy, steadfastness, obduracy, doggedness, strength of will, strength of purpose, resoluteness, pertinacity, staunchness • *Sheer tenacity is crucial to career success.*

tenancy 1 = **lease**, residence, occupancy, holding, renting, possession, occupation • *Check the terms of your tenancy closely.*
2 = **period of office**, tenure, incumbency, time in office • *Baroness Thatcher's nine-year tenancy*

tenant = **leaseholder**, resident, renter, occupant, holder, inhabitant, occupier, lodger, boarder, lessee • *obligations on the landlord for the benefit of the tenant*

tend[1] 1 = **be inclined**, be likely, be liable, have a tendency, be apt, be prone, trend, lean, incline, be biased, be disposed, gravitate, have a leaning, have an inclination • *Lighter cars tend to be noisy.*
2 = **favour**, lean, be biased, gravitate, show a preference for • *Artists and intellectuals often tend towards left-wing views.*

tend[2] 1 = **take care of**, look after, care for, keep, watch, serve, protect, feed, handle, attend, guard, nurse, see to, nurture, minister to, cater for, keep an eye on, wait on, watch over • *For years he tended her in her illness.*
OPPOSITES: ignore, overlook, neglect
2 = **maintain**, take care of, nurture, cultivate, manage • *The grey-haired lady dug and tended her garden.*
OPPOSITES: ignore, overlook, neglect

tendency 1 = **trend**, drift, movement, turning, heading, course, drive, bearing, direction, bias • *the government's tendency towards secrecy in recent years*
2 = **inclination**, leaning, bent, liability, readiness, disposition, penchant, propensity, susceptibility, predisposition, predilection, proclivity, partiality, proneness • *He has a tendency towards snobbery.*

tender[1] 1 = **gentle**, loving, kind, caring, warm, sympathetic, fond, sentimental, humane, affectionate, compassionate, benevolent, considerate, merciful, amorous, warm-hearted, tenderhearted, softhearted, touchy-feely (*informal*) • *tender, loving care*
OPPOSITES: hard, harsh, tough
2 = **romantic**, moving, touching, emotional, sentimental, poignant, evocative, soppy (*Brit. informal*) • *a tragic, tender love story*
3 = **vulnerable**, young, sensitive, new, green, raw, youthful, inexperienced, immature, callow, impressionable, unripe, wet behind the ears (*informal*) • *He had become attracted to the game at the tender age of seven.*
OPPOSITES: mature, grown-up, experienced
4 = **not tough**, done (*informal*), edible, succulent, chewable, easily chewed • *Cook until the meat is tender.*
OPPOSITES: strong, tough, hard
5 = **sensitive**, painful, sore, smarting, raw, bruised, irritated, aching, inflamed • *My tummy felt very tender.*
6 = **fragile**, delicate, frail, soft, weak, feeble, breakable • *The newborn looked so fragile and tender.*
7 = **difficult**, sensitive, tricky, dangerous, complicated, risky, touchy, ticklish • *Even his continuing presence remains a tender issue.*

tender[2] AS A VERB = **offer**, present, submit, give, suggest, propose, extend, volunteer, hand in, put forward, proffer • *She quickly tendered her resignation.*
▸ IN PHRASES: **tender for something** = **put in a bid for**, quote a price for, give a quote for, give an estimate for, propose a price for • *He tendered for and was awarded the contract.*
▸ AS A NOUN = **offer**, bid, estimate, proposal, suggestion, submission, proffer • *Builders will be asked to submit a tender for the work.*

tenderness 1 = **gentleness**, love, affection, liking, care, consideration, sympathy, pity, humanity, warmth, mercy, attachment, compassion, devotion, kindness, fondness, sentimentality, benevolence, humaneness, amorousness, warm-heartedness, softheartedness, tenderheartedness • *She smiled, politely, rather than with tenderness.*
OPPOSITES: cruelty, insensitivity, harshness
2 = **soreness**, pain, sensitivity, smart, bruising, ache, aching, irritation, inflammation, rawness, sensitiveness, painfulness • *There is still some tenderness on her tummy.*
3 = **succulence**, softness, juiciness • *Protein detected is inversely proportional to the tenderness of the meat.*
4 = **fragility**, vulnerability, weakness, sensitivity, softness, feebleness, sensitiveness, frailness, delicateness • *the vulnerability and tenderness he brings to the role*

tenet = **principle**, rule, doctrine, creed, view, teaching, opinion, belief, conviction, canon, thesis, maxim, dogma, precept, article of faith, kaupapa (*N.Z.*) • *Non-violence is the central tenet of their faith.*

tennis
▹ *See panel* **Tennis terms**

tenor = **meaning**, trend, drift, way, course, sense, aim, purpose, direction, path, theme, substance, burden, tendency, intent, purport • *The whole tenor of discussions has changed.*

tense AS AN ADJECTIVE 1 = **strained**, uneasy, stressful, fraught, charged, difficult, worrying, exciting, uncomfortable, knife-edge, nail-biting, nerve-racking • *the tense atmosphere of the talks*
2 = **nervous**, wound up (*informal*), edgy, strained, wired (*slang*), anxious, under pressure, restless, apprehensive, jittery (*informal*), uptight (*informal*), on edge, jumpy, twitchy (*informal*), overwrought, strung up (*informal*), on tenterhooks, fidgety, keyed up, antsy (*informal*), wrought up, adrenalized • *He had been very tense, but he finally relaxed.*
OPPOSITES: collected, calm, serene

TENNIS TERMS

ace, advantage, approach shot, backhand, ball, baseline, baseliner, break of serve, break point, cannonball, centre line, centre mark, chip, clay court, court, deuce, double fault, doubles, drop shot, fault, foot fault, forecourt, forehand, game, grass court, ground stroke, half-volley, hard court, lawn tennis, let, line call, linesman, lob, love, love game, match, mixed doubles, net, net cord, passing shot, racket, rally, receiver, return, serve and volleyer, server, service, service line, set, set point, sideline, singles, slice, smash, tie-break, topspin, tramline, umpire, undercut, volley

3 = **rigid**, strained, taut, stretched, tight • *She lay, eyes shut, body tense.*
OPPOSITES: relaxed, loose, limp
▸ AS A VERB = **tighten**, strain, brace, tauten, stretch, flex, stiffen • *His stomach muscles tensed.*
OPPOSITES: relax, loosen, slacken

tension 1 = **strain**, stress, nervousness, pressure, anxiety, unease, apprehension, suspense, restlessness, the jitters *(informal)*, edginess • *Smiling relieves tension and stress.*
OPPOSITES: relaxation, serenity, calmness
2 = **friction**, hostility, unease, antagonism, antipathy, enmity, ill feeling • *The tension between the two countries is likely to remain.*
3 = **rigidity**, tightness, stiffness, pressure, stress, stretching, straining, tautness • *Slowly, the tension in his face dispersed.*

tentative 1 = **unconfirmed**, provisional, indefinite, test, trial, pilot, preliminary, experimental, unsettled, speculative, pencilled in, exploratory, to be confirmed, TBC, conjectural • *They have reached a tentative agreement to hold talks next month.*
OPPOSITES: final, confirmed, settled
2 = **hesitant**, cautious, uncertain, doubtful, backward, faltering, unsure, timid, undecided, diffident, iffy *(informal)* • *My first attempts at complaining were very tentative.*
OPPOSITES: confident, assured, bold

tenterhooks IN PHRASES: **on tenterhooks** = **in suspense**, anxious, on edge, keyed up, in an agony of doubt, with bated breath • *He was still on tenterhooks waiting for a decision to be made.*

tenth
▸ RELATED PREFIX: deci-

tenuous 1 = **slight**, weak, dubious, shaky, doubtful, questionable, insignificant, flimsy, sketchy, insubstantial, nebulous • *Links between the provinces were seen to be tenuous.*
OPPOSITES: strong, sound, solid
2 = **fine**, slim, delicate, attenuated, gossamer • *She was holding onto life by a tenuous thread.*

tenure 1 = **occupancy**, holding, occupation, residence, tenancy, possession, proprietorship • *Lack of security of tenure meant that many became homeless.*
2 = **term of office**, term, incumbency, period in office, time • *his short tenure of the Labour leadership*

tepid 1 = **lukewarm**, warmish, slightly warm • *She bent to the tap and drank the tepid water.*
2 = **unenthusiastic**, half-hearted, indifferent, cool, lukewarm, apathetic, half-arsed *(Brit. slang)*, half-assed *(U.S. & Canad. slang)* • *His nomination has received tepid support in the Senate.*
OPPOSITES: keen, eager, enthusiastic

term AS A NOUN 1 = **word**, name, expression, title, label, phrase, denomination, designation, appellation, locution • *What's the medical term for a heart attack?*
2 = **session**, course, quarter *(U.S.)*, semester, trimester *(U.S.)* • *the summer term*
3 = **period**, time, spell, while, season, space, interval, span, duration, incumbency • *a 12-month term of service*
4 = **conclusion**, end, close, finish, culmination, fruition • *Older women are just as capable of carrying a baby to term.*
▸ AS A VERB = **call**, name, label, style, entitle, tag, dub, designate, describe as, denominate • *He had been termed a temporary employee.*

terminal AS AN ADJECTIVE 1 = **fatal**, deadly, lethal, killing, mortal, incurable, inoperable, untreatable • *terminal cancer*
2 = **dying**, incurable, near death • *a hospital for terminal patients*
3 = **final**, last, closing, finishing, concluding, ultimate, terminating • *Endowments pay a terminal bonus at maturity.*
OPPOSITES: first, opening, initial
4 = **end**, extreme • *the terminal part of the vertebrate intestine*
5 = **complete**, total, absolute, utter, real, thorough, downright, out-and-out • *The anti-government uprising had threatened terminal chaos.*
▸ AS A NOUN 1 = **terminus**, station, depot, end of the line • *Only the original ochre facade of the nearby railway terminal remains.*
2 = **workstation**, monitor, PC, VDU, visual display unit • *He sits at a computer terminal 40 hours a week.*

terminate 1 = **end**, stop, conclude, finish, complete, axe *(informal)*, cut off, wind up, put an end to, discontinue, pull the plug on *(informal)*, belay *(Nautical)*, bring *or* come to an end • *Her next remark abruptly terminated the conversation.*
OPPOSITES: start, open, begin
2 = **cease**, end, close, finish, run out, expire, lapse • *His contract terminates at the end of the season.*
3 = **abort**, end • *She finally decided to terminate the pregnancy.*
4 = **end its journey**, stop, finish up • *This train will terminate at Taunton.*

termination 1 = **ending**, end, close, finish, conclusion, wind-up, completion, cessation, expiry, cut-off point, finis, discontinuation • *a dispute which led to the abrupt termination of trade*
OPPOSITES: start, opening, beginning
2 = **abortion**, ending, discontinuation • *You should have a medical after the termination of a pregnancy.*

terminology = **language**, terms, vocabulary, jargon, cant, lingo *(informal)*, nomenclature, patois, phraseology, argot • *medical terminology*

terminus = **end of the line**, terminal, station, depot, last stop, garage • *the London terminus of the Channel Tunnel rail link*

termite
▸ NAME OF HOME: termitarium

terms AS A PLURAL NOUN 1 = **language**, terminology, phraseology, manner of speaking • *The video explains in simple terms how the tax works.*
2 = **conditions**, particulars, provisions, provisos, stipulations, qualifications, premises *(Law)*, specifications • *the terms of the Helsinki agreement*

3 = **relationship**, standing, footing, relations, position, status • *We shook hands and parted on good terms.*
4 = **price**, rates, charges, fee, payment • *They provide favourable terms to shops that invest in their services.*
▸ IN PHRASES: **come to terms** = **come to an agreement**, reach agreement, come to an understanding, conclude agreement • *Even if they came to terms, investors would object to the merger.*
come to terms with something = **learn to live with**, come to accept, be reconciled to, reach acceptance of • *She had come to terms with the fact that she would always be ill.*
in terms of = **with regard to**, concerning, regarding, as to, in connection with, in respect of, as regards, with reference to, in the matter of • *Our goods compete well in terms of quality and reliability.*

terrain = **ground**, country, land, landscape, topography, going • *an eight-hour drive on rough terrain*

terrestrial = **earthly**, worldly, global, mundane, sublunary, tellurian, terrene • *terrestrial life forms*

terrible 1 = **awful**, shocking, appalling, terrifying, horrible, dreadful, horrifying, dread, dreaded, fearful, horrendous, monstrous, harrowing, gruesome, horrid, unspeakable, frightful, hellacious *(U.S. slang)* • *Thousands suffered terrible injuries in the disaster.*
2 = **bad**, awful, dreadful, beastly *(informal)*, dire, abysmal, abhorrent, poor, offensive, foul, unpleasant, revolting, rotten *(informal)*, obscene, hideous, vile, from hell *(informal)*, obnoxious, repulsive, frightful, odious, hateful, loathsome, shitty *(taboo slang)*, godawful *(slang)* • *I have the most terrible nightmares.*
OPPOSITES: great, wonderful, excellent
3 = **ill**, sick, unwell, poorly, rough *(informal)*, faint, crook *(Austral. & N.Z. informal)*, dizzy, lousy *(informal)*, nauseated, queasy, out of sorts, nauseous, off colour *(Brit. informal)*, under the weather *(informal)*, indisposed, peaky, wabbit *(Scot. informal)* • *I did feel terrible at the time but I'm all right now.*
4 = **very bad**, poor, inadequate, awful, appalling *(informal)*, pants *(Brit. informal)*, dreadful, useless *(informal)*, hopeless, pathetic *(informal)*, dire *(informal)*, inferior, duff *(Brit. informal)*, unsatisfactory, lousy *(informal)*, pitiful *(informal)*, laughable, atrocious, abysmal *(informal)*, frightful, substandard, crummy *(informal)*, bodger *or* bodgie *(Austral. slang)* • *She admits her French is terrible.*
5 = **serious**, desperate, severe, extreme, bad, dangerous, insufferable • *He claimed that he had a terrible pain in his head.* • *We are in terrible trouble.*
OPPOSITES: mild, insignificant, paltry
6 = **unkind**, nasty, cruel, off *(informal)*, mean, dirty *(informal)*, unfair, foul, beastly *(informal)*, unacceptable, unpleasant, poisonous, shabby, vile, malicious, low-down *(informal)*, hurtful, out of order *(Brit. informal)*, unwarranted, obnoxious, despicable, spiteful, hateful, mean-spirited, contemptible, shitty *(taboo slang)*, wretched, uncharitable, below the belt, uncalled for, dirty rotten *(informal)* • *It was a terrible thing to do to someone.*
7 = **incorrigible**, right *(Brit. informal)*, real, great, shocking, impossible *(informal)*, extreme, awful, proper *(Brit. informal)*, dreadful, outrageous, fearful *(informal)*, frightful • *She's a terrible flirt – a real man-eater.*
8 = **guilty**, sorry, ashamed, apologetic, chastened, contrite, repentant, guilt-ridden, remorseful, regretful, penitent, shamefaced, full of regret, conscience-stricken, self-reproachful • *He said he felt terrible about cancelling the concert.*

terribly 1 = **very much**, greatly, very, much, dreadfully, seriously, extremely, gravely, desperately, thoroughly, decidedly, awfully *(informal)*, exceedingly • *He has suffered terribly in losing his best friend.*
2 = **extremely**, very, much, greatly, dreadfully, seriously, desperately, thoroughly, decidedly, awfully *(informal)*, exceedingly • *I'm terribly sorry to bother you at this hour.*
3 = **badly**, poorly, dreadfully, incompetently, awfully, appallingly, dismally, pitifully, abysmally, atrociously, diabolically *(informal)*, inexpertly, execrably • *We played terribly that day, and didn't deserve to win.*

terrific 1 = **excellent**, great *(informal)*, wonderful, mean *(slang)*, topping *(Brit. slang)*, fine, brilliant, very good, cracking *(Brit. informal)*, amazing, outstanding, smashing *(informal)*, superb, fantastic *(informal)*, ace *(informal)*, magnificent, fabulous *(informal)*, marvellous, sensational *(informal)*, sovereign, awesome *(slang)*, breathtaking, super *(informal)*, brill *(informal)*, stupendous, bodacious *(slang, chiefly U.S.)*, boffo *(slang)*, jim-dandy *(slang)*, chillin' *(U.S. slang)*, booshit *(Austral. slang)*, exo *(Austral. slang)*, sik *(Austral. slang)*, ka pai *(N.Z.)*, rad *(informal)*, phat *(slang)*, schmick *(Austral. informal)*, beaut *(informal)*, barrie *(Scot. slang)*, belting *(Brit. slang)*, pearler *(Austral. slang)* • *What a terrific idea!*
OPPOSITES: bad, terrible, awful
2 = **great**, huge, vast, enormous, extensive, tremendous, immense, gigantic, colossal, prodigious, stupendous, fuck-off *(offensive taboo slang)*, ginormous *(informal)*, humongous *or* humungous *(U.S. slang)* • *He did a terrific amount of fundraising.*
OPPOSITES: moderate, insignificant, paltry
3 = **intense**, great, huge, terrible, enormous, severe, extreme, awful, tremendous, fierce, harsh, excessive, dreadful, horrific, fearful, awesome, gigantic, monstrous • *There was a terrific bang and a great cloud of smoke.*

terrified = **frightened**, scared, petrified, alarmed, intimidated, awed, panic-stricken, scared to death, scared stiff, scared shitless *(taboo slang)*, terror-stricken, shit-scared *(taboo slang)*, horror-struck, frightened out of your wits • *She was terrified that he would attack her.*

terrify = **frighten**, scare, petrify, alarm, intimidate, terrorize, scare to death, put the fear of God into, make your hair stand on end, fill with terror, make your flesh creep, make your blood run cold, scare the bejesus out of *(informal)*, frighten out of your wits • *The thought of a slow, painful death terrified me.*

terrifying = **frightening**, scary *(informal)*, alarming, appalling, dreadful, menacing, intimidating, fearful, daunting, fearsome, unnerving, hair-raising, baleful • *one of the most terrifying diseases known to man*

territory = **district**, area, land, region, state, country, sector, zone, province, patch, turf *(U.S. slang)*, domain, terrain, tract, bailiwick • *They deny that any of their territory is under rebel control.*

NEW ZEALAND TERRITORIES

Cook Islands	the Ross Dependency	Tokelau *or* Union Islands
Niue		

terror 1 = **fear**, alarm, dread, fright, panic, anxiety, intimidation, fear and trembling • *I shook with terror whenever I flew in an aeroplane.*
2 = **nightmare**, monster, bogeyman, devil, fiend, bugbear, scourge • *the many obscure terrors that haunted the children of that period*
3 = **rascal**, devil, monkey, scamp, horror *(informal)*, troublemaker, imp, tyke *(Brit. informal)*, scally *(Northwest English dialect)*, mischief-maker, perisher *(Brit. informal)*, holy terror *(informal)*, spalpeen *(Irish informal)*, nointer *(Austral. slang)* • *He was a little terror; always had been difficult to control.*

terrorist = **freedom fighter**, bomber, revolutionary, gunman, guerilla, suicide bomber, urban guerilla • *an attempt by a terrorist to plant a bomb on an airliner*

terrorize *or* **terrorise** 1 = **bully**, menace, intimidate, threaten, oppress, coerce, strong-arm *(informal)*, browbeat • *In his childhood he liked to terrorize his young siblings.*
2 = **terrify**, alarm, frighten, scare, intimidate, petrify, scare to death, strike terror into, put the fear of God into, fill with terror, scare the bejesus out of *(informal)*, frighten out of your wits, inspire panic in • *The government had the helicopter gunships to terrorize the population.*

terse 1 = **curt**, abrupt, brusque, short, rude, tart, snappy, gruff • *His tone was terse as he asked the question.*
OPPOSITES: polite, chatty
2 = **concise**, short, brief, clipped, neat, to the point, crisp, compact, summary, condensed, incisive, elliptical, laconic, succinct, pithy, monosyllabic, gnomic, epigrammatic, aphoristic, sententious • *He issued a terse statement, saying the decision will be made on Monday.*
OPPOSITES: lengthy, rambling, roundabout

test AS A VERB 1 = **check**, try, investigate, assess, research, prove, analyse, experiment with, try out, verify, assay, put something to the proof, put something to the test • *Test the temperature of the water with your wrist.*
2 = **examine**, put someone to the test, put someone through their paces • *He tested him on verbs and gave him a forfeit for each one he got wrong.*
3 = **challenge**, try, tax, stretch, put a strain on, make demands on • *He was testing me, to see how I would cope.*
▸ AS A NOUN 1 = **trial**, research, check, investigation, attempt, analysis, assessment, proof, examination, evaluation, acid test • *High levels of dioxin were confirmed by scientific tests.*
2 = **examination**, paper, assessment, evaluation • *Only 922 pupils passed the test.*
3 = **measure**, standard, proof, barometer, yardstick, touchstone, litmus test • *The test of any society is how it treats its minorities.*
▸ IN PHRASES: **put something to the test** = **test**, try, tax, put pressure on, put a strain on • *Sooner or later life will put the relationship to the test.*

testament 1 = **proof**, evidence, testimony, witness, demonstration, tribute, attestation, exemplification • *His house is a testament to his Gothic tastes.*
2 = **will**, last wishes • *a codicil to my will and testament*

testicles = **balls** *(taboo slang)*, nuts *(taboo slang)*, bollocks *or* ballocks *(taboo slang)*, rocks *(U.S. taboo slang)*, family jewels *(slang)*, cojones *(Spanish)* • *It is important for men to examine their testicles for abnormalities.*
▸ RELATED ADJECTIVE: testicular
▸ RELATED MANIA: orchidomania

testify AS A VERB 1 = **bear witness**, state, swear, certify, declare, witness, assert, affirm, depose *(Law)*, attest, corroborate, vouch, evince, give testimony, asseverate • *Several eye witnesses testified that they had seen the fight.*
OPPOSITES: dispute, contradict, disprove
2 = **give evidence**, attest, bear witness, be a witness, give your testimony, make a deposition, depone *(Scots Law)* • *Would she be willing to testify in court?*
▸ IN PHRASES: **testify to something** = **prove**, show, indicate, evidence, reveal, establish, confirm, demonstrate, bear out, substantiate, bespeak, corroborate, attest to, bear witness to, give proof of • *Excavations testify to the presence of cultivated inhabitants.*

testimonial = **reference**, recommendation, credential, character, tribute, certificate, endorsement, commendation • *She couldn't expect him to give testimonials to her ability.*

testimony 1 = **evidence**, information, statement, witness, profession, declaration, confirmation, submission, affirmation, affidavit, deposition, corroboration, avowal, attestation • *His testimony was an important element of the case.*
2 = **proof**, evidence, demonstration, indication, support, manifestation, verification, corroboration • *Her living room piled with documents is a testimony to her dedication to her work.*

testing = **difficult**, trying, demanding, taxing, challenging, searching, tough, exacting, formidable, rigorous, strenuous, arduous • *The most testing time is the early months of your return to work.*
OPPOSITES: easy, undemanding, simple

testy = **irritable**, cross, grumpy, crabbed, impatient, snappy, sullen, touchy, bad-tempered, petulant, irascible, cantankerous, peppery, tetchy, ratty *(Brit. & N.Z. informal)*, quarrelsome, chippy *(informal)*, fretful, short-tempered, waspish, peevish, quick-tempered, splenetic, snappish, liverish, captious • *Ben's getting a little testy in his old age.*

tetchy = **irritable**, cross, grumpy, crabbed, impatient, snappy, sullen, touchy, bad-tempered, petulant, irascible, cantankerous, peppery, ratty *(Brit. & N.Z. informal)*, testy, quarrelsome, chippy *(informal)*, fretful, short-tempered, waspish, peevish, quick-tempered, splenetic, snappish, liverish, captious • *You always get tetchy when you're hungry.*

tête-à-tête = **private conversation**, talk, chat, parley, cosy chat, private word, confab *(informal)* • *the usual tête-à-tête between the Queen and the Prime Minister*

tether AS A NOUN = **leash**, rope, lead, bond, chain, restraint, fastening, shackle, fetter, halter • *The eagle sat on a tether, looking fierce.*
▸ AS A VERB = **tie**, secure, bind, chain, rope, restrain, fasten, shackle, leash, fetter, manacle • *He dismounted, tethering his horse to a tree.*
▸ IN PHRASES: **at the end of your tether** = **exasperated**, exhausted, at your wits' end, finished, out of patience, at the limit of your endurance • *She was emotionally at the end of her tether.*

text 1 = **contents**, words, content, wording, body, matter, subject matter, main body • *The photographs enhance the clarity of the text.*
2 = **words**, wording • *A CD-ROM can store up to 250,000 pages of text.*
3 = **transcript**, script • *the text of Dr. Runcie's speech*
4 = **reference book**, textbook, source, reader • *reluctant readers of GCSE set texts*
5 = **written work**, book, printed work, narrative • *Woman functions in Nietzsche's texts as something like a symbol.*
6 = **passage**, extract, line, sentence, paragraph, verse • *I'll read the text aloud first.*
7 = **subject**, matter, topic, argument, theme, thesis, motif • *His work served as the text of secret debates.*
▹ *See panel* **Text messaging abbreviations and symbols**

TEXT MESSAGING EMOTICONS

Emoticon	Meaning
:-)	happy
:-))	cheerful
:-)))	really happy
:-()	smiling with mouth open
8-)	smiling with glasses
D:-)	smiling with baseball cap
;-)	winking
:-*	kissing
:-(	sad
:'-(	crying
:-C	very sad
:-@	screaming
:-O	shocked or surprised

TEXT MESSAGING ABBREVIATIONS AND SYMBOLS

Abbreviation or symbol	Meaning
A3	anytime, anywhere, anyplace
AAM	as a matter of fact
AFAIK	as far as I know
AFK	away from keyboard
al2gethr	altogether
ALrIt	all right
ATB	all the best
ATK	at the keyboard
ATM	at the moment
ATTN	attention
B	be
B4	before
BAK	back at keyboard
BBL	be back later
BCNU	be seeing you
BFN *or* B4N	bye for now
BK *or* COZ	because
BF	boyfriend
BR	bathroom
BRB	be right back
BRT	be right there
BS	bullshit
BWD	backward
BY	busy
C	see
CIAO	goodbye
CMIIW	correct me if I'm wrong
CU	see you
CUL8R	see you later
CYA	see you
EVR	ever
EZ	easy
FC	fingers crossed
FONE	phone
4	for *or* four
4EVA	for ever
F2T	free to talk
FWD	forward
FWIW	for what it's worth
FYI	for your information
GAL	get a life
G9	genius
GF	girlfriend
GG	good game
GGG *or* GGL	giggle
GMTA	great minds think alike

Abbreviation or symbol	Meaning
GR8	great
HAND	have a nice day
H8	hate
HD	hold
IC	I see
IDD	indeed
ILU	I love you
IMHO	in my humble *or* *honest* opinion
IMNSHO	in my not so humble opinion
IMO	in my opinion
IOW	in other words
IRL	in real life
IRW	in the real world
IFYWIMAITYD	if you know what I mean and I think you do
K	okay
KISS	keep it simple, stupid
KIT	keep in touch
L8	late
L8R	later
LDR	long-distance relationship
LO	hello
LOL	laughing out loud
LTNS	long time no see
LUV	love
LZ	loser
M8	mate
MSG	message
MT	empty
MTG	meeting
NE	any
NE1	anyone
Njoy	enjoy
NO1	no-one
NRN	no reply necessary
OFN	often
OIC	oh I see
PCM	please call me
PLS	please
PLU	people like us
PPL	people
PRT	party
PRW	parents are watching

Abbreviation or symbol	Meaning
Q	queue
QL	cool
QT	quiet
R	are
RGDS	regards
ROFL	rolling on floor laughing
ROFLOL	rolling on floor laughing out loud
ROTFL	rolling on the floor laughing
ROTFLOL	rolling on the floor laughing out loud
RUOK	are you OK?
SIT	stay in touch
SK8	skate
SOHF	sense of humour failure
SOM1	someone
THX *or* TX	thanks
Ti2GO	time to go
2	to, too, *or* two
2DAY	today
2MORO	tomorrow
2NITE	tonight
TTYL	talk to you later
TXT	text
U	you
U2	you too
U4E	yours for ever
UR	you are *or* your
W8	wait
WADYA	what do you
WAN2	want to
WAN2TLK	want to talk?
WB	welcome back
WK	week
WKND	weekend
WIV	with
W/O	without
WOT	what
WTG	way to go!
X	kiss
XLNT	excellent
XOXO	hugs and kisses

textiles = **materials**, fabrics, cloths • *decorative textiles for the home*

texture = **feel**, quality, character, consistency, structure, surface, constitution, fabric, tissue, grain, weave, composition • *It is used in moisturisers to give them a silky texture.*

thank 1 = **say thank you to**, express gratitude to, show gratitude to, show your appreciation to • *I thanked them for their long and loyal service.*
2 = **blame**, hold responsible • *I have you to thank for this.*

thankful = **grateful**, pleased, relieved, obliged, in (someone's) debt, indebted, appreciative, beholden • *I'm just thankful that I've got a job.*
OPPOSITES: ungrateful, thankless, unappreciative

thankless = **unrewarding**, unappreciated • *Soccer referees have a thankless task.*
OPPOSITES: rewarding

thanks AS A PLURAL NOUN = **gratitude**, appreciation, thanksgiving, credit, recognition, acknowledgment, gratefulness • *They accepted their certificates with words of thanks.*
▸ AS AN INTERJECTION = **thank you**, cheers, ta, bless you, TY (*S.M.S.*), THX (*S.M.S.*), TNZ (*S.M.S.*), THNQ (*S.M.S.*), T/Y (*S.M.S.*) • *Thanks. You've been great.*
▸ IN PHRASES: **thanks to** = **because of**, through, due to, as a result of, owing to, by reason of • *Thanks to recent research, effective treatment is available.*

thaw = **melt**, dissolve, soften, defrost, warm, liquefy, unfreeze • *The snow hasn't had a chance to thaw.*
OPPOSITES: freeze, chill, harden

theatre AS A NOUN 1 = **playhouse**, auditorium, coliseum, amphitheatre • *When we went to the theatre it was a very big event.*
2 = **arena**, setting, site, scene, field *or* sphere *or* place of action • *The area has often been a theatre of war.*
3 = **hall**, room, auditorium • *a well-equipped library and the main lecture theatre*
▸ IN PHRASES: **the theatre = acting**, the stage, drama, the boards *(informal)*, show business, show biz *(informal)*, performing on the stage, the dramatic arts • *You can move on to work in the films and the theatre.*
▸ RELATED MANIA: theatromania
▹ *See panel* **Theatre terms**

theatrical 1 = **dramatic**, stage, Thespian, dramaturgical • *major theatrical productions*
2 = **exaggerated**, dramatic, melodramatic, histrionic, affected, camp *(informal)*, mannered, artificial, overdone, unreal, pompous, stilted, showy, ostentatious, hammy *(informal)*, ceremonious, stagy, actorly *or* actressy • *In a theatrical gesture he clamped his hand over his eyes.*
OPPOSITES: natural, unpretentious, simple

theft = **stealing**, robbery, thieving, fraud, rip-off *(slang)*, swindling, embezzlement, pilfering, larceny, purloining, thievery • *Art theft is now part of organized crime.*

theme 1 = **motif**, leitmotif, recurrent image, unifying idea • *The need to strengthen the family has become a recurrent theme.*
2 = **subject**, idea, topic, matter, argument, text, burden, essence, thesis, subject matter, keynote, gist • *The novel's central theme is the conflict between men and women.*

then 1 = **at that time**, in those days, at that point, at that moment, on that occasion, at that point in time • *I never worried about money then.*
2 = **after that**, later, next, afterwards, subsequently • *Add the oil and then the scallops.*
3 = **in that case**, that being so, that being the case, it follows that, under those circumstances • *If the answer is yes, then we must decide on appropriate action.*
4 = **in addition**, also, as well, moreover, besides, furthermore, what's more, on top of that, to boot, additionally, over and above that • *We have to do a lot of reading, and then there's our ongoing work.*

theological = **religious**, ecclesiastical, doctrinal, divine • *theological books*

theorem = **proposition**, statement, formula, rule, principle, thesis, hypothesis, deduction, dictum • *He postulated a theorem and proved it.*

theoretical *or* **theoretic** 1 = **abstract**, pure, speculative, ideal, impractical • *theoretical physics*
OPPOSITES: applied, practical, realistic
2 = **hypothetical**, academic, notional, unproven, conjectural, postulatory • *There is a theoretical risk, but there is seldom a problem.*

theorize *or* **theorise** = **speculate**, conjecture, hypothesize, project, suppose, guess, formulate, propound, blue-sky • *We can theorize about their minds by watching them behave.*

theory AS A NOUN 1 = **hypothesis**, philosophy, system of ideas, plan, system, science, scheme, proposal, principles, ideology, thesis • *He produced a theory about historical change.*
OPPOSITES: fact, experience, practice
2 = **belief**, feeling, speculation, assumption, guess, hunch, presumption, conjecture, surmise, supposition • *There was a theory that he wanted to marry her.*
▸ IN PHRASES: **in theory = in principle**, on paper, in an ideal world, in the abstract, hypothetically, all things being equal • *School dental services exists in theory, but in practice there are few.*

therapeutic = **beneficial**, healing, restorative, good, corrective, remedial, salutary, curative, salubrious, ameliorative, analeptic, sanative • *It's so therapeutic, a bit like meditation.*
OPPOSITES: damaging, destructive, harmful

therapist = **psychologist**, analyst, psychiatrist, shrink *(informal)*, counsellor, healer, psychotherapist, psychoanalyst, trick cyclist *(informal)* • *My therapist helped me feel my anger.*

therapy 1 = **remedy**, treatment, cure, healing, method of healing, remedial treatment • *anti-cancer therapy*
2 = **psychotherapy**, analysis, psychoanalysis • *He's having therapy to conquer his phobia.*

thereabouts = **so**, something like that, give or take a bit, plus or minus a few • *She told us her age was 48 or thereabouts.*

thereafter = **after that**, then, next, afterwards, subsequently, following that • *Inflation will fall and thereafter so will interest rates.*

therefore = **consequently**, so, thus, as a result, hence, accordingly, for that reason, whence, thence, ergo • *Muscles need lots of fuel and therefore burn lots of calories.*

thesaurus = **wordbook**, wordfinder • *I refer to my thesaurus a lot when I'm writing songs.*

thesis 1 = **proposition**, theory, hypothesis, idea, view, opinion, proposal, contention, line of argument • *This thesis does not stand up to close inspection.*
2 = **dissertation**, paper, treatise, essay, composition, monograph, disquisition • *He was awarded his PhD for a thesis on industrial robots.*
3 = **premise**, subject, statement, proposition, theme, topic, assumption, postulate, surmise, supposition • *His central thesis is that crime is up because children do not learn self-control.*

thick AS AN ADJECTIVE 1 = **bulky**, broad, big, large, fat, solid, substantial, hefty, plump, sturdy, stout, chunky, stocky, meaty, beefy, thickset • *He folded his thick arms across his chest.*

THEATRE TERMS

act	downstage	greasepaint	opera house	script	stage whisper
backstage	dramatis personae	greenroom	orchestra *or* orchestra pit	soliloquy	stalls
catastrophe	entr'acte	ham	overact	soubrette	theatre-in-the-round
chorus	entrance	house	prompt	speech	Thespian
circle	exit	juvenile	prompter	stage	understudy
Comédie Française	first night	leading lady	prop	stage direction	unities
coup de théâtre	first-night nerves	leading man	proscenium arch	stage door	upstage
crush bar	flat	lines	resting	stage fright	wings
cue	flies	monologue	role	stagehand	
curtain	fluff	noises off	scene	stage left	
curtain call	front of house	off-Broadway	scene dock *or* bay	stage manager	
curtain-raiser	gallery	off-off-Broadway	scenery	stage right	
curtain speech	gods	offstage		stage-struck	

OPPOSITES: thin, narrow, slight
2 = wide, across, deep, broad, in extent *or* diameter • *The folder was two inches thick.*
3 = luxuriant, heavy, dense, abundant, lush • *She inherited our father's thick, wavy hair.*
4 = dense, close, heavy, deep, compact, impenetrable, lush • *He led the rescuers through the thick undergrowth.*
5 = heavy, heavyweight, dense, chunky, bulky, woolly • *She wore a thick tartan skirt.*
6 = opaque, heavy, dense, impenetrable • *The smoke was blueish-black and thick.*
7 = viscous, concentrated, stiff, condensed, clotted, coagulated, gelatinous, semi-solid, viscid • *The sauce is thick and rich.*
OPPOSITES: clear, thin, runny
8 = crowded, full, packed, covered, filled, bursting, jammed, crawling, choked, crammed, swarming, abundant, bristling, brimming, overflowing, seething, thronged, teeming, congested, replete, chock-full, bursting at the seams, chock-a-block • *The area is so thick with people that the police close the streets.*
OPPOSITES: clear, empty
9 = husky, rough, hoarse, distorted, muffled, croaking, inarticulate, throaty, indistinct, gravelly, guttural, raspy, croaky • *His voice was thick with bitterness.*
OPPOSITES: clear, sharp, thin
10 = strong, marked, broad, decided, rich, distinct, pronounced • *He answered questions in a thick accent.*
OPPOSITES: slight, faint, vague
11 = stupid, slow, dull, dense, insensitive, dozy (*Brit. informal*), dopey (*informal*), moronic, obtuse, brainless, blockheaded, braindead (*informal*), dumb-ass (*informal*), thickheaded, dim-witted (*informal*), slow-witted • *How could she have been so thick?*
OPPOSITES: bright, sharp, clever
12 = friendly, close, intimate, familiar, pally (*informal*), devoted, well in (*informal*), confidential, inseparable, on good terms, chummy (*informal*), hand in glove, buddy-buddy (*slang, chiefly U.S. & Canad.*), palsy-walsy (*informal*), matey *or* maty (*Brit. informal*) • *You're thick with the girl, aren't you?*
OPPOSITES: distant, hostile, unfriendly
▸ **AS A NOUN = middle**, centre, heart, focus, core, midst, hub • *I enjoy being in the thick of things.*

thicken **1 = set**, condense, congeal, cake, gel, clot, jell, coagulate, inspissate (*archaic*) • *Keep stirring until the sauce thickens.*
OPPOSITES: thin, weaken, dilute
2 = deepen, become more involved, become more complicated, become more mysterious • *'Find anything?' he asked. 'Yeah. The plot thickens,' I said.*

thicket **= wood**, grove, woodland, brake, clump, covert, hurst (*archaic*), copse, coppice, spinney (*Brit.*) • *a bamboo thicket*

thickness **1 = width**, depth, breadth, broadness, extent • *a sheet of glass of negligible thickness*
2 = density, heaviness, denseness • *the tumbling thickness of his hair*

thickset **= stocky**, sturdy, burly, strong, heavy, muscular, bulky, beefy (*informal*), well-built, stubby, brawny, powerfully built • *his stout, thickset figure*
OPPOSITES: gaunt, bony, scrawny

thick-skinned **= insensitive**, tough, callous, hardened, hard-boiled (*informal*), impervious, stolid, unfeeling, case-hardened, unsusceptible • *He was thick-skinned enough to cope with it.*
OPPOSITES: sensitive, touchy, thin-skinned

thief **= robber**, crook (*informal*), burglar, stealer, bandit, plunderer, mugger (*informal*), shoplifter, embezzler, pickpocket, pilferer, swindler, purloiner, housebreaker, footpad (*archaic*), cracksman (*slang*), larcenist • *The thieves snatched the camera.*

QUOTATIONS
Thieves respect property. They merely wish the property to become their property that they may more perfectly respect it
[G.K. Chesterton *The Man who was Thursday*]

PROVERBS
Set a thief to catch a thief

thieve **= steal**, nick (*slang, chiefly Brit.*), rob, pinch (*informal*), poach, plunder, half-inch (*old-fashioned slang*), embezzle, blag (*slang*), pilfer, snitch (*slang*), purloin, filch, have sticky fingers (*informal*), peculate • *These people can't help thieving.*

thievery **= stealing**, theft, robbery, mugging (*informal*), burglary, plundering, shoplifting, embezzlement, thieving, pilfering, larceny, banditry, home invasion (*Austral. & N.Z.*) • *Fountain pens caused much thievery in the classroom.*

thieving **AS A NOUN = theft**, stealing, robbery, burglary, shoplifting, embezzlement, pilfering, larceny, home invasion (*Austral. & N.Z.*) • *an ex-con who says he's given up thieving*
▸ **AS AN ADJECTIVE = dishonest**, bent (*informal*), crooked (*informal*), light-fingered, larcenous, thievish • *a thieving grocer who put sand in the sugar*

thigh
▸ **RELATED ADJECTIVES:** femoral, crural

thighbone
▸ **TECHNICAL NAME:** femur

thin **AS AN ADJECTIVE 1 = narrow**, fine, attenuate, attenuated, threadlike • *A thin cable carries the signal to a computer.*
OPPOSITES: thick, heavy, bulky
2 = slim, spare, lean, slight, slender, skinny, light, meagre, skeletal, bony, lanky, emaciated, spindly, underweight, scrawny, lank, undernourished, skin and bone, scraggy, thin as a rake • *a tall, thin man with grey hair*
OPPOSITES: heavy, fat, stout
3 = wafer-thin, paper-thin, papery • *The recipe makes about 5 dozen thin biscuits.*
4 = watery, weak, diluted, dilute, runny, rarefied, wishy-washy (*informal*) • *The soup was thin and clear.*
OPPOSITES: strong, concentrated, viscous
5 = meagre, sparse, scanty, poor, scattered, inadequate, insufficient, deficient, paltry • *The crowd had been thin for the first half of the match.*
OPPOSITES: adequate, abundant, plentiful
6 = fine, delicate, flimsy, sheer, transparent, see-through, translucent, skimpy, gossamer, diaphanous, filmy, unsubstantial • *Her gown was thin and she shivered from the cold.*
OPPOSITES: heavy, thick, substantial
7 = unconvincing, inadequate, feeble, poor, weak, slight, shallow, insufficient, superficial, lame, scant, flimsy, scanty, unsubstantial • *The evidence is thin, and to some extent, ambiguous.*
OPPOSITES: strong, convincing, substantial
8 = weak, faint, feeble, small, low, soft, high-pitched, reedy • *Her thin voice rose high in complaint.*
9 = wispy, thinning, sparse, scarce, scanty • *She had pale thin yellow hair.*
▸ **AS A VERB 1 = prune**, trim, cut back, weed out • *It would have been better to thin the trees over several winters.*
2 = dilute, water down, weaken, attenuate • *Aspirin thins the blood, letting it flow more easily.*

thing **AS A NOUN 1 = object**, article, implement, machine, device, tool, instrument, mechanism, apparatus, gadget, gizmo (*informal*), contrivance, whatsit (*informal*), doo-dah (*informal*), thingummy (*informal*), thingummyjig (*informal*) • *What's that thing in the middle of the fountain?*
2 = substance, stuff, element, being, body, material, fabric,

texture, entity • *The Earth is mainly made of iron and silicon and things like that.*
3 = **concept**, idea, notion, conception • *Literacy isn't the same thing as intelligence.*
4 = **matter**, issue, subject, thought, concern, worry, topic, preoccupation • *There were far more serious things on my mind.*
5 = **affair**, situation, state of affairs, state, circumstance, scenario • *This war thing is upsetting me.*
6 = **fact**, detail, particular, point, factor, piece of information • *The first thing parents want to know is what sex the baby is.*
7 = **feature**, point, detail, something, particular, factor, item, aspect, facet • *If you could change one thing about yourself, what would it be?*
8 *often plural* = **task**, job, activity, act, undertaking, deed, chore, piece of business • *He will give you a list of things to do.*
9 = **happening**, event, incident, proceeding, phenomenon, occurrence, eventuality • *A strange thing happened.*
10 = **phobia**, fear, complex, horror, terror, hang-up (*informal*), aversion, neurosis, bee in your bonnet (*informal*) • *She had a thing about spiders.*
11 = **obsession**, liking, preoccupation, mania, quirk, fetish, fixation, soft spot, predilection, idée fixe (*French*) • *He's got a thing about red hair.*
12 = **remark**, comment, statement, observation, declaration, utterance, pronouncement • *No, some things are better left unsaid.*
13 *often plural* = **possessions**, stuff, gear, belongings, goods, effects, clothes, luggage, baggage, bits and pieces, paraphernalia, clobber (*Brit. slang*), odds and ends, chattels, impedimenta • *She told him to take his things and not come back.*
14 = **equipment**, gear, tool, stuff, tackle, implement, kit, apparatus, utensil, accoutrement • *He forgot his shaving things.*
15 = **circumstances**, the situation, the state of affairs, matters, life, affairs • *Everyone agrees things are getting better.*
▸ IN PHRASES: **the thing** = **fashionable**, trendy (*informal*), in fashion, in, popular, cool (*informal*), with it (*informal*), hip (*informal*), in vogue, all the rage, du jour (*French*), the in thing (*informal*), the new, culty • *Mobile phones are the thing these days.*
your thing = **your cup of tea** (*informal*), what you like, your bag (*informal*), what turns you on (*informal*), what interests you, what floats your boat (*informal*) • *Nightclubs are just not my thing!*

think AS A VERB 1 = **believe**, hold that, be of the opinion, conclude, esteem, conceive, be of the view • *I think there should be a ban on tobacco advertising.*
2 = **anticipate**, expect, figure (*U.S. informal*), suppose, imagine, guess (*informal, chiefly U.S. & Canad.*), reckon (*informal*), presume, envisage, foresee, surmise • *I think he'll do a great job for us.*
3 = **judge**, consider, estimate, reckon, deem, regard as • *She thought he was about seventeen years old.*
4 = **ponder**, reflect, contemplate, deliberate, brood, meditate, ruminate, cogitate, rack your brains, be lost in thought, cerebrate • *She closed her eyes for a moment, trying to think.*
5 = **remember**, recall, recollect, review, think back to, bring to mind, call to mind • *I was trying to think what else we had to do.*
6 = **consider**, contemplate, think about, weigh up, mull over, chew over, entertain the idea, give thought to, deliberate about • *He was thinking of taking legal action against her.*
▸ AS A NOUN = **ponder**, consideration, muse, assessment, reflection, deliberation, contemplation • *I'll have a think about that.*
▸ IN PHRASES: **think about something** *or* **someone** = **ponder**, consider, mull over, have in mind, weigh up, chew over (*informal*), reason over, turn over in your mind, revolve in your mind • *I have often thought about this problem.*
think better of something = **change your mind about**, reconsider, decide against, think again, go back on, think twice about, repent, have second thoughts about • *He opened his mouth to protest. Then he thought better of it.*
think much of *or* **a lot of something** *or* **someone** = **have a high opinion of**, value, respect, admire, esteem, rate (*slang*), hold in high regard, attach importance to, set store by, think highly of • *We think a lot of him, and believe he could go a long way.*
think nothing of something 1 = **have no compunction about**, have no hesitation about, take in your stride • *I thought nothing of betting £1,000 on a horse.*
2 = **consider unimportant**, set no store by, regard as routine • *One of his friends kept coming to the house, but I thought nothing of it.*
think something over = **consider**, contemplate, ponder, reflect upon, give thought to, consider the pros and cons of, weigh up, rack your brains about, chew over (*informal*), mull over, turn over in your mind • *She says she needs time to think it over.*
think something up = **devise**, create, imagine, manufacture, come up with, invent, contrive, improvise, visualize, concoct, dream up, trump up • *'Where did you get that idea?' 'I just thought it up.'*

QUOTATIONS
I think, therefore I am
[René Descartes *Le Discours de la Méthode*]

thinkable = **possible**, conceivable, imaginable, likely, reasonable, feasible, within the bounds of possibility • *At the same time, language makes thinkable the unreal and unreasonable.*
OPPOSITES: impossible, unlikely, inconceivable

thinker = **philosopher**, intellect (*informal*), wise man, sage, brain (*informal*), theorist, mastermind, mahatma • *some of the world's greatest thinkers*

thinking AS A NOUN = **reasoning**, thoughts, philosophy, idea, view, position, theory, opinion, conclusions, assessment, judgment, outlook, conjecture • *There was a strong theoretical dimension to his thinking.*
▸ AS AN ADJECTIVE = **thoughtful**, intelligent, cultured, reasoning, sophisticated, rational, philosophical, reflective, contemplative, meditative, ratiocinative • *Thinking people on both sides will applaud this book.*

thin-skinned = **sensitive**, vulnerable, easily hurt, touchy, soft, tender, susceptible, chippy (*informal*), hypersensitive, quick to take offence • *He is too thin-skinned to survive the presidential campaign.*
OPPOSITES: tough, insensitive, callous

third-rate = **mediocre**, bad, inferior, indifferent, poor, duff (*Brit. informal*), shoddy, poor-quality, low-grade, no great shakes (*informal*), chickenshit (*U.S. slang*), not much cop (*informal*), cheap-jack, half-pie (*N.Z. informal*), of a sort *or* of sorts, ropey *or* ropy (*Brit. informal*), bodger *or* bodgie (*Austral. slang*) • *a third-rate movie*

thirst AS A NOUN 1 = **dryness**, thirstiness, drought, craving to drink • *Instead of tea or coffee, drink water to quench your thirst.*
2 = **craving**, hunger, appetite, longing, desire, passion, yen (*informal*), ache, lust, yearning, eagerness, hankering, keenness • *their ever-growing thirst for cash*
OPPOSITES: dislike, loathing, aversion
▸ IN PHRASES: **thirst for something** = **crave**, want, desire, long for, covet, wish for, yearn for, lust after, hanker for, have your heart set on, hunger for *or* after • *We all thirst for the same things.*

thirsty 1 = **parched**, dry, dehydrated • *If a baby is thirsty, it feeds more often.*

2 *with* **for = eager for**, longing for, hungry for, dying for, yearning for, lusting for, craving for, thirsting for, burning for, hankering for, itching for, greedy for, desirous of, avid for, athirst for • *People should understand how thirsty for revenge they are.*

thirteen
▸ RELATED PHOBIA: triskaidecaphobia

thorax
▸ RELATED ADJECTIVE: thoracic

thorn AS A NOUN **= prickle**, spike, spine, barb • *Roses will always have thorns, but with care they can be avoided.*
▸ IN PHRASES: **thorn in your side = irritation**, nuisance, annoyance, trouble, bother, torture, plague, curse, pest, torment, hassle *(informal)*, scourge, affliction, irritant, bane • *She's a real thorn in his side.*

thorny 1 = prickly, spiky, spiny, pointed, sharp, barbed, bristly, spinous, bristling with thorns • *thorny hawthorn trees*
2 = troublesome, difficult, problematic(al), trying, hard, worrying, tough, upsetting, awkward, unpleasant, sticky *(informal)*, harassing, irksome, ticklish, vexatious • *the thorny issue of immigration policy*

thorough 1 = comprehensive, full, complete, sweeping, intensive, in-depth, exhaustive, all-inclusive, all-embracing, leaving no stone unturned • *We are making a thorough investigation.*
OPPOSITES: cursory, half-hearted, haphazard
2 = careful, conscientious, painstaking, efficient, meticulous, exhaustive, scrupulous, assiduous • *The men were expert, thorough and careful.*
OPPOSITES: careless, sloppy, lackadaisical
3 = complete, total, absolute, utter, perfect, entire, pure, sheer, outright, downright, unqualified, out-and-out, unmitigated, arrant, deep-dyed *(usually derogatory)* • *I was a thorough little academic snob.*
OPPOSITES: partial, superficial, incomplete

thoroughbred = purebred, pedigree, pure-blooded, blood, full-blooded, of unmixed stock • *a thoroughbred stallion*
OPPOSITES: hybrid, mongrel, half-breed

thoroughfare 1 = road, way, street, highway, roadway, passageway, avenue • *a busy thoroughfare*
2 = access, way, passage

thoroughly 1 = carefully, completely, fully, comprehensively, sweepingly, efficiently, inside out, meticulously, painstakingly, scrupulously, assiduously, intensively, from top to bottom, conscientiously, exhaustively, leaving no stone unturned • *a thoroughly researched and illuminating biography*
OPPOSITES: carelessly, haphazardly, half-heartedly
2 = fully, completely, throughout, inside out, through and through • *Food must be reheated thoroughly.*
3 = completely, quite, totally, perfectly, entirely, absolutely, utterly, to the full, downright, to the hilt, without reservation • *We returned home thoroughly contented.*
OPPOSITES: partly, somewhat, in part

though AS A CONJUNCTION **= although**, while, even if, despite the fact that, allowing, granted, even though, albeit, notwithstanding, even supposing, tho' *(U.S. or poetic)* • *He's very attractive, though he certainly isn't a ladykiller.*
▸ AS AN ADVERB **= nevertheless**, still, however, yet, nonetheless, all the same, for all that, notwithstanding • *I like him. He makes me angry sometimes, though.*

thought 1 = thinking, consideration, reflection, deliberation, regard, musing, meditation, contemplation, introspection, rumination, navel-gazing *(slang)*, cogitation, brainwork, cerebration • *After much thought I decided to end my marriage.*
2 = opinion, view, belief, idea, thinking, concept, conclusion, assessment, notion, conviction, judgment, conception, conjecture, estimation • *It is my thought that the situation will be resolved.*
3 = consideration, study, attention, care, regard, scrutiny, heed • *He had given some thought to what she had told him.*
4 = intention, plan, idea, design, aim, purpose, object, notion • *They had no thought of surrendering.*
5 = hope, expectation, dream, prospect, aspiration, anticipation • *He had now banished all thought of retirement.*
6 = concern, care, regard, anxiety, sympathy, compassion, thoughtfulness, solicitude, attentiveness • *They had no thought for others who might get hurt.*

QUOTATIONS

Thought flies and words go on foot
[Julien Green *Journal*]

Learning without thought is labour lost; thought without learning is perilous
[Confucius *Analects*]

thoughtful 1 = reflective, pensive, contemplative, meditative, thinking, serious, musing, wistful, introspective, rapt, studious, lost in thought, deliberative, ruminative, in a brown study • *He was looking very thoughtful.*
OPPOSITES: shallow, superficial
2 = considerate, kind, caring, kindly, helpful, attentive, unselfish, solicitous • *a thoughtful and caring man*
OPPOSITES: selfish, insensitive, inconsiderate
3 = profound, serious, deep, intelligent, philosophical, weighty, meaty, pithy, studious • *a thoughtful and scholarly book*

thoughtless 1 = inconsiderate, rude, selfish, insensitive, unkind, uncaring, indiscreet, tactless, impolite, undiplomatic • *a minority of thoughtless and inconsiderate people*
OPPOSITES: thoughtful, considerate, tactful
2 = unthinking, stupid, silly, careless, regardless, foolish, rash, reckless, mindless, negligent, inadvertent, ill-considered, tactless, absent-minded, imprudent, slapdash, neglectful, heedless, slipshod, inattentive, injudicious, remiss, unmindful, unobservant, ditsy *or* ditzy *(slang)* • *It was thoughtless of her to mention it.*
OPPOSITES: wise, intelligent, prudent

thousand
▸ RELATED ADJECTIVE: millenary
▸ RELATED PREFIX: kilo-

thrall = slavery, bondage, servitude, enslavement, subjugation, serfdom, subjection, vassalage, thraldom • *Our children will be even more in the thrall of the silicon chip.*

thrash AS A VERB **1 = defeat**, beat, hammer *(informal)*, stuff *(slang)*, tank *(slang)*, crush, overwhelm, slaughter *(informal)*, lick *(informal)*, paste *(slang)*, rout, maul, trounce, clobber *(slang)*, run rings around *(informal)*, wipe the floor with *(informal)*, make mincemeat of *(informal)*, blow someone out of the water *(slang)*, drub, beat someone hollow *(Brit. informal)* • *They thrashed their opponents 5-nil.*
2 = beat, wallop, whip, hide *(informal)*, belt *(informal)*, leather, tan *(slang)*, cane, lick *(informal)*, paste *(slang)*, birch, flog, scourge, spank, clobber *(slang)*, lambast(e), flagellate, horsewhip, give someone a (good) hiding *(informal)*, drub, take a stick to, beat *or* knock seven bells out of *(informal)* • *'Liar!' she screamed, as she thrashed the child.*
3 = thresh, flail, jerk, plunge, toss, squirm, writhe, heave, toss and turn • *He collapsed on the floor, thrashing his legs about.*
▸ IN PHRASES: **thrash something out = settle**, resolve, discuss, debate, solve, argue out, have out, talk over • *an effort to thrash out differences about which they have strong feelings*

thrashing 1 = defeat, beating, hammering *(informal)*, hiding *(informal)*, pasting *(slang)*, rout, mauling, trouncing, drubbing • *She dropped only 8 points in her thrashing of the former champion.*
2 = beating, hiding *(informal)*, belting *(informal)*, whipping,

tanning *(slang)*, lashing, caning, pasting *(slang)*, flogging, drubbing, chastisement • *She knew if she was caught she would get a thrashing.*

thread AS A NOUN 1 = **strand**, fibre, yarn, filament, line, string, cotton, twine • *a hat embroidered with golden threads*
2 = **theme**, motif, train of thought, course, direction, strain, plot, drift, tenor, story line • *the thread running through the book*
▸ AS A VERB 1 = **move**, pass, inch, ease, thrust, meander, squeeze through, pick your way • *She threaded her way back through the crowd.*
2 = **pass**, move, push, work, inch, ease, string, thrust, poke • *Thread the shock absorber through the large opening.*

threadbare 1 = **shabby**, worn, frayed, old, ragged, worn-out, scruffy, tattered, tatty, down at heel • *She sat cross-legged on a square of threadbare carpet.*
OPPOSITES: new, good, smart
2 = **hackneyed**, common, tired, stale, corny *(slang)*, stock, familiar, conventional, stereotyped, commonplace, well-worn, trite, clichéd, overused, cliché-ridden • *the government's threadbare domestic policies*
OPPOSITES: new, different, original

threat 1 = **danger**, risk, hazard, menace, peril • *the threat of tropical storms*
2 = **threatening remark**, menace, commination, intimidatory remark • *He may be forced to carry out his threat to resign.*
3 = **possibility**, prospect, likelihood, chance, risk, danger, probability • *The company was reprieved from the threat of closure.*
4 = **warning**, foreshadowing, foreboding • *The people who lived there felt a permanent sense of threat.*

threaten 1 = **intimidate**, bully, menace, terrorize, warn, cow, lean on *(slang)*, pressurize, browbeat, make threats to • *He tied her up and threatened her with a knife.*
OPPOSITES: protect, guard, defend
2 = **endanger**, jeopardize, put at risk, imperil, put in jeopardy, put on the line • *The newcomers directly threaten the livelihood of current workers.*
OPPOSITES: protect, guard, defend
3 = **be imminent**, hang over, be in the air, loom, be in the offing, hang over someone's head, impend • *Plants must be covered with a leaf-mould if frost threatens.*

threatening 1 = **menacing**, bullying, intimidatory, terrorizing, minatory, comminatory • *The police should have charged them with threatening behaviour.*
2 = **ominous**, sinister, forbidding, grim, baleful, inauspicious, bodeful • *a threatening atmosphere of rising tension and stress*
OPPOSITES: promising, encouraging, reassuring

three
▸ RELATED ADJECTIVE: ternary
▸ RELATED PREFIXES: tri-, ter-

three-dimensional = **solid**, rounded, holographic, stereoscopic, stereographic • *software which creates three-dimensional images*

threesome = **trio**, trinity, trilogy, triplet, triad, triumvirate, troika, triptych, triplex, trine, triune • *We often all go out as a threesome.*

threshold 1 = **entrance**, doorway, door, doorstep, sill, doorsill • *He stopped at the threshold of the bedroom.*
2 = **start**, beginning, opening, dawn, verge, brink, outset, starting point, inception • *We are on the threshold of a new era in astronomy.*
OPPOSITES: end, close, finish
3 = **limit**, margin, starting point, minimum • *She has a low threshold of boredom, and needs constant stimulation.*
▸ RELATED ADJECTIVE: liminal

thrift = **economy**, prudence, frugality, saving, parsimony, carefulness, good husbandry, thriftiness • *They were rightly praised for their thrift and enterprise.*
OPPOSITES: waste, squandering, extravagance

thrifty = **economical**, prudent, provident, frugal, saving, sparing, careful, parsimonious • *My mother taught me to be thrifty.*
OPPOSITES: extravagant, wasteful, prodigal

thrill AS A NOUN 1 = **pleasure**, charge *(slang)*, kick *(informal)*, glow, sensation, buzz *(slang)*, high, stimulation, tingle, titillation, flush of excitement • *I remember the thrill of opening presents on Christmas morning.*
OPPOSITES: boredom, tedium, monotony
2 = **trembling**, throb, shudder, flutter, fluttering, tremor, quiver, vibration • *He felt a thrill of fear, of adrenaline.*
▸ AS A VERB = **excite**, stimulate, arouse, move, send *(slang)*, stir, flush, tingle, electrify, titillate, give someone a kick • *The electric atmosphere both thrilled and terrified him.*

thrilled = **pleased**, excited, delighted, happy, contented, satisfied, glad, tickled, gratified, over the moon *(informal)*, chuffed *(Brit. slang)*, euphoric, rapt, tickled pink *(informal)* • *I was so thrilled to get a good report from him.*

thrilling = **exciting**, gripping, stimulating, stirring, sensational, rousing, riveting, electrifying, hair-raising, rip-roaring *(informal)* • *a thrilling encounter with wildlife in its natural state*
OPPOSITES: boring, dull, tedious

thrive = **prosper**, do well, flourish, increase, grow, develop, advance, succeed, get on, boom, bloom, wax, burgeon, grow rich, have legs *(informal)* • *Today his company continues to thrive.*
OPPOSITES: fail, decline, wither

thriving = **successful**, doing well, flourishing, growing, developing, healthy, booming, wealthy, blooming, prosperous, burgeoning, going strong • *He now owns a thriving antique business.*
OPPOSITES: failing, unsuccessful, ailing

throat = **gullet**, windpipe, oesophagus, crop, maw, craw, trachea, pharynx • *She had a sore throat.*
▸ RELATED ADJECTIVES: guttural, gular, jugular

throaty = **hoarse**, husky, gruff, low, deep, thick, guttural • *A broad smile and a throaty chuckle were his on-screen trademarks.*

throb AS A VERB 1 = **pulsate**, pound, beat, pulse, thump, palpitate • *His head throbbed.*
2 = **vibrate**, pulse, resonate, pulsate, reverberate, shake, judder *(informal)* • *The engines throbbed.*
▸ AS A NOUN 1 = **pulse**, pounding, beat, thump, thumping, pulsating, palpitation • *The bruise on his stomach ached with a steady throb.*
2 = **vibration**, pulse, throbbing, resonance, reverberation, judder *(informal)*, pulsation • *His head jerked up at the throb of the engine.*

throes AS A PLURAL NOUN = **pains**, spasms, pangs, fit, stabs, convulsions, paroxysm • *The animal twitched in its final death throes.*
▸ IN PHRASES: **in the throes of something** = **in the midst of**, in the process of, suffering from, struggling with, wrestling with, toiling with, anguished by, agonized by, in the pangs of • *The country is in the throes of a general election.*

thrombosis = **blood clot**, embolism, infarction, coronary thrombosis, embolus • *Thinning of the blood reduces the chances of thrombosis.*

throng AS A NOUN = **crowd**, mob, horde, press, host, pack, mass, crush, jam, congregation, swarm, multitude, concourse, assemblage • *An official pushed through the throng.*
▸ AS A VERB 1 = **crowd**, flock, congregate, troop, bunch, herd, cram, converge, hem in, mill around, swarm around • *the multitudes that throng around the Pope*
OPPOSITES: separate, break up, disperse
2 = **pack**, fill, crowd, press, jam • *They throng the beaches in July and August.*
3 = **rush**, pour, stream, press, flow • *The crowds thronged into the mall.*

throttle 1 = **strangle**, choke, garrotte, strangulate • *He tried to throttle her with wire.*
2 = **suppress**, inhibit, stifle, control, silence, gag • *The overvaluation of sterling is throttling industry.*

through AS A PREPOSITION 1 = **via**, by way of, by, between, past, in and out of, from end to end of, from one side to the other of • *The path continues through a tunnel of trees.*
2 = **because of**, by way of, by means of, by virtue of, with the assistance of, as a consequence or result of • *the thought of someone suffering through a mistake of mine*
3 = **using**, via, by way of, by means of, by virtue of, with the assistance of • *I got it cheap through a friend in the trade.*
4 = **during**, throughout, in the middle of, for the duration of, in • *trips at home and abroad all through the year*
5 = **to**, up to and including • *open Monday through Sunday from 7 till 10*
▸ AS AN ADVERB 1 = **from one side to the other**, past, from one end to the other, in and out the other end • *She stood back to allow him to pass through.*
2 = **the whole time**, throughout, continuously, non-stop, constantly, all the time, from start to finish, without a break, without an interruption • *He worked right through.*
▸ AS AN ADJECTIVE 1 *with* **with** = **finished with**, done with, having had enough of • *I'm through with women.*
2 = **completed**, done, finished, ended, terminated • *It would guarantee employment once her schooling was through.*
3 = **non-stop**, direct, express • *a through train*
▸ IN PHRASES: **through and through** = **completely**, totally, fully, thoroughly, entirely, altogether, wholly, utterly, to the core, unreservedly • *People assume they know me through and through as soon as we meet.*

throughout AS A PREPOSITION 1 = **right through**, all through, everywhere in, for the duration of, during the whole of, through the whole of, from end to end of • *The same themes are repeated throughout the film.*
2 = **all over**, all through, everywhere in, through the whole of, over the length and breadth of • *He now runs projects throughout Africa.*
▸ AS AN ADVERB 1 = **from start to finish**, right through, the whole time, all the time, from the start, all through, from beginning to end • *The concert wasn't bad, but people talked throughout.*
2 = **all through**, right through, in every nook and cranny • *Throughout, the walls are white.*

t

throw AS A VERB 1 = **hurl**, toss, fling, send, project, launch, cast, pitch, shy, chuck *(informal)*, propel, sling, lob *(informal)*, heave, put • *He spent hours throwing a tennis ball against a wall.*
2 = **toss**, fling, chuck *(informal)*, cast, hurl, sling, heave, put • *He threw his jacket onto the back seat.*
3 = **bring down**, fell, floor, prostrate • *He threw me to the ground and started to kick me.*
4 = **dislodge**, unseat, upset, overturn, hurl to the ground • *The horse reared, throwing its rider.*
5 = **cast**, project, give off, send, emit, radiate • *The sunlight threw hard-edged shadows on the ground.*
6 = **direct**, shoot, cast, give, dart, bestow on • *She turned and threw a suggestive grin at him.*
7 = **deliver**, land • *Everything was fine until someone threw a punch.*
8 = **organize**, give, host, arrange, put on, plan, provide, jack up *(N.Z. informal)* • *Why not throw a party for your friends?*
9 = **operate**, flick, switch on, click on, engage • *He threw the switch to light the illuminations.*
10 = **confuse**, baffle, faze, astonish, confound, unnerve, disconcert, perturb, throw you out, throw you off, dumbfound, discompose, put your off your stroke, throw you off your stride, unsettle • *He threw me by asking if I went in for martial arts.*
11 = **shape**, form, fashion, mould • *It's not at all simple to throw a pot.*
▸ AS A NOUN = **toss**, pitch, fling, put, cast, shy, sling, lob *(informal)*, heave • *One of the judges thought it was a foul throw.*
▸ IN PHRASES: **a throw** = **each**, for one, apiece, per item • *He offered people lifts at 50p a throw.*
throw someone off 1 = **disconcert**, unsettle, faze, throw *(informal)*, upset, confuse, disturb, put you off your stroke, throw you off your stride • *I lost my first serve in the first set; it threw me off a bit.*
2 = **escape from**, lose, leave behind, get away from, evade, shake off, elude, outrun, outdistance, give someone the slip, show a clean pair of heels to • *He threw off his pursuers by pedalling across the state line.*
throw someone out = **expel**, eject, evict, dismiss, get rid of, oust, kick out *(informal)*, show the door to, turf out *(Brit. informal)*, give the bum's rush to *(slang)*, kiss off *(slang, chiefly U.S. & Canad.)* • *I wanted to kill him, but instead I just threw him out.*
throw something away 1 = **discard**, dump *(informal)*, get rid of, reject, scrap, axe *(informal)*, bin *(informal)*, ditch *(slang)*, junk *(informal)*, chuck *(informal)*, throw out, dispose of, dispense with, jettison, cast off • *I never throw anything away.*
2 = **waste**, lose, blow *(slang)*, squander, fritter away, fail to make use of, make poor use of • *Failing to tackle the problem would be throwing away an opportunity.*
throw something off = **cast off**, shake off, rid yourself of, free yourself of, drop, abandon, discard • *a country ready to throw off the shackles of its colonial past*
throw something on = **slip into**, dress in, pull on, put something on quickly, don quickly • *He stumbled out of bed and threw on his clothes.*
throw something out 1 = **discard**, dump *(informal)*, get rid of, reject, scrap, bin *(informal)*, ditch *(slang)*, junk *(informal)*, chuck *(informal)*, throw away, dispose of, dispense with, jettison, cast off • *Never throw out milk that is about to go off.*
2 = **emit**, radiate, give off, diffuse, disseminate, put forth • *a workshop throwing out a pool of light*
throw something up 1 = **throw together**, jerry-build, run up, slap together • *Scrap metal dwellings are thrown up in any available space.*
2 = **produce**, reveal, bring to light, bring forward, bring to the surface, bring to notice • *These studies have thrown up some interesting results.*
3 = **give up**, leave, abandon, quit, chuck *(informal)*, resign from, relinquish, renounce, step down from *(informal)*, jack in • *He threw up his job as party chairman.*
throw up = **vomit**, be sick, spew, puke *(slang)*, chuck *(Austral. & N.Z. informal)*, heave, regurgitate, disgorge, retch, barf *(U.S. slang)*, chunder *(slang, chiefly Austral.)*, upchuck *(U.S. slang)*, do a technicolour yawn *(slang)*, toss your cookies *(U.S. slang)* • *He threw up over a seat next to me.*

throwaway 1 = **disposable**, one-use, expendable • *Now they are producing throwaway razors.*
2 = **casual**, passing, offhand, careless, understated, unthinking, ill-considered • *a throwaway remark she later regretted*

thrush
▸ RELATED ADJECTIVE: turdine

thrust AS A VERB 1 = **push**, force, shove, drive, press, plunge, jam, butt, ram, poke, propel, prod, impel • *They thrust him into the back of a jeep.*
2 = **shove**, push, shoulder, lunge, jostle, elbow or shoulder your way • *She thrust her way into the crowd.*
3 *often with* **through** *or* **into** = **stab**, stick, jab, pierce • *How can I thrust a knife into my son's heart?*
▸ AS A NOUN 1 = **stab**, pierce, lunge • *Two of the knife thrusts were fatal.*
2 = **push**, shove, poke, prod • *a thrust of his hand that sent the lad reeling*

3 = **momentum**, impetus, drive, motive power, motive force, propulsive force • *It provides the thrust that makes the craft move forward.*
4 = **gist**, meaning, idea, point, force, sense, import, substance, drift, essence, marrow, nub, pith • *The main thrust of the film is its examination of religious values.*
5 = **attack**, drive, charge, push, assault, raid, invasion, offensive, sally, onslaught, foray, sortie, incursion, military advance • *a thrust into territory seized by Iranian forces*
▸ **IN PHRASES: thrust something upon someone** = **impose upon**, force upon, inflict upon, press upon, push upon • *The role of Queen was thrust upon her.*

thud **AS A NOUN** = **thump**, crash, knock, smack, clump, wallop *(informal)*, clunk, clonk • *She tripped and fell with a sickening thud.*
▸ **AS A VERB** = **thump**, crash, knock, smack, clump, wallop *(informal)*, clunk, clonk • *She ran upstairs, her bare feet thudding on the wood.*

thug = **ruffian**, hooligan, tough, heavy *(slang)*, killer, murderer, robber, gangster, assassin, bandit, mugger *(informal)*, cut-throat, bully boy, bruiser *(informal)*, boot boy, tsotsi *(S. African)* • *the cowardly thugs who mug old people*

thumb **AS A NOUN** = **digit** • *She bit her thumb, not looking at me.*
▸ **AS A VERB** 1 = **handle**, finger, mark, soil, maul, mess up, dog-ear • *a well-thumbed copy of Who's Who*
2 = **hitch**, request *(informal)*, signal for, hitchhike • *Thumbing a lift once had a carefree image.*
▸ **IN PHRASES: all thumbs** = **clumsy**, inept, cack-handed *(informal)*, maladroit, butterfingered *(informal)*, ham-fisted *(informal)*, unco *(Austral. slang)* • *Can you open this? I'm all thumbs.*
thumb through something = **flick through**, browse through, leaf through, glance at, turn over, flip through, skim through, riffle through, scan the pages of, run your eye over • *He had the drawer open and was thumbing through files.*
thumbs down = **disapproval**, refusal, rejection, no, rebuff, negation • *Brokers have given the firm the thumbs down.*
thumbs up = **approval**, go-ahead *(informal)*, acceptance, yes, encouragement, green light, affirmation, O.K. *or* okay *(informal)* • *The film got a general thumbs up from the critics.*
▸ **TECHNICAL NAME:** pollex
▸ **RELATED ADJECTIVE:** pollicical

thumbnail = **brief**, short, concise, quick, compact, succinct, pithy • *thumbnail guides and all the tips on top destinations*

thump **AS A NOUN** 1 = **blow**, knock, punch, rap, smack, clout *(informal)*, whack, swipe, wallop *(informal)* • *He felt a thump on his shoulder.*
2 = **thud**, crash, bang, clunk, thwack • *There was a loud thump as the horse crashed into the van.*
▸ **AS A VERB** 1 = **strike**, hit, punch, pound, beat, knock, deck *(slang)*, batter, rap, chin *(slang)*, smack, thrash, clout *(informal)*, whack, swipe, clobber *(slang)*, wallop *(informal)*, lambast(e), belabour, lay one on *(slang)*, beat *or* knock seven bells out of *(informal)* • *He thumped me, nearly knocking me over.*
2 = **thud**, crash, bang, thwack • *She thumped her hand on the witness box.*
3 = **throb**, pound, beat, pulse, pulsate, palpitate • *My heart was thumping wildly.*

thumping = **huge**, massive, enormous, great, impressive, tremendous, excessive, terrific, thundering *(slang)*, titanic, gigantic, monumental, mammoth, colossal, whopping *(informal)*, stellar *(informal)*, exorbitant, gargantuan, fuck-off *(offensive taboo slang)*, elephantine, humongous *or* humungous *(U.S. slang)* • *The gloom deepened after a thumping £145 million loss.*
OPPOSITES: insignificant, negligible, petty

thunder **AS A NOUN** 1 = **thunderclap**, roll of thunder, thunder crack, peal of thunder • *frequent thunder and lightning, and torrential rain*
2 = **rumble**, crash, crashing, boom, booming, explosion, rumbling, pealing, detonation, cracking • *The thunder of the sea on the rocks.*
▸ **AS A VERB** 1 = **rumble**, crash, blast, boom, explode, roar, clap, resound, detonate, reverberate, crack, peal • *the sound of the guns thundering in the fog*
2 = **shout**, roar, yell, bark, bellow, declaim • *'It's your money. Ask for it!' she thundered.*
3 = **rail**, curse, fulminate • *He started thundering about feminists and liberals.*
▸ **RELATED PHOBIA:** brontophobia, tonitrophobia

thunderous = **loud**, noisy, deafening, booming, roaring, resounding, tumultuous, ear-splitting • *The audience responded with thunderous applause.*

thunderstruck = **amazed**, astonished, astounded, floored *(informal)*, shocked, stunned, staggered, paralysed, dazed, taken aback, petrified, aghast, bowled over *(informal)*, open-mouthed, gobsmacked *(Brit. slang)*, dumbfounded, flabbergasted *(informal)*, nonplussed, flummoxed, rooted to the spot, struck dumb, left speechless, knocked for six *(informal)* • *I was thunderstruck – it was like magic!*

thus 1 = **in this way**, so, like this, as follows, like so, in this manner, in this fashion, to such a degree • *She explained her mistake thus.*
2 = **therefore**, so, hence, consequently, accordingly, for this reason, ergo, on that account • *women's access to the basic means of production, and thus to political power*

thwack **AS A NOUN** = **smack**, blow, whack, bash *(informal)*, thump, clout *(informal)*, swipe, wallop *(informal)* • *a sharp thwack across the arm that left fingermarks for ages*
▸ **AS A VERB** = **smack**, hit, bash *(informal)*, thump, beat, deck *(slang)*, chin *(slang)*, clout *(informal)*, flog, whack, swipe, wallop *(informal)*, lambast(e), beat *or* knock seven bells out of *(informal)* • *He just thwacked me on the back of the head with a ruler.*

thwart = **frustrate**, stop, foil, check, defeat, prevent, oppose, snooker, baffle, hinder, obstruct, impede, balk, outwit, stymie, cook someone's goose *(informal)*, put a spoke in someone's wheel *(informal)* • *They were doing all they could to thwart the terrorists.*
OPPOSITES: help, support, assist

tic = **twitch**, jerk, spasm • *She developed a tic in her left eye.*

tick[1] **AS A NOUN** 1 = **check mark**, mark, line, stroke, dash • *Place a tick in the appropriate box.*
2 = **click**, tap, tapping, clicking, clack, ticktock • *He sat listening to the tick of the grandfather clock.*
3 = **moment**, second, minute, shake *(informal)*, flash, instant, sec *(informal)*, twinkling, split second, jiffy *(informal)*, trice, half a mo *(Brit. informal)*, two shakes of a lamb's tail *(informal)*, bat of an eye *(informal)* • *I'll be back in a tick.*
▸ **AS A VERB** 1 = **mark**, indicate, mark off, check off, choose, select • *Please tick here if you do not want to receive such mailings.*
2 = **click**, tap, clack, ticktock • *A clock ticked busily from the kitchen counter.*
▸ **IN PHRASES: tick over** = **idle** • *He sat in the car with the engine ticking over.*
tick someone off 1 = **scold**, rebuke, tell off *(informal)*, lecture, carpet *(informal)*, censure, reprimand, reproach, berate, chide, tear into *(informal)*, reprove, upbraid, take to task, read the riot act to, bawl out *(informal)*, chew out *(U.S. & Canad. informal)*, tear off a strip *(Brit. informal)*, haul over the coals *(informal)*, give a rocket *(Brit. & N.Z. informal)* • *His mum ticked him off when they got home.*
2 = **annoy**, bother, bug *(informal)*, irritate, disturb, aggravate, gall, irk, get on your nerves *(informal)*, get up your nose *(informal)*, get your back up *(informal)*, hack you off *(informal)* • *I just think it's rude and it's really ticking me off.*
tick something off = **mark off**, check off, put a tick at • *He ticked off my name on a piece of paper.*

tick²
▸ **RELATED ADJECTIVE:** acaroid

ticket 1 = **voucher**, pass, coupon, card, slip, certificate, token, chit • *They were queueing to get tickets for the football match.*
2 = **label**, tag, marker, sticker, card, slip, tab, docket • *a price ticket*
3 = **notice**, notification • *a parking ticket*

tickle 1 = **stroke**, pet, chuck, touch lightly • *I was tickling him, and he was laughing and giggling.*
2 = **amuse**, delight, entertain, please, divert, gratify, titillate • *The story really tickled me.*
OPPOSITES: bore, annoy, irritate
3 = **stimulate**, interest, excite, appeal to, arouse, captivate • *Interesting words tickle the imagination.*

ticklish = **difficult**, sensitive, delicate, tricky, nice, critical, uncertain, awkward, risky, unstable, thorny, touchy, unsteady • *the ticklish question of the future of the EU*

tide **AS A NOUN** 1 = **current**, flow, stream, course, ebb, undertow, tideway • *They used to sail with the tide.*
2 = **course**, direction, trend, current, movement, tendency, drift • *They talked of reversing the tide of events.*
▸ **IN PHRASES: tide someone over** = **keep you going**, see you through, keep the wolf from the door, keep your head above water, bridge the gap for • *He wanted to borrow some money to tide him over.*

tidings = **news**, report, word, message, latest *(informal)*, information, communication, intelligence, bulletin, gen *(Brit. informal)* • *He hated always being the bearer of bad tidings.*

tidy **AS AN ADJECTIVE** 1 = **neat**, orderly, ordered, clean, trim, systematic, spruce, businesslike, well-kept, well-ordered, shipshape, spick-and-span, trig *(archaic or dialect)*, in apple-pie order *(informal)* • *Having a tidy desk can sometimes seem impossible.*
OPPOSITES: disordered, messy, untidy
2 = **organized**, neat, fastidious, methodical, smart, efficient, spruce, businesslike, well-groomed, well turned out • *She wasn't a tidy person.*
3 = **considerable**, large, substantial, good, goodly, fair, healthy, generous, handsome, respectable, ample, largish, sizable *or* sizeable • *The opportunities are there to make a tidy profit.*
OPPOSITES: little, small, tiny
▸ **AS A VERB** = **neaten**, straighten, put in order, order, clean, groom, spruce up, put to rights, put in trim • *She made her bed and tidied her room.*
OPPOSITES: disorder, mess up, dirty

tie **AS A VERB** 1 = **fasten**, bind, join, unite, link, connect, attach, knot, truss, interlace • *He tied the ends of the plastic bag together.*
OPPOSITES: loose, undo, unfasten
2 = **tether**, secure, rope, moor, lash, make fast • *She tied her horse to a fence post.*
3 = **do up**, knot, make a bow in, make a knot in • *He pulled on his heavy shoes and tied the shoelaces.*
4 = **restrict**, limit, confine, hold, bind, restrain, hamper, hinder • *I wouldn't like to be tied to catching the last train home.*
OPPOSITES: free, release
5 = **relate**, link, connect, unite, join, couple, marry • *My social life and business life are closely tied.*
6 = **draw**, be even, be level, be neck and neck, match, equal • *Both teams had tied on points and goal difference.*
▸ **AS A NOUN** 1 = **fastening**, binding, link, band, bond, joint, connection, string, rope, knot, cord, fetter, ligature • *little empire-line coats with ribbon ties*
2 = **necktie**, cravat, neckerchief • *He had taken off his jacket and loosened his tie.*
3 = **bond**, relationship, connection, duty, commitment, obligation, liaison, allegiance, affinity, affiliation, kinship • *She had family ties in France.*
4 = **draw**, dead heat, deadlock, stalemate • *The first game ended in a tie.*
5 = **match**, game, contest, fixture, meeting, event, trial, bout • *They'll meet the winners of the first-round tie.*
6 = **encumbrance**, restriction, limitation, check, handicap, restraint, hindrance, bind *(informal)* • *It's a bit of a tie, going there every Sunday.*
▸ **IN PHRASES: tie in with something** 1 = **link**, relate to, connect, be relevant to, come in to, have a bearing on • *subjects which tie in with whatever you enjoy about painting*
2 = **fit in with**, coincide with, coordinate with, harmonize with, occur simultaneously with • *Our wedding date had to tie in with Dave's leaving the army.*
tie someone down = **restrict**, inhibit, constrain, cramp, shackle, cramp someone's style • *We'd agreed from the beginning not to tie each other down.*
tie something up 1 = **secure**, lash, tether, make fast, moor, attach, rope • *I had tied the boat up in the marina and furled my sail.*
2 = **conclude**, settle, wrap up *(informal)*, end, wind up, terminate, finish off, bring to a close • *They hope to tie up a deal within the next few weeks.*
3 = **commit**, invest something long-term, make something unavailable • *Don't tie all your capital up in property.*
tie something *or* **someone up** = **bind**, restrain, pinion, truss up • *Don't you think we should tie him up and put a guard over him?*

TIES AND CRAVATS

ascot	dicky bow	rebozo
bertha	falling band	scarf
black tie	fichu	school tie
boa	foulard	stock
bow tie	kerchief	stole
carcanet *(archaic)*	madras	white tie
comforter *(chiefly Brit.)*	muffler	Windsor tie
cravat	neckcloth	
	neckerchief	

tied up = **busy**, occupied, engaged, engrossed, kept busy • *He's tied up with his new book.*

tie in *or* **tie-in** = **link**, connection, relation, relationship, association, tie-up, liaison, coordination, hook-up • *There's no tie-in to the woman's death at all.*

tier = **row**, bank, layer, line, order, level, series, file, rank, storey, stratum, echelon • *an auditorium with tiers of seats around and above it*

tie-up = **link**, association, connection, relationship, relation, liaison, tie-in, coordination, hook-up, linkup • *The deal is expected to result in a tie-up between the two companies.*

tiff = **quarrel**, row, disagreement, words, difference, dispute, scrap *(informal)*, falling-out *(informal)*, squabble, petty quarrel • *She was walking home after a tiff with her boyfriend.*

tiger
▸ **NAME OF FEMALE:** tigress
▸ **NAME OF YOUNG:** cub

tight 1 = **close-fitting**, narrow, cramped, snug, constricted, close • *His jeans were too tight.*
OPPOSITES: loose, spacious
2 = **secure**, firm, fast, fixed • *Keep a tight grip on my hand.*
3 = **taut**, stretched, tense, rigid, stiff • *Pull the elastic tight and knot the ends.*
OPPOSITES: relaxed, slack
4 = **compact**, compacted, dense, compressed, unyielding • *She curled up in a tight ball.*

5 = **limited**, small, tiny, narrow, restricted, confined, uncomfortable, inadequate, compact, minimal, cramped, constricted, poky • *so many people in such a tight space*
6 = **strict**, stringent, severe, tough, harsh, stern, rigid, rigorous, uncompromising, inflexible, unyielding • *tight control of media coverage*
OPPOSITES: easy-going, liberal, lenient
7 = **sealed**, watertight, impervious, sound, proof, hermetic • *Cover with foil and the lid to ensure a tight seal.*
OPPOSITES: open, loose, porous
8 = **close**, even, well-matched, near, hard-fought, evenly-balanced • *It was a very tight match.*
OPPOSITES: overwhelming, runaway, uneven
9 = **miserly**, mean, stingy, close, sparing, grasping, parsimonious, niggardly, penurious, tightfisted, tight-arse *(taboo slang)*, tight-arsed *(taboo slang)*, tight-ass *(U.S. taboo slang)*, tight-assed *(U.S. taboo slang)*, tight as a duck's arse *(taboo slang)* • *Are you so tight you won't even spend a few quid?*
OPPOSITES: generous, lavish, extravagant
10 = **difficult**, tough, dangerous, tricky, sticky *(informal)*, hazardous, troublesome, problematic, precarious, perilous, worrisome, ticklish • *They teach you to use your head and get out of a tight spot.*
11 = **drunk**, intoxicated, pissed *(Brit., Austral. & N.Z. slang)*, flying *(slang)*, bombed *(slang)*, stoned *(slang)*, wasted *(slang)*, smashed *(slang)*, hammered *(slang)*, steaming *(slang)*, wrecked *(slang)*, out of it *(slang)*, plastered *(slang)*, blitzed *(slang)*, lit up *(slang)*, stewed *(slang)*, pickled *(informal)*, bladdered *(slang)*, under the influence *(informal)*, tipsy, legless *(informal)*, paralytic *(informal)*, sozzled *(informal)*, steamboats *(Scot. slang)*, tiddly *(slang, chiefly Brit.)*, off your face *(slang)*, half cut *(Brit. slang)*, zonked *(slang)*, blotto *(slang)*, inebriated, out to it *(Austral. & N.Z. slang)*, three sheets to the wind *(slang)*, in your cups, rat-arsed *(taboo slang)*, blatted *(Brit. slang)*, boozed-up *(informal)*, dronkverdriet *(S. African)*, elephants *(Austral. slang)*, broken *(S. African informal)*, boozed-up *(slang)*, kaylied *(Brit. slang)*, langered *(Irish slang)*, lashed *(Brit. slang)*, mashed *(Brit. slang)*, mullered *(slang)*, ossified *(Irish slang)*, sat *(S. African)*, stukkend *(S. African slang)*, trashed *(slang)*, Brahms and Liszt *(slang)*, half seas over *(Brit. informal)*, bevvied *(dialect)*, pie-eyed *(slang)* • *He laughed loudly. There was no doubt he was tight.*
OPPOSITES: sober
12 = **scarce**, scant, meagre, in short supply, low, limited, scanty • *Money has been fairly tight in our household.*
13 = **succinct**, economic, concise, to the point, crisp, terse, laconic, pithy, well structured, short and sweet • *the tight writing and upbeat performances of the play*

tighten 1 = **close**, narrow, strengthen, squeeze, harden, constrict • *He answered by tightening his grip on her shoulder.*
OPPOSITES: slacken, ease off, let out
2 = **stretch**, strain, tense, tauten, stiffen, rigidify • *He flung his whole weight back, tightening the rope.*
OPPOSITES: relax, loosen, slacken
3 = **fasten**, secure, screw, fix • *I used my thumbnail to tighten the screw.*
OPPOSITES: unscrew, unfasten, unbind
4 = **contract**, narrow, constrict, become tight, become narrow • *Her throat had tightened and she couldn't speak.*
5 = **purse**, narrow, compress, screw up, pucker • *Martha tightened her lips and shook her head.*
6 = **increase**, heighten, toughen (up), beef up *(informal)*, crank up *(informal)*, scale up, make stricter, make more rigorous • *They have tightened security along the border.*

tight-fisted = **miserly**, mean, stingy, close, tight, sparing, grasping, parsimonious, niggardly, penurious, close-fisted, tight-arse *(taboo slang)*, tight-arsed *(taboo slang)*, mingy *(Brit. informal)*, tight-ass *(U.S. taboo slang)*, tight-assed *(U.S. taboo slang)*, snoep *(S. African informal)*, tight as a duck's arse *(taboo slang)* • *the government's tight-fisted monetary policy*

tight-lipped = **secretive**, reticent, uncommunicative, reserved, quiet, silent, mute, taciturn, close-mouthed, unforthcoming, close-lipped • *Officials are tight-lipped about launching an attack.*

tile
▸ **RELATED ADJECTIVE:** tegular

till[1] = **cultivate**, dig, plough, work, turn over • *freshly-tilled fields*

till[2] = **cash register**, cash box, cash drawer • *He checked the register. There was money in the till.*

tilt **AS A VERB** 1 = **slant**, tip, slope, list, lean, heel, incline, cant • *The boat instantly tilted, filled and sank.*
2 = **angle**, tip, lean, incline • *She tilted her head back to look at him.*
▸ **AS A NOUN** 1 = **inclination**, nod • *an apologetic tilt of the head*
2 = **slope**, angle, inclination, list, pitch, incline, slant, cant, camber, gradient • *the tilt of the earth's axis*
3 = **bid for**, crack at • *His first tilt at Parliament came in 1994.*
4 = **joust**, fight, tournament, lists, clash, set-to *(informal)*, encounter, combat, duel, tourney • *The crowd cheered and the tilt began.*

timber 1 = **beams**, boards, planks • *a bird nestling in the timbers of the roof*
2 = **wood**, logs • *These forests have been exploited for timber since Saxon times.*

timbre = **tone**, sound, ring, resonance, colour, tonality, tone colour, quality of sound • *His voice had a deep timbre.*

time **AS A NOUN** 1 = **period**, while, term, season, space, stretch, spell, phase, interval, span, period of time, stint, duration, length of time, time frame, timeline • *For a long time I didn't tell anyone.*
2 = **occasion**, point, moment, hour, stage, instance, instant, point in time, juncture • *It seemed like a good time to tell her.*
3 = **age**, days, era, year, date, generation, duration, epoch, chronology, aeon • *The design has remained unchanged since the time of the pharaohs.*
4 = **experience**, life, conditions, circumstances • *I was having a hard time in school.*
5 = **tempo**, beat, rhythm, measure, metre • *A reel is in four-four time.*
6 = **lifetime**, day, life, season, duration, life span, allotted span • *I wouldn't change anything if I had my time again.*
7 = **heyday**, prime, peak, hour, springtime, salad days, best years or days • *He was a very good jockey in his time.*
▸ **AS A VERB** 1 = **measure**, judge, clock, count • *He timed each performance with a stop-watch.*
2 = **schedule**, set, plan, book, programme, set up, fix, arrange, line up, organize, timetable, slate *(U.S.)*, fix up, prearrange • *We had timed our visit for March 7.*
3 = **regulate**, control, calculate • *an alarm timed to go off every hour on the hour*
▸ **IN PHRASES:** **ahead of time** = **early**, earlier than expected, with time to spare, in good time • *The train arrived well ahead of time.*
ahead of your *or* **its time** = **revolutionary**, pioneering, avant-garde, futuristic, ground-breaking, ultra-modern, innovatory, trailblazing • *His designs were ahead of their time.*
all the time = **constantly**, always, continually, ever, throughout, continuously, at all times, for the duration, perpetually, ceaselessly, without a break, twenty-four-seven *(informal)* • *She keeps nagging me about my smoking all the time.*
at one time = **once**, previously, formerly, for a while, hitherto, once upon a time • *At one time, 400 people lived in the village.*
at the same time 1 = **simultaneously**, together, at once, all together, as a group, in concert, in unison, concurrently • *The three men arrived at the same time.*

t

2 = **nevertheless**, still, even so, yet, regardless, nonetheless, all the same, notwithstanding, in any event, be that as it may • *I was afraid of her, but at the same time I really liked her.*
at times = **sometimes**, occasionally, from time to time, now and then, on occasion, once in a while, every now and then, every so often • *The debate was highly emotional at times.*
behind the times = **out of date**, old-fashioned, outdated, square *(informal)*, dated, obsolete, out of fashion, antiquated, outmoded, passé, old hat, out of style • *That idea is about 20 years behind the times.*
for the time being = **for now**, meanwhile, meantime, in the meantime, temporarily, for the moment, for the present, pro tem, for the nonce • *The situation is calm for the time being.*
from time to time = **occasionally**, sometimes, now and then, at times, on occasion, once in a while, every now and then, every so often • *Her daughters visited her from time to time.*
in good time 1 = **on time**, early, ahead of schedule, ahead of time, with time to spare • *We always make sure we're home in good time for the programme.*
2 = **promptly**, quickly, rapidly, swiftly, speedily, with dispatch • *Ninety-three per cent of the students received their loans in good time.*
in no time = **quickly**, rapidly, swiftly, in a moment, in a flash, speedily, in an instant, apace, before you know it, in a trice, in a jiffy *(informal)*, in two shakes of a lamb's tail *(informal)*, before you can say Jack Robinson • *At his age he'll heal in no time.*
in time 1 = **on time**, on schedule, in good time, at the appointed time, early, with time to spare • *I arrived in time for my flight to London.*
2 = **eventually**, one day, ultimately, sooner or later, someday, in the fullness of time, by and by • *He would sort out his own problems in time.*
many a time = **frequently**, often, many times, repeatedly, over and over (again), again and again, time and (time) again, on many occasions • *I've been to that house many a time.*
on time = **punctual(ly)**, prompt(ly), on schedule, in good time, on the dot • *Don't worry, she'll be on time.* • *The train arrived on time and she stepped out.*
time after time = **repeatedly**, many times, over and over again, often, frequently, persistently, on many occasions • *He escaped from jail time after time.*
time and again = **over and over again**, repeatedly, time after time • *Time and again political parties have failed to tackle this issue.*
▸ **RELATED ADJECTIVE:** temporal

QUOTATIONS

But meanwhile it is flying, irretrievable time is flying
[Virgil *Georgics*]

Time is the best medicine
[Ovid *Remedia Amoris*]

Every instant of time is a pinprick of eternity
[Marcus Aurelius *Meditations*]

Wait for that wisest of Counsellors, Time
[Pericles]

To every thing there is a season, and a time
to every purpose under heaven:
A time to be born, and a time to die ...
A time to love, and a time to hate;
A time of war, and a time of peace
[*Bible: Ecclesiastes*]

Come what may,
Time and the hour runs through the roughest day
[William Shakespeare *Macbeth*]

time the subtle thief of youth
[John Milton *Sonnet 7*]

Remember that time is money
[Benjamin Franklin *Advice to a Young Tradesman*]

Men talk of killing time, while time quietly kills them
[Dion Boucicault *London Assurance*]

The innocent and the beautiful have no enemy but time
[W.B. Yeats *in memory of Eva Gore-Booth and Con Markiewicz*]

Time goes, you say? Ah, no!
Alas, Time stays, we go
[Henry Austin Dobson *The Paradox of Time*]

Time rushes by and yet time is frozen. Funny how we get so exact about time at the end of life and at its beginning
[Sister Helen Prejean]

PROVERBS

Time and tide wait for no man
Time flies (tempus fugit)
Time is a great healer
Time will tell

▹ *See panel* **Time**

time-honoured = **long-established**, traditional, customary, old, established, fixed, usual, ancient, conventional, venerable, age-old • *The beer is brewed in the time-honoured way here.*
timeless = **eternal**, lasting, permanent, enduring, abiding, immortal, everlasting, ceaseless, immutable, indestructible, undying, ageless, imperishable, deathless, changeless • *There is a timeless quality to his best work.*
OPPOSITES: passing, temporary, ephemeral
timely = **opportune**, appropriate, well-timed, prompt, suitable, convenient, at the right time, judicious, punctual, propitious, seasonable • *These outbreaks are a timely reminder that the disease persists.*
OPPOSITES: inconvenient, ill-timed, untimely
timetable AS A NOUN 1 = **schedule**, programme, agenda, list, diary, calendar, order of the day • *The timetable was hopelessly optimistic.*
2 = **syllabus**, course, curriculum, programme, teaching programme • *Latin was not included on the timetable.*
▸ AS A VERB = **schedule**, plan, arrange, organize, set, book, programme, set up, line up, slate *(informal)*, slot in, fix up, prearrange • *I had nothing timetabled around this lunch-break.*
timid = **nervous**, shy, retiring, modest, shrinking, fearful, cowardly, apprehensive, coy, diffident, bashful, mousy, timorous, pusillanimous, faint-hearted, irresolute • *A timid child, she had learnt obedience at an early age.*
OPPOSITES: confident, brave, bold
timorous = **timid**, nervous, shy, retiring, frightened, shrinking, fearful, trembling, cowardly, apprehensive, coy, diffident, bashful, mousy, pusillanimous, faint-hearted, irresolute • *He is a reclusive, timorous creature.*
OPPOSITES: confident, daring, bold
tin
▸ **RELATED ADJECTIVES:** stannic, stannous
tincture 1 = **essence**, concentrate, extract, solution, infusion • *a few drops of tincture of iodine*
2 = **tinge**, trace, hint, colour, touch, suggestion, shade, flavour, dash, stain, smack, aroma, tint, hue, soupçon *(French)* • *Her courtesy carried a tincture of disdain.*
tinge AS A NOUN 1 = **tint**, colour, shade, cast, wash, stain, dye, tincture • *His skin had an unhealthy greyish tinge.*
2 = **trace**, bit, drop, touch, suggestion, dash, pinch, smack, sprinkling, smattering, soupçon *(French)* • *Could there have been a slight tinge of envy in her voice?*
▸ AS A VERB 1 = **tint**, colour, shade, stain, dye • *The living room was tinged yellow by the sunlight.*
2 = **suffuse**, touch, flavour, modify, sour, imbue • *His homecoming was tinged with sadness.*
tingle AS A VERB = **prickle**, sting, itch, tickle, have goose pimples • *The backs of her thighs tingled.*
▸ AS A NOUN 1 = **prickling**, stinging, itch, itching, tickle, tickling, pins and needles *(informal)* • *I felt a sudden tingle in my fingers.*
2 = **thrill**, quiver, shiver • *a sudden tingle of excitement*

t

TIME

Related vocabulary

calends *or* kalends	day	intercalary	lunar month	nones	week
civil day	Gregorian calendar	Julian calendar	lunar year	Roman calendar	year
civil year	ides	leap year	month	synodic month	

Gregorian calendar

January	March	May	July	September	November
February	April	June	August	October	December

Jewish calendar

Tishri	Kislev	Shevat	Nisan	Sivan	Av
Cheshvan	Tevet	Adar	Iyar	Tammuz	Elul

Muslim calendar

Muharram	Rabia I	Jumada I	Rajab	Ramadan	Dhu'l-Qa'dah
Safar	Rabia II	Jumada II	Shaban	Shawwal	Dhu'l-Hijjah

French revolutionary calendar

Vendémiaire	Frimaire	Pluviôse	Germinal	Prairial	Thermidor
Brumaire	Nivôse	Ventôse	Floréal	Messidor	Fructidor

Time zones

Atlantic Daylight Time	Eastern Daylight Time	Newfoundland Standard Time
Atlantic Standard Time	Eastern Standard Time	Pacific Daylight Time
British Summer Time	Greenwich Mean Time	Pacific Standard Time
Central Daylight Time	Mountain Daylight Time	Yukon Daylight Time
Central European Time	Mountain Standard Time	Yukon Standard Time
Central Standard Time	Newfoundland Daylight Time	

tinker = **meddle**, play, toy, monkey, potter, fiddle *(informal)*, dabble, mess about, muck about *(Brit. slang)* • *Instead of admitting their error, they just tinkered with the problem.*

tinkle AS A VERB **1** = **ring**, chime, jingle, ping, ding, jangle, chink, peal, clink • *The bell tinkled as the door opened.*
2 = **splash**, babble, burble, purl, plash *(literary)* • *We strolled past tinkling fountains and perfumed gardens.*
▸ AS A NOUN **1** = **ring**, chime, jingle, ping, ding, jangle, chink, peal, clink • *the icy tinkle of the bell as he entered*
2 = **splash**, babble, burble, purl, plash *(literary)* • *the tinkle of a Japanese water garden*
3 = **call**, ring *(Brit. informal)*, buzz *(informal)*, bell *(Brit. informal)*, phone call, telephone call • *I'll give you a tinkle around five.*

tinny **1** = **jangling**, thin, metallic, jingling, jangly, jingly, plinky • *the tinny sound of a radio playing a pop song*
2 = **flimsy**, cheap, thin, inferior, shoddy, poor-quality, low-grade, tawdry, trashy, insubstantial, gimcrack, rubbishy, jerry-built, cheapjack • *a cheap car with tinny bodywork*

tinpot = **second-rate**, second-class, paltry, miserable, pathetic, inferior, worthless, unimportant, Mickey Mouse *(slang)*, measly *(informal)*, wretched, two-bit *(U.S. & Canad. slang)*, toytown *(slang)*, poxy *(slang)*, chickenshit *(U.S. slang)*, pants *(slang)*, twopenny-halfpenny • *The island is ruled by a tinpot dictator.*

tinsel = **showy**, flashy, gaudy, cheap, plastic *(slang)*, superficial, sham, tawdry, ostentatious, trashy, specious, gimcrack, meretricious, pinchbeck • *the tinsel image of a movie star*

tint AS A NOUN **1** = **shade**, colour, tone, hue, cast • *Its large leaves often show a delicate purple tint.*
2 = **dye**, wash, stain, rinse, tinge, tincture • *You've had a tint on your hair.*
3 = **hint**, touch, trace, suggestion, shade, tinge • *His words had more than a tint of truth to them.*
▸ AS A VERB = **dye**, colour, stain, rinse, tinge, tincture • *Eyebrows can be tinted with the same dye.*

tiny = **small**, little, minute, slight, mini, wee, miniature, trifling, insignificant, negligible, microscopic, diminutive, petite, puny, pint-sized *(informal)*, infinitesimal, teeny-weeny, Lilliputian, dwarfish, teensy-weensy, pygmy *or* pigmy • *Though she was tiny, she had a very loud voice.*
OPPOSITES: great, huge, giant

tip[1] AS A NOUN **1** = **end**, point, head, extremity, sharp end, nib, prong • *She poked and shifted things with the tip of her walking stick.*
2 = **peak**, top, summit, pinnacle, crown, cap, zenith, apex, spire, acme, vertex • *After dusk, the tip of the cone will light up.*
3 = **cap**, cover, ferrule • *the protective plastic tip of a shoelace*
▸ AS A VERB = **cap**, top, crown, surmount, finish • *a missile tipped with three war-heads*

tip[2] AS A NOUN **1** = **gratuity**, gift, reward, present, sweetener *(informal)*, perquisite, baksheesh, pourboire *(French)* • *I gave the barber a tip.*
2 = **hint**, suggestion, piece of information, piece of advice, gen *(Brit. informal)*, pointer, piece of inside information, heads up *(U.S. & Canad.)* • *A good tip is to buy the most expensive lens you can afford.*
▸ AS A VERB **1** = **reward**, remunerate, give a tip to, sweeten *(informal)* • *Do you think it's customary to tip the waiters?*
2 = **predict**, back, recommend, think of • *He was widely tipped for success.*

tip[3] AS A VERB **1** = **pour**, drop, empty, dump, drain, spill, discharge, unload, jettison, offload, slop *(informal)*, slosh *(informal)*, decant • *She took the plate and tipped the contents into the bin.*
2 = **dump**, empty, ditch *(slang)*, unload, pour out • *the costs of tipping rubbish in landfills*
3 = **tilt**, lean, angle, bend, cock, incline • *She tipped her head back to breathe.*
▸ AS A NOUN = **dump**, midden, rubbish heap, refuse heap • *I took a load of rubbish and grass cuttings to the tip.*

▸ **IN PHRASES: tip over** = **topple over**, overturn, slant, capsize • *We grabbed it just as it was about to tip over.*
tip off = **advise**, warn, caution, forewarn, give a clue to, give a hint to, tip someone the wink *(Brit. informal)* • *He tipped police off on his carphone.*
tip something over = **overturn**, upset, capsize, cant, upend, topple over • *She tipped the table over in front of him.*

tip-off = **hint**, word, information, warning, suggestion, clue, pointer, inside information, word of advice, heads up *(U.S. & Canad.)* • *He was arrested after a tip-off to police by a member of the public.*

tipple AS A VERB = **drink**, imbibe, tope, indulge *(informal)*, swig, quaff, take a drink, bevvy *(dialect)*, bend the elbow *(informal)*, go on the piss *(taboo slang)* • *You may be tempted to tipple unobserved.*
▸ AS A NOUN = **alcohol**, drink, booze *(informal)*, poison *(informal)*, liquor, John Barleycorn • *My favourite tipple is a glass of port.*

tipsy = **tiddly** *(slang, chiefly Brit.)*, fuddled, slightly drunk, happy *(informal)*, merry *(Brit. informal)*, mellow, woozy *(slang, chiefly Brit.)* • *I'm feeling a bit tipsy.*

tirade = **outburst**, diatribe, harangue, abuse, lecture, denunciation, invective, fulmination, philippic • *She launched into a tirade against the authorities.*

tire 1 = **exhaust**, drain, fatigue, weary, fag *(informal)*, whack *(Brit. informal)*, wear out, wear down, take it out of *(informal)*, knacker *(slang)*, enervate • *If driving tires you, take the train.*
OPPOSITES: restore, revive, refresh
2 = **flag**, become tired, fail, droop • *He tired easily, and was unable to sleep well at night.*
3 = **bore**, weary, exasperate, annoy, irritate, harass, hassle *(informal)*, aggravate *(informal)*, irk, get on your nerves *(informal)*, piss you off *(taboo slang)*, hack you off *(informal)* • *That subject tires me.*

tired 1 = **exhausted**, fatigued, weary, spent, done in *(informal)*, flagging, all in *(slang)*, drained, sleepy, fagged *(informal)*, whacked *(Brit. informal)*, worn out, drooping, knackered *(slang)*, drowsy, clapped out *(Brit., Austral. & N.Z. informal)*, enervated, ready to drop, dog-tired *(informal)*, zonked *(slang)*, dead beat *(informal)*, tuckered out *(Austral. & N.Z. informal)*, asleep or dead on your feet *(informal)* • *He is tired and he has to rest after his long trip.*
OPPOSITES: fresh, lively, energetic
2 = **bored**, fed up, weary, sick, annoyed, irritated, pissed *(Brit., Austral. & N.Z. slang)*, exasperated, pissed off *(taboo slang)*, irked, hoha *(N.Z.)* • *I was tired of being a bookkeeper.*
OPPOSITES: keen on, enthusiastic about, fond of
3 = **hackneyed**, stale, well-worn, old, stock, familiar, conventional, corny *(slang)*, threadbare, trite, clichéd, outworn • *I didn't want to hear one of his tired excuses.*
OPPOSITES: original, innovative, imaginative

tireless = **energetic**, vigorous, industrious, determined, resolute, indefatigable, unflagging, untiring, unwearied • *He was a tireless worker for justice.*
OPPOSITES: tired, exhausted, fatigued

tiresome = **boring**, annoying, irritating, trying, wearing, dull, tedious, exasperating, monotonous, laborious, uninteresting, irksome, wearisome, vexatious • *the tiresome old lady next door*
OPPOSITES: stimulating, exhilarating, interesting

tiring = **exhausting**, demanding, wearing, tough, exacting, fatiguing, wearying, strenuous, arduous, laborious, enervative • *It had been a long and tiring day.*

tissue 1 = **matter**, material, substance, stuff, structure • *As we age we lose muscle tissue.*
2 = **paper**, wipe, paper handkerchief, wrapping paper • *a box of tissues*
3 = **series**, pack, collection, mass, network, chain, combination, web, accumulation, fabrication, conglomeration, concatenation • *It was all a tissue of lies which ended in his resignation.*

titan = **giant**, superman, colossus, leviathan • *the country's two richest business titans*

titanic = **gigantic**, huge, giant, massive, towering, vast, enormous, mighty, immense, jumbo *(informal)*, monstrous, mammoth, colossal, mountainous, stellar *(informal)*, prodigious, stupendous, fuck-off *(offensive taboo slang)*, herculean, elephantine, Brobdingnagian, humongous *or* humungous *(U.S. slang)* • *a titanic struggle between two visions of the future*

titbit *or (esp. U.S.)* **tidbit** 1 = **delicacy**, goody, dainty, morsel, treat, snack, choice item, juicy bit, bonne bouche *(French)* • *She offered him titbits; a chicken drumstick, some cheese.*
2 = **piece**, item, scrap, bit, morsel, juicy bit • *titbits of gossip gleaned from the corridors of power*

tit for tat AS A NOUN = **retaliation**, like for like, measure for measure, an eye for an eye, a tooth for a tooth, blow for blow, as good as you get • *a dangerous game of tit for tat*
▸ AS AN ADJECTIVE = **retaliatory**, revenge, reciprocal • *a round of tit-for-tat expulsions*

tithe = **tax**, levy, duty, assessment, tribute, toll, tariff, tenth, impost • *The early church prescribed a tithe for its members.*

titillate = **excite**, stimulate, arouse, interest, thrill, provoke, turn on *(slang)*, tease, tickle, tantalize • *food to titillate the most jaded of palates*

titillating = **exciting**, stimulating, interesting, thrilling, arousing, sensational, teasing, provocative, lurid, suggestive, lewd • *deliberately titillating lyrics*

titivate = **smarten up**, make up, refurbish, do up *(informal)*, prank, preen, touch up, tart up *(Brit. slang)*, doll up *(slang)*, primp, gussy up *(slang, chiefly U.S.)*, prink, pimp up, pimp out

title AS A NOUN 1 = **heading**, name, caption, label, legend, inscription • *The book was first published under the title 'A Place for Us'.*
2 = **publication**, book, offering • *a publisher with 50 new titles a year*
3 = **name**, designation, epithet, term, handle *(slang)*, nickname, denomination, pseudonym, appellation, sobriquet, nom de plume, moniker *or* monicker *(slang)* • *Her husband was honoured with the title 'Sir Denis'.*
4 = **championship**, trophy, laurels, bays, crown, honour • *He has retained his title as world chess champion.*
5 = **ownership**, right, claim, privilege, entitlement, tenure, prerogative, freehold • *He never had title to the property.*
▸ AS A VERB = **name**, call, term, style, label, tag, designate • *a new book titled 'The Golden Thirteen'*

titled = **upper-class**, noble, patrician, blue-blooded, well-born, highborn • *Her mother was a titled lady.*

titter = **snigger**, laugh, giggle, chuckle, chortle *(informal)*, tee-hee, te-hee • *Mention sex therapy and most people will titter with embarrassment.*

tittle-tattle = **gossip**, rumour, dirt *(U.S.)*, goss *(informal)*, hearsay, jaw *(slang)*, chatter, babble, cackle, twaddle, prattle, natter, blather, chitchat, blether, idle chat, yackety-yak *(slang)*, yatter *(informal)*, clishmaclaver *(Scot.)* • *tittle-tattle about the private lives of celebrities*

titular = **in name only**, so-called, token, theoretical, puppet, honorary, nominal, putative • *He is titular head, and merely signs laws occasionally.*
OPPOSITES: real, true, actual

toad
▸ RELATED ADJECTIVE: batrachian
▸ NAME OF YOUNG: tadpole
▸ RELATED PHOBIA: batrachophobia
▷ *See panel* **Amphibians**

toady AS A NOUN = **sycophant**, creep *(slang)*, hanger-on, minion, flunkey, parasite, fawner, jackal, spaniel, lackey, crawler *(slang)*, yes man, brown-noser *(taboo slang)*, flatterer,

truckler, lickspittle, ass-kisser *(U.S. & Canad. taboo slang)*, apple polisher *(U.S. slang)*, groveller, bootlicker *(informal)* • *Life was too short to become a toady to a megalomaniac.*
▸ **AS A VERB** = **fawn on**, flatter, grovel, creep, crawl, cringe, pander to, suck up to *(informal)*, curry favour with, butter up, kiss someone's ass *(U.S. & Canad. taboo slang)*, brown-nose *(taboo slang)*, kowtow to, bow and scrape, lick someone's boots, kiss the feet of, lick someone's arse *(taboo slang)*, be obsequious to • *They came backstage, cooing and toadying to him.*
OPPOSITES: oppose, rebel

toast[1] 1 = **brown**, grill, crisp, roast • *Toast the bread lightly on both sides.*
2 = **warm (up)**, heat (up), thaw, bring back to life • *a bar with an open fire for toasting feet after a day skiing*

toast[2] **AS A NOUN** 1 = **tribute**, drink, compliment, salute, health, pledge, salutation • *We drank a toast to Miss Jacobs.*
2 = **favourite**, celebrity, darling, talk, pet, focus of attention, hero *or* heroine, blue-eyed boy *or* girl *(Brit. informal)* • *She was the toast of Paris.*
▸ **AS A VERB** = **drink to**, honour, pledge to, salute, drink (to) the health of • *They toasted her with champagne.*

QUOTATIONS
Here's tae us; wha's like us?
Gey few, and they're a' deid
[Scottish toast]

tobacco

QUOTATIONS
There's nothing like tobacco; it is the passion of all decent men; a man who lives without tobacco does not deserve to live
[Molière *Don Juan*]
A cigarette is the perfect type of a perfect pleasure. It is exquisite, and it leaves one unsatisfied. What more can one want?
[Oscar Wilde *Picture of Dorian Gray*]
Pernicious weed! whose scent the fair annoys,
Unfriendly to society's chief joys
[William Cowper *Conversation*]
A custom loathsome to the eye, hateful to the nose, harmful to the brain, dangerous to the lungs, and in the black, stinking fume thereof, nearest resembling the horrible Stygian smoke of the pit that is bottomless
[James I *A Counterblast to Tobacco*]

today 1 = **this day**, before tomorrow, this morning, this afternoon, this evening, this very day • *Can you get that done today, please?*
2 = **nowadays**, these days, just now, now, currently, at present, at this time, at the present time, in these times, in this day and age, in the present climate • *He thinks pop music today is as exciting as ever.*

to-do = **fuss**, performance *(informal)*, disturbance, bother, stir, turmoil, unrest, flap *(informal)*, quarrel, upheaval, bustle, furore, uproar, agitation, commotion, rumpus, tumult, brouhaha, ruction *(informal)*, hue and cry, hoo-ha • *Just like him to make such a to-do about it.*

toenail
▸ **TECHNICAL NAME:** unguis
▸ **RELATED ADJECTIVES:** ungual, ungular

together **AS AN ADVERB** 1 = **collectively**, jointly, closely, as one, with each other, in conjunction, side by side, mutually, hand in hand, as a group, in partnership, in concert, in unison, shoulder to shoulder, cheek by jowl, in cooperation, in a body, hand in glove • *Together they swam to the ship.*
OPPOSITES: individually, independently, separately
2 = **at the same time**, simultaneously, in unison, as one, (all) at once, en masse, concurrently, contemporaneously, with one accord, at one fell swoop • *'Yes,' they said together.*
▸ **AS AN ADJECTIVE** = **self-possessed**, calm, composed, well-balanced, cool, stable, well-organized, well-adjusted, grounded • *She was very headstrong, and very together.*

toil **AS A NOUN** = **hard work**, industry, labour, effort, pains, application, sweat, graft *(informal)*, slog, exertion, drudgery, travail, donkey-work, elbow grease *(informal)*, blood, sweat, and tears *(informal)* • *It is only toil which gives meaning to things.*
OPPOSITES: inertia, inactivity, idleness
▸ **AS A VERB** 1 = **labour**, work, struggle, strive, grind *(informal)*, sweat *(informal)*, slave, graft *(informal)*, go for it *(informal)*, slog, grub, bend over backwards *(informal)*, drudge, go for broke *(slang)*, push yourself, bust a gut *(informal)*, give it your best shot *(informal)*, break your neck *(informal)*, work like a dog, make an all-out effort *(informal)*, work like a Trojan, knock yourself out *(informal)*, do your damnedest *(informal)*, give it your all *(informal)*, work your fingers to the bone, rupture yourself *(informal)* • *Boys toiled in the hot sun to finish the wall.*

TOBACCO

Tobacco types

broadleaf, Burley, canaster, caporal, chewing tobacco, cigar binder, cigar filler, cigar wrapper, Cuban cigar leaf, dark air-cured, filler, fire-cured, flue-cured, makhorka, Maryland, perique, rappee, shag, snout *(Brit. slang)*, snuff, Sumatra, Turkish, Virginia

Types of cigar and cigarette

breva, cheroot, cigarillo, claro, concha, corona, Havana, imperiale, maduro, Manila, panatella, perfecto, puritano, roll-up, roll-your-own, stogy, tailor-made *(slang)*

Pipes

briar, calabash *(rare)*, clay pipe, corncob pipe, churchwarden, hookah *or* hubble-bubble, meerschaum, peace pipe

General smoking terms

ash, ashtray, bowl, butt, cigarette case, cigarette holder, cigarette paper, dottle, filter tip, flint, humidor, lighter, makings *(slang)*, matches, pigtail, pipe, pipe cleaner, pipe rack, plug, rollings *(slang)*, smoking jacket, smoking compartment, smoking room, snuffbox, splint, stem, tobacconist, tobacco pouch

2 = **struggle**, trek, slog, trudge, push yourself, fight your way, drag yourself, footslog • *He had his head down as he toiled up the hill.*

toilet 1 = **lavatory**, bathroom, loo *(Brit. informal)*, bog *(slang)*, gents *or* ladies, can *(U.S. & Canad. slang)*, john *(slang, chiefly U.S. & Canad.)*, head(s) *(Nautical slang)*, throne *(informal)*, closet, privy, cloakroom *(Brit.)*, urinal, latrine, washroom, powder room, ablutions *(Military informal)*, crapper *(taboo slang)*, dunny *(Austral. & N.Z. old-fashioned informal)*, water closet, khazi *(slang)*, pissoir *(French)*, little boy's room *or* little girl's room *(informal)*, (public) convenience, W.C., bogger *(Austral. slang)*, brasco *(Austral. slang)* • *She made him flush the pills down the toilet.*
2 = **bathroom**, washroom, gents *or* ladies *(Brit. informal)*, privy, outhouse, latrine, powder room, water closet, pissoir *(French)*, ladies' room, little boy's *or* little girl's room, W.C. • *I ran to the toilet, vomiting.*

token AS A NOUN 1 = **symbol**, mark, sign, note, evidence, earnest, index, expression, demonstration, proof, indication, clue, representation, badge, manifestation • *He sent her a gift as a token of his appreciation.*
2 = **voucher**, coupon, chit, credit note • *£10 book tokens*
3 = **disc**, counter, chip • *The older phones only accept tokens.*
▸ AS AN ADJECTIVE = **nominal**, symbolic, minimal, hollow, superficial, perfunctory • *weak token gestures with no real consequences*

tolerable 1 = **bearable**, acceptable, allowable, supportable, endurable, sufferable • *He described their living conditions as tolerable.*
OPPOSITES: unacceptable, intolerable, unbearable
2 = **fair**, O.K. *or* okay *(informal)*, middling, average, all right, ordinary, acceptable, reasonable, good enough, adequate, indifferent, not bad *(informal)*, mediocre, so-so *(informal)*, run-of-the-mill, passable, unexceptional, fairly good, fair to middling • *Is there anywhere tolerable to eat in town?*
OPPOSITES: bad, awful, dreadful

tolerance 1 = **broad-mindedness**, charity, sympathy, patience, indulgence, forbearance, permissiveness, magnanimity, open-mindedness, sufferance, lenity • *his tolerance and understanding of diverse human nature*
OPPOSITES: discrimination, prejudice, intolerance
2 = **endurance**, resistance, stamina, fortitude, resilience, toughness, staying power, hardness, hardiness • *She has a high tolerance for pain.*
3 = **resistance**, immunity, resilience, non-susceptibility • *Your body will build up a tolerance to most drugs.*

QUOTATIONS
Live and let live
[J.C.F. Schiller *Wallenstein's Camp*]
Tolerance is only another name for indifference
[W. Somerset Maugham]
Tolerance should really be only a temporary attitude; it must lead to recognition
[Goethe]

tolerant = **broad-minded**, understanding, sympathetic, open-minded, patient, fair, soft, catholic, charitable, indulgent, easy-going, long-suffering, lax, lenient, permissive, magnanimous, free and easy, forbearing, kind-hearted, unprejudiced, complaisant, latitudinarian, unbigoted, easy-oasy *(slang)* • *They need to be tolerant of different points of view.*
OPPOSITES: authoritarian, strict, intolerant

tolerate 1 = **endure**, stand, suffer, bear, take, stomach, undergo, swallow, hack *(slang)*, abide, put up with *(informal)*, submit to, thole *(Scot.)* • *She can no longer tolerate the position that she's in.*
2 = **allow**, accept, permit, sanction, take, receive, admit, brook, indulge, put up with *(informal)*, condone, countenance, turn a blind eye to, wink at • *I will not tolerate breaches of the code of conduct.*
OPPOSITES: ban, veto, forbid
3 = **consume**, eat, stomach, digest, take • *I can't tolerate fatty or high-cholesterol meals.*

toleration 1 = **acceptance**, endurance, indulgence, sanction, allowance, permissiveness, sufferance, condonation • *They urged toleration of mixed marriages.*
2 = **religious freedom**, freedom of conscience, freedom of worship • *his views on religious toleration, education and politics*

toll[1] AS A VERB 1 = **ring**, sound, strike, chime, knell, clang, peal • *Church bells tolled and black flags fluttered.*
2 = **announce**, call, signal, warn of • *Big Ben tolled the midnight hour.*
▸ AS A NOUN = **ringing**, ring, tolling, chime, knell, clang, peal • *the insistent toll of the bell in the church tower*

toll[2] 1 = **charge**, tax, fee, duty, rate, demand, payment, assessment, customs, tribute, levy, tariff, impost • *Opponents of motorway tolls say they would force cars onto smaller roads.*
2 = **damage**, cost, loss, roll, penalty, sum, number, roster, inroad • *There are fears that the death toll may be higher.*
3 = **adverse effects**, price, cost, suffering, damage, penalty, harm • *Winter takes its toll on your health.*

tomb = **grave**, vault, crypt, mausoleum, sarcophagus, catacomb, sepulchre, burial chamber • *the tomb of the Unknown Soldier*

tombstone = **gravestone**, memorial, monument, marker, headstone • *What were the words inscribed on his tombstone?*

tome = **book**, work, title, volume, opus, publication • *a hefty legal tome*

tomfoolery 1 = **foolishness**, messing around *(informal)*, shenanigans, clowning, stupidity, larks *(informal)*, fooling around *(informal)*, silliness, idiocy, skylarking *(informal)*, horseplay, buffoonery, childishness • *Were you serious, or was that a bit of tomfoolery?*
OPPOSITES: seriousness, sobriety
2 = **nonsense**, rot, malarkey, tosh *(slang, chiefly Brit.)*, rubbish, pants *(slang)*, trash, bunk *(informal)*, bilge *(informal)*, twaddle, baloney *(informal)*, claptrap *(informal)*, hogwash, poppycock *(informal)*, inanity, balderdash, bosh *(informal)*, stuff and nonsense, hooey *(slang)*, tommyrot, bunkum *or* buncombe *(chiefly U.S.)*, bizzo *(Austral. slang)*, bull's wool *(Austral. & N.Z. slang)* • *That sounds like post-modernist toomfoolery.*

tomorrow

QUOTATIONS
Take therefore no thought for the morrow; for the morrow shall take thought for the things of itself
[Bible: St. Matthew]
After all, tomorrow is another day
[Margaret Mitchell *Gone with the Wind*]

PROVERBS
Tomorrow never comes

tone AS A NOUN 1 = **pitch**, stress, volume, accent, force, strength, emphasis, inflection, intonation, timbre, modulation, tonality • *He spoke in a low tone to her.*
2 = **volume**, timbre, tonality • *the clear tone of the bell*
3 = **character**, style, approach, feel, air, effect, note, quality, spirit, attitude, aspect, frame, manner, mood, drift, grain, temper, vein, tenor • *The tone of the letter was very friendly.*
4 = **colour**, cast, shade, tint, tinge, hue • *Each brick also varies slightly in tone.*
5 = **note**, beep • *a dialling tone*
▸ AS A VERB = **harmonize**, match, blend, suit, go well with • *Her sister toned with her in a turquoise print dress.*
▸ IN PHRASES: **tone something down** 1 = **moderate**, temper, soften, restrain, subdue, play down, dampen, mitigate, modulate, soft-pedal *(informal)* • *He toned down his militant statement after the meeting.*

2 = reduce, moderate, soften, lessen • *He was asked to tone down the spices and garlic in his recipes.*
tone something up = get into condition, trim, shape up, freshen, tune up, sharpen up, limber up, invigorate, get in shape • *Regular exercise will tone up your stomach muscles.*

tongue **1 = language**, speech, vernacular, talk, dialect, idiom, parlance, lingo *(informal)*, patois, argot • *They feel passionately about their native tongue.*
2 = utterance, voice, speech, articulation, verbal expression • *her sharp wit and quick tongue*
▸ **TECHNICAL NAME:** lingua
▸ **RELATED ADJECTIVES:** lingual, glottal

tongue-lashing = scolding, talking-to *(informal)*, rebuke, reprimand, lecture, wigging *(Brit. slang)*, slating *(informal)*, reproach, ticking-off *(informal)*, dressing-down *(informal)*, telling-off *(informal)*, reproof • *After a cruel tongue-lashing, he threw the girl out of the group.*

tongue-tied = speechless, dumb, mute, inarticulate, dumbstruck, struck dumb, at a loss for words • *In their presence I became self-conscious and tongue-tied.*
OPPOSITES: articulate, chatty, talkative

tonic = stimulant, boost, bracer *(informal)*, refresher, cordial, pick-me-up *(informal)*, fillip, shot in the arm *(informal)*, restorative, livener, analeptic, roborant • *We are spending twice as much on health tonics as five years ago.*

tonsil
▸ **RELATED ADJECTIVES:** tonsillar, tonsillary, amygdaline

too **1 = also**, as well, further, in addition, moreover, besides, likewise, to boot, into the bargain • *Depression may be expressed physically too.*
2 = excessively, very, extremely, overly, unduly, unreasonably, inordinately, exorbitantly, immoderately, over- • *I'm afraid you're too late; she's gone.*

tool **AS A NOUN** **1 = implement**, device, appliance, apparatus, machine, instrument, gadget, utensil, contraption, contrivance • *The best tool for the purpose is a pair of shears.*
2 = means, agency, vehicle, medium, agent, intermediary, wherewithal • *The video has become an invaluable teaching tool.*
3 = puppet, creature, pawn, dupe, stooge *(slang)*, jackal, minion, lackey, flunkey, hireling, cat's-paw • *He became the tool of the security services.*
▸ **AS A VERB** **= make**, work, cut, shape, chase, decorate, ornament • *We have a beautifully tooled glass replica of it.*
▹ *See panel* **Tools**

tooth
▸ **RELATED ADJECTIVE:** dental
▸ **RELATED PHOBIA:** odontophobia

TEETH

canine	foretooth	premolar
incisor *or*	molar	wisdom tooth

toothsome = appetizing, nice, sweet, tempting, delicious, tasty, agreeable, luscious, savoury, palatable, dainty, delectable, mouthwatering, yummy *(slang)*, scrumptious *(informal)*, yummo *(Austral. slang)* • *toothsome honey-sweetened gingerbread*

top **AS A NOUN** **1 = peak**, summit, head, crown, height, ridge, brow, crest, high point, pinnacle, culmination, meridian, zenith, apex, apogee, acme, vertex • *I came down alone from the top of the mountain.*
OPPOSITES: base, foot, bottom
2 = upper part, upper layer, upper surface • *Bake the biscuits until the tops are lightly browned.*
3 = lid, cover, cap, cork, plug, stopper, bung • *the plastic tops from aerosol containers*
4 = t-shirt, shirt, jersey, jumper, sweater, blouse, sweat shirt • *Look at my new top.*
5 = first place, head, peak, lead, highest rank, high point • *The USA will be at the top of the medals table.*
6 = highest level, utmost extent • *He shouted to us at the top of his voice.*
7 = shoots, leaves, stem, stalk • *Rabbits have eaten the lettuces and the tops of the carrots.*
▸ **AS AN ADJECTIVE** **1 = highest**, upper, loftiest, furthest up, uppermost, topmost • *Our new flat was on the top floor.*
2 = leading, best, first, highest, greatest, lead, head, prime, finest, crowning, crack *(informal)*, elite, superior, dominant, foremost, pre-eminent • *He was the top student in physics.*
OPPOSITES: worst, lowest, bottom
3 = chief, most important, principal, most powerful, highest, lead, head, ruling, leading, main, commanding, prominent, notable, sovereign, eminent, high-ranking, illustrious • *I need to have the top people in this company work together.*
4 = prime, best, select, first-class, capital, quality, choice, excellent, premier, superb, elite, superior, top-class, A1 *(informal)*, top-quality, first-rate, top-notch *(informal)*, grade A, top-grade • *a candlelit dinner at a top restaurant*
5 = maximum, greatest, utmost, maximal, topmost • *The car-ferry has a top speed of forty-two knots.*
▸ **AS A VERB** **1 = lead**, head, command, be at the top of, be first in • *What happens if the socialists top the poll?*
2 = exceed, go beyond, surpass, cap, outstrip, surmount • *Imports topped £10 billion last month.*
3 = cover, coat, garnish, finish, crown, cap, overspread • *To serve, top the fish with cooked leeks.*
4 = surpass, better, beat, improve on, cap, exceed, best, eclipse, trump, go beyond, excel, transcend, outstrip, outdo, outshine, go one better than • *How are you ever going to top that?*
OPPOSITES: fall short of, fail to equal, not be as good as
5 = reach the top of, scale, mount, climb, conquer, crest, ascend, surmount • *As they topped the hill he saw the town in the distance.*
▸ **IN PHRASES: over the top = excessive**, too much, going too far, inordinate, over the limit, a bit much *(informal)*, uncalled-for, immoderate • *The special effects are a bit over the top, but I enjoyed it.*
top something up **1 = fill (up)**, refresh, recharge, refill, replenish, freshen • *He topped her glass up, complaining that she was a slow drinker.*
2 = supplement, boost, add to, enhance, augment • *The bank topped up their loan to £5000.*

topic = subject, point, question, issue, matter, theme, text, thesis, subject matter • *They offer tips on topics such as home safety.*

topical = current, popular, contemporary, up-to-date, up-to-the-minute, newsworthy • *They discuss topical issues within a Christian framework.*

topmost = highest, top, supreme, upper, loftiest, uppermost • *the topmost branches of a gigantic oak tree*
OPPOSITES: lowest, bottom, bottommost

topple **1 = fall over**, fall, collapse, tumble, overturn, capsize, totter, tip over, keel over, overbalance, fall headlong • *He released his hold and toppled slowly backwards.*
2 = knock over, upset, knock down, tip over • *Wind and rain toppled trees and electricity lines.*
3 = overthrow, overturn, bring down, oust, unseat, bring low • *the revolution which toppled the regime*

topsy-turvy = confused, upside-down, disorderly, chaotic, messy, mixed-up, jumbled, inside-out, untidy, disorganized, disarranged • *The world has turned topsy-turvy in my lifetime.*
OPPOSITES: ordered, organized, orderly

torch **AS A NOUN** **1 = flashlight**, light, lamp, beacon • *She shone a torch over the terrified faces.*

TOOLS

Allen key, alligator, auger, awl, axe, ball-peen hammer, beetle, billhook, bit, bitstock, bodkin, bolster, borer, bosh, brace and bit, broach, broad, burin, bushhammer, centre punch, chaser, chisel, claw hammer, clink, clippers, cold chisel, comb, comber, countersink, cradle, croze, diamond point, dibble, drawknife *or* drawshave, dresser, drift *or* driftpin, drill, drill press, drove *or* drove chisel, edge tool, eyeleteer, facer, file, fillet, firmer chisel, flange, flatter, float, floatcut file, fork, former, fraise, froe *or* frow, fuller, gab, gad, gavel, gimlet, gouger, graver, gympie *(Austral.)*, hack, hack hammer, half-round chisel, hammer, hammer drill, hob, hoe, hone, icebreaker, ice pick, jackhammer, jointer, jumper, kevel, knapping hammer, mallet, mattock, maul, mitre square, monkey wrench, nibbler, nippers, padsaw, percussion tool, pestle, pick, piledriver, pitching tool, plane, pliers, ploughstaff, pneumatic hammer, power drill, pruning hook, punch, rabble, rake, rawhide hammer, ripple, rocker, rounder, router, sander, saw, sax, scorper, screwdriver, screw tap, scriber, scutch, scythe, shave, shears, sickle, slasher *(Austral. & N.Z.)*, sledgehammer, snake, slick, soldering iron, spade, spanner, spider, spitsticker, spud *or* spudder, stiletto, stylus, swage, tack hammer, tilt hammer, triphammer, trepan, trowel, wimble, wrench

2 = **firebrand**, brand, taper, flaming stick • *They lit a torch and set fire to the chapel's thatch.*

▸ **AS A VERB** = **set fire to**, burn, ignite, set on fire, kindle, set alight, incinerate, destroy by fire, set light to, reduce to ashes, put a match to • *The rioters torched the local library.*

torment AS A VERB 1 = **torture**, pain, distress, afflict, rack, harrow, crucify, agonize, excruciate • *At times, memories returned to torment her.*

OPPOSITES: delight, reassure, comfort

2 = **tease**, annoy, worry, trouble, bother, provoke, devil *(informal)*, harry, plague, irritate, hound, harass, hassle *(informal)*, aggravate *(informal)*, persecute, pester, vex, bedevil, chivvy, give someone grief *(Brit. & S. African)*, lead someone a merry dance *(Brit. informal)* • *My older brother used to torment me by singing it to me.*

▸ **AS A NOUN** 1 = **suffering**, distress, misery, pain, hell, torture, agony, anguish • *He spent days in torment while they searched for her.*

OPPOSITES: joy, happiness, bliss

2 = **trouble**, worry, bother, plague, irritation, hassle *(informal)*, nuisance, annoyance, bane, pain in the neck *(informal)* • *the torments of being a writer*

torn 1 = **cut**, split, rent, ripped, ragged, slit, lacerated • *a torn photograph*

2 = **undecided**, divided, uncertain, split, unsure, wavering, vacillating, in two minds *(informal)*, irresolute • *I know the administration was very torn on this subject.*

tornado = **whirlwind**, storm, hurricane, gale, cyclone, typhoon, tempest, squall, twister *(U.S. informal)*, windstorm • *The tornado tossed homes around like litter.*

torpid = **inactive**, lazy, sluggish, languid, slow, dull, passive, numb, motionless, stagnant, inert, slow-moving, lethargic, apathetic, lymphatic, drowsy, listless, indolent, languorous, somnolent, lackadaisical, slothful, benumbed, fainéant • *He led a lazy, torpid life at the weekends.*

torpor = **inactivity**, apathy, inertia, lethargy, passivity, laziness, numbness, sloth, stupor, drowsiness, dullness, sluggishness, indolence, languor, listlessness, somnolence, inertness, stagnancy, accidie *(Theology)*, inanition, torpidity, acedia *(Theology)* • *The sick person gradually falls into a torpor.*

OPPOSITES: energy, go, vigour

torrent 1 = **stream**, flow, rush, flood, tide, spate, cascade, gush, effusion, inundation • *A torrent of water rushed into the reservoir.*

2 = **downpour**, flood, shower, deluge, rainstorm • *The rain came down in torrents.*

3 = **outburst**, stream, barrage, hail, spate, outpouring, effusion • *He directed a torrent of abuse at me.*

torrential = **heavy**, relentless, severe, teeming, copious • *Torrential rain left thousands stranded last night.*

torrid 1 = **hot**, tropical, burning, dry, boiling, flaming, blistering, stifling, fiery, scorched, scorching, sizzling, arid, sultry, sweltering, parched, parching, broiling • *the torrid heat of a Spanish summer*

2 = **passionate**, intense, sexy *(informal)*, hot, flaming, erotic, ardent, steamy *(informal)*, fervent • *He is locked in a torrid affair with a mystery older woman.*

torso = **body**, trunk • *Lower your torso one inch, and stretch up with your arms.*

tortoise

▸ RELATED ADJECTIVES: chelonian, testudinal

▹ *See panel* **Reptiles**

tortuous 1 = **winding**, twisting, meandering, bent, twisted, curved, crooked, indirect, convoluted, serpentine, zigzag, sinuous, circuitous, twisty, mazy • *a tortuous mountain route*

2 = **complicated**, involved, misleading, tricky, indirect, ambiguous, roundabout, deceptive, devious, convoluted, mazy • *long and tortuous negotiations*

OPPOSITES: direct, straightforward, open

torture AS A VERB 1 = **torment**, abuse, persecute, afflict, martyr, scourge, molest, crucify, mistreat, ill-treat, maltreat, put on the rack • *Police are convinced she was tortured and killed.*

OPPOSITES: comfort, soothe, console

2 = **distress**, torment, worry, trouble, pain, rack, afflict, harrow, agonize, give someone grief *(Brit. & S. African)*, inflict anguish on • *He would not torture her further by arguing.*

▸ **AS A NOUN** 1 = **ill-treatment**, abuse, torment, persecution, martyrdom, maltreatment, harsh

treatment • *alleged cases of torture and murder by security forces*
2 = **agony**, suffering, misery, anguish, hell, distress, torment, heartbreak • *Waiting for the result was torture.*
OPPOSITES: delight, pleasure, bliss

TORTURE

INSTRUMENTS OF TORTURE

boot	pilliwinks	thumbscrew
brake	Procrustean bed	wheel
cat-o'-nine-tails	rack	
iron maiden	scourge	

TYPES OF TORTURE

bastinado	gauntlet	water cure
Chinese water torture	strappado	water torture
	waterboarding	

toss AS A VERB 1 = **throw**, pitch, hurl, fling, project, launch, cast, shy, chuck *(informal)*, flip, propel, sling, lob *(informal)* • *He screwed the paper up and tossed it into the fire.*
2 = **throw back**, jerk, jolt • *Gasping, she tossed her hair out of her face.*
3 = **flip**, spin, flick • *We tossed a coin to decide who would go out and buy buns.*
4 = **shake**, turn, mix, stir, tumble, agitate, jiggle • *Toss the apple slices in the mixture.*
5 = **heave**, labour, rock, roll, pitch, lurch, jolt, wallow • *The small boat tossed about in the high seas like a cork.*
6 = **thrash (about)**, twitch, wriggle, squirm, writhe • *I felt as though I'd been tossing and turning all night.*
▸ AS A NOUN = **throw**, cast, pitch, shy, fling, lob *(informal)* • *Decisions are almost made with the toss of a die.*

tot AS A NOUN 1 = **infant**, child, baby, toddler, mite, wean *(Scot.)*, little one, sprog *(slang)*, munchkin *(informal, chiefly U.S.)*, rug rat *(slang)*, littlie *(Austral. informal)*, ankle-biter *(Austral. slang)*, tacker *(Austral. slang)* • *They may hold a clue to the missing tot.*
2 = **measure**, shot *(informal)*, finger, nip, slug, dram, snifter *(informal)*, toothful • *a tot of dark rum*
▸ IN PHRASES: **tot something up** 1 = **add up**, calculate, sum (up), total, reckon, compute, tally, enumerate, count up • *Now tot up the points you've scored.*
2 = **accumulate**, gather, acquire, build up, amass, stockpile, accrue, mount up • *He has totted up a huge list of convictions.*

total AS A NOUN = **sum**, mass, entirety, grand total, whole, amount, aggregate, totality, full amount, sum total • *The companies have a total of 1,776 employees.*
OPPOSITES: part, subtotal, individual amount
▸ AS AN ADJECTIVE 1 = **entire**, full, whole, complete, combined, overall, comprehensive, gross • *The total cost of the project would be more than $240 million.*
2 = **complete**, absolute, utter, whole, perfect, entire, sheer, outright, all-out, thorough, unconditional, downright, undisputed, consummate, unqualified, out-and-out, undivided, overarching, unmitigated, thoroughgoing, arrant, deep-dyed *(usually derogatory)* • *The car was in a total mess.* • *I mean I'm not a total idiot.*
OPPOSITES: part, limited, partial
▸ AS A VERB 1 = **amount to**, make, come to, reach, equal, run to, number, add up to, correspond to, work out as, mount up to, tot up to • *Their exports will total £85 million this year.*
2 = **add up**, work out, sum up, compute, reckon, tot up • *They haven't totalled the exact figures.*
OPPOSITES: deduct, subtract
3 = **wreck**, crash, destroy, smash, write off *(Brit.)*, demolish, prang *(Brit. informal)*, damage beyond repair, kennet *(Austral. slang)*, jeff *(Austral. slang)* • *I broke my collar bone and totalled the bike.*

totalitarian = **dictatorial**, authoritarian, one-party, oppressive, undemocratic, monolithic, despotic, tyrannous • *a cruel, corrupt and totalitarian government*
OPPOSITES: popular, democratic, autonomous

totality 1 = **entirety**, unity, fullness, wholeness, completeness, entireness • *He did not want to reform the system in its totality.*
2 = **aggregate**, whole, entirety, all, total, sum, sum total • *We must take into consideration the totality of the evidence.*

totally = **completely**, entirely, absolutely, quite, perfectly, fully, comprehensively, thoroughly, wholly, utterly, consummately, wholeheartedly, unconditionally, to the hilt, one hundred per cent, unmitigatedly • *Young people want something totally different from the old ways.*
OPPOSITES: partly, somewhat, in part

totter 1 = **stagger**, stumble, reel, sway, falter, lurch, wobble, walk unsteadily • *He tottered to the fridge to get another beer.*
2 = **shake**, sway, rock, tremble, quake, shudder, lurch, waver, quiver, vibrate, teeter, judder • *The balconies begin to tremble and totter in the smoke and fumes.*
3 = **be unstable**, falter, be insecure, be shaky, be precarious, be unsteady, be on the point of collapse • *The property market is tottering.*

touch AS A VERB 1 = **feel**, handle, finger, stroke, brush, make contact with, graze, caress, fondle, lay a finger on, palpate • *Her tiny hand gently touched my face.*
2 = **come into contact**, meet, contact, border, brush, come together, graze, adjoin, converge, be in contact, abut, impinge upon • *Their knees were touching.*
3 = **handle**, use, move, hold, pick up, disturb, interfere with, tamper with, toy with, fiddle with, meddle with, lay a hand on, lay a finger on, play about *or* around with • *Don't touch any of my things!*
4 = **tap**, hit, strike, push, pat • *As the aeroplane came down, the wing touched a pile of rubble.*
5 = **deal with**, do, handle, take care of, see to, attend to • *When he began restoring the house, nothing had been touched for 40 years.*
6 = **affect**, mark, involve, strike, get to *(informal)*, influence, inspire, impress, get through to, have an effect on, make an impression on • *a guilt that in some way touches everyone*
7 = **consume**, take, drink, eat, partake of • *He doesn't drink much, and he never touches drugs.*
8 = **move**, upset, stir, disturb, melt, soften, tug at someone's heartstrings *(often facetious)*, leave an impression on • *It has touched me deeply to see how these people live.*
9 = **match**, rival, equal, compare with, parallel, come up to, come near, be on a par with, be a match for, hold a candle to *(informal)*, be in the same league as • *No one can touch these girls for professionalism.*
10 = **ask**, approach, beg, borrow from • *Now is the time to touch him for a loan.*
11 = **get involved in**, use, deal with, handle, have to do with, utilize, be a party to, concern yourself with • *Some sports wouldn't touch tobacco advertising.*
12 = **reach**, hit *(informal)*, come to, rise to, arrive at, attain, get up to • *The winds had touched storm-force the day before.*
▸ AS A NOUN 1 = **contact**, push, stroke, brush, press, tap, poke, nudge, prod, caress, fondling • *Even a light touch on the face can trigger this pain.*
2 = **feeling**, feel, handling, physical contact, palpation, tactility • *Our sense of touch is programmed to diminish with age.*
3 = **detail**, feature, addition, accessory, nicety • *Small touches to a room like flowers can give it vitality.*

4 = **bit**, spot, trace, drop, taste, suggestion, hint, dash, suspicion, pinch, smack, small amount, tinge, whiff, jot, speck, smattering, intimation, tincture • *She thought she might have a touch of flu.*
5 = **style**, approach, method, technique, way, manner, characteristic, trademark, handiwork • *The striker was unable to find his scoring touch.*
6 = **awareness**, understanding, acquaintance, familiarity • *They've lost touch with what is happening in the country.*
7 = **communication**, contact, association, connection, correspondence • *In my job one tends to lose touch with friends.*
8 = **skill**, ability, flair, art, facility, command, craft, mastery, knack, artistry, virtuosity, deftness, adroitness • *You don't want to lose your touch. You should get some practice.*
9 = **influence**, hand, effect, management, direction • *This place is crying out for a woman's touch.*
▸ **IN PHRASES: touch and go** = **risky**, close, near, dangerous, critical, tricky, sticky *(informal)*, hazardous, hairy *(slang)*, precarious, perilous, nerve-racking, parlous • *It was touch and go whether we'd go bankrupt.*
touch down = **land**, arrive, come down, put down, alight, come to rest, come down to earth, come in to land, make a landing • *Spacecraft Columbia touched down yesterday.*
touch on *or* **upon something** = **refer to**, cover, raise, deal with, mention, bring in, speak of, hint at, allude to, broach, make allusions to • *The film touches on these issues, but only superficially.*
touch someone up = **fondle**, grope *(informal)*, molest, feel up, goose *(informal)*, paw *(informal)*, maul *(informal)*, cop a feel *(U.S. informal)* • *They surrounded me and started touching me up.*
touch something off 1 = **trigger (off)**, start, begin, cause, provoke, set off, initiate, arouse, give rise to, ignite, stir up, instigate, spark off, set in motion, foment • *The massacre touched off a new round of violence.*
2 = **ignite**, light, fire, set off, detonate, put a match to • *set enormous fuel fires raging, or touch off explosions*
touch something up 1 = **enhance**, revamp, renovate, patch up, brush up, gloss over, polish up, retouch, airbrush, titivate, give a face-lift to • *He got up regularly to touch up the painting.*
2 = **improve**, perfect, round off, enhance, dress up, finish off, embellish, put the finishing touches to • *Use these tips to touch up your image.*
▸ **RELATED ADJECTIVES:** haptic, tactile, tactual
▸ **RELATED PHOBIA:** haptophobia

touched 1 = **moved**, affected, upset, impressed, stirred, disturbed, melted, softened, swayed • *I was touched to hear that he finds me engaging.*
2 = **mad**, crazy, nuts *(slang)*, daft *(informal)*, batty *(slang)*, cuckoo *(informal)*, barmy *(slang)*, nutty *(slang)*, bonkers *(slang, chiefly Brit.)*, loopy *(informal)*, crackpot *(informal)*, out to lunch *(informal)*, gonzo *(slang)*, not all there, doolally *(slang)*, off your trolley *(slang)*, up the pole *(informal)*, soft in the head *(informal)*, not right in the head, off your rocker *(slang)*, nutty as a fruitcake *(slang)*, wacko *or* whacko *(informal)*, off the air *(Austral. slang)* • *They thought I was a bit touched.*

touching = **moving**, affecting, sad, stirring, tender, melting, pathetic, poignant, heartbreaking, emotive, pitiful, pitiable, piteous • *the touching tale of a wife who stood by the husband she loved*

touchstone = **standard**, measure, par, criterion, norm, gauge, yardstick • *Job security has become the touchstone of a good job.*

touchy 1 = **oversensitive**, irritable, bad-tempered, cross, crabbed, grumpy, surly, petulant, irascible, tetchy, ratty *(Brit. & N.Z. informal)*, testy, chippy *(informal)*, thin-skinned, grouchy *(informal)*, querulous, peevish, quick-tempered, splenetic, easily offended, captious, pettish, toey *(N.Z. slang)* • *She is very touchy about her past.*
OPPOSITES: pleasant, indifferent, thick-skinned
2 = **delicate**, sensitive, tricky, risky, sticky *(informal)*, thorny, knotty, ticklish • *a touchy subject*

tough **AS AN ADJECTIVE** 1 = **strong**, determined, aggressive, high-powered, feisty *(informal, chiefly U.S. & Canad.)*, hard-nosed *(informal)*, self-confident, unyielding, carnivorous *(informal)*, hard as nails, two-fisted, self-assertive, badass *(slang, chiefly U.S.)* • *She is tough and ambitious.*
OPPOSITES: soft, weak, delicate
2 = **hardy**, strong, seasoned, fit, strapping, hardened, vigorous, sturdy, stout, stalwart, resilient, brawny, hard as nails • *He's small, but he's tough, and I expect him to do well in the match.*
3 = **violent**, rough, vicious, ruthless, pugnacious, hard-bitten, ruffianly, two-fisted, badass *(slang, chiefly U.S.)* • *He shot three people, earning his reputation as a tough guy.*
4 = **rough**, wild, criminal, violent, lawless, badass *(slang, chiefly U.S.)* • *She doesn't seem to be cut out for this tough neighbourhood.*
OPPOSITES: soft, gentle, tender
5 = **harsh**, hard, awful, grim, unpleasant, bleak, austere, spartan, straitened • *She had a pretty tough childhood.*
6 = **strict**, severe, stern, hard, firm, exacting, adamant, resolute, draconian, intractable, inflexible, merciless, unforgiving, unyielding, unbending • *He announced tough measures to limit the money supply.*
OPPOSITES: easy, soft, lenient
7 = **hard**, difficult, exhausting, troublesome, uphill, strenuous, arduous, thorny, laborious, irksome • *Whoever wins the election is going to have a tough job.*
8 = **difficult**, hard, puzzling, baffling, troublesome, perplexing, thorny, knotty • *It was a tough decision but I think we made the right one.*
OPPOSITES: easy, easy-peasy *(slang)*
9 = **resilient**, hard, resistant, durable, strong, firm, solid, stiff, rigid, rugged, sturdy, inflexible, cohesive, tenacious, leathery, hard-wearing, robust • *tough leather boots and trousers*
OPPOSITES: delicate, soft, fragile
10 = **chewy**, fibrous, leathery, stringy, sinewy, gristly • *The steak was tough and the peas were like bullets.*
▸ **AS A NOUN** = **ruffian**, heavy *(slang)*, rough *(informal)*, bully, thug, hooligan, brute, rowdy, bravo, bully boy, bruiser *(informal)*, roughneck *(slang)*, boot boy, tsotsi *(S. African)* • *Three burly toughs elbowed their way to the front.*

toughen 1 = **harden**, season, strengthen, reinforce, temper, fortify, thicken, stiffen, coarsen, rigidify • *laminated and toughened glass*
2 = **make stricter**, tighten, stiffen, beef up *(informal)*, toughen up, make more severe • *Talks are underway to toughen trade restrictions.*
3 = **harden**, strengthen, fortify, brutalize, inure, steel, case-harden, harshen, make resilient • *people who have been toughened by their daily circumstances*

tour **AS A NOUN** 1 = **circuit**, course, round • *the first official cricket tour of South Africa for 22 years*
2 = **journey**, expedition, excursion, trip, progress, outing, jaunt, junket, peregrination • *week five of my tour of European cities*
3 = **visit**, inspection, ramble, walk round, walkabout • *a guided tour of a ruined Scottish castle*
4 = **stint**, turn, shift, stretch, spell, period of service, period of enlistment • *His tour of duty in Ireland changed him.*
▸ **AS A VERB** 1 = **travel round**, holiday in, travel through, journey round, trek round, go on a trip through • *A few years ago they toured the country in a roadshow.*
2 = **visit**, explore, go round, inspect, walk round, drive

round, sightsee • *You can tour the site in modern coaches fitted with videos.*

tourist = **traveller**, journeyer, voyager, tripper, globetrotter, holiday-maker, sightseer, excursionist • *foreign tourists*

QUOTATIONS

You perceive I generalize with intrepidity from single instances. It is the tourist's custom
[Mark Twain]

tournament 1 = **competition**, meeting, match, event, series, contest • *Here is a player capable of winning a world tournament.*
2 = **joust**, the lists, tourney • *a medieval tournament with displays of archery, armour and combat*

tousled = **dishevelled**, disordered, tangled, ruffled, messed up, rumpled, disarranged, disarrayed • *a woman with tousled hair, faded jeans and a baggy jacket*

tout AS A VERB 1 = **recommend**, promote, endorse, support, tip, urge, approve, praise, commend, big up *(slang, chiefly Caribbean)*, speak well of • *the advertising practice of using performers to tout products*
2 = **praise**, tip, promote, urge, endorse, big up *(slang, chiefly Caribbean)* • *He was being touted as the most interesting thing in pop.*
3 = **solicit**, canvass, drum up, bark *(U.S. informal)*, spiel • *He visited several foreign countries to tout for business.*
▸ AS A NOUN = **seller**, solicitor, barker, canvasser, spieler • *a ticket tout*

tow AS A VERB = **drag**, draw, pull, trail, haul, tug, yank, hale, trawl, lug • *He was using the vehicle to tow his trailer.*
▸ AS A NOUN = **drag**, pull, haul, tug • *I can give you a tow if you want.*
▸ IN PHRASES: **in tow** = **accompanying**, following, in attendance, by your side, in convoy, in your charge, under your protection • *There she was on my doorstep with child in tow.*

towards 1 = **in the direction of**, to, for, on the way to, on the road to, en route for • *She walked down the corridor towards the foyer.*
2 = **with the aim of**, for, in order to achieve, in order to obtain, so as to achieve • *They're working towards a hostage release hopefully by Saturday.*
3 = **regarding**, about, concerning, respecting, in relation to, with regard to, with respect to, apropos • *You must develop your own attitude towards religion.*
4 = **just before**, nearing, close to, coming up to, almost at, getting on for, shortly before • *There's a forecast of cooler weather towards the end of the week.*
5 = **for**, as a contribution to, as a help to • *He gave them £50,000 towards a house.*

tower AS A NOUN 1 = **column**, pillar, turret, belfry, steeple, obelisk • *an eleventh-century house with 120-foot high towers*
2 = **stronghold**, castle, fort, refuge, keep, fortress, citadel, fortification • *troops occupied the first two floors of the tower*
▸ AS A VERB *often with* **over** = **rise**, dominate, loom, top, mount, rear, soar, overlook, surpass, transcend, ascend, be head and shoulders above, overtop • *He stood up and towered over her.*

towering 1 = **tall**, high, great, soaring, elevated, gigantic, lofty, colossal • *towering cliffs of black granite*
2 = **impressive**, imposing, supreme, striking, extraordinary, outstanding, magnificent, superior, paramount, surpassing, sublime, stellar *(informal)*, prodigious, transcendent • *a towering figure in British politics*
3 = **intense**, violent, extreme, excessive, burning, passionate, mighty, fiery, vehement, inordinate, intemperate, immoderate • *I saw her in a towering rage only once.*

town = **city**, settlement, municipality, dorp *(S. African)* • *The town is under indefinite curfew.*
▸ RELATED ADJECTIVES: oppidan, urban

QUOTATIONS

God made the country, and man made the town
[William Cowper *The Task*]

toxic = **poisonous**, deadly, lethal, harmful, pernicious, noxious, septic, pestilential, baneful *(archaic)* • *the cost of cleaning up toxic waste*
OPPOSITES: safe, harmless, invigorating

toxin = **poison**, venom • *Tests showed increased levels of toxins in fish.*

toy AS A NOUN 1 = **plaything**, game, doll • *He was really too old for children's toys.*
2 = **trinket**, trifle, bauble, gimcrack, gewgaw, knick-knack • *Computers have become household toys.*
▸ IN PHRASES: **toy with something** 1 *usually with* **with** = **play with**, consider, trifle with, flirt with, dally with, entertain the possibility of, amuse yourself with, think idly of • *He toyed with the idea of going to China.*
2 = **fiddle with**, finger, play with, twiddle • *He picked up a pencil and toyed with it idly.*

trace AS A NOUN 1 = **bit**, drop, touch, shadow, suggestion, hint, dash, suspicion, tinge, trifle, whiff, jot, tincture, iota • *Wash them in cold water to remove all traces of sand.*
2 = **remnant**, remains, sign, record, mark, evidence, indication, token, relic, vestige • *The church has traces of fifteenth-century frescoes.*
3 = **track**, trail, footstep, path, slot, footprint, spoor, footmark • *He disappeared mysteriously without a trace.*
▸ AS A VERB 1 = **search for**, follow, seek out, track, determine, pursue, unearth, ascertain, hunt down • *I first went there to trace my roots.*
2 = **find**, track (down), discover, trail, detect, unearth, hunt down, ferret out, locate • *Police are anxious to trace a man seen leaving the house.*
3 = **outline**, chart, sketch, draw, map out, depict, mark out, delineate • *I traced the course of the river on the map.*
4 = **copy**, map, draft, outline, sketch, reproduce, draw over • *She learnt to draw by tracing pictures from story books.*

track AS A NOUN 1 = **path**, way, road, route, trail, pathway, footpath • *We set off once more, over a rough mountain track.*
2 = **course**, line, path, orbit, trajectory, flight path • *following the track of a hurricane*
3 = **running track**, course, circuit *(Brit.)*, racecourse • *the athletics track*
4 = **line**, rail, tramline • *A woman fell onto the railway track.*
5 = **song**, recording, piece, number • *He has produced two of the tracks on this album.*
▸ AS A VERB = **follow**, pursue, chase, trace, tail *(informal)*, dog, shadow, trail, stalk, hunt down, follow the trail of • *He thought he had better track this creature and kill it.*
▸ IN PHRASES: **keep track of something** *or* **someone** = **keep up with**, follow, monitor, watch, keep an eye on, keep in touch with, keep up to date with • *It's hard to keep track of time here.*
lose track of something *or* **someone** = **lose**, lose sight of, misplace • *It's so easy to lose track of who's playing who and when.*
on track = **on course**, on time, on target, on schedule • *He believes the talks are still on track.*
stop something *or* **someone in its** *or* **their tracks** = **bring to a standstill**, freeze, petrify, transfix, immobilize, stop someone dead, rivet to the spot • *His remark stopped me in my tracks*
track something *or* **someone down** = **find**, catch, capture, apprehend, discover, expose, trace, unearth, dig up, hunt down, sniff out, bring to light, ferret out, run to earth *or* ground • *They are doing all they can to track down terrorists.*

tracks = **trail**, marks, impressions, traces, imprints, prints • *He suddenly noticed tyre tracks on the bank ahead.* • *The killer returned to the scene to cover his tracks.*

tract[1] = **area**, lot, region, estate, district, stretch, quarter, territory, extent, zone, plot, expanse • *A vast tract of land is ready for development.*

tract[2] = **treatise**, essay, leaflet, brochure, booklet, pamphlet, dissertation, monograph, homily, disquisition, tractate • *She produced a feminist tract, 'Comments on Birth Control'.*

tractable = **manageable**, obedient, compliant, willing, yielding, tame, amenable, submissive, docile, controllable, biddable, persuadable, governable • *He could easily manage his tractable younger brother.*
OPPOSITES: defiant, stubborn, headstrong

traction = **grip**, resistance, friction, adhesion, purchase • *Rubber soles offer good traction on court.*

trade **AS A NOUN** 1 = **commerce**, business, transactions, buying and selling, dealing, exchange, traffic, truck, barter • *The ministry has control over every aspect of foreign trade.*
2 = **job**, employment, calling, business, line, skill, craft, profession, occupation, pursuit, line of work, métier, avocation • *He was a jeweller by trade.*
3 = **exchange**, deal, swap, interchange • *It wouldn't exactly have been a fair trade.*
▸ **AS A VERB** 1 = **deal**, do business, buy and sell, exchange, traffic, truck, bargain, peddle, barter, transact, cut a deal, have dealings • *They had years of experience trading with the west.*
2 = **exchange**, switch, swap, barter • *They traded land for goods and money.*
3 = **operate**, run, deal, do business • *The company is thought to be trading at a loss.*
▸ **IN PHRASES: trade on something** = **capitalize on**, use, milk, exploit, take advantage of, profit from, make use of, cash in on *(informal)* • *He was a man who traded on the achievements of others.*
▸ **RELATED ADJECTIVE:** mercantile

trademark 1 = **logo**, stamp, motif, emblem, sign, device, seal, badge, crest, hallmark, insignia, trade name, monogram • *The fabric carries a Pure New Wool trademark.*
2 = **characteristic**, trait, speciality, hallmark, quirk, peculiarity, idiosyncrasy • *the spiky punk hairdo that became her trademark*

trader = **dealer**, marketer, buyer, broker, supplier, merchant, seller, purveyor, merchandiser • *traders at the Stock Exchange*

tradesman = **craftsman**, workman, artisan, journeyman, skilled worker • *I would have made a good tradesman – particularly a carpenter.*

tradition 1 = **customs**, institution, ritual, folklore, lore, praxis, tikanga *(N.Z.)* • *a country steeped in tradition*
2 = **established practice**, custom, convention, habit, ritual, unwritten law • *She has carried on the family tradition of giving away plants.*
3 = **style**, movement, method • *They're marvellous pictures in the tradition of Gainsborough.*

traditional 1 = **old-fashioned**, old, established, conventional, standard, fixed, usual, transmitted, orthodox, accustomed, customary, ancestral, long-established, unwritten, time-honoured, unadventurous • *Traditional teaching methods can put students off learning.*
OPPOSITES: new, modern, revolutionary
2 = **folk**, old, historical • *traditional Indian music*

traduce = **malign**, abuse, knock *(informal)*, rubbish *(informal)*, run down, smear, blacken, slag (off) *(slang)*, detract, misrepresent, denigrate, disparage, decry, revile, vilify, slander, dump on *(slang, chiefly U.S.)*, deprecate, depreciate, defame, bad-mouth *(slang, chiefly U.S. & Canad.)*, speak ill of, drag through the mud, calumniate, asperse • *We have been traduced in the press as xenophobic bigots.*

traffic **AS A NOUN** 1 = **transport**, movement, vehicles, transportation, freight, coming and going • *There was heavy traffic on the roads.*
2 = **traffic jam**, jam, hold-up, congestion, gridlock, bottleneck, tailback, snarl-up • *He phoned in to say he was stuck in traffic.*
3 = **transportation**, shipping, transport, freight, conveyancing • *The ferries can cope with the traffic of goods and passengers.*
4 = **trade**, dealing, commerce, buying and selling, business, exchange, truck, dealings, peddling, barter, doings • *traffic in illicit drugs*
▸ **AS A VERB** *often with* **in** = **trade**, market, deal, exchange, truck, bargain, do business, buy and sell, peddle, barter, cut a deal, have dealings, have transactions • *Anyone who trafficked in illegal drugs was brought to justice.*

traffic jam = **hold-up**, jam, congestion, gridlock, bottleneck, tailback, snarl-up • *He was delayed in a traffic jam.*

tragedy 1 = **disaster**, catastrophe, misfortune, adversity, calamity, affliction, whammy *(informal, chiefly U.S.)*, bummer *(slang)*, grievous blow • *They have suffered an enormous personal tragedy.*
OPPOSITES: success, fortune, joy
2 = **tragic drama**, play • *a classic Greek tragedy*

QUOTATIONS

Tragedy is clean, it is restful, it is flawless
[Jean Anouilh *Antigone*]

Tragedy ought to be a great kick at misery
[D.H. Lawrence *letter*]

All tragedies are finish'd by a death,
All comedies are ended by a marriage
[Lord Byron *Don Juan*]

The world is a comedy to those that think, a tragedy to those that feel
[Horace Walpole, Fourth Earl of Orford *Letters*]

tragic *or* **tragical** 1 = **distressing**, shocking, sad, awful, appalling, fatal, deadly, unfortunate, disastrous, dreadful, dire, catastrophic, grievous, woeful, lamentable, ruinous, calamitous, wretched, ill-starred, ill-fated • *the tragic loss of so many lives*
OPPOSITES: lucky, satisfying, fortunate
2 = **sad**, miserable, dismal, pathetic, heartbreaking, anguished, mournful, heart-rending, sorrowful, doleful, pitiable • *She is a tragic figure.*
OPPOSITES: happy, comic, cheerful
3 = **dreadful**, terrible, awful, galling, grievous, regrettable, abject, deplorable, lamentable, wretched, vexatious • *This is a tragic waste of such a young life.*

trail **AS A NOUN** 1 = **path**, track, route, way, course, road, pathway, footpath, beaten track • *He was following a broad trail through the trees.*
2 = **series**, line, train, row, chain, string, stream, succession • *He left a trail of clues at the scenes of his crimes.*
3 = **tracks**, path, mark, marks, wake, trace, scent, footsteps, footprints, spoor • *They would take no action except that of following her trail.*
4 = **wake**, stream, tail, slipstream • *the high vapour trail of an aircraft*
5 = **train**, series, chain, aftermath • *The blast left a 200-metre trail of wreckage.*
6 = **scent**, track, spoor • *The whales come close to shore, on the trail of squid.*
▸ **AS A VERB** 1 = **follow**, track, chase, pursue, dog, hunt, shadow, trace, tail *(informal)*, hound, stalk, keep an eye on, keep tabs on *(informal)*, run to ground • *Two detectives were trailing him.*
2 = **drag**, draw, pull, sweep, stream, haul, tow, dangle, droop • *She came down the stairs, trailing the coat behind her.*
3 = **lag**, follow, drift, wander, linger, trudge, fall behind, plod, meander, amble, loiter, straggle, traipse *(informal)*, dawdle, hang back, tag along *(informal)*, bring up the rear, drag yourself • *I spent a long afternoon trailing behind him.*

4 = **lose**, be down, be behind, fall behind, lag behind, drop behind • *He scored again leaving Dartford trailing 2-0 at the break.*
5 = **creep**, slide, crawl, slither, slink • *ivy trailing over the concrete*
6 = **advertise**, announce, preview, hype *(informal)*, publicise • *a previously trailed live TV appearance*
▸ **IN PHRASES: trail away** *or* **off** = **fade away** *or* **out**, sink, weaken, diminish, decrease, dwindle, shrink, lessen, subside, fall away, peter out, die away, tail off, taper off, grow weak, grow faint • *'But he of all men...' her voice trailed away.*

train **AS A VERB 1** = **instruct**, school, prepare, improve, coach, teach, guide, discipline, rear, educate, drill, tutor, rehearse • *We train them in bricklaying and other building techniques.*
2 = **study**, learn, qualify, be taught, prepare, take instruction • *a lawyer who has trained with a good quality City firm*
3 = **exercise**, prepare, work out, practise, do exercise, get into shape • *They have spent a year training for the race.*
4 = **coach**, exercise, drill, rehearse, prepare, make ready, make fit • *a man who trained hundreds of dogs*
5 = **aim**, point, level, position, direct, focus, sight, line up, turn on, fix on, zero in, bring to bear • *She trained her binoculars on the horizon.*
▸ **AS A NOUN 1** = **locomotive**, railway train • *We can catch the early-morning train.*
2 = **convoy**, file, rank, string, column, queue, succession, caravan, procession, progression, cavalcade • *a long train of oil tankers*
3 = **sequence**, series, chain, string, set, course, order, cycle, trail, succession, progression, concatenation • *a train of events which would culminate in tragedy*
4 = **tail**, trail, appendage • *a velvet dress, bias cut with a train*
5 = **retinue**, following, entourage, court, staff, household, suite, cortège • *Toby arrived with his train of medical students*

trainer 1 = **coach**, manager, guide, adviser, tutor, instructor, counsellor, guru, handler • *She went to the gym with her trainer.*
2 = **training shoe**, sneaker *(U.S.)*, running shoe, sports shoe • *For many, wearing the fashionable kind of trainers is all-important.*

training = **instruction**, practice, schooling, grounding, education, preparation, exercise, working out, body building, tutelage • *He had no formal training as a decorator.* • *He will soon be back in training for next year.*

traipse *or* **trapse** *(Informal)* **AS A VERB** = **trudge**, trail, tramp, slouch, drag yourself, footslog • *He traipsed from one doctor to another.*
▸ **AS A NOUN** = **trudge**, trek, tramp, slog, long walk • *It's rather a long traipse from here. Let's take a bus.*

trait = **characteristic**, feature, quality, attribute, quirk, peculiarity, mannerism, idiosyncrasy, lineament • *Creativity is a human trait.*

traitor = **betrayer**, deserter, turncoat, deceiver, informer, renegade, defector, Judas, double-crosser *(informal)*, quisling, apostate, miscreant, fifth columnist, snake in the grass *(informal)*, back-stabber, fizgig *(Austral. slang)* • *Some say he's a traitor to the working class.*
OPPOSITES: supporter, defender, loyalist

traitorous = **treacherous**, unfaithful, disloyal, false, untrue, renegade, faithless, double-crossing *(informal)*, double-dealing, seditious, perfidious, apostate, treasonable • *the betrayal of men by their most traitorous companions*
OPPOSITES: true, constant, loyal

trajectory = **path**, line, course, track, flight, route, flight path • *the trajectory of an artillery shell*

tramp **AS A VERB 1** = **trudge**, march, stamp, stump, toil, plod, traipse *(informal)*, walk heavily • *They put on their coats and tramped through the fallen snow.*
2 = **hike**, walk, trek, roam, march, range, ramble, slog, rove, go walkabout *(Austral.)*, yomp, footslog • *He spent a month tramping in the hills around Balmoral.*
▸ **AS A NOUN 1** = **vagrant**, bum *(informal)*, derelict, drifter, down-and-out, hobo *(chiefly U.S.)*, vagabond, bag lady *(chiefly U.S.)*, dosser *(Brit. slang)*, derro *(Austral. slang)* • *an old tramp who slept rough in our neighbourhood*
2 = **tread**, stamp, footstep, footfall • *the slow, heavy tramp of feet on the staircase*
3 = **hike**, march, trek, ramble, slog • *He had just come from a day-long tramp on some wild moor.*
4 = **slut**, tart, slag *(Brit. slang)*, slapper *(Brit. slang)*, scrubber *(Brit. & Austral. slang)*, trollop, sloven, slattern, hornbag *(Austral. slang)* • *Look at her. She's a tramp, getting undressed with the shades open.*

trample 1 *often with* **on, upon,** *or* **over** = **stamp**, crush, squash, tread, flatten, run over, walk over • *I don't want people trampling on the grass.*
2 = **crush**, squash, flatten, run over • *Many people were trampled in the panic that followed.*

trance = **daze**, dream, spell, ecstasy, muse, abstraction, rapture, reverie, stupor, unconsciousness, hypnotic state • *Like a man in a trance, he made his way back to the rooms.*

tranquil 1 = **peaceful**, quiet, calm, serene, still, cool, pacific, composed, at peace, sedate, placid, undisturbed, restful, untroubled, unperturbed, unruffled, unexcited, chilled *(informal)* • *The place was tranquil and appealing.*
2 = **calm**, quiet, peaceful, serene, still, cool, pacific, composed, sedate, placid, undisturbed, restful, untroubled, unperturbed, unruffled, unexcited, chilled *(informal)* • *She settled into a life of tranquil celibacy.*
OPPOSITES: troubled, excited, busy

tranquillity *or (U.S. (sometimes))* **tranquility 1** = **peace**, calm, quiet, hush, composure, serenity, stillness, coolness, repose, rest, calmness, equanimity, quietness, peacefulness, quietude, placidity, restfulness, sedateness • *The hotel is a haven of peace and tranquillity.*
2 = **calm**, peace, composure, serenity, stillness, coolness, repose, calmness, equanimity, quietness, peacefulness, quietude, placidity, imperturbability, restfulness, sedateness • *He has a tranquillity and maturity that I desperately need.*
OPPOSITES: upset, noise, agitation

tranquillize = **calm**, sedate, knock out, lull, drug, quiet, relax, compose, soothe, quell, pacify, stupefy, settle your nerves • *The powerful drug is used to tranquillize patients.*
OPPOSITES: trouble, upset, agitate

tranquillizer *or* **tranquilliser** *or (U.S.)* **tranquilizer** = **sedative**, opiate, barbiturate, downer *(slang)*, red *(slang)*, bromide • *100 tablets of a powerful tranquillizer*

transact = **carry out**, handle, conduct, do, manage, perform, settle, conclude, negotiate, carry on, accomplish, execute, take care of, discharge, see to, prosecute, enact • *This would free them to transact business across the state lines.*

transaction 1 = **deal**, matter, affair, negotiation, business, action, event, proceeding, enterprise, bargain, coup, undertaking, deed, occurrence • *plans to disclose a business transaction with British Telecommunications*
2 = **conducting**, negotiation, performance, handling, settling, conduct, organization, clinching, execution, thrashing out • *Entertaining facilitates the transaction of business.*
3 *plural* = **records**, minutes, affairs, proceedings, goings-on *(informal)*, annals, doings • *the transactions of the Metallurgical Society of Great Britain*

transcend = **surpass**, exceed, go beyond, rise above, leave behind, eclipse, excel, outstrip, outdo, outshine, overstep, go above, leave in the shade *(informal)*, outrival, outvie • *issues like EU membership that transcend party loyalty*

t

transcendence *or* **transcendency** = **greatness**, excellence, superiority, supremacy, ascendancy, pre-eminence, sublimity, paramountcy, incomparability, matchlessness • *the absolute transcendence of God over all human knowledge and work*

transcendent = **unparalleled**, unique, extraordinary, superior, exceeding, sublime, consummate, unrivalled, second to none, pre-eminent, transcendental, incomparable, peerless, unequalled, matchless • *the idea of a transcendent God who stood apart from mankind*

transcribe 1 = **write out**, reproduce, take down, copy out, note, transfer, set out, rewrite • *Every telephone call will be recorded and transcribed.*
2 = **translate**, interpret, render, transliterate • *He decided to transcribe the work for piano.*

transcript = **copy**, record, note, summary, notes, version, carbon, log, translation, manuscript, reproduction, duplicate, transcription, carbon copy, transliteration, written version • *They wouldn't let me have a transcript of the interview.*

transfer AS A VERB 1 = **move**, carry, remove, transport, shift, transplant, displace, relocate, transpose, change • *The person can be transferred from wheelchair to seat with relative ease.*
2 = **hand over**, give, commit, surrender, pass on, transmit, convey, assign, divert, turn over, relinquish, entrust, consign, devolve, make over, cede, redirect, sign over • *Certain kinds of property are transferred automatically.*
▸ AS A NOUN 1 = **transference**, move, removal, handover, change, shift, transmission, translation, displacement, relocation, transposition • *Arrange for the transfer of medical records to your new doctor.*
2 = **move**, sale, switch, handover, relocation, movement • *Gascoigne's transfer to the Italian club, Lazio*

transfigure = **change**, convert, transform, alter, metamorphose, transmute • *They are transfigured by the healing powers of art.*

transfix = **stun**, hold, fascinate, paralyse, petrify, mesmerize, hypnotize, stop dead, root to the spot, engross, rivet the attention of, spellbind, halt *or* stop in your tracks • *We were all transfixed by the images of war.*
OPPOSITES: bore, tire, fatigue

transform 1 = **change**, convert, alter, translate, reconstruct, metamorphose, transmute, renew, transmogrify (*jocular*) • *the speed at which your body transforms food into energy*
2 = **make over**, overhaul, revamp, remake, renovate, remodel, revolutionize, redo, transfigure, restyle • *A cheap table can be transformed by an attractive cover.*

transformation 1 = **change**, conversion, alteration, metamorphosis, transmutation, renewal, transmogrification (*jocular*) • *the transformation of an attic room into a study*
2 = **revolution**, radical change, makeover, sea change, revolutionary change, transfiguration • *He has undergone a personal transformation.*

transgress 1 = **misbehave**, sin, offend, break the law, err, lapse, fall from grace, go astray, be out of order, do *or* go wrong • *If a politician transgresses, it is his own fault.*
2 = **go beyond**, exceed, infringe, overstep, break, defy, violate, trespass, contravene, disobey, encroach upon • *He had transgressed the boundaries of good taste.*

transgression = **crime**, wrong, fault, error, offence, breach, sin, lapse, violation, wrongdoing, infringement, trespass, misdemeanour, misdeed, encroachment, misbehaviour, contravention, iniquity, peccadillo, infraction • *tales of the candidate's alleged past transgressions*

transience = **briefness**, brevity, shortness, impermanence, ephemerality, evanescence, transitoriness, fleetingness, momentariness, fugacity, fugitiveness • *the superficiality and transience of the club scene*

transient = **brief**, passing, short-term, temporary, short, flying, fleeting, short-lived, fugitive, momentary, ephemeral, transitory, evanescent, impermanent, here today and gone tomorrow, fugacious • *the transient nature of high fashion*
OPPOSITES: lasting, long-term, permanent

transit AS A NOUN = **movement**, transfer, transport, passage, travel, crossing, motion, transportation, carriage, shipment, traverse, conveyance, portage • *They halted transit of EU livestock.*
▸ AS A VERB = **pass**, travel, cross, journey, traverse, move • *They have been allowed back into Kuwait by transitting through Baghdad.*
▸ IN PHRASES: **in transit** = **en route**, on the way, on the road, on the move, in motion, on the go (*informal*), on the journey, while travelling, during transport, during passage • *We cannot be held responsible for goods lost in transit.*

transition = **change**, passing, development, shift, passage, conversion, evolution, transit, upheaval, alteration, progression, flux, metamorphosis, changeover, transmutation, metastasis • *a period of transition*

transitional 1 = **changing**, passing, fluid, intermediate, unsettled, developmental, transitionary • *a transitional period following a decade of civil war*
2 = **temporary**, working, acting, short-term, interim, fill-in, caretaker, provisional, makeshift, make-do, stopgap, pro tem • *a meeting to set up a transitional government*

transitory = **short-lived**, short, passing, brief, short-term, temporary, fleeting, transient, flying, momentary, ephemeral, evanescent, impermanent, here today and gone tomorrow, fugacious • *Most teenage romances are transitory.*
OPPOSITES: lasting, long-term, permanent

translate 1 = **render**, put, change, convert, interpret, decode, transcribe, construe, paraphrase, decipher, transliterate • *Only a small number of his books have been translated into English.*
2 = **put in plain English**, explain, make clear, clarify, spell out, simplify, gloss, unravel, decode, paraphrase, decipher, elucidate, rephrase, reword, state in layman's language • *Translating IT jargon is the key to the IT director's role.*
3 = **convert**, change, turn, transform, alter, render, metamorphose, transmute, transfigure • *Your decision must be translated into specific actions.*
4 = **transfer**, move, send, relocate, carry, remove, transport, shift, convey, transplant, transpose • *The local-government minister was translated to Wales.*

translation 1 = **interpretation**, version, rendering, gloss, rendition, decoding, transcription, paraphrase, transliteration • *his excellent English translation of 'Faust'*
2 = **conversion**, change, rendering, transformation, alteration, metamorphosis, transfiguration, transmutation • *the translation of these goals into classroom activities*

QUOTATIONS

Translations, like wives, are seldom faithful if they are in the least attractive
[Roy Campbell *The Poetry Review*]

Some hold translation not unlike to be
The wrong side of a Turkish tapestry
[Julia Ward Howe *Familiar Letters*]

translator = **interpreter**, transcriber, paraphraser, decipherer, linguist, metaphrast, paraphrast, transliterator • *The translator has perfectly captured the style of the original.*

translucent = **semitransparent**, clear, limpid, lucent, diaphanous, pellucid • *The building is roofed entirely with translucent plastic.*

transmigration = **reincarnation**, movement, journey, passage, migration, rebirth, metempsychosis • *the doctrine of the transmigration of souls*

transmission 1 = **transfer**, spread, spreading, communication, passing on, circulation, dispatch, relaying, mediation, imparting, diffusion, transference, dissemination, conveyance, channeling • *the transmission of knowledge and skills*
2 = **broadcasting**, showing, putting out, relaying, sending • *The transmission of the programme was brought forward.*
3 = **programme**, broadcast, show, production, telecast, podcast • *A webcast is a transmission using the internet.*

transmit 1 = **broadcast**, put on the air, televise, relay, send, air, radio, send out, disseminate, beam out, podcast • *letters begging them to transmit the programme daily*
2 = **pass on**, carry, spread, communicate, take, send, forward, bear, transfer, transport, hand on, convey, dispatch, hand down, diffuse, remit, impart, disseminate • *mosquitoes that transmit disease to humans*

transmute = **transform**, change, convert, alter, metamorphose, transfigure, alchemize • *She ceased to think as anger transmuted into passion.*

transparency 1 = **photograph**, slide, exposure, photo, picture, image, print, plate, still • *The first colour photo was a transparency of a tartan ribbon.*
2 = **clarity**, translucency, translucence, clearness, limpidity, transparence, diaphaneity, filminess, diaphanousness, gauziness, limpidness, pellucidity, pellucidness, sheerness • *It is a condition that affects the transparency of the lenses.*
OPPOSITES: opacity, murkiness, cloudiness
3 = **frankness**, openness, candour, directness, forthrightness, straightforwardness • *openness and transparency in the government's decision-making*
OPPOSITES: ambiguity, vagueness
4 = **obviousness**, explicitness, plainness, distinctness, unambiguousness, apparentness, patentness, perspicuousness • *the transparency of pricing with the euro*
OPPOSITES: obscurity, vagueness, unclearness

transparent 1 = **clear**, sheer, see-through, lucid, translucent, crystal clear, crystalline, limpid, lucent, diaphanous, gauzy, filmy, pellucid • *a sheet of transparent coloured plastic*
OPPOSITES: thick, unclear, opaque
2 = **frank**, open, direct, straight, straightforward, candid, forthright, unequivocal, unambiguous, plain-spoken • *striving to establish a transparent parliamentary democracy*
OPPOSITES: mysterious, vague, unclear
3 = **blatant**, obvious, patent, manifest, brazen, shameless, flagrant, undisguised, barefaced, unconcealed • *He thought he could fool people with transparent deceptions.*
4 = **obvious**, plain, apparent, visible, bold, patent, evident, distinct, explicit, easy, understandable, manifest, recognizable, unambiguous, undisguised, as plain as the nose on your face *(informal)*, perspicuous • *The meaning of their actions is transparent.*
OPPOSITES: hidden, uncertain, mysterious

transpire 1 = **become known**, emerge, come out, be discovered, come to light, be disclosed, be made public • *It transpired that he had left his driving licence at home.*
2 = **happen**, occur, take place, arise, turn up, come about, come to pass *(archaic)* • *Nothing is known about what transpired at the meeting.*

transplant 1 = **implant**, transfer, graft • *The operation to transplant a kidney is now fairly routine.*
2 = **transfer**, take, bring, carry, remove, transport, shift, convey, fetch, displace, relocate, uproot • *Marriage had transplanted her from London to Manchester.*
3 = **replant**, relocate, uproot, repot • *Seed it directly rather than having to transplant seedlings.*

transport AS A VERB 1 = **convey**, take, run, move, bring, send, carry, bear, remove, ship, transfer, deliver, conduct, shift, ferry, haul, fetch • *There's no petrol so it's difficult to transport goods.*
2 = **enrapture**, move, delight, entrance, enchant, carry away, captivate, electrify, ravish, spellbind • *I have never seen any man so completely transported by excitement.*
3 = **exile**, banish, deport, sentence to transportation • *He was transported to Italy and interned.*
▸ AS A NOUN 1 = **vehicle**, wheels *(informal)*, transportation, conveyance • *Have you got your own transport?*
2 = **transference**, carrying, shipping, delivery, distribution, removal, transportation, carriage, shipment, freight, haulage, conveyance, freightage • *Safety rules had been breached during transport of radioactive fuel.*
3 *often plural* = **ecstasy**, delight, heaven, happiness, bliss, euphoria, rapture, enchantment, cloud nine *(informal)*, seventh heaven, ravishment • *transports of joy*
OPPOSITES: blues *(informal)*, dumps *(informal)*, despondency
4 = **frenzy**, fit, passion, fervour, rhapsody, paroxysm • *in a great transport of rage*

transpose 1 = **transplant**, move, transfer, shift, displace, relocate, reposition • *Genetic engineers transpose bits of material from one organism to another.*
2 = **interchange**, switch, swap, reorder, change, move, exchange, substitute, alter, rearrange • *Many people inadvertently transpose the digits of the code.*

transverse = **crossways**, diagonal, oblique, crosswise, athwart • *one of the table's transverse supports*

transvestite = **cross-dresser**, drag queen, trannie *(informal, chiefly Brit.)*, ladyboy, T.V. *(informal)* • *My wife accepted I was a transvestite but I abused her tolerance.*

trap AS A NOUN 1 = **snare**, net, booby trap, gin, toils *(old-fashioned)*, pitfall, noose, springe • *He came across a bird caught in a trap.*
2 = **ambush**, set-up *(informal)*, device, lure, bait, honey trap, ambuscade *(old-fashioned)* • *He failed to keep the appointment after sensing a police trap.*
3 = **trick**, set-up *(informal)*, deception, ploy, ruse, artifice, trickery, subterfuge, stratagem, wile, device • *He was trying to decide whether the question was a trap.*
4 = **problem**, snare, prison, cage, net • *The government is caught in a trap of its own making.*
5 = **mouth**, gob *(Brit. informal)*, cakehole *(Brit. informal)*, jaws, kisser *(informal)*, lips, chops *(informal)*, maw, yap *(informal)* • *Shut your trap!*
▸ AS A VERB 1 = **catch**, snare, ensnare, entrap, take, corner, bag, lay hold of, enmesh, lay a trap for, run to earth *or* ground • *The locals were trying to trap and kill the birds.*
2 = **trick**, fool, cheat, lure, seduce, deceive, dupe, beguile, gull, cajole, ensnare, hoodwink, wheedle, inveigle • *Were you trying to trap her into making an admission?*
3 = **capture**, catch, arrest, seize, take, lift *(slang)*, secure, nail *(informal)*, collar *(informal)*, nab *(informal)*, apprehend, take prisoner, take into custody • *To trap the killer they had to play him at his own game.*
4 = **imprison**, confine, cut off, close in, hem in, shut in • *The aircraft cartwheeled, trapping both men.*

trapped = **caught**, cornered, snared, ensnared, stuck *(informal)*, netted, surrounded, cut off, at bay, in a tight corner, in a tight spot, with your back to the wall • *He froze like a trapped animal.*

trappings = **accessories**, trimmings, paraphernalia, finery, things, fittings, dress, equipment, gear, fixtures, decorations, furnishings, ornaments, livery, adornments, panoply, accoutrements, fripperies, bells and whistles, raiment *(archaic or poetic)*, bling *(slang)* • *His family evidently loved the trappings of power.*

trash AS A NOUN 1 = **nonsense**, rubbish, garbage *(informal)*, rot, balls *(taboo slang)*, bull *(slang)*, shit *(taboo slang)*, pants *(slang)*, crap *(slang)*, bullshit *(taboo slang)*, hot air *(informal)*, tosh *(slang, chiefly Brit.)*, pap, cobblers *(Brit. taboo slang)*, bilge *(informal)*, drivel, twaddle, tripe *(informal)*, guff *(slang)*,

t

moonshine, hogwash, malarkey, hokum *(slang, chiefly U.S. & Canad.)*, piffle *(informal)*, poppycock *(informal)*, inanity, balderdash, bosh *(informal)*, eyewash *(informal)*, kak *(S. African taboo slang)*, trumpery, tommyrot, foolish talk, horsefeathers *(U.S. slang)*, bunkum *or* buncombe *(chiefly U.S.)*, bizzo *(Austral. slang)*, bull's wool *(Austral. & N.Z. slang)* • *Don't read that awful trash.*
OPPOSITES: reason, sense, significance
2 = **litter**, refuse, waste, rubbish, sweepings, junk *(informal)*, garbage, dross, dregs, dreck *(slang, chiefly U.S.)*, offscourings • *The yards are overgrown and cluttered with trash.*
3 = **scum**, rabble, dross, lowest of the low, riffraff, dregs of society, rubbish, canaille *(French)* • *He hit out at what he called 'Anti-Semitic trash'.*
▸ **AS A VERB** 1 = **wreck**, damage, destroy, ruin, mar, spoil, deface, vandalize, total *(informal)*, kennet *(Austral. slang)*, jeff *(Austral. slang)* • *Would they trash the place when the party was over?*
2 = **criticise**, attack, abuse, insult, knock *(informal)*, pan *(informal)*, condemn, hammer *(informal)*, slam *(informal)*, rubbish *(Brit. informal)*, savage, roast *(informal)*, slate *(Brit. informal)*, censure, crucify *(informal)*, slag off *(Brit. informal)*, flay, bad-mouth *(chiefly U.S.)*, lambaste, take to pieces *(informal)*, give a bad press to, take *or* pull apart *(informal)* • *Why did the candidates spend so much time trashing each other?*

trashy = **worthless**, cheap, inferior, shabby, flimsy, shoddy, tawdry, tinsel, thrown together, crappy *(slang)*, meretricious, rubbishy, poxy *(slang)*, chickenshit *(U.S. slang)*, catchpenny, cheap-jack *(informal)*, of a sort *or* of sorts • *I was reading some trashy romance novel.*
OPPOSITES: excellent, outstanding, first-class

trauma 1 = **shock**, suffering, worry, pain, stress, upset, strain, torture, distress, misery, disturbance, ordeal, anguish, upheaval, jolt • *I'd been through the trauma of losing a house.*
2 = **injury**, damage, hurt, wound, agony • *spinal trauma*

traumatic = **shocking**, upsetting, alarming, awful, disturbing, devastating, painful, distressing, terrifying, scarring, harrowing
OPPOSITES: relaxing, calming, therapeutic

traumatize = **devastate**, disturb, overwhelm, distress, dismay, knock for six *(informal)*, deeply upset • *young children traumatized by their parents' deaths*

travail = **toil**, suffering, pain, stress, labour, grind *(informal)*, effort, tears, strain, distress, sweat, hard work, slavery, hardship, slog, exertion, drudgery • *He did whatever he could to ease their travail.*

travel **AS A VERB** 1 = **go**, journey, proceed, make a journey, move, walk, cross, tour, progress, wander, trek, voyage, roam, ramble, traverse, rove, take a trip, make your way, wend your way • *You can travel to Helsinki tomorrow.*
2 = **be transmitted**, move, advance, proceed, get through • *Light travels at around 300 million metres per second.*
3 = **go fast**, race, hurry, hasten, whizz, hurtle, burn rubber, go hell for leather *(informal)*, tear along, belt along, bomb along *(informal)*, whip along, hotfoot it, go like a bat out of hell *(informal)*, go at breakneck speed, go rapidly, go like (greased) lightning • *The horse was really travelling.*
▸ **AS A NOUN** *usually plural* = **journey**, wandering, expedition, globetrotting, walk, tour, touring, movement, trip, passage, voyage, excursion, ramble, peregrination • *He collects things for the house on his travels.*
▸ **RELATED ADJECTIVE:** itinerant
▸ **RELATED MANIA:** dromomania
▸ **RELATED PHOBIA:** hodophobia

QUOTATIONS
Travel, at its best, is a process of continually conquering disbelief
[Michael Palin *Pole to Pole*]
Travel is glamorous only in retrospect
[Paul Theroux]
In America there are two classes of travel – first class and with children
[Robert Benchley]
They change their clime, but not their minds, who rush across the sea
[Horace *Epistles*]
Whenever I prepare for a journey I prepare as though for death
[Katherine Mansfield *Journal*]
For my part, I travel not to go anywhere, but to go. I travel for travel's sake. The great affair is to move
[Robert Louis Stevenson *Travels with a Donkey*]
Airplane travel is nature's way of making you look like your passport photo
[Al Gore]
PROVERBS
Travel broadens the mind

traveller 1 = **voyager**, tourist, passenger, journeyer, explorer, hiker, tripper, globetrotter, holiday-maker, wayfarer, excursionist • *Many air travellers suffer puffy ankles during long flights.*
2 = **gypsy**, migrant, wanderer, tinker, tramp, transient, nomad, itinerant, drifter, vagrant, Romany, vagabond, New Age traveller, wayfarer • *The whole idea of being a traveller is being self-sufficient.*
3 = **travelling salesman**, representative, rep, salesman, sales rep, commercial traveller, agent • *My father was a commercial traveller who migrated from Scotland.*

travelling = **itinerant**, moving, touring, mobile, wandering, unsettled, roaming, migrant, restless, roving, nomadic, migratory, peripatetic, wayfaring • *troupes of travelling actors*

traverse 1 = **cross**, go across, travel over, make your way across, cover, range, bridge, negotiate, wander, go over, span, roam, ply • *I traversed the narrow pedestrian bridge.*
2 = **cut across**, pass over, stretch across, extend across, lie across • *a steep-sided valley traversed by streams*

travesty = **mockery**, distortion, parody, caricature, sham, send-up *(Brit. informal)*, spoof *(informal)*, perversion, takeoff *(informal)*, lampoon, burlesque • *If he couldn't prepare his case properly, the trial would be a travesty.*

trawl **AS A VERB** = **search**, go, look, check, wade *(informal)*, sift • *They are trawling through the records of thousands of petty thieves.*
▸ **AS A NOUN** = **search**, look, check, hunt, glance • *Any trawl through their interviews will reveal incisive statements.*

treacherous 1 = **disloyal**, deceitful, untrustworthy, duplicitous, false, untrue, unreliable, unfaithful, faithless, double-crossing *(informal)*, double-dealing, perfidious, traitorous, treasonable, recreant *(archaic)* • *The President spoke of the treacherous intentions of the enemy.*
OPPOSITES: true, reliable, loyal
2 = **dangerous**, tricky, risky, unstable, hazardous, icy, slippery, unsafe, unreliable, precarious, deceptive, perilous, slippy *(informal or dialect)* • *The current of the river is fast-flowing and treacherous.*
OPPOSITES: safe, reliable

treachery = **betrayal**, infidelity, treason, duplicity, disloyalty, double-cross *(informal)*, double-dealing, stab in the back, perfidy, faithlessness, perfidiousness • *He was wounded by the treachery of old friends.*
OPPOSITES: loyalty, allegiance, reliability

tread **AS A VERB** = **step**, walk, march, pace, stamp, stride, hike, tramp, trudge, plod • *She trod casually, enjoying the sensation of bare feet on grass.*
▸ **AS A NOUN** = **step**, walk, pace, stride, footstep, gait, footfall • *We could hear their heavy tread and an occasional coarse laugh.*

t

▸ **IN PHRASES: tread on something 1 = crush underfoot**, step on, stamp on, trample (on), stomp on, squash, flatten • *Oh sorry, I didn't mean to tread on your foot.*
2 = **repress**, crush, suppress, subdue, oppress, quell, bear down on, subjugate, ride roughshod over • *Paid lawyers would tread on the farmers' interests.*

treason = **disloyalty**, mutiny, treachery, subversion, disaffection, duplicity, sedition, perfidy, lese-majesty, traitorousness • *Queen of England for nine days, she was beheaded for treason.*
OPPOSITES: loyalty, allegiance, fidelity

QUOTATIONS
Treason doth never prosper, what's the reason
For if it prosper, none dare call it treason
[Sir John Harington *Epigrams*]

treasonable = **disloyal**, false, subversive, treacherous, seditious, mutinous, perfidious, traitorous, treasonous • *They were brought to trial for treasonable conspiracy.*
OPPOSITES: reliable, loyal, faithful

treasure **AS A NOUN** 1 = **riches**, money, gold, fortune, wealth, valuables, jewels, funds, cash, wonga (*slang*), taonga (*N.Z.*) • *It was here, the buried treasure, she knew it was.*
2 = **objet d'art**, masterpiece, work of art, valuable object • *The house was full of art treasures.*
3 = **angel**, darling, find, star (*informal*), prize, pearl, something else (*informal*), jewel, gem, paragon, one in a million (*informal*), one of a kind (*informal*), nonpareil • *Charlie? Oh he's a treasure, loves children.*
4 = **darling**, angel, precious, pride and joy, apple of your eye, best *or* greatest thing since sliced bread (*informal*) • *They found out that their little treasure was a vicious murderer.*
▸ **AS A VERB** = **prize**, value, worship, esteem, adore, cherish, revere, venerate, hold dear, love, idolize, set great store by, dote upon, place great value on • *She treasures her memories of those joyous days.*

treasury 1 = **funds**, money, capital, finances, resources, assets, revenues, exchequer, coffers, wonga (*slang*) • *reconciling accounts with the central bank and its treasury*
2 = **storehouse**, bank, store, vault, hoard, cache, repository • *He had been compiling a treasury of jokes.*
3 = **rich source**, fund, mine, storehouse, repository, treasure house *or* trove • *These records are a treasury of information.*
4 = **anthology**, collection, digest, compilation, compendium, miscellany • *a treasury of stories for six-year-olds*

treat **AS A VERB** 1 = **behave towards**, deal with, handle, act towards, use, consider, serve, manage, regard, look upon • *He treated most women with indifference.*
2 = **take care of**, minister to, attend to, give medical treatment to, doctor (*informal*), nurse, care for, medicate, prescribe medicine for, apply treatment to • *An experienced nurse treats all minor injuries.*
3 = **cure**, heal, remedy, make better • *For centuries it was used to treat indigestion.*
4 = **prime**, cover, process, prepare • *About 70% of the area is treated with insecticide.*
5 *often with* **to** = **provide**, give, buy, stand (*informal*), pay for, entertain, feast, lay on, regale, wine and dine, take out for, foot *or* pay the bill • *She was always treating him to ice cream.*
6 = **deal with**, consider, study, cover, discuss, review, handle, go into, refer to, tackle, investigate, explore, analyse, critique, touch on • *a working method for treating subjects in the theatre*
7 = **negotiate**, bargain, consult, have talks, confer, come to terms, parley, make a bargain, make terms • *They assumed we were treating with the rebels.*
▸ **AS A NOUN** 1 = **entertainment**, party, surprise, gift, celebration, feast, outing, excursion, banquet, refreshment • *a birthday treat*
2 = **present**, gift, luxury, indulgence, delicacy, extravagance, goodie (*informal*), titbit, little something • *He never failed to return without a special treat for them.*
3 = **pleasure**, delight, joy, thrill, satisfaction, enjoyment, gratification, source of pleasure, fun • *It's a real treat to see someone doing justice to the film.*
▸ **IN PHRASES: treat of something** = **deal with**, discuss, go into, be concerned with, touch upon, discourse upon • *part of Christian theology that treats of the afterlife*

treatise = **paper**, work, writing, study, essay, thesis, tract, pamphlet, exposition, dissertation, monograph, disquisition • *Locke's treatise on Civil Government*

treatment 1 = **care**, medical care, nursing, medicine, surgery, therapy, healing, medication, therapeutics, ministrations • *Many patients are not getting the treatment they need.*
2 = **cure**, remedy, medication, medicine • *a new treatment for eczema*
3 *often with* **of** = **handling**, dealings with, behaviour towards, conduct towards, management, reception, usage, manipulation, action towards • *She was shocked at his treatment of her.*
4 = **presentation**, handling, coverage, investigation, analysis, consideration, examination, interpretation, exploration, critique • *criticism of the media's treatment of the affair*

treaty = **agreement**, pact, contract, bond, alliance, bargain, convention, compact, covenant, entente, concordat • *negotiations over a 1992 treaty on global warming*

tree
▸ **RELATED ADJECTIVES:** arboreal, arboreous

QUOTATIONS
The tree is known by its fruit
[*Bible: St. Matthew*]
I think that I shall never see
A poem lovely as a tree
[Joyce Kilmer *Trees*]
Of all the trees that grow so fair,
Old England to adorn,
Greater are none beneath the Sun,
Than Oak, and Ash, and Thorn
[Rudyard Kipling *Puck of Pook's Hill*]

▹ *See panel* **Trees**

trek **AS A NOUN** 1 = **slog**, tramp, long haul, footslog • *It's a bit of a trek, but it's worth it.*
2 = **journey**, hike, expedition, safari, march, odyssey • *He is on a trek through the South Gobi desert.*
▸ **AS A VERB** 1 = **journey**, march, range, hike, roam, tramp, rove, go walkabout (*Austral.*) • *trekking through the jungles*
2 = **trudge**, plod, traipse (*informal*), footslog, slog • *They trekked from shop to shop looking for knee-length socks.*

trellis = **framework**, mesh, grille, lattice, tracery, latticework, espalier, trelliswork • *Sweet peas can be trained to grow up a trellis.*

tremble **AS A VERB** 1 = **shake**, shiver, quake, shudder, quiver, teeter, totter, quake in your boots, shake in your boots *or* shoes • *He began to tremble all over.*
2 = **vibrate**, rock, shake, quake, wobble, oscillate • *He felt the earth tremble under him.*
▸ **AS A NOUN** = **shake**, shiver, quake, shudder, wobble, tremor, quiver, vibration, oscillation • *I'll never forget the tremble in his hand.*

trembling
▸ **RELATED PHOBIA:** tremophobia

tremendous 1 = **huge**, great, towering, vast, enormous, terrific, formidable, immense, awesome, titanic, gigantic, monstrous, mammoth, colossal, whopping (*informal*), stellar (*informal*), prodigious, stupendous, gargantuan, fuck-off (*offensive taboo slang*) • *I felt a tremendous pressure on my chest.*
OPPOSITES: little, small, tiny

t

TREES

acacia
akee
alder
almond
aloe
angophora (*Austral.*)
Antarctic beech
apple
apricot
ash
aspen
balsa
banana
bangalay *or* bastard mahogany (*Austral.*)
bangalow (palm) *or* piccabean (*Austral.*)
banyalla *or* tallowwood (*Austral.*)
banyan
baobab *or* boab
bat's wing coral-tree (*Austral.*)
bay
beech
beefwood (*Austral.*)
belah *or* black oak (*Austral.*)
berrigan *or* bitterbush (*Austral.*)
bimble box (*Austral.*)
birch
bitterbark (*Austral.*)
black bean *or* Moreton Bay chestnut
blackbutt (*Austral.*)
black pine *or* matai (*Austral.*)
black wattle (*Austral.*)
blackwood *or* mudgerabah (*Austral.*)
blanket-leaf (*Austral.*)
bloodwood (*Austral.*)
bonsai
boree (*Austral.*)
bottle tree (*Austral.*)
box
brazil
brigalow (*Austral.*)
bulwaddy (*Austral.*)
bunya *or* bunya-bunya (pine)
burrawang *or* zamia (*Austral.*)
butternut
cabbage tree (palm) (*Austral.*)
cacao
cadagi (*Austral.*)
cajuput (*Austral.*)
camphor laurel (*Austral.*)
carbeen *or* Moreton Bay ash (*Austral.*)
carob
cashew
cassia
casuarina *or* native oak (*Austral.*)
cedar
cedar of Lebanon
celery pine (*Austral.*)
cherry
chestnut
cinnamon
citrus
coachwood (*Austral.*)
coco
coconut
coolabah
coral tree (*Austral.*)
cork oak
cork tree
cypress
date palm
deal
dogwood
Douglas fir
ebony
elder
elm
eucalyptus
eumung (*Austral.*)
fig
fir
firewheel tree (*Austral.*)
flame tree *or* Illawarra flame tree (*Austral.*)
flooded gum (*Austral.*)
ghost gum (*Austral.*)
gidgee *or* stinking wattle (*Austral.*)
golden wattle (*Austral.*)
grapefruit
grasstree *or* black boy (*Austral.*)
grey gum (*Austral.*)
groundash
ground oak
guava
gum (tree)
gympie
hawthorn
hazel
hemlock
hickory
holly
hoop pine (*Austral.*)
hornbeam
horse chestnut
huon pine (*Austral.*)
ilex
ironbark
iron gum
ironwood
jacaranda
jarrah (*Austral.*)
Judas tree
juniper
karri
kauri
kentia palm (*Austral.*)
kurrajong (*Austral.*)
laburnum
larch
laurel
lemon
lilac
lilly pilly (*Austral.*)
lime
lind
linden
lotus
macadamia, bauple nut, *or* Queensland nut (*Austral.*)
macrocarpa
magnolia
mahogany
mallee (*Austral.*)
mango
mangrove
manuka, kahikatoa, *or* kanuka (*N.Z.*)
maple
marri (*Austral.*)
melaleuca
mimosa
monkey puzzle *or* Chile pine
Moreton Bay fig (*Austral.*)
mountain ash
mugga (*Austral.*)
mulberry
myall (*Austral.*)
Norfolk Island pine (*Austral.*)
nutmeg
oak
olive
orange
osier
palm
papaya
paperbark
pawpaw *or* papaw
peach
pear
peppermint gum (*Austral.*)
persimmon
pine
plane
plum
pomegranate
poplar
pussy willow
quandong (*Austral.*)
quince
radiata pine, insignis pine, *or* Monterey pine (*Austral.*)
raffia
redwood
rivergum (*Austral.*)
rosewood
rowan
sandalwood
sassafras
Scots fir
Scots pine
scribbly gum (*Austral.*)
sequoia
silky oak (*Austral.*)
silver birch
snow gum (*Austral.*)
spotted gum (*Austral.*)
spruce
stinging tree *or* gympie nettle (*Austral.*)
stringy-bark
sycamore
tamarind
Tasmanian blue gum (*Austral.*)
teak
tea-tree
umbrella tree
walnut
wandoo (*Austral.*)

t

TREES (CONTINUED)

wattle	willow	yew
weeping willow	wirilda *(Austral.)*	ylang-ylang
white ash	witch	yucca
whitebeam	witch elm	
wilga *(Austral.)*	yellow box *(Austral.)*	

2 = **excellent**, great, wonderful, brilliant, mean *(slang)*, topping *(Brit. slang)*, cracking *(Brit. informal)*, amazing, extraordinary, fantastic *(informal)*, ace *(informal)*, incredible, fabulous *(informal)*, marvellous, exceptional, terrific *(informal)*, sensational *(informal)*, sovereign, awesome *(slang)*, super *(informal)*, brill *(informal)*, bodacious *(slang, chiefly U.S.)*, boffo *(slang)*, jim-dandy *(slang)*, chillin' *(U.S. slang)*, booshit *(Austral. slang)*, exo *(Austral. slang)*, sik *(Austral. slang)*, rad *(informal)*, phat *(slang)*, schmick *(Austral. informal)*, beaut *(informal)*, barrie *(Scot. slang)*, belting *(Brit. slang)*, pearler *(Austral. slang)* • *I thought it was absolutely tremendous.*
OPPOSITES: average, ordinary, terrible
3 = **deafening**, crashing, booming, roaring, thundering, resounding, thunderous, very loud, ear-splitting, ear-piercing • *Suddenly there was a tremendous explosion.*

tremor 1 = **shake**, shaking, tremble, trembling, shiver, quaking, wobble, quiver, quivering, agitation, vibration, quaver • *He felt a tremor in his arm.*
2 = **earthquake**, shock, quake *(informal)*, tremblor *(U.S. informal)* • *The minute-long tremor measured 6.8 on the Richter Scale.*

tremulous 1 = **trembling**, shaking, nervous, shivering, shaky, wavering, quivering, vibrating, quavering, unsteady, trembly *(informal)*, aflutter, aquiver, quivery • *The old man's voice was tremulous.*
2 = **timid**, excited, afraid, frightened, scared, nervous, anxious, fearful, agitated, jittery *(informal)*, jumpy, agog, antsy *(informal)* • *All she could manage was a tremulous smile.*

trench = **ditch**, cut, channel, drain, pit, waterway, gutter, trough, furrow, excavation, earthwork, fosse, entrenchment • *Dig a trench at least 2ft deep.*

trenchant 1 = **scathing**, pointed, cutting, biting, sharp, keen, acute, severe, acid, penetrating, tart, pungent, incisive, hurtful, sarcastic, caustic, astringent, vitriolic, acerbic, piquant, mordant, acidulous, mordacious • *He was shattered by the trenchant criticism.*
OPPOSITES: kind, soothing, appeasing
2 = **clear**, driving, strong, powerful, effective, distinct, crisp, explicit, vigorous, potent, energetic, clear-cut, forceful, emphatic, unequivocal, salient, well-defined, effectual, distinctly defined • *His comment was trenchant and perceptive.*
OPPOSITES: obscure, vague, unclear

trend AS A NOUN 1 = **tendency**, swing, drift, inclination, current, direction, flow, leaning, bias • *a trend towards part-time employment*
2 = **fashion**, craze, fad *(informal)*, mode, look, thing, style, rage, vogue, mania • *The record may well start a trend.*
▸ AS A VERB = **tend**, turn, head, swing, flow, bend, lean, incline, veer, run • *Unemployment is still trending down.*

trendy AS AN ADJECTIVE = **fashionable**, in *(slang)*, now *(informal)*, latest, with it *(informal)*, flash *(informal)*, stylish, in fashion, in vogue, up to the minute, modish, voguish, culty, schmick *(Austral. informal)*, funky • *a trendy London night club*
▸ AS A NOUN = **poser** *(informal)*, pseud *(informal)* • *an example of what happens when you get a few trendies in power*

trepidation = **anxiety**, fear, worry, alarm, emotion, excitement, dread, butterflies *(informal)*, shaking, disturbance, dismay, trembling, fright, apprehension, tremor, quivering, nervousness, disquiet, agitation, consternation, jitters *(informal)*, cold feet *(informal)*, uneasiness, palpitation, cold sweat *(informal)*, perturbation, the heebie-jeebies *(slang)* • *It was with some trepidation that I viewed the prospect.*
OPPOSITES: confidence, calm, composure

trespass AS A VERB 1 = **intrude**, infringe, encroach, enter without permission, invade, poach, obtrude • *They were trespassing on private property.*
2 *often with* **against** = **sin**, offend, transgress, commit a sin • *Forgive those who trespass against us.*
▸ AS A NOUN 1 = **intrusion**, infringement, encroachment, unlawful entry, invasion, poaching, wrongful entry • *You could be prosecuted for trespass.*
2 = **sin**, crime, fault, error, offence, breach, misconduct, wrongdoing, misdemeanour, delinquency, misdeed, transgression, misbehaviour, iniquity, infraction, evildoing, injury • *Forgive us our trespasses.*

trespasser = **intruder**, unwelcome visitor, invader, poacher, infringer, interloper • *Trespassers will be prosecuted.*

tress *often plural* = **hair**, lock, curl, braid, plait, pigtail, ringlet • *her long, burnished blonde tresses*

triad = **threesome**, triple, trio, trinity, trilogy, triplet, triumvirate, triptych, trine, triune • *the triad of responsibilities: teaching, research and service*

trial AS A NOUN 1 = **hearing**, case, court case, inquiry, contest, tribunal, lawsuit, appeal, litigation, industrial tribunal, court martial, legal proceedings, judicial proceedings, judicial examination • *New evidence showed that he lied at the trial*
2 = **test**, testing, experiment, evaluation, check, examination, audition, assay, dry run *(informal)*, assessment, proof, probation, appraisal, try-out, test-run, pilot study, dummy run • *They have been treated with drugs in clinical trials.*
3 = **hardship**, suffering, trouble, pain, load, burden, distress, grief, misery, ordeal, hard times, woe, unhappiness, adversity, affliction, tribulation, wretchedness, vexation, cross to bear • *the trials of adolescence*
4 = **nuisance**, drag *(informal)*, bother, plague *(informal)*, pest, irritation, hassle *(informal)*, bane, pain in the neck *(informal)*, pain in the arse *(taboo slang)*, vexation, thorn in your flesh *or* side • *The whole affair has been a terrible trial for us all.*
▸ AS AN ADJECTIVE = **experimental**, probationary, testing, pilot, provisional, exploratory • *a trial period*
▸ AS A VERB = **test**, experiment with, try out, put to the test, put through its paces, carry out trials on • *The drug is being trialled at a Brisbane hospital.*

triangular = **three-sided**, three-cornered, trilateral, triangle-shaped • *cottages around a triangular green*

tribe 1 = **race**, ethnic group, people, family, class, stock, house, division, blood, seed *(chiefly biblical)*, sept, gens, clan, caste, dynasty, hapu *(N.Z.)*, iwi *(N.Z.)* • *three hundred members of the Xhosa tribe*
2 = **crowd**, company, group, party, bunch *(informal)*, body, army, host, band, pack, crew *(informal)*, load *(informal)*, drove, gang, mob, flock, herd, horde, posse *(informal)*, bevy • *a tribe of cyclists*

tribulation = **trouble**, care, suffering, worry, trial, blow, pain, burden, distress, grief, misery, curse, ordeal, hardship, sorrow, woe, hassle *(informal)*, misfortune, bad luck,

unhappiness, heartache, adversity, affliction, bummer *(slang)*, wretchedness, vexation, ill fortune, cross to bear • *the trials and tribulations of everyday life*
OPPOSITES: rest, ease, joy

tribunal = **hearing**, court, trial, bar, bench, industrial tribunal, judgment seat, judicial examination • *The tribunal found that he had been unfairly dismissed.*

tribute 1 = **accolade**, testimonial, eulogy, recognition, respect, gift, honour, praise, esteem, applause, compliment, gratitude, acknowledgment, commendation, panegyric, encomium, laudation • *The song is a tribute to Elvis Presley.*
OPPOSITES: blame, criticism, complaint
2 = **testimony to**, evidence of, indication of, proof of, manifestation of, attestation of • *His success has been a tribute to his hard work.*

trice = **moment**, second, minute, shake *(informal)*, flash, instant, tick *(Brit. informal)*, twinkling, split second, jiffy *(informal)*, twinkling of an eye, two shakes of a lamb's tail *(informal)*, bat of an eye *(informal)* • *She was back in a trice.*

trick AS A NOUN 1 = **joke**, put-on *(slang)*, gag *(informal)*, stunt, spoof *(informal)*, caper, prank, frolic, practical joke, antic, jape, leg-pull *(Brit. informal)*, cantrip *(Scot.)* • *We are playing a trick on a man who keeps bothering me.*
2 = **deception**, trap, fraud, con *(slang)*, sting *(informal)*, manoeuvre, dodge, ploy, scam *(slang)*, imposition, gimmick, device, hoax, deceit, swindle, ruse, artifice, subterfuge, canard, feint, stratagem, wile, imposture, fastie *(Austral. slang)* • *That was a really mean trick.*
3 = **sleight of hand**, device, feat, stunt, juggle, legerdemain • *He shows me card tricks.*
4 = **secret**, skill, device, knack, art, hang *(informal)*, technique, know-how *(informal)*, gift, command, craft, expertise • *She showed me all the tricks of the trade.*
5 = **illusion**, deception, mirage, optical illusion • *It appears to be on fire, but it's just a trick of the light.*
6 = **mannerism**, habit, characteristic, trait, quirk, peculiarity, foible, idiosyncrasy, practice, crotchet • *all her little tricks and funny voices*
▸ AS A VERB = **deceive**, trap, have someone on, take someone in *(informal)*, fool, cheat, con *(informal)*, kid *(informal)*, stiff *(slang)*, sting *(informal)*, mislead, hoax, defraud, dupe, gull *(archaic)*, delude, swindle, impose upon, bamboozle *(informal)*, hoodwink, put one over on *(informal)*, pull the wool over someone's eyes, pull a fast one on *(informal)*, scam *(slang)* • *He'll be upset when he finds out how you tricked him.*
▸ IN PHRASES: **do the trick** = **work**, fit the bill, have effect, achieve the desired result, produce the desired result, take care of the problem, be effective *or* effectual, do the business *(informal)* • *Sometimes a few choice words will do the trick.*
trick something *or* **someone out** *or* **up** = **dress up**, do up *(informal)*, deck out, get up *(informal)*, decorate, array *(literary)*, adorn, ornament, embellish, apparel *(literary)*, festoon, attire, garb, bedeck *(literary)*, doll up *(slang)*, rig out, accoutre • *The children were tricked out as princes and princesses.*

QUOTATIONS
I know a trick worth two of that
[William Shakespeare *Henry IV, part I*]

trickery = **deception**, fraud, cheating, con *(informal)*, hoax, pretence, deceit, dishonesty, swindling, guile, double-dealing, skulduggery *(informal)*, chicanery, hanky-panky *(informal)*, hokum *(slang, chiefly U.S. & Canad.)*, monkey business *(informal)*, funny business, jiggery-pokery *(informal, chiefly Brit.)*, imposture • *They will resort to trickery in order to impress their clients.*
OPPOSITES: honesty, openness, candour

trickle AS A VERB = **dribble**, run, drop, stream, creep, crawl, drip, ooze, seep, exude, percolate • *A tear trickled down his cheek.*
▸ AS A NOUN = **dribble**, drip, seepage, thin stream • *There was not so much as a trickle of water.*

trickster = **deceiver**, fraud, cheat, joker, hoaxer, pretender, hustler *(U.S. informal)*, con man *(informal)*, impostor, fraudster, swindler, practical joker, grifter *(slang, chiefly U.S. & Canad.)*, chiseller *(informal)*, rorter *(Austral. slang)*, rogue trader • *The veteran trickster had made a fortune in his 40 years of fraud.*

tricky 1 = **difficult**, sensitive, complicated, delicate, risky, sticky *(informal)*, hairy *(informal)*, problematic, thorny, touch-and-go, knotty, dicey *(informal)*, ticklish • *This could be a very tricky problem.*
OPPOSITES: clear, easy, simple
2 = **crafty**, scheming, subtle, cunning, slippery, sly, deceptive, devious, wily, artful, foxy, deceitful • *They could encounter some tricky political manoeuvring.*
OPPOSITES: open, direct, genuine

trifle AS A NOUN 1 = **knick-knack**, nothing, toy, plaything, bauble, triviality, bagatelle, gewgaw • *He had no money to spare on trifles.*
2 *often plural* = **unimportant matter** *or* **thing**, trivia, technicality, minutiae • *He doesn't let such trifles worry him.*
3 = **very small amount**, pittance, piddling amount *(informal)*, peanuts *(informal)* • *He begged hard for a trifle to pay for a room.*
▸ IN PHRASES: **a trifle** = **slightly**, a little, a bit, somewhat, rather, moderately, marginally, a shade, to some degree, on a small scale, to some extent *or* degree • *He found both locations just a trifle disappointing.*

QUOTATIONS
a snapper-up of unconsidered trifles
[William Shakespeare *The Winter's Tale*]

trifle with = **toy**, play, flirt, mess about, dally, wanton, play fast and loose *(informal)*, coquet, amuse yourself, palter • *'Don't trifle with me,' was my attitude.*

trifling = **insignificant**, small, tiny, empty, slight, silly, shallow, petty, idle, trivial, worthless, negligible, unimportant, frivolous, paltry, minuscule, puny, measly, piddling *(informal)*, inconsiderable, valueless, nickel-and-dime *(U.S. slang)*, footling *(informal)* • *The guests had each paid £250, no trifling sum.*
OPPOSITES: large, major, significant

trigger 1 = **bring about**, start, cause, produce, generate, prompt, provoke, set off, activate, give rise to, elicit, spark off, set in motion • *the incident which triggered the outbreak of the First World War*
OPPOSITES: stop, bar, prevent
2 = **set off**, trip, activate, set going • *The thieves must have triggered the alarm.*

trim AS AN ADJECTIVE 1 = **neat**, nice, smart, compact, tidy, orderly, spruce, dapper, natty *(informal)*, well-groomed, well-ordered, well turned-out, shipshape, spick-and-span, trig *(archaic or dialect)*, soigné *or* soignée • *The neighbours' gardens were trim and neat.*
OPPOSITES: disorderly, messy, untidy
2 = **slender**, fit, slim, sleek, streamlined, shapely, svelte, willowy, lissom • *The driver was a trim young woman of about thirty.*
3 = **smart**, sharp *(informal)*, elegant, crisp, stylish, chic, spruce, dapper, natty *(informal)*, spiffy *(informal)*, schmick *(Austral. informal)* • *with his trim suit and his aura of good living*
▸ AS A VERB 1 = **cut**, crop, clip, dock, shave, barber, tidy, prune, shear, pare, lop, even up, neaten • *My friend trims my hair every eight weeks.*
2 = **decorate**, dress, array, adorn, embroider, garnish, ornament, embellish, deck out, bedeck, beautify, trick out, edge, border, pipe, fringe, hem • *jackets trimmed with crocheted flowers*
3 = **cut back**, reduce, decrease, cut down, prune, curtail,

scale down, slim down, pare down, make reductions in, make cutbacks in, retrench on, dock • *They looked at ways they could trim these costs.*

4 = **shorten**, condense, abbreviate, abridge, telescope, truncate • *The document has been trimmed as it passes through different hands.*

5 *often with* **off** = **remove**, cut (off), take off, cut back, chop off, shave off, hack off, lop off, nip off • *First cut off about half the roots and trim the longest leaves.*

▸ **AS A NOUN** 1 = **decoration**, edging, border, piping, trimming, fringe, garnish, frill, embellishment, adornment, ornamentation • *a white satin scarf with black trim*

2 = **condition**, form, health, shape *(informal)*, repair, fitness, wellness, order, fettle • *He is already getting in trim for the big day.*

3 = **cut**, crop, trimming, clipping, shave, pruning, shearing, tidying up • *His hair needed a trim.*

trimming **AS A NOUN** = **decoration**, edging, border, piping, fringe, garnish, braid, frill, festoon, embellishment, adornment, ornamentation • *the lace trimming on her satin nightgown*

▸ **AS A PLURAL NOUN** 1 = **extras**, accessories, garnish, ornaments, accompaniments, frills, trappings, paraphernalia, appurtenances • *a Thanksgiving dinner of turkey and all the trimmings*

2 = **clippings**, ends, cuttings, shavings, brash, parings • *Use any pastry trimmings to decorate the apples.*

trinity = **threesome**, triple, trio, trilogy, triplet, triad, triumvirate, triptych, trine, triune • *The hotel is owned by a trinity of Japanese corporations.*

trinket = **ornament**, bauble, knick-knack, piece of bric-a-brac, nothing, toy, trifle, bagatelle, gimcrack, gewgaw, bibelot, kickshaw • *She sold trinkets to tourists.*

trio = **threesome**, triple, trinity, trilogy, triplet, triad, triumvirate, triptych, trine, triune • *classy songs from a Texas trio*

trip **AS A NOUN** 1 = **journey**, outing, excursion, day out, run, drive, travel, tour, spin *(informal)*, expedition, voyage, ramble, foray, jaunt, errand, junket *(informal)*, awayday • *On the Thursday we went out on a day trip.*

2 = **stumble**, fall, slip, blunder, false move, misstep, false step • *Slips, trips and falls were monitored using a daily calendar.*

▸ **AS A VERB** 1 *often with* **up** = **stumble**, fall, fall over, slip, tumble, topple, stagger, misstep, lose your balance, make a false move, lose your footing, take a spill • *She tripped and broke her hip.*

2 = **skip**, dance, spring, hop, caper, flit, frisk, gambol, tread lightly • *They tripped along without a care in the world.*

3 = **take drugs**, get high *(informal)*, get stoned *(slang)*, get loved-up *(informal)*, get off your face *(slang)*, turn on *(slang)* • *One night I was tripping on acid.*

4 = **activate**, turn on, flip, release, pull, throw, engage, set off, switch on • *He set the timer, then tripped the switch.*

▸ **IN PHRASES: trip someone up** = **catch out**, trap, confuse, unsettle, disconcert, throw you off, wrongfoot, put you off your stride • *Your own lies will trip you up.*

trip up = **blunder**, make a mistake, slip up *(informal)*, make a faux pas, go wrong, lapse, boob *(Brit. slang)*, err, miscalculate • *He has tripped up in Parliament before.*

tripe = **nonsense**, rot, trash, twaddle, balls *(taboo slang)*, bull *(slang)*, rubbish, shit *(taboo slang)*, pants *(slang)*, crap *(slang)*, garbage *(informal)*, bullshit *(taboo slang)*, hot air *(informal)*, tosh *(slang, chiefly Brit.)*, bollocks *(Brit. taboo slang)*, pap, cobblers *(Brit. taboo slang)*, bilge *(informal)*, drivel, guff *(slang)*, moonshine, claptrap *(informal)*, hogwash, hokum *(slang, chiefly U.S. & Canad.)*, piffle *(informal)*, poppycock *(informal)*, inanity, balderdash, bosh *(informal)*, eyewash *(informal)*, trumpery, tommyrot, foolish talk, horsefeathers *(U.S. slang)*, bunkum *or* buncombe *(chiefly U.S.)*, bizzo *(Austral. slang)*, bull's wool *(Austral. & N.Z. slang)* • *I've never heard such a load of tripe in all my life.*

triple **AS AN ADJECTIVE** 1 = **treble**, three times, three times as much as • *The kitchen is triple the size it used to be*

2 = **three-way**, threefold, tripartite • *Germany, Austria and Italy formed the Triple Alliance.*

▸ **AS A VERB** = **treble**, triplicate, increase threefold • *I got a great new job and my salary tripled.*

triplet = **threesome**, triple, trio, trinity, trilogy, triad, triumvirate, trine, triune • *Goldsmith's triplet of rural virtues*

tripper = **tourist**, holiday-maker, sightseer, excursionist, journeyer, voyager • *when the shops shut and the trippers go home*

trite = **unoriginal**, worn, common, stock, ordinary, tired, routine, dull, stereotyped, hack, pedestrian, commonplace, stale, banal, corny *(slang)*, run-of-the-mill, threadbare, clichéd, uninspired, hackneyed, bromidic • *The movie is teeming with trite and obvious ideas.*

OPPOSITES: new, interesting, original

triumph **AS A NOUN** 1 = **success**, victory, accomplishment, mastery, hit *(informal)*, achievement, smash *(informal)*, coup, belter *(slang)*, sensation, feat, conquest, attainment, smash hit *(informal)*, tour de force *(French)*, walkover *(informal)*, feather in your cap, smasheroo *(slang)* • *Cataract operations are a triumph of modern surgery.*

OPPOSITES: defeat, failure, disaster

2 = **joy**, pride, happiness, rejoicing, elation, jubilation, exultation • *Her sense of triumph was short-lived.*

▸ **AS A VERB** 1 *often with* **over** = **succeed**, win, overcome, prevail, best, dominate, overwhelm, thrive, flourish, subdue, prosper, get the better of, vanquish, come out on top *(informal)*, carry the day, take the honours • *a symbol of good triumphing over evil*

OPPOSITES: lose, fall, fail

2 = **rejoice**, celebrate, glory, revel, swagger, drool, gloat, exult, jubilate, crow • *the euphoria, the sense of triumphing together as a nation*

triumphant 1 = **victorious**, winning, successful, dominant, conquering, undefeated • *the triumphant team*

OPPOSITES: beaten, defeated, embarrassed

2 = **celebratory**, rejoicing, jubilant, triumphal, proud, glorious, swaggering, elated, exultant, boastful, cock-a-hoop • *his triumphant return home*

trivia = **minutiae**, details, trifles, trivialities, petty details • *They talked about such trivia as their favourite fast food.*

OPPOSITES: basics, essentials, core

trivial = **unimportant**, little, small, minor, slight, everyday, petty, meaningless, commonplace, worthless, trifling, insignificant, negligible, frivolous, paltry, incidental, puny, inconsequential, trite, inconsiderable, valueless, nickel-and-dime *(U.S. slang)*, wanky *(taboo slang)*, chickenshit *(U.S. slang)* • *I don't like to visit the doctor just for something trivial.*

OPPOSITES: important, serious, significant

QUOTATIONS

What mighty contests rise from trivial things

[Alexander Pope *The Rape of the Lock*]

triviality 1 = **insignificance**, frivolity, smallness, pettiness, worthlessness, meaninglessness, unimportance, littleness, slightness, triteness, paltriness, inconsequentiality, valuelessness, negligibility, much ado about nothing • *news items of quite astonishing triviality*

OPPOSITES: value, worth, importance

2 = **trifle**, nothing, detail, technicality, petty detail, no big thing, no great matter • *He accused me of making a great fuss about trivialities.*

OPPOSITES: essential, rudiment

PROVERBS

Little things please little minds

trivialize = **undervalue**, underestimate, play down, minimize, scoff at, belittle, laugh off, make light of, underplay • *They continue to trivialize the world's environmental problems.*

trollop = slut, prostitute, tart *(informal)*, whore, slag *(Brit. slang)*, wanton, working girl *(facetious slang)*, harlot, hussy, streetwalker, loose woman, fallen woman, scrubber *(Brit. & Austral. slang)*, strumpet, floozy *(slang)*, slattern, hornbag *(Austral. slang)* • *He behaved towards her as though she was a trollop.*

troop AS A NOUN 1 = **group**, company, team, body, unit, band, crowd, pack, squad, gathering, crew *(informal)*, drove, gang, bunch *(informal)*, flock, herd, contingent, swarm, horde, multitude, throng, posse *(informal)*, bevy, assemblage • *She was aware of a little troop of travellers watching them.*
2 *plural* = **soldiers**, men, armed forces, servicemen, fighting men, military, army, soldiery • *the deployment of more than 35,000 troops from a dozen countries*
▸ AS A VERB 1 = **plod**, trail, tramp, trudge, traipse, drag yourself, schlep *(U.S. informal)* • *They all trooped back to the house for a rest.*
2 = **flock**, march, crowd, stream, parade, swarm, throng, traipse *(informal)* • *The VIPs trooped into the hall and sat down.*

trophy 1 = **prize**, cup, award, bays, laurels • *They could win a trophy this year.*
2 = **souvenir**, spoils, relic, memento, booty, keepsake • *lines of stuffed animal heads, trophies of his hunting hobby*

tropical = hot, stifling, lush, steamy, humid, torrid, sultry, sweltering • *He was unused to the tropical climate.*
OPPOSITES: cold, cool, freezing

trot AS A VERB = **run**, jog, scamper, lope, go briskly, canter • *I trotted down the steps and out to the shed.*
▸ AS A NOUN = **run**, jog, lope, brisk pace, canter • *He walked briskly, but without breaking into a trot.*
▸ IN PHRASES: **on the trot = one after the other**, in a row, in succession, without break, without interruption, consecutively • *She lost five games on the trot.*
trot something out = repeat, relate, exhibit, bring up, reiterate, recite, come out with, bring forward, drag up • *Was it really necessary to trot out the same old stereotypes?*

troubadour = minstrel, singer, poet, balladeer, lyric poet, jongleur • *melodies like a medieval troubadour's laments*

trouble AS A NOUN 1 = **bother**, problems, concern, worry, stress, difficulty *(informal)*, anxiety, distress, grief *(Brit. & S. African)*, irritation, hassle *(informal)*, strife, inconvenience, unease, disquiet, annoyance, agitation, commotion, unpleasantness, vexation • *You've caused a lot of trouble.*
2 = **shortcoming**, problem, failing, fault, weakness, defect, imperfection, weak point • *Your trouble is that you can't take the rejection.*
3 *often plural* = **distress**, problem, suffering, worry, pain, anxiety, grief, torment, hardship, sorrow, woe, irritation, hassle *(informal)*, misfortune, heartache, disquiet, annoyance, agitation, tribulation, bummer *(slang)*, vexation • *She tells me her troubles. I tell her mine.*
OPPOSITES: pleasure, comfort, happiness
4 = **ailment**, disease, failure, complaint, upset, illness, disorder, disability, defect, malfunction • *He had never before had any heart trouble.*
5 = **disorder**, fighting, row, conflict, bother, grief *(Brit. & S. African)*, unrest, disturbance, to-do *(informal)*, discontent, dissatisfaction, furore, uproar, scuffling, discord, fracas, commotion, rumpus, breach of the peace, tumult, affray *(Law)*, brouhaha, ructions, hullabaloo *(informal)*, kerfuffle *(Brit. informal)*, hoo-ha *(informal)*, biffo *(Austral. slang)*, boilover *(Austral.)* • *Riot police are being deployed to prevent any trouble.*
OPPOSITES: peace, agreement, unity
6 = **problem**, bother, concern, pest, irritation, hassle *(informal)*, nuisance, inconvenience, irritant, cause of annoyance • *He's no trouble at all, but his brother is rude and selfish.*
7 = **effort**, work, thought, care, labour, struggle, pains, bother, grief *(Brit. & S. African)*, hassle *(informal)*, inconvenience, exertion • *You've saved us a lot of trouble by helping.*
OPPOSITES: facility, ease, convenience
8 = **difficulty**, hot water *(informal)*, predicament, deep water *(informal)*, spot *(informal)*, danger, mess, dilemma, scrape *(informal)*, pickle *(informal)*, dire straits, tight spot • *a charity that helps women in trouble with the law*
9 = **malfunction**, failure, fault, breakdown, dysfunction • *The multi-million-pound jet developed engine trouble.*
▸ AS A VERB 1 = **bother**, worry, upset, disturb, distress, annoy, plague, grieve, torment, harass, hassle *(informal)*, afflict, pain, fret, agitate, sadden, perplex, disconcert, disquiet, pester, vex, perturb, faze, give someone grief *(Brit. & S. African)*, discompose, put *or* get someone's back up, hack you off *(informal)* • *Is anything troubling you?*
OPPOSITES: please, calm, relieve
2 = **afflict**, hurt, bother, cause discomfort to, pain, grieve • *The ulcer had been troubling her for several years.*
3 = **inconvenience**, disturb, burden, put out, impose upon, discommode, incommode • *'Good morning. I'm sorry to trouble you.'*
OPPOSITES: relieve
4 = **take pains**, take the time, make an effort, go to the effort of, exert yourself • *He yawns, not troubling to cover his mouth.*
OPPOSITES: avoid, dodge

QUOTATIONS
Man is born unto trouble
[*Bible: Job*]
Double, double, toil and trouble
[William Shakespeare *Macbeth*]
PROVERBS
Never trouble trouble till trouble troubles you

troubled 1 = **anxious**, concerned, worried, upset, bothered, disturbed, distressed, dismayed, uneasy, unsettled, agitated, disconcerted, apprehensive, perturbed, ill at ease, discomposed • *She sounded deeply troubled.*
2 = **difficult**, unsettled, problematic, stressful, hard, dark, tough • *There is much we can do to help this troubled country.*

troublemaker = mischief-maker, firebrand, instigator, agitator, bad apple *(U.S. informal)*, rabble-rouser, agent provocateur *(French)*, stirrer *(informal)*, incendiary, rotten apple *(Brit. informal)*, meddler, stormy petrel • *powers to expel suspected troublemakers*
OPPOSITES: appeaser, arbitrator, peace-maker

troublesome 1 = **bothersome**, trying, taxing, demanding, difficult, worrying, upsetting, annoying, irritating, tricky, harassing, oppressive, arduous, tiresome, inconvenient, laborious, burdensome, hard, worrisome, irksome, wearisome, vexatious, importunate, pestilential, plaguy *(informal)* • *The economy has become a troublesome problem for the party.*
OPPOSITES: easy, simple, calming
2 = **disorderly**, violent, turbulent, rebellious, unruly, rowdy, recalcitrant, undisciplined, uncooperative, refractory, insubordinate • *Parents may find that a troublesome teenager becomes unmanageable.*
OPPOSITES: disciplined, obedient, well-behaved

trough = manger, crib, water trough • *The old stone cattle trough still sits by the entrance.*

trounce = defeat someone heavily *or* **utterly**, beat, thrash, slaughter *(informal)*, stuff *(slang)*, tank *(slang)*, hammer *(informal)*, crush, overwhelm, lick *(informal)*, paste *(slang)*, rout, walk over *(informal)*, clobber *(slang)*, run rings around *(informal)*, wipe the floor with *(informal)*, make mincemeat of, blow someone out of the water *(slang)*, give someone a hiding *(informal)*, drub, beat someone hollow

(*Brit. informal*), give someone a pasting (*slang*) • *Australia trounced France by sixty points to four.*

troupe = **company**, group, band, cast, ensemble • *a troupe of travelling actors*

trouper = **performer**, player, actor, theatrical, entertainer, artiste, thespian • *Like the old trouper he is, he timed his entrance perfectly.*

trousers = **slacks**, pants (*U.S.*), strides (*chiefly Austral. informal*), kecks (*Brit. informal*) • *He was smartly dressed in a shirt, dark trousers and boots.*
▷ *See panel* **Trousers and shorts**

truancy = **absence**, shirking, skiving (*Brit. slang*), malingering, absence without leave • *Schools need to reduce levels of truancy.*

truant AS A NOUN = **absentee**, skiver (*Brit. slang*), shirker, dodger, runaway, delinquent, deserter, straggler, malingerer • *She became a truant at the age of ten.*
▸ AS AN ADJECTIVE = **absent**, missing, skiving (*Brit. slang*), absent without leave, A.W.O.L. • *Neither the parents nor the truant students showed up at court.*
▸ AS A VERB = **absent yourself**, play truant, skive (*Brit. slang*), bunk off (*slang*), desert, run away, dodge, wag (*dialect*), go missing, shirk, malinger, bob off (*Brit. slang*) • *In his fourth year he was truanting regularly.*
▸ IN PHRASES: **play truant** = **stay away from school**, be absent, truant, skive off (*Brit. informal*), bunk off (*Brit. informal*), not go to school • *She was in trouble over playing truant.*

truce = **ceasefire**, break, stay, rest, peace, treaty, interval, moratorium, respite, lull, cessation, let-up (*informal*), armistice, intermission, cessation of hostilities • *The fighting has given way to an uneasy truce.*

truck 1 = **lorry**, juggernaut, HGV (*Brit.*), heavy goods vehicle, pick-up, van, dumper, pick-up truck, articulated lorry, dumper truck, pantechnicon (*old-fashioned*), tipper truck, bakkie (*S. African*) • *Now and then they heard the roar of a heavy truck.*
2 = **dealings**, business, association, contact, relations, communication, traffic, connection, transactions, intercourse, trade • *He would have no truck with deceit.*

truculent = **hostile**, defiant, belligerent, bad-tempered, cross, violent, aggressive, fierce, contentious, combative, sullen, scrappy (*informal*), antagonistic, pugnacious, ill-tempered, bellicose, obstreperous, itching *or* spoiling for a fight (*informal*), aggers (*Austral. slang*), arsey (*Brit., Austral. & N.Z. slang*) • *She turned from truculent tot to sullen teenager.*
OPPOSITES: civil, gentle, amiable

trudge AS A VERB = **plod**, trek, tramp, traipse (*informal*), march, stump, hike, clump, lumber, slog, drag yourself, yomp, walk heavily, footslog • *We had to trudge up the track back to the station.*
▸ AS A NOUN = **tramp**, march, haul, trek, hike, slog, traipse (*informal*), yomp, footslog • *We were reluctant to start the long trudge home.*

true AS AN ADJECTIVE 1 = **correct**, right, accurate, exact, precise, valid, legitimate, factual, truthful, veritable, bona fide, veracious • *Everything I had heard about him was true.*
OPPOSITES: made-up, false, pretended
2 = **actual**, real, natural, pure, genuine, proper, authentic, dinkum (*Austral. & N.Z. informal*) • *I allowed myself to acknowledge my true feelings.*
3 = **faithful**, loyal, devoted, dedicated, firm, fast, constant, pure, steady, reliable, upright, sincere, honourable, honest, staunch, trustworthy, trusty, dutiful, true-blue, unswerving • *He was always true to his wife.*
OPPOSITES: unfaithful, false, untrue
4 = **exact**, perfect, correct, accurate, proper, precise, spot-on (*Brit. informal*), on target, unerring • *The score is usually a true reflection of events on the pitch.*
OPPOSITES: incorrect, inaccurate, awry
5 = **rightful**, legal, recognized, valid, legitimate, authorized, lawful, bona fide, de jure (*Law*) • *He was found to be the true owner of the suitcase.*
6 = **sincere**, real, genuine, unaffected, heartfelt, from the heart, unfeigned, unpretended • *God's anger could only be averted by true repentance.*
▸ AS AN ADVERB 1 = **truthfully**, honestly, veritably, veraciously, rightly • *Does the lad speak true?*
2 = **precisely**, accurately, on target, perfectly, correctly, properly, unerringly • *Most of the bullets hit true.*
▸ IN PHRASES: **come true** = **happen**, be realized, come to pass, become reality, occur, be granted • *Many of his predictions are coming true.*

PROVERBS
Many a true word is spoken in jest

true-blue = **staunch**, confirmed, constant, devoted, dedicated, loyal, faithful, orthodox, uncompromising, trusty, unwavering, dyed-in-the-wool • *He is true-blue when it comes to football.*

truism = **cliché**, commonplace, platitude, axiom, stock phrase, trite saying • *the truism that nothing succeeds like success*

truly 1 = **genuinely**, really, correctly, truthfully, rightly, in fact, precisely, exactly, legitimately, accurately, in reality, in truth, beyond doubt, without a doubt, authentically, beyond question, factually, in actuality, veritably, veraciously • *a truly democratic system*
OPPOSITES: falsely, mistakenly, incorrectly
2 = **really**, very, greatly, indeed, seriously (*informal*), extremely, to be sure, exceptionally, verily • *a truly splendid man*
3 = **faithfully**, firmly, constantly, steadily, honestly, sincerely, staunchly, dutifully, loyally, honourably, devotedly, with all your heart, with dedication, with devotion, confirmedly • *He truly loved his children.*
4 = **sincerely**, really, genuinely, honestly, surely, actually, certainly, in fact, indeed, absolutely, undoubtedly, positively, in reality, categorically, without a doubt, assuredly, verily, in actuality • *I truly never minded caring for him.*

trump AS A VERB = **outdo**, top, cap, surpass, score points off, excel • *The Socialists tried to trump this with their slogan.*
▸ IN PHRASES: **trump something up** = **invent**, create, make up, manufacture, fake, contrive, fabricate, concoct,

t

TROUSERS AND SHORTS

bell-bottoms
Bermuda shorts
bloomers
breeches
buckskins
Capri pants
cargo pants
chinos
churidars
combats
corduroys
culottes
cycling shorts
denims
drainpipes
dungarees
flannels
flares
galligaskins
hipsters *or* (*U.S.*) hip-huggers
hot pants
jeans
jodhpurs
Kachera
knickerbockers
lederhosen
leggings
Levis (*trademark*)
loon pants
overalls
Oxford bags
palazzo pants
pantaloons
pedal pushers
plus fours
pyjamas
riding breeches
salopettes
shalwar
ski pants
slacks
slops
smallclothes
spatterdashes
stovepipes
toreador pants
trews
trouse (*Brit.*)
trunk hose

cook up *(informal)* • *He insists that charges against him have been trumped up.*

trumped up = **invented**, made-up, manufactured, false, fake, contrived, untrue, fabricated, concocted, falsified, cooked-up *(informal)*, phoney *or* phony *(informal)* • *He was put on trial facing trumped up spy charges.*

OPPOSITES: real, sound, genuine

trumpet AS A NOUN 1 = **horn**, clarion, bugle • *Picking up his trumpet, he gave it a quick blow.*

2 = **roar**, call, cry, bay, bellow • *One of the elephants gave a trumpet.*

▸ AS A VERB = **proclaim**, advertise, extol, tout *(informal)*, announce, publish, broadcast, crack up *(informal)*, sound loudly, shout from the rooftops, noise abroad • *He is trumpeted as the dance talent of his generation.*

OPPOSITES: hide, conceal, keep secret

▸ IN PHRASES: **blow your own trumpet** = **boast**, crow, brag, vaunt, sing your own praises, big yourself up *(slang, chiefly Caribbean)* • *The cameramen have good reason to blow their own trumpets.*

truncate = **shorten**, cut, crop, trim, clip, dock, prune, curtail, cut short, pare, lop, abbreviate • *I'm going to truncate the time I spend at work.*

OPPOSITES: extend, stretch, lengthen

truncheon = **club**, staff, stick, baton, cudgel, mere *(N.Z.)*, patu *(N.Z.)* • *He swung his truncheon at him, knocking him to the ground.*

trunk 1 = **stem**, stock, stalk, bole • *toadstools growing on fallen tree trunks*

2 = **chest**, case, box, crate, bin, suitcase, locker, coffer, casket, portmanteau, kist *(Scot. & Northern English dialect)* • *He had left most of his records in a trunk in the attic.*

3 = **body**, torso • *Simultaneously, raise your trunk 6 inches above the ground.*

4 = **snout**, nose, proboscis • *It could exert the suction power of an elephant's trunk.*

truss AS A VERB *often with* **up** = **tie**, secure, bind, strap, fasten, tether, pinion, make fast • *She trussed him with the bandage and gagged his mouth.*

▸ AS A NOUN 1 = **support**, pad, bandage • *For a hernia he introduced the simple solution of a truss.*

2 = **joist**, support, stay, shore, beam, prop, brace, strut, buttress, stanchion • *the bridge's arched, lightweight steel truss*

trust AS A NOUN 1 = **confidence**, credit, belief, faith, expectation, conviction, assurance, certainty, reliance, credence, certitude • *There's a feeling of warmth and trust here.*

OPPOSITES: fear, doubt, distrust

2 = **responsibility**, duty, obligation • *She held a position of trust, which was generously paid.*

3 = **custody**, care, guard, protection, guardianship, safekeeping, trusteeship • *The British Library holds its collection in trust for the nation.*

▸ RELATED ADJECTIVE: fiducial

▸ AS A VERB 1 = **believe in**, have faith in, depend on, count on, bank on, lean on, rely upon, swear by, take at face value, take as gospel, place reliance on, place your trust in, pin your faith on, place *or* have confidence in • *'I trust you completely,' he said.*

OPPOSITES: doubt, suspect, distrust

2 = **entrust**, commit, assign, confide, consign, put into the hands of, allow to look after, hand over, turn over, sign over, delegate • *I'd been willing to trust my life to him.* • *savers who are hesitant of trusting their money to the vagaries of the stock market*

3 = **expect**, believe, hope, suppose, assume, guess *(informal)*, take it, presume, surmise, think likely • *We trust that they are considering our suggestion.*

trustee = **administrator**, agent, keeper, custodian, executor, fiduciary *(Law)*, depository, executrix, steward • *Astonishingly, the trustees don't know where the money is either.*

trustful *or* **trusting** = **unsuspecting**, simple, innocent, optimistic, naive, confiding, gullible, unwary, unguarded, credulous, unsuspicious • *She has an open, trusting nature.*

OPPOSITES: guarded, cautious, suspicious

trustworthy = **dependable**, responsible, principled, mature, sensible, reliable, ethical, upright, true, honourable, honest, staunch, righteous, reputable, truthful, trusty, steadfast, level-headed, to be trusted • *He is a trustworthy, level-headed teacher.*

OPPOSITES: irresponsible, unreliable, untrustworthy

trusty = **reliable**, dependable, trustworthy, responsible, solid, strong, firm, true, steady, faithful, straightforward, upright, honest, staunch • *a trusty member of the crew*

OPPOSITES: irresponsible, unreliable, dishonest

truth AS A NOUN 1 = **reality**, fact(s), real life, actuality • *Is it possible to separate truth from fiction?*

OPPOSITES: unreality, lie, legend

2 = **truthfulness**, fact, accuracy, honesty, precision, validity, legitimacy, authenticity, correctness, sincerity, verity, candour, veracity, rightness, genuineness, exactness, factuality, factualness • *There is no truth in this story.*

OPPOSITES: error, inaccuracy, falsity

3 = **fact**, law, reality, certainty, maxim, verity, axiom, truism, proven principle • *It's a universal truth that we all die eventually.*

4 = **the fact of the matter**, what really happened, gospel truth, God's truth, the honest truth, the case • *I must tell you the truth about this.*

5 = **honesty**, principle, honour, virtue, integrity, goodness, righteousness, candour, frankness, probity, rectitude, incorruptibility, uprightness • *His mission is to uphold truth, justice and the American way.*

OPPOSITES: deception, deceit, dishonesty

▸ IN PHRASES: **in truth** = **actually**, really, in fact, in reality, as a matter of fact, to tell the truth, in actual fact, in point of fact, if truth be told • *In truth, we were both unhappy.*

▸ RELATED ADJECTIVES: veritable, veracious

QUOTATIONS

Truth sits upon the lips of dying men
[Matthew Arnold *Sohrab and Rustum*]

Beauty and Truth, though never found, are worthy to be sought
[Robert Williams Buchanan *To David in Heaven*]

'Beauty is truth, truth beauty,' – that is all
Ye know on earth, and all ye need to know
That is all
[John Keats *Ode on a Grecian Urn*]

What is truth? said jesting Pilate; and would not stay for an answer
[Francis Bacon *Essays*]

Truth can never be told so as to be understood, and not believed
[William Blake *Proverbs of Hell*]

Truth never hurts the teller
[Robert Browning *Fifine at the Fair*]

Truth is within ourselves
[Robert Browning *Paracelsus*]

'Tis strange – but true; for truth is always strange;
Stranger than fiction
[Lord Byron *Don Juan*]

I maintain that Truth is a pathless land, and you cannot approach it by any path whatsoever, by any religion, by any sect
[Jiddu Krishnamurti *speech*]

It is the customary fate of new truths to begin as heresies and to end as superstitions
[T.H. Huxley *Science and Culture*]

The first casualty when war comes is truth
[Philander Chase Johnson *Shooting Stars*]

There was things that he stretched, but mainly he told the truth
[Mark Twain *The Adventures of Huckleberry Finn*]
The truth is rarely pure, and never simple
[Oscar Wilde *The Importance of Being Earnest*]
The truth is a terrible weapon of aggression. It is possible to lie, and even to murder, for the truth
[Alfred Adler *The Problem of Neurosis*]
The truth which makes men free is for the most part the truth which men prefer not to hear
[Herbert Agar *A Time for Greatness*]
When you have eliminated the impossible, whatever remains, however improbable, must be the truth
[Sir Arthur Conan Doyle *The Sign of Four*]
The truth shall make you free
[*Bible: St. John*]
When you want to fool the world, tell the truth
[Otto von Bismarck]
It is always the best policy to speak the truth, unless of course you are an exceptionally good liar
[Jerome K. Jerome]
Irrationally held truths may be more harmful than reasoned errors
[T.H. Huxley *Science and Culture*]
Truth is the cry of all, but the game of the few
[Bishop George Berkeley *Siris*]
Truth lies within a little and certain compass, but error is immense
[Henry St. John, 1st Viscount Bolingbroke *Reflections upon Exile*]

PROVERBS
There is truth in wine (in vino veritas)

truthful 1 = **honest**, frank, candid, upfront *(informal)*, true, straight, reliable, faithful, straightforward, sincere, forthright, trustworthy, plain-spoken, veracious • *We are all fairly truthful about our personal lives.*
OPPOSITES: lying, false, dishonest
2 = **true**, correct, accurate, exact, realistic, precise, literal, veritable, naturalistic • *They had not given a truthful account of what actually happened.*
OPPOSITES: made-up, false, untrue

truthfulness = **honesty**, truth, openness, sincerity, candour, frankness, veracity, trustworthiness, genuineness, forthrightness, candidness, lack of deceit • *I can say, with absolute truthfulness, that I did not injure her.*

try AS A VERB 1 = **attempt**, seek, aim, undertake, essay, strive, struggle, endeavour, have a go, go for it *(informal)*, make an effort, have a shot *(informal)*, have a crack *(informal)*, bend over backwards *(informal)*, do your best, go for broke *(slang)*, make an attempt, move heaven and earth, bust a gut *(informal)*, give it your best shot *(informal)*, have a stab *(informal)*, break your neck *(informal)*, exert yourself, make an all-out effort *(informal)*, knock yourself out *(informal)*, have a whack *(informal)*, do your damnedest *(informal)*, give it your all *(informal)*, rupture yourself *(informal)* • *He secretly tried to block her advancement in the Party.*
2 = **experiment with**, try out, put to the test, test, taste, examine, investigate, sample, evaluate, check out, inspect, appraise • *It's best not to try a new recipe on such an important occasion.*
3 = **judge**, hear, consider, examine, adjudicate, adjudge, pass judgement on • *The case was tried in Tampa, a changed venue with an all-white jury.*
4 = **tax**, test, trouble, pain, stress, upset, tire, strain, drain, exhaust, annoy, plague, irritate, weary, afflict, sap, inconvenience, wear out, vex, irk, make demands on, give someone grief *(Brit. & S. African)* • *She really tried my patience.*
▸ **AS A NOUN** = **attempt**, go *(informal)*, shot *(informal)*, effort, crack *(informal)*, essay, stab *(informal)*, bash *(informal)*, endeavour, whack *(informal)* • *I didn't really expect anything, but it was worth a try.*
▸ **IN PHRASES: try something out** = **test**, experiment with, appraise, put to the test, taste, sample, evaluate, check out, inspect, put into practice • *She knew I wanted to try the boat out at the weekend.*

trying = **annoying**, hard, taxing, difficult, tough, upsetting, irritating, fatiguing, stressful, aggravating *(informal)*, troublesome, exasperating, arduous, tiresome, vexing, irksome, wearisome, bothersome • *The whole business has been very trying.*
OPPOSITES: easy, simple, straightforward

tsar *or* **czar** 1 = **ruler**, leader, emperor, sovereign, tyrant, despot, overlord, autocrat • *Princess Anne is related to the Tsar of Russia.*
2 = **head**, chief, boss, big cheese *(informal)*, baas *(S. African)*, head honcho *(informal)*, sherang *(Austral. & N.Z.)* • *He was appointed 'drugs tsar' by Bill Clinton.*

tubby = **fat**, overweight, plump, stout, chubby, obese, portly, roly-poly, podgy, corpulent, paunchy • *He looks tubby and in need of some exercise.*

tuberculosis = **TB**, consumption *(literary)* • *She spent two years in a sanatorium recovering from tuberculosis.*

tubular = **cylindrical**, tube-like, pipe-like, tubiform • *a table with chrome tubular legs*

tuck AS A VERB 1 = **push**, stick, stuff, slip, ease, insert, pop *(informal)* • *He tried to tuck his shirt inside his trousers.*
2 = **pleat**, gather, fold, ruffle • *Pin and tuck back pieces together with right sides facing.*
3 *sometimes with* **away** = **hide**, store, conceal, stash *(informal)*, secrete, stow • *She folded the letter and tucked it behind a book.*
▸ **AS A NOUN** 1 = **food**, eats *(slang)*, tack *(informal)*, scoff *(slang)*, grub *(slang)*, kai *(N.Z. informal)*, nosh *(slang)*, victuals, comestibles, nosebag *(slang)*, vittles *(obsolete or dialect)* • *The wags from the rival house were ready to snaffle his tuck.*
2 = **fold**, gather, pleat, pinch • *a tapered tuck used to take in fullness and control shape in a garment*
▸ **IN PHRASES: tuck in** = **eat up**, get stuck in *(informal)*, eat heartily, fall to, chow down *(slang)* • *Tuck in, it's the last hot food you'll get for a while.*
tuck into something = **devour**, dig into *(informal)*, get stuck into *(informal)*, shift *(Brit. informal)*, consume, hoover *(informal)*, scoff (down) *(informal)*, put away *(informal)*, gobble up, polish off *(informal)*, wolf down, get round the outside of *(informal)*, get your laughing gear round *(informal)* • *She tucked into a breakfast of bacon and eggs.*
tuck someone in = **make snug**, wrap up, put to bed, bed down, swaddle • *I read her a story and tucked her in.*

tuft = **clump**, bunch, shock, collection, knot, cluster, tussock, topknot • *He had a small tuft of hair on his chin.*

tug AS A VERB 1 = **pull**, drag, pluck, jerk, yank, wrench, lug • *A little boy tugged at her sleeve excitedly.*
2 = **drag**, pull, haul, tow, lug, heave, draw • *She tugged him along by his arm.*
▸ **AS A NOUN** = **pull**, jerk, yank, wrench, drag, haul, tow, traction, heave • *My head was snapped backwards by a tug on my air hose.*

tuition = **training**, schooling, education, teaching, lessons, instruction, tutoring, tutelage • *The courses will give the beginner personal tuition.*

tumble AS A VERB 1 = **fall**, drop, topple, plummet, roll, pitch, toss, stumble, flop, trip up, fall head over heels, fall headlong, fall end over end • *The dog had tumbled down the cliff.*
2 = **fall steeply** *or* **sharply**, fall, decline, crash *(informal)*, slide, slump, decrease, plummet, nosedive, take a dive, drop rapidly • *House prices have tumbled by almost 30 per cent.*
3 = **cascade**, fall, flow, pour, stream, spill • *Waterfalls crash and tumble over rocks.*

4 = hurry, rush, bound, pile, scramble, scuttle, scurry • *I love tumbling into my apartment and slamming the door.*
5 = tousle, ruffle, mess up, rumple, muss (up) *(U.S. informal)*, disarrange, dishevel, make untidy, disorder, muss *(U.S. & Canad.)* • *Her hair was tumbled and her nose scarlet with sunburn.*
▸ **AS A NOUN 1 = fall**, drop, roll, trip, collapse, plunge, spill, toss, stumble, flop, headlong fall • *He injured his knee in a tumble from his horse.*
2 = jumble, riot • *her tumble of golden locks*
▸ **IN PHRASES: tumble to something = realize**, get *(informal)*, see, understand, recognize, take in, perceive, grasp, figure out *(informal)*, comprehend, twig *(Brit. informal)*, get the message *(informal)*, savvy *(U.S. informal)*, apprehend, latch on to *(informal)*, suss *(Brit. informal)*, get the picture *(informal)*, catch on to *(informal)*, cotton on to *(informal)*, get wise to *(informal)*, get your head around *(informal)* • *He hasn't yet tumbled to the fact that his wife's cheating on him.*

tumbledown = dilapidated, ruined, crumbling, shaky, disintegrating, tottering, ramshackle, rickety, decrepit, falling to pieces • *bare hills and dusty tumbledown villages*
OPPOSITES: firm, sound, stable

tummy = stomach, belly, abdomen, corporation *(informal)*, pot, gut *(informal)*, paunch, tum *(informal)*, spare tyre *(informal)*, breadbasket *(slang)*, potbelly • *Your baby's tummy should feel warm, but not hot.*

tumour or *(U.S.)* **tumor = growth**, cancer, swelling, lump, carcinoma *(Pathology)*, sarcoma *(Medical)*, neoplasm *(Medical)* • *He died of a brain tumour.*

tumult 1 = disturbance, trouble, chaos, turmoil, storms, upset, stir, disorder, excitement, unrest, upheaval, havoc, mayhem, strife, disarray, turbulence, ferment, agitation, convulsions, bedlam • *the recent tumult in global financial markets*
2 = clamour, row, outbreak, racket, din, uproar, fracas, commotion, pandemonium, babel, hubbub, hullabaloo • *Round one ended to a tumult of whistles, screams and shouts.*
OPPOSITES: peace, quiet, silence

tumultuous 1 = turbulent, exciting, confused, disturbed, hectic, stormy, agitated • *the tumultuous changes in Eastern Europe*
OPPOSITES: still, quiet, calm
2 = wild, excited, riotous, unrestrained, violent, raging, disorderly, fierce, passionate, noisy, restless, unruly, rowdy, boisterous, full-on *(informal)*, lawless, vociferous, rumbustious, uproarious, obstreperous, clamorous • *Delegates greeted the news with tumultuous applause.*

tune AS A NOUN 1 = melody, air, song, theme, strain(s), motif, jingle, ditty, melody line • *She was humming a merry little tune.*
2 = harmony, pitch, euphony • *It was an ordinary voice, but he sang in tune.*
▸ **AS A VERB 1 = tune up**, adjust, bring into harmony • *They were quietly tuning their instruments.*
2 = regulate, adapt, modulate, harmonize, attune, pitch • *He will rapidly be tuned to the keynote of his new associates.*
▸ **IN PHRASES: change your tune = change your attitude**, reconsider, think again, change your mind, have a change of heart, take a different tack, do an about-face • *He changed his tune, saying that the increase was experimental.*
in tune with something = in accord, in line, in keeping, harmonious, in concert, in agreement, in step, consonant, in sympathy • *His change of direction seems more in tune with the times.*
out of tune with something = at odds *(informal)*, out of step, at variance, in disagreement, not in harmony, out of kilter • *The campaigners were out of tune with most ordinary people.*

tuneful = melodious, musical, pleasant, harmonious, melodic, catchy, consonant *(Music)*, symphonic, mellifluous, easy on the ear *(informal)*, euphonious, euphonic • *Melodic and tuneful, his songs made me weep.*
OPPOSITES: clashing, harsh, discordant

tuneless = discordant, clashing, harsh, dissonant, atonal, cacophonous, unmusical, unmelodious, unmelodic • *Someone walked by singing a tuneless song.*
OPPOSITES: pleasing, musical, melodious

tunnel AS A NOUN = passage, underpass, passageway, subway, channel, hole, shaft • *two new railway tunnels through the Alps*
▸ **AS A VERB = dig**, dig your way, burrow, mine, bore, drill, excavate • *The rebels tunnelled out of a maximum security jail.*

turbulence = confusion, turmoil, unrest, instability, storm, boiling, disorder, upheaval, agitation, commotion, pandemonium, tumult, roughness • *a region often beset by religious turbulence*
OPPOSITES: rest, peace, quiet

turbulent 1 = wild, violent, disorderly, agitated, rebellious, unruly, rowdy, boisterous, anarchic, tumultuous, lawless, unbridled, riotous, undisciplined, seditious, mutinous, ungovernable, uproarious, refractory, obstreperous, insubordinate • *six turbulent years of rows and reconciliations*
2 = stormy, rough, raging, tempestuous, boiling, disordered, furious, unsettled, foaming, unstable, agitated, tumultuous, choppy, blustery • *I had to have a boat that could handle turbulent seas.*
OPPOSITES: still, quiet, calm

turf AS A NOUN 1 = grass, green, sward • *They shuffled slowly down the turf towards the cliff's edge.*
2 = sod, divot, clod • *Lift the turfs carefully – they can be re-used elsewhere.*
3 = area or **sphere of influence**, territory, province, preserve, patch *(Brit. informal)*, domain, manor *(Brit. informal)*, home ground, stamping ground, bailiwick *(informal)* • *Their turf was Paris: its streets, theatres, homes and parks.*
▸ **IN PHRASES: the turf = horse-racing**, the flat, racecourse, racetrack, racing • *He has sent out only three winners on the turf this year.*
turf someone out = throw out, evict, cast out, kick out *(informal)*, fire *(informal)*, dismiss, sack *(informal)*, bounce *(slang)*, discharge, expel, oust, relegate, banish, eject, dispossess, chuck out *(informal)*, fling out, kiss off *(slang, chiefly U.S. & Canad.)*, show someone the door, give someone the sack *(informal)*, give someone the bum's rush *(slang)*, give someone his or her P45 *(informal)*, kennet *(Austral. slang)*, jeff *(Austral. slang)* • *stories of people being turfed out and ending up on the streets*

turgid = pompous, inflated, windy, high-flown, pretentious, grandiose, flowery, overblown, stilted, ostentatious, fulsome, bombastic, grandiloquent, arty-farty *(informal)*, fustian, orotund, magniloquent, sesquipedalian, tumid • *He used to make dull, turgid and boring speeches.*

turmoil AS A NOUN = confusion, trouble, violence, row, noise, stir, disorder, chaos, disturbance, upheaval, bustle, flurry, strife, disarray, uproar, turbulence, ferment, agitation, commotion, pandemonium, bedlam, tumult, hubbub, brouhaha • *the political turmoil of 1989*
OPPOSITES: rest, peace, quiet
▸ **IN PHRASES: in turmoil = in a state of confusion**, spinning, reeling, all over the place *(informal)*, disorientated, at sixes and sevens, in a whirl • *Your mind is in turmoil.*

turn AS A VERB 1 *sometimes with* **round = change course**, swing round, wheel round, veer, move, return, go back, switch, shift, reverse, swerve, change position • *He turned abruptly and walked away.*
2 = rotate, spin, go round (and round), revolve, roll, circle,

wheel, twist, spiral, whirl, swivel, pivot, twirl, gyrate, go round in circles, move in a circle • *As the wheel turned, the potter shaped the clay.*
3 = **go round**, come round, negotiate, pass, corner, pass around, take a bend • *The taxi turned the corner of the lane and stopped.*
4 = **bend**, curve, meander, wind, twist, snake, loop, zigzag • *the corner where our street turns into the main road*
5 = **perform**, do, carry out, execute • *They were turning somersaults and cartwheels in the courtyard.*
6 = **flick through**, thumb, skim, browse, flip through • *He turned the pages of a file in front of him.*
7 *with* **into** = **change**, transform, fashion, shape, convert, alter, adapt, mould, remodel, form, mutate, refit, metamorphose, transmute, transfigure • *She turned the house into a beautiful home.*
8 = **become**, get, grow, come to be, go • *The police think that things could turn nasty.*
9 = **make**, produce, generate, yield • *The firm will still be able to turn a modest profit.*
10 = **reach**, become, hit *(informal)*, pass, get to • *He aimed to accumulate a million dollars before he turned thirty.*
11 = **shape**, form, fashion, cast, frame, construct, execute, mould, make • *finely-turned metal*
12 = **sicken**, upset, nauseate • *The true facts will turn your stomach.*
13 = **sprain**, hurt, injure, strain, twist, rick, wrench • *I had to come off because I turned my ankle in the first half.*
14 = **go bad**, go off *(Brit. informal)*, curdle, go sour, become rancid • *milk starting to turn in the refrigerator*
15 = **make rancid**, spoil, sour, taint • *They are stupid and ugly enough to turn milk.*
▸ **AS A NOUN** 1 = **rotation**, turning, cycle, circle, revolution, spin, twist, reversal, whirl, swivel, pivot, gyration • *The rear sprocket will turn only twice for one turn of the pedals.*
2 = **change of direction**, bend, curve, change of course, shift, departure, deviation • *You can't do a right-hand turn here.*
3 = **bend**, corner, twist, zigzag, dog-leg • *There was a hairpin turn in the road.*
4 = **junction**, turning, crossroads, turnoff • *the journey to the turn on the A4*
5 = **direction**, course, tack, swing, tendency, drift, bias • *The scandal took a new turn today.*
6 = **opportunity**, go, spell, shot *(informal)*, time, try, round, chance, period, shift, crack *(informal)*, succession, fling, stint, whack *(informal)* • *Let each child have a turn at fishing.*
7 = **stroll**, airing, walk, drive, ride, spin *(informal)*, circuit, constitutional, outing, excursion, promenade, jaunt, saunter • *I think I'll just go up and take a turn round the deck.*
8 = **deed**, service, act, action, favour, gesture • *He did you a good turn by resigning.*
9 = **shock**, start, surprise, scare, jolt, fright • *It gave me quite a turn.*
10 = **inclination**, talent, gift, leaning, bent, bias, flair, affinity, knack, propensity, aptitude • *She has a turn for gymnastic exercises.*
11 = **act**, show, performance, piece, routine, number • *the most brilliant comic turn in television history*
▸ **IN PHRASES: at every turn** = **repeatedly**, always, constantly, all the time, continually, again and again, over and over again, recurrently, twenty-four-seven *(informal)* • *Their operations were hampered at every turn.*
by turns = **alternately**, in succession, turn and turn about, reciprocally • *His tone was by turns angry and aggrieved.*
in turn = **one at a time**, one by one, in succession, one after another • *There were cheers for each person as they spoke in turn.*
take a turn for the better = **get better**, improve, pick up, recover, rally, revive, look up, perk up, turn the corner • *His fortunes belatedly took a turn for the better.*
take a turn for the worse = **deteriorate**, decline, worsen, get worse, go downhill *(informal)*, retrogress • *Her condition took a sharp turn for the worse.*
to a turn = **perfectly**, correctly, precisely, exactly, just right • *sweet tomatoes roasted to a turn*
turn against someone = **become hostile to**, become disillusioned with, become disenchanted with, take a dislike to, become unsympathetic to • *They turned against me when someone said I'd been insulting them.*
turn back = **go back**, return, retreat, retrace your steps • *They were very nearly forced to turn back.*
turn in = **go to bed**, go to sleep, hit the sack *(slang)*, retire for the night, hit the hay *(slang)* • *Would you like some tea before you turn in?*
turn of events = **development**, incident, circumstance, occurrence, happening • *He was hurt and confused by the turn of events.*
turn of mind = **bent**, tendency, bias, inclination, disposition, way of thinking, propensity, aptitude • *She was of a rational turn of mind.*
turn of phrase = **expression**, term, phrase, idiom, choice of words • *What a strange turn of phrase that is!*
turn off = **branch off**, leave, quit, depart from, deviate, change direction, take a side road, take another road • *He turned off only to find that he was trapped in the main square.* • *The truck turned off the main road along the gravelly track.*
turn on someone = **attack**, assault, fall on, round on, lash out at, assail, lay into *(informal)*, let fly at, lose your temper with • *The demonstrators turned on the police.*
turn on something = **depend on**, hang on, rest on, hinge on, be decided by, balance on, be contingent on, pivot on • *It all turns on what his real motives are.*
turn out 1 = **prove to be**, transpire, become apparent, happen, emerge, become known, develop, roll up, come to light, crop up *(informal)* • *It turned out that I knew the person who got shot.*
2 = **end up**, happen, result, work out, evolve, come to be, come about, transpire, pan out *(informal)*, eventuate • *Things don't always turn out the way we expect.*
3 = **come**, be present, turn up, show up *(informal)*, go, appear, attend, gather, assemble, put in an appearance • *Thousands of people turned out for the funeral.*
turn over = **overturn**, tip over, flip over, upend, be upset, reverse, capsize, keel over • *The buggy turned over and she was thrown out.*
turn someone against something *or* **someone** = **make hostile to**, set against, prejudice against, alienate from, drive a wedge between, influence against, estrange from, cause to dislike, cause to be unfriendly towards • *This job has turned me against this sort of violent programme.*
turn someone away = **send someone away**, reject, repel, rebuff, cold-shoulder, send someone packing *(informal)*, give someone the brush-off *(informal)*, refuse admittance to • *Turning these people away would be an inhumane action.*
turn someone in = **hand someone over**, denounce, inform on, blow the whistle on *(informal)*, shop *(Brit. informal)*, finger *(U.S. informal)*, betray, sell out, split on *(informal)*, grass on *(Brit. informal)*, rat on *(informal)*, peach on *(informal)*, squeal on *(informal)*, dob in *(Austral. slang)* • *There would be strong incentives to turn someone in to the police.*
turn someone off = **repel**, bore, put someone off, disgust, offend, irritate, alienate, sicken, displease, nauseate, gross someone out *(U.S. slang)*, disenchant, lose your interest • *Aggressive men turn me off completely.*
turn someone on = **arouse**, attract, excite, thrill, stimulate, please, press someone's buttons *(slang)*, work someone up, titillate, ring someone's bell *(U.S. slang)*, arouse someone's desire • *The body that turns men on doesn't have to be perfect.*

turn someone onto something = introduce to, show, expose, inform about, initiate into, get you started with • *She turned me on to this really interesting website.*
turn someone out = expel, drive out, evict, throw out, fire *(informal)*, dismiss, sack *(informal)*, axe *(informal)*, discharge, oust, relegate, banish, deport, put out, cashier, unseat, dispossess, kick out *(informal)*, cast out, drum out, show the door, turf out *(Brit. informal)*, give someone the sack *(informal)*, give someone the bum's rush *(slang)*, kiss off *(slang, chiefly U.S. & Canad.)*, give someone his or her P45 *(informal)*, kennet *(Austral. slang)*, jeff *(Austral. slang)* • *It was a monastery but the authorities turned all the monks out.*
turn something *or* **someone back = drive back**, repel, beat off, repulse, force back, beat back, put someone *or* something to flight, fight back • *Police attempted to turn back protesters.*
turn something down 1 = refuse, decline, reject, spurn, rebuff, say no to, repudiate, abstain from, throw something out • *I thanked him for the offer but turned it down.*
2 = lower, soften, reduce the volume of, mute, lessen, muffle, quieten, diminish • *The police told the DJs to turn down the music.*
turn something in = hand in, return, deliver, give back, give up, hand over, submit, surrender, tender • *He told her to turn in her library books.*
turn something off = switch off, turn out, put out, stop, kill, cut out, shut down, unplug, flick off • *She had turned off the light to go to sleep.*
turn something on = switch on, put on, activate, start, start up, ignite, kick-start, set in motion, energize • *Why haven't you turned the lights on?*
turn something on someone = aim at, point at, level at, train on, direct at • *He tried to turn the gun on me.*
turn something out 1 = turn off, put out, switch off, extinguish, disconnect, unplug, flick off • *I'll play till they come round to turn the lights out.*
2 = produce, make, process, finish, manufacture, assemble, put together, put out, bring out, fabricate, churn out • *They have been turning out great furniture for 400 years.*
turn something over 1 = flip over, flick through, leaf through • *She was turning over the pages of the directory.*
2 = consider, think about, contemplate, ponder, reflect on, wonder about, mull over, think over, deliberate on, give thought to, ruminate about, revolve • *You could see her turning things over in her mind.*
3 = hand over, transfer, deliver, commit, give up, yield, surrender, pass on, render, assign, commend, give over • *The lawyer turned over the release papers.*
4 = start up, warm up, activate, switch on, crank, set something in motion, set something going, switch on the ignition of • *I squeezed into the seat and turned the engine over.*
turn something up 1 = find, reveal, discover, expose, come up with, disclose, unearth, dig up, bring to light • *Investigations have never turned up any evidence.*
2 = increase, raise, boost, enhance, intensify, amplify, increase the volume of, make louder • *I turned the volume up.*
turn to someone = appeal to, go to, approach, apply to, look to, resort to, have recourse to • *There was no one to turn to, no one to tell.*
turn to something = take up, take to, resort to, have recourse to • *They are now turning to recycling in large numbers.*
turn up 1 = arrive, come, appear, show up *(informal)*, show *(informal)*, attend, put in an appearance, show your face • *He turned up on Christmas Day with a friend.*
2 = come to light, be found, show up, pop up, materialize, appear • *The rare spoon turned up in an old house in Devon.*

PROVERBS
One good turn deserves another
A bad penny always turns up

turncoat = traitor, renegade, defector, seceder, deserter, apostate, backslider, recreant *(archaic)*, tergiversator, rat *(informal)* • *His one-time admirers now accused him of being a turncoat.*
turning 1 = turn-off, turn, junction, crossroads, side road, exit • *Take the next turning on the right.*
2 = bend, turn, curve • *a turning in the river*
turning point = crossroads, critical moment, decisive moment, change, crisis, crux, moment of truth, point of no return, moment of decision, climacteric, tipping point • *The vote marks something of a turning point in the war.*
turn-off = turning, turn, branch, exit, side road • *They slowed down. There was a turn-off just ahead.*
turnout = attendance, crowd, audience, gate, assembly, congregation, number, throng, assemblage • *It was a marvellous afternoon with a huge turnout of people.*
turnover 1 = output, business, production, flow, volume, yield, productivity, outturn *(rare)* • *The company had a turnover of £3.8 million.*
2 = movement, replacement, coming and going, change • *Short-term contracts increase staff turnover.*
turpentine
▸ **RELATED ADJECTIVE:** terebinthine
turpitude = wickedness, evil, corruption, criminality, depravity, immorality, iniquity, badness, viciousness, villainy, degeneracy, sinfulness, foulness, baseness, vileness, nefariousness • *a beacon of morality in a sea of turpitude*
turtle
▸ **RELATED ADJECTIVES:** chelonian, testudinal
▹ *See panel* **Reptiles**
tussle **AS A VERB 1 = fight**, battle, struggle, scrap *(informal)*, contend, wrestle, vie, brawl, grapple, scuffle • *They ended up tussling with the security staff.*
2 = argue, row *(Brit. informal)*, clash, dispute, disagree, quarrel, squabble, wrangle • *Officials tussled over who had responsibility for it.*
▸ **AS A NOUN 1 = fight**, scrap *(informal)*, brawl, scuffle, battle, competition, struggle, conflict, contest, set-to *(informal)*, bout, contention, fray, punch-up *(Brit. informal)*, fracas, shindig *(informal)*, scrimmage, shindy *(informal)*, bagarre *(French)*, biffo *(Austral. slang)* • *The referee booked him for a tussle with the goalie.*
2 = argument, row *(Brit. informal)*, clash, disagreement, contention, quarrel, squabble, war of words, contretemps • *a legal tussle over who gets custody of the children*
tutelage = guidance, education, instruction, preparation, schooling, charge, care, teaching, protection, custody, tuition, dependence, patronage, guardianship, wardship • *This period of tutelage was indispensable for the territories.*
tutor **AS A NOUN = teacher**, coach, instructor, educator, guide, governor, guardian, lecturer, guru, mentor, preceptor, master *or* mistress, schoolmaster *or* schoolmistress • *He surprised his tutors by failing the exam.*
▸ **AS A VERB = teach**, educate, school, train, coach, guide, discipline, lecture, drill, instruct, edify, direct • *She was at home, being tutored with her brothers.*
tutorial **AS A NOUN = seminar**, lesson, individual instruction • *Methods of study include lectures, tutorials and practical work.*
▸ **AS AN ADJECTIVE = teaching**, coaching, guiding, instructional • *Students may seek tutorial guidance.*
TV = television, telly *(Brit. informal)*, the box *(Brit. informal)*, receiver, the tube *(slang)*, television set, TV set, small screen *(informal)*, gogglebox *(Brit. slang)*, idiot box *(slang)* • *I prefer going to the cinema to watching TV.* • *The TV was on.*
twaddle = nonsense, rubbish, rot, garbage *(informal)*, balls *(taboo slang)*, bull *(slang)*, shit *(taboo slang)*, pants *(slang)*, gossip, crap *(slang)*, trash, chatter, bullshit *(taboo slang)*, hot air *(informal)*, tosh *(slang, chiefly Brit.)*, waffle *(informal, chiefly*

Brit.), pap, cobblers (Brit. taboo slang), bilge (informal), drivel, tripe (informal), guff (slang), tattle, moonshine, verbiage, gabble, claptrap (informal), gobbledegook (informal), hogwash, hokum (slang, chiefly U.S. & Canad.), rigmarole, blather, piffle (informal), poppycock (informal), inanity, balderdash, bosh (informal), eyewash (informal), trumpery, tommyrot, foolish talk, horsefeathers (U.S. slang), bunkum or buncombe (chiefly U.S.), bizzo (Austral. slang), bull's wool (Austral. & N.Z. slang) • *He was baffled by the intellectual twaddle.*

tweak AS A VERB 1 = **twist**, pull, pinch, jerk, squeeze, nip, twitch • *He tweaked my ear roughly.*
2 = **adjust**, improve, alter, adapt, modify, refine, make adjustments to, make improvements to, make alterations to, change • *The system should get better as engineers tweak its performance.*
▸ AS A NOUN 1 = **twist**, pull, squeeze, pinch, jerk, nip, twitch • *a tweak on the ear*
2 = **modification**, change, improvement, adjustment, adaptation, alteration, refinement • *no radical changes – just a tweak here and there*

twee 1 = **sweet**, pretty, cute, sentimental, quaint, dainty, cutesy (informal, chiefly U.S.), bijou, precious • *twee musical boxes shaped like cottages*
2 = **sentimental**, over-sentimental, soppy (Brit. informal), mawkish, affected, precious • *Although twee at times, the script is well-constructed.*

twelve
▸ RELATED ADJECTIVE: duodecimal
▸ RELATED PREFIX: dodeca-

twenty
▸ RELATED ADJECTIVES: vicenary, vigesimal
▸ RELATED PREFIX: icosa-

twiddle = **fiddle with**, adjust, finger, play with, juggle, wiggle (informal), twirl, jiggle, monkey with (informal) • *He twiddled a knob on the dashboard.*

twig[1] = **branch**, stick, sprig, offshoot, shoot, spray, withe • *There was a slight sound of a twig breaking underfoot.*

twig[2] = **understand**, get, see, find out, grasp, make out, rumble (Brit. informal), catch on (informal), comprehend, fathom, tumble to (informal) • *By the time she'd twigged what it was all about, it was too late.*

twilight AS A NOUN 1 = **dusk**, evening, sunset, early evening, nightfall, sundown, gloaming (Scot. or poetic), close of day, evo (Austral. slang) • *They returned at twilight and set off for the bar.*
OPPOSITES: morning, dawn, sunrise
2 = **half-light**, gloom, dimness, semi-darkness • *the deepening autumn twilight*
3 = **decline**, last years, final years, closing years, autumn, downturn, ebb, last phase • *Now they are both in the twilight of their careers.*
OPPOSITES: height, peak, climax
▸ AS AN ADJECTIVE 1 = **evening**, dim, darkening, evo (Austral. slang) • *the summer twilight sky*
2 = **declining**, last, final, dying, ebbing • *the twilight years of the Hapsburg Empire*
▸ RELATED ADJECTIVE: crepuscular

twin AS A NOUN = **double**, counterpart, mate, match, fellow, clone, duplicate, lookalike, likeness, ringer (slang), corollary • *the twin of the chair she had at the cottage*
▸ AS A VERB = **pair**, match, join, couple, link, yoke • *The borough is twinned with Kasel in Germany.*
▸ AS AN ADJECTIVE 1 = **identical**, matched, matching, double, paired, parallel, corresponding, dual, duplicate, twofold, geminate • *the twin spires of the cathedral*
2 = **closely related**, parallel, corresponding, complementary, closely linked, equivalent • *the twin concepts of liberty and equality*

twine AS A NOUN = **string**, cord, yarn, strong thread • *a ball of twine*
▸ AS A VERB 1 = **twist together**, weave, knit, braid, splice, interweave, plait, entwine, interlace, twist • *He twined his fingers into hers.*
2 = **coil**, wind, surround, bend, wrap, twist, curl, loop, spiral, meander, encircle, wreathe • *These strands of molecules twine around each other.*

twinge 1 = **pang**, twitch, tweak, throe (rare), twist • *I would have twinges of guilt occasionally.*
2 = **pain**, sharp pain, gripe, stab, bite, twist, stitch, pinch, throb, twitch, prick, spasm, tweak, tic • *the occasional twinge of indigestion*

twinkle AS A VERB = **sparkle**, flash, shine, glitter, gleam, blink, flicker, wink, shimmer, glint, glisten, scintillate, coruscate • *At night, lights twinkle in distant villages across the valleys.*
▸ AS A NOUN 1 = **sparkle**, light, flash, spark, shine, glittering, gleam, blink, flicker, wink, shimmer, glimmer, glistening, scintillation, coruscation • *A kindly twinkle came into his eyes.*
2 = **moment**, second, shake (informal), flash, instant, tick (Brit. informal), twinkling, split second, jiffy (informal), trice, two shakes of a lamb's tail (informal) • *Hours can pass in a twinkle.*

twinkling or **twink** = **moment**, second, flash, instant, tick (Brit. informal), twinkle, split second, jiffy (informal), trice, two shakes of a lamb's tail (informal), shake (informal), bat of an eye (informal) • *And then in a twinkling all vanished away.*

twirl AS A VERB 1 = **twiddle**, turn, rotate, wind, spin, twist, revolve, whirl • *She twirled an empty glass in her fingers.*
2 = **turn**, whirl, wheel, spin, twist, pivot, gyrate, pirouette, turn on your heel • *Several hundred people twirl around the dance floor.*
▸ AS A NOUN = **turn**, spin, rotation, whirl, wheel, revolution, twist, pirouette, gyration • *with a twirl of his silver-handled cane*

twist AS A VERB 1 = **coil**, curl, wind, plait, wrap, screw, twirl • *She twisted her hair into a bun.*
2 = **intertwine**, wind, weave, braid, interweave, plait, entwine, twine, wreathe, interlace • *The fibres are twisted together during spinning.*
3 = **turn (round)**, rotate, swivel (round), pivot, spin (round), revolve, skew (round) • *Hold your arms straight out and twist to the right and left.*
4 = **distort**, screw up, contort, mangle, mangulate (Austral. slang) • *The car was left a mess of twisted metal.*
OPPOSITES: straighten, untwist
5 = **sprain**, turn, rick, wrench • *He fell and twisted his ankle.*
6 = **wind**, turn, bend, curve, snake, weave, worm, loop, swerve, meander, zigzag, corkscrew • *The road twists and turns between pleasant little cottages.*
OPPOSITES: straighten, unravel, unwind
7 = **misrepresent**, distort, misquote, alter, change, pervert, warp, falsify, garble • *It's a shame the way the media can twist your words.*
8 = **squirm**, wriggle, writhe • *He tried to twist out of my grasp.*
9 = **wring**, squeeze, knead, mangle, mangulate (Austral. slang) • *She sat there twisting her handkerchief for a while.*
▸ AS A NOUN 1 = **surprise**, change, turn, development, revelation • *This little story has a twist in its tail.*
2 = **development**, emphasis, variation, slant • *The battle of the sexes took on a new twist.*
3 = **wind**, turn, spin, swivel, twirl • *The bag is resealed with a simple twist of the valve.*
4 = **coil**, roll, curl, hank, twine • *the bare bulb hanging from a twist of flex*
5 = **curve**, turn, bend, loop, arc, kink, zigzag, convolution, dog-leg, undulation • *the twists and turns of the existing track*

t

6 = **trait**, fault, defect, peculiarity, bent, characteristic, flaw, deviation, quirk, eccentricity, oddity, aberration, imperfection, kink, foible, idiosyncrasy, proclivity, crotchet • *If only she could alter this personality twist.*
7 = **sprain**, turn, pull, jerk, wrench • *A twist of the ankle denied him a place on the substitutes' bench.*

twisted 1 = **perverted**, sick *(informal)*, evil, corrupt, corrupted, distorted, abnormal, warped, unhealthy, degenerate, deviant, wicked, sadistic, depraved, debased, debauched, aberrant, pervy *(informal)* • *the workings of a twisted mind*
2 = **crumpled**, crushed, distorted, warped, buckled, deformed, misshapen • *The three survivors sat 300 yards from the twisted wreckage.*
3 = **crooked**, contorted, lopsided, wry • *a wry, twisted smile*

twit = **fool**, idiot, jerk *(slang, chiefly U.S. & Canad.)*, charlie *(Brit. informal)*, dope *(informal)*, clown, ass, plank *(Brit. slang)*, berk *(Brit. slang)*, prick *(derogatory slang)*, wally *(slang)*, prat *(slang)*, plonker *(slang)*, geek *(slang)*, chump *(informal)*, oaf, simpleton, airhead *(slang)*, dipstick *(Brit. slang)*, dickhead *(slang)*, gonzo *(slang)*, schmuck *(U.S. slang)*, dork *(slang)*, nitwit *(informal)*, blockhead, ninny, divvy *(Brit. slang)*, pillock *(Brit. slang)*, halfwit, silly-billy *(informal)*, nincompoop, dweeb *(U.S. slang)*, putz *(U.S. slang)*, weenie *(U.S. informal)*, eejit *(Scot. & Irish)*, thicko *(Brit. slang)*, dumb-ass *(slang)*, gobshite *(Irish taboo slang)*, numpty *(Scot. informal)*, doofus *(slang, chiefly U.S.)*, fuckwit *(taboo slang)*, juggins *(Brit. informal)*, dickwit *(slang)*, nerd *or* nurd *(slang)*, numbskull *or* numskull, twerp *or* twirp *(informal)*, dorba *or* dorb *(Austral. slang)*, bogan *(Austral. slang)* • *a pompous twit who loved the sound of his own voice*

twitch AS A VERB 1 = **jerk**, blink, flutter, jump, squirm • *His left eyelid twitched involuntarily.*
2 = **pull (at)**, snatch (at), tug (at), pluck (at), yank (at) • *He twitched his curtains to check on callers.*
▸ AS A NOUN = **jerk**, tic, spasm, twinge, jump, blink, flutter, tremor • *He developed a nervous twitch.*

twitter AS A VERB 1 = **chirrup**, whistle, chatter, trill, chirp, warble, cheep, tweet • *There were birds twittering in the trees.*
2 = **chatter**, chat, rabbit (on) *(Brit. informal)*, gossip, babble, gab *(informal)*, prattle, natter, jabber, blather, prate • *They were twittering excitedly about their new dresses.*
▸ AS A NOUN = **chirrup**, call, song, cry, whistle, chatter, trill, chirp, warble, cheep, tweet • *She would waken to the twitter of birds.*

t

two
▸ RELATED ADJECTIVES: binary, double, dual
▸ RELATED PREFIXES: bi-, di-

two-edged = **ambiguous**, ambivalent, backhanded, double-edged, equivocal • *The effect of the laws was two-edged.*

two-faced = **hypocritical**, false, deceiving, treacherous, deceitful, untrustworthy, insincere, double-dealing, duplicitous, dissembling, perfidious, Janus-faced • *He had been devious and two-faced.*
OPPOSITES: frank, genuine, honest

tycoon = **magnate**, capitalist, baron, industrialist, financier, fat cat *(slang, chiefly U.S.)*, mogul, captain of industry, potentate, wealthy businessman, big cheese *(old-fashioned slang)*, plutocrat, big noise *(informal)*, merchant prince • *a self-made property tycoon*

type 1 = **kind**, sort, class, variety, group, form, order, style, species, breed, strain, category, stamp, kidney, genre, classification, ilk, subdivision • *There are various types of the disease.*
2 = **print**, printing, face, case, characters, font, fount • *The correction has already been set in type.*
3 = **sort of person**, sort, type of person • *She was certainly not the type to murder her husband.*

typhoon = **storm**, tornado, cyclone, tempest, squall, tropical storm • *She had to endure being in a typhoon for 67 hours.*

typical 1 = **archetypal**, standard, model, normal, classic, stock, essential, representative, usual, conventional, regular, characteristic, orthodox, signature, indicative, illustrative, archetypical, stereotypical • *such typical schoolgirl pastimes as horse-riding and reading*
OPPOSITES: unique, unusual, unexpected
2 = **characteristic**, in keeping, in character, true to type • *That's just typical of you, isn't it?*
3 = **average**, normal, usual, conventional, routine, regular, orthodox, predictable, run-of-the-mill, bog-standard *(Brit. & Irish slang)* • *not exactly your typical Sunday afternoon stroll*

typify = **represent**, illustrate, sum up, characterize, embody, exemplify, personify, incarnate, epitomize • *These buildings typify the rich extremes of the local architecture.*

tyrannical *or* **tyrannic** = **oppressive**, cruel, authoritarian, dictatorial, severe, absolute, unreasonable, arbitrary, unjust, autocratic, inhuman, coercive, imperious, domineering, overbearing, magisterial, despotic, high-handed, peremptory, overweening, tyrannous • *He killed his tyrannical father with a blow to the head.*
OPPOSITES: understanding, democratic, liberal

tyrannize = **oppress**, bully, dictate to, intimidate, coerce, enslave, terrorize, subjugate, browbeat, ride roughshod over, rule with an iron hand, domineer over, have someone under your thumb • *fathers who tyrannize their families*

tyranny = **oppression**, cruelty, dictatorship, authoritarianism, reign of terror, despotism, autocracy, absolutism, coercion, high-handedness, harsh discipline, unreasonableness, imperiousness, peremptoriness • *I'm the sole victim of her tyranny.*
OPPOSITES: understanding, democracy, liberality

QUOTATIONS
Tyranny is always better organised than freedom
[Charles Péguy *Basic Verities*]

tyrant = **dictator**, bully, authoritarian, Big Brother, oppressor, control freak, despot, autocrat, absolutist, martinet, slave-driver, Hitler • *Since 1804 the country has been mostly ruled by tyrants.*

QUOTATIONS
The hand of vengeance found the bed
To which the purple tyrant fled;
The iron hand crushed the tyrant's head,
And became a tyrant in his stead
[William Blake *The Grey Monk*]

Tyrants seldom want pretexts
[Edmund Burke *letter to a Member of the National Assembly*]

Nature has left this tincture in the blood,
That all men would be tyrants if they could
[Daniel Defoe *The History of the Kentish Petition*]

When he laughed, respectable senators burst with laughter,
And when he cried the little children died in the streets
[W.H. Auden *Epitaph on a Tyrant*]

tyro *or* **tiro** = **beginner**, novice, apprentice, learner, neophyte, rookie *(informal)*, greenhorn *(informal)*, catechumen • *a tyro journalist*

Uu

ubiquitous = **ever-present**, pervasive, omnipresent, all-over, everywhere, universal • *She is the most ubiquitous media personality around.*

ugly 1 = **unattractive**, homely (*chiefly U.S.*), plain, unsightly, unlovely, unprepossessing, not much to look at, no oil painting (*informal*), ill-favoured, hard-featured, hard-favoured, fugly (*chiefly U.S. & Austral.*) • *She makes me feel dowdy and ugly.*
OPPOSITES: pretty, beautiful, attractive
2 = **unpleasant**, shocking, terrible, offensive, nasty, disgusting, revolting, obscene, hideous, monstrous, vile, distasteful, horrid, repulsive, frightful, objectionable, disagreeable, repugnant • *an ugly scene*
OPPOSITES: pleasant, agreeable
3 = **bad-tempered**, nasty, sullen, surly, threatening, dangerous, angry, forbidding, menacing, sinister, ominous, malevolent, spiteful, baleful, bodeful • *He's in an ugly mood today.*
OPPOSITES: friendly, peaceful, good-natured

QUOTATIONS
Ugliness is superior to beauty, because ugliness lasts
[Serge Gainsbourg]

ulcer = **sore**, abscess, gathering, peptic ulcer, gumboil • *In addition to headaches, you may develop stomach ulcers.*

ulterior = **hidden**, secret, concealed, personal, secondary, selfish, covert, undisclosed, unexpressed • *She had an ulterior motive for trying to help Stan.*
OPPOSITES: obvious, plain, apparent

ultimate AS AN ADJECTIVE 1 = **final**, eventual, conclusive, last, end, furthest, extreme, terminal, decisive • *He said it is still not possible to predict the ultimate outcome.*
2 = **fundamental**, basic, primary, radical, elemental • *the ultimate cause of what's happened*
3 = **supreme**, highest, greatest, maximum, paramount, most significant, superlative, topmost • *Of course the ultimate authority remained the presidency.*
4 = **worst**, greatest, utmost, extreme • *Treachery was the ultimate sin.*
5 = **best**, greatest, supreme, optimum, quintessential • *the ultimate luxury foods*
▸ AS A NOUN = **epitome**, height, greatest, summit, peak, extreme, perfection, the last word • *This hotel is the ultimate in luxury.*

ultimately 1 = **finally**, eventually, in the end, after all, at last, at the end of the day, sooner or later, in the fullness of time, in due time • *a tough but ultimately worthwhile struggle*
2 = **fundamentally**, essentially, basically, primarily, at heart, deep down • *Ultimately, Bismarck's revisionism scarcely affected British interests.*

ultra- = **extremely**, excessively, fanatically, radically, rabidly, immoderately • *an ultra-ambitious executive*

ultra-modern = **advanced**, progressive, avant-garde, futuristic, ahead of its time, modernistic, neoteric (*rare*) • *a wide range of ultra-modern equipment*

umbrage IN PHRASES: **take umbrage** = **take offence**, be hurt, be angry, be offended, be upset, be wounded, be put out, be annoyed, bridle, be insulted, take exception, be miffed (*informal*), be indignant, be resentful, be disgruntled, be aggrieved, be affronted, get the hump (*Brit. informal*), be piqued, be riled (*informal*), get huffy, go in a huff, take something personally, have your nose put out of joint (*informal*), take something amiss, get your hackles up • *He takes umbrage against anyone who criticises him.*

umbrella AS A NOUN 1 = **brolly** (*Brit. informal*), parasol, sunshade, gamp • *Harry held an umbrella over Dawn.*
2 = **cover**, protection, guardianship, backing, support, charge, care, agency, responsibility, guidance, patronage, auspices, aegis, safe keeping, protectorship • *under the moral umbrella of the United Nations*
▸ AS AN ADJECTIVE = **coalition**, united, combined, affiliated, confederate, amalgamated • *an umbrella group comprising almost a hundred parties*
▸ RELATED ENTHUSIAST: brolliologist

umpire AS A NOUN = **referee**, judge, ref (*informal*), arbiter, arbitrator, moderator, adjudicator, umpie (*Austral. slang*) • *The umpire's decision is final.*
▸ AS A VERB = **referee**, judge, adjudicate, arbitrate, call (*Sport*), moderate, mediate • *He umpired for school football matches.*

umpteen = **very many**, numerous, countless, millions, gazillions (*informal*), considerable, a good many, a thousand and one, ever so many • *He has produced umpteen books, plays and television series.*

unabashed = **unembarrassed**, blatant, brazen, confident, bold, unconcerned, undaunted, undismayed, unblushing, unawed • *He seems unabashed by his recent defeat.*
OPPOSITES: embarrassed, mortified, abashed

unable *with* **to** = **incapable**, inadequate, powerless, unfit, unfitted, not able, impotent, not up to, unqualified, ineffectual, not equal to • *The military may feel unable to hand over power.*
OPPOSITES: able, effective, capable

unabridged = **uncut**, complete, full-length, whole, unexpurgated, unshortened, uncondensed • *the unabridged version of 'War and Peace'*

unacceptable = **intolerable**, unsatisfactory, unreasonable, off (*Brit. informal*), bad, poor, terrible, offensive, not on (*informal*), unpleasant, inappropriate, unwelcome, unsuitable, disgraceful, undesirable, improper, distasteful, out of order (*informal*), obnoxious, deplorable, displeasing, unseemly, objectionable, disagreeable, a bit much (*informal*), beyond the pale, inadmissible, insufferable, a bit off (*Brit. informal*), insupportable, impermissible, a bit thick (*Brit. informal*) • *She left her husband because of his unacceptable behaviour.*
OPPOSITES: acceptable, desirable, agreeable

unaccompanied 1 = **alone**, on your own, by yourself, solo, lone, unescorted • *Kelly's too young to go unaccompanied.*
2 = **unattended**, abandoned, left alone, unguarded, unwatched • *Unaccompanied bags are either searched or removed.*

unaccountable 1 = **inexplicable**, mysterious, baffling, odd, strange, puzzling, peculiar, incomprehensible, inscrutable, unfathomable, unexplainable • *He had an unaccountable change of mind.*
OPPOSITES: understandable, accountable, comprehensible
2 = **not answerable**, exempt, not responsible, free, unliable • *Economic policy should not be run by an unaccountable committee.*

unaccounted for = **missing**, lost, mislaid, unexplained, not explained • *About £50 million from the robbery is still unaccounted for.*

unaccustomed 1 = **unfamiliar**, unusual, unexpected, new, special, surprising, strange, remarkable, unprecedented, uncommon, out of the ordinary, unwonted • *He comforted me with unaccustomed gentleness.*
OPPOSITES: regular, usual, familiar
2 *with* **to** = **not used to**, unfamiliar with, unused to, not given to, a newcomer to, a novice at, inexperienced at, unversed in, unpractised in, a newbie to *(slang)* • *They were unaccustomed to such military setbacks.*
OPPOSITES: used to

unadorned = **plain**, simple, severe, stark, straightforward, restrained, unfussy, unembellished, unornamented, bare-bones • *The room is typically simple and unadorned.*

unadulterated 1 = **uncontaminated**, pure, unprocessed • *unadulterated food produced without artificial chemicals*
2 = **sheer**, complete, total, pure, absolute, utter, downright, unqualified, out-and-out, unmitigated, thoroughgoing, unalloyed • *It was pure, unadulterated hell.*

unadventurous = **cautious**, careful, wary, safe, stay-at-home, tentative, prudent, timid, hesitant, circumspect, cagey *(informal)*, timorous, chary, unenterprising • *He was a willing player but rather unadventurous.*
OPPOSITES: daring, bold, adventurous

unaffected[1] = **natural**, genuine, unpretentious, simple, plain, straightforward, naive, sincere, honest, unassuming, unspoilt, unsophisticated, dinkum *(Austral. & N.Z. informal)*, artless, ingenuous, without airs, unstudied • *this unaffected, charming couple*
OPPOSITES: affected, pretentious, mannered

unaffected[2] *often with* **by** = **impervious to**, unchanged, untouched, unimpressed, unmoved, unaltered, not influenced, unresponsive to, unstirred • *She seemed totally unaffected by what she'd drunk.*
OPPOSITES: changed, touched, affected

unafraid = **fearless**, confident, daring, intrepid, unshakable, dauntless, unfearing • *a reputation for being tough and unafraid*
OPPOSITES: afraid, alarmed, frightened

unaided AS AN ADJECTIVE = **alone**, solo, single-handed, unaccompanied, without help • *She took her first unaided steps yesterday.*
▸ AS AN ADVERB = **alone**, solo, single-handed, unaccompanied, without help • *an attempt to reach the North Pole unaided*

unalterable = **unchangeable**, unchanging, immutable, fixed, permanent, steadfast, immovable, invariable • *an unalterable fact of life*
OPPOSITES: changing, variable, changeable

unanimity = **agreement**, accord, consensus, concert, unity, harmony, chorus, unison, assent, concord, one mind, concurrence, like-mindedness • *All decisions would require unanimity.*
OPPOSITES: difference, division, disagreement

unanimous 1 = **agreed**, united, in agreement, agreeing, at one, harmonious, like-minded, concordant, of one mind, of the same mind, in complete accord • *Editors were unanimous in their condemnation of the proposals.*
OPPOSITES: split, divided, differing
2 = **united**, common, concerted, solid, consistent, harmonious, undivided, congruent, concordant, unopposed • *the unanimous vote for Hungarian membership*
OPPOSITES: split, divided

unanimously = **without exception**, by common consent, without opposition, with one accord, unitedly, nem. con. • *The executive committee voted unanimously to reject the proposals.*

unannounced AS AN ADVERB = **unexpectedly**, unexpected, out of the blue • *He had just arrived unannounced from South America.*
▸ AS AN ADJECTIVE = **unexpected**, unforeseen, unheralded • *an unannounced visit*

unanswerable 1 = **insoluble**, unexplainable, unresolvable, unascertainable, insolvable • *They would ask their mother unanswerable questions.*
2 = **indisputable**, undeniable, irrefutable, conclusive, absolute, incontrovertible, unarguable, incontestable • *The argument for recruiting McGregor was unanswerable.*

unanswered = **unresolved**, open, unsettled, undecided, disputed, in doubt, vexed, up in the air • *Some of the most important questions remain unanswered.*

unappetizing = **unpalatable**, disgusting, unsavoury, unpleasant, unattractive, distasteful, tasteless, repulsive, off-putting *(Brit. informal)*, unappealing, insipid, vapid, uninviting, yucko *(Austral. slang)* • *cold and unappetizing chicken*
OPPOSITES: tempting, delicious, appetizing

unapproachable 1 = **unfriendly**, reserved, withdrawn, distant, cool, remote, chilly, aloof, frigid, unsociable, offish *(informal)*, standoffish • *I think a lot of people find dentists very unapproachable.*
OPPOSITES: friendly, cordial, sociable
2 = **inaccessible**, remote, out-of-the-way, out of reach, unreachable, un-get-at-able *(informal)* • *Central Asia was virtually unapproachable until this century.*

unarmed = **defenceless**, helpless, unprotected, without arms, unarmoured, weaponless • *Thirteen unarmed civilians died in that attack.*
OPPOSITES: armed, protected, strengthened

unashamed = **blatant**, open, frank, plain, clear, visible, honest, overt, candid, avowed, undisguised, unconcealed • *I grinned at him in unashamed delight.*

unasked = **voluntarily**, without prompting, off your own bat, of your own accord • *His advice, offered to her unasked, was to stay at home.*

unassailable 1 = **undeniable**, indisputable, irrefutable, sound, proven, positive, absolute, conclusive, incontrovertible, incontestable • *His legal position is unassailable.*
OPPOSITES: uncertain, doubtful, dubious
2 = **invincible**, impregnable, invulnerable, secure, well-defended • *Liverpool football club are still looking unassailable.*

unassertive = **meek**, timid, unassuming, retiring, backward, self-effacing, diffident, bashful, mousy, timorous, aw-shucks • *completely out of character to her normal unassertive self*
OPPOSITES: confident, aggressive, assertive

unassuming = **modest**, quiet, humble, meek, simple, reserved, retiring, unpretentious, unobtrusive, self-effacing, diffident, unassertive, unostentatious • *She has a gentle, unassuming manner.*
OPPOSITES: pretentious, audacious, conceited

unattached 1 = **single**, available, unmarried, on your own, by yourself, a free agent, not spoken for, left on the shelf, footloose and fancy-free, unengaged • *Those who are*

u

unattached may find that a potential mate is very close.
2 *often with* **to = independent (from)**, unaffiliated (to), nonaligned (to), free (from), autonomous (from), uncommitted (to) • *There's one nursery which is unattached to any school.*
OPPOSITES: attached (to), affiliated (to), aligned (to)

unattended 1 = **abandoned**, left alone, unguarded, ignored, disregarded, not cared for, unwatched • *An unattended bag was spotted near the platform at Gatwick.*
2 = **alone**, on your own, unaccompanied, unescorted, unwatched • *Never leave young children unattended.*

unattractive = **ugly**, homely *(U.S.)*, plain, hideous, grotesque, unsightly, displeasing, unappealing, unlovely, unprepossessing, plain-looking, ugly-looking, no oil painting *(informal)*, ill-favoured, as ugly as sin *(informal)*, short on looks *(informal)*, fugly *(chiefly U.S. & Austral.)* • *I'm 27, have a good job and I'm not unattractive.*

unauthorized = **illegal**, unofficial, unlawful, unconstitutional, unwarranted, off the record, under-the-table, unapproved, unsanctioned • *the unauthorized use of a military vehicle*
OPPOSITES: official, legal, sanctioned

unavailing = **useless**, unsuccessful, ineffective, futile, vain, idle, pointless, fruitless, unproductive, abortive, ineffectual, to no purpose, of no avail, bootless • *a brave but unavailing fight against a terminal illness*
OPPOSITES: successful, effective, productive

unavoidable = **inevitable**, inescapable, inexorable, sure, certain, necessary, fated, compulsory, obligatory, bound to happen, ineluctable • *Managers said the job losses were unavoidable.*

unaware = **ignorant**, unconscious, oblivious, in the dark *(informal)*, unsuspecting, uninformed, unknowing, heedless, unenlightened, unmindful, not in the loop *(informal)*, incognizant • *She was unaware that she was being filmed.*
OPPOSITES: knowing, aware, conscious

unawares 1 = **by surprise**, unprepared, off guard, suddenly, unexpectedly, abruptly, aback, without warning, on the hop *(Brit. informal)*, caught napping • *The suspect was taken unawares.*
OPPOSITES: prepared, on the lookout, forewarned
2 = **unknowingly**, unwittingly, unconsciously • *They were entertaining an angel unawares.*
OPPOSITES: knowingly, wittingly

unbalanced 1 = **deranged**, disturbed, unstable, touched, mad, crazy, barking *(slang)*, eccentric, insane, irrational, erratic, lunatic, demented, unsound, unhinged, loopy *(informal)*, out to lunch *(informal)*, barking mad *(slang)*, gonzo *(slang)*, not all there, doolally *(slang)*, off your trolley *(slang)*, up the pole *(informal)*, non compos mentis *(Latin)*, not the full shilling *(informal)*, wacko *or* whacko *(informal)*, a sausage short of a fry-up *(slang)*, off the air *(Austral. slang)*, daggy *(Austral. & N.Z. informal)* • *He was shown to be mentally unbalanced.*
2 = **biased**, one-sided, prejudiced, unfair, partial, partisan, unjust, inequitable • *unbalanced and unfair reporting*
3 = **irregular**, not balanced, lacking • *unbalanced and uncontrolled diets*
4 = **shaky**, unstable, wobbly • *The Logan Air BAe 46 was noticeably unbalanced.*
OPPOSITES: balanced, stable

unbearable = **intolerable**, insufferable, unendurable, too much *(informal)*, unacceptable, oppressive, insupportable • *I was in terrible, unbearable pain.*
OPPOSITES: tolerable, bearable, endurable

unbeatable 1 = **unsurpassed**, matchless, unsurpassable • *These resorts remain unbeatable in terms of price.*
2 = **invincible**, unstoppable, indomitable, unconquerable • *The opposition was unbeatable.*

unbeaten = **undefeated**, winning, triumphant, victorious, unsurpassed, unbowed, unvanquished, unsubdued • *He's unbeaten in 20 fights.*

unbecoming 1 = **unattractive**, unflattering, unsightly, unsuitable, incongruous, unsuited, ill-suited • *an unbecoming dress hurriedly stitched from cheap cloth*
2 = **unseemly**, inappropriate, unfit, offensive, improper, tasteless, discreditable, indelicate, indecorous, unbefitting • *Those involved had performed acts unbecoming of university students.*
OPPOSITES: seemly, decent, proper

unbelief 1 = **atheism**, scepticism, freethinking, godlessness, irreligion, paganism, heathenism, nonbelief • *Its purpose was to study atheism and unbelief.*
2 = **disbelief**, scepticism, incredulity, doubt, distrust, mistrust, dubiety • *He wore on his face an expression of amazed unbelief.*
OPPOSITES: trust, belief, faith

QUOTATIONS
To choose unbelief is to choose mind over dogma, to trust in our humanity instead of all these dangerous divinities
[Salman Rushdie *Imagine No Heaven*]

unbelievable 1 = **wonderful**, excellent, superb, fantastic *(informal)*, mean *(slang)*, great *(informal)*, topping *(Brit. slang)*, bad *(slang)*, cracking *(Brit. informal)*, crucial *(slang)*, smashing *(informal)*, magnificent, fabulous *(informal)*, divine *(informal)*, glorious, terrific *(informal)*, splendid, sensational *(informal)*, mega *(slang)*, sovereign, awesome *(slang)*, colossal, super *(informal)*, wicked *(informal)*, def *(slang)*, brill *(informal)*, stupendous, bodacious *(slang, chiefly U.S.)*, boffo *(slang)*, jim-dandy *(slang)*, chillin' *(U.S. slang)*, booshit *(Austral. slang)*, exo *(Austral. slang)*, sik *(Austral. slang)*, rad *(informal)*, phat *(slang)*, schmick *(Austral. informal)*, beaut *(informal)*, barrie *(Scot. slang)*, belting *(Brit. slang)*, pearler *(Austral. slang)* • *His guitar solos are just unbelievable.*
OPPOSITES: bad, terrible, awful
2 = **incredible**, impossible, unthinkable, astonishing, staggering, questionable, improbable, inconceivable, preposterous, unconvincing, unimaginable, outlandish, far-fetched, implausible, beyond belief, jaw-dropping, eye-popping *(informal)*, cock-and-bull *(informal)* • *I find it unbelievable that people can accept this sort of behaviour.*
OPPOSITES: possible, likely, believable

unbeliever = **atheist**, sceptic, disbeliever, agnostic, infidel, doubting Thomas • *They come as unbelievers and go away with a new faith in life.*

unbelieving = **sceptical**, doubting, suspicious, doubtful, dubious, unconvinced, disbelieving, incredulous, distrustful • *He looked at me with unbelieving eyes.*
OPPOSITES: believing, convinced, credulous

unbend 1 = **relax**, loosen up, lighten up *(slang)*, unwind, chill out *(slang, chiefly U.S.)*, let up, take it easy, slacken, cool it *(slang)*, unbutton *(informal)*, ease up, let it all hang out *(slang)*, let yourself go, become informal • *In her dying days, the old Queen unbent a little.*
2 = **straighten**, unwind, uncoil, uncurl • *Joy unbent slowly and eased her spine.*

unbending = **inflexible**, strict, rigid, firm, tough, severe, stubborn, hardline, uncompromising, resolute, intractable, unyielding • *her unbending opposition to the old regime*

unbiased = **fair**, just, objective, neutral, open-minded, equitable, impartial, disinterested, even-handed, dispassionate, unprejudiced • *The researchers were expected to be unbiased.*
OPPOSITES: unfair, prejudiced, biased

unbidden AS AN ADVERB = **spontaneously**, unprompted, freely, unwanted, voluntarily, willingly, uninvited, unasked for • *The name came unbiddden to his mind.*

▸ **AS AN ADJECTIVE** = **spontaneous**, free, voluntary, uninvited, willing, unwanted, unwelcome, unforced, unasked, unprompted • *uncensored mental images and unbidden thoughts*

unbind = **free**, undo, loosen, release, set free, untie, unchain, unfasten, unstrap, unclasp, unshackle, unloose, unfetter, unyoke, unbridle • *Many cultures have strict rules about women displaying unbound hair.*
OPPOSITES: tie, bind, fasten

unblemished 1 = **spotless**, immaculate, impeccable, perfect, pure, unsullied, untarnished • *his unblemished reputation as a man of honour and principle*
OPPOSITES: stained, flawed, tarnished
2 = **perfect**, flawless, spotless, unstained, unflawed, unspotted • *Be sure to select firm, unblemished fruit.*

unblinking = **steady**, unwavering, unflinching, cool, calm, fearless, impassive, unafraid, unemotional, emotionless, unfaltering, unshrinking • *an expressionless, unblinking stare*

unborn = **expected**, awaited, embryonic, in utero *(Latin)* • *her unborn baby*

unbounded = **unlimited**, endless, infinite, limitless, vast, absolute, lavish, uncontrolled, unchecked, boundless, unbridled, unrestrained, immeasurable, unconstrained • *an unbounded capacity to imitate and adopt the new*
OPPOSITES: limited, bounded, restricted

unbreakable = **durable**, indestructible, shatterproof, lasting, strong, solid, resistant, rugged, armoured, toughened, nonbreakable, infrangible • *Tableware for outdoor use should ideally be unbreakable.*
OPPOSITES: delicate, fragile, brittle

unbridled = **unrestrained**, uncontrolled, unchecked, violent, excessive, rampant, unruly, full-on *(informal)*, wanton, riotous, intemperate, ungovernable, unconstrained, licentious, ungoverned, uncurbed • *a tale of lust and unbridled passion*

unbroken 1 = **intact**, whole, undamaged, complete, total, entire, solid, untouched, unscathed, unspoiled, unimpaired • *Against all odds her glasses remained unbroken after the explosion.*
OPPOSITES: broken, damaged, cracked
2 = **continuous**, uninterrupted, constant, successive, endless, progressive, incessant, ceaseless, unremitting • *The ruling party has governed the country for an unbroken thirty years.*
OPPOSITES: occasional, interrupted, irregular
3 = **undisturbed**, uninterrupted, sound, fast, deep, profound, untroubled, unruffled • *We maintained an almost unbroken silence.*
4 = **untamed**, wild, undomesticated • *The car plunged like an unbroken horse.*
5 = **unbeaten**, undefeated, unsurpassed, supreme, unrivalled, second to none, unmatched, matchless • *Her Olympic record stands unbroken.*

u

unburden **AS A VERB** 1 = **reveal**, confide, disclose, lay bare, unbosom • *He had to unburden his soul to somebody.*
2 = **unload**, relieve, discharge, lighten, disencumber, disburden, ease the load of • *The human touch is one of the surest ways of unburdening stresses.*
▸ **IN PHRASES: unburden yourself** = **confess**, come clean about *(informal)*, get something off your chest *(informal)*, tell all about, empty yourself, spill your guts about *(slang)*, make a clean breast of something, cough *(slang)* • *Many came to unburden themselves of emotional problems.*

unburdened = **unrestricted**, unhindered, unencumbered, unhampered, unfettered • *She could enjoy life unburdened by marriage.*

uncalled-for = **unnecessary**, unjustified, unwarranted, inappropriate, needless, unwelcome, unjust, gratuitous, unprovoked, undeserved • *Leo's uncalled-for remarks about her cousin*
OPPOSITES: necessary, deserved, justified

uncanny 1 = **weird**, strange, mysterious, queer, unearthly, eerie, supernatural, unnatural, spooky *(informal)*, creepy *(informal)*, eldritch *(poetic)*, preternatural • *I had this uncanny feeling that Alice was warning me.*
2 = **extraordinary**, remarkable, incredible, unusual, fantastic, astonishing, exceptional, astounding, singular, miraculous, unheard-of, prodigious • *The hero bears an uncanny resemblance to Kirk Douglas.*

uncaring = **unconcerned**, indifferent, negligent, unmoved, unsympathetic, uninterested, unresponsive, unfeeling • *this uncaring attitude towards the less well off*

unceasing = **continual**, constant, incessant, continuing, endless, continuous, persistent, perpetual, never-ending, unending, ceaseless, unremitting, nonstop, unfailing • *After a few minutes, I was plunged into unceasing activity.*
OPPOSITES: occasional, irregular, periodic

unceremoniously = **rudely**, hastily, hurriedly, summarily, suddenly, dismissively, perfunctorily, discourteously • *He had to be bundled unceremoniously out of the way.*

uncertain 1 = **unsure**, undecided, at a loss, vague, unclear, doubtful, dubious, ambivalent, hazy, hesitant, vacillating, in two minds, undetermined, irresolute • *He stopped, uncertain how to put the question tactfully.*
OPPOSITES: sure, certain, positive
2 = **doubtful**, undetermined, unpredictable, insecure, questionable, ambiguous, unreliable, precarious, indefinite, indeterminate, incalculable, iffy *(informal)*, changeable, indistinct, chancy, unforeseeable, unsettled, unresolved, in the balance, unconfirmed, up in the air, unfixed, conjectural • *Students all over the country are facing an uncertain future.*
OPPOSITES: decided, certain, known

uncertainty 1 = **unpredictability**, precariousness, state of suspense, ambiguity, unreliability, fickleness, inconclusiveness, chanciness, changeableness • *a period of political uncertainty*
OPPOSITES: predictability, conclusiveness
2 = **doubt**, confusion, dilemma, misgiving, qualm, bewilderment, quandary, puzzlement, perplexity, mystification • *The magazine ignores all the uncertainties males currently face.*
OPPOSITES: confidence, assurance, certainty
3 = **hesitancy**, hesitation, indecision, lack of confidence, vagueness, irresolution • *There was a hint of uncertainty in his voice.*
4 = **unsureness**, doubt, scepticism, ambivalence, disquiet, indecision, vagueness, hesitancy, vacillation, lack of conviction, irresolution, dubiety, doubtfulness • *There is genuine uncertainty about the party's future plans.*

unchangeable = **unalterable**, fixed, immutable, strong, permanent, stable, constant, inevitable, irreversible, steadfast, immovable, invariable, changeless • *an almost unchangeable system of laws and customs*
OPPOSITES: variable, changeable, shifting

unchanged = **static**, fixed, frozen, stable, constant, steady, unaltered, unvarying • *For many years prices have remained virtually unchanged.*

unchanging = **constant**, eternal, perpetual, lasting, continuing, permanent, enduring, unchanged, abiding, immutable, imperishable, unvarying, changeless, unfading • *eternal and unchanging truths*

uncharacteristic = **unusual**, atypical, uncommon, out of the ordinary, unrepresentative • *an uncharacteristic lack of modesty*

uncharitable = **unkind**, mean, cruel, insensitive, unfriendly, merciless, unforgiving, unsympathetic, stingy, unfeeling, ungenerous, unchristian, hardhearted • *an uncharitable assessment of the reasons for the failure*
OPPOSITES: kind, generous, charitable

uncharted = **unexplored**, unknown, undiscovered, strange, virgin, unfamiliar, unplumbed, not mapped

• *a largely uncharted area of medical science*

unchecked = **uncontrolled**, out of control, rampant, out of hand, full-on *(informal)*, unbridled, riotous, unrestrained, running wild, undisciplined, untrammelled, ungoverned, uncurbed • *Brutality and lawlessness are allowed to go unchecked.*

uncivil = **impolite**, rude, bad-mannered, surly, gruff, churlish, bearish, disrespectful, brusque, boorish, uncouth, discourteous, ill-bred, unmannerly, ill-mannered • *The shock of being addressed in such an uncivil tone was too much.*
OPPOSITES: civil, mannerly, polite

uncivilized 1 = **primitive**, wild, savage, barbarian, illiterate, uneducated, barbaric, barbarous • *non-Western countries which did not wish to appear backward or uncivilized*
2 = **uncouth**, gross, vulgar, coarse, philistine, churlish, brutish, unsophisticated, beyond the pale, boorish, uncultivated, unpolished, uncultured, unmannered • *mutual accusations of uncivilized behaviour*

uncle
▸ RELATED ADJECTIVE: avuncular

unclean 1 = **dirty**, soiled, foul, contaminated, polluted, nasty, filthy, defiled, impure, scuzzy *(slang, chiefly U.S.)*, skanky *(slang)*, festy *(Austral. slang)* • *By bathing in unclean water, they expose themselves to contamination.*
OPPOSITES: clean, pure, spotless
2 = **immoral**, corrupt, impure, evil, dirty, nasty, foul, polluted, filthy, scuzzy *(slang, chiefly U.S.)* • *unclean thoughts*

unclear 1 = **uncertain**, unknown, doubtful, confused, vague, unsettled, in doubt, unsure, ambiguous, unresolved, in the balance, indefinite, debatable, up in the air, indeterminate, open to question, undetermined • *It is unclear how much popular support they have.*
OPPOSITES: evident, intelligible, determinate
2 = **unsure**, confused, doubtful, vague, dubious, wavering, unresolved, hesitant, undecided, hazy, indecisive, vacillating, in two minds, equivocating, irresolute • *He is still unclear about his own future.*

uncomfortable 1 = **uneasy**, troubled, disturbed, embarrassed, distressed, awkward, out of place, self-conscious, disquieted, ill at ease, discomfited, like a fish out of water • *The request for money made them feel uncomfortable.*
OPPOSITES: relaxed, comfortable, at ease
2 = **painful**, awkward, irritating, hard, rough, troublesome, disagreeable, causing discomfort • *Wigs are hot and uncomfortable to wear constantly.*
3 = **awkward**, strained, embarrassing, tense, charged, embarrassed, tickly *(informal)*, unpleasant, uneasy, barro *(Austral. slang)* • *There was another long and uncomfortable silence.*

uncommitted = **undecided**, uninvolved, nonpartisan, nonaligned, free, floating, neutral, not involved, unattached, free-floating, (sitting) on the fence • *The allegiance of uncommitted voters will be crucial.*

uncommon 1 = **rare**, unusual, odd, novel, strange, bizarre, curious, peculiar, unfamiliar, scarce, queer, singular, few and far between, out of the ordinary, infrequent, thin on the ground • *Cancer of the breast in young women is uncommon.*
OPPOSITES: common, regular, usual
2 = **extraordinary**, rare, remarkable, special, outstanding, superior, distinctive, exceptional, unprecedented, notable, singular, unparalleled, noteworthy, inimitable, incomparable • *Both are blessed with an uncommon ability to fix things.*
OPPOSITES: average, ordinary, everyday

uncommonly 1 = **exceptionally**, very, extremely, remarkably, particularly, strangely, seriously *(informal)*, unusually, peculiarly, to the nth degree • *Mary was uncommonly good at tennis.*
2 *used in negative constructions* = **rarely**, occasionally, seldom, not often, infrequently, hardly ever, only now and then, scarcely ever • *Not uncommonly, family strains may remain hidden behind complaints.*

uncommunicative = **reticent**, reserved, withdrawn, close, short, guarded, retiring, silent, shy, secretive, curt, taciturn, unresponsive, unforthcoming, tight-lipped • *My daughter is very difficult, uncommunicative and moody.*
OPPOSITES: forthcoming, chatty, talkative

uncomplicated = **simple**, clear, easy, straightforward, direct, accessible, elementary, effortless, painless, trouble-free, facile, unsophisticated, undemanding, unchallenging, idiot-proof, unexacting • *It must be a very uncomplicated arrangement.*

uncompromising 1 = **inflexible**, strict, rigid, decided, firm, tough, stubborn, hardline, die-hard, inexorable, steadfast, unyielding, obstinate, intransigent, unbending, obdurate, stiff-necked • *Mrs Thatcher was a tough and uncompromising politician.*
2 = **unrelenting**, ruthless, relentless, tough, cruel, merciless, pitiless, unsparing, unsoftened • *a film of uncompromising brutality*

unconcern = **indifference**, detachment, nonchalance, apathy, lack of interest, remoteness, insouciance, aloofness, uninterestedness • *Her feelings had gone from blithe unconcern to anxiety.*

unconcerned = **untroubled**, relaxed, unperturbed, nonchalant, easy, careless, not bothered, serene, callous, carefree, unruffled, blithe, insouciant, unworried, not giving a toss *(informal)* • *Paul was unconcerned about what he had done.*
OPPOSITES: concerned, worried, anxious

unconditional = **absolute**, full, complete, total, positive, entire, utter, explicit, outright, unlimited, downright, unqualified, unrestricted, out-and-out, plenary, categorical, unreserved • *The leader of the revolt made an unconditional surrender.*
OPPOSITES: limited, qualified, partial

unconnected 1 = **separate**, independent, unrelated, divided, detached, disconnected, not related • *I can't believe that those two murders are unconnected.*
2 = **incoherent**, disconnected, disjointed, irrelevant, meaningless, illogical, nonsensical • *The knowledge turned in unconnected fragments in his head.*
OPPOSITES: connected, coherent, relevant

unconquerable = **invincible**, unbeatable, indomitable, enduring, irresistible, irrepressible, insurmountable, unyielding, undefeatable • *a celebration of art, beauty and the unconquerable human spirit*

unconscionable 1 = **criminal**, unethical, amoral, unprincipled, unfair, unjust • *He calls the reductions an unconscionable threat to public safety.*
2 = **excessive**, outrageous, unreasonable, extreme, extravagant, preposterous, exorbitant, inordinate, immoderate • *Some child-care centres were charging unconscionable fees.*

unconscious AS AN ADJECTIVE 1 = **senseless**, knocked out, out cold *(informal)*, out, stunned, numb, dazed, blacked out *(informal)*, in a coma, comatose, stupefied, asleep, out for the count *(informal)*, insensible, dead to the world *(informal)* • *By the time ambulancemen arrived, he was unconscious.*
OPPOSITES: conscious, awake, sensible
2 = **unaware**, ignorant, oblivious, unsuspecting, lost to, blind to, in ignorance, unknowing • *Mr Battersby was apparently quite unconscious of their presence.*
OPPOSITES: aware, conscious, alert
3 = **unintentional**, unwitting, unintended, inadvertent, accidental, unpremeditated • *'You're well out of it,' he said with unconscious brutality.*
OPPOSITES: planned, conscious, intentional

4 = **subconscious**, automatic, suppressed, repressed, inherent, reflex, instinctive, innate, hard-wired, involuntary, latent, subliminal, unrealized, gut *(informal)* • *an unconscious desire expressed solely during sleep*

▸ IN PHRASES: **the unconscious** = **subconscious mind**, self, ego, psyche, id, subconscious, unconscious mind, superego, inner self, inner man *or* woman • *Freud examined the content of the unconscious.*

QUOTATIONS

The images of the unconscious place a great responsibility upon a man. Failure to understand them, or a shirking of ethical responsibility, deprives him of his wholeness and imposes a painful fragmentariness on his life

[Carl Jung *Memories, Dreams, Reflections*]

unconsciousness = **insensibility**, oblivion, blackout, coma, numbness, stupor, torpor, blankness, senselessness, stupefaction, unawareness • *He knew that he might soon lapse into unconsciousness.*

uncontrollable 1 = **unmanageable**, violent, strong, wild, mad, furious, frantic, irresistible, carried away, unruly, irrepressible, ungovernable, beside yourself, like one possessed • *When he lost his temper, he was uncontrollable.*
2 = **violent**, wild, unruly, unmanageable, ungovernable • *The situation could become uncontrollable.*

uncontrolled 1 = **unrestrained**, violent, wild, undisciplined, furious, out of control, rampant, out of hand, unruly, boisterous, unchecked, full-on *(informal)*, unbridled, riotous, running wild, untrammelled, ungoverned, lacking self-control, uncurbed, unsubmissive • *His uncontrolled behaviour disturbed the whole class.*
OPPOSITES: controlled, disciplined, restrained
2 = **unchecked**, unrestrained, ungoverned, uncurbed • *the central bank's uncontrolled printing of money*

unconventional 1 = **unusual**, unorthodox, odd, eccentric, different, individual, original, out there *(slang)*, bizarre, way-out *(informal)*, informal, irregular, bohemian, far-out *(slang)*, idiosyncratic, off-the-wall *(slang)*, oddball *(informal)*, individualistic, out of the ordinary, offbeat, left-field *(informal)*, freakish, atypical, nonconformist, wacko *(slang)*, outré, boho, uncustomary, daggy *(Austral. & N.Z. informal)* • *He was known for his unconventional behaviour.*
OPPOSITES: normal, regular, conventional
2 = **unorthodox**, original, unusual, irregular, atypical, different, uncustomary • *The vaccine had been produced by an unconventional technique.*
OPPOSITES: normal, regular, usual

unconvinced = **sceptical**, doubtful, disbelieving, doubting, cynical, dubious, incredulous, mistrustful, unbelieving, unpersuaded • *Most consumers seem unconvinced that the recession is over.*

unconvincing = **implausible**, unlikely, lame, suspect, thin, weak, dubious, questionable, hard to believe, feeble, improbable, flimsy, fishy *(informal)*, specious, cock-and-bull *(informal)*, unpersuasive • *He was given the usual unconvincing excuses.*
OPPOSITES: likely, convincing, believable

uncooperative = **unhelpful**, difficult, awkward, unreasonable, obstructive, unresponsive, cussed *(informal)*, bloody-minded *(Brit. informal)*, inconsiderate, unsupportive, disobliging, unaccommodating • *a bunch of stupid, cranky, uncooperative old fools*
OPPOSITES: helpful, obliging, accommodating

uncoordinated 1 = **clumsy**, awkward, ungainly, bungling, lumbering, inept, bumbling, graceless, heavy-footed, maladroit, clodhopping *(informal)*, all thumbs, ungraceful, butterfingered *(informal)*, unco *(Austral. slang)* • *They were unsteady on their feet and rather uncoordinated.*
2 = **disorganized**, confused, chaotic, disordered, muddled, jumbled, haphazard, unorganized, unsystematic, unmethodical • *Government action has been half-hearted and uncoordinated.*

uncouth = **coarse**, rough, gross, awkward, crude, rude, clumsy, vulgar, rustic, barbaric, unseemly, ungainly, boorish, gawky, unrefined, loutish, graceless, uncultivated, uncivilized, clownish, oafish, ill-mannered, lubberly • *that oafish, uncouth person*
OPPOSITES: elegant, refined, cultivated

uncover 1 = **reveal**, find, discover, expose, encounter, turn up, detect, disclose, unveil, come across, unearth, dig up, divulge, chance on, root out, unmask, lay bare, make known, blow the whistle on *(informal)*, bring to light, smoke out, take the wraps off, blow wide open *(slang)*, stumble on *or* across • *Auditors said they had uncovered evidence of fraud.*
OPPOSITES: hide, conceal, suppress
2 = **open**, unveil, unwrap, show, strip, expose, bare, lay bare, lift the lid, lay open • *When the seedlings sprout, uncover the tray.*

uncritical = **undiscriminating**, unthinking, undiscerning, indiscriminate, unfussy, easily pleased, unselective, unperceptive, unexacting • *the view of women as uncritical purchasers of advertised products*
OPPOSITES: critical, discriminating, discerning

unctuous 1 = **obsequious**, smooth, slick, plausible, oily, gushing, fawning, suave, glib, ingratiating, insincere, sycophantic, smarmy *(Brit. informal)* • *the kind of unctuous tone that I've heard at diplomatic parties*
2 = **oily**, creamy, greasy, oleaginous • *Goose fat gives the most unctuous flavour.*

undaunted = **undeterred**, unflinching, not discouraged, not put off, brave, bold, courageous, gritty, fearless, resolute, gallant, intrepid, steadfast, indomitable, dauntless, undismayed, unfaltering, nothing daunted, undiscouraged, unshrinking • *Although the forecast was for rain, the crowd were undaunted.*

undecided 1 = **unsure**, uncertain, uncommitted, torn, doubtful, dubious, wavering, hesitant, ambivalent, dithering *(chiefly Brit.)*, in two minds, irresolute, swithering *(Scot.)* • *She was still undecided as to what career she wanted to pursue.*
OPPOSITES: decided, sure, certain
2 = **unsettled**, open, undetermined, vague, pending, tentative, in the balance, indefinite, debatable, up in the air, moot, iffy *(informal)*, unconcluded • *The release date for his record is still undecided.*
OPPOSITES: definite, decided, settled

undefiled = **immaculate**, pure, impeccable, flawless, clear, clean, spotless, squeaky-clean, chaste, unblemished, virginal, unsullied, sinless, unstained, unsoiled, unspotted • *It was a noble soul that had assumed an undefiled body.*
OPPOSITES: impure, soiled, stained

undefined 1 = **unspecified**, indefinite, indeterminate, vague, unclear, unsettled, woolly, unexplained, imprecise, non-specific, undetermined, inexact, unspecific, unfixed • *a strict guarantee to hold prices for an undefined period*
OPPOSITES: exact, precise, specified, clear, defined
2 = **indistinct**, blurred, vague, obscure, dim, shadowy, indefinite, misty, hazy, indistinguishable, blurry, nebulous, formless, barely perceptible • *blurry lines and undefined borders*

undemonstrative = **reserved**, formal, distant, stiff, contained, cold, withdrawn, restrained, aloof, reticent, impassive, unresponsive, stolid, unemotional, uncommunicative, unaffectionate • *Lady Ainslie is an undemonstrative woman.*
OPPOSITES: warm, friendly, demonstrative

undeniable = **certain**, evident, undoubted, incontrovertible, clear, sure, sound, proven, obvious, patent, manifest, beyond (a) doubt, unassailable, indisputable,

u

irrefutable, unquestionable, beyond question, incontestable, indubitable • *Her charm is undeniable.*
OPPOSITES: uncertain, doubtful, dubious

under AS A PREPOSITION 1 = **below**, beneath, underneath, on the bottom of • *A path runs under the trees.*
OPPOSITES: up, over, above
2 = **subject to**, liable to, controlled by, bound by, under the control of, at the mercy of, constrained by • *I'm rarely under pressure at work.*
3 = **subordinate to**, subject to, reporting to, directed by, governed by, inferior to, secondary to, subservient to, junior to • *I am the new manager and you will be working under me.*
4 = **included in**, belonging to, subsumed under, comprised in • *under section 4 of the Family Law Reform Act*
5 = **less than**, below, not as much as • *jobs for those under 65*
6 = **undergoing**, receiving, in the process of • *the Channel tunnel now under construction*
▸ AS AN ADVERB = **below**, down, beneath, downward, to the bottom • *A hand came from behind and pushed his head under.*
OPPOSITES: up, over, above
▸ RELATED PREFIX: sub-

underclothes = **underwear**, lingerie, undies *(informal)*, smalls *(informal)*, undergarments, unmentionables *(humorous)*, underclothing, underthings, underlinen, broekies *(S. African informal)* • *I want to buy some underclothes for a friend of mine.*
▹ *See panel* **Underwear**

undercover = **secret**, covert, clandestine, private, hidden, intelligence, underground, spy, concealed, confidential, hush-hush *(informal)*, surreptitious • *an undercover operation designed to catch drug smugglers*
OPPOSITES: open, plain, visible

undercurrent 1 = **undertone**, feeling, atmosphere, sense, suggestion, trend, hint, flavour, tendency, drift, murmur, tenor, aura, tinge, vibes *(slang)*, vibrations, overtone, hidden feeling • *a deep undercurrent of racism in British society*
2 = **undertow**, tideway, riptide, rip, rip current, crosscurrent, underflow • *He tried to swim after him but the strong undercurrent swept them apart.*

undercut 1 = **charge less than**, undersell, underbid, charge a lower price than • *The firm will be able to undercut its competitors.*
2 = **underprice**, sell cheaply, sell at a loss, undersell, sacrifice, undercharge • *Prices were undercut and profits collapsed.*
3 = **weaken**, undermine, subvert, threaten, impair, debilitate • *Popular support would be undercut by political developments.*

underdeveloped = **developing**, third-world • *public health problems in the underdeveloped world*

underdog = **weaker party**, victim, loser, little fellow *(informal)*, outsider, fall guy *(informal)* • *Most of the crowd were cheering for the underdog to win.*

underestimate 1 = **undervalue**, understate, underrate, diminish, play down, minimize, downgrade, miscalculate, trivialize, rate too low, underemphasize, hold cheap, misprize • *Never underestimate what you can learn from a group of like-minded people.*
OPPOSITES: exaggerate, overstate, overestimate
2 = **underrate**, undervalue, belittle, sell short *(informal)*, not do justice to, rate too low, set no store by, hold cheap, think too little of • *The first lesson I learnt was never to underestimate the enemy.*
OPPOSITES: overestimate, overrate

undergo = **experience**, go through, be subjected to, stand, suffer, bear, weather, sustain, endure, withstand, submit to • *New recruits have been undergoing training in recent weeks.*

underground AS AN ADVERB 1 = **below ground**, in the earth, under the earth, below the surface • *Solid low-level waste will be disposed of deep underground.*
2 = **in hiding**, behind closed doors, in secrecy, undercover, out of sight, in seclusion • *Opposition leaders are working underground.*
▸ AS AN ADJECTIVE 1 = **subterranean**, basement, lower-level, sunken, covered, buried, below the surface, below ground, subterrestrial • *a rundown shopping area with an underground car park*
2 = **secret**, undercover, covert, hidden, guerrilla, revolutionary, concealed, confidential, dissident, closet, subversive, clandestine, renegade, insurgent, hush-hush *(informal)*, surreptitious, cloak-and-dagger, hugger-mugger, insurrectionist, hole-and-corner, radical • *accused of organising and financing an underground youth movement*
3 = **avant-garde**, alternative, experimental, innovative, ground-breaking • *a film about the underground music scene in Los Angeles*
▸ IN PHRASES: **the underground** 1 = **the tube** *(Brit.)*, the subway, the metro • *The underground is ideal for getting to work in Milan.*
2 = **the Resistance**, partisans, freedom fighters, the Maquis • *U.S. dollars were smuggled into the country to aid the underground.*

undergrowth = **scrub**, brush, underwood, bracken, brambles, briars, underbrush, brushwood, underbush • *plunging through the undergrowth*

underhand = **sly**, secret, crooked *(informal)*, devious, sneaky, secretive, fraudulent, treacherous, dishonest, deceptive, clandestine, unscrupulous, crafty, unethical, furtive, deceitful, surreptitious, stealthy, dishonourable, below the belt *(informal)*, underhanded • *The Prime Minister had been involved in underhand financial deals.*
OPPOSITES: open, legal, honest

underline 1 = **emphasize**, stress, highlight, bring home, underscore, accentuate, point up, give emphasis to, call *or* draw attention to • *The report underlined his concern that standards were at risk.*
OPPOSITES: play down, minimize, make light of
2 = **underscore**, mark, italicize, rule a line under • *Take two pens and underline the positive and negative words.*

underling = **subordinate**, inferior, minion, servant, slave, cohort *(chiefly U.S.)*, retainer, menial, nonentity, lackey, hireling, flunky, understrapper • *underlings who do the dirty work*

underlying 1 = **fundamental**, basic, essential, root, prime, primary, radical, elementary, intrinsic, basal • *To stop a problem, you have to understand its underlying causes.*
2 = **hidden**, concealed, lurking, veiled, latent • *hills with the hard underlying rock poking through the turf*

undermine 1 = **weaken**, sabotage, subvert, compromise, disable, debilitate, disempower • *They are accused of trying to undermine the government.*
OPPOSITES: promote, sustain, reinforce
2 = **damage**, weaken, threaten, hurt, injure, impair, sap, put the kibosh on *(informal)*, throw a spanner in the works of *(Brit. informal)* • *This will undermine their chances of success.*
OPPOSITES: strengthen, reinforce, fortify

underneath AS A PREPOSITION = **beneath**, below, at the bottom of • *a table for two underneath the olive trees*
▸ AS AN ADVERB = **inside**, secretly, in your heart, in your heart of hearts, in your innermost thoughts • *Underneath, Sofia was deeply committed to her husband.*
▸ AS AN ADJECTIVE = **underside**, base, bottom • *the underneath mechanism of the engine*
▸ AS A NOUN = **bottom**, base, underside • *The liquid formed on the underneath of the top plate.*

undernourished = **malnourished**, starving, underfed • *People who are undernourished also lack reserves of energy.*

underpinning = **support**, base, foundation, footing, groundwork, substructure • *the economic underpinning of ancient Mexican society*

underprivileged = **disadvantaged**, poor, deprived, in need, impoverished, needy, badly off, destitute, in want, on the breadline • *helping underprivileged children to learn to read*

underrate = **underestimate**, discount, undervalue, belittle, disparage, fail to appreciate, not do justice to, set (too) little store by, misprize • *He underrated the seriousness of William's head injury.*
OPPOSITES: exaggerate, overvalue, overestimate

underside = **bottom**, base, underneath • *the underside of the car*

undersized = **stunted**, underdeveloped, small, tiny, miniature, squat, atrophied, underweight, teeny-weeny, dwarfish, teensy-weensy, runty, runtish, pygmy *or* pigmy • *undersized and underweight babies*
OPPOSITES: big, huge, giant

understand 1 = **comprehend**, get, take in, perceive, grasp, know, see, follow, realize, recognize, appreciate, be aware of, penetrate, make out, discern, twig *(Brit. informal)*, fathom, savvy *(slang)*, apprehend, conceive of, suss *(Brit. informal)*, get to the bottom of, get the hang of *(informal)*, tumble to *(informal)*, catch on to *(informal)*, cotton on to *(informal)*, make head or tail of *(informal)*, get your head round • *I think you understand my meaning.*
2 = **sympathize with**, appreciate, be aware of, be able to see, take on board *(informal)*, empathize with, commiserate with, show compassion for • *Trish had not exactly understood his feelings.*
3 = **believe**, hear, learn, gather, think, see, suppose, notice, assume, take it, conclude, fancy, presume, be informed, infer, surmise, hear tell, draw the inference • *I understand you've heard about David.*

QUOTATIONS
In the long course of history, having people who understand your thought is much greater security than another submarine
[J. William Fulbright *speaking of the Fulbright scholarship programme*]

understandable 1 = **reasonable**, natural, normal, justified, expected, inevitable, legitimate, logical, predictable, accountable, on the cards *(informal)*, foreseeable, to be expected, justifiable, unsurprising, excusable, pardonable • *His unhappiness was understandable.*
2 = **comprehensible**, clear, straightforward, coherent, lucid, user-friendly, easy to understand, crystal clear, unambiguous, intelligible, digestible, perspicuous • *He writes in a simple and understandable way.*

u

understanding AS A NOUN 1 = **perception**, knowledge, grasp, sense, know-how *(informal)*, intelligence, judgment, awareness, appreciation, insight, skill, penetration, mastery, comprehension, familiarity with, discernment, proficiency • *They have to have a basic understanding of computers.*
OPPOSITES: ignorance, incomprehension, obtuseness
2 = **sympathy**, consideration, sensitivity, love, concern, humanity, affection, warmth, tolerance, goodwill, compassion, kindness, empathy, tenderness, neighbourliness, humanitarianism, fellow feeling, considerateness, kind feeling, kind-heartedness • *We would like to thank them for their patience and understanding.*
OPPOSITES: insensitivity
3 = **agreement**, deal, promise, arrangement, accord, contract, bond, pledge, bargain, pact, compact, concord, gentlemen's agreement • *We had not set a date but there was an understanding between us.*
OPPOSITES: dispute, disagreement
4 = **belief**, view, opinion, impression, interpretation, feeling, idea, conclusion, notion, conviction, judgment, assumption, point of view, perception, suspicion, viewpoint, hunch, way of thinking, estimation, supposition, sneaking suspicion, funny feeling • *It is my understanding that this has been going on for many years.*
▸ AS AN ADJECTIVE = **sympathetic**, kind, compassionate, considerate, kindly, accepting, patient, sensitive, forgiving, discerning, tolerant, responsive, perceptive, forbearing • *Her boss, who was very understanding, gave her time off.*
OPPOSITES: insensitive, unsympathetic, inconsiderate

QUOTATIONS
Shallow understanding from people of good will is more frustrating than absolute misunderstanding from people of ill will
[Martin Luther King Jr. *Letter from Birmingham Jail*]
The ill and unfit choice of words wonderfully obstructs the understanding
[Francis Bacon *Novum Organum*]
I shall light a candle of understanding in thine heart, which shall not be put out
[Bible: II Esdras]

understate = **play down**, diminish, minimize, downgrade, talk down *(informal)*, sell short *(informal)*, soft-pedal *(informal)*, underemphasize • *The government chooses to understate the increase in prices.*
OPPOSITES: exaggerate, overstate, talk up *(informal)*

understatement 1 = **euphemism**, trivialization • *To say I'm disappointed is an understatement.*
2 = **restraint**, reserve, subtlety, delicacy, underplaying, understatedness, underemphasis • *typical British understatement*

understood 1 = **assumed**, presumed, accepted, taken for granted • *The management is understood to be very unwilling to agree.*
2 = **implied**, implicit, unspoken, inferred, tacit, unstated • *The technical equality of all officers was understood.*

understudy = **stand-in**, reserve, substitute, double, sub, replacement, fill-in • *He was an understudy to Charlie Chaplin on a tour of the USA.*

undertake 1 = **take on**, embark on, set about, commence, try, begin, attempt, tackle, enter upon, endeavour to do • *She undertook the arduous task of monitoring the elections.*
2 = **agree**, promise, contract, guarantee, engage, pledge, covenant, commit yourself, take upon yourself • *He undertook to edit the text himself.*

undertaker = **funeral director**, mortician *(U.S.)* • *I went out of the room to telephone a doctor and an undertaker.*

undertaking 1 = **task**, business, operation, project, game, attempt, effort, affair, venture, enterprise, endeavour • *Organizing the show has been a massive undertaking.*
2 = **promise**, commitment, pledge, word, vow, assurance, word of honour, solemn word • *British Coal gave an undertaking that it was maintaining the pits.*

undertone 1 = **murmur**, whisper, low tone, subdued voice • *Well-dressed clients were talking in polite undertones as they ate.*
2 = **undercurrent**, suggestion, trace, hint, feeling, touch, atmosphere, flavour, tinge, vibes *(slang)* • *The sobbing voice had an undertone of anger.*

undervalue = **underrate**, underestimate, minimize, look down on, misjudge, depreciate, make light of, set no store by, hold cheap, misprize • *We must never undervalue freedom.*
OPPOSITES: exaggerate, overvalue, overrate

underwater = **submerged**, submarine, immersed, sunken, undersea, subaqueous, subaquatic • *underwater camera equipment*

underway = **in progress**, going on, started, begun, in business, in motion, in operation, afoot • *An investigation is underway to find out how the disaster happened.*

underwear = **underclothes**, lingerie, undies *(informal)*, smalls *(informal)*, undergarments, unmentionables (*humorous*), underclothing, underthings, underlinen, broekies (*S. African informal*), underdaks (*Austral. slang*) • *a change of underwear*

▷ *See panel* **Underwear**

underweight = **skinny**, puny, emaciated, undernourished, skin and bone (*informal*), undersized, half-starved, underfed • *Nearly a third of the children were severely underweight.*

underworld 1 = **criminals**, gangsters, organized crime, gangland (*informal*), criminal element • *a wealthy businessman with underworld connections*

2 = **nether world**, hell, Hades, the inferno, nether regions, infernal region, abode of the dead • *Persephone, goddess of the underworld*

▸ RELATED ADJECTIVES: chthonian, chthonic

underwrite = **finance**, back, fund, guarantee, sponsor, insure, ratify, subsidize, bankroll (*U.S. informal*), provide security, provide capital for • *a special agency to underwrite small business loans*

undesirable = **unwanted**, unwelcome, disagreeable, objectionable, offensive, disliked, unacceptable, dreaded, unpopular, unsuitable, out of place, unattractive, distasteful, unsavoury, obnoxious, repugnant, unpleasing, unwished-for • *A large group of undesirable strangers crashed her party.*

OPPOSITES: welcome, acceptable, desirable

undeveloped = **potential**, immature, embryonic, in embryo • *damage to the undeveloped foetus*

undignified = **unseemly**, inappropriate, unsuitable, improper, unbecoming, unrefined, inelegant, ungentlemanly, beneath you, unladylike, indecorous, infra dig (*informal*), lacking dignity, beneath your dignity • *All this public outpouring is so undignified.*

OPPOSITES: becoming, seemly, dignified

undisciplined = **uncontrolled**, wild, unruly, wayward, wilful, unrestrained, disobedient, obstreperous • *a noisy and undisciplined group of students*

OPPOSITES: controlled, disciplined, restrained

undisclosed = **unrevealed**, unpublished, unannounced, secret • *The company has been sold for an undisclosed amount.*

undisguised = **obvious**, open, evident, complete, patent, utter, explicit, manifest, transparent, blatant, overt, unmistakable, out-and-out, wholehearted, thoroughgoing, unconcealed, unfeigned • *He looked down at Bauer in undisguised disgust.*

OPPOSITES: secret, hidden, disguised

undisputed = **acknowledged**, accepted, recognized, undeniable, sure, certain, conclusive, unchallenged, undoubted, indisputable, unquestioned, irrefutable, not disputed, incontrovertible, uncontested, beyond question, incontestable, freely admitted • *the undisputed fact that he had broken the law*

OPPOSITES: questioned, disputed

undistinguished = **ordinary**, mediocre, unremarkable, everyday, pedestrian, indifferent, commonplace, vanilla (*informal*), so-so (*informal*), prosaic, run-of-the-mill, unimpressive, unexciting, unexceptional, no great shakes (*informal*), nothing to write home about (*informal*) • *his short and undistinguished career as an art student*

OPPOSITES: striking, impressive

undisturbed 1 = **untouched**, not moved • *Peonies react badly to being moved and are best left undisturbed.*

OPPOSITES: moved, interfered with

2 = **quiet**, still, calm, peaceful, serene, tranquil, restful • *the undisturbed waters of the lake*

3 = **uninterrupted**, without interruption • *I can spend the whole day undisturbed at the warehouse.*

OPPOSITES: interrupted

4 = **unperturbed**, untroubled, calm, collected, composed, serene, tranquil, sedate, placid, unfazed (*informal*), unruffled, equable, unbothered, unagitated • *Victoria was strangely undisturbed by this news.*

OPPOSITES: troubled, excited

undivided 1 = **complete**, full, whole, total, entire, concentrated, exclusive, thorough, wholehearted, undistracted • *Adults rarely give the television their undivided attention.*

2 = **united**, whole, entire, unanimous, concerted, solid • *Mandela said, 'We want a united, undivided South Africa.'*

undo 1 = **open**, unfasten, loose, loosen, unlock, unwrap, untie, disengage, unbutton, disentangle, unstrap, unclasp • *I managed to undo a corner of the parcel.*

2 = **reverse**, cancel, offset, wipe out, neutralize, invalidate, annul, nullify • *It would be difficult to undo the damage that had been done.*

3 = **ruin**, defeat, destroy, wreck, shatter, upset, mar, undermine, overturn, quash, subvert, bring to naught • *Their hopes of a victory were undone by a goal from John Barnes.*

undoing = **downfall**, weakness, curse, trouble, trial, misfortune, blight, affliction, the last straw, fatal flaw • *His lack of experience may prove to be his undoing.*

undone[1] = **unfinished**, left, outstanding, not done, neglected, omitted, incomplete, passed over, unfulfilled, not completed, unperformed, unattended to • *She left nothing undone that needed attention.*

OPPOSITES: done, finished, complete

undone[2] = **ruined**, destroyed, overcome, hapless, forlorn, prostrate, wretched • *He is undone by his lack of inner substance.*

undoubted = **certain**, sure, definite, confirmed, positive, obvious, acknowledged, patent, evident, manifest, transparent, clear-cut, undisputed, indisputable,

UNDERWEAR

Balmoral
basque
bloomers
body
body stocking
boxer shorts
bra
briefs
broekies (*S. African*)
bustle
camiknickers
camisole
chemisette
combinations
corselet
corset
crinoline
drawers
foundation garment
French knickers
garter
girdle
G-string
half-slip *or* waist-slip
jockstrap *or* athletic support
knickers
liberty bodice
lingerie
long johns
pannier
panties
pants
panty girdle
petticoat
shift
shorts *or* undershorts (*chiefly U.S. & Canad.*)
singlet (*chiefly Brit.*)
step-ins
string vest
suspender *or* (*U.S.*) garter
suspender belt *or* (*U.S.*) garter belt
teddy
thermals
trunks
underpants
undershirt
underskirt
vest, undervest, undershirt, T-shirt (*U.S. & Canad.*), *or* (*Austral.*) singlet
Y-fronts

unquestioned, unquestionable, incontrovertible, indubitable, nailed-on *(slang)* • *The event was an undoubted success.*

undoubtedly = **certainly**, definitely, undeniably, surely, of course, doubtless, without doubt, unquestionably, unmistakably, assuredly, beyond question, beyond a shadow of (a) doubt • *He is undoubtedly a great player*

undreamed-of *or* **undreamt-of** = **unimagined**, inconceivable, incredible, astonishing, unexpected, miraculous, unheard-of, unforeseen, unsuspected, unthought-of • *They have freedoms that were undreamed-of even ten years ago.*

undress AS A VERB = **strip**, strip naked, disrobe, take off your clothes, peel off, doff your clothes • *She went out, leaving Rachel to undress and have her shower.*

▸ AS A NOUN = **nakedness**, nudity, disarray, deshabille • *Every cover showed a woman in a state of undress.*

undressed = **naked**, stripped, stark naked, in the raw *(informal)*, disrobed, starkers *(Brit. informal)*, unclothed, in the buff *(informal)*, au naturel *(French)*, in the altogether *(informal)*, buck naked *(U.S. informal)*, unclad *(formal)*, bollock-naked *(Brit. taboo slang)*, in the nuddy *(informal)* • *Fifteen minutes later he was undressed and in bed.*

undue = **excessive**, too much, inappropriate, extreme, unnecessary, extravagant, needless, unsuitable, improper, too great, disproportionate, unjustified, unwarranted, unseemly, inordinate, undeserved, intemperate, uncalled-for, overmuch, immoderate • *It might give them undue influence over the coming negotiations.*

OPPOSITES: due, necessary, appropriate

undulate = **wave**, roll, surge, swell, ripple, rise and fall, billow, heave • *the waves undulating like oceanic dunes*

unduly = **excessively**, overly, too much, unnecessarily, disproportionately, improperly, unreasonably, extravagantly, out of all proportion, inordinately, unjustifiably, overmuch, immoderately • *He appealed to firms not to increase their prices unduly.*

OPPOSITES: moderately, reasonably, duly

undying = **eternal**, everlasting, perpetual, continuing, permanent, constant, perennial, infinite, unending, indestructible, undiminished, imperishable, deathless, inextinguishable, unfading, sempiternal *(literary)* • *Dianne declared her undying love for Sam.*

OPPOSITES: fleeting, short-lived, ephemeral

unearth 1 = **discover**, find, reveal, expose, turn up, uncover, bring to light, ferret out, root up • *No evidence has yet been unearthed.*

2 = **dig up**, excavate, exhume, dredge up, disinter • *Fossil hunters have unearthed the bones of an elephant.*

unearthly 1 = **eerie**, strange, supernatural, ghostly, weird, phantom, uncanny, spooky *(informal)*, nightmarish, spectral, eldritch *(poetic)*, preternatural • *The sound was so serene that it seemed unearthly.*

2 = **unreasonable**, ridiculous, absurd, strange, extraordinary, abnormal, unholy *(informal)*, ungodly *(informal)* • *They arranged to meet at the unearthly hour of seven in the morning.*

unease 1 = **anxiety**, apprehension, nervousness, distress, angst, disquiet, trepidation, uneasiness, sense of foreboding, disquietude • *He tried to appear casual, but he couldn't conquer his unease.*

2 = **dissatisfaction**, dismay, discontent, disappointment, unhappiness, displeasure • *the depth of public unease about the economy*

uneasiness = **anxiety**, apprehension, misgiving, worry, doubt, alarm, suspicion, nervousness, disquiet, agitation, qualms, trepidation, perturbation, apprehensiveness, dubiety • *I felt a great uneasiness about meeting her again.*

OPPOSITES: ease, calm, serenity

uneasy 1 = **anxious**, worried, troubled, upset, wired *(slang)*, nervous, disturbed, uncomfortable, unsettled, impatient, restless, agitated, apprehensive, edgy, jittery *(informal)*, perturbed, on edge, ill at ease, restive, twitchy *(informal)*, like a fish out of water, antsy *(informal)*, discomposed • *He looked uneasy and refused to answer questions.*

OPPOSITES: relaxed, comfortable, calm

2 = **precarious**, strained, uncomfortable, tense, awkward, unstable, shaky, insecure, constrained • *An uneasy calm has settled over Los Angeles.*

3 = **disturbing**, upsetting, disquieting, worrying, troubling, bothering, dismaying • *This is an uneasy book.*

uneconomic = **unprofitable**, loss-making, non-profit-making, nonpaying, nonviable • *the closure of uneconomic factories*

OPPOSITES: economic, profitable, productive

uneducated 1 = **ignorant**, illiterate, unread, unschooled, unlettered, untaught • *Though an uneducated man, Chavez was not a stupid one.*

OPPOSITES: educated, literate, schooled

2 = **uncultured**, philistine, uncultivated, vulgar, benighted, lowbrow • *It looks amateurish to the uneducated eye.*

unemotional = **impassive**, cold, reserved, cool, indifferent, apathetic, unresponsive, phlegmatic, unfeeling, passionless, undemonstrative, unexcitable, unimpressionable • *British men are often seen as being reserved and unemotional.*

OPPOSITES: emotional, sensitive

unemployed = **out of work**, redundant, laid off, jobless, idle, on the dole *(Brit. informal)*, out of a job, workless, resting *(of an actor)* • *Have you been unemployed for over six months?*

OPPOSITES: working, in work, having a job

unending = **perpetual**, constant, endless, eternal, continual, never-ending, interminable, incessant, everlasting, ceaseless, unremitting, unceasing • *the country's seemingly unending cycle of political violence*

unendurable = **unbearable**, intolerable, insufferable, too much *(informal)*, overpowering, insupportable, more than flesh and blood can stand • *He had not expected the pain to be unendurable.*

OPPOSITES: tolerable, bearable

unenthusiastic = **indifferent**, uninterested, apathetic, bored, neutral, unimpressed, lukewarm, unmoved, blasé, unresponsive, nonchalant, half-arsed *(Brit. slang)*, half-assed *(U.S. & Canad. slang)*, half-hearted • *Mrs Thatcher was regarded as unenthusiastic about green issues.*

OPPOSITES: interested, excited

unenviable = **unpleasant**, disagreeable, undesirable, painful, uncomfortable, unwanted, thankless, unwished-for, uncoveted • *She had the unenviable task of making the first few phone calls.*

OPPOSITES: pleasant, agreeable

unequal 1 = **disproportionate**, uneven, unbalanced, unfair, irregular, unjust, inequitable, ill-matched • *the unequal power relationships between men and women*

2 = **different**, differing, dissimilar, unlike, varying, variable, disparate, unmatched, not uniform • *These pipes appear to me to be all of unequal length.*

OPPOSITES: like, similar, identical

3 *with* **to** = **not up to**, not qualified for, inadequate for, insufficient for, found wanting in, not cut out for *(informal)*, incompetent at • *Her critics say that she has proved unequal to the task.*

unequalled *or (U.S.)* **unequaled** = **incomparable**, supreme, unparalleled, paramount, transcendent, unrivalled, second to none, pre-eminent, inimitable, unmatched, peerless, unsurpassed, matchless, beyond compare, without equal, nonpareil • *We offer an unequalled level of service.*

unequivocal = **clear**, absolute, definite, certain, direct,

straight, positive, plain, evident, black-and-white, decisive, explicit, manifest, clear-cut, unmistakable, unambiguous, cut-and-dried *(informal)*, incontrovertible, indubitable, uncontestable, nailed-on *(slang)* • *Richardson's unequivocal commitment to fair play*
OPPOSITES: vague, ambiguous, noncommittal

unerring = **accurate**, sure, certain, perfect, exact, impeccable, faultless, infallible, unfailing • *These designs demonstrate her unerring eye for colour and detail.*

unethical = **immoral**, wrong, improper, illegal, dirty, unfair, shady *(informal)*, dishonest, unscrupulous, under-the-table, unprofessional, disreputable, underhand, unprincipled, dishonourable, not cricket *(informal)* • *I thought it was unethical for doctors to operate upon their wives.*
OPPOSITES: legal, moral

uneven 1 = **rough**, bumpy, not flat, not level, not smooth • *He staggered on the uneven surface of the car park.*
OPPOSITES: even, level, flat
2 = **irregular**, unsteady, fitful, variable, broken, fluctuating, patchy, intermittent, jerky, changeable, spasmodic, inconsistent • *He could hear that her breathing was uneven.*
3 = **unequal**, unfair, one-sided, ill-matched • *It was an uneven contest.*
4 = **lopsided**, unbalanced, asymmetrical, odd, out of true, not parallel • *a flat head accentuated by a short, uneven crew-cut*

uneventful = **humdrum**, ordinary, routine, quiet, boring, dull, commonplace, tedious, monotonous, unremarkable, uninteresting, unexciting, unexceptional, ho-hum *(informal)*, unmemorable, unvaried • *The return journey was uneventful, the car running perfectly.*
OPPOSITES: interesting, exciting, eventful

unexceptional = **ordinary**, mediocre, unremarkable, normal, usual, conventional, pedestrian, commonplace, insignificant, run-of-the-mill, undistinguished, unimpressive, bog-standard *(Brit. & Irish slang)*, common or garden *(informal)*, no great shakes *(informal)*, nothing to write home about *(informal)* • *a pretty unexceptional bunch of players*
OPPOSITES: unusual, impressive

unexpected = **unforeseen**, surprising, unanticipated, chance, sudden, astonishing, startling, unpredictable, accidental, abrupt, out of the blue, unannounced, fortuitous, unheralded, unlooked-for, not bargained for • *His death was totally unexpected.*
OPPOSITES: expected, anticipated, foreseen
PROVERBS
Expect the unexpected

unexpectedly = **surprisingly**, remarkably, unusually, incredibly, extraordinarily, startlingly, unpredictably, jaw-droppingly • *Moss had clamped an unexpectedly strong grip on his arm.*

unexpressive = **expressionless**, blank, impassive, vacant, inscrutable, emotionless, inexpressive • *Frido's voice was unexpressive as he continued.*

unfailing 1 = **continuous**, endless, persistent, unlimited, continual, never-failing, boundless, bottomless, ceaseless, inexhaustible, unflagging • *He continued to appear in the office with unfailing regularity.*
2 = **reliable**, constant, dependable, sure, true, certain, loyal, faithful, staunch, infallible, steadfast, tried and true • *He had the unfailing care and support of Erica, his wife.*
OPPOSITES: unreliable, undependable, inconstant

unfair 1 = **unreasonable**, unjustified, out of order *(Brit. informal)*, undeserved, unjustifiable, uncalled for, a bit thick *(Brit. informal)*, unmerited, unwarrantable, wrong • *The union said it was unfair to expect workers to accept pay restraints.*
2 = **biased**, prejudiced, unjust, one-sided, partial, partisan, arbitrary, discriminatory, bigoted, inequitable • *Some have been sentenced to long prison terms after unfair trials.*
3 = **unscrupulous**, crooked *(informal)*, dishonest, unethical, wrongful, unprincipled, dishonourable, unsporting • *nations involved in unfair trade practices*
OPPOSITES: just, fair, ethical

unfaithful 1 = **faithless**, untrue, two-timing *(informal)*, adulterous, fickle, inconstant, unchaste • *She was frequently left alone by her unfaithful husband.*
OPPOSITES: faithful, constant
2 = **disloyal**, false, treacherous, deceitful, faithless, perfidious, traitorous, treasonable, false-hearted, recreant *(archaic)* • *They denounced him as unfaithful to the traditions of the Society.*
OPPOSITES: true, loyal, faithful

unfaltering = **steady**, unfailing, unwavering, firm, persevering, resolute, tireless, steadfast, indefatigable, unflinching, unswerving, unflagging, untiring • *Thomas Covenant's stride went on, as unfaltering as clockwork.*

unfamiliar 1 = **strange**, new, unknown, different, novel, unusual, curious, alien, out-of-the-way, uncommon, little known, unaccustomed, beyond your ken • *She grew many plants that were unfamiliar to me.*
OPPOSITES: familiar, well-known, accustomed
2 *with* **with** = **unacquainted with**, a stranger to, unaccustomed to, inexperienced in, uninformed about, unversed in, uninitiated in, unskilled at, unpractised in, unconversant with • *She speaks no Japanese and is unfamiliar with Japanese culture.*
OPPOSITES: experienced in, familiar with, acquainted with

unfashionable = **passé**, out of date, outmoded, out, square *(informal)*, old-fashioned, dated, unpopular, obsolete, out of fashion, antiquated, old hat, behind the times, unhip *(slang)*, out of the ark *(informal)* • *Wearing fur has become deeply unfashionable.*
OPPOSITES: fashionable, stylish, trendy *(Brit. informal)*

unfasten = **undo**, open, loosen, separate, detach, unlock, disconnect, untie, unstrap, unclasp, uncouple, unlace • *Reaching down, he unfastened the latch on the gate.*

unfathomable 1 = **baffling**, incomprehensible, inexplicable, deep, profound, esoteric, impenetrable, unknowable, abstruse, indecipherable • *How unfathomable and odd is life!*
2 = **immeasurable**, bottomless, unmeasured, unplumbed, unsounded • *Her eyes were black, unfathomable pools.*

unfavourable *or (U.S.)* **unfavorable** 1 = **adverse**, bad, unfortunate, disadvantageous, threatening, contrary, unlucky, ominous, untimely, untoward, unpromising, unsuited, inauspicious, ill-suited, inopportune, unseasonable, unpropitious, infelicitous • *Unfavourable economic conditions were blocking a recovery.*
2 = **hostile**, negative, unfriendly, inimical • *First reactions have been distinctly unfavourable.*
OPPOSITES: warm, positive, friendly

unfeeling = **callous**, insensitive, heartless, cold, cruel, hardened, stony, inhuman, unsympathetic, uncaring, apathetic, pitiless, hardhearted • *an unfeeling bully who used his huge size to frighten people*
OPPOSITES: kind, sensitive

unfeigned = **genuine**, sincere, real, natural, pure, unaffected, heartfelt, unforced, wholehearted, dinkum *(Austral. & N.Z. informal)* • *I could tell from his unfeigned astonishment that he knew nothing.*

unfettered = **uncontrolled**, free, unlimited, unchecked, unbridled, unrestrained, untrammelled, unconstrained, unconfined, unshackled • *Unfettered free trade is an ideal, never achieved.*

unfinished 1 = **incomplete**, uncompleted, half-done, lacking, undone, in the making, imperfect, unfulfilled, unaccomplished • *Jane Austen's unfinished novel*

2 = **natural**, rough, raw, bare, crude, unrefined, unvarnished, unpolished • *unfinished wood ready for you to varnish or paint*
OPPOSITES: finished, polished, smooth

unfit 1 = **out of shape**, feeble, unhealthy, debilitated, flabby, decrepit, in poor condition, out of trim, out of kilter • *Many children are so unfit they are unable to do basic exercises.*
OPPOSITES: fit, healthy, in good condition
2 = **incapable**, inadequate, incompetent, no good, useless, not up to, unprepared, ineligible, unqualified, untrained, ill-equipped, not equal, not cut out • *They were utterly unfit to govern America.*
OPPOSITES: able, qualified, capable
3 = **unsuitable**, inadequate, inappropriate, useless, not fit, not designed, unsuited, ill-adapted • *I can show them plenty of houses unfit for human habitation.*
OPPOSITES: appropriate, suitable, acceptable

unflagging = **constant**, steady, tireless, fixed, persistent, staunch, persevering, unremitting, indefatigable, unfailing, unceasing, untiring, unfaltering, undeviating, unwearied • *He was sustained by the unflagging support of his family.*

unflappable = **imperturbable**, cool, collected, calm, composed, level-headed, unfazed *(informal)*, impassive, unruffled, self-possessed, not given to worry • *Professional life-savers need to be calm and unflappable.*
OPPOSITES: nervous, excitable, twitchy *(informal)*

unflattering 1 = **blunt**, critical, honest, candid, warts and all, uncomplimentary • *He depicted the town's families in an unflattering light.*
2 = **unattractive**, plain, unbecoming, unprepossessing • *The knee-length dresses were unflattering and ugly.*

unfledged = **inexperienced**, immature, callow, young, green, raw, undeveloped, untried • *new-hatched, unfledged courage*

unflinching = **determined**, firm, steady, constant, bold, stalwart, staunch, resolute, steadfast, unwavering, immovable, unswerving, unshaken, unfaltering, unshrinking • *The armed forces had pledged their unflinching support and loyalty.*
OPPOSITES: shaken, scared, wavering

unfold 1 = **develop**, happen, progress, grow, emerge, occur, take place, expand, work out, mature, evolve, blossom, transpire, bear fruit • *The outcome depends on conditions as well as how events unfold.*
2 = **reveal**, tell, present, show, describe, explain, illustrate, disclose, uncover, clarify, divulge, narrate, make known • *Mr Wills unfolds his story with evident enjoyment.*
3 = **open**, spread out, undo, expand, flatten, straighten, stretch out, unfurl, unwrap, unroll • *He quickly unfolded the blankets and spread them on the mattress.*

unforeseen = **unexpected**, unanticipated, unpredicted, surprise, surprising, sudden, startling, accidental, abrupt, out of the blue, unlooked-for, unenvisaged • *Due to unforeseen circumstances, the show has been cancelled.*
OPPOSITES: expected, predicted

unforgettable = **memorable**, impressive, extraordinary, exceptional, striking, notable, never to be forgotten, fixed in the mind • *A visit to the Museum is an unforgettable experience.*

unforgivable = **inexcusable**, indefensible, unpardonable, disgraceful, shameful, deplorable, unjustifiable, unwarrantable • *These people are animals and what they did was unforgivable.*
OPPOSITES: justifiable, allowable

unfortunate 1 = **disastrous**, calamitous, inopportune, adverse, untimely, unfavourable, untoward, ruinous, ill-starred, infelicitous, ill-fated • *Through some unfortunate accident, the information reached me a day late.*
OPPOSITES: fortunate, auspicious, opportune
2 = **regrettable**, deplorable, lamentable, inappropriate, unsuitable, ill-advised, unbecoming • *the unfortunate incident of the upside-down Canadian flag*
OPPOSITES: appropriate, becoming
3 = **unlucky**, poor, unhappy, doomed, cursed, hopeless, unsuccessful, hapless, luckless, out of luck, wretched, star-crossed, unprosperous • *charity days to raise money for unfortunate people*
OPPOSITES: happy, lucky, fortunate

unfortunately = **unluckily**, sadly, alas, regrettably, worse luck *(informal)*, woefully, unhappily, sad to say, lamentably, sad to relate • *Unfortunately, my time is limited.*

unfounded = **groundless**, false, unjustified, unproven, unsubstantiated, idle, fabricated, spurious, trumped up, baseless, without foundation, without basis • *The allegations were totally unfounded.*
OPPOSITES: proven, confirmed, justified

unfrequented = **isolated**, deserted, lonely, remote, solitary, uninhabited, sequestered, off the beaten track, godforsaken, unvisited • *The reference library is quite unfrequented as a rule.*

unfriendly 1 = **hostile**, cold, distant, sour, chilly, aloof, surly, antagonistic, disagreeable, quarrelsome, unsociable, ill-disposed, unneighbourly • *She spoke in a loud, rather unfriendly voice.*
OPPOSITES: warm, friendly, amiable
2 = **unfavourable**, hostile, inhospitable, alien, inauspicious, inimical, uncongenial, unpropitious, unkind • *We got an unfriendly reception from the hotel-owner.*
OPPOSITES: hospitable, congenial, auspicious

unfurl 1 = **open**, unfold, open out, blossom • *two weeks later when the leaves unfurl*
2 = **unfold**, develop, progress • *as the dramatic changes in Europe continue to unfurl*

ungainly = **awkward**, clumsy, inelegant, lumbering, slouching, gawky, uncouth, gangling, loutish, uncoordinated, ungraceful, lubberly, unco *(Austral. slang)* • *Paul swam in his ungainly way to the side of the pool.*
OPPOSITES: elegant, graceful

ungodly 1 = **wicked**, corrupt, sinful, vile, immoral, depraved, profane, blasphemous, godless, irreligious, impious • *My folks had nothing to do with ungodly people.*
2 = **unreasonable**, outrageous, unearthly, dreadful, horrendous, intolerable, unseemly, unholy *(informal)* • *at the ungodly hour of 4.00am*

ungovernable 1 = **unruly**, rebellious, unmanageable, refractory • *The country has become ungovernable.*
2 = **uncontrollable**, wild, unrestrainable • *He was filled with an ungovernable rage.*

ungracious = **bad-mannered**, rude, churlish, offhand, impolite, discourteous, uncivil, ill-bred, unmannerly • *I was often rude and ungracious in refusing help.*
OPPOSITES: civil, mannerly

ungrateful = **unappreciative**, thankless, unthankful, heedless, unmindful, ingrate *(archaic)* • *I don't mean to sound ungrateful in any way.*
OPPOSITES: grateful, thankful

unguarded 1 = **unprotected**, vulnerable, defenceless, undefended, open to attack, unpatrolled • *The U-boat entered in through a narrow unguarded eastern entrance.*
2 = **careless**, rash, unwary, foolhardy, thoughtless, indiscreet, unthinking, ill-considered, imprudent, heedless, incautious, undiplomatic, impolitic, uncircumspect • *He was tricked by a reporter into an unguarded comment.*
OPPOSITES: guarded, careful, cautious

unhappiness 1 = **sadness**, depression, misery, gloom, sorrow, melancholy, heartache, despondency, blues, dejection, wretchedness, low spirits • *There was a lot of unhappiness in my adolescence.*
2 = **discontent**, dissatisfaction, displeasure, uneasiness,

vexation, discontentment • *He has signalled his unhappiness with the government's decision.*

QUOTATIONS
He felt the loyalty we all feel to unhappiness – the sense that that is where we really belong
[Graham Greene *The Heart of the Matter*]
Unhappiness is best defined as the difference between our talents and our expectations
[Edward de Bono]

unhappy 1 = **sad**, depressed, miserable, down, low, blue, gloomy, melancholy, mournful, dejected, despondent, dispirited, downcast, long-faced, sorrowful, disconsolate, crestfallen, down in the dumps *(informal)* • *Her marriage is in trouble and she is desperately unhappy.*
OPPOSITES: happy, cheerful, joyful
2 = **unlucky**, unfortunate, hapless, luckless, cursed, wretched, ill-omened, ill-fated • *I have already informed your unhappy father of your expulsion.*
OPPOSITES: lucky, fortunate
3 = **displeased**, discontented, disgruntled, disappointed, dissatisfied, disapproving of • *He has been unhappy with his son's political leanings.*
OPPOSITES: pleased, satisfied
4 = **inappropriate**, awkward, clumsy, unsuitable, inept, ill-advised, tactless, ill-timed, injudicious, infelicitous, malapropos, untactful • *The legislation represents in itself an unhappy compromise.*
OPPOSITES: becoming, suitable, apt

QUOTATIONS
Those who are unhappy have no need for anything in this world but people capable of giving them their attention
[Simone Weil *Waiting on God*]

unharmed = **unhurt**, safe, unscathed, whole, sound, intact, untouched, in one piece *(informal)*, undamaged, uninjured, safe and sound, without a scratch, unscarred • *The car was a write-off, but everyone escaped unharmed.*
OPPOSITES: hurt, injured

unhealthy 1 = **harmful**, detrimental, unwholesome, noxious, deleterious, insanitary, noisome, insalubrious • *the unhealthy environment of a coal mine*
OPPOSITES: healthy, beneficial, wholesome
2 = **sick**, sickly, unwell, poorly *(informal)*, weak, delicate, crook *(Austral. & N.Z. informal)*, ailing, frail, feeble, invalid, unsound, infirm, in poor health • *a poorly dressed, unhealthy looking fellow with a poor complexion*
OPPOSITES: well, fit, healthy
3 = **weak**, unsound, ailing • *a clear sign of an unhealthy economy*
OPPOSITES: strong, healthy, robust
4 = **unwholesome**, morbid, bad, negative, corrupt, corrupting, degrading, undesirable, demoralizing, baneful *(archaic)* • *an unhealthy obsession with secrecy*
OPPOSITES: wholesome, positive, moral

unheard-of 1 = **unprecedented**, inconceivable, undreamed of, new, novel, unique, unusual, unbelievable, singular, ground-breaking, never before encountered, unexampled • *In those days, it was unheard-of for a woman to work after marriage.*
2 = **shocking**, extreme, outrageous, offensive, unacceptable, unthinkable, disgraceful, preposterous, outlandish • *the unheard-of rate of a bottle of rum for $30*
3 = **obscure**, unknown, undiscovered, unfamiliar, little known, unsung, unremarked, unregarded • *an unheard-of comic waiting for his big break to come along*

unheeded = **ignored**, disregarded, overlooked, forgotten, neglected, unnoticed, disobeyed, unobserved, untaken, unfollowed • *The advice of experts went unheeded.*
OPPOSITES: heeded, regarded

unheralded 1 = **unknown**, unrecognized, unsung, unnoticed, unpublicized, unacclaimed, unproclaimed • *They are inviting talented, but unheralded film-makers.*
2 = **unexpected**, out of the blue, surprise, unforeseen, unannounced • *The complete reversal of this policy was unheralded.*

unhinge = **unbalance**, confuse, derange, disorder, unsettle, madden, craze, confound, distemper *(archaic)*, dement, drive you out of your mind • *The stress of war temporarily unhinged him.*

unhinged = **deranged**, mad, crazy *(informal)*, wild, mental *(informal)*, bananas *(informal)*, manic, insane, crazed, lunatic, maniac, demented, unbalanced, potty *(informal)*, uncontrolled, bonkers *(informal)*, off your head *(informal)*, off your rocker *(informal)*, a sausage short of a fry-up *(slang)*, off the air *(Austral. slang)* • *Tell him I'm menopausal and unhinged.*

unholy 1 = **shocking**, awful, appalling, dreadful, outrageous, horrendous, unearthly, ungodly *(informal)* • *The economy is still in an unholy mess.*
2 = **evil**, vile, wicked, base, corrupt, immoral, dishonest, sinful, heinous, depraved, profane, iniquitous, ungodly, irreligious • *He screamed unholy things at me.*
OPPOSITES: godly, religious, holy

unhurried = **leisurely**, easy, slow, calm, deliberate, easy-going, sedate, slow-paced, slow and steady • *The islands are peaceful, with an unhurried pace of life.*
OPPOSITES: rushed, hurried

unhurt = **uninjured**, safe, intact, unscathed, unharmed, whole, sound, untouched, in one piece *(informal)*, undamaged, safe and sound, without a scratch, unscarred • *The lorry driver escaped unhurt, but a pedestrian was injured.*

unhygienic = **insanitary**, dirty, filthy, unhealthy, foul, contaminated, polluted, noxious, unclean, impure, unwholesome, unsanitary, disease-ridden, skanky *(slang)*, germ-ridden, festy *(Austral. slang)* • *Parts of the shop were very dirty and unhygienic.*

unidentified 1 = **unknown**, unfamiliar, unrecognized, mysterious, unmarked, unclassified • *He was shot this morning by unidentified intruders at his house.*
OPPOSITES: known, familiar
2 = **unnamed**, anonymous, unrevealed, nameless • *based on the comments of anonymous and unidentified sources*
OPPOSITES: named, identified

unification = **union**, uniting, alliance, combination, coalition, merger, federation, confederation, fusion, amalgamation, coalescence • *The ultimate aim is to bring about the unification of Albania and Kosovo.*

uniform AS A NOUN 1 = **regalia**, suit, livery, colours, habit, regimentals • *He was dressed in his uniform for parade.*
2 = **outfit**, dress, costume, attire, gear *(informal)*, get-up *(informal)*, ensemble, garb • *Mark's is the uniform of the young male traveller.*
▸ AS AN ADJECTIVE 1 = **consistent**, unvarying, similar, even, same, matching, regular, constant, equivalent, identical, homogeneous, unchanging, equable, undeviating • *Chips should be cut into uniform size and thickness.*
OPPOSITES: varying, irregular, inconsistent
2 = **alike**, similar, identical, like, same, equal, selfsame • *Along each wall stretched uniform green metal filing cabinets.*

uniformity 1 = **regularity**, similarity, sameness, constancy, homogeneity, evenness, invariability • *Caramel was used to maintain uniformity of colour in the brandy.*
2 = **monotony**, sameness, tedium, dullness, flatness, drabness, lack of diversity • *the dull uniformity of the houses*

unify = **unite**, join, combine, merge, consolidate, bring together, fuse, confederate, amalgamate, federate • *He said he would seek to unify the Party and win the next election.*
OPPOSITES: separate, split, divide

unimaginable = **inconceivable**, incredible, unbelievable, unthinkable, impossible, fantastic, unheard-of, mind-boggling *(informal)*, indescribable, ineffable, beyond your

u

wildest dreams • *The children here have lived through unimaginable horrors.*

unimaginative 1 = **prosaic**, dull, matter-of-fact, dry, ordinary, routine, predictable, tame, pedestrian, uninspired, unromantic, unoriginal, uncreative • *Her second husband was a steady, unimaginative corporate lawyer.*
2 = **unoriginal**, banal, uninspired, usual, ordinary, routine, dull, predictable, tame, pedestrian, derivative, commonplace, vanilla *(informal)*, lifeless, prosaic, hackneyed, unromantic, uncreative • *Film critics called it a monumentally unimaginative movie.*
OPPOSITES: original, creative

unimpeachable = **beyond criticism**, blameless, unquestionable, perfect, impeccable, faultless, unassailable, squeaky-clean, unblemished, beyond question, unchallengeable, irreproachable, unexceptionable, above reproach • *He said all five were men of unimpeachable character.*
OPPOSITES: reprehensible, blameworthy

unimpeded = **unhindered**, open, free, unchecked, unrestrained, untrammelled, unconstrained, unhampered, unblocked • *U.N. aid convoys have unimpeded access to the city.*
OPPOSITES: restrained, hindered

unimportant = **insignificant**, minor, petty, trivial, slight, irrelevant, worthless, trifling, paltry, immaterial, inconsequential, low-ranking, of no consequence, nickel-and-dime *(U.S. slang)*, of no account, nugatory, not worth mentioning, of no moment • *It was an unimportant job, and paid very little.*
OPPOSITES: major, important

uninhabited = **deserted**, waste, barren, desolate, abandoned, empty, desert, lonely, unsettled, vacant, unoccupied, unpopulated, untenanted • *an uninhabited island in the North Pacific*

uninhibited 1 = **unselfconscious**, natural, relaxed, open, free, frank, informal, liberated, spontaneous, instinctive, candid, free and easy, unreserved, unrepressed • *a commanding and uninhibited entertainer*
OPPOSITES: shy, inhibited
2 = **unrestrained**, uncontrolled, unchecked, free, unrestricted, unbridled, unconstrained, uncurbed • *The dancing is uninhibited and as frenzied as an aerobics class.*
OPPOSITES: restrained, inhibited

uninspired = **unexciting**, banal, unimaginative, stock, ordinary, dull, indifferent, commonplace, vanilla *(informal)*, stale, prosaic, uninspiring, humdrum, uninteresting, unoriginal • *The script was singularly uninspired.*
OPPOSITES: original, exciting

uninspiring = **unexciting**, boring, dull, flat, dry, plain, pedestrian, mundane, dreary, drab, prosaic, humdrum, uninteresting, insipid, spiritless, as dry as dust • *His speech on the economy was uninspiring.*
OPPOSITES: exciting, inspiring

unintelligent = **stupid**, obtuse, dull, slow, thick, foolish, dense, dozy *(Brit. informal)*, unthinking, gormless *(Brit. informal)*, brainless, empty-headed, unreasoning, braindead *(informal)*, dumb-ass *(slang)* • *He was abusive of Hemingway as an unintelligent philistine.*
OPPOSITES: bright, sharp

unintelligible = **incomprehensible**, incoherent, inarticulate, meaningless, muddled, jumbled, unfathomable, illegible, indistinct, indecipherable • *He muttered something unintelligible.* • *pages inscribed with unintelligible characters*
OPPOSITES: clear, understandable

unintentional = **accidental**, involuntary, unintended, casual, unconscious, unwitting, fortuitous, inadvertent, unthinking, unpremeditated, undesigned • *There are moments of unintentional humour.*
OPPOSITES: intended, conscious

uninterested = **indifferent**, unconcerned, apathetic, bored, distant, listless, impassive, blasé, unresponsive, uninvolved, incurious • *unhelpful and uninterested shop staff*
OPPOSITES: interested, involved, concerned

uninteresting = **boring**, dull, tedious, flat, dry, commonplace, dreary, drab, tiresome, monotonous, uninspiring, humdrum, uneventful, mind-numbing, unexciting, ho-hum *(informal)*, wearisome, unenjoyable, as dry as dust • *Why did he choose these pale, nerveless, uninteresting people?*
OPPOSITES: interesting, exciting

uninterrupted 1 = **continuous**, constant, steady, sustained, continual, unbroken, undisturbed, unending, nonstop • *five years of rapid and uninterrupted growth*
2 = **clear**, open, unrestricted, unobstructed, unlimited, unhindered, unhampered • *Diners can enjoy an uninterrupted view of the garden.*

uninvited = **unasked**, unbidden, unwanted, not asked, unwelcome, not invited • *He came uninvited to one of Stein's parties.*

uninviting = **unattractive**, off-putting *(Brit. informal)*, unappealing, unpleasant, undesirable, repellent, repulsive, disagreeable, unwelcoming, unappetizing, untempting • *The restaurant looked dilapidated and uninviting.*
OPPOSITES: appealing, inviting

union 1 = **trade union**, guild, workers' association • *Women often benefit from joining a union.*
2 = **joining**, uniting, unification, combination, coalition, merger, mixture, blend, merging, integration, conjunction, fusion, synthesis, amalgamating, amalgam, amalgamation • *The Romanian majority in the province voted for union with Romania.*
3 = **alliance**, league, association, coalition, federation, confederation, confederacy, Bund • *the question of which countries should join the currency union*
4 = **marriage**, match, wedlock, matrimony • *Even Louis began to think their union was not blessed.*
5 = **intercourse**, coupling, copulation, the other *(informal)*, nookie *(slang)*, coitus, rumpy-pumpy *(slang)*, coition • *the joys of sexual union*

PROVERBS
Union is strength

unique 1 = **distinct**, special, exclusive, peculiar, only, single, lone, solitary, one and only, sui generis • *The area has its own unique language, Catalan.*
2 = **unparalleled**, unrivalled, incomparable, inimitable, unmatched, peerless, unequalled, matchless, without equal, nonpareil, unexampled • *She was a woman of unique talent and determination.*
3 *with* **to** = **exclusive to**, particular to, peculiar to, found only in, characteristic of, typical of • *This interesting and charming creature is unique to Borneo.*

unison **IN PHRASES: in unison** 1 = **simultaneously**, at the same time, as one, in concert, all at once, at the same moment, at one and the same time • *Michael and the landlady nodded in unison.*
2 = **together**, unanimously, in agreement, in harmony, in accord, cooperatively, unitedly • *The international community is ready to act in unison against him.*

unit 1 = **entity**, whole, item, feature, piece, portion, module • *Agriculture was based in the past on the family as a unit.*
2 = **section**, company, group, force, detail, division, cell, squad, crew, outfit, faction, corps, brigade, regiment, battalion, legion, contingent, squadron, garrison, detachment, platoon • *a secret military unit*
3 = **measure**, quantity, measurement • *The liver can only burn up one unit of alcohol in an hour.*
4 = **part**, section, segment, class, element, component, constituent, module, tutorial • *designed for teachers to plan a study unit on marine mammals*

unite 1 = **join**, link, combine, couple, marry, wed, blend, incorporate, merge, consolidate, unify, fuse, amalgamate, coalesce, meld • *They have agreed to unite their efforts to bring peace.*
OPPOSITES: part, separate, split
2 = **cooperate**, ally, join forces, league, band, associate, pool, collaborate, confederate, pull together, join together, close ranks, club together • *The two parties have been trying to unite since the New Year.*
OPPOSITES: part, break, split

united 1 = **in agreement**, agreed, unanimous, one, like-minded, in accord, of like mind, of one mind, of the same opinion • *Every party is united on the need for parliamentary democracy.*
2 = **combined**, leagued, allied, unified, pooled, concerted, collective, affiliated, in partnership, banded together • *the first elections in a united Germany for fifty-eight years*

unity 1 = **union**, unification, coalition, federation, integration, confederation, amalgamation • *the future of European economic unity*
2 = **wholeness**, integrity, oneness, union, unification, entity, singleness, undividedness • *The deer represents the unity of the universe.*
OPPOSITES: division, separation, disunity
3 = **agreement**, accord, consensus, peace, harmony, solidarity, unison, assent, unanimity, concord, concurrence • *Speakers at the rally mouthed sentiments of unity.*
OPPOSITES: division, disagreement, discord

QUOTATIONS
We must indeed all hang together, or, most assuredly, we shall all hang separately
[Benjamin Franklin *on his signing of the Declaration of Independence*]
All for one; one for all
[Alexandre Dumas *The Three Musketeers*]
By uniting we stand, by dividing we fall
[John Dickinson *The Patriot's Appeal*]

universal 1 = **widespread**, general, common, whole, total, entire, catholic, unlimited, ecumenical, omnipresent, all-embracing, overarching, one-size-fits-all • *proposals for universal health care*
2 = **global**, worldwide, international, pandemic • *universal diseases*

universality = **comprehensiveness**, generalization, generality, totality, completeness, ubiquity, all-inclusiveness • *The vignettes have a universality that makes them irresistible.*

universally 1 = **without exception**, uniformly, everywhere, always, invariably, across the board, in all cases, in every instance • *a universally accepted point of view*
2 = **widely**, internationally, everywhere, worldwide, globally • *The disadvantage is that it is not universally available.*

universe = **cosmos**, space, creation, everything, nature, heavens, the natural world, macrocosm, all existence • *Einstein's equations showed the Universe to be expanding.*

QUOTATIONS
The more the universe seems comprehensible, the more it also seems pointless
[Steven Weinberg *The First Three Minutes*]
The universe is not hostile, nor yet is it friendly. It is simply indifferent
[Revd. John H. Holmes *A Sensible Man's View of Religion*]
Had I been present at the Creation, I would have given some useful hints for the better ordering of the universe
[attributed to Alfonso 'the Wise', King of Castile]
Now, my own suspicion is that the Universe is not only queerer than we suppose, but queerer than we *can* suppose
[J.B.S. Haldane *Possible Worlds*]

university

QUOTATIONS
The use of a university is to make young gentlemen as unlike their fathers as possible
[Woodrow Wilson]

unjust = **unfair**, prejudiced, biased, wrong, one-sided, partial, partisan, unjustified, wrongful, undeserved, inequitable, unmerited • *campaigning against racist and unjust immigration laws*
OPPOSITES: just, fair, equitable

unjustifiable = **inexcusable**, wrong, indefensible, unforgivable, unacceptable, outrageous, unjust, unjustified, unpardonable, unwarrantable • *Using these missiles to down civilian aircraft is unjustifiable.*

unjustified = **wrong**, indefensible, inexcusable, unacceptable, outrageous, unjust, unforgivable, unjustifiable, unpardonable, unwarrantable • *The commission concluded that the police action was unjustified.*

unkempt 1 = **uncombed**, tousled, shaggy, ungroomed • *His hair was unkempt and filthy.*
2 = **untidy**, scruffy, dishevelled, disordered, messy, sloppy *(informal)*, shabby, rumpled, bedraggled, slovenly, blowsy, sluttish, slatternly, disarranged, ungroomed, disarrayed, frowzy, daggy *(Austral. & N.Z. informal)* • *an unkempt old man*
OPPOSITES: trim, neat, tidy

unkind = **cruel**, mean, nasty, spiteful, harsh, malicious, insensitive, unfriendly, inhuman, unsympathetic, uncaring, thoughtless, unfeeling, inconsiderate, uncharitable, unchristian, hardhearted • *All last summer he'd been unkind to her.*
OPPOSITES: kind, caring, benevolent

unkindness = **cruelty**, spite, malice, insensitivity, harshness, inhumanity, meanness, ill will, malevolence, spitefulness, maliciousness, hardheartedness, unfeelingness • *He realized the unkindness of the remark.*
OPPOSITES: charity, sympathy

QUOTATIONS
This was the most unkindest cut of all
[William Shakespeare *Julius Caesar*]

unknown 1 = **strange**, new, undiscovered, uncharted, unexplored, virgin, remote, alien, exotic, outlandish, unmapped, untravelled, beyond your ken • *a perilous expedition, through unknown terrain*
2 = **undisclosed**, secret, unspecified, unrevealed, concealed, undetermined, undivulged • *The proposed target of the bomb is unknown.*
3 = **unidentified**, mysterious, anonymous, unnamed, nameless, incognito • *Unknown thieves had forced their way into the apartment.*
4 = **obscure**, little known, minor, humble, unfamiliar, insignificant, lowly, unimportant, unheard-of, unsung, inconsequential, undistinguished, unrenowned • *He was an unknown writer.*
OPPOSITES: famous, known, celebrated
5 = **unheard of**, unprecedented, unfamiliar, new, novel, strange, exotic • *A hundred years ago coronary heart disease was virtually unknown.*

unlawful = **illegal**, criminal, illicit, banned, forbidden, prohibited, outlawed, illegitimate, unlicensed, under-the-table, unauthorized, against the law, actionable • *employees who believe their dismissal was unlawful*

unleash = **release**, let go, let loose, free, untie, unloose, unbridle • *Then he unleashed his own, unstoppable attack.*

unlettered = **uneducated**, ignorant, illiterate, unlearned, untutored, unschooled, untaught • *Such misconceptions have not been confined to the unlettered masses.*
OPPOSITES: educated, literate

unlike 1 = **different from**, dissimilar to, not resembling, far from, not like, distinct from, incompatible with, unrelated

to, distant from, unequal to, far apart from, divergent from, not similar to, as different as chalk and cheese from *(informal)* • *She was unlike him in every way except her eyes.*
OPPOSITES: similar to, like, related to
2 = **contrasted with**, not like, in contradiction to, in contrast with *or* to, as opposed to, differently from, opposite to • *Unlike aerobics, walking entails no expensive fees.*

unlikely 1 = **improbable**, doubtful, remote, slight, faint, not likely, unimaginable • *A military coup seems unlikely.*
OPPOSITES: odds-on, likely, probable
2 = **unbelievable**, incredible, unconvincing, implausible, questionable, cock-and-bull *(informal)* • *I smiled sincerely, to encourage him to buy this unlikely story.*
OPPOSITES: possible, plausible, believable

unlimited 1 = **infinite**, endless, countless, great, vast, extensive, immense, stellar *(informal)*, limitless, boundless, incalculable, immeasurable, unbounded, illimitable • *An unlimited number of copies can be made from the original.*
OPPOSITES: limited, finite, bounded
2 = **total**, full, complete, absolute, unconditional, unqualified, unfettered, unrestricted, all-encompassing, unconstrained • *You'll also have unlimited access to the swimming pool.*
OPPOSITES: limited, restricted, constrained

unload 1 = **empty**, clear, unpack, dump, discharge, off-load, disburden, unlade • *Unload everything from the boot and clean it thoroughly.*
2 = **unburden**, relieve, lighten, disburden • *He unloaded the horse where the track dead-ended.*

unlock 1 = **open**, undo, unfasten, release, unbolt, unlatch, unbar • *She unlocked the case and lifted out the vase.*
2 = **discover**, uncover, unearth, lay bare, bring to light, blow wide open *(slang)* • *He dedicated his life to unlocking the secrets of the universe.*

unlooked-for = **unexpected**, unforeseen, unanticipated, chance, surprise, surprising, out of the blue, fortuitous, undreamed of, unpredicted, unthought-of, unhoped-for • *This unlooked-for opportunity couldn't be lost.*

unloved = **uncared-for**, neglected, unwanted, rejected, disliked, unpopular, spurned, forsaken, loveless, uncherished • *I think she feels desperately unloved at the moment.*
OPPOSITES: liked, wanted

unlucky 1 = **unfortunate**, unhappy, disastrous • *Argentina's unlucky defeat by Ireland*
OPPOSITES: happy, lucky, fortunate
2 = **ill-fated**, doomed, inauspicious, ominous, untimely, unfavourable, cursed, ill-starred, ill-omened • *13 was to prove an unlucky number.*

QUOTATIONS

now and then
there is a person born
who is so unlucky
that he runs into accidents
which started to happen
to someone else

[Don Marquis *archys life of mehitabel*]

unmanageable 1 = **cumbersome**, inconvenient, unwieldy, demanding, awkward, bulky, clunky *(informal)*, difficult to handle, unhandy • *The city school system is unmanageable.*
OPPOSITES: manageable, wieldy
2 = **uncontrollable**, difficult, wild, out of hand, disruptive, unruly, troublesome, intractable, boisterous, fractious, undisciplined, stroppy *(Brit. slang)*, incorrigible, refractory, obstreperous • *The signs are that indulged children tend to become unmanageable.*
OPPOSITES: manageable, compliant

unmanly = **effeminate**, soft *(informal)*, weak, feeble, sissy, womanish, camp *(informal)* • *Your partner may feel that it is unmanly to cry.*

unmarried = **single**, unattached, unwed, maiden, bachelor, on the shelf, celibate, unwedded • *a childless unmarried professional woman*

unmask = **reveal**, expose, uncover, discover, disclose, unveil, show up, lay bare, bring to light, uncloak • *Elliott unmasked the master spy and traitor.*

unmatched = **unequalled**, supreme, unparalleled, paramount, consummate, unrivalled, second to none, incomparable, peerless, unsurpassed, matchless, beyond compare • *a landscape of unmatched beauty*

unmentionable = **taboo**, forbidden, unspeakable, shocking, obscene, indecent, disgraceful, shameful, scandalous, X-rated *(informal)*, frowned on, disreputable, immodest, unutterable • *Has he got some unmentionable disease?*

unmerciful = **merciless**, brutal, ruthless, relentless, hard, cruel, heartless, implacable, uncaring, inhumane, remorseless, pitiless, unfeeling, unsparing • *The two men were set upon in an unmerciful and relentless attack.*
OPPOSITES: humane, merciful

unmistakable = **clear**, certain, positive, decided, sure, obvious, plain, patent, evident, distinct, pronounced, glaring, manifest, blatant, conspicuous, palpable, unequivocal, unambiguous, indisputable • *The unmistakable smell of marijuana drifted down.*
OPPOSITES: uncertain, unclear, doubtful

unmitigated 1 = **unrelieved**, relentless, unalleviated, intense, harsh, grim, persistent, oppressive, unbroken, unqualified, unabated, undiminished, unmodified, unredeemed • *She leads a life of unmitigated misery.*
2 = **complete**, absolute, utter, perfect, rank, sheer, total, outright, thorough, downright, consummate, out-and-out, thoroughgoing, arrant, deep-dyed *(usually derogatory)* • *A senior policeman had called him an unmitigated liar.*

unmoved 1 = **unaffected**, indifferent, impassive, cold, untouched, unimpressed, unconcerned, unresponsive, unfeeling, dry-eyed, unstirred • *She carried on criticizing me in this vein, but I was unmoved.*
OPPOSITES: moved, concerned
2 = **inflexible**, firm, resolute, determined, resolved, steadfast, unwavering, unshaken, undeviating • *She appealed to the authorities but they were unmoved.*
OPPOSITES: flexible, adaptable
3 = **fast**, firm, steady, in place, in position • *The great mound of cargo was unmoved.*
OPPOSITES: shifted

unnamed 1 = **anonymous**, unknown, unidentified, unrevealed • *The cash comes from an unnamed source.*
2 = **nameless**, obscure, untitled, undesignated, innominate • *unnamed comets and asteroids*

unnatural 1 = **abnormal**, odd, strange, unusual, extraordinary, bizarre, perverted, queer, irregular, perverse, supernatural, uncanny, outlandish, unaccountable, anomalous, freakish, aberrant • *The altered landscape looks unnatural and weird.*
OPPOSITES: normal, ordinary, typical
2 = **false**, forced, artificial, studied, laboured, affected, assumed, mannered, strained, stiff, theatrical, contrived, self-conscious, feigned, stilted, insincere, factitious, stagy, phoney *or* phony *(informal)* • *She gave him a bright, determined smile which seemed unnatural.*
OPPOSITES: natural, genuine, sincere
3 = **inhuman**, evil, monstrous, wicked, savage, brutal, ruthless, callous, heartless, cold-blooded, fiendish, unfeeling • *Murder is an unnatural act.*
OPPOSITES: humane, loving, caring

unnecessary = **needless**, excessive, unwarranted, useless, pointless, not needed, redundant, wasteful, gratuitous, superfluous, wanton, expendable, surplus to requirements,

uncalled-for, dispensable, unneeded, nonessential, inessential, unmerited, to no purpose, unrequired, supererogatory • *The slaughter of whales is unnecessary and inhuman.*
OPPOSITES: needed, required, essential

unnerve = **shake**, upset, disconcert, disturb, intimidate, frighten, rattle *(informal)*, discourage, dismay, daunt, disarm, confound, fluster, faze, unman, demoralize, unhinge, psych out *(informal)*, throw off balance, dishearten, dispirit • *The news about Dermot had unnerved me.*
OPPOSITES: encourage, strengthen, hearten

unnerving = **disconcerting**, disturbing, upsetting, embarrassing, awkward, distracting, dismaying, off-putting *(Brit. informal)*, barro *(Austral. slang)* • *her unnerving habit of touching people she was speaking to*

unnoticed = **unobserved**, disregarded, unseen, ignored, overlooked, neglected, undiscovered, unheeded, unrecognized, unremarked, unperceived • *I tried to slip up the stairs unnoticed.*
OPPOSITES: noticed, observed

unobtrusive = **inconspicuous**, quiet, unassuming, retiring, modest, humble, restrained, subdued, low-key, meek, unpretentious, keeping a low profile, self-effacing, unnoticeable, unostentatious • *He managed the factory with unobtrusive efficiency.*
OPPOSITES: prominent, noticeable

unoccupied 1 = **empty**, vacant, uninhabited, untenanted, tenantless • *The house was unoccupied at the time of the explosion.*
2 = **idle**, unemployed, inactive, disengaged, at leisure, at a loose end • *Portraits of unoccupied youths and solitary females predominate.*

unofficial 1 = **unconfirmed**, off the record, unsubstantiated, private, personal, unauthorized, undocumented, uncorroborated • *Unofficial estimates speak of at least two hundred dead.*
2 = **unauthorized**, informal, unsanctioned, casual, wildcat • *Rail workers have voted to continue their unofficial strike.*

unorthodox 1 = **unconventional**, unusual, irregular, abnormal, off-the-wall *(slang)*, out there *(slang)*, heterodox, unwonted, uncustomary • *His methods were unorthodox, and his lifestyle eccentric.*
OPPOSITES: traditional, conventional
2 = **irregular**, illegal, improper, inappropriate, unsuitable • *Journalists obtained confidential documents in an unorthodox manner.*
3 = **nonconformist**, heretical, dissenting, renegade, heterodox, dissentient, uncanonical • *his expression of unorthodox religious beliefs*

unpaid 1 = **voluntary**, free, volunteer, honorary, gratuitous, unrewarded, unsalaried, unremunerative • *Even unpaid work for charity is better than nothing.*
2 = **owing**, due, outstanding, unsettled, owed, payable, to be paid, overdue, in the red, in arrears, not discharged • *The bills remained unpaid because of a dispute.*

unpalatable 1 = **unpleasant**, distasteful, disagreeable, bitter, offensive, unattractive, horrid, unsavoury, displeasing, repugnant • *I began to learn the unpalatable truth about John.*
OPPOSITES: pleasant, agreeable
2 = **uneatable**, unsavoury, inedible, unappetizing • *a lump of dry, unpalatable cheese*
OPPOSITES: appetizing, tasty

unparalleled = **unequalled**, exceptional, unprecedented, rare, unique, singular, consummate, superlative, unrivalled, incomparable, unmatched, peerless, unsurpassed, matchless, beyond compare, without equal • *His book was an unparalleled success.*

unpardonable = **unforgivable**, indefensible, inexcusable, outrageous, disgraceful, shameful, scandalous, deplorable, unjustifiable • *an unpardonable lack of discipline*

unperturbed = **calm**, untroubled, unfazed *(informal)*, cool, collected, composed, poised, tranquil, placid, unruffled, self-possessed, unworried, unflustered, undismayed, as cool as a cucumber • *Ruiz seemed totally unperturbed by the events unfolding around him.*
OPPOSITES: worried, troubled

unpleasant 1 = **nasty**, bad, horrid, distressing, annoying, irritating, miserable, troublesome, distasteful, obnoxious, unpalatable, displeasing, repulsive, objectionable, disagreeable, abhorrent, irksome, unlovely, execrable • *They tolerated what they felt was an unpleasant situation.*
OPPOSITES: nice, lovely, pleasant
2 = **obnoxious**, disagreeable, vicious, malicious, rude, mean, cruel, poisonous, unattractive, unfriendly, vindictive, venomous, mean-spirited, inconsiderate, impolite, unloveable, ill-natured, unlikable *or* unlikeable • *He was very unpleasant indeed.*
OPPOSITES: good-natured, likable *or* likeable, congenial
3 = **unappetizing**, disgusting, revolting, bitter, offensive, foul, sour, rotten, sickening, vile, unsavoury, unpalatable, nauseating, repugnant, off-putting, unappealing, rancid, uninviting, yucko *(Austral. slang)* • *an unpleasant taste of cheap coffee*
OPPOSITES: delicious, tasty, appetizing

unpleasantness 1 = **hostility**, animosity, antagonism, bad feeling, malice, rudeness, offensiveness, abrasiveness, argumentativeness, unfriendliness, quarrelsomeness, ill humour *or* will • *Most offices are riddled with sniping and general unpleasantness.*
OPPOSITES: friendliness, pleasantness, good humour *or* will
2 = **nastiness**, awfulness, grimness, trouble, misery, woe, ugliness, unacceptability, dreadfulness, disagreeableness, horridness • *the unpleasantness of surgery and chemotherapy*
OPPOSITES: delight, acceptability, pleasantness

unpolished 1 = **crude**, rough, unfinished, rude, sketchy, rough and ready, unworked, unfashioned • *Much of the prose is unpolished.*
2 = **unrefined**, unsophisticated, uncouth, vulgar, uncultivated, uncivilized, uncultured • *an uncouth and unpolished yokel*

unpopular = **disliked**, rejected, unwanted, avoided, shunned, unwelcome, undesirable, unattractive, detested, out of favour, unloved, out in the cold, cold-shouldered, not sought out, sent to Coventry *(Brit.)* • *I was unpopular in high school.*
OPPOSITES: popular, liked, wanted

unprecedented 1 = **unparalleled**, unheard-of, exceptional, new, original, novel, unusual, abnormal, singular, ground-breaking, unrivalled, freakish, unexampled • *Such a move is unprecedented.*
2 = **extraordinary**, amazing, remarkable, outstanding, fantastic, marvellous, exceptional, phenomenal, uncommon • *The scheme has been hailed as an unprecedented success.*

unpredictable = **extraordinary**, erratic, changeable, variable, chance, random, doubtful, unstable, unreliable, fickle, hit-and-miss *(informal)*, iffy *(informal)*, hit-or-miss *(informal)*, inconstant, unforeseeable, fluky *(informal)*, scattershot • *Britain's notoriously unpredictable weather*
OPPOSITES: reliable, predictable

unprejudiced 1 = **impartial**, fair, objective, just, balanced, unbiased, even-handed, fair-minded, nonpartisan, uninfluenced • *There must be a few honest and unprejudiced lawyers around.*
OPPOSITES: unfair, prejudiced
2 = **tolerant**, liberal, open-minded, progressive, enlightened, unbiased, free-thinking, broad-minded, unbigoted • *an independent, free-thinking and unprejudiced group*
OPPOSITES: biased, bigoted

unprepared 1 = **taken off guard**, caught napping *(informal)*, unready, surprised, unaware, unsuspecting, taken aback, caught on the hop *(Brit. informal)* • *We were completely unprepared.*
2 = **unwilling**, reluctant, loath, opposed, resistant, averse, disinclined, indisposed • *He was unprepared to co-operate, or indeed to communicate.*
3 = **improvised**, spontaneous, off the cuff *(informal)*, ad-lib, extemporaneous • *The actual comedy is unprepared.*

unprepossessing = **unattractive**, unpleasant, unappealing, unsightly, uninviting, scuzzy *(informal)* • *We found the tastiest tapas in the most unprepossessing bars.*

unpretentious = **modest**, simple, plain, homely, humble, straightforward, honest, unaffected, unassuming, unobtrusive, unspoiled, unostentatious, unimposing • *The Tides Inn is both comfortable and unpretentious.*
OPPOSITES: pretentious, showy

unprincipled = **dishonest**, corrupt, crooked, immoral, tricky, unscrupulous, devious, unethical, unprofessional, amoral, deceitful, underhand, dishonourable, unconscionable • *the unprincipled behaviour of the prosecutor's office*
OPPOSITES: honest, moral

unproductive 1 = **useless**, futile, fruitless, vain, idle, ineffective, worthless, unprofitable, unrewarding, valueless, unavailing, otiose, bootless, unremunerative, inefficacious • *They are aware much of their time and effort is unproductive.*
OPPOSITES: effective, useful
2 = **barren**, sterile, infertile, dry, fruitless, unprolific • *increasingly unproductive land*
OPPOSITES: productive, fertile

unprofessional 1 = **unethical**, unfitting, improper, lax, negligent, unworthy, unseemly, unprincipled • *He was also fined $150 for unprofessional conduct.*
2 = **amateurish**, amateur, incompetent, inefficient, cowboy *(informal)*, inexperienced, untrained, slapdash, slipshod, inexpert • *He rubbished his team for another unprofessional performance.*
OPPOSITES: professional, expert, skilful

unprofitable 1 = **uneconomic**, unrewarding, profitless, worthless, unproductive, unremunerative • *unprofitable state-owned industries*
OPPOSITES: profitable, money-making
2 = **fruitless**, useless, pointless, futile, vain, unproductive, unavailing, unfruitful, profitless, bootless • *an endless, unprofitable argument*
OPPOSITES: profitable, constructive

unpromising = **inauspicious**, discouraging, ominous, unfavourable, doubtful, gloomy, adverse, unpropitious, infelicitous • *His business career had distinctly unpromising beginnings.*

unprotected 1 = **vulnerable**, helpless, defenceless, unarmed, unguarded, undefended, open to attack, pregnable • *an unprotected girl, going along that river walkway in the dark*
OPPOSITES: protected, safe
2 = **exposed**, naked, unshielded, open, unsheltered • *exposure of unprotected skin to the sun*
OPPOSITES: shielded

unqualified 1 = **unfit**, incapable, incompetent, not up to, unprepared, ineligible, ill-equipped, not equal to • *She was unqualified for the job.*
2 = **unconditional**, complete, total, absolute, utter, outright, thorough, downright, consummate, unrestricted, out-and-out, categorical, unmitigated, unreserved, thoroughgoing, without reservation, arrant, deep-dyed *(usually derogatory)* • *The event was an unqualified success.*

unquestionable = **certain**, undeniable, indisputable, clear, sure, perfect, absolute, patent, definite, manifest, unmistakable, conclusive, flawless, unequivocal, faultless, self-evident, irrefutable, incontrovertible, incontestable, indubitable, beyond a shadow of doubt, nailed-on *(slang)* • *a man of unquestionable integrity*
OPPOSITES: uncertain, doubtful, dubious

unravel 1 = **break up**, fail, collapse, go wrong, fall apart, come apart (at the seams) • *When she returned to America, the marriage unravelled.*
2 = **solve**, explain, work out, resolve, interpret, figure out *(informal)*, make out, clear up, suss (out) *(slang)*, get to the bottom of, get straight, puzzle out • *She wanted to unravel the mystery of her husband's disappearance.*
3 = **undo**, separate, disentangle, free, unwind, extricate, straighten out, untangle, unknot • *He could unravel knots that others could not even attempt.*

unreadable 1 = **turgid**, heavy going, badly written, dry as dust • *Most computer ads used to be unreadable.*
2 = **illegible**, undecipherable, crabbed • *She scribbled an unreadable address on the receipt.*

unreal 1 = **imaginary**, make-believe, illusory, fabulous, visionary, mythical, fanciful, fictitious, intangible, immaterial, storybook, insubstantial, nebulous, dreamlike, impalpable, chimerical, phantasmagoric • *There are few more unreal worlds than that of the celebrity.*
2 = **absurd**, ridiculous, preposterous, amazing, nonsensical • *Car parking's so expensive nowadays it's unreal.*

unrealistic 1 = **impractical**, romantic, improbable, unworkable, theoretical, half-baked *(informal)*, quixotic, impracticable, starry-eyed • *their unrealistic expectations of parenthood*
OPPOSITES: practical, sensible
2 = **unauthentic**, unreal, non-naturalistic, unlifelike • *an unrealistic portrayal*

unreasonable 1 = **biased**, arbitrary, irrational, illogical, blinkered, opinionated, headstrong • *The strikers were being unreasonable in their demands.*
OPPOSITES: flexible, open-minded, fair-minded
2 = **excessive**, steep *(informal)*, exorbitant, unfair, absurd, extravagant, unjust, too great, undue, preposterous, unwarranted, far-fetched, extortionate, uncalled-for, immoderate • *unreasonable increases in the price of petrol*
OPPOSITES: fair, reasonable, moderate

unrecognizable = **unidentifiable**, disguised, incognito, changed, altered, unknowable • *With a wig and a false moustache I was unrecognizable.*
OPPOSITES: identifiable, recognizable

unrefined 1 = **raw**, crude, untreated, unfinished, unpolished, unpurified • *the price of unrefined oil as it comes out of the ground*
2 = **coarse**, unsophisticated, uncultured, rude, vulgar, boorish, inelegant • *an unrefined boor*

unrelated 1 = **unconnected**, different, dissimilar, unlike, not related • *Two of them died from entirely unrelated causes.*
2 = **irrelevant**, unconnected, extraneous, beside the point, inappropriate, inapplicable, unassociated, not germane • *Two other detectives have been suspended in an unrelated matter.*

unrelenting 1 = **merciless**, tough, ruthless, relentless, cruel, stern, inexorable, implacable, intransigent, remorseless, pitiless, unsparing • *in the face of severe opposition and unrelenting criticism*
2 = **steady**, constant, continuous, endless, perpetual, continual, unbroken, incessant, unabated, ceaseless, unremitting, unwavering • *an unrelenting downpour of rain*

unreliable 1 = **inaccurate**, unconvincing, implausible, mistaken, false, uncertain, fake, deceptive, erroneous, unsound, fallible, specious, delusive • *The figures were unreliable because the sample sizes were too small.*
OPPOSITES: accurate, infallible
2 = **undependable**, irresponsible, untrustworthy, unstable, treacherous, disreputable, not conscientious • *She had*

proved to be an unreliable witness and had lied to police.
OPPOSITES: reliable, dependable

unremitting = **constant**, continuous, relentless, perpetual, continual, unbroken, incessant, diligent, unabated, unwavering, indefatigable, remorseless, assiduous, unceasing, sedulous, unwearied • *boarding school, where I spent six years of unremitting misery* • *thanks to his unremitting efforts*

unrepentant = **impenitent**, shameless, incorrigible, abandoned, hardened, callous, obdurate, unregenerate, not contrite, unremorseful, unrepenting • *She was unrepentant about her strong language and abrasive remarks.*
OPPOSITES: sorry, ashamed

QUOTATIONS
Farewell, remorse! All good to me is lost;
Evil, be thou my good
[John Milton *Paradise Lost*]

unreserved = **total**, full, absolute, complete, entire, unlimited, unconditional, unqualified, wholehearted, without reservation • *Charles displays unreserved admiration for his grandfather.*

unresolved = **undecided**, unsettled, undetermined, vague, doubtful, pending, unanswered, unsolved, up in the air, moot, open to question, problematical, yet to be decided • *A territorial dispute with El Salvador remains unresolved.*

unrest = **discontent**, rebellion, dissatisfaction, protest, turmoil, upheaval, strife, agitation, discord, disaffection, sedition, tumult, dissension • *The real danger is civil unrest in the east of the country.*
OPPOSITES: rest, peace, calm

unrestrained = **uncontrolled**, uninhibited, unbridled, free, natural, abandoned, unlimited, unchecked, inordinate, unhindered, intemperate, unbounded, unconstrained, immoderate, unrepressed • *There was unrestrained joy on the faces of the people.*
OPPOSITES: restrained, inhibited

unrestricted 1 = **unlimited**, open, free, absolute, free-for-all *(informal)*, unregulated, freewheeling *(informal)*, unhindered, unbounded, uncircumscribed • *The Commissioner has unrestricted access to all the files.*
2 = **clear**, open, unobstructed • *Nearly all seats have an unrestricted view.*

unrivalled = **unparalleled**, incomparable, unsurpassed, supreme, unmatched, peerless, unequalled, matchless, beyond compare, without equal, nonpareil, unexcelled • *He had an unrivalled knowledge of south Arabian society.*

unruffled 1 = **calm**, cool, collected, peaceful, composed, serene, tranquil, sedate, placid, undisturbed, unmoved, unfazed *(informal)*, unperturbed, unflustered • *Anne had remained unruffled, very cool and controlled.*
2 = **smooth**, even, level, flat, unbroken • *the unruffled surface of the pool*

unruly = **uncontrollable**, wild, unmanageable, disorderly, turbulent, rebellious, wayward, rowdy, intractable, wilful, lawless, fractious, riotous, headstrong, mutinous, disobedient, ungovernable, refractory, obstreperous, insubordinate • *It's not good enough just to blame the unruly children.*
OPPOSITES: manageable, obedient, docile

unsafe 1 = **dangerous**, risky, hazardous, threatening, uncertain, unstable, insecure, unreliable, precarious, treacherous, perilous, unsound • *Critics claim the trucks are unsafe.*
OPPOSITES: safe, secure, reliable
2 = **vulnerable**, threatened, exposed, unprotected, defenceless, open to attack • *In the larger neighbourhood, I felt very unsafe.*

unsaid = **unspoken**, tacit, unexpressed, undeclared, unstated, unvoiced, left to the imagination, unuttered • *Some things, Donald, are better left unsaid.*

unsanitary = **unhygienic**, dirty, filthy, unhealthy, sordid, squalid, unclean, insanitary, insalubrious, infected, skanky *(slang)*, scungy *(Austral. & N.Z.)*, germ-ridden, festy *(Austral. slang)* • *diseases caused by unsanitary conditions*

unsatisfactory = **not good enough**, inadequate, unacceptable, poor, disappointing, weak, pathetic, insufficient, unsuitable, mediocre, deficient, unworthy, displeasing, not up to scratch *(informal)*, no great shakes *(informal)*, not much cop *(Brit. slang)*, not up to par • *The inspectors said a third of lessons were unsatisfactory.*
OPPOSITES: sufficient, acceptable

unsavoury 1 = **unpleasant**, nasty, obnoxious, offensive, revolting, distasteful, repellent, repulsive, objectionable, repugnant • *The sport has long been associated with unsavoury characters.*
2 = **unappetizing**, unpalatable, distasteful, sickening, disagreeable, nauseating • *unsavoury school meals*
OPPOSITES: tasty, palatable, appetizing

unscathed = **unharmed**, unhurt, uninjured, whole, sound, safe, untouched, unmarked, in one piece, unscarred, unscratched • *He emerged unscathed apart from a severely bruised finger.*

unscrupulous = **unprincipled**, corrupt, crooked *(informal)*, ruthless, improper, immoral, dishonest, unethical, exploitative, dishonourable, roguish, unconscionable, knavish, conscienceless, unconscientious • *These kids are being exploited by very unscrupulous people.*
OPPOSITES: principled, moral, honourable

unseat 1 = **depose**, overthrow, oust, remove, dismiss, discharge, displace, dethrone • *It is not clear who was behind the attempt to unseat the President.*
2 = **throw**, unsaddle, unhorse • *She was unseated on her first ride.*

unseemly = **improper**, inappropriate, unsuitable, out of place, undignified, disreputable, unbecoming, unrefined, out of keeping, discreditable, indelicate, in poor taste, indecorous, unbefitting • *It would be unseemly for judges to receive pay increases.*
OPPOSITES: becoming, seemly, proper

unseen 1 = **unobserved**, undetected, unperceived, lurking, unnoticed, unobtrusive • *I can now accept that there are unseen forces at work.*
2 = **hidden**, concealed, invisible, veiled, obscure • *playing computer games against unseen opponents*

unselfish = **generous**, selfless, noble, kind, liberal, devoted, humanitarian, charitable, disinterested, altruistic, self-sacrificing, magnanimous, self-denying • *As a player he was unselfish, a true team man.*

unsettle = **disturb**, trouble, upset, throw *(informal)*, bother, confuse, disorder, rattle *(informal)*, agitate, ruffle, unnerve, disconcert, unbalance, fluster, perturb, faze, throw into confusion, throw off balance, discompose, throw into disorder, throw into uproar • *The presence of the two policemen unsettled her.*

unsettled 1 = **unstable**, shaky, insecure, disorderly, unsteady • *Britain's unsettled political scene also worries some investors.*
2 = **restless**, tense, uneasy, troubled, shaken, confused, wired *(slang)*, disturbed, anxious, agitated, unnerved, flustered, perturbed, on edge, restive, adrenalized • *To tell the truth, I'm a bit unsettled tonight.*
3 = **unresolved**, undecided, undetermined, open, doubtful, debatable, up in the air, moot • *They were in the process of resolving all the unsettled issues.*
4 = **uninhabited**, unoccupied, unpopulated, unpeopled • *Until very recently Texas was an unsettled frontier.*
5 = **inconstant**, changing, unpredictable, variable, uncertain, changeable • *Despite the unsettled weather, we had a marvellous weekend.*

6 = **owing**, due, outstanding, pending, payable, in arrears • *Liabilities related to unsettled transactions are recorded.*

unsettling = **disturbing**, worrying, troubling, upsetting, alarming, distressing, dismaying, disconcerting, disquieting • *The prospect of change of this kind has an unsettling effect.*

unshakeable *or* **unshakable** = **firm**, staunch, resolute, sure, certain, fixed, secure, constant, absolute, unassailable, well-founded, steadfast, unwavering, immovable, unswerving • *She had an unshakeable faith in human goodness.*
OPPOSITES: shaky, insecure

unsightly = **ugly**, unattractive, repulsive, unpleasant, revolting *(informal)*, hideous, horrid, disagreeable, unprepossessing, fugly *(chiefly U.S. & Austral.)* • *My mother has had unsightly varicose veins for years.*
OPPOSITES: pretty, beautiful, attractive

unskilled = **unprofessional**, inexperienced, unqualified, untrained, uneducated, amateurish, cowboy *(informal)*, untalented • *Most of those who left the province to work abroad were unskilled.*
OPPOSITES: professional, skilled, expert

unsociable = **unfriendly**, cold, withdrawn, retiring, distant, hostile, chilly, reclusive, inhospitable, introverted, unsocial, uncongenial, standoffish, unforthcoming, unneighbourly • *I am by no means an unsociable person.*
OPPOSITES: friendly, outgoing

unsolicited = **uninvited**, unwelcome, gratuitous, unasked for, volunteered, voluntary, spontaneous, unforced, uncalled-for, unsought, unrequested • *Being ex-directory won't necessarily keep unsolicited calls away.*

unsophisticated 1 = **simple**, plain, uncomplicated, straightforward, unrefined, uninvolved, unspecialized, uncomplex • *music of a crude kind which unsophisticated audiences enjoyed*
OPPOSITES: advanced, complex, complicated
2 = **naive**, innocent, inexperienced, unworldly, unaffected, childlike, natural, artless, ingenuous, guileless • *She was quite unsophisticated in the ways of the world.*

unsound 1 = **flawed**, faulty, weak, false, shaky, unreliable, invalid, defective, illogical, erroneous, specious, fallacious, ill-founded • *The thinking is muddled and fundamentally unsound.*
2 = **unstable**, shaky, insecure, unsafe, unreliable, flimsy, wobbly, tottering, rickety, unsteady, not solid • *The church was structurally unsound.*
OPPOSITES: strong, sound, stable
3 = **unhealthy**, unstable, unbalanced, diseased, ill, weak, delicate, ailing, frail, defective, unwell, deranged, unhinged • *He was rejected as an army conscript as being of unsound mind.*

unsparing 1 = **lavish**, liberal, generous, abundant, prodigal, bountiful, open-handed, unstinting, profuse, munificent, ungrudging, plenteous • *He was unsparing with his devotion to the team.*
2 = **severe**, ruthless, relentless, hard, harsh, stern, rigorous, stringent, uncompromising, unforgiving, inexorable, implacable, cold-blooded, unmerciful • *He is unsparing in his criticism.*

unspeakable = **dreadful**, shocking, appalling, evil, awful, overwhelming, horrible, unbelievable, monstrous, from hell *(informal)*, inconceivable, unimaginable, repellent, abysmal, frightful, heinous, odious, indescribable, loathsome, abominable, ineffable, beyond words, execrable, unutterable, inexpressible, beyond description, hellacious *(U.S. slang)*, too horrible for words • *the unspeakable horrors of chemical weapons*

unspecified = **unnamed**, unknown, unidentified, uncertain, mysterious, obscure, vague, arbitrary, undecided, indefinite, nameless, indeterminate, undefined, unstated, undetermined, unquantified, unfixed, undesignated • *He was arrested on unspecified charges.*

unspectacular = **average**, mediocre, unremarkable, middling, normal, ordinary, indifferent, commonplace, plodding, run-of-the-mill, undistinguished, uneventful, inconspicuous, workaday, unexceptional, nothing out of the ordinary, unmemorable • *His progress at school had been unspectacular.*

unspoiled *or* **unspoilt** 1 = **unchanged**, preserved, untouched, perfect, intact, unaffected, unharmed, undamaged, unblemished, unimpaired • *I made the offshore trip to the unspoiled island of Cozumel.*
OPPOSITES: changed, touched
2 = **natural**, unaffected, unassuming, innocent, wholesome, artless, unstudied • *the world's most unspoiled pop kids*

unspoken 1 = **unsaid**, silent, mute, wordless, voiceless, unuttered • *His face was expressionless, but Alex felt the unspoken criticism.*
2 = **tacit**, understood, assumed, implied, implicit, taken for granted, inferred, undeclared, unstated, unexpressed, not spelt out, left to the imagination, not put into words • *There had been an unspoken agreement between them.*
OPPOSITES: spoken, declared

unstable 1 = **changeable**, volatile, unpredictable, variable, fluctuating, unsteady, fitful, inconstant • *The situation is unstable and potentially dangerous.*
OPPOSITES: stable, steady, constant
2 = **insecure**, shaky, precarious, unsettled, wobbly, tottering, rickety, unsteady, not fixed • *a house built on unstable foundations*
3 = **unpredictable**, irrational, erratic, inconsistent, unreliable, temperamental, capricious, changeable, untrustworthy, vacillating • *He was emotionally unstable.*
OPPOSITES: rational, level-headed, stable

unsteady 1 = **unstable**, shaky, insecure, unsafe, precarious, treacherous, rickety, infirm • *a slightly unsteady item of furniture*
2 = **reeling**, wobbly, tottering • *The boy was unsteady, staggering around the room.*
3 = **erratic**, unpredictable, volatile, unsettled, wavering, unreliable, temperamental, changeable, vacillating, flighty, inconstant • *She knew the impact an unsteady parent could have on a young girl.*

unstinted = **lavish**, liberal, generous, full, ample, abundant, plentiful, prodigal, bountiful, unstinting, profuse • *unstinted praise for the relaxed, original cooking*

unstinting = **lavish**, liberal, generous, full, ample, abundant, plentiful, prodigal, bountiful, profuse, unstinted • *The task was made easier by the unstinting help extended to me.*

unsubstantiated = **unconfirmed**, unproven, unsupported, speculative, questionable, spurious, groundless, open to question, uncorroborated, conjectural, unestablished, unattested • *unsubstantiated rumours about his private life*
OPPOSITES: proven, established

unsuccessful 1 = **failed**, useless, ineffective, vain, futile, fruitless, unproductive, abortive, unavailing, bootless • *a second unsuccessful operation on his knee*
OPPOSITES: productive, worthwhile
2 = **unlucky**, losing, defeated, frustrated, unfortunate, foiled, hapless, balked, luckless, ill-starred • *The unsuccessful competitors left with nothing.*
OPPOSITES: winning, triumphant

unsuitable = **inappropriate**, unacceptable, unfit, unfitting, out of place, improper, incompatible, ineligible, incongruous, unseemly, out of character, unsuited, unbecoming, out of keeping, unseasonable, unbefitting, inapt, infelicitous, inapposite • *Amy's shoes were unsuitable for walking any distance.*
OPPOSITES: fitting, appropriate

unsullied = **immaculate**, stainless, impeccable, clean, pure, untouched, pristine, spotless, squeaky-clean, unblemished, untainted, untarnished, uncorrupted, undefiled, unsoiled, unblackened • *the combined talents of intellect, experience and unsullied reputation*

unsung = **unacknowledged**, unrecognized, unappreciated, unknown, neglected, anonymous, disregarded, unnamed, uncelebrated, unhonoured, unacclaimed, unhailed • *They are among the unsung heroes of our time.*

unsure 1 = **lacking in confidence**, hesitant, apprehensive, insecure, unconfident, unassured, lacking assurance • *hesitant unsure performances from all the orchestra*
OPPOSITES: sure, confident
2 = **doubtful**, sceptical, dubious, suspicious, hesitant, undecided, unconvinced, distrustful, in a quandary, mistrustful, irresolute • *Fifty-two per cent were unsure about the idea.*
OPPOSITES: decided, sure

unsurpassed = **supreme**, unparalleled, unrivalled, exceptional, paramount, consummate, superlative, transcendent, second to none, incomparable, peerless, unequalled, matchless, nonpareil, unexcelled, without an equal • *The quality of Smallbone furniture is unsurpassed.*

unsurprising = **predictable**, expected, understandable, predicted, foreseeable, only to be expected, not unexpected • *It is unsurprising that he remains so hated.*

unsuspecting = **trusting**, naive, gullible, unsuspicious, innocent, unconscious, confiding, inexperienced, off guard, unwary, credulous, ingenuous, trustful, unwarned • *selling junk bonds to thousands of unsuspecting depositors*

unswerving = **firm**, staunch, steadfast, constant, true, direct, devoted, steady, dedicated, resolute, single-minded, unwavering, unflagging, untiring, unfaltering, undeviating • *her unswerving belief in her father's innocence*

unsympathetic 1 = **insensitive**, callous, heartless, hard, cold, harsh, cruel, indifferent, unkind, unmoved, unconcerned, apathetic, soulless, unresponsive, unfeeling, uncompassionate, compassionless *(rare)*, stony-hearted, unpitying • *an unsympathetic doctor*
OPPOSITES: sensitive, kind
2 = **unsavoury**, nasty, unpleasant, unattractive, obnoxious, objectionable, disagreeable • *a very unsympathetic main character*
3 *with* **to** = **against**, anti, opposed to, set against, disapproving of, antagonistic towards, ill-disposed towards, unsupportive of • *I'm highly unsympathetic to what you are trying to achieve.*

untamed = **wild**, fierce, savage, unbroken, uncontrollable, feral, barbarous, untameable, undomesticated, not broken in • *acting like wild, untamed animals*

untangle 1 = **disentangle**, unravel, sort out, extricate, straighten out, untwist, unsnarl • *trying to untangle several reels of film*
OPPOSITES: tangle, muddle, entangle
2 = **solve**, clear up, straighten out, understand, explain, figure out *(informal)*, clarify, unravel, fathom, get to the bottom of, elucidate, suss out *(informal)*, puzzle out • *Lawyers began trying to untangle the complex affairs of the bank.*
OPPOSITES: confuse, complicate, muddle

untarnished = **unstained**, immaculate, impeccable, spotless, clean, pure, glowing, squeaky-clean, unblemished, unsullied, unimpeachable, unsoiled, unspotted • *Her reputation abroad has remained largely untarnished.*

untenable = **unsustainable**, indefensible, unsound, groundless, weak, flawed, shaky, unreasonable, illogical, fallacious, insupportable • *He claimed the charges against him were untenable.*
OPPOSITES: sound, justified, reasonable

unthinkable 1 = **impossible**, out of the question, inconceivable, unlikely, not on *(informal)*, absurd, unreasonable, improbable, preposterous, illogical • *Her strong Catholic beliefs made abortion unthinkable.*
2 = **inconceivable**, incredible, unbelievable, unimaginable, beyond belief, beyond the bounds of possibility • *Monday's unthinkable tragedy*

unthinking 1 = **thoughtless**, insensitive, tactless, rude, blundering, inconsiderate, undiplomatic • *He doesn't say those silly things that unthinking people say.*
2 = **impulsive**, senseless, unconscious, mechanical, rash, careless, instinctive, oblivious, negligent, unwitting, witless, inadvertent, heedless, unmindful • *Bruce was no unthinking vandal.*
OPPOSITES: deliberate, careful, conscious

untidy 1 = **messy**, disordered, chaotic, littered, muddled, cluttered, jumbled, rumpled, shambolic, bedraggled, unkempt, topsy-turvy, higgledy-piggledy *(informal)*, mussy *(U.S. informal)*, muddly, disarrayed • *Clothes were thrown in the luggage in an untidy heap.*
OPPOSITES: neat, tidy, orderly
2 = **unkempt**, dishevelled, tousled, disordered, messy, ruffled, scruffy, rumpled, bedraggled, ratty *(informal)*, straggly, windblown, disarranged, mussed up *(informal)*, daggy *(Austral. & N.Z. informal)* • *a thin man with untidy hair*
3 = **sloppy**, messy *(informal)*, slovenly, slipshod, slatternly • *I'm untidy in most ways.*
OPPOSITES: systematic, methodical

untie = **undo**, free, release, loosen, unfasten, unbind, unstrap, unclasp, unlace, unknot, unmoor, unbridle • *Nicholas untied the boat from her mooring.*

until AS A PREPOSITION 1 = **till**, up to, up till, up to the time, as late as • *consumers who have waited until after the Christmas holiday*
2 = **before**, up to, prior to, in advance of, previous to, pre- • *The traffic laws don't take effect until the end of the year.*
▸ AS A CONJUNCTION 1 = **till**, up to, up till, up to the time, as late as • *I waited until it got dark.*
2 = **before**, up to, prior to, in advance of, previous to • *The EC will not lift its sanctions until that country makes changes.*

untimely 1 = **early**, premature, before time, unseasonable • *His mother's untimely death had a catastrophic effect on him.*
OPPOSITES: timely, seasonable
2 = **ill-timed**, inappropriate, badly timed, inopportune, unfortunate, awkward, unsuitable, inconvenient, mistimed, inauspicious • *Your readers would have seen the article as at best untimely.*
OPPOSITES: appropriate, convenient, well-timed

untiring = **tireless**, constant, persistent, patient, dogged, determined, devoted, steady, dedicated, staunch, persevering, incessant, unremitting, indefatigable, unflagging, unfaltering, unwearied • *an untiring fighter for justice, democracy and tolerance*

untold 1 = **indescribable**, unthinkable, unimaginable, unspeakable, undreamed of, unutterable, inexpressible • *This might do untold damage to her health.*
2 = **countless**, incalculable, innumerable, myriad, numberless, uncounted, uncountable, unnumbered, measureless • *the glittering prospect of untold riches*
3 = **undisclosed**, unknown, unrevealed, private, secret, hidden, unrelated, unpublished, unrecounted • *the untold story of children's suffering*

untouched 1 = **unharmed**, intact, unscathed, undamaged, unhurt, uninjured, safe and sound, without a scratch • *Amongst the rubble, there was one building that remained untouched.*
2 = **unmoved**, indifferent, unaffected, unimpressed, unconcerned, dry-eyed, unstirred • *He was completely untouched by her tears.*
OPPOSITES: moved, touched

3 = **unspoilt**, pristine, virgin, natural, perfect, unaffected, unpolluted • *one of the world's last untouched islands*
4 = **unconsumed**, uneaten, undrunk, surplus, unwanted, left over • *The coffee was untouched, the toast had cooled.*

untoward = **unfavourable**, unfortunate, disastrous, adverse, contrary, annoying, awkward, irritating, unlucky, inconvenient, untimely, inauspicious, inimical, ill-timed, vexatious, inopportune • *The surveyor's report didn't highlight anything untoward.*

untrained = **amateur**, inexperienced, unskilled, green, raw, unqualified, uneducated, untutored, unschooled, unpractised, untaught • *It is nonsense to say we have untrained staff dealing with emergencies.*
OPPOSITES: trained, experienced

untried = **untested**, new, unproved, in the experimental stage, novel, unattempted, unessayed • *a long legal battle through untried areas of law*

untroubled = **undisturbed**, unconcerned, unperturbed, cool, calm, steady, peaceful, composed, serene, tranquil, sedate, placid, unfazed *(informal)*, unflappable *(informal)*, unruffled, unworried, unflustered, unstirred, unagitated • *She remained untroubled by the reports.*
OPPOSITES: concerned, worried

untrue 1 = **false**, lying, wrong, mistaken, misleading, incorrect, inaccurate, sham, dishonest, deceptive, spurious, erroneous, fallacious, untruthful • *The allegations were completely untrue.*
OPPOSITES: right, true, correct
2 = **unfaithful**, disloyal, deceitful, treacherous, two-faced, faithless, false, untrustworthy, perfidious, forsworn, traitorous, inconstant • *untrue to the basic tenets of socialism*
OPPOSITES: constant, loyal, faithful

untrustworthy = **unreliable**, treacherous, deceitful, false, tricky, slippery, untrue, dishonest, fickle, devious, unfaithful, capricious, two-faced, disloyal, faithless, fair-weather, fly-by-night *(informal)*, undependable, not to be depended on, untrusty • *His opponents still say he's a fundamentally untrustworthy figure.*
OPPOSITES: reliable, loyal

untruth 1 = **lie**, fabrication, falsehood, fib, story, tale, fiction, deceit, whopper *(informal)*, porky *(Brit. slang)*, pork pie *(Brit. slang)*, falsification, prevarication • *The Authority accused estate agents of using blatant untruths.*
2 = **lying**, perjury, duplicity, falsity, mendacity, deceitfulness, untruthfulness, inveracity *(rare)*, truthlessness • *I have never uttered one word of untruth.*

u

untruthful = **dishonest**, lying, false, deceptive, hypocritical, fibbing, deceitful, dissembling, mendacious • *Some people may be tempted to give untruthful answers.*
OPPOSITES: true, honest

untutored 1 = **uneducated**, ignorant, untrained, illiterate, unlearned, unschooled, unversed • *This untutored mathematician had an obsession with numbers.*
2 = **unsophisticated**, simple, inexperienced, unrefined, artless, unpractised • *The wrangling of trade disputes can baffle the untutored eye.*

unused 1 = **new**, untouched, remaining, fresh, intact, immaculate, pristine • *unused containers of food and drink*
2 = **remaining**, leftover, unconsumed, left, available, extra, unutilized • *Throw away any unused cream when it has reached the expiry date.*
3 *with* **to** = **unaccustomed to**, new to, unfamiliar with, not up to, not ready for, a stranger to, inexperienced in, unhabituated to • *Mother was entirely unused to such hard work.*

unusual 1 = **rare**, odd, strange, extraordinary, different, surprising, novel, bizarre, unexpected, curious, weird *(informal)*, unfamiliar, abnormal, queer, phenomenal, uncommon, out of the ordinary, left-field *(informal)*, unwonted • *rare and unusual plants*
OPPOSITES: usual, familiar, common
2 = **extraordinary**, unique, remarkable, exceptional, notable, phenomenal, uncommon, singular, unconventional, out of the ordinary, atypical • *He was an unusual man with great business talents.*
OPPOSITES: normal, typical, average

unusually AS AN ADVERB = **exceptionally**, especially, remarkably, extraordinarily, abnormally, uncommonly • *this year's unusually harsh winter*
▸ AS AN ADJECTIVE = **surprisingly**, oddly, strangely, peculiarly, uncommonly • *Unusually among British prime ministers, he was not a man of natural authority.*

unutterable = **indescribable**, extreme, overwhelming, unimaginable, unspeakable, ineffable, beyond words • *An unutterable sadness swept over her.*

unvarnished = **plain**, frank, honest, candid, simple, pure, bare, naked, straightforward, stark, sincere, pure and simple, unadorned, unembellished • *The full unvarnished truth about the Duke should be made public.*

unveil = **reveal**, publish, launch, introduce, release, display, broadcast, demonstrate, expose, bare, parade, exhibit, disclose, uncover, bring out, make public, flaunt, divulge, lay bare, make known, bring to light, put on display, lay open, put on show, put on view • *Mr Werner unveiled his new strategy this week.*
OPPOSITES: hide, disguise, conceal

unwanted 1 = **undesirable**, unacceptable, unpopular, unwelcome, terrible, appalling, unfortunate, disastrous, intolerable, unfavourable, undesired • *The city plan would promote unwanted development in the suburbs.*
OPPOSITES: wanted, needed
2 = **unloved**, rejected, disliked, useless, shunned, outcast, forsaken, superfluous, surplus to requirements, friendless, unneeded, uncared for, de trop *(French)*, uncherished • *I was unhappy at home because I felt unwanted and unloved.*
3 = **leftover**, surplus, untouched, unused, going begging, uneaten, unconsumed • *Community purchases of unwanted beef create a new beef mountain.*
4 = **unwelcome**, uninvited, unsolicited, unasked • *From now on he would be an unwanted guest in the Embassy.*

unwarranted = **unnecessary**, unjustified, indefensible, wrong, unreasonable, unjust, gratuitous, unprovoked, inexcusable, groundless, uncalled-for • *an unwarranted interference in the country's internal affairs*

unwary = **careless**, rash, reckless, hasty, thoughtless, unguarded, indiscreet, imprudent, heedless, incautious, uncircumspect, unwatchful • *The hilly roads were slick enough to cause unwary drivers to skid.*
OPPOSITES: cautious, wary, discreet

unwavering = **steady**, consistent, staunch, determined, dedicated, resolute, single-minded, steadfast, immovable, unswerving, unshakable, unflagging, unshaken, untiring, unfaltering, undeviating • *She has been encouraged by the unwavering support of her family.*

unwelcome 1 = **disagreeable**, unpleasant, undesirable, distasteful, displeasing, thankless • *This report will come as unwelcome news to the government.*
OPPOSITES: pleasing, acceptable, wanted, welcome
2 = **unwanted**, unpopular, undesirable, rejected, excluded, unacceptable, uninvited, unwished for • *She was deliberately making him feel unwelcome.*
OPPOSITES: wanted, welcome, popular

unwell = **ill**, poorly *(informal)*, sick, crook *(Austral. & N.Z. informal)*, ailing, unhealthy, sickly, out of sorts, off colour, under the weather *(informal)*, in poor health, at death's door, indisposed, green about the gills • *He felt unwell as he was being driven back to his office.*
OPPOSITES: well, fine, healthy

unwholesome 1 = **harmful**, unhealthy, noxious, deleterious, junk *(informal)*, tainted, poisonous, insanitary, insalubrious, unnourishing • *a chemically reactive ecologically unwholesome substance*
OPPOSITES: healthy, beneficial
2 = **wicked**, bad, evil, corrupting, perverting, degrading, immoral, depraving, demoralizing, maleficent • *My desire to be rich was an insane, unwholesome desire.*
OPPOSITES: moral, edifying

unwieldy 1 = **bulky**, massive, hefty, clumsy, weighty, ponderous, ungainly, clunky *(informal)* • *They came panting up to his door with their unwieldy baggage.*
2 = **awkward**, cumbersome, inconvenient, burdensome, unmanageable, unhandy • *His firm must contend with the unwieldy Russian bureaucracy.*

unwilling 1 = **disinclined**, reluctant, averse, loath, slow, opposed, resistant, not about, not in the mood, indisposed • *Initially the government was unwilling to accept the defeat.*
OPPOSITES: willing, eager, inclined
2 = **reluctant**, grudging, unenthusiastic, resistant, involuntary, averse, demurring, laggard *(rare)* • *He finds himself an unwilling participant in school politics.*
OPPOSITES: willing, voluntary, eager

unwillingness = **reluctance**, resistance, refusal, opposition, objection, aversion, slowness, backwardness, diffidence, coyness, disinclination • *their unwillingness to accept responsibility for mistakes*

unwind 1 = **relax**, wind down, take it easy, slow down, sit back, calm down, take a break, loosen up, quieten down, let yourself go, mellow out *(informal)*, make yourself at home, outspan *(S. African)* • *It helps them to unwind after a busy day at work.*
2 = **unravel**, undo, uncoil, slacken, disentangle, unroll, unreel, untwist, untwine • *One of them unwound a length of rope from around his waist.*

unwise = **foolish**, stupid, silly, rash, irresponsible, reckless, senseless, short-sighted, ill-advised, foolhardy, inane, indiscreet, ill-judged, ill-considered, imprudent, inadvisable, asinine, injudicious, improvident, impolitic • *It would be unwise to expect too much.*
OPPOSITES: wise, sensible, shrewd

unwitting 1 = **unintentional**, involuntary, inadvertent, chance, accidental, unintended, unplanned, undesigned, unmeant • *It had been an unwitting blunder on his part.*
OPPOSITES: intended, deliberate, intentional
2 = **unknowing**, innocent, unsuspecting, unconscious, unaware, ignorant • *We're unwitting victims of the system.*
OPPOSITES: knowing, conscious, witting

unwonted = **unusual**, rare, extraordinary, unexpected, peculiar, unfamiliar, uncommon, singular, unheard-of, out of the ordinary, infrequent, unaccustomed, atypical, seldom seen, uncustomary • *He replied with unwonted irritation.*

unworkable = **impracticable**, unfeasible, unachievable, impossible, out of the question, unattainable • *Washington is unhappy with the peace plan, which it views as unworkable.*

unworldly 1 = **naive**, innocent, unsophisticated, green, trusting, raw, inexperienced, idealistic, wet behind the ears *(informal)*, as green as grass • *Stephen is a little unworldly about such matters.*
2 = **spiritual**, religious, metaphysical, transcendental, nonmaterialistic • *Their minds were occupied by more unworldly matters.*

unworthy 1 = **undeserving**, not good enough, not fit, not worth, ineligible, not deserving • *You may feel unworthy of the attention and help people offer you.*
OPPOSITES: fit, deserving, worthy
2 = **dishonourable**, base, contemptible, degrading, disgraceful, shameful, disreputable, ignoble, discreditable • *Aren't you amazed by how loving the father is to his unworthy son?*
OPPOSITES: honourable, commendable, creditable
3 *with* **of** = **unbefitting**, beneath, unfitting to, unsuitable for, inappropriate to, improper to, out of character with, out of place with, unbecoming to • *His accusations are unworthy of a prime minister.*

unwritten 1 = **oral**, word-of-mouth, unrecorded, vocal • *the unwritten stories of his infancy and childhood*
2 = **understood**, accepted, tacit, traditional, conventional, silent, customary, implicit, unformulated • *They obey the one unwritten rule that binds them all – no talking.*

unyielding 1 = **firm**, tough, rigid, hardline, uncompromising, determined, relentless, adamant, stubborn, staunch, resolute, intractable, inflexible, inexorable, steadfast, obstinate, unwavering, immovable, unbending, obdurate, stiff-necked • *his unyielding attitude on this subject*
OPPOSITES: yielding, compromising
2 = **hard**, firm, solid, stiff, inflexible, unbending, unmoving, non-flexible, unpliable • *He sat on the edge of an unyielding armchair.*
OPPOSITES: yielding, flexible

up IN PHRASES: **ups and downs** = **fluctuations**, changes, vicissitudes, moods, ebb and flow • *Every relationship has a lot of ups and downs.*

up-and-coming = **promising**, ambitious, go-getting *(informal)*, pushing, eager • *Phoenix, at that time, was an up-and-coming actor.*

upbeat = **cheerful**, positive, optimistic, promising, encouraging, looking up, hopeful, favourable, rosy, buoyant, heartening, cheery, forward-looking • *Neil's colleagues say he was actually in a joking, upbeat mood.*

upbraid = **scold**, rebuke, reprimand, blame, condemn, lecture, carpet *(informal)*, censure, reproach, berate, castigate, chide, admonish, tear into *(informal)*, read someone the riot act, tell someone off *(informal)*, reprove, take someone to task, tick someone off *(informal)*, excoriate, chew someone out *(U.S. & Canad. informal)*, bawl someone out *(informal)*, dress someone down *(informal)*, tear someone off a strip *(Brit. informal)*, give someone a rocket *(Brit. & N.Z. informal)*, slap someone on the wrist, rap someone over the knuckles • *Eleanor upbraided him for things he'd left undone.*

upbringing = **education**, training, breeding, rearing, care, raising, tending, bringing-up, nurture, cultivation • *Martin's upbringing shaped his whole life.*

upcoming = **forthcoming**, coming, approaching, imminent, expected, future, prospective, impending • *We'll face a tough fight in the upcoming election.*

update 1 = **bring up to date**, improve, correct, renew, revise, upgrade, amend, overhaul, streamline, modernize, rebrand • *an updated edition of the book*
2 = **brief**, advise, inform, report to, fill in, notify, clue in *(informal)*, apprise, bring up to date, explain the situation to, give details to, keep posted, bring up to speed *(informal)* • *We'll update you on the day's top news stories.*

up-front *or* **up front** AS AN ADJECTIVE 1 = **open**, frank, honest, candid, direct, above board • *You can't help being biased so you may as well be up front about it.*
2 = **advance**, initial, introductory • *up-front charges*
▸ AS AN ADVERB = **in advance**, initially, beforehand • *Some companies charge a fee up front.*

upgrade 1 = **improve**, better, update, reform, add to, enhance, refurbish, renovate, remodel, make better, modernize, spruce up, ameliorate • *Medical facilities are being reorganized and upgraded.*
2 = **promote**, raise, advance, boost, move up, elevate, kick upstairs *(informal)*, give promotion to • *He was upgraded to security guard.*
OPPOSITES: degrade, downgrade, demote

upheaval = **disturbance**, revolution, disorder, turmoil, overthrow, disruption, eruption, cataclysm, violent change • *Algeria has been going through political upheaval.*

U

uphill AS AN ADJECTIVE 1 = **ascending**, rising, upward, mounting, climbing • *a long, uphill journey*
OPPOSITES: descending, downhill, lowering
2 = **arduous**, hard, taxing, difficult, tough, exhausting, punishing, gruelling, strenuous, laborious, wearisome, Sisyphean • *It had been an uphill struggle to achieve what she wanted.*
▸ AS A NOUN = **difficulty**, problem, trouble, dilemma, headache (*informal*), hassle (*informal*), can of worms (*informal*) • *This job has been a real uphill.*

uphold 1 = **support**, back, defend, aid, champion, encourage, maintain, promote, sustain, advocate, stand by, stick up for (*informal*) • *upholding the artist's right to creative freedom*
2 = **confirm**, support, sustain, endorse, approve, justify, hold to, ratify, vindicate, validate • *The crown court upheld the magistrate's decision.*

upkeep 1 = **maintenance**, running, keep, subsistence, support, repair, conservation, preservation, sustenance • *The money will be used for the estate's upkeep.*
2 = **running costs**, expenses, overheads, expenditure, outlay, operating costs, oncosts (*Brit.*) • *subsidies for the upkeep of kindergartens and orphanages*

uplift AS A VERB = **improve**, better, raise, advance, inspire, upgrade, refine, cultivate, civilize, ameliorate, edify • *Art was created to uplift the mind and the spirit.*
▸ AS A NOUN = **improvement**, enlightenment, advancement, cultivation, refinement, enhancement, enrichment, betterment, edification • *literature intended for the uplift of the soul*

uplifted 1 = **raised**, erect, elevated, held high, upraised, upthrust • *her white, uplifted chin*
2 = **inspired**, encouraged, cheered, stimulated, stirred up, enthused, enlivened, elated, gladdened • *a smile so radiant that he felt uplifted by it*

uplifting = **inspiring**, moving, touching, affecting, warming, stirring, cheering, heart-warming • *a charming and uplifting love story*

upmarket = **prestigious**, important, prominent, esteemed, high-quality, notable, renowned, prestige, eminent, reputable • *She chose an upmarket agency aimed at professional people.*

upper 1 = **topmost**, top • *There is a smart restaurant on the upper floor.*
OPPOSITES: lower, bottom
2 = **higher**, high • *the muscles of the upper back and chest*
OPPOSITES: low, lower
3 = **superior**, senior, higher-level, greater, top, important, chief, most important, elevated, eminent, higher-ranking • *the upper echelons of the Army*
OPPOSITES: low, lower, inferior

upper class AS A NOUN = **aristocracy**, nobility, gentry, peerage, ruling class, upper crust (*informal*), elite, haut monde (*French*) • *Many of the British upper-classes are no longer very rich.*
▸ AS AN ADJECTIVE = **aristocratic**, upper-class, noble, high-class, patrician, top-drawer, blue-blooded, highborn • *All of them came from wealthy, upper-class families.*

uppermost 1 = **top**, highest, topmost, upmost, loftiest, most elevated • *John was on the uppermost floor of the three-storey gatehouse.*
OPPOSITES: lowest, bottom, lowermost
2 = **supreme**, greatest, chief, leading, main, primary, principal, dominant, paramount, foremost, predominant, pre-eminent • *Protection of sites is of uppermost priority.*
OPPOSITES: least, slightest, humblest

uppity = **conceited**, cocky, swanky (*informal*), self-important, overweening, bumptious, bigheaded (*informal*), on your high horse (*informal*), uppish (*Brit. informal*), full of yourself, too big for your boots or breeches (*informal*) • *She wasn't uppity or big-headed; she was so natural and relaxed.*

upright 1 = **vertical**, straight, standing up, erect, on end, perpendicular, bolt upright • *He moved into an upright position.*
OPPOSITES: flat, horizontal, lying
2 = **honest**, good, principled, just, true, faithful, ethical, straightforward, honourable, righteous, conscientious, virtuous, trustworthy, high-minded, above board, incorruptible, unimpeachable • *a very upright, trustworthy man*
OPPOSITES: corrupt, dishonest, dishonourable

uprising = **rebellion**, rising, revolution, outbreak, revolt, disturbance, upheaval, mutiny, insurrection, putsch, insurgence • *a popular uprising against the authoritarian government*

uproar 1 = **commotion**, noise, racket, riot, confusion, turmoil, brawl, mayhem, clamour, din, turbulence, pandemonium, rumpus, hubbub, hurly-burly, brouhaha, ruction (*informal*), hullabaloo, ruckus (*informal*), bagarre (*French*) • *The announcement caused uproar in the crowd.*
2 = **protest**, outrage, criticism, complaint, objection, fuss, stink (*informal*), outcry, furore, hue and cry • *The announcement could cause an uproar in the United States.*

uproarious 1 = **riotous**, wild, rowdy, disorderly, loud, noisy, turbulent, boisterous, tumultuous, unrestrained, tempestuous, rollicking, gleeful, clamorous • *He had spent several uproarious evenings at the Embassy Club.*
OPPOSITES: quiet, peaceful
2 = **hilarious**, hysterical, very funny, side-splitting, killing (*informal*), rip-roaring (*informal*), convulsive (*informal*), rib-tickling, screamingly funny • *regaling the family with uproarious imitations of the local dialect*
OPPOSITES: serious, sad

uproot 1 = **displace**, remove, exile, disorient, deracinate • *the trauma of uprooting them from their homes*
2 = **pull up**, dig up, root out, weed out, rip up, grub up, extirpate, deracinate, pull out by the roots • *fallen trees which have been uprooted by the storm*

upset AS AN ADJECTIVE 1 = **distressed**, shaken, disturbed, worried, troubled, hurt, bothered, confused, unhappy, gutted (*Brit. informal*), put out, dismayed, choked (*informal*), grieved, frantic, hassled (*informal*), agitated, ruffled, cut up (*informal*), disconcerted, disquieted, overwrought, discomposed • *They are terribly upset by the breakup of their parents' marriage.*
2 = **sick**, queasy, bad, poorly (*informal*), ill, gippy (*slang*) • *Larry is suffering from an upset stomach.*
3 = **overturned**, toppled, upside down, capsized, spilled, tumbled, tipped over • *an upset cart with one wheel off*
▸ AS A VERB 1 = **distress**, trouble, disturb, worry, alarm, bother, dismay, grieve, hassle (*informal*), agitate, ruffle, unnerve, disconcert, disquiet, fluster, perturb, faze, throw someone off balance, give someone grief (*Brit., S. African*), discompose • *She warned me not to say anything to upset him.*
2 = **tip over**, overturn, capsize, knock over, spill, topple over • *bumping into him, and almost upsetting the ginger ale*
3 = **mess up**, spoil, disturb, change, confuse, disorder, unsettle, mix up, disorganize, turn topsy-turvy, put out of order, throw into disorder • *I was wondering whether that might upset my level of concentration.*
4 = **defeat**, overcome, conquer, overthrow, triumph over, get the better of, be victorious over • *Chang upset world No 1 Pete Sampras in Saturday's semi-finals.*
▸ AS A NOUN 1 = **distress**, worry, trouble, shock, bother, disturbance, hassle (*informal*), disquiet, agitation, discomposure • *a source of continuity in times of worry and upset*
2 = **reversal**, surprise, shake-up (*informal*), defeat, sudden

change • *She caused a major upset when she beat last year's finalist.*
3 = **illness**, complaint, disorder, bug *(informal)*, disturbance, sickness, malady, queasiness, indisposition • *Paul was unwell last night with a stomach upset.*

upshot = **result**, consequence, outcome, end, issue, event, conclusion, sequel, finale, culmination, end result, payoff *(informal)* • *So the upshot is we're going for lunch on Friday.*

upside down *or* **upside-down** AS AN ADVERB = **wrong side up**, bottom up, on its head • *The painting was hung upside down.*
▸ AS AN ADJECTIVE 1 = **inverted**, overturned, upturned, on its head, bottom up, wrong side up • *Tony had an upside-down map of Britain on his wall.*
2 = **confused**, disordered, chaotic, muddled, jumbled, in disarray, in chaos, topsy-turvy, in confusion, higgledy-piggledy *(informal)*, in disorder • *the upside-down sort of life that we've had*
▸ IN PHRASES: **turn something upside down** = **ransack**, search, go through, comb, scour, rummage through, rake through, turn something inside out, fossick through *(Austral. & N.Z.)* • *I've turned the place upside down, but cannot find it.*

upstage = **outshine**, top, eclipse, overshadow, surpass, transcend, outstrip, outdo, outclass, be superior to, be head and shoulders above, leave *or* put in the shade • *He had a younger brother who always publicly upstaged him.*

upstanding = **honest**, principled, upright, honourable, good, moral, ethical, trustworthy, incorruptible, true • *You look like a nice upstanding young man.*
OPPOSITES: bad, corrupt, immoral

upstart = **social climber**, nobody, nouveau riche *(French)*, parvenu, arriviste, non-person, status seeker • *an upstart who had come from nowhere*

upsurge = **increase**, rise, growth, boost, escalation, upturn • *an upsurge in oil prices*

uptight = **tense**, wired *(slang)*, anxious, neurotic, uneasy, prickly, edgy, on the defensive, on edge, nervy *(Brit. informal)*, adrenalized • *Penny never got uptight about exams.*

up-to-date 1 = **modern**, fashionable, trendy *(Brit. informal)*, in, newest, now *(informal)*, happening *(informal)*, current, with it *(informal)*, stylish, in vogue, all the rage, up-to-the-minute, having your finger on the pulse • *This production is bang up-to-date.*
OPPOSITES: old fashioned, dated, out of date
2 *often with* **on** *or* **with** = **informed about**, up on, aware of, in touch with, familiar with, acquainted with, knowledgeable about, conversant with, au fait with, up to speed on, plugged-in to *(slang)*, au courant with • *We'll keep you up to date with any news.*

upturn = **rise**, increase, boost, improvement, recovery, revival, advancement, upsurge, upswing • *There has been a modest upturn in most parts of the industry.*

upward 1 = **uphill**, rising, ascending, climbing • *She started once again on the steep upward climb.*
2 = **rising**, climbing, ascending, mounting • *Figures show a clear upward trend from the mid-Eighties.*

upwards 1 = **up**, skywards, heavenwards • *Hunter nodded again and gazed upwards in fear.*
2 *with* **of** = **above**, over, more than, beyond, exceeding, greater than, in excess of • *projects worth upwards of 200 million pounds*

urban = **civic**, city, town, metropolitan, municipal, dorp *(S. African)*, inner-city • *Most urban areas are close to a park.*

urbane = **sophisticated**, cultured, polished, civil, mannerly, smooth, elegant, refined, cultivated, cosmopolitan, civilized, courteous, suave, well-bred, debonair, well-mannered • *In conversation, he was suave and urbane.*
OPPOSITES: rude, gauche, boorish

urbanity = **sophistication**, culture, polish, charm, grace, courtesy, elegance, refinement, civility, worldliness, suavity, mannerliness • *He had all the charm and urbanity of the trained diplomat.*

urchin = **ragamuffin**, waif, guttersnipe, brat, mudlark *(slang)*, gamin, street Arab *(offensive)*, young rogue • *We were in the bazaar with all the little urchins watching us.*

urge AS A VERB 1 = **beg**, appeal to, exhort, press, prompt, plead, put pressure on, lean on, solicit, goad, implore, enjoin, beseech, pressurize, entreat, twist someone's arm *(informal)*, put the heat on *(informal)*, put the screws on *(informal)* • *They urged parliament to approve plans for their reform programme.*
2 = **advocate**, suggest, recommend, advise, back, support, champion, counsel, insist on, endorse, push for • *He urged restraint on the security forces.*
OPPOSITES: discourage, deter, dissuade
▸ AS A NOUN = **impulse**, longing, wish, desire, fancy, drive, yen *(informal)*, hunger, appetite, craving, yearning, itch *(informal)*, thirst, compulsion, hankering • *He had an urge to open a shop of his own.*
OPPOSITES: reluctance, aversion, disinclination
▸ IN PHRASES: **urge someone on** = **drive on**, push, encourage, force, press, prompt, stimulate, compel, induce, propel, hasten, constrain, incite, egg on, goad, spur on, impel, gee up • *She had a strong and supportive sister who urged her on.*

urgency = **importance**, need, necessity, gravity, pressure, hurry, seriousness, extremity, exigency, imperativeness • *It is a matter of utmost urgency.*

urgent 1 = **crucial**, desperate, pressing, great, important, crying, critical, immediate, acute, grave, instant, compelling, imperative, top-priority, now or never, exigent, not to be delayed • *There is an urgent need for food and water.*
OPPOSITES: minor, trivial, unimportant
2 = **insistent**, earnest, determined, intense, persistent, persuasive, resolute, clamorous, importunate • *His mother leaned forward and spoke to him in urgent undertones.*
OPPOSITES: casual, apathetic, lackadaisical

urinate = **pee**, wee, piss *(taboo slang)*, leak *(slang slang)*, tinkle *(Brit. informal)*, piddle *(informal)*, spend a penny *(Brit. informal)*, make water, pass water, wee-wee *(informal)*, micturate, take a whizz *(slang, chiefly U.S.)* • *A puppy will want to urinate frequently as he has a small bladder.*

urine
▸ RELATED ADJECTIVE: uretic

usable = **serviceable**, working, functional, available, current, practical, valid, at your disposal, ready for use, in running order, fit for use, utilizable • *blackened, but still usable, cooking pots and other objects*

usage 1 = **phraseology**, terminology, parlance, mode of expression, way of speaking *or* writing • *Certain words may not even be in modern usage.*
2 = **use**, operation, employment, running, control, management, treatment, handling • *Parts of the motor wore out because of constant usage.*
3 = **practice**, method, procedure, form, rule, tradition, habit, regime, custom, routine, convention, mode, matter of course, wont • *a fruitful convergence with past usage and custom*

use AS A VERB 1 = **employ**, utilize, make use of, work, apply, operate, exercise, practise, resort to, exert, wield, ply, put to use, bring into play, find a use for, avail yourself of, turn to account • *Officials used loud hailers to call for calm.*
2 *sometimes with* **up** = **consume**, go through, exhaust, spend, waste, get through, run through, deplete, squander, dissipate, expend, fritter away • *You used all the ice cubes and didn't put the ice trays back.*
3 = **take advantage of**, exploit, manipulate, abuse, milk, profit from, impose on, misuse, make use of, cash in on *(informal)*, walk all over *(informal)*, take liberties with

• *Be careful she's not just using you.*

▸ **AS A NOUN 1** = **usage**, employment, utilization, operation, application • *research related to microcomputers and their use in classrooms*

2 = **service**, handling, wear and tear, treatment, practice, exercise • *Holes had developed, the result of many years of use.*

3 = **purpose**, call, need, end, point, cause, reason, occasion, object, necessity • *You will no longer have a use for the car.*

4 = **good**, point, help, service, value, benefit, profit, worth, advantage, utility, mileage *(informal)*, avail, usefulness • *There's no use you asking me any more questions about that.*

▸ **IN PHRASES: use something up** = **consume**, drain, exhaust, finish, waste, absorb, run through, deplete, squander, devour, swallow up, burn up, fritter away • *They aren't the ones who use up the world's resources.*

used = **second-hand**, worn, not new, cast-off, hand-me-down *(informal)*, nearly new, shopsoiled, reach-me-down *(informal)*, preloved *(Austral. slang)* • *Would you buy a used car from this man?*

OPPOSITES: new, brand-new, unused

used to = **accustomed to**, familiar with, in the habit of, given to, at home in, attuned to, tolerant of, wont to, inured to, hardened to, habituated to • *I'm used to having my sleep interrupted.*

useful = **helpful**, effective, valuable, practical, of use, profitable, of service, worthwhile, beneficial, of help, fruitful, advantageous, all-purpose, salutary, general-purpose, serviceable • *The police gained useful information about the organisation.*

OPPOSITES: useless, ineffective, worthless

usefulness = **helpfulness**, value, worth, use, help, service, benefit, profit, utility, effectiveness, convenience, practicality, efficacy • *His interest lay in the usefulness of his work.*

useless 1 = **worthless**, of no use, valueless, pants *(slang)*, ineffective, impractical, fruitless, unproductive, ineffectual, unworkable, disadvantageous, unavailing, bootless, unsuitable • *He realised that their money was useless in this country.*

OPPOSITES: useful, practical, valuable

2 = **pointless**, hopeless, futile, vain, idle, profitless • *She knew it was useless to protest.*

OPPOSITES: worthwhile, profitable

3 = **inept**, no good, hopeless, weak, stupid, pants *(slang)*, incompetent, ineffectual • *He was useless at any game with a ball.*

usher AS A VERB = **escort**, lead, direct, guide, conduct, pilot, steer, show • *They were quickly ushered away.*

▸ **AS A NOUN** = **attendant**, guide, doorman, usherette, escort, doorkeeper • *He did part-time work as an usher in a theatre.*

▸ **IN PHRASES: usher something in** = **introduce**, launch, bring in, precede, initiate, herald, pave the way for, ring in, open the door to, inaugurate • *a unique opportunity to usher in a new era of stability in Europe*

usual = **normal**, customary, regular, expected, general, common, stock, standard, fixed, ordinary, familiar, typical, constant, routine, everyday, accustomed, habitual, bog-standard *(Brit. & Irish slang)*, wonted • *She's smiling her usual, friendly smile.*

OPPOSITES: rare, unusual, extraordinary

usually = **normally**, generally, mainly, commonly, regularly, mostly, routinely, on the whole, in the main, for the most part, by and large, most often, ordinarily, as a rule, habitually, as is usual, as is the custom, USU *(S.M.S.)* • *The best information about hotels usually comes from friends.*

usurp = **seize**, take over, assume, take, appropriate, wrest, commandeer, arrogate, infringe upon, lay hold of • *Did she usurp his place in his mother's heart?*

utensil = **implement**, tool, instrument, aid, machine, device, mechanism, appliance, apparatus, gadget, gimmick *(informal)*, contraption, gizmo *(informal)*, contrivance • *The technique uses a single utensil to cook and serve.*

utilitarian = **functional**, useful, practical, plain, efficient, sensible, pragmatic, unpretentious, soulless, serviceable, unadorned, workaday • *Bruce's office is a corner one, utilitarian and unglamorous.*

utility = **usefulness**, use, point, benefit, service, profit, fitness, convenience, mileage *(informal)*, avail, practicality, efficacy, advantageousness, serviceableness • *He inwardly questioned the utility of his work.*

utilize = **use**, employ, deploy, take advantage of, resort to, make the most of, make use of, put to use, bring into play, have recourse to, avail yourself of, turn to account • *Sound engineers utilize a range of techniques.*

utmost AS AN ADJECTIVE 1 = **greatest**, highest, maximum, supreme, extreme, paramount, pre-eminent • *Security matters are treated with the utmost seriousness.*

2 = **farthest**, extreme, last, final, outermost, uttermost, farthermost • *The break-up tested our resolve to its utmost limits.*

▸ **AS A NOUN** = **best**, greatest, maximum, most, highest, hardest • *I'm going to do my utmost to climb as fast and as far as I can.*

utopia = **paradise**, heaven, Eden, bliss, perfect place, Garden of Eden, Shangri-la, Happy Valley, seventh heaven, ideal life, Erewhon • *We weren't out to design a contemporary utopia.*

utopian AS AN ADJECTIVE = **perfect**, ideal, romantic, dream, fantasy, imaginary, visionary, airy, idealistic, fanciful, impractical, illusory, chimerical • *He was pursuing a utopian dream of world prosperity.*

▸ **AS A NOUN** = **dreamer**, visionary, idealist, Don Quixote, romanticist • *Kennedy had no patience with dreamers or liberal utopians.*

utter[1] = **say**, state, speak, voice, express, deliver, declare, mouth, breathe, pronounce, articulate, enunciate, put into words, verbalize, vocalize • *They departed without uttering a word.*

utter[2] = **absolute**, complete, total, perfect, positive, pure, sheer, stark, outright, all-out, thorough, downright, real, consummate, veritable, unqualified, out-and-out, unadulterated, unmitigated, thoroughgoing, arrant, deep-dyed *(usually derogatory)* • *A look of utter confusion swept across his handsome face.*

utterance 1 = **speech**, words, statement, comment, opinion, remark, expression, announcement, observation, declaration, reflection, pronouncement • *the Queen's public utterances*

2 = **speaking**, voicing, expression, breathing, delivery, ejaculation, articulation, enunciation, vocalization, verbalization, vociferation • *the simple utterance of a few platitudes*

utterly = **totally**, completely, absolutely, just, really, quite, perfectly, fully, entirely, extremely, altogether, thoroughly, wholly, downright, categorically, to the core, one hundred per cent, in all respects, to the nth degree, unqualifiedly • *The new laws coming in are utterly ridiculous.*

u-turn *or* **U-turn** = **reversal**, turnaround, change of heart, about-turn *(Brit.)*, backtracking, shift, sea change, about-face, retraction, change of mind, turnround, change of plan, volte-face, turnabout, reversal of policy, paradigm shift • *a humiliating U-turn by the Prime Minister*

Vv

vacancy 1 = **opening**, job, post, place, position, role, situation, opportunity, slot, berth *(informal)*, niche, job opportunity, vacant position, situation vacant • *They had a vacancy for a temporary secretary.*
2 = **room**, space, available accommodation, unoccupied room • *The hotel only has a few vacancies left.*

vacant 1 = **empty**, free, available, abandoned, deserted, to let, for sale, on the market, void, up for grabs, disengaged, uninhabited, unoccupied, not in use, unfilled, untenanted • *They came upon a vacant house.*
OPPOSITES: taken, full, occupied
2 = **unfilled**, unoccupied • *The post has been vacant for some time.*
OPPOSITES: taken, occupied, engaged
3 = **blank**, vague, dreamy, dreaming, empty, abstracted, idle, thoughtless, vacuous, inane, expressionless, unthinking, absent-minded, incurious, ditzy *or* ditsy *(slang)* • *She had a dreamy, vacant look on her face.*
OPPOSITES: lively, animated, thoughtful

vacate 1 = **leave**, quit, move out of, give up, withdraw from, evacuate, depart from, go away from, leave empty, relinquish possession of • *He vacated the flat and went back to stay with his parents.*
2 = **quit**, leave, resign from, give up, withdraw from, chuck *(informal)*, retire from, relinquish, renounce, walk out on, pack in *(informal)*, abdicate, step down from *(informal)*, stand down from • *He recently vacated his post as Personnel Director.*

vacation AS A NOUN = **holiday(s)**, leave, break, rest, tour, trip, time off, recess, hols *(informal)*, leave of absence, furlough, mini-break, awayday, schoolie *(Austral.)*, acumulated day off *or* ADO *(Austral.)* • *During his vacation he visited Russia.*
▸ AS A VERB = **holiday**, visit, travel, tour, stay, be on holiday, take a break, sojourn, take a holiday, stop over • *He was vacationing in Jamaica and could not be reached.*

vaccinate = **inoculate**, inject, protect, immunize • *Have you had your child vaccinated against whooping cough?*

vaccine = **inoculation**, injection, immunization • *Anti-malarial vaccines are now undergoing trials.*

vacillate = **waver**, hesitate, dither *(chiefly Brit.)*, haver, sway, falter, be doubtful, fluctuate, be uncertain, be unsure, teeter, oscillate, be undecided, chop and change, seesaw, blow hot and cold *(informal)*, temporize, hum and haw, be unable to decide, keep changing your mind, shillyshally *(informal)*, be irresolute *or* indecisive, swither *(Scot.)*, be unable to make up your mind *(chiefly Brit.)*, dillydally • *She is vacillating over whether or not to marry him.*

vacillating = **indecisive**, irresolute, hesitant, uncertain, faltering, wavering, unresolved, oscillating, in two minds *(informal)*, shillyshallying *(informal)* • *He has proved weak, indecisive and vacillating.*

vacillation = **indecisiveness**, hesitation, irresolution, wavering, dithering *(chiefly Brit.)*, fluctuation, unsteadiness, inconstancy, shillyshallying *(informal)*, irresoluteness • *The Prime Minister was pilloried for vacillation and weakness.*

QUOTATIONS
Some praise at morning what they blame at night;
But always think the last opinion right
[Alexander Pope *An Essay on Criticism*]

PROVERBS
Don't change horses in midstream

vacuity = **inanity**, stupidity, emptiness, blankness, vapidity, vacuousness, brainlessness, unintelligence, inaneness • *the vacuity of current pop music*

vacuous = **vapid**, stupid, inane, blank, vacant, unintelligent • *the usual vacuous comments from the chat-show host*

vacuum AS A NOUN 1 = **gap**, lack, absence, space, deficiency, void • *The collapse of the army left a vacuum in the area.*
2 = **emptiness**, space, void, gap, empty space, nothingness, vacuity • *The spinning turbine creates a vacuum.*
3 = **vacuum cleaner**, Hoover *(trademark)*, vac *(Brit. informal)* • *Get the breakfast and take the vacuum round the house before the boys wake.*
▸ AS A VERB = **vacuum-clean**, hoover • *I vacuumed the carpets today.*

QUOTATIONS
Nature abhors a vacuum
[François Rabelais *Gargantua*]

vagabond AS A NOUN = **tramp**, bum *(informal)*, drifter, vagrant, migrant, rolling stone, wanderer, beggar, outcast, rover, nomad, itinerant, down-and-out, hobo *(U.S.)*, bag lady *(chiefly U.S.)*, wayfarer, dosser *(Brit. slang)*, knight of the road, person of no fixed address, derro *(Austral. slang)* • *He had lived as a vagabond, begging for food.*
▸ AS A MODIFIER = **vagrant**, drifting, wandering, homeless, journeying, unsettled, roaming, idle, roving, nomadic, destitute, itinerant, down and out, rootless, footloose, fly-by-night *(informal)*, shiftless • *his impoverished, vagabond existence*

vagary *usually plural* = **whim**, caprice, unpredictability, sport, urge, fancy, notion, humour, impulse, quirk, conceit, whimsy, crotchet, sudden notion • *a coat as a provision against the vagaries of the weather* • *his fairly wide experience of women's vagaries*

vagina = **vulva**, pussy *(taboo slang)*, cunt *(taboo slang)*, box *(taboo slang)*, hole *(taboo slang)*, crack *(taboo slang)*, snatch *(taboo slang)*, fanny *(Brit. taboo slang)*, beaver *(taboo slang)*, muff *(taboo slang)*, twat *(taboo slang)*, quim *(Brit. taboo)*, yoni, minge *(Brit. taboo slang)*, punani *(taboo slang)* • *Sperm are ejaculated into the vagina during intercourse.*

vagrancy = **homelessness**, roaming, roving, rootlessness, nomadism, itinerancy, vagabondism • *Vagrancy and begging are commonplace in London.*

vagrant **AS A NOUN** = **tramp**, bum *(informal)*, drifter, vagabond, rolling stone, wanderer, beggar, derelict, itinerant, down-and-out, hobo *(U.S.)*, bag lady *(chiefly U.S.)*, dosser *(Brit. slang)*, pikey *(Brit. slang)*, person of no fixed address, derro *(Austral. slang)* • *He lived on the street as a vagrant.*
▸ **AS AN ADJECTIVE** = **vagabond**, drifting, wandering, homeless, journeying, unsettled, roaming, idle, roving, nomadic, destitute, itinerant, down and out, rootless, footloose, fly-by-night *(informal)*, shiftless • *the terrifying subculture of vagrant alcoholics*
OPPOSITES: settled, fixed, rooted

vague 1 = **unclear**, indefinite, hazy, confused, loose, uncertain, doubtful, unsure, superficial, incomplete, woolly, imperfect, sketchy, cursory • *Her description of her attacker was very vague.*
OPPOSITES: clear, specific, exact
2 = **imprecise**, unspecified, generalized, rough, loose, ambiguous, hazy, equivocal, ill-defined, non-specific, inexact, obfuscatory, inexplicit • *His answer was deliberately vague.*
3 = **absent-minded**, absorbed, abstracted, distracted, unaware, musing, vacant, preoccupied, bemused, oblivious, dreamy, daydreaming, faraway, unthinking, heedless, inattentive, unheeding • *She had married a charming but rather vague Englishman.*
4 = **indistinct**, blurred, unclear, dim, fuzzy, unknown, obscure, faint, shadowy, indefinite, misty, hazy, indistinguishable, amorphous, indeterminate, bleary, nebulous, out of focus, ill-defined, indiscernible • *He could just make out a vague shape in the distance.*
OPPOSITES: clear, distinct, well-defined
5 = **indefinite**, uncertain, undecided, unconfirmed, pending, speculative, unresolved, indeterminate, yet to be decided • *the team's vague plans to start up a regular magazine*

vaguely 1 = **slightly**, rather, sort of *(informal)*, kind of *(informal)*, a little, a bit, somewhat, moderately, faintly, dimly, to some extent, kinda *(informal)* • *The voice was vaguely familiar.*
2 = **absent-mindedly**, evasively, abstractedly, obscurely, vacantly, inattentively • *'What did you talk about?' 'Oh, this and that,' she replied vaguely.*
3 = **roughly**, loosely, indefinitely, carelessly, in a general way, imprecisely • *'She's back there,' he said, waving vaguely behind him.*

vagueness 1 = **impreciseness**, ambiguity, obscurity, looseness, inexactitude, woolliness, undecidedness, lack of preciseness • *the vagueness of the language used in the text*
OPPOSITES: precision, clarity, preciseness
2 = **absent-mindedness**, abstraction, forgetfulness, confusion, inattention, disorganization, giddiness, dreaminess, befuddlement, empty-headedness • *her deliberately affected vagueness*

vain **AS AN ADJECTIVE** 1 = **futile**, useless, pointless, unsuccessful, empty, hollow, idle, trivial, worthless, trifling, senseless, unimportant, fruitless, unproductive, abortive, unprofitable, time-wasting, unavailing, nugatory • *They worked all night in a vain attempt to finish on schedule.*
OPPOSITES: successful, profitable, worthwhile
2 = **conceited**, narcissistic, proud, arrogant, inflated, swaggering, stuck-up *(informal)*, cocky, swanky *(informal)*, ostentatious, egotistical, self-important, overweening, vainglorious, swollen-headed *(informal)*, pleased with yourself, bigheaded *(informal)*, peacockish • *She's a shallow, vain and self-centred woman.*
OPPOSITES: modest, humble, meek
▸ **IN PHRASES:** **in vain** 1 = **useless**, to no avail, unsuccessful, fruitless, wasted, vain, ineffectual, without success, to no purpose, bootless • *All her complaints were in vain.*
2 = **uselessly**, to no avail, unsuccessfully, fruitlessly, vainly, ineffectually, without success, to no purpose, bootlessly • *He hammered the door, trying in vain to attract her attention.*

vale = **valley**, dale, glen, hollow, depression, dell, dingle, strath *(Scot.)*, cwm *(Welsh)*, coomb • *a small vale sheltering under mist-shrouded hills*

valediction = **farewell**, goodbye, leave-taking, adieu, vale *(Latin)*, sendoff *(informal)* • *She raised her hand in valediction.*

valedictory = **farewell**, leaving, parting, last, final, going away, departing • *making his valedictory address after two years as chairman*

valet = **manservant**, man, attendant, gentleman's gentleman • *He stayed on to serve his master as valet and then butler.*

valiant = **brave**, heroic, courageous, bold, worthy, fearless, gallant, intrepid, plucky, doughty, indomitable, redoubtable, dauntless, lion-hearted, valorous, stouthearted • *valiant attempts by neighbours and firemen to rescue them*
OPPOSITES: fearful, cowardly, timid

valid 1 = **sound**, good, reasonable, just, telling, powerful, convincing, substantial, acceptable, sensible, rational, logical, viable, credible, sustainable, plausible, conclusive, weighty, well-founded, cogent, well-grounded • *Both sides have made valid points.*
OPPOSITES: weak, false, unfounded
2 = **legal**, official, legitimate, correct, genuine, proper, in effect, authentic, in force, lawful, bona fide, legally binding, signed and sealed • *For foreign holidays you will need a valid passport.*
OPPOSITES: illegal, unofficial, invalid

validate 1 = **confirm**, prove, certify, substantiate, corroborate • *The evidence has been validated by historians.*
2 = **authorize**, endorse, ratify, legalize, authenticate, make legally binding, set your seal on *or* to • *Give the retailer your winning ticket to validate.*

validity 1 = **soundness**, force, power, grounds, weight, strength, foundation, substance, point, cogency • *Some people deny the validity of this claim.*
2 = **legality**, authority, legitimacy, right, lawfulness • *They now want to challenge the validity of the vote.*

valley = **hollow**, dale, glen, vale, depression, dell, dingle, strath *(Scot.)*, cwm *(Welsh)*, coomb • *a wooded valley set against the backdrop of Monte Rosa*

valour *or (U.S.)* **valor** = **bravery**, courage, heroism, spirit, boldness, gallantry, derring-do *(archaic)*, fearlessness, intrepidity, doughtiness, lion-heartedness • *He was decorated for valour in the war.*
OPPOSITES: fear, cowardice, timidity

valuable **AS AN ADJECTIVE** 1 = **useful**, important, profitable, worthwhile, beneficial, valued, helpful, worthy, of use, of help, invaluable, serviceable, worth its weight in gold • *The experience was very valuable.*
OPPOSITES: useless, trivial, pointless
2 = **treasured**, esteemed, cherished, prized, precious, held dear, estimable, worth your weight in gold • *She was a valuable friend and an excellent teacher.*
3 = **precious**, expensive, costly, dear, high-priced, priceless, irreplaceable • *valuable old books*
OPPOSITES: cheap, inexpensive, worthless
▸ **AS A PLURAL NOUN** = **treasures**, prized possessions, precious items, heirlooms, personal effects, costly article • *Leave your valuables in the hotel safe.*

valuation = **costing**, price, estimate, value, evaluation, quotation • *The valuations reflect prices at 1 April 1999.*

value **AS A NOUN** 1 = **importance**, use, benefit, worth, merit, point, help, service, sense, profit, advantage, utility, significance, effectiveness, mileage *(informal)*, practicality, usefulness, efficacy, desirability, serviceableness • *Studies are needed to see if these therapies have any value.*
OPPOSITES: insignificance, uselessness, worthlessness

2 = **cost**, price, worth, rate, equivalent, market price, face value, asking price, selling price, monetary worth • *The value of his investment has risen by more than 100%.*

▸ **AS A PLURAL NOUN** = **principles**, morals, ethics, mores, standards of behaviour, code of behaviour, (moral) standards • *a return to traditional family values*

▸ **AS A VERB** 1 = **appreciate**, rate, prize, regard highly, respect, admire, treasure, esteem, cherish, think much of, hold dear, have a high opinion of, set store by, hold in high regard *or* esteem • *Do you value your best friend enough?*

OPPOSITES: underestimate, disregard, undervalue

2 *with* **at** = **evaluate**, price, estimate, rate, cost, survey, assess, set at, appraise, put a price on • *I have had my jewellery valued for insurance purposes.* • *cocaine valued at $53 million*

valued = **appreciated**, prized, esteemed, highly regarded, loved, dear, treasured, cherished • *a valued member of the team*

valueless 1 = **pointless**, worthless, futile, miserable, useless, in vain, ineffective, senseless, fruitless, to no avail, purposeless, of no earthly use • *I felt my existence was totally valueless.*

2 = **worthless**, useless, no good, trifling, unsaleable, of no value • *Money became virtually valueless with the collapse of the economy.*

vamp **AS A NOUN** = **seductress**, siren, femme fatale *(French)*, temptress, Mata Hari, mantrap *(informal)* • *a vamp in a figure-hugging black dress*

▸ **AS A VERB** = **seduce**, tempt, lure, lead on, flirt with, toy with, beguile, chat up *(informal)*, make up to, trifle with, make eyes at • *the scene in which the hero is vamped by a brunette siren*

vandal = **hooligan**, ned *(Scot. slang)*, delinquent, rowdy, lager lout, graffiti artist, boot boy, yob *or* yobbo *(Brit. slang)*, cougan *(Austral. slang)*, scozza *(Austral. slang)*, bogan *(Austral. slang)* • *The phone box had been destroyed by vandals.*

vanguard = **forefront**, front line, cutting edge, leaders, front, van, spearhead, forerunners, front rank, trailblazers, advance guard, trendsetters • *Students have been in the vanguard of revolutionary change in China.*

OPPOSITES: back, rear, rearguard

vanilla = **ordinary**, standard, regular, common, stock, simple, normal, typical, conventional, routine, everyday, down-to-earth, workaday, bog-standard *(informal)* • *I've just got a plain vanilla insurance policy.*

vanish 1 = **disappear**, become invisible, be lost to sight, dissolve, evaporate, fade away, melt away, disappear from sight, exit, evanesce • *The aircraft vanished without trace.*

OPPOSITES: appear, materialize, come into view

2 = **die out**, disappear, pass away, end, fade, dwindle, cease to exist, become extinct, disappear from the face of the earth • *Dinosaurs vanished from the earth millions of years ago.*

vanity 1 = **pride**, arrogance, conceit, airs, showing off *(informal)*, pretension, narcissism, egotism, self-love, ostentation, vainglory, self-admiration, affected ways, bigheadedness *(informal)*, conceitedness, swollen-headedness *(informal)* • *Men who use steroids are motivated by sheer vanity.*

OPPOSITES: modesty, humility, self-deprecation

2 = **futility**, uselessness, worthlessness, emptiness, frivolity, unreality, triviality, hollowness, pointlessness, inanity, unproductiveness, fruitlessness, unsubstantiality, profitlessness • *the futility of human existence and the vanity of wealth*

OPPOSITES: value, worth, importance

QUOTATIONS

I've only been in love with a beer bottle and a mirror
[Sid Vicious]

Vanity is a vital aid to nature: completely and absolutely necessary to life. It is one of nature's ways to bind you to the earth
[Elizabeth Smart *Necessary Secrets*]

Vanity, like murder, will out
[Hannah Cowley *The Belle's Stratagem*]

Possibly, more people kill themselves and others out of hurt vanity than out of envy, jealousy, malice or desire for revenge
[Iris Murdoch *The Philosopher's Pupil*]

Vanity of vanities, all is vanity
[*Bible: Ecclesiastes*]

We are so vain that we even care for the opinion of those we don't care for
[Marie von Ebner-Eschenbach]

vanquish = **defeat**, beat, conquer, reduce, stuff *(slang)*, master, tank *(slang)*, overcome, crush, overwhelm, put down, lick *(informal)*, undo, subdue, rout, repress, overpower, quell, triumph over, clobber *(slang)*, subjugate, run rings around *(informal)*, wipe the floor with *(informal)*, blow out of the water *(slang)*, put to flight, get the upper hand over, put to rout • *a happy ending in which the hero vanquishes the monsters*

vapid = **dull**, boring, insipid, flat, weak, limp, tame, bland, uninspiring, colourless, uninteresting, wishy-washy *(informal)* • *the minister's young and rather vapid wife*

vapour *or (U.S.)* **vapor** = **mist**, fog, haze, smoke, breath, steam, fumes, dampness, miasma, exhalation • *a cloud of poisonous vapour*

variable = **changeable**, unstable, fluctuating, shifting, flexible, wavering, uneven, fickle, temperamental, mercurial, capricious, unsteady, protean, vacillating, fitful, mutable, inconstant, chameleonic • *Weather conditions are variable and change from day to day.*

OPPOSITES: stable, constant, unchanging

variance **AS A NOUN** = **difference**, contrast, discrepancy, variation, disagreement, contradiction, inconsistency, deviation, divergence, incongruity, dissimilarity • *the variances in the stock price*

OPPOSITES: agreement, similarity

▸ **IN PHRASES: at variance** = **in disagreement**, conflicting, at odds, in opposition, out of line, at loggerheads, at sixes and sevens *(informal)*, out of harmony • *Many of his statements are at variance with the facts.*

variant **AS AN ADJECTIVE** = **different**, alternative, modified, derived, exceptional, divergent • *There are so many variant spellings of this name.*

▸ **AS A NOUN** = **variation**, form, version, development, alternative, adaptation, revision, modification, permutation, transfiguration, aberration, derived form • *Bulimia was once seen as a variant of anorexia.*

variation 1 = **alternative**, variety, modification, departure, innovation, variant • *This delicious variation on an omelette is easy to prepare.*

2 = **variety**, change, deviation, difference, diversity, diversion, novelty, alteration, discrepancy, diversification, departure from the norm, break in routine • *Every day without variation my grandfather ate a plate of ham.*

OPPOSITES: uniformity, tedium, monotony

3 *often plural* = **difference**, contrast, distinction, discrepancy, disparity, dissimilarity, dissimilitude • *local variations in price and availability*

varied = **different**, mixed, various, diverse, assorted, miscellaneous, sundry, motley, manifold, heterogeneous • *a varied range of dishes suitable for vegetarians*

OPPOSITES: similar, uniform, unvarying

variegated = **mottled**, pied, streaked, motley, many-coloured, parti-coloured, varicoloured • *variegated grey and green leaves*

variety 1 = **diversity**, change, variation, difference, diversification, heterogeneity, many-sidedness, multifariousness • *people who like variety in their lives and enjoy trying new things*

OPPOSITES: similarity, uniformity, monotony
2 = **range**, selection, assortment, mix, collection, line-up, mixture, array, cross section, medley, multiplicity, mixed bag *(informal)*, miscellany, motley collection, intermixture • *a store selling a wide variety of goods*
3 = **type**, sort, kind, make, order, class, brand, species, breed, strain, category • *She grows 12 varieties of old-fashioned roses.*

QUOTATIONS
Variety's the very spice of life,
That gives all its flavour
[William Cowper *The Task*]
PROVERBS
Different strokes for different folks

various AS A DETERMINER = **different**, assorted, miscellaneous, varied, differing, distinct, diverse, divers *(archaic)*, diversified, disparate, sundry, heterogeneous • *He plans to spread his capital between various bank accounts.*
OPPOSITES: same, similar, alike
▸ AS AN ADJECTIVE = **many**, numerous, countless, several, abundant, innumerable, sundry, manifold, profuse • *The methods employed are many and various.*

varnish AS A NOUN = **lacquer**, polish, glaze, japan, gloss, shellac • *The varnish comes in six natural shades.*
▸ AS A VERB 1 = **lacquer**, polish, glaze, japan, gloss, shellac • *The painting still has to be varnished.*
2 = **polish**, decorate, glaze, adorn, gild, lacquer, embellish • *The floors have all been varnished.*

vary 1 = **differ**, be different, be dissimilar, disagree, diverge, be unlike • *As the rugs are all handmade, each one varies slightly.*
2 = **change**, shift, swing, transform, alter, fluctuate, oscillate, see-saw • *women whose moods vary according to their menstrual cycle*
3 = **alternate**, mix, diversify, reorder, intermix, bring variety to, permutate, variegate • *Try to vary your daily diet to include all the major food groups.*
4 = **modify**, change, alter, adjust • *The colour can be varied by adding filters.*

varying 1 = **different**, contrasting, inconsistent, varied, distinct, diverse, assorted, disparate, dissimilar, distinguishable, discrepant, streets apart • *Reporters gave varying figures on the number of casualties.*
2 = **changing**, variable, irregular, inconsistent, fluctuating • *The green table lamp flickered with varying intensity.*
OPPOSITES: fixed, consistent, unchanging

vassal = **serf**, slave, bondsman, subject, retainer, thrall, varlet *(archaic)*, bondservant, liegeman • *the vassal's oath of homage to his lord*

vast = **huge**, massive, enormous, great, wide, sweeping, extensive, tremendous, immense, mega *(slang)*, unlimited, gigantic, astronomical, monumental, monstrous, mammoth, colossal, never-ending, prodigious, limitless, boundless, voluminous, fuck-off *(offensive taboo slang)*, immeasurable, unbounded, elephantine, ginormous *(informal)*, vasty *(archaic)*, measureless, illimitable, humongous or humungous *(U.S. slang)* • *farmers who own vast stretches of land*
OPPOSITES: small, tiny, microscopic

vastly = **hugely**, enormously, immensely, massively, prodigiously, monumentally, stupendously • *The jury has heard two vastly different accounts of what happened.*

vat = **tub**, tank, barrel, vessel, drum, container, butt, bin, basin, cask, keg, receptacle, tun • *food cooked in huge vats of boiling fat*

vault[1] 1 = **strongroom**, repository, depository • *The money was in storage in bank vaults.*
2 = **crypt**, tomb, catacomb, cellar, mausoleum, charnel house, undercroft • *He ordered that Matilda's body should be buried in the family vault.*
3 = **arch**, roof, ceiling, span • *the vault of a magnificent cathedral*

vault[2] = **jump**, spring, leap, clear, bound, hurdle • *Ned vaulted over the low wall.*

vaulted = **arched**, domed, cavernous, hemispheric • *the pillars soaring to the vaulted ceiling high above them*

vaunted = **boasted about**, flaunted, paraded, shown off, made much of, bragged about, crowed about, exulted in, made a display of, prated about • *Their much-vaunted security procedure hadn't worked.*

veer = **change direction**, turn, swerve, shift, sheer, tack, be deflected, change course • *small potholes which tend to make the car veer to one side or the other*

vegetable
▹ *See panels* **Potatoes; Vegetables**

vegetate = **stagnate**, idle, loaf, exist, do nothing, deteriorate, languish, moulder, go to seed, be inert, veg out *(slang, chiefly U.S.)* • *He spends all his time vegetating in front of the TV.*
OPPOSITES: grow, develop

vegetation = **plants**, flora, greenery, foliage, plant life, verdure, herbiage *(rare)* • *The inn has a garden of semi-tropical vegetation.*

vehemence = **forcefulness**, force, violence, fire, energy, heat, passion, emphasis, enthusiasm, intensity, warmth, vigour, zeal, verve, fervour, eagerness, welly *(slang)*, ardour, earnestness, keenness, fervency • *He spoke loudly and with more vehemence than he had intended.*
OPPOSITES: indifference, apathy, inertia

vehement = **strong**, fierce, forceful, earnest, powerful, violent, intense, flaming, eager, enthusiastic, passionate, ardent, emphatic, fervent, impassioned, zealous, forcible, fervid • *There has been widespread and vehement condemnation of the attack.*
OPPOSITES: moderate, lukewarm, half-hearted

vehicle 1 = **conveyance**, machine, motor vehicle, means of transport • *a vehicle which was somewhere between a tractor and a truck*
2 = **medium**, means, channel, mechanism, organ, apparatus, means of expression • *Her art became a vehicle for her political beliefs.*
▸ RELATED PHOBIA: ochophobia
▹ *See panels* **Aircraft; Bicycles; Boats and ships; Carriages and carts; Types of vehicle**

veil AS A NOUN 1 = **mask**, cover, shroud, film, shade, curtain, cloak • *She swathed her face in a veil of decorative muslin.*
2 = **screen**, mask, disguise, blind • *the chilling facts behind this veil of secrecy*
3 = **film**, cover, curtain, cloak, shroud • *He recognized the coast of England through the veil of mist.*
▸ AS A VERB = **cover**, screen, hide, mask, shield, disguise, conceal, obscure, dim, cloak, mantle • *Her hair swept across her face, as if to veil it.*
OPPOSITES: reveal, display, expose

veiled = **disguised**, implied, hinted at, covert, masked, concealed, suppressed • *He made a veiled threat to withdraw his support if we continued.*

vein 1 = **blood vessel** • *Many veins are found just under the skin.*
2 = **mood**, style, spirit, way, turn, note, key, character, attitude, atmosphere, tone, manner, bent, stamp, humour, tendency, mode, temper, temperament, tenor, inclination, disposition, frame of mind • *He also wrote several works in a lighter vein.*
3 = **streak**, element, thread, suggestion, strain, trace, hint, dash, trait, sprinkling, nuance, smattering • *The song has a vein of black humour running through it.*
4 = **seam**, layer, stratum, course, current, bed, deposit, streak, stripe, lode • *a rich deep vein of copper in the rock*
▸ TECHNICAL NAME: vena
▸ RELATED ADJECTIVE: venous

velocity = **speed**, pace, rapidity, quickness, swiftness, fleetness, celerity • *the velocity at which the planets orbit*

velvety = **soft**, smooth, downy, delicate, mossy, velvet-like • *the velvety fur on the cat's ears*

V

VEGETABLES

ackee
adjigo *or* warran (*Austral.*)
asparagus
aubergine *or* (*esp U.S., Canad. & Austral.*) eggplant
baby corn
bean sprout
beef tomato
beetroot *or* beet
bok choy, Chinese leaf, Chinese cabbage, *or* pak-choi
broad bean
broccoli
Brussels sprout *or* sprout
butternut
cabbage
calabrese
calalu
cardoon
carrot
cauliflower
celeriac
celery
chard
chayote
cherry tomato
chicory
chive
choko
collard
corn on the cob
cos *or* (*U.S. & Canad.*) romaine
courgette *or* (*U.S., Canad. & Austral.*) zucchini
cress
cucumber
endive
fennel
finocchio
frisee
gherkin
globe artichoke
greens
horseradish
iceberg lettuce
Jerusalem artichoke
kale *or* kail
kohlrabi
lamb's lettuce *or* corn salad
leek
lettuce
marrow squash
okra, lady's finger, *or* bhindi
onion
orache
parsnip
pea
pepper, capsicum, *or* (*U.S.*) bell pepper
pe-tsai cabbage
pimento
potato
puha *or* rauriki (*N.Z.*)
radicchio
radish
salsify *or* oyster plant
savoy cabbage
shallot
silver beet
sorrel
Spanish onion
spinach
spring greens
spring onion, salad onion, scallion (*chiefly U.S.*), *or* syboe (*Scot.*)
squash
swede
sweet corn *or* (*chiefly U.S.*) corn
sweet potato, batata, *or* (*N.Z.*) kumera
turnip
vegetable marrow
yam

venal = **corrupt**, bent (*slang*), crooked (*informal*), prostituted, grafting (*informal*), mercenary, sordid, rapacious, unprincipled, dishonourable, corruptible, purchasable • *venal and totally corrupt politicians*
OPPOSITES: principled, upright, honest

vendetta = **feud**, dispute, quarrel, enmity, bad blood, blood feud • *This cartoonist has a personal vendetta against the President.*

vendor = **seller**, dealer, trader, retailer, supplier, merchant, stockist, shopkeeper, hawker, salesperson, shop assistant, tradesman, pedlar, shopman, shopwoman • *There are over four-hundred street vendors in the capital.*

veneer 1 = **mask**, show, façade, front, appearance, guise, pretence, semblance, false front • *He was able to fool people with his veneer of intellectuality.*
2 = **layer**, covering, finish, facing, film, gloss, patina, laminate, cladding, lamination • *bath panels fitted with a mahogany veneer*

venerable = **respected**, august, sage, revered, honoured, wise, esteemed, reverenced • *a venerable old man with white hair*

venerate = **respect**, honour, esteem, revere, worship, adore, reverence, look up to, hold in awe • *My father venerated General Eisenhower.*
OPPOSITES: mock, disregard, scorn

veneration = **respect**, esteem, reverence, worship, awe, deference, adoration • *Churchill was held in veneration in his lifetime.*

vengeance AS A NOUN = **revenge**, retaliation, reprisal, retribution, avenging, an eye for an eye, settling of scores, requital, lex talionis • *She wanted vengeance for the loss of her daughter.*
OPPOSITES: pardon, forgiveness, absolution
▸ IN PHRASES: **with a vengeance** = **to the utmost**, greatly, extremely, to the full, and no mistake, to the nth degree, with no holds barred • *The problem has returned with a vengeance.*

QUOTATIONS
Vengeance is mine; I will repay, saith the Lord
[*Bible: Romans*]

vengeful = **unforgiving**, relentless, avenging, vindictive, punitive, implacable, spiteful, retaliatory, rancorous, thirsting for revenge, revengeful • *He was stabbed to death by his vengeful wife.*

venial = **forgivable**, minor, slight, trivial, insignificant, allowable, excusable, pardonable • *If he had faults, they were venial ones.*

venom 1 = **malice**, hate, spite, bitterness, grudge, gall, acidity, spleen, acrimony, rancour, ill will, malevolence, virulence, pungency, malignity, spitefulness, maliciousness • *There was no mistaking the venom in his voice.*
OPPOSITES: love, charity, benevolence
2 = **poison**, toxin, bane • *snake handlers who grow immune to snake venom*

venomous 1 = **malicious**, vindictive, spiteful, hostile, savage, vicious, malignant, virulent, baleful, rancorous • *He made a venomous personal attack on his opponent.*
OPPOSITES: loving, compassionate, benevolent
2 = **poisonous**, poison, toxic, virulent, noxious, baneful (*archaic*), envenomed, mephitic • *The adder is Britain's only venomous snake.*
OPPOSITES: harmless, nontoxic, nonpoisonous

vent AS A NOUN = **outlet**, opening, hole, split, aperture, duct, orifice • *There was a small air vent in the ceiling.*
▸ AS A VERB = **express**, release, voice, air, empty, discharge, utter, emit, come out with, pour out, give vent to, give expression to • *She telephoned her best friend to vent her frustration.*
OPPOSITES: repress, curb, hold back

ventilate 1 = **aerate**, fan, cool, refresh, air-condition, freshen, oxygenate • *The pit is ventilated by a steel fan.*
2 = **discuss**, air, bring out into the open, talk about, debate, examine, broadcast, sift, scrutinize, make known • *Following a bereavement, people need a safe place to ventilate their feelings.*

V

TYPES OF VEHICLE

aircraft
ambulance
articulated lorry
autocycle
autorickshaw
barrow
bicycle
Black Maria
boat
breakdown van
bulldozer
bus
cab
cabriolet
camion
camper van
car
caravan
carriage
Caterpillar *(trademark)*
chaise
charabanc *(Brit.)*
chariot
coach
combine harvester
Conestoga wagon *(U.S. & Canad.)*
coupé
cycle
delivery van
Dormobile *(trademark)*
double-decker *(chiefly Brit.)*
dray
dump truck
dustcart
estate car
fire engine
fork-lift truck
four-wheel drive
gritter *(Brit.)*
hansom cab
hatchback
hog *(informal)*
Humvee
hybrid car
jaunting car
JCB *(trademark)*
Jeep *(trademark)*
jet ski
jinricksha
jitney *(U.S. rare)*
kart *or* go-kart
kibitka
komatik
koneke *(N.Z.)*
landaulet
light engine
limousine
litter
locomotive
lorry
low-loader
luge
milk float
minibus
moped
motorbicycle
motorbike
motorbus
motorcar
motor caravan
motorcycle
motor scooter
motor vehicle
off-road vehicle
omnibus
paddock-basher *(Austral. slang)*
panda car *(Brit.)*
pantechnicon *(Brit.)*
people carrier, people mover, *or (U.S.)* minivan
pick-up *(Austral. & N.Z.) or* utility truck
police car
postbus
post chaise
pram
racing car
railcar
ratha
rickshaw
roadroller
road train *(Austral.)*
rocket
scooter
scout car
shandrydan
ship
single-decker *(Brit.)*
skibob
sledge
sleigh
Sno-Cat *(trademark)*
snowmobile
snow plough
space capsule
spacecraft
space probe
spaceship
space shuttle
sports car
stagecoach
steamroller
sulky
SUV *or* sports utility vehicle
tandem
tank
tank engine *or* locomotive
tanker
tarantass
taxi
telega
three-wheeler
tipper truck *or* lorry
toboggan
tonga
touring car
traction engine
tractor
trail bike
trailer
train
tram, tramcar, *or (U.S. & Canad.)* streetcar *or* trolley car
travois
tricycle
troika
trolley
trolleybus
troop carrier
truck
tuk-tuk
tumbrel
unicycle
van
wagon
wagonette
wheelbarrow

venture AS A VERB **1 = go**, travel, journey, set out, wander, stray, plunge into, rove, set forth • *Few Europeans had ventured beyond the Himalayas.*
2 = dare, presume, have the courage to, be brave enough, hazard, go out on a limb *(informal)*, take the liberty, stick your neck out *(informal)*, go so far as, make so bold as, have the temerity *or* effrontery *or* nerve • *Each time I ventured to speak, I was ignored.*
3 = put forward, offer, suggest, present, air, table, advance, propose, volunteer, submit, bring up, postulate, proffer, broach, posit, moot, propound, dare to say • *We were warned not to make fools of ourselves by venturing an opinion.*
▸ AS A NOUN **= undertaking**, project, enterprise, chance, campaign, risk, operation, activity, scheme, task, mission, speculation, gamble, adventure, exploit, pursuit, fling, hazard, crusade, endeavour • *a Russian-American joint venture*

PROVERBS
Nothing ventured, nothing gained

venturesome = daring, enterprising, adventurous, spirited, bold, courageous, fearless, intrepid, plucky, doughty, daredevil • *a venturesome entrepreneur who was determined to succeed*

veracity 1 = accuracy, truth, credibility, precision, exactitude • *We have total confidence in the veracity of our research.*
2 = truthfulness, integrity, honesty, candour, frankness, probity, rectitude, trustworthiness, uprightness • *He was shocked to find his veracity being questioned.*

verbal 1 = **spoken**, oral, word-of-mouth, unwritten
2 = **verbatim**, literal • *We have a verbal agreement with our suppliers.*

verbally = **orally**, vocally, in words, in speech, by word of mouth • *He has difficulty expressing himself verbally.*

verbatim AS AN ADVERB = **exactly**, to the letter, word for word, closely, precisely, literally, faithfully, rigorously, in every detail, letter for letter • *The president's speeches are reproduced verbatim in the state-run newspapers.*
▸ AS AN ADJECTIVE = **word for word**, exact, literal, close, precise, faithful, line by line, unabridged, unvarnished, undeviating, unembellished • *He gave me a verbatim report of the entire conversation.*

verbiage = **verbosity**, repetition, tautology, redundancy, circumlocution, prolixity, periphrasis, pleonasm • *His writing is full of pretentious and self-indulgent verbiage.*

verbose = **long-winded**, wordy, garrulous, windy, diffuse, prolix, tautological, circumlocutory, periphrastic, pleonastic • *When drunk, he becomes pompous and verbose.*
OPPOSITES: short, brief, concise

verbosity = **long-windedness**, rambling, verbiage, wordiness, prolixity, garrulity, logorrhoea, loquaciousness, windiness, verboseness • *the pedantry and verbosity of his public speeches*

verdant = **green**, lush, leafy, grassy, fresh, flourishing • *a small verdant garden with a view over Paris*

verdict = **decision**, finding, judgment, opinion, sentence, conclusion, conviction, adjudication, pronouncement • *The jury returned a unanimous guilty verdict.*

verge AS A NOUN 1 = **brink**, point, edge, threshold • *Carole was on the verge of tears.*
2 = **border**, edge, margin, limit, extreme, lip, boundary, threshold, roadside, brim • *The car pulled over on to the verge, off the road.*
▸ IN PHRASES: **verge on something** = **come near to**, approach, border on, resemble, incline to, be similar to, touch on, be more or less, be tantamount to, tend towards, be not far from, incline towards • *a fury that verges on madness*

verifiable = **provable**, demonstrable, testable, attestable, evincible • *This is a not a romantic notion but verifiable fact.*

verification = **proof**, confirmation, validation, corroboration, authentication, substantiation • *There is no independent verification of this story.*

verify 1 = **check**, confirm, make sure, examine, monitor, check out *(informal)*, inspect • *A clerk simply verifies that the payment and invoice amount match.*
2 = **confirm**, prove, substantiate, support, validate, bear out, attest, corroborate, attest to, authenticate • *The government has not verified any of these reports.*
OPPOSITES: disprove, deny, dispute

verisimilitude = **realism**, authenticity, credibility, resemblance, likeness, semblance, plausibility, likeliness • *Computer animation is costly at this level of visual verisimilitude.*

veritable = **positive**, real, absolute, sheer, indisputable, categorical, incontrovertible • *a veritable feast of Christmas TV entertainment*

verity = **fact**, truth, reality, gospel (truth), certainty, actuality, naked truth • *the undeniable verities of life*

vernacular AS A NOUN *with* **the** = **speech**, jargon, idiom, parlance, cant, native language, dialect, patois, argot, vulgar tongue • *To use the vernacular of the day, Peter was square.*
▸ AS AN ADJECTIVE = **colloquial**, popular, informal, local, common, native, indigenous, vulgar • *dialects such as black vernacular English*

versatile 1 = **adaptable**, flexible, all-round, resourceful, protean, multifaceted, many-sided, all-singing, all-dancing • *He stood out as one of the game's most versatile athletes.*
OPPOSITES: limited, fixed, unadaptable
2 = **all-purpose**, handy, functional, variable, adjustable, all-singing, all-dancing • *a versatile piece of equipment*
OPPOSITES: limited

verse 1 = **poetry**, poems, lyrics, rhyme, balladry, poesy *(archaic)*, versification • *a slim volume of verse*
2 = **stanza**, section, stave, canto, part • *This verse describes the three signs of spring.*
3 = **poem**, rhyme, ode, lyric, composition, ballad, sonnet • *He wrote a verse about her pride and sense of accomplishment.*

versed *with* **in** = **knowledgeable**, experienced, skilled, seasoned, qualified, familiar, practised, accomplished, competent, switched-on *(informal)*, tasty *(Brit. informal)*, acquainted, well-informed, proficient, sussed *(Brit. slang)*, well up *(informal)*, conversant • *Page is versed in many styles of jazz.*
OPPOSITES: ignorant, inexperienced, unskilled

version 1 = **form**, variety, variant, sort, kind, class, design, style, model, type, brand, genre • *Ludo is a version of an ancient Indian racing game.*
2 = **adaptation**, edition, interpretation, form, reading, copy, rendering, translation, reproduction, portrayal • *The English version is far inferior to the original French text.*
3 = **account**, report, side, description, record, reading, story, view, understanding, history, statement, analysis, take *(informal, chiefly U.S.)*, construction, tale, impression, explanation, interpretation, rendering, narrative, chronicle, rendition, narration, construal • *She went public with her version of events.*

versus 1 = **as opposed to** • *Profits are up by only 15% versus the 25% we expected.*
2 = **against**, v. • *Italy versus Japan is turning out to be a well-matched competition.*

vertex = **top**, crown, summit, pinnacle, apex, height, crest, culmination, zenith, extremity, apogee, acme • *the vertex of the triangle*

vertical = **upright**, sheer, perpendicular, straight (up and down), erect, plumb, on end, precipitous, vertiginous, bolt upright • *The climber inched up a vertical wall of rock.*
OPPOSITES: level, flat, horizontal

vertigo = **dizziness**, giddiness, light-headedness, fear of heights, loss of balance, acrophobia, loss of equilibrium, swimming of the head • *He had a dreadful attack of vertigo at the top of the tower.*

verve = **enthusiasm**, energy, spirit, life, force, punch *(informal)*, dash, pep, sparkle, zip *(informal)*, vitality, animation, vigour, zeal, gusto, welly *(slang)*, get-up-and-go *(informal)*, élan, brio, vivacity, liveliness, vim *(slang)* • *He played with great style and verve.*
OPPOSITES: reluctance, indifference, apathy

very AS AN ADVERB = **extremely**, highly, greatly, really, deeply, particularly, seriously *(informal)*, truly, absolutely, terribly, remarkably, unusually, jolly *(Brit.)*, wonderfully, profoundly, decidedly, awfully *(informal)*, acutely, exceedingly, excessively, noticeably, eminently, superlatively, uncommonly, surpassingly • *I am very grateful to you for all your help.*
▸ AS AN ADJECTIVE 1 = **exact**, actual, precise, same, real, express, identical, unqualified, selfsame • *Those were his very words to me.*
2 = **ideal**, perfect, right, fitting, appropriate, suitable, spot on *(Brit. informal)*, apt, just the job *(Brit. informal)* • *the very person we need for the job*
3 = **mere**, simple, plain, nothing more than • *The very sound of a telephone ringing evoked fear.*

vessel 1 = **ship**, boat, craft, barque *(poetic)* • *a Moroccan fishing vessel*
2 = **container**, receptacle, can, bowl, tank, pot, drum, barrel, butt, vat, bin, jar, basin, tub, jug, pitcher, urn, canister, repository, cask • *plastic storage vessels*
▹ *See panel* **Boats and ships**

vest AS A VERB
▸ IN PHRASES: **vest in something** *or* **someone** *usually passive* = **place**, invest, entrust, settle, lodge, confer, endow, bestow, consign, put in the hands of, be devolved upon • *All the authority was vested in one man.*
vest with something *usually passive* = **endow with**, furnish with, entrust with, empower with, authorize with • *The mass media has been vested with considerable power.*

vestibule = **hall**, lobby, foyer, porch, entrance hall, portico, anteroom • *A tiled vestibule leads to an impressive staircase.*

vestige 1 = **remnant**, remains, trace, relic, track, token, remainder, residue • *the last vestiges of a great and ancient kingdom*
2 = **trace**, sign, hint, scrap, evidence, indication, suspicion, glimmer • *She had lost every vestige of her puppy fat.*

vestigial 1 = **rudimentary**, undeveloped, incomplete, imperfect, non-functional • *The grass snake has vestigial limbs.*
OPPOSITES: developed, complete, perfect
2 = **surviving**, lasting, remaining, enduring, persisting, lingering, abiding, residual, leftover • *vestigial remains of this ancient custom*

vet AS A NOUN = **veterinary surgeon**, veterinarian *(U.S.)*, animal doctor • *You should take that cat to the vet.*
▸ AS A VERB = **check**, examine, investigate, check out, review, scan, look over, appraise, scrutinize, size up *(informal)*, give the once-over *(informal)*, pass under review • *He was not allowed to read any book until his father had vetted it.*

veteran AS A NOUN = **old hand**, master, pro *(informal)*, old-timer, past master, trouper, warhorse *(informal)*, old stager • *Graf was already a tennis veteran at the age of 21.*
OPPOSITES: novice, beginner, apprentice
▸ AS A MODIFIER = **long-serving**, seasoned, experienced, old, established, expert, qualified, mature, practised, hardened, adept, proficient, well trained, battle-scarred, worldly-wise • *Tony Benn, the veteran Labour MP and former Cabinet Minister*

veto AS A NOUN = **ban**, dismissal, rejection, vetoing, boycott, embargo, prohibiting, prohibition, suppression, knock-back *(informal)*, interdict, declination, preclusion, nonconsent • *congressmen who tried to override the president's veto of the bill*
OPPOSITES: approval, go-ahead *(informal)*, ratification
▸ AS A VERB = **ban**, block, reject, rule out, kill *(informal)*, negative, turn down, forbid, boycott, prohibit, disallow, put a stop to, refuse permission to, interdict, give the thumbs down to, put the kibosh on *(slang)* • *De Gaulle vetoed Britain's application to join the EEC.*
OPPOSITES: pass, approve, endorse

vex = **annoy**, bother, irritate, worry, trouble, upset, disturb, distress, provoke, bug *(informal)*, offend, needle *(informal)*, plague, put out, tease, torment, harass, hassle *(informal)*, aggravate *(informal)*, afflict, fret, gall, agitate, exasperate, nettle, pester, displease, rile, pique, peeve *(informal)*, grate on, get on your nerves *(informal)*, nark *(Brit., Austral. & N.Z. slang)*, give someone grief *(Brit. & S. African)*, get your back up, put your back up, hack you off *(informal)* • *Everything about that man vexes me.*
OPPOSITES: please, comfort, soothe

vexation 1 = **annoyance**, frustration, irritation, dissatisfaction, displeasure, exasperation, chagrin, pique, aggravation *(informal)* • *He kicked the broken machine in vexation.*
2 = **problem**, difficulty, hassle *(informal)*, worry, trouble, upset, bother, headache *(informal)*, nuisance, misfortune, uphill *(S. African)*, irritant, thorn in your flesh • *the tribulations and vexations we have to put up with*

vexatious = **annoying**, trying, irritating, worrying, disappointing, upsetting, distressing, provoking, unpleasant, teasing, tormenting, harassing, nagging, aggravating *(informal)*, afflicting, troublesome, exasperating, disagreeable, burdensome, worrisome, irksome, bothersome • *the vexatious behaviour of petty-minded officials*
OPPOSITES: calming, soothing, agreeable

vexed 1 = **annoyed**, upset, irritated, worried, troubled, bothered, confused, disturbed, distressed, provoked, put out, fed up, tormented, pissed *(Brit., Austral. & N.Z. slang)*, harassed, aggravated *(informal)*, afflicted, agitated, ruffled, exasperated, perplexed, nettled, pissed off *(taboo slang)*, miffed *(informal)*, displeased, riled, peeved *(informal)*, hacked off *(U.S. slang)*, out of countenance, tooshie *(Austral. slang)*, hoha *(N.Z.)* • *He was vexed by the art establishment's rejection of his work.*
2 = **controversial**, disputed, contested, moot, much debated, hot-button *(informal)* • *Later the minister raised the vexed question of refugees.*

via 1 = **through**, by way of, by, by means of • *Mr Baker will return home via Britain and France.*
2 = **using**, by means of, with the help of • *Translators can now work via e-mail.*

viable = **workable**, practical, feasible, suitable, realistic, operational, applicable, usable, practicable, serviceable, operable, within the bounds of possibility • *commercially viable products*
OPPOSITES: impossible, unworkable, impracticable

vibes *sometimes singular* 1 = **feelings**, emotions, response, reaction • *I don't like the guy – I have bad vibes about him.*
2 = **atmosphere**, aura, vibrations, feeling, emanation • *a club with really good vibes*

vibrant 1 = **energetic**, dynamic, sparkling, vivid, spirited, storming, alive, sensitive, colourful, vigorous, animated, responsive, electrifying, vivacious, full of pep *(informal)* • *Tom was drawn to her by her vibrant personality.*
2 = **vivid**, bright, brilliant, intense, clear, rich, glowing, colourful, highly-coloured • *His shirt was a vibrant shade of green.*

vibrate 1 = **shake**, tremble, shiver, fluctuate, quiver, oscillate, judder *(informal)* • *Her whole body seemed to vibrate with terror.*
2 = **throb**, pulse, resonate, pulsate, reverberate • *The noise vibrated through the whole house.*

vibration 1 = **shaking**, shake, trembling, quake, quaking, shudder, shuddering, quiver, oscillation, judder *(informal)* • *The vibration dislodged the pins from the plane's rudder.*
2 = **throbbing**, pulse, thumping, hum, humming, throb, resonance, tremor, drone, droning, reverberation, pulsation • *They heard a distant low vibration in the distance.*

vicar = **priest**, minister, pastor, cleric, clergyman, father, divine, curate, churchman, padre *(informal)*, holy man, man of God, man of the cloth, ecclesiastic, father confessor • *the vicar of the local parish*

vicarious = **indirect**, substitute, surrogate, by proxy, empathetic, at one remove • *people who use television as a vicarious form of social life*

vice 1 = **fault**, failing, weakness, limitation, defect, deficiency, flaw, shortcoming, blemish, imperfection, frailty, foible, weak point, infirmity • *Having the odd flutter on the horses is his only vice.*
OPPOSITES: good point, strong point, talent
2 = **wickedness**, evil, corruption, sin, depravity, immorality, iniquity, profligacy, degeneracy, venality, turpitude, evildoing • *offences connected with vice, gaming and drugs*
OPPOSITES: virtue, morality, honour

viceroy
▸ RELATED ADJECTIVE: viceregal

vice versa = **the other way round**, conversely, in reverse, contrariwise • *We've the utmost confidence in him and vice versa.*

vicinity AS A NOUN = **neighbourhood**, area, district, precincts, locality, environs, neck of the woods *(informal)*, purlieus • *Police say the killer may still be in this vicinity.*
▸ IN PHRASES: **in the vicinity of** = **about**, around, nearly, near, approaching, close to, roughly, something like, just about, just over, more or less, just under, close on, in the region of, getting on for *(Brit. informal)*, in the neighbourhood of • *I'm going to save somewhere in the vicinity of $100 million .*

vicious 1 = **savage**, brutal, violent, bad, dangerous, foul, cruel, ferocious, monstrous, vile, atrocious, diabolical, heinous, abhorrent, barbarous, fiendish • *He suffered a vicious attack by a gang of youths.*
OPPOSITES: kind, friendly, gentle
2 = **depraved**, corrupt, wicked, infamous, degraded, worthless, degenerate, immoral, sinful, debased, profligate, unprincipled • *a vicious criminal incapable of remorse*
OPPOSITES: good, upright, virtuous
3 = **malicious**, vindictive, spiteful, mean, cruel, venomous, bitchy *(informal)*, defamatory, rancorous, backbiting, slanderous • *a vicious attack on an innocent woman's character*
OPPOSITES: complimentary, appreciative, congratulatory

viciousness 1 = **savagery**, cruelty, brutality, ferocity, ruthlessness, sadism, inhumanity, barbarity, bestiality, fierceness, bloodthirstiness • *the intensity and viciousness of this attack*
OPPOSITES: mercy, kindness, gentleness
2 = **malice**, spite, malevolence, vindictiveness, bitterness, venom, rancour, bitchiness *(slang)*, malignity, spitefulness, maliciousness • *the razor-sharp viciousness of his remarks*
OPPOSITES: goodwill, graciousness
3 = **depravity**, evil, wickedness, vice, corruption, criminality, immorality, profligacy, badness, sinfulness • *The book romanticizes the viciousness of organized crime.*
OPPOSITES: virtue, goodness

vicissitude *often plural* = **variation**, change, shift, change of fortune, life's ups and downs *(informal)* • *stiffening himself to withstand life's vicissitudes*

victim AS A NOUN 1 = **casualty**, sufferer, injured party, fatality • *an organisation representing victims of the accident*
OPPOSITES: survivor
2 = **prey**, patsy *(slang, chiefly U.S. & Canad.)*, sucker *(slang)*, dupe, gull *(archaic)*, stooge, sitting duck *(informal)*, sitting target, innocent • *the victim of a particularly cruel hoax*
OPPOSITES: attacker, offender, culprit
3 = **scapegoat**, sacrifice, martyr, fall guy *(informal)*, whipping boy • *A sacrificial victim was thrown to the judicial authorities.*
▸ IN PHRASES: **fall victim to something** = **fall ill with**, develop, catch, contract, pick up, succumb to, be overcome by, become infected with, be stricken with, come *or* go down with • *In the early 1960s, she fell victim to Alzheimer's disease.*

QUOTATIONS
He is brought as a lamb to the slaughter
[*Bible: Isaiah*]

victimize *or* **victimise** = **persecute**, bully, pick on, abuse, harass, discriminate against, lean on, have it in for *(informal)*, push around, give a hard time, demonize, have a down on *(informal)*, have your knife into • *People victimize others in order to exert power and maintain control.*

victor = **winner**, champion, conqueror, first, champ *(informal)*, vanquisher, top dog *(informal)*, prizewinner, conquering hero • *to the victor the spoils*
OPPOSITES: failure, loser, also-ran

victorious = **winning**, successful, triumphant, first, champion, conquering, vanquishing, prizewinning • *He played for the victorious Argentinian side in the World Cup.*
OPPOSITES: losing, defeated, unsuccessful

victory = **win**, success, triumph, the prize, superiority, conquest, laurels, mastery, walkover *(informal)* • *His players deserved this famous victory.*
OPPOSITES: defeat, failure, loss

victuals = **food**, supplies, stores, provisions, eats *(slang)*, meat, bread, rations, tack *(informal)*, grub *(slang)*, kai *(N.Z. informal)*, nosh *(slang)*, edibles, comestibles, nosebag *(slang)*, vittles *(obsolete)*, viands, eatables • *The fleet carries victuals only for six weeks.*

vie *with* **with** *or* **for** = **compete**, struggle, contend, contest, strive, be rivals, match yourself against • *The two candidates are vying for the support of the New York voters.*

view AS A NOUN 1 *sometimes plural* = **opinion**, thought, idea, belief, thinking, feeling, attitude, reckoning, impression, notion, conviction, judgment, point of view, sentiment, viewpoint, persuasion, way of thinking, standpoint • *You should make your views known to your local MP.*
2 = **scene**, picture, sight, prospect, aspect, perspective, landscape, outlook, spectacle, panorama, vista • *The view from our window was one of beautiful countryside.*
3 = **vision**, sight, visibility, perspective, eyeshot, range *or* field of vision • *A group of riders came into view.*
4 = **study**, review, survey, assessment, examination, scan, inspection, look, scrutiny, contemplation • *a concise but comprehensive view of basic economics*
▸ AS A VERB 1 = **regard**, see, consider, judge, perceive, treat, estimate, reckon, deem, look on, adjudge, think about *or* of • *America was viewed as a land of golden opportunity.*
2 = **look at**, see, inspect, gaze at, eye, watch, check, regard, survey, witness, clock *(Brit. slang)*, examine, observe, explore, stare at, scan, contemplate, check out *(informal)*, behold, eyeball *(slang)*, gawp at, recce *(slang)*, get a load of *(informal)*, spectate, take a dekko at *(Brit. slang)* • *The mourners filed past to view the body.*
▸ IN PHRASES: **in view of** = **considering**, taking into account, in the light of, bearing in mind, keeping in mind, mindful of, taking into consideration, taking note of • *In view of the circumstances, his achievement is remarkable.*
on view = **on show**, showing, displayed, on display, on exhibition • *An exhibition of contemporary sculpture is on view at the gallery.*
with a view to = **with the aim** *or* **intention of**, in order to, so as to, in the hope of • *She joined a dating agency with a view to finding a husband.*

viewer = **watcher**, observer, spectator, onlooker, couch potato *(informal)*, TV watcher, one of an audience • *The series is watched by around 19 million viewers every week.*

viewpoint = **point of view**, perspective, angle, position, attitude, stance, slant, belief, conviction, feeling, opinion, way of thinking, standpoint, vantage point, frame of reference • *The novel is written from the murderer's viewpoint.* • *What's your viewpoint on this issue?*

vigilance = **watchfulness**, alertness, caution, observance, circumspection, attentiveness, carefulness • *Drugs are a problem that requires constant vigilance.*

vigilant = **watchful**, alert, on the lookout, careful, cautious, attentive, circumspect, wide awake, on the alert, on your toes, wakeful, on your guard, on the watch, on the qui vive, Argus-eyed, keeping your eyes peeled *or* skinned *(informal)* • *Police warned the public to be vigilant and report anything suspicious.*
OPPOSITES: slack, careless, inattentive

vigorous 1 = **strenuous**, energetic, arduous, hard, taxing, active, intense, exhausting, rigorous, brisk • *Avoid vigorous exercise for a few weeks.*
2 = **spirited**, lively, energetic, active, intense, dynamic, sparkling, animated, forceful, feisty *(informal)*, spanking, high-spirited, sprightly, vivacious, forcible, effervescent, full of energy, zippy *(informal)*, spunky *(informal)* • *The choir and orchestra gave a vigorous performance of Haydn's oratorio.*

OPPOSITES: feeble, lethargic, apathetic
3 = **strong**, powerful, robust, sound, healthy, vital, lively, flourishing, hardy, hale, hearty, lusty, virile, alive and kicking, red-blooded, fighting fit, full of energy, full of beans *(informal)*, hale and hearty, fit as a fiddle *(informal)* • *He was a vigorous, handsome young man.*
OPPOSITES: weak, frail, feeble

vigorously 1 = **energetically**, hard, forcefully, strongly, all out, eagerly, with a vengeance, strenuously, like mad *(slang)*, lustily, hammer and tongs, with might and main • *She shivered and rubbed her arms vigorously.*
2 = **forcefully**, strongly, vehemently, strenuously • *The police vigorously denied that excessive force had been used.*

vigour or *(U.S.)* **vigor** = **energy**, might, force, vitality, power, activity, spirit, strength, snap *(informal)*, punch *(informal)*, dash, pep, zip *(informal)*, animation, verve, gusto, dynamism, welly *(slang)*, oomph *(informal)*, brio, robustness, liveliness, vim *(slang)*, forcefulness • *He lacks the vigour of a normal, healthy teenager.* • *He played with great vigour.*
OPPOSITES: weakness, apathy, inertia

vile 1 = **wicked**, base, evil, mean, bad, low, shocking, appalling, ugly, corrupt, miserable, vicious, humiliating, perverted, coarse, degrading, worthless, disgraceful, vulgar, degenerate, abject, sinful, despicable, depraved, debased, loathsome, contemptible, impure, wretched, nefarious, ignoble • *a vile and despicable crime*
OPPOSITES: pure, noble, honourable
2 = **disgusting**, foul, revolting, offensive, nasty, obscene, sickening, horrid, repellent, repulsive, noxious, nauseating, repugnant, loathsome, yucky *or* yukky *(slang)*, yucko *(Austral. slang)* • *the vile smell of his cigar smoke*
OPPOSITES: lovely, pleasant, agreeable

vilification = **denigration**, abuse, defamation, invective, calumny, mudslinging, disparagement, vituperation, contumely, aspersion, scurrility, calumniation • *Clare did not deserve the vilification she was subjected to.*

vilify = **malign**, abuse, denigrate, knock *(informal)*, rubbish *(informal)*, run down, smear, slag (off) *(slang)*, berate, disparage, decry, revile, slander, dump on *(slang, chiefly U.S.)*, debase, defame, bad-mouth *(slang, chiefly U.S. & Canad.)*, traduce, speak ill of, pull to pieces *(informal)*, calumniate, vituperate, asperse • *He was vilified and forced into exile.*
OPPOSITES: honour, praise, esteem

villain 1 = **evildoer**, criminal, rogue, profligate, scoundrel, wretch, libertine, knave *(archaic)*, reprobate, miscreant, malefactor, blackguard, rapscallion, caitiff *(archaic)*, wrong 'un *(Austral. slang)* • *As a copper, I've spent my life putting villains like him away.*
2 = **baddy** *(informal)*, antihero • *Darth Vader, the villain of the Star Wars trilogy*
OPPOSITES: hero, heroine, goody

villainous = **wicked**, evil, depraved, mean, bad, base, criminal, terrible, cruel, vicious, outrageous, infamous, vile, degenerate, atrocious, inhuman, sinful, diabolical, heinous, debased, hateful, scoundrelly, fiendish, ruffianly, nefarious, ignoble, detestable, blackguardly, thievish • *Richard III, one of Shakespeare's most villainous characters*
OPPOSITES: good, moral, virtuous

villainy = **wickedness**, crime, vice, sin, atrocity, delinquency, criminality, depravity, iniquity, turpitude, baseness, devilry, knavery, rascality • *They justify their villainy in the name of their high ideals.*

vindicate 1 = **clear**, acquit, exonerate, absolve, let off the hook, exculpate, free from blame • *The director said he had been vindicated by the expert's report.*
OPPOSITES: accuse, blame, condemn
2 = **support**, uphold, ratify, defend, excuse, justify, substantiate • *Subsequent events vindicated his policy.*

vindication 1 = **exoneration**, pardon, acquittal, dismissal, discharge, amnesty, absolution, exculpating, exculpation • *He insisted on a complete vindication from the libel jury.*
2 = **support**, defence, ratification, excuse, apology, justification, assertion, substantiation • *He called the success a vindication of his party's economic policy.*

vindictive = **vengeful**, malicious, spiteful, relentless, resentful, malignant, unrelenting, unforgiving, implacable, venomous, rancorous, revengeful, full of spleen • *a vindictive woman desperate for revenge*
OPPOSITES: generous, forgiving, merciful

vintage **AS A NOUN** 1 = **harvest**, year, crop, yield • *This wine is from one of the best vintages of the decade.*
2 = **era**, period, origin, sort, type, generation, stamp, epoch, ilk, time of origin • *a Jeep of World War Two vintage*
▸ **AS AN ADJECTIVE** 1 = **high-quality**, best, prime, quality, choice, select, rare, superior • *Gourmet food and vintage wines are also part of the service.*
2 = **classic**, old, veteran, historic, heritage, enduring, antique, timeless, old-world, age-old, ageless • *This is vintage comedy at its best.* • *vintage, classic and racing cars*

violate 1 = **break**, infringe, disobey, transgress, ignore, defy, disregard, flout, rebel against, contravene, fly in the face of, overstep, not comply with, take no notice of, encroach upon, pay no heed to, infract • *They violated the ceasefire agreement.*
OPPOSITES: respect, honour, obey
2 = **invade**, infringe on, disturb, upset, shatter, disrupt, impinge on, encroach on, intrude on, trespass on, obtrude on • *These journalists were violating her family's privacy.*
3 = **desecrate**, profane, defile, abuse, outrage, pollute, deface, dishonour, vandalize, treat with disrespect, befoul • *Police are still searching for the people who violated the graves.*
OPPOSITES: respect, honour, revere
4 = **rape**, molest, sexually assault, ravish, abuse, assault, interfere with, sexually abuse, indecently assault, force yourself on • *He broke into a woman's home and attempted to violate her.*

violation 1 = **breach**, abuse, infringement, contravention, abuse, trespass, transgression, infraction • *This is a flagrant violation of state law.*
2 = **invasion**, intrusion, trespass, breach, disturbance, disruption, interruption, encroachment • *Legal action will be initiated for defamation and violation of privacy.*
3 = **desecration**, sacrilege, defilement, profanation, spoliation • *This violation of the church is not the first such incident.*
4 = **rape**, sexual assault, molesting, ravishing *(old-fashioned)*, abuse, sexual abuse, indecent assault, molestation • *the violation of women in war*

violence 1 = **brutality**, bloodshed, savagery, fighting, terrorism, frenzy, thuggery, destructiveness, bestiality, strong-arm tactics *(informal)*, rough handling, bloodthirstiness, murderousness • *Twenty people were killed in the violence.*
2 = **force**, power, strength, might, ferocity, brute force, fierceness, forcefulness, powerfulness • *The violence of the blow forced the hammer through his skull.*
3 = **intensity**, passion, fury, force, cruelty, severity, fervour, sharpness, harshness, vehemence • *'There's no need,' she snapped with sudden violence.*
4 = **power**, turbulence, wildness, raging, tumult, roughness, boisterousness, storminess • *The house was destroyed in the violence of the storm.*

QUOTATIONS
All they that take the sword shall perish with the sword
[Bible: St. Matthew]
Violence is one of the most fun things to watch
[Quentin Tarantino at the screening of Pulp Fiction in Cannes]

Keep violence in the mind
Where it belongs
[Brian Aldiss *Barefoot in the Head*]

violent 1 = **brutal**, aggressive, savage, wild, rough, fierce, bullying, cruel, vicious, destructive, ruthless, murderous, maddened, berserk, merciless, bloodthirsty, homicidal, pitiless, hot-headed, thuggish, maniacal, hot-tempered • *He was a violent man with a drink and drugs problem.*
OPPOSITES: gentle, peaceful, mild
2 = **sharp**, hard, powerful, forceful, strong, fierce, fatal, savage, deadly, brutal, vicious, lethal, hefty, ferocious, death-dealing • *She had died from a violent blow to the head.*
3 = **intense**, acute, severe, biting, sharp, extreme, painful, harsh, excruciating, agonizing, inordinate • *He had violent stomach pains.*
4 = **passionate**, intense, extreme, strong, wild, consuming, uncontrollable, vehement, unrestrained, tempestuous, ungovernable • *his violent, almost pathological jealousy*
5 = **fiery**, raging, fierce, flaming, furious, passionate, peppery, ungovernable • *I had a violent temper and was always in fights.*
6 = **powerful**, wild, devastating, strong, storming, raging, turbulent, tumultuous, tempestuous, gale force, blustery, ruinous, full of force • *That night a violent storm arose and wrecked most of the ships.*
OPPOSITES: calm, gentle, mild

VIP = **celebrity**, big name, public figure, star, somebody, lion, notable, luminary, bigwig *(informal)*, leading light *(informal)*, big shot *(informal)*, personage, big noise *(informal)*, big hitter *(informal)*, heavy hitter *(informal)*, man *or* woman of the hour • *The event was attended by such VIPs as Prince Charles and President Clinton.*

virago = **harridan**, fury, shrew, vixen, scold, battle-axe *(informal)*, termagant *(rare)*, Xanthippe, ballbreaker *(slang)* • *Violent wives are too easily dismissed as hysterical, man-hating viragos.*

virgin AS A NOUN = **maiden**, maid *(archaic)*, damsel *(archaic)*, girl *(archaic)*, celibate, vestal, virgo intacta • *I was a virgin until I was twenty-four years old.*
▸ AS AN ADJECTIVE 1 = **untouched**, immaculate, fresh, new, pure, unused, pristine, flawless, unblemished, unadulterated, unsullied • *Within 40 years there will be no virgin forest left.*
OPPOSITES: spoiled, used, dirty
2 = **pure**, maidenly, chaste, immaculate, virginal, unsullied, vestal, uncorrupted, undefiled • *a society in which men still prize virgin brides*
OPPOSITES: corrupted, defiled, impure

virginal 1 = **chaste**, pure, maidenly, virgin, immaculate, celibate, uncorrupted, undefiled • *She had always been a child in his mind, pure and virginal.*
2 = **immaculate**, fresh, pristine, white, pure, untouched, snowy, undisturbed, spotless • *linen tablecloths of virginal white*

virginity = **chastity**, maidenhead, maidenhood • *She lost her virginity when she was 20.*

virile = **manly**, masculine, macho, strong, male, robust, vigorous, potent, forceful, lusty, red-blooded, manlike • *a tall, virile man with rugged good looks*
OPPOSITES: camp *(informal)*, unmanly, effeminate

virility = **masculinity**, manhood, potency, vigour, machismo • *Children are considered a proof of a man's virility.*
OPPOSITES: impotence, effeminacy, unmanliness

virtual = **practical**, near, essential, implied, indirect, implicit, tacit, near enough, unacknowledged, in all but name • *He was a virtual prisoner in his own home.*

virtually = **practically**, almost, nearly, in effect, in essence, as good as, to all intents and purposes, in all but name, for all practical purposes, effectually • *After the divorce she was left virtually penniless.*

virtue AS A NOUN 1 = **goodness**, honour, integrity, worth, dignity, excellence, morality, honesty, decency, respectability, nobility, righteousness, propriety, probity, rectitude, worthiness, high-mindedness, incorruptibility, uprightness, virtuousness, ethicalness • *His mother was held up to the family as a paragon of virtue.*
OPPOSITES: vice, evil, corruption
2 = **merit**, strength, asset, plus *(informal)*, attribute, good quality, good point, strong point • *His chief virtue is patience.*
OPPOSITES: failing, drawback, shortcoming
3 = **advantage**, benefit, merit, credit, usefulness, efficacy • *There is no virtue in overexercising.*
4 = **chastity**, honour, virginity, innocence, purity, maidenhood, chasteness • *His many attempts on her virtue were all unavailing.*
OPPOSITES: promiscuity, unchastity
▸ IN PHRASES: **by virtue of** = **because of**, in view of, on account of, based on, thanks to, as a result of, owing to, by reason of, by dint of • *Mr Olaechea has British residency by virtue of his marriage.*

QUOTATIONS
Virtue is the fount whence honour springs
[Christopher Marlowe *Tamburlaine the Great*]
Virtue is its own reward
[Cicero *De Finibus*]
Virtue is like a rich stone, best plain set
[Francis Bacon *Essays*]
For 'tis some virtue, virtue to commend
[William Congreve]
Virtue could see to do what Virtue would
By her own radiant light, though sun and moon
Were in the flat sea sunk
[John Milton *Comus*]
Against the threats
Of malice or of sorcery, or that power
Which erring men call chance, this I hold firm,
Virtue may be assailed, but never hurt,
Surprised by unjust force, but not enthralled
[John Milton *Comus*]
It is queer how it is always one's virtues and not one's vices that precipitate one into disaster
[Rebecca West *There Is No Conversation*]
The weakest of all weak things is a virtue which has not been tested in the fire
[Mark Twain *The Man That Corrupted Hadleyburg*]

virtuosity = **mastery**, skill, brilliance, polish, craft, expertise, flair, panache, éclat • *At that time, his virtuosity on the trumpet had no parallel in jazz.*

virtuoso AS A NOUN = **master**, artist, genius, maestro, magician, grandmaster, maven *(U.S.)*, master hand • *Canada's foremost piano virtuoso, Glenn Gould*
▸ AS A MODIFIER = **masterly**, brilliant, dazzling, bravura *(Music)* • *a virtuoso performance by a widely-respected musician*

virtuous 1 = **good**, moral, ethical, upright, honourable, excellent, pure, worthy, honest, righteous, exemplary, squeaky-clean, blameless, praiseworthy, incorruptible, high-principled • *The president is portrayed as a virtuous family man.*
OPPOSITES: evil, corrupt, immoral
2 = **chaste**, pure, innocent, celibate, spotless, virginal, clean-living • *a prince who falls in love with a beautiful and virtuous maiden*
OPPOSITES: loose, promiscuous, impure
3 = **self-righteous**, pleased with yourself, smug • *I cleaned the flat, which left me feeling very virtuous.*

virulent 1 = **vicious**, vindictive, bitter, hostile, malicious, resentful, acrimonious, malevolent, spiteful, venomous, rancorous, splenetic, envenomed • *A virulent personal campaign is being waged against him.*
OPPOSITES: kind, warm, benign

2 = **deadly**, lethal, toxic, poisonous, malignant, pernicious, venomous, septic, infective, injurious, baneful *(archaic)* • *A virulent form of the disease has appeared in Belgium.*
OPPOSITES: harmless, innocuous, nontoxic

viscera
▸ RELATED ADJECTIVES: splanchic, visceral

viscous = **thick**, sticky, gooey *(informal)*, adhesive, tenacious, clammy, syrupy, glutinous, gummy, gelatinous, icky *(informal)*, gluey, treacly, mucilaginous, viscid • *a viscous, white, sticky liquid*

visible = **perceptible**, noticeable, observable, clear, obvious, plain, apparent, bold, patent, to be seen, evident, manifest, in sight, in view, conspicuous, unmistakable, palpable, discernible, salient, detectable, not hidden, distinguishable, unconcealed, perceivable, discoverable, anywhere to be seen • *The meadows are hardly visible from the house.* • *a visible effort to control himself*
OPPOSITES: hidden, concealed, invisible

vision 1 = **image**, idea, dream, plans, hopes, prospect, ideal, concept, fancy, fantasy, conception, delusion, daydream, reverie, flight of fancy, mental picture, pipe dream, imago *(Psychoanalysis)*, castle in the air, fanciful notion • *I have a vision of a society free of exploitation and injustice.*
2 = **hallucination**, illusion, apparition, revelation, ghost, phantom, delusion, spectre, mirage, wraith, chimera, phantasm, eidolon • *She heard voices and saw visions of her ancestors.*
3 = **sight**, seeing, eyesight, view, eyes, perception • *The disease causes blindness or serious loss of vision.*
4 = **foresight**, imagination, perception, insight, awareness, inspiration, innovation, creativity, intuition, penetration, inventiveness, shrewdness, discernment, prescience, perceptiveness, farsightedness, breadth of view • *The government's lack of vision could have profound economic consequences.*
5 = **picture**, dream, sight, delight, beauty, joy, sensation, spectacle, knockout *(informal)*, beautiful sight, perfect picture, feast for the eyes, sight for sore eyes, pearler *(Austral. slang)*, beaut *(Austral. & N.Z. slang)* • *The girl was a vision in crimson organza.*

QUOTATIONS
Your old men shall dream dreams, your young men shall see visions
[*Bible: Joel*]
Where there is no vision, the people perish
[*Bible: Proverbs*]

visionary AS AN ADJECTIVE 1 = **idealistic**, romantic, unrealistic, utopian, dreaming, speculative, impractical, dreamy, unworkable, quixotic, starry-eyed, with your head in the clouds • *His ideas were dismissed as mere visionary speculation.*
OPPOSITES: realistic, pragmatic
2 = **prophetic**, mystical, divinatory, predictive, oracular, sibylline, mantic, vatic *(rare)*, fatidic *(rare)* • *visionary experiences and contact with spirit beings*
3 = **imaginary**, fantastic, unreal, fanciful, ideal, idealized, illusory, imaginal *(Psychoanalysis)*, chimerical, delusory • *the visionary worlds created by fantasy writers*
OPPOSITES: real, actual, mundane
▸ AS A NOUN 1 = **idealist**, romantic, dreamer, daydreamer, utopian, enthusiast *(archaic)*, theorist, zealot, Don Quixote • *Visionaries see the world not as it is but as it could be.*
OPPOSITES: cynic, realist, pragmatist
2 = **prophet**, diviner, mystic, seer, soothsayer, sibyl, scryer, spaewife *(Scot.)* • *shamans, mystics and religious visionaries*

visit AS A VERB 1 = **call on**, go to see, drop in on *(informal)*, stop by, look up, call in on, pop in on *(informal)*, pay a call on, go see *(U.S.)*, swing by *(informal)*
2 = **stay at**, stay with, spend time with, pay a visit to, be the guest of • *I want to visit my relatives in Scotland.*
3 = **stay in**, see, tour, explore, take in *(informal)*, holiday in, go to see, stop by, spend time in, vacation in *(U.S.)*, stop over in • *He'll be visiting four cities, including Cagliari in Sardinia.*
4 = **afflict**, attack, smite, trouble, haunt, befall, assail, descend upon • *a house of sickness or infection, such as one visited by the plague*
▸ AS A NOUN 1 = **call**, social call • *Helen recently paid me a visit.*
2 = **trip**, stop, stay, break, tour, holiday, vacation *(informal)*, stopover, sojourn, awayday • *the Pope's visit to Canada*
▸ IN PHRASES: **visit something on** *or* **upon someone** *usually passive* = **inflict on**, execute, impose on, wreak on, bring down upon • *the sufferings visited on the people by the country's regime*

visitation 1 = **apparition**, vision, manifestation, appearance, materialization • *He claims to have had a visitation from the Virgin Mary.*
2 = **inspection**, survey, examination, visit, review, scrutiny • *House-to-house visitation has been authorized by the Board of Health.*

visitor 1 = **guest**, caller, company, visitant, manu(w)hiri *(N.Z.)* • *The other day we had some visitors from London.*
2 *often plural* = **tourist**, vacationer *(U.S.)*, holidaymaker, sightseer, pilgrim, daytripper • *Thousands of visitors flock to see this historical monument.*

vista = **view**, scene, prospect, landscape, panorama, perspective • *an endless vista of snow peaks and shadowed valleys*

visual 1 = **optical**, optic, ocular • *the way our brain processes visual information*
2 = **observable**, visible, perceptible, discernible • *There was no visual evidence to support his claim.*
OPPOSITES: invisible, imperceptible, unnoticeable

visualize *or* **visualise** = **picture**, imagine, think about, envisage, contemplate, conceive of, see in the mind's eye, conjure up a mental picture of • *He could not visualize her as a child.*

vital 1 = **essential**, important, necessary, key, basic, significant, critical, radical, crucial, fundamental, urgent, decisive, cardinal, imperative, indispensable, requisite, life-or-death, must-have • *a blockade which could cut off vital oil and gas supplies*
OPPOSITES: unnecessary, trivial, unimportant
2 = **lively**, vigorous, energetic, spirited, dynamic, animated, vibrant, forceful, sparky, vivacious, full of beans *(informal)*, zestful, full of the joy of living • *It is tragic to see how the disease has diminished a once vital person.*
OPPOSITES: lethargic, apathetic, listless

vitality = **energy**, vivacity, sparkle, go *(informal)*, life, strength, pep, stamina, animation, vigour, exuberance, welly *(slang)*, brio, robustness, liveliness, vim *(slang)*, lustiness, vivaciousness • *He fell in love with her for her vitality and sense of fun.*
OPPOSITES: apathy, inertia, lethargy

vitiate 1 = **spoil**, mar, undermine, impair, injure, harm, devalue, water down, blemish, invalidate, crool *or* cruel *(Austral. slang)* • *electoral abuses which could vitiate the entire voting process*
2 = **corrupt**, contaminate, pollute, pervert, blight, taint, sully, deprave, debase, defile • *His otherwise admirable character is vitiated by his pride.*

vitriolic = **venomous**, scathing, malicious, acid, bitter, destructive, withering, virulent, sardonic, caustic, bitchy *(informal)*, acerbic, envenomed, dripping with malice • *There was a vicious and vitriolic attack on him in the tabloids.*

vituperation = **abuse**, vilification, invective, blame, censure, rebuke, reprimand, flak *(informal)*, reproach, tongue-lashing, fault-finding, castigation, obloquy, scurrility • *racist speeches full of vituperation, slander and prejudice*
OPPOSITES: praise, approval, acclaim

V

vituperative = **abusive**, vitriolic, virulent, insulting, harsh, withering, malign, belittling, sardonic, derogatory, scurrilous, defamatory, censorious, opprobrious, denunciatory, calumniatory • *one of journalism's most vituperative critics*

vivacious = **lively**, spirited, vital, gay, bubbling, sparkling, cheerful, jolly, animated, merry, upbeat *(informal)*, high-spirited, ebullient, chirpy *(informal)*, sparky, scintillating, sprightly, effervescent, full of life, full of beans *(informal)*, frolicsome, sportive, light-hearted • *a beautiful, vivacious and charming young woman*
OPPOSITES: boring, dull, lifeless

vivacity = **liveliness**, life, energy, spirit, pep, sparkle, animation, high spirits, welly *(slang)*, gaiety, brio, ebullience, effervescence, sprightliness • *She danced past, bubbling with vivacity.*
OPPOSITES: apathy, inertia, listlessness

vivid 1 = **clear**, detailed, realistic, telling, moving, strong, affecting, arresting, powerful, sharp, dramatic, stirring, stimulating, haunting, graphic, distinct, lively, memorable, unforgettable, evocative, lucid, lifelike, true to life, sharply-etched • *Last night I had a vivid dream which really upset me.*
OPPOSITES: vague, unclear, unmemorable
2 = **bright**, brilliant, intense, clear, rich, glowing, colourful, highly-coloured • *a vivid blue sky*
OPPOSITES: cool, pale, dull
3 = **lively**, strong, dynamic, striking, spirited, powerful, quick, storming, active, vigorous, energetic, animated, vibrant, fiery, flamboyant, expressive, vivacious, zestful • *one of the most vivid personalities in tennis*
OPPOSITES: quiet, ordinary, routine

vividness 1 = **clarity**, realism, intensity, sharpness, immediacy, distinctness, graphicness • *the vividness of characterisation in the play*
2 = **brightness**, brilliance, intensity, glow, richness, strength, radiance, brilliancy, resplendence • *the startling vividness of colours in his surroundings*

vixen = **shrew**, fury, spitfire, virago, harpy, scold, harridan, termagant *(rare)*, hellcat, Xanthippe, ballbreaker *(slang)* • *She claims she has been caricatured as a vampish vixen by the press.*

viz = **namely**, that is to say, to wit, videlicet • *two places where you can meet men, viz evening classes and supermarkets*

vocabulary 1 = **language**, words, lexicon, word stock, word hoard • *Children need to read to improve their vocabularies.*
2 = **wordbook**, dictionary, glossary, lexicon • *I could not find this word in my small Italian-English vocabulary.*

vocal 1 = **outspoken**, frank, blunt, forthright, strident, vociferous, noisy, articulate, expressive, eloquent, plain-spoken, clamorous, free-spoken • *He has been very vocal in his displeasure over the decision.*
OPPOSITES: reserved, quiet, silent
2 = **spoken**, voiced, uttered, oral, said, articulate, articulated, put into words • *a child's ability to imitate rhythms and vocal sounds*

vocal cords
▸ TECHNICAL NAME: glottis
▸ RELATED ADJECTIVE: glottal

vocalist = **singer**, soloist, crooner, chanteuse *fem.*, songster or songstress • *the band's lead vocalist*

vocation = **profession**, calling, job, business, office, trade, role, post, career, mission, employment, pursuit, life work, métier • *the levels of knowledge and skill required for success in many vocations*

QUOTATIONS
Many are called, but few are chosen
[Bible: St. Matthew]

vociferous = **outspoken**, vocal, strident, noisy, shouting, loud, ranting, vehement, loudmouthed *(informal)*, uproarious, obstreperous, clamorous, clamant • *a vociferous opponent of Conservatism*
OPPOSITES: still, quiet, silent

vogue AS A NOUN = **fashion**, trend, craze, style, the latest, the thing *(informal)*, mode, last word, the rage, passing fancy, dernier cri *(French)* • *the new vogue for herbal medicines*
▸ AS AN ADJECTIVE = **fashionable**, trendy *(Brit. informal)*, in, now *(informal)*, popular, with it *(informal)*, prevalent, up-to-the-minute, modish, the new, du jour *(French)*, voguish, culty • *The word 'talisman' has become a vogue word in sports writing.*
▸ IN PHRASES: **in vogue** = **popular**, big, fashionable, all the rage, happening, accepted, current, cool, in favour, stylish, up to date, in use, prevalent, up to the minute, modish, the new, du jour *(French)*, trendsetting, culty, schmick *(Austral. informal)* • *Pale colours are in vogue this season.*

voice AS A NOUN 1 = **tone**, sound, language, articulation, power of speech • *Miriam's voice was strangely calm.*
2 = **utterance**, expression, words, airing, vocalization, verbalization • *The crowd gave voice to their anger.*
3 = **opinion**, will, feeling, wish, desire • *the voice of the opposition*
4 = **say**, part, view, decision, vote, comment, input • *Our employees have no voice in how our company is run.*
5 = **instrument**, medium, spokesman *or* spokeswoman, agency, channel, vehicle, organ, spokesperson, intermediary, mouthpiece • *He claims to be the voice of the people.*
▸ AS A VERB = **express**, say, declare, air, raise, table, reveal, mention, mouth, assert, pronounce, utter, articulate, come out with *(informal)*, divulge, ventilate, enunciate, put into words, vocalize, give expression *or* utterance to • *Scientists have voiced concern that the disease could be passed to humans.*
▸ RELATED ADJECTIVE: vocal

voice box
▸ TECHNICAL NAME: larynx
▸ RELATED ADJECTIVE: laryngeal

void AS AN ADJECTIVE 1 = **invalid**, null and void, inoperative, useless, ineffective, worthless, ineffectual, unenforceable, nonviable • *The elections were declared void by the former military ruler.*
2 *with* **of** = **devoid of**, without, lacking, free from, wanting, bereft of, empty of, bare of, destitute of, vacant of • *His face was void of emotion as he left the room.*
▸ AS A NOUN 1 = **gap**, space, lack, want, hole, blank, emptiness • *His death has created a void which will never be filled.*
2 = **emptiness**, space, vacuum, oblivion, blankness, nullity, vacuity • *the limitless void of outer space*
▸ AS A VERB = **invalidate**, nullify, cancel, withdraw, reverse, undo, repeal, quash, revoke, disallow, retract, repudiate, negate, rescind, annul, abrogate, countermand, render invalid, abnegate • *The Supreme Court voided his conviction for murder.*
▸ RELATED PHOBIA: kenophobia

volatile 1 = **changeable**, shifting, variable, unsettled, unstable, explosive, unreliable, unsteady, inconstant • *There have been riots before and the situation is volatile.*
OPPOSITES: stable, constant, steady
2 = **temperamental**, erratic, mercurial, up and down *(informal)*, fickle, whimsical, giddy, flighty, over-emotional, inconstant • *She has a volatile temperament.*
OPPOSITES: calm, consistent, reliable
3 = **unstable**, explosive, inflammable, labile *(technical)*, eruptive • *when volatile chemicals explode*

volcano
▹ *See panel* Volcanoes

volition AS A NOUN = **free will**, will, choice, election, choosing, option, purpose, resolution, determination, preference, discretion • *committing crimes of violence through cold, premeditated volition*

V

VOLCANOES

Antisana	Elgon	Huascarán	Llaima	Popocatépetl	Tolima
Apo	El Misti	Iliamna	Mauna Kea	Santa Maria	Tristan da Cunha
Askja	Erciyas Dagi	Ixtaccihuatl	Mauna Loa	Semeru	Tungurahua
Cameroon	Erebus	Katmai	Mayon	Soufrière	Vesuvius
Chimborazo	Etna	Kazbek	Mount St. Helens	Stromboli	
Citlaltépetl	Fuji	Kenya	Nevado de Colima	Suribachi	
Corcovado	Haleakala	Kilauea	Nevado de Toluca	Taal	
Cotopaxi	Hekla	Krakatoa	Paricutín	Tambora	
Egmont	Helgafell	Lassen Peak	Pelée	Teide	

▸ **IN PHRASES: of your own volition = of your own free will**, voluntarily • *Mr Coombes had gone to the police of his own volition.*

volley = **barrage**, blast, burst, explosion, shower, hail, discharge, bombardment, salvo, fusillade, cannonade • *It's still not known how many died in the volleys of gunfire.*

voluble = **talkative**, garrulous, loquacious, forthcoming, articulate, fluent, glib, blessed with the gift of the gab • *Bert is a voluble, gregarious man.*
OPPOSITES: reticent, taciturn, unforthcoming

volume 1 = **amount**, quantity, level, body, total, measure, degree, mass, proportion, bulk, aggregate • *the sheer volume of traffic on our motorways*
2 = **capacity**, size, mass, extent, proportions, dimensions, bulk, measurements, magnitude, compass, largeness, cubic content • *When water is frozen it increases in volume.*
3 = **book**, work, title, opus, publication, manual, tome, treatise, almanac, compendium • *a slim volume of English poetry*
4 = **loudness**, sound, amplification • *He came round to complain about the volume of the music.*
▸ RELATED ADJECTIVE: cubical

voluminous 1 = **large**, big, full, massive, vast, ample, bulky, billowing, roomy, cavernous, capacious • *She was swathed in a voluminous cloak.*
OPPOSITES: small, tiny, skimpy
2 = **copious**, extensive, prolific, abundant, plentiful, profuse • *this author's voluminous writings and correspondence*
OPPOSITES: inadequate, insufficient, scanty

voluntarily = **willingly**, freely, by choice, without being asked, without prompting, lief *(rare)*, on your own initiative, of your own free will, off your own bat, of your own accord, of your own volition • *I would never leave this country voluntarily.*

voluntary 1 = **intentional**, intended, deliberate, planned, studied, purposed, calculated, wilful, done on purpose • *a voluntary act undertaken in full knowledge of the consequences*
OPPOSITES: involuntary, unintentional, instinctive
2 = **optional**, discretionary, up to the individual, open, unforced, unconstrained, unenforced, at your discretion, discretional, open to choice, uncompelled • *The extra course in Commercial French is voluntary.*
OPPOSITES: forced, obligatory, enforced
3 = **unpaid**, volunteer, free, willing, honorary, gratuitous, pro bono *(Law)* • *In her spare time she does voluntary work for the homeless.*

volunteer AS A NOUN = **subject**, participant, case, patient, guinea pig *(informal)* • *the youngest volunteer in the experiment*
▸ AS A VERB 1 = **offer**, step forward, offer your services, propose, let yourself in for *(informal)*, need no invitation, present your services, proffer your services, put yourself at someone's disposal • *Aunt Mary volunteered to clean up the kitchen.*
OPPOSITES: refuse, withdraw
2 = **suggest**, advance, put forward, venture, tender • *His wife volunteered an ingenious suggestion.*

voluptuous 1 = **buxom**, shapely, curvaceous, erotic, ample, enticing, provocative, seductive *(informal)*, well-stacked *(Brit. slang)*, full-bosomed • *a voluptuous, well-rounded lady with glossy red hair*
2 = **sensual**, luxurious, self-indulgent, hedonistic, sybaritic, epicurean, licentious, bacchanalian, pleasure-loving • *a life of voluptuous decadence*
OPPOSITES: Spartan, celibate, abstemious

vomit 1 = **be sick**, throw up *(informal)*, spew, chuck *(Austral. & N.Z. informal)*, heave *(slang)*, puke *(slang)*, retch, barf *(U.S. slang)*, chunder *(slang, chiefly Austral.)*, belch forth, upchuck *(U.S. slang)*, do a technicolour yawn, toss your cookies *(U.S. slang)* • *Any dairy product made him vomit.*
2 *often with* **up** = **bring up**, throw up, regurgitate, chuck (up) *(slang, chiefly U.S.)*, emit *(informal)*, eject, puke *(slang)*, disgorge, sick up *(informal)*, spew out *or* up • *She vomited up all she had just eaten.*

voracious 1 = **gluttonous**, insatiable, ravenous, hungry, greedy, ravening, devouring • *For their size, stoats are voracious predators.*
2 = **avid**, prodigious, insatiable, uncontrolled, rapacious, unquenchable • *He was a voracious reader.*
OPPOSITES: moderate, temperate, self-controlled

vortex = **whirlpool**, eddy, maelstrom, Charybdis *(literary)*, gyre, countercurrent • *a vortex of encircling winds*

vote AS A NOUN 1 = **poll**, election, ballot, referendum, popular vote, plebiscite, straw poll, show of hands • *They took a vote and decided not to do it.*
2 = **right to vote**, franchise, voting rights, suffrage, say, voice, enfranchisement • *Before that, women did not even have the vote.*
▸ AS A VERB 1 = **cast your vote**, ballot, go to the polls, mark your ballot paper • *Over half of the electorate did not vote in the last general election.*
2 = **judge**, declare, pronounce, decree, adjudge • *They voted him Player of the Year.*
3 = **suggest**, propose, recommend, move, table, advocate, submit • *I vote that we ask him to come with us.*
▸ IN PHRASES: **vote someone in** = **elect**, choose, select, appoint, return, pick, opt for, designate, decide on, settle on, fix on, plump for, put in power • *The Prime Minister was voted in by a huge majority.*
vote someone out = **depose**, dismiss, discharge, oust, turn out, kick out *(informal)*, eject, dislodge, push out, boot out *(informal)*, unseat, dethrone, remove from office, turf out *(Brit. informal)*, drum out *(informal)*, remove from power, give someone the boot *(informal)* • *They joined forces to vote her out of office.*

voucher = **ticket**, token, coupon, pass, slip, chit, chitty *(Brit. informal)*, docket • *The winners will each receive a voucher for a pair of cinema tickets.*

vouch for 1 = **guarantee**, back, certify, answer for, swear to, stick up for *(informal)*, stand witness, give assurance of, asseverate, go bail for • *Kim's mother agreed to vouch for Maria and get her a job.*
2 = **confirm**, support, affirm, attest to, assert, uphold • *I cannot vouch for the accuracy of the story.*

V

vouchsafe = **grant**, accord, yield, cede, confer on, favour someone with, deign to give, condescend to give • *He vouchsafed them a little more brandy.*

vow AS A NOUN = **promise**, commitment, pledge, oath, profession, troth *(archaic)*, avowal • *Most people still take their marriage vows seriously.*

▸ AS A VERB = **promise**, pledge, swear, commit, engage, affirm, avow, bind yourself, undertake solemnly • *She vowed that some day she would return to live in France.*

voyage AS A NOUN = **journey**, travels, trip, passage, expedition, crossing, sail, cruise, excursion • *He aims to follow Columbus's voyage to the West Indies.*

▸ AS A VERB = **travel**, journey, tour, cruise, steam, take a trip, go on an expedition • *The boat is currently voyaging through the Barents Sea.*

vulgar 1 = **tasteless**, common, flashy, low, gross, nasty, gaudy, tawdry, cheap and nasty, common as muck • *The decor is ugly, tasteless and vulgar.*

OPPOSITES: elegant, tasteful, high-brow

2 = **crude**, dirty, rude, low, blue, nasty, naughty, coarse, indecent, improper, suggestive, tasteless, risqué, off colour, ribald, indelicate, indecorous • *an oaf with a taste for racist and vulgar jokes*

3 = **uncouth**, boorish, unrefined, impolite, ill-bred, unmannerly • *He was a vulgar old man, but he never swore in front of women.*

OPPOSITES: sophisticated, refined, polite

4 = **vernacular**, native, common, general, ordinary • *translated from Latin into the vulgar tongue*

QUOTATIONS

It's worse than wicked, my dear, it's vulgar
[Punch]

vulgarity 1 = **tastelessness**, bad taste, grossness, tawdriness, gaudiness, lack of refinement • *I hate the vulgarity of this room.*

OPPOSITES: good taste, tastefulness

2 = **crudeness**, rudeness, coarseness, crudity, ribaldry, suggestiveness, indelicacy, indecorum • *a comedian famous for his vulgarity and irreverence*

OPPOSITES: decorum

3 = **coarseness**, roughness, boorishness, rudeness, loutishness, oafishness, uncouthness • *For all his apparent vulgarity, Todd had a certain raw charm.*

OPPOSITES: sophistication, refinement, good manners

vulnerable 1 = **susceptible**, helpless, unprotected, defenceless, exposed, weak, sensitive, tender, unguarded, thin-skinned • *criminals who prey on the more vulnerable members of our society*

OPPOSITES: immune, insensitive, impervious

2 = **exposed**, open, unprotected, defenceless, accessible, wide open, open to attack, assailable • *Their tanks would be vulnerable to attack from the air.*

OPPOSITES: guarded, unassailable, well-protected

Ww

wacky = **unusual**, odd, wild, strange, out there *(slang)*, crazy, silly, weird, way-out *(informal)*, eccentric, unpredictable, daft *(informal)*, irrational, erratic, Bohemian, unconventional, far-out *(slang)*, loony *(slang)*, kinky *(informal)*, off-the-wall *(slang)*, unorthodox, nutty *(slang)*, oddball, zany, goofy *(informal)*, offbeat *(informal)*, freaky *(slang)*, outré, gonzo *(slang)*, screwy *(informal)*, wacko *or* whacko *(informal)*, off the air *(Austral. slang)* • *a wacky new comedy series*

wad 1 = **bundle**, roll, bankroll *(U.S. & Canad.)*, pocketful • *a wad of banknotes*
2 = **mass**, ball, lump, hunk, piece, block, plug, chunk • *a wad of cotton wool*
3 = **plug**, twist, chew, quid • *He spat out a great wad of tobacco.*

wadding = **padding**, filling, stuffing, lining, packing, filler • *a sleeping bag lined with wadding*

waddle = **shuffle**, shamble, totter, toddle, rock, stagger, sway, wobble • *a fat woman waddling down the street*

wade AS A VERB 1 = **paddle**, splash, splash about, slop • *The boys were wading in the cold pool nearby.*
2 = **walk through**, cross, ford, pass through, go across, travel across, make your way across • *We had to wade the river and then climb out of the valley.*
▸ IN PHRASES: **wade in** = **move in**, pitch in, dive in *(informal)*, set to work, advance, set to, get stuck in *(informal)*, buckle down • *I waded in to help, but I got pushed aside.*
wade into someone = **launch yourself at**, charge at, attack, rush, storm, tackle, go for, set about, strike at, assail, tear into *(informal)*, fall upon, set upon, lay into *(informal)*, light into *(informal)* • *The troops waded into the protesters with batons.*
wade into something = **get involved in**, tackle, pitch in, interfere in, dive in, plunge in, get stuck into • *The Stock Exchange yesterday waded into the debate on stamp duty.*
wade through something = **plough through**, trawl through, labour at, work your way through, toil at, drudge at, peg away at • *scientists who have to wade through tons of data*

waffle AS A VERB 1 *often followed by* **on** = **chatter**, rabbit (on) *(Brit. informal)*, babble, drivel, prattle, jabber, gabble, rattle on, verbalize, blather, witter on *(informal)*, blether, run off at the mouth *(slang)*, prate, earbash *(Austral. & N.Z. slang)* • *some guy on TV waffling about political correctness*
2 = **waver**, hesitate, falter, fluctuate, dither *(chiefly Brit.)*, vacillate, seesaw, blow hot and cold *(informal)*, be indecisive, hum and haw, be unable to decide, be irresolute, shillyshally *(informal)*, be unable to make up your mind, swither *(Scot.)* • *He waffled on abortion and gay rights.*
▸ AS A NOUN = **prattle**, nonsense, hot air *(informal)*, twaddle, padding, prating, gibberish, jabber, verbiage, blather, wordiness, verbosity, prolixity, bunkum *or* buncombe *(chiefly U.S.)*, bizzo *(Austral. slang)*, bull's wool *(Austral. & N.Z. slang)* • *I'm tired of his smug, sanctimonious waffle.*

waft AS A VERB 1 = **drift**, float, be carried, be transported, coast, flow, stray, glide, be borne, be conveyed • *The scent of roses wafted through the open window.*
2 = **transport**, bring, carry, bear, guide, conduct, transmit, convey • *A slight breeze wafted the heavy scent of flowers past her.*
▸ AS A NOUN = **current**, breath, puff, whiff, draught, breeze • *A waft of perfume reached Ingrid's nostrils.*

wag[1] AS A VERB 1 = **wave**, shake, swing, waggle, stir, sway, flutter, waver, quiver, vibrate, wiggle, oscillate • *The dog was barking and wagging its tail wildly.*
2 = **waggle**, wave, shake, flourish, brandish, wobble, wiggle • *He wagged a disapproving finger at me.*
3 = **shake**, bob, nod • *She wagged her head in agreement.*
▸ AS A NOUN 1 = **wave**, shake, swing, toss, sway, flutter, waver, quiver, vibration, wiggle, oscillation, waggle • *The dog gave a responsive wag of his tail.*
2 = **nod**, bob, shake • *a wag of the head*

wag[2] = **joker**, comic, wit, comedian, clown, card *(informal)*, kidder *(informal)*, jester, dag *(N.Z. informal)*, prankster, buffoon, trickster, humorist, joculator *or (fem.)* joculatrix • *My dad's always been a bit of a wag.*

wage AS A NOUN *often plural* = **payment**, pay, earnings, remuneration, fee, reward, compensation, income, allowance, recompense, stipend, emolument • *efforts to set a minimum wage well above the poverty line*
▸ AS A PLURAL NOUN = **rewards**, returns, deserts, retribution, just deserts, requital • *He was reaping the wages of sin.*
▸ AS A VERB = **engage in**, conduct, pursue, carry on, undertake, practise, prosecute, proceed with • *the three factions that had been waging a civil war*

QUOTATIONS
For the labourer is worthy of his hire
[Bible: St. Luke]

wager AS A VERB = **bet**, chance, risk, stake, lay, venture, put on, pledge, gamble, hazard, speculate, punt *(chiefly Brit.)* • *People had wagered a good deal of money on his winning the championship.*
▸ AS A NOUN = **bet**, stake, pledge, gamble, risk, flutter *(Brit. informal)*, ante, punt *(chiefly Brit.)*, long shot • *punters placing wagers on the day's racing*

waggle = **wag**, wiggle, wave, shake, flutter, wobble, oscillate • *He was waggling his toes in his socks.*

waif = **stray**, orphan, outcast, urchin, foundling • *The child was a poor, emaciated waif living rough on the streets.*

wail AS A VERB 1 = **cry**, weep, grieve, lament, keen, greet *(Scot. or archaic)*, howl, whine, deplore, bemoan, bawl, bewail, yowl, ululate • *The woman began to wail for her lost child.*

2 = **scream**, cry, yell, howl, shriek, screech, yelp • *She began to wail that she was hungry.*
3 = **howl**, scream, roar, cry • *The wind wailed outside the closed window.*
▸ **AS A NOUN** = **cry**, moan, sob, howl, keening, lament, bawl, lamentation, yowl, ululation • *Wails of grief were heard as visitors filed past the site of the disaster.*

wait AS A VERB 1 = **stay**, remain, stop, pause, rest, delay, linger, hover, hang around *(informal)*, dally, loiter, tarry • *I waited at the corner for the lights to go green.*
OPPOSITES: go, leave, quit
2 = **stand by**, delay, hold on *(informal)*, hold back, wait in the wings, mark time, hang fire, bide your time, kick your heels, cool your heels • *Let's wait and see what happens.*
3 = **be postponed**, be suspended, be delayed, be put off, be put back, be deferred, be put on hold *(informal)*, be shelved, be tabled, be held over, be put on ice *(informal)*, be put on the back burner *(informal)* • *I want to talk to you but it can wait.*
▸ **AS A NOUN** = **delay**, gap, pause, interval, stay, rest, halt, hold-up, lull, stoppage, hindrance, hiatus, entr'acte • *After a long wait, someone finally picked up the phone.*
▸ **IN PHRASES: wait around** = **hang around**, linger, loiter, hover around, mark time, skulk around, loaf around • *I waited around to speak to the doctor.*
wait for *or* **on something** *or* **someone** = **await**, expect, look forward to, hope for, anticipate, look for • *I'm still waiting for a reply from him.*
wait on *or* **upon someone** = **serve**, tend to, look after, take care of, minister to, attend to, cater to • *The owner of the restaurant himself waited on us.*
wait up = **stay awake**, stay up, keep vigil • *I waited up for you till three in the morning.*

PROVERBS
Don't count your chickens before they are hatched
Don't cross the bridge till you come to it

waiter = **attendant**, server, flunkey, steward, servant • *The waiter brought them their bill.*

waitress = **attendant**, server, stewardess, servant

waive 1 = **give up**, relinquish, renounce, forsake, drop, abandon, resign, yield, surrender, set aside, dispense with, cede, forgo • *He pled guilty to the charges and waived his right to appeal.*
OPPOSITES: claim, demand, press (for)
2 = **disregard**, ignore, discount, overlook, set aside, pass over, dispense with, brush aside, turn a blind eye to, forgo • *The council has agreed to waive certain statutory planning regulations.*

waiver = **renunciation**, surrender, remission, abdication, giving up, resignation, denial, setting aside, abandonment, disclaimer, disavowal, relinquishment, eschewal, abjuration • *He had to sign a waiver of his constitutional rights.*

wake[1] AS A VERB 1 = **awake**, stir, awaken, come to, arise, get up, rouse, get out of bed, waken, bestir, rouse from sleep, bestir yourself • *It was still dark when I woke.*
OPPOSITES: fall asleep, go to sleep, sleep
2 = **awaken**, arouse, rouse, waken, rouse someone from sleep • *She went upstairs at once to wake the children.*
3 = **evoke**, recall, excite, renew, stimulate, revive, induce, arouse, call up, awaken, rouse, give rise to, conjure up, stir up, rekindle, summon up, reignite • *Seeing him again upset her, because it woke painful memories.*
▸ **AS A NOUN** = **vigil**, watch, funeral, deathwatch, tangi *(N.Z.)* • *A funeral wake was in progress.*
▸ **IN PHRASES: wake someone up** = **activate**, stimulate, enliven, galvanize, fire, excite, provoke, motivate, arouse, awaken, animate, rouse, mobilize, energize, kindle, switch someone on, stir someone up • *He needs a shock to wake him up a bit.*
wake up to something = **realize**, understand, recognize, appreciate, grasp, conceive, comprehend, become aware of, twig *(Brit. informal)*, get the message, apprehend, catch on to *(informal)*, become conscious of, be cognizant of • *She woke up to the fact that she could not compete with her sister.*

wake[2] AS A NOUN = **slipstream**, wash, trail, backwash, train, track, waves, path • *Dolphins sometimes play in the wake of the boats.*
▸ **IN PHRASES: in the wake of** = **in the aftermath of**, following, because of, as a result of, on account of, as a consequence of • *The move comes in the wake of new measures brought in by the government.*

wakeful = **sleepless**, restless, insomniac, unsleeping, disturbed • *Wakeful babies often continue to need little sleep as they grow older.*
OPPOSITES: asleep, dormant

waken 1 = **awaken**, wake, stir, wake up, stimulate, revive, awake, arouse, activate, animate, rouse, enliven, galvanize • *Have a cup of coffee to waken you.*
2 = **wake up**, come to, get up, awake, awaken, be roused, come awake • *I dozed off and I only wakened when she came in.*
OPPOSITES: fall asleep, go to sleep, sleep

Wales = **Cymru** *(Welsh)*, Cambria *(Latin)* • *the Secretary of State for Wales*

walk AS A VERB 1 = **stride**, wander, stroll, trudge, go, move, step, march, advance, pace, trek, hike, tread, ramble, tramp, promenade, amble, saunter, take a turn, traipse *(informal)*, toddle, make your way, mosey *(informal)*, plod on, perambulate, footslog • *They walked in silence for a while.*
2 = **travel on foot**, go on foot, hoof it *(slang)*, foot it, go by shanks's pony *(informal)* • *When I was your age I walked five miles to school.*
3 = **escort**, take, see, show, partner, guide, conduct, accompany, shepherd, convoy, usher, chaperon • *He offered to walk me home.*
▸ **AS A NOUN** 1 = **stroll**, hike, ramble, tramp, turn, march, constitutional, trek, outing, trudge, promenade, amble, saunter, traipse *(informal)*, breath of air, perambulation • *He often took long walks in the hills.*
2 = **route**, course, beat, path, circuit • *a two-mile coastal walk*
3 = **gait**, manner of walking, step, bearing, pace, stride, carriage, tread • *Despite his gangling walk, George was a good dancer.*
4 = **path**, pathway, footpath, track, way, road, lane, trail, avenue, pavement, alley, aisle, sidewalk *(chiefly U.S.)*, walkway *(chiefly U.S.)*, promenade, towpath, esplanade, footway, berm *(N.Z.)* • *a covered walk consisting of a roof supported by columns*
▸ **IN PHRASES: walk all over someone** 1 = **take advantage of**, abuse, milk, exploit, manipulate, misuse, impose upon, run rings around *(informal)*, take liberties with, play on *or* upon • *She lets her children walk all over her.*
2 = **defeat heavily** *or* **utterly**, beat, thrash, trounce, stuff *(slang)*, tank *(slang)*, hammer *(informal)*, crush, overwhelm, slaughter *(informal)*, lick *(informal)*, paste *(slang)*, rout, walk over *(informal)*, clobber *(slang)*, run rings around *(informal)*, wipe the floor with *(informal)*, make mincemeat of, beat hollow *(Brit. informal)*, drub, give a hiding to *(informal)*, give a pasting to *(slang)* • *We're not going to walk all over our European opponents.*
walk in on someone = **interrupt**, disturb, intrude on, barge in on *(informal)*, butt in on • *His wife walked in on him making love.*
walk off *or* **away with something** 1 = **steal**, take, lift *(informal)*, nick *(slang, chiefly Brit.)*, appropriate, trouser *(slang)*, pinch *(informal)*, poach, swipe *(slang)*, knock off *(slang)*, half-inch *(old-fashioned slang)*, blag *(slang)*, pilfer, misappropriate, purloin, filch, thieve, peculate • *Someone's walked off with my coat.*
2 = **win**, get, gain, collect, achieve, pick up, obtain, acquire,

attain, procure, come away with • *He walked off with a £2,000 prize.*
walk of life = area, calling, business, line, course, trade, class, field, career, rank, employment, province, profession, occupation, arena, sphere, realm, domain, caste, vocation, line of work, métier • *In this job you meet people from all walks of life.*
walk out 1 = leave suddenly, storm out, get up and go, flounce out, vote with your feet, make a sudden departure, take off *(informal)* • *Mr Mason walked out during the performance.*
2 = go on strike, strike, revolt, mutiny, stop work, take industrial action, down tools, withdraw your labour • *Industrial action began this week, when most of the staff walked out.*
walk out on someone = abandon, leave, desert, strand, betray, chuck *(informal)*, run away from, forsake, jilt, run out on *(informal)*, throw over, leave high and dry, leave in the lurch • *Her husband walked out on her.*

PROVERBS
We must learn to walk before we can run

walker = hiker, rambler, backpacker, wayfarer, footslogger, pedestrian • *disturbance to nesting birds caused by walkers and climbers*

walking
▸ RELATED PHOBIA: basophobia

walkout = strike, protest, revolt, stoppage, industrial action • *Moderate unions have refused to join the walkout.*

walkover = pushover, easy victory, breeze *(U.S. & Canad. informal)*, cinch *(slang)*, picnic *(informal)*, landslide, child's play *(informal)*, piece of cake *(informal)*, doddle *(Brit. slang)*, snap *(informal)*, no-brainer *(informal)*, cakewalk *(informal)*, duck soup *(U.S. slang)*, piece of piss *(Brit. slang)* • *The next general election is unlikely to be a walkover for the government.*
OPPOSITES: labour, grind *(informal)*, struggle

walkway = path, alley, footpath, way, road, walk *(chiefly U.S.)*, track, path, lane, trail, avenue, pavement, aisle, pathway, sidewalk *(chiefly U.S.)*, promenade, towpath, esplanade, footway, berm *(N.Z.)* • *The hotel is linked to the terminal by a covered walkway.*

wall AS A NOUN **1 = partition**, divider, room divider, screen, panel, barrier, enclosure • *We're going to knock down the dividing wall to give us one big room.*
2 = barricade, rampart, fortification, bulwark, blockade, embankment, parapet, palisade, stockade, breastwork • *The Romans breached the city walls and captured the city.*
3 = barrier, obstacle, barricade, obstruction, check, bar, block, fence, impediment, hindrance • *I appealed for help but met the usual wall of silence.*
▸ IN PHRASES: **drive someone up the wall = infuriate**, madden, exasperate, get on your nerves *(informal)*, anger, provoke, annoy, irritate, aggravate *(informal)*, incense, enrage, gall, rile, drive you crazy *(informal)*, nark *(Brit., Austral. & N.Z. slang)*, be like a red rag to a bull, make your blood boil, get your goat *(slang)*, drive you insane, make your hackles rise, raise your hackles, piss your off *(taboo slang)*, send you off your head *(slang)*, get your back up, make you see red *(informal)*, put your back up, hack you off *(informal)* • *That tuneless humming of his drives me up the wall.*
go to the wall = fail, close down, go under, go out of business, fall, crash, collapse, fold *(informal)*, be ruined, go bust *(informal)*, go bankrupt, go broke *(informal)*, go into receivership, become insolvent • *Even big companies are going to the wall these days.*
off the wall = comical, eccentric, wacky *(slang)*, oddball *(informal)*, funny, out there *(slang)*, crazy, loony *(slang)*, nutty *(slang)*, zany, madcap, goofy *(informal)*, kooky *(U.S. informal)*, clownish, wacko *or* whacko *(informal)*, off the air *(Austral. slang)* • *his particular brand of off-the-wall humour*
wall someone up = enclose, confine, detain, imprison, lock up, constrain, put away, incarcerate, jail • *He was walled up in a tiny cell and left to die.*
wall something up = close, block off *or* up, secure, seal, shut up • *They had walled up the room for fear of infection.*
wall something *or* someone in = enclose, surround, bound, fence, hedge, encompass, encircle, encase, impound, pen in, circumscribe, hem in, shut in • *The garden is walled in to create a feeling of privacy.*
▸ RELATED ADJECTIVE: mural

wallet = purse, pocketbook, notecase, pouch, case, holder, money-bag • *I took a business card from my wallet and handed it to him.*

wallop AS A VERB **1 = hit**, beat, strike, knock, belt *(informal)*, deck *(slang)*, bang, batter, bash *(informal)*, pound, chin *(slang)*, smack, thrash, thump, paste *(slang)*, buffet, clout *(informal)*, slug, whack, swipe, clobber *(slang)*, pummel, tonk *(slang)*, lambast(e), lay one on *(slang)*, beat *or* knock seven bells out of *(informal)* • *Once she walloped me over the head with a frying pan.*
2 = beat, defeat, slaughter, thrash, best, stuff *(slang)*, worst, tank, hammer *(informal)*, crush, overwhelm, lick *(informal)*, paste *(slang)*, rout, walk over *(informal)*, trounce, clobber *(slang)*, vanquish, run rings around *(informal)*, wipe the floor with *(informal)*, make mincemeat of, blow out of the water *(slang)*, drub, beat hollow *(Brit. informal)*, defeat heavily *or* utterly • *England were walloped by Brazil in the finals.*
▸ AS A NOUN **= blow**, strike, punch, thump, belt *(informal)*, bash, sock *(slang)*, smack, clout *(informal)*, slug, whack, swipe, thwack, haymaker *(slang)* • *With one brutal wallop, Clarke sent him flying.*

wallow 1 = revel, indulge, relish, savour, delight, glory, thrive, bask, take pleasure, luxuriate, indulge yourself • *All he wants to do is wallow in self-pity.*
OPPOSITES: avoid, give up, refrain from
2 = roll about, lie, tumble, wade, slosh, welter, splash around • *Hippos love to wallow in mud.*

wan 1 = pale, white, washed out, pasty, faded, bleached, ghastly, sickly, bloodless, colourless, pallid, anaemic, discoloured, ashen, sallow, whitish, cadaverous, waxen, like death warmed up *(informal)*, wheyfaced • *He looked wan and tired.*
OPPOSITES: bright, healthy, glowing
2 = dim, weak, pale, faint, feeble • *The lamp cast a wan light through the swirls of fog.*

wand = stick, rod, cane, baton, stake, switch, birch, twig, sprig, withe, withy • *a magician's wand*

wander AS A VERB **1 = roam**, walk, drift, stroll, range, cruise, stray, ramble, prowl, meander, rove, straggle, traipse *(informal)*, go walkabout *(Austral.)*, mooch around *(slang)*, stravaig *(Scot. & Northern English dialect)*, knock about *or* around, peregrinate • *He wandered aimlessly around the garden.*
2 = stray, roam, digress, get sidetracked, go off at a tangent • *She allowed her mind to wander to other things.*
▸ AS A NOUN **= excursion**, turn, walk, stroll, cruise, ramble, meander, promenade, traipse *(informal)*, mosey *(informal)*, peregrination • *Let's go for a wander round the shops.*
▸ IN PHRASES: **wander off = stray**, roam, go astray, lose your way, drift, depart, rove, straggle • *The child wandered off and got lost.*
wander off something = deviate, diverge, veer, swerve, digress, go off at a tangent, go off course, lapse • *He has a tendency to wander off the point when he's talking.*

wanderer = traveller, rover, nomad, drifter, ranger, journeyer, gypsy, explorer, migrant, rolling stone, rambler, voyager, tripper, itinerant, globetrotter, vagrant, stroller, vagabond, wayfarer, bird of passage • *His father, a restless wanderer, abandoned the family.*

wandering = **itinerant**, travelling, journeying, roving, drifting, homeless, strolling, voyaging, unsettled, roaming, rambling, nomadic, migratory, vagrant, peripatetic, vagabond, rootless, wayfaring • *a band of wandering musicians*

wanderlust = **restlessness**, itchy feet *(informal)*, urge to travel, unsettledness • *His wanderlust would not allow him to stay long in one spot.*

wane AS A VERB 1 = **decline**, flag, weaken, diminish, fall, fail, drop, sink, fade, decrease, dim, dwindle, wither, lessen, subside, ebb, wind down, die out, fade away, abate, draw to a close, atrophy, taper off • *His interest in her began to wane.*
OPPOSITES: rise, increase, grow
2 = **diminish**, decrease, dwindle • *The sliver of a waning moon was high in the sky.*
OPPOSITES: increase, grow, wax
▸ IN PHRASES: **on the wane** = **declining**, dropping, fading, weakening, dwindling, withering, lessening, subsiding, ebbing, dying out, on the way out, on the decline, tapering off, obsolescent, on its last legs, at its lowest ebb • *His career prospects were clearly on the wane.*

wangle = **contrive**, engineer, fix *(informal)*, arrange, manipulate, work *(informal)*, manoeuvre, pull off, fiddle *(informal)*, bring off, finagle *(informal)* • *He managed to wangle a free ticket for me.*

want AS A VERB 1 = **wish for**, desire, fancy, long for, crave, covet, hope for, yearn for, thirst for, hunger for, pine for, hanker after, set your heart on, feel a need for, have a yen for *(informal)*, have a fancy for, eat your heart out over, would give your eyeteeth for • *My husband really wants a new car.*
OPPOSITES: have, own, possess
2 = **feel like**, desire, fancy, feel the need for, feel up to, feel inclined to, have the inclination for • *Do you want another cup of coffee?*
3 = **need**, demand, require, call for, have need of, stand in need of • *The grass wants cutting.*
4 = **should**, need, must, ought • *You want to look where you're going, mate.*
5 = **desire**, fancy, long for, crave, wish for, yearn for, thirst for, hanker after, burn for • *Come on, darling. I want you.*
6 = **love**, prize, treasure, adore, cherish, dote on, hold dear • *Children should be wanted and planned.*
7 = **lack**, need, require, be short of, miss, be deficient in, be without, fall short in • *Our team still wants one more player.*
▸ AS A NOUN 1 = **lack**, need, absence, shortage, deficiency, famine, default, shortfall, inadequacy, scarcity, dearth, paucity, shortness, insufficiency, non-existence, scantiness • *The men were daily becoming weaker for want of rest.*
OPPOSITES: plenty, excess, abundance
2 = **poverty**, need, hardship, privation, penury, destitution, neediness, hand-to-mouth existence, indigence, pauperism, pennilessness, distress • *He said they were fighting for freedom from want.*
OPPOSITES: ease, comfort, wealth
3 = **wish**, will, need, demand, desire, requirement, fancy, yen *(informal)*, longing, hunger, necessity, appetite, craving, yearning, thirst, whim, hankering • *The company needs to respond to the wants of our customers.*

wanting 1 = **deficient**, poor, disappointing, inadequate, pathetic, inferior, insufficient, faulty, not good enough, defective, patchy, imperfect, sketchy, unsound, substandard, leaving much to be desired, not much cop *(Brit. slang)*, not up to par, not up to expectations, bodger or bodgie *(Austral. slang)* • *He examined her work and found it wanting.*
OPPOSITES: good, enough, adequate
2 = **lacking**, missing, absent, incomplete, needing, short, shy • *I feel as if something important is wanting in my life.*
OPPOSITES: full, complete, saturated

wanton AS AN ADJECTIVE 1 = **wilful**, needless, senseless, unjustified, willed, evil, cruel, vicious, deliberate, arbitrary, malicious, wicked, purposeful, gratuitous, malevolent, spiteful, unprovoked, groundless, unjustifiable, uncalled-for, motiveless • *the unnecessary and wanton destruction of our environment*
OPPOSITES: called-for, justified, provoked
2 = **promiscuous**, immoral, shameless, licentious, fast, wild, abandoned, loose, dissipated, lewd, profligate, debauched, lustful, lecherous, dissolute, libertine, libidinous, of easy virtue, unchaste • *Women behaving with the same sexual freedom as men are considered wanton.*
OPPOSITES: Victorian, rigid, puritanical
▸ AS A NOUN = **slut**, tart, whore, slag *(Brit. slang)*, swinger *(informal)*, harlot, slapper *(Brit. slang)*, loose woman, scrubber *(Brit. & Austral. slang)*, strumpet, trollop, woman of easy virtue, hornbag *(Austral. slang)* • *His wife had shown herself to be a shameless wanton.*

war AS A NOUN 1 = **conflict**, drive, attack, fighting, fight, operation, battle, movement, push, struggle, clash, combat, offensive, hostilities, hostility, warfare, expedition, crusade, strife, bloodshed, jihad, enmity, armed conflict • *matters of war and peace*
OPPOSITES: accord, peace, treaty
2 = **campaign**, drive, attack, operation, movement, push, mission, offensive, crusade • *the war against organized crime*
▸ AS A VERB = **fight**, battle, clash, wage war, campaign, struggle, combat, contend, go to war, do battle, make war, take up arms, bear arms, cross swords, conduct a war, engage in hostilities, carry on hostilities • *The two tribes warred to gain new territory.*
OPPOSITES: co-operate, make peace, co-exist
▸ RELATED ADJECTIVES: belligerent, martial

QUOTATIONS

War is nothing but the continuation of politics by other means
[Karl von Clausewitz *On War*]

Politics is war without bloodshed while war is politics with bloodshed
[Mao Tse-tung *On Protracted War*]

There was never a good war, or a bad peace
[Benjamin Franklin]

War makes rattling good history; but Peace is poor reading
[Thomas Hardy *The Dynasts*]

He that makes a good war makes a good peace
[George Herbert *Outlandish Proverbs*]

O I know they make war because they want peace; they hate so that they may live; and they destroy the present to make the world safe for the future. When have they not done and said they did it for that?
[Elizabeth Smart *Necessary Secrets*]

For what can war but endless war still breed?
[John Milton *Sonnet, On the Lord General Fairfax*]

Above all, this book is not concerned with Poetry,
The subject of it is War, and the Pity of War.
The Poetry is in the Pity
[Wilfred Owen *Poems (preface)*]

As long as war is regarded as wicked, it will always have its fascination. When it is looked upon as vulgar, it will cease to be popular
[Oscar Wilde *The Critic as Artist*]

In war, whichever side may call itself the victor, there are no winners, but all are losers
[Neville Chamberlain]

War is too serious a matter to entrust to military men
[Georges Clemenceau]

War is like love, it always finds a way
[Bertolt Brecht *Mother Courage and Her Children*]

During the time men live without a common power to keep them all in awe, they are in that condition which is called war; and such a war as is of every man against every man
[Thomas Hobbes *Leviathan*]
History is littered with the wars which everybody knew would never happen
[Enoch Powell *speech to the Conservative Party Conference*]
Let slip the dogs of war
[William Shakespeare *Julius Caesar*]
War is the trade of kings
[John Dryden *King Arthur*]
The quickest way of ending a war is to lose it
[George Orwell *Shooting an Elephant*]
Sometime they'll give a war and nobody will come
[Carl Sandburg *'The People, Yes'*]
Since war begins in the minds of men, it is in the minds of men that the defences of peace must be constructed
[*Constitution of UNESCO*]
The next war will be fought with atom bombs and the one after that with spears
[Harold Urey]
War will cease when men refuse to fight
[*pacifist slogan*]
After each war there is a little less democracy to save
[Brooks Atkinson *Once Around the Sun*]
What if someone gave a war and Nobody came?
Life would ring the bells of Ecstasy and Forever be Itself again
[Allen Ginsberg *The Fall of America*]
In the fall the war was always there but we did not go to it any more
[Ernest Hemingway *Men Without Women*]

PROVERBS
All is fair in love and war

warble AS A VERB = **sing**, trill, chirp, twitter, chirrup, make melody, pipe, quaver • *A flock of birds was warbling in the trees.*
▸ AS A NOUN = **song**, trill, quaver, twitter, call, cry, chirp, chirrup • *the soft warble of her speaking voice*

war cry = **battle cry**, rallying cry, war whoop, slogan • *Armed warriors burst into the clearing, shrieking war cries.*

ward AS A NOUN 1 = **room**, department, unit, quarter, division, section, apartment, cubicle • *A toddler was admitted to the emergency ward.*
2 = **district**, constituency, area, division, zone, parish, precinct • *Canvassers are focusing on marginal wards in this election.*
3 = **dependant**, charge, pupil, minor, protégé • *Richard became Burton's legal ward and took his name by deed poll.*
▸ IN PHRASES: **ward someone off** = **drive off**, resist, confront, fight off, block, oppose, thwart, hold off, repel, fend off, beat off, keep someone at bay, keep someone at arm's length • *She may have tried to ward off her assailant.*
ward something off 1 = **avert**, turn away, fend off, stave off, avoid, block, frustrate, deflect, repel, forestall • *A rowan cross was hung over the door to ward off evil.*
2 = **parry**, avert, deflect, fend off, avoid, block, repel, turn aside • *He lifted his hands as if to ward off a blow.*

warden 1 = **steward**, guardian, administrator, superintendent, caretaker, curator, warder, custodian, watchman, janitor • *He was a warden at the local parish church.*
2 = **jailer**, prison officer, guard, screw *(slang)*, keeper, captor, turnkey *(archaic)*, gaoler • *The prisoners seized three wardens.*
3 = **governor**, head, leader, director, manager, chief, executive, boss *(informal)*, commander, ruler, controller, overseer, baas *(S. African)* • *A new warden took over the prison.*
4 = **ranger**, keeper, guardian, protector, custodian, official • *a safari park warden*

warder *or* **wardress** = **jailer**, guard, screw *(slang)*, warden, prison officer, keeper, captor, custodian, turnkey *(archaic)*, gaoler • *The inmates of the jail have taken a prison warder hostage.*

wardrobe 1 = **clothes cupboard**, cupboard, closet *(U.S.)*, clothes-press, cabinet • *Hang your dress up in the wardrobe.*
2 = **clothes**, outfit, apparel, clobber *(Brit. slang)*, attire, collection of clothes • *splurging on an expensive new wardrobe of clothes*

warehouse = **store**, depot, storehouse, repository, depository, stockroom • *He worked in a freight warehouse, lifting and carrying heavy loads.*

wares = **goods**, produce, stock, products, stuff, commodities, merchandise, lines • *Vendors displayed their wares in baskets on the ground.*

warfare = **war**, fighting, campaigning, battle, struggle, conflict, combat, hostilities, strife, bloodshed, jihad, armed struggle, discord, enmity, armed conflict, clash of arms, passage of arms • *There are fears that the dispute could develop into open warfare.*
OPPOSITES: accord, peace, treaty

warily 1 = **cautiously**, carefully, discreetly, with care, tentatively, gingerly, guardedly, circumspectly, watchfully, vigilantly, cagily *(informal)*, heedfully • *He backed warily away from the animal.*
OPPOSITES: rashly, hastily, carelessly
2 = **suspiciously**, uneasily, guardedly, sceptically, cagily *(informal)*, distrustfully, mistrustfully, charily • *The two men eyed each other warily.*

wariness 1 = **caution**, care, attention, prudence, discretion, deliberation, foresight, vigilance, alertness, forethought, circumspection, mindfulness, watchfulness, carefulness, caginess *(informal)*, heedfulness • *Extreme wariness is the safest policy when dealing with these substances.*
OPPOSITES: negligence, oblivion, carelessness
2 = **suspicion**, scepticism, distrust, mistrust • *the country's obsessive wariness of foreigners*

QUOTATIONS
Call no man foe, but never love a stranger
[Stella Benson *This is the End*]

warlike = **belligerent**, military, aggressive, hostile, martial, combative, unfriendly, antagonistic, pugnacious, argumentative, bloodthirsty, hawkish, bellicose, quarrelsome, militaristic, inimical, sabre-rattling, jingoistic, warmongering, aggers *(Austral. slang)*, biffo *(Austral. slang)* • *The Scythians were a fiercely warlike people.*
OPPOSITES: friendly, pacific, peaceful

warlock = **magician**, witch, wizard, sorcerer, conjuror, mage *(archaic)*, enchanter, necromancer • *knights who confront fiery dragons and wicked warlocks*

warlord = **military leader**, general • *a dictator and warlord who had oppressed his people*

warm AS AN ADJECTIVE 1 = **balmy**, mild, temperate, pleasant, fine, bright, sunny, agreeable, sultry, summery, moderately hot • *The weather was so warm I had to take off my jacket.*
OPPOSITES: cold, cool, freezing
2 = **cosy**, snug, toasty *(informal)*, comfortable, homely, comfy *(informal)* • *Nothing beats coming home to a warm house.*
3 = **moderately hot**, heated • *A warm bath will help to relax you.*
OPPOSITES: cold, cool, freezing
4 = **thermal**, winter, thick, chunky, woolly • *Some people can't afford warm clothes.*
OPPOSITES: cool
5 = **mellow**, relaxing, pleasant, agreeable, restful • *The basement hallway is painted a warm yellow.*
6 = **affable**, kindly, friendly, affectionate, loving, happy, tender, pleasant, cheerful, hearty, good-humoured,

W

amiable, amicable, cordial, sociable, genial, congenial, hospitable, approachable, amorous, good-natured, likable or likeable • *We were instantly attracted by his warm personality.*
OPPOSITES: cold, cool, unfriendly
7 = **near**, close, hot, near to the truth • *Am I getting warm? Am I right?*
▸ **AS A VERB** = **warm up**, heat, thaw (out), heat up • *She went to warm her hands by the fire.*
OPPOSITES: cool, freeze, cool down
▸ **IN PHRASES: warm down** = **cool down**, relax, unwind, wind down, cool off, stretch down • *He always warms down after training.*
warm something *or* **someone up** 1 = **heat**, thaw, heat up • *He blew on his hands to warm them up.*
2 = **rouse**, stimulate, stir up, animate, interest, excite, provoke, turn on *(slang)*, arouse, awaken, exhilarate, incite, whip up, galvanize, put some life into, get something *or* someone going, make something *or* someone enthusiastic • *They went on before us to warm up the audience.*
warm to someone = **take to**, begin to like, get on with, be taken with, become friendly with, hit it off with, conceive an affection for, grow attracted to, become on good terms with • *As we got to know him, we gradually warmed to him.*
warm to something = **become enthusiastic about**, become excited about, become supportive of, grow animated about • *At first I was shocked, but I soon warmed to the idea.*
warm up 1 = **become warm**, improve, brighten, get hotter • *The weather has warmed up a bit.*
2 = **limber up**, exercise, stretch, get ready, loosen up, prepare • *Make sure you warm up before you start the exercises.*

warm-blooded = **homeothermic** *or* **homeothermal** *(technical)* • *the theory that dinosaurs were warm-blooded*

warm-hearted = **kindly**, loving, kind, warm, gentle, generous, tender, pleasant, mild, sympathetic, affectionate, compassionate, hearty, cordial, genial, affable, good-natured, kind-hearted, tender-hearted • *a good-natured and warm-hearted woman loved by everyone*
OPPOSITES: mean, hard, cold-hearted

warmonger = **hawk**, aggressor, belligerent, militarist, jingoist, sabre-rattler • *The president was denounced by many as a dangerous warmonger.*

warmth 1 = **heat**, snugness, warmness, comfort, homeliness, hotness • *She went in, drawn by the warmth of the fire.*
OPPOSITES: cold, chill, coolness
2 = **affection**, feeling, love, goodwill, kindness, tenderness, friendliness, cheerfulness, amity, cordiality, affability, kindliness, heartiness, amorousness, hospitableness, fondness • *He greeted us both with warmth.*
OPPOSITES: hostility, indifference, austerity

warn 1 = **notify**, tell, remind, inform, alert, tip off, give notice, make someone aware, forewarn, apprise, give fair warning • *They warned him of the dangers of sailing alone.*
2 = **advise**, urge, recommend, counsel, caution, commend, exhort, admonish, put someone on his *or* her guard • *My mother warned me not to interfere.*

warning **AS A NOUN** 1 = **caution**, information, advice, injunction, notification, caveat, word to the wise • *health warnings on cigarette packets*
2 = **notice**, notification, word, sign, threat, tip, signal, alarm, announcement, hint, alert, tip-off *(informal)*, heads up *(U.S. & Canad.)* • *The soldiers opened fire without warning.*
3 = **omen**, sign, forecast, indication, token, prediction, prophecy, premonition, foreboding, portent, presage, augury, foretoken, rahui *(N.Z.)* • *a warning of impending doom*
4 = **reprimand**, talking-to *(informal)*, caution, censure, counsel, carpeting *(Brit. informal)*, rebuke, reproach, scolding, berating, ticking-off *(informal)*, chiding, dressing down *(informal)*, telling-off *(informal)*, admonition, upbraiding, reproof, remonstrance • *He was given a severe warning from the referee.*
5 = **example**, lesson, caution, deterrent, message, moral • *I hope that your story acts as a warning to other people.*
▸ **AS AN ADJECTIVE** = **cautionary**, threatening, ominous, premonitory, admonitory, monitory, bodeful • *Pain can act as a warning signal that something is wrong.*

warp **AS A VERB** 1 = **distort**, bend, twist, buckle, deform, disfigure, contort, misshape, malform • *Rainwater had warped the door's timber.*
2 = **become distorted**, bend, twist, contort, become deformed, become misshapen • *Plastic can warp in the sun.*
3 = **pervert**, twist, corrupt, degrade, deprave, debase, desecrate, debauch, lead astray • *Their minds have been warped by their experiences.*
▸ **AS A NOUN** = **twist**, turn, bend, defect, flaw, distortion, deviation, quirk, imperfection, kink, contortion, deformation • *small warps in the planking*

warrant **AS A VERB** 1 = **call for**, demand, require, merit, rate, commission, earn, deserve, permit, sanction, excuse, justify, license, authorize, entail, necessitate, be worthy of, give ground for • *The allegations are serious enough to warrant an investigation.*
2 = **guarantee**, declare, assure, pledge, promise, maintain, ensure, secure, swear, uphold, underwrite, affirm, certify, attest, vouch, avouch • *The ship owner must warrant that his vessel is seaworthy.*
▸ **AS A NOUN** 1 = **authorization**, permit, licence, permission, security, authority, commission, sanction, pledge, warranty, carte blanche • *Police have issued a warrant for his arrest.*
2 = **justification**, reason, grounds, defence, basis, licence, rationale, vindication, authority • *There is some warrant for his behaviour.*
3 = **ticket**, token, coupon, voucher, chit • *I'll have a travel warrant issued for you later today.*

warranty = **guarantee**, promise, contract, bond, pledge, certificate, assurance, covenant • *The equipment comes with a twelve-month warranty.*

warring = **hostile**, fighting, conflicting, opposed, contending, at war, embattled, belligerent, combatant, antagonistic, warlike, bellicose, ill-disposed • *He has called on the country's warring factions to end hostilities.*

warrior = **soldier**, combatant, fighter, gladiator, champion, brave, trooper, military man, fighting man, man-at-arms • *the 13th-century warrior, Genghis Khan*

wart = **growth**, lump, tumour, carbuncle, protuberance, verruca, excrescence • *the virus which produces warts on the skin*

wary 1 = **suspicious**, sceptical, mistrustful, suspecting, guarded, apprehensive, cagey *(informal)*, leery *(slang)*, distrustful, on your guard, chary, heedful • *My mother always told me to be wary of strangers.*
2 = **watchful**, careful, alert, cautious, prudent, attentive, vigilant, circumspect, heedful • *Keep a wary eye on children when they are playing near water.*
OPPOSITES: rash, reckless, careless

wash **AS A VERB** 1 = **clean**, scrub, sponge, rinse, scour, cleanse • *He got a job washing dishes in a pizza parlour.*
2 = **launder**, clean, wet, rinse, dry-clean, moisten • *The colours will fade a little each time you wash the shirt.*
3 = **rinse**, clean, scrub, lather • *It took a long time to wash the mud out of his hair.*
4 = **bathe**, bath, shower, take a bath *or* shower, clean yourself, soak, sponge, douse, freshen up, lave *(archaic)*, soap, scrub yourself down • *There was a sour smell about him, as if he had not washed for days.*
5 = **lap**, break, dash, roll, flow, surge, splash, slap, ripple,

swish, splosh, plash • *The sea washed against the shore.*
6 = carry, sweep, take, move, conduct, transport, convey • *The force of the water washed him back into the cave.*
7 = move, overcome, touch, upset, stir, disturb, perturb, surge through, tug at someone's heartstrings *(often facetious)* • *A wave of despair washed over him.*
8 *used in negative constructions* **= be plausible**, stand up, hold up, pass muster, hold water, stick, carry weight, be convincing, bear scrutiny • *All those excuses simply won't wash with me.*
▸ **AS A NOUN 1 = laundering**, cleaning, clean, cleansing • *That coat could do with a good wash.*
2 = bathe, bath, shower, dip, soak, scrub, shampoo, rinse, ablution • *She had a wash and changed her clothes.*
3 = backwash, slipstream, path, trail, train, track, waves, aftermath • *The wash from a passing ship overturned their dinghy.*
4 = splash, roll, flow, sweep, surge, swell, rise and fall, ebb and flow, undulation • *The steady wash of waves on the shore calmed me.*
5 = coat, film, covering, layer, screen, coating, stain, overlay, suffusion • *He painted a wash of colour over the entire surface.*
▸ **IN PHRASES: wash something away = erode**, corrode, eat into, wear something away, eat something away • *The topsoil is washed away by flood rains.*
wash something *or* **someone away = sweep away**, carry off, bear away • *Flood waters washed him away.*
wash something off = scrub off, remove, wipe off, rinse off, sponge off • *Sometimes he would forget to wash off his camouflage paint.*
wash something out = clean out, wipe out, rinse out, scrub out, sanitize, purify, disinfect, sponge out • *It was my job to wash out the fish tank.*
wash something up 1 = do, clean, scrub, rinse • *I bet you wash up their plates, too.*
2 = strand, ground, beach, wash ashore, cast away • *seaweed which had been washed up on a beach*
wash up = do the washing up, wash the dishes, do the dishes • *I ran some hot water and washed up.*

washed out 1 = pale, light, flat, mat, muted, drab, lacklustre, watery, lustreless • *The room was now dull and flat with washed-out colours.*
2 = wan, drawn, pale, pinched, blanched, haggard, bloodless, colourless, pallid, anaemic, ashen, chalky, peaky, deathly pale • *She tried to hide her washed-out face behind large, dark glasses.*
3 = faded, bleached, blanched, colourless, stonewashed • *a washed-out blue denim jacket*
4 = exhausted, drained, worn-out, tired-out, spent, drawn, done in *(informal)*, all in *(slang)*, fatigued, wiped out *(informal)*, weary, knackered *(slang)*, clapped out *(Austral. & N.Z. informal)*, dog-tired *(informal)*, zonked *(slang)*, dead on your feet *(informal)* • *She looked washed-out and listless.*
OPPOSITES: alert, lively, refreshed

washing
▸ **RELATED MANIA:** ablutomania

washout 1 = failure, disaster, disappointment, flop *(informal)*, mess, fiasco, dud *(informal)*, clunker *(informal)* • *The concert was a total washout.*
OPPOSITES: success, winner, victory
2 = loser, failure, incompetent, no-hoper, saddo *(Brit. slang)* • *As a husband, he's a complete washout.*

wasp
▸ **RELATED ADJECTIVE:** vespine
▸ **NAME OF HOME:** vespiary, bike
▹ *See panel* **Ants, bees and wasps**

waspish = bad-tempered, cross, irritable, grumpy, touchy, petulant, waxy *(informal, chiefly Brit.)*, ill-tempered, irascible, cantankerous, peppery, crabbed, tetchy, ratty *(Brit. & N.Z. informal)*, testy, chippy *(informal)*, fretful, peevish, crabby, splenetic, crotchety *(informal)*, snappish, liverish, captious, pettish • *Her tone was somewhat waspish and abrupt.*
OPPOSITES: pleasant, cheerful, good-natured

waste AS A VERB 1 = squander, throw away, blow *(slang)*, run through, lavish, misuse, dissipate, fritter away, frivol away *(informal)* • *We can't afford to waste money on another holiday.*
OPPOSITES: save, protect, preserve
2 *followed by* **away = wear out**, wither, deplete, debilitate, drain, undermine, exhaust, disable, consume, gnaw, eat away, corrode, enfeeble, sap the strength of, emaciate • *a cruel disease which wastes the muscles*
▸ **AS A NOUN 1 = squandering**, misuse, loss, expenditure, extravagance, frittering away, lost opportunity, dissipation, wastefulness, misapplication, prodigality, unthriftiness • *The whole project is a complete waste of time and resources.*
OPPOSITES: saving, economy, thrift
2 = rubbish, refuse, debris, sweepings, scrap, litter, garbage, trash, leftovers, offal, dross, dregs, leavings, offscourings • *This country produces 10 million tonnes of toxic waste every year.*
3 *usually plural* **= desert**, wilds, wilderness, void, solitude, wasteland • *the barren wastes of the Sahara*
▸ **AS AN ADJECTIVE 1 = unwanted**, useless, worthless, unused, leftover, superfluous, unusable, supernumerary • *suitable locations for the disposal of waste products*
OPPOSITES: needed, necessary, utilized
2 = uncultivated, wild, bare, barren, empty, devastated, dismal, dreary, desolate, unproductive, uninhabited • *Yarrow can be found growing wild on waste ground.*
OPPOSITES: cultivated, developed, productive
▸ **IN PHRASES: lay something waste = devastate**, destroy, ruin, spoil, total *(slang)*, sack, undo, trash *(slang)*, ravage, raze, kennet *(Austral. slang)*, jeff *(Austral. slang)*, despoil, wreak havoc upon, depredate *(rare)* • *The war has laid waste large regions of the country.*
waste away = decline, dwindle, wither, perish, sink, fade, crumble, decay, wane, ebb, wear out, atrophy • *People dying from cancer grow thin and visibly waste away.*

PROVERBS
It's no use making shoes for geese

wasted 1 = useless, unnecessary, pointless, needless • *I'm sorry you had a wasted journey.*
2 = missed, lost, blown *(informal)*, neglected, squandered • *a wasted opportunity to help*
3 = emaciated, weak, weakened, withered, frail, skeletal, shrivelled, shrunken, atrophied, scrawny, wizened • *exercises designed to help build up his wasted limbs*

wasteful = extravagant, lavish, prodigal, profligate, ruinous, spendthrift, uneconomical, improvident, unthrifty, thriftless • *the wasteful consumption of fuel*
OPPOSITES: sparing, economical, thrifty

wasteland = wilderness, waste, wild, desert, void • *Pollution has already turned vast areas into a wasteland.*

waster = layabout, loser, good-for-nothing, shirker, piker *(Austral. & N.Z. slang)*, drone, loafer, skiver *(Brit. slang)*, idler, ne'er-do-well, wastrel, malingerer, saddo *(Brit. slang)*, bludger *(Austral. & N.Z. informal)* • *His brother is just a useless waster.*

wastrel 1 = layabout, loser, shirker, good-for-nothing, piker *(Austral. & N.Z. slang)*, drone, loafer, waster, skiver *(Brit. slang)*, idler, ne'er-do-well, malingerer, saddo *(Brit. slang)*, bludger *(Austral. & N.Z. informal)* • *Her husband is a workshy, good-for-nothing wastrel.*
2 = spendthrift, squanderer, prodigal, profligate • *a wastrel who squandered his entire fortune*

watch AS A VERB 1 = look at, observe, regard, eye, see, mark, view, note, check, clock *(Brit. slang)*, stare at, contemplate, check out *(informal)*, look on, gaze at, pay attention to, eyeball *(slang)*, peer at, leer at, get a load of *(informal)*, feast your eyes on, take a butcher's at *(Brit.*

W

informal), take a dekko at *(Brit. slang)* • *The man was standing in the doorway watching him.*
2 = **spy on**, follow, track, monitor, keep an eye on, stake out, keep tabs on *(informal)*, keep watch on, keep under observation, keep under surveillance • *I had the feeling we were being watched.*
3 = **guard**, keep, mind, protect, tend, look after, shelter, take care of, safeguard, superintend • *Parents can't be expected to watch their children 24 hours a day.*
4 = **be careful about**, mind, consider, be aware of, take into account, bear in mind, attend to, pay attention to, keep in mind, pay heed to, exercise caution over • *Watch your diet and try to avoid too much salt.*
▸ **AS A NOUN** 1 = **wristwatch**, timepiece, pocket watch, clock, chronometer, chronograph • *He looked at his watch and checked the time.*
2 = **guard**, eye, attention, supervision, surveillance, notice, observation, inspection, vigil, lookout, vigilance • *Keep a close watch on him while I'm gone.*
▸ **IN PHRASES: watch out for something** *or* **someone** = **keep a sharp lookout for**, look out for, be alert for, be on the alert for, keep your eyes open for, be on your guard for, be on (the) watch for, be vigilant for, keep a weather eye open for, be watchful for, keep your eyes peeled *or* skinned for *(informal)* • *We had to watch out for unexploded mines.*
watch out *or* **watch it** *or* **watch yourself** = **be careful**, look out, be wary, be alert, be on the lookout, be vigilant, take heed, have a care, be on the alert, watch yourself, keep your eyes open, be watchful, be on your guard, mind out, be on (the) watch, keep a sharp lookout, keep a weather eye open, keep your eyes peeled *or* skinned *(informal)*, pay attention • *Watch out if you're walking home after dark.*
watch over something *or* **someone** 1 = **look after**, protect, guard, defend, preserve, shelter, shield, keep safe, stand guard over • *Guards were hired to watch over the houses as they were being built.*
2 = **superintend**, oversee, preside over, keep an eye on, direct • *a monitoring centre to watch over arms control*

PROVERBS
A watched kettle never boils

watchdog 1 = **guardian**, monitor, inspector, protector, custodian, scrutineer • *the government's consumer watchdog, the Office of Fair Trading*
2 = **guard dog** • *A good watchdog can be a faithful friend as well as a deterrent to intruders.*

watcher = **viewer**, witness, observer, spy, spectator, looker-on, onlooker, lookout, fly on the wall • *A perceptive watcher would have realised something was wrong.*

watchful = **alert**, attentive, vigilant, observant, guarded, suspicious, wary, on the lookout, circumspect, wide awake, on your toes, on your guard, on the watch, on the qui vive, heedful • *Children swam at the pool, under the watchful eye of the lifeguards.*
OPPOSITES: unaware, reckless, careless

watchman = **guard**, security guard, security man, custodian, caretaker • *He worked for ten years as a watchman in a factory.*

watchword = **motto**, slogan, maxim, byword, rallying cry, battle cry, catch phrase, tag-line, catchword, catchcry *(Austral.)* • *Caution has always been one of Mr Allan's watchwords.*

water **AS A NOUN** 1 = **liquid**, aqua, Adam's ale *or* wine, H_2O, wai *(N.Z.)* • *Could I have a glass of water, please?*
2 *often plural* = **sea**, main, waves, ocean, depths, briny • *the open waters of the Arctic Ocean*
▸ **AS A VERB** 1 = **sprinkle**, spray, soak, irrigate, damp, hose, dampen, drench, douse, moisten, souse, fertigate *(Austral.)* • *Water the plants once a week.*
2 = **get wet**, cry, weep, become wet, exude water • *His eyes were watering from the smoke.*
▸ **IN PHRASES: hold water** = **be sound**, work, stand up, be convincing, hold up, make sense, be logical, ring true, be credible, pass the test, be plausible, be tenable, bear examination *or* scrutiny • *This argument simply doesn't hold water.*
in hot water = **in trouble**, in a mess • *This remark landed him in hot water with the press.*
pour cold water on *or* **over something** = **dismiss**, reject, discount, discard, disregard, pooh-pooh • *My boss was quick to pour cold water on my suggestion.*
water something down 1 = **dilute**, add water to, put water in, weaken, water, doctor, thin, adulterate • *He always waters his whisky down before drinking it.*
2 = **moderate**, weaken, temper, curb, soften, qualify, tame, mute, play down, mitigate, tone down, downplay, adulterate, soft-pedal • *The government has no intention of watering down its social security reforms.*
▸ **RELATED ADJECTIVES:** aquatic, aqueous
▸ **RELATED PREFIXES:** hydro-, aqua-
▸ **RELATED MANIA:** hydromania
▸ **RELATED PHOBIA:** hydrophobia, aquaphobia

QUOTATIONS
Water, water, every where,
And all the boards did shrink;
Water, water, every where,
Nor any drop to drink.
[Samuel Taylor Coleridge *The Ancient Mariner*]
Water taken in moderation cannot hurt anybody
[Mark Twain *Notebook*]

WATER SPORTS

aquabobbing	rowing	swimming
canoeing	sailing	water polo
canoe polo	skin diving	water-skiing
diving	surfing	windsurfing
parasailing	swimming	yachting
powerboat racing	synchronized	

waterfall = **cascade**, fall, cataract, chute, linn *(Scot.)*, force *(Northern English dialect)* • *Angel Falls, the world's highest waterfall*

WATERFALLS

Angel Falls	Kaieteur Falls	Sutherland Falls
Churchill Falls	Niagara Falls	Tysse
Cleve-Garth	Ormeli	Vestre Mardola
Cuquenan	Pilao	Victoria Falls
Iguaçú Falls	Ribbon	Yellowstone Falls
Itatinga	Roraima	Yosemite Falls

waterlogged = **soaked**, saturated, drenched, sodden, streaming, dripping, sopping, wet through, wringing wet, droukit *or* drookit *(Scot.)* • *The football match is off because of a waterlogged pitch.*

waterproof **AS AN ADJECTIVE** = **watertight**, water-resistant, impermeable, water-repellent, coated, proofed, waxed, weatherproof, damp-proof, rubberized • *The tent is completely waterproof.*
▸ **AS A NOUN** = **raincoat**, mac *(Brit. informal)*, anorak, mackintosh, oilskin, cagoule, sou'wester • *Put on your waterproof, it's raining!*
▸ **AS A PLURAL NOUN** = **oilskins**, oilies *(informal)* • *He was wearing waterproofs over his clothes.*

watershed = **turning point**, defining moment, pivotal moment, tipping point • *Her election in 1990 was a watershed in Irish politics.*

watertight 1 = **waterproof**, hermetically sealed, sealed, water-resistant, sound, coated, impermeable, weatherproof, water-repellent, damp-proof, rubberized • *The batteries are enclosed in a watertight compartment.*
OPPOSITES: leaky
2 = **foolproof**, firm, sound, perfect, conclusive, flawless, undeniable, unassailable, airtight, indisputable, impregnable, irrefutable, unquestionable, incontrovertible • *The police had a watertight case against their suspect.*
OPPOSITES: weak, uncertain, flawed

watery 1 = **pale**, thin, weak, faint, feeble, washed-out, wan, colourless, anaemic, insipid, wishy-washy *(informal)* • *A watery light began to show through the branches.*
2 = **diluted**, thin, weak, dilute, watered-down, tasteless, runny, insipid, washy, adulterated, wishy-washy *(informal)*, flavourless, waterish • *a plateful of watery cabbage soup*
OPPOSITES: concentrated, industrial-strength *(chiefly humorous)*, strong
3 = **wet**, damp, moist, soggy, humid, marshy, squelchy • *a wide watery sweep of marshland*
4 = **liquid**, fluid, aqueous, hydrous • *There was a watery discharge from her ear.*
5 = **tearful**, moist, weepy, lachrymose *(formal)*, tear-filled, rheumy • *Emma's eyes were red and watery.*

wave AS A VERB 1 = **signal**, sign, gesture, gesticulate • *He waved to us from across the street.*
2 = **guide**, point, direct, indicate, signal, motion, gesture, nod, beckon, point in the direction • *The policeman waved to us to go on.*
3 = **brandish**, swing, flourish, wield, wag, move something to and fro, shake • *The protesters were waving banners and shouting.*
4 = **flutter**, flap, stir, waver, shake, swing, sway, ripple, wag, quiver, undulate, oscillate, move to and fro • *Flags were waving gently in the breeze.*
▸ AS A NOUN 1 = **gesture**, sign, signal, indication, gesticulation • *Paddy spotted Mary Anne and gave her a cheery wave.*
2 = **ripple**, breaker, sea surf, swell, ridge, roller, comber, billow • *the sound of waves breaking on the shore*
3 = **curl**, coil, kink, undulation, loop • *His fingers touched the thick waves of her hair.*
4 = **vibration**, ripple, resonance, tremor, reverberation, judder, pulsation • *The blast wave crushed his breath.*
5 = **surge**, welling up, rush, flood, thrill, stab, shiver, feeling, tingle, spasm, upsurge, frisson • *She felt a wave of grief flood over her.*
6 = **outbreak**, trend, rash, upsurge, sweep, flood, tendency, surge, ground swell • *the current wave of violence in schools*
7 = **stream**, flood, surge, spate, current, movement, flow, rush, tide, torrent, deluge, upsurge • *the wave of immigrants flooding into the country*
▸ IN PHRASES: **make waves** = **cause trouble**, stir up trouble • *If I start making waves I'll end up getting the sack.*
wave something *or* **someone aside** *or* **away** = **dismiss**, reject, ignore, discount, disregard, play down, shrug off, spurn, rebuff, brush aside, repudiate, pooh-pooh *(informal)*, treat with contempt • *Rachel waved aside his protests.*
wave something *or* **someone down** = **flag down**, stop, signal, summon, shout to • *He vainly attempted to wave down a taxi.*

wavelength IN PHRASES: **on the same wavelength** = **in tune**, the same, similar, alike, cut from the same cloth, like two peas in a pod • *We get on well because we're on the same wavelength.*

waver 1 = **hesitate**, dither *(chiefly Brit.)*, vacillate, be irresolute, falter, fluctuate, seesaw, blow hot and cold *(informal)*, be indecisive, hum and haw, be unable to decide, shillyshally *(informal)*, be unable to make up your mind, swither *(Scot.)* • *Some military commanders wavered over whether to support the coup.*
OPPOSITES: determine, resolve, be decisive
2 = **flicker**, wave, shake, vary, reel, weave, sway, tremble, wobble, fluctuate, quiver, undulate, totter • *The shadows of the dancers wavered on the wall.*

wavy = **curving**, curly, kinked, curling, rippled, undulating • *She had short, wavy brown hair.*

wax AS A VERB 1 = **increase**, rise, grow, develop, mount, expand, swell, enlarge, fill out, magnify, get bigger, dilate, become larger • *Portugal and Spain had vast empires which waxed and waned.*
OPPOSITES: contract, decline, wane
2 = **become fuller**, become larger, enlarge, get bigger • *One should plant seeds and cuttings when the moon is waxing.*
3 = **become**, get, grow, come to be, turn • *He waxed eloquent about the discovery of new worlds.*
▸ IN PHRASES: **wax lyrical** = **enthuse**, rave, gush, get carried away, become enthusiastic • *He waxed lyrical about the loyalty of his employees.*

waxen = **pale**, white, ghastly, wan, bloodless, colourless, pallid, anaemic, ashen, whitish • *His skin was waxen and pale and his eyes were sunken.*

way AS A NOUN 1 = **method**, means, system, process, approach, practice, scheme, technique, manner, plan, procedure, mode, course of action • *Freezing is a great way to preserve most foods.*
2 = **manner**, style, fashion, mode • *He had a strange way of talking.*
3 = **aspect**, point, sense, detail, feature, particular, regard, respect, characteristic, facet • *In some ways, we are better off than we were before.*
4 *often plural* = **custom**, manner, habit, idiosyncrasy, style, practice, nature, conduct, personality, characteristic, trait, usage, wont, tikanga *(N.Z.)* • *You'll have to get used to my mother's odd little ways.*
5 = **route**, direction, course, road, path • *Can you tell me the way to the station?*
6 = **access**, street, road, track, channel, route, path, lane, trail, avenue, highway, pathway, thoroughfare • *He came round the back way.*
7 = **journey**, approach, advance, progress, passage • *She said she'd pick me up on her way to work.*
8 = **room**, opening, space, elbowroom • *The ranks of soldiers parted and made way for her.*
9 = **distance**, length, stretch, journey, trail • *We've a long way to go yet.*
10 = **condition**, state, shape *(informal)*, situation, status, circumstances, plight, predicament, fettle • *He's in a bad way, but he'll live.*
11 = **will**, demand, wish, desire, choice, aim, pleasure, ambition • *It's bad for a child to get its own way all the time.*
▸ IN PHRASES: **by the way** = **incidentally**, in passing, in parenthesis, en passant, by the bye • *By the way, how did your seminar go?*
get in the way of something = **interfere with**, hamper, hinder, obstruct, impede, be a drag upon *(informal)* • *She never let her feelings get in the way of her job.*
give way 1 = **collapse**, give, fall, crack, break down, subside, cave in, crumple, fall to pieces, go to pieces • *The whole ceiling gave way and fell in on us.*
2 = **concede**, yield, back down, make concessions, accede, acquiesce, acknowledge defeat • *I knew he'd give way if I nagged enough.*
give way to something = **be replaced by**, be succeeded by, be supplanted by • *The numbness gave way to anger*
on the way *or* **on your way** = **coming**, approaching, en route, in transit, close, near, travelling, proceeding, imminent • *He's on his way here now.*

W

under way = in progress, going, started, moving, begun, on the move, in motion, afoot, on the go *(informal)* • *A full-scale security operation is now under way.*
way of life 1 = customs, practices, traditions, rituals, conventions, unwritten laws, tikanga *(N.Z.)* • *the traditional way of life of the Yanomami Indians*
2 = habit, second nature • *cities where violence is a way of life*
ways and means = capability, methods, procedure, way, course, ability, resources, capacity, tools, wherewithal • *discussing ways and means of improving productivity*

PROVERBS
The longest way round is the shortest way home

wayfarer = traveller, walker, trekker, wanderer, journeyer, gypsy, rover, voyager, nomad, itinerant, globetrotter, bird of passage • *40,000 motels catering for weary wayfarers*
waylay 1 = attack, surprise, hold up, ambush, set upon, lie in wait for, catch • *The trucks are being waylaid by bandits.*
2 = accost, stop, intercept, pounce on, swoop down on • *He was forever waylaying me for chats in the corridor.*
way-out = outlandish, eccentric, unconventional, unorthodox, advanced, wild, out there *(slang)*, crazy, bizarre, weird, progressive, experimental, avant-garde, far-out *(slang)*, off-the-wall *(slang)*, oddball *(informal)*, offbeat, freaky *(slang)*, outré, wacko or whacko *(informal)*, off the air *(Austral. slang)* • *Some of his suggestions are pretty way-out.*
wayward = erratic, unruly, wilful, unmanageable, disobedient, contrary, unpredictable, stubborn, perverse, rebellious, fickle, intractable, capricious, obstinate, headstrong, changeable, flighty, incorrigible, obdurate, ungovernable, self-willed, refractory, insubordinate, undependable, inconstant, mulish, cross-grained, contumacious, froward *(archaic)* • *wayward children with a history of behavioural problems*
OPPOSITES: reliable, obliging, obedient
weak 1 = feeble, exhausted, frail, debilitated, spent, wasted, weakly, tender, delicate, faint, fragile, shaky, sickly, languid, puny, decrepit, unsteady, infirm, anaemic, effete, enervated • *I was too weak to move my arms and legs.*
OPPOSITES: strong, tough, healthy
2 = deficient, wanting, poor, lacking, inadequate, pathetic, faulty, substandard, under-strength • *His eyesight had always been weak.*
OPPOSITES: able, effective, capable
3 = ineffectual, pathetic, cowardly, powerless, soft, impotent, indecisive, infirm, spineless, boneless, timorous, weak-kneed *(informal)*, namby-pamby, irresolute • *a weak man who let his wife walk all over him*
OPPOSITES: firm, resolute
4 = slight, faint, feeble, pathetic, shallow, hollow • *He managed a weak smile and said, 'Don't worry about me.'*
5 = faint, soft, quiet, slight, small, low, poor, distant, dull, muffled, imperceptible • *Her voice was so weak we could hardly hear her.*
OPPOSITES: powerful, loud
6 = fragile, brittle, flimsy, unsound, fine, delicate, frail, dainty, breakable • *The animals escaped through a weak spot in the fence.*
7 = unsafe, exposed, vulnerable, helpless, wide open, unprotected, untenable, defenceless, unguarded • *The trade unions are in a very weak position.*
OPPOSITES: safe, secure, invulnerable
8 = unconvincing, unsatisfactory, lame, invalid, flimsy, inconclusive, pathetic • *The evidence against him was too weak to hold up in court.*
OPPOSITES: powerful, convincing, obvious
9 = tasteless, thin, diluted, watery, runny, insipid, wishy-washy *(informal)*, under-strength, milk-and-water, waterish • *a weak cup of tea*
OPPOSITES: strong, potent, tasty
10 = dim, pale, faint, muted, feeble, dull, wan • *The light was so weak we could barely see anything.*

QUOTATIONS
The weakest goes to the wall
[William Shakespeare *Romeo and Juliet*]

weaken 1 = reduce, undermine, moderate, diminish, temper, impair, lessen, sap, mitigate, invalidate, soften up, take the edge off, disempower • *Her opponents believe that her authority has been fatally weakened.*
OPPOSITES: increase, improve, boost
2 = wane, fail, diminish, dwindle, lower, flag, fade, give way, lessen, abate, droop, ease up • *Family structures are weakening and breaking up.* • *The storm was finally beginning to weaken.*
OPPOSITES: increase, grow, improve
3 = sap the strength of, tire, exhaust, debilitate, depress, disable, cripple, incapacitate, enfeeble, enervate • *Malnutrition weakens the patient.*
OPPOSITES: strengthen, revitalize, invigorate
4 = dilute, cut, thin, water down, debase, thin out, adulterate • *a glass of whisky weakened with soda*
weakling = sissy, drip *(informal)*, coward, wimp *(informal)*, wet *(Brit. informal)*, mouse, jessie *(Scot. slang)*, pussy *(slang, chiefly U.S.)*, doormat *(slang)*, wuss *(slang)*, milksop • *a craven weakling with no backbone or moral fibre*
weakness 1 = frailty, fatigue, exhaustion, fragility, infirmity, debility, feebleness, faintness, decrepitude, enervation • *Symptoms of anaemia include weakness and fatigue.*
OPPOSITES: strength, power, health
2 = liking, appetite, penchant, soft spot, passion, inclination, fondness, predilection, proclivity, partiality, proneness • *Carol has a great weakness for ice cream.*
OPPOSITES: dislike, hatred, aversion
3 = powerlessness, vulnerability, impotence, meekness, irresolution, spinelessness, ineffectuality, timorousness, cravenness, cowardliness • *People are always taking advantage of his weakness.*
4 = inadequacy, deficiency, transparency, lameness, hollowness, implausibility, flimsiness, unsoundness, tenuousness • *She was quick to spot the weakness in his argument.*
5 = failing, fault, defect, deficiency, flaw, shortcoming, blemish, imperfection, Achilles' heel, chink in your armour, lack • *His main weakness was his violent temper.*
OPPOSITES: advantage, strength, strong point
▸ RELATED PHOBIA: asthenophobia

PROVERBS
A chain is no stronger than its weakest link

weak-willed = irresolute, soft, feeble, indecisive, infirm, spineless, wimpish *(informal)*, weak-kneed *(informal)*, feeble-minded, namby-pamby, weak-minded, wussy *(slang)* • *He is too weak-willed to stop smoking.*
weal = mark, scar, welt, ridge, streak, stripe, wheal, wale, contusion • *the red weals left across his chest by the whip*
wealth 1 = riches, fortune, prosperity, affluence, goods, means, money, funds, property, cash, resources, substance, possessions, big money, big bucks *(informal, chiefly U.S.)*, opulence, top dollar *(informal)*, megabucks *(U.S. & Canad. slang)*, lucre, wonga *(slang)*, pelf • *The discovery of oil brought untold wealth to the island.*
OPPOSITES: poverty, deprivation, penury
2 = property, funds, capital, estate, assets, fortune, possessions • *His personal wealth is estimated at over 50 million dollars.*
3 = abundance, store, plenty, richness, bounty, profusion, fullness, cornucopia, plenitude, copiousness • *The city boasts a wealth of beautiful churches*
OPPOSITES: want, need, lack
▸ RELATED MANIA: plutomania

QUOTATIONS

In every well-governed state, wealth is a sacred thing; in democracies it is the only sacred thing
[Anatole France *L'Île des pingouins*]

It is easier for a camel to go through the eye of a needle, than for a rich man to enter the kingdom of God
[*Bible: St. Mark*]

I am rich beyond the dreams of avarice
[Edward Moore *The Gamester*]

wealthy = **rich**, prosperous, affluent, well-off, loaded *(slang)*, comfortable, flush *(informal)*, in the money *(informal)*, opulent, well-heeled *(informal)*, well-to-do, moneyed, quids in *(slang)*, filthy rich, rolling in it *(slang)*, on Easy Street *(informal)*, stinking rich *(slang)*, made of money *(informal)*, minted *(Brit. slang)* • *a wealthy international businessman*
OPPOSITES: broke *(informal)*, short, poor

weapon

QUOTATIONS

The only arms I allow myself to use, silence, exile, and cunning
[James Joyce *A Portrait of the Artist as a Young Man*]

Our swords shall play the orators for us
[Christopher Marlowe *Tamburlaine the Great*]

Weapons are like money; no one knows the meaning of *enough*
[Martin Amis *Einstein's Monsters*]

▹ *See panels* **Bombs; Guns; Missiles; Swords and other weapons with blades; Types of club; Weapons**

wear AS A VERB 1 = **be dressed in**, have on, dress in, be clothed in, carry, sport *(informal)*, bear, put on, clothe yourself in • *He was wearing a dark-green uniform.*
2 = **show**, present, bear, display, assume, put on, exhibit • *Millson's face wore a smug expression.*
3 = **deteriorate**, fray, wear thin, become threadbare • *The living room carpet is beginning to wear.*
4 = **last**, survive, endure, hold up, bear up, prove durable, resist wear, stand up to wear • *Casual shoes need to wear well.*
5 = **accept** *(Brit. informal)*, take, allow, permit, stomach, swallow *(informal)*, brook, stand for, fall for, put up with *(informal)*, countenance • *I asked if I could work part-time, but the company wouldn't wear it.*
▸ AS A NOUN 1 = **clothes**, things, dress, gear *(informal)*, attire, habit, outfit, costume, threads *(slang)*, garments, apparel, garb, raiments • *The shops stock an extensive range of beach wear.*
2 = **usefulness**, use, service, employment, utility, mileage *(informal)* • *You'll get more wear out of a car if you look after it properly.*
3 = **damage**, wear and tear, use, erosion, friction, deterioration, depreciation, attrition, corrosion, abrasion • *a large, well-upholstered armchair which showed signs of wear*
OPPOSITES: repair, maintenance, conservation
▸ IN PHRASES: **wear down** = **be eroded**, erode, be consumed, wear away • *Eventually the parts start to wear down.*
wear off 1 = **subside**, disappear, fade, weaken, diminish, decrease, dwindle, wane, ebb, abate, peter out, lose strength, lose effect • *Her initial excitement soon began to wear off.*
2 = **rub away**, disappear, fade, abrade • *The paint is discoloured and little bits have worn off.*
wear on = **pass**, progress, proceed, go by *or* past, lapse, elapse • *As the days wore on Brad became increasingly depressed.*
wear out = **deteriorate**, become worn, become useless, wear through, fray • *Eventually the artificial joint wears out and has to be replaced.*
wear someone down = **undermine**, reduce, chip away at *(informal)*, fight a war of attrition against, overcome gradually • *his sheer persistence in wearing down the opposition*
wear someone out = **exhaust**, tire, fatigue, weary, impair, sap, prostrate, knacker *(slang)*, frazzle *(informal)*, fag someone out *(informal)*, enervate • *The past few days had really worn him out.*
wear something down = **erode**, grind down, consume, impair, corrode, grind down, rub away, abrade • *Rabbits wear down their teeth with constant gnawing.*
wear something out = **erode**, go through, consume, use up, wear holes in, make worn • *He wore his shoes out wandering around the streets.*
wear well = **last**, stand up, endure, hold up, bear up, be durable • *These shoes haven't worn very well.*

weariness = **tiredness**, fatigue, exhaustion, lethargy, drowsiness, lassitude, languor, listlessness, prostration, enervation • *Overcome with weariness, he collapsed.*
OPPOSITES: drive, energy, vitality

wearing = **tiresome**, trying, taxing, tiring, exhausting, fatiguing, oppressive, exasperating, irksome, wearisome • *She finds his continual demands very wearing.*
OPPOSITES: light, easy, refreshing

wearisome = **tedious**, trying, wearing, boring, exhausting, dull, annoying, fatiguing, troublesome, oppressive, exasperating, tiresome, monotonous, prosaic, humdrum, burdensome, uninteresting, mind-numbing, irksome, bothersome, vexatious • *a long and wearisome task*
OPPOSITES: interesting, stimulating

weary AS AN ADJECTIVE 1 = **tired**, exhausted, drained, worn out, spent, done in *(informal)*, flagging, all in *(slang)*, fatigued, wearied, sleepy, fagged *(informal)*, whacked *(Brit. informal)*, jaded, drooping, knackered *(slang)*, drowsy, clapped out *(Austral. & N.Z. informal)*, enervated, ready to drop, dog-tired *(informal)*, zonked *(slang)*, dead beat *(informal)*, asleep *or* dead on your feet *(informal)* • *She sank to the ground, too weary to walk another step.*
OPPOSITES: fresh, stimulated, energetic
2 = **fed up**, bored, sick *(informal)*, discontented, impatient, indifferent, jaded, sick and tired *(informal)*, browned-off *(informal)* • *He was growing weary of his wife's constant complaints.*
OPPOSITES: patient, excited, amused
3 = **tiring**, taxing, wearing, arduous, tiresome, laborious,

WEAPONS

Projectile weapons

ballista	catapult	grapeshot	onager	torpedo
bazooka	crossbow	gun	quarrel	trebuchet
blowpipe	fléchette	longbow	rifle grenade	

Miscellaneous weapons

biological warfare	club	germ warfare	Mace *(trademark)*	pepper spray
bomb	death ray	Greek fire	mustard gas	poison gas
chemical warfare	flame-thrower	knuckle-duster	napalm	

W

irksome, wearisome, enervative • *a long, weary journey in search of food and water*
OPPOSITES: exciting, refreshing, invigorating
▸ **AS A VERB** 1 = **grow tired**, tire, sicken, have had enough, become bored • *He had wearied of teaching in state universities.*
2 = **bore**, annoy, plague, sicken, jade, exasperate, vex, irk, try the patience of, make discontented • *Her nagging and criticism wearied him so much that he left her.*
OPPOSITES: interest, excite, amuse
3 = **tire**, tax, burden, drain, fatigue, fag *(informal)*, sap, wear out, debilitate, take it out of *(informal)*, tire out, enervate • *Her pregnancy wearied her to the point of exhaustion.*
OPPOSITES: stimulate, revive, invigorate

wearying = **tiring**, trying, taxing, grinding, wearing, heavy, tough, draining, exhausting, punishing, exacting, fatiguing, rigorous, gruelling, sapping, arduous, laborious, back-breaking, enervating • *the wearying hours of scrubbing and polishing*

weasel
▸ **RELATED ADJECTIVE:** musteline
▸ **NAME OF MALE:** whittret

weather AS A NOUN = **climate**, conditions, temperature, forecast, outlook, meteorological conditions, elements • *I don't like hot weather much.*
▸ **AS A VERB** 1 = **toughen**, season, wear, expose, harden • *The stones have been weathered by centuries of wind and rain.*
2 = **withstand**, stand, suffer, survive, overcome, resist, brave, endure, come through, get through, rise above, live through, ride out, make it through *(informal)*, surmount, pull through, stick it out *(informal)*, bear up against • *The company has weathered the recession.*
OPPOSITES: yield to, surrender to, give in to
▸ **IN PHRASES: under the weather** = **ill**, unwell, poorly *(informal)*, sick, rough *(informal)*, crook *(Austral. & N.Z. informal)*, ailing, not well, seedy *(informal)*, below par, queasy, out of sorts, nauseous, off-colour *(Brit.)*, indisposed, peaky, ropy *(Brit. informal)*, wabbit *(Scot. informal)* • *I'm feeling a bit under the weather today.*

QUOTATIONS
Summer has set in with its usual severity
[Samuel Taylor Coleridge]
'Tis the hard grey weather
Breeds hard English men
[Charles Kingsley *The Three Fishers*]
weather: the climate of an hour
[Ambrose Bierce *The Devil's Dictionary*]
PROVERBS
Red sky at night, shepherd's delight; red sky in the morning, shepherd's warning

▹ *See panels* **Regions of the atmosphere; Types of cloud; Weather; Winds**

weathered = **weather-beaten**, worn, crumbling, eroded, bleached, discoloured • *the weathered bricks of an old farmhouse*

weave 1 = **knit**, twist, intertwine, plait, unite, introduce, blend, incorporate, merge, mat, fuse, braid, entwine, intermingle, interlace • *She then weaves the fibres together to make the traditional Awatum basket.*
2 = **zigzag**, wind, move in and out, crisscross, weave your way • *The cyclists wove in and out of the traffic.*
3 = **create**, tell, recount, narrate, make, build, relate, make up, spin, construct, invent, put together, unfold, contrive, fabricate • *The author weaves a compelling tale of life in London during the war.*
4 = **incorporate**, work, include, mix, blend, integrate, merge, interlace • *She weaves imaginative elements into her poems.*

web 1 = **cobweb**, spider's web • *He was caught like a fly in a web.*
2 = **mesh**, net, netting, screen, webbing, weave, lattice, latticework, interlacing, lacework • *a delicate web of fine lace*
3 = **tangle**, series, network, mass, chain, knot, maze, toils, nexus • *a complex web of financial dealings*
▸ **RELATED ADJECTIVE:** retiary

wed 1 = **get married to**, espouse, get hitched to *(slang)*, be united to, plight your troth to *(old-fashioned)*, get spliced to *(informal)*, take as your husband or wife • *In 1952 he wed his childhood sweetheart.*
OPPOSITES: divorce, separate from, part from
2 = **get married**, marry, be united, tie the knot *(informal)*, take the plunge *(informal)*, get hitched *(slang)*, get spliced *(informal)*, become man and wife, plight your troth *(old-fashioned)* • *The pair wed in a secret ceremony in front of just nine guests.*
OPPOSITES: part, split (up), divorce
3 = **unite**, combine, bring together, amalgamate, join, link, marry, ally, connect, blend, integrate, merge, unify, make one, fuse, weld, interweave, yoke, coalesce, commingle • *a film which weds stunning visuals and a first-class score*
OPPOSITES: split (up), divide, sever

wedded 1 = **married**, marital, nuptial, conjugal, connubial • *a romantic fantasy of wedded bliss*
2 *with* **to** = **devoted to**, dedicated to, hell-bent on, obsessive about, fixated on, fanatical about • *law enforcement agencies wedded to heavy-handed methods*

wedding = **marriage**, nuptials, wedding ceremony, marriage ceremony, marriage service, wedding service, nuptial rite, espousals • *A lot of women only marry in church for the traditional white wedding.*

wedge AS A VERB = **squeeze**, force, lodge, jam, crowd, block, stuff, pack, thrust, ram, cram, stow • *He wedged himself between the door and the radiator.*
▸ **AS A NOUN** = **block**, segment, lump, chunk, triangle, slab, hunk, chock, wodge *(Brit. informal)* • *a wedge of cheese*

wedlock = **marriage**, matrimony, holy matrimony, married state, conjugal bond • *One in every four children are now born outside wedlock.*

wee = **little**, small, minute, tiny, miniature, insignificant, negligible, microscopic, diminutive, minuscule, teeny, itsy-bitsy *(informal)*, teeny-weeny, Lilliputian, titchy *(Brit. informal)*, teensy-weensy, pygmy *or* pigmy • *Fancy being so scared of a wee spider!*

weed
▸ **IN PHRASES: weed something** *or* **someone out AS A VERB** = **eliminate**, remove, shed, get rid of, eradicate, dispense with, uproot, root out, separate out, extirpate • *He is keen to weed out any applicants whom he believes to be frauds.*

weedy = **weak**, thin, frail, skinny, feeble, ineffectual, puny, undersized, weak-kneed *(informal)*, namby-pamby, nerdy *or* nurdy *(slang)* • *a neurotic, weedy little man*

week
▸ **RELATED ADJECTIVES:** hebdomadal, hebdomadary

weekly AS AN ADJECTIVE = **once a week**, hebdomadal, hebdomadary • *her weekly visit to her parents' house*
▸ **AS AN ADVERB** = **every week**, once a week, by the week, hebdomadally • *The group meets weekly.*

weep 1 = **cry**, shed tears, sob, whimper, complain, keen, greet *(Scot. or archaic)*, moan, mourn, grieve, lament, whinge *(informal)*, blubber, snivel, ululate, blub *(slang)*, boohoo • *She began to weep, tears running down her face.*
OPPOSITES: celebrate, delight, rejoice
2 = **run**, fester, suppurate, exude pus • *The skin can crack and weep.*

weepy AS AN ADJECTIVE = **tearful**, crying, weeping, sobbing, whimpering, close to tears, blubbering, lachrymose, on the verge of tears • *After her mother's death she was depressed and weepy for months.*
▸ **AS A NOUN** = **tear-jerker** *(informal)* • *The film is an old-fashioned weepy with fine performances by both stars.*

WEATHER

Weather descriptions

arctic, baking, balmy, bland, blistering, blustery, breezy, clammy, clear, clement, close, cloudy, cold, dirty, dreich (*Scot.*), drizzly, dry, dull, filthy, fine, foggy, foul, freezing (*informal*), fresh, hazy, hot, humid, icy, inclement, mild, misty, muggy, nippy, overcast, parky (*informal*), perishing (*informal*), rainy, raw, scorching (*informal*), showery, snowy, sticky, stormy, sultry, sunny, thundery, tropical, wet, windy, wintry

Weather phenomena

acid rain, ball lightning, breeze, cloud, cold snap, cyclone, drizzle, dust devil, dust storm, fog, freeze, gale, gust, haar (*Scot.*), hail, heatwave, hurricane, ice, lightning, mist, peasouper (*chiefly Brit.*), precipitation, pressure, rain, sandstorm, sheet lightning, shower, sleet, smirr (*Scot.*), snow, squall, storm, sunshine, tempest (*literary*), thaw, thunder, tidal wave, tornado, tsunami, typhoon, waterspout, whirlwind, wind, willy-willy (*Austral.*), zephyr

Meteorological terms

anticyclone, cold front, cyclone, depression, front, heat-island, isallobar, isobar, lee wave, occluded front, ridge, scud, synoptic chart, thermal, trough, virga, warm front

Gatherers of weather data

dropsonde, meteorograph, Meteorological Office, pilot balloon, radiosonde, weather ship, weather station, weatherman, weatherwoman

Measuring instruments

Instrument	Phenomenon measured
anemometer	wind velocity
anemoscope	wind direction
atmometer	rate of water evaporation into atmosphere
barograph	atmospheric pressure
barometer	atmospheric pressure
baroscope	atmospheric pressure
hygrometer	humidity
maximum-minimum thermometer	temperature variation
nephoscope	cloud velocity, altitude, and direction of movement
psychrometer	humidity
rain gauge	rainfall and snowfall
rawinsonde	atmospheric wind velocity
Stevenson's screen	temperature
sunshine recorder	hours of sunshine
thermometer	temperature
weathercock	wind direction
weather vane	wind direction
wet-and-dry-bulb thermometer	humidity
wind gauge	wind velocity
wind tee	wind direction

weigh AS A VERB **1 = have a weight of**, tip the scales at (*informal*) • *His wife weighs over 22 stone.*
2 = measure the weight of, put someone *or* something on the scales, measure how heavy someone *or* something is • *They counted and weighed the fruits.*
3 = consider, study, examine, contemplate, evaluate, ponder, mull over, think over, eye up, reflect upon, give thought to, meditate upon, deliberate upon • *He is weighing the possibility of filing charges against the doctor.*
4 = compare, balance, contrast, juxtapose, place side by side • *We must weigh the pros and cons of each method.*
5 = matter, carry weight, cut any ice (*informal*), impress, tell, count, have influence, be influential • *His opinion doesn't weigh much with me, I'm afraid.*
▸ IN PHRASES: **weigh on someone = oppress**, burden, depress, distress, plague, prey, torment, hang over, bear down, gnaw at, cast down, take over • *The separation weighed on both of them.*
weigh someone down 1 = burden, overload, encumber, overburden, tax, weight, strain, handicap, saddle, hamper • *The soldiers were weighed down by their heavy packs.*
2 = oppress, worry, trouble, burden, depress, haunt, plague, get down, torment, take control of, hang over, beset, prey on, bear down, gnaw at, cast down, press down on, overburden, weigh upon, lie heavy on • *He could not shake off the guilt that weighed him down.*
weigh someone up = assess, judge, gauge, appraise, eye someone up, size someone up (*informal*) • *As soon as I walked into his office I could see him weighing me up.*
weigh something out = measure, dole out, apportion, deal out • *I weighed out portions of tea and sugar.*

weight AS A NOUN **1 = heaviness**, mass, burden, poundage, pressure, load, gravity, tonnage, heft (*informal*), avoirdupois • *Try to reduce the weight of the load.*
2 = load, mass, ballast, heavy object • *Straining to lift heavy weights can cause back injury.*
3 = importance, force, power, moment, value, authority, influence, bottom, impact, import, muscle, consequence, substance, consideration, emphasis, significance, sway, clout (*informal*), leverage, efficacy, mana (*N.Z.*),

persuasiveness • *That argument no longer carries much weight.*
4 = **burden**, pressure, load, strain, oppression, albatross, millstone, encumbrance • *He heaved a sigh of relief. 'That's a great weight off my mind.'*
5 = **preponderance**, mass, bulk, main body, most, majority, onus, lion's share, greatest force, main force, best *or* better part • *The weight of evidence suggests that he is guilty.*
▸ **AS A VERB** 1 *often with* **down** = **load**, ballast, make heavier • *The body was weighted down with bricks.*
2 = **bias**, load, slant, unbalance • *The electoral law is still heavily weighted in favour of the ruling party.*
3 = **burden**, handicap, oppress, impede, weigh down, encumber, overburden • *His life was a struggle, weighted with failures and disappointments.*
▹ *See panel* **Weights and measures**

WEIGHTS AND MEASURES

IMPERIAL SYSTEM

Linear	**Square**	**Weight**
mile	square mile	ton
furlong	acre	hundredweight
rod	square rod	stone
yard	square yard	pound
foot	square foot	ounce
inch	square inch	–
mil	–	–
Land	**Volume**	**Liquid volume**
square mile	cubic yard	gallon
acre	cubic foot	quart
square rod	cubic inch	pint
square yard	–	fluid ounce

METRIC SYSTEM

Linear	**Square**	**Weight**
kilometre	square kilometre	tonne
metre	square metre	kilogram
centimetre	square centimetre	gram
millimetre	square millimetre	–
Land	**Volume**	**Liquid volume**
square kilometre	cubic metre	litre
hectare	cubic decimetre	millilitre
are	cubic centimetre	–
–	cubic millimetre	–

weighty 1 = **important**, serious, significant, critical, crucial, considerable, substantial, grave, solemn, momentous, forcible, consequential, portentous • *Surely such weighty matters merit a higher level of debate?*
OPPOSITES: minor, petty, unimportant
2 = **heavy**, massive, dense, hefty *(informal)*, cumbersome, ponderous, burdensome • *Simon lifted a weighty volume from the shelf.*
3 = **onerous**, taxing, demanding, difficult, worrying, crushing, exacting, oppressive, burdensome, worrisome, backbreaking • *the weighty responsibility of organizing the entire event*

weird 1 = **strange**, odd, unusual, bizarre, ghostly, mysterious, queer, unearthly, eerie, grotesque, supernatural, unnatural, far-out *(slang)*, uncanny, spooky *(informal)*, creepy *(informal)*, eldritch *(poetic)* • *I had such a weird dream last night.*
OPPOSITES: natural, normal, regular
2 = **bizarre**, odd, strange, unusual, queer, grotesque, unnatural, creepy *(informal)*, outlandish, freakish • *I don't like that guy – he's really weird.*
OPPOSITES: common, natural, ordinary

weirdo *or* **weirdie** = **eccentric**, nut *(slang)*, freak *(informal)*, flake *(slang, chiefly U.S.)*, crank *(informal)*, loony *(slang)*, nutter *(Brit. slang)*, oddball *(informal)*, crackpot *(informal)*, nutcase *(slang)*, headcase *(informal)*, headbanger *(informal)*, queer fish *(Brit. informal)* • *All the other kids at school thought I was a weirdo.*

welcome **AS A VERB** 1 = **greet**, meet, receive, embrace, hail, usher in, say hello to, roll out the red carpet for, offer hospitality to, receive with open arms, bid welcome, karanga *(N.Z.)*, mihi *(N.Z.)* • *Several people came out to welcome me.*
OPPOSITES: refuse, reject, slight
2 = **accept gladly**, appreciate, embrace, approve of, be pleased by, give the thumbs up to *(informal)*, be glad about, express pleasure *or* satisfaction at • *They welcomed the move but felt it did not go far enough.*
▸ **AS A NOUN** = **greeting**, welcoming, entertainment, reception, acceptance, hail, hospitality, salutation • *There was a wonderful welcome waiting for him when he arrived.*
OPPOSITES: slight, rejection, exclusion
▸ **AS AN ADJECTIVE** 1 = **pleasing**, wanted, accepted, appreciated, acceptable, pleasant, desirable, refreshing, delightful, gratifying, agreeable, pleasurable, gladly received • *a welcome change from the usual routine*
OPPOSITES: unacceptable, unpleasant, unwelcome
2 = **wanted**, at home, invited • *I was really made to feel welcome.*
OPPOSITES: rejected, excluded, unwanted
3 = **free**, invited • *Non-residents are welcome to use our facilities.*

weld **AS A VERB** 1 = **join**, link, bond, bind, connect, cement, fuse, solder, braze • *It's possible to weld stainless steel to ordinary steel.*
2 = **unite**, combine, blend, consolidate, unify, fuse, meld • *The miracle was that Rose had welded them into a team.*
▸ **AS A NOUN** = **joint**, bond, seam, juncture • *The weld on the outlet pipe was visibly fractured.*

welfare 1 = **wellbeing**, good, interest, health, security, benefit, success, profit, safety, protection, fortune, comfort, happiness, prosperity, prosperousness • *Above all we must consider the welfare of the children.*
2 = **state benefit**, support, benefits, pensions, dole *(slang)*, social security, unemployment benefit, state benefits, Jobseeker's Allowance, JSA, pogey *(Canad.)* • *proposed cuts in welfare*

well[1] **AS AN ADVERB** 1 = **skilfully**, expertly, adeptly, with skill, professionally, correctly, properly, effectively, efficiently, adequately, admirably, ably, conscientiously, proficiently • *All the team members played well.*
OPPOSITES: badly, incompetently, incorrectly
2 = **satisfactorily**, nicely, smoothly, successfully, capitally, pleasantly, happily, famously *(informal)*, splendidly, agreeably, like nobody's business *(informal)*, in a satisfactory manner • *I thought the interview went very well.*
OPPOSITES: badly, wrongly, poorly
3 = **thoroughly**, completely, fully, carefully, effectively, efficiently, rigorously • *Mix all the ingredients well.*
4 = **intimately**, closely, completely, deeply, fully, personally, profoundly • *How well do you know him?*
OPPOSITES: somewhat, slightly, vaguely
5 = **carefully**, closely, minutely, fully, comprehensively, accurately, in detail, in depth, extensively, meticulously, painstakingly, rigorously, scrupulously, assiduously, intensively, from top to bottom, methodically, attentively, conscientiously, exhaustively • *This is obviously a man who's studied his subject well.*
6 = **favourably**, highly, kindly, warmly, enthusiastically, graciously, approvingly, admiringly, with admiration, appreciatively, with praise, glowingly, with approbation • *He speaks very well of you.*

OPPOSITES: unfavourably, coldly, unkindly
7 = **considerably**, easily, very much, significantly, substantially, markedly • *Franklin did not turn up until well after midnight.*
8 = **fully**, highly, greatly, completely, amply, very much, thoroughly, considerably, sufficiently, substantially, heartily, abundantly • *I am well aware of how much she has suffered.*
9 = **possibly**, probably, certainly, reasonably, conceivably, justifiably • *The murderer may well be someone who was close to the victim.*
10 = **decently**, right, kindly, fittingly, fairly, easily, correctly, properly, readily, politely, suitably, generously, justly, in all fairness, genially, civilly, hospitably • *My parents always treated me well.*
OPPOSITES: unfairly, unjustly, unsuitably
11 = **prosperously**, comfortably, splendidly, in comfort, in (the lap of) luxury, flourishingly, without hardship • *We manage to live very well on our combined salaries.*
12 = **harmoniously**, nicely, pleasantly, happily, politely, famously *(informal)*, amicably, amiably, agreeably, peaceably, genially, like a house on fire *(informal)* • *Her friends all get on well together.*
▸ **AS AN ADJECTIVE** 1 = **healthy**, strong, sound, fit, blooming, robust, hale, hearty, in good health, alive and kicking, fighting fit *(informal)*, in fine fettle, up to par, fit as a fiddle, able-bodied, in good condition • *I hope you're well.*
OPPOSITES: poorly, ill, sick
2 = **satisfactory**, good, right, fine, happy, fitting, pleasing, bright, useful, lucky, proper, thriving, flourishing, profitable, fortunate • *He was satisfied that all was well.*
OPPOSITES: wrong, unsuccessful, unsatisfactory
3 = **advisable**, useful, proper, prudent, agreeable • *It would be well to check the facts before you speak out.*
OPPOSITES: inadvisable, unfitting, improper
▸ **IN PHRASES:** **as well** = **also**, too, in addition, moreover, besides, to boot, into the bargain • *I like the job, and the people I work with are very nice as well.*
as well as = **including**, along with, in addition to, not to mention, at the same time as, over and above • *food and other goods, as well as energy supplies such as gas and oil*

well² **AS A NOUN** 1 = **hole**, bore, pit, shaft • *the cost of drilling an oil well*
2 = **waterhole**, source, spring, pool, fountain, fount • *I had to fetch water from the well.*
3 = **source**, fund, mine, treasury, reservoir, storehouse, repository, fount, wellspring • *a man with a well of experience and insight*
▸ **AS A VERB** 1 = **flow**, trickle, seep, run, issue, spring, pour, jet, burst, stream, surge, discharge, trickle, gush, ooze, seep, exude, spurt, spout • *Blood welled from a gash in his thigh.*
2 = **rise**, increase, grow, mount, surge, swell, intensify • *He could feel the anger welling inside him.*

well advised = **wise**, advised, sensible, prudent • *The party would be well advised to talk to the government.*

well-balanced 1 = **sensible**, rational, level-headed, well-adjusted, together *(slang)*, sound, reasonable, sober, sane, judicious, grounded • *a sensible, well-balanced individual*
OPPOSITES: volatile, unstable, unbalanced
2 = **healthy**, balanced, mixed, varied, sensible • *a well-balanced diet*
3 = **well-proportioned**, proportional, graceful, harmonious, symmetrical • *Intervals of depth are essential to a well-balanced composition.*

well-behaved = **obedient**, good, disciplined, restrained, orderly, respectful, law-abiding, compliant, amenable, submissive, docile, dutiful, deferential, tractable, acquiescent, biddable • *The children have been surprisingly well-behaved all day.*
OPPOSITES: disobedient, bad, disorderly

well-being = **welfare**, good, interest, health, benefit, advantage, comfort, happiness, prosperity • *His work emphasized the emotional as well as the physical well-being of the patient.*

well-bred 1 = **polite**, ladylike, well-brought-up, well-mannered, cultured, civil, mannerly, polished, sophisticated, gentlemanly, refined, cultivated, courteous, gallant, genteel, urbane, courtly • *She was too well-bred to make personal remarks.*
OPPOSITES: base, rude, ill-bred
2 = **aristocratic**, gentle, noble, patrician, blue-blooded, well-born, highborn • *He was clearly of well-bred stock.*

well-built = **burly**, big, strong, powerful, strapping, hefty, muscular, sturdy, stout, bulky, stocky, hulking, beefy *(informal)*, brawny, thickset • *The suspect is well built, of medium height, and with dark hair.*

well-dressed = **smart**, elegant, stylish, chic, spruce, dapper, well turned out, dressed to kill, dressed up to the nines, soigné *or* soignée, schmick *(Austral. informal)* • *all the clothes deemed necessary for a well-dressed young lady*

QUOTATIONS
The sense of being well-dressed gives a feeling of inward tranquillity which religion is powerless to bestow
[Miss C. F. Forbes]

well-fed 1 = **well-nourished**, healthy, in good condition • *The animals were sleek and well-fed.*
2 = **plump**, rounded, fat, stout, chubby, fleshy, portly, rotund, podgy • *a short, well-fed man with a round red face*

well-founded = **justifiable**, justified, reasonable, valid, warranted, legitimate, credible, plausible, defensible, well grounded, supportable • *We must respond to well-founded criticism with a willingness to change.*

well-groomed = **smart**, trim, neat, tidy, spruce, well-dressed, dapper, well turned out, soigné *or* soignée • *well-groomed young men in expensive suits*

well-heeled = **prosperous**, rich, wealthy, affluent, loaded *(slang)*, comfortable, flush *(informal)*, well-off, in the money *(informal)*, opulent, well-to-do, moneyed, well-situated, in clover *(informal)*, minted *(Brit. slang)* • *The price tag is out of reach of all but the most well-heeled.*

well-informed = **educated**, aware, informed, acquainted, knowledgeable *or* knowledgable, understanding, switched-on *(informal)*, well-educated, in the know *(informal)*, sussed *(Brit. slang)*, well-read, conversant, au fait *(French)*, in the loop *(informal)*, well-grounded, au courant *(French)*, clued-up *(informal)*, cognizant *or* cognisant, well-versed • *a man who was well-informed about world events*

well-known 1 = **famous**, important, celebrated, prominent, great, leading, noted, august, popular, familiar, distinguished, esteemed, acclaimed, notable, renowned, eminent, famed, illustrious, on the map, widely known • *He liked to surround himself with attractive or well-known people.*
2 = **familiar**, common, established, popular, everyday, widely known • *It is a well-known fact that smoking can cause lung cancer.*

well-mannered = **polite**, civil, mannerly, gentlemanly, gracious, respectful, courteous, genteel, well-bred, ladylike • *She is a well-mannered, polite child.*

well-nigh = **almost**, nearly, virtually, practically, next to, all but, just about, more or less • *Finding a rug that's just the right colour can be well-nigh impossible.*

well-off 1 = **rich**, wealthy, comfortable, affluent, loaded *(slang)*, flush *(informal)*, prosperous, well-heeled *(informal)*, well-to-do, moneyed, minted *(Brit. slang)* • *My family was quite well-off.*
OPPOSITES: broke *(informal)*, short, poor
2 = **fortunate**, lucky, comfortable, thriving, flourishing, successful • *Compared to some of the people in my ward, I feel quite well off.*

well-paid = **lucrative**, paying, profitable, productive, fruitful, high-income, money-making, gainful, remunerative • *I have an interesting, well-paid job with good career prospects.*

well-read = **educated**, cultured, scholarly, widely read, switched-on *(informal)*, well informed, sussed *(Brit. slang)*, erudite, studious, bookish, swotty *(Brit. informal)* • *He was clever, well-read and interested in the arts.*

well-spoken = **articulate**, refined, polite, nicely spoken, posh-sounding *(Brit. informal)* • *I remember her as a quiet, hard-working, well-spoken girl.*

wellspring = **fountainhead**, source, origin, fount, wellhead • *Nature has always been the wellspring of her art.*

well-thought-of = **respected**, admired, esteemed, revered, highly regarded, venerated, of good repute • *his desire to be well thought of by everyone*
OPPOSITES: despised, scorned, disdained

well-timed = **timely**, appropriate, suitable, judicious, opportune, propitious, seasonable • *One well-timed word from you may be all it takes to change his mind.*

well-to-do = **rich**, wealthy, affluent, well-off, loaded *(slang)*, comfortable, flush *(informal)*, prosperous, well-heeled *(informal)*, moneyed, minted *(Brit. slang)* • *two well-educated girls from well-to-do homes*
OPPOSITES: broke *(informal)*, poor, ruined

well-worn 1 = **stale**, tired, stereotyped, commonplace, banal, trite, hackneyed, overused, timeworn • *To use a well-worn cliché, she does not suffer fools gladly.*
2 = **shabby**, worn, faded, ragged, frayed, worn-out, scruffy, tattered, tatty, threadbare • *He was dressed casually in a sweater and well-worn jeans.*

welt = **mark**, scar, ridge, streak, stripe, weal, wheal, wale, contusion • *He had a red welt on the side of his face where Pringle's blow had landed.*

welter = **jumble**, confusion, muddle, hotchpotch, web, mess, tangle • *the welter of information available on the internet*

wend IN PHRASES: **wend your way** = **go**, move, travel, progress, proceed, make for, direct your course • *sleepy-eyed commuters who wended their way to work*

west
▸ RELATED ADJECTIVES: occidental, Hesperian

wet AS AN ADJECTIVE 1 = **damp**, soaked, soaking, dripping, saturated, moist, drenched, watery, soggy, sodden, waterlogged, moistened, dank, sopping, aqueous, wringing wet • *He rubbed his wet hair with a towel.*
OPPOSITES: dried, dry, hardened
2 = **rainy**, damp, drizzly, showery, raining, pouring, drizzling, misty, teeming, humid, dank, clammy • *It was a miserable wet day.*
OPPOSITES: fine, dry, sunny
3 = **feeble**, soft, weak, silly, foolish, ineffectual, weedy *(informal)*, spineless, effete, boneless, timorous, namby-pamby, irresolute, wussy *(slang)*, nerdy *or* nurdy *(slang)* • *I despised him for being so wet and spineless.*
▸ AS A VERB = **moisten**, spray, damp, dampen, water, dip, splash, soak, steep, sprinkle, saturate, drench, douse, irrigate, humidify, fertigate *(Austral.)* • *Wet the fabric with a damp sponge before ironing.*
OPPOSITES: dry, dehydrate, parch
▸ AS A NOUN 1 = **rain**, rains, damp, drizzle, wet weather, rainy season, rainy weather, damp weather • *They had come in from the cold and the wet.*
OPPOSITES: dry weather, fine weather
2 = **moisture**, water, liquid, damp, humidity, condensation, dampness, wetness, clamminess • *splashing around in the wet of the puddles*
OPPOSITES: dryness

wetland = **marsh**, moss *(Scot. & Northern English dialect)*, swamp, bog, slough, fen, quagmire, morass, muskeg *(Canad.)* • *wetlands rich in plants, insects and birds*

wetness = **damp**, water, wet, liquid, moisture, humidity, condensation, dampness, sogginess, clamminess • *I felt the wetness of my damp clothes against my skin.*

whack AS A VERB = **strike**, hit, beat, box, belt *(informal)*, deck *(slang)*, bang, rap, slap, bash *(informal)*, sock *(slang)*, chin *(slang)*, smack, thrash, thump, buffet, clout *(informal)*, slug, cuff, swipe, clobber *(slang)*, wallop *(informal)*, thwack, lambast(e), lay one on *(slang)*, beat *or* knock seven bells out of *(informal)* • *Someone whacked him on the head with a baseball bat.*
▸ AS A NOUN 1 = **blow**, hit, box, stroke, belt *(informal)*, bang, rap, slap, bash *(informal)*, sock *(slang)*, smack, thump, buffet, clout *(informal)*, slug, cuff, swipe, wallop *(informal)*, wham, thwack • *He gave the donkey a whack across the back with a stick.*
2 = **share**, part, cut *(informal)*, bit, portion, quota, allotment • *I pay a sizeable whack of capital gains tax.*
3 = **attempt**, go *(informal)*, try, turn, shot *(informal)*, crack *(informal)*, stab *(informal)*, bash *(informal)* • *Let me have a whack at trying to fix the car.*

whacking = **huge**, big, large, giant, enormous, extraordinary, tremendous, gigantic, great, monstrous, mammoth, whopping *(informal)*, prodigious, fuck-off *(offensive taboo slang)*, elephantine, humongous *or* humungous *(U.S. slang)* • *Your coat's got a whacking great tear up the back.*

whale
▸ RELATED ADJECTIVE: cetacean
▸ NAME OF MALE: bull
▸ NAME OF FEMALE: cow
▸ NAME OF YOUNG: calf
▸ COLLECTIVE NOUNS: school, gam, run

WHALES AND DOLPHINS

baleen whale	narwhal
beluga	pilot whale, black whale, *or* blackfish
blue whale *or* sulphur-bottom	porpoise
bottlenose dolphin	right whale *or (Austral.)* bay whale
bowhead	rorqual
dorado	sei whale
Greenland whale	sperm whale *or* cachalot
greyback *or* grey whale	toothed whale
humpback whale	whalebone whale
killer whale, grampus, *or* orca	white whale
minke whale	

wharf = **dock**, pier, berth, quay, jetty, landing stage • *There were three teenagers fishing from the wharf.*

whatsit = **thingummy**, whatever it is *(informal)*, whatchamacallit *(informal)*, what's-its-name, thingummyjig *(informal)*, oojamaflip *(informal)*, thing • *'She's a whatsit.' 'A masochist?' 'That's the word.'*

wheedle = **coax**, talk, court, draw, persuade, charm, worm, flatter, entice, cajole, inveigle • *He managed to wheedle some more money out of me.*

wheel AS A NOUN = **disc**, ring, hoop • *a bicycle wheel*
▸ AS A VERB 1 = **push**, trundle, roll • *He wheeled his bike into the alley beside the house.*
2 = **turn**, swing, spin, revolve, rotate, whirl, swivel • *He wheeled around to face her.*
3 = **circle**, orbit, go round, twirl, gyrate • *A flock of crows wheeled overhead.*
▸ IN PHRASES: **at** *or* **behind the wheel** = **driving**, steering, in the driving seat, in the driver's seat • *He persuaded his wife to say she was at the wheel when the car crashed.*

wheeze AS A VERB = **gasp**, whistle, cough, hiss, rasp, catch your breath, breathe roughly • *His chest problems made him wheeze constantly.*
▸ AS A NOUN 1 = **gasp**, whistle, cough, hiss, rasp • *He puffed up the stairs, emitting a wheeze at every breath.*
2 = **trick**, plan, idea, scheme, stunt, ploy, expedient, ruse • *He came up with a clever wheeze to get round the problem.*

whelp
▸ COLLECTIVE NOUN: litter

whereabouts = **position**, situation, site, location • *The police are anxious to hear of this man's whereabouts.*

wherewithal = **resources**, means, money, funds, capital, supplies, ready (*informal*), essentials, ready money • *She didn't have the financial wherewithal to start a new business.*

whet = **stimulate**, increase, excite, stir, enhance, provoke, arouse, awaken, animate, rouse, quicken, incite, kindle, pique • *a delicious aroma which whetted our appetites*
OPPOSITES: depress, dull, suppress

whiff AS A NOUN 1 = **smell**, hint, scent, sniff, aroma, odour, draught, niff (*Brit. slang*) • *He caught a whiff of her perfume.*
2 = **stink**, stench, reek, pong (*Brit. informal*), niff (*Brit. slang*), malodour, hum (*slang*) • *the nauseating whiff of rotting flesh*
3 = **trace**, suggestion, hint, suspicion, bit, drop, note, breath, whisper, shred, crumb, tinge, jot, smidgen (*informal*), soupçon • *Not a whiff of scandal has ever tainted his private life.*
4 = **puff**, breath, flurry, waft, rush, blast, draught, gust • *At the first whiff of smoke, the alarm will go off.*
▸ AS A VERB = **stink**, stench, reek, pong (*Brit. informal*), niff (*Brit. slang*), hum (*slang*) • *These socks whiff a bit, don't they?*

while AS A CONJUNCTION = **at the same time as**, during the time that, for the period that • *Her parents look after her daughter while she works.*
▸ AS A NOUN = **time**, period, stretch, spell, patch (*Brit. informal*), interval, period of time, stint • *They walked on in silence for a while.*
▸ IN PHRASES: **while something away** = **pass**, spend, kill, occupy, use up, beguile • *She whiled away the hours watching old movies on TV.*

whim = **impulse**, sudden notion, caprice, fancy, sport, urge, notion, humour, freak, craze, fad (*informal*), quirk, conceit, vagary, whimsy, passing thought, crotchet • *We decided, more or less on a whim, to sail to Morocco.*

whimper AS A VERB = **cry**, moan, sob, weep, whine, whinge (*informal*), grizzle (*informal, chiefly Brit.*), blubber, snivel, blub (*slang*), mewl • *She lay at the bottom of the stairs, whimpering in pain.*
▸ AS A NOUN = **sob**, moan, whine, snivel • *David's crying subsided to a whimper.*

whimsical = **fanciful**, odd, funny, unusual, fantastic, curious, weird, peculiar, eccentric, queer, flaky (*slang, chiefly U.S.*), singular, quaint, playful, mischievous, capricious, droll, freakish, fantastical, crotchety, chimerical, waggish • *He had an offbeat, whimsical sense of humour.*

W

whine AS A VERB 1 = **cry**, sob, wail, whimper, sniffle, snivel, moan • *He could hear a child whining in the background.*
2 = **complain**, grumble, gripe (*informal*), whinge (*informal*), moan, cry, beef (*slang*), carp, sob, wail, grouse, whimper, bleat, grizzle (*informal, chiefly Brit.*), grouch (*informal*), bellyache (*slang*), kvetch (*U.S. slang*) • *She's always calling me to whine about her problems.*
▸ AS A NOUN 1 = **cry**, moan, sob, wail, whimper, plaintive cry • *His voice became a pleading whine.*
2 = **drone**, note, hum • *the whine of air-raid sirens*
3 = **complaint**, moan, grumble, grouse, gripe (*informal*), whinge (*informal*), grouch (*informal*), beef (*slang*) • *Her conversation is one long whine about her husband.*

whinge AS A VERB = **complain**, moan, grumble, grouse, gripe (*informal*), beef (*slang*), carp, bleat, grizzle (*informal, chiefly Brit.*), grouch (*informal*), bellyache (*slang*), kvetch (*U.S. slang*) • *people who whinge about their alleged misfortunes*
▸ AS A NOUN = **complaint**, moan, grumble, whine, grouse, gripe (*informal*), grouch, beef (*slang*) • *It must be depressing having to listen to everyone's whinges.*

whip AS A NOUN = **lash**, cane, birch, switch, crop, scourge, thong, rawhide, riding crop, horsewhip, bullwhip, knout, cat-o'-nine-tails • *Prisoners were regularly beaten with a whip.*
▸ AS A VERB 1 = **lash**, cane, flog, beat, switch, leather, punish, strap, tan (*slang*), thrash, lick (*informal*), birch, scourge, spank, castigate, lambast(e), flagellate, give a hiding (*informal*) • *He was whipped with a studded belt.*
2 = **dash**, shoot, fly, tear, rush, dive, dart, whisk, flit • *I whipped into a parking space.*
3 = **whisk**, beat, mix vigorously, stir vigorously • *Whip the cream until it is thick.*
4 = **incite**, drive, push, urge, stir, spur, provoke, compel, hound, prod, work up, get going, agitate, prick, inflame, instigate, goad, foment • *an accomplished orator who could whip a crowd into hysteria*
5 = **beat**, thrash, trounce, wipe the floor with (*informal*), best, defeat, stuff (*slang*), worst, overcome, hammer (*informal*), overwhelm, conquer, lick (*informal*), rout, overpower, outdo, clobber (*slang*), take apart (*slang*), run rings around (*informal*), blow out of the water (*slang*), make mincemeat out of (*informal*), drub • *Our school can whip theirs at football and rugby.*
▸ IN PHRASES: **whip someone up** = **rouse**, excite, provoke, arouse, stir up, work up, agitate, inflame • *McCarthy whipped up Americans into a frenzy of anti-Communist activity.*
whip something out = **pull out**, produce, remove, jerk out, show, flash, seize, whisk out, snatch out • *Bob whipped out his notebook.*
whip something up = **instigate**, trigger, provoke, rouse, stir up, incite, kindle, foment • *He accused his opponent of whipping up anti-foreign sentiments.*

whipping = **beating**, lashing, thrashing, caning, hiding (*informal*), punishment, tanning (*slang*), birching, flogging, spanking, the strap, flagellation, castigation, leathering • *Whenever we misbehaved, we were given a whipping.*

whirl AS A VERB 1 = **spin**, turn, circle, wheel, twist, reel, rotate, pivot, twirl • *Hearing a sound behind her, she whirled round.*
2 = **rotate**, roll, twist, revolve, swirl, twirl, gyrate, pirouette • *The smoke whirled and grew into a monstrous column.*
3 = **feel dizzy**, swim, spin, reel, go round • *My head whirled in a giddiness like that of intoxication.*
▸ AS A NOUN 1 = **revolution**, turn, roll, circle, wheel, spin, twist, reel, swirl, rotation, twirl, pirouette, gyration, birl (*Scot.*) • *the whirl of snowflakes in the wind*
2 = **bustle**, round, series, succession, flurry, merry-go-round • *Her life is one long whirl of parties.*
3 = **confusion**, daze, dither (*chiefly Brit.*), giddiness • *My thoughts are in a complete whirl.*
4 = **tumult**, spin, stir, agitation, commotion, hurly-burly • *I was caught up in a terrible whirl of emotion.*
▸ IN PHRASES: **give something a whirl** = **attempt**, try, have a go at (*informal*), have a crack at (*informal*), have a shot at (*informal*), have a stab at (*informal*), have a bash at, have a whack at (*informal*) • *Why not give acupuncture a whirl?*

whirlpool = **vortex**, eddy, maelstrom, Charybdis (*literary*) • *The upturned boat was swept towards a yawning whirlpool.*

whirlwind AS A NOUN 1 = **tornado**, hurricane, cyclone, typhoon, twister (*U.S.*), dust devil, waterspout • *They scattered like leaves in a whirlwind.*
2 = **turmoil**, chaos, swirl, mayhem, uproar, maelstrom, welter, bedlam, tumult, hurly-burly, madhouse • *a whirlwind of frenzied activity*
▸ AS A MODIFIER = **rapid**, short, quick, swift, lightning, rash, speedy, hasty, impulsive, headlong, impetuous • *He got*

married after a whirlwind romance.
OPPOSITES: considered, measured, unhurried

whisk AS A VERB 1 = **rush**, sweep, hurry • *I was whisked away in a police car.*
2 = **pull**, whip *(informal)*, snatch, take • *The waiter whisked our plates away.*
3 = **speed**, race, shoot, fly, career, tear, rush, sweep, dash, hurry, barrel (along) *(informal, chiefly U.S. & Canad.)*, sprint, dart, hasten, burn rubber *(informal)*, go like the clappers *(Brit. informal)*, hightail it *(U.S. informal)*, wheech *(Scot. informal)* • *She whisked out of the room.*
4 = **flick**, whip, sweep, brush, wipe, twitch • *The dog whisked its tail around in excitement.*
5 = **beat**, mix vigorously, stir vigorously, whip, fluff up • *Whisk together the sugar and the egg yolks.*
▸ AS A NOUN 1 = **flick**, sweep, brush, whip, wipe • *With one whisk of its tail, the horse brushed the flies off.*
2 = **beater**, mixer, blender • *Using a whisk, beat the mixture until it thickens.*

whisky = **Scotch**, malt, rye, bourbon, firewater, John Barleycorn, usquebaugh *(Gaelic)*, barley-bree *(Scot.)* • *a glass of whisky*

QUOTATIONS
Freedom and Whisky gang thegither!
[Robert Burns *The Author's Earnest Cry and Prayer*]
a torchlight procession marching down your throat
[John L. O'Sullivan (of whisky)]

WHISKIES

blend	Irish whiskey	shebeen *(Irish)*
blended whisky	malt whisky	single malt
bourbon	poteen	sour mash
corn whisky	redeye *(U.S. slang)*	vatted malt
grain whisky	rye	
hokonui *(N.Z.)*	Scotch	

whisper AS A VERB 1 = **murmur**, breathe, mutter, mumble, purr, speak in hushed tones, say softly, say sotto voce, utter under the breath • *'Keep your voice down,' I whispered.*
OPPOSITES: shout, roar, yell
2 = **gossip**, hint, intimate, murmur, insinuate, spread rumours • *People started whispering that the pair were having an affair.*
3 = **rustle**, sigh, moan, murmur, hiss, swish, sough, susurrate *(literary)* • *The leaves whispered and rustled in the breeze.*
▸ AS A NOUN 1 = **murmur**, mutter, mumble, undertone, low voice, soft voice, hushed tone • *Men were talking in whispers in the corridor.*
2 = **rumour**, report, word, story, hint, buzz, gossip, dirt *(U.S. slang)*, goss *(informal)*, innuendo, insinuation, scuttlebutt *(U.S. slang)* • *I've heard a whisper that he is planning to resign.*
3 = **rustle**, sigh, sighing, murmur, hiss, swish, soughing, susurration *or* susurrus *(literary)* • *the slight whisper of the wind in the grass*
4 = **hint**, shadow, suggestion, trace, breath, suspicion, fraction, tinge, whiff • *There is a whisper of conspiracy about the whole affair.*

whit = **bit**, drop, piece, trace, scrap, dash, grain, particle, fragment, atom, pinch, shred, crumb, mite, jot, speck, modicum, least bit, iota • *It does not make one whit of difference what we do.*

white AS AN ADJECTIVE 1 = **pale**, grey, ghastly, wan, pasty, bloodless, pallid, ashen, waxen, like death warmed up *(informal)*, wheyfaced • *He turned white and began to stammer.*
2 = **silver**, grey, snowy, grizzled, hoary • *an old man with white hair*
▸ IN PHRASES: **whiter than white** = **immaculate**, innocent, virtuous, saintly, clean, pure, worthy, noble, stainless, impeccable, exemplary, spotless, squeaky-clean, unblemished, untainted, unsullied, irreproachable, uncorrupted • *A man in his position has to be seen as being whiter than white.*
▹ *See panel* **Shades from black to white**

white-collar = **clerical**, office, executive, professional, salaried, nonmanual • *White-collar workers are working longer and longer hours.*

whiten 1 = **pale**, blanch, go white, turn pale, blench, fade, etiolate • *His face whitened as he heard the news.*
OPPOSITES: colour, darken
2 = **bleach**, lighten • *toothpastes that whiten the teeth*
OPPOSITES: darken, blacken, stain

whitewash AS A VERB = **cover up**, conceal, suppress, camouflage, make light of, gloss over, extenuate, airbrush • *The administration is whitewashing the regime's actions.*
OPPOSITES: reveal, expose, disclose
▸ AS A NOUN = **cover-up**, deception, camouflage, concealment, smoke and mirrors, extenuation • *The report's findings were condemned as total whitewash.*

whiting
▸ COLLECTIVE NOUN: pod

whittle AS A VERB = **carve**, cut, hew, shape, trim, shave, pare • *Chitty sat in his rocking chair whittling a piece of wood.*
▸ IN PHRASES: **whittle something away** = **undermine**, reduce, destroy, consume, erode, eat away, wear away, cut down, cut, decrease, prune, scale down • *I believe the Government's aim is to whittle away the Welfare State.*
whittle something *or* **someone down** = **reduce**, cut down, cut, decrease, prune, scale down • *He had whittled the twenty interviewees down to two.*

whizz AS A VERB = **speed**, race, career, hurtle, bomb, tear, rush, flash, belt *(slang)*, zoom • *A car whizzed past.*
▸ AS A NOUN = **expert**, professional, master, pro *(informal)*, specialist, ace *(informal)*, buff *(informal)*, wizard, virtuoso, hotshot *(informal)*, past master, dab hand *(Brit. informal)*, wonk *(informal)* • *Simon's a whizz at card tricks.*

whizz kid = **prodigy**, talent, genius, mastermind, whizz *(informal)*, boffin *(Brit. informal)*, rocket scientist *(informal, chiefly U.S.)*, wunderkind, wonder kid, child genius, phenom *(U.S. informal)*, up-and-comer *(informal)* • *a computing whizz kid*

whole AS A NOUN 1 = **total**, all, lot, everything, aggregate, sum total, the entire amount • *Taken as a percentage of the whole, it has to be a fairly minor part.*
2 = **unit**, body, piece, object, combination, unity, entity, ensemble, entirety, fullness, totality • *The different components combine to form a complete whole.*
OPPOSITES: part, bit, piece
▸ AS AN ADJECTIVE 1 = **complete**, full, total, entire, integral, uncut, undivided, unabridged, unexpurgated, uncondensed • *I have now read the whole book.*
OPPOSITES: cut, divided, partial
2 = **undamaged**, intact, unscathed, unbroken, good, sound, perfect, mint, untouched, flawless, unhurt, faultless, unharmed, in one piece, uninjured, inviolate, unimpaired, unmutilated • *I struck the glass with all my might, but it remained whole.*
OPPOSITES: broken, damaged
3 = **healthy**, well, better, strong, sound, fit, recovered, healed, cured, robust, hale, in good health, in fine fettle, able-bodied • *the woman who was made whole by touching the hem of Jesus's garment*
OPPOSITES: diseased, ill, sick
▸ AS AN ADVERB = **in one piece**, in one • *Snakes swallow their prey whole.*
▸ IN PHRASES: **on the whole** 1 = **all in all**, altogether, all things considered, by and large, taking everything into

W

consideration • *On the whole, I think it's better if I don't come with you.*
2 = **generally**, in general, for the most part, as a rule, chiefly, mainly, mostly, principally, on average, predominantly, in the main, to a large extent, as a general rule, generally speaking • *On the whole, women are having children much later these days.*

wholehearted = **sincere**, complete, committed, genuine, real, true, determined, earnest, warm, devoted, dedicated, enthusiastic, emphatic, hearty, heartfelt, zealous, unqualified, unstinting, unreserved, unfeigned • *He deserves our wholehearted support in this matter.*
OPPOSITES: reserved, cool, half-hearted

wholesale AS AN ADJECTIVE = **extensive**, total, mass, sweeping, broad, comprehensive, wide-ranging, blanket, outright, far-reaching, indiscriminate, all-inclusive • *the wholesale destruction of life on this planet*
OPPOSITES: limited, restricted, confined
▸ AS AN ADVERB = **extensively**, comprehensively, across the board, all at once, indiscriminately, without exception, on a large scale • *The army was burning down houses and killing villagers wholesale.*

wholesome **1** = **moral**, nice, clean, pure, decent, innocent, worthy, ethical, respectable, honourable, uplifting, righteous, exemplary, virtuous, apple-pie *(informal)*, squeaky-clean, edifying • *It was all good, wholesome fun.*
OPPOSITES: blue, evil, corrupt
2 = **healthy**, good, strengthening, beneficial, nourishing, nutritious, sanitary, invigorating, salutary, hygienic, healthful, health-giving • *The food was filling and wholesome.*
OPPOSITES: rotten, unhealthy, putrid

wholly **1** = **completely**, totally, perfectly, fully, entirely, comprehensively, altogether, thoroughly, utterly, heart and soul, one hundred per cent *(informal)*, in every respect • *The accusation is wholly without foundation.*
OPPOSITES: partly, relatively, somewhat
2 = **solely**, only, exclusively, without exception, to the exclusion of everything else • *societies which rely wholly on farming to survive*

whoop AS A VERB = **cry**, shout, scream, cheer, yell, shriek, hoot, holler *(informal)* • *The audience whooped and cheered with delight.*
▸ AS A NOUN = **cry**, shout, scream, cheer, yell, shriek, hoot, holler *(informal)*, hurrah, halloo • *A wild frenzy of whoops and yells arose outside.*

whopper **1** = **big lie**, fabrication, falsehood, untruth, tall story *(informal)*, fable • *He's always telling whoppers about his sex life.*
2 = **giant**, monster, jumbo *(informal)*, mammoth, colossus, leviathan, crackerjack *(informal)* • *As comets go, it is a whopper.*

whopping = **gigantic**, great, big, large, huge, giant, massive, enormous, extraordinary, tremendous, monstrous, whacking *(informal)*, mammoth, prodigious, fuck-off *(offensive taboo slang)*, elephantine, humongous *or* humungous *(U.S. slang)* • *Planned spending amounts to a whopping $31.4 billion.*

whore AS A NOUN = **prostitute**, hooker *(U.S. slang)*, tart *(informal)*, streetwalker, tom *(Brit. slang)*, brass *(slang)*, slag *(Brit. slang)*, hustler *(U.S. & Canad. slang)*, call girl, courtesan, working girl *(facetious slang)*, harlot, loose woman, fallen woman, scrubber *(Brit. & Austral. slang)*, strumpet, trollop, lady of the night, cocotte, woman of easy virtue, demimondaine, woman of ill repute, fille de joie *(French)*, demirep *(rare)* • *There were pimps and whores standing on every street corner.*
▸ AS A VERB **1** = **prostitute yourself**, solicit, hustle *(U.S. & Canad. slang)*, walk the streets, sell yourself, be on the game *(slang)*, sell your body • *women who have to whore in order to survive*
2 = **sleep around**, womanize, wanton *(informal)*, wench *(archaic)*, fornicate, lech *or* letch *(informal)* • *His eldest son gambled, whored and drank.*

whorehouse = **brothel**, bordello, cathouse *(U.S. slang)*, knocking-shop *(Brit. slang)*, house of prostitution, bagnio *(rare)*, disorderly house, house of ill fame *or* repute • *the madam of a high-class whorehouse in New Hampshire*

whorl = **swirl**, spiral, coil, twist, vortex, helix, corkscrew • *The plant has dense whorls of red-purple flowers.*

wicked **1** = **bad**, evil, corrupt, vile, guilty, abandoned, foul, vicious, worthless, shameful, immoral, scandalous, atrocious, sinful, heinous, depraved, debased, devilish, amoral, egregious, abominable, fiendish, villainous, unprincipled, nefarious, dissolute, iniquitous, irreligious, black-hearted, impious, unrighteous, maleficent, flagitious • *She flew at me, shouting how evil and wicked I was.*
OPPOSITES: good, principled, virtuous
2 = **mischievous**, playful, impish, devilish, arch, teasing, naughty, cheeky, rascally, incorrigible, raffish, roguish, rakish, tricksy, puckish, waggish • *She has a delightfully wicked sense of humour.*
OPPOSITES: good, mannerly, well-behaved
3 = **agonizing**, terrible, acute, severe, intense, awful, painful, fierce, mighty, dreadful, fearful, gut-wrenching • *A wicked pain shot through his injured elbow.*
4 = **harmful**, terrible, intense, mighty, crashing, dreadful, destructive, injurious • *The wind gets so wicked you want to stay indoors while the sea rages.*
OPPOSITES: pleasant, mild, harmless
5 = **expert**, great *(informal)*, strong, powerful, masterly, wonderful, outstanding, remarkable, ace *(informal)*, first-class, marvellous, mighty, dazzling, skilful, A1 *(informal)*, adept, deft, adroit • *John's a wicked tennis player. He always wins.*

QUOTATIONS
There is no peace unto the wicked
[Bible: Isaiah]

wickedness = **evil**, wrong, sin, curse, wrongdoing, depravity, immorality, iniquity, badness, viciousness, sinfulness, turpitude, baseness, malignity, heinousness, maleficence • *moral arguments about the wickedness of nuclear weapons* • *They have sunk to new levels of wickedness.*

wide AS AN ADJECTIVE **1** = **spacious**, broad, extensive, ample, roomy, commodious • *The doorway should be wide enough to allow wheelchair access.*
OPPOSITES: tight, confined, cramped
2 = **baggy**, full, loose, ample, billowing, roomy, voluminous, capacious, oversize, generously cut • *Wear the shirt loose over wide trousers.*
3 = **expanded**, dilated, fully open, distended • *His eyes were wide with disbelief.*
OPPOSITES: closed, shut
4 = **broad**, comprehensive, extensive, wide-ranging, large, catholic, expanded, sweeping, vast, immense, ample, inclusive, expansive, exhaustive, encyclopedic, far-ranging, compendious • *The brochure offers a wide choice of hotels and holiday homes.*
OPPOSITES: narrow, restricted
5 = **extensive**, general, far-reaching, overarching • *The case has attracted wide publicity.*
6 = **large**, broad, vast, immense • *the wide variation in the ages and backgrounds of the candidates*
7 = **distant**, off, away, remote, off course, off target • *The shot was several feet wide.*
▸ AS AN ADVERB **1** = **fully**, completely, right out, as far as possible, to the furthest extent • *He opened his mouth wide.*
OPPOSITES: partly, narrowly, partially
2 = **off target**, nowhere near, astray, off course, off the mark • *The big striker fired wide and missed an easy goal.*

▸ **IN PHRASES: wide awake** 1 = **conscious**, fully awake, roused, wakened • *I could not relax and was still wide awake after midnight.*
2 = **alert**, vigilant, on the ball *(informal)*, aware, keen, wary, watchful, observant, on the alert, on your toes, on the qui vive, heedful • *You need to stay alert and wide awake to avoid accidents as you drive.*

wide-eyed 1 = **naive**, green, trusting, credulous, simple, innocent, impressionable, unsophisticated, ingenuous, wet behind the ears *(informal)*, unsuspicious, as green as grass • *He told tall stories to a wide-eyed group of tourists.*
2 = **staring**, spellbound, gobsmacked *(Brit. slang)*, dumbfounded, agog, agape, thunderstruck, goggle-eyed, awe-stricken • *She was wide-eyed in astonishment.*

widen 1 = **broaden**, expand, enlarge, dilate, spread, extend, stretch, open wide, open out *or* up • *He had an operation to widen an artery in his heart.*
OPPOSITES: reduce, narrow, shrink
2 = **get wider**, spread, extend, expand, broaden, open wide, open out *or* up • *The river widens considerably as it begins to turn east.*
OPPOSITES: contract, narrow, shrink

wide-open 1 = **outspread**, spread, outstretched, splayed, fully open, fully extended, gaping • *He came towards her with his arms wide open in welcome.*
2 = **unprotected**, open, exposed, vulnerable, at risk, in danger, susceptible, defenceless, in peril • *The virus leaves the body wide open to infection.*
3 = **uncertain**, unsettled, unpredictable, up for grabs *(informal)*, indeterminate, anybody's guess *(informal)* • *The match was still wide open at half-time.*

wide-ranging = **far-reaching**, sweeping, broad, widespread, extensive, pervasive, significant • *a package of wide-ranging economic reforms*

widespread = **common**, general, popular, sweeping, broad, extensive, universal, epidemic, wholesale, far-reaching, prevalent, rife, pervasive, far-flung • *There is widespread support for the proposals.* • *Food shortages are widespread.*
OPPOSITES: local, limited, rare

width = **breadth**, extent, span, wideness, reach, range, measure, scope, diameter, compass, thickness, girth • *The width of the road has been increased to 20 ft.*

wield 1 = **brandish**, flourish, manipulate, swing, use, manage, handle, employ, ply • *He was attacked by an assailant wielding a kitchen knife.*
2 = **exert**, hold, maintain, exercise, have, control, manage, apply, command, possess, make use of, utilize, put to use, be possessed of, have at your disposal • *He remains chairman, but wields little power in the company.*

wife = **spouse**, woman *(informal)*, partner, mate, squeeze *(informal)*, bride, old woman *(informal)*, old lady *(informal)*, little woman *(informal)*, significant other *(U.S. informal)*, better half *(humorous)*, her indoors *(Brit. slang)*, helpmate, helpmeet, (the) missis *or* missus *(informal)*, vrou *(S. African)*, bidie-in *(Scot.)*, wahine *(N.Z.)*, wifey *(informal)*, Wag *(Brit. informal)* • *He married his wife Jane 37 years ago.*
▸ **RELATED ADJECTIVE:** uxorial

QUOTATIONS

If you get a good wife you'll become happy; if you get a bad one, you'll become a philosopher
[Socrates]

Wives are young men's mistresses, companions for middle age, and old men's nurses
[Francis Bacon]

An ideal wife is any woman who has an ideal husband
[Booth Tarkington]

I... chose my wife, as she did her wedding gown, not for a fine glossy surface, but such qualities as would wear well
[Oliver Goldsmith *The Vicar of Wakefield*]

My fairest, my espoused, my latest found,
Heaven's last best gift, my ever new delight
[John Milton *Paradise Lost*]

best image of myself and dearer half
[John Milton *Paradise Lost*]

wigeon
▸ **COLLECTIVE NOUNS:** bunch, company, knob, flight

wiggle AS A VERB 1 = **jerk**, shake, twitch, wag, jiggle, waggle • *She wiggled her fingers to attract his attention.*
2 = **squirm**, twitch, writhe, shimmy • *A little worm was wiggling on the pavement.*
▸ **AS A NOUN** = **jerk**, shake, twitch, wag, squirm, writhe, jiggle, waggle, shimmy • *With a wiggle of her hips, she slid out of her skirt.*

wild AS AN ADJECTIVE 1 = **untamed**, fierce, savage, ferocious, unbroken, feral, undomesticated, free, warrigal *(Austral. literary)* • *The organization is calling for a total ban on the trade of wild animals.*
OPPOSITES: broken, tame, domesticated
2 = **uncultivated**, natural, native, indigenous • *The lane was lined with wild flowers.*
OPPOSITES: planted, farmed, cultivated
3 = **desolate**, empty, desert, deserted, virgin, lonely, uninhabited, godforsaken, uncultivated, uncivilized, trackless, unpopulated • *one of the few wild areas remaining in the South East*
OPPOSITES: urban, inhabited, populated
4 = **stormy**, violent, rough, intense, raging, furious, howling, choppy, tempestuous, blustery • *The recent wild weather has caused millions of pounds' worth of damage.*
5 = **excited**, mad *(informal)*, crazy *(informal)*, eager, nuts *(slang)*, enthusiastic, raving, frantic, daft *(informal)*, frenzied, hysterical, avid, potty *(Brit. informal)*, delirious, agog • *The children were wild with excitement.*
OPPOSITES: uninterested, unenthusiastic
6 = **uncontrolled**, violent, rough, disorderly, noisy, chaotic, turbulent, wayward, unruly, rowdy, boisterous, lawless, unfettered, unbridled, riotous, unrestrained, unmanageable, impetuous, undisciplined, ungovernable, self-willed, uproarious • *When drunk, he became wild and violent.*
OPPOSITES: ordered, controlled, calm
7 = **mad** *(informal)*, furious, fuming, infuriated, incensed, enraged, very angry, irate, livid *(informal)*, in a rage, on the warpath *(informal)*, hot under the collar *(informal)*, beside yourself, tooshie *(Austral. slang)*, off the air *(Austral. slang)* • *When I told him what I had done, he was wild.*
8 = **outrageous**, fantastic, foolish, rash, extravagant, reckless, preposterous, giddy, madcap, foolhardy, flighty, ill-considered, imprudent, impracticable • *I was just a kid and full of wild ideas.*
OPPOSITES: practical, realistic, logical
9 = **dishevelled**, disordered, untidy, unkempt, tousled, straggly, windblown, daggy *(Austral. & N.Z. informal)* • *They were alarmed by his wild hair and staring eyes.*
10 = **passionate**, mad *(informal)*, ardent, fervent, zealous, fervid • *She's just wild about him.*
11 = **uncivilized**, fierce, savage, primitive, rude, ferocious, barbaric, brutish, barbarous • *the wild tribes which still roam the northern plains with their horse herds*
OPPOSITES: advanced, civilized
▸ **IN PHRASES: the wilds** = **wilderness**, desert, wasteland, middle of nowhere *(informal)*, backwoods, back of beyond *(informal)*, uninhabited area • *They went canoeing in the wilds of Canada.*
run wild 1 = **grow unchecked**, spread, ramble, straggle • *The front garden is running wild.*
2 = **go on the rampage**, stray, rampage, run riot, cut loose, run free, kick over the traces, be undisciplined, abandon all restraint • *She lets her children run wild.*

W

wilderness 1 = **wilds**, waste, desert, wasteland, uncultivated region • *He looked out over a wilderness of mountain, lake and forest.*
2 = **tangle**, confusion, maze, muddle, clutter, jumble, welter, congeries, confused mass • *The neglected cemetery was a wilderness of crumbling gravestones and parched grass.*

wildlife = **flora and fauna**, animals, fauna • *People were concerned that wildlife could be affected by the pesticides.*

wile AS A NOUN = **cunning**, craft, fraud, cheating, guile, artifice, trickery, chicanery, craftiness, artfulness, slyness • *His wit and wile has made him one of the sharpest politicians in the Cabinet.*
▸ AS A PLURAL NOUN = **ploys**, tricks, devices, lures, manoeuvres, dodges, ruses, artifices, subterfuges, stratagems, contrivances, impositions • *She never hesitated to use her feminine wiles to get her own way.*

wilful or **willful** 1 = **intentional**, willed, intended, conscious, voluntary, deliberate, purposeful, volitional • *Wilful neglect of the environment has caused this problem.*
OPPOSITES: unconscious, accidental, unintentional
2 = **obstinate**, dogged, determined, persistent, adamant, stubborn, perverse, uncompromising, intractable, inflexible, unyielding, intransigent, headstrong, obdurate, stiff-necked, self-willed, refractory, pig-headed, bull-headed, mulish, froward *(archaic)* • *a spoilt and wilful teenager*
OPPOSITES: yielding, compromising, obedient

will AS A NOUN 1 = **determination**, drive, aim, purpose, commitment, resolution, resolve, intention, spine, backbone, tenacity, willpower, single-mindedness, doggedness, firmness of purpose • *He lacked the will to confront her.*
2 = **wish**, mind, desire, pleasure, intention, fancy, preference, inclination • *He was forced to leave the country against his will.*
3 = **choice**, decision, option, prerogative, volition • *the concept of free will*
4 = **decree**, wish, desire, command, dictate, ordinance • *He has submitted himself to the will of God.*
5 = **testament**, declaration, bequest(s), last wishes, last will and testament • *Attached to his will was a letter he had written just before his death.*
▸ AS A VERB 1 = **decree**, order, cause, effect, direct, determine, bid, intend, command, resolve, bring about, ordain • *They believed they would win because God had willed it.*
2 = **wish**, want, choose, prefer, desire, elect, opt, see fit • *Say what you will about him, but he's always been a good provider.*
3 = **bequeath**, give, leave, transfer, gift, hand on, pass on, confer, hand down, settle on • *She had willed all her money to her brother, Frank.*
▸ IN PHRASES: **at will** = **as you please**, at your discretion, as you think fit, at your pleasure, at your desire, at your whim, at your inclination, at your wish • *Some yoga practitioners can slow their heart-rates down at will.*
▸ RELATED ADJECTIVES: voluntary, volitive

PROVERBS
Where there's a will there's a way

willing 1 = **inclined**, prepared, happy, pleased, content, in favour, consenting, disposed, favourable, agreeable, in the mood, compliant, amenable, desirous, so-minded, nothing loath • *There are some questions which they will not be willing to answer.*
OPPOSITES: reluctant, unwilling, averse
2 = **ready**, game *(informal)*, eager, enthusiastic • *He had plenty of willing volunteers to help him clear up.*
OPPOSITES: reluctant, unwilling, grudging

willingly = **readily**, freely, gladly, happily, eagerly, voluntarily, cheerfully, with pleasure, without hesitation, by choice, with all your heart, lief *(rare)*, of your own free will, of your own accord • *I would willingly die for my children.*
OPPOSITES: reluctantly, grudgingly, unwillingly

willingness = **inclination**, will, agreement, wish, favour, desire, enthusiasm, consent, goodwill, disposition, volition, agreeableness • *The leaders have expressed their willingness to compromise.*
OPPOSITES: disagreement, reluctance, loathing

willowy = **slender**, slim, graceful, supple, lithe, limber, svelte, lissom(e), sylphlike • *She was a slim, willowy woman in her late thirties.*

willpower = **self-control**, drive, resolution, resolve, determination, grit, self-discipline, single-mindedness, fixity of purpose, firmness of purpose *or* will, force *or* strength of will • *She doesn't have the willpower to give up smoking.*
OPPOSITES: weakness, uncertainty, apathy

willy-nilly 1 = **whether you like it or not**, necessarily, of necessity, perforce, whether or no, whether desired or not, nolens volens *(Latin)* • *We were dragged willy-nilly into the argument.*
2 = **haphazardly**, at random, randomly, without order, without method, without planning, any old how *(informal)* • *The papers were just bundled into the drawers willy-nilly.*

wilt 1 = **droop**, wither, sag, shrivel, become limp *or* flaccid • *The roses wilted the day after she bought them.*
2 = **weaken**, sag, languish, droop • *She began to wilt in the morning heat.*
3 = **wane**, fail, sink, flag, fade, diminish, dwindle, wither, ebb, melt away, lose courage • *Their resolution wilted in the face of such powerful opposition.*

wily = **cunning**, designing, scheming, sharp, intriguing, arch, tricky, crooked, shrewd, sly, astute, deceptive, crafty, artful, shifty, foxy, cagey *(informal)*, deceitful, underhand, guileful, fly *(slang)* • *He is an experienced and wily old statesman.*
OPPOSITES: simple, dull, straightforward

wimp = **weakling**, wet *(Brit. slang)*, mouse, drip *(informal)*, coward, jessie *(Scot. slang)*, pussy *(slang, chiefly U.S.)*, jellyfish *(informal)*, sissy, doormat *(slang)*, pussycat *(Brit. informal)*, wuss *(slang)*, milksop, softy *or* softie • *He's a total wimp, incapable of standing up for himself.*

win AS A VERB 1 = **be victorious in**, succeed in, prevail in, come first in, finish first in, be the victor in, gain victory in, achieve first place in • *He does not have any reasonable chance of winning the election.*
OPPOSITES: lose, fail in, suffer defeat in
2 = **be victorious**, succeed, triumph, overcome, prevail, conquer, come first, finish first, carry the day, sweep the board, take the prize, gain victory, achieve mastery, achieve first place, carry all before you • *Our team is confident of winning again this year.*
OPPOSITES: lose, fall, fail
3 = **gain**, get, receive, land, catch, achieve, net, earn, pick up, bag *(informal)*, secure, collect, obtain, acquire, accomplish, attain, procure, come away with • *The first correct entry will win the prize.*
OPPOSITES: lose, miss, forfeit
▸ AS A NOUN = **victory**, success, triumph, conquest • *Arsenal's run of eight games without a win*
OPPOSITES: beating, loss, defeat
▸ IN PHRASES: **win someone over** *or* **round** = **convince**, influence, attract, persuade, convert, charm, sway, disarm, allure, prevail upon, bring *or* talk round • *He had won over a significant number of his opponents.*
win through = **succeed**, make it *(informal)*, triumph, do well, thrive, flourish, be successful, make good, prosper, make the grade *(informal)*, make your mark *(informal)*, gain your end • *Stick to your principles, and you will win through.*

PROVERBS
You can't win them all

wince AS A VERB = **flinch**, start, shrink, cringe, quail, recoil, cower, draw back, blench • *He tightened his grip on her arm until she winced in pain.*

▸ **AS A NOUN** = **flinch**, start, cringe • *She gave a wince at the memory of their first date.*

wind[1] **AS A NOUN 1** = **air**, blast, breath, hurricane, breeze, draught, gust, zephyr, air-current, current of air • *During the night the wind had blown down the fence.*
2 = **flatulence**, gas, flatus • *tablets to treat trapped wind*
3 = **breath**, puff, respiration • *A punch in the stomach knocked the wind out of me.*
4 = **nonsense**, talk, boasting, hot air, babble, bluster, humbug, twaddle *(informal)*, gab *(informal)*, verbalizing, blather, codswallop *(informal)*, eyewash *(informal)*, idle talk, empty talk, bizzo *(Austral. slang)*, bull's wool *(Austral. & N.Z. slang)* • *You're just talking a lot of wind.*
▸ **IN PHRASES: get wind of something** = **hear about**, learn of, find out about, become aware of, be told about, be informed of, be made aware of, hear tell of, have brought to your notice, hear on the grape vine *(informal)* • *I don't want the press to get wind of our plans at this stage.*
in the wind = **imminent**, coming, near, approaching, on the way, looming, brewing, impending, on the cards *(informal)*, in the offing, about to happen, close at hand • *By the mid-1980s, economic change was in the wind again.*
put the wind up someone = **scare**, alarm, frighten, panic, discourage, unnerve, scare off, frighten off, scare the bejesus out of *(informal)* • *I had an anonymous letter that really put the wind up me.*
▸ **RELATED ADJECTIVE:** aeolian
▸ **RELATED PHOBIA:** anemophobia

PROVERBS
It's an ill wind that blows nobody any good

wind[2] **AS A VERB 1** = **meander**, turn, bend, twist, curve, snake, ramble, twist and turn, deviate, zigzag • *The Moselle winds through some 160 miles of tranquil countryside.*
2 = **wrap**, twist, reel, curl, loop, coil, twine, furl, wreathe • *She wound the sash round her waist.*
3 = **coil**, curl, spiral, encircle, twine • *The snake wound around my leg.*
▸ **IN PHRASES: wind down 1** = **calm down**, unwind, take it easy, unbutton *(informal)*, put your feet up, de-stress *(informal)*, outspan *(S. African)*, cool down *or* off • *I need a drink to help me wind down.*
2 = **subside**, decline, diminish, come to an end, dwindle, tail off, taper off, slacken off • *The relationship was winding down by more or less mutual agreement.*
wind someone up 1 = **irritate**, excite, anger, annoy, exasperate, nettle, work someone up, pique, make someone nervous, put someone on edge, make someone tense, hack you off *(informal)* • *This woman kept winding me up by talking over me.*
2 = **tease**, kid *(informal)*, have someone on *(informal)*, annoy, rag *(informal)*, rib *(informal)*, josh *(informal)*, vex, make fun of, take the mickey out of *(informal)*, send someone up *(informal)*, pull someone's leg *(informal)*, jerk *or* yank someone's chain *(informal)* • *You're joking. Come on, you're just winding me up.*
wind something down = **coil**, reduce, relax, lessen, slacken, bring something to a close *or* end, wind something up • *Foreign aid workers have already begun to wind down their operation.*
wind something up 1 = **end**, finish, settle, conclude, tie up, wrap up, finalize, bring to a close, tie up the loose ends of *(informal)* • *The President is about to wind up his visit to Somalia.*
2 = **close down**, close, dissolve, terminate, liquidate, put something into liquidation • *The bank seems determined to wind up the company.*
wind up = **end up**, be left, find yourself, finish up, fetch up *(informal)*, land up, end your days • *You're going to wind up a bitter and lonely old man.*
▹ *See panel* **Winds**

windbag = **bore**, boaster, gossip, prattler, loudmouth *(informal)*, braggart, blether *(Scot.)*, bigmouth *(slang)*, gasbag *(informal)*, blowhard *(informal)*, bullshitter *(taboo slang)*, bullshit artist *(taboo slang)*, tattletale *(chiefly U.S. & Canad.)*, figjam *(Austral. slang)* • *He's just a boring old windbag.*

winded = **out of breath**, panting, puffed, breathless, gasping for breath, puffed out, out of puff, out of whack *(informal)* • *He fell to the ground and lay there, winded.*

windfall = **godsend**, find, jackpot, bonanza, stroke of luck, manna from heaven, pot of gold at the end of the rainbow • *If you had a windfall of £5000, how would you spend it?*
OPPOSITES: disaster, misfortune, bad luck

winding = **twisting**, turning, bending, curving, crooked, spiral, indirect, roundabout, meandering, tortuous, convoluted, serpentine, sinuous, circuitous, twisty, anfractuous, flexuous • *a long and winding road*
OPPOSITES: even, level, straight

window 1 = **aperture**, casement • *He opened the window to let in some air.*
2 = **space**, opening, gap, blank • *Tell her I've got a window in my diary later on this week.*
▸ **RELATED ADJECTIVE:** fenestral

windpipe = **throat**
▸ **TECHNICAL NAME:** trachea
▸ **RELATED ADJECTIVES:** tracheal, tracheate

windswept 1 = **exposed**, bare, bleak, windy, desolate, unprotected, windblown, blowy • *the remote and windswept hillside*
2 = **dishevelled**, disordered, messy, untidy, unkempt, tousled, windblown, disarranged, mussed up *(U.S.)* • *windswept hair*

wind-up = **joke**, gag *(informal)*, lark, prank, jest, practical joke • *At first I didn't believe it and thought it was a wind-up by one of my mates.*

windy = **breezy**, wild, stormy, boisterous, blustering, windswept, tempestuous, blustery, gusty, inclement, squally, blowy • *It was a windy, overcast day.*
OPPOSITES: still, calm, smooth

wine
▸ **RELATED ADJECTIVE:** vinaceous
▸ **RELATED MANIA:** oenomania
▸ **RELATED ENTHUSIAST:** oenophile
▸ **RELATED ADJECTIVE:** vinous

QUOTATIONS
A sight of the label is worth fifty years' experience
[Michael Broadbent *Wine Tasting*]
God made only water, but man made wine
[Victor Hugo *Les Contemplations*]
Wine is the drink of the gods, milk the drink of babies, tea the drink of women, and water the drink of beasts
[John Stuart Blackie]
When the wine is in, the wit is out
[Thomas Becon *Catechism*]
strong brother in God and last companion, Wine
[Hilaire Belloc *Heroic Poem upon Wine*]
Look not thou upon the wine when it is red, when it giveth his colour in the cup... at the last it biteth like a serpent, and stingeth like an adder
[Bible: Proverbs]
Give strong drink unto him that is ready to perish, and wine unto those that be of heavy hearts
[Bible: Proverbs]
Wine, madame, is God's next best gift to man
[Ambrose Bierce *The Devil's Dictionary*]

PROVERBS
There is truth in wine (in vino veritas)

▹ *See panel* **Grapes used in making wine; Wines**

wing AS A NOUN 1 = **organ of flight**, pinion *(poetic)*, pennon *(poetic)* • *The bird flapped its wings furiously.*

WINDS

Wind	Location	Wind	Location
berg wind	South Africa	levanter	W Mediterranean
bise	Switzerland	libeccio	Corsica
bora	Adriatic Sea	meltemi *or* etesian wind	NE Mediterranean
buran	central Asia	mistral	S France to Mediterranean
Cape doctor	Cape Town, South Africa	monsoon	S Asia
chinook	Washington & Oregon coasts	nor'wester	Southern Alps, New Zealand
		pampero	S America
föhn	N slopes of the Alps	simoom *or* simoon	Arabia & N Africa
harmattan	W African coast	sirocco	N Africa to S Europe
khamsin	Egypt	tramontane	W coast of Italy

Beaufort scale

Beaufort number	Wind force	Speed (kph)	Speed (knots)	Characteristics
0	Calm	less than 1	less than 1	smoke goes straight up; sea like a mirror
1	Light air	1-5	1-3	smoke blows in the wind; sea ripples, but without foam crests
2	Light breeze	6-11	4-6	wind felt on the face; leaves rustle; small wavelets; wave crests have a glassy appearance and do not break
3	Gentle breeze	12-19	7-10	light flag flutters; leaves in constant motion; large wavelets; wave crests begin to break; scattered white horses
4	Moderate breeze	20-28	11-16	dust and loose paper blown about; small branches move; small waves, becoming larger; white horses fairly frequent
5	Fresh	29-38	17-21	small trees sway; moderate waves; white horses frequent
6	Strong	39-49	22-27	hard to use umbrellas; large waves begin to form; white foam crests more extensive
7	Near gale	50-61	28-33	hard to walk into; whole trees in motion; sea heaps up; white foam from breaking waves begins to be blown along the direction of the wind
8	Gale	62-74	34-40	twigs break off trees; moderately high waves; edges of crests begin to break off into spindrift; foam is blown along the direction of the wind
9	Strong gale	75-88	41-47	slates lost; high waves; crests of waves begin to topple, tumble and roll over; spray may affect visibility
10	Storm	89-102	48-55	trees uprooted; considerable structural damage; very high waves; the surface of the sea takes on a white appearance; visibility affected
11	Violent storm	103-117	56-63	widespread damage; exceptionally high waves; small and medium-size ships may be lost to view behind the waves; visibility affected
12	Hurricane	118 and over	64 and over	violent, massive damage; the air is filled with foam and spray; visibility very seriously affected

2 = annexe, part, side, section, extension, adjunct, ell *(U.S.)* • *We were given an office in the empty west wing of the building.* **3 = faction**, grouping, group, set, side, arm, section, camp, branch, circle, lobby, segment, caucus, clique, coterie, schism, cabal • *the liberal wing of the Democratic party*
▸ **AS A VERB 1 = fly**, soar, glide, take wing • *Several birds broke cover and went winging over the lake.*
2 = hurry, fly, race, speed, streak, zoom, hasten, hurtle • *He was soon winging his way home to rejoin his family.*
3 = wound, hit, nick, clip, graze • *He shot at the bird but only managed to wing it.*
▸ **IN PHRASES: wing it = improvise**, ad lib, play it by ear, busk it *(informal)*, extemporize • *I'd forgotten my notes so I just had to wing it.*

wink **AS A VERB 1 = blink**, bat, flutter, nictate, nictitate • *Brian winked an eye at me, giving me his seal of approval.*
2 = twinkle, flash, shine, sparkle, gleam, shimmer, glimmer • *From the hotel window, they could see lights winking on the bay.*
▸ **AS A NOUN 1 = blink**, flutter, nictation, nictitation • *Diana gave me a reassuring wink.*
2 = twinkle, flash, sparkle, gleam, blink, glimmering, glimmer • *In the distance, he noticed the wink of a red light.*
▸ **IN PHRASES: in the wink of an eye = quickly**, in a moment, in a second, in a flash, in an instant, in a split second, in the blink of an eye *(informal)*, in a jiffy *(informal)*, in a twinkling, in two shakes of a lamb's tail *(informal)* • *It was all over in the wink of an eye.*
wink at something = condone, allow, ignore, overlook, tolerate, put up with *(informal)*, disregard, turn a blind eye to, blink at, connive at, pretend not to notice, shut your eyes to • *Corrupt police have been known to wink at crimes in return for bribes.*

winkle **AS A VERB**
▸ **IN PHRASES: winkle someone out = force someone out**, dislodge, extricate, smoke out, prise someone out • *He somehow managed to winkle Picard out of his room.*
winkle something out = extract, dig out, draw out, extricate, prise out, worm out • *They will go to any lengths to winkle out information.*

winner = victor, first, champion, master, champ *(informal)*, conqueror, vanquisher, prizewinner, conquering hero • *She will present the trophies to the winners.*
OPPOSITES: loser, failure, flop *(informal)*

winning **AS AN ADJECTIVE 1 = victorious**, first, top,

WINES

Wines

Amarone
Asti Spumante
Bairrada
Bandol
Banyuls
Barbaresco
Barbera d'Albi
Barbera d'Asti
Barolo
Barsac
beaujolais
beaujolais nouveau
Bereich Bernkastel
Bergerac
blanc de blancs
Blanquette de Limoux
Bordeaux
Bourgogne
Bourgueil
Brouilly
Brunello di Montalcino
Bucelas
Bull's Blood *or* Egri Bikaver
Burgundy
Cahors
canary
Carema
Cava
Chablis
Chambertin
Champagne
chardonnay
chianti
Colheita Port
claret
Condrieu
Constantia
Corbières
Coteaux du Tricastin
Côte de Beaune-Villages
Côte Rôtie
Côtes du Rhône
Crémant d'Alsace
Crémant de Loire
Crozes-Hermitage
crusted port
Dão
Entre-Deux-Mers
Faugères
Fitou
Fleurie
Frascati
Fumé Blanc
Gaillac
Gattinara
Gavi
Gevrey-Chambertin
Gigondas
Grange Hermitage
Graves
Hermitage
hock
jerepigo
Jurançon
lachryma Christi
Lambrusco
Liebfraumilch
Lirac
Liqueur Muscat
Liqueur Tokay
Mâcon
Mâcon-Villages
Madeira
Málaga
Margaux
Marsala
Médoc
Meursault
Minervois
Monbazillac
Montepulciano d'Abruzzo
montilla
Moscato d'Asti
Moselle
muscadet
Muscat de Beaumes-de-Venise
muscatel
Niersteiner
Nuits-Saint-Georges
Orvieto
Parrina
Pauillac
Pessac-Léognan
Pinot Grigio
Piesporter
Pomerol
Pommard
port
Pouilly-Fuissé
Pouilly-Fumé
Quarts de Chaume
Quincy
retsina
Rhine wine
riesling
Rioja
Roero
Rosé d'Anjou
Rosso Conero
Rüdesheimer
Rueda
Rully
sack
Saint-Émilion
Saint-Estèphe
Saint-Julien
Saint-Véran
Salice Salentino
Sancerre
Saumur
Sauternes
scuppernong
sherry
straw wine
Tavel
Teroldego Rotaliano
Tokaji
Tokay-Pinot Gris
Valdepeñas
Valpolicella
Verdicchio
Vinho Verde
vin ordinaire
Vino Nobile di Montepulciano
Vosne-Romanée
Vouvray

Wine-producing areas

	Country		Country		Country
Ahr	Germany	Goulburn Valley	Australia	Penedès	Spain
Alsace	France	Hawkes Bay	New Zealand	Piedmont	Italy
Alto Adige *or* Südtirol	Italy	Hessiches Bergstrasse	Germany	–	Portugal
Anjou	France	–	Greece	Provence	France
–	Argentina	–	Hungary	Rheingau	Germany
–	Austria	Hunter Valley	Australia	Rheinhessen	Germany
Barossa Valley	Australia	Languedoc	France	Rheinpfalz	Germany
Baden	Germany	Loire	France	Rhône	France
Bordeaux	France	Marlborough	New Zealand	Ribera del Duro	Spain
–	Bulgaria	Margaret River	Australia	Rioja	Spain
Burgundy	France	Martinborough	New Zealand	–	Romania
California	U.S.A.	McLaren Vale	Australia	Sicily	Italy
Chablis	France	Mendocino	U.S.A.	Sonoma	U.S.A.
Champagne	France	Mittelrhein	Germany	–	South Africa
Chianti	Italy	–	Moldavia	–	Switzerland
–	Chile	Mornington Peninsula	Australia	Touraine	France
Clare Valley	Australia	Mosel-Saar-Ruwer	Germany	Tuscany	Italy
Coonawarra	Australia	Nahe	Germany	Umbria	Italy
Côte d'Or	France	Napa Valley	U.S.A.	Valdepeñas	Spain
Finger Lakes	U.S.A.	Navarra	Spain	Veneto	Italy
Franken	Germany	New York State	U.S.A.	Washington State	U.S.A.
Friuli	Italy	Oregon	U.S.A.	Württemberg	Germany
Gisborne	New Zealand	Padthaway	Australia	Yarra Valley	Australia

Wine terms

abbocatto
AC *or* appellation contrôlée
amabile
amontillado
AOC *or* appellation d'origine contrôlée
aszú
Ausbruch
Auslese
Baumé
Beerenauslese
botrytis
botrytized
Brix
brut
cream
crianza
cru bourgeois
cru classé
cuvée
demi-sec
dessert wine
DOC *or* denominazione di origine controllata
DOCG *or* denominazione di origine controllata e garantita
dolce
dry
Einzellage
Eiswein
erzeugerabfüllung
estate bottled
flor
fino
fortified wine
garrafeira
grand cru
gran reserva
Grosslage
halbtrocken
Kabinett
late harvest
LBV *or* Late-Bottled Vintage (Port)
malmsey
malolactic fermentation
manzanilla
medium
medium-dry
medium-sweet
méthode champenoise

WINE TERMS (CONTINUED)

moelleux	premier cru	Ruby Port	table wine	vieilles vignes
mousseux	puttonyos	sec	Tafelwein	vigneron
noble rot	QbA, Qualitätswein	secco	tannin	vignoble
NV *or* non-vintage	bestimmter	second wine	Tawny Port	vin de pays
Oechsle	Anbaugebiet, *or*	Sekt	terroir	vin de table
oloroso	Qualitätswein	sin crianza	tinto	vin doux naturel
organic	QmP *or* Qualitätswein	Sigle Quinta Port	trocken	vin gris
pale cream	mit Prädikat	solera	Trockenbeerenauslese	vino da tavola
passito	recioto	sparkling wine	*or* TBA	vintage
pétillant	récolte	Spätlese	varietal	Weingut
plonk	reserva	spumante	VDQS *or* Vin Délimité	Weissherbst
pourriture noble	rosé	sur lie	de Qualité Supérieure	Winzergenossenschaft
prädikat	riserva	sweet	vendage tardive	

successful, unbeaten, conquering, triumphant, undefeated, vanquishing, top-scoring, unvanquished • *The winning team returned home to a heroes' welcome.*
2 = **charming**, taking, pleasing, sweet, attractive, engaging, lovely, fascinating, fetching, delightful, cute, disarming, enchanting, endearing, captivating, amiable, alluring, bewitching, delectable, winsome, prepossessing, likable *or* likeable • *She had great charm and a winning personality.*
OPPOSITES: offensive, unpleasant, unattractive
▸ **AS A PLURAL NOUN** = **spoils**, profits, gains, prize, proceeds, takings, booty • *The poker player collected his winnings and left.*

winnow **AS A VERB** = **separate**, fan, divide, sift • *a device which winnows wheat, separating the chaff from the seed*
▸ **IN PHRASES: winnow something** *or* **someone out** = **separate**, part, screen, select, divide, sort out, comb, sift, cull • *Most of the faulty products were winnowed out by these processes.*

winsome = **charming**, taking, winning, pleasing, pretty, fair, sweet, attractive, engaging, fascinating, pleasant, fetching, cute, disarming, enchanting, endearing, captivating, agreeable, amiable, alluring, bewitching, delectable, comely, likable *or* likeable, fit (*Brit. informal*) • *She gave him her most winsome smile.*

winter
▸ **RELATED ADJECTIVES:** brumal, hibernal, hiemal

winter sport

WINTER SPORTS

Alpine skiing	figure skating	ski jumping
biathlon	luge	slalom
bobsleigh	Nordic skiing	snowboarding
curling	Nordic walking	speed skating
downhill racing	skating	super-G
ice dancing	skibobbing	tobogganing
ice hockey	skiing	
ice skating *or*	skijoring	

wintry 1 = **cold**, freezing, frozen, harsh, icy, chilly, snowy, frosty, hibernal • *The wintry weather continues to sweep across the country.*
OPPOSITES: warm, bright, pleasant
2 = **unfriendly**, cold, cool, remote, distant, bleak, chilly, frigid, cheerless • *Melissa gave him a wintry smile and walked on without a word.*

wipe **AS A VERB** 1 = **clean**, dry, polish, brush, dust, rub, sponge, mop, swab • *She wiped her hands on the towel.*
2 = **erase**, remove, take off, get rid of, take away, rub off, efface, clean off, sponge off • *Gleb wiped the sweat from his face.*
▸ **AS A NOUN** = **rub**, clean, polish, brush, lick, sponge, mop, swab • *I'll give the surfaces a wipe with some disinfectant.*
▸ **IN PHRASES: wipe something up** = **clean something up**, mop something up, sop something up • *I spilled my coffee and Mom leaned across me to wipe it up.*
wipe something *or* **someone out** = **destroy**, eliminate, take out (*slang*), massacre, slaughter, erase, eradicate, blow away (*slang, chiefly U.S.*), obliterate, liquidate (*informal*), annihilate, efface, exterminate, expunge, extirpate, wipe from the face of the earth (*informal*), kill to the last man, kennet (*Austral. slang*), jeff (*Austral. slang*) • *a fanatic who is determined to wipe out anyone who opposes him*

wire **AS A NOUN** 1 = **cable**, lead, flex • *I ripped out the telephone wire.*
2 = **cable**, telegraph, telex, radiogram • *I sent him a wire congratulating him.*
▸ **AS A VERB** = **send**, cable, telegraph • *I'm wiring you some money.*

wiry 1 = **lean**, strong, tough, thin, spare, skinny, stringy, sinewy • *a wiry and athletic young man*
OPPOSITES: fat, weak, flabby
2 = **stiff**, rough, coarse, curly, kinky, bristly • *wiry black hair*

wisdom 1 = **understanding**, learning, knowledge, intelligence, smarts (*slang, chiefly U.S.*), judgment, insight, enlightenment, penetration, comprehension, foresight, erudition, discernment, sagacity, sound judgment, sapience • *a man respected for his wisdom and insight*
OPPOSITES: stupidity, foolishness
2 = **knowledge**, learning, philosophy, scholarship, lore • *Semitic wisdom, religion and faith*
3 = **prudence**, reason, sense, intelligence, logic, circumspection, astuteness, judiciousness • *Many have expressed doubts about the wisdom of the decision.*
OPPOSITES: bêtise (*rare*), nonsense, folly
▸ **RELATED ADJECTIVE:** sagacious
▸ **RELATED MANIA:** sophomania

QUOTATIONS

Knowledge comes, but wisdom lingers
[Alfred, Lord Tennyson *Locksley Hall*]

Wisdom denotes the pursuing of the best ends by the best means
[Francis Hutcheson *Inquiry into the Original of our Ideas of Beauty and Virtue*]

The art of being wise is the art of knowing what to overlook
[William James *Principles of Psychology*]

Be wiser than other people if you can, but do not tell them so
[Lord Chesterfield]

wise enough to play the fool
[William Shakespeare *Twelfth Night*]

The price of wisdom is above rubies
[*Bible: Job*]

Some folks are wise, and some are otherwise
[Tobias Smollett *Roderick Random*]
But where shall wisdom be found? And where is the place of understanding?
[*Bible: Job*]
Wisdom is the principal thing; therefore get wisdom; and with all thy getting get understanding
[*Bible: Proverbs*]
It is the province of knowledge to speak and it is the privilege of wisdom to listen
[Oliver Wendell Holmes *The Poet at the Breakfast-Table*]
PROVERBS
Don't teach your grandmother to suck eggs

wise **AS AN ADJECTIVE** 1 = **sage**, knowing, understanding, aware, informed, clever, intelligent, sensible, switched-on (*informal*), enlightened, shrewd, discerning, perceptive, well-informed, sussed (*Brit. slang*), erudite, sagacious, sapient, clued-up (*informal*), grounded • *She has the air of a wise woman.*
OPPOSITES: stupid, silly, foolish
2 = **sensible**, sound, politic, informed, reasonable, clever, intelligent, rational, logical, shrewd, prudent, judicious, well-advised • *She had made a very wise decision.*
OPPOSITES: stupid, silly, unwise
▸ **IN PHRASES: put someone wise = inform**, tell, alert, warn about, notify of, apprise of, tip off about, clue in *or* up about (*informal*), let into the secret about • *He took me aside and put me wise to the rumours.*
wise to = aware of, familiar with, acquainted with, cognizant of • *Consumers are becoming wise to the tricks of the marketing trade.*
QUOTATIONS
The stupid neither forgive nor forget; the naive forgive and forget; the wise forgive but do not forget
[Thomas Szasz *The Second Sin*]
PROVERBS
It's a wise child that knows its own father
A word to the wise is enough
It is easy to be wise after the event

wisecrack **AS A NOUN** = **joke**, sally, gag (*informal*), quip, jibe, barb, jest, witticism, smart remark, pithy remark, sardonic remark • *He kept making wisecracks about her weight.*
▸ **AS A VERB** = **joke**, quip, jibe, jest, tell jokes, be facetious • *He soon had them in stitches as he wisecracked with old Hollywood friends.*

wish **AS A NOUN** 1 = **desire**, liking, want, longing, hope, urge, intention, fancy (*informal*), ambition, yen (*informal*), hunger, aspiration, craving, lust, yearning, inclination, itch (*informal*), thirst, whim, hankering • *Clearly she had no wish for his company.*
OPPOSITES: dislike, reluctance, aversion
2 = **request**, will, want, order, demand, desire, command, bidding, behest (*literary*) • *The decision was made against the wishes of the party leader.*
▸ **AS A VERB** 1 = **want**, feel, choose, please, desire, think fit • *We can dress as we wish nowadays.*
2 = **require**, ask, order, direct, bid, desire, command, instruct • *I will do as you wish.*
3 = **bid**, greet with • *He wished me a good morning.*
▸ **IN PHRASES: wish for = desire**, want, need, hope for, long for, crave, covet, aspire to, yearn for, thirst for, hunger for, hanker for, sigh for, set your heart on, desiderate • *They both wished for a son to carry on the family business.*
PROVERBS
The wish is father to the thought
If wishes were horses, beggars would ride

wishy-washy 1 = **feeble**, weak, bland, ineffective, ineffectual, insipid, vapid, jejune • *I can't stand indecisive, wishy-washy men.*
2 = **pale**, bland, wan, pallid, insipid • *She always dresses in wishy-washy pastel colours.*

wisp = **piece**, twist, strand, thread, shred, snippet • *She smoothed away a wisp of hair from her eyes.*

wispy 1 = **straggly**, fine, thin, frail, wisplike • *Grey wispy hair straggled down to her shoulders.*
2 = **thin**, light, fine, delicate, fragile, flimsy, ethereal, insubstantial, gossamer, diaphanous, wisplike • *a wispy chiffon dress*

wistful = **melancholy**, longing, dreaming, sad, musing, yearning, thoughtful, reflective, dreamy, forlorn, mournful, contemplative, meditative, pensive, disconsolate • *There was a wistful look in his eyes when he spoke of his childhood.*

wit **AS A NOUN** 1 = **humour**, fun, quips, banter, puns, pleasantry, repartee, wordplay, levity, witticisms, badinage, jocularity, facetiousness, drollery, raillery, waggishness, wittiness • *Bill was known for his biting wit.*
OPPOSITES: gravity, seriousness, sobriety
2 = **humorist**, card (*informal*), comedian, wag, joker, dag (*N.Z. informal*), punster, farceur (*French*), epigrammatist • *a man who fancied himself as a great wit*
3 = **cleverness**, mind, reason, understanding, sense, brains, smarts (*slang, chiefly U.S.*), judgment, perception, wisdom, insight, common sense, intellect, comprehension, ingenuity, acumen, nous (*Brit. slang*), discernment, practical intelligence • *The information is there for anyone with the wit to use it.*
OPPOSITES: ignorance, folly, stupidity
▸ **IN PHRASES: at your wits' end = in despair**, lost, stuck (*informal*), stumped, baffled, bewildered, at a loss, at the end of your tether • *I just can't think what to do – I'm at my wits' end.*
QUOTATIONS
True wit is nature to advantage dress'd,
What oft was thought, but ne'er so well expressed
[Alexander Pope *An Essay on Criticism*]
Brevity is the soul of wit
[William Shakespeare *Hamlet*]
Next to being witty yourself, the best thing is being able to quote another's wit
[Christian N. Bovee]
Wit is the epitaph of an emotion
[Friedrich Nietzsche *Menschliches, Allzumenschliches*]

witch = **enchantress**, magician, hag, crone, occultist, sorceress, Wiccan, necromancer • *an evil witch who had cast a spell on the prince*
QUOTATIONS
witch: (1) An ugly and repulsive old woman, in a wicked league with the devil. (2) A beautiful and attractive young woman, in wickedness a league beyond the devil
[Ambrose Bierce *The Devil's Dictionary*]

witchcraft = **magic**, spell, witching, voodoo, the occult, wizardry, black magic, enchantment, occultism, sorcery, incantation, Wicca, the black art, witchery, necromancy, sortilege, makutu (*N.Z.*) • *She was found guilty of witchcraft and burned at the stake.*

witch doctor = **shaman**, healer, sangoma (*S. African*) • *He believed the village witch doctor had put a curse on him.*

with = **accompanied by**, in the company of, escorted by, WIV (*S.M.S.*), w/ (*S.M.S.*) • *She came with her two children.*

withdraw 1 = **remove**, pull, take off, pull out, extract, take away, pull back, draw out, draw back • *Cassandra withdrew her hand from Roger's.* • *He reached into his pocket and withdrew a piece of paper.*
2 = **take out**, extract, draw out • *They withdrew 100 dollars from their bank account.*
3 = **retreat**, go, leave (*informal*), retire, depart, pull out, fall back, pull back, back out, back off, cop out (*slang*), disengage from • *Troops withdrew from the country last March.*
OPPOSITES: go on, advance, progress

W

4 = go, leave, retire, retreat, depart, make yourself scarce, absent yourself • *The waiter poured the wine and then withdrew.*
5 = pull out, leave, drop out, secede, disengage, detach yourself, absent yourself • *The African National Congress threatened to withdraw from the talks.*
6 = retract, recall, take back, revoke, rescind, disavow, recant, disclaim, abjure, unsay • *He withdrew his remarks and said he had not intended to cause offence.*

withdrawal 1 = **removal**, ending, stopping, taking away, abolition, elimination, cancellation, termination, extraction, discontinuation • *the withdrawal of foreign aid*
2 = exit, retirement, departure, pull-out, retreat, exodus, evacuation, disengagement • *the withdrawal of troops from Eastern Europe*
3 = departure, retirement, exit, secession • *his withdrawal from government in 1946*
4 = retraction, recall, disclaimer, repudiation, revocation, disavowal, recantation, rescission, abjuration • *The charity insists on a withdrawal of the accusations.*

withdrawn = **uncommunicative**, reserved, retiring, quiet, silent, distant, shy, shrinking, detached, aloof, taciturn, introverted, timorous, unforthcoming • *Her husband had become withdrawn and moody.*
OPPOSITES: open, forward, outgoing

wither 1 = **wilt**, dry, decline, shrink, decay, disintegrate, perish, languish, droop, shrivel, desiccate • *Farmers have watched their crops wither because of the drought.*
OPPOSITES: develop, thrive, flourish
2 = waste, decline, shrink, shrivel, atrophy • *His leg muscles had withered from lack of use.*
3 = fade, decline, wane, perish • *His dream of being a famous footballer withered and died.*
OPPOSITES: increase, develop, succeed
4 = humiliate, blast, shame, put down, snub, mortify, abash • *Mary withered me with a glance.*

withering 1 = **scornful**, blasting, devastating, humiliating, snubbing, blighting, hurtful, mortifying • *She launched a withering attack on the Press.*
2 = destructive, killing, devastating, deadly, murderous, death-dealing, slaughterous • *The forces were unable to withstand the withering artillery barrages.*

withhold 1 = **keep secret**, keep, refuse, hide, reserve, retain, sit on *(informal)*, conceal, suppress, hold back, keep back • *Police withheld the victim's name until her relatives had been informed.*
OPPOSITES: give (out), accord, reveal
2 = hold back, check, resist, suppress, restrain, repress, keep back • *She could not withhold a scornful comment as he passed.*
OPPOSITES: release, reveal, expose

W

within = **inside**, in, surrounded by, enclosed by, within the bounds *or* confines of • *A small tent stood within a thicket of trees.*

with it = **fashionable**, in *(informal)*, happening *(informal)*, the latest *(informal)*, modern, swinging *(slang)*, progressive, stylish, trendy *(Brit. informal)*, up-to-date, in vogue, up-to-the-minute, modish, schmick *(Austral. informal)*, funky • *Don't you hate it when old people try to be with it and trendy?*

without = **lacking**, wanting, needing, requiring, short of, in need of, deprived of, destitute of, w/o *(S.M.S.)* • *Many people are still without power and heating because of the floods.*

withstand = **resist**, take, face, suffer, bear, weather, oppose, take on, cope with, brave, confront, combat, endure, defy, tolerate, put up with *(informal)*, thwart, stand up to, hold off, grapple with, hold out against, stand firm against • *A politician has to be able to withstand criticism from the Press.*
OPPOSITES: give way to, give in to

witless = **foolish**, crazy, stupid, silly, dull, daft *(informal)*, senseless, goofy *(informal)*, idiotic, dozy *(Brit. informal)*, inane, loopy *(informal)*, crackpot *(informal)*, moronic, obtuse, unintelligent, empty-headed, asinine, imbecilic, braindead *(informal)*, dumb-ass *(slang)*, halfwitted, rattlebrained *(slang)* • *clueless, witless and one-dimensional pop stars*

witness AS A NOUN 1 = **observer**, viewer, spectator, looker-on, watcher, onlooker, eyewitness, bystander, beholder • *No witnesses of the crash have come forward.*
2 = testifier, deponent, attestant • *Eleven witnesses were called to testify.*
▸ AS A VERB 1 = **see**, mark, view, watch, note, notice, attend, observe, perceive, look on, be present at, behold *(archaic or literary)* • *Anyone who witnessed the attack is urged to contact the police.*
2 = countersign, sign, endorse, validate • *Ask a friend to witness your signature on the application.*
▸ IN PHRASES: **bear witness** 1 = **confirm**, show, prove, demonstrate, bear out, testify to, be evidence of, corroborate, attest to, be proof of, vouch for, evince, betoken, be a monument to, constitute proof of • *Many of his poems bear witness to the years he spent in India.*
2 = give evidence, testify, depose, give testimony, depone • *His mother bore witness in court that he had been at home that night.*
▸ RELATED ADJECTIVE: testimonial

witter = **chatter**, chat, rabbit (on) *(Brit. informal)*, babble, waffle *(informal, chiefly Brit.)*, cackle, twaddle, clack, burble, gab *(informal)*, prattle, tattle, jabber, blab, gabble, blather, blether, prate, earbash *(Austral. & N.Z. slang)* • *She witters on about her boyfriend all the time.*

witticism = **quip**, sally, pun, one-liner *(slang)*, riposte, pleasantry, repartee, epigram, play on words, bon mot, clever remark, witty remark • *This witticism produced a burst of raucous laughter.*

witty = **humorous**, gay, original, brilliant, funny, clever, amusing, lively, sparkling, ingenious, fanciful, whimsical, droll, piquant, facetious, jocular, epigrammatic, waggish • *one of those genuinely witty speakers to whom one could listen for hours*
OPPOSITES: boring, stupid, dull

wizard 1 = **magician**, witch, shaman, sorcerer, occultist, magus, conjuror, warlock, mage *(archaic)*, enchanter, necromancer, thaumaturge *(rare)*, tohunga *(N.Z.)* • *Merlin, the legendary wizard who worked magic for King Arthur*
2 = genius, star, expert, master, ace *(informal)*, guru, buff *(informal)*, adept, whizz *(informal)*, prodigy, maestro, virtuoso, boffin *(Brit. informal)*, hotshot *(informal)*, rocket scientist *(informal, chiefly U.S.)*, wiz *(informal)*, whizz kid *(informal)*, wonk *(informal)*, maven *(U.S.)*, fundi *(S. African)*, up-and-comer *(informal)* • *a mathematical wizard at Harvard University*

wizardry 1 = **expertise**, skill, know-how *(informal)*, craft, mastery, cleverness, expertness • *a piece of technical wizardry*
2 = magic, witching, witchcraft, voodoo, enchantment, occultism, sorcery, the black art, witchery, necromancy, conjuration, sortilege • *Hogwarts School of Witchcraft and Wizardry*

wizened = **wrinkled**, lined, worn, withered, dried up, shrivelled, gnarled, shrunken, sere *(archaic)* • *a little wizened old fellow with no teeth*
OPPOSITES: rounded, smooth, swollen

wobble AS A VERB 1 = **shake**, rock, sway, tremble, quake, waver, teeter, totter, seesaw • *The ladder wobbled on the uneven ground.*
2 = tremble, shake, vibrate • *My voice wobbled with nerves.*
3 = hesitate, waver, fluctuate, dither *(chiefly Brit.)*, be undecided, vacillate, shillyshally *(informal)*, be unable to make up your mind, swither *(Scot.)* • *He dithered and wobbled when questioned on his policies.*
▸ AS A NOUN 1 = **unsteadiness**, shake, tremble, quaking

• *He rode off on his bicycle with only a slight wobble.*
2 = unsteadiness, shake, tremor, vibration • *There was a distinct wobble in her voice when she replied.*

wobbly **1 = unstable**, shaky, unsafe, uneven, teetering, unbalanced, tottering, rickety, unsteady, wonky *(Brit. slang)* • *I was sitting on a wobbly plastic chair.*
2 = unsteady, weak, unstable, shaky, quivery, all of a quiver *(informal)* • *His legs felt wobbly after the long flight.*
3 = shaky, unsteady, tremulous • *'I want to go home,' she said in a wobbly voice.*

woe **1 = misery**, suffering, trouble, pain, disaster, depression, distress, grief, agony, gloom, sadness, hardship, sorrow, anguish, misfortune, unhappiness, heartache, heartbreak, adversity, dejection, wretchedness • *He listened to my tale of woe.*
OPPOSITES: pleasure, fortune, happiness
2 = problem, trouble, trial, burden, grief, misery, curse, hardship, sorrow, misfortune, heartache, heartbreak, affliction, tribulation • *He did not tell his friends about all his woes.*

woebegone **= gloomy**, low, blue, troubled, sad, miserable, forlorn, mournful, dejected, downcast, grief-stricken, lugubrious, long-faced, sorrowful, wretched, disconsolate, funereal, crestfallen, doleful, downhearted, down in the dumps *(informal)*, cheerless, hangdog, down in the mouth *(informal)*, chapfallen • *She sniffed and looked quite woebegone.*

woeful **1 = wretched**, sad, unhappy, tragic, miserable, gloomy, grieving, dismal, pathetic, afflicted, pitiful, anguished, agonized, disconsolate, doleful, pitiable • *those woeful people to whom life had dealt a bad hand*
OPPOSITES: happy, delighted, contented
2 = sad, distressing, tragic, miserable, gloomy, dismal, pathetic, harrowing, heartbreaking, grievous, mournful, plaintive, heart-rending, sorrowful, doleful, piteous • *a woeful ballad about lost love*
OPPOSITES: happy, joyful, light-hearted
3 = pitiful, mean, bad, poor, shocking, sorry, disappointing, terrible, awful, appalling, disastrous, inadequate, dreadful, miserable, hopeless, rotten *(informal)*, pathetic, catastrophic, duff *(Brit. informal)*, feeble, disgraceful, lousy *(slang)*, grievous, paltry, deplorable, abysmal, lamentable, calamitous, shitty *(taboo slang)*, wretched, pitiable, godawful *(slang)*, not much cop *(Brit. slang)* • *the team's recent woeful performance*

wolf **AS A VERB** *often with* **down = devour**, stuff, bolt, cram, hoover *(informal)*, scoff *(slang)*, gulp, gobble, pack away *(informal)*, gorge on, gollop • *I was in the changing-room wolfing down tea and sandwiches.*
OPPOSITES: bite, peck, nibble
▸ **AS A NOUN = womanizer**, seducer, Don Juan, Casanova, philanderer, Lothario, lecher, lady-killer, lech *or* letch *(informal)* • *My grandfather is still an old wolf.*
▸ **RELATED ADJECTIVE:** lupine
▸ **NAME OF FEMALE:** bitch
▸ **NAME OF YOUNG:** cub, whelp
▸ **COLLECTIVE NOUNS:** pack, rout, herd

woman **1 = lady**, girl, miss, female, bird *(slang)*, dame *(slang)*, sheila *(Austral. & N.Z. informal)*, vrou *(S. African)*, maiden *(archaic)*, chick *(slang)*, maid *(archaic)*, gal *(slang)*, lass, lassie *(informal)*, wench *(facetious)*, adult female, she, charlie *(Austral. slang)*, chook *(Austral. slang)*, wahine *(N.Z.)* • *No woman in her right mind would ever want to go out with you.*
ho *(U.S. derogatory slang)*
OPPOSITES: man, boy, guy *(informal)*
2 = girlfriend, girl, wife, partner, mate, lover, squeeze *(informal)*, bride, mistress, spouse, old lady *(informal)*, sweetheart, significant other *(U.S. informal)*, ladylove, bidie-in, wifey *(informal)* • *I know my woman will never leave me, whatever I do.*
3 = maid, domestic, char *(informal)*, housekeeper, lady-in-waiting, chambermaid, handmaiden, charwoman, maidservant, female servant • *Catriona had been nagging him to get a woman in to clean once a week.*
▸ **RELATED PREFIXES:** gyn- or gyno-, gynaeco-
▸ **RELATED MANIA:** gynomania
▸ **RELATED PHOBIA:** gynophobia

QUOTATIONS

The meaning of what it is to be a woman has never been more open-ended and therefore more filled with anxiety
[Nancy Friday *What is a Real Woman?*]

Women have served all these centuries as looking-glasses possessing the magic and delicious power of reflecting the figure of man at twice its natural size
[Virginia Woolf *A Room of One's Own*]

The individual woman is required ... a thousand times a day to choose either to accept her appointed role and thereby rescue her good disposition out of the wreckage of her self-respect, or else follow an independent line of behavior and rescue her self-respect out of the wreckage of her good disposition
[Jeannette Rankin]

When a woman behaves like a man why doesn't she behave like a nice man?
[Edith Evans]

The great question that has never been answered, and which I have not yet been able to answer, despite my thirty years of research into the feminine soul, is 'What does a woman want?'
[Sigmund Freud]

A woman can look both moral and exciting – if she also looks as if it was quite a struggle
[Edna Ferber]

I think being a woman is like being Irish ... Everyone says you're important and nice, but you take second place all the same
[Iris Murdoch *The Red and the Green*]

Fickle and changeable always is woman
[Virgil *Aeneid*]

A man is as old as he's feeling,
A woman as old as she looks
[Mortimer Collins *The Unknown Quantity*]

Men play the game, women know the score
[Roger Woddis]

A complete woman is probably not a very admirable creature. She is manipulative, uses other people to get her own way, and works within whatever system she is in
[Anita Brookner]

One is not born a woman; one becomes one
[Simone de Beauvoir *The Second Sex*]

Woman was God's second blunder
[Friedrich Nietzsche *Der Antichrist*]

Being a woman is of special interest only to aspiring male transsexuals. To actual women it is merely a good excuse not to play football
[Fran Lebowitz *Metropolitan Life*]

A woman seldom writes her mind but in her postscript
[Sir Richard Steele *The Spectator*]

A woman without a man is like a fish without a bicycle
[attributed to Gloria Steinem]

Frailty, thy name is woman!
[William Shakespeare *Hamlet*]

A woman, especially, if she have the misfortune of knowing anything, should conceal it as well as she can
[Jane Austen *Northanger Abbey*]

A woman who thinks she is intelligent demands equal rights with men. A woman who is intelligent does not
[Colette]

W

Whatever women do they must do twice as well as men to be thought half as good. Luckily this is not difficult
[Charlotte Whitton]
All women become like their mothers. That is their tragedy. No man does. That's his
[Oscar Wilde *The Importance of Being Earnest*]
When women go wrong, men go right after them
[Mae West]
Women – one half of the human race at least – care fifty times more for a marriage than a ministry
[Walter Bagehot *The English Constitution*]
Women can't forgive failure
[Anton Chekhov *The Seagull*]
Women are really much nicer than men: no wonder we like them
[Kingsley Amis *A Bookshop Idyll*]
Any woman who chooses to behave like a full human being should be warned that the armies of the status quo will treat her as something of a dirty joke
[Gloria Steinem *Outrageous Acts and Everyday Rebellions*]
There are only three things to be done with a woman. You can love her, suffer for her, or turn her into literature
[Lawrence Durrell *Justine*]
If all men are born free, how is it that all women are born slaves?
[Mary Astell *Some Reflections upon Marriage*]
Good women always think it is their fault when someone else is being offensive. Bad women never take the blame for anything
[Anita Brookner *Hotel du Lac*]
O fairest of creation, last and best
Of all God's works
[John Milton *Paradise Lost*]

PROVERBS
A woman's place is in the home
Hell hath no fury like a woman scorned
A woman's work is never done

womanhood 1 = **adulthood**, maturity • *a young girl on the threshold of womanhood*
2 = **women**, womankind, womenfolk, the female sex, womenkind • *a fine example of modern womanhood*

womanizer = **philanderer**, wolf *(informal)*, seducer, Don Juan, Casanova, Lothario, lecher, lady-killer, lech *or* letch *(informal)* • *He had a reputation as a womanizer and gambler.*

womankind = **women**, womenfolk, the female sex, womenkind • *Childbearing is womankind's chief role in life.*

womanly 1 = **feminine**, motherly, female, warm, tender, matronly, ladylike • *the accepted womanly qualities of compassion and unselfishness*
2 = **curvaceous**, ample, voluptuous, shapely, curvy *(informal)*, busty *(informal)*, buxom, full-figured, Rubenesque, Junoesque • *a womanly figure*

womb
▸ **TECHNICAL NAME:** uterus
▸ **RELATED ADJECTIVE:** uterine

wonder **AS A VERB** 1 = **think**, question, doubt, puzzle, speculate, query, ponder, inquire, ask yourself, meditate, be curious, conjecture, be inquisitive • *I wonder what he's up to.* • *We were wondering where you were.*
2 = **be amazed**, stare, marvel, be astonished, gape, boggle, be awed, be flabbergasted *(informal)*, gawk, be dumbstruck, stand amazed • *I wondered at the arrogance of the man.*
▸ **AS A NOUN** 1 = **amazement**, surprise, curiosity, admiration, awe, fascination, astonishment, bewilderment, wonderment, stupefaction • *'How did you know that?' Bobby exclaimed in wonder.*
2 = **phenomenon**, sight, miracle, spectacle, curiosity, marvel, prodigy, rarity, portent, wonderment, nonpareil • *a fascinating lecture on the wonders of nature*

SEVEN WONDERS OF THE ANCIENT WORLD

Colossus of Rhodes
Hanging Gardens of Babylon
Mausoleum of Halicarnassus
Pharos of Alexandria
Phidias' statue of Zeus at Olympia
Pyramids of Egypt
Temple of Artemis at Ephesus

wonderful 1 = **excellent**, mean *(slang)*, great *(informal)*, topping *(Brit. slang)*, brilliant, cracking *(Brit. informal)*, outstanding, smashing *(informal)*, superb, fantastic *(informal)*, tremendous, ace *(informal)*, magnificent, fabulous *(informal)*, marvellous, terrific, sensational *(informal)*, sovereign, awesome *(slang)*, admirable, super *(informal)*, brill *(informal)*, stupendous, out of this world *(informal)*, tiptop, bodacious *(slang, chiefly U.S.)*, boffo *(slang)*, jim-dandy *(slang)*, chillin' *(U.S. slang)*, booshit *(Austral. slang)*, exo *(Austral. slang)*, sik *(Austral. slang)*, rad *(informal)*, phat *(slang)*, schmick *(Austral. informal)* • *I've always thought he was a wonderful actor.*
OPPOSITES: bad, average, terrible
2 = **remarkable**, surprising, odd, strange, amazing, extraordinary, fantastic, incredible, astonishing, staggering, eye-popping *(informal)*, marvellous, startling, peculiar, awesome, phenomenal, astounding, miraculous, unheard-of, wondrous *(archaic or literary)*, awe-inspiring, jaw-dropping • *This is a wonderful achievement for one so young.*
OPPOSITES: common, usual, ordinary

wondrous = **wonderful**, strange, amazing, extraordinary, fantastic, incredible, marvellous, awesome, miraculous, awe-inspiring, jaw-dropping • *a wondrous vast land of lakes and forests*

wonky 1 = **askew**, squint *(informal)*, awry, out of alignment, skewwhiff *(Brit. informal)* • *The wheels of the trolley kept going wonky.*
2 = **shaky**, weak, wobbly, unsteady, infirm • *He's got a wonky knee.*

wont **AS AN ADJECTIVE** = **accustomed**, used, given, in the habit of • *Both have made mistakes, as human beings are wont to do.*
▸ **AS A NOUN** = **habit**, use, way, rule, practice, custom • *Keith woke early, as was his wont.*

woo 1 = **seek**, cultivate, try to attract, curry favour with, seek to win, solicit the goodwill of • *The bank wooed customers by offering low interest rates.*
2 = **court**, chase, pursue, spark *(rare)*, importune, seek to win, pay court to, seek the hand of, set your cap at *(old-fashioned)*, pay your addresses to, pay suit to, press your suit with • *The penniless author successfully wooed and married Roxanne.*

wood **AS A NOUN** 1 = **timber**, planks, planking, lumber *(U.S.)* • *The floor is made of polished wood.*
2 = **woodland**, trees, forest, grove, hurst *(archaic)*, thicket, copse, coppice, bushland • *After dinner they went for a walk through the wood.*
3 = **firewood**, fuel, logs, kindling • *We gathered wood for the fire.*
▸ **IN PHRASES:** **out of the wood(s)** *used in negative constructions* = **safe**, clear, secure, in the clear, out of danger, home and dry *(Brit. slang)*, safe and sound • *The nation's economy is not out of the woods yet.*
▸ **RELATED ADJECTIVES:** ligneous, sylvan, xyloid
▸ **RELATED MANIA:** hylomania
▹ *See panel* **Types of wood**

woodcock
▸ **COLLECTIVE NOUN:** fall

wooded = **tree-covered**, forested, timbered, woody, sylvan *(poetic)*, tree-clad • *a wooded valley*

TYPES OF WOOD

African mahogany
afrormosia
alerce
amboyna
apple
ash
assegai
balsa
basswood
baywood
beech
beefwood
birch
black walnut
bog oak
boxwood
brazil
bulletwood
butternut
cade
calamander
camwood
candlewood
cedar
cherry
chestnut
citron wood
coachwood
corkwood
crabwood
cypress
durmast
eaglewood
ebony
elm
fiddlewood
fir
gaboon
gopher wood
greenheart
guaiacum
gumwood
hackberry
hardwood
hazel
hemlock
hickory
hornbeam
iroko
ironwood
jacaranda
jelutong
kauri
kiaat
kingwood
koa
lancewood
larch
locust
mahogany
maple
marblewood
nutwood
oak
olive
orangewood
padauk
Paraná pine
partridge-wood
pear
persimmon
pine
pitch pine
poon
poplar
pulpwood
quassia
quebracho
red cedar
red fir
red gum
red oak
ribbonwood
rosewood
sandalwood
sandarac
sappanwood
sasswood
satinwood
Scots pine
shagbark *or* shellbark
sneezewood
softwood
spotted gum
spruce
stinkwood
sumach
sycamore
tamarack
tamarind
teak
thorn
toon
torchwood
tulipwood
tupelo
walnut
western red cedar
white cedar
white pine
whitewood
willow
yellowwood
yew
zebrawood

wooden 1 = **made of wood**, timber, woody, of wood, ligneous • *the shop's bare brick walls and wooden floorboards* 2 = **awkward**, stiff, rigid, clumsy, lifeless, stilted, ungainly, gauche, gawky, inelegant, graceless, maladroit • *The film is marred by the wooden acting of the star.*
OPPOSITES: flowing, elegant, graceful
3 = **expressionless**, empty, dull, blank, vacant, lifeless, deadpan, colourless, glassy, unresponsive, unemotional, emotionless, spiritless • *It's hard to tell from his wooden expression whether he's happy or sad.*

woodland = **forest**, trees, woods, wood, bushland • *the strip of woodland which bordered the stream*

woodwork = **carpentry**, joinery • *Joseph instructs a class in woodwork.*

wool AS A NOUN 1 = **fleece**, hair, coat • *These shawls are made from the wool of mountain goats.*
2 = **yarn** • *a ball of wool*
▸ IN PHRASES: **dyed in the wool** = **hardened**, confirmed, settled, fixed, uncompromising, inflexible, diehard, inveterate, unshakeable, unchangeable • *He is a dyed-in-the-wool socialist.*
pull the wool over someone's eyes = **deceive**, kid (*informal*), trick, fool, take in (*informal*), con (*slang*), dupe, delude, bamboozle (*informal*), hoodwink, put one over on (*slang*), pull a fast one on someone (*informal*), lead someone up the garden path (*informal*) • *a phony psychic who pulled the wool over everyone's eyes*

woolly *or (U.S. (sometimes))* **wooly** AS AN ADJECTIVE
1 = **woollen**, fleecy, made of wool • *She wore a woolly hat with pompoms.*
2 = **vague**, confused, clouded, blurred, unclear, muddled, fuzzy, indefinite, hazy, foggy, nebulous, ill-defined, indistinct • *It is no good setting vague, woolly goals – we need a specific aim.*
OPPOSITES: clear, obvious, precise
3 = **downy**, hairy, shaggy, flocculent • *The plant has silvery, woolly leaves.*
▸ AS A NOUN = **sweater**, jersey, jumper, pullover • *Bring a woolly – it can get cold here at night.*

woozy = **dizzy**, confused, rocky (*informal*), bemused, dazed, wobbly, nauseated, unsteady, tipsy, befuddled • *The fumes made us feel a bit woozy.*

word AS A NOUN 1 = **term**, name, expression, designation, appellation (*formal*), locution, vocable • *The word 'ginseng' comes from the Chinese word 'Shen-seng'.*
2 = **chat**, tête-à-tête, talk, discussion, consultation, chitchat, brief conversation, colloquy, confabulation, confab (*informal*), heart-to-heart, powwow (*informal*) • *James, could I have a quick word with you?*
3 = **comment**, remark, expression, declaration, utterance, brief statement • *I'd like to say a word of thanks to everyone who helped me.*
4 = **message**, news, latest (*informal*), report, information, account, notice, advice, communication, intelligence, bulletin, dispatch, gen (*Brit. informal*), communiqué, intimation, tidings, heads up (*U.S. & Canad.*) • *There is no word from the authorities on the reported attack.*
5 = **promise**, guarantee, pledge, undertaking, vow, assurance, oath, parole, word of honour, solemn oath, solemn word • *He simply cannot be trusted to keep his word.*
6 = **command**, will, order, go-ahead (*informal*), decree, bidding, mandate, commandment, edict, ukase (*rare*) • *I want nothing said about this until I give the word.*
7 = **rumour**, talk, gossip, goss (*informal*), hearsay, the word on the street (*informal*) • *The word is that he's planning to retire.*
▸ AS A PLURAL NOUN 1 = **remark**, comment, statement, observation, declaration, utterance, pronouncement • *I was devastated when her words came true.*
2 = **text**, script, lyrics • *Can you hear the words on the album?*
▸ AS A VERB = **express**, say, state, put, phrase, utter, couch, formulate • *If I had written the letter, I might have worded it differently.*
▸ IN PHRASES: **have words** = **argue**, fight, row, clash, disagree, fall out (*informal*), feud, quarrel, squabble, wrangle, bicker, have a row, lock horns, cross swords, be at each other's throats, have a tiff (*informal*), have a barney (*Brit. informal*) • *We had words and she stormed out.*
in a word = **briefly**, in short, in a nutshell, to sum up, succinctly, concisely, not to put too fine a point on it, to put it briefly • *'Don't you like her?' 'In a word – no.'*
the last word 1 = **final say**, ultimatum • *Our manager has the last word on all major decisions.*
2 = **summation**, finis • *We'll let this gentleman have the last word.*
the last word in something = **epitome**, newest, best, latest, crown, cream, rage, ultimate, vogue, perfection, mother of all (*informal*), quintessence, crème de la crème (*French*), ne plus ultra (*Latin*), dernier cri (*French*) • *The spa is the last word in luxury.*

word for word *or* **word-for-word 1 = verbatim**, precisely, exactly, faithfully, to the letter, line for line, letter-for-letter • *He repeated the whole conversation word for word.*
2 = verbatim, direct, strict, accurate, exact, precise, faithful, literal, unadulterated, unabridged, unvarnished, undeviating, unembellished • *a word-for-word account of what had been said*
▸ **RELATED ADJECTIVES:** lexical, verbal
▸ **RELATED MANIA:** verbomania
▸ **RELATED PHOBIA:** logophobia

QUOTATIONS

In the beginning was the Word
[*Bible: St. John*]

Words are, of course, the most powerful drug used by mankind
[Rudyard Kipling]

For words, like Nature, half reveal
And half conceal the Soul within
[Alfred, Lord Tennyson]

'When I use a word,' Humpty Dumpty said in a rather scornful tone, 'it means just what I choose it to mean – neither more nor less.'
[Lewis Carroll *Through the Looking-Glass*]

Words just say what you want them to say; they don't know any better
[A.L. Kennedy *The Role of Notable Silences in Scottish History*]

and once sent out, a word takes wing beyond recall
[Horace *Epistles*]

Words are the physicians of a mind diseased
[Aeschylus *Prometheus Bound*]

Thought flies and words go on foot
[Julien Green *Journal*]

How often misused words generate misleading thoughts
[Herbert Spencer *Principles of Ethics*]

Words are the tokens current and accepted for conceits, as moneys are for values
[Francis Bacon *The Advancement of Learning*]

Words are wise men's counters, they do but reckon by them
[Thomas Hobbes *Leviathan*]

Oaths are but words, and words but wind
[Samuel Butler *Hudibras*]

wording = phraseology, words, language, phrasing, terminology, choice of words, mode of expression • *The wording is so vague that no-one knows what it actually means.*

wordplay = puns, wit, punning, repartee, witticisms • *He amused friends and colleagues with his clever wordplay.*

wordy = long-winded, rambling, windy, diffuse, garrulous, discursive, loquacious, verbose, prolix, pleonastic *(rare)* • *His speech is full of wordy rhetoric.*
OPPOSITES: short, brief, to the point

work AS A VERB 1 = be employed, do business, have a job, earn a living, be in work, hold down a job • *I want to work, I don't want to be on welfare.*
2 = labour, sweat, slave, toil, slog (away), drudge, peg away, exert yourself, break your back • *My father worked hard all his life.*
OPPOSITES: play, relax, laze
3 = function, go, run, operate, perform, be in working order • *The pump doesn't work and we have no running water.*
OPPOSITES: be broken, be out of order
4 = succeed, work out, pay off *(informal)*, be successful, be effective, do the trick *(informal)*, do the business *(informal)*, get results, turn out well, have the desired result, go as planned, do the business *(informal)* • *Most of these diets don't work.*
5 = accomplish, cause, create, effect, achieve, carry out, implement, execute, bring about, encompass, contrive • *Modern medicine can work miracles.*
6 = handle, move, excite, manipulate, rouse, stir up, agitate, incite, whip up, galvanize • *a performer with the ability to work an audience*
7 = cultivate, farm, dig, till, plough • *Farmers worked the fertile valleys.*
8 = operate, use, move, control, drive, manage, direct, handle, manipulate, wield, ply • *I learnt how to work the forklift.*
9 = manipulate, make, form, process, fashion, shape, handle, mould, knead • *Work the dough with your hands until it is very smooth.*
10 = progress, move, force, manoeuvre, make your way • *Rescuers were still working their way towards the trapped men.*
11 = move, twitch, writhe, convulse, be agitated • *His face was working in his sleep.*
12 = contrive, handle, fix *(informal)*, swing *(informal)*, arrange, exploit, manipulate, pull off, fiddle *(informal)*, bring off • *Some clever people work it so that they never have to pay taxes.*
▸ **AS A NOUN 1 = employment**, calling, business, job, line, office, trade, duty, craft, profession, occupation, pursuit, livelihood, métier • *What kind of work do you do?*
OPPOSITES: play, holiday, unemployment
2 = effort, industry, labour, grind *(informal)*, sweat, toil, slog, exertion, drudgery, travail *(literary)*, elbow grease *(facetious)* • *This needs time and a lot of hard work.*
OPPOSITES: rest, ease, leisure
3 = task, jobs, projects, commissions, duties, assignments, chores, yakka *(Austral. & N.Z. informal)* • *I used to take work home, but I don't do it any more.*
4 = handiwork, doing, act, feat, deed • *Police say the bombing was the work of extremists.*
5 = creation, performance, piece, production, opus, achievement, composition, oeuvre *(French)*, handiwork • *In my opinion, this is Rembrandt's greatest work.*
▸ **IN PHRASES: out of work = unemployed**, on the street, jobless, idle, on the dole *(Brit. informal)*, out of a job • *A third of the population is out of work.*

work on someone = persuade, influence, manipulate, sway, put pressure on, coax, lean on, cajole, soften up, put the squeeze on someone *(informal)*, twist someone's arm *(informal)* • *She's working on her dad to give her the money for the trip.*

work out 1 = happen, go, result, develop, come out, turn out, evolve, roll up, pan out *(informal)* • *Things didn't work out as planned.*
2 = succeed, flourish, go well, be effective, prosper, go as planned, prove satisfactory, do the business *(informal)* • *I hope everything works out for you in your new job.*
3 = exercise, train, practise, drill, warm up, do exercises • *I work out at a gym twice a week.*

work out at something = amount to, come to, reach, add up to, reach a total of • *The price per pound works out at £3.20.*

work someone up = excite, move, spur, wind up *(informal)*, arouse, animate, rouse, stir up, agitate, inflame, incite, instigate, get someone all steamed up *(slang)* • *By now she had worked herself up so much that she couldn't sleep.*

work something out 1 = solve, find out, resolve, calculate, figure out, clear up, suss (out) *(slang)*, puzzle out • *It took me some time to work out what was going on.*
2 = plan, form, develop, arrange, construct, evolve, devise, elaborate, put together, formulate, contrive • *Negotiators are due to meet today to work out a compromise.*

work something up = generate, rouse, instigate, foment, enkindle • *Malcolm worked up the courage to ask his grandfather for help.*
▸ **RELATED MANIA:** ergasiomania
▸ **RELATED PHOBIA:** ergasiophobia

W

QUOTATIONS

I just don't happen to think [work]'s an appropriate subject for an ethic

[Barbara Ehrenreich *Goodbye to the Work Ethic*]

Work expands so as to fill the time available for its completion

[N. Northcote Parkinson *Parkinson's Law*]

I mean, really: *Why work? Simply to buy more stuff?*

[Douglas Coupland *Generation X*]

Work is the curse of the drinking classes

[Oscar Wilde]

Work is the great cure of all maladies and miseries that ever beset mankind

[Thomas Carlyle]

If any would not work, neither should he eat

[*Bible: II Thessalonians*]

All that matters is love and work

[attributed to Sigmund Freud]

Anyone can do any amount of work, provided it isn't the work he is supposed to be doing

[Robert Benchley]

PROVERBS

All work and no play makes Jack a dull boy

workable = **viable**, possible, practical, feasible, practicable, doable • *This isn't a workable solution to the problem.*
OPPOSITES: impossible, useless, unworkable

workaday = **ordinary**, common, familiar, practical, routine, everyday, commonplace, mundane, prosaic, run-of-the-mill, humdrum, bog-standard *(Brit. & Irish slang)* • *an escape from the tedium of the workaday world*
OPPOSITES: different, special, extraordinary

worker = **employee**, hand, labourer, workman, craftsman, artisan, tradesman, wage earner, proletarian, working man *or* working woman • *Wages have been frozen and workers laid off.*

QUOTATIONS

The proletarians have nothing to lose but their chains. They have a world to win. Workers of all countries unite!

[Marx & Engels *The Communist Manifesto*]

workforce = **employees**, staff, personnel, human resources, manpower, labour force • *a country where half the workforce is unemployed*

working AS AN ADJECTIVE **1** = **employed**, labouring, in work, in a job • *Like most working women, I use a lot of convenience foods.*
2 = **functioning**, going, running, operating, active, operative, operational, functional, usable, serviceable, in working order • *the oldest working steam engine in the world*
3 = **effective**, useful, practical, sufficient, adequate • *I used to have a good working knowledge of French.*
▸ AS A NOUN = **operation**, running, action, method, functioning, manner, mode of operation • *computer systems which mimic the workings of the human brain*
▸ AS A PLURAL NOUN = **mine**, pit, shaft, quarry, excavations, diggings • *housing which was built over old mine workings*

workman = **labourer**, hand, worker, employee, mechanic, operative, craftsman, artisan, tradesman, journeyman, artificer *(rare)* • *The workmen were building a fence around the area.*

PROVERBS

A bad workman always blames his tools

workmanlike = **efficient**, professional, skilled, expert, masterly, careful, satisfactory, thorough, tasty *(Brit. informal)*, skilful, adept, painstaking, proficient • *craftsmen who do a consistent, workmanlike job*
OPPOSITES: cowboy *(informal)*, careless, amateurish

workmanship = **skill**, work, art, technique, manufacture, craft, expertise, execution, artistry, craftsmanship, handiwork, handicraft • *a carpenter who prided himself on the quality of his workmanship*

work of art = **masterpiece**, magnum opus, master work • *a collection of works of art of international importance*

workout = **exercise**, training, drill, warm-up, training session, practice session, exercise session • *Have a 35-minute aerobic workout three times a week.*

works **1** = **factory**, shop, plant, mill, workshop • *the belching chimneys of the steel-works at Corby*
2 = **writings**, productions, output, canon, oeuvre *(French)* • *the complete works of Milton*
3 = **deeds**, acts, actions, doings • *a religious order who dedicated their lives to prayer and good works*
4 = **mechanism**, workings, parts, action, insides *(informal)*, movement, guts *(informal)*, machinery, moving parts, innards *(informal)* • *The box held what looked like the works of a large clock.*

workshop **1** = **seminar**, class, discussion group, study group, masterclass • *She runs a writing workshop for women.*
2 = **factory**, works, shop, plant, mill • *a small workshop for repairing secondhand motorcycles*
3 = **workroom**, studio, atelier • *He got a job in the workshop of a local tailor.*

world AS A NOUN **1** = **earth**, planet, globe, earthly sphere • *It's a beautiful part of the world.*
2 = **mankind**, man, men, everyone, the public, everybody, humanity, human race, humankind, the race of man • *The world was shocked by this heinous crime.*
3 = **sphere**, system, area, field, environment, province, kingdom, realm, domain • *The publishing world had never seen an event quite like this.*
4 = **life**, nature, existence, creation, universe, cosmos • *Be happy, in this world and the next!*
5 = **planet**, star, orb, heavenly body • *conditions which would support life on other worlds*
6 = **period**, times, days, age, era, epoch • *What was life like for the ordinary man in the medieval world?*
▸ IN PHRASES: **a world of** = **a huge amount of**, a mountain of, a wealth of, a great deal of, a good deal of, an abundance of, an enormous amount of, a vast amount of • *They may look alike but there's a world of difference between them.*
for all the world = **exactly**, just like, precisely, in every way, to all intents and purposes, just as if, in every respect • *He looked for all the world as if he was dead.*
on top of the world = **overjoyed**, happy, ecstatic, elated, over the moon *(informal)*, exultant, on cloud nine *(informal)*, cock-a-hoop, in raptures, beside yourself with joy, stoked *(Austral. & N.Z. informal)* • *After his win, he was on top of the world.*
out of this world = **wonderful**, great *(informal)*, excellent, superb, fantastic *(informal)*, incredible, fabulous *(informal)*, marvellous, unbelievable, awesome *(slang)*, indescribable, bodacious *(slang, chiefly U.S.)*, booshit *(Austral. slang)*, exo *(Austral. slang)*, sik *(Austral. slang)*, rad *(informal)*, phat *(slang)*, schmick *(Austral. informal)* • *The food in this place is simply out of this world.*
think the world of someone = **love**, treasure, worship, adore, dote on, hold someone dear, have great affection for • *I thought the world of my father.*

QUOTATIONS

The world began without man, and it will end without him

[Claude Lévi-Strauss *Tristes Tropiques*]

All the world's a stage

[William Shakespeare *As You Like It*]

The world's mine oyster

[William Shakespeare *The Merry Wives of Windsor*]

world-class = **first-rate**, top, prime, excellent, outstanding, superb, elite, exceptional, superlative, A1 *or* A-one *(informal)*, mean *(slang)*, booshit *(Austral. slang)*, exo *(Austral. slang)*, sik *(Austral. slang)*, rad *(informal)*, phat *(slang)*,

W

schmick *(Austral. informal)* • *He was determined to become a world-class tennis player.*

worldly 1 = **earthly**, lay, physical, fleshly, secular, mundane, terrestrial, temporal, carnal, profane, sublunary • *It is time you woke up and focused your thoughts on more worldly matters.*
OPPOSITES: heavenly, spiritual, divine
2 = **materialistic**, grasping, selfish, greedy, avaricious, covetous, worldly-minded • *He has repeatedly criticized Western churches as being too worldly.*
OPPOSITES: moral, unworldly, nonmaterialistic
3 = **worldly-wise**, knowing, experienced, politic, sophisticated, cosmopolitan, urbane, blasé, well versed in the ways of the world • *He was worldly and sophisticated, quite unlike me.*
OPPOSITES: innocent, naive, unsophisticated

QUOTATIONS
Be wisely worldly, be not worldly wise
[Francis Quarles *Emblems*]

worldly-wise = **experienced**, knowing, worldly, sophisticated • *A more worldly-wise man would have seen through him at once.*
OPPOSITES: innocent, naive, inexperienced

world-view = **outlook**, views, attitude, perspective, point of view, viewpoint, standpoint, frame of mind • *Many artists express their world-view in their work.*

worldwide = **global**, general, international, universal, ubiquitous, omnipresent, pandemic • *Doctors fear a worldwide epidemic of this disease.*
OPPOSITES: national, local, limited

worm
▸ **RELATED ADJECTIVES:** vermiform, vermicular
▸ **RELATED PHOBIA:** helminthophobia

worn 1 = **ragged**, shiny, frayed, shabby, tattered, tatty, threadbare, the worse for wear • *an elderly man in well-cut but worn clothes*
2 = **haggard**, lined, drawn, pinched, wizened, careworn • *A sudden smile lit up his worn face.*
3 = **exhausted**, spent, tired, fatigued, wearied, weary, played-out *(informal)*, worn-out, jaded, tired out • *She looked tired and worn.*

worn out *or* **worn-out** 1 = **worn**, done, used, broken-down, ragged, useless, rundown, frayed, used-up, shabby, tattered, tatty, threadbare, decrepit, clapped out *(Brit., Austral. & N.Z. informal)*, moth-eaten • *Always replace worn-out tyres with the same brand.*
2 = **exhausted**, spent, done in *(informal)*, tired, all in *(slang)*, fatigued, wiped out *(informal)*, weary, played-out, knackered *(slang)*, prostrate, clapped out *(Austral. & N.Z. informal)*, tired out, dog-tired *(informal)*, zonked *(slang)*, shagged out *(Brit. slang)*, fit to drop, jiggered *(dialect)*, dead *or* out on your feet *(informal)* • *I was exhausted – worn out by the strain I'd been under.*
OPPOSITES: rested, fresh, refreshed
3 = **obsolete**, old, stock, stereotyped, commonplace, stale, overworked, antiquated, corny *(informal)*, well worn, trite, clichéd, hackneyed, overused, time-worn • *The problem will be solved by common sense, not worn-out religious dogmas.*

worried = **anxious**, concerned, troubled, upset, afraid, bothered, frightened, wired *(slang)*, nervous, disturbed, distressed, tense, distracted, uneasy, fearful, tormented, distraught, apprehensive, perturbed, on edge, ill at ease, overwrought, fretful, hot and bothered, unquiet, antsy *(informal)* • *I'm not worried about the future.*
OPPOSITES: quiet, calm, unworried

worrisome = **disturbing**, worrying, upsetting, distressing, troublesome, disquieting, vexing, perturbing, irksome, bothersome • *Worrisome rumours of war were beginning to spread.*

worry **AS A VERB** 1 = **be anxious**, be concerned, be worried, obsess, brood, fret, agonize, feel uneasy, get in a lather *(informal)*, get in a sweat *(informal)*, get in a tizzy *(informal)*, get overwrought • *I worry about my daughter constantly.*
OPPOSITES: be unconcerned, be unperturbed, be apathetic
2 = **trouble**, upset, harry, bother, disturb, distress, annoy, plague, irritate, tease, unsettle, torment, harass, hassle *(informal)*, badger, hector, disquiet, pester, vex, perturb, tantalize, importune, make anxious • *'Why didn't you tell us?' 'I didn't want to worry you.'*
OPPOSITES: comfort, calm, soothe
3 = **attack**, bite, kill, tear, go for, harry, savage, harass, lacerate, gnaw at • *The dog was shot dead by a farmer for worrying sheep.*
▸ **AS A NOUN** 1 = **anxiety**, concern, care, fear, trouble, misery, disturbance, torment, woe, irritation, unease, apprehension, misgiving, annoyance, trepidation, perplexity, vexation • *His last years were overshadowed by financial worry.*
OPPOSITES: comfort, calm, peace of mind
2 = **problem**, care, trouble, trial, bother, plague, pest, torment, irritation, hassle *(informal)*, annoyance, vexation • *Robert's health had always been a worry to his wife.*

worrying = **disturbing**, trying, taxing, difficult, upsetting, alarming, grave, distressing, tricky, unpleasant, dismaying, sticky *(informal)*, traumatic, unsettling, daunting, harassing, troublesome, problematic, harrowing, prickly *(informal)*, disquieting, niggling, thorny, perturbing, worrisome, nerve-wracking, bothersome, vexatious • *the worrying trend of anorexia among younger girls*

worsen 1 = **deteriorate**, decline, sink, decay, get worse, degenerate, go downhill *(informal)*, go from bad to worse, take a turn for the worse, retrogress • *The security forces had to intervene to prevent the situation from worsening.*
OPPOSITES: improve, recover, mend
2 = **aggravate**, damage, exacerbate, make worse • *These options would actually worsen the economy and add to the deficit.*
OPPOSITES: improve, enhance, upgrade

worship **AS A VERB** 1 = **revere**, praise, respect, honour, adore, glorify, reverence, exalt, laud, pray to, venerate, deify, adulate • *people who still worship the pagan gods*
OPPOSITES: mock, ridicule, dishonour
2 = **love**, adore, idolize, put on a pedestal • *The children worship their father.*
OPPOSITES: despise, disdain, spurn
▸ **AS A NOUN** = **reverence**, praise, love, regard, respect, honour, glory, prayer(s), devotion, homage, adulation, adoration, admiration, exaltation, glorification, deification, laudation • *The temple had been a centre of worship of the goddess Hathor.*

worth 1 = **value**, price, rate, cost, estimate, valuation • *The total worth of the Australian sharemarket is now close to $520 billion.*
OPPOSITES: worthlessness
2 = **merit**, value, quality, importance, desert(s), virtue, excellence, goodness, estimation, worthiness • *She did not appreciate her husband's true worth until he was gone.*
OPPOSITES: wretchedness, unworthiness
3 = **usefulness**, value, benefit, quality, importance, utility, excellence, goodness • *The client has little means of judging the worth of the advice he is given.*
OPPOSITES: futility, insignificance, uselessness

worthless 1 = **valueless**, poor, miserable, trivial, trifling, paltry, trashy, measly, wretched, two a penny *(informal)*, rubbishy, poxy *(slang)*, nickel-and-dime *(U.S. slang)*, wanky *(taboo slang)*, a dime a dozen, nugatory, chickenshit *(U.S. slang)*, negligible • *This piece of old junk is totally worthless.*
OPPOSITES: valuable, precious, profitable
2 = **useless**, meaningless, pointless, futile, no use, insignificant, unimportant, ineffectual, unusable, unavailing, not much cop *(Brit. slang)*, inutile, not worth a hill of beans *(chiefly U.S.)*, negligible, pants *(slang)* • *Training is worthless unless there is proof that it works.*
OPPOSITES: important, significant, useful

3 = **good-for-nothing**, base, abandoned, useless, vile, abject, despicable, depraved, contemptible, ignoble • *Murphy was an evil, worthless man.*
OPPOSITES: decent, worthy, honourable

worthwhile = **useful**, good, valuable, helpful, worthy, profitable, productive, beneficial, meaningful, constructive, justifiable, expedient, gainful • *The study did not produce any worthwhile results.*
OPPOSITES: useless, vain, trivial

worthy AS AN ADJECTIVE = **praiseworthy**, good, excellent, deserving, valuable, decent, reliable, worthwhile, respectable, upright, admirable, honourable, honest, righteous, reputable, virtuous, dependable, commendable, creditable, laudable, meritorious, estimable • *worthy members of the community*
OPPOSITES: useless, dubious, disreputable
▸ AS A NOUN = **dignitary**, notable, luminary, bigwig *(informal)*, big shot *(informal)*, personage, big hitter *(informal)*, heavy hitter *(informal)* • *The event brought together worthies from many fields.*
OPPOSITES: nobody, punter *(informal)*, pleb
▸ IN PHRASES: **be worthy of** = **deserve**, rate, earn, justify, merit, qualify for, warrant, have a right to, be deserving of, have a claim to *or* on • *a cause which is worthy of our support*

would-be = **budding**, potential, so-called, professed, dormant, self-styled, latent, wannabe *(informal)*, unfulfilled, undeveloped, self-appointed, unrealized, manqué, soi-disant *(French)*, quasi- • *a book that provides encouragement for would-be writers*

wound AS A NOUN 1 = **injury**, cut, damage, hurt, harm, slash, trauma *(Pathology)*, gash, lesion, laceration • *Six soldiers are reported to have died of their wounds.*
2 *often plural* = **trauma**, injury, shock, pain, offence, slight, torture, distress, insult, grief, torment, anguish, heartbreak, pang, sense of loss • *Her experiences have left deep psychological wounds.*
▸ AS A VERB 1 = **injure**, cut, hit, damage, wing, hurt, harm, slash, pierce, irritate, gash, lacerate • *The driver of the bus was wounded by shrapnel.*
2 = **offend**, shock, pain, hurt, distress, annoy, sting, grieve, mortify, cut to the quick, hurt the feelings of, traumatize • *He was deeply wounded by the treachery of his closest friends.*

QUOTATIONS
what wound did ever heal but by degrees?
[William Shakespeare *Othello*]

wounding = **hurtful**, pointed, cutting, damaging, acid, bitter, slighting, offensive, distressing, insulting, cruel, savage, stinging, destructive, harmful, malicious, scathing, grievous, barbed, unkind, pernicious, caustic, spiteful, vitriolic, trenchant, injurious, maleficent • *wounding remarks about her appearance*

wound up = **tense**, strained, wired *(slang)*, nervous, anxious, restless, edgy, jittery *(informal)*, uptight *(informal)*, on edge, jumpy, twitchy *(informal)*, overwrought, fidgety, keyed up, adrenalized • *I was too wound up to sleep.*

wraith = **ghost**, spirit, shade *(literary)*, phantom, spectre, spook *(informal)*, apparition, revenant, eidolon, kehua *(N.Z.)* • *She believed herself to have been visited by wraiths from the afterlife.*

wrangle AS A VERB = **argue**, fight, row, dispute, scrap, disagree, fall out *(informal)*, contend, quarrel, brawl, squabble, spar, bicker, have words, altercate • *The two parties are still wrangling over the timing of the election.*
▸ AS A NOUN = **argument**, row, clash, dispute, contest, set-to *(informal)*, controversy, falling-out *(informal)*, quarrel, brawl, barney *(informal)*, squabble, bickering, tiff, altercation, slanging match *(Brit.)*, turf war *(informal)*, angry exchange, argy-bargy *(Brit. informal)*, bagarre *(French)* • *He was involved in a legal wrangle with the Health Secretary.*

wrap AS A VERB 1 = **cover**, surround, fold, enclose, roll up, cloak, shroud, swathe, muffle, envelop, encase, sheathe, enfold, bundle up • *She wrapped the baby in a blanket.*
OPPOSITES: open, strip, uncover
2 = **pack**, package, parcel (up), tie up, gift-wrap • *Harry had wrapped some presents for the children.*
OPPOSITES: unpack, unwrap
3 = **bind**, wind, fold, swathe • *She wrapped a handkerchief round her bleeding hand.*
OPPOSITES: unwind
▸ AS A NOUN = **cloak**, cape, stole, mantle, shawl • *a model wearing a leopard-print wrap*
▸ IN PHRASES: **wrap something up** 1 = **giftwrap**, pack, package, enclose, bundle up, enwrap • *We spent the evening wrapping up Christmas presents.*
2 = **end**, conclude, wind up, terminate, finish off, round off, tidy up, polish off, bring to a close • *NATO defence ministers wrap up their meeting in Brussels today.*
wrap up = **dress warmly**, muffle up, wear something warm, put warm clothes on • *Make sure you wrap up warmly before you go out.*

wrapped up *usually with* **in** = **absorbed (in)**, lost (in), involved (in), preoccupied (with), immersed (in), engrossed (in), rapt (in) • *He's too wrapped up in his career.*

wrapper = **cover**, case, paper, packaging, wrapping, jacket, envelope, sleeve, sheath • *an unsmoked cigar in its cellophane wrapper*

wrath = **anger**, passion, rage, temper, fury, resentment, irritation, indignation, ire, displeasure, exasperation, choler • *His action incurred the wrath of animal rights activists.*
OPPOSITES: delight, pleasure, satisfaction

QUOTATIONS
I was angry with my friend,
I told my wrath, my wrath did end.
I was angry with my foe,
I told it not, my wrath did grow
[William Blake *A Poison Tree*]
nursing her wrath to keep it warm
[Robert Burns *Tam o' Shanter*]
wrath: anger of a superior quality and degree, appropriate to exalted characters and momentous occasions
[Ambrose Bierce *The Devil's Dictionary*]

wrathful = **angry**, raging, furious, choked, pissed *(taboo slang)*, infuriated, incensed, enraged, indignant, pissed off *(taboo slang)*, irate, displeased, incandescent, wroth *(archaic)*, tooshie *(Austral. slang)* • *He feared his stern and wrathful father.*
OPPOSITES: happy, pleased

wreak 1 = **create**, work, cause, visit, effect, exercise, carry out, execute, inflict, bring about • *Violent storms wreaked havoc on the coast.*
2 = **unleash**, express, indulge, vent, gratify, give vent to, give free rein to • *He wreaked vengeance on the men who had betrayed him.*

wreath = **garland**, band, ring, crown, loop, festoon, coronet, chaplet • *She wore a wreath of jasmine flowers in her hair.*

wreathe 1 = **surround**, envelop, encircle, enfold, coil around, writhe around, enwrap • *Cigarette smoke wreathed her face.*
2 = **festoon**, wind, crown, wrap, twist, coil, adorn, intertwine, interweave, entwine, twine, engarland • *The temple's huge columns were wreathed in laurels.*

wreck AS A VERB 1 = **destroy**, break, total *(slang)*, smash, ruin, devastate, mar, shatter, spoil, demolish, sabotage, trash *(slang)*, ravage, dash to pieces, kennet *(Austral. slang)*, jeff *(Austral. slang)* • *Vandals wrecked the garden.*
OPPOSITES: build, create, save
2 = **spoil**, blow *(slang)*, ruin, devastate, shatter, undo, screw

up *(informal)*, cock up *(Brit. slang)*, fuck up *(offensive taboo slang)*, play havoc with, crool or cruel *(Austral. slang)* • *His life has been wrecked by the tragedy.*
OPPOSITES: save, fulfil, make possible
3 = **run aground**, strand, shipwreck, run onto the rocks • *His ship was wrecked off the coast of Ireland.*
▸ **AS A NOUN** 1 = **shipwreck**, derelict, hulk, sunken vessel • *the wreck of a sailing ship*
2 = **ruin**, mess, destruction, overthrow, undoing, disruption, devastation, desolation • *a broken man contemplating the wreck of his life*
OPPOSITES: saving, creation, preservation
3 = **remains**, pieces, ruin, fragments, debris, rubble, hulk, wrack • *Mark was dragged from the burning wreck of his car.*
4 = **accident**, smash, pile-up • *He was killed in a car wreck.*

wren
▸ **NAME OF FEMALE:** jenny

wrench **AS A VERB** 1 = **twist**, force, pull, tear, rip, tug, jerk, yank, wring, wrest • *They wrenched open the passenger door and got into the car.*
2 = **sprain**, strain, rick, distort • *He had wrenched his ankle badly in the fall.*
▸ **AS A NOUN** 1 = **twist**, pull, rip, tug, jerk, yank • *The rope stopped his fall with a wrench that broke his neck.*
2 = **sprain**, strain, twist • *We are hoping the injury is just a wrench.*
3 = **blow**, shock, pain, ache, upheaval, uprooting, pang • *I knew it would be a wrench to leave home.*
4 = **spanner**, adjustable spanner, shifting spanner • *He took a wrench from his toolbox.*

wrest 1 = **seize**, take, win, extract • *He has been trying to wrest control from the central government.*
2 = **pull**, force, strain, seize, twist, extract, wrench, wring • *She wrested the suitcase from the chauffeur's grasp.*

wrestle = **fight**, battle, struggle, combat, contend, strive, grapple, tussle, scuffle • *The boys wrestled with each other in the garden.*

wretch 1 = **poor thing**, unfortunate, poor soul, poor devil *(informal)*, miserable creature • *Before the wretch had time to reply, he was shot.*
2 = **scoundrel**, rat *(informal)*, shit *(taboo slang)*, worm, bastard *(offensive)*, villain, rogue, bugger *(taboo slang)*, outcast, swine, rascal, son-of-a-bitch *(slang, chiefly U.S. & Canad.)*, asshole *(U.S. & Canad. taboo slang)*, profligate, turd *(taboo slang)*, vagabond, ruffian, motherfucker *(taboo slang, chiefly U.S.)*, cur, rotter *(slang, chiefly Brit.)*, scumbag *(slang)*, good-for-nothing, miscreant, bad egg *(old-fashioned or informal)*, blackguard, mother *(taboo slang, chiefly U.S.)*, cocksucker *(taboo slang)*, asswipe *(U.S. & Canad. taboo slang)*, wrong 'un *(Austral. slang)* • *I think he's a mean-minded, vindictive old wretch.*

W

wretched 1 = **unfortunate**, poor, sorry, hapless, pitiful, luckless, star-crossed, pitiable • *wretched people living in abject poverty*
2 = **unhappy**, depressed, distressed, miserable, gloomy, hopeless, dismal, pathetic, worthless, melancholy, pitiful, forlorn, abject, woeful, dejected, downcast, disconsolate, funereal, crestfallen, doleful, down in the dumps *(informal)*, pitiable, cheerless, woebegone, comfortless, brokenhearted • *The wretched look on the little girl's face melted his heart.*
OPPOSITES: happy, contented, cheerful
3 = **worthless**, poor, sorry, miserable, pathetic, inferior, paltry, deplorable • *What a wretched excuse!*
OPPOSITES: great, successful, excellent
4 = **shameful**, mean, low, base, shabby, vile, low-down *(informal)*, paltry, despicable, contemptible, scurvy, crappy *(slang)*, poxy *(slang)* • *Politicians – I hate the whole wretched lot of them.*
OPPOSITES: decent, worthy, admirable
5 = **ill**, poorly, sick, crook *(Austral. & N.Z. informal)*, sickly, unwell, off colour *(Brit. informal)*, under the weather *(informal)* • *The flu was making him feel absolutely wretched.*

wriggle **AS A VERB** 1 = **jiggle**, turn, twist, jerk, squirm, writhe • *The audience were fidgeting and wriggling in their seats.*
2 = **wiggle**, jerk, wag, jiggle, waggle • *She pulled off her shoes and stockings and wriggled her toes.*
3 = **crawl**, snake, worm, twist and turn, zigzag, slink • *Bauman wriggled along the passage on his stomach.*
▸ **AS A NOUN** = **twist**, turn, jerk, wag, squirm, wiggle, jiggle, waggle • *With a wriggle, he freed himself from her grasp and ran off.*
▸ **IN PHRASES:** **wriggle out of something** = **twist**, avoid, duck, dodge, extricate yourself from, talk your way out of, worm your way out of • *The government is trying to wriggle out of its responsibilities.*

wring = **twist**, force, squeeze, extract, screw, wrench, coerce, wrest, extort • *He hoped to put pressure on the British and wring concessions from them.*

wrinkle **AS A NOUN** 1 = **line**, fold, crease, furrow, pucker, crow's-foot, corrugation • *His face was covered with wrinkles.*
2 = **crease**, gather, fold, crumple, furrow, rumple, pucker, crinkle, corrugation • *He noticed a wrinkle in the material.*
▸ **AS A VERB** = **crease**, line, gather, fold, crumple, ruck, furrow, rumple, pucker, crinkle, corrugate • *I wrinkled the velvet.* • *The skin around her eyes had begun to wrinkle.*
OPPOSITES: level, press, smooth

wrinkled 1 = **lined**, furrowed, shrivelled, wizened, weather-beaten, crinkly, time-worn • *I looked older and more wrinkled than ever.*
2 = **creased**, crumpled, rumpled, crinkled • *His suit was wrinkled and he looked very tired.*

wrist
▸ **TECHNICAL NAME:** carpus
▸ **RELATED ADJECTIVE:** carpal

writ = **summons**, document, decree, indictment, court order, subpoena, arraignment • *He issued a writ against one of his critics.*

write **AS A VERB** 1 = **record**, copy, scribble, take down, inscribe, set down, transcribe, jot down, put in writing, commit to paper, indite, put down in black and white • *Write your name and address at the top of the page.*
2 = **compose**, create, author, draft, pen, draw up • *She wrote articles for magazines in Paris.*
3 = **correspond**, get in touch, keep in touch, write a letter, drop a line, drop a note, e-mail • *Why didn't you write and let me know you were coming?*
▸ **IN PHRASES:** **write something off** 1 = **wreck**, total *(slang)*, crash, destroy, trash *(slang)*, smash up, damage beyond repair • *John's written off four cars. Now he sticks to public transport.*
2 = **cancel**, shelve, forget about, cross out, score out, give up for lost • *The President persuaded the West to write off Polish debts.*
write something *or* **someone off** = **disregard**, ignore, dismiss, regard something *or* someone as finished, consider something *or* someone as unimportant • *He is fed up with people writing him off because of his age.*

writer = **author**, novelist, hack, columnist, scribbler, scribe, essayist, penman, wordsmith, man of letters, penpusher, littérateur, penny-a-liner *(rare)* • *detective stories by American writers*

QUOTATIONS
The wise writer ... writes for the youth of his own generation, the critics of the next, and the schoolmasters of ever afterward
[F. Scott Fitzgerald *Some Sort of Epic Grandeur*]
Some editors are failed writers – but so are most writers
[T.S. Eliot]

Writers, like teeth, are divided into incisors and grinders
[Walter Bagehot *Estimates of some Englishmen and Scotchmen*]

▹ *See panels* **Diarists; Dramatists; Novelists; Poets; Writers**

writhe = squirm, struggle, twist, toss, distort, thrash, jerk, wriggle, wiggle, contort, convulse, thresh • *He was writhing on the floor in agony.*

writing AS A NOUN **1 = script**, hand, print, printing, fist *(informal)*, scribble, handwriting, scrawl, calligraphy, longhand, penmanship, chirography • *It's a little difficult to read your writing.*
2 = document, work, book, letter, title, opus, publication, literature, composition, belle-lettre • *Althusser's writings are focused mainly on France.*
▸ IN PHRASES: **writing on the wall = omen**, sign, warning, signal, portent, forewarning, ill omen • *We should have seen the writing on the wall and guessed what was coming.*
▸ RELATED MANIAS: graphomania, scribomania
▸ RELATED PHOBIA: graphophobia

QUOTATIONS

Writing, at its best, is a lonely life
[Ernest Hemingway *speech, accepting the Nobel Prize for Literature*]

I think writing does come out of a deep well of loneliness and a desire to fill some kind of gap
[Jay McInerney]

Would you not like to try all sorts of lives – one is so very small – but that is the satisfaction of writing – one can impersonate so many people
[Katherine Mansfield *letter*]

wrong AS AN ADJECTIVE **1 = amiss**, faulty, unsatisfactory, not right, defective, awry • *Pain is the body's way of telling us that something is wrong.*
2 = incorrect, mistaken, false, faulty, inaccurate, untrue, erroneous, off target, unsound, in error, wide of the mark, fallacious, off base *(U.S. & Canad. informal)*, off beam *(informal)*, way off beam *(informal)* • *That was the wrong answer – try again.*
3 = inappropriate, incorrect, unfitting, unsuitable, unhappy, not done, unacceptable, undesirable, improper, unconventional, incongruous, unseemly, unbecoming, indecorous, inapt, infelicitous, malapropos • *I'm always embarrassing myself by saying the wrong thing.*
OPPOSITES: becoming, seemly, correct
4 = bad, criminal, illegal, evil, unfair, crooked, unlawful, illicit, immoral, unjust, dishonest, wicked, sinful, unethical, wrongful, under-the-table, reprehensible, dishonourable, iniquitous, not cricket *(informal)*, felonious, blameworthy • *It was wrong of you to leave her alone in the house.*
OPPOSITES: just, godly, moral
5 = defective, not working, faulty, out of order, awry, askew, out of commission • *We think there's something wrong with the computer.*
6 = opposite, inside, reverse, inverse • *Iron the t-shirt on the wrong side to prevent damage to the design.*
▸ AS AN ADVERB **1 = incorrectly**, badly, wrongly, mistakenly, erroneously, inaccurately • *You've spelled my name wrong.*
OPPOSITES: squarely, correctly, truly
2 = amiss, astray, awry, askew • *Where did we go wrong with our children?*

WRITERS

Children's writers

Louisa May Alcott *(U.S.)*
Hans Christian Andersen *(Danish)*
Lynn Reid Banks *(English)*
J(ames) M(atthew) Barrie *(Scottish)*
Judy Blume *(U.S.)*
Enid (Mary) Blyton *(English)*
Elinor M(ary) Brent-Dyer *(English)*
Lewis Carroll *(English)*
Babette Cole *(British)*
Eoin Colfer *(Irish)*
Susan Coolidge *(U.S.)*
Karen Cushman *(U.S.)*
Roald Dahl *(British)*
Anne Digby *(English)*
Dr Seuss *(U.S.)*
Anne Fine *(English)*
Kenneth Grahame *(Scottish)*
Laura Ingalls Wilder *(U.S.)*
Mick Inkpen *(English)*
Robin Jarvis *(English)*
Diana Wynne Jones *(Welsh)*
Dick King-Smith *(English)*
C(live) S(taples) Lewis *(English)*
A(lan) A(lexander) Milne *(English)*
Michael Morpurgo *(English)*
Jill Murphy *(English)*
E(dith) Nesbit *(English)*
Terry Pratchett *(English)*
Philip Pullman *(English)*
Chris Riddell *(English)*
J K Rowling *(British)*
Louis Sachar *(U.S.)*
Paul Stewart *(English)*
Noel Streatfield *(English)*
Jacqueline Wilson *(English)*

Short story writers

Giovanni Boccaccio *(Italian)*
Jorge Luis Borges *(Argentinian)*
Stephen Crane *(U.S.)*
Arthur Conan Doyle *(British)*
Joel Chandler Harris *(U.S.)*
Nathaniel Hawthorne *(U.S.)*
Washington Irving *(U.S.)*
Carson McCullers *(U.S.)*
Katherine Mansfield *(N.Z.-British)*
W(illiam) Somerset Maugham *(English)*
(Henri René Albert) Guy de Maupassant *(French)*
Herman Melville *(U.S.)*
H(ector) H(ugh) Munro *(Scottish)*
O. Henry *(U.S.)*
Dorothy Parker *(U.S.)*
Edgar Allan Poe *(U.S.)*

Non-fiction writers

Joseph Addison *(English)*
Aesop *(Greek)*
Roger Ascham *(English)*
James Boswell *(Scottish)*
John Bunyan *(English)*
Edmund Burke *(British)*
Jane Welsh Carlyle *(Scottish)*
Thomas Carlyle *(Scottish)*
William Godwin *(English)*
Marcus Tullius Cicero *(Roman)*
William Cobbett *(English)*
Desiderius Erasmus *(Dutch)*
Edward Gibbon *(English)*
William Hazlitt *(English)*
R.H. Hutton *(English)*
Thomas Jefferson *(U.S.)*
Jerome K(lapka) Jerome *(English)*
Samuel Johnson *(English)*
Margery Kempe *(English)*
Lord Chesterfield *(English)*
John Lyly *(English)*
Thomas Malory *(English)*
Michel Eyquem de Montaigne *(French)*
Tom Paine *(English-U.S.)*
Samuel Pepys *(English)*
François Rabelais *(French)*
John Ruskin *(English)*
Richard Steele *(English)*
Leslie Stephen *(English)*
Thomas Traherne *(English)*
Izaak Walton *(English)*
Mary Wollstonecraft *(English)*

W

▸ **AS A NOUN 1 = wickedness**, injustice, unfairness, inequity, immorality, iniquity, sinfulness • *He doesn't seem to know the difference between right and wrong.*
OPPOSITES: good, virtue, morality
2 = offence, injury, crime, abuse, error, sin, injustice, grievance, infringement, trespass, misdeed, transgression, infraction, bad *or* evil deed • *I intend to right the wrong done to you.*
OPPOSITES: favour, good turn, good deed
▸ **AS A VERB = mistreat**, abuse, hurt, injure, harm, cheat, take advantage of, discredit, oppress, malign, misrepresent, dump on *(slang, chiefly U.S.)*, impose upon, dishonour, ill-treat, shit on *(taboo slang)*, maltreat, ill-use • *She felt she had been wronged.*
OPPOSITES: help, support, treat well
▸ **IN PHRASES: get someone wrong = misunderstand**, mistake, misinterpret, misread, misconstrue, get the wrong idea, misapprehend • *Don't get me wrong. I like him, but I know he can be a pain at times.*
go wrong 1 = fail, flop *(informal)*, fall through, come to nothing, miscarry, misfire, come to grief *(informal)*, go pear-shaped *(informal)* • *Nearly everything that could go wrong has gone wrong.*
2 = make a mistake, boob *(Brit. slang)*, err, slip up *(informal)*, go astray • *I think I've gone wrong somewhere in my calculations.*
3 = break down, fail, malfunction, misfire, cease to function, conk out *(informal)*, go on the blink *(slang)*, go kaput *(informal)*, go phut *(informal)* • *If your video recorder goes wrong, you can have it repaired.*
4 = lapse, sin, err, fall from grace, go astray, go to the bad, go off the straight and narrow *(informal)* • *We condemn teenagers who go wrong and punish those who step out of line.*
in the wrong = guilty, mistaken, at fault, off course, off target, in error, to be blamed, off beam *(informal)*, blameworthy • *He didn't argue because he knew he was in the wrong.*

QUOTATIONS

A man should never be ashamed to own he has been in the wrong, which is but saying, in other words, that he is wiser today than he was yesterday
[Alexander Pope *Miscellanies*]

PROVERBS

Two wrongs don't make a right

wrongdoer = offender, criminal, villain, culprit, sinner, delinquent, trespasser *(archaic)*, miscreant, malefactor, evildoer, transgressor, lawbreaker, perp *(U.S. & Canad. informal)* • *ways to punish the wrongdoer so he will not offend again*

wrongdoing = crime, vice, corruption, guilt, misconduct, delinquency, wickedness, iniquity, illegality, villainy, lawbreaking, malefaction • *The authorities haven't found any evidence of criminal wrongdoing.*

wrongful = improper, illegal, unfair, inappropriate, unlawful, illicit, immoral, unjust, illegitimate, unethical, groundless • *his protest at what he claims is his wrongful conviction for murder*
OPPOSITES: just, legal, rightful

wrong-headed 1 = mistaken, wrong, false, incorrect, faulty, misguided, erroneous, off target, unsound, in error, fallacious • *I realise now that my thinking was wrong-headed and immature.*
2 = obstinate, dogged, contrary, stubborn, perverse, inflexible, wilful, intransigent, obdurate, self-willed, refractory, pig-headed, bull-headed, mulish, cross-grained, froward *(archaic)* • *The Government persists in its blind, wrong-headed approach to prisons and crime.*

wrongly = incorrectly, falsely, mistakenly, by mistake, erroneously, in error, inaccurately, fallaciously • *He was wrongly diagnosed as having a bone tumour.*

wry 1 = ironic, dry, mocking, sarcastic, sardonic, droll, pawky *(Scot.)*, mordacious • *a wry sense of humour*
2 = contorted, twisted, crooked, distorted, warped, uneven, deformed, awry, askew, aslant, skewwhiff *(Brit. informal)* • *She cast a wry grin in his direction.*
OPPOSITES: even, level, straight

W

xenophobia = **racism**, nationalism, bigotry, isolationism, racial hatred, ethnocentrism, jingoism, racialism, racial intolerance, ethnocentricity • *a wave of xenophobia*

xenophobic = **racist**, nationalist, bigoted, parochial, insular, isolationist, ethnocentric, racialist, ethnocentrist • *Stalin was obsessively xenophobic.*

Xerox *(trademark)* **AS A NOUN** = **photocopy**, copy, reproduction, duplicate • *He enclosed a Xerox of the advert.* ▸**AS A VERB** = **photocopy**, copy, reproduce, run off, print, replicate, duplicate, make a Xerox of *(trademark)* • *I should have simply Xeroxed this sheet for you.*

Xmas = **Christmas**, Noel, festive season, Yule *(archaic)*, Yuletide *(archaic)*, Christmastime, Christmastide, Crimbo *(Brit. informal)* • *It would be nice to have my dad home for Xmas.*

QUOTATIONS

'Twas the night before Christmas, when all through the house
Not a creature was stirring, not even a mouse
[Clement C. Moore *A Visit from St. Nicholas*]

X-ray = **radiograph**, x-ray image • *An x-ray clearly shows the fracture.*

Yy

ya = **yes**, yeah *(informal)*, sure, okay, aye *(Scot. informal)*, affirmative *(formal)*, uh-huh *(slang)*, yebo *(S. African informal)* • *'Are you coming now?' 'Ya.'*

yacht = **boat**, ship, cutter, sloop, ketch, sailboat • *His yacht sank last summer.*

yahoo = **philistine**, savage, lout, beast, barbarian, brute, rowdy, hoon *(Austral. & N.Z.)*, roughneck *(slang)*, boor, churl, yob *or* yobbo *(Brit. slang)*, cougan *(Austral. slang)*, scozza *(Austral. slang)*, bogan *(Austral. slang)* • *a typical City merchant banking yahoo*

yak = **gossip**, go on, gab *(informal)*, rabbit (on) *(Brit. informal)*, run on, jaw *(slang)*, chatter, spout, waffle *(informal, chiefly Brit.)*, yap *(informal)*, tattle, jabber, blather, chew the fat *(slang)*, witter on *(informal)*, run off at the mouth • *He and Cosby had a chance to yak.*

yank AS A VERB = **pull**, tug, jerk, seize, snatch, pluck, hitch, wrench • *She yanked the child back into the house.*
▸ AS A NOUN = **pull**, tug, jerk, snatch, hitch, wrench, tweak • *Grabbing his ponytail, Shirley gave it a yank.*

yap AS A VERB 1 = **yelp**, bark, woof, yip *(chiefly U.S.)* • *The little dog yapped frantically.*
2 = **talk**, go on, rabbit (on) *(Brit. informal)*, gossip, jaw *(slang)*, chatter, spout, babble, waffle *(informal, chiefly Brit.)*, prattle, jabber, blather, run off at the mouth *(slang)*, earbash *(Austral. & N.Z. slang)* • *She keeps yapping at me about Joe.*
▸ AS A NOUN = **bark**, yelp, woof, yip *(chiefly U.S.)* • *a high-pitched terrier yap*

yard 1 = **courtyard**, court, garden, backyard, quadrangle • *I saw him standing in the yard.*
2 = **workshop**, works, plant, industrial unit • *a railway yard*

yardstick = **standard**, measure, criterion, gauge, benchmark, touchstone, par • *an exceptional vintage by any yardstick*

yarn 1 = **thread**, fibre, cotton, wool • *vegetable-dyed yarn*
2 = **story**, tale, anecdote, account, narrative, fable, reminiscence, urban myth, tall story, urban legend, cock-and-bull story *(informal)* • *Doug has a yarn or two to tell me about his trips into the bush.*

yawn = **gape**, open, split • *The gulf between them yawned wider than ever.*

yawning = **gaping**, wide, huge, vast, wide-open, cavernous • *a yawning budget deficit*

yeah = **yes**, sure, okay, aye *(Scot. informal)*, affirmative *(formal)*, uh-huh *(slang)*, ya *(S. African)*, yebo *(S. African informal)* • *Yeah, alright, I'll come.*

year AS A NOUN = **twelve months**, calendar year, twelve month period • *She's done quite a bit of work this last year.*
▸ AS A PLURAL NOUN = **old age**, age, senility, dotage, senescence, second childhood, eld *(archaic)* • *His advanced years have made him absent-minded.*
▸ IN PHRASES: **year in, year out** = **again and again**, always, repeatedly, over and over (again), continuously, time and (time) again, time after time, unfailingly, recurrently • *Year in, year out, nothing changes.*
▸ RELATED ADJECTIVE: annual

yearly AS AN ADJECTIVE = **annual**, each year, every year, once a year • *a yearly meeting*
▸ AS AN ADVERB = **annually**, every year, by the year, once a year, per annum • *interest is paid yearly*

yearn *often with* **for** = **long**, desire, pine, pant, hunger, ache, lust, crave, covet, itch, languish, hanker after, have a yen for *(informal)*, eat your heart out over, set your heart upon, suspire *(archaic or poetic)*, would give your eyeteeth for • *He yearned for freedom.*

yearning = **longing**, wish, desire, need, burning, urge, yen *(informal)*, pining, hunger, hungering, inclination, eagerness, hankering • *He spoke of his yearning for another child.*

yell AS A VERB = **scream**, shout, cry out, howl, call out, wail, shriek, screech, squeal, bawl, holler *(informal)*, yelp, call at the top of your voice • *He was out there shouting and yelling.*
OPPOSITES: whisper, mutter, murmur
▸ AS A NOUN = **scream**, cry, shout, roar, howl, shriek, whoop, screech, squeal, holler *(informal)*, yelp, yowl • *He let out a yell.*
OPPOSITES: whisper, mutter, murmur

yellow AS A NOUN = **lemon**, gold, amber • *a symphony of reds and yellows*
▸ AS AN ADJECTIVE 1 = **lemon**, gold, amber, yellowish, yellowy • *The walls have been painted bright yellow.*
2 = **cowardly**, spineless, gutless, chicken *(informal)*, craven *(informal)*, faint-hearted, yellow-bellied *(informal)*, lily-livered • *You yellow dogs!*
▸ RELATED ADJECTIVE: xanthous
▹ *See panel* **Shades of yellow**

yelp AS A VERB 1 = **bark**, howl, yap, yip *(chiefly U.S.)*, yowl • *Her dog yelped and came to heel.*
2 = **cry**, shout, scream, yell, wail, screech, squeal • *wrenching my ankle so hard that I yelped in pain*
▸ AS A NOUN = **cry**, shout, scream, yell, wail, screech, squeal • *She gave a yelp of pain.*

yen = **longing**, desire, craving, yearning, passion, hunger, ache, itch, thirst, hankering • *Mike had a yen to try cycling.*

yes = **yeah** *(informal)*, sure, okay, aye *(Scot. informal)*, affirmative *(formal)*, uh-huh *(slang)*, ya *(S. African)*, yup *(informal)*, yebo *(S. African informal)* • *'Are you a friend of his?' 'Yes'.*

yet AS AN ADVERB 1 = **so far**, until now, up to now, still, as yet, even now, thus far, up till now, up to the present time • *They haven't finished yet.*
2 = **now**, right now, just now, so soon, already • *Don't get up yet.*
3 = **still**, further, in addition, as well, moreover, besides, to boot, additionally, over and above, into the bargain • *This weekend yet more uniformed soldiers were posted at official buildings.*
▸ AS A CONJUNCTION = **nevertheless**, still, however, for all that, notwithstanding, just the same, be that as it may • *I don't eat much, yet I am a size 16.*

yield AS A VERB 1 = **bow**, submit, give in, surrender, give way,

SHADES OF YELLOW

almond	butternut	eau de nil	lemon	ochre	topaz
amber	canary yellow	ecru	magnolia	old gold	tortoiseshell
beige	champagne	eggshell	maize	primrose	
bisque	cinnamon	gamboge	mustard	saffron	
bistre	citron	gold *or* golden	nankeen	straw	
buff	daffodil	jasmine	oatmeal	tea rose	

succumb, cave in *(informal)*, capitulate, knuckle under, resign yourself • *She yielded to general pressure.*
OPPOSITES: resist, hold out
2 = **relinquish**, resign, hand over, surrender, turn over, part with, make over, cede, give over, bequeath, abdicate, deliver up • *He may yield control.*
OPPOSITES: keep, maintain, retain
3 = **surrender**, give up, give in, concede defeat, cave in *(informal)*, throw in the towel, admit defeat, accept defeat, give up the struggle, knuckle under, raise the white flag, lay down your arms, cry quits • *Their leader refused to yield.*
4 = **produce**, give, provide, pay, return, supply, bear, net, earn, afford, generate, bring in, furnish, bring forth • *400,000 acres of land yielded a crop worth $1.75 billion.*
OPPOSITES: use, consume, use up
▸ **AS A NOUN** 1 = **produce**, crop, harvest, output • *improving the yield of the crop*
2 = **profit**, return, income, revenue, earnings, takings • *the yield on a bank's investment*
OPPOSITES: loss, consumption, input
▸ **IN PHRASES: yield to something** = **comply with**, agree to, concede, allow, grant, permit, go along with, bow to, consent to, accede to • *Television officials had yielded to demands.*

yielding 1 = **soft**, pliable, springy, elastic, resilient, supple, spongy, unresisting, quaggy • *the soft yielding cushions*
2 = **submissive**, obedient, compliant, docile, easy, flexible, accommodating, pliant, tractable, acquiescent, biddable • *women's yielding nature*
OPPOSITES: stubborn, perverse, obstinate

yob *or* **yobbo** = **thug**, hooligan, lout, heavy *(slang)*, tough, rough *(informal)*, rowdy, yahoo, hoon *(Austral. & N.Z. slang)*, hoodlum, ruffian, roughneck *(slang)*, boot boy, tsotsi *(S. African)*, cougan *(Austral. slang)*, scozza *(Austral. slang)*, bogan *(Austral. slang)* • *Violent and dangerous yobs deserve to be locked up.*

yoke AS A NOUN 1 = **oppression**, slavery, bondage, servitude, service, burden, enslavement, serfdom, servility, vassalage, thraldom • *People are suffering under the yoke of capitalism.*
2 = **harness**, coupling, tackle, chain, collar, tack • *He put a yoke around his body and pulled along the cart.*
▸ **AS A VERB** 1 = **unite**, join, link, tie, bond, bind, connect • *They are yoked by money and votes.*
2 = **harness**, join, couple, link, tie, connect, bracket, hitch • *a plough team of eight oxen yoked in pairs*

yokel = **peasant**, hick *(informal, chiefly U.S. & Canad.)*, rustic, countryman, hillbilly, boor, country cousin, hayseed *(U.S. & Canad. informal)*, bushie *or* bushy *(Austral. & N.Z. informal)*, clodhopper *(informal)*, (country) bumpkin • *a local yokel*

young AS AN ADJECTIVE 1 = **immature**, juvenile, youthful, little, growing, green, junior, infant, adolescent, callow, unfledged, in the springtime of life • *I was still too young to understand what was going on.*
OPPOSITES: adult, mature, old
2 = **early**, new, undeveloped, fledgling, newish, not far advanced • *the larvae, the young stages of the worm*
OPPOSITES: old, developed, advanced
▸ **AS A NOUN** = **offspring**, baby, litter, family, issue, brood, little onesy, progeny • *The hen may not be able to feed its young.*
OPPOSITES: parent, adult, grown-up

youngster = **youth**, girl, boy, kid *(informal)*, lad, teenager, juvenile, cub, young person, lass, young adult, pup *(informal, chiefly Brit.)*, urchin, teenybopper *(slang)*, young shaver *(informal)*, young 'un *(informal)* • *Other youngsters are not so lucky.*

yourself IN PHRASES: by yourself 1 = **on your own**, independently, solo, single-handedly, unaided, without help, unassisted, without assistance, under your own steam, off your own bat • *I'd rather do it by myself, thanks.*
2 = **alone**, separately, on your own, singly, unaccompanied, friendless, unescorted, on your tod *(slang)*, companionless, in a solitary state • *He was sitting all by himself.*

youth 1 = **immaturity**, adolescence, early life, young days, boyhood *or* girlhood, salad days, juvenescence • *the comic books of my youth*
OPPOSITES: age, maturity, old age
2 = **youthfulness**, youngness, freshness • *The team is now a good mixture of experience and youth.*
3 = **boy**, lad, youngster, kid *(informal)*, teenager, young man, adolescent, teen *(informal)*, stripling, young shaver *(informal)* • *gangs of youths who broke windows and looted shops*
OPPOSITES: grown-up, adult, pensioner
4 = **young people**, the young, the younger generation, teenagers, the rising generation • *He represents the opinions of the youth of today.*
OPPOSITES: old people, the old, the aged

QUOTATIONS

Youth's a stuff will not endure
[William Shakespeare *Twelfth Night*]

Young men have more virtue than old men; they have more generous sentiments in every respect
[Dr. Johnson]

Youth, which is forgiven everything, forgives itself nothing: age, which forgives itself anything, is forgiven nothing
[George Bernard Shaw *Maxims for Revolutionists*]

Whom the gods love dies young
[Menander *Mouostichoi*]

Bliss was it in that dawn to be alive,
But to be young was very heaven
[William Wordsworth *The Prelude*]

Youth is a disease that must be borne with patiently!
Time, indeed, will cure it
[R.H. Benson]

I've never understood why people consider youth a time of freedom and joy. It's probably because they have forgotten their own
[Margaret Atwood *Hair Jewelry*]

Hope I die before I get old
[Pete Townshend *My Generation*]

PROVERBS

Youth must be served

youthful 1 = **young**, juvenile, childish, immature, boyish, pubescent, girlish, puerile • *youthful enthusiasm and high spirits*
OPPOSITES: old, aged, elderly
2 = **vigorous**, fresh, active, young looking, young at heart, spry • *I'm a very youthful 50.*
OPPOSITES: ancient, over the hill, tired

Zz

zany = **comical**, crazy, nutty *(slang)*, funny, eccentric, wacky *(slang)*, loony *(slang)*, oddball *(informal)*, madcap, goofy *(informal)*, kooky *(U.S. informal)*, out there *(slang)*, clownish, wacko *or* whacko *(informal)*, off the air *(Austral. slang)* • *the zany humour of the Marx Brothers*

zap = **hit**, shoot, blast, kill, destroy, stun, neutralize • *A guard zapped him with the stun gun.*

zeal = **enthusiasm**, passion, zest, fire, spirit, warmth, devotion, verve, fervour, eagerness, gusto, militancy, fanaticism, ardour, earnestness, keenness, fervency • *his zeal for teaching*
OPPOSITES: indifference, apathy, coolness

zealot = **fanatic**, enthusiast, extremist, militant, maniac, fiend *(informal)*, bigot • *He was forceful but by no means a zealot.*

zealous = **enthusiastic**, passionate, earnest, burning, spirited, keen, devoted, eager, militant, ardent, fanatical, fervent, impassioned, rabid, fervid • *She was a zealous worker for charitable bodies.*
OPPOSITES: indifferent, apathetic, unenthusiastic

zenith = **height**, summit, peak, top, climax, crest, high point, pinnacle, meridian, apex, high noon, apogee, acme, vertex • *His career is now at its zenith.*
OPPOSITES: base, bottom, lowest point

zero AS A NOUN **1** = **nought**, nothing, nil, naught, cipher • *a scale ranging from zero to seven*
2 = **zilch**, nil, nothing, zip *(U.S. slang)*, nada *(U.S. informal)*, bugger all *(slang)*, fuck all *(taboo slang)*, sweet FA *(informal)*, sweet Fanny Adams *(informal)* • *A man's sperm count drops to zero.*
3 = **rock bottom**, the bottom, an all-time low, a nadir, as low as you can get, the lowest point *or* ebb • *My spirits were at zero.*
▸ IN PHRASES: **zero in on something 1** = **zoom in on**, focus on, aim at, train on, home in on • *He raised the binoculars again and zeroed in on an eleventh-floor room.*
2 = **focus on**, concentrate on, home in on, pinpoint on, converge • *Critics have zeroed in on his weakness.*

zero hour = **moment of truth**, crisis, turning point, vital moment, appointed hour, moment of decision, tipping point • *Your zero hour has arrived.*

zest 1 = **enjoyment**, love, appetite, relish, interest, joy, excitement, zeal, gusto, keenness, zing *(informal)*, delectation • *He has a zest for life and a quick intellect.*
OPPOSITES: loathing, indifference, aversion
2 = **flavour**, taste, savour, kick *(informal)*, spice, relish, smack, tang, piquancy, pungency • *Lemon oil adds zest to your cuppa.*
3 = **rind**, skin, peel, outer layer • *the zest and juice of the lemon*

zigzag = **winding**, wiggly, wavy, meandering, snaking, crooked, zigzagging, twisty, squiggly • *a zigzag pattern*

zing = **vitality**, go *(informal)*, life, energy, spirit, dash, pep, zip *(informal)*, animation, vigour, zest, welly *(slang)*, oomph *(informal)*, brio, liveliness, pizzazz *or* pizazz *(informal)* • *He just lacked that extra zing.*

zip AS A VERB = **speed**, shoot, fly, tear, rush, flash, dash, hurry, barrel (along) *(informal, chiefly U.S. & Canad.)*, buzz, streak, hare *(Brit. informal)*, zoom, whizz *(informal)*, hurtle, pelt, burn rubber *(informal)* • *My craft zipped along the bay.*
▸ AS A NOUN = **energy**, go *(informal)*, life, drive, spirit, punch *(informal)*, pep, sparkle, vitality, vigour, verve, zest, gusto, welly *(slang)*, get-up-and-go *(informal)*, oomph *(informal)*, brio, zing *(informal)*, liveliness, vim *(slang)*, pizzazz *or* pizazz *(informal)* • *He gave the choreography his usual class and zip.*
OPPOSITES: apathy, inertia, lethargy

zodiac

SIGNS OF THE ZODIAC

Aquarius (the Water Carrier)	Libra (the Scales)
Aries (the Ram)	Pisces (the Fishes)
Cancer (the Crab)	Sagittarius (the Archer)
Capricorn (the Goat)	Scorpio (the Scorpion)
Gemini (the Twins)	Taurus (the Bull)
Leo (the Lion)	Virgo (the Virgin)

▸ *See panel* **Chinese animal years**

zone = **area**, region, section, sector, district, territory, belt, sphere, tract • *The area has been declared a disaster zone.*

zoology
QUOTATIONS
The city is not a concrete jungle, it is a human zoo
[Desmond Morris *The Human Zoo*]
▸ *See panel* **Zoology**

zoom 1 = **speed**, shoot, fly, tear, rush, flash, dash, barrel (along) *(informal, chiefly U.S. & Canad.)*, buzz, streak, hare *(Brit. informal)*, zip *(informal)*, whizz *(informal)*, hurtle, pelt, burn rubber *(informal)* • *A police car zoomed by.*
2 = **rise**, rocket, soar, escalate, shoot up, climb • *The economy sank and inflation zoomed.*

CHINESE ANIMAL YEARS

Chinese	English	Years				
Shu	Rat	1960	1972	1984	1996	2008
Niu	Ox	1961	1973	1985	1997	2009
Hu	Tiger	1962	1974	1986	1998	2010
Tu	Hare	1963	1975	1987	1999	2011
Long	Dragon	1964	1976	1988	2000	2012
She	Serpent	1965	1977	1989	2001	2013
Ma	Horse	1966	1978	1990	2002	2014
Yang	Sheep	1967	1979	1991	2003	2015
Hou	Monkey	1968	1980	1992	2004	2016
Ji	Cock	1969	1981	1993	2005	2017
Gou	Dog	1970	1982	1994	2006	2018
Zhu	Boar	1971	1983	1995	2007	2019

ZOOLOGY

Branches of zoology

arachnology
archaeozoology
cetology
entomology
ethology
herpetology
ichthyology
malacology
mammalogy
myrmecology
ophiology
ornithology
palaeozoology
primatology
protozoology
zoogeography
zoography
zoometry
zootomy

Zoology terms

abdomen
aestivation
amphibian
antenna
anterior
appendage
arachnid
arthropod
biped
bivalve
carnivore
caudal
chordate
chrysalis
cocoon
coelenterate
coelom
colony
crustacean
decapod
dipteran
dorsal
echinoderm
edentate
fin
gastropod
gill
herbivore
hibernation
imago
insectivore
invertebrate
larva
lepidopteran
marsupial
metamorphosis
migration
omnivore
parenchyma
passerine
pectoral
placenta
posterior
predator
prey
primate
protozoan
pupa
quadruped
raptor
reptile
rodent
ruminant
segment
skeleton
spawn
spine
sucker
thorax
ventral
vertebrate

Zoologists

Georges Cuvier *(French)*
Charles (Robert) Darwin *(English)*
Richard Dawkins *(British)*
Hans Adolf Eduard Driesch *(German)*
Gerald (Malcolm) Durrell *(British)*
Charles Sutherland Elton *(British)*
Karl von Frisch *(Austrian)*
Paul Kammerer *(Austrian)*
Alfred Charles Kinsey *(U.S.)*
Jean Baptiste Pierre Antoine de Monet Lamarck *(French)*
Edwin Ray Lankester *(English)*
Konrad Zacharias Lorenz *(Austrian)*
Peter Brian Medawar *(English)*
Thomas Hunt Morgan *(U.S.)*
Nikolaas Tinbergen *(British)*
Alfred Russel Wallace *(British)*
Solly Zuckerman *(British)*

Supplement

Reports and Presentations

Contents

Writing reports

A report is a document that presents information about an investigation or a body of research. It should have a clear structure. This structure should enable specific pieces of information to be located easily by the reader. Reports are used in many areas of business, including accounting, finance, management, and marketing, as well as in scientific research work.

Initial planning

Before starting to write any report, there are a number of questions you need to be able to answer. The answers to these questions will largely define the approach you take when putting together the report.

▷ *what is the purpose of the report?*
Ideally, you should be able to summarize the purpose in one sentence
▷ *is there an outline or remit for the report?*
If there is, the purpose of the report should be clear
▷ *who will read the report?*
Reports can be written for internal and external office use, for professionals in a particular field, or for members of the public, for instance shareholders in a large corporation
▷ *will the report be formal or informal?*
This largely depends on who the report is written for
▷ *is there a timescale for completion of the report?*
▷ *is there a word limit for the report?*
▷ *are you the sole author of the report?*
▷ *how will you undertake research for the report?*
Research can take a number of forms: consulting reference sources, previous reports on the subject, and the internet; interviewing professionals in the area of research; asking colleagues for information; or undertaking new market research
▷ *how will the report be presented?*
The report could be for internal use only, or widely distributed inside and outside the work environment. The prospective readership will affect the design, approach, and style of the whole report.

When you have answered these questions, you will be in a position to organize the subject matter for your report into sections.

Organizing the report into sections

The organization or layout of the report must make it as easy as possible for readers to get to the information they need. By subdividing the report into sections, you should be able to accommodate all the information in a clear, straightforward fashion.

The following list covers all the section headings for a major report, but smaller or less important reports may not require all of them.

Title page

This page includes the report title, the author's name, and the date of completion or release. If the report has more than one author, consider putting the authors' names in alphabetical order. Alternatively, it may be more appropriate to place the main or most prestigious author first. Remember that, unless alphabetical, the order of names sends out messages about seniority or the level of contribution of each person.

Abstract

A short summary of the report, including aims, methods, conclusions, and any recommendations. Scientific research abstracts generally appear in library files or journals of abstracts. As they don't appear with the main report in these instances, they need to be comprehensible in isolation.

Contents

A list of the sections within the report, along with their corresponding page numbers.

Introduction

This explains the purpose of the report and the methods used in its or background compilation.The introduction should be concise and explain:

- ▷ what the subject of the report is
- ▷ who commissioned the report
- ▷ what the background to the commissioning of the report is
- ▷ what the method of working in compiling the report was
- ▷ what the main sources are

Main body of the report

This contains the information you have collected for the report in a number of clearly headed sections. Ensure that each section is treated in a similar way and that the most important information always comes first within a section. See **Presentation** below for more details.

Conclusions

A brief, easy-to-understand section giving an overview of the results gained from the information given in the main body of the report.

Recommendations

A section detailing possible action points and strategies for improvement in the light of the conclusions.

Appendices

These contain additional information or samples omitted from the main body of the text but which are relevant to the report as a whole.

Notes

These give details that would be too cumbersome to include in the main text. Clear cross-reference superscript numbers should appear within the text, immediately after the information to which the note refers. The notes should appear in numerical order in the Notes section.

Bibliography

This is an alphabetical listing, normally by author, of all the sources used in the report. For example:

Stirling, E.Q., 2004. *Bovine Anatomy Revisited*. 2nd ed. Jersey: Hursto Press

Wilson, J., 2002. Better milking practices. *Farm and Field*, 24 (3), 36–38.

As you can see, each source should have the following information, though the order can be varied slightly but consistently, depending on the system used:

▷ the author's name
▷ the date of publication
▷ the title of the book, newspaper, or journal, or the website address
▷ the title of the newspaper or journal article, if appropriate
▷ any edition number, other than the first edition of a book
▷ the name of the publisher of the journal or magazine

Presentation

All reports need to be as clear as possible. If they are not, readers will lose interest in their contents. Ways of making information easily accessible include:

▷ Organizing information into different sections (see **Organizing the report into sections**), giving each one a clear heading.
▷ Breaking up larger sections into manageable subsections, each with its own subheading. Bear in mind that the longer a section is, the less likely it is that it will be fully read. Sections and subsections should be numbered as follows:

1. [section heading]
1.1 [subsection heading]
1.2 [subsection heading] etc
2. [section heading]
2.1 [subsection heading] etc

▷ Maintaining consistency in the presentation of similar information.
▷ Paying attention to the numbering of sections and appendices.
▷ If appropriate, adding simple graphs, tables, and illustrations.
These break up the text and often provide a quick, easy-to-understand

overview of the information.

▷ Putting large and unwieldy amounts of data into appendices, so as not to interrupt the flow of the text.

▷ Using a clear typeface for all of the text in the report. The reader wants to take in the essential points of the report as quickly as possible.

SUMMARY

▷ Know the subject and purpose of the report

▷ Know who is going to read the report

▷ Set out the report in clearly defined sections

▷ Make the essential points and conclusions as clear as possible

Giving presentations

As with writing reports, one of the keys to giving a good presentation is organizing your material. Your subject should be clearly stated, logically thought through, and explained interestingly enough to hold your audience's attention.

Notes

▷ don't learn your presentation by heart or write it down word for word. Such strategies usually result in boring delivery. Instead, make notes to refer to during the presentation so that you have something to prompt you

▷ write the notes on numbered index cards. You can then move each card to the bottom of the pile when you have used it and will always keep your place

Content

▷ try to start with something exciting but relevant to make your audience sit up and take notice. A short, telling anecdote can be useful for this

▷ give an introductory outline of your presentation, and make sure you keep to this. Avoid introducing a completely new subject without warning halfway through, or changing the tone of your presentation

▷ use links to lead logically from one section to the next: *while we're on the subject of; in view of; as for; before moving on to; in spite of*

▷ provide specific examples. These give the audience something to think about, and can be a source for a later question-and-answer session

▷ if you are presenting an argument, build from the weakest point to the strongest

▷ include a few light jokes or puns, but always ensure that they are appropriate to the presentation subject and to the audience

▷ don't be afraid to express your opinions. When you are expressing opinion rather than stating facts, remember to make this clear by using expressions such as *I believe that*; *in my opinion*; *to my mind*. You can show how strong your beliefs are by slightly amending some of these expressions: *I firmly believe that*; *I strongly believe that*; *we are absolutely certain that*; *we are pretty sure that*

▷ consider including some aspect of audience participation. Some degree of interaction tends to make a presentation more interesting

▷ end the presentation with a brief recap of the main points and a strong, persuasive conclusion

Visual aids

▷ use visual aids to illustrate your presentation, but ensure that they are simple, useful and clearly visible from the back of the room. Well-explained, well-chosen and simple visual aids are more effective than under-explained, complicated visual aids. Avoid having too many visual aids since constant changes can be distracting. Be careful not to stand in front of any visuals

▷ if you have access to a computer, you might consider using a presentation program such as PowerPoint®. Keep the number of slides to a minimum, with no more than a few concise bullet points to each slide

▷ if you are providing handouts, ensure you have made enough copies for everyone beforehand. Remember too that you must allow some time for the handouts to be received and viewed before you continue your presentation

Practice and timing

▷ try recording your presentation beforehand. This will help you get your timing and pacing right. It will also allow you to check that you sound clear and confident, that you are not mumbling or talking too fast

▷ if you can enlist the help of a supportive friend or family member, try out your presentation in front of them and ask for comments on any distracting habits you may have, such as fiddling with your hair or endlessly repeating a particular expression

▷ before the event, make sure you run through your presentation exactly as you intend to do it on the day, complete with any visuals and handouts. Time how long it takes and tailor it as necessary to fit the time allotted for it. It is very important to ensure that it does not overrun

Venue

▷ if you are using a computer or overhead projector for your presentation, ensure that you have time to find out how to work it before the presentation
▷ make sure that there are enough seats for your audience
▷ familiarize yourself with the venue and its acoustics, to ensure that you feel comfortable speaking in it and that you are able to project your voice across the whole room

You, your body and your voice

▷ if you feel nervous before giving your presentation, practise deep breathing and rehearse your opening sentences
▷ if you are very nervous, standing behind a lectern may help you feel less vulnerable, as well as giving you something to lean on and somewhere to place your notes
▷ as you give your presentation, stand straight and keep you chin up as you speak. A strong, positive posture will both improve your confidence and convince the audience that you have something interesting to say
▷ look round all the faces in the audience with sweeping glances. Look members of the audience very briefly in the eye when you can, avoiding looking at any one individual for too long
▷ speak sincerely and with warmth
▷ subtly vary your tone of voice to add interest, but make sure that you do not overdo this
▷ vary your pace, but never talk too quickly as you may well lose your audience if you do
▷ pause slightly between points to show the audience when you are about to move on to a different subject. Allow pauses for audience reaction
▷ smile from time to time where appropriate. It will help you feel more relaxed and it will encourage a bond with your audience
▷ do not be put off if you make a mistake during the presentation. Apologize quickly and move on

SUMMARY

Three helpful steps to remember when planning your presentation:
▷ Say what you are going to say.
▷ Say it.
▷ Say what you've said.

- if you are using a computer or overhead projector for your presentation, ensure that you have time to find out how to work it before the presentation
- make sure that there are enough seats for your audience
- familiarize yourself with the venue and its acoustics, to ensure that you feel comfortable speaking in it and that you are able to project your voice across the whole room

You, your body and your voice

- if you feel nervous before giving your presentation, practise deep breathing and rehearse your opening sentences
- if you are very nervous, standing behind a lectern may help you feel less vulnerable, as well as giving you something to lean on and somewhere to place your notes
- as you give your presentation, stand straight and keep your chin up as you speak. A strong, positive posture will both improve your confidence and convince the audience that you have something interesting to say
- look round at the faces in the audience with sweeping glances. Look members of the audience very briefly in the eye when you can, avoiding looking at any one individual for too long
- speak sincerely and with warmth
- subtly vary your tone of voice to add interest, but make sure that you do not overdo this
- vary your pace, but never talk too quickly as you may well lose your audience if you do
- pause slightly between points to show the audience when you are about to move on to a different subject. Allow pauses for audience reaction
- smile from time to time where appropriate. It will help you feel more relaxed and it will encourage a bond with your audience
- do not be put off if you make a mistake during the presentation. Apologize quickly and move on

SUMMARY

Three helpful steps to remember when planning your presentation:
- Say what you are going to say.
- Say it.
- Say what you've said.